GRANGER'S
INDEX TO POETRY

GRANGER'S INDEX TO POETRY

FIFTH EDITION, COMPLETELY REVISED AND ENLARGED, INDEXING ANTHOLOGIES PUBLISHED THROUGH JUNE 30, 1960

EDITED BY WILLIAM F. BERNHARDT

COLUMBIA UNIVERSITY PRESS
MORNINGSIDE HEIGHTS NEW YORK 1962

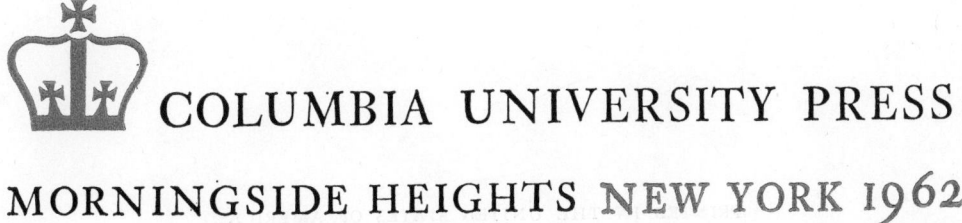

FIFTH EDITION, COMPLETELY REVISED AND ENLARGED
First printing 1962
Third printing 1966

PRINTED IN THE UNITED STATES OF AMERICA

PREFACE

A NEW edition of GRANGER'S INDEX TO POETRY needs no introduction to those thousands of readers who have made use of the previous editions published in the past fifty-eight years. However, a few general remarks about the format of this new edition are perhaps in order.

On the whole, the Fifth Edition of GRANGER'S INDEX makes no departures from the scheme devised for the Fourth Edition, so that librarians familiar with that volume will have no difficulty in using the new edition. As in the previous volume, titles and first lines are combined into one TITLE AND FIRST LINE INDEX. Once more, no prose selections in anthologies have been indexed. Anthologies containing both prose and poetry have been included only when the poetry selections constitute one fourth or more of the whole.

The SUBJECT INDEX has been expanded from its beginnings in the Fourth Edition, and it is hoped that the added headings will increase the usefulness of this particular section of the volume.

The Fifth Edition indexes a total of 574 volumes of anthologies. In this total, each revised edition of an anthology is counted as a separate volume. From the Fourth Edition, 400 volumes have been retained; this number represents books in print or standard volumes which are still frequently used in many libraries. Doubtless certain omitted anthologies may still be on the active list in some libraries, and for this reason librarians may wish to retain copies of the previous edition for reference. In addition, 64 volumes from the supplement published in 1957 (which indexed anthologies published between 1951 and 1955) have been carried over to the new edition, and 110 new volumes have been added for the first time. For those anthologies retained from the Fourth Edition and the 1957 Supplement, the earlier symbols are again used. No new symbol duplicates a symbol used before.

A note of explanation is necessary to account for the absence from the title page of the name of Raymond J. Dixon, under whose capable editorship the Fourth Edition and the 1957 Supplement went to press. Mr. Dixon expected to serve as editor for this new edition, and had in fact given some attention to the matter of content and had actually supervised some of the preliminary operations, but illness forced him to withdraw from the project.

There remains only the pleasant task of thanking those persons whose interest and endeavor contributed so much toward the making of the present edition. An accompanying page lists the names of those responsible for undertaking the arduous and time-consuming jobs involved in a project as large and as complicated as this: marking and checking the anthologies involved, filing, eliminating the symbols of omitted anthologies, and finally the important process of editing the thousands of cards on which the entries were typed. To these persons goes the credit for completing the minute, demanding, and often tedious tasks involved in the compilation of a major reference book.

A word of special thanks is due to Eleanor T. Smith, Coordinator of Adult Services at the Brooklyn Public Library, and to Milton Metcalf, Chief of that library's Language and Literature Division, and his staff for their suggestions regarding out-of-print anthologies considered for omission.

The Libraries of Columbia University and the New York Public Library greatly facilitated our work by lending us many volumes for extended periods of time.

Dr. William Bridgwater, Editor in Chief of Columbia University Press, was most generous of his advice and guidance amid the crush of his other responsibilities. Once again, Eugenia Porter, head of the Production Department, handled matters of design and production with her customary expertness. A special vote of thanks is due to Alice R. Stoddard for her administrative assistance in the early stages of work, to Ronald Schreiber for his aid in collecting the anthologies to be considered for inclusion and for his editing of the SUBJECT INDEX, and to Elva D. Hoover for her expert proofreader's eye that saved many a blunder from being perpetuated in print. Finally, to all those whose names are listed on the facing page the editor acknowledges his thankfulness.

W. F. B.

November 29, 1961

CONTENTS

PREFACE v

EXPLANATORY NOTES x

ABBREVIATIONS xi

KEY TO SYMBOLS xiii

TITLE AND FIRST LINE INDEX 1

AUTHOR INDEX 1609

SUBJECT INDEX 1969

EXPLANATORY NOTES

THE TITLE AND FIRST LINE INDEX is the principal index and must be used in connection with both the AUTHOR INDEX and the SUBJECT INDEX.

In the TITLE AND FIRST LINE INDEX initial capitals in the important words of the titles distinguish titles from first lines. Symbols are listed after both titles and first lines. However, more complete information as to translators, acts and scenes, abridgments, and variant titles is given in the title entries.

When the title and first line of a poem are the same, only the title entry has been indexed. When they are so nearly the same as to be adjacent, again only the title has been indexed, with the first line added in quotation marks and in parentheses to the title entry.

In the arrangement of the title entries, indention is important. Single indention indicates a selection from the work named above; double indention with parentheses indicates a variant title.

Because the Mother Goose rhymes are so much better known by first lines than by the artificial and varying titles given to them in various collections, only their first lines have been included in the TITLE AND FIRST LINE INDEX.

In such titles as "Ode," "Poem," "Song," "Sonnet," too frequent to be distinctive, the first line is added to the title given in the anthology (e.g., Ode: "We are the music-makers"). The title is then alphabeted by first line under "Ode," "Poem," etc.

Titles and first lines beginning with "O" and "Oh" have been filed, as in previous editions, as if all were spelled "O," and are alphabeted according to the words which follow.

"Mac," "Mc," and "M' " are filed as if all were spelled "Mac."

Arabic and Chinese names in the AUTHOR INDEX are filed as if written in one word (e.g., "Al-Dabbaj" comes after "Alcuin" and before "Aldana" and "Li Lung Yü" comes after "Lillington" and before "Lily"). Japanese names are more of a problem. Old-style Japanese names are handled in the same way as Chinese names (i.e., as if written in one word), while modern Japanese names are usually inverted in the Western manner for filing purposes. Japanese names in the AUTHOR INDEX are handled in agreement with this practice.

A KEY TO SYMBOLS is provided, with dates and editions added after titles of anthologies.

ABBREVIATIONS

abr.	abridged
ad.	adapted
add.	additional
arr.	arranged
at.	attributed
Bk.	book
br.	brief
c.	copyright
ch.	chapter
comp.	compiled *or* compiler
comps.	compilers
cond.	condensed
diff.	different
Eng.	English
fr.	from
frag.	fragment
incl.	included *or* including
introd.	introduction *or* introductory
ll.	lines
Mid.	Middle
misc.	miscellaneous
mod.	modernized *or* modern
N.T.	New Testament
O.T.	Old Testament
orig.	original
pant.	pantomime
par.	paraphrase *or* paraphrased
pr.	prose
prol.	prologue
pseud.	pseudonym
Pt.	part
rev.	revised
sc.	scene
Sec.	section
sel.	selection
sels.	selections
sl.	slightly
st.	stanza
sts.	stanzas
tr.	translator, translation, *or* translated
trs.	translators *or* translations
var.	various
vers.	version *or* versions
wr.	wrong *or* wrongly

KEY TO SYMBOLS

Note: The date or number of an edition given in parentheses after a symbol in the Title and First Line Index [e.g., BoCaPo (1948 ed.), HBV (8th ed.), OBEV (1st ed.), OBEV (new ed.)] indicates that the poem appears in that particular edition only.

AA	American Anthology, An, 1787–1900. *Edmund Clarence Stedman, ed.* (c.1900) Houghton Mifflin Company
ABF	American Ballads and Folk Songs. *John A. Lomax and Alan Lomax, comps.* (1934, reissue, 1946) The Macmillan Company
ABS	American Ballads and Songs. *Louise Pound, ed.* (c.1922) Charles Scribner's Sons
ACP	Anthology of Catholic Poets, An. *Shane Leslie, ed.* (1926, rev. ed., 1953) The Macmillan Company, *later pub. by* The Newman Press
ADAH	Arbor Day (Our American Holidays Series). *Robert Haven Schauffler, ed.* (1909) Dodd, Mead & Company
AEV	Anthology of English Verse, An. *John Drinkwater, ed.* (1924) Houghton Mifflin Company
AlBD	All the Best Dog Poems. *Edwin Burtis, comp.* (c.1946) Thomas Y. Crowell Company
AlDL	All Day Long. *Pamela Whitlock, comp.* (1954) Oxford University Press
ALV	Anthology of Light Verse, An. *Louis Kronenberger, ed.* (c.1935) The Modern Library
AmP	American Poetry (American Literary Forms). *Karl Shapiro, ed.* (c.1960) Thomas Y. Crowell Company
AmPo	American Poetry (Living Masterpieces of American Literature, Vol. IV). *Randall Stewart and Dorothy Bethurum, eds.* (c.1954) Scott, Foresman and Company
AmPP	American Poetry and Prose. *Norman Foerster, ed.* (3d ed., c.1947; 4th ed., c.1957) Houghton Mifflin Company
AmSS	American Sea Songs and Chanteys. *Frank Shay, ed.* (c.1948) W. W. Norton & Company. Edition of 1924, published by Doubleday, Doran & Company, had title Iron Men and Wooden Ships
AnAmPo	Anthology of American Poetry, An. *Alfred Kreymborg, ed.* (2d rev. ed., 1941) Tudor Publishing Company. Edition of 1930 had title Lyric America. *See* LA
AnCL	Anthology of Contemporary Latin-American Poetry. *Dudley Fitts, ed.* (Rev. and enl. ed., c.1947) New Directions

AnEC — Ancient English Christmas Carols, MCCCC to MDCC. *Edith Rickert, ed.* (1928) Chatto & Windus

AnEnPo — Anthology for the Enjoyment of Poetry. *Max Eastman, ed.* (1939) Charles Scribner's Sons

AnFE — Anthology of Famous English and American Poetry, An. *William Rose Benét and Conrad Aiken, eds.* (c.1945) The Modern Library

AnFP — Anthology of French Poetry from Nerval to Valéry in English Translation, An. *Angel Flores, ed.* (1958) Doubleday Anchor Books

AnGP — Anthology of German Poetry from Hölderlin to Rilke in English Translation, An. *Angel Flores, ed.* (1960) Anchor Books

AnIL — Anthology of Irish Literature, An. *David H. Greene, ed.* (c.1954) The Modern Library

AnIV — Anthology of Irish Verse, An. *Padraic Colum, ed.* (Rev. ed., 1948) Liveright Publishing Corporation

AnMP — Anthology of Mexican Poetry. *Octavio Paz, comp.* (c.1958) Indiana University Press

AnNE — Anthology of the New England Poets, An; from Colonial Times to the Present Day. *Louis Untermeyer, ed.* (c.1948) Random House

AnNoLy — Anthology of Norwegian Lyrics. *Charles Wharton Stork, ed. and tr.* (1942) Princeton University Press, American-Scandinavian Foundation

AnNZ — Anthology of New Zealand Verse, An. *Robert Chapman and Jonathan Bennett, comps.* (1956) Oxford University Press

AnOE — Anthology of Old English Poetry, An. *Charles W. Kennedy, tr.* (1960) Oxford University Press

AnSL — Anthology of Swedish Lyrics, from 1750 to 1925. *Charles Wharton Stork, ed. and tr.* (1930) American-Scandinavian Foundation

AnSpL 1–2 — Anthology of Spanish Literature in English Translation, An, Vols. I–II. *Seymour Resnick and Jeanne Pasmantier, eds.* (c.1958) Frederick Ungar Publishing Company

AOAH — Armistice Day (Our American Holiday Series). *A. P. Sanford and Robert Haven Schauffler, eds.* (1927) Dodd, Mead & Company

APA — American Poetry, 1671–1928. *Conrad Aiken, ed.* (c.1929) The Modern Library. Revised edition of 1944 has title A Comprehensive Anthology of American Poetry. *See* CoAnAm

APW — American Poetry from the Beginning to Whitman. *Louis Untermeyer, ed.* (1931) Harcourt, Brace and Company

ArmLP — Armenian Legends and Poems. *Zabelle C. Boyajian, comp.* (1916, reissue, 1959) Columbia University Press

AS — American Songbag, The. *Carl Sandburg, comp.* (c.1927, reissue, 1936) Harcourt, Brace and Company

AtBAP — Atlantic Book of British and American Poetry, The. *Edith Sitwell, ed.* (c.1958) Little, Brown & Company

ATP — Approaches to Poetry. *Walter Blair and W. K. Chandler, eds.* (1935,

	2d ed., c.1953) D. Appleton-Century Company, *later pub. by* Appleton-Century-Crofts
AV	Answering Voice, The; Love Lyrics by Women. *Sara Teasdale, comp.* (New ed., 1928) The Macmillan Company
AWP	Anthology of World Poetry, An. *Mark Van Doren, ed.* (Rev. and enl. ed., 1936) Reynal & Hitchcock
BaBo	Ballad Book, The. *MacEdward Leach, ed.* (1955) Harper & Brothers
BANP	Book of American Negro Poetry, The. *James Weldon Johnson, ed.* (Rev. ed., 1931) Harcourt, Brace and Company
BAP	Book of American Poetry, The. *Edwin Markham, comp.* (1934) William H. Wise & Company. Included in Anthology of the World's Best Poems. *Edwin Markham, comp.* (Memorial ed., 6 vols., 1948) William H. Wise & Company
BAV	Book of American Verse, A (The World's Classics). *A. C. Ward, ed.* (1935) Oxford University Press
BBV	Boy's Book of Verse, The. *Helen Dean Fish, comp.* (1923, rev. ed., 1951) Frederick A. Stokes Company, *later pub. by* J. B. Lippincott Company
BCEP	Book of Classic English Poetry, The, 600–1830. *Edwin Markham, comp.* (1934) William H. Wise & Company. Included in Anthology of the World's Best Poems. *Edwin Markham, comp.* (Memorial ed., 6 vols., 1948) William H. Wise & Company
BEL	Book of English Literature, A. *Franklyn Bliss Snyder and Robert Grant Martin, eds.* (3d ed., 1933) The Macmillan Company
BeLS	Best Loved Story Poems. *Walter E. Thwing, ed.* (c.1941, reissue, 1948) Garden City Publishing Company
BePJ	Beautiful Poems on Jesus. *Basil Miller, comp.* (1948) Beacon Hill Press
BeR	Before the Romantics. *Geoffrey Grigson, ed.* (1946) George Routledge & Sons
BHV	Book of Heroic Verse, A (Everyman's Library). *Arthur Burrell, comp.* (1920) E. P. Dutton & Company
BLA	Bird-Lovers' Anthology, The. *Clinton Scollard and Jessie B. Rittenhouse, comps.* (1930) Houghton Mifflin Company
BlG	Blue and the Gray, The; the Best Poems of the Civil War. *Claudius Meade Capps, ed.* (c.1943) Bruce Humphries
BLP	Book of Living Poems, A. *William R. Bowlin, ed.* (1934) Albert Whitman & Company
BLPA	Best Loved Poems of the American People, The. *Hazel Felleman, ed.* (1936) Garden City Publishing Company
BLRP	Best Loved Religious Poems, The. *James Gilchrist Lawson, comp.* (1933) Fleming H. Revell Company
BLV	Book of Living Verse, The. *Louis Untermeyer, ed.* (c.1932) Har-

court, Brace and Company. For the revised editions of 1939 and 1945, *see* BoLiVe

BMEP Book of Modern English Poetry, The. *Edwin Markham, comp.* (1934) William H. Wise & Company. Included in Anthology of the World's Best Poems. *Edwin Markham, comp.* (Memorial ed., 6 vols., 1948) William H. Wise & Company

BoAN 1–2 Books of American Negro Spirituals, The; including The Book of American Negro Spirituals and The Second Book of Negro Spirituals. *James Weldon Johnson, ed.* (c.1925, 1926, 2 vols. in 1, 1940, reissue, 1944) The Viking Press

BoAu Book of Australian and New Zealand Verse, A. *Walter Murdoch, ed.* (Rev. ed., 1945, reissue, 1949) Oxford University Press. Edition of 1918 had title The Oxford Book of Australasian Verse

BoAV Book of Australian Verse, A. *Judith Wright, ed.* (1956) Oxford University Press

BoCaPo Book of Canadian Poetry, The. *A. J. M. Smith, ed.* (c.1943, rev. ed., c.1948) The University of Chicago Press

BoChLi Book of Children's Literature, A. *Lillian Hollowell, ed.* (c.1939, 2d ed., c.1950) Rinehart & Company

BoDaBa Book of Danish Ballads, A. *Axel Olrik, ed.* (1939) Princeton University Press, American-Scandinavian Foundation

BoDS Book of Danish Verse, A Second. *Charles Wharton Stork, tr.* (1947) Princeton University Press, American-Scandinavian Foundation

BoFr Book of Friendship, The. *Elizabeth Selden, comp.* (1947) Houghton Mifflin Company

BoHiPo Book of Historical Poems, A. *William R. Bowlin, comp.* (1939) Albert Whitman & Company

BOHV Book of Humorous Verse, The. *Carolyn Wells, comp.* (Rev. and enl. ed., 1934, reissue, 1947) Garden City Publishing Company

BOL Book of Lullabies, A. *Elva S. Smith, comp.* (c.1925) Lothrop, Lee & Shepard Company

BoLiVe Book of Living Verse, The. *Louis Untermeyer, ed.* (Rev. ed., c.1939, new [rev.] ed., c.1945) Harcourt, Brace and Company. For the edition of 1932, *see* BLV

BoN Book of Nonsense, The. *Roger Lancelyn Green, ed.* (c.1956) E. P. Dutton & Company

BoR Book of Russian Verse, A. *C. M. Bowra, ed.* (c.1943, reissue, 1947) Macmillan & Company

BoRS Book of Russian Verse, A Second. *C. M. Bowra, ed.* (1948) Macmillan & Company

BoSA Book of South African Verse, A. *Guy Butler, comp.* (1959) Oxford University Press

BoTP Book of a Thousand Poems, The. *Jeannie Murray MacBain, ed.* (1942) Evans Brothers

BoW	Book of the Winter, A. *Edith Sitwell, comp.* (c.1951) The Vanguard Press
BPN	British Poets of the Nineteenth Century. *Curtis Hidden Page and Stith Thompson, eds.* (New ed., 1929) Benj. H. Sanborn & Company
BPP	Book of Personal Poems, A. *William R. Bowlin, comp.* (1936) Albert Whitman & Company
BrBE	Broadway Book of English Verse, The; from the Fourteenth Century to the Present Day. *William Bowyer Honey, ed.* (4th ed., 1946) George Routledge & Sons. Edition of 1939 had title The Sacred Fire
BrR	Bridled with Rainbows. *Sara Brewton and John E. Brewton, eds.* (1949) The Macmillan Company
BSV	Book of Scottish Verse, A (The World's Classics). *R. L. Mackie, ed.* (1934) Oxford University Press
BTP	Book of Treasured Poems, A. *William R. Bowlin, comp.* (1928) Albert Whitman & Company
CaAE	Cassell's Anthology of English Poetry. *Margaret Flower and Desmond Flower, eds.* (2d ed., 1946) Cassell and Company
CAG	Cap and Gown; a Treasury of College Verse, Fourth Series. *R. L. Paget, comp.* (1931) L. C. Page & Company
CaP	Canadian Poetry in English (Canadian Literature Series). *Bliss Carman, Lorne Pierce, and V. B. Rhodenizer, eds.* (Rev. and enl. ed., c.1954) The Ryerson Press. Edition of 1935 had title Our Canadian Literature. *See* OCL
CAW	Catholic Anthology, The. *Thomas Walsh, ed.* (Rev. ed., 1932, reissue, 1939) The Macmillan Company
CBE	Chilswell Book of English Poetry, The. *Robert Bridges, comp.* (1924, reissue, 1937) Longmans, Green & Company
CBOV	College Book of Verse, The, 1250–1925. *Robert M. Gay, comp.* (1927) Houghton Mifflin Company. Same as Riverside Book of Verse
CBPC	Cambridge Book of Poetry for Children, The. *Kenneth Grahame, ed.* (1933) G. P. Putnam's Sons
CDC	Caroling Dusk; an Anthology of Verse by Negro Poets. *Countee Cullen, ed.* (1927) Harper & Brothers
CenHV	Century of Humorous Verse, A, 1850–1950 (Everyman's Library). *Roger Lancelyn Green, ed.* (1959) E. P. Dutton & Company
CenL	Century of Lyrics, A, 1550–1650. *D. C. Whimster, ed.* (1938) Edward Arnold & Company
CEP	Collection of English Poems, A, 1660–1800. *Ronald S. Crane, ed.* (1932) Harper & Brothers
CG	Children's Garland, The. *Coventry Patmore, comp.* (1862, reissue, 1906, 1930) The Macmillan Company
CH	Come Hither. *Walter de la Mare, comp.* (Rev. ed., 1928, new ed., 1948, 3d ed., 1957) Alfred A. Knopf

ChBR	Christmas Bells Are Ringing; a Treasury of Christmas Poetry. *Sara Brewton and John E. Brewton, eds.* (c.1951) The Macmillan Company
ChER	Choice of English Romantic Poetry, A. *Stephen Spender, ed.* (1947) The Dial Press
ChIP	Christ in Poetry. *Thomas Curtis Clark and Hazel Davis Clark, eds.* (c.1952) Association Press
ChLP	Chinese Love Poems. *D. J. Klemer, ed.* (c.1959) Doubleday & Company
ChMo	Chief Modern Poets of England and America. *Gerald DeWitt Sanders and John Herbert Nelson, eds.* (3d ed., c.1943) The Macmillan Company. For the edition of 1936, *see* CMP
ChMP	Chatto Book of Modern Poetry, The, 1915–1955. *C. Day Lewis and John Lehmann, eds.* (New ed., 1959) Chatto & Windus
ChrBoLe	Christmas Book of Legends and Stories, The. *Elva Sophronia Smith and Alice Isabel Hazeltine, eds.* (c.1944) Lothrop, Lee & Shepard Company. For the edition of 1915, *see* CLS
ChTr	Cherry-Tree, The. *Geoffrey Grigson, comp.* (c.1959) Phoenix House
CIV	Cat in Verse, The. *Carolyn Wells and Louella D. Everett, comps.* (1935) Little, Brown & Company
CLS	Christmas in Legend and Story. *Elva Sophronia Smith and Alice Isabel Hazeltine, eds.* (1915) Lothrop, Lee & Shepard Company. For the edition of 1944, *see* ChrBoLe
CMP	Chief Modern Poets of England and America. *Gerald DeWitt Sanders and John Herbert Nelson, eds.* (Rev. ed., 1936) The Macmillan Company. For the edition of 1943, *see* ChMo
COAH	Christmas (Our American Holidays Series). *Robert Haven Schauffler, ed.* (1907) Dodd, Mead & Company
CoAnAm	Comprehensive Anthology of American Poetry, A. *Conrad Aiken, ed.* (c.1944) The Modern Library. Edition of 1929 had title American Poetry, 1671–1928. *See* APA
CoBA	College Book of American Literature, A. *Milton Ellis, and others, eds.* (2d ed., c.1949) American Book Company
CoBE	College Book of English Literature. *James Edward Tobin, and others, comps.* (c.1949) American Book Company
CoBMV	College Book of Modern Verse, A. *James K. Robinson and Walter B. Rideout, eds.* (c.1958) Row, Peterson and Company
CoEV	Collected English Verse. *Margaret Bottrall and Ronald Bottrall, eds.* (1946) Sidgwick & Jackson
CoMu	Common Muse, The; an Anthology of Popular British Ballad Poetry, XVth–XXth Century. *Vivian de Sola Pinto and Allan Edwin Rodway, eds.* (1957) Philosophical Library
CoSo	Cowboy Songs and Other Frontier Ballads. *John A. Lomax and Alan*

	Lomax, eds. (Rev. and enl. ed., 1938, reissue, 1948) The Macmillan Company. For the edition of 1916, *see* CSF
CoSP	Contemporary Spanish Poetry; Selections from Ten Poets. *Eleanor L. Turnbull, tr.* (1945) The Johns Hopkins Press
CoV	Conscious Voice, The; an Anthology of American Poetry from the Seventeenth Century to the Present (The American Heritage Series). *Albert D. Van Nostrand and Charles H. Watts II, eds.* (c.1959) The Liberal Arts Press
CP	Contemporary Poetry. *Marguerite Wilkinson, ed.* (c.1923, reissue, 1942) The Macmillan Company
CPG	Canadian Poets. *John W. Garvin, ed.* (Rev. ed., 1926) McClelland & Stewart
CrMA	Criterion Book of Modern American Verse, The. *W. H. Auden, ed.* (c.1956) Criterion Books
CSF	Cowboy Songs and Other Frontier Ballads. *John A. Lomax, comp.* (New ed., 1916) The Macmillan Company. For the revised edition of 1944, *see* CoSo
CV	Contemporary Verse. *A. Marion Merrill and Grace E. W. Sprague, eds.* (New ed., 1936) Little, Brown & Company
DaM	Dark of the Moon; Poems of Fantasy and the Macabre. *August Derleth, ed.* (1947) Arkham House
DD	Days and Deeds; a Book of Verse. *Burton Egbert Stevenson and Elizabeth B. Stevenson, comps.* (1931) Doubleday, Doran & Company
DDA	Desk Drawer Anthology, The. *Alice Roosevelt Longworth and Theodore Roosevelt, comps.* (1937) Doubleday, Doran & Company
DiM	Distaff Muse, The; an Anthology of Poetry Written by Women. *Clifford Bax and Meum Stewart, comps.* (1949) Hollis & Carter
EBSV	Edinburgh Book of Scottish Verse, The, 1300–1900. *W. Macneile Dixon, ed.* (1910) Oxford University Press
EG	English Galaxy of Shorter Poems, The. *Gerald Bullett, ed.* (1934) The Macmillan Company
EiPP	Eighteenth Century Poetry and Prose. *Louis I. Bredvold, Alan D. McKillop, and Lois Whitney, eds.* (2d ed., c.1956) The Ronald Press Company
ElL	Elizabethan Lyrics. *Norman Ault, ed.* (3d ed., c.1949) William Sloane Associates. Paperback edition of 1960 published by G. P. Putnam's Sons
ElSeCe	Elizabethan and Seventeenth-Century Lyrics. *Matthew W. Black, ed.* (1938) J. B. Lippincott Company
EM 1–2	English Masterpieces, 700–1900, Vols. I–II. *H. W. Herrington, ed.* (Rev. ed., 1937) W. W. Norton & Company. Vol. I: From the Beginnings through the Eighteenth Century; Vol. II: The Nineteenth Century

EmBrPo — Eminent British Poets of the Nineteenth Century. *Paul Robert Lieder, ed.* (2 vols. in 1, 1938) Harper & Brothers

EnL — English Literature; a College Anthology. *Donald B. Clark, Leon T. Dickinson, Charles M. Hudson, and George B. Pace, eds.* (c.1960) The Macmillan Company

EnLi 1–2 — English Literature and Its Backgrounds, Vols. I–II. *Bernard D. N. Grebanier and Stith Thompson, eds.* (c.1939) *Bernard D. Grebanier, Samuel Middlebrook, Stith Thompson, and William Watt, eds.* (Rev. ed., c.1949) The Dryden Press

EnLit — English Literature; a Period Anthology. *Albert C. Baugh and George William McClelland, eds.* (c.1954) Appleton-Century-Crofts

EnLoPo — English Love Poems. *John Betjeman and Geoffrey Taylor, comps.* (1957) Faber and Faber

EnLP — English Lyric Poetry (Living Masterpieces of English Literature, Vol. III). *Dorothy Bethurum and Randall Stewart, eds.* (c.1954) Scott, Foresman and Company

EnRP — English Romantic Poetry and Prose. *Russell Noyes, ed.* (1956) Oxford University Press

EnSB — English and Scottish Ballads (The Poetry Bookshelf). *Robert Graves, ed.* (1957) The Macmillan Company

EnSW — English, Scottish, and Welsh Landscape, 1700–c.1860 (New Excursions into English Poetry). *John Betjeman and Geoffrey Taylor, comps.* (1944) Frederick Muller

EOAH — Easter (Our American Holidays Series). *Susan Tracy Rice and Robert Haven Schauffler, eds.* (1916) Dodd, Mead & Company

EPN — English Poetry of the Nineteenth Century. *G. R. Elliott and Norman Foerster, eds.* (1923, reissue, 1954) The Macmillan Company

EPP — English Prose and Poetry. *John Matthews Manly, comp.* (1926) Ginn and Company

EPS — English Poetry of the Seventeenth Century. *Roberta Florence Brinkley, ed.* (1936, rev. ed., c.1942) W. W. Norton & Company

ERP — English Romantic Poets. *James Stephens, Edwin L. Beck, and Royall H. Snow, eds.* (1933) American Book Company

ES — English Sonnets. *Arthur T. Quiller-Couch, ed.* (1936) Thomas Y. Crowell Company

ESPB — English and Scottish Popular Ballads. *Helen Child Sargent and George Lyman Kittredge, eds., from the collection of Francis James Child.* (c.1904, 1932, reissue, 1947) Houghton Mifflin Company

EtPaEn — Eternal Passion in English Poetry. *Edith Wharton and Robert Norton, comps.* (1939) D. Appleton-Century Company

EtS — Eternal Sea, The; an Anthology of Sea Poetry. *W. M. Williamson, ed.* (c.1946) Coward-McCann

EV 1–5 — English Verse (The World's Classics), Vols. I–V. *W. Peacock, ed.* (1928–1931) Oxford University Press. Vol. I: Early Lyrics to

Shakespeare; Vol. II: Campion to the Ballads; Vol. III: Dryden to Wordsworth; Vol. IV: Sir Walter Scott to Elizabeth Barrett Browning; Vol. V: Longfellow to Rupert Brooke

ExPo Exploring Poetry. *M. L. Rosenthal and A. J. M. Smith, eds.* (c.1955) The Macmillan Company

FaBoBe Family Book of Best Loved Poems, The. *David L. George, ed.* (c.1952) Hanover House

FaBoCh Faber Book of Children's Verse, The. *Janet Adam Smith, comp.* (1953) Faber and Faber

FaBoEn Faber Book of English Verse, The. *John Hayward, ed.* (1958) Faber and Faber

FaBoMo Faber Book of Modern Verse, The. *Michael Roberts, ed.* (2d ed., 1951, with a supplement of poems chosen by Anne Ridler) Faber and Faber

FaBoTw Faber Book of Twentieth Century Verse, The; an Anthology of Verse in Britain, 1900–1950. *John Heath-Stubbs and David Wright, eds.* (1953) Faber and Faber

FaFP Family Album of Favorite Poems, The. *P. Edward Ernest, ed.* (c.1959) Grosset & Dunlap

FAOV Father; an Anthology of Verse. *Margery Doud and Cleo M. Parsley, comps.* (1931) E. P. Dutton & Company

FaPON Favorite Poems Old and New. *Helen Ferris, ed.* (c.1957) Doubleday & Company

FiBHP Fireside Book of Humorous Poetry, The. *William Cole, ed.* (1959) Simon and Schuster

FiMAP Fifteen Modern American Poets. *George P. Elliott, ed.* (c.1956) Rinehart & Company

FiP Fifteen Poets; Chaucer to Arnold. (1941) Oxford University Press

FOAH Flag Day (Our American Holidays Series). *Robert Haven Schauffler, ed.* (1912) Dodd, Mead & Company

FoS Formal Spring; French Renaissance Poems. *R. N. Currey, tr.* (1950) Oxford University Press

FTB Four & Twenty Blackbirds. *Helen Dean Fish, ed.* (1937) Frederick A. Stokes Company, *later pub. by* J. B. Lippincott Company

GA Great Americans, as Seen by the Poets. *Burton Egbert Stevenson, ed.* (1933) J. B. Lippincott Company

GaP Gaily We Parade. *John E. Brewton, comp.* (c.1940, reissue, 1944) The Macmillan Company

GBV Girl's Book of Verse, The. *Mary Gould Davis, comp.* (1922, rev. ed., 1952) Frederick A. Stokes Company, *later pub. by* J. B. Lippincott Company

GDAH Graduation Day (Our American Holidays Series). *A. P. Sanford and Robert Haven Schauffler, eds.* (1930) Dodd, Mead & Company

GEPC Great English Poets. *Oscar James Campbell and J. F. A. Pyre, comps.* (1928) F. S. Crofts & Company

GFA Golden Flute, The. *Alice Hubbard and Adeline Babbitt, comps.* (c.1932) The John Day Company

GN Golden Numbers. *Kate Douglas Wiggin and Nora Archibald Smith, eds.* (1902) Doubleday, Doran & Company

GoBC Golden Book of Catholic Poetry, The. *Alfred Noyes, ed.* (c.1946) J. B. Lippincott Company

GoBP Golden Book of Poetry, The. *Jane Werner, ed.* (c.1949) Simon and Schuster

GoSl Golden Slippers; an Anthology of Negro Poetry for Young Readers. *Arna Bontemps, comp.* (4th ed., c.1941) Harper & Brothers

GoTL Golden Treasury of Longer Poems, The (Everyman's Library). *Ernest Rhys, ed.* (1939, rev. ed., 1949) J. M. Dent & Sons

GoTP Golden Treasury of Poetry, The. *Louis Untermeyer, ed.* (c.1959) Golden Press

GoTS Golden Treasury of Scottish Poetry, The. *Hugh MacDiarmid, ed.* (1941) The Macmillan Company

GoYe Golden Year, The; the Poetry Society of America Anthology, 1910–1960. *Melville Cane, John Farrar, and Louise Townsend Nicholl, eds.* (1960) The Fine Editions Press

GrCo 1–2 Great Companions, Vols. I–II. *Robert French Leavens and Mary Agnes Leavens, comps.* (1927–1941) The Beacon Press

GrL Greek Literature in Translation. *Whitney Jennings Oates and Charles Theophilus Murphy, eds.* (1944) Longmans, Green and Company

GrPE Greek Poetry for Everyman. *F. L. Lucas, ed. and tr.* (1951) The Macmillan Company

GrPo Greek Poets, The. *Moses Hadas, ed.* (c.1953) The Modern Library

GrR Greek Reader, The. *A. L. Whall, ed.* (1943) Doubleday, Doran & Company

GTBS Golden Treasury of the Best Songs and Lyrical Poems in the English Language. *Francis Palgrave, comp.* (1929) Oxford University Press

GTBS-D Golden Treasury of the Best Songs and Lyrical Poems in the English Language, The. *Francis Turner Palgrave, comp. With additional poems selected by C. Day Lewis.* (1954) William Collins Sons & Company

GTBS-W F. T. Palgrave's The Golden Treasury of the Best Songs and Lyrical Poems (A Mentor Book). *Revised and enlarged by Oscar Williams.* (c.1953) The New American Library

GTIV Golden Treasury of Irish Verse, A. *Lennox Robinson, ed.* (1925) The Macmillan Company

GTML Golden Treasury of Modern Lyrics, The. *Laurence Binyon, comp.* (New ed., 1924) The Macmillan Company

GTSE Golden Treasury (Everyman's Library). *Francis T. Palgrave, comp.* (1934) E. P. Dutton & Company

GTSL Golden Treasury of Songs and Lyrics, The. *Francis T. Palgrave, comp.* (Rev. and enl. ed., 2 vols. in 1, 1928, reissue, 1944) The Macmillan Company

HaMV Harrap Book of Modern Verse, The (Harrap's Modern English Series). *Maurice Wollman and Kathleen B. Parker, comps.* (1959) George G. Harrap & Company

HBMV Home Book of Modern Verse, The. *Burton Egbert Stevenson, ed.* (1925, 2d ed., c.1953) Henry Holt and Company

HBV Home Book of Verse, The. *Burton Egbert Stevenson, ed.* (6th ed., c.1926, 8th ed., c.1949, 2 vols.) Henry Holt and Company

HBVY Home Book of Verse for Young Folks, The. *Burton Egbert Stevenson, ed.* (Rev. and enl. ed., 1929) Henry Holt and Company

HeT Heroic Tales in Verse. *E. J. Pratt, ed.* (c.1941, reissue, 1945) The Macmillan Company of Canada

HH Highdays and Holidays. *Florence Adams and Elizabeth McCarrick, comps.* (1927) E. P. Dutton & Company

HiLiAm High Lights in American Literature. *Ola Pauline Srygley, and others, eds.* (c.1940) Banks Upshaw and Company

HiLiEn High Lights in English Literature. *Ola Pauline Srygley and Otsie Vernona Betts, eds.* (c.1940) Banks Upshaw and Company

HOAH Hallowe'en (Our American Holidays Series). *Robert Haven Schauffler, ed.* (1933) Dodd, Mead & Company

HoPM How Does a Poem Mean? (An Introduction to Literature, Part III). *John Ciardi, ed.* (c.1959) Houghton Mifflin Company

In Praise of Nuns. *See* PraNu

IAP Introduction to American Poetry, An. *Frederick C. Prescott and Gerald DeWitt Sanders, eds.* (1932) F. S. Crofts & Company

IcP Icelandic Poems and Stories. *Richard Beck, ed.* (c.1943) Princeton University Press, American-Scandinavian Foundation

IDAH Independence Day (Our American Holidays Series). *Robert Haven Schauffler, ed.* (1912) Dodd, Mead & Company

IHA I Hear America Singing. *Ruth Barnes, comp.* (1937) John C. Winston Company

ImOP Imagination's Other Place; Poems of Science and Mathematics. *Helen Plotz, comp.* (c.1955) Thomas Y. Crowell Company

InMe Innocent Merriment; an Anthology of Light Verse. *Franklin P. Adams, comp.* (c.1942) McGraw-Hill Book Company

InP Introduction to Poetry, An. *Jay B. Hubbell and John O. Beaty, eds.* (Rev. ed., c.1936, reissue, 1949) The Macmillan Company

InPo Introduction to Poetry. *Mark Van Doren, ed.* (c.1951) William Sloane Associates, *later pub. by* The Dryden Press

InvP Invitation to Poetry; a Round of Poems from John Skelton to Dylan

Thomas. *Lloyd Frankenberg, ed.* (1956) Doubleday & Company

IrPN Irish Poets of the Nineteenth Century (The Muses' Library). *Geoffrey Taylor, ed.* (c.1951) Harvard University Press

ISi I Sing of a Maiden; the Mary Book of Verse. *Sister M. Thérèse, ed.* (1947) The Macmillan Company

JAWP Junior Anthology of World Poetry, A. *Mark Van Doren and Garibaldi M. Lapolla, eds.* (1929) Albert & Charles Boni. *Same as* WBP

JKCP Joyce Kilmer's Anthology of Catholic Poets. *Joyce Kilmer, ed.* (New ed., 1926, reissue, 1939) Liveright Publishing Corporation. *With a new supplement by James Edward Tobin.* (c.1955) Doubleday & Company (Image Books). Edition of 1917 had title Dreams and Images; an Anthology of Catholic Poetry

KiLC Kings, Lords, & Commons; an Anthology from the Irish. *Frank O'Connor, ed. and tr.* (1959) Alfred A. Knopf

KN Knapsack, The; a Pocket-Book of Prose and Verse. *Herbert Read, ed.* (1939, 7th ed., 1947) George Routledge & Sons

LA Lyric America, 1630–1930. *Alfred Kreymborg, ed.* (1930) Coward-McCann. Revised editions of 1935 and 1941 have title An Anthology of American Poetry. *See* AnAmPo

LaA Late Augustans, The; Longer Poems of the Later Eighteenth Century (The Poetry Bookshelf). *Donald Davie, ed.* (c.1958) The Macmillan Company

LaNeLa Lays of the New Land; Stories of Some American Poets and Their Work. *Charlie May Simon, ed.* (c.1943) E. P. Dutton & Company

LaP Latin Poetry in Verse Translation; From the Beginnings to the Renaissance. *L. R. Lind, ed.* (c.1957) Houghton Mifflin Company

LauV Laughing Verse. *Fairfax Downey, comp.* (c.1946) Thomas Y. Crowell Company

LBAH Lincoln's Birthday (Our American Holidays Series). *Robert Haven Schauffler, ed.* (1909) Dodd, Mead & Company

LBAP Little Book of American Poets, The, 1787–1900. *Jessie B. Rittenhouse, ed.* (1915, reissue 1929) Houghton Mifflin Company

LBBV Little Book of Modern British Verse, The. *Jessie B. Rittenhouse, comp.* (1924) Houghton Mifflin Company

LBMV Little Book of Modern Verse, The. *Jessie B. Rittenhouse, ed.* (1913) Houghton Mifflin Company. *See also* SBMV *and* TBM

LBN Little Book of Necessary Nonsense, A. *Burges Johnson, comp.* (1929) Harper & Brothers

LEAP Le Gallienne Book of English and American Poetry, The. *Richard Le Gallienne, ed.* (2 vols. in 1, 1935) Garden City Publishing Company. First published, by Boni & Liveright, as The Le Gallienne Book of English Verse (c.1922) and The Le Gallienne Book of American Verse (c.1925)

LH Lyra Heroica. *William Ernest Henley, ed.* (1934) Charles Scribner's Sons

LHV Little Book of American Humorous Verse, A. *T. A. Daly, comp.* (1926) David McKay Company

LiA Limits of Art, The (Bollingen Series). *Huntington Cairns, ed.* (c.1948) Pantheon Books

LiBL Little Book of Limericks, The. *H. I. Brock, comp.* (c.1947) Duell, Sloan and Pearce

LiL Little Laughter, A. *Katherine Love, comp.* (c.1957) Thomas Y. Crowell Company

LiTA Little Treasury of American Poetry, A. *Oscar Williams, ed.* (1948) Charles Scribner's Sons

LiTB Little Treasury of British Poetry, A. *Oscar Williams, ed.* (1951) Charles Scribner's Sons

LiTG Little Treasury of Great Poetry, A, English and American. *Oscar Williams, ed.* (1947) Charles Scribner's Sons

LiTL Little Treasury of Love Poems, A. *John Holmes, ed.* (1950) Charles Scribner's Sons

LiTM Little Treasury of Modern Poetry, A, English and American. *Oscar Williams, ed.* (1946, rev. ed., c.1950) Charles Scribner's Sons

LiTW Little Treasury of World Poetry, A. *Hubert Creekmore, ed.* (1952) Charles Scribner's Sons

LO Love. *Walter de la Mare, ed.* (1946) William Morrow & Company

LoBV London Book of English Verse, The. *Herbert Read and Bonamy Dobrée, comps.* (1949, 2d rev. ed., 1952) The Macmillan Company

LoEn Love's Enchantment; Story Poems and Ballads. *Helen Ferris, comp.* (c.1944) Doubleday, Doran & Company

LoGBV Looking Glass Book of Verse, The. *Janet Adam Smith, comp.* (c.1959) Looking Glass Library. Revised edition of FaBoCh

LoPo Love Poems, Old and New. *Catharine Connell, comp.* (c.1943) Random House

LoPS Love Poems of Six Centuries. *Helen Husted, ed.* (c.1950) Coward-McCann

LPS 1–3 Library of Poetry and Song, Vols. I–III. *William Cullen Bryant, ed.* (Rev. and enl. ed., 1925) Doubleday, Doran & Company

LS Lyric South, The. *Addison Hibbard, ed.* (1928) The Macmillan Company

LyMA Lyrics of the Middle Ages. *Hubert Creekmore, ed.* (c.1959) Grove Press

LyPI Lyric Poetry of the Italian Renaissance; an Anthology with Verse Translations. *L. R. Lind, comp.* (1954) Yale University Press

MaC Magic Circle, The; Stories and People in Poetry. *Louis Untermeyer, ed.* (c.1952) Harcourt, Brace and Company

MAP Modern American Poetry. *Louis Untermeyer, ed.* (5th rev. ed., c.1936) Harcourt, Brace and Company. For the sixth and seventh revised editions, *see* MoAmPo

MAPA Modern American Poets. *Conrad Aiken, ed.* (1927) The Modern Library. Enlarged edition of 1944 has title Twentieth-Century American Poetry. *See* TwAmPo

MaPo Major Poets, The; English and American. *Charles M. Coffin, ed.* (c.1954) Harcourt, Brace and Company

MaRV Masterpieces of Religious Verse. *James Dalton Morrison, ed.* (c.1948) Harper & Brothers

MBP Modern British Poetry. *Louis Untermeyer, ed.* (4th rev. ed., c.1936) Harcourt, Brace and Company. For the fifth and sixth revised editions, *see* MoBrPo

MC My Country. *Burton Egbert Stevenson, ed.* (1932) Houghton Mifflin Company

MCCG Magic Casements. *George S. Carhart and Paul A. McGhee, comps.* (1926, reissue, 1948) The Macmillan Company

MDAH Memorial Day (Our American Holidays Series). *Robert Haven Schauffler, ed.* (1911) Dodd, Mead & Company

MeEV Medieval English Verse and Prose, in Modernized Versions. *Roger Sherman Loomis and Rudolph Willard, eds.* (c.1948) Appleton-Century-Crofts

MeLP Metaphysical Lyrics & Poems of the Seventeenth Century. *Herbert J. C. Grierson, ed.* (1921, reissue, 1947) Oxford University Press

MeMeAg Merry Meet Again. *Elizabeth Hough Sechrist, ed.* (c.1941) Macrae-Smith-Company

MePo Metaphysical Poets, The. *Helen Gardner, ed.* (c.1957) Penguin Books

MeRV Mentor Book of Religious Verse, The. *Horace Gregory and Marya Zaturenska, eds.* (c.1956) The New American Library

MiAP Mid-Century American Poets. *John Ciardi, ed.* (c.1950) Twayne Publishers

MiCF Mid-Century French Poets. *Wallace Fowlie, ed. and tr.* (c.1955) Twayne Publishers

MiFP Mirror for French Poetry, A, 1840–1940. *Cecily Mackworth, ed.* (1947) George Routledge & Sons

MM Modern Muse, The. Published for the English Association. (1934) Oxford University Press

MoAB Modern American & Modern British Poetry. *Louis Untermeyer, ed., in consultation with Karl Shapiro and Richard Wilbur.* (Rev., shorter ed., c.1955) Harcourt, Brace and Company

MOAH Mothers' Day (Our American Holidays Series). *Susan Tracy Rice, comp., Robert Haven Schauffler, ed.* (1915) Dodd, Mead & Company

MoAmPo Modern American Poetry. *Louis Untermeyer, ed.* (6th rev. ed., c.1942; mid-century ed. [7th rev. ed.], c.1950) Harcourt, Brace and Company. For the fifth revised edition, *see* MAP

MOAP Masterpieces of American Poets. *Mark Van Doren, ed.* (1936) Garden City Publishing Company. Editions of 1932 and 1940, published by Little, Brown & Company, have title American Poets, 1630–1930

MoAuPo Modern Australian Poetry. *H. M. Green, comp.* (2d ed., rev., 1952) Melbourne University Press

MOB Magic of Books, The (Our American Holidays Series). *A. P. Sanford and Robert Haven Schauffler, eds.* (1929) Dodd, Mead & Company

MoBrPo Modern British Poetry. *Louis Untermeyer, ed.* (5th rev. ed., c.1942; mid-century ed. [6th rev. ed.], c.1950) Harcourt, Brace and Company. For the fourth revised edition, *see* MBP

MoGP Modern Greek Poetry. *Rae Dalven, tr. and ed.* (c.1949) Gaer Associates

MooP Moorish Poetry; a Translation of The Pennants, an Anthology Compiled in 1243 by the Andalusian Ibn Sa'id. *A. J. Arberry, ed. and tr.* (1953) Cambridge University Press

MoP Modern Poet, The. *Gwendolen Murphy, ed.* (1938, reissue, 1947) Sidgwick & Jackson

MoPo Modern Poetry; American and British. *Kimon Friar and John Malcolm Brinnin, eds.* (c.1951) Appleton-Century-Crofts

MoPW Modern Poets' World, The (The Poetry Bookshelf). *James Reeves, ed.* (1957) William Heinemann

MoShBr Moon Is Shining Bright as Day, The; an Anthology of Good-humored Verse. *Ogden Nash, ed.* (c.1953) J. B. Lippincott Company

MoSiPe More Silver Pennies. *Blanche Jennings Thompson, comp.* (c.1938) The Macmillan Company

MotAn Mothers' Anthology, The. *William Lyon Phelps, comp.* (1941) Doubleday, Doran & Company

MoVE Modern Verse in English, 1900–1950. *David Cecil and Allen Tate, eds.* (c.1958) The Macmillan Company

MoWP Modern Welsh Poetry. *Keidrych Rhys, ed.* (1954) Faber and Faber

MPB My Poetry Book. *Grace Thompson Huffard, Laura Mae Carlisle, and Helen Ferris, comps.* (1934, rev. ed., c.1956) John C. Winston Company

MuM Music Makers, The; an Anthology of Recent American Poetry. *Stanton A. Coblentz, comp.* (c.1945) Bernard Ackerman

MuP Music of Poetry, The. *Alfred H. Body, comp.* (1940) Thomas Nelson & Sons

MW Magic World, A. *Margery Gordon and Marie B. King, eds.* (1930) D. Appleton–Century Company

MyFE My Favourite English Poems. *John Masefield, ed.* (1950) The Macmillan Company

NA Nonsense Anthology, A. *Carolyn Wells, ed.* (c.1930) Charles Scribner's Sons. Paperback edition of 1958 published by Dover Publications

NAMP New Anthology of Modern Poetry, A. *Selden Rodman, ed.* (1938) Random House, *later pub. by* The Modern Library

NBE New Book of English Verse, The. *Charles Williams, and others, eds.* (1936) The Macmillan Company

NeAP New American Poetry, The, 1945–1960. *Donald M. Allen, ed.* (c.1960) Grove Press

NeBP New British Poets, The. *Kenneth Rexroth, ed.* (1949) New Directions

NeHB New Home Book of Best Loved Poems, The. *Richard Charlton MacKenzie, ed.* (c.1946) The Blakiston Company

NeIP New Irish Poets. *Devin A. Garrity, ed.* (1948) The Devin-Adair Company

NeLNL New Land, New Language; an Anthology of Australian Verse. *Judith Wright, comp.* (1957) Oxford University Press

NeMA New Modern American & British Poetry, The. *Louis Untermeyer, ed.* (Mid-century ed. [4th ed.], c.1950) Harcourt, Brace and Company

NePA New Pocket Anthology of American Verse from Colonial Days to the Present, The. *Oscar Williams, ed.* (c.1955) World Publishing Company

NePoAm New Poems by American Poets. *Rolfe Humphries, ed.* (1953) Ballantine Books

NePoAm-2 New Poems by American Poets #2. *Rolfe Humphries, ed.* (1957) Ballantine Books

NePoEA New Poets of England and America. *Donald Hall, Robert Pack, and Louis Simpson, eds.* (c.1957) Meridian Books

NeTW New Treasury of War Poetry, The; Poems of the Second World War. *George Herbert Clarke, ed.* (c.1943) Houghton Mifflin Company

NLK Nature Lover's Knapsack, The. *Edwin Osgood Grover, ed.* (c.1927, enl. ed., c.1947) Thomas Y. Crowell Company

NoCaPo North Carolina Poetry. *Richard Gaither Walser, ed.* (c.1941, rev. ed., 1951) Garrett & Massie

NP New Poetry, The. *Harriet Monroe and Alice Corbin Henderson, eds.* (New ed., rev. and enl., 1932, reissue 1947) The Macmillan Company

NV New Voices. *Marguerite Wilkinson, ed.* (New ed., rev. and enl., 1928) The Macmillan Company

OAEP Oxford Anthology of English Poetry, An. *Howard Foster Lowry and Willard Thorp, eds.* (c.1935, 2d ed., 1956) Oxford University Press

OBAV Oxford Book of American Verse, The. *Bliss Carman, ed.* (1927, reissue, 1935) Oxford University Press. For the edition of 1950, edited by F. O. Matthiessen, *see* OxBA

OBB Oxford Book of Ballads, The. *Arthur Quiller-Couch, ed.* (1910, reissue, 1927, 1946) Oxford University Press

OBEC Oxford Book of Eighteenth Century Verse, The. *David Nichol Smith, ed.* (1926) Oxford University Press

OBEV Oxford Book of English Verse, The. *Sir Arthur Quiller-Couch, ed.* (1st ed., 1900, new ed., rev. and enl., 1939) Oxford University Press

OBMV Oxford Book of Modern Verse, The, 1892–1935. *William Butler Yeats, ed.* (1936) Oxford University Press

OBRV Oxford Book of Regency Verse, The, 1798–1837. *H. S. Milford, ed.* (1928) Oxford University Press. Edition of 1935 has title Oxford Book of English Verse of the Romantic Period, 1798–1837

OBS Oxford Book of Seventeenth Century Verse, The. *H. J. C. Grierson and G. Bullough, eds.* (1934) Oxford University Press

OBSC Oxford Book of Sixteenth Century Verse, The. *E. K. Chambers, comp.* (1932) Oxford University Press

OBVV Oxford Book of Victorian Verse, The. *Arthur Quiller-Couch, comp.* (1912, reissue, 1925) Oxford University Press

OCL Our Canadian Literature. *Bliss Carman and Lorne Pierce, eds.* (Rev. ed., 1935) The Ryerson Press. Revised edition of 1954 has title Canadian Poetry in English. *See* CaP

OHFP One Hundred and One Famous Poems. *Roy J. Cook, comp.* (1929, rev. ed., c.1958) Reilly & Lee Company

OHIP Our Holidays in Poetry. *Mildred P. Harrington and Josephine H. Thomas, comps.* (1929, reissue, 1935, 1950) The H. W. Wilson Company

OlF Old Favorite Songs and Hymns. *Richard Charlton MacKenzie, ed.* (c.1946) Garden City Publishing Company

OnAP 100 American Poems (A Penguin Signet Book). *Selden Rodman, ed.* (c.1948) The New American Library

OnCuPl Onions and Cucumbers and Plums; 46 Yiddish Poems in English. *Sarah Zweig Betsky, ed.* (1958) Wayne State University Press

OnHM 100 Modern Poems. *Selden Rodman, comp.* (1949) Pellegrini & Cudahy

OnHT One Hundred and Ten Favorite Children's Poems. *H. G. Platt, ed.* (c.1943) Reilly & Lee Company

OnPC One Hundred Poems from the Chinese. *Kenneth Rexroth, tr.* [1956] New Directions

OnPJ One Hundred Poems from the Japanese. *Kenneth Rexroth, tr.* [1955] New Directions

OnPM One Thousand and One Poems of Mankind; Memorable Short Poems from the World's Chief Literatures. *Henry W. Wells, comp.* (c.1953) Tupper and Love

OnPP 100 Poems about People. *Elinor Parker, comp.* (c.1955) Thomas Y. Crowell Company

OnSP 100 Story Poems. *Elinor Parker, comp.* (c.1951) Thomas Y. Crowell Company

OnYI 1000 Years of Irish Poetry. *Kathleen Hoagland, ed.* (c.1947) The Devin-Adair Company

OQP 1000 Quotable Poems. *Thomas Curtis Clark, ed.* (1937) Willett, Clark and Company, *later pub. by* Harper & Brothers. *Includes* QP-1 *and* QP-2

OtMeF Other Men's Flowers. *A. P. Wavell, Earl Wavell, comp.* (1944) Jonathan Cape

OTPC One Thousand Poems for Children. *Roger Ingpen, ed.* (Rev. and enl. ed., 1923) *Elizabeth Hough Sechrist, ed.* (1946) Macrae-Smith-Company

OuHeWo Our Heritage of World Literature. *Stith Thompson and John Gassner, eds.* (Rev. ed., c.1942, 2 books in 1) The Dryden Press. Book One, Literature in Translation; Book Two, Literature in Our Own Tongue. Also published separately

OuSiCo Our Singing Country; a Second Volume of American Ballads and Folk Songs. *John A. Lomax and Alan Lomax, comps.* (1941, reissue, 1949) The Macmillan Company

OxBA Oxford Book of American Verse, The. *F. O. Matthiessen, ed.* (1950) Oxford University Press. For the edition of 1927, edited by Bliss Carman, *see* OBAV

OxBG Oxford Book of Greek Verse in Translation, The. *T. F. Higham and C. M. Bowra, eds.* (1938) Oxford University Press

OxBI Oxford Book of Irish Verse, The; XVIIth Century–XXth Century. *Donagh MacDonagh and Lennox Robinson, comps.* (1958) Oxford University Press

OxBoCh Oxford Book of Christian Verse, The. *Lord David Cecil, ed.* (1940) Oxford University Press

OxBoLi Oxford Book of Light Verse, The. *W. H. Auden, ed.* (1938, repr., with corr., 1939) Oxford University Press

OxNR Oxford Nursery Rhyme Book, The. *Iona Opie and Peter Opie, comps.* (1955) Oxford University Press

PA Parody Anthology, A. *Carolyn Wells, comp.* (1904) Charles Scribner's Sons

PaA Patriotic Anthology, The. *Introduced by Carl Van Doren.* (c.1941) Doubleday, Doran & Company

PAH Poems of American History. *Burton Egbert Stevenson, ed.* (Rev. ed., 1922) Houghton Mifflin Company

PaOS Pageant of Old Scandinavia, A. *Henry Goddard Leach, ed.* (1946) Princeton University Press, American-Scandinavian Foundation

PAP Poems of American Patriotism. *Brander Matthews, ed.* (Rev. and enl. ed., 1922) Charles Scribner's Sons

PC Poetry Cure, The. *Robert Haven Schauffler, comp.* (1925) Dodd, Mead & Company

PCD Poet's Craft, The *Helen Fern Daringer and Anne Thaxter Eaton, comps.* (1935) World Book Company

PCH Poems for the Children's Hour. *Josephine Bouton, comp.* (c.1927, 1945). The Platt & Munk Company

PCN Poems, Chiefly Narrative. *W. L. MacDonald and F. C. Walker, eds.* (New rev. ed., 1938, reissue 1945) J. M. Dent & Sons. Edition of 1925 had title Narrative English Poems

PeBoSo Penguin Book of Sonnets, The. *Carl Withers, ed.* (1943) Penguin Books

PECK Poems Every Child Should Know. *Mary E. Burt, ed.* (1904) Grosset & Dunlap

PeCV Penguin Book of Canadian Verse, The. *Ralph Gustafson, ed.* (c.1958) Penguin Books

PEDC Pieces for Every Day the Schools Celebrate. *Norma H. Deming and Katharine I. Bemis, comps.* (Enl. ed. 1931, rev. and enl. ed., 1949) Noble & Noble, Publishers

PEOR Pieces for Every Occasion. *Caroline B. Le Row, comp.* (Rev. and enl. ed., 1927) Noble & Noble, Publishers

PeP Persian Poems; an Anthology of Verse Translations (Everyman's Library). *A. J. Arberry, ed.* (1954) J. M. Dent & Sons

PFE Poems for Enjoyment. *Elias Lieberman, ed.* (1931) Harper & Brothers

PFY Poems for Youth. *William Rose Benét, comp.* (1925) E. P. Dutton & Company

PG Poet's Gold. *David Ross, ed.* (c.1933, rev. and enl. ed., 1945) The Macaulay Company, *later pub. by* Dial Press. (2d rev. ed., 1956) The Devin-Adair Company

PGD Poems for the Great Days. *Thomas Curtis Clark and Robert Earle Clark, comps.* (c.1948) Abingdon-Cokesbury Press

PIAE Poetry: Its Appreciation and Enjoyment. *Louis Untermeyer and Carter Davidson, eds.* (1934) Harcourt, Brace and Company

PIR Poems I Remember. *John Kieran, comp.* (c.1942, reissue, 1945) Doubleday, Doran & Company

Po Poem, The; a Critical Anthology. *Josephine Miles, ed.* (1959) Prentice-Hall

PoC Poet's Cat, The. *Mona Gooden, comp.* (1946) George G. Harrap & Company

PoD Poems of Death (New Excursions into English Poetry). *Phoebe Pool, comp.* (1945) Frederick Muller

PoE Poems in English, 1530–1940. *David Daiches and William Charvat, eds.* (c.1950) The Ronald Press Company

PoEL 1–5 Poets of the English Language, Vols. I–V. *W. H. Auden and Norman*

Holmes Pearson, eds. (1950) The Viking Press. Vol. I: Langland to Spenser; Vol. II: Marlowe to Marvell; Vol. III: Milton to Goldsmith; Vol. IV: Blake to Poe; Vol. V: Tennyson to Yeats

PoeMoYo Poems for Modern Youth. *Adolph Gillis and William Rose Benét, eds.* (c.1938) Houghton Mifflin Company

PoeT Poems of To-Day. Published for the English Association. (1915, reissue, 1948) Sidgwick & Jackson

PoF Poetry of Flight, The. *Selden Rodman, ed.* (c.1941) Duell, Sloan and Pearce

PoFr Poetry of Freedom, The. *William Rose Benét and Norman Cousins, eds.* (c.1945) Random House, *later pub. by* The Modern Library

PoFS Poems for Study; a Critical and Historical Introduction. *Leonard Unger and William Van O'Connor, eds.* (c.1953) Rinehart & Company

PoHN Poems of the Hundred Names; a Short Introduction to Chinese Poetry. *Henry H. Hart, ed.* (3d ed., c.1954) Stanford University Press. Originally published in 1933 as The Hundred Names

PoLFOT Poetry from Literature for Our Time, Third Edition. *Harlow O. Waite and Benjamin P. Atkinson, eds.* (c.1958) Henry Holt and Company

PoLi Poetry and Life; an Anthology of English Catholic Poetry. *F. J. Sheed, comp.* (1942) Sheed and Ward

PoLJ Poetry of Living Japan, The. *Takamichi Ninomiya and D. J. Enright, eds.* [1958] Grove Press

PoMa Poems for a Machine Age. *Horace J. McNeil, ed.* (c.1941) McGraw-Hill Book Company. Edition of 1949, published by the Globe Book Company, has title Living Poetry

PoMS Poems of Magic and Spells. *William Cole, ed.* (c.1960) World Publishing Company

PoN Poetry Now. *G. S. Fraser, ed.* (1956) Faber and Faber

PoNe Poetry of the Negro, The, 1746–1949. *Langston Hughes and Arna Bontemps, eds.* (1949) Doubleday & Company

PoOW Poems of the Old West; a Rocky Mountain Anthology. *Levette J. Davidson, ed.* (c.1951) The University of Denver Press

PoP Poet Physicians; an Anthology of Medical Poetry Written by Physicians. *Mary Lou McDonough, comp.* (1945) Charles C Thomas, Publisher

PoRA Poems to Read Aloud. *Edward Hodnett, ed.* (c.1957) W. W. Norton & Company

PoRh Pocketful of Rhymes, A. *Katherine Love, ed.* (c.1946) Thomas Y. Crowell Company

PoRL Poems for Red Letter Days. *Elizabeth Hough Sechrist, comp.* (c.1951) Macrae Smith Company

POT Poems of Today. *Alice Cecilia Cooper, ed.* (1924) Ginn and Company. For new enlarged edition of 1939, *see* PoTo

POTE Poems of Our Time, 1900–1942 (Everyman's Library). *Richard Church and M. M. Bozman, eds.* (1945) J. M. Dent & Sons

Poems of Our Time, 1900–1960 (Everyman's Library). *Richard Church, Mildred Bozman, and Edith Sitwell, eds.* (1959) J. M. Dent & Sons

PoTo Poems of Today. *Alice Cecilia Cooper, ed.* (New enl. ed., c.1939) Ginn and Company. For the edition of 1924, *see* POT

PoToHe Poems That Touch the Heart. *A. L. Alexander, comp.* (c.1941, new, enl. ed., c.1956) Garden City Publishing Company

POTT Poetry of the Transition, 1850–1914. *Thomas Marc Parrott and Willard Thorp, eds.* (1932) Oxford University Press

PoVP Poetry of the Victorian Period. *George Benjamin Woods and Jerome Hamilton Buckley, eds.* (Rev. ed., c.1955) Scott, Foresman and Company

PPL Pinafore Palace. *Kate Douglas Wiggin and Nora Archibald Smith, eds.* (1907) Doubleday, Doran & Company

PR Patrician Rhymes. *Clinton Scollard and Jessie B. Rittenhouse, eds.* (1932) Houghton Mifflin Company

PraNu Praise of Nuns, In. *James M. Hayes, ed.* (c.1942) E. P. Dutton & Company

PraP Prayer Poems. *O. V. Armstrong and Helen Armstrong, comps.* (c.1942) Abingdon-Cokesbury Press

PreP Preface to Poetry. *Charles W. Cooper, in consultation with John Holmes.* (c.1946) Harcourt, Brace and Company

PrPoCR Prose and Poetry of the Continental Renaissance in Translation. *Harold Hooper Blanchard, ed.* (2d ed., 1955) Longmans, Green and Company

PrWP Presenting Welsh Poetry. *Gwyn Williams, ed.* (c.1959) Faber and Faber

PRWS Posy Ring, The. *Kate Douglas Wiggin and Nora Archibald Smith, eds.* (1903, reissue, 1935) Doubleday, Doran & Company

PSO Poems for Special Days and Occasions. *Thomas Curtis Clark, comp.* (1930) Harper & Brothers

PTA 1–2 Poems Teachers Ask For, Vols. I–II. [1925?] F. A. Owen Publishing Company

PtOT Poets of Our Time. *Eric Gillett, comp.* (1932, reissue, 1939) Thomas Nelson and Sons

PtP Poet to Poet; a Treasury of Golden Criticism. *Houston Peterson and William S. Lynch, eds.* (1945) Prentice-Hall

PtPa Poets of the Pacific; Second Series. *Yvor Winters, ed.* (c.1949) Stanford University Press

PYM Poetry of Youth. *Edwin Markham, comp.* (1935) William H. Wise

& Company. Included in Anthology of the World's Best Poems. *Edwin Markham, comp.* (Memorial ed., 6 vols., 1948) William H. Wise & Company

QP 1–2 Quotable Poems, Vols. I–II. *Thomas Curtis Clark and Esther A. Gillespie, comps.* (1928–1931) Willett, Clark and Company. For the one-volume edition, *see* OQP

QS Questing Spirit, The; Religion in the Literature of Our Time. *Halford E. Luccock and Frances Brentano, eds.* (c.1947) Coward-McCann

RAR Ring-a-Round. *Mildred P. Harrington, comp.* (1930) The Macmillan Company

REAL Readings in English and American Literature. *Gerald E. Seboyar, comp.* (2d ed., c.1945) F. S. Crofts & Company

ReaPo Reading Poems. *Wright Thomas and Stuart Gerry Brown, eds.* (1941) Oxford University Press

ReEn Renaissance England; Poetry and Prose from the Reformation to the Restoration. *Roy Lamson and Hallett Smith, eds.* (c.1956) W. W. Norton & Company. Edition of 1942 had title The Golden Hind

ReIE Renaissance in England, The; Non-dramatic Prose and Verse of the Sixteenth Century. *Hyder E. Rollins and Herschel Baker, comps.* (c.1954) D. C. Heath and Company

ReMP Reading Modern Poetry (Key Editions). *Paul Engle and Warren Carrier, eds.* (c.1955) Scott, Foresman and Company

ReTS Reciter's Treasury of Scenes and Poems, The. *Ernest Guy Pertwee, ed.* (1934, reissue, 1946) George Routledge & Sons

RG Rainbow Gold. *Sara Teasdale, comp.* (1922) The Macmillan Company

RiBV Rinehart Book of Verse, The. *Alan Swallow, ed.* (c.1952) Rinehart & Company

RIS Rainbow in the Sky. *Louis Untermeyer, ed.* (c.1935) Harcourt, Brace and Company

RO Romantics, The. *Geoffrey Grigson, ed.* (1942) George Routledge & Sons

RoL Roman Literature in Translation. *George Howe and Gustave Adolphus Harrer, eds.; revised by Albert Suskin.* (Rev. ed., c.1959) Harper & Brothers

RuPo Russian Poetry, 1917–1955. *Jack Lindsay, ed. and tr.* (1957) The Bodley Head

SaFP Saint Francis and the Poet; Poems on Saint Francis of Assisi, 1200 A.D. to the Present. *Elizabeth B. Patterson, ed.* (1956) The Devin-Adair Company

SAS Sugar and Spice. *Mary Wilder Tileston, comp.* (1928, reissue, 1942) Little, Brown & Company

SaSa	Saucy Sailor and Other Dramatized Ballads, The. *Alice M. G. White and Janet E. Tobitt, comps.* (1940) E. P. Dutton & Company
SBMV	Second Book of Modern Verse, The. *Jessie B. Rittenhouse, ed.* (1919) Houghton Mifflin Company. *See also* LBMV *and* TBM
	Second Book of Danish Verse, A. *See* BoDS
	Second Treasury of the Familiar, A. *See* TreFS
SCC	Songs of the Cattle Trail and Cow Camp. *John A. Lomax, comp.* (c.1919, new ed., 1950) The Macmillan Company, *later pub. by* Duell, Sloan and Pearce
SDH	Stardust and Holly; Poems and Songs of Christmas. *Dorothy Middlebrook Shipman, comp.* (1932) The Macmillan Company
SeCePo	Seven Centuries of Poetry; Chaucer to Dylan Thomas. *A. N. Jeffares, ed.* (1955) Longmans, Green & Company
SeCeV	Seven Centuries of Verse, English & American. *A. J. M. Smith, ed.* (2d ed., rev. and enl., c.1957) Charles Scribner's Sons
SeCL	Seventeenth Century Lyrics. *Norman Ault, ed.* (2d ed., c.1950) William Sloane Associates
SeCSL	Seventeenth Century Songs and Lyrics. *John P. Cutts, ed.* (1959) University of Missouri Press
SeCV 1–2	Seventeenth-Century Verse and Prose, Vols. I–II. *Helen C. White, Ruth C. Wallerstein, and Ricardo Quintana, eds.* (c.1951, 1952) The Macmillan Company. Vol. I: 1600–1660; Vol. II: 1660–1700
SeEP	Seventeenth-Century English Poetry (The Harper English Literature Series). *R. C. Bald, ed.* (c.1959) Harper & Brothers
SG	Sailor's Garland, A. *John Masefield, ed.* (New ed., 1924) The Macmillan Company
ShBV 1–4	Sheldon Book of Verse, The, Books I–IV. *P. G. Smith and J. F. Wilkins, comps.* (1959) Oxford University Press
ShGoBo	Shorter Golden Book of Narrative Verse, The. *Frank Jones, ed.* (1943) Blackie & Son
ShS	Shantymen and Shantyboys; Songs of the Sailor and Lumberman. *William Main Doerflinger, comp.* (1951) The Macmillan Company
SiB	Silver Branch, The; a Collection of the Best Old Irish Lyrics, Variously Translated. *Seán O'Faoláin, comp.* (1938) The Viking Press
SiCE	Sixteenth-Century English Poetry (The Harper English Literature Series). *Norman E. McClure, ed.* (c.1954) Harper & Brothers
SiPS	Silver Poets of the Sixteenth Century (Everyman's Library). *Gerald Bullett, ed.* (1947) J. M. Dent and Sons
SiSoSe	Sing a Song of Seasons. *Sara Brewton and John E. Brewton, eds.* (c.1955) The Macmillan Company
SiTL	Silver Treasury of Light Verse, The (A Mentor Book). *Oscar Williams, ed.* (c.1957) The New American Library
SN	Songs of Nature. *John Burroughs, comp.* (1901) Garden City Publishing Company. Edition of 1938 has title Book of Songs of Nature

SoAF	Songs of American Folks. *Satis N. Coleman and Adolph Bregman, eds.* (c.1942) The John Day Company
SoAmSa	Songs of American Sailormen. *Joanna C. Colcord, ed.* (Enl. and rev. ed., c.1938) W. W. Norton & Company. Edition of 1924, published by the Bobbs-Merrill Company, had title Roll and Go, Songs of American Sailormen
SoLD	Songs from the Land of Dawn. *Lois J. Erickson, tr.* (c.1949) Friendship Press
SoV	Soldiers' Verse (New Excursions into English Poetry). *Patric Dickinson, comp.* (1945) Frederick Muller
SP	Silver Pennies. *Blanche Jennings Thompson, comp.* (1925) The Macmillan Company
SPP	Southern Poets. *Edd Winfield Parks, ed.* (1936) American Book Company
StaSt	Stars to Steer By. *Louis Untermeyer, ed.* (c.1941) Harcourt, Brace and Company
StDa	Steamboatin' Days; Folk Songs of the River Packet Era. *Mary Wheeler, comp.* (1944) Louisiana State University Press
StJW	Story of Jesus in the World's Literature, The. *Edward Wagenknecht, ed.* (c.1946) Creative Age Press
StPo	Story Poems, New and Old. *William Cole, ed.* (c.1957) World Publishing Company
StVeCh	Story and Verse for Children. *Miriam Blanton Huber, ed.* (c.1940, reissue, 1947; rev. ed., c.1955) The Macmillan Company
SUS	Sung under the Silver Umbrella. *Association for Childhood Education.* (1935) The Macmillan Company
TBM	Third Book of Modern Verse, The. *Jessie B. Rittenhouse, ed.* (1927) Houghton Mifflin Company. *See also* LBMV *and* SBMV
TCAP	Three Centuries of American Poetry and Prose. *Alphonso Gerald Newcomer, Alice E. Andrews, and Howard Judson Hall, eds.* (Rev. ed., 1929) Scott, Foresman and Company
TCEP	Twelve Centuries of English Poetry and Prose. *Alphonso Gerald Newcomer, Alice E. Andrews, and Howard Judson Hall, comps.* (Rev. ed., 1928) Scott, Foresman and Company
TCPD	Twentieth-Century Poetry. *John Drinkwater, Henry Seidel Canby, and William Rose Benét, eds.* (1929) Houghton Mifflin Company
TeCS	Ten Centuries of Spanish Poetry; an Anthology in English Verse with Original Texts. *Eleanor L. Turnbull, ed.* (c.1955) The Johns Hopkins Press
ThWaDe	This Way, Delight; a Book of Poetry for the Young. *Herbert Read, ed.* (c.1956) Pantheon Books
TIP	Treasury of Irish Poetry, A. *Stopford A. Brooke and T. W. Rolleston, eds.* (Rev. and enl. ed., 1932) The Macmillan Company

TiPo	Time for Poetry. *May Hill Arbuthnot, comp.* (General ed., c.1952, rev. ed., c.1959) Scott, Foresman and Company
TMEV	Treasury of Middle English Verse; Selected and Rendered into Modern English. *Margot Robert Adamson, comp.* (1930) E. P. Dutton & Company
TOAH	Thanksgiving (Our American Holidays Series). *Robert Haven Schauffler, ed.* (1907) Dodd, Mead & Company
TOP	Types of Poetry. *Jacob Zeitlin and Clarissa Rinaker, comps.* (1926, reissue, 1946) The Macmillan Company
TrAS	Treasury of American Song, A. *Olin Downes and Elie Siegmeister, comps.* (2d ed., rev. and enl., 1943) Alfred A. Knopf
TrCh	Translations from the Chinese. *Arthur Waley, tr.* (c.1941) Alfred A. Knopf
TreF	Treasury of the Familiar, A. *Ralph L. Woods, ed.* (c.1942, reissue, 1945) The Macmillan Company
TreFS	Treasury of the Familiar, A Second. *Ralph L. Woods, ed.* (1950) The Macmillan Company
TrFP	Treasury of French Poetry, A. *Alan Conder, ed. and tr.* [1951] Harper & Brothers
TrGrPo	Treasury of Great Poems, English and American, A. *Louis Untermeyer, ed.* (1942, rev. and enl. ed., 1955) Simon and Schuster
TriL	Triumph of Life, The; Poems of Consolation for the English-speaking World. *Horace Gregory, ed.* (c.1943) The Viking Press
TrJP	Treasury of Jewish Poetry, A. *Nathan Ausubel and Marynn Ausubel, eds.* (c.1957) Crown Publishers
TrPWD	Treasury of Poems for Worship and Devotion, A. *Charles L. Wallis, ed.* (c.1959) Harper & Brothers
TrRV	Treasury of Russian Verse, A. *Avrahm Yarmolinsky, ed.* (1949) The Macmillan Company
TSW	This Singing World. *Louis Untermeyer, ed.* (1923) Harcourt, Brace and Company
TSWC	This Singing World for Younger Children. *Louis Untermeyer, ed.* (1926) Harcourt, Brace and Company
TuPP	Tudor Poetry and Prose. *J. William Hebel, Hoyt H. Hudson, Francis R. Johnson, A. Wigfall Green, and Robert Hoopes, eds.* (c.1953) Appleton-Century-Crofts. Copyright (in part) 1929 by F. S. Crofts & Company under title Poetry of the English Renaissance
TVC	Treasury of Verse for Little Children, A. *M. G. Edgar, ed.* (Rev. and enl. ed., 1927, new ed., 1946) Thomas Y. Crowell Company
TVSH	Treasury of Verse for School and Home, A. *M. G. Edgar and Eric Chilman, comps.* (1936) Grosset & Dunlap
TwAmPo	Twentieth-Century American Poetry. *Conrad Aiken, ed.* (c.1944) The Modern Library. Edition of 1927 had title Modern American Poets. *See* MAPA

TwCaPo Twentieth Century Canadian Poetry. *Earle Birney, ed.* (c.1953) The Ryerson Press

TwCrTr Two Creative Traditions in English Poetry. *Seymour M. Pitcher, and others, eds.* (1939) Farrar & Rinehart

TwCV Twentieth Century Verse. *Ira Dilworth, ed.* (1945) Clarke, Irwin & Company

TwGV Twentieth-Century German Verse. *Herman Salinger, ed. and tr.* (1952) Princeton University Press

TwHP Two Hundred Poems. *Ricardo Quintana, ed.* (1947) Longmans, Green and Company

TwP 12 Poets. *Glenn Leggett, ed.* (c.1958) Rinehart & Company

TwSpPo 12 Spanish American Poets. *H. R. Hays, ed. and tr.* (1943) Yale University Press

TyEnPo Types of English Poetry. *Rudolf Kirk and Clara Marburg Kirk, eds.* (1940) The Macmillan Company

UnPo Understanding Poetry. *Cleanth Brooks and Robert Penn Warren, eds.* (c.1938, 3d ed., c.1960) Henry Holt and Company, *later pub. by* Holt, Rinehart and Winston

UnS Untune the Sky; Poems of Music and the Dance. *Helen Plotz, comp.* (c.1957) Thomas Y. Crowell Company

UnW Unseen Wings; the Living Poetry of Man's Immortality. *Stanton A. Coblentz, comp.* (1949) The Beechhurst Press

UTS Under the Tent of the Sky. *John E. Brewton, comp.* (1937) The Macmillan Company

VA Victorian Anthology, A, 1837–1895. *Edmund Clarence Stedman, ed.* (c.1895) Houghton Mifflin Company

ViBoFo Viking Book of Folk Ballads of the English-speaking World, The. *Albert B. Friedman, ed.* (1956) The Viking Press

ViBoPo Viking Book of Poetry of the English-speaking World, The. *Richard Aldington, ed.* (c.1941; rev., mid-century ed., 1959, in 2 vols.) The Viking Press

ViP Victorian Poetry; Clough to Kipling. *Arthur J. Carr, ed.* (c.1959) Rinehart & Company

ViPo Victorian Poetry. *E. K. Brown, ed.* (1942) Thomas Nelson and Sons

ViPP Victorian Poetry and Poetics. *Walter E. Houghton and G. Robert Stange, eds.* (c.1959) Houghton Mifflin Company

VLEP Victorian and Later English Poets. *James Stephens, Edwin L. Beck, and Royall H. Snow, eds.* (1934) American Book Company

VOD Verse of Our Day. *Margery Gordon and Marie B. King, eds.* (Rev. ed., c.1931, 2d rev. ed., c.1935) Appleton-Century-Crofts

WaaP War and the Poet . . . from Ancient Times to the Present. *Richard Eberhart and Selden Rodman, eds.* (1945) The Devin-Adair Company

WaKn Way of Knowing, A; a Collection of Poems for Boys. *Gerald D. McDonald, comp.* (c.1959) Thomas Y. Crowell Company

WaL Wagon of Life, The, and Other Lyrics by Russian Poets of the Nineteenth Century. *Sir Cecil Kisch, tr.* (1947) Oxford University Press

WaP War Poets, The; an Anthology of the War Poetry of the 20th Century. *Oscar Williams, ed.* (c.1945) The John Day Company

WBLP World's Best-loved Poems, The. *James Gilchrist Lawson, comp.* (1927) Harper & Brothers

WBP World's Best Poems, The. *Mark Van Doren and Garibaldi M. Lapolla, eds.* (c.1929, 1946) Albert & Charles Boni, *later pub. by* The World Publishing Company. *Same as* JAWP

WGRP World's Great Religious Poetry, The. *Caroline Miles Hill, ed.* (1934) The Macmillan Company

WHA Winged Horse Anthology, The. *Joseph Auslander and Frank Ernest Hill, eds.* (1929) Doubleday, Doran & Company

WhBS Where Birds Sing. *Ada L. F. Snell, comp.* (c.1959) Bookman Associates

WhC What Cheer; an Anthology of American and British Humorous and Witty Verse. *David McCord, ed.* (c.1945) Coward-McCann

WHL With Harp and Lute. *Blanche Jennings Thompson, comp.* (1935) The Macmillan Company

WhP White Pony, The; an Anthology of Chinese Poetry from the Earliest Times to the Present Day. *Robert Payne, ed.* (c.1947) The John Day Company

WOAH Washington's Birthday (Our American Holidays Series). *Robert Haven Schauffler, ed.* (1910) Dodd, Mead & Company

WoL World Literature. *Arthur E. Christy and Henry W. Wells, eds.* (c.1947) American Book Company

WP Way of Poetry. *John Drinkwater, comp.* (1922) Houghton Mifflin Company

YaCaBo Yale Carol Book, The. *H. Frank Bozyan and Sidney Lovett, eds.* (1944) Yale University Press

YaD Yankee Doodles. *Ted Malone, ed.* (c.1943) McGraw-Hill Book Company. Edition of 1948, published by the Garden City Publishing Company, has title The All-American Book of Verse

YeAr Year Around, The; Poems for Children. *Alice I. Hazeltine and Elva S. Smith, comps.* (c.1956) Abingdon Press

YT Yesterday and Today. *Louis Untermeyer, ed.* (c.1926) Harcourt, Brace and Company

WaKn — Way of Knowing, A; a Collection of Poems for Boys. *Gerald D. McDonald, comp.* (c.1959) Thomas Y. Crowell Company

WaL — Wagon of Life, The, and Other Lyrics by Russian Poets of the Nineteenth Century. *Sir Cecil Kisch, tr.* (1947) Oxford University Press

WaP — War Poets, The: an Anthology of the War Poetry of the 20th Century. *Oscar Williams, ed.* (c.1945) The John Day Company

WBLP — World's Best-loved Poems, The. *James Gilchrist Lawson, comp.* (1927) Harper & Brothers

WBP — World's Best Poems, The. *Mark Van Doren and Garibaldi M. Lapolla, eds.* (c.1929, 1946) Albert & Charles Boni, later pub. by The World Publishing Company. Same as LiWP?

WGRP — World's Great Religious Poetry, The. *Caroline Miles Hill, ed.* (1934) The Macmillan Company

WHA — Winged Horse Anthology, The. *Joseph Auslander and Frank Ernest Hill, eds.* (1929) Doubleday, Doran & Company

WhBS — Where Birds Sing. *Ada L. F. Snell, comp.* (c.1959) Bookman Associates

WhC — What Cheer; an Anthology of American and British Humorous and Witty Verse. *David McCord, ed.* (c.1945) Coward-McCann

WHL — With Harp and Lute. *Blanche Jennings Thompson, comp.* (1935) The Macmillan Company

WhP — White Pony, The; an Anthology of Chinese Poetry from the Earliest Times to the Present Day. *Robert Payne, ed.* (c.1947) The John Day Company

WOAH — Washington's Birthday (Our American Holidays Series). *Robert Haven Schauffler, ed.* (1910) Dodd, Mead & Company

WoL — World Literature. *Arthur E. Christy and Henry W. Wells, eds.* (c.1947) American Book Company

WP — Way of Poetry. *John Drinkwater, comp.* (1922) Houghton Mifflin Company

YaCaBo — Yale Carol Book, The. *H. Frank Bozyan and Sidney Lovett, eds.* (1944) Yale University Press

YaD — Yankee Doodles. *Ted Malone, ed.* (c.1943) McGraw-Hill Book Company. Edition of 1948, published by the Garden City Publishing Company, has title The All American Book of Verse.

YeAr — Year Around, The; Poems for Children. *Alice I. Hazeltine and Elva S. Smith, comps.* (c.1956) Abingdon Press

YT — Yesterday and Today. *Louis Untermeyer, ed.* (c.1926) Harcourt, Brace and Company

TITLE AND FIRST LINE INDEX

A, A, A, A,/ Nunc Gaudet Ecclesia. *Unknown.* AnEC
A, A, A, A,/ Nunc Gaudet Maria. *Unknown.* *See* Nunc Gaudet Maria.
A. A violent order is disorder. Connoisseur of Chaos. Wallace Stevens. LiTM (rev. ed.); MoPo; Po
A. Apple Pie. Edward Lear. *See* Nonsense Alphabet, A ("A was once an apple-pie").
A, B, C. Charles Stuart Calverley. *See* Alphabet, The.
A. B. C., An [*or* The]. Chaucer. CoBE
(La Prière de Nostre Dame, *mod. vers. by* Anselm M. Townsend.) ISi
Well of Pity, The, *sel.* PoLi
A B C. Eliza Cook. OTPC (1923 ed.)
A B C. *Unknown, tr. fr. German.* SAS
A B C Bunny, The. Wanda Gág. TiPo
A B C D. *Unknown.* OxNR
A, B, C, D, E, F, G,/ Little Robin Redbreast sitting on a tree. *Unknown.* OxNR
A, B, C, D, E, F, G. The Alphabet. *Unknown.* PCH
A B C you know. A B C. *Unknown, tr. fr. German.* SAS
A B C's in Green. Leonora Speyer. DD; HBMV; HBVY; NLK; OHIP; OQP; QP-1
A black, E white, I red, U green, O blue. Vowels. Arthur Rimbaud, *tr. by* Louise Varèse. AnFP
A black, E white, I red, U green, O blue—I'll tell. Voyels. Arthur Rimbaud, *tr. by* Norman Cameron. MiFP
A. C. S. Alexander M. Stephen. CPG
A celuy que pluys eyme en mounde. Lines from Love Letters. *Unknown.* OBEV (new ed.)
A Clymène. Paul Verlaine, *tr. fr. French by* Arthur Symons. AWP; JAWP; WBP
A Cushla Gal Mo Chree. Michael Doheny. TIP
A Dieu! and Au Revoir. John Oxenham. MaRV
A dis, a dis, a green grass. Green Grass. *Unknown.* BoTP; CH; LO; OxBoLi; OxNR
A.E.F. Carl Sandburg. CoBA; HBMV; MAP; MoAB; MoAmPo; TCAP; WaaP
A. E. Housman and a Few Friends. Humbert Wolfe. FiBHP; WhC
A E I O U. Swift. BoTP
A Fauxbourg. George Croly. *Fr.* Paris in 1815. OBRV
A for Apple, big and red. The A B C Bunny. Wanda Gág. TiPo
A for the animals out in the stable. An Alphabet of Christmas. *Unknown.* ChBR
A! [*or* Ah!] fredome [*or* freedom] is a noble thing! Freedom. John Barbour. *Fr.* The Bruce. BSV; EBSV; EV-1; FaBoCh; GoTS· LoGBV; OBEV; PoFr; TrGrPo; ViBoPo
A Ha Ha Ha! This World Doth Passe. *Unknown.* AtBAP; PoEL-2
(Idle Fyno.) ChTr
A ho! A ho!/ Love's horn doth blow. Love Goes a-Hawking [*or* Song]. Thomas Lovell Beddoes. *Fr.* The Bride's Tragedy. ChER; VA
A. "I was a Have." B. "I was a 'Have-not.'" "Equality of Sacrifice." Kipling. *Fr.* Epitaphs of the War. FaBoTw; OAEP (2d ed.)
A is an angel of blushing eighteen. The Alphabet [*or* A, B, C]. Charles Stuart Calverley. HBV; SiTL
A is an apple, sour and green. *Unknown.* WhC
A is for Acting, the shantyboys' life. The Shantyboys' Song. Kenneth Zwicker. ShS
A Is for Alpha: Alpha Is for A. Conrad Aiken. NePA
A is for apple tree, sweet with bloom. Arbor Day Alphabet. Ada Simpson Sherwood. ADAH
A is for ax, and that we all know. The Lumberman's Alphabet. *Unknown.* ShS
A is to begin with, and A began with Adam. Genesis of Vowels. James Broughton. CrMA
A. J. J. A. E. Housman. More Poems, XLII. BoFr
A Jovino: El Melancólico, *abr.* Juan Meléndez Valdés, *tr. fr. Spanish by* Elizabeth Selden. BoFr
A. L. G. William Channing Gannett. GrCo-2
A la Belle Etoile. Sara Hamilton Birchall. NLK
A la Carte. Kenneth Fearing. ChMo
A-la-lo, my son is a beauty! *Unknown.* BOL
A la Malibran. Alfred de Musset. *See* Malibran.
A la promenade. Paul Verlaine, *tr. fr. French by* Arthur Symons. AWP
A Mhic, ná Meabhraigh Eigse. *Unknown, tr. fr. Irish by* Máire MacEntee. OxBI
"A, my dere, a, my dere Son." Mary Weeps for Her Child. *Unknown.* OxBoLi
A! My Herte, A! What Aileth The. Sir Thomas Wyatt. AtBAP
A putta putta putt. Riding in a Motor Boat. Dorothy W. Baruch. FaPON; MPB
A Quoi Bon Dire. Charlotte Mew. HBMV
A. R. U., *with music.* *Unknown.* AS
A sè stesso. Giacomo Leopardi, *tr. fr. Italian by* Lorna de' Lucchi. AWP; JAWP; WBP
A Solis Ortus Cardine. Ford Madox Ford. ViBoPo
A soun tres chere et special. Lines from Love Letters. *Unknown.* OBEV (new ed.)
A Terre. Wilfred Owen. LiTM (rev. ed.); WaP
A' the boys of merry Lincoln. Hugh of Lincoln. *Unknown.* OBB
A was an ape. Nonsense Alphabet. Edward Lear. SAS
A was an apple-pie;/ B bit it. Mother Goose. BoChLi; OTPC; OxNR; PCH
A was an apple pie. The Alphabet. Kate Greenaway. HBVY
A was an archer, who shot at a frog. Tom Thumb's Alphabet. *Unknown.* HBV; HBVY; OTPC; OxNR; SiTL
A was once an apple-pie. Nonsense Alphabet [*or* A. Apple Pie]. Edward Lear. PPL; SUS; TiPo
A ye wha are sae guid yoursel. *See* O ye wha are sae guid yoursel.
Aa the skippers of bonny Lothen. Young Allan. *Unknown.* ESPB
Aage and Else. *Unknown, tr. fr. Danish by* E. M. Smith-Dampier. BoDaBa
(Aager and Eliza, *tr. unknown.*) LyMA
Aaron. George Herbert. MeLP; MePo; OAEP; OBS; PoFS; TwCrTr
Aaron Burr. Stephen Vincent Benét. InMe
Aaron Burr's Wooing. Edmund Clarence Stedman. GA; PAH
Aaron Hatfield. Edgar Lee Masters. *Fr.* Spoon River Anthology. LiTA; NP
Aaron Stark. E. A. Robinson. MoAB; MoAmPo (1950 ed.); TwP
Aastrid. Kristofer Janson, *tr. fr. Norwegian by* Charles W. Stork. AnNoLy
Abalone, *with music.* *Unknown.* AS
Abandonado, El, *with music.* *Unknown, tr. fr. Spanish by* Frank Dobie. ABF; AS
Abandoned. Madison Cawein. YT
Abandoned Adobe, An. Rose Henderson. VOD
Abandoned Brothel. C. R. Holmes. PtPa
Abandoned Dog, The. Théodore Agrippa d'Aubigné, *tr. fr. French by* Elizabeth Selden. BoFr
Abandoned on the beach. Yosano Akiko, *tr. fr. Japanese by* Kenneth Rexroth. LiTW
Abandoned Roads. Amy May Rogers. DDA
Abandoned Towpath, An. Elias Lieberman. PFE; PoeMoYo
Abandoning an Alien Country. Pushkin, *tr. fr. Russian by* Babette Deutsch. TrRV
(To ——: "Bound for your far-off native shore," *tr. by* Maurice Baring.) BoR
Abba-labba-lá. David Stefánsson, *tr. fr. Icelandic by* Skuli Johnson. IcP
Abbé Liszt, The/ Hit the piano with his fist. Liszt. E. C. Bentley. *Fr.* Biography for Beginners. UnS
Abbess, The ("The abbess was of noble blood"). Sir Walter Scott. *Fr.* Marmion, II. GoBC; PraNu
Abbey, The. José M. Eguren, *tr. fr. Spanish by* Thomas Walsh. CAW
Abbey Asaroe. William Allingham. GTIV; OnYI; OxBI
Abbey Walk, The. Robert Henryson. BSV
Abbie Ben Adams, *parody.* Carolyn Wells. CIV
Abbot, The, *sel.* Sir Walter Scott.
Life. BPN
Abbot arose, and closed his book, The. The Red Fisherman. Winthrop Mackworth Praed. PCN
Abbot of Canterbury, The. *Unknown.* *See* King John and the Abbot of Canterbury.
Abbot of Derry, The. John Bennett. HBMV; TBM
Abbot of Inisfalen, The. William Allingham. GN; HBV; MW
Abbreviated Interviews with a Few Disgruntled Literary Celebrities. Reed Whittemore. FiBHP
Abdelazer, *sel.* Aphra Behn.
Song: "Love in fantastic [*or* fantastique] triumph sate [*or*

Abdelazer (*continued*)
satt].” AtBAP· EV-3; HBV; OBEV; TrGrPo; ViBoPo
(Love Armed.) ElSeCe; SeCL
(Love in Fantastic[k] Triumph [Sate].) DiM; OAEP; OnPM
(Song: Love Arm'd [*or* Armed].) CaAE; CoEV; OBS
Abdication of Fergus Mac Roy, The. Sir Samuel Ferguson. AnIL
Abdul A-Bul-Bul A-Mir. *Unknown.* TreF
(Abdul, the Bulbul Ameer, *with music.*) AS
(Abdullah Bulbul Amir.) BLPA; StPo
(Ballade of Ivan Petrofsky Skevar, Ye, *with music.*) ABF
Abdul Aziz one day. Scurvy Entertainment. Abu Abd Allah. MooP
Abe Lincoln stood at the White House gate. Lord Lovel (B *vers., parody*). *Unknown.* ViBoFo
Abel. Demetrios Capetanakis. AtBAP; WaaP
Abel, my brother, you sleep. Cain and Abel. Itzik Manger. OnCuPl
Abélard Tells His Love to Héloïse. Herbert E. Palmer. POTE
Abelard was: God is. Sic et Non. Herbert Read. FaBoTw
Abenamar, Abenamar. *Unknown, tr. fr. Spanish by* Robert Southey. AnSpL-1; AWP; OuHeWo
(Abenamar, *tr. by* James Young Gibson.) TeCS
Abertawy. Walter Savage Landor. EmBrPo
Abhrain an Bhuideil. Joseph Sheridan Le Fanu. *See* Drunkard to His Bottle, A.
Abide in Me, *sel.* Harriet Beecher Stowe.
“Soul alone, like a neglected harp, The.” ChIP
Abide with Me. Henry F. Lyte. BCEP, *sel.;* BLRP; BPP; FaBoBe; FaFP; HBV; MaRV; NeHB; PECK; TreF; VA; WBLP; WGRP
(“Abide with me: fast falls the eventide.”) OlF
Abide with me, O Christ; Thou must not go. It Is toward Evening. *Unknown.* BePJ
Abide with Us. Horatius Bonar. BePJ; VA
Abiding Love, The. John White Chadwick. BLPA; FaBoBe; NeHB
(Auld Lang Syne.) MaRV; WGRP
Abishag. Jacob Fichman, *tr. fr. Hebrew by* Sholom J. Kahn. TrJP
Abishag. Rainer Maria Rilke, *tr. fr. German by* Jethro Bithell. AWP
Abishag. André Spire, *tr. fr. French by* Emanuel Eisenberg. TrJP
Abla. Antara, *tr. fr. Arabic by* E. Powys Mathers. *Fr.* The Mu'allaqát. AWP; JAWP; LiTW; WBP
Abnegation. Christina Rossetti. *See* If There Be Any One.
Aboard at a Ship's Helm. Walt Whitman. MOAP; NePA; OxBA
Aboard the *Sea-Swallow.* Edward Dowden. TIP
Aboard this trolley I become again. Rush Hour. Joachim Smet. QS
Abode Divine. Al-Rusafi, *tr. fr. Arabic by* A. J. Arberry. MooP
Abode of the nightingale is bare, The. Alone. Walter de la Mare. ChTr; EnLoPo
Abolitionist, The. Robert Conquest. PoN
Abolitionist Hymn, *with music. Unknown.* TrAS
Abominable Snow Men, The. Frank Belknap Long. DaM
Aboriginal Mother's Lament, An. Charles Harpur. MOAH; VA
Aboriginal Sin. John Hay. NePoAm-2
Abortive tears! Thaw. Jean Starr Untermeyer. AtBAP
Abou Ben Adhem. Leigh Hunt. BCEP; BeLS; BLPA; BoFr; BTP; CaAE; CBE; CBPC; CG; DD; EnLi-2; EnRP; EPN; ERP; EV-4; FaBoBe; FaFP; GBV (1952 ed.); GN; GoTP; GrCo-1; HBV; HBVY; HiLiEn; LEAP; LPS-3; MaRV; MCCG; MW; NeHB; OBEV (new ed.); OBVV; OHFP; OnHT; OnSP; OQP; OTPC; PC; PECK; PIR; PTA-1; PYM; QP-1; RIS; StVeCh (1940 ed.); TCEP; TreF; TVSH; WBLP; WGRP
(Abou Ben Adhem and the Angel.) EnLit; FaPON
Abou Ben Adhem's name led all the rest. Holy Order. J. B. Boothroyd. FiBHP
About a fierce highwayman my story I will tell. Brennan on the Moor. *Unknown.* OuSiCo
About a well-spring, in a little mead. Of Three Damsels in a Meadow. John Payne. OBVV
About an Allegory. Walter Conrad Arensberg. AnAmPo; LA
About ane bank, where birdis on bewis. May-Morn and Cupid. Alexander Montgomerie. *Fr.* The Cherry and the Slae. EBSV; GoTS
About Animals. Hilda Conkling. UTS
About Buttons. Dorothy Aldis. MoSiPe
About fifty years since, in the days of our daddies. Paddy's Metamorphosis. Thomas Moore. OnYI
About Glenkindie and his man. Glenkindie. William Bell Scott. HBV; VA
About her head or floating feet. My Father's Child. “Stuart Sterne.” AA
About him was a ruinous fair place. Sir William Watson. *Fr.* The Prince's Quest. BMEP
About his brow the laurel and the bay. A Man. Clinton Scollard. OHIP; PEDC
About its lip winds ivy, ivy flecked. The Cup. Theocritus. *Fr.* Idylls. OxBG
About me the night, moonless, wimples the mountains. Vancouver Lights. Earle Birney. CaP; TwCV
About my temples go triumphant bays. Ovid. *Fr.* Elegies. ReIE
About Savannah. *Unknown.* PAH
About suffering they were never wrong. Musée des Beaux Arts. W H. Auden. ChMo; ChMP; CoBMV; EnL; ExPo; FaFP; LiTB; LiTG; LiTM; MaPo; MoAB; MoPo; NePA; OAEP (2d ed.); PG (1955 ed.); PoFS; PoLFOT; PoRA; SeCePo; SeCeV; TrGrPo (rev. ed.); TwHP
About the august and ancient Square. Oxford Nights. Lionel Johnson. EnLit
About the chambers of my heart. *See* About the little chambers of my heart.
About the chilly, ragged lawns they lie. Autumn Leaves. Minnie Case Hopkins. OQP; QP-2
About the dog days folks complain. A Dog Day. Rachel Field. SiSoSe
About the Fairies. Jean Ingelow. BoTP
About the fashions of the day. Hug Me Tight. John Kendall. WhC
About the field they piped right. Tyrle, Tyrlow, Tyrle, Tyrlow. *Unknown.* AnEC; MeRV
About the flowerless land adventurous bees. Spring Song. John Davidson. BMEP
About the heights, soft clouds, a few. Alfred Domett. *Fr.* Ranolf and Amohia. AnNZ
About the hilltop how the clouds are cool. Summer Days. Roy Daniells. CaP
About the holy Cittie rowles a flood. Giles Fletcher. *Fr.* Christ's Victory and Triumph: Christ's Triumph after Death. EPS
About the little chambers of my heart. Gone. Mary Elizabeth Coleridge. HBV; MBP; OBEV (new ed.); OBVV; OQP; QP-2; TOP
About the Shark, phlegmatical one. The Maldive Shark. Herman Melville. AmP; AmPP (4th ed.); APW; LoGBV; NePA; OxBA; PoEL-5; PoFS
About the Shelleys. *Unknown, quoted by* Wordsworth. WhC
About the sweet bag of a bee. The Bag of the Bee. Robert Herrick. OAEP
About the time of Christmas. Jane Conquest. *Unknown.* PTA-1
About the time when Christ was born. Baile and Aillinn. W. B. Yeats. GTML
About the year of one B.C. Jonah and the Whale. *Unknown.* BLPA
About their prince each took his wonted seat. Pluto's Council. Tasso. *Fr.* Godfrey of Bulloigne. OBSC
About This, *sel.* Vladimir Mayakovsky, *tr. fr. Russian by* Jack Lindsay.
Man Seven Years Standing, The. RuPo
About this lady many fruitful trees. The Lady with the Unicorn. Vernon Watkins. LiTB
About this time when dusk falls like a shutter. Adolescents in the Dusk. Iain Fletcher. FaBoMo
About thy roseate cheeks is floating. Lydia. Leconte de Lisle. TrFP
About with this brimmer my bullyes. *Unknown.* SeCSL
About Women. H. Phelps Putnam. AnFE; CoAnAm; MAP; MoAmPo (1942 ed.); TwAmPo
About Yule, when the wind blew cool [*or* cule]. Young Waters. *Unknown.* EBSV; EnLit; ESPB; OBB; ReaPo; TOP
Above, a mountain ten thousand feet high. Alarm at First Entering the Yang-tze Gorges. Po Chü-i. TrCh
Above a rough altar, coarse cement all. La Mambo dans le Hounfort. Charles F. Pressoir. PoNe
Above a Snow. Juan Ramón Jiménez, *tr. fr. Spanish by* Eleanor L. Turnbull. TeCS
Above a stretch of still unravaged weald. The Garden Party. Donald Davie. NePoEA
Above a world entrapped by fear. The Forgotten Star. Thomas Curtis Clark. PGD
Above and below the ship, this blue. Becalmed. John Blight. BoAV
Above, below, in sky and sod. The Over-Heart. Whittier. OQP; QP-2; WGRP
Above dark cities build. To Young Dreamers. Lucia Trent. OQP; QP-2
Above his grave the grass and snow. Longfellow. Thomas Bailey Aldrich. GA
Above lone woodland ways that led. The Whippoorwill. Madison Cawein. MW
Above me passed an angel winged and white. Apparition. Victor Hugo. TrFP
Above me the abbey, grey arches on the cliff. Cædmon. Norman Nicholson. FaBoTw
Above my face is a map. The Cloud-Mobile. May Swenson. GoTP

Above my head the shields are stained with rust. The Lamp of Poor Souls. Marjorie Pickthall. CPG; HBV; TwCV
Above on the bare mountain. Little Town. Federico García Lorca. CoSP; OnPM
Above our isle. Surprise. *Unknown.* SoLD
Above St. Irénée. Duncan Campbell Scott. VA
Above Salerno. Ada Foster Murray. HBV
Above the Battle. Mark Van Doren. MOAP
Above the Battle's Front. Vachel Lindsay. StJW
Above the cannon's roar we hear His voice. Look Up. Martha Snell Nicholson. BePJ
Above the city, where I dwell, guarding it close, runs an embattled wall. The City Wall. Eunice Tietjens. NP
Above the cloistral valley. The Sleeper. Clinton Scollard. HBV; MuM; OBAV
Above the clouds. The Moon. Azumamaro. OnPM
Above the Crags that fade and gloom. From a Window in Princes Street. W. E. Henley. BPN; POTT
Above the crestward-climbing pines. The Trumpet of the Dawn. Clinton Scollard. NLK
Above the Dark. Jarl Hemmer, *tr. fr. Swedish by* Charles W. Stork. AnSL
Above the Dock. T. E. Hulme. FaBoMo
Above the forest of the parakeets. The Bird with the Coppery, Keen Claws. Wallace Stevens. AnFE; APA; CoAnAm; CoV
Above the fresh ruffles of the surf. The Sea. Hart Crane. Voyages, I. ChMo; CrMA; OxBA; Po; ReaPo
Above the graves of countless millions slain. In the Name of Our Sons. Dorothy Gould. PGD
Above the height of Mikasa in Kasuga. Wine and the Moon. *Unknown. Fr.* Manyo Shu. OnPM
Above the hemispheres there floats. The Elements. Oscar Williams. NAMP
Above the High. Geoffrey Grigson. EnLoPo
Above the Hills of Time. Thomas Tiplady. MaRV
Above the Lake of Galilee. Immortal Words. Aline Badger Carter. ChIP
Above the last squeak-squeal of wheels. Climbers. Earle Birney. TwCaPo
Above the laughter, O sea. The Signal. Eugenio Florit. OnPM; TwSpPo
Above the petty passions of the crowd. The Metempsychosis. Thomas Bailey Aldrich. UnW
Above the pine trees. Cazador (Hunter). Federico García Lorca. Po
Above the pines the moon was slowly drifting. Dickens in Camp. Bret Harte. HBV; IAP; LBAP; LEAP; LPS-2; PoRL; TCAP
Above the place where children play. A Sussex Legend. Charles Dalmon. BoTP
Above the pools, above the valley of fears. Elevation. Baudelaire. AWP
Above the quiet dock in midnight. Above the Dock. T. E. Hulme. FaBoMo
Above the quiet valley and unrippled lake. Spring Oak. Galway Kinnell. NePoAm
Above the road to Bethlehem. The Road to Bethlehem. Watson Kirkconnell. MaRV
Above the roaring waters of the gorge. The Old Forge. Clinton Scollard. PoTo
Above the rocking waters' ripples fiercely stand. Cimmerian Twilight, III. Maximilian Aleksandrovich Voloshin. TrRV
Above the shouting of the gale. Bag-Pipes at Sea. Clinton Scollard. LBMV; NLK (1947 ed.)
Above the sleeping pool the reeds are stirred. Towards the Past. Henri de Régnier. TrFP
Above the Stable. Nona Keen Duffy. BrR; ChBR
Above the stately roofs, wind-lifted, high. The Flags on Fifth Avenue. Christopher Morley. VOD (1931 ed.)
Above the sunset's many-tinted bar. The Evening Star. Grace Blackburn. CPG
Above the surface of this low, mean sphere. Random Thoughts. Bahar. PeP
Above the unfathomed deep. The Precipice. John Banister Tabb. AmP
Above the voiceful windings of a river. At the Grave of Henry Vaughan. Siegfried Sassoon. ChMo; ChMP; CMP; POTE; PtP; TriL
Above the water, in her rocky niche. The Strawberry Plant. Ruth Pitter. DiM; POTE
Above the waters, like a hoary giant. The Rock. Hovhannes Hovhannessian. ArmLP
Above the weary waiting world. Christmas Song. Bliss Carman. PeCV; StJW
Above the world the bronze-winged eagle flew. The Eagle. Arthur Guiterman. QS
Above them spread a stranger sky. The Indian's Welcome to the Pilgrim Fathers. Lydia Huntley Sigourney. AA; DD
Above these bleak Wyoming plains. Winter Juniper. Joseph Langland. NePoEA
Above us hangs the jewelled night. Waking. John Le Gay Brereton. BoAu
Above us the clouds are weaving and unweaving. The Clouds. Lu Yu. WhP
Above white clouds I hear sweet. Kyoroku, *tr. fr. Japanese by* Lois J. Erickson. SoLD
Above yon sombre [*or* somber] swell of land. The Plough [*or* Plow]. Richard Henry Horne. HBV; OBEV; OBVV; VA; WP
Abraham. Edmund Vance Cooke. QS
Abraham and Isaac. Genesis, XXII: 1–13, Bible, *O.T.* EnLi-1 (1949 ed.); OuHeWo
Abraham Davenport. Whittier. AmPP; AnNE; CBOV; CoBA; CoV; DDA; IAP; MOAP; OBAV
Abraham Lincoln. A. S. Ames. OHIP
Abraham Lincoln. Joseph Auslander. YaD
Abraham Lincoln. Rosemary Benét *and* Stephen Vincent Benét. NAMP; TiPo; YeAr
Abraham Lincoln. Joel Benton. DD; LBAH
Abraham Lincoln. Virginia Frazer Boyle. BAP
Abraham Lincoln. Henry Howard Brownell. GN, *abr.;* LBAH
Abraham Lincoln. Bryant. BlG; DD; GA; GDAH; MC; PaA; PAH
(Death of Lincoln, The.) AmP; BAV; CoBA; HH; IAP; InP; RiBV
(To the Memory of Abraham Lincoln.) BoHiPo; LBAH; OHIP
Abraham Lincoln. Samuel Valentine Cole. OHIP; PEDC
Abraham Lincoln. Rose Terry Cooke. LBAH
Abraham Lincoln *sels.* John Drinkwater.
"Kinsmen, you shall behold." TwCV
"Wind blows in the night, A." MM
Abraham Lincoln. James Russell Lowell. *Fr.* Ode Recited at the Harvard Commemoration, July 21, 1865. GDAH; LPS-3; PAP; PEOR, *sel.*
(Lincoln.) AnNE
(Martyr Chief, The.) LBAH
(Our Martyr-Chief.) OHIP; PEDC
("Such was he, our Martyr-Chief.") InP
Abraham Lincoln. Mildred Plew Meigs. TiPo
Abraham Lincoln. Francesca Falk Miller. PEDC
Abraham Lincoln. Frank Moore. LBAH
Abraham Lincoln. Florence Evelyn Pratt. LBAH
Abraham Lincoln. Edmund Clarence Stedman. GA; PAH
Abraham Lincoln ("Not as when some great captain falls"). Richard Henry Stoddard. AA; FaBoBe; GDAH; PAH
(Horatian Ode, An.) LBAH
Abraham Lincoln ("This man whose homely face"). Richard Henry Stoddard. DD; GN; HH; LBAH; OHIP; OTPC (1946 ed.); PEDC; PGD; PSO
(Lincoln's Birthday.) PoRL
Abraham Lincoln. Tom Taylor, *sometimes wr. at. to* Mark Lemon *and to* Shirley Brooks. BMEP, *abr.;* BoHiPo, *4 sts.;* DDA; GA; HBV; LBAH; LPS-3; MCCG; PaA; PAH; PTA-1; VA
Abraham Lincoln. Robert Whitaker. GA; HH
Abraham Lincoln, the dear president. The Dear President. John James Piatt. DD; GA; MC; PAH
Abraham Lincoln, the Master. Thomas Curtis Clark. OHIP; PEDC
(Master, The.) OQP; QP-2
Abraham Lincoln Walks at Midnight. Vachel Lindsay. AmPP; AnFE; ATP (1935 ed.); BoHiPo; CaAE; CoAnAm; CoBA; CP; FaFP; FaPON; GrCo-2; HBV; InP; LaNeLa; LiTA; MAP; MaRV; MC; MCCG; MoAmPo; MOAP; MoVE; MPB; NAMP; NP; OBAV; OHFP; OHIP; OnPP; OQP; OxBA; PaA; PAH; PEDC, *abr.;* PFE; PG (1945 ed.); PoRL, *6 sts.;* QP-2; SBMV; TCAP; TreF; TriL; VOD
Abraham Lincoln was ten feet tall. Abraham Lincoln. Joseph Auslander. YaD
Abraham Lincoln's Christmas Gift. Nora Perry. LBAH
Abraham's Daughter, *with music.* Septimus Winner. TrAS
Abram Brown, *with music. Unknown.* SoAmSa
Abrim with Dionysos' wine. Moero, *tr. fr. Greek by* W. C. Lawton. GrPo
Abroad. Sophus Claussen, *tr. fr. Danish by* Charles W. Stork. BoDS
Abroad and at Home. Swift. WhC
Abroad on a winter's night there ran. A Christmas Legend. Frank Sidgwick. OHIP; WP
Abroad the royal banners fly. Vexilla Regis. Fortunatus. CAW; WHL
Abroad Thoughts from Home. Donald Hall. NePoEA
Abruptly mounting her ramshackle wheel. In War Time. W. H. Auden. TwHP
Absâl Tempts Salámán. Jami, *tr. fr. Persian by* Edward Fitzgerald. *Fr.* Salámán and Absál. PeP
Absalom and Achitophel, Pt. I. Dryden. CEP; EiPP; EM-1; EnLi-1; EPS; GEPC; LiA; OAEP; REAL; SeCV-2; SeEP; TOP
Sels.
Achitophel. AWP, *br. sel.;* BCEP, *br. sel.;* EPP; EV-3; JAWP; SeCePo; WBP; WHA, *br. sel.*
(Character of the Earl of Shaftesbury, *br. sel.*) LPS-3

Absalom and Achitophel (*continued*)
(Characters from the Satires: Achitophel.) InPo
(Earl of Shaftesbury, The.) FaBoEn
(False Achitophel, The.) FiP
(Lord Shaftesbury.) LoBV
("Of these the false Achitophel was first.") AtBAP; PoEL-3; ViBoPo
(Shaftesbury.) NBE; OBS
English in 1680, The. NBE
"In pious times, ere [*or* e'er] priestcraft did begin." BrBE; TyEnPo, *longer sel.*
"Inhabitants of old Jerusalem, The." TCEP
(Popish Plot, The, *br. sel.*) ACP
"Numerous host of dreaming saints succeed, A." EPP
(Crowd and Buckingham, The.) NBE
(Duke of Buckingham, The.) FaBoEn
"This Plot, which failed for want of common sense." CoBE
Titus Oates. NBE
Zimri. AnFE; AWP; BCEP; EV-3; JAWP; LPS-3; SeCePo; ShBV-4; WBP
(Characters from the Satires: Zimri.) InPo
(Duke of Buckingham, The.) CoEV
("How happy had he been, if Destiny," *longer sel.*) BrBE
("In the first rank of these did Zimri stand.") PoFS; ViBoPo
(Malcontents, The.) OBS
Absalom and Achitophel, Pt. II, *sels.* Nahum Tate *and* John Dryden.
"Levi, thou art a load, I'll lay thee down." Dryden. AtBAP; SeEP
"Next these, a troop of buisy spirits press." Dryden. CEP; SeCV-2
Og and Doeg. Dryden. AWP; BeR; FiP, *shorter sel.;* JAWP; WBP
(Characters from the Satires: Og and Doeg.) InPo
("Doeg though without knowing.") PoEL-3
Thomas Shadwell the Poet, *2 ll.* Dryden. ChTr
Absence. Matthew Arnold. Switzerland, VI. PoVP; ViPP
("In this fair stranger's eyes of grey.") OAEP
Absence. John Arthur Blaikie. VA
Absence. Robert Bridges. OBEV (1st ed.)
("When my love was away.") EG; LO
Absence. Chang Chiu-ling, *tr. fr. Chinese by* Henry H. Hart. PoHN
Absence. John Hoskins, *sometimes at. to* John Donne. EV-2; LEAP; LiTL; LoPo, *abr.;* MeLP; UnPo (1st ed.)
("Absence, heare my protestation.") EG
(Ode: "Absence, hear thou.") ElL; ElSeCe; ReEn; TuPP
(Present in Absence.) GTBS; GTBS-D; GTBS-W; GTSE; GTSL
(That Time and Absence Proves Rather Helps than Hurts to Loves.) OBEV (1st ed.)
Absence. Richard Jago. BCEP; HBV; OBEV
Absence. Frances Anne Kemble. LPS-1; NeHB
What Shall I Do? *sel.* PoToHe (new ed.)
Absence ("Here, ever since you went abroad"). Walter Savage Landor. OBEV (1st ed.); TOP
Absence ("Ianthe! you resolve to cross the sea"). Walter Savage Landor. EnRP
("Ianthe, you resolve to cross the sea.") OBVV
(Lyrics to Ianthe.) BPN
Absence. Claude McKay CDC
Absence. Charlotte Mew. ChMP; MoAB; MoBrPo
Absence. Shakespeare. *See* Sonnets, LVII.
Absence. William Shenstone. A Pastoral Ballad, Pt. I. OBEC
Absence. Sir Philip Sidney. SiPS
Absence ("Western wind"). *Unknown. See* Western Wind, When Wilt Thou Blow?
Absence ("When I think on the happy days"). *Unknown.* GTSL; LPS-1
Absence, The. Sylvia Townsend Warner. MBP; MoBrPo
Absence. Nathaniel Parker Willis. MOAH
Absence absenting causeth me to complain. Sir Thomas Wyatt. SiPS
Absence and Presence. Fulke Greville. Caelica, XLV[XLIV]. OBSC
("Absence, the noble truce.") PoEL-1
Absence, hear thou my [*or* hear my *or* hear thou this] protestation. Absence [*or* Ode *or* Present in Absence *or* That Time and Absence Proves . . .]. John Hoskins, *sometimes at. to* John Donne. EG; ElL; ElSeCe; EV-2; GTBS; GTBS-D; GTBS-W; GTSE; GTSL; LEAP; LiTL; LoPo; MeLP; OBEV (1st ed.); ReEn; TuPP; UnPo (1st ed.)
Absence of Occupation ("Lucrative offices are seldom lost"). William Cowper. *Fr.* Retirement. OBEC
Absence of occupation is not rest. The Pledge of Cheerfulness. William Cowper. *Fr.* Retirement. BPP
Absence, the noble truce. Absence and Presence. Fulke Greville. Caelica, XLV[XLIV]. OBSC; PoEL-1

Absent Creation. D. S. Savage. NeBP
Absent face, remote and sharp, as far, An. The Beaches, III. "Robin Hyde." AnNZ
Absent Friend, An. Sappho, *tr. fr. Greek by* C. M. Bowra. GrL; OxBG
Absent Friends. Ibn Hazm, *tr. fr. Arabic by* A. J. Arberry. MooP
Absent from thee, I languish still. A Song [*or* Return]. Earl of Rochester. AEV; CoEV; EnLoPo; EPS; FaBoEn; LO; LoBV; MePo; OBEV; OBS; PoFS; SeCePo; SeCL; SeCV-2; SeEP; ViBoPo
Absent Minded Birch Tree, The. Kathleen Millay. PEDC
Absent Soldier Son, The. Sydney Dobell. MOAH
Absent Yet Present. Sir Edward Bulwer-Lytton. LoPS; OBVV; UnPo
Absinthe-Drinker, The. Arthur Symons. FaBoTw
Absolute, The. Hugh Wilgus Ramsaur. MuM
Absolute and Abitofhell. Ronald Arbuthnott Knox. CenHV
Absolute Explains. The. Thomas Hardy. MM
Absolute knowledge I have none. Source of News. *Unknown.* TreF
Absolute, pity the visionless. Address to an Absolute. Roy McFadden. NeIP
Absolution. Martha Lindstedt. CAG
Absolution. Siegfried Sassoon. NV
Absolution. Edward Willard Watson. AA
Absolvers, The. Robert Southey. *Fr.* A Vision of Judgement. EnRP; ERP
Abstemia. Gelett Burgess. NA
Abstinence and Desire. Blake. *Fr.* Gnomic Verses. OnPM
("Abstinence sows sand all over.") ExPo; TrGrPo
(Poems from MSS.) ViBoPo
Abstinent Lover, The. Abul Bahr, *tr. fr. Arabic by* A. J. Arberry. MooP
Abstrosophy. Gelett Burgess. CenHV; NA
Abt Vogler. Robert Browning. BEL; BMEP; BPN; CoBE; EM-2; EmBrPo; EPN; GEPC; GoTL; HBV; OAEP; PoVP; TOP; TriL; VA; ViPo; ViPP; VLEP; WGRP
Sels.
"Builder and maker Thou." OQP; QP-1
Music. GrCo-1
"Therefore to whom turn I but to thee, the ineffable Name?" MaRV; ReTS, *longer sel.*
Abu Nowas for the Barmacides. *Unknown, tr. fr. Arabic by* E. Powys Mathers. *Fr.* The Thousand and One Nights. AWP
Abune the braes I see him stand. An Ochil Farmer [*or* The Farmer of Westerha']. James Logie Robertson. EBSV; POT
Abused Lover Seeth His Folly and Entendeth to Trust No More, The. Sir Thomas Wyatt. ReIE
Abusive Snatches. *Unknown, tr. fr. Old Irish.* SiB
Abyss. Gerard Manley Hopkins. *See* No Worst, There Is None.
Acacia Leaves, The. Allen Upward. *Fr.* Scented Leaves from a Chinese Jar. NP
Academic. Theodore Roethke. CrMA; MiAP
Academic Discourse at Havana. Wallace Stevens. MoPo
Academic Visit to the Continent, An. Richard Porson. *See* Epigram on an Academic Visit to the Continent.
Academy. Sister Mary Jeremy. JKCP (1955 ed.)
Academy at Venice. Thc. Arthur Hugh Clough. BHV
Acadia, *sels.* Joseph Howe.
"In ev'ry thought, in ev'ry wish I own." CaP
Indian Massacre, The. BoCaPo
Accents in Alsace, *sels.* Gertrude Stein. AtBAP
Alsace or Alsatians.
Watch on the Rhine, The.
Accept each gift, though it be small. Lines for a Wedding Gift. Wesley Trimpi. NePoEA
Accept My Full Heart's Thanks. Ella Wheeler Wilcox. PoToHe
Accept Our Tribute. Isaac Watts. BePJ
Accept the counsel that I offer, lady. Take Life as It Comes. Euripides. OxBG
Accept the holy mounds of incense, Juno of her birth. Intercession on Sulpicia's Birthday, to Her Guardian Spirit. Tibullus. LaP
Accept the sacrifice I made. Sacrifice. Al-Tutili. MooP
Accept, thou shrine of my dead saint. The Exequy [*or* Exequy on His Wife] Henry King. AEV; AtBAP; ATP; BrBE; CoEV; EPS (1942 ed.); EV-2; FaBoEn; InvP; KN; LiTL; LoBV; MeLP; MePo; OBEV; OBS; PoEL-2; ReEn; SeCePo; SeCL; SeEP; ViBoPo; WHA
Acceptable Sacrifice, The. Micah, VI: 6–8, Bible, *O.T.* GrCo-1
(What Doth the Lord Require?) MaRV
Acceptance. Robert Frost. ChMo; CMP; MOAP; OxBA
Acceptance. Langston Hughes. NePoAm-2
Acceptance. Willard Wattles. OQP; QP-1; SBMV
(Comrades of the Cross.) HBMV
Acceptation. Margaret Junkin Preston. MC; PAH
Accepted and Will Appear. "Parmenas Mix." BOHV
Accident happens, An. Jean Cocteau. *Fr.* The Crucifixion. MiCF

Accident in Art. Richard Hovey. HBV; PreP
Accidents will happen—still, in time. A Bedtime Story. Robert Mezey. NePoEA
Accidian. Henry Charles Beeching. OBVV
Acclamation, An. Sir John Davies. *Fr.* Nosce Teipsum. OxBoCh; TuPP
Accompanied by clamor and by noise. Power. Grace Noll Crowell. PoMa
Accomplished Facts. Carl Sandburg. WHA
"According to the Mighty Working." Thomas Hardy. ChMo; OnPM; ReMP
According to Thy Gracious Word. James Montgomery. MaRV
According to [*or* to the] tradition. The Tryst. Christopher Morley. ALV; BOHV; HBMV
Accordingly Medea Met Jason in the Temple of Hecate. Apollonius Rhodius, *tr. fr. Greek by* F. L. Lucas. *Fr.* Argonautica, III. GrPE
Accordionist. Vladimir Kazin, *tr. fr. Russian by* Jack Lindsay. RuPo
Account Me Not. Henry Longan Stuart. JKCP (1955 ed.)
Account of the Greatest English Poets, An, *sel.* Addison. PtP
"Since, dearest Harry, you will needs request."
Accountability. Paul Laurence Dunbar. AnAmPo; LA; YaD
Accounte of W. Canynge's Feast, The. Thomas Chatterton. EnLi-2; EPP
Accumulation triumphant. Festivity. Jorge Guillén. CoSP
Accursed, The. Baudelaire, *tr. fr. French by* F. P. Sturm. LiTW
Accursed be love . . . *See* Accurst Be Love.
Accursèd power which stands on Privilege, The. On a Great [*or* General] Election. Hilaire Belloc. MoVE; OxBoLi; WhC
Accursed the man, whom fate ordains, in spite. The Pains of Education. Charles Churchill. SiTL
Accurst Be Love. Thomas Lodge. ElSeCe
("Accursed [*or* Accurst] be love and they that trust his trains.") CaAE; SiCE
Accurst the hour, the day, the month, the year. Exile in Rome. Joachim du Bellay. Regrets, XXV. TrFP
Accusation of the Inward Man, The. Edward Taylor. *Fr.* God's Determinations. LiTA
Accuse me not, beseech thee, that I wear. Sonnets from the Portuguese, XV. Elizabeth Barrett Browning. DiM
Accuse me thus: that I have scanted all. Sonnets, CXVII. Shakespeare. PeBoSo
Accusèd though I be without desert. Sir Thomas Wyatt. SiPS
Ace—Pride of parents. The Airman's Alphabet. W. H. Auden. *Fr.* Journal of an Airman. NAMP; PoF
Aceldama. Longfellow. StJW
Achaeans Renew the Battle, The. Homer, *tr. fr. Greek by* F. L. Lucas. *Fr.* The Iliad, IV. GrPE
Achaemenides once, Menippus now they call him. Fortune's Freehold. *Unknown.* GrPE
Achaians Have Got Troy, upon This Very Day, The. Aeschylus, *tr. fr. Greek by* Richmond Lattimore. *Fr.* Agamemnon. WaaP
Acharnians, The, *sels.* Aristophanes, *tr. fr. Greek.*
Dicaeopolis and the Case for the Enemy, *tr. by* Benjamin Bickley Rogers. GrR
"First, I detest the Spartans most extremely," *tr. by* John Hookham Frere. GrPo
Plea for the Enemy, A, *tr. by* Benjamin Bickley Rogers. OxBG
Poet and the People, The, *tr. by* Benjamin Bickley Rogers. OxBG
(Poet and His Public, The.) GrR
Ache is easy, An. Longing's length. Poem of Quietness, III. Robert Herring. MoWP
Ache of wide millions, The. Return of a Reaper. Alan Creighton. CaP
Acheloos (the River-God). Angelos Sikelianos, *tr. fr. Modern Greek by* Rae Dalven. MoGP
Achievement. Morris Abel Beer. PFE; PoMa
Achievement. Berta Hart Nance. MaRV
Achilles, *sel.* John Gay.
Song: "Think of dress in ev'ry light," *fr.* III. OBEC
(Think of Dress in Every Light.) InvP
Achilles. Ernest Myers. OBVV; PtP
Achilles. Pindar. *tr. fr. Greek by* C. J. Billson. *Fr.* Isthmian Odes, VIII. GrR
Achilles and Agamemnon; the Fatal Feud. Homer, *tr. fr. Greek by* the Earl of Derby. *Fr.* The Iliad, I. GrR
("Have you the face to utter such a threat, most grasping Atrides?" *longer sel., tr. by* George Ernle.) GrPo
("O tyrant, armed with insolence and pride," *tr. by* William Hyde Appleton.) PoFr
Achilles and Lycaon. Homer, *tr. fr. Greek. Fr.* The Iliad, XXI. GrR, *tr. by* the Earl of Derby; OxBG, *shorter sel., tr. by* C. M. Bowra
(Achilles Refuses to Spare Lycaon's Life, *shorter sel., pr. tr. by* A. T. Murray.) LiA
(Achilles to Lycaon, *shorter sel., tr. by* Richmond Lattimore.) LiTW; WaaP
Achilles and Patroclus. Homer, *tr. fr. Greek by* Sir William Marris. *Fr.* The Iliad, XVI. OxBG
("Meanwhile Patroclus stood beside his friend," *tr. by* Bryant.) GrPo
(Patroclus to Achilles, *tr. by* the Earl of Derby.) GrR
Achilles and the Scamander. Homer. *See* Scamander the River God.
Achilles and Thetis. Homer. *See* Achilles' Remorse.
Achilles' Arms. Homer, *tr. fr. Greek by* F. L. Lucas. *Fr.* The Iliad, XIX. GrPE
Achilles' baneful wrath resound, O goddess that impos'd. Homer. *Fr.* The Iliad, I. ReIE
Achilles Deatheridge. Edgar Lee Masters. MaC; PoMa
Achilles Goes Forth to Battle. Homer, *tr. fr. Greek by* George Chapman. *Fr.* The Iliad, XIX. EV-1
Achilles on the Rampart. Homer, *tr. fr. Greek by* Tennyson. *Fr.* The Iliad, XVIII. OxBG
(Achilles over the Trench, *tr. by* F. L. Lucas.) GrPE
(Achilles' Shout, *tr. by* Tennyson.) LiA
("So saying, light-foot Iris past away," *tr. by* Tennyson.) GrPo
Achilles' Prayer. Homer, *tr. fr. Greek by* the Earl of Derby. *Fr.* The Iliad, XVI. OxBG
("Achilles then within his tent withdrew," *tr. by* the Earl of Derby.) GrPo
(Prayer of Achilles, The, *pr. tr. by* Andrew Lang, Walter Leaf, *and* Ernest Myers.) GrR
Achilles rais'd his spear, in act to strike. Achilles and Lycaon. Homer, *tr. by* the Earl of Derby. *Fr.* The Iliad, XXI. GrR
Achilles Refuses to Spare Lycaon's Life. Homer. *See* Achilles and Lycaon.
Achilles Rejects the Embassy. Homer, *tr. fr. Greek by* F. L. Lucas. *Fr.* The Iliad, IX. GrPE
Achilles' Remorse. Homer, *tr. fr. Greek by* F. L. Lucas. *Fr.* The Iliad, XVIII. GrPE
(Achilles and Thetis, *shorter sel., tr. by* Sir William Marris.) OxBG
(So Ends the Wrath of Achilles, *tr. by* William Cowper.) GrR
Achilles' Reply to the Embassy. Homer. *See* Achilles Unreconciled.
Achilles' Shield. Homer. *See* Shield of Achilles, The.
Achilles' Shout. Homer. *See* Achilles on the Rampart.
Achilles Shows Himself in the Battle by the Ships. Homer, *tr. fr. Greek by* George Chapman. *Fr.* The Iliad, XVIII. OBS
Achilles then within his tent withdrew. Achilles' Prayer. Homer, *tr. by* the Earl of Derby. *Fr.* The Iliad, XVI. GrPo; OxBG
Achilles to Lycaon. Homer. *See* Achilles and Lycaon.
Achilles Unreconciled. Homer, *tr. fr. Greek by* the Earl of Derby. *Fr.* The Iliad, IX. GrR
(Achilles' Reply to the Embassy, *abr., tr. by* Maurice Hewlett.) OxBG
("Most valiant and noble Odysseus, seeing Atrides," *tr. by* George Ernle.) GrPo
Achitophel. Dryden. *Fr.* Absalom and Achitophel, Pt. I. AWP, *br. sel.*; BCEP, *br. sel.*; EPP; EV-3; JAWP; SeCePo; WBP; WHA, *br. sel.*
(Character of the Earl of Shaftesbury, *br. sel.*) LPS-3
(Characters from the Satires: Achitophel.) InPo
(Earl of Shaftesbury, The.) FaBoEn
(False Achitophel, The.) FiP
(Lord Shaftesbury.) LoBV
("Of these the false Achitophel was first.") AtBAP; PoEL-3; ViBoPo
(Shaftesbury.) NBE; OBS
Acis and Galatea, *sels.* John Gay
Love in Her Eyes Sits Playing. EnLi-1 (1949 ed.); EV-3; OBFC; OnPM; ViBoPo
(Song: "Love in her eyes sits playing.") FaBoEn; LoPo
O Ruddier than the Cherry. LiTL; ViBoPo
(Song: "O ruddier than the cherry.") CaAE; EV-3; HBV; OBEC; OBEV (1st ed.)
Acknowledgment. Sidney Lanier. PeBoSo
("Now at thy soft recalling voice I rise.") CBOV
Acknowledgment (of a Locket Received), An. Henry King. CoEV
Acme and Septimius. Catullus, *tr. fr. Latin by* Abraham Cowley. AWP; LiA
Acolyte, The. James Rorty. MOAP
Acolyte. Mary Brent Whiteside. LS
Acoma, *sel.* Edgar Lee Masters.
Hymn to the Sun. ChMo; CMP
Acon and Rhodope; or, Inconstancy. Walter Savage Landor. BPN
Aconite, The. A. M. Graham. BoTP
Acorn, The. *Unknown.* BoTP
Acorn and the Pumpkin, The. La Fontaine, *tr. fr. French by* Elizur Wright. BoChLi

Acorns. Edith King. GFA; RAR
Acquaintance. David Morton. MCCG
Acquainted with the Night. Robert Frost. AmP; ChMo; ChTr; CoBMV; CoV; InP; LiTM; NP; MaPo; NePA; PoFS; PoLFOT; TwP; VOD (1935 ed.)
Acre of Grass, An. W. B. Yeats. GTBS-D; POTE
Acre of land between the shore and the hills, An. For These. Edward Thomas. TCPD
Acrobat. Rachel Field. *Fr.* A Circus Garland. StVeCh
Acrobat on the border of the sea, An. The Woman That Had More Babies than That. Wallace Stevens. LiTA
Across clear drops of dew. Bunya no Asayasu, *tr. fr. Japanese by* I. W. Furukami. LiTW
Across Illinois. John Stoltze. PoMa; POT; PoTo
Across its wastes a universe I trod. Search. T. Moore Atkinson. ChIP
Across my loom of years there fell a shadow, gaunt and gray. The Shadow on the Loom. Nellie Burget Miller. OQP; QP-2
Across my seventy years. Deathbed. Eric Robertson Dodds. MM
Across the ages they come thundering. Say This of Horses. Minnie Hite Moody. DDA; PoeMoYo
Across the azure spaces. The Winds of God. Clinton Scollard. PoRL
Across the barrage, the cities of Europe remember. Homage of War. Bruce Williamson. NeIP
Across the bitter centuries I hear the wail of men. Thy Kingdom Come [*or* A Page from America's Psalter]. Willard Wattles. BPP; OQP; QP-2
Across the bristled and sallow fields. The Hawk. Raymond Knister. BoCaPo
Across the cool stones, every day. To a Snail in the Cemetery. Sara Henderson Hay. DDA
Across the crests of the naked hills. Laramie Trail. Joseph Mills Hanson. PoOW
Across the dark linked loveliness of lakes. Dawn. "Æ." BEL
Across the Delaware. Will Carleton. MC; PAH
Across the desert dry as bone. The Upas Tree. Pushkin. LiTW
Across the dewy lawn she treads. Paean. Jonathan Henderson Brooks. CDC
Across the Door. Padraic Colum. HBV
Across the drifted square from street and lane. Independence Square, Christmas, 1783. Arthur Guiterman. PEDC
Across the eastern sky has glowed. The Crowing of the Red Cock. Emma Lazarus. AA; HBV; OBAV
Across the edges of the world there blows a wind. The Spring of God. William Alexander Percy. *Fr.* In April Once. OQP; QP-2
Across the empty garden-beds. The Sailing of the *Sword.* William Morris. BPN; CoBE; EmBrPo; OAEP; OBVV; PoVP; TCEP; VLEP
Across the Fens. Gilbert Thomas. HaMV
Across the Fields. Walter Crane. VA
Across the fields as green as spinach. The Lady with the Sewing-Machine. Edith Sitwell. NV
Across the fields like swallows fly. Across the Fields. Walter Crane. VA
Across the fields of yesterday. Sometimes. Thomas S. Jones, Jr. BAP; BLP; HBV; InP; LBMV; LEAP; MaRV; OQP; PoMa; POT; PoTo; QP-2
Across the fields the neighbors go. The Night Meeting. Adaline H. Tatman. DDA
Across the Fields to Anne. Richard Burton. HBV; LBMV; POT; PoTo; PR
Across the floor flits the mechanical toy. Cirque d'Hiver. Elizabeth Bishop. FiMAP; LiTA; MiAP
Across the foaming river. The Bridge. Frederick Peterson. HBV; OBAV
Across the forest of Delay. Ballade: The Hostelry of Thought. Charles d'Orléans. LyMA
Across the gap made by our English hinds. August. William Morris. *Fr.* The Earthly Paradise. BPN
Across the gardens of Life they go. Love and Time. Beatrix Demarest Lloyd. AA
Across the German Ocean. Little Gottlieb. Phoebe Cary. OTPC (1946 ed.); TVC; TVSH
Across the grass I see her pass;/ She comes with tripping pace. The Milkmaid. Austin Dobson. HBV
Across the grass I see her pass,/ She walks with stately grace. To My Little Daughter. E. J. Francis Davies. FAOV
Across the heath, the monolith's pubic arch. Sonnet. Alfred Jarry. MiFP
Across the hills of Arcady. To Arcady. Charles Buxton Going. HBV; LBAP; PR
Across the lonely beach we flit. *See* Across the narrow beach we flit.
Across the long-curved bight or bay. Epistemology of Poetry. Robert Conquest. PoLFOT
Across the moorlands of the Not. Moorlands of the Not. *Unknown.* NA
Across the mud the line drags on and on. Ration Party. John Manifold. WaP
Across the narrow [*or* lonely] beach we flit. The Sandpiper. Celia Thaxter. AA; BAP; BBV (1923 ed.); BLA; BoChLi; BTP; DD; DDA; FaBoBe; FaPON; GN; HBV; HBVY; LBAP; LEAP; LPS-2; MPB; MW; PECK; SN; UTS; WBLP
Across the noisy street. Ballade of the Thrush. Austin Dobson. BLA
Across the page of history. Lincoln Leads. Minna Irving. HH; OHIP
Across the pearly distance. Autumn Haze. Richard Kendall Munkittrick. PoRL
Across the places deep and dim. The Road to Anywhere. Bert Leston Taylor. HBMV; MPB; TSW; TSWC
Across the plain the wind whines through the sage. The Snowstorm. Pearl Riggs Crouch. PoOW
Across the roaring ocean, with heart and with eye of flame. Catullus, *tr. fr. Latin by* Grant Allen. LaP
Across the round field, under the dark male tower. The Lovers. Alex Comfort. NeBP
Across the sands of Syria. The Legend of the First Cam-u-el. Arthur Guiterman. ALV; BAP; BOHV; CenHV; PFE; PoeMoYo; PYM
Across the school-ground it would start. The House at Evening. William Rose Benét. TBM
Across the sea a land there is. A Land across the Sea. William Morris. *Fr.* The Earthly Paradise. VA
Across the sea, along the shore. "What Went Ye Out for to See?" Arthur Hugh Clough. PoVP; StJW
Across the seas of Wonderland to Mogadore we plodded. Forty Singing Seamen. Alfred Noyes. AnFE; BBV; BEL; BMEP; BoChLi; ChMo; CMP; CV; GBV; GDAH; NV; PCN; PYM; ShBV-1; StPo; TOP
Across the shaken bastions of the year. Sonnets of a Portrait Painter, XLVII. Arthur Davison Ficke. AnAmPo; LA
Across the shimmering meadows. The Hawthorn Tree. Willa Cather. HBMV
Across the silent stream. From the Hills of Dream. "Fiona Macleod." MoSiPe
Across the sky run streaks of white light, aching. Before Olympus. John Gould Fletcher. MAP; MoAmPo
Across the snow the silver bells. Silver Bells. Hamish Hendry. BoTP
Across the snow the water-color blue. Refugee in New England. Frances Frost. BoFr; NeTW
Across the sombre prairie sea. Prairie. Herbert Bates. AA
Across the Stony Mountains, o'er the desert's drouth and sand. The Crisis. Whittier. PAH
Across the storm-swept plain. A Traveler Caught in a Storm. Kiokusui. GaP
Across the swiffling waves they went. The Cruise of the *P.C.* *Unknown.* NA
Across the thick and the pastel snow. By the Lake. Edith Sitwell. *Fr.* Façade. AV
Across the vast blue-shadow-sweeping plain. Taoping. James Elroy Flecker. SoV
Across the way my neighbor's windows shine. Intolerance. Molly Anderson Haley. DDA; MaRV
Across the Western Ocean, *with music. Unknown.* AmSS; AS; SoAmSa
Across the wrack besprinkled bay. The Glaucous-Gull's Death. Daniel James O'Sullivan. NeIP
Across the years he could recall. The Secret Heart. Robert P. Tristram Coffin. PoRL; TwCV
Across thousands of mountains no birds fly. Ice in a Stream. Liu Tsung-yuan. OnPM; WhP
Acroteleutium, I told you all our plan within. Plautus. *Fr.* Miles Gloriosus. LaP
A-Cruising We Will Go. *Unknown.* AmSS
Act V (Midnight). Thomas Bailey Aldrich. PFY
Act of Love. Nicholas Moore. NeBP
Actaeon. Rayner Heppenstall. FaBoTw
Actaeon. *Unknown. See* I Would I Were Actaeon.
Actaeon, *sel.* William Wilkins.
"It was on the Mount Cithaeron." TIP
Actea. Sir Rennell Rodd. VA
Action. James Oppenheim. TrJP
Action Rhyme. E. M. Adams. BoTP
Action will furnish belief—but will that belief be the true one? The Real Question. Arthur Hugh Clough. *Fr.* Amours de Voyage. BPN
Actions. Marcel Schwob, *tr. fr. French by* William Brown Meloney. TrJP
Actor, An. "Peter Pindar." BOHV
Actor's dead, and memory alone, The. J. B. Henry Cuyler Bunner. AA
Actress of emotional roles, An. The Tattooed Man. Harry B. Smith. *Fr.* The Idol's Eye. InMe; LauV
Acts, The, *sels.* Bible, *N.T.*
"Chief captain commanded him to be brought into the castle, The," XXII: 24-30. PoFr
Paul on the Road to Damascus, IX: 3-6. TreF
Actual evidence I have none. When the War Will End. Reginald Arkell. InMe
Actual Willow. Winifred Welles. MAP

Actuality. Sir John Suckling. *See* Doubt of Martyrdom, A.
Ad. Kenneth Fearing. ChMo
Ad Castitatem. Francis Thompson. PoLi
Ad Chloen, M.A. Mortimer Collins. BOHV; HBV
Ad Cinerarium. Victor Plarr. MBP
Ad Coelum. Harry Romaine. BLPA; FaBoBe; NeHB
Ad Collegium Wintoniensem. John Heath. TuPP
Ad Curiosum Lectorem. Thomas Bastard. SiCE
Ad Deum. George Chapman. ReIE
Ad Domnulam Suam. Ernest Dowson. HBV; PG
Ad Eandem. Thomas Bastard. SiCE
Ad Finem. Heine, *tr. fr. German by* Elizabeth Barrett Browning. AWP; JAWP; WBP
Ad Finem. Ella Wheeler Wilcox. BLPA
Ad Gulielmum Shakespeare. John Weever. ReIE; SiCE; TuPP
Ad Gulielmum Warner. John Weever. ReIE
Ad Henricum Wottonem ("Wotton my little Bere dwells on a hill"). Thomas Bastard. SiCE
Ad Henricum Wottonum ("Wotton, the country and the country swain"). Thomas Bastard. SiCE
Ad Jo. [*or* Io.] Marston & [*or* et] Ben. Jonson [*or* Johnson *or* Ionson]. John Weever. ReIE; SiCE; TuPP
Ad Judaeos Mactatores Stephani. Richard Crashaw, *tr. fr. Latin by* D. C. Allen. Epigrammata Sacra, I, 38. LaP
Ad Lectorem ("How quickly doth the reader pass away"). Thomas Bastard. SiCE; TuPP
Ad Lectorem ("If my books easy of digestion be"). Thomas Bastard. SiCE
Ad Lectorem ("Reader, my book flies low, and comes not near"). Thomas Bastard. SiCE
Ad Lectorem ("Reader, there is no biting in my verse"). Thomas Bastard. SiCE
Ad Lectorem. John Weever. ReIE
Ad Lesbiam. Catullus, *tr. fr. Latin by* Niall Sheridan. OxBI
Ad Leuconoen. Franklin P. Adams, *after the Latin of* Horace. AWP; JAWP; WBP
Ad Leuconoen. Francis Sylvester Mahony. IrPN
Ad Majorem Dei Gloriam. Frederick George Scott. MaRV; VA
Ad Majorem Hominis Gloriam. John Gould Fletcher. MAP; MoAmPo
Ad Manus Puellae. Ernest Dowson. *See* Your Hands.
Ad Mariam. Sister Mary Edwardine. WHL
Ad Matrem. Julian Fane. HBV
Ad Matrem Amantissimam et Carissimam Filii in Aeternum Fidelitas. John Myers O'Hara. SBMV
Ad Matrem, in Caelis. Charles L. O'Donnell. WHL
Ad Matrem in Coelis. Linda Lyon Van Voorhis. GoBC
Ad Michaelem Drayton. John Weever. ReIE
Ad Ministram. Thackeray, *after the Latin of* Horace. HBV (Persicos Odi.) OBEV (new ed.)
Ad Modernos Epigrammatistas. John Heath. SiCE; TuPP
Ad Musam. Sir John Davies. ReIE; SiCE
Ad Patriam, *sel.* William Dudley Foulke.
"Land of my heart,/ What future is before thee?" PGD
Ad Patriam. Clinton Scollard. PaA; PAH; PEDC
(Land of Our Fathers.) MC
Ad Persephonen. Franklin P. Adams. InME
Ad Reginam Elizabetham ("Live long Elisa, that the wolf of Spain"). Thomas Bastard. SiCE
Ad Reginam Elizabetham ("Mother of England, and sweet nurse of all"). Thomas Bastard. SiCE
Ad Samuelem Daniel. John Weever. ReIE
Ad Samuelem Danielem. Thomas Bastard. SiCE
Ad Tho. Bastardum Epigrammatistam. John Heath. TuPP
Ad Xanthium Phoceum. Franklin P. Adams, *after the Latin of* Horace. AWP; JAWP; WBP
Ad Zoilum. John Heath. TuPP
Adagio. Bo Bergman, *tr. fr. Swedish by* Charles W. Stork. AnSL
Adam. *Unknown.* *See* Adam Lay Ibounden.
Adam/ Had 'em. On [*or* Lines on] the Antiquity of Microbes. Strickland Gillilan. InP; PIAE; PreP; WhC
Adam, a brown old vulture in the rain. Ancient History. Siegfried Sassoon. SoV
Adam and Eve. Itzig Manger, *tr. fr. Yiddish by* Jacob Sonntag. TrJP
Adam and Eve ("Now Morn her rosie steps in th' eastern clime"). Milton. *Fr.* Paradise Lost, V. LiA
Adam and Eve ("So passed they naked on, nor shunned the sight"). Milton. *Fr.* Paradise Lost, IV. SeCePo
Adam and Eve ("Two of far nobler shape, erect and tall"). Milton. *See* Adam and Eve in the Garden.
Adam and Eve. Karl Shapiro. AmP; FiMAP; ReMP
Sels.
Recognition of Eve, The. MoAB
Sickness of Adam, The. CoBMV; MoAB
Adam and Eve in the Garden. Milton. *Fr.* Paradise Lost, IV. EV-2
(Adam and Eve.) LPS-2
(Man and Woman Made One Unity.) BCEP
(Satan Looks upon Adam and Eve in Paradise.) TreFS
Adam at first was formed of dust. The Whore on the Snow Crust. *Unknown.* OnAP
Adam Bell, Clim of the Clough, and William of Cloudesly. *Unknown.* ESPB; OBB
Adam Describing Eve. Milton. *Fr.* Paradise Lost, VIII. LPS-1
Adam, First Man of Men. Milton. *Fr.* Paradise Lost, VIII. MaPo
Adam in the Garden Pinnin' Leaves, *with music.* *Unknown.* OuSiCo
Adam Lay Ibounden [*or* I-bowndyn *or* Ibowndyn *or* Ybounden *or* Ybownden]. *Unknown.* AnEC; AtBAP; BoW; CaAE; ChTr; CoEV; EG; GoBC; LO; NBE; OAEP; OnPM; OxBoCh; OxBoLi; PoEL-1; PoLi; SeCeV
(Adam.) CH; LiA
(Adam Lay Bound.) LyMA
("O Felix Culpa.") ACP; CAW
Adam, Lilith, and Eve. Robert Browning. BPN; HBV; PoVP; ViPP; VLEP
Adam our father was in bliss. O Flos de Jesse Virgula. *Unknown.* AnEC
Adam Posed. Countess of Winchilsea. Po
Adam scriveyn, if ever it thee bifalle. Chaucers Word[e]s unto Adam, His Owne Scriveyn. Chaucer. BEL; EM-1
Adam stood by the sleeping lion. Eden. F. R. Scott. TwCaPo
Adam the goodliest man of men since born. A Scene in Paradise. Milton. *Fr.* Paradise Lost, IV. GN
Adam to Eve. Milton. *Fr.* Paradise Lost, IX. LPS-1
Adam, walking in the summer garden. Lord of Eden. Marie de L. Welch. AnAmPo
Adam was my grandfather. For All Blasphemers. Stephen Vincent Benét. AtBAP; OxBA
Adam, who thought himself immortal still. The Discovery. Monk Gibbon. BMEP; OnYI
Adamastor, whom Camoens and the sea. David Wright. *Fr.* A Voyage to Africa. BoSA
Adams and Liberty. Robert Treat Paine. MC; PAH
Adam's Curse. W. B. Yeats. CoBMV; Po
Adam's Footprint. Vassar Miller. NePoEA
Adam's Hymn in Paradise. Joost van den Vondel, *tr. fr. Dutch by* Sir John Bowring. WGRP
(Hymn of Adam.) CAW
Adam's Morning Hymn [in Paradise]. Milton. *Fr.* Paradise Lost, V. LPS-2; WGRP
(Morning Hymn in Paradise.) GrCo-1
(Morning Hymn of Adam, *abr.*) TrPWD
(Morning Hymn of Adam and Eve.) OxBoCh; TCEP
(These Are Thy Glorious Works.) BrBE; MaRV
Adam's Race. Sadi, *tr. fr. Persian by* Edward B. Eastwick. LiTW
Adam's Song of the Visible World, *much abr.* Ridgely Torrence. TrPWD
Adam's Wonder. George O'Neil. NP
Adapt Thyself. Shem-Tob ben Joseph Palquera, *tr. fr. Hebrew by* Rabbi Ettelson. TrJP
Adare, *sel.* John Francis O'Donnell.
"Morn comes freshly from the east, The." IrPN
Add but a handle. The Fan. Sokan. GFA
Adder, The. Theognis, *tr. fr. Greek by* F. L. Lucas. GrPE
Addict, The. Larry Rubin. GoYe
"Addio!" "Addio!" The guide and the guide's wife. Climbing a Mountain. James Reeves. MoP
Addison. Pope. *See* Atticus.
Addison's Funeral in the Abbey. Thomas Tickell. *Fr.* To the Earl of Warwick on the Death of Mr. Addison. BeR
Additional Verses to "Hail Columbia." Oliver Wendell Holmes. PAH
Address, The. *Unknown.* PCH
Address Not Known. John Heath-Stubbs. ChMP
Address of Death to Thomas De Roiste, The. *Unknown, tr. fr. Irish by* Douglas Hyde. TIP
Address of Richard III to His Army, The. Shakespeare. King Richard III, *fr.* V, iii. UnPo (1st ed.)
Address of Ruth to Naomi. Ruth, Bible, *O.T.* *See* Intreat Me Not to Leave Thee.
Address of Welcome. Maurice James Craig. *Fr.* Three Cat Poems. PoC
Address to a Child during a Boisterous Winter Evening. Dorothy Wordsworth. OTPC (1923 ed.)
Wind, The, *sel.* BoTP
Address to a Haggis. Burns. EBSV; ViBoPo
Address to a Lady. Burns. *See* O Wert Thou in the Cauld Blast.
Address to a Mummy. Horace Smith. HBV; TVSH
(Address to the Mummy at Belzoni's Exhibition.) LPS-2
Address to an Absolute. Roy McFadden. NeIP
Address to Bellona and King James V. John Bellenden. EBSV
Address to Death. Afanasi Afanasievich Fet, *tr. fr. Russian by* Babette Deutsch. TrRV
Address to His Elbow-Chair, New Cloath'd, An. William Somervile. CEP; OBEC
Address to Liberty. William Cowper. IDAH
Address to My Soul. Elinor Wylie. AnFE; APA; AWP; CoAnAm; LiTM; MOAP; OxBA; PoFr

Address to Plenty, *sel.* John Clare.
"'Tis not great, what I solicit." OBRV
Address to the Body. Francis Maguire. JKCP (1955 ed.)
Address to the Crown. Charles L. O'Donnell. GoBC
Address to the Deil. Burns. BCEP; CEP; DaM; EBSV; EiPP; EM-1; EnRP; EPP; EV-3; GoTS; OAEP; PoE; PoEL-4; REAL; TCEP; TyEnPo; UnPo (1st ed.)
Address to the Doomed, *sel.* George Dillon.
"Say it is life that matters. Say the bone," I. NP
Address to the Moon. Keats. *Fr.* Endymion, III. ERP
Address to the Mummy at Belzoni's Exhibition. Horace Smith. *See* Address to a Mummy.
Address to the New Year Dinah Maria Mulock Craik. PEDC; PEOR
Address to the Ocean. Byron. *See* Ocean, The.
Address to the Ocean. "Barry Cornwall." LPS-2
Address to the Scholars of New England. John Crowe Ransom. AmPP; LiTM (rev. ed.); NePA
Address to the Soul Occasioned by a Rain, An. Edward Taylor. CoV; OxBA; Po; PoEL-3
Address to the Toothache. Burns. BCEP, *much abr.*; BOHV; LPS-3
Address to Tragedy. Olga Berggolts, *tr. fr. Russian by* Jack Lindsay. RuPo
Address to the Unco Guid, or the Rigidly Righteous. Burns. AnFE; BEL; BoLiVe; CBOV; CEP; CoBE; EiPP; EM-1; EnLit; EnRP; EPP; HBV; LoBV; OAEP; OBEC; PIR; PoFr; SeCeV; TCEP, *abr.*; TOP; TreFS; TrGrPo; ViBoPo
(To the Unco Guid.) LPS-3
"Then gently scan your brother man," *2 sts.* MaRV
Address to the Woodlark. Burns. BCEP
Address to Venus. Lucretius, *tr. fr. Latin by* Spenser. *Fr.* De Rerum Natura *and fr.* The Faerie Queene, IV, 10. AnEnPo; AWP
(Prayer to Venus.) EIL
Addressed to a Young Lady. William Cowper. *See* To a Young Lady.
Addressed to Haydon. Keats. EM-2; EmBrPo; EnRP; ERP
(Great Spirits Now on Earth Are Sojourning.) BPN; PeBoSo
(Sonnet: Addressed to Haydon.) GEPC
Ad-dressing of Cats, The. T. S. Eliot. GoTP
Adela Cathcart, *sel.* George Macdonald.
Sir Lark and King Sun, *fr. ch.* 16. HBV; HBVY; OTPC
Adelaide Crapsey. Carl Sandburg. HBMV
Adelaide Neilson. William Winter. AA
Adelgitha. Thomas Campbell. CG
Adelheid. Paul the Deacon, *tr. fr. Latin by* Howard Mumford Jones. LaP
Adelita, *with music.* Unknown, *tr. fr. Spanish by* F. S. Curtis, Jr. AS
Adelphos. Manuel Machado, *tr. fr. Spanish by* Beatrice Gilman Proske. AnSpL-2
Adepts, The. Lawrence Durrell. *Fr.* Eight Aspects of Melissa. NeBP
Adeste Fideles. *Unknown. See* O Come, All Ye Faithful.
Adieu. Edmund John Armstrong. TIP
Adieu. Thomas Carlyle. HBV; OBRV; VA
Adieu. Eleanor Elizabeth Montgomery. VA
Adieu. Pierre de Ronsard, *tr. fr. French by* Alan Conder. TrFP
Adieu, adieu, fair Annie, he did say. Fair Annie (B *vers.*). *Unknown.* BaBo
Adieu, Adieu! My Native Shore. Byron. *See* Childe Harold's Farewell to England.
Adieu, dear object of my love's excess. Orinda to Lucasia Parting, October, 1661, at London. Katherine Philips. OBS
Adieu, fair isle! I love thy bowers. Farewell to Cuba. Maria Gowen Brooks. AA
Adieu, Farewell, Earth's Bliss [*or* Blisse]! Thomas Nashe. *Fr.* Summer's Last Will and Testament. AtBAP; CH; EIL; ElSeCe; InvP; LoBV; OAEP; PoD; PoE; ReaPo; SiCE; TuPP; ViBoPo
(Death's Summons.) HBV
(Dust Hath Closed Helen's Eye.) SeCePo
(In a Time of Pestilence.) HoPM; PoFS; TrGrPo
(In Plague Time.) FaBoCh; LoGBV; OBSC; RiBV
(In Time of Pestilence [1593].) CoEV; LiTG; MeRV; OBEV; OtMeF; PIAE
(Lament in Time of Pestilence, A.) EV-2
(Litany in Time of Plague, A.) BEL; EnLi-1 (1949 ed.); PoRA; ReEn
(Lord, Have Mercy on Us.) ChTr
(Song.) FaBoEn; MyFE; PoEL-2
Adieu, fond love, farewell you wanton powers. The Farewell to Love. Beaumont *and* Fletcher. TriL
"Adieu, for now I've made an end." John Gower. *Fr.* Confessio Amantis: Conclusion. MeEV
Adieu, kind Life, though thou hast often been. Departure. May Riley Smith. AA
Adieu Love, Untrue Love. *Unknown. See* Faithless Shepherdess, The.
"Adieu [*or* Adiew], madame [*or* madam], my mother dear." Lord Maxwell's [Last] Good-Night. *Unknown.* EBSV; ESPB (B *vers.*); OBB
Adieu, O Daisy of Delight! Adieu [*or* He Bids Adieu] to His Mistress. Alexander Montgomerie. EBSV; LO
Adieu, O Soldier,/ You of the rude campaigning. Adieu to a Soldier. Walt Whitman. BoFr
Adieu, sweet Angus, Maeve, and Fand. The Passing of the Shee. J. M. Synge. OnYI; TIP
Adieu to a Soldier. Walt Whitman. BoFr
Adieu to Belashanny [*or* Ballyshannon]! where I was bred and born. The Winding Banks of Erne [*or* Adieu to Belashanny]. William Allingham. AnIV; GTIV; IrPN; OxBI; TIP
Adieu to Bon County, *with music. Unknown.* ABF
Adieu to France. John Hunter-Duvar. *Fr.* De Roberval. VA
Adieu to His Mistress. Alexander Montgomerie. EBSV
(He Bids Adieu to His Mistress.) LO
Adieu to the Stone Walls, *with music. Unknown.* OuSiCo
Adieu? why so? deare Castaminda stay. *Unknown.* SeCSL
Adieux à Marie Stuart. Swinburne. EmBrPo; PoVP
Adina. Harold Telemaque. PoNe
Adios. Donald C. Babcock. NePoAm-2
Adios. Joaquin Miller. OQP; QP-2
Adjectives. Moishe Nadir, *tr. fr. Yiddish by* Joseph Leftwich. TrJP
Adjuration. Charles Enoch Wheeler. PoNe
Adjustment. Whittier. WGRP
Adlatts parke is wyde and broad. Will Stewart and John. *Unknown.* ESPB
Adlestrop. Edward Thomas. AlDL; CH; GTBS; GTBS-W; LBBV; LiTB; LiTM; MM; NP; OBEV (new ed.); PoeMoYo; ShBV-2; TCPD; TwCV
Admirable New Northern Story of Two Constant Lovers, The. *Unknown.* SG
Admiral, Admiral, sailing home. The Homing. John Jerome Rooney. AA
Admiral Benbow. *Unknown.* EnSB; SG
Admiral Byrd. Ogden Nash. InMe; YaD
Admiral Death. Sir Henry Newbolt. BHV; LBBV
Admiral Hosier's Ghost. Richard Glover. EV-3; HBV; SG; ViBoPo
Admiral Rodney's Triumph on the 12th of April. *Unknown.* SG
Admirals All. Sir Henry Newbolt. ShGoBo; TVSH
Admiral's Caravan, The, *sel.* Charles Edward Carryl.
Plaint of the Camel, The. AnAmPo; BoTP; FaPON; HBV; HBVY; LA; OTPC (1946 ed.); PCN; PoeMoYo; PoRh; SP; StVeCh; UTS
(Camel's Complaint, The.) GoBP
(Camel's Lament, The.) GoTP
Admiral's Ghost, The. Alfred Noyes. BBV; PoMS; TiPo (1952 ed.)
Admire thy wreath? And wherefore should I not. To a Plagiarist. Moses ibn Ezra. TrJP
Admit the ruse to fix and name her chaste. The Romantic. Louise Bogan. NP
Admit thou darlinge of myne eyes. *Unknown.* SeCSL
Admonition. John Peale Bishop. TwAmPo
Admonition. John L. Bonn. JKCP (1955 ed.)
Admonition. Philip Stack. BLPA
Admonition before Grief. Hazel Hall. NP
Admonition for Spring. L. A. MacKay. BoCaPo; CaP; PeCV; TwCV
Admonition to a Traveller. Wordsworth. GTBS; GTBS-D; GTBS-W; GTSE; GTSL
Admonition to Young Lassies, An. Alexander Montgomerie. BSV; EBSV
Admonitions Margaret Bell Houston. MoSiPe
Adolescence. P. K. Page. BoCaPo (1948 ed.); CaP; TwCaPo
Adolescence. Sappho, *tr. fr. Greek by* Walter Petersen. GrR
Adolescents in the Dusk. Iain Fletcher. FaBoMo
Adolicus; that's a creeper rug, its small. The Houses, III. "Robin Hyde." AnNZ
Adolphus Elfinstone. Gelett Burgess. GaP; PoRL
Adonais. Will Wallace Harney. AA; HBV
Adonais; an Elegy on the Death of John Keats. Shelley. AEV; AtBAP; ATP; BCEP, *abr.*; BEL; BoLiVe; BPN; ChER; EM-2; EmBrPo; EnL; EnLi-2; EnLit; EnRP; EPN; EPP; ERP; EV-4; FiP, *much abr.*; GEPC; GoTL; HBV; HoPM; LiA; LoBV; MaPo; MCCG; NBE, *abr.*; OAEP; OBRV; PIAE, *abr.*; PoE; PoEL-4; PtP; REAL; ReaPo; TOP; TrGrPo; TriL; TwCrTr; UnPo (1st ed.); ViBoPo, *abr.*; WHA; WoL. *abr.*
Sels.
"Alas! that all we love." OHIP
Go Thou to Rome. ChTr
(Grave of Keats, The.) TCEP
"He has outsoared the shadow of our night." CoEV
"He is made one with Nature." WGRP
"Here pause: these graves are all too young as yet." MyFE
"One remains, the many change and pass, The." InP
(Lumen de Lumine.) GoBC

One with Nature ("He lives, he wakes"). MaRV
"Peace, peace! he is not dead, he doth not sleep." BoFr; FaBoEn; LEAP; LO; UnW
(Against Oblivion.) TreFS
(He Is Not Dead.) MaRV
Adonis. Hilda Doolittle ("H. D."). AWP; BAV; InPo; JAWP; LiTA; MOAP; PFE; TBM; WBP
Adonis. Sappho, *tr. fr. Greek by* H. De Vere Stacpoole. GrR
Adonis in Slumber. Keats. *Fr.* Endymion, II. ERP
(Cast Asleep.) BCEP
(Sleeping Youth, A.) SeCePo
Adonis-like, gored by the rough world's wound. Ideal Passion, XLI. George Edward Woodberry. MOAP
Adonis Song, The. Theocritus, *tr. fr. Greek by* R. C. Trevelyan. *Fr.* Idylls. GrR
Adoration. Mme Guyon. WGRP
Adoration. David Morton. MaRV
Adoration. Christopher Smart. *See* Mermaid's Pap, The.
Adoration of the Disk by King Akhnaten and Princess Nefer Neferiu Aten. *Unknown, tr. fr. Egyptian by* Robert Hillyer. *Fr.* The Book of the Dead. AWP; JAWP; WBP
"Cattle roam again across the field, The," *sel.* FaPON
Adoration of the Shepherds, The. St. Luke, Bible, *N.T.* ChrBoLe (II: 1-16); CLS (II: 1-20)
(Birth of Jesus, The, II: 1-20.) EM-1
(Christmas Eve, II: 8-14.) ChBR; GaP; PCH; SiSoSe
(Christmas Story, The, II: 8-14.) MaRV
(First Christmas, The.) OTPC (1946 ed.) (II: 8-16); PoRL (II: 8-16); TreFS (II: 1-19)
(Tidings of Great Joy, II: 8-14.) FaPON
Adoration of the Wise Men, The. Cecil Frances Alexander. COAH; HBVY; PRWS
Adoro Te Devote. St. Thomas Aquinas, *tr. fr. Latin.* CAW, *tr. by* Dom F. Cabrol; WHL, *abr., tr. unknown*
Adown a quiet glen where the gowan-berries glisten. The Haunted Hazel. James B. Dollard. CPG; OCL
Adown the leafy lane we two. A Memory. D. MacAleese. TIP
A-down the road and gun in hand. Whiskey Bill; a Fragment. *Unknown.* SCC
Adrasta, *sel.* John Jones.
Come, Lovers, Bring Your Cares. SeCL; TuPP
Adrian Block's Song. Edward Everett Hale. PAH
Adriani Morientis ad Animam Suam. Emperor Hadrian. *See* To His Soul.
Adrift. Elizabeth Dickinson Dowden. WGRP
Adsum. Richard Henry Stoddard. AA; TCAP
Adulterous medley of contraries. His Epitaph. Tristan Corbière. TrFP
Advance of the Trojans, The. Homer, *tr. fr. Greek by* William Cowper. *Fr.* The Iliad. III. OxBG
("But when the bands were mustered round their leaders on each side," *tr. by* F. L. Lucas.) GrPE
(Trojans and Greeks, *tr. by* the Earl of Derby.) GrR
Advance your choral motions now. Song: To the Masquers Representing Stars [*or* The Stars Dance]. Thomas Campion. *Fr.* The Lords' Mask. LoBV; OBSC
Advantage of the Outside, The. Richard Eberhart. NePA
Advantages of living with two cultures, The. Bonne Entente. F. R. Scott. FiBHP; PeCV; SiTL
Advent. Brother Antoninus. NeAP
Advent. W. H. Auden. *Fr.* For the Time Being. OAEP (2d ed.)
Advent. John Gould Fletcher. MAP; MaRV; MoAmPo
Advent. Jorge Guillén, *tr. fr. Spanish by* Eleanor L. Turnbull. CoSP
Advent. F. W. H. Myers. *Fr.* Saint Paul. MaRV
Advent. Christina Rossetti. PoVP; VLEP
Advent Lyrics, *sels* *Unknown, tr. fr. Anglo-Saxon by* Charles W. Kennedy. *Fr.* Christ I. AnOE
"Bless earth with Thine Advent, O Saviour Christ!" VIII.
"Hail, O most worthy in all the world!" IX.
"O holy Jerusalem, Vision of peace," III.
". . . to the King./ Thou art the wall-stone the workers rejected," I.
Advent of Spring. Tu Fu, *tr. fr. Chinese.* WhP
Adventure. Harry Behn. TiPo (1959 ed.)
Adventure. Laura Benét. GaP; HBMV; RAR; TSW; TSWC
Adventure. Henry Holcomb Bennett. BoHiPo
Adventure. Adelaide Crapsey. NP
Adventure. Thomas Wade Earp. PoMa
Adventure. Mary Fullerton. BoAV
Adventure. Guy Mason. CaP
Adventure. Grace Fallow Norton. HBMV
Adventure. William Alexander Percy. LS
Adventure. Nancy Byrd Turner. StVeCh (1955 ed.)
Adventurer, The. José Moreno Villa, *tr. fr. Spanish by* Eleanor L. Turnbull. CoSP
Adventurer, The. Odell Shepard. HBMV; OBAV
Adventurers, The. May Byron. GA; HBV
Adventures of Huckleberry Finn, The, *sel.* "Mark Twain."
Ode to Stephen Dowling Bots, Dec'd. FiBHP
Adventures of Isabel. Ogden Nash. AlDL; CenHV; MoAmPo; MoShBr; NeMA; TiPo (1959 ed.)
Adventures of Johnny Newcome in the Navy, The, *sels.* John Mitford.
Fight, The. SG
Gale of Wind, A. SG
Adventures of Master F. I. [*or* F. J.], The, *sels.* George Gascoigne.
And If I Did, What Then? ElL; FaBoEn; PoEL-1; ReIE
(Farewell, A.) LoBV; OBSC
"As some men say there is a kind of seed." ReIE
"Fair Bersabe the bright, once bathing in a well." ReIE
Adventures of my separate bark, The. Charles Madge. *Fr.* Poem by Stages. BoSA
Adventures of Simon Swaugum, a Village Merchant, The. Philip Freneau. PoEL-4
Adventures of Tom Sawyer, The, *sel.* "Mark Twain."
Missouri Maiden's Farewell to Alabama, A, *fr. ch.* 21. InMe
Adventurous bird walking upon the air. The Bird. Edwin Muir. POTE
Advertisement of a Lost Day. Lydia Huntley Sigourney. WBLP
Advice. Gwendolyn B. Bennett. CDC
Advice. Walter Savage Landor. HBV; VA
Advice, The. Sir Walter Ralegh. SiPS
Advice. Hugh Rhodes. GoTP
Advice. Earl of Roscommon. *Fr.* An Essay on Translated Verse. BeR
Advice, The. Charles Sackville. *See* Song: "Phyllis, for shame, let us improve."
Advice. A. M. Sullivan. PFE
Advice against Travel. James Clarence Mangan. OBVV
Advice for a Journey. Sidney Keyes. SoV
Advice from an Expert. John Kieran. InMe
Advice to a Blue-Bird. Maxwell Bodenheim. HBMV; MAP; MoAmPo (1942 ed.)
Advice to a Boy. Robinson Kay Leather. LEAP
Advice to a Buttercup. Maxwell Bodenheim. LEAP
Advice to a Clansman. *Unknown, tr. fr. Gaelic by* Thomas Pattison. EBSV
Advice to a Forest. Maxwell Bodenheim. TrJP
Advice to a Girl. Thomas Campion. CoBE; EnLit; GTSL; HBV; LiTL; LoPo
(Never Love [Unless You Can].) EG; ElL; ElSeCe; LoBV; ReEn; SiCE; TrGrPo; TuPP; TyEnPo; ViBoPo
Advice to a Lady in Autumn. Earl of Chesterfield. CEP; OBEC
Advice to a Lover. S. Charles Jellicoe. HBV
Advice to a Lover. Menander. *See* Plight of a Forsaken Lover.
Advice to a Lover. Sir John Suckling. *See* Why So Pale and Wan?
Advice to a Lover. *Unknown.* *See* Sea Hath Many Thousand Sands, The.
Advice to a Raven in Russia, December, 1812. Joel Barlow. AmPP (4th ed.); APW; NePA; OxBA
Advice to a Young Man (of Letters) Who Doesn't Know How to Take Care of Himself. Irwin Edman. InMe
Advice to a Young Romanticist. Allen Tate. TBM
Advice to an Old Beauty. Thomas Parnell. *Fr.* An Elegy: To an Old Beauty. BeR
Advice to Bores. Abraham ibn Chasdai, *tr. fr. Hebrew by* Joseph Chotzner. TrJP
Advice to Hotheads. Samuel ben Elhanan Isaac Archevolti of Padua, *tr. fr. Hebrew by* A. B. Rhine. TrJP
Advice to Julia, *sels.* Henry Luttrell.
After the Wedding. IrPN
Dress. OBRV
Honeymoon, The. OBRV
Lovers and Friends. OBRV
Peace, The. OBRV
Advice to Kyrnos. Theognis. *See* Eugenics.
Advice to Leesome Merriness. Sir Richard Maitland. EBSV
Advice to Small Children. Edward Anthony. GoTP
Advice to the Ladies of London in the Choice of Their Husbands. *Unknown.* CoMu
Advice to the Old Beaux. Sir Charles Sedley. BeR; CEP; SeCV-2
Advice to the Same ("Who doth desire that chaste his wife should be"). Sir Philip Sidney. *See* Truth Doth Truth Deserve.
Advice to Travelers. Walker Gibson. NePoAm-2
Advice to Worriers. George S. Kaufman. ALV; PC
Advice to Young Naturalists. Laura E. Richards. LiL
Advices from Rexroth's Bestiary. Kenneth Rexroth. *See* Bestiary, A.
Ae boat anerlie nou. Largo. Sidney Goodsir Smith. NeBP
Ae day a clock wad brag a dial. The Clock and Dial. Allan Ramsay. CBOV
Ae Fond Kiss. Burns. AnFE; BCEP; BEL; BSV; CEP; EBSV; EiPP; EM-1; EnLi-2; EnLit; EnRP; EPP; EtPaEn; EV-3; HBV; LEAP; OAEP; OBEC; OBEV;

Ae Fond Kiss (*continued*)
OuHeWo; PoEL-4; REAL; ReaPo; SeCeV; TyEnPo; WHA
(Ae Fond Kiss, and Then We Sever.) LO; ViBoPo
(Ae Fond Kiss before We Part.) LPS-1
(Farewell to Nancy.) FaFP; LoPS; TreF; WoL
Ae Happy Hour. Alexander Laing. EBSV
Ae time that I our flownrie life appraisit. Frae the Second Canzone o Dante's "Vita Nuova." Dante, *tr. into Scots by* Douglas Young. *Fr.* La Vita Nuova. LyPI
Ae weet forenicht i' the yow-trummle. The Watergaw. "Hugh MacDiarmid." GoTS; NeBP
Aedh Tells of the Rose in His Heart. W. B. Yeats. *See* Lover Tells of the Rose in His Heart, The.
Aedh Wishes for the Cloths of Heaven. W. B. Yeats. MBP; MoBrPo; NeMA; OBEV (new ed.); OBVV; PoeT; PtOT; TwCV
(He Wishes for the Cloths of Heaven.) ChMo; CMP; EPP; SP
Aegean Islands 1940–41. Bernard Spencer. NeBP
Aeglamour Seeks His Shepherdess. Ben Jonson. *See* Here She Was Wont to Go.
Aeglamour's Lament. Ben Jonson. *See* Here She Was Wont to Go.
Aeliana's Ditty. Henry Chettle. *See* Wily Cupid.
Aella; a Tragycal Enterlude, *sels.* Thomas Chatterton.
Minstrel's Song. BLV; CG; HBV; LEAP; LoBV; LPS-1; TrGrPo, *sl. abr.*; WHA
(Minstrel's Roundelay, The, *sl. abr.*) BCEP
(Mynstrelles Songe.) AnFE; BEL; CEP; EiPP; EnLi-2; EnLoPo; EnRP; EV-3; OBEC
(O, Sing unto My Roundelay, *abr.*) CH
(Roundelay.) CBOV; WP
(Song: "O sing unto my roundelay.") ATP (1935 ed.), *sl. abr.*; LiTL; LO, *abr.*
(Song from "Aella.") LiA; LiTG; OBEV; TOP
Mynstrelles Songe: "Angelles bee wrogte to bee of neidher kynde." EnLoPo
Song of the Three Minstrels. TrGrPo
("Budding floweret blushes at the light, The.") ViBoPo
(Mynstrelles Songe.) EnRP
(There Lacketh Somethynge Stylle, *abr.*) EV-3
Autumn Fruits, *2 sts.* RO
Aeneas and Dido. Virgil, *tr. fr. Latin. Fr.* The Aeneid, IV. LaP, *tr. by* Rolfe Humphries; RoL, *longer sel., tr. by* Theodore C. Williams
Aeneas at the Site of Rome. Virgil, *tr. fr. Latin by* Rolfe Humphries. *Fr.* The Aeneid, VIII. LaP
Aeneas at Washington. Allen Tate. LiTA; MoPo; MoVE; NePA; OxBA
Aeneas dead, Ascanius reign'd; Ascanius dead, his brother. William Warner. *Fr.* Albion's England. ReIE
Aeneid. Claire McAllister. NePA
Aeneid, The. John William Mackail. PtP
Aeneid, The, *sels.* Virgil, *tr. fr. Latin.*
Aeneas and Dido, *fr.* IV. LaP, *tr. by* Rolfe Humphries; RoL, *longer sel., tr. by* Theodore C. Williams
Aeneas at the Site of Rome, *fr.* VIII, *tr. by* Rolfe Humphries. LaP
Battle of Actium, *fr.* VIII, *tr. by* Dryden. OBS
Blest Abode, A, *fr.* VI, *tr. by* Theodore C. Williams. GrCo-1
"But now the wounded queen. with heavy care," *fr.* IV, *tr. by* the Earl of Surrey. ReIE
Camilla, *fr.* VII, *tr. by* Rolfe Humphries. LaP
Death of Turnus, The, *abr., fr.* XII, *tr. by* Dryden. WoL
Departure of Aeneas from Dido, *fr.* IV, *tr. by* the Earl of Surrey. TCEP
Destruction of Troy, The, *fr.* II, *tr. by* Sir John Denham. SeCV-1
Dido among the Shades, *fr.* VI, *tr. by* Dryden. OBS
Dido to Aeneas, *fr.* IV. *tr. by* Richard Stanyhurst. AnIV
Dido's Hunting, *fr.* IV, *tr. by* the Earl of Surrey. OBSC
(Fourth Book of Virgil, The.) ReEn
Entrance to Hell, The, *fr.* VI, *tr. into Middle English by* Gawin Douglas. GoTS
Entrance to Tartarus, The, *fr.* VI, *tr. into Middle English by* Gawin Douglas. BSV
Fall of Troy, The, II, *tr. by* Theodore C. Williams. RoL
"Full soon the Queen this crafty sleight 'gan smell," *fr.* IV, *tr. by* the Earl of Surrey. EnLit
"I that my slender oaten pipe in verse was wont to sound," *fr.* I, *tr. by* Thomas Phaer. ReIE
Ibant Obscuri; Vision of Aeneas, *fr.* VI, *tr. by* Robert Bridges. LaP
"It was then night; the sounde and quiet slepe," *fr.* IV, *tr. by* the Earl of Surrey. PoEL-1
Jupiter Sends a Fury to Baffle Turnus in Battle, *fr.* XII, *pr. tr. by* H. R. Fairclough. LiA
Lower World, The (the Sibyl Speaks), *fr.* VI, *tr. by* Rolfe Humphries. LaP
Marcellus, *fr.* VI, *tr. by* Dryden. OBS
"Night: and tired creatures over all the world," *fr.* IV, *tr. by* Rolfe Humphries. LaP
On Some Verses of Virgil, *fr.* VIII, *tr. by* James Rhoades. LiA
Rang'd on the Line Opposed, Antonius Brings, *fr.* VIII, *tr. by* Dryden. WaaP
Sad Dido, *fr.* IV, *tr. by* Sidney Godolphin. LiA
Shipwreck of the Trojans; Landing at Carthage, I, *tr. by* Theodore C. Williams. RoL
Sixth Book of the Aeneis, The, *tr. by* Dryden. SeCV-2
Sunt Lacrimae Rerum, *fr.* I, *tr. by* James Rhoades. LiA
"Then from the seas the dawning gan arise," *fr.* IV, *tr. by* the Earl of Surrey. ReEn
"Then Mercury 'gan bend him to obey," *fr.* IV, *tr. by* the Earl of Surrey. ViBoPo
"They whisted all, with fixèd face attent," *fr.* II, *tr. by* the Earl of Surrey. EnLi-1; EPP
(Certain Books of Virgil's Aeneis.) TuPP
(Second Book of Virgil's Aeneid, The.) SiCE; SiPS
(Translation from Virgil's Aeneid.) LiTB
Venus the Goddess, *br. sel. fr.* I, *pr. tr. by* H. R. Fairclough. LiA
Vision of Rome's Destiny, *fr.* VI, *tr. by* Dryden. RoL
Welcome to the Sun, *fr.* XII, *tr. by* Gawin Douglas. ACP
"With tentive list'ning each wight was settled in hark'ning," *fr.* II, *tr. by* Richard Stanyhurst. ReIE
With Wound Still Fresh, *fr.* VI, *pr. tr. by* H. R. Fairclough. LiA
Aeolian Harp. William Allingham. OnYI; TIP
Aeolian Harp, An. "Michael Field." VA
Aeolus, *sel.* Euripides, *tr. fr. Greek by* C. M. Bowra.
Old Men, The. OxBG
Aeons of history float. Prisoner. Marguerite George. GoYe
Aerial City, The. Afanasi Afanasievich Fet, *tr. fr. Russian by* Babette Deutsch. TrRV
Aeronaut to His Lady, The. Frank Sidgwick. WhC
Aeroplane, The. Hart Crane. *Fr.* The Bridge: Cape Hatteras. VOD (1935 ed.)
Aeroplane. Mary McB. Green. TiPo
Aeroplane, The. Jeannie Kirby. BoTP
Aeschylean Chorus, An. Aristophanes, *tr. fr. Greek by* T. F. Higham. *Fr.* The Frogs. OxBG
Aeschylos and Sophocles. Walter Savage Landor. BPN; PtP
Aeschylus. Aeschylus. *See* Epitaph for Himself.
Aesop. Andrew Lang. VA
Aesop, *sel.* Sir John Vanbrugh.
Nightingale, The. SeCL
Aesop at Play. Phaedrus, *tr. fr. Latin by* Christopher Smart. AWP; JAWP; WBP
Aesop, mine author, makis mentioun. The Taill of the Uponlandis Mous and the Burges Mous. Robert Henryson. BSV; EV-1
Aesthete, The. Callimachus, *tr. fr. Greek by* F. L. Lucas. GrPE
Aesthete, The. W. S. Gilbert. *See* Bunthorne's Song.
Aesthete to the Rose, The. *Unknown.* PA
Aesthetics. Gerardo Diego, *tr. fr. Spanish* by Eleanor L. Turnbull. CoSP
Aestivation. Oliver Wendell Holmes. *Fr.* The Autocrat of the Breakfast Table, *ch.* 11. AmPP; AnNE; BOHV; InMe; NA; REAL; WhC
(Intramural Aestivation, or Summer in Town, by a Teacher of Latin.) ChTr
Aestuary, An. George Croly. IrPN
Aetate XIX. Herman Charles Merivale. OBVV; VA
Æthelstan [*or* Athelstan] King,/ Lord among Earls. The Battle of Brunanburh. *Unknown, tr. by* Tennyson. BEL; CoBE; EnLit; ExPo; TrGrPo; WaaP
Æthelstan King, lord of eorls. The Battle of Brunanburh. *Unknown, tr. by* Charles W. Kennedy. AnOE
Aeternae Memoriae Patris, *sel.* Léon Paul Fargue, *tr. fr. French by* Eugene Jolas.
"Since then, there has been always, suspended on my brow and hurting me." MiFP
Aeterne Rerum Conditor. St. Ambrose, *tr. fr. Latin by* J. V. Cunningham. LaP
Aethiopus Lotus. Richard Crashaw, *tr. fr. Latin by* D. C. Allen. Epigrammata Sacra, I, 9. LaP
Aethra's Intercession. Euripides, *tr. fr. Greek by* Arthur S. Way. *Fr.* Suppliants. GrR
Aëtius at Châlons, September, 451. Arthur William Ryder. MuM
Aetna. Pindar, *tr. fr Greek by* H. T. Wade-Gery *and* C. M. Bowra. *Fr.* Pythian Odes, I. GrR
Aetna—I've been up Vesuvius. To Mount Aetna. Tristan Corbière. AnFP
Afar from you and very near to care. Sonnet XVIII. Marqués de Santillana. AnSpL-1
Afar in the Desert. Thomas Pringle. BoSA; HBV; LPS-1
Afar on the Floodways. *Unknown. Fr.* The Seafarer. PoLi
Afar the hunt in vales below has sped. Meeting of Orion and Artemis. Richard Henry Horne. *Fr.* Orion. VA
Affable Irregular, An. The Road at My Door. W. B. Yeats. Meditations in Time of Civil War, V. LiTB; SoV
Affaire d'Amour. Margaret Deland. HBV

Affairs of the world are all hurry and trouble, The. Poems Translated from the Chinese. *Unknown, tr. by* John Francis Davis. RO
Affection and Desire. Sir Walter Ralegh. *See* Conceit Begotten by the Eyes.
Affectionate Shepherd, The, *sel.* Richard Barnfield.
Daphnis to Ganymede. ElL; ThWaDe
Affection's charm no longer gilds. The Personified Sentimental. Bret Harte. NA
Affections, Instincts, Principles, and Powers. Written in Butler's Sermons. Matthew Arnold. MeRV
Affections lose their object; Time brings forth. Sonnet to an Octogenarian. Wordsworth. BPN; EmBrPo
Affidavit in Platitudes. E. B. White. InMe
Affinities. Baudelaire. *See* Correspondences.
Affinities. Heine, *tr. fr. German by* Herman Salinger. AnGP
Affinity. "Ricketty Kate." MoAuPo
Affinity. R. S. Thomas. HaMV; PoN
Affinity, The. Anna Wickham. BMEP; HBMV; MBP; MoBrPo
Affinity with the Stars. Dante, *tr. fr. Italian by* Wendell Phillips Stafford. *Fr.* Divina Commedia: Paradiso. GrCo-2
Affirmation, An. Minot Judson Savage. MaRV
Affirmations (I-III). Peter Viereck. MiAP
Affliction. Lamentations, III: 1–15, Bible, *O.T.* TrJP
Affliction. Sir John Davies. *Fr.* Nosce Teipsum. CoEV; OBSC
Affliction ("Broken in pieces all asunder"). George Herbert. LoBV
Affliction ("When first Thou didst entice"). George Herbert. CoEV; EPS; EV-2; LiTB; MaPo; MeLP; MePo; NBE; OBS; OxBoCh
Affliction. W. Wesley Trimpi. PtPa
Affliction. Henry Vaughan. PoP
Affliction of Margaret, The. Wordsworth. BPN; EmBrPo; EnRP; ERP; EV-3; GEPC; GTBS; GTBS-D; GTBS-W; GTSE; GTSL; MotAn; OBRV; PoEL-4
Affliction of Richard, The. Robert Bridges. TriL
Afforestation. E. A. Wodehouse. FiBHP
Affronting fool, subdue your transient light. To a Critic of Tennyson. Ambrose Bierce. BAP
Afield, afield, out in the open field! How the Grain Grows. *Unknown.* OnPM
Afloat on the Lake. Shen Yü Ch'iu, *tr. fr. Chinese by* Henry H. Hart. PoHN
Afloat; We Move. Delicious! Arthur Hugh Clough. *Fr.* Dipsychus. PoVP; ViPP
Afoot. Sir Charles G. D. Roberts. CaP; HBV; NLK; OCL; VA
Afoot. Cicely Fox Smith. NLK
Afoot and light-hearted I take to the open road. Song of the Open Road [*or* Afoot and Light-hearted *or* The Open Road]. Walt Whitman. APW; AtBAP; FaFP; GTSE; HBVY; IAP; LEAP; MAP; MoAmPo; NeMA; NePA; NLK; OQP; PC; PoMa; QP-2; StaSt; TiPo; ViBoPo; WHA
Afore the Lammas tide. The Scottish Widow's Lament. Thomas Smibert. EBSV
Aforetime, by the waters wan. Roast Swan Song. *Unknown.* LiTW
Aforetime, fruitfulness and tilth were here. Deserted Farms. Richard Burton. AnAmPo; LA
Afraid? Of whom am I afraid? Emily Dickinson. EOAH (Afraid.) OHIP
Africa. Lewis Alexander. CDC
Africa. *Unknown.* MaRV; StJW
African Affair, The. Bruce McM. Wright. PoNe
African Chief, The. Bryant. AnNE; BLPA; PTA-2; TreFS
African Dance. Langston Hughes. FaPON; MoSiPe; TiPo (1952 ed.)
African Moonrise. Roy Campbell. CoBE
African Night. Jessie Lemont. MuM
African Song, An. Thomas Chatterton. LoBV; RO
Afrikaans Homestead. Peter Jackson. BoSA
Afro-American Fragment. Langston Hughes. PoNe
"Aften [*or* Aft] hae I playd [*or* played] at the cards and the dice." The Rantin Laddie. *Unknown.* BaBo (A *and* B *vers.*); ESPB
After. Theodora Bates. CAG
After. Robert Browning. BLV; BMEP; BoLiVe; TrGrPo (Avenger Speaks, The.) EG
After. Florence Earle Coates. AOAH
After. Caroline Grayson. BLRP
After. Amory Hare. MuM
After. Ralph Hodgson. ChMo; CMP; MBP; MoBrPo
After. Philip Bourke Marston. HBV
After. Lizette Woodworth Reese. HBV; LS
After a banquet. The Cynneddf. Rolfe Humphries. CrMA
After a Dolmetsch Concert. Arthur Upson. LBMV; PFY; PoeMoYo
After a Game of Squash. Samuel L. Albert. GoYe; NePoAm-2
After a hundred years. Emily Dickinson. AWP; FaBoEn; InPo; MOAP; MoPo; OxBA
After a Journey. Thomas Hardy. AtBAP; ChMP; CoEV; EnLoPo; FaBoEn; GTBS-D; MoPW; MoVE; PoEL-5
After a Lecture on Keats. Oliver Wendell Holmes. AA; OBAV; PtP; ViBoPo
After a light shower, the pools, muddy green in color. Mid-July Twilight, Eight o'Clock. Jules Laforgue. AnFP
After a Little While. James Ryder Randall. CAW
After a Parting. Alice Meynell. PoVP
After a Rain. Lucy Cherry Crisp. NoCaPo (rev. ed.)
After a Retreat. Robert Hugh Benson. JKCP
After a soiree, with his dark head bent. Hazlitt Sups. Katharine Day Little. GoYe
After a sunrise heavy with unease. The Blizzard. Lenore A. Pratt. TwCaPo
After a Symphony Concert. Katharine Shepard Hayden. MuM
After a thousand mazes overgone. Adonis in Slumber [*or* Cast Asleep *or* A Sleeping Youth]. Keats. *Fr.* Endymion, II. BCEP; ERP; SeCePo
After a Time. Catherine Davis. NePoEA
After All. Donald Jeffrey Hayes. CDC
After All. Thomas S. Jones, Jr. VOD
After All. Arthur Upson. PR
After All. William Winter. PAP
After all,/ One country, brethren! One Country. Frank Lebby Stanton. AA; PaA
After All and After All. Mary Carolyn Davies. GaP; MPB; SP; TiPo (1952 ed.)
After all and after all. After All. Donald Jeffrey Hayes. CDC
After all, freedom is theirs. Sea-Gulls. Tatsuji Miyoshi. PoLJ
After All Splendors. Mary Brent Whiteside. LS
After all you are weary of this oldtime world. Zone. Guillaume Apollinaire. AnFP
After an Interval. Walt Whitman. AA
After Anacreon. Lew Welch. NeAP
After Annunciation. Anna Wickham. MBP; MoBrPo
After Apple-picking. Robert Frost. AmP; AmPo; AnAmPo; AnNE; BrBE; CoBMV; CoV; LA; LEAP; LiTA; MAP; MoAB; MoAmPo; MoPo; MoVE; NP; OnAP; OxBA; ReaPo; ReMP; RiBV; SBMV; UnPo; ViBoPo; WoL
After, at sea a tall ship did appeare. The Visions of Petrarch, II. *Tr. by* Spenser. EnLi-1
After Aughrim. Arthur Gerald Geoghegan. BoHiPo; OnYI; TIP
After Aughrim. Emily Lawless. GTIV; OBEV (new ed.); OxBI
After Battle. Duncan Campbell Scott. AOAH; TwCV
After Battle ("Better to live on beggar's bread"). *Unknown, tr. fr. Sanskrit by* Sir Edwin Arnold. *Fr.* Bhagavad-Gita. MaRV
After Battle ("When after many battles past"). *Unknown.* MaRV
After being beaten. Satirical Poems on Daimyos, V. Issa. PoFr
After Being Separated for a Long Time. Li Po, *tr. fr. Chinese by* Florence Ayscough *and* Amy Lowell. ChLP
After Blenheim. Robert Southey. *See* Battle of Blenheim, The.
After Bombardment. John Pudney. WaP
After Browning. *Unknown.* PA
After careful meditation. Thomas Love Peacock. *Fr.* Crotchet Castle. ALV
After Christmas. W. H. Auden. *Fr.* For the Time Being. MoAB; MoBrPo (1950 ed.) (Well, So That Is That.) LiTA
After Christmas. Consuelo Valencia. MaRV
After Christmas a Landlord Remembers. Elizabeth J. Coatsworth. StJW (Reminiscences of a Landlord.) ChrBoLe
After-Christmas Poem. Elizabeth-Ellen Long. ChBR
After Collecting the Autumn Taxes. Po Chü-i, *tr. fr. Chinese by* Arthur Waley. TrCh
After-Comers, The Robert Trail Spence Lowell. AA
After completing a book for one now dead. Indian Summer. William Ellery Leonard. *Fr.* Two Lives, Pt. III. PG (1945 ed.)
After Construing. A. C. Benson. VA
After Corunna. Charles Wolfe. *See* Burial of Sir John Moore after Corunna.
After Dark Vapours [*or* Vapors] Have Oppressed Our Plains. Keats. BPN; EmBrPo; ERP; EV-4 (After Dark Vapours.) EnRP (Sonnet: After Dark Vapors.) AtBAP
After day's persistent labor. Panacea. Georgia B. Gierasch. MuM
After Death. R. A. K. Mason. AnNZ
After Death. Fanny Parnell. AnIV; GTIV; OBVV; OnYI; OxBI; VA (Post-Mortem.) PoFr; TIP
After Death. Charles Francis Richardson. AA

After Death. Christina Rossetti. EnLi-2; POTT; PoVP; UnW; VA; VLEP
After Death. Swinburne. ViP
After Death in Arabia, *abr.* Sir Edwin Arnold. *Fr.* Pearls of the Faith. BMEP; EOAH; HBV; VA; WGRP
"Farewell, friends! yet not farewell," *sel.* MaRV
After Dilettante Concetti. Henry Duff Traill. BOHV; CenHV; HBV
After dinner Erasmus. E. C. Bentley. *Fr.* Biography for Beginners. CenHV
After Disaster. Lizette Woodworth Reese. TBM
After Dunkirk. Alun Lewis. SoV
After Galen. Oliver St. John Gogarty. OBMV; PoRA
After Getting Drunk Becoming Sober in the Night. Po Chü-i, *tr. fr. Chinese by* Arthur Waley. TrCh
After Goethe. Mikhail Yurevich Lermontov, *tr. fr. Russian by* Sir Cecil Kisch. WaL
After Gray Vigils, Sunshine in the Heart. George Santayana. Sonnets, XLIX. MAP; MoAmPo; MOAP; WHA
After great pain a formal feeling comes. Emily Dickinson. CoBA; CoV; InPo; LiTA; LiTG; MAP; MaPo; MoAB; MoAmPo; MOAP; MoPo; MoVE; NePA; Po; PoE; ReMP; RiBV; TwP; UnPo
After great storms the calm returns. Sir Thomas Wyatt. SiPS
After Harvest. Stefan George, *tr. fr. German by* Herman Salinger. *Fr.* Das Jahr der Seele. TwGV
After He Had Gone. Sylvia Townsend Warner. MBP; MoBrPo
After Hearing the Prime Minister, April 27th, 1941. Richard Elwes. NeTW
After Heine. Nikolai Alekseyevich Nekrasov, *tr. fr. Russian by* Sir Cecil Kisch. WaL
After Horace. A. D. Godley. BOHV
After hot loveless nights, when cold winds stream. The Sisters. Roy Campbell. ChMP; FaBoTw; MoVE; OBMV
After Hour. Sydney King Russell. MuM
After I ate my dinner then I ate. Confession of a Glutton. Don Marquis. AlBD
After I got religion and steadied down. "Butch" Weldy. Edgar Lee Masters. *Fr.* Spoon River Anthology. NePA
After I had seen/ That spectacle. He Remembers the Vista of a Towering Peak. Wordsworth. *Fr.* The Prelude, I. LiA
After Jena. Thomas Hardy. *Fr.* The Dynasts, Pt. II, Act I, sc. vii. WaaP
After Laughter. Grace Buchanan Sherwood. GoYe
After-Life. Pindar. *See* Life after Death.
After Light and the shaping of Land he came. The Elder Brother (Poem for All Good and Loyal Dogs). Elma Dean. NeMA
After lilacs come out. Lilacs. Hilda Conkling. NP; TBM
After London. John Dynham Cornish Pellow. GTBS
After long, after vague leagues. Sonata and Destructions. "Pablo Neruda." AnCL
After long journey in sun. Ear Is Not Deaf. Irene Dayton. GoYe
After Long Rain. Wang Wei, *tr. fr. Chinese.* WhP
After Long Silence. W. B. Yeats. CaAE; EnLoPo; GTBS-W; HoPM; LiTL; LiTM; OBMV; POTE; TwP; UnPo
After long storms' [*or* stormes] and tempests' sad assay. Amoretti, LXIII. Spenser. BEL; EnLit; FaBoEn; OAEP; OBSC; PeBoSo; SiCE
After long struggle I find joy at last. The Gospel of Consolation. Havelock Ellis. PoP
After long thirty years re-met. Epitaph. Sylvia Townsend Warner. BLV
After Looking into Carlyle's Reminiscences. Swinburne. ViPo
After Love. Arthur Symons. LEAP; NeHB
After Lunch. Po Chü-i, *tr. fr. Chinese by* Arthur Waley. TrCh
After Mardi Gras. Sister Mary Honora. NePoAm-2
After Margrave died, nothing/ Seemed worth while. History of a Literary Movement. Howard Nemerov. NePoEA
After Midnight. Charles Vildrac, *tr. fr. French by* Jethro Bithell. AWP; JAWP; WBP
After Missing the Recluse on the Western Mountain. Ch'iu Wei, *tr. fr. Chinese by* Witter Bynner. BoFr
After much eating, drinking, speaking ill. Timocreon. Simonides. GrL; OxBG
After Music. Josephine Preston Peabody. AA
After night's thunder [slumber, *wr.*] far away had rolled. Haymaking. Edward Thomas. AnFE; MBP; MoAB; MoBrPo; SeCePo
After one moment when I bowed my head. The Convert. G. K. Chesterton. GoBC; InP; JKCP (1926 ed.)
After Pain. Marjorie Meeker. NP
After Parting. Sara Teasdale. TOP
After Passing the Examination. Po Chü-i, *tr. fr. Chinese by* Arthur Waley. AlDL; Po; TrCh
After Rain. Eleanor Farjeon. BoChLi
After Rain. Archibald Lampman. CPG
After Rain. Tu Fu, *tr. fr. Chinese by* Chi Hwang Chu *and* Edna Worthley Underwood. OnPM
After rain, through afterglow, the unfolding fan. Train Ride. John Wheelwright. AnFE; CoAnAm; MoPo; TriL; TwAmPo
After Reading "Ajax." William Johnson Cory. PtP
After Reading Homer. Digby Mackworth Dolben. GoBC
After Reading in a Letter Proposals for Building a Cottage. John Clare. EV-4; OBRV
After Reading Milne. Ruth Powell. PCD
After Reading Psalms XXXIX, XL, etc. Thomas Hardy. NBE
After Reading St. John the Divine. Gene Derwood. LiTM; NePA
After Reading Saint Teresa, Luis de Leon and Ramon Lull. Muna Lee. CAW
After Reading "Tamburlaine the Great." Sir William Watson. BMEP; PtP, *sl. diff.* (From "Epigrams.") LEAP
After Reading the Reviews of "Finnegans Wake." Melville Cane. WhC
After Reading Twenty Years of Grantland Rice. Don Skene. InMe
After Ronsard. Charles Williams. GTBS; TCPD
After St. Augustine. Mary Elizabeth Coleridge. MaRV; MeRV; TriL; TrPWD
After Seeing Her in a Dream. Nalan Hsinteh, *tr. fr. Chinese.* ChLP
After six days Jesus taketh with him. The Transfiguration. St. Matthew, Bible, *N.T.* GrCo-2
After Six Thousand Years. Victor Hugo, *tr. fr. French by* Selden Rodman. WaaP
After Snow. Anne Blackwell Payne. NoCaPo
After so long a race as I have run. Amoretti, LXXX. Spenser. PeBoSo; ReEn; ReIE; SiCE
After so many deaths to breathe again. Variations on a Theme by George Herbert. Marya Zaturenska. TrPWD
After So Much Loss. Laura Riding. MoP
After Some Day of Decision. Reed Whittemore. NePoEA
After some days of heat. A Sudden Squall. David Gascoyne. AlDL
After Soufrière. "Michael Field." MBP
After Speaking of One Dead a Long Time. Padraic Colum. GoYe
After Storm. David Morton. HBMV
After such years of dissension and strife. Epigram [*or* Natural Tears *or* Dust to Dust]. Thomas Hood. FiBHP; GoTP; HBV
After Summer. Philip Bourke Marston. HBV; VA
After Sunset. William Allingham. IrPN
After Sunset. Grace Hazard Conkling. AnAmPo; BAP; EPN; HBMV; LA; MaRV; NLK; NV; SBMV; VOD; YT
After Sunset, *sel.* Swinburne.
"If light of life outlive the set of sun," III. BEL; EPN; EPP; OQP; QP-1
After supper stand a while. Rhymes to Remember. *Unknown.* StaSt
After the Agony in the Garden. Daryl Hine. PeCV
After the Annunciation. Eileen Duggan. ISi
After the Armistice I was at Tours. First World War. Kenneth Slade Alling. NePoAm
After the Ball. Charles Kassell Harris. TreF
After the Battle. Thomas Moore. ERP; TIP
After the Battle. Shakespeare. King Henry V, *fr.* IV, vii-viii. BHV
After the Battle. Richard Chenevix Trench. VA
After the Battle. George Sylvester Viereck. GoYe
After the blast of lightning from the East. The End. Wilfred Owen. CH; ES; HBMV; MeRV; MoVE; PeBoSo
After the brief bivouac of Sunday. The Stenographers. P. K. Page. BoCaPo; CaP; PeCV; TwCaPo
After the Burial. James Russell Lowell. AA; BAP; CoBA; IAP; TCAP; TOP; UnPo
After the Centennial. Christopher Pearse Cranch. PAH
After the centres' naked files, the basic line. The Lines. Randall Jarrell. CrMA
After the Chariot-Race. Homer, *tr. fr. Greek by* Pope. *Fr.* The Iliad, XXIII. OxBG
(Sequel to the Chariot Race, *pr. tr. by* Lang, Leaf, *and* Myers.) GrR
After the Club-Dance. Thomas Hardy. At Casterbridge Fair, III. BEL; EmBrPo; EnLi-2 (1949 ed.); EnLit; PoVP
After the coffee and the cognac at the garden table. Valmondois. Clark Mills. NeTW
After the Comanches. *Unknown.* PAH
After the comfortable words come these. Sursum Corda. Annie Lake Townsend. OQP; QP-1
After the Curfew. Oliver Wendell Holmes. IAP
After the dark of night. Daybreak. Walter de la Mare. AlDL
After the darkness and storm. After. Caroline Grayson. BLRP
After the darkness, dawning. After. Earle Coates. AOAH

After the day is over. **The Tales the Barbers Tell.** Morris Bishop. ALV
After the Dazzle of Day. Walt Whitman. NePA
After the emotion of rain. This Morning. Hildegarde Flanner. NP
After the experience of waves. Ground Swell. G. Stanley Koehler. NePoAm-2
After the eyes that looked, the lips that spake. Lincoln at Gettysburg. Bayard Taylor. *Fr.* The Gettysburg Ode. BlG; LBAH; OHIP; PAH
After the Fair. Thomas Hardy. At Casterbridge Fair, VII. BEL; ChMo; CMP; EmBrPo; EnLi-2 (1949 ed.); EnLit; PoVP
After the Festival. Stefan George, *tr. fr. German by* Carol North Valhope *and* Ernst Morwitz. LiTW
After the fierce midsummer all ablaze. Friendship after Love. Ella Wheeler Wilcox. AV; ReaPo
After the Fire. Oliver Wendell Holmes. MC; PAH
After the first powerful plain manifesto. The Express. Stephen Spender. AlDL; AnFE; BBV (1951 ed.); EnL; EnLi-2 (1949 ed.); EnLit; ExPo; LiTM; MBP; MoAB; MoBrPo; MoVE; NAMP; NeMA; PoLFOT; ReaPo; SeCeV; ShBV-3
After the Flood. Arthur Rimbaud, *tr. fr. French.* BoW, *tr. by* Helen Rootham; MiFP, *tr. by* Ramon Guthrie
After the Fourth of July. M. Phelps Dawson. DD
After the Funeral. Dylan Thomas. CoBMV; FaBoMo; GTBS-W; MaPo; MoVE; OAEP (2d ed.); ReMP
(In Memory of Ann Jones.) CoEV; LiTB; MoAB; MoBrPo (1950 ed.); MoPo; MoWP; NeBP; PoE
After the Gale. Robert Bridges. *See* Upon the Shore.
After the honey drops of pearly showers. The Rose. William Hammond. OBS
After the Hunt. Detlev von Liliencron, *tr. fr. German by* Ludwig Lewisohn. AWP
After the Kiss. Rofu Miki, *tr. fr. Japanese by* Takamichi Ninomiya *and* D. J. Enright. PoLJ
After the Last Bulletins. Richard Wilbur. MoAB; NePoAm; TrGrPo (rev. ed.); ViBoPo (1958 ed.)
After the leaves have fallen, we return. The Plain Sense of Things. Wallace Stevens. CoV
After the lights and after the rumba and after the bourbon. A Charm for Cantinflas. Muriel Rukeyser. FiMAP
After the Martyrdom. Scharmel Iris. ChIP; MaRV
After the May time and after the June time. Midsummer. Ella Wheeler Wilcox. HBV
After the Order of Melchisedec. Robert Norwood. CPG; MaRV
After the Pangs of a Desperate Lover. Dryden. *Fr.* An Evening's Love, II, i. OAEP; ViBoPo
(Song: "After the pangs of a desperate lover.") FaBoEn
After the Party. William Wise. FaPON
After the Persian. Louise Bogan. NePoAm
After the Plague. *Unknown, tr. fr. Arabic by* Sir Charles Lyall. LiTW
After the planes unloaded, we fell down. The Dead in Europe. Robert Lowell. NePA; NePoEA; OxBA
After the Pleasure Party. Herman Melville. PoEL-5
After the Quarrel. Paul Laurence Dunbar. CDC
After the Quarrel. Adam Lindsay Gordon. OBVV
After the Rain. Thomas Bailey Aldrich. LPS-2
After the Rain. Edward A. Collier. BLRP
After the Rain. Tristan Corbière, *tr. fr. French by* Kenneth Koch *and* Georges Guy. AnFP
After the Rain. Virgil, *tr. fr. Latin by* Dryden. *Fr.* Georgics, I. BeR
After the rain comes on the lawn. Mister Angleworm. —— Manchester. GFA
After the rain the mossy house-steps are green. Descriptive Poem. Han Wu. OnPM
After the rare arch-poet Jonson died [*or* dy'd]. Upon M. Ben. Jonson, Epigram. Robert Herrick. HoPM; OAEP; PtP
After the Round-up. *At. to* D. J. White. *See* When the Work's All Done This Fall.
After the Sea-Ship. Walt Whitman. NePA; SG
After the sea, the harbor. Sequence. Edgar Daniel Kramer. BLRP
After the shameful trial in the hall. The Ninth Hour. Caroline Hazard. ChIP; OQP; QP-1
After the Show. Sam Harrison. NeIP
After the Shower. Archibald Lampman. CaP; OCL
After the siege and the assault of Troy. Sir Gawain and the Green Knight. *Unknown.* BEL; EM-1; EnLit
After the squealing brass. Saint's Parade. Robert Layzer. NePoEA
After the stars were all hung separately out. The Book of How. Merrill Moore. BoLiVe (1939 ed.); MAP; MoAmPo; NeMA
After the Storm. Elizabeth Bartlett. GoYe
After the storm. The Monk Noin, *tr. fr. Japanese by* Kenneth Rexroth. OnPJ
After the Storm. Thackeray. *Fr.* The White Squall. PRWS
After the sun has turned him, for the space of fifty days. Autumn. Hesiod. *Fr.* Works and Days. GrPE
After the Supper and Talk. Walt Whitman. APW; MAP; MoAmPo; MOAP
After the Surprising Conversions. Robert Lowell. CoBMV; FiMAP; NePoEA; SeCeV
After the thorns I came to the first page. The Sleeping Beauty; Variation of the Prince. Randall Jarrell. FiMAP
After the Thought of Saint Francis. Sister Mary Maura. SaFP
After the Tyrant's Death. Alcaeus, *tr. fr. Greek by* Walter Petersen. GrR
After the Visit. Thomas Hardy. FaBoEn; GTBS-D
After the War. Richard Le Gallienne. MC; PAH
After the Wedding. Henry Luttrell. *Fr.* Advice to Julia. IrPN
After the whipping, he crawled into bed. Portrait of a Boy. Stephen Vincent Benét. HBMV; MCCG; MW; NeMA; PoMa; TCAP
After the whistle's roar has bellowed and shuddered. Night Landing. John Gould Fletcher. Down the Mississippi, VI. ChMo; LiTA
After the Winter. Claude McKay. BANP; GoSl; PoNe
After the winter thawed away, I rose. The Assignation. James Wright. NePoEA
After the Wise Men went, and the strange star. The Vigil of Joseph. Elsa Barker. NV; StJW
After their first brief vernal intercourse. The Muse. Thomas Blackburn. PoN
After these weeks at sea, my native land. Durban Revisited. R. N. Currey. BoSA
After They Have Tired [of the Brilliance of Cities]. Stephen Spender. AtBAP; BrBE; FaBoMo; LiTM; TwCV
After those reverend papers, whose soule is. To Sir H. W. [*or* Wotton] at His Going Ambassador to Venice. John Donne. MeLP; OBS; SeEP
After-Thought. *See* Afterthought.
After Tschaikowsky. Wallace Gould. AnAmPo; LA
After Twenty Years. Ramón de Campoamor, *tr. fr. Spanish by* J. D. M. Ford. *Fr.* Doloras. AnSpL-2
After Two Years. Richard Aldington. BLV; CP; GTML; GTSL; HBV; LBBV; LEAP; MBP; MoBrPo; NV; PG; WHA
After Vacation. *Unknown.* PEOR
After volcanoes husht [*or* Over dead craters, hushed] with snows. The Christ of the Andes. Edwin Markham. AOAH; BoFr; PEDC; PoRL
After we, dear friends, have drunk together. Friends Drinking Together. Lady Otomo of Sakanoye. OnPM
After we fled away from the shuddering dock. On the Way to the Island. David Ferry. NePoAm-2
After we'd left off loving, long after that. The People, I. "Robin Hyde." AnNZ
After Wings. Sarah M. B. Piatt. AA; HBV; LBAP
After Winter. Carolyn Sherwin Bailey. PCH
After Winter. Sterling Brown. GoSl; PoNe
After Woman, The. Francis Thompson. EmBrPo; ISi; TCPD
After Work. John Oxenham. MaRV
After your mother says good night. Pepita. Alfred de Musset. TrFP
Afterglow, The. Basho, *tr. fr. Japanese by* Harold Gould Henderson. WoL
(Haiku: "Summer grass," *tr. by* Kenneth Rexroth.) OnPJ
Aftermath, The. Euripides, *tr. fr. Greek by* Richmond Lattimore. *Fr.* Iphigenia in Aulis. WaaP
Aftermath. Margaret McCulloch. PGD
Aftermath. Sydney King Russell. UnW
Aftermath. Siegfried Sassoon. AnFE; AOAH; GTSL; HiLiEn; MaRV; MBP; MCCG; MoBrPo; NeMA; PoeMoYo; TCEP; TrJP; ViBoPo; WaP
"Do you remember," *sel.* BMEP
Afternoon. Fannie Stearns Davis. POT; PoTo
Afternoon. George Dillon. PFE
Afternoon. Wendell Phillips Garrison. *Fr.* Post-Meridian. AA
Afternoon, The/ Flutters and dies. Nox Mortis. Paul Bewsher. PtOT
Afternoon: Amagansett Beach. John Hall Wheelock. MoVE; NePA
Afternoon Call. Donald Davidson. LS
Afternoon foreclosing, see, The. The Swimmer. Irving Layton. PeCV
Afternoon in a Church. Raymond Kresensky. ChIP
Afternoon in a Tree. Sister Maris Stella. GoBC
Afternoon in Anglo-Ireland. Bruce Williamson. NeIP
Afternoon in Artillery Walk, An; Mary Milton Loquitur. Leonard Bacon. AnAmPo; ATP; LA; PreP
Afternoon in Florence. Elizabeth Jennings. PoN
Afternoon in the Tropics. Rubén Darío, *tr. fr. Spanish by* Pauline Cook. LiTW
Afternoon like dead skin, The; now heat bores. Portoferraio. Alan Ross. PoN
Afternoon of a Faun, The. Stéphane Mallarmé. *See* Après-Midi d'un faune, L'.
Afternoon on a Hill. Edna St. Vincent Millay. BAP; BoTP; FaPON; LEAP; MPB; NLK; OxBA; POT; PoTo;

Afternoon on a Hill (*continued*)
SBMV; StVeCh (1955 ed.); TiPo (1952 ed.); TSW; TSWC; VOD
Afternoon on the Water. Johan Sebastian Cammermeyer Welhaven, *tr. fr. Norwegian by* Charles W. Stork. AnNoLy
Afternoon Tea. Arthur Guiterman. TCAP; TOP
Afternoon with Grandmother. Barbara A. Huff. FaPON
Afternoon with heavy hours, The. The Traveler. Allen Tate. LiTM; MM
After-Song. Richard Watson Gilder. *Fr.* The New Day. AA; LBAP; TrPWD
After-Thought. Wordsworth. The River Duddon, XXXIV. EnL; EnRP; EPN; FaBoEn; MeRV; SeCePo
(After-Thought Appended to "The River Duddon.") EM-2
(After-Thought—River Duddon.) ES
(After-Thought to "The River Duddon.") BPN; OAEP; OBRV; PIAE; TCEP
("I thought or thee. my partner and my guide.") EnLi-2; EPP
(Sonnet: "I thought of thee . . .") CoEV
(Valedictory Sonnet to the River Duddon.) OBEV
Afterthoughts. *Unknown, tr. fr. Greek by* Jack Lindsay. *Fr.* Homeric Hymns. OxBG
Afterthoughts of Donna Elvira. Carolyn Kizer. NePoAm-2
Afterward. Mary Matheson. CaP
Afterward. Elizabeth Stuart Phelps Ward. HBV
Afterward he may take thought. *See* Afterwards he may . . .
Afterward, soon as the chaste Persephone hither and thither. Homer. *Fr.* The Odyssey, XI. GrPo
Afterwards. Peter Baker. NeTW
Afterwards. "Violet Fane." HBV; OBVV; VA
Afterwards. Mahlon Leonard Fisher. MuM; SBMV
Afterwards. Federico Garcia Lorca, *tr. fr. Spanish by* Eleanor L. Turnbull. CoSP
Afterwards. Thomas Hardy. AnFE; BEL; CaAE; CH; ChMP; ChTr; EnLi-2 (1949 ed.); EPP; FaBoEn; KN; LiTB; LiTG; LiTM (rev. ed.); MBP; MM; MoAB; MoBrPo; MoVE; NAMP; PoEL-5; PoLFOT; POTE; ReTS; SeCeV; ShBV-3; TrGrPo; TwCV; ViBoPo; ViPP; VLEP; VOD; YT
("When the present has latched its postern behind my tremulous stay.") EG
Afterwards. Frances Ridley Havergal. BLRP
Afterwards. Mary Dixon Thayer. GFA
Afterwards [*or* Afterward] he may take thought. The Airman. W. R. Rodgers. PoD; WaP
Afterwards, let us make riddles. Riddles. Patrick F. Kirby. GoBC
Afton Water. Burns. *See* Flow Gently, Sweet Afton.
Again. Frantisek Halas, *tr. fr. Czech by* Karl W. Deutsch. WaaP
Again. Charlotte Mew. MBP; MoAB; MoBrPo; NeMA
Again a child, where childhood rov'd, I run. Ebenezer Elliott. *Fr.* Spirits and Men. EnSW
Again among the Hills, *abr.* Richard Hovey. NLK
Again and again I make the intolerable journey. The Repeated Journey. Thomas McGrath. NePoEA
Again and then again . . . the year is born. New Year's Day. Robert Lowell. NePoEA
Again at Christmas did we weave. In Memoriam A. H. H., LXXVIII. Tennyson. BPN; EM-2; EmBrPo; EnL; EnLi-2; EnLit; EPN; GEPC; OAEP; ViPo; VLEP
Again, beside this silver rivulet's shore. John Leyden. *Fr.* Scenes of Infancy. EnSW
Again Columbia's stripes, unfurl'd. *Enterprise* and *Boxer. Unknown.* PAH
Again, Dear Lord, we meet. Sabbath Morning Worship. Dwight Edwards Marvin. PraP
Again for You. Sister Mary Catherine. JKCP (1955 ed.)
Again God plants the tree of doom. Mutans Nomen Evae. Eric Gill. CAW
Again has come the spring-time. April. Samuel Longfellow. SN
Again I hear that creaking step. My Familiar. John Godfrey Saxe. AnNE; APW; HBV; PR; TreFS
Again I reply to the triple winds. January. William Carlos Williams. MAP; MoAB; MoAmPo; NP
"Again I Saw Another Angel." Margaret L. Woods. UnW
Again I see my bliss at hand. Meeting. Matthew Arnold. *Fr.* Switzerland. OAEP; ViPP
Again, I see you, ah my queen. Juana. Alfred de Musset. AWP; JAWP; WBP
Again it was the task of faithful Zyd. The Death of Kais. Nizami. *Fr.* Laili and Majnún. PeP
Again maternal Autumn grieves. Mater Dolorosa. John Banister Tabb. AnAmPo; LA; StJW
Again next spring when the heath blows white and pink. Sun Orchids. Douglas Stewart. NeLNL
Again on the morrow morning doth Sigurd the Volsung ride. Sigurd Rideth to the Glittering Heath. William Morris. *Fr.* The Story of Sigurd the Volsung. PoEL-5
Again, pale noiseless prophetess of night. To the Evening Star. Edgar Fawcett. OBAV

Again, perhaps and only once again. In Memoriam; Lady Blessington. Walter Savage Landor. TriL
Again Rejoicing Nature Sees. Burns. SN
(Song: "Again rejoicing Nature sees.") HBV
Again, Sappho. Mary Brent Whiteside. LS
Again the copses glow out yonder. Nelly. Nikolai Tikhonov. RuPo
Again the doleful fall is here. Tuberculosis. Victor Robinson. PoP
Again the native hour lets down the locks. More Sonnets at Christmas, I. Allen Tate. LiTA; LiTM; NePA; PeBoSo; PreP; WaP
Again the Story Is Told. Ada Jackson. MaRV
Again the summer-fevered skies. Garfield's Ride at Chickamauga. Hezekiah Butterworth. BIG; GA; PAH
Again the veld revives. Namaqualand after Rain. William Plomer. BoSA
Again the violet of our early days. Spring. Ebenezer Elliott. EV-4; LPS-2
Again, the year's decline, midst storms and floods. Robert Bloomfield. *Fr.* The Farmer's Boy. OBRV
Again they muster from the far-off hillside. After Vacation. *Unknown.* PEOR
Again thy birthday dawns, O man beloved. Lincoln's Birthday. Ida Vose Woodbury. LBAH; PEOR
Again today, Lord,/ Let me write. A Song of Daily Life. Utako Hayashi. SoLD
Again we climb the little hill—again. Pilgrimage. Catherine Parmenter. PEDC
Again we smelled for days on end. Again. Frantisek Halas. WaaP
Again your kindly, smiling face I see. Mother. Max Ehrmann. PoToHe
Against a Second Coming, *sel.* Sidney Keyes.
Walking Woman, The. AtBAP; POTE
Against an Atheist. Sir John Harington, *after the Latin of* Martial. SiCE
Against an Extreme Flatterer That Preached at Bath on the Queen's Day the Fortieth Year of Her Reign. Sir John Harington. SiCE
Against Artifice. Sir Philip Sidney. *See* Astrophel and Stella: Sonnets, XV.
Against Blame of Women. Gerald, Earl of Desmond, *tr. fr. Late Middle Irish by* the Earl of Longford. AnIL
Against Despair. Sister Mary Ada. JKCP (1955 ed.)
Against each perfect note I bear all thought. For W. A. Mozart. Edgar Bowers. PtPa
Against Feasting. Sir John Harington. SiCE
Against Fruition. Sir John Suckling. NBE
Against Fulfillment of Desire. *Unknown.* TrGrPo
Against Garnesche, *sel.* John Skelton.
"What, have you kithed you a knight." ViBoPo
Against Gaudy, Bragging, Undoughty Daccus. John Davies of Hereford. SiCE
Against God I daily offend by frailty. Of Rebellion. John Heywood. ReIE
Against Hope. Abraham Cowley. *Fr.* The Mistress. GTBS-W; LiTB; LiTG; LoBV; MeLP; OBS; SeCV-1
Against Idleness and Mischief. Isaac Watts. *See* How Doth the Little Busy Bee.
Against Illuminations. Archibald MacLeish. MOAP
Against Indifference. Charles Webbe. HBV; LoPS; OBEV (More Love or More Disdain.) SeCL
Against Irresolution. Richard Crashaw. OxBCh
Against Knowledge in Loving. Michael Drayton. *See* Idea: "Why should your fair eyes . . ."
Against Mosquitoes. Meleager, *tr. fr. Greek by* Dudley Fitts. LiTW
Against Mustolphus His Lying. John Davies of Hereford. SiCE
Against my love shall be, as I am now. Sonnets, LXIII. Shakespeare. OBSC; PeBoSo; ReEn; SiCE
Against My Will I Take My Leave, *in mod. Eng. Unknown.* TMEV
Against my will was I married. "Ho There, Death!" *Unknown.* OnPM
Against Oblivion. Shelley. *See* He Is Not Dead.
Against Paulus. Sir John Harington. SiCE
Against Platonick Love. *Unknown.* OBS
Against Quarrelling and Fighting. Isaac Watts. *See* Let Dogs Delight to Bark and Bite.
Against Romanticism. Kingsley Amis. NePoEA
Against Suspicion, *sel.* Mark Akenside.
Benevolence. OBEC
Against that time (if ever that time come). Sonnets, XLIX. Shakespeare. PeBoSo
Against the balcony railing I leaned by night. Moonrise. Annette von Droste-Hülshoff. AnGP
Against the burly air I strode. Genesis. Geoffrey Hill. NePoEA; PoLFOT; PoN
Against the Cold. Witter Bynner. MAP; MoAmPo (1942 ed.)
Against the Court of Rome. Petrarch, *tr. fr. Italian by* Sir Thomas Wyatt. Sonnets to Laura: To Laura in Life, CVII. LiTW; LyMA

Against the Demos. Theognis, *tr. fr. Greek by* F. L. Lucas. GrPE
Against the Dispraisers of Poetry. Richard Barnfield. SiCE; TuPP
Against the False Magicians. Thomas McGrath. NePoEA
Against the Fantastical Attire That Many Ladies Wear Nowadays. John Davies of Hereford. SiCE
Against the Fear of Death, *sels.* Lucretius, *tr. fr. Latin by* Dryden. *Fr.* De Rerum Natura, III.
"As for the dog, the furies, and their snakes." PoD
"For thou shalt sleep, and never wake again." PoD
"What has this bugbear death to frighten man." AWP; JAWP; WBP
Against the flare and descant of the gas. Warning to a Guest. John Holloway. NePoEA
Against the green flame of the hawthorn-tree. On Hampstead Heath. W. W. Gibson. EPN; HBV; NP
Against the guide of Truth. Epigram V. *Unknown. Fr.* Duel with Verses over a Great Man. TrJP
Against the Hope of Reconstruction. F. T. Marinetti, *tr. fr. Italian by* Selden Rodman. OnHM
Against the huge black door of the night. The Guest. Jorge Carrera Andrade. AnCL
Against the lamp I sit by the south window. Sitting at Night. Po Chü-i. WhP
Against the planks of the cabin side. Sea Song. "Laurence Hope." AV; BMEP; LBBV
Against the pure, reflective tiles. My Six Toothbrushes. Phyllis McGinley. GoYe
Against the rigors of an austere season. The Bird. Sister Mary Thérese. JKCP (1955 ed.)
Against the swart magnolia's sheen. Carolina Spring Song. Hervey Allen. BAP; HBMV; TBM
Against the Thieves of Liddesdale. Sir Richard Maitland. BSV
(Aganis the Thievis of Liddisdale.) EBSV; GoTS
Against the Wall. Aline Kilmer. FAOV; NV
Against the wall of this sky. Elegy on an Empty Skyscraper. John Gould Fletcher. AmP
Against the window pane. Summer Rain. Sir Herbert Read. LiTM; POTE
Against the world I closed my heart. White Magic. Arthur Symons. POTT; VLEP
Against Them Who Lay Unchastity to the Sex of Women. William Habington. *Fr.* Castara, II. ElSeCe; MePo; OBS; SeEP
Against this lantern, shrill, alone. The Memorial: 1914–1918. Edmund Blunden. SoV
Against this wrong of the Teutonic might. The Arsenal of the Lord. William Stanley Braithwaite. PoNe
Against Time. Louis Untermeyer. MoAmPo (1942 ed.)
Against time and the damages of the brain. Prologue. James Agee. *Fr.* Let Us Now Praise Famous Men. OnAP
Against Unworthy Praise. W. B. Yeats. AnFE
Against Women: Satire VI, *abr.* Juvenal, *tr. fr. Latin by* Dryden. *Fr.* The Satires. LiTW
Against Women either Good or Bad. Thomas Norton. ElL; ViBoPo
(Man May Live Thrice Nestor's Life, A.) InvP
Against Women's Fashions. John Lydgate. ACP
Against Writers That Carp at Other Men's Books. Sir John Harington. *See* Critics and Cooks.
Agamede's Song. Arthur Upson. *Fr.* The City. LBMV; LEAP
Agamemnon, *sels.* Aeschylus, *tr. fr. Greek.*
Achaians Have Got Troy, upon This Very Day, The, *tr. by* Richmond Lattimore. WaaP
Beacons, The. GrR, *tr. by* E. D. A. Morshead; OxBG, *tr. by* Walter Headlam
Case for the Defense, A, *tr. by* G. M. Cookson. GrR
Cassandra, *tr. by* Gilbert Murray. GrR
Cassandra Prepares to Die, *tr. by* Louis MacNeice. OxBG
Cassandra's Lament, *tr. by* Richmond Lattimore. LiTW
Chorus: "Great Fortune is an hungry thing," *tr. by* Gilbert Murray. AWP; JAWP; WBP
Chorus: "O Zeus our king and Night our friend," *tr. by* Louis MacNeice. LiTW
"Dead are not to rise, The," *tr. by* J. S. Blackie. PoFr
Death of Agamemnon, The, *tr. by* George Thomson. LiA
"From Ida fleet Hephaestus shot the spark," *tr. by* J. S. Blackie. GrPo
God of War, Money Changer of Dead Bodies, The, *tr. by* Richmond Lattimore. WaaP
Helen, *tr. by* Jack Lindsay. OxBG
(Helen; and the Wages of War, *tr. by* E. D. A. Morshead.) GrR
Human Responsibility, *tr. by* E. D. A. Morshead. GrR
Hymn to Zeus, *tr. by* Gilbert Murray. WGRP
If I Were to Tell of Our Labours, Our Hard Lodging, *tr. by* Louis MacNeice. WaaP
Menelaus Abandoned, *tr. by* E. D. A. Morshead. LiA
Purple Carpet, The, *tr. by* Walter Headlam. OxBG
Sacrifice of Iphigenia, The. GrR, *tr. by* G. M. Cookson; LiA, *shorter sel., tr. by* George Thomson; OxBG, *tr. by* Jack Lindsay
Sin and Satiety, *tr. by* E. D. A. Morshead. GrR
"So much he mourns the queen beyond the seas," *tr. by* J. C. Wordsworth. GrPo
Welcome to Agamemnon, *tr. by* Walter Headlam. LiA; OxBG
(Clytemnestra, *longer sel., tr. by* G. M. Cookson.) GrR
Agamemnon and Nestor. Shakespeare. *Fr.* Troilus and Cressida, I, iii. EV-1
Agamemnon; Peace Offerings to Achilles. Homer, *tr. fr. Greek by* Maurice Hewlett. *Fr.* The Iliad, IX. GrR
Agamemnon's Children. Euripides. *See* Tidings of Home.
Agamemnon's Tomb. Sacheverell Sitwell. LiTB; OBMV
"One by one, as harvesters," *sel.* MoBrPo
Aganis the Thievis of Liddisdale. Sir Richard Maitland. *See* Against the Thieves of Liddesdale.
Agatha. Alfred Austin. HBV; VA
Agathe, Aged Five. *Unknown, tr. fr. Latin by* F. L. Lucas. *Fr.* Carmina Epigraphica. LaP
Agathon, *sel.* George Edward Woodberry.
Song of Eros. AA; HBV
Age, The. Herbert Edwin Clarke. VA
Age. Abraham Cowley, *after the Greek of* Anacreon. AWP; JAWP; OnPM; WBP
Age. *At. to* H. S. Fritsch *and to* Edward Tuck. *See* How Old Are You?
Age. Richard Garnett. VA
(Sonnet: Age.) OBVV
Age. Walter Savage Landor. PoEL-4
Age. Sir Thomas More. TuPP
Age. *At. to* Edward Tuck *and to* H. S. Fritsch. *See* How Old Are You?
Age. William Winter. HBV
Age after age our bird through incense flies. Bird, Bird. Gene Derwood. LiTA; PeBoSo
Age and Youth. Shakespeare. *See* Crabbed Age and Youth.
Age being mathematical, these flowers, An. Tulips. Padraic Colum. ImOP
Age cannot reach me where the veils of God have shut me in. Immortality. Susan L. Mitchell. GTIV; OnYI
Age cannot wither her, nor custom stale. Her Infinite Variety [*or* A Shakespeare Gallery: Cleopatra]. Shakespeare. *Fr.* Antony and Cleopatra, II, ii. EV-1; MaC
Age cannot wither her whom not gray hairs. Evening. Wendell Phillips Garrison. *Fr.* Post-Meridian. AA
Age Demanded, The ("For this agility chance found"). Ezra Pound *Fr.* Hugh Selwyn Mauberley. CoBMV; CoV; LiTA; LiTM (rev. ed.); MoPo
Age demanded an image, The. Ezra Pound. Hugh Selwyn Mauberley, II. CoBMV; CoV; InPo; LiTA; LiTM (rev. ed.); MOAP; MoPo; OnAP
Age in her embraces past, An. The Mistress; a Song [*or* His Mistress]. Earl of Rochester. AtBAP; EPS; MePo; NBE; OBS; OnPM; ViBoPo
Age in Prospect. Robinson Jeffers. BLV; BoLiVe; MAP; MoAB; MoAmPo; NeMA
Age in Youth. Trumbull Stickney. MAP; MoAmPo (1942 ed.); MOAP
Age Intercedes for Youth. Rachel Annand Taylor. EBSV
Age is a quality of mind. How Old Are You? [*or* Age]. *At. to* Edward Tuck *and to* H. S. Fritsch. DDA; PoRL; PoToHe
Age is dull and mean, The. Men creep. For Righteousness' Sake. Whittier. CoV; PoEL-4
Age Is Great and Strong, The. Victor Hugo, *tr. fr. French by* W. J. Robertson. WGRP
Age Is Opportunity. Longfellow. *Fr.* Morituri Salutamus. QP-2
("For age is opportunity no less.") PoToHe (new ed.)
Age Not to Be Rejected. Robert Herrick. *See* To a Gentlewoman Objecting to Him His Gray Hairs.
Age of a Dream, The. Lionel Johnson. OBMV; TIP; ViPP
Age of Children Happiest, The. Earl of Surrey. *See* How No Age Is Content.
Age of Herbert & Vaughan, The. Edmund Blunden. PtP
Age of Wisdom, The. Thackeray. *Fr.* Rebecca and Rowena. ALV; BMEP, *sl. abr.;* HBV; LEAP; LPS-1; VA; WhC
(Love at Two Score.) PoVP
Age with devouring fingers spareth naught. Rome. Marcelino Menéndez y Pelayo. CAW
"Age, with Stealing Steps . . ." George Crabbe. *Fr.* Tales of the Hall, X. BCEP; LEAP
(Approach of Age, The.) LPS-1
Ageanax. Edward Cracroft Lefroy. *Fr.* Echoes from Theocritus. OBVV
Aged Aged Man. The. "Lewis Carroll." *See* White Knight's Song, The.
Aged Carle, The. Sir Walter Scott. *See* Time.
Aged catch their breath, The. Preface. W. H. Auden. *Fr.* The Sea and the Mirror. LiTA; SeCeV
Aged Cities. Frederick William Faber. BMEP
Aged Couple Gives Thanks, An. Lois Givens Vaughan. PraP
Aged Fisherman. Witter Bynner. GoYe
Aged Indian, The. *Unknown.* ABS
Aged Lover Renounceth Love, The. Thomas, Lord Vaux. ElL; ElSeCe; OAEP; PoEL-1; ReEn; SiCE; TuPP

Aged Lover Renounceth Love (*continued*)
(I Loathe That I Did Love.) RiBV
(Image of Death, The.) GoTL; OBSC; PoLi
Aged man, that mowes [*or* mows] these fields. A Dialogue betwixt Time and a Pilgrim[e]. Aurelian Townsend. CoEV; MePo; NBE; OBS; PoEL-2; SeEP
Aged man, when he beheld winter approaching, The. The Acacia Leaves. Allen Upward. NP
Aged Man Who Loved to Doze Away, An. Walter Savage Landor. BPN
Aged Ninety Years. Wilbert Snow. AnAmPo; LA
Aged Stranger, The. Bret Harte. AA; CaAE; LHV; MaC; MAP; MoAmPo (1942 ed.); NeMA; TreFS
Aged Writer, An. Roy McFadden. NeIP
Ageing king, the warrior, The. The Treason of Ganelon. Elise Aylen. NeTW
Ageless Christ, The. B. L. Byer. BePJ
Ageless shadows fall, The. Paul to Peter and John. Marjorie E. Johnson. UnW
Ageless, the Mantinean woman speaks. ". . . Discourse Heard One Day . . ." Donald C. Babcock. NePoAm-2
Ages. Friedrich Hölderlin, *tr. fr. German by* Iwan Goll. OnPM
Ages of Man, The. Charles Heavysege. BoCaPo
Ages of Man, The. Hesiod, *tr. fr. Greek by* Sir William Marris. OxBG
Ages of Man, The. *At. to* Abraham ibn Ezra, *tr. fr. Hebrew by* Nina Davis Salaman. TrJP
Aghadoe. John Todhunter. AnIL; AnIV; GTIV; OBEV (1st ed.); OBVV; OxBI; PoVP
Agile noisy jungle flower he flies, An. Pretty Polly. E. Merrill Root. BLA; MAP
Agincourt. Michael Drayton. BEL; BeLS; BHV; EIL; EV-1; FaBoBe; FaBoCh; GoTL; HBV; LEAP; LH; LoGBV; MCCG; OBEV; OnSP; ShBV-1; TCEP; WHA
(Ballad of Agincourt. The [*or* A].) BCEP; KN; PoRA; ReaPo
(Battle of Agincourt, The.) GN; LPS-2; TVSH
(His Ballad of Agincourt.) ElSeCe
(Ode to the Cambro-Britons [*or* -Britans *or* -Britains] and Their Harp, His Ballad of Agincourt.) EnLi-1; EPP; TwHP
(To the Cambro-Britons [*or* -Britains] and Their Harp, His Ballad of Agincourt.) AEV; AnFE; CaAE; EnL; OAEP; OBS; ReEn; ReIE; SeEP; TOP; TriL; TuPP; TyEnPo
Agincourt. Shakespeare. *See* King Henry before the Field of Saint Crispian.
Agincourt ("Agincourt, Agincourt!"). *Unknown.* OTPC (1923 ed.)
Agincourt Song of Victory ("Our king went forth to Normandy"). *Unknown.* MuP
Aging Coquette, The. John Trumbull. *Fr.* The Progress of Dulness. AnNE
Agitation of the air, An. End of Summer. Stanley Kunitz. CrMA
Agitato Ma Non Troppo. John Crowe Ransom. OxBA
Aglaia. Nicholas Breton. *Fr.* The Passionate Shepherd. OBSC
Aglaura, *sels.* Sir John Suckling.
Song: "No, no, fair heretic[k], it needs must be," *fr.* IV, i. AtBAP; LiTL; LoBV; OBS; ReEN; RiBV; SeEP
Why So Pale and Wan [Fond Lover]? *fr.* IV, ii. AEV; ALV; AnFE; AWP; BBV (1923 ed.); BCEP; BEL; BLV; CenL; CoBE; EG; ElSeCe; EM-1; EnL; EnLi-1; EnLit; EPP; HoPM; InPo; JAWP; LiTG; LiTL; LoPo; LPS-1; MCCG; OBEV; OBS; OtMeF; OuHeWo; PoFS; PoMa; PoRA; ReaPo; RiBV; SeCePo; SeCL; ShBV-4; TOP; TreFS; TrGrPo; TyEnPo; ViBoPo; WBP; WHA
(Advice to a Lover.) CBOV
(Constant Lover, The.) NeHB; PG
(Encouragements to a Lover.) BTP; FaFP; GTBS; GTBS-D; GTBS-W; GTSE; GTSL; PYM
(Orsames' Song.) AnEnPo
(Song: "Why so pale and wan, fond lover?") CaAE; EnLoPo; EPS; EV-2; HBV; InP; LEAP; LoBV; MePo; PoE; PoEL-3; PoeMoYo; ReEn; SeCV-1; SeEP; TCEP; TwHP
(Why So Pale?) OnPM
Aglow are the temples with burnt sacrifices. Croesus. Bacchylides. GrR
Agnes. Ibsen, *tr. fr. Norwegian by* Charles W. Stork. *Fr.* Brand. AnNoLy
Agnes. Henry Francis Lyte. ATP (1935 ed.); GTSL
Agnes and the Hill-Man. *Unknown, tr. fr. Danish by* William Morris. BPN; PoVP; VLEP
Agnes and the Merman. *Unknown, tr. fr. Danish by* E. M. Smith-Dampier. BoDaBa
Agnes lived with geraniums on the window-sills. Short Short Story. Josephine Jacobsen. NePoAm-2
Agnes, my delicate butterfly. Agnes. Ibsen. *Fr.* Brand. AnNoLy
Agnes she walked on the edge of the steep. Agnes and the Merman. *Unknown.* BoDaBa
Agnes, thou child of harmony, now fled. Whither. Philip Becker Goetz. AA
Agnes went through the meadows a-weeping. Agnes and the Hill-Man. *Unknown, tr. by* William Morris. BPN; PoVP; VLEP
Agnostic, The. Xenophanes, *tr. fr. Greek by* F. L. Lucas. GrPE
Agnostic's Creed, The. Walter Malone. HBV
ΑΓΝΩΣΤΩι ΘΕΩι (To an Unknown God). Thomas Hardy. MoPo
(Agnosto Theo.) WGRP
Agnus Dei. Victor Kinon, *tr. fr. French by* Richard C. Savage. CAW
Agog, in rain house-deep. Apologia. Jean Garrigue. LiTA
Agonie, The. George Herbert. MePo; NBE
Agony is gone; his pain and care, The. The Suicide. Hugh Wilgus Ramsaur. UnW
Agony of God, The. Georgia Harkness. MaRV
Agreed that all these birds. All These Birds. Richard Wilbur. FiMAP; Po
Agricultural Irish Girl, The. *Unknown.* OnYI
Agriculture; a Poem, *sel.* Robert Dodsley.
"See where the farmer, with a master's eye." EnSW
Agrippina, *sel.* Thomas Gray.
Rape of Helen, The. RO
Aguinaldo. Bertrand Shadwell. PAH
Ah, a bud! all blue and white. Blossoms. Mary Fenollosa. PCH
Ah, ah the falce fatall tale I read. *Unknown.* SeCSL
Ah! Ah! There! What a strange fire! Cassandra. Aeschylus. *Fr.* Agamemnon. GrR
Ah, all the sands of the earth lead unto heaven. Persian Miniature. William Jay Smith. MoVE
Ah, Are You Digging on My Grave? Thomas Hardy. CaAE; EnLi-2; EnLit, EPP; MBP; MoAB; MoBrPo; PoLFOT; PoVP; PreP; TCEP; TyEnPo
Ah, Be Not False. Richard Watson Gilder. AA; HBV; HBVY
Ah, be not vain! In yon flower-bell. Dewdrop, Wind and Sun [*or* The Dewdrop]. Joseph Skipsey. OBVV; VA
Ah, bed! the field where joy's peace some do see. Astrophel and Stella, XCVIII. Sir Philip Sidney. EnLoPo; ReEn; SiPS
Ah, Ben!/ Say how or when. An Ode for Ben Jonson [*or* An Ode for Him *or* To Ben Jonson]. Robert Herrick. AWP; BCEP; BEL; CBOV; CoBE; EG; ElSeCe; EM-1; EnLi-1; EnLit; EPS; EV-2; InPo; InvP; JAWP; LEAP; LoBV; LPS-3; MaPo; OAEP; OBS; PIR; PoE; PoFS; PreP; PtP; RiBV; SeCV-1; SeEP; TOP; TrGrPo; TwHP; UnPo; WBP
Ah, bird,/ our love is never spent. Cuckoo Song. Hilda Doolittle ("H. D."). ChMo; CMP; TwCV
Ah, blackbird, thou art satisfied. The Blackbird. *Unknown.* AnIL; OnYI
Ah, blessedness of work! the aimless mind. Work. Louis James Block. AA
Ah, Bring It Not. Dollie Radford. VA
Ah, broken is the golden bowl! the spirit flown forever! Lenore. Poe. AA; AmP; AmPo; AmPP; AnFE; APA; BAP; CoAnAm; CoBA; IAP; LiTA; MOAP; SPP; TreFS; WHA
Ah, but could your eyes. The Ship. Ibn Safar. MooP
Ah! but the third one, ah! but the third. The Judgment of Paris. *Unknown.* OtMeF
Ah, can you never still. Owl Sinister. Rose O'Neill. BLA
Ah! cease this kind persuasive strain. Ode to a Friend. William Mason. OBEC
Ah changed and cold, how changed and very cold. Dead before Death. Christina Rossetti. EmBrPo
Ah Chloris [*or* Cloris]! that [*or* could] I now could [*or* but] sit. Child and Maiden [*or* Song *or* To Chloris]. Sir Charles Sedley. *Fr.* The Mulberry Garden, III, ii. EV-3; GTBS; GTBS-D; GTBS-W; GTSE; GTSL; HBV; LiTL; LPS-1; OAEP; OBEV; OBS; SeCL; SeCV-2; TOP; ViBoPo
Ah, Christ, I love you rings to the wild sky. Sonnets at Christmas, II. Allen Tate. AmP; GTBS-W; LiTA; LiTM; NePA; ReMP
Ah, Clemence! when I saw thee last. La Grisette. Oliver Wendell Holmes. AA; HBV; IAP
Ah Cloris! that I now could sit. *See* Ah Chloris . . .
Ah, clover has such a mouth of honey. Clover. Helge Rode. BoDS
Ah come to town de udder night. Old Dan Tucker. Daniel Decatur Emmett. SoAF
"Ah, could I but be understood!" Appreciated. Edward Rowland Sill. PR
Ah, could I [*or* I could] lay me down in this long grass. Journey. Edna St. Vincent Millay. NLK; TCAP; VOD
"Ah, could thy grave at home, at Carthage, be!" Monica's Last Prayer. Matthew Arnold. MeRV
Ah! County Guy, the hour is nigh. County Guy [*or* A Serenade *or* Song]. Sir Walter Scott. *Fr.* Quentin Durward. BCEP; BEL; BPN; CH; EBSV; EmBrPo; EPN;

EtPaEn; EV-4; GTBS; GTBS-D; GTBS-W; GTSE; GTSL; LPS-1; OAEP; OBRV; TCEP; TOP
Ah Cupid, I mistook thee. Francis Davison. EG
Ah, Dear Heart. *Unknown.* TuPP
Ah! dear one, we were young so long. Alas, So Long! Dante Gabriel Rossetti. PoVP
Ah! dearest love, sweet home of all my fears. Keats. *Fr.* Ode to Fanny. ChER
Ah, deck not out thine own heart's evil springs. Arraignment of Helen. Euripides. *Fr.* Trojan Women. GrR
Ah, did he climb, that man, nigher to heaven than I. Dark Rapture. "Æ." SeCePo
Ah, did you once see Shelley plain. Memorabilia. Robert Browning. BEL; BMEP; BoLiVe; BPN; CBPC; EmBrPo; EnLi-2; EnLit; EPN; FaBoEn; FiP; GEPC; GTBS-W; HBV; LEAP; LoBV; OAEP; PIR; PoeMoYo; PoVP; PtP; PYM; SeCePo; TCEP; TOP; TwP; VA; ViPo; ViPP; VLEP; WHA
Ah, drink again. Lethe. Edna St. Vincent Millay. PG
Ah, drops of gold in whitening flame. To Daisies. Francis Thompson. HBV
Ah, Eros does not always smite. Eros Does Not Always Smite. "Michael Field." BoFr; LBBV
Ah, Fading Joy. Dryden. *Fr.* The Indian Emperor, IV, iii. ChTr; FiP; LoBV; OAEP; ViBoPo
("Ah, fading joy, how quickly art thou past!") ElSeCe; MaPo
(Song: "Ah, fading joy!") BeR; EPS (1942 ed.); FaBoEn; TCEP
Ah! fair and lovely bloom the flowers of youth. Youth and Age. Mimnermus. AWP; OnPM
Ah! fair face gone from sight. Lionel Johnson. *Fr.* In Memory. FaBoEn; PoEL-5
Ah faire [*or* fair] Zenocrate, divine Zenocrate. Fair Is Too Foul an Epithet. Christopher Marlowe. *Fr.* Tamburlaine, Pt. I, Act V, sc. ii. AtBAP; LiTB; NBE; PoEL-2; ViBoPo
Ah Faustus,/ Now hast thou but one bare hour [*or* hower] to live. Christopher Marlowe. *Fr.* Dr. Faustus. AtBAP; BoLiVe; CBOV; ChTr; LiA; MyFE; NBE; PoEL-2; ShBV-4; TrGrPo; ViBoPo; WHA
Ah! First snow! Transient Beauty. Basho. OnPM
Ah, Flood of Life on which I am a wave. Watson Kirkconnell. *Fr.* The Tide of Life. CaP
Ah, flow on, flow on. Sail Peacefully Home. Simeon Frug. TrJP
Ah for pittie, wil rancke Winters rage. Februarie. Spenser. *Fr.* The Shepheardes Calender. EPP
Ah for the throes of a heart sorely wounded! The Damsel. Omar b. Abi Rabi'a. AWP; LiTW
Ah! fredome [*or* freedom] is a noble thing! *See* A! fredome is a noble thing!
Ah! friends, friends,/ These are the things we do not like to know. E. A. Robinson. *Fr.* Captain Craig. BoFr
Ah! from mine eyes the tears unbidden start. Sonnet: On a Distant View of England. William Lisle Bowles. CEP
Ah! gentle, fleeting, wavering sprite. On the Soul. Emperor Hadrian, *tr. by* Byron. WoL
Ah, gentle lady! must I go. Chanson: Leaving on Crusade. Thibaut of Champagne. LyMA
Ah gentle shepherd, thine the lot to tend. John Dyer. *Fr.* The Fleece. PoEL-3
Ah, gentle, tender lady mine. The Chronicle of the Drum. Thackeray. ViBoPo
Ah! Give Me, Lord, the Single Eye. Augustus Montague Toplady. OxBoCh
Ah, give us back our dear dead Land of Dreams. The Land of Dreams. Henry Martyn Hoyt. HBMV
Ah God, How Good She Is to See. Charles d'Orléans, *tr. fr. French by* Alan Conder. TrFP
Ah God, how lovely Lady Sloe looked walking through the square! Lady Sloe. Juan Ruiz, Archpriest of Hita. TeCS
Ah God, how much I envy thee. The Lark. Pierre de Ronsard. TrFP
Ah, God! To have a breast like that. The White Rooster. George O'Neil. PoeMoYo; TCPD
Ah, Golden Eyes, to win you yet. Golden Eyes. Rufinus. GrL
Ah got a hook an' you got a line, Honey. The Crawdad Song. *Unknown.* SoAF
Ah, great it is to believe the dream. The Dream. Edwin Markham. OQP; QP-1
Ah, had I ever thought the world would care. Sonnet. Petrarch. *Fr.* Sonnets to Laura: To Laura in Death. LyPI
Ah, had you seen the Coolun. *See* O had you seen the Coolun.
Ah, Happiness: Who called you "Earandel." A Song of Happiness. Ernest Rhys. NP
Ah, happy blindness! Enion sees not the terrors of the uncertain. It Is Not So with Me. Blake. *Fr.* Vala; or, The Four Zoas. SeCePo
Ah, happy who have seen Him, whom the world. Francis W. Bourdillon. *Fr.* A Lost God. WGRP
Ah, happy youths, ah, happy maid. On a Picture by Poussin Representing Shepherds in Arcadia. John Addington Symonds. FaBoBe; HBV
Ah hate to see de evenin' sun go down. St. Louis Blues. W. C. Handy. NAMP
Ah, help, my Daemon, that hast served me well! Francis Thompson. *Fr.* Sister Songs. VLEP
Ah! here is the beauteous Moon at full. Complaint of the Moon in the Provinces. Jules Laforgue. TrFP
Ah, here it is! the sliding rail. The Crooked Footpath. Oliver Wendell Holmes. *Fr.* The Professor at the Breakfast Table. HBV; TreF
"Ah! Here's the little round thing my papa talks into." A Telephone Message. *Unknown.* PEOR
Ah, how I pity the young dead who gave. The Young Dead. Edith Wharton. AOAH
Ah, how I wish I could sleep. *Unknown, tr. fr. Spanish by* Eleanor L. Turnbull. TeCS
Ah, how poets sing and die! Dunbar. Anne Spencer. BANP; CDC
Ah, How Sweet It Is to Love. Dryden. *Fr.* Tyrannick Love, IV, i. EnLi-1; HBV; HoPM; LEAP; LiTL; LPS-1; MaPo; OBEV (1st ed.); ViBoPo
(Song: "Ah, how sweet it is to love.") EiPP; EPS (1942 ed.); FaBoEn
Ah How the Throat of a Girl. Archibald MacLeish. *Fr.* Conquistador. AtBAP
Ah, I could lay me down in this long grass. *See* Ah, could I lay me down . . .
Ah, I know what happiness is! Poem. Blanche Taylor Dickinson. CDC
Ah! I remember Stillwater, as it were yesterday. Arnold at Stillwater. Thomas Dunn English. GA; PAH
Ah I remember well (and how can I). A Reminiscence of Early Love. Samuel Daniel. *Fr.* Hymen's Triumph. EV-1
Ah, if man's boast and man's advance be vain. Doves. Louise Imogen Guiney. BLA; PC
Ah! if we only dreamed how close they stand. Comfort. May Doney. HBMV
Ah! I'm feared thou's come too sooin. To a Daisy. John Hartley. VA
Ah, in the long procession of our life. Annie Charlotte Dalton. *Fr.* Flame and Adventure. CPG
Ah in the thunder air. Trees in the Garden. D. H. Lawrence. MBP; MoAB; MoBrPo; Po
Ah, it is you, it is you, eternal name without date. Death. Vicente Aleixandre. CoSP
Ah, Jack it was, and with him little Jill. Jack and Jill. Harriet S. Morgridge. *Fr.* Mother Goose Sonnets. AA
Ah, June is here, but where is May? Unfulfilment. Frances Louisa Bushnell. AA
Ah, lad, if I could only say. Unsaid. Josephine Preston Peabody. PR
Ah! lay by your lute. Wit Predominant. Thomas Rymer. *Fr.* Edgar. SeCL
Ah! leave, my lord, in this your flowering age. Sonnet: The Dream. Gaspara Stampa. LyPI
Ah! leave the smoke, the wealth, the roar. Ballade to Theocritus, in Winter [*or* To Theocritus . . .] Andrew Lang. InP; PC; VA
Ah, Leipsydrion, thou hast betrayed them. Leipsydrion. *Unknown.* OxBG
Ah, let us go, whom nature gave firm minds and courage fast. The Draught of Life. Abu-l-Ala al-Maarri. LiTW
Ah! liberal-handed lady, though. The Good Tradition. *Unknown.* AnIL
Ah Liberty, so lovely, so denied! Petrarch. *Fr.* Sonnets to Laura: To Laura in Life. PrPoCR
Ah, life is good! and good thus to behold. Summons. Arthur Davison Ficke. Sonnets of a Portrait Painter, XIV. HBMV
Ah! light lovely lady with delicate lips aglow. At Mass. *Unknown, tr. by* Robin Flower. GTIV; OxBI
Ah! little flower, upspringing, azure-eyed. Fruitionless. Ina Donna Coolbrith. AA; LBAP
Ah, little mill, you're rumbling still. An Oxford Idyll. Thomas Edward Brown. PoVP; VLEP
Ah little recks the laborer. Walt Whitman. *Fr.* Song of the Exposition. IAP
Ah, little road, all whirry in the breeze. The Road. Helene Johnson. BANP; CDC; GoSl; PoNe
Ah! little they know of true happiness, they whom satiety fills. Labor Song. Denis Florence MacCarthy. *Fr.* The Bell-Founder. DD; LPS-2
Ah, London, London! our delight. A Ballad of London. Richard Le Gallienne. BMEP; HBMV; MBP
Ah lonely isles, fragments of earth, that with his thunder. The Desolation of the Cyclades. Antipater of Thessalonica. GrPE
Ah! long ago since I or thou. Before and After. Oliver Madox Brown. VA
Ah, look./ How sucking their last sweetness from the air. The Divers. Peter Quennell. MBP; MoBrPo; MoVE; TCPD
Ah, Love, but a day. James Lee's Wife. Robert Browning. EPN, *sel.;* ViPP
Ah Love! could you and I with Him conspire. A Wish.

Ah Love! could you and I with Him conspire (*continued*) Omar Khayyám, *tr. by* Edward Fitzgerald. *Fr.* The Rubáiyat. OnPM
Ah, Love, I cannot die, I cannot go. Rispetto. Agnes Mary Frances Robinson. Tuscan Cypress, XV. AV; HBMV
Ah, Love, Let Us Be True. Matthew Arnold. *Fr.* Dover Beach. OQP; QP-2
Ah! Love, my master, hear me swear. Of His Death. Meleager. AWP
Ah love, the sweet spring blossoms cling. Spring Song. Dollie Radford. DiM
Ah, love, the teacher we decried. A Pure Hypothesis. May Kendall. VA
Ah, love, there is no better life than this. Swinburne. *Fr.* Laus Veneris. PIAE
Ah love! where is thy abydinge? *Unknown.* SeCSL
Ah, lovely Devon. Oh, to Be in England Now the Weather's There! *Unknown.* SiTL
Ah! make a shady garden of my heart. The Nun's Heart. *Unknown.* PraNu
"Ah, Marianson, my beauteous dame." Marianson. *Unknown, tr. by* William McLennan. BoCaPo
Ah! marvel not if when I come to die. For He Had Great Possessions. Richard Middleton. HBV
Ah! Matt.: old age has brought to me. Senex to Matt. Prior. James Kenneth Stephen. *Fr.* Two Epigrams. BOHV; CenHV; FiBHP; WhC
Ah, me!/ There lives no mortal who is truly free. "I Shame to Wear a Heart So White." Euripides. *Fr.* Hecuba. GrR
Ah me!/ Would that a mortal's curse could reach to God! The Leave-taking of Artemis. Euripides. *Fr.* Hippolytus. GrR
Ah Me! Am I the Swaine. George Wither. OBS
Ah, me! and is it come, the end of all. The End of Troy. Euripides. *Fr.* Trojan Women. OxBG
Ah me, but it might have been! On a Nankin Plate. Austin Dobson. PoVP
Ah Me, Do You Remember Still. Agnes Mary Frances Robinson. WHA
(Italian Garden, An.) LBBV
Ah me, dread friends of mine—Love, Time, and Death. Love, Time and Death. Frederick Locker-Lampson. HBV
Ah me! full sorely is my heart forlorn. The Schoolmistress. William Shenstone. CEP; EiPP; EPP; EV-3; GoTL; LaA
Ah, me! I know how like a golden flower. The Grand Ronde Valley. Ella Higginson. AA
Ah me, if I grew sweet to man. The Tragic Mary Queen of Scots. "Michael Field." EnLoPo; GTML; MBP; OBMV; TCPD
Ah me, my friend! it will not, will not last! Elegy: He Complains How Soon the Pleasing Novelty of Life Is Over [*or* Elegy XI]. William Shenstone. CEP; OBEC; RO
Ah me, once Archeades pressed near and ever nearer. Bittersweet. Asclepiades. GrPE
Ah me the hand upon the body. Legerdemain. Kenneth Mackenzie. BoAV
Ah Me! The Mighty Love. George Frederick Cameron. CaP; CPG; OCL
Ah me! the rain has a sadder sound. The Soldier in the Rain. Julia L. Keyes. BlG
Ah me! to many deaths decreed. To Many Deaths Decreed. John Crowne. *Fr.* Regulus. SeCL
Ah me! when mallows in the garden die. Soliloquy. Moschus. GrR
Ah, me! when shall I marry me? Song. Goldsmith. GTIV
Ah me! Why may not love and life be one? Love and Life. Henry Timrod. *Fr.* Most Men Know Love but as a Part of Life. OQP; QP-2
Ah, Melanippus, why dost thou lament to me? To Melanippus. Alcaeus. GrR
Ah! might I in some humble Kentish dale. Lines Written at Cambridge, to W. R., Esquire. Phineas Fletcher. ElL
Ah, misty Geraneia, ill crag, thou shouldst stand facing. Lost at Sea. Simonides. GrPE
Ah, moment not to be purchased. Bayard Taylor. *Fr.* The Sunshine of the Gods. AA
Ah, more than any priest, O soul, we too believe in God. Walt Whitman. *Fr.* Passage to India. WGRP
Ah mother of a mighty race. Bryant. *See* O Mother of a Mighty Race.
Ah, Mother Russia, never yet have I. Freedom. Nikolai Alekseyevich Nekrasov. TrRV
Ah, mourn, thou loved retreat! Thomas Warton, the Younger. *Fr.* Ode to a Friend on His Leaving a Favourite Village in Hampshire. EnSW
Ah Music, thou sweet sprite. To Music. William Kean Seymour. HBMV
Ah, my beloved, how I love your sisters. Your Sisters. Karl Asplund. AnSL
Ah, my dear angry [*or* deare angrie] Lord. Bitter-sweet. George Herbert. OxBoCh; TrPWD
Ah, my dear father and my parent sweet. His Apology of His Good Father. Gabriel Harvey. *Fr.* Greene's Memorial. ReIE
"Ah, my dear Son," said Mary, "ah, my dear." This Endernight I Saw a Sight [*or* A Dream Carol]. *Unknown.* AnEC; BOL
Ah my deare angrie Lord. *See* Ah, my dear angry Lord.
Ah My Dere ("Ah my dere, ah my dere Son"). *Unknown.* *See* This Endernight I Saw a Sight (" 'Ah, my dear Son' ").
Ah, my God,/ What might I not have made of thy fair world. We Needs Must Love the Highest. Tennyson. *Fr.* Idylls of the King: Guinevere. MaRV
Ah! my heart, ah! what aileth thee. To His Heart. Sir Thomas Wyatt. OBSC; SiPS
Ah, my heart grieves. The Bow. Al-Buqaira. MooP
Ah! my heart is weary waiting. Summer Longings. Denis Florence MacCarthy. HBV; LPS-2
Ah, my heart, the storm and sadness! Liebesweh. Dora Wilcox. BoAu
Ah my Perilla! dost [*or* do'st] thou grieve to see. To Perilla. Robert Herrick. AtBAP; ElSeCe; OBS; ReaPo; SeCV-1; SeEP; UnPo (1st ed.)
Ah, my sweet sweeting. My Sweet Sweeting. *Unknown.* CH; LO; LoPs; LPS-1
Ah, my young princes! ah, my tender babes! Shakespeare. King Richard III, *fr.* IV, iv. MotAn
Ah Night! blind germ of days to be. A Ballad of High Endeavor. *Unknown.* BOHV; NA
Ah! no, no, it is nothing, surely nothing at all. The Wind. William Morris. DaM; PoVP; VLEP
Ah! not because our Soldier died before his field was won. Raglan. Sir Edwin Arnold. VA
Ah! on Thanksgiving Day, when from East and from West. The Pumpkin. Whittier. DD; LPS-2; OHIP; PoRL; TOAH
"Ah, Poor Faun, Poor Faun!" Archias of Mytilene, *tr. fr. Greek by* F. L. Lucas. GrPE
Ah! poor intoxicated little knave. To a Fly. "Peter Pindar." BOHV
Ah! poor Psyche, born mid shadows in this earthly vale of strife. Psyche. Viktor Rydberg. AnSL
Ah, ra, chickera. *Unknown.* OxNR
Ah, rest to the morrow, for many the sorrow. Rebel Mother's Lullaby. Shane Leslie. BOL
Ah, Robin. William Cornish. ElSeCe
"Ah Robin,/ Jolly Robin." Sir Thomas Wyatt. SiPS
Ah, Robin, gentle Robin. Ah, Robin. William Cornish. ElSeCe
Ah, sad and strange, as in dark summer dawns. Tennyson. *Fr.* The Princess, Pt. II. LoPS
Ah! sad are they who know not love. Song from the Persian. Thomas Bailey Aldrich. LBAP; OBAV
Ah! sad wer we as we did peace. The Turnstile. William Barnes. CH; OBVV
Ah! say you so, bold sailor. The Herald Crane. Hamlin Garland. BLA; HBV; SN
Ah, see the fair chivalry come, the companions of Christ! Te Martyrum Candidatus. Lionel Johnson. ACP; CAW; GTIV; HBV; JKCP; MuP; OBMV; OxBoCh; PoLi; TIP
Ah, see what a wonderful smile again! Slumber-Songs of the Madonna, V. Alfred Noyes. BOL
"Ah, Spring, sweet Spring, chief pride of Nature!" Spring. Prince Vyazemsky. TrRV
Ah stay! ah turn! ah whither would you fly. Song. Congreve. *Fr.* The Fair Penitent (*by* Nicholas Rowe). AtBAP; LoBV; OBEC
Ah stay thy treacherous hand, forbear to trace. Verses on Sir Joshua Reynolds's Painted Window at New College, Oxford. Thomas Warton, the Younger. CEP; OBEC; PoEL-3
Ah, stern cold man. A Woman and Her Dead Husband. D. H. Lawrence. NP
Ah, Sun, ah, Moon. The Sun and the Moon. *Unknown.* WhP
Ah! Sunflower [Weary of Time]. Blake. *Fr.* Songs of Experience. AtBAP; AWP; BLV; EG; EiPP; EnLi-2; EnLit; EnRP; EV-3; ExPo; GTBS-D; GTBS-W; InPo; JAWP; LEAP; MaPo; NBE; OAEP; OBEC; OuHeWo; PoE; PoEL-4; ReaPo; RiBV; SeCeV; ShBV-4; TCEP; TOP; UnPo; ViBoPo; WBP
(Sunflower, The.) BEL; BoLiVe; ChTr; PoFS; TrGrPo
Ah, sure, without the childher, now, I don't know what I'd do at all. The Childher. Denis A. McCarthy. CV
Ah, sweet Content, where is thy mild abode? Sonnet [*or* Content]. Parthenophil and Parthenophe, LXVI. Barnabe Barnes. ElL; ElSeCe; ES; OBSC; PeBoSo; ReEn; TuPP
Ah, Sweet Is Tipperary. Denis A. McCarthy. CV; HBV; POT; PoTo
Ah, sweet is youth!—but always eld. Youth of All Blessings Best. Euripides. *Fr.* Heracles. GrR
"Ah, sweet Kitty Neil, rise up from that wheel." Kitty Neil

[or Dance Light]. John Francis Waller. HBV; LPS-1; TIP; VA
Ah, sweet, thou little knowest how. Serenade. Thomas Hood. HBV
Ah! take those lips away; no more. Deadly Kisses. Pierre de Ronsard. AWP
Ah tell me why you turn and fly. Take Her, Break Her. Anacreon. GrL; OxBG
Ah, that day!—do you remember?—with its flood of sun and rain. That Day. Poul la Cour. BoDS
Ah, that she kisses and forgets so soon! Villanelle of Poor Pierrot. Walter Adolphe Roberts. PFE
Ah, that warm February morning! Workers. Arthur Rimbaud. AnFP
Ah! the May was grand this mornin'! The Song of the Thrush. T. A. Daly. BAP; MAP; NeMA
Ah! the morning is grey. Chimney-Tops. *Unknown.* BoTP
Ah! the Sighs. William Cornish. TuPP
Ah, the world hath [or has] many a Horner. Jack Horner. Adeline D. T. Whitney. *Fr.* Mother Goose for Grown Folks. LPS-3
Ah, then how sweetly closed those crowded days! Boyhood. Washington Allston. LPS-1; MOAH
Ah, there be souls none understand. Sea-blown. Joaquin Miller. LBAP
Ah, there is no abiding! Change. Mary Elizabeth Coleridge. MoVE
Ah, there's nothing half so sweet as when the seed is in the ground. Aristophanes. *Fr.* Peace. GrPo
Ah! there's the lily, marble pale. The Rose of May. Mary Howitt. HBV
Ah, those hours when by-gone sages. Half Hours with the Classics. H. J. DeBurgh. BOHV; InMe
Ah, those who love not God. God's Justice. Nagata. SoLD
Ah thou memorial of my best-beloved. The Burial Urn. Sophocles. *Fr.* Electra. GrR
Ah! thou, too. Dante, Shakespeare, Milton. Sydney Dobell. *Fr.* Balder. VA
Ah, through the open door. Spring Morning. D. H. Lawrence. MBP; MoAB; MoBrPo
Ah! To be all alone in a little cell. The Desire for Hermitage. *Unknown.* AnIL; SiB
Ah, to be by Mooni now. Mooni. Henry C. Kendall. BoAu
Ah truly I deem purblind was the skill. If Music Might but Assuage. Euripides. *Fr.* Medea. GrR
Ah, vale of woe, of gloom and darkness moulded. Song. Rachel Morpurgo. TrJP
Ah voices sweet as honey, ah maiden songs divine. The Old Poet to His Maiden Choir. Alcman. GrPE
Ah, wasteful woman, she who may. Unthrift [or Wasteful Woman or Preludes, I]. Coventry Patmore. *Fr.* The Angel in the House. BMEP; GoBC; HBV; POTT
Ah, we are neither heaven nor earth, but men. John Masefield. *Fr.* Sonnets ("Long long ago"). EPN; PoeMoYo
Ah! weak and wide astray! Blake. *Fr.* Jerusalem. OBRV
Ah, weary! I am called the laughing devil. Malzah Speaks. Charles Heavysege. *Fr.* Saul. BoCaPo
Ah, well, Friend Death, good friend thou art. Helen Hunt Jackson. *Fr.* Habeas Corpus. OHIP
Ah! well I love these books of mine. My Books. *Unknown.* DDA
Ah, well I remember that long summer's day. The Baltimore Grays. *Unknown.* BIG
Ah, well it is—since she is gone. Reply. Hartley Coleridge. OBRV
Ah, well-a-day, my lady! My Lady Fair. Martha Day Fenner. MeMeAg
Ah, were it so we ever. No Appeasement. Kaj Munk. BoDS
Ah! were she pitiful as she is fair. Fawnia [or In Praise of His Loving and Best-beloved Fawnia]. Robert Greene. *Fr.* Pandosto. AtBAP; EG; ElSeCe; ES; HBV; OBEV; OBSC; PeBoSo; PoEL-2; TrGrPo; ViBoPo
Ah! what a weary race my feet have run. Sonnet: To the River Lodon [or Loddon]. Thomas Warton, the Younger. CEP; CoBE; OBEC; ViBoPo
Ah, what a web/ Of gray, inconsequential-seeming threads! Lift Up the Curtain. Hermann Hagedorn. *Fr.* The Heart of Youth. QS
Ah, what are strength and beauty? Hymn. Synesius. CAW
Ah, what are these you draw ashore. But Still Intrepid Icarus. Louise Crenshaw Ray. MuM
Ah! What Avails the Sceptred Race! Walter Savage Landor. *See* Rose Aylmer.
Ah, what can ail thee, wretched wight [or knight-at-arms]. *See* O what can ail thee, knight-at-arms.
Ah, what can ever be more stately and admirable to me than mast-hemmed Manhattan? Walt Whitman. *Fr.* Crossing Brooklyn Ferry. AA
Ah, what if Time forgot to light the stars. World-Ruin. Hugh Wilgus Ramsaur. MaRV; MuM
Ah, what is life?—what is joy?—but Aphrodite the golden? "Gather Ye Rosebuds." Mimnermus. GrPE
Ah! what is love? It is a pretty thing. The Shepherd's Wife's Song [or The Shepherd and the King]. Robert Greene. *Fr.* Greene's Mourning Garment. CoEV; EG; ElL; ElSeCe; EnLit; EPP; EV-1; HBV; LoBV; LPS-1; OBSC; PG; ReEn; SiCE; TOP; TuPP; ViBoPo
Ah, what joy/ Can out-joy this. Suave Mari Magno. Sophocles. OxBG
Ah! what joy, the bagpipe and the flute. Paul Fort. *Fr.* Ballad of the Bells. WoL
Ah, what of life! Does no one answer me? Life's Brevity. Francisco de Quevedo y Villegas. TeCS
Ah! what pleasant visions haunt me. The Secret of the Sea [or The Galley of Count Arnaldos]. Longfellow. AnNE; CBPC; EtS; GoTP; IAP; OBEV (new ed.); OBVV; RIS; TCAP
Ah, what rapture! to banish the past. The Song of the Billows. Nils Collett Vogt. AnNoLy
Ah! what time wilt thou come? when shall that cry [or crie]. The Dawning. Henry Vaughan. CAW; EV-2; MePo; MeRV; OxBoCh; ReEn; TrPWD
Ah! What Woes Are Mine. Edmond O'Ryan, *tr. fr. Modern Irish by* Charlotte Brooke. OnYI
Ah! when our wedded life begun. The New House a-Gettèn Wold. William Barnes. RO
Ah, when the means are gone that buy this praise. Shakespeare. *Fr.* Timon of Athens, II, ii. MyFE
Ah! when will this long weary day have end. Spenser. *Fr.* Epithalamion. LO
Ah! whence yon glare. War. Shelley. *Fr.* Queen Mab, IV. LPS-2
Ah, where, Kincora! is Brian the Great? *See* Oh, where, Kincora! is Brian the Great?
Ah! where must needy poet seek for aid. Swift. *Fr.* A Description of a City Shower. ViBoPo
Ah wherefore with infection should he live. Sonnets, LXVII. Shakespeare. PeBoSo; SiCE
Ah! whither doost thou now, thou greater Muse. Two Cantos of Mutabilitie. Spenser. *Fr.* The Faerie Queene. ReEn
Ah whither, Love, wilt thou now carrie me? An Hymne in Honour of Beautie. Spenser. GEPC; ReEn; SiCE
Ah! who can tell how hard it is to climb. The Minstrel, I. James Beattie. CEP; EiPP
Ah! who has seen the mailèd lobster rise. Wonders of Nature. *Unknown.* BOHV
Ah, whom can we deem happier. The Grasshopper. Remy Belleau. TrFP
Ah! why hath Nature to so hard a heart. Amoretti, XXXI. Spenser. PeBoSo
"Ah, why," said Ellen, sighing to herself. Springtime with One Love. Wordsworth. *Fr.* The Excursion, VI. LiA
Ah! why those piteous sounds of woe. The Forlorn One. "Thomas Ingoldsby." BOHV
Ah! why will my dear little girl be so cross. Washing and Dressing. Ann Taylor. SAS
Ah, with the Grape my fading Life provide. Omar and Death [or Ritual of the Grape]. Omar Khayyám, *tr. by* Edward Fitzgerald. *Fr.* The Rubáiyát. GTBS-W; GTSE; OBEV; OBVV; OnPM
Ah! with what freedom [or freedome] could I once have pray'd. The Sigh. Nathaniel Wanley. OBS; OxBoCh
Ah with what heart of wonder, on calm and windless days. Dolphin and Seal. Oppian. *Fr.* Halieuticks. GrPE
Ah! without the moon, what white nights. Without the Moon. Jules Laforgue. LiTW
Ah Woe Is Me. Propertius, *tr. fr. Latin by* F. A. Wright. Elegies, I, 1. AWP
Ah woe is me for pleasure that is vain. Vanity of Vanities. Christina Rossetti. POTT
Ah woe is me, of passion naught I knew. Ah Woe Is Me. Propertius. AWP
Ah, worshipped one, ah, faithful Spring. One Distant April. Gertrude Hall. LBAP
Ah! would that poets could write. Austin Dobson. Christopher Morley. PtP
Ah yah, tair um bam, boo wah. Jungle Mammy Song. *Unknown.* AS
Ah, Yes, I Wrote It. Gelett Burgess. *See* Cinq Ans Après.
Ah, Yes, I Wrote the "Purple Cow." Gelett Burgess. *See* Cinq Ans Après.
Ah, yes—the fight! Well, messmates, well. The Sea Fight. *Unknown.* LPS-2
"Ah, yes, the works are busy on the Hook." A Hook for Leviathan. Norman Cameron. ChMP
Ah! yesterday was dark and drear. Dare Quam Accipere. Mathilde Blind. OBVV
Ah! Yet Consider It Again! Arthur Hugh Clough. BPN; EPN; PoVP; TOP; VA; VLEP
(Old Things Need Not Be Therefore True.) ViPP
Ah, you are cruel. Neighbors. Anne Spencer. CDC
Ah, you mistake me, comrades, to think that my heart is steel! Arnold at Stillwater. Thomas Dunn English. GA; PAH
Ah, you night, you. Russian Song. Anton Delvieg. BoRS
Ah (You Say), This Is Holy Wisdom. Hilda Doolittle ("H. D."). *Fr.* Tribute to the Angels. CrMA; MeRV
Ah! You who wakened in my child's soul. Women of Suli. "Myrtiotissa." MoGP

Ah, young men have less sorrow—a harder lot, and cheerless. The Maid's Complaint. Agathias Scholasticus. GrPE
Ah, Your White-as-Lily Fingers. Heine, *tr. fr. German by* Vernon Watkins. AnGP
Aha! a traitor in the camp. To a Usurper. Eugene Field. FAOV
Aha! I've caught you there again! Dog in Chair. Margaret Mackprang Mackay. AlBD
Aha! these rounded shoulders. Punishment. Emil Aarestrup. BoDS
Ahab Mohammed. James Matthew Legaré. AA
Ahkoond of Swat, The. George Thomas Lanigan. *See* Threnody, A: "What, what, what . . ."
Ahkoond [*or* Ahkond] of Swat, The. Edward Lear. *See* Akond of Swat, The.
Ah'm Broke an' Hungry, *with music.* Lawrence Gellert. TrAS
Ah'm goin' whah nobody knows my name, Lawd, Lawd. Levee Moan (A *and* B *vers.*). *Unknown.* AS
Ah'm gonna build mahself a raft. De [*or* The] Blues Ain' Nothin'. *Unknown.* AS; TrAS
Ah'm sick, doctor-man, Ah'm sick! Calling the Doctor. John Wesley Holloway. BANP; IHA
Ahmed. James Berry Bensel. AA
Ahoy and ahoy, birds! Wings and Wheels. Nancy Byrd Turner. StVeCh (1955 ed.); SUS; TiPo
"Ahoy! and O-ho! and it's who's for the ferry?" Twickenham Ferry. Théophile Marzials. HBV; VA
A-Hunting. Jennie Dunbar. BoTP
A-Hunting We Will Go. Henry Fielding. *Fr.* Don Quixote in England, II. CBOV; HBV; LPS-2; OTPC (1923 ed.); ViBoPo
(Hunting Song.) CEP; OBEC; OxBoLi
(Song: A-Hunting We Will Go.) EV-3
A-hunting went the noble knight. Mudarra and Rodrigo. *Unknown.* LyMA; TeCS
Ai, ai, my small red man. Song of Welcome. Hermia Harris Fraser. BoCaPo; CaP
Ai Ai Thinks of the Man She Loves. Ting Liu Niang, *tr. fr. Chinese by* Florence Ayscough *and* Amy Lowell. ChLP
Aid me, Bellona, while the dreadful fight. The Battle [*or* Battel] of the Summer Islands. Edmund Waller. CEP; EPS (1942 ed.); ReEn; SeCV-1
Aid to Self-Knowledge. Menander, *tr. fr. Greek by* John Addington Symonds. GrR
Aideen. *Unknown, tr. fr. Irish by* Frank O'Connor. KiLC
Aideen's Grave, *sel.* Sir Samuel Ferguson.
"They heaved the stone, they heap'd the cairn." TIP
Aidenn. Katrina Trask. AA
Aiken Drum. *Unknown.* BoN; FaBoCh; LoGBV; OxNR
Aileen Aroon. Gerald Griffin. *See* Eileen Aroon.
Ailill the king is vanished. The Downfall of Heathendom. *Unknown.* KiLC
Ailing Parent, The. Lora Dunetz. NePoAm-2
Aim, The. Sir Charles G. D. Roberts. MaRV; PeCV
Aim of Life, The. Philip James Bailey. *Fr.* Festus. LPS-3; OQP; QP-2
(Country Town, A, 4 *ll.*) PoToHe (new ed.)
(We Live in Deeds.) BMEP; MaRV
Aim Was Song, The. Robert Frost. HH; NP
Aiming from clocks and space. Into Life. Stephen Spender. TwHP
Aimirgin's Invocation. *At. to* Amergin. *See* Invocation to Ireland.
Aimless. Louis Palagyi, *tr. fr. Hungarian by* Watson Kirkconnell. TrJP
Aimless business of your feet, The. Cecidit, Cecidit Babylon Magna! Theodore Maynard. JKCP
Aimless darting arrow, An. Rimas, II. Gustavo Adolfo Bécquer. TeCS
Ain' but de one thing I done wrong. Rosie. *Unknown.* ABF
Ain' Go'n to Study War No Mo', *with music.* *Unknown.* AS
Ain' No Mo' Cane on de Brazis, *with music.* *Unknown.* ABF
Ain't Education Grand? Jean Gillespie. DDA
Ain't Gonna Rain, *with music.* *Unknown.* AS
Ain't Got No Place to Lay My Head, *with music.* *Unknown.* StDa
Ain't It Awful, Mabel? John Edward Hazzard. BOHV
Ain't it fierce to be so beautiful. Beautiful. *Unknown.* ABF
"Ain't It Fine Today!" Douglas Malloch. *See* It's Fine Today.
Ain't It Hard to Be a Right Black Nigger, *with music.* *Unknown.* OuSiCo
Ain't it nice at set o' sun. At the Sorghum-bilin'. James Larkin Pearson. NoCaPo
Ain't Nature Commonplace! Arthur Guiterman. FiBHP; InMe
Ain't that a pity, oh Lawd. The Gold Dust Fire. *Unknown.* StDa
Ain't Workin' Song, *with music.* *Unknown.* OuSiCo
Air. Edwin Denby. CrMA
Air. Kathleen Raine. MoAB
Air: "I ne'er could any luster see." Sheridan. *Fr.* The Duenna. HBV
Air and Angels. John Donne. *See* Aire and Angells.
Air comes forth this morning, The. Little Song in the Air. Genaro Estrada. AnCL
Air cool and soft, The. Chaka. F. T. Prince. BoSA
Air grows pure and clear, The. Ode to Francisco Salinas. Luis de León. AnSpL-1
Air has in it the smell of young leaves, The. Spring Morning. Coley B. Taylor. *Fr.* Chinoiseries. PFE
Air in Spring, The. Basil Dowling. AnNZ
Air is clear, The. The Fragrant Blossoms. Tzu Yeh. PoHN
Air is filled with sunlight, The. Spring. Thorsteinn Gislason. IcP
Air is full of a farewell, The. On Leaving Ullswater. Kathleen Raine. NeBP
Air is full of diamond dust tonight, The. Frozen Fire. Floris Clarke McLaren. CaP
Air is keen, The; Yule-tide is at the door. The Old Inn. Karle Wilson Baker. VOD
Air is like a butterfly, The. Easter. Joyce Kilmer. MPB; NP; TiPo
Air is soft and balmy, The. In April. Emily Gail Arnold. PEDC
Air is still, The—the night is dark. The Fisherman's Light. Susanna Moodie. BoCaPo
Air is sweetest that a thistle guards, The. Variations: The Air Is Sweetest That a Thistle Guards. James Merrill. NePoEA
Air is thick with nerves and smoke, The: pens tremble in sweating hands. University Examinations in Egypt. D. J. Enright. MoPW
Air is whipped by the frequent rain-drops, The. Boris Pasternak, *tr. fr. Russian by* C. M. Bowra. BoRS
Air is white and winds are crying, The. Snow Storm. Sister Mary Madeleva. GoBC
Airmail Arrives, The. Ethel Romig Fuller. PoTo
Air Mail, Special. Sister Mary Philip. JKCP (1955 ed.)
Air of Coolness Plays upon His Face, An. Sarah N. Cleghorn. PC
Air of June Sings, The. Edward Dorn. NeAP
Air Plant, The (Grand Cayman, W.I.). Hart Crane. MAP; MoAB; MoAmPo
Air Raid, The. Archibald MacLeish. PoF
Air Raid. John Allan Wyeth. PoP
Air revealed a glimmering form, The. On a Night of Stars. Leah Bodine Drake. UnW
Air Sentry, The. Patrick Barrington. CenHV
Air Strikes Chill, The. Osip Emilyevich Mandelstamm, *tr. fr. Russian by* Babette Deutsch. TrRV
Air was calm, the sun was low, The. On the Victory of Poland and Her Allies over the Sultan Osman, 1621. Casimir Sarbiewski. CAW
Air was full of withered leaves, The. The Flying Dead. Rose O'Neill. TBM
Air was washed with silver as night went, The. The Gift of Poets. Alice Hunt Bartlett. BAP
Air, which is not anything. Elements. Carolyn Wilson Link. GoYe
Airborn. Louis Grudin. PG (1955 ed.)
Aircrews have had it and the war goes on. "For Whom the Bell Tolls." Gavin Ewart. WaP
Aire and Angells [*or* Angels]. John Donne. AtBAP; BoW; MeLP; MePo; OBS; SeCV-1
(Air and Angels.) MeRV; PoFS; TuPP
("Twice or thrice had I loved thee.") EG
Airedale, erect beside the chauffeur of a Rolls-Royce, An. Fashions in Dogs. E. B. White. FiBHP
Airly Beacon. Charles Kingsley. EtPaEn; EV-5; GTBS; GTML; GTSL; HBV; OBEV; PoVP
Airmail. *See* Air Mail.
Airman, The. W. R. Rodgers. PoD; WaP
Airman's Alphabet, The. W. H. Auden. *Fr.* Journal of an Airman. NAMP; PoF
Airman's Certificate—No. 39289—U.S. Civil Aeronautics Authority. A. Fleming MacLiesh. Exploration by Air, III. PoF
Airman's Prayer, An. Hugh R. Brodie. MaRV
(Sergeant's Prayer, A.) PGD
Airmen's Hymn, The. Harry Webb Farrington. MaRV
Airplane, The. Rowena Bastin Bennett. FaPON; GFA; OTPC (1946 ed.)
Airplane, The. Annette Wynne. GFA
Airplane has gigantic wings, An. The Airplane. Rowena Bastin Bennett. FaPON; GFA; OTPC (1946 ed.)
Airplane taxied to the station's gate, The. First Flight. Robert P. Tristram Coffin. PoMa
Airplane taxis down the field, The. Taking Off. Mary McB. Green. TiPo
Airs! that wander and murmur round. The Siesta. *Unknown.* AnSpL-1; AWP; JAWP; WBP
Airship. Hy Sobiloff. NePA
Airy as leaves blown by the autumn storm. Kittens. Michael Scot. PoC

Airy, fairy Lilian. Lilian. Tennyson. HBV; PoVP; VLEP
Airy Nothings. Shakespeare. *See* Our Revels Now Are Ended.
Aishah Schechinah. Robert Stephen Hawker. ACP (1926 ed.); EV-4; GoBC; ISi; NBE; OxBoCh
Aisle of a Temple, The. Congreve. *Fr.* The Mourning Bride. II, i. EV-3
Aisling. Austin Clarke. AnIV
Aix-la-Chappelle, 1945. Edgar Bowers. NePoEA
Aiyee ("Aiyee, so handsome!"). *Unknown, tr. fr. Chinese.* WhP
Ai-yee! My yellow-bird-woman. Beat against Me No Longer. Lew Sarett. NP
Aizmirstai Mihlai. Arthur Berthold. CAG
Ajanta. Muriel Rukeyser. FiMAP; LiTA; LiTM; MiAP; MoAB; MoAmPo (1950 ed.); TwAmPo
Aja's Lament over His Dead Wife, *abr.* Kalidasa, *tr. fr. Sanskrit by* Arthur W. Ryder. LiTW
Ajax, *sels.* Sophocles, *tr. fr. Greek.*
Ajax! to All Farewell, *tr. by* Robert Whitelaw. GrR
(Universal Change, *tr. by* Charles Stuart Calverley.) LiTW; OxBG
Bitterness, *br. sel., tr. by* F. Storr. LiA
Ajax's Death, *tr. by* F. Storr. LiA
(Ajax, before His Suicide, *tr. by* F. Storr.) LiTW
(Before Death, *tr. by* Robert Whitelaw.) OxBG
(O Welcome! Gentle Death, *tr. by* Robert Whitelaw.) GrR
Calchas the Seer, *tr. by* Robert Whitelaw. GrR
Chorus: "Fair Salamis, the billow's roar," *tr. by* Winthrop Mackworth Praed. AWP; JAWP; WBP
"Cursed Be He Who First Taught Grecians War," *tr. by* Lewis Campbell. GrR
Musings on Man's Sad Estate, *tr. by* Lewis Campbell. GrR
Tecmessa, *tr. by* Robert Whitelaw. GrR
Tecmessa's Fruitless Plea, *tr. by* Robert Whitelaw. GrR
"Thou that makest high heaven thy chariot course," *tr. by* Edward Bulwer-Lytton. GrPo
Unpalatable Truths, *tr. by* Lewis Campbell. GrR
Ajax and Ulysses. James Shirley. *See* Contention of Ajax and Ulysses, The.
Ajax, before His Suicide. Sophocles. *See* Ajax's Death.
Ajax Covers the Flight of the Greeks. Homer, *tr. fr. Greek by* William Cowper. *Fr.* The Iliad, XI. GrR
(Ajax in the Fight, *tr. by* William Cowper.) OxBG
("But now Zeus throned in the highest made Ajax' heart turn cold," *shorter sel., tr. by* F. L. Lucas.) GrPE
("But the eternal father throned on high," *tr. by* William Cowper.) GrPo
Ajax on the Decks. Homer, *pr. tr. fr. Greek by* Andrew Lang, Walter Leaf *and* Ernest Myers. *Fr.* The Iliad, XV. OxBG
Ajax Prays for Light. Homer, *tr. fr. Greek by* the Earl of Derby. *Fr.* The Iliad, XVII. LiA
Ajax! to All Farewell! Sophocles, *tr. fr. Greek by* Robert Whitelaw. *Fr.* Ajax. GrR
(Universal Change, *tr. by* Charles Stuart Calverley.) LiTW; OxBG
Ajax's Death. Sophocles, *tr. fr. Greek by* F. Storr. *Fr.* Ajax. LiA
(Ajax, before His Suicide, *tr. by* F. Storr.) LiTW
(Before Death, *tr. by* Robert Whitelaw.) OxBG
(O Welcome! Gentle Death, *tr. by* Robert Whitelaw.) GrR
Akathistos Hymn, The. *Unknown, tr. fr. Greek by* Vincent McNabb. ISi
Akbar's Dream, *sel.* Tennyson.
Hymn: "Once again thou flamest heavenward, once again we see thee rise." PoVP
Akhnaton. Thomas S. Jones, Jr. AnAmPo; LA
Akinetos. Richard Henry Horne. *Fr.* Orion. VA
Akond of Swat, The. Edward Lear. ALV; CenHV; FaBoCh; FiBHP; GoTP; LauV; LiL; OnPP; SiTL
(Ahkoond [*or* Ahkond] of Swat, The.) BOHV; NA; RIS
Al Aaraaf. Poe. AmP
Sels.
Song: "Neath blue-bell or streamer." APA
('Neath Blue-Bell or Streamer.) AmPP (3d ed.); IAP
(Song from "Al Aaraaf.") AmPP (4th ed.); AnFE; CoAnAm; NePA; OxBA
Ligeia ("Ligeia! Ligeia!/ My beautiful one!") APW
Song: "Spirit! that dwellest where." CoBA
(Song of Nesace.) APW
Sonnet to Science. Prologue. AmP; AmPo; AmPP; AnAmPo; AnFE; CoBA; CoV; NePA; OnAP; OxBA
(Sonnet: To Science.) APA; CoAnAm; IAP; LA; MOAP
(To Science.) PeBoSo; SPP
Al-Maumin. Sir Edwin Arnold. BoFr
Al Nist by the Rose. *Unknown.* AtBAP
Al the Meryere. *Unknown. See* All the Merrier Is That Place.
Ala, mala, mink, monk. *Unknown.* OxNR
Alabado, *with music. Unknown, tr. fr. Spanish.* TrAS
Alabama, The. Maurice Bell. PAH
Alabama. Julia Tutwiler. BlG; PoRL
Alabama, The. *Unknown.* ShS, *2 vers., with music;* SoAmSa, *with music*
Alabama, Alabama,/ We will aye be true to thee. Alabama. Julia Tutwiler. BlG; PoRL
Alabama Bound. *Unknown. See* I'm Alabama Bound.
Alabama Earth (at Booker Washington's Grave). Langston Hughes. GoSl
Alabama, good-bye! I love thee well! A Missouri Maiden's Farewell to Alabama. "Mark Twain." InMe
Alack-a-day!/ I'm carried clean away. Black but Comely. Asclepiades. GrR
Alack, what poverty my Muse brings forth. Sonnets, CIII. Shakespeare. PeBoSo
Aladdin. James Russell Lowell. AnNE; APW; BAV; BBV (1951 ed.); BLP; HBV; MW; NeHB; OBAV; PoMS; PYM; StVeCh (1940 ed.); WaKn
Aladdin and the Jinn. Vachel Lindsay. AnAmPo; AnFE; APA; ChMo; CMP; CoAnAm; GTBS-W; LA; LiTM; NP; NV; OnPP; TBM
(Poems about the Moon [VI].) MAPA; TwAmPo
Aladdin Throws Away His Lamp. Elias Lieberman. PoMa
Alamance. Seymour W. Whiting. PAH
Alarm and time clock still intrude too early. And on This Shore. M. Carl Holman. PoNe
Alarm at First Entering the Yang-tze Gorges. Po Chü-i, *tr. fr. Chinese by* Arthur Waley. TrCh
Alarm in 1645, An, *sel.* Thomas Jordan.
Cavalier's Lullaby for His Mistress, A. SeCL
Alarmed Skipper, The. James Thomas Fields. BOHV; EtS; GoTP; HBV; LHV; YaD
(Nantucket Skipper, The.) AmSS; DDA; LPS-3
Alarming Progress of Luxury in New England, The. Benjamin Tompson. *See* Prologue: "Times wherein old Pompion, The."
Alarum, The. Sylvia Townsend Warner. MBP; MoBrPo
Alas! Phoebe Cary. LBAP
Alas! Sadi, *tr. fr. Persian by* L. Cranmer-Byng. *Fr.* The Gulistan. AWP; WoL
Alas! *Unknown.* IHA
Alas,/ Autumn wind! Song of the Samma. Haruo Sato. PoLJ
Alas!/ In vain I listen. To One Who Has Passed. Wu Ti. PoHN
Alas—a Sea Song. Frances B. Stone. CAG
Alas, Alack! Walter de la Mare. FaPON; GFA; MPB; PoRh; TiPo
Alas, alas, Miss X: twenty years! To Miss X, Buried in the West Wind. Rafael Alberti. CoSP
Alas, alas, quo' bonnie Heck. The Last Dying Words of Bonnie Heck. William Hamilton. EBSV
Alas, Alas, the Winter. Edith Lovejoy Pierce. MuM
Alas! alas! thou turn'st in vain. Claim to Love. Giovanni Battista Guarini. AWP
Alas! and am I born for this. On Liberty and Slavery. George Moses Horton. PoNe
Alas! and did my Saviour bleed. Isaac Watts. OlF
Alas, and well-a-day! they are talking of me still. A Maori Girl's Song. Alfred Domett. OBVV
Alas, Chao of Nippon—you who left the Imperial City. The Poet Mourns His Japanese Friend. Li Po. FoFr
Alas, dear heart! what hope had I. Love Me Again. *Unknown.* ElL
Alas! for all the pretty women who marry dull men. Meditation at Kew. Anna Wickham. AnEnPo; FaBoTw; MBP; MoBrPo
"Alas for grim old age! Alas for youth!" I cry. The Years. Theognis. GrPE
Alas for him that for any of the vile rude world's estates. He Who Forsakes the Clerkly Life. *Unknown. Fr.* The Life of St. Cellach of Killala. OnYI
Alas for him who never sees. Whittier. *Fr.* Snow-bound. InP
Alas for me, who loved a falcon well. Sonnet: A Lady Laments for Her Lost Lover. *Unknown.* AWP
Alas! for Peter not a helping hand. George Crabbe. *Fr.* The Borough, Letter XXII. OBRV
Alas! for Saturn's days of gold. William Morris. *Fr.* The Life and Death of Jason, X. EmBrPo
Alas! for the going of swiftness, for the feet of the running of thee. Johnny, I Hardly Knew Ye: In Swinburnese, *parody.* Robert Yelverton Tyrrell. OnYI
Alas for the voyage, O High King of Heaven. Farewell [*or* Colum-Cille's Farewell] to Ireland. *At. to* St. Columcille, *tr. by* Douglas Hyde. AnIV; AWP; JAWP; LiTW; WBP
Alas! for them, their day is o'er. Indians. Charles Sprague. *Fr.* Centennial Ode. GN
Alas for Youth. Firdausi, *tr. fr. Persian by* R. A. Nicholson. AWP; JAWP; LiTW; WBP
Alas, Fra Giacomo. Fra Giacomo. Robert Buchanan. LPS-3
Alas, have I not pain enough, my friend. Astrophel and Stella, XIV. Sir Philip Sidney. ReEn; SiPS; TuPP; TwHP

Alas! how can I sleep? who truly loves. Thomas Middleton. *Fr.* Blurt, Master Constable. LO

Alas! how dismal is my tale. The Curse of Doneraile. Patrick O'Kelly. OnYI

Alas, how easily things go wrong! Sweet Peril. George Macdonald. BLPA; FaBoBe; NeHB; TreFS

Alas! how frail and weak a little boat. A Summer Storm. Lord Alfred Douglas. JKCP (1926 ed.)

Alas! how full of fear. Prophets in Their Time [*or* The Fate of the Prophets]. Longfellow. *Fr.* Christus; a Mystery. GrCo-2; WGRP

Alas! How Light a Cause May Move. Thomas Moore. *Fr.* Lalla Rookh. LPS-1

Alas, how right the ancient saying is. The Old Men. Euripides. *Fr.* Aeolus. OxBG

Alas, How Soon the Hours Are Over. Walter Savage Landor. *See* Plays.

Alas, I am a heavy child. Stout. Rue Carpenter. RIS

Alas, I am so faint I may not stand. The Desertion of Beauty and Strength. *Unknown. Fr.* Everyman. ACP

Alas, Kind Element. Léonie Adams. MoVE

Alas! Madam, for Stealing of a Kiss. Sir Thomas Wyatt. OAEP

Alas, man's care, and O the vacuity. Satires, I. Persius. LaP

Alas! my Child, where is the Pen. The Hen. Oliver Herford. LBN; NA

Alas! my dear friend, what a state of affairs! Epistle of Condolence. Thomas Moore. OnYI

Alas, My God. Thomas Shepherd. *Fr.* For Communion with God. OxBoCh

("Alas, my God, that we should be," *shorter sel.*) TrPWD

Alas, My Heart. Sir Edward Dyer. ElSeCe

("Alas, my heart, mine eye hath wrongèd thee.") SiCE

(Corydon to His Phyllis.) ElL

Alas, my heart is black. The New Heart. *Unknown.* WGRP

Alas, my heart! mine eye hath wrongèd thee. Alas, My Heart [*or* Corydon to His Phyllis]. Sir Edward Dyer. ElL; ElSeCe; SiCE

Alas! my Lord is going. Comfort in Extremity. Christopher Harvey. OxBoCh

Alas, my love, ye [*or* you] do me wrong. My Lady Greensleeves [*or* Lady Greensleeves *or* A New Courtly Sonnet]. *Unknown.* AtBAP; EV-2; LoGBV; PoEL-2; WP. *See also* Greensleeves was all my joy.

Alas, my Postumus, our years. To Postumus. Horace. Odes, II, 14. LiTW; OuHeWo

Alas! my son, you little know. Wedlock. Jenny Grahame. LiTL

Alas, my worthy master honourable. *See* Allas! my worthy maister honorable.

Alas, O King of Kings. The Song of the Heads. *Unknown.* KiLC

Alas! our pleasant moments fly. On Parting. Edward Coote Pinkney. APW; SPP

Alas! our young affections run to waste. Desire and Disillusion. Byron. *Fr.* Childe Harold's Pilgrimage. EPN

Alas, poor Death, where is thy glory? A Dialogue Anthem. George Herbert. StJW

Alas, poor heart, I pity thee. Medieval Norman Songs, IX. *Unknown, tr. by* John Addington Symonds. AWP

Alas, poor man, what hap have I. Sir Thomas Wyatt. SiPS

Alas! Poor Queen. Marion Angus. GoTS

"Alas!" said he, "were I but always borne." Endymion Chooses Mortal Love. Keats. *Fr.* Endymion. ERP

Alas! shall ever I see again. Two Remember Dawn. Heinrich von Morungen. LyMA

Alas so all things now do hold their peace. A Complaint by Night of the Lover Not Beloved [*or* Night]. Earl of Surrey, *after* Petrarch. AWP; CaAE; ElL; ElSeCe; FaBoEn; LoBV; OBSC; OuHeWo; ReEn; SiCE; SiPS; TuPP

Alas, So Long! Dante Gabriel Rossetti. PoVP

Alas! that all we loved of him should be. Shelley. *Fr.* Adonais. OHIP

Alas! that ever [*or* evyr] that speche was spoken [*or* spokyn]. *Unknown. Fr.* Eva's Lament. AtBAP; EnLoPo

Alas! that liquid look, that lovely face! Petrarch. *Fr.* Sonnets to Laura: To Laura in Death. PrPoCR

Alas! that men must see. Love and Death. Margaret Deland. AA; HBV

Alas, that my heart is a lute. My Heart Is a Lute. *At. to* Lady Anne Lindsay *and to* Lady Blanche Elizabeth Lindsay. HBV; VA

Alas! the endowment of immortal power. These Helps Solicit. Wordsworth. *Fr.* The Excursion, IV. GrCo-2

Alas the grief, and deadly woful smart. Sir Thomas Wyatt. SiPS

Alas! the love of women! it is known. The Love of Women. Byron. *Fr.* Don Juan, II. BCEP; CoBE

Alas, the moon should ever beam. The Water Lady. Thomas Hood. CH; HBV; RO; VA; ViBoPo

Alas! the rolling [*or* weary] hours pass slow. The Countersign. *Unknown.* BlG; MDAH

Alas! they had been friends in youth. The Quarrel of Friends [*or* Friendship]. Samuel Taylor Coleridge. *Fr.* Christabel. BoFr; CBE; LEAP; LO; LPS-1; MCCG; OBRV

Alas, thy poor beast's body hangs for the winds to batter. "Ah, Poor Faun, Poor Faun!" Archias of Mytilene. GrPE

Alas, 'tis true I have gone here and there. Sonnets, CX. Shakespeare. EM-1; EnLi-1 (1949 ed.); EPP; EtPaEn; EV-1; MaPo; NBE; OAEP; OBSC; PeBoSo; PoE; ReEn; ReIE; SiCE; ViBoPo

Alas, unhappy land; ill-fated spot. Dirge of the Moolla of Kotal. George Thomas Lanigan. BOHV; NA

Alas! what boots it with incessant care. Milton. *Fr.* Lycidas. PC

Alas! what pity 'tis that regularity. Toby Tosspot. George Colman. LPS-3

Alas, what pleasure, now the pleasant spring. A Canzon Pastoral in Honor of Her Majesty. Edmund Bolton. TuPP

Alas! What Shall I Do for Love? Henry VIII, King of England. PrWP

Alas, whence came this change of looks? Astrophel and Stella, LXXXVI. Sir Philip Sidney. SiPS

Alas! who knows or cares, my love. Laura's Song. Oliver Madox Brown. OBVV; VA

Alas, with what tormenting fire. Chorus [*or* Of Death]. Robert Garnier, *tr. by* the Countess of Pembroke. *Fr.* Antonius. ElL; TuPP

"Alas, you native berry." Lament of the Troops on the Death of Peter the Great. *Unknown.* BoFr

Alaska. Joaquin Miller. PAH

Alaska. *Unknown.* PoRL

Alastor; or, The Spirit of Solitude. Shelley. BCEP, *abr.*; BEL; BPN; CBE; EmBrPo; EnLi-2 (1949 ed.); EnRP; ERP; EV-4; GEPC; OAEP; TCEP

Sels.

"As an eagle grasped." ChER

"Earth, ocean, air, belovèd brotherhood!" FiP; MeRV

(Invocation.) WHA

(Invocation to Nature.) EPN

"Poet wandering on, through Arabie, The." UnW

"There was a Poet whose untimely tomb." EPP

Alba, *sel.* Robert Tofte.

Love's Labour Lost. ElL

Alba Innominata. *Unknown, tr. fr. Provençal by* Ezra Pound. AWP; LiTW

Albanians still sleep, glutted, weary, The. Aristotelis Valaoritis. *Fr.* Athanase Diakos. MoGP

Albatross, The. Baudelaire, *fr. French.* AnFP, *tr. by* Kate Flores; EnLi-2, *tr. by* Frances Winwar; OnPM, *tr. by* Lilian Spencer Walker; ReMP, *tr. by* Warren Carrier; TrFP, *tr. by* Alan Conder; WoL, *tr. by* George Dillon

Albatross. Charles Burgess. NePoAm-2

Albatross, The. William Pember Reeves. AnNZ

Albatross. Charles Warren Stoddard. AA; BLA; EtS; SN

Albeit the Venice girls get praise. Ballad of the Women of Paris. Villon, *tr. by* Swinburne. AWP; JAWP; OuHeWo; WBP

"Albemarle" Cushing. James Jeffrey Roche. PAH

Albert Sidney Johnston. Kate Brownlee Sherwood. BlG; GA; MC; PAH

Albert Sidney Johnston. Francis Orrery Ticknor. PAH

Albert the Good. Tennyson. *Fr.* Idylls of the King: Dedication. BMEP

Alberta, Let Yo' Hair Hang Low, *with music. Unknown.* StDa

Alberto Rojas Jiménez Comes Flying. "Pablo Neruda," *tr. fr. Spanish by* H. R. Hays. TwSpPo

Albi, Ne Doreas, *wr.* [Doleas]. Horace, *tr. fr. Latin by* Austin Dobson. Odes, I, 33. AWP

Albion and Albanius, *sels.* Dryden.

Nereids Rise Out of the Sea and Sing, Tritons Dance. BeR

Song of the River Thames, A. FaBoEn

(Song of Thamesis.) TCEP

Albion's England, *sels.* William Warner.

"Aeneas dead, Ascanius reign'd; Ascanius dead, his brother," *fr. Bk.* II, *ch.* 13. ReIE

"Eight Henry, heir indubitate of York and Lancaster," *fr. Bk.* VIII, *ch.* 38. TuPP

Fate of Narcissus, The, *fr. Bk.* IX, *ch.* 46. OBSC

"Now of the conqueror this isle had Brutain unto name," *fr. Bk.* III, *ch.* 14. ReIE

"Of world-admired Drake," *fr. Bk.* XI, *ch.* 71. SG

"Spaniard's long time care, The," *fr. Bk.* IX, *ch.* 49. SG

Albuera. Thomas Hardy. *Fr.* The Dynasts, Pt. II, Act VI, sc. iv. WaaP

Album, The. C. Day Lewis. ChMP; EnLoPo; FaBoEn; OxBI

Album Verses. Oliver Wendell Holmes. *Fr.* The Autocrat of the Breakfast Table, *ch.* 1. AmPP

Alcaeus of Messene. Philip V, King of Macedon, *tr. fr. Greek by* J. H. Merivale. OxBG

Alcaics; to H. F. B. Robert Louis Stevenson. OBEV (new ed.); OBVV; ShBV-3

("Brave lads in olden musical centuries.") EG

Alcestis, *sels.* Euripides, *tr. fr. Greek.*

Alcestis' Final Hour, *tr. by* Gilbert Murray. GrR

Bereavement, *tr. by* C. M. Bowra. OxBG

Farewell: "Boat two-oared, upon water, A," *tr. by* Gilbert Murray. GrR
Hospitality, *tr. by* Robert Browning. OxBG
("Hence Loathèd Melancholy . . ." *tr. by* Gilbert Murray.) GrR
It Is a Gracious House and Ever Was, *tr. by* Dudley Fitts *and* Robert Fitzgerald. LiTW
Necessity, *tr. by* Gilbert Murray. GrR
"O much-enduring heart and hand of mine!" *tr. by* Robert Browning. GrPo
(Death the Enemy.) OxBG
Strength of Fate, The, *tr. by* A. E. Housman. AWP; JAWP; WBP
To Alcestis, *tr. by* Richard Aldington. OxBG
(Praise of a Heroine, *tr. by* Gilbert Murray.) GrR
"Why look'st so solemn and so thought-absorbed?" *tr. by* Robert Browning. GrPo
Alcestis. Isabel Williams Verry. GoYe
Alcestis in Ely. Nicholas Moore. NeBP
Alchemist, The. Louise Bogan. AWP; MAP; MoAmPo; MOAP
Alchemist, The, *sels.* Ben Jonson.
"Come on, sir. Now, you set your foot on shore," *fr.* II, i–ii. AtBAP; PoEL-2
(Here's the Rich Peru.) LiA
"I have blown, sir,/ Hard for your worship," *fr.* II, ii. LO
"I will have all my beds blown up, *fr.* II, ii. NBE
"No. I'll have no bawds," *fr.* II, ii. ViBoPo
Alchemist, The. Ezra Pound. LiTA; NePA
Alchemy. Francis Carlin. JKCP
Alchemy. Ibn Abil Khayal, *tr. fr. Arabic* by A. J. Arberry. MooP
Alchemy. Adelaide Love. PGD
Alchemy of Words, The. Arthur Rimbaud, *tr. fr. French by* Bert M-P. Leefmans. AnFP
Alcibiades to a Jealous Girl. Arthur Davison Ficke. HBMV
Alcilia, *sel.* "J. C."
Frailty of Beauty, The. ElL
Alciphron and Leucippe. Walter Savage Landor. OBEV; RO
Alcohol. Louis MacNeice. LiTM
Alcoholic Goblins. Thomas Jefferson Savage. PoP
Alcove at Sunrise, An. Victor Hugo, *tr. fr. French by* Alan Conder. TrFP
Alcyone. Frances Laughton Mace. AA; LEAP
Aldaran. Annie Campbell Huestis. CPG
Aldebaran at Dusk. George Sterling. PFY; TCPD
Alder by the river, The. Spring. Celia Thaxter. BoChLi; DD; HH; OTPC (1946 ed.); PRWS; RAR
Aldfrid's Itinerary through Ireland. *Unknown, tr. fr. Middle Irish by* James Clarence Mangan. OnYI
Ale. W. H. Davies. PC
Alec Yeaton's Son. Thomas Bailey Aldrich. EtS; FAOV
Aleppo. Ibn Kharuf, *tr. fr. Arabic by* A. J. Arberry. MooP
Alex, perhaps a colour of which neither of us had dreamt. Letter to Alex Comfort. Dannie Abse. FaBoTw
Alexander and Campaspe, *sels.* John Lyly.
Apelles' Song: "Cupid and my Campaspe played," *fr.* III, v. ATP; EM-1; EnLi-1; EnLit; EPP; NeHB; OuHeWo; TOP; TrGrPo
(Alexander and Campaspe.) ElSeCe
(Cards and Kisses.) BCEP; HoPM; LiTL; OBEV
(Cupid and Campaspe.) AtBAP; BEL; BLV; BTP; ElL; EV-1; GTBS; GTBS-D; GTBS-W; GTSE; GTSL; HBV; LEAP; LiTG; LPS-1; SeCeV; UnPo (1st ed.); WHA
(Cupid and My Campaspe.) PoRA
(Cupid and My Campaspe Played [*or* Play'd].) CenL; ExPo; KN; OAEP; PECK; ReaPo; ReEn; SiCE; TuPP; ViBoPo
(Song by Apelles.) ALV; CaAE
(Song of Apelles.) OBSC
Serving Men's Song, A: "O! for a bowl of fat Canary," *fr.* I, iii. *Also in* A Mad World, My Masters (*by* Thomas Middleton). ALV; OBSC
Trico's Song: "What bird so sings," *fr.* V, i. OBSC; RiBV; TrGrPo
(Spring, The.) CH
(Spring's Welcome.) AnEnPo; BCEP; BEL; EPP; OBEV; TOP
(To Welcome in the Spring.) EV-1
(What Bird So Sings.) EG; ElL; SiCE; ThWaDe; TuPP; ViBoPo
Alexander and the Pirate. John Gower. *Fr.* Confessio Amantis, III. EV-1
Alexander Campbell, *sel.* Vachel Lindsay.
My Fathers Came from Kentucky. HBMV
Alexander Graham Bell Did Not Invent the Telephone. Robert P. Tristram Coffin. TiPo (1959 ed.)
Alexander Jannai. C. P. Cavafy, *tr. fr. Modern Greek by* Simon Chasen. TrJP
Alexander Pope at Stanton Harcourt. Sidney Keyes. *Fr.* Sour Land. FaBoTw
Alexander Selkirk during His Solitary Abode in the Island of Juan Fernandez. William Cowper. *See* Verses Supposed to Be Written by Alexander Selkirk . . .
Alexander the Great. *Unknown.* CH
Alexander Throckmorton. Edgar Lee Masters. *Fr.* Spoon River Anthology. BAP; SBMV
Alexander's Feast; or, The Power of Music [*or* Musique]. Dryden. ACP; AEV; AnFE; ATP; BCEP; BEL; BLV; BoLiVe; BrBE; CaAE; CEP; CoBE; EiPP; EM-1; EnL; EnLi-1; EnLit; EPP; EPS; EV-3; FiP; GEPC; GN, *sts.* 1–2; GoBC; GTBS; GTBS-D; GTBS-W; GTSE; GTSL; HBV; LEAP, *sts.* 1–2; LH; LiA; LiTB; LoBV; LPS-3; OAEP; OBS; OtMeF, *st.* 1; OuHeWo; PIAE; PoE; PreP; REAL; SeCeV; SeCV-2; SeEP; TCEP; TOP; TrGrPo; TwCrTr; TyEnPo; WHA
War, *br. sel.* TreFS
Alexandra, *sels.* Lycophron, *tr. fr. Greek by* Lord Royston. GrPo
"But when athwart the empty-vaulted heaven."
"Greece/ For this one crime, aye for this one, shall weep."
"Mark then my words, for I will speak, O King."
"Now Mars showers down a fiery sleet, and winds."
Out of Lycophron ("What shall become of Man so wise"), *tr. by* Sir Charles Sedley. BeR
"Then woes, and wars, and wasting tides of blood."
"Visions of glory, crowd not on my soul."
Alexandria. Lawrence Durrell. MoVE; PoN
Alexandrian Erotic Fragment. *Unknown, tr. fr. Greek.* GrPo
Alexandrian Songs, *sels.* Mikhail Alekseyevich Kuzmin, *tr. fr. Russian by* Babette Deutsch.
"Dying is sweet," II. TrRV
"How I love the world in all its beauty," I. TrRV
Alexis Calls Me Cruel. José Iglesias, *tr. fr. Spanish by* Bryant. AnSpL-2
Alexis, here she stayed; among these pines. Sonnet [*or* Spring Bereaved *or* Primitiae]. William Drummond of Hawthornden. EBSV; ElL; ElSeCe; ES; HBV; LO; OBEV; OBS
Alf of Odderskerry. *Unknown, tr. fr. Danish by* E. M. Smith-Dampier. *Fr.* Hervarar Saga. BoDaBa
Alfred, a Masque, *sel.* James Thomson *and* David Mallet.
Rule, Britannia! *fr.* II, v. Thomson. AEV; BEL; BHV; CEP; EiPP; EnLi-2 (1949 ed.); EnLit; EPP; EV-3; GTBS; GTBS-D; GTBS-W; GTSE; GTSL; HBV; LEAP; LPS-2; OAEP; OBEC; PoFr; TCEP; TreF; WBLP
(Ode, An: "When Britain first, at heaven's command.") CaAE
Alfred de Musset. *Unknown.* RIS
Alfred, Lord Tennyson. Reed Whittemore. SiTL
Alfred Tennyson. Wilfrid Scawen Blunt. PtP; VLEP
Alfred the Harper. John Sterling. BeLS; LPS-2
Alfred was a ninny. Alfred, Lord Tennyson. Reed Whittemore. SiTL
Algebra of Divorce. L. F. Gerlach. PtPa
Algeciras Seen over a Stormy Sea. Ibn Malik of Granada, *tr. fr. Arabic by* A. J. Arberry. MooP
Algy Met a Bear. *Unknown.* FaPON
(Algy.) MoShBr
Alhama. *Unknown, tr. fr. Spanish by* Byron. LH
(Ay de mi Alhama.) AnSpL-1
(Moorish King Who Lost Alhama, The.) LyMA
(Very Mournful Ballad on the Siege and Conquest of Alhama, A.) TeCS
Alhambra, The. Francisco Martínez de la Rosa, *tr. fr. Spanish by* Longfellow. AnSpL-2
Alibi. Hughes Mearns. *Fr.* Later Antigonishes. InMe
Alice. Herbert Bashford. HBV
Alice. Charles Cotton. *Fr.* Resolution in Four Sonnets . . . Concerning Four Rural Sisters. TrGrPo
("Alice is tall and upright as a pine.") EG
(Concerning Four Rural Sisters.) PeBoSo
(Resolution in Four Sonnets . . .) PoEL-3
(Two Rural Sisters.) EnLoPo
Alice B., *with music.* *Unknown.* AS
Alice Brand. Sir Walter Scott. *Fr.* The Lady of the Lake, IV. BeLS; EmBrPo; HBV; HBVY; OTPC (1946 ed.); TVSH
(Ballad: Alice Brand.) EV-4
Alice Clay and Sally Mitchell. Marion Strobel. DDA
Alice, dear, what ails you. A Frosty Night. Robert Graves. CH; MBP; MoAB; MoBrPo
Alice Fell. Wordsworth. BEL; BeLS; CG; OTPC
Alice grown lazy, mammoth but not fat. Last Days of Alice. Allen Tate. AmP; AtBAP; MOAP; OxBA; UnPo
Alice in Cambridge. R. C. Evarts. CAG
Alice is tall and upright as a pine. Alice [*or* Two Rural Sisters]. Charles Cotton. *Fr.* Resolution in Four Sonnets . . . Concerning Four Rural Sisters. EG; EnLoPo; PeBoSo; PoEL-3; TrGrPo
Alice of Monmouth, *sel.* Edmund Clarence Stedman.
Cavalry Song. LPS-2; PEOR
Alice Ray. Sarah Josepha Hale. AA
Alice Where Art Thou. W. Guernsey. OlF
Alice's Adventures in Wonderland, *sels.* "Lewis Carroll."

Alice's Adventures in Wonderland (*continued*)
Evidence Read at the Trial of the Knave of Hearts, *fr. ch.* 12. FaFP; LiTG; OxBoLi; SiTL
(Important Evidence.) ViP
Father William, *fr. ch.* 5. BLV; BOHV; FaPON; FiBHP; GoTP; HBV; HoPM; InMe; LBN; LiL; LiTB; LiTG; MBP; MW; OnPP; OTPC (1946 ed.); PA; PC; PCD; PECK; PIR; PoRA; PoVP; PYM; RIS; SiTL; StaSt; TOP; TreF; TrGrPo; TSW; TSWC; WaKn
(You Are Old, Father William.) ALV; BoChLi; BTP; KN; PoeMoYo; ShBV-2; TiPo; WhC
How Doth the Little Crocodile, *fr. ch.* 2. BoChLi; FaBoCh; FaFP; FaPON; LiL; LoGBV; MoShBr; MPB; OTPC (1946 ed.); PreP; PYM; TiPo; TreFS; WaKn; WhC; YT
(Crocodile, The.) EnLi-2 (1949 ed.); GFA; GoTP; HoPM; MBP; PA; PoFS; TrGrPo
Lobster Quadrille, The [*or* A], *fr. ch.* 10. BoChLi; BoTP; FaPON; MoShBr; OTPC (1946 ed.); PA; PCD; PCH; PRWS; RAR; RIS; SAS; StVeCh; UTS
(Mock Turtle's Song, The.) ChTr; MPB (1956 ed.); PoVP
(Quadrille, A.) EnLi-2
(Whiting and the Snail, The.) HBV; HBVY
(" 'Will you walk a little faster?' said a whiting to a snail.") TiPo (1952 ed.)
Long and a Sad Tale, A, *fr. ch.* 3. ViP
Of Alice in Wonderland, *introd.* VA
Speak Roughly to Your Little Boy, *fr. ch.* 6. FaBoCh
Turtle Soup, *fr. ch.* 10. BrR; InMe; PA
Twinkle, Twinkle, Little Bat! *fr. ch.* 7. WhC
(Bat, The.) PA
Voice of the Lobster, The, *fr. ch.* 10. SAS; SiTL
(Lobster, The.) BoN
Alice's Supper. Laura E. Richards. MPB
Alicia's Bonnet. Elisabeth Cavazza Pullen. AA
Alien. Helen Frazee-Bower. HBMV
Alien. Ann Louise Hayes. PtPa
Alien. Archibald MacLeish. EtS
Alien, The. Charles Murray. MM
Alien. Mary Brent Whiteside. SaFP
Alien to the Earth. Lilith Lorraine. UnW
Alienation. Harry Kemp. BAP; HBMV
Alienation of an Old Friend. *Unknown, tr. fr. Chinese by* William Jennings. BoFr
Aliens. Phebe Ann Clarke. MuM
Alike, beneath thine eye. A Bryant Alphabet. *Comp. by* Caroline B. Le Row. PEOR
Alike in green or snowy pride. Stockholm in White. Daniel Fallström. AnSL
Aliscamp, The. Frédéric Mistral, *tr. fr. Provençal by* Harriet Waters Preston. CAW
Alison. *Unknown. See* Alisoun.
Alison and Willie. *Unknown.* BaBo; ESPB
Alison Gross. *Unknown.* FaBoCh; OBB
(Allison Gross.) BaBo; CH; ESPB
Alisoun. Chaucer. *Fr.* The Canterbury Tales: The Miller's Tale. CoEV
Alisoun. *Unknown.* AtBAP; BLV, *Middle English and mod. vers.*; MeEV, *mod. by* Mabel Van Duzee; PoEL-1
(Alison.) CBOV; EV-1; OBEV
(Alysoun.) BEL; CoBE; EnL; EnLi-1; EnLit; EPP; GoBC; LiA; TyEnPo
(Bytuene Mershe and Averil.) AtBAP; EnL; EnLit; ViBoPo
Aliud. Thomas Freeman. TuPP
Alive for Evermore. Amos Niven Wilder. MaRV
Alive in space against his will. The Noise of Leaves. George Dillon. NLK (1947 ed.)
Alive where I lie and hide. The Veteran. Louis O. Coxe. MoVE
All. Antoni Slonimski, *tr. fr. Polish.* PoFr, *tr. by* Marion Moore Coleman; TrJP, *tr. by* Wanda Dynowska
All. Cyril G. Taylor. ReTS
All, The. *Unknown, tr. fr. Sanskrit by* Joseph Nadin Rawson. *Fr.* The Upanishads. OnPM
All a green willow, willow, willow. A Green Willow Is My Garland. John Heywood. CoBE; EIL
"All aboard! All aboard!" is the cry. Shearing. David McKee Wright. AnNZ
All Aboard for Bombay. Leroy F. Jackson. BrR
All Adam's race are members of one frame. Adam's Race. Sadi. LiTW
All after pleasures as I rid [*or* rode] one day. Christmas. George Herbert. AnEC; CBE; EV-2; OxBoCh; SeCV-1; TriL
All afternoon the passion of heaven spent. The Divine Fantasy. John Hall Wheelock. LEAP
All, All. Baudelaire, *tr. fr. French by* George Dillon. WoL
All, All a-Lonely. *Unknown.* ChTr; OxBoLi
("Three little children sitting on the sand.") ExPo
All, all for immortality. Walt Whitman. *Fr.* Song of the Universal. MaRV
All, All of a Piece Throughout. Dryden. *Fr.* The Secular Masque. ChTr; GTBS-W
(Chorus: "All, all of a piece throughout.") BeR; OnPM; ViBoPo
All, all that was once mine is mine for ever. Afanasi Fet, *tr. fr. Russian by* Oliver Elton. BoR
All, all was cheerless to the horizon's bound. Wordsworth. *Fr.* Guilt and Sorrow. EnSW
All alone—alone,/ Calm, as on a kingly throne. Solitude. Edward Rowland Sill. AnNE
All alone as I strayed by the banks of the river. The Lost Jimmie Whalen. *Unknown.* ABF
All alone on the hillside. The "Grey Horse Troop." Robert W. Chambers. HBV; PAH
All alone this fellow found. Menander. *Fr.* Arbitrants. GrPo
All Alone Tree, The. F. O'Neil Gallagher. PCH
All along the backwater. Duck's [*or* Ducks'] Ditty. Kenneth Grahame. *Fr.* The Wind in the Willows. BoTP; FaPON; MoShBr; MPB; OTPC (1946 ed.); PCH; PoRh; RAR; SUS; TiPo; UTS; WaKn; WhBS
All along the Brazos River. Texas. Henry van Dyke. GDAH
All along the valley, stream that flashest white. In the Valley of Cauteretz. Tennyson. BPN; EmBrPo; EPN; OBVV; PoVP; TCEP; TOP; UnW; ViPo; VLEP
All are architects of Fate. The Builders. Longfellow. BTP; FaFP; IAP; MaRV; OHFP; PTA-1; TCAP; TreFS
All are asleep, heart so true. *Unknown. Fr.* Two Songs. LyMA
All are but parts of one stupendous whole. Pope. *Fr.* An Essay on Man, Epistle I. WGRP
All are keen. Aideen. *Unknown.* KiLC
All are not moralists, like Southey, when. The Lake Poets. Byron. *Fr.* Don Juan, III. UnPo (1st ed.)
All are not taken; there are left behind. Consolation. Elizabeth Barrett Browning. OBEV (1st ed.); PoVP; VLEP
All are sleeping, my sad heart. *Unknown, tr. fr. Spanish by* Eleanor L. Turnbull. TeCS
All around him Patmos lies. Patmos. Edith M. Thomas. HBV
All around the cobbler's bench. Pop! Goes the Weasel. *Unknown.* OlF
All around the house is the jet black night. *See* All round the house is the jet-black night.
All around the kitchen, cocky doodle doodle doo. Cocky Doodle Doodle Doo. *Unknown.* OuSiCo
All around the mulberry bush. Mother Goose. OTPC (1946 ed.)
All Around the Town, *sels.* Phyllis McGinley.
"B's the Bus." FaPON; TiPO
(B.) LiL
"C is for the Circus." TiPo
"E is the Escalator." TiPo
(E.) LiL
"F is the fighting firetruck." FaPON
"J's the jumping Jay-walker." FaPON; TiPo (1952 ed.)
"P's the proud Policeman." TiPo
"R is for the Restaurant." TiPo (1959 ed.)
"U is for Umbrellas." TiPo
"W's for Windows." TiPo
All as a Sea, the World No Other Is. *Unknown.* ReIE
"All Ashore!" Leonidas of Tarentum, *tr. fr. Greek by* Walter Leaf. GrR
All at Sea. Frederick Moxon. BOHV
All Awry. Justin Richardson. SiTL
All Beauteous Things. Robert Bridges. *See* I Love All Beauteous Things.
All Beautiful the March of Days. Frances Whitmarsh Wile. MaRV
All beautiful things bring sadness, nor alone. Sonnet. Richard Chenevix Trench. VA
All Bells in Paradise. *Unknown. See* Over Yonder's a Park.
All beneath the white-rose tree. The Three Captains. *Unknown.* AWP
All bones but yours will rattle when I say. The Sea-Serpent. James Robinson Planché. NA
All buildings are but monuments of death. Epigram: Fatum Supremum [*or* Fatum Supremum]. *Unknown.* OBS; SeCL
All Busy. *Unknown.* CBPC
(Busy Day, A.) PCH
(Cock's on the Housetop, The.) OTPC (1946 ed.)
(Summer.) RIS
All but Blind. Walter de la Mare. BMEP; FaPON; HBMV; MBP; MoAB; MoBrPo; ShBV-2; UnPo (1st ed.); WaKn
All but unutterable Name! The Divine Presence. Aubrey Thomas De Vere. *Fr.* May Carols. BMEP; GoBC; MaRV
All by the sides of the wild wide river. Cradle Song. Alice Cary. BOL
All children sound the same. The Core. John Holmes. MiAP
All Christians and lay-elders too. The Four-legg'd Elder; or, A Horrible Relation of a Dog and an Elder's Maid. Sir John Birkenhead. CoMu
All Clowns Are Masked. Delmore Schwartz. The Repetitive Heart, III. LiTA; OxBA; ViBoPo

All colors fade away. Beyond. Father Dies. Abraham Sutskever. OnCuPl
All crying, "We will go with you, O Wind!" Misgiving. Robert Frost. TBM
All day/ The bird sits in his cage. Issa, *tr. fr. Japanese by* Lois J. Erickson. SoLD
All day a pilgrim had I gone. At Lexington. Benjamin Sledd. BIG
All day a steady snow had drifted down. The Slide at the Empire Mine. Harriet L. Wason. PoOW
All day across the sagebrush flat. The Sheep-Herder. Badger Clark. IHA; SCC
All day, all night, we hear, we feel. Standard Forgings Plant. William Stephens. NAMP
All day and all day, as I sit at my measureless turning. The Mother's Song. Virginia Woodward Cloud. AA
All day and every day the sea shone, steeped in its blueness. When I Was Young. Alun Llywelyn-Williams. PrWP
All day and many days I rode. A Wish. Hamlin Garland. AA
All day and night, save winter, every weather. Aspens. Edward Thomas. ChMP
All day beneath the bleak, indifferent skies. Prometheus. W. W. Gibson. EPN
All day cars mooed and shrieked. Klaxon. James Reaney. TwCaPo
All day from that deep well of life within. Alone into the Mountain. Katharine Lee Bates. ChIP; MaRV; StJW
All day has the battle raged. King Olaf's Death-Drink. Longfellow. *Fr.* The Saga of King Olaf. AmPP (4th ed.)
All day he drowses by the sail. The Golden Journey. William Vaughn Moody. MOAP
All day he stood at Weeping Cross. Karl. Charles Spear. AnNZ
All day he toils, with zeal severe. The Scholar's Sweetheart. Edgar Fawcett. PR
All day I bar you from my slightest thought. Compensation. Lizette Woodworth Reese. HBMV
All day I did the little things. The Blue Bowl. Blanche Bane Kuder. BLPA; FaBoBe; NeHB
All day I follow. The Plowman [*or* The Ploughman]. Raymond Knister. BoCaPo; PeCV; TwCaPo
All day I have been completely alone, and now the night. Separation. D. S. Savage. NeBP
All day I have been waiting for your smile. Spendthrift. Vega Curl. CAG
All Day I Hear [the Noise of Waters]. James Joyce. Chamber Music, XXXV. FaBoCh; LoGBV; MBP; MoBrPo; NP; OnYI; PIAE; PoRA; TIP
(Noise of Waters, The.) FaPON; TiPo (1959 ed.); TSW
All day I hear them tapping in the street. Footsteps. Otto Freund. MuM
All day I heard your high heart-broken laughter. The Swallow. Pamphilus. OxBG
All day I tell my rosary. Love's Rosary. Alfred Noyes. HBV
All day I watch the stretch of burning sand. Le Repos en Egypte; the Sphinx. Agnes Repplier. CAW; ISi; JKCP; StJW
All day in exquisite air. Larks. Katharine Tynan. GTIV; OnYI; TIP
All day in Mother's garden here. Bedtime. Helen Coale Crew. GFA
All day it had been raining; now, the leaves. Hunt. Melvin Walker La Follette. NePoEA
All Day It Has Rained. Alun Lewis. PoN
All day, knowing you dead. The Hours. John Peale Bishop. MoVE; OxBA
All day long/ The sun shines bright. The Night Sky. *Unknown.* BoTP
All day long/ The gray rain beating. Rain. "Seumas O'Sullivan." OnYI
All day long and every day. The Chapel in Lyoness. William Morris. BPN; EmBrPo; PoVP; ViPo; VLEP
All day long I have been working. Madonna of the Evening Flowers. Amy Lowell. BAV; ChMo; CMP; MAP; MM; MoAmPo; NeMA; OBAV; PoeMoYo; SBMV; TOP
All day long I lean on the pavilion balustrade. Prune Flowers. Lu Yu. WhP
All day long I played in an orchard. And of Laughter That Was a Changeling. Elizabeth Rendall. HBMV
All day long in the city's canyon street. Who Follow the Flag. Henry van Dyke. FOAH
All day long in the scorching weather. London River. Frederic Edward Weatherly. TVSH
All day long in the spindrift swinging. To a Petrel. Cale Young Rice. BLA
All day long o'er the ocean I fly. The Sea Gull. *Unknown.* GFA; RAR
All day long on the highway. The Highway. Louise Driscoll. HBV
All day long on the prairie I ride. The Cowboy. *Unknown.* CoSo (B *vers.*); CSF
All day long roved Hiawatha. The Famine. Longfellow. *Fr.* The Song of Hiawatha. BAV; IAP
All day long the guns at the forts. The Surrender of New Orleans. Marion Manville. PAH
All day long the storm of battle through the startled valley swept. The Drummer-Boy's Burial. *Unknown.* LPS-2
All day long the traffic goes. In Lady Street. John Drinkwater. WP
All day long till the west was red. Making Port. J. T. McKay. EtS
All day low clouds and slanting rain. The Old Clock. John Charles McNeill. NoCaPo
All day my sheep have mingled with yours. Shepherdess. Norman Cameron. Three Love Poems, III. FaBoTw
All day my songs. Song of the Long River. Constance Lindsay Skinner. AV; CPG; TBM
All day my wife, the maid[s], the men. After Christmas a Landlord Remembers [*or* Reminiscences of a Landlord]. Elizabeth J. Coatsworth. ChrBoLe; StJW
All day on the prairie in the saddle I ride. The Cowboy. *Unknown.* CoSo (A *vers.*); CSF
All day she hurried to get through. Mis' Smith. Albert Bigelow Paine. BOHV
All day she lay in deep oblivious dream. Feodor Ivanovich Tyutchev, *tr. fr. Russian by* Sir Cecil Kisch. WaL
All day she sits behind a bright brass rail. The Travel Bureau. Ruth Comfort Mitchell. HBMV; PoeMoYo; VOD
All day, so long as arms had power. The Labourer. Aleksey Khomyakov. BoR
All day that metronome, thrice gallant heart. Dirge for Two Clavichords and Bowler Hat. Kendrick Smithyman. AnNZ
All day the coast of Africa was seen. To Naples. H. B. Mallalieu. WaP
All day the great guns barked and roared. Molly Pitcher. Laura E. Richards. GA; MC; PAH; YaD
All day the low-hung clouds have dropped. An April Day. Caroline Anne Bowles. PEOR; TVSH
All day the stormy wind has blown. Take Heart. Edna Dean Proctor. BLP; HBV; LBAP
All day the unnatural barking of dogs. The Dog. Valentin Iremonger. NeIP
All day the waves assailed the rock. Waves. Emerson. AA
All day Theseus marched, and all th' ensuing night. The Knight's Tale. Chaucer. *Fr.* The Canterbury Tales. BEL; GEPC; TOP
All day they loitered by the resting ships. The *Wanderer.* John Masefield. MCCG; TCEP
All day this spring—the first he's known. The Rabbit. Camilla Doyle. MBP; PIAE; StaSt
All day to watch the blue wave curl and break. On Lynn Terrace. Thomas Bailey Aldrich. IAP
All day we had ridden through scarred, tawny hills. Spain, 1809. F. L. Lucas. HaMV
All day we have sat and watched the shadows' feet. Cerne Abbas. Hal Summers. HaMV
All day with anxious heart and wondering ear. Voices. Louis Untermeyer. PC
All Devils Fading. Martin Seymour Smith. PoN
All do not love in clotting fields to sweat. Edges of the Sea. William Diaper. *Fr.* Nereides. BeR
All down the years the fragrance came. The Cedars. Josephine Preston Peabody. NV
All down the years thy tale has rolled. To Homer. John Malcolm Bulloch. ATP (1935 ed.)
All dripping in tangles green. The Tuft of Kelp. Herman Melville. ChTr; RO
All during a night/ Of anxiety I wait. The Monk Shun-e, *tr. fr. Japanese by* Kenneth Rexroth. OnPJ
All Earthly Beauty Hath One Cause [and Proof]. Robert Bridges The Growth of Love, XXXV. ChMo; CMP; PoVP; ViP
All earthly loves to me are of the earth. Ideal Passion, VIII. George Edward Woodberry. MOAP
All else for use, One only for desire. Deo Optimo Maximo. Louise Imogen Guiney. TrPWD
All else I love. but this abhor. Her Only Flaw. Rufinus. OxBG
All else shall die; voices alone live on. Voices. Homer C. House. MuM
All-embracing, The. Frederick William Faber. *See* There's a Wideness in God's Mercy.
All endeavor to be beautiful. Primer of Plato. Jean Garrigue. MoVE
All evening, while the summer trees were crying. Evening in Summer [*or* While the Summer Trees Were Crying *or* Time, the Faithless]. Valentin Iremonger. AnIV; NeIP; OxBI
All eyes were on Enceladus's face. Hyperion's Arrival [*or* Entrance of Hyperion *or* Hyperion and Saturn]. Keats. *Fr.* Hyperion. BrBE; OBRV; ReTS; SeCePo
All Fellows, *sel.* Laurence Housman.
"Dear love, when with a two-fold mind." WGRP

All Flesh. Francis Thompson. PoeT
All Flesh Is Grass. Isaiah, XL: 6–8, Bible, *O.T.* TrJP
All flesh is grass and so are feathers too. Epitaph on Lady Ossory's Bullfinch. Horace Walpole. ChTr
"All folks hev some soft spot." Pa's Soft Spot. D. A. Ellsworth. FAOV
All folks who pretend to religion and grace. The Place of the Damn'd. Swift. BeR
All Fools' Day. *Unknown.* PoRL; SiSoSe
(April Fool's Day.) PCH
("First of April, some do say, The.") BoTP
All for Love. Byron. *See* Stanzas Written on the Road between Florence and Pisa.
All for Love, *sels.* Dryden.
Cleopatra, *fr.* III. BeR
Cleopatra and Antony, *fr.* II. FiP
"How I loved/ Witness, ye days and nights," *fr.* II. LO
("Witness, ye days and nights, and all ye hours.") LoPS
"Portents and prodigies are grown so frequent," *fr.* I. AtBAP
(Wild Weather.) BoW
"She comes. She's here," *fr.* III. MyFE
All French folk, whereso'er ye be. If I Were King. Justin Huntly M'Carthy, *par. fr. the French of* Villon. *Fr.* If I Were King. HBV
All furnish'd, all in arms. Armed [*or* The King's Army]. Shakespeare. King Henry IV, Pt. I, *fr.* IV, i. BHV; LiA
All gather from the village here. Where Is Dominga? Francisco de Sá de Miranda. OnPM
All gentlemen and yeomen good. Robin Hood and the Shepherd. *Unknown.* ESPB
All glorious as the Rainbow's birth. Young Love. Gerald Massey. OBVV
All glory cannot vanish from the hills. The Passing of the Forest. William Pember Reeves. AnNZ
All glory, laud and honor. Theodulph of Orleans, *tr. fr. Latin by* John Mason Neale. OlF
All Goats. Elizabeth J. Coatsworth. PoMa; TCPD
All God's Chillun Got Wings. *Unknown.* BoAN-1, *with music;* OlF; TreFS
(Goin' to Walk All ovah God's Heb'n.) HiLiAm
(I Got a Robe.) SiTL
All gods were deathless once. All mortals knew. Chant Royal of Love. Michael Lewis. PIAE
All Gold. *Unknown, tr. fr. Irish by* Frank O'Connor. KiLC
All Gone. C. Day Lewis. FaBoMo
All good things have not kept aloof. To ——. Tennyson. OBRV
All Grasses Are Yellow. *Unknown, tr. fr. Chinese.* WhP
All Greece hates/ the still eyes in the white face. Helen. Hilda Doolittle ("H. D."). BAV; CBOV; FaBoTw; MAP; MoAmPo; MoVE; PreP
All Greece is headstone to Euripides. Euripides [*or* Epitaph on Euripides]. *At. to* Thucydides. GrR; OxBG
"All green things on the earth, bless ye the Lord!" Benedicite. Anna Callender Brackett. AA
All grim and soiled and brown with tan. The Reformer. Whittier. CoV; LPS-2
All hail! Holy Mary, our hope and our joy! The Irish Reaper's Harvest Hymn. John Keegan. TIP
All hail, inexorable lord! To Ruin. Burns. CoBE
All Hail, the Pageant of the Years. John Haynes Holmes. MaRV
All hail the power of Jesus' name! Coronation. Edward Perronet. HBV; MaRV; OlF; TreFS; WGRP
All hail, thou glorious morn. Washington's Birthday. Charles S. Davis. HH
All Hail, Thou Noble Guest. Martin Luther, *tr. fr. German by* Arthur Tozer Russell *and* Catherine Winkworth. TrPWD
All hail! thou noble land. America to Great Britain. Washington Allston. AA; HBV; LEAP; LPS-2; PaA
All hail to Pennsylvania. Pennsylvania. Helen Hall Bucher. PoRL
All hail to the day when the Britons came over. The Flag of Old England. Joseph Howe. BoCaPo
All Hail to the Days That Merit More Praise, *with music.* Thomas D'Urfey, *and others.* YaCaBo
All hail to the ruins, the rocks and the shores! The Ocean. James Montgomery. LPS-2
All hail to the State that we honor. The State We Honor. Fanny J. Crosby. PoRL
All hail! Unfurl the Stripes and Stars! God Save Our President. Francis de Haes Janvier. PaA; PAH
All hail, ye tender martyr-flowers. The Holy Innocents. Prudentius. CAW
All Hallow Eve. Carolyn Wells. DD
All hands at work, my boys and maids. Flaming Torches. Horace, *tr. by* Thomas Creech. *Fr.* Odes, IV, 11. BeR
All Hands Unmoor! William Falconer. *Fr.* The Shipwreck. EtS
All harmony, all marvel, she. The Beauty. Pushkin. BoR
All Hearts Are Not Disloyal. Henry T. Tuckerman. APW
All Heaven Is Blazing Yet. Christina Rossetti. ViP
All heavy minds. Sir Thomas Wyatt. EG; SiPS
All her devils here tonight. All Devils Fading. Martin Seymour Smith. PoN
All her melancholy frowns. Tippler's Philosophy. *Unknown, tr. by* Thomas Girdlestone. GrR
All Here. Oliver Wendell Holmes. IAP
All his life long did he love. Point of Flame. Jules Supervielle. TrFP
All hollow vaults and dungeons sealed from sight. Sacred Night. Michelangelo. OnPM
All holy influences dwell within. The "Children's Crusade" [*or* The Children Band]. Sir Aubrey De Vere. ES; OBEV
All honest folk throughout the land. *Unknown. Fr.* La Carmagnole. PoFr
"All honor to him who shall win the prize [*or* fight]." For Those Who Fail. Joaquin Miller. BTP; CBPC; MaRV; OQP; PC; PoToHe; QP-2; TSW; TSWC
All honor to that day which long ago. Washington's Birthday. Arthur J. Burdick. OHIP
All honor to woman, the sweetheart, the wife. Woman. Fitz-Greene Halleck. PR
All houses wherein men have lived and died. Haunted Houses. Longfellow. AnNE; UnW
All how silent and how still. Noon. John Clare. ERP; EV-4; OBRV; SeCePo
All human progress up to God. The Martyr's Hymn. Francis H. Rose. MaRV
All human race wou'd fain be wits. Swift. *Fr.* On Poetry; a Rhapsody. BeR; PoEL-3
All human things are subject to decay. Life's Brevity. Simonides. OnPM
All human [*or* humane] things are subject to decay. MacFlecknoe. Dryden. AnFE; AtBAP; ATP (1953 ed.); BEL; CEP; CoBE; CoEV; EiPP; EnLi-1; EnLit; EV-3; ExPo; FiP; GEPC; MaPo; NBE; OAEP; OBS; OxBoLi; Po; PoE; PoFS; PtP; ReaPo; SeCV-2; SeEP; SiTL; TCEF; TrGrPo; TwHP; ViBoPo
All Hushed and Still within the House. Emily Brontë. FaBoCh
All hushed the trees are waiting. Tree Shadows. *Unknown.* GFA
All I can give you is broken-face gargoyles. Broken-Face Gargoyles. Carl Sandburg. MAP; MoAmPo; OxBA
All I can offer now is a cracked china jug. Winter Offering. D. S. Savage. LiTB; LiTM; NeBP
All I can say is—I saw it! Natural Magic. Robert Browning. BPN; PoVP; VLEP
All I could see from where I stood. Renascence. Edna St. Vincent Millay. AmPP; BAV; ChMo; CMP; FaFP; HBV; LBMV; MAP; MoAB; MoAmPo; NeMA; NePA; NV; OHFP; PFY; TCPD; TwAmPo
All I Do, de Church Keep a-Grumblin', *with music. Unknown.* BoAN-2
"All I do is dole out minutes." Gallop, Gallop to a Rhyme. Monica Shannon. SiSoSe
All I have got of wealth and wisdom, I. Confession. Kenneth Mackenzie. BoAV
All I need to make me happy. *Unknown.* GoTP
All I want in this creation. Black-eyed Susie. *Unknown.* ABF
All Ignorance Toboggans into Know. E. E. Cummings. AmPP; OxBA; WaP
All Impelled Onward Alike. Robert Blair. *Fr.* The Grave. EV-3
All impulses of soul and sense. Samuel Taylor Coleridge. *Fr.* Love. LO
All in a Garden Green. W. E. Henley. OBMV
All in a garden green. *Unknown.* LO
All in All. Edith Nesbit. PoFr
All in All. John Banister Tabb. OQP; QP-2
All in All. Tennyson. *See* In Love, If Love Be Love.
All in Green Went My Love Riding. E. E. Cummings. ChMo; CoBA; InPo; LiTA; LiTM; MOAP; NePA; OxBA; PoRA; ThWaDe
(Song: "All in green went my love riding.") TCPD; ViBoPo
All in our marriage garden. Our Wee White Rose. Gerald Massey. *Fr.* The Mother's Idol Broken. HBV; LPS-1
All in Red. Eileen Mathias. BoTP
All in the April evening [morning, *wr.*]. Sheep and Lambs. Katharine Tynan. AnIV; BoTP; GTIV; HBV; JKCP; MBP; OBEV; OBVV; OnYI; OTPC (1946 ed.); OxBI; PoRL; PRWS; StJW; VA; WHL
All in the Downs. Tom Hood. ALV; CenHV
All in the Downs the fleet was moored [*or* moor'd]. Black-eyed Susan [*or* Sweet William's Farewell to Black-eyed Susan]. John Gay. BeLS; CEP; CoEV; EiPP; EPP; EtS; EV-3; GTBS; GTBS-D; GTBS-W; GTSE; GTSL; HBV; LPS-1; OBEC; TreFS
All in the golden weather, forth let us ride today. The King's Highway. John Steven McGroarty. DDA; HBV; MW; NLK; POT; PoTo

All in the gorgeous dawn of day. Black Bill's Honey-Moon. Alfred Noyes. *Fr.* Tales of the Mermaid Tavern, III. PCN
All in the groves of dragon-fungus. The Chickamungus. James Reeves. GoTP
All in the leafy darkness, when sleep had passed. Care. Virginia Woodward Cloud. AA; HBV; LBAP
All in the lilac-rain. In the Lilac-Rain. Edith M. Thomas. HBV
All in the merry month of May. Barbara Allen [*or* Barbara Allen's Cruelty]. *Unknown.* BLV; FaBoBe; MaC
All in the morning early. The Blue Boy in London. William Brighty Rands. OTPC
All in the morning, long ere day. Queen Bengerd. *Unknown.* BoDaBa
All in the pleasant afternoon. The Lost Playmate. Abbie Farwell Brown. HBVY
All in the pleasant evening, together comers we. *See* All in this pleasant evening . . .
All in the town were still asleep. The Little Dog's Day. Rupert Brooke. ShBV-1
All in their lofty bower so still. Medelwold and Sidselille. *Unknown.* BaBo
All in this pleasant evening, together come are we. Old May Song. *Unknown.* AtBAP; BoTP; CH; HH
All-intellectual eye, our solar round. James Thomson. *Fr.* To the Memory of Sir Isaac Newton. ImOP
All Is Best. Milton. *Fr.* Samson Agonistes. SeCePo
("All is best, though we oft doubt.") MyFE; OBEV; OBS
(Choruses from "Samson Agonistes.") SeCeV
(Epilogue.) FaBoEn
(Final Chorus.) ExPo
(Last Chorus.) ShBV-4
All is changing now—it seems as though all must be parted. Goethe. *Fr.* Hermann and Dorothea. PoFr
All is divine/ which the Highest has made. The Queen of Seasons. Cardinal Newman. GoBC
All is dust, and a mocking dream. Futility. Glycon, *tr. by* J. A. Pott. OxBG
All is dust, and all is laughter. Glycon, *tr. fr. Greek by* the Earl of Cromer. GrPo
All is dying; hearts are breaking. Unchanging Jesus. Karl Johann Philipp Spitta. BLRP
All is erased; leaving this slendering pine. The Pine. Gertrude MacGregor Moffat. CPG
All is far/ And long gone by. Lament. Rainer Maria Rilke. AnGP
All Is Hidden, Naught Concealed. Grace Margaret Robertson. MuM
All is of God! If He but wave his hand. The Two Angels. Longfellow. PTA-2
All is over! fleet career. The Last Leap. Adam Lindsay Gordon. BoAu
All is phantom that we mid fare. Phantasy. *Unknown.* ACP
All is quiet and the desert moon. Guard. Michael C. Martin. WaP
All Is Sold ("All is sold, all is lost, all is plundered"). "Anna Akhmatova," *tr. fr. Russian by* Babette Deutsch. OnPM; TrRV
("All is sold, all betrayed, all is looted," *tr. by* C. M. Bowra.) BoR
(Now All Is Sold, *tr. by* Jack Lindsay.) RuPo
All is still/ Under the pines. Under the Pines. Arthur S. Bourinot. BoCaPo
All is still and restful now. Sleep, Baby Dear. *Unknown.* BOL
All is still in the sweetest rest. Slumber Song. *Unknown.* BOL
All is the same still. Earth and heaven locked in. Emily Brontë. C. Day Lewis. ChMP
All Is Vanity. *Unknown, at. to* Philip Rosseter. HBV
(Vanity of Vanities.) BLV
("Whether men do laugh or weep.") ElSeCe; OBSC
All Is Vanity. John Webster. *See* All the Flowers of the Spring.
All Is Vanity. Countess of Winchilsea. *See* Soldier's Death, The.
All Is Well. Arthur Hugh Clough. BEL; BPN; EmBrPo; EnLi-2; EPN; PoVP; TCEP; VLEP
(Whate'er You Dream with Doubt Possest.) OAEP
All joy is God's own gift. Both Are Blessing. Egi. SoLD
All joys upon him! for he is my friend. Beaumont *and* Fletcher. *Fr.* The Maid's Tragedy. BoFr
All June I bound the rose in sheaves. One Way of Love. Robert Browning. BPN; EmBrPo; GEPC; HBV; OtMeF; PoVP; TOP; VA; VLEP
All kings, and all their favourites [*or* favorites]. The Anniversary [*or* The Anniversarie]. John Donne. AEV; AnFE; BrBE; CoEV; ElSeCe; EnLP; EPS; ExPo; HoPM; LiTB; LiTG; MeLP; MePo; OAEP; OBS; ReaPo; ReIE; SeCeV; SeCV-1; SeEP; TuPP; UnPo (1st ed.)
All knights of the green cathedral, in armour. The Captains. Nikolai Gumilev. BoR
All landscapes are his land. A Wealthy Man. William Allingham. IrPN
All Last Night. Lascelles Abercrombie. FaBoTw; HBV
All leapt to chariot. The Chariot Race. Homer. *Fr.* The Iliad, XIII. EV-1
All lesser reasons for loving die away. Come to Birth. Abbie Huston Evans. NePoAm
All Life. Paul Eluard, *tr. fr. French by* Glauco Cambon. OnPM
All Life Moving to One Measure. W. W. Gibson. ChMo; CMP; PoeMoYo
(Daily Bread.) LEAP
All life, tumbled together in a storm. For Posterity. Kathleen Raine. NeBP
All look and likeness caught from earth. Phantom. Samuel Taylor Coleridge. DaM; LO; NBE; PoEL-4; TriL; UnW
All looks be pale, hearts cold as stone. A Lamentation [*or* Lament for Prince Henry]. Thomas Campion. CH; OHIP; TriL
All love at first, like generous wine. Love. Samuel Butler. SeCL
All loved and lovely women dear to rhyme. Immortals. David Morton. HBV
All Lovely Things. Conrad Aiken. *See* All Lovely Things Will Have an Ending.
All Lovely Things. Richard Aldington. NeMA
All lovely things: a bell across the snow. A Joy as Old as Breathing. Etta May Van Tassel. JKCP (1955 ed.)
All Lovely Things I Love. John Peale Bishop. CAG
All Lovely Things Will Have an Ending. Conrad Aiken. ChMo; CMP; ReaPo; TwCV
(All Lovely Things.) PoRA
All lovers are campaigners, and Cupid has his wars. Every Lover Is a Soldier. Ovid. *Fr.* Amores, I, 9. RoL
All-loving, The. Robert Browning. *Fr.* An Epistle Containing the Strange Medical Experience of Karshish, the Arab Physician. MaRV; OQP; QP-1
("So, the All-great were the All-loving too.") ChIP
All Mah Sins Been Taken Away. *Unknown.* *See* Mary Wore Three Links of Chain.
All meet here with us, finally. Ostriches & Grandmothers! LeRoi Jones. NeAP
All men are brothers and each people is my own. My Song to the Jewish People. Leib Olitski. TrJP
All Men Are Free! Elliott Napier. BoAu; InP
All men know it, the young when the enemy in them. The Fear of Dying. John Holmes. MiAP
All men speak ill of thee, unlucky Tree! Larch Trees. Frederick William Faber. EnSW
All mortal men, this day rejoice. Easter Day. Jasper Heywood. ReIE
All moveless stand the ancient cedar-trees. In the Dark. George Arnold. HBV
All moves within the visual frame. A Monument. Charles Madge. FaBoMo
All moving things to other things do move. The Immortality of the Soul. Sir John Davies. *Fr.* Nosce Teipsum. EV-2
All music, sauces, feasts, delights and pleasures. Measure. Thomas Traherne. *Fr.* Christian Ethics. BLV; UnS
All must be used. Barracks Apt. 14. Theodore Weiss. NePoAm-2
All my ambition will in you be crown'd. One Long Nuptial Day. Dryden. *Fr.* Secret Love. BeR
All my green years and golden prime of man. Petrarch. *Fr.* Sonnets to Laura: To Laura in Death. PrPoCR
All My Heart This Night Rejoices. Paul Gerhardt, *tr. fr. German by* Catherine Winkworth. MaRV
All my hurts. Musketaquid. Emerson. IAP; MOAP
All my life I never spent. Debauch. Ibn Rashiq. MooP
All my life I played, and all were fond of me. Agathe, Aged Five. *Unknown.* *Fr.* Carmina Epigraphica. LaP
All my life they have told me. More Letters Found near a Suicide. Frank Horne. BANP
All my love for my sweet. Song. John Hall Wheelock. NP
All My Luve, Leave Me Not. *Unknown.* GoTS; MeRV
All my past life is mine no more. Love and Life. Earl of Rochester. BLV; CaAE; CEP; EG; ElSeCe; EnLoPo; EPP; EPS; EV-3; FaBoEn; HBV; LiTL; LoBV; MePo; OBEV; OBS; PoEL-3; PreP; SeCL; SeCV-2; SeEP; TrGrPo; ViBoPo
All my pleasure is in catching of birds. The English Schoolboy. John Heywood. *Fr.* The Play of the Weather. ACP
All my senses, like beacon's flame. Caelica, LVI. Fulke Greville. InvP; PoEL-1
All my sheep/ Gather in a heap. Last Words before Winter. Louis Untermeyer. GoTP; MAP; MoAmPo; NeMA
All my stars forsake me. Song of the Night at Daybreak. Alice Meynell. CH; PoVP; VA
All my thoughts always speak to me of Love. Divided Thoughts. Dante. *Fr.* La Vita Nuova. AWP; OnPM
All my uncles put on beards of grey. Grey Uncles. Ephraim Auerbach. OnCuPl
All names I will not mention, as you may understand. Lumberjacks and Teamsters. *Unknown.* OuSiCo

All nature has a feeling: woods, fields, brooks. Eternity of Nature. John Clare. MeRV
All Nature Has a Voice to Tell. J. Gilchrist Lawson. BLRP
All nature is a temple where the alive. Correspondences. Baudelaire. AWP; LiTW
All Nature seems at work. Slugs leave their lair. Work without Hope. Samuel Taylor Coleridge. BEL; BoTP; 4 *ll.*; BPN; EM-2; EmBrPo; EnLi-2; EnRP; EPN; ERP; ES; EV-4; FiP; HBV; LEAP; LoBV; OBEV; OBRV; OQP; PeBoSo; PG; QP-2; RO; TCEP
All nature teem'd with harmony divine. The Birth of Rustem. Firdausi. *Fr.* Shah Namah. PeP
All Needs Met. J. H. Sammis. BLRP
All night a noise of leaping fish. The Fisher. Roderic Quinn. BoAV
All night a wind of music. Fragment. Thomas Lovell Beddoes. CaAE
All night around the Thorn Tree. The Fairy Tree. Temple Lane. StJW
All night between my dreams the thought of you. Flight. Helen Frazee-Bower. *Fr.* Two Married. HBMV
All night had shout of men and cry. Easter Night. Alice Meynell. ChIP; OHIP; StJW; WP
All night he sits and plays at solitaire. Expatriate. Mary Brown Onstott. PoMa
All night I could not sleep. A "Tzu-yeh" Song. *Unknown.* ChLP; OnPM; TrCh
All Night I Heard. Gertrude MacGregor Moffat. CaP; CPG; OCL
All night I muse, all day I cry. Sighs. *Unknown.* LO; SeCL
All night I raced the moon. Laurence Dakin. *Fr.* Tancred, II, i. CaP
All night I thought on those wise men who took. Twelfth Night. John Peale Bishop. UnPo (3d ed.)
All night I watched awake for morning. Dawn-Angels. Agnes Mary Frances Robinson. HBV; VA
All night I wearied utterly of the pillow of darkness. In a Wood Clearing. Wilson MacDonald. CaP; OCL
All night, in May, dogs barked in the hollow woods. Eidolon. Robert Penn Warren. FiMAP
All Night Long. Stephen Vincent Benét. LoPo; LoPS
All Night Long, *with music. Unknown.* AS
All night long. The Coming of Autumn. Ch'ien Lin. PoHN
All night long and every night. Young Night Thought. Robert Louis Stevenson. GaP; NeHB; RIS
All night long the pine-trees wait. Christmas Eve. Mary Mapes Dodge. SDH
All night long through the starlit air and the stillness. The Cattle of His Hand. Wilbur Underwood. AA; WGRP
All night rain fell. The Old Adam. William Rose Benét. MOAP; YaD
All night the crickets chirp. Crickets at Dawn. Leonora Speyer. PFY
All Night the Lone Cicada. Sir Charles G. D. Roberts. CPG; PC
All night the maid reposes in the cave. Ariosto. *Fr.* Orlando Furioso, III. PrPoCR
All night the sinister moth has lain. Unholy Garden. Leila Jones. PIAE
All night the small feet of the rain. April. Dora Sigerson Shorter. HBMV; HBVY
All night the water has worked without pause. The Cocks. Boris Pasternak. LiTW
All night there had sought in vain. The Reminder. Léonie Adams. MoVE
All night they fought north of Hsiangkiang. Song at the Frontier. Hsu Hun. WhP
All night they marched, the infantrymen under pack. 1935. Stephen Vincent Benét. MAP; MoAmPo; NeMA
All night they toiled, those men of Galilee. Launch Out into the Deep. Ida Norton Munson. ChIP
All night they whine upon their ropes and boom. Nocturne of the Wharves. Arna Bontemps. BANP
All night under the moon. For G. W. W. Gibson. LO; LoPS
All night upon the guarded hill. The Defence of Lawrence. Richard Realf. MC; PAH
All night, without the gates of slumber lying. On a Steamship. Upton Sinclair. MaRV
All now is o'er, the torches out. Oh, Thou, My Lover. Victor Hugo. *Fr.* Hernani. LiA
All of a sudden bicycles are toys. A Certain Age. Phyllis McGinley. NePoAm-2
All of a sudden the big nasturtiums. The Big Nasturtiums. Robert Beverly Hale. PoMS; SiTL
All of heaven in my hands. A Star Map. Sara Teasdale. TCAP
All of Her. Samuel L. Albert. NePoAm-2
All of Roses. D. H. Lawrence. *See* River Roses.
All of the flowers are going to bed. Flower Lullaby. Addie Litchfield. BOL
All of them the wind took, all of them the light lured. Alone. Hayyim Nahman Bialik. TrJP
All of thine that cannot die, The. Grief. Byron. *Fr.* And Thou Art Dead as Young and Fair. LiA
All of us—/ stones, people, glass slivers in the sun. Text. Aaron Zeitlin. OnCuPl
All of Us Always Turning Away for Solace. Delmore Schwartz. The Repetitive Heart, I. OxBA
All Offices of Heav'n so well she knows. Dryden. *Fr.* Eleonora. NBE
All One in Christ. John Oxenham. *See* Brothers of the Faith.
All or Nothing. Theognis, *tr. fr. Greek by* J. M. Edmonds. GrR
All other joys of life he strove to warm. Modern Love, IV. George Meredith. EmBrPo; GTBS-D; OAEP; VA; ViPo
All otherwise to me my thoughts portend. A Hero in Despair. Milton. *Fr.* Samson Agonistes. BHV
All Our Griefs to Tell. John Newton. BePJ
All Our Joy Is Enough. Geoffrey Scott. OBMV; TwCV
All our stones like as much sun as possible. Forecast. Josephine Miles. CrMA
All out of doors looked darkly in at him. An Old Man's Winter Night. Robert Frost. AmPP; AnAmPo; AnEnPo; AnNE; AWP; BLV; BoLiVe; CoBA; HBMV; JAWP; LA; MAP; MoAB; MoAmPo; MOAP; MoVE; NP; NV; OnPP; OxBA; PoMa; WBP
All over America last Sunday afternoon goes your Symphony No. 7. Take a Letter to Dmitri Shostakovitch. Carl Sandburg. NeTW
All over America railroads ride through roses. Landscape as Metal and Flowers. Winfield Townley Scott. HoPM; MiAP
All-over Love. Abraham Cowley. *Fr.* The Mistress. LiTL; SeCL
All Over the World. Geoffrey Johnson. HaMV
All over the world. Waiting Mothers. Anne Zucker. PEDC
All over the world, I wonder, in lands that I never have trod. Meditations of a Hindu Prince. Sir Alfred Comyn Lyall. VA; WGRP
All over this unsettled country, bands/ Of wild and unowned horses roam. Wild Horse Jerry's Story. Sarah Elizabeth Howard. PoOW
All overgrown by cunning moss. For Charlotte Brontë. Emily Dickinson. CoBA
All overgrown with bush and fern. Boston Common—Three Pictures. Oliver Wendell Holmes. TCAP
All own the young Silvia is fatally fair. Young Silvia. — De La Sale. SeCL
All Paths Lead to You. Blanche Shoemaker Wagstaff. BLPA; FaBoBe; NeHB
All peacefully gliding. The Rapid. Charles Sangster. CaP; CPG; OCL
All people that on earth do dwell. The Hundredth Psalm [*or* Old Hundredth *or* Scotch Te Deum]. William Kethe. MaRV; OtMeF; WGRP
All people with me, I am sure will agree. Bounteous Poverty. Aristophanes. *Fr.* Plutus. GrR
All perished—brides and infants. Song of a Jewish Boy. "M. J." TrJP
All places that the eye of heaven visits. Banishment. Shakespeare. King Richard II, *fr.* I, iii. EV-1
All poor men and humble. Poverty. *Unknown.* SDH
All-powerful had angel tribes, The. The Fall of Satan. Cædmon(?). *Fr.* Genesis. TCEP
All-powerful Ruler of angels, The. Fall of Angels and of Man. Cædmon(?). *Fr.* Genesis. PoLi
All praise to Thee, my God, this night. An Evening Hymn. Thomas Ken. OBS
All Quiet along [*or* on] the Potomac. Ethel Lynn Beers, *sometimes at. to* Lamar Fontaine. *See* Picket-Guard, The.
"All ready?" cried the captain. The Slave-Ships. Whittier. APW
All Revelation. Robert Frost. MoPo; NePA
All right, I may have lied to you and about you. Love 20¢ the First Quarter Mile. Kenneth Fearing. LoPS
All right now, boys. Sis Joe. *Unknown.* OuSiCo
All Roads Lead to Death. *Unknown, tr. fr. Greek by* F. L. Lucas. GrPE
All roads that lead to God are good. The Goal. Ella Wheeler Wilcox. BLP; MaRV; OQP; QP-1
All rose before the aged apparition. The Apparition. Blake. *Fr.* America. BoW
All round the borders where the pansie blue. Flowers and Vegetables. William Julius Mickle. *Fr.* The Concubine. RO
All round [*or* around] the house is the jet-black night. Shadow March. Robert Louis Stevenson. HOAH
All Ruin Is the Same. Emanuel Litvinoff. WaP
All Saints. Wyn Griffith. MoWP
All Saints'. Edmund Yates. BOHV; HBV; SiTL
All-Saints' Eve. Leah Bodine Drake. DaM
All sate, and audience gave. Thersites Out of Bounds. Homer. *Fr.* The Iliad, II. GrR
All Scottish legends did his fancy fashion. Robert Burns. William Alexander. HBV
All sea is still the sea: why vainly blame. Drowned in Harbour. Antipater of Thessalonica. OxBG

All Seasons in One. *Unknown.* TrGrPo
("April is in my mistress' face.") EG; OBSC; ReEn; SiCE
All Seasons Shall Be Sweet. Samuel Taylor Coleridge. *Fr.* Frost at Midnight. BoTP
("Therefore all seasons shall be sweet to thee.") EnSW
All-seeing Gods, The. Longfellow. *Fr.* The Masque of Pandora. OQP; QP-2
All Service Ranks the Same with God. Robert Browning. *Fr.* Pippa Passes, Introd. BEL; MaRV; OQP; QP-1
(New Year's Hymn.) BMEP; HiLiEn; TCEP
(Service.) TrGrPo; TSW
(Song: "All service ranks the same with God.") LoBV
All singers have shadows. The Green Singer. Shaw Neilson. BoAu
All smatterers are more brisk and pert. Smatterers. Samuel Butler. BOHV
All sorts of grain which our land doth yield. The Plymouth Harvest. William Bradford. PCH
All Souls. Katharine Tynan. BMEP; MBP
All Souls' Day. Siegfried Sassoon. QS
All Souls' Eve. Mary E. Mannix. GoBC
All Souls' Night. Frances Cornford. Two Poems, II. EnLoPo
All Souls' Night. Dora Sigerson Shorter. DaM; TIP; VA
All Souls' Night. W. B. Yeats. *Fr.* A Vision. MoVE; ReMP
All souls that struggle and aspire. Whittier. *Fr.* The Shadow and the Light. TrPWD
All Sounds Have Been as Music. Wilfred Owen. AlDL
All southern vices, Heav'n be prais'd, are here. A Plant That Will Not Grow. Dryden. *Fr.* Aureng-Zebe: Prologue. BeR
All storms whatever move my love. On the Altai. Aleksandr Yashin. RuPo
All strangest things the multitudinous years. Universal Change. Sophocles. *Fr.* Ajax. LiTW; OxBG
All suddenly a stormy whirlwind blew. The Mask of Cupid [*or* The Procession of Cupid]. Spenser. *Fr.* The Faerie Queene, III. NBE; OBSC
All-sufficient Christ, The. Bernice W. Lubke. BLRP
All summer long the people knelt. At the President's Grave. Richard Watson Gilder. GA; PAH
All summer watch the children in the public garden. A Prospect of Children. Lawrence Durrell. *Fr.* Eight Aspects of Melissa. NeBP
All Sung. Richard Le Gallienne. OBVV
All that a man might ask, thou hast given me, England. A Petition. Robert Ernest Vernède. InP
All that hate me whisper together against me. Psalm XLI, Bible, *O.T.* BoFr
All that have two or but one ear. The Four-legg'd Quaker. *Unknown.* CoMu
All, that he came to give. A Friend. Lionel Johnson. BoFr; CaAE; HBV; JKCP; PoeT; VLEP
All that I am to Earth belongs. Life's Testament, XI. William Baylebridge. BoAV
All that I ask. My Desk. Humbert Wolfe. YT
All that I dream. Sunset on the Spire. Elinor Wylie. CoBA
All that I got from love. A Poem about Love. G. S. Fraser. NeBP
All that I had I brought. Exchanges. Ernest Dowson. OBMV
All that I know/ Of a certain star. My Star. Robert Browning. BEL; BMEP; BoLiVe; EmBrPo; EPN; EPP; FaPON; GEPC; HBV; OAEP; OTPC (1946 ed.); OuHeWo; PC; PIAE; PoVP; StaSt; TOP; TrGrPo; UnPo (1st ed.); ViPo; ViPP
All that I know of you is that you wore. The True Romance. Herbert Jones. HBMV
All that I may swynk or swet. Care Away. *Unknown.* OxBoLi
All That Is, and Can Delight. Robert Farren. OxBI
All that is finished, finished, finished. Aleksandr Blok, *tr. fr. Russian by* C. M. Bowra. BoR
All That Is Left. Basho, *tr. fr. Japanese by* Curtis Hidden Page. WaaP
("Old battle field, fresh with spring flowers again.") AWP; LiTW; PFE
All that is moulded of iron. Woodworkers' Ballad. Herbert Edward Palmer. HaMV; OBEV (new ed.)
All That 'Lieve in Christian Lay. *Unknown.* AnEC
All That Matters. Edgar A. Guest. ATP
All That Matters. Walter Sorell. GoYe
All that matters is to be at one with the living God. Pax. D. H. Lawrence. MaRV
All that night I walked alone and wept. Gethsemane. Arna Bontemps. CDC
All That Summer. Lora Dunetz. NePoAm-2
All that was beautiful and just. In the Streets of Catania. Roger Casement. AnIV
All that we know of April is her way. Acquaintance. David Morton. MCCG
All that we say returns. Recompense. John Richard Moreland. OQP; QP-2
All that we see, about, abroad. On the Universality and Other Attributes of the God of Nature. Philip Freneau. AmP
All that we see has changes. Returning Home. Joseph von Eichendorff. AnGP
All that which Egypt whilom did devise. Ruins of Rome, VIII. Joachim du Bellay. OnPM
All that which lies outside our sort of why. Objects. W. H. Auden. NePoAm-2
All that you see here, stranger, where great Rome now stands. Propertius. Elegies, IV, 1. LaP
All That's Bright Must Fade. Thomas Moore. OxBI
All That's Past. Walter de la Mare. AnFE; BrBE; CaAE; CoBE; CoEV; GTML; InP; MM; MoAB; NP; OAEP (2d ed.); OBMV; PG (1945 ed.); PoeMoYo; PoeT; POTE; POTT; SeCeV; ShBV-4; ThWaDe; TrGrPo; TwCV; ViBoPo; WHA
All the afternoon there has been a chirping of birds. Free Fantasia on Japanese Themes. Amy Lowell. MAP; MoAmPo
All the apostles of freedom, I've hated them all my life. Goethe. *Fr.* Venetian Epigrams. PoFr
All the bells of heaven may ring. A Child's Laughter. Swinburne. BPN; EmBrPo; EPN; HBV; PoVP; PRWS; TCEP; TOP; VLEP
All the bells were ringing. The Broken Doll. Christina Rossetti. *Fr.* Sing-Song. MPB; TiPo
All the birds have come again. Spring's Arrival. *Unknown.* FaPON
All the books in all this world. Books. Hermann Hesse. TwGV
All the boys of merry Lincoln. Hugh of Lincoln. *Unknown.* ACP
All the breath and the bloom of the year in the bag of one bee. Summum Bonum. Robert Browning. BPN; EmBrPo; EnLi-2 (1949 ed.); EPN; GEPC; GTML; GTSL; HBV; LEAP; LiTL; LoPo; NeHB; OHFP; PG (1955 ed.); PoVP; VLEP
All the Cats. Kate Greenaway. SAS
All the complicated details. Winter Trees. William Carlos Williams. NP
All the earth a hush of white. Nocturne. Amelia Josephine Burr. HBV
All the Farewells. Byron Vazakas. MoPo
All the Flowers of the Spring. John Webster. *Fr.* The Devil's Law Case. AtBAP; BrBE; CaAE; EG; ElL; EV-2; ExPo; GTBS-W; LiTB; LiTG; OBS; PoEL-2; PoFS; PoRA; SiCE; ViBoPo
(All Is Vanity.) CoEV
(Burial, The.) CH; LoBV
(Nets to Catch the Wind.) BLV; TrGrPo
(Song: "All the flowers of the spring.") HBV
(Vanitas Vanitatum.) BCEP; BEL; LEAP; OBEV; PoFr, *last 4 ll.*
All the forms are fugitive. Emerson. *Fr.* Woodnotes, II. WGRP
All the foul fiends and demons of the air. Static. Rolfe Humphries. UnS
All the full-moon night in the coomb. In the Night of the Full Moon. Carl Busse. AWP
All the ghosts I ever knew. An April Ghost. Lizette Woodworth Reese. AV; DaM
All the glorious Spring makes me color blind. Sorrow. Marie Tello Phillips. GoYe
All the Heaven. Petronius, *tr. fr. Latin by* Walter K. Kelly. OnPM
All the heavy days are over. A Dream of a Blessed Spirit. W. B. Yeats. PoeT; TIP
All the here and all the there. Our Two Worthies. John Crowe Ransom. LS; SPP
All the Hills and Vales Along. Charles Hamilton Sorley. EnLit; FaBoCh; HBMV; MBP; MoBrPo; SoV
(Route March.) POTE
All the Hosts of Heaven. Simeon ben Isaac ben Abun of Mainz, *tr. fr. Hebrew by* Nina Davis Salaman. TrJP
All the house was asleep. Sly Santa Claus. Mrs. C. S. Stone. COAH
All the islands have run away. Islands. Rachel Field. GFA
All the lands are filled with soldiers. Hushaby. McLandburgh Wilson. BOL
All the lanes are lyric. Spring. Norman Gale. NLK
All the Little Hoofprints. Robinson Jeffers. Po
All the long August afternoon. In August. William Dean Howells. GN; PoRL
All the long day the robin on the spray. In the Midst of Life. Dora Sigerson Shorter. GTIV
All the long night. The Happy Farmer. Tse Nan. OnPM; PoHN
All the maidens are in the street! Apart. *Unknown.* OnPM
All the men of Harbury go down to the sea in ships. Harbury. Louise Driscoll. BAP; LEAP; POT; PoTo; SBMV
All the Merrier Is That Place. *Unknown.* AnEC
(Al the Meryere.) AtBAP; BoW
("Al the meryere is that place.") NBE
All the Mowgli Stories, *sel.* Kipling.
Only Son, The. VLEP

All the names I know from nurse. The Flowers. Robert Louis Stevenson. FaPON; MPB
All the night/ And all day long. Blacksmith. B. K. Pyke. BoTP
All the night sleep came not upon my eyelids. Sapphics [*or* Sappho]. Swinburne. AnEnPo; BPN; EmBrPo; GTML; Po; PoEL-5; POTT; PoVP; PtP; TOP; ViP; ViPo; VLEP
All the others translate: the painter sketches. The Composer. W. H. Auden. UnS
All the Pretty Little Horses. *Unknown.* ABF, *with music;* OxBoLi
All the promises of the world are lies. The Promises of the World. Moses ibn Ezra. *Fr.* The World's Illusion. TrJP
All the Road to Egypt. Katharine Lee Bates. ChrBoLe
All the Robin Redbreasts. Valentines to My Mother (1885). Christina Rossetti. BoChLi; DD; MOAH
All the roses are but one rose. The Only Rose. Juan Ramón Jiménez. OnPM
All the Saturdays met one day. The Saturdays' Party in Fairyland. Mary Carolyn Davies. TVC; TVSH
All the scenery in the north. The Snow. Mao Tse-tung. WhP
All the selves that have been slain. Fugue. R. A. K. Mason. OnPM
All the sheets are clacking, all the blocks are whining. A Young Man's Fancy [*titled* Third Mate *in* Masefield's "Poems"]. *At. to* R. E. McGowan *by* John Masefield. SG
All the ships of the world come here. In an Oriental Harbour. Cale Young Rice. VOD
All the skippers o Scarsburgh. Young Allan. *Unknown.* BaBo
All the small birds in good greenwood. The Ballad of the Eagle. *Unknown.* BoDaBa
All the Smoke. Eli Siegel. FiBHP
All the soldiers marching along. Remembering Day. Mary Wright Saunders. DD; HH; MeMeAg; OTPC (1946 ed.); PEDC; YeAr
All the songs here sung. Envoy. Martin Armstrong. QS
All the starlings in our town. The Tree of Starlings. Grace Hazard Conkling. BLA
All the starlings in the world. In the Lane. L. A. G. Strong. HaMV
All the storm has rolled away. On the Bridge. Arthur Reed Ropes. VA
All the streets are a-shine with rain. Rain in the City. Rachel Field. GFA
All the time they were praying. The Death Bed. Waring Cuney. CDC; PoNe
All the trees they are so high. The Trees So High. *Unknown.* OBB; OxBoLi; PoD; SiTL
All the voices of the wood called "Muriel!" Then I Saw What the Calling Was. Muriel Rukeyser. FiMAP
All the way back, the moon. The Moon. Kotomichi. OnPM
All the way my Saviour leads me. Fanny Crosby. OlF
All the way to Tir na n'Og are many roads that run. The King of Ireland's Son. Nora Hopper. AnIL
All the whole world is living without war. Canzone: He Speaks of His Condition through Love. Folcachiero de' Folcachieri. AWP
All the wide air was trawled for cloud. L'Ile du Levant; the Nudist Colony. Barbara Howes. NePoAm-2
All the wide world now I sway. The Birds' Life. Aristophanes. *Fr.* The Birds. OxBG
All the wise men that ever were, by aught that I can witness. Poverty Not All Loss. William Langland. *Fr.* The Vision of Piers Plowman. PoLi
All the women tell me. The Old Reveller. *Unknown. Fr.* Anacreontea. GrPE
All the words that I utter. Where My Books Go. W. B. Yeats. OBEV; OBVV
All the World. *Unknown, tr. fr. Hebrew by* Israel Zangwill. TrJP
All the world is now at peace. The Elusive Dove, 1946. Norman R. Jaffray. LauV
All the world over, I wonder, in lands that I never have trod. Meditations of a Hindu Prince. Sir Alfred Comyn Lyall. VA; WGRP
All the world shall come to serve Thee. All the World. *Unknown.* TrJP
All the World's a Stage. Palladas, *tr. fr. Greek by* Robert Bland. OxBG
("This life a theatre we well may call.") GrPo
All the World's a Stage. Sir Walter Ralegh. *See* On the Life of Man.
All the World's a Stage. Shakespeare. *Fr.* As You Like It, II, vii. FiP; GoTP; LEAP; LiTB; LiTG; PIR; TrGrPo (Life.) BCEP; PYM
(Seven Ages of Man, The.) CBE; EV-1; FaFP; GTBS-W; LPS-2; OQP; QP-2; TreF; TVSH
All the world's malice, all the spite of fate. Sonnets; a Sequence of Profane Love. XIII [XVI]. George Henry Boker. MOAP
All the year we travel. The Crossroads. Catherine Parmenter. PEDC
All the young men. Mediocracy. Caryll Houselander. JKCP (1955 ed.)
All their pipes were still. Praise of Spenser. William Browne. *Fr.* Britannia's Pastorals, Bk. II, Song 1. EV-2
All these and more came flocking; but with looks/ Down-cast. Mustering the Hosts of Hell. Milton. *Fr.* Paradise Lost, I. BCEP; MyFE
All these are your essence, you are their flesh and their force. Dick Diespecker. *Fr.* Between Two Furious Oceans. CaP
All These Birds. Richard Wilbur. FiMAP; Po
All these on whom the sacred seal was set. An Unbeliever. Anna Hempstead Branch. MaRV; NV; PFY; WGRP
All these reasons for honoring this man. Walt Whitman. Zona Gale. GA
All these things are in my mind also, lady; but I fear still. Hektor to Andromache. Homer. *Fr.* The Iliad, VI. WaaP
All these years I have remembered a night. Grievance. Amy Lowell. ViBoPo (1941 ed.)
All things announce her coming and her praise. Celebration of Love. James McAuley. MoAuPo
All Things Are a Flowing. R. P. Blackmur. TwAmPo
All things are best when first begun. I Love the Beginning of All Rain. Geoffrey Scott. POTE
All things are changed save thee—thou art the same. To the Spirit of Poetry. Philip Bourke Marston. VA
All Things Are Current Found. Henry David Thoreau. *Fr.* A Week on the Concord and Merrimack Rivers. AnNE; OnPM; ViBoPo; WoL
All things are doubly fair. Art. Théophile Gautier, *tr. by* George Santayana. AWP; JAWP; LiA; LiTW; WBP; WoL
All things are hushed, as Nature's self lay dead. Midnight. Dryden. ACP
All Things Are Sentient. Gérard de Nerval, *tr. fr. French by* Alan Conder. TrFP
All things are wonderful to him. The Eyes of Wonder. Jessie Corrigan Pegis. JKCP (1955 ed.)
All Things Be Dear but Poor Mens Labour; or, The Sad Complaint of Poor People. "L. W." CoMu
All Things Bright and Beautiful. Cecil Frances Alexander. BoChLi (1950 ed.); MaRV; NeHB; OHIP; OlF; PRWS; PTA-1; StVeCh; TVC, *abr.*
(All Things Beautiful, *abr.*) PEDC; RAR
(Creation, The.) FaPON; MeMeAg; MPB; OTPC
All things burn with the fire of God. Revelation. Verne Bright. BLRP; OQP; QP-1; WBLP
All things change, we are told, in this world of change and sorrow. Four Folk-Songs in Hokku Form, 3. *Unknown.* LiTW
All Things Drink. Thomas Stanley, *after the Greek of* Anacreon. *See* Fruitful Earth Drinks Up the Rain.
All Things except Myself I Know. Villon, *tr. fr. French by* Henry Carrington. BOHV
All things God can do, but this thing He will not. Judgment and Mercy. Dorothy L. Sayers. *Fr.* The Devil to Pay. MaRV
All Things Have Savour [*or* Savor]. *Unknown.* LiTG; SiTL
All things have their own shelter. The Poor Scholars. Tao Yuan-ming. WhP
All things have their time; as for me I crave but a moment. Omnia Tempus Habent. "The Archpoet of Cologne." LaP
All things he saw, even to the ends of the earth. Gilgamesh. *Tr. by* William Ellery Leonard. WoL
All things in Nature are beautiful types to the soul that will read them. Correspondences. Christopher Pearse Cranch. IAP
All things journey: sun and moon. Song of the Zincali. "George Eliot." *Fr.* The Spanish Gypsy. VA
All things must die. Guitar Song. Martha Barris. CAG
All things return, Nietzsche said. The Recurrence. Edwin Muir. MoPo
All Things Revive save the Lover. Thomas Lodge. *See* Sonnet: "O shady vales . . ."
All things shall die and decay, but the kingdom of Allah endureth. His Face Is Forever. *Unknown.* OnPM
All things shall have an end: the more and less. Gilboa. Victor Starbuck. *Fr.* Saul, King of Israel. MuM
All things slip from me, sinking into darkness. Ecstasy. Vilhelm Krag. AnNoLy
All things that are on earth shall wholly pass away. The Love of God. Bernard Rascas, *tr. by* Bryant. CAW; LPS-2; WGRP
All things that pass. Passing and Glassing. Christina Rossetti. FaBoEn; VA
All things that please another displease me. Desperate. Cino da Pistoia. LyMA; LyPI
All things thou bringest, Hesper, that the bright Dawn did part. Evensong. Sappho. GrPE
All Things to All Men. Theognis, *tr. fr. Greek by* T. F. Higham. GrL; OxBG
All things turned to Orpheus' hand. The Greater Music. Theodore Weiss. NePoAm-2
All things uncomely and broken, all things worn out and old. The Lover [*or* Aedh] Tells of the Rose in His Heart.

W. B. Yeats. ChMo; CMP; CoBE; EnLi-2 (1949 ed.); GTML; MBP; MoBrPo; POTT; ViBoPo
All Things Wait upon Thee. Christina Rossetti. GN
All things whate'er they be. Being Underived. Dante, *tr. by* Longfellow. *Fr.* Divina Commedia: Paradiso. CAW
All things will change and come aright. Tragic Tale. Boris Pasternak. RuPo
All This Is Ended. Rupert Brooke. *See* Dead, The ("These hearts were woven").
All this is one. My Faith. Ananda Acharya. WGRP
All this is vanity. Peace. Brian Vrepont. BoAu
All this night shrill chanticleer [*or* chanticler]. Chanticleer [*or* Sun of Righteousness]. William Austin. AnEC; CenL; MeRV; OxBoCh; SeCL
All this (said she) we know. Achilles Shows Himself in the Battle by the Ships. Homer. *Fr.* The Iliad, XVIII. OBS
All this smacking. Just a Smack at Smacking. *Unknown.* SiTL
All this stood on her and was the world. The Grownup. Rainer Maria Rilke. AnGP
All This Time This Song Is Best. *Unknown.* AnEC; RiBV (Three Christmas Carols, 3.) ACP
All This World's Riches. Spenser. *See* Amoretti, XV.
All those dark days in spring when we would sew. Compensation. Ruth Comfort Mitchell. PEDC
All those Germans. Some Europeans. *Unknown.* SiTL
All those treasures that lie in the little bolted box whose tiny space is. Slow Movement. William Carlos Williams. NP
All those who journey, soon or late. Gethsemane. Ella Wheeler Wilcox. MaRV; OQP; PSO; QP-1
All those who seek Thee tempt Thee. I Would Comprehend Thee. Rainer Maria Rilke. OnPM
All thoughts, all passions, all delights. Love [*or* Genevieve]. Samuel Taylor Coleridge. BCEP; BEL; BeLS; BPN; ChER; EM-2; EmBrPo; EnRP; EPN; ERP; EV-4; GTBS; GTBS-D; GTBS-W; GTSE; GTSL; HBV; LEAP; LiTL; LoBV; LPS-1; OAEP; OBEV; TOP
All thro' the breathing night there seemed to flow. A Venetian Night. Hugo von Hofmannsthal. AWP; JAWP; WBP
All thro' the Year. *Unknown.* BLRP
All through an empty place I go. The Loss of Love. Countee Cullen. PoNe
All through life I see a cross. The Christian Paradox. Walter Chalmers Smith. MaRV
All through my fevered nights their grey ghosts came. Visitation. David Morton. PFE
All through that summer at ease we lay. The Castle. Edwin Muir. LiTB
All through the day I toil for little gods. Daedalus Sings in the Dusk; before the Skyline of New York. Virginia McCormick. LS
All through the deep blue night. The Fountain. Sara Teasdale. CMP; VOD
All through the garden I went and went. The Butterbean Tent. Elizabeth Madox Roberts. LS; StVeCh; SUS
All through the golden weather. A Song of Autumn. Sir Rennell Rodd. HBV
All through the Night ("Sleep, my love, and peace attend thee"). Harold Boulton. OlF; TreFS
All through the Night ("Sleep, my babe, lie still and slumber"). *Unknown.* FaPON (Welsh Lullaby.) GoTP
All through the night I can hear the sound of dancers. Harbor Water. Beatrice Ravenel. Tidewater, II. LS
All through the night in silence they come and go. Charing Cross. Cecil Roberts. HBMV
All through the night the happy sheep. The Happy Sheep. Wilfrid Thorley. GFA; PCH
All through the Stranger's Wood. Isaac Leibush Peretz, *tr. fr. Yiddish by* Joseph Leftwich. TrJP
All through the sultry hours of June. My Thrush. Mortimer Collins. BLA; HBV; OTPC (1923 ed.)
All through the windless night the clipper rolled. John Masefield. *Fr.* Dauber, VI. AnFE; ChMo; CMP
All told the gray world. The Tall Toms. Edwin Honig. NePA
All too long the night. The Banished Lover. Al-Mustazhir. MooP
All Too Slowly. Lucia Trent. ChIP
All travail of high thought. The Beginnings of Faith. Sir Lewis Morris. WGRP
All travellers at first incline. Stella's Birthday [Written A.D. 1720[-21]. Swift. CBOV; EV-3; OxBI; PoEL-3
All truths wait in all things. Walt Whitman. Song of Myself, XXX. PFY; PoLFOT
All uncompelled, weightless as the notes. Cædmon. George Garrett. NePoAm-2
All under the Leaves, and the Leaves of Life. *Unknown. See* Seven Virgins. The.
All unseen the Master walketh. My Grace Is Sufficient for Thee. *Unknown.* BePJ
All up and down in shadow-town. The Shadows. Frank Dempster Sherman. AA
All Virgil's idyls end in sunsets; pale. The Voice. Edmund Wilson. TwAmPo
All vision fades, but splendor does not fail. Samuel Roth. NV
All was play, all was sport. *Unknown. Fr.* The Combat of Ferdiad and Cuchulain. OnYI
All we have achieved, the machine threatens to rule. Sonnets to Orpheus, Pt. II, X. Rainer Maria Rilke, *tr. by* Jessie Lemont. OnPM
All we have gained the machine threatens. Sonnets to Orpheus, Pt. II, X. Rainer Maria Rilke, *tr. by* M. D. Herter Norton. PoFr
All we make is enough. All Our Joy Is Enough. Geoffrey Scott. OBMV; TwCV
All week, the maid tells me, bowing. A Walk in Kyoto. Earle Birney. GoYe
All Will Be Well. Amory Hare. TBM
All will go right—will go right—will go right. *Unknown. Fr.* Ça ira! PoFr
All winter long you listened for the boom. The Stoic; for Laura von Courten. Edgar Bowers. NePoEA; PtPa
All winter through I bow my head. The Scarecrow. Walter de la Mare. MBP; MoBrPo; PoeT; ShBV-1
All wisdom and renown are worth. Summer Interlude. Lionel Stevenson. CaP
All women born are so perverse. Triolet. Robert Bridges. ChMo; CMP; HBV; PoVP; SeCePo
All Wool. Abbie Farwell Brown. TiPo (1952 ed.)
All work and no play makes Jack a dull boy. *Unknown.* OxNR
All worldly shapes shall melt in gloom. The Last Man. Thomas Campbell. BSV; EnRP; EV-4; OBRV; UnW
All worlds lie folded in the arms of power. Power. Edwin Markham. GrCo-2
All ye poets of the age. Namby Pamby. Henry Carey. EV-3
All Ye That Go Astray. Moses ibn Ezra, *tr. fr. Hebrew by* Solomon Solis-Cohen. *Fr.* The World's Illusion. TrJP
All ye that handle harp and viol and pipe. Chorus. Moses Hayyim Luzzatto of Padua. *Fr.* Unto the Upright Praise. TrJP
All ye that labor! Every broken man. Optimist. James Stephens. ChMo; CMP
All ye that learnèd hours beguile. Mike. F. C. W. Hiley. PoC
All ye that lovely lovers be. Harvester's Song [*or* Harvestmen a-Singing]. George Peele. *Fr.* The Old Wives' Tale. BLV; EPP; TrGrPo
All Ye That Pass. Dante, *tr. fr. Italian by* Dante Gabriel Rossetti. La Vita Nuova, II. LiTW; LyMA ("All ye that pass along Love's trodden way.") AWP; JAWP; WBP
"All Ye That Pass By." John Masefield. ChMo; CMP
All ye, who far from town, in rural hall. On a Wet Summer. John Codrington Bampfylde. EnSW; ES
All ye who love the springtime. The Dawning o' the Year. Mary Elizabeth McGrath Blake. AA; LBAP
All ye woods, and trees, and bowers. The God of Sheep [*or* Song to Pan *or* To Pan]. John Fletcher. *Fr.* The Faithful Shepherdess, V, v. BLV; CenL; ElL; EV-2; FaBoCh; LoGBV; TrGrPo
All yee forsaken lovers come & pitty my distress. *Unknown.* SeCSL
All you lords of Scottland ffaire. Tom Potts. *Unknown.* ESPB
All you possessed with indepressed spirits. Hymnus in Noctem. George Chapman. *Fr.* The Shadow of Night. TuPP
All you that are enamored of my name. Demos. E. A. Robinson. CoV; NP
All You That Are Good Fellows. *Unknown.* AnEC
All you that are to mirth inclin'd, come tarry here a little while. The Country Girl's Policy; or, The Cockney Outwitted. *Unknown.* CoMu
All you that delight to spend some time. Little John a Begging. *Unknown.* BaBo; ESPB (B *vers.*)
All you that desire to here of a jest. The Unfortunate Miller; or, The Country Lasses Witty Invention. *Unknown.* CoMu
All You That in This House Be Here. AnEC (Old English Carol.) OHIP
All you that pass along. The Dumb Maid. *Unknown.* CoBE
All you that to feasting and mirth are inclined. Old Christmas Returned. *Unknown.* COAH; GN; OHIP
All you that weep, all you that mourn. Resurrexit. Henry Longan Stuart. CAW
All young men should take note of the case. Limerick. M. B. Thornton. LiBL
All Your Fortunes We Can Tell Ye. Ben Jonson. *Fr.* The Gypsies Metamorphosed. ChTr
All yow that crye O hone! O hone! A Lementable New Ballad upon the Earle of Essex Death. *Unknown.* CoMu
Allá en El Rancho Grande, *with music. Unknown, tr. fr. Spanish.* ABF
Allah. Siegfried August Mahlmann, *tr. fr. German by* Longfellow. AWP
Allah. *Unknown, tr. fr. Arabic by* Sir Edwin Arnold. OnPM
Allah Akbar!/ All things vanish after brief careering. Night Is Nearing. James Clarence Mangan, *after the Persian.* IrPN

"Allah!" Bi-'smi-'llah! Say that God is one. Allah. *Unknown.* OnPM
Allah gives light in darkness. Allah. Siegfried August Mahlmann. AWP
Allah, the Artificer. *Unknown, tr. fr. Arabic by* Sir Edwin Arnold. OnPM
Allah's Tent. Arthur Colton. HBV
Allalu Mo Wauleen. *Unknown.* AnIV
Allan Water. Matthew Gregory Lewis. HBV; OTPC (1923 ed.)
Allas! my worthy maister honorable. Lament for Chaucer. Thomas Hoccleve. *Fr.* De Regimine Principum. OBEV; PtP
Allas the Wo! Allas, the peynes stronge. Chaucer. *Fr.* The Canterbury Tales: The Knight's Tale. LO
Allatoona. *Unknown.* PAH
Alle beon he blithe. King Horn. *Unknown.* EPP
Alle Vögel Sind Schon Da. Frances Chesterton. UnS
Allegory, An: "Portal as of shadowy adamant, A." Shelley. EmBrPo
Allegory of the Adolescent and the Adult. George Barker. LiTB
Allegory of Torment. "Pablo de Rokha," *tr. fr. Spanish by* H. R. Hays. AnCL
Allegra Agonistes. Grace Fallow Norton. NP
Allegro. "McM." InMe
Allegro Maëstoso. W. E. Henley. *Fr.* London Voluntaries. ViP
Alleluia, Alleluia,/ De Virgine Maria. *Unknown.* AnEC
Alleluia! Alleluia!/ Deo Patri Sit Gloria. *Unknown.* AnEC
Alleluia, Alleluia ("Now may we mirthes make"). *Unknown.* AnEC
Alleluia, Alleluia, Alleluia ("Salvator mundi, Domine"). *Unknown.* AnEC
Alleluia, Alleluia, Alleluia, Now Sing We. *Unknown.* AnEC
Alleluia! Alleluia! Finished is the battle now. Resurgam. *Unknown.* EOAH
Allen-a-Dale. Sir Walter Scott. *Fr.* Rokeby, III. BCEP; BPN; EmBrPo; EnRP; ERP; OTPC (1946 ed.); StPo; TOP; TVSH
Allenby Enters Jerusalem. Stephen Chalmers. PoMa
Allendale Dog. Lilian Bowes-Lyon. DiM
Allergy. Walker Gibson. NePoAm
Alley Cat. Esther Valck Georges. DDA
Alley Cat. Frank Stevens. CIV
Alley Cat, An. Nancy Byrd Turner. CIV; PoeMoYo
Alli Veri Figlioli Delle Muse. *Unknown.* *Fr.* Zepheria. ReIE; TuPP
Alliance of Education and Government, The, *abr.* Thomas Gray. CEP
Alliances. Nathalia Crane. MAP
Allie ("Allie, call the birds in"). Robert Graves. FaPON
Alligator, The. Beatrice Ravenel. LS; TCPD
Allison Gross. *Unknown.* *See* Alison Gross.
Alliteration; or, The Siege of Belgrade. *Unknown, at. to* Alaric A. Watts. *See* Siege of Belgrade, The.
Allons! after the great Companions, and to belong to them! Human Progress. Walt Whitman. GrCo-1
Allow no personality to stamp. The Manner. Sir Osbert Sitwell. MoP
All's dust, all's laughter, all's nonentity. Life's a Jest. Glycon. GrPE
All's ill and will be so. The Wind Is Ill. John Malcolm Brinnin. LiTA
All's over, then: does truth sound bitter. The Lost Mistress. Robert Browning. AEV; EmBrPo; EV-5; FaBoEn; FiP; GTSE; HBV; LiA; OBEV; OBVV; PoVP; VLEP
All's peace to-day at Beecher Isle. Beecher Island. Arthur Chapman. PoOW
All's Vast. Francis Thompson. *See* Heart, The.
All's Well! William Allen Butler. HBV
All's Well. Thomas Dibdin. *Fr.* The British Fleet. LPS-2
All's Well. Harriet McEwen Kimball. AA
(Evening Prayer, An.) PraP
All's Well. William A. Quayle. MaRV
All's Well! *Unknown.* *See* Now Is Well and All Things Aright.
All's Well. David A. Wasson. BAP
All's Well. Whittier. OBVV
All's Well That Ends Well, *sels.* Shakespeare.
For I the Ballad Will Repeat, *fr.* I, iii. ViBoPo
Love's Memory, *fr.* I, i. LPS-1
"Nay, a mother:/ Why not a mother?" *fr.* I, iii. MotAn
All's Well That Ends Well ("A friend of mine"). *Unknown.* BOHV; FaFP; SiTL
Allusion to Horace, An. The 10th Satire of the 1st Book. Earl of Rochester. OBS; SeEP
Alma Mater, *with music.* Robert Dye. PreP
Alma Mater. Mary Elizabeth Osborn. NePoAm
Alma Mater. Sir Arthur Quiller-Couch. OBVV; PoeT
Alma Mater, Forget Me. William Cole. FiBHP
Alma Mater's Roll. Edward Everett Hale. AA
Alma; or, The Progress of the Mind, *sel.* Matthew Prior.
"My simple System shall suppose." NBE
Alma Redemptoris. *Unknown.* WHL
Alma Redemptoris Mater. *At. to* Hermanus Contractus, *tr. fr. Latin by* Winfred Douglas. ISi
Alma Redemptoris Mater ("As I lay upon a night"). *Unknown.* *See* My Thought Was on a Maid So Bright.
Almae Matres. Andrew Lang. BSV; OBVV; POTT; TOP
Almeria. Ibn Safar, *tr. fr. Arabic by* A. J. Arberry. MooP
Almería. "Pablo Neruda," *tr. fr. Spanish by* Angel Flores. LiTW; WaaP
Almeria river. Almeria. Ibn Safar. MooP
Almighty and all [*or* al] merciable queen [*or* quene]. An A. B. C. [*or* La Prière de Nostre Dame *or* The Well of Pity]. Chaucer. CoBE; ISi; PoLi
Almighty and all present Power. An Airman's [*or* A Sergeant's] Prayer. Hugh R. Brodie. MaRV; PGD
Almighty Builder, bless, we pray. The Cornerstone. Edward A. Church. MaRV
Almighty crowd, thou shorten'st all dispute. Vox Populi. Dryden. *Fr.* The Medal. OBS
Almighty Framer of the skies! A Hymn for Christmas Day. Thomas Chatterton. MaRV; OTPC (1923 ed.)
Almighty God grants you this wondrous life. To My Children. John J. Burchenal. FAOV
Almighty God, may thoughts of Thee. A Pastor's Prayer. Grace E. Troy. PraP
Almighty God, our Father of heaven above. Pater and Credo. *Unknown.* TMEV
Almighty God, the Wonderful. That's Jesus! Grace B. Renfrow. BePJ
Almighty God, unchangeable. Prayer to the Crucifix. Mossén Juan Tallante. CAW
Almighty God, Whose Justice Like a Sun. Hilaire Belloc. Sonnets, XXI. TrPWD
(Sonnet: "Almighty God, whose justice like a sun.") QS
Almighty Lord, with One Accord. M. Woolsey Stryker. MaRV
Almighty Maker God! Sincere Praise. Isaac Watts. CEP; TrPWD
Almighty, Well of Light. Prison Songs, III. *Unknown.* TMEV
Almighty! What Is Man? Solomon ibn Gabirol, *tr. fr. Hebrew by* Emma Lazarus. TrJP
Almighty Will, The. Robert Louis Stevenson. *Fr.* It Is Not Yours, O Mother, to Complain. GrCo-1
Almighty Wisdom made the land. The Sea Is His. Edward Sandford Martin. EtS
Almond Blossom. Sir Edwin Arnold. GN; HBV; LPS-2; OTPC
Almond Blossoms. Charles Dalmon. *Fr.* Three Pictures. TSW; TSWC
Almond Blossoms of Chao Village, The. Po Chü-i, *tr. fr. Chinese by* Henry H. Hart. PoHN
Almond groves of Samarkand, The. The East a-Callin'. Oscar Wilde. *Fr.* Ave Imperatrix! OtMeF
Almond Tree, The. Georgios Drossinis, *tr. fr. Modern Greek by* Rae Dalven. MoGP
Almond tree has bought herself a dress, The. Spring & Co. Jorge Carrera Andrade. AnCL
Almost. Rachel Field. SUS
Almost a girl it was and issued forth. Four Sonnets to Orpheus. Rainer Maria Rilke, *tr. by* M. D. Herter Norton. *Fr.* Sonnets to Orpheus. LiTW
Almost a girl it was, then, issuing. Rainer Maria Rilke, *tr. by* W. D. Snodgrass. *Fr.* Sonnets to Orpheus. ReMP
Almost afraid they led her in. Transfigured. Sarah Morgan Bryan Piatt. AA
Almost before the sun has touched the fields. City Wife. Dorothy Livesay. BoCaPo (1943 ed.)
Almost emptied of sound and light. Great Silence. Sister Mary St. Virginia. JKCP (1955 ed.)
Almost ere enmity began. Judas. Edward Davison. NV
Almost happy now, he looked at his estate. Voltaire at Ferney. W. H. Auden. LiTA
Almost reluctant, we approach the block. Thumbprint. Celeste Turner Wright. MuM; PreP
Almost the body leads the laggard soul. Grieve Not for Beauty. Witter Bynner. *Fr.* The New World. NP
Almost two thousand years ago today. Easter Message. John Van Brakle. ChIP
Alms, *sel.* Robert Herrick.
"Give, if thou canst, an alms," *2 ll.* MyFE
Alms. Josephine Preston Peabody. POT; PoTo
Alms House, The. George Crabbe. *Fr.* The Borough, Letter XVIII. NBE
("Your plan I love not; with a number you.") LO
Alms in Autumn. Rose Fyleman. NLK; PCH
Alms to the highwayman in pursuit! Hours. Tristan Corbière. AnFP
Almswomen. Edmund Blunden. GTBS; LBBV; OBMV; POTE; ShBV-3
Alnwick Castle. Fitz-Greene Halleck. AA; IAP; LPS-2
Aloe Plant, The. Henry Harbaugh. BLPA
Aloft he guards the starry folds. The Eagle of the Blue. Herman Melville. AA

Aloft in Heavenly Mansions, Doubleyou One. The Playboy of the Demi-World; 1938. William Plomer. FaBoTw
Aloft, in secret veins of air. Waldeinsamkeit. Emerson. APW; HBV; IAP; OBAV; SN; WGRP
Aloft, the ponderous arches of the bridge. Morning in the Market. Nora Archibald Smith. VOD
Aloft upon an old basaltic crag. Kane. Fitz-James O'Brien. LPS-3; PAH
Aloft we all must go oh. John Dameray. *Unknown.* ShS
Aloha. William Griffith. HBMV
Aloha Oe. Don Blanding. PoToHe (new ed.)
Alone. Hayyim Nahman Bialik, *tr. fr. Hebrew by* Jessie Sampter. TrJP
Alone. Chu Shu Chen, *tr. fr. Chinese by* Kenneth Rexroth. OnPC
Alone. Walter de la Mare. ChTr; EnLoPo
Alone. John Farrar. BoChLi; GaP; GFA; MPB; YeAr
Alone. Robert Finch. CaP; PeCV
Alone. Stella Gibbons. AlDL
Alone. Hermann Hesse, *tr. fr. German by* Herman Salinger. TwGV
Alone. Francis Jammes, *tr. fr. French by* J. F. Mullen. CAW
Alone. James Joyce. InvP; NP
Alone. Elsie Laurence. CaP
Alone. Li Lung Yü, *tr. fr. Chinese by* Henry H. Hart. PoHN
Alone. Itzik Manger. *tr. fr. Yiddish by* Sarah Zweig Betsky. OnCuPl
Alone. Joseph Paget-Fredericks. StVeCh
Alone. Poe. *See* From Childhood's Hour.
Alone. Sappho. *See* Night.
Alone. Siegfried Sassoon. BLV; BoLiVe; MBP; MoBrPo; TrGrPo (1942 ed.); YT
(When I'm Alone.) OBMV; POTE; ShBV-3
Alone. Carolyn Spencer. MuM
Alone. *Unknown.* NA
Alone. Carolyn Wells. PoToHe
Alone. Hubert Witheford. AnNZ
Alone?/ In wilderness of lofty, virgin trees. Abraham Lincoln. Francesca Falk Miller. PEDC
Alone, above Manila's bay. Captain Colin P. Kelly, Jr. Robert Nathan. NeTW
Alone, alone, about a dreadful wood. Advent. W. H. Auden. *Fr.* For the Time Being. OAEP (2d ed.)
Alone! Alone! I sit in the solitudes of the moonshades. Alone. *Unknown.* NA
Alone amid the forest of his soul. Alone. Francis Jammes. CAW
Alone and ever weary with dark care. Sonnet. Petrarch. *Fr.* Sonnets to Laura: To Laura in Life. LyPI
Alone as I went up and doun. The Abbey Walk. Robert Henryson. BSV
Alone by the Hearth. George Arnold. HBV
Alone by the Lake. Verner von Heidenstam, *tr. fr. Swedish by* Charles W. Stork. AnSL
Alone, dear Lord, to sacrifice you go. Good Friday. Peter Abelard. LyMA
Alone far in the wilds and mountains I hunt. Song of Myself, X. Walt Whitman. CoBA; SeCeV
Alone, from your dim cell you shall look forth; behold and see. Munition-Maker. Laura Simmons. PIAE
Alone God Sufficeth. St. Theresa of Avila, *tr. by* Longfellow. *See* Santa Teresa's Book-Mark.
Alone, head pillowed on the mother heart. Voices. Alexander M. Stephen. CPG
Alone here on the mountain. On Gredos. Miguel de Unamuno. TeCS
Alone I sit at eventide. Our Native Birds. Nathan Haskell Dole. BOHV
Alone I stay; for I am lame. A Board School Pastoral. May Kendall. VA
Alone I wait, till her twilight gate. Reverie. "Laurence Hope." LoPo
Alone I walk a trackless land. Loneliness. Ignace M. Ingianni. MuM
Alone I walked the ocean strand. A Name in the Sand. Hannah Flagg Gould. AA; PECK
Alone in April. James Branch Cabell. HBMV
Alone in Her Beauty. Tu Fu, *tr. fr. Chinese by* Witter Bynner. ChLP
Alone in Rome. Why, Rome is lonely too. Written at Rome. Emerson. IAP
Alone, in silence, at a certain time of night. A Local Train of Thought. Siegfried Sassoon. AtBAP
Alone in Spring. Caroline Giltinan. LS; TBM
Alone in the dreary, pitiless street. Nobody's Child. Phila H. Case. PTA-2; TreF
Alone in the hot sun. The Song Maker. Kingsley Fairbridge. BoSA
Alone in the Night. Li Ch'ing-chao, *tr. fr. Chinese by* Kenneth Rexroth. OnPC
Alone in the night. Stars. Sara Teasdale. BoChLi; CP; FaPON; HBMV; NP; SP; TiPo; YT
Alone in this desert under the cold moon. If I Forget Thee. Emanuel Litvinoff. TrJP
Alone into the Mountain. Katharine Lee Bates. ChIP; MaRV; StJW
Alone of gods Death has no love for gifts. Inexorable Death. Aeschylus. *Fr.* Niobe. OxBG
Alone, on gold-red lanes of autumn light. On His Departed Wife. Hitomaro. UnW
Alone on Lykaion since man hath been. Mt. Lykaion [*or* Alone on Lykaion]. Trumbull Stickney. *Fr.* Sonnets from Greece. AnAmPo; AnFE; APA; CoAnAm; LA; MAF; MoAmPo (1942 ed.); MOAP; MoVE; NePA; OxBA; TrGrPo
Alone on the hill where the sun goes down. Box-Car Letters. Karle Wilson Baker. InP
Alone on the lawn. The Dancing Cabman. J. B. Morton. AlDL; MoShBr; ShBV-4
Alone on the shore in the pause of the night-time. The Full Heart. Robert Nichols. HBMV; LEAP; NLK (1947 ed.)
Alone one noon on a sheet of igneous rock. Myths. Guy Butler. BoSA
Alone, thought-sick, I pace where none has been. Petrarch. *Fr.* Sonnets to Laura: To Laura in Life. PrPoCR
Alone to sacrifice Thou goest, Lord. Good Friday; the Third Nocturn. Peter Abelard. LiTW
Alone, upon a summer's eve. Swansong on the Moorlands. Steingrímur Thorsteinsson. IcP; LiTW
Alone upon my hill-top. The Hill-Top. Clark Ashton Smith. MuM
Alone, upon the broad, low bench, he sits. To Borglum's Seated Statue of Abraham Lincoln. B. Jordan. OHIP
Alone upon the housetops, to the North. The Love Song of Har Dyal. Kipling. EtPaEn; GBV; OtMeF
Alone walking. The Bailey Beareth the Bell Away. *Unknown.* SeCePo
Alone was I born,/ a comfort to my folk. Christ Tells of His Passion. Cynewulf. *Fr.* Christ. PoLi
Alone we are born/ And die alone. High Country Weather. James K. Baxter. AnNZ
Alone with God for one sweet solemn hour. The Quiet Hour. Louise Hollingsworth Bowman. BLRP
Alone, yet never lonely. Lindbergh. Aline Michaelis. DD; GA
Along a river-side, I know not where. The Washers of the Shroud. James Russell Lowell. CoBA; HBV; IAP; PAH; PAP; TCAP
Along a road/ Not built by man. Rain Clouds. Elizabeth-Ellen Long. BrR
Along Ancona's hills the shimmering heat. Poppies in the Wheat. Helen Hunt Jackson. AA; BAP; LEAP; OBAV; PFY
Along by the sea and the river. Barcarola. Joan Zorro. LyMA
Along came the F. F. V., the fastest on the line. The Wreck on the C. & O.; or, The Death of Jack Hinton. *Unknown.* ABF
Along her tranquil way she went. Unwedded. Ada Foster Murray. AV
Along Highway 40, blare. The Shape of Autumn. Virginia Russ. GoYe
Along in September comes Toe River Fair. An Episode. Muriel Earley Sheppard. IHA
Along its front no sabers shine. A Holmes Alphabet. *Comp. by* Caroline B. Le Row. PEOR
Along my ways of life you never came. Sonnets, XII. Muna Lee. HBMV; NP
Along old terraces where blinds tent the masonry. The Sun. Baudelaire. MiFP
Along Shore. Herbert Bashford. AA
Along the avenues of cypresses. Giorno dei Morti. D. H. Lawrence. MeRV; POTE; SeCePo; ShBV-4; TriL
Along the Beach. Robert Browning. James Lee's Wife, IV. VLEP
Along the beach the great Achilles went. The Wrath of Achilles. Homer. *Fr.* The Iliad, XIX. BBV (1923 ed.)
Along the blushing borders, bright with dew. Spring Flowers. James Thomson. *Fr.* The Seasons: Spring. AtBAP; OBEC
Along the country roadside, stone on stone. Stone Walls. Julie Mathilde Lippmann. AA
Along the crowded streets I walk and think. Pulvis et Umbra. Agnes Mary Frances Robinson. UnW
Along the dark aisles. The Way of the Cross. Leonard Feeney. WHL
Along the dark and silent night. The Bell-Man. Robert Herrick. CH; HOAH; OBS; PCD
Along the dark wet lanes of golden light. A Drunken Man on Highgate Hill. Paul Hasluck. MoAuPo
Along the earth and up the sky. Pandora's Songs. William Vaughn Moody. *Fr.* The Fire-Bringer. GBV; MOAP
Along the East River and the Bronx. Ode to Walt Whitman. Federico García Lorca. KN
Along the Field as We Came By. A. E. Housman. A Shropshire Lad, XXVI. BPN; HBV; LiTL; MBP; MoAB; MoBrPo; OAEP; POTT; PoVP; ViPo

Along the forest path she walks with me. Phantoms and Spring. Gunnar Reiss-Andersen. AnNoLy

Along the frozen lake she comes. Our Skater Belle. *Unknown.* LPS-2

Along the garden terrace, under which. Modern Love, XXXVII. George Meredith. ViPo

Along the garden ways just now. A Love Symphony. Arthur O'Shaughnessy. HBV; VLEP

Along the graceless grass of town. A Dead Harvest. Alice Meynell. MoVE; PoeT

Along the grass sweet airs are blown. A New Year's Burden. Dante Gabriel Rossetti. AtBAP

Along the grave green downs, this idle afternoon. On Scratchbury Camp. Siegfried Sassoon. HaMV

Along the greening road of spring. The Skull. Charles Edward Eaton. NoCaPo (rev. ed.)

Along the high-street in Cologne. Marizibill. Guillaume Apollinaire. AnFP

Along the just-returning green. Wonder and a Thousand Springs. William Alexander Percy. HBMV

Along the lane beside the mead. A Pastoral. Norman Gale. HBV

Along the line of smoky hills. Indian Summer. Wilfred Campbell. BoCaPo (1948 ed.); CaP; OCL

Along the Noisy Streets. Pushkin, *tr. fr. Russian by* Babette Deutsch. TrRV
(Stanzas: "When down the loud streets I go straying," *tr. by* C. M. Bowra.) BoR

Along the pastoral ways I go. A Holiday. Lizette Woodworth Reese. AA; OBAV

Along the path that skirts the wood. The Three Musicians. Aubrey Beardsley. ACP (1926 ed.); JKCP (1926 ed.)

Along the Potomac ("When I was small, a woman died"). Emily Dickinson. OnPM

Along the Rand in eighty-five. Johannesburg. William Plomer. BoSA

Along the Road. Robert Browning Hamilton. BLPA; BPP; NeHB; TreFS
(Pleasure and Sorrow.) MaRV

Along the road all shapes must travel by. Prolonged Sonnet. Simone dall' Antella. AWP

Along the road where I had suffered much. The Kiss. Franz Werfel. BoFr

Along the roadside, like the flowers of gold. Prelude. Whittier. *Fr.* Among the Hills. CoBA; OxBA; PoEL-4; TOP

Along the roof-line, sharp and red. My Jack. John Francis O'Donnell. IrPN

Along the Sacred Road I strolled one day. The Bore. Horace. *Fr.* Satires. ATP

Along the sand of the beach. Manuel Altolaguirre, *tr. fr. Spanish by* Eleanor L. Turnbull. CoSP

Along the sea-edge, like a gnome. The Sandpiper. Witter Bynner. BLA; HBMV; WhBS

Along the sea shore, surf-beaten and brown. Sing Ho for the Herring. Grace Blackburn. CPG

Along the serried coast the Southerly raves. Sea-Grief. Dowell O'Reilly. BoAu

Along the shore of the Great Bitter Lake. Commandos Embarking. George Whalley. TwCaPo

Along the shore the slimy brine-pits yawn. The Witch's Whelp. Richard Henry Stoddard. AA; AnAmPo; LA; LEAP

Along the Strand. Alfred Mombert, *tr. fr. German by* Jethro Bithell. TrJP

Along the tangled path and in the red. Elegy. Manuel José Othón. AnMP

Along the thousand roads of France. The Good Joan. Lizette Woodworth Reese. FaPON; MoShBr; MPB; SP; TiPo (1952 ed.); VOD; WHL

Along the water front, in years before. Water Front. Jennie M. Palen. MuM

Along the Wind. Chard Powers Smith. TBM

Along the wind-swept platform, pinched and white. Morning Express. Siegfried Sassoon. HaMV; ShBV-3

Along the woodland path we took. Where You Passed. Amelia Josephine Burr. HBMV

Along these low pleached lanes, on such a day. On a Country Road. Swinburne. *Fr.* A Midsummer Holiday. BPN; PoVP; TOP; VLEP

Along this path he walked, great Washington. At Mount Vernon. Thomas Curtis Clark. PGD

Alons au bois le may cueillir. Charles d'Orléans, *tr. fr. French by* W. E. Henley. AWP; JAWP; PreP; WBP

Alonso to Ferdinand. W. H. Auden. *Fr.* The Sea and the Mirror. MoPo

Alonzo the Brave and Fair Imogine. Matthew Gregory Lewis. *Fr.* The Monk. LPS-3

Aloof. Christina Rossetti. The Thread of Life, I. BLV; BoLiVe; ES; OBEV; OBVV; TrGrPo; TyEnPo; YT
(Irresponsive Silence of the Land, The.) MBP
(Thread of Life, The.) FaBoEn; VA

Aloof, aloof, and come no near. The Sea Mark. John Smith. SPP

Aloof, and aloof, and steady I steer. Sir Francis Drake Reviv'd. Sir William Davenant. *Fr.* The History of Sir Francis Drake. SG

Aloof as aged kings. Day's Ending. Sara Teasdale. ChMo; CMP

Aloof upon [*or* within] the day's immeasured dome. The Black Vulture. George Sterling. AnAmPo; BAP; BLA; HBV; LA; LBMV; LEAP; MAP; MoAmPo (1942 ed.); MOAP; NP; NV; OBAV; PFY; PoMa; PoTo; TCAP; TCPD

Aloud for her son Eros, Cypris cries. Moschus, *tr. fr. Greek by* H. H. Chamberlin. GrPo

Alow and aloof. The Windy Night. Thomas Buchanan Read. GN

Alpha and Omega. Frederic William Henry Myers. *Fr.* Saint Paul. OQP; QP-1

Alphabet, The. Charles Stuart Calverley. HBV
(A, B, C.) SiTL

Alphabet, An. Charles Edward Carryl. LBN

Alphabet, The. Kate Greenaway. HBVY

Alphabet, The ("A, B, C, D, E, F, G"). *Unknown.* PCH

Alphabet of, The/ the trees. The Botticellian Trees. William Carlos Williams. AmP; LiTA; NP

Alphabet of Christmas, An. *Unknown.* ChBR

Alphabet rejoiced to hear, The. A Literary Squabble. James Robinson Planché. CenHV

Alphabetical Song on the Corn Law Bill. *Unknown.* OxBoLi

Alpheus and Arethusa. Eugene Howell Daly. AA

Alpine Descent. Wordsworth. *See* Simplon Pass, The.

Alpine Flowers The. Lydia Huntley Sigourney. AnAmPo; LA

Alpine Heights. Friedrich Adolph Krummacher, *tr. fr. German by* Charles T. Brooks. LPS-2

Alpine Village, An. Anne Goodwin Winslow. LS

Alps of Poetry, The ("Fir'd at first sight with what the muse imparts"). Pope. *Fr.* An Essay on Criticism, Pt. II. BeR
(Heights of Arts, The.) LiA

Alps on Alps. Pope. *See* Little Learning, A.

Already. Stephen Spender. FaBoMo

Already batter'd, by his lee they lay. The Sea Battle. Dryden *Fr.* Annus Mirabilis. FiP

Already blushes in [*or* on] thy cheek. Nemesis. Emerson. AtBAP; MOAP

Already, close by our summer dwelling. An Invitation to the Country. Bryant. ADAH; SN

Already fallen plum-bloom stars the green. The Poor Man's Pig. Edmund Blunden. CoEV; MBP; MoBrPo

Already I grow weary thinking how. Sonnet. Petrarch. *Fr.* Sonnets to Laura: To Laura in Life. LyPI

Already I'm upon the bridge that leads. Starting on the Journey. Verner von Heidenstam. AnSL

Already in the dew-wrapped vineyards dry. Among the Orchards. Archibald Lampman. PeCV

Already in the east the amorous star. Petrarch. *Fr.* Sonnets to Laura: To Laura in Life. PrPoCR

Already it's late summer. Sun-bathers go. The Divine Insect. John Hall Wheelock. GoYe

Already our kingdoms are beginning to totter. Charles Rann Kennedy. *Fr.* The Terrible Meek. ChIP

Already the dry leaves fall from the trees. What the Swallows Say. Théophile Gautier. TrFP

Already the slim crocus stirs the snow. Joy. Oscar Wilde. *Fr.* Humanitad. PCH

Already, through the splendour ere the morn. Virgil's Farewell to Dante. Dante. *Fr.* Divina Commedia: Purgatorio. FaBoTw

Already was Tithonus' mistress fair. Dante. *Fr.* Divina Commedia: Purgatorio, IX. EnLi-1

Already we were on the boat, already I was sailing. Fate. Henri Michaux. MiCF

Already you are beginning to become. Already. Stephen Spender. FaBoMo

Alsace or Alsatians. Gertrude Stein. *Fr.* Accents in Alsace. AtBAP

Also sprach Zarathustra, *sel.* Nietzsche, *tr. fr. German by* Thomas Common.
Seven Seals, The. LiA

Also Ulysses once—that other war. Kilroy. Peter Viereck. MoAmPo (1950 ed.); NeMA; OnAP; PoRA

Alta Quies. A. E. Housman. *See* Parta Quies.

Altar, The. George Herbert. ATP; ElSeCe; EPS; PoFS; ReEn; SeCV-1; TrGrPo

Altar, The. Jean Starr Untermeyer. BAP; HBMV

Altar and Sacrifice to Disdain for Freeing Him from Love, An. *Unknown.* ReIE; SiCE

Altar Boy, The. Leonard Feeney. WHL

Altar of Liberty. Sophia Mavroidi Papadaky, *tr. fr. Modern Greek by* Rae Dalven. MoGP

Altars, The. *sel.* Kostes Palamas, *tr. fr. Modern Greek by* Rae Dalven.
Fathers, The. MoGP

Altar Smoke. Rosalie Grayer. GoTP

Altars. Bernard Freeman Trotter. MaRV

Altarwise by Owl-Light. Dylan Thomas. CoBMV

(Sonnet: "Altarwise by owl-light in the halfway-house.") LiTM
(Two Sonnets.) MoAB; MoBrPo (1950 ed.)
Alter? When the hills do. Emily Dickinson. AnNE; OBAV; PIAE; TCAP
(Alter?) LoPS
(Constant.) AA; FaBoBe; LEAP
Alteram Partem. Arthur Hugh Clough. BPN; PoVP; VLEP
Altered look about the hills, An. Emily Dickinson. OxBA
(April.) NLK
Alternating Nocturne. José Juan Tablada, *tr. fr. Spanish by* Samuel Beckett. AnMP
Alternative. Charles Bruce. BoCaPo
Alternative Endings to an Unwritten Ballad. Paul Dehn. FiBHP
Although a gem be cast away. On True Worth. Sadi. LiTW
Although as yet my cure be incomplete. Retractions, I. James Branch Cabell. HBMV
Although beneath this grave-mound thy white bones now are lying. A Hound [*or* The Hound's Grave]. Simonides. GrL; GrPE; OxBG; WoL
Although crowds gathered once if she but showed her face. Fallen Majesty. W. B. Yeats. InP; PoeMoYo
Although from falsehood I with all my will. Petrarch. *Fr.* Sonnets to Laura: To Laura in Life. PrPoCR
Although I am sorely vexed by an old friend's leaving the city. Life at Rome. Juvenal. Satires, III. LaP
Although I can see him still. The Fisherman. W. B. Yeats. CoBMV; NP; ShBV-4
Although I do not hope to turn again. T. S. Eliot. Ash Wednesday, VI. FaBoEn
Although I do not know. Saigyo Hoshi, *tr. fr. Japanese by* Arthur Waley. AWP
Although I enter not. At the Church Gate. Thackeray. *Fr.* Pendennis. BMEP; EPN; HBV; LoPo; LPS-1; VA
Although I had a check. Earl of Surrey. SiPS
Although I hide it. Taira no Kanemori, *tr. fr. Japanese by* Kenneth Rexroth. OnPJ
Although I put away his life. Emily Dickinson. CoBA; MAP; MoAmPo; PoLFOT
Although I shelter from the rain. The Lamentation of the Old Pensioner. W. B. Yeats. MaPo
Although I transmigrate from friend to friend. Ideal Passion, VII. George Edward Woodberry. MOAP
Although I turned my head. Continuing Love. Ibn Rashiq. MooP
Although in the main I am like other men. My Irish Great-Grandfather, Patrick O'Flyng. Homer C. House. DDA
Although it is a cold evening. At the Fishhouses. Elizabeth Bishop. FiMAP; MoVE
Although it is not plainly visible to the eye. Fujiwara no Toshiyuki, *tr. fr. Japanese by* Arthur Waley. *Fr.* Kokin Shu AWP; JAWP; WBP; PFE, *tr. wr. at. to* Curtis H. Page
Although it may appear archaic. Eppur Si Muove? Robert Hillyer. GoYe
Although my clothes are fine and gay. Clothes. Abbie Farwell Brown. PPL
Although my eyes may never see. My Galilees. Belle Chapman Morrill. MaRV
Although my years be not yet two-and-twenty. Why Plague Me, Loves? Asclepiades. OxBG
Although she feeds me bread of bitterness. America. Claude McKay. AnAmPo; CDC; LA; PoFr; PoNe; TCPD
Although the bed, by hollow shadowing. A Simpler Thing, a Chair. Robert Mezey. NePoEA
Although the Borgias/ Were rather gorgeous. Important People. Louis Untermeyer, *and others.* StaSt
Although the lattice had dropped loose. The Bride's Prelude. Dante Gabriel Rossetti. SeCePo
Although the night is damp. The Firefly Lights His Lamp. *Unknown.* MPB
Although the sheath of my song. Constant Friend. Emilio Prados. CoSP
Although the ship's bell marks the time, it is. Concert at Sea. Hubert Creekmore. WaP
Although the snow still lingers. Last Snow. Andrew Young. AIDL; MoBrPo (1942 ed.); POTE; StaSt
Although the words of men suffice. How Sleep the Brave. Donald F. Drummond. PtPa
Although thy hand and faith and good works too. Change. John Donne. Elegies, III. LiTG; ViBoPo
Although Tormented. Kalonymos ben Judah, *tr. fr. Hebrew.* TrJP
Although with lives, submerged and brief. Coral Islands. Louis Ginsberg. OQP; QP-2
Although you died in a distant land. Vigil. Marjorie Freeman Campbell. CaP
Although your charms are many. To Natalie. Morrie Ryskind. HBMV
Altitude. Lola Ridge. NP
Altogether, hermanos. Penance by Whipping. *Tr. by* Mary Austin. APW
Alton Locke, *sels.* Charles Kingsley.
Alton Locke's Song, 1848. PoFr
(People's Song, 1849.) BMEP
Sands of [*or* o'] Dee, The. BBV (1923 ed.); BeLS; BLP; BMEP; BoChLi; CBE; CBOV; CBPC; CG; CH; DaM; EV-5; FaPON; GBV (1952 ed.); GN; GTBS; GTBS-D; GTML; GTSE; GTSL; HBV; LEAP; LPS-2; MCCG; MPB; MuP; MW; NeHB; OBEV (1st ed.); OnSP; OTPC; PECK; PFE; PoMS; PoVP; RG; ShBV-2; TreF; TSW; TSWC; TVSH; UnW; VA; WBLP; WP
(O Mary, Go and Call the Cattle Home!) PIR
Alton Locke's Song, 1848. Charles Kingsley. *See* Alton Locke.
Altruism. David Starr Jordan. OQP; QP-2
Alulvan. Walter de la Mare. GBV (1952 ed.); MoVE
Alumnus Football, *sels.* Grantland Rice.
"For when the One Great Scorer comes." MaRV
"You'll find the road is long and rough, with soft spots far apart." TreFS
Alvar's Address to the Spirits of the Dead. Samuel Taylor Coleridge. *Fr* Remorse (Osorio), III, i. EmBrPo
Alvorada: "Arise, friend sleeping in the dawn so chilly." Nuño Fernández Torneol, *tr. fr. Portuguese by* Seth G. Thornton. LyMA
Alvorada: "Girl arose so lovely, The." Dinis, King of Portugal, *tr. fr. Portuguese by* Seth G. Thornton. LyMA
Always ("Always/ We'll go further without ever advancing"). Guillaume Apollinaire, *tr. fr. French by* R. G. Stern. AnFP
Always. Harrison Smith Morris. OBAV
Always a "little boy" to her. Her Little Boy. *Unknown.* PEDC
Always alone in sleep. The Little Death. Carolyn Wilson Link. MuM
Always alone, star-told? Man. Samuel Greenberg. CrMA
Always at dusk, the same tearless experience. The Eyes of My Regret. Angelina Weld Grimké. CDC
Always at evening when a horseman passed. Sagebrusher's Wife. Howard McKinley Corning. MuM
Always Battling. Thomas O'Brien. NeIP
Always before Your Voice [My Soul]. E. E. Cummings. AnFE; CoAnAm; CoBA; LiTA; MAP; MoAmPo; MOAP; NePA; TwAmPo
(Song: "Always before your voice . . .") APA; TBM
Always Comes Evening. Robert Ervin Howard. DaM
Always do right. Right. "Mark Twain." BoHiPo
Always driven, always in the bite of the blast. And Yet We Are Here! Karl Wolfskehl. TrJP
Always Finish. *Unknown.* BLPA; FaBoBe; NeHB; WBLP
Always for the First Time. André Breton, *tr. fr. French by* Wallace Fowlie. MiCF
Always have these clear sounds been in your ear. Poem for You. Robert Pack. NePoEA
Always He feared you. The Crowd. Irene McKeighan. ChIP; MaRV
Always he sits in his accustomed place. Habitué. Helen Frith Stickney. GoYe
Always, here where I sleep, I hear the sound of the sea. The Sound of the Sea. John Hall Wheelock. EtS
Always I am mourning. I Grieve for Beauty Wasted. Grace Noll Crowell. LS
Always—I tell you this they learned. House Fear. Robert Frost. *Fr* The Hill Wife. BAP; ChMo; CMP; IAP; MOAP; NP; SBMV
Always in the Parting Year. Else Lasker-Schüler, *tr. fr. German by* Ralph Manheim. TrJP
Always I've loved this lonely hill, whose trees. Infinity. Giacomo Leopardi. UnW
Always remembering always remembering. Be Still. William Closson Emory. NP; PoeMoYo
Always Right. Eugene Field. TCAP
Always the dead seem unsuccessful. War Dead. Patrick Anderson. BoCaPo (1943 ed.)
Always the Following Wind. W. H. Auden. MBP; MoBrPo
Always the ghost of these will wake again. Oxford Bells. Sister Maris Stella. GoBC
Always the heavy air. The Lion House. John Hall Wheelock. BAP; HBMV; TBM
Always the Melting Moon Comes. Margot Osborn. CaP
Always the month of April fills. April. Isobel McFadden. MaRV
Always the path leads back. Finale. Douglas Le Pan. TwCaPo
Always the same, when on a fated night. The Onset. Robert Frost. AmP; AnNE; ChMo; CMP; CoBMV; CP; IAP; MoAB; MoAmPo; NeMA; OBAV; OxBA; TBM
Always there is someone who has turned away. The Hermit. Howard Moss. NePoAm
Always too eager for the future, we. Next, Please. Philip Larkin. NePoEA
Always waiting at the back of my mind. Landscape with Children. Sister Maris Stella. JKCP (1955 ed.)
Always we are following a light. The Lamp of Life. Amy Lowell. MaRV
Always well behaved am I. Grisette Dines. Antoinette Deshoulières. CIV

Always with us, always with us. I Am with You Alway. Edwin Henry Nevin. BePJ
Alyona. Aleksandr Yashin, *tr. fr. Russian by* Jack Lindsay. RuPo
Alysoun ("Bytuene Mersh and Averil"). *Unknown. See* Alisoun.
Alysoun ("Lenten ys come with love to towne"). *Unknown. See* Lenten Is Come.
Am I a king, that I should call my own. From My Arm-Chair. Longfellow. BLPA
Am I a soldier of the cross. Isaac Watts. OlF
Am I a stone, and not a sheep. Good Friday. Christina Rossetti. ChIP; MaRV; MeRV; PoEL-5; StJW; TriL; ViP
Am I alone. Recitation and Song [*or* Bunthorne's Recitative and Song]. W. S. Gilbert. *Fr.* Patience. CoBE; MBP; PoVP; WoL
Am I alone—or is it you, my friend? Toussaint L'Ouverture. E. A. Robinson. PoNe
Am I, am I beautiful? Virelay. Eustache Deschamps. FoS
Am I despised [*or* despis'd] because, you say. To a Gentlewoman Objecting to Him His Gray Hairs [*or* Age Not to Be Rejected]. Robert Herrick. MyFE; OBS
Am I failing? For no longer can I cast. Modern Love, XXIX. George Meredith. EmBrPo; ViPo
Am I getting gray at this early day. Getting Gray. William Green Brownson. PoP
Am I mad, O noble Festus. The Distracted Puritan. Richard Corbet. OxBoLi
Am I sadly cast aside. The Slave's Complaint. George Moses Horton. NoCaPo
Am I sincere? I say I dote. To Anthea, Who May Command Him Anything. Alfred Cochrane. HBV
Am I so soon grown tired?—yet this old sky. So Soon Tired. Richard Le Gallienne. BMEP
Am I the one who in these fateful days. Citizen. Kondrati Ryleyev. TrRV
Am I the slave they say. Soggarth Aroon. John Banim. GoBC; TIP; VA
Am I Thy Gold? Edward Taylor. Sacramental Meditations, VI. AmPP (4th ed.)
("Am I thy gold? Or purse, Lord, for thy wealth.") NePA; OxBA
(Meditation Six.) AtBAP; LiTA
Am I to set my life upon a throw. A Well-bred Man. William Cowper. BPP
Am I with you, or you with me. Songs in Absence, XI. Arthur Hugh Clough. EmBrPo; EPN
Am not I in blessed case. My Dear Lady. *Unknown. Fr.* The Trial of Treasure. EIL; TuPP
Amantium Irae. Ernest Dowson. HBV
Amantium Irae. Richard Edwards. BOL; EIL; EV-1; HBV; KN; LEAP; LoBV; OBEV
(Amantium Irae Amoris Redintegratio [*or* Redintigratio] [Est].) OBSC; PoE; ReEn; ReIE; SiCE; TuPP
Amaranth, The. Coventry Patmore. The Angel in the House, II, xii, 2. LoBV (1949 ed.)
Amarantha sweet and fair. To Amarantha, That She Would Dishevel Her Hair. Richard Lovelace. BLV; EG; HBV; HoPM; LiTL; LO; MePo; OBEV; PoFS; SeCV-1; TrGrPo; ViBoPo
Amaranthine flower beds stretching to. Brussels. Arthur Rimbaud. AnFP
A-Marching to Quebec. *Unknown.* APW
Amarillis [*or* Amaryllis]. Thomas Campion. *See* I Care Not for These Ladies.
Amarillis teare thy haire. *Unknown.* SeCSL
Amaryllis. E. A. Robinson. TwP
Amaryllis. *Unknown, tr. fr. Spanish by* Sir John Bowring. TeCS
Amaryllis I did woo. George Wither. EG
Amasis. Laurence Binyon. OBVV
Amateur Bard on Woman, The. *Unknown.* PC
Amateur Botanist, The. Franklin P. Adams. PreP
Amateur, driving too fast, An. Aristophanes, *tr. by* F. A. Wright. *Fr.* The Wasps. LiBL
Amateur Flute, The. *Unknown.* PA
Amaturus. William Johnson Cory. EV-5; GTBS; GTML; HBV
A-Maying, a-Playing. Thomas Nashe. *Fr.* Summer's Last Will and Testament. EIL
(Clownish Song, A.) OBSC
Amaze. Adelaide Crapsey. AnAmPo; LA
Amazing, Beauteous Change! Philip Doddridge. LPS-2
Amazing Facts about Food. *Unknown.* BOHV
Amazing Grace, *with music. Unknown.* ABF
Amazing monster! that, for aught I know. A Fish Answers [*or* Fish to Man]. Leigh Hunt. *Fr.* The Fish, the Man, and the Spirit. FiBHP; MoShBr
Amazing sight, the Savior stands. Henry Alline. *Fr.* Christ Inviting Sinners to His Grace. CaP
Ambassador Puser the ambassador. Memorial Rain. Archibald MacLeish. AnFE; BLV; BoLiVe; CoAnAm; CoBA; LiTA; MAP; MoAB; MoAmPo; PoLFOT; TwAmPo; TwCV; TwHP
Amber. Holger Drachmann, *tr. fr. Danish by* Charles Wharton Stork. BoDS; LiTW
Amber Bead, The. Robert Herrick. ChTr
Amber Beads. Audrey Alexandra Brown. CaP
Amber Lands. Tom MacInnes. BoCaPo; CPG
Amber morning floats a tree, The. Adam's Wonder. George O'Neil. NP
Amber the wine. At the Party. Freda Laughton. NeIP
Ambience of Love, The. Isidore Schneider. PG (1933 ed.)
Ambiguous Dog, The. Arthur Guiterman. AlBD; PoMa
Ambiguous Lines. *Unknown. See* I Saw a Peacock.
Ambiguous Time, I heard you sighing. Montgomery. J. C. Hall. ChMP
Ambition. Edith Agnew. GaP; TiPo
Ambition. W. H. Davies. MBP; MoBrPo; TrGrPo
Ambition. J. Hinckley. CAG
Ambition, *abr.* Samuel Johnson. *Fr.* The Vanity of Human Wishes. BHV
Ambition. Aline Kilmer. HBMV; LHV; SBMV; WHL
Ambition. Christopher Marlowe. *Fr.* Tamburlaine the Great, Pt. I, Act II, sc. vi. CoEV
Ambition. Thomas Nashe. EV-2
Ambition. Anne Blackwell Payne. GFA
Ambition. Shakespeare, *and probably* John Fletcher. *See* Higher Loyalty, The.
Ambition—following down this far-famed slope. Sonnet. Wordsworth. SoV
Ambitious Dreams. Joseph Marie Soulary, *tr. fr. French by* Alan Conder. TrFP
Ambitious Gorgons, wide-mouthed Lamians. John Marston. *Fr.* Satire V. ViBoPo
Ambitious Mouse, The. John Farrar. PCH; TSW
Ambitious Nile, thy banks deplore. De Rosis Hibernis. Sir Edmund Gosse. VA
Ambracian Cleombrotus. The Zealous Platonist. Callimachus. GrR
Ambrose. James Russell Lowell. TCAP
Ambuscade. Hugh McCrae. BoAV
Ambuscade, The. Florence Cecilia Roberts. UnW
Ambushed by Angels. Gustav Davidson. GoYe
Amelia Mixed the Mustard. A. E. Housman. WhC
Amen. A. C. Benson. OBVV
Amen. Frederick G. Browning. BLRP
Amen. Georg Trakl, *tr. fr. German by* Kate Flores. *Fr.* Rosary Songs. AnGP
Amen of the Rocks, The. Christian Gellert, *tr. fr. German.* PEOR
"Amend Me and Punish Me Not," *in mod. Eng. Unknown.* TMEV
Amendment. Thomas Traherne. SeCV-2
Amends for Ladies, *sel.* Nathaniel Field.
Rise, Lady Mistress, Rise! EIL; TuPP
(Matin Song.) HBV
(Song: "Rise Lady Mistress, rise.") OBS
Amends to Nature. Arthur Symons. BMEP; CBOV; GTML; GTSL; HBMV; PoVP; YT
Amends to the Tailors and Soutars. William Dunbar. BSV
America. Donald C. Babcock. NePoAm
America. Arlo Bates. *Fr.* The Torch-Bearers. AA; PaA
"America, last hope of man and truth," *sel.* PGD
America. Stephen Vincent Benét. *Fr.* John Brown's Body: Invocation. PoeMoYo
America. George Berkeley. *Fr.* On the Prospect of Planting Arts and Learning in America. BeR
America, *sels.* Blake.
Apparition, The. BoW
Morning Comes, The. RO
(Empire Is No More.) EnRP
America ("O mother of a mighty race"). Bryant. *See* O, Mother of a Mighty Race.
America. Florence Earle Coates. PEDC
America. Arthur Cleveland Coxe. *Fr.* England and America. MC; PAH
America. Sydney Dobell. EPN; EPP; OBVV; ShGoBo
"Nor force nor fraud shall sunder us!" *sel.* BMEP; ES; HBV; PaA
America. Alfred Kreymborg. NP
America. Claude McKay. AnAmPo; CDC; LA; PoFr; PoNe; TCPD
America. Raúl Otero Reiche, *tr. fr. Spanish by* Donald Devenish Walsh. AnCL
America. Samuel Francis Smith. AA; BoHiPo; DD; FaBoBe; FaFP; FaPON; GFA; HBV; HBVY; HH; IDAH; LEAP; MaRV, *with add. st. by* Longfellow; MC; OlF; OnHT; OTPC; PaA; PECK; PEDC; PoFr; PoRL; TCAP; TreF; WBLP; YaD
America. Bayard Taylor. *Fr.* National Ode, Read at the Celebration in Independence Hall, Philadelphia, July 4, 1876. AA; FOAH; HiLiAm; PoFr
(Liberty's Latest Daughter.) IDAH
America. Henry van Dyke. HiLiAm
America; a Prophecy. Blake. *See* America.
America always! American Feuillage. Whitman. Po

America! dear brother land! Greeting from England. *Unknown.* PAH
America First. G. Ashton Oldham. MaRV; PGD
America for Me. Henry van Dyke. BAP; BLPA; BTP; CV; FAFP; GA; HBVY; MC; MPB; OHFP; OTPC (1946 ed.); PaA; PCD; PYM; SP; TreFS; WBLP
(Home Thoughts from Europe.) POT; PoTo
"I know that Europe's wonderful, yet something seems to lack." *sel.* MaRV
America, give heed:/ this is no flight of herons or of angels. Wings over Europe. María Olimpia de Obaldía. BoFr
America Greets an Alien. *Unknown.* PGD; PSO
(Welcome over the Door of an Old Inn.) PoToHe (new ed.)
America has nourished wiser sons. The Prophet. Thomas Curtis Clark. HH; PEDC
"America, I Love You." Bert Kalmar *and* Harry Ruby. FiBHP; InMe
America Is Corn. Robert P. Tristram Coffin. WaKn
America, last hope of man and truth. Arlo Bates. *Fr.* The Torch-Bearers. PGD
America, my country, can the mind. Emerson. *Fr.* Journals. AmPP
America, my own! National Song. William Henry Venable. DD; MC; PAH
America, My Sweet. Jacinto Fombona Pachano, *tr. fr. Spanish by* H. R. Hays. TwSpPo
America, O Power benign, great hearts revere your name. Land of the Free. Arthur Nicholas Hosking. BLPA; PaA
America Prays. Arthur Gordon Field. PGD
America Remembers, *sel.* Paul Engle.
"Here by this midland lake," *much abr.* NAMP
America Resurgent. Wendell Phillips Stafford. MC
America the Beautiful. Katharine Lee Bates. AOAH; BLP; BLPA; CP; CV; DD; FaBoBe; FaFP; FaPON; GrCo-1; HBMV; HBVY; HiLiAm; MaRV; MC; MCCG; MPB; MW; NeHB; OBAV; OlF; OQP; OTPC (1946 ed.); PaA; PCH; PEDC; PoRL; POT; PoTo; PSO; QP-1; TreF; WBLP; WGRP; YaD
America, the Homeland! What America Means to Me. Letta Eulalia Thomas. HiLiAm
America, the land beloved. The name of Washington. Arthur Gordon Field. PGD
America! thou fractious nation. A Proclamation. *Unknown.* PAH
America to England. George Edward Woodberry. AA
America to Great Britain. Washington Allston. AA; HBV; LEAP; LPS-2; PaA
America, unbend that troubled brow! To Thee, My Country. Louise Burton Laidlaw. PAH
America was forests. America Was Schoolmasters. Robert P. Tristram Coffin. WaKn
America Was Promises. Archibald MacLeish. ChMo; PoLFOT
"America was promises—to whom?/ Jefferson knew," *sel.* PoFr
America Was Schoolmasters. Robert P. Tristram Coffin. WaKn
American Boy, The. *Unknown.* PEDC
American Cradle-Song. Robert J. Burdette. BOL
American Feuillage. Whitman. Po
American Flag, The. Joseph Rodman Drake. AA; APW; BAP; BAV; DD, *much abr.;* DDA; FaBoBe; FaFP; FOAH; GN; HBV; HBVY; HH; IAP; LBAP; LEAP; LPS-2; MaRV; MC; OBAV; OnHT; OTPC, *abr.;* PaA; PAH; PAP; PGD, *abr.;* PIR; PoFr; PTA-1; TCAP; TreF; TVSH; WBLP
(Ode to the American Flag.) PEOR
American Flag, The. Lena E. Faulds. HH
American Flag, The. Charles Constantine Pise. CAW
American Freedom, The. Matthew Biller. PoRL
American frigate, a frigate of fame, An. Paul Jones' Victory. *Unknown.* TrAS
American frigate from Baltimore came, An. Paul Jones. *Unknown.* GA; PAH
American Girl, An. Brander Matthews. AA
American Girl and the War, The. Hester L. Anderson. CAG
American Hero, The. Nathaniel Niles. IAP; PoFr; WaaP
(Bunker Hill, *with music.*) TrAS
American History. Marguerite Janvrin Adams. PoRL
American History. W. R. Moses. LiTA
American Independence. Francis Hopkinson. PAH
American Independence. Alfred Billings Street. PEDC
American Indian, The. *Unknown.* FiBHP; SiTL
(Indian, The.) LiTG
American jump, American jump. *Unknown.* OxNR
American land is a land of freedom, The. The American Freedom. Matthew Biller. PoRL
American Laughter. Kenneth Allan Robinson. PaA; TreFS
American Letter. Archibald MacLeish. AmPP; CoV; OxBA; PoLFOT
American Love-Ode, An. Thomas Warton, the Elder. CEP
American muse, whose strong and diverse heart. Invocation. Stephen Vincent Benét. *Fr.* John Brown's Body. CrMA; MPB; NP; PaA
American Names. Stephen Vincent Benét. AmP; BoLiVe (1945 ed.); DDA; InP; LaNeLa; LoGBV; NP; OxBA; PG; WaKn; YaD
American, One of the Roughs, a Kosmos, An. *Unknown.* PA
American Patriot's Prayer, The. *Unknown.* PAH
American Primitive. William Jay Smith. NePoAm; NePoEA
American Rhapsody (4). Kenneth Fearing. MoAmPo; PoLFOT; TrGrPo (1942 ed.)
American Soldier, The. Philip Freneau. MOAP
American Soldier's Hymn, The. *Unknown.* PAH
American Spring Song. Sherwood Anderson. NP
American Takes a Walk, An. Reed Whittemore. MoVE
American to France, An. Alice Duer Miller. HBMV
American Traveller, The. "Orpheus C. Kerr." BOHV; WhC
American Vineyard. Mildred Cousens. GoYe
American Yarns. Carl Sandburg. *See* They Have Yarns.
Americans All. Minna Irving. PEDC
Americans, rejoice. Old Song Written during Washington's Life. *Unknown.* OHIP
America's Answer. R. W. Lillard. BLPA; HH; PEDC
(America's Reply.) POT
America's Gospel. James Russell Lowell. MaRV; PGD
America's Prosperity. Henry van Dyke. PGD
(They Tell Me Thou Art Rich.) PSO
America's Reply. R. W. Lillard. *See* America's Answer.
America's Welcome Home. Henry van Dyke. AOAH; MC
Americus, as he did wend. The Noble Tuck-Man. Jean Ingelow. NA
Ametas and Thestylis Making Hay-Ropes. Andrew Marvell. ALV; InvP; SeCL
Amherst Train, The. Emily Dickinson. *See* I like to see it lap the miles.
Amico Suo. Herbert P. Horne. VA
Amid all Triads let it be confest. Epigram. Richard Garnett. OBVV
Amid my bale I bathe in bliss. A Strange Passion of a Lover. George Gascoigne. ElSeCe; EnLit; ReEn; ReIE; SiCE; TuPP
Amid the boundless and unknown. Home. Sidney Royse Lysaght. *Fr.* Old Landmarks. GrCo-2
Amid the cares of married strife. Tell Her So. *Unknown.* PoToHe (new ed.)
Amid the chapel's chequered gloom. Heliotrope. Harry Thurston Peck. AA; HBV; LEAP; PR
Amid the cloistered gloom of Aachen's aisle. The Opening of the Tomb of Charlemagne. Sir Aubrey De Vere. HBV
Amid the clouds of battle-smoke. He'll See It When He Wakes. Frank Lee. MDAH
Amid the fairest things that grow. Her Dwelling-Place. Ada Foster Murray. HBV; LEAP
Amid the foremost, towering in the van. Hesiod. *Fr.* Theogony. GrPo
Amid the garden's fragrance laid. Ode: Allusion to Horace. Mark Akenside. CEP
Amid the immense broad brownness of the sands. The Wreck. John Gould Fletcher. TCAP
Amid the loud ebriety of war. The *Birkenhead.* Sir Henry Yule. LH
Amid the nut grove, still and brown. The Faerie's Child. Thomas Caulfield Irwin. OnYI
Amid the Shadows. Antero de Quental, *tr. fr. Portuguese by* S. Griswold Morley. UnW
Amid the shining swords and lances. Fragment. Sharaf al-Din. MooP
Amid the thunders of the falling Dark. The Coat of Fire. Edith Sitwell. FaBoTw; OAEP (2d ed.)
Amid the turbulent waters. The Turbulent Waters. *Unknown.* WhP
Amid this hot green glowing gloom. Interlude. Edith Sitwell. MoAB; MoBrPo; NeMA
Amidst the fairest mountain tops. Cynthia. Sir Edward Dyer. OBEC
Amidst the rage of civil strife. Molly Odell on Her Birthday. Jonathan Odell. IAP
Amidst these scenes, O Pilgrim, seek'st thou Rome! Rome in Her Ruins. Francisco de Quevedo y Villegas. AnSpL-1; TeCS
Amidst Thuringia's wooded hills she dwelt. St. Elizabeth of Hungary. Whittier. MeRV
Amidst thy sacred effigies. The Emancipation Group. Whittier. LBAH
Aminta, *sels.* Tasso, *tr. fr. Italian.*
Birds and Plants of Love, The, *tr. by* the Countess of Winchilsea. BeR
Golden Age, The. AWP, *tr. by* Leigh Hunt; LyPI, *tr. by* Henry Reynolds (John Reynolds, *wr.*)
(Pastoral, A: "O happy golden age," *tr. by* Samuel Daniel.) OBSC; PoEL-2; ReEn; ReIE
Amintas and Claudia; or, The Merry Shepherdess. *Unknown.* CoMu
Amintor oh thou faithless swane. *Unknown.* SeCSL
Amitié Amoureuse. Luc Grimard, *tr. fr. French by* Edna Worthley Underwood. PoNe

Amo, Amas. John O'Keeffe. ChTr
("*Amo, amas,/* I love a lass.") LO
(Jingle.) IrPN
Among a race high-handed, strong of heart. The Non-Combatant. Sir Henry Newbolt. SoV
Among All Lovely Things My Love Had Been. Wordsworth. *See* Glow-Worm, The.
Among all the myths and masks and make-believes. Charles Madge. *Fr.* Poem by Stages. BoSA
Among Foes. Nietzsche, *tr. fr. German by* Paul Victor Cohn. PoFr
Among His Books. Robert Southey. *See* My Days among the Dead Are Past.
Among his books he sits all day. A Tragedy. Edith Nesbit. HBV
Among other things profiting in our tongue. John Heywood. *Fr.* A Dialogue Containing the Number of the Effectual Proverbs in the English Tongue. ReIE
Among poppies in a field of maize. Death in the Corn. Detlev von Liliencron. WaaP
Among School Children. W. B. Yeats. AnIL; ATP (1953 ed.); ChMo; ChMP; CMP; CoBMV; CoEV; EnLP; FaBoEn; LiTB; LiTG; LiTM (rev. ed.); MaPo; MBP; MoAB; MoBrPo; MoVE; OAEP (2d ed.); PoVP; ReMP; RiBV; SeCeV; TrGrPo; TwHP; UnPo
Among Shadows. Arthur Davison Ficke. NP
Among that band of Officers was one. Wordsworth. *Fr.* The Prelude. ChER
Among the ancient tombs both high and low. On an Ancient Tomb East of the Village. Po Chü-i. WhP
Among the anthropophagi. Funebrial Reflections. Ogden Nash. CenHV; ImOP
Among the Beautiful Pictures. Alice Cary. *See* Pictures of Memory.
Among the black trees spider-webbed. The Tenants. Leah Bodine Drake. DaM
Among the bumble-bees in red-top hay. Adelaide Crapsey. Carl Sandburg. HBMV
Among the cigarettes and the peppermint creams. Far West. A. J. M. Smith. BoCaPo (1948 ed.); PeCV
Among the contemporaries of Shakespeare. Clerihews. E. C. Bentley. OnPP
Among the Daffadillies. Giles Farnaby. OAEP
Among the Dead. Congreve. *Fr.* The Mourning Bride, II, iii. BeR
(Temple, The.) LiA
Among the dwellings framed by birds. A Wren's Nest. Wordsworth. CG
Among the Embers. Mimnermus, *tr. fr. Greek by* John Addington Symonds. GrR
Among the Ferns. Edward Carpenter. E[illegible]P; WGRP, *abr.*
"I lay among the ferns," *sel.* OQP; QP-2
"Among the few things/ I brought with me." A Cross on a Hill [*or* Symbol of Hope]. Carl S. Weist. BePJ; ChIP
Among the flowers, among the lilies. Idyll. Jean Vauquelin de la Fresnaye. TrFP
Among the fox-red fallen leaves I surprised him. Snap. The Squirrel. Ian Serraillier. AlDL
Among the guests who often stayed. Shelley. *Fr.* Peter Bell the Third. ChER
Among the Heather. William Allingham. IrPN
Among the Hills, *sels.* Whittier.
"For weeks the clouds had raked the hills." SN
Prelude: "Along the roadside, like the flowers of gold." CoBA; OxBA; PoEL-4; TOP
Among the hills of Athol he was born. The Wanderer. Wordsworth. *Fr.* The Excursion, I. EnRP
Among the iodoform, in twilight-sleep. The Leg. Karl Shapiro. MoAB; MoAmPo (1950 ed.); NeMA; TrGrPo (rev. ed.); UnPo (3d ed.)
Among the legends sung or said. The Wishing Bridge. Whittier. PTA-2
Among the level valley lands. Song. Aleksey Merzlyakov. BoRS
Among the mad, none madder; and in the company. "Hurler avec les Loups." Theognis. GrPE
Among the maple-buds we hear the tones. April. Lloyd Mifflin. *Fr.* The Fields of Dawn. ADAH; SN
Among the meadows ot the countryside. The Old-fashioned Garden. John Russell Hayes. AA
Among the Millet. Archibald Lampman. CaP; OCL
Among the Mountains I Had Lost My Way. Christian Morgenstern, *tr. fr. German by* Eileen Hutchins *and* Ursula Grahl. AnGP
Among the mountains I wandered and saw blue haze and red crag and was amazed. The Poor. Carl Sandburg. NP
Among the Nuts. *Unknown.* BoTP; TVC; TVSH
Among the Orchards. Archibald Lampman. PeCV
Among the people who work at small trades. In the Land of Magic. Henri Michaux. LiTW
Among the pickled foetuses and bottled bones. "Siene Mi Fe'; Disfecemi Maremma." Ezra Pound. *Fr.* Hugh Selwyn Mauberley. CoBMV; CoV; LiTA; LiTM (rev. ed.); MoPo
Among the pines we ran and called. Monologue at Midnight. Robert Penn Warren. PreP
Among the priceless gems and treasures rare. Pastel. Francis Saltus Saltus. AA; OBAV
Among the rest by Fortune overthrown. How Shore's Wife . . . Was by King Richard Despoiled of All Her Goods and Forced to Do Open Penance. Thomas Churchyard. *Fr.* A Mirror for Magistrates. ReIE
Among the Rocks. Robert Browning. James Lee's Wife, VII. BLV; BoLiVe; BPN; VLEP
(Ancient Doctrine, The.) OBVV
"O good gigantic smile," *sel.* EPN; YT
Among the Sand-Hills. William Alexander. TIP
Among the signs of autumn I perceive. Tall Ambrosia. Henry David Thoreau. PoEL-4
Among the silver cornstalks. Eve. Robert L. Wolf. HBMV
Among the smoke and fog of a December afternoon. Portrait of a Lady. T. S. Eliot. AnAmPo; BAP; CoAnAm; HBMV; LA; LiTG; MAP; MAPA; MoAmPo (1942 ed.); MOAP; NP; PoLFOT; ReaPo; TBM; TCPD; TwAmPo; TwHP
Among the Spruces. Frederick George Scott. OCL
Among the Stars. Wordsworth. *See* Crescent Boat, The.
Among the stars on a tower I was standing. Flash in the Gulf. Jules Laforgue. TrFP
Among the sullen peaks she stood at bay. The Mountain Woman. DuBose Heyward. AnAmPo; LA; LS; MuM; NP; OnPP; TBM; TCAP
Among the thistles on the hill. Little Sorrow. "Marian Douglas." SAS; TVC; TVSH
Among the thousand, thousand spheres that roll. Alcyone. Frances Laughton Mace. AA; LEAP
Among the Violets, Fair Lilies and Roses. *Unknown.* SeCL
(Dying Damsel's Doleful Destiny, The.) SeEP
Among the wondrous ways of men and time. Sequence of Sonnets on the Death of Robert Browning, V. Swinburne. BPN
Among the woods and tillage. Yattendon. Sir Henry Newbolt. HBMV; WP
Among the Worst of Men That Ever Lived. Henry David Thoreau. PoEL-4
Among their graven shapes to whom. Fitz-Greene Halleck. Whittier. LPS-3
Among These Turf-Stacks. Louis MacNeice. LiTB; LiTM; SeCePo; WaP
(Turf-Stacks.) OBMV; ShBV-4
Among Those Killed in the Dawn Raid Was a Man Aged One Hundred. Dylan Thomas. InPo; MoPo
Among those mountain-skirts a league away. The Lough. William Allingham. IrPN
Among those things that make our love complete. Consummation. Elsa Barker. *Fr.* The Spirit and the Bride. HBMV
Among thy fancies tell me this. The Kiss. Robert Herrick. LPS-1
Among twenty snowy mountains. Thirteen Ways of Looking at a Blackbird. Wallace Stevens. CoBMV; CoV; LiTM; MAPA; OnAP; PoFS; TwAmPo
Amongst the mourners that attend his hearse. Charles Cotton. ReEn
Amongst the princely paragons. A Princely Ditty in Praise of the English Rose. Thomas Deloney. BoTP
Amongst the pure ones all. The Quaker's Song. *Unknown.* CoMu
Amor Habet Superos. *Unknown, tr. fr. Latin by* George F. Whicher. *Fr.* Carmina Burana. LaP
Amor Ineluctabilis. *At. to* Joshua Sylvester. *See* Were I as Base as Is the Lowly Plain.
Amor Mundi. Christina Rossetti. EmBrPo; MeRV; PoEL-5; POTT; PoVP; ViP; ViPo; VLEP
Amor Mysticus. Sister Marcela de Carpio de San Félix, *tr. fr. Spanish by* John Hay. AnSpL-1; AWP; CAW; JAWP; LiTW; WBP
Amor Omnipotens. Apollonius Rhodius, *tr. fr. Greek by* George Allen. *Fr.* Argonautica, III. OxBG
Amor Profanus. Ernest Dowson. PoVP; UnW; VLEP
Amor que te tenia, El, *with music.* *Unknown, tr. fr. Spanish.* ABF
Amores, *sels.* Ovid, *tr. fr. Latin.*
Every Lover Is a Soldier, *fr.* I, 9, *tr. by* Kirby Flower Smith. RoL
"Graecinus (well I wot) thou touldst me once," II, 10, *tr. by* Christopher Marlowe. LaP
"I meane not to defend the scapes of any," II, 4, *tr. by* Christopher Marlowe. LaP
"In summers heate and mid-time of the day," I, 5, *tr. by* Christopher Marlowe. LaP
"Now ore the sea from her old Love comes she," I, 13, *tr. by* Christopher Marlowe. LaP
"Old Wood, stands uncut of long yeares space, An," III, 1, *tr. by* Christopher Marlowe. LaP
To a Janitor, I, 6, *tr. by* George Howe. RoL
Amoret. Mark Akenside. HBV; OBEV
Amoret. Congreve. ElSeCe; GTIV; ViBoPo

(Hue and Cry after Fair Amoret, A.) BCEP; CEP; EV-3; OBEC; OBEV
Amoretti (*Complete*, I-LXXXVIII). Spenser. PeBoSo
Sels.
I. "Happy ye leaves! when as those lily [*or* lilly] hands." ATP; BEL; CoBE; EnLi-1; EnLit; LoBV; Po; ReEn; ReIE; SiCE
(To His Book.) ES
III. "The sovereign beauty which I do admire." ATP; HBV; OAEP; TwHP
("Soverayne beauty which I doo admyre, The.") PoEL-1; SiCE
IV. "New yeare forth looking out of Ianus gate." ReEn
V. "Rudely thou wrongest my dear heart's desire." ElL; ReIE; SiCE
VII. "Fayre eyes, the myrrour of my mazed hart." REAL
VIII. "More than most fair[e], full of the living fire." BoLiVe; EPP; HBV; OAEP; TrGrPo
(Your Power.) BLV
IX. "Long while I sought to what I might compare." PoE; TwHP
XIII. "In that proud port which her so goodly graceth." EV-1; ReIE
XV. "Ye tradeful[l] merchants, that with weary toil [*or* toyle]." BoLiVe; LiTB; LiTG; ReEn; ReIE; SiCE; TCEP; TrGrPo
(All This World's Riches.) LiTL
(His Love's Riches.) BLV
XVI. "One day as I unwarily did gaze." ReEn
XVIII. "The rolling wheel, that runneth often round." TwHP
XIX. "The merry cuckoo [*or* cuckow], messenger [*or* messinger] of spring." ES; EV-1; OBSC; ReEn; ReIE; RiBV
XXI. "Was it the work[e] of Nature or of Art." ReaPo
(Art of Eyes, The.) LiTL
XXII. "This holy season, fit to fast and pray." ES; ReEn; SiCE
XXIII. "Penelope, for her Ulysses' [*or* Ulisses] sake." CoBE; ReaPo; ReEn; ReIE
XXIV. "When I behold that beauty's [*or* beauties] wonderment." BEL; HBV
XXVI. "Sweet is the rose, but grows [*or* growes] upon a brere [*or* brier]." ElL; ReEn
(Sweet and Sour.) HBV
XXVII. "Fair Proud! now tell me, why should fair be proud?" ES
XXVIII. "The laurel leaf which you this day do wear." ReIE
XXX. "My love is like to ice, and I to fire." ATP; BoLiVe; LiTB; LiTG; LiTL; PG (1955 ed.); TrGrPo
(Ice and Fire.) BLV
XXXIII. "Great wrong I do[e], I can it not deny." ReEn; ReIE
XXXIV. "Like [*or* Lyke] as a ship, that through the ocean wide [*or* wyde]." AnFE; BEL; BrBE; CoBE; EnLi-1; EnLit; EPP; ES; EtS; HBV; KN; OBSC; PIAE; PoFS; REAL; ReaPo; ReEn; ReIE; SiCE; TwHP
XXXVI. "Tell me when shall these wearie woes haue end." AEV
XXXVII. "What guile [*or* guyle] is this, that those her golden tresses." ElSeCe; EV-1; InP; LiTL; LoPS; OBSC; ReEn; SiCE; TCEP; TrGrPo
XL. "Mark when she smiles with amiable cheer." OBSC
(April Smile.) ES
(When She Smiles.) CBOV
XLI. "Is it her nature or is it her will." OAEP
XLIV. "When those renoumed noble peers of Greece." ReIE
XLVI. "When my abodes prefixed time is spent." PoFS
XLVII. "Trust not the treason of those smiling looks." BoLiVe; LO; TrGrPo
(Golden Hook, The.) BLV
LIV. "Of this world's theatre in which we stay." ReEn; ReIE
LV. "So soft as I her beauty do[e] behold." BoLiVe; ElSeCe; HBV; SiCE; TrGrPo
(Another Element.) BLV
LVI. "Fayre ye be sure, but cruell and unkind." EnLit
LXI. "The glorious image of the Maker's beauty." SiCE; TCEP
LXII. "The weary year[e] his race now having run." OBSC; ReaPo; ReIE; SiCE
LXIII. "After long storm[e]s and tempests sad assay." BEL; EnLit; FaBoEn; OAEP; OBSC; SiCE
LXIV. "Comming to kisse her lyps (such grace I found)." LoBV
LXV. "The doubt which ye misdeem, fair love, is vain." SiCE
LXVII. "Like [*or* Lyke] as a huntsman after weary chase [*or* chace]." BoLiVe; BrBE; ES; OAEP; PoEL-1; ReEn; RiBV; SeCePo; SiCE; TrGrPo; TwHP
(Tamed Deer, The.) BLV
LXVIII. "Most glorious Lord of life [*or* lyfe]! that on this day." ATP; BrBE; ElL; ES; EV-1; HBV; LiTB; MeRV; OBEV; OxBoCh; PeBoSo; PoE; ReEn; ReIE; SeCeV; SiCE; TrPWD
(Easter.) CAW; CoEV; StJW
(Easter Morning.) DD; EOAH; MaRV; OHIP
(So Let Us Love.) BLV
LXIX. "The famous warriors of the antique [*or* anticke] world." CoBE; ReEn; SiCE
LXX. "Fresh spring, the herald of love's mighty king." AWP; BEL; CaAE; ChTr; ElL; ElSeCe; EnLit; ES; FaBoEn; HBV; JAWP; LEAP; LiTB; OBEV; OBSC; OnPM; PoFS; ReEn; ReIE; SeCeV; SiCE; TOP; ViBoPo; WBP
(Make Haste, Sweet Love.) LiTL
LXXI. "I joy to see how in your drawn work." SiCE
LXXII. "Oft when my spirit doth spre[a]d her bolder wing[e]s." EG; EnLi-1; LEAP; OAEP; OBSC; RiBV; SiCE
LXXIII. "Being my[e]self [*or* my selfe] captived [*or* captyved] here in care." BrBE; CoBE; LoBV
LXXV. "One day I wrote her name upon the strand." AnFE; ATP; AWP; BEL; BoLiVe; CoBE; ElL; ElSeCe; EnLi-1; EnLit; ES; FiP; HBV; JAWP; LEAP; LiTB; LiTG; LiTL; OAEP; PG (1955 ed.); PoE; PoFS; PreP; REAL; ReaPo; ReEn; ReIE; SeCeV; SiCE; TOP; ViBoPo; WBP
(Her Name Upon the Strand.) SeCePo
LXXVII. "Was it a dream, or did I see it plain?" ReIE
LXXVIII. "Lacking my love, I go from place to place." ElL; ViBoPo
LXXIX. "Men call you fair [*or* fayre], and you do[e] credit it." ATP; AWP; BEL; EnLi-1; FaBoBe; HBV; JAWP; LiTL; PoFS; ReIE; SiCE; TOP; WBP
(True Fair, The.) CBOV
LXXX. "After so long a race as I have run." ReEn; ReIE; SiCE
LXXXI. "Fair is my love, when her fair golden hairs [*or* heares]." ElL; ElSeCe; LiTL; LoPo; PIAE; PoE
LXXXII. "Joy of my life! full oft for loving you." BEL; ReIE
LXXXV. "The world that cannot deeme of worthy things." ReEn
LXXXVI. "Venemous toung, tipt with vile adders sting." ReEn
LXXXVII. "Since I did leave the presence of my love." EG; ReEn
LXXXVIII. "Like as the culver, on the barèd bough." EG; ES
Amoris Finis. George Frederick Cameron. CPG
Amorist, The. Nahum Tate. SeCL
Amorous Bigot, The, *sel.* Thomas Shadwell.
Fire of Love, The, *at. to* Shadwell *and to* Charles Sackville, Earl of Dorset. SeCL
Amorous Dialogue between John and His Mistress, An. *Unknown.* CoMu
Amorous M. A., An. Limerick. *Unknown.* LiBL
Amorous of Laura's Loveliness. Sister Juana Inés de la Cruz, *tr. fr. Spanish by* Samuel Beckett. AnMP
Amorous Temper, An. John Trumbull. *See* Tom Brainless Seeks a Wife.
Amorous War, The, *sel.* Jasper Mayne.
Time. OBEV; SeCL
(First Song, Sung by Two Amazons, The.) SeEP
("Time is the feather'd thing.") EG
Amorous Worms' Meat, The. Petrarch, *tr. fr. Italian by* Anna Maria Armi. Sonnets to Laura: To Laura in Death, XXXVI. LiTW
Amos, *sel.* Bible, *O.T.*
O Ye That Would Swallow the Needy, VIII:4-10. TrJP
Amour, *sel.* Paul Verlaine, *tr. fr. French by* Denis Devlin.
Parsifal. LiA
Amours, Les, *sels.* Joachim du Bellay, *tr. fr. French by* Alan Conder. TrFP
Blameless Kiss, The, XV.
Contemplation, XXV.
On His Deafness, XXVI.
Upon the Same ("I yearn more hungrily to see your face"), XXVII.
Amours de Cassandre, *sels.* Pierre de Ronsard, *tr. fr. French by* Curtis Hidden Page. PrPoCR
"As the young stag, when lusty Spring supreme."
"Come, boy, and where the grass is thickest pied."
"Ere Love from barren Chaos drew the skies."
"I dragged my life along with sullen sighs."
"Maid of fifteen, in childlike beauty dight."
"Take thou this rose, sweet even as thou art."
(Take Thou This Rose, *tr. by* Alan Conder.) TrFP
"This is the wood my holy angel-child."
"To think one thought a hundred hundred ways."
"When Nature formed Cassandra, who should move."
(Nature Adorned Cassandra, *tr. by* Alan Conder.) TrFP
Amours de Marie, *sels.* Pierre de Ronsard, *tr. fr. French.*
"As in the gardens, all through May, the rose," *tr. by*

Amours de Marie (*continued*)
Andrew Lang. PrPoCR
(As When the Rose, *tr. by* Alan Conder.) TrFP
(His Lady's Tomb, *tr. by* Andrew Lang.) AWP; JAWP; WBP
"Fair flower of fifteen springs, that still," *tr. by* Andrew Lang. PrPoCR
(To His Young Mistress.) AWP; OuHeWo
"Hide this one night thy crescent, kindly Moon," *tr. by* Andrew Lang. PrPoCR
(To the Moon.) AWP, *tr. by* Andrew Lang; TrFP, *tr. by* Alan Conder
"Marie, arise, my indolent sweet saint!" *tr. by* Curtis Hidden Page. PrPoCR
(Wake Up, Marie, *tr. by* Alan Conder.) TrFP
"Twain that were foes, while Mary lived, are fled," *tr. by* Andrew Lang. PrPoCR
(His Lady's Death.) AWP
"When the beauteous spring I see," *tr. by* Curtis Hidden Page. PrPoCR
Amours de Voyage. Arthur Hugh Clough. EmBrPo, *abr.;* ViPP
Sels.
"*Dulce* it is, and *decorum*, no doubt, for the country to fall," Canto II, ii. OAEP; SoV
Envoi: "So go forth to the world." BPN
"Is it illusion? or does there a spirit from perfecter ages," Canto II, *introd.* EPN
Juxtaposition, Canto III, vi. VA
Letter from Rome, A, Canto I, v. LoBV
"Now supposing the French or the Neapolitan soldier," Canto II, iv. SoV
On Montorio's Height, Canto III, xi. BPN
"Over the great windy waters, and over the clear-crested summits," Canto I, *introd.* EPN
(En Route.) BPN
Pantheon, Canto I, viii. BPN
Real Question, The, *fr.* Canto V, ii. BPN
"Rome disappoints me still; but I shrink and adapt myself to it," Canto I, ii. EPN
(Rome.) BPN
Rome Is Fallen, I Hear, Canto V, vi. BEL
(Sceptic Moods.) BPN
"Victory! Victory!—Yes! ah, yes, thou republican Zion," Canto II, vi. SoV
"Whither depart the souls of the brave that die in the battle," *fr.* Canto V, vi. OAEP
"Will they fight? They say so," Canto II, iii. SoV
"Yes, as I walk I behold, in a luminous, large intuition," Canto III, vii. GTBS-D
"Yes, we are fighting at last, it appears," Canto II, v. SoV
Amours Diverses, Les, *sels.* Pierre de Ronsard, *tr. fr. French.* PrPoCR
"Another Winter comes. The last comes soon, I know," *tr. by* Curtis Hidden Page.
"More closely than the clinging vine," *tr. by* Andrew Lang.
Amphiaraus. Aeschylus, *tr. fr. Greek by* Gilbert Murray. *Fr.* Seven against Thebes. GrR
Amphibian. Robert Browning. *See* Prologue: "Fancy I had to-day, The."
Amphibious Crocodile. John Crowe Ransom. AnAmPo; LA
Amphimachos the Dandy. Vincent McHugh. NePoAm-2
Amphipolis. Antipater of Thessalonica, *tr. fr. Greek by* Sir William Marris. OxBG
Amphitryon, *sels.* Dryden.
Fair Iris and Her Swain, *fr.* IV, i. ViBoPo
Song: "Fair Iris I love, and hourly I die," *fr.* IV, i. AWP; JAWP; LiTL; WBP; WoL
(Fair Iris I Love.) InPo; OnPM
(Mercury's Song to Phaedra.) CEP; EPS (1942 ed.); LoPS; PoEL-3; SeCV-2
Amphitryon, *sels.* Plautus, *tr. fr. Latin.*
"Then the armies came out," *tr. by* F. A. Wright. LaP
Vertue, *tr. by* Sir Thomas Elyot. LiA
Amphora, The. "Feodor Sologub," *tr. fr. Russian by* Babette Deutsch *and* Avrahm Yarmolinsky. AWP; JAWP; WBP
(In a Gay Jar.) OnPM; TrRV
(Jar, The, *tr. by* C. M. Bowra.) BoR
"Ample heaven of fabrik sure, The." A Summer's Day. Alexander Hume. *Fr.* Summer Day. CH
Ample make this bed. Emily Dickinson. AtBAP; MAP; MoAB; MoAmPo; OxBA; PoEL-5
Ampler Circumscription, The. William Baylebridge. BoAV
Am'rous youth, whose tender breast, The. To My Lord Buckhurst, Very Young, Playing with a Cat. Matthew Prior. PoC
Amsterdam. Francis Jammes, *tr. fr. French by* Jethro Bithell. AWP; JAWP; WBP
Robinson Crusoe Returns to Amsterdam, *sel.* FaPON
Amulet. Ibn Sa'id of Alcala la Real, *tr. fr. Arabic by* A. J. Arberry. MooP
Amulet of Love, The. Michelangelo, *tr. fr. Italian by* John Addington Symonds. OnPM
Amusements. George Crabbe. *Fr.* The Borough, Letter IX. OBRV
Amusing Myself. Li Po, *tr. fr. Chinese.* WhP
Amwell; a Descriptive Poem, *sel.* John Scott of Amwell.
"How picturesque/ The slender group of airy elm." EnSW
Amy. James Matthew Legaré. AA
Amy Elizabeth Ermyntrude Annie. Queenie Scott-Hopper. BoTP; TiPo (1952 ed.)
Amy Wentworth. Whittier. BeLS; IAP; MOAP
Amycus. Theocritus, *tr. fr. Greek by* Charles Stuart Calverley. *Fr.* Idylls. OxBG
Amynta. Sir Gilbert Elliot. HBV
(My Sheep I Neglected.) EBSV
Amyntas. Tasso. *See* Aminta.
Amyntas Led Me to a Grove. Aphra Behn. *Fr.* The Dutch Lover. DiM
(Willing Mistress, The.) ViBoPo
Amyntas; or, The Impossible Dowry, *sel.* Thomas Randolph, *tr. fr. Latin by* Leigh Hunt.
Fairies' Song. ALV; EPP; LPS-3; PoMS
(Fairy Song.) HBV
(Song of Fairies Robbing an Orchard.) OBRV
Amyntichus the aged, when his fisher's days were ended. Farewell to the Sea. Macedonius. GrPE
Amyntor. Thomas Godfrey. IAP
Amyntor, son of Philip, lies. Greater Love. Antipater of Sidon. OxBG
An' Charlie he's my darling. Charlie He's My Darling. *Unknown, wr.* [Burns]. ALV; CH. *See also* 'Twas on a Monday morning.
An der Beach, an der Beach. An Unserer Beach. Kurt M. Stein. InMe
An' I couldn't hear nobody pray, O, Lord. I Couldn't Hear Nobody Pray. *Unknown.* BoAN-1
An' noo ance mair the Lomon'. Hughie's Advice to Dauvit to Enjoy the Fine Weather. James Logie Robertson. BSV
An' O, for ane-and-twenty, Tam! O, for Ane-and-Twenty. Burns. BSV
An' the thought of us each was the boat; och, however'd she stand it at all. Misther Denis's Return. Jane Barlow. *Fr.* Th' Ould Master. TIP
An Thou Were My Ain Thing. Allan Ramsay. EBSV; EiPP; EV-3; ViBoPo, 5 *sts.*
An Unserer Beach. Kurt M. Stein. InMe
An' zoo o' Monday we got drough. Easter Monday. William Barnes. PoVP
Anabasis, *sels.* "St.-J. Perse," *tr. fr. French by* T. S. Eliot.
"For my soul engaged in far matters," Pt. V.
(Three Sections from "Anabasis.") LiTW
I Have Built Myself, with Honour and Dignity, Pt. I. AtBAP
Song: "I have halted my horse by the tree of the doves." (Three Sections from "Anabasis.") LiTW
Song: "Under the bronze leaves a colt was foaled." AtBAP
(Three Sections from "Anabasis.") LiTW
Such Is the Way of the World, Pt. IV. AtBAP; MiFP
(Thus Was the City Founded.) OnHM
We Shall Not Dwell Forever in These Yellow Lands, Pt. VII. AtBAP
Anabasis. Eithne Wilkins. NeBP
Anacreon. Gutierre de Cetina, *tr. fr. Spanish by* Paul T. Manchester. AnSpL-1
Anacreon to the Sophist. "B. H." InMe
Anacreon's Dove. Samuel Johnson, *after the Greek of* Anacreon. AWP; JAWP; WBP
Anacreon's Tomb. *Unknown, tr. fr. Greek by* Evelyn Baring, Earl of Cromer. OxBG
Anacreontea. *Unknown.* *See* Anacreontics.
Anacreontic. Robert Herrick. OAEP; OnPM; OxBoLi; WoL
Anacreontic. Theophilus Hunter Hill. NoCaPo
Anacreontic. Francisco Martinez de la Rosa, *tr. fr. Spanish by* James Kennedy. AnSpL-2
Anacreontic. Thomas Parnell. GTIV
Anacreontic on Drinking. Abraham Cowley. *See* Drinking.
Anacreontics [*or* Anacreontea]. *Unknown, tr. fr. Greek by* Byron *and others.* GrL; GrPE; GrPo; GrR; OuHeWo; OxBG
Anactoria. Swinburne. EmBrPo
Sels.
"For who shall change with prayers or thanksgivings." AtBAP
"Thee too the years shall cover; thou shalt be." ViBoPo
Analogous to floral pageantry. Land of the Free. Sister Mary Honora. NePoAm-2
Analogy. Edith Dorothea Morrell. DDA
Analysis of Love, The. Sir Herbert Read. FaBoMo; LiTG
"Nature has perpetual tears," *sel.* MBP; MoBrPo (1942 ed.)
Anansi son name Stan'-up-stick. Sweet Riley. *Unknown.* BaBo
Anastasia, fair blossom of the Garden of the Graces. The Bride of Sixteen. Julianus. GrPE
Anastasis. Albert E. S. Smythe. CaP; CPG; OCL

Anathemata, The, *sels.* David Jones.
Rite and Fore-Time. AtBAP
"Stands a lady/ on a mountain." PrWP
Anatole France at Eighty. Gladys Oaks. AnAmPo; LA
Anatomie of the World, An. John Donne. *See* Anatomy of the World. An.
Anatomy Lesson. Ilo Orleans. RIS
Anatomy o Winter, The. Hesiod, *tr. fr. Greek into Scottish by* Robert Garioch. *Fr.* Works and Days. PoN
Anatomy of a Lover, The. George Gascoigne. ReIE
Anatomy of Baseness, The, *sel.* John Andrews.
To the Detracted. ElL. 8 *ll.*; LO, 16 *ll.*; SeEP
Anatomy of Happiness, The. Ogden Nash. LiTA; LiTM; SiTL
Anatomy of Humor, The. Morris Bishop. InMe; WhC
Anatomy of Melancholy, The, *sels.* Robert Burton.
Authors Abstract of Melancholy, The. OBS; SeCL
"Dost ask (my dear) what service I will have?" *after the Latin of* Terence. LO
Anatomy [*or* Anatomie] of the World, An; the First Anniversary. John Donne. EnLP; EPS, *abr.*; NBE, *abr.*
Sels.
Doth Not a Tenarif, or Higher Hill. ChTr
"How witty's ruin! how importunate." ReEn
New Philosophy, The. ExPo
"She, she is dead." MyFE
"So did the world from the first hour decay." TuPP
"When that rich Soule which to her heaven is gone." SeCV-1; SeEP
Anatomye, *sel.* John Halle.
"But chieflye the anatomye." PoP
Anaxagoras' ward was as true as his lord. Euripides. Alexander Aetolus. OxBG
"Ancestor remote of Man, The." Man and the Ascidian. Andrew Lang. HBV
Ancestors, The. Judith Wright. BoAV
Ancestral Burden. Alfonsina Storni, *tr. fr. Spanish by* Richard O'Connell. AnCL
Ancestral Dwellings, The. Henry van Dyke. CV; HiLiAm; PoMa; VOD
Ancestral Ghosts. John W. Garvin. CPG
Ancestral Houses. W. B. Yeats. Meditations in Time of Civil War, I. ChMP; LiTB; MoVE
Ancestry. Stephen Crane. The Black Riders, XXII. AA; LEAP
("Once I saw mountains angry.") MOAP
Ancestry. William A. Donaghy. JKCP (1955 ed.)
Anchises. Blanaid Salkeld. OxBI
Anchor: "Oft I must strive with wind and wave." *Unknown, tr. fr. Anglo-Saxon by* Charles W. Kennedy. *Fr.* Riddles. AnOE
Anchor is weighed, and the sails they are set, The. Away, Rio! *Unknown.* AmSS; LoGBV
Anchor Song. Kipling. PIR
Anchorage, The. Pat Wilson. AnNZ
Anchored to the Infinite. Edwin Markham. CV; MaRV; OQP; QP-1
Anchor's Aweigh, The, *with music. Unknown.* ShS
Ancient. "Æ." SeCePo
Ancient Adage. *Unknown, tr. fr. German.* PIAE
Ancient and leaden-lidded he treads. Chameleon. Anthony Delius. BoSA
Ancient and Modern Muses, The. Francis Turner Palgrave. VA
Ancient ape, once on a time, An. Uncivilized. Edmund Vance Cooke. BAP
Ancient Ballad of Chevy-Chase, The. *Unknown. See* Chevy Chase.
Ancient Barbarossa, the Kaiser Frederick old, The. Barbarossa. Friedrich Rückert. AWP
Ancient Beautiful Things, The. Fannie Stearns Davis. AV; BAP; SBMV
Ancient bridge, and a more ancient tower, An. My House. W. B. Yeats. Meditations in Time of Civil War, II. LiTB
Ancient Castle, An. William Morris. *See* Ladies' Gard.
Ancient cavern, huge and wide, An. The Cavern and the Hut. John Hookham Frere. OTPC (1923 ed.)
Ancient chestnut's blossoms threw, An. Alciphron and Leucippe. Walter Savage Landor. OBEV; RO
Ancient Christmas Carol, An. *Unknown. See* "I sing of a Maiden."
Ancient Doctrine, The. Robert Browning. *See* Among the Rocks.
Ancient fortress sprung between, An. Leper Island. Patricia Avis. PoN
Ancient greybeard shoulders on his load, The. Sonnet. Petrarch. *Fr.* Sonnets to Laura: To Laura in Life. LyPI
Ancient History. Siegfried Sassoon. SoV
Ancient Idyl, The; Europa and Her Mother. Walter Savage Landor. NBE
Ancient Lights. Austin Clarke. OxBI
Ancient long-horned bovine, An. The Last Longhorn. *At. to* R. W. Hall. CoSo; CSF
Ancient Lullaby. Gerald Griffin. IrPN
Ancient Mansion, The. George Crabbe. *Fr.* Posthumous Tales. EnSW; EV-3
Spring to Winter, *sel.* ChTr
Ancient Mariner, The. Samuel Taylor Coleridge. *See* Rime of the Ancient Mariner, The.
Ancient Mariner, The, *parody. Unknown.* PA
Ancient memories buried lie, The. Cadences: Minor. John Payne. VA
Ancient Music. Ezra Pound. CoV; LiTM; NePA; OxBA; PoE; ReaPo; SiTL
Ancient of Days. William Croswell Doane. AA
Ancient of days! august Athena! where. The Ruins of Athens. Byron. *Fr.* Childe Harold's Pilgrimage, II. CBOV
Ancient of Days forever is young, The. From the Conflict of Convictions. Herman Melville. APW
Ancient of Days, Who sittest, throned in glory. Ancient of Days. William Croswell Doane. AA
Ancient pages of the Talmud. The Talmud. Simeon Frug. TrJP
Ancient Person, for whom I. A Song of a Young Lady to Her Ancient Lover. Earl of Rochester. BeR; MePo
Ancient Phyllis. Congreve. *Fr.* The Double-Dealer. SeCL
Ancient Poem. *Unknown, tr. fr. Chinese by* Alan Lee Simms. ChLP
Ancient Prayer, An. T. H. B. Webb. *See* Prayer, A: "Give me a good digestion, Lord."
Ancient Prophecy, An. Philip Freneau. PAH
Ancient Race, The. Michael Tormey. JKCP (1926 ed.); TIP
Ancient readers of heaven's book, Th'. Ode: Of Cynthia. *Unknown.* OBSC; SiCE
Ancient Sacrifice, The. Mahlon Leonard Fisher. AnAmPo; LA
Ancient Sage, The. Tennyson. EPN; ViPP; VLEP
Sels.
Cling to Faith. OQP; QP-1
Faith ("Thou canst not prove the Nameless"). MaRV
"Thou canst not prove that thou art body alone." WGRP
Ancient songs pass deathward mournfully, The. Choricos. Richard Aldington. CBOV; HBMV; LBBV; NP
Ancient Sorrow. Giosuè Carducci, *tr. fr. Italian by* Glauco Cambon. OnPM
Ancient sowed an acorn from His mind, The. Oak. Philip Child. CaP
Ancient spiders with a flutter spread, The. One Night. Juan Ramón Jiménez. AnSpL-2
Ancient story I'll tell you anon, An. King John and the Abbot of Canterbury. *Unknown.* BLV; BoChLi; BOHV; BoTP; CG; EnSB; EV-2; GN; GoTP; HBV; LPS-3; OBB; OnSP; OTPC; RG; StaSt; TrGrPo
Ancient Tear, The. Luis G. Urbina, *tr. fr. Spanish by* Samuel Beckett. AnMP
Ancient terrible tree. The Ancient Tree. Marjorie Allen Seiffert. BAP
Ancient Thought, The. Watson Kerr. WGRP
Ancient to Ancients, An. Thomas Hardy. AEV; BMEP; ChMo; ChMP; CMP; CoBMV; LiTM (rev. ed.); MoPo; MoVE; PoVP; TCPD; TOP; TriL; TwCV
Ancient Track, The. Howard Phillips Lovecraft. DaM
Ancient Tree, The. Marjorie Allen Seiffert. BAP
Ancient Trees, The. Blake. *See* Hear the Voice of the Bard.
Ancient Winter. Salvatore Quasimodo, *tr. fr. Italian by* Glauco Cambon. OnPM
Ancients, The. Ch'en Tzu-ang, *tr. fr. Chinese.* WhP
And a clam caught my little finger. The Little Girl That Lost a Finger. "Gabriela Mistral." AnCL; FaPON
And a day will come, a black day! The Prophet. Kostes Palamas. *Fr.* The Twelve Songs of the Gypsy. MoGP
And a dog, lying there, lifted its head and pricked its ears. Homer. *Fr.* The Odyssey, XVII. LO
And a great sign appeared in heaven. A Woman Clothed with the Sun. Apocalypse (Revelation), Bible, *N.T.* (*Douay vers.*) ISi
And a youth said, Speak to us of Friendship. On Friendship. Kahlil Gibran. *Fr.* The Prophet. BoFr
And Achilles made at him, for his heart was filled. The Last Fight. Homer. *Fr.* The Iliad, XXII. OxBG
And after all, it's there for the listening. The Oracle of Delphi. Adèle Naudé. BoSA
And after April, when May follows. The Wise Thrush. Robert Browning. *Fr.* Home Thoughts from Abroad. BLA; WhBS
And after Calvary, a garden, green. They Saw and Believed. Esther Lloyd Hagg. ChIP
And after he has come to hide. Compensation. Phoebe Cary. OQP; QP-1
And after these came others—arguing. The Excuses. Ferid ed-Din Attar. *Fr.* The Bird Parliament. PeP
And all is well, tho' faith and form. In Memoriam A. H. H., CXXVII. Tennyson. BEL; BPN; CoBE; EmBrPo; EnLi-2; EPN; GEPC; HBV; OAEP; TCEP; ViPo; VLEP

"And All the While the Sky Is Falling . . ." Lora Dunetz. NePoAm
And all the while they mocked him and reviled. The Martyr. Natalie Flohr. ChIP; PGD
And Already the Minutes. Conrad Aiken. Priapus and the Pool, V [VI]. InPo; MOAP
And an old priest said, Speak to us of Religion. Of Religion. Kahlil Gibran. *Fr.* The Prophet. GrCo-2
And answer made King Arthur, breathing hard. Tennyson. *Fr.* Morte d'Arthur. ReTS
And are ye one of Hermitage. The Inquiry. Thomas Hardy. At Casterbridge Fair. V. BEL; EmBrPo; EnLi-2 (1949 ed.); EnLit; PoVP
And [*or* But] are ye [*or* you] sure the news is true? The Sailor's Wife [*or* The Mariner's Wife *or* There's Nae Luck about the House]. William Julius Mickle, *also at. to* Jean Adam. BeLS; BSV; CBOV; EPP; EV-3; GN; GTBS; GTBS-D; GTBS-W; GTSE; GTSL; HBV; LO; LPS-1; OBEC; ViBoPo
And Art Thou Come, Blest Babe? *Unknown.* OxBoCh
And art thou come to this at last. Alexander McLachlan. *Fr.* To an Indian Skull. CaP
And art thou fallen and lowly laid. Lament for Tabby. *Unknown.* CIV
And art thou wearied with the sun. Refreshment. Anyte. GrR
And as Dame Fame was in laudation. Stephen Hawes. *Fr.* The Pastime of Pleasure. ReIE
And as for me, though that my wit be lite [*or* thogh that I can but lyte]. Chaucer. *Fr.* The Legend of Good Women. CH; ViBoPo
And as he journeyed, he came near Damascus. Paul on the Road to Damascus. The Acts, Bible, *N.T.* TreF
And as I did awake of my sueving. William Dunbar. *Fr.* The Golden Targe. NBE
And as I sat, the briddes herkning thus. *Unknown.* *Fr.* The Flower and the Leaf. DiM
And as I thus sadly amonge them avysid. The House of Fame. John Skelton. Fr. The Garlande of Laurell. NBE
And as, my friend, you ask me what makes me sad and still. Utah Carroll. *Unknown.* CoSo; CSF
And as she backward cast her busy eye. Be Bold. Spenser. *Fr.* The Faerie Queene, III. MyFE
And as the moisture, which the thirsty earth. The Immortality of the Soul. Sir John Davies. *Fr.* Nosce Teipsum. EV-2
And as we spoke the Nicene Creed we were called out. Barnfire during Church. Robert Bly. NePoEA
And as we walked the grass was faintly stirred. Hawks. James Stephens. BMEP; HBMV; NP; PYM
And as ye would that men should do to you. On Compassion. St. Luke, Bible, *N.T.* BoFr
And at Lake Geneva, which is in Wisconsin. At Lake Geneva. Richard Eberhart. LiTA
And at last when I go. Daily Prayer. Marion Strobel. NP
And Atlas' seven daughters, named from him. The Daughters of Atlas. Aeschylus. OxBG
And before hell mouth; dry plain. Ezra Pound. *Fr.* Canto XVI. ExPo; MoPo
And, behold, a certain lawyer stood up, and tempted him. The Good Samaritan. St. Luke, Bible, *N.T.* TreF
. . . And behold thrones were kingless, and men walked. The Day of Liberty. Shelley. *Fr.* Prometheus Unbound, III, iv. EPN
And, behold, two of them went that same day to a village called Emmaus. On the Road to Emmaus. St. Luke, Bible, *N.T.* TreFS
. . . And blest are those. Fortune's Finger. Shakespeare. *Fr.* Hamlet, III, ii. BLP
And by her side went Eros, and Passion followed fast. The Coming of Aphrodite. Hesiod. *Fr.* Theogony. GrPE
And by "his kind" this scoundrel means no less. Lawyer in Search of Six Poets. *Unknown.* SiTL
And Can the Physician Make Sick Men Well. *Unknown.* *Fr.* Robin Goodfellow, Pt. II. AtBAP
(Lily, Germander, and Sops-in-Wine.) AnFE
(Song: "And can the physician make sick men well?") ElL; LoBV; ThWaDe
And canst thou find God in the crystal sphere. Immanence. F. Barrie Flint. OQP; QP-1
And canst thou, Mother, for a moment think. To My Mother. Henry Kirke White. MOAH
And children slowly grow with their deep eyes. Ballad of the Outer Life. Hugo von Hofmannsthal, *tr. by* Michael Hamburger. AnGP
And children still grow up with longing eyes. Twilight of the Outward Life. Hugo von Hofmannsthal, *tr. by* Peter Viereck. OnHM
And Dancing. Ivy O. Eastwick. MPB (1956 ed.)
And David lamented with this lamentation over Saul and over Jonathan his son. David's Lament. *Fr.* Second Samuel, Bible, *O.T.* ChTr
And day by day, the more the tide of ether. The Earth. Lucretius. *Fr.* De Rerum Natura, V. LiA
And Death Shall Have No Dominion. Dylan Thomas. ChMP; CoBE; ExPo; LiTM; MaPo; MoAB; MoBrPo (1950 ed.); MoVE; NeBP; OAEP (2d ed.); OnHM; PoD; POTE; SeCePo; ShBV-4
And deep-eyed children cannot long be children. Ballad of the Outer Life. Hugo von Hofmannsthal. AWP; JAWP; LiTW; TrJP; WBP
And Dick said, "Look what I have found!" Crescent Moon. Elizabeth Madox Roberts. SUS; TiPo (1952 ed.)
And did ever a man go black with sun in a Belgian swamp. Nigger. Karl Shapiro. OxBA
And Did Those Feet in Ancient Time. Blake. *Fr.* Milton. AEV; AtBAP; ATP; AWP; BCEP; BEL; CaAE; EG; EiPP; EM-1; EnRP; FaBoCh; InPo; JAWP; LEAP; LoBV; LoGBV; MaRV; OAEP; OBRV; PG (1945 ed.); PIR; PoE; PoEL-4; PoFS; PoRA; PreP; ReaPo; SeCeV; StJW; TOP; TyEnPo; UnPo (1st ed.); ViBoPo; WBP; WGRP; WP
(Building of Jerusalem, The.) TVSH
(Building of the New Jerusalem, The.) MuP
(Chariot of Fire.) OnPM
(Jerusalem.) BBV (1951 ed.); BoTP; CoEV; GTBS-W; OBEV (new ed.); OtMeF; ShBV-2; WaaP
(New Jerusalem, A [*or* The].) BLV; BoLiVe; CBE; EV-3; FaBoEn; LiTB; LiTG; PIAE; RiBV; TrGrPo
(Preface to "Milton.") AnFE; CEP; NeHB
(Song: "And did those feet in ancient time.") WoL
(Stanzas from "Milton.") EnLi-2; EnLit
(Till We Have Built Jerusalem.) OQP; QP-2
And did thy sapphire shallop slip. To a New-born Baby Girl. Grace Hazard Conkling. HBV
And did you not hear of a jolly young waterman. The Jolly Young Waterman. Charles Dibdin. EV-3
And did you not hear of a mirth that befell. Away to Twiver, Away, Away! *Unknown.* ElL
"And did you once see Shelley plain?" A Travelogue; Clovelly. Carolyn Wells. InMe
And did young Stephen sicken. Ode to Stephen Dowling Bots, Dec'd. "Mark Twain." *Fr.* The Adventures of Huckleberry Finn. FiBHP
And didst thou die, dear Mother of our Life? Our Lady's Death. Benjamin Dionysius Hill. JKCP
And didst Thou love the race that loved not Thee? Kinsman. Jean Ingelow. MaRV
And do I see some cause a hope to feed. Astrophel and Stella, LXVI. Sir Philip Sidney. ReEn; SiPS
And do our loves all perish with our frames? Immortality. Richard Henry Dana. AA; WGRP
And Do They So? Henry Vaughan. ReEn
("And do they so? have they a sense.") MeLP; OBS
(Rom. Cap. 8. Ver. 19.) SeEP
And dost thou faithlessly abandon me? The Unrealities. Schiller. AWP; WoL
And dost thou, holy Shepherd, leave. Hymn on the Ascension. Luis de León. AnSpL-1
And doun on knes anoon-ryght I me sette. This Fresshe Flour. Chaucer. *Fr.* The Legend of Good Women. SeCePo
And down in the horrible tower I heard the door. Ugolino. Dante. *Fr.* Divina Commedia. Inferno. LiA
And Dust to Dust. Charles David Webb. NePoAm-2
And Each Man's Leave. Roland Robinson. NeLNL
. . . And either Tropic now/ 'Gan thunder. Calm and Sinless Peace. Milton. *Fr.* Paradise Regained, IV. LiA
And Ellen, when the graybeard years. To Ellen. Emerson. IAP; MOAP; TOP
"And even our women," lastly grumbles Ben. The Girl of All Periods. Coventry Patmore. VA
And even silence found a tongue. John Clare. *Fr.* Secret Love. LO
And ever as I see the starres to fall. Spenser. *Fr.* Daphnaida. PoD
And ever must I fan this fire? Camoens. Herman Melville. PtP; ViBoPo
And every beast of beating heart grew bold. Shelley. *Fr.* The Witch of Atlas. MyFE
And every prodigal greatness. The Flowering Urn. Laura Riding. FaBoMo; LiTA
And fast beside there trickled softly downe. Spenser. *Fr.* The Faerie Queene, II. PC
And first Morency, far famed water, you. Standish O'Grady. *Fr.* The Emigrant. CaP
And first, the lamp-posts whose burning match-heads. Jewish Main Street. Irving Layton. CaP
And first: To make my observation right. The Politician and Mr. Gay. Swift. *Fr.* To Mr. Gay. BeR
And, first, within the porch and jawes of hell. The Porch of Hell. Thomas Sackville. *Fr.* Induction to "The Mirror for Magistrates." EV-1
And for the soul,/ if it is to know itself. Argonautica. George Seferis. OnHM
"And forasmuch that he made Nature." Stephen Hawes. *Fr.* The Pastime of Pleasure. ReIE

And forth h' is brought unto th' accomplishment. Samuel Daniel. *Fr.* The Civil Wars, II. ReIE

. . . & Forty-second Street. Archibald MacLeish. CoBA

And fra his folk wist he was dead. Bannockburn. John Barbour. *Fr.* The Bruce. EBSV

And Freedom rear'd in that august sunrise. Tennyson. *Fr.* The Poet. PoFr

And from a northern coast the Lovers watch'd. Three Fragments, I. William Allingham. IrPN

And from Sardes her/ thoughts. Arignota Remembers. Sappho. LiTW

And from the windy West came two-gunned Gabriel. Sonnets, V. Dylan Thomas. LiTM

And glad to find, on again looking at it. Quayside. Robert Graves. FaBoMo

And God Created the Great Whales. Milton. *Fr.* Paradise Lost, VII. EtS

And God saw that the wickedness of man was great in the earth. Noah and the Flood. Genesis, Bible, *O.T.* OuHeWo

And God spake all these words, saying. The Ten Commandments. Exodus, Bible, *O.T.* TreF

And God stepped out on space. The Creation. James Weldon Johnson. BANP; CDC; GoSl; MAP; MaRV; MoAmPo; NP; NV; PoNe; PreP; QS; TiPo (1952 ed.); YaD

And Grow. John Hay. WaP

And Gwydion said to Math, when it was spring. The Wife of Llew. Francis Ledwidge. LBBV; LEAP; MBP; PoMS

And haply, bason'd in some unsunn'd cleft. Samuel Taylor Coleridge. *Fr.* To a Young Friend. ChER

And hark! how blithe the throstle sings! Let Nature Be Your Teacher. Wordsworth. *Fr.* The Tables Turned. MaRV

And hast thou sought thy heavenly home. Casa Wappy. David Macbeth Moir. LPS-1

And hasten Og and Doeg to rehearse. Og and Doeg [*or* Characters from the Satires]. Dryden. *Fr.* Absalom and Achitophel, Pt. II. AWP; InPo; JAWP; WBP

And have the bright immensities. Via Lucis. Howard Chandler Robbins. MaRV; OQP; QP-2

And have we done with war at last? Two Fusiliers. Robert Graves. BoFr

"And have you any children?" Peniny and the Silken Lady. Lucy Cherry Crisp. NoCaPo (rev. ed.)

And have you been to Borderland? Borderland. Herman Knickerbocker Viele. PR

"And having taken bread, he broke it." Holy Week. Phoebe Smith Bachelder. ChIP

And He Answered Them Nothing. Richard Crashaw. MePo

And he cast it down, down, on the green grass. The New Ghost. Fredegond Shove. ChMP; HBMV; MoVE; NV; OxBoCh; TwCV

And he said, A certain man had two sons. The Prodigal Son. St. Luke, Bible, *N.T.* EM-1; TreF

And he said to himself. Between Worlds. Carl Sandburg. MoAmPo (1950 ed.)

And he shall charm and soothe, and breathe and bless. Christ's Reign of Peace. Stephen Phillips. ChIP

And he showed me a pure river of water of life. There Shall Be No Night. Revelation, Bible, *N.T.* TrGrPo

And he went unto Ramah. There he met. The Dance of Saul with the Prophets. Saul Tchernichowsky. TrJP

And he who was righteous loomed radiant, striding. Lot's Wife. "Anna Akhmatova." TrRV

And heed not them that warn or chide thee. The Rosy Days Are Numbered. Moses ibn Ezra. *Fr.* Wine-Songs. TrJP

"And her, Alcinous chose his royal mate." Arete; Portrait of a High-born Matron. Homer, *tr. by* Pope. *Fr.* The Odyssey, VII. GrR

And here face down beneath the sun. You, Andrew Marvell. Archibald MacLeish. AmP; AmPP; AnAmPo; AnEnPo; AnFE; APA; AWP; BLV; BoLiVe; ChMo; CMP; CoAnAm; CoBA; CoBMV; CoV; GTBS-W; HoPM; InP; InPo; LA; LiTA; LiTM; MAP; MoAB; MoAmPo; MOAP; MoVE; NeMA; NP; OxBA; PoeMoYo; PoLFOT; PoMa; PoRA; ReaPo; TCPD; TrGrPo; TwAmPo; TwHP; ViBoPo; WoL

And here is the end of it all, and we count the loss. Eyeless and Limbless and Shattered. Cecil Roberts. *Fr.* Charing Cross. BMEP

And here, sweet friend, I go my way. Adios. Joaquin Miller. OQP; QP-2

And Here the Hermit Sat, and Told His Beads. William Ellery Channing. OnAP

And here the precious dust is laid [*or* layd]. Maria Wentworth [*or* The Inscription on the Tomb[e] of the Lady Mary Wentworth]. Thomas Carew. ATP; CoEV; MeLP; MePo; OBS; SeCV-1; SeEP; TriL

And here the Singer for his art. Tennyson. *Fr.* The Charge of the Heavy Brigade at Balaclava: Epilogue. BPN

And here where all is waste and wild. Syracuse. Elizabeth J. Coatsworth. TBM

And here's good luck to the shanty boys. Lumberjacks and Teamsters. *Unknown.* OuSiCo

And here's the happy bounding flea. The Flea [*or* The Happy Bounding Flea]. Roland Young. SiTL; WaKn; WhC

And him beside rides fierce revenging Wrath. Spenser. *Fr.* The Faerie Queene, I. MyFE

And Him evermore I beheld. Follow Me. Longfellow. PGD

And His Name Shall Be Called Wonderful. Martha Snell Nicholson. BePJ

And his son Judas, who was called Maccabeus. Judas Maccabeus. First Maccabees, Bible, Apocrypha. TrJP

And hither Pallas flew; and left the Maid. Nausicaa and Odysseus; the Meeting. Homer, *tr. by* George Chapman. *Fr.* The Odyssey, VI. GrR

And how will fancy lead his life to-day? New Day. Harold Monro. ChMo; CMP

And I am only a little man. A Little Man. *Unknown.* SiTL

"And I fare you well, Lady Ouncebell." Lord Lovel (A *vers.*). *Unknown.* ABS; BaBo; ESPB

And I have come upon this place. L'An Trentiesme de Mon Eage (*or* Age) [*or* In My Thirtieth Year]. Archibald MacLeish. AnFE; APA; CoAnAm; LiTM; MAP; MoAmPo; MoVE; NePA; NP; TBM; TriL; TwAmPo

And I have felt/ A presence. Wordsworth. *Fr.* Lines Composed a Few Miles above Tintern Abbey. UnW

And I have learned how diving's done. Fantasia. Dorothy Livesay. BoCaPo (1948 ed.); TwCV

And I Have Loved Thee, Ocean! Byron. *See* Ocean, The.

And I Have Seen Again the Marvelous Child. Paul Verlaine, *tr. fr. French by* Vernon Watkins. AnFP (Sonnet.) LiTW; MiFP

"And I, if I Be Lifted Up, Shall Draw All Men." E. P. Dickie. MaRV ("If I Be Lifted Up.") ChIP

And I mankind/ Have not in mind. My Love That Mourneth for Me. John Gwynneth. AnEC

And I said, Oh that I had wings like a dove. *Fr.* Psalm LV, Bible, *O.T.* BoFr

And I said to myself I will build a house. The Little House. Struthers Burt. NoCaPo

And I said to the man who stood at the gate of the year. M. Louise Haskins. *Fr.* The Gate of the Year. MaRV; TreFS

And I saw a great white throne. The Last Judgment. Revelation, Bible, *N.T.* TreF

And I saw a new heaven and a new earth. The New Jerusalem. Revelation, Bible, *N.T.* EM-1; TrGrPo

And I thought of how impossibly alone we were. After a Game of Squash. Samuel L. Albert. GoYe; NePoAm-2

And I wake in the darkness and find darkness paled to defulgent light. Werewolf. Arthur Inman. DaM

And I will war, at least in words (and—should). His Politics. Byron. *Fr.* Don Juan, IX. GEPC

And ich bowede my body and bihelde al aboute. A Vision of Nature. William Langland. *Fr.* The Vision of Piers Plowman. PoEL-1

And if an eye may save or slay. Sir Thomas Wyatt. SiPS

And If at Last. Louise Labé, *tr. fr. French by* Frederic Prokosch. LiTW

And if by such bright tokens. To Our Lady, the Ark of the Covenants. Raymond E. F. Larsson. ISi

And if Fate remember later, and come to claim her due. Carpe Diem. "Laurence Hope." OtMeF

And if he ever should come back. The Last Words. Maeterlinck. AWP; JAWP; WBP

And if he should come again. Ylen's Song. Richard Hovey. *Fr.* The Birth of Galahad. AA

"And if he's gone away," said she. Story. Dorothy Parker. InMe; MaC

And if his sun depart. Love's Storm. Ibn Sa'id of Alcala la Real. MooP

And if I came not again. An Old Song. Fannie Stearns Davis. AV

And If I Did, What Then? George Gascoigne. *Fr.* The Adventures of Master F. I. EIL; FaBoEn; PoEL-1; ReIE (Farewell, A.) LoBV; OBSC

And if I hadde y-taken for to wryte. The Death of Troilus. Chaucer. *Fr.* Troilus and Criseyde. PoD

And if I have a soldier's head. *Unknown.* *Fr.* Penitentes. SiB

And if I loved you Wednesday. Thursday. Edna St. Vincent Millay. InMe; PR

And if, my friend, you'd have it end. They Part. Dorothy Parker. ALV

And if my heart be scarred and burned. Incurable. Dorothy Parker. PR

And if some day. Thomas Hardy. EG

And if the dead, and the dead/ Of spirit now join. The Conspirators. Frederic Prokosch. LiTM; NAMP; NePA; WaP

And if tomorrow shall be sad. Today. *Unknown.* OQP; QP-2

And if tonight my soul may find her peace. Shadows. D. H. Lawrence. BrBE; OAEP (2d ed.)

And if ye stand in doubt/ Who brought this rhyme about. John Skelton. *Fr.* Colin Clout. ReEn

And, if you asked of him to say. Charles Stuart Calverley. *Fr.* Gemini and Virgo. FiBHP
And if you meet the Canon of Chimay. Concerning Geffray Teste Noire. William Morris. PoVP; ViPo; VLEP
And I'll have him sing how once a king, of wilful malice bent. Summer Joys. Theocritus. *Fr.* Idylls. LiA
And in Her Morning. Jessica Powers. ISi
And in September, O what keen delight. Of the Months: September. Folgore da San Geminiano. AWP
And in strange lands. I Shall Remember. H. D. Carberry. PoNe
And in that faroff age when Amphitryoniades. Propertius. Elegies, IV, 9. LaP
And in that land dwells a king. Sir Cawline. *Unknown.* ESPB
And in the frosty season, when the sun. On the Frozen Lake [*or* Skating]. Wordsworth. *Fr.* The Prelude. FaBoCh; GN; GoTP; InP; LoGBV; MyFE; PoMa; ShBV-3
"And in the Grave We're Safe, Surely." *Unknown, tr. fr. Greek by* F. L. Lucas. GrPE
And in the Hanging Gardens. Conrad Aiken. MAP; MAPA; MoAB; MoAmPo; MOAP
And in the midst of all a fountaine stood. The Bower of Bliss. Spenser. *Fr.* The Faerie Queene, II. CH
And, in the night, the Spirit came. The Messenger. Alfred Noyes. GoBC
And in the nights of winter. Macaulay. *Fr.* Horatius. AlDL
And in the sixth month, the angel Gabriel was sent from God. Mary and Gabriel. St. Luke, Bible, *N.T.* (*Douay vers.*). ISi
And is he gone, whom these arms held but now. Quaerit Jesum Suum Maria. Richard Crashaw. ACP; CAW
And Is It Night? *Unknown.* ElL
And is the swallow gone? The Departure of the Swallow. William Howitt. LPS-2; VA
And is there care in heaven? and is there love. Ministering Angels [*or* The Bright Squadrons *or* Guardian Angels *or* Heavenly Aid]. Spenser. *Fr.* The Faerie Queene, II. CBE; GoBC; LPS-2; MaRV; OBSC; OxBoCh; PC
And is this—Yarrow!—This the stream. Yarrow Visited [1814]. Wordsworth. BEL; BPN; EM-2; EmBrPo; EnLi-2; EnRP; ERP; GEPC; GTBS; GTBS-D; GTBS-W; GTSL; HBV
And Ishmael crouch'd beside a crackling briar. Ishmael. Herbert Edward Palmer. OBEV (new ed.); POTE
And it came to pass after these things, that God did tempt Abraham. Abraham and Isaac. Genesis, Bible, *O.T.* EnLi-1 (1949 ed.); OuHeWo
And It Came to Pass at Midnight. Yannai, *tr. fr. Hebrew.* TrJP
And it came to pass in an eveningtide. David and Bathsheba [*or* David and Uriah, the Hittite]. Second Samuel, Bible, *O.T.* EM-1; OuHeWo
And it came to pass in those days. The Adoration of the Shepherds [*or* The Birth of Jesus *or* The First Christmas]. St. Luke, Bible, *N.T.* ChrBoLe; CLS; EM-1; TreFS
And it fayrlye befell so fayr me bethought. *Unknown.* NBE
And it shall come to pass in the day that the Lord shall give thee rest. Isaiah, Bible, *O.T.* PoFr
And it shall come to pass in the end of days. In the End of Days. Isaiah, Bible, *O.T.* TrJP
And it shall come to pass in the latter days. Swords and Plowshares. Isaiah, Bible, *O.T.* GrCo-1
And it shall come to pass when the days shall grow long. When the Days Shall Grow Long. Hayyim Nahman Bialik. TrJP
And it was I who had a dream. Happiness. Grethe Heltberg. BoDS
And it was in the winter. Contrast. Charles Granville Hamilton. ChIP
And it was night to morning, and the cocks full oft they crew. The Cid's Farewell to His Wife. *Unknown. Fr.* The Cid. AnSpL-1
And it's fare you well, fare you well. Runagate Runagate. Robert E. Hayden. PoNe
And it's ladies to the center. Shoot the Buffalo. *Unknown.* ABF
And it's Quarter Less Twain. Soundings at Memphis. *Unknown.* StDa
And Jephthah vowed a vow unto the Lord. Jephthah's Daughter. Judges, Bible, *O.T.* OuHeWo
And Jesus answered them, saying, The hour is come. Children of the Light. St. John, Bible, *N.T.* WoL
And Jesus said, A certain man had two sons. St. Luke, Bible, *N.T.* LO
And Jesus said unto them, I am the bread of life. I Am the Bread of Life. St. John, Bible, *N.T.* TreFS
And Jesus Wept. Matthew Bridges. BePJ
And Job spake, and said: Let the day perish wherein I was born. Job, Bible, *O.T.* BrBE
And just by crossing the short sea. Channel Crossing. George Barker. ChMP
And King Olaf heard the cry. King Olaf's Return. Longfellow. *Fr.* The Saga of King Olaf. AmPP (4th ed.)
And ladders leaning against damson trees. The Looker-on. Frank Kendon. POTE
And last of all/ Camilla rode, leading her troops on horseback. Camilla. Virgil. *Fr.* The Aeneid, VII. LaP
And learn O voyager to walk. The Seafarer. Archibald MacLeish. CoV; TwHP
And Left Me Stranded on a Hush. Doyle Hennessy. JKCP (1955 ed.)
"And Left the Thorn." Thymocles, *tr. fr. Greek by* F. L. Lucas. GrPE
And let the canakin clink, [clink]. Shakespeare. *Fr.* Othello, II, iii. LiBL
And Lightly, like the Flowers. Pierre de Ronsard, *tr. fr. French by* W. E. Henley. AWP; PIAE
And like a dying lady, lean and pale. The Moon [*or* The Waning Moon]. Shelley. AnFE; BLV; BoLiVe; CBE; CH; ChER; FaBoCh; LoGBV; OBEV; PIAE; TrGrPo
And like the riptide riven reef-swirls. Reef Wrack. Clement B. Christesen. BoAu
And like thy father sing in tunefulness. A Barren Soul. Joseph Ezobi. *Fr.* The Silver Bowl. TrJP
And lo! it shines upon the cities. Epilogue. Margarita Aliger. *Fr.* Your Victory. TrRV
And, lo! leading a blessed host comes one. Lincoln. Harriet Monroe. *Fr.* Commemoration Ode. AA
And lo! the Dame Xiména came with her daughters twain. His Wife and Daughters Come to the Exiled One. *Unknown. Fr.* The Cid. TeCS
And lo! the sea that fleets about the land. *See* For lo! the sea that fleets about the land.
"And Lo, the Star!" Molly Anderson Haley. PGD
And long it irked his father when he tried. The Taming of Pegasus [*or* Bellerophon]. Pindar. *Fr.* Olympian Odes, XIII. GrR; OxBG
And Los beheld the mild Emanation, Jerusalem, eastward bending. In Deadly Fear. Blake. *Fr.* Jerusalem. SeCePo
And Love Hung Still. Louis MacNeice. LiTL; LoPo; LoPS; MoBrPo
"And Man is left alone with Man." 'Tis well! At the Worst. Israel Zangwill. WGRP
And many a dark and youthful night. Night and Day. Ibn Darraj. MooP
And many an endless, endless lake. Wordsworth. *Fr.* Ruth. MyFE
And Mary rising up in those days. Mary and Elizabeth. St. Luke, Bible, *N.T.* (*Douay vers.*). ISi
And Mary said, "Before the void was filled." Ex Maria Virgine. Norbert Engels. ISi
And Mary said: My soul doth magnify the Lord. The Magnificat. St. Luke, Bible, *N.T.* (*Douay vers.*). ISi
And Mary stood beside the cross! Her soul. Mary at the Cross. Clyde McGee. BPP; MaRV; PGD
And mathematics, fresh as May. Edmund Blunden. *Fr.* Reliques. ImOP
And may my humble dwelling stand. Matthew Green. *Fr.* The Spleen. LoBV
And me happiest when I compose poems. The Birth of Tragedy. Irving Layton. PeCV
And Medon answer made, the man of skill. Penelope Forlorn. Homer. *Fr.* The Odyssey, IV. OxBG
And mightier grew the joy to meet full-faced. Swimming. Swinburne. *Fr.* Tristram of Lyonesse. GN
And Monelle said: I will speak to you of actions. Actions. Marcel Schwob. TrJP
And Monelle said: I will speak to you of moments. Moments. Marcel Schwob. TrJP
And Monelle said: I will speak to you of things dead. Things Dead. Marcel Schwob. TrJP
And mony ane sings o' grass, o' grass. *Unknown. Fr.* The Birth of Robin Hood. ViBoPo
And more to lulle him in his slumber soft. Spenser. *Fr.* The Faerie Queene, I. PC
And much fruit, the swan. See in the Midst of Fair Leaves. Marianne Moore. MoAB
And must I say that God is Christ. Faith. Edwin McNeill Poteat. ChIP; MaRV
And must the old priest wake with fright. The Priest and the Pirate. Hervey Allen. LS
. . . And my dear one sat in the shadows; very softly she wept. Ford Madox Ford. *Fr.* On Heaven. ViBoPo
And my poor fool is hang'd! No, no, no life! Death of Lear [*or* My Poore Foole]. Shakespeare. *Fr.* King Lear, V, iii. FiP; LiA; PoD
And my roan: a brand. The Roan. Ibn Khafaja. MooP
And my young sweetheart sat at board with me. Idyl. Alfred Mombert. AWP; JAWP; WBP
And Naomi said/ Unto her two daughters-in-law. Naomi and Ruth. Ruth, Bible, *O.T.* TrJP
And natheless there is no man. *Unknown.* LO
And nature, the old nurse, took. The Manuscripts of God. Longfellow. *Fr.* The Fiftieth Birthday of Agassiz. MaRV
And near some river-mouth—shoal—marshy-wide. Alfred Domett. *Fr.* Ranolf and Amohia. AnNZ

And Nestor, the Gerenian knight, replied. At Pylos. Homer. *Fr.* The Odyssey, III. OxBG
And new Philosophy calls all in doubt. The New Philosophy. John Donne. *Fr.* An Anatomy of the World. ExPo
And next in order sad Old Age we found. Old Age. Thomas Sackville. *Fr.* Induction to "The Mirror for Magistrates." BCEP
And Nicodemus came by night. Nicodemus. Harry Kemp. OQP; QP-2
And Nimrod cried aloud, "Lord, I am he." Anna Hempstead Branch. *Fr.* Nimrod. BAP
And "No" she answered to his plea. Ballad of the Huntsman. Selma Robinson. PIAE
And none but Love their woeful hap did rue. *Unknown.* *Fr.* Love Winged My Hopes. LO
And nor will these tears be the last. Nor Will These Tears Be the Last. Goethe. LiTW
"And Now . . ." J. B. Boothroyd. FiBHP
And now all nature seemed in love. On a [or the] Bank as I Sat a-Fishing [or A Description of the Spring or A May Day]. Sir Henry Wotton. CH; ElSeCe; EV-2; LoBV; MyFE; OBS; SeCL; WP
And now another day is gone. An Evening Prayer. Isaac Watts. MeMeAg
And now arriving at the isle, he springs. Homer. *Fr.* The Odyssey, V. GrPo
And now at last I come to it: spring. Spring, etc. Reed Whittemore. WaKn
And now at length the joyful time drew on. Endymion's Convoy. Michael Drayton. *Fr.* Endimion and Phoebe. OBSC
And now before the new-built shrine. Horace. Odes, I, 31. LaP
And now, behold! as at the approach of the morning. The Celestial Pilot. Dante. *Fr.* Divina Commedia: Purgatorio. WGRP
And now behold your tender nurse, the air. The Dancing of the Air. Sir John Davies. *Fr.* Orchestra. LPS-2
And now Cyllenian Hermes summon'd forth. The Last Journey of the Wooers [or Limbo; the Shades of the Suitors]. Homer. *Fr.* The Odyssey, XXIV. GrR; OxBG
And now Duke William marèshall'd his band. Thomas Chatterton. *Fr.* Battle of Hastings. TCEP
And Now Dwell Thou, I Pray. Christian Morgenstern, *tr. fr. German by* R. G. L. Barrett. AnGP
And now farewell, my friend. To John Fiorini. C. R. Holmes. PtPa
And now four days the sun had seen our woes. The Great Fire. Dryden. *Fr.* Annus Mirabilis. FiP
And now gentlemen. The Base of All Metaphysics. Walt Whitman. BoFr; CaAE; NePA
And, now gives Time, her states description. George Chapman. *Fr.* Euthymiae Raptus. PoEL-2
And now he slinks through dark Oblivion's gate. Harry Thurston Peck. *Fr.* Jefferson Davis. BoHiPo
And now I go with the departing sun. Amoris Finis. George Frederick Cameron. CPG
And now I have another lad! The Danger of Writing Defiant Verse. Dorothy Parker. InMe
And now I shall speak my word to the men of peace. I Announce the Kingdom of the Star. Jacinto Fombona Pachano. TwSpPo
And now in age I bud again. George Herbert. *Fr.* The Flower. BCEP
And now, kind friends, what I have wrote. What I Have Wrote. Julia A. Moore. FiBHP; SiTL
And now Love sang: but his was such a song. Willowwood, 2. Dante Gabriel Rossetti. The House of Life, L. BPN; EmBrPo; OAEP; POTT; PoVP; ReaPo; TCEP; ViP; ViPo; VLEP
And now, man-slaughtering Pallas tooke in hand. The End of the Suitors. Homer. *Fr.* The Odyssey, XXII. OBS
And now methinks I could e'en chide myself. To His Mistress' Skull. Cyril Tourneur. Fr. The Revenger's Tragedy. CoEV; PoD; ViBoPo
"And now, my clerks who go in fur or feather." Saint Francis Endeth His Sermon. Louise Imogen Guiney. SaFP
And now, O shaken from thine antique throne. Francis Thompson. *Fr.* Ode to the Setting Sun. VLEP
And now on lonely walks by hill and lake. William Ellery Leonard. *Fr.* Two Lives, Pt. III. MOAP
And now only I still remain to gather the strands. The Final Soliloquy. Colin Thiele. *Fr.* Burke and Wills. NeLNL
And now, perchd prowdlie on the topmost spray. Evening. William Julius Mickle. *Fr.* The Concubine. RO
"And now," said the Governor, gazing abroad on the piled-up store. The First Thanksgiving Day. Margaret Junkin Preston. HiLiAm; MC; PAH
And now she cleans her teeth into the lake. Camping Out. William Empson. FaBoMo; MoVE
And now, since thou hast nerved thee for the act. Clytemnestra's Dream. Aeschylus. *Fr.* Choephoroe. GrR
And now spring. Tanka, VI. Lewis Alexander. CDC
And now take thought, my sonnet, who is he. Sonnets of the Months: Conclusion. Folgore da San Gemignano. AWP; LyPI
And now th'art set wide ope, the speare's sad art. I Am the Door. Richard Crashaw. OAEP
And now that man prepares for doom. Interlude. Idris Davies. MoWP
And now the cypress stature of Salámán. Absál Tempts Salámán. Jami. *Fr.* Salámán and Absál. PeP
And now the dawn was breaking and morning coming on. Dawn in the Town. *Unknown.* *Fr.* The Cid. TeCS
And now the earth they had spurned rose up against them in anger. The Flight. C. Day Lewis. *Fr.* A Time to Dance. FaBoMo
And now the herald came, leading with care. The Minstrel Worthy of His Hire. Homer. *Fr.* The Odyssey, VIII. GrR
And now the Lady Gundelil. Sir Palle's Bridal. *Unknown.* BoDaBa
And now the long, long lines of the Nation's graves. For Decoration Day, II. Rupert Hughes. AA; MDAH
And now the maiden Hero walked to Aphrodite's temple. Musaeus. *Fr.* Hero and Leander. GrPo
And now the prayer is over and the mass in its due course. The Farewell. *Unknown.* *Fr.* The Cid. TeCS
And now the sea-scoured temptress, having failed. The Re-Birth of Venus. Geoffrey Hill. NePoEA
And now the silver-footed Queen had her ascension made. Visit of Thetis to Hephaistos. Homer. *Fr.* The Iliad, XVIII. GrR
And now the swain young Svejdal. Young Svejdal. *Unknown.* BoDaBa
And now the trembling light. Shoreham. Samuel Palmer. RO
And Now There Is Nothing Left. George Barker. LiTM (rev. ed.)
("And now there is nothing left to celebrate.") NeBP
And now they nigh approachèd to the stead. The Mermaids. Spenser. *Fr.* The Faerie Queene, II, 12. ChTr
And now 'tis time; for their officious haste. Heroic [or Heroique] Stanzas. Dryden. CEP; SeCV-2
And now, to all the other memories. Threnody for a Pet Cat. Mazie V. Caruthers. CIV
"And now to God the Father," he ends. In Church. Thomas Hardy. *Fr.* Satires of Circumstance. MoAB; MBP; MoBrPo
And now to proceed: since I have explained in what way everything might come to pass. Evolution of Life and Society. Lucretius. *Fr.* De Rerum Natura. RoL
And now to the abbyss I pass. Andrew Marvell. *Fr.* Appleton House. AtBAP
And now to what remains!—Since I've resolved. Origins of Vegetable and Animal Life. Lucretius, *tr. by* William Ellery Leonard. *Fr.* De Rerum Natura. OuHeWo
And now, unveil'd, the toilet stands display'd. The Toilet [or Belinda's Morning]. Pope. *Fr.* The Rape of the Lock. BCEP; BrBE; CoEV; ExPo; LEAP; LPS-2; OBEC
And now we climb this bare eroded hill. Dombashawa. Peter Jackson. BoSA
And now we will write the praises of our Lady. Weddase Maryam. *Unknown.* ISi
And now what are we? unbelievers both. In Doubt of Doubt. Robert Browning. *Fr.* Bishop Blougram's Apology. MaRV
And now what monarch would not gardener be. To Amanda Walking in the Garden. Nicholas Hookes. SeCL
And Now Where're He Strays. Richard Crashaw. LiTG
And now, with gleams of half-extinguished thought. Wordsworth. *Fr.* Tintern Abbey. ViBoPo
And now you live dispersed on ribbon roads. T. S. Eliot. *Fr.* The Rock. TiPo
And O and O,/ The daisies blow. Song of Spring. Keats. BoTP
And oh! if he should come again one day. If He Should Come Again. Maeterlinck. MiFP
"And Oh!—That the Man I Am Might Cease to Be." D. H. Lawrence. BrBE
And O the Wind. Witter Bynner. VOD
And, oh! there lives within my heart. A Hope. Anne Brontë. MaRV
And oh, to think the sun can shine. Adelaide Neilson. William Winter. AA
And Odysseus of many counsels answered him saying. Homer. *Fr.* The Odyssey, IX. GrL
And of Laughter That Was a Changeling. Elizabeth Rendall. HBMV
And oft he traced the uplands, to survey. James Beattie. *Fr.* The Minstrel. EnSW
And oft I did refrain. Continence. Ibn Faraj. MooP
And oft, while wonder thrill'd my breast, mine eyes. Waterspout. Luis de Camões. EtS
And on her lover's arm she leant. The Departure. Tennyson. *Fr.* The Day-Dream. LPS-1; TriL
And on My Eyes Dark Sleep by Night. "Michael Field." OBMV

And on that day, upon the heavenly scarp. Psalm VI [*or* Upon the Heavenly Scarp]. A. M. Klein. *Fr.* The Psalter of Avram Haktani. BoCaPo; PeCV

And on the wall was limned a mouldering corse. On the Wall. Immanuel di Roma. TrJP

And on This Shore. M. Carl Holman. PoNe

And once again a face has fled away. Indolent Heart. Franz Werfel. BoFr

And once again I was within that house. The Dream. John Peale Bishop. LiTA; LiTM (rev. ed.)

And once, in some swamp-forest, these. Coal Fire. Louis Untermeyer. GoTP

And once more the necromancer. The White Kite. *Unknown.* *Fr.* Song of Quetzalcoatl. LiTW

And one morning while in the woods. Between the World and Me. Richard Wright. PoNe

And One Shall Live in Two. Jonathan Henderson Brooks. PoNe

"And one that dips with me the sop."—"Not I!" Judas. Howard McKinley Corning. ChIP

And Only Our Shadow Walks with Us. Eithne Wilkins. NeBP

And/Or. Clarence Day. WhC

And over his head/ Birds without number are flying. Orpheus. Simonides. GrL; OxBG

And owe we not these visions. Philip Pendleton Cooke. *Fr.* The Power of the Bards. SPP

And Paris be it or Helen dying. Fragment on [*or* of] Death. Villon, *tr. by* Swinburne. AWP; OuHeWo

And Pergamos,/ City of the Phrygians. Chorus. Euripides. *Fr.* Iphigenia in Aulis. AWP; LiTW

And Phoebus stooped under the craggy roof. Hymn to Mercury [*or* Pocket-Cattle-Thief]. *Unknown.* *Fr.* Homeric Hymns. GrPo; GrR; LiTW

"And pray, who are you?" The Tax-Gatherer. John Banister Tabb. GN; UTS

And Rest in a Flame. Francis Maguire. JKCP (1955 ed.)

"And ride in triumph through Persepolis!" Christopher Marlowe. *Fr.* Tamburlaine the Great, Pt. I, Act II, sc. v. BCEP; MyFE; TrGrPo; WHA

And rise, O moon, from yonder down. Tennyson. *Fr.* In Memoriam A. H. H.: Epilogue. BrBE; EPP; LEAP; OAEP; RiBV

And round these men spread the sub-tropic latitudes. Anthony Delius. *Fr.* The Great Divide. BoSA

And Ruth said, "Intreat [*or* Entreat] me not to leave thee." Intreat Me Not to Leave Thee [*or* Address of Ruth to Naomi]. Ruth, Bible, *O.T.* GBV (1952 ed.); LO; TreF

And said I that my limbs were old. Love. Sir Walter Scott. *Fr.* The Lay of the Last Minstrel, III. BSV; EV-4; LPS-2

And Saul's servants said unto him, Behold now, an evil spirit. Saul, David, and Jonathan. First Samuel *and* Second Samuel, Bible, *O.T.* BoFr

And "Science" said. The Dunce. Walter de la Mare. ImOP

And seeing the multitudes, he went up into a mountain. The Sermon on the Mount. St. Matthew, Bible, *N.T.* EM-1; OuHeWo; ReIE; TreF; WoL

And shall I then the fact deny? Sir Eustace Grey. George Crabbe. MyFE

And shall I weep that Love's no more. Le Roi Est Mort. Agnes Mary Frances Robinson. OBVV

And shall one woman rule me all my years. Gather Ye Roses. Johannes Secundus. Elegies, I, 5. LaP

And Shall Trelawny Die? Robert Stephen Hawker. *See* Song of the Western Men, The.

And she clothed her in vesture floating in many a lovely fold. The Vesting of Aphrodite. *Unknown.* *Fr.* Homeric Hymns. GrR

And she has trod before me in these ways! In Her Paths. Francis Thompson. VLEP

And she is with me—years roll, I shall change. Andromeda. Robert Browning. *Fr.* Pauline. OBRV

And She Washed His Feet with Her Tears, and Wiped Them with the Hairs of Her Head. Sir Edward Sherburne, *after the Italian of* Giambattista Marini. AEV; ChTr; MeLP; MeRV; OBS; OxBoCh; SeCL; SeEP (Magdalen, The.) ACP; GoBC

And should my soul be torn with grief. My Bible. Edgar A. Guest. *Fr* My Books and I. MaRV

And Simeon blessed them, and said to Mary his mother. Mary and Simeon. St. Luke, Bible, *N.T.* (*Douay vers.*). ISi

And since he rowed his father home. The Blind Rower. W. W. Gibson. POTT

And since to live men labour, only knowing. Labour. V. Sackville-West. *Fr.* The Land. TwCV

And sitting down they watched him there. Gambler [*or* He Was a Gambler Too]. G. A. Studdert-Kennedy. ChIP; MaRV; QS

And sleeps thy heart when flower and tree. Summer. Johannes Carl Andersen. BoAu

And slowly answered Arthur from the barge. Tennyson. *Fr.* Morte D'Arthur (*also in* Idylls of the King: The Passing of Arthur). FaBoEn; GTSL

And so! already here thou art upon the table. Before a Corpse. Manuel Acuña. PoP

And so an easier life our Cyclops drew. The Cyclops. Theocritus, *tr. by* Elizabeth Barrett Browning. Idylls, XI. AWP; EnLi-1; JAWP; OuHeWo; WBP

And so, Anne Everard, in those leafy Junes. Anne's Book. Mary Webb. OnPP

And So at Last. David Starr Jordan. MaRV

And so befell that once upon a day. The Friar's Tale. Chaucer. *Fr.* The Canterbury Tales. BCEP

And so bifel, whan comen was the tyme. Chaucer. *Fr.* Troilus and Criseyde, I. EPP

And so, dishonest ghost, you found not Heaven. To a Spirit Seen in a Dream. Lord Dunsany. UnW

And so, farewell for ever. George Chapman. *Fr.* The Tragedy of Charles, Duke of Byron. MyFE

And so he called her Pigeon. Husband Betrayed. John Crowe Ransom. TwAmPo

And so he groan'd, as one by beauty slain. The Indian Maid. Keats. *Fr.* Endymion, IV. ERP

And so I must lose her whose mind. Prothalamium. Donagh MacDonagh. NeIP

And so it came to that last day. The Wanderer: St. James' Grove. William Carlos Williams. TwAmPo

And So It Goes. Thad Stem, Jr. NoCaPo (rev. ed.)

And so, like most young poets, in a flush. The Ferment of New Wine. Elizabeth Barrett Browning. *Fr.* Aurora Leigh, I. VA

And so, one day when the tide was away out. The Farewell. Pat Wilson. AnNZ

And so our royal relative is dead! A Dirge Concerning the Late Lamented King of the Cannibal Islands. William Augustus Croffut. BOHV; InMe

And So the Day Drops By. Frederick Goddard Tuckerman. AnNE

And so the Mother, shutting up the duty-book. Seven-year-old Poet. Arthur Rimbaud. OnHM

And so the river moves. The Lost Children. Richard Eberhart. NePoAm-2

And so the wrinkled squaw began. Lionel Haweis. *Fr.* Tsoqalem, the Cowichan Monster. CPG

And so to a chambre full solacious. Dame Music. Stephen Hawes. *Fr.* The Pastime of Pleasure. PoEL-1

And so unto the End of Graves came he. Estunt the Griff. Kipling. PA

And so we labored all the good night long. At the Last. Vincent David Engels. CAW

And so we two came where the rest have come. The Question. F. T. Prince. ChMP

And so when a year had passed, as the circling seasons sped. Birth of the Muses. Hesiod. *Fr.* Theogony. GrR

And so, when the time came. In Memoriam. Frank A. Collymore. PoNe

And so, with feet God meant should cling. To a Bird on a Downtown Wire. Hilton Ross Greer. BLA

And so you find them somewhat thin. The Old Songs. Sir Owen Seaman. InMe

And so you found that poor room dull. Appearances. Robert Browning. BPN; PoVP

And so your head aches friend? Inscription for a Smyrna Privy. Agathias Scholasticus. LyMA

And softe he cougheth with a semysoun. Young Woman. Chaucer. *Fr.* The Canterbury Tales: The Miller's Tale. BoW

And some, to be large cyphers in a state. Pleased with an Empty Swelling. Swift. *Fr.* Ode to Dr. William Sancroft. BeR

And sometimes in the cool night I see you are an animal. Ode for Soft Voice. Michael McClure. NeAP

And sometimes the speech. Invisible Trumpets Blowing. E. J. Pratt. *Fr.* Brébeuf and His Brethren. CaP

And, star and system rolling past. Tennyson. *Fr.* In Memoriam A. H. H.: Epilogue. ImOP

And still the night of history gives birth. On Rereading Shelley. Bryllion Fagin. MuM

And still the picnickers come on. Sunday in the Park. William Carlos Williams. *Fr.* Paterson. CrMA

And still they come and go: and this is all I know. Picture-Show. Siegfried Sassoon. ChMo; CMP

And still upon my cheek I feel their breath. Evanescence. Hugo von Hofmannsthal. AnGP

And still we climbed. On the Palisades. Louis Untermeyer. POT; PoTo

And such did Paris come/ Unto Atrides' home. Menelaus Abandoned. Aeschylus. *Fr.* Agamemnon. LiA

And Suddenly It's Evening. Salvatore Quasimodo, *tr. fr. Italian by* Glauco Cambon. OnPM

And suddenly the flowing night stands still. Burning Bush. Louis Untermeyer. MAP

And summer mornings the mute child, rebellious. Eleven. Archibald MacLeish. ChMo; CMP; PoLFOT

And take the garland from your head, Menecthenus! The Eve of the Festival. Stefan George. AnGP

And Tangi and his tribe thus much had gained. Alfred Domett. *Fr.* Ranolf and Amohia. AnNZ

And tears burst forth from those aged eyelids. Jason's Father Sees His Returning Son. Pindar. *Fr.* Odes. LiA

And thanne cam Covetyse; I can him not descryve. Covetousness. William Langland. *Fr.* The Vision of Piers Plowman. CoEV

And that is all I really have to say. The Epilogue of the Wandering Jew. Colin Newbury. AnNZ

And that wild tremor, is it with thee still? When the Ecstasy Has Passed. Euripides. *Fr.* Bacchae. GrR

And that's what sits upon its torse. A Tail for the Horse. *Unknown.* SiTL

And the Age Ended. W. H. Auden. ExPo

And the betrayers of language. Ezra Pound. *Fr.* Canto XIV. MoPo

And the child grew, and waxed strong in spirit. The Child of Nazareth. St. Luke, Bible, *N.T.* ChrBoLe

And the children of Israel were fruitful. The Child Moses. Exodus, Bible, *O.T.* OuHeWo

And the corn singing Millennium! Background with Revolutionaries. Archibald MacLeish. Frescoes for Mr. Rockefeller's City, VI. ReaPo; TwHP; UnPo

And the day arrives at last, my friends. Nightmare of a Cook. Chester Kallman. CrMA

And the Dead. Sean Jennett. NeBP

And the Earth Rebelled. Yuri Suhl, *tr. fr. Yiddish by* Max Rosenfeld. TrJP

And the first grey [*or* gray] of morning fill'd the east. Sohrab and Rustum. Matthew Arnold. BEL; BPN; EmBrPo; EPN; EPP; EV-5; GEPC; HeT; PoVP; REAL; ShBV-2; TCEP; TOP; TyEnPo; ViPo; ViPP; VLEP

And the glorious son of Hippolochus answered him. The Story of Bellerophon. Homer. *Fr.* The Iliad, VI. OxBG

And the Greatness of These. J. R. Perkins. OQP; QP-2

And the high majesty of Paul's. The Wind-Fiend. W. E. Henley. *Fr.* London Voluntaries. BMEP

And the ladies dress in silk. On the High Cost of Dairy Products. James McIntyre. FiBHP

"And the Life Everlasting." Percy Clough Ainsworth. MaRV

And the Lord God whispered and said to me. Angela Morgan. *Fr.* God Prays. OQP; QP-1

And the Lord said, Simon, Simon. Jesus, Judas, and Peter. St. Luke, Bible, *N.T.* BoFr

And the Lord said to Moses. *Unknown.* SiTL

And the Lord said unto Samuel, How long wilt thou mourn for Saul. David and Goliath. First Samuel, Bible, *O.T.* TreFS

And the Mother, closing the exercise book. Poets Seven Years Old. Arthur Rimbaud. AnFP

And the news. "Andrei Bely." *Fr.* Christ Is Risen. TrRV

And the next who came in was a sailor. When Johnson's Ale Was New. *Unknown.* ShS

And the other creatures on the face of the earth. God's Little Creatures: Foreword. Joaquin Antonio Peñalosa. SaFP

And the raying sun from behind breaks out east. Heraclitus in the West. Charles G. Bell. NePoAm

And the Sabbath drew on. The First Easter. St. Luke, Bible, *N.T.* EOAH

And the sea parted before and closed again behind. The Discovery. Charles Brasch. *Fr.* Genesis. AnNZ

And the traveller hopes: "Let me be far from any/ Physician." Journey to Iceland. W. H. Auden. BrBE

And the trunk: "So sweet those words to me that I." Pier delle Vigne. Dante. *Fr.* Divina Commedia: Inferno. HoPM

And the voice that was calmer [*or* softer] than silence said. James Russell Lowell. *Fr.* The Vision of Sir Launfal, Pt. II. ChIP; MaRV

And the whole multitude of them arose. The Death of Jesus. St. Luke, Bible, *N.T.* TreF

And the word of the Lord came unto me, saying. Unfaithful Shepherds. Ezekiel, Bible, *O.T.* WoL

"And the Word Was Made Flesh." Laurence Housman. MaRV

And the World's Face. Julian Symons. WaP

And their faces were pale. Departure. Guillaume Apollinaire. OnPM

And then/ He made the stars also. Stars. Florence S. Edsall. MoSiPe

And then came Iris as a messenger. Homer. *Fr.* The Iliad, III. GrPo

And Then Her Burial. Merrill Moore. MAP; MoAmPo (1942 ed.)

And then I pressed the shell. The Shell. James Stephens. AlDL; BLV; BoTP; CH; ChMo; CMP; EPP; MBP; MM; MoAB; MoBrPo; MoShBr; MoVE; NeMA; PoeMoYo; POT; POTE; PoTo; YT

And then I sat me down, and gave the rein. Sonnets, II. Gustave Rosenhane. AWP; JAWP; WBP

And Then No More. Friedrich Rückert, *tr. fr. German by* James Clarence Mangan. AnIV; BLPA; GTIV; IrPN

And then one day Hershey played by the door. You Are a Jew! Delmore Schwartz. *Fr.* Genesis. TrJP

And then she saw me creeping. Fossils. James Stephens. OnYI

And Then There. Frantisek Halas, *tr. fr. Czech by* Michael Flach. LiTW

And then went down to the ship. Canto I. Ezra Pound. AmPP; AtBAP; CoBMV; CoV; LiTA; MAP; MoAB; MoAmPo; MoVE; SeCeV; TrGrPo (rev. ed.)

And there a lovely cloistered court he found. The Lady of the Land. William Morris. *Fr.* The Earthly Paradise. EPP; TOP; VLEP

And there appeared a great wonder in heaven. Revelation, Bible, *N.T.* CAW

And there followed him a great company of people. St. Luke, Bible, *N.T.* LO

And there I found a gray and ancient ass. Pegasus Lost. Elinor Wylie. MAP; MoAmPo; NeMA

And there I saw the seed upon the mountain. Preludes to Definition, I. Conrad Aiken. TwAmPo

And there illustrious Vulcan also wrought. Homer. *Fr.* The Iliad, XVIII. GrPo

And there is little Selma. Selma. Herman Wildenvey. AnNoLy

And There Shall Be No More Death, *sel.* Ruth Gilbert. "That which the long scythe whispered to the grass." AnNZ

And There Shall Come Forth. Isaiah, Bible, *O.T. See* Rod of Jesse, The.

And there she's leand her back to a thorn. The Cruel Mother. *Unknown.* ESPB

And there two runners did the sign abide. Atalanta's Race. William Morris. *Fr.* The Earthly Paradise. BEL; BMEP; BPN; EV-5; LPS-1

"And There Was a Great Calm." Thomas Hardy. ChTr; LiTM

And there was grass on the floor of the temple. Ezra Pound. *Fr.* Canto XXI. MoPo

And there was great mourning in Israel in every place. Great Mourning. First Maccabees, Bible, Apocrypha. TrJP

And there we were together again. The Return of Morgan and Fingal. E. A. Robinson. TOP

And there were in the same country shepherds abiding in the field. The Adoration of the Shepherds [*or* The First Christmas *or* Christmas Eve *or* Tidings of Great Joy]. St. Luke, Bible, *N.T.* ChBR; FaPON; GaP; MaRV; OTPC (1946 ed.); PCH; PoRL; SiSoSe

And there were spring-faced cherubs that did sleep. The Sea of Death. *Unknown.* CH

And there will be just as rich fruits to cull. After Death. R. A. K. Mason. AnNZ

And There Will I Be Buried. Thomas Davidson. BSV; EBSV

And therefore praise I even the most high. James Branch Cabell. *Fr.* Retractions. HBMV

And therefore since I have out-liv'd the date. The Writer's Tragedy. Samuel Daniel. *Fr.* The Tragedie of Philotas. LiA

And therewith cast [*or* there-with kest] I doun mine eye again. The Dawn of Love [*or* Walking under the Tour]. James I, King of Scotland. *Fr.* The Kingis Quair. EBSV; SeCePo

And these all night upon the bridge of war. The Trojan Camp-Fires. Homer. *Fr.* The Iliad, VIII. OxBG

And these few precepts in thy memory. Polonius' Advice to Laertes [*or* This above All]. Shakespeare. *Fr.* Hamlet, I, iii. GN; PoeMoYo; TrGrPo

And these mountains which my eyes have seen. The Seven Metal Mountains. Enoch, Bible, Pseudepigrapha. TrJP

And they, and all, in one loud symphony. Shelley. *Fr.* The Revolt of Islam, V. PoFr

And they have thrust our shattered dead away in foreign graves. The Martyrs of the Maine. Rupert Hughes. PAH

And They Shall Beat Their Swords into Plowshares. Micah, IV: 1-5, Bible, *O.T.* TreF

And they, the Ionians, whose first-born minds. Ideal Passion, XXVII. George Edward Woodberry. MOAP

And they who tell me of the nightingale. Ideal Passion, XVIII. George Edward Woodberry. MOAP

And this, at intervals in language bright. Maria Gowen Brooks. *Fr.* Zophiel; or, The Bride of Seven. BAV

And this comely dame. John Skelton. *Fr.* Elinor Rumming. ViBoPo

And this freedom will be the freedom of all. A Free Nation. Edwin Markham. MaRV

And this I hate—not men, nor flag, nor race. The Hymn of Hate. Joseph Dana Miller. PGD; PSO

And this is England! June's undarkened green. This Is England. Laurence Binyon. BoTP

"And this is freedom!" cried the serf; "At last." Bondage. "Owen Innsley." AA

And this is [*or* is to *or* Here's to] good old Boston. A Boston Toast. John Collins Bossidy. BLPA; BoHiPo; CenHV; GoTP; HBV; NeHB; TreFS; WhC; YaD

And this is Marathon—this sweep of plain. Marathon. Clinton Scollard. VOD

And this is the song that the white woman sings. Goosey

And this is the song (*continued*)
Goosey Gander—by Various Authors (Kipling's Version). William Percy French. CenHV
And this is the way the baby woke. The Way the Baby Woke. James Whitcomb Riley. AA
And this is to good old Boston. *See* And this is good old Boston.
And this our life exempt from public haunt. Good in Everything. Shakespeare. *Fr.* As You Like It, II, i. PoToHe
And this place our forefathers made for man! The Dungeon. Samuel Taylor Coleridge. *Fr.* Remorse (Osorio), V. MCCG
And this reft house is that the which he built. The House That Jack Built. Samuel Taylor Coleridge. BOHV; PA
And this same pallid moon tonight. Red Moon. Norman Bethune. PoP
And this was she! the peerless and the bright. Lines. Miss Holford. DiM
And those two young ladies of Birmingham. Limerick. *Unknown.* LiBL
And those who husbanded the golden grain. Omar Khayyám, *tr. by* Edward Fitzgerald. *Fr.* The Rubáiyát. PoFr
And thou, America,/ For the scheme's culmination. Walt Whitman. *Fr.* Song of the Universal, IV. PGD
And thou America,/ Thy offspring towering e'er so high. Walt Whitman. *Fr.* Song of the Exposition, VIII. GA
And Thou Art Dead, as Young and Fair. Byron. AtBAP; BPN; EM-2; EmBrPo; ERP; EV-4; PoEL-4; TOP
(Elegy on Thyrza.) GTBS; GTBS-D; GTBS-W; GTSE; GTSL
Sels.
Grief, *last 5 ll.* LiA
Poems to Thyrza, *2 sts.* PoD
And thou art gone, most loved, most honored friend! On the Late S. T. Coleridge. Washington Allston. AA
And thou art now no longer near! To the Parted One. Goethe. AWP; JAWP; WBP
"And Thou Beside Me Singing in the Wilderness." Theocritus, *tr. fr. Greek by* F. L. Lucas. *Fr.* Idylls, VIII. GrPE
And thou, blest star of Europe's darkest hour. Pitt. Reginald Heber. BHV
And Thou, Expectant . . . Amado Nervo, *tr. fr. Spanish by* Samuel Beckett. AnMP
And thou hast walked about (How strange a story!). Address to a Mummy. Horace Smith. HBV; LPS-2; TVSH
And thou, O Life, the lady of all bliss. Newborn Death, 2. Dante Gabriel Rossetti. The House of Life, C. BPN; EmBrPo; PoVP; ViPo
And Thou, O Lord! by whom are seen. Whittier. *Fr.* The Eternal Goodness. TrPWD
And thou, O Virgin, Daughter, Mother, Bride. Appeal for Illumination. Luigi Pulci, *tr. by* Byron. *Fr.* Il Morgante maggiore. ISi
And thou that art the flower of virgins all. Invocatio ad Mariam. Chaucer. *Fr.* The Canterbury Tales: The Prologue to the Second Nun's Tale. ISi
And thou wert beaten then at Waterloo? To Napoleon in Exile. Walter Channing. PoP
And thou wert sad—yet I was not with thee. Lines on Hearing That Lady Byron Was Ill. Byron. EmBrPo
And Thou! whom earth still holds, and will not yield. Wordsworth. William Wilberforce Lord. *Fr.* Ode to England. AA
And Thou Would'st Not! Winifred Stoddard LeBar. ChIP
And though my soul mix with the fatal ways. Ideal Passion, IX. George Edward Woodberry. MOAP
And Three Hundred and Sixty-six in Leap Year. Ogden Nash. NePA
And thus a moon roll'd on, and fair Haidée. Juan and Haidée. Byron. *Fr.* Don Juan, II. MaPo
And thus all-expectant abiding I waited not long, for soon. He Heard Her Sing. James Thomson. VA
And thus as we were talking to and fro. Complaint of the Common Weill of Scotland. Sir David Lindsay. GoTS
And thus at times, in Crete, the women there. Bas-Relief. Sappho. GrR
And thus I went wide-where, walking myn one. A Dream. William Langland. *Fr.* The Vision of Piers Plowman. CoEV
And thus she spoke to the bright Marygold of Leutha's Vale. The Marigold. Blake. *Fr.* Visions of the Daughters of Albion. AtBAP
And thus they fought; the iron clangour pierc'd. The Immortal Steeds [*or* The Horses] of Achilles. Homer. *Fr.* The Iliad, XVII. GrR; OxBG
And timid, funny, brisk little bunny. Christina Rossetti. *Fr.* Sing-Song. TiPo
. . . And to Dione came. The Plight of Wounded Aphrodite. Homer. *Fr.* The Iliad, V. GrR
And to the Young Men. Merrill Moore. BLV; BoLiVe (1939 ed.); MAP; MoAmPo; PreP
And, truly, I would rather be struck dumb. Keats. *Fr.* Endymion. ViBoPo
And truth, you say, is all divine. Realism. A. C. Benson. VA
And, unfortunately. The Nine Monsters. César Vallejo. TwSpPo
. . . And Uriel to his charge. Milton. *Fr.* Paradise Lost, IV. BrBE
And was it true,/ The stranger standing so. The Annunciation. John Duffy. ISi
And was not death a lusty struggler. Of a Cozener. John Hoskins. TuPP
And was the day of my delight. In Memoriam A. H. H., XXIV. Tennyson. EmBrPo; EnLi-2; EPN; GEPC; ViPo; VLEP
And was there not a king somewhere who said. She Says, Being Forbidden. Leonora Speyer. AV
And wasna he a roguey. The Piper o' Dundee. *Unknown.* EBSV
And we love Art for Art's sake. Art for Art's Sake. Marc Blitzstein. *Fr.* The Cradle Will Rock. TrJP
And we might trust these youths and maidens fair. Youth, Love, and Death. Philip James Bailey. *Fr.* Festus. VA
And welcom now (Great Monarch) to your own. Dryden. *Fr.* Astraea Redux. OBS
And well our Christian sires of old. Christmas. Sir Walter Scott. *Fr.* Marmion. ERP
And whan that he was slayn in this manere. The Assumption of Troilus. Chaucer. *Fr.* Troilus and Criseyde. CoEV
And what are you that, missing you. The Philosopher. Edna St. Vincent Millay. ChMo; CMP; PR; TOP
And what I seek I know not. Edmund John. *Fr.* Symphonie Symbolique. BCEP
And what is beauty? It is a going-home. Sonnet. Arthur Davison Ficke. MuM
And what is death? Death. James Oppenheim. WGRP
And what is faith? The anchored trust that at the core of things. Sam Walter Foss. *Fr.* The Higher Catechism. OQP; QP-1
And what is love? Misunderstanding, pain. Epigram. J. V. Cunningham. NePoAm
And what is so rare as a day in June? June [*or* A Day in June]. James Russell Lowell. *Fr.* The Vision of Sir Launfal. BBV; FaBoBe; FaFP; FaPON; GoTP; HiLiAm; NePA; OBAV; PoeMoYo; PoRL; PYM; StaSt; StVeCh (1955 ed.)
And what, my thoughtless Sons, should fire you more. Britannia's Empire. James Thomson. *Fr.* Britannia. OBEC
And what of her that took. So Great a Sweetness. W. B. Yeats. *Fr.* Friends. LiA
And what of Hodge, and where stood he. Hodge in the Strife. Maurice Hewlett. *Fr.* The Song of the Plow. PoFr
And What Shall You Say? Joseph Seamon Cotter, Jr. BANP; CDC; GrCo-1; PoNe; QS
And What Sordello Would See There. Robert Browning. *Fr.* Sordello. MyFE
And What though Winter Will Pinch Severe. Sir Walter Scott. *Fr.* Old Mortality. EnRP
(Cavalier Song.) BPN
And what were roses. Perfume? for I do. Sonnet. E.E. Cummings. NP
And when, accoutred in your mail. The Handsome Knight. Mu'tamid, King of Seville. MooP
And when he saw the multitude he went up into a mountain. St. Matthew, Bible, *N.T.* ReIE
And when he was himself again, she questioned him withal. *Unknown.* *Fr.* Tsar Lazar and Tsaritsa Militsa. PoFr
And when her broken thoughts went following after. Seven Sad Sonnets, V. Mary Aldis. HBMV
And when his youth was in its flowery spring. A Bride to the Victor. Pindar. *Fr.* Olympian Odes, I. GrR
And When I Am Entombèd. Emerson. ViBoPo
And When I Lamented. Heine, *tr. fr. German by* Emma Lazarus. *Fr.* Homeward Bound. TrJP
And when I pay death's duty. Poem. Robin Blaser. NeAP
And when, immortal mortal, droops your head. To My Godchild—Francis M. W. M. Francis Thompson. JKCP; PC
"And when it comis to the ficht." Bannockburn [*or* Bruce Addresses His Army]. John Barbour. *Fr.* The Bruce, XIII. EBSV; GoTS
And, when it was darkest, I came to a strong City. The Strong City. Alfred Noyes. *Fr.* The Last Voyage. GoBC
And when—its force expended. After the Storm. Thackeray. *Fr.* The White Squall. PRWS
And when Joseph came home. Genesis, Bible, *O.T.* LO
And when my work is over, to Cheyenne then I'll head. Dodge City, the End of the Trail. *Unknown.* CoSo
And when new regions prompt their feet to roam. Timothy Dwight. *Fr.* Greenfield Hill. Po
And when religious sects ran mad. Intolerance. Winthrop Mackworth Praed. MaRV
And when Saul saw David go forth against the Philistine. First Samuel, Bible, *O.T.* LO

And when Sir Gelis de Argenté. Bannockburn. John Barbour. *Fr.* The Bruce. EBSV
And when the eyes of love. Courtship. Ibn Sa'id of Alcala la Real. MooP
And when the kings were in the field,—their squadrons in array. The Battle of Simancas. Gonzalo de Berceo. *Fr.* The Life of San Millán. TeCS
And when the people saw that Moses delayed to come down. The Golden Calf. Exodus, Bible, *O.T.* GrCo-1
And when the rain had gone away. The Cricket. Marjorie Barrows. BoChLi (1950 ed.)
And when the scandalmongers strove. Revenge. Hamda. MooP
And when the sun puts out his lamp. To the Mountains. Henry David Thoreau. PoEL-4
And when the travellers by night. The Benefactor. Ibn Sara. MooP
And When They Fall. James J. Montague. HBMV
And when they see me coming. Beware of Larry Gorman. Larry Gorman. ShS
And when this work all brought was to an end. Now Welcome Summer. Chaucer. *Fr.* The Parlement of Foules. PoLi
And when thou hast on foot the purblind hare. Poor Wat. Shakespeare. *Fr.* Venus and Adonis. OBSC; UnPo (1st ed.)
And when thy heart is resting. Emily Brontë. LO
And when upon the morn. Serpent Curls. Ibn Jakha. MooP
And when you passed, for all to seek. The Wine-Bearer. Habib. MooP
And when you search through wounded France. Until You Pass. A. Newberry Choyce. BoHiPo
And when you walk the world lifts up its head. To a Very Beautiful Lady. Ruthven Todd. NeBP
"And where have you been, my Mary." The Fairies of the Caldon Low. Mary Howitt. BeLS; HBV; HBVY; OTPC; PRWS; TVC; TVSH
"And where now, Bayard, will thy footsteps tend?" Bayard Taylor. Whittier. DD; GA; HBV
"And whither would you lead me then?" Ballad. Sir Walter Scott. *Fr.* Rokeby, V. ERP
And who has seen the moon, who has not seen. Moonrise. D. H. Lawrence. GTBS-W; LiTM; NP; TriL
And who is this? A man whose heart. Alienation of an Old Friend. *Unknown.* BoFr
And Who Shall Tell? Mae Winkler Goodman. MuM
And who will lead the way? Love Comes. Ernest Crosby. OQP; QP-2
And why not? He spoke wisely. Poem for M. A. J. D. Davies Aberpennar. MoWP
And why not I, as hee. To Himselfe and the Harpe. Michael Drayton. OBS
And why so coy? what is your rose. *Unknown.* SeCSL
And why this vault and tomb? Wiston Vault. Katherine Philips. DiM
And why to me this, thou lame lord of fire. An Execration upon Vulcan. Ben Jonson. ReEn
And Will He [*or* A'] Not Come Again? Shakespeare. *Fr.* Hamlet. IV, v. EG; InPo; PoEL-2; ViBoPo (Ophelia's Songs, 1.) AnFE; TrGrPo
And will they cast the altars down. In Portugal, 1912. Alice Meynell. OxBoCh
"And will you cut a stone for him." The Stone. W. W. Gibson. CV; LBBV; MBP; MoBrPo; NeMA
And wilt thou have me fashion into speech. Sonnets from the Portuguese, XIII. Elizabeth Barrett Browning. BPN; DiM
And wilt thou leave [*or* wylt thow leve] me thus? An Earnest Suit to His Unkind Mistress Not to Forsake Him [*or* The Appeal *or* The Lover's Appeal]. Sir Thomas Wyatt. AtBAP; BEL; EG; ElL; ElSeCe; EnLit; EnLoPo; GoBC; GTBS; GTBS-D: GTBS-W; GTSE; GTSL; LiTL; LoBV; LPS-1; OAEP; OBEV; OBSC; ReEn; ReIE; SiCE; SiPS; TOP; TuPP
And wilt thou pluck my fair son from mine age? Shakespeare. King Richard II. *fr.* V, ii. MotAn
And with a sigh deep-drawn. The Vow of Vengeance. Homer. *Fr.* The Iliad, XVIII. GrR
And with her words Iris cast sweet desire. Helen. Homer. *Fr.* The Iliad, III. GrR
And with No Language but a Cry. Amos Niven Wilder. MaRV; QS
And worth the blossoms that acacias. Poplar Tree. Padraic Colum. NePoAm
And Would You See My Mistress' Face. *At. to* Thomas Campion. EV-2; OAEP; OBSC
And wouldst Thou, Holy Shepherd, leave. At the Ascension. Luis de León, *tr. by* Thomas Walsh. CAW
And wylt thow leve me thus. *See* And wilt thou leave me thus.
And ye maun braid your yellow hair. Song. Swinburne. *Fr.* Mary Stuart. BPN
And ye shall [*or* sall] walk in silk attire. The Siller Croun. Susanna Blamire. AV; DiM; HBV; LPS-1
And Yet. Arthur B. Rhinow. BLRP
And Yet. Errol B. Sloan. BLRP
And yet all this were challenge to be strong. William Ellery Leonard. *Fr.* Two Lives, Pt. III. MOAP
And yet, because thou overcomest so. Sonnets from the Portuguese, XVI. Elizabeth Barrett Browning. BPN; OAEP; ViPo
And yet but lately have I seen, e'en here. A Winter-Piece. Ambrose Philips. SeCePo
And yet, dear heart! remembering thee. Whittier. *Fr.* Snowbound. MaRV
And Yet Fools Say. George S. Holmes. PoeMoYo; VOD (1935 ed.)
And yet how lovely in thine age of woe. Greece. Byron. *Fr.* Childe Harold's Pilgrimage, II. EV-4; LPS-2; OBRV
And yet I cannot reprehend the flight. To Delia, XXXII. Samuel Daniel. ES; HBV; OAEP; OBEV
And yet I really must complain. The Modern Traveller. Hilaire Belloc. OtMeF
And yet perchance, were the circumstance. Margery Daw. Daniel Henry Holmes. BAP
And yet the southern whale does sometime come. The Whales. Marguerite Young. ReMP
—And yet this great wink [wing, *wr.*] of eternity. Voyages, II. Hart Crane. AnFE; BLV; BoLiVe (1939 ed.); CoAnAm; CoBMV; ExPo; FaBoEn; GTBS-W; LiTM; MAP; MoAB; MoAmPo; MoPo; MoVE; NAMP; NePA; NP; Po; PoFS; ReaPo; TwAmPo; UnPo (3d ed.); ViBoPo (1958 ed.)
And yet to-night, to-night—when all my wealth. Tennyson. *Fr.* The Lover's Tale. VLEP
And Yet We Are Here! Karl Wolfskehl, *tr. fr. German by* Carol North Valhope *and* Ernst Morwitz. TrJP
And yet what joy it were for me. Oscar Wilde. *Fr.* Rome Unvisited. VLEP
And yet, what of the sorrowing years. Oracles, II. Lionel Johnson. VLEP
And you are gone, my King. I am alone. The King's Dancer. Hilda Mary Hooke. CPG
And you are "mad" poor friend? Aye, so we say. A Meeting and a Memory. Habberton Lulham. PoP
And You as Well Must Die, Belovèd Dust. Edna St. Vincent Millay. Unnamed Sonnets, VIII. BAP; GTBS-W; NP; PoRA
And you, O most of all. Enemies. R. D. N. Wilson. GTIV
And you, Robert Bridges, you made your last will. Robert Bridges. Humbert Wolfe. PtP
And You, Seas. "St.-J. Perse," *tr. fr. French by* Wallace Fowlie. *Fr.* Seamarks. MiCF
And You Shall Deal the Funeral Dole. Sir Walter Scott. *See* Claud Halcro's Song.
"And you, Sir Poet, shall you make, I pray." The Poet and the Child. Winifred Howells. AA
And you who love, you who attach yourselves. Conrad Aiken. *Fr.* Time in the Rock. ViBoPo
And you, ye stars. Matthew Arnold. *Fr.* Empedocles on Etna, II. VA
And your eyes look on me. Epistle for Spring. R. Ellsworth Larsson. CAW
Andalusian Cradle-Song. Thomas Bailey Aldrich. *Fr.* Mercedes. BOL
Andalusian merchant, that returns, The. *Unknown.* *Fr.* Wonders. FaBoCh
Andalusian Sereno. The. Francis Saltus Saltus. AA
Andante, ma Non Assai. Rufinus Domesticus, *tr. fr. Greek by* Dudley Fitts. LiTW
Andean Crossing. Alejandro Peralta, *tr. fr. Spanish by* Muna Lee. AnCL
Andirons were the dragons, The. The Castle in the Fire. Mary Jane Carr. BrR
André. Charlotte Fiske Bates. MC; PAH
Andre. Gwendolyn Brooks. TiPo (1959 ed.)
Andrea del Sarto. Robert Browning. ATP; BEL; BMEP; BPN; CoBE; EM-2; EmBrPo; EnL; EnLi-2; EnLit; EPN; GEPC; HBV; MaPo; OAEP; PIAE; PoE; PoEL-5; PoVP; PreP; REAL; ReaPo; TOP; TyEnPo; ViPo; ViPP; VLEP; WHA
Andreas, *sels.* *Unknown, tr. fr. Anglo-Saxon.*
Christ to the Sufferer. PoLi
St. Andrew's Voyage to Mermedonia, *tr. by* Charles W. Kennedy. AnOE
André's Request to Washington. Nathaniel Parker Willis. MC; PAH
André's Ride. Augustus Henry Beesly. HBV
Andrew. Thomas William Parsons. AA
Andrew and Maudlin, Rebecca and Will. A Ballad of Andrew and Maudlin. *Unknown.* CoMu
Andrew Jackson. Stephen Vincent Benét. InMe
Andrew Jackson. Donald Davidson. *Fr.* The Tall Men. SPP
Andrew Jackson. Martha Keller. GoTP; MaC
Andrew Jackson/ Was an Anglo-Saxon. *Unknown.* RIS
Andrew Jackson/ Was Anglo-Saxon. Important People. Louis Untermeyer, *and others.* StaSt
Andrew Lammie. *Unknown.* ESPB
Andrew M'Crie. Robert Fuller Murray. CenHV

Andrew Magrath's Reply to John O'Tuomy. Andrew Magrath, *tr. fr. Modern Irish by* John O'Daly, *vers. by* James Clarence Mangan. OnYI
Andrew Rose, *with music.* *Unknown.* SoAmSa
Andrew Rykman's Prayer, *sels.* Whittier.
"If there be some weaker one." MaRV
"Make my mortal dreams come true." TrPWD
"Pardon, Lord, the lips that dare." TrPWD
Andro and His Cutty Gun. *Unknown.* EBSV
Andromache, *sels.* Euripides, *tr. fr. Greek.*
Chorus: Kings of Troy, The, *tr. by* George Allen. OxBG; WaaP
Gone Are Ilium's Kings, *tr. by* Arthur S. Way. GrR
Monogamy, *tr. by* M. Wodhull. GrR
Murder of Neoptolemus, The, *tr. by* Hugh Owen Meredith. GrR
"O ye inhabitants of Sparta, the whole human race loathes you," *pr. tr. by* Moses Hadas *and* J. H. McLean. GrPo
Peleus, *tr. by* Hugh Owen Meredith. GrR
Plague the Meddling Female, A, *tr. by* Hugh Owen Meredith. GrR
Andromache. Homer, *pr. tr. fr. Greek by* Samuel Butler. *Fr.* The Iliad, XXII. OxBG
(Andromache the Desolate, *pr. tr. by* Andrew Lang, Walter Leaf, *and* Ernest Myers.) GrR
("So she spoke in tears but the wife of Hektor had not yet/ heard," *tr. by* Richmond Lattimore.) GrPo
Andromache, I think of you!—This small river. The Swan. Baudelaire. AnFP
Andromache Learns of Her Son's Fate. Euripides, *tr. fr. Greek by* Arthur S. Way. *Fr.* Trojan Women. LiA
Andromache the Desolate. Homer. *See* Andromache.
Andromache's Wedding. Sappho, *tr. fr. Greek by* George Allen. GrL; OxBG
Andromeda. Thomas Bailey Aldrich. AA
Andromeda. Robert Browning. *Fr.* Pauline. OBRV
Andromeda, *sel.* Euripides, *tr. fr. Greek.*
"Holy Night!/ How long is the road of thy horses." OxBG
Andromeda. Gerard Manley Hopkins. FaBoMo; LiTB
Andromeda, *sels.* Charles Kingsley.
Andromeda and the Sea-Nymphs. VA
Pallas in Olympus. CBOV
Andromeda. James Jeffrey Roche. AA; HBV; JKCP
Andromeda and the Sea-Nymphs. Charles Kingsley. *Fr.* Andromeda. VA
Andromeda, by Perseus saved and wed. Aspecta Medusa. Dante Gabriel Rossetti. BPN; EmBrPo; PoVP
Ane Ballat of Our Lady. William Dunbar. EBSV
(Ballad of Our Lady.) ACP; CAW; ISi, *mod. vers. by* E. M. Clerke
Ane Ballat of the Feignèd Friar of Tungland. William Dunbar. EBSV
Ane by Ane. George Macdonald. EBSV
Ane doolie season [*or* sessoun] to ane careful [*or* cairfull] dyte. The Testament of Cresseid: Prologue. Robert Henryson. BSV; GoTS
Ane Sang of the Birth of Christ, with the Tune of Baw Lula-law [*or* Lula Low]. John Wedderburn, *after the German of* Martin Luther. AnEC
"My saul and life stand up and see," *sel.* BSV; ChTr
Ane Satyre [*or* Satire] of the Threi [*or* Three] Estaitis. Sir David Lindsay. *See* Satire of the Three Estates, The.
Ane Supplication in Contemptioun of Syde Taillis, *abr.* Sir David Lindsay. GoTS
Anear the centre of that northern crest. Melancholia [*or* Melencolia]. James Thomson. The City of Dreadful Night, XXI. AnEnPo; BMEP; FaBoEn; MBP; NBE; OAEP; POTT; VA
Anecdote for Fathers. Wordsworth. EmBrPo; EnRP; FAOV
Anecdote of Men by the Thousand. Wallace Stevens. Po
Anecdote of the Jar. Wallace Stevens. CoBMV; CoV; ExPo; GTBS-W; LiTA; MoAB; MoAmPo; MOAP; MoVE; NePA; OxBA
Anecdote of the Sparrow. Robert Pack. NePA
Anemones for Miss Austen. Bernard Bergonzi. HaMV; PoN
Anew He is wounded! The barbs of His wounding. The Wounded Christ-Heart. "George Klingle." PSO
Angel, The ("I asked a thief . . ."). Blake. *See* I Asked a Thief.
Angel, The ("I dreamt a dream!"). Blake. *Fr.* Songs of Experience. CH; EiPP; EnRP
Angel, The. Alfred Hayes. TrJP
Angel, The. Mikhail Lermontov, *tr. fr. Russian.* BoR, *tr. by* V. de S. Pinto; TrRV, *tr. by* Babette Deutsch; WaL, *tr. by* Sir Cecil Kisch
Angel: "My work is done." Cardinal Newman. *Fr.* The Dream of Gerontius. GoBC
Angel: "Softly and gently, dearly-ransom'd soul." Cardinal Newman. *Fr.* The Dream of Gerontius. OxBoCh
Angel. Pushkin, *tr. fr. Russian by* C. M. Bowra. BoR
Angel and the girl are met, The. The Annunciation. Edwin Muir. MeRV
Angel and the Rose, The. Carlos Oquendo de Amat, *tr. fr. Spanish by* H. R. Hays. AnCL
Angel and the Shepherds, The. *Unknown, tr. fr. Flemish by* Alfred R. Bellinger. ChrBoLe
Angel at the Ford, The. William James Dawson. VA
Angel Cadotte was mischievous, more roguish. The Miscreant Angel. Lew Sarett. FAOV
Angel came by night, The. Adsum. Richard Henry Stoddard. AA; TCAP
Angel came with lilies three, The. Annunciation to All Women. Agnes C. Foote. ChIP
Angel choirs on high are singing. Joys of Heaven. Thomas à Kempis. CAW
Angel Describes Truth, An. Ben Jonson. *Fr.* Hymenaei. OBS
Angel Enclosed, An. Li Yu, *tr. fr. Chinese by* Hsiung Ting. WhP
Angel found a daisy where it lay, An. The Daisy. Virna Sheard. CPG
Angel Gabriel, The. *Unknown.* OBB
Angel, hast thou betrayed me? Long ago. Vers la Vie. Arthur Upson. HBV
Angel Heurtebise, *sel.* Jean Cocteau, *tr. fr. French by* Wallace Fowlie.
"Angel Heurtebise, with unbelievable/ Brutality." MiCF
Angel in the Apple Tree, The. Winifred Welles. StVeCh
Angel in the Cloud, The, *sels.* Edwin Wiley Fuller.
Flight. NoCaPo
Man Is a Prisoner. NoCaPo
Angel in the House, The, *sels.* Coventry Patmore.
Abdication, The, *fr.* I, xii.
(Honoria's Surrender.) VA
Amaranth, The, II, xii, 2. LoBV (1949 ed.)
Attainment, The, I, iii, 4. OBVV
(Preludes, II.) GoBC
Constancy [Rewarded], II, xi, 4. OBVV
Courtesy, *fr.* I, xi, 2. OBVV
Dance, The, *fr.* I, xi.
("My memory of Heaven awakes!") EG
Dean, The, *fr.* I, vi.
(Dean's Consent, The.) VA
Foreign Land, The, II, ix, 2. HBV
(Woman.) OBVV
Going to Church, *fr.* I, x. LoBV
Hono[u]r and Desert, II, iv, 1. HBV
Impossibility, The, *fr.* I, i, 1. PoVP
Joyful Wisdom, The, I, x, 1. HBV
Kiss, The, II, viii, 3. ALV; EnLoPo; FiBHP; LiTL; OBVV; PC
(Sly Thoughts.) LPS-1
Life of Life, I, viii, 1. EPP
Love at Large, I, ii, 2. HoPM; PoVP
Love in Action, *fr.* II, x. EG
Love Serviceable, I, vi, 3. EnLoPo; MaRV
Lover, The, I, iii. 1. EPP; EV-5; PoVP
Love's Reality, fr. I, i, 1. PoVP
Married Lover, The, II, xii, 1. EPN; EV-5; GoBC; GTBS; HBV; LiTL; LoPS; OBEV; PIAE; POTT; PoVP; TrGrPo; VA
("Why, having won her, do I woo?") EG
Nearest the Dearest, II, i, 4. HBV
"Once more I came to Sarum Close," *fr.* I, i. EnSW
Poet's Confidence, The, I, i, 3. POTT
Revelation, The, I, viii, 2. EnLoPo; EPP; POTT
("Idle poet, here and there, An.") EG; ViBoPo
"Love wakes men, once a life-time each," *sel.* LO
Revulsion, The, *fr.* II, vii.
('Twas When the Spousal Time of May.) EV-5
Rose of the World, The, I, iv, 1. HBV; LPS-1
Sensuality, *fr.* I, ix, 2. OBVV
Shame, *fr.* I, ix, 2. OBVV
Spirit's Epochs, The, I, viii, 3. EPP; GoBC
("Not in the crises of events.") EG
Tribute, The, I, iv, 2. HBV; LPS-1
Unthrift, I, iii, 3. HBV; POTT
(Preludes, I.) GoBC
(Wasteful Woman.) BMEP
Wedding Sermon The, II, xi 3. PoVP
Angel, king of streaming morn. Sun. Henry Rowe. OBEV
Angel-Nocturne. Xavier Villaurrutia, *tr. fr. Spanish by* Dudley Fitts. AnCL
Angel of Dawn, The. Julian S. Cutler. PEOR
Angel of Death, The, *sel.* Johan Olof Wallin, *tr. fr. Swedish by* Charles W. Stork.
"I am the Strong One, and I have power." AnSL
Angel of God, my guardian dear. To the Guardian Angel. *Unknown.* WHL
Angel of Life, The. Richard Rowe. BoAu
Angel of Numerals, The. Rafael Alberti, *tr. fr. Spanish by* Eleanor L. Turnbull. AnSpL-2; CoSP
Angel of Patience, The. Whittier, *after the German.* LPS-1; WGRP
Angel of Perugino, An. Arthur Symons. VLEP
Angel of poets,/ Tell us how. Prayer for All Poets at This Time. Irwin Edman. TrPWD

Angel of the Agony. Cardinal Newman. *Fr.* The Dream of Gerontius. OxBoCh
Angel of the flowers, one day, The. The Moss Rose. Friedrich Adolph Krummacher. LPS-2
Angel of the Lord declared unto Mary, The. Angelus Domini. *Unknown.* WHL
Angel of words, in vain I have striven with thee. A Child Asleep. Walter de la Mare. POTE
Angel or Woman. Thomas Parnell. *See* Song: "When thy beauty appears."
Angel, robed in spotless white, An. Dawn. Paul Laurence Dunbar. GoSl; PoNe
Angel Roll de Stone Away, De, *with music. Unknown.* BoAN-2
Angel sets at my place, An. Palm. Paul Valéry. AnFP
Angel Singing, An. Blake. MeMeAg; RIS
(Two Songs, The.) CBOV
Angel song still trembles, The. After Christmas. Consuelo Valencia. MaRV
Angel Sons, The. Vachel Lindsay. TCAP
Angel Spirits of Sleep. Robert Bridges. CH
(Spirits.) OBEV; OBVV
Angel spoke and tried to hold, The. Joseph's Suspicion. Rainer Maria Rilke. ReMP
Angel swoops, like eagle on his prey, An. The Rebel. Baudelaire. LiA
Angel that presided o'er my birth, The. Injunction. Blake. *Fr.* Gnomic Verses. BLV; BoLiVe; OBRV; TrGrPo
Angel thus til him can sai [*or* to him did say], An. The Flight into Egypt. *Unknown. Fr.* Cursor Mundi. CoBE; EPP
Angel Touched Your Forehead, An. Ernst von der Recke, *tr. fr. Danish by* Charles W. Stork. BoDS
Angel Unawares, An. *Unknown.* BLRP; MaRV
Angel Voices. Mary B. Stevenson. ChIP
Angel voices, ever singing. Francis Pott. OlF
Angel was flying through night's deep blue, An. The Angel. Mikhail Lermontov, *tr. by* V. de S. Pinto. BoR
Angel was winging his way through the night, An. The Angel. Mikhail Lermontov, *tr. by* Babette Deutsch. TrRV
Angelic Chorus, The. D. J. Donahoe. JKCP
Angelic figures gliding in the stream. The Stream of Life. W. W. E. Ross. BoCaPo
Angelic Guidance. Cardinal Newman. GoBC
Angelic host. MS. of St. Martial of Limoges. *Tr. by* Helen Waddell. TriL
Angelic Service. Winifred M. Letts. CV
Angelic Vilancete, The. Gil Vicente. *Fr.* The Auto of the Four Seasons. CAW
Angelica and the Ork. Ariosto, *tr. fr. Italian by* Sir John Harington. *Fr.* Orlando Furioso, X. OBSC
Angelica, when she had won again. Ariosto, *tr. by* William Stewart Rose. *Fr.* Orlando Furioso, XIX. PrPoCR
Angelina. Paul Laurence Dunbar. HBV; VOD
Angelina, you who know how to sew, and you who embroider, Jane. The Dead Grenadier. Pedro Juan Vignale. AnCL
Angelles bee wrogte to bee of neidher kynde. Mynstrelles Songe. Thomas Chatterton. *Fr.* Aella. EnLoPo
Angelo Orders His Dinner. Bayard Taylor. BOHV; PA
Angels, The. William Drummond of Hawthornden. AnEC; COAH; GN; HBV
(Angels for the Nativity of Our Lord, The.) OxBoCh
(Nativitie, The.) OBS
Angels. Gertrude Hall. *See* How Shall We Tell an Angel.
Angels above us hover, The Our Dead Heroes. Morton Bryan Wharton. BlG
Angels angels in the sky. White Snow. Guillaume Apollinaire. AnFP
Angels are bright still, though the brightest fell. Lucifer. D. H. Lawrence. OAEP (2d ed.)
Angels are stooping, The. A Cradle Song. W. B. Yeats. BOL; POTE; TSW
Angels, as well as birds, on silent wing. On Angels. W. W. E. Ross. BoCaPo
Angels at Hamburg, The. Randall Jarrell. AmP
Angels at the foot. Watching Angels. Christina Rossetti. *Fr.* Sing-Song. EmBrPo; PPL
Angels bending, The. The Empty Cradle. José Selgas y Carrasco. CAW
Angels Came a-Mustering, The. *Unknown, tr. fr. Hebrew by* Israel Zangwill. TrJP
Angels' eyes, whom veils cannot deceive, The. Of the Blessed Sacrament of the Altar. Robert Southwell. OBEV (new ed.)
Angels for the Nativity of Our Lord, The. William Drummond of Hawthornden. *See* Angels, The.
Angels, from the Realms of Glory. James Montgomery. OlF; YaCaBo, *with music*
(Good Tidings of Great Joy to All People.) HBV
(Nativity.) MaRV; OBRV
Angels guide him now, The. In Memory of a Child. Vachel Lindsay. InP
Angels have talked with him, and showed him thrones. The Mystic. Tennyson. OAEP
Angels in Heab'n Gwineter Write My Name, De, *with music. Unknown.* BoAN-2
Angels in high places, The. Azrael. Robert Gilbert Welsh. BAP; HBV; LBMV; MaRV; OQP; QP-1
Angels of Buena Vista, The. Whittier. BeLS; PAH; TCAP
Angels of the Spring. Robert Stephen Hawker. *See* Are They Not All Ministering Spirits?
Angels of the sunlight clothe, The. Desideria. Lionel Johnson. VLEP
Angels received his dying breath. On the Death of a Journalist. Roy Campbell. CoBE
Angels, Roll the Rock Away! Thomas Scott. BePJ
Angels' Song, The. Edmund Hamilton Sears. *See* It Came upon the Midnight Clear.
Angel's Story, The. Adelaide Anne Procter. DD
Angels, thy old friends, there shall greet thee. The Good Woman Made Welcome in Heaven. Richard Crashaw. CBPC
Angels to the shepherds sang, The. A Carol. Fred E. Weatherly. YeAr
Angel's voice rose recently cut. The Angel and the Rose. Carlos Oquendo de Amat. AnCL
Angels We Have Heard on High. *Unknown.* TreFS; YaCaBo, *with music*
Angels, where you soar. A Prayer. Alfred Noyes. BMEP
Angel's Whisper, The. Samuel Lover. BOL; LPS-1; OnYI; PRWS
Angelus. Carmen Alicia Cadilla, *tr. fr. Spanish by* Dudley Fitts. AnCL
Angelus, The. Florence Earle Coates. HBV
Angelus, The. Gerardo Diego, *tr. fr. Spanish by* Eleanor L. Turnbull. CoSP
Angelus, The. Frances Laughton Mace. PEOR
Angelus, The. Edwin Markham. GrCo-2
True Work Is Worship, *sel.* MaRV
Angelus. "Yehoash," *tr. fr. Yiddish by* Elbert Aidline. LiTW
Angelus Domini. *Unknown.* WHL
Angelus-Time near Dublin. William Bedell Stanford. NeIP
Anger. Charles *and* Mary Lamb. FaBoBe; HBV; HBVY; OTPC (1923 ed.)
Anger. César Vallejo, *tr. fr. Spanish by* H. R. Hays. TwSpPo
Anger in its time and place. Anger. Charles *and* Mary Lamb. FaBoBe; HBV; HBVY; OTPC (1923 ed.)
Anger of Christ, The. Richard Watson Gilder. StJW
Anger of Samson, The. Alfred de Vigny, *pr. tr. fr. French.* LiA
Anger that breaks a man into children. Anger. César Vallejo. TwSpPo
Angina Pectoris. W. R. Moses. LiTA
Angler, The. Bhartrihari. *tr. fr. Sanskrit by* Paul Elmer More. LiTW
Angler, The (*in* Izaak Walton's The Compleat Angler). John Chalkhill. HBV; LPS-2
Angler. Isabel Fiske Conant. PC
Angler, The, *sel.* David Moir.
"Early a-foot,/ On public roads." EnSW
Angler, The. Thomas Buchanan Read. LPS-2
Angler named Ezekiel Hutt, An. Haulage. E. E. Nott-Bower. WhC
Angler's Ballad, The. Charles Cotton. CEP
Angler's Invitation, The. Thomas Tod Stoddart. GN; HBV
(Come when the Leaf Comes, *2 sts.*) AlDL
Angler's Reveille, The. Henry van Dyke. *Fr.* The Toiling of Felix. BBV (1923 ed.); GN; PYM; StVeCh
Angler's Song, The (*in* Izaak Walton's The Compleat Angler). William Basse. CenL; ElSeCe; OBS
Angler's Song, The. John Dennys. *Fr.* The Secrets of Angling. ElL
("Let me live harmlessly, and near the brink.") MyFE
Angler's Song, The ("Man's life is but vain") (*in* Izaak Walton's The Compleat Angler). *Unknown.* AlDL; SeCL
Angler's Tent, The, *sel.* "Christopher North."
"How leapt our hearts, when from an airy height." EnSW
Angler's Trysting-Tree, The. Thomas Tod Stoddart. LPS-2
Angler's Vindication, The Thomas Tod Stoddart. EBSV
Angler's Wish, An. Henry van Dyke. AA; ADAH; DDA; LEAP; MMV; OBAV; SN
(When Tulips Bloom.) VOD
Angler's Wish, The. Izaak Walton. *Fr.* The Compleat Angler. HBV; LPS-2; SeCL
Angleworm. Herbert Cahoon. SiTL
Anglian Tradition, The. *Unknown, tr. fr. Anglo-Saxon by* Francis B. Gummere. *Fr.* Beowulf *and* Widsith. PaOS
Angling. James Thomson. *Fr.* The Seasons: Spring. LPS-2
Anglo-Eire Vignette. Patric Stevenson. NeIP
Anglo-Irishman's Complaint, An. *Unknown.* AnIL
Anglo-Norman Carol. *Unknown. See* Lordings, Listen to Our Lay.
Anglo-Saxon. E. L. Mayo. MiAP
Anglosaxon Street. Earle Birney. BoCaPo
Angry future like a winter builds, The. Poem on Hampstead Heath. Louis Adeane. NeBP
Angry Kynges, The. Seneca, *tr. fr. Latin by* Thomas Heywood. *Fr.* Hercules Furens, IV. LiA

Angry Word, An. Margaret E. Bruner. PoToHe
Angry young husband called Bicket, An. Limerick. John Galsworthy. CenHV
Anguish. Adelaide Crapsey. PFE
Anguish. Stéphane Mallarmé, *tr. fr. French.* AnFP, *tr. by* Kate Flores; AWP, *tr. by* Arthur Symons
Anguish, The. Edna St. Vincent Millay. BAP; ChMo; CMP; NeMA
Anguish. José Moreno Villa, *tr. fr. Spanish by* Eleanor J. Turnbull. CoSP
Anguish. Paul Verlaine, *tr. fr. French by* Kate Flores. AnFP
Anguish knows but one melody. Duet. Erik Blomberg. AnSL
Anguish of the earth absolves our eyes, The. Absolution. Siegfried Sassoon. NV
Anguishes of poets are, The. Poets Easily Consoled. Christopher Morley. LHV
Angus Armstrong. W. W. Gibson. *Fr.* Casualties. VOD
Angus McGregor. Lew Sarett. PoMa
Anima Christi. St. Ignatius Loyola, *tr. fr. Latin.* WHL
Animal Crackers. Christopher Morley. BoChLi; FaPON; GFA; MPB; OTPC (1946 ed.); PCD; RAR; SP; SUS; TiPo; UTS
Animal Critics, The. Swift. *Fr.* To Mr. Congreve. BeR
Animal Fair. Philip Booth. NePoAm-2
Animal Fair. *Unknown.* AS, *with music;* BLPA; FaBoBe; GoTP; MoShBr; SiTL; YaD
Animal Howl, The. "M. J.," *tr. fr. Polish by* A. Glanz-Leyeless. TrJP
Animal Store, The. Rachel Field. AIBD; GoBP; OTPC (1946 ed.); TiPo; UTS
Animal that I am, I come to call. The Man in the Dress Suit. Robert L. Wolf. HBMV
Animal Tranquillity and Decay. Wordsworth. *See* Old Man, An.
Animals, The. Josephine Jacobsen. GoYe
Animals, The. Edwin Muir. MoPW
Animals. Walt Whitman. *Fr.* Song of Myself, XXXII. EV-5; FaFP; GTBS-W; LiTG; MCCG; SiTL
(Beasts, The.) HBV; OBVV; PC
("I think I could turn.") AnEnPo; LoBV; PG (1955 ed.); PoMa; TrGrPo; WGRP
Animals are my friends and my kin and my playfellows. About Animals. Hilda Conkling. UTS
Animals came in two by two, The. One More River. *Unknown.* SiTL
Animals Ill with the Plague, The. La Fontaine, *tr. fr. French by* Alan Conder. TrFP
Animals in the Ark, The. *Unknown. Fr.* The Deluge. ChTr
Animals will never know, The. If They Spoke. Mark Van Doren. ImOP
Animated glass that drawest nigh. Grievous Peril of a Gallant in Moth Metaphor. Luis de Sandoval y Zapata. AnMP
Animula. T. S. Eliot. AmPP; ChMo; LiTB; MAP; MoAmPo (1942 ed.); MoPW; MoVE; PoLFOT; TwAmPo; TwP
Animula Blandula Vagula. Emperor Hadrian. *See* To His Soul.
Animula Vagula, *sels.* Leonard Bacon.
"There is dogwood in my soul," XXVII. NV
"This is the road." TCPD
Animula Vagula. A. Y. Campbell. HBMV
Animus et Corpus. Ralph Gustafson. BoCaPo (1948 ed.)
Ankle's chief end is exposiery, The. The Limeratomy: The Ankle. Anthony Euwer. HBMV
Ann, Ann!/ Come! quick as you can! Alas, Alack! Walter de la Mare. FaPON; GFA; MPB; PoRh; TiPo
Ann Rutledge. Edwin Markham. MW; TBM
Ann Rutledge. Edgar Lee Masters. *See* Anne Rutledge.
Ann stood and watched the combers race to shore. Andrew Merkel. *Fr.* Tallahassee. CaP
Anna. Burns. TrGrPo
Anna Elise, she jumped with surprise. *Unknown.* BoN; LiL; OxNR
Anna-Marie, Love, Up Is the Sun. Sir Walter Scott. *Fr.* Ivanhoe, *ch.* 40. EmBrPo; ViBoPo
Anna Susanna. *Unknown.* SAS
Annabel Lee, *parody.* Stanley Huntley. BOHV; PA
Annabel Lee. Poe. AA; AmP; AmPo; AmPP; AnFE; APA; APW; AWP; BAP; BAV; BBV; BeLS; BLPA; BLV; BoLiVe; BTP; CaAE; CH; CoAnAm; CoBA; DDA; EtS; EV-5; FaFP; FaPON; GoTP; GTBS-W; GTSE; HBV; HBVY; HoPM; IAP; InPo; JAWP; LEAP; LiTA; LiTG; LiTL; LoEn; LoGBV; LoPo; LPS-1; MaC; MCCG; MOAP; MPB; MW; NeHB; NePA; OBAV; OBEV (1st ed.); OBVV; OtMeF; OTPC, *abr.;* OuHeWo; OxBA; PCD; PG; PIR; PoFS; PTA-2; PYM; SeCeV; SPP; StaSt; StPo; StVeCh; TCAP; TOP; TreF; TrGrPo; TVSH; ViBoPo; WBP; WBLP; YT
Annales, *sel.* Ennius, *tr. fr. Latin by* John Wight.
Like a Shower of Rain. LaP; WaaP
Annan Water *Unknown.* BaBo; CBOV; CH; EV-2; HBV; OBB
Annar-Mariar's Christmas Shopping. Eleanor Farjeon. ChBR
Anne. Lizette Woodworth Reese. AA; PR
Anne Boleyn. Barbara Bingley. ReTS
Anne Grenville, Countess Temple, Appointed Poet Laureate to the King of the Fairies. Horace Walpole. *See* Countess Temple, Appointed Poet Laureate.
Anne Hathaway ("Would ye be taught, ye feathered throng"). *Unknown, sometimes at. to* Shakespeare. LPS-3
Anne Hutchinson's Exile. Edward Everett Hale. PAH
Anne [*or* Ann] Rutledge. Edgar Lee Masters. *Fr.* Spoon River Anthology. AmP; BAP; ChMo; CMP; CP; FaFP; InPo; LiTA; LiTM (rev. ed.); LoPo; MAP; MoAmPo; MoVE; NeHB; NeMA; NePA; NP; NV; OHFP; OxBA; PaA; PG (1945 ed.); PYM; SBMV; TCAP; TrGrPo; VOD
Anne's Book Mary Webb. OnPP
Annette Myers; or, A Murder in St. James's Park. *Unknown.* OxBoLi
Annie. Guillaume Apollinaire, *tr. fr. French by* Dudley Fitts. AnFP
Annie and Rhoda, sisters twain. The Sisters. Whittier. AWP; InPo; MOAP
Annie and Willie's Prayer. Sophia P. Snow. BeLS; BLPA; PTA-2
Annie Bolanny. *Unknown.* ChTr
Annie Breen, *with music. Unknown.* CoSo
Annie Ferguson. Mary W. Findlater. DiM
Annie Laurie. William Douglas, *revised by* Lady John Scott. BTP; EBSV; EtPaEn; FaBoBe; FaFP; GN; GTBS-W; HBV; InP; LiTG; LiTL; LPS-1; MCCG; OIF; OTPC; PECK; PYM; SiTL; TreF; WBLP
Annie McConkus. Amy Belle Adams. StaSt
Annie Shore and Johnnie Doon. Patrick Orr. BANP; HBV
Annie's Garden. Eliza Lee Follen. PPL
Annihilation. Conrad Aiken. BLV; CrMA; LO; MAP; MoAB; MoAmPo
Anniversaries. Aldous Huxley. LBBV
Anniversary [*or* Anniversarie], The. John Donne. AEV; AnFE; BrBE; CoEV; ElSeCe; EnLP; EPS; ExPo; HoPM; LiTB; LiTG; MeLP; MePo; OAEP; OBS; ReaPo; ReIE; SeCeV; SeCV-1; SeEP; TuPP; UnPo (1st ed.)
"Only our love hath no decay," *sel.* LO
Anniversary. Stefan George, *tr. fr. German by* Reginald H. Phelps. AnGP
Anniversary, An. William Knox Johnson. TIP
Anniversary, An. Richard Lovelace. LoBV
Anniversary, The. Sir Ronald Ross. PoP
Anniversary. Leonora Speyer. LoPS
Anniversary of Antonia Pozzi's Death by Suicide. Vittorio Serini, *tr. fr. Italian by* Glauco Cambon. OnPM
Anniverse, The. Henry King. NBE
Anno Domini. John Bellenden. ACP (1926 ed.)
Anno 1829. Heine, *tr. fr. German by* Charles Stuart Calverley. AWP; JAWP; WBP; WoL; LiTW, *tr. by* Louis Untermeyer
Anno Santo. Stephen Spender. FaBoMo
Annot Lyle's Song: "Birds of Omen." Sir Walter Scott. *Fr.* The Legend of Montrose, VI. EmBrPo; EnRP
Announce it here with triple leading. Rarae Aves. Franklin P. Adams. WhC
Announced by all the trumpets of the sky. The Snowstorm. Emerson. AA; AmP; AmPo; AmPP; AnNE; APW; BAP; BAV; BLV; BoLiVe; CoBA; FaBoBe; GTBS-D; GTBS-W; IAP; InP; LaNeLa; LEAP; LiTA; LiTG; LPS-2; MOAP; NePA; OBAV; OHFP; OnAP; OTPC; OuHeWo; OxBA; PCH; PG (1945 ed.); PIAE; PoE; PoEL-4; PoeMoYo; PoFS; PYM; TCAP; TiPo; TrGrPo; YT
Announcement. Elizabeth J. Coatsworth. *See* Conquistador.
Annual Drama, The. Walt Whitman. *Fr.* The Return of the Heroes. GrCo 1
Annual Gaiety. Wallace Stevens. MAP; MoAB; MoAmPo
Annual Legend. Winfield Townley Scott. GTBS-W; LiTA; LiTM; WaP
Annual Solution, The. Edwin Meade Robinson. InMe
Annuity, The. George Outram. BOHV; BSV; EBSV; HBV
Annul Wars. Nahman of Bratzlav, *tr. fr. Hebrew by* Jacob Sloan. TrJP
Annunciation, The. Margaret Devereaux Conway. ISi; JKCP (1955 ed.)
Annunciation, The. Abraham Cowley. *Fr.* Davideis. OxBoCh
Annunciation. John Donne. ISi; OBS
Annunciation, The. John Duffy. ISi
Annunciation. Ken Etheridge. MoWP
Annunciation, The. Edwin Muir. MeRV
Annunciation, The. St. Nerses, *tr. fr. Armenian by* W. H. Kent. ISi
Annunciation, The. Adelaide Anne Procter. JKCP
Annunciation. Rainer Maria Rilke, *tr. fr. German by* J. B. Leishman. MeRV
Annunciation, The. John Banister Tabb. ISi
Annunciation, The. *Unknown, tr. fr. German.* ISi
Annunciation Night. Katherine E. Conway. CAW; ChIP
Annunciation Night. Abby Maria Hemenway. *Fr.* Mary of Nazareth. ISi
Annunciation to All Women. Agnes C. Foote. ChIP

Annus Mirabilis, *sels.* Dryden.
Bees. BeR
"But ah! how unsincere are all our joys!" SeEP
Fire of London, The. ChTr; EV-3; FaBoEn, *shorter sel.*
Fourth Day's Battle, The. OBS
Great Fire, The. FiP
New London, The. FaBoCh; OBS
(London.) SeCePo
"Night came, but without darkness or repose." BeR
Sea Battle, The. FiP
"Yet London, empress of the northern clime." ViBoPo
Annus Mirabilis. Laurence Housman. LBBV; PoeT
Anodyne, The. Sarah N. Cleghorn. OQP; PC; QP-2
Anodyne, An. Thomas Ken. OxBoCh
Anon out of the earth a fabric huge. Pandemonium and Its Architect. Milton. *Fr.* Paradise Lost, I. PoFS; TreFS
Anonymous. John Banister Tabb. AA; BAP; LEAP; OBAV
Anonymous Alba. *Unknown, tr. fr. French by* Stanley Burnshaw. OuHeWo
Anonymous as cherubs. Two Voices in a Meadow. Richard Wilbur. NePoAm-2; UnPo (3d ed.)
Anonymous Lieutenant, The. Clark Mills. NeTW
Anonymous—nor needs a name. Anonymous. John Banister Tabb. AA; BAP; LEAP; OBAV
Anonymous Speech. Jorge Carrera Andrade, *tr. fr. Spanish by* H. R. Hays. TwSpPo
Anonymous Valentine, The. Wilbur D. Nesbit. OnHT
Another [Beggar Poem] ("For one copper"). Issa, *tr. fr. Japanese by* Max Bickerton. PoFr
Another. Richard Lovelace. AtBAP; PoEL-3
Another [Epigram]. Matthew Prior. *See* Epigram: "Yes, every Poet is a Fool."
Another age ground down by civil strife! The Horrors of Civil War. Horace. WoL
Another Altar. Edmund Blunden. MoPW
Another armoured animal—scale. The Pangolin. Marianne Moore. CoBMV; CrMA
Another Beggar Poem ("A bleak day!"). Issa, *tr. fr. Japanese by* Max Bickerton. PoFr
Another Charm. Robert Herrick. OTPC (1923 ed.)
Another Cross. John Masefield. *Fr.* The Everlasting Mercy. MaRV
Another Cynical Variation. "Helen." InMe
Another Dark Lady. E. A. Robinson. LoPo; TwP
Another Dawn. Bernard Mandeville. *Fr.* A Description of the Morning. BeR
Another day is numbered with the past. At Evening. *Unknown.* BOL
Another day its course hath run. Evening Hymn for a Child. John Pierpont. BOL
Another dreadful tale of woe as I will here unfold. Annette Myers; or, A Murder in St. James's Park. *Unknown.* OxBoLi
Another Element. Spenser. *See* Amoretti, LV.
Another Fan (of Mademoiselle Mallarmé). Stéphane Mallarmé, *tr. fr. French by* Joseph Bennett. AnFP
(Miss Mallarmé's Fan, *tr. by* Alan Conder.) TrFP
Another four I've left yet to bring on. Spring. Anne Bradstreet. *Fr.* The Four Seasons of the Year. TCAP
Another Generation. J. C. Squire. HBMV
Another good cow-puncher has gone to meet his fate. Charlie Rutledge [*or* Rutlage]. *Unknown, at. to* D. J. White (D. J. O'Malley). CoSo; CSF
Another Grace for a Child ("Here a little child I stand"). Robert Herrick. *See* Grace for a Child.
Another Grace for a Child ("What God gives, and what we take"). Robert Herrick. *See* Grace for Children.
Another guest that winter night. Prophetess. Whittier. *Fr.* Snow-bound. AA
Another knight smote Saint Thomas in that self wound. Becket's Diadem. *Unknown.* ACP
Another Lament of Lord Pierrot. Jules Laforgue, *tr. fr. French by* Joseph Bennett. AnFP
Another Little Drink, *with music. Unknown.* TrAS, *with* Old Zip Coon.
Another might have spared your pride. What I Have. Robert Farren. JKCP (1955 ed.)
Another nickel in the slot. A Hero in the Land of Dough. Robert Clairmont. WaKn; WhC
Another night, and yet no tidings come. The Parting of King Philip and Marie. John Westland Marston. *Fr.* Marie de Meranie. VA
Another, of Another Mind ("A king, oh boon for my aspiring mind!"). "F M." TuPP
Another, of Another Mind ("The greatest kings do least command content"). *Unknown.* TuPP
Another, of His Cynthia. Fulke Greville. *See* Of His Cynthia.
Another of the Same. Sir Walter Ralegh. SiPS
Another of the Same. Excellently Written by a Most Woorthy Gentleman. *At. to* Sir Edward Dyer. *See* Epitaph on Sir Philip Sidney.
Another Plum-Cake. Ann Taylor. *See* Plum-Cake, The.
Another ray of light hath fled, another Southern brave. Cleburne. *Unknown.* BlG
Another Reply to "In Flanders Fields." C. B. Galbreath, *sometimes at. to* J. A. Armstrong. BLPA
(In Flanders Fields, an Answer.) HH; PTA-1
Another sate near him, whose harp of gold. Fenton Johnson. *Fr.* The Vision of Lazarus. BANP
Another scorns the homespun thread of rhymes. Satire VI. Joseph Hall. *Fr.* Virgidemiarum. SiCE; TuPP
Another side, umbrageous grots and caves. Paradise. Milton. *Fr.* Paradise Lost, IV. OBS
Another Song: "It is I that am under sorrow at this time." William Ross, *tr. fr. Gaelic.* GoTS
Another Song: "Though heaven's gate of light uncloses." Victor Hugo, *tr. fr. French by* H. B. Favnie. LiA
Another Sonnet to Black Itself. Lord Herbert of Cherbury. SeEP
Another Spirit Advances. Jules Romains, *tr. fr. French by* Joseph T. Shipley. AWP; JAWP; MiFP; WBP
Another Spring. Tu Fu, *tr. fr. Chinese by* Kenneth Rexroth. OnPC
Another squall! The Rain-beaten Cathedral. Kotaro Takamura. PoLJ
Another star 'neath time's horizon dropped. To the Memory of Hood. James Russell Lowell. PtP
Another Time. W. H. Auden. OxBA
Another Tribute to Wyatt ("In the rude age, when knowledge was not rife"). Earl of Surrey. SiPS
Another Villon-ous Variation. Don Marquis. HBMV
Another Way. Ambrose Bierce. AA; BAP; LEAP; LHV
Another Way. Andrew Lang. UnW
Another Way of Love. Robert Browning. BPN; EmBrPo; GEPC; PoVP; VLEP
Another Weeping Woman. Wallace Stevens. MoVE; NP
Another While. Morris Rosenfeld, *tr. fr. Yiddish.* TrJP
Another Winter comes. The last comes soon, I know. Pierre de Ronsard. *Fr.* Les Amours Diverses. PrPoCR
Another writes because his father writ. Edward Young. SiTL
Another Year. Frances Ridley Havergal. *See* Another Year Is Dawning.
Another Year. Thomas O'Hagan. PEDC; PEOR
Another year! another deadly blow! November, 1806. Wordsworth. BPN; OBRV; PoFr; SoV
Another year! another year! One More Year. A. Norton. PEOR
Another year has struck the vibrant chime. Washington. Mae Winkler Goodman. PGD
Another year I enter. A New Year's Promise. *Unknown.* BLRP
Another Year Is Dawning. Frances Ridley Havergal. PraP; WBLP
(Another Year.) BLRP
Another year passed over—gone. Another Year. Thomas O'Hagan. PEDC; PEOR
Anselmo Speaks ("There is no peace on earth today save the peace in the heart"). Edna St. Vincent Millay. *Fr.* Conversation at Midnight. TwCV
Anster Fair, *sels.* William Tennant.
On the Road to Anster Fair. OBRV
"Saffron-elbow'd Morning up the slope, The." EnSW
Answer, The. Sara Hamilton Birchall. NLK
Answer, An. George Frederick Cameron. CPG
Answer. Mary Elizabeth Colman. BoCaPo (1943 ed.)
Answer. Isabel Fiske Conant. TBM
Answer, The. "Katherine Hale." CPG
Answer. Harriet Hoock. WHL
Answer, The. Robinson Jeffers. ChMo; GoYe; PoLFOT
Answer, The. Orrick Johns. NP
Answer, An. Henry S. Leigh. YT
Answer, An. Sir Tobie Matthew. SeCL
("Say, but did you love so long?") SeCV-1
Answer. Merrill Moore. NeMA
Answer. Thomas Osbert Mordaunt. *See* Sound, Sound the Clarion.
Answer, The. Isobel Pagan. DiM
Answer, The. Earl of Rochester. EPS
Answer. Leonora Speyer. PG (1945 ed.)
Answer, The. Sara Teasdale. LEAP; NP; NV; TCPD
Answer for Hope. Richard Crashaw. *See* For Hope.
Answer that ye made to me, my dear, The. Sir Thomas Wyatt. SiPS
Answer to a Child's Question. Samuel Taylor Coleridge. CBE; CG; DD; EmBrPo; EnRP; ERP; EV-4; FaBoBe; HBV; HBVY; LPS-2; MeMeAg; NeHB; OTPC; PEDC; PRWS; RAR; ThWaDe; TVC; UTS
(Birds, The.) BoTP
(What the Birds Say.) CBPC
Answer to a Worldly One. Li Po, *tr. fr. Chinese by* C. W. Luh. OnPM
Answer to Chloe [*or* Cloe] Jealous. Matthew Prior. ALV; ElSeCe; OBEC; SeCePo; SeCL
(Better Answer [to Cloe Jealous], A.) AWP; CEP; EiPP; EV-3; ExPo; FaBoEn; InPo; JAWP; PoE; PoEL-3; SeCeV; TCEP; TOP; WBP

Answer to Chloe [or Cloe] Jealous (continued)
("Dear Cloe, how blubber'd is that pretty face.") NBE
(To Chloe [or Cloe] Jealous [a Better Answer].) HBV; LiTL; LO; ViBoPo
Answer to Defiance; the Earthquake. Aeschylus, tr. fr. Greek by Gilbert Murray. Fr. Prometheus Bound. GrR
Answer to Marlowe. Sir Walter Ralegh. See Nymph's Reply to the Shepherd, The.
Answer to Master Wither's Song. Ben Jonson. BOHV; InMe; PA
Answer to "Rock Me to Sleep," An. Unknown. PTA-1
Answer to the Cuckold's Complaint, An. Unknown. See Scolding Wives Vindication, The.
Answer to the Parson, An. Blake. OxBoLi
(Epigram: An Answer to the Parson.) SiTL
Answer to Ting Yuan Ch'en, An. Ou-yang Hsiu, tr. fr. Chinese by Kenneth Rexroth. OnPC
Answer to Twenty-one Years, An. Unknown. See Little Willie's My Darlin'.
Answer you, Sirs? Do I understand aright? Giuseppe Caponsacchi. Robert Browning. The Ring and the Book, VI. PoVP; VLEP
Answered Prayer, The. Annie Johnson Flint. PraP
Answered Prayer. Myra Goodwin Plantz. PraP
Answered Thus by Sir P. S. Sir Philip Sidney. TuPP
Answering Vice-Prefect Chang. Wang Wei, tr. fr. Chinese by Witter Bynner and Kiang Kang-hu. OuHeWo
Answers, The. Robert Clairmont. GoTP; SiTL; WhC
(When Did the World Begin.) WaKn
Answers. Elizabeth Jennings. NePoEA
Ant, The. Al-Tulaitili, tr. fr. Arabic by A. J. Arberry. MooP
Ant, The. Oliver Herford. LBN
Ant and shrew. The Translation. Mark Van Doren. TCPD
Ant and the Cricket, The. Unknown. GoTP; HBV; HBVY; OnHT; OTPC (1923 ed.); PRWS; TVSH
Ant Battle. Glenn Ward Dresbach. MuM
Ant Explorer, The. C. J. Dennis. NeLNL
Ant on the tablecloth, An. Departmental. Robert Frost. AmP; AmPP; AnNE; GoYe; HoPM; MoAB; MoAmPo; OnAP; PoLFOT
And that puts aside his wings, The. Wings. Charles G. Blanden. PoTo
Ant Village, The. Marion Edey. FaPON; TiPo
Ant was running in the grass, An. The Wandering Ant. Corydon Bell. RAR
Antagonist, The. David Ferry. NePoAm-2
Antagonists, The. Muriel Rukeyser. Fr. Ninth Elegy. FiMAP
Ante-Bellum Sermon, An. Paul Laurence Dunbar. YT
Ante Mortem. Robinson Jeffers. CoV; MAP; MoAmPo; MoVE
Antechapel where the statue stood, The. Solitude. Wordsworth. Fr. The Prelude, III. LiA
Antelope. William Jay Smith. TiPo (1959 ed.)
Antelopes, The. James K. Baxter. AnNZ
Antenora. "Hugh MacDiarmid." SeCePo
Anteroom, The. Denise Levertov. NeBP
Anteros. William Johnson Cory. OBVV
(Dirge, A: "Naiad, hid beneath the bank.") BMEP
Anteros. Gérard de Nerval, tr. fr. French. AnFP, tr. by Barbara Howes; TrFP, tr. by Alan Conder
Anthem for Doomed Youth. Wilfred Owen. AnFE; BLV; BoLiVe; CBOV; ChTr; CoBMV; EnLi-2 (1949 ed.); ES; FaBoMo; FaFP; GTBS-D; GTBS-W; GTML; GTSL; HBMV; LBBV; LiTM; MaRV; MBP; MoAB; MoBrPo; MoPW; MoVE; NeMA; NP; OAEP (2d ed.); OBEV (new ed); PoE; PoeMoYo; POTE; SeCePo; ShBV-4; TrGrPo; ViBoPo; VOD (1931 ed.); WaP; WHA
Anthem of Earth, An, sel. Francis Thompson.
"What is this Man, thy darling kissed and cuffed." BrBE
Anthill, The ("The anthill lay unsheltered in the sun"). Donald C. Babcock. NePoAm
Anthologist, The. Anderson M. Scruggs. DDA
Anthologistics. Arthur Guiterman. InMe; WhC
Anthony Munday unto All Young Gentlemen in Commendation of this Gallery and Workmen Thereof. Anthony Munday. ReIE
Anthony O'Daly. James Stephens, after the Irish of Anthony Raftery. BoFr
Anthony Wayne. Arthur Guiterman. TiPo (1959 ed.)
Anthropomorphism. Xenophanes, tr. fr. Greek by F. L. Lucas. GrPE
Anthropos apteros for days. The Labyrinth. W. H. Auden. GTBS-W; LiTA; LiTM (rev. ed.); NePA; SiTL
Anti-Symbolist, The. Sidney Keyes. MoPo
Anti-aircraft seen from a certain distance. Dam Neck, Virginia. Richard Eberhart. LiTA; MoAB; WaP
Antichrist, or the Reunion of Christendom; an Ode. G. K. Chesterton. SeCePo
Antichrist, playing his lissome flute and merry. Armageddon. John Crowe Ransom. LiTA
Anticipation. Lord De Tabley. GTBS-D
Anticipation. Amy Lowell. LEAP
Anticipation. Joseph Tusiani. GoYe
Anticipations and Recollections, sel. Samuel Bartlett Parris.
"Go to the sick man's bedside—mark how dim." PoP
Antidote. Alcaeus. tr. fr. Greek by John Addington Symonds. GrR
Antigone, sel. Robert Garnier, pr. tr. fr. French.
Oedipus. fr. I, i. LiA
Antigone. George Meredith. TwCrTr
Antigone, sels. Sophocles, tr. fr. Greek.
Antigone Entombed Alive, tr. by Gilbert Murray. GrR
(Buried Alive, tr. by Robert Whitelaw.) OxBG
As It Was in the Beginning Is Now and Ever Shall Be, tr. by Lewis Campbell. GrR
Choral Ode: "Wonders are many, and none is more wonderful than man," pr. tr. by Richard C. Jebb. PreP
(Choral Ode from "Antigone," tr. by Dudley Fitts and Robert Fitzgerald.) LiTW
(Man; Creation's Masterpiece, tr. by Gilbert Murray.) GrR
("Many the forms of life," tr. by E. H. Plumptre.) GrPo
(What a Piece of Work Is a Man, tr. by F. L. Lucas.) OxBG
Evils of Money, The, tr. by Lewis Campbell. GrR
Last Journey, The, tr. by T. F. Higham. OxBG
Love, Conquering and Unconquerable, tr. by J. S. Phillimore. GrR
(Power of Love, The.) LiA
(Unconquerable Love.) OxBG
Nuptials of Haemon and Antigone, The, tr. by Gilbert Murray. GrR
"O Love, in every battle victor owned," tr. by E. H. Plumptre. GrPo
Omniscience Granted to No Man, tr. by Lewis Campbell. GrR
State versus Conscience, The, tr. by Gilbert Murray. GrR
(Higher Command, The, tr. unknown.) MaRV
(Undying Law, The, tr. by C. M. Bowra.) OxBG
Victory over Aggressors, tr. by Gilbert Murray. GrR
(Thebes of the Seven Gates, longer sel., tr. by Dudley Fitts and Robert Fitzgerald.) WaaP
Void of a Joyless Heart, The, tr. by Gilbert Murray. GrR
Antigone and Helen—would they laugh. Two Sonnets. David P. Berenberg. HBMV
Antigone Entombed Alive. Sophocles, tr. fr. Greek by Gilbert Murray. Fr. Antigone. GrR
(Buried Alive, tr. by Robert Whitelaw.) OxBG
Antigonish. Hughes Mearns. InMe; WhC
(Case, A.) LiTM; SiTL
(Little Man, The.) StaSt
(Little Man Who Wasn't There, The.) FaFP; FaPON
Antimenidas. Alcaeus, tr. fr. Greek by Sir William Marris. OxBG
Antinous. Quentin Stevenson. POTE (1959 ed.)
Antipater of Thessalonica. Kenneth Rexroth. CrMA
Antiphon: "Let all the world in every [or ev'ry] corner sing." George Herbert. CBE; EPS (1942 ed.); EV-2; PreP
Antiphonal, An. Psalms, Bible, O.T. See Twenty-fourth Psalm, The.
Antiphony. William Morris. See Song from "Ogier the Dane."
Antiplatonick, The. John Cleveland. MePo
Antiquary. John Donne. TuPP
Antiquary, The. Martial, tr. fr. Latin by Paul Nixon. LiTW; RoL
Antiquary, The, sels. Sir Walter Scott.
Harlaw, fr. ch. 40. BSV; EnLi-2
(Herring, The, st. 1.) BOHV
("Herring loves the merry moonlight, The.") FaBoCh; LoGBV
(Oysters, The, st. 1.) RIS
(Red Harlaw, The.) LH
Time, fr. ch. 10. BPN; EmBrPo
(Aged Carle, The.) OAEP
(Omnipotent, The.) LH
(Why Sit'st [or Sitt'st] Thou by That Ruin'd [or Ruined] Hall.) EnRP; EPN
Antique. Arthur Rimbaud, tr. fr. French by Frederick Morgan. AnFP
Antique Carved Figures. Raymond E. F. Larsson. JKCP (1955 ed.)
Antique Dresden Porcelain, Marked "Do Not Handle." Blanche D. Small. DDA
Antique Glimpses, sel. Thomas Caulfield Irwin.
"Grey-faced Spirit! let us sit." IrPN
Antique Harvesters. John Crowe Ransom. AnFE; APA; CoAnAm; CoBMV; CrMA; FaBoEn; InPo; MAP; MM; MoAB; MoAmPo; MOAP; OxBA; WoL
Antique Shop. Carl Carmer. FaPON; MoSiPe
Antiques of old Auctus will bore me to death, The. The Antiquary. Martial. LiTW; RoL
Antiquities of Rome, sels. Joachim du Bellay, tr. fr. French by Alan Conder. TrFP
Destruction, XIII.
Immortality. XXXII.

Kingship, XVI.
Relics, XXX.
Revolt, XII.
Ruined Glories, XXVII.
Antiquity of Freedom, The. Bryant. AA; AnNE; APW; CoBA; CoV; IAP; IDAH; TOP
"Oh Freedom! thou art not, as poets dream," *sel.* PoFr
Antiseptic Baby and the Prophylactic Pup, The. Strictly Germ-proof. Arthur Guiterman. BAP; BLPA; BOHV; HBV; PC; PFE; PoeMoYo; TCAP; TreF; TrJP; YaD
Antlered being, belling one. Crazy Sweeney's Song of the Woods. *Unknown. Fr.* Sweeney the Mad. LyMA
Ant-ology. Christian Morgenstern, *tr. fr. German by* R. F. C. Hull. AnGP
Antonio. Laura E. Richards. MoShBr; PoRh; TiPo (1959 ed.)
Antonio and Mellida, *sel.* John Marston.
"My thoughts are fixed." ViBoPo
Antonio, Antonio,/ Was tired of living alonio. Antonio. Laura E. Richards. MoShBr; PoRh; TiPo (1959 ed.)
Antonio Sarto ees buildin' a wall. The Blossomy Barrow. T. A. Daly. LHV
Antonio Torres Heredia. The Arrest of Antoñito el Camborio in the Streets of Seville. Federico García Lorca. PoFr
Antonio's Revenge, *sel.* John Marston.
Prologue: "Rawish dank of clumsy winter ramps, The." CoEV; LoBV; NBE; ViBoPo
Antonius, *sel.* Robert Garnier, *tr. fr. French by* the Countess of Pembroke.
Chorus: "Alas, with what tormenting fire." TuPP
(Of Death.) ElL
Antony and Cleopatra (3 *sonnets*). José Maria de Heredia, *tr. fr. French by* Henri Coulette. NePoEA
Antony and Cleopatra, 1 *sonnet, tr. by* Alan Conder. TrFP
Antony and Cleopatra. William Haines Lytle. *See* Antony to Cleopatra.
Antony and Cleopatra, *sels.* Shakespeare.
Cleopatra, *fr.* II, ii. CoEV; KN; LiTB; LiTG; LiTL; LPS-2
("Barge she sat in, like a burnish'd throne, The.") BoHiPo
(Cleopatra and Her Barge.) TreF
(Cleopatra's Barge.) PoFS; TrGrPo
(Enobarbus' Description of Cleopatra.) PreP
(From "Antony and Cleopatra.") LEAP
(Royal Barge, A.) BCEP
Cleopatra's Lament, *fr.* V, ii. UnPo
Come, Thou Monarch of the Vine, *fr.* II, vii. BEL; OAEP; OnPM; ViBoPo
(Drinking Song, A.) OBSC
Death of Cleopatra, *fr.* V, ii. FiP; TreFS
(Cleopatra's Death.) TrGrPo
(Deaths of Antony and Cleopatra.) CBOV
("Give me my robe, put on my crown.") AtBAP; LoPS; NBE
(I am Fire, and Ayre.) LiA
"Eros thou yet behold'st me?" *fr.* IV, xii. PoD
Eternal Feminine, The, II, v. LiA
Her Infinite Variety, *fr.* II, ii. EV-1
(Shakespeare Gallery, A: Cleopatra.) MaC
"I am dying Egypt, dying," *fr.* IV, xiii. EtPaEn, *br. sel.;* LoPS
(Death of Antony.) FiP
(Deaths of Antony and Cleopatra.) CBOV
Lament: "O! wither'd is the garland of the war," *br. sel. fr.* IV, xiii. KN
"Let Rome in Tiber melt, and the wide arch," *br. sel. fr.* I, i. EtPaEn
"My desolation does begin to make," *br. sel. fr.* V, ii. NBE
"No more, but in a woman, and commanded," *fr.* IV, xiii. NBE
"Oh Sunne,/ Burne the great sphere thou mov'st in," *fr.* IV, xv. AtBAP
"Oh, thou day o' the world," *br. sel. fr.* IV, viii. EtPaEn
"Unarme, Eros, the long dayes task is done," *fr.* IV, xii. NBE
Antony and Octavius, *sel.* Walter Savage Landor.
Corruption of Power, The, *fr.* sc. xii. RO
Antony to Cleopatra. William Haines Lytle. AA; BeLS; HBV; OBAV; OnPP
(Antony and Cleopatra.) BLPA; LPS-1; NeHB; TreF
Antony's Oration, *abr.* Shakespeare. *Fr.* Julius Caesar, III, ii. TrGrPo
(Antony's Oration over Caesar's Body.) LiTB; TreF
(Antony's Oration over the Body of Caesar.) EV-1; LPS-3, *abr.*
("Friends, Romans, countrymen," *abr.*) PIR
(I Come to Bury Caesar.) WHA
(Mark Antony's Oration, *shorter sel.*) BCEP; PYM
Antrim. Robinson Jeffers. CoV
Ants. Alfred Kreymborg. MAPA
Ants. Ramón López Velarde, *tr. fr. Spanish.* AnMP, *tr. by* Samuel Beckett; TwSpPo, *tr. by* H. R. Hays
Ant's a centaur in his dragon world, The. Pull Down Thy Vanity. Ezra Pound. *Fr.* Canto LXXXI. FaBoEn; MeRV
Ants are walking under the ground, The. The People. Elizabeth Madox Roberts. GoBP: TiPo
Anvil, The—God's Word. John Clifford. BLPA; NeHB; OQP; PoToHe (new ed.); QP-1
(Anvil, The.) BPP
(Anvil of God's Word, The.) BLRP
(God's Word.) MaRV
(Hammers and Anvil.) WBLP
Anvil of God's Mercy, The. Anna Hamilton Wood. OQP; QP-2
Anvil of God's Word, The. John Clifford. *See* Anvil, The—God's Word.
Anxiety, *sel.* Emerson.
"Some of your hurts you have cured." MaRV
Anxiety of a Young Lady to Get Married. *Unknown, tr. fr. Chinese by* James Legge. OuHeWo
Anxious Dead, The. John McCrae. BTP; CPG; OCL; OHIP; PoP
Anxious worry once I had, An. Sic Semper Tyrannis. Aldis Dunbar. DDA
Any Bird. Ilo Orleans. RIS
Any Father to Any Son. Francis Burdett Money-Coutts. OBVV
"Any floozie." Overheard at a Sculpture Show at a Museum. *Unknown.* SiTL
Any honest housewife would sort them out. The Poets. Robert Graves. MoPW
Any Husband or Wife. Carol Haynes. *See* Any Wife or Husband.
Any Lover, Any Lass. Richard Middleton. HBV; OBVV
Any Man's Advice to His Son. Kenneth Fearing. ChMo; PoLFOT
Any road leads anywhere. Roads. Katharine Knight. TVSH
Any Saint, *abr.* Francis Thompson. EmBrPo; MBP; MoBrPo
Any Size We Please. Robert Frost. CoV
Any Sunset. Louis Untermeyer. GoTP
Any time you hears da cheers and tables crack. Signs of Rain. Edward Jenner, *ad. by* Alex Rogers. StaSt
Any Town. Charles Norman. BAP
Any way the old world goes. The Song on the Way. *Unknown.* BrR; MPB
Any Wife or Husband. Carol Haynes. BLPA; NeHB
(Any Husband or Wife.) PoToHe
Any Wife to Any Husband. Robert Browning. BPN; EmBrPo; EtPaEn; FaBoEn; GEPC; OtMeF; PoVP
Any Woman. Hazel Hall. MAP; MoAmPo (1942 ed.)
Anyhow, anyhow, anyhow my Lord! I'm Gwine Up to Heab'n Anyhow. *Unknown.* BoAN-2
Anyone Lived in a Pretty How Town. E. E. Cummings. ChMo; CoBMV; LiTA; LiTM; MoAB; MoPo; Po; PoLFOT; ShBV-3; TwAmPo
Any One Will Do. *Unknown.* BOHV
Anywhere Out of the World. Baudelaire, *tr. fr. French by* William M. Davis. AnFP
Aodh Ruadh O'Domhnaill. Thomas McGreevy. AnIV; OBMV; OxBI
(Red Hugh.) OnYI
Aoibhinn, a leabhráin, do thriall. *Unknown, tr. fr. Irish.* AnIV, *tr. by* Flann O'Brien; OxBI, *tr. by* Brian O Nolan
Apache in Ambush, The. Bailey Millard. BAP
Apart. *Unknown, tr. fr. Russian by* W. R. S. Ralston. OnPM
Apartment House. Gerald Raftery. PoMa
Apathy. Paul Verlaine *tr. fr. French by* Muriel Kittel. AnFP
Ape, The. La Fontaine, *tr. fr. French by* Elizur Wright. OnPM
Ape, The. Roland Young. WhC
Ape and the Key, The. Mary W. Findlater. DiM
Apelles' Song. John Lyly. *Fr.* Alexander and Campaspe, III v. ATP; EM-1; EnLi-1; EnLit; EPP; NeHB; OuHeWo; TOP; TrGrPo
(Alexander and Campaspe.) ElSeCe
(Cards and Kisses.) BCEP; HoPM; LiTL; OBEV
(Cupid and Campaspe.) AtBAP; BEL; BLV; BTP; EIL; EV-1; GTBS; GTBS-D; GTBS-W; GTSE; GTSL; HBV; LEAP; LiTG; LPS-1; SeCeV; UnPo (1st ed.); WHA
(Cupid and My Campaspe.) PoRA
(Cupid and My Campaspe Played [*or* Play'd].) CenL; ExPo; KN; OAEP; PECK; ReaPo; ReEn; SiCE; TuPP; ViBoPo
(Song by Apelles.) ALV; CaAE
(Song of Apelles.) OBSC
Apelles the Painter. Leonidas of Tarentum, *tr. fr. Greek by* Lord Neaves. OnPM
Apeneck Sweeney spreads his knees. Sweeney among the Nightingales. T. S. Eliot. AnEnPo; AnFE; APA; BLV; BoLiVe; ChMo; ChMP; CMP; CoAnAm; CoBMV; CoEV; EnL; EnLit; FaBoMo; InPo; InvP; LiTA; LiTM; MAP; MAPA; MaPo; MoAmPo (1942 ed.); MOAP; MoVE; NePA; NP; OAEP (2d ed.); OBMV; OxBA; ReaFo; ReMP; SeCeV; TwAmPo; TwHP
Apes and Ivory. Alfred Noyes. TSW; TSWC

Apes yawn and adore their fleas in the sun, The. The Jaguar. Ted Hughes. POTE (1959 ed.)
Apethorpe. Julian Fane. EnSW
Apex. Nate Salsbury. InMe; WhC
Aphrodite. "Æ." LBBV
Aphrodite and the Knife-Grinder. Carl Snoilsky, *tr. fr. Swedish by* Charles W. Stork. AnSL
Aphrodite, daughter of Zeus, undying. To Aphrodite. Sappho. GrPE
Aphrodite has a son. The Voyage of Love. Cercidas. GrL; OxBG
Aphrodite of Praxiteles, The. *Unknown, tr. fr. Greek by* Humbert Wolfe. OxBG
Aphrodite on Ida. *Unknown. See* Vesting of Aphrodite, The.
Apis his fellow-boxers here have set. The Champion's Statute. Lucilius. GrPE
Apocalypse. Bible, *N.T. See* Revelation.
Apocalypse. Theodore Maynard. JKCP
Apocalypse. John Frederick Nims. MiAP
Apocalypse. Richard Realf. PaA; PAP
Apocalyptic roll out of the East. The Hymn of Armageddon. George Sylvester Viereck. LPS-1
Apocrypha. Bible, *O.T. See* Baruch; Ecclesiasticus; First Maccabees; Judith; Second Maccabees; Tobit; Wisdom of Solomon, The
Apocrypha. Babette Deutsch. HBMV
Apocryphal Apocalypse. John Wheelwright. MoVE
Apocryphal Soliloquies. Louis Untermeyer. TCPD
(Goliath and David.) TrJP
Apoem I. Henri Pichette, *tr. fr. French by* Richard Wilbur. LiTW
Apollo. Matthew Arnold. *See* Callicles' Song.
Apollo. Thomas Holley Chivers. APW; MOAP; SPP
Apollo Alone Approves. Mark Turbyfill. NP
Apollo and Daphne. Ovid, *tr. fr. Latin by* Gilbert Highet. *Fr.* Metamorphoses, I. LaP
Apollo and Daphne. W. R. Rodgers. LiTB
Apollo and Daphne, *sel.* Paul Whitehead.
Hunting Song. OBEC; OxBoLi
Apollo Confounds the Furies. Aeschylus, *tr. fr. Greek by* Gilbert Murray. *Fr.* Eumenides. GrR
Apollo Destroys the Wall. Homer, *tr. fr. Greek by* the Earl of Derby. *Fr.* The Iliad, XV. OxBG
Apollo great, whose beams the greater world do light. Hymn to Apollo. Sir Philip Sidney. EPP
Apollo hearing this, passed quickly on. The Cattle-Thief. *Unknown. Fr.* Homeric Hymns. OxBG
Apollo kept my father's sheep. A Daughter of Admetus. T. Sturge Moore. FaBoTw
Apollo once a yeare may merry be. *Unknown.* SeCSL
Apollo sings, his harpe resounds; give roome. Upon Master Fletchers Incomparable Playes. Robert Herrick. OBS; PtP
Apollo the Betrayer. Euripides, *tr. fr. Greek by* C. M. Bowra. *Fr.* Ion. OxBG
Apollo then, with sudden scrutiny and gloomless eyes. Keats. *Fr.* Hyperion. NBE; OBRV
Apollonius, *sel.* Apostolos Melachrinos, *tr. fr. Modern Greek by* Rae Dalven.
Playing the Lyre. MoGP
Apollo's Song. Ben Jonson. *Fr.* The Masque of Augurs. LoBV
Apollo's Song. John Lyly. *See* Daphne.
Apollyonists, The. Phineas Fletcher. *See* Locusts, or Apollyonists, The.
Apologia. Jean Garrigue. LiTA
Apologia. David Gascoyne. ChMP
Apologia. Oscar Wilde. PoVP
Apologia pro Poemate Meo. Wilfred Owen. ChMP; CoBE; CoBMV; LBBV; LiTM (rev. ed.); MBP; MoAB; MoBrPo; NeMA; NP; PoFr; TwCV
Apologia pro Vita Sua. Samuel Taylor Coleridge. EnRP
Apologie for Having Loved Before, An. Edmund Waller. *See* Apology for Having Loved Before, An.
Apology, The. Emerson. AmPP (3d ed.); BAV; CoBA; IAP; OBAV; PG (1945 ed.)
Apology. Ibn al-Haddad, *tr. fr. Arabic by* A. J. Arberry. MooP
Apology. Amy Lowell. AV; BLV; BoLiVe; NP; OBAV; SBMV; VOD
Apology. John McClure. LS; TBM
Apology. Vassar Miller. NePoEA
Apology, An: "Of Heaven or Hell I have no power to sing." William Morris. *Fr.* The Earthly Paradise. AWP; BEL; BLPA; BPN; CoBE; EmBrPo; EnLi-2; EnLit; EPN; GTBS; GTBS-W; GTSL; InP; OAEP; POTT; PoVP; TCEP; TOP; ViP; ViPP; VLEP
(Earthly Paradise, The: Prologue.) OtMeF
(Idle Singer, The, *abr.*) BMEP
("Of Heaven or Hell I have no power to sing.") EPP; LiTB; LoBV; ViBoPo, *abr.;* ViPo
(Prelude to "The Earthly Paradise.") LEAP
(Prologue: "Of Heaven or Hell . . .") FaBoEn
(Prologue to "The Earthly Paradise.") BrBe
(Singer's Prelude, The.) HBV; VA
Apology. Richard Wilbur. NePoAm
Apology for Actors, An, *sel.* Thomas Heywood.
Author to his Booke, The. OBS
Apology for Bad Dreams. Robinson Jeffers. AmP; AmPP; AnFE; CoAnAm; CoBMV; LiTA; MAP; MoAB; MoAmPo; MOAP; OnAP; OxBA; SeCeV; TwAmPo
Apology [*or* Apologie] for Having Loved Before, An. Edmund Waller. MePo; OAEP
Apology for Love. Boccaccio, *tr. fr. Italian by* Dryden. LiTW; LyMA
Apology for Vagrants. John Langhorne. *Fr.* The Country Justice. OBEC
Apology of the Young Scientists. Celia Dimmette. GoYe
Apology to a Small Dog. Teddy Webb. AlBD
Apology to the Harp, An. Thomas D'Arcy McGee. GTIV
Apology: Why Do I Write Today? William Carlos Williams. OxBA
Apon the midsummer evin, mirriest of nichtis. *See* Upon the midsummer even
Apostasy. Aus of Kuraiza, *tr. fr. Arabic by* Hartwig Hirschfeld. TrJP
Apostasy. Mary Mills. NePoAm
Apostasy, The, *sel.* Thomas Traherne.
"One star/ Is better far." CoBE
Apostate, The. A. E. Coppard. OBMV
Apostle, citizen, and artisan! Love's Cosmopolitan. Annie Matheson. OBVV
Apostles of the hidden sun. The Last Supper. Oscar Williams. FaFP; GTBS-W; LiTA; LiTM; NePA; TwAmPo
Apostles of the risen Christ, go forth! His Glory Tell. Horatius Bonar. BePJ
Apostrophe to a Pram Rider. E. B. White. InMe
Apostrophe to Death. Caelius Sedulius, *tr. fr. Latin by* George Sigerson. *Fr.* Carmen Paschale. OnYI
Apostrophe to the Island of Cuba. James Gates Percival. PAH
Apostrophe to the Ocean. Byron. *See* Ocean, The.
Apostrophic Notes from the New-World Physics. E. B. White. ImOP
Apotheosis, *abr.* Joseph Bajza, *tr. fr. Hungarian by* William N. Loew. PoFr
Apotheosis. Jules Laforgue, *tr. fr. French by* Vernon Watkins. AnFP
Apotheosis. Alexander M. Stephen. OCL
Apparel of green woods and meadows gay. On Revisiting Cintra after the Death of Catarina. Luis de Camões. AWP
Apparelled as a Paynim in pilgrim's wise. The Palmer. William Langland. *Fr.* The Vision of Piers Plowman. ACP; CAW
Apparent Failure. Robert Browning. PoVP; VLEP
"It's wiser being good than bad." *sel.* BMEP; MaRV; PC
Apparently the Nibelungs. Operatic Note. Melville Cane. UnS
Apparently with no surprise. Emily Dickinson. AmPo; AmPP; AnFE; AnNE; APA; CoAnAm; TrGrPo
(Death and Life.) OnPM
(Frost, The.) CoBA
Apparition. John Peale Bishop. MoVE
Apparition, The. Blake. *Fr.* America. BoW
Apparition, The. John Donne. AtBAP; ElSeCe; EnLoPo; EnLP; ExPo; LoBV; MePo; OBEV (new ed.); OBS; ReEn; SeCV-1; SeEP; ViBoPo
Apparition. John Erskine. HBMV
Apparition. W. E. Henley. *Fr.* In Hospital. BEL; EnLi-2 (1949 ed.); POTT; PoVP; TCEP; TrGrPo
Apparition. Victor Hugo, *tr. fr. French by* Alan Conder. TrFP
Apparition. Stéphane Mallarmé, *tr. fr. French by* Kate Flores. AnFP
Apparition, The. Stephen Phillips. GTML; MBP; OBEV (new ed.); OBVV
(Dream, A [*or* The]). BMEP; LBBV; MaRV; PoeMoYo
Apparition of His Mistress Calling Him to Elysium [*or* Elizium], The. Robert Herrick. ExPo; SeCV-1
Apparition of Splendor. Marianne Moore. NePoAm
Apparition of these faces in the crowd, The. In a Station of the Metro. Ezra Pound. AmP; CoV; ExPo; InP; MAP; MoAB; MoAmPo; NeMA; OxBA; UnPo
Apparition of War. Joel Barlow. *Fr.* The Columbiad. APW
Apparitions. Thomas Bailey Aldrich. BAP; UnW
Apparitions. Robert Browning. *See* Such a Starved Bank of Moss.
Apparitions. Thomas Curtis Clark. BPP; MaRV; OQP; PGD; QP 1
(It Shall Not Be Again!) PEDC; PoRL; PSO
Apparitions. Alice Corbin. NP
Apparitions, The. W. B. Yeats. LiTM (rev. ed.); PoFS
Apparuit. Ezra Pound. APA; CoAnAm; TwAmPo
Appeal, The. Emily Brontë. EmBrPo; LoBV
("If grief for grief can touch thee.") EnLoPo
Appeal, The. Walter Savage Landor. VA
(Lyrics to Ianthe.) BPN
(Remain.) OBEV (1st ed.)
(Remain, Ah Not in Youth Alone.) OAEP
Appeal, An. Swinburne. BPN

Appeal, The. Sir Thomas Wyatt. *See* Earnest Suit to His Unkind Mistress Not to Forsake Him, An.
Appeal for Are to the Sextant of the Old Brick Meetinouse, A. Arabella M. Willson. BOHV
(To the "Sextant.") LPS-3
Appeal for Illumination. Luigi Pulci, *tr. fr. Italian by* Byron. *Fr.* Il Morgante maggiore. ISi
Appeal of Phoenix, The. Homer, *tr. fr. Greek by* George Ernle. *Fr.* The Iliad, IX. OxBG
(Old Knight Phoenix, The, *pr. tr. by* Lang, Leaf *and* Myers.) GrR
Appeal to Cats in the Business of Love, An. Thomas Flatman. EnLoPo
Appeal to Harold, The. H. C. Bunner. AA
Appeal to the Goddess A, An. Thomas Ybarra. CAG
Appearances. Robert Browning. BPN; PoVP
Appeared/ The princess with that merry child Prince Guy. Athulf and Ethilda. Sir Henry Taylor. *Fr.* Edwin the Fair. LPS-1
Appeasement of Demeter, The. George Meredith. EnLi-2
Appendix Vergiliana. *Tr. fr. Latin by* Helen Waddell. DiM
Appian Way, The. Geoffrey Johnson. JKCP (1955 ed.)
Appile Tree, De. Joel Chandler Harris. IHA; TSW; TSWC
Applauding youths laughed with young prostitutes. The Harlem Dancer. Claude McKay. BANP; MAP
Apple, The Lady Margaret Sackville. OBVV
Apple and Mole. Donald Davidson. MAP; MoAmPo (1942 ed.)
Apple and Rose. Karle Wilson Baker. FAOV
Apple-Barrel, The. Edwin L. Sabin. DD
Apple-Barrel of Johnny Appleseed, The. Vachel Lindsay. MAP; MoAmPo; NeMA; OxBA
Apple, beech and cedar fair. Song. *Unknown.* ADAH
Apple Blossom. Kate Louise Brown. GFA; OTPC (1946 ed.)
Apple Blossoms. Ralph Bergengren. GFA
Apple Blossoms. Ludvig Holstein, *tr. fr. Danish by* Charles W. Stork. BoDS
Apple Blossoms. Lucy Larcom. YeAr
Apple Blossoms. Helen Adams Parker. BoTP
Apple Blossoms. Arthur L. Phelps. CPG
Apple Blossoms. Helen Wing. GFA
Apple blossoms, budding, blowing. Apple Blossoms. Lucy Larcom. YeAr
Apple blossoms grow so high, The. Apple Blossoms. Helen Wing. GFA
Apple blossoms look like snow. A Comparison. John Farrar. BrR; FaPON; MPB; TSW
Apple Dumplings and a King. "Peter Pindar." OBEC
Apple-Elf, The. Sheila E. Braine. GFA
Apple Gathering, An. Christina Rossetti. PoVP; TCEP
Apple-green west and an orange bar. "Frost To-Night." Edith M. Thomas. BLP; CP; LBMV; MCCG; NV; PCD; POT; PoTo
Apple Harvest. Helen Leuty. BoTP
Apple Howling Songs ("Here stands a good apple tree"). *Unknown.* OTPC (1923 ed.)
(Two Apple-howling Songs, 1.) PCH
Apple Howling Songs ("Here's to thee, old apple tree"). *Unknown.* OTPC (1923 ed.)
("Here's to thee, old apple tree.") OxNR
(Two Apple-howling Songs, 2.) PCH
Apple Orchard in the Spring, The. William Wesley Martin. GN; OTPC
Apple orchard smells like wine, An. Wise. Lizette Woodworth Reese. HBV; LBAP
Apple Peeler. Robert Francis. CrMA; NePoAm
Apple-Pie and Cheese. Eugene Field. LHV
Apple-pie, apple-pie. *Unknown.* OxNR
Apple Rhyme, The. Madeleine Nightingale. BoTP
Apples ripen under yellowing leaves, The. Sonnet. Thomas Caulfield Irwin. IrPN
Apple Season. Frances Frost. BrR; SiSoSe
Apple-Seed John. Lydia Maria Child. DD, *abr.;* GA, *abr.;* OHIP; OTPC
Apple Song. Frances Frost. FaPON; TiPo (1959 ed.)
Apple Tree, The. Beatrice Curtis Brown. SiSoSe
Apple-Tree, The. Nancy Campbell. AnIV; NP
Apple Tree, The. Oliver St. John Gogarty. AIDL; QS
Apple Tree, The. *Unknown, tr. fr. Armenian by* Zabelle C. Boyajian. ArmLP
Apple Tree. The. Brian Vrepont. BoAu
Apple tree can grieve my spirit so, An. Spring Apple Tree. "Igor Severyanin." TrRV
Apple tree there groweth, An. Le Pommier doux. *Unknown, tr. by* William McLennan. BoCaPo
Apple trees are hung with gold, The. Endymion. Oscar Wilde. HBV; VLEP
Apple-trees, with burdens of white bloom, The. Messengers. Charles Hanson Towne. CAW
Apples. Lisel Mueller. NePoAm-2
Apples. Lizette Woodworth Reese. YT
Apples. Swift. *Fr.* Verses for Fruitwomen. AnIV; OnYI
Apples along the highway strewn. Wayfaring. Richard Le Gallienne. TVSH
Apples are ripe in the orchard, The. After All. William Winter. PAP
Apples are seasoned, The. Apple Song. Frances Frost. FaPON; TiPo (1959 ed.)
Apples falling from the tree, The. Night Magic. Amelia Josephine Burr. MPB; SP
Apples in New Hampshire. Marie Gilchrist. PoMa
Apples of gold the Hero dropt. Good Luck. Oliver St. John Gogarty. JKCP (1926 ed.)
Appleton House Andrew Marvell. *See* Upon Appleton House.
Applied Astronomy. Esther B. Tiffany. PR
Apply for the position (I've forgotten now for what). In Order To. Kenneth Patchen. Po
Appoggiatura. Donald Jeffrey Hayes. PoNe
Appointed in the newe moon. Jason and Medea. John Gower. *Fr.* Confessio Amantis. ACP
Appointed lot has come upon me, mother, The. Farewell to My Mother. "Plácido," *tr. by* Bryant. BANP
Appointed winners in a long-stretch'd game, The. To-Day and Thee. Walt Whitman. NePA
Appointment, The. Sully-Prudhomme, *tr. fr. French by* Arthur O'Shaughnessy. OxBI
Appointment, An. W. B. Yeats. AnEnPo; PoFr
Appointment in Doctor's Office. Josephine Miles. FiMAP
Appollyon. George Rostrevor Hamilton. SoV
Appomattox. MacKinlay Kantor. AnAmPo
Appomattox (On the Death of Grant). Ben D. House. BIG
Appraisal. Sara Teasdale. MAP; MoAmPo
Appreciated. Edward Rowland Sill. PR
Appreciation. Thomas Bailey Aldrich. AA
Appreciation. George Meredith. EmBrPo; ViBoPo
Appreciation à la Mode. Armel O'Connor. SaFP
Apprehension. James Anderson Fraser. MaRV; OQP; QP-2
Apprehension. *Unknown, tr. fr. Sanskrit by* Douglas Ainslie. OBVV
Apprentice Boy The. *Unknown.* ABS
Apprenticed. Jean Ingelow. *Fr.* Songs of the Night Watches. LiTL; OBVV
("Come out and hear the waters shoot . . .") AIDL
Approach, The. Thomas Traherne. OxBoCh
"O Lord I wonder at thy Lov," *sel.* TrPWD
Approach and bring from Araby the blest. Kneel to the Lord. Christopher Smart. *Fr.* On the Goodness of the Supreme Being. BeR
Approach, for what we seek is here! Matthew Arnold. *Fr.* Stanzas from the Grande Chartreuse. BMEP
Approach of Age, The. George Crabbe. *See* "Age, with Stealing Steps . . ."
Approach of Age, The. Shakespeare. *See* Sonnets, XII.
Approach of Evening. George Croly. IrPN
Approach of Pharaoh, The. Cædmon (?), *tr. fr. Anglo-Saxon by* C. W. Kennedy. *Fr.* Genesis. ACP; WaaP
(Coming of Pharaoh, The.) CAW
Approach of Spring. John Clare. ERP
Approach of the Fairies, The. Shakespeare. *See* Now the Hungry Lion Roars.
Approach of Winter, The. Jules Laforgue, *tr. fr. French by* Joseph Bennett. AnFP
(Winter Is Coming, *tr. by* Alan Conder.) TrFP
Approach of Winter, The. Thomas Sackville. *Fr.* Induction to "The Mirror for Magistrates." CoEV
(Winter, *shorter sel.*) EIL; SeCePo
Approach of Winter. James Thomson. *Fr.* The Seasons: Winter. OBEC
Approach this court with deference. On Entering a Forest. Elinor Lennen. PGD
Approaches. George Macdonald. MaRV; OQP; QP-1
Approaching America. J. C. Squire. HBMV
Approaching by the gate (Class of '79). Views of the Favorite Colleges. John Malcolm Brinnin. LiTA; MoAB; OnHM
Approaching God. Amos Bronson Alcott. IAP
Approved by works of love and might. Summer. Aubrey Thomas De Vere. *Fr.* The Year of Sorrow: Ireland, 1849. TIP
Appuldurcombe Park. Amy Lowell. ChMo; CMP
Après. Arthur J. Munby. LPS-3
Après-Midi d'un faune, L'. Stéphane Mallarmé, *tr. fr. French by* Aldous Huxley. AWP; LiTW; MiFP
(Afternoon of a Faun, The.) AnFP, *tr. by* Frederick Morgan; LiA, *tr. by* Aldous Huxley; ReMP, *tr. by* Roger Fry
"Après Moi le Déluge." *Unknown, tr. fr. Greek.* GrPE, *tr. by* F. L. Lucas; OxBG, *tr. by* A. J. Butler
Apricot Tree, The. Ibn A'isna, *tr. fr. Arabic by* A. J. Arberry. MooP
April. Obadiah Cyrus Auringer. AA
April. Remy Belleau, *tr. fr. French.* AWP, *tr. by* Andrew Lang; TrFP, *tr. by* Alan Conder
(Sweet Month of April, The, *tr. by* Henry F. Cary.) RO
April. Godfrey Fox Bradby. ShBV-1
April. Vidame de Chartres, *tr. fr. French by* Swinburne. AWP
April. John Vance Cheney. NLK
April. Emily Dickinson. *See* Altered look about the hills, An.

April. Emerson. ViBoPo
April. Theodosia Garrison. DD; HBMV; MPB; NLK; TCAP; VOD
April. Florence Hamilton. BAP; PYM
April. Thomas S. Jones, Jr. VOD
April. Mary Sinton Leitch. LS
April ("When the warm sun, that brings"). Henry Wadsworth Longfellow. ADAH
April ("Again has come the spring-time"). Samuel Longfellow. SN
April. Robert Loveman. AA
April. Isobel McFadden. MaRV
April. Lloyd Mifflin. *Fr.* Fields of Dawn. ADAH; SN
April. John Francis O'Donnell. IrPN
April. Sir Herbert Read. *Fr.* Eclogues. BrBE
April. Ted Robinson. GoTP
April. Dora Sigerson Shorter. HBMV; HBVY
April [*or* Aprill]. Spenser. *Fr.* The Shepheardes Calender. EnLi-1; PoEL-1; ReEn; ReIE; SiCE
Sels.
Ditty, A: "See where she sits upon the grassie greene," 6 *sts.* OBEV
("See where she sits upon the grassy green," 2 *sts.*) ViBoPo
Elisa. CoEV; OBSC
(Hobbinol's Lay of Fair Elisa.) ElSeCe
("Ye dayntye Nymphs, that in this blessed Brooke.") AtBAP
April. Francis Sweeney. JKCP (1955 ed.)
April. Sara Teasdale. FaPON; GFA; OTPC (1946 ed.); PCH; StVeCh; TiPo; TSW; YeAr
April. Eunice Tietjens. YeAr
April. Jaime Torres Bodet, *tr. fr. Spanish by* Blanca López Castellón. AnCL
April. Sir William Watson. *See* Song: "April, April."
April Adoration, An. Sir Charles G. D. Roberts. HBV
April again and it is a year again. Elegy. Sidney Keyes. FaBoMo; WaP
April—and Dying. Anne Reeve Aldrich. AA
April and May. Emerson. *Fr.* May-Day. GN; OHIP
April and May. Anne Robinson. MeMeAg; SUS
April, April,/ Laugh thy girlish laughter. Song [*or* April]. Sir William Watson. BLV; BMEP; BoTP; CaAE; DD; GN; GoTP; HBV; HBVY; LBBV; LEAP; MBP; MoBrPo (1942 ed.); NLK; OBVV; PoRL; PYM; TreF; TrGrPo; TSW; TSWC; YT
April! April! Are You Here? Dora Read Goodale. PTA-2
April cold with dropping rain. April and May. Emerson. *Fr.* May-Day. GN; OHIP
April comes with sudden showers. April's Coming. Lancaster Pollard. NLK
April Day, An. Caroline Anne Bowles. PEOR; TVSH
April Day, An. Joseph Seamon Cotter, Jr. CDC
April Days. Tennyson. *See* In Memoriam A. H. H.: "Dip down upon the northern shore."
April Earth, The. Max Eastman. AnEnPo
April, 1885. Robert Bridges. BrBE; ChMo; CMP
April Fantasie. Ellen Mackay Hutchinson Cortissoz. AA
April Fool. Elizabeth J. Coatsworth. YeAr
April Fool. Eleanor Hammond. GFA
April Fools. Katherine Brégy. JKCP (1955 ed.)
April Fool's Day. *Unknown.* *See* All Fools' Day.
April Ghost, An. Lizette Woodworth Reese. AV; DaM
April goes out as May comes in. *Unknown, tr. fr. Spanish by* Eleanor L. Turnbull. TeCS
April had come, brimful. Yellow Spring. Juan Ramón Jiménez. TeCS
April in England. Robert Browning. *See* Home Thoughts from Abroad.
April in the Hills. Archibald Lampman. CPG
April Inventory. W. D. Snodgrass. NePoEA
April is a laundress. April and May. Anne Robinson. MeMeAg; SUS
April is in my mistress' face. All Seasons in One. *Unknown.* EG; OBSC; ReEn; SiCE; TrGrPo
April is no month for burials. Rite of Spring. Leo Kennedy. CaP
April is the cruellest [*or* cruelest] month, breeding. The Burial of the Dead. T. S. Eliot. The Waste Land, I. AmPo; AmPP; AtBAP; ATP (1953 ed.); CoBMV; EnLit; FaBoMo; LiTA; LiTM; MoAB; MoAmPo (1950 ed.); MoPo; MoVE; NePA; OAEP (2d ed.); OxBA; ReaPo; ReMP; UnPo (3d ed.)
April Love. Ernest Dowson. PG
April Moment. Arthur Davison Ficke. *See* Come Forth! for Spring Is Singing in the Boughs.
April, month without a peer. April. Remy Belleau. TrFP
April Morning, An. Bliss Carman. CV; DD; GBV; HBMV; HBVY; NV; VOD
April Morning. George Elliston. NLK
April Morning, An. Wordsworth. *See* It Was an April Morning.
April Mortality. Léonie Adams. AnAmPo; LA; MAP; MoAB; MoAmPo; MOAP; TrGrPo, 2 *sts.*
April Music. Clinton Scollard. NLK
April, 1940. Patrick Maybin. NeIP
April, 1941. Vera Bax. DiM
April, 1942. Mark Van Doren. WaP
April—North Carolina. Harriet Monroe. SBMV
April now walks the fields again. April on the Battlefields. Leonora Speyer. AOAH; OBAV; SBMV
April of Our Desire. Lola Ridge. MAP; MoAmPo (1942 ed.)
April of the Ages, The. Digby Mackworth Dolben. GoBC
April on the Battlefields. Leonora Speyer. AOAH; OBAV; SBMV
April on Tweed. Andrew Lang. EBSV
(Trout-fishing on Tweed.) POT
April, pride of woodland ways. April. Remy Belleau. AWP
April Puddle. Rowena Bennett. TiPo (1959 ed.)
April Rain. Mathilde Blind. HBV
April Rain. Robert Loveman. BAP; BoTP; DD; HBV; HBVY; LEAP; MaRV; NLK; POT; PoTo; RIS; SUS; TrJP
(Rain Song, The.) MPB; OQP; QP-1; WBLP
April Rain Song. Langston Hughes. FaPON; PoRh; SUS; TiPo
April rain, the April rain, The. April Rain. Mathilde Blind. HBV
April Rise. Laurie Lee. GTBS-D; OnHM
April Showers. Mary E. Wilkins Freeman. PTA-2
April Showers. James Stephens. TiPo (1959 ed.)
April Smile. Spenser. *See* Amoretti, XL.
April Speaks. Lloyd Mifflin. POT; PoTo
April, sweet month, the daintiest of all. The Sweet Month of April. Remy Belleau, *tr. by* Henry F. Cary. RO
April Theology. John G. Neihardt. LEAP
April this year, not otherwise. Song of a Second April. Edna St. Vincent Millay. ChMo; CMP; LoPo; OxBA
April, up on a twig a leaftuft stands. First Warm Days. Edwin Denby. GTBS-W; LiTM; PeBoSo
April walks beside me still in budded cloak of brown. Hurdy-Gurdy Days. Martha Haskell Clark. MPB
April Weather. Bliss Carman. NLK
April Weather. Jessie McDermott. OTPC (1946 ed.); PCH
April Weather. Lizette Woodworth Reese. DD; HBMV; LS; NLK; PoTo; SPP; VOD
April, when I heard. Renewal. Charles Hanson Towne. CV; NLK
April whispered this to me. The Secret. John Richard Moreland. NLK; OQP; QP-2
April Winds. Michael Lewis. TSW; TSWC
(In Spring.) StaSt
April winds are magical, The. April. Emerson. ViBoPo
April world is misted with emerald and gold, The. Gypsy-Heart [*or* Gipsy-Heart]. Katharine Lee Bates. HBMV; NLK; POT; PoTo
Aprill. Spenser. *See* April.
April's Amazing Meaning. George Dillon. MAP; MoAmPo (1942 ed.); TBM
April's Coming. Lancaster Pollard. NLK
Apron of Flowers, The. Robert Herrick. *See* To Gather Flowers Sappha Went.
Aquae in Vinum Versae. Richard Crashaw, *tr. fr. Latin by* D. C. Allen. Epigrammata Sacra, I, 96. LaP
Aquarium. Eugenio Florit, *tr. fr. Spanish by* H. R. Hays. TwSpPo
Aquarium. José Gorostiza, *tr. fr. Spanish by* Donald Devenish Walsh. AnCL
Aquarium, An. Amy Lowell. PFY
Ar, these is 'appy days! An' 'ow they've flown. The Stoush o' Day. C. J. Dennis. NeLNL
Arab, The. Charles Stuart Calverley. LPS-3
Arab Love-Song, An. Francis Thompson. AWP; BMEP; LBBV; LEAP; LoPo; LoPS; MBP; MoAB; BoBrPo; OtMeF; POTE; POTT; VLEP; VOD (1935 ed.); YT
("Hunchèd camels of the night, The.") EG
Arab Song. Richard Henry Stoddard. AA; OBAV
Arab to His Favorite Steed, The. Caroline E. S. Norton. BeLS; LPS-2; TreFS
(Arab's Farewell to His Horse.) BLPA
Arab to the Palm, The. Bayard Taylor. LPS-2
Arabia. Walter de la Mare. GTBS; HBMV; POTE; PtOT; TCPD; WHA; WP
Arabia, in our fields threw down her Spanish rocks. Roland. Napoléon Peyrat. LiA
Arabian Nights. *Unknown.* *See* Thousand and One Nights, The.
Arabian Proverb ("He who knows . . ."). *Unknown, tr. fr. Arabic.* TreF
(He Who Knows.) BLPA; GoTP; NeHB
(Philosophic Advice.) PFE
Arabian Shawl, The. Katherine Mansfield. *Fr.* Two Nocturnes. HBMV
Arabs. Alfred Kreymborg. MAPA; TwAmPo
Arab's Farewell to His Horse. Caroline E. S. Norton. *See* Arab to His Favorite Steed, The.
Arachne. Rose Terry Cooke. AA; AnAmPo; LA

Arachne. William Empson. InvP; MoVE; OBMV
Arac's Song. W. S. Gilbert. *Fr.* Princess Ida. FiBHP; WhC
Aran ("Aran of the many stags"). *Unknown, tr. fr. Old Irish by* Seán O'Faoláin. SiB
Araphoe. *Unknown. See* Buckskin Joe.
Araucana, La, *much abr.* Alonso de Ercilla y Zúñiga, *tr. fr. Spanish by* Paul Thomas Manchester *and* Charles Maxwell Lancaster. OuHeWo
Welcome of the Young Cacique, The, *sel., fr.* XXXVI, *tr. by* Elizabeth Selden. BoFr
Araxes Came Devouringly. Hovhannes Hovhannessian, *tr. fr. Armenian by* Zabelle C. Boyajian. ArmLP
Araygnement of Paris, The. George Peele. *See* Arraignment of Paris.
Arbasto, *sels.* Robert Greene.
In Time We See That Silver Drops. ReIE; SiCE
(Doralicia's Song.) LoBV; OBSC
Whereat Erewhile I Wept, I Laugh. EIL
Arbitrants, *sels.* Menander, *tr. fr. Greek by* F. G. Allinson. GrPo
"All alone this fellow found."
"Sinless saint I was, mine eyes on honour fixed, The!"
Arbor Amoris. Villon, *tr. fr. French by* Andrew Lang. AWP
Arbor Day. Dorothy Brown Thompson. SiSoSe
Arbor Day Alphabet. Ada Simpson Sherwood. ADAH
Arbor Day Exercise, An. Bryant, *and others. Fr. various poems.* ADAH
Arbor Day Song. Mary A. Heermans. ADAH; HH
Arbor Day Tree, An. *Unknown.* ADAH; DD; HH; MeMeAg; OHIP
Arbor Una Nobilis. Sister Thomas Aquinas. JKCP (1955 ed.)
Arbor Vitae. Coventry Patmore. The Unknown Eros, II, iii. GoBC; LoBV; SeCePo; ViP
Arboreal ape, The. A Hymn Not in Favor of Evolution. Catherine Graham Miller. CAG
Arbutus. Adelaide Crapsey. MoAmPo (1942 ed.)
Arcades, *sels.* Milton.
Song: "Nymphs and shepherds, dance no more." AtBAP; ElSeCe; FiP; SeCL; ViBoPo
Song: "O'er [*or* O're] the smooth enamel[l]ed green." AtBAP; BLV; BoLiVe; ElSeCe; InPo; LEAP; LoBV; OBEV; SeCL; ThWaDe; TrGrPo; ViBoPo
Arcadia, *sels.* Sir Philip Sidney.
Country Song, A: "Lad Philisides, The." OBSC; SiPS
Cupid. SiPS
Double Sestine. AtBAP; LiTB; PoEL-1
(Sestina.) LiTG
(Strephon and Klaius.) CoEV
("Ye goat-herd gods, that love the grassy mountains.") SiCE
Echo. SiPS
Epithalamium: "Let mother earth now deck[e] herself[e] in flowers." EV-1; SiPS
Geron and Histor. SiPS
Get Hence Foule Griefe. AtBAP; PoEL-1
(Contentment.) SiPS
Graven Thoughts. SiPS
In Vain, Mine Eyes. SiPS
"Lock up, fair lids, the treasure of my heart." SiCE
(Sleep.) OBSC; SiPS
(Sonnet: "Lock up, fair lids, the treasure of my heart.") EG; EIL
Love and Jealousy. SiPS
Love and Reason. SiPS
Loved I Am, and Yet Complaine of Love. PoEL-1
(Complaint of Love.) SiPS
Madrigal: "Why dost thou haste away." EG; OBSC; SiPS
"My sheep are thoughts, which I both guide and serve." SiCE; SiPS
(Dorus His Comparisons.) CaAE; ReIE
My True Love Hath My Heart [and I Have His]. AtBAP; BLV; BoLiVe; CH; CoBE; EG; FaBoBe; HBV; LiTG; LiTL; LoPo; LoPS; MaPo; OAEP; OnPM; PeBoSo; PoE; PoEL-1; ReEn; SeCeV; SiCE; TrGrPo; ViBoPo
(Arcadian Duologue.) SiPS
(Bargain, The.) CBE; EV-1; OBEV; OtMeF; PG; TreFS
(Ditty, A.) AWP; ElSeCe; GTBS; GTBS-D; GTBS-W; GTSE; GTSL; InPo; JAWP; PoRL; TOP
(Ditty: Heart Exchange.) EnLit
(Friendship.) ES
(From "The Arcadia." LEAP
(Heart Exchange.) LiTB; LoBV
(Just Exchange.) FaBoEn
(Shepherdess' Song.) CaAE
(Song: "My true love hath my heart.") EnLi-1
(Sonnet: "My true love hath my heart.") EIL; WHA
(True Love.) ALV; ChTr; OBSC
Night. SiPS
("O Night, the ease of care.") NBE
O Sweet Woods (*three sonnets*). AtBAP; CoBE, *first sonnet;* KN, 16 *ll., diff.;* PeBoSo, *second sonnet;* PoEL-1; TuPP
(Delight of Solitariness, The.) LiTB
(Dorus's Song.) LoBV
("O sweet woods the delight of solitariness!") SiCE
(Solitariness.) OBSC; SiPS
O Words Which Fall Like Summer Dew on Me. MaPo
(Rural Poesy.) EIL; ElSeCe
Old Age. SiPS
Sapphics. SiPS
Shepherd Song: "As I my little flock on Ister bank." SiPS
"Such maner time there was." NBE
Shepherd's Tale, A. SiPS
Since So Mine Eyes. SiPS
Sweeter Saint I Serve, A. SiPS
Tale for Husbands, A. SiPS
Truth Doth Truth Deserve. HBV; LiTL
(Advice to the Same.) SiPS
"What length of verse can serve brave Mopsa's good to show." ReIE
What Tongue Can Her Perfections Tell? SiPS
When Two Suns Do Appear. SiPS
Why Fear to Die? SiPS
Wronged Lover, The. SiPS
Arcadia was of old (said he) a state. Rhotus on Arcadia. John Chalkhill. *Fr.* Thealma and Clearchus. OBS
Arcadian Duologue. Sir Philip Sidney. *See* My True Love Hath My Heart.
Arcana Sylvarum. Charles De Kay. AA
Arch Armadillo, The. Carolyn Wells. PCH
Archaeological Picnic, The. John Betjeman. EnLoPo
Archaeologist of the Future, The. Leonard Bacon. WhC
Archaeology of Love, The. Richard Murphy. EnLoPo; PoN
Archaic Apollo. William Plomer. ChMP
Archaic Torso of Apollo. Rainer Maria Rilke, *tr. fr. German by* Vernon Watkins. LiTW
(Torso of an Archaic Apollo, *tr. by* C. F. MacIntyre.) MeRV
Archangel, The. Byron. *See* At the Gate of Heaven.
Archbishop Tait. *Unknown.* ChTr
Archduke's wife a German princess with a jaw, The. Aria in Austria. Marie Luhrs. PIAE
Archeanassa. Asclepiades, *tr. fr. Greek by* Robert Allason Furness. GrR; OxBG
Archedike. Simonides, *tr. fr. Greek by* Walter Leaf. GrL; OxBG
(On the Daughter of Hippias, son of Pisistratus.) GrR
Archer, The. Clinton Scollard. FaPON; GaP
Archer, The. A. J. M. Smith. PeCV
Archer, The. *Unknown, tr. fr. Sanskrit by* Douglas Ainslie. OBVV
Archer is wake, The! Peace on Earth. William Carlos Williams. LiTA; MAP; NP; PFY; TBM; TCPD; ViBoPo
Archer, the Archer, The. The Archer. *Tr. by* Douglas Ainslie. OBVV
Archers of the King. Sister Mary Genoveva. GoBC
Archery. Ibn Sa'id of Alcala la Real, *tr. fr. Arabic by* A. J. Arberry. MooP
Arches. Helen Hoyt. NP
Arches of a bridge my eyes. Manuel Altolaguirre, *tr. fr. Spanish by* Eleanor L. Turnbull. CoSP
Arches on arches! as it were that Rome. The Coliseum. Byron. *Fr.* Childe Harold's Pilgrimage, IV. BCEP; BEL; CoBE; EPN; EV-4; LPS-2; TCEP
Archibald Higbie. Edgar Lee Masters. *Fr.* Spoon River Anthology. InP; NP
Archibald MacLeish Suspends the Five Little Pigs, *parody.* Louis Untermeyer. MoAmPo
Archie o' [*or* of] Cawfield. *Unknown.* BaBo (A *and* B *vers.*); ESPB (A *and* B *vers.*); OBB (*diff. vers.*)
Archilochus's seaside tomb you see. A Slanderer. *Unknown.* OnPM
Archimago's Hermitage. Spenser. *Fr.* The Faerie Queene, I, i. BCEP
Archin' here and arrachin' there. Water Music. "Hugh MacDiarmid." GoTS
Archipelago, The. Friedrich Hölderlin, *tr. fr. German by* Stephen Stepanchev. AnGP
Architect, The. Molly Anderson Haley. ChIP
Architects of Dream. Lucia Trent. PGD
Architects plant their imagination, weld their poems on rock. Earthfast. A. S. J. Tessimond. POTE
Archons of Athens, topped by the tettix, see, I return! Pheidippides. Robert Browning. MW
Archpriest's Prayer, The. Juan Ruiz, Archpriest of Hita, *tr. fr. Spanish by* Elisha K. Kane. *Fr.* The Book of Good Love. AnSpL-1
Archy a Low Brow. Don Marquis. *Fr.* Archys Life of Mehitabel. WhC
Archy and Mehitabel, *sels.* Don Marquis.
Archy Confesses. FiBHP
Ballade: "Outcast bones from a thousand biers." WhC
Cheerio My Deario ShBV-4
Flattered Lightning Bug, The. StPo
Hen and the Oriole, The. FiBHP; TwCV
Mehitabel Sings a Song. InMe
Old Trouper, The. MoP
Song of Mehitabel, The. FiBHP; TreFS

Archy and Mehitabel (*continued*)
Wail of Archy, The, *sel.*
"Gods I am pent in a cockroach." FiBHP
Warty Bliggens, the Toad. FiBHP
Archy Confesses. Don Marquis. *Fr.* Archy and Mehitabel. FiBHP
Archy Experiences a Seizure. Don Marquis. *Fr.* Archys Life of Mehitabel. WhC
(Hero Cockroach, The.) TSW; TSWC
Archy, the Cockroach, Speaks. Don Marquis. *Fr.* Certain Maxims of Archy. FaPON
Archygrams. Don Marquis. *Fr.* Archys Life of Mehitabel. WhC
Archys Autobiography. Don Marquis. *Fr.* Archys Life of Mehitabel. CrMA
Archys Last Name. Don Marquis. *Fr.* Archys Life of Mehitabel. CrMA
Archys Life of Mehitabel, *sels.* Don Marquis.
Archy a Low Brow. WhC
Archy Experiences a Seizure. WhC
(Hero Cockroach, The.) TSW; TSWC
Archygrams. WhC
Archys Autobiography. CrMA
Artists Shouldn't Have Offspring. CrMA
Ballade of the Under Side. InvP
Arcite's Farewell. Chaucer, *mod. vers. by* John Hall Wheelock. *Fr.* The Canterbury Tales: The Knight's Tale. LiTL
Arctic Agrarian. Louis Untermeyer. PIAE
Arctic Indian's Faith, The. Thomas D'Arcy McGee. BoCaPo (1943 ed.)
Arctic Moon, The. Joaquin Miller. *Fr.* The Yukon. MAP; MoAmPo (1942 ed.)
Arctic moon hangs overhead, The. The Wolf Cry. Lew Sarett. FaPON; PoMa
Arctic Tern in a Museum. Mary Effie Lee Newsome. PoNe
Arctic Vision, An. Bret Harte. MC; PAH
Arcturus in Autumn. Sara Teasdale. AV; MOAP; NP; NV; TBM
Arcturus is his other name. Emily Dickinson. StaSt
Arcum Conteret. Sister Mary Thérèse. PraNu
Ardan Mór. Francis Ledwidge. AnIV; AWP; GTIV; JAWP; WBP
(Herons, The.) ACP; AlDL; OnYI; OxBI
Ardelia to Melancholy. Countess of Winchilsea. DiM
Arden of Feversham, *sel. Unknown.*
"Ungentle Alice, thy sorrow is my sore." LO
Ardor. Gamaliel Bradford. HBMV
Ardor. Jorge Guillén, *tr. fr. Spanish by* Eleanor L. Turnbull. CoSP
Ardor [*or* Ardour] and Memory. Dante Gabriel Rossetti. The House of Life, LXIV. PoVP; ViPo
Ardour of red flame is thine, The. Lionel Johnson. *Fr.* The Dark Angel. LO
Are all the birds imprisoned there. Alle Vögel Sind Schon Da. Frances Chesterton. UnS
Are friends delight or pain? Emily Dickinson. BoFr
Are lovers full of fire? Upon His Timorous Silence in Her Presence. Francis Davidson. EG; TuPP
". . . Are not molesters of women" the book says. Pocket Guide for Servicemen. Hubert Creekmore. WaP
Are the Children at Home? Margaret E. Sangster. HBV; LPS-1; MotAn
Are the desolate, dark weeks. These. William Carlos Williams. CoBMV; MoAB; MoAmPo; OxBA
". . . Are the horns of the hall on fire?" The Battle of Finnsburg. *Unknown.* AnOE
Are the living so much use. At the Cenotaph. "Hugh MacDiarmid." NAMP
"Are the reindeer in the rain, dear?" Conversation between Mr. and Mrs. Santa Claus. Rowena Bennett. ChBR; SiSoSe; TiPo (1959 ed.)
Are there favoring ladies above thee? Valse Jeune. Louise Imogen Guiney. AA
Are there no roses in your garden. Jardin des Fleurs. Charles David Webb. NePoAm-2
Are these the honors they reserve for me. Columbus in Chains. Philip Freneau. MC; PAH
Are these the tracks of some unearthly friend. Angelic Guidance. Cardinal Newman. GoBC
Are they clinging to their crosses. Antichrist, or the Reunion of Christendom; an Ode. G. K. Chesterton. SeCePo
Are They Dancing. Edward Dorn. NeAP
Are They Not All Ministering Spirits? Robert Stephen Hawker. CoBE; EPN; EV-4; GoBC; HBV; OBEV (1st ed.)
(Angels of the Spring.) NLK
Are They Shadow[e]s [That We See]? Samuel Daniel. *Fr.* Tethys' Festival. AtBAP; ATP; ElL; ExPo; InvP; LoBV; SeCeV; TuPP
("Are they shadows that we see?") CH; ElSeCe; SiCE
(Eidola.) LO
(Shadows.) EV-1; OBSC; RiBV
(Song: "Are they shadowes that we see?") PoEL-2
Are thine eyes weary? is thy heart too sick. November. William Morris. *Fr.* The Earthly Paradise. EmBrPo; EPN; GTML; GTSL; ViPo; ViPP
. . . Are we devils? Are we men? Saint Francis. Tennyson. *Fr.* Locksley Hall Sixty Years After. SaFP
Are we mere pieces in the hand. Fate. James Fenimore Cooper. HBMV
Are we not all of race divine. Patriots of Mankind. Christopher Smart. PoFr
Are We Not the People, *sel.* Al-Samau'al ibn Adiya, *tr. fr. Arabic by* Hartwig Hirschfeld.
"Now listen to boasting which leaves the heart dazed." TrJP
Are we not the progeny. Royal Pride. Al-Nasir. MooP
Are we, then, wholly fallen? Can it be. Freedom. James Russell Lowell. PaA
Are Women Fair? *At. to* Francis Davison. BOHV; HBV
Are ye all there? Are ye all there. Stars in My Country's Sky—Are Ye All There? Lydia H. Sigourney. FOAH
Are ye so strong, O kings, O strong men? Nay. Swinburne. *Fr.* A Year's Burden, 1870. PoFr
Are you a giant, great big man, or is your real name Smith? Big Smith. Juliana Horatia Ewing. TVC; TVSH
"Are you afraid of change—of death?" Caterpillars' Conversation. Mary W. Findlater. DiM
Are you alive? The Pool. Hilda Doolittle ("H. D."). ExPo; NP
Are you almost disgusted with life, little man? How to Be Happy. *Unknown.* BLPA
"Are you asleep?" After the Kiss. Rofu Miki. PoLJ
Are you asleep, Mother? Mary's Vision. *Unknown.* ISi
Are you astonished to be told. To Madame Lullin. Voltaire. TrFP
"Are you awake." Haunting Fingers. Thomas Hardy. MaPo
Are you awake? Do you hear the rain? Rain at Night. Helen Hoyt. LiTM; NP
"Are you awake, Gemelli." Star-Talk. Robert Graves. AlDL; HBMV; MBP; MoBrPo; PtOT; RG; TCPD; TwCV; WP
Are you dreaming of Christmas? Christmas 1942. Robert Nathan. PoFr
"Are you flying through the night." The Fire-Fly. John Banister Tabb. UTS
"Are you ready for your steeple-chase, Lorraine, Lorraine, Lorèe?" Lorraine [*or* Lorraine Lorèe]. Charles Kingsley. BBV; PoVP; VA
"Are you ready, O Virginia." The Call to the Colors. Arthur Guiterman. FOAH; PaA; PAH
Are you sheltered, curled up and content by your world's warm fire? For the New Year. Edwin Markham. OQP; QP-1
Are you standing at "Wit's End Corner." Wit's End Corner. Antoinette Wilson. BLRP
Are You the New Person Drawn toward Me? Walt Whitman. BoFr; NePA
Are You There? Strickland Gillilan. PoToHe (new ed.)
Are you tir'd? Rosamond at Woodstock. Swinburne. *Fr.* Rosamond. VA
Are you truly too weak to remember the time that seemed blessed? Infinite Time. Hugo von Hofmannsthal. AnGP
Are you very weary? Rest a little bit. Rest. *Unknown.* PoToHe
"Are you waking?" shout the breezes. Christmas Bells. George Cooper. HH; MeMeAg
Are you washed in the blood. For His Sake. Annie Denman. BePJ
Are you worsted in a fight? Laugh It Off. Henry Rutherford Elliot. WBLP
Are your rocks shelter for ships. The Shrine. Hilda Doolittle ("H. D."). AnAmPo; LA; MAPA; NP
Are zebras black with broad white stripes. Zebra. William Jay Smith. TiPo (1959 ed.)
Areiopagus, The; a Higher Justice Come to Dwell among Men. Aeschylus, *tr. fr. Greek by* Lewis Campbell. *Fr.* Eumenides. GrR
Areopagitica, *sel.* Milton.
"This is true liberty," *tr. fr. the Greek of* Euripides. PoFr
Ares. Albert Ehrenstein, *tr. fr. German by* Babette Deutsch *and* Avrahm Yarmolinsky. TrJP
Ares at last has quit the field. Under Which Lyre. W. H. Auden. MoAB; MoBrPo (1950 ed.); PoLFOT
Ares, in might surpassing, gold-helmeted charioteer. Hymn to Ares. *Unknown.* *Fr.* Homeric Hymns. GrPE
Ares is blind, and with unseeing eyes. The God of War. Sophocles. OxBG
Arete; Portrait of a High-born Matron. Homer, *tr. fr. Greek by* Pope. *Fr.* The Odyssey, VII. GrR
Aretemias. E. A. Robinson, *after the Greek of* Antipater of Sidon.
(Variations of Greek Themes, VII.) MOAP
Arethusa, The. Prince Hoare. LH; SG; TVSH
Arethusa. Shelley. BPN; EmBrPo; EnRP; EPN; EV-4; GN; HBV; OBRV; TVSH
Arethusa sends this message to her husband Lycotas. Propertius. Elegies, IV, 3. LaP
Aretina's Song. Sir Henry Taylor. VA

Aretousa much desires that the day turn to night. Vincenzo Kornaros. *Fr.* Erotokritos. MoGP
Argalus and Parthenia, *sels.* Francis Quarles.
 Authour's Dreame, The. OBS
 Hos Ego Versiculos. CaAE; CenL; OBS; SeEP. *See also* Man's Mortality, *sl. diff. vers. at. to* Simon Wastell, *fr.* Microbiblion.
Argentina in one swing of the bell skirt. The Beautiful Train. William Empson. MoVE
Arglwydd Arwain. William Williams. *See* Guide Me, O Thou Great Jehovah.
Argonaut, The; or, Lost Adventurer. Philip Freneau. MOAP
Argonautica, *sels.* Apollonius Rhodius, *tr. fr. Greek.*
 Accordingly Medea Met Jason in the Temple of Hecate, *fr.* III, *tr. by* F. L. Lucas. GrPE
 Amor Omnipotens, *fr.* III, *tr. by* George Allen. OxBG
 (She Tells Him How to Win the Fleece, *tr. by* F. L. Lucas.) GrPE
 Eros and His Mother, *fr.* III, *tr. by* George Allen. OxBG
 Hylas, *fr.* I, *tr. by* George Allen. OxBG
 Jason's Sowing and Reaping, *fr.* III, *tr. by* George Allen. OxBG
 "Long did the heroes with King Phineus bide," *fr.* II, *tr. by* L. P. Chamberlayne. GrPo
 Medea Betrayed, *fr.* IV, *tr. by* George Allen *and* T. F. Higham. OxBG
 Medea's Dream, *fr.* III, *tr. by* George Allen. OxBG
 Medea's Hesitation, *fr.* III, *tr. by* George Allen. OxBG
 Medea's Parting Words, *fr.* III, *tr. by* George Allen. OxBG
 Medea's Passion, *fr.* III, *tr. by* Arthur S. Way. GrR
 Meeting of Medea and Jason, The, *fr.* III, *tr. by* Arthur S. Way. GrR
 ("But Medea—her thoughts unto nought else turned," *longer sel., tr. by* Arthur S. Way.) GrL
 (Meeting, The, *tr. by* George Allen.) OxBG
 Moving Rocks, The, *fr.* IV, *tr. by* George Allen *and* C. M. Bowra. OxBG
 "Now as she lay upon her couch awhile," *fr.* III, *tr. by* J. C. Wordsworth. GrPo
 Remorse, *fr.* III, *tr. by* George Allen. OxBG
 (Heart-Searchings of Medea, The, *tr. by* F. L. Lucas.) GrPE
 ("Now over earth was spread the veil of night," *tr. by* J. C. Wordsworth.) GrPo
 (Vigil and Remorse, *tr. by* Arthur S. Way.) GrR
Sailing of Argo, The, *fr.* I. GrPE, *tr. by* F. L. Lucas; GrR, *tr. by* Arthur S. Way; OxBG, *tr. by* George Allen
 Slaying of the Earth-born, The, *fr.* III, *tr. by* Arthur S. Way. GrR
 "So did he chide with the band; was none dared meet his eye," *fr.* I, *tr. by* Arthur S. Way. GrPo
 "So to the sacred wood those two drew nigh," *fr.* IV, *tr. by* J. C. Wordsworth. GrPo
 "Sorry prophet this, a witless seer, A," *fr.* III, *tr. by* J. C. Wordsworth. GrPo
 "Sudden transport seiz'd the melting maid, A," *fr.* III, *tr. by* Francis Fawkes. GrPo
 "To deck with honours due the bridal bed," *fr.* IV, *tr. by* Francis Fawkes. GrPo
Argonautica. George Seferis, *tr. fr. Modern Greek by* Rex Warner. OnHM
Argonauts, The. Apollonius Rhodius. *See* Argonautica.
Argonauts, The. Pindar. *See* Quest of the Golden Fleece, The.
Argument, The. Archibald MacLeish. *Fr.* Conquistador. AtBAP
Argument, An. Thomas Moore. EnLoPo
Argument. Mildred Weston. PoMa; WhC
Argument of His Book, The. Robert Herrick. AtBAP; AWP; BEL; BLV; BoLiVe; CoBE; ElSeCe; EM-1; EnL; EnLi-1; EnLit; EPS; HBV; InP; InPo; InvP; OAEP; OBS; PoE; PoEL-3; PoRA; ReEn; SeCePo; SeCeV; SeCV-1; SeEP; TrGrPo; TyEnPo; ViBoPo; WHA
 (Argument of This Book, *abr.*) HBVY
 (Hesperides.) MyFE
 (His Theme.) LEAP
 ("I sing of brooks, of blossomes, birds, and bowers.") BrBE
Argument, An—Of the Passion of Christ. Thomas Merton. CrMA
Argument of This Book. Robert Herrick. *See* Argument of His Book, The.
Argument on Immortality. Lenore G. Marshall. BoFr
Argumentum ad Hominem. Hyam Plutzik. FiMAP
Argus ("Argus was a puppy"). Eleanor Farjeon. GBV (1952 ed.)
Aria for Flute and Oboe. Joseph Langland. NePoEA
Aria in Austria. Marie Luhrs. PIAE
Ariana. Franklin Benjamin Sanborn. AA
Arid Land. Federico García Lorca, *tr. fr. Spanish by* Eleanor L. Turnbull. CoSP
Arid Lands, The. Herbert Bashford. AA
Aridity. "Michael Field." OBMV; OxBoCh
Ariel. David Campbell. NeLNL
Ariel in the Cloven Pine. Bayard Taylor. AA; TCAP
Ariel to Miranda.—Take. With a Guitar, to Jane [*or* To a Lady with a Guitar]. Shelley. BEL; BPN; EmBrPo; EnRP; EPN; ERP; EtPaEn; GTBS; GTBS-D; GTBS-W; GTSE; GTSL; HBV
Arielle Grierson. Edgar Lee Masters. *Fr.* The New Spoon River. ChMo; CMP
Ariel's Dirge. Shakespeare. *See* Ariel's Song: "Full fathom five . . ."
Ariel's Last Song. Shakespeare. *See* Ariel's Song: "Where the bee sucks."
Ariel's Song: "Come unto these yellow sands." Shakespeare. *Fr.* The Tempest, I, ii. CBE; EG; EV-1; FaBoCh; GN; LoBV; LoGBV; MCCG; MPB (1956 ed.); PCH; RAR; ThWaDe
 ("Come unto these yellow sands.") AEV; AnFE; AtBAP; BEL; BoTP; CH; ElL; EM-1; InPo; KN; OBSC; OTPC (1923 ed.); PoEL-2; SiCE; TOP; TwHP; ViBoPo
 (Fairy Land.) BCEP; OBEV
 (Fairy Life, The, 2.) GTSL
 (Fairy Songs.) HBV
 (Shakespeare's Fairies: They Dance and Play.) CBPC
 (Song of Ariel.) CG
 (Songs from "The Tempest.") LEAP
Ariel's Song: "Full fathom five thy father lies." Shakespeare. *Fr.* The Tempest, I, ii. BoLiVe; CoEV; EG; EV-1; FaBoEn; GN; LoBV; PFE; SeCePo
 (Ariel's Dirge.) ThWaDe
 (Ditty: "Full fadom five thy father lies.") LiA
 (Fairy Land.) BCEP; OBEV
 ("Full fathom five thy father lies.") AnFE; AtBAP; ATP; BEL; CaAE; CenL; ChTr; ElL; ElSeCe; EM-1; EnLi-1; ExPo; FaBoCh; GTSL; HoPM; InPo; KN; LiTB; LiTG; LoGBV; MaPo; OAEP; OBSC; OTPC; OuHeWo; PIR; PoEL-2; PoRA; ReaPo; SeCeV; ShBV-1; SiCE; TOP; TwHP; TwP; TyEnPo; ViBoPo; WHA
 (Sea Dirge, A.) AnEnPo; BLV; CBOV; CBPC; CG; EPP; EtS; GTBS; GTBS-D; GTBS-W; GTSE; HBV; MCCG; TrGrPo
 (Song: "Full fathom five thy father lies." BrBE; NeHB
 (Songs from the Plays.) AWP; JAWP; WBP
 (Songs from "The Tempest.") LEAP; SG
Ariel's Song: "Where the bee sucks." *Fr.* The Tempest, V, i. AnEnPo; CaAE; EG; EV-1; GN; HOAH; MCCG; PCD; PFE; RAR
 (Ariel's Last Song.) CBE
 (Fairy Land.) BCEP; OBEV
 (Fairy Life, The, 1.) GTSL
 (Fairy Songs.) HBV; HBVY; RIS
 (Fairy's Life, A.) PCH
 (Shakespeare's Fairies: Ariel Sings.) CBPC
 (Songs from the Plays.) AWP; JAWP; WBP
 (Songs from "The Tempest.") LEAP
 ("Where the bee sucks, there suck I.") AnFE; BEL; BoTP; CH; ElL; EM-1; EnLi-1; EnLit; EPP; InPo; KN; MPB; OBSC; OTPC; PIR; PoRh; ReaPo; SeCeV; SiCE; ThWaDe; TiPo; TOP; TyEnPo; UTS; ViBoPo; WHA
Arignota Remembers. Sappho, *tr. fr. Greek by* Olga Marx *and* Ernst Morwitz. LiTW
Arion. Pushkin, *tr. fr. Russian by* Babette Deutsch. TrRV
Arion Anadyomenos. Ronald Bottrall. CoEV; MoP
Arion, when through tempest's cruel wrack. Amoretti, XXXVIII. Spenser. PeBoSo
Arise and go now to the city of slaughter. The City of Slaughter. Hayyim Nahman Bialik. TrJP
Arise! Arise! Louis Untermeyer. StaSt
Arise arise, faire Sun restore the daye. *Unknown.* SeCSL
Arise, beloved, let us go. *Unknown, tr. fr. Modern Greek by* Rae Dalven. MoGP
Arise, friend sleeping in the dawn so chilly. Alvorada. Nuño Fernández Torneol. LyMA
Arise, Get Up, My Dear Love. *Unknown.* TuPP
 ("Arise, get up, my dear love, rise, make haste, begone thee!") ReEn
Arise (I commun'd with my self) arise. Knowledge; Solomon Discourses. Matthew Prior. *Fr.* Solomon on the Vanity of the World. BeR
Arise, My Love, My Fair One. The Song of Solomon, II: 8–14, Bible, *O.T.* LoPo
Arise, my slumbering soul! arise. Soul and Country. James Clarence Mangan. VA
Arise, O soul, and gird thee up anew. A Challenge. James Benjamin Kenyon. AA
Arise, Saint Aodh, and find, on rising. The Scribe. F. R. Higgins. JKCP (1926 ed.)
Arise, shine, for thy light is come. Zion Redeemed. Isaiah, Bible, *O.T.* LiA
Arise—'tis the day of our Washington's glory. Crown Our Washington. Hezekiah Butterworth. DD; HH; PEDC; PEOR; PoRL; WOAH
Arise up on thy feet, O Quiet Heart. He Biddeth Osiris to

Arise up on thy feet (*continued*)
Arise from the Dead. *Unknown. Fr.* Book of the Dead. AWP
Arise, ye kings of Macha. *Unknown. Fr.* The Combat of Ferdiad and Cuchulain. OnYI
Arise, ye Sons of Britain, in chorus join and sing. The Battle of Trafalgar. *Unknown.* SG
Arise, yes, yes, arise, O thou my dust. The Resurrection. Friedrich Gottlieb Klopstock. EOAH
Arise, you who will not be bondslaves. Ch'i Lai'. Shih Ee. PoFr
Arisen at Last. Whittier. IAP
Aristeides. Antipater of Sidon, *tr. fr. Greek by* Charles Whibley. AWP
Aristion, so swift once to toss her tresses curling. The Dead Dancer. Thyillus. GrPE
Aristippus, *sel.* Thomas Randolph. Drinking Song. SeCL
Aristocrats. Keith Douglas. NePoEA
Aristocrats of Labor. W. Stewart. *Fr.* The True Aristocrat. OQP; PGD; PSO; QP-1
Ariston had a sling, wherewith he got. A Stalker of Geese. *Unknown.* OxBG
Arithmetic. Carl Sandburg. ImOP; WaKn
"Arithmetic is where numbers fly like pigeons in and out of your head," *sel.* FaPON
Arizona. Margaret Rowe Clifford. PoRL
Arizona. Sharlot Mabridth Hall. PAH
Arizona. *Unknown.* ABF
Arizona Boys and Girls, The. *Unknown.* CoSo, *with music;* CSF
Arizona Nights. Berta Hart Nance. HiLiAm
Arizona Poems, *sels.* John Gould Fletcher.
Mexican Quarter, II. ChMo; CMP; NP; TCPD
Rain in the Desert, VI. TCPD
(Rain in the Street.) NP
Windmills, The, IV. CrMA; NV; PoMa; PoTo; TCPD
Ark, The. Milton. *Fr.* Paradise Lost, XI. EtS
Ark, The. Jones Very. IAP
Ark and the *Dove,* The. Daniel Sargent. EtS
Ark of the Covenant. Louise Townsend Nicholl. ImOP
Arkansas Traveler, The. *At. to* Sanford C. Faulkner. PoRL
Arkansaw Traveler, The. *Unknown. See* State of Arkansas, The.
Arkham. Robert Ervin Howard. DaM
Arlington. David McKee Wright. AnNZ
Arlington Cemetery Looking toward the Capitol. Winthrop Palmer. GoYe
Arlo Will. Edgar Lee Masters. *Fr.* Spoon River Anthology. ChMo; CMP; LiTA; NP
Arm, arm, arm, arm! the scouts are all come in. The Joy of Battle. John Fletcher. *Fr.* The Mad Lover. CenL; ElL; EV-2; LH
Armada, The. Macaulay. BeLS; BHV; FaBoCh; LH; LoGBV; OBRV; OTPC (1923 ed.); ShBV-2; TVSH; WBLP
(Armada, The; a Fragment.) EV-4; GN; HBV
(Spanish Armada, The.) CG
England's Standard, *sel.* OtMeF
Armada, *sel.* Swinburne.
England. LH
Armada, The. *Unknown, at. to* William Warner. *See* Defeat of the Spanish Armada, The.
Armada of Thirty Whales An. Daniel G. Hoffman. NePA
Armadillo, The. Lesley Gordon. GFA
Armageddon. Sir Edwin Arnold. PTA-2
Armageddon. John Crowe Ransom. LiTA
Armageddon, *sel.* Francis Reginald Scott.
Shock, The. BoCaPo (1948 ed.)
Armand Dussault. Wilson MacDonald. WhC
Arm'd year—year of the struggle. Eighteen Sixty-one. Walt Whitman. CoV; IAP; TCAP
Armed. Shakespeare. *See* King's Army, The.
Armenian maidens, come and view. The Lily of Shavarshan. Leo Alishan. ArmLP
Armenian Poet's Prayer, The. Alexander Dzadourian, *tr. fr. Armenian by* Zabelle C. Boyajian. ArmLP
Armenia's Love to Shakespeare. Zabelle C. Boyajian. ArmLP
Armful, The. Robert Frost. ChMo; CMP
Armida, the Sorceress. Tasso, *tr. fr. Italian by* Edward Fairfax. *Fr.* Jerusalem Delivered, IV. EnLi-1
Armies joined, The; I saw the Prince of Peace. The Retreat from Heaven. J. A. R. McKellar. MoAuPo
Arming of Pigwiggen, The. Michael Drayton. *Fr.* Nymphidia; or, The Court of Fairy. GN; OTPC
(Pigwiggen.) BoTP
(Pigwiggen Arms Himself.) MoShBr
(Pigwiggen Prepares for the Fight with King Oberon.) EV-1
Armipotent lady, Bellona serene. Address to Bellona and King James V. John Bellenden. EBSV
Armistice. Charles Buxton Going. AOAH; DD; HBMV; PEDC
Armistice. Sophie Jewett. AA
Armistice. Eunice Mitchell Lehmer. PGD; PSO
Armistice. Thomas Lodge. *See* For Pity, Pretty Eyes, Surcease.
Armistice. Margaret E. Sangster. PEDC
Armistice Day. Mary Carolyn Davies. AOAH
Armistice Day. Roselle Mercier Montgomery. MC; PoRL
Armistice Day. Lucia Trent. PGD
(Armistice Day, 1926.) AOAH
Armistice Day, 1918–1928. Nancy Byrd Turner. AOAH
Armistice Day, 1926. Lucia Trent. *See* Armistice Day.
Armistice Day Vow. Dorothy Gould. PGD
Armistice Night. Curtis Wheeler. HH
Armor of ants is bright in the sun, The. Ant Battle. Glenn Ward Dresbach. MuM
Armor the Bud. Frances Frieseke. JKCP (1955 ed.)
Armorer's Song, The. Harry Bache Smith. AA; OHIP
(Armourer's Song, The.) MW
Armory, The. Alcaeus, *tr. fr. Greek by* James S. Easby-Smith. GrR
(Armoury, An, *tr. by* Gilbert Highet.) OxBG; WaaP
Armour's Undermining Modesty. Marianne Moore. CoBMV
Arms and the Boy. Wilfred Owen. AnEnPo; FaFP; GTBS-W; LiTB; LiTM; MBP; MoAB; MoBrPo; NAMP; NP; OAEP (2d ed.); WaP
Arms and the heroes signalised in fame. Passage to India. Luis de Camões. *Fr.* The Lusiads. WoL
Arms and the leader I sang whose piety. Sonnet. Tasso. LyPI
Arms and the man I sing, and sing for joy. Epigram. J. V. Cunningham. NePoAm
Arms and the man I sing, who first made way. Shipwreck of the Trojans; Landing at Carthage. Virgil. The Aeneid, I. RoL
Arms and the Muse. Milton. *See* When the Assault Was Intended to the City.
Arms of the people! This way! Menace and siege. Ode of the Sun to the People's Army. "Pablo Neruda." TwSpPo
Arms of the sea are extended, The. A Delusion of Reference. R. A. D. Ford. PeCV
Arms reversed and banners craped. A Dirge for McPherson. Herman Melville. BlG; GA; PAH; PoEL-5
Armstrong at Fayal, The. Wallace Rice. PAH
Army, The. Abu Zaid, *tr. fr. Arabic by* A. J. Arberry. MooP
Army Corps on the March, An. Walt Whitman. AmPo; APW; CoBA; IAP; MOAP; TCAP
Army Correspondent's Last Ride. George Alfred Townsend. AA; MDAH
Army is gathering from near and from far, The. Marching Along. William B. Bradbury. BlG
Army, Navy. *Unknown.* OxNR
Army of Despair, The. John Chalmers DaCosta. PoP
Army of grey rats devours our land, An. The Rats. Albrecht Haushofer. *Fr.* Sonnets from Moabite Prison. TwGV
Army of the Dead, The. William Rose Benét. QS
Army of the Potomac, *abr.* Joaquin Miller. PEOR
Army of the Red Cross, The. Katrina Trask. PEDC
Army of the Sidhe, The. Lady Gregory. SP
Army of Xerxes, The. Delphic Oracle, *tr. fr. Greek by* A. D. Godley. OxBG
Army was ours that spring, The. Landing in England. North Pickenham. Coman Leavenworth. *Fr.* Norfolk Memorials. LiTA
Arnold. *Unknown. See* Arnold, the Vile Traitor.
Arnold at Stillwater. Thomas Dunn English. GA; PAH
Arnold, Master of the *Scud.* Bliss Carman. EtS
Arnold, the Vile Traitor. *Unknown.* GA; PAH
Arnold von Winkelried. James Montgomery. BeLS; PECK
(Make Way for Liberty.) LPS-2; PoFr, *abr.;* TreFS
(Patriot's Pass-Word, The.) HBV
Arnold's Departure. Philip Freneau. MOAP
Around, above my bed, the pitch-dark fly. Truth. Howard Nemerov. MoVE
Around, above the world of snow. February. James Berry Bensel. GoTP
Around and around a dusty little room. Margaret Johnson. SAS
Around Assisi's convent gate. St. Francis' Sermon to the Birds. Longfellow. OTPC
Around Cape Horn, *with music. Unknown.* AmSS
Around her fountain which flows. Circe's Palace. T. S. Eliot. CAG
Around Me Rose the Phantoms of the Dark. Gerald Massey. *Fr.* Only a Dream. UnW
Around me the images of thirty years. The Municipal Gallery Revisited. W. B. Yeats. BoFr; LiTB
Around my garden the little wall is low. Losing a Slave-Girl. Po Chü-i. AWP; TrCh
Around our necks may some one lay. Marigold and Myrrh. Alcaeus. GrR
Around the bend we streaked it with the leaders swingin' wide. The Oro Stage. H. H. Knibbs. IHA
Around the Child. Walter Savage Landor. BCEP; HBV
Around the Corner. Charles Hanson Towne. PoToHe
Around the Fish; after Paul Klee. Howard Moss. MoPo
Around the headland, at the end. The Lives of Gulls and Children. Howard Nemerov. FiMAP; NePoEA

Around the house the flakes fly faster. Birds at Winter Nightfall. Thomas Hardy. MBP; MoBrPo
Around the magnet, Faraday. Induced Current. Herbert Mayo. PoMa
Around the rick, around the rick. *Unknown.* OxNR
Around the rocky headlands, far and near. The Sea's Voice. William Prescott Foster. EtS
Around the Sun. Katharine Lee Bates. NV
Around the upper edges the winding ivy runs. The Cup. Theocritus. *Fr.* Idylls. GrR
Around the vase of Life at your slow pace. The Vase of Life. Dante Gabriel Rossetti. The House of Life, XCV. PoVP; ViPo
Around the weedy grass-grown fields. I Planted Little Trees To-Day. James B. Carrington. PEDC
Around the World. Kate Greenaway. MeMeAg; OTPC; PPL
(In Go-Cart So Tiny.) FaPON; SAS; TiPo
Around their legs girl athletes twist. Girl Athletes. Haniel Long. HBMV
Around this lovely valley rise. Midsummer. John Townsend Trowbridge. AA; DD; HBV; HBVY; OBAV
Around thy tomb, O bard divine! To Anacreon. Antipater of Sidon. GrPo
Around us lies a world invisible. Lone-Land. John Banister Tabb. OQP; QP-2
Around us summer wrote its last farewell. September Afternoon. Margaret Haley Carpenter. GoYe
"Around us the night closes dense as a wood." A Soldier's Wife. Gerald Massey. UnW
Around us unaware the solemn night. Enlargement. Helena Coleman. CPG
Around were all the roses red. Spleen. Paul Verlaine, *tr. by* Ernest Dowson. AWP; EnLi-2; JAWP; OnPM; WBP
"Arouse, arouse, ye drowsy sleepers." The Drowsy Sleeper. *Unknown.* ABS
Arouse, arouse, ye friends of right. The World Hymn. J. Gilchrist Lawson. WBLP
A-Roving. Victor Daley. BoAu
A-Roving. *Unknown. See* Fair Maid of Amsterdam, The.
Arques—Afternoon. Arthur Symons. PoVP
Arraigned, poor captive at the bar I stand. Fidessa, More Chaste than Kind, V. Bartholomew Griffin. ReIE; SiCE; TuPP
Arraignment, *sel.* William Rose Benét.
"What did you do with the world that you bade us to bow to anew?" MaRV
Arraignment. Helen Gray Cone. AA
Arraignment. Lizette Woodworth Reese. VOD
Arraignment of a Lover, The. George Gascoigne. EV-1; ReIE; SiCE
(Gascoigne's Arraignment.) ReEn; TuPP
Arraignment of Helen. Euripides, *tr. fr. Greek by* Gilbert Murray. *Fr.* Trojan Women. GrR
Arraignment of Paris, The, *sels.* George Peele.
Dirge: "Welladay, welladay, poor Colin." EIL
(Shepherd's Dirge, The.) OBSC
Fair and Fair. EIL; EV-1; OBEV; ViBoPo
("Fair and fair, and twice so fair.") ElSeCe; ReaPo; ReEn; SiCE; TCEP; TuPP
(Cupid's Curse.) BEL; LiA; TOP
(Song of Oenone and Paris.) OBSC
(Song of Paris and Oenone.) EPP
Not Iris in Her Pride. ViBoPo
(Peeping Flowers.) EV-1
O Gentle Love. EIL
(Colin, the Enamored Shepherd, Singeth This Passion of Love.) ReIE
(Colin's Passion of Love.) OBSC
Oenone's Complaint. EIL; OBSC
Arran. *Unknown. tr. fr. Irish by* Kuno Meyer. FaBoCh; LoGBV; ChTr. *tr. by* Kenneth Jackson
Arrange the scene with only a shade of difference. An Incident. Douglas Le Pan. PeCV
Arranged by two's as peaches are. Nine Nectarines and Other Porcelain. Marianne Moore. OxBA
Arrest of Antoñito el Camborio in the Streets of Seville, The. Federico García Lorca, *tr. fr. Spanish by* A. L. Lloyd. PoFr
Arrest of Oscar Wilde at the Cadogan Hotel, The. John Betjeman. InvP; LiTM (rev. ed.); SiTL
Arrested like marble horses. A Frieze. John Peale Bishop. MoPo
Arrival, The. William Rose Benét. QS
Arrival, The. Kostes Palamas, *tr. fr. Modern Greek by* Rae Dalven. *Fr.* The Twelve Songs of the Gypsy. MoGP
Arrival and Departure. Charles Eglington. BoSA
Arrival at Santos. Elizabeth Bishop. FiMAP
Arrival of a Guest, The. Tu Fu, *tr. fr. Chinese by* Soame Jenyns. WoL
Arrival of the Crusaders, The. St. Nerses, *tr. fr. Armenian by* Zabelle C. Boyajian. ArmLP
Arrival of the Family at Valencia. *Unknown, tr. fr. Spanish by* R. Selden Rose *and* Leonard Bacon. *Fr.* The Cid. TeCS
Arrival of the Greenhorn, The. *Unknown.* IHA
Arriv'd now at our ship, we launch'd, and set. Ulysses Hears the Prophecies of Tiresias. Homer. *Fr.* The Odyssey, XI. LoBV
Arrived at last,/ The prince, with living water. Vision of Rome's Destiny. Virgil. *Fr.* The Aeneid, VI. RoL
Arrived from scattered cities, several lands. Shipment to Maidenek. Ephim G. Fogel. TrJP
Arrived upon the downs of asphodel. Classic Encounter. "Christopher Caudwell." POTE
Arriving at Hsün-yang (*two poems*). Po Chü-i, *tr. fr. Chinese by* Arthur Waley. TrCh
"Bend of the river brings into view two triumphal arches, A."
"We are almost come to Hsün-yang: how my thoughts are stirred."
Arrogance Repressed. John Betjeman. FiBHP
Arrogant Frog and the Superior Bull, The. Guy Wetmore Carryl. StPo
Arrogant kings with envious lust [*or* with hate and lust]. The Coins of Love. John Richard Moreland. *Fr.* What of the Night? ChIP; MaRV
Arrow, The. Richard Henry Stoddard. *See* Flight of the Arrow, The.
Arrow, The. Clarence Urmy. HBMV
Arrow, The. W. B. Yeats. EG
Arrow and the Song, The. Longfellow. AA; AnAmPo; AnNE; BAP; BBV (1951 ed.); BTP; DD; FaFP; HBV; HBVY; IAP; LA; LEAP; MaRV; NeHB; OBAV; OnHT; OQP; OTPC; PECK; PG; PoToHe (new ed.); PTA-1; PYM; QP-2; TCAP; TreF; TSWC; TVSH
Arrow, feathery, alive, An. Mocking Bird. Witter Bynner. VOD; WhBS
Arrowhead mingled with black ash, brown powdered bones, watery-reddish stains, The. Song of the Arrowhead. Li Ho. WhP
Arrows of Chimpoko are tipped with hawks' feathers, The. Dark Night, the Wild Geese Fly High. Lu Lun. WhP
Arrows of Love. Bhartrihari, *tr. fr. Sanskrit by* Arthur W. Ryder. OnPM
Arrowtown. Denis Glover. AnNZ
Ars Gratia Artis. Keats. *Fr.* The Fall of Hyperion, I. LiA
("None can usurp this height," *longer sel.*) OBRV
Ars Poetica. Horace, *tr. fr. Latin.*
(Art of Poetry, The.) EnLi-1, *tr. by* the Earl of Roscommon; LaP. *tr. by* John G. Hawthorne; RoL, *tr. by* Philip Francis
Ars Poetica. Archibald MacLeish. AmP; AmPP; AWP; CoBMV; CoV; ExPo; HoPM; InP; InPo; LiTA; LiTM; MAP; MoAB; MoAmPo; MOAP; NeMA; NP; OxBA; PreP; ReMP; SeCeV; TBM; TwHP
("Poem should be palpable and mute, A.") NAMP
Ars Poetica. Victor van Vriesland, *tr. fr. Dutch by* Adriaan J. Barnouw. TrJP
Ars Victrix. Austin Dobson, *after* Théophile Gautier. BMEP; HBV; HBVY; MBP; MoBrPo (1942 ed.); POTT; PoVP; PreP; VA; VLEP
"O Poet, then, forbear," *sel.* InP
Arsenal at Springfield, The. Longfellow. AmPP; AnNE; APW; CoBA; CoV; DD, *abr.*; GTBS; HBV; IAP; MCCG; TCAP; WaaP
Sels.
"Were half the power, that fills the world with terror." PGD
When War Shall Be No More. MaRV
Arsenal of the Lord, The. William Stanley Braithwaite. PoNe
Arsinoë's Cats. Rosamund Marriott Watson. CIV; PoC
Art. Emerson. PEOR
Art. Théophile Gautier, *tr. fr. French by* George Santayana. AWP; JAWP; LiA; LiTW; WBP; WoL; TrFP, *tr. by* Alan Conder
Art. Apollon Nikolayevich Maikov, *tr. fr. Russian by* Babette Deutsch. TrRV
Art. Herman Melville. APW; PoFS; ViBoPo
Art. Alfred Noyes. OBEV (new ed.)
Art. Sir Gilbert Parker. *Fr.* A Lover's Dairy. VA
Art. Lilla Cabot Perry. AA
Art. José Asunción Silva, *tr. fr. Spanish by* Thomas Walsh. CAW
Art. James Thomson. EmBrPo
Sels.
"If you have a carrier-dove," II. EPP
"Singing is sweet; but be sure of this," III. EnLi-2
"What precious thing are you making fast," I. EnLi-2; OBVV; PoVP
Art. *Unknown.* BLPA
Art above Nature; to Julia. Robert Herrick. BrBE; EM-1
Art and Life. Leonardo da Vinci, *tr. fr. Italian by* Edward McCurdy. GrCo-1
Art and Life. Lola Ridge. HBMV
Art and Nature. Francisco de Medrano, *tr. fr. Spanish by* Longfellow. OnPM

Art for Art's Sake. Marc Blitzstein. *Fr.* The Cradle Will Rock. TrJP
Art has taught this man to writhe in marble. Carrara. Philip Murray. NePoAm
Art is unmade/ To nature and the wild again. An Open Air Performance of "As You Like It." E. J. Scovell. ChMP
Art Master, An. John Boyle O'Reilly. AA
Art of Biography, The. E. C. Bentley. *Fr.* Biography for Beginners. CenHV; FiBHP
Art of Book-keeping, The. Laman Blanchard. BOHV
Art of Book-keeping, The. *At. to* Thomas Hood. LPS-3; MOB
Art of Bringing Up Children, The, *sel.* Scevola de Sainte-Marthé.
"'Twas a sage said it, and the saying's good." PoP
Art of Cookery, The. William King. BeR
Art of Eyes, The. Spenser. *See* Amoretti, XXI.
Art of Love, The. Samuel Butler. *Fr.* Hudibras. FaBoEn
Art of Love, The. Sir John Suckling. *See* Song: "Honest lover whosoever."
Art of lying is you cannot stand, The. Just a Fishing Smack at Empson. George Barker. SiTL
"Art of Our Necessities Is Strange, The." Forrest Izard. WhC
Art of Poetry, The. Nicolas Boileau-Despréaux. *See* Art poétique, L'.
Art of Poetry, The. Horace. *See* Ars Poetica.
Art of Poetry, The. Vicente Huidobro, *tr. fr. Spanish by* Milton Ben Davis. AnCL
Art of Poetry, The. Paul Verlaine. *See* Art poétique.
Art of Politicks, The, *sel.* James Bramston.
Time's Changes, *abr.* OBEC
Art of Preserving Health, The, *sels.* John Armstrong.
Blest Winter Nights, *fr.* III. OBEC
Building a Home. LPS-2
Home of the Naiads, The, *fr.* II. OBEC
Art of Succeeding, The. Johan Henrik Kellgren, *tr. fr. Swedish by* Charles W. Stork. AnSL
Art of Writing, The. Pope. *Fr.* An Essay on Criticism. BCEP
("But most by numbers judge a poet's song.") AnFE; EV-3; InP
(Poetical Numbers.) OBEC; SeCePo
Art poétique, L', *sels.* Nicholas Boileau-Despréaux, *tr. fr. French by* Sir William Soames *and* John Dryden.
Fantastick Mind, The, *fr.* III. BeR
"Lucilius was the man, who, bravely bold," II. EnLi-1
"Rash author, 'tis a vain presumptuous crime," I. EnLi-1
Art poétique. Paul Verlaine, *tr. fr. French by* Arthur Symons. AWP
(Art of Poetry, The, *tr. by* Muriel Kittel.) AnFP
Art thou a Statist in the van. A Poet's Epitaph. Wordsworth. BPN; EmBrPo; EnRP; GEPC; OBRV; UnPo (1st ed.)
Art thou alive? It cannot be. On a Lady with Foul Breath. Thomas Parnell. PoE
Art Thou Dejected? Edward Young. *Fr.* Night Thoughts, VIII. GrCo-1
Art Thou Gone in Haste? *Unknown. Fr.* The Thracian Wonder. EIL; LO; OxBoLi; ThWaDe
("Art thou gon in haste Ile not forsake thee," *longer vers.*) SeCSL
(Chase, The.) CH
(Pursuit of Love.) ChTr
Art thou Heywood with the mad, merry wit? Of Heywood. John Heywood. ReIE; SiCe; TuPP
Art thou in love? it cannot be? *Unknown.* SeCSL
Art thou indeed among these. An Appeal. Swinburne. BPN
Art Thou Lonely? John Oxenham. PoToHe
Art thou not hungry for thy children, Zion? To Zion. Judah Halevi. AWP; JAWP; WBP
Art thou not lovely? Abélard Tells His Love to Héloïse. Herbert E. Palmer. POTE
Art thou pale for weariness. The Moon [*or* To the Moon]. Shelley. AnFE; BLV; BoLiVe; BPN; ChER; EmBrPo; EnRP; EPN; EV-4; GTBS; GTBS-D; GTBS-W; GTSE; GTSL; LoBV; MCCG; OBEV; OnPM; PIAE; TrGrPo; ViBoPo
Art thou poor, yet hast thou golden slumbers? The Happy Heart [*or* Content *or* O Sweet Content *or* Sweet Content *or* The Basket-Maker's Song]. Thomas Dekker. *Fr.* The Pleasant Comedy of Patient Grissell, I, i. AtBAP; BBV (1923 ed.); BEL; BLV; CBE; CBOV; CenL; CH; EG; EIL; ElSeCe; EnLi-1; EnLit; EPP; EV-2; GTBS; GTBS-D; GTBS-W; GTSE; GTSL; HBV; LEAP; LoBV; LPS-2; OAEP; OBEV; OBSC; OtMeF; PG; ShBV-2; SiCE; TCEP; ThWaDe; TOP; TrGrPo; TuPP; TVSH; ViBoPo; WHA; WoL
Art thou some wingèd Sprite, that, fluttering round. To a Maple Seed. Lloyd Mifflin. AA; ADAH
Art Thou That She. *Unknown.* ElSeCe; OnPM; SeCL; SeCSL; ViBoPo
Art thou the bird whom man loves best. The Redbreast Chasing a Butterfly. Wordsworth. CG; OTPC
"Art thou the grave of Charidas?" Dialogue with the Dead. Callimachus. OxBG
Art Thou the Same. Frances Dorr Tatnall. AA
Art Thou Weary? John Mason Neale, *after the Greek of* St. Stephen the Sabaite. BPP; CAW; LPS-2
(Art Thou Weary, Art Thou Troubled.) MaRV
Artegall and Radigund. Spenser. *Fr.* The Faerie Queene, V, 5. OBSC
"Artemidora! Gods invisible." The Death of Artemidora. Walter Savage Landor. *Fr.* Pericles and Aspasia. BEL; BPN; EnRP; EPN; ERP; InP; SeCeV; VA; ViBoPo
Artemis. Gérard de Nerval, *tr. fr. French.* AnFP, *tr. by* Barbara Howes; LiTW, *tr. by* Hubert Creekmore; TrFP, *tr. by* Alan Conder
Artemis Prologizes. Robert Browning. AnEnPo; LoBV (2d ed.)
Artemis Visits the Cyclopes. Callimachus, *tr. fr. Greek by* T. F. Higham. OxBG
Arthur. Ogden Nash. FiBHP
Arthur. William Winter. AA
"Thou idol of my constant heart," *sel.* LEAP
Arthur, king most wroth, heard that Modred. **Arthur's Last Battle** Layamon. *Fr.* The Brut. BEL
Arthur o'Bower has broken his band[s]. The Wind [*or* The High Wind] *Unknown.* ChTr; FaBoCh; LoGBV; OxNR
Arthur, to Robert, made a sign. The Nest. Mary Elliott. OTPC (1923 ed.)
Arthur turns into Tuscany when the time is favorable. *Unknown, tr. fr. Middle English. Fr.* Morte Arthure. MeEV
Arthur went to Cornwall. Layamon. *Fr.* The Brut. EPP
Arthur's Disillusionment. Tennyson. *Fr.* Idylls of the King. TreFS
Arthur's Dream. Layamon, *tr. fr. Middle English. Fr.* The Brut. MeEV
Arthur's Last Fight. Layamon, *tr. fr. Middle English. Fr.* The Brut. MeEV
(Arthur's Last Battle, *pr. tr.*) BEL
Artichoke, The. Ibn al-Talla, *tr. fr. Arabic by* A. J. Arberry. MooP
Articles of War. Dunstan Thompson. WaP
Articulate Thrush. Lew Sarett. BLA
Artificer, The. Ewart Milne. PoN
Artificial Beauty. Lucian, *tr. fr. Greek by* William Cowper. AWP; JAWP; OnPM; WBP
Artillery [*or* Artillerie]. George Herbert. MaPo; PoEL-2; SeCV-1
Artillery Shoot. James Forsyth. WaP
Artisan, The. Alice Brown. TrPWD
Artist, The. Henry Bellamann. LS
Artist. Aleksandr Blok, *tr. fr. Russian by* C. M. Bowra. BoR
Artist, The. Arthur Grissom. AA
Artist, The. Oscar Levertin, *tr. fr. Swedish by* Charles W. Stork. AnSL
Artist. Ernestine Mercer. InMe
Artist, The. Sir Walter Raleigh. WhC
Artist. "Joseph Upper." MuM
Artist, The. William Carlos Williams. HoPM
Artist and Ape. Gordden Link. GoYe
Artist and his luckless wife, The. The Artist. Sir Walter Raleigh. WhC
Artistically weather-proof. On Moving into a Skylight Room. Sister Rita Agnes. JKCP (1926 ed.)
Artists, The. Jalal ed-Din Rumi, *tr. fr. Persian by* Sir James Redhouse. PeP
Artist's Last Word, The. Parrhasius, *tr. fr. Greek by* F. L. Lucas. GrPE
Artists Shouldn't Have Offspring. Don Marquis. *Fr.* Archys Life of Mehitabel. CrMA
Arts Lough. George Arthur Greene. TIP
Arts of Death, The. Blake. *Fr.* The Four Zoas. CoEV
Art's use; what is it but to touch the springs. Art. Sir Gilbert Parker. *Fr.* A Lover's Diary. VA
Arvia, east of the morning. Invitation. Ridgely Torrence. NP
As a bathtub lined with white porcelain. The Bath Tub. Ezra Pound. ReaPo
As a Beam o'er the Face of the Waters May Glow. Thomas Moore BCEP
As a [*or* For] beauty I'm not a great star [*or* I am not a star]. Limerick [*or* My Face *or* The Face]. Anthony Euwer. *Fr.* The Limeratomy. BOHV; FaFP; GoTP; HBMV; HBV; HBVY; InvP; LiBL; LiTM; NePA; SiTL; TreF; TSWC; WhC
As a Bell in a Chime. Robert Underwood Johnson. AA
As a Blossom Sweet and Rosy. Robert Began, *tr. fr. Welsh by* Alfred Perceval Graves. BOL
As a boy old bachelors and old maid. Henry Ditch. Edgar Lee Masters. *Fr.* The New Spoon River. LEAP
As a Boy with a Richness of Needs I Wandered. Clifford Dyment. HaMV
As a child holds a pet. Port Bou. Stephen Spender. MoPo
As a corpse face in shadow of a shrub. Sagittarius or the Archer. Joseph Gordon Macleod. NP

As a couple of good soldiers were walking one day. The Soldier's Amen. *Unknown.* BIG
As a dancer dancing in a shower of roses before her King. The Joys of Art. Rachel Annand Taylor. OBVV
As a dare-gale skylark scanted in a dull cage. The Caged Skylark. Gerard Manley Hopkins. ChMo; LiTM; MBP; MoAB; MoBrPo; MoPo; OBMV; RiBV; ViPP
As a decrepit father takes delight. Sonnets, XXXVII. Shakespeare. PeBoSo
As a drenched drowned bee. A Baby Asleep after Pain. D. H. Lawrence. LBBV; NP; TCEP
As a fond mother, when the day is o'er. Nature. Longfellow. AA; AmPP (3d ed.); AnNE; APW; BLP; BLV; CBOV; CoBA; CoV; ES; FaBoBe; HBV; IAP; InP; LEAP; MaRV; MotAn; OBAV; PFE; PIAE; PoeMoYo; PoMa; TOP; TrGrPo; WHA
As a friend to the children, commend me the Yak. The Yak. Hilaire Belloc. ALV; BOHV; FaPON; HBVY; InMe; LauV; MBP; MoBrPo, MPB; NA; PCH; PoRh; StaSt; TreFS; TSW; TSWC; UTS
As a gem set in gold. Other Days. Fu Yüan. PoHN
As a gray rose-leaf that is fading white. H. C. Bunner. *Fr.* Triumph. BAP
As a guest who may not stay. In Memory of James T. Fields. Whittier. OBVV
As a hundred winds on Morven. James Macpherson. *Fr.* Fingal, III. BCEP
As a little child I come. Rest. Irene Rutherford McLeod. AV
As a Man Soweth. Goethe, *tr. fr. German.* MaRV
As a mote in at a minster door, so mighty were its jaws. Jonah. *Unknown. Fr.* Patience. ACP
As a naked man I go. The Waste Places [*or* In Waste Places]. James Stephens. CBOV; ChMo; CMP; GTML; GTSL; HBV; MBP; MoAB; MoBrPo; MoVE; NP; NV; PoFr, ReaPo; TCPD
As a perfume doth remain. Memory. Arthur Symons. LBBV
As a Plane Tree by the Water. Robert Lowell. CoBMV; CrMA; GTBS-W; LiTM (rev. ed.); MoAB; MoAmPo (1950 ed.); NePA; NePoEA; OxBA; TrGrPo (rev. ed.); UnPo (3d ed.)
As a rule, man is a fool. Man Is a Fool. *Unknown.* FaFP; SiTL
As a Seal upon Thy Heart. The Song of Solomon, Bible, *O.T.* *See* Love.
As a seed deeply sheathed within a cone. Sonnet. Phyllis Reid. DiM
As a signet of carbuncle in a setting of gold. Music. Ecclesiasticus, Bible, Apocrypha. TrJP
As a sloop with a sweep of immaculate wing on her delicate spine. Buick. Karl Shapiro. CoBA; HoPM; MiAP; MoAB; TrGrPo (rev. ed.); ViBoPo (1958 ed.)
As a soul from whom companionships subside. Starved Rock. Edgar Lee Masters. ChMo; CMP
As a stream that runs to sea. Bonds. Laurence Housman. MaRV
As a twig trembles, which a bird. She Came and Went. James Russell Lowell. AA; BAP; CoBA; HBV; IAP; LBAP; LEAP; TCAP; ViBoPo
As a wave that steals when the winds are stormy. The Lay of Macaroni. Bayard Taylor. PA
As a white candle. The Old Woman. Joseph Campbell. AWP; BMEP; CBOV; CP; EPP; GoBC; GTIV; HBMV; JAWP; LBBV; MBP; MCCG; MoBrPo; MotAn; NeHB; NeMA; NP; NV; OnYI; OxBI; POTE; PoToHe (new ed.); TIP; ViBoPo; WBP; YT
As a woman who stands on an echoing beach. No Nice Girl's Song. Robert Herring. MoWP
As a young child the wisest could adore him. W. H. Auden. *Fr.* In Time of War. ChMo
As a young Child, whose Mother, for a jest. The Child's Purchase. Coventry Patmore. CoBE; ISi; NBE
As a young lobster roamed about. The Lobster. *Unknown.* GoTP
As Adam Early in the Morning. Walt Whitman. OxBA
As Aesop was with boys at play. Aesop at Play. Phaedrus. AWP; JAWP; WBP
As after noon one summer's day. Cupid Mistaken. Matthew Prior. ALV; InMe; ViBoPo
As all fanatics preach, so all men write. How Men Write. Samuel Butler. BeR
As Always. James F. Gallagher. JKCP (1955 ed.)
As Amoret with Phyllis Sat. Sir Carr Scrope. *Fr.* The Man of Mode (*by* Sir George Etherege). SeCL
As an eagle grasped/ In folds of the green serpent. Shelley. *Fr.* Alastor. ChER
As an intruder I trudged with careful innocence. Old Mansion [*or* Southern Mansion]. John Crowe Ransom. MoP; OxBA
As an Old Mercer. Mahlon Leonard Fisher. HBV
As an unperfect actor on the stage. Sonnets, XXIII. Shakespeare. BEL; EM-1; EnL; EtPaEn; HBV; InvP; OAEP; PeBoSo; REAL; ReEn; SiCE
As And to Aus, and Aus to Bis. The Passionate Encyclopedia Britannica Reader to His Love. "Maggie." InMe
As Ann came in one summer's day. The Sleeper. Walter de la Mare. MBP; MoAB; MoBrPo; SeCeV; YT
As Arthur is to England. Lee. Archibald Rutledge. LS
As at noon[e] Dulcina rested. Dulcina [*or* On Dulcina *or* The Shepherd's Wooing Dulcina]. *At. to* Sir Walter Ralegh. ALV; CoMu; TuPP
As at Thy Portals Also Death. Walt Whitman. MOAH; TCAP
As back we look across the ages. Lincoln's Birthday. Nathan Haskell Dole. GA
As balmy as the breath of her you love. Fragment. Dante Gabriel Rossetti. RO
As beautiful Kitty one morning was tripping. Kitty of Coleraine. *At. to* Charles Dawson Shanly, *also to* Edward Lysaght. BOHV; HBV; LPS-1; MCCG; OnYI; StPo; TIP
As bees, that when the skies are calm and fair. Bees and Monks. John Hookham Frere. *Fr.* King Arthur and His Round Table. OBRV
As beneath the moon I walked. The Whisperers. W. W. Gibson. CMP; HBV
As between Gentlemen's Gentlemen. Aristophanes, *tr. fr. Greek by* Benjamin Bickley Rogers. *Fr.* The Frogs. GrR
As billows upon billows roll. The Surrender at Appomattox. Herman Melville. MC; PAH
As birds are fain to build their nests. April on Tweed [*or* Trout-fishing on Tweed]. Andrew Lang. EBSV; POT
As Birds Are Fitted to the Boughs. Louis Simpson. NePoEA
As birds their infant brood protect. Jehovah-Shammah. William Cowper. MeRV
As biting Winter flies, lo, Spring with sunny skies. To Lucius Sestius. Horace. Odes, I, 4. OuHeWo
As black as ink and isn't ink. *Unknown.* OxNR
As boring as the fact of a marvelous friend. The Rainy Season. William Meredith. NePoEA
As boy, I thought myself a clever fellow. Disillusion. Byron. *Fr.* Don Juan, IV. GEPC
As boys begin their dancing to Apollo. The Sailing of the Argo. Apollonius Rhodius. *Fr.* Argonautica. OxBG
As bronze may be much beautified. Fragment: The Abyss of War. Wilfred Owen. POTE
As burnish'd gold, such are my sovereign's hears. Robert Tofte. *Fr.* Laura. ReIE
"As Busy as I Tan Be." A. B. Carroll. FAOV
As butterflies are but winged flowers. The Ways of Time. W. H. Davies. ChMo; CMP
As by occasion late, towards Brutus' city old. A Winter's Morning Muse. Thomas Howell. SiCE
As, by some tyrant's stern command. The Lawyer's Farewell to His Muse. Sir William Blackstone. EV-3
As by the dead we love to sit. Emily Dickinson. NePA
As by the intrument she took her place. Virtuosa. Mary Ashley Townsend. AA
As by the Shore at Break of Day. Thomas Moore. LPS-2
As Careful Merchants. William Browne. *Fr.* Britannia's Pastorals, II. ElSeCe
As Catholics make of the Redeemer. Brand Speaks. Ibsen. *Fr.* Brand, I. WGRP
As cedars beaten with continual storms. George Chapman. *Fr.* Bussy d'Ambois, I, i. ViBoPo
As certain as color. Ono no Komachi, *tr. fr. Japanese by* Kenneth Rexroth. OnPJ
As changed to his essential Self by Time. The Tomb of Edgar Poe. Stéphane Mallarmé. TrFP
As children lost and wandering. The New Year. Roy G. Pearce. PoP
As chimes that flow o'er shining seas. Far-away. George Sigerson. JKCP (1926 ed.); TIP
As Chloe [*or* Cloe] came into the room t'other day. A Lover's Anger. Matthew Prior. LO; LoPS; SeCL
As clever Tom Clinch, while the Rabble was bawling. Clever Tom Clinch Going to Be Hanged. Swift. CEP; CoMu; SeCeV
As convicts go, when it is time, to cells. The Convict. Anthony Frisch. CaP
As cruel as a Turk: whence came. On Mammon. Herman Melville. *Fr.* Clarel. OxBA
As Cupid in a garden strayed. The Bee. *Unknown.* TrAS
As custome was, the pepill far and neir. The Assembly of the Gods. Robert Henryson. *Fr.* The Testament of Cresseid. PoEL-1
As Day Begins to Wane. Helena Coleman. BoCaPo (1943 ed.); CaP; CPG
As day did darken on the dewless grass. The Wind at the Door. William Barnes. AtBAP; EV-4; LO; PoEL-4; RO
As Dew in April. *See* I Sing of a Maiden.
As doctors give physic by way of prevention. For My Own Monument. Matthew Prior. CEP; HBV; LoBV; OBEC; OBEV
As does his heart who travels far from home. To a Young Child. Eliza Scudder. AA
As dolphins coming up to take the sun. The Moving Rocks. Apollonius Rhodius. *Fr.* Argonautica. OxBG

As dolphins love the wave and hawks the air. Words. Mary Josephine Benson. CPG
As down by Banna's banks I strayed. Mailligh Mo Stor. George Ogle. IrPN
As Down in the Sunless Retreats. Thomas Moore. BCEP
As down the road [*or* street] she wambled slow. Bessie Bobtail. James Stephens. ChMo; CMP; NP; TIP
As down the wide indifferent streams I went. The Drunken Boat. Arthur Rimbaud. MiFP
As Down the Woodland Ways. Sir Charles G. D. Roberts. TwCaPo
As due by many titles I resign[e]. Resignation to God. John Donne. Holy Sonnets, II. EPS; EV-2; MePo; NBE; OBS; SeEP
As dyed in blood the streaming vines appear. Woodbines in October. Charlotte Fiske Bates. AA
As, each in turn, the Old Years rise and gird them up to go. The Lost Days. "Susan Coolidge." PSO
As, even today, the airman, feeling the plane sweat. Icarus. Valentin Iremonger. NeIP; OnYI; OxBI
As evening slowly spreads his mantle hoar. Ode Written at Vale-Royal Abbey in Cheshire. Thomas Warton, the Younger. CoBE
As far as human need exists. Love. Charles Russell Wakeley. OQP; QP-1
As fast as thou shalt wane, so fast thou grow'st. Sonnets, XI. Shakespeare. PeBoSo
As flame streams upward, so my longing thought. He Made Us Free. Maurice Francis Egan. AA; JKCP
As flits the restless bee around the fair. A Thought. Juan Meléndez Valdés. TeCS
As flow the rivers to the sea. Inheritance. "Æ." ChMo; CMP; EPN; PoVP; TIP
As fly the shadows o'er the grass. The Irish Wolf-Hound. Denis Florence MacCarthy. *Fr.* The Foray of Con O'Donnell. SN; VA
As for my life, I've led it. A Placid Man's Epitaph. Thomas Hardy. MBP; MoBrPo
As for the dog, the furies, and their snakes. Against the Fear of Death. Lucretius, *tr. by* Dryden. *Fr.* De Rerum Natura, III. PoD
As Fowlers Lie in Wait. Jeremiah, V: 26–31, Bible, *O.T.* TrJP
As Freedom Is a Breakfastfood. E. E. Cummings. AnFE; ChMo; CoAnAm; LiTA; LiTM; OxBA; TwAmPo
As from my window at first glimpse of dawn. At the Dawn. Alice Macdonald Kipling. MaRV
As from our dream we died away. Parting. "Æ." GTIV; PoVP
As from the house your mother sees. To Any Reader. Robert Louis Stevenson. MOB
As from the moist and gelid sleep. George Darley. *Fr.* Nepenthe. OnYI
As from the sultry town, oppressed. A Character. Thomas Caulfield Irwin. TIP
As frosty age renews the early fire. Indian Summer. Erle Reiter Hannum. CAG
As gay for you to take your father's ax. To a Young Wretch. Robert Frost. NeMA
As gillyflowers do but stay. A Lady Dying in Childbed. Robert Herrick. EG
As Glycera was perfect, so. The Grammar of Love. Martial, *tr. by* Pott *and* Wright. ALV
As good enough as a feast: yea, God save it. Of Enough and a Feast. John Heywood. SiCE; TuPP
As good to write, as for to lie and groan. Astrophel and Stella, XL. Sir Philip Sidney. SiPS; TuPP
As growth of form or momentary glance. Transfigured Life. Dante Gabriel Rossetti. The House of Life, LX. BPN; PoVP; ViPo
As hags hold sabbaths, not for joy but spite. Pope. *Fr.* Moral Essays. ExPo
As hang two mighty thunderclouds. The Guns in the Grass. Thomas Frost. MC; PAH
As Happy Dwellers by the Seaside Hear. Celia Thaxter. EtS
As hath been, lo, these many generations. First Travels of Max. John Crowe Ransom. MAP; MoAmPo
As he climbs down our hill, my kestrel rises. Esyllt. Glyn Jones. MoWP
As he goes whistling down his fourteenth year. Boy Fourteen. Amanda Benjamin Hall. MuM
As he had often done before. The Story of the Inky Boys. Heinrich Hoffmann. BoN
As He Is. W. H. Auden. MoPo
As he lived in the daytime and only one day. Truth of Two. Pedro Salinas. CoSP
As he that loves oft looks on the dear form. On the "Vita Nuova" of Dante. Dante Gabriel Rossetti. EmBrPo; PoVP
As he trudg'd along to school. The Story of Johnny Head-in-Air. Heinrich Hoffmann. BoN; TiPo
As He Walked with Us. Harry Webb Farrington. ChIP
As he was speaking, she with lips apart. Stephen Phillips. *Fr.* Marpessa. BrBE
As hearts have broken, let young hearts break. Little Dirge. Jean Starr Untermeyer. HBMV
As Helen Once. Muna Lee. HBMV; TBM
As Hermes once took to his feathers light. A Dream, after Reading Dante's Episode of Paolo and Francesca [*or* On a Dream]. Keats. EnRP; EV-4; PtP; RO
As his great wings the albatross. Albatross. Charles Burgess. NePoAm-2
As his movements twist and wind. The Dancer. Ibn Kharuf. MooP
As home again I travelled regretfully through London. Town Maid. Clifford Bax. POTE
As honest Jacob on a night. The Patriarch. Burns. CoMu
As I a fare had lately past. The Ferryman, Venus, and Cupid. Michael Drayton. *Fr.* The Muses' Elysium. CG
As I am a rhymer. On My Joyful Departure from the City of Cologne. Samuel Taylor Coleridge. InvP; WhC
As I am now, so you must be. *Unknown.* WhC
As I approach. The Monk Noin, *tr. fr. Japanese by* Kenneth Rexroth. OnPJ
As I cam in by Dunidier. The Battle of Harlaw. *Unknown.* EBSV; ESPB
"As I cam in by Glasgow [*or* boney Glassgow] town." Glasgow Peggie. *Unknown.* BaBo; ESPB
As I cam thro the Garrioch land. The Battle of Harlaw (B *vers.*). *Unknown.* ESPB
As I came by a green forest-side. A Carol of Hunting. *Unknown.* AnEC
As I came by the way. Man, Move Thy Mind, and Joy This Feast. *Unknown.* AnEC
As I Came Down from Lebanon. Clinton Scollard. AA; AnAmPo; BAP; HBV; LA; LBMV; LEAP; POT; PoTo
As I came down into the Place of Spain. Fame. Leonard Bacon. PoeMoYo
As I Came Down Mount Tamalpais. Clarence Urmy. AA; HBMV
As I came down the Bowery. Can't You Dance the Polka? *Unknown.* SoAmSa
As I came down the hillside. Despair. Edward Bliss Reed. HBMV
As I came down to the long street by the water. South Street. Francis E. Falkenbury. EtS; PFY; PoeMoYo; VOD (1935 ed.)
As I came in by Fiddich-side. Willie Macintosh. *Unknown.* ESPB (B *vers.*)
As I came in from the green South Downs. The Wealthy Shepherd. Louise Morey Bowman. CPG
As I Came O'er Cairney Mount. *Unknown.* CoMu
As I came out of the New York Public Library. Nuns in the Wind. Muriel Rukeyser. FiMAP
As I Came Over the Grey, Grey Hills. Joseph Campbell. AnIL
As I came over the humpbacked hill. The Green Fiddler. Rachel Field. BoChLi; StPo
As I came over the rise by Stewart's ash. Country Miracle. Abbie Huston Evans. LiTM
As I came over Windy Gap. Running to Paradise. W. B. Yeats. BLV; BoLiVe; OxBoLi
As I came past the Brimham Rocks. The Song of Nidderdale. Dorothy Una Ratcliffe. HBMV
As I came round the harbor buoy. The Long White Seam. Jean Ingelow. GN; HBV; OTPC; VA
As I came thro' Sandgate. The Keel Row [*or* Weel]. May the Keel Row. *Unknown.* EV-4; WP
As I Came through the Desert. James Thomson. *Fr.* The City of Dreadful Night, IV. LiTB
("As I came through the desert thus it was.") EPP, *abr.*; LiTG; MBP, *abr.*; PoEL-5
(Nightmare, *abr.*) BLV
As I came to the edge of the woods. Come In. Robert Frost. AmPP; AnNE; GTBS-W; LiTA; LiTM; MaPo; MoAB; MoAmPo; NeMA; ReMP; RiBV; TrGrPo; TwCV; UnPo (3d ed.)
As I came to the sea wall that August day. On the Sea Wall. C. Day Lewis. SeCePo
As I came up the sandy road that lifts above the sea. The Spell. Henry Martin Hoyt. HBMV
As I came wandering down Glen Spean. The Emigrant Lassie. John Stuart Blackie. VA
As I contrive to slumber by your will. Conopion. Callimachus. GrL
As I descended black, impassive rivers. The Drunken Boat. Arthur Rimbaud. AnFP
As I did roam the other day. Thomas of Erceldoune. *Unknown.* MeEV
As I did walk abroad one time. The Mourning Conquest. *Unknown.* CoMu
As I did walke my selfe alone. King James and Brown. *Unknown.* ESPB
As I drive to the junction of lane and highway. At Castle Boterel. Thomas Hardy. CoEV; FaBoEn; GTBS-D; MoVE
As I Ebb'd with the Ocean of Life. Walt Whitman. LoBV; OnAP

As I gaed down the water side. Ca' the Yowes. Isobel Pagan. TCEP
As I gae*c* in yon greenwood-side. The Duke of Athole's Nurse. *Unknown.* BaPo
As I Gird On for Fighting. A. E. Housman. Last Poems, II. ChMo; CMP; EmBrPo; TwCV
As I Go on My Way. Strickland Gillilan. MaRV
As I Grew Older. Langston Hughes. BANP
As I Grow Old. Douglas Malloch. BPP
As I Grow Old. *Unknown.* MaRV; OQP; PraP; QP-2
As I grow old it seems that I. As I Grow Old. Douglas Malloch. BPP
As I have seene when on the breast of Thames. Praise of Poets. William Browne. *Fr.* Britannia's Pastorals, II, Song 2. OBS
As I in darkness lay the other night. God's Voice. Charles Augustin Sainte-Beuve. TrFP
As I in hoary [*or* hoarie] winter's night stood shivering in the snow. The Burning Babe [*or* A Carol]. Robert Southwell. ACP; AEV; AnEC; AnFE; AtBAP; BEL; BLV; BoW; CAW; CH; COAH; CoBE; CoEV; EG; ElL; ElSeCe; EM-1; EnLit; EPP; EV-1; FaBoCh; FaBoEn; GoBC; HBV; HoPM; LiTB; LiTG; LoBV; LoGBV; MaRV; MePo; OBEV; OBSC; OxBoCh; PoEL-2; PoLi; ReEn; ReIE; SDH; SeCePo; SiCE; StJW; TCEP; TOP; TrGrPo; TuPP; UnPo (1st ed.); ViBoPo
As I kissed Agathon, my soul. Ecstasy. Plato. GrPE
As I lay asleep in Italy. The Mask of Anarchy. Shelley. CoEV; EM-2; EmBrPo; EnRP
As I lay awake in the white moonlight. Sleepyhead. Walter de la Mare. TiPo
As I Lay Dreaming Abed. John McClure. LS
As I lay dying on my bed. Aftermath. Sydney King Russell. UnW
As I lay in a winter's night. The Debate of the Body and the Soul. *Unknown.* CoBE
As I lay in the early sun. Song. Edward Shanks. BMEP
As I Lay Musing ("As I lay musing all alone"). *Unknown.* CoMu
(Friar in the Well, The, A *and* B *vers.*) ESPB
As I lay musing all alone/ upon my resting bed. The Poore Man Payes for All. *Unknown.* CoMu
As I Lay Quiet. Margaret Widdemer. GoYe
As I lay sleeping. *Unknown.* EG; LO; TrGrPo
As I lay upon a night. My Thought Was on a Maid So Bright [*or* Alma Redemptoris Mater]. *Unknown.* AnEC; ISi
As I Lay with My Head in Your Lap Camerado. Walt Whitman. IAP; OxBA
As I Laye a-Thynkynge. "Thomas Ingoldsby." HBV
(Last Lines.) OBVV
As I lie dreaming, visions of the night. Upon the Whirlwind. Antero de Quental. UnW
As I lie in bed. A Prayer. Joseph Seamon Cotter, Jr. BANP
As I lie roofed in, screened in. On the Porch. Harriet Monroe. BAP; NP
As I look back upon your first embrace. Surrender. Amelia Josephine Burr. HBV
As I looked on my husband, and felt my last thread was spun. Johannes Barbucallus, *tr. fr. Greek by* William Stebbing. GrPo
As I looked out of my window. Run Along, You Little Dogies. *Unknown.* OuSiCo
As I looked out one May morning. The Princess and the Gypsies. Frances Cornford. StPo
As I Me Walk'd in One Morning. *Unknown.* TwHP
As I my little flock on Ister bank. Shepherd Song. Sir Philip Sidney. *Fr.* Arcadia. SiPS
As I once in wanton play. *Unknown, tr. fr. Greek by* Abraham Cowley. GrPo
As I one ev'ning sat before my cell. Artillery [*or* Artillerie]. George Herbert. MaPo; PoEL-2; SeCV-1
As I Out Rode This Enders Night. *Unknown.* AnEC
As I passed [*or* pass'd] by a river side. The Carnal and the Crane. *Unknown.* AnEC; ESPB; OBB; StJW
As I passed by Tom Sherman's bar-room. The Cowboy's Lament (A *vers.*). *Unknown.* ViBoFo
As I Pondered in Silence. Walt Whitman. IAP; LEAP; WHA
As I proceeded down along impassive rivers. The Drunken Boat. Arthur Rimbaud. LiA; LiTW
As I ride, as I ride. Through the Metidja to Abd-el-Kadr. Robert Browning. BPN; EmBrPo; GEPC; PoVP
As I rode down the arroyo through yuccas [*or* yucas] belled with bloom. In the Mohave. Patrick Orr. BANP; LiTM; NV
As I rode out one evening down by a river side. Two Lovers Discoursing. *Unknown.* ShS
As I rode this latter day. Five Joys. *Unknown.* TMEV
As I rose in the early dawn. Wanderers. James Hebblethwaite. BoAu; NeLNL
As I rose like a lover from the ravished sea. To a Poet Who Has Never Travelled. Charles Causley. POTE (1959 ed.)
As I roved out, at Faha, one morning. The Maid of Cloghroe. *Unknown.* TIP
As I roved out impatiently. In the Ringwood. Thomas Kinsella. OxBI
As I roved out on a May morning. Johnny's the Lad I Love. *Unknown.* AnIV; GTIV; OxBoLi
As I roved out on a summer's morning. Sweet Castle Hyde [*or* Castle Hyde]. Edward Kenealy. IrPN; OnYI; RO
As I roved out one summer's morning, speculating most curiously. Colleen Rue. *Unknown.* OnYI
As I row over the plain. Fujiwara no Tadamichi, *tr. fr. Japanese by* Kenneth Rexroth. OnPJ
As I rummaged thro' [*or* through] the attic. My Trundle Bed. J. G. Baker. BLPA; FaBoBe
As I said to myself I will build a house. The Little House. Struthers Burt. NoCaPo
As I sail home to Galveston. A Sailor's Song. Hazel Harper Harris. EtS
As I Sat Alone by Blue Ontario's Shore. Walt Whitman. *See* By Blue Ontario's Shore.
As I Sat at My Spinning-Wheel. *Unknown.* CoMu
As I sat at the café I said to myself. Spectator ab Extra. Arthur Hugh Clough. *Also in* Dipsychus. ALV; FiBHP; LiTG; OxBoLi; SeCePo; SiTL; ViPP
As I sat by my fire one night. Heard on the Roof at Midnight. Leah Bodine Drake. DaM
As I sat by my window last evening. Miss Foggerty's Cake. *Unknown.* BLPA
As I sat down t' play a game o' coon can. Po' Boy. *Unknown.* TrAS
As I sat down to a game o' coon-can. The Penitentiary Blues. *Unknown.* SoAF
As I sat down to breakfast in state. The Country Clergyman's Trip to Cambridge. Macaulay. OxBoLi
As I sat musing by the frozen dyke. The Song of Soldiers. Walter de la Mare. SoV
As I Sat on a Sunny Bank. *Unknown.* *See* I Saw Three Ships.
As I Sat under a Sycamore Tree. *Unknown.* *See* I Saw Three Ships.
As I Set Down to Play Tin-Can. *Unknown.* *See* Po' Boy.
As I sit at the loom. Weaving. Tzu Yeh. PoHN
As I sit looking out of a window of the building. The Instruction Manual. John Ashbery. NeAP
As I sit on a log here in the woods among the clean-faced beeches. Choir Practice. Ernest Crosby. AA
As I sit with others, at a great feast, suddenly, while the music is playing. Thought. Walt Whitman. MaRV; MeRV
As I stand by the cross on the lone mountain's crest. The Two Ships. Bret Harte. MaRV
As I start for a saunter, I turn and say. When He Goes to Play with the Boys. Strickland Gillilan. PEDC
As I stole out of Babylon beyond the stolid warders. Out of Babylon. Clinton Scollard. TBM
As I stood at the door. The College of Surgeons. James Stephens. AnIL
As I Stood by Yon Roofless Tower. Burns. *See* Vision, The.
As I stray'd o'er the common on Cork's rugged border. Mary Le More. George Nugent Reynolds. OnYI
As I strolled out one evening, out for a night's career. The Fire Ship. *Unknown.* AmSS
As I sunk the lobster-pots. Fisherman's Luck. W. W. Gibson. EtS
As I suppose, and as I suppose. *Unknown.* SiTL
As I threw the last log on the hearth. March of the Spirit. Angelos Sikelianos. MoGP
As I up rose in a morning. Mother, White as Lily Flower. *Unknown.* AnEC
As I walk through the streets. Prayer. F. S. Flint. CP; NV; TrPWD
As I Walk'd by Myself. *Unknown.* *See* As I Walked by Myself.
As I walk'd out one evening just as the sun went down. *See* As I walked out one evening just as the sun went down.
As I walk'd [*or* walked] thinking through a little grove. Catch: On a Wet Day. Franco Sacchetti, *tr. by* Dante Gabriel Rossetti. AWP; JAWP; WBP
As I Walked [*or* Walk'd] by Myself. *Unknown.* ChTr; OTPC (1923 ed.); OxNR; SiTL
(As I Walked, 1 *st.*) MPB (1956 ed.)
(Song on King William III, A.) NA
As I walked down by the river. A Ballad for Katharine of Aragon. Charles Causley. FaBoTw; NePoEA
As I walked down the waterside. The Sleepers. W. H. Davies. AnFE; BMEP; ChMo; CMP; LBBV; PoeMoYo; POTT; PYM; TwCV; WoL
As I walked fforth one morninge. Christopher White. *Unknown.* ESPB
As I walked me this endurs day. Here I Sit Alone. *Unknown.* OxBoCh
As I Walked Out in the Streets of Laredo. *Unknown.* *See* Cowboy's Lament, The.
As I walked out in yonder dell. The Elfin Knight (B *vers.*). *Unknown.* ViBoFo

As I walked out of St. James's Hospital. The Bad Girl's Lament. *Unknown.* ViBoFo
As I walked out one cold winter night. The Lass of Roch Royal (C *vers.*). *Unknown.* ViBoFo
As I Walked Out One Evening. W. H. Auden. AtBAP; ChMP; LiTM; OAEP (2d ed.); PoD; PoFS; POTE; SeCeV; UnPo (3d ed.)
(Song: As I Walked Out One Evening.) MoAB; MoBrPo (1950 ed.)
As I walked [*or* walk'd] out one evening just as the sun went down. The Shanty-Boy and the Farmer's Son. *Unknown.* ABF; APW; IHA
As I walked out one evening late, a-drinking of sweet wine. My Old True Love. *Unknown.* OuSiCo
As I walked out one May morning. The Bold Fisherman. *Unknown.* BaBo
As I walked out one morning down by the Sligo dock. Yellow Meal. *Unknown.* ShS
As I walked out [*or* was a-walking] one morning for pleasure. Whoopee Ti Yi Yo, Git Along, Little Dogies [*or* Git Along, Little Dogies]. *Unknown.* ABF; ABS; AmPP; AS; CoSo; CSF; FaPON; IHA; InP; MoShBr; MPB; OTPC (1946 ed.); StVeCh; TiPo; TreF; TSW; TSWC; WaKn
As I walked out one morning in May,/ Just before the break of day. Archie o Cawfield (B *vers.*). *Unknown.* BaBo
As I walked out one morning in May,/ For my recreation. The Lass of Mohea. *Unknown.* SoAmSa
As I walked out one night, it being dark all over. The Sailor's Return. *Unknown.* LO; OxBoLi
As I walked out one summer's evening. John Riley. *Unknown.* OuSiCo
As I walked out that sultry night. Full Moon. Robert Graves. FaBoEn; POTE
As I walked out upon the road one day. Poor Old Man. *Unknown.* ShS
As I walked over Stony Hill. Ozark Song. Dennis Murphy. BAP
As I walked over the hill [*or* hills] one day. A Nursery Song. Ann A. G. Carter. BOL; MOAH; OTPC (1923 ed.); PPL; RAR; SAS
As I walked the heights of Meelin on a tranquil autumn day. The Fairy Harpers. James B. Dollard. CaP; CPG; OCL
As I walked thinking through a little grove. *See* As I walk'd thinking . . .
As I walked through my garden. Butterfly. Hilda Conkling. NP; TiPo
As I walked through the rumorous streets. Vistas. Odell Shepard. HBMV; NV; QS
As I walked through Tom Sherman's bar-room. The Dying Cowboy. *Unknown.* ABS
As I walked under the African moon. Lament. George Malcolm. NeTW
As I wandered in the forest. Wild Flower's Song. Blake. BoTP
As I wandered over the city through the night. Irradiations, XXV. John Gould Fletcher. LEAP
As I wandered round the homestead. My Mother's Prayer. T. C. O'Kane. BLPA; FaBoBe
As I was a-gwine [*or* goin'] down the road. Turkey in the Straw. *Unknown.* AS; FaFP; TrAS; TreFS; YaD
As I was a-roaming for pleasure one day. The Little Mohee. *Unknown.* BaBo
As I was a-walkin'/ All by the seashore. Little Mohee. *Unknown.* AmSS
As I was a-walkin' [*or* a-walking *or* walking] down Paradise Street. Blow the Man Down. *Unknown.* ABF; AmSS (*vers.* II); AS; IHA; SoAmSa (B *vers.*)
As I was a-walking/ One morning in spring. The Lark in the Morning. *Unknown.* ChTr
As I was a-walking [*or* walking] mine alane. Archie of [*or* o'] Cawfield. *Unknown.* ESPB (B *vers.*); OBB
As I was a-walking on Westminster Bridge. *Unknown.* OxNR
As I was a-walking one morning down by the Clarence Dock. Heave Away, *vers.* I. *Unknown.* ShS
As I was a-walking one morning for pleasure. *See* As I walked out one morning for pleasure.
As I was a-walking the other day. The Shoemaker. *Unknown.* FaPON; GFA
As I was a-walking upon my wedding-day. The Drownèd Lover. Lady Margaret Sackville. AV
As I was carving images from clouds. Opifex. Thomas Edward Brown. OBVV; PoVP
As I was cast in my first [*or* ffirst] sleepe. Young Andrew. *Unknown.* ESPB; OBB
As I was climbing Ardan Mór [*or* The Herons]. Francis Ledwidge. ACP; AlDL; AnIV; AWP; GTIV; JAWP; OnYI; OxBI; WBP
As I was coming down the stair. *Unknown.* BoN; CenHV
As I was driving my waggon one day. Gee Ho, Dobin. *Unknown.* CoMu
As I was falling down the stair. Later Antigonishes. Hughes Mearns. InMe
As I was goin' down the road. *See* As I was a-gwine down the road.
As I was going along, long, long [*or* along, along]. Mother Goose. OxNR; TiPo (1952 ed.)
As I was going by candlelight. Copper Song. Ethel Talbot Scheffauer. PoMS
As I was going by Charing Cross. *Unknown.* CH; FaBoCh; LoGBV; OxNR; RIS
As I was going o'er London Bridge. *Unknown.* OxNR; SiTL
As I was going o'er Tipple Tine. *Unknown.* OxNR
As I was going o'er Westminster bridge. *Unknown.* OTPC (1946 ed.); PPL
As I was going out one day. *Unknown.* BoN
As I was going to Banbury. *Unknown.* OxNR
As I was going to Bethlehem-town. Bethlehem-Town. Eugene Field. WBLP
As I was going to Derby,/ Upon a market day. The Derby Ram [*or* The Ram]. *Unknown.* BoN; LiL; OxNR; SiTL; ViBoFo
As I was going to Derby, all on a market day. The Wonderful Derby Ram. *Unknown.* BoTP
As I was going to Derby, 'twas on a market day. Derby Ram. *Unknown.* SoAmSa
As I was going to St. Ives. Mother Goose. BoChLi; HBV; HBVY; OTPC; OxNR; PPL; RIS; SiTL; StVeCh
As I was going to sell my eggs. *Unknown.* OxNR
As I was going to town. Me Alone. Lula Lowe Weeden. CDC
As I was going up Pippen Hill. *Unknown.* OxNR
As I was going up the hill. Jack the Piper. *Unknown.* ChTr; OxNR
As I was going [*or* a-walking] up the stair. Antigonish [*or* A Case *or* The Little Man Who Wasn't There]. Hughes Mearns. FaFP; FaPON; InMe; LiTM; SiTL; StaSt; WhC
As I was hiking past the woods, the cool and sleepy summer woods. Out There Somewhere. H. H. Knibbs. BLPA
As I Was Laying on the Green. *Unknown.* FiBHP; SiTL; WhC
As I was letting down my hair. The Lady with Technique. Hughes Mearns. *Fr.* Later Antigonishes. FiBHP; InMe; SiTL; WhC
As I was lumberin' down the street. Louisiana Girls. *Unknown.* ABF
As I was lumb'ring down de street. Lubly Fan. Cool White. TrAS
As I was marching in Flanders. Comrades. W. W. Gibson. BEL; ChMo; CMP
As I was on the high-road. Wet or Fine. Amory Hare. HBMV
As I was out upon the road one day. Sacramento, *vers.* II. *Unknown.* ShS
As I was out walking for pleasure one day. Little Mohee. *Unknown.* APW
As I was passing by. The Vine. Mu'tamid, King of Seville. MooP
As I was playing on the green. *Unknown.* WhC
As I was robbing Chelsea Bank. Later Antigonishes. Hughes Mearns. InMe
As I was rumbling through the mountain rift. Reward of Virtue. Arthur Guiterman. InMe
As I was sitting in my chair. The Perfect Reactionary. Hughes Mearns. SiTL; WhC
As I was, so be ye. Epitaph. *Unknown.* TreFS
As I Was Standing in the Street. *Unknown.* SiTL
As I was strolling down a woodland way. Down a Woodland Way. Mildred Howells. AA
As I was travelling one morning in May. The Bachelor's Lay. *Unknown.* OuSiCo
As I was wa'kin' all alone. The Wee Wee Man. *Unknown.* *See* As I was walking mine alane.
As I Was Walkin' down Wexford Street, *with music.* *Unknown.* AS
As I was walkin' th' jungle round, a-killin' of tigers an' time. A Ballad. Guy Wetmore Carryl. BOHV; InMe; PA
As I was walking all alane [*or* alone]. The Twa Corbies. *Unknown.* AnFE; BaBo (B *vers.*); BCEP; BoLiVe; BSV; CaAE; CBOV; CH; CoEV; DaM; EBSV; EnL; EnLi-1; EnLit; EnSB; ESPB; EV-2; ExPo; FaBoCh; GoTS; GTBS; GTBS-D; GTBS-W; GTSE; GTSL; HBV; InP; InPo; LEAP; LH; LiTL; LO; LoGBV; OBB; OBEV; Po; SeCePo; SeCeV; ShBV-2; StPo; TOP; ViBoFo (B *vers.*)
As I was walking all alone. The Wee Wee Man. *Unknown.* *See* As I was walking mine alane.
As I was walking along in the fields. *Unknown.* BoN
As I was walking down Paradise Street. *See* As I was a-walkin' down Paradise Street.
As I was walking I met a woman. An Old Air. F. R. Higgins. AnIL
As I was walking in a field of wheat. *Unknown.* OxNR
As I was walking in the Park. The Neutral. Wrenne Jarman. DiM

As I was walking mine alane. Archie o' Cawfield. *Unknown.* *See* As I was a-walking mine alane.
As I was walking [*or* wa'kin' *or* wa'king] mine alane [*or* all alone]. The Wee Wee Man. *Unknown.* BaBo; CH; DaM; ESPB; FaBoCh; OBB; OTPC (1946 ed.)
As I was walking out upon the road one day. Sacramento, *vers.* III. *Unknown.* ShS
As I was walking up the stair. *See* As I was going up the stair.
As I was walking up the street. O Mally's Meek, Mally's Sweet. Burns. GN; HBV; OTPC
As I watch the moon. Oe no Chisato, *tr. fr. Japanese by* Kenneth Rexroth. OnPJ
As I watch the moonbeams' gentle riot. In the Moonlight. Jens Peter Jacobsen. BoDS
As I watched the unlikely ones at the bar. Dramas of the Rose. James Schevill. FiMAP
As I went a-walking all by the seashore. The Little Mohee. *Unknown.* ABF
As I went a-Walking down Ratcliffe Highway, *2 vers., with music.* *Unknown.* ShS
As I Went a-Walking One Fine Summer's Evening, *with music.* *Unknown.* OuSiCo
As I Went By. Rose O'Neill. BAP
As I went by a dyer's door. The Dyer. *Unknown.* ChTr; OxNR
As I went down by Hastings Mill I lingered in my going. Hastings Mill. Cicely Fox Smith. HBV; WaKn
As I went down the hill along the wall. Meeting and Passing. Robert Frost. CoV; MaPo; OxBA
As I went down the hill I heard. The Voice. Norman Gale. HBV; OHIP
As I went down the village green. Ducks. Norman Ault. BoTP
As I went down through Dublin City. Dublin; the Old Squares. Padraic Colum. NePoAm
As I went down to Darby town. The Ram of Darby. *Unknown.* OuSiCo
As I went down to Dymchurch Wall. In Romney Marsh. John Davidson. BSV; EV-5; GoTS; GTBS; GTBS-D; LBBV; OBVV; PC; PoeT; POTE; ShBV-3; ViBoPo
As I went down to Rotten Lake I remembered. Rotten Lake Elegy. Muriel Rukeyser. MoPo; NePA
As I went down to the old depot. The Maid Freed from the Gallows (D *vers.*). *Unknown.* ViBoFo
As I went dreaming. The Poplars. "Seumas O'Sullivan." GTIV
As I went lonely up the stair. On the Stair. Annie Campbell Huestis. UnW
As I went out a Crow. The Last Word of a Bluebird. Robert Frost. FaPON; StVeCh (1955 ed.); TiPo; WhBS
As I Went Out for a Ramble, *with music.* *Unknown.* OuSiCo
As I went out one evening. The Mermaid. *Unknown.* OuSiCo
As I went out one morning to breathe the morning air. Lolly Too-Dum. *Unknown.* OuSiCo
As I went out to walk. Country Tune. Elizabeth Riddell. BoAV; NeLNL
As I went out walking for pleasure one day. The Pretty Mohea. *Unknown.* ABS
As I went over London Bridge. Riddle. *Unknown.* ChTr
As I went over the Far Hill. Beyond Rathkelly. Francis Carlin. HBMV; PR; SBMV
As I went over the water. *Unknown.* BoN; OxNR; SiTL
As I went over Tipple Tyne. Riddle. *Unknown.* ChTr
As I Went Singing over the Earth. Mary Elizabeth Coleridge. UnS
(Bird, The.) AlDL
As I Went through a Garden Green. *Unknown.* AnEC
As I went through the [*or* a] garden gap. Mother Goose. BoChLi; HBV; HBVY; OTPC; PPL; RIS
As I went through the tangled wood. The Haughty Aspen. Nora Archibald Smith. ChrBoLe; CLS; SDH
As I went to Bonner. *Unknown.* BoN; OxBoLi; OxNR; SiTL
As I went to Totnam. The Maid of Tottenham. *Unknown.* CoMu
As I went to Walsingham. Francis' New Jig. George Attowell. ReIE
As I went up by Heartbreak Road. Heartbreak Road. Helen Gray Cone. BAP; HBMV
As I went up the Brandy hill. *Unknown.* OxNR
As I went up the garden. *Unknown.* BoTP
As I went up to Craigbilly Fair. Craigbilly Fair. *Unknown.* ChTr
"As I went up to London." Going Up to London. Nancy Byrd Turner. GaP; HBMV; MW; PC
As I went walking. Song in Spring. Louis Ginsberg. YeAr
As I went walking one March day. One March Day. *Unknown.* PCH
As I wer readen ov a stwone. The Readen ov a Head-Stwone [*or* The Head-Stone]. William Barnes. CH; HBV; OBVV
As I were a-walking upon a fine day. Because I Were Shy. *Unknown.* StPo
As I'd Nothing Else to Do. Herbert Fry. TreFS
As if Awakened, Summoned. Wordsworth. *Fr.* The Prelude. AtBAP
As if he were a vision that would fade. Mephibosheth. Nathaniel Parker Willis. MOAH
As if it had ev'n twenty thousand faces. Thomas Traherne. *Fr.* On Leaping over the Moon. AlDL
As if it were. Merritt Parkway. Denise Levertov. NeAP
As if stone Caesar shook. Fragment. Hugh McCrae. BoAV
As if the storm meant him. Why Are Ye Afraid, O Ye of Little Faith? Richard Crashaw. MeRV
As if the sun had trodden down the sky. Heat. John Gould Fletcher. Down the Mississippi, II. ChMo; CMP; LiTA
As if you could not leave the jug alone! The Broken Jug. William Barnes. PoVP
As I'm French born, I'm pained to say. Quatrain. Villon. TrFP
As I'm sitting all alone in the gloaming. Bantry Bay. James Lyman Molloy. OnYI
As imperceptibly as grief. Emily Dickinson. AmPo; ExPo; FaBoEn; LiTA; LiTM (rev. ed.); PoEL-5; PoFS; RiBV
As in a Dusky and Tempestuous Night. William Drummond of Hawthornden. BSV; EV-2; LO, 4 *ll.*
(Sonnet: "As in a duskie and tempestuous night.") FaBoEn; OBS
As in a Picture-Book. Fannie Stearns Davis. TBM
As in a porch of stars we stand; the night. The Porch of Stars. Laurence Binyon. LHV
As in a Rose-Jar. Thomas S. Jones, Jr. POT; PoTo; VOD
As in a royal army, led by a king. Christ's Coming to Judgment. Thomas Dekker. AnEnPo
As in a theater, the eyes of men. Gentle Richard. Shakespeare. King Richard II, *fr.* V, ii. LiA
As in a Watteau fete of rose and silver blue. The Tempest. Marya Zaturenska. MoAmPo; TrGrPo (1942 ed.)
As in her ancient mistress' lap. Familiarity Dangerous. Vincent Bourne, *tr. by* William Cowper. PoC
As in old days of mellow candle-light. Candle-Light. Thomas S. Jones, Jr. VOD
As in old dungeon under marble thrones. William Ellery Leonard. *Fr.* Two Lives, Pt. III. MOAP
As in Silks My Julia Goes. Robert Herrick. *See* Upon Julia's Clothes.
As in smooth oil the razor best is whet. Epigram. *Unknown.* HBV
As in some countries, far remote from hence. Idea, L. Michael Drayton. ReIE
As in some old and simple village street. Noon-Tide. Thomas S. Jones, Jr. VOD
As in the age of shepherd king and queen. Dans l'allée. Paul Verlaine. AWP
As in the boughs of a tall poplar-tree. Wind in the Poplars. Sophocles. OxBG
As in the cool air'd road I come by. My Love's Guardian Angel. William Barnes. AtBAP; PoEL-4; RO
As in the depths of an ancient cavern. The Ancient Tear. Luis G. Urbina. AnMP
As in the gardens, all through May, the rose. His Lady's Tomb. Pierre de Ronsard. *Fr.* Amours de Marie. AWP; JAWP; PrPoCR; WBP
As in the greatest of societies. Proemium I. Everard Guilpin. *Fr.* Skialetheia. ReIE; SiCE
As in the house I sate. Poverty. Thomas Traherne. ElSeCe; OxBoCh
As in the Midst of Battle There Is Room. George Santayana. Sonnets, XXV. AnFE; APA; AWP; BAP; CoAnAm; JAWP; LBMV; LEAP; LiTM (1946 ed.); MAP; MoAmPo; MOAP; NePA; ReaPo; WBP
As in the night I restless lie. An Anodyne. Thomas Ken. OxBoCh
As in the Night We See the Sparks Revived. *Unknown.* ReIE
As in the street, smug, hideously bland. The Chastisement of Tartufe. Arthur Rimbaud. TrFP
As in the sunshine of the morn. Butterfly and the Snail. John Gay. CG
As in the Woodland I Walk. Richard Le Gallienne. CV
As in your innocent eyes last night. Birthday Poem, November 4th. John Thompson, Jr. WaP
As inward love breeds outward talk. The Angler's Song. William Basse. CenL; ElSeCe; OBS
As it befel[l] [*or* itt beffell] in midsummertime. Sir Andrew Barton. *Unknown.* BaBo; EnSB; ESPB; EV-2; OBB; ViBoFo
As it befell on a bright holiday. The Bitter Withy. *Unknown.* ChTr
As it befell upon one time. Hughie Grame. *Unknown.* ESPB
As It Began to Dawn. George Edward Hoffman. ChIP
As it fell on a holy-day. John Dory. *Unknown.* BHV; ESPB; SG
As it fell one [*or* on one] holy-day. Little Musgrave and Lady Barnard. *Unknown.* BaBo (A *vers.*); ESPB; OBB; ViBoFo
As it fell out on a high holy day. Little Musgrave and Lady Barnard. *Unknown.* InvP

As it fell out on a holy day. The Bitter Withy. *Unknown.* AnEC; BaBo; OAEP; ViBoFo
As it fell out on a long summer's day. Fair Margaret and Sweet William. *Unknown.* BLV; ESPB; OBB; TOP
As it fell out one May morning. The Holy Well. *Unknown.* AnEC; FaBoCh; LoGBV; OBB; OxBoCh
As it fell out upon a day. Dives [*or* Diverus] and Lazarus [*or* Lazarus]. *Unknown.* ATP; BaBo; ESPB; OBB; SaSa
As It Fell upon a Day. Richard Barnfield. *See* Nightingale, The.
As it is true that I, like all, must die. Scene-Shifter Death. Mary Devenport O'Neill. NeIP
As It Looked Then. E. A Robinson. MaPo; NePA
As It Was. Lilla Cabot Perry. Meeting after Long Absence, II. AA; OBAV
As It Was in the Beginning Is Now and Ever Shall Be. Sophocles, *tr. fr. Greek by* Lewis Campbell. *Fr.* Antigone. GrR
As it/ Were tissue of silver. Fate Defied. Adelaide Crapsey. NP; NV; SBMV; VOD (1935 ed.); YT
As it were upon the sea. Under the wind's hand. The Desert Travellers. L. D. Lerner. BoSA
As itt beffell in m[i]dsumer-time. *See* As it befel . . .
As Jack walked out of London city, no one on Jack to take pity. Jack the Jolly Tar. *Unknown.* BaBo
As Jesus and his followers. The Boy Out of Church. Robert Graves. TCPD
As Jock the Leg and the merry merchant. Jock the Leg and the Merry Merchant. *Unknown.* ESPB
As Joe Gould says. E. E. Cummings. FiBHP
As Joseph Was a-Walking. *Unknown.* BoTP; CLS; DD; OHIP; PCH; StVeCh; ViBoPo
(Cherry-Tree Carol, The.) AnEC; ChrBoLe
(Christmas Carol.) COAH; GN; HBV; HBVY; HH; OTPC
As Jove the Olympian (who both I and you know). The Political Balance. Philip Freneau. IAP
As junco is with winter. Different Winter. Louise Townsend Nicholl. NePoAm-2
As Kingfishers Catch Fire, Dragonflies Draw Flame. Gerard Manley Hopkins. ExPo; FaBoMo; LiTM; ViP
(Immanent, The.) ES
(What I Do Is Me.) MoAB; MoBrPo
As Lambs into the Pen. Dorothy Wellesley. FaBoTw
As landscapes richen after rain, the eye. Foliage of Vision. James Merrill. MoPo
As late I journeyed o'er the extensive plain. Life. Samuel Taylor Coleridge. BPN; EmBrPo; EnRP
As late I rambled in the happy fields. Sonnet: To a Friend Who Sent Me Some Roses. Keats. GEPC
As late I sought the spangled bowers. Odes of Anacreon, *tr. by* Thomas Moore. OuHeWo
As lately I traveled. The Seaman's Compass. Laurence Price. SG
As laurel leaves that cease not to be green. The Promise of a Constant Lover. *Unknown.* EIL; ReIE
As life runs on, the road grows strange. Sixty-eighth Birthday. James Russell Lowell. PoEL-5
As Life What Is So Sweet. *Unknown.* SeCL
As life's unending column pours. The Two Armies. Oliver Wendell Holmes. TCAP
As Like the Woman as You Can. W. E. Henley. HBV
As lily-blooms that quiver. Erik Axel Karlfeldt. *Fr.* Flower-Songs. AnSL
As lily grows up easily. Peggy Mitchell. Anthony Raftery. GTIV
As Lise however my mother was white. The Black Man's Son. Oswald Durand. PoNe
As little children in a darkened hall. Wayside Music. Charles Henry Crandall. SDH
As little Jenny Wren/ Was sitting by the shed. *Unknown.* OxNR
As lonely I strayed by the banks of the river. Lost Jimmie Whalen. *Unknown.* BaBo
As long ago we carried to your knees. *See* As years ago we carried . . .
As long as Fame's imperious music rings. Three Quatrains. E. A. Robinson. TwP
As long as I go forth on ships that sail. A Seaman's Confession of Faith. Harry Kemp. TrPWD
As long as I live. Me. Walter de la Mare. FaPON; TiPo (1959 ed.)
As long as I looked good to you. Horace à la Mode. "J. C. C. H., Jr." CAG
As long as men for fellow men face death and falter not. The Ballad of "La Tribune." Archibald MacMechan. CPG
As long as the blade has never. Shame. Arthur Rimbaud. AnFP
As long as you never marry me, and I never marry you. Warning. Margaret Widdemer. PR
As Love and I, late harbour'd in one inn. Love's Proverbs [*or* A Play with Proverbs]. Michael Drayton. Idea, LIX. ES; EV-1
As Love is cause of joy. Love. Anthony Munday. *Fr.* Zellanto, the Fountain of Fame. OBSC
As lovers, banished from their lady's face. Before Her Portrait in Youth. Francis Thompson. EmBrPo; EPN
As loving hind that (hartless) wants her deer. A Letter to Her Husband, Absent upon Publick Employment. Anne Bradstreet. OxBA
As low in Cupid's garden for pleasure I did walk. The Prentice Boy. *Unknown.* ABS
As Lucy Went a-Walking. Walter de la Mare. RIS
As mad sexton's bell, tolling. Song on the Water. Thomas Lovell Beddoes. EG; ERP; FaBoCh; LoGBV; PoE
As man and his motor have brought it about. Streamlined Stream-Knowledge. Arthur W. Bell. WhC
As many as the leaves fall from the tree. The Golden Apples. William Morris. *Fr.* The Earthly Paradise. EPN
As Many Questions as Answers. Laura Riding. MoP
As Mary and Willie sat by the sea shore. Mary and Willie. *Unknown.* ABS
As May Margaret sat in her bowerie, in her bower all alone. Sweet William's Ghost. *Unknown.* HOAH
As Memnon's marble harp renowned of old. Delights of Fancy. Mark Akenside. *Fr.* The Pleasures of Imagination, I. LPS-3
"As men from men." Despondency Corrected. Wordsworth. *Fr.* The Excursion, IV. EnRP
As men talk in a dream so Corinth all. Wide-spreaded Night. Keats. *Fr.* Lamia. LiA
As men who fight for home and child and wife. Battle of Oriskany. Charles D. Helmer. PAH
As men who see a city fitly planned. Proofs of Buddha's Existence. *Unknown.* WGRP
As mountain peaks that tower above the plain. Pioneers. Gertrude B. Gunderson. DDA
As my hand dropt a seed. Sowing Seed. Laurence Binyon. POTE
As my lady was in her daisy garden. The Spanish Man. F. R. Higgins. JKCP (1926 ed.)
As nature works in all things to an end. George Chapman. *Fr.* The Tragedy of Caesar and Pompey. NBE
As near beauteous Boston lying. A New Song. *Unknown.* PAH
As near Porto-Bello lying. Admiral Hosier's Ghost. Richard Glover. EV-3; HBV; SG; ViBoPo
As newer comers crowd the fore. The Superseded. Thomas Hardy. TOP
As Night Comes On. Cecil Cobb Wesley. GoYe
As night drew on, and, from the crest. Winter Night [*or* The Fireside]. Whittier. *Fr.* Snow-bound. MW; TrGrPo; YT
As Ocean Holds the Globe. Feodor Ivanovich Tyutchev, *tr. fr. Russian by* Babette Deutsch. TrRV
(As Ocean's Stream, *diff. tr., by* Babette Deutsch *and* Avrahm Yarmolinsky.) AWP
As o'er my latest book I pored. Printer's Error. P. G. Wodehouse. FiBHP
As o'er the cold sepulchral stone. Lines Written in an Album at Malta. Byron. InP
As o'er the hill we roam'd at will. Wanderers. Charles Stuart Calverley. CenHV
As o'er the world came trailing. Bacchanal. Ibn Baqi. MooP
As oft as I behold and see. Earl of Surrey. SiPS
As oft I doe record. *Unknown.* SeCSL
As often as we thought of her. Neighbors. E. A. Robinson. ChMo; CMP; CP; NV
As on a branch, in May, we see the rose. Sonnet. Pierre de Ronsard. FoS
As on a dark guitar. Ballad of Love and Blood. Angel Miguel Queremel. AnCL
As on a daye Clorinda fayre was bathinge. *Unknown.* SeCSL
As on a green hillock. On a Green Hillock. Howard Ramsden. MuM
As on Euphrates shady banks we lay. Paraphrase on the Psalms of David: Psalm CXXXVII. George Sandys. OBS
As on my bed at dawn I mused and pray'd. The Lattice at Sunrise. Charles Tennyson Turner. OBVV; VA
As on the bank the poor fish lies. The Restless Heart. *Unknown.* WGRP
As on the fiery lightning followeth the thunder. The Rise of Dictatorship. Solon. GrPE
As on the first day of Creation. Nirvana. Dmitri Sergeyevich Merezhkovsky. TrRV
As on the gauzy wings of fancy flying. Oliver Wendell Holmes. *Fr.* The Iron Gate. AA
As on the Heather. Reinmar von Hagenau, *tr. fr. German by* Jethro Bithell. AWP
As on the hedge they danced one night. Wild Marjorie. "Jean Lorrain." CAW
As on the night before this happy morn. Christmas Day. George Wither. AnEC
As on the wrathful, roaring sea a great. Kingship. Joachim du Bellay. Antiquities of Rome, XVI. TrFP
"As once Hippolytus from Athens fled." Paradise. Dante. *Fr.* Divina Commedia. EnLi-1

As once I played beside the sea. The Tides. Thomas Tapper. GFA

As once, if not with light regard. Ode on the Poetical Character. William Collins. CEP; EiPP; EnRP; OAEP; PoEL-3; PoFS

As once the sons of earth in mad revolt. Revolt. Joachim du Bellay. Antiquities of Rome, XII. TrFP

As one advances up the slow ascent. Solitude. Philip Henry Savage. AA

As one, at midnight, wakened by the call. Prelude [*or* Proem]. W. W. Gibson. LBBV; MBP; MoBrPo

As one by one the singers of our land. The Succession. Frances Laughton Mace. AA

As one dark morn I trod a forest glade. The Forest Glade. Charles Tennyson Turner. VA

As One Finding Peace. Sister Mary Madeleva. JKCP

As One Finding Peace. Sister Mary of the Visitation. JKCP (1926 ed.)

As one long lost in no-man's-land of war. On Reading Keats in Wartime. Karl Shapiro. MuM; PtP

As one sees on the branch in the month of May the rose. Roses. Pierre de Ronsard. LiTW

As one that ere a June day rise. Eastward. Swinburne. *Fr.* Songs before Sunrise. CBOV

As one that for a weary space has lain. The Odyssey. Andrew Lang. BMEP; ES; GTBS-D; HBV; InP; LEAP; LoBV; OBEV; OBVV; OtMeF; PC; PFE; PoeMoYo; PoRA; POTT; PoVP; PtP; TOP; VA; ViBoPo; VOD; WHA; YT

As One Who Bears beneath His Neighbor's Roof. Robert Hillyer. MAP; MoAmPo

As one who came with ointments sweet. Spikenard. Laurence Housman. TrPWD

As one who cleaves the circumambient air. Timon of Archimedes. Charles Battell Loomis. NA

As one who cons at evening o'er an album all alone. An Old Sweetheart of Mine. James Whitcomb Riley. BLPA; OBAV; TreFS

As one who, destined from his friends to part. To My Books. William Roscoe. MOB

As one who follows a departing friend. Last Days. Elizabeth Stoddard. AA; AnAmPo; LA

As one who hangs down-bending from the side. A Dedicated Spirit. Wordsworth. *Fr.* The Prelude. SeCePo

As one who has sailed across an unknown sea. The Solitary. Rainer Maria Rilke. TrJP

As one who held herself apart. Sister. Whittier. *Fr.* Snow-bound. AA

As one who late hath lost a friend adored. Sonnet. Mary Tighe. DiM

As one who lingers over some old store. Sonnet. Phyllis Reid. DiM

As one who, long by wasting sickness worn. Hope. William Lisle Bowles. EnRP

As one who long hath fled with panting breath. Victor and Vanquished. Longfellow. CoBA; CoV

As one who, long in populous city pent. Eve and the Serpent [*or* Satan Beholds Eve]. Milton. *Fr.* Paradise Lost, IX. BLV; PoFS

As one who, long in thickets and in brakes. The Garden. William Cowper. The Task, III. CEP; EiPP

As one who strives from some fast steamer's side. O. M. B. Ford Madox Brown. VA

As one who walks in sleep, up a familiar lane. The Road. John Gould Fletcher. HBMV; TSW

As One Who Wanders into Old Workings. C. Day Lewis. FaBoMo; LiTM (rev. ed.)

As one whose country is distraught with war. Conflict. Caroline Clive. OBVV

As one would stand who saw a sudden light. Love's Outset. Sir Gilbert Parker. *Fr.* A Lover's Diary. VA

As other men, so I myself do muse. Idea, IX. Michael Drayton. EnLi-1 (1949 ed.); ReEn; SiCE; TuPP

As Others See Us. Burns. *Fr.* To a Louse. MaRV

As our king lay musing on his bed. King Henry Fifth's Conquest of France. *Unknown.* BaBo (A *vers.*); ESPB

As over English earth I gaze. English Earth. Laurence Binyon. NeTW

As over muddy shores a dragon flock. The Fear. Lascelles Abercrombie. OBMV

As over the fresh grass her golden feet. Sonnet. Petrarch. *Fr.* Sonnets to Laura: To Laura in Life. LyPI

As Oyster Nan Stood by Her Tub. *Unknown.* CoMu

As painters, men of knowledge in their art. Nature the Artist. Empedocles. OxBG

As patience paints the flower red, so grass. And Grow. John Hay. WaP

As pearls slip off a silken string and fall into the sea. Song of Summer Days. Virna Sheard. OCL

As pilot well expert in perilous wave. The Cave of Mammon. Spenser. *Fr.* The Faerie Queene, II. PoEL-1

As pioneering children, when no rain. Wagon Train. E. L. Mayo. MiAP

As pools beneath stone arches take. Invocation. John Drinkwater. HBMV; NP

As power and wit will me assist. Sir Thomas Wyatt. SiPS

As prounde Bayard ginneth for to skip. Chaucer. *Fr.* Troilus and Criseyde, I. MyFE

As Pure Water. *Unknown, tr. fr. Sanskrit by* Joseph Nadin Rawson. *Fr.* The Upanishads. OnPM

As Puritans they prominently wax. A Certain People. George Meredith. EmBrPo

As rays around the source of light. St. Stephen's Day. John Keble. CoBE

As reason ruled my reckless mind. Filius Regis Mortuus Est et Resurexit. *Unknown.* TMEV

As Red Men Die. E. Pauline Johnson. CPG

As rising from the vegetable World. James Thomson. *Fr.* The Seasons: Spring. PoEL-3

As, rising on its purple wing. Transient Beauty. Byron. *Fr.* The Giaour. LPS-1

As Rivers of Water in a Dry Place. Anna Bunston de Bary. HBMV

As rivers seek the sea. Confluents. Christina Rossetti. BPN

As Rochefoucauld [*or* Rochefoucault] his maxims drew. Verses on the Death of Dr. Swift. Swift. CEP; CoBE; EiPP; LoBV; NBE; PoEL-3; PoFS; TriL

As rock to sun or storm. Poem. Niall Sheridan. OnYI

As round as an apple, as deep as a cup. Mother Goose. OxNR; PPL; StVeCh (1940 ed.); TiPo

As round the pine-clad top of Morna's hill. A Distant Prospect of the City of Armagh. James Stuart. *Fr.* Morna's Hill. IrPN

As salt resolved in the ocean. Jalal ed-Din Rumi, *tr. fr. Persian by* A. J. Arberry. PeP

As sea-foam blown of the winds, as blossom of brine that is drifted. Home, Sweet Home, with Variations, II. H. C. Bunner. BOHV; CenHV; InMe; PA

As Severn lately in her ebbs that sank. The Severn. Michael Drayton. *Fr.* The Baron's War, I. ChTr

As shadows cast by cloud and sun. Christmas [*or* The Holy Star] Bryant. BePJ; ChIP; MaRV

As Shakespeare couldn't write his plays. By Deputy. Arthur St. John Adcock. CenHV

As She Feared It Would Be. Lilla Cabot Perry. Meeting after Long Absence, I. AA; OBAV

As shepherd and shepherdess, how many summers had we. Out of That Sea. David Ferry. NePoAm-2

As shining sand-drift. Epitaphs, XXXII. Lady Margaret Sackville. HBMV

As ships, becalmed [*or* becalm'd] at eve, that lay. Qua Cursum Ventus. Arthur Hugh Clough. BEL; BPN; EmBrPo; EnLi-2; EnLit; EPN; EPP; EtS; EV-5; GTBS; GTML; HBV; LPS-1; OAEP; OBEV (new ed.); OBVV; PoVP; TCEP; TOP; VA; ViP; ViPo; ViPP; VLEP

As sickly plants betray a niggard earth. The Alliance of Education and Government. Thomas Gray. CEP

As silent as a mirror is believed. Legend. Hart Crane. InPo; MOAP; MoVE; OxBA; TwAmPo

As simple an act. Way Out West. LeRoi Jones. NeAP

As Sir Launfal made morn through the darksome gate. Sir Launfal and the Leper. James Russell Lowell. *Fr.* The Vision of Sir Launfal, Pt. I. GN; OTPC

As Slow Our Ship. Thomas Moore. *See* Journey Onwards, The.

As soft as silk, as white as milk. Mother Goose. HBV; HBVY; OTPC (1946 ed.); OxNR; PPL

As some brave Admiral, in former war. The Maim'd Debauchee. Earl of Rochester. PoEL-3; UnPo (3d ed.)

As some day it may happen that a victim must be found. Ko-Ko's Song [*or* They'll None of 'em Be Missed]. W. S. Gilbert. *Fr.* The Mikado. EnLi-2 (1949 ed.); LiTB; PoVP; SiTL

As some fond virgin, whom her mother's care. Epistle to [Miss *or* Mrs.] Martha Blount on Her Leaving Town after the Coronation [*or* To a Young Lady]. Pope. BrBE; CaAE; CEP; ExPo; OBEC; PoEL-3; SeCeV

As some lone miser visiting his store. Real Happiness. Goldsmith. *Fr.* The Traveller. OBEC

As some men say there is a kind of seed. George Gascoigne. *Fr.* The Adventures of Master F. I. ReIE

As Some Mysterious Wanderer of the Skies. Henry Jerome Stockard. AA

As some new ghost, that wanders to and fro. Sonnets; a Sequence of Profane Love, XXXIII. George Henry Boker. MOAP

As some red rosebud in the darkness born. The Seventeenth Kiss: Neaera's Lips. Johannes Secundus. LaP

As some true chief of men, bowed down with stress. The Sun's Shame, 2. Dante Gabriel Rossetti. The House of Life, XCIII. PoVP; ViPo

As sometimes in a dead man's face. In Memoriam A. H. H., LXXIV. Tennyson. BPN; EmBrPo; EPN; GEPC; LiTB; LiTG; ReaPo; ViPo; VLEP

As soon/ As a squirrel. Song for Thrift Week. Mildred Weston. WhC

As Soon as Ever Twilight Comes. Walter de la Mare. SiSoSe

As soon as I begin to overtake. Sonnet. Louise Labé. FoS
As soon as I passed out of my first youth. Plautus. *Fr.* Mercator. LaP
As soon as I saw before me the sons of Huyayy. Bragging Song. *Unknown.* LiTW
As soon as I withdraw to take my rest. Dreams. Louise Labé. TrFP
As soon as I'm in bed at night. Mrs. Brown. Rose Fyleman. BoTP; GaP; TiPo
As soon as the fire burns red and low. The Sleepy Song. Josephine Daskam Bacon. BOL; OTPC (1946 ed.); PCH; PPL; RAR; StVeCh; SUS; UTS
As soon as the idea of the Flood had abated. After the Flood. Arthur Rimbaud, *tr. by* Helen Rootham. BoW
As soon as the idea of the Flood was assuaged. After the Flood. Arthur Rimbaud, *tr. by* Ramon Guthrie. MiFP
As squirrels store their autumn hoard. Man and His Books. Eiluned Lewis. DiM
As star that shines dependent upon star. Places of Worship. Wordsworth. GEPC
As supple as a tiger's skin. The Prayer Rug. Sara Beaumont Kennedy. HBMV; VOD
As sure as we have a fatherland. Fellow-Citizens. Verner von Heidenstam. AnSL
As sweet as the breath that goes. Unsung. Thomas Bailey Aldrich. UnW
As tapering pines, still stately watchers. Suspense. William J. Grace. JKCP (1955 ed.)
As Tate grows old some child will fondle him. From Gestures to the Dead. John Wheelwright. MoVE
As the bee through the garden ranges. God. Emerson. *Fr.* Woodnotes, II. OQP; QP-2
As the black storm upon the mountain-top. Residence in London. Wordsworth. *Fr.* The Prelude, VII. ERP; NBE; PoEL-4
As the brown mowers strode across the field. The Swathe Uncut. John Hewitt. NeIP
As the cat/ climbed over. Poem. William Carlos Williams. FaPON; InvP; ThWaDe
As the child knows not if his mother's face. From Dawn to Noon. Dante Gabriel Rossetti. The House of Life, LXXX. PoVP; ViPo
As the child, to cool his red and tortured head. The Lice-Seekers. Arthur Rimbaud. TrFP
As the clouds that are so light. The Clouds That Are So Light. Edward Thomas. FaBoTw
As the coin of her ear-ring. June Song of a Man Who Looks Two Ways. Leslie Daiken. NeIP
As the Crow Flies, *sel.* Samuel Hoffenstein.
"How much we pay to say, *Je suis.*" WhC
As the dark shades of autumn fly over hills of grass. James Macpherson. *Fr.* Fingal, II. BCEP
As the dawn flushes the vast desert-sands. The Sentry. W. W. Gibson. NeTW
As the dawn was breaking the Sambhur belled. Hunting-Song of the Seeonee Pack. Kipling. AlDL
As the Day Breaks. Ernest McGaffey. AA
As the days grow longer. Mother Goose. PPL
As the Dead Prey upon Us. Charles Olson. NeAP
As the dead year is clasped by a dead December. New Year's Resolve. Ella Wheeler Wilcox. PEOR
As the deep blue of heaven brightens into stars. God's Promises. *Unknown.* BLRP
As the earth looks up adoring. Phaon to Sappho. Marian Osborne. CPG
As the fish that leaps from the river. Fugitive Beauty. John Gould Fletcher. ChMo; CMP
As the flight of a river. Absent yet Present. Sir Edward Bulwer-Lytton. LoPS; OBVV; UnPo
As the gambler drew his bow. Iberian God. Antonio Machado. TeCS
As the golden grass burns out. September Evening, 1938. William Plomer. SeCePo
As the hand moves over the harp, and the strings speak. Inspiration. *Unknown.* *Fr.* Solomon. WGRP
As the hart panteth after the water brooks. Psalm XLII, Bible, *O.T.* AWP; JAWP; TrJP; TrGrPo; WGRP; WoL
As the Holly Groweth Green. Henry VIII, King of England. *See* Green Groweth the Holly.
As the hyacinth high on the mountains under the shepherds' tread. Lost Maidenhead. Sappho. GrPE
As the immense dew of Florida. Nomad Exquisite. Wallace Stevens. AtBAP
As the inhastening tide doth roll. The Visiting Sea. Alice Meynell. GTML; LoPS
As the insect from the rock. The Making of Man. John White Chadwick. AA; LBAP
As the kindling glances. The Voice. Matthew Arnold. GEPC; GTML; ViPP
As the Liberty lads o'er the sea. Song for the Luddites. Byron. PoFr
As the marsh-hen secretly builds on the watery sod. Sidney Lanier. *Fr.* The Marshes of Glynn. BAP; MaRV; OQP; QP-1
As the mists rise in the dawn. Fujiwara no Sadayori, *tr. fr. Japanese by* Kenneth Rexroth. OnPJ
As the moon sinks on the mountain-edge. Far beyond Us. *Unknown.* OnPM
As the mother bird to the waiting nest. Rhapsody. Florence Earle Coates. AV
As the mute nightingale in closest groves. The Nightingale [*or* To the Blessed Virgin Mary]. Gerald Griffin. CAW; JKCP; OnYI
As the Old Year seeks the shadows. New Year Prayer. Edgar Daniel Kramer. PEDC; PraP
As the poorest may borrow some treasure. To My Father. Grace Denio Litchfield. FAOV
As the proud horse with costly trappings gay. Shortening Sail. William Falconer. *Fr.* The Shipwreck, II. EtS; SG
As the racing circle closed in like a lasso. Ceremonial Hunt. Elizabeth J. Coatsworth. *Fr.* The Painted Desert. PoeMoYo
As the rain falls. Rain. William Carlos Williams. CoBMV
As the Sculptor. Toyohiko Kagawa, *tr. fr. Japanese.* OQP; QP-2
As the skull of man grows broader. Don Marquis. *Fr.* The God-Maker, Man. OQP; QP-1
As the slanting sun drowsed lazily. Cape Coloured Batman. Guy Butler. BoSA
As the soft yield of water cleaves obstinate stone. Lesson of Water. *Unknown, at. to* Lao-tzu. *Fr.* Tao Teh King. OnPM
As the sown field with tender green doth swarm. Relics. Joachim du Bellay. Antiquities of Rome, XXX. TrFP
As the stars go out so let me go. Wilson MacDonald. *Fr.* The Last Portage. MaRV
As the sun rose. Pigeons Just Awake. Hilda Conkling. YT
As the sunbeams stream through liberal space. Emerson. *Fr.* Woodnotes, II. ADAH; OHIP
As the swallow down there flits over the sea. Three Threads of Gold. Leconte de Lisle. TrFP
As the sweet apple reddens, high up against the sky. The Maid Unwed. Sappho. GrPE
As the Team's Head-Brass. Edward Thomas. ExPo
As the through-train of words with white-hot whistle. Express. W. R. Rodgers. MoVE
As the Tide Comes In. Cale Young Rice. NLK; VOD
As the train went out and you stood so white. Goodbye. Nordahl Grieg. AnNoLy
As the transatlantic tourists. The Doves of Venice. Laurence Hutton. AA
As the Twig Is Bent. Pope. *Fr.* Moral Essays, Epistle I. TreF
As the uncertain twittering of the birds. Sonnet: Grief. Thomas Holley Chivers. SPP
As the war-trumpet drowns the rustic flute. Pindar. Antipater of Sidon. AWP
As the weeders went trimming the corn young and green. The Legend of Babe Jesus and the Weeders. *Unknown.* ChrBoLe
As the wind at play with a spark. Louisa May Alcott. Louise Chandler Moulton. AA
As the wise men of old brought gifts. The Gift. William Carlos Williams. NePoAm-2
As the World Turns. Swift. OTPC (1946 ed.); RIS
As the years go by/ The old familiar faces. Lonely Old Age. Yüan Chen. PoHN
As the years go by, give me but peace. Answering Vice-Prefect Chang. Wang Wei. OuHeWo
As the young phoenix, duteous to his sire. Renewal. "Michael Field." DiM; OBVV
As the young stag, when lusty Spring supreme. Pierre de Ronsard. *Fr.* Amours de Cassandre. PrPoCR
As their sides they swayed. Beauty's Armoury. Al-Hadrami. MooP
As there I left the road in May. The Surprise. William Barnes. PoVP
As there is music uninform'd by art. To My Honor'd Friend Sir Robert Howard, on His Excellent Poems. Dryden. EiPP
As they came in by the Eden side. The Slaughter of the Laird of Mellerstain. *Unknown.* ESPB
As They Fell. Edward A. Blount, Jr. PoP
As they join their various voices. The Birds. Blossius Aemilius Dracontius. CAW
As they sat sipping their glasses in the courtyard. Dinner at the Hotel de la Tigresse Verte. Donald Evans. AnAmPo; LA
As they talked a dog lying there lifted head and pricked his ears. The Dog Argos. Homer, *pr. tr. by* T. E. Lawrence. *Fr.* The Odyssey, XVII. OxBG
As they were thus talking, a dog that had been lying asleep. The Old Hound Argos. Homer, *pr. tr. by* Samuel Butler. *Fr.* The Odyssey, XVII. GrR
As this blind rose, no more than a whim of the dust. This Blind Rose. Humbert Wolfe. CaAE

As this comes in/ Call you. The Lute in the Attic. Kenneth Patchen. OnHM
As Thomas was cudgel'd one day by his wife. Abroad and at Home. Swift. WhC
As those of old drank mummia. Mummia. Rupert Brooke. CMP
As those we love decay, we die in part. Verses Occasioned by the Death of Dr. Aikman [*or* On the Death of a Particular Friend *or* Finis]. James Thomson. BSV; CoEV; OBEC; OBEV
As those who are not athletic at breakfast day by day. Nature Morte. Louis MacNeice. ChMo
As though a thousand vampires, from the day. Nightmare. Clark Ashton Smith. DaM
As though all the stars should fall down, putrified. My Poem to the Children Killed in the War in Spain. José Ramón Heredia. AnCL
As though he could hold all in consciousness. Elegy against a Latter Day. Kendrick Smithyman. AnNZ
As though in the tender summer I were lost. In the Pioneer Camp. "Anna Akhmatova." RuPo
As threads spilling dew-drops. The Dolphins. Hamish Maclaren. EtS
As thro' [*or* through] the Land at Eve We Went. Tennyson. *Fr.* The Princess, Pt. I. AnFE; AtBAP; BPN; EV-5; GTBS; GTBS-W; LiTB; LiTG; LiTL; MaRV; OBVV; PoVP; TreFS; VA
(Reconciliation, The.) HBV
(Songs from "The Princess.") MotAn; OAEP; ViPo; VLEP
(We Kiss'd Again with Tears.) PoToHe
As through the palms ye wander. The Lullaby. Lope de Vega. CAW
As through the void we went I heard his plumes. The Doors. Lloyd Mifflin. AA; LEAP
As through the Wild Green Hills of Wyre. A. E. Housman. A Shropshire Lad, XXXVII. BoFr; BPN; CBE; PoVP
As thus my spleen upon the view I fed. The Ancient Mansion. George Crabbe. EV-3
As thus the snows arise, and foul and fierce. The Lost Shepherd. James Thomson. *Fr.* The Seasons: Winter. CoBE; SeCePo
As Thy Day Thy Strength Shall Be. *Unknown.* PEOR
As Thy Days. Grant Colfax Tullar. BLRP
As Thy Days So Shall Thy Strength Be. "George Klingle." BLRP
As thy friend's face, with shadow of soul o'erspread. Life the Beloved. Dante Gabriel Rossetti. The House of Life, XCVI. BPN; PoVP; ViPo
As Time Goes On. Emilio Adolfo von Westphalen, *tr. fr. Spanish by* H. R. Hays. AnCL
As Time One Day by Me Did Pass. Henry Vaughan. MeLP; SeCV-1
As to a bird's song she were listening. Deaf. H. C. Bunner. AA
As to a sacrament/ Quiet I go. Love's Language. Donagh MacDonagh. NeIP
As to Being Alone. James Oppenheim. PoMa; TrJP
As to democracy, fellow-citizens. John Hancock Otis. Edgar Lee Masters. *Fr.* Spoon River Anthology. PoFr; TOP
As to Eyes. Franklin P. Adams. PR
As to His Choice of Her. Wilfrid Scawen Blunt. *See* To Manon, as to His Choice of Her.
As to kidnap the Congress has long been my aim. General Howe's Letter. *Unknown.* PAH
As to marshals, and statesmen, and all their whole lineage. French Cookery. Thomas Moore. *Fr.* The Fudge Family in Paris. OBRV
As to naps. Perambulator Poems, VI. David McCord. WhC
As to the blooming prime. To Favonius. Edmund Bolton. OBSC
As to the seer in ancient time. A Prayer for Teachers. Marguerite Emilio. OQP; PraP; QP-2
As to the Weather. *Unknown.* BOHV
As to thine image oft my thoughts would yield. To Jean Paul. August, Graf von Platen. BoFr
As Toilsome I Wander'd [*or* Wandered] Virginia's Woods. Walt Whitman. AmPo; AmPP (3d ed.); BLP; HBV; IAP; InP; LO; PCD; PFE; SeCeV; TCAP; TVSH; ViBoPo
As Tom and his wife were discoursing one day. Too Candid by Half. John Godfrey Saxe. HBV
As Tom the Porter went up Ludgate-Hill. Tom the Porter. John Byrom. CEP
As Tommy Snooks and Bessy [*or* Bessie] Brooks. Mother Goose. BoChLi; HBV; HBVY; OTPC; OxNR; PCH; PPL, *sl. diff.;* RIS, *sl. diff.*
As towering through the height. The Eagle (to Hiero of Syracuse). Bacchylides. GrPE
As trails a sadly wounded deer the hound. The Quarry. Juan Boscán. LiTW
As treading some long corridor. My Soul and I. Charles Buxton Going. MaRV
As Troylus did rejoice. To His Friend Riding to Londonward. George Turberville. ReIE
As true as I was born into. Halfway. Maxine W. Kumin. GoYe
As True as Thy Faith, This Riddle Thus Saith. Thomas Tusser. *See* Praise of Husbandry, The.
As tuned harp-strings sad noates take. *Unknown.* SeCSL
As Turpin was riding across a [*or* the] moor. Turpin [*or* Dick Turpin] and the Lawyer. *Unknown.* ABS; ViBoFo
As twilight fell. I Saw a Ghost. Joan Boilleau. TiPo
As two men were a-walking, down by the sea-side. The Duke of Grafton. *Unknown.* ChTr
As two whose love, first foolish, widening scope. Know in Vain. Dante Gabriel Rossetti. The House of Life, LXV. BPN; EmBrPo; EnLi-2; EPP; PoVP; TCEP; ViPo
As unconcernedly it flows. The Spring Called Parthenius. Hesiod. OxBG
As unto blowing roses summer dews. Love against Love. David A. Wasson. LPS-3
As unto Francis poverty. Brother Juniper. Blanche Mary Kelly. GoBC; JKCP
As unto heaven thou'rt soaring. At the Assumption. Luis de León. CAW
"As unto the bow the cord is." Hiawatha's Wooing. Longfellow. *Fr.* The Song of Hiawatha. BeLS; IAP; TreFS
As up by Kennetside I rode. An Old Thought. Maurice Hewlett. *Fr.* The Song of the Plow. PoFr
As Venus from her mother's bosom rose. Apelles the Painter. Leonidas of Tarentum. OnPM
As Vesta was from Latmos Hill descending. *Unknown.* OAEP
As virtuous men pass [*or* passe] mildly away. A Valediction Forbidding Mourning. John Donne. CoBE; CoEV; ElSeCe; EM-1; EnL; EnLi-1; EnLit; EnLP; EPS; EtPaEn; ExPo; FaBoEn; HoPM; LEAP; LiTB; MaPo; MeLP; MePo; NBE; OAEP; OBS; Po; PoEL-2; PoFS; ReaPo; ReEn; ReIE; RiBV; SeCeV; SeCV-1; SeEP; TCEP; TuPP; TwP; TyEnPo; UnPo
As vonce I valked by a dismal swamp. The Old Cove. Henry Howard Brownell. PAH
As warm north rain breaks over suburb houses. Rocket Show. James K. Baxter. AnNZ
As watchers couched beneath a Bantine oak. The Last Ode. Kipling. MeRV
As water rained upon a height. As Pure Water. *Unknown. Fr.* The Upanishads. OnPM
As we come marching, marching, in the beauty of the day. Bread and Roses. James Oppenheim. OQP; QP-1
As We Dance Round. *Unknown.* CH; HH
As we entered by that door. Dirge of the Lone Woman. Mary M. Colum. AnIV
As we get older we do not get any younger. Chard Whitlow. Henry Reed. FiBHP; LiTM (rev. ed.); OnHM; PoN; SiTL
As We Grow Older. Grantland Rice. DDA
As We Grow Older. Rollin J. Wells. PoToHe
(Growing Old.) WBLP
(Growing Older.) BLPA
As we hammer out iron we shall hammer out new days. Tomorrow. Regino Pedroso. AnCL; PoFr
As we lay musing in our beds. The Mermaid. *Unknown.* BaBo; ESPB
As we look at these gay flowers. Rondel. Charles d'Orléans. FoS
As We Pray. John Keble. *Fr.* Oh, Timely Happy, Timely Wise. MaRV; PraP
As we rowed from our ships and set foot on the shore. The Savages. Josephine Miles. FiMAP
As We Rush, as We Rush in the Train. James Thomson. Sunday at Hampstead, X. EBSV; EmBrPo; EV-5; GTBS; GTBS-W; POTT; PoVP; ViBoPo
(As We Rush.) LiTG
(In the Train.) BoTP; LoPo; OBEV; PCD
As we sailed down the Chyannel of old Engeland. Let Go the Reef Tackle. *Unknown.* ShS
As we sailed on the water blue. Whisky Johnny. *Unknown.* ABF; AS
As we the withered ferns. Ballade of Dead Friends. E. A. Robinson. AA
As we wax older on this earth. "The Things That Are More Excellent." Sir William Watson. OHFP
As we went up the narrow stair. In the Shadows. Leah Bodine Drake. DaM
As We Were a-Sailing. *Unknown.* SG
As we were walking. The Mask. *Unknown.* BoFr
As Weary Pilgrim [Now at Rest]. Anne Bradstreet. AnNE; IAP; PoEL-3; TCAP
(Longing for Heaven.) AnFE; APA; APW; CoAnAm; LiTA; MOAP
As well be dead as Egypt is. Dead Enchantress. Harold Vinal. PR
As wet as a fish—as dry as a bone. Similes [*or* Comparisons]. *Unknown.* BOHV; GoTP; HBVY

As When a Man ("As when a man, that sails in a balloon"). Tennyson. A Dream of Fair Women, *first 4 sts. of orig. vers.* ChER; OBRV

As when a scout. New Worlds. Milton. *Fr.* Paradise Lost, III. OBS

As when a traveller, forced to journey back. Parting. William Johnson Cory. EV-5

As when a tree's cut down, the secret root. Prologue to "The Tempest." Dryden. EiPP; EnL; PoE; RiBV

As when a vulture on Imaus bred. Milton. *Fr.* Paradise Lost, III. HoPM

As, when a wave begins to whiten in mid-sea. The Stateliest Measure. Virgil. *Fr.* Georgics. LiA

As when a wretch (who conscious of his crime). Priam and Achilles. Homer, *tr. by* Pope. *Fr.* The Iliad, XXIV. OBEC

As when abroad some celebrated Fair. Oppian. *Fr.* Halieuticks. GrPo

As when desire, long darkling, dawns, and first. Bridal Birth. Dante Gabriel Rossetti. The House of Life, II. BMEP; BPN; EmBrPo; OAEP; POTT; PoVP; RiBV; ViPo; VLEP

As when far off the warbled strains are heard. La Fayette. Samuel Taylor Coleridge. BPN; EmBrPo; EnRP

As when from his mountain-outlook a goatherd spies a cloud. The Achaeans Renew the Battle. Homer. *Fr.* The Iliad, IV. GrPE

As when, from the splendid thundering organ, high. The Source of the Danube. Friedrich Hölderlin. AnGP

As when great shipwrecks mark the tempest's might. The Guileful Ocean. Lucretius. *Fr.* De Rerum Natura, II. LiA

As when, high up the mountains, through the endless woodland ways. Homer. *Fr.* The Iliad, II. GrPE

As when it happeneth that some lovely town. Content and Resolute. William Drummond of Hawthornden. ES

As when, of amorous night uncertain birth. A Summer Storm. Charles Whitehead. OBRV

As when, on Carmel's sterile steep. The Little Cloud. John Howard Bryant. LPS-2

As when one layeth/ His worn-out robes away. Death. *Unknown. Fr.* Bhagavad-Gita. MaRV

As when some dire usurper Heav'n provides. The Fire of London. Dryden. *Fr.* Annus Mirabilis. ChTr

As when some skilful cook, to please each guest. On a Miscellany of Poems to Bernard Lintott. John Gay. CEP; EiPP

As when the billow gathers fast. The Two Hosts. Homer. *Fr.* The Iliad, IV. OxBG

As when the deep lies heaving with a great swell, silently. Nestor's Doubt. Homer. *Fr.* The Iliad, XIV. GrPE

As when the hand some mimic form would paint. A Fragment from St. Gregory Nazianzen. Cardinal Newman. PraNu

As when the moon hath comforted the night. George Chapman. *Fr.* The Conspiracy of Charles, Duke of Byron. ViBoPo

As when the moon, refulgent lamp of night. A Homeric Moonlight. Homer, *tr. by* Pope. *Fr.* The Iliad, VIII. BeR

As When the Rose. Pierre de Ronsard. *See* His Lady's Tomb.

As when the scepter dangles from the hand. Sonnets, XLII. George Santayana. ATP; MOAP

. . . As when the sun new-risen. Lucifer. Milton. *Fr.* Paradise Lost, I. UnPo (1st ed.)

As when the winds, ascending by degrees. Strife, War's Sister, Urges on the Host. Homer. *Fr.* The Iliad, IV. GrR

As when two men have loved a woman well. Lost on Both Sides. Dante Gabriel Rossetti. The House of Life, XCI. BPN; GTML; GTSL; PoVP; SeCePo; ViPo; ViPP

As when, upon a trancèd summer-night. Keats. *Fr.* Hyperion, I. ViBoPo

As when we wake from some enchanted sleep. Burial. Struthers Burt. UnW

As wildly ranged the tea-imbibing throng. Afternoon Tea. Arthur Guiterman. TCAP; TOP

As William and Mary stood by the seashore. Love in Disguise. *Unknown.* CSF

As wine that with its own weight runs, is best. Poetry and Wine. Samuel Butler. BeR

As, with enforced yet unreluctant pace. The Social Future. John Kells Ingram. OnYI

As with Gladness Men of Old. William Chatterton Dix. MaRV

As with My Hat. Samuel Johnson. LBN

As with varnish red and glistening. Casualty. W. E. Henley. *Fr.* In Hospital. PoVP

As withereth the primrose by the river. A Palinode. Edmund Bolton ElL; ElSeCe; InvP; OBSC; PoEL-2; SiCE; TuPP

As Wulfstan said on another occasion. Speech for the Repeal of the McCarran Act. Richard Wilbur. NePoAm

As Ye Came from the Holy Land. *Unknown, sometimes at. to* Sir Walter Ralegh. *See* As You Came from the Holy Land.

As Ye Do It unto These. *Unknown.* ChIP

As ye go through these palm-trees. A Song of the Virgin Mother. Lope de Vega, *tr. by* Ezra Pound. AWP; JAWP; LiTW; WBP

As ye see, a mountaine lion fare. Sarpedon's Speech. Homer, *tr. by* Chapman. *Fr.* The Iliad, XII. OBS

As years [*or* long] ago we carried to your knees. Dedication. Kathleen Norris. *Fr.* Mother. MOAH; PoToHe

As years do grow, so cares increase. To Mistress Anne Cecil, upon Making Her a New Year's Gift. William Cecil, Lord Burghley. ElL; OBSC; PrWP

As yet, the girl was but a child. On the Death of a Young Girl. Evariste de Parny. TrFP

As yet the trembling year is unconfirmed. Spring. James Thomson. *Fr.* The Seasons. EnSW

As yet there's not a snowdrop fain. "Blackie." John Joy Bell. TVSH

As Yonder Lamp. Charles Whitehead. *See* Lamp, The.

As You [*or* Ye] Came from the Holy Land. *Unknown, sometimes at. to* Sir Walter Ralegh. AtBAP; CBOV; ChTr; EG; ElL; ElSeCe; EnLoPo; EV-1; KN; LiTL; LoBV; OBEV; PG; PoFL-2; ReEn; ReIE; SiCE; TrGrPo; TuPP; ViBoPo
(Holy Land of Walsinghame, The.) EnSB
(Lover's Complaint, A.) FaBoEn
(Pilgrim to Pilgrim.) TCEP
(Walsinghame.) FaBoCh; LiTB; LoGBV; OBSC; SeCeV; UnPo (1st ed.)

As you drank deep as Thor, did you think of milk or wine? Fish Food. John Wheelwright. AnFE; CoAnAm; LiTA; OnAP; TwAmPo

As you know, the kangaroo. Advices from Rexroth's Bestiary. Kenneth Rexroth. *Fr.* A Bestiary. SiTL

As You Like It, *sels.* Shakespeare.
All the World's a Stage, *fr.* II, vii. FiP; GoTP; LEAP; LiTB; LiTG; PIR; TrGrPo
(Life.) BCEP; PYM
(Seven Ages of Man, The.) CBE; EV-1; FaFP; GTBS-W; LPS-2; OQP; QP-2; TreF; TVSH
Blow, Blow, Thou Winter Wind, *fr.* II, vii. AnFE; ATP (1935 ed.); BCEP; BEL; BoFr; BoLiVe; BTP; CBE; CH; ChTr; CoBE; EG; ElL; ElSeCe; EM-1; EnLi-1 (1949 ed.); EnLit; EPP; EV-1; FaFP; GTBS; GTBS-D; GTBS-W; GTSE; GTSL; HBV; InPo; LiTB; LiTG; LO; LPS-1; MaPo; MCCG; OAEP; OBEV; OBSC; OQP; OTPC; OuHeWo; PFE; PG (1945 ed.); PIR; PoEL-2; PYM; QP-2; ReaPo; RG; SeCeV; ShBV-1; SiCE; TCEP; TOP; TVSH; TyEnPo; UnPo (1st ed.); ViBoPo; WaKn; WHA
(Bitter Song.) BLV
(Blow, Thou Winter Wind.) TreF
(Ingratitude.) BBV; PECK
(Man's Ingratitude.) CBOV
(Song: "Blow, blow, thou winter wind.") CaAE; CBE; FiP
(Song of the Holly.) COAH
(Songs from "As You Like It," 2.) LEAP
(Songs from the Plays.) AWP; JAWP; WBP
(Songs of the Greenwood.) TrGrPo
(Two Songs by Amiens, 1.) BoLiVe
Constant Service of the Antique World, The ("I have five hundred crowns"), *fr.* II, iii. EV-1
"Fool, A, a fool! I met a fool i' the forest," *fr.* II, vii. PIR
(Motley's the Only Wear.) TrGrPo
"Good shepherd, tell this youth what 'tis to love," *abr., fr.* V, ii. LO
If it do come to pass, *fr.* II, v. ViBoPo
It Was a Lover and His Lass, *fr.* V, iii. BEL; CBE; CH; EG; ElL; ElSeCe; EM-1; EnL; EnLi-1; EnLit; EV-1; ExPo; GTBS; GTBS-D; GTBS-W; GTSE; GTSL; HBV; InPo; LiTB; LiTG; LiTL; LO; LoBV; OBEV; PIR; PoRA; ReaPo; ShBV-1; SiCE; SiTL; TOP; ViBoPo
(Country Song.) TrGrPo
(Love in Spring-Time.) MCCG
(Lovers Love the Spring.) BLV
(Pages' Song, The.) OBSC; SeCePo
(Song: "It was a lover and his lass.") FiP
(Song of the Two Pages.) BoLiVe
(Songs from "As You Like It.") LEAP
(Songs from the Plays.) AWP; JAWP; WPB
Love Dissembled, *fr.* III, v. LPS-1
Old Age of Temperance, *fr.* II, iii. LPS-2
Orlando's Rhymes, *fr.* III, ii. OBSC
Under the Greenwood Tree, *fr.* II, v. ADAH; AnFE; BBV (1923 ed.); BCEP; BEL; BLV; BoTP; CBE; CBOV; CH; EG; ElL; ElSeCe; EM-1; EnLi-1; EnLit; EPP; ExPo; FaBoBe; FaFP; FaPON; GBV; GN; GTBS; GTBS-D; GTBS-W; GTSE; GTSL; HoPM; InPo; KN; LiTB; LiTG; MCCG; MPB; OAEP; OBEV; OBSC; OHIP; OTPC; OuHeWo; PCH; PFE; PIR; PYM; RG; SeCeV; ShBV-2; SiCE; TCEP; TiPo; TOP; TreFS; TVSH; TyEnPo; ViBoPo; WHA; WoL
(Call of the Woods, The.) CBPC
(Greenwood. The.) EV-1

(Greenwood Tree, The.) RIS
(In the Greenwood.) AnEnPo
(Song: "Under the greenwood tree.") CG; FiP; REAL
(Songs from the Plays.) AWP; JAWP; WBP
(Songs of the Greenwood.) TrGrPo
(Two Songs by Amiens, 2.) BoLiVe
Uses of Adversity, The, *fr.* II, i. LiTB; TreFS; TrGrPo
(Banished Duke [Living in the Forest] Speaks to His Retainers, The.) CBE; LiTG
(Forest of Arden, The, *sl. abr.*) EV-1
(Good in Everything, *much abr.*) PoToHe
("Now, my co-mates and brothers in exile.") PIR
(Sermons in Stones.) GrCo-1
(Sweet Are the Uses of Adversity, *6 ll.*) MaRV
Wedding Is Great Juno's Crown, *fr.* V, iv. ViBoPo
What Shall He Have That Kill'd the Deer? *fr.* IV, ii. KN; OBSC; ViBoPo
As you love me, let there be. A Dieu! and Au Revoir. John Oxenham. MaRV
As you sit there at your ease. Une Marquise. Austin Dobson. BPN
As you—so I. To the Sea. Cally Monrad. AnNoLy
As you were out a-riding. The Balloon Man. —— Morton. GFA
As young Aurora, with crystal hail. Ane Ballat of the Feignèd Friar of Tungland. William Dunbar. EBSV
Ascend, descend the spiral stair. The Gulls; Provincetown Harbor Benjamin Albert Botkin. CAG
Ascension, The. Joseph Beaumont. OxBoCh
Ascension, The Luis de León, *tr. fr. Spanish by* Aubrey F. G. Bell. TeCS
(At the Ascension, *tr. by* Thomas Walsh.) CAW
(Hymn on the Ascension, *tr. by* George Ticknor.) AnSpL-1
Ascension, The. Edwin Markham. StJW
Ascension, The, and the Assumption. Ramón López Velarde, *tr. fr. Spanish by* H. R. Hays. TwSpPo
Ascension Day. Sheila Kaye-Smith. CAW
Ascension-Day. Henry Vaughan. OxBoCh
Ascension Hymn. The Venerable Bede. *See* Hymn of Glory Let Us Sing, A.
Ascension Hymn. Jean Baptiste de Santeuil, *tr. fr. French by* Allan G. McDougall. CAW
Ascension-Hymn. Henry Vaughan. *See* They Are All Gone.
Ascent. Charles G. Blanden. OQP; QP-2
Ascent of F 6, The, *sel.* W. H. Auden *and* Christopher Isherwood.
"At last the secret is out, as it always must come in the end." NAMP; SeCePo
Ascent to the Sierras. Robinson Jeffers. AmPP (3d ed.); LoGBV; MOAP; OxBA
Ascention. John Donne. OBS
Asclepiades the miser, about his chamber peering. The Miser's Entertainment. Lucilius. GrPE
Asclepias, child of passion, bright eyes like the calm sea's blue. The Siren. Meleager. GrPE
Asclepius. Pindar, *tr. fr. Greek by* C. J. Billson. *Fr.* Pythian Odes, III. GrR; OxBG
Ascot Waistcoat. David McCord. FiBHP
A-settin' on the ice till my feet got cold. Sweet Thing: The Crawdad Song. *Unknown.* OuSiCo
Ash and the Oak, The. Louis Simpson. NePoAm
Ash-heap of four cultures. Conon in Alexandria. Lawrence Durrell. MoPo
Ash on an Old Man's Sleeve. T. S. Eliot. *Fr.* Four Quartets: Little Gidding. FaBoTw; GTBS-W; PoFS
Ash tree is the only one, The. The Timid Ash Tree. Kathleen Millay. PEDC
Ash Trees. *Unknown, tr. fr. Chinese.* ChLP
Ash Wednesday. T. S. Eliot. AmPP; AnFE; ChMo; CoAnAm; CoBMV; LiTA; LiTG; MoAB; MoAmPo; MoPo; OxBA; Po; SeCeV; TwAmPo
Sels.
"Although I do not hope to turn again," VI. FaBoEn
"Because I do not hope to turn again," I. ATP (1953 ed.); CMP; OxBoCh; TwHP
"If the lost word is lost, if the spent word is spent," V. BrBE; OxBoCh
"Lady, three white leopards sat under a juniper-tree," II. LO; LoBV
(Salutation.) AnAmPo; LA; TCPD
"Who walked between the violet and the violet," IV. BrBE
Ash Wednesday. John Erskine. NV
Ash Wednesday. Rosa Zagnoni Marinoni. PoRL; WHL
Ashamed at times that I am silent. The Praises of Laura Transcend His Poetic Power. Petrarch. *Fr.* Sonnets to Laura: To Laura in Life. EnLi-1; OuHeWo
Ashamed of Jesus. Joseph Grigg. BePJ
("Jesus, and shall it ever be.") OIF
Ashby. John Reuben Thompson. AA; BIG
Ashcake. Thomas Nelson Page. AA; OBAV
Ashen feelers of the frigid morrow, The. The Specter. Ernst Hardt. AWP
Ashes. Heine. *See* Sag', wo ist dein schönes Liebchen.
Ashes in the fire stir, The. The Fireside Kitten. Elizabeth J. Coatsworth. CIV
Ashes in the Sea, The. George Sterling. LBMV
Ashes of Glory. Augustus Julian Requier. BIG
Ashes of Life. Edna St. Vincent Millay. AV; FaBoBe; HBV; LiTL; NP
Ashes of Roses. Elaine Goodale Eastman. AA; HBV; OBAV
Ashes of Soldiers. Walt Whitman. TCAP
Ashes of the Christmas Tree. Yetza Gillespie. ChBR
Ashes on the Slide. Eugene Field. BBV (1923 ed.)
Ashokan. Dachine Rainer. NePoAm
Ashore. "Laurence Hope." BMEP; HBV; LEAP
Asia. Shelley. *Fr.* Prometheus Unbound, II, v. PoFS; ViBoPo
(Asia's Response.) TCEP
(Asia's Song.) ATP (1935 ed); UnPo (1st ed.)
(My Soul Is an Enchanted Boat.) PC
(To a Singer.) CBPC
Asian Birds. Robert Bridges. VA
Asian Desert. Dorothy Wellesley. OBMV
Asian Muse, The, a stranger fair! On the Ingenious Mr. Jones's Elegant Translations . . . of Eastern Poetry. John Scott of Amwell. PtP
Asia's Response. Shelley. *See* Asia.
Asia's Song. Shelley. *See* Asia.
Asides. Paul Valéry, *tr. fr. French by* William Jay Smith. AnFP
Asides on the Oboe. Wallace Stevens. CoV; MoAB; MoAmPo
Asinaria, *sel.* Plautus, *tr. fr. Latin by* F. A. Wright.
"This trade of mine, dear boy." LaP
A-Sitting on a Gate. "Lewis Carroll." *See* White Knight's Song, The.
Ask and Have. Samuel Lover. HBV; PFE; TreFS
(How to Ask and Have.) BOHV
Ask and it shall be given. Choice. Ellen Coit Elliott. OQP; QP-2
Ask, and Ye Shall Receive. Mrs. Havens. BLRP
Ask any question in this town. "Round Cape Horn." *Unknown.* EtS
Ask God to give thee skill. Sympathy. Anna E. Hamilton. OQP; QP-1
Ask if I love thee? Oh, smiles cannot tell. Margaret to Dolcino. Charles Kingsley. HBV
Ask, is it well, O thou consumed of fire. The Burning of the Law. Meïr of Rothenburg. TrJP
Ask, Is Love Divine. George Meredith. EmBrPo; EPP
Ask Me No More. Thomas Carew. *See* Ask Me No More Where Jove Bestows.
Ask Me No More. Tennyson. *See* Ask me no more: the moon may draw the sea.
Ask me no more: I've had enough Chablis. To an Importunate Host. *Unknown.* BOHV; PA
Ask me no more: the moon may draw the sea. Tennyson. *Fr.* The Princess, Pt. VI. AnFE; AtBAP; BoLiVe; BPN; EM-2; EmBrPo; EnLi-2; EnLit; EPN; GEPC; GTBS-W; HBV; LiTB; MaPo; MotAn; OAEP; PIR; PoEL-5; PoVP; REAL; TrGrPo; VA; ViPo; ViPP; VLEP
Ask me no more; the moon may draw the sea. Lines to a Book Borrower. "F. C." MOB
Ask Me No More Where Jove Bestows. Thomas Carew. AEV; AWP; BCEP; BEL; CoBE; EG; ElSeCe; EnLit; JAWP; LiTL; OAEP; PoRA; SeCePo; SeCL; TOP; TrGrPo; TyEnPo; ViBoPo; WBP; WHA
(Song, A: "Ask [*or* Aske] me no more where Jove bestows.") AtBAP; ATP (1953 ed.); CaAE; CH; CoEV; EnLoPo; EPP; EPS; FaBoEn; FaFP; GTBS-W; HBV; HoPM; InPo; LEAP; LiTB; LiTG; LO; LoBV; MeLP; MePo; NeHB; OBEV; OBS; PG; PIAE; PoE; PoEL-3; PoFS; RiBV; SeCV-1; SeEP; TCEP; TrGrPo; TwHP; WP
Ask me no more, why there appears. Pyms Anarchy. *At. to* Thomas Jordan. OBS
Ask me not what my love shall do or be. The Separation. Abraham Cowley. EPS (1942 ed.)
Ask me why I live among the green mountains? Answer to a Worldly One. Li Po. OnPM
Ask me why I peer. Walls. Marjorie Meeker. PC
Ask me why I send you here. The Primrose. Robert Herrick. EM-1; EV-2; HBV; OBEV; ViBoPo
Ask night how it feels to be dark. To Be Black, to Be Lost. Hannah Kahn. GoYe
Ask No Return. Horace Gregory. Chorus for Survival, XIV. MAP; MoAmPo; TrGrPo (1942 ed.)
(Chorus for Survival, XIV.) ChMo; TwAmPo
Ask Not One Least Word of Praise. Robert Browning. *Fr.* Ferishtah's Fancies, IV. BPN; VLEP
Ask not overmuch for fair. He That Loves a Rosy Check. Heinrich von Rugge. AWP; JAWP; WBP
Ask not the cause why sullen spring. Song to a Fair Young Lady Going Out of [the] Town in the Spring [*or* To a Fair Young Lady . . .]. Dryden. AEV; ElSeCe; EV-3; HBV; LiTL; MaPo; OBEV; OBS; SeCL; SeEP
Ask not why sorrow shades my brow. Montross. Charles Cotton. SeCL

Ask nothing more of me, sweet. The Oblation. Swinburne. BPN; EmBrPo; EnLit; EtPaEn; HBV; LEAP; POTT; PoVP; VLEP
Ask of your soul this question, What is strength? Strength. Jessie Wilmore Murton. ChIP; MaRV; OQP; QP-2
Ask the Empresse of the night. The Magnet. Thomas Stanley. MePo
Ask what love is? It is a passion. A True Description of Love. *Unknown.* TuPP
Ask you what provocation I have had? Satire [*or* In Defence of Satire *or* Provocation to Satire]. Pope. *Fr.* Epilogue to the Satires, Dialogue II. BeR; CoBE; OBEC
Asked of Echo, t'other day. Echo. John Godfrey Saxe. BoHV; LPS-3; PTA-1; PTA-2
Asked the Traveller of the Tomb. Leonidas of Tarentum, *tr. fr. Greek by* Walter Leaf. GrR
Asking Forgiveness. Arthur Symons. BMEP; LEAP
Aslant the shoulder of each prisoner. Sara Bard Field. *Fr.* Barabbas. PoFr
Asleep. Alcman, *tr. fr. Greek by* Olga Marx *and* Ernst Morwitz. LiTW
Asleep. Witter Bynner. *Fr.* Chapala Poems. NP
Asleep. Wilfred Owen. POTE
Asleep. William Winter. AA; OBAV
Asleep at last! For fourscore years. Oliver Wendell Holmes. William Hamilton Hayne. DD; GA
Asleep at the Switch. George Hoey. BeLS; PTA-1
Asleep in Jesus. Margaret Mackay. BePJ
("Asleep in Jesus! blessed sleep!") OlF
Asleep in the Bosom of Youth. Judah Halevi, *tr. fr. Hebrew by* Nina Salaman. LiTW
Asleep, my Love? Shakespeare. *Fr.* A Midsummer Night's Dream, V, i. LBN
Asleep or waking is it? for her neck. Laus Veneris. Swinburne. EmBrPo; PoVP; ViPP
Asleep within the deadest hour of night. To ——. Robert Nichols. HBMV; MBP
A-sleepin' at length on the sand. The Sea Serpant. Wallace Irwin. FiBHP
Asmodai. Geoffrey Hill. NePoEA
Asolando, *sels.* Robert Browning.
Epilogue: "At the midnight in the silence of the sleep-time." AEV; BEL; BMEP; BoLiVe; BPN; CoBE; EM-2; EmBrPo; EnL; EnLi-2; EnLit; EPN; EPP; FaBoEn; FiP; GEPC; GTSL; HBV; HBVY; HiLiEn; InP; LEAP; MaRV; OAEP; OBVV; OHFP; OQP; OuHeWo; PC; PoeMoYo; PoVP; QP-1; TCEP; TOP; TrGrPo; VA; ViBoPo; ViPo; ViPP; VLEP
(One Who Never Turned His Back, *2 sts. only.*) GrCo-2
Prologue: "Poet's age is sad, The." PoVP; ViPo; ViPP
Aspatia's Song. Beaumont *and* Fletcher. *Fr.* The Maid's Tragedy, II, i. AWP; BCEP; BLV; CBOV; EV-2; HBV; InPo; JAWP; LEAP; OBEV; OBS; PIAE; TOP; TrGrPo; WBP
(Dirge: "Lay a garland on my hearse.") EPP
(I Died True.) CH
(Lay a Garland on My Hearse.) AtBAP; CenL; ElL; ElSeCe; InP; OAEP; SiCE; TuPP; ViBoPo; WHA
Aspecta Medusa. Dante Gabriel Rossetti. BPN; EmBrPo; PoVP
Aspects of the Pines. Paul Hamilton Hayne. AA; AmPP (3d ed.); AnAmPo; HBV; HiLiAm; IAP; LA; SPP; TCAP
Aspens. Edward Thomas. ChMP
Aspens and the maple now, The. Valentine's Day. Aileen Fisher. YeAr
Asperius Nihil Est Humili cum Surgat in Altum. Henry Parrot. SiCE
Asphalt morning found him; he was dead, The. Raccoon on the Road. Joseph Payne Brennan. GoYe
Aspiration. Emily Dickinson. *See* We never know how high we are.
Aspiration. William Drennan. IrPN
Aspiration. Eileen Duggan. JKCP (1955 ed.)
Aspiration. Ibn Hani, *tr. fr. Arabic by* A. J. Arberry. MooP
Aspiration. Mary Lamb. *See* Maternal Lady with the Virgin Grace.
Aspiration, The. John Norris. LoBV; MeRV; OxBoCh
"How long, great God, how long must I," *sel.* BeR
Aspiration. John Banister Tabb. LO
Aspiration. Edward William Thomson. OBVV
Aspiration. George Wither. MaRV
Ass, The. Edwin Allan. WhC
Ass, The. Moses Mendes *Fr.* The Chaplet. TrJP
Ass, The/ is decidedly middlecrass. The Ass. Edwin Allan. WhC
Ass and the Flute, The. Tomás de Iriarte, *tr. fr. Spanish by* James Kennedy. AnSpL-2
Ass-Face. Edith Sitwell. OBMV
Ass in a depressive state, An. The Two Asses. Christian Morgenstern. AnGP
Ass in the Lion's Skin, The. Aesop, *rhymed tr. fr. Greek by* William Ellery Leonard. AWP; JAWP; LiTW; WBP
Ass Speaks, The. Katharine Tynan. MaRV
Ass will with his long ears fray, An. Maggots of Flattery. Samuel Butler. BeR
Assassination, The. Robert Hillyer. AnNE; MoAmPo; TrGrPo (1942 ed.)
Assault, The. Byron. *Fr.* The Siege of Corinth. EV-4
Assault, The. Robert Nichols. BMEP; MCCG
Assault Heroic, The. Robert Graves. NV
Assault on the Fortress, The. Timothy Dwight. PAH
Assemble, all ye maidens, at the door. Elegy on a Lady, Whom Grief for the Death of Her Betrothed Killed. Robert Bridges. CoBMV; LEAP; OBEV (new ed.); OBVV; PoeT; POTT
Assembling of the Fays, The. Joseph Rodman Drake. *Fr.* The Culprit Fay. GN
Assembly; Harlem School. Eugene T. Maleska. GoYe
Assembly of the Gods, The. Robert Henryson. *Fr.* The Testament of Cresseid. PoEL-1
Assert ten barren love day made. A Play on Words. Eugene Field. WhC
Asses milk, half a pint, take at seven, or before. Advice to a Lady in Autumn. Earl of Chesterfield. CEP; OBEC
Assignation, The, *sel.* Dryden.
Long betwixt Love and Fear. LiTL; SeCL; ViBoPo
(Song: "Long betwixt love and fear Phillis tormented.") SeEP
Assignation, The. Imr el Kais, *tr. fr. Arabic by* Howard Mumford Jones. LiTW
Assignation, The, *sel.* Poe
To One in Paradise. AA; AmPo; AnFE; APA; APW; BLV; BoLiVe; CoAnAm; CoBA; GTBS-D; HBV; IAP; LBAP; LEAP; LiTA; MOAP, *abr.*; NePA; OBAV; OBEV (new ed.); OBRV; OBVV; PG; PIR, *abr.*; SPP; TCAP, *abr.*; TrGrPo; TriL; UnW; ViBoPo; WHA; YT
Assignation, The. James Wright. NePoEA
Assisi. Alfred Noyes. GoBC; SaFP
Assist me, ye muses, (whose harps are in tune). The Progress of Balloons. Philip Freneau. IAP
Assistance, The. Paul Blackburn. NeAP
Association Copy. Paula Kurth. JKCP (1955 ed.)
Assorted Relishes. Richard Armour. WhC
Assuagement. Sister Claude of Jesus. JKCP (1955 ed.)
Assumpta Est Maria. Liam Brophy. ISi
Assumpta Maria. Francis Thompson. ISi
Assumption, The. Sir John Beaumont. ACP (1952 ed.); CAW; GoBC
Assumption, The. John Gilland Brunini. ISi
Assumption, The. St. Nerses, *tr. fr. Armenian by* W. H. Kent. CAW
Assumption, The. John Banister Tabb. ISi
Assumption of the Virgin, The. Luis de León, *tr. fr. Spanish by* Longfellow. AnSpL-1
(At the Assumption, *tr. by* Thomas Walsh.) CAW
Assumption of Troilus, The. Chaucer. *Fr.* Troilus and Criseyde. CoEV
Assunpink and Princeton. Thomas Dunn English. MC; PAH
Assurance, An. Nicholas Breton. OBSC
Assurance. Grace Noll Crowell. PoRL
Assurance. George Herbert. OxBoCh
Assurance. Ida Norton Munson. PGD
Assurances. Walt Whitman. IAP
Assured of worthiness we do not dread. Internal Harmony. George Meredith. EPN
Assured that you are doomed to die. The Tomb of Sardanapalus. *Unknown.* OxBG
Assyrian came down like the [*or* a] wolf on the fold, The. The Destruction of Sennacherib. Byron. ATP; BCEP; BEL; BeLS; BHV; BLPA; BLV; BoLiVe; BPN; BTP; CaAE; CBPC; CG; CoBE; EM-2; EmBrPo; EnLi-2; EnLit; EnRP; ERP; EV-4; FaBoBe; FaBoCh; FaFP; FaPON; GEPC; GN; GoTP; HBV; HiLiEn; InP; LH; LiA; LiTG; LoGBV; LPS-2; MaRV; MCCG; MPB (1956 ed.); MuP; NeHB; OAEP; OTPC; OuHeWo; PCD; PECK; PIR; Po; PoE; PreP; REAL; RG; ShBV-1; TCEP; TOP; TreF; TVSH; TwCrTr; WBLP; WGRP
Assyrian King in peace, with foul desire, The. Sardanapalus [*or* The Portrait of Henry VIII]. Earl of Surrey. ACP (1952 ed.); SiPS
Assyrian Lion, The. Leah Bodine Drake. MuM
Astarte Syriaca. Dante Gabriel Rossetti. PoVP
Aster ("Thou gazest on the stars"). Plato, *tr. fr. Greek.* OxBG
Aster ("Thou wert the morning-star among the living"). Plato. *See* Morning and Evening Star.
Asteria. W. Wesley Trimpi. PtPa
Asterisk, The. *Unknown.* DDA
Astonished Listener Hears the Radio Announcer Bat Out the Long Balls of Verbs. Nouns and Adjectives, An. James Schevill. FiMAP
Astonished poplars hide. Paysage Moralisé. John Hollander. NePoEA
Astonished stood Lucrece and Nara. Lucrece and Nara. Laura Riding. FaBoMo

Astraea. Emerson. AnNE; TCAP
Astraea. Whittier. AA; IAP
Astraea at the Capitol. Whittier. PAH
Astraea Redux. Dryden. CEP
  Sels.
  "And welcom now (Great Monarch)." OBS
  "Now with a general peace the world was blest." OBS
Astral Fates, The. Samuel Butler. *Fr.* Hudibras. BeR
Astride on steel. Motorcycle. Benjamin Sturgis Pray.
  GoYe
Astride the pivot of the world. Seesaw. Gerardo Diego.
  CoSP; LiTW
Astrologer's Song, An. Kipling. MBP; MoBroPo; NeMA
Astrology. Sennett Stephens. PR
Astronomer, The. Kevin F. Doherty. JKCP (1955 ed.)
Astronomers should treat of stars and comets. Ode. "Peter
  Pindar." PoP
Astrophel. Spenser. LiA
  (Death of Astrophel, The.) EV-1
Astrophel and Stella. Sir Philip Sidney. SiPS, *Sonnets,*
  I–CVIII, and 9 Songs
  Sonnets:
  I.   "Loving in truth, and fain in verse my love to show."
       AEV; AnFE; AWP; BCEP; BEL; CoBE; EG; ElSeCe;
       EnL; EnLi-1; EnLit; EPP; EV-1; FaBoEn; GTBS-W;
       HBV; InPo; JAWP; LEAP; LiTB; LiTG; LoPo; MaPo;
       OAEP; OBSC; PeBoSo; Po; PoFS; ReaPo; ReEn;
       ReIE; SeCePo; SeCeV; SiCE; SiPS; TCEP; TOP;
       TrGrPo; TuPP; TwHP; ViBoPo; WBP
       (Look into Thy Heart.) LiTL
       ("Loving in truth and fayne my love in verse to show.")
       NBE
  II. "Not at first sight, nor [yet] with a dribbed shot."
       ElSeCe; MaPo; ReEN; ReEn; ReIE; SiCE; SiPS; TuPP
  III. "Let dainty wits cry on the sisters nine." OBSC;
       ReEn; ReIE; SiCE; SiPS; TuPP
  IV. "Virtue, alas, now let me take some rest." MaPo;
       ReEn
  V.   "It is most true, that eyes are form'd [or formed] to
       serve." MaPo; OBSC; ReEn; SiCE; SiPS; TuPP;
       TwHP
  VI. "Some lovers speak, when they their muses entertain."
       PeBoSo; ReEn; ReIE; SiPS; TuPP
  VII. "When nature made her chief work, Stella's eyes."
       ElSeCe; ReEn; ReIE; SiCE; SiPS; TuPP
  X.   "Reason, in faith thou art well serv'd, that still."
       MaPo; ReEn; SiCE; SiPS
  XI. "In truth, O Love, with what a boyish kind." EIL;
       ElSeCe; InvP; ReEn; SiCE; SiPS
  XII. "Cupid, because thou shin'st in Stella's eyes." ReEn;
       SiPS
  XIV. "Alas, have I not pain enough, my friend." ReEn;
       SiPS; TuPP; TwHP
  XV. "You that do search for every purling spring."
       CoBE; EPP; EV-1; OBSC; ReEn; ReIE; SiCE; SiPS;
       TuPP
       (Against Artifice.) ES
  XVIII. "With what sharp checks I in myself am shent."
       ReEn; SiPS
  XX. "Fly, fly, my friends, I have my death wound; fly."
       MaPo; ReIE; SiPS; TuPP
  XXI. "Your words, my friend (right healthful caustics),
       blame." PeBoSo; ReEn; ReIE; SiCE; SiPS; TuPP
  XXII. "In highest way of heaven the sun did ride." OBSC;
       SiPS
  XXIII. "The curious wits, seeing dull pensiveness." EV-1;
       ReEn; SiPS
  XXIV. "Rich fools there be, whose base and filthy heart."
       OAEP; ReEn; ReIE; SiCE; SiPS; TuPP
  XXV. "The wisest scholar of the wight most wise." ReEn;
       SiPS
  XXVI. "Though dusty wits dare scorn astrology." ReEn;
       SiPS
  XXVII. "Because I oft in dark abstracted guise." ReEn;
       SiCE; SiPS
  XXVIII. "You that with allegory's curious frame." ReEn;
       ReIE; SiCE; SiPS; TuPP
  XXX. "Whether the Turkish new moon minded be." ReEn;
       ReIE; SiPS; TuPP
  XXXI. "With how sad steps, O Moon, thou climb'st the
       skies!" AEV; AnEnPo; AnFE; AtBAP; AWP; BEL;
       BLV; BoLiVe; CaAE; CBOV; CH; ChTr; CoBE; CoEV;
       EG; EIL; ElSeCe; EnL; EnLi-1; EnLit; EPP; ERP;
       EV-1; FaBoEn; GTSL; HBV; InvP; JAWP; LEAP;
       LiTL; LPS-1; MaPo; OAEP; OBSC; PeBoSo; PoE;
       PoEL-1; PoeMoYo; ReaPo; ReEn; ReIE; RiBV; SeCeV;
       SiCE; SiPS; TCEP; TOP; TrGrPo; TuPP; TwHP;
       ViBoPo; WRP; WHA
       (His Lady's Cruelty.) OBEV
       (Moon, The.) ES; LoBV
       (To the Moon.) LiTG; PIAE
  XXXII. "Morpheus, the lively son of deadly sleep." ReEn;
       SiPS
  XXXIII. "I might—unhappy word—O me, I might."
       OBSC; ReEn; SiPS; TuPP
  XXXIV. "Come, let me write. And to what end? To ease."
       ReIE; SiPS; TuPP
  XXXV: "What may words say, or what may words not
       say." ReIE; SiCE; SiPS; TuPP
  XXXVII. "My mouth doth water, and my breast doth
       swell." ReEn; ReIE; SiPS; TuPP
  XXXIX. "Come, sleep, O sleep, the certain knot of peace."
       AnFE; BCEP; BEL; BLV; BoLiVe; CaAE; CoBE;
       CoEV; EIL; ElSeCe; EnL; EnLi-1; EnLit; EPP; EV-1;
       HBV; InP; LEAP; LiTG; MyFE; OAEP; OBSC;
       PeBoSo; PoE; PoFS; ReaPo; ReEn; ReIE; SiCE; SiPS;
       TreFS; TrGrPo; TuPP; TwHP; ViBoPo; WHA
       (Sleep.) ES; GTSL; LoBV; LPS-3; OBEV; PIAE
       (To Sleep.) PC; ShBV-4
  XL. "As good to write as for to lie and groan." SiPS;
       TuPP
  XLI. "Having this day my horse, my hand, my lance."
       AnFE; ATP; BEL; CoBE; EG; ElSeCe; EnL; EnLit;
       EPP; OAEP; OBSC; PeBoSo; PoFS; ReEn; ReIE;
       SiCE; SiPS; TOP; TuPP
       (Lists, The.) ES
       (Stella Looked On.) CBOV
  XLV. "Stella oft sees the very face of woe." PoE; ReEn;
       SiCE; SiPS; TuPP
  XLVII. "What, have I thus betrayed my liberty [or liber-
       tie]?" AtBAP; PoEL-1; ReEn; SiPS
       (Yoke of Tyranny, The.) TrGrPo
  XLVIII. "Soul's Joy, bend not those morning stars from
       me." MaPo; SiPS
  XLIX. "I on my horse, and Love on me, doth try." ReEn;
       SiPS
  L.   "Stella, the fullness of my thoughts of thee." ReEn;
       SiPS
  LII. "A strife is grown between Virtue and Love." ReEn;
       SiPS
  LIII. "In martial sports I had my cunning tried." ReEn;
       ReIE; SiPS
  LIV. "Because I breathe not love to every one." BoLiVe;
       ElSeCe; OAEP; OBSC; PeBoSo; ReEn; SiCE; SiPS;
       TOP; TrGrPo; TuPP
       (Love's Silence.) LPS-1
       (Magpies and Swans.) BLV
  LV. "Muses, I oft invoked your holy aid." SiPS; TuPP
  LVI. "Fie, school of patience, fie! Your lesson is." ReEn;
       SiPS
  LVII. "Woe having made, with many fights, his own."
       ReEn; SiPS
  LVIII. "Doubt there hath been, when with his golden
       chain." ReEn; SiPS
  LIX. "Dear, why make you more of a dog than me?"
       OAEP; SiPS
  LXII. "Late tired with woe, even ready for to pine."
       EnLit; HBV; ReEn; SiPS
  LXIII. "O grammar rules, O now your virtues show."
       PeBoSo; SiPS; TuPP
  LXIV. "No more, my dear, no more these counsels try."
       BEL; CoBE; ElSeCe; HBV; NBE; OBSC; ReEn; SiCE;
       SiPS; TOP; TuPP
  LXVI. "And do I see some cause a hope to feed." ReEn;
       SiPS
  LXVII. "Hope, art thou true, or dost thou flatter me?"
       ReEn; SiPS
  LXVIII. "Stella, the only planet of my light." OBSC;
       ReEn; SiPS
  LXIX. "O joy too high for my low style [or stile] to
       show!" BoLiVe; EV-1; MaPo; PoFS; ReEn; SiCE;
       SiPS; TrGrPo; TuPP
       (Conditional Surrender.) BLV
  LXX. "My Muse may well grudge at my heavenly joy."
       ReEn; SiPS
  LXXI. "Who will in fairest book of Nature know." MaPo;
       ReEn; ReIE; SiCE; SiPS
  LXXII. "Desire, though thou my olde companion art."
       NBE; ReEn; SiPS
  LXXIII. "Love still a boy and oft a wanton is." EG;
       HBV; MyFE; OAEP; ReEn; SiPS
  LXXIV. "I never drank of Aganippe well." OBSC; ReEn;
       ReIE; SiCE; SiPS; TuPP
  LXXVI. "She comes, and streight therewith her shining
       twins do move." ReIE; SiPS
  LXXIX. "Sweet kiss, thy sweets I fain would sweetly in-
       dite." ReEn; SiPS
  LXXXII. "Nymph of the garden where all beauties be."
       InvP; SiPS
  LXXXIV. "Highway, since you my chief Parnassus be."
       CaAE; EIL; OAEP; OBSC; ReEn; SiPS
       (Highway, The.) Ev-1; GTBS-W; LiTB; LiTG; OBEV
       (Road, The.) ES
       (Via Amoris.) GTSL
  XC. "Stella, think not that I by verse seek fame." ElSeCe;
       EnLit; OBSC; ReEn; SiCE; SiPS; TuPP

Astrophel and Stella (*continued*)
XCII. "Be your words made, good Sir, of Indian ware." ReEn; SiPS
XCIV. "Grief, find the words; for thou hast made my brain." ReEn; SiPS
XCVI. "Thought, with good cause thou likest so well the night." ReEn; SiPS
XCVII. "Dian, that fain would cheer her friend the Night." ReEn; SiPS
XCVIII. "Ah, bed! the field where joy's peace some do see." EnLoPo; ReEn; SiPS
XCIX. "When far-spent night persuades each mortal eye." MaPo; OBSC; ReEn; SiPS
C. "O tears, no tears, but rain from Beauty's skies." ReIE; SiPS
CIII. "O happy Thames [*or* happie Tems] that didst my Stella bear[e]." EV-1; HBV; ReEn; SiPS
CIV. "Envious wits, what hath been mine offence." SiPS; TuPP
CVII. "Stella since thou so right a princess[e] art." EV-1; HBV; MaPo; ReEn; SiPS
CIX. "Thou blind man's mark, thou fool's self-chosen snare." *Sometimes considered part of* Astrophel and Stella; *also in* Certain Sonnets. SiCE; TuPP; ViBoPo
(Desire.) LiTB; LiTG; PeBoSo; SiPS; TrGrPo
CX. "Leave me, O love, which reachest but to dust." *Sometimes considered part of* Astrophel and Stella; *also in* Certain Sonnets. BCEP; BrBE; CoEV; EG; ElL; ElSeCe; EnLit; ExPo; LEAP; LiTB; LiTG; MaPo; OAEP; OxBoCh; PoE; PoRA; ReaPo; ReEn; ReIE; RiBV; SeCePo; SeCeV; SiCE; TOP; TriL; TrPWD; TuPP; TyEnPo; ViBoPo; WHA
(Farewell, A.) CBOV; UnPo (1st ed.)
(Farewell World.) FaBoEn
(Love.) PeBoSo
(Splendidis Longum Valedico Nugis.) ES; EV-1; LO; OBEV; OBSC; SiPS
Songs.
First Song: "Doubt you to whom my muse these notes intended [*or* entendeth]." AtBAP; ElSeCe; EV-1; HBV; OBSC; PoFS; ReIE; SiCE; SiPS; TCEP; TuPP
(To Stella.) ElL; WHA
(To You! To You!) LiTL
Second Song: "Have I caught my heavenly jewel."
(Stella Sleeping.) SiPS
Third Song: "If Orpheus' voice [*or* voyce] had force." PoEL-1; ReIE; SiPS
Fourth Song: "Only [*or* Onely] joy, now here you are." AtBAP; ElL; InvP; LEAP; OBSC; ReEn; ReIE; SiCE; SiPS; TuPP
Sixth Song: "O you that hear[e] this voice." NBE; OBSC; SiPS
Eighth Song: "In a grove most rich of shade." OBSC; SiPS
(Eighth Sonnet, The.) OAEP
Ninth Song: "Go, my flock, go get you hence." SiPS
Tenth Song: "O dear life, when shall it be?" SiPS
Eleventh Song: "Who is it that this dark[e] night." AtBAP; ElL; EnLi-1; EV-1; OBSC; PoEL-1; ReEn; ReIE; SiCE; TuPP; ViBoPo; WoL
(Dialogue, A.) EG
(Lovers' Dialogue.) SiPS
(Underneath My Window.) SeCePo
(Voices at the Window.) CBOV; OBEV
Astrophel's Love Is Dead. Sir Philip Sidney. *See* Ring Out Your Bells.
Asunder shall the clouds be rolled. The Day of Judgment. Dugald Buchanan. GoTS
A-swell within her billowed skirts. The Mad Woman of Punnet's Town. L. A. G. Strong. MBP; MoBrPo
Asylum. John Freeman. OBMV
At a Bach Concert. Adrienne Cecile Rich. NePoEA
At a Burial. Sir William Watson. MaRV
At a certain time in life it becomes essential. Cartier at St. Malo. Francis Webb. *Fr.* A View of Montreal. BoAV
At a Concert of Music. Conrad Aiken. ChMo; CMP; MAP; MoAB; MoAmPo; UnS
At a Country Dance in Provence. Harold Monro. OBVV
At a Country Fair. John Holmes. MoShBr
At a Cowboy Dance. James Barton Adams. HBV; IHA; PoOW; SCC
(Idaho Cowboy Dance, An.) ABF
At a dinner so various, at such a repast. The Retaliation. Goldsmith. CEP; OAEP; TCEP; TOP
At a gay reception given in a mansion grand and old. The Moth and the Flame. George Taggert. TreF
At a Hasty Wedding. Thomas Hardy. ViP
At a high mountaines foot, whose lofty crest. A Cave; Pool's Hole, Derbyshire. Charles Cotton. Fr. The Wonders of the Peake. BeR
At a House in Hampstead. Thomas Hardy. EmBrPo
At a Loss. James L. Weil. GoYe
At a Lunar Eclipse. Thomas Hardy. MoPW; POTE; TOP
At a Parade. F. T. Prince. NeBP; WaP
At a pleasant evening party I had taken down to supper. Ferdinando and Elvira. W. S. Gilbert. BOHV; FiBHP; LBN; NA; PC
At a posterne forth they gan to ryde. John Lydgate. *Fr.* The Story of Thebes. EPP
At a pot-house bar as I chanced to pass. What the Trumpeter Said. Sebastian Evans. VA
At a round-up on the Gila. The Legend of Boastful Bill. Badger Clark. SCC
At a Solemn Music [*or* Musick]. Milton. BCEP; BrBE; EG; EV-2; ExPo; GTBS; GTBS-D; GTBS-W; GTSE; GTSL; HBV; LoBV; OAEP; OBEV; OBS; PoE; PoEL-3; SeCeV; SeCL; SeEP; TOP
(Blest Pair of Sirens.) OxBoCh
"Blest pair of sirens, pledges of heaven's joy," *sel.* UnS
At a university women's sort of charity fair. The Fortune Teller. John Holmes. NePoAm-2
At a Vacation Exercise. Milton. OBS
At a Window. Carl Sandburg. ChMo; CMP; FaBoBe; HBMV; LEAP; NP; PCD; PoToHe; TrPWD
At a Window Sill. Christopher Morley. OBAV
At Aberdeen. *Unknown. See* Epitaph: "Here lie I, Martin Elginbrodde."
At All Times. Alice Reynolds Flower. PraP
At an Old Battlefield. Umaki, *tr. fr. Japanese by* Asataro Miyamori. OnPM
At anchor in Hampton Roads we lay. The *Cumberland.* Longfellow. AA; AnNE; APW; BoHiPo; EtS; IAP; LH; MC; PaA; PAH; PAP
At Assisi. William Vaughn Moody. *Fr.* Song-Flower and Poppy. LEAP; SaFP
At Atri in Abruzzo, a small town. The Bell of Atri. Longfellow. *Fr.* Tales of a Wayside Inn. MW
At Babiloyne whilom fil it thus. The Story of Thisbe of Babylon, Martyr. Chaucer. *Fr.* The Legend of Good Women. TCEP
At Bacharach on Rhine-bank. Lore Lay. Clemens Brentano. AnGP
At Baia. Hilda Doolittle ("H. D."). AnFE; APA; CoAnAm; LiTA; MAPA; MOAP; NP; TwAmPo
At beauty's bar as I did stand. The Arraignment of a Lover [*or* Gascoigne's Arraignment]. George Gascoigne. EV-1; ReEn; ReIE; SiCE; TuPP
At Beckwith in the pass below Chilcoot. In the Pass. Clinton Scollard. TBM
At Bedtime. Mariana Griswold Van Rensselaer. HBMV
At Beecher's Island. John G. Neihardt. *Fr.* The Song of the Indian Wars. TCPD
At Beltane, when ilk body bownis. Peblis to the Play. *Unknown.* EBSV; GoTS
At Benediction. Eleanor Rogers Cox. JKCP
At Best. John Boyle O'Reilly. AA; LBAP
At Bethlehem. John Banister Tabb. The Child, I. AA
(Child at Bethlehem, The.) PRWS
At birth a witch laid on me monstrous spells. The Singer in the Mist. Robert Ervin Howard. DaM
At Bjerregaard's Grave. Henrik Wergeland, *tr. fr. Norwegian by* Charles W. Stork. AnNoLy
At break of day I chanced to stray. The Oul' Grey Mare. *Unknown.* AnIV
At Breakfast. I. M. Mills. BoTP
At breakfast a husband is cheery or blue. Sentimental Journey. "Elspeth." WhC
At Brill on the hill. *Unknown.* OxNR
At Burgos. Arthur Symons. VLEP
At Cambridge. Audrey McGaffin. NePoAm
At Candle-lightin' Time. Paul Laurence Dunbar. HOAH; IHA
At Carbis Bay. Arthur Symons. PoVP
At Carcassonne. Winfred Ernest Garrison. OQP; QP-2
At Casterbridge Fair. Thomas Hardy. BEL; EmBrPo; EnLit; PoVP
Sels.
After the Fair, VII. ChMo; CMP
Ballad-Singer, The, I. ChMo; LO
Former Beauties, II. FaBoEn; OBMV
At Castle Boterel. Thomas Hardy. CoEV; FaBoEn; GTBS-D; MoVE
At Castle Wood. Emily Brontë. ViBoPo; VLEP
At Cato's Head in Russel Street. On a Fly-Leaf of a Book of Old Plays. Walter Learned. PR
At Ceuta I cast aside. Algeciras Seen over a Stormy Sea Ibn Malik of Granada. MooP
At Ch'ang-an—a full foot of snow. An Early Levée. Po Chü-i. TrCh
At Chappaqua. Joel Benton. AA
At Christmastide. Laura Simmons. PGD
At Christmas Time. Mary Brennan Clapp. GFA
At Christmas time so long ago. The Little Fir Tree. Margaret Rose. BoTP
At Church Next Sunday. *Unknown.* BLRP
At clear dawn I comb my white hairs. On a Pine Tree Shown to Me by the Taoist Scholar Li. Tu Fu. WhP
At Close of Day. Stephan G. Stephansson, *tr. fr. Icelandic by* Jakobina Johnson. IcP

At Cockcrow. Lizette Woodworth Reese. TrPWD
At Common Dawn. Vivian Locke Ellis. CH
At cool of day, with God I walk. Eventide. Caroline Atherton Briggs Mason. MaRV; TreFS
At counters where I eat my lunch. Marble-Top. E. B. White. FiBHP; WhC
At Court. Spenser. *Fr.* Mother Hubberds Tale. PoFr
At court I met it, in clothes brave enough. On Something That Walks [*or* Walkes] Somewhere. Ben Jonson. CoBE; SeCV-1; TuPP
At Creçy by Somme in Ponthieu. Creçy. Francis Turner Palgrave. BeLS; HBV
At Dawn. Rose Fyleman. BoChLi
At Dawn. Victor Hugo, *tr. fr. French by* Alan Conder. OnPM; TrFP
At Dawn. José Moreno Villa, *tr. fr. Spanish by* Eleanor L. Turnbull. CoSP
At Dawn. Arthur Symons. VLEP
At Dawn. Charles Williams. FaBoTw
At dawn amid colored clouds I left White Emperor City. Leaving White Emperor City at Dawn. Li Po. WhP
"At dawn," he said, "I bid them all farewell." The Volunteer. Elbridge Jefferson Cutler. AA; IDAH; MDAH
At dawn I rode to escort the Doctors of Art. Escorting Candidates to the Examination Hall. Po Chü-i. TrCh
At dawn I sighed to see my hairs fall. On His Baldness. Po Chü-i. TrCh
At dawn in her kennel of rye-stalks. Song about a Bitch. Sergei Yesenin. BoRS
At dawn of day I saw a man. The Drunkard's Doom. *Unknown.* AS
At Dawn of the Year. "George Klingle." PGD; PSO
At dawn she lay with her profile at that angle. Daybreak. Stephen Spender. LiTL; POTE
At dawn she sought the Saviour slain. Mary Magdalene. Richard Burton. BPP; ChIP
At dawn the dark birds flew. The Ninth of April. Otto Gelsted. PoFr
At dawn, the joyful choir of bells. Ave Maria Bells. Charles Warren Stoddard. ISi; JKCP
At dawn the reading of the Word. Dawn. Tanikado. SoLD
At dawn the ridge emerges massed and dun. Attack. Siegfried Sassoon. MBP; MCCG; MoBrPo; PoMa
At dawn they launched the ships; and all went well. Audrey Alexandra Brown. *Fr.* Laodamia. TwCV
At dawn to-day I thought I'd bring thee roses. The Roses of Saadi. Marceline Desbordes-Valmore. TrFP
At dawn to-morrow, when the world grows pale. To His Dead Daughter. Victor Hugo. TrFP
At dawn, when England's childish tongue. Dandelion. Annie Rankin Annan. HBV
At Dawning. Nelle Richmond Eberhart. OlF
At daybreak there spread through the heavens. The Aerial City. Afanasi Afanasievich Fet. TrRV
At daybreak, when the falcon claps his wings. Ballad Written for a Bridegroom. Villon, *tr. by* Swinburne. AWP
At de feet o' Jesus. Feet o' Jesus. Langston Hughes. NP
At Dead Low Water. Allen Curnow. AnNZ
At Dead o' the Night, Alanna. James B. Dollard. CPG
At dead of night, when mortals lose. The Ungrateful Cupid. John Hughes. CG
At Delos. Duncan Campbell Scott. BoCaPo; PeCV
At Dingle Bank. Edward Lear. WhC
At dinner, she is hostess, I am host. Modern Love, XVII. George Meredith. EnLit; OAEP; POTT; VA; ViP; ViPo
At Dirty Dick's and Sloppy Joe's. W. H. Auden. *Fr.* The Sea and the Mirror. FaBoTw
At Dover Cliffs. William Lisle Bowles. *See* Dover Cliffs.
At dusk, alone, among tall trees he stood. The Traveler. Joseph Corson Miller. UnW
At dusk it is. Mrs. Southern's Enemy. Sir Osbert Sitwell. AtBAP
At dusk the narrow street is a landscape in Limbo. The Narrow Street. Menotti del Picchia. AnCL
At dusk the torrid day grew pale with mood elusive. Aleksey Konstantinovich Tolstoy, *tr. fr. Russian by* Sir Cecil Kisch. WaL
At dusk they heard the roar. King Philip's Men. Audrey Alexandra Brown. BoCaPo
At dusk, upon my heart. Bell across the Snow. Rofu Miki. PoLJ
At each moment we rise vainly from the dead. Vain Cry; Lydian Campaign, 1941. Glauco Cambon. OnPM
At early dawn I marked them in the sky. The Pelican. James Montgomery. *Fr.* The Pelican Island. LPS-2
At early dawn I once had been. The Dawning of the Day. *Unknown.* OnYI; TIP
At early dawn through London you must go. Prescription for a Spring Morning. John Davidson. *Fr.* Fleet Street Eclogues. CBPC; LEAP
At Early Morn. Binga Dismond, *fr. the French of* Catulle Mendes. PoNe
At Ease. Walter de la Mare. ChMP
At Easter Time. Charles G. Blanden. PSO
At Easter Time. Laura E. Richards. BoChLi; DD; EOAH; HH; MPB; OHIP; OTPC (1946 ed.)
At Ecelin. Robert Browning. *Fr.* Sordello. MyFE
At Eden's gateway, downward spying. Angel. Pushkin. BoR
At eight o'clock in the evening. Baboon. Charles Hanson Towne. BAP; LEAP
At Eighty. "Katherine Hale." OCL
At Eighty-seven. Dachine Rainer. NePoAm
At Eighty-three, *sel.* Thomas Durley Landels.
"Thank God for life, with all its endless store." MaRV
At Epidaurus. Lawrence Durrell. LiTB; MoPo
At Eutaw Springs the valiant died. To the Memory of the Brave Americans [*or* Eutaw Springs]. Philip Freneau. AA; AmP; AmPP; BeLS; CoBA; IAP; MOAP; NeHB; PaA; PAH; PAP; TCAP; TriL
"At eve should be the time," they said. Datur Hora Quieti. Robert Stephen Hawker. GoBC
At eve the horse is freed of plough and wain. An Evening Falls. James Stephens. SUS
At Even. Frederic Manning. NP
At even o' Hallowmas no sleep I sought. The Spell. John Gay. DD; HOAH
At even unexpectedly. The Passers By. Al-Radi Billah. MooP
At Even, when the Sun Was Set. Henry Twells. MaRV
At Evening. *Unknown.* BOL
At Evening. Dora Wilcox. BoAu
At evening. A Patio. Jorge Luis Borges. TwSpPo
At evening and at morning. A Wood-Path. Bliss Carman. MM
At evening when I go to bed. Daisies. Frank Dempster Sherman. GoBP; RAR; TSW; TVC; TVSH
At evening when the lamp is lit. The Land of Story-Books. Robert Louis Stevenson. CBPC; FaBoBe; FaPON; GoTP; HBV; HBVY; MOB; MPB; NeHB; OTPC; PoVP; PRWS; TiPo; TreFS; TSW; TSWC
At Eventide. *Unknown, tr. fr. German by* Robert Bridges. MaRV
At eventide the autumnal woods. Grodek. Georg Trakl. AnGP
At eventime I walk beside. Rain at Night. Lu Ying Su. PoHN
At every heart-beat. Time. "Æ." ChMo; CMP
At every pelourinho's ledge. Don Juan in Portugal. Florence Wilkinson Evans. TBM
At every stroke his brazen fins do take. The Whale. John Donne. *Fr.* The Progress of the Soul. ChTr
At Ferns Castle. Padraic Colum. NePoAm
At fifteen I went with the army. Old Poem [*or* Return]. *Unknown.* LiTW; TrCh
At First. Nigel Heseltine. MoWP
At first a dusky wreath they seem to rise. The Coming of the Rain. James Thomson. *Fr.* The Seasons: Spring. EPP
At first cock-crow. The Neighbors. Theodosia Garrison. HBMV; UnW
At first he stirs uneasily in sleep. Dog at Night. Louis Untermeyer AlBD; GoTP; PoeMoYo; StaSt
At first I feared the color of the dark. The Pulse of Darkness. John Fandel. JKCP (1955 ed.)
At first I prayed for Light. The Larger Prayer. Ednah Dow Cheney. BLRP; MaRV; OQP; PraP; QP-1; WGRP
At first I thought a pest. Armour's Undermining Modesty. Marianne Moore. CoBMV
At first I thought some animal, wounded. Near Barbizon. Galway Kinnell. NePoAm-2
At first I thought there was a superfine. Fleming Helphenstine. E. A. Robinson. TwP
At first I went apart. And now I see. Tammuz. Rayner Heppenstall. WaP
At first, in that place, at all times, above the earth. The Walam Olum. *Unknown.* WoL
At first she thought it a fantastic dream. Ballade of Charon and the River Girl. J. B. Morton. WhC
At first the river's very small. The Growing River. Rodney Bennett. BoTP
At first there all sea-water on the top land. On the Creation and Ontogony. *Unknown.* *Fr.* Wallam Olum. LiTA
At first we sat imprisoned in this place. Conversation in Black and White. May Sarton. GoYe
At five in the afternoon. Lament for the Death of a Bullfighter [*or* Lament for Ignacio Sanchez Mejias]. Federico García Lorca. CoSP; LiTW; ReMP
At five o'clock he milks the cow. The Breakfast Song. Emilie Poulsson. HBVY
At five o'clock one April morn. The Orphans. W. W. Gibson. CP
At Flores in the Azores Sir Richard Grenville lay. The *Revenge* [*or* A Ballad of the Fleet]. Tennyson. BBV; BEL; BeLS; BPN; EnLi-2; EnLit; EM-2; EmBrPo; EPN; FaBoCh; GDAH; GEPC; GTML; HBV; HiLiEn; HoPM; LH; MaC; MCCG; OAEP; OnHT; OTPC; PCD; PCN; PECK; PoRA; PoVP; ShBV-1; TCEP; TOP; UnPo (1st ed.); ViPo; VLEP
At Fontainebleau. Arthur Symons. VA

At Fotheringay. Robert Southwell. PoEL-2
(Decease, Release. Dum Morior, Orior.) SiCE
Sels.
Martyrdom of Mary, Queen of Scots, The. ACP
On the Execution of Mary, Queen of Scots. MeRV
At four in the morning the smoke of the forded river. While We Slept. David Wolff. AnAmPo; TrJP
At four o'clock. Roosters. Elizabeth Bishop. CrMA; FiMAP; LiTM; NePA; OnHM
At four o'clock in the morning. Waking Time. Ivy O. Eastwick. SiSoSe; TiPo (1959 ed.)
At Fourscore. Eben E. Rexford. MotAn
At Francis Allen's on the Christmas eve. The Epic (Introduction to "Morte d'Arthur"). Tennyson. EmBrPo; PoVP; ViPP; VLEP
At Fredericksburg (December 13, 1862). John Boyle O'Reilly. BIG; MC; PAH
At full my huge Leviathan shall rise. Leviathan. Edward Young. *Fr.* A Paraphrase on Part of the Book of Job. BeR
"At Fyvie's yetts there grows a flower." Andrew Lammie. *Unknown.* ESPB
At Gibraltar (*Sonnets I and* II). George Edward Woodberry. AA; AnAmPo; BAP; GN; LA; LBMV; LEAP
"England, I stand on thy imperial ground," *sel.* HBV
At Glastonbury. Henry Kingsley. *See* Magdalen.
At Glendalough lived a young saint. St. Kevin. Samuel Lover. OnYI
At Gold Hill Monastery. Su T'ung-po, *tr. fr. Chinese by* Kenneth Rexroth. OnPC
At Golgotha I stood alone. Edwin John Ellis. *Fr.* Himself. OBMV
At Graduating Time. *Unknown.* DD; PEDC; PEOR; PoRL
At Grass. Philip Larkin. HaMV; NePoEA; PoN
At Great Torrington, Devon. *Unknown.* SiTL
At Gull Lake, August, 1810. Duncan Campbell Scott. BoCaPo
At half-past three a single bird. Emily Dickinson. MoAmPo (1950 ed.); MOAP; OxBA
At half-past three he gets around to hear. The Busy Music Critic. Bert Leston Taylor. LauV
At Haroun's court it chanced, upon a time. The World's Way. Thomas Bailey Aldrich. HBV; LHV
At Harvest. Joseph Campbell. NP
At hawthorn-time in Wiltshire travelling. Lob. Edward Thomas. MoVE
At her doorway Mrs. Mayle. The Lavender Bush. Elizabeth Fleming. BoTP
At Her Fair Hands. Walter Davison. *See* How Can the Heart Forget Her.
At Her Grave. Arthur O'Shaughnessy. PoVP; VA
At Her Window. Frederick Locker-Lampson. HBV; LEAP; OBEV (1st ed.); OBVV
At High Mass. Robert Hugh Benson. CAW
At hint of spring I have you back again. Two Songs in Spring, II. Thomas S. Jones, Jr. VOD
At His Feet. Lois R. Carpenter. BePJ
At His Grave. Alfred Austin. VA
At his heart stood/ the poisoned point. Death in Battle. *Unknown.* *Fr.* The Battle of Maldon. PoLi
At his hour, the muttering sea crawled up! The Tide. Joseph William Holden. NoCaPo
At His Table. Bertha Gerneaux Woods. PraP
At his word we flew/ To search. The Nuptials of Haemon and Antigone. Sophocles. *Fr.* Antigone. GrR
At Home. Christina Rossetti. PoVP; UnW; VA; VLEP
At Home alone, O Nomades. Home, Sweet Home, with Variations, IV. H. C. Bunner. BOHV; CenHV; InMe; PA
At Home among the Stars ("This prospect vast, what is it?"). Edward Young. *Fr.* Night Thoughts, IX. GrCo-1
At home, as in no other city, here. Oxford. Keith Douglas. NePoEA
At Home in Heaven. James Montgomery. HBV; VA
(Forever with the Lord.) LPS-2
At home, in my flannel gown, like a bear to its floe. 90 North. Randall Jarrell. CoBMV; FiMAP; MoAB; MoPo; MoVE
At-Home in Sparta, An. Homer, *pr. tr. fr. Greek by* Samuel Butler. *Fr.* The Odyssey, IV. GrR
At home it seems to be the rule. Ma's Tools. *Unknown.* DDA; PEDC
At Hooker's Tomb. John Keble. ES
At Hsin-feng an old man—four-score and eight. The Old Man with the Broken Arm. Po Chü-i. TrCh
At Husking Time. E. Pauline Johnson. POT; VA
At insular café tables under awnings. Green Coconuts. Lawrence Durrell. FaBoMo
At Ithaca. Hilda Doolittle ("H. D."). AnAmPo; LA; MM
At its own distance. Siciliana; the Landings at Gela. G. Stanley Koehler. NePoAm-2
At I-ye Temple. Po Chü-i, *tr. fr. Chinese by* Ching Ti. WhP
At Jerusalem. Edna Dean Proctor. BPP
At John's, up at Sandhills, 'tis healthy and dry. Hill and Dell. William Barnes. EnSW
At Kew. Alfred Noyes. *See* Go Down to Kew in Lilac-Time.
At Knaresborough. Donald Davie. NePoEA
At Lagos you knew sad faced girls. Langston Hughes. Jacques Roumain. PoNe
At Lake Geneva. Richard Eberhart. LiTA
At Lanier's Grave. John Banister Tabb. AmP
At Last. Paul Hamilton Hayne. EOAH
At Last. Philip Bourke Marston. VA
At Last. Sir Lewis Morris. VA
At Last. Richard Henry Stoddard. HBV
At Last. Katrina Trask. AA
At Last. Whittier. NeHB, *abr.;* OQP, *abr.;* PraP, *abr.;* QP-2, *abr.;* TreFS; TrPWD; WGRP
(To Paths Unknown.) MaRV
At last! Alone! There is no longer anything to be heard. At One o'Clock in the Morning. Baudelaire. AnFP
At last, beloved Nature! I have met. Sonnet [*or* Elusive Nature]. Henry Timrod. SN; SPP
At last comes such a love that gossip that I conceal it. To Cerinthus. Sulpicia. LaP
At last he sleeps alone, but to his bier. The Wake. Robert Avrett. UnW
At last her face was turned to him who knew. Seven Sad Sonnets, II. Mary Aldis. HBMV
At last his sail-broad vannes. Milton. *Fr.* Paradise Lost, II. BrBE
At last I have a Sabine farm. My Sabine Farm. Eugene Field. InMe
At last I have ceased repining, at last I accept my fate. The Agnostic's Creed. Walter Malone. HBV
At last I have found the spring where everything is hidden. A Retreat in the Mountains. Chu Wan. WhP
At last I left the open sea behind. Venetian Sonnets, I. August, Graf von Platen. AnGP
At last I put off love. He Abjures Love. Thomas Hardy. NBE
At last Jeane come down stairs, a-drest. Jeane's Wedden Day in Mornen. William Barnes. PoVP
At last, my old inveterate foe. Ardelia to Melancholy. Countess of Winchilsea. DiM
At last, O thou serene retreat. To Retirement. Luis de León. TrJP
At last our dull Earth listens. Earth Listens. Katharine Lee Bates. PGD; PSO
At last she calls to mind where hangs a piece. Troy Depicted. Shakespeare. *Fr.* The Rape of Lucrece. OBSC
At last, so faire a ladie did I spie. The Visions of Petrarch. *Tr. by* Spenser. EnLi-1
At last the beautiful Palm Sunday comes. Palm Sunday. Francis Jammes. CAW
At last the bird that sang [*or* sung] so long. Good Friday Night. William Vaughn Moody. APA; CBOV; StJW; TCAP
At last the dawn throws the forest in relief. After the Agony in the Garden. Daryl Hine. PeCV
At last the four year storm of fratricide. The Sawing of the Dragon. John G. Neihardt. *Fr.* The Song of the Indian Wars. TCAP
At Last the Secret Is Out. W. H. Auden *and* Christopher Isherwood. *Fr.* The Ascent of F 6. NAMP; SeCePo
At last the toil encumbered days. Indian Summer. J. P. Irvine. SN
At last to be identified! Resurgam. Emily Dickinson. WGRP
At last we are met—but I hope with no other. The Pacific Engagement. *Unknown.* *Fr.* Bungiana. WhC
At last we parley: we so strangely dumb. Modern Love, XLVI. George Meredith. EmBrPo; EnLit; ViPo
At last withdraw your cruelty. Sir Thomas Wyatt. SiPS
At last you yielded up the album, which. Lines on a Young Lady's Photograph Album. Philip Larkin. EnLoPo; PoN
At Least. Charles Churchill. *Fr.* The Times. BeR
At least, it was a life of swords. Comrades. Lionel Johnson. HBV
At Least to Be at Peace. August, Graf von Platen, *tr. fr. German by* Edwin Morgan. AnGP
At Leeds. *Unknown.* WhC
At length a reverend sire among them came. The Ark. Milton. *Fr.* Paradise Lost, XI. EtS
At length, by so much importunity pressed [*or* press'd]. The Lover; a Ballad. Lady Mary Wortley Montagu. CEP; LO; OBEC
At length I saw a lady within call. Iphigenia [*or* Helen and Iphigenia]. Tennyson. *Fr.* A Dream of Fair Women. BHV; TwCrTr
At length my chariot wheel about the mark hath found the way. Arthur Golding. ReIE
At length the finished garden to the view. James Thomson. *Fr.* The Seasons: Spring. ViBoPo
At length the freshening western blast. Flodden. Sir Walter Scott. *Fr.* Marmion, VI. BHV
At length the term's ending. A Letter. Sir Arthur Quiller-Couch. CenHV
At length their long kiss severed, with sweet smart. Nuptial Sleep. Dante Gabriel Rossetti. The House of Life, VI. BrBE; LoBV; PeBoSo; ViPo; ViPP

At length there dawns the glorious day. Brotherhood. Ozora Stearns Davis. MaRV

At length they came into a larger space. The Cave of Mammon. Spenser. *Fr.* The Faerie Queene, II, 7. FiP

At length 'tis done, the glorious conflict's done. On the Late Successful Expedition against Louisbourg. Francis Hopkinson. PAH

At length we have settled a pastor. Wanted, a Minister's Wife. *Unknown.* BLPA; TreFS

At length with jostling, elbowing and the aid. At the Gate of Heaven. Byron. *Fr.* The Vision of Judgment. OBRV

At Les Eboulements. Duncan Campbell Scott. SG; VA

At Lexington. Benjamin Sledd. BlG

At liberty I sit and see. The Lover in Liberty Smileth at Them in Thraldom, That Sometime Scorned His Bondage. *Unknown.* EIL; ElSeCe

At Lincoln. Oscar Fay Adams. AA

At Lincoln's Grave. Maurice Thompson. *Fr.* Lincoln's Grave. GA

At London in England, not a very long time. Saint Erkenwald. *Unknown.* MeEV

At Loschwitz above the city. The Birch-Tree at Loschwitz. Amy Levy. AV; TrJP

At Lulworth Cove a Century Back. Thomas Hardy. ChMP

At Magnolia Cemetery. Henry Timrod. AA; AmP; AnAmPo; LA; LBAP; OBAV; PoeMoYo; TCAP (Decoration Day at Charleston.) DD (Hymn for Memorial Day.) MDAH (Magnolia Cemetery.) BAP; PaA (Ode: "Sleep sweetly in your humble graves.") AmPP; BAV; BlG; BoHiPo; HBV; LPS-2; OxBA; SPP (Ode Sung on the Occasion of Decorating the Graves of the Confederate Dead, at Magnolia Cemetery, Charleston, S.C.) IAP; MC; MOAP

At Manly. Leonard Mann. MoAuPo

At Marshfield. William Cleaver Wilkinson. *Fr.* Webster, an Ode. AA

At Mass. *Unknown, tr. fr. Irish by* Robin Flower. GTIV; OxBI

At Melville's Tomb. Hart Crane. ATP (1953 ed.); CaAE; CoBMV; InPo; MOAP; NePA; OnAP; Po; ReMP; TriL; UnPo

At Memphis Station. Johannes V. Jensen, *tr. fr. Danish by* S. Foster Damon. WoL

At midday they looked up and saw their death. Three Memorial Sonnets, III. George Barker. WaP

At Midnight. Frank Dempster Sherman. AA; MAP

At midnight by the stream I roved. Lewti. Samuel Taylor Coleridge. BPN; EmBrPo; EnRP; ERP; EV-4

At midnight Death dismissed the chancellor. Lines on the Death of Bismarck. John Jay Chapman. PoEL-5

At midnight, death's and truth's unlocking-time. The Crystal. Sidney Lanier. AmP; PtP; TCAP

At midnight from the zenith burst a light. The Angelic Chorus. D. J. Donahoe. JKCP

At midnight, in his guarded tent. Marco Bozzaris. Fitz-Greene Halleck. AA; BAP; BeLS; GN; HBV; HoPM; IAP; LEAP; LPS-2; OBAV; OnHT; PECK; PFY; PIR; TCAP; TreF; WBLP

At midnight in the alley. The Tomcat. Don Marquis. BAP; CIV; DDA; LEAP; PoeMoYo; PoMa; PoRA

At midnight, in the garden never planted. They Also Stand . . . Merrill Moore. CrMA

At midnight, in the month of June. The Sleeper. Poe. AA; AmPo; AmPP; AnFE; APA; APW; BAP; CoAnAm; CoBA; IAP; InP; LiTA; NePA; OBAV; OBVV; OxBA; PoEL-4; PoFS; ReaPo; TCAP; TrGrPo; UnPo (1st ed.)

At midnight in the silence of the sleep-time. *See* At the midnight . . .

At midnight, through my dream, the signals dread. The Blind. Thomas Walsh. BAP

At midnight when cattle are sleeping. The Cowboy's Meditation. *Unknown.* CoSo; CSF

At Midnight's Hour I Raised My Head. Henry David Thoreau. PoEL-4

At Mrs. Appleby's. Elizabeth Upham McWebb. BrR; SiSoSe; StVeCh (1955 ed.); TiPo

At morn, at noon, at twilight dim. Hymn [or Hymn of the Angelus]. Poe. CAW; IAP; ISi

At morn I plucked a rose and gave it Thee. A Rose in Jericho. Christina Rossetti. MeRV

At morn to kneel before Him. My Task. Hayashi. SoLD

At Morning an Iris. Patrick Evans. NeBP

At morning from the coldness of Mount Brandon. Aisling. Austin Clarke. AnIV

At morning the pale pigeons come in a band. Pigeons. George Dillon. BLA; WhBS

At morning's call. Our Hymn. Oliver Wendell Holmes. BOIIV

At morning's dawn Hermione appears. Colluthus. *Fr.* Rape of Helen. GrPo

At most mischief. Sir Thomas Wyatt. SiPS

At Mount Vernon. Thomas Curtis Clark. PGD

At my casement I sat by night, while the wind remote in dark valleys. Epilogue. Aubrey Thomas De Vere. IrPN

At My Father's Grave. Matthias Claudius, *tr. fr. German by* Ralph Marcus. WoL

At My Whisper. Lyle Donaghy. AnIV

At my windowpane a bird. That Is All I Heard. "Yehoash." TrJP

At Nazareth. Katharine Lee Bates. StJW

At Nebra, by the Unstrut. The Inn of Care. Samuel Waddington. OBVV; VA

At Night. Winifred Adams Burr. UnW

At Night ("My brain is like the ravaged shores"). Frances Cornford. MBP; MoBrPo

At Night ("On moony nights the dogs bark shrill"). Frances Cornford. StaSt; TSW; TSWC

At Night. Joseph von Eichendorff, *tr. fr. German by* Mabel Cotterell. WoL

At Night. Alice Meynell. CH; EV-5; HBV; LBBV; LiTL; LoPo; NV; OBVV; PoeT; POTT (To W. M.) GoBC

At Night. George Edgar Montgomery. AA

At Night. Anne Blackwell Payne. GFA; UTS

At Night. Sergei Smirnov, *tr. fr. Russian by* Jack Lindsay. RuPo

At night, alone, the animals came and shone. The Animals. Josephine Jacobsen. GoYe

At night, as drough the mead I took my way. To Me. William Barnes. PoEL-4

At night, by the fire. Domination of Black. Wallace Stevens. AmPP; AnFE; CoAnAm; CoBMV; MAP; MAPA; MoAB; MoAmPo; OxBA; TwAmPo

At night I dreamt I was back in Ch'ang-an. Dreaming That I Went with Lu and Yu to Visit Yüan Chen. Po Chü-i. BoFr; TrCh

At night in each other's arms. Love's Vision. Edward Carpenter. WGRP

At night, in my dream, I stoutly climbed a mountain. A Dream of Mountaineering. Po Chü-i. TrCh

At Night in the Wood. Nancy M. Hayes. BoTP; TVSH (Night in the Wood, A.) TVC

At night the painted mimicries. At Night. Winifred Adams Burr. UnW

At night through the city in a song. For Them All. John Hall Wheelock. HBMV; TSW; TSWC

At night what things will stalk abroad. Lux in Tenebris. Katharine Tynan. GTIV; OxBI; TIP; TrPWD

At night when ale is in. Of Drunkenness. George Turberville. TuPP

At night when I am tired of play. Bed Time. Ella Young. BoChLi (1950 ed.)

At night when sick folk wakeful lie. The Dead Coach. Katharine Tynan. HBV; VA

At night, when the black water-hen. The Heron. John Lyle Donaghy. NeIP

At night when there are no lights my city is a man who arises. The Lame One. Sherwood Anderson. AnAmPo; LA

At night you came and took my hand and we wandered. Dreaming of Yüan Chen. Po Chü-i. TrCh

At Nightfall. Charles Hanson Towne. BLPA; FaBoBe; NeHB (Nightfall.) PoToHe (new ed.)

At Nightfall, on the Wall of Paris. Victor Hugo, *tr. fr. French by* Alan Conder. TrFP

At nightfall they carried the stranger dead into the house. Wayfaring. George Trakl. AnGP

At nine in the morning there passed a church. Faintheart in a Railway Train. Thomas Hardy. EnLoPo

At nine o'clock the bus snouts cityward. Nine o'Clock. Louis Simpson. PoNe

At Nine Rivers, in the tenth year, in winter,—heavy snow. Releasing a Migrant "Yen" (Wild Goose). Po Chü-i. TrCh

At noon I watched. Immensity. John Hall Wheelock. BAP

At noon of night, and at the night's pale end. Apparitions. Thomas Bailey Aldrich. BAP; UnW

At noon she left her cavern cell. Imogen—in Wales. Thomas Caulfield Irwin. IrPN

At noon the elfin flakes began to fall. Snowfall. Marjorie Meeker. TBM

At noon they buried her. The day was fair. Death on the Rancherie. Emily Leavens. TwCaPo

At noon, Tithonus, withered by his singing. The Wedding. Conrad Aiken. AnAmPo; ChMo; CMP; TCPD

At noon, within the dusty town. Birch Stream. Anna Boynton Averill. LPS-2; SN

At once all the inanimate things burst out singing. The Desk. Wen Yi-tuo. WhP

At once, from hence, my lines and I depart. To Mr. T. W. John Donne. BoFr

At once I hate and love as well. Catullus, *tr. fr. Latin by* M. H. Tattersall. LaP

At once in blacke I disrespected walkt. On a Maide of Honour Seene by a Schollar in Sommerset Garden. Thomas Randolph. MePo

At once, she went, and found the Cyclopes. Artemis Visits the Cyclopes. Callimachus. OxBG

At once with him they rose. Hell. Milton. *Fr.* Paradise Lost, II. OBS
At One o'Clock in the Morning. Baudelaire, *tr. fr. French by* Bert M-P. Leefmans. AnFP
At one o'clock the wind with sudden shift. The Shipwreck. Byron. *Fr.* Don Juan, II. MCCG
At one point of the journey, a memorable one. A Valentine. Hal Summers. ChMP
At one the Apocalypse had spoken. Karl Shapiro. Recapitulations, II. FiMAP
At Palomar. Sister Mary Edwardine. JKCP (1955 ed.)
At Paris, hard by the Maine barriers. Thackeray. *Fr.* The Chronicle of the Drum. OtMeF
At Paris it was, at the opera there. Aux Italiens. "Owen Meredith." BeLS; BLPA; BMEP; FaBoBe; HBV; LPS-1; PTA-2; TreFS; VA
At Parting. Heine, *tr. fr. German by* Dwight Durling. AnGP
At Parting. Swinburne. HBV; POTT; ViBoPo; VLEP
At Parting. *Unknown.* SeCL
At Pei-mang how they rise to Heaven. The Desecration of the Han Tombs. Chang Tsai. TrCh
At Penshurst. Edmund Waller. EPS; OAEP; PoFS; ReEn
(At Penshurst Another.) SeCV-1
At Piccadilly Circus. Vivian de Sola Pinto. OBMV
At play in April skies that spread. The Swallow. John Burroughs. BLA
At Polwart on the Green. Polwart on the Green. Allan Ramsay. CEP
At Port Royal. Whittier. PAH, *abr.*; PAP
Song of the Negro Boatman, *sel.* GN
At Prayer Meeting. Margaret E. Sangster. PraP
At Prime Jesus was y-led. William of Shoreham. *Fr.* Hours of the Passion. ACP; CAW
At Pylos. Homer, *tr. fr. Greek by* J. W. Mackail. *Fr.* The Odyssey, III. OxBG
At Quebec. Jean Blewett. CaP; OCL
At Quincey's moat [*or* mote] the straggling [*or* squandering] village ends. Almswomen. Edmund Blunden. GTBS; LBBV; OBMV; POTE; ShBV-3
At Rest in the Blast. Marianne Moore. MoAB; MoAmPo (1950 ed.)
At Richmond the people walked along by the river. Mr. Symons at Richmond, Mr. Pope at Twickenham. Julian Symons. WaP
At Rochecoart,/ Where the hills part. Provincia Deserta. Ezra Pound. CrMA; OxBA; TCPD
At Sagamore the Chief lies low. Sagamore. Corinne Roosevelt Robinson. BAP; HBMV; PoRL
At Saint-Germain. Léon Paul Fargue, *tr. fr. French by* Wallace Fowlie. MiCF
At Saint Patrick's Purgatory. *At. to* Donnchadh mor O'Dala, *tr. fr. Middle Irish by* Seán O'Faoláin. AnIL; LiTW; LyMA; OnYI; SiB
At Sainte-Marguerite. Trumbull Stickney. LiTA; MoVE; OxBA; TwAmPo
At Ste. Thérèse. S. Frances Harrison. BoCaPo (1943 ed.)
At School-Close. Whittier. PoRL; PTA-1
At school I sometimes read a book. My Education. James Kenneth Stephen. WhC
At Sea. Allan Cunningham. *See* Wet Sheet and a Flowing Sea, A.
At Sea. D. H. Rogers. AnNZ
At Sea. John T. Trowbridge. EtS
At Sestos, Hero dwelt; Hero the fair[e]. Hero the Fair[e]. Christopher Marlowe. *Fr.* Hero and Leander. FaBoEn; WHA
At Set of Sun. "George Eliot." *See* Count That Day Lost.
At Set of Sun. Mary Ashley Townsend. AA
At setting day and rising morn. Song. Allan Ramsay. HBV; LPS-1
At seven, when I go to bed. A Child's Thought. Robert Louis Stevenson. BoTP
At Seventy-two, *sel.* Thomas Dunn English.
"'Tis nearly over; in this darkening hour." PoP
At Shakespeare's Grave. Irving Browne. AA
At Shelley's birth. To Shelley. John Banister Tabb. AA; LBAP
At Singing Time. Anne P. L. Field. MOAH
At six—I well remember when. Growing Old. "Vandyke Brown." PR
At six o'clock we were waiting for coffee. A Miracle for Breakfast. Elizabeth Bishop. AmP; FiMAP; LiTA; MiAP
At sixteen years she knew no care. Butterflies. John Davidson. HBV; LEAP
At Sparta; Helen and Menelaus. Homer. *See* Helen, Menelaos, and Memories of Troy.
At Sparta; Menelaus and Proteus. Homer, *pr. tr. fr. Greek by* S. H. Butcher *and* Andrew Lang. *Fr.* The Odyssey, IV. OxBG
At Stadacona half the sky. Cartier Arrives at Stadacona. William T. Allison. CPG
At steeplecock height. Quebec. Eldon Grier. PeCV
At Stiklestad, ranged. Tord Foleson. Per Sivle. AnNoLy
At Stratford-on-Avon. Mackenzie Bell. VA
At summer eve, when Heaven's ethereal bow. Thomas Campbell. *Fr.* The Pleasures of Hope. EnRP
At Sunrise. Rosa Zagnoni Marinoni. PoToHe
At sunrise, swimming [*or* striking] out to sea. The Voice. W. W. Gibson. CV; TCPD
At Sunset. Ivy O. Eastwick. BoTP
At Sunset. Louis V. Ledoux. HBV
At Sunset. Steingrímur Thorsteinsson, *tr. fr. Icelandic by* Jakobina Johnson. IcP
At Sunset. Wordsworth. *See* It Is a Beauteous Evening . . .
At sunset my brown nightingales. Nightingales. Grace Hazard Conkling. HBMV
At sunset our white butterflies. Lullaby. Joseph Russell Taylor. BOL
At sunset under the low clouds, clustered like rocks. Fairytales. Peter Hellings. MoWP
At table yonder sits the man we seek. At the Mermaid Inn. Charles Lotin Hildreth. AA
At Tara [*or* Tarah] today, in this awful hour. St. Patrick's Hymn before Tara [*or* Tarah]. James Clarence Mangan. EnRP; GoBC
At Tea. Thomas Hardy. Satires of Circumstance, I. EPP; PoVP; TyEnPo
At Thames faire port. Praise of Poets. William Browne. *Fr.* Britannia's Pastorals, II, Song 1. OBS
At that time, saith the Lord, they shall bring out the bones. Peace! and There Is No Peace. Jeremiah, Bible, *O.T.* WoL
At the Airport. John Malcolm Brinnin. MoAB
At the Altar-Rail. Thomas Hardy. Satires of Circumstance, IX. MBP; MoAB; MoBrPo; PoVP
At the Aquarium. Max Eastman. AnAmPo; BAP; FaPON; HBMV; LA; LEAP; OTPC (1946 ed.); PoMa; StaSt; WGRP
At the Ascension. Luis de León. *See* Ascension, The.
At the Assumption. Luis de León. *See* Assumption of the Virgin, The.
At the Back of the North Wind, *sel.* George Macdonald.
Baby, The, *fr. ch.* 23. FaPON; HBV; HBVY; LPS-1; MPB; OTPC; PTA-1; RAR; TreF; TVC; TVSH; VA
(Where Did You Come From?) BLPA; FaFP
At the back of the pompous houses. Green Crosses. Abbie Farwell Brown. CV
At the Ball Game. Roswell Martin Field. InMe
At the Ball Game. William Carlos Williams. *See* Crowd at the Ball Game, The.
At the banquet tables of our social gatherings, I was ridiculed. Propertius. Elegies, III, 25. LaP
At the barren heart of midnight. Nocturn. W. E. Henley. In Hospital, XXVII. BPN
At the Battery Sea-Wall. Clifford James Laube. GoYe
At the beginning of the meat. Po, Po, Po, Po,/ [I] Love Brawn and So Do Mo. *Unknown.* AnEC
At the beginning of winter a cold chill falls. The Nineteen Han Poems, XII. *Unknown, tr. fr. Chinese.* WhP
At the beginning of winter a cold spirit comes. Old Chinese Poem [*or* Seventeen Old Poems, 16]. *Unknown, tr. by* Arthur Waley. BoFr; TrCh
At the black wood's corner, not one green bud. Pluviose. Julian Bell. ChMP
At the bottom of the river. The Curve. Bocho Yamamura. PoLJ
At the Bottom of the Well. Louis Untermeyer. MAP
At the break of Christmas Day. The Waits. Margaret Deland. COAH; DD; HH
At the breast of Poesy. Poesy. Paul Valéry. TrFP
At the British Museum. Richard Aldington. BLV; MBP; MoBrPo
At the British War Cemetery, Bayeux. Charles Causley. POTE (1959 ed.)
At the Cannon's Mouth. Herman Melville. PAH
At the Carnival. Anne Spencer. BANP; CDC; PoNe
At the Cedars. Duncan Campbell Scott. BoCaPo; CaP; CPG; OCL; PCN; VA
At the Cenotaph. "Hugh MacDiarmid." NAMP
At the Cenotaph. Siegfried Sassoon. ChMo; CMP
(Make Them Forget). MaRV
At the Church Gate. Thackeray. *Fr.* Pendennis, *ch.* 32. BMEP; EPN; HBV; LoPo; LPS-1; VA
At the Circus. Dorothy Aldis. TiPo (1952 ed.); UTS
Bare-Back Rider.
Elephants, The.
Seals, The.
At the close of a winter day. The Rhyme of the Three Captains. Kipling. BeLS
At the Close of Day. Iku Takenaka, *tr. fr. Japanese by* Takamichi Ninomiya *and* D. J. Enright. PoLJ
At the close of the day when the hamlet is still. James Beattie. *Fr.* The Hermit. EV-3; LPS-3
At the Closed Gate of Justice. James David Corrothers. BANP
At the Comedy. Arthur Stringer. HBV
At the Convent Gate. Austin Dobson. VLEP

At the corner of the rue de la Verrerie. The Neighborhood of Saint-Merri. Robert Desnos. MiCF
At the corner of Wood Street, when daylight appears. The Reverie of Poor Susan [*or* Poor Susan's Dream]. Wordsworth. BPN; CBE; CBPC; CH; EM-2; EmBrPo; EnRP; GEPC; GTBS; GTBS-D; GTBS-W; GTSE; GTSL; HBV; MCCG; MW; OTPC (1923 ed.); OxBoLi; ShBV-1
At the creation God made women's natures. Some Women. Semonides. OxBG
At the cross her station keeping. Stabat Mater [Dolorosa]. *At. to* Jacopone da Todi, *tr. fr. Latin by* Richard Mant *and* Edward Caswall. OlF; TreFS; WGRP; WHL
At the Cross thy station keeping. St. Monica. Francis Thompson. MeRV
At the Crossroad. Itzik Manger, *tr. fr. Yiddish by* Sarah Zweig Betsky. OnCuPl
At the Crossroad Lies Buried. Heine, *tr. fr. German by* Vernon Watkins. AnGP
At the crossroad the summer wind sings. At the Crossroad. Itzik Manger. OnCuPl
At the Crossroads. Richard Hovey. BAP; BBV (1951 ed.); BLP; BoFr, *abr.*; CP; HBV; LBAP; MAP; MoAmPo (1942 ed.); NeMA; PFY; PoMa; PYM
At the cross-roads I came upon the delinquent moon. Templeogue. Blanaid Salkeld. NeIP
At the cry of the first bird. The Crucifixion. *Unknown.* GTIV; OnYI; OxBI
At the dance in the village. Mairgread ni Chealleadh. Edward Walsh. IrPN
At the Dark Hour. Paul Dehn. WaP
At the Dawn. Alice Macdonald Kipling. MaRV
At the dawn I seek Thee. Morning Song. Solomon ibn Gabirol. TrJP
At the dead centre of the boundless plain. The Riders. Edwin Muir. *Fr.* Variations on a Time Theme. MoP; MoVE
At the Discharge of Cannon Rise the Drowned. Hubert Witheford. AnNZ
At the Dog Show. Christopher Morley. AlBD; MoShBr; MPB
At the Door. Lillie Fuller Merriam. PoToHe
At the door of his hut sat Massasoit. The Peace Message. Burton Egbert Stevenson. PAH
At the door on summer evenings. Hiawatha's Childhood [*or* Firefly Song]. Longfellow. *Fr.* The Song of Hiawatha. BoTP; PCD
At the Doors. "Der Nistor," *tr. fr. Yiddish by* Joseph Leftwich. TrJP
At the Draper's. Thomas Hardy. Satires of Circumstance, XII. EnLi-2 (1949 ed.); MBP; MoAB; MoBrPo
At the Dreamland Gate. Mary E. Wilkins Freeman. BOL
At the earliest ending of winter. Not Ideas about the Thing but the Thing Itself. Wallace Stevens. ViBoPo (1958 ed.)
At the edge of all the ages. The Song of Finis. Walter de la Mare. MoBrPo
At the Edge of the Bay. Thomas Caldecot Chubb. EtS
At the Edge of the Day. Clarence Urmy. HBMV
At the edge of the shore sits a yellow-haired girl. The Embroidery on the Kerchief. Kostas Krystallis. MoGP
At the end I will bellow my challenge. Phantoms. Harry McGuire. CAW
At the end of a full day of walking we found. Passion. Galway Kinnell. NePoAm
At the end of a long-walled garden. The Cottage Hospital. John Betjeman. MoVE; UnPo (3d ed.)
At the end of my yard there is a vat. Riddle. *Unknown.* ChTr
At the End of Play. Bertel Gripenberg, *tr. fr. Swedish by* Charles W. Stork. AnSL
At the End of Spring. Po Chü-i, *tr. fr. Chinese by* Arthur Waley. TrCh
At the end of the battle. Masses. César Vallejo. TwSpPo
At the end of the bough. Sweet Apple. James Stephens. ChMo; CMP
At the End of the Day. Richard Hovey. HBVY; LBMV; PC; StaSt; YT
At the End of the Way. Verner von Heidenstam, *tr. fr. Swedish by* Charles W. Stork. AnSL
At the End of Things. Arthur Edward Waite. WGRP
At the end will be but rust. The Empty Soul. Walter R. Bowie. MaRV
At the entrance, there where all roads begin. Song of Thomas, Departed. "Winétt de Rokha." AnCL
At the equinox when the earth was veiled in a late rain. Continent's End. Robinson Jeffers. AnFE; AWP; CoAnAm; ImOP; InPo; JAWP; MOAP; ReMP; TwAmPo; WBP
At the farthest point of the cold bright azure sky. Fantasia under the Clear Sky. Kenji Miyazawa. PoLJ
At the feast of Belshazzar and a thousand of his lords. The Handwriting on the Wall. Knowles Shaw. BLPA
At the Fireside. Afanasi Afanasievich Fet, *tr. fr. Russian.* TrRV, *tr. by* Babette Deutsch; WaL, *tr. by* Sir Cecil Kisch
At the first hour from dawn. Journey through the Night. John Holloway. NePoEA
At the first hour, it was as if one said, "Arise." Spring. John Gould Fletcher. NV; PFY; SBMV
At the first peep of dawn she roused me! The Wanderer: Paterson—the Strike. William Carlos Williams. MAPA; TwAmPo
At the first stepping-stone, the past of water. The Stepping Stones. Conrad Aiken. CrMA
At the Fishhouses. Elizabeth Bishop. FiMAP; MoVE
At the Fishing Settlement. Alistair Campbell. AnNZ
At the Florists' Feast in Norwich. Matthew Stevenson. SeCL
(Stay! O stay! Ye Winged Howers.) AEV
At the focus of thought there is no face. The Crystal Skull. Kathleen Raine. FaBoMo; NeBP
At the foot of a great pine, in the wild country. Reconciliation. John Hall Wheelock. CrMA
At the foot of the south mountain I sow beans. Living in the Country. Tao Yuan-ming. WhP
At the foot of yon mountain, where the fountain doth flow. Red River Shore. *Unknown.* ABF; CoSo
At the Fountain. Marcabrun, *tr. fr. French by* Harriet Waters Preston. AWP; JAWP; WBP
At the Front. John Erskine. HBMV
At the Frontier. Tu Fu, *tr. fr. Chinese.* WhP
At the game which is my life. The Game. Conrado Nalé Roxlo. AnCL; OnPM
At the Garden Gate. David McCord. FaPON; RIS; StaSt
At the Garden Rail. A. M. Buckton. BoSA
At the Gate. Chaucer. *Fr.* Troilus and Criseyde. SeCePo
At the Gate of Heaven. Byron. *Fr.* The Vision of Judgment. OBRV
(Archangel, The.) LoBV
(Where He Gazed a Gloom Pervaded, *br. sel.*) LiA
At the gate of old Granada, when all its bolts are barred. The Lamentation for Celin. *Unknown, tr. by* John Gibson Lockhart. AWP; JAWP; OuHeWo; PoFr; WBP
At the gate of the West I stand. "Scum o' the Earth." Robert Haven Schauffler. CP; GDAH; HBV; IDAH; LBMV; NV; OBAV; PaA; PC; PoFr; POT; PoTo; TCAP
At the Goal. Christina Rossetti. OQP; QP-1
At the Grand Canyon. George Sterling. MuM
At the Grave of a Land-Shark. Ernest G. Moll. WhC
At the Grave of Burns [1803]. Wordsworth. Memorials of a Tour in Scotland, 1803, II. BEL; BPN; EM-2; EmBroPo; EnLi-2; EnRP; ERP; GEPC; PtP
At the Grave of Cecil Rhodes. Peter Jackson. BoSA
At the Grave of Champernowne. John Albee. HBV
At the Grave of Dante Gabriel Rossetti. Mackenzie Bell. VA
At the Grave of Henry James. W. H. Auden. LiTA; MoPo
At the Grave of Henry Vaughan. Siegfried Sassoon. ChMo; ChMP; CMP; POTE; PtP; TriL
At the Grave of My Grandfather. Pearce Young. PtPa
At the Grave of Poe. Clinton Scollard. GA
At the Grave of Selvaggia. Cino da Pistoia. *See* Sonnet: Of the Grave of Selvaggia.
At the Grave of Walker. Joaquin Miller. AA; AnAmPo; AnFE; APA; CoAnAm; LA; OBAV
At the Great Wall of China. Edmund Blunden. HaMV
At the great water's edge/ Golden Narcissus lies. Narcissus. Alistair Campbell. AnNZ
At the grey dawn, amongst the falling leaves. A Bird from the West. Dora Sigerson Shorter. OBVV
At the Hacienda. Bret Harte. AA; OBAV
At the Hawk's Well, *sel.* W. B. Yeats.
Salt Sea Wind. LiA
At the head of Wear Water, about twelve at noon. The North Country Collier. *Unknown.* SG
At the Heart. Mark Antony De Wolfe Howe. PC
At the heart of the cyclone tearing the sky. The Place of Peace. Edwin Markham. MaRV; OQP; QP-2
At the high ridge. The Wooden Christ. Martha Foote Crow. ChIP; StJW
At the inn there was no room. The Loan of a Stall. James L. Duff. ISi
At the Instance of a Noble Lady. John Skelton. CaAE
At the Keyhole. Walter de la Mare. MBP; MoAB; MoBrPo
At the king's gate the subtle noon. Coronation. Helen Hunt Jackson. AA; BeLS; GN; HBV; LBAP; OBAV; PFY; TCAP
At the Lamb's high feast we sing. Praise to the Lamb. *Unknown.* EOAH
At the Last. Richard Doddridge Blackmore. *See* Dominus Illuminatio Mea.
At the Last. Witter Bynner. TwAmPo
At the Last. Vincent David Engels. CAW
At the Last. "Fiona Macleod," VLEP
At the Last. Philip Bourke Marston. HBV; VA
At the last, tenderly. The Last Invocation [*or* The Imprisoned Soul]. Walt Whitman. AmP; AnFE; APA; APW; BLV; BoLiVe; CoAnAm; GTBS-D; HBV; IAP; LBAP; MAP; MaRV; MoAmPo; MOAP; NeMA; OBEV; OnAP; OQP; OxBA; PoEL-5; QP-1; RiBV; TCAP; TOP; TrGrPo; TrPWD; WGRP

At the last tumult of the railroad. Anniversary of Antonia Pozzi's Death by Suicide. Vittorio Serini. OnPM
At the Lavender Lantern. Charles Divine. HBMV
At the Leap of the Waters. Edward F. Garesché. JKCP
At the Lincoln Memorial. William E. Brooks. OQP; QP-2
At the Lincoln Tomb. John H. Bryant. PGD
At the long meadow's end, where the road runs. The Pond. Howard Nemerov. FiMAP
At the Lord's table waiting, robed and stoled. An Incident. Frederick Tennyson. GoBC
At the Lowest Ebb of Night. Robert P. Tristram Coffin. MuM
At the Manor House. Christian Winther, *tr. fr. Danish by* Charles W. Stork. BoDS
At the Mermaid, *sel.* Robert Browning.
My Sun Sets to Rise Again. MaRV
At the Mermaid Cafeteria. Christopher Morley. BAP; PFY; PoeMoYo
At the Mermaid Inn. Charles Lotin Hildreth. AA
At the Mid Hour of Night. Thomas Moore. AnIV; CBOV; EV-4; FaBoEn; GoBC; GTBS; GTIV; GTSE; GTSL; HBV; LEAP; OAEP; OBEV; OBRV; OxBI; PoEL-4; TIP; TreFS; UnW; ViBoPo
("At the mid hour of night, when stars are weeping, I fly.") GTBS-D; GTBS-W
At the Mid Hour of Night. *Unknown, tr. fr. Greek by* Thomas Stanley. GrL; OxBG; WoL
At the mid-hour of twilight, in the time. Mary. Tavallali. PeP
At the midnight in the silence of the sleep-time. Epilogue. Robert Browning. *Fr.* Asolando. AEV; BEL; BMEP; BoLiVe; BPN; CoBE; EM-2; EmBrPo; EnL; EnLi-2; EnLit; EPN; EPP; FaBoEn; FiP; GEPC; GTSL; HBV; HBVY; HiLiEn; InP; LEAP; MaRV; OAEP; OBVV; OHFP; OQP; OuHeWo; PC; PoeMoYo; PoVP; QP-1; TCEP; TOP; TrGrPo; VA; ViBoPo; ViPo; ViPP; VLEP
At the midsummer, when the hay was down. Four Years. Dinah Maria Mulock Craik. HBV
At the Moon's Eclipse. Robert P. Tristram Coffin. NeTW
At the muezzin's call for prayer. Ad Coelum. Harry Romaine. BLPA; FaBoBe; NeHB
At the Name of Jesus. Caroline Maria Noel. OlF
At the New Year. Kenneth Patchen. AnFE; CoAnAm; TwAmPo
At the Ninth Hour. John Lancaster Spalding. *Fr.* God and the Soul. AA
At the old concert hall on the Bowery. She Is More to Be Pitied than Censured William B. Gray. BeLS; BLPA; TreF
At the one shot. The Caged Eagle's Death Dream. Robinson Jeffers. PoF
At the Pantomime. Oliver Wendell Holmes. AnNE
At the Party. Freda Laughton. NeIP
At the Place of the Roman Baths. "Richard Scrace." CaP; CPG; OCL
At the Place of the Sea. Annie Johnson Flint. BLPA; OQP; QP-2
(Red Sea Place in Your Life, The.) BLRP
At the Poem Society a black-haired man stands up to say. Fresh Air. Kenneth Koch. NeAP
At the Portal. Frances Ridley Havergal. BLRP
At the President's Grave. Richard Watson Gilder. GA; PAH
At the Rendezvous. A. W. Schack von Staffeldt, *tr. fr. Danish by* Charles W. Stork. BoDS
At the report agony like dark mist clouded his eyesight. Homer. *Fr.* The Iliad, XVIII. GrPo
At the rise of summer a hundred beasts and trees. The Beginning of Summer. Po Chü-i. TrCh
At the River's Edge. Li Po, *tr. into English by* James Whitall *fr. the Chinese-to-French translation of* Judith Gautier. ChLP
At the Road-House. Bliss Carman. MOB
At the round earth's imagin'd [*or* imagined] corners, blow. Holy Sonnets, VII. John Donne. AnEnPo; AtBAP; ATP (1953 ed.); ChTr; CoBE; CoEV; ElSeCe; EnLP; EPS; EV-2; ExPo; FaBoEn; InPo; LiTB; LiTG; LoBV; MaPo; MeLP; MePo; MyFE; NBE; OAEP; OBS; OxBoCh; PeBoSo; Po; PoD; PoEL-2; PoFS; ReaPo; ReEn; SeCeV; SeCV-1; SeEP; ShBV-4; TriL; TuPP; TwCrTr; TwHP; TwP; ViBoPo
At the rude goodness. Vernal Showers. David O'Neil. AnAmPo; LA
At the safari's end a porter. H. C. Bosman. *Fr.* The Luck in the Square Stone. BoSA
At the Salon. Florence Wilkinson Evans. HBV
At the Saturday Club. Oliver Wendell Holmes. AmPP (3d ed.); CoBA; IAP
At the Seaside. George Ewart Evans. MoWP
At the Seaside. Robert Louis Stevenson. FaPON; GFA; MPB (1956 ed.); OTPC; StVeCh (1940 ed.); SUS; TiPo
At the Ship. R. P. Lister. FiBHP
At the Shrine. Richard Kendall Munkittrick. AA; OBAV
At the side of my husband, Eliza Spaulding. Donald Burnie. PaA
At the siege of Belle Isle. *Unknown.* OxNR
At the Sign of the Cock. Sir Owen Seaman. BOHV; PA
At the silken sign of the poppy. Where Dreams Are Sold. Jean Graham. OCL
At the Slackening of the Tide. James Wright. UnPo (3d ed.)
At the Sorghum-Bilin'. James Larkin Pearson. NoCaPo
At the source of my forces my memory. All Life. Paul Eluard. OnPM
At the Stage-Door. Arthur Symons. LEAP; POTT
At the stars thou gazest, Aster. The Young Astronomer. Plato. GrPE; GrR
At the Stevenson Fountain. Wallace Irwin. POT; PoTo
At the Sunrise in 1848. Dante Gabriel Rossetti. BPN; PoVP
At the Symphony. Robert Nathan. HBMV; MAP; PoRL; TSW
At the Theater. Rachel Field. FaPON; GFA; MPB
At the Theater. A. P. Herbert. FiBHP
At the time of parting. Translations from Modern Japanese Poetry. Takeko Kujo. PFE
At the time when blossoms. A "Tzu-yeh" Song. *Unknown.* ChLP; TrCh
At the time when blossoms fall from the cherry-tree. Summer Song. Wu Ti. AlDL
At the Tomb of Rachel. "Yehoash," *tr. fr. Yiddish by* Isidore Goldstick. TrJP
At the Tomb of Washington. Clinton Scollard. DD; GA; MC; OHIP; PEDC
At the Tombs of the House of Savoy. William Jay Smith. NePoAm-2
At the Top of My Voice. Vladimir Mayakovsky, *tr. fr. Russian by* Herbert Marshall. OnHM
Sels.
"Let fame," *tr. by* Babette Deutsch. TrRV
"My verse will reach you," *tr. by* Babette Deutsch. LiTW; TrRV
At the top of the house the apples are laid in rows. Moonlit Apples. John Drinkwater. BoTP; OBMV; PoRA; TCPD
At the Top of the Road. Charles Buxton Going. HBV
At the Turning of the Tide. James Harold Manning. CPG
At the village emporium in Woodstock. Limerick. Frederick Winsor. WhC
At the Washing of My Son. Su T'ung-po, *tr. fr. Chinese by* Kenneth Rexroth. OnPC
At the Water. Elizabeth Madox Roberts. LS
At the wayside well I stooped down for to drink. Haunted. Helen Lanyon. GTIV
At the Wedding March. Gerard Manley Hopkins. PoLi; ViP
At the wedding of Shon Maclean. The Wedding of Shon Maclean. Robert Buchanan. EBSV
At the western window I paused from writing rescripts. Being on Duty All Night in the Palace and Dreaming of Hsien-yu Temple. Po Chü-i. TrCh
At the wheel plied Mariline. Mariline. Charles Sangster. BoCaPo
At the White Mass. Lilies. Padraic Colum. NePoAm
At the wicket. The Rush Hour. Fuyuhiko Kitagawa. PoLJ
At the Window. Praxilla, *tr. fr. Greek by* T. F. Higham. OxBG
At the window ledge concealing. Saint. Stéphane Mallarmé. AnFP
At the Worst. Israel Zangwill. WGRP
At the "Ye That Do Truly." Charles Williams. OxBoCh
At the Zoo. A. A. Milne. FaPON; TiPo (1959 ed.)
At the Zoo. Anne May Smith. PCH
At the Zoo. Israel Zangwill. TrJP
At thee the Mocker sneers in cold derision. The Maid of Orleans. Schiller. AWP; JAWP; WBP
At Thermopylae. Simonides. *See* Thermopylae.
At these high words great heaven began to shake. A Prayer Brings Rain. Tasso, *tr. by* Edward Fairfax. *Fr.* Godfrey of Bulloigne. OBSC
At these two men well may we churchmen scoff. Simon and Judas. Kenneth W. Porter. ChIP
At thieves I bark'd, at lovers wagg'd my tail. Epitaph on the Lap-Dog of Lady Frail. John Wilkes. ALV
At thirteen I followed the army and garrisoned a border town. Song of a Soldier. "Monk of Eight Fingers." WhP
At Thirty Years. Byron. *Fr.* Don Juan, I. FiP
(Labuntur Anni, *longer sel.*) BPN
At This Farewell. Wordsworth. *See* Dear Native Regions.
At This Moment of Time. Delmore Schwartz. TwAmPo
At this the last yet second meeting. The Encounter. Lawrence Durrell. *Fr.* Eight Aspects of Melissa. NeBP
At Tide Water. Sir Charles G. D. Roberts. PeCV
At Timber Line. Frank H. Mayer. PoOW
At Timberline. Richard Leon Spain. MuM
At times a breath. Mystery. George Sterling. MuM
At times, concealed by cunning clouds in the reaches. Sunset. Victor Hugo. TrFP
At times I am fast confined by my Master. A Storm. *Unknown.* *Fr.* Riddles. EnLi-1; OuHeWo
At times I lie stretched out, and never rise. Victor Hugo. *Fr.* Paroles sur la dune. LiA

At times I resort, beyond man's discerning. Wind. *Unknown. Fr.* Riddles. AnOE
At times I travel in tracks undreamed of. A Storm, II. *Unknown. Fr.* Riddles. OuHeWo
At times 'mid daily toils and tumults unrelenting. Aleksey Konstantinovich Tolstoy, *tr. fr. Russian by* Sir Cecil Kisch. WaL
At times the air is sad. Sad Air. Carmen Alicia Cadilla. AnCL
At times these walls enchanted fade, it seems. My Library. Henry Jerome Stockard. NoCaPo
At times, when all's asleep, I contemplate. Celestial Fête. Victor Hugo. TrFP
At times when we're walking. Underground Rumbling. James S. Tippett. GFA
At times with self (when self is gripped anew). William Ellery Leonard. *Fr.* Two Lives, Pt. III. MOAP
At Timon's Villa. Pope. *See* Timon's Villa.
At Torcello. Arthur Hugh Clough. *See* Help, Sure Help.
At Trumpyngtoun nat fer from Cantebrigge. The Reeve's Tale. Chaucer. *Fr.* The Canterbury Tales. ViBoPo
At Twelfth Night twilight now. Twelfth Night. Philip Booth. NePoEA
At twelve bell answers bell. Angelus-Time near Dublin. William Bedell Stanford. NeIP
At Twilight. Peyton Van Rensselaer. AA
At twilight time, when the lamps are lit. Coyote [*or* Father Coyote]. George Sterling. DDA; PoTo
At twilight, when I am alone with my thoughts. Evening. Stephan G. Stephansson. IcP
At two o'clock in the morning, if you open your window and listen. The Dawn Wind. Kipling. POT; PoTo
At Vallauris and Vence, Picasso and Matisse. Picasso and Matisse. Robert Francis. NePoAm
At Venice. Arthur Hugh Clough. ViPo
In the Piazza at Night.
On the Lido.
At Villequier. Victor Hugo, *tr. fr. French by* Alan Conder. TrFP
At Viscount Nelson's lavish funeral. 1805. Robert Graves. ChMP; FaBoCh; HaMV; LoGBV
At Waking. Ethelwyn Wetherald. CPG
At War. Charles Madge. FaBoMo
At Warm Springs. William Rose Benét. PoRL
At Wednesbury there was a cocking. Wednesbury Cocking. *Unknown.* EnSB
At Welbedacht. A. M. Buckton. BoSA
At what a great cost God gave to the world. He's Come! The Saviour Has Come! Alice Mortenson. BePJ
At whiles (yea oftentimes) I muse over. Dante. *Fr.* La Vita Nuova. AWP; JAWP; WBP
At Whose Sheltering Shall the Day Sea. W. S. Graham. FaBoMo
At Willie's wedding o' the green. Jenny Dang the Weaver. Sir Alexander Boswell. EBSV
At Winter's End. Sister Mary Madeleva. JKCP
At Woodlawn I heard the dead cry. The Lost Son. Theodore Roethke. CoBMV; FiMAP; MiAP; MoPo; NePA; ReMP; TrGrPo (rev. ed.)
At Woodward's Gardens. Robert Frost. ImOP
At Wu Shan, of an autumn night. The Fireflies. Tu Fu. OnPM; PoHN
At Year's-End. Richard Wilbur. LiTM (rev. ed.); MiAP; NePA
(Years-End.) FiMAP; NePoEA
At Your Service; the Panama Gang. Berton Braley. BLPA
At your voice,/ Panic, despair, flee away. Contagion of Courage. Matthew Arnold. *Fr.* Rugby Chapel. MaRV
Atalanta. Maurice Thompson. OBAV
Atalanta in Calydon. Swinburne. ViPo
Sels.
Before the Beginning of Years. BEL; EnL; EPN; FaFP; HBV; LiTB; LiTG; OAEP; PoFS; PoVP; PreP; TyEnPo; ViPP; VLEP; WHA
(Chorus: "Before the beginning of years.") EnLit; GTBS-D; GTBS-W; LoBV; MBP; OBVV; PIR; REAL; ViP
(Chorus from "Atalanta.") OBEV (new ed.)
(Choruses from "Atalanta in Calydon.") AEV; EnLi-2; GTSE; LiA; POTT; ViBoPo
(Life of Man, The.) BMEP; BPN; EmBrPo; TOP
(Making of Man, The.) GDAH
(Man.) BLV; BoLiVe; TrGrPo
Death of Meleager, The. BMEP; BPN; OBVV; PoVP; VLEP
Final Chorus: "Who shall contend," *br. sel.* BPN
"Maiden, and mistress of the months and stars." PoEL-5
(Invocation.) PoVP
Not as with Sundering of the Earth. PoVP; VLEP
(Fate) BPN; EmBrPo
"O that I now, I too were."
(Nature.) BPN; EmBrPo
Sweet wise death of old men honorable, The."
(Fortunate Dead, The.) EmBrPo
We Have Seen Thee, O Love. BEL; PoVP; VLEP, *abr.*
(Chorus: "We have seen thee, O Love.") VA
(Choruses from "Atalanta in Calydon.") EnLi-2; LiA
(Love and Love's Mates.) BMEP, *abr.;* BPN, *abr.;* EmBrPo
When the Hounds of Spring [Are on Winter's Traces]. BLV; BoLiVe; CoBE; EnL; FaBoBe; HBV; LiTB; MBP; PIAE; PoFS; PoVP; TreF; TrGrPo; TyEnPo; ViPP; VLEP
(Chorus: "When the hounds of spring are on winter's traces.") AnFE; AWP; CaAE; CBOV; CoEV; EnLit; EPN; EPP; ExPo; FaBoEn; InPo; JAWP; LEAP; LPS-2; OBEV; OuHeWo; PIR; Po; REAL; RG, *abr.;* SeCeV; ShBV-4; TCEP; TOP; VA; ViP; WBP
(Chorus from "Atalanta.") EV-5; GTSL
(Choruses from "Atalanta in Calydon.") EnLi-2; LiA; ViBoPo
(Hounds of Spring, The.) BEL; BMEP; YT
(Huntsmen's Chorus.) GTML
(Youth of the Year, The.) BPN; EmBrPo
"Who hath given man speech?"
(Choruses from "Atalanta in Calydon.") ViBoPo
Atalanta in Camden-Town. "Lewis Carroll." ALV; CenHV; PA
Atalanta's Defeat. William Morris. *Fr.* The Earthly Paradise. VA
Atalanta's Race. William Morris. *Fr.* The Earthly Paradise. BEL; BMEP, *much abr.;* BPN; EV-5; LPS-1, *much abr.;* ViPo
Atalanta's Victory. William Morris. *Fr.* The Earthly Paradise. VA
Ataraxia. Bert Leston Taylor. HBMV; InMe
Atavism. Cale Young Rice. BAP; UnW
Atavism. Elinor Wylie. AnEnPo; HBMV; NP; TCAP
Athalie, *sel.* Racine, *tr. fr. French by* Charles Randolph.
Chorus: "God whose goodness filleth every clime, The." CAW; WGRP
Athanese Diakos, *sel.* Aristotelis Valaoritis, *tr. fr. Modern Greek by* Rae Dalven.
"Albanians still sleep, glutted, weary, The." MoGP
Atharva-Veda. *Unknown. See* Vedic Hymns.
Athassel Abbey. Louise Imogen Guiney. OBAV
Atheist and the Acorn, The. Countess of Winchilsea. WP
Atheist Buries His Son, The. Abu'l-Atahija, *tr. fr. Arabic by* Henry Baerlein. LiTW
Atheist's Tragedy, The, *sels.* Cyril Tourneur.
"Cease that harsh musick; we are not pleas'd with it," *fr.* V, i. AtBAP
"His body lies interred within this mold," *fr.* III, i. SiCE
(Epitaph on a Soldier.) ElL
Walking Next Day upon the Fatal Shore, *fr.* II, i. ViBoPo; WaaP
(Drowned Soldier, A.) BHV
Soldier's Death, A, *shorter sel.* SeCePo
Atheist's Wail, The. Dorothy Ducas. QS
Athelstan King. Battle of Brunanburh. *Unknown, tr. fr. Anglo-Saxon by* Tennyson. See Æthelstan King.
Athena's Faith. Aeschylus, *tr. fr. Greek by* E. H. Plumptre. *Fr.* Eumenides. LiA
Athenian Aeschylus, Euphorion's son,/ In fertile Gela lies. An Epitaph for Himself. Aeschylus, *tr. by* Hugh Macnaghten. GrL; GrPo
Athenian Aeschylus, Euphorion's son,/ This tomb at Gela holds. Aeschylus. Aeschylus (Simonides, *wr.*), *tr. by* Lord Neaves. OnPM
Athenian Dead, The. Simonides, *tr. fr. Greek by* T. F. Higham. GrL; OxBG; WoL
(Dead of Athens at Chalcis, The, *tr. by* F. L. Lucas.) GrPE
Athenian Monument, The. Simonides, *tr. fr. Greek by* William C. Lawton. GrL; OxBG
(On Those Who Fell at Plataea, *tr. by* Walter Leaf.) GrR; PoFr
Athenians, ye who are trying this first cause. The Areiopagus; a Higher Justice Come to Dwell among Men. Aeschylus, *tr. by* Lewis Campbell. *Fr.* Eumenides. GrR
Athens. Kostas Kariotakis, *tr. fr. Modern Greek by* Rae Dalven. MoGP
Athens. Milton. *Fr.* Paradise Regained, IV. OBS
(Athens the Eye of Greece, *shorter sel.*) TwCrTr
("Look once more ere we leave this specular Mount," *shorter sel.*) SeEP; ViBoPo
(Satan's Survey of Greece, *shorter sel.*) EV-2
(Vision of Athens, *shorter sel.*) TOP
Athens, *sel.* Rita Boumy Pappas, *tr. fr. Modern Greek by* Rae Dalven.
"Athens is critically ill." MoGP
Athens. Pindar, *tr. fr. Greek by* F. L. Lucas. GrPE
Athens. Nicephorus Vrettakos, *tr. fr. Modern Greek by* Rae Dalven. MoGP
Athens, a fragile kingdom by the foam. Triumph. John Crowe Ransom. HBMV
Athens is critically ill. Rita Boumy Pappas. *Fr.* Athens. MoGP

Athens. It is midnight. Athens. Nicephorus Vrettakos. MoGP
Athens the Eye of Greece. Milton. *See* Athens.
Athirst for insects, butterflies. Summer. Boris Pasternak. BoRS
Athirst in spirit, through the gloom. The Prophet. Pushkin. AWP; JAWP; LiTW; TrRV; WBP; WGRP
Athlete, virtuoso. For One Who Would Not Take His Life in His Hands. Delmore Schwartz. NAMP
Athleticism. Xenophanes, *tr. fr. Greek by* F. L. Lucas. GrPE
Athol Cummers. James Hogg. EBSV
Athulf and Ethilda. Sir Henry Taylor. *Fr.* Edwin the Fair. LPS-1
Athulf's Death Song. Thomas Lovell Beddoes. *Fr.* Death's Jest Book, IV, iii. VA
Athwart the harbour lingers yet. Sunrise along Shore. L. M. Montgomery. CPG
Athwart the jangling of our creeds is heard. Come, Follow Me! Thomas Curtis Clark. ChIP
Athwart the sky a lowly sigh. London. John Davidson. BSV; PoeT; VA
Athwart the sod which is treading for God. Francis Thompson. *Fr.* A Judgment in Heaven. CoBE
Athwart the sunrise of our western day. Achilles. Ernest Myers. OBVV; PtP
Athwart the whirling hailstones, through the darkness of December. The Goatherds' Thank-Offering. Leonidas of Tarentum. GrPE
Atisket, Atasket. *Unknown.* *See* Itiskit, Itaskit.
"Atkins." George Meredith. PoVP; SoV
Atlantic. Eugenio Florit, *tr. fr. Spanish by* H. R. Hays. TwSpPo
Atlantic. George Rostrevor Hamilton. NeTW
Atlantic and Pacific I have sailed. Travels. W. W. Gibson. PtOT
Atlantic Charter; 1942. Francis Brett Young. *Fr.* The Island. BBV (1951 ed.)
(Atlantic Charter, A.D. 1620–1942.) TiPo (1952 ed.)
Atlantic City Waiter. Countee Cullen. BAP
Atlantic is a stormy moat, and the Mediterranean, The. The Eye. Robinson Jeffers. CoBMV; CrMA; FaBoEn; GTBS-W; LiTA; LiTM; OxBA; WaP
Atlantic Moonrise. Vivian L. Virtue. PoNe
Atlantid islands, phantom-fair. Frederick William Henry Myers. *Fr.* Teneriffe. OBVV
Atlantides, The. Henry David Thoreau. *Fr.* A Week on the Concord and Merrimack Rivers. MOAP; ViBoPo
Atlantis. W. H. Auden. FaBoTw
Atlantis. Gordon Bottomley. AEV; POTE; PtOT; TCPD
Atlantis. Hart Crane. *Fr.* The Bridge. AnFE; AtBAP; CoAnAm; CoV; LiTA; LiTM; MOAP; MoPo; NePA; TwAmPo
Atlantis Regained. Edwin Björkman. NoCaPo (1941 ed.)
Atli sent of old to Gunnar. Attila the Hun. *Unknown.* *Fr.* The Elder Edda. PaOS
Atoll in the Mind, The. Alex Comfort. FaBoMo; GTBS-W; LiTB; LiTM; POTE; SeCePo
Atom, The. Thomas Thornely. QS
Atom from Atom. Emerson. *Fr.* Fragments on Nature and Life. ImOP
("Atom from atom yawns as far.") TiPo (1959 ed.)
Atomic Courtesy. Ethel Jacobson. FaFP; LiTM (rev. ed.); SiTL
Atoms are small things, The. Lucillius, *tr. fr. Greek by* Ralph Gladstone. GrPo
Atoms as old as stars. The Voice. Sara Teasdale. ChMo; CMP; NV
Atonement. Margaret E. Bruner. MaRV; PoToHe
Atonement, The. Gerald Gould. POTE
Atonement. Marie LeNart. ChIP; OQP; QP-1
Atonement, The. Milton. *Fr.* Paradise Lost, III. OBS
Atonement? Lord, who doth atone today? Atonement. Marie LeNart. ChIP; OQP; QP-1
Atossa. Matthew Arnold. *See* On the Death of a Favorite Canary.
Atri in Abruzzo, a small town. The Bell of Atri. Longfellow. *Fr.* Tales of a Wayside Inn. MW
Atrides Goes into Battle. Homer, *tr. fr. Greek by* George Chapman. *Fr.* The Iliad, XI. KN
Atropos. John Myers O'Hara. AnAmPo; BAP; LA; SBMV
Attack, The. Thomas Buchanan Read. PAH
Attack. Siegfried Sassoon. MBP; MCCG; MoBrPo; PoMa
Attack me, Father, now. Prayer for Peace. Johnstone G. Patrick. TrPWD
Attack on Finnsburg, The. *Unknown, tr. fr. Anglo-Saxon by* Francis B. Gummere. BEL
Attainment. Madison Cawein. WGRP
Attainment. Ferid ed-Din Attar, *tr. fr. Persian by* Edward Fitzgerald. *Fr.* The Bird-Parliament. PeP
Attainment, The. Coventry Patmore. The Angel in the House, I, iii, 3. OBVV
(Preludes, II.) GoBC
Attainment. Algernon Tassin. AA
Attainment. Ella Wheeler Wilcox. OQP; QP-2; WGRP
Attend [*or* Come], all ye who list to hear our noble England's praise. The Armada [*or* The Spanish Armada]. Macaulay, BeLS; BHV; CG; EV-4; FaBoCh; GN; HBV; LH; LoGBV; OBRV; OTPC (1923 ed.); ShBV-2; TVSH; WBLP
Attend my fable if your ears be clean. Roy Campbell. *Fr.* The Wayzgoose. BoSA
Attend my lays, ye ever honour'd nine. Hymn to the Morning. Phillis Wheatley. BAV
Attend, my Muse, and, if you can, approve. In Praise of Young Girls. Raymond Asquith. OtMeF
Attend my words, my gentle knave. Stans Puer ad Mensam. Sir Walter Raleigh. WhC
Attend you and give ear awhile. The Honour of Bristol. *Unknown.* EV-2; LH; SG
Attendant angel, mark this one. Mill Girl. James K. Baxter. AnNZ
Attendants. David Morton. SDH
Attentive eyes, fantastic heed. A Poet. Thomas Hardy. VLEP
Atthis, our own loved Anactoria. The Lost Friend. Sappho. GrPE
Attic, The. Charles Bruce. *Fr.* The Flowing Summer. CaP
Attic, The. Richard Eberhart. *Fr.* Burr Oaks. MoAB
Attic, The. Rose Fyleman. PCH
Attic and the cedar chest—nostalgia! The Attic. Richard Eberhart. *Fr.* Burr Oaks. MoAB
Attic maid! with honey fed. A Swallow. Euenus, *tr. by* William Cowper. OxBG; WoL
Attic room that houses me, The. The Little House. John Richard Moreland. LS
Attic window's in the ceiling, The. The Attic. Rose Fyleman. PCH
Atticus. Pope. *Fr.* Epistle to Dr. Arbuthnot. AWP; JAWP; MaPo; OBEC; SeCePo; ShBV-4; WBP; WHA
(Addison.) BCEP; LPS-3
(Characters from the Satires: Atticus.) InPo
("Peace to all such! but were there One whose fires.") PoFS; ViBoPo
(Portrait of Atticus.) UnPo (1st ed.)
Attila the Hun. *Unknown, tr. fr. Icelandic by* Henry Adams Bellows. *Fr.* The Elder Edda. PaOS
Attila's spirit rides again the red roads of the East. Ave, Vita Nostra! Clifford James Laube. ISi
Attired in black, spangled with flames of fire. The Spirit of Night. Thomas Rogers. ElL
Attis. Catullus, *tr. fr. Latin by* Horace Gregory. LiA
Attitude of Youth, The. John Gould Fletcher. NeTW
Attitudes for a New Zealand Poet, III. Allen Curnow. AnNZ
Attractions of a Fashionable Irish Watering-Place, The. Francis Sylvester Mahony. IrPN
Au Jardin. Ezra Pound. MOAP
Au Revoir. Alexander Robertson. MM
Aubade. Madison Cawein. SPP
(Morning Serenade.) HBV
Aubade. Sir William Davenant. *See* Lark Now Leaves His Wat'ry Nest, The.
Aubade. William Empson. FaBoTw; LiTB
Aubade. Ibn Hani, *tr. fr. Arabic by* A. J. Arberry. MooP
Aubade. Louis MacNeice. ViBoPo
Aubade. Shakespeare. *See* Hark! Hark! the Lark.
Aubade. Edith Sitwell. ExPo; InP; MBP; MoAB; MoBrPo; NeMA; NP; PoRA; TrGrPo, *abr.*
Aubade: Dick, the Donkey-Boy. Sir Osbert Sitwell. HaMV
Aubade for Hope. Robert Penn Warren. MAP; MoAmPo
Aubergines. Ibn Sara, *tr. fr. Arabic by* A. J. Arberry. MooP
Auburn. Goldsmith. *See* Village, The ("Sweet Auburn . . .").
Aucassin and Nicolete. Francis William Bourdillon. HBV
Aucassin and Nicolete. *Unknown, tr. fr. French by* Andrew Lang. OuHeWo; WoL
Aucassin and Nicolette. Edmund Clarence Stedman. *See* Provençal Lovers.
"Auchanachie Gordon is bonny and braw." Lord Saltoun and Auchanachie. *Unknown.* BaBo; ESPB
Auction. John Holmes. WaKn
Auction, The. "Richard Scrace." CPG
Auction Sale—Household Furnishings. Adele de Leeuw. PoToHe (new ed.)
Auctioneer of parting, The. Emily Dickinson. PoEL-5
Audaces Fortuna Iuvat. George Gascoigne. CaAE
Audacious painters have nine worthies made. In Decium. Sir John Davies. TuPP
Auditors In. Patrick Kavanagh. OxBI
Auf dem Wasser zu Singen. Stephen Spender. EnLoPo
Auf meiner Herzliebsten Äugelein. Heine, *tr. fr. German by* Richard Garnett. AWP
Auf Wiedersehen. Donald Jeffrey Hayes. CDC
Auf Wiedersehen, *sel.* Longfellow.
"It were a double grief." OQP; QP-2
Auf Wiedersehen. James Russell Lowell. AA; BAV; CoBA; HBV; IAP; LPS-1; PR; TCAP
Auguries. Blake. *See* Robin Redbreast, A.
Auguries of Innocence. Blake. AnFE; AtBAP; BLV, *abr.*; BoLiVe, *abr.*; BrBE, *much abr.*; CoBE, 4 *ll.*; EiPP;

EnLi-2, 4 *ll.;* EnLit, 4 *ll.;* EnRP; FaBoCh, *abr.;* FaBoEn; FaFP; GTBS-W; ImOP, 4 *ll.;* InP, 4 *ll.;* KN; LiTB; LiTG; LoBV; LoGBV, *abr.;* MaRV, *abr.;* OAEP; OBRV, *abr.;* OtMeF; PIAE, *much abr.;* Po; PoEL-4; PoFr, *abr.;* PoFS; RiBV; SeCeV; TOP, *sl. abr.;* TreFS, 4 *ll.;* TrGrPo, *abr.;* TriL; TyEnPo; UnW, 4 *ll.;* ViBoPo, 4 *ll.;* WoL
(Augury of Innocence, An, 4 *ll.*) OnPM
(To See a World.) GoTP
("To see a world in a grain of sand.") BEL, 4 *ll.;* EG, *much abr.;* EM-1, *abr.;* EPP, 4 *ll.;* LO, *much abr.;* WGRP, *much abr.;* WHA, 4 *ll.*
Sels.
Life ("Joy and woe are woven fine"), *br. sel.* CBE
Robin Redbreast, A, *much abr.* SiSoSe; UTS
(Auguries, *much abr.*) MuP
(Our Lesser Kindred, *abr.*) BCEP
("Robin redbreast in a cage, A," *sl. abr.*) OxBoLi
(Things to Remember, *br. sel.*) RIS
(Three Things to Remember, *br. sel.*) BLA; CBPC; FaPON; MoShBr; OTPC (1946 ed.); PCD
Augus' meetin' 's over now, De. 'Ligion. John Charles McNeill. NoCaPo
August. Eunice Fallon. BoTP
August. William D. Gallagher. APW; SN
August. Francis Ledwidge. OxBI
August. Michael Lewis. GoTP
August. Lu Yu, *tr. fr. Chinese by* Pai Chwen-yu. WhP
August. Louis MacNeice. ChMo; FaBoEn; LiTM
August. Charles Mair. BoCaPo; CPG
August. William Morris. *Fr.* The Earthly Paradise. BPN
August ("The sixth was August"). Spenser. *Fr.* The Faerie Queene, VII, 7. GN
August ("Tell me, Perigot"). Spenser. *Fr.* The Shepheardes Calender. OAEP; ReEn
Perigot and Willie's [*or* Willye's] Roundelay, *sel.* ElSeCe; EV-1
(It Fell upon a Holy Eve.) PoE
(Perigot and Willye.) LoBV
(Roundelay, A: "It fell upon a holy eve.") ElL
August. Swinburne. AtBAP
August. Celia Thaxter. FaPON; SN; YeAr
August. Helen Maria Winslow. YeAr
August. Elinor Wylie. AnEnPo; BAV; MAP; MoAB; MoAmPo; NeMA; PIAE; PoeMoYo
August Afternoon. Marion Edey. YeAr
August Afternoon, An. J. P. Irvine. SN
August and on the vine eight melons sleeping. Eight Melons. Malcolm Cowley. TwAmPo
August Evening. Olive Tilford Dargan. NoCaPo
August for the People. W. H. Auden. WaP
August is a lazy girl. August Smiles. Elizabeth J. Coatsworth. SiSoSe
August Is Nearly Over. Louis MacNeice. *Fr.* Autumn Journal. ChMo
August Meeting, The. John Charles McNeill. NoCaPo (rev. ed.)
August Midnight, An. Thomas Hardy. EmBrPo; PoMa
August Mood, An. Duncan Campbell Scott. PC
August Moonrise. Sara Teasdale. TCAP
August Night. Elizabeth Madox Roberts. YeAr
August Night. Sara Teasdale. MAP; MoAmPo; NV; TBM
August Night, 1953. Elizabeth B. Harrod. NePoEA
August, 1914. John Masefield. HBV
August, revered,/ Our nation's sire. His Task—and Ours. Dorothy Gould. PGD
August Smiles. Elizabeth J. Coatsworth. SiSoSe
August 'twas the twenty fifth. Bars Fight. Lucy Terry. PoNe
August Weather. Katharine Tynan. TIP
Augustus was a chubby lad. The Story of Augustus Who Would Not Have Any Soup. Heinrich Hoffmann. BoN; HBV; HBVY; MoShBr; OnHT; OTPC; TiPo
Auld Daddy Darkness. James Ferguson. BLP; BOL; HBV; HBVY; PCH; PRWS; RG
Auld Deil cam to the man at the pleugh, The. The Farmer's Curst Wife (B *vers.*). *Unknown.* ESPB
Auld House, The. Lady Nairne. HBV; MotAn; OTPC (1923 ed.)
Auld Kirk o' Scotland, The. George Murray. EBSV
Auld Lang Syne. Burns. AWP; BCEP; BEL; BSV; CaAE; CBE; CBOV; CEP; CoBE; EBSV; EiPP; EM-1; EnLi-2; EnLit; EnRP; EV-3; FaFP; GoTS; GTBS-W; HBV; HiLiEn; InP; InPo; JAWP; LEAP; LiTB; LiTG; LiTL; LPS-1; MCCG; NeHB; OAEP; OBEC; OBEV; OlF; OuHeWo; PC; PoE; PreP, *with music;* PYM; SiTL; TCEP; TOP; TreF; WBP
(Goal of Life, The.) LH
Auld Lang Syne. John White Chadwick. *See* Abiding Love, The.
Auld Man's Mear's Dead, The. Patrick Birnie. GoTS
Auld Matrons. *Unknown.* BaBo; ESPB
Auld Noah was at hame wi' them a'. Parley of Beasts. "Hugh MacDiarmid." LO; MoBrPo; OBMV
Auld Robin Gray. Lady Anne Lindsay. AV; BCEP; BeLS; BSV; CBE; CBOV; CH; DiM; EBSV; EV-3; GoTS; GTBS; GTBS-D; GTBS-W; GTSE; GTSL; HBV; LPS-1; OBEC; OBEV; OnPP; TCEP; ViBoPo
Auld Seceder Cat, The. *Unknown.* SiTL
Auld Wife [Sat at Her Ivied Door], The. Charles Stuart Calverley. *See* Ballad: "Auld wife sat at her ivied door, The."
Auncient Acquaintance, Madam, The. John Skelton. PoEL-1
Aunt Alice has a birthday. Shops. John Farrar. PCH
Aunt Eliza. Harry Graham. ALV; ChTr; FaFP; NA; SiTL; WhC
(Four Ruthless Rhymes.) MaC
Aunt Eliza's Slow Ear. Winifred Welles. GaP
Aunt Helen. T. S. Eliot. TwP
Aunt Jane. Herbert Asquith. GaP
Aunt Jane Allen. Fenton Johnson. GoSl; PoNe
Aunt Jane's in such a hurry. Aunt Jane. Herbert Asquith. GaP
Aunt Mary; a Christmas Chant. Robert Stephen Hawker. JKCP; OHIP
(Modryb Marya—Aunt Mary.) AnEC
Aunt Maud. Harry Graham. *See* Waste.
Aunt Nerissa's Muffin. Wallace Irwin. FiBHP
Aunt Selina. Carol Haynes. HBMV; HBVY; MPB
Aunt Tabitha. Oliver Wendell Holmes. CenHV; PTA-1
Aunt Zillah Speaks. Herbert Palmer. FaBoTw
Auntie, did you feel no pain. Some Ruthless Rhymes, III. Harry Graham. CenHV; SiTL
Aunties know all about fairies. Grown-ups. Rose Fyleman. HH
Auntie's Skirts. Robert Louis Stevenson. MPB (1956 ed.); PoVP
Auras of Delight. Coventry Patmore. The Unknown Eros, II, xi. ACP; CAW; LoBV; OBVV
Aurelia. Robert Nichols. OBMV; POTE
Aureng-Zebe, *sels.* Dryden.
Epilogue: "Pretty task, A; and so I told the fool." SeEP
Prologue to "Aureng-Zebe." ATP; CEP; EiPP; FiP; OBS; OxBoLi; SeCeV; SiTL
(Prologue: "Our Author by experience finds it true.") SeCV-2; SeEP
Plant That Will Not Grow, A, *fr.* Prologue. BeR
When I Consider Life, *fr.* IV, i. FiP
(Life a Cheat.) BCEP
Aureole. Helene Magaret. BPP
Aurora. Emily Dickinson. *See* Of bronze and blaze.
Aurora, *sels.* Earl of Stirling.
"I envy not Endymion now no more," Sonnet XXIX. ElL
"I swear, Aurora, by thy starry eyes," Sonnet X. EV-2
"Let others of the world's decaying tell," Sonnet XCVIII. ElL
"O happy Tithon!" Song IX, *sts.* 1–2. OBEV
"Oh, if thou knew'st how thou thyself dost harm," Sonnet XXXIII. ElL; EV-2
(To Aurora.) EBSV; GTBS; GTBS-D; GTBS-W; GTSE; GTSL
(Two in One.) ES
"Then whilst that Latmos did contain her bliss," Sonnet XXVIII. ViBoPo
"When in her face mine eyes I fix," Madrigal I. ElL
Aurora Leigh, *sels.* Elizabeth Barrett Browning.
Aurora Leigh Discovers Books ("Books, books, books!"), *fr.* I. MOB
Books ("Or else I sat on in my chamber green"), *fr.* I. VA
"But poets should/ Exert a double vision," *fr.* V. VLEP
By Solitary Fires, *fr.* V. VA
England, *fr.* I. VA
(Sweetness of England, The, *longer sel.*) EV-4
Ferment of New Wine, The, *fr.* I. VA
Glory in the Commonplace, *fr.* VII. MaRV
"I dared to rest, or wander," *fr.* I. EnSW
Man, *fr.* I. BCEP
Motherless, *fr.* I. MOAH; VA
"Nowise beautiful/ Was Marian Erle," *fr.* III. VLEP
Paris, *fr.* VI ViP
Poets, The, *fr.* I. VA
Reading, *fr.* I. GN; HH
("Good from a Book.") PoRL
Romney and Aurora, *fr.* IX. VA
" 'There is none good save God,' said Jesus Christ," *fr.* IV. VLEP
Traveling South toward Italy, *fr.* VII. BCEP
"Truth, so far, in my book; the truth which draws," *fr.* VII. WGRP
"Where There Is No Vision," *fr.* II, *abr.* MaRV
Aurora rous'd by some damn'd cock. Another Dawn. Bernard Mandeville. *Fr.* A Description of the Morning. BeR
Aurore Pradère, *with music. Unknown, tr. fr. French.* ABF
Auspex. James Russell Lowell. AmPP (3d ed.); AnFE; AnNE; APA; APW; BLV; CBOV; CoAnAm; GTBS-W; HBV; IAP; LBAP; MOAP; NePA; OBVV; PoEL-5

Auspice of Jewels. Laura Riding. FaBoMo; LiTA
Austere and lovely Vega, you have gazed. Sonnet in Sorrow. B. Y. Williams. MuM
Austere My Verse. "Feodor Sologub." *See* Austere the Music of My Songs.
Austere, removed, grave as the thought of death. Snow. Humbert Wolfe. TwCV
Austere the Music of My Songs. "Feodor Sologub," *tr. fr. Russian by* Babette Deutsch *and* Avrahm Yarmolinsky. AWP
(Austere My Verse, *rev. tr. by* Babette Deutsch.) TrRV
Austerity of Poetry. Matthew Arnold. BEL; BMEP; BPN; EM-2; EmBrPo; EnLi-2; EPN; OAEP; OBVV; PoFS; PoVP; PtP; TCEP; TOP; VLEP
(Jacopone da Todi.) CAW; GoBC
Austin Dobson. Christopher Morley. PtP
Australasia, *sel.* William Charles Wentworth.
"Celestial poesy! whose genial sway." BoAu
Australia. A. D. Hope. BoAV; MoAuPo; OnHM
Australia. Eve Langley. BoAV
Australia. Bernard O'Dowd. BoAu; NeLNL
Australia. Dowell O'Reilly. BoAu
Australia, *abr.* John Laurence Rentoul. PoFr
Australia Day, 1942; in Memoriam W. J. Miles. Ian Mudie. BoAu
Australia, 1894. William Gay. BoAu
Australia is a part of us. Soldier Overseas. Leonard Mann. BoAu
Australia, 1905. Archibald T. Strong. *Fr.* Sonnets of the Empire. BoAu
Australia, 1914. Archibald T. Strong. *Fr.* Sonnets of the Empire. BoAu
Australia to England. Archibald T. Strong. *Fr.* Sonnets of the Empire. BoAu; PoFr
Australian, The. Arthur Adams. BoAu
Australian Federation. William Gay. BoAu; PoFr
Australian Girl, An. Ethel Castilla. VA
Australian Spring. Hugh McCrae. BoAu
Australian Symphony, An. G. Essex Evans. BoAu
Austrian Archduke, assaulted and assailed, An. The War: A–Z. John R. Edwards. BOHV
Austrian Army, An. *Unknown, at. to* Alaric A. Watts. *See* Siege of Belgrade, The.
Aut Caesar aut Nullus. Lilian White Spencer. CAW; TBM
Author and God of freedom, Thou dost plant. The Spirit of Freedom. *Unknown.* PoFr
Author Loving These Homely Meats, The. John Davies of Hereford. ElL; ElSeCe
(Buttered Pippin-Pies.) ChTr
(Homely Meats.) FaBoCh; LoGBV
Author of Light. Thomas Campion. AtBAP; MeRV
("Author of light, revive my dying spright.") SiCE
Author of the "Pobble," The. Edward Lear. *See* How Pleasant to Know Mr. Lear.
Author to a Daughter of Nine Years Old, The. Sir John Harington, *after the Latin of* Martial. SiCE
Author to Her Book, The. Anne Bradstreet. AmPP; IAP; NePA; OxBA
Author to His Booke, The. Thomas Heywood. *Fr.* An Apology for Actors. OBS
Author to Queen Elizabeth, in Praise of Her Reading, The. Sir John Harington. SiCE
Author Writes His Own Epitaph, The. Edward Thompson. MM
Authority. William Reed Huntington. AA
Author's Abstract of Melancholy, The. Robert Burton. *Fr.* The Anatomy of Melancholy. OBS; SeCL
Authors and actors and artists and such. Bohemia. Dorothy Parker. CrMA; NAMP
Author's Entreaty for His Lay. Eysteinn Asgrímsson, *tr. fr. Icelandic by* Eirik Magnusson. *Fr.* Lilya. ISi
Author's Epitaph, The. *Unknown.* FiBHP
Author's Epitaph, The, Made by Himself the Night before His Death. Sir Walter Ralegh. *See* Conclusion, The.
Author's Last Words to His Students, The. Edmund Blunden. PtOT
Author's Life, The. Thomas Tusser. ReIE
Author's Miseries, The, *abr.* Pope. *Fr.* Epistle to Dr. Arbuthnot. BCEP
Author's Purpose, The. Byron. *Fr.* Don Juan, IV. EPN
("Nothing so difficult as a beginning.") BEL; BPN; CoBE; EM-2; EnRP; PoFS
(Romantic to Burlesque, *shorter sel.*) FiP
Author's Resolution [in a Sonnet], The. George Wither. *See* Shall I, Wasting in Despair.
Authour's Dreame, The. Francis Quarles. *Fr.* Argalus and Parthenia. OBS
Auto of the Bark of Purgatory, The, *sel.* Gil Vicente, *tr. fr. Spanish by* Aubrey F. G. Bell.
Song of the Three Angels. CAW
Auto of the Four Seasons, The, *sel.* Gil Vicente, *tr. fr. Spanish by* Aubrey F. G. Bell.
Angelic Vilancete, The. CAW
Auto Wreck. Karl Shapiro. LiTM; MiAP; MoVE; NePA; ReMP
Autobiographical. A. M. Klein. BoCaPo
Autobiography. John Gould Fletcher. MOAP
Autobiography, An. Bairam at Tunisie, *tr. fr. Turkish by* Herbert Howarth *and* Ibrahim Shukrallah. LiTW
Autobiography. Lu Yu, *tr. fr. Chinese by* Pai Chwen-yu. WhP
Autobiography. Louis MacNeice. FaBoTw
Autobiography. Dorothy Parker. WhC
Autobiography, An. Ernest Rhys. OBEV (new ed.); OBVV; POTE; PrWP; VA
Autochthon. Sir Charles G. D. Roberts. CaP; OCL; SN; VA
Autocrat of the Breakfast Table, The, *sels.* Oliver Wendell Holmes.
Aestivation, *fr. ch.* 11. AmPP; AnNE; BOHV; InMe; NA; REAL; WhC
Album Verses, *fr. ch.* 1. AmPP
Chambered Nautilus, The, *fr. ch.* 4. AA; AmP; AmPP; AnAmPo; AnNE; APW; BAP; BAV; BTP; DD; EOAH; EtS; EV-5; FaBoBe; FaFP; GN; GTBS; GTBS-W; HBV; HBVY; HoPM; IAP; IHA; LA; LBAP; LEAP; LiTA; LPS-2; MaRV; MCCG; NeHB; NePA; OBAV; OBVV; OHFP; OQP; OTPC; OuHeWo; PCD; PECK; PG (1955 ed.); PIR; PoEL-5; PoP; PTA-1; QP-1; TCAP; TreF; TVSH; UnPo (1st ed.); WGRP; YT
(More Stately Mansions, *last st.*) GrCo-1
Contentment, *fr. ch.* 11. AmPP (4th ed.); AnNE; BOHV; HBV; HiLiAm; IAP; InMe; OnPP; OxBA; PIR; PR; REAL; TCAP; TOP; TreF
Deacon's Masterpiece, The; or, The Wonderful "One-Hoss Shay," *fr. ch.* 11. AmP; AmPP; AnNE; APW; BBV (1923 ed.); BOHV; CoBA; DDA; EV-5; FaFP; HBV; HBVY; IAP; InMe; LHV; LiTA; LoGBV; MOAP; MoShBr; NePA; OBAV; OHFP; OnHT; OnSP; OTPC; OxBA; Po; PoRA; REAL; RIS; SiTL; StPo; StVeCh; TCAP; WBLP; YT
(Logical Story, A—The Deacon's Masterpiece; or, The Wonderful "One-Hoss Shay.") BAP; LEAP
(One-Hoss Shay, The; or, The Deacon's Masterpiece.) LPS-3; PIR; TreF
(Wonderful "One-Hoss Shay," The.) BeLS; FaBoBe; PYM; YaD
Latter-Day Warnings, *fr. ch.* 1. IAP; OnAP; PCD
Living Temple, The, *fr. ch.* 7. AA; AmPP (3d ed.)
Voiceless, The, *fr. ch.* 12. AA; BAP; CoBA; IAP; TCAP; ViBoPo
Autograph, An. James Russell Lowell. AA
Autograph, An. Whittier. AA
Autolycus [*or* Autolycus' Songs]. Shakespeare. *See* Jog On, Jog On *and* Lawn as White as Driven Snow *and* When Daffodils Begin to Peer.
Autolycus' Song (in Basic English). Richard L. Greene. WhC
Automaton whose stiffened gesture writes. Record Perpetual Loss. Mary Stanley. AnNZ
Automobile, The. Percy MacKaye. AnAmPo; BAP; LA; LBMV; LEAP; PoeMoYo
Automobile and the Cat, The. Elizabeth J. Coatsworth. DDA
Automobile Mechanics. Dorothy W. Baruch. FaPON; TiPo
Automobiles/ In a row. Stop—Go. Dorothy W. Baruch. FaPON; SUS; TiPo
Autonomous. Mark Van Doren. LiTA; PG (1955 ed.)
Autosonic Door. Dorothy Brown Thompson. GoYe
Autres Bêtes, Autres Mœurs. Ogden Nash. *See* Turtle, The.
Autumn. Antipater of Sidon, *tr. fr. Greek by* Robert Allason Furness. GrR
Autumn. Guillaume Apollinaire, *tr. fr. French by* W. S. Merwin. AnFP
Autumn. Roy Campbell. JKCP (1955 ed.); MBP; MoBrPo; OBMV; POTE; TrGrPo (1942 ed.)
Autumn. Bliss Carman. VOD
Autumn. William Herbert Carruth. MPB
Autumn ("I love the fitful gust"). John Clare. BoTP, 3 *sts.*; EnSW; GTBS-D; MW; PCH, 2 *sts.*; WP
("I love the fitful gust that shakes.") EG
Autumn ("The thistledown's flying"). John Clare. PoEL-4
Autumn. Edwin Curran. HBMV; TSW
Autumn. Walter de la Mare. GTBS-D; POTE
(Lost Playmate, The.) OTPC (1923 ed.)
Autumn. Aubrey Thomas De Vere. *Fr.* The Year of Sorrow: Ireland, 1849. TIP
Autumn. Emily Dickinson. *See* Morns are meeker than they were, The
Autumn, The. William Davis Gallagher. *Fr.* Autumn in the West. LPS-2
Autumn. José Gorostiza, *tr. fr. Spanish by* H. R. Hays. TwSpPo
Autumn. Hesiod, *tr. fr. Greek by* F. L. Lucas. *Fr.* Works and Days. GrPE
Autumn. Florence Hoatson. BoTP
Autumn ("The autumn is old"). Thomas Hood. LPS-2; PTA-2

Autumn ("I saw old Autumn in the misty morn"). Thomas Hood. ERP; EV-4; LiTB; OBEV; PCD; ViBoPo
(Ode: Autumn.) OBRV; PoEL-4; VA
(Ode to Autumn.) HBV
Autumn. T. E. Hulme. FaBoMo; LoBV; MBP; MoBrPo (1942 ed.); SeCePo; ViBoPo
Autumn. Thomas Caulfield Irwin. IrPN
Autumn. Kalidasa, *tr. fr. Sanskrit by* Arthur W. Ryder. *Fr.* The Seasons. AWP; JAWP; WBP
Autumn. Nikolai Karamzin, *tr. fr. Russian by* Sir John Bowring. BoRS
Autumn. Arthur A. Knipe. GFA
Autumn. Walter Savage Landor. *See* Mild Is the Parting Year.
Autumn. Mary Leapor. *Fr.* Colinetta. BeR
Autumn. Detlev von Liliencron, *tr. fr. German by* Ludwig Lewisohn. AWP; JAWP; WBP
Autumn ("Thou comest, Autumn, heralded by the rain"). Longfellow. BAV; OBVV
Autumn ("With what a glory comes"). Longfellow. BAV
Autumn ("Like a fairy spirit I leave the gate of the city"). Lu Yu, *tr. fr. Chinese by* Pai Chwen-yu. WhP
Autumn ("The village wine is sweet and sour"). Lu Yu, *tr. fr. Chinese by* Pai Chwen-yu. WhP
Autumn. Itzig Manger, *tr. fr. Yiddish by* Joseph Leftwich. TrJP
Autumn. Lloyd Mifflin. *Fr.* The Fields of Dawn. SN
Autumn. John Richard Moreland. LS
Autumn. Nagata, *tr. fr. Japanese by* Lois J. Erickson. SoLD
Autumn. Thomas Nashe. *Fr.* Summer's Last Will and Testament. ElL; LoBV; OBSC; RiBV; TrGrPo
("Autumn hath all the summer's fruitful treasure.") CenL; TuPP
(Winter, Plague and Pestilence.) BLV
Autumn. *Tr. fr. Irish by* Frank O'Connor. *See* Growing Old.
Autumn. Hans Hartvig Seedorff Pedersen, *tr. fr. Danish by* Charles W. Stork. BoDS
Autumn. Pushkin, *tr. fr. Russian by* Max Eastman. AnEnPo; AWP; TrRV, *tr. by* Babette Deutsch
Autumn. Forrest Reid. GTIV
Autumn. Rainer Maria Rilke, *tr. fr. German.* AnGP, *tr. by* Kate Flores; MoAuPo, *tr. by* James McAuley; OnPM, *tr. by* Jessie Lemont; TrJP, *tr. by* C. F. MacIntyre.
Autumn. Elizabeth Madox Roberts. AnAmPo; LA; YaD
Autumn. W. R. Rodgers. NeBP
Autumn ("Care flieth"). Christina Rossetti. EmBrPo
Autumn ("I dwell alone"). Christina Rossetti. EmBrPo
Autumn. Siegfried Sassoon. NP
Autumn. Shelley. *See* Autumn; a Dirge.
Autumn. Alexander Smith. *See* Sea-Marge.
Autumn. William Jay Smith. NePoAm
Autumn. Spenser. *Fr.* The Faerie Queene, VII, 7. GN; HOAH
Autumn. James Stephens. ChMo; CMP
Autumn. Su T'ung-po, *tr. fr. Chinese by* Kenneth Rexroth. OnPC
Autumn. Rabindranath Tagore. WGRP
Autumn. Allen Tate. Seasons of the Soul, II. MoVE
Autumn. Tennyson. *See* In Memoriam A. H. H.: "Calm is the morn without a sound."
Autumn. James Thomson. *Fr.* The Seasons. CEP
Sels.
"But see the fading many-colour'd woods." EnRP; EnSW; LoBV
"Fled in the blasted verdure." OAEP
Lavinia. OBEC
Love of Nature. OBEC
Moonlight in Autumn, *abr.* OBEC
Moonlight, 6 *ll.* BeR
Stag Hunt, The. LPS-2
Storm in Harvest. EPP
Autumn. Meta E. B. Thorne. *Fr.* Songs of the Seasons. PEOR
Autumn. Rietta Trimm. CAG
Autumn! Nancy Byrd Turner. YeAr
Autumn ("Autumn's good, a cosy season"). *Unknown, tr. fr. Irish by* Frank O'Connor. KiLC
Autumn ("Now wither rose and lily flower"). *Unknown.* TMEV
Autumn. Jean Starr Untermeyer. HBMV; MAP; MCCG; MoAmPo; NeMA; PFY; SBMV
Autumn. Sir William Watson. LEAP; OBVV
Autumn. Frances Winwar. GoYe
Autumn. Sergei Aleksandrovich Yesenin, *tr. fr. Russian.* BoRS, *tr. by* C. M. Bowra; TrRV, *tr. by* Babette Deutsch
Autumn; a Dirge. Shelley. AEV; CG; HBV
(Autumn.) CH; OTPC; WP
Autumn along the Beaches. John Hall Wheelock. AnAmPo; LA
Autumn already, Epicles! and bright. Autumn. Antipater of Sidon. GrR
Autumn; an Ode. Charles Gullans. NePoEA
Autumn and Death. Amy Lowell. TBM
Autumn, and I Would Go Back to You. Ronald Hambleton. BoCaPo
Autumn and the elms unleaving. Autumn Is a Season. James F. Cotter. JKCP (1955 ed.)
Autumn and Winter. Thomas Chatterton. *Fr.* Elegy to the Memory of Mr. Thomas Philips of Fairford. RO
Autumn at Taos. D. H. Lawrence. BrBE
Autumn, Autumn, give me of your crimson. A Song in Autumn. Theodosia Garrison. NLK
Autumn, autumn, you thought I was not spying. Autumn. John Richard Moreland. LS
Autumn Bird. Howard McKinley Corning. MAP; MoAmPo (1942 ed.)
Autumn Breeze, An. William Hamilton Hayne. AA
Autumn Change, An. Charles Sangster. *Fr.* The Happy Harvesters. BoCaPo
Autumn Chant. Edna St. Vincent Millay. BAP; CP
Autumn, chestnut mare, quietly stirs. Autumn. Sergei Yesenin. BoRS
Autumn chrysanthemums have the loveliest colors, The. Chrysanthemums. Tao Yuan-ming. WhP
Autumn cicada, The. Haiku. Joso. OnPJ
Autumn, cloud blades on the horizon. Clear after Rain. Tu Fu. OnPC
Autumn Color. Tom Robinson. YeAr
Autumn comes, a maiden fair, The. Autumn. Kalidasa. *Fr.* The Seasons. AWP; JAWP; WBP
Autumn comes on slippered feet. Autumn's Fete. Alice Sutton McGeorge. YeAr
Autumn Complaint. Nikolaus Lenau, *tr. fr. German by* Dwight Durling. AnGP
Autumn constellations, The. Moon Festival. Tu Fu. OnPC
Autumn Countryside. Tu Fu, *tr. fr. Chinese by* Hsieh Wen Tung. WhP
Autumn Cricket, An. Clinton Scollard. MuM
Autumn, Crystal Eye. Margot Ruddock. OBMV
Autumn Dawn. Antonio Machado, *tr. fr. Spanish by* Jean Rogers Longland. TeCS
Autumn Day. Rainer Maria Rilke, *tr. fr. German by* C. F. MacIntyre. TrJP
(Autumn's Day, *tr. by* Kate Flores.) AnGP
Autumn Day, An. Margaret E. Sangster. PEOR
Autumn Daybreak. Edna St. Vincent Millay. LaNeLa
Autumn departs; but still his mantle's fold. Fading Autumn. Sir Walter Scott. *Fr.* The Lord of the Isles, I. EV-4
Autumn Eve. Amelia Andriello. SiSoSe
Autumn Evening. John Clare. ThWaDe
Autumn Evening. Feodor Ivanovich Tyutchev, *tr. fr. Russian.* BoRS, *tr. by* C. M. Bowra; OnPM, *tr. by* Babette Deutsch; TrRV, *tr. by* Babette Deutsch
Autumn evening. Haiku. Basho. OnPJ
Autumn Evening beside the Lake. Li Ch'ing-chao, *tr. fr. Chinese by* Kenneth Rexroth. OnPC
Autumn Fancies. *Unknown.* FaPON; MPB; StVeCh
Autumn Fashions. Edith M. Thomas. DD; YeAr
Autumn Fields. Elizabeth Madox Roberts. BrR
Autumn Fires. Robert Louis Stevenson. BrR; GFA; SUS; TiPo; YeAr
Autumn Flitting, An. George Cotterell. VA
Autumn, Forsake These Hills. Frank Ernest Hill. PoMa
Autumn frosts will lie upon the grass, The. Wild Peaches, II. Elinor Wylie. LiTA; NAMP; OxBA
Autumn Fruits. Thomas Chatterton. *Fr.* Aella. RO
Autumn Fruits. Joachim du Bellay, *tr. fr. French by* Alan Conder. Olive, XXXII. TrFP
Autumn Garden, An. Bliss Carman. HBV; NLK
Autumn Gloves. Mildred D. Shacklett. GFA
Autumn has changed to spring since I last wrote. The Letters. Lawrence Lee. MuM
Autumn has come. The Monk Eikei, *tr. fr. Japanese by* Kenneth Rexroth. OnPJ
Autumn has come invisibly. Fujiwara no Toshiyuki, *tr. fr. Japanese by* Kenneth Rexroth. OnPJ
Autumn hath all the summer's fruitful treasure. Autumn [*or* Winter, Plague and Pestilence]. Thomas Nashe. *Fr.* Summer's Last Will and Testament. BLV; CenL; ElL; LoBV; OBSC; RiBV; TrGrPo; TuPP
Autumn Haze. Richard Kendall Munkittrick. PoRL
Autumn Healing. Jean Ward. LaNeLa
Autumn Hour. George Chapman. JKCP (1955 ed.)
Autumn House, The. George M. Brady. OnYI
Autumn Idleness. Dante Gabriel Rossetti. The House of Life, LXIX. PoVP; ViPo; ViPP; VLEP
Autumn in Carmel. George Sterling. TBM
Autumn, in her scarlet cloak. Carouse. Charles Hanson Towne. NLK; VOD
Autumn in King's Hintock Park. Thomas Hardy. PoVP
Autumn in Oregon is wet as spring. Smith, of the Third Oregon, Dies. Mary Carolyn Davies. SBMV
Autumn in the Highlands. Arthur Hugh Clough. GTSE
Autumn, in the second year of the Sovereign Land. Journey to the North. Tu Fu. WhP

Autumn in the West. William Davis Gallagher. AA; AnAmPo; LA
Autumn, The, *sel.* LPS-2
Autumn in Wartime. Gilean Douglas. MuM
Autumn Is a Season. James F. Cotter. JKCP (1955 ed.)
Autumn is a train that travels. Autumn Train. Mildred D. Shacklett. GFA
Autumn is for older men. Adios. Donald C. Babcock. NePoAm-2
Autumn is here. The beech leaves strew the lawn. W. H. Auden. *Fr.* Letter to Lord Byron. MoP
Autumn is in the air. London Interior. Harold Monro. ChMo; CMP
Autumn is old, The. Autumn. Thomas Hood. LPS-2; PTA-2
Autumn is only winter in disguise. Against the Cold. Witter Bynner. MAP; MoAmPo (1942 ed.)
Autumn is weary, halt, and old. The October Redbreast. Alice Meynell. MBP; MoBrPo
Autumn Journal, *sels.* Louis MacNeice.
August Is Nearly Over. ChMo
"Conferences, adjournments, ultimatums." WaP
Good-bye Now, Plato and Hegel. OnHM
"Nightmare leaves fatigue." AnIL
Now We Are Back to Normal. ChMo
Sleep Serene, Avoid the Backward. ChMo
These Days Are Misty, Insulated. ChMo
Autumn Journey. Denise Levertov. NeBP
Autumn Leaves. W. Hodgson Burnet. PoMa
Autumn Leaves. Janie Screven Heyward. HBMV; MPB
Autumn Leaves. Minnie Case Hopkins. OQP; QP-2
Autumn Leaves. Lu Lun, *tr. fr. Chinese by* Henry H. Hart. PoHN
Autumn Leaves. Margaret P. Sutphen. PCH
Autumn Leaves. Toshiyuki, *tr. fr. Japanese by* Basil Hall Chamberlain. OnPM
Autumn Leaves, The. *Unknown.* NA
Autumn Leaves. Angelina Wray. PTA-2
Autumn leaves are falling, The. The Autumn Leaves. *Unknown.* NA
Autumn Love. Aleksandr Blok, *tr. fr. Russian by* C. M. Bowra. BoR
Autumn Love. Ibycus, *tr. fr. Greek by* Olga Marx *and* Ernst Morwitz. LiTW
Autumn Love. John Crowe Ransom. SPP
Autumn loved and ailing. Sick Autumn. Guillaume Apollinaire. TrFP
Autumn Memories. George Francis Savage-Armstrong. VA
Autumn met me to-day as I walked over Castle Hill. The Stand-to. C. Day Lewis. SoV
Autumn Moon. Chisato, *tr. fr. Japanese by* Basil Hall Chamberlain. OnPM
Autumn Moon. Wang I, *tr. fr. Chinese by* Henry H. Hart. PoHN
Autumn Morning, An. *Unknown.* BoTP
Autumn Morning. Adeline White. BoTP
Autumn Morning at Cambridge. Frances Cornford. HBMV; MoVE; OBVV; TCPD
Autumn Movement. Carl Sandburg. NP; SBMV
Autumn Night. Evelyn Scott. AnAmPo; LA
Autumn night is clear, The. Stars and Moon on the River. Tu Fu. OnPC
Autumn 1940. W. H. Auden. LiTA
Autumn on the Beaches. Sara Teasdale. PoTo
Autumn orchids and the silver pennies, The. The Junior Arbiter of Fate. Chu Yuan. *Fr.* The Nine Songs. WhP
Autumn Park, An. David Gascoyne. MoPo
Autumn Ploughing. Hesiod, *tr. fr. Greek by* F. L. Lucas. *Fr.* Works and Days. GrPE
Autumn Races. Emilie Blackmore Stapp. GFA
Autumn Rain, The. Hubbard Fulton Page. NoCaPo
Autumn Rain. Yin Shin, *tr. fr. Chinese by* Henry H. Hart. PoHN
Autumn Refrain. Wallace Stevens. LiTA
Autumn Riddle, An. *Unknown.* OTPC (1946 ed.)
Autumn Road, An. Glenn Ward Dresbach. HBMV
Autumn Robin, The. John Clare. BoTP
Autumn Rose-Tree, An. Michael Earls. JKCP
Autumn seems to cry for thee, The. Helen. "Susan Coolidge." AA
Autumn Song, An. Bliss Carman. *See* Vagabond Song, A.
Autumn Song. Edward Dowden. OnYI
Autumn Song. William Griffith. BAP
Autumn Song. Philip Clark Horton. CAG
Autumn Song. Elizabeth-Ellen Long. SiSoSe
Autumn Song. Nyleen Newton. CAG
Autumn Song. Margaret Rose. BoTP
Autumn Song. Dante Gabriel Rossetti. BPN; ViBoPo; VLEP
Autumn Song. Edmund Clarence Stedman. DD
(Going a-Nutting.) BBV (1923 ed.); GN
Autumn Song. Johann Ludwig Tieck, *tr. fr. German by* James Clarence Mangan. AWP
Autumn Song. *Unknown, tr. fr. Old Irish by* Padraic Colum. SiB
Autumn Song. Paul Verlaine, *tr. fr. French by* Gerard Previn Meyer. LiTW
Autumn Sunset. Wang Shih Cheng, *tr. fr. Chinese by* Henry H. Hart. PoHN
Autumn: the ninth year of Yüan Ho. The Temple. Po Chü-i. OBMV
Autumn Thoughts. Lu Yu, *tr. fr. Chinese by* Kenneth Rexroth. OnPC
Autumn-time has come, The. My Triumph. Whittier. AnNE; BHV; IAP; TCAP
Autumn time is with us, The. Autumn in the West. William Davis Gallagher. AA; AnAmPo; LA; LPS-2
Autumn Train. Mildred D. Shacklett. GFA
Autumn Twilight. Henri de Réginer, *tr. fr. French by* L. R. Lind. LiTW
Autumn Valentine. Dorothy Parker. NeMA
Autumn Walk, An. Witter Bynner. GoYe
Autumn was cold in Plymouth town. Her Picture. Ellen Mackay Hutchinson Cortissoz. AA; LBAP
Autumn Wind, The. Wu Ti, *tr. fr. Chinese by* Arthur Waley. FaBoCh; LoGBV; TrCh
—— *Tr. into English by* James Whitall *fr. the French translation of* Judith Gautier. ChLP
(Autumn Winds, The.) WhP
Autumn Wind, The. Autumn Rain. Yin Shin. PoHN
Autumn wind awakes and calls aloud, The. Hallow Even. Carrie Ward Lyon. HOAH
Autumn wind blows mournfully, The. At an Old Battlefield. Umaki. OnPM
Autumn wind came stealing. The Thief. Irene F. Pawsey. BoTP
Autumn wind, The—oh, hear it howl! Hallowe'en. Arthur Cleveland Coxe. DD
Autumn wind rises, The,/ white clouds are flying before it. The Autumn Wind. Wu Ti. *tr. by* James Whitall. ChLP
Autumn wind rises; white clouds fly. The Autumn Wind. Wu Ti *tr. by* Arthur Waley. FaBoCh; LoGBV; TrCh
Autumn Winds, The. Wu Ti. *See* Autumn Wind, The.
Autumn wind's a pirate, The. Pirate Wind. Mary Jane Carr. BrR; SiSoSe
Autumn winds rise and the white clouds fly, The. The Autumn Winds. Wu Ti. WhP
Autumn wins you best by this its mute. Scene in a Garden. Robert Browning. *Fr.* Paracelsus, I. PCH
Autumn with chilling touch draws swiftly near. Nature's Miracle. David Fallon. POT; PoTo
Autumn Woods. Bryant. AnNE; PTA-1
Autumn Woods. James S. Tippett. BoChLi; SUS; TiPo
Autumnal, The. John Donne. Elegies, IX. EPS (1942 ed.); ReEn; TuPP; ViBoPo
(Autumnall, The.) NBE; PoEL-2; SeCV-1
(Elegy IX: The Autumnal[l].) AtBAP; EnL; EnLP; OAEP; SeEP
Autumnal. Marie Emilie Gilchrist. TBM
Autumnal. Ann Louise Hayes. PtPa
Autumnal Aria, *sel.* Juan Ramón Jiménez, *tr. fr. Spanish by* Alice Jane McVan.
"Idly sings the shepherd," XVIII. AnSpL-2
Autumnal Clouds. John Gould Fletcher. MAPA
Autumnal Consummation. Patric Stevenson. NeIP
Autumnal Evening, An. "Fiona Macleod." GBV
Autumnal Love. Georgy Ivanovich Chulkov, *tr. fr. Russian by* Babette Deutsch. TrRV
Autumnal Song. Walter Savage Landor. *See* Very True, the Linnets Sing.
Autumnal Spring Song. Vassar Miller. NePoEA
Autumnall. Joseph Bennett. NePA
Autumnall, The. John Donne. *See* Autumnal, The.
Autumn's attrition. Then this world laid waste. A Girl in the Snow. Robert Conquest. PoLFOT
Autumn's Fete. Alice Sutton McGeorge. YeAr
Autumn's good, a cosy season. Autumn. *Unknown.* KiLC
Autumn's Mirth. Samuel Minturn Peck. GN
Autumn's Processional. Dinah Maria Mulock Craik. GN
Autumnus. Joshua Sylvester. ElL; LO; OBS; SeEP; UnPo (1st ed.)
Aux Carmélites. Katharine Tynan. OnYI
Aux Italiens. "Owen Meredith." BeLS; BLPA; BMEP; FaBoBe; HBV; LPS-1; PTA-2; TreFS; VA
Aux taureaux Dieu cornes donne. Peter Parasol. Wallace Stevens. NP
'Av 'ee met a Cornish miner. The Cornish Miner. Walter F. Gries. IHA
Avalanche, The. Pushkin, *tr. fr. Russian by* W. A. Morison. BoRS
Avalon. Thomas Holley Chivers. AnFE; APA; CoAnAm; MOAP
Avalon. Donald Davidson. LS
Avalon. Audrey McGaffin. NePoAm
Avarice. George Herbert. LiTB; PeBoSo
("Money, thou bane of bliss and source of woe.") GTBS-W
Avarice. William Langland. *See* Covetousness.

Avarice. Luis de León, *tr. fr. Spanish by* Audrey F. G. Bell. WoL

Avaricious Angel, The. Rafael Alberti, *tr. fr. Spanish by* Eleanor L. Turnbull. CoSP

Avaro ("Avaro sick is seen to shiver"). John Swanwick Drennan. IrPN

Avast, honest Jack! now, before you get mellow. The Battle of Erie. *Unknown.* GA; PAH

Avaunt, I charge you! Get ye from my door! Apollo Confounds the Furies. Aeschylus. *Fr.* Eumenides. GrR

Ave. Ada Foster Murray. GA

Ave. Dante Gabriel Rossetti. EmBrPo; GoBC; ISi; OxBoCh; POTT; ViPo; VLEP

Ave, *in mod. Eng. Unknown.* (Three Devout Fragments, 2.) TMEV

Ave atque Vale. Dryden. *Fr.* Sigismonda and Guiscardo. OBS

Ave atque Vale. Thomas S. Jones, Jr. HBV
"You found the green before the Spring was sweet," *sel.* VOD

Ave atque Vale. Swinburne. BMEP; CaAE; EnLi-2; LEAP; LiA; OAEP; OBEV; POTT; PoVP; PtP; ViBoPo; ViP; ViPP; VLEP

Ave atque Vale. Rosamund Marriott Watson. HBV; VA

Ave, Caesar! W. E. Henley. In Hospital, XIV. POTT

Ave Caesar. Robinson Jeffers. MoVE; OxBA

Ave Crux, Spes Unica! Edward Shillito. ChIP; MaRV; OQP; QP-2

Ave Eva. John Wheelwright. MoPo

Ave Imperatrix! Oscar Wilde. HBV; VA
East a-Callin', The, *sel.* OtMeF

Ave Maria. Byron. *Fr.* Don Juan, III. ERP, *9 sts.*; ISi, *2 sts.*; MCCG, *6 sts.*
(Devotion, *7 sts.*) GEPC

Ave Maria. Henriette Charasson, *tr. fr. French by* Frederic Thompson. CAW; ISi

Ave Maria. Hart Crane. *Fr.* The Bridge. AtBAP; CoV; LiTA; MoPo; NePA

Ave Maria. John Jerome Rooney. JKCP

Ave Maria. Sir Walter Scott. *See* Hymn to the Virgin.

Ave Maria! *in mod. Eng. Unknown.* TMEV

Ave Maria Bells. Charles Warren Stoddard. ISi; JKCP

Ave Maria! blessèd be the hour! Ave Maria [*or* Devotion]. Byron. *Fr.* Don Juan, III. GEPC; ISi; MCCG

Ave Maria Gratia Plena. Oscar Wilde. ACP (1926 ed.); CAW; ChIP; ISi; JKCP (1926 ed.); StJW

Ave Maria! Maiden mild! Hymn to the Virgin [*or* Ave Maria]. Sir Walter Scott. *Fr.* The Lady of the Lake, III. EnRP; GoBC; ISi

Ave Maria! o'er the earth and sea. Evening. Byron. *Fr.* Don Juan, III. LPS-2

Ave Maris Stella ("Ave maris stella,/ The star in the sea"). *Unknown.* AnEC

Ave, Maris Stella ("Hail, Thou star of ocean"). *Unknown, tr. fr. Latin.* WHL

Ave Maris Stella ("Star of ocean fairest"). *Unknown, tr. fr. Latin.* ISi

Ave! Nero Imperator. Duffield Osborne. AA

Ave Regina ("Hail, O Queen of heaven enthroned"). *Unknown, tr. fr. Latin.* WHL

Ave Regina Coelorum ("Queen of the heavens, we hail thee"). *Unknown, tr. fr. Latin by* Winfred Douglas. ISi

Ave Sanctissima! *Unknown.* WHL

Ave Verum Corpus Natum, *abr. Unknown, tr. fr. Latin.* WHL

Ave, Vita Nostra! Clifford James Laube. ISi

'Ave you 'eard o' the Widow at Windsor. The Widow at Windsor. Kipling. OAEP (2d ed.)

Avenge, O Lord. Milton. *See* On the Late Massacre in Piedmont.

Avenger Speaks, The. Robert Browning. *See* After.

Avengers, The. Robert Graves. HBMV

Avengers, The. Edwin Markham. MAP; MoAmPo; NeMA

Avenging Daughters, The. *Unknown, tr. fr. Danish by* E. M. Smith-Dampier. BoDaBa; LiTW; LyMA

Avenging Sword, The. *Unknown, tr. fr. Danish by* E. M. Smith-Dampier. BoDaBa

Avenue in Savernake Forest. William Lisle Bowles. EnSW

Avenue of the Allies, The. Alfred Noyes. PoFr

Avenue of Trees, The. Tsurayuki, *tr. fr. Japanese by* Basil Hall Chamberlain. OnPM

Average. P. K. Page. TwCaPo

Average Man, The. William Langland, *mod. by* Henry W. Wells. *Fr.* The Vision of Piers Plowman. PoLi

Average Man, The. Margaret E. Sangster. WBLP

Avert, High Wisdom, never vainly wooed. On the Danger of War. George Meredith. CoBE; EmBrPo; EPN

Avesta. *See* Gathas.

Aviator, The. Aleksandr Blok, *tr. fr. Russian by* Payson Loomis. OnHM; PoF

Avocat Patelin, L'. *Unknown. See* Lawyer Patelin.

Avoid extreams and shun the fault of such. Pope. *Fr.* An Essay on Criticism. NBE

Avoid the friend who's parasitic. Bad Company. Abu Amr. MooP

Avoid the reeking herd. The Eagle and the Mole. Elinor Wylie. AnFE; APA; AWP; BLV; BoLiVe; CBOV; ChMo; CoAnAm; CoBA; GTBS-W; HBMV; LiTA; LiTM; MAP; MM; MoAB; MoAmPo; MOAP; NeMA; NP; NV; PG; PoE; PoeMoYo; TCPD; TSW; TwAmPo; ViBoPo; WHA

Avoid, you strollers in the dark street. Against Illuminations. Archibald MacLeish. MOAP

Avon, The. Henry Jacobs. AnNZ

Avondale Mine Disaster, The. *Unknown.* BaBo; ViBoFo

Avowal. A. M. Sullivan. JKCP (1926 ed.)

Aw, quit yer cryin', kid—I know it's tough. Cell-Mates. Louis Untermeyer. HBMV

Aw, Sally Brown, I been a long while a-courtin' ya. Sally Brown, *vers.* II. *Unknown.* ShS

Awaiting the Barbarians. C. P. Cavafy, *tr. fr. Modern Greek by* Rae Dalven. MoGP

Awaits no solar quadriga. The Welcome. Freda Laughton. NeIP

Awake! Song of Solomon, IV: 16, Bible, *O.T.* FaPON
("Awake! oh, north wind.") SUS

Awake! W. R. Rodgers. LiTM (rev. ed.); WaP

Awake! Walther von der Vogelweide, *tr. fr. German by* Jethro Bithell. AWP; JAWP; OnPM; WBP
(Awake! The Day Is Coming Now.) WoL

Awake, Aeolian lyre, awake. The Progress of Poesy. Thomas Gray. ATP; AWP; BEL; CBOV; CEP; CoBE; EiPP; EM-1; EnLi-2 (1949 ed.); EnLit; EnRP; EPP; EV-3; GTBS; GTBS-D; GTBS-W; GTSE; GTSL; HBV; OAEP; OBEC; OBEV; PIAE; PoFS; TCEP; ViBoPo

Awake, alone, aware. Insomniac Poem. Ron Loewinsohn. NeAP

Awake and praise, O dwellers in the dust! The Resurrection. John Gilland Brunini. MaRV

Awake, arise,/ Pull out your eyes. *Unknown.* OxNR

Awake, arise, rally, friends! The Destruction of Leire. *Unknown.* PaOS

Awake! arise! shake off thy dreams! To My Native Land. James Clarence Mangan. AnIL; IrPN

Awake! arise! the hour is late! A Longfellow Alphabet. *Comp. by* Caroline B. Le Row. PEOR

Awake! arise, ye men of might! To Arms. Park Benjamin. PAH

Awake! Awake! Sir William Davenant. *See* Lark Now Leaves His Wat'ry Nest, The.

Awake! Awake! Ruskin. *Fr.* Song of the Dawn. HBV
("Awake! awake! the stars are pale.") PoFr

Awake! Awake! The Bells. William Young. *Fr.* Wishmakers' Town. AA

Awake! awake! Aristophanes. *Fr.* The Birds. GrPo

Awake, awake, Deborah. Judges, Bible, *O.T.* PoFr

Awake! awake! my gallant friends. The Battle of Tippecanoe. *Unknown.* GA; PAH

"Awake, awake, my little boy!" The Land of Dreams. Blake. BeLS; BOL; CBPC; CH; OBRV

Awake, Awake, My Lyre! Abraham Cowley. *See* Supplication, A.

Awake, awake, O Church of God! The Clarion-Call. *Unknown.* BLRP

Awake! awake! the stars are pale, the east is russet gray. Awake! Awake! Ruskin. *Fr.* Song of the Dawn. HBV; PoFr

Awake, Awake, Thou Heavy Sprite. Thomas Campion. EV-2; SiCE

Awake, awake, you weary sleepers. Rules of the Road. *Unknown.* SoAmSa

Awake but not yet up, too early morning. Out of Sleep. Allen Curnow. AnNZ

Awake, fair[e] Muse; for I intend. An Ode. William Browne. OBS; SeEP

Awake! flower of the forest, sky-treading bird of the prairie. Calling-One's-Own. *Unknown.* NV

Awake! for Morning in the bowl of Night. Rubáiyát of Omar Khayyám, *tr. by* Edward Fitzgerald. CaAE; GTBS-D; LoBV; OxBI; PeP; PoFS; PreP; ShBV-4.
See also Wake! for the Sun who scattered into flight.

Awake from slumbering lethargy! To His Muse. Edward Benlowes. *Fr.* Theophila; or, Love's Sacrifice. SeCL

Awake! Glad Heart! Henry Vaughan. *See* Christ's Nativity.

Awake (great Sir) the Sun shines heer. On New-Years Day 1640. To the King. Sir John Suckling. SeCV-1

Awake, Mine Eyes! *Unknown.* ElL

Awake, My Fair. Judah Halevi, *tr. fr. Hebrew by* Alice Lucas. TrJP

Awake, My Heart [to Be Loved]. Robert Bridges. EtPaEn; HBV; MBP; MoAB; MoBrPo; OBEV (new ed.); OBVV; PoeT; VA; VLEP

Awake, My Lute! C. S. Lewis. BoN; CenHV

Awake, my mate! Hark! the Hoopoe's Call. Aristophanes. *Fr.* The Birds. GrR

Awake, my St. John! leave all meaner things. An Essay on

Awake, my St. John! (*continued*)
Man. Pope. BEL; CEP; EiPP; EnL; EnLi-1; EPP; GEPC; OAEP; PIAE; PoEL-3; REAL; TCEP; TOP
Awake, My Soul! Philip Doddridge. WGRP
("Awake, my soul, stretch every nerve.") OlF
Awake, My Soul. Moses ibn Ezra, *tr. fr. Hebrew by* Solomon Solis-Cohen. *Fr.* Wine-Songs. TrJP
Awake, My Soul ("Awake, my soul, and with the sun"). Thomas Ken. *See* Morning Hymn.
Awake, my soul, and come away. A Hymn for Christmas Day. Jeremy Taylor. AnEC
Awake, my soul, let's to the tavern go. Awake, My Soul. Moses ibn Ezra. *Fr.* Wine-Songs. TrJP
Awake, O, north wind. Song of Solomon, Bible, *O.T.* FaPON; SUS
Awake!—the crimson dawn is glowing. Thirty-first of May. Frederick Tennyson. VA
Awake! the dawn is on the hills! Aubade [*or* Morning Serenade]. Madison Cawein. HBV; SPP
Awake! The Day Is Coming Now. Walther von der Vogelweide. *See* Awake!
Awake thee, my Bessy, the morning is fair. Song. Jeremiah Joseph Callanan. IrPN; OnYI
Awake thee, my lady-love! Morning-Song [*or* Serenade]. George Darley. *Fr.* Sylvia; or, The May Queen. HBV; VA
Awake, thou wintry earth. Easter Hymn. Thomas Blackburn. HH
Awake, ye forms of verse divine! The National Paintings. Fitz-Greene Halleck *and* Joseph Rodman Drake. *Fr.* The Croaker Papers. AA
Awake, ye nations, slumbering supine. Sonnets Written in the Fall of 1914. George Edward Woodberry. HBV; MC; PAH
Awakened, I behold through dewy leaves. Sonnet. Thomas Caulfield Irwin. IrPN
Awakened War God, The. Margaret Widdemer. WGRP
Awakening, The. Conrad Aiken. The Kid, VII. MoVE
Awakening. Rose Terry Cooke. EOAH
Awakening, The. Robert Creeley. NeAP
Awakening, The. Don Marquis. HBMV
Awakening, The. Angela Morgan. OHIP
Awakening. Margaret E. Sangster. AA; PTA-2
Awakening from Drunkenness on a Spring Day. Li Po, *tr. fr. Chinese.* WhP
Awakening of Dermuid, The. Austin Clarke. *Fr.* The Vengeance of Finn. AnIV
Awakening of Epimenides, The, *sel.* Goethe, *tr. fr. German by* F. Melian Stawell *and* Nora Purtscher-Wydenbruck.
"Up my brothers! Set all men free!" PoFr
Awakening of Man, The. Robert Browning. *See* Man's Destiny.
Awakening of Spring, The. Ku Shih, *tr. fr. Chinese by* Henry H. Hart. PoHN
Awaking early from your winter's sleep. To an Early Plum. Hsieh Hsieh. PoHN
Award. Gertrude Callaghan. JKCP (1955 ed.)
Aware. D. H. Lawrence. MBP; MoBrPo
Awareness. Miriam Teichner. BLP; MaRV; OQP; QP-1
Awareness is on us, now, of the several heavens. Chorus for Easter. David Morton. MaRV
Away. Walter de la Mare. ChMo
Away. Max Ehrmann. PoToHe
Away. James Whitcomb Riley. BLRP, *abr.;* LPS-1; MaRV; WGRP, *abr.*
(He Is Not Dead.) BLPA; NeHB
(He's Just Away.) BLP
Away across the yellow plain. A Mexican Lullaby. Grace Hazard Conkling. BOL
Away, airy comber of comets! Small Death to Laugh. Tristan Corbière. AnFP
Away and away. Dreaming of My Dead Wife. Su T'ung-po. WhP
Away and away I sail in my light boat. Boating in Autumn. Lu Yu. TrCh
Away, Away! Shelley. *Fr.* To Jane: The Invitation. GoTP
Away! away! The Complaint. Mark Akenside. OBEV
Away, away, from men and towns. Away, Away! Shelley. *Fr.* To Jane: The Invitation. GoTP
Away, away in the Northland. A Legend of the Northland. Phoebe Cary. GoTP; HBV; HBVY; OTPC; PTA-2; RIS
Away! away! through the sightless air. Song of the Lightning. George W. Cutter. LPS-3
Away, Away, Vex Me No More. *Unknown.* SeCL
Away, away, ye men of rules. *Unknown, tr. fr. Greek by* Thomas Moore. GrPo
Away back yonder when years were few. Choice. James Larkin Pearson. NoCaPo
Away beyond the Jarboe house. Strange Tree. Elizabeth Madox Roberts. BoChLi; FaPON; MPB; NP; SP
Away by the haunts of the Yang-tse-boo. The Rhyme of the Kipperling. Sir Owen Seaman. CenHV
Away, Delights! Beaumont *and* Fletcher. *Fr.* The Captain, III, iv. ElL; OBEV; ViBoPo
("Away, delights! go seek some other dwelling.") LO
(Farewell, False Love!) TriL
(Sad Song, The.) FaBoEn
Away down Home. John Charles McNeill. NoCaPo
Away down South in old Tennessee. A Long Time Ago, *vers.* I. *Unknown.* ShS
Away down South where I was born. A Long Time Ago. *Unknown.* ShS, *vers.* II; SoAmSa
Away, for we are ready to a man! The Golden Journey to Samarkand: Epilogue (*also in* Hassan). James Elroy Flecker. CP; ShBV-3
Away from friends, away from home. The Wanderer's Grave. Rufus B. Sage. PoOW
Away from home I am nothing. Womankind. Sophocles. OxBG
Away from London. Pope. *Fr.* An Epistle to Martha Blount on Her Leaving Town after the Coronation. BeR
Away from the town, in the safe retreat. A Lesson in Geography. Frances Wynne. TIP
Away, haul away,/ Rock and roll me over. Haul Away, Joe, *vers.* I. *Unknown.* ShS
Away, haul away, boys, haul away together. Haul Away O. *Unknown.* SG
Away, haul away, Oh, haul and sing together. Haul Away Joe. *Unknown.* SoAmSa
Away, haul away, Oh, haul away together. Haul Away, Joe. *Unknown.* AmSS
Away, haunt thou not me. In a Lecture-Room. Arthur Hugh Clough. BPN; EmBrPo; EPN; PoVP; TCEP; VA; ViPo; VLEP
Away in a Manger. Martin Luther. *See* Cradle Hymn, A.
Away; let nought to love displeasing. Winifreda. *Unknown.* EV-2; HBV; OBEC; OBEV (new ed.)
Away my verse! and never fear. To His Verse [*or* Lyrics, to Ianthe]. Walter Savage Landor. BPN; OBVV
Away out in old Texas, that great Lone Star State. Only a Cowboy. *Unknown.* CoSo; CSF
Away out yonder in Arizony. Whoppers. John A. Lomax. OuSiCo
Away, Rio! *Unknown.* AmSS, *with music;* LoGBV
Away the horde rode, in a storm of hail. The Uncertain Battle. David Gascoyne. SoV
Away! the moor is dark beneath the moon. Stanzas—April, 1814 [*or* Remorse]. Shelley. BPN; BrBE; CaAE; CBE; ChER; EM-2; EmBrPo; EnRP; ERP; FiP; LoBV; MyFE; OAEP; OBEV
Away thou fondling motley humorist. Satires, I. John Donne. OAEP
Away to the Brook. The Angler's Ballad. Charles Cotton. CEP
Away to Twiver, Away, Away! *Unknown.* ElL
Away, useless trifles! Of the Sad Lot of the Humanists in Paris. George Buchanan. GoTS
Away, 'way off 'cross the seas and such. The Little Toy Land of the Dutch. *Unknown.* GFA; MPB; OTPC (1946 ed.)
Away We Go. Aileen Fisher. TiPo (1959 ed.)
Away with Bloodshed. A. E. Housman. WhC
Away with learning! Away with grieving! Tao Teh Ching, V. *Unknown, tr. fr. Chinese.* WhP
Away with recipes in books. Ancient Adage [*or* Old German Mottos]. *Unknown.* PIAE; StaSt
Away with sages! Away with wise men! Tao Teh Ching, XX. *Unknown, tr. fr. Chinese.* WhP
Away with silks, away with lawn. Clothes Do but Cheat and Cozen Us. Robert Herrick. ALV; LoPS
Away with these self-loving lads. Of [*or* Song to] His Cynthia [*or* Cynthia]. Fulke Greville. Caelica, LII. AtBAP; ElL; ElSeCe; OBSC; ReIE; RiBV; SiCE; TuPP; ViBoPo
Away with this cash. *Unknown.* SeCSL
"Away with you, away with you, James de Grant!" James Grant. *Unknown.* ESPB
Away with your fictions of flimsy romance. The First Kiss of Love. Byron. HBV
Away, ye gay landscapes, ye gardens of roses! Lachin y Gair. Byron. BPN
Away yee barb'rous woods; how ever yee be plac't. Michael Drayton. *Fr.* Polyolbion: Third Song. OBS
Away, Your Touch Is Everywhere. Eve Merriam. LoPS
Aw'd by her own rash words she was still: and her eyes to the seaward. Andromeda and the Sea-Nymphs. Charles Kingsley. *Fr.* Andromeda. VA
Aweary Am I. Abu-l-Ala al-Maarri, *tr. fr. Arabic by* R. A. Nicholson. AWP; LiTW
Awesome are the works of God. The Works of God. Moses ibn Ezra. TrJP
Awesome thing happened, An. The Specter's Tale. Yetza Gillespie. DaM
Awful Lot to Fishin', An. R. C. Calloway. DDA
Awful Responsibility, An. Keith Preston. WhC
Awful shadow of some unseen Power, The. Hymn to Intellectual Beauty. Shelley. AnEnPo; AnFE; BCEP; BEL; BoLiVe; BPN; CoBE; EM-2; EmBrPo; EnL; EnLi-2; EnLit; EnRP; EPN; EPP; ERP; GEPC; OAEP; OBRV;

OuHeWo; Po; PoE; PoFS; REAL; ReTS; TOP; TwCrTr; TyEnPo; UnPo (1st ed.)
Awful tempest mashed the air, An. A Tempest. Emily Dickinson. MCCG
Awhile, O Dawn-star [*or* Daystar] of the living. The Young Astronomer Dead. Plato. GrPE; GrR
Awhile their route they silent made. Lake Coriskin. Sir Walter Scott. *Fr.* The Lord of the Isles, III. EV-4
Awkward was she yesterday. The Maiden. Peter Hille. AWP
Awltho I no how 2 and fro. My Own Simplified Spelling. E. V. Knox. SiTL
A-Working on the Railway. Arthur H. Clark. IHA
Awright, awright, ev'rybody get ready. Steel Laying Holler. *Unknown.* ABF
Axa, Fátima, and Marién. *Unknown, tr. fr. Spanish by* Jean Rogers Longland. AnSpL-1
(Song, *tr. at. to* Jean Willard Burnham.) LiTW
("Three Moorish girls I loved," *tr. by* Jean Rogers Longland.) TeCS
Axe, The. Isabella Valancy Crawford. VA
(Axe of the Pioneer, The.) CaP; OCL
Axe Has Cut the Forest Down, The. Elizabeth J. Coatsworth. BrR; MPB (1956 ed.)
(Wilderness is Tamed, The.) FaPON; StVeCh
Axe-Helve, The. Robert Frost. AmPo; CoV; OxBA
Axe in the Wood, The. Clifford Dyment. POTE
Axe of the Pioneer, The. Isabella Valancy Crawford. *See* Axe, The.
Axle Song. Mark Van Doren. MoPo; TwAmPo
Axolotl, The. David McCord. FiBHP; WhC
Ay, an old story, yet it might. A Legend. May Kendall. VA
Ay and No. John Gay. CBOV
Ay ant lak pie-plant pie so wery vell. Sonnet on Stewed Prunes. William F. Kirk. WhC
Ay, ay, and away she goes. Highland Laddie. *Unknown.* ShS
Ay, beshrew you, by my fay. Mannerly Margery Milk and Ale. John Skelton. ReEn
Ay, but I know. Unrequited Love. Shakespeare. *Fr.* Twelfth Night, II, iv. LPS-1
Ay, but to Die. Shakespeare. *Fr.* Measure for Measure, III, i. BCEP
("Ay [*or* Aye], but to die, and go we know not where.") BrBE; PoD
Ay "Conspiracy" and "Tyrant." Vogue of the Tar-Brush. Aristophanes. *Fr.* The Wasps. GrR
Ay de mi Alhama. *Unknown. See* Alhama.
Ay! drop the treacherous mask! throw by. Butler's Proclamation. Paul Hamilton Hayne. PAH
Ay, Dwainie!—My Dwainie! Dwainie. James Whitcomb Riley. *Fr.* Flying Islands of the Night. AA
Ay, from the first my soul was outward-bound. Ideal Passion, XII. George Edward Woodberry. MOAP
Ay, gnaw me to my root. The Vine to the Goat. Euenus. OxBG
Ay, guitarrist of the roots. Romanza of the Guitarrist. Raúl Otero Reiche. AnCL
Ay, here such valorous deeds were done. Waterloo. Winthrop Mackworth Praed. SoV
Ay, if a madman could have leave. Lines. Keats. PoP
Ay, it is fitting on this holiday. Ode in Memory of the American Volunteers Fallen for France. Alan Seeger. PAH
Ay, let it rest! And give us peace. The Gospel of Peace. James Jeffrey Roche. PAH
Ay Me, Alas. *Unknown.* FaBoCh; LoGBV
(Ay Me, Alas, Heigh Ho!) CH
(Madrigals, 3.) OxBoLi; SiTL
Ay me alas! the beautiful bright hair. Canzone: His Lament for Selvaggia. Cino da Pistoia. AWP; JAWP; WBP
Ay me, ay me! I sigh to see the scythe afield. A Proper Sonnet, How Time Consumeth All [Earthly] Things [*or* Sic Transit]. *Unknown, at. to* Thomas Proctor. BLV; ChTr; EIL; OBSC; PoD; SiCE; TrGrPo; TuPP
Ay me, ay me, the mallow in the mead. Nox Est Perpetua una Dormienda. *Unknown. Fr.* Lament for Bion. OxBG
Ay me! for aught that ever I could [*or* I could ever] read. The Course of True Love. Shakespeare. *Fr.* A Midsummer Night's Dream, I, i. LPS-1; TreFS; WHA
"Ay, not at home, then, didst thou say?" A Call on Sir Walter Raleigh. Sarah M. B. Piatt. AA
Ay, Oliver! I was but seven, and he was eleven. Echo and the Ferry. Jean Ingelow. CBPC
Ay, once I dreamed of an age-wide sea. Walter de la Mare. *Fr.* Dreams. UnW
Ay or Nay? Ralph Schomberg. *Fr.* The Judgment of Paris. TrJP
Ay, shout and rave, thou cruel sea. Herndon. S. Weir Mitchell. PAH
Ay, since beyond these walls no heavens there be. Herbert Trench. *Fr.* To Arolilia. LO
Ay [*or* Aye], tear her tattered ensign down! Old Ironsides. Oliver Wendell Holmes. AA; AmPP (3d ed.); AnNE; APW; BBV; BLPA; BTP; CoBA; DD; EtS; FaBoBe; FaFP; FaPON; GA; GDAH; GN; HBV; HBVY; IAP; LPS-2; MaC; MC; MCCG; MOAP; NeHB; OnHT; OTPC; OuHeWo; PaA; PAH; PAP; PECK; PIR; PoRL; PTA-1; PYM; TCAP; TreF; TVSH; YaD
Ay—There It Is. Emily Brontë. ChER
Ay, this is freedom!—these pure skies. The Hunter of the Prairies. Bryant. AA
Ay [*or* Aye], thou art welcome, heaven's delicious breath! October. Bryant. IAP; PEOR
Ay, 'Tis Thus. *Unknown, tr. fr. Hebrew by* Israel Zangwill. TrJP
Ay, 'twas here, on this spot. Atalanta in Camden-Town. "Lewis Carroll." ALV; CenHV; PA
Ay! Unto thee belong. Theocritus. Annie Fields. AA; LBAP
Ay Waukin, O. Burns. EBSV
Aye and 'tis worth the hearing. The Sausage-Seller's Triumph. Aristophanes. *Fr.* The Knights. GrR
Aye, edge the trees in white. February. Ann Louise Hayes. PtPa
Aye, I was one with moon-touched, whispering leaves. Fulfillment. Cathleen Keegan. UnW
Aye, lads, aye, we fought 'em. Off Manilly. Edmund Vance Cooke. PAH
Aye, master! fine old trees! Robert Southey. *Fr.* The Old Mansion. EnSW
Aye me can love and bewtie soe conspire. *Unknown.* SeCSL
Aye, on the shores of darkness there is light. Keats. *Fr.* To Homer. PC
"Aye, squire," said Stevens, "they back him at evens!" How We Beat the Favo[u]rite. Adam Lindsay Gordon. OtMeF; VA
Aye, tear her tattered ensign down! *See* Ay, tear her tattered ensign down!
Aye, the Jute's a sturdy lad. The Jutlander. Steen Steensen Blicher. BoDS
Aye, there it is; that's just what I was saying. Sky-Riding on a Beetle. Aristophanes. *Fr.* The Peace. GrR
Aye, thou art welcome, heaven's delicious breath! *See* Ay, thou art welcome . . .
Aye Waukin' O! *Unknown.* BSV; GoTS
Ayee! Ai! This is [*or* This] heavy earth on our shoulders. Burying Ground by the Ties. Archibald MacLeish. Frescoes for Mr. Rockefeller's City, III. AmPP (4th ed.); MAP; MoAmPo; NAMP; ReaPo; UnPo; WoL
Aylmer's Field, *sels.* Tennyson.
Leolin and Edith. GN
"Never, since our bad earth became one sea." VLEP
"Whisper half reveal'd her to herself, A." EnSW
Ayme, Ayme, I Sigh to See the Scythe Afield. *Unknown.* *See* Proper Sonnet, A, How Time Consumeth . . .
Azalea, The. Coventry Patmore. The Unknown Eros, I, vii. GoBC; POTT; PoVP; ViP; VLEP
Azaleas. Muda, *tr. fr. Japanese by* Lois J. Erickson. SoLD
Azaleas—whitest of white! White Azaleas. Harriet McEwen Kimball. AA; HBV
Azra, The. Heine, *tr. fr. German by* John Hay. AWP; JAWP; WBP
Azrael. Longfellow. Tales of a Wayside Inn: The Spanish Jew's Tale, Pt. III. AnAmPo; LA
Azrael. Gertrude Huntington McGiffert. BAP
Azrael. Robert Gilbert Welsh. BAP; HBV; LBMV; MaRV; OQP; QP-1
Aztec City, The. Eugene Fitch Ware. AA; HBV
Azur'd vault, the crystal circles bright, The. *See* Azured vault, the crystal . . .
Azure, The. Stéphane Mallarmé, *tr. fr. French by* Kate Flores. AnFP
Azure! behold me . . . I come from the caverns of death. Helen. Paul Valéry, *tr. by* Andrew Chiappe. AnFP
Azure sky, An/ All star bestrewn. Christmas. *Unknown.* BoTP
Azure, 'tis I, come from Elysian shores. Hélène (Helen, the Sad Queen). Paul Valéry, *tr. by* Janet Lewis. Po
Azure, 'tis I, from the caves of death withdrawn. Helen, the Sad Queen. Paul Valéry, *tr. by* Joseph T. Shipley. AWP; CAW; JAWP; WBP
Azure! 'tis I . . . I come from death's own caves. Helen. Paul Valéry, *tr. by* Alan Conder. TrFP
Azured [*or* Azur'd] vault, the crystal circles bright, The. Heaven and Earth [*or* Sonnet]. James I, King of England. ChTr; EIL; SeCePo
Azzoomm, azzoomm loud and strong. Riding in an Airplane. Dorothy W. Baruch. FaPON

B

B. Larry Eigner. NeAP
B. Phyllis McGinley. *See* B's the Bus.
Ba-ba, black wool. Chorus. William Brighty Rands. *Fr.* Topsy-turvy World. BoN; PIAE

Baa, baa, black sheep, have you any wool? Mother Goose. BoChLi; FaBoBe; FaFP; HBV; HBVY; OTPC; OxNR; PCH; PPL; RIS; SAS; SiTL; StVeCh; TiPo
Baal Shem Tov. A. M Klein. CaP; TrJP
Bab-Lock-Hythe. Laurence Binyon. MoVE; PoeT
Babbitt and the Bromide, The. Ira Gershwin. *Fr.* Funny Face. ALV
Babbitt, your tribe is passing away. The Virginians Are Coming Again. Vachel Lindsay. NP
Babbling current fails, A. Trust Thy Last Friend against the World. *Unknown.* BoFr
Babe, The. Monk Gibbon. OxBI
Babe is born all of a May, A. Three Christmas Carols, I [*or* Nowell, Ell, Ell, Ell]. *Unknown.* ACP; AnEC
Babe is born, to bliss us bring, A Now Sing We with Angelis. *Unknown.* AnEC
Babe Jesu lying/ On my little pallet lonely. Saint Ita's Fosterling. *At. to* St. Ita. OnYI
Babe Jesus is here. The Little Lord Jesus. *Unknown.* ChrBoLe
Babe of Bethlehem, The. Henry Beer. BePJ
Babe of Bethlehem, The. Condé Benoist Pallen. JKCP
Babel and Bethel. Frank Buchanan. QS
Babel Falls. Anna Hempstead Branch. *Fr.* Nimrod, V. TCPD
Babes in the Wood [*or* Woods], The ("My dear, do you know/ How, a long time ago"). *Unknown.* ABS, *sl. abr.;* OTPC (1946 ed.); RIS
("My dear, do you know how a long time ago.") PPL
Babes in the Wood [*or* Woods], The ("Now ponder well, you parents dear"). *Unknown.* EV-2; HBV; HBVY; OTPC (1923 ed.)
(Children in the Wood, The.) CG; EnSB; OBB; OnSP
Babes in the Woods, The. Bret Harte. BAV
Babiaantje, The F. T. Prince. BoSA; ChMP
Babie, The. Jeremiah Eames Rankin, *wr. at. to* Hugh Miller. AA; HBV; LPS-1; PECK; PTA-2
Babies haven't any hair. More Hair. Samuel Hoffenstein. SiTL
Baboon. Charles Hanson Towne. BAP; LEAP
Babushka; a Russian Legend. Edith M. Thomas. ChrBoLe; OTPC (1946 ed.); SDH
(Babouscka.) MPB
Baby, The. Mary Raymond Shipman Andrews. DDA
Baby. Elaine Goodale Eastman. AA
Baby. Florence Kiper Frank. HBMV
Baby, The. Sir William Jones, *after the Sanskrit of* Kalidasa. BCEP; LPS-1; PIR; TreFS
(Epigram: "On parent knees, a naked new-born child.") OBEV
(Moral Tetrastich, A.) OBEC; PrWP
(On Parent Knees [a Naked New-born Child].) HBV; TriL
(To an Infant Newly Born.) CBOV
Baby, The. George Macdonald. *Fr.* At the Back of the North Wind, *ch.* 23. FaPON; HBV; HBVY; LPS-1; MPB; OTPC; PTA-1; RAR; TreF; TVC; TVSH; VA
(Where Did You Come From?) BLPA; FaFP
Baby, The. Ann Taylor. DD, *abr.;* MOAH; OHIP
Baby,/ You shall be free. Kadia the Young Mother Speaks. Jessie Sampter. TrJP
Baby and I/ Were baked in a pie. *Unknown.* BoN; OxNR
Baby and Mary. *Unknown.* NA
Baby Asleep after Pain, A. D. H. Lawrence. LBBV; NP; TCEP
Baby at Play. *Unknown.* HBV; HBVY; OTPC
("Brow bender.") PPL
Baby, baby bright. Cradle Songs, I. Swinburne. BOL
Baby, baby dear. Cradle Songs, II. Swinburne. BOL
Baby, baby, hush-a-bye. A Lullaby. Laurence Alma-Tadema. BOL
Baby, baby, lay your head. Good Night. Jane Taylor. BoChLi; BOL; CBPC; HBV; HBVY; OTPC; PPL; RAR; SAS, *st.* 1
Baby, baby, naughty baby. *Unknown.* OxNR
Baby, baby, ope your eye. Good-Morning. *Unknown.* SAS
Baby Beds. *Unknown.* BoTP
Baby Bell. Thomas Bailey Aldrich. HBV; LPS-1
Baby born in Bethlehem. Little Child of Mary. H. T. Burleigh. StJW
Baby bye. The Fly. Theodore Tilton. RIS
Baby child of Mary, The. Lullaby. *Unknown.* BOL
Baby Christ, when He was born, The. The Birthday of the Lord. Mary Jane Carr. ChBR
Baby Cobina. Gladys May Casely Hayford. CDC
Baby Corn. Lydia Avery Coonley Ward. GFA; PRWS
Baby cry. Christina Rossetti. *Fr.* Sing-Song. EmBrPo
Baby Dear. Samuel Lover. BOL; OTPC (1946 ed.)
Baby dear, good-night, good-night. *Unknown.* SAS
Baby found a caterpillar, The. The Caterpillar Appeal. Julia Ann Rogers. DDA
Baby Girl, The. Eugenio Florit, *tr. fr. Spanish by* Donald Devenish Walsh. AnCL
Baby Goes Out to Tea. *Unknown.* SAS
Baby Goes to Boston, The. Laura E. Richards. GoBP; SAS; TiPo
Baby Hare The. Meleager, *tr. fr. Greek by* F. L. Lucas. GrPE; GrR
Baby in the Basket, The. Emily Carter. SAS
Baby is a sailor boy. Swing, Cradle, Swing. George Cooper. BOL
Baby is sailing away in a boat. The Cradle Boat. John Keynton. BOL
Baby King Jesus came down to His own, The. Christmas Legend. Edna Randolph Worrell. ChBR
Baby-Land. George Cooper. *See* Babyland.
Baby Lapp's Ride. *Unknown.* SAS
Baby laughed—and through the car, The. A Street Car Miracle. Minnie Leona Upton. POT
Baby Livingston. *Unknown.* OBB
Baby Lon. *Unknown. See* Babylon; or, The Bonnie Banks o' Fordie.
Baby Louise. Margaret Eytinge. LPS-1
Baby loves to play with me. Hide and Seek. Phyllis Drayson. BoTP
Baby lying on his mother's breast, A. Man's Pillow. Irving Browne. AA; LEAP
Baby Making Cakes. *Unknown.* SAS
Baby May. William Cox Bennett. HBV; LPS-1; OTPC (1923 ed.); VA
Baby Mine. Kate Greenaway. RAR
Baby moon, a canoe, a silver papoose canoe, The. Early Moon. Carl Sandburg. LaNeLa; MOAP; PG
Baby mustn't frown. The Gravel Path. Laurence Alma-Tadema. PPL; RAR
Baby new to earth and sky, The. In Memoriam A. H. H., XLV. Tennyson. EmBrPo; EnLi-2; EPN; GEPC; ViPo; VLEP
Baby, O baby, fain you are for bed. Cradle Song. Louis Esson. BoAu
Baby of Saint Brigid, The. Francis Carlin. PraNu
Baby on Her Travels. *Unknown.* SAS
Baby Running Barefoot. D. H. Lawrence. MoPW
Baby sat on the window-seat. Baby and Mary. *Unknown.* NA
Baby, see the flowers! In a Garden. Swinburne. BOL; PRWS; VLEP
Baby Seed Song. Edith Nesbit. BoChLi; DD; FaPON; HBV; HBVY; MPB; OTPC; PCH; PRWS; RAR; SP; TVC; TVSH
Baby Seeds. *Unknown.* MeMeAg; OTPC (1946 ed.); PCH
Baby Show, De. Wilson MacDonald. WhC
Baby sits in her cradle, The. Silent Baby. Ellen Bartlett Currier. LPS-1
Baby, Sleep. Christina Rossetti. *Fr.* Sing-Song. OTPC (1946 ed.)
("Lie a-bed.") BOL
Baby, sleep! shadows creep. Cradle Song of a Soldier's Wife. T. T. Barker. BOL
Baby Sleeps. Samuel Hinds. HBV; LPS-1
Baby Song, A. Elizabeth Stoddard. BOL
Baby-Song. Tennyson. *See* What Does Little Birdie Say?
Baby takes to her bed at night, The. Household Gods. J. H. Macnair. DDA; PoMa; POT; PoTo
Baby Toes. Carl Sandburg. FaPON; LaNeLa; SUS; TSW
Baby Verse, A ("Tit-tat-toe,/ My first go"). *Unknown.* BoTP
("Tit, tat, toe.") OxNR
Baby wants a lullaby. Lullaby. William Brighty Rands. BOL; PPL
Baby wants his breakfast. Baby's Breakfast. Emilie Poulsson. HBV; HBVY; PPL; RAR
Baby was lonely with mother away. An Erris Fairy. Hal D'Arcy. BOL
Baby was sleeping, A. The Angel's Whisper. Samuel Lover. BOL; LPS-1; OnYI; PRWS
Baby watched a ford, whereto, A. Wagtail and Baby. Thomas Hardy. HBMV
Baby wept, The. Baby Sleeps. Samuel Hinds. HBV; LPS-1
Baby Zulma's Christmas Carol. Augustus Julian Requier. LPS-1
Babyhood. Josiah Gilbert Holland. *See* Cradle Song: "What is the little one thinking about?"
Babyland [*or* Baby-Land]. George Cooper. BoTP; HBV; HBVY; OTPC; PPL
Babylon. "Æ." HBMV; PtOT; TwCV
Babylon. Robert Graves. HBMV; TwCV
Babylon. Ralph Hodgson. HBMV; TCEP
Babylon. Robert Eyres Landor. *Fr.* The Impious Feast, I. OBRV
Babylon. Virgil Markham. BAP
Babylon. A. G. Stephens. BoAu
Babylon. Viola Taylor. HBV
Babylon ("King and Queen of Cantelon"). *Unknown.* ChTr
Babylon ("There were three ladies lived in a bower"). *Unknown. See* Babylon; or, The Bonnie Banks o' Fordie.
Babylon and Sion (Goa and Lisbon). Luis de Camões, *tr. fr. Portuguese by* Richard Garnett. AWP; WoL

Babylon has fallen! Aye; but Babylon endures. Babylon. A. G. Stephens. BoAu
Babylon; or, The Bonnie Banks o' Fordie. *Unknown.* BaBo (*A and B vers.*); EnLi-1; ESPB; TOP
(Baby Lon.) SeCePo
(Babylon.) OBB
Babylonia, *sel.* "Owen Meredith."
Tempora Acta. VA
Babylonian Sorrows. Heine, *tr. fr. German by* Herman Salinger. AnGP
Baby's Bath, The. Sarah Jane S. Harrington. RAR
Baby's been in Sleepyland. Sleepyland. Laura E. Richards. SAS
Baby's Birthday, The. Eliza Lee Follen. PPL
Baby's brain is tired of thinking. A Boston Lullaby. James Jeffrey Roche. BOHV; BOL
Baby's Breakfast. Emilie Poulsson. HBV; HBVY; PPL; RAR
Baby's cradle with no baby in it, A. Christina Rossetti. *Fr.* Sing-Song. EmBrPo
Baby's Death, A. Swinburne. TCEP; VLEP
Baby's Debut, The. Horace Smith *and* James Smith. ALV; BOHV; EV-4; OBRV
Baby's Evening-Song. Edith M. Thomas. BOL
Baby's Eyes, A. Swinburne. Etude Réaliste, III. TSW
(Etude Réaliste.) BMEP; BPN; EPP; GN; HBV; OuHeWo; PoVP; VA
Baby's Feet, A. Swinburne. Etude Réaliste, I. FaPON; InP; TSW; TSWC
(Etude Réaliste.) BMEP; BPN; EPP; GN; HBV; OuHeWo; PoVP; VA
Baby's Hands. Gomei, *tr. fr. Japanese.* MPB
Baby's hands in Bethlehem, A. The Hands of Christ. Leslie Savage Clark. ChIP; MaRV
Baby's hands, like rosebuds furled, A. Etude Réaliste, II. Swinburne. BMEP; BPN; EPP; GN; HBV; OuHeWo; PoVP; VA
Baby's in Jail; the Animal Day Plays Alone. Charles Henri Ford. MoVE
Baby's Omar, The. Carolyn Wells. PA
Baby's Shoes. William Cox Bennett. LPS-1
Baby's Skies. Mary C. Bartlett. MOAH
Baby's Soliloquy, A. *Unknown.* PA
Baby's Way. Rabindranath Tagore. MOAH
Bacaote to Alexis. Gillespie Evans. CAG
Baccalaureate. David McCord. WhC
Bacchae, *sels.* Euripides, *tr. fr. Greek.*
On Cithaeron, *tr. by* Gilbert Murray. OxBG
"On tongues uncurbed by reverent awe," *tr. by* J. C. Wordsworth. GrPo
Prelude to Revel, *tr. by* H. H. Milman. GrR
Revel, The, *tr. by* Gilbert Murray. GrR
Song of the Bacchanals, *tr. by* Gilbert Murray. GrR
(Bacchanal, *shorter sel., tr. by* T. F. Higham.) OxBG
(Home of Aphrodite, The, *shorter sel., tr. by* Gilbert Murray.) AWP
"This Is Alone Life, Joy, Empire and Victory," *tr. by* Gilbert Murray. GrR
(Where Shall Wisdom Be Found? *abr., tr. by* Gilbert Murray.) OxBG; UnS, 6 *ll.*
When the Ecstasy Has Passed, *tr. by* Gilbert Murray. GrR
Bacchanal. Ibn Baqi, *tr. fr. Arabic by* A. J. Arberry. MooP
Bacchanalia; or, The New Age. Matthew Arnold. BPN; EmBrPo; GEPC; PoVP; VLEP
Bacchanalian Verse, A. Robert Herrick. BEL
Bacchanals. Euripides. *See* Bacchae.
Bacchante to Her Babe, The. Eunice Tietjens. HBMV; NP; NV
Bacchante's Offering, The. Callimachus, *tr. fr. Greek by* G. M. Young. GrL
Bacchus. Emerson. AmP; AmPo; AmPP; AnAmPo; AnFE; AnNE; APA; APW; AWP; BAV; CoAnAm; CoV; HBV; LA; LBAP; LEAP; LiTA; MOAP; OBEV; OxBA; PoEL-4; RiBV; ViBoPo
Bacchus. Thomas Love Peacock. *Fr.* Rhododaphne. OBRV
Bacchus. Frank Dempster Sherman. BAP; LBMV; MAP
Bacchus by the lonely ocean. Bacchus. Thomas Love Peacock. *Fr.* Rhododaphne. OBRV
Bacchus in Tuscany, *sels.* Francesco Redi, *tr. fr. Italian.*
Bacchus's Opinion of Wine, and Other Beverages, *tr. by* Leigh Hunt. AWP
Bacchus on Beverages, *tr. by* Leigh Hunt, *shorter sel.* LiTW
"Oh how widely wandereth he." PoP
Bacchus must now his power resign. A Drinking-Song. Henry Carey. OBEV
Bacchus, the father of drunken Nowls. The Man in the Moon Drinks Clarret. *Unknown.* CoMu
Bacchus's Opinion of Wine, and Other Beverages. Francesco Redi, *tr. fr. Italian by* Leigh Hunt. *Fr.* Bacchus in Tuscany. AWP
Bacchus on Beverages, *shorter sel.* LiTW
Bacchylides. George Meason Whicher. AA
"Bachelor bears compare combine." Dream Verses. Edith Nesbit. BoN
Bachelor Hall. Eugene Field. BLPA
Bachelor's Ballade, The. David Fisher Parry. InMe
Bachelors' Buttons. Maud Morin. BoTP
Bachelor's Dream, The. Thomas Hood. BOHV
Bachelor's Hall. John Finley. HBV; LPS-3
Bachelor's Lay, The, *with music.* *Unknown.* OuSiCo
Bachelor's Maid. John Gay. *Fr.* Work for a Cooper. BeR
Bachelor's Mono-Rhyme, A. Charles Mackay. BOHV
Bachelor's Soliloquy, The. *Unknown.* PA
Bachelor's Song, The. Thomas Flatman. *See* On Marriage.
Back. W. W. Gibson. ChMo; CMP; GTSL; LBBV; MaRV; PoeMoYo
(Black.) BMEP; PYM
Back and Forth. Lucy Sprague Mitchell. FaPON
Back and Side Go Bare, Go Bare. *At. to* William Stevenson. *Fr.* Gammer Gurton's Needle. BEL; EG; ElSeCe; EM-1; EnLi-1; InvP; LiTB; OAEP; PoRA; ReEn; RiBV; SiCE; TOP; TuPP; ViBoPo
(Good Ale.) LPS-3
(I Cannot Eat but Little Meat.) ExPo
(In Praise of Ale.) TrGrPo
(Jolly Good Ale [and Old].) EV-1; HBV; LEAP; OBEV; SeCeV; SiTL
(Of Jolly Good Ale and Old.) ElL
(Song of Ale, A.) AnFE; OBSC; UnPo (1st ed.)
Back arching: so. The Water-Wheel. Abu Abd Allah. MooP
Back behind the mirror is another pussy-cat. The Looking-Glass Pussy. Margaret Widdemer. RAR; UTS
Back from the front there came. George Henry Boker. *Fr.* Before Vicksburg. PEOR
Back from the trebly crimsoned field. Wanted—a Man. Edmund Clarence Stedman. IAP; PAH
Back Home. Harriet Monroe. PFE
Back Home Again. Grantland Rice. BoHiPo
Back in the Return. Huw Menai. MoWP
Back in the years when Phlagstaff, the Dane, was monarch. The Rejected "National Hymns," I. "Orpheus C. Kerr." BOHV; InMe; PA
Back now to their source will the sacred streams be mounting. The Dawn of Woman's Day. Euripides. *Fr.* Medea. GrR
Back of Chicago the open fields—were you ever there? Evening Song. Sherwood Anderson. NP
Back of God, The. J. R. Perkins. MaRV; OQP; QP-2
Back of the beating hammer. The Thinker. Berton Braley. BLPA; BTP; MW; NeHB; OQP; PEDC; PoMa; POT; PoTo; QP-1; StVeCh (1940 ed.); WBLP
Back of the loaf is the snowy flour. Our Daily Bread [*or* "Give Us This Day Our Daily Bread"]. Maltbie D. Babcock. BPP; MaRV; OQP; QP-1
Back of this door is the fabled star. For a Library Door. Theda Kenyon. MOB
Back out of all this now too much for us. Directive. Robert Frost. CoBMV; CrMA; LiTA; LiTM (rev. ed.); MoAB; MaPo; NePA; SeCeV
Back Road Farm. Charles Bruce. CaP
Back Room Joys. Justin Richardson. FiBHP
Back she came through the trembling dusk. Folk-Song. Louis Untermeyer. HBV
Back side of Albany stands Lake Champlain. Siege of Plattsburg. *Unknown.* ABF
Back thro' the hills I hurried home. Ballad of the Banshee. James B. Dollard. CPG
Back through clouds. Train Tune. Louise Bogan. NePoAm
Back to Dublin. R. A. D. Ford. CaP
Back to Griggsby's Station. James Whitcomb Riley. BLPA
Back to our shores he comes from the sad strand. League of Nations. Nancy Byrd Turner. AOAH
Back to the bewildering vision. Kinship. Sir Charles G. D. Roberts. CaP; OCL
Back to the flower-town, side by side. In Memory of Walter Savage Landor. Swinburne. BPN; EmBrPo; HBV; PoEL-5; PoFS; POTT; PoVP; PtP; VA; ViP; VLEP
Back to the Ghetto. Jacob Glatstein, *tr. fr. Yiddish by* Joseph Leftwich. TrJP
Back to the green deeps of the outer bay. The Herring Weir. Sir Charles G. D. Roberts. *Fr.* Songs of the Common Day. PeCV
Back to the sun he ploughed the mead. The Laborer. Evan Thomas. PSO
Back where the Old Gods dream there is no pain. Song from a Masque. Margaret Widdemer. TBM
Backbiter, The. Simonides, *tr. fr. Greek by* F. L. Lucas. GrPE
Backdrop is a misty form, The. September Morning. Eduard Mörike. AnGP
Background with Revolutionaries. Archibald MacLeish. Frescoes for Mr. Rockefeller's City, VI. ReaPo; TwHP; UnPo
Backstair Ballad. David McCord. BOHV
Backward—Forward. *Unknown.* BLRP

Backward, turn backward, film guy in your flight. Two Parodies. *Unknown.* CoSo

Backward, turn backward, O time, in your flight. Rock Me to Sleep. Elizabeth Akers Allen. AA; BLPA; DD; FaBoBe; FaFP; LPS-1; MOAH; MotAn; NeHB; OBAV; PTA-1; TreF; WBLP

Backward, turn backward, O Time with your wheels. Two Parodies. *Unknown.* CoSo

Backward we look regretful, forward we glance with dread. Resurgam. W. Nelson Bitton. BLRP

Backwoods Hero, A, *sel.* Alexander McLachlan.
"Where yonder ancient willow weeps." CaP

Backwoodsman, The, *sel.* James Kirke Paulding.
"Glory and Danger ever are allied." BAV

Bacon and Eggs. A. P. Herbert. WhC

Bacon's Epitaph, Made by His Man. *Unknown.* AnAmPo; APW; IAP; LA; PAH; SPP

Bad Boy, The, *with music. Unknown.* CoSo
(Root Hog or Die, *with music.*) CSF

Bad Company. Abu Amr, *tr. fr. Arabic by* A. J. Arberry. MooP

Bad Dreams. Robert Browning. OAEP; PoVP

Bad Girl's Lament, The. *Unknown.* ViBoFo

Bad Kittens, The. Elizabeth J. Coatsworth. FaPON; MoSiPe; MPB; PoeMoYo; PoRL; YT

Bad Luck to This Marching. Charles James Lever. OnYI

Bad Man Ballad, *with music. Unknown.* ABF
(Late One Night, *diff. vers., with music.*) StDa

Bad Man from the Brazos, The. *Unknown.* CoSo

Bad Season Makes the Poet Sad, The. Robert Herrick. LiTB; OAEP; SeCeV; UnPo (1st ed.)

Bad Squire, The. Charles Kingsley. *See* Rough Rhyme on a Rough Matter, A.

Bad Times. Joseph Beaumont. MaRV

Badger. John Clare. EnRP; ExPo; LiTB; PoE; PoEL-4; UnPo (3d ed.)

Badgers, The. Eden Phillpotts. BoTP

Badminton. Sir Alfred Comyn Lyall. *Fr.* Studies at Delhi. OBVV

Bad-tempered Wife, The. *Unknown. See* Farmer's Curst Wife, The.

Baffled. Rose Macaulay. AlDL

Baffled and beaten back she works on still. Melancholia. James Thomson. *Fr.* The City of Dreadful Night, XXI. CoEV

Baffled Knight, The. *Unknown.* BaBo; ESPB; ViBoFo
(There was a Knight and He Was Young.) CoMu

Bag of the Bee, The. Robert Herrick. OAEP

Bag of Tools, A. R. L. Sharpe. BLPA; MaRV; NeHB; PoToHe (new ed.); YaD
(Builders, *sl. diff.*) DDA

Baggage Coach Ahead, The. Gussie L. Davis. *See* In the Baggage Coach Ahead.

Baggot Street Deserta. Thomas Kinsella. PoN

Bagheera's Song. Kipling. *Fr.* The Second Jungle Book. PoFr

Bagley Wood. Lionel Johnson. AnFE; VLEP

Bagpipe Man, The. Nancy Byrd Turner. BoChLi; GaP; TiPo

Bagpipe Music. Louis MacNeice. ExPo; LiTB; LiTM; OAEP (2d ed.); OnYI; PoE; ReaPo; SeCePo; SeCeV; SiTL; ViBoPo (1958 ed.)

Bag-Pipes at Sea. Clinton Scollard. LBMV; NLK (1947 ed.)

Bah! I have sung women in three cities. Cino. Ezra Pound. ReaPo

Baharistan, *sel.* Jami, *tr. fr. Persian.*
Fragment: "Though decked the tray." CIV

Baiamai's Never-failing Stream. William Hart-Smith. BoAV

Bailada: "Let's dance now, all of us, all of us, oh my maidens." Airas Núñez, *tr. fr. Portuguese by* Seth G. Thornton. LyMA

Baile and Aillinn. W. B. Yeats. GTML

Bailey Beareth the Bell Away, The. *Unknown. See* Maidens Came, The.

Bailiff's Daughter of Islington, The. *Unknown.* BaBo (A *vers.*); ESPB; EV-2; GN; GoTP; HBV; LoEn; OAEP; OBB; OnSP; OTPC; OxBoLi; ReaPo; SaSa, *with music;* ViBoFo, *with music*
(Bayliffe's Daughter of Islington, The.) WP
(Love Token, The, B *vers.*) BaBo

Bairnies cuddle doon at nicht, The. Cuddle Doon. Alexander Anderson. BOL; BTP; GN; HBV; OHFP; VA

Bairns i' their beds, worn oot wi' nae wark, The. What the Auld Fowk Are Thinkin. George Macdonald. BSV

Bait [*or* Baite], The. John Donne. AnEnPo; EnLP; EPS (1942 ed.); HoPM; LiTL; OAEP; PoRA; ReaPo; TuPP; WhC

Baith Gude and Fair and Womanly. *Unknown.* GoTS

Bajazet, *sel.* Racine, *tr. fr. French.*
"Here, Osmyn, we may reason unobserv'd," *fr.* I, i. LiA

Baker's Boy, The. Mary Effie Lee Newsome. CDC; GoSl

Baker's Duzzen Uv Wize Sawz, A. Edward Rowland Sill. FaBoBe; FaFP; HBV; HBVY; InMe; SiTL; TreFS

Bakers have perfumed the dawn, The. Sun. Iwan Goll. OnPM

Baker's Reply to the Needle Peddler, The. *Unknown.* SiTL
("I need not your needles.") OxNR

Baker's Tale, The. "Lewis Carroll." *Fr.* The Hunting of the Snark, III. BoChLi; MBP; PoVP

Balaam. John Keble. OBVV

Balaam's Blessing. Numbers, XXIV; 5-9, Bible, *O.T.* TrGrPo

Balade: "Hyd[e], Absolon, thy gilte tresses clere." Chaucer. *Fr.* The Legend of Good Women. AtBAP; AWP; BrBE; ChTr; FiP; InPo; JAWP; LiTG; LoBV; OBEV; SeCeV; WBP
(Ballade.) LyMA
(Hyd, Absolon, Thy Gilte Tresses Clere.) ExPo
(Of His Lady, *sl. diff.*) EG

Balade de [*or* of] Bon Conseyl [*or* Conseil *or* Conseill]. Chaucer. BEL; BLV; EPP; LiTG; TrGrPo; ViBoPo
(Ballad of Good Counsel.) ACP; CAW; GoBC, *sl. mod. vers. by* Wordsworth
(Ballade of Good Counsel, *mod. by* Henry van Dyke.) BLV; TrGrPo
(Good Counse[i]l of Chaucer.) BCEP; EV-1
(Truth.) AWP; EM-1; GrCo-1; MaPo; MyFE; PoLi; TyEnPo
("Truth Shall Make You Free, The.") CBOV
(Written on His Deathbed.) LEAP

Balaklava. Alexander Beaufort Meek. LPS-2

Balance. Melanie Hyman. PtPa

Balance, The. George Sterling. PC

Balance of Europe, The. Pope. SeCeV; TOP

Balancing of gaudy broad pavilions, The. Irradiations, IV [VI]. John Gould Fletcher. AnFE; APA; MAPA; TwAmPo

Balancing spaces are not disturbed, The. The Known Soldier. Kenneth Patchen. WaaP

Balankin was as gude a mason. Lamkin (B *vers.*). *Unknown.* ESPB

Balaustion's Adventure, *sel.* Robert Browning.
"So were we at destruction's very edge." PtP

Balboa. Nora Perry. PAH

Balcon, Le. Baudelaire, *tr. fr. French by* Lord Alfred Douglas. AWP

Balcony Scene, The. Shakespeare. *See* He Jests at Scars . . .

Balcony with Birds, A. Howard Moss. NePoEA

Bald-bare, bone-bare, and ivory yellow: skull. The U.S. Sailor with the Japanese Skull. Winfield Townley Scott. FiMAP; MiAP; PreP; WaP

Bald-headed Tyrant, The. Mary E. Vandyne. BOHV

Bald heads forgetful of their sins. The Scholars. W. B. Yeats. TwP

Bald Old Woman, The. *Tr. fr. Chinese by* I. T. Headland. GaP

Balder, *sels.* Sydney Dobell.
Chanted Calendar, A. BoTP; DD; GBV; GTSE; HBV; HBVY; OBEV; RG; WP
(Procession of the Flowers.) GN; OTPC
(Spring's Procession.) CBPC
Cradle Song of Amy. BOL
Dante, Shakespeare, Milton. VA
Mother's Song, A. BOL
Sea Ballad. VA
This Dear English Land. EV-5
"Thought, Labor, Patience." BMEP

Balder Dead, *sels.* Matthew Arnold.
Burning of Balder's Ship, The. BMEP
(Incremation, The.) VA
"Gods held talk together, group'd in knots, The." BPN
Second Asgard, The. FiP

Balder's Wife. Alice Cary. AA; AnAmPo; LA

Baldness and the Swan. Winfield Townley Scott. FiMAP

Baldy Bane. W. S. Graham. NePoEA

Baldy Green. *Unknown.* PoOW

Balearic Idyll. Frederick Packard. FiBHP

Balefire kindled in the night, A. Carlyle and Emerson. Montgomery Schuyler. AA; PoMa

Balin and Balan. Tennyson. *See* Idylls of the King.

Balkis. Lascelles Abercrombie. *Fr.* Emblems of Love: Judith. BMEP; HBV; LEAP
(Song: "Balkis was in her marble town.") MBP; MoBrPo

Ball. Kate Greenaway. PCH

Ball, The ("The ball no question makes of ayes and noes"). Omar Khayyám, *tr. fr. Persian by* Edward Fitzgerald. *Fr.* The Rubáiyát. OnPM

Ball of fire shoots through the tamarack, A. The Scarlet Tanager. Joel Benton. AA; BLA

Ball Poem, The. John Berryman. MoAmPo (1950 ed.)

Ball will bounce, but less and less, A. Juggler. Richard Wilbur. AmP; FiMAP; LiTM (rev. ed.); MoAB; NePA; NePoEA

Ballad: A.D. 1400. Charles Kingsley. *See* Ballad of Earl Haldan's Daughter, The.

Ballad: Alice Brand. Sir Walter Scott. *See* Alice Brand.

Ballad: " 'And whither would you lead me then?' " Sir Walter Scott. *Fr.* Rokeby, V. ERP

Ballad, A: "As I was walkin' th' jungle round, a-killin' of tigers and time." Guy Wetmore Carryl. BOHV; PA
Ballad: "Auld wife sat at her ivied door, The." Charles Stuart Calverley. BOHV; CenHV; EV-5; FiBHP; HBV; InMe; MuP; OnSP; PA; PC; PCD; PoVP; SiTL; TSW; WhC
(Auld Wife [Sat at Her Ivied Door], The.) EnLi-2 (1949 ed.); NA; PIAE
Ballad: "Dark forests clothe the mountain-side." Raffi, *tr. fr. Armenian by* Zabelle C. Boyajian. ArmLP
Ballad, A: "Druid Urien had daughters seven, The." Sir Walter Scott. BHV
Ballad: "Follow, follow me into the South." Marjorie Allen Seiffert. HBMV
Ballad: "He, before the captain, still and silent stood." Ivan Sergeyevich Turgenev, *tr. fr. Russian by* Sir Cecil Kisch. WaL
Ballad: "He did not kill." Jacob Glatstein, *tr. fr. Yiddish by* Sarah Zweig Betsky. OnCuPl
Ballad: "He pulled a flower." Leonard Cohen. PeCV
Ballad: "He said: 'The shadows darken down.'" May Kendall. HBV
Ballad: "In the summer even." Harriet Prescott Spofford. HBV; LBAP
Ballad: "It was not in the winter." Thomas Hood. *See* Time of Roses.
Ballad: La Belle Dame sans Merci. Keats. *See* La Belle Dame sans Merci.
Ballad: "Lady of Heaven, Regent of the earth." Villon. *See* His Mother's Service to Our Lady.
Ballad: "Mother mine, Mother mine, what do you see?" Annemarie Ewing. NePoAm
Ballad: "Oh, come my joy, my soldier boy." Henry Treece. WaP
Ballad: "O! shairly ye hae seen my love." William Soutar. NeBP
Ballad: "O what is that sound which so thrills the ear." W. H. Auden. MaC; MBP; MoAB; MoBrPo; PoFr; ViBoPo (1958 ed.); WaP
(O What Is That Sound.) HaMV; LiTB
(O What Is That Sound Which So Thrills the Ear.) AnFE; ExPo; PoE; SoV
Ballad: "Of all the girls that e'er were seen." John Gay. CoMu
Ballad: "On high by the sea sat a beautiful maid." Mikhail Yurevich Lermontov, *tr. fr. Russian by* Sir Cecil Kisch. WaL
Ballad: "Roses in my garden, The." Maurice Baring. HBV
Ballad: "Spring it is cheery." Thomas Hood. ERP; VA
(What Can an Old Man Do but Die?) LPS-1
Ballad: Time of Roses. Thomas Hood. *See* Time of Roses.
Ballad: "'Twas when the seas were roaring." John Gay. *Fr.* The What D'Ye Call It. CEP; EV-3; HBV; ViBoPo
Ballad: White Rose. Sacheverell Sitwell. POTE (1959 ed.)
Ballad against Long-loving, A, *in mod. Eng.* *Unknown.* TMEV
Ballad against the Enemies of France. Villon, *tr. fr. French by* Swinburne. AWP; PoFr
Ballad by Hans Breitmann. Charles Godfrey Leland. *See* Ballad of the Mermaid.
Ballad for a Boy, A. William Johnson Cory. PECK
(Two Captains, The.) LH
Ballad for Gloom. Ezra Pound. LiTM (rev. ed.); MAP; MoAmPo; NeMA; NePA; OBVV
Ballad for Katharine of Aragon, A. Charles Causley. FaBoTw; NePoEA
Ballad from the Seven Dials Press, A. *Unknown.* CoMu
Ballad in Blank Verse of the Making of a Poet, A, *sels.* John Davidson.
Greenock. BSV
Man as God. BMEP
Ballad in Blonde Hair Foretold. Robert Bagg. NePoAm-2
Ballad, A, in the Manner of R–dy–rd K–pl–ng, *parody.* Guy Wetmore Carryl. InMe
Ballad Monger, The, *abr.* John Gay. *Fr.* The Shepherd's Week. EV-3
Ballad of a Bridal. Edith Nesbit. VA
Ballad of a Bun, A. Sir Owen Seaman. CenHV
Ballad of a Child. John G. Neihardt. SBMV
Ballad of a Famous Fisherman, A. Lyon Sharman. CPG
Ballad of a Lost House. Leonora Speyer. TBM
Ballad of a Nun, A. John Davidson. BeLS; BMEP; EnLit; HBMV; LBBV; LEAP; MBP; MoBrPo; PoVP; VLEP
Ballad of a Strange Thing. H. Phelps Putnam. MAP; MoAmPo (1942 ed.); MOAP; MoVE; OxBA; TCPD
Ballad of a Wedding, A. Sir John Suckling. *See* Ballad upon a Wedding, A.
Ballad of Adam's First, The. Leland Davis. HBMV
Ballad of Agincourt. Michael Drayton. *See* Agincourt.
Ballad of All the Trades, A. *Unknown.* CoMu
Ballad of Andrew, The. Kostas Varnalis, *tr. fr. Modern Greek by* Rae Dalven. MoGP
Ballad of Andrew and Maudlin, A. *Unknown.* CoMu
Ballad of Another Ophelia. D. H. Lawrence. ChTr; CoBMV; MoVE
Ballad of Antiquaries, A. Austin Dobson. POTT
Ballad of Baby Bunting, The. Henry S. Leigh. BOL
Ballad of Beau Brocade, The. Austin Dobson. EV-5
Ballad of Bedlam. *Unknown.* NA
Ballad of Billie Potts, The. Robert Penn Warren. AmPP (3d ed.); MoAmPo (1950 ed.); OxBA
Ballad of Bouillabaisse, The. Thackeray. ALV; BOHV; EV-5; HBV; InMe; OBEV (new ed.); OBVV; PoVP; VA; ViBoPo
Ballad of Bunker Hill, The. Edward Everett Hale. MC; PAH
Ballad of Burdens, A. Swinburne. BPN; EmBrPo; EnLi-2; PIR; PoVP; VLEP
Ballad of Camden Town, The. James Elroy Flecker. EnLit; HBV
Ballad of Captain Kidd, The. *Unknown.* *See* Captain Kidd.
Ballad of Cassandra Brown, The. Helen Gray Cone. BOHV; InMe
Ballad of Ch'ang Kan, A. Li Po, *tr. fr. Chinese by* Soame Jenyns. ChLP
Ballad of Charity, The. Charles Godfrey Leland. BOHV; InMe
Ballad of Chickamauga, The. Maurice Thompson. BlG; MC; PAH
Ballad of Chicken Bill, The. F. E. Vaughn. PoOW
Ballad of Christmas, A. Walter de la Mare. SDH; StJW
Ballad of College Days, A. *Unknown.* CAG
Ballad of Coronado's Quest. Jessie Wilmore Murton. MuM
Ballad of Culinary Frustration. Phyllis McGinley. FiBHP
Ballad of Dansekar the Dutchman, A. *Unknown.* SG
Ballad of Davy Crockett, The, *with music.* *Unknown.* ABF
Ballad of Dead Girls. Dana Burnet. OBAV
Ballad of Dead Ladies, A ("I wonder in what Isle of Bliss"). Justin Huntly M'Carthy. *See* I Wonder in What Isle of Bliss.
Ballad of Dead Ladies, The. Villon, *tr. fr. French by* Dante Gabriel Rossetti. ALV; ATP (1935 ed.); AWP; BEL; EnLi-2; EPP; ExPo; FaFP; GoBC; HBV; InP; JAWP; LiA; LO; OuHeWo; PIR; PoFS; PoRA; POTT; PoVP; PreP; TOP; VA; ViBoPo; ViP; ViPP; VLEP; WBP
(Ballade of Dead Ladies, *tr. by* Andrew Lang.) HBV; LEAP; PIAE
(Ballade of Fair Ladies of Olden Time, *tr. by* Alan Conder.) TrFP
(Ballade of the Women of the Past, *tr. by* Ralph N. Currey.) FoS
Ballad of Death, A. Swinburne. PoVP; VLEP
Ballad of Douglas Bridge. Francis Carlin. AnIV; BoFr; GTIV; HBMV; OxBI
Ballad of Downal Baun. Padraic Colum. SUS
Ballad of Dowsabell, The. Michael Drayton. *See* Cassamen and Dowsabel.
Ballad of Dreamland, A. Swinburne. BPN; EmBrPo; EPN; HBV; PoVP; TCEP; VLEP
(Ballade of Dreamland, A.) MBP
Ballad of Earl Haldan's Daughter, The. Charles Kingsley. EV-5; OTPC
(Ballad: A.D. 1400.) GN
Ballad of East and West, The. Kipling. AnFE; BBV (1951 ed.); BEL; BeLS; BoFr; BPN; ChMo; CP; FaBoBe; HBV; HiLiEn; LBBV; LH; MaC; PIR; POT; PoTo; PoVP; PTA-2; PYM; ShGoBo; TCEP; TSW; TSWC; VA
"O East is East, and West is West, and never the twain shall meet," *br. sel.* MaRV
Ballad of Emma Samson, A. John Trotwood Moore. BlG
Ballad of Father Gilligan, The. W. B. Yeats. AnIV; CV; EnLit; HBV; InP; InPo; MBP; MoBrPo; NeMA; OnYI; PCN; PoRA; POTT; TVSH; TwP; WaKn; WHL
(Father Gilligan.) TSW; TSWC
Ballad of Federico Garcia Lorca. Luis Cardoza y Aragón, *tr. fr. Spanish by* Donald Devenish Walsh. AnCL
Ballad of Fisher's Boarding-House, The. Kipling. PIR; PoRA
Ballad of François Villon, A. Swinburne. BEL; BMEP; BPN; EmBrPo; EnLi-2; PFE; PIR; PoEL-5; PoRA; PoVP; PtP; ViP; ViPP; VLEP
Ballad of Good Counsel. Chaucer. *See* Balade de Bon Conseyle.
Ballad of Halfmoon Bay, The, *sel.* Keith Sinclair.
"Edward Edwards was a castaway sealer." AnNZ
Ballad of Hampstead Heath, The. James Elroy Flecker. MoBrPo
Ballad of Heaven, A. John Davidson. BeLS; BMEP; EnLit; HBMV; MeRV; PoVP; TCEP; UnW; VA; VLEP
Ballad of Hell, A. John Davidson. AnEnPo; AnFE; BLV; CBOV; HoPM; MBP; MoBrPo; PoVP; WHA
Ballad of Heroes, A. Austin Dobson. BLP; GA; HBV; HBVY; InP; OHIP; PEOR; PoRL; POT; PoTo
Ballad of High Endeavor, A. *Unknown.* BOHV; NA
Ballad of Hope and Fear. Charles Madge. FaBoMo
Ballad of Human Life. Thomas Lovell Beddoes. BeLS; VA
Ballad of Imitation, The. Austin Dobson. HBV; VLEP

Ballad of Ishmael Day, The. *Unknown.* PAH
Ballad of Jack and Jill, The. Anthony C. Deane. *See* Here Is the Tale.
Ballad of Jack Monroe, The. Jesse Edgar Middleton. CPG
Ballad of Jenny the Mare, The. Edward Fitzgerald. EV-5
Ballad of John Cable and Three Gentlemen. W. S. Merwin. NePoEA
Ballad of John Camplejohn. Bliss Carman. LEAP
Ballad of John Silver, A. John Masefield. BoChLi (1939 ed.); CV; MPB; PtOT; TSW; TSWC
Ballad of Johnny Appleseed, A. Helmer O. Oleson. SiSoSe; TiPo (1959 ed.)
Ballad of Judas Iscariot, The. Robert Buchanan. BMEP; DaM; HBV; VA
Ballad of Keith of Ravelston, The. Sydney Dobell. *Fr.* A Nuptial Eve. BMEP; HBV; LEAP; OBEV; OBVV; TOP; UnW
(Keith of Ravelston.) CH; DaM; EV-5; GTBS
"Ravelston, Ravelston," *sel.* LO
Ballad of Kynd [*or* Kind] Kittok, The. William Dunbar. GoTS; OxBoLi; TMEV, *in mod. Eng.*
Ballad of "La Tribune," The. Archibald MacMechan. CPG
Ballad of Lieutenant Miles. Clinton Scollard. MC
(Deed of Lieutenant Miles, The.) PAH
Ballad of Life, A. Swinburne. HBV; PoVP; VLEP
Ballad of London, A. Richard Le Gallienne. BMEP; HBMV; MBP
Ballad of Love and Blood. Angel Miguel Queremel, *tr. fr. Spanish by* Rolfe Humphries. AnCL
Ballad of Low-lie-down. Madison Cawein. HBV
Ballad of Manila Bay, A. Sir Charles G. D. Roberts. GA; PAH
Ballad of Marjorie, A. Dora Sigerson Shorter. TIP
Ballad of Moll Magee, The. W. B. Yeats. TwP
Ballad of Nails, The. Nikolai Tikhonov, *tr. fr. Russian by* Jack Lindsay. RuPo
Ballad of New Orleans, The. George Henry Boker. PAH
Ballad of O'Bruadir, The. F. R. Higgins. EtS; OBMV
Ballad of Old Doc Higgins. Leonora Speyer. PFE
Ballad of Oriana, The. Tennyson. EmBrPo
Ballad of Oriskany, The. Obadiah Cyrus Auringer. AA
Ballad of Orleans, A. Agnes Mary Frances Robinson. HBV; VA
Ballad of Our Lady. William Dunbar. *See* Ane Ballat of Our Lady.
Ballad of Our Lady. *Tr. fr. the Spanish of the* Penitentes *by* Mary Austin. APW
Ballad of Paco Town, The. Clinton Scollard. PAH
Ballad of Past Meridian, A. George Meredith. EmBrPo; EV-5; POTT; PoVP
Ballad of Persse O'Reilly, The. James Joyce. *Fr.* Finnegans Wake. LiTB; SiTL
Ballad of Poor Chimney Sweeps. Villon, *tr. fr. French by* John Payne. WoL
Ballad of Private Chadd, The. A. A. Milne. CenHV
Ballad of Prose and Rhyme, The. Austin Dobson. *See* Ballade of Prose and Rhyme, The.
Ballad of Reading Gaol, The. Oscar Wilde. AnFE; BeLS; BMEP; EnLi-2; EnLit; HBV; LEAP; LiTG, *much abr.*; OBMV, *abr.*; OnYI; OtMeF, *abr.*; PIR, *sl. abr.*; PoVP; TCEP, *much abr.*; TreF
(Ballad of Reading Jail, The.) VLEP
Sels.
"He did not wear his scarlet coat," *fr.* I *and* II. MBP; MoBrPo
Hope ("We did not dare to breathe a prayer"), *br. sel. fr.* III. MaRV
"I know not whether Laws be right," V. ACP (1926 ed.); MaRV, 7 *sts.*
(In Prison, 3 *sts.*) OQP; QP-2
"I never saw a man who looked/ With such a wistful eye," *fr.* II. PoFr
"In Debtor's Yard the stones are hard," III, *abr.* ViBoPo
In Reading Gaol by Reading Town, VI. FaFP; LiTB
"There is no chapel on the day," *fr.* IV. GTIV; OxBI
Yet Each Man Kills the Thing He Loves, *fr.* I. LO, 3 *sts.*; TrGrPo, 14 *sts. fr.* I *and* II; WHA, *br. sel.*
Ballad of Red Fox, The. Melvin Walker La Follette. NePoEA
Ballad of Redhead's Day, A. Richard Butler Glaenzer. MC; PAH
Ballad of Remembrance, A. Robert E. Hayden. PoNe
Ballad of Riding, A. Marjorie Allen Seiffert. NP
Ballad of St. Thomas, A. Charles A. Brady. JKCP (1955 ed.)
Ballad of Sally in Our Alley, The. Henry Carey. *See* Sally in Our Alley.
Ballad of Sarsfield, A. Aubrey Thomas De Vere. GoBC; HBV
Ballad of Sea Fardingers, Describing Evil Fortune, A. *Unknown.* SG
Ballad of Semmerwater, The. Sir William Watson. PoVP
Ballad of Sir Brian and the Three Wishes, The. Newman Levy. FiBHP
Ballad of Sir John Franklin, A. George Henry Boker. AA; HBV
Ballad of Sir Patrick Spens. *Unknown.* *See* Sir Patrick Spens.
Ballad of Sister Anne, The. Sir Osbert Sitwell. AtBAP
Ballad of Sweet P, The. Virginia Woodward Cloud. PAH
Ballad of the Angel, The. Theodosia Garrison. HBV
Ballad of the Armada, A. Austin Dobson. *See* Ballad to Queen Elizabeth, A.
Ballad of the Banshee. James B. Dollard. CPG
Ballad of the Battle of Gibeon, The. G. K. Chesterton. YT
Ballad of the Bells. *sel.* Paul Fort, *tr. fr. French by* Joseph T. Shipley.
"Ah! what joy, the bagpipe and the flute." WoL
Ballad of [*or* to] the *Billycock*, The. Anthony C. Deane. ALV; BMEP; NeMA; TSW
Ballad of the Boat, The. Richard Garnett. CG; HBV; VA
Ballad of the *Bolivar*, The. Kipling. CaAE; EPP; TCEP
Ballad of the Boll Weevil, The. *Unknown.* *See* Ballet of de Boll Weevil, De.
Ballad of the Bore, The. Austin Dobson. VLEP
Ballad of the Boston Tea-Party, A. Oliver Wendell Holmes. MC; PaA; PAH; PoFr, *abr.*
Ballad of the Bushman. Eileen Duggan. CoBE
Ballad of the Canal. Phoebe Cary. BOHV
Ballad of the Captains, A. E. J. Brady. EtS
Ballad of the Cats of Bygone Time. Michael Scot. PoC
Ballad of the Children of the Czar, The. Delmore Schwartz. MiAP; OnHM
Ballad of the Circus, A. Charles Hanson Towne. CV
Ballad of the *Clampherdown*, The. Kipling. PECK; PIR
Ballad of the Common Man (for the Jefferson Memorial). Alfred Kreymborg. PoFr
Ballad of the Conemaugh Flood, A. Hardwicke Drummond Rawnsley. PAH
Ballad of the Courtier and the Country Clown, A. *Unknown.* CoMu
Ballad of the Cross, The. Theodosia Garrison. HBMV; HBVY; NV
Ballad of the Dark Ladie, The. Samuel Taylor Coleridge. BPN; EmBrPo; EnRP; ERP; PreP
Ballad of the Days of the Messiah. A. M. Klein. TrJP
Ballad of the Despairing Husband. Robert Creeley. NeAP
Ballad of the Doorstone. Louise Ayres Garnett. TBM
Ballad of the Eagle, The. *Unknown, tr. fr. Danish by* E. M. Smith-Dampier. BoDaBa
Ballad of the Emeu, The. Bret Harte. BOHV
Ballad of the Epiphany. Charles Dalmon. HBMV; TSW
Ballad of the Equinox. Vernon Watkins. PrWP
Ballad of the Erie Canal. *Unknown.* ABF; IHA
Ballad of the Faded Field. Robert Burns Wilson. AA
Ballad of the Faithful Clerk. Albert Stillman. InMe
Ballad of the Fiddler, The. "Seumas O'Sullivan." MPB
Ballad of the Fleet, A. Tennyson. *See Revenge*, The.
Ballad of the Fox. *Unknown.* *See* Fox, The.
Ballad of the Foxhunter, The. W. B. Yeats. CMP; EnLit
Ballad of the French Fleet, A. Longfellow. AA; HBV; MC; PAH
Ballad of the Gibbet. Villon. *See* Epitaph in Form of a Ballad, The.
Ballad of the Good Lord Nelson, A. Lawrence Durrell. LiTM; OnHM; PoN; SiTL
Ballad of the Goodly Fere. Ezra Pound. BAP; BLV; CAW; ChMo; CMP; CoV; HBV; LEAP; LiTA; LiTM; MAP; MoAB; MoAmPo; NePA; NP; PoRA; PreP; ReaPo; TCPD; TrGrPo
Ballad of the Güije. Nicolás Guillén, *tr. fr. Spanish by* H. R. Hays. TwSpPo
Ballad of the Happy Christmas Wind. Sister Mary Madeleva. ChrBoLe
Ballad of the Harp-Weaver, The. Edna St. Vincent Millay. MaC; StPo; YT
Ballad of the Holy Evening Bread, The. Itzik Manger, *tr. fr. Yiddish by* Sarah Zweig Betsky. OnCuPl
Ballad of the Huntsman. Selma Robinson. PIAE
Ballad of the *Ivanhoe*, The. Bill Adams. BBV; PYM
Ballad of the Jabberwock, The. Leah Bodine Drake. DaM
Ballad of the King's Jest, The. Kipling. GBV
Ballad of the Lady Lorraine, The. Padraic Gregory. ReTS
Ballad of the Lakes, A. Laura E. McCully. CPG
Ballad of the Lincoln Penny. Alfred Kreymborg. YaD
Ballad of the Little Black Hound. Dora Sigerson Shorter. OnYI; StPo
Ballad of the Londoner. James Elroy Flecker. EnLoPo
Ballad of the Long-legged Bait. Dylan Thomas. CoBMV; SeCeV
Ballad of the Lords of Old Time. Villon, *tr. fr. French by* Swinburne. AWP; JAWP; WBP
Ballad of the Mermaid. Charles Godfrey Leland. FiBHP; LauV
(Ballad by Hans Breitmann.) BOHV; CenHV
(Ritter Hugo.) LPS-3
Ballad of the Merry Ferry, The. Emma Rounds. MPB; RIS

Ballad of the Outer Life. Hugo von Hofmannsthal, *tr. fr. German by* Jethro Bithell. AWP; JAWP; LiTW; TrJP; WBP; AnGP, *tr. by* Michael Hamburger
(Twilight of the Outward Life, *tr. by* Peter Viereck.) OnHM
Ballad of the Oysterman, The. Oliver Wendell Holmes. AmPP; AnAmPo; AnNE; BOHV; EtS; FaFP; HBV; HBVY; LA; MCCG; MOAP; MoShBr; OnSP; PCD; PoeMoYo; PYM; TreFS; YT
Ballad of the Primitive Jest. Andrew Lang. BOHV
(Ballade of the Primitive Jest.) HBV
Ballad of the Prodigal Son, The. "W. H. S." CAG
Ballad of the Quest, The. Virna Sheard. CPG
Ballad of the Rag-Bag Heart. Marjorie Allen Seiffert. AV
Ballad of the Rising in the North, A. *Unknown.* ACP
Ballad of the River Duero. Gerardo Diego, *tr. fr. Spanish by* Eleanor L. Turnbull. CoSP
Ballad of the *Rover,* The. Archibald MacMechan. CPG; OCL
Ballad of the Sailor Ben. Jack Mitchell.
(Hints on Writing Verse.) PCD
Ballad of the Spanish Civil Guard. Federico García Lorca, *tr. fr. Spanish.* CoSP, *tr. by* Eleanor L. Turnbull; LiTW, *tr. by* Lysander Kemp
Ballad of the Strange and Wonderful Storm of Hail, A. *Unknown.* CoMu
Ballad of the Tempest. James Thomas Fields. BeLS; EtS; FaBoBe; HBV (8th ed.); PTA-2; YaD
(Captain's Daughter, The.) FaFP; HBV (6th ed.); HBVY; PECK
(Tempest, The.) LPS-2; TreF
Ballad of the Thanksgiving Pilgrim. Clinton Scollard. TOAH
Ballad of the Two Grandfathers. Nicolás Guillén, *tr. fr. Spanish by* H. R. Hays. TwSpPo
Ballad of the War, A. George Herbert Sass. BIG
Ballad of the Western Island in the North Country. *Unknown, tr. fr. Chinese by* Arthur Waley. TrCh
Ballad of the White Horse, The, *sels.* G. K. Chesterton.
"Before the gods that made the gods." ACP (1952 ed.); ReTS
Harp of Alfred, The. MoVE
Songs of Guthrum and Alfred, The. HBV
King Alfred Answers the Danes. OxBoCh
"To sweat a slave to a race of slaves." PoFr
"Up over windy wastes." BMEP; LEAP
Ballad of the Women of Paris. Villon, *tr. fr. French by* Swinburne. AWP; JAWP; OuHeWo; WBP
Ballad of Thread for a Needle. Marjorie Allen Seiffert. TBM
Ballad of Trees and the Master, A. Sidney Lanier. AA; ADAH; AmP; AnAmPo; BAV; BTP; CAW; ChIP; CoBA; CoV; DDA; GoBC; GTBS-W; HBV; IAP; LA; LaNeLa; LBAP; LiTA; MAP; MaRV; MoAmPo (1942 ed.); OBAV; OQP; OxBA; PC; PFE; PFY; PoEL-5; PoeMoYo; PoRL; QP-1; SPP; StJW; TCAP; TOP; WGRP; WHL
(Cross, The.) BePJ
(Trees and the Master, The.) NLK
Ballad of Tristram, The. *Unknown, tr. fr. Icelandic by* Watson Kirkconnell. PaOS
Ballad of True Thomas, The. *Unknown. See* Thomas the Rhymer.
Ballad of Two Seas. George Sterling. MOAP
Ballad of Val-ès-Dunes, The, *sel.* Hilaire Belloc.
"Horse from Cleres and Valery, The." AlDL
Ballad of William Sycamore, The. Stephen Vincent Benét. AnAmPo; BLV; BoLiVe; HBMV; LA; MAP; MoAmPo; MOAP; MPB; OnSP; PFY; PoRA; PoTo; PreP; TBM; TCAP
Ballad of Wise Men, A. George M. P. Baird. ChrBoLe; SDH
Ballad of Wonder, A. Eleanor Slater. MaRV
Ballad of Yukon Jake, The. Edward E. Paramore, Jr. BeLS; BLPA; NeHB
Ballad on the Taxes, A. Edward Ward. OxBoLi; SiTL
Ballad Riding in the North, A. *Unknown.* ACP
Ballad Singer, The. Thomas Hardy. At Casterbridge Fair, I. BEL; ChMo; EmBrPo; EnLi-2 (1949 ed.); EnLit; LO; PoVP
Ballad to a Traditional Refrain. Maurice James Craig. SeCePo
Ballad to Queen Elizabeth, A. Austin Dobson. ALV; GTBS; MuP; OBVV; ShBV-2; TVSH
(Ballad of the Armada, A.) LH
Ballad to the *Billycock,* The. Anthony C. Deane. *See* Ballad of the *Billycock,* The.
Ballad to the Tune of Bateman, A. Sir Charles Sedley. CoMu
Ballad to William of Nassau. *Unknown, tr. fr. Dutch by* A. J. Barnouw. PoFr, *7 sts.*
Ballad upon a Wedding, A. Sir John Suckling. AtBAP; EPS; EV-2; HBV, *sl. abr.;* InvP; LEAP; LoBV; NBE; OBS; ReEn; SeCeV; SeCL; ViBoPo
(Ballad of a Wedding, A.) LiA
(Ballade upon a Wedding, A.) CoMu; SeCV-1; SeEP
(Wedding, A.) BOHV
Sels.
Bride, The ("Her feet beneath her petticoat"). BLV; LPS-1, *abr.;* TrGrPo
"Maid, The (and thereby hangs a tale)." LO; LoPS
Ballad upon the Popish Plot, A. John Gadbury. CoMu
Ballad Walking in Sleep. Federico García Lorca, *tr. fr. Spanish by* Eleanor L. Turnbull. CoSP
(Somnambulant Ballad, *tr. by* Warren Carrier.) ReMP
(Somnambule Ballad, *tr. by* J. L. Gili *and* Stephen Spender.) AnSpL-2
(Somnambulistic Ballad, *tr. by* Roy Campbell *and* Mary Campbell.) LiTW; OnHM
Ballad Warning Men to Beware of Deceitful Women, A, *sel.* John Lydgate.
"Women, of kinde, have conditions three." LO
Ballad with an Ancient Refrain. *Unknown.* NA
Ballad Written for a Bridegroom. Villon, *tr. fr. French by* Swinburne. AWP
Ballade: Hostelry of Thought, The. Charles d'Orléans, *tr. fr. French by* Barbara Howes. LyMA
Ballade: "Hyde, Absalon, thy gilte tresses clere." Chaucer. *See* Balade: "Hyd, Absolon . . ."
Ballade: "I die of thirst beside the fountain's brim." Villon, *tr. fr. French by* Ralph N. Currey. FoS
Ballade: "Looking one day toward the coast of France." Charles d'Orléans, *tr. fr. French by* William Stirling. LiTW
Ballade: "One day I asked my heart." Charles d'Orléans, *tr. fr. French by* Ralph N. Currey. FoS
Ballade: "Outcast bones from a thousand biers." Don Marquis. *Fr.* Archy and Mehitabel. WhC
Ballade: "Pretty maid she died, she died, in love-bed as she lay, The." Paul Fort, *tr. fr. French by* Frederick York Powell. AWP; JAWP; WBP
(Pretty Maid, The.) OBMV
Ballade by the Fire. E. A. Robinson. InP; PFE; POT; PoTo
Ballade Catalogue of Lovely Things, A. Richard Le Gallienne. CBOV; CP; HBMV; PIAE; POT; PoTo
Ballade de Marguerite. *Unknown, tr. fr. French by* Oscar Wilde. AWP; JAWP; WBP
Ballade d'une Grande Dame. G. K. Chesterton. OxBoLi
Ballade for Peace, *sl. abr.* Charles d'Orléans, *tr. fr. French by* Ralph N. Currey. FoS
Ballade in a Bad Temper. Louis MacNeice. PoFr
Ballade Made in the Hot Weather. W. E. Henley. AnFE; MBP; MoBrPo; POTT
(Made in the Hot Weather.) GN
Ballade Morale. Neil Tracy. BoCaPo
Ballade of a Book-Reviewer, A. G. K. Chesterton. PtOT
Ballade of a Conspicuous Omission from "The Book of Humorous Verse." Carolyn Wells. BOHV
Ballade of a Friar. Clément Marot. *See* Friar Lubin.
Ballade of a Ship. E. A. Robinson. TSW; TSWC
Ballade of a Summer Hotel. "Junia." WhC
Ballade of a Toyokuni Color-Print. W. E. Henley. BPN; PoVP
Ballade of Adaptation, The. Brander Matthews. PC
Ballade of an Anti-Puritan, A. G. K. Chesterton. BOHV
Ballade of Andrew Lang. Dugald Sutherland MacColl. CenHV
Ballade of Any Father to Any Son, A. J. C. Squire. PIAE; WhC
Ballade of Ballade-Mongers, A. Augustus M. Moore. BOHV; PA
Ballade of Big Plans. Dorothy Parker. InMe
Ballade of Blue China. Andrew Lang. BMEP; PoVP; TSW; TSWC
(Of Blue China.) VA
Ballade of Busy Doctors, A. James Newton Matthews. PoP
Ballade of Charon and the River Girl. J. B. Morton. WhC
Ballade of Christmas Ghosts. Andrew Lang. COAH; SDH
Ballade of Dead Actors. W. E. Henley. ALV; InP; OBMV; PFE; POTT; PoVP; VLEP
Ballade of Dead Cities. Sir Edmund Gosse. BMEP
Ballade of Dead Friends. E. A. Robinson. AA
Ballade of Dead Ladies. Villon. *See* Ballad of Dead Ladies, The.
Ballade of Dime Novels. Arthur Guiterman. PFE
Ballade of Diminishing Control, A. J. C. Squire. WhC
Ballade of Dreamland, A. Swinburne. *See* Ballad of Dreamland, A.
Ballade of Evolution, A. Grant Allen. ATP (1935 ed.)
Ballade of Expansion. Hilda Johnson. PAH
Ballade of Fact and Fiction, The. Brander Matthews. PFE
Ballade of Fair Ladies of Olden Time. Villon. *See* Ballad of Dead Ladies, The
Ballade of Faith. Tom MacInnes. CaP; OCL
Ballade of Forgotten Loves. Arthur Grissom. BOHV
Ballade of Good Counsel. Chaucer. *See* Balade de Bon Conseyl.
Ballade of Hell and of Mrs. Roebeck. Hilaire Belloc. MoVE
Ballade of His Choice of a Sepulcher. Andrew Lang. BSV; POTT; PoVP
(Of His Choice of a Sepulchre.) VA

Ballade of Illegal Ornaments. Hilaire Belloc. ACP (1952 ed.)
Ballade of Islands, A. Lucy Catlin Robinson. AA
Ballade of Ivan Petrofsky Skevar, Ye. *Unknown. See* Abdul A-Bul-Bul A-Mir.
Ballade of Ladies' Names. W. E. Henley. HBV
Ballade of Middle Age. Andrew Lang. HBV; LEAP
Ballade of Muhammad Din Tilai. *Unknown, tr. fr. Pushtu by* E. Powys Mathers. PG (1945 ed.)
Ballade of My Lady's Beauty. Joyce Kilmer. HBV; LBMV; LEAP; PR
Ballade of 1933, A. Franklin P. Adams. PIAE
Ballade of Old Loves, A. Carolyn Wells. COAH
Ballade of Playing Cards, A. Gleeson White. VA
Ballade of Primitive Man. Andrew Lang. *See* Double Ballade of Primitive Man.
Ballade of Prose and Rhyme, The. Austin Dobson. LEAP; MBP; MoBrPo (1942 ed.); PIAE
(Ballad of Prose and Rhyme, The.) POTT
Ballade of Queen's Lace. Richard Le Gallienne. CV
Ballade of Remembered Roses. George Macy. PIAE
Ballade of Schopenhauer's Philosophy. Franklin P. Adams. HBMV
Ballade of Soporific Absorption. J. C. Squire. InMe
Ballade of Spring. W. E. Henley. PIAE; TSW
Ballade of Spring's Unrest, A. Bert Leston Taylor. PoMa; YT
Ballade of Suicide, A. G. K. Chesterton. ALV; BOHV; FiBHP; HBV; InMe; JKCP (1955 ed.)
Ballade of the Ancient Wheeze. Nate Salsbury *and* Newman Levy. InMe
Ballade of the Dreamland Rose. Brian Hooker. HBMV
Ballade of the Engaged Young Man. Richard Kendall Munkittrick. PR
Ballade of the Gibbet. Villon. *See* Epitaph in Form of a Ballad, The.
Ballade of the Golfer in Love. Clinton Scollard. BOHV
Ballade of the Goth. Sir Walter Raleigh. WhC
Ballade of the Grotesque, A. G. K. Chesterton. PIAE
Ballade of the Hanged Men. Villon. *See* Epitaph in Form of a Ballad.
Ballade of the Harrowing of Hell. D. B. Wyndham Lewis. CoBE; JKCP (1955 ed.)
Ballade of the Heresiarchs. Hilaire Belloc. MoVE
Ballade of the Higher Learning, A. *Unknown.* CAG
Ballade of the Mystic and the Mud. Tom MacInnes. CPG
Ballade of the Nurserie, A. John Twig. NA
Ballade of the Poetic Life. J. C. Squire. OBMV; WhC
Ballade of the Pompadour's Fan. Austin Dobson. *See* On a Fan That Belonged to the Marquise de Pompadour.
Ballade of the Primitive Jest. Andrew Lang. *See* Ballad of the Primitive Jest.
Ballade of the Road Unknown. Richard Le Gallienne. CV
Ballade of the Scottyshe Kynge, A. John Skelton. CoMu
Ballade of the Southern Cross. Andrew Lang. InP
Ballade of the Things That Remain. Richard Le Gallienne. PFE
Ballade of the Thrush. Austin Dobson. BLA
Ballade of the Unchanging Beauty. Richard Le Gallienne. InP; PFE
Ballade of the Under Side. Don Marquis. *Fr.* Archys Life of Mehitabel. InvP
Ballade of the Women of the Past. Villon. *See* Ballad of Dead Ladies, The.
Ballade of Unfortunate Mammals. Dorothy Parker. ALV; BOHV; InMe
Ballade of Youth and Age. W. E. Henley. PoVP
Ballade of Youth Remaining. Tom MacInnes. CPG
Ballade on Eschatology. Sister Mary Madeleva. GoYe
Ballade That Villon Made at the Request of His Mother to Intercede with Our Lady. Villon. *See* His Mother's Service to Our Lady.
Ballade to My Psychoanalyst. Kenneth Lillington. FiBHP
Ballade to Our Lady. Sebastian Brant, *tr. fr. German by* Alexander Barclay. *Fr.* The Ship of Fools. ISi
Ballade to Our Lady of Czestochowa. Hilaire Belloc. ACP (1952 ed.); ISi; QS
Ballade to Theocritus, in Winter. Andrew Lang. InP; PC
(To Theocritus, in Winter.) VA
Ballade un Peu Banale. A. J. M. Smith. SiTL
Ballade upon a Wedding, A. Sir John Suckling. *See* Ballad upon a Wedding, A.
Ballade Written during Captivity in England. Charles d'Orléans, *tr. fr. French by* Alan Conder. LyMA; TrFP
Ballads of the Last Prince, The, *sel.* Ernest Rhys.
Mountain Liberty. PoFr
Ballads on Napoleon, *sels. Unknown.*
Hop-o-My-Thumb. CoBE
Island, The. CoBE
Ballata 7: "Being in thought of love I came upon." Guido Cavalcanti, *tr. fr. Italian by* Ezra Pound. LyPI
(Ballata: He Reveals His Increasing Love for Mandetta, *tr. by* Dante Gabriel Rossetti, *shorter sel.*) AWP
Ballata: Concerning a Shepherd-Maid. Guido Cavalcanti, *tr. fr. Italian by* Dante Gabriel Rossetti. AWP
Ballata: Flowers and Love. Boccaccio, *tr. fr. Italian by* Richard Aldington. *Fr.* The Decameron. LyPI
Ballata: He Reveals His Increasing Love for Mandetta. Guido Cavalcanti. *See* Ballata 7: "Being in thought of love I came upon."
Ballata: He Will Gaze upon Beatrice. Dante, *tr. fr. Italian by* Dante Gabriel Rossetti. AWP; JAWP; LyPI; WBP
(Sonnet: "Because mine eyes can never have their fill.") GoBC
Ballata: His Talk with Certain Peasant-Girls. Franco Sacchetti, *tr. fr. Italian by* Dante Gabriel Rossetti. AWP
Ballata: In Exile at Sarzana. Guido Cavalcanti, *tr. fr. Italian by* Dante Gabriel Rossetti. AWP; JAWP; WBP
Ballata 11: Last Song; from Exile. Guido Cavalcanti, *tr. fr. Italian by* G. S. Fraser. LyPI
Ballata 5: "Light do I see within my Lady's eyes." Guido Cavalcanti, *tr. fr. Italian by* Ezra Pound. LyPI
Ballata: Of a Continual Death in Love. Guido Cavalcanti, *tr. fr. Italian by* Dante Gabriel Rossetti. AWP
Ballata: Of His Lady among Other Ladies. Guido Cavalcanti. *See* Ballata: "With other women I beheld my love."
Ballata 12: Of Love's Power. Guido Cavalcanti, *tr. fr. Italian by* Hubert Creekmore. LyPI
(Ballata of Love's Power.) LiTW
Ballata: Of True and False Singing. *Unknown, tr. fr. Italian by* Dante Gabriel Rossetti. AWP
(Ballata of True and False Spring.) UnS
(True and False Singing.) OnPM
Ballata: One Speaks of the Beginning of His Love. *Unknown, tr. fr. Italian by* Dante Gabriel Rossetti. AWP
Ballata: "Since all my life out of my death derives." Guido Cavalcanti, *tr. fr. Italian by* Hubert Creekmore. LyMA
Ballata 9: "There in a woodland, to my thought more bright." Guido Cavalcanti, *tr. fr. Italian by* G. S. Fraser. LyPI
Ballata: "Welcome to May." Angelo Poliziano, *tr. fr. Italian by* L. R. Lind. LyPI
Ballata: "With other women I beheld my love." Guido Cavalcanti, *tr. fr. Italian by* Dante Gabriel Rossetti. OnPM
(Ballata: Of His Lady among Other Ladies.) AWP
Ballata of Love's Power. Guido Cavalcanti. *See* Ballata 12: Of Love's Power.
Ballata of Myrrha's Eyes. Angelo Poliziano, *tr. fr. Italian by* John Addington Symonds. LiTW
(Three Ballate, II.) AWP
Ballata of True and False Spring. *Unknown. See* Ballata: Of True and False Singing.
Ballet. Palladas, *tr. fr. Greek by* F. L. Lucas. GrPE
Ballet [*or* Ballit] of de [*or* the] Boll Weevil, De (*diff. versions*). *Unknown.* ABF, *with music;* AS, *with music;* IHA; ViBoFo (A *vers.;* B *vers., with music*)
(Ballad of the Boll Weevil, The, *with music.*) TrAS
(Boll Weevil, The, *with music.*) SoAF
(Boll Weevil Song, The.) APW; AS; SPP
Ballet of the Fifth Year, The. Delmore Schwartz. MoAB; OxBA
Ballet Song of Mary, A. Eizabeth Madox Roberts. MAP; MoAmPo; NP
Balliol Rooks, The. Frederick S. Boas. BLA
Balloon Man, The. Dorothy Aldis. TiPo
Balloon Man. Hazel I. Dannecker. PoMa
Balloon Man, The. Rose Fyleman. BoTP; SUS
Balloon Man, The. E. Herbert. BoTP
Balloon Man, The. —— Morton. GFA
Balloon Man. Jessica Nelson North. GaP
Balloon over the Rhondda. Roland Mathias. MoWP
Balloon Seller, The. Elizabeth Fleming. BoTP
Ballot, The. John Pierpont. AA; InP; LEAP; PoRL
Ballroom Dancing Class. Phyllis McGinley. MoShBr
Ball's Bluff. Herman Melville. BAV; SoV
Ball's lost, lost, gone. The Lost Ball. Lucy Sprague Mitchell. TiPo (1959 ed.)
Bally. Arthur Rimbaud, *tr. fr. French by* Frederick Morgan. AnFP
Ballyhoo for a Mendicant. Carlton Talbott. AnAmPo; LA
Ballykinlar, May, 1940. Patrick Maybin. NeIP
Ballyshannon foundered off the coast of Cariboo, The. Etiquette. W. S. Gilbert. BOHV; CenHV; EnLi-2; FaBoCh; FiBHP; MaC
Ballytullagh. William Allingham. *Fr.* Laurence Bloomfield in Ireland. IrPN
Ballyvourney. Thomas Boyd. GTIV
Balme. Spenser. *Fr.* The Faerie Queene, I, 11. CH
Balmy South a gentle sigh releases, The. A Greeting. Jónas Hallgrímsson. IcP
Balmy warmth comes wafted o'er the seas, A. Farewell to Bithynia. Catullus. OuHeWo
Baloo, baloo, my wee, wee thing. Cradle Song. Richard Gall. BOL; EBSV
Baloo, loo, lammy, now baloo, my dear. Lullaby. Lady Nairne. HBV

Baloo, My Bairnie, Fa' Asleep. James Smith. BOL
Balooloo, My Lammie. Lady Nairne. BOL
Lullaby, *sel.* HBV
Balow. *Unknown.* EV-1; LO; MotAn; OBEV
(By-low.) BLV, *abr.*; CBOV
(By-low, My Babe, *abr.*) TrGrPo
(Lady Anne Bothwell's Lament.) BOL; HBV; LPS-1
Balow, my babe, weep not for me. The New Balow. *Unknown.* CoMu
Balsam buds are bluer, The. On Clingman Dome. Olive Tilford Dargan. LS; NoCaPo; VOD
Balthasar's Song. Shakespeare. *See* Sigh No More, Ladies.
Baltimore Grays, The. *Unknown.* BIG
Balulalow. James, John, *and* Robert Wedderburn. LoBV; OxBoCh
(Cradle Song: "O my deir hert, young Jesus sweit.") OBEV
(Nativity Carol.) BOL
Bamboo Briars, The. *Unknown.* ABS
Ban of Time there is no disobeying, The. Lament. Gelett Burgess. InMe
Banana. Charles G. Bell. NePoAm-2
Bananas ripe and green, and ginger-root. The Tropics in New York. Claude McKay. GoSl; PoNe
Banbury Fair. Edith G. Millard. BoTP
Band, The. ——John. GFA
Band blares, The. Circus. Eleanor Farjeon. MPB; SUS; UTS
Band in the Pines, The. John Esten Cooke. AA; SPP
Band makes a tunnel of the open street. The Bands and the Beautiful Children. P. K. Page. PeCV
Band o' Gideon, De. *Unknown.* APW; BoAN-1, *with music*
Band of beggars out to view, A. Kohei, *tr. fr. Japanese by* Lois J. Erickson. SoLD
Band of Gideon, The. Joseph S. Cotter, Jr. BANP; CDC
Band of Military Officers, A. Wordsworth. *Fr.* The Prelude, IX. EnLi-2
Band of the bold were gathered together, The. The Parting of the Red Sea. *Unknown. Fr.* Exodus. AnOE
Band Played On, The. John F. Palmer. TreF
Band was playing "Dixie" when he marched, marched away, The. The Volunteer. Frank L. Stanton. MDAH
Bandage Is Red, The. John Ackerson. MuM
Bandit, The. Rowena Porter Baker. CAG
Bandit Peter Mancino's Death, The. *Unknown. tr. fr. Italian by* Maria Graham. CAW
Bandit's Grave, The. Charles Pitt. SCC
Bandog, The. Walter de la Mare. TiPo
Bands and the Beautiful Children, The. P. K. Page. PeCV
Bands of dark and bands of light. Travellers' Song. George Macdonald. BSV
Bands were playing in the street, The. Flag and Cross. Alfred J. Hough. FOAH
Bandusia, Stainless Mirror ("O fons Bandusiae"). Horace, *tr. fr. Latin by* Charles Stuart Calverley. Odes, III, 13. OnPM
Bane of Poverty, The. Theognis, *tr. fr. Greek by* T. F. Higham. GrL; OxBG
Baneful company of friends I fear, The. Persian Maxim. Sadi. BoFr
Bang on your platter. Weight Gainer. Edgar A. Guest. OnHT
Bangidero, *with music. Unknown.* SoAmSa
Bangkolidye. Barry Pain. BOHV
Banished, The. Arturo Serrano Plaja, *tr. fr. Spanish by* Rolfe Humphries. PoFr
Banished, dispossessed dead, The. Litany of the Rooms of the Dead. Franz Werfel. TrJP
Banished Duke [Living in the Forest] Speaks to His Retainers, The. Shakespeare. *See* Uses of Adversity, The.
Banished Duke of Grantham, The. *Unknown.* EnSB
Banished Lover, The. Al-Mustazhir, *tr. fr. Arabic by* A. J. Arberry. MooP
Banishment, The. Milton. *Fr.* Paradise Lost, XII. OBS
Banishment. Shakespeare. King Richard II, *fr.* I, iii. EV-1
Banishment from Paradise. Milton. *Fr.* Paradise Lost, XII. TreFS
Banishment of the Cid, The. *Unknown, tr. fr. Spanish by* R. Selden Rose *and* Leonard Bacon. *Fr.* The Cid. AnSpL-1; TeCS
Banisht!/ It greev'd me much to heare the sentence. John Webster. *Fr.* The White Devil, I, i. AtBAP
Banjo Boomer. Wallace Stevens. WaKn
Banjo of the Past, The. Howard Weeden. AA
Banjo Player, The. Fenton Johnson. AnAmPo; BANP; GoSl; LA; PoNe
Bank of the Arkansaw, The, *with music. Unknown.* OuSiCo
Bank Thief, The. J. R. Farrell. BeLS; BLPA
Bankers Are Just like Anybody Else, except Richer. Ogden Nash. ATP (1953 ed.); LiTA
Bankis of Helicon, The. Alexander Montgomerie. EBSV
Bankrupt, The. Thomas Otway. *Fr.* Venice Preserved. EV-3
Bankrupt. Cortlandt W. Sayres. PoToHe (new ed.)
Banks o' Doon, The. Burns. BLV; BoLiVe; BSV; CaAE; CBOV; CEP; EBSV; EnLi-2; InP; LoBV; LPS-1; MCCG; NeHB; OBEC; OBEV; OtMeF; OuHeWo; PECK; PoMa; TCEP; TreFS; TrGrPo; ViBoPo; WBLP; WHA; WP
(Bonie Doon.) BEL; EPP; HiLiEn; REAL
(Bonnie Doon.) BCEP; CoEV; EnLit; HBV; LEAP; SN
(False Love.) LiTL
(Ye Banks and Braes [o' Bonnie Doon].) AtBAP; CH; EiPP; EV-3; GTSE; GTSL; OlF
(Ye Flowery Banks [o' Bonnie Doon].) AWP; CEP; EG; EM-1; EnRP; GTBS; GTBS-D; GTBS-W; InPo; JAWP; OAEP; OBEC; PoEL-4; ReaPo; TOP; TyEnPo; WBP
Banks of Banna, The. George Ogle. IrPN
Banks of Dundee, The. *Unknown.* BaBo
Banks of Gaspereaux, The. *Unknown.* BaBo
(Banks of the Gaspereaux, The.) ShS
Banks of Newfoundland, The, *with music. Unknown.* ShS; SoAmSa
Banks of Sacramento, The, *with music. Unknown.* AmSS; AS
(Banks of the Sacramento.) SG
Banks of the Gaspereaux, The. *Unknown. See* Banks of Gaspereaux, The.
Banks of the Pamanaw, The. *Unknown.* ABF
Banks of the Roses, The, *with music. Unknown.* ShS
Banks of the Sacramento. *Unknown. See* Banks of Sacramento, The.
Banner of America. Denis A. McCarthy. CV
Banner of England, not for a season, O banner of Britain, hast thou. The Defence of Lucknow. Tennyson. BeLS; BPN
Banner of Freedom high floated unfurled, The. The *United States* and *Macedonian. Unknown.* PAH
Banner of the Cross, The. George Washington Doane. BePJ
Banner of the Jew, The. Emma Lazarus. AA; OBAV; TrJP
Bannerman of the Dandenong. Alice Werner. TVSH
Banners of the King go forth, The. Vexilla Regis Prodeunt. Venantius Fortunatus. LaP
Bannockburn. John Barbour. *Fr.* The Bruce, XII, XIII, *and* XX. EBSV
Bannockburn. Burns. *See* Scots Wha Hae.
Bannockburn. Sir Walter Scott. *Fr.* The Lord of the Isles, VI. BSV
Banquet, The, *sel.* Dante, *tr. fr. Italian by* Howard Nemerov. "Ye intelligences, turning the third sphere." LyMA; LyPI
Banquet, The. Louise Driscoll. MaRV
Banquet, The. Keats. *Fr.* Lamia. SeCePo
Banquet-cups, of many a hue and shape, The. The Respite. Maria Gowen Brooks. *Fr.* Zophiel; or, The Bride of Seven. AA
Banquet at the Tso Family Manor. Tu Fu, *tr. fr. Chinese by* Kenneth Rexroth. OnPC
Banquet Song. Edwin Osgood Grover. PR
Bansha Peeler wint won night, A. The Peeler and the Goat. *Unknown.* AnIL
Ban-Shee, The. William Allingham. TIP
Banshee, The. John Todhunter. OnYI; VA
Bantam Husband, The. *Unknown. See* Petit Mari, Le.
Bantams in Pine-Woods. Wallace Stevens. AtBAP; InPo; MOAP; MoVE; OxBA; SeCeV
Bantry Bay. James Lyman Molloy. OnYI
Banty Tim. John Hay. DDA; LPS-3; MAP; MoAmPo (1942 ed.)
Baptism, The. Leonard Aaronson. FaBoTw
Baptism. Claude McKay. AnEnPo; PoNe
Baptist, The. William Drummond of Hawthornden. *See* For the Baptist.
Baptist, Baptist, is my name. Gabriel's Trumpet. *Unknown.* StDa
Baptist's Sonnet, The. William Drummond of Hawthornden. *See* For the Baptist.
Bar, The. *Unknown.* PoToHe (new ed.)
Bar at Night, A. Sakutaro Hagiwara, *tr. fr. Japanese by* Katue Kitasono. LiTW
Bar is crossed, The: but Death—the pilot—stands. Becalmed. John Banister Tabb. AA
Bar Kochba. Emma Lazarus. TrJP
Bar of steel—it is only, A. Carl Sandburg. *Fr.* Smoke and Steel. PoeMoYo; VOD (1935 ed.)
Bar-Z on a Sunday Night. Percival Combes. SCC
Barabas in His Counting-House. Christopher Marlowe. *Fr.* The Jew of Malta. CoEV
("Fye, what a trouble tis to count this trash.") NBE
Barabbas. William E. Brooks. BPP
Barabbas, *sels.* Sara Bard Field. PoFr
"Aslant the shoulder of each prisoner," *fr.* III.
"In secret mountain fastnesses we stored," *fr.* I.
Barabbas, Judas Iscariot. The Morning After. Dorothy Wellesley. OBMV

Barabbas Speaks. Edwin McNeill Poteat. MaRV
Barbara. Ruth Comfort Mitchell. VOD
Barbara. Alexander Smith. BMEP; BSV; GoTS; GTBS; HBV; OBEV (1st ed.); OBVV
Barbara Allen [*or* Allan]. *Unknown.* ABS (B *vers.*); BeLS, *diff. vers.*; BSV; EBSV; EnSB; FaFP; MaC; TrAS, *with music;* TreF; TyEnPo; ViBoFo (A *and* C *vers.;* B *vers., with music*)
(Barbara Allen's Cruelty.) BCEP; BLV, *abr.;* CBOV, *abr.;* FaBoBe; HBV; LEAP; OBB; OBEV; OnSP; OTPC (1923 ed.); ViBoPo
(Barbara Ellen.) IHA
(Barbery Allen, A *vers.*) ABS
(Barbra Allen, *with music.*) AS
(Bonny Barbara Allan.) AWP; BaBo (A, B, *and* C *vers.*); BEL; BoLiVe; CH, *abr.;* CoBE; EM-1; EnLi-1 (1949 ed.); EnLit: ESPB (A *and* B *vers.*); InPo; JAWP; LiTB; LiTL; LoEn; OuHeWo; ReaPo; RiBV; TOP; TrGrPo; WBP
(Bonny Barbara Ellen.) Po
(Sir John Graeme and Barbara Allan.) OxBoLi
Barbara, child, with luminous face. Barbara. Ruth Comfort Mitchell. VOD
Barbara Ellen. *Unknown. See* Barbara Allen.
Barbara Frietchie. Whittier. AmPP (3d ed.); AnNE; BAV; BBV; BeLS; BoTP; DD; EV-5; FaBoBe; FaFP; FaPON; GA; GN; GoTP; HBV; HBVY; IAP; LEAP; LH; LPS-2; MaC; MC; MW; NeHB; OnHT; OnSP; OTPC; PaA; PAH; PAP; PECK; PTA-1; PYM; REAL; RIS; ShGoBo; StVeCh (1940 ed.); TreF; TrGrPo; TVSH; WBLP; YaD; YT
Barbarian. Arthur Rimbaud, *tr. fr. French by* Hubert Creekmore. LiTW
Barbarians. James Stephens. ChMo; CMP
Barbarossa, *sel.* Giovanni Battista Niccolini, *tr. fr. Italian by* William Dean Howells.
"When will you dream,/ You Germans." PoFr
Barbarossa. Friedrich Rückert, *tr. fr. German.* AWP
Barbarous Chief, The. Ella Wheeler Wilcox. PEOR
Barb'd blossom of the guarded gorse. A Song of Winter. Emily Davis Pfeiffer. PrWP; VA
Barbed Wire. Eithne Wilkins. NeBP
Barber, barber, shave a pig. Mother Goose. BoChLi; BoN; GaP; HBV; HBVY; OTPC; OxNR; RIS
Barber Shaved the Mason, The. *Unknown.* OTPC (1923 ed.); OxNR
Barber shop is blank, The. Through the Barber Shop Window. Violet Anderson. CaP
Barber, Spare Those Hairs. John Love, Jr. YaD
Barbered woman's man, A. Contemporaries. Richard Hovey. MAP; MoAmPo (1942 ed.)
Barberries. Mary Aldis. HBMV
Barberries ripe. Chant for Skippers. Katharine Gallagher. SiSoSe
Barber's, The. Walter de la Mare. GaP; MPB; PCH; RAR; SUS
Barber's Cry, *with music. Unknown.* TrAS
Barbery Allen. *Unknown. See* Barbara Allen.
Barbra Allen. *Unknown. See* Barbara Allen.
Barcarola: "Along by the sea and the river." Joan Zorro, *tr. fr. Portuguese by* Seth G. Thornton. LyMA
Barcarola: "Whenever I see waves surging." Roy Fernández, *tr. fr. Portuguese by* Seth G. Thornton. LyMA
Barcarole. Johan Ludvig Heiberg, *tr. fr. Danish by* Charles W. Stork. BoDS
Barcarole. Sigbjörn Obstfelder, *tr. fr. Norwegian by* Charles W. Stork. AnNoLy
Barcarole of James Smith, The. Herbert S. Gorman. HBMV
Barclay of Ury. Whittier. IAP; LPS-2; TCAP
Bard, The. Blake. *See* Hear the Voice of the Bard.
Bard, The. Thomas Gray. BEL; BHV; CEP; EiPP; EM-1; EnL; EnLi-2; EnRP; EV-3; GTBS; GTBS-D; GTBS-W; GTSE; GTSL; LH; OAEP; OBEC; Po; PoFr, *abr.;* ShBV-4; TOP
Sels.
Curse upon Edward. BCEP; OBEV
"On a rock, whose haughty brow." SeCePo
Bard Ethell, The, *abr.* Aubrey Thomas De Vere. TIP
Bard has sung, God never formed a soul, The. Disappointment. Maria Gowen Brooks. *Fr.* Zophiel; or, The Bride of Seven. LPS-1
Bard is buried here, not strong, but sweet, A. The Epitaph of Eusthenes. Edward Cracroft Lefroy. *Fr.* Echoes from Theocritus. AWP; OBVV
Bard of Auld Lang Syne, The. James Main Dixon. POT
Bard of Love, The. *Unknown, tr. fr. Greek by* Byron. OuHeWo
Bard of the Fleece, whose skilful genius made. To the Poet, John Dyer. Wordsworth. PtP
Bard there was, and that a worthy wight, A. For Maister Geoffrey Chaucer. Robert Hillyer. PtP
Bard! to no brave chief belonging. The Fight of the Forlorn. George Darley. TIP
Bardolph, be blythe: Nim, rowse thy vaunting veines. The Death of Falstaff. Shakespeare. King Henry V, *fr.* II, iii. LiA
Bards, The. Robert Graves. FaBoMo; GTBS-W; LiTM (rev. ed.); SeCePo; ViBoPo (1958 ed.)
(Lust in Song.) OxBI; ViBoPo (1941 ed.)
Bard's Chant. James Shirley. *Fr.* Saint Patrick for Ireland. ACP
Bard's Epitaph, A. Burns. EiPP; EPP; InP; LPS-3; PIR
Bards falter in shame, their running verse, The. The Bards [*or* Lust in Song]. Robert Graves. ViBoPo. *See also* Their cheeks are blotched for shame, their running verse.
Bards of brow funereal. Mystical Poets. Amado Nervo. CAW
Bards of Passion and of Mirth. Keats. *See* Ode: "Bards of Passion and of Mirth."
Bards of the Future! you that come. On the Future of Poetry. Austin Dobson. PoVP; VLEP
Bard's Song, The. Sir Robert Stapylton. SeCePo
Bard's Song. Nikolai Yazykov, *tr. fr. Russian by* C. M. Bowra. BoRS
Bards We Quote, The. Bert Leston Taylor. HBMV; WhC
Bare Almond Trees. D. H. Lawrence. MoP
Bare-bosom'd Night. Walt Whitman. *See* Earth at Night.
Bare Days. Evgeni Baratynsky, *tr. fr. Russian by* W. A. Morison. BoRS
Bare skin is my wrinkled sack. The Shrouded Stranger. Allen Ginsberg. NeAP
Bare though it seemed at first, this close-built cell. In Chains. Albrecht Haushofer. *Fr.* Sonnets from Moabite Prison. TwGV
Bare twisted shrubbery without a drop of water, The. General Quiroga Rides to Death in a Carriage. Jorge Luis Borges. TwSpPo
Bare Winter owns the earth at last. Winter Life and Scenery. Thomas Caulfield Irwin. IrPN
Bareback. William Haskell Simpson. *Fr.* In Arizona. NP
Bare-Back Rider. Dorothy Aldis. *Fr.* At the Circus. UTS
Barefoot and ragged, with neglected hair. On a Fair Beggar. Philip Ayres. ElSeCe; EnLoPo; LO; OBS; SeCL; SeEP
Barefoot Boy, A. James Whitcomb Riley. FaFP
Barefoot Boy, The. Whittier. AA; AmPP (3d ed.); AnNE; BAP; CoBA; FaBoBe; CN; GTBS-W; HBV; HBVY; IAP; LaNeLa; LBAP; LEAP; LiTA; LPS-1; MOAP; NeHB; OBAV; OBVV; OHFP; OnPP; OTPC; PIR; PoeMoYo; PTA-1; PYM; SN; TCAP; TreF; WBLP, *abr.*
"Blessings on thee, little man," *sel.* FaPON
Barefoot Boy, A! I mark him at his play. A Barefoot Boy. James Whitcomb Riley. FaFP
Barefoot Days. Rachel Field. FaPON; YeAr
Barefoot friar all in brown, A. The Irish Franciscan. Rosa Mulholland. CAW; SaFP
Barefoot I went and made no sound. The Viper. Ruth Pitter. AlDL; FaBoTw
Barefoot vagabond on a stone, A. On My Wander Flute. Abraham Sutskever. OnCuPl
Barefoot without a stitch she walks. Dance with Banderillas. Richard Duerden. NeAP
Barefooted boys scud up the street. A Sudden Shower. James Whitcomb Riley. PRWS
Barefooted Friar, The. Sir Walter Scott. *Fr.* Ivanhoe, *ch.* 17. EmBrPo; EV-4
Barefooted, in his hood and cloak of brown. The Friar. Julián del Casal. CAW; SaFP; WHL
Barely a twelvemonth after. The Horses. Edwin Muir. HaMV
Bargain, A. Abbie Farwell Brown. CV
Bargain, The. Anna Bunston de Bary. MaRV
Bargain. Louise Driscoll. HBMV
Bargain, The. Sir Philip Sidney. *See* My True Love Hath My Heart.
Bargain, The. Neidhart von Reuental, *tr. fr. German by* Jethro Bithell. LiTW
Bargain Basement. F. T. Macartney. MoAuPo
Bargain Sale, A. S. E. Kiser. PoToHe (new ed.)
Barge, The. Rose Fyleman. BrR
Barge glided, The. Vision. Israel Zangwill. TrJP
Barge she sat in, like a burnish'd throne, The. Cleopatra [*or* A Royal Barge]. Shakespeare. *Fr.* Antony and Cleopatra, II, ii. BCEP; BoHiPo; CoEV; KN; LEAP; LiTB; LiTG; LiTL; LPS-2; PoFS; PreP; TreF; TrGrPo
Barge Wife, A. John Farrar. TBM
Bark and boom of guns and shrieking flight, The. The Silent Stars. Eric H. Daniell. MaRV
Bark leaps love-fraught from the land, The. The Thousand Islands. Charles Sangster. *Fr.* The St. Lawrence and the Saguenay. BoCaPo
Bark of Clanranald, The. Alexander MacDonald, *tr. fr. Gaelic by* Alexander Nicolson. EBSV
(Birlinn Chlann-Raghnaill, *tr. by* "Hugh MacDiarmid.") GoTS
Bark that bare me through foam and squall. Boatman's Hymn. *At. to* Andrew Magrath. OnYI

Bark that held the prince went down, The. He Never Smiled Again. Felicia Dorothea Hemans. HBV
Barking sound the shepherd hears, A. Fidelity. Wordsworth. AlBD; CG; PECK
Barley-break. Sir John Suckling. SeCV-1
Barley Fields, The. Jean Blewett. OCL
Barley-Mowers' Song, The. Mary Howitt. OTPC (1923 ed.)
Barn, The. Edmund Blunden. GTML; MBP; MoBrPo; SeCePo
Barn, The. Elizabeth J. Coatsworth. AnNE; ChBR; GoTP; UTS
Barn, The. Stephen Spender. HaMV
Barn in Winter, The. Claire Harris MacIntosh. CaP
Barn-Swallow, The. William Sargent. RIS
Barnabe Rich, Gentleman Soldier, in Praise of the Author. Barnabe Rich. ReIE
Barnaby Bloggin. Drinking Vessels. Laura E. Richards. LiL
Barnacle, The. A. P. Herbert. RIS
Barnacle Bill the Sailor. *Unknown.* *See* Abram Brown.
Barnacles. Sidney Lanier. IAP; OQP; PECK; QP-1; TCAP
Barney Bodkin broke his nose. *Unknown.* BoN; OxNR; SiTL
Barney McGee. Richard Hovey. BAP, *st.* 1; BOHV; HBV; InMe; TreFS
Barney O'Hea. Samuel Lover. OnYI; TIP
Barney's Invitation. Philip Freneau. IAP; PAH
Barnfire during Church. Robert Bly. NePoEA
Barnfloor and Winepress. Gerard Manley Hopkins. ACP; CAW
Barnyard, The. Maud Burnham. PCH; PPL; TiPo
Barnyard Song, *with music. Unknown.* TrAS
("I had a cat and the cat pleased me.") OxNR
Baron hath the landward park, the fisher hath the sea, The. The Sea Fowler. Mary Howitt. VA
Baron o' [*or* of] Brackley, The. *Unknown.* BaBo; EBSV; ESPB (A *and* B *vers.*); OBB
Baron o Leys, The. *Unknown.* ESPB
Baron of Smaylho'me rose with day, The. The Eve of St. John. Sir Walter Scott. BPN; DaM; EmBrPo; EnRP; EPN; EV-4; PoEL-4
Baron Renfrew's Ball. Charles Graham Halpine. PAH
Barons Bold, The. William Johnson Fox. PoFr; VA
Baron's Last Banquet, The. Albert Gorton Greene. AA; BeLS; LPS-1
Baron's War, The, *sel.* Michael Drayton.
Severn, The, *fr.* I. ChTr
Baroque Comment. Louise Bogan. CrMA
Baroque Wall-Fountain in the Villa Sciarra, A. Richard Wilbur. NePoEA
Barque is floating, water-sodden, A. The Floating Barque. *Tr. by* Florence Randal Livesay. CPG
Barque is small, the ocean vast, The. During the Storm. Théophile Gautier. TrFP
Barque of phosphor. Fabliau of Florida. Wallace Stevens. NP
Barrack-Room Ballads, *sel.* Kipling.
Dedication: "Beyond the path of the outmost sun through utter darkness hurled." ViPP
Barrack-square, washed clean with rain, The. In Barracks. Siegfried Sassoon. FaBoTw
Barrack Yard, The. Nettie Palmer. NeLNL
Barracks Apt. 14. Theodore Weiss. NePoAm-2
Barred Islands. Philip Booth. NePoEA
Barrel-Organ, The. Alfred Noyes. BMEP; ChMo; CMP; EnLit; HBV; MBP; MCCG; MoBrPo; NeMA, *sl. abr.;* PFE; PoeMoYo; PoRA; PYM; TCEP; TreF, *sl. abr.;* TwCV; VOD
Go Down to Kew in Lilac-Time, *sel.* BoTP
(At Kew.) TVSH
Barrels of blue potato spray, The. Spraying the Potatoes. Patrick Kavanagh. OxBI
Barren "Rachel," *tr. fr. Hebrew by* L. V. Snowman. TrJP
Barren Battlefield, The. Homer, *tr. fr. Greek by* F. L. Lucas. *Fr.* The Iliad, XIX. GrPE
Barren Easter, The. Clinton Scollard. EOAH
Barren Moors, The. William Ellery Channing. AA
Barren Soul, A. Joseph Ezobi, *tr. fr. Hebrew by* D. I. Friedmann. *Fr.* The Silver Bowl. TrJP
Barren Spring. Dante Gabriel Rossetti. The House of Life, LXXXIII. BPN; FaBoEn; NBE; PoEL-5; PoVP; ViPo; VLEP
Barren Stone. Nicolás Guillén, *tr. fr. Spanish by* Langston Hughes. PoNe
Barricade—a wall—a stronghold, A. The Breech. Michael McClure. NeAP
Barricades, The. Denise Levertov. NeBP
Barrier, The. Louis Lavater. MoAuPo
Barrier, The. Claude McKay. BANP
Barrier. John Frederick Nims. JKCP (1955 ed.)
Barrier. Dorothy Quick. MuM; UnW
Barrier stone has rolled away, The. Easter. Edwin L. Sabin. DD; HH; OHIP; PoRL
Bars Fight. Lucy Terry. PoNe
Bars of Fate, The. Ellen M. H. Gates. BLP
Bart Hinch. August Derleth. DaM
Barter. Marie Blake. PoToHe (new ed.)
Barter. Earle V. Eastwood. OQP; QP-1
Barter. Sara Teasdale. ChMo; CMP; FaPON; MCCG; MPB; OBAV; OQP; OTPC (1946 ed.); PVS; QP-2; SP; TreFS; VOD
Barter. Margaret Widdemer. HBMV; WGRP
Barter Our Northern Darkness. Nigel Heseltine. MoWP
Barthélémon at Vauxhall. Thomas Hardy. UnS
Bartholdi Statue, The. Whittier. PaA; PAH
Bartholomew. Norman Gale. HBV; HBVY; OTPC; RAR; SP
Bartholomew Benjamin Bunting. The Singular Sangfroid of Baby Bunting. Guy Wetmore Carryl. NA
Bartholomew is very sweet. Bartholomew. Norman Gale. HBV; HBVY; OTPC; RAR; SP
Bartholomew, my brother. St. Bartholomew's on the Hill. Bliss Carman. NLK
Bartimeus. Laura Simmons. ChIP
Bartol. Amos Bronson Alcott. AA
Baruch, *sel.* Bible, Apocrypha.
Path of Wisdom, The, III: 9–IV: 4. TrJP
Bas Bleu, *sel.* Hannah More.
Conversation. OBEC
Bas-Relief. Carl Sandburg. CrMA; MOAP
Bas-Relief. Sappho, *tr. fr. Greek by* H. De Vere Stacpoole. GrR
Base Details. Siegfried Sassoon. MBP; MoBrPo; NeMA; TwCV
Base of All Metaphysics, The. Walt Whitman. BoFr; CaAE; NePA
Baseball's Sad Lexicon. Franklin P. Adams. FaFP; InMe; TreFS
Bashful Earthquake, The, *sel.* Oliver Herford.
Earth. BTP
(Proem: "If this little world tonight.") AA; TPH
Basia. Thomas Campion. *See* Turn Back, You Wanton Flyer.
Basic Communication. Thomas Hornsby Ferril. NePoAm-2
Basil, rosemary, rue and lavender! Saint Teresa. Thomas S. Jones, Jr. PraNu
Basilisk, The. Philip Child. CaP
Basket Maker's Song. Thomas Dekker. *See* Happy Heart, The.
Basket of roses for the Royal House of David, A. A Gift of Flowers. Leonard Feeney. WHL
Baskets of ripe fruit in air. Gardener Janus Catches a Naiad. Edith Sitwell. MBP; MoAB; MoBrPo
Basking in peace in the warm spring sun. The Romance of the Carpet. Robert J. Burdette. BOHV
Bast. William Rose Benét. HBMV; PoC
Bastard, The, *sels.* Richard Savage.
Bastard's Lot, The. OBEC
On Himself. BeR
Bastille, The. William Cowper. *Fr.* The Task, V. RO
Bat, The. "Lewis Carroll." *See* Twinkle, Twinkle, Little Bat!
Bat, The. Ruth Pitter. AlDL
Bat, The. Theodore Roethke. GoTP
Bat, bat, come under my hat. Mother Goose. OTPC; OxNR
Batch of freshmen came to Cobweb College, A. Cobweb College. Kenneth Leslie. BoCaPo
Batchelor leads an easy life, A. Good & Bad Wives. *Unknown.* CoMu
Batchelors Song, The. Thomas Flatman. CEP
Batchin'. S. Omar Barker. IHA
Bath, The. Harry Graham. CenHV
Bath, The. Joel Oppenheimer. NeAP
Bath-maidens all of Pallas, hither away! For the Bath of Pallas. Callimachus. GrR
Bath Tub. *See* Bathtub.
Bathe me O God in thee, mounting to thee. Walt Whitman. *Fr.* Passage to India. TrPWD
Bather in a Painting, A. Ashton Greene. NePoAm
Bathers, The. Arthur Hugh Clough. *Fr.* The Bothie of Tober-na-Vuolich. VA
("There is a stream.") EV-5
Bathers. Terence Tiller. ChMP; FaBoMo; NeBP
Bather's Dirge, The. Tennyson Minor. PA
Bathing. John Keble. OTPC (1923 ed.)
Bathing. James Thomson. *Fr.* The Seasons: Summer. LPS-2
Bathing Children, The. Viktor Rydberg, *tr. fr. Swedish by* Charles W. Stork. AnSL
Bathing Girl, A. Johannes V. Jensen, *tr. fr. Danish by* Charles W. Stork. BoDS
Bathing of Oisin's Head, The. *Unknown, tr. fr. Early Modern Irish by* Eoin MacNeill. AnIL
Bathing of Pallas, The. Callimachus, *tr. fr. Greek by* F. L. Lucas. GrPE
Baths of Rome and Babylon. A City Song. John Hanlon Mitchell. CaP; OCL

Bathsheba: to whom none ever said scat. Epitaph. Whittier. CIV
Bathsheba came out to the sun. Telling the Bees. Lizette Woodworth Reese. AA; LEAP
Bathsheba's Song. George Peele. *See* Bethsabe's Song.
Bath Tub, The. Ezra Pound. ReaPo
Bathtub Bay. Lenore Riggs. GFA
Bathtub Gin. Philip H. Rhinelander. WhC
Bathymeter. William Hart-Smith. BoAV
Batrachomyomachia, *sel. Unknown, tr. fr. Greek by* Thomas Parnell.
"To fill my rising song with sacred fire." GrPo
(Battle of the Frogs and Mice, The.) GrL
Bats, The. Robert Hillyer. GoYe
Bats. Mary Effie Lee Newsome. GoSl
Batson, *with music. Unknown.* OuSiCo
Battarias. Miltiades Malakassis, *tr. fr. Modern Greek by* Rae Dalven. MoGP
Battel of the Summer-Islands, The. Edmund Waller. *See* Battle of the Summer Islands, The.
Batter my heart, three-person'd God; for, you. Holy Sonnets, XIV. John Donne. AnEnPo; AnFE; BLV; BoLiVe; CaAE; CoEV; EnL; EnLP; EPS; ExPo; FaFP; GoBC; GTBS-W; LiTB; LiTG; MaPo; MaRV; MeLP; MePo; NBE; OAEP; OBS; OxBoCh; PeBoSo; Po; PoE; PoEL-2; PoFS; ReEn; RiBV; SeCePo; SeCeV; SeCV-1; SeEP; TrGrPo; TrPWD; TuPP; TwCrTr; TwP
Batter'd, wreck'd old man, A. Prayer of Columbus. Walt Whitman. AmPP (4th ed.); APW; ATP; WGRP
Batteries Out of Ammunition. Kipling. *Fr.* Epitaphs of the War. PoVP
Battery grides and jingles, The. The Day's March. Robert Nichols. LBBV
Battery Moving Up to a New Position from Rest Camp: Dawn. Robert Nichols. QS
Battery Park. Leonard Cline. PR
Batte's Song: "Love is the heaven's fair [*or* fayre] aspèct." Michael Drayton. *Fr.* The Shepherd's Garland, Eclogue VII. LO; NBE
Batte's Song: "What is love but the desire." Michael Drayton. *Fr.* The Shepherd's Garland, Eclogue VII. LoBV
Battle. Al-Tutili, *tr. fr. Arabic by* A. J. Arberry. MooP
Battle, The. Chu Yuan, *tr. fr. Chinese by* Arthur Waley. TrCh; WaaP
Battle. Robinson Jeffers. *See* May–June, 1940.
Battle, The. Macaulay. *Fr.* Lays of Ancient Rome. BHV
Battle, The ("By this, though deep the evening fell"). Sir Walter Scott. *See* Flodden.
Battle, The ("Not far advanc'd was morning day"). Sir Walter Scott. *See* Marmion: Marmion and Douglas.
Battle: Hit. W. W. Gibson. *See* Hit.
Battle Autumn of 1862, The. Whittier. BlG; MC; PAH
Battle Ballad, A. Francis Orrery Ticknor. BlG; PAH
Battle between the Angels and the Anarchs, *much abr.* Milton. *Fr.* Paradise Lost, VI. BCEP
Battle Cry. John G. Neihardt. BAP; HBMV
Battle Cry, A. Lee Shippey. MaRV
Battle Cry. William Henry Venable. PAH
Battle Cry of Freedom, The. George Frederick Root. FaBoBe; FOAH; OlF; PaA; PAH; PoFr; TreFS; YaD
Battle Eve of the [Irish] Brigade, The. Thomas Osborne Davis. AnIV; OnYI
Battle-Flag of Sigurd, The. Dora Greenwell. OBVV
Battle grows more hard and harder yet, The. The Last Battle. *Unknown. Fr.* The Song of Roland. LiTW
Battle Hymn. Michael Altenburg, *tr. fr. German by* Catherine Winkworth. WGRP
(Battle-Song of Gustavus Adolphus, The.) LPS-2
Battle Hymn of the American Republic. Julia Ward Howe. *See* Battle Hymn of the Republic.
Battle Hymn of the Chinese Revolution (1912). *Unknown, tr. fr. Chinese.* PoFr
Battle Hymn of the Republic. Julia Ward Howe. AA; AnAmPo; AnFE; APA; APW; BAP; BAV; BBV (1923 ed.); BLPA; BoHiPo; CH; CoAnAm; CoBA; DD; DDA; FaBoBe; FaFP; FaPON; GN; GoTP; HBV; HBVY; IAP; InP; LA; LBAP; LEAP; LiTG; LPS-2; MaRV; MC; MDAH; NeHB; NePA; OBAV; OHIP; OlF; OnAP; OQP; OTPC; PaA; PAH; PAP; PIR; PoFr; PYM; QP-1; RG; TCAP; TOP; TrAS, *with music;* TreF; TVSH; WBLP; WGRP; YaD
(Battle Hymn of the American Republic.) CBPC; OBVV; OtMeF
Battle Hymn of the Spanish Rebellion. L. A. Mackay. BoCaPo
(Battle Hymn of the Spanish Republic.) OnPM
Battle in the Clouds, The. William Dean Howells. PAH
Battle is fought and won, The. Scanderbeg. Longfellow. *Fr.* Tales of a Wayside Inn. PFY
Battle of Actium. Virgil, *tr. fr. Latin by* Dryden. *Fr.* The Aeneid, VIII. OBS
Battle of Agincourt. Michael Drayton. *See* Agincourt.
Battle of Ai, The. Timothy Dwight. *Fr.* The Conquest of Canaan. BAP
Battle of Argoed Llwyfain, The. Taliesin, *tr. fr. Welsh by* Gwyn Williams. PrWP
Battle of Baltimore, The. *Unknown.* PAH
Battle of Bannockburn, The. John Barbour. *Fr.* The Bruce, XIII. BSV
Battle of Bath, The. Layamon, *tr. fr. Middle English. Fr.* The Brut. MeEV
Battle of Beal' and Duine. Sir Walter Scott. *Fr.* The Lady of the Lake, VI. TCEP, *abr.*
(Beal' an Dhuine.) LPS-2
Battle of Bennington, The. Thomas P. Rodman. GA, *abr.;* MC; PAH
Battle of Blenheim, The. Robert Southey. BCEP; BeLS; BoChLi; BOHV; BTP; EnLit; EnRP; EPN; ERP; GN; GoTP; HBV; HBVY; InMe; LPS-2; MCCG; MW; NeHB; OBRV; OnSP; OTPC; PCN; PECK; PIR; SoV; StVeCh (1940 ed.); TCEP; TOP; TreF; TrGrPo; TVSH; WBLP
(After Blenheim.) BBV; BLV; CG; EV-4; GTBS; GTBS-D; GTBS-W; GTSE; GTSL; PC; PIAE; PoeMoYo; PYM
"Now tell us what 'twas all about," *sel.* OQP; QP-2
Battle of Bridgewater, The. *Unknown.* PAH
Battle of Brunanburh. *Unknown, tr. fr. Anglo-Saxon by* Tennyson. BEL; CoBE; EnLit; ExPo; TrGrPo; WaaP
—— *Tr. by* Charles W. Kennedy. AnOE
—— *Tr. by* Stith Thompson. EnLi-1 (1949 ed.)
Battle of Bunker Hill, The. *Unknown.* PAH
Battle of Bunker's Hill, The. Frederick S. Cozzens. PTA-2
Battle of Charleston Harbor, The. Paul Hamilton Hayne. MDAH; PAH
Battle of Charlestown, The. Henry Howard Brownell. PAH
Battle of Erie, The. *Unknown.* GA, *abr.;* PAH
Battle of Eutaw, The. William Gilmore Simms. PAH
Battle of Finnsburg, The. *Unknown, tr. fr. Anglo-Saxon by* Charles W. Kennedy. AnOE
Battle of Gettysburg, The. Stephen Vincent Benét. *Fr.* John Brown's Body. BeLS
Battle of Harlaw, The. *Unknown.* EBSV (A *vers.*); ESPB (A *and* B *vers.*)
Battle of Hastings, *sel.* Thomas Chatterton.
"And now Duke William." TCEP
Battle of Hohenlinden, The. Thomas Campbell. *See* Hohenlinden.
Battle of Ivry, The. Macaulay. *See* Ivry.
Battle of Kegs, The. Francis Hopkinson. *See* Battle of the Kegs, The.
Battle of Killiecrankie, The, *abr.* William E. Aytoun. TVSH
Battle of King's Mountain, The. *Unknown.* PAH; SPP
Battle of La Prairie, The. William Douw Schuyler-Lighthall. MC; PAH; VA
Battle of Lake Champlain, The. Philip Freneau. PAH
Battle of Lake Regillus, The, *sels.* Macaulay. *Fr.* Lays of Ancient Rome.
Battle, The. BHV
Death of Herminius, The. OtMeF
Fight in the Centre, The. OtMeF
"Men said he saw strange visions." UnW
War-Horse, The. BHV
Battle of Lena, The. *Unknown, tr. fr. Danish by* E. M. Smith-Dampier. BoDaBa
Battle of Lexington, The. Sidney Lanier. *Fr.* The Psalm of the West. PAP
Battle of Lookout Mountain, The. George Henry Boker. MC; PAH
Battle of Lovell's Pond, The. Longfellow. PAH
Battle of Maldon, The. *Unknown, tr. fr. Anglo-Saxon.* AnOE, *tr. by* Charles W. Kennedy; EPP; LiA, *pr. tr. by* R. K. Gordon
Sels.
Death in Battle. PoLi
"Wilt thou hear, O sailor, what this people say?" PoFr
Battle of Manila, The. Richard Hovey. PAH
Battle of Monmouth, The. Thomas Dunn English. PAH
Battle of Monmouth, The. "R. H." PAH
Battle of Morris' Island, The. *Unknown.* PAH
Battle of Murfreesboro, The. Kinahan Cornwallis. PAH
Battle of Muskingum, The. William Harrison Safford. PAH
Battle of Naseby, The. Macaulay. EV-4; GTBS; HBV; OBRV; ShBV-3; TVSH; VA
(Naseby.) BHV; LPS-2
Battle of Navarino, The. *Unknown.* CoMu
Battle of New Orleans, The. Thomas Dunn English. GA, *abr.;* PAH; PAP
Battle of Oriskany. Charles D. Helmer. PAH
Battle of Otterbourne [*or* Otterburn], The. *Unknown.* BaBo (A *and* B *vers.*); BSV; EBSV; EM-1; EPP; ESPB (A, B, and C *vers.*); EV-2; FaBoCh; GoTS; HBV; OBB, *mod. Eng.*
Fey, *sel.* OtMeF
Battle of Peace, The. Wilson MacDonald. MaRV
Battle of Philiphaugh, The. *Unknown.* ESPB
Battle of Plattsburg, The. *Unknown.* PAH

Battle of Plattsburg Bay, The. Clinton Scollard. GA; MC; PAH
Battle of Point Pleasant, The. *Unknown.* ABS
Battle of Queenstown, The. William Banker, Jr. PAH
Battle of Salamis, The. Aeschylus. *See* Salamis.
Battle of Simancas, The. Gonzalo de Berceo, *tr. fr. Spanish by* Longfellow. *Fr.* The Life of San Millán. TeCS
Battle of Somerset. Cornelius C. Cullen. PAH
Battle of Stonington on the Seaboard of Connecticut, The. Philip Freneau. PAH
Battle of the Angels, *much abr.* Milton. *Fr.* Paradise Lost, VI. LPS-2
(Beginning of the Battle of the Angels, The, *much abr., shorter sel.*) BCEP
Battle of the Baltic, The. Thomas Campbell. BHV; CoBE; EBSV; EnRP; EPP; ERP; EV-4; GN; GTBS; GTBS-D; GTBS-W; GTSE; GTSL; HBV; LH; OBEV; OTPC (1923 ed.); TVSH
Battle of the *Bonhomme Richard* and the *Serapis.* Walt Whitman. *See* Sea-Fight, A.
Battle of the Books, The. Callimachus, *tr. fr. Greek by* T. F. Higham. OxBG
Battle of the Cowpens, The. Thomas Dunn English. PAH; PAP
Battle of the Curetes and Aetolians. Homer, *tr. fr. Greek by* Pope. *Fr.* The Iliad, IX. LiA
Battle of the Frogs and Mice, The. *Unknown, tr. fr. Greek by* Thomas Parnell. *Fr.* Batrachomyomachia. GrL
("To fill my rising song with sacred fire.") GrPo
Battle of the Jarama, The. "Pablo Neruda," *tr. fr. Spanish by* Angel Flores. WaaP
Battle of the Kegs, The. Francis Hopkinson. BAV; IAP; OnAP; PaA; TCAP
(Battle of Kegs, The.) HiLiAm
(British Valor Displayed.) PAH
Battle of the King's Mill. Thomas Dunn English. MC; PAH
Battle of the Lake Regillus, The. Macaulay. *See* Battle of Lake Regillus, The.
Battle of the Pekes and the Pollicles, The, and the Intervention of the Great Rumpus Cat. T. S. Eliot. AlBD
Battle [*or* Battel] of the Summer Islands, The. Edmund Waller. CEP
"Aid me, Bellona, while the dreadful fight," I. EPS (1942 ed.); ReEn; SeCV-1
Battle of Tippecanoe, The. *Unknown.* GA, *abr.;* PAH
Battle of Trafalgar, The. *Unknown.* SG
Battle of Trenton, The. *Unknown.* IDAH; MC; PAH; PAP
Battle of Valparaiso, The. *Unknown.* PAH
Battle of Waterloo. Byron. *See* Waterloo ("There was a sound . . .").
Battle-Piece. Hesiod, *tr. fr. Greek by* Arthur S. Way. *Fr.* Shield of Heracles. GrR
Battle-Plane in France, A. O. C. A. Child. PaA
Battle Rainbow, The. John Reuben Thompson. BlG
Battle rent a cobweb diamond-strung, The. Range-finding. Robert Frost. MaPo; SoV
Battle Sleep. Edith Wharton. VOD
Battle-smoke still fouled the day, The. The Red Cross Nurse. Edith M. Thomas. PEDC
Battle Song. Ebenezer Elliott. BCEP; EV-4; LH; OBEV (1st ed.); OBRV
Battle Song. Ibn Farsan, *tr. fr. Arabic by* A. J. Arberry. MooP
Battle Song. Robert Burns Wilson. MC; PAH
Battle-Song of Failure. Amelia Josephine Burr. HBMV
Battle-Song of Gustavus Adolphus, The. Michael Altenburg. *See* Battle Hymn.
Battle-Song of the *Oregon.* Wallace Rice. PaA; PAH
Battle Within, The. Christina Rossetti. *See* Who Shall Deliver Me?
Battledores. Fitz-James O'Brien. PR
Battlefield, The. Bryant. AA; CBOV; CoBA; IAP; LPS-2; MDAH; TCAP
Sels.
Good Fight, The. BPP
Truth, Crushed to Earth. BAP; NeHB; OQP; QP-2
("Truth crushed to earth shall rise again.") MaRV
(Truth, the Invincible.) TreF
Battle-Field, The. Emily Dickinson. *See* They dropped like flakes, they dropped like stars.
Battlefield, The. Lloyd Mifflin. PAH
Battles? No! Agonies! And before the agonies. César Vallejo. *Fr.* Hymn to the Volunteers of the Republic. PoFr
Battles nor songs can from oblivion save. Immortality. Lizette Woodworth Reese. AA; BAP; HBMV; HBVY; LEAP; POT; PoTo
Battles of the Centaurs, *sel.* Sacheverell Sitwell.
Centaurs and Lapithae. AtBAP
Battus, though bound from drinking wine of late. Ebrius Dissimulans. Henry Parrot. TuPP
Baucis. Erinna. *See* Erinna to Her Friend.
Baucis and Philemon. Ovid, *tr. fr. Latin by* Dryden. *Fr.* Metamorphoses, VIII. AWP; JAWP; RoL; WBP; WoL
(Philemon and Baucis, *tr. by* Arthur Golding.) OBSC
Baucis and Philemon. Swift. CEP; CG, *abr.;* EiPP; GN, *abr.;* GoTL; KN; OBEC; OTPC (1946 ed.); StPo
Baudelaire. Eugene Lee-Hamilton. BMEP; LEAP
Baudelaire. Humbert Wolfe. PtP
Bavarian Gentians. D. H. Lawrence. AtBAP; CaAE; FaBoCh; FaBoMo; LiTB; LoGBV; OAEP (2d ed.); PoE; SeCeV; TriL; TwCV; UnPo (3d ed.); ViBoPo
Bavarian Roadside. Leonora Speyer. NV
Baviad, The, *sel.* William Gifford.
Della Cruscans, The. OBEC
Bavieca. *Unknown, tr. fr. Spanish by* John Gibson Lockhart. AnSpL-1
Bawl of a steer, The. The Cowboy's Life. *At. to* James Barton Adams. CoSo; CSF; MPB; POT; PoTo; TiPo
Bawloo, my bonnie baby, bawlililu. The Last Cradle Song. James Hogg. BOL
"Bay Billy." Frank H. Gassaway. PTA-1; TVSH
Bay, The; December. Frederick Mortimer Clapp. VOD (1935 ed.)
Bay Fight, The. Henry Howard Brownell. GA, *abr.;* PaA; PAH; PAP, *abr.*
"Three days through sapphire seas we sailed," *sel.* PFY
Bay is bluer than all the sky, The. A Sea Spell. Fannie Stearns Davis. VOD
Bay is gouged by the wind, The. Green Lions. Douglas Stewart. AnNZ
Bay is not blue but somber yellow, The. Self-Criticism in February. Robinson Jeffers. AmPP; CoV
Bay is set with ashy sails, The. At Les Eboulements. Duncan Campbell Scott. SG; VA
Bay of Biscay, The. Andrew Cherry. LPS-2
Bay of Guanabara. Menotti del Picchia, *tr. fr. Portuguese by* Dudley Poore. AnCL
Bay of Tsunu, The. Kakinomoto no Hitomaro, *tr. fr. Japanese by* Kenneth Rexroth. OnPJ
Bay Violets. Sister Maris Stella. GoBC
Bay was bronze with sunset, and so light, The. Wings. William Rose Benét. PoMa
Bayadere, The. Francis Saltus Saltus. AA; OBAV
Bayard Taylor, *abr.* Thomas Bailey Aldrich. GA
Bayard Taylor. Longfellow. DD; GA; MOB
Bayard Taylor. Whittier. DD; GA; HBV
Baying Hounds, The. Mary Gilmore. BoAV
Bayliffe's Daughter of Islington, The. *Unknown. See* Bailiff's Daughter of Islington, The.
Bayonet, The. Shawn O'Leary. MoAuPo
Be a god, your spirit cried. To William Blake. Olive Tilford Dargan. HBMV
Be absolute for death; either death or life. Fear of Death [*or* Life and Death]. Shakespeare. *Fr.* Measure for Measure, III, i. CoEV; KN; NBE
Be aisy an' list to a chune. Tim the Dragoon. Sir Arthur Quiller-Couch. WhC
Be all his servants, female, young, and fair. At Least. Charles Churchill. *Fr.* The Times. BeR
Be always in time. *Unknown.* OxNR
Be anxious if Christ presses on your life. If Any Man Would Come after Me. Edwin McNeill Poteat. ChIP
Be assured, the Dragon is not dead. Vanity. Robert Graves. CoEV
Be Beautiful, Noble, like the Antique Ant. José Garcia Villa AnFE; CoAnAm; TwAmPo
(Be Beautiful.) CrMA
Be Bold. Spenser. *Fr.* The Faerie Queene, III, 11. MyFE
Be brave, faint heart. Optimism. Newton Mackintosh. BOHV
Be careful what/ You say or do. Zoo Manners. Eileen Mathias. BoTP
Be Comforted. Tennyson. *Fr.* The Death of the Duke of Clarence and Avondale. MaRV
Be composed—be at ease with me—I am Walt Whitman. To a Common Prostitute. Whitman. AnAmPo; APW; LA; LEAP; MAP; MoAmPo; ViBoPo
Be dark, be deep, wait there for me between. The Upper Lake. Francis Stuart. NeIP
Be dead, then—die—be of another world. Emptiness. John Ransom Palmer. PoP
Be Different to Trees. Mary Carolyn Davies. DD; FaPON; HBMV; HBVY; MPB
(Be Deferent to Trees.) OHIP
Be Drunk. Baudelaire, *tr. fr. French by* William M. Davis. AnFP
Be dumb ye infant chimes, thump not the metal. Great Tom. Richard Corbet. OxBoLi
Be ever meek and humble, nor essay. The Meek and the Proud. Abraham ibn Chasdai. TrJP
Be extra careful by this door. The Whisperer. Mark Van Doren. AnFE; CoAnAM; LoPS; MAP; MoAmPo; TwAmPo
Be famous then. Athens the Eye of Greece. Milton. *Fr.* Paradise Regained, IV. TwCrTr
Be for a little while eternal. O Mors Aeterna. Horace Gregory. ChMo
Be gentle/ When you touch bread. Bread. *Unknown.* MaRV

Be gentle to the comma with its curly little tail. Comma Caution. Harold Willard Gleason. DDA
Be glad all ye that luvaris been. Welcome to May. *Unknown.* EBSV
Be glad in heart, grow great before the Lord. A Brave-hearted Maid. *Unknown.* ISi; PoLi
Be glad, lordings, be ye more and less. Puer Nobis Natus Est. *Unknown.* AnEC
Be he God, or be he man. Eros: Deus Catholicus. Euripides. *Fr.* Hippolytus. GrR
Be his memory forever green and rich. Baal Shem Tov. A. M. Klein. CaP; TrJP
Be Hopeful. Strickland Gillilan. PoToHe
Be humble, you will be whole. *Unknown, tr. fr. Chinese.* Tao Teh Ching, VII. WhP
Be Hush'd. Thomas Hastings. BOL
Be in me as the eternal moods. Δώρια (Doria). Ezra Pound. LEAP; MAP; MoAB; MoAmPo; MoVE; NP; TBM; ViBoPo
Be it not mine to steal the cultured flower. Simple Nature. George John Romanes. HBV
Be it right or wrong[e], these men among[e]. The Nut-brown Maid [*or* Nutbrown Mayde *or* Nutbrowne Maide]. *Unknown.* CBOV; EPP, *sl. diff.*; EV-1; LiTL; MeEV; OBB; OBEV; OBSC; TCEP
Be just, and fear not. For a Patriot. Shakespeare. King Henry VIII, *fr.* III, ii. PGD
Be Kind. Margaret Courtney. PoToHe
Be kind and tender to the Frog. The Frog. Hilaire Belloc. BMEP; BoChLi; BOHV; FaBoBe; FaPON; FiBHP; GoBP; HBV; InMe; LiL; MoShBr; MPB; NA; PoeMoYo; TSW
Be Kind Promptly. *Unknown, tr. fr. Greek by* Lord Neaves. OnPM
Be kind to all dumb animals. Humane Thought. Rebecca McCann. DDA; YaD
Be kind to her O Time. To End her Fear. John Freeman. OBMV
Be kind to the panther! for when thou wert young. Kindly Advice [*or* The Panther]. *Unknown.* BOHV; NA
Be kind to thy father; for when thou wert young. Be Kind. Margaret Courtney. PoToHe
Be kind unto these three, O King! Eileen, Diarmuid and Teig. James Stephens. BoFr
Be life what it has been, and let us hold. To His Wife. Decimus Magnus Ausonius. AWP; JAWP; WBP
Be like the Bird. Victor Hugo, *tr. fr. French.* FaPON; OTPC (1946 ed.); SUS; TiPo; UTS (Wings.) MaRV
"Be like the hummingbird," they said. Hummingbird. Violet Alleyn Storey. PoMa
Be like the twisted polyp that coiling round a boulder. Protective Colouring. Theognis. GrPE
Be married, senses mine, hearing and touch and sight. The Harmonious Vision of the Earth. Paul Fort. MiFP
Be Merciful. John T. McFarland. OQP; PraP; QP-2
Be Merry All That Be Present. *Unknown.* AnEC
Be merry, be merry, I pray you, be merry every one. Be Merry. *Unknown.* AnEC
Be merry, man! and tak nocht far in mind. Hermes the Philosopher. William Dunbar. EBSV
Be Mine, and I Will Give Thy Name. William Cox Bennett. VA
Be near Me. Aleksandr Kovalenkov, *tr. fr. Russian by* V. de S. Pinto. BoRS
Be near me when my light is low. In Memoriam A. H. H., L. Tennyson. AnFE; AtBAP; BEL; CoBE; EM-2; EmBrPo; EnL; EnLi-2; EPN; GEPC; LiTB; LiTG; OAEP; PoE; PoEL-5; PoFS; ReaPo; TOP; UnPo; ViPo; VLEP
Be near to me, O white shadowless Light of my soul's swift venture. Psalm to the Holy Spirit. A. M. Sullivan. TrPWD
Be no word spoken. Hide away. Silentium. Feodor Tyutchev. BoR
Be not afeard [*or* afeared *or* affeard]; the isle is full of noises [*or* noyses]. Caliban [*or* Caliban on the Island *or* To Dream Again]. Shakespeare. *Fr.* The Tempest, III, ii. AtBAP; CoEV; FiP; TrGrPo; UnS
Be Not Afraid. Robert Nathan. GBV (1952 ed.)
Be Not Afraid. Walt Whitman. *Fr.* The Song of the Open Road. MaRV
Be not afraid, O Dead, be not afraid. Struthers Burt. *Fr.* The Land. AOAH; DD; HBMV
Be not afraid of every stranger. A Spell. George Peele. *Fr.* The Old Wives' Tale. ChTr
Be not afraid to pray—to pray is right. Prayer. Hartley Coleridge. ES; MaRV; OQP; QP-1; VA
Be not angry with me that I bear. Apology. Amy Lowell. AV; BLV; BoLiVe; NP; OBAV; SBMV; VOD
Be not astonished—nay. Whisper in Agony. Jules Supervielle. TrFP
Be not deceived, my brother. John Ford. *Fr.* 'Tis Pity She's a Whore. PoD
Be not dismayed, whate'er betide. God's Goodness. C. D. Martin. WBLP
Be not frighted with our fashion. All Your Fortunes We Can Tell Ye. Ben Jonson. *Fr.* The Gypsies Metamorphosed. ChTr
Be not proud. nor coye nor cruell. *Unknown.* SeCSL
Be not proud pritty one. *Unknown.* SeCSL
Be Not Silent. David ben Meshullam, *tr. fr. Hebrew.* TrJP
Be not so desolate. Promise. "Æ." ChMo; CMP; POTE; TCEP; TwCV
Be not sparing. Herrings. Swift. *Fr.* Verses for Fruitwomen. AnIV; OnYI
Be not too certain, life! The Hill. Horace Holley. WGRP
Be not too proud, imperious Dame. The Defiance. Thomas Flatman. AEV; CEP; OBS
Be not too quick to carve our rhyme. A Song. Herbert P. Horne. LEAP
Be not too wise, nor too foolish. Instructions of King Cormac. Cormac, King of Cashel. PoToHe (new ed.)
Be nothing in this book construed. To the Dead Doughboys. William Ellery Leonard. AOAH
Be nought dismayed that her unmovèd mind. Amoretti, VI. Spenser. PeBoSo
Be of Good Cheer. St. John, XVI: 1–33, Bible, *N.T.* WoL
Be of Good Cheer; I Have Overcome the World, 19–33. TreFS
Be our daily bread withheld, be it given. Thanksgiving. Amos Niven Wilder. MaRV
Be Patient. "George Klingle." PoToHe
Be patient, heart; you can't have all your due. Unselfish Suitor. Theognis. GrR
Be patient, Life, when Love is at the gate. Dialogue. Walter Conrad Arensberg. SBMV
Be patient, O be patient! Put your ear against the earth. Patience. William James Linton. VA
Be pitiful, my God! Mea Culpa. "Ethna Carbery." CAW; JKCP; TrPWD
Be present at our table, Lord. Table Graces, or Prayers. *Unknown.* BLRP
Be proud—I'll bear with you. Fidelity. Ibn Zaydun. MooP
Be proud New-York of your prize domes. . . . & Forty-second Street. Archibald MacLeish. CoBA
Be proud you people of these graves. City of Monuments. Muriel Rukeyser. NAMP
Be quick, be quick, my eyes, my ears. Harvesting. Selma Robinson. InMe
Be Quiet; Fear Not. Frances Ridley Havergal. *See* Thy Presence.
"Be quiet, good Trusty." Trusty Learning A, B, C. Eliza Lee Follen. SAS
Be quiet now, my beating heart. The Mountain Comes to Mahomet. Helene Mullins. MuM
Be rootfast. Never yield. Last Rally. Clifford J. Laube. JKCP (1955 ed.)
Be sad, be cool, be kind. The Long Shadow of Lincoln. Carl Sandburg. MoAmPo (1950 ed.)
Be secret, heart, and if your dreams have come. Sonnet. Anna Virginia Mitchell. OQP; QP-2
Be She Fair as Lilies Be. *Unknown.* SeCL
Be silent, secret [*or* hidden], and conceal. Silentium. Feodor Ivanovich Tyutchev. LiTW; OnPM; TrRV; WoL
Be staid; be careful; and be not too free. Week-end. Harold Monro. SeCePo
Be Still. William Ward Ayer. BLRP
Be Still. William Closson Emory. NP; PoeMoYo
Be Still. Mani Leib, *tr. fr. Yiddish by* Sarah Zweig Betsky. OnCuPl
Be Still. Katharina von Schlegel, *tr. fr. German by* Jane L. Borthwick. MaRV
Be still and know that I am God! Be Still. William Ward Ayer. BLRP
Be Still as You Are Beautiful. Patrick MacDonogh. AnIV; LoPS; NeIP; OxBI
Be still, be still, don't speak out loud. Be Still. Mani Leib. OnCuPl
Be still: be still: nor dare. A Holy Hill. "Æ." AWP; JAWP; WBP
Be still, Mr. Wind, be still! Take Care. Rose Waldo. GFA
Be still, my heart, and listen. Khristna and His Flute. "Laurence Hope." HBV
Be still, my little, dancing feet. A Song of Diligence. Helen Frazee-Bower. HBMV
Be Still, My Soul. Archilochus, *tr. fr. Greek by* C. M. Bowra. GrL; OxBG (Sursum Corda, *tr. by* F. L. Lucas.) GrPE
Be Still, My Soul, Be Still. A. E. Housman. A Shropshire Lad, XLVIII. AnFE; BMEP; ChMo; CMP; MoAB; MoBrPo; OAEP; PIAE; POTT; PoVP; TrGrPo; TwP
Be still, my soul: the Lord is on thy side. Be Still. Katharina von Schlegel. MaRV
Be still, sad soul, be still. Resignation. Seumas MacManus. JKCP

Be Still. The Hanging Gardens Were a Dream. Trumbull Stickney. AnAmPo; AnFE; APA; CoAnAm; LA; LBMV; LiTA; MOAP; NePA; TwAmPo
Be still, while the music rises about us. At a Concert of Music. Conrad Aiken. ChMo; CMP; MAP; MoAB; MoAmPo; UnS
Be still, ye wooded cliffs and waterfalls. Pan. *Unknown.* RAR
Be Strong! Maltbie Davenport Babcock. BLPA; FaBoBe; FaFP; MaRV; NeHB; OHFP; OQP; PTA-1; QP-1; WBLP
Be Strong. William James Price. LPS-1
Be Strong. Adelaide Anne Procter. MaRV
Be Strong! Duncan Campbell Scott. PC
Be strong in faith and courage: ever true. Be Strong. William James Price. LPS-1
Be strong O warring soul! For very sooth. Be Strong! Duncan Campbell Scott. PC
Be strong to hope, O Heart! Be Strong. Adelaide Anne Procter. MaRV
Be strong! We are not here to play. Be Strong! Maltbie Davenport Babcock. BLPA; MaRV; NeHB; OHFP; OQP; PTA-1; QP-1; WBLP
Be Swift O Sun. R. A. K. Mason. AnNZ
Be Thankful unto Him. Psalms, C, Bible, *O.T.* *See* Thanksgiving.
Be the Best of Whatever You Are. Douglas Malloch. BLPA; YaD
Be the mistress of my choice. What Kind of Mistress He Would Have. Robert Herrick. TrGrPo
Be the New Year sweet and short. Prosit Neujahr. George Santayana. InMe
Be then your counsels, as your subject, great. To the Federal Convention. Thomas Dwight. PAH
Be this the fate/ Of the man who would shut his gate. A Curse on a Closed Gate. James H. Cousins. AnIV
Be Thou/ The home of my thoughts, dear Lord. Home of My Thoughts. Marie Barton. PraP
Be thou at peace this night. Nocturne. Edward Davison. CH; SoV
Be thou guardian of the weak. Joseph B. Gilder, *wr. at. to* Jeannette L. Gilder. *Fr.* The Parting of the Ways. AA; HBV; MaRV; OQP; PAH; QP-2
Be Thou My Guide. Florence Earle Coates. TrPWD
Be thou my priestess, who hast ever stood. To Nature. Mahlon Leonard Fisher. AnAmPo; LA
Be Thou my vision, O Lord of my heart. A Prayer. *Unknown.* OnYI
Be thou praised, my Lord, with all Thy creatures. Praise of Created Things. St. Francis of Assisi. FaPON; GBV (1952 ed.)
Be thy duty high as angels flight. Duty Our Ladder. Robert Leighton. OQP; QP-2
Be to her, Persephone. Prayer to Persephone. Edna St. Vincent Millay. *Fr.* Memorial to D. C. BAP; NP; PoeMoYo
Be True. Horatius Bonar. FaBoBe; GN; HBV; MaRV (Honesty.) HBVY
(Thou Must Be True.) OQP; QP-2
Be True. Shakespeare. *See* Polonius' Advice to Laertes.
Be Useful, *abr.* George Herbert. GN
Be vengeance wholly left to powers divine. Conversion [*or* The World Well Lost *or* Worldly Vanity]. Dryden. *Fr.* The Hind and the Panther, III. ACP; CAW; FiP; PoLi
Be versatile, my Kyrnos; make a blend. All Things to All Men. Theognis. GrL; OxBG
"Be well assured, wife, all these things in my kind cares are weighed." Hector to Andromache. Homer. *Fr.* The Iliad. ReEn
Be wise as thou art cruel; do not press. Sonnets, CXL. Shakespeare. PeBoSo
Be wise, my Sorrow; oh, more tranquil be! Meditation. Baudelaire. AnFP
Be wise to-day; 'tis madness to defer. Procrastination. Edward Young. *Fr.* Night Thoughts, I. AnEnPo; BCEP; EV-3; LPS-3; OBEC
Be with me, Beauty, for the fire is dying. On Growing Old. John Masefield. BEL; BMEP; ChMo; CMP; CoBE; FaFP; HBMV; InP; LBBV; LiTB; LiTM; MBP; MoAB; MoBrPo; PG; PoRA; ReaPo; TreFS; ViBoPo; VOD; WHA
Be with me, laughter, when the last, thin shout. Recompense. Wade Oliver. PoP
Be with me, Luis de San Angel, now. Ave Maria. Hart Crane. *Fr.* The Bridge. AtBAP; CoV; LiTA; MoPo; NePA
Be with me now, leaving the Isle of Pelops. Alcaeus, *tr. fr. Greek by* Richmond Lattimore. GrPo
Be with us, Lord, at eventide. Grace at Evening. Edwin McNeill Poteat. ChIP; TrPWD
Be with us, Lord, today. Soul-feeding Hyacinths. Corinne Farley. ChIP
Be Ye Also Ready. Bryant. *Fr.* Thanatopsis. MaRV
Be Ye in Love with April-Tide. Clinton Scollard. AA; HBV; PR
Be you still, be you still, trembling heart. To His Heart, Bidding It Have No Fear. W. B. Yeats. PC
Be your words made, good Sir, of Indian ware. Astrophel and Stella, XCII. Sir Philip Sidney. ReEn; SiPS
Beach. Glyn Jones. MoWP
Beach Burial. Kenneth Slessor. BoAV; MoAuPo
Beach Fire. Frances M. Frost. TiPo
Beach of old bones—the tide gasps. Evil Landscape. Tristan Corbière. AnFP
Beach Queen. David Campbell. BoAV
Beachcomber, The. W. H. Oliver. AnNZ
Beached on the meadow, close by the sea's/ Accustomed lap. The Old Boat. Lenore Pratt. CaP
Beaches, The, *sels.* "Robin Hyde." AnNZ
"Absent face, remote and sharp, as far, An," III.
"Close under here, I watched two lovers once," VI.
"This is my secret, this is the chord most perfectly strung," V.
Beachy Head, *sel.* Charlotte Smith.
"Where woods of ash, and beech." EnSW
Beacon, The, *sel.* Joanna Baillie.
Fisherman's Song. EBSV; EV-3
Beacon Light. Leslie Savage Clark. ChIP; PGD
Beacons, The. Aeschylus, *tr. fr. Greek.* *Fr.* Agamemnon. GrR, *tr. by* E. D. A. Morshead; OxBG, *tr. by* Walter Headlam
Beacons, The. Henry Hart Milman. *Fr.* Samor. OBRV
Bead Mat, The. Walter de la Mare. MoPW
Beagles. W. R. Rodgers. FaBoTw; OnYI
Beagle's Cry, The. *Unknown, tr. fr. Late Middle Irish by* Eoin MacNeill. OnYI
Beal' an Dhuine. Sir Walter Scott. *See* Battle of Beal' an Duine.
Beam of Light, A. John Jerome Rooney. AA
Beams from your forest built my little house. To My Country. Marguerite Wilkinson. AOAH
Bean-vine twines around the hemp-stalk, The. The Bride's Song. Tu Fu. ChLP
Beanfield, The. John Clare. BoTP; WP
Bear, The. Robert Frost. AmP; MAP; MoAB; MoAmPo
Bear, The. Vladimir Lugovskoi, *tr. fr. Russian by* Jack Lindsay. RuPo
Bear from me to Khurásán, Zephyr, a kindly word. Message. Nasir-i Khusrau. PeP
Bear him, comrades, to his grave. The Burial of Barber. Whittier. PAH
Bear Hunt, The. Margaret Widdemer. FaPON; GoBP; MPB; UTS
Bear in mind/ That death is a drum. Drum. Langston Hughes. MAP; MoAmPo
Bear in the Hill, The, *with music.* *Unknown.* ABF
Bear me no grudge, spectators, if, a beggar. A Plea for the Enemy. Aristophanes. *Fr.* The Acharnians. OxBG
Bear of Dalby, The. *Unknown, tr. fr. Danish by* E. M. Smith-Dampier. BoDaBa
Bear on, proud billows; Boreas blow. Mr. Le Strange His Verses in the Prison at Linn. Sir Roger L'Estrange. SeCL
Bear puts both arms around the tree above her, The. The Bear. Robert Frost. AmP; MAP; MoAB; MoAmPo
Bear that breath[e]s [*or* breaks] the northern blast, The. Upon a Wasp Chilled with Cold. Edward Taylor. AmPP (4th ed.); AtBAP; FaBoEn; GTBS-W; PoEL-3
Bear the love of my heart to my land far away. The Fair Hills of Eire. Padraic Colum. CP
Bear, the Monkey, and the Hog, The. Tomás de Iriarte, *tr. fr. Spanish by* James Kennedy. AnSpL-2
Bear the News, Mary, *with music.* *Unknown.* ABF
Bear Up Awhile. James Thomson. MaRV
Bear went over the mountain, A. Mother Goose. StVeCh (1955 ed.)
Bear with me, Master, when I turn from Thee. Prayer. Edith Lovejoy Pierce. ChIP; TrPWD
Bear, with whom a Piedmontese, A. The Bear, the Monkey, and the Hog. Tomás de Iriarte. AnSpL-2
Beard, The. Ibn al-Hajj, *tr. fr. Arabic by* A. J. Arberry. MooP
Bearded grass waves in the summer breeze, The. Death and Night. James Benjamin Kenyon. AA
Bearded Oaks. Robert Penn Warren. AmP; AnFE; CoAnAm; FiMAP; LiTM; MoAmPo (1950 ed.); MoVE; OnHM; ReMP
Bearded prawn's a lively instance made, The. Prawn and Pearl. William Diaper. *Fr.* Nereides; or, Sea-Eclogues. BeR
Beardless Youth. Ibn Iyad, *tr. fr. Arabic by* A. J. Arberry. MooP
Bearer of Freedom's holy light. Democracy. Whittier. PoFr; StaSt
Bearer's Song. Miu Hsi, *tr. fr. Chinese by* Arthur Waley. TrCh
Bears. Arthur Guiterman. PoRA

Bears. Adrienne Cecile Rich. NePoEA
Bear's Song, The. *Tr. fr. Haida Indian song by* Constance Lindsay Skinner. AWP; JAWP; WBP
Beast and bird must bow aside. Epilogue for a Masque of Purcell. Adrienne Cecile Rich. NePoEA
Beast in View. Muriel Rukeyser. FiMAP
Beasts, *sel.* Paul Engle.
"That was a shocking day." ReMP
Beasts, The. Walt Whitman. *See* Animals.
Beasts. Richard Wilbur. CrMA; FiMAP; NePoAm
Beasts, Birds, and Fishes. Adelaide O'Keeffe. OTPC (1923 ed.)
Beasts' Confession, The. Swift. ATP (1935 ed.); CEP; EiPP; EV-3; PIAE; TOP
Beasts in field are glad, and have not wit, The. Sir William Watson. Epigrams, XXXII. LEAP
Beasts in the Tower, The. Charles *and* Mary Lamb. OTPC (1923 ed.)
Beasts in their major freedom. Beasts. Richard Wilbur. CrMA; FiMAP; NePoAm
Beasts onely capable of sense, enjoy. John Ford. *Fr.* The Broken Heart. PoEL-2
Beat against Me No Longer. Lew Sarett. NP
Beat—beat—beat—drums—beat. Drums of Haiti. Marcus B. Christian. GoSl
Beat! Beat! Drums! Walt Whitman. APW; ATP (1935 ed.); CoBA; DDA; IAP; LaNeLa; LH; MDAH; MOAP; TCAP
Beat hell out of it. Paterson; Episode 17. William Carlos Williams. OxBA
Beat on, proud billows [*or* billowes]; Boreas blow. Loyalty Confin'd [*or* In Prison *or* Liberty and Requiem of an Imprisoned Royalist]. Sir Roger L'Estrange. EV-2; LPS-3; OBS; SeCL
Beat on the drum and be without fear. Doctrine. Heine. AnGP
Beat on the Tom-toms, and scatter the flowers. The Bride. "Laurence Hope." HBV
Beat the drums of skins. War Comes. Zalman Schneour. TrJP
Beat the drums of tragedy for me. Fantasy in Purple. Langston Hughes. BANP; CDC; TBM
Beat the knife on the plate and the fork on the can. Going In to Dinner. Edward Shanks. OBMV
Beata l'Alma. Sir Herbert Read. LiTG
Beata Solitudo. Ernest Dowson. POTT; PoVP
Beaten and a baffled man, A. The Black Knight. John Todhunter. OBVV; PoVP
Beaten, beaten, beaten, beaten. The Copper Song. Hermia Harris Fraser. CaP
Beaten by jagged rocks to steam. The Avalanche. Pushkin. BoRS
Beaten Path, The. Anne Goodwin Winslow. HBMV; TBM
Beati Mortui. Louise Imogen Guiney. LBAP
Beati Oculi Qui Vident. Richard Crashaw, *tr. fr. Latin by* D. C. Allen. Epigrammata Sacra, I, 76. LaP
Beati Omnes. Psalms, CXXVIII, Bible, *O.T., tr. by* Thomas Sternhold. ReIE; SiCE
Beatific Sea, The. Thomas Campbell. EtS
Beating heart! we come again. At Her Window. Frederick Locker-Lampson. HBV; LEAP; OBEV (1st ed.); OBVV
Beating of the guns grows louder, The. The Assault. Robert Nichols. BMEP; MCCG
Beatitudes, The. St. Matthew, V, Bible, *N.T. Fr.* The Sermon on the Mount. GrCo-1 (3–12); TrGrPo (3–10)
(Beatitudes of Jesus, The.) MaRV (3–12)
Beatitudes for a Housewife. Mary Mae Oesch. PoToHe (new ed.)
Beatrice. Baudelaire, *tr. fr. French by* Stephen Stepanchev. AnFP
Beatrice, *sel.* Joseph Sheridan Le Fanu.
Hymn: "Hush! oh ye billows." OnYI
Beatrice. Oscar Levertin, *tr. fr. Swedish by* Charles W. Stork. AnSL
Beatrice Cenci in Her Cell. Shelley. *Fr.* The Cenci, V, iv. ReTS
Beatrice is gone up into high Heaven. Sonnet. Dante, *tr. by* Dante Gabriel Rossetti. *Fr.* La Vita Nuova. GoBC
Beatrice to Dante. Dante, *tr. fr. Italian by* M. B. Anderson. *Br. sel. fr.* Divina Commedia: Paradiso, V. GrCo-1
Beatrice's Last Words. Shelley. *Fr.* The Cenci, V, iv. FiP
Beatus Vir. Psalms, I, Bible, *O.T., tr. by* Thomas Sternhold. ReIE; SiCE
Beatus Vir. Richard Le Gallienne. HBMV; OHIP; PoTo
Beau, The. Martial, *tr. fr. Latin by* Paul Nixon. RoL
Beaufort Exile's Lament, The. *Unknown.* BIG
Beauing, belling [*or* belle-ing], dancing, drinking. The Rakes of Mallow. *Unknown.* GTIV; IrPN; OnYI
Beaumont and Fletcher. Swinburne. *Fr.* Sonnets on English Dramatic Poets. PoVP
Beauregard. Catherine Anne Warfield. GA; MC; PaA; PAH
Beau's Receipt for a Lady's Dress, The. *Unknown.* CoMu
Beau's Reply. William Cowper. FaBoCh; OTPC (1923 ed.); PRWS
Beauté, La. Baudelaire. *See* Beauty.
Beauteous Ethel's father has, The. A Piazza Tragedy. Eugene Field. FiBHP
Beautie, and the life, The. *See* Beauty, and the life, The.
Beautie, I know, is good, and bloud is more. Ben Jonson. *Fr.* Epistle to Elizabeth, Countess of Rutland. FaBoEn
Beautie sate bathing by a Spring. *See* Beauty sat bathing by a spring.
Beautie, sweet love, is like the morning dewe. *See* Beauty, sweet love, is like the morning dew.
Beauties Arouse Love. André Chénier, *pr. tr. fr. French.* LiA
Beauties, Have Ye Seen This Toy. Ben Jonson. *Fr.* The Hue and Cry after Cupid. OAEP
(Beauties, Have Ye Seen.) TuPP
(Cupid.) BOHV, *abr.*; InMe
(Venus' Runaway.) HBV; ReEn
Beauties of Santa Cruz, The, *sels.* Philip Freneau.
"From the vast caverns of old ocean's bed." AmPP (4th ed.); IAP
"Sick of thy northern glooms, come shepherd, seek." CoBA
Beautiful. W. A. Bixler. WBLP
Beautiful, The. W. H. Davies. POTE
Beautiful, The. John Aylmer Dorgan. AA
Beautiful, *with music. Unknown.* ABF
Beautiful always the littoral line. The Innocent. Gene Derwood. NePA; WaP
Beautiful am I, oh, mortals, like a dream of stone! Beauty. Baudelaire. AnFP
Beautiful American Word, Sure, The. Delmore Schwartz. CrMA; LiTA
Beautiful and happy girl, A. Memories. Whittier. CoBA; IAP; OBVV; TCAP
Beautiful and rich is an old friendship. Old Friendship. Eunice Tietjens. NP
Beautiful are the fingers of the loved one. When She Plays upon the Harp or Lute. Moses ibn Ezra. TrJP
Beautiful as a tiered cloud. Clipper-Ships. John Gould Fletcher. CP
Beautiful as the flying legend of some leopard. Judith of Bethulia. John Crowe Ransom. CrMA; FaBoMo; LiTA; LiTM (rev. ed.); LS; MM; MoPo; NePA; SPP
Beautiful as the pomegranate is the white face of Ophrah. The Hot Flame of My Grief. Moses ibn Ezra. TrJP
Beautiful, Beautiful Mother, give. Immaculate Palm. Joseph Joel Keith. ISi
Beautiful bird at the casement sings, A. A Slumber Song. A. Holcombe Aiken. BOL
Beautiful bird, in as your wings as vivid. To the Rosella in the Poinsettia Tree. James Picot. BoAV
"Beautiful body made of ivory." Conrad Aiken. *Fr.* Variations, XIV. PG (1945 ed.)
Beautiful Boy, The. *Unknown, tr. fr. Arabic by* E. Powys Mathers. *Fr.* The Thousand and One Nights. LiTW
Beautiful boy, like a faun here in loneliness roaming, who art thou? Narcissus; a Pompeian Bronze. Vyacheslav Ivanovich Ivanov. TrRV
Beautiful Changes, The. Richard Wilbur. FiMAP
Beautiful, delicate bright gazelle, The. Love-Song. W. J. Turner. OBMV
Beautiful Dreamer. Stephen Collins Foster. OlF
Beautiful Evelyn Hope is dead. Evelyn Hope. Browning. AEV; BLV; BMEP; BoLiVe; BPN; CaAE; EmBrPo; EPP; GEPC; HBV; LEAP; LPS-1; MaPo; OuHeWo; PIR; PoVP; PYM; TCEP; TrGrPo; VA; ViPo; VLEP
Beautiful face of a child. Three Portraits of Prince Charles. Andrew Lang. PoVP; VA
Beautiful faces are those that wear. Beautiful Things. Ellen Palmer Allerton. BLPA; NeHB; WBLP
Beautiful Foreign Land. Joseph von Eichendorff, *tr. fr. German by* Mabel Cotterell. AnGP
Beautiful Gift, The. Grace Noll Crowell. PEDC
Beautiful girl said something in your praise, A. To a Friend on His Marriage. F. T. Prince. LiTM
Beautiful glooms, soft dusks in the noonday fire. Sidney Lanier. *Fr.* The Marshes of Glynn. PFY
Beautiful grape wine, the night-glittering cups, The. The Song of Liangchow. Wang Han. WhP
Beautiful habitations, auras of delight! Auras of Delight. Coventry Patmore. *Fr.* The Unknown Eros. ACP; CAW; LoBV; OBVV
Beautiful Hands. Ellen M. H. Gates. TreF
Beautiful Horses, The. Donald Hall. NePoAm-2
Beautiful Hsi-shih, The. Wang Wei, *tr. fr. Chinese by* Witter Bynner *and* Kiang Kang-hu. OuHeWo
Beautiful is she. The Abstinent Lover. Abul Bahr. MooP
Beautiful is she, this woman. Love Song. *Tr. by* Constance Lindsay Skinner. AWP; JAWP; WBP
Beautiful is the large church. Churches. *Unknown.* MaRV
Beautiful Is the Loved One. Moses ibn Ezra, *tr. fr. Hebrew by* Solomon Solis-Cohen. TrJP
Beautiful lady named Psyche, A. Limerick. *Unknown.* LiBL; LiTG; SiTL; WhC
Beautiful Land, The. Eric Chilman. TVSH

Beautiful Land of Nod, The. Ella Wheeler Wilcox. BOL
Beautiful Lie the Dead. Stephen Phillips. LBBV; MBP; POTE
Beautiful lily!/ So gently unfolding. Beautiful Lily. Alice Mortenson. BePJ
Beautiful lily, dwelling by still rivers. Flower-de-Luce. Longfellow. TCAP
Beautiful Meals. T. Sturge Moore. BoTP; TCPD; WP
Beautifull Mistress, A. Thomas Carew. OBS
("If when the sun at noon displays.") EG
(Song: Beautiful Mistress, A.) SeEP
Beautiful mother is bending, The. Nativity Song. Jacopone da Todi. OHIP
Beautiful must be the mountains whence ye come. Nightingales. Robert Bridges. AtBAP; BLA; BLV; CaAE; ChMo; CMP; CoBMV; EnLi-2 (1949 ed.); ExPo; FaBoEn; GTBS; GTML; HBMV; LEAP; LiTB; LiTM; MBP; MoAB; MoBrPo; MoPo; OBEV; OBMV; OBVV; Po; PoeMoYo; PoVP; ReaPo; RiBV; SeCeV; TrGrPo; TwCV; UnPo; ViP; VLEP; VOD
Beautiful, my delight. To Be Sung on the Water. Louise Bogan. MoVE
Beautiful Necessity, The, *sel.* Claude Bragdon.
Point, the Line, the Surface and Sphere, The, *2 ll.* ImOP
Beautiful Negress, The. Ruth Pitter. MoVE
Beautiful Night, A. Thomas Lovell Beddoes. *Fr.* Fragments Intended for the Dramas. ChER; ERP; LoBV
Beautiful Night, A. Naoyoshi, *tr. fr. Japanese by* Asataro Miyamori. OnPM
Beautiful, O beautiful—/ In all the mountain passes. The April of the Ages. Digby Mackworth Dolben. GoBC
Beautiful place is the town of Lo-yang, A. Lo-yang. Emperor Ch'ien Wen-ti. AtBAP; AWP; JAWP; TrCh; WBP
Beautiful Proud Sea. Sara Teasdale. NP
Beautiful rain falls, the unheeded angel, The. In Time. Kathleen Raine. NeBP
Beautiful Saviour. Charlotte M. Kruger. BePJ
Beautiful? Sir, you may say so. Thar isn't her match in the country. Chiquita. Bret Harte. AA; IHA; MW; PFE; PFY
Beautiful Snow, *parody. Unknown.* PA
Beautiful Snow, The. John Whittaker Watson. BLPA; LPS-1; TreF; WBLP
Beautiful soup, so rich and green. Turtle Soup. "Lewis Carroll." *Fr.* Alice's Adventures in Wonderland. BrR; InMe; PA
Beautiful Spirit of Life. Ode to the Spirit of Life. James Harold Manning. CPG
Beautiful spoils! borne off from vanquisht [*or* vanquish'd] death! Rose Aylmer's Hair, Given by Her Sister. Walter Savage Landor. BPN; TriL; VA
Beautiful, sublime, and glorious. The Sea. Bernard Barton. LPS-2
Beautiful sun that giveth us light. Beautiful. W. A. Bixler. WBLP
Beautiful, tender, wasting away for sorrow. Luscious and Sorrowful. Christina Rossetti. PoEL-5; SeCePo
Beautiful Things. Ellen Palmer Allerton. BLPA; NeHB; WBLP
Beautiful, tragical faces. Piccadilly. Ezra Pound. BAP; LEAP
Beautiful Train, The. William Empson. MoVE
Beautiful Virgin! clothèd with the sun. To the Virgin Mary. Petrarch. Sonnets to Laura, Canzone VIII. CAW
Beautiful vision! how bright it rose. The Reign of Peace. Eliza Thornton. PEDC
Beautiful was the night. Behind the black wall of the forest. Moonlight on the Prairie. Longfellow. *Fr.* Evangeline. LPS-2
Beautiful, which mocked his fond pursuing, The. The Beautiful. John Aylmer Dorgan. AA
Beautiful Woman, The. Tu Fu, *tr. fr. Chinese by* Soame Jenyns. WoL
Beautiful woman, a cup of wine, and a garden, A. Joy of Life. Moses ibn Ezra. *Fr.* The Book of Tarshish. TrJP
Beautiful Women. Walt Whitman. LEAP
Beautiful World, The. W. L. Childress. OHIP
Beautiful world of huts. Victory of Guernica. Paul Eluard. MiCF
Beautiful world of new, superber birth, that rises to my eyes. Walt Whitman. *Fr.* Thou Mother with Thy Equal Brood. PoFr
Beautiful Young Nymph Going to Bed, A. Swift. BeR
Beautifully Janet slept. Janet Waking. John Crowe Ransom. AmP; AnAmPo; ExPo; LA; MAP; MoAB; MoAmPo; ReaPo; ThWaDe
Beauty. Abu Hafs, *tr. fr. Arabic by* A. J. Arberry. MooP
Beauty. Kenneth Slade Alling. HBMV
Beauty. Baudelaire, *tr. fr. French.* AnFP, *tr. by* Bert M-P. Leefmans; LO, *tr. by* Alan Conder; OnPM, *tr. by* Arthur Symons; TrFP, *tr. by* Alan Conder
(Beauté, La, *tr. by* Lord Alfred Douglas.) AWP; JAWP; WBP
Beauty. Laurence Binyon. MBP; MoBrPo
Beauty. Abraham Cowley. AnFE; BLV; CoEV; LiTB; PoEL-2; SiTL; TrGrPo
Beauty. E-Yeh-Shure'. FaPON; TiPo
Beauty, The, *sel.* Thomas Hardy.
"I hate my beauty in the glass." LO
Beauty. Peter Hille, *tr. fr. German by* Jethro Bithell. AWP
Beauty. Edward Hovell-Thurlow. LPS-3
Beauty. Keats. *See* Thing of Beauty, A.
Beauty. Christopher Marlowe. *See* Poet's Pen, The.
Beauty ("I have seen dawn and sunset"). John Masefield. BEL; LoPS; PoeT
Beauty, The. Pushkin, *tr. fr. Russian by* Maurice Baring. BoR
Beauty. Isaac Rosenberg. TrJP
Beauty. Sappho. *See* One Girl.
Beauty. Mary Craig Sinclair. OQP; QP-2
Beauty. Alexander Smith. VA
Beauty ("So every spirit, as it is most pure"). Spenser. *Fr.* An Hymne in Honour of Beautie. LPS-3
Beauty ("What time this world's great workmaster did cast"). Spenser. *Fr.* An Hymne in Honour of Beautie. OBSC
(Soul Is Form, *abr.*) GoBC
("What time this world's great workmaster," *abr.*) EPP
Beauty. Joel Elias Spingarn. HBMV
Beauty. Thomas Stanley, *after the Greek of* Anacreon. AWP; JAWP; PG (1945 ed.); WBP
(Horns to Bulls Wise Nature Lends.) GrPo; OnPM
Beauty. Edward Thomas. NP
Beauty. Miguel de Unamuno, *tr. fr. Spanish by* Eleanor L. Turnbull. TeCS
Beauty ("Beauty is but a vain and doubtful good"). *Unknown.* The Passionate Pilgrim, XIII. OBSC
Beauty. William Winter. LPS-3
Beauty. Elinor Wylie. NP; OxBA
Beauty—a beam, nay, flame. Fading Beauty. Giambattista Marini. AWP
Beauty, a silver dew that falls in May. Epigram. *Unknown.* OBSC
Beauty, Alas, Where Wast Thou Born. *At. to* Thomas Lodge *and to* Robert Greene. ElL
Beauty all stainless, a pearl of a maiden, A. The Geraldine's Daughter. Egan O'Rahilly. AnIL; IrPN; OnYI
Beauty and Duty. Dante, *tr. fr. Italian by* Dante Gabriel Rossetti. PIAE
(Sonnet: Of Beauty and Duty.) AWP; JAWP; WBP
Beauty and Duty. Ellen S. Hooper. *See* Duty.
Beauty and Terror. Lesbia Harford. MoAuPo
Beauty and the Artist. Michelangelo, *tr. fr. Italian by* John Addington Symonds. PoFr
Beauty and the Beast. Edwin Björkman. NoCaPo (1941 ed.)
Beauty [*or* Beautie], and the life, The. Madrigal [*or* Her Passing]. William Drummond of Hawthornden. AtBAP; EBSV; ElL; ElSeCe; OBEV; PoEL-2; TriL
Beauty and Truth. Emily Dickinson. *See* I died for beauty.
Beauty, arise, show forth thy glorious shining! A Bridal Song [*or* Beauty, Arise!]. Thomas Dekker, *and others. Fr.* The Pleasant Comedy of Patient Grissell. ElL; OBSC; TrGrPo; TuPP
Beauty as a Shield. Elsie Robinson. BLPA; PoToHe (new ed.)
Beauty at the Plough. Arthur Joseph Munby. *Fr.* Dorothy; a Country Story. VA
Beauty Bathing. Anthony Munday. *See* To Colin Clout.
Beauty blue and beauty white. Shopping Day. Orrick Johns. InMe
Beauty calls and gives no warning. Evensong. Ridgely Torrence. HBV; LBMV; LEAP; OBAV
Beauty Clear and Fair. John Fletcher. *Fr.* The Elder Brother, III, v. BEL; EPP; HoPM; LO; OAEP; OBEV; SeCL; SeEP; ViBoPo
(Beauty Cleere and Fair.) AtBAP
(Song: "Beauty clear and fair.") OBS
Beauty crowds me till I die. Emily Dickinson. LEAP
Beauty does not walk through lovely days. Beauty and Terror. Lesbia Harford. MoAuPo
Beauty Everywhere. Albert Durrant Watson. CPG
Beauty Extolled [*or* Extoll'd]. *Unknown, at. to* Henry Noel *and to* William Strode. ChTr; CoEV; OBS
("Gaze not on swans in whose soft breast.") LO
(On His Mistress.) PoEL-2
Beauty glittering. The Down. Ibn Rashiq. MooP
Beauty goes out to meet a greater beauty. Dying. Jessie Holt. ChIP; PGD
Beauty growing on a thorn. Chiaroscuro. John B. Thompson. OQP; QP-2
Beauty had first my pride. The Star. Willoughby Weaving. HBMV; HBVY
Beauty in Rags. Ibn al-Arabi, *tr. fr. Arabic by* A. J. Arberry. MooP
Beauty in woman; the high will's decree. Sonnet: He Compares All Things with His Lady. Guido Cavalcanti, *tr. by* Dante Gabriel Rossetti. AWP

Beauty in Worship. *Unknown. Fr.* A Poem, in Defence of the Decent Ornaments of Christ-Church . . . OBS
Beauty is a lily. Reflection. Lew Sarett. MoSiPe
Beauty Is a Lovely Sweet. *Unknown.* SiCE; TuPP
Beauty Is a Witch. Shakespeare. *Fr.* Much Ado about Nothing, II, i. TrGrPo
Beauty is but a flower. Death's Summons. Thomas Nashe. *Fr.* Summer's Last Will and Testament. CBOV; LO
Beauty Is but a Painted Hell. Thomas Campion. AtBAP; TyEnPo
Beauty is but a passenger; she will not. Vale. Patrick Mary Plunkett. JKCP (1955 ed.)
Beauty is but a vain and doubtful good. Beauty. *Unknown.* The Passionate Pilgrim, XIII. OBSC
Beauty Is Elsewhere. Boyce House. HiLiAm
Beauty Is Ever to the Lonely Mind. Robert Nathan. HBMV; MuM
Beauty is fashioned out of mud. Viaticum. Herbert S. Gorman. TBM
Beauty is gone from the hills, the high brooks are forsaken. Vespers. Ian Maxwell. MoAuPo
Beauty is gull. The Bull. Francis Maguire. JKCP (1955 ed.)
Beauty Is Most at Twilight's Close. Pär Lagerkvist, *tr. fr. Swedish by* G. Kenneth Laycock. LiTW
Beauty Is Not Bound. Thomas Campion. *See* Give Beauty All Her Right.
Beauty is not caused—it is. Emily Dickinson. LiTA
Beauty is seen. Beauty. E-Yeh-Shure'. FaPON; TiPo
Beauty is still immortal in our eyes. The Immortal. Marjorie Pickthall. CaP; OCL
Beauty like hers is genius. Not the call. Genius in Beauty. Dante Gabriel Rossetti. The House of Life, XVIII. BPN; EmBrPo; EnLit; InP; OAEP; POTT; PoVP; TOP; ViP; ViPo; VLEP
Beauty may be the path to highest good. The Straight Road. Ellen Hooper. HBV
Beauty no more the subject be. Song. Thomas Nabbes. *Fr.* Hannibal and Scipio. SeCL; TuPP
Beauty, no other thing is, then a beam[e]. The Definition of Beauty. Robert Herrick. NBE; Po
Beauty of, The/ the terrible faces. Apology: Why Do I Write Today? William Carlos Williams. OxBA
Beauty of Israel is slain, The. David's Lament [*or* How Are the Mighty Fallen *or* Lament over Saul]. Second Samuel, Bible, *O.T.* AWP; BHV; LiTW; LO; ShBV-3; TrGrPo; WaaP
Beauty of ladies of compassionate heart. Sonnet. Guido Cavalcanti. LyPI
Beauty of Terror, The. Blake. *See* Tiger, The.
Beauty of the autumn leaf, The. Wisdom. Jay Paul. CAG
Beauty of the brook is miniature, The. The Brook. Fynette Fiske. CAG
Beauty of the northern dawns, The. The Christine. John Hay. AA
Beauty of the Stars, The. Moses ibn Ezra, *tr. fr. Hebrew by* Solomon Solis-Cohen. TrJP
Beauty of the World, The. William Brighty Rands. UnW
Beauty of the World. Frank Wilmot. MM; MoAuPo
Beauty of the world hath made me sad, The. The Wayfarer. Padraic Pearse. OxBI
Beauty of Things, The. Robinson Jeffers. CoV
Beauty of This Earth. Martin Opitz, *tr. fr. German by* Werner Heider. LiTW
Beauty on a Western Balcony. Luis de Sandoval y Zapata, *tr. fr. Spanish by* Samuel Beckett. AnMP
Beauty Paramount. Sir William Killigrew. *Fr.* Selindra. SeCL
Beauty Persists. Struthers Burt. NoCaPo (1941 ed.)
Beauty Rohtraut. Eduard Mörike, *tr. fr. German by* George Meredith. AWP; JAWP; WBP; WoL
Beauty sat [*or* Beautie sate] bathing by a spring. To Colin Clout [*or* Beauty Bathing *or* Beauty Sat Bathing *or* Colin]. Anthony Munday. *Fr.* Primaleon of Greece. CenL; ElL; ElSeCe; EV-1; GTBS; GTBS-D; GTBS-W; GTSE; GTSL; OAEP; OBEV; OBSC; PG (1955 ed.); TuPP; ViBoPo
"Beauty sometime, in all her glory crowned." Idea's Mirrour, IX. Michael Drayton. NBE
Beauty still walketh on the earth and air. Beauty. Alexander Smith. VA
Beauty [*or* Beautie], sweet love, is like the morning dew. Sonnet [*or* Beauty, Time, and Love *or* Beauty's Lease]. Samuel Daniel. To Delia, XLII [XLVII]. ElL; ElSeCe; ES; FaBoEn; HBV; OBEV; OBSC; TuPP; ViBoPo
Beauty That All Night Long, A. Jalal ed-Din Rumi, *tr. fr. Persian by* R. A. Nicholson. AWP; LiTW
Beauty! thou are a wanderer on the earth. Behold, O Aspasia! I Send You Verses. Walter Savage Landor. *Fr.* Pericles and Aspasia. LoBV; ViBoPo
Beauty, thou wild fantastic ape. Beauty. Abraham Cowley. AnFE; BLV; CoEV; LiTB; PoEL-2; SiTL; TrGrPo
Beauty, Time, and Love (7 *sonnets*). Samuel Daniel. *Fr.* To Delia. OBEV
Beauty, Too, Seeks Surrender. Jessica Powers. JKCP (1955 ed.)
Beauty Unbound. Thomas Campion. *See* Give Beauty All Her Right.
Beauty—what is it? A perfume without name. Epitaph for the Poet V., III. Arthur Davison Ficke. HBMV
Beauty which all men admire. *Unknown.* SeCSL
Beauty will not let me rest. Pitiless Beauty. John Hall Wheelock. LEAP
Beauty with the flame shawl, do not repulse me. Ghazal of Isa Akhun Zada. *Unknown, tr. fr. Pushtu by* E. Powys Mathers. PG (1945 ed.)
Beauty, your name sounds strange and sad. April, 1941. Vera Bax. DiM
Beauty's a Flower. "Moira O'Neill." BMEP; MBP
Beauty's Armoury. Al-Hadrami, *tr. fr. Arabic by* A. J. Arberry. MooP
Beauty's Glass. Samuel Daniel, *after the French of* Philippe Desportes. OnPM
(To Delia, XXXIV, *sl. diff.*) ReIE
Beauty's Hands Are Cool. Karle Wilson Baker. GoYe
Beauty's Lease. Samuel Daniel. *See* Sonnet: "Beauty, sweet love . . ."
Beauty's Nomads. Vyacheslav Ivanov, *tr. fr. Russian by* C. M. Bowra. BoR
Beauty's Pageant. Dante Gabriel Rossetti. The House of Life, XVII. BPN; PoVP; ViPo
Beauty's Paradigm. Pierre de Ronsard, *tr. fr. French by* Alan Conder. *Fr.* Sonnets pour Hélène. TrFP
("See love, whose kingdom as the world is ample," *tr. by* Humbert Wolfe.) PrPoCR
Beauty's Power. *Unknown, tr. fr. Greek by* F. L. Lucas. *Fr.* Anacreontea. GrPE
Beauty's pure native gems, ye quivering hairs! Nancy's Hair. Walter Savage Landor. TriL
Beauty's Queen. Kisa'i of Merv, *tr. fr. Persian by* R. A. Nicholson. LiTW
Beauty's Self. *Unknown. See* My Love in Her Attire Doth Show Her Wit.
Beauty's Soliloquy during Her Honeymoon, A. Thomas Hardy. PoVP
Beaver Brook. James Russell Lowell. IAP; TCAP
"Hushed with broad sunlight lies the hill," *sel.* CoBA
Beaver Island Boys, The, *with music. At. to* Daniel Malloy. OuSiCo
Beaver roars hoarse with meltin' snows. Mr. Hosea Biglow to the Editor of the Atlantic Monthly. James Russell Lowell. *Fr.* The Biglow Papers, 2d series, No. X. PoEL-5
Beaver Sign. Kenneth Porter. NePoAm
Becalmed. John Blight. BoAV
Becalmed. John Banister Tabb. AA
Because. Edward Fitzgerald. HBV
Because. Sara Teasdale. ChMo; CMP
Because a curious dream ruined your heart. Memorandum to Saint Francis—April 16. Sister Mary Francis. SaFP
Because a lady asks me, I would tell. Canzone: A Lady Asks Me. Guido Cavalcanti. LyPI
Because a thin-lipped ancestor. New England Gothic. Rachel Field. QS
Because a woman's lips were red. History. "Paul Tanaquil." HBMV
"Because, because," the sound of the hard road said. Proud, Unhoped-for Light. Raymond Holden. MAP; MoAmPo (1942 ed.)
Because, dear Christ, your tender, wounded arm. Brier. E. Pauline Johnson. MaRV
Because, dear Lord, their way is rought and steep. Prayer for Shut-Ins. Ruth Winant Wheeler. PoToHe (new ed.)
Because hate is legislated. Entry April 28. Walter Benton. LoPS
Because he had spoken harshly to his mother. Revelation. Robert Penn Warren. AnFE; CoAnAm; FiMAP; LiTA; MoPo; NePA; TwAmPo
Because he is so very small. On the Death of His Child. Okura, *tr. by* Mabel Lorenz Ives. PFE
Because he is young. Okura, *tr. fr. Japanese by* Arthur Waley. *Fr.* Manyo Shu. AWP; JAWP; LiTW; WBP
Because He Lives. Adele Lathrop. BLRP
Because he puts the compromising chart. Zola. E. A. Robinson. CoV; MoVE; NePA; OxBA; TwP
Because he seemed to walk with an intent. James Thomson. *Fr.* The City of Dreadful Night. EnLit
Because he was a butcher and thereby. Reuben Bright. E. A. Robinson. AmP; AnNE; CoV; MAP; MaPo; MoAB; MoAmPo; NePA; TCAP; TrGrPo; TwP
Because Heaven's cost is Hell, and perfect joy. Cost. Richard Watson Gilder. StJW
Because his soup was cold, he needs must sulk. House-Mates. Leon Gellert. MoAuPo
Because I am a woman, I must be. I Must Be Silent. Anne Blackwell Payne. NoCaPo

Because I am bewildered, because I must decide. Herod. W. H. Auden. *Fr.* For the Time Being. OnHM
Because I am idolatrous and have besought. Epigram. Ernest Dowson. ACP; BrBE
"Because I am mad about women." The Wild Old Wicked Man. W. B. Yeats. AnIL; AtBAP
Because I bid her clean the pots for supper. The Land of Heart's Desire. W. B. Yeats. PoVP
Because I breathe not love to every one. Sir Philip Sidney. Astrophel and Stella, LIV. BLV; BoLiVe; ElSeCe; LPS-1; OAEP; OBSC; PeBoSo; ReEn; SiCE; SiPS; TOP; TrGrPo; TuPP
Because I could not stop for Death. Emily Dickinson. AmP; AmPo; AmPP (4th ed.); AnAmPo; AnNE; AWP; CoV; ExPo; GTBS-W; InPo; LA; MaPo; MoAB; MoAmPo; MOAP; MoPo; MoVE; NePA; OBAV; OxBA; PoE; PoEL-5; ReMP; SeCeV; TriL; TwP; UnPo (3d ed.) (Chariot, The.) AnFE; APA; BPP; CoAnAm; LiA; LiTA; LiTM; MAPA; MaRV, *st.* 1; OQP; PoFS; QP-2; TreFS; TwAmPo; WGRP
Because I coveted courage. Courage. Virginia Moore. PC
Because I craved a gift too great. Compensation. Theodosia Garrison. PC
Because I do not always know. A Prayer for Charity. Edwin O. Kennedy. TrPWD
Because I do not hope to turn again. Ash Wednesday. T. S. Eliot. AmPP; AnFE; ATP (1953 ed.); ChMo; CMP; CoAnAm; CoBMV; LiTA; LiTG; MoAB; MoAmPo; MoPo; OxBA; OxBoCh; Po; SeCeV; TwAmPo; TwHP
Because I feel that [*or* Because the angels], in the Heavens above. To My Mother. Poe. AnAmPo; APW; DD; IAP; LA; LaNeLa; MaRV; MCCG; MOAH; MotAn; NePA; OxBA
Because I had loved so deeply. Compensation. Paul Laurence Dunbar. BAP; HBV; LBAP; LEAP; PoNe
Because I have been given much. Because of Thy Great Bounty. Grace Noll Crowell. OQP; QP-2; TrPWD
Because I have called to you. Calls. Carl Sandburg. NP
Because I have loved life, I shall have no sorrow to die. A Song of Living. Amelia Josephine Burr. HBV; OBAV; POT; PoTo
Because I have made light of death. Death. Alan Mackintosh. LBBV
Because I heard His ways were just. Text. Sara Henderson Hay. QS
Because I Liked You Better. A. E. Housman. EnLit
Because I Live. Evelyn Ames. GoYe
Because I love her. Gerald Bullett. LO
Because I love, I weep. Song. Mary Carolyn Davies. TBM
Because I oft in dark abstracted guise. Astrophel and Stella, XXVII. Sir Philip Sidney. ReEn; SiCE; SiPS
Because I once beat you up. For a Far-out Friend. Gary Snyder. NeAP
Because I set no snare. Michael's Song. W. W. Gibson. BoTP
Because I think not ever to return. Ballata: In Exile at Sarzana. Guido Cavalcanti. AWP; JAWP; WBP
Because I used to shun. The Spark. Joseph Mary Plunkett. AnIV; AWP; JAWP; TIP; WBP
Because I waddle when I walk. The Dachshund. Edward Anthony. GoTP
Because I was content with these poor fields. Musketaquid. Emerson. CoBA; IAP; MOAP
Because I Were Shy. *Unknown.* StPo
Because in tender majesty. I Thank My God. G. A. Studdert-Kennedy. PSO
Because in the hour of the morning-star. The Hour of the Morning-Star. John Hall Wheelock. PR
Because in these so malcontented times. Against Paulus. Sir John Harington. SiCE
Because mine eyes can never have their fill. Ballata: He Will Gaze upon Beatrice [*or* Sonnet]. Dante, *tr. by* Dante Gabriel Rossetti. AWP; GoBC; JAWP; LyPI; WBP
Because My Faltering Feet. Hilaire Belloc. Sonnets, XVII. OxBoCh
(Her Faith.) GoBC
(Sonnet.) POTE
Because My Grief Seems Quiet and Apart. Robert Nathan. MAP
(Sonnet: "Because my grief seems quiet and apart.") BAP; TrJP
Because my joy is less than joy. Courage. Helen Frazee-Bower. HBMV
Because my life has lain so close to thine. Thus Far. Sophie Jewett. LBAP
Because my will is simple as a window. The Blessed Virgin Mary Compared to a Window. Thomas Merton. ISi
Because of body's hunger are we born. Sehnsucht. Anna Wickham. BMEP; MBP; MoBrPo; TwCV
Because of Clothes. Laura Riding. LiTA
Because of Her Who Flowered So Fair. Leonard Feeney. *Fr.* Song for a Listener. ISi
Because of one small low-laid head all crowned. Through Sorrow to Service. *Unknown.* MaRV
Because of one whose footstep never fell. The Harper. Helene Mullins. TBM
Because of someone's death. The Night They Kept Vigil in the South. Jorge Luis Borges. AnCL
Because of the light of the moon. Alchemy. Francis Carlin. JKCP
Because of the memory of one we held dear. In a Province. F. T. Prince. BoSA; MoVE
Because of Thee. Rabindranath Tagore. Gitanjali, IV. GrCo-1
Because of Thy Great Bounty. Grace Noll Crowell. OQP; QP-2; TrPWD
Because of You. W. Cestrian. OQP; QP-2
Because of You. Sophia Almon Hensley. HBV
Because of you I bear aloft the standard. Because of You. W. Cestrian. OQP; QP-2
Because of you we will be glad and gay. Julian Grenfell. Maurice Baring. HBMV; POTE
Because of your firm faith, I kept the track. The Stimulus of Friendship. *Unknown.* OQP; QP-1
Because on the branch that is tapping my pane. In the Hospital. Arthur Guiterman. MaRV; SBMV; VOD; WGRP
Because one creature of his breath. Pandora's Songs, III. William Vaughn Moody. *Fr.* The Fire-Bringer. MOAP
Because our lives are cowardly and sly. The Road. James Stephens. HBMV; PoeMoYo; VOD
Because our talk was of the cloud-control. Secret Parting. Dante Gabriel Rossetti. The House of Life, XLV. EtPaEn; PoVP; ViPo
Because out of corruption burns the rose. Nature. Laurence Binyon. BMEP; CBE
Because river-fog. River-Fog. Kiyowara Fukayabu. *Fr.* Shui Shu. AWP; FaPON; JAWP; LiTW; WBP
Because some men in khaki coats. A Lullaby. G. R. Glasgow. BOL
Because somewhere there was a man in a candystripe silk shirt. Homage to the Empress of the Blues. Robert E. Hayden. PoNe
Because that you are going. Emily Dickinson. MoAmPo
Because the angels in the Heavens above. *See* Because I feel that, in the Heavens above.
Because the blood of Christ/ spurted upon my eyes. Christian's Poem. Jorge de Lima. AnCL
Because the day that stretches out for me. A Nurse's Prayer. Ruth Winant Wheeler. PraP
Because the earth is vast and dark. Home for Love. John Freeman. TCPD
Because the mind is growing cold. William Morris. Idris Davies. MoWP
Because the misery of some great men. Sonnet. Owen Barfield. PtOT
Because the Old French *chatepelose* meant hairy cat. D-9. James Schevill. FiMAP
Because the paint is not the shadow of branches. Camouflage. John Manifold. WaP
Because the plum trees on the peak. The Mountain Top. Hitomaro. PFE
Because the rose must fade. Song. Richard Watson Gilder. HBV
Because the shadows deepen'd verily. At the Last. Philip Bourke Marston. HBV; VA
Because, the singer of an age, he sang. Shakespeare. Agnes Lee. NP
Because the snow is deep. The Fox. Kenneth Patchen. AnAmPo
Because the Spirit of Delight has laid. As One Finding Peace. Sister Mary of the Visitation. JKCP (1926 ed.)
Because the upper and the nether stones. To a Baffled Idealist. J. G. E. Hopkins. JKCP (1926 ed.); MaRV
Because the warm honey. Sanctuary. Bruce Boyd. NeAP
Because the years are few, I must be glad. The Debt. Katharine Lee Bates. OQP; QP-1
Because there is safety in derision. The Apparitions. W. B. Yeats. LiTM (rev. ed.); PoFS
Because they could not give it too much ground. In a Bird Sanctuary. Richard Wilbur. FiMAP
Because they thought his doctrines were not just. Shelley. Paul Hamilton Hayne. SPP; TCAP
Because thou canst not see. The Philosopher to His Mistress. Robert Bridges. ChMo; CMP; LiTM (rev. ed.); OAEP; PoEL-5; POTT; VLEP
Because thou hast the power and own'st the grace. Elizabeth Barrett Browning. Sonnets from the Portuguese, XXXIX. BPN; VA
Because thou wast the daughter of a king. To Saint Catherine. Henry Constable. GoBC
Because thro' twenty times ten million years. My Instant. Mary Sinton Leitch. LS
Because to-day is some religious festival. She Turns the Dolls' Faces to the Wall. W. B. Yeats. Upon a Dying Lady, III. LiTB
Because upon the first glad Easter day. Easter Light. Ida Norton Munson. ChIP

Because upon the rocks I snatch my rest. The Traveller. Ono no Komachi. PFE
Because we broke their statues. Ionian Song. C. P. Cavafy. MoGP
Because We Do Not See. *Unknown.* BLRP
Because we felt there could not be. God's Acre. Witter Bynner. AnEnPo; SBMV
Because we love bare hills and stunted trees. Hound Voice. W. B. Yeats. POTE
Because ye have broken your own chain. The Curse. Elizabeth Barrett Browning. *Fr.* A Curse for a Nation. PoVP
Because you are old and departing I have wetted my handkerchief. Seeing Hsia Chan Off by River. Po Chü-i. WhP
Because you are simple people, kindly and romantic. Fourth Act. Robinson Jeffers. LiTA; WaP
Because You Care. Frank Crane. PoToHe (new ed.)
Because you have no fear to mingle. To a Sparrow. Francis Ledwidge. BLA; HBMV; TSW; VOD; WhBS
Because you have thrown of your Prelate Lord. On the New Forcers of Conscience under the Long Parliament. Milton. PoFr
Because you left her name unnamed. Joseph Mary Plunkett. Wilfrid Meynell. ISi
Because you made me glad, I was the net. Affirmations. Peter Viereck. MiAP
Because you passed, and now are not. A Ballad of Heroes. Austin Dobson. BLP; GA; HBV; HBVY; InP; OHIP; PEOR; PoRL; POT; PoTo
Because your voice was at my side. Chamber Music, XVII. James Joyce. ReaPo
Becket, *sel.* Tennyson.
"O I see now/ Your purpose is to fright me." ReTS
Becket's Diadem. *Unknown.* ACP
Beclouded. Emily Dickinson. *See* Sky is low, the clouds are mean, The.
Bed, The. James Merrill. NePoEA
Bed, The. John Owen, *tr. fr. Latin by* Thomas Harvey. *Fr.* Four Epigrams. PrWP
Bed Charm. *Unknown.* See Matthew, Mark, Luke, and John.
Bed during Exams. Clara Warren Vail. PA
Bed in Summer. Robert Louis Stevenson. GFA; OnHT; OTPC; PCH; PoVP; RIS; StVeCh
Bed is the boon for me! Old Lizette on Sleep. Agnes Lee. HBMV
Bed Is Too Small. Elizabeth J. Coatsworth. DDA
Bed of ashes and a half-burned brand, A. Morning in Camp. Herbert Bashford. AA; BAP; POT
Bed of Campanula, A. "John Crichton." CaP; OCL
Bed of Love, The. William Hamilton. *Fr.* The Braes of Yarrow. BeR
Bed Time. *See* Bedtime.
Bed was made, the room was fit, The. A Camp [*or* Camper's Night Song *or* God's Green Inn]. Robert Louis Stevenson. *Fr.* Travels with a Donkey. BBV; MW; VLEP
Bedbug. *Unknown.* GoSl
Bedouin Song. Bayard Taylor. AA; AmP; AnAmPo; BAP; FaBoBe; GBV; HBV; IAP; LA; LBAP; LoPo; MCCG; NeHB; OBAV; PFY; TCAP
(Bedouin Love-Song.) BBV; LPS-1; PIR
Bedouins of the Skies, The. James Benjamin Kenyon. AA
Bed-ridden, laid by an age's malady. Final Poem. Robert Bhain Campbell. MoPo; NePA
Beds of Fleur-de-Lys, The. Charlotte Perkins Gilman. AA
Beds were all untouch'd by hand or tool, The. Thomas Hood. *Fr.* The Haunted House. RO
Bedside. Francis Reginald Scott. BoCaPo (1948 ed.)
Bed-Time. Laurence Alma-Tadema. BoTP
Bedtime. Helen Coale Crew. GFA
Bedtime. Francis Robert St. Clair Erskine, Earl of Rosslyn. HBV; HBVY; PRWS; VA
Bedtime. Eleanor Farjeon. TiPo
Bed-Time. *At. to* Thomas Hood. BOL; BoTP; OTPC (1946 ed.)
Bed-Time. Ralph M. Jones. HBMV
Bed Time. Ella Young. BoChLi (1950 ed.)
Bedtime Prayer. Henry van Dyke. PraP
Bed-Time Song. Emilie Poulsson. BOL; HBV; HBVY
Bed-Time Story. Melville Cane. GoTP
Bedtime Story, A. Robert Mezey. NePoEA
Bedtime's come fu' little boys. Lullaby. Paul Laurence Dunbar. BoChLi; GoSl; LBAP; MPB; StVeCh (1940 ed.); TSW; TSWC; VOD
Bee, The ("Like trains of cars"). Emily Dickinson. AnNE; GN; MoAB; MoAmPo (1950 ed.); NeMA; OTPC
Bee, The. John Fandel. GoYE
Bee, The. Charles Fitzgeffrey. *Fr.* Sir Francis Drake. EIL
Bee, The. Henry Hawkins. ACP
Bee, The ("As Cupid in a garden strayed"), *with music. Unknown.* TrAS
Bee, The. ("Summer's nectar-gathering bee"). *Unknown.* SeCL
Bee, The. ("There is a little gentleman"). *Unknown.* PCH
Bee, The. Paul Valéry, *tr. fr. French by* Alan Conder. TrFP
Bee, The. Isaac Watts. *See* How Doth the Little Busy Bee.
Bee and the Cuckoo, The. Tomás de Iriarte, *tr. fr. Spanish by* George H. Devereux. BoChLi
Bee and the Lily, The. Thomas Westwood. TVC; TVSH
Bee-balm for humming-birds. Garden Song. Arthur Guiterman. MoSiPe
Bee baw babby lou, on a tree top. *Unknown.* BOL
Bee baw bunting. *Unknown.* BOL
Bee-Boy's Song, The. Kipling. VLEP
Bee in amber hides, yet gleams unspoiled, The. Martial, *tr. fr. Latin by* Geoffrey Johnson. Epigrams, IV, 32. LaP
Bee is a rover, The. The Happy World [*or* Brown Bee]. William Brighty Rands. MeMeAg; OTPC (1946 ed.); PCH; PPL; StVeCh (1940 ed.)
Bee is not afraid of me, The. Emily Dickinson. LaNeLa
Bee Is Such a Busy Soul, The. *Unknown.* SiTL
Bee-Keeper, A. *Unknown, tr. fr. Greek by* J. A. Pott. OxBG
Bee-Master. V. Sackville-West. HaMV; PtOT
Bee-Orchis, The. Andrew Young. ChTr
Bee quick my boyes drinke off your wine. *Unknown.* SeCSL
Bee Sets Sail, A. Katharine Morse. UTS
Bee, the Ant, and the Sparrow, The. Charles Cotton. RIS
Bee to the heather, The. Song. Sir Henry Taylor. OBVV
Beech, The. Theodore Daeubler, *tr. fr. German by* Glauco Cambon. OnPM
Beech Leaves. James Reeves. AlDL
Beech leaves are silver, The. October. Richard Aldington. *Fr.* Epigrams. PFE
Beech, The, says: my power is the foliage. The Beech. Theodore Daeubler. OnPM
Beech Trees. Sister Mary Madeleva. BBV (1951 ed.)
Beech Tree's Petition, The. Thomas Campbell. ADAH; GTSL; HBV; SN
Beecher Island. Arthur Chapman. PoOW
Beeches, without order seemly. Christopher Smart. *Fr.* St. Philip and St. James. RO
Beefsteak When I'm Hongry, *with music. Unknown.* StDa
Beeg Irish cop dat walk hees beat. Two 'Mericana Men. T. A. Daly. CV; MPB
Beehive. Jean Toomer. PoNe
Beëlzebub Rises to Speak. Milton. *Fr.* Paradise Lost, II. UnPo (1st ed.)
Been All aroun' the Whole Roun' Worl', *with music. Unknown.* StDa
Been in dat jailhouse, expectin' a fine. Sun Gonna Shine in My Door Some Day. *Unknown.* OuSiCo
Been in the Pen So Long, *with music. Unknown.* AS
Been on the hummer since ninety-four. A. R. U. *Unknown.* AS
Been to Pike's Peak, lost all my dimes. Soliloquy of the Returned Gold Adventurer. *Unknown.* PoOW
Beeny Cliff. Thomas Hardy. PoVP; TwHP
Beer. George Arnold. AA; LEAP
Beer. Charles Stuart Calverley. CenHV
"But hark! a sound is stealing on my ear," *sel.* FiBHP
Beer. Julian the Apostate, *tr. fr. Greek by* T. F. Higham. OxBG
Beer. *Unknown. See* Limerick: "Man to whom illness was chronic, A."
Beer and Skittles. Diana Barrett. StaSt
Bees. Marchette Chute. BoChLi (1950 ed.)
Bees. Dryden. *Fr.* Annus Mirabilis. BeR
Bees, The. Monk Gibbon. OnYI
Bees. Richard R. Kirk. PIAE
Bees, The. Lola Ridge. FaPON; MPB
Bees. Frank Dempster Sherman. PPL
Bees about the Linden-tree, The. November's Cadence. James Carnegie. EBSV
Bees and Monks. John Hookham Frere. *Fr.* King Arthur and His Round Table. OBRV
Bees are busy in their murmurous search, The. Nesting Time. Archibald Lampman. CPG
Bees! Bees! Hark to your bees! The Bee-Boy's Song. Kipling. VLEP
Bees before Winter. Merrill Moore. RIS
Bees build in the crevices, The. The Stare's Nest by my Window. W. B. Yeats. Meditations in Time of Civil War, VI. LiTB
Bees don't care about the snow. Bees. Frank Dempster Sherman. PPL
Bee's fixed hexagon, The. "Come, Sleep . . ." Louise Bogan. OnAP
Bees in the clover are making honey, and I am making my hay, The. The Mower in Ohio. John James Piatt. AA
Bees of Christ, The. Clifford J. Laube. JKCP (1955 ed.)
Bees of Middleton [*or* Myddleton] Manor, The. May Probyn. GoBC; JKCP; VA
Bees over the gooseberry bushes. The Bees. Lola Ridge. FaPON; MPB
Bees' Song, The. Walter de la Mare. LiL; OTPC (1946 ed.); WhC; YT
Beethoven. Florence Ellenwood Allen. CAG

Beethoven. Edward Carpenter. PoMa
Beethoven. Roden Noel. BMEP
Beethoven. John Todhunter. TIP
Beethoven Andante, A. Grace Hazard Conkling. PFY
Beethoven's Death Mask. Stephen Spender. CaAE; UnS
Beetle, The. Vicente Aleixandre, *tr. fr. Spanish by* Eleanor L. Turnbull. CoSP
Beetle, The. Edith King. GFA
Beetle, The. James Whitcomb Riley. PCD
"Shrilling locust slowly sheathes, The," *sel.* FaPON
Beetle loves his unpretending track, The. Wordsworth. *Fr.* Liberty. FiBHP
Befind, wilt thou not come with me. The Fairy Midir's Invitation to Etain. *Unknown.* SiB
Before, *sel.* Robert Browning.
"Our wars are wars of life, and wounds of love." ChIP; StJW
Before. W. E. Henley. In Hospital, IV. BEL; BMEP; BPN; EnLi-2; MBP; MoBrPo; PoVP; OuHeWo; TCEP; ViP
Before. Mary Sinton Leitch. OQP; QP-2
Before a Corpse. Manuel Acuña, *tr. fr. Spanish.* AnMP, *tr. by* Samuel Beckett; PoP, *tr. by* E. S. Green *and* H. Von Lowenfels
Before a Statue of Achilles. George Santayana. HBV
Before a Statue of Apollo. Saul Tchernichowsky, *tr. fr. Hebrew by* Sholom J. Kahn. LiTW
(Before the Statue of Apollo, *tr. by* L. V. Snowman.) TrJP
Before Action. Leon Gellert. BoAV
Before Action. W. W. Gibson. BEL; ChMo; CMP; TOP; TwCV; VOD (1931 ed.)
Before Action. William Noel Hodgson. MaRV; PC; WGRP
Before Agincourt. Shakespeare. *Fr.* King Henry V, *prologue to* IV. ChTr
Before all Time, before all worlds. Namdev. *Fr.* Everlasting to Everlasting. MaRV
Before and After. Oliver Madox Brown. VA
Before and after Marriage. Anne Campbell. PoToHe (new ed.)
Before Ararat. J. Redwood Anderson. QS
Before Bannockburn. Burns. *See* Scots Wha Hae.
Before Bedtime. John Charles McNeill. NoCaPo
Before beginning, and without an end. The Power That Moves to Good. Arnold. GrCo-2
Before Christ left the Citadel of Light. His Laureate. Joyce Kilmer. StJW
Before Dante's Tomb, where the sun dedicates his everburning rays. Dante's Scourge. Sumako Fukao. PoLJ
Before Dawn. Melville Cane. *See* Dawn Has Yet to Ripple In.
Before Dawn. Elinor Chipp. HBMV
Before Dawn. Walter de la Mare. AlDL; ChrBoLe
Before Dawn. Swinburne. PIR; VLEP
Before Dawn in the Woods. Marguerite Wilkinson. HBMV; LEAP; PC
Before Day. Siegfried Sassoon. WGRP
Before Death. Sophocles. *See* Ajax's Death.
Before Disaster. Yvor Winters. HoPM
Before Exile. Louise Mack. BoAu
Before God's footstool to confess. Success. *Unknown.* PoToHe
Before he embarks on shipboard. Three Dangers. *Unknown.* OnPM
Before he pass'd from mortal view. Solemn Rondeau. Charles Dent Bell. OBVV
Before heaven and earth existed there was in nature a primordial substance. Tao. Lao-tse, *tr. by* Walter Gorn Old. GrCo-2
Before Heaven and Earth were born. *Unknown, tr. fr. Chinese.* Tao Teh Ching, IV. WhP
Before her flew Affliction, girt in storms. Herculean Silence. George Chapman. *Fr.* Euthymiae Raptus; *or,* The Teares of Peace. EV-1
Before Her Portrait in Youth. Francis Thompson. EmBrPo; EPN
Before her supper where she sits. The Daughter at Evening. Robert Nathan. HBMV; TSW
Before Him weltered like a shoreless sea. Judgment Day. William Dean Howells. AA; PFY
Before I began to burn. Interval with Fire. Dorothy Livesay. CaP
Before I brand a brother. Before. Mary Sinton Leitch. OQP; QP-2
Before I came across the sea. The Native Irishman. *Unknown.* OnYI
Before I close my eyes in sleep. An Evening Prayer. Bernard Barton. BOL
Before I die I may be great. Vista. Marguerite Wilkinson. *Fr.* Songs of an Empty House. SBMV
Before I got my eye put out. Emily Dickinson. LiTA; LiTM (rev. ed.)
Before I joined the army. Death and the Fairies. Patrick MacGill. HBMV; LBBV
Before I knew how cruel. Gossip. Lexie Dean Robertson. MoSiPe
Before I knew, the Dawn was on the road. The Road to Dieppe. John Finley. MCCG
Before I Knocked and Flesh Let Enter. Dylan Thomas. FaBoTw
Before I melt. The Snowflake. Walter de la Mare. AlDL
Before I saw the spring. Spring in Hiding. Frances Frost. YeAr
Before I see another day. The Complaint of a Forsaken Indian Woman. Wordsworth. NBE
Before I sigh my last gasp[e], let me breath[e]. The Will. John Donne. ATP (1935 ed.); EM-1; EnLP; EPS (1942 ed.); LiA; LiTB; LiTG; LPS-3; MePo; SeEP; TOP; TuPP
Before I stumbled. Francis Carlin. HBMV
Before I trust my fate to thee. A Woman's Question[s]. Adelaide Anne Procter. AV; BMEP; HBV; LiTL; LO; LPS-1; VA
Before I was a travelled bird. Regarding (1) the U. S. and (2) New York. Franklin P. Adams. HBMV
Before I woke I knew her gone. The Flower of Flame. Robert Nichols. OBMV
Before Invasion, 1940. John Betjeman. MoVE
Before It Is Too Late. George Bancroft Griffith. MOAH
Before It Is Too Late. Frank Herbert Sweet. PoToHe (new ed.)
Before man came. Stone Mountain. Mary Brent Whiteside. HiLiAm; LS
Before man came to blow it right. The Aim Was Song. Robert Frost. HH; NP
Before Man parted for this earthly strand. Revolutions. Matthew Arnold. EmBrPo; EPN; PoVP; VLEP
Before Man's labouring wisdom gave me birth. The Ship and Her Makers. John Masefield. CoBE
Before March. Archibald MacLeish. PIAE
Before Marching, and After. Thomas Hardy. AOAH
Before me grew the human soul. The Clearer Self. Archibald Lampman. UnW
Before me you bowed as before an altar. Homage. Helen Hoyt. AnAmPo; AV; LA; NV
Before My Face the Picture Hangs. Robert Southwell. *See* Upon the Image of Death.
Before my lady's window gay. Medieval Norman Songs, IV. *Unknown, tr. by* John Addington Symonds. AWP
Before my light goes out for ever if God should give me a choice of graces. Impenitentia Ultima. Ernest Dowson. HBV; POTT; VLEP
Before night falls, the bumblebees are ringing. Farewell in Memory of F. O. Haeller. Franz Staude. BoFr
Before Olympus. John Gould Fletcher. MAP; MoAmPo
Before our barbed and tangled wire, long time a dead man lay. Brothers. Heinrich Lersch. TwGV
Before our eyes a pageant rolled. After the Centennial. Christopher Pearse Cranch. PAH
Before our lady came on earth. Song from "The Hill of Venus." William Morris. *Fr.* The Earthly Paradise. POTT; PoVP; VLEP
Before our lives divide forever. The Triumph of Time. Swinburne. EmBrPo; EtPaEn; PoVP; ViPo; ViPP; VLEP
Before our trenches at Cambrai. Cambrai and Marne. Sir Charles G. D. Roberts. CPG
Before Parting. Burns. *See* My Bonnie Mary.
Before Pilate. Leslie Savage Clark. ChIP
Before proud Rome's imperial throne. Caractacus. Bernard Barton. LPS-2
Before Rain. *Tr. fr. Navaho Indian by* Mary Austin. APW
Before remembrance we moved here, withheld. The Font in the Forest. Léonie Adams. CrMA
Before Saint Anne. The Good Bishop. *Unknown.* CAW; WGRP
Before St. Francis' burg I wait. At Assisi. William Vaughn Moody. *Fr.* Song-Flower and Poppy. LEAP; SaFP
Before Salamis. William Bedell Stanford. NeIP
Before Sedan. Austin Dobson. BPN; LPS-2; MBP; MoBrPo (1942 ed.); NeMA; TreFS
Before Sentence Is Passed. R. P. Blackmur. LiTA
Before she first had smiled or looked with calm. E. J. Scovell. *Fr.* The First Year. FaBoMo
Before she has her floor swept. Portrait by a Neighbor. Edna St. Vincent Millay. FaPON; GaP; MoShBr; MPB; SP; TiPo; TSW; TSWC
Before she saw him in the wood. The Quickening. Stella Weston Tuttle. GoYe
Before she went from grieving. Apples. Lizette Woodworth Reese. YT
Before sheep came, before my fathers drove. Frances Frost. *Fr.* Woman of This Earth. AnAmPo
Before Sleep. Prudentius, *tr. fr. Latin by* Helen Waddell. LiTW; TriL
Before Sleep. Anne Ridler. NeBP
Before Sleeping. *Unknown.* *See* Matthew, Mark, Luke and John.

Before Spring. P. A. Ropes. BoTP
Before Sunrise in Winter. Edward Rowland Sill. AA
Before that my loved one. Apprehension. *Tr. by* Douglas Ainslie. OBVV
Before the altar in his heart he knelt. The Dissenter. Lillian M. Swenson. ChIP
Before the Anaesthetic; or, A Real Fright. John Betjeman. SeCePo
Before the Aragva at Night. Nikolai Tikhonov, *tr. fr. Russian by* Jack Lindsay. RuPo
Before the Barn-Door Crowing. John Gay. *Fr.* The Beggar's Opera. BeR
(Song: "Before the barn-door crowing.") PoEL-3
Before the Battle. Thomas Moore. EV-4
Before the battle soldiers fight the fear. Ghostly Battles. Glenn Ward Dresbach. TBM
Before the Beginning. Christina Rossetti. OxBoCh
(Last Prayer.) OBVV
Before the Beginning of Years. Swinburne. *Fr.* Atalanta in Calydon. BEL; EnL; EPN; FaFP; HBV; LiTB; LiTG; OAEP; PoFS; PoVP; PreP; TyEnPo; ViPP; VLEP; WHA
(Chorus: "Before the beginning of years.") EnLit; GTBS-D; GTBS-W; LoBV; MBP; OBVV; PIR; REAL; ViP
(Chorus from "Atalanta.") OBEV (new ed.)
(Choruses from "Atalanta in Calydon.") AEV; EnLi-2; GTSE; LiA; POTT; ViBoPo
(Life of Man, The.) BMEP; BPN; EmBrPo; TOP
(Making of Man, The.) GDAH
(Man.) BLV; BoLiVe; TrGrPo
Before the beginning Thou hast foreknown the end. Before the Beginning [*or* Last Prayer]. Christina Rossetti. OBVV; OxBoCh
Before the Carnival. Thom Gunn. NePoEA
Before the cathedral in grandeur rose. How the Great Guest Came [*or* The Great Guest Comes]. Edwin Markham. BeLS; BLPA; WBLP
Before the Coming of the Planes That Burn the Cities. Otto D'Sola, *tr. fr. Spanish by* Angel Flores. AnCL
Before the Crucifix. Princess Gabrielle Wrede, *tr. fr. German by* Robert Huntington. StJW
Before the dawn is yet the day. Music. Agnes Mary Frances Robinson. UnW
Before the dawn of history. The Woman Always Pays. "H. T. R." CAG
Before the dawn-wind swept the troubled sky. A Vision. Geoffrey Dearmer. HBMV
Before the door. A Peasant Song. *Unknown.* ChLP
Before the earth with glittering seas was girded. Perpetual Vows. Sister Mary Angelita. PraNu
Before the ending of the day. *At. to* St. Ambrose, *tr. fr. Latin by* John Mason Neale. OlF
Before the Fair. Anna Hempstead Branch. PR
Before the Feast of Shushan. Anne Spencer. BANP
Before the glare o' dawn I rise. The Shearer's Wife. Louis Esson. BoAu
Before the gods that made the gods. G. K. Chesterton. *Fr.* The Ballad of the White Horse. ACP (1952 ed.); ReTS
Before the grass is out the people are out. William Carlos Williams. *Fr.* Paterson. ReMP
Before the Great Void, we burn the fragrant incense. To Purity and Truth. *Unknown.* TrJP
Before the Ikon of the Mother of God. Constantine of Rhodes, *tr. fr. Greek by* G. R. Woodward. ISi
Before the Laureate's Day. Pindar, *tr. fr. Greek by* C. J. Billson. *Fr.* Isthmian Ode, II. GrR
Before the listening world behold him stand. The Violin. Richard Watson Gilder. PoRL
Before the living bronze Saint-Gaudens made. *See* Before the solemn bronze . . .
Before the mansion lay a lucid lake. The Lake at Newstead. Byron. *Fr.* Don Juan. GEPC
Before the Mirror. Swinburne. OBVV
"Glad, but not flush'd with gladness," *sel.* OBEV (new ed.)
Before the Paling of the Stars. Christina Rossetti. *See* Christmas Carol, A: "Before the paling of the stars."
Before the Pavilion. Li Yu, *tr. fr. Chinese by* Hsiung Ting. WhP
Before the Peak of Returning Joy the sand was like snow. A Song of War. Li Po. WhP
Before the Rain. Thomas Bailey Aldrich. GN; LPS-2
Before the Rain. Amélie Rives. AA
Before the regal chariot, as it past. Processional. Stesichorus. GrR
Before the Roman Came to Rye. G. K. Chesterton. *See* Rolling English Road, The.
Before the seas and mountains were brought forth. The Burden of Time. Frederick George Scott. CPG
Before the shadows slew the sun the kites were soaring free. The King and the Oak. Robert Ervin Howard. DaM
Before the sixth day of the next new year. A Prognostication upon Cards and Dice. Sir Walter Ralegh. SiPS
Before the Snow. Andrew Lang. VOD
Before the solemn [*or* living] bronze Saint-Gaudens made. An Ode in Time of Hesitation. William Vaughn Moody. AmPP; AnFE; APA; ATP; CoAnAm; HBV; LBMV; OxBA; PaA; PAH; TOP
Before tne sonne had guilde the morne of silved daij. *Unknown.* SeCSL
Before the spring had flowered away full summer burst in middle May. A Berkshire Holiday. Clifford Bax. TCPD
Before the Squall. Arthur Symons. PoVP; VLEP
Before the starry threshold of Jove's court. Prologue of the Attendant Spirit in Comus. Milton. *Fr.* Comus. CBE
Before the Statue of Apollo. Saul Tchernichowsky. *See* Before a Statue of Apollo.
Before the stirring of the notes at the lecture. Madonna of the Dons. Arthur MacGillivray. ISi; JKCP (1955 ed.)
Before the Storm. Albert Samuel Davis. CAG
Before the Storm. Richard Dehmel, *tr. fr. German by* Ludwig Lewisohn. AWP; JAWP; WBP
Before the stout harvesters falleth the grain. The Summer Shower. Thomas Buchanan Read. CG
Before the sun rose at yester-dawn. Kitty Bhan. Edward Walsh. ACP
Before the swan in waters blue has sunken. Death's Delight. Joseph von Eichendorff. AnGP
Before the urchin well could go. The Fair Thief. Charles Wyndham. HBV
Before the world was made. Words in the Wilderness. Sister Claude of Jesus. JKCP (1955 ed.)
Before there was in Egypt any sound. Monadnock through the Trees. E. A. Robinson. InP; TOP
Before there were houses, there were the wild hills and the blind wind. A Lodging for the Night. James Rorty. MOAP
Before there were pineapples, peaches, or plums. How the Feud Started. Arthur Guiterman. AlBD
Before they closed him in the tomb. Five Days and Nights. Vera Inber. RuPo
Before they come I hear their talk. People Going By. Elizabeth Madox Roberts. GaP
Before this coiling planet shall be cold. Edna St. Vincent Millay. Epitaph for the Race of Man, I. AmP
Before this generous time. The Finding of Love. Robert Graves. TCPD
Before this time another year, I may be gone. Oh, Lawd, How Long? *Unknown.* ABF
Before this, when I was stationed at Hsün-yang. On Being Removed from Hsün-yang and Sent to Chung-chou. Po Chü-i. TrCh
Before those golden altar-lights we stood. Victory. Alfred Noyes. BEL
Before Thy cross I'm kneeling. Before the Crucifix. Princess Gabrielle Wrede. StJW
Before Thy cross, O Saviour, we confess. Hymn to the Perfect. Edith Lovejoy Pierce. ChIP
Before thy door too long of late. Extremum Tanain. Horace. Odes. III, 10. AWP; JAWP; WBP
Before thy grisly front no man may stand. Christus Triumphans. Condé B. Pallen. CAW
Before thy radiance fails. Two Voices. Paul Verlaine. TrFP
"Before thy time thy temples will grow grey." Cassandra Speaks. Pierre de Ronsard. TrFP
Before Time was, and vast, insensate void. The Great Word. Estelle Duclo. BAP
Before us in the sultry dawn arose. The Slave. Richard Henry Horne. VA
Before Vespasian's regal throne. Death of Gaudentis. "Harriet Annie." WBLP
Before Vicksburg. George Henry Boker. PAH; PEOR, *sl. abr.*
Before Waterloo. Thomas Hardy. *Fr.* The Dynasts, Pt. III, Act VI, sc. viii. MoAB; PoVP; WaaP
(Chorus: "Yea, the coneys are scared by the thud of hoofs.") LoBV
("Eyelids of eve fall together at last, The," *longer sel.*) EPP
(Field of Waterloo, The.) FaBoCh; LoGBV
Before we came the moon-soaked dews were here. Prelude to Cricket. Thomas Moult. POTE
Before we shall again behold. Song. Sir William Davenant. MeLP; MePo; MeRV; OBS; SeEP; TriL
Before Winter. Frederick R. McCreary. MAP
Before you bid, for Christmas' sake. For Them. Eleanor Farjeon. ChBR
Before You Came. Marjorie Meeker. AV
Before you kissed me only winds of heaven. The Kiss. Sara Teasdale. CMP; HBV
Before You Now, My Tyrant-Sorrow. Stefan George, *tr. fr. German by* Peter Viereck. AnGP
Before you praise spring's advent, note. Quatrain. Tu Fu. WhP
Before you thought of spring. The Bluebird. Emily Dickinson. BLA; WhBS

Before you touch the bolt that locks this gate. Spoken at a Castle Gate. Donald Davidson. MAP; MoAmPo (1942 ed.)
Before your tiger roar was heard. Chang Liang. Li Po. PoFr
Beforehand. Witter Bynner. HBMV
Befriend the friends you have, and go. Giving and Taking. Hesiod. *Fr.* Works and Days. OxBG
Beg Parding. *Unknown.* ChTr
Bega. Marjorie Pickthall. CaP; OCL
Begetting of Cain, The. Hyam Plutzik. FiMAP
Beggar, The. Margaret E. Bruner. PoToHe
Beggar, The. H. L. Doak. HBMV
Beggar. F. S. Flint. MBP; MoBrPo (1942 ed.)
Beggar, The. Thomas Moss. LPS-1
Beggar, The. Tao Yuan-ming, *tr. fr. Chinese by* Yang Yeh-tzu. WhP
Beggar. Terence Tiller. PoN
Beggar died last night, A; his soul. Of Charity. Arthur Symons. VLEP
Beggar does not sulk in grime, The. The Dwarf. W. Wesley Trimpi. PtPa
Beggar for God, A. John Stigall. PraNu
. . . "Beggar," he sayes. Little John a Begging. *Unknown.* ESPB
Beggar lad, The—dies early. Emily Dickinson. MeRV
Beggar Laddie, The. *Unknown.* ESPB
Beggar Maid, The. Tennyson. BeLS; BoTP; BPN; CG; EmBrPo; HBV; OTPC; PoVP; TCEP; WP
Beggar to Burgher. A. R. D. Fairburn. AnNZ
Beggar, to Mab the Fairy Queen, The. Robert Herrick. OTPC (1923 ed.)
Beggar to the graveyard hied, A. Poverty. *Unknown. Fr.* The Panchatantra. AWP; PoFr
Beggars. Rhys Carpenter. HBMV
Beggars. Francis Davidson. CH
Beggars. Ella Higginson. AA; LBAP
Beggars, The. Margaret Widdemer. NP
Beggars' Bush, *sel.* John Fletcher.
Cast Our Caps and Cares Away, *fr.* II, i. SiCE; TuPP; ViBoPo
Beggar's Child, The. Padraic Colum. GTIV
Beggar's Opera, The, *sels.* John Gay.
Before the Barn-Door Crowing, *fr.* II, i. BeR
(Song: "Before the barn-door crowing.") PoEL-3
"Fox may steal your hens, sir, A," *fr.* I, i. CEP
"How happy could I be with either," *fr.* II, ii. ViBoPo
"If the heart of a man is deprest with cares," *fr.* II, i. CEP
(If the Heart of a Man.) ATP (1935 ed.)
(Song: "If the heart of a man . . .") CaAE
"Let us take the road," *fr.* II, i. ATP (1935 ed.); CEP
"Man may escape from rope and gun," *fr.* II, ii. CEP
"O Polly, you might have toy'd and kist," *fr.* I, i. EnLoPo
Song: "Can love be controll'd by advice?" LoBV
Song: "If any wench Venus's girdle wear," *fr.* I, i. PoEL-3
Song: "Thus when the swallow, seeking prey," *fr.* II, ii. PoEL-3
"Through all the employments of life," *fr.* I, i. CEP
Were I Laid on Greenland's Coast, *fr.* I, i. AtBAP; CEP
(Macheath and Polly.) LoBV
(Over the Hills and Far Away.) ATP (1935 ed.); EnLi-1 (1949 ed.)
(Song: "Were I laid on Greenland's coast.") BeR; CaAE; OBEC; OxBoLi; PoEL-3; SeCeV
"Youth's the season made for joys," *fr.* II, i. CEP
(Song.) EV-3; OBEC
Beggar's Rhyme. *Unknown.* ChBR; GaP; PCH; SDH
("Christmas is coming, the geese are getting fat.") OxNR; TiPo (1952 ed.)
Beggar's Serenade. John Heath-Stubbs. NeBP
Beggar's Soliloquy, The. George Meredith. EmBrPo
Begging Another, on Colour of Mending the Former. Ben Jonson. *Fr.* A Celebration of Charis. LO; LoPS; OAEP; PoEL-2; TuPP
(Kiss, The.) AtBAP
Begin Again. "Susan Coolidge." MaRV
(New Every Morning.) BLP
Begin again. There is no law which says. Five Epigrams, 1. Donald Hall. NePoAm-2
Begin, my tongue, some heavenly theme. Isaac Watts. OlF
Begin the Beguine. Cole Porter. PreP
Begin the Day with God ("Every morning lean thine arms awhile"). *Unknown.* MaRV
Begin the day with God. With God. *Unknown.* PraP
Begin unto my God with timbrels. ". . . With Timbrels." Judith, Bible, Apocrypha. TrJP
Beginner, The. Kipling. *Fr.* Epitaphs of the War. FaBoTw; LiA
Beginners. Walt Whitman. AA; IAP
Beginning and the End, The. *Unknown, tr. fr. Icelandic by* Henry Adams Bellows. *Fr.* The Elder Edda. LiTW, *abr.;* LyMA; PaOS
(Voluspo.) AWP
Beginning My Studies. Walt Whitman. OxBA
Beginning of an Undergraduate Poem. *Unknown.* SiTL
Beginning of Creation, The. Cædmon(?), *tr. fr. Anglo-Saxon by* F. B. Gummere. *Fr.* Genesis. BCEP
Beginning of Day, The. Euripides, *tr. fr. Greek.* OxBG
Beginning of Love, The. Keats. *Fr.* Isabella; or, The Pot of Basil. UnPo (1st ed.)
Beginning of Summer, The. Po Chü-i, *tr. fr. Chinese by* Arthur Waley. TrCh
Beginning of the Battle of the Angels, The. Milton. *See* Battle of the Angels.
Beginning of the People, The. *Unknown, tr. fr. Chinese.* WhP
Beginning of the Wrath, The. Homer, *tr. fr. Greek by* Sir William Marris. *Fr.* The Iliad, I. OxBG
Beginnings of Civilization. Lucretius, *tr. fr. Latin by* William Ellery Leonard. *Fr.* De Rerum Natura (Of the Nature of Things). OuHeWo
Beginnings of Day, The. William Diaper. *Fr.* Dryades; or, The Nymphs Prophecy. BeR
Beginnings of Faith, The. Sir Lewis Morris. WGRP
Beg-Innish. J. M. Synge. GTIV; MBP; MoBrPo; NeMA; OnYI; OxBI
Begon thou fatall fyery feaver. *Unknown.* SeCSL
"Begone!" the north wind cries. December. Victor Hugo. TrFP
"Begone, thou fond presumptuous Elf." The Waterfall and the Eglantine. Wordsworth. OTPC
Begone, you, sir. Here, shepherd, call your dog. The Shepherd Dog of the Pyrenees. Ellen Murray. PoRL
Begonias. Su T'ung-po, *tr. fr. Chinese by* Kenneth Rexroth. OnPC
Begotten by the meeting of rock with rock. Sea Holly. Conrad Aiken. LiTM; MAPA; NePA; TCPD
Behave Yoursel' before Folk. Alexander Rodger. BOHV; EBSV; HBV; LPS-1
Behaviour of Money. Bernard Spencer. LiTB
Behind Devaney's barn I saw. A Little Pig Asleep. Leroy F. Jackson. BrR
Behind him lay the gray [*or* great] Azores. Columbus. Joaquin Miller. AA; AmPP (3d ed.); BAP; BBV; BeLS; BTP; CBPC; DD; DDA; EtS; FaBoBe; FaFP; FaPON; GN; HBV; HBVY; IAP; LBAP; LEAP; MC; MCCG; MPB; NeHB; NeMA; OBAV; OHFP; OnSP; OQP; OTPC (1946 ed.); PaA; PAH; PCD; PECK; PEDC; PFY; PGD; PoeMoYo; PoRL; PTA-1; PYM; QP-1; StaSt; StVeCh; TiPo (1952 ed.); TreF; TSW; TSWC; WaKn; YaD; YeAr; YT
Behind me dips eternity. Emily Dickinson. WoL
Behind me lie the clumping streets. Battery Park. Leonard Cline. PR
Behind me lies the mistress of the East. The Pilgrim. Eleanor Downing. JKCP
Behind me the house was asleep. Happening. Edwin Honig. NePA
Behind me you must go, behind me. Demon. Aleksandr Blok. BoR
Behind my father's house. Gai lon la, gai le rosier. *Unknown.* BoCaPo (1948 ed.)
Behind the Arras, *sel.* Bliss Carman.
"I like the old house." BAP
Behind the board fence at the banker's house. The Last Antelope. Edwin Ford Piper. PCN; PoMa; TCPD
Behind the Closed Eye. Francis Ledwidge. MCCG; VOD
Behind the docks and under the bridge. Warehouses. Frederick Mortimer Clapp. VOD (1935 ed.)
Behind the Door. Bert Leston Taylor. LHV
Behind the granite church. Fugue. Constance Carrier. GoYe
Behind the hilltop drops the sun. Evening Songs, IV. John Vance Cheney. AA
Behind the House Is the Millet Plot. Muna Lee. *See* Melilot.
Behind the Line. Edmund Blunden. ChMP
Behind the Log, *sel.* E. J. Pratt.
"Whatever doubt the eye might have imposed." TwCaPo
Behind the Manor lies the mere. En roulant ma boule. *Unknown.* BoCaPo
Behind the pinions of the Seraphim. The Garden. Thomas S. Jones, Jr. Four Sonnets, III. SBMV
Behind the Plough. James H. Cousins. OxBI
Behind the tree, behind the house, behind the stars. Seen in a Glass. Kathleen Raine. ChMP
Behind the wall of St. John's in the city. The Garden at St. John's. May Swenson. NePoEA
Behind the Waterfall. Winifred Welles. PoMS; StVeCh; TiPo
Behind the wattle-woven house. St. Christopher of the Gael. "Fiona Macleod." CLS
Behind the wild-bird's throat. Wood-Thrush. John Hall Wheelock. NePoAm
Behind thee leave thy merchandise. God Hide the Whole World in Thy Heart. Emerson. *Fr.* Woodnotes, I. OQP; QP-2
Behind thy pasteboard, on thy battered hack. Don Quixote. Austin Dobson. HBV; HBVY; PC

Behind this mist of whispering soft lace. City Rain. Lola Mallet. DDA
Behind yon hills where Lugar flows. My Nanie, O [*or* Song: My Nanie, O]. Burns. EBSV; EnLi-2
Behold a critic, pitched like the *castrati.* Pipling. Theodore Roethke. NePA; SiTL
Behold! a giant am I! The Windmill. Longfellow. MoShBr; TVSH
Behold a hag whom life denies a kiss. Opportunity. Madison Cawein. AA
Behold a little [*or* helpless *or* seely *or* silly] tender babe. New Prince, New Pomp [*or* Humble Pomp]. Robert Southwell. AnEC; CenL; COAH; EG; EV-1; GN; GoTP; MaRV; OBSC; OHIP; ReIE; SDH; SiCE; StJW; ThWaDe; TriL; TuPP
Behold! a new white world! A New Year. Dora Sigerson Shorter. YeAr
Behold a rev'rend sire, whom want of grace. A Reverend Sire. Pope. *Fr.* Moral Essays. BeR
Behold, a seely [*or* silly] tender babe. *See* Behold a little tender babe.
Behold, a stranger's at the door! Christ at the Door. *Unknown.* BePJ
Behold a virgin shall conceive, and bear a son. The Messiah. Isaiah, Bible, *O.T.* AWP
Behold a woman! Whitman's Mother [*or* The Justified Mother of Men]. Walt Whitman. *Fr.* Faces. APW; OHIP
Behold a Wonder Here! *Unknown.* ALV; OBSC; TrGrPo (Miracle, The.) BLV
"Behold another singer!" Criton said. "Song, to the Gods, Is Sweetest Sacrifice." Annie Fields. AA
Behold Fiammetta, shown in vision here. Fiammetta. Dante Gabriel Rossetti. VLEP
Behold, four Kings in majesty rever'd. The Playing Cards. Pope. *Fr.* The Rape of the Lock. ChTr
Behold from sluggish winter's arm. Primo Vere. Giosuè Carducci. AWP; JAWP; WBP
Behold, God is great, and we know him not. Job, Bible, *O.T.* ImOP
Behold great Neptunes risen from the deep. *At. to* Henry Hughes. SeCSL
Behold her Seven Hills loom white. Resurge San Francisco. Joaquin Miller. PAH
Behold her, single in the field. The Solitary Reaper [*or* The Reaper]. Wordsworth. AEV; AnEnPo; AnFE; AtBAP; ATP; AWP; BCEP; BEL; BLV; BoLiVe; BPN; BrBE; CBE; CBOV; CH; ChER; CoBE; CoEV; EG; EM-2; EmBrPo; EnL; EnLi-2; EnLit; EnLP; EnRP; EPN; EPP; ERP; EV-3; ExPo; FaBoCh; FaBoEn; FiP; GBV; GEPC; GN; GTBS; GTBS-D; GTBS-W; GTSE; GTSL; HBV; HiLiEn; HoPM; InP; InPo; JAWP; KN; LEAP; LiA; LiTB; LiTG; LiTL; LoBV; MaPo; MCCG; OAEP; OBEV; OBRV; OnPP; OTPC; OuHeWo; PCD; PIAE; PoE; PoEL-4; PoeMoYo; PoFS; PoRA; PYM; REAL; ReaPo; RG; RiBV; SeCeV; ShBV-3; TCEP; ThWaDe; TOP; TreF; TrGrPo; TwHP; TwP; TyEnPo; UnPo; UnS; WBP; WHA; WP
Behold Him now as He Comes! The Real Christ. Richard Watson Gilder. *Fr.* The Passing of Christ. ChIP; MaRV; OQP; QP-1
Behold him, priests, and though he stink of sweat. George Gascoigne. *Fr.* The Steel Glass. ReEn
Behold how from her lair the youthful llama. A Llyric of the Llama. Burges Johnson. LauV
Behold, how good and how pleasant it is for brethren to dwell in unity! To Dwell Together in Unity. Psalm CXXXIII, Bible, *O.T.* AWP; JAWP; OnPM; TrJP
Behold how yonder reed. The Reed. Abul Hajjaj. MooP
Behold, I gathered mine offenses. The Caravan. Hovhannes Blouz. CAW
Behold, I have a weapon. Othello's Remorse. Shakespeare. *Fr.* Othello, V, ii. LPS-3
Behold, I show you a mystery. The Mystery of Death. First Corinthians, Bible, *N.T.* BBV (1951 ed.)
Behold! in various throngs the scribbling crew. Byron. *Fr.* English Bards and Scotch Reviewers. EnRP
"Behold," in vision said. The New Year. Frederick Lucian Hosmer. GrCo-2
Behold it once again, the old familiar place. Home. Nikolai Nekrasov. BoR
Behold, Lord, Thou Didst Tear from Me. Antonio Machado, *tr. fr. Spanish by* Eleanor L. Turnbull. TeCS
Behold me waiting—waiting for the knife. Before. W. E. Henley. In Hospital, IV. BEL; BMEP; BPN; EnLi-2; MBP; MoBrPo; OuHeWo; PoVP; TCEP; ViP
Behold, My Cross Was Gone! Alice Mortenson. BePJ
Behold, My Servant. Isaiah, Bible, *O.T.* *See* Servant of God, The.
Behold, newcomer, liberty is dead. Ilya Ehrenburg, *tr. fr. Russian by* Y. Hornstein. BoRS
Behold, O Aspasia! I Send You Verses. Walter Savage Landor. *Fr.* Pericles and Aspasia. LoBV
Behold, O Man. Spenser. *Fr.* The Faerie Queene, II, 6. EIL
Behold, O noble Lady, O Mother piteous. Prayer to Santa Maria del Vade. Juan Ruiz, Archpriest of Hita. CAW
Behold, O world, the toiling man. Edwin Markham. *Fr.* The Toiler. PGD
Behold, of dreams the best will I tell. The Dream of the Rood. *Unknown.* CAW
Behold once more with serious labor here. To the Reader. Samuel Daniel. OBSC; SiCE
Behold our first great warrior of the sea. John Paul Jones. Richard Watson Gilder. PoRL
Behold Pelides with his yellow hair. Before a Statue of Achilles. George Santayana. HBV
Behold poor Clito's humble cot. Contentment. Leonidas of Tarentum. GrR
Behold, slow-settling o'er the lurid grove. The Storm. James Thomson. *Fr.* The Seasons: Summer. LoBV
Behold that vale, whose sides are cloth'd with wood. James Hurdis. *Fr.* A Landscape. EnSW
Behold the birds. God Provides. St. Matthew, Bible, *N.T.* BLRP
Behold the brand of beauty tossed! The Dancer. Edmund Waller. BLV; PoFS; TrGrPo
Behold the child. Pope. *Fr.* An Essay on Man, Epistle II. BeR
Behold the cot! where thrives th' industrious swain. George Crabbe. *Fr.* The Parish Register, I. OBRV
Behold, the days come, saith the Lord. A New Covenant. Jeremiah, Bible, *O.T.* GrCo-2
Behold the Deeds! H. C. Bunner. ALV; BOHV; HBV; InMe; LEAP; LHV; PA
Behold the duck. The Duck. Ogden Nash. MoShBr; WhC
Behold the fatal day arrive! Swift. *Fr.* Verses on the Death of Dr. Swift. ViBoPo
Behold, the grave of a wicked man. Why? Stephen Crane. The Black Riders, XXV. AA; LEAP
Behold, the horsemen are galloping along the Szechuan road. Horsemen on the Great Szechuan Road. Ts'en Ts'an. WhP
Behold the man alive in me. Ecce Homo. Witter Bynner. WGRP
Behold the mansion reared by Daedal Jack! The Domicile of John [*or* The Modern House That Jack Built]. *Unknown, sometimes at. to* Pope. InMe; LPS-3; PA
Behold the Master passeth by! William Walsham How. OIF
Behold the Meads. Guillaume de Poitiers, *tr. fr. French by* Harriet Waters Preston. AWP; OuHeWo
Behold the mighty dinosaur. The Dinosaur. Bert Leston Taylor. ImOP; LHV; PoMa
Behold! the mother bird. The Assumption. John Banister Tabb. ISi
Behold the portal: open wide it stands. The Garden Where There Is No Winter. Louis James Block. AA
Behold the purple tendrils of your vine. Christus Vitis ad Vinitorem Patrem. Richard Crashaw. Epigrammata Sacra, I, 61. LaP
Behold the ravens on the trees. Contentment. Benjamin Schlipf. BLRP
Behold the reed of scorn. Two Easter Lilies. John Banister Tabb. StJW
Behold the rocky wall. Two Streams. Oliver Wendell Holmes. *Fr.* The Professor at the Breakfast Table. PEOR
Behold, the rosy dawn. The Nymphs' Song. Michael Drayton. *Fr.* The Muses' Elysium. SeCL
Behold the Saviour of mankind. The Saviour. Samuel Wesley. BePJ
Behold the sea. The Sea. Emerson. *Fr.* Sea-Shore. LPS-2
"Behold, the sower went forth to sow." Parables from Nature. St. Mark, Bible, *N.T.* GrCo-1
Behold the tyrants that oppressed your land. Orestes Goes Mad. Aeschylus. *Fr.* Choephoroe. OxBG
Behold the vast cavalcades of horses. Sonnets, I. Feng Chih. *Fr.* Twenty-seven Sonnets. WhP
Behold the wicked little barb. The Question Mark. Persis Greely Anderson. PoMa; WhC
Behold the wonders of the mighty deep. The Sea. *Unknown.* NA
Behold the world's great wonder. Hymn to the Sun. George Darley. TIP
Behold the young, the rosy spring. Spring. Thomas Moore. LPS-2
Behold them all, dew-sprinkled, standing there! The Rose of Roses. Adam Oehlenschläger. BoDS
Behold This Dreamer. Elizabeth Bartlett. NePoAm-2
Behold, This Dreamer Cometh! Gustaf Fröding, *tr. fr. Swedish by* Charles W. Stork. AnSL
Behold this fleeting world, how all things fade. An Epitaph of the Death of Nicholas Grimald. Barnabe Googe. ReIE; SiCE; TriL; TuPP
Behold this needle, when the arctic stone. On the Needle of a Sundial. Francis Quarles. OBS; TrGrPo
Behold this ruin! 'Twas a skull. To a Skeleton. *Unknown.* BLPA; BMEP; LPS-3
Behold, thou art fair, my love. The Song of Solomon, Bible, *O.T.* LoPS; TrJP; WoL

Behold through the veil of distance a pleasing image. Jonathan. "Rachel." TrJP
"Behold Thy Mother and Thy Brother," *in mod. Eng.* William Heribert. TMEV
Behold, Tibullus lies/ Here burnt. Robert Herrick. *Fr.* To Live Merrily, and to Trust to Good Verses. PoD
Behold upon the swelling seas. A-Cruising We Will Go. *Unknown.* AmSS
Behold, we go up to Jerusalem again. Lent. Miriam LeFevre Crouse. ChIP
Behold, we have gathered together our battleships, near and afar. "Mene, Mene, Tekel, Upharsin." Madison Cawein. PAH
Behold, we stand at many doors and knock. The Untried Door. Edward Shillito. ChIP
Behold what furies still. Chorus. Samuel Daniel. *Fr.* Cleopatra. LoBV
Behold what homage to his idol paid. With Petrarch's Sonnets. Walter Savage Landor. InP
Behold where beauty walks with peace! A California Christmas. Joaquin Miller. OBAV
Behold where on the Aegean shore a city stands. Vision of Athens. Milton. *Fr.* Paradise Regained, IV. TOP
Behold with wondering eyes. The Rising Sun. Al-Haitham. MooP
Behold within our Hayden Planetarium. Ode to the Hayden Planetarium. Arthur Guiterman. ImOP
Behold, within the leafy shade. The Sparrow's Nest [*or* A Sister]. Wordsworth. BPN; EmBrPo; EnRP; ERP; WP
"Behold yon arching doors." A Blest Abode. Virgil. *Fr.* The Aeneid, VI. GrCo-1
Behold yon azure dome, the sapphire sky. Divine Providence. Sadi. PeP
Behold yon hill, how it is swell'd with pride. Describes the Place where Cynthia Is Sporting Herself. Philip Ayres. EnLoPo
Behold yon mountain's hoary height. To Thaliarchus [*or* Ode to Thaliarchus *or* Winter]. Horace. Odes, I, 9. AWP, JAWP; LiTW; PreP; RoL; WBP
Behold yon new-born infant, griev'd. The Ignorance of Man. James Merrick. OxBoCh
Behold you not this globe, this golden bowl. Thomas Dekker. *Fr.* Old Fortunatus. ViBoPo
Behold Your King! Frances Ridley Havergal. BePJ
Beholding God. Walt Whitman. *Fr.* Song of Myself, XLVIII. GrCo-1
Beholding youth and hope in mockery caught. The Sun's Shame, 1. Dante Gabriel Rossetti. The House of Life, XCII. PoVP; ViPo
Behramgur first discovered rhyme, men say. Goethe. *Fr.* West-Eastern Divan. BoFr
Being. Jacob Glatstein, *tr. fr. Yiddish by* Jacob Sloan. *Fr.* The Bratzlav Rabbi to His Scribe. LiTW
Being a Daughter. Mary Carolyn Davies. FAOV
Being a Gypsy. Barbara Young. BrR
(Being Gypsy.) TiPo (1952 ed.)
Being a man, ask not release from pain. Menander, *tr. fr. Greek by* John Addington Symonds. GrPo
Being a pleasant song made of a sailor. The Fair Maid's Choice or the Seaman's Renown. *Unknown.* SG
Being a woman, I am/ not more than man nor less. The Wife Speaks. Mary Stanley. AnNZ
Being Beauteous. Arthur Rimbaud, *tr. fr. French by* Angel Flores. AnFP
Being born the lowest of the low. Satirical Poems on Daimyos, IV. Issa. PoFr
Being but man, forbear to say. The Turn of a Dragonfly's Wing. Simonides. GrL; OxBG
Being but Men. Monk Gibbon. VOD (1935 ed.)
Being cleaves the moonlit air, A. Hans Christian Andersen. Sir Edmund Gosse. VA
Being Danish. Kaj Munk, *tr. fr. Danish by* Charles W. Stork. BoDS
Being Forsaken of His Friend He Complaineth. "E. S." EIL
("Why should I longer long to live.") SiCE
Being Gypsy. Barbara Young. *See* Being a Gypsy.
Being Her Friend. John Masefield. BMEP; BoFr; GTSL
Being homeward bound on the mighty deep. Lady Franklin's Lament, *vers.* I. *Unknown.* ShS
Being Importunate, at the Length He Obtaineth. Richard Edwards. TuPP
Being in thought of love I came upon. Ballata 7. Guido Cavalcanti, *tr. by* Ezra Pound. LyPI
Being in thought of love, I chanced to see. Ballata: He Reveals His Increasing Love for Mandetta. Guido Cavalcanti, *tr. by* Dante Gabriel Rossetti. AWP
Being myself [*or* myeself *or* my selfe] captived [*or* captyved] here in care. Amoretti, LXXIII. Spenser. BrBE; CoBE; LoBV; PeBoSo
Being now completely wet through to the skin. Wet Through. Hal Summers. HaMV
Being now three or four years more than sixty. The World's Wonders. Robinson Jeffers. NePA
Being on Duty All Night in the Palace and Dreaming of Hsien-yu Temple. Po Chü-i, *tr. fr. Chinese by* Arthur Waley. TrCh
Being one day at my window all alone. The Visions. Petrarch, *tr. by* Spenser. *Fr.* Sonnets to Laura: Songs. AWP; EnLi-1; JAWP; WBP
Being out of heart with government. An Appointment. W. B. Yeats. AnEnPo; PoFr
Being perplexed, I say. Guide Me. *Unknown.* PraP
Being Scorned, and Disdained, He Inveighs against His Lady. *Unknown.* SiCE
Being set, let's sport a while, my fair. Thomas Randolph. *Fr.* A Pastoral Courtship. ViBoPo
Being set on the idea. Atlantis. W. H. Auden. FaBoTw
Being Sick. Jimmy Garthwaite. BrR
Being slowly lifted up, thou long black arm. On Seeing a Piece of Our Artillery Brought into Action. Wilfred Owen. LiTM (1946 ed.)
Being so tired, it is hard to hide from you. A Man Walks in the Wind. Maurice Lesemann. AnAmPo; LA; LiTL
Being suspicious of great happiness. Being Unused to Joyous Consciousness. Delmore Schwartz. FiMAP
Being to Timelessness as It's to Time. E. E. Cummings. NePA
Being Underived. Dante, *tr. by* Longfellow. *Fr.* Divina Commedia: Paradiso. CAW
Being Unused to Joyous Consciousness. Delmore Schwartz. FiMAP
Being Visited by a Friend during Illness. Po Chü-i, *tr. fr. Chinese by* Arthur Waley. TrCh
Being Young. John Holmes. HiLiAm
Being your slave what should I do[e] but tend. Sonnets, LVII. Shakespeare. EG; ES; EtPaEn; EV-1; GTBS; GTBS-D; GTBS-W; GTSE; GTSL; LiA; LiTL; LoPo; LoPS; OBEV; PeBoSo; PoEL-2; ViBoPo; WoL
Bel m'es quan lo vens m'alena. Arnaut Daniel, *tr. fr. Provençal by* Harriet Waters Preston. AWP; JAWP; LiTW; WBP
(Canso: "Softly sighs the April air.") LyMA
Belagcholly Days. *Unknown.* BOHV; LPS-3; StaSt
Belated Sunflowers. Mikhail Alexandrovich Zenkevich, *tr. fr. Russian by* Avrahm Yarmolinsky. TrRV
Belated Violet, A. Oliver Herford. AA
Belden Hollow. Leslie Nelson Jennings. GoYe
Beleaguered Cities. F. L. Lucas. HaMV; POTE
Beleaguered City, The. Longfellow. CG; IAP; TriL; UnW
Belfast; High Street. Padraic Colum. NePoAm
Belfry, The. Laurence Binyon. CH
Belfry of Bruges, The. Longfellow. HBV
Sels.
Carillon. CoBA; IAP; LPS-2
"In the market place." EV-5
Belfry Pigeon. Nathaniel Parker Willis. LPS-2
Belgian Lullaby, A. Martha S. Gielow. BOL
Belgravians came down on the queen in her hold, The. The Rout of Belgravia. "Jon Duan." PA
Belief. Ruth Fitch Bartlett. InMe
Belief. Josephine Miles. FiMAP
Believe! And if, while standing under a shower. To My Children. Marion Strobel. NP
Believe and Take Heart. John Lancaster Spalding. AA; JKCP
"Believe in me," the Prophet cried. Infallibility. Thomas Stephens Collier. AA
Believe Me, Dearest Susan, *with music. Unknown.* SoAmSa
Believe Me, if All Those Endearing Young Charms. Thomas Moore. AnFE; BCEP; BEL; BLPA; EnLi-2 (1949 ed.); EnLit; EnRP; ERP; FaBoBe; FaFP; GTBS-W; HBV; InP; LiTB; LiTG; LiTL; LoPo; LPS-1; MCCG; NeHB; OBRV; OlF; OnYI; PIR; PoEL-4; PreP; SiTL; TreF; WBLP
Believe me, knot of gristle, I bleed like a tree. Give Way, Ye Gates. Theodore Roethke. FiMAP
Believe me, Love, this vagrant life. To Cordelia [*or* To His Wife]. Joseph Stansbury. BAV; BoCaPo (1948 ed.); CaP
Believe me not, friend, when in grief's unreason. Aleksey Konstantinovich Tolstoy, *tr. fr. Russian by* C. M. Bowra. BoR
Believe me, O Eteocles my son. Jocasta. Euripides. *Fr.* Phoenician Maidens. GrR
Believe me, sir, I'd like to spend whole days. Martial, *tr. fr. Latin by* J. V. Cunningham. Epigrams, II, 5. LaP
Believe Not. Isaac Leibush Peretz, *tr. fr. Yiddish by* Solomon Liptzin. TrJP
Believe Not Him. *Unknown.* SeCL
Believe not that the world is for naught, made. Believe Not. Isaac Leibush Peretz. TrJP
Believe thou, O my soul. Samuel Taylor Coleridge. *Fr.* Religious Musings. RO
Belinda. Pope. *Fr.* The Rape of the Lock, II. CBOV
Belinda in her dimity. A Song to Belinda. Theodosia Garrison. VOD

Belinda lived in a little white house. The Tale of Custard the Dragon. Ogden Nash. FaPON; GoBP; GoTP; PoRA; ShBV-1; TiPo (1959 ed.)
Belinda's Fan. Samuel Minturn Peck. PR
Belinda's Morning. Pope. *See* Toilet, The.
Belinda's Recovery from Sickness. William Broome. OBEV (1st ed.)
Belinda's Window. Margaret Widdemer. PEDC
Belisarius. Longfellow. BAV; PoEL-5
Beliza shade your shining eyes. *Unknown.* SeCSL
Bell, The. W. H. Davies. ChMo; CMP
Bell, The. James Rorty. BLP; PC
Bell, A. Clinton Scollard. AA; SDH; VOD
Bell across the Snow. Rofu Miki, *tr. fr. Japanese by* Takamichi Ninomiya *and* D. J. Enright. PoLJ
Bell at Evening, A. K'ung Hsiang Shu, *tr. fr. Chinese by* Henry H. Hart. PoHN
Bell-Birds. Henry C. Kendall. BoAu
Bell-Birds. Benjamin F. Musser. SaFP
Bell-Bottom Trousers. *Unknown.* AmSS
Bell Buoy, The. Kipling. BLP; PIR; POTT
Bell-Founder, The, *sel.* Denis Florence MacCarthy.
Labor Song. DD; LPS-2
Bell horses, bell horses,/ What time of day? A London Clock [*or* What Time of Day?]. Mother Goose. BoTP; OxNR; PCH; SiSoSe; TiPo
Bell in the convent tower hung, The. The Book of Hours of Sister Clotilde. Amy Lowell. APA
Bell in the Night, The. Hsi P'ei Lan, *tr. fr. Chinese by* Henry H. Hart. PoHN
Bell-Man. *See* Bellman.
Bell My Wife. *Unknown. See* Old Cloak, The.
Bell of Atri, The. Longfellow. *Fr.* Tales of a Wayside Inn: The Sicilian's Tale, Pt. II. MW
Bell of the Hermitage, The. *Unknown, tr. fr. Old Irish.* CAW
Bell-Ringers, The. James Rorty. MOAP
Bell-rope that gathers God at dawn, The. The Broken Tower. Hart Crane. AmP; CoBMV; GTBS-W; MeRV; MoAB; MoPo; MoVE; OnAP; OxBA; Po; TrGrPo (rev. ed.); TriL
Bell sound flies as though he had, A. Bim, Bam, Bum. Christian Morgenstern. AnGP
Bell Speech. Richard Wilbur. MoAB; MoVE
Bell strikes one, The: we take no note of time. Time [*or* The Lapse of Time]. Edward Young. *Fr.* Night Thoughts. BCEP; LPS-3
Bell struck one, and shook the silent tower, The. Fair Eleanor. Blake. DaM
Bell that tolls my syllables can tell, The. S.S. *City of Benares.* G. S. Fraser. NeBP; OnHM
Bell Tower. Léonie Adams. AnAmPo; LA; MAP; MoAB; MoAmPo
Belle, *with music. Unknown.* OuSiCo
Belle-de-nuit. Ignace Nau, *tr. fr. French by* Edna Worthley Underwood. PoNe
Belle Isis; Ballad of a Rose. Sacheverell Sitwell. Rosario d'Arabeschi; Poems and Rose Portraits, I. POTE (1959 ed.)
Belle of the Balkans, The. Newman Levy. ALV; FiBHP
Belle of the Ball-Room, The. Winthrop Mackworth Praed. Every-Day Characters, III. ALV; EnRP; EPP; ERP; HBV; InMe; ViBoPo, *2 sts.*
(Belle of the Ball, The.) BOHV; LPS-3
Bellerophon, *sel.* Euripides, *tr. fr. Greek by* J. A. Symonds.
There Are No Gods. OxBG
Bellerophon. George Meredith. EPP
Bellerophon. Pindar. *See* Taming of Pegasus, The.
Bellies bitter with drinking. Final Chorus. Archibald MacLeish. *Fr.* Panic. MAP; MoAmPo
Bell-Man, The. Robert Herrick. CH; HOAH; OBS; PCD
Bellman of Night, if I about shall go. Cock-Crow. Robert Herrick. MyFE
Bellman's Good-Morrow, The. *Unknown.* PoLi
Bellman's Song, The [*or* A]. *Unknown.* CenL; ElL; ElSeCe; SeCePo
Bellow of good Master Bull, The. Ballade un Peu Banale. A. J. M. Smith. SiTL
Bells, The. Guillaume Apollinaire, *tr. fr. French by* Alan Conder. TrFP
Bells, The. Antonio Fogazzaro, *tr. fr. Italian.* CAW
Bells, The, *parody.* "Judy." PA
Bells, The. Poe. AA; AmPo; AmPP (3d ed.); APW; BBV; CoBA; CoV; FaFP; GN; HBV; HiLiAm; IAP; LiTA; LPS-2; NeHB; NePA; OBAV; OHFP; OTPC; PCD; PCH, *st.* 1; PFE; PG (1945 ed.); PIAE; PIR; PoeMoYo; PYM; ShBV-1; TCAP; TreF; TVSH; WBLP
"Hear the sledges with the bells," *sel.* FaPON
Bells. Duncan Campbell Scott. CaP; OCL
Bells, The. *Unknown.* BOHV; FiBHP
Bells, The. William Young. *Fr.* Wishmakers' Town. AA
Bells across the Snow. Frances Ridley Havergal. COAH
Bells and sighs, bells slowly tolling. Spring in the Convent. Sergei Gorodetsky. BoRS
Bells are tolling, The. Tolling Bells. Lady Kasa. OnPM
Bells assault the maiden air, The. Ou Phrontis. Charles Causley. AtBAP; NePoEA; PoN
Bells at Midnight, The. Thomas Bailey Aldrich. PAH
Bells, back from Rome but yestermorn, break forth. Easter. Paul Verlaine. TrFP
Bell's Dream, *abr.* Frederic Edward Weatherly. OTPC
Bells for John Whiteside's [Whitesides', *wr.*] Daughter. John Crowe Ransom. AmP; AmPP; AnFE; ChMo; CoAnAm; CoBMV; CrMA; GTBS-D; InP; InPo; LiTA; LiTM (rev. ed.); LS; MAP; MoAB; MoAmPo; MOAP; MoVE; NePA; NP; OxBA; ReMP; TwAmPo; UnPo (3d ed.)
Bells have wide mouths and tongues, but are too weak. Upon a Ring of Bells. Bunyan. CH
Bells in the Country. Robert Nathan. BrR; HBMV; OTPC (1946 ed.); PCH; TSW
Bells in the Rain. Elinor Wylie. PC; YT
Bells in this steeple drip with sound when ushering a bride. Reflection for a Sunday Morning. Leo Kennedy. OCL
Bells of Cadiz clashed for them, The. Spanish Ledges. Crosbie Garstin. ReTS
Bells of Christmas, The. Clinton Scollard. SDH
Bells of Heaven, The. Ralph Hodgson. BoTP; ChMo; CMP; GTBS-W; LiTM; MBP; MoAB; MoBrPo; OBEV (new ed.); OtMeF; PC; QS; ShBV-1; SiSoSe; SP; TwCV; UTS; WP
Bells of London, The. *Unknown.* BoTP; BrR; HBV; HBVY; PCH; PoRA; SiTL; WP
("Gay go up and gay go down.") OTPC; OxNR; PPL
(London Bells.) ChTr; LiTB; LiTG; OxBoLi
Bells of Lynn, The. Longfellow. AA
Bells of Mount Vernon are ringing to-day, The. Washington's Birthday. Hezekiah Butterworth. PTA-2
Bells of New Year. Arthur Gordon Field. PGD
Bells of Oria, The. The Bells. Antonio Fogazzaro. CAW
Bells of Osenèy, The. Chanson of the Bells of Osenèy. Cale Young Rice. AnFE; APA; CoAnAm; HBV; SBMV
Bells of Ostend, The. William Lisle Bowles. *See* Sonnet: At Ostend, July 22, 1787.
Bells of Peace, The. Aileen Fisher. SiSoSe
Bells of Ste. Anne des Monts, The. Leo Cox. CaP
Bells of San Blas, The. Longfellow. AmP; AmPP (3d ed.); IAP; OxBA
Bells of San Gabriel, The. Charles Warren Stoddard. CAW; JKCP
Bells of Shandon, The. Francis Sylvester Mahony. ACP; AnIV; BCEP; CAW; CH; ChTr; GoBC; HBV; IrPN; LPS-2; OBEV; OBRV; OBVV; TIP; TreFS; UnPo
(Shandon Bells, The.) EV-4; GTBS; OnYI; ShBV-2; VA
Bells of Sunday rang us down, The. Song. John Ciardi. WaP
Bells of Youth, The. "Fiona Macleod." BoTP; ReTS
Bells of Yule. Tennyson. *See* In Memoriam, A. H. H.: "Time draws near the birth of Christ, The."
Bells ring clear as bugle note, The. Christmas Morning. Joaquin Miller. MaRV
Bells their Christmas message send o'er earth, The. Perpetual Christmas. Arthur Gordon Field. PGD
Bellville, *sel.* Wetenhall Wilkes.
Pigeon House, A. BeR
Belonging to Summer. Mildred D. Shacklett. GFA
Belov'd of all to whom that Muse is dear. To Joseph Joachim. Robert Bridges. TriL
Belovèd. Elizabeth Barrett Browning. *See* Belovèd, my Belovèd . . .
Beloved, The. Hafiz, *tr. fr. Persian by* R. A. Nicholson. PeP
Beloved, The. May Probyn. GoBC
Beloved, The. Sappho, *tr. fr. Greek by* F. L. Lucas. GrPE
Beloved, The. Theognis, *tr. fr. Greek by* F. L. Lucas. GrPE
Beloved, The. Katharine Tynan. HBV
Beloved! amid the earnest woes. To F——. Poe. IAP
Beloved Brothers in our Lord Jesus Christ. Sermon to the Fishes. Joaquin Antonio Peñalosa. SaFP
Beloved, do you pity not my doleful case. Lament of the Mangaire Sugach. Andrew Magrath. OnYI; TIP
Belovèd friends! More glorious times than ours. To My Friends. Schiller. AWP; LiTW
Belovèd, from the Hour That You Were Born. Corinne Roosevelt Robinson. HBMV
Beloved, gaze in thine own heart. The Two Trees. W. B. Yeats. MaPo; POTE; TIP
Beloved, glorious, blest. Synesius, *tr. fr. Greek by* L. P. Chamberlayne. GrPo
Belovèd, It Is Morn. Emily Henrietta Hickey. CAW; GoBC; JKCP; OnYI; VA
(Song: "Belovèd, it is morn.") OBVV
Beloved land is yon land in the east, A. Deirdre's Farewell to Scotland. *Unknown.* OnYI
Beloved, let our love be quite. Let Our Love Be. Samuel Hoffenstein. PR

Beloved, let us love: love is of God. Love Is of God. Horatius Bonar. MaRV
Beloved, Let Us Once More Praise the Rain. Conrad Aiken. Preludes to Attitude, VIII. LiTA; TwAmPo
Beloved, may your sleep be sound. Lullaby. W. B. Yeats. EnLP; FaBoTw; OBMV; POTE
Belovèd, my Belovèd, when I think. Sonnets from the Portuguese, XX. Elizabeth Barrett Browning. AV; BPN; CoBE; EmBrPo; EPP; MaRV; OAEP; TOP; VA; ViP; ViPo
Belovèd one, for thy sweet sake. The Exile's Song. *Unknown.* ArmLP
Beloved person must I think, The. Ki no Akimine. *Fr.* Kokin Shu. AWP
Beloved, the black swans of my eyes. Birds. Hildegarde Flanner. NP
Beloved, there is nothing I can say. A Cold Wind Blows. Zoe Kincaid Brockman. NoCaPo
Beloved, thou hast bought me many flowers. Sonnets from the Portuguese, XLIV. Elizabeth Barrett Browning. BPN; OAEP; ViP; ViPo
Belovèd, till the day break. Envoi. Josephine Preston Peabody. SBMV
Beloved to me is that land to the East. Deirdre Looks Back at Scotland. *Unknown.* SiB
Beloved to the Spouse, The. William Baldwin. *See* Christ to His Spouse.
Beloved Vagabond, The. W. G. Tinckom-Fernandez. NLK
Beloved, you may be as all men say. The Illusion of Love. Sarojini Naidu. MM
Below, Ferndale squats in a gash of cwm. Rhondda. Meurig Walters. MoWP
Below lies one whose name was traced in sand. My Epitaph. David Gray. MaRV; OBVV; VA
Below me the Caucasus. Lone on the height. The Caucasus. Pushkin. BoRS
Below me trees unnumber'd rise. John Dyer. *Fr.* Grongar Hill. FaBoEn
Below my pretty love I lie. Song of the Witless Boy. Hugh McCrae. MM
Below my watchtower window, over the scarecrow-sticked. The Coastguardsman in the Fog. James Schevill. FiMAP
Below the ancient plane. Sad Love. Tavallali. PeP
Below the City of P'ing. Li Ho, *tr. fr. Chinese by* Ho Chih-yuan. WhP
Below the dawn-flushed sky, where the green billow lies. A Nereid. Pushkin. TrRV
Below the down the stranded town. A Cinque Port. John Davidson. PoeT; ReTS; TVSH
Below the hall/ The pine-trees grow. The Pine-Trees in the Courtyard. Po Chü-i. TrCh
Below the Heights. Walter Herries Pollock. VA
Below the Old House. William Bell Scott. EBSV
Below, the river scrambled like a goat. God's Little Mountain. Geoffrey Hill. NePoEA
Below the surface of the earth a face appearing. A Sick Face below the Surface of the Earth. Sakutaro Hagiwara. PoLJ
Below the thunders of the upper deep. The Kraken. Tennyson. GTBS-D; NBE; OBRV; Po; PoEL-5; PoVP; ViPP; VLEP
Below the Waggoner's feet. Aratus. *Fr.* Phaenomena. GrPo
Below this music, grave and slow. Receive, Beloved. Virginia Earle. JKCP (1955 ed.)
Belphegor; or, The Marriage of the Devil, *sel.* John Wilson. Were I to Take Wife. SeCL
Belshazzar's Feast. Daniel, V: 1-31, Bible, *O.T.* MuP, *abr.*; TreF
Belvoir Castle. George Crabbe. CaAE
Ben-Arabie was the Camel. Exile. Virna Sheard. PeCV
Ben Backstay. *Unknown.* AmSS
Ben Battle was a soldier bold. Faithless Nelly [*or* Nellie] Gray. Thomas Hood. BOHV; EnRP; ERP; HBV; InMe; InP; LPS-3; NA; PIR; ShBV-2; SiTL; SoV; TOP; TreF; TSW
Ben Bluff. Thomas Hood. BOHV
Ben Bolt. Thomas Dunn English. AA; FaBoBe; FaFP; HBV; LEAP; OBAV; TreF
(Oh! Don't You Remember Sweet Alice.) OlF
Ben Dorain. Duncan Ban MacIntyre. *See* Praise of Ben Dorain, The.
Ben Franklin munched a loaf of bread while walking down the street. Benjamin Franklin. Rosemary Benét *and* Stephen Vincent Benét. FaPON; TiPo
Ben Franklin's Head (1728). Mark Antony De Wolfe Howe. WaKn
Ben-Hur, *sel.* Lew Wallace.
Song: "Wake not, but hear me, love!" AA
Ben Jonson. Swinburne. Sonnets on English Dramatic Poets (1590-1650), III. BEL; EmBrPo; PeBoSo; PoVP; PtP; VLEP
Ben Jonson Entertains a Man from Stratford. E. A. Robinson. AmPP; APA; ATP; CoAnAm; IAP; MAP; MAPA; MoAB; MoAmPo; MOAP; MoPo; TwAmPo
"You are a friend then, as I make it out," *sel.* InP
Ben Jonson's Commonplace Book. Lucius Cary. LPS-3
Ben Jonson's [*or* Johnsons] Sociable Rules for the Apollo. Ben Jonson, *tr. fr. Latin by* Alexander Brome. SeCV-1; TuPP
Ben Karshook's Wisdom. Robert Browning. BPN; PoVP
Ben Milam. William H. Wharton. PAH
Benares. Jorge Luis Borges, *tr. fr. Spanish by* H. R. Hays. TwSpPo
Bench, the sewermouth, the hydrant placed, The. Northern Boulevard. Edwin Denby. CrMA
Bench-legged Fyce, The. Eugene Field. AlBD
Benches are broken, the grassplots brown and bare, The. South End. Conrad Aiken. MoVE; OxBA
Bend as the Bow Bends. Conrad Aiken. ChMo
Bend back thy bow, O Archer, till the string. The Archer. A. J. M. Smith. PeCV
Bend low again, night of summer stars. Summer Stars. Carl Sandburg. YeAr
Bend low, O dusky night. To-Night. Louise Chandler Moulton. AA; OBAV
Bend now thy body to the common weight. The Breaking. Margaret Steele Anderson. HBV; SBMV
Bend of the river brings into view two triumphal arches, A. Arriving at Hsün-yang, 1. Po Chü-i. TrCh
Bend willow, willow bend down deep. Willow Bend and Weep. Herbert Clark Johnson. PoNe
Bendemeer. Thomas Moore. *See* By Bendemeer's Stream.
Bending above the spicy woods which blaze. October. Helen Hunt Jackson. TCAP
Bending over/ I stain the sections of a brain. Hospital Verses. Mokichi Saito. PoP
Bending sails shall whiten on the sea, The. The Ships. Theodore Maynard. EtS
Beneath a churchyard yew. O Sweet Anne Page [*or* Slender's Ghost]. William Shenstone. EiPP; SeCePo
Beneath a goblin yew-tree's shade. Immortals in Exile. Arthur Davison Ficke. PFY
Beneath a holm repaired two jolly swains. Corydon and Thyrsis. Virgil. Eclogues, VII. AWP
Beneath a myrtle shade. Song of the Zambra Dance [*or* the Zambra Dance]. Dryden. *Fr.* The Conquest of Granada. AtBAP; CEP; OAEP; PoEL-3; SeCV-2
Beneath a palm-tree by a clear cool spring. A Lesson of Mercy. George Murray. VA
Beneath a shaggy pine. The Devil's Swing. "Feodor Sologub." TrRV
Beneath a shivering canopy reclined. Noontide. John Leyden. LPS-2
Beneath a venerable yew. The Ravens, the Sexton, and the Earthworm. John Gay. NBE
Beneath an Indian palm a girl. The Palm-Tree and the Pine. Richard Monckton Milnes. EV-5; HBV
Beneath blue skies of her own country. On the Death of Amalia Riznich. Pushkin. BoR
Beneath Her Native Skies. Pushkin, *tr. fr. Russian by* Babette Deutsch. TrRV
(On the Death of Amalia Riznich, *tr. by* C. M. Bowra.) BoR
Beneath my palm trees, by the river side. Procession of Bacchus. Keats. *Fr.* Endymion, IV. TwCrTr; ViBoPo
Beneath my window in a city street. The Steam Shovel. Eunice Tietjens. NP; PoeMoYo
Beneath our consecrated elm. Washington [*or* New-come Chief]. James Russell Lowell. *Fr.* Under the Old Elm. GA; LPS-3; MC
Beneath our feet and o'er our head. The Holy Field. Henry Hart Milman. OxBoCh
Beneath our feet, the shuddering bogs. On Yes Tor. Sir Edmund Gosse. AlDL; CH
Beneath Pont Mirabeau flows the Seine. Pont Mirabeau. Guillaume Apollinaire. MiFP
Beneath Such Rains. James E. Warren, Jr. ChIP
Beneath the azure of her native skies she dropped. Beneath Her Native Skies. Pushkin. TrRV
Beneath the barren artifice of red. City Girl. Maxwell Bodenheim. HBMV
Beneath the blistering tropical sun. Wheeler's Brigade at Santiago. Wallace Rice. MC
Beneath the bloodstained lintel I with my children stand. The Mother's Trust. *Unknown.* PraP
Beneath the branch of the green may. Medieval Norman Songs, XIII. *Unknown, tr. by* John Addington Symonds. AWP; JAWP; WBP
Beneath the branches of the olive yard. Etruscan Tombs. Agnes Mary Frances Robinson. WIIA
Beneath the brown, lustrous haze. Reflection. Margaret Allonby. BoSA
Beneath the burning brazen sky. The Ute Lover. Hamlin Garland. AA; OBAV; PFY
Beneath the Cross. Elizabeth Cecilia Clephane. MaRV
("Beneath the cross of Jesus.") OlF

Beneath the curious gaze of all the dead. The Gown. Mary Carolyn Davies. HBMV
Beneath the Cypress Shade. Thomas Love Peacock. *See* Grave of Love, The.
Beneath the deep my broken timbers lie. The Spirit of the *Bluenose.* Claire Harris MacIntosh. CaP
Beneath the evening gold. Golden. Francisco A. de Icaza. AnMP
Beneath the Flag. *Unknown.* FOAH; HH
Beneath the Forms of Outward Rite. James A. Blaisdell. MaRV
Beneath the fourteen pointed arches. Cataclysm. N. H. Brettell. BoSA
Beneath the golden cope of dawn. The Shepherd of Meriador. Wilfred Rowland Childe. HBMV
Beneath the hot midsummer sun. His Mother's Songs. *Unknown.* PTA-2
Beneath the loveliest dream there coils a fear. Theodore Watts-Dunton. *Fr.* The Coming of Love. BMEP; LEAP
Beneath the low-hung night cloud. The *Three Bells* [of Glasgow]. Whittier. EtS; PECK
Beneath the Memnonian shadows of Memphis, it rose from the slime. The Reed. Henry Bernard Carpenter. AA
Beneath the midnight moon of May. The Night Watch. William Winter. AA
Beneath the ocean's sapphire lid. The Gardens of the Sea. George Sterling. EtS
Beneath the orange tree. Lola. Federico García Lorca. CoSP
Beneath the poplars o'er the sacred pool. The Suppliant. Sir Edmund Gosse. TCPD
Beneath the poplar's shadow lay me. Song. Nathaniel Lee. *Fr.* Sophonisba; or, Hannibal's Overthrow. BeR
Beneath the sagging roof. Hugh Selwyn Mauberley, X. Ezra Pound. CoBMV; CoV; LiTA; LiTM (rev. ed.); MoPo
Beneath the Sanctuary Lamp. Elenita Thompson Kirkpatrick. PraNü
Beneath the sand-storm John the Pilgrim prays. John the Pilgrim. Theodore Watts-Dunton. MaRV
Beneath the shade of an olive tree the young infanta fair. The Lovely Infanta. *Unknown.* AnSpL-1
Beneath the shaded calm of his cottage now. Evening Fantasy. Friedrich Hölderlin. LiTW
Beneath the shadow of dawn's aërial cope. Hope and Fear. Swinburne BPN; EmBrPo; EPP; EV-5; FaBoBe; HBV; PoVP; VA
Beneath the Shadow of the Cross. Samuel Longfellow. BePJ
Beneath the silent chambers of the earth. Hell. Abraham Cowley. *Fr.* Davideis, I. OxBoCh; SeEP
Beneath the softly falling snow. The Changing Road. Katharine Lee Bates. HBV
Beneath the stars a man alone. Nocturne. Georg Trakl. TwGV
Beneath the train the miles are folded by. El Poniente. Ruth Comfort Mitchell. PoeMoYo; VOD
Beneath the warrior's helm, behold. On an Intaglio Head of Minerva. Thomas Bailey Aldrich. HBV; InMe; LPS-3; PR
Beneath the Wattle Boughs. Frances Gill. VA
Beneath these alien stars. Pioneer Woman. Vesta Pierce Crawford. PoOW
Beneath these fruit-tree boughs that shed. The Green Linnet. Wordsworth. AEV; AtBAP; BPN; EmBrPo; EnRP; EPN; ERP; EV-3; GEPC; GTBS; GTBS-D; GTBS-W; GTSE; GTSL; HBV; OTPC
Beneath these poppies buried deep. Epitaph on Robert Southey [*or* a Well-known Poet]. Thomas Moore. InMe; SiTL
Beneath these sun-warm'd pines among the heather. A South Coast Idyll. Rosamund Marriott Watson. OBVV
Beneath this morning's glazed and dusty sun. The Shadow Line. George S. Greene. CAG
Beneath this narrow jostling street. Fleet Street. Arthur Adams. BoAu
Beneath this silent stone is laid. Epitaph on a Talkative Old Maid. Benjamin Franklin. WhC
Beneath this starry arch On, On, Forever. Harriet Martineau. VA
Beneath this stone, a lump of clay. Epitaphs. *Unknown.* SiTL
Beneath this stone lies one good man; and when. An Epitaph. W. H. Davies. ChMP
Beneath this stone our baby lies. *Unknown.* WhC
Beneath this stony roof reclined. Retirement [*or* Inscription in a Hermitage]. Thomas Warton, the Younger. HBV; LPS-2; SN
Beneath this turf by pious love interred. Epitaph on a Pet Mocking Bird. William Gaston. NoCaPo
Beneath this turfy mound. Epitaph on a Pet Dog. Joachim du Bellay. FoS
Beneath this world of stars and flowers. The Idea. Agnes Mary Frances Robinson. UnW
Beneath those buttressed walls with lichens grey. Below the Old House. William Bell Scott. EBSV
Beneath those rugged elms, that yew-tree's shade. Thomas Gray. *Fr.* Elegy Written in a Country Churchyard. BHV
Beneath thy spell, O radiant summer sea. The Sea's Spell. Susan Marr Spalding. AA; EtS
Beneath Thy Wing. Hayyim Nahman Bialik, *tr. fr. Hebrew by* Helena Frank. TrJP
Beneath Time's roaring cannon. When the Mississippi Flowed in Indiana. Vachel Lindsay. Three Poems about Mark Twain, II. ChMo; CMP
Beneath yon birch with silver bark. The Ballad of the Dark Ladie. Samuel Taylor Coleridge. BPN; EmBrPo; EnRP; ERP; PreP
Beneath yon ruined abbey's moss-grown piles. The Solemn Noon of Night. Thomas Warton, the Younger. *Fr.* The Pleasures of Melancholy. OBEC; SeCePo
Beneathe an ancient oake one daye. A Christmas Legend. Oliver Herford. PoMS
Benedicite. Anna Callender Brackett. AA
Benedicite. Whittier. IAP; LPS-1; MOAP
Benedicite, What Dremid I This Night? *Unknown.* *See* Dream, A ("Benedicite, what dreamed I this night?").
Benedict Brosse. S. Frances Harrison. *Fr.* Down the River. CPG
Benedictine Garden, A. Alice Brown. HBV
Benedictine Ultima, The. *Unknown, tr. fr. Latin.* CAW
Benedictio Domini. Ernest Dowson. CAW; JKCP; POTT
Benediction. Baudelaire, *tr. fr. French by* Stephen Stepanchev. AnFP
Benediction. Numbers, VI: 24–26, Bible, *O.T.* TrGrPo (Blessing of the Priests.) TrJP
Benediction. Valery Yakovlevich Bryusov, *tr. fr. Russian.* BoR, *tr. by* C. M. Bowra; TrRV, *tr. by* Babette Deutsch
Benediction. Donald Jeffrey Hayes. PoNe
Benediction. Georgia Douglas Johnson. GoSl
Benediction. Stephen Phillips. *Fr.* Herod. MaRV
Benediction. Mark Turbyfill. NP; TBM
Benedictus. St. Luke, I: 68–79, Bible, *N.T.* MaRV
Benefactor, The. Ibn Sara, *tr. fr. Arabic by* A. J. Arberry. MooP
Beneficence. Sadi, *tr. fr. Persian by* Stephen Weston. PeP
Benevolence. Mark Akenside. *Fr.* Against Suspicion. OBEC
Benevolence. Siraj, *tr. fr. Arabic by* A. J. Arberry. MooP
Benjamin. Ogden Nash. NePA; SiTL
Benjamin Franklin [1706–1790]. Rosemary Benét *and* Stephen Vincent Benét. FaPON; TiPo
Benjamin Franklin. Florence Earle Coates. GA
Benjamin Franklin Hazard. Edgar Lee Masters. *Fr.* The New Spoon River. TCAP
Benjamin Pantier. Edgar Lee Masters. *Fr.* Spoon River Anthology. AlBD
Benjamin's Lamentations, The. *Unknown.* SG
Bennie's kisses left me cold. Georgie Porgie. Franklin P. Adams. HBMV
Bennington. W. H. Babcock. PAH
Benny Havens, Oh! —— O'Brien. ABF
Bent and heavy with rain. Roadside near Moscow. R. A. D. Ford. PeCV; TwCaPo
Bent double, like old beggars under sacks. Dulce et Decorum Est. Wilfred Owen. AnFE; CoBMV; FaBoTw; InP; InvP; LiTB; LiTM (rev. ed.); MBP; MoAB; MoBrPo; MoPW; OAEP (2d ed.); ShBV-3; TwCV; WaP
Bent Sae Brown. The. *Unknown.* ESPB
Benvenuto Cellini. Carl Snoilsky, *tr. fr. Swedish by* Charles W. Stork. AnSL
Benvenuto's Valentine. Elinor Wylie. AV
Beowulf. *Unknown, tr. fr. Anglo-Saxon.* BEL (*sl. abr., tr. by* Francis B. Gummere); EM-1 (*abr., tr. by* J. Duncan Spaeth); EnL (*pr. tr. by* Chauncey B. Tinker); EnLi-1 (*mod. vers., sl. abr., by* J. Duncan Spaeth); EnLit (*pr. tr. by* Albert C. Baugh); OuHeWo (Prologue *and* I-XXXI, *pr. tr. by* Chauncey B. Tinker); TCEP (*abr., tr. by* Benjamin Thorpe); TOP (*pr. tr. by* Chauncey B. Tinker); ViBoPo (Prologue, *tr. by* C. K. Scott-Moncrieff)
Sels.
Anglian Tradition, The, *tr. by* Francis B. Gummere. PaOS
Beowulf and Wiglaf Slay the Dragon, *tr. by* Charles W. Kennedy. AnOE
Beowulf's Death, *tr. by* Charles W. Kennedy. AnOE
Beowulf's Fight in the Enchanted Mere, *tr. by* C. K. Scott-Moncrieff. KN
Death-going of Scyld, *tr. by* Francis B. Gummere. BCEP
Death of Grendel's Mother, The, *tr. and ad. by* Chauncey B. Tinker. EPP
Fire-Dragon and the Treasure, The, *tr. by* Charles W. Kennedy. AnOE
Funeral Pyre, The, *tr. by* Charles W. Kennedy. AnOE
Haunt of Grendel, The. *tr. by* Francis B. Gummere. BCEP
Lay of Finn, The, *tr. by* Charles W. Kennedy. AnOE

Slaying of Grendel, The, *tr. by* Chauncey B. Tinker. EPP (Slaughter of Grendel by Beowulf, The, *tr. by* Charles W. Kennedy.) LiTW
Tale of Sigemund, The, *tr. by* Charles W. Kennedy. AnOE
Beowulf. Richard Wilbur. CrMA
Beowulf and Wiglaf Slay the Dragon. *Unknown, tr. fr. Anglo-Saxon by* Charles W. Kennedy. *Fr.* Beowulf. AnOE
Beowulf's Death. *Unknown, tr. fr. Anglo-Saxon by* Charles W. Kennedy. *Fr.* Beowulf. AnOE
Beppo. Byron. BEL
Italy, *sel.* OBRV; SeCePo
Bequest of His Heart, A. Alexander Scott. *See* Hence, Hairt.
Bequest to My Daughters. Lawrence Lee. FAOV
Berceuse Ariettes, *sel.* Alfred Kreymborg.
"Our window is stained." PG (1955 ed.)
Berceuse for Birds. Joseph Auslander. BLA
Bereaved. Emily Dickinson. CoBA
Bereaved. James Whitcomb Riley. AA; BAP; LBAP; LEAP; MaRV; OBAV
Bereaved Maid, The. *Unknown. See* Falcon, The.
Bereaved of all, I went abroad. Trying to Forget. Emily Dickinson. MAPA; TwAmPo
Bereaved Swan, The. Stevie Smith. FaBoTw
Bereavement. Euripides, *tr. fr. Greek by* C. M. Bowra. *Fr.* Alcestis. OxBG
Bereavement of the Fields. Wilfred Campbell. CaP; OCL
Bereft. Robert Frost. AnFE; AtBAP; CoAnAm; LiTM; MAP; MoAB; MoAmPo; OxBA; TwAmPo
Berg, The. Herman Melville. AmP; AtBAP; LiTA; PoEL-5; PoFS
Berkshire Holiday, A. Clifford Bax. TCPD
Berkshires in April. Clement Wood. SBMV; VOD
Bermuda Suite. Winfield Townley Scott. MiAP
"Flared down from broken cloud the calipered light," V. FiMAP
Bermudas. Andrew Marvell. AlDL; AtBAP; AWP; BrBE; CaAE; CEP; CH; ChTr; CoBE; CoEV; ElSeCe; EnL; EPS; ExPo; FaBoCh; FaBoEn; GN; HBV; InPo; KN; LoBV; LoGBV; MePo; OAEP; OBEV; OBS; PAH; PoE; PoFS; ReEn; RiBV; SeCeV; SeCL; SeEP; TriL; TwHP; TyEnPo; ViBoPo
(In Exile.) LH
(Song of the Emigrants.) OxBoCh
(Song of the Emigrants in Bermuda.) EV-2; GTBS; GTBS-D; GTBS-W; GTSE; GTSL; LPS-2; OTPC (1923 ed.); ShBV-3
Bernál Díaz's Preface to His Book. Archibald MacLeish. *Fr.* Conquistador. AmPP (3d ed.)
"We saw that city on the inland sea," *sel.* AtBAP
Bernard reads late, alone; and twilight falls. The Vision of St. Bernard. M. Whitcomb Hess. ISi
Bernardo del Carpio. Felicia Dorothea Hemans. PTA-2
Bernardo's March to Roncesvalles. *Unknown, tr. fr. Spanish by* Longfellow. AnSpL-1
Berries. Walter de la Mare. AtBAP; BoChLi; MBP; MoBrPo; OnSP; RG; StaSt; TiPo
Berrying. Emerson. AtBAP
Bert Kessler. Edgar Lee Masters. *Fr.* Spoon River Anthology. AnFE; APA; CoAnAM
Bertrand and Raton—a monkey and a cat. The Monkey and the Cat. La Fontaine. CIV
Bertrand Hume. Edgar Lee Masters. *Fr.* The New Spoon River. LEAP
Beset Wife, The. Robert Farren. OxBI
Beset with doubts, in agony. The Oracle. Walther von der Vogelweide. LyMA
Beshrew that heart that makes my heart to groan. Sonnets, CXXXIII. Shakespeare. InvP; PeBoSo; ReIE
Beside a Balance Wheel. MacKnight Black. NP
Beside a chapel I'd a room looked down. Dread. J. M. Synge. MBP; MoBrPo
Beside a green meadow a stream used to flow. The Cow and the Ass. Jane Taylor. BoTP; OTPC (1923 ed.)
Beside a hill there is a still. Good Ol' Mountain Dew. *Unknown.* ABF
Beside a massive gateway built up in years gone by. Waiting by the Gate. Bryant. TCAP
Beside a primrose 'broider'd rill. Phyllis Lee. Oliver Herford. BOHV
Beside a runnel build my shed. After Reading in a Letter Proposals for Building a Cottage. John Clare. EV-4; OBRV
Beside a Spring. Johan Ludvig Runeberg, *tr. fr. Swedish by* Charles W. Stork. AnSL
Beside a Stream. Hamda, *tr. fr. Arabic by* A. J. Arberry. MooP
Beside dim wharves, the battered ships are dreaming. Old Ships. Louis Ginsberg. HBMV
Beside he was a shrewd philosopher. Hudibras the Sectarian. Samuel Butler. *Fr.* Hudibras. SeCePo
Beside her ashen heath she sate her down. The Fortunate One. Harriet Monroe. AA
Beside her oven of clay and stone she stands. The Oven. Frank Oliver Call. CPG; OCL
Beside his heavy-shouldered team. Bullocky. Judith Wright. BoAV; MoAuPo; NeLNL; SeCePo
Beside his wife at Passover in spring. Passover Eve. Fania Kruger. GoYe; QS
Beside Lilia Dead. Sister Mary Catherine. JKCP (1955 ed.)
Beside me,—in the car,—she sat. Natura Naturans. Arthur Hugh Clough. ViP
Beside me there is resting. The Dead Bee. Nathalia Crane. MAP; MoAmPo (1942 ed.)
Beside that lake whose wave is hushed to hear. The Conquistador. *Unknown.* DDA
Beside that tent and under guard. Geronimo. Ernest McGaffey. AA; PAH
Beside the Bed. Charlotte Mew. AnEnPo; BLV; MBP; MoAB; MoBrPo; NeMA; NP; TrGrPo
Beside the bed where parting life was laid. The Village Preacher. Goldsmith. *Fr.* The Deserted Village. TrGrPo
Beside the Blackwater. Norreys Jephson O'Conor. HBMV
Beside the crater and the tattered palm. The Dead in Melanesia. Randall Jarrell. MiAP
Beside the dead I knelt for prayer. Christus Consolator. Rossiter W. Raymond. HBV; MaRV; OQP; QP-1
Beside the empty sepulcher she lingered. Mary. "W. B." ChIP; PSO
Beside the grey sea-shingle, here at the cross-roads' meeting. The Spring of Hermes. Anyte. GrPE; GrR
Beside the haunted lake where nereids seem. Mademoiselle Richarde. Edith Sitwell. MoVE
Beside the Lake. Wang Wei, *tr. fr. Chinese.* WhP
Beside the landsman knelt a dame. The Manor Lord. George Houghton. AA
Beside the lone river. Little Big Horn. Ernest McGaffey. GA; PAH
Beside the Mead of Memories. The Dead Quire. Thomas Hardy. OAEP; POTT
Beside the Moldau's rushing stream. The Beleaguered City. Longfellow. CG; IAP
Beside the mountain roads, the men. Blue Smoke. Frances Frost. SiSoSe
Beside the old hall-fire—upon my nurse's knee. Fairy Days. Thackeray. GoTP; OTPC (1946 ed.)
Beside the pale water. The Pool. Fritz S. Burnell. BoAu
Beside the pleasant Mill of Trompington. Wordsworth. *Fr.* The Prelude. OBRV
Beside the pounding cataracts. The City of the End of Things. Archibald Lampman. BoCaPo; VA
Beside the rail, despite the gale. The Missing Link. Oliver Herford. CenHV
Beside the Railway Track. *Unknown.* PEOR
Beside the reckless music of a line of waterfalls. A Dynasty. Witter Bynner. PtOT
Beside the river stands the hundred-foot tower. On the Tower Overlooking the River. Po Chü-i. WhP
Beside the rivers of the midnight town. Madrigal. John Frederick Nims. MiAP
Beside the Sea. Ella Higginson. OTPC (1946 ed.)
Beside the stolid opaque flow. The Gravel-Pit Field. David Gascoyne. NeBP; PoN
Beside the sycamore, in hesitating. Within an Emerald. Salvador Díaz Mirón. AnMP
Beside the ungathered rice he lay. The Slave's Dream. Longfellow. AnNE; CoBA; GTBS; IAP; MOAP; OBVV; PoNe; PYM; TSW; TSWC
Beside yon church, that beams a modest ray. Church and School. Timothy Dwight. *Fr.* Greenfield Hill. AmPP (3d ed.)
Beside yon straggling fence that skirts the way. The Village Schoolmaster [*or* The Schoolmaster]. Goldsmith. *Fr.* The Deserted Village. BTP; CBOV; OBEC; OTPC (1946 ed.); ShBV-2; TrGrPo; TVSH
Besides the autumn poets sing. Emily Dickinson. OxBA
Besieged. Zalman Schneour, *tr. fr. Yiddish by* Joseph Leftwich. TrJP
Besieged Heart, The. Sir John Suckling. *See* Siege, The.
Besom-Man, The. Joseph Campbell. OnYI
Bess and Her Spinning-Wheel. Burns. BSV
Bess the Gawkie. James Muirhead. EBSV
Bessie Bell and Mary Gray. Mother Goose. *See* Bessy Bell and Mary Gray.
Bessie Bell and Mary Gray (*ballad*). *Unknown.* BSV; CBOV; EBSV; OBB
(Bessy Bell and Mary Gray.) ESPB; ViBoFo
Bessie Bobtail. James Stephens. ChMo; CMP; NP; TIP
Bessie Brown, M.D. Samuel Minturn Peck. BOHV; LauV; PR
Bessy [*or* Bessie] Bell and Mary Gray. Mother Goose. OTPC (1923 ed.); OxNR; PCH; PPL; RIS
Bessy Bell and Mary Gray (*ballad*). *Unknown. See* Bessie Bell and Mary Gray.
Best, The. Elizabeth Barrett Browning. OBVV
Best. Rose Fyleman. BrR

Best, The. Carl Sandburg. *Fr.* The People, Yes. MaRV
Best and brightest, come away! To Jane: The Invitation [*or* The Invitation *or* The Invitation to Jane]. Shelley. AlDl; CH; EmBrPo; EPN; ERP; GTBS; GTBS-D; GTBS-W; GTSE; GTSL; HBV; OBEV; OBRV; OTPC; PC; SeCeV; SN
Best Days. Pseudo-Hipponax, *tr. fr. Greek by* J. M. Edmonds. OxBG
Best Firm, The. Walter G. Doty. HBV; HBVY; RIS
Best Friend, The. W. H. Davies. OBMV
Best Game the Fairies Play, The. Rose Fyleman. GFA; GoBP; TiPo (1952 ed.); YT
Best Memorial, The. Agathias Scholasticus, *tr. fr. Greek by* George Allen. OxBG
Best Not to Be Born. Archias, *tr. fr. Greek by* William Hay. OnPM
Best of All, The. Fanny Crosby. BLRP
Best of All, The. Margaret G. Rhodes. BoTP
Best of All. *Unknown.* WBLP
Best of All. J. M. Westrup. BoTP
Best of all things is water; but gold, like a gleaming fire. Pindar. *Fr.* Olympian Odes. GrPo
Best of artists hath no thought to show, The. Sonnet: To Vittoria Colonna. Michelangelo. LyPI
Best of life is nearest, The: he who grieves. Today. Celeste Turner Wright. MuM
Best preacher is the heart, The. The Best. Carl Sandburg. *Fr.* The People, Yes. MaRV
Best Religion, The. Heine, *tr. fr. German by* Emma Lazarus. *Fr.* Tannhäuser. TrJP
Best Road of All, The. Charles Hanson Towne. HBMV; NLK; OQP; POT; PoTo; QP-2
Best Song as It Seems to Me, The. *Unknown.* CoBE
Best That I Have, The. Juan Ramón Jiménez, *tr. fr. Spanish by* Eleanor L. Turnbull. TeCS
Best time for making a voyage, The. Sailing Weather. Hesiod. *Fr.* Works and Days. OxBG
Best Time of All, The. Nancy Byrd Turner. GFA
Best Treasure, The. John J. Moment. MaRV
Best Way, The. Walter C. Smith. EBSV
Bestiary. A. M. Klein. BoCaPo
Bestiary, A, *sels.* Kenneth Rexroth.
Deer. HoPM
Herring. HoPM
Kangaroo.
(Advices from Rexroth's Bestiary.) SiTL
Lion. HoPM
Racoon. FiBHP
(Advices from Rexroth's Bestiary.) SiTL
Trout.
(Advices from Rexroth's Bestiary.) SiTL
Wolf.
(Advices from Rexroth's Bestiary.) SiTL
You. HoPM
Bestiary, The, *sels. Unknown, tr. fr. Middle English.* MeEV
Eagle's Nature, The.
Lion's Nature, The.
Serpent's Nature, The.
Whale's Nature, The.
Bestowal of the Poem. Stéphane Mallarmé, *tr. fr. French by* R. G. Stern. AnFP
Bestowed in Farewell. Tu Mu, *tr. fr. Chinese by* Soame Jenyns. ChLP
Bête Humaine. Francis Brett Young. CH; HBMV
Beth Gêlert. William Robert Spencer. BeLS; GoTP; OnSP; OTPC; TreFS
(Beth Gêlert or the Grave of the Grayhound.) BLPA; LPS-2
Bethel. A. J. H. Duganne. PAH
Bethesda. Arthur Hugh Clough. BPN; EmBrPo; PoVP
(Bethesda; a Sequel.) VLEP
Bethink you next, what sort of days I pass. Electra. Sophocles. *Fr.* Electra. GrR
Bethinking Himself of His End, Writeth Thus. Thomas, Lord Vaux. *See* Latter Day, The.
Bethlehem. William Canton. BoTP; YeAr
Bethlehem. Bliss Carman, *ad. fr. the French of* Yvette Guilbert. SDH
Bethlehem. Harry Webb Farrington. OQP; QP-2
Bethlehem. Arthur Ketchum. ChrBoLe
Bethlehem. Clinton Scollard. *See* Little Town, The.
Bethlehem. Katharine Tynan. SDH
Bethlehem of Judea. *Unknown.* ChBR
Bethlehem Road, The. Ida Norton Munson. ChIP
Bethlehem Star, The, Shines On! Alice Mortenson. BePJ
Bethlehem-Town ("As I was going to Bethlehem-town"). Eugene Field. WBLP
"Unto a Child in Bethlehem-town," *sel.* PGD
Bethou Me, Said Sparrow. Wallace Stevens. Notes toward a Supreme Fiction, XVI. CrMA; LiTM (rev. ed.); NePA
("Bethou me, said sparrow, to the crackled blade.") MoPo
Bethsabe's Song. George Peele. *Fr.* David and Bethsabe, I, i. ATBAP; ATP; CoEV; OBSC; OxBoLi; SeCeV
(Bathsheba's Song.) InPo
(Bethsabe Bathing.) ElL; ExPo; LoBV; TrGrPo
(Bethsabe, Bathing, Sings.) BLV
("Hot sun, cool fire, tempered with sweet air.") ElSeCe; LO; PoEL-2; SiCE; TuPP
Betrayal. Hester H. Cholmondeley. MaRV; OQP; QP-1
(Still as of Old.) PGD
Betrayal, The. Alice Furlong. AnIV
Betrayal, The. Sidney Lanier. *Fr.* The Jacquerie. AA
Betrayal. Ibn Sa'id of Alcala la Real, *tr. fr. Arabic by* A. J. Arberry. MooP
Betrayal. John Banister Tabb. ACP
Betrayal. *Unknown.* OQP; QP-1
Betrayal. Sir Thomas Wyatt. *See* How Should I Be So Pleasant.
Betrayal of the Rose, The. Edith M. Thomas. AA
Betrayed. Lizette Woodworth Reese. TBM
Betrayed by friend dragged from the garden hailed. Ecce Homunculus. R. A. K. Mason. AnNZ
Betrothal, The. Edna St. Vincent Millay. NP; PG
Betrothed, The. Kipling. HBV
Betrothed, The, *sel.* Sir Walter Scott.
Woman's Faith, *fr. ch.* 20. ViBoPo
Betrothed Anew. Edmund Clarence Stedman. LPS-2
Betsey Trotwood's Cat. Louella C. Poole. CIV
Betsinda's Bun. Thackeray. *Fr.* The Rose and the Ring. BoN
Betsy from Pike. *Unknown. See* Sweet Betsy from Pike.
Betsy Jane's Sixth Birthday. Alfred Noyes. SiSoSe
Betsy's Battle-Flag. Minna Irving. DD; GA; MC; PAH; PEDC; PoRL
Better a Day of Faith. Henry Burke Robins. MaRV
Better Answer (to Cloe Jealous), A. Matthew Prior. *See* Answer to Chloe Jealous.
Better to be early and have to wait. Rhymes to Remember. *Unknown.* StaSt
. . . Better be with the dead. Shakespeare. *Fr.* Macbeth, III, ii. PIR
Better Eros, The. Asclepiades, *tr. fr. Greek by* Robert Guthrie MacGregor. OnPM
Better go outdoors now, shut the door on trouble. First Concerns. Abbie Huston Evans. NP
Better in the Wild. Bhartrihari, *tr. fr. Sanskrit by* Arthur W. Ryder. OnPM
Better it were, my brother. Man to Man. John McClure. HBMV
Better late than never: yea, mate. Of Late and Never. John Heywood. TuPP
Better music ne'er was known. Beaumont *and* Fletcher. *Fr.* The Knight of the Burning Pestle. SiCE; TuPP
Better never trouble Trouble. Trouble. David Keppel. FaFP; TreF; WBLP
Better not to go back to the village. The Malefic Return. Ramón López Velarde. AnMP
Better one bird in hand than ten in the wood. Of Birds and Birders. John Heywood. SiCE
Better Part, The. Matthew Arnold. BPN; ChIP; EM-2; EPN; GrCo-1; MaRV; PoVP; StJW; TOP; ViPP; VLEP
Better Part, The. Bhartrihari, *tr. fr. Sanskrit by* Arthur W. Ryder. OnPM
Better Part, The. Theognis. *See* Despair.
Better Part of Valour, The. Archilochus. *See* Poet's Shield, The.
Better Path, The. Ecclesiastes, VII: 1-5, Bible, *O.T.* TreFS
(It Is Better . . . 1-9.) TrJP
Better Resurrection, A. Christina Rossetti. HBV; OxBoCh; POTT; PoVP; StJW; TrPWD; ViPo; VLEP
Better than Gold ("Better than grandeur . . ."). Abram J. Ryan, *at. also to* Alexander Smart. FaFP; MaRV; PoToHe; PTA-1
Better than granite, Spoon River. Aaron Hatfield. Edgar Lee Masters. *Fr.* Spoon River Anthology. LiTA; NP
Better the empty sorrow in the dark. Night of Rain. Bernice Kenyon. HBMV
Better the Vase Be Broken. Stanton A. Coblentz. MuM
Better to Be Brave. Lucillius, *tr. fr. Greek by* Lord Neaves. OnPM
Better to drink life in one flaming hour. Advice. A. M. Sullivan. PFE
Better to dwell in mountains wild. Better in the Wild. Bhartrihari. OnPM
Better to live on beggar's bread. After Battle. *Unknown. Fr.* Bhagavad-Gita. MaRV
Better to see your cheek grown hollow. Madman's Song. Elinor Wylie. BAP; MAP; MoAB; MoAmPo; MoSiPe; PoRA
Better trust all and be deceived. Faith [*or* Trust]. Frances Anne Kemble. FaBoBe; HBV; LPS-3; MaRV; NeHB; OBVV; VA
Better Unborn. *Unknown, tr. fr. Greek by* F. L. Lucas. GrPE
Better Way, The. "Susan Coolidge." PaA
Better, Wiser and Happier. Ella Wheeler Wilcox. WBLP

Betty and the Bear. *Unknown.* PTA-2
Betty at the Party. Mary E. Bradley. BoTP
Betty Botter bought some butter. *Unknown.* OxNR; SiTL
Betty by the Sea. Ronald McCuaig. BoAV
Betty Perrin. A. E. Coppard. MBP; MoBrPo (1942 ed.)
Betty Pringle [Had a Little Pig]. *Unknown.* OTPC (1923 ed.); PPL
Betty told Dupree, "Daddy, I want a diamond ring." *Unknown.* OuSiCo
Betty Zane. Thomas Dunn English. GA; PAH
Between a sunny bank and the sun. Two Houses. Edward Thomas. ChMP; FaBoCh; LoGBV
Between Adam and me the great difference is. Upon Being Obliged to Leave a Pleasant Party. Thomas Moore. BOHV
Between Attention and Attention. W. H. Auden. ReaPo
Between Brielle and Manasquan. Oliver St. John Gogarty. OnYI
Between broad fields of wheat and corn. The Stranger on the Sill. Thomas Buchanan Read. PTA-2
Between decision and ensuing act. Birdwatcher. Henry Treece. WaP
Between extremities. Vacillation. W. B. Yeats. EnLP; MoVE
Between fearful feathers, between the nights. Alberto Rojas Jiménez Comes Flying. "Pablo Neruda." TwSpPo
Between fields of popcorn. "America, I Love You." Bert Kalmar *and* Harry Ruby. FiBHP; InMe
Between God's Eyelashes. José Garcia Villa. CrMA
Between life and life's image, battling. Allegory of Torment. "Pablo de Rokha." AnCL
Between long rows of figures lurk. A Book of Economics. Haniel Long. BAP
Between me and the rising sun. Cobwebs. E. L. M. King. BoTP
Between me and the sunset, like a dome. The Man against the Sky. E. A. Robinson. AmPP; APA; ChMo; CMP; CoAnAm; CoBMV; CoV; IAP; LiTA; MAPA; MOAP; MoVE; NAMP; OxBA; TwAmPo
Between me and the sunset, the whole of life. The Present Evening. Eugenio Florit. TwSpPo
Between Midnight and Morning. Sir Owen Seaman. *See* Victory.
Between my eyes and her so thin the screen. Ideal Passion, XXXVII. George Edward Woodberry. HBMV; MOAP
Between my love and me there runs a thread. Sonnets. Irene Rutherford McLeod. HBMV
Between my suppertime and bed. A Busy Person. Alfarata Hilton. PCH
Between my thighs an extraordinary. From Knees Up, Muvver Brown, I. H. L. R. Edwards. MoWP
Between Namur and Liège. Wordsworth. EPN; MCCG
Between Nose and Eyes a strange contest arose. The Nose and the Eyes [*or* Dispute between Nose and Eyes *or* Report of an Adjudged Case]. William Cowper. BOHV; LPS-3; MPB; OTPC
Between our eastward and our westward sea. Northumberland. Swinburne. VLEP
Between such animal and human heat. The Partner. Theodore Roethke. *Fr.* Four for Sir John Davies. NePA; NePoAm
Between the amber portals of the sea. The Peach Tree. Edith Sitwell. NP
Between the avenue of cypresses. Service of All the Dead. D. H. Lawrence. NP; TCEP
Between the Battles. Francis Sherman. BoCaPo (1943 ed.)
Between the blue that burned the swimming bay. Hylas. L. A. Mackay. BoCaPo
Between the cliffs of brick and stone. The White Brigade. John Macy. MDAH
Between the dark and the daylight. The Children's Hour. Longfellow. AA; AmP; AnNE; CoBA; FaBoBe; FaFP; FAOV; FaPON; GoTP; HBV; HBVY; IAP; LaNeLa; LPS-1; MPB; NeHB; OHFP; OnHT; OTPC; PCH; PIR; PoEL-5; PTA-1; PYM; TCAP; TreF; TSW; TSWC; WBLP
Between the earth and the drowned platinum. The Battle of the Jarama. "Pablo Neruda." WaaP
Between the erect and solemn trees. The Temple of the Trees. J. D. C. Pellow. PGD
Between the falling leaf and rose-bud's breath. The Term of Death. Sarah Morgan Bryan Piatt. AA
Between the first pangs and the last of love. This Little Vigil. Charles G. Bell. NePoAm
Between the fosse and inner wall. The Defender. Arthur M. Sampley. GoYe
Between the gardening and the cookery. A Bookshop Idyll. Kingsley Amis. NePoEA
Between the Graves. Harriet Prescott Spofford. PEOR
Between the gray pastures and the dark wood. *See* Between the grey . . .
Between the green bud and the red. Prelude to "Songs before Sunrise." Swinburne. EmBrPo; PoVP; TCPD; ViP; ViPo
Between the grey [*or* gray] pastures and the dark wood. The Valley of White Poppies. "Fiona Macleod." MoSiPe; PoVP
Between the hands, between the brows. Love-Lily. Dante Gabriel Rossetti. AtBAP; BPN; EmBrPo; POTT; PoVP; VLEP
Between the hill and the brook, ook, ook. The Rabbits. *Unknown, tr. fr. German.* PCH; PPL; SAS
Between the legs. The Mother. Raymond Souster. PeCV
Between the Lines. W. W. Gibson. HiLiEn; MCCG
Between the moondawn and the sundown here. On the Cliffs. Swinburne. BPN; EmBrPo
Between the moonlight and the fire. Ballade of Christmas Ghosts. Andrew Lang. COAH; SDH
Between the mountains and the sea. Santa Barbara. Francis Fisher Browne. AA
Between the pleasant lands, the sunlit places. Program Note on Sibelius. Donald Babcock. UnS
Between the Porch and the Altar. Robert Lowell. FiMAP; MiAP; NePoEA
Between the rail of woven brass. Two Sermons. Austin Dobson. VLEP
Between the railway and the mine. The Blackberry. Norman Nicholson. MoBrPo (1950 ed.); NeMA
Between the Rapids. Archibald Lampman. VA
Between the rice swamps and the fields of tea. The Quarry. William Vaughn Moody. AnAmPo; LA
Between the roadside and the wood. A Windflower. Bliss Carman. VA
Between the roses. Five Roses. Jacinto Verdaguer, *tr. by* Thomas Walsh. CAW
Between the rough hills of gabbro and the cold sea. In Our Time. Michael Roberts. WaP
Between the Showers. Amy Levy. VA
Between the solemn portico's. Miranda's Supper. Elinor Wylie. TCPD
Between the spaces. The Dark-red Shadow-Spots. Yumei Kanbara. LiTW
Between the Sunken Sun and the New Moon. Paul Hamilton Hayne. AA; HiLiAm; LEAP
Between the Sunset and the Sea. Swinburne. *See* Mary Beaton's Song.
Between the Traveller and the Setting Sun. Henry David Thoreau. PoEL-4
Between the upland orchard, the pink of the chilled peach limbs. Winter Noon. James Rorty. MOAP
Between the World and Me. Richard Wright. PoNe
Between their sandspit ends. Barred Islands. Philip Booth. NePoEA
Between thirty and forty, one is distracted by the Five Lusts. On Being Sixty. Po Chü-i. AWP; TrCh
Between Two Furious Oceans, *sels.* Dick Diespecker.
"All these are your essence, you are their flesh and their force." CaP
"You have asked me, 'What am I?' " TwCaPo
Between Two Loves. T. A. Daly. BOHV; MAP; MoAmPo (1942 ed.); PoeMoYo; PoMa; StVeCh (1940 ed.); VOD
Between two russet [*or* golden] tufts of summer grass. Lying in the Grass. Sir Edmund Gosse. LBBV; OBVV; PoeT; TCEP; TOP; VA
Between two stones is a trickling spring. The Spring. Théophile Gautier. TrFP
Between two unknown trees I stood. Fantasy in a Forest. Leah Bodine Drake. MuM
Between two worlds life hovers like a star. Life. Byron. *Fr.* Don Juan, XV. GEPC
Between us lie/ The mountains and the plain. With One Swift Thought. Sister Maryanna. JKCP (1955 ed.)
Between wise men and fools, among things many. Of Difference between Wise Men and Fools. John Heywood. ReIE
Between Worlds. Carl Sandburg. MoAmPo (1950 ed.)
Betwix twelve houris and eleven. Amends to the Tailors and Soutars. William Dunbar. BSV
"Betwixt a Sleep and a Sleep." Macedonius, *tr. fr. Greek by* F. L. Lucas. GrPE
Betwixt and Between. Hugh Lofting. GaP
Betwixt mine eye and heart a league is took. Sonnets, XLVII. Shakespeare. PeBoSo
Betwixt old March and April gay. Alysoun. *Unknown.* EPP
Betwixt the actual and unseen, alone. Beethoven. Edward Carpenter. PoMa
Betwixt the quarters, flows a golden sea. Battle of Actium. Virgil, *tr. by* Dryden. *Fr.* The Aeneid, VIII. OBS
Betwixt the stirrop and the ground. Gravestones, III. *Unknown.* OtMeF
Betwixt two billows of the downs. The Winnowers. Robert Bridges. OAEP; POTT; TVSH
Beverley Maid and the Tinker, The. *Unknown.* CoMu
Bewail with me, all ye that have professed. On the Death of Phillips. *Unknown.* OBSC
Bewailing [*or* Bewailling] in my chamber thus allone. He Sees His Beloved [*or* The Coming of Love]. James I,

Bewailing in my chamber thus allone (*continued*)
King of Scotland. *Fr.* The Kingis Quair. BSV; GoTS; LEAP; PoEL-1
Beware! Archilochus, *tr. fr. Greek by* A. C. Benson. GrR
Beware. *Tr. fr. German by* Longfellow. PR
Beware. Dora Sigerson Shorter. GTSL; GTML
Beware, Aristotelian man. Caution. Donald F. Drummond. PtPa
Beware, beware the snare of "victory." Victory. Roger Axford. PGD
Beware Fair Maid[e]. *Unknown, at. to* Joshua Sylvester. OBS; RiBV
"Beware lest, Love, too often with your stings." *Unknown, tr. fr. Greek by* Humbert Wolfe. PIAE
Beware, my friend, of fiends and their grimaces. Sonnet to a Cat. Heine. CIV
Beware of a pirate who will scuttle your ship. Convention. Alfred Kreymborg. MAPA
Beware of Larry Gorman, *with music.* Larry Gorman. ShS
Beware of Sirens. —— Bewe. ReIE
("When sage Ulysses sailed by.") SiCE
Beware Our Loving Dog. Lucretia Penny. AlBD
Beware, rash boy, beware! Beware! Archilochus. GrR
Beware the Cuckoo. E. G. Moll. BoAV
Beware the deadly Sitting habit. Cave Sedem! Theodore F. McManus. HBV
Beware! The Israelite of old, who tore. The Warning. Longfellow. CoBA
Beware the January month: beware. Hesiod. *Fr.* Works and Days. GrPo
Beware the Jealous Hand. Meleager, *tr. fr. Greek by* Robert Allason Furness. GrR
Beware the lurking scorpion, friend. A Scorpion under Every Stone. *Unknown.* OxBG
Beware the month of Lenaion—foul days. Winter. Hesiod. *Fr.* Works and Days. OxBG
Beware the wolves of Egremont. The Wolves of Egremont. Dorothy Quick. DaM
Beware, Wass. Davies Aberpennar. MoWP
Bewhiskered raticide, whose velvet paw. The Eternal Question. D. B. Van Buren. CIV
Bewick and Graham. *Unknown.* BaBo; ESPB
Bewick Finzer. E. A. Robinson. AnNE; BoLiVe (1945 ed.); ChMo; CMP; CoBMV; MAP; MoAB; MoAmPo; NeMA; TwP
Bewildered Arab, The. Jami. *See* Simple Arab, The.
Bewildered Guest, The. William Dean Howells. BAP
Bewildered in the morning down dry roads. The Bullocks. Alex Comfort. FaBoTw
Bewildered with the broken tongue. Words in Time. Archibald MacLeish. CrMA; NePA; PoRA
Bewitched. W. H. Davies. AlDL
Bewitched. Walter de la Mare. PoMS
Bewitching Drowned. Vicente Huidobro, *tr. fr. Spanish by* Joseph Staples. AnCL
Bewteis of the Fute-Ball, The. *Unknown.* GoTS
Beyond. Thomas S. Jones, Jr. TBM
Beyond. Hannah Parker Kimball. AA
Beyond. John Gibson Lockhart. MaRV
Beyond. John Richard Moreland. UnW
Beyond, The. Ella Wheeler Wilcox. MaRV
Beyond a hundred years and more. Pope at Twickenham. Charles Kent. PtP; VA
"Beyond a sky-swept crest of hills." Bernard Freeman Trotter. *Fr.* Smoke. CPG
Beyond Arcturus and the Pleiades. White Splendor. Leslie Savage Clark. ChIP
Beyond, beyond the mountain line. Dreams. Cecil Frances Alexander. OnYI; TIP
Beyond Biology. Robert Francis. NePoAm
Beyond Connecticut, beyond the Sea. John Peale Bishop. SPP
Beyond Debate. Hervey Allen. LS
Beyond Electrons. Adelaide P. Love. OQP; QP-2
Beyond Good and Evil. George Edward Woodberry. TCPD
Beyond Kerguelen. Henry C. Kendall. BoAu
Beyond my window in the night. A Town Window. John Drinkwater. BoTP; GTBS; NeMA; PoeT; POT; PoTo
Beyond Nagel's Funeral Parlor. The Elizabethans Called It Dying. James Schuyler. NeAP
"Beyond Ortygia there lies an isle." The Tale of Eumaeus. Homer. *Fr.* The Odyssey, XV. GrPE
Beyond Possession. Elizabeth Jennings. NePoEA
Beyond Rathkelly. Francis Carlin. HBMV; PR; SBMV
Beyond Recall. Mary E. Bradley. AA
Beyond Religion. Lucretius, *tr. fr. Latin by* William Ellery Leonard. *Fr.* De Rerum Natura. AWP
"Whilst human kind/ Throughout the lands lay miserably crushed," *sel.* PoFr
Beyond the blue rim of the world. Hesperides. Harry Kemp. NLK
Beyond the blue, the purple seas. The Hunter. Walter James Turner. HBMV; PtOT
Beyond the bourn of mortal death and birth. At Last. Katrina Trask. AA
Beyond the Chiltern coast, this church. Edlesborough. Anne Ridler. NeBP
Beyond the common lot who lusts to live. Old Age the Friendless. Sophocles. *Fr.* Oedipus at Colonus. GrR
Beyond the corn-rows from our Barracks stood. The Quaker Meeting-House. William Ellery Leonard. PFY
Beyond the cypress unexpected drifts. Samarian Nights. Yaakov Fichman. LiTW
Beyond the desolate expanse of plain. Then and Now. George Sterling. PoMa
Beyond the doorway of the tiny room. Blue Homespun. Frank Oliver Call. *Fr.* A Sonnet Series of French Canada. CaP; CPG; OCL
Beyond the eagle-haunted mist that wreathes. The Condor's Sleep. Leconte de Lisle. TrFP
Beyond the East Gate. *Unknown, tr. fr. Chinese.* WhP
Beyond the East the sunrise, beyond the West the sea. Wander-Thirst [*or* Wanderlust]. Gerald Gould. BMEP; HBV; NLK; PoMa; POT; PoTo; StaSt; TiPo; TSW; TSWC; TVSH
Beyond the edge of the world, past crater terrain. The Antelopes. James K. Baxter. AnNZ
Beyond the End. Denise Levertov. NeAP
Beyond the famous river Utva. Field of Tears. *Unknown.* OnPM
Beyond the Farthest Horizon, *abr.* Sidney Royse Lysaght. GrCo-2
Beyond the ferry water. Ferry Hinksey. Laurence Binyon. CBE; HBV
Beyond the Final Breath. Lilith Lorraine. UnW
Beyond the frontiers lie the hard winters and the raging winds. To the Tune of "Horses Drinking by the Great Wall." Li Shih-ming. WhP
Beyond the Grave. Margaret E. Bruner. AlBD; PoToHe
Beyond the great valley an odd instructive rising. Ascent to the Sierras. Robinson Jeffers. AmPP (3d ed.); LoGBV; MOAP; OxBA
Beyond the guns in Libya the Roman trumpets sound. Peace Is Only an Interlude. Ruth Guthrie Harding. MuM
Beyond the harbour drift. Harbour Music. Edward Thompson. MM
Beyond the hollow sunset, ere a star. In the Bay. Swinburne. BMEP; VLEP
Beyond the Horizon. Robert Freeman. BPP; MaRV; OQP; QP-2
Beyond the hour we counted rain that fell. Old Countryside. Louise Bogan. LiTA; MOAP; NePA; NP; TwAmPo
Beyond the Hunting Woods. Donald Justice. NePoEA
Beyond the last horizon's rim. The Hills of Rest. Albert Bigelow Paine. HBV; MaRV; OQP; POT; PoTo; QP-2; WGRP
Beyond the Last Lamp. Thomas Hardy. MoVE; PoVP; TwCV
Beyond the little [*or* narrow] window. The Tree-Top Road. May Riley Smith. HBV; MaRV; NLK
Beyond the low marsh-meadows and the beach. The Pines and the Sea. Christopher Pearse Cranch. AA; AnAmPo; HBV; LA; LEAP
Beyond the moor and mountain crest. The West. A. E. Housman. POTT
Beyond the murk that swallows me. Irene Rutherford McLeod. *Fr.* The Rebel. WGRP
Beyond the narrow window. *See* Beyond the little window.
Beyond the open grating between walls. Graveyard in the City. Luis Cernuda. CoSP
Beyond the pale of memory. Amor Profanus. Ernest Dowson. PoVP; UnW; VLEP
Beyond the path of the outmost sun through utter darkness hurled. Dedication. Kipling. *Fr.* Barrack-Room Ballads. ViPP
Beyond the Potomac. Paul Hamilton Hayne. BlG; PAH
Beyond the Profit of Today. *Unknown.* PoToHe (new ed.)
Beyond the sea a land of heroes lies. Salutation. George Sylvester Viereck. LPS-1
Beyond the sea, I know not where. Vivérols. David Starr Jordan. AA
Beyond the seas they say there is another earth. Ma Wei. Li Shang-yin. WhP
Beyond the Smiling and the Weeping. Horatius Bonar. HBV; LPS-1
(Little While, A.) VA
Beyond the sphere which spreads to widest space. La Vita Nuova, XXIX [*or* Sonnet]. Dante, *tr. by* Dante Gabriel Rossetti. AWP; JAWP; LyPI; OnPM; OuHeWo; WBP
Beyond the Stars. Charles Hanson Towne. UnW
Beyond the sunset and the amber sea. Ode to Sleep. Paul Hamilton Hayne. TCAP
Beyond the Tapestries. Norma Farber. GoYe
Beyond the Tower. Wen T'ing-yun, *tr. fr. Chinese.* WhP
Beyond the vague Atlantic deep. Our Mother Tongue [*or* An Envoy to an American Lady]. Richard Monckton Milnes. GN; OTPC; VA
Beyond the Veil. Henry Vaughan. *See* They Are All Gone.
Beyond the Violet Rays. Helena Coleman. CPG

Beyond the Vulgar Reach. Sappho, *tr. fr. Greek by* J. M. Edmonds. GrR
Beyond the war-clouds and the reddened ways. The Morning Breaks [*or* The Coming Day]. John Oxenham. MaRV; OQP; QP-1
Beyond the white dust flushed by the carriers. Patrol; Buonamary. Bernard Gutteridge. WaP
Beyond these chilling winds and gloomy skies. Heaven. Nancy Woodbury Priest. LPS-2
Bhagavad [*or* Bhagavat]-Gita, *sels. Unknown, tr. fr. Sanskrit.*
After Battle, *tr. by* Sir Edwin Arnold. MaRV
Considerations of Murder, *tr. by* Swami Prabhavananda *and* Christopher Isherwood. LiTW
Death ("As when one layeth/ His worn-out robes away"), *tr. by* Sir Edwin Arnold. MaRV
Debate between Arjuna and Sri Krishna, *tr. by* Swami Prabhavananda *and* Christopher Isherwood. WaaP
Eternal Self, The, *tr. by* Charles Johnston. WoL
Give Me Your Whole Heart, *tr. by* Swami Prabhavananda *and* Christopher Isherwood. MaRV
"Never the spirit was born," *tr. by* Sir Edwin Arnold. MaRV
Transfiguration, The, *tr. by* Sir Edwin Arnold. OuHeWo
Union with the Eternal, *tr. by* Charles Johnston. GrCo-1
Wise, The, *tr. by* Sir Edwin Arnold. OQP; QP-2
Bianca among the Nightingales. Elizabeth Barrett Browning. ViPo
Bible, The, *sel.* David Levi, *tr. fr. Italian by* Mary A. Craig. "Thou, Zion, old and suffering." TrJP
Bible, The. Sir Walter Scott. *See* Book of Books, The.
Bible, The. Thomas Traherne. LoBV (1949 ed.)
Bible, A ("A stern destroyer"). *Unknown, tr. fr. Anglo-Saxon by* Stith Thompson. *Fr.* Riddles. EnLi-1; OuHeWo
Bible, The ("When I am tired, the Bible is my bed"). *Unknown.* OQP; QP-1
Bible, The. Whittier. *Fr.* Miriam. MaRV; NeHB; OQP; QP-1
(Book Our Mothers Read, The.) BLRP
(Knowledge.) PoToHe (new ed.)
Bible My Mother Gave Me, The. *Unknown.* PTA-2
Bible of the Race, The. James Russell Lowell. OQP; QP-1
Bible Stories. Lizette Woodworth Reese. BrR; MoSiPe; MPB; StJW; TSW; TSWC
Bible Stories. *Unknown.* LiTG
Bibliolatres. James Russell Lowell. IAP
God Is Not Dumb, *sel.* MaRV; OQP; QP-1; WGRP
Bibliomaniac's Prayer, The. Eugene Field. AA
"Biby's" Epitaph. *Unknown.* FiBHP
Bicycling Song. Henry Charles Beeching. *See* Going down Hill on a Bicycle.
Bid Adieu to Maidenhood. James Joyce. Chamber Music, XI. LiTG; LiTL; OBEV (new ed.)
(Bid Adieu, Adieu, Adieu.) GTIV; OnYI
(Bid Adieu to Girlish Days.) HBV
Bid me go asleep: I scorn it with my heels. Samuel Rowlands. SiCE
Bid me live, and I will live. *See* Bid me to live . . .
Bid me not go where neither suns nor showers. A Valediction. William Cartwright. EG; ElSeCe; OBS; SeCL; SeEP
Bid me remember, O my gracious Lord. Mary Elizabeth Coleridge. *Fr.* Death. TrPWD
Bid Me Sin No More. Charles Wesley. BePJ
Bid me to live [*or* love], and I will live. To Anthea, Who May Command Him Anything [*or* To Anthea]. Robert Herrick. BLV; BoLiVe; CaAE; CoBE; ElSeCe; EM-1; EnLit; EPS; EV-2; GTBS; GTBS-D; GTBS-W; GTSE; GTSL; HBV; LEAP; LH; LoBV; NeHB; OAEP; OBEV; OBS; PIAE; ReEn; SeCL; SeCV-1; SeEP; TOP; TrGrPo; TwHP; TyEnPo; ViBoPo
Bid not farewell for fate can ne're divorce. *Unknown.* SeCSL
Bid the din of battle cease! The Message of Peace. Julia Ward Howe. PGD; PSO
Biddy, Biddy, *with music. Unknown.* OuSiCo
Bide thou thy time! The Patient Church. Cardinal Newman. GoBC
Bi-focal. Hal Porter. BoAV
Biftek aux Champignons. Henry Augustin Beers. AA; HBV; PR
Big and Little Things. Alfred H. Miles. OTPC (1923 ed.)
Big Arm-Chair, The. "E. H. R." GFA
Big Baboon, The. Hilaire Belloc. InP; MBP; MoBrPo; MoShBr; RIS
Big Bell in Zion, The. Theodore Henry Shackleford. BANP
Big Bethel Church, De. Joel Chandler Harris. *Fr.* Uncle Remus, His Songs and His Sayings. LEAP
Big Billie Potts was big and stout. The Ballad of Billie Potts. Robert Penn Warren AmPP (3d ed.); MoAmPo (1950 ed.); OxBA
Big black nigger, lying on the log. When de Good Lord Sets You Free. *Unknown.* ABF
Big blue overcoat and breeches red as red. Paris Again. *Unknown.* AOAH
Big blue-jean, the summer-bored boy next door, The. Carry Me Back. John Holmes. NePoAm-2
Big Boat's up the Rivuh, *with music. Unknown.* StDa
Big boat's up the rivuh an' she won't come down. Ferd Herold Blues. *Unknown.* StDa
Big Boss Speaks, The. Nate Salsbury. LauV
Big box,/ Little box. *Unknown.* OxNR
Big boys had run off and left him, The. And So It Goes. Thad Stem, Jr. NoCaPo (rev. ed.)
Big Brother. Elizabeth Madox Roberts. FaPON; GaP; MPB
Big Chief Wotapotami. David McCord. WhC
Big Clock, The. *Unknown.* TiPo
Big doors of the country barn stand open and ready, The. Song of Myself, IX. Walt Whitman. CoV
Big Engines, The. Chorus. Jack Kerouac. *Fr.* Mexico City Blues. NeAP
Big Fat Woman, *with music. Unknown.* OuSiCo
Big feet,/ Black feet. Feet. Irene Thompson. BoTP
Big Five-Gallon Jar, The, *with music. Unknown.* ShS
Big grey elephant, A. Just Jumbo. Eileen Mathias. BoTP
Big guns again. Imperator Victus. Hart Crane. OxBA
Big house,/ Little house. *Unknown.* OxNR
Big iron horse with lifted head. The Little Boy to the Locomotive. Benjamin R. C. Low. HBMV
Big Jim. *Unknown.* ABF
Big-lipped Negro. Nicolás Guillén, *tr. fr. Spanish by* H. R. Hays. TwSpPo
Big mountains sit still in the afternoon light, The. Sinners. D. H. Lawrence. ViBoPo
Big Mystical Circus, The. Jorge de Lima, *tr. fr. Portuguese by* Dudley Poore AnCL
Big Nasturtiums, The. Robert Beverly Hale. PoMS; SiTL
Big Rock Candy Mountain[s], The. *Unknown.* APW; ChTr; MaC
Big Rug, The. Po Chü-i, *tr. fr. Chinese by* Arthur Waley. TrCh
Big Smith. Juliana Horatia Ewing. TVC; TVSH
Big Swing-Tree Is Green Again, The. Mary Jane Carr. BrR; SiSoSe
Big Thompson Canon. Jean Milne Gower. PoOW
Big trucks for steel beams. Trucks. James S. Tippett. FaPON; GFA
Big trucks with apples. Country Trucks. Monica Shannon. BrR; FaPON; TiPo (1950 ed.)
Big-uddered piebald cattle low. Christmas Holiday. Alun Lewis. PrWP
Big Wind. Theodore Roethke. InvP; ViBoPo (1958 ed.)
Big yam taters in de sandy lan'. Sandy Lan'. *Unknown.* ABF
Big yellow trolley limbers along. There Are So Many Ways of Going Places. Leslie Thompson. FaPON
Bigamist born in Zambezi, A. Lessons in Limericks, I. David McCord. InMe
Bigerlow, *with music. Unknown.* AS
Bigger Day, The. G. E. Bishop. WBLP
Bigler, The (*diff. versions*), *with music. Unknown.* AmSS; OuSiCo
(*Bigler's* Crew, The.) IHA
(Cruise of the *Bigler,* The, *with music.* SoAmSa
Biglow Papers, The, *sels.* James Russell Lowell.
1st Series, No. 1.
Letter from Mr. Ezekiel Biglow of Jaalam to the Hon. Joseph T. Buckingham, A ("Thrash away, you'll hev to rattle"). AmPP; OxBA; TCAP
(Biglow Papers, The.) IAP
(Ez for War, *abr.*) APW
(Mr. Hosea Biglow Speaks.) PAH
("Thrash away, you'll hev to rattle.") CoBA
(To a Recruiting Sergeant.) AnNE
War, *sel., 1 st.* MaRV
1st Series, No. II.
Letter from Mr. Hosea Biglow to the Hon. J. T. Buckingham, A ("This kind o' sogerin' "). OxBA
1st Series, No. III.
What Mr. Robinson Thinks. AA; AmPP; AnNE; APW, *abr.;* BAP, *abr.;* BOHV; DDA; HBV; IAP; IHA; InMe; LHV; LPS-3; PAH; TOP; YaD
(Biglow Papers, The.) LEAP
1st Series, No. V.
Debate in the Sennit, The. GA, *abr.;* HBV; PAH
1st Series, No. VI.
Pious Editor's Creed, The. AnNE; IAP; PIAE; REAL; TOP
(Candidate's Creed, The, *abr.*) BOHV; YaD
(From "The Biglow Papers.") MOAP
1st Series, No. VII.
Letter from a Candidate for the Presidency, A ("Dear Sir,—You wish to know my notions").
(Candidate's Letter, The.) AA
2d Series, Introduction.
Courtin', The. AA; AmPP; AnNE; APW; BeLS; BOHV; CoBA; EV-5; HBV; HiLiAm; IAP; IHA; InMe; LHV; LPS-3; MOAP; MCCG; MW; OBAV; OBVV; PTA-2; REAL; StVeCh; TCAP; TreFS; YT
2d Series, No. II.

Biglow Papers, The (*continued*)
Mason and Slidell; a Yankee Idyll, *sel.*
Jonathan to John. CoBA; IAP; PaA; PAH; PAP
2d Series, No. VI.
Sunthin' in the Pastoral Line. AmPP (3d ed.); APW, *abr.*; CoBA; IAP; PFY, *abr.*
(Spring, *abr.*) MCCG
Bobolink, The, *very br. sel.* BLA
"I, country-born an' bred, know where to find." SN
2d Series, No. X.
Mr. Hosea Biglow to the Editor of the Atlantic Monthly. AA, *abr.*; IAP; PoEL-5
(Hosea Biglow's Lament, *abr.*) PFY
Bigness of cannon, The. La Guerre. E. E. Cummings. MAP; MoAB; MoAmPo
Bigot. Eleanor Slater. MaRV
Bile Dem Cabbage Down, *with music.* *Unknown.* SoAF
Bill/ Was ill. Careless Talk. Mark Hollis. FiBHP
Bill and Joe. Oliver Wendell Holmes. AA; HBV; IAP; LPS-1; PCD
Bill Boram, *sel.* Robert Norwood.
"Bill Boram was the bad man." CPG
Bill dug a well. A Narrative. Theodore Spencer. NeMA; WaKn; WhC
Bill Haller's Dance. Robert V. Carr. PoOW
Bill Jones was cynical and sad. Jim and Bill. Franklin P. Adams. LHV
Bill Jupp lies 'ere, aged sixty year. From the Greek Anthology. L. A. G. Strong. WhC
Bill Manning. Joseph I. C. Clarke. JKCP (1926 ed.)
Bill Martin and Ella Speed, *with music.* *Unknown.* ABF
Bill of Complaint, The Chaucer. LyMA
Bill Peters, the Stage Driver. *Unknown.* CoSo; CSF; IHA
(Bill Peters.) TSW; TSWC
Bill the Bachelor lived by himself. Bachelors' Buttons. Maud Morin. BoTP
Bill [*or* Billy] Venero. *Unknown.* CoSo, *with music;* CSF
Billiards. Walker Gibson. NePoAm
Billowing sea of sand no eye can span, A. The Elephants. Leconte de Lisle. TrFP
Billows swarmed, impeding, The. The Ship in Storm. Ibn Darraj. MooP
Billowy headlands swiftly fly, The. Battle-Song of the *Oregon.* Wallace Rice. PaA; PAH
Bill's in the Legislature. James Barton Adams. *See* Billy, He's in Trouble.
Billy. Harry Graham. *See* Tenderheartedness.
Billy Barlow, *with music.* *Unknown.* OuSiCo
Billy Boy. Dorothy King. BoTP
Billy Boy. *Unknown.* ABF, *with music;* ABS; BLPA; IHA; SiTL
("Where have ye [*or* you] been all the day,/ Billy Boy?") LO; OxNR
Billy Boy, Billy Boy, where are you riding to? Billy Boy. Dorothy King. BoTP
Billy Budd, Foretopman, *sel.* Herman Melville.
Billy in the Darbies. AmPP (4th ed.); AtBAP; ExPo; KN; LoBV; OxBoLi; PoEL-5
Billy Goat, The. Anyte, *tr. fr. Greek by* F. A. Wright. GrR
Billy Goat would like to chew, The. Billy Goats Chew. Richard W. Emery. GoBP
Billy goat's a handsome gent, The. The Goat. Roland Young. WhC
Billy Goats Chew. Richard W. Emery. GoBP
Billy, He's in Trouble. James Barton Adams. DDA; YaD
(Bill's in the Legislature.) PTA-2
Billy, in one of his nice new sashes. Tenderheartedness [*or* Billy *or* Some Ruthless Rhymes]. Harry Graham. CenHV; FaFP; LiTM; MaC; SiTL; WhC
Billy in the Darbies. Herman Melville. *Fr.* Billy Budd, Foretopman. AmPP (4th ed.); AtBAP; ExPo; KN; LoBV; OxBoLi; PoEL-5
Billy Peg-Leg's Fiddle. Bill Adams. *See* Peg-Leg's Fiddle.
Billy the Kid ("Billy was a bad man"). *Unknown.* ABF; CoSo; CSF
Billy the Kid ("I'll sing you a true song of Billy the Kid"). *Unknown.* ABF, *with music;* CoSo, *with music;* FaBoBe; SoAF, *with music*
Billy Venero heard them say. Bill [*or* Billy] Venero. *Unknown.* CoSo; CSF
Billy was a bad man. Billy the Kid. *Unknown.* ABF; CoSo; CSF
Billy's dead, and gone to glory—so is Billy's sister Nell. Billy's Rose. George R. Sims. PTA-2
Billy's Rose. George R. Sims. PTA-2
Bim, Bam, Bum. Christian Morgenstern, *tr. fr. German by* Lola Gruenthal. AnGP
Bind us the Morning, mother of the stars. Thefts of the Morning. Edith M. Thomas. AA
Binding of Isaac, The. Itzik Manger, *tr. fr. Yiddish by* Sarah Zweig Betsky. OnCuPl
Bindlestiff. Edwin Ford Piper. HBMV; MAP
Bind-Weed. "Susan Coolidge." GN; OTPC (1923 ed.)
Bingen on the Rhine. Caroline Elizabeth Sarah Norton. BeLS; BLPA; HBV; LPS-2; NeHB; PTA-1; TreF; WBLP
Bingo. *Unknown.* CH; OTPC (1946 ed.)
(Bobby Bingo.) RIS
Bingo Has an Enemy ("Bingo is kind and friendly"). Rose Fyleman. TiPo; UTS
Binnorie; or, The Two Sisters. *Unknown.* *See* Two Sisters, The.
Binsey Poplars (Felled 1879). Gerard Manley Hopkins. CoBMV; EG; MoVE; TwCV; UnPo (3d ed.)
Biographer, The. Louise Lamprey. DDA
Biography. Charles Bruce. CaP; PeCV
Biography. Jorge Carrera Andrade, *tr. fr. Spanish by* H. R. Hays. TwSpPo
Biography. Jacob Glatstein, *tr. fr. Yiddish by* Sarah Zweig Betsky. OnCuPl
Biography. A. M. Klein. TrJP
Biography. John Masefield. ChMo; CMP
Biography. Mavor Moore. TwCaPo
Biography. Aleksey Nedogonov, *tr. fr. Russian by* Jack Lindsay. RuPo
Biography. "Jan Struther." InMe
Biography for Beginners, *sels.* E. C. Bentley.
"After dinner Erasmus." CenHV
"Art of Biography, The." CenHV; FiBHP
"Dr. Clifford." CenHV
"Great Duke of Wellington, The." CenHV
"If only Mr. Roosevelt." CenHV
"Intrepid Ricardo, The." CenHV
"John Stuart Mill." FiBHP
(J. S. Mill.) BOHV; OxBoLi; WhC
Liszt. UnS
"Mr. Bernard Shaw." CenHV
"Mr. Hilaire Belloc." CenHV
"People of Spain think Cervantes, The." CenHV; FiBHP
(Miguel de Cervantes.) LauV
Sir Christopher Wren. BOHV; CenHV; FiBHP; InMe; LauV; LiTG; MoShBr; ShBV-3; SiTL; WhC
(Important People, 8.) StaSt
Sir Humphry Davy. CenHV; ImOP; LauV; ShBV-3
"Sir Walter Raleigh." CenHV
"What I like about Clive." CenHV
(Clive.) ShBV-3
(Lord Clive.) BOHV; MoShBr; OxBoLi; WhC
"Younger Van Eyck, The." FiBHP
Biography for the Use of the Birds. Jorge Carrera Andrade, *tr. fr. Spanish by* Donald Devenish Walsh. AnCL
Biography of an Agnostic. Louis Ginsberg. TrJP
Biologic Face, The. "L. B." CAG
Bion's Lament for Adonis. Bion. *See* Lament for Adonis.
Birch begins to crack its outer sheath, The. A Young Birch. Robert Frost. LiTA
Birch Stream. Anna Boynton Averill. LPS-2; SN
Birch-Tree, The. James Russell Lowell. BAV
Birch-Tree at Loschwitz, The. Amy Levy. AV; TrJP
Birch Trees. John Richard Moreland. DD; HBMV; HBVY; OHIP
Birches, The. Walter Prichard Eaton. StVeCh
Birches. Robert Frost. AmPo; AmPP; AnNE; ChMo; CMP; CoBA; CoV; CP; CV; HaMV; HBMV; HiLiAm; IAP; LEAP; LiTA; LiTM; LoGBV; MAP; MAPA; MCCG; MoAB; MoAmPo; MoVE; NeMA; OxBA; PFY; PIAE; PoFS; PoRA; PreP; SBMV; TCPD; TOP; TreF; TrGrPo; TwAmPo; TwCV; UnPo (3d ed.)
Birches that dance on the top of the hill, The. Parenthood. John Farrar. FAOV; MPB; OHIP
Birch-Wood. Leo Cox. BoCaPo (1943 ed.)
Bird, The. William Allingham. OTPC
Bird, The. Mary Elizabeth Coleridge. *See* As I Went Singing over the Earth.
Bird, A. Emily Dickinson. *See* Bird came down the walk, A.
Bird, The. Robert Greacen. NeIP
Bird, The. Samuel Hoffenstein. FiBHP
Bird, The. Jorge de Lima, *tr. fr. Portuguese by* Dudley Poore. AnCL; LiTW
Bird, The. Max Michelson. NP; TrJP
Bird, The. Edwin Muir. POTE
Bird, The. Pushkin, *tr. fr. Russian by* Sir Cecil Kisch. WaL
Bird, The. Rabindranath Tagore, *tr. fr. Bengali by* Rabindranath Tagore. LiTW
Bird, The. Sister Mary Thérèse. JKCP (1955 ed.)
Bird, The. Henry Vaughan. AtBAP; EPS; LoBV; OBEV (new ed.); PoEL-2; SeCL; SeCV-1
Bird, The. Countess of Winchilsea. EiPP
Bird, The. Andrew Young. POTE
Bird, a man, a loaded gun, A. *Unknown.* WhC
Bird and Brook, *sel.* Sir Samuel Ferguson.
"Bird that pipest on the bough." IrPN
Bird and the Tree, The. Ridgely Torrence. BAP; CBOV; HBMV; MAP; MoAmPo (1942 ed.); NP; NV; PoFr; PoNe; TBM
Bird appears a thoughtless thing, A. Crumbs to the Birds. Charles *and* Mary Lamb. OTPC

Bird at Dawn, The. Harold Monro. BLA; BoTP; GoTP; MoBrPo (1950 ed.); WhBS
Bird at Night. Marion Ethel Hamilton. GoYe
Bird Bath, The. Florence Hoatson. BoTP
Bird, Bird. Gene Derwood. LiTA; PeBoSo
Bird came down the walk, A. Emily Dickinson. AnAmPo; CoBA; InvP; LA; MaPo; MoAmPo; MOAP; MoShBr; MoVE; OxBA; PG; PoRA; PoRh; SeCeV; TiPo; TwP
(Bird, A.) FaPON, 8 *ll.;* MPB; StVeCh, 8 *ll.;* UTS
(In the Garden.) AnFE; APA; CoAnAm; LiTA; LiTM (rev. ed.); MAPA; TwAmPo
Bird Catcher. *See* Birdcatcher.
Bird flew tangent-wise to the open window, A. The Bird. Robert Greacen. NeIP
Bird from the West, A. Dora Sigerson Shorter. OBVV
Bird has flared his wingtips on the reef, The. The Froward Gull. Donald F. Drummond. PtPa
Bird has little, A—only a feather. Only a Little. Dora Read Goodale. PEOR
Bird in a Cage, The. William Lisle Bowles. TVC
Bird in a Cage, The, *with music.* *Unknown.* AS
Bird in my bower, A. Song. Francis Howard Williams. AA
Bird in Search of a Cage, A. Robert Pack. NePoEA
Bird in the Corn, The. Old Crow. John Drinkwater. WP
Bird in the Hand, A. Frederic E. Weatherly. BOHV; VA
Bird in the Room, The. Rudolph Chambers Lehmann. HBMV; HBVY
Bird kept saying that birds had once been men, The. On an Old Horn. Wallace Stevens. LiTA
Bird, Let Loose in Eastern Skies, The. Thomas Moore. HBV; OTPC (1923 ed.)
Bird may curve across the sky, A. Flight. Hazel Hall. AnAmPo; LA; MAP; MoAmPo (1942 ed.)
Bird Music. James Rorty. BLA
Bird-Notes. Johan Sebastian Cammermeyer Welhaven, *tr. fr. Norwegian by* Charles W. Stork. AnNoLy
Bird of Paradise, The. Laura Benét. BLA; PFY
Bird of Paradise, The. W. H. Davies. AtBAP; MoVE
Bird of slumber thought, The. Eyelashes. Ibn al-Hammara. MooP
Bird of the bitter bright gray golden morn. A Ballad of François Villon. Swinburne. BEL; BMEP; BPN; EmBrPo; EnLi-2; PFE; PIR; PoEL-5; PoRA; PoVP; PtP; ViP; ViPP; VLEP
Bird of the fierce delight. To a Sea-Gull. Arthur Symons. BLA; PoVP
Bird of the Sea. Euripides, *tr. fr. Greek by* Gilbert Murray. *Fr.* Iphigenia in Tauris. OxBG
(O Halcyon Bird.) GrR
Bird of the spray, the tree of bones. Loss. Randall Jarrell. FiMAP
Bird of the wilderness. The Skylark. James Hogg. ATP; BLA; BSV; CBPC; DD; EBSV; EV-3; GN; HBV; HBVY; LPS-2; OTPC; PECK; PIR; SN; TVSH
Bird of Time. Gustav Davidson. MuM
Bird of Time, The. Omar Khayyám, *tr. fr. Persian by* Edward Fitzgerald. *Fr.* The Rubáiyát. OnPM
("Come, fill the cup, and in the fire of spring.") CBOV; InP; TreF; WGRP
(Fifteen Rubáiyát.) LiTW
Bird Omens. Stefan George, *tr. fr. German by* Charles E. Passage. AnGP
Bird or Beast? Christina Rossetti. BPN
("Did any bird come flying.") EG
Bird-Parliament, The, *sels.* Ferid ed-Din Attar, *tr. fr. Persian by* Edward Fitzgerald. PeP
Attainment.
Excuses, The.
Nightingale, The.
Parrot, The.
Prelude: "Once on a time from all the Circles seven."
Ring-Dove, The.
Bird-Pastoral. Aristophanes. *See* Birds' Life, The.
Bird ran up the onyx steps of night, A. Fantasy. Louis Untermeyer. TSW
Bird Raptures. Christina Rossetti. ViPo; VLEP
Bird-Scarer's Song, The. *Unknown.* CBPC
Bird Sings at Night, A. Hildegrade Flanner. BLA
Bird sings the selfsame song, A. The Selfsame Song. Thomas Hardy. ChMo; CMP; TOP
Birdsong. Blake. *See* Nightingale and Flowers.
Bird Song. John Hay. NePoAm-2
Bird Song. Alfred Noyes. *See* You That Sing in the Blackthorn.
Bird Song. Laura E. Richards. HBV
Bird-Song. Mary Dixon Thayer. CAW
Bird that discoursest from yon poplar bough. Sonnet. James Clarence Mangan. IrPN
Bird that flies to climates crisper, The. Spring. Oscar Williams. LiTA
Bird that I don't know, A. A Country Life. Randall Jarrell. MiAP; MoAmPo (1950 ed.); NoCaPo (rev. ed.)
Bird that pipest on the bough. Sir Samuel Ferguson. *Fr.* Bird and Brook. IrPN
Bird Trades. *Unknown.* DD; HH
Bird Was Singing, A. Dietmar von Aist, *tr. fr. German by* Jethro Bithell. AWP; LiTW
Birdwatcher. Henry Treece. WaP
Bird watchers top my honors list. Up from the Egg; the Confessions of a Nuthatch Avoider. Ogden Nash. FiBHP
Bird with a Broken Wing, The. Hezekiah Butterworth. *See* Broken Pinion, The.
Bird with the Coppery, Keen Claws, The. Wallace Stevens. AnFE; APA; CoAnAm; CoV
Bird Wounded by an Arrow, The. La Fontaine, *tr. fr. French by* Elizur Wright. OnPM
Birdcatcher, The. Ralph Hodgson. AtBAP; MBP; MoBrPo; NeMA
Bird-Catcher, The. Elizabeth Turner. OTPC (1923 ed.)
Birdcatcher's Song. William John Courthope. *Fr.* The Paradise of Birds. VA
Birdie. Eliza Lee Follen. OTPC; SAS
"Birdie, Birdie, will you pet?" The Bird. William Allingham. OTPC
Birdie in the Cradle. *Unknown.* BOL
Birdie with a yellow bill, A. Time to Rise. Robert Louis Stevenson. BoChLi; InP; MeMeAg; OTPC (1946 ed.); PCH; PoVP; RIS; SiSoSe; StVeCh; UTS
Birdies' Breakfast, The. *Unknown.* BoTP
Birdies may sleep, but the winds must wake, The. Song of the Little Winds. Laura E. Richards. BOL
Birdies with Broken Wings. Mary Mapes Dodge. *See* Mother.
Birdless heaven, seadusk, one lone star, A. Tutto è Sciolto. James Joyce. MM; OBMV; OxBI; TriL
Bird-men, the devil's alloy in their metal. In the Vale of Glamorgan. Huw Menai. MoWP
Birds, The, *sels.* Aristophanes, *tr. fr. Greek.*
"Awake! awake!" *tr. by* John Hookham Frere. GrPo
Birds' Life, The, *tr. by* H. F. Cary. OxBG
(Bird-Pastoral, *tr. by* Benjamin Bickley Rogers.) GrR
Building of Cloudcuckoocity, The, *tr. by* T. F. Higham. OxBG
(Building of Cloudcuckoobury, The, *tr. by* Benjamin Bickley Rogers.) GrR
Chorus Hymeneal, *tr. by* Benjamin Bickley Rogers. GrR
Chorus of Birds, *tr. by* Swinburne. AWP; JAWP; WBP; WoL, *tr. by* Benjamin Bickley Rogers
(Grand Chorus of Birds, *tr. by* Swinburne.) PoEL-5
(Hymn of the Birds.) GrR, *tr. by* Benjamin Bickley Rogers; OxBG, *tr. by* Swinburne
Hoopoe's Call, The, *tr. by* T. F. Higham. OxBG
(Hark! the Hoopoe's Call, *tr. by* Benjamin Bickley Rogers.) GrR
Life of Men, The, *tr. by* John Hookham Frere. RO
"Nothing can be more delightful than the having wings to wear!" *tr. by* John Hookham Frere. GrPo
"To the judges of the prize, we wish to mention in a word," *tr. by* John Hookham Frere. GrPo
Wedding Chant, The, *tr. by* T. F. Higham. OxBG
Birds, The. Hilaire Belloc. JKCP
Birds, The. Blake. CH; OBRV
Birds, The. Samuel Taylor Coleridge. *See* Answer to a Child's Question.
Birds. W. H. Davies. ChMo; CMP
Birds. Geoffrey Dearmer. PtOT
Birds, The. Blossius Aemilius Dracontius, *tr. fr. Latin by* Thomas Walsh. CAW
Birds. Hildegarde Flanner. NP
Birds, The. Herbert S. Gorman. BLA; TBM
Birds. Robinson Jeffers. BLA; CoBMV; MOAP; TwAmPo; TwCV
Birds. James Montgomery. *Fr.* The Pelican Island. LPS-2
Birds, The. Ogden Nash. *Fr.* The Carnival of Animals. UnS
Birds. "Moira O'Neill." BLA; HBV
Birds. "Seumas O'Sullivan." OxBI
Birds, The. J. C. Squire. BLA; BMEP; HBMV
Birds. Richard Henry Stoddard. AA; HBV; LBAP; TCAP
Birds, The ("From out of a wood did a cuckoo fly"). *Unknown, tr. fr. Czech.* ChrBoLe
Birds ("Wild pigeon of the leaves"). *Unknown, tr. fr. Arabic by* E. Powys Mathers. *Fr.* The Thousand and One Nights. AWP; LiTW
Birds All Singing. Norman MacCaig. ChMP
Birds all the sunny day. Nest Eggs. Robert Louis Stevenson. EBSV
Birds and bees and butterflies. Out of Doors. E. North. BoTP
Birds and Francis, The. Louis Untermeyer. SaFP
Birds and Plants of Love, The. Tasso, *tr. fr. Italian by* the Countess of Winchilsea. *Fr.* Aminta. BeR
Birds and the Pheasant, The. *Unknown.* PA
Birds are coming home soon, The. The Coming of Spring. *Unknown.* PEDC
Birds are singing round my window. Birds. Richard Henry Stoddard. AA; HBV; LBAP; TCAP
Birds at Winter Nightfall. Thomas Hardy. MBP; MoBrPo

Birds, Bags, Bears, and Buns. *Unknown. See* Common Cormorant, The.
Birds' Ball, The. Charles William Bardeen. BLPA
Birds, Beasts and Bugs. *Unknown.* APW
Birds, companions more unknown. On the Death of a Favourite Canary. Matthew Arnold. *Fr.* Poor Matthias. BLA; PC
Birds' Courting Song, The, *with music. Unknown.* TrAS
(Birds' Courting, The.) APW
Bird's egg, a green branch, A. That's June. Mary F. Butts. YeAr
Birds engulf hard pebbles to grind the grain in their crops. The First Lamp. Pien Chih-lin. WhP
Bird's Epitaph, A. Martin Armstrong. *See* On a Little Bird.
Birds feed on birds, beasts on each other prey. Wretched Man. Earl of Rochester. *Fr.* A Satire against Mankind. SeCePo
Birds Go By, The. Shaw Neilson. MoAuPo
Birds go fluttering in the air, The. The Silent Snake. *Unknown.* BoTP; FaPON; TiPo (1959 ed.)
Birds have been singing today, The. In February. John Addington Symonds. DD; PRWS; YeAr
"Birds have hid, the winds are low, The." John Vance Cheney. Evening Songs, I. AA
Birds in April. W. E. Henley. YT
Birds in Spring. Thomas Nashe. *See* Spring, the Sweet Spring.
Birds in Spring. James Thomson. *Fr.* The Seasons: Spring. OBEC
Birds in Summer. Mary Howitt. HH; MPB; OTPC; PRWS
Birds in the Fens. Michael Drayton. Polyolbion, Song 25. ChTr
Birds in the Flax. Stanley Snaith. HaMV
"Birds in the high Hall-garden." Tennyson. *Fr.* Maud. BPN; CBOV; EV-5; GEPC; OTPC (1923 ed.)
Birds in the Night. Lionel H. Lewin. BOL
Birds in the world were waking. Long Ago. Siegfried Sassoon. AlDL
Birds in their nests are softly calling. Lullaby. Grace Mitchell. BOL
Birds in their oratory of leaves. Per Diem et per Noctem. Mary Stanley. AnNZ
Birds, joyous birds of the wandering wing! The Birds of Passage. Felicia Dorothea Hemans. OTPC
Birds' Lament. John Clare. PoEL-4
Birds' Life, The. Aristophanes, *tr. fr. Greek by* H. F. Cary. *Fr.* The Birds. OxBG
(Bird-Pastoral, *tr. by* Benjamin Bickley Rogers.) GrR
Bird's Nest, A. Elizabeth Akers Allen. PEDC
Bird's Nest, The. John Drinkwater. StVeCh
Bird's Nest, The. Elizabeth Turner. OHIP; OTPC (1923 ed.); RAR
Birdsnest, A, built on the palm of the high-/ Most bough. Lightness. Richard Wilbur. FiMAP
Bird's Nest in Winter, A. "John Crichton." CPG
Birds' Nests. Millicent Seager. BoTP
Birds' Nests. *Unknown.* BoTP; MPB; RAR; TVSH
Birds of a feather will flock together. *Unknown.* GoTP
Birds of Bethlehem, The. Richard Watson Gilder. AA
Birds of God, The. Euripides. *See* O for the Wings of a Dove.
Birds of Killingworth, The. Longfellow. *Fr.* Tales of a Wayside Inn: The Poet's Tale. APW; IAP; OxBA; PCN
"Do you ne'er think that wondrous beings these?" *sel.* WBLP
Birds of omen dark and foul. Annot Lyle's Song. Sir Walter Scott. *Fr.* The Legend of Montrose. EmBrPo; EnRP
Birds of Passage, *sel.* Steen Steensen Blicher, *tr. fr. Danish by* Charles W. Stork.
Prelude: "Time draws nigh when I shall go forth, The." BoDS
Birds of Passage. Felicia Dorothea Hemans. OTPC
Birds of Passage. Esaias Tegnér, *tr. fr. Swedish by* Charles W. Stork. AnSL
Birds of Passage, *sel.* Walt Whitman.
In This Earth Perfection. OQP; QP-2
Birds of Prey. Leconte de Lisle, *tr. fr. French by* Alan Conder. TrFP
Birds of Rhiannon, The. Euros Bowen, *tr. fr. Welsh by* Gwyn Williams. PrWP
Birds of Scotland, The. Hugh Macdonald. SN
Birds of the air, they sing it, The. Song. John Vance Cheney. NLK
Birds of Tin, The. Charles Madge. NeBP
Birds of Whitby, The. Thomas S. Jones, Jr. BLA
Birds on a Telegraph Wire. Carl Snoilsky, *tr. fr. Swedish by* Charles W. Stork. AnSL
Birds on the School Windowsill, The. Evelyn Dainty. BoTP
Birds Praise the Advent of the Saviour, The. *Unknown.* SDH
Birds' Rondel, The. Chaucer. *See* Roundel, A: "Now welcom, somer, with thy sonne softe."
Birds sit and sing among the flowers. Shou, *tr. fr. Japanese by* Lois J. Erickson. SoLD
Birds sleeping gently, The. Alice Where Art Thou. W. Guernsey. OlF
Bird's Song at Morning. William James Dawson. VA
Bird's Song in April. Clinton Scollard. PEOR
Bird's Song in Spring. Edith Nesbit. *See* Child's Song in Spring.
Bird's Song, the Sun, and the Wind, The. Sir Charles G. D. Roberts. VA
Birds that float upon a wave. Sea-Birds. Elinor MacArthur. BLA
Birds that were gray in the green are black in the yellow. September. "Seranus." VA
Birds, the free tenants of land, air, and ocean. Birds. James Montgomery. *Fr.* The Pelican Island. LPS-2
Birds their love-notes warble, The. Alice Ray. Sarah Josepha Hale. AA
Birds their quire apply, The; airs, vernal airs. The Eternal Spring. Milton. GN
Birds to wanton in the air desire, The. Madrigal: The Restless Lover. Francisco de Quevedo TeCS
Birds trailed him with their ardent wings. Thoreau. Genevieve Taggard. PoTo
Birdsong. *See* Bird Song.
Birdwatcher. *See* Bird Watcher.
Birkenhead, The. Sir Henry Yule. LH
"Not with the cheer of battle," *sel.* OtMeF
Birks of Aberfeldy [*or* Aberfeldie], The. Burns. EBSV; ViBoPo
Birks of Invermay, The. David Mallet. EBSV
(Birks of Endermay, The.) OBEC
Birlinn Chlann-Raghnaill. Alexander MacDonald. *See* Bark of Clanranald, The.
Birmingham. Louis MacNeice. ChMo; MBP; MoAB; MoBrPo
Birr, A! a whirr! a salmon's on. The Taking of the Salmon. Thomas Tod Stoddart. EBSV
Birth. George Burt Lake PoP
Birth, The. Don Marquis. NV
Birth. Grace Raymond. AA
Birth. E. Merrill Root. TBM
Birth, A. Muriel Rukeyser. FiMAP
Birth. Georg Trakl, *tr. fr. German by* Christopher Middleton. AnGP
Birth and Death. Thomas Wade. VA
Birth and Death of Pain, The, *sel.* Silas Weir Mitchell.
"Birth of pain, The! Let centuries roll away." PoP
Birth-Bond, The. Dante Gabriel Rossetti. The House of Life, XV. BPN; EmBrPo; HBV; OAEP; POTT; PoVP; ViPo
Birth by Anesthesia. George Scarbrough. GoYe
Birth-Dues. Robinson Jeffers. MAP; MoAB; MoAmPo
Birth in a Narrow Room, The. Gwendolyn Brooks. PoNe
Birth of Arachne, the Spider, The. James Schevill. FiMAP
Birth of Arthur, The. Layamon, *tr. fr. Middle English. Fr.* The Brut. MeEV
Birth of Australia, The. Percy Russell. VA
Birth of Christ, The. Tennyson. *See* In Memoriam A. H. H.: "Time draws near the birth of Christ, The."
Birth of Galahad, The, *sel.* Richard Hovey.
Ylen's Song. AA
Birth of Hermes, The. *Unknown, tr. fr. Greek by* Shelley. *Fr.* Homeric Hymns. GrR
Birth of Jesus, The. St. Luke, Bible, *N.T. See* Adoration of the Shepherds, The.
Birth of Lucifer, The. John Gould Fletcher. MAP; MoAmPo
Birth of pain, The! Let centuries roll away. Silas Weir Mitchell. *Fr.* The Birth and Death of Pain. PoP
Birth of Robin Hood, The. *Unknown.* OBB; ViBoPo, *last 2 sts.*
(Willie and Earl Richard's Daughter, A, B, *and* C *vers.*) ESPB
Birth of Rustem, The. Firdausi, *tr. fr. Persian by* Joseph Champion. *Fr.* Shah Namah. PeP
Birth of Saint Patrick, The. Samuel Lover. BOHV; DD; HBV; LPS-3; PoRL
Birth of Salámán, The. Jami, *tr. fr. Persian by* Edward Fitzgerald. *Fr.* Salámán and Absál. PeP
Birth of Speech, The. Hartley Coleridge. VA
Birth of the Flowers, The. Mary McNeil Fenollosa. OQP; QP-1
Birth of the Muses, The. Hesiod, *tr. fr. Greek by* Arthur S. Way. *Fr.* Theogony. GrR
Birth of the Squire, The; an Eclogue. John Gay. BeR; PoEL-3
Birth of Tragedy, The. Irving Layton. PeCV
Birth of Venus, The. *Unknown.* EtS
Birth seems like chance, and life appears uncertain. Lincoln. Rembrandt William B. Ditmars. HBMV
Birth Song of Christ, The. Edmund H. Sears. *See* Christmas Song.
Birthday, The, *sels.* Caroline Anne Bowles.
Cuckoo Clock, The. LPS-2

"Say with a friend we contemplate some scene." EnSW
Birthday, The. Witter Bynner. FAOV
Birthday, A. Rachel Field. SiSoSe; TiPo (1959 ed.)
Birthday, A. Christina Rossetti. AV; AWP; BLV; BMEP; BoLiVe; BPN; CBOV; CH; CoBE; EmBrPo; EnLi-2; EPP; EtPaEn; EV-5; FaFP; GTBS; GTSE; GTSL; HiLiEn; InvP; JAWP; LEAP; LiTB; LiTG; LiTL; LoBV; LoPS; MBP; OAEP; OBEV; OBVV; OuHeWo; PCD; PIAE; PoE; POTT; PoVP; ShBV-4; ThWaDe; TOP; TreFS; TrGrPo; TSW; TSWC; TyEnPo; ViBoPo; ViP; ViPo; VLEP; WBP; WHA; YT
("My heart is like a singing bird.") EG; PFE
Birthday. Jean Starr Untermeyer. MAP; MoAmPo (1942 ed.)
Birthday Again. Fuyue Anzai, *tr. fr. Japanese by* Takamichi Ninomiya *and* D. J. Enright. PoLJ
Birthday Child, The. Rose Fyleman. FaPON; SiSoSe
Birthday Crown, The. William Alexander. OBVV
Birthday Gift. Ethel Barnett de Vito. AlBD
Birthday Gift, A. Christina Rossetti. PRWS
Birthday Gifts. Herbert Asquith. SiSoSe
Birthday of Catharine Tufton, The, *sel.* Countess of Winchilsea.
Portrait, The. OBEC
Birthday of Daniel Webster. Oliver Wendell Holmes. DD; GA
Birthday of the Lord, The. Mary Jane Carr. ChBR
Birthday Poem for Thomas Hardy. C. Lay Lewis. CoBMV
Birthday Poem, November 4th. John Thompson, Jr. WaP
Birthday Prayer, A. John Finley. TrPWD
Birthday Song, A. Richard Watson Gilder. PoRL
Birthday Song. Nahabed Kouchak, *tr. fr. Armenian by* Zabelle C. Boyajian. ArmLP
Birthday Song, A (Composed . . . in Honour of . . the King's Birthday, June 4, 1777). Jonathan Odell. BoCaPo (1948 ed.); IAP
Birthday Sonnet. Elinor Wylie. BLV; BoLiVe; MAP; MoAB; MoAmPo; OnPM; TriL
Birthday Wish, A. Dorothy Nell McDonald. PoToHe (new ed.)
Birthdays. Marchette Chute. SiSoSe; StVeCh
Birthdays from the ocean one desert april noon. That "Craning of the Neck." Isabella Gardner. NePA
Birthdays? yes, in a general way. Imitation of Robert Browning. James Kenneth Stephen. InMe; PA
Birthnight Candle, A. John Finley. POT; PoTo
Birthplace, The. Robert Frost. LoGBV
Birthplace Revisited. Gregory Corso. NeAP
Birthright. John Drinkwater. AlDL; CH; HBV; LBBV; MM; POTE; WHA
Birthright, The. Eiluned Lewis. AlDL; DiM
(We Who Were Born.) FaPON; TiPo (1959 ed.)
Bishop among the Plotters, The. Charles Churchill. *Fr.* The Duellist. BeR
Bishop and His Portmanteau, The. *Unknown.* ALV
Bishop Blougram's Apology. Robert Browning. BrBE, *abr.;* OtMeF, *abr.;* PoEL-5; ViPo; ViPP
Sels.
Common Problem, The. OQP; QP-1
In Doubt of Doubt. MaRV
"When the fight begins within himself." MaRV
Bishop Boundary-rides His Diocese, The. Allen Curnow. *Fr.* Not in Narrow Seas. AnNZ
Bishop Butler of Kilcash. *Unknown.* OnYI
Bishop Doane on His Dog ["Cluny"]. William Croswell Doane, *wr. at. to* George Washington Doane. AlBD; BBV (1951 ed.); BLPA; FaBoBe; NeHB
Bishop Hatto. Robert Southey. *See* God's Judgment on a Wicked Bishop.
Bishop of Rum-ti-Foo, The. W. S. Gilbert. CenHV; PoVP
Bishop Orders His Tomb at Saint Praxed's Church, The. Robert Browning. ATP; AWP; BEL; BMEP; BoLiVe; BPN; CoEV; CP; EM-2; EmBrPo; EnL; EnLi-2; EnLit; EPN; ExPo; FiP; GEPC; GTSE; HBV; MaPo; MyFE; OAEP; OtMeF; Po; PoD; PoE; PoVP; SeCeV; ShBV-4; TwCrTr; TwP; VA; ViBoPo; ViPo; ViPP; VLEP
Bishop tells us, The: "When the boys come back." "They." Siegfried Sassoon. BMEP; ChMo; CMP; HBMV; MaRV
Bishop's Harp, The. Robert Mannyng. ACP
Bishop's See, The. *Unknown.* CoMu
Bismarck. K. G. Ossian-Nilsson, *tr. fr. Swedish by* Charles W. Stork. AnSL
Bison, The. Hilaire Belloc. NA
Bisy larke, messager of day, The. *See* Busy larke, messager of daye, The.
Bit of color against the blue, A. A Song for Our Flag. Margaret E. Sangster. FaFP
Bit of Colour, A. Horace Smith. BoTP
Bit of jungle in the street, A. Alley Cat. Esther Valck Georgns. DDA
Biter Bit, The. William Edmonstoune Aytoun. BOHV; InMe; PA
Bits of song—what else? Hokku. Yone Noguchi. NP
Bitten. Mark Van Doren. AnAmPo; LA
Bitter and beautiful, sing no more. To the Sea. Sara Teasdale. ChMo; CMP
Bitter, bitter/ Is my fate. Misery. Shao Ch'ang Heng. OnPM
Bitter Bread and Weak Wine. Jean Starr Untermeyer. TBM
Bitter-cold year comes to an end, The. The Cold Year. Tao Yuan-ming. WhP
Bitter Herb, The. Jeanne Robert Foster. SBMV
Bitter in sooth is the wind to-night. The Viking. Whitley Stokes. OnYI
Bitter Love, A. Li Po, *tr. fr. Chinese by* Witter Bynner. ChLP
Bitter Meditation. Byron. *Fr.* Childe Harold's Pilgrimage, IV. ERP
(Love.) EPP
(Love Unseen.) RO
("Oh Love! no habitant of earth thou art.") ViBoPo
Bitter pine cone may be eaten, The. The Empty Purse. Tu Fu. WhP
Bitter Purple Willows, The. Allen Upward. *Fr.* Scented Leaves from a Chinese Jar. NP
Bitter Question. Arthur R. Macdougall, Jr. PGD
Bitter Sanctuary. Harold Monro. ChMo; CMP; FaBoMo; LiTB; OBMV
Bitter Song. Shakespeare. *See* Blow, Blow, Thou Winter Wind.
Bitter-sweet. Asclepiades, *tr. fr. Greek by* F. L. Lucas. GrPE
Bitter-sweet. George Herbert. OxBoCh; TrPWD
Bitter-sweet, *sels.* Josiah Gilbert Holland.
Cradle Song: "What is the little one thinking about?" BOL; HBV; LPS-1; PCD
(Babyhood.) AA
Hymn: "For summer's bloom and autumn's blight." TrPWD
Song of Faith. WGRP
Bitter-sweet. Elisabeth Scollard. TBM
Bitter-sweet is the ailment called love. Sophocles, *tr. fr. Greek by* Moses Hadas. GrPo
Bitter the storm to-night. The Vikings. *Unknown.* ChTr
Bitter was it, Oh to view. *Unknown. Fr.* A Lament for the Priory of Walsingham. ChTr
Bitter Withy, The. *Unknown.* AnEC; BaBo; ChTr; OAEP; ViBoFo, *with music*
Bitterly they fought, for that planet room. The Inexorable. Huw Menai. MoWP
Bittern, The. Roberta Teale Swartz. WhBS
Bitterness. V. Sackville-West. TCPD
Bitterness. Sophocles, *tr. fr. Greek by* F. Storr. *Fr.* Ajax. LiA
Bitterness of days like these we know, The. Salutamus. Sterling A. Brown. CDC
Bitters. Lizette Woodworth Reese. DaM
Bitwene Mersh and Averil. *Unknown. See* Alisoun.
Bivouac. Alun Lewis. ChMP
Bivouac of the Dead, The. Theodore O'Hara. AA; AnAmPo; AOAH; BIG; BLPA; BoHiPo; DD, *much abr.;* GA, *much abr.;* HBV; HH; LA; LBAP; MC; MDAH, *abr.;* NeHB; OBAV; PaA; PAH; PAP; PTA-2; SPP; TCAP; TreF
"Muffled drum's sad roll has beat, The," *sel.* PoRL
Bivouac on a Mountain Side. Walt Whitman. AA; AmP; AmPo; APW; ChTr; CoBA; CoV; IAP; MDAH; MOAP; OxBA; Po; TCAP
Bixby's Landing. Robinson Jeffers. MOAP
Bizarre Deity, dark as infernal nights. Sed Non Satiata. Baudelaire. OnPM
Black. W. W. Gibson. *See* Back.
Black *A*, white *E*, red *I*, green *U*, blue *O*. Vowels. Arthur Rimbaud. TrFP
Black absence hides upon the past. Stanzas. John Clare. EnLoPo
Black, all black are their horses. Ballad of the Spanish Civil Guard. Federico García Lorca. CoSP
Black and Blue Eyes. Thomas Moore. LPS-1
Black and Gold. Nancy Byrd Turner. MPB; TiPo; YeAr
Black and White. Esther Lilian Duff. HBMV
Black and White Shuffle. Harry Elmore Hurd. WhC
Black Angel. Lewis Thompson. AtBAP
Black as a battering-ram the massive head. Buffalo. Roy Daniells. CaP
Black as a chimney is his face. "Sooeep!" Walter de la Mare. BoTP
Black Ashes. Martha Haskell Clark. NLK
Black Ball Line, The, *with music. Unknown.* ABF; AmSS; SoAmSa, *diff. vers.*
(Blow, Boys, Blow, *vers.* IV, *diff. vers.*) ShS
Black beamy hairs, which so seem to arise. To Her Hair. Lord Herbert of Cherbury. SeEP
Black beauty, which above that common light. Sonnet of Black Beauty. Lord Herbert of Cherbury. AtBAP; BoW; ElSeCe MePo; SeCL; SeEP
Black Betty, *with music. Unknown.* ABF
Black Bill's Honey-Moon, *abr.* Alfred Noyes. *Fr.* Tales of the Mermaid Tavern, III. PCN

Black Bird. *See* Blackbird.
Black, black, the sheen of his back and shoulders. Toro. W. S. Merwin. NePA
Black Book of Carmarthen, The, *sels. Unknown, tr. fr. Welsh.*
Englyn, *tr. by* Gwyn Williams. PrWP
On Christians, Mercy Will Fall, *tr. by* D. M. Lloyd. PrWP
Song of the Graves, The, *tr. by* Ernest Rhys. BMV
Winter, *tr. by* Kenneth Jackson. PrWP
Wisdom in Winter, *tr. by* Gwyn Williams. PrWP
Black Boy. Carl Carmer. AnAmPo; LA
Black Boy. Norman Rosten. TrJP
Black boy rose from his bed, The. Samuel. Alan Paton. BoSA
Black boy, the night hides you. Black Boy. Norman Rosten. TrJP
Black Boys, The. James Boyd. MuM
Black Bread. "Eduard Bagritsky." *See* Piece of Black Bread, A.
Black brother, think you life so sweet. Time to Die. Ray Garfield Dandridge. BANP
Black Bunny. William Brighty Rands. CBPC
Black but Comely. Asclepiades, *tr. fr. Greek by* Robert Allason Furness. GrR
Black Cat. Lora Dunetz. NePoAm-2
Black cat among roses, A. The Garden by Moonlight. Amy Lowell. NP; PFY; TOP; YT
Black cat, black cat, with the lucky white spot at your neck. Black Cat. Lora Dunetz. NePoAm-2
Black Cat Crossed His Luck, De. James D. Corrothers. CIV
Black Cat in Prunus-Tree. Joseph Braddock. PoC
Black cat yawns, The. The Cat. Mary Britton Miller. BoChLi; StVeCh; SUS; TiPo; UTS
Black Christ, The. Arthur Shearly Cripps. BoSA
Black Christmas. DuBose Heyward. LS
Black city is mute and as if in meditation, The. Militarism. Joseph Eliyia. MoGP
Black clouds and mists and sullen night. Hymn for Morning. Prudentius. *Fr.* Cathemerinon. LaP
Black clouds press on the city; the city would seem to be destroyed. Die for His Majesty. Li Ho. WhP
Black clouds spread over the sky. Looking from the Pavilion over the Lake. Su T'ung-po. OnPC
Black Cottage, The. Robert Frost. AmPo; AmPP; CoBA; CV; OnAP
"Black" Country, The. D. J. Enright. HaMV
Black Crispus Attucks taught/ Us how to die. Dark Symphony. Melvin B. Tolson. PoNe
Black crosses on the skyline, like a squad heedless of levies. Erris Coast, 1943. Hugh Connell. NeIP
Black Diamond. Nikolai Stepanovich Gumilev, *tr. fr. Russian by* Babette Deutsch. TrRV
Black door gapes and the black wall rises, The. Lines Written in the Realization That I Must Die. Robert Ervin Howard. DaM
Black Dot, The. Gérard de Nerval. *See* Dark Blot, The.
Black dusk growing. The Twelve. Aleksandr Blok. BoRS
Black earth tipples rain, The. *Unknown, tr. fr. Greek by* Sir Edwin Arnold. GrPo
Black earth's always drinking, The. "Come, Fill the Cup." *Unknown. Fr.* Anacreontea. GrPE
Black enormous cat, A. Cloud Fantasies, I. Christian Morgenstern. OnPM
Black-eyed Susan. John Gay. EPP; EtS; GTBS; GTBS-D; GTBS-W; GTSE; GTSL; HBV; LPS-1; TreFS
(Song: Black-eyed Susan.) EV-3
(Sweet William's Farewell to Black-eyed Susan.) BeLS; CEP; CoEV; EIPP; OBEC
Black-eyed Susie, *with music. Unknown.* ABF
Black Eyes. Avetis Isahakian, *tr. fr. Armenian by* Zabelle C. Boyajian. ArmLP
Black eyes if you seem dark. To Her Eyes. Lord Herbert of Cherbury. OBS
Black eyes, in your dark orbs doth lie. Upon Black Eyes, and Becoming Frowns. James Howell. SeCL
Black Finger, The. Angelina W. Grimké. PoNe
Black fool, why winter here? These frozen skies. Advice to a Raven in Russia, December, 1812. Joel Barlow. AmPP (4th ed.); APW; NePA; OxBA
Black Friday. Louella C. Poole. CIV
Black Frost. May Folwell Hoisington. LPS-1
Black Gal, De, *with music. Unknown.* ABF
Black grows the sudden sky, betokening rain. Sudden Shower. John Clare. EV-4; OBRV
Black Hair. Muhammadji, *tr. fr. Persian by* E. Powys Mathers. LiTW
Black-haired gaunt Paulinus, The. Edwin and Paulinus. *Unknown.* LPS-2
Black haw is in flower again, The. Song from the Traffic. Margaret Bell Houston. LS
Black horse came to visit us, A. Snow on the East Wind. Lord Dunsany. MBP; MoBrPo (1942 ed.)
Black Horse with a White Breast, A. Ibn Sa'id of Alcala la Real, *tr. fr. Arabic by* A. J. Arberry. MooP
Black I am and much admired. *Unknown.* OxNR
Black in the fog and in the snow. Waifs and Strays. Arthur Rimbaud. WoL
Black is no color; white is all of sense. Five Epigrams, 4. Donald Hall. NePoAm-2
Black [*or* Blacke] is the beauty of the brightest day. Divine Zenocrate [*or* To Entertain Divine Zenocrate *or* The Death of Zenocrate]. Christopher Marlowe. *Fr.* Tamburlaine the Great, Pt. II. AtBAP; BoW; ChTr; PoD; ViBoPo; WHA
Black is the night they are marching through. What Though the Dark! Archie Edwards. BePJ
Black is what the prisons are. The African Affair. Bruce McM. Wright. PoNe
Black Jack David come ridin' through the woods. The Gypsy Laddie (B *vers.*). *Unknown.* ViBoFo
Black Jack Davy [*or* Davie]. *Unknown. See* Wraggle Taggle Gipsies, The.
Black Knight, The. John Todhunter. OBVV; PoVP
Black Leopard, The. Frances Crawford. PtPa
Black, long-tailed, The/ one then. The Yellow Season. William Carlos Williams. MoAB; MoAmPo (1950 ed.)
Black Madonna, The. Albert Rice. CDC
Black Magdalens. Countee Cullen. BANP; BAP; QS
Black magnet of hate has sucked up our flight, The. The Man without a Road, X. Erik Lindegren. LiTW
Black Mammies. John Wesley Holloway. BANP; MotAn
Black Mammy's Lullaby, 1855. Wightman F. Melton. BOL
Black Man Talks of Reaping, A. Arna Bontemps. BANP; CDC; PoNe
Black Man's Son, The. Oswald Durand, *tr. fr. French by* Edna Worthley Underwood. PoNe
Black Marigolds. Bilhana, *formerly at. to* Chauras, *tr. fr. Sanskrit by* E. Powys Mathers. AWP; LiTW, *abr.*
Sels.
Death Sends Me the Flickering of Powdery Lids. OnPM
Her Mouth Carelessly Scented. OnPM
I Have a Need. OnPM
I Have No Surety. OnPM
I Know My Princess. OnPM
I Know That I Have Savoured. OnPM
I Love Long Black Eyes. OnPM
I Mind That I Went Round with Men and Women. OnPM
I Mind the Coming. OnPM
I Mind the Time of the Falling of Blossoms. OnPM
I See Her. OnPM
I See the Heavy Startled Hair. OnPM
I Seem to See My Prison Walls. OnPM
If I See in My Soul. OnPM
If My Girl with Lotus Eyes. OnPM
Love Is a God. OnPM
My Eyes That Hurry to See. OnPM
Pleased Intimacy, The. OnPM
She Swims Back in the Crowning Hour. OnPM
She with Young Limbs. OnPM
Spread We Our Nets. OnPM
Stainless Fair Appearance, The. OnPM
When All My Heavy Heart. OnPM
Woodcutter and the Fisherman Turn Home, The. OnPM
Black Messengers, The. César Vallejo, *tr. fr. Spanish by* H. R. Hays. TwSpPo
Black Militia of the Pen, The. Edward Young. *Fr.* Epistles to Mr. Pope Concerning the Authors of the Age. BeR
Black milk of the dawn we drink it evenings. Death Fugue. Paul Celan. TrJP
Black mountains pricked with pointed pine. The Watershed. Alice Meynell. POTE; POTT
Black night./ White snow. The Twelve. Aleksandr Aleksandrovich Blok. AWP; LiTW; PoFr; TrRV
Black night bends down upon the tangled woods. In the Forest. Alexander Petofi. LiTW
Black night came down in rain and wrath and storm, The. Sing Thou, My Soul. Theodosia Garrison. CAW
Black night without, and blacker night within. Rachel. Ruth Gilbert. AnNZ
Black-nosed kitten will slumber all the day, A. Choosing a Kitten. *Unknown.* StVeCh
Black November Turkey, A. Richard Wilbur. FiMAP; MoAB
Black on flat water past the jonquil lawns. The Black Swan. James Merrill. MoPo
Black-out. Robinson Jeffers. LiTA; LiTM (rev. ed.); NePA; WaP
Black Panther, The. John Hall Wheelock. BAP; HBMV; LiTG; LiTM; PFY
Black pitchy night, companion of my woe. Sonnet. Michael Drayton. Idea's Mirrour, LXX [XLV]. LoBV; OBSC; ReIE; SiCE; TuPP
Black Poplar-Boughs. John Freeman. HBMV
Black Prince, The. Sir Walter Scott. *Fr.* Rob Roy. CBPC
Black reapers with the sound of steel on stones. Reapers. Jean Toomer. CDC
Black, Red, and Gold, *sel.* Ferdinand Freiligrath, *tr. fr. German by* J. L. Joynes.
"True Freedom breaks the yokes that gall." PoFr

Black Regiment, The. George Henry Boker. GN; HBV; LPS-2; PAH; PAP
Black Riders, The, *sels.* Stephen Crane.
Black Riders, The, I (*title poem*). AA; AmP; MOAP; TCAP
Blades of Grass, The ("In heaven/ Some little blades of grass"), XVIII. AmP; BAP; MAP; MaRV; MoAmPo; NeMA; PoeMoYo; PYM; TCAP
Heart, The ("In the desert/ I saw a creature"). III. HoPM; MAP; MoAmPo; NeMA
(Eating.) BAP
"I met a seer," XXXVI. CoBA
(Book of Wisdom, The.) HoPM; MAP; MoAmPo
I Saw a Man [Pursuing the Horizon], XXIV. BAP; CoBA; HoPM; LiTA; LoGBV; MAP; MoAmPo; NeMA; NePA; PoeMoYo
I Stood upon a High Place, IX. AmP; LiTA; NePA
It Was Wrong to Do This, Said the Angel, LIV. AmP; LiTA; NePA
Learned Man, A, XX. LiTA; MoAmPo (1950 ed.); NePA
Man Saw a Ball of Gold in the Sky, A. XXXV. AmP; LiTA; NePA
Many Workmen, XXXI. LiTA; NePA
"On the horizon the peaks assembled," XXXVII. MOAP
"Once I saw mountains angry," XXII. MOAP
(Ancestry.) AA; LEAP
"Sage lectured brilliantly, The," LVIII. AnAmPo; LA; YaD
'Scaped ("Once I knew a fine song"), LXV. AA
"Two or three angels," XXXII. AnAmPo; LA
Why? ("Behold the grave of a wicked man"), XXV. AA; LEAP
"Youth in apparel that glittered, A," XXVII. AnAmPo; LA; LiTA; MoAmPo (1950 ed.); NePA
(Content.) AA; LEAP
Black riders came from the sea. The Black Riders, I. Stephen Crane. AA; AmP; MOAP; TCAP
Black Rock, The. John Gould Fletcher. SPP; TCPD
Black Rock of Kiltearn, The. Andrew Young. FaBoTw
Black Rose, The. Clement Wood. TBM
Black Sailor's Chanty. Charles Keeler. EtS
Black Sheep. Richard Burton. AA; BPP; HBV; LBMV; OBAV
Black spruce and Norway pine. Pare Lorentz. *Fr.* The River. NAMP
Black swallows swooping or gliding. The Skaters. John Gould Fletcher. MAP; MoAmPo; NeMA; PFY; PoMa
Black Swan, The. Randall Jarrell. FiMAP
Black Swan, The. James Merrill. MoPo
Black Swans. Carl Snoilsky, *tr. fr. Swedish by* Charles W. Stork. AnSL
Black Tail Range, The, *with music.* *Unknown.* CoSo
Black Tambourine. Hart Crane. CoBMV; NAMP; OxBA; PoNe
Black texture of the leafy trees, engraved. Three Fragments, III. William Allingham. IrPN
Black Thing. *Unknown.* CoMu
Black Tower, The. W. B. Yeats. ChMo
Black Tragedy lets slip her grim disguise. Masks. Thomas Bailey Aldrich. AA
Black velvet where a shining diamond. Black Diamond. Nikolai Stepanovich Gumilev. TrRV
Black Virgin, The. G. K. Chesterton. ISi
Black Vulture, The. George Sterling. AnAmPo; BAP; BLA; HBV; LA; LBMV; LEAP; MAP; MoAmPo (1942 ed.); MOAP; NP; NV; OBAV; PFY; PoMa; PoTo; TCAP; TCPD
Black Wall-Flower, The. Frances Anne Kemble. VA
Black wave the trees in the forest. Adventure. Laura Benét. GaP; HBMV; RAR; TSW; TSWC
Black we are but [*or* though] much admired. *Unknown.* OTPC (1946 ed.); RIS
Black wings and white in the hollow. Behind the Plough. James H. Cousins. OxBI
Black within and red without. Mother Goose. BoChLi; OxNR; PPL; RIS
Black Your Shoes, Your Honour? *Unknown.* PCH
("Here's Finiky Hawkes.") OxNR
Blackberry, The. Norman Nicholson. MoBrPo (1950 ed.); NeMA
Blackberry Fold. *Unknown.* *See* Squire and Milkmaid.
Blackberry Girl, The. Nancy Dennis Sproat. BLPA
Blackberry Winter. John Crowe Ransom. OnHM; OxBA; PoRA
Blackbird, A. Marcus Argentarius, *tr. fr. Greek by* Sir William Marris. LiTW; OxBG
Blackbird, The. William Barnes. EV-4; GTSE; HBV
Blackbird, The. Henry Charles Beeching. OBVV
Blackbird, The. Alice Cary. BLA; LBAP
Blackbird, The. Dinah Maria Mulock Craik. BoTP; GoTP
Blackbird, The. Phyllis Drayson. BoTP
Blackbird, The. John Drinkwater. BLA; TVSH; WP
Blackbird, The. Théophile Gautier, *tr. fr. French by* Alan Conder. TrFP
Blackbird, The. W. E. Henley. Echoes, XVIII. BLA; BPN; BTP; EPP; HBV; LoPo; MBP; MoBrPo; NeMA; PoeMoYo; TrGrPo; TSW; TSWC
(To A. D.) AnFE; BEL; BPN; HoPM; LoPS; OuHeWo; POTT; PoVP; TOP; ViBoPo; VOD
Blackbird, The. A. E. Housman. *See* When Smoke Stood Up from Ludlow.
Blackbird, The. Tennyson. OTPC; SN
Blackbird, The. Frederick Tennyson. HBV; LPS-2; VA
Blackbird, The ("Ah, blackbird, thou art satisfied"). *Unknown, tr. fr. Middle Irish by* Kuno Meyer. AnIL; OnYI
Blackbird, The. ("In midst of woods or pleasant grove"). *Unknown.* *See* In Midst of Woods.
Blackbird, The ("On a fair summer's morning of soft recreation"). *Unknown.* OnYI
Blackbird, The. Humbert Wolfe. BLA; BoTP; FAOV; FaPON; HBMV; HBVY; MPB; NLK; PCH; StVeCh; SUS; TiPo; TSW; UTS
Blackbird, blackbird in the cage. The Bird and the Tree. Ridgely Torrence. BAP; CBOV; HBMV; MAP; MoAmPo (1942 ed.); NP; NV; PoFr; PoNe; TBM
Blackbird by Belfast Lough, The. *Unknown, tr. fr. Irish by* Frank O'Connor. KiLC
Blackbird darted through the boughs, The. The Bird. Andrew Young. POTE
Blackbird flew down to the almond tree, A. Opposites. José Moreno Villa. CoSP; OnPM
Blackbird in the Town, The. Oliver St. John Gogarty. PoP
Blackbird of Derrycairn, The ("Stop, stop and listen"). Austin Clarke, *after the Irish.* NeIP
Blackbird of Derrycairn, The ("Sweetly sung"). *Unknown, tr. fr. Old Irish by* Seán O'Faoláin. SiB
Blackbird of Litir Lone, The. On Not Hearing the Birds Sing in Ireland. Padraic Colum. NePoAm
Black bird of my heart, whose breasts are oranges. Three Haitian Creole Moods. Emile Roumer. OnHM
Blackbird Song, The. Marjory Christmas. ReTS
Blackbird Suddenly, A. Joseph Auslander. BAP; BLA; MaRV; MPB; NLK; PC; PIAE; PoRL; TiPo; VOD
Black-bird whistles from the thorny brake, The. Birds in Spring. James Thomson. *Fr.* The Seasons: Spring. OBEC
Blackbirds in the Rain. Joyce Horner. WhBS
Blackbird's Nest. The. *Unknown.* *See* Deserted Home, The.
Blackbird's Song, The. *Unknown, tr. fr. Old Irish by* George Sigerson. TIP
Blackcap, madcap. Chickadees. Edith M. Thomas. BLA
Blackcaps pipe among the reeds. The. Before the Rain. Amélie Rives. AA
Blacke is the beauty of the brightest day. *See* Black is the beauty of the brightest day.
Blacken thy heavens, Jove. Prometheus. Goethe. AWP; JAWP; WBP; WoL
Blackened and bleeding, helpless, panting, prone. Chicago. Bret Harte. PAH
"Blackie." John Joy Bell. TVSH
Blackmwore Maidens. William Barnes. EPN; EV-4; GTBS; HBV; PoVP; ShBV-3; VA
Blackness behind. A Black Horse with a White Breast. Ibn Sa'id of Alcala la Real. MooP
Black'on frowns east on Maidon. After the Club-Dance. Thomas Hardy. At Casterbridge Fair, III. BEL; EmBrPo; EnLi-2 (1949 ed.); EnLit; PoVP
Blackpool Breezes. *Unknown.* CoMu
Blacksmith. B. K. Pyke. BoTP
Blacksmith, The. *Unknown, tr. fr. German.* SAS
Blacksmith did not hobble here, The. Old Hundred. Mark Van Doren. UnS
Blacksmith of Limerick, The. Robert Dwyer Joyce. TIP
Blacksmith Pain. Otto Julius Bierbaum, *tr. fr. German by* Jethro Bithell. AWP; JAWP; WBP
Blacksmiths, The. *Unknown, tr. fr. Middle English by* George B. Pace. EnL
Blacksmith's boy went out with a rifle, The. Legend. Judith Wright. BoAV
Blacksmith's Serenade, The. Vachel Lindsay. StPo
Blacktail Deer. Lew Sarett. NP
Blade I bear, The. Harmodius and Aristogeiton. *Unknown.* GrL; OxBG
Blade is sharp, the reaper stout, The. Theology. Joyce Kilmer. TSW; TSWC
Blade of Grass Sings to the River, The. Leah Goldberg, *tr. fr. Hebrew by* Robert Friend. TrJP
Blades of Grass, The. Stephen Crane. The Black Riders, XVIII. AmP; BAP; MAP; MaRV; MoAmPo; NeMA; PoeMoYo; PYM; TCAP
Blades of Harden, The. Will H. Ogilvie. *Fr.* Whaup o' the Rede. GoTS
Bladud had one son, Leir was he called. Leir and His Daughters. Layamon. *Fr.* The Brut. MeEV
Bladyn's Song of Cloten. Charles M. Doughty. *Fr.* The Dawn in Britain. PoEL-5
Blake. John Gould Fletcher. InP

Blake saw a treeful of angels at Peckham Rye. Mad Blake. William Rose Benét. BAP; HBMV; SBMV
Blame Not My Cheeks. Thomas Campion. EG; EV-2; UnPo
Blame Not My Lute. Sir Thomas Wyatt. ElL; ElSeCe; ReEn; ReIE; RiBV; SiCE; SiPS; TuPP
(Lute Obeys, The.) OBSC
Blame Not the Gods! Homer, *pr. tr. fr. Greek by* S. H. Butcher *and* Andrew Lang. *Fr.* Odyssey. GrR
Blameless Kiss, The. Joachim du Bellay, *tr. fr. French by* Alan Conder. Les Amours, XV. TrFP
Blaming Sons. T'ao Ch'ien, *tr. fr. Chinese by* Arthur Waley. Twelve Poems, 5. TrCh
Blaming the bitterness of this sorrow, Perikles, no man. Archilochus, *tr. fr. Greek by* Richmond Lattimore. GrPo
Blanaid's Song ("Blanaid loves roses"). Joseph Campbell. OxBI
Blanche comme la neige, *with music.* *Unknown, tr. fr. French.* OuSiCo
Blancheflour and Jellyflorice. *Unknown.* ESPB
Bland many-eyed walls, The. Prevailing Winds. Lee Anderson. TwAmPo
Blank Book Letter, The. Samuel Greenberg. LiTA
"Blank Misgivings of a Creature Moving About in Worlds Not Realized." Arthur Hugh Clough. EmBrPo
Sels.
"Here am I yet, another twelvemonth spent," I. VLEP
"How often sit I, poring o'er," V. EPN; GTBS-D; VLEP
(Blank Misgivings.) BPN
"Though to the vilest things beneath the moon," II. VLEP
"Well, well—Heaven bless you all," III. VLEP
"Yes, I have lied, and so must walk my way," IV. VLEP
Blare of trumpet and roll of drum! The Victor. William Young. HBMV
Blast . . . 1875, The. Robert Louis Stevenson. POTT
Blast from Freedom's Northern hills, upon its Southern way, The. Massachusetts to Virginia. Whittier. AmPP; AnNE; CoBA; IAP; WoL
Blast! if the sun desert these shores! Michael and Christine. Arthur Rimbaud. AnFP
Blast of War, The. Shakespeare. *See* Once More unto the Breach . . .
Blast of Wind, A, a Momentary Breath. Barnabe Barnes. *See* Life of Man, The.
Blasted and bored and undermined. The Chalk-Cliff. Andrew Young. POTE
Blasted Herb, The. Meshech Weare. PAH
Blasted with sighs, and surrounded with teares [*or* tears]. Twicknam [*or* Twickenham] Garden. John Donne. CaAE; EnLoPo; EPS; LoBV; MeLP; MePo; OBS; PoEL-2; PoFS; ReIE; SeEP; TuPP
Blasts of Autumn drive the winged seeds, The. Spring. Shelley. *Fr.* The Revolt of Islam. EV-4
Blauen Veilchen der Äugelein, Die. Heine. *See* Withered Heart, The.
Blazing Heart, The. Alice Williams Brotherton. AA
Blazing sun has made the armor hot, The. Pause on the March. Sergey Orlov. TrRV
Blazon Columbia's emblem. Columbia's Emblem. Edna Dean Proctor. GN
Bleak, bony-grey, its twisted branches rise. The Dead Tree. Arthur Davison Ficke. MuM
Bleak day, A! Another Beggar Poem. Issa. PoFr
Bleak-faced Winter, with his braggart winds, The. Australian Spring. Hugh McCrae. BoAu
Bleak the February light. Kingdom of Heaven. Léonie Adams. MAP; MoAB; MoAmPo
Bleak wind is riding on the waves, A. Gray. Oscar Williams. NLK
Bleat of Protest. Mildred Weston. FiBHP
Bleeding Heart Aflame, A. James M. Hayes. PraNu
Blend of mirth and sadness, smiles and tears, A. Lincoln [*or* The Masterpiece]. Walter Malone. InP; PGD; PSO
Blend of stubborn English oak, A. My Mother. Mahlon Leonard Fisher. NV
Blenheim. Addison. *Fr.* The Campaign. OBEC
("But O, my Muse.") EPP
Blennerhassett's Island. Thomas Buchanan Read. *Fr.* The New Pastoral. PAH
Bless, Dear Saviour, This Child. Thomas Beck. BePJ
Bless earth with Thine Advent, O Saviour Christ! Advent Lyrics, VIII. *Unknown.* *Fr.* Christ I. AnOE
Bless Him ("Bless Him, O constant companions"). *Unknown, tr. fr. Hebrew by* Israel Abrahams. TrJP
Bless love and hope. Full many a withered year. Love and Hope. Dante Gabriel Rossetti. The House of Life, XLIII. PoVP; ViPo
Bless the Blessed Morn. Horatius Bonar. BePJ
Bless the Dear Old Verdant Land. Denis Florence MacCarthy. VA
Bless the four corners of this house. House Blessing. Arthur Guiterman. BrR; MaRV; PraP; TiPo; TrPWD
Bless the Lord, O my soul; and all that is within me. Psalm CIII, Bible, *O.T.* AWP; JAWP; PC; TiPo (1952 ed.); WGRP
Bless the Lord, O my soul. O Lord my God, Thou art very great. Psalm CIV, Bible, *O.T.* OHIP; TrJP; WGRP
Bless Thou this year, O Lord! Prayer [*or* A Prayer for a Happy New Year]. A. S. C. Clarke. BLRP; PGD; PSO
Bless with the splendor white of God's new shrine. Mother Mary Xavier. Francis P. Donnelly. PraNu
Bless you, bless you, bonnie [*or* burnie] bee. *Unknown.* BoTP; OxNR; SAS
Bless'd art Thou, O Lord of all. Prayer before Sleep. Alice Lucas. TrJP
Bless'd be the great! for those they take away. Pope. *Fr.* Epistle to Dr. Arbuthnot. PtP
Blessed. Soné, *tr. fr. Hebrew by* David Kuselewitz. TrJP
Blessed. *Unknown.* OQP; PraP; QP-2
(How God Answers.) MaRV
Blessed Agitator, The. Lucia Trent. ChIP
Blessed are the eyes that see. My Peace I Give unto You. G. A. Studdert-Kennedy. MaRV
Blessed are the poor in spirit. The Beatitudes. St. Matthew, Bible, *N.T.* ExPo; GoTP; GrCo-1; MaRV; TrGrPo
Blessèd Are They. Yevgeny Abramovich Boratynsky, *tr. fr. Russian by* Harold Furth. TrRV
Blessed Are They. Wilhelmina Stitch. PoToHe
Blessed are they of the Easter faith. Easter Beatitudes. Clarence M. Burkholder. BLRP
Blessed are they that have eyes to see. Some Blesseds. John Oxenham. WGRP
Blessèd are they that righteousness proclaim! Blessèd Are They. Yevgeny Abramovich Boratynsky. TrRV
Blessed are they who are pleasant to live with. Blessed Are They. Wilhelmina Stitch. PoToHe
Blessed are they who sow but do not reap. Blessed. Soné. TrJP
Blessed are those who have not seen. In Stratis Viarum. Arthur Hugh Clough. PoVP; VLEP
Blessed art Thou, O God our Lord. Blessings for Chanukah. Jessie E. Sampter. TiPo (1952 ed.)
Blessed Art Thou, O Lord. *Unknown, tr. fr. Hebrew by* Theodor H. Gaster. *Fr.* The Dead Sea Scrolls. TrJP
Blessed art thou that fearest God. Beati Omnes. Psalm CXXVIII, Bible, *O.T., tr. by* Thomas Sternhold. ReIE; SiCE
Blessed be God who made such pretty birches. Courtesy. Daniel Sargent. DDA; MW
Blessed Be That Lady Bright. *Unknown.* AnEC
Blessed be that maid Mary. Eia Jesus Hodie. *Unknown.* AnEC
Blessed be the English and all their ways and works. Jobson's Amen. Kipling. AnFE; POTT; VLEP
Blessed Be the Holy Will of God. *Unknown, tr. fr. Modern Irish by* Douglas Hyde. OnYI
Blessed Be the Hour. Walther von der Vogelweide, *tr. fr. German by* Margarete Münsterberg. LyMA
Blessed be the Lord God of Israel; for he hath visited and redeemed his people. Benedictus. St. Luke, Bible, *N.T.* MaRV
Blessed be this place. Blood and the Moon. W. B. Yeats. CaAE; EnLP; TwHP
Blessed be thou, Lady. Salve Regina! *Unknown.* TMEV
Blessed be your name, my God. Paul Claudel. *Fr.* Five Grand Odes. OnHM
Blessed Bible, sacred treasure. The Best of All. Fanny Crosby. BLRP
Blessed Bird, as I You Say, A. *Unknown.* AnEC
Blessed, blessed is all nature. Morning Worship. Henrik Wergeland. AnNoLy
Blessed by the baptism of the deep. Wonder Books. Carrie Ward Lyon. MOB
Blessed cooling fount thou art, A. The Tear. Kristján Jónsson. IcP
Blessed Damozel, The. Dante Gabriel Rossetti. AEV; AnFE; AWP; BEL; BLV; BMEP; BoLiVe; BPN; CaAE; CBOV; CoBE; CoEV; EmBrPo; EnL; EnLi-2; EnLit; EPN; EPP; EV-5; GBV; GoTL; GTBS; GTML; GTSL; HBV; HiLiEn; LEAP; LiTB; LiTG; LoBV; LPS-3, *abr.;* OAEP; OBEV; OBVV; OHFP; OuHeWo; PC; PIAE; PIR, *abr.;* PoE; PoEL-5; POTT; PoVP; REAL; ReaPo; SeCeV; ShBV-4; TCEP; TOP; TrGrPo; TSW; TSWC; TyEnPo; VA; ViP; ViPo; ViPP; VLEP; WHA
Blessed Face, The. Ray Palmer. *See* Jesus, These Eyes Have Never Seen.
Blessed Is God ("Blessed is God that liveth forever"). *Tr. fr. Greek by* D. C. Simpson. Tobit, XIII, Bible, Apocrypha. TrJP
Blessed is he who, far from cities, rather. Contentment. Olivier de Magny. TrFP
Blessed is she whose daily tasks are a labor of love. Beatitudes for a Housewife. Mary Mae Oesch. PoToHe (new ed.)
Blessed is the man, O Virgin Mary. St. Bonaventure. *Fr.* Psalter of the Blessed Virgin Mary. ISi
Blessed is the man that beholdeth the face of a friend in a far country. The Face of a Friend. Henry van Dyke. OQP; QP-2

Blessed is the man that walketh not in the counsel of the ungodly. The Godly and the Ungodly. Psalm I, Bible, *O.T.* AWP; EnLi-1; HiLiEn; JAWP; TreF; WGRP; WoL
Blessed land of Judea! thrice hallowed of song. Palestine. Whittier. WBLP
Blessed Little Jesus of the Cradle. A Christmas Prayer. Lucy Embury. ChrBoLe
Blessed Match, The. Hannah Senesh, *tr. fr. Yiddish.* TrJP
Blessed May Thou Be, Sweet Jesus. *At. to* Richard Smert. AnEC
Blessed morn has come again, The. Snow—a Winter Sketch. Ralph Hoyt. LPS-2
Blessed Name, The. George W. Bethune. BLRP
Blessed of the Lord Be His Land. Deuteronomy, XXXIII: 13–16, Bible, *O.T.* BrR
(Give Ear, O Ye Heavens.) PCH
Blessed Offendo[u]r: who thyself hast tried [*or* haist try'd]. To Saint Mary Magdalen. Henry Constable. LoBV (2d ed.); PoEL-2
Blessed poster girl leaned out, The. The Poster Girl. Carolyn Wells. HBV; InMe; FA
Blessed Road, The. Charles Buxton Going. ChIP
Blessed Saint Winefride, at thy fair shrine. Saint Winefride. C. W. Barraud. PraNu
Blessed Spot, A. Abulfadhel Ahmed, *tr. fr. Arabic by* Leigh Hunt. OnPM
Blessed story of the Christ, The. The Babe of Bethlehem. Henry Beer. BePJ
Blessed Task, The. Harriet McEwen Kimball. BePJ
Blessed the Dead in Spirit, our brave dead. Beati Mortui. Louise Imogen Guiney. LBAP
Blessed the match that was burned. The Blessed Match. Hannah Senesh. TrJP
Blessed thou, Simon. Poems by the Roadside. St. Matthew, Bible, *N.T.* CAW
Blessed Trinity have pity! Childless. Giollabhrighde Mac Conmidhe. KiLC
Blessed Virgin Compared to the Air We Breathe, The. Gerard Manley Hopkins. ISi; MoPo; OxBoCh; PoLi
Blessed Virgin Mary Compared to a Window, The. Thomas Merton. ISi
Blessed Virgin's Expostulation, The. Nahum Tate. ISi
Blessed with a joy that only she. The Gift of God. E. A. Robinson. AnAmPo; CoBMV; CP; MAP; MAPA; MoAB; MoAmPo; OxBA; TCPD; TwAmPo
Blessèd, yet sinful one, and broken-hearted! To Mary Magdalen. Bartholome Leonardo de Argensola. CAW
Blessing, The. Mary Colborne-Veel. BoAu
Blessing for the Blessed, A. Laurence Alma-Tadema. BOL; BoTP; PRWS
(Sunset.) GFA
Blessing Mrs. Larkin. Margery Mansfield. GoYe
Blessing of Columcille, The. Thomas S. Jones, Jr. Sonnets of the Saints, I. TBM
Blessing of Saint Francis, The. St. Francis of Assisi. SaFP
Blessing of St. Francis, The. Sister Maura. CaP; SaFP
Blessing of the Dead, The. *Unknown, tr. fr. Greek by* F. L. Lucas. GrPE
Blessing of the Priests. Numbers, Bible, *O.T. See* Benediction.
Blessing of Toil. Samuel Ellsworth Kiser. PEDC
Blessing on Little Boys. Arthur Guiterman. DDA; TBM; TrPWD
Blessing on the Dance, A. Irwin Russell. *See* Blessing the Dance.
Blessing on you, Mrs. Larkin, for planting my trees, A! Blessing Mrs. Larkin. Margery Mansfield. GoYe
Blessing over Food. Hayyim Nahman Bialik. YeAr
Blessing the Dance. Irwin Russell. *Fr.* Christmas-Night in the Quarters. AnAmPo; LA
(Blessing on the Dance, A.) SPP
Blessing the Hounds. Mary Winter. GoYe
Blessings at Table. *Unknown.* PraP
Blessings for Chanukah. Jessie E. Sampter. TiPo (1952 ed.)
Blessings, in abundance come. The Good-Night or Blessing. Robert Herrick. ALV
Blessings of Peace. Bacchylides, *tr. fr. Greek by* Walter Headlam. GrR
(Peace.) OxBG
Blessings on Doneraile. Patrick O'Kelly. OnYI
Blessings on the hand of women! The Hand That Rocks the Cradle Is the Hand That Rules the World. William Ross Wallace. FaFP; TreF; WBLP
Blessings on thee, little man. The Barefoot Boy. Whittier. AA; AmPP (3d ed.); AnNE; BAP; CoBA; FaBoBe; FaPON; GN; GTBS-W; HBV; HBVY; IAP; LaNeLa; LBAP; LEAP; LiTA; LPS-1; MOAP; NeHB; OBAV; OBVV; OHFP; OnPP; OTPC; PIR; PoeMoYo; PTA-1; PYM; SN; TCAP; TreF; WBLP
Blessings That Remain, The. Annie Johnson Flint. BLRP
Blest Abode, A ("Behold yon arching doors"). Virgil, *tr. fr. Latin by* Theodore C. Williams. *Fr.* The Aeneid, VI. GrCo-1
Blest are the pure in heart. Purity of Heart. John Keble. *Fr.* The Purification. BLRP
Blest as the Immortal Gods. Sappho. *See* To a Bride.
Blest be God/ Who did create. Blessing over Food. Hayyim Nahman Bialik. YeAr
Blest be the bastard's birth! thro' wond'rous ways. On Himself. Richard Savage. *Fr.* The Bastard. BeR
Blest be the bric-a-brac that still survives. In the Shadowy Whatnot Corner. Robert Hillyer. NePoAm
Blest be the God of love. Even-Song. George Herbert. FaBoEn
Blest Be the Tie That Binds. John Fawcett. HBV; OlF
Blest beyond earth's bliss, with heaven I deem him. To a Bride. Sappho. GrL; OxBG; WoL
Blest, Blest and Happy He. *Unknown.* GoTS
Blest he who, like Ulysses, breasts the foam. My House. Joachim du Bellay. Regrets, XXXI. TrFP
Blest he who thinks on human destiny. At Dawn. Victor Hugo. OnPM; TrFP
Blest infant bud, whose blossom-life. The Burial of an Infant. Henry Vaughan. OAEP
Blest is he that seeketh rest. The Tree of the Cross. "Angelus Silesius." CAW
Blest is the man who never lent. The Patriot. Thomas Godfrey. PoFr
Blest Leaf! whose aromatic gales dispense. In Imitation of Pope. Isaac Hawkins Browne. *Fr.* A Pipe of Tobacco. OBEC
Blest pair of sirens, pledges of heav'ns [*or* heaven's] joy. At a Solemn Music [*or* Musick]. Milton. BCEP; BrBE; EG; EV-2; ExPo; GTBS; GTBS-D; GTBS-W; GTSE; GTSL; HBV; LoBV; OAEP; OBEV; OBS; OxBoCh; PoE; PoEL-3; SeCeV; SeCL; SeEP; TOP; UnS
Blest Retirement. Goldsmith. *Fr.* The Deserted Village. OBEC
Blest Spirit of Calm that dwellest in these woods! Charles Sangster. *Fr.* Sonnets Written in the Orillia Woods. PeCV
Blest Statesman He, Whose Mind's Unselfish Will. Wordsworth. EPN
Blest the Infant Babe. Wordsworth. *Fr.* The Prelude. AtBAP
Blest, who upon night's bed can lie. Elegy. Nikolai Yazykov. BoRS
Blest Winter Nights. John Armstrong. *Fr.* The Art of Preserving Health, III. OBEC
Blight. Arna Bontemps. BANP
Blight. Emerson. BAV; CDC; IAP
Blight rests in your face, The. To a Publisher . . . Cut-out. LeRoi Jones. NeAP
Blighted Love. Luís de Camões, *tr. fr. Portuguese by* Lord Strangford. LPS-1
"Blighters." Siegfried Sassoon. FaBoTw; MoVE
Blin' Man Stood on de Road [*or* Way] an' Cried, De. *Unknown.* ABF; BoAN-1, *with music*
(Blind Man, *with music.*) TrAS
Blind. John Kendrick Bangs. MaRV; OQP; POT; PoToHe; QP-1
Blind. Fanny Crosby. MaRV
Blind. Harry Kemp. BAP; HBMV; NLK; PFY; PoMa; POT; PoTo; SBMV
Blind. Norman V. Pearce. MaRV; PoToHe
Blind, The. Thomas Walsh. BAP
Blind as the song of birds. Lines to a Blind Girl. Thomas Buchanan Read. AA
Blind Bartimeus. Longfellow. ChIP
(Jericho's Blind Beggar.) WBLP
Blind Beggar of Alexandria, The, *sel.* George Chapman.
"Twentie are making for my head tyres and gownes." NBE
Blind Beggar's Daughter of Bednall-Green, The. *Unknown.* EV-2; LoEn; OBB; OTPC (1923 ed.), *sl. abr.*
(Blind Beggar of Bednall Green, The, *diff. vers.*) BaBo
Blind Boy, The. Colley Cibber. CEP; CG; GTBS; GTBS-D; GTBS-W; GTSE; GTSL; HBV; LPS-1; NeHB; OBEC; PRWS; TreFS; TVSH
Blind Boy's Pranks, The. William Thom. EBSV; EV-4; OBEV
Blind but Happy. Fanny Crosby. MaRV
Blind Child, The. *Unknown.* MaRV
Blind child, A. Haiku. Kikaku. OnPJ
Blind Date. Conrad Aiken. MoVE; ViBoPo (1958 ed.)
Blind door yawing to the snow, A. The Farm, 1871. Archibald MacLeish. ChMo; CMP
Blind Girl, The. Marjorie Cole. CAG
Blind Girl, The. Nathalia Crane. MAP; MCCG; MoAmPo (1942 ed.); PFE
Blind girl singing on the radio, A. Singing in the Dark. Irma Wassall. PoNe
Blind god Plutus, better far. The God of Wealth. Timocreon. OxBG
Blind Highland Boy, The. Wordsworth. OTPC
Blind, I Speak to the Cigarette. Joanne de Longchamps. GoYe
Blind lamentation in the wind, moon-days of winter. South Wind. Georg Trakl. AnGP

Blind Louise. George Washington Dewey. AA
Blind Love. Shakespeare. *See* Sonnets, CXLVIII.
Blind Man, The. Nazhun, *tr. fr. Arabic by* A. J. Arberry. MooP
Blind Man, The. Margaret E. Sangster. PoToHe
Blind Man. *Unknown. See* Blin' Man Stood on de Road an' Cried, De.
Blind Man at the Fair, The. Joseph Campbell. AnIV; AWP; JAWP; TIP; WBP
Blind man, blind man. *Unknown.* OxNR
Blind Man Lay beside the Way, *with music. Unknown.* AS
Blind Man's Cries. Tristan Corbière, *tr. fr. French by* Kenneth Koch *and* Georges Guy. AnFP
(Cries Out of Blindness, *tr. by* Harold Rosenberg.) LiTW
Blind Man's Morning, The. Viola Meynell. MoBrPo (1942 ed.)
Blind men add the figures, draw the maps, The. Great Powers Conference. Edith Lovejoy Pierce. PGD
Blind Men and the Elephant, The. Sana'i, *tr. fr. Persian by* E. G. Browne. PeP
Blind Men and the Elephant, The. John Godfrey Saxe. AnNE; APW; BBV (1951 ed.); BLPA; BoTP; FaBoBe; GoTP; HBV; HBVY; MaC; MaRV; MW; NeHB; OTPC; PCD; PoeMoYo; PoToHe (new ed.); PreP; StPo; StVeCh (1940 ed.); TreF; TSW; TVSH; WBLP
Blind minstrel, come. Robert Norwood. *Fr.* The Man of Kerioth. CPG
Blind Musicians, The. *Unknown, tr. fr. Chinese.* WhP
Blind Nun, The. Thomas S. Jones, Jr. PraNu
Blind Old Man, The. *Unknown, tr. fr. Greek by* T. F. Higham. *Fr.* Homeric Hymns. OxBG
Blind Peddler [*or* Pedlar], The. Sir Osbert Sitwell. BMEP; MBP; MoBrPo (1942 ed.)
Blind Preacher, The. Yakov Polonsky, *tr. fr. Russian by* J. S. Phillimore. BoR
Blind Psalmist, The. Elizabeth Clementine Kinney. AA
Blind Rower, The. W. W. Gibson. POTT
Blind Sailor, The. Theodore Goodridge Roberts. CPG
Blind Singer, The. Friedrich Hölderlin, *tr. fr. German by* J. B. Leishman. LiA; LiTW
Blind Student, The. Edmund John Armstrong. TIP
Blind Thamyris, and blind Maeonides. Ode to the Human Heart. Laman Blanchard. BOHV; InMe; NA
Blinded and deafened by the seas. Meditation. Blanaid Salkeld. OnYI
Blinded Bird, The. Thomas Hardy. AnFE; BMEP; ChMo; CMP; LiTM (rev. ed.); MeRV; VLEP
Blinded parson gingering down the neo-Gothic steps, A. The Four. Geoffrey Grigson. WaP
Blindfolded and alone I stand. Not As I Will. Helen Hunt Jackson. OQP; QP-2
Blinding July sun [*or* Blinding sun] at ten o'clock, The. The Church. Edwin Ford Piper. GrCo-1; WGRP
Blinding lust for honors, money-greeds, The. On Human Ambitions. Lucretius. *Fr.* De Rerum Natura, III. LaP
Blinding of Tiresias, The. Callimachus, *tr. fr. Greek by* Robert Allason Furness. OxBG
(Sacrilege of Tiresias, The, *abr.*) GrR
Blinding spot burned on the snow, A. Mistress of the Matchless Mine. Clyde Robertson. PoOW
Blindman's Buff. Peter Viereck. MiAP; MoAmPo (1950 ed.)
Blindness. Sophocles, *tr. fr. Greek by* J. T. Sheppard. *Fr.* Oedipus Rex. OxBG
Blindness of Samson, The. Milton. *Fr.* Samson Agonistes. LiTB; UnPo
(Samson on His Blindness.) LPS-1
Bliss for which our spirits pine, The. The True Heaven. Paul Hamilton Hayne. WGRP
Bliss of summer's magic spell, The. Summer. Thøger Larsen. BoDS
Blissful Bane. Pierre de Ronsard, *tr. fr. French by* Alan Conder. TrFP
"Blissful," quoth [*or* said] I, "can [*or* may] this be true?" The Queen of Courtesy. *Unknown. Fr.* The Pearl. ACP; CAW; ISi
Blissful, they turned them to go: but the fair-tressed Pallas Athenė. Pallas in Olympus. Charles Kingsley. *Fr.* Andromeda. CBOV
Blissit mot be the heye goddis all. James I, King of Scotland. *Fr.* The Kingis Quair. AtBAP
Blistered and dry was the desert I trod. The Palm. Roy Campbell. MBP; MoBrPo
Blith and Bonny Country Lass, A. Thomas Lodge. *Fr.* Rosalynde. ALV
(Corydon's Song.) ReIE
Blithe Mask, The. Dollett Fuguet. MaRV
Blithe playmate of the summer time. To a Humming Bird in a Garden. George Murray. SN; VA
Blithe the bright dawn found me. John O'Dwyer of the Glen. Thomas Furlong. AnIV
Blizzard, The. Lenore A. Pratt. TwCaPo
Bloated Biggaboon, The. Henry Cholmondeley-Pennell. NA
Block City. Robert Louis Stevenson. FaPON; MPB; OnHT; PCH; TiPo
Block the cannon; let no trumpets sound! Sunset Horn. Myron O'Higgins. PoNe
Blockade of the senses! Mail steamers from the Levant! The Approach of Winter. Jules Laforgue. AnFP
Blockader, The. DuBose Heyward. LS
Blockhead and Beehive, The, *sel.* Christopher Smart. Poet, The. BeR
Blocking the Pass. Charles Madge. MoP
Blondel. Clarence Urmy. AA; HBMV; PFY
Blondie Goes to Heaven. *Unknown.* OtMeF
Blood. Ray Bremser. NeAP
Blood and the Moon. W. B. Yeats. CaAE; EnLP; TwHP
Blood-Guilty, The. Empedocles, *tr. fr. Greek by* T. F. Higham. OxBG
Blood hath been shed ere now, i' the olden time. Shakespeare. *Fr.* Macbeth, III, iv. MyFE
Blood Horse, The. "Barry Cornwall." BCEP; GN; HBV; LPS-2; OTPC; VA
Blood Is Thicker than Water. Wallace Rice. PaA; PAH
Blood locked as I am, sun bound, and hot as a pistol. Life Must Burn. John Hay. NePoAm
Blood on a Stone. Francisco Méndez, *tr. fr. Spanish by* Donald Devenish Walsh. AnCL
Blood on the Saddle, *with music. Unknown, at. to* Everett Cheetham. SoAF
(Trail End, *at. to* Everett Chatham.) CoSo
Blood-Red Ring Hung round the Moon, A. John E. Logan. VA
Blood-red trillium in a pocket. Red Trillium. "John Crichton." CPG
Blood thirsty care goe packe. *Unknown.* SeCSL
Blood, wine, and glee. The Dance of the Sword. *Unknown.* WaaP
Bloodhound Speaks, The. Edward Anthony. AlBD
(Bloodhound, The.) GoTP
Bloodhounds look like sad old judges, The. Nice Day for a Lynching. Kenneth Patchen. PoNe
Blood-Root. "E. S. F." SN
Blood-strained Banders, The, *with music. Unknown.* OuSiCo
Bloody and a sudden end, A. John Kinsella's Lament for Mrs. Mary Moore. W. B. Yeats. AtBAP; EnLP; LiTM; MoAB; OAEP (2d ed.); SiTL
Bloody Bill. D. M. Ross. AnNZ
Bloody Brother, The, *sels.* John Fletcher, *and others.*
Drink To-Day [and Drown All Sorrow], *fr.* II, ii. ElSeCe; EnLit; HBV; OAEP; ViBoPo
(Drinking Song.) EIL; TuPP
(Song, The: "Drink to-day and drown all sorrow.") SeEP
Take, O Take, Those Lips Away, *fr.* V, ii; *st.* 1 *also in* Shakespeare's Measure for Measure. AtBAP; FaBoEn; HBV; LEAP; LPS-1; PoEL-2; TuPP
(Hide, Oh, Hide Those Hills, *st.* 2.) ViBoPo
Bloody Conquests of Mighty Tamburlaine, The. Christopher Marlowe. *See* Tamburlaine the Great.
Bloody Cranesbill on the Dunes. E. J. Scovell. ChMP
Bloody Injians, The. *Unknown.* CoSo
(Fragment, A: "I'd rather hear a rattler rattle.") CSF
Bloody Sire, The. Robinson Jeffers. ChMo; LiTM; NePA
Bloody Sword, The. Ibn al-Zaqqaq, *tr. fr. Arabic by* A. J. Arberry. MooP
Bloody trunk [*or* Bloudy trunck] of him who did possess[e], The. The Fall. Sir Richard Fanshawe. *Fr.* Il Pastor Fido. MePo; OBS
Bloom. Alfred Kreymborg. HBMV; TSW
Bloom Hoists Its Banner, The. José Gorostiza, *tr. fr. Spanish by* H. R. Hays. TwSpPo
Bloom is result. To meet a flower. Emily Dickinson. PoEL-5
Bloom of Age. Abu Yahya, *tr. fr. Arabic by* A. J. Arberry. MooP
Bloom of tenderer flowers is past, The. Winter. Kalidasa. *Fr.* The Seasons. AWP
Bloom the Jasmines. William Shenstone. LiA
Blooming of the White Thorn, The. Edith M. Thomas. CLS; ChrBoLe
Blossom, The. Blake. OTPC (1923 ed.); ThWaDe
Blossom, The. John Donne. AWP; ElSeCe; EV-2; InPo; LiTB; SeEP; UnPo (1st ed.)
(Blossome, The.) MeLP; OBS
"But thou which lov'st to be," *sel.* LO
Blossom, The. Shakespeare. *See* On a Day—Alack the Day!
Blossom of the almond trees. Almond Blossom. Sir Edwin Arnold. GN; HBV; LPS-2; OTPC
Blossom of the Soul, The. Robert Underwood Johnson. AA
Blossom on the plum. March. Nora Hopper. HBV
Blossom Time. Wilbur Larremore. AA
Blossome, The. John Donne. *See* Blossom, The.
Blossoms. Mary Fenollosa. PCH
Blossoms. Otomo Yakamochi, *tr. fr. Japanese by* Ishii *and* Obata. OnPM

Blossoms and Storm. Sadaiye, *tr. fr. Japanese by* H. G. Henderson. OnPM
Blossoms are open, The. The Call of Spring. Pao Lin Hui. PoHN
Blossoms dropped before we really saw them, The. The Quick. Sean Jennett. NeBP
Blossoms fall like snowflakes, The. Butterflies. Chu Miao Tuan. PoHN
Blossoms of babies. Handfuls. Carl Sandburg. NP
Blossoms of Lo Yang, The. Ting Liu Niang, *tr. fr. Chinese by* Florence Ayscough *and* Amy Lowell. ChLP
Blossoms of the plum. Tanka. *Unknown.* InP
Blossoms she gave him—indeed, they were fair, The. To My Daughter. H. C. Bunner. FAOV
Blossomy Barrow, The. T. A. Daly. LHV
"Blot as Black as Death, A." Euripides, *tr. fr. Greek by* Gilbert Murray. *Fr.* Electra. GrR
Blot in the 'Scutcheon, A, *sel.* Robert Browning.
There's a Woman like a Dewdrop. BPN
(Earl Mertoun's Song.) HBV; OBEV
Blou Northerne Wynd. *Unknown. See* Blow, Northern Wind.
Bloudy trunck of him who did possesse, The. *See* Bloody trunk of him who did possess, The.
Blouzelinda's Death. John Gay. *Fr.* The Shepherd's Week: Friday. BeR
Blouzelinda's Funeral. John Gay. *Fr.* The Shepherd's Week: Friday. OBEC
Blow, blow over me, sweet-scented breath. Wind of the Prairie. Grace Clementine Howes. GoYe
Blow, blow! The winds are so hoarse they cannot blow. The Winter Storms. Sir William Davenant. SeCL
Blow, Blow, Thou Winter Wind. Shakespeare. *Fr.* As You Like It, II, vii. AnFE; ATP (1935 ed.); BCEP; BEL; BoFr; BoLiVe; BTP; CBE; CH; ChTr; CoBE; EG; ElL; ElSeCe; EM-1; EnLi-1 (1949 ed.); EnLit; EPP; EV-1; GTBS; GTBS-D; GTBS-W; GTSE; GTSL; HBV; InPo; LiTB; LiTG; LO; LPS-1; MaPo; MCCG; OAEP; OBEV; OBSC; OQP; OTPC; OuHeWo; PFE; PG (1945 ed.); PIR; PoEL-2; PYM; QP-2; ReaPo; RG; SeCeV; ShBV-1; SiCE; TCEP; TOP; TVSH; TyEnPo; UnPo (1st ed.); ViBoPo; WaKn; WHA
(Bitter Song.) BLV
(Blow, Thou Winter Wind.) FaFP; TreF
(Ingratitude.) BBV; PECK
(Man's Ingratitude.) CBOV
(Song: "Blow, blow, thou winter wind.") CaAE; CBE; FiP
(Song of the Holly.) COAH
(Songs from "As You Like It," 2.) LEAP
(Songs from the Plays.) AWP; JAWP; WBP
(Songs of the Greenwood.) TrGrPo
(Two Songs by Amiens, 1.) BoLiVe
Blow, Boys, Blow ("Blow, my bullies, I long to hear you"). *Unknown.* IHA; ShS (*vers.* I)
Blow, Boys, Blow ("I served my time in the Black Ball Line"). *Unknown. See* Black Ball Line, The.
Blow, Boys, Blow ("Now, it's blow, you winds"). *Unknown.* ShS (*vers.* III)
Blow, Boys, Blow ("A Yankee ship came down the river"), *with music. Unknown.* ShS (*vers.* II); SoAmSa; TrAS
(Blow, Bullies, Blow, *diff. vers.*) AmSS, *with music;* SG
Blow, Bugle! Thomas Curtis Clark. PGD
Blow, Bugle, Blow. Tennyson. *See* Bugle Song, The.
Blow, bugle, blow! Bugle Song of Peace. Thomas Curtis Clark. PEDC; PSO; WBLP; WGRP
Blow, Bugles, Blow. John Steven McGroarty. DD; HBV; PaA
Blow, Bullies, Blow. *Unknown. See* Blow, Boys, Blow.
Blow cold against the flame. Incarnation. Edith Lovejoy Pierce. MaRV; MuM
Blow colder, wind, and drive. The Wind. Edward Shanks. AIDL
Blow gently over my garden. The Beloved. Katharine Tynan. HBV
Blow gently passion in my faire ones breast. *Unknown.* SeCSL
Blow, golden trumpets, sweet and clear. Easter Music. Margaret Wade Deland. ChIP; HH; OQP; PoRL; QP-1
Blow High, Blow Low. Charles Dibdin. EV-3; HBV
Blow Me Eyes! Wallace Irwin. BOHV; HBMV; InMe; StPo
Blow, my bullies, I long to hear you. Blow, Boys, Blow. *Unknown.* IHA
Blow, Northern Wind. *Unknown.* OBEV
(Blou Northerne Wynd.) AtBAP
Blow, northern winds! December. Louisa Parsons Hopkins. PEOR
Blow on me, wind, from west and south. Song of the Spring Days. George Macdonald. BSV
Blow on the embers, an' sigh at the sparkles! A Bud in the Frost. "Moira O'Neill." GTIV; POTE
Blow out the dying candles one by one. Threnody. Richmond Lattimore. CAG
Blow out, you bugles, over the rich dead! The Dead. Rupert Brooke. 1914, III. AOAH; BEL; GrCo-1; GTML; LBBV; LEAP; MCCG; NV; OQP; PoFr; QP-1; TCEP; TreF; VOD; WGRP
Blow, shepherds, blow your pipes, with gladsome glee resounding. *Unknown.* ReEn; SiCE
Blow softly, bugles, for our honoured dead. Taps at Twilight. Arthur Stringer. NeTW
Blow Softly, Thrush. Joseph Russell Taylor. BLA; HBV
Blow, summer wind, from yonder ocean blow. Spring. Thomas Caulfield Irwin. IrPN
Blow the fife and clarinet. Jonathan Bing Dances for Spring. Beatrice Curtis Brown. GoBP; SiSoSe
Blow the fire, blacksmith. *Unknown.* OxNR
Blow the Man Down. *Unknown.* ABF, *with music;* AmSS, *2 vers., with music;* AS, *diff. vers., with music;* IHA, *sl. diff. vers.;* PYM; SG; ShS, *5 vers., with music;* SoAmSa (A, B, *and* C *vers.*), *with music;* TrAS, *with music*
Blow the Winds, I-ho! *Unknown.* OxBoLi
Blow [*or* Blowe] there, sweet Zephyrus [*or* Zephirus]! where thou shalt find[e]. Song. *Unknown.* SeCL; SeCSL
Blow, Thou Winter Wind. Shakespeare. *See* Blow, Blow, Thou Winter Wind.
Blow trumpet, for the world is white with May. Trumpet Song [*or* The War Song]. Tennyson. *Fr.* Idylls of the King: The Coming of Arthur. BHV; BPN
Blow, wind, blow! Winter Night. Mary Frances Butts. OTPC; PRWS; RAR; TiPo (1952 ed.)
Blow, wind, blow. A Wintry Lullaby. Laurence Alma-Tadema. BOL
Blow, wind, blow! And go, mill, go! Mother Goose. BrR; CBPC; HBV; OTPC; OxNR; PCH; PPL; StVeCh; TiPo
Blow, wind, blow, sing through yard and shroud. A Christmas Song. William Cox Bennett. COAH; VA
Blow, Winds. Shakespeare. *Fr.* King Lear, III, ii. TrGrPo; WHA
("Blow windes, and crack your cheeks; rage, blow.") AtBAP
(Father's Fury, A, *longer sel.*) BCEP
Blow, Ye Winds. *Unknown.* AmSS, *with music;* IHA; SoAmSa, *with music*
Blow Your Trumpets, Angels. John Donne. *See* Sonnet: "At the round earth's imagin'd corners, blow."
Blowe there sweet Zephirus where thou shalt finde. *See* Blow there, sweet Zephyrus . . .
Blowing Bubbles. William Allingham. GN
(Bubble, The.) OnYI
Blown [*or* Blowne] in the morning, thou shalt fade ere noon [*or* noone]. A Rose [*or* The Rose of Life]. Sir Richard Fanshawe. *Fr.* Il Pastor Fido. AWP; ES; HBV; OBEV; OBS; PoEL-2; SeCePo; SeCL; SeEP; TeCS
Blows the Wind To-Day. Robert Louis Stevenson. *See* To S. R. Crockett.
Bludy Serk, The. Robert Henryson. CaAE; EBSV; OBEV (1st ed.); OxBoCh
Blue and buff; and the tramp of feet. The Dreamers. Martha Haskell Clark. VOD (1931 ed.)
Blue and Gold. Ibn Burd, *tr. fr. Arabic by* A. J. Arberry. MooP
Blue and Gold. Dora Wilcox. MM
Blue and the Gray, The. Francis Miles Finch. AA; BAP; BlG; BLPA; BTP; CoBA; DD, *abr.;* FaBoBe; GA, *abr.;* HBV; HH; IAP; LBAP; LEAP; LPS-2; MC; MDAH; NeHB; OBAV; PaA; PAH; PAP; PCD; PEDC; PTA-1; TreF; WBLP
Blue and the Gray, The ("Each thin hand resting on a grave"). *Unknown.* MDAH
Blue and the Gray, The ("A mother's gift to her country's cause"). *Unknown.* ABS
Blue and White. Mary Elizabeth Coleridge. OBEV (new ed.); OBVV
Blue and white are the heavens. Two Folk Songs, 1. *Unknown.* LiTW
Blue are the beautiful skies! Sweeping the Skies. Elizabeth Anna Hart. CenHV
Blue are the twilight heavens above the hill. May Night. William Ellery Leonard. AOAH
Blue-black Nubian plucking oranges, A. Color. W. W. Gibson. InP; NP
Blue Blood. James Stephens, *after* O'Bruaidar. MBP; MoAB; MoBrPo; OBMV; OxBI
Blue, blue is the sea to-day. A December Day. Robert Fuller Murray. EBSV
Blue, blue is your collar. The Collar. *Unknown.* WhP
Blue Bottle, *with music. Unknown.* OuSiCo
Blue Bowl, The. Blanche Bane Kuder. BLPA; FaBoBe; NeHB
Blue Boy in London, The. William Brighty Rands. OTPC
Blue, brown, blue: sky, sand, sea. Irradiations, XVIII. John Gould Fletcher. ChMo; CMP

Blue-Butterfly Day. Robert Frost. BAP; NeMA
Blue Closet, The. William Morris. BPN; EmBrPo; PoVP; TCEP; VA; ViPo; ViPP; VLEP
Blue dome above us, marvellous hive. The First Snowfall. Charles Warren Stoddard. PraNu
Blue drifted the sea; the waters of the sun. The Sea. Herman Gorter. LiTW
Blue Duck, The. Lew Sarett. NP
Blue dusk, The, ran between the streets: my love was winged within my mind. Babylon. "Æ." HBMV; PtOT; TwCV
Blue dusk, that brings the dewy hours. A Toad. Edgar Fawcett. SN
Blue Ey'd Mary. *Unknown.* CoMu
Blue-eyed and bright of face but waning fast. Staff-Nurse: New Style. W. E. Henley. *Fr.* In Hospital. PoVP
Blue-eyed phantom far before, A. Christina Rossetti. EG
Blue-eyed was Elf the minstrel. The Harp of Alfred. G. K. Chesterton. *Fr.* The Ballad of the White Horse. MoVE
Blue eyes, against the whiteness pressed. Songs for Fragoletta, IV. Richard Le Gallienne. HBV
Blue eyes looking up at me. Songs for Fragoletta, II. Richard Le Gallienne. HBV
Blue, faded purple, horizon mount, The. Peace. Samuel Greenberg. CrMA
Blue-Fly, The. Robert Graves. MoVE
Blue Funk. Joel Oppenheimer. NeAP
Blue Girls. John Crowe Ransom. AmP; AnFE; APA; ChMo; ChTr; CoAnAm; HoPM; LiTA; LiTL; MAP; MoAB; MoAmPo; MoPW; MoVE; NP; ReMP; SPP; TBM; TwAmPo
Blue Ghosts. Stanley Snaith. ChMP
Blue gulf all around us. Burial of the Dane. Henry Howard Brownell. AA; HBV; LBAP; LEAP; OBAV
Blue Hen's Chickens, The. Arthur Guiterman. PaA
Blue Hepatica. "John Crichton." CPG
Blue Heron, The. Theodore Goodridge Roberts. BoCaPo; CaP; PeCV; TwCaPo
Blue Heron, The. Maurice Thompson. BLA
Blue Hills, The. Philip Francis Little. GTIV
Blue Hills beneath the Haze. Charles Goodrich Whiting. AA; OBAV
Blue Homespun. Frank Oliver Call. *Fr.* A Sonnet Series of French Canada. CaP; CPG; OCL
Blue Horse, The. Melvin Walker La Follette. NePoEA
Blue Horses, The. J. P. McAuley. BoAV
Blue Hussars. Nikolai Aseyev, *tr. fr. Russian by* Jack Lindsay. RuPo
Blue in the west the mountain stands. Vickery's Mountain. E. A. Robinson. MAP; MoAmPo
Blue is Our Lady's colour. Blue and White. Mary Elizabeth Coleridge. OBEV (new ed.); OBVV
Blue is the sea: a glittering incredible blue. High Noon; Galveston Beach. Stanley E. Babb. HiLiAm
Blue is true. *Unknown.* GoTP
Blue Island Intersection. Carl Sandburg. MAP; MoAmPo; PIAE
Blue Jay, The. Louise Driscoll. BLA; VOD
Blue Jay. Leonora Speyer. BLA; WhBS
Blue-Jay, The. Susan Hartley Swett. PRWS
Blue jay, fly to my windowsill! Invitation. Harry Behn. FaPON
Blue jay scuffling in the bushes follows, The. On the Move. Thom Gunn. ShBV-4; UnPo (3d ed.)
Blue Juniata, *sels.* Malcolm Cowley.
Blue Juniata. MAP; MoAmPo (1942 ed.)
Farm Died, The. MAP; MoAmPo (1942 ed.)
Mine No. 6. InP; MAP; MoAmPo (1942 ed.)
Urn, The. AnAmPo; LA; MoVE; NP
William Wilson. AnAmPo; LA; MoVE
Winter; Two Sonnets. MAP; MoAmPo (1942 ed.)
Blue laguna rocks and quivers, The. Port of Holy Peter. John Masefield. AtBAP; OBMV; POTE; ShBV-2
Blue Larkspur. Sister Mariella. JKCP (1955 ed.)
Blue Men of the Minch, The. Donald A. MacKenzie. EBSV
Blue Moonshine. Francis G. Stokes. NA
Blue mountains to the north of the walls. Taking Leave of a Friend. Li Po, *tr. by* Ezra Pound. CoAnAm; PoFS; TwAmPo
Blue Persian. Isabel Fiske Conant. CIV
Blue Peter. Stanislaus Lynch. OnYI
Blue, pink and yellow houses, and, afar. Tropical Town. Salomón de la Selva. BAP; HBV
Blue Ribbon at Amesbury, A. Robert Frost. NePA
Blue Ribbon Cats. Lalia Mitchell Thornton. CIV
Blue Ridge, The. Harriet Monroe. HBMV
Blue robe on their shoulders, A. The Seven Fiddlers. Sebastian Evans. PoMS; RIS
Blue sea, blue sky, blue eggs. Reflection in Blue. David McCord. MoAmPo (1942 ed.)
Blue shadows lay upon the crater's rim. The Abominable Snow Men. Frank Belknap Long. DaM
Blue Shoes. Kate Greenaway. MPB; RAR
Blue skies and bluer sea with its white teeth showing. Sand Dunes and Sea. John Richard Moreland. HBMV
Blue skies are over Cotswold. Cotswold Love. John Drinkwater. POT; PoTo
Blue skies bend and are about her furled, The. Roma Mater Sempaeterna. Shaemas O'Sheel. JKCP
Blue sky, blue noon, and the secret line is flung. The Sounding. Conrad Aiken. CrMA
Blue sky, green fields, and lazy yellow sun! Spring Passion. Joel Elias Spingarn. HBV
Blue Sleigh. Winfield Townley Scott. NePoAm; PG (1955 ed.)
Blue Smoke. Frances Frost. SiSoSe
Blue Squills. Sara Teasdale. ChMo; CMP; HBMV; NP; SBMV; TCAP; TwCV; VOD
Blue Symphony, The. John Gould Fletcher. AnAmPo; ChMo; CMP; LA; MAPA; NP; TwAmPo
Blue-Tail Fly, The [*or* De]. *Unknown.* FaFP; SiTL; SoAF, *with music;* ViBoFo
Blue Valentine, A. Joyce Kilmer. ISi; JKCP; LHV
Blue veins. Dorothy: Her Hands. Alfred Kreymborg. AnAmPo; LA
Blue wallpaper has lost its hue, The. In an Empty House. Ivan Alekseyevich Bunin. TrRV
Blue water . . . a clear moon. Nocturne. Li Po. OnPM
Blue waters of the ocean with the endless sky above you. A Sea Song. John Richard Moreland. DDA; LS
Blue waves are sleeping, The. Serenade. Jeremiah Joseph Callanan. IrPN; OnYI
Blue wave's slumber and the rocky brow, The. Olive Grove. James Merrill. NePoAm
Blue waves within the stone. The Immobile Wind. Yvor Winters. NP
Blue Woman. *Unknown.* APW
(When a Woman Blue, *with music.*) AS
Bluebeard. Edna St. Vincent Millay. BAV
Bluebeard's Closet. Rose Terry Cooke. AA; OBAV
Bluebell, The. Emile Brontë. OTPC (1923 ed.)
Bluebell. Geoffrey Taylor. NeIP
Bluebell is the sweetest flower, The. The Bluebell. Emily Brontë. OTPC (1923 ed.)
Bluebells. Walter de la Mare. MPB
Bluebells. Olive Enoch. BoTP
Bluebells. Juliana Horatia Ewing. BoTP
Bluebells. Lucia Clark Markham. HBMV
Bluebells. P. A. Ropes. BoTP
Bluebells [*or* Blue Bells] of Scotland, The. *Unknown, sometimes at. to* Mrs. Grant of Laggan. HBV; OIF; OTPC; PECK; TreFS
(O Where, Tell Me Where.) EBSV
Bluebird, The. Thomas Bailey Aldrich. *Fr.* Spring in New England. BLA; SN
Bluebird. Hilda Conkling. GFA
Bluebird, The. Emily Dickinson. BLA; WhBS
Bluebird, The. Emily Huntington Miller. GFA; MPB; OTPC (1946 ed.); PRWS; PTA-1; RAR
Bluebird, The. Eben Eugene Rexford. *See* Sign of Spring, A.
Bluebird, The. Maurice Thompson. BLA
Blue-Bird, The. Alexander Wilson. AA; HiLiAm
Bluebird lives in yonder tree, A. To Miguel de Cervantes Saavadra. Richard Kendall Munkittrick. AA
Bluebirds. Helen Merrill Egerton. CPG
Blue-Flag in the Bog, The. Edna St. Vincent Millay. AnAmPo; LA
Blues Ain' Nothin', The [*or* De], *with music. Unknown.* AS; TrAS
Blues for Bessie. Myron O'Higgins. PoNe
Bluff King Hal was full of beans. Henry VIII. Eleanor *and* Herbert Farjeon. OnPP; StPo
Blum. Dorothy Aldis. MoShBr
Blueprint. D. B. Steinman. GoYe
Blurb, The. Richard Armour. SiTL
Blurred tombstone, hidden in the woods. Elegy to the Lost and Already Blurred by Time. Xavier Abril. AnCL
Blurt, Master Constable, *sels.* Thomas Middleton.
"Alas! how can I sleep? who truly loves." LO
"Love for such a cherry lip." EG; ElSeCe; ViBoPo
(Lips and Eyes.) HBV
(Song: "Love for such a cherry lip.") ElL
Midnight. ElL; SeCePo
Song: Love Is like a Lamb. AtBAP
True Love Ditty, A. ElL
Blush as of roses, A. La Marais du Cygne. Whittier. PAH
Blush is on the flower, and the bloom is on the tree, The. My Own Cáilin Donn. George Sigerson. FaBoBe; HBV
Blush Not Redder than the Morning. Nathaniel Lee. *Fr.* Caesar Borgia. SeCL
Blushing rose and purple flower, The. Song [*or* A Song of Pleasure]. Philip Massinger. *Fr.* The Picture, III, v. LiTL; SeCL; ViBoPo
Blyth, blyth, blyth was she. Andro and His Cutty Gun. *Unknown.* EBSV
Blythe bell, that calls to bridal halls. A Thought. Walter Savage Landor. VA

Blythe young Bess to Jean did say. Bess the Gawkie. James Muirhead. EBSV
Blythesome Bridal, The. *Unknown.* EBSV
Boabdil. José Zorrilla, *tr. fr. Spanish by* James Kennedy. AnSpL-2
Boadicea. William Cowper. BCEP; BeLS; BHV; CG; EV-3; HBV; LEAP; LH; LPS-2; OTPC
Boar Is Dead, The. *Unknown.* AnEC
Board Meets, The. John Gloag. FiBHP
Board School Pastoral, A. May Kendall. VA
Boarding nettings are triced for fight, The. Jack Creamer. James Jeffrey Roche. GA; MC; PAH
Boar's Head Carol, The. *Unknown.* COAH; MeEV, *diff. vers.*
(Boar's Head in Hand Bear I, The.) AnEC
Boar's Head in hand bring I, The. A Carol Bringing in the Boar's Head. *Unknown.* AnEC
Boar's head in hand I bring, The. Hey, Hey, Hey, Hey,/ The Boar's Head Is Armëd Gay. *Unknown.* AnEC
Boar's head [*or* Borys hede] that we bring here, The. In Die Nativitatis [*or* A Christmas Carol]. *Unknown.* AnEC; EnLit
Boast Not, Proud English. Roger Williams. *Fr.* A Key into the Language of America. AmPP (4th ed.)
Boast not your fresh unmingled sweets. On Her Absence. Thomas Rymer. SeCL
Boast of heraldry, the pomp of power, The. Thomas Gray. *Fr.* Elegy Written in a Country Churchyard. LO
Boasting Drunk in Dodge, The. *Unknown.* CoSo
Boasting of Sir Peter Parker, The. Clinton Scollard. PAH
Boat, The. Rose Fyleman. BrR
Boat, The. Joseph Addison Richards. *See* Master of My Boat, The.
Boat a boat haste to the ferry, A. *Unknown.* SeCSL
Boat, beneath a sunny sky, A. Of Alice in Wonderland. "Lewis Carroll." *Fr.* Alice's Adventures . . . , *introd.* VA
Boat-Haven, Co Mayo. Geoffrey Taylor. NeIP
Boat is chafing at our long delay, The. Song. John Davidson. BMEP; EBSV; OBEV; OBVV
Boat Lost, A. *Unknown, tr. fr. Japanese by* Ishii *and* Obata. OnPM
Boat of hunchback Andrew, The. The Ballad of Andrew. Kostas Varnalis. MoGP
Boat of sandalwood and oars of magnolia, A. Boating Song. Li Po. WhP
Boat on the Sea, A. Ethel Turner. BoAu
Boat on the Serchio, The, *sel.* Shelley.
"Stars burnt out in the pale blue air, The." MyFE
Boat ploughed on, The. Going Back to School. Stephen Vincent Benét. LaNeLa
Boat Sails Away, The. Kate Greenaway. MoShBr
Boat Song. Sir Walter Scott. *Fr.* The Lady of the Lake, II. BEL; BHV; EBSV; EnLi-2 (1949 ed.); EV-4; OAEP; PoEL-4
(Hail to the Chief Who in Triumph Advances!) BCEP, *sl. abr.*; BPN; EmBrPo; EnRP
(Song of Clan-Alpine.) LPS-2
Boat two-oared upon water, A; I see, I see. Farewell! Euripides. *Fr.* Alcestis. GrR
Boatie Rows, The. John Ewen. EBSV
Boating in Autumn. Lu Yu, *tr. fr. Chinese by* Arthur Waley. TrCh
Boating Song. *At. to* St. Columban, *tr. fr. Latin by* Jack Lindsay. LaP
Boating Song. Li Po, *tr. fr. Chinese.* WhP
Boatman, The. Christina Rossetti. *See* Ferry Me across the Water.
Boatman, The. *Unknown, tr. fr. Gaelic by* Thomas Pattison. EBSV
Boatman of Kinsale, The. Thomas Osborne Davis. VA
Boatman's Hymn. *At. to* Andrew Magrath, *tr. fr. Modern Irish by* Sir Samuel Ferguson. OnYI
Boatman's Song, The. Thomas Hardy. *See* Night of Trafalgar, The.
Boats. Rowena Bastin Bennett. GFA; TiPo
Boats Are Afloat, The. Chu Hsi, *tr. fr. Chinese by* Kenneth Rexroth. OnPC
Boats at Night. Edward Shanks. CH; MCCG; POTE
Boats go out and the boats come in, The. The Fisher's Widow. Arthur Symons. HBV; PoMa
Boats in a Fog. Robinson Jeffers. AmPP; OxBA; TCPD
Boats of Slumberland, The. *Unknown.* BOL
Boats Sail on the Rivers [*or* River]. Christina Rossetti. *Fr.* Sing-Song. BoChLi; BoTP; BrR; CoBE; OTPC (1946 ed.); PCH; PoRh; PoVP; RAR; RIS; StVeCh; TiPo; TSW
(Rainbow, The.) GFA
Boats that carry sugar. Freight Boats. James S. Tippett. BrR; FaPON; GFA; MPB; StVeCh (1955 ed.)
Boats that sail in Nancy's fleet, The. Bathtub Bay. Lenore Riggs. GFA
Boats upon the river, The. River Boats. *Unknown.* MW
Boatswain! Shakespeare. *Fr.* The Tempest, I, i. SG
Boaz Asleep ("Boaz lay down, with weariness outworn"). Victor Hugo, *tr. fr. French by* Alan Conder. TrFP
Bob Anderson, My Beau. *Unknown.* PAH
Bob has blown a hundred eggs. Eggs. Herbert Asquith. BrR
Bob Sawyer. *Unknown.* SG
Bob Southey! You're a poet—Poet-laureate. Dedication [*or* Southey and Wordsworth]. Byron. *Fr.* Don Juan. BEL; BoLiVe; BPN; EnLi-2 (1949 ed.); EnLit; EnRP; ERP; EV-4; FiP; InP; LoBV; OAEP; PoFS; PtP; TrGrPo
Bob Stanford. *Unknown.* CoSo; CSF
Bob was bathing in the Bay. Some Ruthless Rhymes, V. Harry Graham. CenHV
Bob went lookin' for a job. Plain Bob and a Job. James W. Foley. PTA-1
Bob White. George Cooper. DD; GoTP; HBVY; OTPC (1946 ed.); StVeCh (1940 ed.)
(Bobwhite.) MPB
Bob White. Dora Read Goodale. BLA; WhBS
Bobbily Boo and Wollypotump. Laura E. Richards. LiL
Bobby. Gelett Burgess. LauV
(Ego Sum.) InMe
Bobby Bingo. *Unknown. See* Bingo.
Bobby Blue. John Drinkwater. FaPON; GaP
Bobby Shafto. *Unknown.* PTA-1
Bobby Shaftoe's [*or* Shafto's *or* Shafto has] gone to sea. Mother Goose. AtBAP; BoChLi; BrR; HBV; MPB, (1956 ed.); OnHT; OTPC; OxNR; PPL; RIS
Bobby's First Poem. Norman Gale. FiBHP; MoShBr
Bobolink, The. Thomas Hill. HBV; LPS-2; SN
Bobolink, The. James Russell Lowell. *Fr.* The Biglow Papers, 2d Series, No. VI. BLA
Bobolink! that in the meadow. The Bobolink. Thomas Hill. HBV; LPS-2; SN
Bobolinks, The. Christopher Pearse Cranch. AA; GN, *abr.*; OTPC, *abr.*
Bobwhite. *See* Bob White.
Boddynge flourettes bloshes atte the lyghte, The. *See* Budding floweret blushes . . .
Bodies that gleam like rare bronze in the fire. The War Dance. Robert V. Carr. PoOW
Bodiless amid bodies, The. Omnipresent Self. *Unknown. Fr.* The Upanishads. OnPM
Bodiless, nameless God. Prayer of the Young Stoic. Stephen P. Dunn. TrPWD
Bodily Beauty. George Rostrevor Hamilton. HBMV
Body, The. John Freeman. TCPD
Body, The. Rachel Annand Taylor. GTML
Body and Soul. Abul Fadl, *tr. fr. Arabic by* A. J. Arberry. MooP
Body and Soul. Shakespeare. *See* Sonnets, CXLVI.
Body and Spirit. W. H. Davies. AtBAP
Body and Spirit I surrendered whole. The Wonder. Kipling. *Fr.* Epitaphs of the War. PoVP
Body, if age or uppish soul. Address to the Body. Francis Maguire. JKCP (1955 ed.)
Body is not fallen like the soul, The. Piero della Francesca. Anne Ridler. FaBoMo; PoN
Body is not spent, The. Phlegm. W. Wesley Trimpi. PtPa
Body, long oppressed, The. This corruptible. Elinor Wylie. AnFE; CoAnAm; MAP; MoAB; MoAmPo; TwAmPo
Body my house. Question. May Swenson. NePoEA
Body of Jesus. Arthur Cleveland Coxe. BePJ
Body of John. R. A. K. Mason. AnNZ
Body of Man, The. Sir Charles Scott Sherrington. PoP
Body of Summer, The. "Odysseus Elytis," *tr. fr. Modern Greek by* Kimon Friar. LiTW
Body of the Queen. Donald Evans. AnAmPo; LA
Body Politic, The. Donald Hall. NePoEA
Body Remember. C. P. Cavafy, *tr. fr. Modern Greek by* Rae Dalven. MoGP
"Body snatchers! they have come, The." The Ghost's Complaint. *Unknown.* BoHiPo
Body's Beauty. Dante Gabriel Rossetti. The House of Life, LXXVIII. ATP (1953 ed.); BMEP; BPN; EnL; HBV; POTT; PoVP; TrGrPo; ViP; ViPo; ViPP; VLEP
(Lilith.) EmBrPo; PoEL-5
(Sonnets from "The House of Life.") LEAP
Body's Eye, The. Anne Welsh. BoSA
Body's Freedom. Helen Neville. NePA
Body's rest, the quiet of the heart, The. Sleep. Thomas Sackville. *Fr.* Induction to "The Mirror for Magistrates." CBOV
Body's Speech, The. Donal MacCarthy, First Earl Clancarty, *tr. fr. Irish by* Frank O'Connor. KiLC
Boer War, The. William Plomer. BoSA
Bofors A.A. Gun, The. Gavin Ewart. WaP
Bog Lands, The. William A. Byrne. AnIV; JKCP (1926 ed.)
Bogac Bán. Darrell Figgis. AnIV
Boggy Creek. *Unknown. See* Buffalo Skinners, The.
Bohemia. Dorothy Parker. CrMA; NAMP
Bohemian Cradle-Song. *Unknown.* BOL
Bohemian Girl, The, *sels.* Alfred Bunn.

Bohemian Girl, The (*continued*)
I Dreamt that I Dwelt in Marble Halls. OlF
When Other Lips and Other Hearts. TreF
(Then You'll Remember Me.) OlF
Bohemian Hymn, The. Emerson. APW; IAP; MOAP; OQP; PFY; QP-1; WGRP
Bohemond and Tancred and Raymond St. Giles. God Wills It. Richard F. Grady. JKCP (1955 ed.)
Bohernabreena. Leslie Daiken. OnYI
Bohunkus. *Unknown.* YaD
Boiling Tea. Su T'ung-po, *tr. fr. Chinese by* Yu Min-chuan. WhP
Boke of Phyllyp Sparowe. John Skelton. *See* Phyllyp Sparowe.
Boke of Two Ladies, *sel.* David Morton.
Petition for a Miracle. ISi
Bold, amiable, ebon outlaw, grave and wise! To a Crow. Robert Burns Wilson. AA
Bold as thou art, ere now thou hast had thy boisterous throat. Timotheus. *Fr.* Persae. GrPo
Bold Captain of the Body-Guard. Zagonyi. George Henry Boker. GA; PAH
Bold Daniels [*or* Bold Manan]. *Unknown.* SoAmSa
Bold Dragoon, The. Sir Walter Scott. BHV
Bold Fisherman, The. *Unknown.* BaBo
Bold Hathorne. *Unknown.* *See* Cruise of the *Fair American,* The.
Bold Lanty was in love, you see, with lively Rosie Carey. Lanty Leary. *Unknown.* ChTr
Bold McCarthy. *Unknown.* *See City of Baltimore,* The.
Bold Manan. *Unknown.* *See* Bold Daniels.
Bold Manning, *with music. Unknown.* ShS
Bold o'er the sea with spreading sail. Olaf Trygveson. Björnstjerne Björnson. AnNoLy
Bold Peddler [*or* Pedlar] and Robin Hood, The. *Unknown.* BaBo; ESPB
Bold Phelim Brady, the Bard of Armagh. *Unknown.* OnYI
Bold *Princess Royal,* The, *with music. Unknown.* ShS (2 *vers.*)
(Fair *Princess Royal,* The, *with music.*) SoAmSa
Bold Privateer, The. *Unknown.* SG
Bold Robert Emmet. Tom Maguire. OnYI
Bold Robin has robed him in ghostly attire. Robin Hood and the Grey Friars. Thomas Love Peacock. *Fr.* Maid Marian. EV-4
Bold Satirist, The, *abr.* Horace, *tr. fr. Latin by* Philip Francis. WoL
Boldest man with something on his conscience, The. Conscience Doth Make Cowards of Us All. Menander. OxBG
Boldness[e] in Love. Thomas Carew. EV-2; MePo; SeCL; SeCV-1; SeEP
(Mark How the Bashful Morn [in Vain].) EG; LiTL
Boll Weevil [Song], The. *Unknown.* *See* Ballet of de Boll Weevil, De
Boll-weevil's coming, and the winter's cold. November Cotton Flower. Jean Toomer. CDC
Bologna, and Byron. Samuel Rogers. *Fr.* Italy. OBRV
Bolshevik who never gave heed to queen or to king, A. Dain do Eimhir, XXX. Sorley Maclean. NeBP
Bolster'd with down, amid a thousand wants. Erasmus Darwin. *Fr.* The Botanic Garden: The Loves of the Plants. PoP
Bolsum Brown, *with music. Unknown.* AS
Bolt and bar, bolt and bar. Plautus. *Fr.* Curculio. LaP
Bolt and bar the front door. Hallowe'en. Molly Capes. HOAH; MoSiPe
Bolt and bar the shutter. Mad as the Mist and Snow. W. B. Yeats. AtBAP; ChTr
Bomb That Fell on America, The. Herman Hagedorn. QS
Bombardment, The. Amy Lowell. NV; YT
Bombardment of Bristol, The. *Unknown.* PAH
Bombay. Josephine Miles. FiMAP
Bombed Happiness, The. Stephen Spender. ChMo
Bombed in London. Kipling. *Fr.* Epitaphs of the War. PoVP
Bomber, The. Robert Lowell. WaaP
Bomber, The. Brian Vrepont. BoAV
Bomber climb out on the roof. The Bomber. Robert Lowell. WaaP
Bombers. C. Day Lewis. ChMo; MoAB
Bombing Casualties in Spain. Sir Herbert Read. FaBoTw
"Bon jour, Madame Sans Souci." Madame Sans Souci. *Unknown.* BOHV
Bonac. John Hall Wheelock. MoVE
Bondage. "Owen Innsley." AA
Bondage. Joan Lamburn. DiM
Bondmen of Mizraim/ Were our fathers. Flowering without End. Stefan Zweig. *Fr.* Jeremiah. TrJP
Bonds. Laurence Housman. MaRV
Bonduca, *sel.* John Fletcher.
"Had we a difference with some petty isle." PoFr
Bone-aged is my white horse. Song [*or* Song—Talysarn]. Brenda Chamberlain. MoWP; NeBP; NeIP
Bone, God Wot, A. *Unknown.* AnEC
Bone Thoughts on a Dry Day. George Starbuck. GoYe
Bone-white, bane-white, throttles tight. Landscape of Evil. Tristan Corbière. MiFP
"Boneless tongue, so small and weak, The." The Tongue. *Unknown.* PoToHe (new ed.); WBLP
Bones. Walter de la Mare. FiBHP
Bones of a French Lady in a Museum. Richard Gillman. NePoAm
Bones of Chuang Tzu, The. Chang Heng, *tr. fr. Chinese by* Arthur Waley. AtBAP; AWP
Bones of the children cried out upon the mountain, The. On the Mountain. M. K. Joseph. AnNZ
Boney ("Boney was a warrior"), *with music. Unknown.* AmSS; ShS (2 *vers.*); SoAmSa, *sl. diff. vers.*
(John François.) SG
Bonfire, The. Robert Frost. InvP
Bonfire of Kings. Donald Evans. AnAmPo; LA
Bonhomme Richard and *Serapis,* The. Philip Freneau. GA, *abr.;* PAH
(On the Memorable Victory by Captain Paul Jones.) IAP
Bonie Doon. Burns. *See* Banks o' Doon, The.
Bonie lassie, will ye go. *See* Bonnie lassie . . .
Bonie Lesley. Burns. *See* Bonnie Lesley.
Bonne Entente. F. R. Scott. FiBHP; PeCV; SiTL
Bonnie Annie. *Unknown.* ESPB (A *and* B *vers.*); OBB (*combined vers.* A *and* B, *sl. diff.*)
Bonnie Banks o' Fordie, The. *Unknown.* *See* Babylon; or, The Bonnie Banks o' Fordie.
Bonnie Banks o' Loch Lomond, The. *Unknown, at. to* Lady John Scott. EBSV; OlF
(Loch Lomond.) TreFS
Bonnie Bessie Lee. Robert Nicoll. VA
Bonnie Black Bess. *Unknown.* *See* My Bonny Black Bess.
Bonnie Blue Flag, The ("Come, brothers! rally for the right"). Annie Chambers Ketchum. FOAH; PaA; PAH
Bonnie Blue Flag, The ("We are a band of brothers"). Harry McCarthy. BlG, *abr.;* SPP
Bonnie, bonnie bairn who sits poking in the ase, The. Castles in the Air. James Ballantine. HBV
Bonnie Bower. *Unknown.* *See* Lament of the Border Widow, The.
Bonnie Broukit Bairn, The. "Hugh MacDiarmid." FaBoCh; GoTS
Bonnie Bruckit Lassie, The. James Tytler. EBSV
Bonnie Charlie's now awa. Will Ye No Come Back Again? Lady Nairne. DiM; ShBV-1
Bonnie Doon. Burns. *See* Banks o' Doon, The.
Bonnie Dundee. Sir Walter Scott. *See* Bonny Dundee.
Bonnie Earl of Murray [*or* Moray], The. *Unknown.* *See* Bonny Earl of Murray, The.
Bonnie George Campbell. *Unknown.* AWP; BEL; BLV; BoLiVe; CBOV; CH; EBSV; EnLit; EnRP; ERP; HBV; InPo; TCEP
(Bonny George Campbell.) BSV; GoTS; OBB; OxBoLi; PCD, *shorter vers.;* ViBoPo
(Bonnie [*or* Bonny] James Campbell.) BaBo (A *and* B *vers.*); ESPB (A, B, C *and* D *vers.*)
Bonnie House o' [*or* of] Airlie, The. *Unknown.* BaBo (A *and* B *vers.*); EBSV; ESPB; OBB; OBEV
Bonnie James Campbell. *Unknown.* *See* Bonnie George Campbell.
Bonnie Jeanie. J. B. Morton. ShBV-4
Bonnie [*or* Bonny] Kilmeny gaed up the glen. Kilmeny. James Hogg. *Fr.* The Queen's Wake. BSV; CBPC; DaM; EBSV; EV-3; GBV; GoTS; HBV; LPS-3; OBEV; OBRV; OnSP
Bonnie [*or* Bonie] lassie, will ye go. The Birks of Aberfeldy [*or* Aberfeldie]. Burns. EBSV; ViBoPo
Bonnie Lesley [*or* Leslie]. Burns. AtBAP; CaAE; GTBS; GTBS-D; GTBS-W; GTSE; GTSL; OBEC; OBEV
(Bonie Lesley.) EPP
(O, Saw Ye Bonnie Lesley?) EV-3; HBV; LPS-1
(Saw Ye Bonie Lesley.) EBSV
Bonnie "No" with smiling looks again, A. An Admonition to Young Lassies. Alexander Montgomerie. BSV; EBSV
Bonnie Prince Charlie. James Hogg. EBSV
Bonnie Wee Thing. Burns. HBV
Bonnie Wood o' Craigie-lea. Robert Tannahill. EBSV
Bonniest Bairn in A' the Warl', The. Robert Ford. GN
Bonniest lass that ye meet neist, The. For A' That an' A' That. *At. to* Robert Burns. CoMu
Bonny Baby Livingston. *Unknown.* BaBo; ESPB (A *and* C *vers.*)
Bonny Barbara Allen. *Unknown.* *See* Barbara Allen.
Bonny Bee Hom. *Unknown.* BaBo; ESPB; OBB, *sl. diff. vers.*
Bonny Birdy, The. *Unknown.* ESPB
Bonny Black Bess. Charles Sackville. SeCL
(Song: "Methinks the poor town has been troubled too long.") CEP; SeCV-2
Bonny Black Bess. *Unknown.* *See* My Bonny Black Bess.
Bonny Blue Flag, The. *See* Bonnie Blue Flag, The.
Bonny, bonny bird I had, A. Richard Brome. *Fr.* The Northern Lass. TuPP

Bonny Bunch of Roses, O, The. *Unknown.* OxBoLi
Bonny burgh is Edinbro', the city brave and bright, A. Edinburgh. Arthur Guiterman. WhC
Bonny Dundee. Sir Walter Scott. *Fr.* The Doom of Devorgoil, II, ii. BEL; BHV; BPN; EBSV; EmBrPo; EnRP; ERP; EV-4; FaBoCh; HBV; LH; LoGBV; OBRV; OxBoLi; SeCeV; TCEP; TOP
(Bonnie Dundee.) OTPC (1923 ed.)
Bonny [*or* Bonnie] Earl of Murray, The. *Unknown.* AnFE; BaBo (A *and* B *vers.*); BEL; EBSV; EnLit; ESPB (A *and* B *vers.*); HBV; OBB; OBEV; OBS; ViBoFo; WP
(Bonny [*or* Bonnie] Earl o' [*or* of] Moray, The.) BSV; FaBoCh; GoTS; LoGBV
Bonny Eloise. C. W. Elliott. BlG
Bonny fine maid of a noble degree, A. Robin Hood and Maid Marian. *Unknown.* BaBo; ESPB
Bonny George Campbell. *Unknown.* *See* Bonnie George Campbell.
Bonny Harvest Moon, The. John Barr of Craigielee. AnNZ
Bonny heir, and the well-faird [*or*-faur'd] heir, The. The Heir of Linne. *Unknown.* BaBo; ESPB (B *vers.*); OBB
Bonny Hind, The. *Unknown.* ESPB; ViBoFo
Bonny James Campbell. *Unknown.* *See* Bonnie George Campbell.
Bonny John Seton. *Unknown.* BaBo; ESPB
Bonny Kilmeny gaed up the glen. *See* Bonnie Kilmeny . . .
Bonny Lass of Anglesey, The. *Unknown.* ESPB (A *and* B *vers.*)
Bonny Lassie O. John Clare. CH
Bonny Lizie Baillie. *Unknown.* BaBo; ESPB
Bonny Tweed for Me, The. William A. Foster. EBSV
Bonum Est Mihi Quod Humiliasti Me, *abr.* Earl of Surrey. SiPS
Boogah Man, The. Paul Laurence Dunbar. VOD
Boogie-woogie Ballads. St. Clair McKelway. PoNe
Book, A ("He ate and drank the precious words"). Emily Dickinson. *See* He ate and drank the precious words.
Book, A [*or* The] ("There is no frigate like a book"). Emily Dickinson. *See* There is no frigate like a book.
Book, The. William Drummond of Hawthornden. *See* Book of the World, The.
Book, The. Winfred Ernest Garrison. OQP; QP-1
Book, A. Hannah More. HH; OTPC; PoRL
(Riddle, A: Book, A.) GN
Book, A. Lizette Woodworth Reese. YeAr
Book, The. Henry Vaughan. EnL; EPS; EV-2; SeCV-1
Book, a friend, a song, a glass, A. William Thompson. *Fr.* The Happy Life. ViBoPo
Book and a jug and a dame, A. Limerick. *Unknown.* LiBL
Book & Bookplate. John Masefield. WhC
Book, Book. Annette Wynne. HH
Book for Christmas, A. Margaret Allonby. BoSA
Book I Held Grew Cold, The. Ernst Toller, *tr. fr. German by* Ashley Dukes. TrJP
Book Is an Enchanted Gate, A. Morris Abel Beer. HH
Book is like a magic box, A. Sing a Song of Books. Nancy Byrd Turner. MOB
Book lay beside his dead belt, A. Little Responsory for a Republican Hero. César Vallejo. TwSpPo
Book may be a flower, A. A Book. Lizette Woodworth Reese. YeAr
Book-Moth. *Unknown.* *See* Book-Worm, A.
Book of a Thousand Nights and a Night, The. *Unknown.* *See* Thousand and One Nights, The.
Book of Books, The. Sir Walter Scott. *Fr.* The Monastery, *ch.* 12. MaRV; NeHB; OQP; QP-1
(Bible, The.) BLRP
(Sir Walter Scott's Tribute.) WBLP
Book of Economics, A. Haniel Long. BAP
Book of Good Love, The, *sels.* Juan Ruiz, Archpriest of Hita, *tr. fr. Spanish.*
Archpriest's Prayer, The, *tr. by* Elisha K. Kane. AnSpL-1
Disputation between the Greeks and the Romans, The, *tr. by* Elisha K. Kane. AnSpL-1
Hymn to the Virgin, *tr. by* Longfellow. AnSpL-1; TeCS
Joys of the Virgin Mary, The, *tr. by* Elisha K. Kane. AnSpL-1
Power of Money, The, *tr. by* Elisha K. Kane. AnSpL-1
Praise of Little Women, *tr. by* Longfellow. AnSpL-1; AWP
"In a little precious stone what splendor meets the eyes!" TeCS
Song of the Mountain Girl, The, *tr. by* Elisha K. Kane. AnSpL-1
Book of guests, A. May it include. For a Guest Book. S. Weir Mitchell. DDA
Book of Hours, The, *sels.* Rainer Maria Rilke, *tr. fr. German by* Jessie Lemont.
"I live my life in circles that grow wide." UnW
"Many have painted her." CAW
Book of Hours of Sister Clotilde, The. Amy Lowell. APA
Book of How, The. Merrill Moore. BoLiVe (1939 ed.); MAP; MoAmPo; NeMA
Book of Leinster, *sel.* Cormac, *tr. fr. Old Irish by* George Sigerson.
Heavenly Pilot, The. OnYI
Book of Life, The. Maurice James Craig. *Fr.* Three Cat Poems. PoC
Book of Life's the book supreme, The. Lines on an Album. Mary Bayard Clarke. NoCaPo
Book of Los, The, *sel.* Blake.
Immortal, The, *fr. ch.* 2. LiTB; LoBV
Book of Odes, The. *Unknown.* *See* Shi King [*or* Book of Odes].
Book of Orm, The, *sel.* Robert Buchanan.
Dream of the World without Death, The. VA
Book of Philip Sparrow, The. John Skelton. *See* Phyllyp Sparowe.
Book of Rights, *sel.* *Unknown, tr. fr. Middle Irish by* James Clarence Mangan.
Testament of Cathaeir Mor, The. OnYI
Book of Songs. *Unknown.* *See* Shi King [*or* Book of Odes].
Book of Tarshish, The, *sel.* Moses ibn Ezra, *tr. fr. Hebrew by* Solomon Solis-Cohen.
Joy of Life. TrJP
Book of the Dead, The, *sels.* George Henry Boker. MOAP
"Hopes, on which our spirits."
"I, sighing o'er the happy past."
"If any good may come to me."
"When I am turned to molding dust."
Book of the Dead, *sels.* *Unknown, tr. fr. Egyptian by* Robert Hillyer.
Adoration of the Disk by King Akhnaten and Princess Nefer Neferiu Aten. AWP; JAWP; WBP
"Cattle roam again across the field, The." FaPON
Dead Man Ariseth and Singeth a Hymn to the Sun, The. AWP; JAWP; WBP
He Approacheth the Hall of Judgment. AWP; JAWP; WBP
He Asketh Absolution of God. AWP
He Biddeth Osiris to Arise from the Dead. AWP
He Cometh Forth into the Day. AWP; JAWP; WBP
He Commandeth a Fair Wind. AWP
He Defendeth His Heart against the Destroyer. AWP
He Embarketh in the Boat of Ra. AWP
He Entereth the House of the Goddess Hathor. AWP
He Establisheth His Triumph. AWP; JAWP; WBP
He Holdeth Fast to the Memory of His Identity. AWP; JAWP; WBP
He Is Declared True of Word. AWP; JAWP; WBP
He Is like the Lotus. AWP; JAWP; WBP
He Is like the Serpent Saka. AWP
He Kindleth a Fire. AWP
He Knoweth the Souls of the East. AWP
He Knoweth the Souls of the West. AWP; JAWP; WBP
He Maketh Himself One with Osiris. AWP
He Maketh Himself One with the God Ra. AWP
He Maketh Himself One with the Only God, Whose Limbs Are the Many Gods. AWP; JAWP; WBP
He Overcometh the Serpent of Evil in the Name of Ra. AWP
He Prayeth for Ink and Palette That He May Write. AWP
He Singeth a Hymn to Osiris the Lord of Eternity. AWP
He Singeth in the Underworld. AWP; JAWP; WBP
He Walketh by Day. AWP; JAWP; WBP
Hymn to Ra, *pr. tr. by* E. A. Wallis Budge. OuHeWo
"I am the past and the present, and I bear," *tr. by* Lindley W. Hubbell. LiTW
Other World, The. AWP; JAWP; WBP
Book of the Duchesse, The, *sels.* Chaucer.
Dream, The. FiP
May Morning. WHA
Book of the Native, The, *sel.* Sir Charles G. D. Roberts.
When the Sleepy Man Comes. HBV; HBVY; MPB
(Sleepy Man.) BOL
Book of the New Year, The. *Unknown.* PEOR
Book of the Two Married Women and the Widow, The. William Dunbar. *See* Tua Mariit Wemen and the Wedo, The.
Book of the World, The. William Drummond of Hawthornden. BSV; EBSV; ElSeCe; ES; HBV; PIAE; TOP
(Book, The.) CH; MCCG; PCD
(Lessons of Nature, The.) CBOV; GTBS; GTBS-D; GTBS-W; GTSE; GTSL
(Of This Fair Volume.) EV-2
(On the Margin Wrought.) SeCePo
(Sonnet: "Of this fair volume which we world do name.") SeCL
Book of Thel, The. Blake. BEL; CEP; ChER; EiPP; EnRP; Po; PoEL-4
Sels.
"Clod of Clay heard the Worm's voice and raised her pitying head, The." LO
Thel's Motto ("Does the eagle know what is in the pit?"). ChTr; LO

Book of Thel, The (*continued*)
"Why cannot the ear be closed to its own destruction?" FaBoEn
Book of Verses underneath the bough, A. Omar Khayyám, *tr by* Edward Fitzgerald. *Fr.* The Rubáiyát. AnFE; EG; GTBS-W; HoPM; LiTL; LoPo; OBEV; OBVV; OnPM; OQP; PC; QP-2; SeCePo; SeCeV; SiTL; YT
Book of Wisdom, The. Stephen Crane. The Black Riders, XXXVI. HoPM; MAP; MoAmPo
("I met a seer.") CoBA
Book Our Mothers Read, The. Whittier. *See* Bible, The.
Book Review. David Ross. PG (1945 ed.)
Book was dull, its pictures, The. The Bride. Ralph Hodgson. AEV; HBMV; InP; TCPD
Book was writ of late called *Tetrachordon,* A. On the Detraction Which Followed upon My Writing Certain Treatises. Milton. EM-1; SeCeV
Book which thou dost read, it is, The. To Fidentinus. Martial, *tr. by* Timothe Kendall. TuPP
Book you may buy for a shilling, A. Barter. Earle V. Eastwood. OQP; QP-1
Booker Washington Trilogy, The, *sels.* Vachel Lindsay.
John Brown, II. AnAmPo; LA; MAP; MoAmPo; NP; TBM; TriL
Simon Legree—a Negro Sermon, I. CoBA; HBMV; InMe; LiTA; LoGBV; MoVE; NAMP; NePA; PCN; PFY; ShBV-2
("Legree's big house was white and green.") LA
(Negro Sermon, A: Simon Legree.) AnAmPo; ATP (1935 ed.); MAP; MoAmPo; PFY
Book-Lover. Ralph Bergengren. FAOV
Book Lover, The. Clinton Scollard. MOB
Bookra. Charles Dudley Warner. AA; HBV; LBAP
Books. Elizabeth Barrett Browning. *Fr.* Aurora Leigh, I. VA
Books. Ch'en Shih-tao, *tr. fr. Chinese.* WhP
Books. Hilda Conkling. HH; MOB
Books. George Crabbe. *Fr.* The Library. EV-3, *abr.;* OBEC
Books. Eleanor Farjeon. YeAr
Books. Hermann Hesse, *tr. fr. German by* Herman Salinger. TwGV
Books. John Higgins. LPS-3
Books. Joseph Joel Keith. StVeCh (1955 ed.)
Books. Robert Leighton. MOB
Books. Nancy Byrd Turner. MOB
Books. *Unknown.* LPS-3
Books. Florence Van Cleve. DDA; HH
Books. Wordsworth. *Fr.* The Prelude, V. ERP; PoEL-4
Books a Substantial World. Wordsworth. *Fr.* Personal Talk. MOB
Books and Love. Carl David af Wirsén, *tr. fr. Swedish by* Charles W. Stork. AnSL
Books and the Man I sing, the first who brings. Pope. *Fr.* The Dunciad. CEP
Books are bridges. Golden Spurs. Virginia Scott Miner. PoRL; SiSoSe; StaSt
Books Are Keys. Emilie Poulsson. HH; SiSoSe
Books are more than words. Books. Joseph Joel Keith. StVeCh (1955 ed.)
Books Are Soldiers. Annette Wynne. HH
Books, books, books! Aurora Leigh Discovers Books. Elizabeth Barrett Browning. *Fr.* Aurora Leigh. MOB
Books, books, books, and the treasure they hold. Books. Nancy Byrd Turner. MOB
Books, books, that I love so. Books. Hilda Conkling. HH; MOB
Books composed before our day, The. Prolog. John Gower. *Fr.* Confessio Amantis. MeEV
Books grow clear upon the shelf, The. Her Second Song. James K. Baxter. Cressida, IX. AnNZ
Books I have are made of lead, The. Convalescence, VIII. David McCord. WhC
Books say well, my Brothers, The! each man's life. Nirvana. Sir Edwin Arnold. *Fr.* Light of Asia. VA
Bookshop Idyll, A. Kingsley Amis. NePoEA
Bookworm, The. Walter de la Mare. TiPo (1959 ed.)
Bookworm, The. J. M. Moore. CAG
Bookworm, The. Su T'ung-po, *tr. fr. Chinese by* Henry H. Hart. PoHN
Book-Worm, A [*or* The]. *Unknown, tr. fr. Anglo-Saxon. Fr.* Riddles. CoBE; EnLi-1, *tr. by* Stith Thompson
(Book-Moth: "Moth ate a word, A. To me it seemed," *tr. by* Charles W. Kennedy.) AnOE
("Moth ate words, A. To me that seemed," *tr. by* Harold S. Stine.) EnLit
Book-Worms, The. Burns. ChTr; FiBHP; RO
Bookworm's Content, A. Thomas Sheridan. MOB
Boolee, the Bringer of Life. Mary Gilmore. BoAV
Boom, cannon, boom to all the winds and waves! Our Country Saved. James Russell Lowell. *Fr.* Ode Recited at the Harvard Commemoration, July 21, 1865. IDAH
Boomerang, The. Carrie May Nichols. PoToHe
Boon, A. William Meredith. NePoEA
Boon Companion, The. Oliver St. John Gogarty. *See* To a Boon Companion.
Boon nature scattered, free and wild. Flowers and Trees. Sir Walter Scott. *Fr.* The Lady of the Lake. EV-4
Boon Nature to the woman bows. The Tribute. Coventry Patmore. *Fr.* The Angel in the House. HBV
Boosting the Booster ("Boost your city, boost your friend"). *Unknown.* WBLP
Boot and a Shoe and a Slipper, A. High and Low. John Banister Tabb. BrR
Boot and Saddle ("Boot, saddle, to horse, and away!"). Robert Browning. Cavalier Tunes, III. CBOV; EmBrPo; EnLi-2; EnLit; MuP; MW; PoVP; PreP; ShBV-1; ViPo
(Cavalier Tune.) PIAE
Booth led boldly with his big bass drum. General William Booth Enters into Heaven. Vachel Lindsay. AmPP; ATP; BAP; BAV; CBOV; ChMo; CMP; CoBA; DDA; FaBoMo; HBV; IAP; InPo; LEAP; LiTA; LiTM; MAP; MaRV; MM; MoAB; MoAmPo; MOAP; MoP; MoPo; NP; OBAV; OnAP; OxBA; PoeMoYo; PYM; ReMP; SBMV; SeCeV; TCPD; TOP; TreFS; TrGrPo; TwCV; WGRP
Boots. Kipling. BLPA; BPN; MBP; MoBrPo; PFE; PoVP; ShBV-2; WHA
Boots,/ Shoes. *Unknown.* OxNR
Boots and Saddles. Nicolas Saboly, *tr. fr. Provençal.* OHIP; SDH
Boots and Shoes. Lilian McCrea. BoTP
Boozer, The. *Unknown. See* Desperado, The.
Bo-Peep, *parody.* Anthony C. Deane. PA
Bo-peep,/ Little Bo-peep. *Unknown.* OxNR
Bo-peeper. *Unknown.* OxNR
Bora Ring. Judith Wright. NeLNL
Bordello squatting motionless. Abandoned Brothel. C. R. Holmes. PtPa
Border. Isabel Fisk Conant. BAP
Border Affair, A. Badger Clark. SCC
Border Ballad. Sir Walter Scott. *Fr.* The Monastery, *ch.* 25. BHV; BPN; EmBrPo; EnLit; EPN; EV-4; GN; HBV; PCD
(Border March.) EBSV; EnRP; PCN
(March, March [Ettrick and Teviotdale].) BSV; ViBoPo
Border River. Alfred Goldsworthy Bailey. CaP
Border Widow's Lament. *Unknown. See* Lament of the Border Widow, The.
Borderland. Herman Knickerbocker Vielé. PR
Bore, The. Horace, *tr. fr. Latin.* Satires, I, 9. ATP, *tr. by* John Conington; EnLi-1, *tr. by* Sir Theodore Martin; OuHeWo, *tr. by* Sir Theodore Martin; RoL, *tr. by* B. L. Ullman
Bore, The. Mark Van Doren. MOAP
Boreas blows on his high wood whistle. In Winter. C. H. Bretherton. InMe
Bored Mirror, The. Syuichi Nagayasu, *tr. fr. Japanese by* Katue Kitasono. LiTW
Bored rain-god spills his irritation over, The. Spleen. Baudelaire. MiFP
Boredom. Mildred Bowers Armstrong. GoBP
Boredom. Ramón de Campoamor, *tr. fr. Spanish. Fr.* Doloras. AnSpL-2, *tr. by* J. D. M. Ford; OnPM, *tr. by* Beatrice Gilman Proske
Boredom. Nalan Hsinteh, *tr. fr. Chinese.* ChLP
Borgia, thou once wert [*or* were] almost too august. On Lucretia Borgia's Hair [*or* On Seeing a Hair of Lucretia Borgia]. Walter Savage Landor. AnFE; BCEP; BPN; EnRP; OAEP; ReaPo; RiBV; TOP; UnPo (1st ed.) VA
Born are we of fire. Mothers and Children. Orrick Johns. AnAmPo; HBMV; LA
Born beautiful, I hear them say. Tears Cost Her Nothing Anyway. Konstantin Simonov. BoRS
Born free, thus we resolve to live. The Oath of Freedom. James Barron Hope. MDAH
Born I was to be old. Anacreontic. Robert Herrick. OAEP; OnPM; OxBoLi; WoL
Born[e] I was to meet with age. On Himself[e]. Robert Herrick. ChTr; SeCV-1
Born in a borrowed cattle shed. Evaluation. Elinor Lennen. OQP; QP-2
Born in a day, full-grown our Nation stood. The Confederacy. Jane T. H. Cross. BlG
Born in a hovel, trained in Hardship's school. Abraham Lincoln. A. S. Ames. OHIP
Born in the garret, in the kitchen bred. A Sketch. Byron. NBE; OBRV
Born Is the Babe. *Unknown.* AnEC
Born, nurtured, wedded, prized, within the pale. La Fayette. Dolly Madison. PaA; PAH
Born of a star, they say. Asteria. W. Wesley Trimpi. PtPa
Born of my voiceless time, your steps. The Footsteps. Paul Valéry. LiTW
Born of Tears. W. H. Davies. GTBS-D

Born of the sorrowful of heart. For Paul Laurence Dunbar [*or* Four Epitaphs, 3]. Countee Cullen. CDC; GoSl
Born of the starry night in her undoing. The Wanderings of Heracles. Sophocles. *Fr.* Trachiniae. GrR
Born on the Colorado. Cowboy to Pitching Bronco [*or* Cowboy Talks to a Pitching Horse]. *Unknown.* ABF; CoSo
Born the child of cities where. Expiation. Paul Verlaine. TrFP
Born with a monocle he stares at life. En Monocle. Donald Evans. AnAmPo; LA; NP
Born with all arms, he sought a separate peace. The Deserter. John Manifold. WaP
Born with the Vices. Thomas d'Urfey. OBS
Born without a Chance. Edmund Vance Cooke. BLPA
Born Yesterday. Philip Larkin. HaMV
Borne-heid demoniac. Defeat o' the Hert. Sidney Goodsir Smith. AtBAP
Borne on a whispered sigh. Fallen Leaves. Kathryn Munro. CaP; OCL
Borne on the wings of time another year. On the Prospect of a Revolution in France. Philip Freneau. IAP
Borodino. Mikhail Lermontov, *tr. fr. Russian by* Frances M. Cornford. BoRS
Borough, The, *sels.* George Crabbe.
"Alas! for Peter not a helping hand," *fr.* Letter XXII. OBRV
Alms House, The, *fr.* Letter XVIII. NBE
("Your plan I love not; with a number you.") LO
Amusements, *fr.* Letter IX. OBRV
"But ere you enter, yon bold Tower survey," *fr.* Letter II. EnSW
"Can scenes like these," *fr.* Letter I. OBRV
Caroline, The, *fr.* Letter XI. SeCePo
Foreshore, The, *fr.* Letter XXII. CoEV
"Thus by himselt compell'd to live each day," *sel.* FaBoEn; SeCePo
General Description, Letter I, *abr.* TCEP
Peter Grimes, Letter XXII. EnRP; PoEL-4
Physic, Letter VII, *abr.* PoP
Poor, The, *fr.* Letter XXII. AEV
Portrait of a Vicar, *fr.* Letter III. RO
Quack Medicines, *fr.* Letter VII. LPS-3
Sea Marsh, *fr.* Letter XXII. RO
Suffolk Shore, The, *fr.* Letter XXIII. RO
Winter Storm at Sea, The, *fr.* Letter I. EtS
(Winter Storm, The, *longer sel.*) EV-3
Borrow and borrow. Rhymes to Remember. *Unknown.* StaSt
"Borrowed." *Unknown.* *See* Cross Was His Own, The.
Borrowed Child, The. Howard Weeden. AA
Borrowed wings on his ankles. Perseus. Louis MacNeice. CoBMV; GTBS-W; LiTM; ReMP
Borrower. Mary Carolyn Davies. *Fr.* A Girl's Songs. SBMV
Borrower of Salt, The. Oscar Williams. *Fr.* Variations on a Theme. LiTA; NePA
Borrowing. Emerson. WhC
Borrowing Trouble. Burns. *Fr.* The Twa Dogs. BLP
Borys hede that we bryng here, The. *See* Boar's head that we bring here, The.
Bos'n Hill. John Albee. AA
Bosom, A, of/ green buds. Mare Nostrum. Joel Oppenheimer. NeAP
Boss I just discovered what. Archys Last Name. Don Marquis. *Fr.* Archys Life of Mehitabel. CrMA
Boss, I saw a picture. Archy a Low Brow. Don Marquis. *Fr.* Archys Life of Mehitabel. WhC
Bossy and the Daisy. Margaret Deland. PPL
Boston. Franklin P. Adams. BoHiPo
Boston ("And this is good old Boston"). John Collins Bossidy. *See* Boston Toast, A.
Boston ("I come from the city of Boston"). *At. to* Samuel C. Bushnell. LiTM; OxBoLi; SiTL. *See also* Boston Toast, A.
Boston. Emerson. BoHiPo, *br. sel.;* MC; PAP
Boston. Sam Walter Foss. *See* Calf-Path, The.
Boston. John Boyle O'Reilly. PAH
Boston ("From Boston harbor we set sail"), *with music.* *Unknown.* SoAmSa
Boston Burglar, The. *Unknown.* ABS, A *vers.;* CSF, *diff. vers.;* ViBoFo
(Charlestown, B *vers.*) ABS
Boston Cats, The. Arthur Macy. CIV
Boston Charlie. Walt Kelly. FiBHP
Boston Come-All-Ye, The, *with music.* *Unknown.* ABF; SoAmSa
(Fishes, The.) TrAS
Boston Common—Three Pictures. Oliver Wendell Holmes. TCAP
Boston Evening Transcript, The. T. S. Eliot. NePA; OnAP
Boston Hymn. Emerson. AnNE; IAP; LaNeLa; LPS-2; MC; PaA; PAH; TCAP; TOP; WGRP
"Word of the Lord, The," *sel.* BAP; DD, *diff. and abr.*
Boston Lullaby, A. James Jeffrey Roche. BOHV; BOL
Boston Nursery Rhymes. Joseph Cook. BOHV; InMe; PA
Boston Symphony Orchestra, The. James Fenimore Cooper. POT; PoTo
Boston Tea Party, The. *Unknown.* *See* New Song, A.
Boston Toast, A ("And this is [*or* is to *or* Here's to] good old Boston"). John Collins Bossidy. BLPA; NeHB; YaD
("And this is good old Boston.") CenHV
(Boston.) BoHiPo; GoTP
(Boston, *sl. diff. vers.:* "I come from the city of Boston.") LiTM (*Unknown*); OxBoLi (*At. to* Samuel C. Bushnell); SiTL (*Unknown*)
(On the Aristocracy of Harvard.) HBV; WhC
(On the Aristocracy of Harvard, *sl. diff. vers.:* "I come from good olde Boston," *at. to* Samuel C. Bushnell.) BOHV
(To Boston.) TreFS
Boswell by my bed. Reading in War Time. Edwin Muir. WaP
Botanic Garden, The, *sels.* Erasmus Darwin.
Pt. I. The Economy of Vegetation.
Immortal Nature, *fr.* Canto IV. OBEC
Steam Power, *fr.* Canto I. BoHiPo; OBEC
Pt. II. The Loves of the Plants.
"Bolster'd with down, amid a thousand wants," *fr.* Canto II. PoP
Fuseli's "Nightmare," *fr.* Canto III. RO
Vegetable Loves, *fr.* Canto I. OBEC; SeCePo
Botany Bay. *Unknown.* ViBoFo
Both Are Blessing. Egi, *tr. fr. Japanese by* Lois J. Erickson. SoLD
Both gazed on sleeping Egypt as they stood. Antony and Cleopatra. José Maria de Heredia. TrFP
Both gentlemen, or yoemen bould. A True Tale of Robin Hood. *Unknown.* ESPB
Both heaven and hell are from the human race. Tale of Eternity. Gerald Massey. BMEP
Both Less and More. Richard Watson Dixon. LoBV
Both old and young, I pray lend an ear. The *Nightingale.* *Unknown.* ShS
Both power and being are denied to us. The Life within Our Forms. Jami. OnPM
Both robb'd of air, we both lie in one ground. Hero and Leander. John Donne. ReIE
Both roof, and floor, and walls were all of gold. Mammon's House. Spenser. *Fr.* The Faerie Queene. MyFE
Both Sides. Mary Abigail Dodge. CIV
Both thou and I alike, my Bacchic urn. On an Urn. Richard Garnett. VA
Bothie of Tober-na-Vuolich, The, *sel.* Arthur Hugh Clough.
Bathers, The. VA
("There is a stream, I name not its name, lest inquisitive tourist.") EV-5
Bothwell, *sel.* Swinburne.
John Knox's Indictment of the Queen. VA
Bothwell Bridge. *Unknown.* BaBo; ESPB
Botticellian Trees, The. William Carlos Williams. AmP; LiTA; NP
Bottle. The. Walter de la Mare. MoPo; POTE
Bottle O! *with music.* *Unknown.* SoAmSa
Bottle of perfume that Willie sent, The. Limerick. *Unknown.* GoTP; TSWC; WhC
"Bottle Should Be Plainly Labeled 'Poison.'" Sara Henderson Hay. GoYe
Bottled, New York. Helene Johnson. GoSl
(Bottled.) CDC
Bottomed by tugging combs of water. The Swan. W. R. Rodgers. NeBP
"Bottoms Up" ad Finem. P. A. Hutchison. CAG
Bough of Babylon. Joseph Auslander. TBM
Bough of the plane tree, where is the clear-beaked bird. Woodcock of the Ivory Beak. Elizabeth Madox Roberts. MAP; MoAmPo
Bough will bend, the leaf will sometime fall, The. Fable. Mary Mills. NePoAm
Boughs do shake and the bells do ring, The. Harvest Song. *Unknown.* BoTP; OxNR
Boughs, the boughs are bare enough, The. Winter with the Gulf Stream. Gerard Manley Hopkins. ExPo; ViP
Bought. Francis Douglas Davison. NeBP
Bought Embrace, A. G. S. Fraser. WaP
Bought Locks. Martial, *tr. fr. Latin by* Sir John Harington. AWP; JAWP; LiTW; OuHeWo; WBP; WoL
Boule's Hop. *Unknown.* IHA
Bounce ball! Bounce ball! Song for a Ball-Game. Wilfrid Thorley. BoTP
Bounce, buckram, velvet's dear. *Unknown.* OxNR
Bound and Wound. *Unknown, tr. fr. Chinese.* WhP
Bound Down to Newfoundland, *with music.* *Unknown.* ShS
Bound for holy Palestine. The Crusade. Thomas Warton, the Younger. EiPP
Bound for Sourabaya! Charles Henry Souter. BoAu
Bound for the Harvest-Home. Theocritus, *tr. fr. Greek by* Walter Headlam. *Fr.* Idylls. OxBG
Bound for your far-off native shore. To ——. Pushkin. BoR

Bound to a boy's swift feet, hard blades of steel. River Skater. Winifred Welles. PoeMoYo
Bound to my heart as Ixion to the wheel. Dirge for the New Sunrise. Edith Sitwell. *Fr.* Three Poems of the Atomic Bomb. AtBAP; MoAB; MoBrPo (1950 ed.); SeCePo
Bound to the Caucasus of my suffering. Maurice Scève. *Fr.* La Délie. LiA
Bound upon the accursed tree. The Crucifixion. Henry Hart Milman. BePJ
Boundaries. Catherine Cate Coblentz. BPP; OQP; QP-1
Boundaries. Jessica Powers. JKCP (1955 ed.)
Boundary Rider, The. Thomas Heney. BoAu
Bounded unbrokenly by summer weather. The Made Lake. Louise Townsend Nicholl. NePoAm-2
Boundless. Leonora Clawson Stryker. MuM
Boundless, immeasurable time is in gardens. Gardens. Jorge Guillén. CoSP
Boundless, the great sea. Magic. Po Chü-i. TrCh
Bounteous Poverty. Aristophanes, *tr. fr. Greek by* Benjamin Bickley Rogers. *Fr.* Plutus. GrR
Bountiful in charity. Praise of Mary. *Unknown.* ISi
Bounty. Abus Salt, *tr. fr. Arabic by* A. J. Arberry. MooP
Bounty. Mary Webb. AlDL
Bounty of Our Age, The. Henry Farley. *See* To See a Quaint Outlandish Fowl.
Bouquet of Belle Scavior. Wallace Stevens. MoAB; MoAmPo
Bourne, The. Christina Rossetti. BLV; FaBoEn; HBV; LoBV; MBP; PIAE; POTT; VLEP
Bourtree, bourtree, crookit rung. The Elder Tree. *Unknown.* ChTr
Bout with Burning. Vassar Miller. NePoEA
Bouton d'Or. Jessie B. Rittenhouse. PR
Bow, The. Al-Buqaira, *tr. fr. Arabic by* A. J. Arberry. MooP
Bow Down, Dear Land. James Russell Lowell. Ode Recited at the Harvard Commemoration, July 21, 1865, XI, *abr., and* XII. DD
Bow down, dear Land, for thou hast found release! My Country. James Russell Lowell. *Fr.* Ode Recited at the Harvard Commemoration, July 21, 1865. GDAH
Bow down: I am the emperor of dreams. The Hashish-Eater. Clark Ashton Smith. DaM
Bow down, my song, before her presence high. Morton Luce. *Fr.* Thysia. HBV
Bow down my soul in worship very low. Russian Cathedral. Claude McKay. CDC; PoNe
Bow Down Your Head and Cry. *Unknown.* CoSo
Bow-Meeting Song, A. Reginald Heber. BCEP
Bow of Zeus has twanged, The. Helen. Aeschylus. *Fr.* Agamemnon. OxBG
Bow-wow, says the dog. *Unknown.* OxNR
Bow, wow, wow,/ Whose dog art thou? Greeting. Mother Goose. OxNR; PCH; PPL; RIS; SAS; StVeCh; TiPo
Bowed by the weight of centuries he leans. The Man with the Hoe. Edwin Markham. AA; AnAmPo; AnFE; APA; BAP; BAV; BLPA; BLV; BTP; CoAnAm; CP; CV; DD; FaFP; GTBS-W; HBV; HiLiAm; LA; LBMV; LEAP; LiTA; LiTM; MAP; MaRV; MCCG; MoAmPo; NAMP; NeHB; NeMA; NV; OBAV; OHFP; OQP; PC; PECK; PEDC; PFE; PFY; PoeMoYo; PoFr; PoMa; POT; PoTo; PreP; PTA-1; PYM; QP-1; TCAP; TCPD; TreF; TrGrPo; VOD; WBLP; WGRP; WoL
Bowels of pitie heare! George Herbert. *Fr.* Longing. BrBE
Bower of Bliss, The. Spenser. *Fr.* The Faerie Queene, II, 12. BCEP, *mod. vers., abr.;* CH; CoEV; FaBoEn; FiP; LoBV; LPS-3; OBSC; PoEL-1
("Eftsoons they heard a most melodious sound.") UnS, *2 sts.;* ViBoPo
(Gather the Rose.) EIL; WHA
("Thence passing forth, they shortly doe arrive.") ATP
Bower of Peace, The. Robert Southey. *Fr.* Ode Written during the War with America, 1814. MC; PAH
Bowers whereat, in dreams, I see, The. To——. Poe. IAP; RO
Bowery, The. Charles Hale Hoyt. TreF; YaD
Bowge of Court, The. John Skelton. ReIE
Bowing Her Head. *Unknown.* BIG
Bowing thyself in dust before a Book. Bibliolatres. James Russell Lowell. IAP
Bowl, The. Earl of Rochester. EV-3
Bowl. Wallace Stevens. NP
Bowl in my hand is the earth, A. The Turquoise Bowl. Kathryn White Ryan. BAP
Bowl of Roses, A. W. E. Henley. BPN; EnLi-2; EPP; MBP; MoBrPo; OuHeWo
Bowl of Wine, A. Ming Ti, *tr. fr. Chinese by* Henry H. Hart. PoHN
Bowlegged peasant and his ox receding, A. Autumn. Guillaume Apollinaire. AnFP
Bowline, The. A. P. Herbert. WhC
Bowman, The. Hugh Chesterman. MW
Bows glided down, and the coast, The. Ballad of the Long-legged Bait. Dylan Thomas. CoBMV; SeCeV
Bows will not avail thee. Archilochus, *tr. fr. Greek by* J. H. Merivale. GrPo
Box-car held a motley group of men, A. The Hobo's Dog. Margaret E. Bruner. AlBD
Box-Car Letters. Karle Wilson Baker. InP
Box cars run by a mile long. Work Gangs. Carl Sandburg. CoBA
Boxer, A. Simonides, *tr. fr. Greek* by Gilbert Highet. OxBG
Boxer Called Panther, A. Reuel Denney. PreP
Boxing. Kipling. *Fr.* Verses on Games. OtMeF
Boy. William Allingham. PRWS
Boy, A. John Ashbery. NeAP
Boy, The. Eugene Field. NA
Boy, The. W. W. Gibson. NeTW
Boy, A. Hugo von Hofmannsthal, *tr. fr. German by* Vernon Watkins. AnGP
Boy. Winifred Welles. NP
Boy, A/ Blew west. In Praise of Johnny Appleseed. Vachel Lindsay. StVeCh
Boy Alexander understands his father to be a famous lawyer, The. Boy and Father. Carl Sandburg. CMP; FAOV
Boy and a Pup, A. Arthur Guiterman. AlBD; MPB; UTS
Boy and Father. Carl Sandburg. CMP; FAOV
Boy and Girl of Plymouth. Helen L. Smith. PTA-2
Boy and His Playthings, The. Anna Maria Lenngren, *tr. fr. Swedish by* Charles W. Stork. AnSL
Boy and His Stomach, A. Edgar A. Guest. OnHT; PTA-1
Boy and His Top, The. John Hookham Frere. OTPC (1923 ed.)
Boy and Tadpoles. Louis Untermeyer. YT
Boy and the Angel, The. Robert Browning. BMEP; EmBrPo; EOAH; EV-5; GEPC; MW; OTPC; PoVP; TCEP; VLEP
Boy and the Flute, The. Björnstjerne Björnson, *tr. fr. Norwegian by* Sir Edmund Gosse. AWP; JAWP; WBP
Boy and the Geese, The. Padraic Fiacc. NeIP
Boy and the Mantle, The. *Unknown.* BaBo; ESPB; OBB
Boy and the Parrot, The. John Hookham Frere. OTPC (1923 ed.)
Boy and the Schoolmaster, The. La Fontaine, *tr. fr. French by* Elizur Wright. WoL
Boy and the Sheep, The. Ann Taylor. *See* Sheep, The.
Boy and the Squirrel, The. F. Hey. SAS
Boy and the Wolf, The. Aesop, *ad. fr. Greek by* Louis Untermeyer. MaC
Boy and the Wolf, The. John Hookham Frere. HBV; HBVY; OnHT; OTPC (1923 ed.)
Boy at the Door. Louis J. Sanker. JKCP (1955 ed.)
Boy, Bare Your Head. Nancy Byrd Turner. PCD; PCH
Boy, bring the jug; I want a wet. Gentlemen Topers. Anacreon. GrR
Boy, bristle thy courage up; for Falstaff he is dead. Shakespeare. King Henry V, *fr.* II, iii. LO
Boy Brittan. Forceythe Willson. MC; PAH
Boy called to his team, The. Late Autumn. Andrew Young. HaMV; MoVE
Boy Christ, The. Helene Mullins. StJW
Boy Columbus, The. *Unknown.* HH; PEDC (1923 ed.)
Boy drove into the city, his wagon loaded down, A. The Little Black-eyed Rebel. Will Carleton. FaPON; GoTP; PAH; PAP; PTA-1
Boy employed to guard the sheep, A. The Boy and the Wolf. Aesop. MaC
Boy Fishing, The. E. J. Scovell. HaMV; ThWaDe
Boy Fourteen. Amanda Benjamin Hall. MuM
Boy from Ballytearim, The. "Moira O'Neill." CP; NV
Boy from his bedroom window, The. The Boy. William Allingham. PRWS
Boy from Hodgensville, The, *abr.* Robertus Love. GA
Boy from Rome, Da. T. A. Daly. FaPON; LBMV; MPB; POT
Boy He Had an Auger, A, *with music.* *Unknown.* AS
Boy, I detest these modern innovations. Persicos Odi. Charles Edmund Merrill, Jr. AA
Boy, I hate their empty shows. Persian Fopperies [*or* Persian Pomp]. Horace, *tr. by* William Cowper. *Fr.* Odes. AWP; EnLi-1; JAWP; OnPM; RoL; WBP; WoL
Boy, I hate this Persian frippery. Frippery. Horace, *tr. by* L. R. Lind. *Fr.* Odes. LiTW
Boy I Love, The. John Townsend Trowbridge. FAOV
Boy in the Dusk. Humbert Wolfe. MM
Boy in the Piney Woods, A. John Henry Boner. NoCaPo
Boy in the Wilderness. Samuel Taylor Coleridge. *See* Fruit Plucker, The.
Boy in the Wind. George Dillon. MAP; MoAmPo (1942 ed.); TBM
Boy Jesus, The. John Banister Tabb. StJW
Boy named Simon sojourned in a dale, A. Simple Simon. Harriet S. Morgridge. *Fr.* Mother Goose Sonnets. AA
Boy of eighteen years 'mid myrtle-boughs, A. Le Jeune Homme Caressant Sa Chimère. John Addington Symonds. OBVV; PoVP
Boy of five years old, serene and gay, A. Dead Child. Lucian. OnPM

Boy of Old Manhattan, A. Morris Abel Beer. HH
Boy of the Ghetto, A. Margaret Widdemer. CV
Boy of the House, The. Jean Blewett. CPG
Boy of Twenty, A. Horace Gregory. NV
Boy Out of Church, The. Robert Graves. TCPD
Boy Playing an Organ. Francis Sweeney. GoBC
Boy, presuming on his intellect, A. At Woodward's Gardens. Robert Frost. ImOP
Boy Reciter, The. David Everett. *See* Tall Oaks from Little Acorns Grow.
Boy Remembers in the Field. Raymond Knister. CaP
Boy Riding Forward Backward. Robert Francis. NePoAm-2
Boy should have an open fireplace, A. A Boy's Need. Herbert Clark Johnson. PoNe
Boy, should you meet a pretty wench. Advice to a Boy. Robinson Kay Leather. LEAP
Boy stood in the supper-room, The. *Unknown.* CenHV
Boy stood on the burning deck, The/ whence all but him had fled. Casabianca. Felicia Dorothea Hemans. BCEP; BeLS; BLPA; CG; EtS; FaBoBe; FaFP; FaPON; GoTP; HBV; HBVY; LH; LPS-2; NeHB; OnSP; OTPC; PECK, PIR; PreP; PTA-2; TreF; TVSH; WBLP
Boy stood on the burning deck, The/ Eating peanuts by the peck. Peanuts. *Unknown.* FaFP; GoTP; SiTL
Boy stood on the burning deck, The,/ His fleece was white as snow. Familiar Lines. *Unknown.* FiBHP
Boy that is good, A. *Unknown.* OxNR
Boy that is truthful and honest, A. The Boy We Want. *Unknown.* WBLP
Boy Was Born at Bethlehem, A. Edward Hilton Young. *See* Christmas.
Boy was born 'mid little things, A. Two Gods. Sam Walter Foss. MaRV
Boy Washington, The. Dorothy Brown Thompson. SiSoSe
Boy We Want, The. *Unknown.* WBLP
Boy wears a grin, The. A Boy and a Pup. Arthur Guiterman. AlBD; MPB; UTS
Boy Who Didn't Pass, The. *Unknown.* PTA-2
Boy, who in my festive home. To His Cup Bearer. Catullus. OnPM
Boy Who Laughed at Santa Claus, The. Ogden Nash. CenHV; MaC; StPo
Boy Who Never Told a Lie, The. *Unknown.* PECK
Boy, whose little, confiding hand. Locomotive to the Little Boy. Benjamin R. C. Low. HBMV
Boy with a Cart, The, *sel.* Christopher Fry.
"In our fields, fallow and burdened, in grass and furrow." LiTB
Boy with a Silver Plow. Dennis Murphy. BAP
Boy with His Hair Cut Short. Muriel Rukeyser. ExPo; FiMAP; MoAB; NAMP; TwAmPo
Boy with the Hoe, The. T. B. Weaver. PTA-2
Boyhood. Washington Allston. LPS-1; MOAH
Boyhood, *sel.* Sir Charles Abraham Elton.
"I stood upon a lawn whose greensward spread." EnSW
Boyhood. Wordsworth. *See* Influence of Natural Objects.
Boyhood Etchings. Walter Adolphe Roberts. PoNe
Boyne Walk, The. F. R. Higgins. OxBI
Boyne Water, The. *Unknown.* AnIV; OnYI; TIP
Boys, The. Oliver Wendell Holmes. BAP; BLP; CoBA; GDAH; HBV; HiLiAm; IAP; LPS-3; PTA-2; PYM; TCAP; WBLP
Boys. Winifred M. Letts. HBMV
Boys. *Unknown.* FAOV
Boys and girls come out to play. *Unknown.* OxNR; RIS
Boys, are ye callin' a toast to-night? Admiral Death. Sir Henry Newbolt. BHV; LBBV
Boys flying kites haul in their white-winged birds. Words. Will Carleton. OQP; QP-2
Boy's green song and the lyric of youth, The. Spring Fragment. Ken Etheridge. MoWP
Boy's heart is a light heart, A. Hero Wanted. Berton Braley. FAOV
Boys in sporadic but tenacious droves. The Horse Chestnut Tree. Richard Eberhart. AtBAP; CrMA; FiMAP; MoAB; NePA; NePoAm; Po
Boy's King, A. S. E. Kiser. FAOV
Boy's Mother, A. James Whitcomb Riley. DD; HBVY; HH; OHIP; OTPC; PoRL; PPL
Boys mount the mossy branches of this tree. Landmark. John Short. PoN
Boys' Names. Eleanor Farjeon. SUS; TiPo
Boy's Need, A. Herbert Clark Johnson. PoNe
Boys of the Island, The, *with music.* "Larry Gorman." ShS
Boys of the Island, The. *Unknown.* IHA
Boys out in the trenches, The. Destroyer Life. *Unknown.* ABF
Boy's Playthings. Leonidas, *tr. fr. Greek by* Lord Neaves. OnPM
Boy's Prayer, A. Henry Charles Beeching. *See* Prayers.
Boy's Prayer. A. B. Ponsonby. MaRV
Boy's Song, A. James Hogg. AlDL; BoChLi; BoTP; BSV; CBPC; CH; EBSV; EV-3; FaPON; GaP; HBV; HBVY; LEAP; LiTG; MoShBr; OBEV; OnHT; OTPC (1946 ed.); PCH; PECK; PoRh; PRWS; PTA-1; RIS; StVeCh (1940 ed.); TVC; TVSH; WaKn; WP
Boy's Song to Mariana. Shakespeare. *See* Take, O Take Those Lips Away.
Boy's Speech, A. *Unknown.* MeMeAg
Boy's Summer Song, A. Paul Laurence Dunbar. SiSoSe
Boy's Trust, A. Leo C. Turner. FAOV
Bozzy and Piozzi, *sel.* "Peter Pindar."
Introduction and Anecdotes. PoEL-3
Brace of sinners, for no good, A. The Pilgrims and the Peas. "Peter Pindar." BOHV; LPS-3
Braced to the temple-foot by Krantas' hand. The Sailor's Dedication. Macedonius. OxBG
Bracelet to Julia, The. Robert Herrick. EV-2; HBV; OBEV; TrGrPo
("Why I tie about thy wrist.") EG
Bracken on the hillside. November. Aileen Fisher. SiSoSe; TiPo (1959 ed.)
Brackish reach of shoal off Madaket, A. The Quaker Graveyard in Nantucket. Robert Lowell. CoBMV; FiMAP; MiAP; MoAB; MoPo; MoVE; NePA; OnAP; OxBA; ReMP; UnPo (3d ed.); ViBoPo (1958 ed.)
Braddock's Defeat. *Unknown.* ABF
Braddock's Fate, with an Incitement to Revenge. Stephen Tilden. PAH
Brady (A *and* B *vers.*), *with music. Unknown.* AS
(Duncan and Brady, *sl. diff., with music.*) OuSiCo
Brady's Bend. Martha Keller. StPo
Braes o' Balquhither, The. Robert Tannahill. EBSV
Braes o' [*or* of] Gleniffer, The. Robert Tannahill. EBSV; EV-4; OBRV
Braes o' Yarrow, The. *Unknown.* *See* Dowie Houms o' Yarrow, The.
Braes of Yarrow, The. William Hamilton. CEP; EBSV; EiPP; EV-3; OBEC
Bed of Love, The, *sel.* BeR
Braes of Yarrow, The. John Logan. BSV; EBSV; EV-3; GTBS; GTBS-D; GTBS-W; GTSE; GTSL; HBV; OBEC
(Thy Braes Were Bonny.) LPS-1
Braggart! Denis Wrafter. OnYI
Braggart March stood in the season's door, The. The Passing of March. Robert Burns Wilson. HBV; SN
Bragging Song. *Unknown, tr. fr. Arabic by* Sir Charles Lyall. LiTW
Brahma. Emerson. AA; AmP; AmPo; AmPP; AnAmPo; AnFE; AnNE; APA; APW; AWP; BAP; BAV; BLV; BoLiVe; CBOV; CoAnAm; CoBA; CoV; DDA; EV-4; GTBS; GTBS-D; GTBS-W; HBV; IAP; InPo; JAWP; LA; LEAP; LiTA; LiTG; LPS-3; MOAP; NePA; OBAV; OBEV; OBVV; OxBA; PFY; Po; PoLFOT; PoRA; REAL; SeCeV; ShBV-4; TCAP; TreF; TrGrPo; UnPo; ViBoPo; WBP; WGRP; WHA; WoL
Brahma. John Gould Fletcher. MOAP
Brahma. Andrew Lang. CenHV
Brahma sleeps. Brahma. John Gould Fletcher. MOAP
Brahma, the World Idea. *Unknown. Fr.* Rigveda. WGRP
Brahma's Answer. Richard Henry Stoddard. LPS-3
Brahmin, fat and debonair, A. Irreverent Brahmin, The. Arthur Guiterman. LHV
Brahms, The. Herbert Morris. NePoAm-2
Braid Claith. Robert Fergusson. BSV; CEP; EBSV; GoTS; OBEC
Brain, The ("The brain within its groove"). Emily Dickinson. CoBA; OnPM
Brain, be ice. Mens Creatrix. Stanley J. Kunitz. NP
Brain forgets, The, but the blood will remember. The Dark Chamber. Louis Untermeyer. LoPS; MAP; MoAmPo; TBM; TOP; WHA
Brain is wider than the sky, The. Emily Dickinson. AmP; AmPP (4th ed.); AnNE; CoV; MAP; MoAB; MoAmPo; OxBA; PoFS; TwP
Brain, the blood, the busy thews, The. Life's Testament, II. William Baylebridge. BoAV
Brain within its groove, The. The Brain. Emily Dickinson. CoBA; OnPM
Braith fach—a half-stone in the scales. The Cat and the Man. Oliver Edwards. PoC
Bramble Jam. Irene F. Pawsey. BoTP
Branch, The. Jones Very. TriL
Branch of myrtle in her happiness, A. Girlhood. Archilochus. GrPE
Branch of the apple-tree from Emain, The. *Unknown. Fr.* The Voyage of Bran. AnIL
Branch of the Sweet and Early Rose. William Drennan. IrPN
Branches interlacing down the street, The. Iced Branches. Kenneth Slade Alling. MuM
Branches of wild cherry! Wild Cherry. Jeanne Robert Foster. TBM
Brand, *sels.* Ibsen, *tr. fr. Norwegian.*
Agnes, *tr. by* Charles W. Stork. AnNoLy
Brand Speaks, *br. sel., tr. by* C. H. Herford. WGRP
Brand Fire New Whaling Song Right from the Pacific Ocean. *Unknown.* EtS

Brand Speaks. Ibsen. *Fr.* Brand. WGRP
Branding, The. Farrukhi, *tr. fr. Persian by* E. G. Browne. PeP
Branding Iron Herd, The. Ralph Rigby. PoOW
Brandish't sword of God before them blaz'd, The. Expulsion from Paradise. Milton. *Fr.* Paradise Lost, XII. ChTr
Branwen, *sel.* Wyn Griffith.
"I have borne too long this burden." MoWP
Braque. M. K. Joseph. AnNZ
Brass band blares, The. Circus. Eleanor Farjeon. BoChLi; MPB; SUS; UTS
Brass Horse, The. Drummond Allison. FaBoTw
Brass Spittoons. Langston Hughes. BANP; MAP; MoAmPo; NeMA
Brasses ("Brass that makes no sound"). Lyon Sharman. CPG
Bratzlav Rabbi to His Scribe, The. Jacob Glatstein, *tr. fr. Yiddish by* Jacob Sloan. TrJP
Being, *sel.* LiTW
Braut von Messina, Die, *sel.* Schiller, *tr. fr. German by* Benjamin W. Wells.
Where Mortals Dwell, *fr.* IV, iv. LiA
Brave and high-souled Pilgrims, you who knew no fears. Thanksgiving Day. Annette Wynne. OHIP
Brave as a falcon and as merciless. To Manon, Comparing Her to a Falcon [*or* The Falcon]. Wilfrid Scawen Blunt. The Love Sonnets of Proteus, II. ACP; OBVV; VA
Brave as the firstborn flame upsprings the statue. At the Salon. Florence Wilkinson Evans. HBV
Brave at Home, The. Thomas Buchanan Read. *Fr.* The Wagoner of the Alleghanies. BLP; HBV; LBAP; LPS-2; MDAH; PAP
Brave English language, you are strong as trees. Rhyme for a Phonetician. Frances Cornford. YT
Brave Epitaph, A. Milton. *Fr.* Samson Agonistes. BHV
("Come, come, no time for lamentations now.") FiP
(Death of Samson.) ChTr
Brave flowers, that I could gallant it like you. A Contemplation upon Flowers. Henry King. ATP (1935 ed.); BLV; CaAE; CenL; EG; ElSeCe; EV-2; HBV; LoBV; MeLP; MePo; OBEV; OBS; PG; PIAE; SeCL; SeEP; TrGrPo
Brave Infant of Saguntum, clear[e]. A Pindaric Ode: To the Immortal Memory of That Noble Pair, Sir Lucius Cary, and Sir Henry Morrison. Ben Jonson. OBS; PoEL-2; PoFS; SeCV-1; SeEP; TuPP
Brave iron, brave hammer, from your sound. Song of the Cyclops. Thomas Dekker. *Fr.* London's Tempe. NBE; ShBV-1; TuPP
Brave lads in olden musical centuries. Alcaics; to H. F. B. Robert Louis Stevenson. EG; OBEV (new ed.); OBVV; ShBV-3
Brave little bird that fears not God, A. The Meadow Lark. Hamlin Garland. AA
Brave Lord Willoughby. *Unknown. See* Lord Willoughby.
Brave men have followed. The Flag Speaks. Emily Greene Balch. PGD
Brave New World. Archibald MacLeish. AmP; OxBA
Brave New World. Shakespeare. *Fr.* The Tempest, V, i. TrGrPo
Brave News from Admiral Vernon. *Unknown.* SG
Brave News Is Come. *Unknown.* OTPC (1923 ed.)
("Brave news is come to town.") OxNR; PPL
Brave nose, whose rubies cost such casks of rare/ White wine and claret. To His Nose. Jean Le Houx, *formerly at. to* Olivier Basselin. FoS
Brave Old Oak, The. Henry Fothergill Chorley. FaBoBe; HBV; LPS-2; PIR
Brave Old Ship, the *Orient,* The. Robert Traill Spence Lowell. AA; FaBoBe
Brave Old World. Elisabeth Lambert. FaFP; SiTL
Brave Paulding and the Spy. *Unknown.* GA, *abr.;* MC; PAH
Brave Spirit, A. George Chapman. *See* Master Spirit, The.
Brave Tars of Old England, The. *Unknown.* SG
Brave Wolfe. *Unknown.* BaBo (A *and* B *vers.*); PAH; TrAS, *with music, sl. diff.;* ViBoFo
Brave young city by the Balboa seas, The. Twilight at the Heights. Joaquin Miller. AA; BAP; LEAP
Brave young Prince a young Princess adores, A. The Essence of Opera. *Unknown.* OnPM
Brave Women of Tann, The. William James Linton. BHV
Brave work, Ivan! Here's a New Year greeting! Ivan. G. D. Martineau. NeTW
Brave-hearted Maid, A. *Unknown, tr. fr. Anglo-Saxon by* Mother Margaret Williams. ISi; PoLi
Braver than sea-going ships with the dawn in their sails. To My Wife. William Rose Benét. PoMa
Bravery. Shakespeare. King Henry IV, Pt. I, *fr.* V, ii. BHV
Bravest Battle, The. Joaquin Miller. *See* Mothers of Men, The.
Bravest names for fire and flames, The. General John. W. S. Gilbert. GoTP; NA
Bravest of brave sweet blossoms in all of the garden-row. Chrysanthemums. Mary Mapes Dodge. PEOR
Bravo of Chao, The. Li Po, *tr. fr. Chinese.* WhP
Bravura. *Unknown, tr. fr. Spanish by* Mary Austin. APW
Braw Lads o' Galla Water. Burns. EBSV
Brawn of England's Lay. John Hunter-Duvar. VA
Brazen Tongue. William Rose Benét. MAP; MoAmPo
Brazier Coals, The. Miguel de Unamuno, *tr. fr. Spanish by* Thomas Walsh. OnPM
(Domestic Scenes.) LiTW; WoL
Brazil. Ronald de Carvalho, *tr. fr. Portuguese by* Dudley Poore. AnCL; WoL
Bread. Stanley Burnshaw. TrJP
Bread. Leslie Savage Clark. ChIP
Bread. A. M. Klein. PeCV
Bread. *Unknown.* MaRV
Bread. H. E. Wilkinson. BoTP
Bread and Butter Letter, A. Alice Duer Miller. VOD
Bread and milk for breakfast. Winter. Christina Rossetti. *Fr.* Sing-Song. EmBrPo; PCH; SAS
Bread and Music. Conrad Aiken. *See* Music I Heard.
Bread and Roses. James Oppenheim. OQP; QP-1
Bread is a lovely thing to eat. Lovely Things. H. M. Sarson. BoTP
Bread-Line, The. Dana Burnet. OBAV
Bread of Brotherhood. Lucia Trent. PGD
Bread of Life, The. Mary A. Lathbury. OQP; QP-1
(Break Thou the Bread of Life.) MaRV
Bread of the World. Reginald Heber. MaRV
Bread that bringeth [*or* giveth] strength I want to give, The. I Shall Not Pass Again This Way. Ellen H. Underwood. BLRP; MaRV; OQP; QP-1; TreF; WBLP
Break, Break, Break. Tennyson. ATP; AWP; BEL; BLV; BMEP; BoLiVe; BPN; BTP; CBE; EG; EM-2; EmBrPo; EnL; EnLi-2; EnLit; EPN; EPP; EtS; FaBoBe; FaBoEn; FiP; GTBS; GTBS-W; GTML; GTSE; GTSL; HBV; InP; InPo; JAWP; LEAP; LiTB; LiTG; LPS-1; MaRV; MCCG; NeHB; OAEP; OTPC; OuHeWo; PFE; PG (1945 ed.); PIAE; PIR; Po; PoE; PoEL-5; PoeMoYo; PoFS; PoRA; PoVP; PTA-2; PYM; REAL; ReaPo; RiBV; ShBV-2; SN; TCEP; TOP; TreF; TrGrPo; TVSH; TwHP; TyEnPo; ViPo; ViPP; VLEP; WBP; WHA; YT
Break, break, break,/ On thy cold, hard stones, O sea! The Bather's Dirge. "Tennyson Minor." PA
Break, break, break, O voice!—let me urge thy plea! The Musical Pitch. *Unknown.* PA
Break Down the Walls. John Oxenham. OQP; QP-1
Break, Fantasy, from thy cave of cloud. Fantasy. Ben Jonson. *Fr.* Vision of Delight. LPS-3
Break forth, break forth, O Sudbury town. Lydia. Lizette Woodworth Reese. AA; OBAV
Break forth in song, ye trees. Centennial Hymn. John Pierpont. AnNE
Break me a bread not made with hands. The Unfaithful. Genevieve Taggard. AV
Break My Heart of Stone. Charles Wesley. BePJ
Break not his sweet repose. A Soldier's Grave. John Albee. AA
Break of Day. John Donne. ElL; EnLP; LiTB; LiTG; LiTL; LoPS; TrGrPo; TuPP; TwP
(Daybreak.) OBEV; TOP
("Stay, O sweet, and do not rise!") EG
Break of Day, The. John Shaw Neilson. BoAu; BoAV
Break of Day in the Trenches. Isaac Rosenberg. CoEV; FaBoMo; MoBrPo; MoP; SeCePo; ViBoPo; WaaP; WaP
"Break off your argument." The Shape of a Bird. Laurence Whistler. MoVE
Break the Heart's Anger, *sel.* Paul Engle.
"I will make a new song of the word," *abr., fr.* Prologue. PoFr
Break the News to Mother. Charles Kassell Harris. TreFS
Break thou my heart, ah, break it. Arab Song. Richard Henry Stoddard. AA; OBAV
Break Thou the Bread of Life. Mary A. Lathbury. *See* Bread of Life, The.
Breake hart in twayne, fayre Ronile may se. *Unknown.* SeCSL
Breakers of Broncos. Lew Sarett. HiLiAm
Breakfast. W. W. Gibson. NV; OBMV
Breakfast. Mary Lamb. OTPC (1923 ed.)
Breakfast and Puss. Ann *or* Jane Taylor. PoC
Breakfast Song, The. Emilie Poulsson. HBVY
Breakfast Time. James Stephens. SUS
Breakfast with Gerard Manley Hopkins. Anthony Brode. FiBHP
Breaking, The. Margaret Steele Anderson. HBV; SBMV
Breaking from under That Thy Cloudy Veil. Lord Herbert of Cherbury. EV-2
(Upon Combing Her Hair.) SeEP
Breaking In a Tenderfoot. *Unknown.* ABS; IHA
Breaking Point. Sylvia Auxier. GoYe
Breaking waves dashed high, The. The Landing of the Pilgrim Fathers in New England [*or* Pilgrim Fathers]. Felicia Dorothea Hemans. BCEP; BeLS; BLPA; BoHiPo; BoTP; DD; ERP; FaBoBe; FaFP; FaPON; GN; GoTP; HBV; HBVY; HH; LH; LPS-2; MaRV; MC; MW; NeHB; OHIP; OnSP; OTPC; PaA; PAH;

PCH; PECK; PGD; PIR; PoRL; PoFr; PTA-1; TreF; WBLP
Breast of my stalwart horse, The. The Meadow. Manuel Altolaguirre. CoSP
Breast to breast in the whirling. Boolee, the Bringer of Life. Mary Gilmore. BoAV
Breastplate of Saint Patrick, The. *At. to* St. Patrick. *See* Deer's Cry, The.
Breath, A ("A breath can fan love's flame to burning"). "Madeline Bridges." AA
Breath o' the grass. Susurro. "Fiona Macleod." *Fr.* Sospiri di Roma. BMEP; VA
Breath of Avon, The. Theodore Watts-Dunton. VA
Breath of Day. Catullus, *tr. fr. Latin by* Sir William Marris. LiA
Breath of dew, and twilight's grace, The. A Friend's Song for Simoisius. Louise Imogen Guiney. PFY; TCPD
Breath of Hampstead Heath. Edith M. Thomas. AA
Breath of life imbued those few dim days, The! Fragment. Jessie Redmond Fauset. CDC
Breath of Night, The. Randall Jarrell. CrMA
Breath of prayer in the morning, A. The Meaning of Prayer. *Unknown.* PraP
Breath of the Briar. George Meredith. POTT
("O briar-scents, on yon wet wing.") EG
Breath of time shall blast the flowry spring, The. Upon the Thought of Age and Death. William Habington. AEV
Breath on the Oat. Joseph Russell Taylor. HBV; PAH
Breathe balmy airs, ye fragrant flowers. Flower-strewn Graves. Samuel Francis Smith. MaRV
Breathe from the gentle South, O Lord. The Waiting Soul. William Cowper. NBE
Breathe Julia, breathe and I'll protest. Of Her Breath. Robert Herrick. EG
Breathe me the ancient words when I shall find. Love's Ritual. Charles Hanson Towne. LBMV
Breathe, Mountain Pan, a joyous note. Alcaeus of Messene, *tr. fr. Greek by* Walter Leaf. GrPo
Breathe not, hid Heart: cease silently. To an Unborn Pauper Child. Thomas Hardy. CoBMV; LiTB; PoLFOT; ReMP; ViBoPo
Breathe on Me, Breath of God. Edwin Hatch. MaRV
Breathe, trumpets, breathe. Requiem. George Lunt. AA; PaA
Breathes There a Man. Samuel Hoffenstein. WhC
("Breathes there a man with hide so tough.") FiBHP
Breathes there a man who claimeth not. Gethsemane. Edmund Leamy. JKCP; OQP; PSO; QP-1
Breathes there a man with hide so tough. Breathes There a Man. Samuel Hoffenstein. FiBHP; WhC
Breathes There the Man [with Soul So Dead]. Sir Walter Scott. *Fr.* The Lay of the Last Minstrel, VI. BBV; BHV; BLPA; CBE; EnRP; ERP; FaFP; InP; LPS-2; MaRV; NeHB; OAEP; OBRV; PGD; PIR; PTA-1; PYM; TreF
(From "The Lay of the Last Minstrel.") LEAP
(Innominatus.) OBEV; TOP
(Love of Country.) BTP; OHFP; OQP; PSO; QP-1; WBLP
(Love of Fatherland.) TVSH
(My Native Land.) GN; MPB (1956 ed.); OnHT; OTPC (1923 ed.); StaSt
(My Own, My Native Land.) EBSV; StVeCh (1940 ed.)
(Native Land.) PIAE; TrGrPo
(Patriotism.) BCEP; EV-4; PCD; PG (1945 ed.)
Breathing do I draw that air to me. Song of Breath. Peire Vidal. AWP; JAWP; WBP
Breathing something German at the end. The Gift to Be Simple. Howard Moss. ImOP
Breathless Awe. Edwin Markham. *See* Third Wonder, The.
Breathless, we flung us on the windy hill. The Hill. Rupert Brooke. CBOV; EnLit; GTML; GTSL; HBV; LEAP; LiTL; LoPo; LoPS; MBP; MoBrPo; POTE; POTT; ViBoPo
Breaths of kissing night and day, The. Dream-Tryst. Francis Thompson. AnFE; EmBrPo; EnLit; GTML; POTT; UnW; VA
Brébeuf and His Brethren, *sels.* E. J. Pratt.
"Fury of taunt was followed by fury of blow, The," *fr.* XII. PeCV; TwCaPo
Invisible Trumpets Blowing, *shorter sel.* CaP
Brébeuf and Lalemant. Alan Sullivan. CPG
Brechva's Harp Song. Ernest Rhys. VA
Bred in a low place, lord of little deeds. A Man of Men. Leonard Charles Van Noppen. PGD
Bred in distant woods, the clown. The Country Clown. John Trumbull. AnAmPo; LA
Bred on the dry land with the winds to race. A Mare. Mnasalcas. OxBG
Bredon Hill. A. E. Housman. A Shropshire Lad, XXI. BEL; BPN; ChMo; CMP; EmBrPo; EnLi-2; LiTL; MBP; MoAB; MoBrPo; NeMA; PoTo; POTT; PoVP; RiBV; TCEP; TCPD; TreF; TwCV; TyEnPo; ViP; ViPo; WHA
(Summer Time on Bredon.) GBV (1952 ed.)
Breech, The. Michael McClure. NeAP
Breeze, The. Al-Husri, *tr. fr. Arabic by* A. J. Arberry. MooP
Breeze, The. *Unknown. See* Summer Breeze.
Breeze and Billow. Albert Durrant Watson. CaP; CPG
Breeze blows o'er the lake, A. Herons. *Unknown.* SUS
Breeze has swelled the whitening sail, The. Song of the Pilgrims. Thomas Cogswell Upham. MC; PAH
Breeze is on the bluebells, The. Bluebells. Juliana Horatia Ewing. BoTP
Breeze of the morn, The. Jalal ed-Din Rumi, *tr. fr. Persian by* A. J. Arberry. PeP
Breeze of the morning, at the hour thou knowest. Love's Language. Hafiz. PeP
Breeze was crisp and the sea lay blue, The. The Pirates' Fight. Joseph Schull. *Fr.* The Legend of Ghost Lagoon. CaP
Breezes went steadily through the tall pines, The. Nathan Hale [*or* Hale in the Bush]. *Unknown.* GA; IAP; PAH; TCAP
Brekeke-kesh, koash, koash. Chorus. Aristophanes, *tr. by* John Hookham Frere. *Fr.* The Frogs. PreP
Brekeke kex ko ax ko ax. The Frogs' Song. Aristophanes, *tr. by* T. F. Higham. *Fr.* The Frogs. OxBG
Brekekekex, ko-ax, ko-ax. The Frog's Song. Aristophanes, *tr. by* Benjamin Bickley Rogers. *Fr.* The Frogs. GrR
Brendan, holy Brendan of the blessed beard. Saint Brendan's Prophecy. *Unknown.* OnYI
Brennan on the Moor. *Unknown.* BaBo; OnYI; OuSiCo, *with music;* ViBoFo, *with music*
Brennbaum. Ezra Pound. *Fr.* Hugh Selwyn Mauberley. CoBMV; CoV; LiTA; LiTM (rev. ed.); MoPo
Brer Tarrypin tired er prom'nadin' roun'. How Brer Tarrypin Learned to Fly. Joel Chandler Harris. TSW; TSWC
Breshkovskaya, *sel.* Elsa Barker.
"Mother of power, my soul goes out to you." BAP
Brest Left Behind. John Chipman Farrar. AOAH; PAH
Bretagne had not her peer. In the province far or near. Lady of Castlenoire. Thomas Bailey Aldrich. BeLS; LoEn
Breughel's Winter. Walter de la Mare. SeCePo
Breviary on the Subway. Leonard McCarthy. JKCP (1955 ed.)
Brevities. Siegfried Sassoon. MoPW
Brewer, A. *Unknown.* WhC
Brewer's Man, The. L. A. G. Strong. FiBHP; WhC
Brewing of Soma, The. Whittier. PoEL-4
Dear Lord and Father of Mankind, *sel.* GrCo-1; MaRV; OlF; PreP, *with music;* TrPWD
Brian O'Linn. *Unknown.* OnYI
Briar-Rose. *Unknown, tr. fr. German by* Louis Untermeyer. RIS
Bricklayer, The. Vasili Kazin, *tr. fr. Russian.* BoR, *tr. by* C. M. Bowra; TrRV, *tr. by* Babette Deutsch
Bricklayer Love. Carl Sandburg. AmP
Bricklayer tells the busdriver, The. The Continuity. Paul Blackburn. NeAP
Bridal Ballad. Poe. IAP; TriL
Bridal Birth. Dante Gabriel Rossetti. The House of Life, II. BMEP; BPN; EmBrPo; OAEP; POTT; PoVP; RiBV; ViPo; VLEP
Bridal Hymn. Catullus, *tr. fr. Latin by* W. H. Mallock. WoL
Bridal Morning. *Unknown. See* Maidens Came, The.
Bridal Night. Don Marquis. TBM
Bridal o 't, The. Alexander Ross. EBSV
Bridal of Queen Dagmar, The. *Unknown, tr. fr. Danish by* E. M. Smith-Dampier. BoDaBa
Bridal Pair, The. William Young. *Fr.* Wishmakers' Town. AA
Bridal Song ("Cynthia, to thy power"). Beaumont *and* Fletcher. *Fr.* The Maid's Tragedy, I, ii. OBEV; TuPP
Bridal Song ("Hold back thy hours"). Beaumont *and* Fletcher. *Fr.* The Maid's Tragedy, I, ii. ElL; LoPS; TrGrPo
(Hold Back Thy Hours.) ViBoPo
("Hold back thy hours, dark Night, till we have done.") EG; ElSeCe; RiBV
Bridal Song ("Now, sleep, bind fast the flood of air"). George Chapman. *Fr.* The Masque of the Middle Temple and Lincoln's Inn. *See* Now, Sleep, Bind Fast.
Bridal Song ("O come, soft rest of cares! come, Night!"). George Chapman. *Fr.* Hero and Leander, Fifth Sestiad. BCEP; OBEV
(Come, Night.) OnPM
("O come, soft rest of cares! come, Night!") EG
(Song.) ViBoPo
Bridal Song. Thomas Dekker, *and others.* *Fr.* The Pleasant Comedy of Patient Grissell, V, ii. OBSC; TrGrPo
(Beauty, Arise!) ElL; TuPP
Bridal Song. Fletcher *and* Shakespeare. *Fr.* The Two Noble Kinsmen, I, i. CBOV; ElL; OBEV; OBSC
("Roses, their sharp spines being gone.") BrBE; CenL; EG; ElSeCe; EV-1; MyFE; ViBoPo
Bridal Song, A. Hugh McCrae. BoAu
Bridal Song, A. Shelley. EV-4; OBRV
Bridal Song to Amala. Thomas Lovell Beddoes. *Fr.* Death's Jest Book, IV, iii. OBVV

Bridal Song to Amala (*continued*)
(Epithalamia.) PoEL-4
(Song: "We have bathed, where none have seen us.") ChER; FaBoEn
(Song[s] at Amala's Wedding.) LoBV; PoE
Bridal Voyage, The. Andreas Munch, *tr. fr. Norwegian by* Charles W. Stork. AnNoLy
Briddes that han left their song, The. Guillaume de Lorris. *Fr.* The Romaunt of the Rose. EG
Bride, The. Henry Alford. OBEV (1st ed.)
(Sonnet: "'Rise,' said the Master.") LPS-1
Bride, The. Ambrose Bierce. AA; LHV
Bride, The. Ralph Hodgson. AEV; HBMV; InP; TCPD
Bride, The. "Laurence Hope." HBV
Bride, A. Meleager, *tr. fr. Greek by* Henry Charles Beeching. GrL; OxBG; WoL
(Bride of Death, The, *tr. by* F. L. Lucas.) GrPE; GrR
Bride, The. Ruth Comfort Mitchell. HBMV
Bride, The. Spenser. *Fr.* Epithalamion. LPS-1
Bride, The. L. A. G. Strong. POTE
Bride, The. Sir John Suckling. *Fr.* A Ballad upon a Wedding. BLV; LPS-1, *abr.*; TrGrPo
Bride cam' out o' the byre, The. Woo'd and Married and A'. *Unknown.* EBSV; EV-3; HBV
Bride in the '30's, A. W. H. Auden. FaBoMo
Bride of Abydos, The. Byron. BPN; EmBrPo; OAEP
Sels.
Know Ye the Land, *fr.* I. BEL; EPP; MCCG
(Land of the Sun, The.) EV-4
(Orient, The.) LPS-2
"Winds are high on Helle's wave, The," *fr.* II. OBRV
Bride of Death, The. Meleager. *See* Bride, A.
Bride of Lammermoor, The, *sels.* Sir Walter Scott.
Lucy Ashton's Song, *fr. ch.* 3. BSV; CBE; EBSV; EnRP; EV-4; GoTS; LEAP; OBEV; OtMeF
(Look Not Thou.) OBRV
True-Love, an Thou Be True. BPN
Bride of Ribe, The. *Unknown, tr. fr. Danish by* E. M. Smith-Dampier. BoDaBa
Bride of Sardis, The. Sappho, *tr. fr. Greek by* Walter Petersen. GrR
Bride of Sixteen, The. Julianus, *tr. fr. Greek by* F. L. Lucas. GrPE
Bride she bound her golden hair, The. Sir Turlough; or, The Churchyard Bride. William Carleton. IrPN; TIP
Bride, The, she wears a white, white rose—the plucking it was mine. Song. Margaret Steele Anderson. SBMV
Bride Song, A ("Through the vales to my love"). Christina Rossetti. EtPaEn
Bride Song ("Too late for love, too late for joy"). Christina Rossetti. *Fr.* The Prince's Progress. EPP; OBEV; OBVV; TOP
(Too Late for Love.) PoVP
Bride to the Victor, A. Pindar. *See* Pelops.
Bridegroom, The. Kipling. *Fr.* Epitaphs of the War. SoV
Bridegroom calls and led by love they go, The. The White Sisters of Culion. Wilbur Underwood. PraNu
Bridegroom dear, to what shall I compare thee? Wedding Songs. Sappho. GrL; OxBG
Bridegroom Dick, *sel.* Herman Melville.
Where's Commander All-a-Tanto? OnAP; PoEL-5
Bridegroom none but death alone. A Bride. Meleager. GrL; OxBG; WoL
Bridegroom of Cana, The. Marjorie Pickthall. BoCaPo; CaP; CPG; OCL
Brides of Enderby, The; or, The High Tide. Jean Ingelow. *See* High Tide on the Coast of Lincolnshire, The.
Bride's Prelude, The. Dante Gabriel Rossetti. SeCePo
Bride's Song, The. Tu Fu, *tr. fr. Chinese by* Edna Worthley Underwood *and* Chi Hwang Chu. ChLP
Bride's Toilette, The. Ellen M. Hutchinson Cortissoz. AA
Bride's Tragedy, The, *sels.* Thomas Lovell Beddoes.
"Dear, I could weep, but that my brain is dry." LO
"Eternal people of the lower world." NBE
Hesperus Sings. VA
("Poor old pilgrim Misery.") EnRP; NBE
Love Goes a-Hawking. VA
(Song: "A ho! A ho!") ChER
Bridge, The. Hart Crane. LiTA
Sels.
Atlantis. AnFE; AtBAP; CoAnAm; CoV; LiTM; MOAP; MoPo; NePA; TwAmPo
Ave Maria. AtBAP; CoV; MoPo; NePA
Cape Hatteras. CoV; OnAP, *abr.*; WoL
Aeroplane, The. VOD (1935 ed.)
"Nasal whine of power whips a new universe, The." MoAB
Power. VOD (1935 ed.)
Power: Cape Hatteras. MAP; MoAmPo
Cutty Sark. AmPP; FaBoMo; NP
Powhatan's Daughter.
Dance, The. AnAmPo; AnFE; CoAnAm; LA; LiTM; MoAB; MoAmPo; OxBA; SeCeV; TwAmPo
Harbor Dawn, The. AmP; CoV; MoPo; NePA; OxBA
Indiana. AnFE; CoAnAm; TwAmPo
River, The. AmP; AmPP; AnFE; CoAnAm; CoBA; CoBMV; CoV; MoAB; MoAmPo; NAMP; OxBA; TwAmPo; ViBoPo (1958 ed.)
"Down, down—born pioneers in time's despite." TrGrPo
"You will not hear it as the sea." ViBoPo (1941 ed.)
Van Winkle. AmP; AmPP; CrMA; MAP; MoAB; MoAmPo; ReMP
Quaker Hill. LiTM (rev. ed.)
Three Songs.
National Winter Garden. AmP; LiTM (rev. ed.); OxBA
To Brooklyn Bridge. AmPP; ChMo; CoBMV; CrMA; ExPo; FaBoEn; GTBS-W; LiTA; LiTM; MoAB; MoAmPo (1950 ed.); MoPo; NePA; OxBA; PoE; ReMP; SeCeV
(Proem: To Brooklyn Bridge.) AmP; CoV
Tunnel, The. AmP; LiTA; LiTG; MAP; MoAB; MoAmPo; MoVE; NePA; OxBA; PoFS; TCPD
Bridge. S. Foster Damon. AnAmPo; LA
Bridge, The. Henry Dumont. PoTo
Bridge, The. Willibald Köhler, *tr. fr. German by* George N. Shuster. CAW
Bridge, The. Longfellow. BPP; CoBA; HBV; IAP; REAL; SN; TCAP; TreF
Bridge, The. Frederick Peterson. HBV; OBAV
Bridge, The. Geoffrey Scott. TwCV
Bridge, The. James Thomson. *See* Oh, What Are You Waiting For.
Bridge, The. Nikolai Tikhonov, *tr. fr. Russian by* Jack Lindsay. RuPo
Bridge, The. Albert Verwey, *tr. fr. Dutch by* A. J. Barnouw. LiTW
Bridge Builder, The. Will Allen Dromgoole. FAOV; MaRV; NeHB; OQP; PoToHe; PTA-2; QP-2; TreFS
(Building the Bridge for Him.) BLP
Bridge Builder, The. Isabel Ecclestone Mackay. CPG
Bridge-Guard in the Karroo. Kipling. BoSA
Bridge Instead of a Wall, A. *Unknown.* PoToHe (new ed.)
Bridge of Arta, The. *Unknown, tr. fr. Modern Greek by* Rae Dalven. MoGP
Bridge of Death, The. *Unknown, tr. fr. French by* Andrew Lang. AWP
Bridge of Sighs, The. Thomas Hood. BCEP; BEL; BeLS; CBOV; EnLi-2; EnLit; EnRP; ERP; EV-4; GTBS; GTBS-D; GTBS-W; GTSE; GTSL; HBV; HoPM; LEAP; LiTG; LPS-1; OBEV; OBVV; PC; PFE; PG; PYM; TreF; VA; WBLP; WHA
Rhymes, 1 *st.* LiA
Bridge, St. James's Park, The. Virginia Graham. DiM
Bridge, The, says: Come across, try me; see how good I am. Potomac Town in February. Carl Sandburg. WaKn
Bridge weaves its arch with pearls, A. The Rainbow—a Riddle. Schiller. OTPC (1946 ed.)
Bridge You'll Never Cross, The. Grenville Kleiser. MaRV
Bridges are for going over water. Over and Under. William Jay Smith. TiPo (1959 ed.)
Bridle-reins hang loose in the hold of his lean left hand, The. The Boundary Rider. Thomas Heney. BoAu
Brief as the Snow. Gertrude MacGregor Moffat. CPG
Brief Autumnal. *Unknown, tr. fr. Greek by* Dudley Fitts. LiTW
Brief, den du geschrieben, Der. Heine, *tr. fr. German by* Louis Untermeyer. ALV
Brief History. Olga Hampel Briggs. GoYe
Brief is Erinna's song, her lowly lay. Erinna. Antipater of Sidon. AWP
Brief life is here our portion. The Celestial Country. Bernard of Cluny. GrCo-1
Brief, on a flying night. Chimes. Alice Meynell. AnFE; BLV; BoTP; CH; MBP; MoBrPo; NP; PoeT; POTT; TSW; TSWC; WHA
Brief Sermon, A. *Unknown.* TreFS
Brier. E. Pauline Johnson. MaRV
Brier-Rose. Hjalmar Hjorth Boyesen. PTA-1
Brier-Wood Pipe, The. Charles Dawson Shanly. LPS-2
"Brigade Must Not Know, Sir, The." *Unknown.* GA; MC; PAH; SPP
Brigadier. *Unknown, tr. fr. French-Canadian folk song by* A. J. M. Smith. BoCaPo (1948 ed.)
Brigham Young (A *and* B *vers.*). *Unknown.* CoSo; CSF
Bright Abandon. Tessa Sweazy Webb. GoYe
Bright amorous e'e where love in ambush lies. Sonnet: To His Mistress. Alexander Montgomerie. EBSV
Bright are the heavens, the narrow bay serene. The Indian's Grave. George J. Mountain. BoCaPo (1943 ed.); CaP
Bright as moon serenely burning. Battle. Al-Tutili. MooP
Bright as the day, and like the morning fair. Chloe [*or* Cloe]. George Granville. BeR; PIAE; SeEP
Bright axe breaks the silence in the wood, The. Tree Felling. George Woodcock. NeBP
Bright babe! Whose awfull beautyes make. In the Glorious Epiphanie of Our Lord God. Richard Crashaw. PoEL-2

Bright baffling Soul, least capturable of themes. To Shakespeare. Thomas Hardy. PtP; VLEP
Bright Be the Place of Thy Soul! Byron. EmBrPo; HoPM
(Stanzas for Music: "Bright be the place.") ERP
Bright be the skies that cover thee. To Laura W——, Two Years Old. Nathaniel Parker Willis. HBV
Bright beach glittering in the morning sun, A. On the Edge of the Pacific. Theodore Maynard. CAW
Bright books! the perspectives to our weak sights. To His Books. Henry Vaughan. EPS (1942 ed.)
Bright breaks the warrior o'er the ocean wave. The Ocean Wanderer. *Unknown.* BOHV; NA
Bright, bright, the gilded magpie mirror. The Mirror. Li Po. ChLP
Bright cap and streamers. Chamber Music, X. James Joyce. ReaPo
Bright cards above the fire bring no friends near. Christmas 1944. Denise Levertov. NeBP
Bright Clouds. Edward Thomas. POTE
Bright Death. "Andrei Bely," *tr. fr. Russian.* BoRS, *tr. by* C. M. Bowra; TrRV, *tr. by* Babette Deutsch
Bright Delusion. Inez Barclay Kirby. MuM
Bright drips the morning from its trophied nets. Sonnet of Fishes. George Barker. FaBoMo
Bright earth moves in destined grooves, The. Final Thoughts on the Weather in England during 1953. David Daiches. SiTL
Bright eyes and laughing lips. Rain. Patrick F. Kirby. GoBC
Bright Eyes, Light Eyes! Daughter of a Fay! The Faery Foster-Mother. Robert Buchanan. VA
Bright Flower! whose home is everywhere. To the Daisy. Wordsworth. BPN; CoBE; EmBrPo; EnRP; EPN; ERP
Bright glows the east with blushing red. The Farm. Jane Taylor. OTPC (1923 ed.)
Bright Hair, Grow Dim. Humbert Wolfe. CaAE
Bright Hillside, The. Rhoda Coghill. NeIP; OxBI
Bright image of the early years. To the Painted Columbine. Jones Very. IAP
Bright Is the Ring of Words. Robert Louis Stevenson. PoVP; TrGrPo
(Words.) GoTP
Bright little maid of St. Thomas, A. Limerick. *Unknown.* HBV
Bright moon illumines the night-prospect, A. Old Chinese Poem [*or* Seventeen Old Poems, 7]. *Unknown.* BoFr; TrCh
Bright moon in love must surely laugh at me, The. To the Tune of "Gathering Mulberry Seeds." Nalan Hsinteh. WhP
Bright moon lifts from the Mountain of Heaven, The. The Moon at the Fortified Pass. Li Po. LiTW; WaaP
Bright moon, oh, how white it shines, The. *Unknown, tr. fr. Chinese by* Arthur Waley. Seventeen Old Poems, 17. TrCh
Bright moon soars over the Mountain of Heaven, The. The Moon over the Mountain Pass. Li Po. WhP
Bright Night, A. *Unknown, tr. fr. Japanese by* Arthur Waley. *Fr.* Manyo Shu. WoL
("Shall we make love.") AWP; LiTW
Bright Offerings from Shepherds. Elizabeth Rowe. *Fr.* A Pastoral in Imitation of Drayton's Second Nymphal. BeR
Bright on the banners of lily and rose. Welcome to the Nations. Oliver Wendell Holmes. IDAH; PAH
Bright Phoebus drove his rapid car amain. The Squabble of the Sea Nymphs or the Sacrifice of the Tuscararoes. Mercy Warren. BAV
Bright portals [*or* portalles] of the sky. An Hymn [*or* Song] of the Ascension. William Drummond of Hawthornden. EPS; OBS; SeCL
Bright Queen of Heaven, God's Virgin Spouse. The Knot. Henry Vaughan. ISi
Bright ran thy line, O Galloway. Lord Galloway. Burns. OxBoLi
Bright rays of lofty Phaeton shine, The. Immortal Springtime and Its Tokens. Bernardo de Balbuena. *Fr.* Grandeza Mexicana. AnMP
Bright sea washed beneath her feet, The. The Return. Annie Fields. AA
Bright seas cast far upon her shore. The Day of Coming Days. Lionel Johnson. POTT
Bright shadows of true rest! some shoots of blisse. Son-Dayes. Henry Vaughan. AtBAP
Bright shine the golden summits in the light. A Calm Sea. Robert Southey. EtS
Bright shines the new tower. The New Tower. *Unknown.* WhP
Bright shines the sun on Clinch's Hill. The Vance Song. Abner Vance. OuSiCo
Bright shines the sun; play, beggars, play! In Praise of a Beggar's Life [*or* A Song in Praise of a Beggar's Life *or* Play, Beggars, Play!]. "A. W." ElL; ElSeCe; OBSC; SiCE; TrGrPo; WHA
Bright shone the lists, blue bent the skies. The Tournament. Sidney Lanier. PECK
Bright silk trappings are onion-green, The. I Pass the Great Hall. Li Ho. WhP
Bright something, sailing down apace, A. Diana. Keats. *Fr.* Endymion, I. BCEP
Bright soule, instruct poore mortalls how to mourne. *Unknown.* SeCSL
Bright spark, shot from a brighter place. The Star [*or* Starre]. George Herbert. AtBAP; MeRV
Bright Sparkles in the Churchyard. *Unknown.* AA
Bright Spirit. Josephine Royle. BAP
Bright Squadrons, The. Spenser. *See* Ministering Angels.
Bright Star. Keats. *See* Bright Star! Would I Were Steadfast as Thou Art.
Bright star of beauty, fairest fair alive. To His Mistress. Richard Barnfield. *Fr.* Cynthia. SiCE; TuPP
Bright star of beauty, on whose eyelids sit. Idea, IV. Michael Drayton. ElSeCe; EPP; HBV; SiCE
Bright Star! Would I Were Steadfast [*or* Stedfast] as Thou Art. Keats. ATP; BEL; BoLiVe; BPN; CoBE; EmBrPo; EnL; EnLi-2; EnLit; EnLoPo; EPN; ERP; ExPo; GTBS; GTBS-D; GTBS-W; GTSE; LiTB; LiTG; LO; MaPo; OuHeWo; PoE; PoFS; ReaPo; SeCeV; ShBV-4; TCEP; TOP; TreFS; TrGrPo; TwHP; TwP; TyEnPo; ViBoPo
(Bright Star.) EM-2; EnRP; EPP; LiTL; LoPo; PeBoSo; PG (1955 ed.); PoeMoYo; PreP; WHA
(His Last Sonnet.) LoBV
(Keats' Last Sonnet.) ES; EV-4
(Last Sonnet.) AnFe; BCEP; BLV; ChER; GTSL; HBV; LEAP; NeHB; OBEV; PIAE
(Sonnet: "Bright star.") AnEnPo; CaAE; FiP; LiA; LoPS; OAEP; PoEL-4; ShBV-4
(Sonnet: Written on a Blank Page in Shakespeare's Poems, Facing "A Lover's Complaint.") EtPaEn; GEPC
(Written on a Blank Page in Shakespeare's Poems [Facing "A Lover's Complaint"].) FaBoEn; OBRV
Bright Stars and Dark. Victor Hugo, *tr. fr. French by* Sir George Young. *Fr.* Les Contemplations. LiA
Bright stars, around the fair Selene peering. The Moon Sappho. GrL; OxBG
Bright stars, light stars. Stars. Rhoda W. Bacmeister. BrR
Bright swords. Bright spears. They blur, blot, the world. Farewell to Han So. Tu Fu. OnPM
Bright, thin, new moon appears, The. New Moon. Tu Fu. OnPC
Bright things of the morning, The. A Lover and His Lass. Ronald Hambleton. BoCaPo
Bright thro' the valley gallops the brooklet. Eros. Coventry Patmore. GTSE
Bright Vision, The. Dryden. *Fr.* The Conquest of Granada. BeR
Bright vocabularies are transient as rainbows. Precious Moments. Carl Sandburg. MAP; MoAmPo
Bright was the morn—the waveless bay. Perry's Victory on Lake Erie. James Gates Percival. PaA; PAP
Bright Was the Morning. Thomas D'Urfey. OBS
Bright water: like the salty tears of infancy. Memory. Arthur Rimbaud. LiTW
Bright waves scour the wound of Carthage, The. Rome Remember. Sidney Keyes. MoAB; PoN
Bright were the mornings first impearl'd. And Jesus Wept. Matthew Bridges. BePJ
Brightest and Best of the Sons of the Morning. Reginald Heber. COAH; GN; HBVY; MaRV; OTPC; SDH; WGRP; YaCaBo, *with music*
(Epiphany.) PoRL
Brightest night of all, The. Revel. Abul Hasan of Santa Maria. MooP
Brightly colored for a new season. Merry-go-round. Oliver Jenkins. GoYe
Brightly for him the future smiled. Mother and Son. Phoebe Cary. MOAH
Brightly lit from above, I am sitting. Stanzas. Vladislav Khodasevich. BoRS
Brightness of a bronze mirror, The. The Mirror. Po Chü-i. WhP
Brightness of Brightness Egan O'Rahilly, *tr. fr. Irish by* Frank O'Connor. KiLC
Brigid, the daughter of Duffy, she wasn't like other young things. Saint Brigid. Denis A. McCarthy. JKCP
Brignall [*or* Brignal] Banks. Sir Walter Scott. *Fr.* Rokeby, III. BCEP; BEL; BPN; EBSV; EmBrPo; EnRP; EPN; ERP; OBEV; PCN; TOP; TyEnPo
(Edmund's Song.) EnLi-2; PoRA
(Outlaw, The.) GTBS; GTBS-D; GTBS-W; GTSE; GTSL; LH; OtMeF
(Song: Brignall Banks.) EV-4
(Song: "O Brignall banks are wild and fair.") HBV; OAEP; OBRV
Brigs of Ayr, The, *sel.* Burns.
"When heavy, dark, continued, a'-day rains." MCCG

Brilliant black eye, The. Black and Blue Eyes. Thomas Moore. LPS-1
Brilliant Day, A. Charles Tennyson Turner. EnSW
Brilliant seaside glitters its farewell, The. A Summer Gone. Howard Moss. NePoEA
Brimming Water. Tu Fu, *tr. fr. Chinese by* Kenneth Rexroth. OnPC
Brindled Hare, The. Thomas S. Jones, Jr. Sonnets of the Saints, II. TBM
Bring a Torch. Jeannette, Isabella. *At. to* Nicolas Saboly, *tr. fr. Provençal.* ChrBoLe; OHIP; YaCaBo, *with music* (Christmas Carol of Provence.) RAR
Bring a yellow ear of corn, then rub, rub, rub. Popping Corn Song. *Unknown.* MeMeAg
Bring cypress, rosemary and rue. Grover Cleveland. Joel Benton. DD; GA; PAH
Bring Daddy home. *Unknown.* OxNR
Bring down the moon for genteel Janet. Goodbye Now; or, Pardon My Gauntlet. Ogden Nash. FiBHP
Bring flowers, to strew again. Ode for Decoration Day. Henry Peterson. MDAH; OHIP; PEOR
Bring flowers to strew His way. Easter. Katharine Tynan. YT
Bring forth the flowers. Song for Decoration Day. Helen C. Bacon. HH
Bring from Big Creek a huge boulder. Henry Cogdal. Edgar Lee Masters. *Fr.* The New Spoon River. ChMo; CMP; TCAP
Bring from the craggy haunts of birch and pine. Song [*or* O Mighty, Melancholy Wind]. John Todhunter. OBVV; OnYI; PoVP; TIP
Bring Games. Vicente Huidobro, *tr. fr. Spanish by* Joseph Staples. AnCL
Bring Good Ale. *Unknown. See* Bring Us in Good Ale.
Bring hemlock, black as Cretan cheese. Epigram. Robert Hillyer. WhC
Bring Home the Poet. Patrick MacDonough. OnYI
Bring, in this timeless grave to throw. A. E. Housman. A Shropshire Lad, XLVI. BrBE; PoVP
Bring Kateen-beug and Maurya Jude. Beg-Innish. J. M. Synge. GTIV; MBP; MoBrPo; NeMA; OnYI; OxBI
Bring me a cherry without a stone. Captain Wedderburn's Courtship (C *vers.*). *Unknown.* BaBo
Bring me a cup of good red wine. Rinaldo. Henry Peterson. AA
Bring me a letter, postman! The Postman. Alice Todd. BoTP
"Bring me a long sharp knife for we are in danger." The Sunflowers. Douglas Stewart. BoAV
Bring me a rose. Grief-in-Idleness. Thomas Lovell Beddoes. *Fr.* Early Fragments. AtBAP
Bring Me Men. Sam Walter Foss. *Fr.* The Coming American. OQP; QP-2
("Bring me men to match my mountains.") BBV (1951 ed.); BLPA; FaBoBe; MaRV; NeHB; PaA; WaKn
Bring me my dead! Tennyson. Thomas Henry Huxley. HBV; VA
"Bring me soft song," said Aladdin. Aladdin and the Jinn. Vachel Lindsay. AnAmPo; AnFE; APA; ChMo; CMP; CoAnAm; GTBS-W; LA; LiTM; MAPA; NP; NV; OnPP; TBM; TwAmPo
Bring Me the Cup. Moses ibn Ezra, *tr. fr. Hebrew by* Solomon Solis-Cohen. *Fr.* Wine-Songs. TrJP
Bring me the sunflower to transplant. The Sunflower. Eugenio Montale. OnPM
Bring me the sunset in a cup. Emily Dickinson. MAP; MoAmPo; NLK (1947 ed.)
Bring me to the blasted oak. Crazy Jane and the Bishop. W. B. Yeats. AtBAP; TwP
Bring me wine, but wine which never grew. Bacchus. Emerson. AmP; AmPo; AmPP; AnAmPo; AnFE; AnNE; APA; APW; AWP; BAV; CoAnAm; CoV; HBV; LA; LBAP; LEAP; LiTA; MOAP; OBEV; OxBA; PoEL-4; RiBV; ViBoPo
Bring myrrh and myrtle bud. Hilda Doolittle ("H. D."). *Fr.* Songs from Cyprus. TwCV
Bring no jarring lute this way. A Woodland Grave. Lord De Tabley. VA
Bring not a wife to your home too soon or too late. Marriage. Hesiod. *Fr.* Works and Days. OxBG
Bring not bright candles, for her eyes. The Dreamer. Walter de la Mare. CMP; OTPC (1923 ed.)
Bring, novelist, your note-book! bring, dramatist, your pen! The Women of Mumbles Head. Clement Scott. PTA-2
Bring, O Morn, thy music! Bring, O night, thy hushes! "Who Wert and Art and Evermore Shalt Be." William Channing Gannett. TrPWD
Bring on the pomp and pride of old Castile. Alfred Noyes. *Fr.* Drake, XI. CAW
Bring out the hemlock! bring the funeral yew! Dirge of the Munster Forest. Emily Lawless. DiM; GTIV; OBVV; OnYI
"Bring out your dead!" The Female Martyr. Whittier. PraNu
Bring snow-white lilies, pallid heart-flushed roses. The Pantheist's Song of Immortality. Constance C. W. Naden. VA
Bring the biggest bath you've seen. The Song of the Bath. Margaret Gibbs. BoTP
Bring the bowl which you boast. Here's a Health to King Charles [*or* Glee for King Charles]. Sir Walter Scott. *Fr.* Woodstock, *ch.* 20. BPN; CoBE; EmBrPo; EPN; TCEP
Bring the comb and play upon it! Marching Song. Robert Louis Stevenson. BoTP; FaPON; OTPC; TiPo; VLEP
Bring the good old banner, boys, the emblem of the free! Flag Song. Sara F. Archer. FOAH
Bring the good old bugle, boys, we'll sing another song. Marching through Georgia. Henry Clay Work. BlG; GA; MDAH; OTPC; PaA; PAH
Bring the laurel crown so bright. At Bjerregaard's Grave. Henrik Wergeland. AnNoLy
Bring them alang, the young, the strang. A Green Yule. Charles Murray. EBSV
Bring Them Not Back. James Benjamin Kenyon. AA
Bring to me then all passionate, crimson flowers. She Plans Her Funeral. Louise Morey Bowman. CaP; CPG; OCL
Bring to me white roses, roses, pinks, and lavender. The Patchwork Quilt. Dora Sigerson Shorter. HBMV
Bring Torches. A. M. Stephen. CaP
Bring Us In Good Ale. *Unknown.* AnEC; CH; EG; ViBoPo
(Bring Good Ale.) SeCePo
Bring where our Beauty lies. Certain Artists Bring Her Dolls and Drawings. W. B. Yeats. Upon a Dying Lady, II. LiTB
Bringer of sun, arrower of evening, star-begetter and moon-riser. Hymnal. Harold Vinal. TrPWD
Bringers. Carl Sandburg. NP
Bringers of the Hemlock. Stanton A. Coblentz. ChIP
Bringing in the Wine. Li Po, *tr. fr. Chinese by* Witter Bynner *and* Kiang Kang-hu. OuHeWo
Bringing Our Sheaves. Elizabeth Akers Allen. HBV
Briseis, the Slave Girl: Tears for Patroclus. Homer, *tr. fr. Greek by* William Cowper. *Fr.* The Iliad, XIX. GrR
("Briseis, fair as golden Venus, saw," *tr. by* the Earl of Derby.) GrPo
Brisk Encounter between a Youngman and His Love, A. *Unknown. See* Wil the Merry Weaver, and Charity the Chamber-Maid.
Brisk methinks I am, and fine. Five Wines. Robert Herrick. BOHV
Brisk wielder of the birch and rule. The Schoolmaster. Whittier. *Fr.* Snow-bound. GoTP
Brisk Wind, A. William Barnes. UnPo (3d ed.)
Brissit brawnis and broken banis. The Bewteis of the Fute-Ball. *Unknown.* GoTS
Bristling beard was his peculiarity, A. His Hirsute Suit. Frank Sidgwick. WhC
Bristowe Tragedie; or, The Dethe of Syr Charles Bawdin. Thomas Chatterton. CEP; EiPP; EnRP; EPP; EV-3; OBEC
Britain's Ida. Phineas Fletcher. *See* Brittain's Ida.
Britannia ("As on the sea-beat shore Britannia sat"), *sels.* James Thomson.
Britannia's Empire. OBEC
War for the Sake of Peace. LPS-2
Britannia ("Rich is thy soil"). James Thomson. *Fr.* The Seasons: Summer. BeR
Britannia Rules of Orthography. "Firth." InMe; WhC
Britannia rules the waves. England and America; On a Parisian Boulevard. James Kenneth Stephen. InMe
Britannia to Columbia. Alfred Austin. *See* To America.
Britannia's Empire. James Thomson. *Fr.* Britannia. OBEC
Britannia's gallant streamers. Yankee Thunders. *Unknown.* PAH
Britannia's Pastorals, *sels.* William Browne.
As Careful Merchants, *fr.* II, Song 3. ElSeCe
Frolic Mariners of Devon, The, *fr.* II, Song 3. ChTr
Gentle Nymphs, Be Not Refusing, *fr.* I, Song 3. ElL; ViBoPo
Glide Soft, Ye Silver Floods, *fr.* II, Song 1. AEV; ElL
(Shepherd's Moan, A.) ElSeCe
Hail, Thou My Native Soil, *fr.* II, Song 3. EPS; EV-2
Memory ("Marina's gone, and now sit I"), 7 *sts. fr.* III, Song 1. HBV
(Celadyne's Song.) OBS
(So Shuts the Marigold Her Leaves, *shorter sel.*) ChTr
Memory ("So shuts the marigold her leaves"), 3 *sts. fr.* III, Song 1. CBOV; EV-2; OBEV
(Since She Is Gone.) LiTL
("So shuts the marigold her leaves.") EG; ViBoPo
"Near to this wood there lay a pleasant mead," *abr., fr.* I, Song 2. EPS
"Now was the Lord and Lady of the May," *abr., fr.* II, Song 5. EPP
Praise of Poets ("At Thames faire port"), *fr.* II, Songs 1 *and* 2. OBS

Praise of Spenser ("All their pipes were still"), *fr.* II, Song 1. EV-2
Shall I Tell You Whom I Love? *fr.* II, Song 2. ElL; EV-2; SeEP
(My Choice.) BCEP; LPS-1
(Song: "Shall I tell you whom I love?") HBV
(What Wight He Loved.) ElSeCe
"Time never can produce," *abr., fr.* II, Song 3. SG
Venus and Adonis, *fr.* II, Song 2. ElL
("Venus, by Adonis' side.") SeEP
Britannia's sons, though slaves ye be. Hymn. John Bramwich. PoFr
British. The. A. S. J. Tessimond. ChMP
British are a funny race, The. Study of a People. H. I. Phillips. LauV
British Church, The. George Herbert. PoE
British Commerce. John Dyer. *Fr.* The Fleece, IV. OBEC
British Commerce. James Thomson. *Fr.* Liberty, IV. OBEC
British Fleet, The, *sel.* Thomas Dibdin.
All's Well. LPS-2
British Grenadier, The ("Come, come fill up your glasses"). *Unknown.* PAH
British Grenadiers, The ("Some talk of Alexander, and some of Hercules"). *Unknown.* HBV; OBEC; OxBoLi
British in branding their betters, The. Lessons in Limericks, II. David McCord. InMe
British Journalist, The. Humbert Wolfe. FiBHP
British Lyon Roused, The. Stephen Tilden. PAH
British Museum Reading Room, The. Louis MacNeice. LiTM; MoAB; MoBrPo; SeCePo; WaP
British Prison Ship, The, *sel.* Philip Freneau.
Hospital Prison Ship, The, *fr.* III. IAP
British Tar, The. W. S. Gilbert. *Fr.* H. M. S. Pinafore. ALV
British Valor Displayed. Francis Hopkinson. *See* Battle of the Kegs, The.
Britomart in the House of Busirane. Spenser. *Fr.* The Faerie Queene, III, 11-12. FiP
Britons and Guests. Edith M. Thomas. PaA
Britons grown big with pride. A Poem Containing Some Remarks on the Present War. *Unknown.* PAH
Brittain's Ida, *sel.* Phineas Fletcher.
Song: "Fond men! whose wretched care the life soon ending." ElL
Brittan's Remembrancer, *sel.* George Wither.
"I know that if thou please thou canst provide." SeCV-1
Brittle Beauty. Earl of Surrey. AnFE; PoFS; TrGrPo
("Brittle beauty, that Nature made so frail.") EnLoPo; SiPS
(Frail Beauty.) BLV
(Frailty and Hurtfulness of Beauty, The.) ElSeCe; HoPM; ReIE; SiCE; TuPP
Brittle World. Lew Sarett. MoSiPe
"Broad acres, sir." You hear them in my talk. At Knaresborough. Donald Davie. NePoEA
Broad-Axe [*or* -Ax], The. Walt Whitman. *Fr.* Song of the Broad-Axe. APW; MAP; MoAmPo
Broad-backed hippopotamus, The. The Hippopotamus. T. S. Eliot. AmPP; AnAmPo; AWP; ChMo; CMP; HoPM; LA; LiTB; LiTM (1946 ed.); MOAP; NAMP; OBMV; TwP
Broad bars of sunset-slanted gold. Ballad of the Faded Field. Robert Burns Wilson. AA
Broad-based, broad-fronted, bounteous, multiform. Ben Jonson. Swinburne. *Fr.* Sonnets on English Dramatic Poets. BEL; EmBrPo; PeBoSo; PoVP; PtP; VLEP
Broad beach, The,/ Sea-wind and the sea's irregular rhythm. Afternoon; Amagansett Beach. John Hall Wheelock. MoVE; NePA
Broad, but not deep, along his rock-chafed bed. Castleconnell. Sir Aubrey De Vere. IrPN
Broad Gold. "Anna Akhmatova," *tr. fr. Russian by* Babette Deutsch. LiTW; TrRV
Broad is the Gate and wide the Path. The Bath. Harry Graham. CenHV
Broad Minded Bishop Rebukes the Verminous Saint Francis, A. G. K. Chesterton. SaFP
Broad shadows fall on all the mountain side. A Sunset at Les Eboulements. Archibald Lampman. BoCaPo
Broad sun, The/ The bright day. The Far-Farers. Robert Louis Stevenson. BoTP
Broadcast, The. John W. Simons. JKCP (1955 ed.)
Broadcast to the Scholars in the Eyrie. David Ross. PG (1945 ed.)
Broadcast widely if you can. Benevolence. Siraj. MooP
Broadcasting. Mildred D. Shacklett. GFA
Broadway. Hermann Hagedorn. DDA; NV
Broadway. Walt Whitman. DDA
Broadway's Canyon. John Gould Fletcher. InP, VOD (1935 ed.)
Brocadōs and Damasks, and Tabbies, and Gawzes. An Excellent New Song on a Seditious Pamphlet. Swift. CoMu
Brock. Charles Sangster. BoCaPo; CPG
Brock; Valiant Leader. John Daniel Logan. CPG
Brocks snuffle from their holt within. The Badgers. Eden Phillpotts. BoTP
Brogan's Lane. Louis Esson. BoAu
Broke an' hungry, ragged an' dirty too. The "Cholly" Blues. *Unknown.* ABF
Broken altar, Lord, thy servant rears. The Altar. George Herbert. ATP; ElSeCe; EPS; PoFS; ReEn; SeCV-1; TrGrPo
Broken and Desolate. John Henry Boner. NoCaPo
Broken Appointment, A. Thomas Hardy. CoEV; EPP; MoPW; OAEP (2d ed.); ViPo; ViPP
Broken as a clown's sunshade. Synthesis. David Evans. MoWP
Broken Balance, The, *sel.* Robinson Jeffers.
"Rain, hail and brutal sun." PIAE
Broken Bodies. Louis Golding. HBMV; MaRV
Broken bones were left to brokenness. Richard Eberhart. *Fr.* Brotherhood of Men. OnHM
Broken Chain, The. Theognis, *tr. fr. Greek by* F. L. Lucas. GrPE
Broken Doll, The. Christina Rossetti. *Fr.* Sing-Song. MPB
("All the bells were ringing.") TiPo
Broken Drake. Lew Sarett. BAP
Broken Drought, The. Robert Frost. CoV
Broken-face Gargoyles. Carl Sandburg. MAP; MoAmPo; OxBA
Broken figure disappears alone, A. Vale—atque Salve. Mark Antony de Wolfe Howe. AOAH
Broken flower-stem, a broken vase, A. The Sources of the Past. Kingsley Amis. PoLFOT
Broken Friendship. Mary Elizabeth Coleridge. BoFr
Broken Heart, The. Thomas Beedome. OBS
Broken Heart, The. John Donne. AtBAP; ElSeCe; LiTL; LoPo; PoFS; ReEn; TuPP
Broken Heart, The, *sels.* John Ford.
"Beasts onely capable of sense, enjoy," *fr.* IV, ii. PoEL-2
Can You Paint a Thought? *fr.* III, ii. AtBAP; InvP; LO; OAEP; PoEL-2; TuPP; ViBoPo
(Song: "Can you paint a thought? or number?") EPP
"Glories, pleasures, pomps, delights, and ease," *fr.* V, iii. ElSeCe; TuPP; ViBoPo
(Broken Heart, A.) OnPM
(Dirge.) EPP; EV-2; LoBV
(Song, A.) OBS
"Oh, no more, no more, too late," *fr.* IV, iii. AtBAP; KN; LO; PoEL-2; TuPP; ViBoPo
(Now Love Dies.) SeCL
(Song.) BrBE; LoBV; OBS; SeCePo; SeEP
Royall Lady, *fr.* V, ii. LiA
"Sure, if we were all sirens, we should sing pitifully," *fr.* IV, ii. PoD
Broken-hearted Gardener, The. *Unknown.* ChTr
Broken in pieces all asunder. Affliction. George Herbert. LoBV
Broken Jug, The. William Barnes. PoVP
Broken moon lay in the autumn sky, The. To ——. Alexander Smith. VA
Broken Mug, The. John Esten Cooke. BlG
Broken Music. Dante Gabriel Rossetti. The House of Life, XLVII. PoVP; VA; ViPo; VLEP
Broken Oar, The. Longfellow. LiA
Broken One, The. John Holmes. MiAP
Broken pillar of the wing jags from the clotted shoulder, The. Hurt Hawks. Robinson Jeffers. AmP; AmPP; AtBAP; BAV; BLV; BoLiVe; ChMo; CMP; CoBA; CoBMV; LiTA; MAP; MoAB; MoAmPo; MOAP; MoVE; NeMA; NP; OxBA; PoLFOT
Broken Pinion, The. Hezekiah Butterworth. MaRV; PTA-2
(Bird with a Broken Wing, The.) WBLP
Broken Pitcher, The. William Edmondstoune Aytoun. BOHV; InMe; PoVP
Broken Ring, The. Joseph von Eichendorff, *tr. fr. German by* Mabel Cotterell. AnGP
Broken Ring, The. *Unknown.* *See* Dark-eyed Canaller.
Broken Song, A. "Moira O'Neill." BMEP; MBP; OBVV; PG (1945 ed.)
Broken Sword, The. Edward Rowland Sill. *See* Opportunity.
Broken Tower, The. Hart Crane. AmP; CoBMV; GTBS-W; MeRV; MoAB; MoPo; MoVE; OnAP; OxBA; Po; TrGrPo (rev. ed.); TriL
Broken Tryst. Paulus Silentiarius, *tr. fr. Greek by* F. L. Lucas. GrPE
Broken Vase, The. Aleksey Nikolayevich Apukhtin, *after the French of* Sully-Prudhomme, *tr. fr. Russian by* Sir Cecil Kisch. WaL
Broken Voices. Lynette Roberts. MoWP
Broken wagon wheel that rots away beside the river, A. Pioneers. Badger Clark. FaBoBe
Broken Water-Wheel, The. Al-Hajjam, *tr. fr. Arabic by* A. J. Arberry. MooP
Broker Cupid. Frank Dempster Sherman. PR
Brome, Brome on Hill. *Unknown.* *Fr.* The Broomfield Hill. AtBAP

Bronc Peeler's Song. *Unknown.* CoSo; CSF
Bronc That Wouldn't Bust, The. *Unknown.* SCC
Broncho Dan halts midway of the stream. A Health at the Ford. Robert Cameron Rogers. AA; FaBoBe
Broncho That Would Not Be Broken, The. Vachel Lindsay. ATP (1935 ed.); BAP; BBV (1951 ed.); ChMo; CMP; CP; CV; LaNeLa; LiTM (rev. ed.); NePA; NV; PFY; TBM; YT
Broncho versus Bicycle. *Unknown.* SCC
Bronx. Joseph Rodman Drake. AnAmPo; LA
Bronze Frog, The. *Unknown, tr. fr. Greek by* Lord Neaves. OnPM
Bronze Head, A. W. B. Yeats. LiTB
Bronze in the rose-dusted twilight. Red-Rock, the Moose-Hunter. Lew Sarett. PFE
Bronze Statuette of Kwan-yin, A. Charles Wharton Stork. GoYe
Brooding beside the waterfall, he saw. The Waterfall. Arthur Davison Ficke. UnW
Brooding for ages in the graven rock. An Old Stone God. Olivia Freeman. UnW
Brooding Grief. D. H. Lawrence. LoBV
Brooding of Sigurd, The. William Morris. *Fr.* The Story of Sigurd the Volsung. SeCePo
Brook, The. Fynette Fiske. CAG
Brook, The. William Wilberforce Lord. AA
Brook, The. Tennyson. *See* Brook, The; an Idyl.
Brook, The. Edward Thomas. MoVE; SeCeV
Brook, The, *sel.* William Bull Wright.
"Through his million veins are poured." AA
Brook, The; an Idyl. Tennyson. EV-5
Sels.
Brook The. Tennyson. BoTP; BPN; CBPC; CG; EmBrPo; EPN; FaPON; GEPC; GN; GTBS; HiLiEn; MCCG; MPB; MW; OnHT; OTPC; PC; PCH; PIR; PTA-1; PYM; RIS; ShBV-2; SN; TVSH; WP
(Brook's Song, The.) FaBoBe; FaFP; HBV; HBVY; TreF
(Song of the Brook, The.) BoChLi; LPS-2; PoVP; VLEP
"I chatter, chatter, as I flow," *abr.* PECK
"I chatter over stony ways," *abr.* GFA
"O Katie, what I suffer'd for your sake!" EnSW
Brook and road, The/ Were fellow-travellers. The Simplon Pass. Wordsworth. *Fr.* The Prelude, VI. BPN; EM-2; ERP; EV-2; InPo; OBRV; PoFS
Brook and the Wave, The. Longfellow. APW
Brook and the Willow Tree, The. *Unknown, tr. fr. Japanese.* GFA
Brook in the City, A. Robert Frost. OxBA; PIAE; TSW; TSWC
Brook in Winter, The. James Russell Lowell. *See* Winter Pictures.
Brook of the Heart, The. Emily Dickinson. *See* Have you got a brook in your little heart.
Brook Song. James Herbert Morse. AA
Brook Song, The. James Whitcomb Riley. CG
Brook That Runs to France, The. John Clair Minot. DD
Brook, would thou couldst flow. Brook Song. James Herbert Morse. AA
Brook wound through the woods behind, The. The Crayfish. Robert Wallace. WaKn
Brookfield. William E. Marshall. CPG
"But see this happy village festival," *sel.* CaP
Brooklet, The. David Gray. EnSW
Brooklet came from the mountain, The. The Brook and the Wave. Longfellow. APW
Brooklyn at Santiago, The. Wallace Rice. PAH
Brooklyn Bridge. Frederick Mortimer Clapp. VOD (1935 ed.)
Brooklyn Bridge, The. Edna Dean Proctor. MC; PAH
Brooklyn Bridge. Sir Charles G. D. Roberts. PAH
Brooklyn Bridge at Dawn. Richard Le Gallienne. HBMV; PoeMoYo; PoTo; VOD
Brooklynese Champion. Margaret Fishback. WhC
Brook's Song, The. Tennyson. *See* Brook, The; an Idyl.
Brooks that flush, The. The Thrush. John Duffy. JKCP (1955 ed.)
Brookside, The. Richard Monckton Milnes. HBV; LPS-1; TreFS; VA
(Song: "I wander'd by the brook-side.") CG
Broom. John Farrar. GFA
Broom, The. Giacomo Leopardi, *tr. fr. Italian.* LiTW, *tr. by* John Heath-Stubbs; WoL, *tr. by* R. C. Trevelyan
Broom and the shovel, the poker, and tongs, The. The Broom, the Shovel, the Poker, and the Tongs. Edward Lear. RAR
Broom Flower, The. Mary Howitt. HBV
Broom, Green Broom. *Unknown. See* Green Broom.
Broom of Cowdenknowes, The ("Oh the broom, the bonnie, bonnie broom"). *Unknown.* EBSV
Broom of Cowdenknows, The ("There was a troop of merry gentlemen," A *vers.*; "It was on an evening sae saft and sae clear," B *vers.*). *Unknown.* ESPB
Broom out the floor now, lay the fender by. June. Francis Ledwidge. CBOV; CP; GTIV; HBMV; NV; OnYI; PIAE; PoeMoYo; TCEP; VOD
Broom that once through Sarah's halls, The. Sarah's Halls. *Unknown.* PA
Broom, the Shovel, the Poker, and the Tongs, The. Edward Lear. RAR
Broomfield Hill, The. *Unknown.* BaBo; ESPB (A *and* B *vers.*); OBB; ViBoFo
("O where were ye, my milk-white steed.") CH
Brome, Brome on Hill, *sel.* AtBAP
Brooms. Dorothy Aldis. GFA
Broomstick Train; or Return of the Witches. Oliver Wendell Holmes. HOAH
(Broomstick Train, The.) MCCG
"Look out! Look out, boys! Clear the track!" *sel.* FaPON; PoMS
Brother, The. *sel.* Charles Abraham Elton.
Landscape of the Heart. RO
"Brother." Virginia Lyne Tunstall. LS
Brother, The. Semyon Yakovlevich Nadson, *tr. fr. Russian by* H. Badanes. TrJP
Brother and Sister. Callimachus, *tr. fr. Greek by* G. M. Young. GrL
Brother and Sister. "Lewis Carroll." ChTr
Brother and Sister, *abr.* "George Eliot." GN
Brother, are the cakes all done? Baby Making Cakes. *Unknown.* SAS
Brother Ass. Eric Irvin. BoAV
Brother Ass and St. Francis. John Banister Tabb. AnAmPo; LA; SaFP
Brother Ass, fretful, slothful. After the Thought of Saint Francis. Sister Mary Maura. SaFP
Brother Beasts. Cale Young Rice. MW
Brother, come!/ And let us go unto our God. And What Shall You Say? Joseph Seamon Cotter, Jr. BANP; CDC; GrCo-1; PoNe; QS
Brother Dog. Luis Aníbal Sánchez, *tr. fr. Spanish by* Muna Lee. CAW; SaFP
Brother Fire. Louis MacNeice. AtBAP; FaBoMo; MoAB; MoPW; OAEP (2d ed.); WaaP
Brother Gian. Cale Young Rice. LS
Brother, I am fire. Kin. Carl Sandburg. BAP; NP
Brother, I come from many seas and lands. Rite at a Brother's Grave. Catullus. OnPM
Brother Indian, The. Roger Williams. *See* Courteous Pagan Shall Condemn, The.
Brother Jonathan's Lament for Sister Caroline. Oliver Wendell Holmes. APW; CoBA; HBV; IAP; MDAH; PaA; PAH
Brother Juniper. Blanche Mary Kelly. GoBC; JKCP
Brother Noah, *with music. Unknown.* AmSS
Brother of mine, good monk with cowlĕd head. Thomas à Kempis. Lizette Woodworth Reese. AA
Brother of the wind and sun bare-shod, The. The Roses of Saint Francis. Thomas S. Jones, Jr. SaFP
Brother, Tell Me of the Battle. T. Manahan. BlG
Brother, thou art gone before us. Burial Hymn. Henry Hart Milman. VA
Brother to the firefly. Morning Light. Mary Effie Lee Newsome. CDC; PoNe
Brother Toper. R. R. Kirk. CAG
Brother Tree. Idealists. Alfred Kreymborg. BAP; CP; NV; PoMa; SBMV; TSW
Brotherhood. Blake. *Fr.* Jerusalem. CoEV
Brotherhood. Ozora Stearns Davis. MaRV
Brotherhood. Edwin Markham. BBV (1951 ed.); MaRV; NeMA; OQP; PEDC; PGD; PoRL; POT; PoTo; QP-1
Brotherhood, *sel.* Sir Lewis Morris.
"There shall come from out this noise of strife and groaning." PGD
Brotherhood. Walt Whitman. *Fr.* Passage to India, III. MW
("Passage to India!/ Lo soul!") PC
Brotherhood is not by the blood certainly, The. Speech to Those Who Say Comrade. Archibald MacLeish. AmPP; BoFr; OxBA; PoLFOT; PreP; ReaPo
Brotherhood of Men, *sel.* Richard Eberhart.
"Broken bones were left to brokenness." OnHM
Brothers. George E. Day. MaRV
Brothers, The. Goethe, *tr. fr. German.* LPS-3
Brothers. Gerard Manley Hopkins. OAEP; POTT
Brothers. James Weldon Johnson. BANP; PreP
Brothers. Heinrich Lersch, *tr. fr. German.* BoFr, *tr. by* Elizabeth Selden; TwGV, *tr. by* Herman Salinger
Brothers. Elias Lieberman. PFE; PoMa
Brothers, The. Charles Sprague. AA
Brothers, The. Wordsworth. ERP
Brothers and men that shall after us be. Ballad [*or* Ballade] of the Gibbet. Villon. AWP; JAWP; WBP; WoL
Brothers and sisters I have many. Which is the Favourite? Charles *and* Mary Lamb. OTPC (1923 ed.)
Brothers in blood! They who this wrong began. To the

United States of America. Robert Bridges. HBV; HiLiEn; PaA; PAH; PoFr
Brothers of the Faith. John Oxenham. ChIP; OQP; QP-1
(All One in Christ.) BLRP
(No East or West.) MaRV
Brothers, this spot is holy! Look around! The Surrender of Burgoyne. James Watts de Peyster. IDAH
Broughty Wa's. *Unknown.* ESPB
Brow austere, a circumspective eye, A. How to Make a Man of Consequence. Mark Lemon. BOHV
Brow bender. Baby at Play. *Unknown.* HBV; HBVY; OTPC; PPL
Brow, brow, brenty. *Unknown.* OxNR
Brow of Nephin, The. *Unknown, tr. fr. Modern Irish by* Douglas Hyde. AnIL
Brown Adam. *Unknown.* ESPB (A *and* B *vers.*); OBB
Brown and Furry. Christina Rossetti. *See* Caterpillar, The.
Brown Baby Cobina, with his large black velvet eyes. Baby Cobina. Gladys May Casely Hayford. CDC
Brown Bear, The. Mary Austin. FaPON; MPB; OTPC (1946 ed.); UTS; WaKn
Brown bed of earth, still fresh and warm with love. Irradiations, VIII [XIV]. John Gould Fletcher. MAPA; TwAmPo
Brown Bee. William Brighty Rands. *See* Happy World, The.
Brown Bird, The. Walt Whitman. *See* Out of the Cradle Endlessly Rocking.
Brown bunny sits inside his burrow. The Rabbit. Edith King. BoTP; GFA; HBMV; StVeCh
Brown-dappled fawn, The. The Fawn in the Snow. William Rose Benét. AnAmPo; LA; MAP; MoAmPo; MOAP
Brown Dwarf of Rügen, The. Whittier. PoMS
Brown earth-line meets gray heaven. In November. Anne Reeve Aldrich. AA
Brown enormous odor he lived by, The. The Prodigal. Elizabeth Bishop. FiMAP; InvP; MoAB
Brown-eyed Lee, *with music.* *Unknown.* CoSo
Brown Eyes. Mrs. S. L. Dempsey. AlBD
Brown eyes,/ Straight nose. Polly. William Brighty Rands. GoTP; OTPC (1923 ed.); PRWS; VA
Brown Frog, The. Mary K. Robinson. BoTP
Brown Girl, The ("I am as brown as brown can be"). *Unknown.* BaBo (A *and* B *vers.*); ESPB (A *and* B *vers.*); OBB
Brown Girl, The, or Fair Eleanor [*or* Ellender]. *Unknown.* *See* Lord Thomas and Fair Annet.
Brown Is My Love. *Unknown.* EIL; ElSeCe
(Brown Is My Love, but Graceful[l].) AtBAP; EG; OBSC
Brown Jug, The. Frances Fawkes, *after* Amaltheus. ViBoPo
Brown lived at such a lofty farm. Brown's Descent. Robert Frost. CV; MAP; MoAmPo; NV; PoRA; StPo; WhC
Brown net of branches, A. Paseo de la Castellana. John Dos Passos. *Fr.* Winter in Castile. VOD (1935 ed.)
Brown o' San Juan. Home, Sweet Home with Variations, III. Henry Cuyler Bunner. BOHV; InMe; PA
Brown of Osawatomie [*or* Ossawatomie]. Whittier. BHV; DD; GA; HBV; LEAP; LPS-2; MC; OTPC; PAH; PIR
Brown owl sits in the ivy bush, The. The Great Brown Owl. Ann Hawkshaw. OTPC (1923 ed.)
Brown Penny. W. B. Yeats. ExPo; FaBoCh; LoGBV
Brown Robin (A *and* B *vers.*). *Unknown.* ESPB
Brown Robin's Confession. *Unknown.* ACP; WHL
(Brown Robyn.) CH
(Brown Robyn's Confession.) ESPB; OBB; SG
Brown round of the continent tonight, The. Australia. Eve Langley. BoAV
Brown, sad-coloured hillside, where the soil, A. The Sower. Sir Charles G. D. Roberts. CaP; OCL
Brown sails of fishing boats. The Fishing Fleet. Lincoln Colcord. HBMV; VOD
Brown Thrush, The. Lucy Larcom. BoChLi; BoTP; DD; FaPON; HBV; HBVY; MPB; OTPC; PEDC; PPL; PTA-1; RAR; RIS; TVC; UTS
Browner than the hazel-husk, swifter than the wind. The Little Fauns of Proserpine. Marjorie Pickthall. OCL
Brownie. A. A. Milne. CBPC
Brownie, Brownie Let Down Your Milk. Christina Rossetti. *Fr.* Sing-Song. RIS
Browning at Asolo. Robert Underwood Johnson. AA; BAP; LEAP
Browning, old fellow, your leaves grow yellow. In a Copy of Browning. Bliss Carman. HBMV
Brown's Descent. Robert Frost. CV; MAP; MoAmPo; NV; PoRA; StPo; WhC
Brown's for Lalage, Jones for Lelia. Ballade of Ladies' Names. W. E. Henley. HBV
Brown's wife, herself a normal type. Family Life. Allan M. Laing. FiBHP
Browny Bee. Irene F. Pawsey. BoTP
Browny Hen, The. Irene F. Pawsey. BoTP
Bruadar and Smith and Glinn. *Tr. fr. Irish by* Douglas Hyde. AnIV
Bruce, The, *sels.* John Barbour.
Bannockburn, *fr.* XII, XIII, XX. EBSV
Battle of Bannockburn, The, *fr.* XIII. BSV
Bruce Addresses His Army, *abr., fr.* XIII. GoTS
Bruce Consults His Men, *fr.* VIII. GoTS
Freedom, *fr.* I BSV; EBSV; EV-1; FaBoCh; GoTS; LoGBV; OBEV; TrGrPo
("A! fredome is a noble thing!") PoFr; ViBoPo
Loyalty, *fr.* I. EBSV
Bruce and the Spider. Bernard Barton. BeLS; LPS-2
Bruce Consults His Men. John Barbour. *Fr.* The Bruce, VIII. GoTS
Bruce [*or* Bruce's Address] to His Army [*or* Men] at Bannockburn. Burns. *See* Scots Wha Hae.
Bruce's March to Bannockburn. Burns. *See* Scots Wha Hae.
Bruised and battered. Tenement Room; Chicago. Frank Marshall Davis. GoSl
Bruised Reed Shall He Not Break, A. Christina Rossetti. *See* I Will Accept.
Brumana. James Elroy Flecker. LBBV; PoeT; POTT
Brushed by the shadows of the dead. Dusk. Guillaume Apollinaire. AnFP
Brushes and paints are all I have. Quatrains. Gwendolyn B. Bennett. CDC
Brushing her hair by candlelight. The Princess. C. Ethel Evans. VOD
Brussels. Arthur Rimbaud, *tr. fr. French by* Louise Varèse. AnFP
Brussels Cross Inscription. *Unknown, tr. fr. Anglo-Saxon by* Chauncey B. Tinker. InP
Brut, The, *sels.* Layamon. *tr. fr. Middle English.*
"Arthur went to Cornwall." EPP
Arthur's Dream. MeEV
Arthur's Last Battle, *orig. and mod. English pr.* BEL
Arthur's Last Fight. MeEV
Battle of Bath, The. MeEV
Birth of Arthur, The. MeEV
Building of London, The. MeEV
King Arthur ("When that Arthur was king"), *12 ll.* LEAP
Leir and His Daughters. MeEV
Prolog, The: "There was a priest in the land." MeEV
Prophecy of Diana, The. MeEV
Round Table, The. EnLi-1, *tr. by* Stith Thompson; MeEV
Brute, The. William Vaughn Moody. PoeMoYo
Bruton Town. *Unknown.* *See* In Brunton Town.
Brutus. Shakespeare. *See* Portrait of Brutus.
Brutus and Portia. Shakespeare. *Fr.* Julius Caesar, II, i. GrCo-2
Brutus has riv'd my heart. Shakespeare. *Fr.* Julius Caesar, IV, iii. BoFr
Brutus held Britain, and Corineus, Cornwall. The Building of London. Layamon. *Fr.* The Brut. MeEV
Brutus, my lord! Brutus and Portia. Shakespeare. *Fr.* Julius Caesar, II, i. GrCo-2
Brutus; or, The Fall of Tarquin, *sel.* John Howard Payne.
Lucius Junius Brutus over the body of Lucretia. LPS-3
Brutus, that brave and complete cavalier. Henry Parrot. SiCE
Brutus took Ignogen and upon the ship led her. The Prophecy of Diana. Layamon. *Fr.* The Brut. MeEV
Bryan, Bryan, Bryan, Bryan. Vachel Lindsay. CrMA; LiTA; OxBA; OxBoLi
Bryan O'Lin had no breeches to wear. Mother Goose. BrR
Bryant. James Russell Lowell. *Fr.* A Fable for Critics. AnNE
("There is Bryant, as quiet, as cool, and as dignified.") CoBA; PtP
Bryant Alphabet, A. *Comp. by* Caroline B. Le Row, *fr. various poems by* Bryant. PEOR
Bryant Dead. Paul Hamilton Hayne. DD; GA
Bryant on His Seventieth Birthday. Whittier. DD; GA
Bryant, whose songs are thoughts that bless. William Cullen Bryant. Fitz-Greene Halleck. PEOR
Bryght as the stern of day begouth to schyne. The Golden [*or* Goldyn] Targe. William Dunbar. BSV; EBSV
Bryng us in good ale, and bryng us in good ale. *See* Bring Us in Good Ale.
B's the Bus. Phyllis McGinley. *Fr.* All Around the Town. FaPON; TiPo
(B.) LiL
Bubble, The. William Allingham. *See* Blowing Bubbles.
Bubble, The. John Banister Tabb. AA
Bubble-blowing. William Canton. TVSH
Bubble-breasted swells the dome. Frascati's. Aldous Huxley. InPo; ViBoPo
Bubble, bubble, light and airy. Bubbles. George H. Shorey. PCH
Bubble of the silver-springing waves, The. The Poetic Land. William Caldwell Roscoe. OBVV
Bubbles. L. Nicholson. BoTP
Bubbles. George H. Shorey. PCH
Bubbling brook doth leap when I come by, The. Nature. Jones Very. AnAmPo; HBV; LA; LPS-2; SN

Bubbling Wine. Abu Zakariya, *tr. fr. Arabic by* A. J. Arberry. MooP
Buccaneer, The, *sel.* Richard Henry Dana.
Island, The. AnNE; LPS-2
Buccaneer, The. Nancy Byrd Turner. TiPo
Buccaneers, The. Young E. Alison. *See* Derelict.
Buck and the Doe, The. *Tr. fr. the Spanish of the* Penitentes *by* Mary Austin. APW
Buck in the Snow, The. Edna St. Vincent Millay. CrMA; NP
Buckee Bene. *Unknown.* CH
Bucket, The. Samuel Woodworth. *See* Old Oaken Bucket, The.
Bucket of Bees, A. David McCord. MAP; MoAmPo (1942 ed.)
Bucket of Sea-Serpents. Howard Ant. GoYe
Bucking Bronco. *Unknown, at. to* Belle Star. ABF; CoSo
(Bucking Broncho.) CSF
(Cowgirl, The, *var., abr.*) CSF
Buckle, The. Walter de la Mare. BrR; PoRh
Bucko-Mate. Samuel Schierloh. GoYe
Buckskin Joe. *Unknown.* CoSo
(Araphoe, or Buckskin Joe.) CSF
Bucolic Funeral. Justo Sierra, *tr. fr. Spanish by* Samuel Beckett. AnMP
Bucoliques, *sel.* André Chénier, *tr. fr. French by* Charles Richard Cammell.
Néère, XIII. LiA
Bucyrus. John Holmes. CrMA; NePoAm
Bud in the Frost, A. "Moira O'Neill." GTIV; POTE
Buddha. Arno Holz, *tr. fr. German by* William Ellery Leonard. AWP
Buddha at Kamakura, The. Kipling. LoBV
Buddha in Glory. Rainer Maria Rilke, *tr. fr. German by* Jessie Lemont. OnPM
Buddhist to His Soul, The. Ch'en Sheng Chi, *tr. fr. Chinese by* Henry H. Hart. PoHN
Budding [*or* Boddynge] floweret blushes at the light, The. Song of the Three Minstrels [*or* Mynstrelles Songe *or* There Lacketh Somethynge Stylle]. Thomas Chatterton. *Fr.* Aella. EnRP; EV-3; TrGrPo; ViBoPo
Budding-Time Too Brief. Evaleen Stein. AA
Budget. "Elspeth." PR
Budget of Paradoxes, A. John Martley. TIP
Budmouth Dears. Thomas Hardy. *Fr.* The Dynasts, Pt. III, Act II, sc. 1. CH; MoVE; PoVP
(Hussar's Song.) TCPD
("When we lay where Budmouth Beach is.") LO
Buds are backward and winter lingers. At Winter's End. Sister Mary Madeleva. JKCP
Buds awake at touch of Spring, The. Spring's Immortality. Mackenzie Bell. VA
Buds of April dare not yet unfold, The. Like an April Day. Johan Sebastian Cammermeyer Welhaven. AnNoLy; LiTW
Buen Matina. Sir John Salusbury. ElL
Buena Vista. Albert Pike. PAH
Buena Vista Battlefield. *Unknown.* CSF
Buffalo. Florence Earle Coates. PAH
Buffalo. Roy Daniells. CaP
Buffalo Bill's/ defunct. Portrait. E. E. Cummings. AmPP; AnNE; CoBA; LiTA; MAP; MoAB; MoAmPo; NePA; UnPo
Buffalo! Buffalo! Call to Freedom. Hazel Harper Harris. PoTo
Buffalo Creek. John Le Gay Brereton. BoAu
Buffalo Dusk. Carl Sandburg. CaAE; TiPo
Buffalo Herds, The. Charles Mair. *Fr.* Tecumseh. VA
Buffalo Hunters, The. *Unknown.* CoSo; CSF; IHA
Buffalo loomed at the far loop of the field, The. The Difference. Winfield Townley Scott. NePoAm
Buffalo Moon and Sun-Go-Under. Reservation. David McCord. WhC
Buffalo Skinners, The. *Unknown.* ABF, *with music;* ABS; AS, *with music;* BaBo; CoSo, *with music;* CSF; ViBoFo
(Boggy Creek, *cowboy vers.*) CoSo
(Jolly Lumbermen, The, *diff. vers., with music.*) TrAS
Buffaloes are gone, The. Buffalo Dusk. Carl Sandburg. CaAE; TiPo
Buffel's Kop. Roy Campbell. ChMP
Bufo. Pope. *Fr.* Epistle to Dr. Arbuthnot. OBEC
Bug, A. Eileen Fisher. GoBP
Bugger Burns, *with music. Unknown.* OuSiCo
Bugle, The. Tennyson. *See* Bugle Song, The.
Bugle and battle-cry are still. Happy Death. John Freeman. HBMV
Bugle calls coiling through the rocky valley. A Northern Legion. Sir Herbert Read. FaBoMo; SeCePo
Bugle echoes shrill and sweet, The. Memorial Day. Joyce Kilmer. MaRV
Bugle Song. Tennyson. *Fr.* The Princess, III. ATP; BEL; BoChLi; BTP; CBOV; EnLit; FaPON; GN; HBV; MCCG; MPB; MW; PCD; PECK; PFE; PG (1945 ed.); PTA-1; RG; StVeCh; TreF; VA
(Blow, Bugle, Blow.) BLV; BMEP; CBPC; ChTr; FaFP; GTBS-W; LiTB; LiTG; OBEV; TSW; TSWC; UnS
(Bugle, The.) LPS-2; ShBV-2
(From "The Princess.") LEAP
(Horns of Elfland, The.) GBV
(Lyrics from "The Princess.") OuHeWo
(Our Echoes Roll from Soul to Soul.) MaRV
(Song: "Splendor [*or* Splendour] falls on castle walls, The.") AlDL; CaAE; ExPo; LoBV; NeHB; ThWaDe; TOP
(Songs from "The Princess.") AWP; EmBrPo; GEPC; InPo; JAWP; OAEP; PIR; ViPo; WBP
(Splendor [*or* Splendour] Falls [on Castle Walls], The.) AnFE; AtBAP; BoLiVe; BPN; CH; CoBE; EM-2; EnL; EnLi-2; EPN; EV-5; FaBoCh; FiP; GTBS; GTBS-D; GTML; GTSL; InP; LoGBV; OBVV; OQP; OTPC; PoE; PoEL-5; PoVP; QP-2; REAL; TCEP; TrGrPo; TVSH; TyEnPo; ViBoPo; ViPP
Bugle Song of Peace. Thomas Curtis Clark. PEDC; PSO; WBLP; WGRP
Bugler, The. F. W. Harvey. BMEP
Bugler boy from barrack (it is over the hill), A. The Bugler's First Communion. Gerard Manley Hopkins. OAEP (2d ed.); POTT; VLEP
Bugler named Dougal MacDougal, A. Edouard. Ogden Nash. LiL; NePA; SiTL
Bugler's First Communion, The. Gerard Manley Hopkins. OAEP (2d ed.); POTT; VLEP
Bugles! And the Great Nation thrills and leaps to arms! The Call of the Bugles. Richard Hovey. AA
Bugle's call, The . . . the drum's low beat. "Disabled"—Armistice Day. Catherine Parmenter. PEDC
Bugles of Dreamland, The. "Fiona Macleod." OTPC (1946 ed.)
Bugles of England were blowing o'er the sea, The. For England. J. D. Burns. BoAu
Bugs. Will Stokes. BBV (1923 ed.); MoShBr
Bugville team was surely up against a rocky game, The. Casey—Twenty Years Later. S. P. McDonald. BLPA
Buick. Karl Shapiro. CoBA; HoPM; MiAP; MoAB; TrGrPo (rev. ed.); ViBoPo (1958 ed.)
Build a Fence of Trust. Mary Frances Butts. OQP; QP-2
(To-Day.) MaRV
Build a house for "Little Friend." "Little Friend's" Grave. Frederick George Scott. BoCaPo
Build a house of gold for Punch. Conrad Aiken. *Fr.* Punch, the Immortal Liar. NP
"Build at Kallundborg by the sea." Kallundborg Church. Whittier. BeLS; GBV
Build for yourself a strong box. Then Laugh. Bertha Adams Backus. BLPA; NeHB; PoToHe (new ed.); WBLP; YaD
Build high your white and dazzling palaces. To February. Ethelwyn Wetherald. VA
Build me a castle of sand. Sand Castles. W. Graham Robertson. CBPC; MPB
"Build me straight, O worthy Master!" The Building of the Ship. Longfellow. AnNE; CoBA; EtS; IAP; LH; MOAP; TCAP
Build on, and make thy castles high and fair. Challenge to Youth. Longfellow. *Fr.* The Castle Builder. MaRV
Build thee more stately mansions, O my soul! More Stately Mansions. Oliver Wendell Holmes. *Fr.* The Chambered Nautilus. GrCo-1
Build your houses, build your houses, build your towns. Beleaguered Cities. F. L. Lucas. HaMV; POTE
Builder, The. Caroline Giltinan. HBMV; LS; TBM
Builder, The. Duncan Campbell Scott. CPG
Builder, The. Francis Sherman. CaP; OCL
Builder, The. *Unknown.* BLPA; MaRV
(Building a Temple.) OQP; QP-2
Builder, The. Willard Wattles. AnAmPo; BAP; HBMV; LA; OQP; PoeMoYo; PYM; QP-1; TBM
Builder and maker Thou, of houses not made with hands! Robert Browning. *Fr.* Abt Vogler. OQP; QP-1
Builder builded a temple, A. The Builder [*or* Building a Temple]. *Unknown.* BLPA; MaRV; OQP; QP-2
Builder eternally of things. Aeterne Rerum Conditor. St. Ambrose. LaP
Builder who first bridged Niagara's gorge, The. Anchored to the Infinite. Edwin Markham. CV; MaRV; OQP; QP-1
Builders. Purd E. Deitz. MaRV
Builders, The. Ebenezer Elliott. VA
Builders. Hortense Flexner. HBMV
Builders, The. Longfellow. BTP; FaFP; IAP; MaRV; OHFP; PTA-1; TCAP; TreFS
Builders. R. L. Sharpe. *See* Bag of Tools, A.
Builders, The. Henry van Dyke. OQP; QP-2
"Grant us the knowledge that we need," *sel.* TrPWD
Builders, The. Judith Wright. SeCePo
Builder's Lesson, A, *sel.* John Boyle O'Reilly.
"How shall I a habit break?" PoToHe (new ed.)
Builders of the State. Richard Watson Gilder. PoRL
Building. Ella Wheeler Wilcox. OQP; QP-1

Building a Home. John Armstrong. *Fr.* The Art of Preserving Health. LPS-2
Building a Skyscraper. Louis Dudek. BoCaPo (1948 ed.)
Building a Skyscraper. James S. Tippett. MPB
Building a Temple. *Unknown. See* Builder, The.
Building for Eternity. N. B. Sargent. BLPA
Building in Stone. Sylvia Townsend Warner. MBP; MoBrPo
Building of Cloudcuckoocity, The. Aristophanes, *tr. fr. Greek by* T. F. Higham. *Fr.* The Birds. OxBG
(Building of Cloudcuckoobury, The, *tr. by* Benjamin Bickley Rogers.) GrR
Building of Jerusalem, The. Blake. *See* And Did Those Feet in Ancient Time.
Building of London, The. Layamon, *tr. fr. Middle English. Fr.* The Brut. MeEV
Building of the *Long Serpent,* The. Longfellow. *Fr.* Tales of a Wayside Inn: The Musician's Tale, Pt. I. EtS
Building of the Nest, The. Margaret E. Sangster. DD; HBV; HBVY
Building of the New Jerusalem, The. Blake. *See* And Did Those Feet in Ancient Time.
Building of the Sea-Wall, The. Lyon Sharman. CPG
Building of the Ship, The. Longfellow. AnNE; CoBA; EtS; IAP; LH; MOAP; TCAP
Sels.
Ship of State, The. BTP; FaBoBe; GrCo-1; HBVY; MaRV; NeHB; OHIP; OQP; PAP; PECK; PSO; QP-1
(Republic, The.) AA; DD; HH; IDAH; LEAP; MC; PAH; WGRP
(Sail on, O Ship of State!) FaPON; PoFr; TreF
(Thou, Too, Sail On.) GDAH
("Thou, too, sail on, O Ship of State!") HiLiAm; PaA; PGD; PTA-1; YaD
"Then the Master with a gesture." OHFP
Building the Bridge for Him. Will Allen Dromgoole. *See* Bridge Builder, The.
Buildings above the leafless trees. Central Park at Dusk. Sara Teasdale. ChMo; CMP
Buildings are fountains jetting [*or* waterfalls of] stone. Waterfalls of Stone. Louis Ginsberg. PIAE; PoMa
Bulb, A. Richard Kendall Munkittrick. AA
Bulbs. Louise Driscoll. MW
Bulbul, The ("Bulbul hummeth like a book, The"). Sir Owen Seaman. NA
Bulbul wail'd, The. "Oh, Rose! all night I sing." Song without a Sound. Sir Edwin Arnold. *Fr.* With Sa'di in the Garden. VA
Bulge of midday. The Dead Nereid. Eugenio Florit. TwSpPo
Bulging rampart streaked with pink and jade, The. The Watchers. Charles Spear. AnNZ
Bulkeley, Hunt, Willard, Hosmer, Meriam, Flint. Hamatreya. Emerson. AmP; AmPo; AmPP; BAV; CoBA; CoV; IAP; MOAP; OnAP; OxBA; PoE; PoEL-4; SeCeV; WoL. *See also* Minott, Lee, Willard, Hosmer . . .
Bull, The. Ralph Hodgson. AnFE; BMEP; ChMo; CMP; EnLi-2 (1949 ed.); EnLit; LiTG; LiTM (rev. ed.); MBP; MoAB; MoBrPo; MoVE; NV; OBMV; ShBV-2; TOP; YT
Bull, The. Freda Laughton. NeIP
Bull, The. Francis Maguire. JKCP (1955 ed.)
Bull, The. V. Sackville-West. DiM
Bull, The. William Carlos Williams. MoVE
Bull be took bad, says old Sam—wunnot fancy 'is fodder, Th'. From My Rural Pen. T. S. Watt. FiBHP
Bull Calf, The. Irving Layton. PeCV
Bull Fight, The. L. Worthington Green. SCC
Bulldog Speaks, The. Edward Anthony. AlBD
Bulldozer, The. Donald A. Stauffer. WaP
Bulletin of Bad Weather. Jorge Carrera Andrade, *tr. fr. Spanish by* H. R. Hays. TwSpPo
Bulletin of the boarding school, The. Under All This Slate. James Hayford. NePoAm-2
Bullocks, The. Alex Comfort. FaBoTw
Bullocky. Judith Wright. BoAV; MoAuPo; NeLNL; SeCePo
Bull's eyes and targets. *Unknown.* OxNR
Bullwhacker, The. *Unknown.* ABF; CoSo; CSF
Bully, The. *At. to the* Earl of Rochester *and to* Thomas D'Urfey. InvP; SeCL
(Song: Noble Name of Spark, The.) SeCePo
(Song: "Room, room for a blade of the town.") BeR
Bully ship and a bully crew, A. Sacramento. *Unknown.* SoAmSa
Bully ship and bully crew, A. Lowlands, *vers.* III. *Unknown.* ShS
Bulrush stood on the river's brim, A. The Vainglorious Oak and the Modest Bulrush. Guy Wetmore Carryl. TSW; TSWC
Bulwark of Home, The. Grace B. Palmer. PraP
Bum. W. Dayton Wedgefarth. AlBD; BLPA; LPS-1
Bumblebeaver, The. Kenyon Cox. *Fr.* Mixed Beasts. RIS; TiPo
Bumblebee. Edna D. Wood. PCH
Bumble-Bee and Clover. *Unknown.* GFA
Bumblebee, I'm sure I like you. Bumblebee. Edna D. Wood. PCH
Bumblebee went flying, A. The Easter Airplane. Carolyn R. Freeman. GFA
Bumble-Bug and Bumble-Bee. Famous Battle of Bumble-Bug and Bumble-Bee. *Unknown.* FTB
Bumper of good liquor, A. Sheridan. *Fr.* The Duenna, II, iii. WhC
Bumpety, bumpety, bump. Fan, the Filly. Wilfrid Thorley. BoTP
Bunch, a Cat. Claude Colleer Abbott. PoC
Bunch of Cowslips, A. *Unknown.* PEOR
Bunch of golden keys is mine, A. Golden Keys. *Unknown.* PTA-1
Bunch of grass, a wild rose, A. That's July. Mary F. Butts. YeAr
Bunch of Roses, A. John Banister Tabb. HBVY; PRWS; SP
Bunch of the boys were whooping it up in the Dixie-Belle, on Lex, A. The Tale of the Dixie-Belle. Frank Chase. InMe
Bunch of the boys were whooping it up in the Malamute saloon, A. The Shooting of Dan McGrew. Robert W. Service. BAP; BeLS; BoCaPo; FaBoBe; FaFP; MaC; NeHB; PoRA; TreF
Bunches of Grapes. Walter de la Mare. BOHV; CBPC; HBV; HBVY; MoShBr; OTPC; PoRh; SUS; TiPo
Bundle is a funny thing, A. Bundles. John Farrar. BrR; ChBR; GFA; PCH; TiPo
Bundle of Letters, A. Frank Dempster Sherman. PR
Bundles. John Farrar. BrR; ChBR; GFA; PCH; TiPo
Bundles. Carl Sandburg. MAP; MoAmPo
Bundles of Firewood, The. *Unknown, tr. fr. Chinese by* E. D. Edwards. ChLP
Bung Yer Eye. *Unknown, at. to* Stewart Edward White. ABF; IHA
(Shanty Boy, The.) CSF
Bungiana, *sel. Unknown.*
Pacific Engagement, The. WhC
Bunhill's Fields. Anne Ridler. NeBP
Bunk-House Orchestra, The. Badger Clark. SCC
Bunker Hill. George Henry Calvert. BeLS; DD, *abr.;* FaBoBe; GA, *abr.;* MC
Bunker Hill. Nathaniel Niles. *See* American Hero, The.
Bunny Rabbit ("Bunny creeps out and caresses his nose"). *Unknown.* BoTP
Buns for Tea. Dorothy M. Richardson. VOD (1935 ed.); YT
Bunthorne's Recitative and Song ("Am I alone"). W. S. Gilbert. *See* Recitation and Song.
Bunthorne's Song ("If you're anxious for to shine"). W. S. Gilbert. *Fr.* Patience. FiBHP; LiTB; SiTL
(Aesthete, The.) ALV; EnLi-2
(Bunthorne's Song: The Aesthete.) ViP
(Song: Bunthorne.) PoVP
Bunyip, The. Douglas Stewart. MoAuPo
Bunyip and the Whistling Kettle, The. John Manifold. LiTB; LiTM; NeLNL; PoMS; SiTL; WaP
Buona vespre! Sleep: Your candle-end. Sleep, Baby, Sleep. Tristan Corbière. AnFP
Buonaparte. Tennyson. PoVP; VLEP
Buonconte Relates His Fate. Dante, *pr. tr. fr. Italian by* Charles Eliot Norton. *Fr.* Divina Commedia: Purgatorio, V. LiA
Buoy-Bell, The. Charles Tennyson Turner. EtS; VA
Burbank with a Baedeker; Bleistein with a Cigar ("Burbank crossed a little bridge"). T. S. Eliot. HBMV; MAP; MoAmPo (1942 ed.)
Burd Ellen and Young Tamlane ("Burd Ellen sits in her bower windowe"). *Unknown.* ESPB
Burd Helen was her mother's dear. Broughty Wa's. *Unknown.* ESPB
Burd Isabel and Earl Patrick. *Unknown.* BaBo; ESPB
Burden, The. "Marianne Farningham." OQP; QP-2
Burden, The. Toyohiko Kagawa. MaRV
Burden, The. Märta af Sillén, *tr. fr. Swedish by* Charles W. Stork. AnSL
Burden of Age, The. Samuel Johnson. *Fr.* The Vanity of Human Wishes. BeR
(Life's Last Scene.) OBEC, *abr.;* SeCePo
Burden of an ancient rhyme, The. Poems, CXL. Walter Savage Landor. PG
Burden of Everyday, The. Buddhadeva Bose, *tr. fr. Bengali by* Buddhadeva Bose. LiTW
Burden of fair women, The. Vain delight. A Ballad of Burdens. Swinburne. BPN; EmBrPo; EnLi-2; PIR; PoVP; VLEP
Burden of Itys, The, *sel.* Oscar Wilde.
"Harmless rabbit gambols with its young, The." VLEP
Burden of Love, The. "Owen Innsley." AA
Burden of Nineveh, The. Dante Gabriel Rossetti. BPN; EmBrPo; OAEP; PoVP; TwCrTr; ViP; VLEP
Burden of Strength, The. George Meredith. EPN
Burden of Time, The. Frederick George Scott. CPG

Burden of Tyre, The, *sel.* Christopher Brennan.
  "Let them devour and be devour'd!" NeLNL
Burdened as you are with misfortune and sorrow. Catullus, *tr. fr. Latin by* Frances Fletcher. LaP
Burdened with years and full of sinfulness. A Prayer for Strength. Michelangelo. OnPM
Burdens. William Haskell Simpson. *Fr.* In Arizona. NP
Burdens of Unrest. Thomas Holley Chivers. SPP
  (Mary's Lament for Shelley, Lost at Sea.) APW
Burdens of Water Jars. Burdens. William Haskell Simpson. *Fr.* In Arizona. NP
Burdock leaves beside the hedge, The. A Brisk Wind. William Barnes. UnPo (3d ed.)
Burgeoning trees are thick with leaves, The. East Wind. Ou-yang Hsiu. OnPC
Burges, *with music. Unknown.* ABF
Burgesses of Calais, The. Laurence Minot. ACP
Burghers' Battle, The. William Morris. BPN; PoVP; VA
Burglar Bill. "F. Anstey." CenHV; FiBHP
Burgraves, Les, *sel.* Victor Hugo, *tr. fr. French by* George Burnham Ives.
  Light and Life, *fr.* Pt. I, sc. iii. LiA
Burgundian Carol. Bernard de la Monnoye, *tr. fr. French by* Percy Dearmer. UnS
  (Patapan.) ChBR
Burial. Struthers Burt. UnW
Burial, The. Kipling. BoSA
Burial, The. John Webster. *See* All the Flowers of the Spring.
Burial. Edward Weismiller. MuM
Burial at Sea. E. J. Pratt. *Fr.* The *Roosevelt* and the *Antinoe.* CaP; OCL; TwCV
Burial Hymn. Henry Hart Milman. VA
Burial in the East. "Pablo Neruda," *tr. fr. Spanish by* Angel Flores. AnCL
Burial of an Infant, The. Henry Vaughan. OAEP
Burial of Barber. Whittier. PAH
Burial of Grant, The. Richard Watson Gilder. MDAH
Burial of Gustaf Fröding, The. Verner von Heidenstam, *tr. fr. Swedish by* Charles W. Stork. AnSL
Burial of King Cormac, The. Sir Samuel Ferguson. AnIL; GTIV; IrPN; OnYI; TIP; TVSH
Burial of Latané, The. John Reuben Thompson. *See* Captain Latané.
Burial of Moses. Cecil Frances Alexander. BeLS; BLPA; BLRP; BPP; GN; HBV; LPS-2; NeHB; OTPC; PTA-2; WBLP
Burial of Robert Browning, The. "Michael Field." VA
Burial of Saint Brendan, The. Padraic Colum. OxBI
Burial of Sir John McKenzie, The. Jessie Mackay. AnNZ
Burial of Sir John Moore after [*or* at] Corunna, The. Charles Wolfe. AnIV; BBV; BCEP; BEL; BHV; BTP; CaAE; CBE; CBPC; ChTr; EnRP; EPN; EPP; ERP; EV-4; FaFP; GN; GTBS; GTBS-D; GTBS-W; GTIV; GTSE; GTSL; HBV; HBVY; InP; LEAP; LiA; LiTG; LPS-3; MaC; MCCG; MW; NeHB; OBEV; OBRV; OnSP; OnYI; OTPC (1923 ed.); OxBI; PCD; PECK; PIR; PoRA; PTA-1; PYM; TCEP; TIP; TOP; TreF; TVSH; WaaP; WBLP; WHA
  (After Corunna.) LH
Burial of the Bachelor, The. *Unknown.* PA
Burial of the Dane, The. Henry Howard Brownell. AA; HBV; LBAP; LEAP; OBAV
Burial of the Dead. John Keble. OBEV (1st ed.)
Burial of the Dead, The. Prudentius, *tr. fr. Latin by* Helen Waddell. LiTW; TriL
Burial of the Linnet. Juliana Horatia Ewing. PRWS
Burial of the Minnisink. Longfellow. DDA; LaNeLa; MOAP
Burial of the Spirit. Richard Hughes. BLV; MBP; MoBrPo
Burial of the Young Love. Waring Cuney. BANP; PoNe
Burial Songs. *Unknown, tr. fr. Chinese by* Arthur Waley.
  Dew on the Garlic-Leaf, The, I. TrCh
  (Burial Song.) WoL
  Graveyard, The, II. TrCh
Burial Urn, The [*or* A]. Sophocles, *tr. fr. Greek. Fr.* Electra. GrR, *tr. by* Sir George Young; OxBG, *tr. by* J. T. Sheppard
Buriall. Henry Vaughan. SeCV-1
Burials, *sels.* George Crabbe. The Parish Register, Pt. III.
  "My record ends." OBRV
  "Next died the Lady who yon Hall possess'd." PoD
  "There was, 'tis said, and I believe, a time." EiPP
Buried Alive. Sophocles. *See* Antigone Entombed Alive.
Buried Child, The. Dorothy Wellesley. Deserted House: Epilogue. GTBS-D; OBMV
Buried City, The. George Sylvester Viereck. LBMV
Buried Fire. Emperor Meiji, *tr. fr. Japanese by* Asataro Miyamori. OnPM
Buried in the shades of horrid night. On His Late Espoused Saint. Sir Kenelm Digby. ACP
Buried in woods we lay, you recollect. Ottima and Sebald, Two Lovers. Robert Browning. *Fr.* Pippa Passes. BMEP
Buried Lady, The. Paul Valéry, *tr. fr. French by* Barbara Howes. AnFP
Buried Lake, The. Allen Tate. CrMA
Buried Life, The. Matthew Arnold. BEL; BMEP; BoLiVe; BPN; EmBrPo; EnL; EnLi-2; EnLit; EPN; ERP; GEPC; LEAP; OAEP; OuHeWo; PoFS; PoVP; SeCeV; VA; ViPP; ViPo; VLEP
Buried Love. Sara Teasdale. ChMo; CMP
Buried statue through the marble gleams, The. Form. Eva Gore-Booth. MaRV; TriL
Buried To-Day. Dinah Maria Mulock Craik. LPS-1
Buried voice bespake Antigone, The. Antigone. George Meredith. TwCrTr
Burke and Wills. Ken Barratt. BoAV
Burke and Wills, *sels.* Colin Thiele. NeLNL
  Final Soliloquy, The.
  Wills Dies in Solitude.
Burlesque of Lope de Vega. Samuel Johnson. *See* If the Man Who Turnips Cries.
Burly and big, his books among. Hodge, the Cat. "Susan Coolidge." CIV
Burly, dozing humble-bee. The Humble-Bee. Emerson. AA; AmPP; AnNE; APW; BAP; CBOV; EV-4; FaPON; GN; HBV; HBVY; HiLiAm; IAP; LaNeLa; LHV; MOAP; OBAV; OTPC; OxBA; PIAE; PYM; REAL; SN; TCAP
Burma Hills. Bernard Gutteridge. WaP
Burman Lover, The. Calder Campbell. *See* Ossian's Serenade.
Burn me, sun, burn me. Clean. Dorothy Mitchell. CAG
Burn me, Tongue of Fire! Paraclete. Jorge de Lima. AnCL; PoFr
Burn on, sweet fire, for I live by that fuel. Parthenophil and Parthenophe, LXXXVII. Barnabe Barnes. TuPP
Burn Out Burn Quick ("Burn out, my life, burn quick"). Abraham Reisen, *tr. fr. Yiddish by* Joseph Leftwich. TrJP
Burn stilly, thou; and come with me. To a Candle. Walter de la Mare. ChMP; GTBS-D
Burn the Stubble! Sidney Lanier. CoV
Burn, wood, burn. Flame Song. Nancy Byrd Turner. MW
Burned Forests. Frank Oliver Call. OCL
Burned in this element. Letter II. W. S. Graham. NePoEA
Burning, *abr.* Gary Snyder. Myths & Texts, III. NeAP
Burning—at first—would be probably worst, The. Heaven and Hell. James Kenneth Stephen. CenHV
Burning angel of light. The Two Angels. Rafael Alberti. CoSP
Burning Babe, The. Robert Southwell. ACP; AEV; AnEC; AnFE; AtBAP; BEL; BLV; BoW; CAW; CH; CoBE; CoEV; EIL; ElSeCe; EM-1; EnLit; EPP; EV-1; FaBoCh; FaBoEn; GoBC; HBV; HoPM; LiTB; LiTG; LoBV; LoGBV; MaRV; MePo; OBEV; OBSC; OxBoCh; PoEL-2; PoLi; ReEn; ReIE; SDH; SeCePo; SiCE; StJW; TCEP; TOP; TrGrPo; TuPP; UnPo (1st ed.); ViBoPo
  ("As I in hoary winter's night stood shivering in the snow.") EG
  (Carol, A: "As I in a hoarie, winter's night.") COAH
Burning Bush. Karle Wilson Baker. HBMV
Burning Bush, The. Exodus, III. 1–14, Bible, *O.T.* GrCo-1
Burning Bush. Martin Feinstein. TrJP
Burning Bush, The. Norman Nicholson. NeBP; SeCePo
Burning Bush. Louis Untermeyer. MAP
Burning candle glows, The. The Candle. Al-Hajjam. MooP
Burning fire, or blowing wind. To Ocean Hazard; Gipsy. Lionel Johnson. VLEP
Burning-Glass, The. "Æ." LEAP
Burning-Glass, The. Walter de la Mare. QS; StJW
Burning Leaves. Charles Edward Eaton. NoCaPo (rev. ed.)
Burning Letters, The. Nikolai Alekseyevich Nekrasov, *tr. fr. Russian by* Sir Cecil Kisch.
Burning Love Letters. Howard Moss. HoPM
Burning of Absál, The. Jami, *tr. fr. Persian by* Edward Fitzgerald. *Fr.* Salámán and Absál. PeP
Burning of Balder's Ship, The. Matthew Arnold. *Fr.* Balder Dead. BMEP
  (Incremation, The.) VA
Burning of Jamestown, The. Thomas Dunn English. PAH
Burning of the Law, The. Mëir of Rothenburg, *tr. fr. Hebrew by* Nina Davis Salaman. TrJP
Burning of the Leaves, The. Laurence Binyon. ChMP; MoVE; POTE
  "Now is the time for the burning of the leaves," *sel.* GTBS-D
Burning of the Temple, The. Isaac Rosenberg. FaBoMo; TrJP
Burning skies are steel, The. Drought. David John Darlow. MM
Burning the Bee-Tree. Ruth Pitter. POTE
Burning the Christmas Greens. William Carlos Williams. CoBMV; MoPo; NePA
Burning the Letters. Randall Jarrell. MiAP; MoAB; MoAmPo (1950 ed.)
Burning upon some hidden shore. The Lighthouse. Marjorie Wilson. BoTP

Burning with love, the shepherd Corydon. Eclogues, II. Virgil. LaP
Burnished with copper light, burnished. Mending the Bridge. Douglas Stewart. AnNZ
Burns. Ebenezer Elliott. *See* Poet's Epitaph, A.
Burns. Fitz-Greene Halleck. AA; LPS-3; TCAP
Burns. Whittier. CoBA; IAP; LPS-3; PtP; TCAP
Burns; an Ode. Swinburne. VLEP
Burns and His Highland Mary, *with music. Unknown.* ShS
Burns's Log Camp, *with music. Unknown.* ShS
Burnt Lands. Sir Charles G. D. Roberts. VA
Burnt lawns and iron-bound pastures. Midsummer. Sybil Horatia Calverley. DiM
Burnt Norton. T. S. Eliot. *Fr.* Four Quartets. AnFE; AtBAP; CoAnAm; LiTG; LiTM (rev. ed.); MoAB; MoAmPo (1950 ed.); MoPo; PoE; TwAmPo; TwHP
Sels.
"Garlic and sapphires in the mud," *fr.* II. GTBS-W
"Words move, music moves," V. UnS; ViBoPo (1958 ed.)
Burnt Ship, A. John Donne. WaaP
Burnt Ships. Ibsen, *tr. fr. Norwegian by* Charles W. Stork. AnNoLy
Burr Oaks, *sel.* Richard Eberhart.
Attic, The. MoAB
Burro, The. J. J. Gibbons. PoOW
Burro Bells in the Moonlight. Glenn Ward Dresbach. PoTo
Burro once, sent by express, A. Advice to Travelers. Walker Gibson. NePoAm-2
Burro with the Long Ears. *Tr. fr. Navajo Indian by* Hilda Faunce Wetherill. FaPON
Burrowing mole lives under the ground, The. The Mole. Edith King. GFA
Burst to bloom, you proud white flower. Chicago. Mildred Plew Meigs. BoHiPo
Bursts from a rending East in flaws. Hard Weather. George Meredith. EmBrPo; EPN; Po; POTT; TyEnPo; ViP; ViPP
Bury Her at Even. "Michael Field." CAW; GTML; OBMV
Bury me close to the Roman Road. The Roman Road. Rachel Annand Taylor. EBSV
Bury me deep when I am dead. Requiescat. Rosamund Marriott Watson. AV; BMEP; HBV; LBBV; LEAP
Bury Me Not on the Lone Prairie. *Unknown. See* Dying Cowboy, The ("Oh, bury me not . . .").
Bury Me Out on the Prairie, *with music. Unknown.* CoSo
"Bury me," the bishop said. St. Swithin. Daniel Henderson. HBMV
Bury the Dragon's Teeth! Bury Them. Henry Howard Brownell. PAH
Bury the Great Duke. Ode on the Death of the Duke of Wellington. Tennyson. BEL; BHV; BMEP, 2 *sts.;* BPN; EM-2; EmBrPo; GEPC; HBV; OBVV; PCD; PoVP; ShGoBo; TOP; TVSH; TyEnPo; UnPo (1st ed.); VA; ViPo; ViPP; VLEP
Bury Them. Henry Howard Brownell. PAH
Bury your heart in some deep green hollow. Saturday Market. Charlotte Mew. HBMV; NV
Bury your love. Death in May. Muriel Newton. NeTW
Burying Ground by the Ties. Archibald MacLeish. Frescoes for Mr. Rockefeller's City, III. AmPP (4th ed.); MAP; MoAmPo; NAMP; ReaPo; UnPo; WoL
Bus, The. "Peter." BoTP
Bus driver,/ Tram driver. We Thank You! L. E. Cox. BoTP
Bus Ride. Selma Robinson. *Fr.* Ferry Ride. FaPON
Bus rides like a room across the night, The. The Sea Dike. M. Vasalis. LiTW
Bus Trip, The. Joel Oppenheimer. NeAP
Bush, The. James Lister Cuthbertson. BoAu
Bush, The, *sels.* Bernard O'Dowd.
Last Stanzas of "The Bush." BoAu
"Where is Australia, singer, do you know?" PoFr
Bush aboon Traquair, The. John Campbell Shairp. EBSV; OBVV
Bush Goblins. H. M. Green. BoAu
Bushed. Earle Birney. PeCV
Bushes lean in the wind, The. Need of an Angel. Raymond Souster. CaP
Bushfeller, The. Eileen Duggan. AnNZ; JKCP (1955 ed.)
Bushman's Song, A. Andrew Barton Paterson. BoAu
Bushman's stature is not great, The. The Fat-buttocked Bushmen. Earnest A. Hooton. WhC
Busie old foole, unruly Sunne. *See* Busy old fool, unruly Sun.
Business and bluebirds waken first in spring. Spring's on the Curb. Hildegarde Flanner. AnAmPo
Business Is Business. Berton Braley. WBLP
Business Man's Prayer, A. William Ludlum. BLRP
Business Men. Ch'en Tzu-ang, *tr. fr. Chinese by* Arthur Waley. OnPM; MoPW; TrCh; WoL
(Men of Affairs.) WhP
Business of the lambing ewes would make me, The. Eagles over the Lambing Paddock. Ernest G. Moll. BoAu
Busk ye, busk ye, my bonny bonny bride. The Braes of Yarrow. William Hamilton of Bangour. CEP; EBSV; EiPP; EV-3; OBEC
Bussy d'Ambois, *sels.* George Chapman.
"As cedars beaten with continual storms," *fr.* I, i. ViBoPo
"Ile sooth his plots: and strow my hate with smiles," *fr.* IV, ii. PoEL-2
Invocation, An: "I long to know," *fr.* V, iii. EV-1; ViBoPo
(Invocation to Spirit.) LiA
"Me thought the Spirit," *fr.* V, iii. NBE
"Now all ye peacefull regents of the night," *fr.* II, ii. LO; NBE; PoEL-2
"Now shall we see, that nature hath no end," *fr.* V, ii. PoEL-2
"Since I am free,/ Offending no just law, let no law make," *fr.* II, i. MyFE
Virtue the Safest Guide, *Fr.* I, i. CoEV
Bust, The. W. H. Davies. MoPW
Bustan, The, *sels.* Sadi, *tr. fr. Persian by* Sir Edwin Arnold.
Dancer, The. AWP; JAWP; OuHeWo; WBP
Great Physician, The. AWP; OuHeWo
Buster's got a popper gun. To China. Leroy F. Jackson. StVeCh (1940 ed.)
Bustle in a house, The. Emily Dickinson. AmPo; AmPP; AnFE; APA; CoAnAm; CoBA; IAP; MaPo; NePA; OBAV; OnPM; OxBA; PoEL-5; TwP
(Death.) BPP; WGRP
(Post Mortem.) BAP
Busy Bee, The. Isaac Watts. *See* How Doth the Little Busy Bee.
Busy Body, The. Rachel Field. InMe
Busy Carpenters. James S. Tippett. StVeCh
Busy, curious, thirsty fly! On a Fly Drinking Out of [*or* from] His Cup [*or* The Flyer *or* To a Fly]. William Oldys. BoHiPo; EG; EV-3; FaFP; GoTP; GTBS-W; LEAP; LiTG; OBEC; OBEV; OTPC (1923 ed.); PoeMoYo; TrGrPo; ViBoPo
Busy Day. James Laughlin. OnHM
Busy Day, A. *Unknown. See* All Busy.
Busy day is over, The. The Happy Hour. Mary Frances Butts. DD; MOAH
Busy Heart, The. Rupert Brooke. HBV; LoPo; MBP; MoBrPo
Busy [*or* Bisy] larke, messager of daye [*or* day], The. Morning in May [*or* Dawn]. Chaucer. *Fr.* The Canterbury Tales: The Knight's Tale. CBOV; LPS-2
Busy Music Critic, The. Bert Leston Taylor. LauV
Busy [*or* Busie] old fool, unruly Sun. The Sun [*or* Sunne] Rising. John Donne. AnFE; AtBAP; BLV; BoLiVe; EG; EnLP; ExPo; GTSE; InvP; LiTB; LiTG; LiTL; LoBV; MeLP; MePo; OAEP; PoE; PoEL-2; PoFr; PoFS; ReEn; ReIE; SeCePo; SeCeV; SeCV-1; SeEP; TrGrPo; TuPP; TwHP; TwP
Busy Person, A. Alfarata Hilton. PCH
Busy Street, A. *Unknown.* DDA
Busy wind is out today, The. My Kite. Beatrice Brown. GFA
Busybody. Loretta Lee. DDA
But a little while ago. Winter and Spring. *Unknown.* BoTP
But Achilles, by the breakers of the loud-thundering sea. The Wraith of Patroclus. Homer. *Fr.* The Iliad, XXIII. GrPE
But Achilles went into his hut. The Prayer of Achilles. Homer. *Fr.* The Iliad, XVI. GrR
But afar on the headland exalted. By the North Sea, VII. Swinburne. PoVP
But after they had taken their fill of meat and drink. Odysseus Spurns Calypso. Homer. *Fr.* The Odyssey, V. GrR
But Agamemnon, as the rites demand. Preparation of the Pyre for Patroclus. Homer. *Fr.* The Iliad, XXIII. UnPo (1st ed.)
But ah! how unsincere are all our joys! The Fire of London. Dryden. *Fr.* Annus Mirabilis. EV-3; SeEP
But ah! let me under some Kentish hill. Phineas Fletcher. *Fr.* The Purple Island. ViBoPo
But, ah! Maecenas is yclad in clay [*or* claye]. Spenser. *Fr.* The Shepheardes Calender: October. MyFE; PoD
But Alcimus and Automedon toiled busily. The Horse Xanthus Warns Achilles. Homer. *Fr.* The Iliad, XIX. GrPE
But all my night has been sleepless! And now, at dawn. The Swallows. Agathias Scholasticus. LiTW
But All the Roses. Claire Goll, *tr. fr. French by* Claire Goll. OnPM
But all too soon, the much-loved father died. His Youth. John Oxenham. StJW
But among the immortals uncontrollable laughter. Homer. *Fr.* The Iliad, I. GrPo
But are ye [*or* you] sure the news is true? *See* And are ye sure the news is true?
But Art Thou Come, Dear Saviour? *Unknown.* OxBoCh
"But as bees or supple-waisted wasps, that love to make." Wasps. Homer. *Fr.* The Iliad, XII. GrPE

But as he shook with passionate desire. George Chapman. *Fr.* Hero and Leander. NBE
But as in a garden a poppy bows its head away. The Death of Gorguthion. Homer. *Fr.* The Iliad, VIII. GrPE
But as o'er some parched mountain sweeps a portentous blaze. Homer. *Fr.* The Iliad, XX *and* XXI. GrPE
But as on a day in winter thickly the flakes of snow. The Storming of the Achaean Wall. Homer. *Fr.* The Iliad, XII *and* XIII. GrPE
But as some star of bale amid night's misty skies. Homer. *Fr.* The Iliad, XI. GrPE
But as they left the dark'ning [*or* darkening] heath. Flodden [*or* Flodden Field]. Sir Walter Scott. *Fr.* Marmion, VI. LiA; NBE
But as they talked, laid near them a dog upraised his head. The Death of Argus. Homer. *Fr.* The Odyssey, XVII. GrPE
But be contented: when that fell arrest. Sonnets, LXXIV. Shakespeare. BoFr; OBSC; PeBoSo; TCEP
But beggars about midsummer go breadless to supper. Prayer for the Poor. William Langland. *Fr.* The Vision of Piers Plowman. PoFr; PoLi
But better hopes inspirit and make blithe. Tasso. *Fr.* Jerusalem Delivered, VI. PrPoCR
But beware the month of Lenaion, ill days of bitter frost. Winter. Hesiod. *Fr.* Works and Days. GrPE
But, breaking day, their several flutes. The Moment. Kendrick Smithyman. AnNZ
But bringing up the rear of this bright host. At the Gate of Heaven [*or* The Archangel *or* Where He Gazed a Gloom Pervaded]. Byron. *Fr.* The Vision of Judgment. LiA; LoBV; OBRV
But chief by numbers of industrious hands. A Nation's Wealth. John Dyer. *Fr.* The Fleece. OBEC
But chief—surpassing all—a cuckoo clock! The Cuckoo Clock. Caroline Anne Bowles. *Fr.* The Birthday. LPS-2
But chieflye the anatomye. John Halle. *Fr.* Anatomye. PoP
But Choose. John Holmes. MiAP
But Christ can give thee heart who loveth thee. Christ Can Give Thee Heart. Christina Rossetti. ChIP
But Delos is pleasant, O Phoebus, above the rest. Ionian Holiday. *Unknown.* *Fr.* Homeric Hymns. OxBG
But do not let us quarrel any more. Andrea del Sarto. Robert Browning. ATP; BEL; BMEP; BPN; CoBE; EM-2; EmBrPo; EnL; EnLi-2; EnLit; EPN; GEPC; HBV; MaPo; OAEP; PIAE; PoE; PoEL-5; PoVP; PreP; REAL; ReaPo; TOP; TyEnPo; ViPo; ViPP; VLEP; WHA
But do thy worst to steal thyself away. Sonnets, XCII. Shakespeare. PeBoSo
But do we truly mourn our soldier dead. For Decoration Day, I. Rupert Hughes. AA; MDAH
But Dulness sits at helm, and in this age. More Dullness. Earl of Rochester. *Fr.* Julian. BeR
"But er I bere thee mochë ferre." The House of Fame. John Skelton. *Fr.* The Garlande of Laurell. NBE
But ere you enter, yon bold Tower survey. George Crabbe. *Fr.* The Borough, Letter II. EnSW
But evening now. Alfred Domett. *Fr.* Ranolf and Amohia. AnNZ
But far astern of Argo her whitening wake was seen. The Sailing of Argo. Apollonius Rhodius. *Fr.* Argonautica, I. GrPE
But fast in heart I hold the lofty fame. The Infant Heracles. Pindar. *Fr.* Nemean Odes. OxBG
But Fear Thou Not, O Jacob. Jeremiah, XLVI: 27–28, Bible, *O.T.* TrJP
But for Lust. Ruth Pitter. FaBoTw
But for your Terror. To Death. Oliver St. John Gogarty. MaRV; OBMV; OtMeF
But Fortune, like some others of her sex. Fortune. Fitz-Greene Halleck. *Fr.* Fanny. LPS-3
But Gebir when he heard of her approach. Walter Savage Landor. *Fr.* Gebir. OBRV
But give me for my soul, those beauteous maids. Those Beauteous Maids. Moses ibn Ezra. TrJP
But Give Me Holly, Bold and Jolly. Christina Rossetti. *Fr.* Sing-Song. BrR; ChBR; TiPo
But give them me, the mouth, the eyes, the brow! Eurydice to Orpheus. Robert Browning. EPN; TriL
But God sent forth a pale and spectral host. Nimrod Wars with the Angels. Anna Hempstead Branch. *Fr.* Nimrod. TCPD
But golden-haired Achilles, biding still. The Childhood of Achilles. Pindar. *Fr.* Nemean Odes. OxBG
But, gracious [*or* gratious] God, how well dost Thou provide. The Church's Testimony [*or* Confession of Faith *or* Conversion]. Dryden. *Fr.* The Hind and the Panther, I. ACP; CAW; PoLi; TrPWD; UnPo (1st ed.)
But grant, in public, men sometimes are shown. Woman's Ruling Passions. Pope. *Fr.* Moral Essays. OBEC
But grant, the virtues of a temp'rate prime. The Burden of Age [*or* Life's Last Scene]. Samuel Johnson. *Fr.* The Vanity of Human Wishes. BeR; OBEC; SeCePo
But, grant thy poetry should find success. John Oldham. *Fr.* A Satire. ViBoPo
But, gratious God, how well dost thou provide. *See* But, gracious God . . .
But half a man's days—and his days were nights. Transfiguration. Swinburne. PeBoSo
But half of me is woman grown. To a Vagabond. Constance Davies Woodrow. CaP; OCL
But happy they! the happiest of their kind! The Connubial Life. James Thomson. *Fr.* The Seasons: Spring. LPS-1
But hark! a sound is stealing on my ear. Charles Stuart Calverley. *Fr.* Beer. FiBHP
But hark; I hear her liquid tone. The Nightingale. Mark Akenside. *Fr.* Ode to the Evening Star. RO
But, hark, 'tis late; the Whistlers knock from Plough. Evening Prayer. Edward Benlowes. *Fr.* Theophila. FaBoEn
But harken, my America, my own. The Errand Imperious. Edwin Markham. PGD
But haste we!—'Tis that merry time of year. Spring. William Allingham. IrPN
But he comes! the Messiah of royalty comes! George the Fourth in Ireland. Byron. OBRV
But he followed the pair to Pawtucket. Limerick [*or* That Nantucket Limerick and What Followed]. *Unknown.* LiTG; TreF
But he his wonted pride. Satan and His Host. Milton. *Fr.* Paradise Lost, I. OBS
But he—to him, who knows what gift is thine. A Sequence of Sonnets on the Death of Robert Browning, IV. Swinburne. BPN
"But hear. If you stay, and the child be born." In the Restaurant. Thomas Hardy. Satires of Circumstance, XI. MBP; MoAB; MoBrPo
But Hector, when he beheld great-hearted Patroklos. The Death of Patroklos. Homer, *tr. by* Lang, Leaf, *and* Myers. *Fr.* The Iliad, XVI. GrR
But Hector, when he saw great-heart Patroclus. The Death of Patroclus. Homer, *tr. by* Sir William Marris. *Fr.* The Iliad, XVI. OxBG
But Hellen now, on new device did stand. Helen, Menelaos, and Memories of Troy. Homer. *Fr.* The Odyssey, IV. GrR
But her knees at his words were loosened and the heart within her breast. The Reunion of Odysseus and Penelope. Homer. *Fr.* The Odyssey, XXIII. GrPE
But here, at starting, I must just premise. John Moultrie. *Fr.* Sir Launfal. OBRV
But here is the finger of God, a flash of the will that can. Music. Robert Browning. *Fr.* Abt Vogler. GrCo-1
But here, my son, so plagued, they cast me forth. The Castaway. Sophocles. *Fr.* Philoctetes. GrR
But His lone cross and crown of thorns. Easter. John Oxenham. OQP; QP-2
"But hold y . . . hold y . . . ," says Robin. The Jolly Pinder of Wakefield. [*or* Robin Hood and the Pinder of Wakefield]. *Unknown.* ESPB; EV-2
But how can I describe the doleful sight. Vision of Sorrow. Thomas Sackville. *Fr.* Induction to "The Mirror for Magistrates." LoBV
But How It Came from Earth. Conrad Aiken. MAP; MoAB; MoAmPo
But how many months [*or* monthes] be in the year [*or* yeere]. Robin Hood and the Curtal Friar. *Unknown.* EM-1; ESPB; EV-2; OBB
But how shall I, unblamed, express. Dress. Henry Luttrell. *Fr.* Advice to Julia. OBRV
But how shall we this union well express? The Soul and the Body [*or* In What Manner the Soul Is United to the Body]. Sir John Davies. *Fr.* Nosce Teipsum. LiTB; OBSC; PoEL-2
But human bodies are sic fools. Borrowing Trouble. Burns. *Fr.* The Twa Dogs. BLP
But "I" being less than soul, of dustier plume. Some Lines in Three Parts, II. Peter Viereck. MoAmPo (1950 ed.)
But I came from the dancing place. Ashore. "Laurence Hope." BMEP; HBV; LEAP
But I Do Not Need Kindness. Gregory Corso. NeAP
But I hae dream'd a dreary dream. Fey. *Unknown.* OtMeF
But I have sinuous shells of pearly hue. The Shells. Walter Savage Landor. *Fr.* Gebir. BCEP
But I perceive how vain. Prophets Exposed. Euripides. *Fr.* Helen. GrR
But I remember when the fight was done. Hotspur's Description of a Fop [*or* The Staff Officer]. Shakespeare. King Henry IV, Pt. I, *fr.* I, iii. LPS-2; OtMeF; PIR
But I Shall Weep. Beatrice Redpath. CaP; OCL
But I think the king of that country comes out from his tireless host. Henry van Dyke. *Fr.* The Gospel of Labor. WGRP
But I *was* dead, an hour or more. Escape. Robert Graves. MBP; MoBrPo
But I was first of all. Tennyson. *Fr.* Idylls of the King: Guinevere. GTSL
But if Our Love Be Dying. "Michael Field." BoFr

But if that I may have truly. Back and Side Go Bare [*or* A Song of Ale]. *At. to* William Stevenson. *Fr.* Gammer Gurton's Needle. AnFE; OBSC; PoRA; UnPo
But if the darkness and corruption leave. Christina Rossetti. *Fr.* Remember. LO
But if thou art late with ploughing, remedy thou hast still. Spring Ploughing. Hesiod. *Fr.* Works and Days. GrPE
But if thou needs will hunt, be ruled by me. Shakespeare. *Fr.* Venus and Adonis. SiCE
But in sunshine ever fair. The Island [*or* Islands] of the Blest. Pindar. *Fr.* Olympian Odes, II. GrR; OxBG
But in the crowding darkness not a word did they say. The Old-Marrieds. Gwendolyn Brooks. PoNe
But in the evening the oppression lifted. W. H. Auden. *Fr.* In Time of War. EnLit
But in the last days it shall come to pass. And They Shall Beat Their Swords into Plowshares. Micah, Bible, *O.T.* TreF
But indignation works where hope is not. France. Wordsworth. *Fr.* The Prelude. ERP
But it could never be true. Devil's Dream. Kenneth Fearing. ChMo; PoLFOT
"But it is not Black," they will tell you, "any longer." The "Black" Country. D. J. Enright. HaMV
But it seems that something has happened that has never happened before. When the Church Is No Longer Regarded. T. S. Eliot. *Fr.* The Rock. MaRV
"But it was even thou . . ." Roundel of Passion-Tide. *Unknown.* CAW
But, knowing now that they would have her speak. The Defence [*or* Defense] of Guenevere. William Morris. EmBrPo; EnL; EnLi-2; EnLit; PoVP; ViP; ViPo; ViPP
But leave the Wise to wrangle, and with me. Omar Khayyám, *tr. by* Edward Fitzgerald. *Fr.* The Rubáiyát. RiBV
But, leaving these vain trifles of men's souls. Christopher Marlowe. *Fr.* Dr. Faustus. MyFE
But let applause be dealt in all we may. Portrait of a Vicar. George Crabbe. *Fr.* The Borough. RO
But let my due feet never fail. Milton. *Fr.* Il Penseroso. PC
But letting go . . . hands, eyes, teeth, body, all ways. The People, IV. "Robin Hyde." AnNZ
But lightly veiling the awful grace. Palm. Paul Valéry. TrFP
But lo! at length the day is lingered out. Francis Thompson. *Fr.* Sister Songs. OBMV; VLEP
But, lo! from forth a copse that neighbours by. The Courser and the Jennet. Shakespeare. *Fr.* Venus and Adonis. OBSC; LoBV
But lo we see, we touch, sayeth John. Of the Holy Eucharist. *Unknown.* ACP (1952 ed.)
But look! o'er the fall see the angler stand. The Angler. Thomas Buchanan Read. LPS-2
But look: the water. This Will Remain. Semyon Osipovich Kirsanov. TrRV
But look ye, Gil, at morning dawn. Mingo. Juan del Encina. AnSpL-1
But looke where sadly the poore wretch comes reading. Shakespeare. *Fr.* Hamlet, II, ii. AtBAP
"But, Lord," she said, "my shoulders still are strong." At the Top of the Road. Charles Buxton Going. HBV
But love whilst that thou may'st [*or* maist] be loved again[e]. Samuel Daniel. To Delia, IX [XXXVII]. AtBAP; EIL; OBSC; SiCE; TuPP
But love's true passion is of immortal happiness. Robert Bridges. *Fr.* The Testament of Beauty. LO
But Man, Proud Man. Shakespeare. *Fr.* Measure for Measure, II, ii. WHA (Man.) BCEP
But meanwhile in the centre. The Fight in the Centre. Macaulay. *Fr.* The Battle of Lake Regillus. OtMeF
But Medea—her thoughts unto nought else turned. Appollonius Rhodius. *Fr.* Argonautica. GrL
But Menelaos also arose among them. Sequel to the Chariot Race. Homer. *Fr.* The Iliad, XXIII. GrR
But mind, but thought—/ If these have been the master part of us. Life and Thought. Matthew Arnold. *Fr.* Empedocles on Etna. FiP
But Minerva fetch'd/ The winds from sea. Homer. *Fr.* The Odyssey, V. EnLi-1
But mortal man/ Was then far hardier in the old champaign. Of Human Progress. Lucretius, *tr. by* William Ellery Leonard. *Fr.* De Rerum Natura (Of the Nature of Things). WoL
But most by numbers judge a poet's song. The Art of Writing [*or* Poetical Numbers]. Pope. *Fr.* An Essay on Criticism. AnFE; BCEP; EV-3; InP; OBEC; SeCePo
But my fate, on some throbbing wheel of God. Fortune Is like the Moon. Sophocles. OxBG
But my good little man, you have made a mistake. To a Boy-Poet of the Decadence. Sir Owen Seaman. CenHV; FiBHP; LEAP
But "nameless somethings" and "unbounded spaces." Roy Campbell. *Fr.* A Veld Eclogue: The Pioneers. BoSA
But never came there Plutus, the blind one. A Visit from Wealth. Hipponax. OxBG
But no, the familiar symbol, as that the/ curtain. Conrad Aiken. *Fr.* Time in the Rock. FaBoMo
But not on a shell, she starts. The Paltry Nude Starts on a Spring Voyage. Wallace Stevens. NP
But not so odd. A Reply. Cecil Browne. SiTL
But not to deal/ Thus closely with thee longer. Dante. *Fr.* Divina Commedia: Paradiso. SaFP
But now a herald, leading the bard beloved, drew near. Odysseus and Demodocus. Homer. *Fr.* The Odyssey, VIII. GrPE
But now—as ravening wolves, with hearts to flinch at nought. Patroclus Goes to Battle. Homer. *Fr.* The Iliad, XVI. GrPE
But now at last the sacred influence. Milton. *Fr.* Paradise Lost, II. BrBE
But now Athenian mountains they descry. William Falconer. *Fr.* The Shipwreck, III. GoTL
But now dejected, languid, listless, low. Delay Has Danger. George Crabbe. *Fr.* Tales of the Hall. EnSW
But now Hektor was come unto the Skaian Gates. Women Who Wait. Homer. *Fr.* The Iliad, VI. GrR
But now more serious let me grow. Matthew Green. *Fr.* The Spleen. PoEL-3
But now, my boys, leave off, and list to me. Rudiments of War. Christopher Marlowe. *Fr.* Tamburlaine the Great. KN
But now my muse, toil'd with continual care. Sonnet. Richard Barnfield. ReIE
But now our Quacks are gamesters, and they play. Quack Medicines. George Crabbe. *Fr.* The Borough. LPS-3
But now the clear bright Moon her zenith gains. Wordsworth. *Fr.* An Evening Walk. RO
But now the dentist cannot die. Andrew Lang. CenHV
But now the Dream has come again, the world is as of old. Dream. Anna Hempstead Branch. SBMV
But now the huntsman takes his usual round. The Beginnings of Day. William Diaper. *Fr.* Dryades; or, The Nymphs Prophecy. BeR
But now the salmon-fishers moist. Carrying Their Coracles. Andrew Marvell. *Fr.* Upon Appleton House. ChTr
But now the second morning from her bower. Christ's Triumph after Death. Giles Fletcher. *Fr.* Christ's Victory and Triumph. EPS
But now the sun, great Hyperion's child. Voyage of the Sun [*or* The Setting Sun]. Stesichorus. GrR; OxBG
But now the sun had pass'd the height of Heaven. The Burning of Balder's Ship [*or* The Incremation]. Matthew Arnold. *Fr.* Balder Dead. BMEP; VA
But now the wholesome music of the wood. The Fire of Heaven. Tennyson. *Fr.* Idylls of the King. EPN
But now the wounded queen, with heavy care. Virgil, *tr. by* the Earl of Surrey. *Fr.* The Aeneid, IV. ReIE
But now there came a flash of hope once more. The Shipwreck. Byron. *Fr.* Don Juan, II. TCEP
But now, when waned the spring, and lambs were fed. Hylas. Theocritus. *Fr.* Idylls. GrR
But now you are mine, all mine. Slumber-Songs of the Madonna, VII. Alfred Noyes. BOL
But now Zeus throned in the highest made Ajax' heart turn cold. Homer. *Fr.* The Iliad, XI. GrPE
But O my God! though grovelling I appear. Aspiration. George Wither. MaRV
But, O my Lord, I thank Thee. Christ and the Common Day. Marguerite Wilkinson. BePJ
But O, my Muse, what numbers wilt thou find. Blenheim. Addison. *Fr.* The Campaign. EPP; OBEC
But O the heavy change, now thou art gon. Milton. *Fr.* Lycidas. PoD
But oh! o'er all, forget not Kilda's race. St. Kilda. William Collins. *Fr.* Ode on the Popular Superstitions of the Highlands. FaBoEn
But oh, the night! oh, bitter-sweet! oh, sweet! Romney and Aurora. Elizabeth Barrett Browning. *Fr.* Aurora Leigh, IX. VA
But Odysseus of many a rede of his rags he stripped him bare. The Slaying of the Suitors. Homer. *Fr.* The Odyssey, XXII. GrR
But Once. *Unknown.* BLP
But Once. Theodore Winthrop. AA
But once I pass this way. The Pilgrim Way. John Oxenham. OQP; QP-1
But once or twice we met, touched hands. A Greeting. Austin Dobson. BoFr; BPN; GTML
But once upon a time. Cranach. Sir Herbert Read. FaBoMo
But one Apocalyptic Lion's whelp (in flesh). There Is No Opera like "Lohengrin." John Wheelwright. OnHM; WhC
But one of the whole mammoth-brood still kept. Keats. *Fr.* Hyperion; a Fragment, I. OBRV
But only three in all God's universe. Sonnets from the Portuguese, II. Elizabeth Barrett Browning. BPN; ES

But only to be memories of spiritual gate. Immortality. Samuel Greenberg. LiTA
But others of the sons of Los build moments and minutes and hours. Blake. *Fr.* Milton, I. NBE
But, our Winter come, in vain. Sir Richard Fanshawe. LO
But peaceful was the night. The Peaceful Night. Milton. *Fr.* On the Morning of Christ's Nativity. ChrBoLe; CLS; FaBoCh; LoGBV
But piteous things we are—when I am gone. Sonnets to Aurelia, III. Robert Nichols. OBMV
"But plett a wand o bonnie birk." Sweet William's Ghost (G *vers.*) *Unknown.* ESPB
But poets should/ Exert a double vision. Elizabeth Barrett Browning. *Fr.* Aurora Leigh, V. VLEP
But quiet to quick bosoms is a hell. Byron. *Fr.* Childe Harold's Pilgrimage, III. PoFr
But quit thy meaner game, indignant Muse. Bryant. *Fr.* The Embargo. CoBA
But Robin he walkes in the g[reene] fforest. Robin Hood and the Butcher. *Unknown.* ESPB
"But see! look up—on Flodden bent." Flodden; the Attack. Sir Walter Scott. *Fr.* Marmion, VI. LH
But see the fading many-coloured woods. Autumn. James Thomson. *Fr.* The Seasons: Autumn. EnRP; EnSW; LoBV
But see this happy village festival. William E. Marshall. *Fr.* Brookfield. CaP
But shall I go mourn for that, my dear? Shakespeare. *Fr.* The Winter's Tale, IV, ii. PoD
But since He heareth prayer at any time. Prayer. *Unknown.* PraP
But since I know thy falsehood and thy pride. Abraham Cowley. LO
But so long as/ This prison-planet. Petar Preradovic. *Fr.* Ode to Slavdom. PoFr
But sometimes let me leave the noisy roads. The Pleasure of Walking through an Alley. John Gay. *Fr.* Trivia; or, The Art of Walking the Streets of London, II. EnLi-1 (1949 ed.)
But souls that of His own good life partake. In Him We Live. Henry More. MaRV
But stay, my thoughts, make end, give fortune way. Sir Walter Ralegh. *Fr.* The Ocean to Cynthia, XI. TuPP
But still did the Mighty Makers. John G. Neihardt. *Fr.* The Poet's Town. OBAV
But Still Intrepid Icarus. Louise Crenshaw Ray. MuM
But stirred was the heart of Odysseus, and the sharp grief rose on high. Laertes. Homer. *Fr.* The Odyssey, XXIV. GrR
But stricken with the high cafard, the town. Anthony Delius. *Fr.* The Great Divide. BoSA
But Tell Me ("But tell me, was there life here, too"). Ilya Ehrenburg, *tr. fr. Russian by* Babette Deutsch. TrRV
"But tell me, you that in this place are happy." His Will Is Our Peace. Dante. *Fr.* Divina Commedia: Paradiso, III. GrCo-2
But Terror's widened bane has been to me. William Ellery Leonard. *Fr.* Two Lives, Pt. III. MOAP
But That from Slow Dissolving Pomps of Dawn. Arthur Hugh Clough. ViPP
But that my lord may plainly understand. George Gascoigne. *Fr.* The Steel Glass. ReEn
"But that was nothing to what things came out." Welsh Incident. Robert Graves. ShBV-3
But that which most I wonder at, which most. Innocence. Thomas Traherne. EPS
But the chaste blackbird, to its partner true. Goldsmith. LO
But the chief/ Are poets. Poets. Mark Akenside. *Fr.* The Pleasures of Imagination, IV. OBEC
But the eternal father throned on high. Ajax Covers the Flight of the Greeks [*or* Ajax in the Fight]. Homer. *Fr.* The Iliad, XI. GrPo; GrR; OxBG
But the majestic river floated on. Oxus. Matthew Arnold. *Fr* Sohrab and Rustum. VA
But the men of the steppes were tougher then by far, naturally. The Life of Primitive Man. Lucretius. *Fr.* De Rerum Natura, V. LaP
But the morn to the noon hath fallen, and the afternoon to the eve. The Brooding of Sigurd. William Morris. *Fr.* The Story of Sigurd the Volsung. SeCePo
But the rain is gone by, and the day's dying out in a splendour. Winter Evening. Katharine Tynan. TIP
But the son of Aison outshone all there in wondrous wise. Medea's Passion. Apollonius Rhodius. *Fr.* Argonautica. GrR
But the vast pile th' amazed vulgar views. The Destruction of Troy. Virgil, *tr. by* Sir John Denham. *Fr.* The Aeneid. SeCV-1
But Thee, but Thee, O sovereign Seer of Time. The Crystal Christ. Sidney Lanier. *Fr.* The Crystal. BePJ; ChIP; MaRV; TrPWD
But then there comes that moment rare. Voices of the Air. Katherine Mansfield. HBMV
But there are richer entanglements. Love and Friendship. Keats. *Fr.* Endymion, I. OBRV
But these were only a few, there were others, too, many others. Trippers. Sir Osbert Sitwell. HaMV
But they that wait upon the Lord shall renew their strength. Isaiah. Bible, *O.T.* TiPo (1952 ed.)
But they who never from the right have strayed. Hesiod. *Fr.* Works and Days. GrPo
But, this I found. Robert Norwood. *Fr.* The Man of Kerioth. CaP
But This Is Also Everlasting Life. Sarah N. Cleghorn. QS
But this is learning; to have skill to throw[e]. Learning. George Chapman. *Fr.* Euthymiae Raptus; or, The Teares of Peace. BrBE; SeCePo
But this is nothing; an eccentric joke. A Red Carpet for Shelley. Elinor Wylie. PtP
But this may not be. Afterthoughts. *Unknown.* *Fr.* Homeric Hymns. OxBG
But this: to know Thy life, without a stain. The True Need. Thomas Curtis Clark. OQP; QP-1
But tho' we must obey when Heav'n commands. Advice. Earl of Roscommon. *Fr.* An Essay on Translated Verse. BeR
But those old bridges claim another look. Jean Ingelow. *Fr.* The Four Bridges. EnSW
But thou, Beth-lehem Ephratah. The Prince of Peace. Micah, Bible, *O.T.* ChrBoLe
But thou, Israel, My servant. Israel, My Servant. Isaiah, Bible, *O.T.* TrJP
But thou, O Sleep, bend down and give. Norman Gale. *Fr.* To Sleep. PC
But thou which lov'st to be. John Donne. *Fr.* The Blossom. LO
But through the livelong night no sleep laid hold. Quintus Smyrnaeus. *Fr.* Posthomerica, X. GrPo
But to have lain upon the grass. In the Meadows at Mantua. Arthur Symons. PoeT
But to His Mother Mary. Milton. *Fr.* Paradise Regained, II. ISi
But to inform the mind and mend the heart. Benjamin Church. *Fr.* The Choice. PoP
But to reach the archimedean point. "Mysticism Has Not the Patience to Wait for God's Revelation." Richard Eberhart. MoPo
But to say something of her moral sense. The Prioress. Chaucer. *Fr.* The Canterbury Tales: Prologue. PraNu
But to tell the white-armed Helen came Iris—shaped was she. Priam and Helen on the Wall. Homer. *Fr.* The Iliad, III. GrPE
But Troy, alas, methought above them all. Troy. Thomas Sackville. *Fr.* Induction to "The Mirror for Magistrates." SeCePo
But, truth to tell, men have another love. Pure Love. Euripides. OxBG
But twelve short years you lived, my son. His Son. Callimachus. AWP; JAWP; WBP
But Two I Love. James M. Hayes. PraNu
But Two There Are . . . C. Day Lewis. OxBI
But unmoved thou. John Donne. *Fr.* Satires, III. NBE
But up soon swims our mullet, lured by the scent; the hook. The Mullet and the Hook. Oppian. *Fr.* Halieuticks. GrPE
But vain the sword and vain the bow. A Tear Is an Intellectual Thing. Blake. *Fr.* The Grey Monk. BCEP; LEAP
But, venture on the darkness; and within. A Fauxbourg. George Croly. *Fr.* Paris in 1815. OBRV
But Venus first. Sister Juana Inés de la Cruz, *tr. fr. Spanish by* Samuel Beckett. *Fr.* First Dream. AnMP
But we by a love, so much refined. John Donne. LO
But We Shall Bloom. Haim Guri, *tr. fr. Hebrew by* David Kuselewitz. TrJP
But well away, so is mine heart woe. To Chaucer. Thomas Hoccleve. *Fr.* De Regimine Principum. ACP
But Whan the Cok. Chaucer. *Fr.* Troilus and Criseide, III. AtBAP
But what, by the fur on your satin sleeves. The Retort Discourteous. Stephen Vincent Benét. HBMV
But what dark flag. Shark's Fin. Eithne Wilkins. NeBP
But what does our proud ign'rance learning call. Our Knowledge. Swift. *Fr.* Ode to Sir William Temple. BeR
But when athwart the empty-vaulted heaven. Lycophron. *Fr.* Alexandra. GrPo
But when Brisëis, bright as Venus, saw. Briseis, the Slave Girl: Tears for Patroclus. Homer. *Fr.* The Iliad, XIX. GrR
But when came early Morning, with fingers rosy-red. The Debate in Ithaca. Homer. *Fr.* The Odyssey, II. GrPE
But when he that beareth his house on his back up the plants doth climb. The Snail's Moving Day. Hesiod. *Fr.* Works and Days. GrR
But when her heart had had its fill of weeping. Penelope Dreams. Homer. *Fr.* The Odyssey, XX. OxBG

But when now they came unto the ford of the fair-flowing river. Homer. *Fr.* The Iliad, XXI. GrPo
But when radiant Dawn with her flashing eyes on the steeps looked down. The Sailing of the Argo. Apollonius Rhodius. *Fr.* Argonautica. GrR
But when that comely he covered his wits. The Temptation of Sir Gawain. *Unknown.* *Fr.* Sir Gawain and the Green Knight. ACP
But when the bands were mustered round their leaders on each side. Homer. *Fr.* The Iliad, III. GrPE
But when the morning's dewy locks drunk up. The End of the Last Fight of the *Revenge.* Gervase Markham. SG
But when the mother of morning, rose-fingered day-dawn, shone. Of Cyclops and the Ram. Homer. *Fr.* The Odyssey, IX. OxBG
But when through Troy's wide city Hector had turned again. Hector and Andromache. Homer. *Fr.* The Iliad, VI. GrPE
But when to Priam's lordly house they came. The Lamentations of the Women. Homer. *Fr.* The Iliad, XXIV. GrR
But when up stalks from the ground House-carrier turns to climb. Summer. Hesiod. *Fr.* Works and Days. GrPE
"But when we were come to the shore and our black ship again." The Kingdom of Death. Homer. *Fr.* The Odyssey, XI. GrPE
But when with her white horses day shone fair. Salamis. Aeschylus. *Fr.* Persians. WaaP
But When Ye Pray. Frances Crosby Hamlet. OQP; QP-1
But where began the change; and what's my crime? Modern Love, X. George Meredith. EnLit; PoEL-5; ViPo
But where shall wisdom be found. Wisdom. Job, Bible, *O.T.* BHV
But where to find the happiest spot below. Home [*or* The First, Best Country]. Goldsmith. *Fr.* The Traveller. GN; LPS-1
But wherefore do not you a mightier way [*or* waie]. Sonnets, XVI. Shakespeare. FaBoEn; PeBoSo
But whether in the uncoloured light of truth. Seven Sonnets, IV. Arthur Hugh Clough. ViPP
"But who art thou, with curious beauty graced." Opportunity. Machiavelli. AWP; JAWP; WBP
But who considers well will find indeed. Andrew Marvell. *Fr.* The Loyal Scot. ViBoPo
But who is this, what thing on [*or* of] sea or land? Delilah. Milton. *Fr.* Samson Agonistes. BoHiPo; SeCePo
But Who the Melodies of Morn Can Tell? James Beattie. *Fr.* The Minstrel, I. EBSV; ViBoPo
(Melodies of Morn, The, *longer sel.*) EV-3
(Morning.) LPS-2
(Nature and the Poets, *longer sel.*) OBEC; SeCePo
But whoso may, thrice happy man him hold. Spenser. *Fr.* An Hymne of Heavenly Beauty. WGRP
But why do I feel so strangely about you? Sphinx. D. H. Lawrence. MoP
"But why do you go?" said the lady, while both sate under the yew. Lord Walter's Wife. Elizabeth Barrett Browning. BeLS; LPS-1
But why then publish? Compliments. Pope. *Fr.* Epistle to Dr. Arbuthnot. LiA
But wine was cheap in old Judea. And bread. Passover. John Beauchamp Thompson. ChIP
But word is come to Warrington. Sir John Butler. *Unknown.* ESPB
But words are things; and a small drop of ink. Fame. Byron. *Fr.* Don Juan, III. GEPC
But yesterday/ I loved. Death of Love. *Unknown.* ChLP; PoHN
But yesterday I met a snake. The Snake. Francis Flagg. DaM
But yesterday she played with childish things. The Dead Child. George Barlow. OBVV; VA
But yesterday the earth drank like a child. A Letter to His Friend Isaac. Judah Halevi. TrJP
But yesterday these few and hoary sheaves. The Two Harvests. Francisco de Medrano. OnPM
But you are tir'd—I'll tell a tale.—"Agreed." Sir Balaam. Pope. *Fr.* Moral Essays. MaPo
But you can Life upon the Poor bestow. To a Good Physician. William Wycherley. ACP
But you should know what Everywoman does. Juvenal, *tr. fr. Latin by* Gilbert Highet. *Fr.* Satires, VI. LaP
But you, Thomas Jefferson. Brave New World. Archibald MacLeish. AmP; OxBA
But you who seek to give and merit fame. Pope. *Fr.* An Essay on Criticism, Pt. I. EnL
"Butch" Weldy. Edgar Lee Masters. *Fr.* Spoon River Anthology. NePA
Butcher Boy, The. *Unknown.* BaBo; ViBoFo
(Butcher's Boy, The.) ABS
Butcher Shop. Jorge Luis Borges, *tr. fr. Spanish by* H. R. Hays. OnPM; TwSpPo
Butchers. Redmond Phillips. NeLNL
Butcher's Boy, The. *Unknown.* *See* Butcher Boy, The.
Buthaina ("Buthaina, if the flower of youth could raise its head anew"). Jamil, *tr. fr. Arabic by* Howard Mumford Jones. LiTW
Butler's Proclamation. Paul Hamilton Hayne. PAH
Butter is in the firkin, and the eggs, The. Getting Ready for Town. Robert P. Tristram Coffin. DDA
Butterbean Tent, The. Elizabeth Madox Roberts. LS; StVeCh; SUS
Buttercup, A. *Unknown.* BoTP
Buttercup Cow. Elizabeth Rendall. TiPo
Buttercup Farm. *Unknown.* SAS
Buttercup nodded and said good-by. August. Celia Thaxter. FaPON; SN; YeAr
Buttercup, the cow, had a new baby calf. The New Baby Calf. Edith H. Newlin. TiPo
Buttercups. Louis Ginsberg. HBVY; YT
Buttercups. Dolly Radford. RIS
Buttercups. Wilfrid Thorley. DD; FaPON; GaP; HBV; HBVY; NLK; OBVV; PC
Buttercups. *Unknown.* BoTP
Buttercups and Daisies. Mary Howitt. BoTP; CBPC; DD; HBV; HBVY, *abr.;* OHIP; OTPC; PECK; TVC
Buttercups and daisies in the meadow. Fairy Gold. John Todhunter. TIP
Buttercups, buttercups stretching for miles. Buttercups. Dolly Radford. RIS
Buttercups, buttercups, what do you hold? Buttercups. Louis Ginsberg. HBVY; YT
Buttercups golden and gay. Buttercups. *Unknown.* BoTP
Buttercups in the sunshine look. A Fairy Song. Elizabeth T. Dillingham. OTPC (1946 ed.); PCH
Buttered Pippin-Pies. John Davies of Hereford. *See* Author Loving These Homely Meats, The.
Butterflies. Chu Miao Tuan, *tr. fr. Chinese by* Henry H. Hart. PoHN
Butterflies. John Davidson, *sometimes at. to* François Coppée. HBV; LEAP
Butterflies. Kageki, *tr. fr. Japanese by* Asataro Miyamori. OnPM
Butterflies. Haniel Long. HBMV
Butterflies, butterflies. Corn-grinding Song. *Tr. fr. Laguna Indian by* Natalie Curtis. AWP; JAWP; SUS; WBP
Butterflies can scarcely find, The. Kyoshi, *tr. fr. Japanese by* Lois J. Erickson. SoLD
Butterflies to Haga faring. Of Haga. Karl Mikael Bellman. AnSL
Butterfly, The. Margaret Avison. BoCaPo; ExPo
Butterfly ("As I walked through my garden"). Hilda Conkling. NP; TiPo
Butterfly ("Butterfly,/ I like the way you wear your wings"). Hilda Conkling. PoRh; TVC; TVSH
Butterfly, The. Alice Archer James. AA
Butterfly. Kwaso, *tr. fr. Japanese by* H. G. Henderson. OnPM
Butterfly, The. Adelaide O'Keeffe. HBV; HBVY
Butterfly, The. Alice Freeman Palmer. HBV; MaRV; POT; PoTo
Butterfly, The. Margaret Rose. BoTP
Butterfly, The. Clinton Scollard. GFA
Butterfly, The. Joseph Skipsey. VA
Butterfly. Mary White Slater. PSO
Butterfly. William Jay Smith. TiPo (1959 ed.)
Butterfly, The. Spenser. *Fr.* Muiopotmos. EV-1
Butterfly. John Banister Tabb. OTPC (1946 ed.); UTS
Butterfly,/ I like the way you wear your wings. Butterfly. Hilda Conkling. PoRh; TVC; TVSH
Butterfly, an idle thing, The. The Butterfly. Adelaide O'Keeffe. HBV; HBVY
Butterfly and the Bee, The. William Lisle Bowles. HBV; HBVY; PECK
Butterfly and the Caterpillar, The. Joseph Lauren. RIS; StaSt
Butterfly and the Snail, The. John Gay. CG
Butterfly, butterfly, brilliant and bright. To a Butterfly. Lady Flora Hastings. OTPC (1923 ed.)
Butterfly, Butterfly, sipping the sand. Butterfly. John Banister Tabb. OTPC (1946 ed.); UTS
Butterfly from flower to flower, The. The Butterfly. Joseph Skipsey. VA
Butterfly in April. Eduard Mörike, *tr. fr. German by* James Edward Tobin. AnGP
Butterfly in Church, A. George Marion McClellan. BANP
Butterfly, one summer morn, A. The Butterfly and the Caterpillar. Joseph Lauren. RIS; StaSt
Butterfly swings on the flower asleep, The. A Sleepy Song. Charles Buxton Going. BOL; RAR; SP; VOD
Butterfly, the cabbage-white, The. The Flying Crooked. Robert Graves. FaBoMo; LiTM (rev. ed.)
Butterfly Weed. Indian Fire. Florence Randal Livesay. CPG
Butterfly's Ball, The. William Roscoe. BoChLi; BoN; CBPC; GoTP; OTPC, *diff. vers.;* TVC; TVSH
Butterfly's First Flight, The. *Unknown.* OTPC
Butterfly's Funeral, The. *Unknown.* OTPC (1923 ed.)

Butternut and walnut. Hillside Pause. Catharine Morris Wright. GoYe
Buttery, sugary, syrupy waffle, A. The Groaning Board. "Pink." InMe
Button to chin. *Unknown.* OxNR
Buttons, a farthing a pair. *Unknown.* OxNR
Buxom Joan. Congreve. *See* Soldier and a Sailor, A.
Buy Me an Ounce and I'll Sell You a Pound. E. E. Cummings. OxBA
Buy my English posies! The Flowers. Kipling. OBVV; PoeT
Buying a Pig. John Heywood. SiCE
Buying Flowers. Po Chü-i, *tr. fr. Chinese by* Ching Ti. WhP
Buz, Quoth the Blue Fly. Ben Jonson. *Fr.* Oberon, the Fairy Prince. NA; TuPP
("Buzz, quoth the blue fly," *sl. diff.*) OxNR
(Catch, A.) EIL
(Sylvan Catch.) BoN
Buzz-saw snarled and rattled in the yard, The. Out, Out. Robert Frost. AmPP (4th ed.); CoV; InP; OxBA; PreP; TCPD; TwP; UnPo
"Buzz!" went the Bee, with a merry din. The Bee and the Lily. Thomas Westwood. TVC; TVSH
Buzzards, The. Martin Armstrong. BLA; HBMV; POTE; TwCV
Buzzards over Pondy Woods, The. Pondy Woods. Robert Penn Warren. MAP; MoAmPo
Buzzing, buzzing, buzzing, my golden-belted bees. The Bees of Middleton Manor. May Probyn. GoBC; JKCP; VA
Buzzy Brown. Leroy F. Jackson. GaP
By a bank as I lay. Dawn. *Unknown.* OBSC
By a Bier-Side. John Masefield. PoeT
By a British Barrow. Andrew Young. NeTW
By a broken-down old dwellin', lookin' somethin' like a shoe. Mandy's Lay. Louis Untermeyer. StaSt
By a Chapel as I Came. *Unknown.* ChTr
By a clear well, within a little field. Of Three Girls and [of] Their Talk. Boccaccio. *Fr.* Sonnets. AWP; JAWP; OnPM; WBP
By a dim road, o'ergrown with dry thin grass. Cut It Down. Mary Elizabeth Coleridge. MoVE
By a dim shore where water darkening. The Reed-Player. Duncan Campbell Scott. OCL; VA
By a dismal Cypress lying. A Song from the Italian. Dryden. *Fr.* Limberham; or, The Kind Keeper. CEP; SeCV-2
By a flat rock on the shore of the sea. The Rock. *Unknown.* ChTr
By a peninsula the painter sat and/ Sketched. Conduct. Samuel Greenberg. CrMA; LiTA
By a peninsula the wanderer sat and sketched. Emblems of Conduct. Hart Crane, *after* Samuel Greenberg. LiTA; LiTM (rev ed.); NAMP; NePA
By a quiet little stream on an old mossy log. The Frog and the Bird. Vera Hessey. BoTP
By a route obscure and lonely. Dream-Land. Poe. AmP; AmPo; AmPP; AnFE; APA; APW; CaAE; CoAnAm; CoBA; CoV; DaM; IAP; LiTA; MOAP; NePA; OxBA; PoFS; UnW
By a silver fountain. Fairy Frolic. Annie Isobel Rentoul. GFA
By a void and soundless river. A Vision of Twilight. Archibald Lampman. UnW
By all the deeds to thy dear glory done. Australia to England. Archibald T. Strong. *Fr.* Sonnets of the Empire. BoAu; PoFr
By all the Dodos! These are thoughts of weight. Dodoism. W. J. Courthope. *Fr.* The Paradise of Birds. OtMeF
By all the glories of the day. Before Action. William Noel Hodgson. MaRV; PC; WGRP
By all thy gloryes willingly I goe. *Unknown.* SeCSL
By all the gods I did not know. Rufinus, *tr. fr. Greek by* Elsie Spoerl. GrPo
By Allah! while the days endure. The Mock Caliph. *Unknown.* EnLi-1
By an alley lined with tumble-down shacks. Mexican Quarter. John Gould Fletcher. Arizona Poems, II. ChMo; CMP; NP; TCPD
By an Ancient Sea. Thomas Curtis Clark. ChIP; QS
By an Ant-Heap. Terence Heywood. BoSA
By an' By. *Unknown.* APW; BoAN-1, *with music*
By an Evolutionist. Tennyson. BEL; EmBrPo; EnLi-2; EPN; PoVP; TCEP
"If my body come from brutes," *2 sts.* MaRV
By an Iris-shadowed Pool. Mary Carolyn Davies. TBM
By an Open Window in Church. Corinne Roosevelt Robinson. BLP; POT; PoTo
By and by. On a Waiter. David McCord. WhC
By April mist. Spring Song. Katharine O'Brien. GoYe
By apt comparisons I thought to praise thee. Missed Again. John T. Durward. JKCP (1926 ed.)
By archy/ the roach that scurries. Ballade of the Under Side. Don Marquis. *Fr.* Archys Life of Mehitabel. InvP
By Arthur's Dale as late I went. Bonny Bee Hom. *Unknown.* BaBo; ESPB; OBB, *sl. diff. vers.*
By ashing sods where shadows mope. The Finding of the Táin. Robert Farren. CoBE
By autumnal walls, shadows are searching there. Limbo. Georg Trakl. AnGP
By, baby bunting. *See* Bye, baby bunting.
By banks where burned awhile the rose. Renascence. Muredach J. Dooher. OnYI
By bars of my prison. The Prisoner. Afanasi Fet. BoR
By Bendemeer's Stream. Thomas Moore. *Fr.* Lalla Rookh. BLP; OTPC (1946 ed.); RG
(Bendemeer.) OBRV
(Girl's Song, A.) CBPC
By Blue Ontario's Shore, *sels.* Walt Whitman.
"Give me the pay I have served for," *fr.* XIV. LEAP
"I listened to the Phantom by Ontario's shore," IX. IAP
Poet, The, IX–XVII. MoAmPo (1950 ed.)
By broad Potomac's silent shore. George Washington. *Unknown.* LPS-3
By broken shafts the greasy river. River Rhondda. Alun Lewis. MoWP
By-by, Lullaby. *Unknown.* AnEC; BOL
By Candlelight. Jules Supervielle, *tr. fr. French by* James Kirkup. MiFP
By candlelight should mortals sup. Candlelight. R. Balfour Daniels. CAG
By Capricorn seas and typhoon. The Green Navies. John Prichard. MoWP
By Cavité on the bay. The Battle of Manila. Richard Hovey. PAH
By chance, at the ball, in the welter. Aleksey Konstantinovich Tolstoy, *tr. fr. Russian by* Sir Cecil Kisch. WaL
By channels of coolness the echoes are calling. Bell-Birds. Henry C. Kendall. BoAu
By Chickamauga's crooked stream the martial trumpets blew. The Ballad of Chickamauga. Maurice Thompson. BlG; MC; PAH
By Cobequid Bay. Alexander Louis Fraser. CaP
By Coelia's Arbor. Sheridan. OnYI
By Cool Siloam's Shady Rill. Reginald Heber. MaRV; OxBoCh; PRWS
By copse and hedgerow, waste and wall. Knapweed. A. C. Benson. HBV; VA
By Cronus' son Poseidon loved and won. Evadne [*or* Evadne and Her Son]. Pindar. *Fr.* Olympian Odes, VI. GrR; OxBG
By daily sipping poison Mithridates used to think. Martial, *tr. fr. Latin by* "T. W. M." Epigrams, V, 76. LaP
By dark severance the apparition head. Painted Head [*or* Painting; a Head]. John Crowe Ransom. CoBMV; CrMA; LiTA; LiTG; LiTM (rev. ed.); MAP; MoAB; MoAmPo; MoPo; MoVE; OxBA; ReMP
By David's mouth, God spoke, "Be still and see that I am God." Canticle of Quietness. Sister Mary Paulinus. JKCP (1955 ed.)
By day. The Jefferson Highway. Sister Mariella. JKCP (1955 ed.)
By day forget your dream, renounce all dreaming! Sacrifice. Hans Egon Holthusen. TwGV
By day Golgotha sleeps, but when night comes. Night at Gettysburg. Don C. Seitz. OHIP
By day my timid passions stand. Serenade. Richard Middleton. HBV; LoP
By day the bat is cousin to the mouse. The Bat. Theodore Roethke. GoTP
By day the fields and meadows cry. The Poet's Call. Thomas Curtis Clark. WGRP
By day, the returning terror of swifts, the scream. Flight. Laurence Whistler. POTE
By day the skyscraper looms in the smoke and sun. Skyscraper. Carl Sandburg. HiLiAm; PoMa; VOD (1935 ed.)
By day . . . tireless smokestacks. Five Towns on the B. and O. Carl Sandburg. OnPM; WoL
By Deputy. Arthur St. John Adcock. CenHV
By desert-deepened wells and chasmed ways. Outlanders. Clark Ashton Smith. DaM
By dint of dart, by push of sharpened spear. A Merry Ballad of Vintners. John Payne. ALV
By divination came the Dorians. In Arcadia. Lawrence Durrell. FaBoMo
By ear, he sd. I, Maximus of Gloucester, to You. Charles Olson. NeAP
By easy slope to west as if it had. Cheyenne Mountain. Helen Hunt Jackson. PoOW
By-Election Idyll. Peter Dickinson. FiBHP
By England's lakes, in grey old age. Matthew Arnold. *Fr.* Stanzas in Memory of the Author of "Obermann." PtP
By every ebb of the river-side. Pisgah. Willard Wattles. WGRP
By every light, in every pose. In God's Eternal Studios. Paul Shivell. *Fr.* The Studios Photographic. HBV
By fate, not option, frugal Nature gave. Xenophanes. Emerson. AnNE; APW
By favorable breezes fanned. Cythère. Paul Verlaine. AWP

By feathers green, across Casbeen. The Phoenix. A. C. Benson. OBEV; OBVV; ShBV-4
By Fiat of Adoration. Oscar Williams. GTBS-W; LiTL; LiTM; NePA
By flowers of china-pink and lily pads. Die Pelzaffen. Charles Spear. AnNZ
By force I live, in will I wish to die. Life Is but Loss. Robert Southwell. SiCE
By Friendship's Ties. Euripides. *See* Pylades.
By Goldsmith's tomb, the City's cry. For a Copy of "The Vicar of Wakefield." Austin Dobson. BPN
By grange and castle when the fields were cool. The Brindled Hare. Thomas S. Jones, Jr. Sonnets of the Saints, II. TBM
By granting charters of peace. An Anglo-Irishman's Complaint. *Unknown.* AnIL
By hard journeys in a dead land. Omphalos; the Well. Seán Jennett. NeIP
By Heaven 'tis false, I am not vain. The Defiance. Aphra Behn. EnLoPo
By heaven's high gift, in case revived were. Concerning Virgil's Aeneids. Nicholas Grimald. ReIE
By Heaven's! 'twas bravely done! Spoken Extempore. Earl of Rochester. SeCePo
By hell 'twas bravely done! what less than this? Satire I: Garnet's Ghost Addressing to the Jesuits. John Oldham. *Fr.* Satires upon the Jesuits. SeEP
By Her Aunt's Grave. Thomas Hardy. Satires of Circumstance, III. MBP; MoAB; MoBrPo; PoVP
By Herndyke Mill there haunts, folks tell. The Silver Bird of Herndyke Mill. Edmund Blunden. GoTL (1949 ed.)
By him lay heavy Sleep, the cousin of Death. Sleep. Thomas Sackville. *Fr.* Induction to "The Mirror for Magistrates." WHA
By his evening fire the artist. Gaspar Becerra. Longfellow. AnNE
By hot noon, in a vale of Dargestan. Dream. Mikhail Lermontov. BoR
By Jove, 'tis done with me, for Isabeau. Rondeau. Vincent Voiture. LiA
By Hsi Tzu Lake. The Wine Shop. Chu Miao Tuan. PoHN
By June our brook's run out of song and speed. Hyla Brook. Robert Frost. AnFE; AnNE; APA; CoAnAm; MAPA; MOAP; TwAmPo
By Killarney's lakes and fells, em'rald isles and winding bays. Killarney. Edmund Falconer. OlF; TreFS
By Logan's streams that rin sae deep. Logan [*or* Logan's] Braes. John Mayne [*wr. at. to* Burns]. BSV; EBSV; MotAn
By Longing I Am Led, *in mod. Eng. Unknown.* TMEV
By loss in play men oft forget. The Gambler's Repentance. Gerald, Baron of Offaly. AnIV
By lost Clonard the river meads still hold. Clonard. Thomas S. Jones, Jr. HBMV; VOD
By love directed, I would choose a wife. The Wife. William Livingston. BAV
. . . By love subsists/ All lasting grandeur, by pervading love. Love. Wordsworth. *Fr.* The Prelude, XIV. RO
By-low, My Babe. *Unknown. See* Balow.
By man came death. Epitaph. Antonia White. DiM
By man forgotten. The Mission Graves. Nora May French. BAP
By man I am forsaken and the world. A Flute. Nobutsuna. OnPM
By many a saint and many a scholar led. Memorial Sonnet. Marjorie Meeker. AnAmPo; LA
By many paths we reach the single goal. From the Foothills. Robert Hillyer. MuM
By Markentura's Flowery Marge. *Unknown.* CSF
By Memory Inspired. *Unknown.* AnIV; GTIV; TIP
By miracles exceeding power of man. Crucifying. John Donne. OBS
By Momba Tracks. Roderic Quinn. NeLNL
By Moscow Self-devoted to a Blaze. Wordsworth. PoFr
By my life I vow. The Vow. Sir Edward Sherburne. SeCL
By Myself. Robert Frost. RIS
By nature's law, what may be, may be now. Procrastination. Edward Young. *Fr.* Night Thoughts. EPP
By Nebo's lonely mountain. Burial of Moses. Cecil Frances Alexander. BeLS; BLPA; BLRP; BPP; GN; HBV; LPS-2; NeHB; OTPC; PTA-2; WBLP
By Night. Philip Jerome Cleveland. BPP; MaRV
By night around my temple grove. Buddha. Arno Holz. AWP
By night on my bed I sought him whom my soul loveth. On My Bed I Sought Him. The Song of Solomon, Bible, *O.T.* TrJP
By night they haunted a thicket of April mist. Spectral Lovers. John Crowe Ransom. SPP; TCPD; TriL
By night we linger'd on the lawn. In Memoriam A. H. H., XCV. Tennyson. AnFE; EmBrPo; EnL; EnSW; EPN; GEPC; LoBV; OAEP; PoEL-5; ReaPo; ViPo; VLEP
By night with flogging whip He rides the breeze. God's Riding. Vincent Starrett. LPS-1
By night within my bed I roamed here and there. The Most Excellent Song Which Was Salomon's. Michael Drayton. *Fr.* The Harmony of the Church. ReIE
By none but me can the tale be told. The White Ship. Dante Gabriel Rossetti. EmBrPo; OnSP; POTT; PoVP
By numbers here from shame or censure free. Poverty in London. Samuel Johnson. *Fr.* London. BeR; ChTr; CoEV; EnLi-1 (1949 ed.); EPP; OBEC; ViBoPo
By One Great Heart. Margaret Deland. OQP; QP-1 (Life.) MaRV; WGRP
By orange grove and palm-tree, we walked the southern shore. Hemlock Mountain. Sarah N. Cleghorn. HBV
By our first strange and fatal[l] interview. On His Mistress [*or* Elegie: On His Mistris]. John Donne. Elegies, XVI. EPS; LiTB; LiTG; LoBV; MeLP; MePo; MyFE; NBE; PoEL-2; ReaPo; ReEn; SeCeV; SeCV-1; SeEP; TriL; TuPP; TwP; ViBoPo
By Parcels Post. George R. Sims. BOHV
By Perfection fooled too long. Perfection. Oliver St. John Gogarty. GTIV
By pillar, post, and trestle. Confirmation for a Rumor. Phyllis McGinley. DDA
By proud New York and its man-piled Matterhorns. Proud New York. John Reed. HBMV; NP
"By Reason of Thy Law." Francis Thompson. VLEP
By Red Bridge grass and flowers overgrow a wilderness. The Red Bridge. Tu Mu. WhP
By Return Mail. Richard Aldridge. NePoAm-2
By right of fires that smelted ore. The Man and the Machine. E. J. Pratt. WoL
By Saint [*or* Saynt] Mary, my lady. To [*or* In Praise of] Mistress [*or* Maystres] Isabel[l] Pennell. John Skelton. *Fr.* The Garlande of Laurell. AtBAP; CH; EG; KN; LiTG; LiTL; LO; OAEP; OBEV (new ed.); OBSC; OxBoLi; PoEL-1; PoFS; SeCeV; TrGrPo; TuPP; ViBoPo
B'y Sara Burned Down, *with music. Unknown.* StDa
By scattered rocks and turbid waters shifting. The Mountain Heart's-Ease. Bret Harte. HBV
By sea and by land. Summer. Richard Burton. *Fr.* Dumb in June. NLK
By seven vineyards on one hill. The Mystic. Witter Bynner. HBV; LBMV; LEAP
By Shaded Wells. Bhartrihari, *tr. fr. Sanskrit by* Paul Elmer More. OnPM
By sloth on sorrow fathered. Lollocks. Robert Graves. ChTr; MoPW
By Solitary Fires. Elizabeth Barrett Browning. *Fr.* Aurora Leigh, V. VA
By some peculiar force centrifugal. To a Book. Elinor Wylie. LiTA
By some sad means, when Reason holds no sway. Philip Freneau. *Fr.* The House of Night. AmPP; PoEL-4
By something formed, I nothing am. In a Glass. Swift. RIS
By special lens, photo-electric cells. A Different Speech. Louise Townsend Nicholl. ImOP
By strangers' coasts and waters, many days at sea. Catullus, *tr. fr. Latin by* Robert Fitzgerald. LaP
By Stubborn Stars, *sels.* Kenneth Leslie.
Sonnet: "Day slipped out of the web of her fog-wet gown." BoCaPo
Sonnet: "My love is sleeping; but her body seems." BoCaPo
Sonnet: "Silver herring throbbed thick in my seine, The." BoCaPo; PeCV; TwCaPo
Sonnet: "Warm rain whispers, but the earth knows best, A." PeCV; TwCaPo
By such an all-embalming summer day. Near Helikon. Trumbull Stickney. AnFE; CoAnAm; LiTA; MOAP; TwAmPo
By that evening window where. Verses for the 60th Birthday of T. S. Eliot. George Barker. ChMP
By That Lake, Whose Gloomy Shore. Thomas Moore. EV-4
By the abortions of the teeming Spring. Litany to Pan. Eden Phillpotts. MBP
By the Alma River. Dinah Maria Mulock Craik. LPS-2
By the Babe Unborn. G. K. Chesterton. AlDL
"By the Babylonish waters." By the Waters of Babylon. Heine. *Fr.* Hebrew Melodies. TrJP
By the beard of the Prophet the Bashaw swore. How We Burned the *Philadelphia.* Barrett Eastman. GA; PaA; PAH
By the Beautiful Sea. Thomas Cole. NePoAm-2
By the Bivouac's Fitful Flame. Walt Whitman. AmPo; BoFr; IAP; MOAP; OxBA; Po; REAL
By the blue sky of a clear vision. Draw the Sword, O Republic. Edgar Lee Masters. AOAH; NV
By the blue taper's trembling light. A Night-Piece on Death. Thomas Parnell. AEV; CEP; EiPP; GTIV; OBEC
By the Bridge. Arthur W. H. Eaton. CPG
By the city dead-house by the gate. The City Dead-House. Walt Whitman. IAP
By the Conemaugh. Florence Earle Coates. PAH
By the cool water the breeze murmurs, rustling. Orchard Song. Sappho. LiTW
By the Cradle. George Macdonald. BOL; OTPC (1946 ed.)

By the cross of expiation/ The Mother stood, and kept her station. Stabat Mater [Dolorosa]. *At. to* Jacopone da Todi. ISi
By the Deep Nine. *At. to* W. Pearce. *See* Heaving the Lead.
By the Earth's Corpse. Thomas Hardy. ChMo; CMP; ViPo
By the edge of the divan. A Song of Self-Pity. Geoffrey Vivien. TwCaPo
By the Fireside. Robert Browning. BMEP; EmBrPo; EV-5; FT; SN, *much abr.;* VLEP
"With me youth led . . . I will speak now," *sel.* LoPS
By the Fireside. Lucy Larcom. LPS-1
By the flow of the inland river. The Blue and the Gray. Francis Miles Finch. AA; BAP; BlG; BLPA; BoPo; BTP; CoBA; DD; FaBoBe; GA; HBV; HH; IAP; LBAP; LEAP; LPS-2; MC; MDAH; NeHB; OBAV; PaA; PAH; PAP; PCD; PEDC; PTA-1; TreF; WBLP
By the fond name that was his own and mine. In Patris Mei Memoriam. John Myers O'Hara. SBMV
By the foot of old Keeper, besides the bohreen. Joseph Sheridan Le Fanu. *Fr.* The Legend of the Glaive. TIP
By the Fountain. Anyte. *See* On a Fountain.
By the glimmer of green and golden. The Passing Year. *Unknown.* PEOR
By the Gray Sea. John Hall Wheelock. TBM
By the Great Wall. Li Po, *tr. fr. Chinese by* Shigeyoshi Obata. ChLP
By the Grey Gulf-Water. A. B. Paterson. TVSH
By the grim grace of the Puritans she had been brought. Sarah Threeneedles. Katharine Lee Bates. BAP; HBMV
By the hoof of the Wild Goat up-tossed. Predestination. Kipling. *Fr.* Plain Tales from the Hills. LoBV
By the hope within us springing. Before the Battle. Thomas Moore. EV-4
By the Isar, in the Twilight. River Roses [*or* All of Roses]. D. H. Lawrence. LEAP; ViBoPo
By the Lake. Lawrence Durrell. *Fr.* Eight Aspects of Melissa. NeBP
By the Lake. Edith Sitwell. *Fr.* Façade. AV
By the lake the orchards lie. Intermezzo. Robert Hillyer. NePoAm
By the lamplit stall I loitered, feasting my eyes. Sight. W. W. Gibson. BMEP; ChMo; CMP; MBP; MoBrPo; NeMA; PoMa
By the light of the Moon God. Dialogue. Prince Yuhara. OnPM
By the little river, still and deep and brown. The Willows. Walter Prichard Eaton. DD; FaPON; HBMV; MPB; MW; OHIP
By the love of the heavenly emperor all things grow as in spring. For My Brother. Su T'ung-po. WhP
By the Margin of the Great Deep. "Æ." CaAE; HBMV; OBEV; OBVV; PoVP
By the margin of the ocean, one morning in the month of June. The Bonny Bunch of Roses O. *Unknown.* OxBoLi
By the merest chance, in the twilight gloom. What My Lover Said. Homer Greene. AA; HBV; TreFS
By the might of the spirit uplifted sheer. Ecstasy. Matthías Jochumsson. IcP
By the Moon We Sport and Play. *Unknown, at. to* John Lyly *and to* Thomas Ravenscroft. *Fr.* The Mayde's Metamorphosis. OTPC; TuPP
(By the Moon.) CH
(Fairy Dances, 1.) ElL
(Fairy Frolic, The.) LEAP; PCH, *longer sel.*
(Urchins' Dance, The.) BoTP
By the North Gate, the wind blows full of sand. Lament of the Frontier Guard. Li Po, *tr. by* Ezra Pound. CoAnAm; CoBMV; TwAmPo; WaaP
By the North Sea. Swinburne. EmBrPo
Sels.
"But afar on the headland exalted," VII. PoVP
"Land that is lonelier than ruin, A," I. PoEL-5; PoVP
By the old Moulmein Pagoda, lookin' eastward to [*or* lazy at] the sea. Mandalay. Kipling. ATP; BEL; BLV; BoLiVe; BPN; ChMo; EnLi-2; EnLit; EPP; HBV; LEAP; LiTB; LiTM (rev. ed.); MBP; MoBrPo; OlF; PIAE; PoVP; PTA-1; ShBV-2; SiTL; StaSt; TCPD; TOP; TreF; TrGrPo; VLEP; YT
By the open highway I betake me. Feodor Ivanovich Tyutchev, *tr. fr. Russian by* Sir Cecil Kisch. WaL
By the Pacific. Herbert Bashford. AA; BAP
By the Pacific Ocean. Joaquin Miller. AA; AnAmPo; LA; MAP; MoAmPo (1942 ed.)
By the path of winter-mutilated clouds you shall reach. Last Song to a Girl of the Waterfront. Otto D'Sola. AnCL
By the pool. Tanka, VII. Lewis Alexander. CDC
By the Pool at the Third Rosses. Arthur Symons. POTT; VLEP
By the Potomac. Thomas Bailey Aldrich. PAH
By the purple haze that lies. Indian Summer. Susanna Moodie. CaP; OCL
By the Rio Grande. The Rio Grande. Sacheverell Sitwell. SeCePo
By the River. Harold Lenoir Davis. NP
By the rivers gently flowing, Illinois, Illinois. Illinois. C. H. Chamberlain. PoRL
By the rivers ot Babylon, there we sat down. Psalm CXXXVII, Bible, *O.T.* AWP; CBOV; ExPo; JAWP; LiTW; OBS; OnPM; PG (1955 ed.); StaSt; TrGrPo; TrJP
By the Road to the Air-Base. Yvor Winters. CrMA; Po
By the Road to the Contagious Hospital. William Carlos Williams. OxBA
(Poem: "By the road . . .") MAP; MoAB; MoAmPo; NeMA; UnPo (3d ed.)
(Spring and All.) CoBMV; ExPo; MoVE
By the roadside, rain or shine. Ragged Robin and Bouncing Bet. Alice Reid. DD
By the rosy cliffs of Devon, on a green hill's crest. Where Love Is. Amelia Josephine Burr. HBV; LoP; SBMV
By the rude bridge that arched the flood. Concord Hymn [*or* Hymn]. Emerson. AA; AmP; AmPo; AmPP; AnAmPo; AnNE; APW; AWP; BAP; BBV; BLPA; BoPo; BTP; CBOV; CoBA; DD; DDA; ExPo; FaBoBe; FaBoEn; FaFP; FaPON; FOAH; GN; GTBS-W; HBV; HBVY; HH; IAP; IDAH; InP; InPo; JAWP; LA; LEAP; LiTA; LiTG; MaRV; MC; MCCG; MOAP; MPB; MW; NeHB; NePA; OHFP; OlF; OnPM; OQP; OTPC; OuHeWo; OxBA; PaA; PAH; PAP; PEDC; PEOR; PG (1945 ed.); PIR; Po; PoFr; PoFS; PoRL; PTA-1; PYM; QP-1; REAL; SeCeV; StVeCh; TCAP; TOP; TreF; TrGrPo; TriL; TVSH; ViBoPo; WaaP; WBP; WoL; YaD; YT
By the ruined arch, where the bougainvillea bled. The World Comes Galloping; a True Story. Robert Penn Warren. Mexico Is a Foreign Country, III. FiMAP
By the rushy-fringèd bank. Milton. *Fr.* Comus. ElSeCe; TOP
By the Salt Margin. Abbie Huston Evans. NePoAm
By the Salpêtrière. Thomas Ashe. VA
By the Sea. Marchette Chute. StVeCh (1955 ed.)
By the Sea. Mary Clemmer. LPS-3
By the Sea. Emily Dickinson. *See* I started early, took my dog.
By the Sea, *parody.* Bayard Taylor. PA
By the Sea. Wordsworth. *See* It Is a Beauteous Evening, Calm and Free.
By the Sea of Galilee. Katharine Lee Bates. ChIP
By the seven stars of her halo. Lady of O. James J. Galvin. ISi
By the shore, a plot of ground. The Ruined Chapel. William Allingham. IrPN; TIP
By the shores [*or* shore] of Gitche [*or* Gitchee] Gumee. Hiawatha's Childhood. Longfellow. *Fr.* The Song of Hiawatha. BoChLi; FaPON; GFA; MPB; OHFP; PECK, PoRh; RAR; ShBV-1; StVeCh; TiPo; TreF; TVSH; WBLP
By the shrouded gleam of the western skies. Keenan's Charge. George Parsons Lathrop. AA; BBV; HBV; MC; MDAH; OBAV; PAH; PAP; PFY
By the side of a green stagnate pool. A Pastoral. G. A. Stevens. CoMu
By the side of a murmuring stream an elderly gentleman sat. The Elderly Gentleman. George Canning. BOHV; NA; PA
By the side of the Hoongting bridge, to the east of the bridge Haelo. Poems Translated from the Chinese. *Unknown, tr. by* John Francis Davis. RO
By the side of the railway track. The Telephone Pole. Karel van den Oever. OnPM
By the sierra gardens. Songs of Several Lands. Antonio Machado. AnSpL-2
By the Statue of King Charles at Charing Cross. Lionel Johnson. BMEP; CaAE; CoBE; GTIV; GTML; HBV; JKCP; LEAP; MBP; MoBrPo; OBEV (new ed.); OBMV; OBVV; PoEL-5; PoeT; POTT; PoVP; ShBV-4; ViP; ViPP; VLEP
By the street's noise muffled, the hammers. Building a Skyscraper. Louis Dudek. BoCaPo (1948 ed.)
By the time you swear you're his. Unfortunate Coincidence. Dorothy Parker. ALV; TreF; WhC
By the Turnstile. John Francis O'Donnell. IrPN
By the vats of Dionysus, where the sacred vine-juice splashes. On an Old Tippleress. *Unknown.* GrPE
By the victory there much honour unto his beard he did. The Cid and the Count of Barcelona. *Unknown.* *Fr.* The Cid. AnSpL-1
By the Waterfall. Friedrich Adler, *tr. fr. German by* Jethro Bithell. TrJP
By the Waters of Babylon. Heine, *tr. fr. German by* Charles Godfrey Leland. *Fr.* Hebrew Melodies. TrJP
By the Waters of Babylon. Edgar Lee Masters. TBM
By the waters of Babylon, there we sat down. *See* By the rivers of Babylon . . .
By the waters of Babylon we sat down and wept. Super Flumina Babylonis. Swinburne. AnFE; LiA; OBVV; PoEL-5· PoFr; PoVP; ViPo; VLEP
By the waters of Life we sat together. An Old Man's Idyl. Richard Realf. AA; HBV; OBAV

By the Way, *sel.* William Allingham.
"You see/ Nestled into a hollow of the downs." EnSW; IrPN
By the Way. Annie Johnson Flint. PraP
By-the-Way. Patrick MacGill. BMEP
By the wayside, on a mossy stone. Old. Ralph Hoyt. AA; LPS-1
By the Weir. W. W. Gibson. MoVE; POTE
By the wide lake's margin I marked her lie. Shelter. Charles Stuart Calverley. PCD
By the Winding River ("Every day on the way home"). Tu Fu, *tr. fr. Chinese by* Kenneth Rexroth. OnPC
By the Winding River ("Everywhere petals are flying"). Tu Fu, *tr. fr. Chinese by* Kenneth Rexroth. OnPC
By the wireless I can hear. Wireless. Rodney Bennett. BoTP
By the Wood. Robert Nichols. ChMP; HBMV; LBBV; NP
By these presents be it known. Countess Temple [*or* Anne Grenville, Countess Temple], Appointed Poet Laureate to the King of the Fairies. Horace Walpole. CEP; OBEC
By these slow shadows and the frosted air. Calvinist Autumnal. Elizabeth B. Harrod. NePoEA
By thine own tears thy song must tears beget. The Song-Throe. Dante Gabriel Rossetti. The House of Life, LXI. BPN; PoVP; ViPo
By this body's lonely ark. To Fear. Clifford J. Laube. JKCP (1926 ed.)
By this bright bank the easy noon. The River Glideth in a Secret Tongue. Anthony Ostroff. NePoAm-2
By this cold shuddering fit of fear. The Glen of Silence. "Hugh MacDiarmid." NeBP
By this he knew she wept with waking eyes. Modern Love, I. George Meredith. AnEnPo; BEL; BMEP; EmBrPo; EnLi-2; EnLit; EnLoPo; HBV; HoPM; LEAP; OAEP; Po; PoEL-5; POTT; PoVP; TyEnPo; ViP; ViPo; ViPP; VLEP
By this, the dreadfull beast drew nigh to hand. The Death of the Dragon. Spenser. *Fr.* The Faerie Queene, I. WHA
By this the sun was all one glitter. Lines. John Masefield. *Fr.* The Everlasting Mercy. GBV
By this, though deep the evening fell. Flodden [*or* The Battle *or* Flodden; the Last Stand]. Sir Walter Scott. *Fr.* Marmion, VI. BSV; LH; PoEL-4; PoFr
By those soft tods of wooll. A Conjuration, to Electra. Robert Herrick. AtBAP; PoEL-3
By Thy Birth, Thou blessed Lord. Blessed May Thou Be, Sweet Jesus. *At. to* Richard Smert. AnEC
By Thy Life I Live. Mme Guyon. MaRV
By thys fyre I warme my handys. The Months. *Unknown.* ChTr
By Tigris, or the streams of Ind. They Had No Poet. Don Marquis. DDA
By vigilance some minds may keep. Invective. Pearce Young. PtPa
By Way of Preface. Edward Lear. *See* How Pleasant to Know Mr. Lear.
By way of pretext. Pretext. Yakamochi. *Fr.* Manyo Shu. AWP; JAWP; LiTW; WBP; WoL
By ways remote and distant waters sped. On the Burial of His Brother [*or* Hail and Farewell]. Catullus. AWP; EnLi-1; JAWP; LiA; OuHeWo; WBP
By weight of the wearying years, and by grievous illness. Epitaphium Felis. John Jortin. PoC
By Wellesbourne and Charlcote ford. Women Singing. Sir Henry Taylor. OBVV
By what astrology of fear or hope. Longfellow. *Fr.* To a Child. FaBoEn
By what bold passion am I rudely led. Sir William Davenant. *Fr.* Gondibert, I. FaBoEn; OBS
By what strange whimsies is a man's fate swayed. Barabbas. William E. Brooks. BPP
By what word's power, the key of paths untrod. Heart's Hope. Dante Gabriel Rossetti. The House of Life, V. BMEP; BPN; EmBrPo; EnLit; EPN; HBV; LEAP; PoVP; ViP; ViPo; VLEP
By Wood and Wold. Adam Lindsay Gordon. BoAu
By woods and water, whose houses are these. The Grand Houses at Lo-yang. Po Chü-i. TrCh
By World Laid Low. *Unknown, tr. fr. Irish.* ChTr
By yon bonnie banks, and by yon bonnie braes. The Bonnie Banks o' Loch Lomond [*or* Loch Lomond]. *Unknown, at. to* Lady John Scott. OlF; TreFS
By Yon Burn Side. Robert Tannahill. HBV
By yon castle wa', at the close of the day. There'll Never Be Peace till Jamie Comes Hame. Burns. CBE
By Zeus!/ Shout word of this. The Grand Canyon. Adelaide Crapsey. PoeMoYo
By Zeus I charge thee, whose clear lightnings shine. Heracles' Errant Love [*or* Heracles]. Sophocles. *Fr.* Trachiniae. GrR; OxPG
By Zeus the Saviour, quite the gentleman. As between Gentlemen's Gentlemen. Aristophanes. *Fr.* The Frogs. GrR
Bye Baby Bunting. Boston Nursery Rhymes. Joseph Cook. BOHV; PA
Bye [*or* By], baby bunting. Mother Goose. BoChLi; HBV; HBVY; OTPC; OxNR; PPL; RIS; SAS; TiPo; StVeCh; TrAS, *with music*
Bye, Baby, Night Is Come. Mary Mapes Dodge. BOL; RAR
Bye-bye. *Unknown. See* When Little Birdie Bye-bye Goes.
Bye, bye, baby bunting/ Your Daddy's gone a-hunting. *Unknown.* OxNR
Bye-low Song, The. *Unknown.* BOL
Bye-o, baby, bye. Mamma's Gone to the Mail Boat. *Unknown.* OuSiCo
Bye O my baby. Sorrow and Woe—English. *Unknown.* BOL
Bygones. Bert Leston Taylor. BOHV; HBMV
Bylo-Land. James B. Kenyon. BOL
Bylo Land. *Unknown.* BOL
By'm By, *with music. Unknown.* AS
Byron. Clyde Walton Hill. LPS-1
Byron, *sel.* Joaquin Miller.
In Men Whom Men Condemn [as Ill]. BAP; HBV; MaRV; MoAmPo (1942 ed.); NeMA; OQP; QP-2
(Byron.) BLP; LBAP; MAP; PC
(Charity.) PoeMoYo
(Lines: "In men whom men condemn as ill.") BBV (1951 ed.)
Byron. Robert Pollok. *Fr.* The Course of Time, IV. LPS-3
Byron! how sweetly sad thy melody! To Byron. Keats. PtP
Byron, the beautiful, the much maligned. Byron. Clyde Walton Hill. LPS-1
Byron the Voluptuary. Sir William Watson. VA
Byron! 'tis thine alone on eagles' pinions. To Lord Byron. Richard Henry Wilde. SPP
Byron's Conspiracy. George Chapman. *See* Conspiracy of Charles, Duke of Byron, The.
Byron's Farewell. Byron. *See* On This Day I Complete My Thirty-sixth Year.
Byron's Latest Verses. Byron. *See* On This Day I Complete My Thirty-sixth Year.
Byron's Tragedy. George Chapman. *See* Tragedy of Charles, Duke of Byron, The.
Byrontown, *with music.* Larry Gorman. ShS
Bystanders, The. Mark Van Doren. MOAP
Bytuene Mersh and Averil. *Unknown. See* Alisoun.
Byzantium. W. B. Yeats. BrBE; CoBMV; CoEV; EnLP; FaBoEn; FaBoMo; GTBS-W; LiTM; LoBV; MaPo; MoAB; MoP; MoPo; OAEP (2d ed.); OnYI; PoE; PoLFOT; ReaPo; SeCePo; SeCeV; TwHP

C

C. C. Rider (A *and* B *vers.*), *with music. Unknown.* AS
C is for the Circus. Phyllis McGinley. *Fr.* All Around the Town. TiPo
C. L. M. John Masefield. BLV; BMEP; BoLiVe; ChMo; CMP; HBV; LiTM; MBP; MoBrPo; MotAn; POTT
(To His Mother, C. L. M.) OBVV
C. S. A. Commissioners, The. *Unknown.* PAH
C Stands for Civilization. Kenneth Fearing. TrJP
Ça ira! *sel. Unknown, tr. fr. French by* John Oxenford.
"All will go right—will go right—will go right," 3 *sts.* PoFr
Ca' the Yowes to the Knowes. Burns. EBSV; EnRP; LPS-1; PoE
(Hark! the Mavis.) OBEV
Ca' the Yowes to the Knowes. Isobel Pagan. EBSV, *sl. diff. vers.*; OBEV; TCEP
Cabin-Kid. Tristan Corbière, *tr. fr. French by* Dudley Fitts. AnFP
Cabin on the mountain side hid in a grassy nook, A. Connla's Well. "Æ." TIP
Cabin Where Lincoln Was Born, The. Robert Morris. GA
Cable Hymn, The. Whittier. PAH
Caboose Thoughts. Carl Sandburg. AnAmPo; ChMo; CMP; IAP; LA; OnAP
Cachalot, The. E. J. Pratt. BoCaPo
"Where Cape Delgado strikes the sea," *sel.* CaP
Cackle, cackle, Mother Goose. *Unknown.* OxNR; SiTL
Cacoëthes Scribendi. Oliver Wendell Holmes. AA; APW; BOHV
Cactus, The. Manuel Bandeira, *tr. fr. Portuguese by* Dudley Poore. AnCL
Cactus. Terence Heywood. BoSA
Cactus, The. *Unknown.* APW
Cactus towers, straight and tall, The. In Mexico. Evaleen Stein. AA
Cacus, if any chance on him to call. In Cacum. Thomas Bastard. SiCE

Cad, The. *Unknown, tr. fr. Old Irish by* Seán O'Faoláin. SiB
Cadences. Samuel T. Clover. POT; PoTo
Cadences. John Payne. VA
Cadenus and Vanessa, *sel.* Swift.
"Cupid tho' all his Darts were lost." OxBI
Cadenza. Miriam Waddington. CaP
Cadgwith. Lionel Johnson. CoBE; GTBS; JKCP; OBVV; PoVP
(Song: "My windows open to the autumn night.") MeRV
"Mary Star of the sea," III. ISi
Cadmus and Harmonia. Matthew Arnold. *Fr.* Empedocles on Etna. OBVV; ViPo
("Far, far from here.") NBE
(Song of Callicles, The.) FiP
Caecus awaked, was told the Sun appeared. Nullum Stimulum Ignavis. Henry Parrot. SiCE
Cædmon. George Garrett. NePoAm-2
Cædmon. Thomas S. Jones, Jr. InP
Cædmon. Norman Nicholson. FaBoTw
Caelia, *sel.* William Browne.
"Fairest, when by the rules of palmistry," III. ElSeCe
Caelia, *sel.* Sir David Murray.
Sonnet: "Ponder thy cares, and sum them all in one." ElL
Caelica, *sels.* Fulke Greville.
"Absence, the noble truce," XLV [XLIV]. PoEL-1
(Absence and Presence.) OBSC
"All my senses, like beacons flame," LVI. PoEL-1
"Away with these self-loving lads," LII. AtBAP; ReIE; SiCE
(Another, of His Cynthia.) TuPP
(Cynthia.) OBSC; RiBV
(Of His Cynthia.) ElL; ElSeCe
(Song to His Cynthia.) ViBoPo
"Caelica, I overnight was finely used," XXXVIII. PeBoSo; TuPP
"Cupid, my little boy, come home again[e]," XXXV. AtBAP; PeBoSo
"Cupid, my pretty boy, leave off thy crying," XXV. AtBAP
"Cupid, thou naughty boy, when thou wert loathed," XII. TuPP
(To Cupid.) ES
"Cynthia, because your horns look divers [*or* diverse] ways," LIV [LV]. ElSeCe; SiCE
"Cynthia, whose glories are at full forever," XVII. ElSeCe
"Downe in the depth of mine iniquity," XCIX [C]. OBS; SiCE
(Down in the Depth.) LiTG
(Saving God, The.) LoBV (2d ed.)
"Earth, The, with thunder torn, with fire blasted," LXXXVII. ElSeCe; PeBoSo; SiCE; TuPP
"Eternal [*or* Eternall] Truth, almighty, infinite," XCVII [XCVIII]. OBS; OxBoCh; SiCE
"Faction, that ever dwells," XXIX.
(Love and Fortune.) OBSC
"Farewell, sweet boy, complain not of my truth," LXXXV.
(Farewell to Cupid.) OBSC
"Fie [*or* Fye] foolish Earth, think [*or* thinke] you the heaven wants glory," XVI. LO; PoEL-1; ReIE; SiCE; TuPP
(Love's Glory.) OBSC
"I, with whose colors [*or* colours] Myra dressed [*or* drest] her head," XXII. AtBAP; EG; ElSeCe; PoE
(Myra.) CoEV; ElL; EV-1; GTBS-W; LoBV; OBEV; OBSC
(To Myra.) LiTB; LiTG; LiTL; ViBoPo
"In the time when herbs and flowers," LXXVI.
(Caelica and Philocell.) OBSC
"In the window of a grange," LXXIV.
(Love and Honour.) OBSC
"Love, the delight of all well-thinking minds," I. OBSC; PoE; SiCE
"Malice and love in their ways opposite," XCV. SiCE
"Man, dreame no more of curious mysteries," LXXXVIII [LXXXIX]. MePo; OBS
"Men that delight to multiply desire," XCIV [XCV]. OBS; SiCE
"More than most fair, full of that heavenly fire," III. ElL; SiCE
(To His Lady.) OBSC
"Nurse-life wheat within his green husk growing, The," XL. PeBoSo
(Youth and Maturity.) ES; OBSC; RiBV
"O false and treacherous Probability," CIII [CIV]. OBS; OxBoCh; RiBV
"Selfe-pitties teares, wherein my hope lyes drown'd," VIII. AtBAP
"Sion lies [*or* Syon lyes] waste, and Thy Jerusalem," CIX [CX]. OxBoCh; PoEL-1; ReIE; SiCE; TriL; TuPP
"Three things there be in man's opinion deare," CV [CVI]. LiTB; LiTG; OBS; PoEL-1; SiCE
"Under a throne I saw a virgin sit," LXXXI [LXXXII]. ReIE; SiCE; TuPP
"Whenas [*or* When as] man's life, the light of human lust." LXXXVII [LXXXVIII]. ElSeCe; GTBS-W; LiTB; MePo; OBS; OxBoCh; PoD; PoEL-1
"Who grace, for zenith had, from which no shadowes grow," LXXXIII [LXXXIV]. PoEL-1
(Despair.) OBSC
"World, that all contains, is ever moving, The," VII. ReIE; SiCE; TuPP
(Change.) CoEV; OBSC
"Wrapp'd [*or* Wrapt] up, O Lord, in man's degeneration," XCVIII [XCIX]. OxBoCh; SiCE
"You little stars [*or* starres] that live in skies [*or* skyes]," IV. ElL; NBE; ReIE; RiBV; SiCE; TuPP
(His Lady's Eyes.) OBSC
"You that seek what life is in death," LXXXIII.
(Time and Eternity.) OBSC
Caelica and Philocell. Fulke Greville. Caelica, LXXVI. OBSC
Caelica, I overnight was finely used. Caelica, XXXVIII. Fulke Greville. PeBoSo; TuPP
Caelius, my Lesbia, that one, that only Lesbia. Whom Lesbia Loved. Catullus. LiTW; RoL
Caesar, *sel.* Thomas Caulfield Irwin.
"Within the dim museum room." TIP
Caesar. Paul Valéry, *tr. fr. French by* C. F. MacIntyre. WaaP
Caesar, afloat with his fortunes! The Turtle. *Unknown.* PAH
Caesar and Pompey. George Chapman. *See* Tragedy of Caesar and Pompey, The.
Caesar Borgia, *sel.* Nathaniel Lee
Blush Not Redder than the Morning. SeCL
Caesar Remembers. William Kean Seymour. HBMV; LBBV; OnPP; PoeMoYo
Caesar, serene Caesar, your foot on all. Caesar. Paul Valéry. WaaP
Caesar, that proud man. Caesar Remembers. William Kean Seymour. HBMV; LBBV; OnPP; PoeMoYo
Caesura. Kenneth Mackenzie. BoAV
Café Scene. Saunders Lewis, *tr. fr. Welsh by* Gwyn Williams. PrWP
Café Society. Theognis, *tr. fr. Greek by* J. M. Edmonds. GrR
Cage, The. Martin Armstrong. BLV; PoFr; POTE
Cage, The. Elizabeth Bartlett. NePoAm-2
Caged Bird, A. Sarah Orne Jewett. BLA; SN
Caged Eagle, The. John Gould Fletcher. ChMo; CMP
Caged Eagle's Death Dream, The. Robinson Jeffers. *Fr.* Cawdor. PoF
Caged in old woods, whose reverend echoes wake. Captivity. Samuel Rogers. FaBoEn
Caged Mongoose, The. Constance Hollar. PoNe
Caged Skylark, The. Gerard Manley Hopkins. ChMo; LiTM; MBP; MoAB; MoPo; MoBrPo; OBMV; RiBV; ViPP
Caiaphas, Pilate and Herod. Fellowship. Elinor Lennen. ChIP
Cailleach Bein-y-Vreich. John Campbell Shairp. VA
Cain. Théodore Agrippa d'Aubigné, *pr. tr. fr. French. Fr.* Les Tragiques. LiA
Cain and Abel. Itzik Manger, *tr. fr. Yiddish by* Sarah Zweig Betsky. OnCuPl
Cain Shall Not Slay Abel Today on Our Good Ground. Malcolm Lowry. BoCaPo (1948 ed.); PeCV
Cairn Builders. "An Pilibin." GTIV
Cairo Jag. Keith Douglas. NePoEA
Caisson Song. Edmund L. Gruber. OlF; TreF
Cakes and Ale. *Unknown. See* I Gave Her Cakes; I Gave Her Ale.
Cakes I have eaten, the wine I have drunk, The. All Is Hidden, Naught Concealed. Grace Margaret Robertson. MuM
Calabash wherein she served my food, The. The Serving Girl. Gladys May Casely Hayford. CDC; GoSl; PoNe
Calais Sands. Matthew Arnold. OAEP
Calchas before the Body of Ajax. James Shirley. *See* Death the Leveller.
Calchas the Seer. Sophocles, *tr. fr. Greek by* Robert Whitelaw. *Fr.* Ajax. GrR
Caldwell of Springfield. Bret Harte. PAH
Caledonian Market, The. William Plomer. ChMP; HaMV
Calendar. Witter Bynner. *Fr.* Chapala Poems. NP
Calendar, A. Sara Coleridge. *See* Garden Year, The.
Calendar, The. *Unknown.* PCH
Calendar Rhyme. Flora Willis Watson. BoTP
Calf in the Goldenrod. Judy Van der Veer. MuM
Calf-Path, The. Sam Walter Foss. CV; DDA; HBV; HBVY
(Boston, *much abr.*) BoHiPo
Calf's Head Meeting, A. Samuel Butler. *Fr.* Hudibras. BeR
Calgary Station. Isabel Ecclestone Mackay. CPG
Caliban ("Be not afeard; the isle is full of noises"). Shake-

speare. *Fr.* The Tempest, III, ii. FiP
("Be not afeard [*or* affeard], the isle is full of noises [*or* noyses]." AtBAP; UnS
(Caliban on the Island.) CoEV
(To Dream Again.) TrGrPo
Caliban in the Coal Mines. Louis Untermeyer. BAP; CP; HBV; LEAP; MAP; MaRV; MoAmPo; NeMA; NV; PoeMoYo; PoMa; TreFS; TrJP
Caliban on the Island. Shakespeare. *See* Caliban.
Caliban upon Setebos. Robert Browning. AWP; BPN; EM-2; EmBrPo; EPN; GEPC; OAEP; PoVP; ViPo; VLEP; WGRP
Calico Pie. Edward Lear. BoN; FaBoCh; FaPON; GoTP; LiL; LoGBV; MPB; SAS; TrGrPo; WhC
Calidore. Keats. EmBrPo
California. Thomas Lake Harris. AA
California. Lydia Huntley Sigourney. MC; PAH
California, *with music. Unknown.* AS
California Christmas, A. Joaquin Miller. OBAV
California Dissonance. James Rorty. MOAP
California Joe. "Captain Jack" Crawford. CoSo; CSF
California Stage Company, The. *Unknown.* CoSo; CSF
California Trail. *Unknown.* CSF
California Vignette, A. Robinson Jeffers. *Fr.* Tamar. PC
Caligula, envying the bright fames. Of the Small Respect Had of Learned Men in General. John Davies of Hereford. SiCE
Caligula, pacing thro' his pillar'd hall. Power. Sir Ronald Ross. TCPD
Caliph and Satan, The. James Freeman Clarke, *versified fr.* Tholuck's *tr. fr. the Persian.* LPS-3
Caliph, I did thee wrong. I hailed thee late. To the Sultan. Sir William Watson. BMEP; LEAP
Caliph's Draught, The. Sir Edwin Arnold. VA
Calisto, *sel.* John Crowne.
Kind Lovers, Love On. InvP
(Song: "Kind lovers, love on.") ALV; SeCL
Call, A. "Æ." NV
Call, The. Björnstjerne Björnson. RAR
Call, The. Thomas Curtis Clark. PGD
Call, The. Daniel Corkery. OnYI
Call, The. Cora D. Fenton. NLK
Call, The. Edgar A. Guest. NLK
Call, The. John Hall. AEV; FaBoEn; LO; MeLP; MePo; OBS; SeCL; ViBoPo
Call, The. George Herbert. MeRV
Call, The. Reginald Wright Kauffman. HBV
Call, The. Edwin Markham. PoTo
Call, The. Charlotte Mew. ChMP; MoP
Call, The. Thomas Osbert Mordaunt. *See* Sound, Sound the Clarion.
Call, The. Katharine Tynan. BMEP
Call, The. *Unknown.* OBEV
"Call All." *Unknown.* BoHiPo; PAH
Call all hands to man the capstan. Rolling Home, *vers.* I. *Unknown.* ShS
Call—call—and bruise the air. Expression. Isaac Rosenberg. MoBrPo
"Call down the hawk from the air." The Hawk. W. B. Yeats. AtBAP
Call for the Robin Redbreast [and the Wren]. John Webster. *Fr.* The White Devil, V, iv. AtBAP; BrBE; CenL; ChTr; ElSeCe; ExPo; FaBoCh; LoGBV; OAEP; PoE; PoEL-2; PoRA; ReaPo; ReEn; SeCePo; SeCeV; SiCE; TuPP; ViBoPo
(Cornelia's Song.) CoEV; OBS; TrGrPo
(Dirge, A: "Call for the robin redbreast and the wren.") AEV; BCEP; BEL; CBOV; ElL; EnLi-1; EV-2; FaBoEn; GTBS; GTSE; GTSL; HBV; KN; LEAP; LiA; LiTB; OBEV; RiBV; ThWaDe; UnPo; WHA
(Funeral Dirge for Marcello.) AnFE
(Land Dirge. A.) BLV; CH; GTBS-D; GTBS-W; LoBV
(Song: "Call for the robin redbreast and the wren.") CaAE; ShBV-3
Call for True Repentance, A. Jeremiah, VII: 1-20, Bible, *O.T.* WoL
Call Him High Shelley Now. Alfred Kreymborg. *See* Man Whom Men Deplore, A.
Call him who loves you to your feast. Neighbours and Kinsfolk. Hesiod. *Fr.* Works and Days. OxBG
Call Home the Heart. Michael Drayton. *See* To His Coy Love.
Call it neither love nor spring madness. Without Name. Pauli Murray. PoNe
Call it not vain; they do not err. Nature's Sympathy with the Poet. Sir Walter Scott. *Fr.* The Lay of the Last Minstrel, V. EV-4; OBRV
"Call Junius!" From the crowd a shadow stalked. At the Gate of Heaven. Byron. *Fr.* The Vision of Judgment. OBRV
Call John the Boatman, *with music. Unknown.* ShS
Call Martha Corey. The Trial. Longfellow. *Fr.* Giles Corey of the Salem Farms. PAH
Call me at the one among your hours. Sonnets to Orpheus, Pt. II, XXIII. Rainer Maria Rilke. AnGP
Call me friend or foe. The Comrade. Lee Wilson Dodd. HBMV
Call me no more. His Lachrimae or Mirth, Turn'd to Mourning. Robert Herrick. SeCV-1; SeEP
Call me no more, O gentle stream. To a River in the South. Sir Henry Newbolt. CH; MM
Call me no more the cursed tree. I Saw Death Slain. William Capell. ChIP
Call Me Not Back from the Echoless Shore. *Unknown.* BLPA
Call Me Not Dead. Richard Watson Gilder. HBV; WGRP
Call me not false, beloved. The Bridegroom. Kipling. *Fr.* Epitaphs of the War. SoV
Call no faith false which e'er has brought. Tolerance. Sir Lewis Morris. OBVV
Call not on comfort lest she come. Passivity. Mary Fullerton. BoAV
Call not thy wanderer home as yet. Germinal. "Æ." MoBrPo; OBEV (new ed.); OBMV; TwCV
Call of Spring, The. Pao Lin Hui, *tr. fr. Chinese by* Henry H. Hart. PoHN
Call of Spring, The. Shih Ch'eng Le, *tr. fr. Chinese by* Henry H. Hart. PoHN
Call of the Bugles, The. Richard Hovey. AA
Call of the Morning, The. George Darley. OnYI
Call of the Plains, The. Ethel MacDiarmid. SCC
Call of the Road, The. Florence Nash. DDA
Call of the Scot, The. Ruth Guthrie Harding. *See* Call to a Scot, The.
Call of the Sea, The. Howard James Savage. CAG
Call of the Spring, The. Alfred Noyes. SUS; VOD
Call of the Wild, The. Robert W. Service. CaP; NLK; OCL
Call of the Woods, The. Shakespeare. *See* Under the Greenwood Tree.
Call off your eyes from care. A Young Man's Exhortation. Thomas Hardy. ViPP
Call on Sir Walter Raleigh, A. Sarah M. Bryan Piatt. AA
Call on thy children of the hill. Carolina. Henry Timrod. PoRL
Call out, celebrate the beam. The Tears of a Muse in America. F. T. Prince. FaBoMo
"Call Rose Costara!" The Night Court. Ruth Comfort Mitchell. BAP; HBV
Call the fire engines out! Turn the hydrants on! Fire. Merrill Moore. MOAP
Call the roller of big cigars. The Emperor of Ice-Cream. Wallace Stevens. AmP; AmPP (4th ed.); CoBMV; CoV; FaBoMo; LiTA; LyMo; MoPo; MoVE; NePA; OxBA; PoFS; ViBoPo (1958 ed.)
Call to a Scot, The. Ruth Guthrie Harding. HBV
(Call of the Scot, The.) BoHiPo
Call to Action, A. Callinus, *tr. fr. Greek by* T. F. Higham. GrL; OxBG; WaaP
("How long will ye slumber? when will ye take heart? *tr. by* H. N. Coleridge.) GrPo
(Rallying Song, *tr. by* H. N. Coleridge.) GrR; PoFr
Call to Arms, A. Mary Raymond Shipman Andrews. MC; PAH
Call to Freedom. Hazel Harper Harris. PoTo
Call to God's Service. Francis William Newman. GrCo-1
Call to Nature and All Men to Praise God, A. Psalms, CXLVIII, Bible, *O.T.* *See* Song of Praise, A.
Call to Pentecost, A. Inez M. Tyler. BLRP
Call to the Colors, The. Arthur Guiterman. FOAH; PaA; PAH
Call to the Strong, The. William Pierson Merrill. BLRP
Call to the swan and bid him bring. Childless. L. A. G. Strong. POTE
Call to the Wild, A. Lord Dunsany. OnYI
Call us not weeds, we are flowers of the sea. Flowers of the Sea. *Unknown.* RO
Callahan. *Unknown.* OuSiCo
Callao. Crosbie Garstin. PoeMoYo
Calle de Toledo, Madrid. John Dos Passos. *Fr.* Winter in Castile. VOD (1935 ed.)
Called Away. Richard Le Gallienne. *See* I Meant to Do My Work Today.
Called Back. Emily Dickinson. *See* Just lost when I was saved!
Called out by fife and drum. Memorial Day. Alma Adams Wiley. PEDC
Called son by many lands. St. Patrick's Treasure. Patrick J. Carroll. JKCP
Caller Herrin'. Lady Nairne. EBSV; EV-3; HBV; MCCG; OBRV
Caller Water, *sel.* Robert Fergusson.
"Whan father Adie first pat spade in." EPP
Callicles' Song. Matthew Arnold. *Fr.* Empedocles on Etna, II. BMEP; BPN; ChTr; EmBrPo; LoBV
(Apollo.) LH; ViPo
(Last Song of Callicles.) VLEP

Callicles' Song (*continued*)
(Song for Apollo.) FiP
(Song of Callicles [on Etna], The.) GTBS; OBEV; OBVV; ShBV-3
("Through the black, rushing smoke-bursts.") PoVP
Callignotus and Ionis. Callimachus, *tr. fr. Greek by* G. M. Young. GrL
Callimachus to Heraclitus. Callimachus, *tr. fr. Greek by* Ralph Marcus. OnPM
Calling, The. Luis Felipe Contardo, *tr. fr. Spanish by* Thomas Walsh. CAW
Calling, The. George Sigerson. JKCP (1926 ed.); TIP
Calling and the melody all night long, The. Chapultepec Park. Muriel Rukeyser. FiMAP
Calling Eagles. Leo Kennedy. TwCaPo
Calling in the Cat. Elizabeth J. Coatsworth. AnAmPo; LA; NeMA
Calling-One's-Own. *Tr. fr. Ojibwa Indian by* Charles Fenno Hoffman. NV
Calling the Doctor. John Wesley Holloway. BANP; IHA
Calling, the heron flies athwart the blue. The Creek-Road. Madison Cawein. AA
Calling the Violet. Lucy Larcom. MPB
Calling to mind, my eyes went long about. The Excuse. Sir Walter Ralegh. SiPS
Calling to mind [*or* minde], since first my love begun. Idea, LI. Michael Drayton. OBSC; PoEL-2; RiBV; SiCE
Calliope, *with music. Unknown.* AS
Calliope,/ As ye may se. Why Were Ye Calliope Embrawdred with Letters of Golde? John Skelton. CaAE
Calloused grass lies hard, The. By the Road to the Air-Base. Yvor Winters. CrMA; Po
Callow young were huddling in the nests, The. Scorned. Alexander Smith. OBVV
Calls. Carl Sandburg. NP
Calm. Stanton A. Coblentz. EtS
Calm, The. John Donne. LoBV; ReEn; ReIE; SeEP; SG; TuPP; TwP
(Calme, The.) MePo
Calm and Full the Ocean. Robinson Jeffers. WaP
Calm and implacable. Imitation. Anthony C. Deane. BOHV; PA
Calm and keen as the Punjab cold. Havildar Ganga Singh, V. C. Stanley Gerald Dunn. MM
Calm and Sinless Peace. Milton. *Fr.* Paradise Regained, IV. LiA
Calm and Storm on Lake Leman. Byron. *See* Lake Leman ("Clear, placid Leman!").
Calm as that second summer which precedes. Charleston. Henry Timrod. AA; AmP; AmPP; CoBA; IAP; MOAP; OBAV; OxBA; PAH; SPP; TCAP
Calm as the Cloudless Heaven. "Christopher North." EtS
Calm circumference of life, The. Strife. Hafiz. PeP
Calm columns diademed. Song of the Columns. Paul Valéry. TrFP
Calm, cool face, The. Suicide's Note. Langston Hughes. CDC
Calm Death, God of crossed hands and passionless eyes. Death. George Pellew. AA
Calm grows the air around. Ode to Salinas. Luis de León. TeCS
Calm is all nature as a resting wheel. Written in Very Early Youth [*or* Twilight]. Wordsworth. BPN; EmBrPo; EnRP; ES
Calm is the fragrant air, and loth to lose. Evening Voluntary. Wordsworth. CaAE
Calm is the landscape when the storm has passed. Peace in the Welsh Hills. Vernon Watkins. ChMP
Calm is the morn without a sound. In Memoriam A. H. H., XI. Tennyson. BoLiVe; BPN; CaAE; ChTr; CoBE; CoEV; EmBrPo; EnLi-2; EnSW; EPN; ExPo; FaBoEn; FiP; GEPC; GTBS-D; GTML; GTSL; LiTB; LPS-1; OAEP; OBEV (1st ed.); PoE; PoEL-5; PoFS; ReaPo; SeCeV; ShBV-4; SN; TrGrPo; TVSH; ViPo; VLEP
Calm martyr of a noble cause. Jefferson Davis. Walker Meriwether Bell. BoHiPo; GA; PAH
Calm Morning at Sea. Sara Teasdale. EtS
Calm Nature's idle spy, I follow. Swallows. Afanasi Afanasievich Fet. OnPM; TrRV
Calm of Evening. Hsieh T'iao, *tr. fr. Chinese by* Henry H. Hart. PoHN
Calm on the bosom of thy God. Dirge [*or* A Death-Hymn]. Felicia Dorothea Hemans. *Fr.* The Siege of Valencia. BCEP; EV-4; HBV; OBEV; OBRV
Calm on the listening ear of night. Christmas Song [*or* The Birth Song of Christ]. Edmund H. Sears. BePJ; COAH; SDH
Calm, sad, secure; behind high convent walls. Nuns of the Perpetual Adoration. Ernest Dowson. BrBE; CaAE; PoVP; PraNu; TOP; TriL; ViPP
Calm Sea, A. Robert Southey. EtS
Calm sinks the Night upon the land. Midnight. Eduard Mörike. AnGP
Calm Soul of All Things. Matthew Arnold. *Fr.* Lines Written in Kensington Gardens. TrPWD; WGRP
(From "Lines Written in Kensington Gardens.") LEAP
(Inward Peace.) MaRV
Calm, strong and gentle Man of Galilee. As He Walked with Us. Harry Webb Farrington. ChIP
Calm the boy sleeps, though death is in the clouds. Infant Noah. Vernon Watkins. NeBP
Calm [*or* Calme] was the day, and through the trembling air [*or* ayre]. Prothalamion. Spenser. AnFE; AtBAP; ATP; AWP; BEL; CaAE; CBOV; ChTr; CoBE; EIL; ElSeCe; EnL; EnLi-1; EnLit; EPP; EV-1; FaBoEn; GEPC; GoTL; GTBS; GTBS-D; GTBS-W; GTSE; GTSL; HBV; InPo; LEAP; LiTB; LiTG; LiTL; LoBV; MaPo; MCCG; OBEV; OBSC; OuHeWo; PoE; ReaPo; ReEn; ReIE; RiBV; SeCePo; ShBV-4; SiCE; TCEP; TOP; TwHP; TyEnPo; UnPo (1st ed.); ViBoPo; WHA
Calm Was the Even [and Clear Was the Sky]. Dryden. *Fr.* An Evening's Love; or, The Mock-Astrologer, IV, i. MaPo; OAEP
(Song: "Calm was the even, and clear was the sky.") CEP; SeCV-2
Calm was the evening and clear was the sky (*longer vers.*). Amintas and Claudia; or, The Merry Shepherdess. *Unknown.* CoMu
Calm was the sea to which your course you kept. To W. P, I. George Santayana. BoFr; OBAV
Calme, The. John Donne. *See* Calm, The.
Calmly as the morning's soft tears shed. On a Lady Sleeping. *Unknown.* SeCL
Calmly beside her tropic strand. Charleston. Paul Hamilton Hayne. BlG; PAH
Calmly, breathe calmly all your music, maids! The Last Music. Lionel Johnson. GTIV; PoVP
Calmly to wait whatever Chance may give. Odes, III, 20. Pierre de Ronsard. PrPoCR
Calmly we walk through this April's day. Time Is the Fire [*or* For Rhoda]. Delmore Schwartz. The Repetitive Heart, IV. LiTA; LiTM; MoAB; MoAmPo; MoVE; OxBA
Calomel. *Unknown.* ABS
Calumny. Frances Sargent Osgood. AA; HBV
Calvary. Mary Hallet. ChIP; PGD
Calvary. William Dean Howells. ChIP; OQP; QP-1
Calvary. Hugh Robert Orr. ChIP
Calvary. E. A. Robinson. AnNE; ChIP; CoBA; MAP; MaRV; MoAmPo; NeMA; OQP; QP-1; QS; StJW; TreFS; TwP; WGRP
Calvary. Libby Stopple. GoYe
Calvary was just one more. Daily Cross. Earl Bigelow Brown. ChIP
Calvary ("Ev'ry time I think about Jesus"), *with music. Unknown.* BoAN-1
Calvary ("I walked alone to my Calvary"). *Unknown.* OQP; QP-2
Calvary and Easter. "Susan Coolidge." OQP; PGD; PSO; QP-1; WBLP
(Easter Song.) BLRP; EOAH
Calvary is a continent. Still the Cross. E. Merrill Root. MaRV; StJW
Calvary's Cry. John William Cunningham. BePJ
Calved from a glacier near Godhaven coast. The Iceberg. E. J. Pratt. *Fr.* The *Titanic.* TwCaPo
Calverly's. E. A. Robinson. LBMV; MOAP
Calvinist Autumnal. Elizabeth B. Harrod. NePoEA
Calvinist in Love, A. Jack R. Clemo. ChMP
Calvus, if any joy from mortal tears. Quintilia Dead. Catullus. OnPM
Calypso. William Carlos Williams. NePoAm-2
Calypsomania. Anthony Brode. FiBHP
Calypso's Island. Homer, *tr. fr. Greek by* George Chapman. *Fr.* The Odyssey, V. GrR; OxBG
Calypso's Island. Archibald MacLeish. MoAB
Cam' Ye By ("Cam' ye by the salmon fishers?"). *Unknown.* AtBAP; CH
Cambrai and Marne. Sir Charles G. D. Roberts. CPG
Cambric Shirt, The. *Unknown. See* Elfin Knight, The.
Cambridge, an outdoor library stack of bricks. Vale. John Ciardi. MiAP
Cambridge and the Alps. Wordsworth. *Fr.* The Prelude, VI. ERP; PoEL-4
("Imagination—here the Power so called.") NBE
Cambridge Ladies, The. E. E. Cummings. *Fr.* Sonnets—Realities. AnAmPo; CoBA; LA; MoPW; MoVE; OxBA; TCPD; ViBoPo (1958 ed.)
Cambridge town is a beleaguered city. The Devourers. Rose Macaulay. PoeT
Cambridge, with whom, my pilot and my guide. To Richard Owen Cambridge. Thomas Edwards. ES
Cambyses, *sel.* Elkanah Settle.
She That with Love Is Not Possessed. SeCL
Camden, most reverend head, to whom I owe. To William Camden. Ben Jonson. AWP; EPS; InPo; OBS; PoFS; ReEn; ReIE; SeCV-1; SeEP; TuPP

Came a roaring bumble-bee. Bumble-Bee and Clover. *Unknown.* GFA
Came an amorous rider. An Encounter in the Field. Li Po. ChLP
Came first, five hundred miles from port. Approaching America. J. C. Squire. HBMV
Came in my full youth to the midnight cave. Ajanta. Muriel Rukeyser. FiMAP; LiTA; LiTM; MiAP; MoAB; MoAmPo (1950 ed.); TwAmPo
Came Jean Brébeuf from Rennes, in Normandy. Brébeuf and Lalemant. Alan Sullivan. CPG
Came, on a Sabbath morn [*or* noon], my sweet. Meet We No Angels, Pansie? Thomas Ashe. HBV; OBEV (1st ed.); OBVV
Came the morning of that day. Sumter. Edmund Clarence Stedman. MC; PAH
Came the relief. "What, sentry, ho!" Relieving Guard. Bret Harte. BTP; LBAP
Came threshing-time, the height of all our seasons. Wrestling. John Crowe Ransom. MoP
Camel. Gene Derwood. NePA
Camel. W. S. Merwin. NePA
Camel. Mary Britton Miller. TiPo (1959 ed.); UTS
Camel, The. Ogden Nash. CenHV; LiL
Camel, at the close of day, The. The Kneeling Camel [*or* Submission and Rest *or* Rest and Work]. Anna Temple Whitney. BLPA; BLRP; MaRV
Camel bells are sounding, The. The Little King. Irene Gass. ChrBoLe
Camel has a funny hump, The. Primer. Samuel Hoffenstein. BOHV
Camel has a single hump, The. The Camel. Ogden Nash. CenHV; LiL
Camel Rider, The. *Unknown, tr. fr. Arabic by* Wilfrid Scawen Blunt. AWP; FaBoTw
Camella Fair. *Unknown.* ElSeCe
Camelot. Charles Dalmon. TCPD
"Camels are coming, The," huzza, huzza! The Camels Have Come. *Unknown.* PoOW
Camel's Complaint, The. Charles Edward Carryl. *See* Plaint of the Camel, The.
Camels Have Come, The. *Unknown.* PoOW
Camel's Hump, The. Kipling. *Fr.* Just-so Stories. BoChLi
Camel's Lament, The. Charles Edward Carryl. *See* Plaint of the Camel, The.
Camel's Nose, The. Lydia Huntley Sigourney. OTPC (1923 ed.); PRWS
Cameo, The. Edna St. Vincent Millay. LiTA; MAP; MoAmPo
Cameos. Jeannette Bliss Gillespy. AA
Forgiven?
Valentine, A.
Camerado, this is no book. Walt Whitman. *Fr.* So Long. LEAP
Cameradós. Bayard Taylor. BOHV; PA
Cameronian Cat, The. *Unknown.* BOHV; CIV
Camilla. Charles Augustus Keeler. AA
Camilla. Virgil, *tr. fr. Latin by* Rolfe Humphries. *Fr.* The Aeneid, VII. LaP
Camille St. Saëns was racked with pains. Introduction. Ogden Nash. *Fr.* The Carnival of Animals. UnS
Camoens. Herman Melville. PtP; ViBoPo
Camoens in the Hospital. Herman Melville. PtP; ViBoPo
Camões, alone, of all the lyric race. Luis de Camões. Roy Campbell. BoSA; FaBoTw
Camomile, The. Al-Buqaira, *tr. fr. Arabic by* A. J. Arberry. MooP
Camouflage. John Manifold. WaP
Camouflage. Helen Frith Stickney. MuM
Camp. Patrick Anderson. BoCaPo (1948 ed.)
Camp, A. Robert Louis Stevenson. *Fr.* Travels with a Donkey. VLEP
(Camper's Night Song.) BBV
(God's Green Inn.) MW
Camp at Night, The. Homer, *tr. fr. Greek by* George Chapman. *Fr.* The Iliad, VIII. LPS-2
(Trojans outside the Walls, The, *sl. longer sel.*) OBS
Camp Chums. Rose Waldo. MPB
Camp-Fire, The. W. Harry Clemons. CAG
Camp Fire Has Gone Out, The. *Unknown.* CSF
Camp in the Prussian Forest, A. Randall Jarrell. MiAP; MoAmPo (1950 ed.); NeMA
Camp within the West, The. Roderic Quinn. BoAu
Campaign, The. Addison. CEP
Blenheim, *sel.* OBEC
("But O, my Muse, what numbers wilt thou find.") EPP
Campaign, The. Frederic Prokosch. NeTW; SoV
Campaign against Wu, The (*two poems*). Wei Wen-ti, *tr. fr. Chinese by* Arthur Waley. TrCh
"In the North-west there is a floating cloud."
"My charioteer hastens to yoke my carriage."
Campaigners, The; or, The Pleasant Adventures at Brussels, *sel.* Thomas D'Urfey.
Scotch Song, *fr.* III, i. CEP
Campañero, The, *with music.* *Unknown.* ShS
Campaspe. John Lyly. *See* Alexander and Campaspe.
Camp-Bell. Winthrop Mackworth Praed. LPS-3
(Charade.) GN
Campbells Are Coming, The. *Unknown.* EBSV; OlF
Campers. Robert Finch. TwCaPo
Camper's Night Song. Robert Louis Stevenson. *See* Camp, A.
Camping Out. William Empson. FaBoMo; MoVE
Camping Song. Bliss Carman. NLK
Campion white, The/ Above the grass. The Lamp Flower. Margaret Cecilia Furse. BoTP
Camp's asleep and thro' the gloom, The. Silhouette in Sepia. Robert V. Carr. PoOW
Camps of Green. Walt Whitman. PoE
Camptown. John Ciardi. WaP
Camptown Races, De, *with music.* Stephen Collins Foster. TrAS
Campus. Margaret E. Sangster. BPP
Can a Maid That Is Well Bred. *Unknown.* TuPP
Can death be faithful or the grave be just. The Resurrection. Nathaniel Wanley. LoBV
Can Doleful Notes to Mesur'd Accents Set. John Danyel. UnS
Can freckled August—drowsing warm and blonde. The Rain-Crow. Madison Cawein. AA; BAP; BLA; LBAP; LEAP
Can he that loves be man. *Unknown.* SeCSL
Can I a craven coward be. Battle Song. Ibn Farsan. MooP
Can I bear to part wi' thee. The Laird o' Lamington. James Hogg. EBSV
Can I believe. Ariosto, *tr. fr. Italian by* "Moira O'Neill." CAW
Can I Forget? Sidney Goodsir Smith. NeBP; SeCePo
Can I forget?—no, never, while my soul. Heaven's Hour. William Winter. LEAP
Can I forget the dismal night, that gave. Addison's Funeral in the Abbey. Thomas Tickell. *Fr.* To the Earl of Warwick on the Death of Mr. Addison. BeR
Can I forget the sickle mune. Can I Forget? Sidney Goodsir Smith. NeBP; SeCePo
Can I forget the sweet days that have been. Days That Have Been. W. H. Davies. PoeT; PrWP
Can I hear your soft step treading. Orpheus and Eurydice. Valery Yakovlevich Bryusov. BoR
Can I not come to Thee, my God, for these. To His Ever-loving God. Robert Herrick. TrPWD
Can I not sin, but thou wilt be. To His Conscience. Robert Herrick. MaPo; OxBoCh; PoEL-3
Can I Not Sing [but Hoy!]. *Unknown.* EV-2; NBE; ViBoPo
(Jolly Shepherd Wat, The.) AnEC; SDH; TMEV, *mod.*
(Jolly Wat.) OBB
(Joly Wat.) AnEnPo
(Shepherd upon a [*or* the] Hill, The.) GoBC; OxBoCh
Can I see another's woe. On Another's Sorrow. Blake. *Fr.* Songs of Innocence. AWP; CEP; EnRP; EV-3; LiTG; MaRV; OTPC (1923 ed.); PoEL-4; ViBoPo
Can I, who have for others oft compiled. Of [*or* On] My Dear Son [*or* Sonne], Gervase Beaumont. Sir John Beaumont. EV-2; OBS; SeCL; SeEP; ViBoPo
"Can it be good to die?" you question, friend. An Answer. George Frederick Cameron. CPG
Can it be possible, when we grow old. No Immortality. Frances Cornford. DiM
Can it be right to give what I can give? Sonnets from the Portuguese, IX. Elizabeth Barrett Browning. BPN; HBV; VA
Can it be that never more. Men on Islands. Padraic Colum. TIP
Can it indeed be, Jove, you have grown old? Petronius, *tr. fr. Latin by* John Peale Bishop. *Fr.* Satyricon. LaP
Can it then be, that the earth loved some city. Subterranean City. Thomas Lovell Beddoes. *Fr.* Fragments Intended for the Dramas. ERP
Can Life Be a Blessing. Dryden. *Fr.* Troilus and Cressida. ATP (1935 ed.); ElSeCe; SeCePo; SeCL; ViBoPo
(Song: "Can life be a blessing.") CEP; SeCV-2; SeEP
Can love be controll'd by advice? Song. John Gay. *Fr.* The Beggar's Opera. LoBV
Can man be free if woman be a slave? Shelley. *Fr.* The Revolt of Islam, II. PoFr
Can scenes like these withdraw thee from thy wood. George Crabbe. *Fr.* The Borough, Letter I. OBRV
Can She Excuse My Wrongs with Virtue's Cloak. *Unknown.* ReIE
Can that hackneyed jade be sane? On an Unpleasant Woman. Catullus. OnPM
Can the depths of the ocean afford you not graves. The Munster War-Song. Richard D'Alton Williams. TIP
Can the lover share his soul. Epithalamium. W. J. Turner. OBMV
Can the Mole Take. C. Day Lewis. OBMV
Can the moving soul be One. Tao Teh Ching, XIX. *Unknown, tr. fr. Chinese.* WhP
Can the single cup of wine. To His Brother Hsing-chien. Po Chü-i. TrCh
Can they still live. Ghosts. J. R. Ackerley. POTE

Can this be Dionysus? How the deuce! Beer. Julian the Apostate. OxBG
Can this be he. Milton. *Fr.* Samson Agonistes. InP
Can this be love men yield me in return. Renewal. Gladys Cromwell. AnAmPo; LA; NP
Can this be the bird to man so good. The Redbreast Chasing a Butterfly. Wordsworth. CG; OTPC
Can this, the world we see today, be real? Motion Picture Show. Ralph Cheyney. MuM
Can tyrants but by tyrants conquer'd be. Byron. *Fr.* Childe Harold's Pilgrimage, IV. PoFr
Can we believe—by an effort. Cities. Hilda Doolittle ("H. D."). ChMo; CMP; ViBoPo (1941 ed.)
Can we fail to be touched by the thought. Sanctuary. J. B. Boothroyd. FiBHP
Can we not consecrate. Love and Sacrifice. Bernard O'Dowd. BoAu; BoAV
Can we not force from widowed [*or* widdowed] Poetry. An Elegie [*or* Elegy] upon the Death of the Deane of Pauls, Dr. John Donne. Thomas Carew. EPS; MeLP; MePo; OBS; PtP; SeCV-1; SeEP
Can ye play me Duncan Gray. Duncan Gray. Burns. CoMu
Can Ye Sew Cushions? *Unknown.* FaBoCh; LoGBV
("O can ye sew cushions?") BOL
Can you dance? Music. Eleanor Farjeon. TiPo (1959 ed.)
Can you forego me? Treat me like a thing. His First Love. Lizette Woodworth Reese. AV
Can you make me a cambric shirt. The Cambric Shirt. *Unknown.* BaBo; OxNR
Can you not now remember. Rejected Odyssey. John Perrin. NeTW
Can you not see her as she sat of old. Hepzibah of the Cent Shop. Virginia McCormick. LS; VOD (1935 ed.)
Can You Paint a Thought? John Ford. *Fr.* The Broken Heart, III, ii. AtBAP; InvP; LO; OAEP; PoEL-2; TuPP; ViBoPo
(Song: "Can you paint a thought? or number?") EPP
Can you picture the decision. Barter Our Northern Darkness. Nigel Heseltine. MoWP
Can you recall an ode to June. A Drawing-Room Ballad. Henry Duff Traill. CenHV
"Can you spare a threepenny bit." War Relief. Oliver Herford. BOHV
Can you the author of our joy. Thomas Campion. *Fr.* A Relation of the Late Royal Entertainment Given by the Lord Knowles. SiCE
Cana. James Freeman Clarke. LPS-2
Canada. Sir Charles G. D. Roberts. BoCaPo; PeCV; PoFr; VA
Canada; Case History. Earle Birney. TwCaPo
Canada Speaks of Britain. Sir Charles G. D. Roberts. NeTW
Canada to England. Marjorie Pickthall. PoFr
Canaday I. O. Ephraim Braley. BaBo; ViBoFo, *with music*
Canadian, The. Jesse Edgar Middleton. CPG; OCL
Canadian Authors Meet, The. F. R. Scott. BoCaPo; WhC
Canadian Boat Song, A. Thomas Moore. CG; EV-4; GoBC; HBV; LPS-2; OBRV
Canadian Boat Song. *Unknown, at. to* John Galt. BLPA; BSV; CaP; EBSV; FaBoCh; GoTS; LoGBV; NBE; OBEV (new ed.); OBRV; OCL
Scotland Yet, 4 *ll.* OtMeF
Canadian Exile, The. Antoine Gerin-Lajoie, *tr. fr. French-Canadian by* John Boyd. CaP
Canadian Farmer. Genevieve Bartole. CaP
Canadian Folk Song. Wilfred Campbell. PCH; VA
Canadian Herd-Boy, The. Susanna Moodie. BoCaPo
Canadian Hunter's Song. Susanna Moodie. VA
Canadian Pine, The. William T. Allison. CPG
Canadian Rossignol, The. Edward William Thomson. CaP; CPG; OCL
Canadian Ski Song. Arthur S. Bourinot. CPG
Canal, The. Aldous Huxley. HBMV
Canaries in the morning, orchestras/ In the afternoon. Academic Discourse at Havana. Wallace Stevens. MoPo
Canary, The. Ogden Nash. FiBHP
Canary, The. Elizabeth Turner. OTPC (1923 ed.)
Canary-birds feed on sugar and seed. The Plaint of the Camel [*or* The Camel's Complaint]. Charles Edward Carryl. *Fr.* The Admiral's Caravan. AnAmPo; BoTP; FaPON; GoBP; GoTP; HBV; HBVY; LA; OTPC (1946 ed.); PCN; PoeMoYo; PoRh; SP; StVeCh; UTS
Cancel the Past. Thomas Michael Kettle. GTIV
Cancelled Itinerary. Frederick Mortimer Clapp. LiTM (rev. ed.)
Cancer Cells, The. Richard Eberhart. HoPM; MiAP
Cancion: "O love, I never, never thought." John II of Castile, *tr. fr. Spanish by* George Ticknor. AWP; JAWP; WBP
Cancion: "Whether you love me." Marqués de Santillana, *tr. fr. Spanish by* John Pierrepont Rice. AnSpL-1
Candid Man, The. Stephen Crane. War Is Kind, IX. MAP; MoAmPo
Candid morn already lifts on high, The. Morning. José Manuel Martínez de Navarrete. AnMP
Candid the Lady was and yet as candid. Simonetta. Angelo Poliziano. *Fr.* La Giostra. LyPI
Candidate: Now, Mr. Echo, will you vote for me? By-Election Idyll. Peter Dickinson. FiBHP
Candidate's Creed, The. James Russell Lowell. *See* Pious Editor's Creed, The.
Candidate's Letter, The ("Dear Sir,—You wish to know my notions"). James Russell Lowell. The Biglow Papers, 1st Series, No. VII. AA
Candle, The. Al-Hajjam, *tr. fr. Arabic by* A. J. Arberry. MooP
Candle, A. Leroy F. Jackson. PCH
Candle, The, a Saint. Wallace Stevens. PoRA
Candle and the Flame, The. George Sylvester Viereck. BAP; LBMV; LEAP
Candle-blossoms of horse-chestnut left, The. What Trinkets? Thomas Hornsby Ferril. NePoAm-2
Candle, candle. Christmas Chant. Isabel Shaw. ChBR; SiSoSe
Candle Flame, The. Janet Lewis. CrMA
Candle Indoors, The. Gerard Manley Hopkins. CoEV; EmBrPo; FaBoMo; GTBS-W; LiTB; LiTM; MeRV; OxBoCh; PeBoSo; PoEL-5; ReMP; ViPP
Candle is enough, A. Heart. Jules Supervielle. MiCF
Candle is out, The. The Lady. Elizabeth J. Coatsworth. InP; MaC
Candle lit in darkness of black waters, A. On the Lake. V. Sackville-West. ChMP; MoVE; OBMV
Candle Song. Anna Elizabeth Bennett. GoYe
Candle, waiter, A! Thank you. A Birthnight Candle. John Huston Finley. POT; PoTo
Candlelight. R. Balfour Daniels. CAG
Candle-Light. Thomas S. Jones, Jr. VOD
Candle Light. John Cowper Powys. LEAP
Candle-lighting Song. Arthur Ketchum. HBMV
Candlemas. Hugh Francis Blunt. JKCP (1955 ed.)
Candlemas. Alice Brown. AA; LBMV; PoRL
Candlemas. *Unknown.* PoRL
Candles. Babette Deutsch. VOD
Candles. Sister Mary Eleanore. JKCP (1955 ed.)
Candles. *Unknown.* GoBC
Candles are lighted, the fire blazes bright, The. The Shadows. Mary Lundie Duncan. OTPC (1923 ed.)
Candles Divine. Morris Abel Beer. MW
Candles gutter and burn out, The. Winter Night. A. R. D. Fairburn. AnNZ
Candles. Red tulips, sixty cents the bunch. Recipe for an Evening Musicale. Phyllis McGinley. UnS; WhC
Candles splutter; and the kettle hums, The. The Still Small Voice. A. M. Klein. PeCV
Candles toppling sideways in tomato-cans. Flash-Lights. Mary Aldis. BAP; NP
Candor. H. C. Bunner. HBV; PR
Candour may be devilish. White Magic. Tom MacInnes. CPG
Candy/ Is dandy. Reflections on Ice-breaking. Ogden Nash. FaFP; LiTM; NePA; ShBV-4; SiTL
Cane. Nicolás Guillén, *tr. fr. Spanish by* Langston Hughes. PoNe
Cane-bottomed Chair, The. Thackeray. FAOV; HBV; OTPC; PoVP
Canis Major. Robert Frost. *Fr.* A Sky Pair. AlBD; AlDL; MAP; MoAB; MoAmPo
Canner, exceedingly [*or* remarkably] canny, A. Limerick. Carolyn Wells. FaPON; HBV; HBVY; LiBL; PoeMoYo; TWS; TWSC; YaD
Cannibal bold of Penzance, A. Limerick. *Unknown.* LiBL
Cannibal Flea, The. Tom Hood. PA
Cannibal Song. Charles Dickens. *Fr.* Holiday Romance. BoN
Cannonade fell still, The. All along the fishhook line. Pickett's Charge. Stephen Vincent Benét. *Fr.* John Brown's Body. PoeMoYo
Cannonball Blues. *Unknown.* *See* White House Blues, The.
Cannon's voice is dumb, The. Peace. Harold Trowbridge Pulsifer. AOAH; MC; PEDC
Canny moment, lucky fit. The Nativity Champ. Sir Walter Scott. *Fr.* Guy Mannering. ChTr; FaBoCh; LoGBV
Canny old codger at Yalta, A. Limerick. *Unknown.* LiBL
Canoe, The. Isabella Valancy Crawford. BoCaPo; OnYI; VA
Canoe. Keith Douglas. NeBP
Canoe returning, The. Nameless Islands. Jorge Carrera Andrade. TwSpPo
Canoe Song at Twilight. Laura E. McCully. CaP; CPG; OCL
Canoe-Trip. Douglas Le Pan. CaP; PeCV; TwCaPo
Canon for Apocreos. The. St. Theodore of Studium, *tr. fr. Greek by* John Mason Neale. CAW
Canonicus and Roger Williams. *Unknown.* PAH
Canonization, The. John Donne. ATP; BEL; BLV; BoLiVe; CoBE; EIL; EM-1; EnL; EnLi-1 (1949 ed.); EnLoPo; EnLP; EPS; EV-2; GTBS-W; GTSE; LiTB; LiTG; LiTL; MaPo; MePo; OBS; Po; PoE; PoEL-2; PoFS; ReEn; ReIE; RiBV; SeCeV; SeCV-1; SeEP; TOP; TrGrPo; TuPP; TwP; ViBoPo
(Canonisation, The.) LoBV; SeCePo

Canons Ashby. David Wright. PoN
Canopus. Bert Leston Taylor. ALV; FiBHP; HBMV; InMe; PIAE; WhC
Canopy of Heav'n is Hung wth sable, The. Very Dark. Nathaniel Lee. *Fr.* The Tragedy of Nero. BeR
Canso: "I cannot see the bright sun's glow." Bernard de Ventadorn, *tr. fr. Provençal by* Barbara Smythe. LyMA
Canso: "Softly sighs the April air." Arnaut Daniel. *See* Bel m'es quan lo vens m'alena.
Canso: "When all the ice and cold and snow." Giraut de Bornelh, *tr. fr. Provençal by* Hubert Creekmore. LyMA
Canso Strait, *with music. Unknown.* ShS
Canst thou by searching find out God? The Eternal Quest [*or* Job's Comforters]. Job, Bible, *O.T.* MaRV; WGRP
Canst thou draw out leviathan with an hook? Leviathan. Job, Bible, *O.T.* TrGrPo
"Canst thou indeed be he that still would sing." Dante. *Fr.* La Vita Nuova. AWP
Canst thou love and lie alone? The Courtier's Good-Morrow to His Mistress. *Unknown.* ElL
Canst thou love me, lady? Love. Charles Stuart Calverley. ALV; FiBHP
Canst thou not minister to a mind diseased? A Mind Diseased [*or* Remorse]. Shakespeare. *Fr.* Macbeth, V, iii. BCEP; MaRV
Canst thou, O cruel, say I love thee not. Sonnets, CXLIX. Shakespeare. PeBoSo
Can't. Harriet Prescott Spofford. DD; GA; MC; PAH
Can't They Dance the Polka! *with music. Unknown.* ShS
Can't You. Gamaliel Bradford. PR
Can't You Dance the Polka? *with music. Unknown.* SoAmSa
Can't You Live Humble? *with music. Unknown.* BoAN-2
Cantaliso in a Bar. Nicolás Guillén, *tr. fr. Spanish by* Langston Hughes. AnCL
Cantata for the Graduation Festival at Upsala, the Sixth of September, 1877. Viktor Rydberg, *tr. fr. Swedish by* Charles W. Stork. AnSL
Cante Hondo. Ellen de Young Kay. NePoEA
Cantelope, The. Bayard Taylor. BOHV; PA
Cantemus Cuncti Melodum. Notker Balbulus, *tr. fr. Latin by* John Mason Neale. CAW
Canterbury. Basil Dowling. AnNZ
Canterbury Pilgrims, The. Chaucer. *See* Canterbury Tales: Prologue.
Canterbury Tales, The, *sels.* Chaucer.
  Prologue. BCEP, *mod. by* Edwin Markham, *much abr.*; BEL; BoLiVe, *abr.*; CoBE, *abr.*; EM-1; EnL, *sl. abr.*; EnLi-1; EnLit; EPP, *abr.*; EV-1; FiP, *much abr.*; GEPC; LiA; MaPo, *much abr.*; OAEP; OuHeWo, *mod. by* J. U. Nicolson; PIAE, *much abr.*; REAL; SeCeV; TCEP, *sl. abr.*; TOP, *much abr.*; TyEnPo, *much abr.*; ViBoPo, *much abr.*; WoL, *abr.*, *mod.*
    (Canterbury Pilgrims, *much abr.*) LPS-2
    Clerk of Oxenford, The. CoEV; OnPP, *mod. by* Frank Ernest Hill
    (Clerk of Oxford, A.) CBOV
    Knight, A. GoTP, *mod. vers. by* Louis Untermeyer
    (Five Pilgrims, *orig.*, *with mod. vers. by* Louis Untermeyer.) BLV
    (Seven Pilgrims. *orig.*, *with mod. vers. by* Louis Untermeyer.) TrGrPo
    (Some Characters from "The Canterbury Tales.") LEAP
    (Three Canterbury Pilgrims, *mod. vers. by* Louis Untermeyer.) MaC
    Miller, A. GoTP, *mod. vers. by* Louis Untermeyer
    Parson, A. CBOV; GrCo-1, *abr.*, *with mod. vers.*
    (Good Parson, The, *mod. vers. by* H. C. Leonard.) MaRV; WGRP
    (Parish Priest, The.) PoLi
    (Poor Parson, The.) ACP; CAW
    (Poure Persoun, The.) GoBC
    Prioress, The. CBOV; PraNu, *shorter sel.*, *mod.*
    Shipman, The. ACP, *mod.*; EtS; SG
    Squire, A. GoTP, *mod. vers. by* Louis Untermeyer
    "Whan that Aprille with his shoures soote." BLV, *orig.*, *with mod. vers. by* Louis Untermeyer; CaAE; ChTr, *much abr.*; GoBC, *much abr.*; InP; PreP, *longer sel.*; TrGrPo, *orig.*, *with mod. vers. by* Louis Untermeyer
    (Than Longen Folk to Goon on Pilgrimages.) ATP; CBOV
    Wife of Bath, A. ATP; CBOV
    (Wife of Bath and the Parson, The, *longer sel.*) NBE
  Clerk's [*or* Clerkes] Tale.
    Chaucer's Envoy to the Story of Patient Griselda, *mod. by* W. W. Skeat. AnEnPo
    (Griselda.) BHV
    (Patient Griselda, *mod. by* Edward Hodnett.) PoRA
  Franklin's Prologue, The. OAEP
  Franklin's Tale, The. OAEP
  Friar's [*or* Freres] Tale, The, *sl. abr.* BCEP, *mod. by* Edwin Markham; BLV, *orig.*, *with mod. vers. by* F. E. Hill; ErLi-1 (1949 ed.), *mod. vers. by* Edwin M. Everett
  Prologue: "This worthy limitour, this noble Frere." EnLi-1 (1949 ed.)
  Introduction to the Man of Law's Prologue. FiP
  Knight's [*or* Knightes] Tale, The. BEL; GEPC; GoTL; TOP
    Arcite's Farewell, *mod. by* John Hall Wheelock. LiTL
    ("Allas the Wo! Allas, the peynes stronge.") LO
    Emily's Prayer to Diana. MyFE
    Morning in May. LPS-2
    (Dawn, *shorter sel.*) CBOV
    Prayer to Venus, *mod. by* John Hall Wheelock. LiTL
    "Whan that Arcite to Thebes comen was." LiA
  Maunciple's Tale, The.
    Lat Take a Cat. ChTr
  Miller's [*or* Milleres] Tale, The. OxBoLi
    Alisoun. CoEV
    Carpenter's Young Wife, The. ExPo
    Young Woman, 3 *ll.* BoW
  Monk's Tale, The.
    Croesus. MyFE
    Tale of Hugelin, Count of Pisa, The. MyFE
  Nun's Priest's [*or* Nonne Preestes] Tale, The. AnFE; AtBAP; BEL; CoBE; EM-1; EnL, *mod. by* Theodore Morrison; EnLi-1; EV-1; GEPC; MaPo; OAEP; OuHeWo, *mod. by* J. U. Nicolson; PIAE; PoEl-1; SeCeV; TCEP, *sl. abr.*; TOP, *abr.*, TrGrPo, *orig.*, *with mod. vers. by* Frank Ernest Hill; TyEnPo
    (Cock and the Fox, The.) LiA
    Chasing the Fox. CoEV
    Murder Will Out. MyFE
    Poor Widow's Cock, The, 6 *ll.* MyFE
    "This Chauntecleer stood hye up-on his toos." FiP
  Pardoner's Tale, The. BEL; CoBE, *sl. abr.*; EM-1, *sl. abr.*; EnL, *mod. by* Theodore Morrison; EnLi-1; EnLit; EV-1; FiP, *abr.*; LiA; OAEP; PoEL-1; RiBV, *mod. by* Frank Ernest Hill
    (Death and the Ruffians, *abr.*, *mod. by* Leigh Hunt.) BCEP
    (Quest for Death, *shorter sel.*) CoEV
    ("These rioters, of whom I make my rime," *mod. vers.*) WHA
    "This ryotoures three, of which I tell." MyFE
  Prioress's Prologue, The. EM-1; OAEP
  Prioress' Tale, The. ACP, *mod.*; BEL; EM-1; GEPC; GoBC, *mod. by* Wordsworth; ISi, *mod. by* Frank Ernest Hill; LoBV; OAEP; OxBoCh
    Invocation: "O mother maid! O maiden-mother free," *mod. by* Frank Ernest Hill. ISi
    (O Mooder Mayde.) BoW
    (Prayer to the Blessed Virgin, *shorter sel.*, *mod.*) CAW
    (Two Invocations of the Virgin, 2, *mod.*) ACP
  Prologue of [*or* to] the Pardoner's Tale. BEL; CoBE; EM-1; EnL, *mod. by* Theodore Morrison; OAEP; RiBV, *mod. by* Frank Ernest Hill
  Prologue cf the Prioresses Tale. AtBAP
  Prologue to Melibeus, *abr.* EM-1
  Prologue to Sir Thopas. EM-1
  Prologue to the Man of Law's Tale FiP
  Reeve's Tale, The.
    "At Trumpyngtoun nat fer from Cantebrigge." ViBoPo
  Second Nun's Tale, The.
    "Thou mayde and mooder," *fr. prologue.*
    (Invocatio ad Mariam, *mod. by* Frank Ernest Hill.) ISi
    ("Thou maid and mother, daughter of thy Son," *mod.*) GoBC
    (Two Invocations of the Virgin, 1, *mod.*) ACP
  Sir Thopas. BEL; EM-1, *abr.*
  Wife of Bath's Prologue, The. EnL, *mod. by* Theodore Morrison, EnLi-1 (1949 ed.); OxBoLi, *abr.*
    (Prologue to the Wife of Bath's Tale, The.) PoEL-1
    "My fifthe housbonde, god his soule blesse," *abr.* FiP
  Wife of Bath's Tale, The. EnL, *mod. by* Theodore Morrison; EnLit
    (Tale of the Wyf of Bathe, The.) REAL
    (Wife of Bath['s Tale], The.) LiA
    "In th' olde dayes of the Kyng Arthour," 25 *ll.* ViBoPo
Cantica: Our Lord Christ *At. to* St. Francis of Assisi, *tr. fr. Italian by* Dante Gabriel Rossetti. AWP; JAWP; WBP
  (Of Order in Our Lord Christ.) CAW; GoBC; SaFP
  (Order.) OnPM
Cantica: Our Lord Christ; of Order. *At. to* Jacopone da Todi, *tr. fr. Italian by* Dante Gabriel Rossetti. LyPI
Canticle. Thomas Edward Brown. VLEP
Canticle. William Griffith. BLA; CP; DD; HBMV; HBVY; NV
Canticle. Michael McClure. NeAP
Canticle. Francis Quarles. *See* My Beloved Is Mine, and I Am His.
Canticle. John Norris. SeCL
  (Second chap. of the Cant. from the 10. Verse to the 13.) SeEP
Canticle de Profundis. Lucy Larcom. MDAH
Canticle for Three Voices *sel.* Paul Claudel, *tr. fr. French by* J. O'Connor.
  "Since you will have it so, I sing the rose." MiFP
Canticle of Bernadette, The, *abr.* *Unknown.* WHL

Canticle of Canticles. Bible, *O.T.* *See* Song of Solomon, The.
Canticle of Creatures, The. St. Francis of Assisi. *See* Canticle of the Sun.
Canticle of Darkness, *sel.* Wilfred Watson.
"Stand gentle in my words." MeRV
Canticle of Quietness. Sister Mary Paulinus. JKCP (1955 ed.)
Canticle of Saint John. Stéphane Mallarmé, *tr. fr. French by* Alan Conder. TrFP
Canticle of the Creatures. St. Francis of Assisi. *See* Canticle of the Sun.
Canticle of the Race. Edgar Lee Masters. ChMo; CMP
Song of Men.
Song of the Human Spirit.
Song of Women.
Canticle of the Sun. St. Francis of Assisi, *tr. fr. Italian by* Matthew Arnold. OuHeWo; ReTS, *tr. unknown;* TreFS; WGRP, *tr. by* Maurice Egan; WHL, *tr. unknown;* WoL, *tr. by* Eleanor L. Turnbull
(Canticle of Creatures, The, *tr. by* Marian Douglas.) SaFP
(Canticle of the Creatures, The, *tr. by* Eleanor L. Turnbull.) LyPI
(Canticle [*or* Song] of the Creatures, *tr. by* Matthew Arnold.) CAW; GoBC; LiTW; MaRV
("Most high, omnipotent, Good Lord," *tr. unknown.*) MeRV
Canticle to the Waterbirds, A. Brother Antoninus. NeAP
Canticus Troili. Chaucer. *See* Song of Troilus.
Cantiga: "Take away from me my eyes." Gil Vicente, *tr. fr. Portuguese by* Seth G. Thornton. LyMA
Cantiga: "White and crimson, cheek and breast." Gil Vicente, *tr. fr. Portuguese and Spanish by* Thomas Walsh. CAW; ISi
Cantiga de Amigo: "On the greening grasses." Pero Meogo, *tr. fr. Portuguese by* Seth G. Thornton. LyMA
Cantiga de Amigo: "When you know you love a sweetheart." Martín Códax, *tr. fr. Portuguese by* Seth G. Thornton. LyMA
Cantiga de Amor: "Fair lady, I see you do complain." Dinis, King of Portugal, *tr. fr. Portuguese by* Seth G. Thornton. LyMA
Cantiga de Santa Maria. Alfonso X, King of Castile and Leon, *tr. fr. Portuguese by* Seth G. Thornton. LyMA
Canto I: "Of Men, nay Beasts; worse, Monsters; worst of all." Phineas Fletcher. *Fr.* The Locusts, or Apollyonists. EPS; SeCV-1; SeEP
Canto I: "And then went down to the ship." Ezra Pound. AmPP; AtBAP; CoBMV; CoV; LiTA; MAP; MoAB; MoAmPo; MoVE; SeCeV; TrGrPo (rev. ed.)
Canto II: "Hang it all, Robert Browning." Ezra Pound. AmPP (4th ed.); AtBAP; CoBMV; MoAB; NePA; OxBA
Canto XIII: "Kung walked/ by the dynastic temple." Ezra Pound. FaBoMo; NP; TwCV
(Kung's Wisdom.) MoP
Canto XIV, *sel.* Ezra Pound.
"And the betrayers of language." MoPo
Canto XV, *sel.* Ezra Pound.
"Skin-flakes, repetitions, erosions." MoPo
Canto XVI, *sel.* Ezra Pound.
"And before hell mouth; dry plain/ and two mountains." ExPo; MoPo
Canto XVII: "So that the vines burst from my fingers." Ezra Pound. ExPo; LoBV; NAMP; OBMV; Po; ReMP
Canto XX, *sel.* Ezra Pound.
"Jungle:/ Glaze green and red feathers, jungle." MoPo
Canto XXI: "Keep the peace, Borso!" Ezra Pound. ChMo; CMP
"And there was grass on the floor of the temple," *sel.* MoPo
Canto XXIX, *sel.* Ezra Pound.
"She is submarine, she is an octopus, she is/ A biological process." MoPo
Canto XLV: "With Usura/ With usura hath no man a house of good stone." Ezra Pound. LiTM (rev. ed.); MoPo; NePA; OnAP; ReMP
Canto XLVII: "Who even dead, yet hath his mind entire!" Ezra Pound. CrMA; MoPo
Canto LXXIX, *sel.* Ezra Pound.
"O Lynx, wake Silenus and Casey." AtBAP; POTE (1959 ed.)
Canto LXXX, *sel.* Ezra Pound.
"Tudor indeed is gone and every rose."
(From "The Pisan Cantos.") FaBoTw
Canto LXXXI, *sels.* Ezra Pound.
"Ant's a centaur in his dragon world, The."
(From "The Pisan Cantos.") FaBoEn
(Pull Down Thy Vanity.) MeRV
"What thou lovest well remains." GTBS-D; MoAB; NePA; OxBA; SeCeV; UnPo (3d ed.); ViBoPo (1958 ed.)
(From "The Pisan Cantos.") FaBoTw
"Yet/ Ere the season died a-cold." MoVE
Canto Amor. John Berryman. MoAmPo (1950 ed.); MoPo; MoVE; NePA
Canto Espiritual. Juan Maragall, *tr. fr. Spanish by* Thomas Walsh. CAW
Cantus. *Unknown.* BSV
Canute the Great, *sel.* "Michael Field."
"She dared not wait." VA
Canvas leaves, the painted trees, The. Midsummer Night's Dream. Byron Vazakas. NePA
Canzo: "When fresh grass-blades and leaves appear." Bernard de Ventadour, *tr. fr. Provençal by* Hubert Creekmore. LiTW
Canzo of Bird-Songs and Love. Arnaut Daniel, *tr. fr. Provençal by* Ezra Pound. LiTW
Canzon Pastoral in Honor of Her Majesty, A. Edmund Bolton. TuPP
Canzone 126: "Clear, fresh, and dulcet streams." Petrarch, *tr. fr. Italian by* Leigh Hunt. Sonnets to Laura: To Laura in Life, Canzone XIV. LyPI
(Canzone: "Clear, fresh, sweet waters," *tr. by* William D. Foulke.) LiTW
Canzone: "Eyes that weep for pity of the heart, The." Dante, *tr. fr. Italian by* Dante Gabriel Rossetti. La Vita Nuova, XIX. LyMA; LyPI
("Eyes that weep for pity of the heart, The.") AWP; OuHeWo; WGRP
Canzone 129: "From thought to thought, from mountain-peak to mountain." Petrarch, *tr. fr. Italian by* Morris Bishop. Sonnets to Laura: To Laura in Life, Canzone XVII. LyPI
Canzone: He Beseeches Death for the Life of Beatrice. Dante, *tr. fr. Italian by* Dante Gabriel Rossetti. AWP; LyPI
Canzone: He Perceives His Rashness in Love. Guido Guinicelli, *tr. fr. Italian by* Dante Gabriel Rossetti. AWP; JAWP; WBP
Canzone: He Rebukes the Evil of That Time, *sel.* Siciliano Inghilfredi, *tr. fr. Italian by* Dante Gabriel Rossetti.
"Let none who have not wisdom govern you." PoFr
Canzone: He Speaks of His Condition through Love. Folcachiero de' Folcachieri, *tr. fr. Italian by* Dante Gabriel Rossetti. AWP
Canzone: His Lament for Selvaggia. Cino da Pistoia, *tr. fr. Italian by* Dante Gabriel Rossetti. AWP; JAWP; WBP
Canzone: His Portrait of His Lady. Fazio degli Uberti, *tr. fr. Italian by* Dante Gabriel Rossetti AWP
Canzone: "It is the evening hour; the rapid sky." Petrarch, *tr. fr. Italian by* Morris Bishop. LyMA; LyPI
Canzone: "Ladies that have intelligence in love." Dante. *See* Ladies That Have Intelligence in Love.
Canzone: "Lady asks me, A/ I speak in season." Guido Cavalcanti, *tr. fr. Italian by* Ezra Pound. LiTW
(Canzone: Lady Asks Me, A, *diff. translation.*) LyPI
Canzone 128: "O my own Italy! though words are vain." Petrarch, *tr. fr. Italian by* Lady Dacre. LyPI
Canzone: Of Distance. Ruggieri d'Amici, *tr. fr. Italian by* John Heath-Stubbs. LyPI
Canzone: Of His Dead Lady. Giacomino Pugliesi, *tr. fr. Italian by* Dante Gabriel Rossetti. AWP; JAWP; WBP
Canzone: Of His Love. Prinzivalle Doria, *tr. fr. Italian by* Dante Gabriel Rossetti. AWP
Canzone: Of the Gentle Heart. Guido Guinicelli, *tr. fr. Italian by* Dante Gabriel Rossetti. AWP; LiTW; LyMA; LyPI
(Of the Gentle Heart.) GoBC; WoL
Canzone: To Love and to His Lady. Guido delle Colonne, *tr. fr. Italian by* Dante Gabriel Rossetti. AWP; LyPI
Canzone: To the Lady Pietra, of Sienna. Dante, *tr. fr. Italian by* John Heath-Stubbs. LiTW
(Sestina 2: To the Lady Pietra of Siena.) LyPI
Canzone: "When shall we learn, what should be clear as day." W. H. Auden. LiTA; LiTM; MoVE
Canzone of the Gentle Heart. Guido Guinicelli. *See* Canzone: Of the Gentle Heart.
Canzonet. *Unknown.* EIL
("See, see, mine own sweet jewel.") EG; LO
Canzonet, to His Coy Love. Michael Drayton. *See* To His Coy Love.
Canzonetta: Bitter Song to His Lady, A. Pier Moronelli di Fiorenza, *tr. fr. Italian by* Dante Gabriel Rossetti. AWP; JAWP; WBP
Canzonetta: He Will Neither Boast Nor Lament to His Lady. Jacopo da Lentino, *tr. fr. Italian by* Dante Gabriel Rossetti. AWP
Canzonetta: Of His Lady and of His Making Her Likeness. Jacopo da Lentino, *tr. fr. Italian by* Dante Gabriel Rossetti. AWP
(Canzonetta: "My lady mine, I send.") LyMA
Canzonetta: Of His Lady in Absence. Giacomino Pugliesi, *tr. fr. Italian by* Dante Gabriel Rossetti. AWP; LyPI
Canzoniere. Petrarch. *See* Sonnets to Laura.
Caoch O'Lynn. Arthur Stringer. CPG
Caoilte. *Unknown, tr. fr. Irish by* Frank O'Connor. KiLC
Caow-hand with a gun or two, A. Western Formula. *Unknown.* PoOW
Cap and Bells, The. W. B. Yeats. BMEP; ChTr; GTSL; LEAP; MBP; MoAB; MoBrPo; OBVV
Cap That Fits. Austin Dobson. TSW; TSWC

Cape Ann. T. S. Eliot. Landscapes, V. KN; LoGBV; ThWaDe
Cape Cod Girls. *Unknown.* AmSS; TrAS, *with music*
Cape Coloured Batman. Guy Butler. BoSA
Cape-Cottage at Sunset. William Belcher Glazier. LPS-2
Cape Hatteras. Hart Crane. *Fr.* The Bridge. CoV; LiTA; OnAP, *abr.*
Sels.
Aeroplane, The. VOD (1935 ed.)
"Nasal whine of power whips a new universe, The." MoAB
Power. MAP; MoAmPo; VOD (1935 ed.), *shorter sel.* (Cape Hatteras: "The nasal whine of power," *longer sel.*) WoL
Cape Horn Gospel—I ("'I was in a hooker once,' said Karlssen"). John Masefield. StPo
Cape Horn Gospel—II ("Jake was a dirty Dago lad"). John Masefield. ShBV-3
Cape of Tempests, The. Luís de Camões. *See* Episode of Adamastor off the Cape of Good Hope.
Capilano ("Capilano, in the canyon"). A. M. Stephen. CaP
Capital, The. W. H. Auden. ChMo; MoPW
Capital ship for an ocean trip, A. A Nautical Ballad [*or* The Walloping Window-Blind]. Charles Edward Carryl. *Fr.* Davy and the Goblin. FaPON; GFA; GoTP; HBV; InMe; LauV; LiL; LBN; MPB; NA; OTPC (1946 ed.); StVeCh; TreFS; WhC. *See also* O, a capital ship for an ocean trip.
Capital Square. Patrick Anderson. BoCaPo
Capitals Are Rocked, The. Nikolai Alekseyevich Nekrasov, *tr. fr. Russian by* Babette Deutsch. OnPM; TrRV; AWP, *tr. by* Babette Deutsch *and* Avrahm Yarmolinsky
"Cap'n." Arthur Wallace Peach. EtS
Cap'n, I Believe, *with music. Unknown.* AS
Cap'n was drunk and he went below, The. Bottle O! *Unknown.* SoAmSa
Capped arbiter of beauty in this street. For the Marriage of Faustus and Helen (III). Hart Crane. FaBoMo; LiTM
Capriccio. Babette Deutsch. HBMV; TSW
Capriccio Dramatico, Il, *sel.* Lorenzo da Ponte, *tr. fr. Italian by* John Mazzinghi.
To an Artful Theatre Manager. TrJP
Caprice. William Dean Howells. ALV; PR
Caprice. Anne Morrow Lindbergh. DDA
Capstan Chantey, A. Edwin James Brady. HBMV
Captain, The, *abr.* John G. C. Brainard. EtS
Captain, The. Dorothea Day. *See* My Captain.
Captain, The, *sels.* Beaumont *and* Fletcher.
Away, Delights! *fr.* III, iv. ElL; OBEV; ViBoPo ("Away, delights! go seek some other dwelling.") LO (Farewell, False Love!) TriL (Sad Song, The.) FaBoEn
Tell me, Dearest, What Is Love? *fr.* II, ii. *Diff. vers., 2 sts., given in* The Knight of the Burning Pestle. ElL; SeEP; ViBoPo (What Is Love?) HBV
Captain, The. Tennyson. TCEP
Captain, The. Jon Manchip White. NePoEA
Captain and the Mermaids, The. W. S. Gilbert. YT
Captain bold, in [*or* from] Halifax, who [*or* that] dwelt in country quarters, A. Unfortunate Miss Bailey [*or* Miss Bailey's Ghost]. George Colman, the Younger. BOHV; FiBHP; OxBoLi; ViBoFo
Captain Bover. *Unknown.* SG
Captain Busby put his beard in his mouth and sucked it. Poems. Philip O'Connor. LiTM
Captain Car; or, Edom o Gordon. *Unknown. See* Edom o' Gordon.
Captain Carpenter. John Crowe Ransom. AnFE; APA; AtBAP; CoAnAm; CoBMV; FaBoMo; GTBS-W; LiTA; LiTG; LiTM; LoBV (2d ed.); MAP; MoAB; MoAmPo; MOAP; MoVE; NePA; OxBA; SeCeV; TwAmPo
Captain Chilver's gone to Sea. The *Benjamin's* Lamentations. *Unknown.* SG
Captain Colin P. Kelly, Jr. Robert Nathan. NeTW
Captain Craig, *sels.* E. A. Robinson.
"Ah! friends, friends." BoFr
"How, forsooth,/ Shall any man, by curses." BoFr
"I doubt if ten men in all Tilbury Town." PoEL-5
"I had a dream last night." PC
"There was a soldier once." BoFr
Captain Death. *Unknown.* CoMu
Captain Enoch. Rachel Field. MW
Captain Glen. *Unknown. See* William Glen.
Captain Guynemer. Florence Earle Coates. AOAH
Captain, I have seen. A Warning for Abraham Lincoln. Jacinto Fombona Pachano. AnCL; PoFr; WoL
Captain Jim Rees an' the Katie, *with music. Unknown.* StDa
Captain Jinks. *Unknown, at. to* T. Maclagan. BLPA; FaFP; OnPP; TreF
Captain Kidd. *Unknown.* ABS; BBV (1923 ed.); IHA; MoShBr, *shorter vers.;* SoAmSa, *longer vers., with music;* TrAS, *with music;* ViBoFo (Ballad of Captain Kidd, The.) AmSS (Captain Robert Kidd, *longer vers.*) ABF
Captain Latané. John Reuben Thompson. BlG (Burial of Latané, The.) PAH
Captain Loredan. Edward King. PFY
"Captain, oh, captain, what will you give me." The Lowdown, Lonesome Low. *Unknown.* OuSiCo
Captain of St. Kitts, The. Beulah May. EtS
Captain of the Northfleet, The. Gerald Massey. BMEP
Captain of the Oberon, The. Francis Webb. *Fr.* A Drum for Ben Boyd. NeLNL
Captain of the *Shannon* came sailing up the bay, The. The *Shannon* and the *Chesapeake.* Thomas Tracy Bouvé. GA; MC; PAH
Captain of the Western wood. Madroño. Bret Harte. AA; OBAV
Captain or Colonel, or Knight in Arms. When the Assault Was Intended to the City [*or* Arms and the Muse]. Milton. EM-1; EPP; ES; EV-2; GTBS; GTBS-D; GTBS-W; GTSE; GTSL; LH; OuHeWo; SeEP; TCEP
Captain Paton's Lament. John Gibson Lockhart. *See* Lament for Capt. Paton.
Captain Quiros and Mr. William Lane. Terra Australis. Douglas Stewart. BoAV; MoAuPo
Captain Reece. W. S. Gilbert. CenHV; FiBHP; GN; HBV; LPS-3; MaC; OTPC
Captain Robert Kidd. *Unknown. See* Captain Kidd.
Captain Rodgers' Cruelty. *Unknown. See* Andrew Rose.
Capt. Sally Tompkins, C. S. A. Beverley Randolph Tucker. PoP
Captain Stood on the Carronade, The. Frederick Marryat. *Fr.* Snarleyyow; or, The Dog Fiend. BBV (1923 ed.); EtS; HBV; OTPC; SG (Old Navy, The.) CBE; CBOV; EV-4; LH; StPo; TVSH
Captain Stratton's Fancy. John Masefield. MBP; MoBrPo; OBEV (new ed.); OnPP
Captain Sword. Leigh Hunt. GN
Captain Ward and the *Rainbow. Unknown.* BaBo; ESPB; ViBoFo (Famous Sea Fight between Captain Ward and the *Rainbow.*) SG
Captain Wattle and Miss Roe. Charles Dibdin. OxBoLi
Captain! we often heretofore. To Our House-Dog Captain. Walter Savage Landor. PoEL-4
Captain Wedderburn's Courtship. *Unknown.* BaBo (A *and* C *vers.*); ESPB (A *and* B *vers.*); ViBoFo (A *and* B *vers.*) (Six Questions, B *vers.*) BaBo
Captain Went Below, The, *frag. Unknown.* AmSS
Captain went to sea at seventeen, The. Clipper Captain. Shirley Barker. WaKn
Captaine, The. John Fletcher. *See* Captain, The.
Captains, The. Nikolai Gumilev, *tr. fr. Russian by* C. M. Bowra. BoR
Captains, The. Walter Adolphe Roberts. PoNe
Captains and conquerors leave a little dust. Epigram. Sir William Watson. BPP
Captain's Daughter, The. James Thomas Fields. *See* Ballad of the Tempest.
Captain's Dream, The. Anne Brontë. UnW
Captain's Feather, The. Samuel Minturn Peck. AA; LBAP
Captains of the Years, The. Arthur R. Macdougall, Jr. ChIP; MaRV; OQP; QP-2
Captain's Table. Witter Bynner. AnFE; CoAnAm
Captain's Walk; Salem. Oliver Jenkins. PoMa
Captive. Peretz Hirshbein, *tr. fr. Yiddish by* Joseph Leftwich. TrJP
Captive, The. Enrique González Martínez, *tr. fr. Spanish by* Edna Worthley Underwood. PoP
Captive, The. Kipling. VLEP
Captive. John Richard Moreland. PoMa
Captive, The. Sappho. *See* Love.
Captive, The. Chang Yu Shu, *tr. fr. Chinese by* Henry H. Hart. PoHN
Captive Bird was gone; —to cliff or moor, The. On Revisiting Dunolly Castle. Wordsworth. PeBoSo
Captive! Is there a hell to him like this? As Red Men Die. E. Pauline Johnson. CPG
Captive Knight. Mikhail Yurevich Lermontov, *tr. fr. Russian by* Babette Deutsch. TrRV
Captive Lion, The. W. H. Davies. ChMo; CMP; PtOT
Captive of Love, A. Ovid, *tr. fr. Latin by* Christopher Marlowe. Elegies, I, 2. AWP
Captive Ships at Manila, The. Dorothy Paul. PAH
Captive snake half dead with fright, A. The Snake and the Mouse. Bhartrihari. OnPM
Captive woman behind the bar. The Captive. Enrique González Martínez. PoP
Captives, The. *Unknown, tr. fr. Ukrainian by* Florence Randal Livesay. PoFr
Captives from the Western Tribes. Po Chü-i, *tr. fr. Chinese by* Ching Ti. WhP
Captives Going Home. *Unknown.* BlG
Captive's Hymn, The. Edna Dean Proctor. PAH

Captivity. Chaucer. Merciles Beaute, I. AEV; LiA
(Merciles Beaute, I.) CaAE; CoEV; LEAP; OBEV (1st ed.)
(Merciless Beauty. I, *mod. vers.*) ACP
(Rondel of Merciles Beautè [*or* Merciless Beauty], A, *orig. and mod. vers. by* Louis Untermeyer.) TrGrPo
Captivity. Samuel Rogers. FaBoEn
Captivity, The; an Oratorio, *sels.* Goldsmith.
Hope, *fr.* II. OBEC
"Hope, like a gleaming taper's light." MaRV
Memory, *fr.* I. OBEC, *sl. diff. vers.*; OBEV; PoP
(Song: "O memory, thou fond deceiver.") ViBoPo
Capture of Athens, The. Oracle, *tr. fr. Greek by* T. F. Higham. OxBG
Capture of Little York. *Unknown.* PAH
Captured. Archibald MacLeish. HBMV
Caput apri defero [*or* differo]. A Carol Bringing in the Boar's Head. *Unknown.* AnEC; TuPP
Caput Mortuum. E. A. Robinson. NP
Car stopped at the wood's edge, The. Deer and Bracken. Stella Gibbons. AlDL
Caractacus. Bernard Barton. LPS-2
Caravan, The. J. Redwood Anderson. TCPD
Caravan, The. Hovhannes Blouz, *tr. fr. Armenian by* Thomas Walsh. CAW
Caravan, The. Madeleine Nightingale. BoTP; GaP; MPB
Caravan from China Comes, A. Richard Le Gallienne. BrR; LBMV; MoSiPe
Caravans. Hal Borland. MoSiPe
Caravans. Emily Patterson. ChIP
Caravans. Josephine Preston Peabody. AA
Caravans. Irene Thompson. BoTP
Caravels of Columbus, The. Elias Lieberman. PEDC (1949 ed.)
Carcassonne. Gustave Nadaud, *tr. fr. French by* John R. Thompson. BLPA; FaBoBe; HBV; MW; NeHB
Carcassonne. Margaret Talbott Stevens. LPS-1
Carceri, soft rain in February, The. Things to Be Loved. Sister Mary Madeleva. SaFP
Card-Dealer, The. Dante Gabriel Rossetti. BPN; EmBrPo; PoVP; ViP; ViPo; VLEP
Card of Invitation to Mr. Gibbon, at Brighthelmstone, A. William Hayley. OBEC
Cardinal, The. Robert Penn Warren. Kentucky Mountain Farm, IV. MoVE
Cardinal and the Dog, The. Robert Browning. AlBD
Cardinal Bird, The. William Davis Gallagher. AA; BLA, *much abr.*; HiLiAm; SN
Cardinal Fisher. John Heywood. ACP
Cardinal, lover of shade. The Cardinal. Robert Penn Warren. Kentucky Mountain Farm, IV. MoVE
Cardinal Manning. Aubrey Thomas De Vere. JKCP; VA
Cardinal Wolsey's Farewell. Shakespeare, *and probably* John Fletcher. *See* Wolsey's Farewell to His Greatness.
Cardinal's Soliloquy, The. Sir Edward Bulwer-Lytton. *Fr.* Richelieu; or, The Conspiracy, III, i. VA
Cardinals were singing in this wood. Lord Cornwallis and a Carolina Spring. Helen Bevington. NoCaPo (rev. ed.)
Cards and Kisses. John Lyly. *See* Apelles' Song.
Care. Virginia Woodward Cloud. AA; HBV; LBAP
Care Away. *Unknown.* OxBoLi
("Care away away away.") NBE
Care away goe thow from me. *Unknown.* SeCSL
Care-Charmer Sleep [Son of the Sable Night]. Samuel Daniel. To Delia, LI. AtBAP; BCEP; CBOV; EV-1; GTSE (XXXV); LiTB; LiTG; LoBV (LIV); PeBoSo; ReaPo; TreFS
("Care-charmer Sleep, son of the sable Night.") ATP (LIV); EG; EnLit (XLV); FaBoEn; GTBS; GTBS-D; GTBS-W; GTSL; HBV; LEAP; LPS-2; OAEP; ReEn (XLV); ReIE (XLIX); SiCE (XLV); TCEP; TOP (XLIX); TuPP; ViBoPo
Delia. CoBE (LIV); ElSeCe (XLV); EnLi-1; TrGrPo
(Prayer to Sleep.) ES
(Sleep.) BLV
(Sonnet.) CoEV; ElL; PoEL-2 (XLIV)
(Sonnets to Delia.) BEL (LII); EPP (LIV); OBSC (XIV)
Care-charmer sleep, sweet ease in restless misery. Sleep. Bartholomew Griffin. Fidessa, More Chaste than Kind, XV. OBSC; ReEn; ReIE; SiCE; TuPP
Care-charming Sleep. John Fletcher. *Fr.* The Tragedy of Valentinian, V, ii. BEL; BLV; KN; OnPM; PC; TrGrPo; ViBoPo
(Care-Charming Sleep, Thou Easer Of All Woes.) AtBAP; BrBE; OAEP; SeEP; TuPP
(Into Slumbers.) SeCePo
(Invocation to Sleep.) AnEnPo; EPP; WHA
(Sleep.) EV-2
(Song: "Care-charming Sleep . .") LoBV; PoEL-2
(Song for the Sick Emperor.) FaBoEn
(Song to Sleep.) OxBoLi
(To Sleep.) EnLi-1; PoRA
Care flieth. Autumn. Christina Rossetti. EmBrPo
Care Is Heavy. Conal O'Riordan. CAW
Carefree. Po T'ing, *tr. fr. Chinese by* Henry H. Hart. PoHN
Careful hen, The. Domestic Birds. James Thomson. *Fr.* The Seasons: Spring. BCEP; LPS-2
Careful Husband, The. *Unknown, tr. fr. Late Middle Irish by* the Earl of Longford. OnYI; OxBI
Careful man I ought to be, A. The Little Chap Who Follows Me. *Unknown.* PoToHe (new ed.)
Careful observers may foretel[l] the Hour. A Description of a City Shower. Swift. BrBE; CEP; CIV; EiPP; EnLi-1 (1949 ed.); ExPo; KN; LoBV; OnYI; PoE; PoFS; SeCePo; SeCeV; UnPo (3d ed.)
Careful Penman, The. *Unknown.* BOHV
Carefully on tiptoe stealing. It Was the Cat. W. S. Gilbert. *Fr.* H.M.S. Pinafore. CIV
Carefully the birch tree. The Absent Minded Birch Tree. Kathleen Millay. PEDC
Careles of love & free from feares. *At. to* Thomas Carew. SeCSL
Careless Content. John Byrom. CEP; EV-3; HBV; OBEC
"I am content, I do not care," *sel.* LO
Careless Delight. Omar Khayyám, *tr. fr. Persian by* Edward Fitzgerald. *Fr.* The Rubáiyát. OnPM
Careless Fairy, The. Nancy Byrd Turner. BoChLi
Careless forever, beautiful proud sea. Beautiful Proud Sea. Sara Teasdale. NP
Careless Gallant, The. Thomas Jordan. CoMu; OxBoLi; SeCL; SiTL
(Coronemus Nos Rosis Antequam Marcescant.) HBV; OBEV
(Epicure, The, Sung by One in the Habit of a Town Gallant.) SeEP
Careless Good Fellow, The. John Oldham. CEP; SeCV-2
Careless I lived, accepting day by day. Epitaph on a Vagabond. Alexander Gray. HBMV
Careless Kittens, The. *Unknown. See* Three Little Kittens.
Careless Love. Stanley Kunitz. WaP
Careless Love, *with music. Unknown.* AS; StDa; TrAS
Careless rhymer, it is true. Chloe, M. A. Mortimer Collins. BOHV
Careless she lies along the Southern Main. Australia, 1905. Archibald T. Strong. *Fr.* Sonnets of the Empire. BoAu
Careless Talk. Mark Hollis. FiBHP
Careless Willie. *Unknown.* FaPON
Cares. *Unknown. See* Out in the Fields with God.
Cares and anxieties. For Sleep When Overtired [*or* Worried]. Sarah N. Cleghorn. OQP; PC; QP-2
Cares of Majesty, The. Shakespeare. *See* Henry IV's Soliloquy on Sleep.
Caresses. Elsa Barker. *Fr.* The Spirit and the Bride. HBMV
Cargoes. John Masefield. AnEnPo; ATP; BEL; BMEP; CaAE; CBE; CBOV; ChMo; CMP; CP; EnLi-2 (1949 ed.); EnLit; ExPo; FaPON; GTBS-D; GTSL; LEAP; LiTM; MBP; MCCG; MoAB; MoBrPo; MuP; NP; NV; OBEV (new ed.); OBMV; OBVV; OtMeF; PCH; PCN; PIAE; PoeMoYo; PoRA; PtOT; SeCeV; ShBV-1; SP; TCEP; TCPD; TiPo (1952 ed.); TOP; TreF; TVSH; VOD; YT
Cargoes of the Radanites. Harry Alan Potamkin. TrJP
Caria and Philistia considered. Cry Faugh! Robert Graves. CoBMV
Caribbean, The. Stephanie Ormsby. PoNe
Carillon, The. Rosalia Castro de Murguía, *tr. fr. Spanish by* Garrett Strange. CAW
Carillon. Longfellow. *Fr.* The Belfry of Bruges. CoBA; IAP; LPS-2
Caring. F. R. Scott. PeCV
Caring for Silkworms. Sung Shih, *tr. fr. Chinese by* Henry H. Hart. PoHN
Caring is loving, motionless. Caring. F. R. Scott. PeCV
Carl Hamblin. Edgar Lee Masters. *Fr.* Spoon River Anthology. AmP; ChMo; CMP; LiTA; LiTM (rev. ed.)
Carle, Now the King's Come. Sir Walter Scott. EBSV
Carlino! what art thou about, my boy? To My Child Carlino. Walter Savage Landor. OBRV
Carlyle and Emerson. Montgomery Schuyler. AA; PoMa
Carlyle combined the lit'ry life. Thomas Carlyle. *Unknown.* FiBHP
Carmagnole, La. *sel. Unknown, tr. fr. French by* John Oxenford.
"All honest folk throughout the land," 6 *sts.* PoFr
Carman's Account of a Law-Suit, A. Sir David Lindsay. BOHV
Carmelite Breaks Silence, A. Sister Miriam. PraNu
Carmen. Newman Levy. ALV; FiBHP
Carmen Bellicosum. Guy Humphreys McMaster. AA; ALV; DD; DDA; GN; HBV; LPS-2; MC; OBAV; PaA; PAH
(Old Continentals, The.) PAP
Carmen Genesis. Francis Thompson. CoBE; PoLi
Carmen Paschale [*or* Easter Song], *sels.* Caelius Sedulius, *tr. fr. Latin.*

Apostrophe to Death, *tr. by* George Sigerson. OnYI
Christ Quiets the Tempest, *tr. by* George Sigerson. OnYI
Hail, Maiden Root, *tr. by* Raymond F. Roseliep. ISi
Invocation: "Eternal God omnipotent! The One," *tr. by* George Sigerson. OnYI
Magi Visit Herod, The, *tr. by* H. T. Henry. CAW
Miracle, The, *tr. by* H. T. Henry. CAW
Slaughter of the Innocents by Order of King Herod, The, *tr. by* George Sigerson. OnYI
Carmen Possum. *Unknown.* BLPA
Carmina Burana, *sels. Unknown, tr. fr. Latin.*
Amor Habet Superos, *tr by* George F. Whicher. LaP
De Ramis Cadunt Folia, *tr. by* Helen Waddell. LaP
(Winter Love Song.) LiTW
Exiit Diluculo, *tr. by* George F. Whicher. LaP
Gaudeamus Igitur, *tr. by* John Addington Symonds. HBV; LaP; WoL
In Taberna Quando Sumus, *tr. by* George F. Whicher. LaP
Juliana, *tr. by* George F. Whicher. LaP
Nobilis, Precor, *tr. by* Basil Blackett. LaP
Noble Wood Displays, The, *tr. by* Jack Lindsay. LaP
O Comes Amoris, Dolor, *tr. by* George F. Whicher. LaP
Obmittamus Studia, *tr. by* Helen Waddell. LaP
Potatores Exquisiti, *tr. by* Basil Blackett. LaP
Suscipe Flos Florem, *tr. by* L. R. Lind. LaP
Tempus Instat Floridum, *tr. by* George F. Whicher. LaP
(Flowering Time.) LyMA
Ver Redit Optatum, *tr. by* George F. Whicher. LaP
Vidi Viridi Phyllida sub Tilia, *tr. by* Rolfe Humphries. LaP
Volo Virum Vivere Viriliter, *tr. by* Helen Waddell. LaP
Carmina Epigraphica, *sels. Unknown, tr. fr. Latin by* F. L. Lucas. LaP
Agathe, Aged Five.
"Lovely as is the rose to men, when first it flowers in spring."
"Mourn not my loss; tears change not destiny."
Old Gentleman of Seventy-seven, An.
"Rich man builds a house, but the wise a tomb, The."
"Short is my say, O stranger. Stay and read."
"Women and wine and baths bring life's decline."
Carnal and Spiritual Love. Michelangelo, *tr. fr. Italian by* John Addington Symonds. OnPM
Carnal and the Crane, The. *Unknown.* AnEC; ESPB; OBB; StJW
Carnations. Ken Etheridge. MoWP
Carnations. Margaret Widdemer. AV
Carnival. J. R. Hervey. AnNZ
Carnival ("Carnival! carnival! Laughter is rife"). Codman Hislop. CAG
Carnival of Animals, The, *sels.* Ogden Nash. UnS
Birds, The.
Introduction: "Camille St. Saëns was racked with pains."
Carnival Song: Song of the Girls and the Tattlers (Cicadas). Lorenzo de' Medici, *tr. fr. Italian by* Richard Aldington. LyPI
Carnival Song: Triumph of Bacchus and Ariadne. Lorenzo de' Medici, *tr. fr. Italian by* Richard Aldington. LyPI
Carol: "All this night shrill chanticler." William Austin. *See* Chanticleer.
Carol, A: "Angels to the shepherds sang, The." Fred E. Weatherly. YeAr
Carol, A: "As I in a hoarie, winter's night." Robert Southwell. *See* Burning Babe, The.
Carol: "Deep in the fading leaves of night." W. R. Rodgers. ChMP; FaBoTw
Carol: "Fire is what's precious now." Alison Boodson. NeBP
Carol: Five Joys of the Virgin, The. *Unknown.* ACP; ISi
Carol: "He came all so still." *Unknown. See* I Sing of a Maiden.
Carol: "I saw a sweet and seemly sight." *Unknown, at. to* John Brackley *See* I Saw a Sweet and Silly Sight.
Carol: "I sing of a Maiden." *See* I Sing of a Maiden.
Carol, A: "Joseph was an old man." Lizette Woodworth Reese. StJW
Carol: "Mary laid her Child among." Norman Nicholson. NeBP; StJW
Carol, A: "Mary the Mother sang to her Son." Lizette Woodworth Reese. HBMV
Carol: "Mary, the mother, sits on the hill." Langdon Elwyn Mitchell. BOL; SDH
(Song: "Mary, the mother . . .") ChrBoLe
Carol: "Month can never forget the year, The." John McClure. HBMV
Carol: "Shepherd and a shepherdess, A." Clément Marot, *tr. fr. French by* Ralph N. Currey. FoS
Carol, A: "Sweet Music, sweeter far." Edmund Bolton. OxBoCh
Carol: "There was a Boy bedded in bracken." John Short. FaBoCh; FaBoTw; LoGBV
Carol: "Three kings from out the Orient." Thomas Edward Brown. VLEP
Carol: "Villagers all, this frosty tide." Kenneth Grahame. *Fr.* The Wind in the Willows. OHIP
(Christmas Carol.) FaPON; MPB
Carol, A: "Vines branching stilly." Louise Imogen Guiney. CAW; OBVV
(Five Carols for Christmastide, II.) ISi
Carol: "We saw Him sleeping in His manger bed." Gerald Bullett. DD; HBVY
(We Saw Him Sleeping.) SDH
Carol: "When the herds were watching." William Canton. DD; HBVY; OHIP; SDH
Carol at the Manger, A. *Unknown. See* Coventry Carol, The.
Carol Bringing in the Boar's Head, A. *Unknown.* AnEC; TuPP
Carol, Brothers, Carol. William A. Muhlenberg. SDH; TiPo (1952 ed.)
Carol, Christians! Christ is here! Christ Is Here. Robert Lowell. BePJ
Carol, every violet has. Epilogue. Alfred Noyes. *Fr.* The Flower of Old Japan. MBP; MoBrPo
Carol for Candlemas Day. *Unknown.* MeRV; SeCL
Carol for Christmas Day, A. *Unknown.* TuPP
(Cast Off All Doubtful Care.) AnEC
Carol for Christmas Day before Dawn, A. Gordon Bottomley. QS
Carol for Christmas Eve, A. Eleanor Farjeon. BoChLi
Carol for His Darling on Christmas Day. Derek Stanford. NeBP
Carol for Saint Stephen's Day, A. *Unknown. See* St. Stephen and Herod.
Carol for Twelfth Day, A. *Unknown.* OHIP; SDH
(" Mark well my heavy doleful tale.") COAH
Carol in Praise of the Holly and Ivy. *Unknown. See* Holly and Ivy Made a Great Party.
Carol Naïve. John McClure. HBMV
Carol of Hunting, A. *Unknown.* AnEC
Carol of Jesus Child. Francis Macnamara. BOL
Carol of Mother Mary, A. *Unknown.* BCEP
Carol of the Birds. *Unknown, tr. fr. French.* OHIP; SDH
(Whence Comes This Rush of Wings?) ChrBoLe
Carol of the Birth of Christ, A. *Unknown.* AnEC
Carol of the Fir Tree, The. Alfred Noyes. SDH
Carol of the Poor Children, The. Richard Middleton. QS
Carol of the Russian Children. *Unknown.* OHIP; SDH
Carol of Three Kings, The. Nora Hopper Chesson. ChrBoLe
Carol round the ruddy hearth, A. For Christmas Day. Eleanor Farjeon. ChBR; TiPo (1952 ed.)
Carol Singers, The. Margaret G. Rhodes. BoTP
Carol to Our Lady: "I sing of a Maiden." *Unknown. See* I Sing of a Maiden.
Carol with Variations. Phyllis McGinley. QS
Carolina. Henry Timrod. BIG; MC; PAH; PoRL; SPP
Carolina ("Carolina! Carolina! Noble name in State and story"). John A. Wagner. BIG
Carolina! Carolina! Heaven's blessings attend her! The Old North State. William Gaston. NoCaPo; PoRL
Carolina Herons Zoe Kincaid Brockman. NoCaPo
Carolina Spring Song. Hervey Allen. BAP; HBMV; TBM
Caroline, The. George Crabbe. *Fr.* The Borough. SeCePo
Caroline Cricket. C. Lindsay McCoy. GFA
Caron oh Caron come away. *Unknown.* SeCSL
Carousal. Ibn Khafaja, *tr. fr. Arabic by* A. J. Arberry. MooP
Carousal. Ibn Safar, *tr. fr. Arabic by* A. J. Arberry. MooP
Carouse. Charles Hanson Towne. NLK; VOD
Carpe Diem. Asclepiades. *See* There Is No Loving after Death.
Carpe Diem. "Laurence Hope." *Fr.* In the Early, Pearly Morning. OtMeF
Carpe Diem. Horace. *See* To Leuconoë.
Carpe Diem. Thomas Lodge. *See* Pluck the Fruit and Taste the Pleasure.
Carpe Diem. Théophile Marzials. VA
Carpe Diem. Shakespeare. *See* O Mistress Mine.
Carpe Diem. Ridgely Torrence. *Fr.* The House of a Hundred Lights AA
Carpe Diem. *Unknown. See* Hey Nonny No!
Carpenter, The. Amy Bruner Almy. ChIP
Carpenter. Leslie Savage Clark. ChIP
Carpenter. Isabel Fiske Conant. StJW
Carpenter, The. Phyllis Hartnoll. ChIP; QS
Carpenter. E. V. Lucas. StVeCh
Carpenter, The. George Macdonald. TrPWD
Carpenter, The. G. A. Studdert-Kennedy. ChIP; OQP; QP-1; StJW
Carpenter, The. Gumpei Yamamuro, *tr. fr. Japanese by* Lois J. Erickson. SoLD
Carpenter Christ. Mildred Fowler Field. PGD
Carpenter of Eternity ("A carpenter, he worked with wood"). E. Merrill Root. ChIP; PGD
Carpenter of Galilee, The. Hilda W. Smith. ChIP; MaRV
Carpenter of Nazareth, The. George Blair. StJW
Carpenter of Nazareth, The. Walter Smith. ChIP
Carpenter was not afraid to die, The. The Divine Rebel. George Scheftel. ChIP

Carpenter, what are you building now? Not Made with Hands. Lilith Lorraine. ChIP
Carpenter's Plane, The. Vasili Kazin, *tr. fr. Russian by* Babette Deutsch. OnPM; TrRV
Carpenter's Son. Annie Johnson Flint. BePJ
Carpenter's Son, The A. E. Housman. A Shropshire Lad, XLVIII. BLV; BoLiVe; BPN; CoBMV; EmBrPo; MoAB; MoBrPo; NeMA; PoVP; ReaPo
Carpenter's Son, The. Kathryn Blackburn Peck. BePJ
Carpenter's Young Wife, The. Chaucer. *Fr.* The Canterbury Tales: The Miller's Tale. ExPo
Carpette Knyghte, Ye. "Lewis Carroll." AlDL
Carrara. Philip Murray. NePoAm
Carriage brushes through the bright, The. Solo for Ear-Trumpet. Edith Sitwell. MBP; MoAB; MoBrPo; NeMA
Carriage from Sweden, A. Marianne Moore. LiTA; LiTM (rev. ed.); MoAB; NePA
Carrickfergus. Louis MacNeice. AnIL; OnYI
Carrier, The. Thomas Hardy. BMEP
Carrier cannot sing today the ballads, The. The Old Sergeant. Forceythe Willson. BIG
Carrier's Address. *Unknown.* PoOW
Carrion, A. Baudelaire, *tr. fr. French by* Allen Tate. AWP; LiTW
Carrion Comfort. Gerard Manley Hopkins. AnFE; AtBAP; CoBE; EmBrPo; EnLi-2; LiTB; LiTG; MaPo; MoP; MoVE; NBE; OAEP; OxBoCh; PoEL-5; PoLi; POTT; PoVP; ViP; ViPo; ViPP
(Sonnet.) CoEV; FaBoEn
(Terrible Sonnets, The, I.) MoPo
Carrion Crow, The. Thomas Lovell Beddoes. *See* Song: "Old Adam, the carrion crow."
Carrion crow sat on an oak, A. Mother Goose. OTPC (1923 ed.); OxNR
Carrion-eater's nobility calls back from God, The. A Dreamed Realization. Gregory Corso. NeAP
Carroll's Sword. *At. to* Dallan MacMore. *See* Song of Carroll's Sword, The.
Carrot has a green fringed top, A. Vegetables. Rachel Field. GFA
Carrouse to the Emperor, the Royal Pole, and the Much-wronged Duke of Lorrain, A. *Unknown.* CoMu
Carrowmore. "Æ." BEL; ChMo; CMP; HBMV
(Gates of Dreamland, The.) HBV
Carry and Kate. William Brighty Rands. *Fr.* Topsy-turvy World. BoN
Carry Her over the Water. W. H. Auden. FaBoTw
Carry Me Back. John Holmes. NePoAm-2
Carry Me Back to Old Virginny. James A. Bland. FaBoBe; FaFP; GoSl; OlF; PoRL; TreF
Carry me out. Discharged. W. E. Henley. *Fr.* In Hospital. BPN; POTT; PoVP; VLEP
Carry me over the long last mile. The Long Last Mile. Lauchlan MacLean Watt. MaRV
Carry On! Thomas Curtis Clark. OQP; QP-2
Carry On! Robert W. Service. HBV; MaRV
Carry your grief alone. Alone. Robert Finch. CaP; PeCV
Carryin' Sacks, *with music. Unknown.* StDa
Carrying Their Coracles. Andrew Marvell. *Fr.* Upon Appleton House. ChTr
Carrying their packages of groceries in particular. Old Men and Old Women Going Home on the Street Car. Merrill Moore. MAP; MoAmPo
Cars Go Fast. Annette Wynne. GFA
Cart that carries hay, The. Farm Cart. Eleanor Farjeon. BrR
Carter from the village drove his wain, A. Babrius, *tr. fr. Greek by* James Davies. GrPo
Carthage. Miriam Allen deFord. MuM
Carthon, a Poem. James Macpherson. EiPP; EnRP
Ossian's Address to the Sun, *sel.* BEL
Carthusians. Ernest Dowson. JKCP; PoVP; TriL
Cartier Arrives at Stadacona. William T. Allison. CPG
Cartier at St. Malo. Francis Webb. *Fr.* A View of Montreal. BoAV
Cartier; Dauntless Discoverer. John Daniel Logan. CPG
Cartoons of slashes on the tide-traced crater. Sonnets, VI. Dylan Thomas. LiTM
Carve me a cherub! All of me head and wings! Louise Hedeen. Edgar Lee Masters. *Fr.* The New Spoon River. LEAP
Carve your name upon a tree. Poem of Circumstance. Jean Cocteau. CAW
Carved by a mighty race whose vanished hands. The Sphinx Speaks. Francis Saltus Saltus. AA; BAP; LEAP; OBAV
Carved Stone, A. *Unknown, tr. fr. Greek by* Lord Neaves. OnPM
Carver, The. Conrad Aiken. *See* See, as the Carver . . .
Caryatid. Léonie Adams. MoVE
Casa d'Amunt. Alastair Reid. NePoEA
Casa Guidi Windows, *sels.* Elizabeth Barrett Browning.
"Cry is up in England, which doth ring, A." *fr.* II. PoVP
Juliet of Nations. VA
(From "Casa Guidi Windows," *br. sel.*) PECK
Sursum Corda. VA
Casa Wappy. David Macbeth Moir. LPS-1
Casabianca. Felicia Dorothea Hemans. BCEP; BeLS; BLPA; CG; EtS; FaBoBe; FaFP; FaPON; GoTP; HBV; HBVY; LH; LPS-2; NeHB; OTPC; OnSP; PECK; PIR; PreP; PTA-2; TreF; TVSH; WBLP
Casa's Dirge. David Macbeth Moir. VA
Cascade, The. Edgell Rickword. ChMP; FaBoTw
Cascade, The. Tadamine, *tr. fr. Japanese by* Basil Hall Chamberlain. OnPM
Cascading streamers down of palest green. Weeping Willow. Richard Aldridge. NePoAm-2
Case, A. Hughes Mearns. *See* Antigonish.
Case for the Defense, A. Aeschylus, *tr. fr. Greek by* G. M. Cookson. *Fr.* Agamemnon. GrR
Case for the Miners, The. Siegfried Sassoon. PoFr
Case History. Arthur W. Bell. WhC
Case is Altered, The, *sel.* Ben Jonson.
"'Tis not to be told/ What servile villainies men will do for gold." LO
Case of the Murdered Bird, The. Luis Cernuda, *tr. fr. Spanish by* Eleanor L. Turnbull. CoSP
Case of Thomas More, The. Sister Mary St. Virginia. GoBC
Casement high and triple-arched there was, A. Keats. *Fr.* The Eve of Saint Agnes. PC
Casements. Isabel Fisk Conant. BAP
Casey at the Bat. Ernest Lawrence Thayer. BBV (1951 ed.); BeLS; BLPA; BOHV; FaBoBe; FaFP; FaPON; HBV; IHA; InMe; LHV; MaC; NeHB; OnSP; PoRA; PreP; PTA-1; PYM; StPo; TreF; YaD
Casey Jones. E. V. Swart. LiTM
Casey Jones *Unknown.* ABF, *with music;* ABS, *sl. abr.;* AmPP; ANL, *diff. vers.;* APW, *diff. vers.;* AS, *with music;* ATP; BeLS; IHA, *sl. abr.;* KN; MaC, *arr. by* T. Lawrence Seibert; OxBoLi; TreF; TrGrPo; ViBoFo (A, B, C, D, E, F, *and* G *vers.*)
(Mama, Have You Heard the News, *diff. vers., with music.*) AS
(Natchul-born Easman, *diff. vers.*) ABF
Casey Jones, befo' he died. Natchul-born Easman. *Unknown.* ABF
Casey Jones has left today. Casey Jones. E. V. Swart. LiTM
Casey Jones was a brave engineer. Casey Jones (D *vers.*) *Unknown.* ViBoFo
Casey Jones was engineer. Casey Jones (F *vers.*). *Unknown.* ViBoFo
Casey Jones was long and tall. Casey Jones (E *vers.*). *Unknown.* ViBoFo
Casey—Twenty Years Later. S. P. McDonald. BLPA
Casey would waltz with a strawberry blonde (*refrain*). The Band Played On. John F. Palmer. TreF
Casey's Daughter at the Bat, *parody.* Al Graham. InMe
Casey's Revenge. James Wilson. BLPA; PTA-1; TreFS
Casey's Table d'Hote. Eugene Field. PoOW
Cashed in his chips. Epitaph for a Man from Virginia City. Kenneth Porter. NePoAm-2
Cashel of Munster. *Unknown, at. to* William English, *tr. fr. Modern Irish by* Sir Samuel Ferguson. AnIV; GTIV; IrPN; OBEV; OBVV; OnYI; OxBI
Casina, *sel.* Plautus, *tr. fr. Latin by* F. A. Wright.
"There's nothing in the world like love." LaP
Casino. W. H. Auden. MoPo; PoLFOT
Casket, The. Nathaniel Wanley. SeCL
Casket Song, A. Shakespeare. *See* Tell Me Where Is Fancy Bred.
Caspar Hauser Song. Georg Trakl, *tr. fr. German by* David Luke. AnGP
Caspar, Melchior, Balthazar. The Gift. Laura Spencer Portor. StJW
Cassamen and Dowsabell. Michael Drayton. *Fr.* The Shepherd's Garland. OBSC
(Ballad of Dowsabell, The.) LoBV
(Eighth Eclogue.) ReEN; TuPP
Cassandra. Aeschylus, *tr. fr. Greek by* Gilbert Murray. *Fr.* Agamemnon. GrR
Cassandra. Louise Bogan. AnAmPo; LA; MAP; MoAmPo; MOAP; MoVE; NP
Cassandra. Euripides, *tr. fr. Greek by* Gilbert Murray. *Fr.* Trojan Women. GrR
Cassandra. Robinson Jeffers. LiTA; LiTM; NePA; WaP
Cassandra. E. A. Robinson. AmPP; ExPo; LiTA; LiTM (rev. ed.); MaPo; NePA; NP; OxBA; PoFr; SeCeV
Cassandra Prepares to Die. Aeschylus, *tr. fr. Greek by* Louis MacNeice. *Fr.* Agamemnon. OxBG
Cassandra Southwick. Whittier. IAP; PAH
Cassandra Speaks. Pierre de Ronsard, *tr. fr. French by* Alan Conder. TrFP
Cassandra, treading the Titanic deck. Captain's Table. Witter Bynner. AnFE; CoAnAm

Cassandra's Lament. Aeschylus, *tr. fr. Greek by* Richmond Lattimore. *Fr.* Agamemnon. LiTW
Cassandra's Song of Celibacy. Gil Vicente, *tr. fr. Spanish by* George Ticknor. AnSpL-1
Cassius Hueffer. Edgar Lee Masters. *Fr.* Spoon River Anthology. OxBA
Cassius Poisons Brutus' Mind. Shakespeare. *Fr.* Julius Caesar, I, ii. TreFS
Cast all your cares on God; that anchor holds. Cast Your Cares on God. Tennyson. *Fr.* Enoch Arden. MaRV
Cast Asleep. Keats. *See* Adonis in Slumber.
Cast away care, he that loves sorrow. Thomas Dekker *and* John Ford. *Fr.* The Sun's Darling. ReEn; TuPP
Cast away those silkne clouds. *Unknown.* SeCSL
Cast Down, but Not Destroyed. *Unknown.* PAH
Cast from a rush, into a running stream. The Great Banquet. Ramón de Campoamor. *Fr.* Doloras. AnSpL-2
Cast Off All Doubtful Care. *Unknown. See* Carol for Christmas Day, A
Cast on the water by a careless hand. The Cocoa Tree. Charles Warren Stoddard. AA; CAW; OBAV
Cast our caps and cares away. John Fletcher. *Fr.* Beggars' Bush. SiCE; TuPP; ViBoPo
Cast Thy Bread upon the Waters. Ecclesiastes, XI: 1-6, Bible, *O.T.* AWP; JAWP; TiPo (1952 ed.), *2 ll.*; WBP
(Life's Uncertainty, XI: 1-10.) TreFS
(Youth and Age, XI: 1-XII: 7.) OuHeWo
Cast wide the folding doorways of the East. From the Night of Forebeing. Francis Thompson. OBVV; OtMeF
Cast Your Cares on God. Tennyson. *Fr.* Enoch Arden. MaRV
Castara, *sels.* William Habington.
Against Them Who Lay Unchastity to the Sex of Women, *fr.* II. ElSeCe; MePo; OBS; SeEP
Castara ("Like the violet, which alone"), *fr.* I. HBV; LiTL
Melancholy, *fr.* II. LoBV
Nox Nocti Indicat Scientiam, *fr.* III. ACP; CAW; CoEV; ElSeCe; EV-2; GoBC; GTSL; HBV; LoBV; MeLP; MePo; MeRV; OBEV; OBS; PoFr; PoLi; SeCL; TriL
(When I Survey the Bright.) OxBoCh
To Castara: Of the Knowledge of Love, *fr.* II. EV-2
To Castara: The Reward of Innocent Love, *fr.* II. EV-2
(Reward of Innocent Love, The.) ACP
(To Castara.) LoBV
To Castara Praying, *fr.* I. MeRV
To Castara, upon Beauty, *fr.* II. CoBE
To Roses in the Bosom of Castara, *fr.* I. ElSeCe; EnLoPo; EV-2; GoBC; HBV; LoBV; MeLP; OBEV; SeCL; SeEP; ViBoPo
Upon Castara's Departure, *fr.* I. SeCL
Upon Thought Castara May Die, *fr.* I. ACP
Castara, see that dust the sportive wind. To Castara, upon Beauty. William Habington. *Fr.* Castara, II. CoBE
Castaway, The. William Cowper. AtBAP; BEL; CEP; CoBE; CoEV; EiPP; EnLi-2; EnLit; EnRP; EV-3; FaBoEn; FiP; GTSL; InPo; NBE; OAEP; OBEC; PoE; PoEL-3; PoFS; TCEP; TOP; TriL; TwHP
Castaway, The. Sophocles, *tr. fr. Greek by* Robert Whitelaw. *Fr.* Philoctetes. GrR
(Philoctetes Deserted, *tr. by* C. M. Bowra.) OxBG
Castaways, The. Marya Zaturenska. TrGrPo (1942 ed.)
Castello. Agnes Mary Frances Robinson. LBBV
Casterbridge Captains, The. Thomas Hardy. EV-5
Castile. Miguel de Unamuno, *tr. fr. Spanish by* Eleanor L. Turnbull. TeCS
Castilian. Elinor Wylie. AnAmPo; HBMV; LA; NAMP; TBM; TCAP; VOD (1935 ed.)
Casting All Your Care upon God, for He Careth for You. Thomas Washbourne. OxBoCh
Casting the times with their strong signs. Richard Crashaw. *Fr.* Sospetto d'Herode, I. EPS (1942 ed.)
Castle, The. Sidney Alexander. PoNe
Castle, The. Edwin Muir. LiTB
Castle, The. Michael Roberts. MoP
Castle and Cottage. Anna Maria Lenggren, *tr. fr. Swedish by* Charles W. Stork. AnSL
Castle Builder, The. La Fontaine, *tr. fr. French.* OTPC
Castle Builder, The, *sel.* Longfellow.
Challenge to Youth ("Build on, and make thy castles high and fair"). MaRV
Castle by the Sea, The. Ludwig Uhland, *tr. fr. German by* Longfellow. AWP; JAWP; UnW; WBP
Castle Howard. Lawrence Toynbee. NeTW
Castle Hyde. Edward Kenealy. *See* Sweet Castle Hyde.
Castle in the Air, The. Thomas Paine. LPS-3
Castle in the Fire, The. Mary Jane Carr. BrR
Castle of Indolence, The, *sels.* James Thomson.
Canto I. BEL; CEP; EiPP; LPS-3, *much abr.*
"Doors that knew no shrill alarming bell, The." *fr.* I. ViBoPo
"In lowly dale, fast by a river's side," *fr.* I. EnRP; EPP; ViBoPo
(Enchanted Ground.) BSV
(Land of Indolence.) OBEC; SeCePo
(Vale of Indolence.) CBOV; EBSV
Indifference to Fortune, *fr.* II. OBEC
"O mortal man, who livest here by toil," *fr.* I. EM-1; EnLi-2 (1949 ed.); EV-3; TCEP
"Pleasing land of drowsy-head it was, A," *fr.* I. BCEP; LEAP
Praise of Industry, The, *fr.* II. OBEC
"Sometimes the pencil, in cool airy halls," *fr.* I. PoEL-3
Sons of Indolence, *fr.* I. OBEC
Witching Song, A, *fr.* I. OBEC
Wondrous Show, A, *fr.* I. OBEC
Castle Ruins, The. William Barnes. VA
Castleconnell. Sir Aubrey De Vere. IrPN
Castled crag of Drachenfels, The. The Rhine. Byron. *Fr.* Childe Harold's Pilgrimage. LPS-2; ViBoPo
Castlehyde. Edward Kenealy. *See* Sweet Castle Hyde.
Castles. A. Glanz-Leyeless, *tr. fr. Yiddish by* Joseph Leftwich. TrJP
Castles and Distances. Richard Wilbur. FiMAP
Castles in the Air. James Ballantine. HBV
Castles in the Air. Thomas Love Peacock. HBV
Castles in the Sand. Dorothy Baker. BoTP
Castles with lofty. Soldier's Song. Goethe. *Fr.* Faust. AWP
Castor and Polydeuces. Alcaeus, *tr. fr. Greek by* C. M. Bowra. OxBG
Castor and Polydeuces. Pindar, *tr. fr. Greek by* C. J. Billson. *Fr.* Nemean Odes. OxBG
(Twin Brothers.) GrR
Casual glance on me, The. Old Essex Door. Agnes McCarthy Hickey. GoYe
Casual Gold. Maud E. Uschold. YeAr
Casual Man, The. Denis Glover. AnNZ
Casual Meeting. Margaret E. Bruner. PoToHe
Casual Song, A. Roden Noel. HBV
Casualties, *sels.* W. W. Gibson. VOD
Angus Armstrong.
Noel Dark.
Philip Dagg.
Ralph Straker.
Casualty. W. E. Henley. *Fr.* In Hospital. PoVP
Casualty. Edwin McNeill Poteat. MaRV
Casualty. Diana Witherby. ChMP
Casuarina. Roland Robinson. BoAV
Cat. Dorothy W. Baruch. SUS; TiPo; UTS
Cat, The. Baudelaire, *tr. fr. French by* Alan Conder. TrFP
Cat, The. Charles Stuart Calverley. *Fr.* Sad Memories. ChTr
Cat, The. Richard Church. AlDL
Cat, A. Jules Lemaitre, *tr. fr. French.* CIV
Cat. Sinclair Lewis. GoTP
Cat, The. Mary Britton Miller. BoChLi; StVeCh; SUS; TiPo; UTS
Cat, The. Walter Adolphe Roberts. CIV; PFE
Cat, The. Christopher Smart. *See* My Cat Jeoffry.
Cat, The. Lytton Strachey. PoC
Cat. "Jan Struther." GoTP
Cat, A. Edward Thomas. PoC
Cat, The. Helen Hay Whitney. GFA
Cat and Crocuses. Eva Martin. PoC
Cat and Lady. Paul Verlaine. *See* Femme et chatte.
Cat and Northern Lights, The. Elizabeth J. Coatsworth. CIV
Cat and the Bird, The. George Canning. ChTr
Cat and the Bird, The. Marvin Solomon. NePoAm-2
Cat and the Fox, The. La Fontaine, *tr. fr. French by* Sir Edward Marsh. PoC
Cat and the Man, The. Oliver Edwards. PoC
Cat and the Moon, The. W. B. Yeats. AlDL; EnLP; ExPo; FaBoCh; InPo; KN; LoGBV; MM; MoP; Po; PoC; PoMS; ShBV-1; ThWaDe
Cat and the Partridge, The. Damocharis the Grammarian, *tr. fr. Greek by* W. Bedell Stanford. PoC
Cat Ballerina Assoluta. Emilie Glen. GoYe
Cat came fiddling out of a barn, A. Mother Goose. BoChLi; BoN; BoTP; OTPC; PCH; PPL; SAS; StVeCh
Cat Changed into a Woman, The. La Fontaine, *tr. fr. French.* CIV
(Cat into Lady, *tr. by* Sir Edward Marsh.) PoC
Cat do not die. For a Siamese Cat. Mairi MacInnes. PoN
Cat I sing, of famous memory. A. A Catalectic Monody. *Unknown.* BOHV; CIV
Cat, if you go outdoors you must walk in the snow. On a Night of Snow. Elizabeth J. Coatsworth. CIV; GoTP; MAP; MoAmPo; MoShBr; MW; PoTo
Cat in distress, A. Verses on a Cat. Shelley. CIV; PoC
Cat in the Snow, The. F. Hey. SAS
Cat into Lady. La Fontaine. *See* Cat Changed into a Woman, The.
Cat is in the parlour, The. Indifference. *Unknown.* BOHV
Cat is walking in my brain, A. The Cat. Baudelaire. TrFP
Cat May Look at a King, A. *Unknown.* OxBoLi
Cat may look on a king, and what of that, A. Of a Cat's Look. John Heywood. SiCE; TuPP

Cat-o'-Nine-Tails, The. John Blight. BoAV; NeLNL
Cat of Cats. Vivien Bulkley. PoC
Cat of Cats, The. William Brighty Rands. *Fr.* The White Princess. CIV
(Kitten Speaks, The.) RIS
(Kitty: What She Thinks of Herself.) CBPC, *abr.*; MoShBr
Cat on the Porch at Dusk. Dorothy Harriman. GoYe
Cat runs races with her tail, The. Signs of Winter. John Clare. PoE; WaKn
Cat sat asleep by the side of the fire, The. *Unknown.* OxNR
Cat sat quaintly by the fire, A. Hearth. Peggy Bacon. FaPON; MPB
Cat sleeps in a chimney jam, The. Before Bedtime. John Charles McNeill. NoCaPo
Cat that comes to my window sill, The. That Cat. Ben King. FiBHP
Cat That Followed His Nose, The. John Kaye Kendall. CenHV
Cat, the Weasel, and the Little Rabbit, The. La Fontaine, *tr. fr. French by* Alan Conder. TrFP
Cat to Her Kittens, A. Eliza Grove. OTPC (1923 ed.)
Cat was once a weaver, The. What the Gray Cat Sings. Arthur Guiterman. MoShBr; MPB; PoMS; PoRL
Cat went here and there, The. The Cat and the Moon. W. B. Yeats. AlDL; EnLP; ExPo; FaBoCh; InPo; KN; LoGBV; MM; MoP; Po; PoC; PoMS; ShBV-1; ThWaDe
Cat! who hast pass'd thy grand climacteric. To a Cat [*or* Sonnet to Mrs. Reynolds' Cat]. Keats. CIV; FaBoCh; PoC
Cataclysm. N. H. Brettell. BoSA
Cataclysm. Catullus, *tr. fr. Latin by* Horace Gregory. LiTW
Cataclysm. Louis Johnson. AnNZ
Catalectic Monody, A. *Unknown.* BOHV; CIV
Cataline, Cato,/ Pericles and Plato. Food for Thought. Michael Lewis. RIS
Catalog. Rosalie Moore. GoTP; StaSt
Catalogue. *Unknown, tr. fr. Greek by* F. L. Lucas. *Fr.* Anacreontea. GrPE
Catalogue. Louis Untermeyer. HBMV
Catalpa Tree. Padraic Colum. NePoAm
"Catamount Tavern," The, is lively to-night. Parson Allen's Ride. Wallace Bruce. GA; MC; PAH
Cataract of Lodore, The. Robert Southey. BOHV; GN; HBV; HiLiEn; LPS-2; OTPC; PEOR; PoeMoYo; PYM; TreFS; WBLP
Catarina to Camoens, *sel.* Elizabeth Barrett Browning.
"Keep my riband, take and keep it." GTSE
Catawba Wine. Longfellow. LHV
Catbird. Stephen Crombie. BLA; WhBS
Catch, A: "Buz, quoth the blue fly." Ben Jonson. *See* Buz, Quoth the Blue Fly.
Catch, A: "Cold's the wind." Thomas Dekker. *See* Cold's the Wind.
Catch, A: "If all be true that I do think." Henry Aldrich. *See* Reasons for Drinking.
Catch, A: "If you were queen of bloaters." Tom Hood. CenHV
Catch, A: "Ne'er trouble thyself at the times or their turnings." *Unknown.* SeCL
Catch: On a Wet Day. Franco Sacchetti, *tr. fr. Italian by* Dante Gabriel Rossetti. AWP; JAWP; WBP
Catch, A: "Once the head is gray." Richard Henry Stoddard. AA; LEAP
Catch, A: "Seamen three!" Thomas Love Peacock. *See* Three Men of Gotham.
Catch, A: "Wisemen were but seven, The." *Unknown.* SeCL; SeEP
(We Are Three.) AlDL
Catch by the Hearth, A. *Unknown.* ChBR; OHIP; RAR
(Christmas Hearth Rhyme.) MeMeAg; PCH
Catch for Singing, A. W. W. Gibson. AnFE
Catch for Spring, A. Robert Nichols. GBV
Catch her and hold her if you can. Defiance. Walter Savage Landor. HBV
Catch him, crow! Carry him, kite! *Unknown.* OxNR
Catechism, The. Walter de la Mare. ChMo
Categorical Courtship. *Unknown.* BOHV; CIV
Caterpillar, The. Robert Graves. TSW
Caterpillar. R. E. Rashley. CaP
Caterpillar. Christina Rossetti. *Fr.* Sing-Song. BoChLi (1950 ed.); BoTP; FaPON; GFA; GoTP; MPB; OTPC (1946 ed.); RIS; StVeCh
(Brown and Furry.) SUS; UTS
Caterpillar and the Ant, The. Allan Ramsay. SeCePo
Caterpillar and the Butterfly, The. José Rosas Moreno, *tr. fr. Spanish by* Bryant. OnPM
Caterpillar Appeal. Julia Ann Rogers. DDA
Caterpillar Tractor, A. *Unknown.* DDA
Caterpillars. John Freeman. ChMP
Caterpillar's Apology for Eating a Favorite Gladiolus, A. Charles Dalmon. TSW
Caterpillars' Conversation. Mary W. Findlater. DiM
Catfish. John Farrar. GFA
Catfish. Oliver Herford. BOHV
Catfish with whiskers that lives in the brook, The. Catfish. John Farrar. GFA
Cat-Goddesses. Robert Graves. MoVE
Cath-Loda, *sel.* James Macpherson.
"Tale of the times of old, A!" BEL
Catharine Plouffe. S. Frances Harrison. *Fr.* Down the River. CPG
Catharsis, The. Alfred Alvarez. PoN
Cathedral, The. Thomas S. Jones, Jr. MaRV
Cathedral, The, *sels.* James Russell Lowell.
Life's Purpose ("This life were brutish did we not sometimes"). MaRV
"Whatsoe'er/ The form of building or the creed professed." ChIP
(Sovereign Emblem, The.) MaRV
Witness of God. OQP; QP-2
Cathedral at Evening, The. Luis Cernuda, *tr. fr. Spanish by* Eleanor L. Turnbull. CoSP
Cathedral by Sea. Norman Levine. PeCV
Cathedral in Trondheim, The. Jakob Thorarensen, *tr. fr. Icelandic by* Watson Kirkconnell. IcP
Cathedral of Rheims, The. Edmond Rostand, *tr. fr. French by* Thomas Walsh. CAW
Cathedral of Rheims, The. Emile Verhaeren, *tr. fr. French by* Joyce Kilmer. CAW
Cathedral of St. Louis, The. Carl Carmer. MoSiPe
Cathedral Verger, The. Margaret Willy. DiM
Cathedral-Walk, The. George Crabbe. *Fr.* Tales of the Hall. EnSW
Cathedrals, etc. Wordsworth. PeBoSo
Cathemerinon, *sels.* Prudentius, *tr. fr. Latin.*
Hymn for Morning, *tr. by* Basil Blackett. LaP
O Noble Virgin, *Hymn XI, verses 53-60, tr. by* Raymond F. Roseliep. ISi
Catherine Kinrade. Thomas Edward Brown. OBVV
Catholic Amen, The. Christopher Smart. *Fr.* A Song to David. GoBC
("He sang of God—the mighty source.") BLV; GBV; GTSL; LiTG
(Song of David, The.) GTBS-W
Catholic Bells, The. William Carlos Williams. OxBA
Catholic Church, The. Dryden. *Fr.* The Hind and the Panther, II. OBS
("One in herself not rent by Schism, but sound.") SeEP
Catholic Faith, The. Kenelm H. Digby. CAW
Catiline, *sel.* George Croly.
Catiline to the Roman Army, *fr.* V, ii. LPS-2
Catkin. *Unknown.* GFA; MPB; OTPC (1946 ed.); TiPo
Catkins, by village folk. Willow. Sylvia Townsend Warner. DiM
Cato, *sels.* Addison.
Cato's Soliloquy [on Immortality], *fr.* V, i. BCEP; MaRV; ReTS; TreFS; WBLP
(Immortality, *br. sel.*) BPP; OQP; QP-1
(Lines: "Soul, secure in her existence, smiles, The," *sel.*) UnW
(Soliloquy on Immortality.) LPS-3
"My voice is still for war," *fr.* II, i. PoFr
(Sempronius' Speech for War.) LPS-2
"Sempronius, why, why wilt thou urge the fate," *fr.* III, v. PoFr
Cato, *sel.* Jonathan Mitchell Sewall.
War and Washington. GA, *much abr.*; PAH
Cato's Address to His Troops in Lybia. Lucan, *tr. fr. Latin by* Nicholas Rowe. *Fr.* Pharsalia. OBEC
Cato's Soliloquy [on Immortality]. Addison. *See* Cato.
Cato's Way of Life. Furius Bibaculus, *tr. fr. Latin by* Geoffrey Johnson. LaP
Cats, The. Baudelaire, *tr. fr. French.* MiFP, *tr. by* J. C. Squire; OnPM, *tr. by* Arthur Symons; PoC, *tr. by* D. S. MacColl
Cats. Edith Richmond Blanchard. CIV
Cats. Francis Scarfe. NeBP
Cats. John Banister Tabb. CIV
Cats. A. S. J. Tessimond. AlDL; HaMV; POTE; ShBV-4
Cats. William Wallace Whitelock. CIV
Cats and Humans—All the Same. Anthony Euwer. CIV
Cat's at the window, and Shock's at the door, The. The Bird-Catcher. Elizabeth Turner. OTPC (1923 ed.)
Cat's Conscience, The. E. V. Lucas. The Nature of the Cat, IV. CIV
Cat's Eye. Paul Engle. PoMa
Cats Have Come to Tea, The. Kate Greenaway. OTPC (1946 ed.); PCH
Cat's Meat. Harold Monro. MoP; OBMV; PoC; TSW; TSWC
Cats, no less liquid than their shadows. Cats. A. S. J. Tessimond. AlDL; HaMV; POTE; ShBV-4
Cats of Baddeck, The. Phoebe Hoffman. CIV
Cats of Kilkenny, The. *Unknown.* GoTP
Cats sleep fat and walk thin. Catalog. Rosalie Moore. GoTP; StaSt

Cats' Tea-Party, The. Frederic Edward Weatherly. MeMeAg; OTPC (1946 ed.); RAR; SAS; TiPo
Cat's World. Bernice Kenyon. CIV
Cattle. Banko, *tr. fr. Japanese.* MPB
Cattle. Frederick Mortimer Clapp. LiTM (1946 ed.)
Cattle. Berta Hart Nance. HiLiAm
Cattle of His Hand, The. Wilbur Underwood. AA; WGRP
Cattle roam again across the field, The. Adoration of the Disk. *Unknown. Fr.* The Book of the Dead. FaPON
Cattle Round-up, The. H. D. C. McLachlan. SCC
Cattle Show. "Hugh MacDiarmid." GoTS; MoBrPo; OBMV
Cattle-Thief, The. *Unknown, tr. fr. Greek by* Shelley. *Fr.* Homeric Hymns. OxBG
Cattle-trains edge along the river, The. Ceiling Unlimited. Muriel Rukeyser. MoAmPo
Catts as other creatures doe, The. *Unknown.* SeCSL
Cattullus of a sparrow sung. On a Little Dog. Martial. AlBD
Catullian Hendecasyllables. Samuel Taylor Coleridge. EtPaEn
Catullus' Translation of the Ode to Anactoria. Catullus. *See* Sappho.
Catwise. Philip Booth. NePoAm-2
Caucasus, The. Pushkin, *tr. fr. Russian by* C. M. Bowra. BoRS
Caucasus lay spread before our gaze, The. Boris Pasternak. *Fr.* Waves. TrRV
"Caudal" Lecture, A. William Sawyer. BOHV
Caughnawaga Beadwork Seller, The. William Douw Lighthall. CaP; OCL
Caught by Chance. T. W. Ramsey. HaMV
Caught in the glib catcher's net. Sockeye Salmon. Ronald Hambleton. BoCaPo; CaP; PeCV
Caught still as Absalom. Chagrin. Isaac Rosenberg. ChMP; MoBrPo; TriL
Caught upon a thousand thorns, I sing. 1934. Richard Eberhart. TwAmPo
Cauld are the ghaisties in yon kirk yaird. Ghaisties. Robert Garioch. NeBP
Cauld blows [*or* blaws] the wind frae north to south. Up in the Mornin' Early [*or* Cold Blows the Wind]. John Hamilton. CH; EBSV
Cauld Kail in Aberdeen. Alexander Gordon. EBSV
Cauld Lad of Hilton, The. *Unknown.* OxBoLi
(Cauld Lad's Song, The.) ChTr
(Ghost's Song, The.) FaBoCh; LoGBV
(Wandering Spectre, The.) AtBAP; CH
Caulker, The. M. A. Lewis. StPo
Cause of Our Joy. Sister Maris Stella. ISi
Cause of the South, The. Abram J. Ryan. LPS-2
Cause of This I Know Not, The. Haniel Long. HBMV; NP
Caution. Donald F. Drummond. PtPa
Caution, A. *Unknown. See* Our Lips and Ears.
Caution to Everybody, A. Ogden Nash. NePA
Caution to Poets, A. Matthew Arnold. PoVP
Cautionary Verses [to Youth of Both Sexes]. Theodore Hook. BOHV; HBV
Cautious and still, mute and absorbed. Chess Knight. Michalis Stasinopoulos. MoGP
Cautious collapsible cow, The. Limerick. *Unknown.* LiBL
Cautious Householder, The. Anaxilas, *tr. fr. Greek by* T. F. Higham. OxBG
Cautious Lovers, The, *sel.* Countess of Winchilsea.
To Silvia. HBV
Cavalier. Richard Bruce. CDC
Cavalier, The. Sir Walter Scott. *Fr.* Rokeby, V. TVSH
(Song: Cavalier, The.) EV-4
Cavalier Song. Sir Walter Scott. *See* And What though Winter Will Pinch Severe.
Cavalier Tunes. Robert Browning. BEL; BLV; BPN; EM-2; EmBrPo; EnLit; EPN; EV-5; GEPC; HBV; MCCG; OAEP; PoVP; PreP; PYM; ShBV-1; TCEP; TOP; VA; VLEP
Sels.
Boot and Saddle, III. CBOV; EnLi-2; MuP; MW; ViPo
(Cavalier Tune.) PIAE
Give a Rouse, II. EnLi-2; EPP; PC; ViPo
(Cavalier Tune, A.) BLV; BoLiVe
Marching Along, I. ATP (1935 ed.); BMEP; EnLi-2; EPP; MW; PIR; ViPo; YT
(From "Cavalier Tunes.") LEAP
Cavalier's Escape, The. George Walter Thornbury. FaBoBe; GN; HBV; MW; OTPC; ShGoBo
Cavalier's Lullaby for His Mistress, A. Thomas Jordan. *Fr.* An Alarm in 1645. SeCL
Cavalier's Song. Robert Graham. *See* If Doughty Deeds.
Cavalier's Song, The. William Motherwell. EBSV; GN; HBV; OTPC
Cavalry Crossing a Ford. Walt Whitman. AA; AmP; AmPo; AmPP; APW; ChTr; CoBA; IAP; MDAH; MOAP; OxBA; Po; TCAP; UnPo (3d ed.)
Cave-Boy, The. Laura E. Richards. FaPON
Cave-Drawing, The. Vernon Watkins. LiTB
Cave of Despair, The. Spenser. *Fr.* The Faerie Queene, I, 9. LoBV
Cave of Mammon, The. Spenser. The Faerie Queene, II, 7. BCEP, 29 *sts.;* FiP, 12 *sts.;* LiA, 3 *sts.;* PoEL-1
(House of Richesse, The, 3 *sts.*) CH
Cave of Sleep, The. Spenser. *See* House of Morpheus, The.
Cave, A; Pool's Hole, Derbyshire. Charles Cotton. *Fr.* The Wonders of the Peake. BeR
Cave Rock is made of toffee. For a Child. Denis Glover. AnNZ
Cave Sedem. Theodore F. MacManus. HBV
Caveat to the Fair Sex, A. Lady Mary Wortley Montagu. DiM
Cavern and the Hut, The. John Hookham Frere. OTPC (1923 ed.)
Caverns and you, cascades. Of the Choice of His Burial-Place. Pierre de Ronsard. LiA
Caves, The. Michael Roberts. ChMP
Caw, Caw. F. Hey. SAS
"Caw," said the rook. Birds' Nests. Millicent Seager. BoTP
Cawdor, *sels.* Robinson Jeffers.
Caged Eagle's Death Dream, The. PoF
Old Man's Dream after He Died, The. CoV
Cawna ("Cawna, o Cawna! deck'd in sable charms"). Thomas Chatterton. *Fr.* Heccar and Gaira. RO
Cawsand Bay. *Unknown.* OBB
(Fine New Ballad of Cawsand Bay, *mod. vers. by* Hamilton Moore.) PC
Cazador (Hunter). Federico García Lorca, *tr. fr. Spanish by* Stephen Spender *and* J. L. Gili. Po
Céad Mile Fáilte, Elim! Gerald Griffin. TIP
Cean Dubh Deelish. *Unknown. See* Dear Dark Head.
Cean Duv Deelish. Dora Sigerson Shorter. GTIV; TIP
Cean-Salla. James Clarence Mangan. OnYI
Cease from grinding, O ye toilers. A Water Mill. Antipater of Thessalonica. OxBG
Cease not thou heavnly voiced glorious creature. *Unknown.* SeCSL
Cease Not to Be a Mystery. Roberta Teale Swartz. TBM
Cease, Paullus, to burden my grave with tears. The Shade of Cornelia Consoles Her Husband. Propertius, *tr. by* H. E. Butler. *Fr.* Elegies. LiA
Cease, Paullus, to oppress my tomb with tears. Propertius, *tr. by* Frances Fletcher. *Fr.* Elegies. LaP
Cease, rude Boreas, blustering railer! The Storm. George Alexander Stevens. LPS-2
Cease, sorrow cease, & doe noe more torment. *Unknown.* SeCSL
Cease that harsh musick; we are not pleas'd with it. Cyril Tourneur. *Fr.* The Atheist's Tragedy, V, i. AtBAP
Cease then nor Order Imperfection name. Whatever Is, Is Right. Pope. *Fr.* An Essay on Man, Epistles I–II. OBEC
Cease thy wishes gentle boy. *Unknown.* SeCSL
"Cease to Do Evil—Learn to Do Well." Denis Florence MacCarthy. TIP
Cease, warrring thoughts, and let his brain. A Lullaby. James Shirley. *Fr.* The Triumph of Beauty. BOL; TuPP
Cease ye this farness; 'bate this pride of you. The Mock Caliph. *Unknown, tr. by* Richard F. Burton. EnLi-1
Ceaselessly the weaver, Time. The Weaver. William H. Burleigh. BLPA
Cecidit, Cecidit Babylon Magna! Theodore Maynard. JKCP
Cecil. Walter de la Mare. BOL
Cedar and jagged fir. The Lonely Land. A. J. M. Smith. CaP; TwCV
Cedar Mountain. Annie Fields. MC; PAH
Cedars, The. Joseph Preston Peabody. NV
Cedars of Lebanon, The. Alphonse Marie Louis de Lamartine, *tr. fr. French by* Toru Dutt. AWP; JAWP; WBP
Cedars of Lebanon, The. Letitia E. Landon. PEOR
Ceiling Unlimited. Muriel Rukeyser. MoAmPo
Ceix and Alceone, *sel.* John Gower. *Fr.* Confessio Amantis.
House of Sleep, The. AtBAP
Celadyne's Song. William Browne. *See* Memory ("Marina's gone . . .").
Celanta at the Well of Life. George Peele. *See* Song at the Well, The.
Celebration, A. May Sarton. NePoAm-2
Celebration for Neptune ("Festo quid potius die"). Horace, *tr. fr. Latin by* Roselle M. Montgomery. Odes, III, 28. LiA
Celebration in the Plaza, The. Adrienne Cecile Rich. NePoEA
Celebration of Charis, A, *sels.* Ben Jonson.
Begging Another, on Colo[u]r of Mending the Former. LO; LoPS; OAEP; PoEL-2; TuPP
(Kiss, The.) AtBAP
Claiming a Second Kiss by Desert. LiTL
"Do but look on her eyes, they do light." LO
Have You Seen a Bright Lily Grow. OTPC (1923 ed.)
(From "Love's Chariot.") LEAP
("Have you seen but a bright lily grow.") EG; FaBoCh; LoGBV; ReEn
(She.) BCEP
(So Sweet Is She.) GN

Celebration of Charis, A (*continued*)
(So White, So Soft, So Sweet.) TrGrPo
(Triumph, The.) LoPS; PG, 8 *ll.*
Her Man Described by Her Own Dictamen. AtBAP; NBE
His Excuse for Loving. PoEL-2; SeCV-1; SeEP; TuPP
How He Saw Her. AtBAP, 4 *ll.*; OAEP; SeCV-1
Triumph of Charis, The. BEL; ElSeCe; EPP; EV-2; ExPo; GoBC; LiTB; LoBV; SeCeV; TCEP; TOP; WHA
(Her Triumph.) AEV; AtBAP; ElL; EPS; FaBoEn; HBV; InPo; LiTL; MaPo; OAEP; Po; PoEL-2; SeCV-1; SeEP; TuPP; TwHP; TyEnPo; ViBoPo
(See the Chariot at Hand Here of Love.) InvP; SiCE
(Triumph, The.) AnFE; CoEV; OBEV
Celebration of Love. James McAuley. MoAuPo
Celebration of Peace. Friedrich Hölderlin, *tr. fr. German by* Francis Golffing *and* Kurt Opitz. AnGP
Celebrations. Austin Clarke. OxBI
Celery. Ogden Nash. FaPON
Celeste Dancing. Frances Sargent Osgood. *See* Dancing Girl, A.
Celestial Bird. Jessica Powers. JKCP (1955 ed.)
Celestial Body. Louise Townsend Nicholl. NePoAm
Celestial choir! enthron'd in realms of light. His Excellency General Washington. Phillis Wheatley. APW; PoNe; TCAP
Celestial City, The. Giles Fletcher. Christ's Victory and Triumph, IV. OBS
Celestial Country, The. Bernard of Cluny. *See* Jerusalem, the Golden.
Celestial Dream. Pierre de Ronsard, *tr. fr. French by* Alan Conder. TrFP
Celestial Hour. Paul Verlaine. *See* White Moon, The.
Celestial Fête. Victor Hugo, *tr. fr. French by* Alan Conder. TrFP
Celestial Love, *sel.* Emerson.
Love's Nobility. TreF
Celestial Love. Michelangelo, *tr. fr. Italian by* John Addington Symonds. AWP; JAWP; WBP
(Sonnet LII: "No mortal object did these eyes behold," *tr. by* Wordsworth.) BoFr; LyPI; RO
Celestial Passion, The. Richard Watson Gilder. AA; AnAmPo; LA; LEAP; OBAV
Celestial Pilot, The. Dante, *tr. fr. Italian by* Longfellow. *Fr.* Divina Commedia: Purgatorio. WGRP
Celestial poesy! whose genial sway. William Charles Wentworth. *Fr.* Australasia. BoAu
Celestial Queen. Jacopo Sannazaro, *tr. fr. Latin by* John C. Eustace. *Fr.* De Partu Virginis. ISi
Celestial Surgeon, The. Robert Louis Stevenson. BBV; BMEP; BPP; EBSV; EPN; GBV (1922 ed.); GoTP; HBV; HBVY; LBBV; MaRV; MBP; MoBrPo; MW; OQP; PC; PIAE; PoeT; PoToHe (new ed.); POTT; PoVP; QP-1; TreFS; TrGrPo; TrPWD; ViBoPo; WGRP
Celestial Wisdom. Juvenal, *tr. fr. Latin by* Samuel Johnson. The Satires, X. AWP; JAWP; WBP
Celestina, *sels.* Fernando de Rojas, *tr. fr. Spanish by* James Mabbe.
Now Sleep, and Take Thy Rest. SeCL
"You birds whose warblings prove." ElSeCe
Celestine. Robert Fitzgerald. MoVE
Celestine Silvousplait Justine de Mouton Rosalie. Propinquity Needed. Charles Battell Loomis. BOHV; InMe; PA
Celia. Thomas Duffett. SeCL
Celia and Belinda. Colley Cibber. *Fr.* Woman's Wit. SeCL
Celia Is Gone. William Browne. SeCL
Celia, my fairest Celia, fell. Charles Cotton. LO
Celia sat beside the seaside. *Unknown.* SiTL
Celia Singing ("Hark, how my Celia"). Thomas Carew. OAEP
Celia Singing ("You that think Love can convey"). Thomas Carew. ElSeCe; EnLit; EPS (1942 ed.); LO; SeCL
(Celia Sings.) EV-2
(Her Sweet Voice.) LiTL
(Song: Celia Singing.) SeEP
("You that think Love can convey.") EG
Celia Threatened. Thomas Carew. *See* Ingrateful Beauty Threatened.
Celia, thy sweet angels face. *At. to* the Countess of Winchilsea. SeCSL
Celia, too late you would repent. Upon a Favour Offered. William Walsh. SeCL
Celia turnes awaye her eyes. *Unknown.* SeCSL
"Celia was laughing. Hopefully I said." Witter Bynner. *Fr.* The New World. NV
Celia, when you bade [*or* bid] me. Night. Witter Bynner. LoPo; LoPS; NP
Celia's Home-coming. Agnes Mary Frances Robinson. OBEV (new ed.); OBVV; VA
Celibacy. Austin Clarke. JKCP (1926 ed.)
Celibate, The. Joan Lamburn. DiM
Celimena, of my heart. Damon and Celimena. Dryden. *Fr.* An Evening's Love. InvP; SeCL
Cell, The. George Rostrevor Hamilton. GTML; TrPWD
Cell-Mates. Louis Untermeyer. HBMV
Cellach's Poem to the Dawn. *Unknown, tr. fr. Old Irish by* Seán O'Faoláin. SiB
Cellar, The. Hilda Conkling. PCH
"Cellini, play the man." King Francis said. Benvenuto Cellini. Carl Snoilsky. AnSL
Cello, The. Richard Watson Gilder. AA
Cello, The. Ernst Josephson, *tr. fr. Swedish by* Charles W. Stork. AnSL
Cello sobs, the symphony begins, The. The Festival. Frederic Prokosch. LiTA; LiTM (1946 ed.); NeTW; WaP
'Cellos, setting forth apart, The. At the Symphony. Robert Nathan. HBMV; MAP; PoRL; TSW
Celt Speaks, The. Arthur Stringer. PoFr
Celtic Cross, The. Thomas D'Arcy McGee. OnYI; VA
Celtic spearman forcing the cromlech-builder's brown daughter, A. Second-best. Robinson Jeffers. CoV
Celtic Twilight, *sel.* W. B. Yeats.
Into the Twilight. BEL; ChMo; CMP; EPN; EV-4; HBV; PC; POTT
Celts, The. Thomas D'Arcy McGee. GTIV; OnYI; OxBI
Celts and Saxons. Thomas Osborne Davis. TIP
Cemeteries are places for departed souls. Lines Written at the Grave of Alexandre [*or* Alexander] Dumas. Gwendolyn B. Bennett. CDC; PoNe
Cemetery, A. Emily Dickinson. *See* This quiet dust was gentlemen and ladies.
Cemetery by the Sea, The. Paul Valéry, *tr. fr. French by* Barbara Gibbs. AnFP; LiTW; OnHM, *tr. by* Selden Rodman
(Graveyard by the Sea, The, *tr. by* Alan Conder.) TrFP
(Marine Cemetery, The, *tr. by* Sidney Alexander.) ReMP
Cemetery Is, The. Audrey McGaffin. NePoAm-2
Cemetery stone New England autumn, The. Voices of Heroes. Horace Gregory. PoFr; TrGrPo (1942 ed.)
Cenci, The. Shelley. EnRP
Sels.
Beatrice Cenci in Her Cell, *fr.* V, iv. ReTS
Beatrice's Last Words, *fr.* V, iv. FiP
Cenotaph. Glaucus, *tr. fr. Greek by* Walter Leaf. OxBG
Cenotaph. Brian Fitzpatrick. MoAuPo
Cenotaph, A. Simonides, *tr. fr. Greek by* T. F. Higham. GrL; OxBG
Cenotaph of Lincoln, The. James T. McKay. OHIP; PSO
Censer of the eglantine was moved, The. A Song of April. Francis Ledwidge. VOD
Censorship. Arthur Waley. WaP
Centaur, The. Theodore Roethke. NePoAm-2
Centaur, The. Poul Sørensen, *tr. fr. Danish by* Charles W. Stork. BoDS
Centaur, The. May Swenson. NePoAm-2
Centaur does not need a horse, The. The Centaur. Theodore Roethke. NePoAm-2
Centaur Song. Hilda Doolittle ("H. D.") MOAP
Centaur, Syren, I foregoe, The. Another. Richard Lovelace. AtBAP; PoEL-3
Centaurs, The. James Stephens. AnEnPo; MM
Centaurs and Lapithae. Sacheverell Sitwell. *Fr.* Battles of the Centaurs. AtBAP
Centaur's Bath, The. Luis G. Urbina, *tr. fr. Spanish by* Samuel Beckett. AnMP
Centaurs' Flight. José Maria de Heredia, *tr. fr. French by* Alan Conder. TrFP
Centennial Hymn. Bryant. PAH
Centennial Hymn. John Pierpont. AnNE
Centennial Hymn, The. Whittier. AA; APW; FOAH; HiLiAm; IDAH; MC; PaA; PAH; TOP
Centennial Meditation of Columbia, The. Sidney Lanier. PAH
Dear Land of All My Love, *sel.* DD; GA; GN; HBVY; MPB; StVeCh
("Long as thine Art shall love true love.") PGD
Centennial Ode, *sel.* Charles Sprague.
Indians. GN
Center of all centers, germ of germs. Buddha in Glory. Rainer Maria Rilke. OnPM
Centipede, The. Samuel Hopkins Adams. InMe
Centipede, A [*or* The]. Mrs. Edward Craster. *See* Centipede Was Happy Quite, A.
Centipede, The. A. P. Herbert. CenHV
Centipede, The. Ogden Nash. FaPON
Centipede is not quite nice, The. The Centipede. A. P. Herbert. CenHV
Centipede Was Happy Quite, A. Mrs. Edward Craster. ALV; LiL
(Centipede, A [*or* The].) GoTP; PCH; PoMa; TiPo (1959 ed.)
(Puzzled Centipede, The.) FaPON; UTS
(Quandary.) TreFS
Central, *sel.* John Curtis Underwood.
"Though men may build their bridges high." PoMa
Central Europe. Norman Cameron. MoPW
Central Park at Dusk. Sara Teasdale. ChMo; CMP
Centuries shall not deflect. To E.A.R. Lola Ridge. NP; TBM

Centuries, since Christ to earthland came, The. His Is the Way. Thomas Curtis Clark. ChIP
Centurion, The. Helen Purcell Roads. ChIP
Century of Couplets, A, *sel.* Richard Chenevix Trench.
"Who praises God the most." OBRV
Century of Peace, A. Guy Bilsford. BoHiPo
Cerelle. Margaret Bell Houston. PoMa
Ceremonial Hunt. Elizabeth J. Coatsworth. *Fr.* The Painted Desert. PoeMoYo
Ceremonial Ode Intended for a University. Lascelles Abercrombie. OBVV
Ceremonies for Candlemas Day, The ("Kindle the Christmas brand"). Robert Herrick. EnLit; EPS; OAEP
(Ceremonies for Christmas Day, The.) COAH
Ceremonies for Candlemas Day, The. Ben Jonson. OAEP
Ceremonies for Candlemas[s] Eve ("Down with the rosemary and bays"). Robert Herrick. EPS; EV-2; OAEP; OBS; OTPC (1923 ed.); SeEP
Ceremonies for Christmas ("Come bring with a noise"). Robert Herrick. COAH; EPS; EV-2; GN; HBV; MuP; OHIP; OTPC (1923 ed.); TiPo (1952 ed.)
(Come Bring with a Noise.) SDH
Ceremonies for Christmas Day, The ("Kindle the Christmas brand"). Robert Herrick. *See* Ceremonies for Candlemas Day.
Ceremony. Vassar Miller. NePoEA
Ceremony. Richard Wilbur. FiMAP; MiAP; Po; ReMP
Ceremony after a Fire Raid. Dylan Thomas. CoBMV; ExPo; MoPo; WaP
Ceremony for Candlemas Day, A ("Down with the rosemary and so"). Robert Herrick. OTPC; PoRL
(Ceremony upon Candlemas Eve.) EPS
Ceremony must be found, The. Speaking of Poetry. John Peale Bishop. LiTA; LiTM (rev. ed.); OxBA
Ceremony upon Candlemas Eve. Robert Herrick. *See* Ceremony for Candlemas Day, A.
Ceres, most bounteous lady, thy rich leas. Shakespeare. *Fr.* The Tempest, IV, i. AtBAP
Ceres! to thee belongs the votive lay. *Unknown. Fr.* Homeric Hymns. GrPo
Cerinthus Forgiven; Once More Tibullus Speaks for the Girl. Tibullus, *tr. fr. Latin by* Hubert Creekmore. LaP
(Sulpicia's Rival.) LiTW
Cerne Abbas. Hal Summers. HaMV
Certain Age, A. Phyllis McGinley. NePoAm-2
Certain American Poets. Odell Shepard. InP; NV
Certain Artists Bring Her Dolls and Drawings. W. B. Yeats. Upon a Dying Lady, II. LiTB
Certain Books of Virgil's Aeneis. Virgil, *tr. fr. Latin by* the Earl of Surrey. *Fr.* The Aeneid, II. TuPP
(Second Boke of Virgiles Aenaeis, The.) SiCE
("They whisted all, with fixèd face attent.") EnLi-1; EPP; SiPS
(Translation from Virgil's Aeneid.) LiTB
Certain Eclogues, *sel.* Alexander Barclay.
Prologue, The: "Famous poets with the muses nine, The." ReIE
Certain lawyer stood up and tempted (Jesus), A. Who Is My Neighbor? St. Luke, Bible, *N.T.* GrCo-1
Certain man in physic skilled, A. Of Fuscus, a Drunkard. Sir Thomas More, *tr. by* Timothe Kendall. TuPP
Certain Maxims of Archy. Don Marquis. InMe
Archy, the Cockroach, Speaks, *sel.* FaPON
Certain Maxims of Hafiz. Kipling. HBV
Maxim: "If he play," *2 ll.* OtMeF
Certain Mercies. Robert Graves. CoBMV
Certain parting does not wait its hour. Penelope. Ursula Wood. SoV
Certain pasha, dead five thousand years, A. A Turkish Legend. Thomas Bailey Aldrich. GN; HBV; HBVY; OTPC (1946 ed.); YT
Certain People, A. George Meredith. EmBrPo
Certain Presbyterian pair, A. The Presbyterian Wedding. *Unknown.* CoMu
Certain Rich Man, A. Theodore Maynard. OQP; QP-2
Certain Saturday, A. Edith Lovejoy Pierce. ChIP
Certain Slant of Light, A. Emily Dickinson. *See* There's a certain slant of light.
Certain tyrant, to disgrace, A. Poe's Critics. John Banister Tabb. BAP
Certain young fellow, named Bobbie, A. Limerick. *Unknown.* LiBL
Certain young gourmet of Crediton, A. Limerick. *Unknown, sometimes at. to* Charles Inge. CenHV; LiBL; WhC
Certain Young Lady, A. Washington Irving. FaBoBe; HBV; OnPP; PR
Certain youthful lady in Thoulouse, A. Sonnet: Of the Eyes of a Certain Mandetta. Guido Cavalcanti. AWP
Certainties. Kenneth W. Porter. ChIP
Certainties. Margaret Widdemer. HBMV
Certainty. Emily Dickinson. *See* I never saw a moor.
Certainty. Evelyn Hardy. HBMV
Certainty Enough. Amelia Jospehine Burr. HBMV
Cervantes, Dostoievsky, Poe. A Poem Intended to Incite the Utmost Depression. Samuel Hoffenstein. BOHV; SiTL
Cervera. Bertrand Shadwell. PAH
César Franck. Joseph Auslander. HBMV
Ceylon. A. Hugh Fisher. HBV
Cézanne. Alfred Kreymborg. BAP; NP
Chace, The, *sel.* William Somervile.
Hare-hunting, *fr.* II. OBEC
Chaeronean Plutarch, to thy deathless praise. Plutarch. Agathias Scholasticus. AWP; GrPo; JAWP; WBP
Chaffinch flies fast, The. Cherry Tree. Ivy O. Eastwick. BoTP
Chaffinch's Nest at Sea, The. William Cowper. OTPC (1923 ed.)
Chagrin. Isaac Rosenberg. ChMP; MoBrPo; TriL
Chagrined, because he saw us flitting past. Satan in Profile. Harold Vinal. MuM
Chahcoal Man, *with music. Unknown.* AS
Chain hangs down with golden fetters, A. A Prologue. Pushkin. BoRS
Chain I gave was fair to view, The. From the Turkish. Byron. HBV
Chain of Princes Street, The. Elizabeth Fleming. PCH
Chain of the sea roars and lashes it, The. Subterranean Days and Nights. "Pablo de Rokha." TwSpPo
Chained by stern duty to the rock of state. Lincoln. S. Weir Mitchell. PAH; PSO
Chained in the market-place he stood. The African Chief. Bryant. AnNE; BLPA; PTA-2; TreFS
Chains. Patrick Carey. SeCL
Chair she sat in, like a burnished throne, The. A Game of Chess. T. S. Eliot. *Fr.* The Waste Land. PreP
Chairoplane Chant. Nancy Byrd Turner. RIS
Chairs. Annette Wynne. GFA
Chaitivel. Marie de France. *See* Chartivel.
Chaka. F. T. Prince. BoSA
Chalcomede Prays to Be Saved from Love. Nonnus, *tr. fr. Greek by* C. M. Bowra. *Fr.* Dionysiaca. OxBG
Chalcomede Wards Off Her Lover. Nonnus, *tr. fr. Greek by* Michael Balkwill. *Fr.* Dionysiaca. OxBG
Chalk-Cliff, The. Andrew Young. POTE
Chalk from Eden. Howard Moss. NePA
Challenge. Sterling A. Brown. CDC
Challenge. Thomas Curtis Clark. MaRV; PGD
Challenge. John Drinkwater. PoMa
Challenge. Harry W. Falconer. PoToHe (1941 ed.)
Challenge, A. James Benjamin Kenyon. AA
Challenge, The. Grenville Kleiser. BLRP
Challenge. Kenton Foster Murray. HBV
Challenge, The. Pope. PoEL-3
Challenge. Sir Walter Scott. *Fr.* Marmion, V. OtMeF
Challenge comes, The. The Challenge. Grenville Kleiser. BLRP
Challenge for Beauty, A, *sel.* Thomas Heywood.
"I remember,/ There lived a Spanish Princess of our name." LO
Challenge of Death, The. Milton. *See* Death.
Challenge of Life, The. Tennyson. *Fr.* Ulysses. MaRV
(Experience.) OQP; QP-2
Challenge of Thor, The. Longfellow. The Saga of King Olaf, 1. AmPP (4th ed.)
Challenge to Youth. Longfellow. *Fr.* The Castle Builder. MaRV
Challengers. Alfred Dorn. GoYe
Chalma, whose excellence is known from far. Flowers and Spice. Thomas Chatterton. *Fr.* Narva and Mored. RO
Chalse a Killey. Thomas Edward Brown. POTT; PoVP
Chamber Music, *sels.* James Joyce.
All Day I Hear [the Noise of Waters], XXXV. FaBoCh; LoGBV; MBP; MoBrPo; NP; OnYI; PIAE; PoRA; TIP
(Noise of Waters, The.) FaPON; TiPo (1959 ed.); TSW
"Because your voice was at my side," XVII. ReaPo
Bid Adieu to Maidenhood, XI. LiTG; LiTL; OBEV (new ed.)
(Bid Adieu, Adieu, Adieu.) GTIV; OnYI
(Bid Adieu to Girlish Days.) HBV
"Bright cap and streamers," X. ReaPo
Goldenhair V. BoTP; ChTr; HBMV; LEAP; MoSiPe
("Lean out of the window.") TwCV
(Song: "Lean out of the window.") POTE
I Hear An Army [Charging upon the Land], XXXVI. AnIV; AWP; ExPo; GTIV; JAWP; JKCP (1926 ed.); LiTL; LiTM; MBP; MoBrPo; NAMP; OxBI; PoRA; POTE; ShBV-4; TwCV; ViBoPo; WBP
"I would in that sweet bosom be," VI. ReMP
"In the dark pine-wood," XX. ReaPo
"My dove, my beautiful one," XIV. TIP
"Now, O now, in this brown land." XXXIII. ReaPo
"O, it was out by Donnycarney," XXXI.
(Song.) MBP; MoBrPo; OBVV
O Sweetheart, Hear You, XVIII. HBMV; LBBV; MBP; MoBrPo; ReaPo
Strings in the Earth, I. CBOV; HBMV; MoBrPo
(Strings in the Earth and Air.) GTIV; OnYI; ReMP

Chamber Music (*continued*)
This Heart That Flutters near My Heart, XXIII. AnIV
What Counsel Has the Hooded Moon, XII. OnYI; OxBI
Chamber over the Gate, The. Longfellow. OBAV
Chamber Scene. Nathaniel Parker Willis. HBV
Chambered Nautilus, The. Oliver Wendell Holmes. *Fr.* The Autocrat of the Breakfast Table, *ch.* 4. AA; AmP; AmPP; AnAmPo; AnNE; APW; BAP; BAV; BTP; DD; EOAH; EtS; EV-5; FaBoBe; FaFP; GN; GTBS; GTBS-W; HBV; HBVY; HoPM; IAP; IHA; LA; LBAP; LEAP; LiTA; LPS-2; MaRV; MCCG; NeHB; NePA; OBAV; OBVV; OHFP; OQP; OTPC; OuHeWo; PCD; PECK; PG (1955 ed.); PIR; PoEL-5; PoP; PTA-1; QP-1; TCAP; TreF; TVSH; UnPo (1st ed.); WGRP; YT
More Stately Mansions, *last st.* GrCo-1
Chambers of Death, The. Edward Young. *Fr.* A Paraphrase on Part of the Book of Job. BeR
Chambers of the mansions of my heart, The. James Thomson. *Fr.* The City of Dreadful Night, X. LEAP
Chameleon. Anthony Delius. BoSA
Chameleon. Paul Engle. CrMA
Chameleon, The. A. P. Herbert. FaPON; PCD
Chameleon. Gordon LeClaire. EtS
Chameleon, The. James Merrick, *after* De la Motte. HBV
Chameleon changes his color, The. The Chameleon. A. P. Herbert. FaPON; PCD
Chameleon, knowing I am near. Chameleon. Paul Engle. CrMA
Chamonix. George Hookham. OBVV
Champagne. Franz Mikael Franzén, *tr. fr. Swedish by* Charles W. Stork. AnSL
Champagne Rosée [*or* Rosé]. John Kenyon. OBEV; OBRV; OBVV; VA
Champion, The. Ibn Baqi, *tr. fr. Arabic by* A. J. Arberry. MooP
Champion of those who groan beneath. To William Lloyd Garrison. Whittier. CoBA; GA; PAH
Champion's Statue, The. Lucilius, *tr. fr. Greek by* F. L. Lucas. GrPE
Champlain; First Canadian. John Daniel Logan. CPG
Chance, The. John Holmes. NePoAm-2
Chance. *Unknown, tr. fr. Greek by* C. M. Bowra. OxBG
Chance and Change. Thomas Campion. *See* What if a Day . . .
Chance Encounter. Katsumi Tanaka, *tr. fr. Japanese by* Takamichi Ninomiya *and* D. J. Enright. PoLJ
Chance-fallen Seed. Marie Emilie Gilchrist. BAP
Chance, in whom men start and end. Chance. *Unknown.* OxBG
Chance Meeting. Hilda Doolittle ("H. D."). MoP
Chance Meetings. Conrad Aiken. BAP
Chance Met. Rosemary Dobson. NeLNL
Chancellor mused as he nibbled his pen, The. Love and War. Arthur Patchett Martin. VA
Chancellor's Gravel-Drive, The. Po Chü-i, *tr. fr. Chinese by* Arthur Waley. TrCh
Chancing upon the Devil in the Doorway. The Devil and the Angel, 1. Rosemary Dobson. BoAV
Chanclebury Ring. Wilfrid Scawen Blunt. MM; PoeT
Chandelier, Le, *sel.* Alfred de Musset, *tr. fr. French.*
Fortunio's Song, *fr.* II. LiA, *tr. by* William Frederic Giese; TrFP, *tr. by* Alan Conder
Chandler Nicholas. Edgar Lee Masters. *Fr.* The New Spoon River. NAMP
Chang Liang. Li Po, *tr. fr. Chinese by* W. J. B. Fletcher. PoFr
Change. Mary Elizabeth Coleridge. MoVE
Change, The. Abraham Cowley. *Fr.* The Mistress. BEL; CoBE; FaBoEn; LO; MeLP; MePo; OBS; ReEn; SeCV-1
Change. John Donne. Elegies, III. LiTG; ViBoPo
Change. Earl of Essex. *See* Change Thy Mind.
Change. Fulke Greville. Caelica, VII. CoEV; OBSC
(Sonnet.) ReIE
("World, that all contains, is ever moving, The.") SiCE; TuPP
Change. William Dean Howells. AA; OBAV
(Sometimes, When after Spirited Debate.) LEAP
Change. Raymond Knister. BoCaPo; CaP; PeCV
Change. Stanley J. Kunitz. NP
Change. Lalia Mitchell Thornton. CIV
Change in the Year, A. Wordsworth. *Fr.* To My Sister. BoTP
Change Is Sweetest of All. Clove Bell. DDA
Change is the circumstance of our delight. The Prism. H. A. Pinkerton. NePoAm
Change of Face, A. Harrison Smith Morris. PR
Change of Heart, A. Valine Hobbs. SiSoSe
Change of Subject, A. Daniel Sargent. JKCP (1955 ed.)
Change Should Breed Change. William Drummond of Hawthornden. *Fr.* Flowers of Sion. BSV; EBSV; OBEV; OxBoCh
("New doth the sun appear.") MeRV
Change-Song, The. Constance Lindsay Skinner. OCL
Change Thy Mind [since She Doth Change]. Earl of Essex. ElL; TuPP
(Change.) OBSC
Changed. Charles Stuart Calverley. ALV; FiBHP
Changed Cross, The. Mrs. Charles Hobart. LPS-2
Changed Woman, The. Louise Bogan. HBMV
Changeful Beauty. *Unknown. See* Love in Her Hair.
Changefulness. Abu Ishaq, *tr. fr. Arabic by* A. J. Arberry. MooP
Changeless. Martha Haskell Clark. NLK
Changeless. Edith Hickman Divell. OQP; QP-2
(In Whom Is No Variableness.) MaRV
Changeless. Alice Meynell. VA
Changeless Shore. Sarah Leeds Ash. GoYe
Changeling. Leah Bodine Drake. DaM; PoMS
Changeling, The. Charlotte Mew. CH; MPB
Changeling, The, *sels.* Thomas Middleton.
"Here we are, if you have any more," *fr.* V, iii. AtBAP; PoEL-2
"What makes your lip so strange?" *fr.* III, iv. AtBAP; PoEL-2
Changeling. Vincent Starrett. DaM
Changeling. Barbara Young. MoSiPe
Changeling Grateful, A. Josephine Preston Peabody. AA
Changelings. Mary Potter Thacher Higginson. AA
Changes. Charles Barter. *Fr.* Stray Memories of Natal and Zululand. BoSA
Changes. Ibn Sa'id of Alcala la Real, *tr. fr. Arabic by* A. J. Arberry. MooP
Changes; or, Love in a Maze, *sel.* James Shirley.
"Melancholy, hence! go get." TuPP
Changing guests, each in a different mood, The. Inclusiveness. Dante Gabriel Rossetti. The House of Life, LXIII. EmBrPo; EnLi-2; PoVP; VA; ViPo
Changing Love. John Gould Fletcher. ChMo; CMP
Changing Road, The. Katharine Lee Bates. HBV
Changing Wind, The. Julian Orde. NeBP
Changing World, The. Jami, *tr. fr. Persian by* F. Hadland Davis. OnPM
Changing Year, The. Lloyd Roberts. DD
Channel Crossing. George Barker. ChMP
Channel Firing. Thomas Hardy. CoBMV; EnL; ExPo; LiTB; MaPo; MoPo; OAEP (2d ed.); PoEL-5; PoFS; PoRA; RiBV; SeCeV; UnPo; ViP; ViPP; WaaP
Channel Passage, A. Rupert Brooke. FaBoTw
Channel Pasage, A. Swinburne. VLEP
Channing. Amos Bronson Alcott. AA
Chanson: Leaving on Crusade. Thibaut of Champagne, *tr. fr. French by* Louisa S. Costello. LyMA
Chanson: "My wand'ring thoughts awake to love anew." Chatelain of Coucy, *tr. fr. French by* Louisa S. Costello. LyMA
Chanson: "There is no comfort to be found for pain." Thibaut of Champagne. *See* Oh, Gentle Beauty.
Chanson d'automne. Paul Verlaine. *See* Chansons d'automne.
Chanson de Chateaulaire. Herbert Gorman. AnAmPo; LA; TCPD
Chanson de Renaud. *Unknown. See* Song of Renaud.
Chanson de Roland. *Unknown. See* Song of Roland, The.
Chanson de Rosemonde. Richard Hovey. HBV
Chanson d'Or. Ann Hamilton. HBMV
Chanson Innocent[e]. E. E. Cummings. FaPON; MAP; MoAB; MoAmPo; MoShBr; NP; ReMP
(In Just-[Spring When the World].) AmPP; ChMo; GoTP; PoLFOT; PreP; ThWaDe
Chanson mystique. *Unknown, tr. fr. French by* Percy Allen. CAW
(Mystic Song, A.) WGRP
Chanson Naïve. John McClure. HBMV
Chanson of the Bells of Oseněy. Cale Young Rice. AnFE; APA; CoAnAm; HBV; SBMV
Chanson sans Paroles. Ernest Dowson. PoVP
Chanson un Peu Naïve. Louise Bogan. HBMV
Chansons d'automme. Paul Verlaine, *tr. fr. French by* Arthur Symons. AWP; JAWP; WBP
(Chanson d'automne.) LiA
(Song of Autumn.) OnPM; WoL
Chant for Reapers. Wilfrid Thorley. OBEV (new ed.); OBVV
Chant for Skippers. Katharine Gallagher. SiSoSe
Chant for the Moon-of-Flowers. Lew Sarett. NV
Chant of dark betrayals, A; song betrayed. Our Thirty Pieces. Harry Kemp. TBM
Chant of Departure; a Missionary's Prayer. Alfred J. Barrett. GoBC; ISi
Chant of Hate against England, A. Ernst Lissauer, *tr. fr. German by* Barbara Henderson. HBV
Hymn of Hate against England, A, *sel.* OtMeF
Chant of Love for England, A. Helen Gray Cone. LBAP; LEAP; VOD
Chant of the Box Cars. Harry Kemp. PoMa
Chant of the Colorado, The. Cale Young Rice. SBMV

Chant of the Ninth Order of Seraphim. Inigo de Mendoza, *tr. fr. Spanish by* Roderick Gill. CAW
Chant of the Old Men in the Woods. Charles Norman. BAP
Chant of the Woman, The. Grace Blackburn. CPG
Chant Out of Doors, A. Marguerite Wilkinson. CP; POT; PoTo; SP; TrPWD
Chant-Pagan. Kipling. BPN; OAEP (2d ed.)
(English Irregular, '90–'02.) CBE; CBOV
Chant Royal from a Copydesk. Rufus Terral. InMe
Chant Royal of High Virtue. Sir Arthur Quiller-Couch. HBV
Chant Royal of Love. Michael Lewis. PIAE
Chant Royal of the Dejected Dipsomaniac. Don Marquis. HBMV
Chant to a Were-Bear. Hermia Harris Fraser, *ad. fr. Haida Indian song.* BoCaPo
Chanted Calendar, A. Sydney Dobell. *Fr.* Balder. BoTP; DD; GBV; GTSE; HBV; HBVY; OBEV; RG; WP
(Procession of the Flowers, The.) GN; OTPC
(Spring's Procession.) CBPC
Chantey of Notorious Bibbers. Henry Morton Robinson. InMe
Chanticleer. William Austin. OxBoCh
(Carol: "All this night shrill chanticler." MeRV; SeCL
(Hymn: "All this night . . .") CenL
(Sun of Righteousness.) AnEC
Chanticleer. John Farrar. GFA; PCH; TiPo; UTS
Chanticleer. Celia Thaxter. PRWS; TVC; TVSH
Chanticleer. Katharine Tynan. HBV; HBVY; MPB; MW; OTPC; TiPO; TSW; TSWC; TVSH
Chanting Cherubs, The—a Group by Greenough. Richard Henry Dana. AA
Chanting the Square Deific. Walt Whitman. PoE
Chants Communal, *sel.* Horace Traubel.
What Can I Do? TrJP
Chants for Socialists, *sel.* William Morris.
March of the Workers, The. BMEP; ViP
Chants, incense, and the glory pass and die. December 26. George Edward Hoffman. PGD
Chanty: "Kneel to the beautiful women who bear us this strange brave fruit." John Masefield. *Fr.* The Tragedy of Pompey the Great. BMEP
Chanty: "When rain falls, I say." Ronald McCuaig. MoAuPo
Chao-Mong-Mu freely laid his hands over the sky. Sermon. Emanuel Carnevali. NP
Chaos. Pope. *See* Conclusion: "In vain, in vain . . ."
Chaos—and the Way Out, *sel.* John Oxenham.
Law of Love, The. OQP; QP-2
Chaos in all the world. The Kingdom of God Is Within You. Toyohiko Kagawa. SoLD
Chaos is tamed and ordered as we ride. In the Subway. Louis Untermeyer. PoeMoYo
Chaos on Her Throne, or the Triumph of Dullness. Pope. *Fr.* The Dunciad: Conclusion. BeR
("She comes! she comes!") NBE
Chapala Poems, *sels.* Witter Bynner. NP
Asleep.
Calendar.
Montezuma.
Web, The.
Chapel in Lyoness, The. William Morris. BPN; EmBrPo; PoVP; ViPo; VLEP
Chapel in the Woods. Mary Newton Baldwin. UnW
Chaperon, The. H. C. Bunner. AA; HBV; MMV
Chaplet, The. Witter Bynner. PFY; PoeMoYo
Chaplet, The, *sels.* Moses Mendes. TrJP
Ass, The.
Philanderer, The.
Chaplet of Cypress, The. Thomas Holley Chivers. APW; MOAP; SPP
Chaplinesque. Hart Crane. ChMo; CrMA; LiTG; LiTM (rev. ed.); OxBA; ReMP
Chaplin's Sad Speech. Rafael Alberti, *tr. fr. Spanish by* Lloyd Mallan. LiTW
Chapman, we find, by thy past-prized fraught. To My Worthy Friend Mr. George Chapman, and His Translated Hesiod. Michael Drayton. PtP
Chapultepec Park. Muriel Rukeyser. FiMAP
Character, A. Charlotte Fiske Bates. AA
Character, A. Blake. *See* Epigram: Character, A.
Character. Emerson. AA; AnFE; AnNE; APA; CoAnAm; IAP; LiTA
Character, A. Thomas Caulfield Irwin. TIP
Character and Talent. Jules Laforgue, *tr. fr. French by* Patricia Terry. OnPM
Character Building. Edward Anthony. GoTP
Character of a Happy Life, The. Sir Henry Wotton. BLV; CBE; DD; EiL; ElSeCe; EV-2; GrCo-1; GTBS; GTBS-D; GTBS-W GTSE; CTSL; HBV; HBVY; LEAP; LiTB; LiTG; LPS-3; MaRV; MCCG; OBEV; OBS; OTPC (1923 ed.); PCD; PoFr; SeEP; ShBV-2; StaSt: TOP; TreF; TrGrPo; TVSH; ViBoPo; WP
(Happy Life, The.) MyFE, *abr.;* PECK
(How Happy Is He Born.) BHV
(Lord of Himself.) LH
Character of Holland, The, *sel.* Andrew Marvell.
"Holland, that scarce deserves the name of land." ChTr
Character of Love Seen as a Search for the Lost, The. Kenneth Patchen. TwAmPo
Character of Sir Robert Walpole, The. Swift. BeR
Character of the Earl of Shaftesbury. Dryden. *See* Achitophel.
Character of the Happy Warrior. Wordsworth. BEL; BoLiVe, *abr.;* BPN; CBE; EM-2; EmBrPo; EnLit; EnLP; EnRP; EPN; ERP; FaBoBe; FaFP; GDAH; GEPC; GrCo-1, *abr.;* HBV; HBVY; HiLiEn; LiTB; LiTG; LoBV; MaRV. *abr.;* OBRV; PTA-1; TOP; TreF
(Happy Warrior, The.) BHV; EV-3; OHFP; OQP, *abr.;* QP-2 *abr.*
Sels.
"Who is the happy warrior? Who is he." BLV
"Whose powers shed round him." PC
Characteristics of a Child Three Years Old. Wordsworth. OBRV
Characterization, A. Sir Henry Taylor. VA
Characters from the Satires: Achitophel. Dryden. *See* Achitophel.
Characters from the Satires: Atticus. Pope. *See* Atticus.
Characters from the Satires: Chloe. Pope. *See* Chloe.
Characters from the Satires: Og and Doeg. Dryden. *See* Og and Doeg.
Characters from the Satires: Sporus. Pope. *See* Sporus.
Characters from the Satires: Wharton. Pope. *Fr.* Moral Essays, Epistle I. InPo
(Wharton.) AWP; JAWP; WBP
Characters from the Satires: Zimri. Dryden. *See* Zimri.
Characters of great and small, The. The Skeleton in the Cupboard. Frederick Locker-Lampson. HBV; VA
Characters of Women: Flavia, Atossa, and Cloe. Pope. *Fr.* Moral Essays, Epistle II. OBEC
Chloe, *sel.* AWP; JAWP; WBP
Characters of Women. Edward Young. *Fr.* Love of Fame, the Universal Passion, V. OBEC
Charade. Winthrop Mackworth Praed. *See* Camp-Bell.
Charcoal-Burner, The. Sir Edmund Gosse. OBVV
Charcoal-Burner, The. Po Chü-i. *See* Charcoal-Seller, The.
Charcoal-Burner's Son, The. Erik Gustaf Geijer, *tr. fr. Swedish by* Charles W. Stork. AnSL; WoL
Charcoal in sacks if you bring ten. Automedon, *tr. fr. Greek by* Norman Douglas. GrPo
Charcoal Man, *with music.* *Unknown.* TrAS
Charcoal-Seller, The. Po Chü-i, *tr. fr. Chinese by* Arthur Waley. TrCh; WoL
(Charcoal-Burner, The, *tr. by* Ching Ti.) WhP
Charcoal Sketch. Michael Scot. PoC
Chard Whitlow. Henry Reed. FiBHP; LiTM (rev. ed.); OnHM; PoN; SiTL
Charge, A. Herbert Trench. HBV; LEAP; OBEV (new ed.); OBVV; TVSH
Charge at Santiago, The. William Hamilton Hayne. MC; PAH
Charge at Waterloo, The. Sir Walter Scott. *Fr.* The Field of Waterloo. PEOR
Charge by the Ford, The. Thomas Dunn English. PAH
Charge of Pickett's Brigade, The. *Unknown.* PTA-2
Charge of the Heavy Brigade at Balaclava, The. Tennyson.
(Heavy Brigade, The.) LH
Sels.
"And here the Singer for his art," *fr.* Epilogue. BPN
I Would That Wars Should Cease, *fr.* Epilogue. AOAH
Charge of the Light Brigade, The. Tennyson. BBV; BEL; BeLS; BHV; BLPA; BPN; CG; EM-2; EmBrPo; EPN; EV-5; FaBoBe; FaFP; FaPON; GEPC; GN; HBV; HBVY; HiLiEn; HoPM; LEAP; LPS-2; MaC; MCCG; NeHB; OHFP; OnHT; OnSP; OTPC; PC; PCD; PECK; PFE; PIR; PoVP; PTA-1; PYM; ShBV-1; TCEP; TOP; TreF; TSWC; TVSH; VA; VLEP; WBLP
Charge the Can Cheerily, *with music.* *Unknown.* AmSS
Charge to Keep I Have, A. Charles Wesley. HBV
Charge to Youth, A. "Æ." *Fr.* On Behalf of Some Irishmen Not Followers of Tradition. GrCo-2
Charing Cross. Cecil Roberts. HBMV
Eyeless and Limbless and Shattered, *sel.* BMEP
Charing Cross Road. Bernard Bergonzi. PoN
Chariot, The. Emily Dickinson. *See* Because I could not stop for Death.
Chariot Axles, The. *Unknown, tr. fr. Chinese by* E. D. Edwards. ChLP
Chariot of Fire. Blake. *See* And Did Those Feet in Ancient Time.
Chariot Race, The. Homer, *tr. fr. Greek by* George Chapman. *Fr.* The Iliad, XIII. EV-1
Chariot-Race, A. Sophocles, *tr. fr. Greek. Fr.* Electra. GrR, *tr. by* Robert Whitelaw; OxBG, *tr. by* J. T. Sheppard
Charioteer. Witter Bynner. AnFE; CoAnAm; TwAmPo
Charioteer, The. Shelley. *Fr.* Prometheus Unbound, II, iv. ShBV-3
("My coursers are fed with the lightning.") OBRV

Charioteer, A. *Unknown, tr. fr. Greek by* George Allen. OxBG
Chariots. Witter Bynner. HBMV
Chariots Go Forth to War, The. Tu Fu, *tr. fr. Chinese.* PoHN, *tr. by* Henry H. Hart; WhP
Chariots of silver and copper, The. Marine. Arthur Rimbaud. AnFP
Charis, guess, and do not miss. Claiming a Second Kiss by Desert. Ben Jonson. *Fr.* A Celebration of Charis. LiTL
Charisius Rebukes Himself. Menander, *tr. fr. Greek by* Gilbert Highet. *Fr.* Epitrepontes. OxBG
Charitas Nimia; or, The Dear Bargain. Richard Crashaw. EPS; MePo; OxBoCh; PoFS; PoLi; ReEn; SeEP
"Lord, what is man?" *sel.* MaRV
Charity. First Corinthians, XIII, Bible, *N.T.* BPP; EM-1; ShBV-4; StVeCh
(Gospel of Love, The.) OuHeWo
(Greatest of These Is Love.) GrCo-1; TrGrPo, *abr.*
(Greatness of Love, The.) MaRV
(Love the Indispensable and Crowning Grace.) PG (1955 ed.)
(St. Paul on Charity.) TreF
("Though I speak with the tongues of men . . . .") BoFr; BrBE; LO; PreP
Charity. George Parsons Lathrop. CAW; JKCP
Charity. Joaquin Miller. *See* In Men Whom Men Condemn.
Charity. Pope. *Fr.* An Essay on Man, III. OBEC
("For forms of government let fools contest.") ViBoPo
Charity. *Unknown, at. to* Edward Wallis Hoch. BLPA; NeHB
(Good and Bad.) TreFS
(Thought to Remember, A, *sl. diff.*) BLP
Charity in Thought. Samuel Taylor Coleridge. WhC
Charlemagne. Longfellow. Tales of a Wayside Inn: The Poet's Tale. Pt. III. AnAmPo; FaFP; LA
Charlemagne carried it far. The Cross. Ruby Weyburn Tobias. ChIP
Charles at the Siege. George Hetherington. AnIV
Charles Augustus Fortescue. Hilaire Belloc. OnPP
Charles Carvilie's Eyes. E. A. Robinson. MaPo; NePA; OxBA
Charles! Charles! my son! What! hast thou left me then? Mourning. Victor Hugo. TrFP
Charles Dickens. Louella C. Poole. POT; PoTo
Charles —for it seems you wish to know. A Gage d'Amour. Austin Dobson. VA
Charles Gave Elizabeth a Dodo. Esther Lilian Duff. DDA
(Of a Certain Green-eyed Monster.) HBMV
Charles Guiteau. *Unknown.* ABS; ViBoFo
Charles Gustavus Anderson, *2 vers., with music. Unknown, at. to* Joseph Keating, Sr. ShS
Charles Lamb. Pakenham Beatty. VA
Charles! my slow heart was only sad. Sonnet to a Friend Who Asked How I Felt When the Nurse First Presented My Infant to Me. Samuel Taylor Coleridge. EnRP; MotAn
Charles O'Malley, the Irish Dragoon, *sels.* Charles Lever.
It's Little for Glory I Care. OnYI
(Mickey Free's Song.) ALV
Larry M'Hale. OnYI; TIP
Widow Malone, The. BOHV; HBV; LPS-3; TIP; TreFS
Charles II Andrew Marvell. *Fr.* Last Instructions to a Painter. OBS
Charles II, *sel.* Douglas Brooke Wheelton Sladen.
Refrain. VA
Charles II of Spain to Approaching Death. Eugene Lee-Hamilton. VA
Charles Sumner. Longfellow. GA; PEOR
Charles the Fifth and the Peasant. Robert Lowell, *after the French of* Paul Valéry. MiAP
Charles the First, *sel.* Shelley.
"Widow bird sate mourning for her love, A," *fr.* sc. v. AtBAP; BoTP; CBE; CG; CH; EPN; EV-4; FaPON; GTBS; GTBS-D; GTBS-W; GTSE; LO; MPB; OBRV; OTPC (1946 ed.); SeCeV
(Song, A.) BPN; FaBoEn; KN; LoBV; PoEL-4; ShBV-1; ThWaDe; WP
(Winter.) BLV; CBOV; PIAE; StaSt
Charles the First, *sel.* William Gorman Wills.
Cromwell and Henrietta Maria. VA
Charles XII. Samuel Johnson. *Fr.* The Vanity of Human Wishes. BCEP; LPS-3, *abr.;* OBEC, *abr.;* PIR
(Charles XII of Sweden.) CoEV
("On what foundation stands the warrior's pride.") ViBoPo
Charleston. Richard Watson Gilder. PAH
Charleston (February, 1865). Paul Hamilton Hayne. BlG; PAH
Charleston. Henry Timrod. AA; AmP; AmPP; CoBA; IAP; MOAP; OBAV; OxBA; PAH; SPP; TCAP
Charleston Garden, A. Henry Bellamann. LS
Charlestown *Unknown. See* Boston Burglar, The.
Charley Barley, butter and eggs. *Unknown.* OxNR
Charley, Charley. *Unknown.* OxNR
Charley Lee. Henry Herbert Knibbs. WaKn
Charley Snyder. *Unknown.* ABF
Charley Warlie had a cow. *Unknown.* OxNR
Charlie Chaplin Went to France. *Unknown, at. to* Carl Withers. FaFP; MoShBr; SiTL
Charlie, he's a young man. *Unknown.* LaNeLa
Charlie, He's My Darling. Burns. ALV; CH; EV-3; ViBoPo
(Charlie Is My Darling.) HBV
Charlie Is My Darling. James Hogg. OTPC (1946 ed.)
Charlie Is My Darling. Lady Nairne. DiM
Charlie Machree. William J. Hoppin. LPS-1
Charlie MacPherson. *Unknown.* ESPB
Charlie Piecan. F. Murray *and* F. Leigh. OxBoLi
Charlie Rutledge [*or* Rutlage]. *Unknown, at. to* D. J. White (D. J. O'Malley). CoSo; CSF
Charlie Wag. *Unknown.* OxNR
Charlotte [*or* Charlottie] liv'd on a mountaintop in a bleak and lonely spot. The Frozen Girl. *Unknown.* AS; IHA
Charm, The. Rupert Brooke. LoPo
Charm, A. Dryden. ChTr
Charm, A ("If ye fear to be affrighted"). Robert Herrick. ChTr
Charm, A ("In the morning when you rise"). Robert Herrick. OTPC (1923 ed.)
Charm. Ben Jonson. *See* Witches' Charms, The.
Charm, A. Kipling. GTML; OtMeF
Charm, A. Christopher Morley. POT; PoTo
Charm, A. Thomas Randolph. *Fr.* The Jealous Lovers. SeCL
Charm, The. Shakespeare. *See* Witches' Song, The.
Charm against a Magpie, A. *Unknown.* ChTr
Charm against Enemies. *Unknown, tr. fr. Irish by* Lady Wilde. JKCP (1926 ed.)
Charm against the Toothache, A. John Heath-Stubbs. NePoEA
Charm for a Sudden Stitch. *Unknown, tr. fr. Anglo-Saxon by* Charles W. Kennedy. AnOE
Charm for Bees, A. *Unknown, tr. fr. Old High German.* CAW
Charm for Cantinflas, A. Muriel Rukeyser. FiMAP
Charm for Spring Flowers, A. Rachel Field. TiPo (1959 ed.)
Charm for Swarming Bees. *Unknown, tr. fr. Anglo-Saxon by* William O. Stevens. EPP
Charm for Unfruitful Land. *Unknown, tr. fr. Anglo-Saxon by* Charles W. Kennedy. AnOE
Charm is a woman's strongest arm. If They Meant All They Said. Alice Duer Miller. BOHV
Charm is the measure of attraction's power. What Is Charm? Louisa Carroll Thomas. BLPA; NeHB
Charm is working, now, The. April. John Vance Cheney. NLK
Charm me asleep, and melt me so. To Music [*or* Musique], to Becalm [*or* Becalme] His Fever. Robert Herrick. ATP; CoEV; EG; ElSeCe; EPS; EV-2; HBV; OBEV; OBS; PIAE; ReEn; SeCL; SeCV-1; TyEnPo; UnS
Charm, or an Allay for Love, A. Robert Herrick. FaBoCh; LoGBV
Charm to Call Sleep, A. Henry Johnstone. PRWS
Charm to Quell a Rival. *Unknown, tr. fr. Sanskrit by* R. J. H. Griffith. *Fr.* The Rigveda. LiTW
Charm to Save Cattle. *Unknown, tr. fr. Russian by* W. R. S. Ralston. OnPM
Charm Verses. *Unknown, tr. fr. Armenian by* Zabelle C. Boyajian. ArmLP
Charmer, on a given straight line. The Collegian to His Bride. *Unknown.* LPS-3
Charming of the East Wind, The. Charles Tennyson Turner. EnSW
Charming Woman, The. Helen Selina Sheridan. ALV; OBRV
Charms. W. H. Davies. CaAE
Charms, The. Emma A. Opper. DD
Charms of Nature, The. Joseph Warton. *Fr.* The Enthusiast; or, The Lover of Nature. OBEC; SeCePo
Charoba at Her Bath. Walter Savage Landor. *Fr.* Gebir. RO
Charon, O Charon, draw thy boat to th' shore. The New Charon. Robert Herrick. ReEn
Chart, The. Walter de la Mare. CoBMV
Chart, The. Michael Lewis. StaSt
Chart of the Pacific. Clifford Gessler. MuM
"Chart Showing Rain, Winds, Isothermal Lines and Ocean Currents." Louise Owen. PFE
Charted Skies, The. Charles L. O'Donnell. MM
Charter of Salvation, The. George Arthur Clarke. MaRV
Chartist Song. Thomas Cooper. VA
Chartivel, *sel.* Marie de France, *tr. fr. French by* Arthur O'Shaughnessy.
Song from "Chartivel." AWP; JAWP; LEAP, *abr.;* LiTW; LyMA; WBP
("Hath any loved you well, down there.") EnLoPo; PoVP

(Sarrazine's Song.) GTIV
(Sarrazine's Song to Her Dead Lover.) HBV
Chartless. Emily Dickinson. *See* I never saw a moor.
Chase, The ("Harp of the North!"). Sir Walter Scott. *See* Harp of the North.
Chase, The ("The stag at eve had drunk his fill"). Sir Walter Scott. *Fr.* The Lady of the Lake, I. LH
(Stag Hunt, The.) LPS-2
Chase, The ("Art thou gone in haste?"). *Unknown. See* Art Thou Gone in Haste?
Chase, The. ("Here's a moccasin track in the drifts"). *Unknown.* SCC
Chase and the Race, The. Adam Lindsay Gordon. *Br. sel. fr.* Ye Wearie Wayfarer, Fytte VII. OtMeF
Chase me, chase me!/ I came to you. The Meeting. Georges Duhamel. BoFr
Chasing the Fox. Chaucer. *Fr.* The Canterbury Tales: The Nun's Priest's Tale. CoEV
Chaste and Lost Lovers, The, *sel.* William Bosworth.
See'st Not, My Love. SeCL
Chaste Arabian Bird, The. Earl of Rochester. SiTL
Chaste as the air whither she's fled. On the Death of Mrs. Elizabeth Filmer. Richard Lovelace. EV-2
Chaste Cloris doth disclose the shames. Cloris and Mertilla. Michael Drayton. *Fr.* The Muses' Elysium. LoBV
Chaste Goddesse, wel wostow that I. Emily's Prayer to Diana. Chaucer. *Fr.* The Canterbury Tales: The Knight's Tale. MyFE
Chaste Maid in Cheapside, A, *sel.* Thomas Middleton.
"Weep eyes, break heart!" TuPP
(Parting.) ElL
Chaste maids which haunt fair Aganippe's well. Lament. William Drummond of Hawthornden. *Fr.* Tears on the Death of Meliades. LoBV
Chastelard, *sels.* Swinburne.
Between the Sunset and the Sea. PoVP
(Love at Ebb.) BPN
(Mary Beaton's Song.) HBV; PIR
Chastelard and Mary Stuart. VA
Chastised Clown, The. Stéphane Mallarmé, *tr. fr. French by* Kate Flores. AnFP
Chastisement of Tartufe, The. Arthur Rimbaud, *tr. fr. French by* Alan Conder. TrFP
Chastity. Milton. *Fr.* Comus. OBS
Château de Monthiers. Katherine Mann. EBSV
Château Papineau. S. Frances Harrison. CaP; OCL; VA
Chatelaine within her tower, A. Her Name. Paul Verlaine. TrFP
Chattanooga. Herman Melville. APW
Chattering and laughing on her way she goes. The American Girl and the War. Hester L. Anderson. CAG
Chattering finch and water-fly. The Skeleton. G. K. Chesterton. FaBoTw
Chattering swallow! what shall we. The Swallow. Thomas Stanley. AWP
Chaucer. Benjamin Brawley. BANP
Chaucer. E. E. Cummings. MeRV
Chaucer. Longfellow. AA; AmP; AmPP; APW; ATP (1935 ed.); AWP; BLV; CBOV; ES; IAP; InPo; InvP; JAWP; LEAP; MOAP; NePA; OBAV; OBEV (new ed.); OBVV; OnPP; OxBA; PeBoSo; PFE; PoRA; PtP; TOP; TrGrPo; WBP
Chaucer is dead; and Gower lies in grave. Against the Dispraisers of Poetry. Richard Barnfield. SiCE; TuPP
Chaucer's Complaint to His Empty Purse. Chaucer. *See* Compleint of Chaucer to His Empty Purse, The.
Chaucer's Envoy to the Story of Patient Griselda. Chaucer, *mod. by* W. W. Skeat. *Fr.* The Canterbury Tales: The Clerk's Tale. AnEnPo
(Griselda.) BHV
Chaucers Word[e]s unto Adam, His Owne Scriveyn. Chaucer. BEL; EM-1
Chaunt no more thy roundelay. To a Linnet. Robert Allan. EBSV
Chavez. Mildred I. McNeal Sweeney. HBV; LBMV; VOD (1935 ed.)
Chayah. Thomas Moult. NV
Che Sara Sara. Victor Plarr. HBV; LBBV
Cheat of Cupid, The; or, The Ungentle Guest. Robert Herrick, *after the Greek of* Anacreon. AWP; PG (1945 ed.); SeCeV
Check James Stephens. AnIL; BMEP; GTSL; HBMV; PoRh; RAR; SiSoSe; SP; SUS; TiPo
(Night, The.) BoTP
(Night Was Creeping.) StVeCh
Cheddar Pinks. Robert Bridges. ChMP; MoVE; POTE; SeCePo
Cheeks as soft as July peaches. Baby May. William Cox Bennett. HBV; LPS-1; OTPC (1923 ed.); VA
Cheer and salute for the Admiral, and here's to the Captain bold, A. The Men behind the Guns. John Jerome Rooney. AA; BLPA; EtS; FaBoBe; HBV; JKCP; MC; PaA; PAH; YaD
Cheer, Boys, Cheer. Charles Mackay. BHV
Cheer of the *Trenton,* The. Walter Mitchell. EtS
Cheer up, all you young men. Brave Wolfe (B *vers.*). *Unknown* BaBo
Cheer Up, My Mates. Abraham Cowley. EV-2
Cheer up, my [*or* ye] young men all [*or* your hearts, young men], let nothing fright you. Brave Wolfe. *Unknown.* BaBo (A *vers.*); PAH; TrAS; ViBoFo
Cheered with this hope, to Paris I returned. Residence in France. Wordsworth. *Fr.* The Prelude. PoEL-4
Cheerfu' supper done, wi' serious face, The. Burns. *Fr.* The Cotter's Saturday Night. BHV; WGRP
Cheerful and industrious beast, A. The Bumblebeaver. Kenyon Cox. *Fr.* Mixed Beasts. RIS; TiPo
Cheerful Horn, The. *Unknown.* CH
Cheerful old bear at the Zoo, A. *Unknown.* GoTP
Cheerfulness Taught by Reason. Elizabeth Barrett Browning. EOAH; PoVP
Cheeriest room, that morn, the kitchen. Flying Jim's Last Leap. Emma Dunning Banks. PTA-2
Cheerily carols the lark. Mad Margaret's Song. W. S. Gilbert. *Fr.* Ruddigore. RIS
Cheerily, on the axe of labour. The Lumbermen. Whittier. BHV
Cheerio My Deario. Don Marquis. *Fr.* Archy and Mehitabel. ShBV-4
Cheer'ly, Man. *Unknown.* AmSS; SoAmSa, *with music*
(Cheer'ly, O! *diff. vers.*) AmSS
Cheese-Mites Asked, The. *Unknown.* WhC
Cheetah. Charles Eglington. BoSA
Cheetie-Poussie-Cattie, O. *Unknown. See* There Was a Wee Bit Mousikie.
Chef whose hat is celluloid and green, A. Owed to Dickens, 1956. Jan Burroway. NePoAm-2
Chelsea Crypt. Robert Herring. MoWP
Chemist to His Love, The ("I love thee, Mary, and thou lovest me"). *Unknown.* BOHV; InMe
Chemistry of Character, The. Elizabeth Dorney. BLPA
Chen, The *Unknown, tr. fr. Chinese by* E. D. Edwards. ChLP
Chengtu. Tu Fu, *tr. fr. Chinese.* WhP
Cheops. James Schevill. FiMAP
Chercheuses de poux, Les. Arthur Rimbaud, *tr. fr. French by* T. Sturge Moore. AWP
(Lice Seekers, The.) AnFP, *tr. by* Kenneth Koch *and* Georges Guy; TrFP, *tr. by* Alan Conder
(Louse-Catchers, The, *tr. by* Roy Campbell.) LiTW; MiFP
"Cherchez Fortune Ailleurs." Theognis, *tr. fr. Greek by* F. L. Lucas. GrPE
Cherish You Then the Hope I Shall Forget. Edna St. Vincent Millay. *See* Sonnet: "Cherish you then . . ."
Cherrie-ripe. Robert Herrick. *See* Cherry-ripe.
Cherries. Zalman Schneour, *tr. fr. Yiddish by* Joseph Leftwich. TrJP
Cherries. Frederic E. Weatherly. SAS
Cherries at the Eta Temple. On the Eta, the Untouchables. Issa. PoFr
Cherry and Pear are white. The Crowns. John Freeman. CH
Cherry and the Slae, The, *sel.* Alexander Montgomerie.
May-Morn and Cupid EBSV
("About ane bank, where birdis on bewis.") GoTS
Cherry-Blossom Wand, The. Anna Wickham. MBP; MoBrPo; TSW; TwCV
Cherry-blossoms, more. Onitsura, *tr. fr. Japanese by* Harold Gould Henderson. LiTW
Cherry Creek store shoulders up to the bridge, The. The Snake Charmer. Muriel Earley Shepperd. IHA
Cherry Fair, A. *Unknown.* ChTr
Cherry flowers. Issa, *tr. fr. Japanese by* Lois J. Erickson. SoLD
Cherry-Pit. Robert Herrick. OAEP
Cherry-red her mouth was. Eleanor. Christina Rossetti. BPN
Cherry-ripe. Thomas Campion. BEL; CBOV; CH; CoBE; EnLi-1; EnLit; EPP; EV-2; ExPo; GTBS; GTBS-D; GTBS-W; GTSE; GTSL; HBV; LEAP; LiTB; LiTG; LiTL; OBEV; PG (1955 ed.); PIAE; SeCeV; TCEP
(There Is a Garden.) AtBAP; TuPP
(There Is a Garden in Her Face.) BLV; CenL; EG; ElL; ElSeCe; EM-1; EnL; FaBoEn; InPo; LPS-1; OAEP; OBSC; PoEL-2; PoFS; PreP; ReaPo; ReEn; RiBV; SiCE; SiTL; ThWaDe; TrGrPo; ViBoPo; WHA
Cherry-ripe. Robert Herrick. CaAE; CH; CoBE; EM-1; EnL; EPP; EV-2; LiTL; OBEV; OTPC (1923 ed.); PoE; PoFS; ReaPo; ShBV-1
(Cherrie-ripe.) SeCV-1
("Cherry-ripe, ripe, ripe, I cry.") EG
Cherry Robbers. D. H. Lawrence. MBP; MoAB; MoBrPo
Cherry Tree. Hermann Claudius, *tr. fr. German by* Herman Salinger. TwGV
Cherry Tree. Ivy O. Eastwick. BoTP
Cherry Tree. Christina Rossetti. YeAr
Cherry Tree. Sacheverell Sitwell. AtBAP
Cherry Tree, The. James Stephens. TCPD

Cherry-Tree Carol, The (*diff. versions*). *Unknown.* ABS; AnEC; AnEnPo; BaBo (*A and B vers.*); BLV; BoLiVe; ChTr; EnSB; ESPB (*A and B vers.*); KN; LoBV; OAEP; OBB; OxBoCh; OxBoLi; SeCeV; StJW; TrGrPo; ViBoFo, *with music*

(Joseph Was an Old Man.) ViBoPo

(Old Christmas Carol, An.) RG

"O I shall be as dead, mother," *sel.* PoD

Cherry-Tree Carol, The: As Joseph Was a-Walking. *Unknown. See* As Joseph . . .

Cherry tree is fragrant with blossoms, The. Spring Night. Coley B. Taylor. *Fr.* Chinoiseries. PFE

Cherry tree's shedding, The. May Morning. Marjorie Barrows. GFA

Cherry Way. Ruth Comfort Mitchell. NV

Cherry year, A. *Unknown.* OxNR

Cherub-Folk, The. Enid Dinnis. CAW

Cherubic Pilgrim, The. "Angelus Silesius," *tr. fr. German.* WGRP

Cherubim, The, *sel.* Thomas Heywood.

"I have wandered like a sheep that's lost." WGRP

Cherubim tune up their instruments, The. Seven Sonnets. Christopher Logue. PoN

Cherwell Water Lily [*or* Waterlily], The. Frederick W. Faber. CAW; GoBC

Chesapeake and the *Shannon,* The. *Unknown.* PAH; ViBoFo, *with music*

Chesapeake Marsh, A. Lizette Woodworth Reese. LS

Chesapeake so bold, The. The *Chesapeake* and the *Shannon.* *Unknown.* PAH; ViBoFo

Cheshire Cat. Kenneth Allott. NeBP

Chess. Ibn Sharaf, *tr. fr. Arabic by* A. J. Arberry. MooP

Chess. John Thompson. BoAu

Chess Knight. Michalis Stasinopoulos, *tr. fr. Modern Greek by* Rae Dalven. MoGP

Chess-Board, The. "Owen Meredith." HBV; LPS-1; OBVV; VA

Chesspieces. Joseph Campbell. OxBI

Chest of Perote, The. Joaquín Arcadio Pagaza, *tr. fr. Spanish by* Samuel Beckett. AnMP

Chester, *with music.* William Billings. TrAS

Chestnut Buds. Evelyn M. Williams. BoTP

Chestnut Casts His Flambeaux [and the Flowers], The. A. E. Housman. Last Poems, IX. AtBAP; ChMo; CMP; EG; EnLit; LiTB; MBP; MoAB; MoBrPo; OBMV; PoLFOT; POTE; POTT; ReaPo; ReMP; TwP; ViP; ViPo

Chestnut Stands. Rachel Field. SiSoSe

Chestnut's a fine tree, The. A Christmas-Tree Song. Rodney Bennett. BoTP

Chevalier de maison rouge, Le, *sel.* Alexandre Dumas, *tr. fr. French by* John Oxenford.

Girondins, The. PoFr

Chevy Chase [*or* Chace]. *Unknown.* BHV; EnLi-1 (1949 ed.); EnSB; EV-2; GN; HBV; LEAP; LH; LiA, *older vers.;* LPS-2, *mod.;* OBB, *older vers.;* PFE, *sl. abr.;* TOP, *abr.;* ViBoFo, *with music;* ViBoPo, *older vers.;* WHA, *older vers.*

(Ancient Ballad of Chevy-Chase, The, *older vers.*) EnRP; KN

(Hunting of the Cheviot, The.) BaBo (*A, B, and C vers.*); BEL, *older vers.;* ESPB (*A and B vers.*); OAEP; TCEP, *older vers.*

Cheyenne, *with music.* *Unknown.* CoSo

Cheyenne Boys. *Unknown.* ABS

Cheyenne Mountain. Helen Hunt Jackson. PoOW

Chez Brébant. Francis Alexander Durivage. AA

Chez Jane. Frank O'Hara. NeAP

Chez Madame. Sam Harrison. NeIP

Chi è questa. Guido Cavalcanti. *See* Sonnet: "Who is she that comes, makyng turn every man's eye."

Ch'i Lai' (March of the Volunteers). Shih Ee, *tr. fr. Chinese by* Li Pao-sheng *and* Liu Liang-mo. PoFr

Chian river brimming over, The. The Stone Drums, II. *Unknown, tr. fr. Chinese by* Yu Min-chuan. WhP

Chiang-nan is a glorious and beautiful land. Song of the Men of Chin-ling. Hsieh T'iao. TrCh

Chiaroscuro. John B. Thompson. OQP; QP-2

Chiaroscuro: Rose. Conrad Aiken. MAPA

Chicago. Sherwood Anderson. NP

Chicago. Bret Harte. PAH

Chicago. Galway Kinnell. NePoAm

Chicago. Mildred Plew Meigs. *See* To Chicago at Night.

Chicago. John Boyle O'Reilly. PAH

Chicago. Carl Sandburg. AmPP; BAP; ChMo; CMP; CoBA; CoV; HBMV; IAP; InP; LEAP; LiTM (rev. ed.); LoGBV; MAP; MoAB; MoAmPo; MOAP; MoVE; NePA; NP; OxBA; PFE; PoeMoYo; PreP; PYM, *abr.;* TCAP; TCPD; TOP; TreF; TwCV; ViBoPo (1958 ed.); YaD

Chicago. Whittier. BAV; MC; PAH; PoRL

Chicago Idyll. E. Merrill Root. AnAmPo; LA; PreP

Chicago Poem. Lew Welch. NeAP

Chick! my naggie. *Unknown.* OxNR

Chickadee. Martha Haskell Clark. BLA; WhBS

Chickadee. The. Hilda Conkling. BoChLi; RAR; TiPo; TSW; TSWC

Chickadee, The. Emerson. *Fr.* The Titmouse. FaPON; GFA; OTPC (1946 ed.); PCH

Chickadee. Marion Mitchell Walker. GFA

Chickadee in the apple tree, The. The Chickadee. Hilda Conkling. BoChLi; RAR; TiPo; TSW; TSWC

Chickadee-dee-dee is not a bird, The. Scarabs for the Living, VII. R P. Blackmur. CoAnAm; TwAmPo

Chickadees, The. John Hay. NePoAm-2

Chickadees. Edith M. Thomas. BLA

Chickamauga. G. T. Ferris. MDAH

Chickamauga. *Unknown.* MDAH

Chickamauga—1898. *Unknown.* MDAH

Chickamungus, The. James Reeves. GoTP

Chicken. Walter de la Mare. NeMA; TiPo

Chicken-skin, delicate, white. On a Fan That Belonged to the Marquise de Pompadour [*or* Ballade of the Pompadour's Fan]. Austin Dobson. ALV; BPN; HBV; LPS-3; OBVV; PFE; PoVP; VA; ViBoPo

Chickens, The. Rose Fyleman. TiPo (1952 ed.)

Chickens, The. *Unknown.* *See* Five Little Chickens.

Chickens a-crowin' [*or* crowin'] on Sourwood Mountain. Sourwood Mountain. *Unknown.* ABF; APW; AS; TrAS

Chickens am a roostin' in de old plum-tree. Sleep, My Little 'Simmin-colored Coon. William H. Plass. BOL

Chickens Are a-Crowing, The, *with music.* *Unknown.* TrAS

Chickens in Trouble. *Unknown, tr. fr. Norwegian by* Emilie Poulsson. PPL

Chickens they are crowing, a-crowing, a-crowing, The. The Chickens Are a-Crowing. *Unknown.* TrAS

Chickory. Zerubavel Gal'ed, *tr. fr. Hebrew.* TrJP

Chide, chide no more away. Expectation [*or* Destiny]. Thomas Stanley. ElSeCe; LoBV; OBS; SeCL; SeEP

Chief captain commanded him to be brought into the castle, The. The Acts, Bible, *N.T.* PoFr

Chief Centurions, The. John Masefield. *Fr.* The Tragedy of Pompey the Great. POTE; TCPD

("Man is a sacred city, built of marvellous earth.") WGRP

Chief defect of Henry King, The. Henry King. Hilaire Belloc. CenHV; HBMV; TSW; TSWC

Chief in thy generation born of men. Dickens. Swinburne. PoVP

Chief of organic numbers! Lines on Seeing a Lock of Milton's Hair. Keats. TriL

Chief, The, replied: "That post shall be my care." Homer, *tr. by* Pope. *Fr.* The Iliad, VI. EPP

Chief, The, reply'd: This time forbids to rest. Homer, *tr. by* Pope. *Fr.* The Iliad, VI. ATP; CEP

Chief [*or* Chiefe] use then in man of that he knows [*or* knowes], The. Man's Service. Fulke Greville. *Fr.* Of Humane Learning. OBS; PoFr; SiCE

Chiefest is water of all things, for streaming. For Hiero, Tyrant of Syracuse. Pindar. *Fr.* Olympian Odes. GrL

Chiefly to Mind Appears. C. Day Lewis. MBP; MoAB; MoBrPo

Chief's Prayer after the Salmon Catch, The. Constance Lindsay Skinner. *Fr.* Songs of the Coast Dwellers. BoCaPo; NP

Chiefs that bow to Capet's reign, The. On the Anniversary of the Storming of the Bastille. Philip Freneau. AmPP (3d ed.); CoBA; IAP

Chieftain Iffucan of Azcan in caftan. Bantams in Pine-Woods. Wallace Stevens. AtBAP; InPo; MOAP; MoVE; OxBA; SeCeV

Chieftain reared his form on high, The. The Battle of Beal' an Duine. Sir Walter Scott. *Fr.* The Lady of the Lake. LPS-2; TCEP

Chieftain, to the Highlands bound, A. Lord Ullin's Daughter. Thomas Campbell. BBV (1923 ed.); BCEP; BeLS; BoTP; CG; EBSV; EnRP; ERP; EV-4; FaPON; GN; GTBS; GTBS-D; GTBS-W; GTSE; GTSL; HBV; HBVY; LoEn; LPS-1; MW; OBRV; OnSP; OTPC; PECK; PYM; TreF; TVSH; WBLP; WP

Chiffons! William Samuel Johnson. HBV

Child, The. Vaughtie Carroll. CAG

Child, The. Sara Coleridge. MotAn; OBEV (1st ed.)

Child, A. Richard Watson Gilder. AA

Child, A. Mary Lamb. *See* Parental Recollections.

Child, The. Rainer Maria Rilke, *tr. fr. German by* Randall Jarrell. AnGP

Child. Carl Sandburg. NV; OQP; QP-1; StJW

Child, The. John Banister Tabb.

I. At Bethlehem. AA

(Child at Bethlehem, The.) PRWS

II. "Where were ye, birds, that bless His name?" AA

III. To His Mother. AA

Child, A. *Unknown, tr. fr. Greek by* J. A. Pott. OxBG

Child, The. George Edward Woodberry. Wild Eden, XXX. AA

Child, A/ Curious and innocent. To R. L. S. [*or* To Robert Louis Stevenson]. W. E. Henley. BPN; MBP; MoBrPo; POTT; VOD
Child,/ You are my brother. The Mists Are Rising Now. Hasye Cooperman. GoYe
Child alone a poet is, The. Babylon. Robert Graves. HBMV; TwCV
Child and Maiden. Sir Charles Sedley. *Fr.* The Mulberry Garden, III, ii. GTBS; GTBS-D; GTBS-W; GTSE; GTSL; LiTL; TOP
("Ah Cloris! that I now could sit.") OAEP; OBS
(Song: "Ah Chloris [*or* Cloris]! that I now could sit.") SeCV-2; ViBoPo
(Song: To Chloris.) EV-3
(To a Very Young Lady.) LPS-1
(To Chloris.) HBV; OBEV; SeCL
Child and Mother. Eugene Field. HH; MOAH; MotAn, *abr.*; MPB
(Mother and I.) CBPC
Child and Poet. Swinburne. BPN; EmBrPo; EnLit; EPN; PoVP
Child and the Book, The. William L. Stidger. BAP
Child and the Fairies, The. *Unknown.* MeMeAg; OTPC (1946 ed.); PCH; PRWS; StVeCh (1940 ed.)
Child and the Mariner, The. W. H. Davies. CH; PCN; POTT
Child and the Piper, The. Blake. *See* Piping Down the Valleys Wild.
Child and the World, The. Kate Douglas Wiggin. PPL
Child and the Year, The. Celia Thaxter. DD; HH; PEOR
Child and Wind. Lola Ridge. BAP
Child Asleep, A. Walter de la Mare. POTE
Child Asleep, A. Elizabeth Madox Roberts. AnAmPo; LA
Child at a Crèche, A. Alice Isabel Hazeltine. ChrBoLe
Child at Bethlehem, The. John Banister Tabb. *See* At Bethlehem.
Child at school who fails to pass, A. The Untutored Giraffe. Oliver Herford. PoMa
Child awaits the angel, The. He stares. The Angel. Alfred Hayes. TrJP
Child, behold the lovely pattern. Mathematics. Lionel Wiggam. PoMa
Child born in the cawl. Naked and Alone. Phyllis Reid. DiM
Child-Burial; Sequel to Battles. Euripides, *tr. fr. Greek by* Gilbert Murray. *Fr.* Trojan Women. GrR
Child, Child. Sara Teasdale. HBV
Child Compassion, The. Margot Ruddock. OBMV
Child Cried at Night, A. Ernst Wiechert, *tr. fr. German by* Herman Salinger. TwGV
Child, do not neglect the garden you inherit. The Fathers. Kostes Palamas. *Fr.* The Altars. MoGP
Child! do not throw this book about! Dedication on the Gift of a Book to a Child [*or* A Foreword]. Hilaire Belloc. HBVY; MOB; TSW; TSWC
Child Dying, The. Edwin Muir. ChMP; FaBoTw; GTBS-D
Child Eros, The. Meleager. *See* Runaway Cupid.
Child fell, turning slowly with arms outstretched like a doll, The. For Brian Priestman. F. R. Scott. TwCaPo
Child for Sale, A. Meleager, *tr. fr. Greek by* Humbert Wolfe. OxBG
(Love for Sale, *tr. by* F. L. Lucas.) GrPE
Child He was, and had not learned to speak, A. The Incarnation. Giles Fletcher. StJW
Child heart. Child of My Heart. Edwin Markham. BAP
Child. I surrender—and hereby declare. To a Staring Baby in a Perambulator. Nancy Byrd Turner. PC
Child: I want mama. Innocent Fears. Gerasimos Markoras. MoGP
Child, I will give you rings to wear. Declaration. Arthur Symons. ViBoPo
Child—in all the flying sky. Poem. Josephine Strongin. AnAmPo; LA
Child in Me, The. May Riley Smith. BAP; SBMV
Child in Our Soul, The. Björnstjerne Björnson, *tr. fr. Norwegian by* Arthur Hubbell Palmer. WoL
Child in the Garden, The. Henry van Dyke. FAOV; HBV; MaRV
Child in the House, The, *abr.* Madison Cawein. FAOV
Child in the Sabbath peace, there, A. A Sunday. Walter de la Mare. POTE
Child in the Street, The. John James Piatt. AA
Child in the Train, The. Eleanor Farjeon. AlDL
Child is thy father dead? Song. Ebenezer Elliott. BCEP
Child, it is sundown. Town Child. Andrew Hewitt. NoCaPo
Child Jesus, The. Francis Quarles. *See* On the Infancy of our Saviour.
Child Jesus in the Garden, The. *Unknown.* ChrBoLe; CLS
Child Jesus to Mary the Rose, The. John Lydgate. CAW; GoBC; ISi
Child-King, The. Morris Wintchevsky, *tr. fr. Yiddish by* Alter Brody. TrJP
Child Labor. Charlotte Perkins Gilman. BAP
Child Looks Out, The. Dorothy Livesay. TwCaPo
Child Maurice. *Unknown. See* Childe Maurice.
Child Moses, The. Exodus, I: 7–II: 15, Bible, *O.T.* OuHeWo
Child most infantine, A. A Child of Twelve. Shelley. *Fr.* The Revolt of Islam. GN
Child-Musician, The. Austin Dobson. BPN; GN
Child, my child, how sound you sleep! Danaë's Lullaby. Andrew Lang. BOL
Child My Choice, A. Robert Southwell. CAW; GoBC; HBV; OxBoCh; PoLi; SiCE
Child Next Door, The. Rose Fyleman. FaPON; GaP; MPB; SP
Child Noryce is a clever young man. Child Maurice (B *vers.*). *Unknown.* ESPB
Child not yet is lulled to rest, The. Cradle Song at Twilight. Alice Meynell. BOL; TCPD
Child of a Day. Walter Savage Landor. MOAH; VA
(Child of a Day, Thou Knowest Not.) BPN
(On a Child.) OBVV
Child of Athens, honey nurtured, wouldst thou for thy feathered brood. Evenus, *tr. fr. Greek by* Norman Douglas. GrPo
Child of Hippias, foremost captain once, The. Archedike [*or* On the Daughter of Hippias]. Simonides. GrL; GrR; OxBG
Child of Loneliness. Norman Gale. WGRP
Child of Mary. *Unknown. See* This Endernight I Saw a Sight.
Child of My Heart. Edwin Markham. BAP
Child of my love! though thou be bright as day. Shadow. Mary Elizabeth Coleridge. PoVP
Child of Nazareth, The. St. Luke, II: 40–52, Bible, *N.T.* ChrBoLe
Child of Peace, The. Selma Lagerlöf, *tr. fr. Swedish by* Charles W. Stork. AnSL
Child of Prayer, A. *Unknown, tr. fr. Japanese by* Lois J. Erickson. SoLD
Child of sin and sorrow. Exhortation. Thomas Hastings. AA
Child of the frightened face. Frightened Face. Marion Strobel. HBMV
Child of the gorgeous East, whose ardent suns. To an Egyptian Boy. H. W. Berry. WhC
Child of the Long Grass. Roy Macnab. BoSA
Child of the Romans. Carl Sandburg. LaNeLa
Child of the sea, marvel of earth, made firm for aye. Delos. Pindar. GrPE
Child of the Sun, in whom his rays appear. La Gialletta Gallante; or, The Sunburn'd Exotique Beauty. Lord Herbert of Cherbury. AtBAP
Child of the Wind with the Harmonica. Nicephorus Vrettakos, *tr. fr. Modern Greek by* Rae Dalven. MoGP
Child of the World. Edna L. S. Barker. GoYe
Child of To-Day, A. James Buckham. AA
Child of Twelve, A. Shelley. *Fr.* The Revolt of Islam. GN
Child of War. Lionel Johnson. SoV
Child on the Judgment Seat, The. Elizabeth Rundle Charles. BLPA; PEOR
Child on Top of a Greenhouse. Theodore Roethke. AtBAP; MiAP
Child Owlet. *Unknown.* ESPB
Child quickens the coy light of a candle, The. Genesis. Ronald Bottrall. CoEV
Child ran alone, A. Memories. Mark Van Doren. MOAP
Child Reads an Almanac, The. Francis Jammes, *tr. fr. French by* Ludwig Lewisohn. AWP; FaPON; JAWP; WBP
Child Said, *What Is the Grass?* A. Walt Whitman. *See* Grass, The.
Child sees sleepy granny spinning wool, The. Granny's Nodding. Victor Hugo. TrFP
Child should always say what's true, A. Whole Duty of Children. Robert Louis Stevenson. HBV; HBVY; NeHB; OTPC; PoVP; SAS; TreFS
Child should have a pocket, A. Pockets. Susan Adger Williams. BrR; DDA
Child sleeps in the daytime, The. Child Waking. E. J. Scovell. PoLFOT; PoN
Child sleeps under a rose-bush fair, A. The Rose-Bush. *Unknown.* LPS-3
Child-Song. Sir Philip Sidney. BOL
Child That Has a Cold, A. Thomas Dibdin. ChTr
Child, the seed, the grain of corn, The. The Almighty Will. Robert Louis Stevenson. GrCo-1
Child-Thought, A. Wilfrid Thorley. PCH
Child to Parents. Viola Meynell. PtOT
Child to the Father, The. Robert Bridges. FAOV
Child to whom my loneliness. Fathers and Sons. Arthur Davison Ficke. FAOV
Child upon the Stair, The. Carolyn Hall. TSW
Child Waking. E. J. Scovell. PoLFOT; PoN
Child, The, was gone: the Mother stood alone. Madonna of the Empty Arms. Maurice Francis Egan. ISi
Child [*or* Childe] Waters. *Unknown.* BaBo; ESPB (A and B *vers.*); OAEP; OBB, *longer vers.*; ViBoFo

Child, weary of thy baubles of to-day. The Human Plan. Charles Henry Crandall. AA
Child, who went gathering the flowers of death. Haroun Al-Rachid for Hearts-Life. *Unknown. Fr.* The Thousand and One Nights. AWP
Child with the hungry eyes. Beggars. Ella Higginson. AA; LBAP
Child, your white face is chanting memories. Elegy. Karel van de Woestijne. LiTW
Childe Harold to the dark tower, L-two. The Letter. John Holmes. NePoAm
Childe Harold's Farewell to England. Byron. *Fr.* Childe Harold's Pilgrimage, I. OHFP
(Adieu, Adieu! My Native Shore.) LPS-1
Childe Harold's Pilgrimage, *sels.* Byron.
"But quiet to quick bosoms is a hell," *fr.* III. PoFr
"Can tyrants but by tyrants conquer'd be," *fr.* IV. PoFr
"Castled crag of Drachenfels, The," *fr.* III. ViBoPo
(Rhine, The.) LPS-2
Childe Harold ("Where rose the mountains, there to him were friends"), *fr.* III. OBRV
Childe Harold's Farewell to England, *fr.* I, *abr.* OHFP
(Adieu! Adieu! My Native Shore.) LPS-1
Coliseum, The, *fr.* IV. BCEP; BEL; EPN; EV-4, *abr.*; LPS-2; TCEP, *abr.*
("Arches on arches! as it were that Rome," *abr.*) CoBE
Desire and Disillusion, *fr.* IV. EPN
Dying Gladiator, The, *fr.* IV. CBE
"Egeria, sweet creation of some heart," *fr.* IV. ViBoPo
"Fair Greece! sad relic of departed worth!" *fr.* II. PoFr
(Greece.) EV-4, *abr.*; LPS-2, *abr.*; OBRV
Fame, *fr.* IV. FiP
Farewell, The: "Oh, thou! in Hellas deem'd of heavenly birth," *fr.* I. EPP
"Ferrara! in thy wide and grass-grown streets," *fr.* IV. PtP
Filial Love, *fr.* IV. LPS-1
He Who Ascends to Mountain-Tops, *fr.* III. OQP; QP-2
(Isolation of Genius, The.) WBLP
"I have not loved the world, nor the world me," *fr.* III. OBRV
(Defiance.) RO
(Poet and the World, The.) SeCePo
"I stood in Venice, on the Bridge of Sighs," *fr.* IV. BPN, *abr.*; EnRP; OAEP, *abr.*; OBRV, *abr.*; ViBoPo, 3 *sts.*
(Refuge in Venice.) ERP
(Venice.) BEL; EV-4; HBV; TCEP, *abr.*
(Venice and Rome, *abr.*) MCCG
(Venice and Sunset, *abr.*) EPN
"Is thy face like thy mother's, my fair child!" III. BEL; BoLiVe, *abr.*; BPN; ChER, *sts.* 1-15; CoBE, *abr.*; EM-2; EmBrPo; EnL; EnLi-2; EnLit, *abr.*; EnRP; ERP; GEPC; OAEP; REAL; TOP
(Canto Third.) EPN
Lake Leman ("Clear, placid Leman!"), *fr.* III. MaPo
(Calm and Storm on Lake Leman, *abr.*) LPS-2
(Night and Storm in the Alps, *abr.*) MCCG
(Night on Lake Leman.) TCEP
Lake Leman ("Lake Leman woos me"), *fr.* III. PoEL-4
(Man and Nature.) EPP
Man-o'-War, The, *fr.* II. SG
"Moon is up, and yet it is not night, The," *fr.* IV. AnFE
Napoleon, *fr.* III. LPS-3; OBRV
Night ("It is the hush of night"), *fr.* III. LoBV
(It Is the Hush of Night.) LiTB
Night (" 'Tis night, when meditation bids us feel"), *fr.* II. LPS-2; SN
"Oh Love! no habitant of earth thou art," *fr.* IV. ViBoPo
(Bitter Meditation.) ERP
(Love.) EPP
(Love Unseen.) RO
Ocean, The, *fr.* IV. BCEP; BLV; CBE; CoEV; EPN; ERP; EV-4; MaPo; MaRV, 9 *ll.*; MCCG; MW, 9 *ll.*; NLK; PIAE; PoEL-4; ShBV-3; TCEP; TrGrPo; UnPo (1st ed.)
(Address to the Ocean.) TreFS
(And I Have Loved Thee, Ocean!) WHA
(Apostrophe to the Ocean.) EtS; GDAH; OHFP; WBLP
(Communion with Nature, 9 *ll.*) GrCo-1
(Deep and Dark Blue Ocean.) ChTr
(Man and Nature: "Oh, that the desert.") EPP
(Nature.) BEL
(Roll On, Thou Deep and Dark Blue Ocean.) AtBAP; BoLiVe; FaPON; FiP
(Sea, The.) FaBoBe; HBV; LiTB; LiTG; LPS-2; PYM; SG
(Solitude, *shorter sel.*) SN
("There is a pleasure in the pathless woods.") InP; OBRV; PreP; ViBoPo
(There Is Pleasure in the Pathless Woods, 9 *ll.*) TreF
(To the Ocean.) GN; LEAP; WGRP
(Where None Intrudes.) PC
Pantheon, The, *fr.* IV. LPS-2
Poet's Impulse, The, *fr.* III. LPS-3
Rome, *fr.* IV. BEL; EPP, *abr.*; MaPo; ShBV-3; TCEP, *abr.*
("Oh Rome! my country! City of the soul!") InP
(On Rome.) ERP
(Rome and Freedom.) EPN
(Ruins of Rome, The, *abr.*) CBOV
Ruins of Athens, The, *fr.* II. CBOV
Sky, Mountains, River! *fr.* III, *abr.* WHA
"Then farewell, Horace; whom I hated so," *fr.* IV. PtP
"There is a tomb in Arqua; rear'd in air," *fr.* IV. PtP
To England, *fr.* IV. WHA
To Ianthe, *Dedication.* FaBoEn
Voltaire and Gibbon, *fr.* III. CoEV; OBRV
Wandering Outlaw, The, *fr.* III. FiP
Waterloo ("There was a sound of revelry by night"), *fr.* III. BHV, *abr.*; BLV, *abr.*; EPP; EV-4; FiP; LPS-2, *abr.*; MCCG; OBRV; PIR; TCEP; TrGrPo; TVSH, *abr.*; WaaP; WHA
(Battle of Waterloo, The.) FaFP; HiLiEn; TreF
(Eve of the Battle of Waterloo, The.) OTPC
(Eve of Waterloo, The.) BBV, *abr.*; BCEP, *abr.*; BeLS, *abr.*; CBPC; FaBoBe; FaBoCh; FaBoEn; HBV; OnSP; OtMeF; PECK, *abr.*; PTA-2, *abr.*; PYM, *abr.*; ShBV-3
(Night before the Battle of Waterloo, The, *abr.*) WBLP
(Night before Waterloo.) BoHiPo; GN, *abr.*
("There was a sound of revelry by night.") AnFE; ViBoPo
Childe [*or* Child] Maurice. *Unknown.* BaBo; BLV, *abr.*; ESPB (A, B, *and* D *vers.*); OBB; TrGrPo, *abr.*; ViBoFo
(Gil Morice, *diff. vers.*) EBSV
"Childe Maurice hunted the Silver Wood," *sel.* HoPM
"Childe Roland to the Dark Tower Came." Robert Browning. AnFE; ATP; BEL; BMEP; BPN; EM-2; EmBrPo; EnL; EPP; GEPC; OAEP; OtMeF; Po; PoVP; SeCeV; TCEP; TOP; TwP; VA; ViPo; ViPP; VLEP
(Childe Roland.) BHV
"My first thought was, he lied in every word," *sel.* PoD
Childe Waters. *Unknown. See* Child Waters.
Childher, The. Denis A. McCarthy. CV
Childhood. Jens Baggesen, *tr. fr. Danish by* Longfellow. AWP; JAWP; WBP
Childhood. Carlos Drummond de Andrade, *tr. fr. Portuguese by* Dudley Poore. AnCL
Childhood. John Erskine. MaRV
Childhood. Louis Ginsberg. RIS
Childhood. Charles Lamb. LPS-1
Childhood. Donagh MacDonagh. NeIP
Childhood. Sir Thomas More. TuPP
Childhood. Edwin Muir. SeCePo
Childhood. Boris Pasternak, *tr. fr. Russian by* Jack Lindsay. *Fr.* 1905. RuPo
Childhood. Rainer Maria Rilke, *ad. fr. German by* Randall Jarrell. AnGP
Childhood, A. Stephen Spender. NeBP
Childhood. John Banister Tabb. HBV
Childhood. Thomas Traherne. TrGrPo
Childhood. Georg Trakl, *tr. fr. German by* Christopher Middleton. AnGP
Childhood. Henry Vaughan. EPS; OxBoCh; SeEP
"I cannot reach it," *sel.* EV-2
Childhood ("Fair seed-time"). Wordsworth. *See* Fair Seed-Time Had My Soul.
Childhood ("When he had left the mountains and received"). Wordsworth. *Fr.* The Prelude, I. CoBE
Childhood alone is glad. With it time flees. The Ages of Man. Charles Heavysege. BoCaPo
Childhood and Age. Diana Witherby. PoN
Childhood and School-Time. Wordsworth. *See* Fair Seed-Time Had My Soul.
Childhood Church, The. Pat Wilson. AnNZ
Childhood Fled. Charles Lamb. EnRP
Childhood of Achilles, The. Pindar, *tr. fr. Greek by* C. J. Billson. *Fr.* Nemean Odes. OxBG
Childhood of James V, The. Sir David Lindsay. *Fr.* The Complaynt of Schir David Lindesay. AtBAP
Childhood of Zeus, The. Moero, *tr. fr. Greek by* T. F. Higham. OxBG
Childhood Reds. Don Blanding. DDA
Childhood's Immunity from Inward Sorrows. Sophocles, *tr. fr. Greek by* Lewis Campbell. *Fr.* Trachiniae. GrR
Childish Game, A. Reinmar von Hagenau, *tr. fr. German.* AWP; JAWP; WBP
Childless. Giollabhrighde Mac Conmidhe, *tr. fr. Irish by* Frank O'Connor. KiLC
Childless. L. A. G. Strong. POTE
Childless Father, The. Wordsworth. CH
(Timothy.) CG
Childless Mother, The. Francis Turner Palgrave. MotAn
Childless Mother's Lullaby, The. Ella Higginson. BOL
Childlike Heart. Ellen Weston Catlin. PGD
Children, The. Charles Monroe Dickinson, *wr. at. to* Charles Dickens. AA; BAP; HBV; LPS-1; PTA-1; PTA-2

Children, The. Clifford Dyment. ChMP
Children. Euripides, *tr. fr. Greek by* T. F. Higham. OxBG; WoL
Children. Walter Savage Landor. DD; MOAH
Children. Longfellow. GTBS; IAP; PTA-2; TCAP
Children. Po Chü-i, *tr. fr. Chinese by* Arthur Waley. TrCh
Children, The. William Soutar. POTE
Children. Swinburne. BMEP; BPN; GrCo-1; POTT; PoVP
(Of Such Is the Kingdom of Heaven.) VLEP
(Upon a Child.) TCEP
Children, The. William Carlos Williams. NePoAm-2
Children and Dogs Are Subject. Elinor Wylie. ChMo
Children and pets, please note. In a Closed Universe. James Hayford. NePoAm-2
Children are at the door. At the Door. Lillie Fuller Merriam. PoToHe
Children are dumb to say how hot the day is. The Cool Web. Robert Graves. AWP; ChMP; GTBS-D
Children are what the mothers are. Children. Walter Savage Landor. DD; MOAH
Children (as such forgive them) have I known. Religious Isolation. Matthew Arnold. EmBrPo; EPN
Children Band, The. Sir Aubrey De Vere. *See* "Children's Crusade," The.
Children, behold the Chimpanzee. The Chimpanzee. Oliver Herford. CenHV; FiBHP; InP; LBN; NA
Children born of fairy stock. I'd Love to Be a Fairy's Child. Robert Graves. BoTP; FaPON; HBVY; TSW; TSWC
Children, Children, Don't Forget. Dora Owen. MPB
Children conceived when two nightgowns. The Submarine Bed. John Peale Bishop. LiTA
Children dear, was it yesterday. Matthew Arnold. *Fr.* The Forsaken Merman. BoTP
Children, do you ever. My Other Me. Grace Denio Litchfield. AA; HBV
Children dreamed the whole night through, The. Christmas Eve. Marguerite Merington. SDH
Children go. Follow Me! Eliza Lee Follen. PPL
Children, if you dare to think. Warning to Children. Robert Graves. FaBoCh; FaFP; GTBS-W; LoGBV; SiTL
Children in the Wood, The. *Unknown. See* Babes in the Wood. The ("Now ponder well").
Children indeed are we—children that wait. We Are Children. Robert Buchanan. VA
Children kept coming one by one, The. The Children We Keep. E. V. Wilson. PTA-2
Children Look at the Parents, The. A. S. J. Tessimond. ChMP
Children March, The. Elizabeth Riddell. MoAuPo
Children model the dust. In a City Square. Eleanor Glenn Wallis. NePoAm-2
Children now awake to birds. Lines for the Margin of an Old Gospel. Sheila Wingfield. ChMP; PoN
Children of Earth. Josephine Johnson. MuM
Children of Francis, 1953. Sister Mary Francis. SaFP
Children of Greenock, The. W. S. Graham. FaBoTw
Children of Heracles [*or* Heraclidae], *sels.* Euripides, *tr. fr. Greek.*
Fortune's Wheel, *tr. by* M. Wodhull. GrR
Macaria and Iolaus. GrR, *tr. by* Arthur S. Way; OxBG, *tr. by* George Allen
Not Peace at any Price, *tr. by* M. Wodhull. GrR
Children of Israel prayed for bread, The. Old Sam's Wife. *Unknown.* ChTr
Children of Light. Robert Lowell. FiMAP; MoAB; OxBA
Children of Lir, The. Katharine Tynan. GTIV
Children of Love. Harold Monro. CMP; MBP; MM; MoBrPo; TwCV
Children of Martha. Gilean Douglas. TwCaPo
Children of my happier prime. Immolated. Herman Melville. APW; ViBoPo
Children of the cold sun and the broken horizon. The City. Ben Maddow. LiTM (1946 ed.); WaP
Children of the Czar, The. The Ballad of the Children of the Czar. Delmore Schwartz. MiAP; OnHM
Children of the dead are going to play, The. Rhenish Autumn. Guillaume Apollinaire. AnFP
Children of the Foam, The. Wilfred Campbell. CPG
Children of the Heavenly King. John Cennick. WGRP
Children of the Light. St. John, XII: 23-36, Bible, *N.T.* WoL
Children of the Night, The. E. A. Robinson. AmPP (4th ed.); OxBA; NePA; QS
L'Envoi, *sel.* GrCo-2; MeRV; TwP
Children of the Poor, The. Victor Hugo, *tr. fr. French by* Swinburne. LiA; LiTW; TrFP, *tr. by* Alan Conder
Children of the Sun. Fenton Johnson. BANP
Children of the Wind. Carl Sandburg. *Fr.* The People, Yes, Sec. 13. StVeCh
Children of the World. Spain, Take from Me this Cup. César Vallejo. AnCL
Children of the world are on the march, The. The Children March. Elizabeth Riddell. MoAuPo
Children of Tomorrow. Zona Gale OQP; QP-2
Children of yesterday, heirs of tomorrow. Song of Hope [*or* Room for Him! Room!]. Mary Artemisia Lathbury. BLPA; ChIP; MaRV
Children picking up our bones. A Postcard from the Volcano. Wallace Stevens. AmPP; LiTA
Children romp within the graveyard's pale, The. Four Epigrams. Sir William Watson. MBP; MoBrPo (1942 ed.)
Children, the house is empty. The Little House. Sir Gilbert Parker. CPG
Children, the Sandbar, That Summer. Muriel Rukeyser. FiMAP
Children today—tomorrow—men! Tomorrow's Men. Georgia Douglas Johnson. GoSl
Children vowed to suicide. The Massacre of the Innocents. André Salmon. MiFP
Children We Keep, The. Mrs. E. V. Wilson. PTA-2
Children were frightened by crescendoes, The. A Fete. Larry Eigner. NeAP
Children were shouting together, The. Frolic. "Æ." BoTP; FaPON; GTML; GTSL; MBP; MoBrPo; OTPC (1946 ed.); TwCV
Children, who extend their smile of crystal. The Bombed Happiness. Stephen Spender. ChMo
Children, ye have not lived, to you it seems. Life. Sarojini Naidu. BPP
Children, you are very little. Good and Bad Children. Robert Louis Stevenson FaBoCh; FaFP; HBV; HBVY; LoGBV; OTPC (1923 ed.); PoVP; TreF; VLEP
Children's Auction, The. Charles Mackay. BMEP
Children's Bells, The. Eleanor Farjeon. BoTP; CH
Children's cat upon the window-sill, The. The Housewife; Winter Afternoon. Karle Wilson Baker. LS
"Children's Crusade," The. Sir Aubrey De Vere. ES
(Children Band, The.) OBEV
Children's Elegy. Muriel Rukeyser. *Fr.* Eighth Elegy. FiMAP
Children's Festival. Tien Ch'ien, *tr. fr. Chinese.* WhP
Children's Ghosts, The. Winifred M. Letts. BMEP; HBMV
Children's Hour, The. Longfellow. AA; AmP; AnNE; CoBA; FaBoBe; FaFP; FAOV; FaPON; GoTP; HBV; HBVY; IAP; LaNeLa; LPS-1; MPB; NeHB; OHFP; OnHT; OTPC; PCH; PIR; PoEL-5; PTA-1; PYM; TCAP; TreF; TSW; TSWC; WBLP
Children's Playground, The. Oscar Williams. SiTL
Children's Song. Ford Madox Ford. HBV
Children's Song, The. Kipling. *See* Land of our Birth.
Children's Song ("The starry light and the lady bright"). *Unknown.* ABS
Children's Song, The ("The swallow has come again"). *Unknown. See* Swallow Song.
Children's Song of the Nativity. Frances Chesterton. *See* How Far Is It To Bethlehem?
Children's voices in the orchard. New Hampshire. T. S. Eliot. Landscapes, I. FaBoCh; KN; LoBV; LoGBV; ThWaDe
Child's a plaything for an hour, A. Parental Recollections [*or* A Child *or* In Memoriam]. Mary Lamb. EV-4; FAOV; GTSL; OBEV; OBRV
Child's Appeal, The. Mamie Gene Cole. MaRV; OQP; QP-2
Child's castle crumbles, The; hot air shimmers. M. K. Joseph. *Fr.* Mercury Bay Eclogue. AnNZ
Child's Christmas Carol, A. Christine Chaundler. BoTP
Child's Christmas Song, A. T. A. Daly. OBAV
Child's cough scratches at my heart—my head, The. New York—December, 1931. Babette Deutsch. ImOP
Child's Day Begins, A. Walter de la Mare. StVeCh
(Child's Day, A, Part II.) TiPo (1952 ed.)
("Softly, drowsily.") SUS
Child's Desire, The. Jemima Luke. *See* I think When I Read That Sweet Story of Old.
Child's Dream, The. *Unknown, tr. fr. Russian by* W. R. S. Ralston. OnPM
Child's Evening Hymn. Sabine Baring-Gould. *See* Now the Day Is Over.
Child's Evening Hymn, A. George Herbert Clarke. BOL
Child's Evening Hymn, A. Francis Turner Palgrave. BOL
Child's Evening Prayer, A. Samuel Taylor Coleridge. *See* Pains of Sleep, The.
Child's Evening Prayer, A. Mary Lundie Duncan. MaRV; OTPC
(Evening Prayer, An.) PraP
(Jesus, Tender Shepherd [Hear Me].) BLRP; PCH
(Tender Shepherd, The.) BOL
Child's Evensong, A. Richard Le Gallienne. BOL
Child's Evensong. Ethel Robb. GFA
Child's eyes to see. The Vision Clear. J. M. Westrup. BoTP
Child's Fancy, A. "A." PRWS
Child's First Grief, The. Felicia D. Hemans. BLPA; NeHB
(First Grief, The.) CH
Child's Future, A. Swinburne. BPN; EmBrPo; EnLi-2
Child's Game, A Karle Wilson Baker. PCD
Child's Grace, A. Burns. BrR; FaPON; MeMeAg; MoShBr; MPB; PCH; PRWS; StVeCh
(Two Graces.) FaBoCh; LoGBV

Child's Grace, A ("Here a little child I stand"). Robert Herrick. *See* Grace for a Child.
Child's hair falls in hay-pale ribbons, The. The Midsummer Meadow. E. J. Scovell. PoN
Child's Heritage, The. John G. Neihardt. FAOV; HBV; NV
Child's Hymn, A. Matilda Betham-Edwards. *See* Child's Prayer, A.
Child's Hymn, The. Mary Howitt. GoTP
Child's Hymn of Praise, A. Jane Taylor. OTPC (1923 ed.)
Child's Kiss, A. Francis Thompson. GTML
Child's Laughter, A. Swinburne. BPN; EmBrPo; EPN; HBV; PoVP; PRWS; TCEP; TOP; VLEP
Child's Morning Prayer, A. Mary Lundie Duncan. OTPC
Child's Morning Prayer, A. Jeannie Kirby. BoTP
Child's Natural History, *sels.* Oliver Herford.
Geese. HBV; LEAP
(Some Geese.) FiBHP; NA
Mon-Goos, The. AA; HBV; LEAP
Seal, A. HBV; HBVY
Yak, The. HBV; HBVY
Child's Offering, A. *Unknown.* MaRV
Child's Pet, A. W. H. Davies. CH; POT
Child's Play of Men, The. Michael Earls. FAOV
Child's Poem. Kay Smith. TwCaPo
Child's Portrait, A. William James Dawson. VA
Child's Prayer, A. Matilda Betham-Edwards. BOL; MeMeAg; OTPC; PRWS
(Child's Hymn, A.) TVC; TVSH
Child's Prayer, A. William Canton. BoTP
Child's Prayer, The. Comte Robert de Montesquiou-Fezensac, *tr. fr. French by* Joseph T. Shipley. CAW
Child's Prayer, A. Siegfried Sassoon. BoTP
Child's Prayer, A. William L. Stidger. PraP
Child's Prayer, A. John Banister Tabb. DDA; FaPON; OBAV; TreF; YaD
(Little Child's Prayer, A.) GaP
Child's Prayer, A. Francis Thompson. DD; HBVY; OHIP; PoRL; SDH; TreFS; TSW; TSWC
(Ex Ore Infantium.) Francis Thompson. BoTP; ChrBoLe; GTSE; HBV; OBVV; PoRh; SUS
(Little Jesus.) EmBrPo; MaRV; POTT; PoVP; StJW; VOD
Child's Prayer, A ("Father, lead me, day by day"). *Unknown.* BLRP
Child's Prayer, A ("Lord, teach a little child to pray"). *Unknown.* BOL
Child's Prayer, A. *At. to* R. J. Weston. *See* Prayer: "Father, we thank thee for the night."
Child's Prayer at Evening, A. Sir Charles G. D. Roberts. BOL
(Domine, Cui Sunt Pleiades Curae.) VA
Child's Present to His Child-Saviour, A. Robert Herrick. *See* To His Saviour, a Child; a Present by a Child.
Child's Purchase, The. Coventry Patmore. The Unknown Eros, II, xvii. CoBE; ISi; NBE
Child's Quest, The. Frances Shaw. NP
Child's Question, The. Emily Dickinson. *See* Will there really be a morning?
Child's Question, A. Emma Huntington Nason. AA
Child's Song, A. William Allingham. *See* Robin Redbreast.
Child's Song. Gerald Gould. BoTP
Child's Song. Kate Greenaway. OTPC (1946 ed.); PCH
(Naughty Blackbird, The.) HBVY
Child's Song. Thomas Moore. AlDL; ERP; GoBC; GTIV; OxBI; SUS; ViBoPo
Child's Song. Swinburne. BPN; GTML; GTSL; OBVV; PoVP
Child's Song in Spring. Edith Nesbit. BoTP; DD; HBV; HH; MeMeAg; MW; OHIP; OTPC; RAR
(Bird's Song in Spring.) PRWS
Child's Song of Christmas, A. Marjorie Pickthall. BOL; BoTP; HBV; HBVY; YeAr
Child's Song Overheard, A. Grace Hazard Conkling. PC
Child's Song to Her Mother, A. Winifred Welles. HBMV
Child's Star, The. John Banister Tabb. PPL
Child's Talk in April. Christina Rossetti. GN; OTPC (1923 ed.)
Child's Thought, A. Robert Louis Stevenson. BoTP
Child's Thought of God A. Elizabeth Barrett Browning. FaPON; MeMeAg; MPB; OTPC; PCH; PRWS; PTA-1
Child's Thought of Harvest, A. "Susan Coolidge." BoChLi (1939 ed.); DD; OHIP; OTPC (1946 ed.)
Child's Winter Evening, A. Gwen John. CH
Child's Wish, A. Abram J. Ryan. AA; CAW; JKCP
Child's Wish Granted, The. George Parsons Lathrop. AA; HBV; JKCP
Child's World, The. William Brighty Rands. *See* Wonderful World, The.
Chill, A. Christina Rossetti. BoTP; PRWS
Chill and harsh the year draws to its close. T'ao Ch'ien, *tr. fr. Chinese by* Arthur Waley. Twelve Poems, 3. TrCh
Chill, chill! Winter. *Unknown.* KiLC
Chill New England sunshine, The. The Death of Goody Nurse. Rose Terry Cooke. PAH
Chill November day was done, The. A Little Goose. Eliza Sproat Turner. BOHV
Chill of the Eve. James Stephens. ChMo; CMP; OnYI
Chill the winter, cold the wind. Solace in Winter. *Unknown. Fr.* Silva Gadelica. TIP
Chilled into a serenity. To an Icicle. Blanche Taylor Dickinson. CDC
Chilled with salt dew, tossed on dark waters deep. A Mermaiden. Thomas Hennell. FaBoTw
Chillingham. Mary Elizabeth Coleridge. BoTP; PoeT
Chillon. Byron. *See* Sonnet on Chillon.
Chilly./ Isn't it chilly! Conversation on an Autumn Night. Shimpei Kusano. PoLJ
Chilly Dovebber with his boadigg blast. Belagcholly Days. *Unknown.* BOHV; LPS-3; StaSt
Chilly Water, *with music. Unknown.* BoAN-2
Chilly Winds, *with music. Unknown.* OuSiCo; TrAS
Chilterns, The. Robert Brooke. MBP; MoBrPo; POTT
Chilterns, The. John Davidson. VLEP
Chime of a bell of gold, The. Songs' End. John Payne. VA
Chimes. Longfellow. OBAV
Chimes. Alice Meynell. AnFE; BLV; BoTP; CH; MBP; MoBrPo; NP; PoeT; POTT; TSW; TSWC; WHA
Chiming a dream by the way. To My Mother. W. E. Henley. PoVP
Chimney, breathing a little smoke, A. February. James Schuyler. NeAP
Chimney Swallows Horatio Nelson Powers. HBV; OTPC (1923 ed.)
Chimney Sweeper, The ("A little black thing among the snow"). Blake. *Fr.* Songs of Experience. AtBAP; BoW; CBOV; EiPP; EnL; EnLi-2 (1949 ed.); EnLit; EV-3
Chimney Sweeper, The ("When my mother died I was very young"). Blake. *Fr.* Songs of Innocence. AtBAP; BCEP; BoW; CEP; CH; EiPP; EnRP; KN
Chimney-Sweeps of Cheltenham, The. Alfred Noyes. VOD
Chimney-Tops. *Unknown.* BoTP
Chimneys, rank on rank, The. Evening. Richard Aldington. MBP; MoBrPo; SeCePo
Chimneys with widebrimmed hats. Ill Humour. Jorge Carrera Andrade. AnCL
Chimpanzee, The. Oliver Herford. FiBHP; InP; LBN; NA
("Children, behold the Chimpanzee.") CenHV
Chimpanzee, The/ Is a most embarrassing animal to see. Muriel Sly. FiBHP
Ch'in Chia's Farewell. Ch'in Chia, *tr. fr. Chinese by* Arthur Waley. ChLP
(Ch'in Chia.) TrCh
(To His Wife.) LiTW
Ch'in Chia's Wife's Reply. *Unknown, tr. fr. Chinese by* Arthur Waley. ChLP; TrCh
Chin in, I doubt the praying mantis prays. The Chance. John Holmes. NePoAm-2
Chinatown Chant. Tom MacInnes. CaP; OCL
Chinese Banyan, The. William Meredith. NePoEA
Chinese Caprice. Théophile Gautier, *tr. fr. French by* Alan Conder. TrFP
Chinese Lullaby. Dorothy Henderson. GaP; GFA; OTPC (1946 ed.)
Chinese Nightingale, The. Vachel Lindsay. AmPP (3d ed.); ChMo; CMP; HBMV; IAP; LiTM (rev. ed.); MAP; MAPA; MoAmPo; NePA; NP; OnSP; SBMV; TCPD
Chinese Nursery Rhyme, A. *Unknown, tr. fr. Chinese by* I. T. Headland. RAR; TVC; TVSH
Chinese Poet, A. Frank Oliver Call. CPG
Chinese Pond. Edmund Blunden. PtOT
Chinese sandmen,/ Wise and creepy. Chinese Lullaby. Dorothy Henderson. GaP; GFA; OTPC (1946 ed.)
Chinoiseries. Amy Lowell. AnAmPo; LA; NP
Falling Snow.
Hoar-Frost.
Reflections.
Chinoiseries. Coley B. Taylor. PFE
Spring Morning
Spring Night.
Chip on His Shoulder, A. *Unknown.* BLPA; WBLP
Chipeta. Eugene Field. PoOW
Chipeta's Ride. John W. Taylor. PoOW
Chipmunk ("The chipmunk thinks I am a tree"). Leigh Hanes. StaSt
Chipmunk. Marie de L. Welch. PoeMoYo
Chippewa Legend, A. James Russell Lowell. BAV; MPB
Chiquita. Bret Harte. AA; IHA; MW; PFE; PFY
Chirruping grasshopper, drunken with dewdrops. A Cicada. Meleager. OxBG
Chirrupy Cricket, The. Martha Banning Thomas. GFA; PCH
Chisel in hand stood a sculptor boy. Life-Sculpture [*or* Sculptors of Life]. George Washington Doane. BAP; BPLA; MaRV; OHFP; OQP; QP-1; WBLP
Chiseled in stone, his image will not fade. Duel. Stepan Petrovich Shchipachev. TrRV
Chiseler, The. Francis X. Maynard. JKCP (1955 ed.)

Chisholm Trail, The. *Unknown. See* Old Chisholm Trail, The.
Chivalry. "Æ." ViBoPo
Chivalry. Euripides, *tr. fr. Greek by* C. M. Bowra. *Fr.* Suppliants. OxBG
Chivalry at a Discount. Edward Fitzgerald. HBV
Chloe. Burns. GN; HBV; OTPC
Chloe. George Granville. PIAE
(Cloe.) BeR; SeEP
Chloe. Charles Mordaunt, Earl of Peterborough. CEP; OBEC
Chloe. Pope. *Fr.* Moral Essays. AWP; JAWP; WBP
(Characters from the Satires: Chloe.) InPo
Chloe. Matthew Prior. LEAP
Chloe Divine. Thomas D'Urfey. HBV; LO; OBEV
Chloe found Amyntas lying. Rondelay [*or* Roundelay]. Dryden. ALV; ElSeCe; MaPo; SeCL; SeEP; ViBoPo
Chloe Is False. Sir Edmund Gosse. TCPD
Chloe, M.A. Mortimer Collins. BOHV
Chloe, thou fliest me like a fawn. To Chloe. Horace, *tr. by* Goldwin Smith. OuHeWo
Chloe, we must not always be in heaven. To Chloe. "Peter Pindar." LPS-1
Chloe, why wish you that your years. To Chloe, Who [for His Sake] Wished Herself Young Enough for Me. William Cartwright. CBOV; ElSeCe; EV-2; HBV; LiTB; LiTL; MePo; OBS; SeCL; SeEP; ViBoPo
Chloe, you shun me like a hind. To Chloe ("Vitas hinnuleo"). Horace, *tr. by* Austin Dobson. AWP; JAWP; WBP
Chloe's a Nymph in flowery groves. Chloe Divine. Thomas D'Urfey. HBV; LO; OBEV
Chloridia, *sel.* Ben Jonson.
Song of Zephyrus and the Spring. EPS (1942 ed.)
Chloris, *sels.* William Smith.
"Colin, my dear and most entire beloved," *dedication.* ReEn
(To the Most Excellent and Learned Shepherd, Colin Clout.) TuPP
"Feed, silly sheep, although your keeper pineth," III. TuPP
"My love, I cannot thy rare beauties place," XVIII. InvP
(Sonnet.) ElL
"When I more large thy praises forth shall show," XLIV. TuPP
"Whole showers of tears to Chloris I will pour," IV. TuPP
Chloris a Constant Comfort. Henry Hughes. SeCL
Chloris and Corydon ("Chloris, a maid of nimble feet"). Sennett Stephens. PR
Chloris and Hylas. Edmund Waller. SeCL
(Chloris and Hilas. Made to a Saraban.) SeCV-1
Chloris Farewell. *At. to* Edmund Waller. OBS
(Song: "Chloris farewell; I now must go.") CEP
Chloris, Forbear Awhile. Henry Bold. ElSeCe; LO; SeCL
Chloris [*or* Cloris], I cannot say your eyes. To Cloris. Sir Charles Sedley. CEP; LO
Chloris, I swear by all I ever swore. Lover's Play of Words. Martial. OnPM
Chloris in the Snow. William Strode. *See* On Chloris Walking in the Snow.
Chloris, it is not thy disdain. *See* Cloris, it is not thy disdaine.
Chloris made my heart to stop. A Winter Madrigal. Morris Bishop. InMe
Chloris. 'Tis Not in Your Power. Sir George Etherege. OBS
Chloris [*or* Cloris], when I to thee present. A Song. *Unknown.* OBS; SeCSL
Chloris, whil'st thou and I were free. A Sonnet. Charles Cotton. BrBE; ViBoPo
Chloris! yourself you so excel. To a Lady Singing a Song of His Own Composing. Edmund Waller. EV-2; ReEn; SeCL; SeEP
Chocolate-Cream. E. V. Lucas. *Fr.* Counsel to Those That Eat. BOHV
Choephoroe, *sels.* Aeschylus, *tr. fr. Greek.*
Clytemnestra's Dream, *tr. by* G. M. Cookson. GrR
Crime of Orestes, The, *tr. by* George Thomson. LiA
"Dies Irae," *tr. by* G. M. Cookson. GrR
Invocation of Agamemnon's Ghost, *tr. by* G. M. Cookson. OxBG
Kilissa, the Nurse, *tr. by* Lewis Campbell. GrR
"Mad Scene, The," *tr. by* G. M. Cookson. GrR
Orestes Goes Mad, *tr. by* G. M. Cookson. OxBG
Choice, The. Thomas Beedome. SeCL
Choice, The, *sel.* Benjamin Church.
"But to inform the mind and mend the heart." PoP
Choice. Emily Dickinson. *See* Of all the souls that stand create.
Choice. Ellen Coit Elliott. OQP; QP-2
Choice. John Farrar. BrR; SiSoSe
Choice, The. Dora Hagemeyer. MuM
Choice. Muna Lee. NV; TBM
Choice, The. John Masefield. Lollingdon Downs, VIII. MBP; MoAB; MoBrPo
(Kings Go By, The.) PoeMoYo
Choice. Angela Morgan. SBMV
Choice. James Larkin Pearson. NoCaPo
Choice, The. John Pomfret. CEP; EiPP; OBEC; PoE; PreP, *abr.;* TOP
Sels.
"If Heaven the grateful liberty would give." PoFS
"Would bounteous Heaven one more indulge, I'd choose." LO
Choice, The. Dante Gabriel Rossetti. The House of Life, LXXI-LXXIII. ATP; BEL; BPN; EmBrPo; EnL; EnLi-2; EPP; HBV; MyFE; OBVV; PIAE; POTT; PoVP; PreP; TOP; ViBoPo; ViPo; VLEP
"Eat thou and drink," LXXI. WHA
"Think thou and act," LXXIII. GTML; OBEV (new ed.); OHIP; WHA
Choice, The. Thomas Traherne. EPS
Choice, The. Katharine Tynan. CP; PoeT
Choice, A. Edward de Vere, Earl of Oxford. *See* Were I a King.
Choice. Anna Wickham. QS
Choice, The. George Wither. OBEV
Choice, The. W. B. Yeats. TwP
Choice in Spoons, A. Joel Barlow. *Fr.* The Hasty Pudding. OnAP
Choice of the Cross, The. Dorothy L. Sayers. *Fr.* The Devil to Pay. MaRV
Choice soul, in whom, as in a glass, we see. The Doom of Beauty. Michelangelo. AWP; JAWP; LiTW; WBP
Choir Boys, The. Heine, *tr. fr. German by* Ezra Pound. *Fr.* Die Heimkehr. LiTW
("Mutilated choir boys, The.") AWP
Choir Invisible, The. "George Eliot." *See* O May I Join the Choir Invisible.
Choir of bright beauties in spring did appear, A. The Lady's Song. Dryden. SeCeV
Choir of Day, The. Blake. *See* Nightingale and Flowers.
Choir Practice. Ernest Crosby. AA
Choir-Boys on Christmas Eve. Louise Townsend Nicholl. TSW
Choirs of Heaven, The. *Unknown. See* Immortal Choirs, The.
Choirs of Heaven are tokened in a harp-string, The. The Counsels of O'Riordan, the Rann Maker. T. D. O'Bolger. AnIV
Choliambs. Persius, *tr. fr. Latin by* Robert A. Brooks. LaP
"Cholly" Blues, The, *with music. Unknown.* ABF
Choo a choo a choo tooth. Cannibal Song. Charles Dickens. *Fr.* Holiday Romance. BoN
Chook, chook, chook, chook, chook. *Unknown.* OxNR
Choose. Carl Sandburg. NP
Choose Flawless Marble, Sculptor. Théodore de Banville, *tr. fr. French by* Alan Conder. TrFP
Choose judiciously thy friends; for to discard them is undesirable. Of Friendship. Charles Stuart Calverley. PA
Choose me your Valentine. To His Mistress. Robert Herrick. ViBoPo
Choose Something like a Star. Robert Frost. AnNE; MoAB; MoAmPo (1950 ed.); NeMA
Choose the darkest part o' the grove. Incantation in "Oedipus." Dryden. TriL
Choose You a Seat 'n' Set Down, *with music. Unknown.* OuSiCo
Choosing. Eleanor Farjeon. TiPo
Choosing a Kitten. *Unknown.* StVeCh
Choosing a Mast. Roy Campbell. CaAE; FaBoTw; GTBS-D; TwCV
Choosing a Name. Mary Lamb. HBV; LPS-1; OTPC (1923 ed.)
Choosing Friends. Theognis. *See* On Choosing Friends.
Choosing Shoes. ffrida Wolfe. BrR; GoBP; SUS; TiPo
Chop-Cherry. Robert Herrick. ALV; EnLoPo; MyFE; SeEP
Chopin Prelude. Eleanour Norton. HBMV
Chopo. *Unknown.* CSF
Choral: "We the proper ancients speak not out of turn," *abr.* Marcus Adeney. *Fr.* Mansong. BoCaPo (1943 ed.)
Choral Ode: "Wonders are many, and none is more wonderful than man." Sophocles, *pr. tr. fr. Greek by* Richard C. Jebb. *Fr.* Antigone. PreP
(Choral Ode: "Numberless are the world's wonders," *tr. by* Dudley Fitts *and* Robert Fitzgerald.) LiTW
(Man; Creation's Masterpiece, *tr. by* Gilbert Murray.) GrR
("Many the forms of life," *tr. by* E. H. Plumtre.) GrPo
(What a Piece of Work Is a Man, *tr. by* F. L. Lucas.) OxBG
Choral Poem: "Land beloved of horsemen, fair, The." Sophocles, *tr. fr. Greek by* Robert Fitzgerald. *Fr.* Oedipus at Colonus. LiTW
Choral Song of Illyrian Peasants. Samuel Taylor Coleridge. *See* Hunting Song.
Choral Symphony Conductor. Carol Coates. CaP
Chorale: "Our Father, whose creative Will." W. H. Auden. *Fr.* For the Time Being. QS
("Our Father, whose creative Will.") TrPWD
Chorale for Autumn. Marya Zaturenska. NP
Chord—very softly sounded—echoing on. Vibrations. Siegfried Sassoon. CaAE
Choric Song: "There is sweet music here that softer falls." Tennyson. *Fr* The Lotos-Eaters. GTML; GTSL; LiTG;

Choric Song (*continued*)
OuHeWo; PC. *st.* 1; ReTS, 4 *sts.*; WHA
(Choric Song of the Lotos-Eaters.) FaFP; GTBS-W; ViBoPo
(Song of the Lotos-Eaters.) BMEP; CBE; CBOV; CoEV; OBEV
Choricos. Richard Aldington. CBOV; HBMV; LBBV; NP
Choristers, The. Bliss Carman. OCL
Choros: "Give me your poppies." Hilda Doolittle ("H. D."). *Fr.* Morpheus. FaBoMo
Chorus: "Alas, with what tormenting fire." Robert Garnier, *tr. fr. French by* the Countess of Pembroke. *Fr.* Antonius. TuPP
(Of Death.) ElL
Chorus: "All, all of a piece throughout." Dryden. *See* All, All of a Piece Throughout.
Chorus: "All ye that handle harp and viol and pipe." Moses Hayyim Luzzatto of Padua, *tr. fr. Hebrew by* Nina Davis Salaman. *Fr.* Unto the Upright Praise. TrJP
Chorus: "And Pergamos." Euripides, *tr. fr. Greek by* Hilda Doolittle ("H. D."). *Fr.* Iphigenia in Aulis. AWP; LiTW
Chorus: "Ba-ba, black wool." William Brighty Rands. *Fr.* Topsy-turvy World. PIAE
("Ba-ba, black wool.") BoN
Chorus: "Before the beginning of years." Swinburne. *See* Before the Beginning of Years.
Chorus: "Behold what furies still." Samuel Daniel. *Fr.* Cleopatra. LoBV
Chorus: "Big Engines, The." Jack Kerouac. *Fr.* Mexico City Blues. NeAP
Chorus: "Brekeke-kesh, koash, koash." Aristophanes. *See* Frogs' Song
Chorus: "Climb at Court for me that will." Seneca, *tr. fr. Latin by* Andrew Marvell. *Fr.* Thyestes. OnPM
("Climb at Court for me that will.") LaP
(Quiet Life, The.) LiTW
(Senec. Traged. ex Thyeste Chor. 2) SeCV-1
Chorus: "Could I take me to some cavern for mine hiding." Euripides. *See* O for the Wings of a Dove.
Chorus: "Doth not our chiefest bliss then lie." Sidney Godolphin. LO
Chorus: "Eagle soars in the summit of Heaven, The." T. S. Eliot. *See* Eagle Soars in the Summit of Heaven, The.
Chorus: "Essence of Existence, The." Jack Kerouac. *Fr.* Mexico City Blues. NeAP
Chorus: "Fair Salamis, the billow's roar." Sophocles. *Fr.* Ajax. AWP; JAWP; WBP
Chorus: "For this one thing above all I would be praised as a man." Sophocles, *tr. fr. Greek by* W. B. Yeats. *Fr.* Oedipus Rex. LiTW
Chorus: "Give away her gowns." Edna St. Vincent Millay. *Fr.* Memorial to D. C. NP
Chorus: "Glenn Miller and I were heroes." Jack Kerouac. *Fr.* Mexico City Blues. NeAP
Chorus: "God whose goodness filleth every clime, The." Racine. *Fr.* Athalie. CAW; WGRP
Chorus: "Got up and dressed up." Jack Kerouac. *Fr.* Mexico City Blues. NeAP
Chorus: "Great fortune is an hungry thing." Aeschylus. *Fr.* Agamemnon. AWP; JAWP; WBP
Chorus: "Hail to the Headlong!" Thomas Love Peacock. *Fr.* Headlong Hall, *ch.* 13. OBRV
Chorus: "He is the Way." W. H. Auden. *Fr.* For the Time Being. AnFE
(He Is the Way.) MaRV
Chorus: "How dost thou wear and weary out thy days." Samuel Daniel. *Fr.* The Tragedie of Philotas. OBSC
Chorus: "If I drink water while this doth last." Thomas Love Peacock. *Fr.* Crotchet Castle, *ch.* 6. ViBoPo
Chorus: "In speculation." A. E. Housman. *Fr.* Fragment of a Greek Tragedy. BMEP
Chorus: "In wonder and time-mists." Lord De Tabley. *Fr.* Philoctetes. PoVP
Chorus: "It is hard for those who have never known persecution." T. S. Eliot. *Fr.* The Rock, Chorus VI. LiTM; QS
Chorus: Kings of Troy, The. Euripides, *tr. fr. Greek by* George Allen. *Fr.* Andromache. WaaP
(Kings of Troy, The.) OxBG
Chorus: "Let th' ayre complayne, and eke the parent great." Seneca, *tr. fr. Latin by* Thomas Newton. *Fr.* Hercules Furens. LaP
Chorus: "Life may change, but it may fly not." Shelley. *Fr.* Hellas. BPN; EmBrPo; EPN
Chorus: "Life of Life! thy lips enkindle." Shelley. *See* Life of Life.
Chorus: Love Song. Euripides, *tr. fr. Greek by* Shelley. *Fr.* Cyclops. AWP; JAWP; WBP
("One with eyes the fairest.") GrPo
Chorus: "Love's multitudinous boneyard." Jack Kerouac. *Fr.* Mexico City Blues. NeAP
Chorus: "Nobody knows the other side." Jack Kerouac. *Fr.* Mexico City Blues. NeAP
Chorus: "Oh, may my constant feet not fail." Sophocles. *See* God and Man.
Chorus: "O Slavery! thou frost of the world's prime." Shelley. *Fr.* Hellas. PoFr
Chorus: "O wearisome condition of humanity." Fulke Greville *See* Chorus Sacerdotum.
Chorus: "O Zeus our king and Night our friend." Aeschylus, *tr. fr. Greek by* Louis MacNeice. *Fr.* Agamemnon. LiTW
Chorus: "Old Man Mose." Jack Kerouac. *Fr.* Mexico City Blues. NeAP
Chorus: "Only awake to Universal Mind." Jack Kerouac. *Fr.* Mexico City Blues. NeAP
Chorus: "Praised be man, he is existing in milk." Jack Kerouac. *Fr.* Mexico City Blues. NeAP
Chorus: "Saints, I give myself up to thee." Jack Kerouac. *Fr.* Mexico City Blues. NeAP
Chorus: "Since you have come thus far." C. Day Lewis. *Fr.* Noah and the Waters. OAEP (2d ed.)
Chorus: "Spring all the Graces of the age." Ben Jonson. *Fr.* Neptune's Triumph. OBS; SeCL
Chorus: "Surely in no benignant mood." William Alexander Percy, *after the Greek.* SPP
Chorus: "Sweet are the ways of death to weary feet." Lord De Tabley. *Fr.* Medea. OBEV (new ed.); OBVV
Chorus: "Then thus we have beheld." Samuel Daniel. *Fr.* Cleopatra. OBSC
Chorus: "Though he believe it, no man is strong." W. H. Auden. *Fr.* Paid on Both Sides. CoEV
Chorus: "'Tis not enough for one that is a wife." Lady Elizabeth Carew. *Fr.* Mariam. LiTL
Chorus: "To throw away the key and walk away." W. H. Auden. *Fr.* Paid on Both Sides. MBP; MoBrPo; PIAE
(To Throw Away the Key.) ChMo
Chorus: "Upward and back to their fountains the sacred rivers are stealing." Euripides. *See* Dawn of Woman's Day, The.
Chorus: "Vain man, born to no happiness." Sidney Godolphin. LoBV
Chorus: "Void that's highly embraceable, The." Jack Kerouac. *Fr.* Mexico City Blues. NeAP
Chorus: "We have seen thee, O love." Swinburne. *See* We Have Seen Thee, O Love.
Chorus: "Welcome to our wond'ring sight." Richard Crashaw. *Fr.* In the Holy Nativity of Our Lord God. MeRV
(Hymn of the Nativity, A.) ChIP
Chorus: "What man is he that yearneth." Sophocles. *See* Old Age.
Chorus: "What sharpe assaultes of cruell Cupids flame." Seneca, *tr. fr. Latin by* John Studley. *Fr.* Medea. LaP
Chorus: "Wheel of the quivering meat, The." Jack Kerouac. *Fr.* Mexico City Blues. NeAP
Chorus: "When love has passed its limits." Euripides, *tr. fr. Greek by* Frederic Prokosch. *Fr.* Medea. LiTW
Chorus: "When the hounds of spring are on winter's traces." Swinburne. *See* When the Hounds of Spring.
Chorus: "Word of the Lord came unto me, The." T. S. Eliot *Fr.* The Rock. LiTB
Chorus: "World's great age begins anew, The." Shelley. *Fr.* Hellas. AtBAP; CoEV; ERP; ExPo; FaBoEn; HBV; InPo; LoBV; MyFE; OAEP; PoE; PoEL-4; RiBV; SeCeV; TCEP; TOP; TwCrTr; WoL
(Choruses from "Hellas.") EnRP
(Final Chorus.) BEL; BoLiVe; BPN; EmBrPo; EPP; OBRV; PoFS; SeCePo
(Hellas.) ChTr; OBEV; ShBV-4
(New World, A.) BLV; TrGrPo
("World's great age begins anew, The.") AWP; BCEP; EM-2; EnLit; EPN; FiP; GEPC; JAWP; LEAP; SoV; TreFS; WBP
Chorus: "Worlds on worlds are rolling ever." Shelley. *Fr.* Hellas. BPN; EmBrPo; EnRP; OAEP
(Worlds on Worlds Are Rolling Ever.) PoFS
"Power from the unknown God, A," *sel.* StJW
Chorus: "Yea, the coneys are scared by the thud of hoofs." Thomas Hardy. *See* Before Waterloo.
Chorus: "You have seen the house built, you have seen it adorned." T. S. Eliot. The Rock, Chorus X. QS
Chorus for Easter. David Morton. MaRV
Chorus for Refusal. Margaret Marks. MAP
Chorus for Survival, *sels.* Horace Gregory. ChMo (I, III, IX, XIV); TwAmPo (XIV)
Ask No Return, XIV. MoAmPo; TrGrPo
"Waking from sleep we heard the Great Lakes' tide," III. AtBAP
Chorus from a Play. W. H. Auden. *See* Doom Is Dark.
Chorus from a Tragedy. Leonard Bacon. ViBoPo
Chorus from "Atalanta in Calydon." Swinburne. *See* Before the Beginning of Years *and* When the Hounds of Spring.
Chorus from "Hellas." Shelley. *See* Chorus: "World's great age begins anew, The."
Chorus Hymeneal. Aristophanes, *tr. fr. Greek by* Benjamin Bickley Rogers. *Fr.* The Birds. GrR
Chorus of Batavian Women. Joost van den Vondel, *tr. fr. Dutch by* Sir John Bowring. WoL
Chorus of Birds. Aristophanes, *tr. fr. Greek by* Swinburne. *Fr.* The Birds. AWP; JAWP; WBP; WoL, *tr. by*

Benjamin Bickley Rogers
(Grand Chorus of Birds.) PoEL-5, *tr. by* Swinburne
(Hymn of the Birds, The.) GrR, *tr. by* Benjamin Bickley Rogers; OxBG, *tr. by* Swinburne
Chorus of Clouds. Aristophanes. *See* Song of the Clouds.
Chorus of Frogs, The. Ann Hawkshaw. OTPC
Chorus of Priests. Fulke Greville. *See* Chorus Sacerdotum.
Chorus of Satyrs, Driving Their Goats. Euripides, *tr. fr. Greek by* Shelley. *Fr.* The Cyclops. AWP; JAWP; WBP
("Where has he of race divine.") GrPo
Chorus of Spirits. George Darley. *Fr.* Sylvia; or, The May Queen. OnYI; VA
Chorus of Spirits: "From unremembered ages we." Shelley. *Fr.* Prometheus Unbound. LoBV
Chorus of the Clouds. Aristophanes. *See* Song of the Clouds.
Chorus of the Elements. Cardinal Newman. *See* Elements.
Chorus of the Furies ("Look, sisters, look!"). Aeschylus, *tr. fr Greek by* John Stuart Blackie. *Fr.* Eumenides. WoL
Chorus of the Furies, The ("Weave the weird dance"). Aeschylus, *tr. fr. Greek by* E. D. A. Morshead. *Fr.* Eumenides. LiA
(Furies' Prayer, The, *tr. by* G. M. Cookson.) OxBG
Chorus of the Winds. Per Daniel Amadeus Atterbom, *tr. fr. Swedish by* Charles W. Stork. AnSL
Chorus of Women. Aristophanes. *See* Male Inconsistency.
Chorus on the Death of Faustus. Christopher Marlowe. *Fr.* Dr. Faustus: Epilogue. LEAP
("Cut is the branch that might have grown full [*or* growne ful] straight.") PoD; ViBoPo
Chorus Primus: Wise Counsellors. Fulke Greville. *Fr.* Mustapha. OBS
Chorus Quintus: Tartarorum. Fulke Greville. *Fr.* Mustapha. OBS
Chorus Sacerdotum. Fulke Greville. *Fr.* Mustapha. ATP (1935 ed.); BrBE; CoEV; FaBoEn; InvP; MePo; NBE; OBS; PoEL-1; RiBV; SeCePo; SiCE; TuPP
(Chorus: "O wearisome condition of humanity!") ViBoPo
(Chorus of Priests.) EV-1
(O Wearisome Condition of Humanity.) EG; LiTB; SeCeV
Chorus Tertius: Of Time: Eternitie. Fulke Greville. *Fr.* Mustapha. OBS
Choruses from "Atalanta in Calydon." Swinburne. *See* Atalanta in Calydon.
Chosen of God. Stefan Zweig, *tr. fr. German by* Eden *and* Cedar Paul. *Fr.* Jeremiah. TrJP
Chosen People, The. W. N. Ewer. ALV; SiTL
(Epigram: "How odd/ Of God.") OtMeF
Choses du soir, *sel.* Victor Hugo, *pr. tr. fr. French. Fr.* L'Art d'être grand-père.
"Some coasting vessels can be seen on the ocean." LiA
Choucoune. Oswald Durand, *tr. fr. French by* Edna Worthley Underwood. PoNe
Chough, The. James Reaney. PeCV
Chough and crow to roost are gone, The. The Outlaw's Song [*or* Song of the Outlaws]. Joanna Baillie. *Fr.* Orra. EBSV; EV-3; OBEV; OBRV; OTPC; PoFr; TVSH
Chough, said a dictionary, The. The Chough. James Reaney. PeCV
Chragan Palace, The. Thomas Terzyan, *tr. fr. Armenian by* Alice Stone Blackwell. ArmLP
Chrismus on the Plantation. Paul Laurence Dunbar. IHA
Christ. Robert Jones Burdette. *Fr.* My Guide. BePJ
Christ, *sels.* Cynewulf, *tr. fr. Anglo-Saxon.*
Christ Tells of His Passion. PoLi
Heaven. PoLi
Last Judgment, The, *tr. by* Charles W. Kennedy. AnOE
(Human Race Comes to Be Judged, The, *diff. tr.*) PoLi
Maiden Ring-adorned, A, *tr. by* Mother Margaret Williams. ISi; PoLi, *shorter sel.*
"Then the Courage-hearted quakes," *abr., tr. by* Stopford Brooke. TCEP
Voyage of Life, The, *tr. by* Charles W. Kennedy. AnOE
("Our life is likest a long sea-voyage," *tr. by* J. Duncan Spaeth.) EnLi-1, *br. sel.*
Christ I. *sels.* *Unknown, tr. fr. Anglo-Saxon by* Charles W. Kennedy. AnOE
Advent Lyrics.
"Bless earth with Thine Advent, O Saviour Christ!" VIII.
"Hail, O most worthy in all the world!" IX.
"O holy Jerusalem, Vision of peace," III.
". . . to the King./ Thou art the wall-stone the workers rejected," I. AnOE
Christ ("Christ for sickness"). *Unknown.* BePJ
Christ, The. Edgar William Whan. ChIP
Christ,/ For the men we pray. The Sacrament of Work. John S. Hoyland. PraP
Christ,/ Grant us this boon. A Prayer for Brotherhood. John S. Hoyland. MaRV
Christ All-sufficient. Frederic W. H. Myers. *Fr.* Saint Paul. MaRV
("Christ, I am Christ's, and let the name suffice you.") ChIP
Christ and His Mother at the Cross. Jacopone da Todi, *tr. fr. Italian by* Thomas Walsh. CAW
Christ and his Mother, heavenly maid. Founder's Day [*or* Dedication]. Robert Bridges. MOAH; OBVV
Christ and Satan, *sels.* Cædmon (?), *tr. fr. Anglo-Saxon.*
Lamentations of the Fallen Angels, *tr. by* Charles W. Kennedy. AnOE
"O thou glory of the Lord! Guardian of Heaven's hosts." LiA
Christ and the Common Day. Marguerite Wilkinson. BePJ
Christ and the Little Ones. Julia Gill. BLPA
Christ and the Mourners. Katherine E. Conway. ChIP; OQP; QP-1
Christ and the Pagan. John Banister Tabb. CAW; JKCP; MeRV
Christ and the Winds. John Banister Tabb. StJW
Christ—and We. Annie Johnson Flint. *See* Jesus Christ—and We.
Christ and We. Robert Herrick. ChIP
(Christ's Incarnation.) StJW
Christ, as a light. James Clarence Mangan. *Fr.* St. Patrick's Hymn before Tara. TriL
Christ at the Door. *Unknown.* BePJ
Christ bears a thousand crosses now. Quatrain. Charles G. Blanden. ChIP; PGD
Christ before Pilate. George Herbert Clarke. StJW
Christ Brought Home. *Unknown.* PoLi
Christ, by dark clouds of worldliness concealed. Prayer before Meat. Una W. Harsen. ChIP; TrPWD
Christ, by Thine own darkened hour. Christ the Comrade. Padraic Colum. CAW; JKCP
Christ came to earth again, and made his plea. The Second Coming. Stanton A. Coblentz. ChIP
Christ Can Give Thee Heart. Christina Rossetti. ChIP
Christ Candle, The. Kate Louise Brown. OTPC (1946 ed.); VOD
(Christmas Candle, The.) PoRL
Christ-Child, The. G. K. Chesterton. *See* Christmas Carol, A: "Christ-Child lay on Mary's lap, The."
Christ-Child, The. St. Gregory of Narek, *tr. fr. Armenian by* Alice Stone Blackwell. ArmLP; CAW
Christ-Child, The. Agnes Lee. BPP
Christ-Child, The. Laura Spencer Portor. StJW
(Christ Child's Christmas, The.) PEDC
Christ Child. Henry Treece. MaRV
Christ Child at Christmas, The. John Drinkwater. QS
Christ-Child Day in Australia, A. Ethel Turner. BoAu
Christ-child lay in the ox's stall, The. Ox and Donkey's Carol. Sister Maris Stella. PoRL
Christ-child lay on Mary's lap, The. A Christmas Carol [*or* The Christ-Child]. G. K. Chesterton. BoTP; ChBR; ChrBoLe; FaFP; GaP; GoBC; HBV; HBVY; MaRV; OHIP; PoRL; StJW; SUS; TiPo (1952 ed.); VOD; WHL
Christ Child's Christmas, The. Laura Spencer Portor. *See* Christ-Child, The.
Christ Church Bells. *At. to* Henry Aldrich. SeCL
Christ claims our help in many a strange disguise. The Man of Sorrows. *Unknown.* ChIP; MaRV; OQP; PGD; QP-2
Christ-Cross Rhyme, A. Robert Stephen Hawker. ACP (1926 ed.); CAW; GoBC; StJW
Christ Crucified. Richard Crashaw. BLV; GoBC; OBEV; PoRL
Christ for a dream was given from the dead. A Christmas Night. John Drinkwater. StJW
Christ for sickness, Christ for health. Christ. *Unknown.* BePJ
Christ, forgive us! Except Ye Repent. J. Franklin Pineo. ChIP
Christ gave a yoke, a sword, a cross. Gifts. Chauncey R. Piety. PGD
Christ God who savest man, save most. Count Gismond. Robert Browning. BEL; BMEP; GEPC; PoVP; ViPP
Christ has no hands but our hands. Jesus Christ—and We [*or* Christ—and We]. Annie Johnson Flint. MaRV; OQP; QP-1
Christ Has Risen. "Susan Coolidge." ChIP
Christ hath a garden walled around. Isaac Watts. FaBoCh; LoGBV
Christ His Cross shall be my speed! A Christ-Cross Rhyme. Robert Stephen Hawker. ACP (1926 ed.); CAW; GoBC; StJW
Christ, I am Christ's and let the name suffice you. Christ All-sufficient. Frederic W. H. Myers. *Fr.* Saint Paul. ChIP; MaRV
Christ, I have walked around your erection. Reality! Reality! What Is It? Richard Eberhart. FiMAP
Christ in Flanders. Lucy Whitmell. PTA-1; QS
Christ in Introspect. Charlotte Brontë. MaRV
Christ in the Andes. Carl John Bostelmann. ChIP
Christ in the City. Frank Mason North. MaRV
(City, The.) WGRP

Christ in the City (*continued*)
(“Where cross the crowded ways of life.”) OlF
Christ in the Street. Jay G. Sigmund. ChIP
Christ in the Universe. Alice Meynell. ACP; CAW; EV-5; GoBC; HBMV; JKCP; MBP; MeRV; MoBrPo; StJW
Christ in Woolworth's. Teresa Hooley. ChIP; DDA; QS; StJW
Christ Inviting Sinners to His Grace, *sel.* Henry Alline.
“Amazing sight, the Saviour stands,” *fr.* Bk. II, Hymn XXXVII. CaP
Christ Is All. Horatius Bonar. BePJ
Christ Is Arisen. Goethe. *See* Easter Chorus.
Christ is born! Tell forth His fame! Tell Forth His Fame. *Unknown.* BePJ
“Christ is come!” the people said. The Second Coming of Christ. Harrington Green. CAG
Christ Is Coming. Heyman Wreford. BePJ
Christ Is Crucified Anew. John Richard Moreland. ChIP; MaRV; PGD
Christ Is Here. Robert Lowell. BePJ
Christ is Risen, *sels.* “Andrei Bely,” *tr. fr. Russian by* Babette Deutsch. TrRV
“And the news,” *st.* 22.
“I know,” *st.* 24.
“Russia,/ My country,” *st.* 23.
Christ Is Risen! Mrs. D. H. Dugan. BLRP
Christ Is Risen! Christoph Christian Sturm. BePJ
“Christ is risen, Christ is risen!” the glad voices glibly say. The Stone. Kenneth W. Porter. ChIP; PSO
Christ is the Fact of facts, the Bible's Theme. The Greatest Person in the Universe. Daniel L. Marsh. BLRP
Christ Is the Substance of the Levitical Priesthood. Isaac Watts. BeR
Christ Jesus was born in a stable. A Christmas Thought. Mrs. Frank A. Breck. BePJ
Christ keep the Hollow Land. Song. William Morris. *Fr.* The Hollow Land. AtBAP; ChTr; PoD; PoEL-5; ThWaDe
Christ keep us all, as He well can. Now Sing We, Sing We: Gloria Tibi, Domine. *Unknown.* AnEC
Christ Liveth in Me. Toyohiko Kagawa, *tr. fr. Japanese by* Lois J. Erickson. SoLD
Christ made a trance on Friday view. Good Friday. *Unknown.* ChTr
Christ maketh to man a fair present. Christ's Gift to Man. *Unknown.* ACP
Christ Militant, The. Thomas Curtis Clark. ChIP
Christ, My Beloved. William Baldwin. ElL; OxBoCh
(Spouse to the Beloved, The.) OBSC
Christ of Common Folks, The. George T. Liddell. BPP; OQP; QP-1
Christ of Everywhere. Henry van Dyke. MaRV
Christ of God, The. Russell E. Kauffman. BePJ
Christ of His gentleness. In the Wilderness. Robert Graves. CH; GTBS-D; MBP; MoAB; MoBrPo; SeCePo; ShBV-3
Christ of Judea, look thou in my heart! Richard Watson Gilder. *Fr.* Credo. TrPWD
Christ of the Andes, The. Florence Earle Coates. BPP; StJW
Christ of the Andes, The. Edwin Markham. AOAH; BoFr; PEDC; PoRL
“O Christ of Olivet, you hushed the wars,” *sel.* TrPWD
“Christ of the Andes,” Christ of Everywhere. Christ of Everywhere. Henry van Dyke. MaRV
Christ of the council chamber. The Ageless Christ. B. L. Byer. BePJ
Christ of the glowing heart and golden speech. The Final Armistice. Frank B. Cowgill. OQP; QP-2
Christ of the market, and the Christmas flare. A Prayer of Penitence. Robert Whitaker. PSO
Christ of the World's Highway, The. Dorothy Clarke Wilson. MaRV
Christ of Velázquez, The, *sels.* Miguel de Unamuno, *tr. fr. Spanish by* Eleanor L. Turnbull. TeCS
“ 'It is finished!' Thou didst cry like the roar,” *fr.* Pt. II.
“Of what art Thou thinking, oh my dead Christ?” *fr.* Pt. I.
Christ on Madison Street. Raymond Kresensky. ChIP
Christ on the Cross (“He that seeth on the rood”). *Unknown.* TMEV
Christ on the Cross (“They raised him on the rood”). *Unknown.* PSO
Christ Our All in All, *sel.* Christina Rossetti.
“Lord, I am here.—But, child, I look for thee.” MeRV; ViP
Christ Our Contemporary. William Charles Braithwaite. MaRV
Christ Our Example in Suffering. James Montgomery. *See* Go to Dark Gethsemane.
Christ placed all rest, and had no resting place. Wondrous Love. Countess of Pembroke. BePJ
Christ Quiets the Tempest. Caelius Sedulius, *tr. fr. Latin by* George Sigerson. *Fr.* Carmen Paschale. OnYI
Christ Speaks. Wade Oliver. MaRV
Christ Tells of His Passion. Cynewulf. *Fr.* Christ. PoLi
Christ the Answer. Richard Watson Gilder, *also at. to* George Macdonald. *See* Doubter, The.
Christ the Carpenter. Leslie L. Haskin. BePJ
Christ the Comrade. Padraic Colum. CAW; JKCP
Christ, the Conqueror, *abr.* Aaron Crossley Hobart Seymour, *wr. at. to* Henry Foster Burder. BePJ
Christ the Consoler. Henry W. Baker. BePJ
Christ, the Fleur-de-Lis. *Unknown.* MeRV
(Sing We All, for Time It Is.) AnEC
Christ, the Good Physician. Charles Wesley. BePJ
Christ the Lord is risen again. Resurrection Hymn. Michael Weiss. BePJ
Christ the Lord Is Risen To-Day. Charles Wesley. *See* Easter Hymn.
Christ the Lord is risen today. Victimae Paschali [Laudes]. Wipo, *tr fr. Latin.* CAW; WHL
“Christ the Lord is risen today,” sons of men and angels say. Easter Hymn [*or* Easter Day *or* For Easter-Day]. Charles Wesley. BePJ; CEP; DD; EOAH; HH; MaRV; OHIP; OlF
Christ the Man. W. H. Davies. ChMo; CMP; MaRV; WGRP
Christ the Mendicant. John Banister Tabb. MOAH
Christ, the Way. George Washington Doane. BePJ
(Way, the Truth, the Life, The.) MaRV
Christ, there is a swarm of bees outside. A Charm for Bees. *Unknown.* CAW
Christ to His Spouse. William Baldwin. ElL; OxBoCh
(Beloved to the Spouse, The.) OBSC
Christ to the Sufferer. *Unknown.* *Fr.* Andreas. PoLi
Christ to Thomas. Richard Crashaw. StJW
Christ took our nature on Him, not that He. Christ and We [*or* Christ's Incarnation]. Robert Herrick. ChIP; StJW
Christ Unconquered, *sel.* Arthur J. Little.
Invocation: “Mother of God, mother of man reborn,” *fr.* Bk. IX. ISi
Christ Walking on the Water. W. R. Rodgers. AnIL; MoAB; OxBI
Christ was born on Christmas day. Christmas Carol. *At. to* Thomas Helmore. OHIP
Christ was dead last eve they said. Good Friday Song. Robert P. Tristram Coffin. QS
Christ was of virgin birth. and, being slain. The Nobler Lesson. Don Marquis. OBAV
Christ was no prisoner of time. No Prisoner of Time. William H. Hudnut, Jr. ChIP
Christ was your lord and captain all your life. To His Father. Robinson Jeffers. PeBoSo
Christ washed the feet of Judas! The Feet of Judas. George Marion McClellan. BANP; PoNe
Christ, when a Child, a garden made. A Legend. Peter Ilich Tchaikovsky, *tr. fr. Russian by* Nathan Haskell Dole. ChIP; MaRV; OHIP; SDH
Christ when He died. Christ's Victory. Richard Crashaw. MaRV; StJW
Christ Whose Glory Fills the Skies. Charles Wesley. *See* Morning Hymn, A.
Christabel. Samuel Taylor Coleridge. BCEP; BEL; BPN; CoBE; EM-2; EmBrPo; EnL; EnLi-2; EnLit; EnRP; EPN; ERP; GoTL; LiA; OAEP; REAL; TOP; WHA
Sels.
“Alas! they had been friends in youth,” *fr.* Pt. II. CBE; LEAP; LO; OBRV
(Friendship, *abr.*) MCCG
(Quarrel of Friends, The.) LPS-1
Christabel, Pt. I. BrBE; CH, *ll.* 1–65; EPP, *ll.* 1–103; EV-4; FiP; NBE, *abr*; OBRV; ShBV-3; TCEP
(“ 'Tis the middle of night by the castle clock.”) SeCePo
Little Child, a Limber Elf, A, *fr.* Pt. II. LoBV; ViBoPo
“Lovely lady, Christabel, The,” *fr.* Pt. I. LO
Christendom. Thomas Traherne. PoEL-2
“Things native sweetly grew,” *sel.* FaBoEn
Christening Remembered, A. Vernon Watkins. FaBoMo
Christian, A. Thomas Russell Ybarra. *See* Christian Is a Man Who Feels, A.
Christian, be up before the end of day. Epistle. Robert Nathan. MaRV
Christian Child. Ferid ed-Din Attar, *tr. fr. Persian by* A. J. Arberry. PeP
Christian, Dost Thou See Them? St. Andrew of Crete, *tr. fr. Greek by* John Mason Neale. MaRV
Christian Ethics, *sels.* Thomas Traherne.
“All music, sauces, feasts, delights and pleasures.” UnS
(Measure.) BLV
Contentment Is a Sleepy Thing. OxBoCh
For Man to Act. OxBoCh
Mankind Is Sick. OxBoCh
“Were all the world a paradice of ease.” MeRV
Christian Freedom. George Matheson. *See* Christ's Bond-servant.
Christian, A! going, gone! The Christian Slave. Whittier. PreP
Christian Is a Man Who Feels, A. Thomas Russell Ybarra. WhC
(Christian, A.) SiTL
Christian Lady and the Moor, The. José Zorrilla, *tr. fr. Spanish by* James Kennedy. AnSpL-2

Christian Life, The. Samuel Longfellow. PraP; WGRP
Christian Militant, The. Robert Herrick. HoPM
Christian Paradox, The. Walter Chalmers Smith. MaRV
Christian Paradox. *Unknown.* MaRV
Christian Pilgrim's Hymn, The. William Williams. *See* Guide Me, O Thou Great Jehovah.
Christian, rise, and act thy creed. Laborare Est Orare. Francis Albert Rollo Russell. MaRV
Christian Slave, The. Whittier. PreP
Christian Soldier, The. G. A. Studdert-Kennedy. MaRV
Christian Year, The, *sel.* John Keble.
What Went Ye Out to See? ViP
Christianity and War. Ernest Crosby. PSO
Christians, Awake, Salute the Happy Morn. John Byrom. *See* Hymn for Christmas Day, A.
Christian's "Good-Night," The. Sarah Doudney. BLPA
Christian's New-Year Prayer, The, *sel.* Ella Wheeler Wilcox.
"If my vain soul needs blows and bitter losses." TrPWD
Christian's Poem. Jorge de Lima, *tr. fr. Portuguese by* Dudley Poore. AnCL
Christians Reply to the Phylosopher, The. Sir William Davenant. MeLP
Life and Death, *sel.* OBS
Christians were on the earth ere Christ was born. An Early Christian. Robert Barnabas Brough. OBVV
Christie's Portrait. Gerald Massey. VA
Christina. Louis MacNeice. OxBI
Christine. John Hay. AA
Christis Kirk of the Green. *Unknown.* EBSV
Christmas. Cecil Frances Alexander. *See* Once in Royal David's City.
Christmas. Margaret Avison. TwCaPo
Christmas. Bryant. ChIP; MaRV
(Holy Star, The.) BePJ
Christmas. Marchette Chute. BrR; ChBR; SiSoSe
Christmas. Rose Terry Cooke. COAH
Christmas. George Herbert. AnEC; CBE; EV-2; OxBoCh; SeCV-1; TriL
Christmas. Gertrude von Le Fort, *tr. fr. German by* Margaret Chanler. ISi
Christmas. Catherine Parmenter. DD; SDH
Christmas. Elizabeth Stanton Rice. StJW
Christmas. Sir Walter Scott. *See* Christmas in the Olden Time.
Christmas. Shakespeare. *See* Gracious Time, The.
Christmas. Betty Scott Stam. BePJ
Christmas. Nahum Tate. *See* While Shepherds Watched Their Flocks by Night.
Christmas. Tennyson. *See* In Memoriam A. H. H.: "Ring out, wild bells . . ."
Christmas. Henry Timrod. MOAP; SPP
Christmas. Nancy Byrd Turner. PraP
Christmas. Thomas Tusser. AnEC
Christmas ("An azure sky,/ All star bestrewn"). *Unknown.* BoTP
Christmas. Edward Hilton Young. SDH; StJW; TSW
(Boy Was Born at Bethlehem, A.) MaRV
Christmas after War. Katharine Lee Bates. SDH
Christmas Amnesty. Edith Lovejoy Pierce. PGD
Christmas and Common Birth. Anne Ridler. FaBoTw
Christmas and Ireland. Lionel Johnson. JKCP
Christmas Antiphon[e], A. Swinburne. CBE; ChIP, *2 sts.;* PGD, *2 sts.;* TrPWD, *abr.*
(Christmas Antiphony, A.) MeRV; TriL
(Peace-Giver, The.) CBPC; MaRV; OTPC (1946 ed.)
Christmas at Babbitt's. Henry Hallam Tweedy. MaRV
Christmas at Indian Point. Edgar Lee Masters. ChMo; CMP; NP
Christmas at Melrose. Leslie Pinckney Hill. BANP
Christmas at Sea. Robert Louis Stevenson. BBV (1951 ed.); CH; EtS; FaBoBe; HBV; MCCG; OBVV; OTPC (1946 ed.); PCN; PoVP; SG; ShBV-2; StaSt; StPo
Christmas Bells. George Cooper. HH; MeMeAg; PEDC
Christmas Bells. John Keble. COAH
Christmas Bells. Longfellow. BLRP; ChIP, *abr.;* COAH; DD; FaFP; FaPON; GoTP; HBV; HBVY; HH; MaRV; MPB; OQP; PEOR; PGD, *abr.;* PoRL; PSO; QP-1; SDH; WBLP
(I Heard the Bells on Christmas Day.) NeHB; OlF
Christmas Bells. Alice Mortenson. BePJ
Christmas Bells. Tennyson. *See* In Memoriam A. H. H.: "Time draws near the birth of Christ, The."
Christmas Bells. *Unknown.* COAH
Christmas bells are ringing sweetly. Christmas Bells. Alice Mortenson. BePJ
Christmas Birthday. Grace Ellen Glaubitz. SiSoSe
Christmas Blessing. Franklin D. Elmer, Jr. ChIP
Christmas Brownie. Rowena Bennett. ChBR
Christmas Calf, The. Judy Van der Veer. BPP
Christmas Candle, The. Kate Louise Brown. *See* Christ Candle, The.
Christmas Carmen, A. Whittier. COAH; SDH
Christmas Carol: "As Joseph was a-walking." *Unknown.* *See* As Joseph Was a-Walking.
Christmas Carol, A: "Before the paling of the stars." Christina Rossetti. EmBrPo
(Before the Paling of the Stars.) ChIP; DD; HBVY; MaRV; OTPC (1946 ed.); SDH; TVSH
(Christmas Daybreak.) GoTP
Christmas Carol, A: "Borys hede that we bryng here, The." *Unknown.* *See* In Die Nativitatis.
Christmas Carol, A: "Christ-child lay on Mary's lap, The." G. K. Chesterton. BoTP; ChBR; ChrBoLe; FaFP; GaP; GoBC; HBV; HBVY; MaRV; OHIP; PoRL; StJW; SUS; TiPo (1952 ed.); VOD
(Christ-Child, The, *abr.*) WHL
Christmas Carol: "Christ was born on Christmas day." *At. to* Thomas Helmore. OHIP
Christmas Carol: "Earth has grown old with its burden of care, The." Phillips Brooks. COAH; HH; MaRV; PEDC; PSO; SDH
Christmas Carol, A: "Everywhere, everywhere Christmas tonight." Phillips Brooks. OHIP; PCH, *st. 1;* SDH
(Christmas Everywhere.) FaFP; GoTP; MaRV; PTA-1
(Everywhere, Everywhere Christmas Tonight.) HH; OTPC; PoRL
Christmas Everywhere, *sel.* BLRP; NeHB; OHFP; QP-1; WBLP
Christmas Carol: "From the starry heav'ns descending." J. R. Newell. BLRP
Christmas Carol, A: "Glory to God on high, and jolly mirth." Francis Quarles. *Fr.* The Shepherd's Oracles. AnEC
Christmas Carol: "God bless the master of this house." *Unknown.* BoTP; BrR; ChBR; MeMeAg; OHIP; OxNR; SiSoSe; StVeCh; TiPo
(Good-bye, *with music.*) YaCaBo
(Grace, A.) MoShBr
Christmas Carol, A: "God rest ye, merry gentlemen." Dinah Maria Mulock Craik. *See* God Rest Ye, Merry Gentlemen.
Christmas Carol, A: "God rest you, merry gentlemen." *Unknown.* *See* God Rest You Merry, Gentlemen.
Christmas Carol, A: "In the bleak mid-winter." Christina Rossetti. AnEC; ChTr; COAH; MBP; OHIP; RG
(In the Bleak Mid-winter.) OxBoCh; StJW; SUS
My Gift, *st. 5.* BrR; ChBR; FaPON; MaRV; MeMeAg; OTPC (1946 ed.); SiSoSe
(Birthday Gift, A.) PRWS
Christmas Carol: "It came upon the midnight clear." Edmund Hamilton Sears. *See* It Came upon the Midnight Clear.
Christmas Carol: "Kings they came from out the south, The." Sara Teasdale. ChrBoLe; SDH; StJW
Christmas Carol, A: "Lacking samite and sable." May Probyn. ACP; CAW; GoBC; HBMV; ISi; OBVV
Christmas Carol: "Land grew bright in a single flower, The." Sister Francisca Josefa del Castillo, *tr. fr. Spanish by* Thomas Walsh. CAW
Christmas Carol: "Listen, lordings, unto me, a tale I will you tell." *Unknown.* COAH
Christmas Carol, The: "Minstrels played their Christmas tune, The." Wordsworth. COAH
Christmas Carol, A: "Night in the far Judean land." Mary A. O'Reilly. JKCP
Christmas Carol, A: "Other night, The." *Unknown.* BLV
Christmas Carol: "Quid petis, O fily." *Unknown.* *See* Quid Petis, O Fili?
Christmas Carol, A: "Shepherds had an Angel, The." Christina Rossetti. *See* Shepherds Had an Angel, The.
Christmas Carol, A: "Shepherds went their hasty way, The." Samuel Taylor Coleridge. ISi; OxBoCh
(Shepherds, The.) StJW
Christmas Carol: "So crowded was the little town." James S. Park. COAH
Christmas Carol, A: "So, now is [*or* has] come our joyfullest [*or* joyful'st *or* joyful] feast." George Wither. AnEC; CenL; ElSeCe; EPS (1942 ed.); OBS; SeEP; UnPo (1st ed.); ViBoPo; WP
(Old Christmas.) EV-2
(Our Joyful Feast.) ChBR; OHIP; SDH; SiSoSe
(So, Now Is Come Our Joyful'st Feast.) COAH
Christmas Carol, A: "There's a song in the air." Josiah Gilbert Holland. AA; COAH; DD; HBVY; PSO; RG; SDH
(There's a Song in the Air!) ChIP; MaRV
Christmas Carol, A: "They leave the land of gems and gold." Sir Aubrey De Vere. COAH
Christmas Carol, A: "Three damsels in the queen's chamber." Swinburne. *See* Three Damsels in the Queen's Chamber.
Christmas Carol, A: "Thys ender nyght." *Unknown.* *See* This Endernight I Saw a Sight.
Christmas Carol, A: "Trees are hung with crystal lamps, The." Christian Burke. COAH
Christmas Carol: "Villagers all, this frosty tide." Kenneth Grahame. *See* Carol: "Villagers all . . ."
Christmas Carol, A: " 'What means this glory 'round our feet.' " James Russell Lowell. ChIP; COAH; DD; PGD; SDH; StJW
Christmas Carol, A: "What sweeter music [*or* musick] can we

Christmas Carol, A (*continued*)
bring." Robert Herrick. AnEC; CBPC; MeRV; MPB; TriL
(Christmas Carol, Sung to the King in the Presence at Whitehall, A.) EV-2
"We see Him come, and know Him ours," 3 *ll.* MyFE
Christmas Carol: "When Christ was born in Bethlehem." *Unknown, tr. fr. Italian by* Longfellow. ChrBoLe; CLS; OHIP
Christmas Carol for Children, A. Martin Luther. COAH; SDH
Christmas Carol of Provence. *At. to* Nicolas Saboly. *See* Bring a Torch, Jeannette, Isabella.
Christmas Carol, Sung to the King in the Presence at Whitehall, A. Robert Herrick. *See* Christmas Carol, A: "What sweeter music can we bring."
Christmas Carols. Gui Barozai, *par. by* Longfellow. BoTP
Christmas Chant. Isabel Shaw. ChBR; SiSoSe
Christmas Child, The. *Unknown, tr. fr. Spanish by* Katharine B. Clay. PCH
Christmas Childhood, A. Patrick Kavanagh. AnIL; OxBI
Christmas Chimes ("Little Penelope Socrates"). *Unknown.* BOHV
Christmas comes. School after Christmas. Wymond Garthwaite. ChBR
Christmas comes but once a year. *Unknown.* OxNR
Christmas Cradlesong, A. Lope de Vega. *See* Madonna, to Her Sleeping Child, The.
Christmas Dawn at Sea, A. Evan Morgan. EtS
Christmas Day, *sel.* Charles Kingsley.
"How will it dawn, the coming Christmas Day?" EnSW
Christmas Day. Margaret E. Sangster. PEDC
Christmas Day. Christopher Smart. Hymns and Spiritual Songs, Hymn XXXII. ChTr
Christmas Day. Charles Wesley. *See* Hark! the Herald Angels Sing.
Christmas Day. George Wither. AnEC
Christmas Day. Andrew Young. AlDL
Christmas Day in the Workhouse. George R. Sims. BeLS; BLPA; PTA-2; TreF
Christmas Day Is Come. Luke Wadding. OxBI
Christmas Day on the Aisne. Ernest E. Blau. CAG
Christmas Day was coming, the Christmas Eve drew near, The. The Little Christmas Tree. "Susan Coolidge." DD; PEDC; PEOR; SDH
Christmas Daybreak. Christina Rossetti. *See* Christmas Carol, A: "Before the paling of the stars."
Christmas declares the glory of the flesh. Christmas and Common Birth. Anne Ridler. FaBoTw
Christmas Dusk. Wilbur D. Nesbit. PEDC
Christmas, 1898. Edward Sandford Martin. DD
Christmas 1898, *sel.* Sir Lewis Morris.
"'Tis nigh two thousand years." TrPWD
Christmas Encyclical. Joseph Auslander. QS
Christmas Eve. St. Luke, Bible, *N.T. See* Adoration of the Shepherds, The.
Christmas Eve. Zoe Kincaid Brockman. NoCaPo
Christmas-Eve. Robert Browning. *See* Christmas-Eve and Easter-Day.
Christmas Eve. Olaf Bull, *tr. fr. Norwegian by* Charles W. Stork. AnNoLy
Christmas Eve. Liam P. Clancy. ISi
Christmas Eve. Charlotte Druitt Cole. BoTP
Christmas Eve. John Davidson. CBPC; MPB; OHIP; SDH
Christmas Eve. Mary Mapes Dodge. SDH
Christmas Eve. John Drinkwater. HBMV
Christmas Eve. Marion Edey. YeAr
Christmas Eve. Eugene Field. BOL; OHIP
Christmas Eve. Robert Herrick. *See* Christmas Eve—Another Ceremony.
Christmas Eve. Florence Hoatson. GFA
Christmas Eve. Marguerite Merington. SDH
Christmas Eve. Catherine Parmenter. PEDC; PGD
Christmas Eve. Edna Kingsley Wallace. BoTP
Christmas Eve. Kate Douglas Wiggin. *See* Romance of a Christmas Card, The.
Christmas-Eve and Easter-Day, *sels.* Robert Browning.
"Earth breaks up, time drops away." ChIP
Life. OQP; QP-2
Rest Remaineth. OQP; PoRL; QP-1
Christmas Eve, and twelve of the clock. The Oxen. Thomas Hardy. BLV; BoLiVe; BoTP; CaAE; CBOV; ChMo; ChrBoLe; CMP; CoBMV; EnL; GTBS-W; GTML; GTSL; HBMV; LiTM; MaPo; MaRV; MBP; MoAB; MoBrPo; OAEP; OTPC (1946 ed.); Po; PoLFOT; POT; PoTo; POTT; PoVP; QS; RiBV; SDH; ShBV-2; StJW; TCPD; TSW; TVSH; TwCV; TwHP; ViPP; VLEP; WP
Christmas Eve—Another Ceremony. Robert Herrick. OHIP
(Christmas Eve.) MuP
Christmas Eve—Another to the Maids. Robert Herrick. OHIP
Christmas Eve; Australia. Karl Shapiro. ReMP
Christmas Eve Choral, A. Bliss Carman. ISi
Christmas Eve in France. Jessie Redmond Fauset. BANP
Christmas Eve in Ireland. Katharine Tynan. ChrBoLe
Christmas Eve in Whitneyville, 1955. Donald Hall. UnPo (3d ed.)
Christmas Eve; Market Square. P. K. Page. TwCaPo
Christmas Eve Meditation. Margaret E. Bruner. MaRV
Christmas Eve under Hooker's Statue. Robert Lowell. NePA; OxBA
Christmas Everywhere. Phillips Brooks. *See* Christmas Carol, A: "Everywhere, everywhere Christmas tonight."
Christmas Exchange, The. Arthur Guiterman. BrR; ChBR
Christmas Fires, The. Anne P. L. Field. COAH
Christmas Folk-Song, A. Lizette Woodworth Reese. ChBR; ChrBoLe; DD; FaPON; GFA; HBMV; HBVY; MPB; NV; OHIP; OTPC (1946 ed.); PoRh; PoRL; RAR; SDH; SP; StJW; SUS; TiPo (1952 ed.); TSW; UTS; VOD
Christmas Ghost-Story, A. Thomas Hardy. EmBrPo; EnLi-2
Christmas "Good Night." Ethel Robb. GFA
Christmas Greeting ("Sing hey! Sing hey!"). *Unknown.* ChBR; MeMeAg; SiSoSe
(Old Christmas Greeting, An.) FaPON; MPB; TiPo
Christmas Greeting ("When Bill gives me a book, I know"). *Unknown.* BrR
Christmas hath made an end. Carol for Candlemas Day. *Unknown.* MeRV; SeCL
Christmas Hearth Rhyme. *Unknown. See* Catch by the Hearth, A.
Christmas Holiday. Alun Lewis. PrWP
Christmas Holly, The. Eliza Cook. COAH; OTPC (1946 ed.); PRWS
Christmas Husbandly Fare. Thomas Tusser. SiCE; TuPP
Christmas Hymn, A. Cecil Frances Alexander. *See* Once in Royal David's City.
Christmas Hymn, A. Alfred Domett. BMEP; COAH; DD; GN; GTBS; HBV; OTPC; TVSH; WGRP
(Christmas Hymn, 1837.) OBVV
(Christmas Hymn, A: Old Style, 1837.) VA
"It is the calm and solemn night," *sel.* PGD
Christmas Hymn, *sel.* St. Ephrem, *tr. fr. Syriac by* W. H. Kent.
Virgin Truly Full of Wonder. ISi
(Christmas Hymn, The.) CAW
Christmas Hymn, A. Richard Watson Gilder. CLS; MaRV; StJW
Christmas Hymn. Sister Juana Inés de la Cruz, *tr. fr. Spanish by* Samuel Beckett. AnMP
Christmas Hymn. Milton. *See* Hymn: "It was the winter wild."
Christmas Hymn, A. *Unknown.* COAH
Christmas Hymn, 1837. Alfred Domett. *See* Christmas Hymn.
Christmas Hymn for Children, A. Josephine Dodge Daskam Bacon. SDH
Christmas Hymn for Lambeth. J. C. Squire. TCPD
Christmas Hymn, A: New Style, *sel.* Alfred Domett.
"To murder one so young!" VA
Christmas Hymn, A: Old Style, 1837. Alfred Domett. *See* Christmas Hymn, A.
Christmas in Carmel. Sister Mary Thérèse. PraNu
Christmas in England. Sir Walter Scott. *See* Christmas in the Olden Time.
Christmas in Freelands. James Stephens. ChMo; CMP
Christmas in India. Kipling. LPS-1
Christmas in lands of the fir tree and pine. Everywhere, Everywhere Christmas Tonight. Phillips Brooks. HH; OTPC; PoRL
Christmas in Olden Time Sir Walter Scott. *See* Christmas in the Olden Time.
Christmas in Provence. Sister Mary Madeleva. WHL
Midnight Mass, II.
Serenade, The, I.
Christmas in the Heart. *Unknown.* ChBR; MaRV; OHIP; SiSoSe
Christmas in the North. Margaret E. Sangster. PEDC
Christmas in the Olden Time. Sir Walter Scott. *Fr.* Marmion, *Introd. to* VI. COAH, *sl. abr.*; EPP; GoBC; LPS-2; OTPC; PCH, 3 *ll.*; PEOR, *abr.*
(Christmas: "And well our Christian sires of old," *abr.*) ERP
(Christmas: "The damsel donned her kirtle sheen," *abr.*) PCH
(Christmas in England, *abr.*) GN
(Christmas in Olden Time.) PoRL
("Heap on more wood!—the wind is chill," 3 *ll.*) TiPo
(Old Christmas-Tide.) ChBR, 3 *ll.*; DD; MPB; SDH; SiSoSe, 3 *ll.*
Christmas in the Woods. Frances Frost. BrR; ChBR; TiPo (1952 ed.)
Christmas Insurrection, A. Anne P. L. Field. COAH
Christmas is a bitter day. David, Aged Four. Mildred Focht. DDA; MaRV
Christmas is coming, the geese are getting fat. Beggar's

Rhyme. *Unknown.* ChBR; GaP; OxNR; PCH; SDH; TiPo (1952 ed.)
Christmas is here. The Mahogany Tree. Thackeray. COAH; HBV; LPS-1; VA
Christmas Is Remembering. Elsie Binns. ChBR; SiSoSe
Christmas Island. Katharine Lee Bates. HBMV; HBVY; TSW
Christmas knows a merry, merry place. Wassail Chorus at the Mermaid Tavern. Theodore Watts-Dunton. BMEP; OBEV (1st ed.)
Christmas Legend, A. Oliver Herford. PoMS
Christmas Legend, A. Frank Sidgwick. OHIP; WP
Christmas Legend. Edna Randolph Worrell. ChBR
Christmas Legends. Denis A. McCarthy. ChBR; ChrBoLe
Christmas Letter from Australia, A. Douglas Brooke Wheelton Sladen. COAH; VA
Christmas Long Ago, A. *Unknown.* PTA-2
Christmas Lullaby, A. John Addington Symonds. AnEC; COAH; PRWS
Christmas Lullaby. Ulrich Troubetzkoy. YeAr
Christmas Lullaby, A. Arthur Weir. BOL
Christmas Meditation. George Macdonald. BSV
Christmas morn, the legends say. Christmas Legends. Denis A. McCarthy. ChBR; ChrBoLe
Christmas Morning. Elsie Melchert Fowler. ChBR
Christmas Morning. Joaquin Miller. MaRV
Christmas Morning. Elizabeth Madox Roberts. ChBR; ChrBoLe; GoTP; LS; MAP; MaRV; MoAmPo; MPB; PCH; PoRh; StJW; StVeCh; SUS; TSW; WHL
Christmas Mystery we now present, A. The Star. Bertha Palmer Lane. ChrBoLe
Christmas Night, A. John Drinkwater. StJW
Christmas Night. Alice Isabel Hazeltine. ChrBoLe
Christmas Night. Marion Lochhead. MaRV
Christmas Night. Hugh MacCawell, *tr. fr. Irish by* Frank O'Connor. KiLC
Christmas Night. Alice Meynell. POTT; StJW
Christmas Night. B. E. Milner. BoTP
Christmas Night. *Unknown. See* Our Lady's Song.
Christmas-Night in the Quarters, *sels.* Irwin Russell.
Blessing the Dance. AnAmPo; LA
(Blessing on the Dance, A.) SPP
Fust Banjo, De. AA; BAP; BLPA; HBV; IHA; LEAP; PFY
(First Banjo, The.) BOHV; LHV; SPP
Christmas Night of '62. William Gordon McCabe. AA
Christmas 1944. Denise Levertov. NeBP
Christmas, 1943. Vera Bax. DiM
Christmas, 1943. James Boyd. NoCaPo (rev. ed.)
Christmas 1942. Eric Irvin. BoAV
Christmas 1942 Robert Nathan. PoFr
Christmas, 1917. Brent Dow Allinson. AOAH
Christmas, 1930. Anderson M. Scruggs. CAW
(Christmas Today.) MaRV; OQP; QP-2
(How Can They Honor Him.) SDH; StJW
Christmas Now Is Past, The. Nicholas Breton. AnEC
Christmas of Long Ago, A. Morton Bryan Wharton. BlG
Christmas on Three Continents. John Peter. BoSA
Christmas once found country squires. Christmas: Past and Present. F. S. Holmes *and* S. H. Stackpole. CAG
Christmas Party, A. Carolyn Sherwin Bailey. PCH
Christmas Party, The. Adeline White. BoTP
Christmas: Past and Present. F. S. Holmes *and* S. H. Stackpole. CAG
Christmas Pastoral. Robert Hillyer. MaRV
Christmas Peal, The. Harriet Prescott Spofford. PEOR
Christmas Prayer, A. Ruby Dell Baugher. PraP
Christmas Prayer. Ralph Spaulding Cushman. MaRV
Christmas Prayer, A. Lucy Embury. ChrBoLe
Christmas Prayer. A. Molly Anderson Haley. PGD; PSO
Christmas Prayer, A. Herbert H. Hines. ChIP; MaRV; OQP; PGD; PSO; QP-1
Christmas Prayer, A. George Macdonald. BOL; SUS
Christmas Prayer. Madeline Morse. PGD; PSO
Christmas Pudding, The. *Unknown.* TiPo (1952 ed.)
Christmas Question, A. Minot J. Savage. PEOR
Christmas Rede. Jane Barlow. OBVV
Christmas Rose. Margaret Evelyn Singleton. ChIP
Christmas Roses. May Riley Smith. PEOR
Christmas Shoppers. Aileen Fisher. ChBR
Christmas Silence, The. Margaret Deland. ChrBoLe; CLS; COAH; OHIP; PRWS; SDH
Christmas Singing. Elsie Williams Chandler. ChBR; SiSoSe
Christmas Snow. John Moore. StaSt
Christmas Song, A. William Cox Bennett. COAH; VA
Christmas Song, A. Teresa Brayton. JKCP
Christmas Song. Bliss Carman. PeCV; StJW
Christmas Song, A. Florence Evelyn Dratt. MaRV; SDH
Christmas Song. Eugene Field, *wr. at. to* Lydia Avery Coonley Ward. COAH; DD; HH; OHIP; PRWS; YeAr
(Song: "Why do the bells of [*or* do bells for] Christmas ring?") BoTP; GaP; GFA; PCH; RAR; TiPo (1952 ed.)
Christmas Song. Laurence Housman. SDH
Christmas Song, A. Tudor Jenks. COAH
Christmas Song. Elizabeth-Ellen Long. ChBR; SiSoSe
Christmas Song. Edmund H. Sears. COAH; SDH
(Birth Song of Christ, The.) BePJ
Christmas Song, A: "Winds through the olive trees softly did blow." *Unknown. See* Long, Long Ago.
Christmas Song, A. Ruth Winant Wheeler. PraP
Christmas Song for Three Guilds, A. G. K. Chesterton. TCPD
Christmas Sonnet, A. E. A. Robinson. CoV; MaRV
Christmas Star, The. Nancy Byrd Turner. MaRV
Christmas star burns overhead, The. Childlike Heart. Ellen Weston Catlin. PGD
Christmas Still Lives. William Hawkes. BePJ
Christmas Story, The. St. Luke, Bible, *N.T. See* Adoration of the Shepherds, The.
Christmas Symbol, The. *Unknown.* OQP; QP-1
Christmas, the Year One, A.D. Sara Henderson Hay. PoRA
Christmas Thought, A. Mrs. Frank A. Breck. BePJ
Christmas Thought, A. Lucy Larcom. PEOR
Christmas Thought about Dickens, A. Bertha S. Scranton. PEOR
Christmas Today. E. G. Reith. PSO
Christmas Today. Anderson M. Scruggs. *See* Christmas, 1930.
Christmas Treasures. Eugene Field. SDH
Christmas Tree, A. William Burford. NePA
Christmas Tree, The. C. Day Lewis. GTBS-D
Christmas Tree, The. Isabel de Savitzsky. BoTP
Christmas Tree. Aileen Fisher. ChBR
Christmas Tree, The. Mary E. Wilkins Freeman. PEDC
Christmas Tree. Vasili Lebedev-Kumach, *tr. fr. Russian by* Jack Lindsay. RuPo
Christmas Tree. The. Edward Shillito. ChIP; OQP; QP-1; SDH
Christmas Tree in the Nursery, The. Richard Watson Gilder. DD; HBVY; OHIP
(Sery.) COAH
Christmas-Tree Song, A. Rodney Bennett. BoTP
Christmas tree stood by the parlor door, The. Golden Cobwebs. Rowena Bennett. ChBR
Christmas Trees, The. Mary Frances Butts. OHIP; PRWS
Christmas Trees. Robert Frost. PoTo
Christmas-Trees. Kenneth Grahame. CBPC
Christmas Trees. Violet Alleyn Storey. SDH; StJW
Christmas Verse, A. "Kay." BoTP
Christmas Wail, A. *Unknown.* PA
Christmas was in the air and all was well. Karma. E. A. Robinson. AmPP; AnNE; ChMo; CMP; CoBMV; MoAB; MoAmPo (1950 ed.)
Christmas Wish, A. Eugene Field. ChBR
Christmas Wish, A. Rose Fyleman. BoTP
Christmas Wish, A. Celia Thaxter. SDH
Christmas-Tide ("Let no mon cum into this hall"). *Unknown.* CBOV
Christmas-Time. Rose Fyleman. ChBR
Christmas Time. Villon, *tr. fr. French by* John Payne. *Fr.* Le Petit Testament. LiA
Christmas time was drawing near. Three Little Babes. *Unknown.* ABS
Christo Paremus Canticam, Excelsis Gloria. *Unknown. See* In Excelsis Gloria.
Christofo Colombo was a hungry man. Mysterious Biography. Carl Sandburg. SiSoSe
Christofo Columbo, *with music. Unknown.* AmSS
Christoph. Charles Spear. AnNZ
Christopher Columbus. Franklin P. Adams. InMe
Christopher Columbus. Rosemary Benét *and* Stephen Vincent Benét. PoRh
Christopher Columbus. Annette Wynne. HH
Christopher Marlowe. Michael Drayton. *Fr.* To Henry Reynolds, of Poets and Poesy. ChTr
Christopher Marlowe. Swinburne. *Fr.* Sonnets on English Dramatic Poets. BEL; PoVP; PtP; TOP; TrGrPo; VLEP
Christopher of the Shenandoah, A. Edith M. Thomas. PAH
Christopher Robin goes. Hoppity. A. A. Milne. TiPo
Christopher White. *Unknown.* ESPB
Christ's Bloody Sweat. Robert Southwell. ReIE
Christ's Bondservant. George Matheson. MaRV
(Christian Freedom.) TrPWD
Christ's Coming in Triumph. Jeremy Taylor. BePJ
(Christ's Coming O Jerusalem in Triumph.) StJW
(Lord, Come Away!) MaRV
Christ's Coming to Judgment. Thomas Dekker. AnEnPo
Christ's Gift to Man. *Unknown.* ACP
Christ's Giving. Anna E. Hamilton. ChIP; OQP; QP-1
Christ's Incarnation. Robert Herrick. *See* Christ and We.
Christ's Nativity. Henry Vaughan. AnEC; AtBAP; COAH; StJW
(Awake! Glad Heart!) GoTP
Christ's Prayer in Gethsemane. *Unknown.* SeCePo
Christ's Reign of Peace. Stephen Phillips. ChIP

Christ's Reply. Edward Taylor. *Fr.* God's Determinations. PoEL-3
Christ's Spirit taketh breath again. Christ Our Contemporary. William Charles Braithwaite. MaRV
Christ's Sympathy. Sir Edward Bulwer-Lytton. BePJ
Christ's Triumph after Death. Giles Fletcher. *See* Christ's Victory and Triumph.
Christ's Triumph over Death. Giles Fletcher. *See* Christ's Victory and Triumph.
Christ's Victory. Richard Crashaw. MaRV; StJW
Christ's Victory and Triumph, *sels.* Giles Fletcher.
Christ's Triumph after Death, IV. EPS
Celestial City, The. OBS
Easter Morn. EIL
"Had I a voice of steel to tune my song." LoBV
Heavenly Jerusalem, The. OxBoCh
Christ's Triumph over Death, III.
On the Crucifixion. OxBoCh
"So down the silver streams of Eridan." LoBV
Christ's Victory in Heaven, I.
Description of Mercy. EV-2
Excellency of Christ. BePJ; MaRV; StJW; WGRP
("He is a path, if any be misled.") ChIP
"She was a Virgin of austere regard." ViBoPo
Christ's Victory on Earth, II.
"His haire was blacke, and in small curls did twine." SeCV-1
"Love is the blossom where there blows." ElSeCe; LO; ViBoPo
(Wooing Song.) EIL; EV-2; HBV; OBEV
"Twice had Diana bent her golden bowe." SeEP
Christ's Victory in Heaven. Giles Fletcher. *See* Christ's Victory and Triumph.
Christ's Victory on Earth. Giles Fletcher. *See* Christ's Victory and Triumph.
Christsmass Carol for Saint Francis' Ears, A. Raymond E. F. Larsson. SaFP
Christus; a Mystery, *sels.* Longfellow.
Flight into Egypt, The, *fr.* II, 3. APW; OBVV
Jesus at Play with His School-Mates, *fr.* II, 3. APW
Love and Hate, *fr.* I, 1st Interlude. MaRV
"My work is finished; I am strong." ChIP
Prophets in Their Time, *fr.* I, Introitus. GrCo-2
(Fate of the Prophets, The.) WGRP
Village School, The, *fr.* II, 3. APW
Christus Consolator. Rossiter W. Raymond. HBV; MaRV; OQP; QP-1
Christus Matthaeum et Discipulos Alloquitur. Sir Edward Sherburne. ACP
Christus Triumphans. Condé Benoist Pallen. CAW
Christus Vitis ad Vinitorem Patrem. Richard Crashaw, *tr. fr. Latin by* D. C. Allen. Epigrammata Sacra, I, 61. LaP
Chromis. Phineas Fletcher. Piscatorie Eclogues, IV. LoBV
Chromis! Mnasil! none appear? Oberon, the Fairy Prince. Ben Jonson. EPS
Chromis my joy, why drop thy rainy eyes? Chromis. Phineas Fletcher. Piscatorie Eclogues, IV. LoBV
Chromium-plated Hat, A; Inlaid with Scenes from Siegfried. Howard Nemerov. FiMAP
Chronicle, The. Abraham Cowley. *See* Chronicle, The; a Ballad.
Chronicle, A. *Unknown.* NA; SiTL
Chronicle, The; a Ballad. Abraham Cowley. BOHV; BrBE; CEP; EV-2; GoTL; LPS-1; SeCV-1; ViBoPo
Chronicle of Meola Creek, The. Keith Sinclair. AnNZ
Chronicle of the Drum, The, *sels.* Thackeray.
"Ah, gentle, tender lady mine!" ViBoPo
"At Paris, hard by the Maine barriers." OtMeF
Chronicle of Wasted Time. Shakespeare. *See* Sonnets, CVI.
Chronicler, The. Alexander Bergman. TrJP
Chronometer, The. A. M. Sullivan. WaKn
Chronos, Chronos, mend thy pace. The Secular Masque. Dryden. ExPo; MaPo; PoEL-3; SeCeV; SeCV-2; SeEP; TCEP
Chrysalis, A. Mary Emily Bradley. AA; HBV; PECK; SN
Chrysalis, The. John James Piatt. InP
Chrysanthemum Legend, The. Arthur Davison Ficke. PoMa
Chrysanthemum Show, The. C. Day Lewis. MoVE
Chrysanthemums. Mary Mapes Dodge. PEOR
Chrysanthemums. F. S. Flint. MBP; MoBrPo (1942 ed.)
Chrysanthemums ("The autumn chrysanthemums have the loveliest colors"). Tao Yuan-ming, *tr. fr. Chinese by* Yang Chi-sing. WhP
Chrysanthemums ("I built my cottage"). Tao Yuan-ming. *See* I Built My Hut.
Chrysanthemums. *Unknown, tr. fr. Japanese by* Lois J. Erickson. SoLD
Chrysanthemums in the Eastern Garden, The. Po Chü-i, *tr. fr. Chinese by* Arthur Waley. TrCh
Chryseis Walter Conrad Arensberg. AnAmPo; LA
Chrysolites and Rubies, [Bacchus Brings], The. Walter Savage Landor. BPN; EmBrPo; EPN
Chrysothemis. Henry Reed. MoVE
Chu K'o. Chu Yuan. *See* Nine Songs, The.
Chuang-tzu, the Monist. Po Chü-i, *tr. fr. Chinese by* Arthur Waley. *Fr.* The Philosophers. TrCh
Chu-ch'en Village. Po Chü-i, *tr. fr. Chinese by* Arthur Waley. TrCh
"Chuff! chuff! chuff!" An' a mountain bluff. A Song of Panama. Damon Runyon. PAH
Chug! Puff! Chug! Tugs. James S. Tippett. FaPON; GFA
Chums. Buson, *tr. fr. Japanese.* GaP
Chums. James William Foley. PTA-2
Chums. Arthur Guiterman. GaP; MPB
Chung Tzu. *Unknown, tr. fr. Chinese.* WhP
Church. Gilberto González y Contreras, *tr. fr. Spanish by* Dudley Fitts. AnCL
Church, The Edwin Ford Piper. GrCo-1; WGRP
Church, The. Jules Romains, *tr. fr. French by* Jethro Bithell. WGRP
Church,/ Chapel. *Unknown.* OxNR
Church and Church-yard at Night. Robert Blair. *Fr.* The Grave. OBEC
("See yonder hallow'd fane! the pious work.") EnSW; ViBoPo
Church and School. Timothy Dwight. *Fr.* Greenfield Hill. AmPP (3d ed.)
Church and the World walked far apart, The. The Church Walking with the World. Mathilda C. Edwards. BLPA
Church Bell in the Night, The. *Unknown, tr. fr. Old Irish by* Kuno Meyer. AnIL
(Church Bell at Night, The, *tr. by* Howard Mumford Jones.) OnYI
Church bells are ringing, The. Sunday up the River, IV. James Thomson. EmBrPo; OAEP
Church bells at Christmas-time, The. Christmas-Time. Rose Fyleman. ChBR
Church bells toll a melancholy round, The. Written in Disgust of Vulgar Superstition. Keats. PeBoSo
Church-Builder, The. Thomas Hardy. BEL
Church Decking at Christmas. Wordsworth. COAH
Church do zeem a touchèn zight, The. Vo'k a-Comen into Church. William Barnes. OxBoCh
Church flings forth a battled shade, The. The Church-Builder. Thomas Hardy BEL
Church-Floor, The. George Herbert. ATP; ExPo; OBS; PoE; SeCePo: SeCeV
(Church-Floore, The.) MeLP
Church Going. Philip Larkin. HaMV; NePoEA; UnPo (3d ed.)
Church has pieces jutting out, The. The Pilaster. Elizabeth Madox Roberts. NP
Church in the Heart, The. Morris Abel Beer. MaRV
(Piety.) PFE
("Who builds a church within his heart.") PoToHe
Church is man when his awed soul goes out, The. What Is the Church? Sam Walter Foss. OQP; QP-1
Church-Monuments. George Herbert. MaPo; RiBV; TriL
Church-Music [or -Musick]. George Herbert. EPS; SeCV-1; UnS
Church of a Dream, The. Lionel Johnson. GTIV; OBMV; PoVP; TIP
Church of Brou, The. Matthew Arnold. EmBrPo
Tomb, The, *sel.* PoVP; TriL
Church of England, The. Dryden. *Fr.* The Hind and the Panther, I. OBS
Church of Graves, The. Robert Blair. *Fr.* The Grave. BeR
Church of the Revolution, The. Hezekiah Butterworth. PAH
Church of the Sacred Heart, The. Ashton Greene. NePoAm
Church Porch, The, *sels.* George Herbert.
Courage. PCD; PCH
Dare to Be True. GoTP
"Lie not; but let thy heart be true to God." EPS (1942 ed.)
Maxims. CBE
On Worship. MaRV
Stanzas from "The Church Porch." TVSH
"Thou whose sweet youth and early hopes enhance." LPS-2
Church Romance, A. Thomas Hardy. FaBoTw
Church Scene, The. Longfellow. *Fr.* Evangeline. TreF
Church Street wears ever a smile, from having watched bright belles. Streets. Douglas Goldring. HBMV
Church Today, The. Sir William Watson. MaRV; QS; WGRP
Church Triumphant. S. Ralph Harlow. MaRV
Church Triumphant, The. John Addington Symonds. *See* Loftier Race, A.
Church Universal, The. Samuel Longfellow. GrCo-1; MaRV; WGRP
Church Walking with the World. Mathilda C. Edwards. BLPA
Church Windows, The. George Herbert. *See* Windows, The.
Church-Windows, The, *abr.* *Unknown.* *Fr.* A Poem, in Defence of the Decent Ornaments of Christ-Church, Oxon. OBS
Churches. *Unknown.* MaRV
Churches of Rome and of England, The. Dryden. *Fr.* The Hind and the Panther, I. ACP
Churchill's Grave. Byron. EmBrPo
Church's One Foundation, The. Samuel J. Stone. MaRV; OIF; WGRP

Church's one foundation, The. Battle Hymn of the Spanish Rebellion [*or* Republic]. Louis Alexander Mackay. BoCaPo; OnPM
Church's Testimony, The. Dryden. *Fr.* The Hind and the Panther, I. ACP; CAW
("But, gratious God, how well dost thou provide.") TrPWD
(Confession of Faith.) UnPo (1st ed.)
(Conversion: "But, gracious God.") PoLi
Churchyard, The. Robert Buchanan. HBV; VA
Churchyard among the Mountains, The. Wordsworth. *Fr.* The Excursion, VII. ERP
Churchyard in Wales, A. *Unknown.* SiTL
("Our life is but a summer's day.") WhC
Churchyard leans to the sea with its dead, The. The Old Churchyard of Bonchurch. Philip Bourke Marston. HBV; OBVV; VA
Churchyard of St. Mary Magdalene, Old Milton. John Heath-Stubbs. NePoEA
Churchyard on the Sands, The. Lord De Tabley. CBOV; CH, *abr.;* GTBS-D, *abr.;* HBV; LoBV
Churl in spirit, up or down, The. In Memoriam A. H. H., CXI. Tennyson. BPN; EmBrPo; EPN; GEPC; ViPo; VLEP
Churl that wants another's fare, The. The Dog in the River. Phaedrus. AWP; JAWP; OnPM; WBP
Chus doth so often to the doctor go. In Chus. *Unknown.* TuPP
Chu-ying was lord of this place and produced this flower. Inscribed on a Jade Tablet of Yu. *Unknown. Fr.* The Fountain of Old Poems. WhP
Ciaran, the Master of Horses and Lands. Joseph Campbell. JKCP (1926 ed.)
Cicada. Libero de Libero, *tr. fr. Italian by* Frederick Mortimer Clapp. LiTW
Cicada, A. Li Shang-yin, *tr. fr. Chinese by* Witter Bynner *and* Kiang Kang-hu. OuHeWo
Cicada, A. Meleager, *tr. fr. Greek by* Walter Headlam. OxBG
Cicada, The. Ou-yang Hsiu, *tr. fr. Chinese by* Arthur Waley. AWP
Cicada (*fr.* Anacreontics). *Unknown, tr. fr. Greek.* GrL, *tr. by* Edmund Blunden; GrPE, *tr. by* F. L. Lucas; GrR, *tr. by* Judson France Davidson; OxBG, *tr. by* Edmund Blunden; OuHeWo, *tr. by* Addison
Cicada, The ("Why, ruthless shepherds"). *Unknown, tr. fr. Greek by* Francis Wrangham. OxBG
Cicada cries out, The. Peasant and Geisha Songs. *Unknown.* LiTW
Cicada Days. Hesiod, *tr. fr. Greek by* T. F. Higham. *Fr.* Works and Days. OxBG
Cicada sings, The/ In the rotten willow. *Unknown, tr. fr. Japanese by* Kenneth Rexroth. OnPJ
Cicada that on tall tree tops. Cicada. *Unknown, tr. by* Judson France Davidson. GrR
Cicadas, The. Aldous Huxley. POTE; TwCV
Cicadas. Richard Wilbur. FiMAP
(Cigales.) NePoEA
Ciceronis Amor. Robert Greene. *See* Tullie's Love.
Cid, The, *sel.* Corneille, *tr. fr. French by* Paul Landis.
Two Lovers in the Toils of Honor. LiTW
Cid, The, *sels. Unknown, tr. fr. Spanish by* R. Selden Rose *and* Leonard Bacon.
Arrival of the Family at Valencia. TeCS
Banishment of the Cid, The. AnSpL-1; TeCS
Cid and the Count of Barcelona, The. AnSpL-1
Cid's Farewell to His Wife, The. AnSpL-1
Cid's Prayer, The. TeCS
Dawn in the Town. TeCS
Farewell, The. TeCS
His Wife and Daughters Come to the Exiled One. TeCS
Pawning the Coffers of Sand. LiTW
Cid and the Count of Barcelona, The. *Unknown, tr. fr. Spanish by* R. Selden Rose *and* Leonard Bacon. *Fr.* The Cid. AnSpL-1
Cid and the Five Moorish Kings, The. *Unknown, tr. fr. Spanish by* John Gibson Lockhart. AnSpL-1
Cid of the West. Edna Dean Proctor. DD; GA
Cider Song, A. G. K. Chesterton. MM
Cid's Farewell to His Wife, The. *Unknown, tr. fr. Spanish by* R. Selden Rose *and* Leonard Bacon. *Fr.* The Cid. AnSpL-1
Cid's Prayer, The. *Unknown, tr. fr. Spanish by* R. Selden Rose *and* Leonard Bacon. *Fr.* The Cid. TeCS
Cid's Rising, The. Felicia D. Hemans. OBRV
Cigales. Richard Wilbur. *See* Cicadas.
Cigar Smoke, Sunday, after Dinner. Louise Townsend Nicholl. NePoAm
Cigarette, The. Jules Laforgue, *tr. fr. French by* William J. Smith. LiTW
Cigarette for the Bambino. Gavin Ewart. WaP
Cigarettes Will Spoil Yer Life, *with music. Unknown.* AS
Cimabuella. Bayard Taylor. PA
Cimmerian Twilight. Maximilian Aleksandrovich Voloshin, *tr. fr. Russian by* Babette Deutsch. TrRV
Cincinnatus of the West, The. Byron. *See* Washington.
Cincirinella Had a Mule. *Unknown, tr. fr. Italian by* Maria Cimino. FaPON
Cinderella's Song. Elizabeth Madox Roberts. PoRh
Cindy. *Unknown.* SoAF, *with music;* TrAS, *with music;* TreFS
Cino. Ezra Pound. ReaPo
Cinq Ans Après. Gelett Burgess. HBV; PoeMoYo; TreFS
(Ah, Yes, I Wrote It.) SiTL
(Ah, Yes, I Wrote the "Purple Cow.") FiBHP
(Nonsense Quatrains.) CenHV
Cinque Port, A. John Davidson. PoeT; ReTS; TVSH
Circassian Song. Mikhail Lermontov, *tr. fr. Russian by* J. S. Phillimore. BoR
Circe. Lord De Tabley. VA
Circe. Austin Dobson. *Fr.* Rose-Leaves. BPN
(To Rose.) PFE
Circe. Homer, *tr. fr. Greek by* F. L. Lucas. *Fr.* The Odyssey, X. GrPE
Circe. Alfred Kreymborg. MAPA
Circe. Louis MacNeice. LO; OBMV
Circe Remembers. Sherman Conrad. CAG
Circean cup, and Epicurus' sty. Sonnet. Luis de Góngora. AnSpL-1
Circe's Palace. T. S. Eliot. CAG
Circle, The. Carol Coates. CaP
Circle, The. Jean Garrigue. LiTA; MoPo
Circle, The. Katharine Welles Wheeler. MuM
Circle of C, The. Lynette Roberts. MoWP
Circle to the left, the old Brass Wagon. Old Brass Wagon. *Unknown.* AS
Circle will remain, of mountain, hill, The. The World's Centre. Ruth Dallas. AnNZ
Circles. Harry Behn. LiL
Circles. Emerson. APW
Circles. Miriam Waddington. BoCaPo (1948 ed.); PeCV
Circles never fully round, but change, The. Perspective of Coordination. Arthur Davison Ficke. NP
Circling Hearths, The. Roderic Quinn. BoAu
Circling on high, in cloudless sky. On the Plains. Francis Brooks. *Fr.* Intaglios. AA
Circling Year, The. Ramona Graham. PTA-2
Circumstance. Thomas Bailey Aldrich. AA
Circumstance. Frederick Locker-Lampson. BOHV
Circumstance. Tennyson. BPP; CG
Circumstance without Pomp. John Kendall. WhC
Circus, The. Fannie Stearns Davis. PCH
Circus. Eleanor Farjeon. BoChLi; MPB; SUS; UTS
Circus, The. Milton Kaplan. GoYe
Circus, The. Elizabeth Madox Roberts. FaPON; GFA; MPB; UTS
Circus, The. E. B. White. InMe
Circus Animals' Desertion, The. W. B. Yeats. ChMo; FaBoTw; LiTB; OAEP (2d ed.)
Circus Clown, The. John Ferguson. MW
"Circus comes this week, The!" The Circus. Fannie Stearns Davis. PCH
Circus Elephant. Kathryn Worth. BrR
Circus Garland, A, *sels.* Rachel Field.
Acrobat. StVeCh
Elephant, The. StVeCh
Epilogue. UTS
Equestrienne. UTS
Girl on the Milk-white Horse, The. StVeCh
Next Day. StVeCh
Parade. StVeCh; UTS
Performing Seal, The. StVeCh; TiPo (1959 ed.); UTS
Circus Parade, The. Olive Beaupré Miller. GFA; TiPo
Circus Parade. James S. Tippett. UTS
Circus-postered Barn, The. Elizabeth J. Coatsworth. MAP; MoAmPo; PoeMoYo
Circus Ship *Euzkera,* The. Walker Gibson. *See* In Memory of the Circus Ship *Euzkera* . . .
Circus was never meant for children, The. The Circus. Milton Kaplan. GoYe
Cirque d'Hiver. Elizabeth Bishop. FiMAP; LiTA; MiAP
Cistern, The. George Seferis, *tr. fr. Modern Greek by* Rae Dalven. MoGP
Cisterns and stones; the fig tree in the wall. Tuscany. V. Sackville-West. PtOT
Cit, a Common-Council-Man by place, The. What Is't to Us? Charles Churchill. *Fr.* Night. SeCePo
Citation and Examination of William Shakespeare, The, *sels.* Walter Savage Landor.
Maid's Lament, The. BPN; EV-4; GTBS; HBV; LPS-1; OBEV; OBRV; OBVV; ReTS; VA
Upon a Sweet-Briar. BPN
Citation for Horace Gregory. Muriel Rukeyser. NAMP
Cities, The. "Æ." OBMV
Cities. Hilda Doolittle ("H. D."). ChMo; CMP; ViBoPo (1941 ed.)
Cities. Boyce House. HiLiAm
Cities. Arthur Rimbaud, *tr. fr. French by* Frederick Morgan. AnFP

Cities and Thrones and Powers. Kipling. *Fr.* Puck of Pook's Hill. CoEV; FaBoEn; GTBS-D; GTML; MoVE; PoEL-5; POTE; POTT; PoVP; SeCeV; ShBV-4; TwCV; ViPP
Cities, The, are mine! The Devil's Meditation. Michael Sweany. MaRV
Cities, The, send to one another saying: "My sons are mad." Vala; or, The Four Zoas. Blake. ViBoPo
Citizen. Louis Grudin. NePA
Citizen. Kondrati Ryleyev, *tr. fr. Russian by* Babette Deutsch. TrRV
Citizen, myself, or personal friend. More Sonnets at Christmas, IV. Allen Tate. LiTM; WaP
Citizen of the World. Joyce Kilmer. OQP; QP-1; StJW
Citizen Turned Gentleman, The, *sel.* Edward Ravenscroft.
I Sigh All the Night. SeCL
Citizens Defend Angiers, The. Shakespeare. *Fr.* King John, II, i. BHV
Citizenship; Form 8889512, Sub-section Q. G. K. Chesterton. OxBoLi
City, The. "Æ." WGRP
City, The. Richard Burton. *See* City of the Dead, The.
City, The. C. P. Cavafy, *tr. fr. Modern Greek by* Rae Dalven. MoGP
City. Langston Hughes. FaPON
(City; San Francisco.) GoSL
City, The. Ben Maddow. LiTM (1946 ed.); WaP
City, The. Frank Mason North. *See* Christ in the City.
City. Jaime Torres Bodet, *tr. fr. Spanish by* Rolfe Humphries. AnCL
City, The. Charles Hanson Towne. *Fr.* Manhattan, XIV. CV; SBMV
City, The, *sels.* Arthur Upson.
Agamede's Song. LBMV; LEAP
Euchenor Chorus. LBMV
City about whose brow the north winds blow. Ottawa. Duncan Campbell Scott. VA
City Afternoon, A. Edith Wyatt. LiTM (1946 ed.); NP
City and Country Life. William Cowper. *Fr.* The Task. CoBE
City and Solitude, *sel.* Kostes Palamas, *tr. fr. Modern Greek by* Rae Dalven
Rose-Fragrance. MoGP
City and the Sea, The. Longfellow. PEOR
City and the Trucks, The. Dorothy Brown Thompson. BrR
City Asleep. Maurice Lesemann. NP
City asleep, avenue bare. Tryst. Stepan Petrovich Shchipachev. RuPo
City Bells. "Thomas Ingoldsby." *Fr.* The Ingoldsby Legends: The Lay of St. Aloy's. LPS-2
City Bird. Theda Kenyon. PoMa
City Birds. Spud Johnson. PoMa
City Butterfly, A. Victor Starbuck. LS
City by Night. Vittorio Sereni, *tr. fr. Italian by* Glauco Cambon. OnPM
City charts. white-veined on crackling blue, The. Vacant Lots. Molly Anderson Haley. BAP
City Child, The. Tennyson. BoTP; OTPC; PRWS
City child, A, rooms are to him no mere places to live in. Ten Years Old. Louis Untermeyer. TSW; TSWC
City Childhood. Selma Robinson. PIAE
City Church, The. "E. H. K." WGRP
City Clerk, The. Thomas Ashe. OBVV
City clocks point out the hours, The. Belfast; High Street. Padraic Colum. NePoAm
City closet is no place for you, A. Old Shoes. Gertrude Ryder Bennett. DDA
City Dead-House, The. Walt Whitman. IAP
City Dwellers all complain, The. August. Michael Lewis. GoTP
City Financier, The/ walks in the gardens. Thrushes. Humbert Wolfe. MBP; MoBrPo; TwCV
City Girl. Maxwell Bodenheim. HBMV
City had withdrawn into itself, The. Christmas Trees. Robert Frost. PoTo
City, The, has fallen; only the hills and rivers remain. Advent of Spring. Tu Fu. WhP
City has streets, The. City Streets and Country Roads. Eleanor Farjeon. BrR; TiPo
City Heiress, The; or, Sir Timothy Treat-All, *sel.* Aphra Behn.
Jolly Swain, A. DiM
City, I never told you yet. To Sydney. Louise Mack. BoAu
City in the Sea, The. Poe. AA; AmP; AmPo; AmPP; AnAmPo; AnEnPo, AnFE; APA; APW; BAP; BLV; BoLiVe; CaAE; CBOV; CoAnAm; CoBA; CoV; FaBoEn; GTBS-D; HBV; IAP; LEAP; LiTA; MOAP; NePA; OBAV; OnAP; OxBA; PoE; PoEL-4; PoFS; ReaPo; RiBV; RO; SPP; TCAP; TrGrPo; ViBoPo; WHA
(Doomed City, The.) OBRV
City is cutting a way, The. New York. Arthur Guiterman. PaA
City is of Night, The; perchance of death. James Thomson. *Fr.* The City of Dreadful Night, I. AnFE; BMEP; EnLit; LiTB; NBE; OAEP; PoEL-5; POTT; PYM; ViBoPo; ViP
City is silent, The. Dawn over the Mountains. Tu Fu. OnPC
City Lieutenant, The. Gustaf Fröding, *tr. fr. Swedish by* Charles W. Stork. AnSL
City-Life. D. H. Lawrence. OAEP (2d ed.)
City Lights. Karle Wilson Baker. PCD
City Lights. Rachel Field. FaPON; GFA
City Magistrate. Defoe. *Fr.* Reformation of Manners. BeR
City Match, The, *sel.* Jasper Mayne.
"We show no monstrous crocodile," *fr.* III, ii. CenL
City Mouse and the Garden Mouse, The. Christina Rossetti. *Fr.* Sing-Song. BoChLi; BoTP; FaBoBe; FaPON; GoTP; HBV; HBVY; MeMeAg; MPB; OTPC; PPL; StVeCh; UTS
(City Mouse and the Country Mouse, The.) PCH
("City mouse lives in a house, The.") SUS; TiPo
City Nature. Esther Pinch. PoMa
City of Baltimore, The, with music. Unknown. ShS
City of Beggars, The. Alfred Hayes. WaP
City of Dreadful Night, The. James Thomson. DaM; EmBrPo; PoVP; VLEP
Sels.
"Anear the centre of that northern crest," XXI. BMEP; FaBoEn; NBE; OAEP; POTT
(Melancholia, 7 *sts.*) AnEnPo; MBP
(Melancholia: "Baffled and beaten back," 5 *sts.*) CoEV
(Melencholia.) VA
"As I came through the desert thus it was," *fr.* IV. EPP, *abr.*; LiTB; LiTG; MBP, *abr.*; PoEL-5
(Nightmare, *abr.*) BLV
"Because he seemed to walk with an intent," II. EnLit
"Chambers of the mansions of my heart, The," *fr.* X. LEAP
"City is of Night, The; perchance of Death," I. AnFE; BMEP; EnLit; LiTB; NBE; OAEP; PoEL-5; POTT; PYM, *abr.*; ViBoPo; ViP
"He stood alone within the spacious square," IV. AnFE; EnLi-2; POTT
"How the moon triumphs through the endless nights!" XVII. BMEP; GTML; GTSL
"I sat me weary on a pillar's base," XX. OAEP; POTT; ViP
(Sphinx, The.) EPN
"Large glooms were gathered in the mighty fane," XIV. OAEP; POTT; ViP
"Of all things human which are strange and wild," XIII. LoBV (XIII–XIV); ViBoPo
"Our isolated units could be brought," XII. ViP
Proem: "Lo, thus, as prostrate, 'In the dust I write.'" EnLit; GoTS; OAEP; POTT; ViBoPo; ViP
City of Christmas, here, I love your season. Christmas Eve; Market Square. P. K. Page. TwCaPo
City of Falling Leaves, The. Amy Lowell. 1777, II. MAPA; SUS; TCPD; TiPo; TwAmPo
City of God. Samuel Johnson. AA; MaRV; WGRP
City of God. R. H. Long. BoAu
City of God, The. Francis Turner Palgrave. MaRV; WGRP
City of God, The. Henry B. Robins. MaRV
City of God, The. Anna Louise Strong. MaRV
City of God, how broad and far. City of God. Samuel Johnson. AA; MaRV; WGRP
City of Light, The. Felix Adler. *See* Hail! the Glorious Golden City.
City of mist and rain and blown grey spaces. Edinburgh. Alfred Noyes. HBV
City of Monuments. Muriel Rukeyser. NAMP
City of Our Hopes, The. Felix Adler. *See* Hail! the Glorious Golden City.
City of Prague, The. William Jeffery Prowse. CenHV
City of Ships. Walt Whitman. APW
City of Slaughter, The. Hayyim Nahman Bialik, *tr. fr. Hebrew by* A. M. Klein. TrJP
City of the Dead, The. Richard Burton. HBV; LEAP
(City, The.) LBAP
City of the End of Things, The. Archibald Lampman. BoCaPo; VA
City of the Plague, The, *sel.* Pushkin, *tr. fr. Russian by* V. de S. Pinto.
Song in Time of Plague. BoRS
City of the Soul, The. Lord Alfred Douglas. HBMV; LBBV, *abr.*
"Each new hour's passage is the acolyte," *sel.* BMEP; MBP; MoBrPo (1942 ed.); WHA
City plum is not a plum, A. Christina Rossetti. *Fr.* Sing-Song. EmBrPo
City Priest. Anne Higginson Spicer. OQP; QP-1
City Rain. Rachel Field. TiPo
City Rain. Lola Mallet. DDA
City Roofs. Charles Hanson Towne. BLPA; CV; SBMV
(Roof-Tops.) PoToHe
City; San Francisco. Langston Hughes. *See* City.

City Show, The. Eleanor Farjeon. GaP
City Shower, A. Swift. *See* Description of a City Shower.
City sleeps in its unconcern, but the highways are awake, The. The City and the Trucks. Dorothy Brown Thompson. BrR
City Song, A. John Hanlon Mitchell. CaP; OCL
City stirred about me softly as air, The. The Hours of the Day. George Dillon. NP
City-Storm. Harold Monro. MBP; MoBrPo
City Streets and Country Roads. Eleanor Farjeon. BrR; TiPo
City to which its prince turns not in compassion, sighs itself away into silence, The. Lamentation of Nippur. *Unknown.* LiTW
City Tramp, The, *sel.* T. P. Cameron Wilson.
In the City. MW
City Tree, The. Isabella Valancy Crawford. CaP; OCL
City Trees. Vere Dargan OQP; PGD; QP-2
City Trees. Edna St. Vincent Millay. FaPON; LaNeLa; PoMa
City Trees. Anderson M. Scruggs. PoMa
City Voice, A. Theodosia Garrison. NLK; VOD
City Wall, The. Eunice Tietjens. NP
City-weary. Edgar A. Guest. NLK
City whence I come, The. The Democratic Way; Pro and Con. Euripides. *Fr.* Suppliants. GrR
City which thou seest no other deem, The. Rome. Milton. *Fr.* Paradise Regained, IV. OBS
City Wife. Dorothy Livesay. BoCaPo (1943 ed.)
City's Crown, The. William Dudley Foulke. GrCo-1; HBMV; MaRV; OQP; QP-2; WGRP
Civil Irish and Wild Irish. Laoiseach Mac an Bhaird, *tr. fr. Late Middle Irish by* Kenneth Jackson. AnIL
Civil War. Friedrich von Hausen, *tr. fr. German by* F. C. Nicholson. LyMA
Civil War, The. Lucan. *See* Pharsalia.
Civil War. Charles Dawson Shanly. BlG; HBV; LPS-2; PAH
Civil War. Mark Van Doren. MoVE
Civil Wars, The, *sels.* Samuel Daniel.
"And forth h' is brought unto th' accomplishment," *fr.* II. ReIE
Death of Talbot, The, *fr.* V. EV-1
"I sing the civil wars, tumultuous broils," *fr.* I. ReIE
Richard II as Captive, *fr.* II. SiCE
Civile, res ago [*or* si ergo]. See, Will, 'Ere's a Go. *Unknown.* ChTr; WhC
Civilian for a pause of hours. Goodmorning with Light. John Ciardi. WaP
Civilization. Stanton A. Coblentz. OQP; QP-2
Civilization. Yüan Chieh, *tr. fr. Chinese by* Arthur Waley. LiTW
Civilized, crying how to be human again: this will tell you how. Signpost. Robinson Jeffers. GoYe; ViBoPo
Civitas Dei. Edith Lovejoy Pierce. MaRV
Clack your beaks you cormorants and kittiwakes. A Canticle to the Waterbirds. Brother Antoninus. NeAP
Clad All in White. Abraham Cowley. *Fr.* The Mistress. SeCV-1
Clad in thick mail he stumbles down the floor. Divers. Robert Haven Schauffler. TBM
Claim That Has the Canker on the Rose, The. Joseph Plunkett. OxBI
Claim to Love. Giovanni Battista Guarini, *tr. fr. Italian by* Thomas Stanley. AWP
Claimed by our patriarchs to have survived. Lament for a Quince Tree Uprooted by the Storm. Tu Fu. WhP
Claiming a Second Kiss by Desert. Ben Jonson. *Fr.* A Celebration of Charis. LiTL
Claiming the Promise. Charles Wesley. BePJ
Clair de Lune. Ford Madox Ford. BMEP
Clair de lune. Luis Palés Matos, *tr. fr. Spanish by* Donald Devenish Walsh. AnCL
Clair de lune. Paul Verlaine, *tr. fr. French by* Arthur Symons. AWP; LiA
(Moonlight.) AnFP, *tr. by* Muriel Kittel; TrFP, *tr. by* Alan Conder
Clais. Sappho, *tr. fr. Greek by* H. De Vere Stacpoole. GrR
Clam, A. *Unknown. See* Nirvana.
Clam Man, The. Burke Boyce. DDA
Clamor of cannon dies down, the furnace mouth of the battle is silent, The. Lincoln. John Gould Fletcher. CMP; HBMV; MAP; MOAP; PFE; SBMV; SP; VOD
Clancy of The Overflow. Andrew Barton Paterson. BoAu
"Clang!" goes the high-framed, feather-tufted gong. "Tan Ta Ra, Cries Mars . . ." David Wagoner. NePoAm-2
Clann Cartie. James Stephens. *See* Wave of Cliona, The.
Clap, clap handies. Mother Goose. PPL
Clap hands, clap hands. *Unknown.* OxNR
Clap hands, Daddy comes. *Unknown.* OxNR
Clap hands, Daddy's coming. *Unknown.* OxNR
Clap hands with festal joy, O holy people. Hymn for Laudes; Feast of Our Lady of Good Counsel. *Unknown.* ISi
Clapping blackness of the wings of pointed cormorants, the great indolent planes, The. The Cycle. Robinson Jeffers. TBM
Clapping her platter stood plump Bess. Chicken. Walter de la Mare NeMA; TiPo
Cl'ar de Kitchen, *with music* *Unknown.* SoAF
Clarastella Distrusting. Robert Heath. SeCL
Clare Coast. Emily Lawless. GTIV; OxBI
Clare de Kitchen. *Unknown.* BLPA
Clarel, *sels.* Herman Melville.
Epilogue: "If Luther's day expand to Darwin's year." AnAmPo; APW; ImOP; LA
Of Rome. OxBA
On Mammon. OxBA
Seedsmen of Old Saturn's Land. AmPP (3d ed.)
Ungar and Rolfe. OxBA
Clare's Dragoons. Thomas Osborne Davis. OnYI
Clari, the Maid of Milan, *sel.* John Howard Payne.
Home, Sweet Home. AA; APW; BAV; BLPA; BoHiPo; FaBoBe; FaFP; HBV; LEAP; LPS-1; MaRV; NeHB; OBAV; OlF; OnHT; OTPC; PECK; TCAP; TreF; WBLP
Claribel. Tennyson. AtBAP; BPN; EmBrPo; PoVP; ViPo; VLEP
Claribel's Way to God, *sel.* Hilda Doolittle ("H. D.").
"I met a friar in a hood." MeRV
Clarimonde. Théophile Gautier, *tr. fr. French by* Lafcadio Hearn. AWP; JAWP; UnW; WBP
Clarion. Thomas O. Mordaunt. *See* Sound, Sound the Clarion.
Clarion-Call, The. *Unknown.* BLRP
Clark Colven and his gay ladie. Clerk Colvill (A *vers.*). *Unknown.* ESPB
Clark Sanders and May Margret. Clerk Saunders. *Unknown.* BaBo; ESPB (A *vers.*)
Clash the cymbals! The Chant of the Woman. Grace Blackburn. CPG
Clasp her and hold her and love her. At Sunset. Louis V. Ledoux. HBV
Clasp you the God within yourself. The Last Round. Anna Wickham. MBP; MoBrPo
Clasped, dear girl, in your embrace. Vanity of Kissing. Bonefonius. OnPM
Clasping of Hands. George Herbert. PoEL-2
Classic Case, A. Gilbert Sorrentino. NeAP
Classic Encounter. "Christopher Caudwell." POTE
Classic Ode, A. Charles Battell Loomis. NA
Classic Scene. William Carlos Williams. AmP; OxBA; WoL
Classic Waits for Me, A. E. B. White. WhC
Classical Criticism. George Lynde Richardson. AA
Classroom in October. Elias Lieberman. GoYe
Claud Halcro's Song: "And you shall deal the funeral dole." Sir Walter Scott. *Fr.* The Pirate, *ch.* 23. BHV; EBSV
(And You Shall Deal the Funeral Dole.) BSV
Clavering. E. A. Robinson. CrMA; HBMV; OxBA
Clavichord, The. May Sarton. UnS
Clay. E. V. Lucas. HBV
Clay Hills. Jean Starr Untermeyer. CP; HBMV; MAP; MoAmPo (1942 ed.); NeMA; NP; NV; PCD
Clean. Dorothy Mitchell. CAG
Clean as a lady. Tulip. Humbert Wolfe. BLV; MBP; MoBrPo; NP; TSW
Clean as the ivoried hoofs of antelopes. Mountain Dawn. Gene Boardman Hoover. StaSt
Clean birds by sevens. A Charm against a Magpie. *Unknown.* ChTr
Clean Clara. William Brighty Rands. BOHV; HBV; HBVY
Clean Clothes. Rafael Arévalo Martínez, *tr. fr. Spanish by* Muna Lee. AnCL
Clean Curtains. Carl Sandburg. TCAP; WoL
Clean de ba'n and sweep de flo'. Uncle Eph's Banjo Song. James Edwin Campbell. BANP
Clean Hands. Austin Dobson. AOAH; TrPWD
Clean is the autumn wind. Verses. Li Po. WhP
Clean Platter, The. Ogden Nash. BOHV
Clean the spittoons, boy. Brass Spittoons. Langston Hughes. BANP; MAP; MoAmPo; NeMA
Cleaning Ship. Charles Keeler. EtS
Cleaning the Candelabrum. Siegfried Sassoon. HaMV
Cleanliness. Charles *and* Mary Lamb. OTPC (1923 ed.); PRWS
Cleanly rush of the mountain air, The. The Dead Knight. John Masefield. CH
Cleanly, sir, you went to the core of the matter. A Correct Compassion. James Kirkup. ChMP; FaBoTw; ImOP; SeCePo
Cleanse [*or* Light] with the burning log of oak. Yule-Tide Fires. *Unknown.* PCD; PCH; SDH
Cleansing. Heinrich Suso Waldeck, *tr. fr. German by* George N. Schuster. CAW
Cleansing Fires. Adelaide Anne Procter. WGRP
Cleanthes of Andros, The. To a Greek Ship in the Port of Dublin. William Bedell Stanford. NeIP

Cleanthus Trilling. Edgar Lee Masters. *Fr.* The New Spoon River. LEAP
("Urge of the seed, The.") OQP; QP-1
Clear after Rain. Tu Fu, *tr. fr. Chinese by* Kenneth Rexroth. OnPC
Clear air and grassy lea. Early Morning at Bargis. Hermann Hagedorn. HBV; NLK
Clear and bright is the splendor. The Day of Cold Food. Li Ch'ing-chao. OnPC
Clear and Cool. Charles Kingsley. *Fr.* The Water Babies. GN; PC
(Song of the River.) LPS-2; SN
(Tide River, The.) HBV; PoVP
Clear and Gentle Stream. Robert Bridges. POT; PoTo
(Elegy: "Clear and gentle stream!") OAEP
Clear and sweet in the crystal weather. Off Banks Peninsula. Denis Glover. AnNZ
Clear Anker [*or* Cleere Ankor], on whose silver-sanded shore. Michael Drayton. Idea, LIII, *also in* Idea's Mirrour. BrBE; TuPP
Clear as air, the western waters. The Grave of Rury. Thomas W. Rolleston. AnIL; AnIV; GTIV; IrPN; OnYI
Clear Autumn. I gaze out. Overlooking the Desert. Tu Fu. OnPC
Clear brown eyes, kindly and alert, The. Portrait. Kenneth Fearing. MoAmPo; OnAP; PoLFOT
Clear, cool, and lovely brook. Here Rules Love. Petrarch, *tr. by* Anna Maria Armi. *Fr.* Sonnets to Laura: To Laura in Life. LiA
Clear cool note of the cuckoo which has ousted the legitimate nest-holder, The. Imitation of Walt Whitman [*or* Sincere Flattery *or* Of W. W. (Americanus)]. James Kenneth Stephen. FiBHP; HBV; InMe; PA; WhC
Clear-cut, alien fault he understood, The. The Abolitionist. Robert Conquest. PoN
Clear Evening after Rain. Tu Fu, *tr. fr. Chinese by* Kenneth Rexroth. OnPC
Clear Eyes ("Clear eyes do dim at last"). Walter de la Mare. MoVE; ViBoPo
Clear eyes, sweet and serene. Madrigal. Gutierre de Cetina. AnSpL-1
Clear, fresh, and dulcet streams. Canzone 126. Petrarch, *tr. by* Leigh Hunt. Sonnets to Laura: To Laura in Life, Canzone XIV. LyPI
Clear, fresh, sweet waters. Canzone. Petrarch, *tr. by* William D. Foulke. Sonnets to Laura: To Laura in Life, Canzone XIV. LiTW
Clear frost succeeds, and thro' the blew serene. James Thomson. *Fr.* Winter. FaBoEn
Clear [*or* Cleere] had the day been from the dawn. A Fine Day [*or* The Sixth Nymphal]. Michael Drayton. *Fr.* The Muses' Elysium. BoTP; CG; GN; LoBV; OBS; OTPC; PCH; TuPP
Clear horizon on this April day, The. Meditations on a Landscape. Maxwell Bodenheim. MOAP
Clear Midnight, A. Walt Whitman. NeMA
Clear night and icy wind. The snow is red. Hialmar's Heart. Leconte de Lisle. TrFP
Clear night in harvest time, A. I Pass the Night at General Headquarters. Tu Fu. OnPC
Clear on the air, their pulsing cadence pealing. Convent Echoes. Helen Louise Moriarty. JKCP
Clear or Cloudy, Sweet as April Showering. *Unknown.* ElL; OBSC
Clear, placid Leman! thy contrasted lake. Lake Leman [*or* Calm and Storm on Lake Leman *or* Night and Storm in the Alps *or* Night on Lake Leman]. Byron. *Fr.* Childe Harold's Pilgrimage, III. LPS-2; MaPo; MCCG; TCEP
Clear ringing of a bell. New Years and Old. Maud Frazer Jackson. PGD; PSO
Clear Rock's Chisholm Trail, *with music. Unknown.* CoSo
Clear the brown path, to meet his coulter's gleam! The Ploughman. Oliver Wendell Holmes. LPS-2
Clear the field for the grand tournament of the nations! The Tournament of Man. Ernest Crosby. PGD
Clear the fountain waters glowing. Vyacheslav Ivanovich Ivanov. *Fr.* Vespers, III. TrRV
Clear—the senses bright—sitting in the black chair—Rocker. Peyote Poem, I. Michael McClure. NeAP
Clear the Track, *with music. Unknown.* SoAmSa
Clear the way and build the road! The Road. Zalman Schneour. TrJP
Clear-toned swan, to the beating of his wings, The. To Apollo. *Unknown. Fr.* Homeric Hymns. OxBG
Clear, unvexed as youth's beginning. Niagara. Nikolaus Lenau. AnGP
Clear water in a brilliant bowl. The Poems of Our Climate. Wallace Stevens. AmP; CoV; MoPo; OxBA; TrGrPo (rev. ed.)
Clear water; like the salt of childhood tears. Memory. Arthur Rimbaud, *tr. by* Wallace Fowlie. LiA; ReMP
Clear water; like the salt of childhood's tears. Memory. Arthur Rimbaud, *tr. by* Louise Varèse. AnFP
Clearer Self, The. Archibald Lampman. UnW
Clearest eyes in all the world they read, The. A Sequence of Sonnets on the Death of Robert Browning, I. Swinburne. BPN
Clearing at Dawn. Li Po, *tr. fr. Chinese by* Arthur Waley. AWP; JAWP; TrCh; WBP
Clearing for the Plough. E. G. Moll. MoAuPo
Clearing in the forest. The Lincoln Child. James Oppenheim. GA; HBMV; MAP; MoAmPo (1942 ed.)
Clearing the Fields. *Unknown, tr. fr. Chinese.* WhP
"Clearly the rest I behold of the dark-ey'd Sons of Achaia." Helen on the Walls of Troy Looking for Her Brothers [*or* Helen Seeks for Her Brothers]. Homer. *Fr.* The Iliad, III. CBOV; LiA
Cleary Pioneer, A. Fred Crewe. DDA; PaA
Cleator Moor. Norman Nicholson. FaBoTw; NeBP
Cleavage. Louise Townsend Nicholl. NePoAm
Cleave ever to the sunnier side of doubt. Cling to Faith. Tennyson. *Fr.* The Ancient Sage. OQP; QP-1
Cleburne. *Unknown.* BIG
Cleere Ankor, on whose silver-sanded shore. *See* Clear Anker, on whose silver-sanded shore.
Cleere had the day bin from the dawne. *See* Clear had the day been from the dawn.
Clefs de la prison, Les, *with music. Unknown.* OuSiCo
Cleitagoras. Leonidas of Tarentum. *See* Dead Shepherd, The.
Clemency. Ibn al-Hajj, *tr. fr. Arabic by* A. J. Arberry. MooP
Clenched little hands like crumpled roses. Slumber-Songs of the Madonna, VI. Alfred Noyes. BOL
Cleombrotus. Callimachus, *tr. fr. Greek by* G. M. Young. GrL
(Zealous Platonist, The, *tr. by* Walter Leaf.) GrR
Cleomenes, *sel.* Dryden.
No, No, Poor Suffering [*or* Suff'ring] Heart, *fr.* II, ii. AtBAP; GTBS-W; LiTB; LiTG; LiTL; LoBV; ViBoPo
(One Happy Moment.) OBEV (new ed.)
(Song: "No, no, poor suff'ring heart no change endeavour.") CEP; SeCV-2; TCEP
Cleon. Robert Browning. GEPC; OAEP; PoVP; TwCrTr; ViPo; ViPP; VLEP
Greece, *br. sel.* OtMeF
Cleon and I. Charles Mackay. LPS-3; MaRV; PTA-2
Cleon the poet (from the sprinkled isles). Cleon [*or* Greece]. Robert Browning. GEPC; OAEP; OtMeF; PoVP; TwCrTr; ViPo; ViPP; VLEP
Cleone to Aspasia. Walter Savage Landor. *Fr.* Pericles and Aspasia, CXIX. BPN
Cleonicos. Edward Cracroft Lefroy. Echoes from Theocritus, XXVII. AWP; JAWP; WBP
Cleopatra, *sels.* Samuel Daniel.
Chorus: "Behold what furies still." LoBV
Chorus: "Then thus we have beheld." OBSC
O Fearfull, Frowning Nemesis. PoEL-2
Cleopatra. Dryden. *Fr.* All for Love. BeR
Cleopatra. Albert Samain, *tr. fr. French by* F. S. Flint. MiFP
Cleopatra ("The barge she sat in"). Shakespeare. *Fr.* Antony and Cleopatra, II, ii. CoEV; KN; LiTB; LiTG; LiTL; LPS-2
("Barge she sat in, like a burnish'd throne, The.") BoHiPo
(Cleopatra and Her Barge.) TreF
(Cleopatra's Barge.) PoFS; TrGrPo
(Enobarbus' Description of Cleopatra.) PreP
(From "Antony and Cleopatra.") LEAP
(Royal Barge, A.) BCEP
Cleopatra. William Wetmore Story. AA; BAP; BAV; OBAV
Cleopatra. Swinburne. BeLS
Cleopatra and Antony. Dryden. *Fr.* All For Love. FiP
Cleopatra and Her Barge. Shakespeare. *See* Cleopatra.
Cleopatra Dying. Thomas Stephens Collier. BLPA; FaBoBe; NeHB
Cleopatra Embarking on the Cydnus. Thomas Kibble Hervey. BCEP
Cleopatra, who thought they maligned her. Limerick. Newton Mackintosh. LiBL; NA
Cleopatra's Barge. Shakespeare. *See* Cleopatra.
Cleopatra's Death. Shakespeare. *See* Death of Cleopatra.
Cleopatra's Lament. Shakespeare. *Fr.* Antony and Cleopatra, V, ii. UnPo
Clergyman, in want, A. Limerick [*or* Rhymes]. Ronald Arbuthnott Knox. OxBoLi; WhC
Clergyman out in Dumont, A. Limerick. Morris Bishop. LiBL; WhC
Clerical Oppressors. Whittier. PAH
Clerihews, *sels.* E. C. Bentley.
"Among the contemporaries of Shakespeare." OnPP
"'I quite realized,' said Columbus." FiBHP; OnPP
"It was a rule of Leonardo da Vinci's." OnPP
"It was a weakness of Voltaire's." OnPP
Clerimont's Song. Ben Jonson. *See* Simplex Munditiis.
Clerk Colvill[e]. *Unknown.* BaBo; EnSB; ESPB (A *and* B *vers.*); ViBoFo
(Clerk Colven.) OBB

Clerk of Oxenford [*or* Oxford], The. Chaucer. *Fr.* The Canterbury Tales: Prologue. CBOV; CoEV; OnPP, *mod. by* Frank Ernest Hill
Clerk Saunders (*diff. versions*). *Unknown.* AnFE; BaBo; BCEP; CoEV; EBSV; ESPB (A, B, *and* F *vers.*); EV-2; LEAP; LO; OAEP; OBB; OBEV; SeCeV; ViBoFo
(Clerk Saunders and May Margaret, *abr.*) PoD
Clerk ther was of Oxenford also, A. The Clerk of Oxenford [*or* Oxford]. Chaucer. *Fr.* The Canterbury Tales: Prologue. CBOV; CoEV; TrGrPo
Clerke of ye Wethere, Ye ("A clerke ther was"), *parody.* *Unknown.* PA
Clerkes Tale, The. Chaucer. *See* Clerk's Tale, The.
Clerks, The. E. A. Robinson. AA; AnNE; MAP; MoAB; MoAmPo; MoVE; NeMA; PoEL-5; TwP
Clerk's [*or* Clerkes] Tale, The, *sel.* Chaucer. *Fr.* The Canterbury Tales.
Chaucer's Envoy to the Story of Patient Griselda, *mod. by* W. W. Skeat. AnEnPo
(Griselda.) BHV
(Patient Griselda, *mod. by* Edward Hodnett.) PoRA
Clerk's Twa Sons o Owsenford, The. *Unknown.* BaBo; ESPB
Clevedon Church. Andrew Lang. BSV; GoTS, *abr.*
Cleveland. William Goldsmith Brown. GA; DD
Cleveland Lyke-Wake Dirge. *Unknown.* *See* Lyke-Wake Dirge, A.
Cleveland's Song: "Farewell! Farewell! the voice you hear." Sir Walter Scott. *Fr.* The Pirate, *ch.* 23. BSV
(Farewell.) LH
(Farewell! Farewell!) EBSV
Cleveland's Song: "Love wakes and weeps." Sir Walter Scott. *Fr.* The Pirate, *ch.* 23. EmBrPo
Clever man builds a city, A. Woman. *Unknown.* *Fr.* Shi King. AWP; LiTW
Clever Tom Clinch Going to Be Hanged. Swift. CEP; CoMu; SeCeV
Click, click! like an elfin musket. Photograph. James J. Galvin. JKCP (1955 ed.)
Click o' the Latch. Nancy Byrd Turner. HBMV
Clickety-clack. Song of the Train. David McCord. FaPON
Cliff, The. John Henry Boner. NoCaPo
Cliff and Cloud. Richard Savage. *Fr.* The Wanderer, V. BeR
Cliff Dwelling, The. Arthur W. Monroe. PoOW
Cliff Klingenhagen. E. A. Robinson. AmP; AmPP; CoBMV; MAP; MoAB; MoAmPo; MOAP; NeMA; TreFS; TwP
Cliff-locked port and a bluff sea wall, A. Reid at Fayal. John Williamson Palmer. PAH
Cliff Rose, The. Ernest Fewster. CaP; OCL
Cliff-Top, The. Robert Bridges. AlDL; BoTP; GFA, *st.* 1
Cliffs,/ Cliffs,/ And a twisted sea. Thorn Piece. Amy Lowell. ChMo; CMP
Cliffs of Dover, The. Felicia Dorothea Hemans. DiM
Cliffs of scarlet cloud gleam in the west. The Return. Tu Fu. LiTW; WhP
Cliffs that rise a thousand feet. Sailing Homeward. Chan Fang-sheng, *tr. by* Arthur Waley. AWP; FaBoCh; JAWP; LoGBV; TrCh; WBP
Cliffside Path, The. Swinburne. EmBrPo
Clifton. Thomas Edward Brown. POTT
Clifton Chapel. Sir Henry Newbolt. OBEV (new ed.); OBVV; TwCV
Climate of Thought, The. Robert Graves. MoAB; ViBoPo (1958 ed.)
Climb. Winifred Welles. BAP; NLK (1947 ed.); NV; PoeMoYo; TSW; TSWC; VOD
Climb at Court for me that will. Chorus [*or* The Quiet Life]. Seneca. *tr. by* Andrew Marvell. *Fr.* Thyestes. LaP; LiTW; OnPM; SeCV-1
Climb, squirrel, climb the oak hard by. Waiting. Victor Hugo. TrFP
Climb then by spiral stairways of cold thought. The Ghost in the Cellarage. John Heath-Stubbs. NeBP
Climb to Glory, *with music.* *Unknown.* SoAF
Climb to Virtue, The. Simonides, *tr. fr. Greek by* C. M. Bowra. GrL; OxBG
Climbers. Earle Birney. TwCaPo
Climbers, The. Elizabeth Jennings. NePoEA
Climbing. Thomas Edward Brown. VLEP
Climbing a Mountain. James Reeves. MoP
Climbing a Mountain. Tao-yün, *tr. fr. Chinese by* Arthur Waley. TrCh
Climbing after Knowledge. Christopher Marlowe. *See* Nature That Framed Us of Four Elements.
Climbing from the Lethal dead. Orpheus. Yvor Winters. MoVE
Climbing sun had drunk the shade, The. Blue Ghosts. Stanley Snaith. ChMP
Climbing the Ling Ying Terrace and Looking North. Po Chü-i, *tr. fr. Chinese by* Arthur Waley. TrCh
Climbing the Terrace of Kuan-yin and Looking at the City. Po Chü-i, *tr. fr. Chinese by* Arthur Waley. TrCh
Climbing through the January snow, into the Lobo canyon. Mountain Lion. D. H. Lawrence. AtBAP; HaMV; MoP; ShBV-2
Climbing to the Light. Charles Mackay. RIS
Climbing Tung Kuan Mountain. Tai Ping, *tr. fr. Chinese by* Henry H. Hart. PoHN
Climbing up the hillside beneath the summer stars. Man in Nature. William Roscoe Thayer. AA
Clime of the brave! the high heart's home. New England. George Denison Prentice. AA
Clime of the unforgotten brave! Greece. Byron. *Fr.* The Giaour. LPS-2; PoFr
Clinch Mountain. *Unknown.* *See* Rye Whiskey.
Cling to Faith. Tennyson. *Fr.* The Ancient Sage. OQP; QP-1
Cling to thy home! if there the meanest shed. Home. Leonidas of Alexandria. LPS-1
Cling together in your dust: the frost. Earthly Love. Joseph Bennett. NePA
Clinging children at their mother's knee, The. A Trial of Orthodoxy. Sir William Watson. ArmLP
Clinging to Thee. *Unknown, tr. fr. Japanese by* Lois J. Erickson. SoLD
Clinical. W. E. Henley. In Hospital, XI. TCEP
Clink, clink, clinkety-clink. The Milkman. *Unknown.* BoTP
Clink of the Ice, The. Eugene Field. InMe
Clinker, The. *Unknown.* PEDC; StVeCh (1940 ed.)
Clinking bell gaed through the town, The. Clerk Saunders and May Margaret. *Unknown.* PoD
Clio. Ernest Rhys. POTE
Clipped Wings. Lew Sarett. PoMa
Clipper, The. Thomas Fleming Day. EtS
Clipper Captain. Shirley Barker. WaKn
Clipper Loitered South, The. John Masefield. *Fr.* Dauber EtS
Clipper Ship *Dreadnaught*, The. *Unknown.* IHA
Clipper Ships. John Anderson. EtS
Clipper-Ships. John Gould Fletcher. CP
Clipper Ships, The. Edgar Lee Masters. TCAP
Clipper Ships and Captains. Rosemary Benét *and* Stephen Vincent Benét. StVeCh (1955 ed.)
Cliques and Critics. Sa'ib of Isfahan, *tr. fr. Persian by* Edward G. Browne. LiTW
Clive. E. C. Bentley. *See* Lord Clive.
Cloak, The. Violet Anderson. CaP
Cloak of Laughter. Abigail Cresson. PoToHe
Cloak of laughter I have worn, The. A Song of Pierrot. Maurice A. Hanline. LEAP
Clock, The. Baudelaire, *tr. fr. French by* Alan Conder. LO; TrFP
Clock, The. Jovan Ducic, *tr. fr. Serbo-Croatian by* Oliver Elton. LiTW
Clock. Harold Monro. MoP
Clock, The. Francis Scarfe. NeBP
Clock, The ("Tick, tock, tick, tock"). *Unknown.* MeMeAg; OTPC (1946 ed.); PCH
Clock, A ("Twelve little figures around me"). *Unknown.* OTPC (1946 ed.)
Clock-a-Clay. John Clare. FaPON; LiTB; LoBV; PoEL-4; SeCeV; ThWaDe; WHA
(Clock-o'-Clay.) BLV; PoFS; TrGrPo
Clock and Dial, The. Allan Ramsay. CBOV
Clock has struck, The! A life has paid the cost. Capt. Sally Tompkins, C.S.A. Beverley Randolph Tucker. PoP
Clock is on the stroke of six, The. Father Is Coming. Mary Howitt. FAOV; OTPC
Clock-o'-Clay. John Clare. *See* Clock-a-Clay.
Clock Shop, The. Jeannette C. Shirk. GFA
Clock stopped, A—not the mantel's. Emily Dickinson. AnFE; APA; CoAnAm; MAPA; MaPo; PoEL-5; TwAmPo
Clock Struck Twelve, The. Antonio Machado, *tr. fr. Spanish by* Eleanor L. Turnbull. TeCS
Clock Symphony. John Frederick Nims. MiAP
Clock ticks slowly, slowly in the hall, The. The Twenty-fourth of December. *Unknown.* PCH
Clocked with the sun and by his journey paced. Homestead —Winter Morning. Mary Ballard Duryee. GoYe
Clocking Hen, The. Ann Hawkshaw. *See* Clucking Hen, The.
Clocks. Louis Ginsberg. PIAE; TrJP
Clocks. Carl Sandburg. CrMA
Clocks are chiming in my heart, The. Past. John Galsworthy. HBV
Clock's Song, The. Rose Hawthorne Lathrop. AA; JKCP
Clock's untiring fingers wind the wool of darkness, The. Cradle Song. Louis MacNeice. MBP; MoAB; MoBrPo
Clock-Winder, The. Thomas Hardy. PoVP
Clockwork beings, winding out their lives. Insects. Isidor Schneider. AnAmPo; LA; TrJP
Clod, The. Edwin Curran. BAP; HBMV
Clod and the Pebble, The. Blake. *Fr.* Songs of Experience. AWP; BEL; BoLiVe; CoEV; EiPP; EM-1; EnL; EnLi-2; EnLit; EnLoPo; EnRP; EPP; FaBoEn; JAWP;

Clod and the Pebble, The (*continued*) LoBV; NBE; OAEP; OBEC; OnPM; OtMeF; TOP; TrGrPo; ViBoPo; WBP
("Love seeketh not itself to please.") LO
Clod of Clay heard the Worm's voice and raised her pitying head, The. Blake. *Fr.* The Book of Thel. LO
Clods of battlefields are red, The. Stanzas from "Elegy for Edward Thomas." Charles Dalmon. POTE
Cloe. George Granville. *See* Chloe.
Cloe, by your command, in verse I write. A Letter from Artemisa in the Town, to Cloe, in the Country. Earl of Rochester. SeCV-2
Cloe Jealous. Matthew Prior. CEP; EiPP
Cloister. Conrad Aiken. Preludes to Attitude, VI. MAP; MoAmPo; MoAB
(Preludes to Attitude.) TwAmPo
(So in the Evening, to the Simple Cloister.) LiTA
Cloister, The. George Allen. MotAn
Cloister. Mother Mary Campion. PraNu
Cloister, The. Richard Le Gallienne. LBBV
Cloister. Charles L. O'Donnell. CAW; SaFP
Cloistered. Alice Brown. AA; BAP; LEAP; MaRV
Cloistered. Mary Carolyn Davies. LEAP
Cloisters, The. Samuel Yellen. NePoAm
Clonard. Thomas S. Jones, Jr. HBMV; VOD
Clonmacnoise. Angus O'Gillan. *See* Dead at Clonmacnois, The.
Clora! Conde Bernardino de Rebolledo, *tr. fr. Spanish by* Sir John Bowring. OnPM
Clora come view my Soul, and tell. The Gallery. Andrew Marvell. MeLP; OBS; ReEn; SeEP
Clora! to church—your sad complaint. Clora! Conde Bernardino de Rebolledo. OnPM
Cloris and Mertilla. Michael Drayton. *Fr.* The Muses' Elysium. LoBV
Cloris, I cannot say your eyes. *See* Chloris, I cannot say your eyes.
Cloris I faine would try to love againe. *Unknown.* SeCSL
Cloris I wish that envye were. *Unknown.* SeCSL
Cloris [*or* Chloris], it is not thy disdaine. Song [*or* To Chloris *or* To the Tune of, in Fayth I Cannot Keepe My Fathers Sheepe]. Sidney Godolphin. BrBE; EG; MeLP; OBS; SeCL
Cloris, since my death doth com from you. *Unknown.* SeCSL
Cloris when I to thee present. *See* Chloris, when I to thee present.
Close all open things, O God! Prayer for Sophistication. Mark Turbyfill. NP
Close as the stars along the sky. Reine d'Amour. Francis Turner Palgrave. GBV (1952 ed.)
Close by a fringed banke I found. *Unknown.* SeCSL
Close by the margin of the brook. Dame Duck's First Lecture on Education [*or* Dame Duck's Lecture to Her Ducklings]. Ann Hawkshaw. DDA; OTPC (1923 ed.); SAS
Close by the threshold of a door nailed [*or* nail'd] fast. The Colubriad. William Cowper. BOHV; CG; CIV; OTPC (1923 ed.); PoC
Close by those meads, for ever crown'd [*or* crowned] with flowers. Pope. *Fr.* The Rape of the Lock. FiP; OxBoLi; WHA
Close Clan, The. Mark Van Doren. GoYe
Close gray sky, A. The Lark. Lizette Woodworth Reese. BLA; GFA; HBMV; NLK; OTPC (1946 ed.); TCAP; VOD
Close her eyes; she must not peep! By the Cradle. George Macdonald. BOL; OTPC (1946 ed.)
Close his eyes; his work is done! Dirge for a Soldier. George Henry Boker. AA; AnFE; APA; CoAnAm; DD; GA; HBV; IAP; LBAP; LEAP; LPS-2; MC; OBAV; OBVV; PaA; PAH; PAP; TCAP; WaaP
Close his eyes with the coins; bind his chin with the shroud. Stephen Vincent Benét. *Fr.* Death-Chant of the Centaurs. LEAP
Close in a cage a bird I'll keep. Riddles, 2. *Unknown.* CoBE
Close in the hollow bank she lies. The Stockdove. Ruth Pitter. HaMV; SeCePo
Close not thy hand upon the innocent joy. Forbearance. "Owen Meredith." PCD
Close now thine eyes, and rest secure. A Good-Night. Francis Quarles. EPS (1942 ed.); OBS; SeCL; SeEP; TrGrPo; TriL
Close of Day, The. Wesley Curtwright. CDC
Close on the edge of a midsummer dawn. A Shadow of the Night. Thomas Bailey Aldrich. AA
Close ranks and ride on! The Riderless Horse. Harold Trowbridge Pulsifer. BAP; MaRV; PC
Close the high-stooped houses stood. Street of Cats. William Rose Benét. PoC
Close thine [*or* thy] eyes, and sleep secure. On a Quiet Conscience. Charles I. King of England. CH; PCD
Close to the breast of night. Life of Life. Johannes Edfelt. LiTW
Close to the frontier of Eternity is my patrimony. The Migrant. Donald C. Babcock. NePoAm
Close to the heart that is throbbing in love for you. A Lullaby. Willis Walton Franz. BOL
Close to the road's impurity. A Primrose by the Wayside. Anna Bunston de Bary. MaRV
Close to the Sacred Heart, it nestles fair. Ladye Chapel at Eden Hall. Eleanor C. Donnelly. JKCP
Close to the sea—so far. Aquarium. Eugenio Florit. TwSpPo
Close to the sod. The Snowdrop. Anna Bunston de Bary. BoTP; HBMV; MaRV
Close under here, I watched two lovers once. The Beaches, VI. "Robin Hyde." AnNZ
Close up the casement, draw the blind. Shut Out That Moon. Thomas Hardy. ChMo; CMP; MoVE; PoD; ViBoPo
Close up the Ranks. Edward S. Van Zile. PEDC
Close-wrapped in living thought I stand. All Souls' Day. Siegfried Sassoon. QS
Close Your Eyes! Arna Bontemps. CDC; PoNe
Close your eyes and lose yourself in darkness. Oblivion. Octavio Paz. AnCL
Closed Door, The. Theodosia Garrison. BLPA; PoToHe
Closed eyes can't see the white roses. Give Them the Flowers Now. Leigh M. Hodges. PTA-2; WBLP
Closed for Good. Robert Frost. MoAmPo (1950 ed.)
Closed in death lies Durandarte. Death of Durandarte [*or* Montesinos and Durandarte]. *Unknown.* LyMA; TeCS
Closely to my heart I hold thee. A Song of Mary. Agnes H. Begbie. BOL
Closer the curtain. Still the sun is flame. With the Caravan. Ina Donna Coolbrith. BAP
Closes and courts and lanes. Song. John Davidson. HBV; PoVP
Closest to men, thou pitying Son of Man. To Jesus of Nazareth. Frederic Lawrence Knowles. TrPWD
Closing Address. *Unknown.* MeMeAg
Closing Doxology, The. Psalms, CL, Bible, *O.T.* (Smith-Goodspeed *tr.*). MaRV
Closing Lines of "Prometheus Unbound." Shelley. *See* Promethean Ideal, The.
Closing of the Rodeo, The. William Jay Smith. NePoEA
Closing Prayer. Johnstone G. Patrick. TrPWD
Closing Scene, The. Thomas Read. AA; HBV; LBAP; LPS-2; SN
Closing the Doors. Irene Pettit McKeehan. MaRV; OQP; QP-1
Closing Year, The. George Denison Prentice. LPS-3
Clote, The (Water-Lily). William Barnes. GTBS-D; PoEL-4
Cloth Cap, The. *Unknown, tr. fr. Chinese.* WhP
Clothed in yellow, red, and green. *Unknown.* OxNR
Clothed in your filmy muslin gown. The Manchy. Charles Marie Leconte de Lisle. LiA
Clother of the lily, Feeder of the sparrow. A Prayer [*or* They Toil Not neither Do They Spin]. Christina Rossetti. OBVV; TrPWD
Clothes. Abbie Farwell Brown. PPL
Clothes Do but Cheat and Cozen Us. Robert Herrick. ALV; LoPS
Clothes-Line, The. Charlotte Druitt Cole. BoTP
Clothes make no sound when I tread ground. A Riddle. *Unknown.* ChTr
Clothing's New Emperor, The. Donald Finkel. NePoEA
Clotted and curdled with light the water gleamed. The Grey Washer by the Ford. Sean Jennett. MeRV
Cloud, The. Salvador Díaz Mirón, *tr. fr. Spanish by* Alice Stone Blackwell. PoFr
Cloud, The. Oliver Herford. BOHV
Cloud. Samuel Hoffenstein. AnAmPo; LA
Cloud, The. Josephine Preston Peabody. LBMV; OBAV
Cloud, The. Pushkin, *tr. fr. Russian by* C. M. Bowra. BoR
Cloud, The. Shelley. ATP; BCEP; BEL; BLV; BoLiVe; BPN; CBOV; ChER; EM-2; EmBrPo; EnL; EnLi-2; EnLit; EnRP; EPN; EPP; ERP; EV-4; FaPON; GEPC; GN; GTBS-W; HBV; ImOP, *abr.*; InP; KN; LiTB; LiTG; LPS-3; MCCG; MPB; MW; OAEP; OBAV; OBRV; OHFP; OTPC; OuHeWo; PCH, *much abr.*; PIAE; PoE; PoEL-4; PTA-1; PYM; RAR, *br. sel.*; ReaFo; RG; RIS, *sts.* 1-2; SeCeV; SN; StaSt, *br. sel*; TCEP; TOP; TreF; TrGrPo; TVSH; TyEnPo; ViBoPo
(Fragments from the Old Masters: The Cloud, *br. sel.*) PoF
Cloud, The. Sara Teasdale. POT; PoTo
Cloud and Wind. Dante Gabriel Rossetti. The House of Life, XLIV. PoVP; ViPo
Cloud assumes fantastic shapes, The. Cloud. Samuel Hoffenstein. AnAmPo; LA
Cloud-backed heron will not move, The. The Heron. Vernon Watkins. ChMP; UnPo (3d ed.)
Cloud-bank lies in a red-gold ring, The. Judith Remembers. Maxwell Anderson. *Fr.* Judith of Minnewaulken. WHA

Cloud by Day, The. Cædmon (?), *tr. fr. Anglo-Saxon by* Benjamin Thorpe. *Fr.* Exodus. TCEP
Cloud-capp'd towers, the gorgeous palaces, The. Our Revels Now Are Ended. Shakespeare. *Fr.* The Tempest, IV, i. MaRV
Cloud Confines, The. Dante Gabriel Rossetti. BEL; EmBrPo; EnLi-2; TCEP; TOP; VLEP
Cloud Country. James Merrill. NePoEA
Cloud doth gather, the green wood roar, The. Thekla's Song. Schiller. *Fr.* The Piccolomini. AWP; JAWP; WBP
Cloud Fantasies, I. Christian Morgenstern, *tr. fr. German by* Babette Deutsch *and* Avrahm Yarmolinsky. OnPM
Cloud House, The. Adrian Mott. GaP
Cloud is hide de moon, but dere's plaintee light above, De. Johnnie's First Moose. William Henry Drummond. CP
Cloud is the post office between continents, The. To Modigliani to Prove to Him That I Am a Poet. Max Jacob. MiCF; TrJP
Cloud lay cradled near the setting sun, A. The Evening Cloud. "Christopher North." HBV; LPS-2
Cloud-maidens that float on forever. Song of the Clouds. Aristophanes. *Fr.* The Clouds. AWP; GrPo
Cloud-Messenger, The, *sel.* Kalidasa, *tr. fr. Sanskrit by* Arthur W. Ryder.
"O cloud, the parching spirit stirs thy pity." LiTW
Cloud-Mobile, The. May Swenson. GoTP
Cloud moved close, A. The Bulk of the wind shifted. The Visitant. Theodore Roethke. UnPo (3d ed.)
Cloud of Carmel, The. Jessica Powers. ISi
Cloud of dust on the long, white road, A. The Teams. Henry Lawson. BoAu; NeLNL
Cloud of Unknowing, The. Philip Murray. NePoAm-2
Cloud-piercing mountains! Chance and Change. Fest. Puritatis. Aubrey Thomas De Vere. *Fr.* May Carols. PoVP
Cloud possessed the hollow field, A. The High Tide at Gettysburg. Will Henry Thompson. AA; BeLS; BlG; BLPA; FaBoBe; HBV; LBAP; LEAP; MC; MDAH; PaA; PAH; PFY; PoFr; TreFS
Cloud-puffball, torn tufts, tossed pillows. That Nature Is a Heraclitean Fire and of the Comfort of the Resurrection. Gerard Manley Hopkins. AtBAP; CoBMV; FaBoMo; LiTB; MaPo; MoAB; MoPo; MoVE; OAEP (2d ed.); PoEL-5; ViP; ViPP
Cloud-riders leap for Normandy. On the Cliff. Hal Summers. ChMP
Cloud storming over cloud. Winds and rain. The Ballad of the Holy Evening Bread. Itzik Manger. OnCuPl
Clouded vision, light obscure. Such Is Love [*or* Love]. Rodrigo Cota de Maguaque. AnSpL-1; OnPM
Clouded with snow. Winter. Walter de la Mare. OBMV
Cloudless night like this, A. A Walk after Dark. W. H. Auden. MaPo
Clouds. Charles R. Angell. LPS-1
Clouds, The, *sels.* Aristophanes, *tr. fr. Greek.*
Old Education, The, *tr. by* George Allen *and* T. F. Higham. OxBG
(Education vs. Fads, *longer sel., tr. by* Benjamin Bickley Rogers.) GrR
"So now let them do with me just what they will," *tr. by* B. D. Walsh. GrPo
Socrates' Experiments, *tr. by* Thomas Mitchell. OxBG
(Lampoon; in the School of Socrates, *longer sel., tr. by* Benjamin Bickley Rogers.) GrR
Song of the Clouds. AWP, *tr. by* Oscar Wilde; GrL, *tr. by* T. F. Higham; OxBG, *tr. by* T. F. Higham
(Chorus of Clouds, *tr. by* Benjamin Bickley Rogers.) GrR
(Chorus of the Clouds, *tr. by* T. F. Higham.) LiTW
("Cloud-maidens that float on forever," *tr. by* Oscar Wilde.) GrPo
Clouds. Norman Ault. HBVY
Clouds. Rupert Brooke. BrBE; GTSL; MoVE; OBEV (new ed.); OBMV; POTE
Clouds. John Jay Chapman. EtS
Clouds, The. William Croswell. AA
Clouds. W. H. Davies. TCEP
Clouds. Gerardo Diego, *tr. fr. Spanish by* Eleanor L. Turnbull. CoSP
Clouds. Frank Ernest Hill. AnAmPo; LA; PoeMoYo; VOD (1935 ed.)
Clouds. Mikhail Lermontov, *tr. fr. Russian.* BoR
Clouds, The. Lu Yu, *tr. fr. Chinese by* Pai Chwen-yu. WhP
Clouds. James Gates Percival. APW
Clouds. Frank Dempster Sherman. OnHT; PRWS; RAR; TVSH
Clouds. *Unknown. wr. at. to* Christina Rossetti. BrR; OTPC (1946 ed.); PCH; StVeCh
(White Sheep, *wr. at. to* W. H. Davies.) BoTP
("White sheep, white sheep.") TiPo
Clouds, The. William Carlos Williams. MoPo
Clouds. Helen Wing. GFA
Clouds across the Canyon. John Gould Fletcher. Grand Canyon of the Colorado, IV. TCPD
Clouds and Sky. Lancaster Pollard. NLK
Clouds are scudding across the moon, The. Storm Song. Bayard Taylor. BBV (1923 ed.); EtS; HBV
Clouds are scurrying and spinning, The. Evil Spirits. Pushkin. TrRV
Clouds are thick and darkly lower, The. Rain and Shine. Brander Matthews. PFE
Clouds, clouds, clouds in the sky. Washerwoman's Song. L. A. G. Strong. YT
Clouds, ever drifting in air. Song [*or* Chorus] of the Clouds. Aristophanes. *Fr.* The Clouds. GrL; LiTW; OxBG
Clouds grow clear, the pine-wood glooms and stills. The. A Summer Evening. Archibald Lampman. PeCV; TwCV
Clouds had made a crimson crown, The. A Moment. Mary Elizabeth Coleridge. BMEP; PoVP
Clouds Have Already Told Me, The. Jacinto Fombona Pachano, *tr. fr. Spanish by* H. R. Hays. TwSpPo
Clouds Have Left the Sky, The. Robert Bridges. CH; EG; PoVP
Clouds have spouted orange leaves, The. Fireworks at the Redentore. Rob Lyle. PoN
Clouds Have Wings, The. Gerald Gould. TCPD
Clouds here and there arisen an hour past noon. Philip Massinger. Swinburne. *Fr.* Sonnets on English Dramatic Poets. EmBrPo; PtP; VLEP
Clouds in the skies above, hastily scurrying. Clouds. Mikhail Lermontov. BoR
Clouds in the sky at twilight. The Violin Calls. Florence Randal Livesay. CaP; CPG; OCL
Clouds in the West. Augustus Julian Requier. BIG
Clouds, lingering yet, extend in solid bars. Composed by the Side of Grasmere Lake [*or* Sonnet: Composed . . .]. Wordsworth. ChER; ERP
Clouds of all hue. Chorus of Clouds. Aristophanes. *Fr.* The Clouds. GrR
Clouds of children round the trough. The Horse-Trough. Richard Hughes. AlDL
Clouds of Evening. Robinson Jeffers. MAP; MoAB; MoAmPo
Clouds of sunset, The. Moonlight on the Han River. Su T'ung-po. PoHN
Clouds or waves? Waves or clouds? A View of the Sea. Mabuchi. OnPM
Clouds spout upon her. Rain on a Grave. Thomas Hardy. CoBMV; EmBrPo; HBV; OAEP
Clouds That Are So Light, The. Edward Thomas. FaBoTw; GTML
Clouds, The, the source of rain, one stormy night. Lost in Heaven. Robert Frost. MAP; MoAmPo
Clouds upon Windless Peaks. Homer, *tr. fr. Greek by* F. L. Lucas. *Fr.* The Iliad, V. GrPE
Clouds weave a shawl, The. Garment. Langston Hughes. GoSl
Clouds were all brushed up and back, The. Snow Advent. Joseph Auslander. DDA; MoSiPe
Clouds, which rise with thunder, slake, The. All's Well. Whittier. OBVV
Clover, The. Margaret Deland. AA; PR
Clover. Lope de Vega, *tr. fr. Spanish by* Jessie Read Wendell. LiTW; TeCS
Clover. Helge Rode, *tr. fr. Danish by* Charles W. Stork. BoDS
Clover. John Banister Tabb. AA; AnAmPo; AnFE; APA; CoAnAm; LA; NLK; OBAV
Clover, dear Christ, what fragrance! Clover. Lope de Vega. LiTW; TeCS
Clover for Breakfast. Frances Frost. StVeCh (1955 ed.)
Clovers, The. Jean Garrigue. MoPo
Clown, The. Tefcros Anthias, *tr. fr. Modern Greek by* Rae Dalven. MoGP
Clown, The. Margaret E. Bruner. PoToHe
Clown. Henri Michaux, *tr. fr. French by* Wallace Fowlie. MiCF
Clown, The. Beatrice Redpath. CPG
Clown Pondi. Sir Osbert Sitwell. PtOT
Clownish Song, A. Thomas Nashe. *See* A-Maying, a-Playing.
Clown's Baby, The. "Margaret Vandegrift." SCC
Clown's Courtship, The. *Unknown. See* Quoth John to Joan.
Clown's Song. Shakespeare. *See* O Mistress Mine.
Cloying sea envelopes man at birth, A. Adventure. Guy Mason. CaP
Club Woman. Phyllis McGinley. QS
Clubby! thou surely art, I ween. Verses on a Cat. Charles Daubeny. CIV; HBV
Cluck, Cluck, *with music. Unknown.* FTB
Clucking Hen, The. Ann Hawkshaw. BoTP; PPL
(Clocking Hen, The.) HBVY; OTPC; SAS
Clue, The. Charlotte Fiske Bates. AA
Clues. Mary Sinton Leitch. LS
Clumps of lilies-of-the-valley, daisies too on either hand. The Bathing Children. Viktor Rydberg. AnSL
Clunton and Clunbury. A. E. Housman. A Shropshire Lad, L. BPN; PoVP; ViPo
(In Valleys of Springs of Rivers.) ViP

Clustering rainbow-grapes. Balloon Man. Jessica Nelson North. GaP
Clusters in Thy vineyard turn to gold, The. O God. Grape-gathering. Abraham Shlonsky. TrJP
Clusters of electric bulbs. The Excavation. Max Endicoff. PoMa
Clyde [*or* Clyde's] Water[s]. *Unknown. See* Mother's Malison, The; *or,* Clyde's Waters.
Clytemnestra. Aeschylus. *Fr.* Agamemnon. *See* Welcome to Agamemnon.
Clytemnestra's Dream. Aeschylus, *tr. fr. Greek by* G. M. Cookson. *Fr.* Choephoroe. GrR
Clytie. André Chénier, *tr. fr. French by* Alan Conder. TrFP
Coach. Eleanor Farjeon. PoRh
Coach,/ Carriage. *Unknown.* OxNR
Coach is at the door at last, The. Farewell to the Farm. Robert Louis Stevenson. BoChLi (1939 ed.); BoTP; FaPON; GaP; MPB; OTPC; TiPo
Coach of Life, The. Pushkin, *tr. fr. Russian by* Babette Deutsch. TrRV
(Coach of Time, The, *tr. by* C. M. Bowra.) BoRS; LiTW
(Wagon of Life, The, *tr. by* Sir Cecil Kisch.) WaL
Coal. Dorothy E. Hanbury Rowe. MM
Coal Fire. Louis Untermeyer. GoTP
Coal Man, The. Hugh Chesterman. GFA
Coal Miner's Child, The. *Unknown. See* Orphan Girl, The.
Coal-Owner and the Pitman's Wife, The. *Unknown.* CoMu
Coals of Fire. A. P. Herbert. ALV
Coarse/ jocosity/ catches the crowd. Archy Confesses. Don Marquis. *Fr.* Archy and Mehitabel. FiBHP
Coast-Guard, The. Emily Huntington Miller. PEOR
Coast Guard's Cottage, The. Elinor Wylie. BoFr
Coast hills at Sovranes Creek, The. The Place for No Story. Robinson Jeffers. CoV
Coast, The—I think it was the coast that I. Juan and Haidee; Ways of Love. Byron. *Fr.* Don Juan, II. EPN
Coast of Peru, The. *Unknown.* EtS; ShS; SoAmSa, *with music, diff. vers.*
Coast-Road, The. Robinson Jeffers. PreP
Coast-Watch, The. W. W. Gibson. NeTW
Coasters, The. Thomas Fleming Day. AA; OBAV; PFY
Coastguardsman in the Fog, The. James Schevill. FiMAP
Coasts. Beatrice Ravenel. Tidewater, I. LS
Coasts of High Barbary, The. *Unknown.* OnSP
Coastwise Lights, The. Kipling. EtS
Coat, A. W. B. Yeats. GTBS-W; LiTG; LiTM (rev. ed.); PoEL-5; TwP
Coat of Faded Gray, The. G. W. Harris. BlG
Coat of Fire, The. Edith Sitwell. FaBoTw; OAEP (2d ed.)
Coat of Mail. 'Asa the Blind, *tr. fr. Arabic by* A. J. Arberry. MooP
Coat of Mail. Ibn Abdul Ghafur, *tr. fr. Arabic by* A. J. Arberry. MooP
Coat of Squirrel fur, many dancing girls, A. Two Songs for General Chao, I. Ts'en Ts'an. WhP
Coaxing a Fairy Fiddler. Monica Shannon. BoChLi
Cobb Would Have Caught It. Robert Fitzgerald. InvP
Cobbe's Prophecies. *Unknown.* NA
Cobbled with stars. Lament for a Man Who Loved God. James Schevill. FiMAP
Cobbler. Peggy Bacon. PoMa
Cobbler, The. Eleanor Alletta Chaffee. GaP; TiPo
Cobbler, The. *Unknown.* BoTP
Cobbler and the Rich Man, The. La Fontaine, *tr. fr. French by* Elizur Wright. OuHeWo
Cobbler bent at his wooden foot, The. John Masefield. *Fr.* Reynard the Fox. ViBoPo
Cobbler, cobbler, mend my shoe. Mother Goose. OxNR; RIS; StVeCh (1940 ed.)
Cobbler in Willow Street, The. George O'Neil. HBMV; VOD
Cobbler sang from morn till night, A. The Cobbler and the Rich Man. La Fontaine. OuHeWo
Cobbler's Song, The. *At. to* George Peele, *also at. to* Charles Tilney. *Fr.* Locrine, II, iii. OBSC
(Strumbo, Dorothy, Trumpart, Cobbling Shoes.) TuPP
("We cobblers lead a merry life.") ElSeCe
Coble o Cargill, The. *Unknown.* ESPB
Coblerone I'm told, A. Mutton and Leather. *Unknown.* CoMu
Cobweb. Winifred Welles. AnAmPo; LA
Cobweb College. Kenneth Leslie. BoCaPo
Cobwebbed men slouching in deep armchairs. What the Madman Sees Looking in the Window. Kay Smith. BoCaPo (1948 ed.)
Cobwebs. E. L. M. King. BoTP
Cobwebs. *Unknown.* GFA
Cobwebs and dust have long. Hut near Desolated Pines. Alistair Campbell. AnNZ
Coca Tree, The. Jacinto Fombona Pachano, *tr. fr. Spanish by* H. R. Hays. TwSpPo
Cocaine Lil. *Unknown.* AS, *with music;* OnAP; TrAS, *with music*
(Cocaine Lil and Morphine Sue.) OxBoLi; SiTL
Cock, The. Eleanor Farjeon. RIS
(For a Cock.) PoRh
Cock, The. Rose Fyleman. UTS
Cock-a-doodle-doo! Richard R. Kirk. LS; TSWC
Cock-a-doodle-doo!/ My dame has lost her shoe. Mother Goose. BoTP; HBVY; OTPC; OxNR; RIS; StVeCh (1940 ed.)
Cock-a-doodle-doo the brass-lined rooster says. Dog. John Crowe Ransom. LiTA
Cock a doodle do! 'tis the bravest game. Cock-throwing. Martin Lluellyn. SeCL
Cock and hens. Eliza Lee Follen. SAS
Cock and his hen perching in the night, A. The Cock and the Hen. John Heywood. ReIE
Cock and the Bull, The. Charles Stuart Calverley. ALV; BOHV; InMe; LPS-3; NA; PA
Cock and the Fox, The. Chaucer. *See* Nun's Priest's Tale, The.
Cock and the Hen, The. John Heywood. ReIE
Cock and the Pearl, The. La Fontaine, *tr. fr. French by* Elizur Wright. OnPM
Cock, cock, cock, cock. Cock and Hens. Eliza Lee Follen. SAS
Cock, cock, cock, cock. *Unknown.* OxNR
Cock-Crow. Abbie Huston Evans. BAP
Cock-Crow, *sl. abr.* Robert Herrick. MyFE
Cock-Crow. Edward Thomas. EPP; MBP; MoAB; MoBrPo; NeMA; PoeMoYo; TCPD
Cock-Crow. *Unknown, tr. fr. Chinese by* E. D. Edwards. ChLP
Cockcrow. Eithne Wilkins. NeBP
Cock-Crow Song. *Unknown, tr. fr. Chinese by* Arthur Waley. LiTW; TrCh
Cock-Crow; Woodstock. Henry Morton Robinson. CAW
Cock-crowing. Henry Vaughan. AtBAP; EPS; MaPo; MePo; NBE; SeCV-1
Cock Crows, The. *Unknown, tr. fr. Chinese.* ChLP; WhP
Cock crows in the morn. The Cocks [*or* Rules of Behavior]. Mother Goose. HBVY; PPL; RIS
Cock crows once, the cock crows twice, The. The New Day. Elizabeth Selden. BoFr
Cock doth crow, The. Mother Goose. OxNR; PCH; TiPo
Cock-Fight, The. Ts'ao Chih, *tr. fr. Chinese by* Arthur Waley. TrCh
Cock had first performed and roused the dogs, The. Morning Overture; Chorus of Dogs. Pearl Strachan. GoTP
Cock has crowed, The. The Cock Crows. *Unknown.* ChLP; WhP
Cock has crowed, says the girl, The. Cock-Crow. *Unknown.* ChLP
Cock is crowing, The. The Farm Yard. Eliza Lee Follen. OTPC (1946 ed.)
Cock is crowing, The. Written in March [*or* In March *or* The Merry Month of March]. Wordsworth. AlDL; BLV; BoChLi; BoTP; BPN; CBPC; CG; DD; EmBrPo; EnRP; FaPON; GoTP; HBV; HBVY; HiLiEn; LiTG; MoShBr; MPB; MW; OnHT; OTPC; PCH; PoRL; PRWS; RG; RIS; ShBV-1; StaSt; SUS; ThWaDe; TiPo; UnPo (3d ed.); WaKn; YeAr
Cock Pheasant, The. *Unknown, tr. fr. Chinese.* WhP
Cock Robin and Jenny Wren. *Unknown.* MeMeAg
Cock Robin got up early. *Unknown.* BoTP; OxNR; RIS
Cock scratch'd up, one day, A. The Cock and the Pearl. La Fontaine. OnPM
Cock shall crow, The. Ditty. Robert Louis Stevenson. TrGrPo; VLEP
Cock stubble-searching pheasant, delicate. Pheasant. Sidney Keyes. HaMV
Cock that crew when Peter lied, The. Cock-Crow; Woodstock. Henry Morton Robinson. CAW
Cock that crowed this dawn up, heard, The. Robert D. Fitzgerald. *Fr.* Copernicus. BoAV
Cock-throwing. Martin Lluellyn. SeCL
Cock Up Your Beaver. Burns. *See* Johnnie, Cock Up Your Beaver.
Cockayne Country. Agnes Mary F. Robinson. OBVV; VA
Cockchafer hums down the rut-rifted lane, The. Young Jenny. John Clare. EnSW; ERP
Cockcrow. *See* Cock-Crow.
Cockerel Sun. Rosemary Dobson. MoAuPo
Cockerel, the Cat, and the Young Mouse, The. La Fontaine, *tr. fr. French by* Elizur Wright. WoL
Cockles and Mussels. *Unknown.* OnYI
("In Dublin's fair city, where the girls are so pretty.") LO
(Molly Malone.) MaC
Cockle-Shell and Sandal-Shoon. Herbert T. J. Coleman. CaP
Cockley Moor, Dockray, Penrith. Norman Nicholson. NeBP
Cockney Enigma on the Letter H. Horace Mayhew. PA
(Travesty of Miss Fanshawe's Enigma.) BOHV
Cockney of the North, The. Harry Graham. CenHV
Cockney Outwitted, The. *Unknown. See* Country Girl's Policy, The.
Cockpit in the Clouds. Dick Dorrance. FaPON; PoMa; TiPo
Cockroach Song. *Unknown. See* Cucaracha, La.

Cockroach stood by the mickle, The. Archy Experiences a Seizure [*or* The Hero Cockroach]. Don Marquis. *Fr.* Archys Life of Mehitabel. TSW; TSWC; WhC
Cocks, The. Boris Pasternak, *tr. fr. Russian by* J. M. Cohen. LiTW
Cocks Are Crowing. Tu Fu, *tr. fr. Chinese by* Pu Hsiang-hsing. WhP
Cocks are crowing, The. Eerily Sweet. Elizabeth J. Coatsworth. ChBR
Cocks crow in the morn. Mother Goose. GoTP; TiPo
Cocks in the north at dawn. Dawn in the Cockloft. José Juan Tablada. AnMP
Cocks of the south were crowing, The. Renaissance. Idris Davies. MoWP
Cock's on the housetop blowing his horn, The. All Busy [*or* A Busy Day *or* Summer]. *Unknown.* CBPC; OTPC (1946 ed.); PCH; RIS
Cock's on the wood pile, The. *Unknown.* OxNR
Cocksure boy in the gloom of the gilded market bends, A. Wreath Makers; Leeds Market. James Kirkup. PoN
Cocktail is a pleasant drink, The. R-e-m-o-r-s-e. George Ade. ALV; FiBHP; LauV
Cocky Doodle Doodle Doo, *with music.* *Unknown.* OuSiCo
Cocky Walkers, The. Mervyn Peake. POTE; ShBV-4
Cocoa Tree, The. Charles Warren Stoddard. AA; CAW; OBAV
Cocola: some torment. To Cocola Fernández del Castillo. José Martí. BoFr
Coconut, The. "Ande." FiBHP
Coco-Nut, A. Toson Shimazaki, *tr. fr. Japanese by* Takamichi Ninomiya *and* D. J. Enright. PoLJ
Cocooning, The. Frédéric Mistral, *tr. fr. French by* Harriet Waters Preston. *Fr.* The Mirèio. AWP; JAWP; WBP; WoL
Cod Liver Ile, *with music.* *Unknown.* OuSiCo
Coda. Dorothy Parker. BOHV; InMe; TreFS
Code, The. Robert Frost. MaC; NP; YT
Code, The. Christopher Morley. LHV
Code arrives, A; language; lingo; slang. Carl Sandburg. *Fr.* Good Morning, America. ReMP
Code of Morals, A. Kipling. OnSP
Code of the Cow Country. S. Omar Barker. PoOW
Codes. Lois Seyster Montross. HBMV
Codfish Shanty, The, *with music.* *Unknown.* SoAmSa
Cod-Fisher, The. Joseph C. Lincoln. EtS
Codicil. Mabel MacDonald Carver. GoYe
Codicil for Pvt. John Hogg's Will. Winfield Townley Scott. FiMAP
Cod-Piece That Will House, The. Shakespeare. *Fr.* King Lear, III, ii. ViBoPo
Codrus, a shepherd lusty, gay, and stout. The Fourth Egloge of Alexander Barclay. Alexander Barclay. ReIE
Coelia, *sels.* William Percy.
"If it be sin so dearly for to love thee," VII. ReIE
"It shall be said I died for Coelia," XIX. ReEn; ReIE; TuPP
(Sonnet.) ElL
"Judg'd by my goddess' doom to endless pain," I. ReIE; TuPP
"Receive these writs, my sweet and dearest friend," XX. ReIE
"Relent, my dear yet unkind Coelia," XVII. TuPP
"What is the fair to whom so long I plead?" XV. ReIE
Coelo et in Terra. Thomas Walsh. JKCP
Coelo Tonantem. Horace, *tr. fr. Latin by* Sir Edward Marsh. Odes, III, 5. SoV
Coeur de Lion to Berengaria. Theodore Tilton. AA
Coffee cups cool on the Vicar's harmonium. A Game of Consequences. Paul Dehn. FiBHP
Coffeepot Face, A. Aileen Fisher. MPB
Coffin, The. Heine, *tr. fr. German by* Louis Untermeyer. AWP; JAWP; WBP
Coffin-Worm, The. Ruth Pitter. MoBrPo; TrGrPo (1942 ed.)
Cogie o' Yill, A. Andrew Shirrefs. EBSV
Cogitabo pro Peccato Meo. William Habington. CoBE
Cogitative Bass Crank, The. Joseph B. Cawthorn. DDA
Coil of browns, A, a whirr! The Crotalus. Bailey Millard. BAP
Coil upon coil, the grave serpent holds. An Equation. Hyam Plutzik. FiMAP
Coin, The. Sara Teasdale. CP; HBMV; SP; TiPo (1952 ed.)
Coin in the Fist. Florence Kerr Brownell. GoYe
Coin of Pity, The. George Meredith. Modern Love, XLIV. VA
Coins of Love, The. John Richard Moreland. *Fr.* What of the Night? MaRV
("Arrogant kings, with envious lust.") ChIP
Cois na Teineadh. T. W. Rolleston. AnIV
Cokaygne. *Unknown.* *See* Land of Cokaigne, The.
Cold. Robert Francis. NePoAm-2
Cold. Margaret Parton. PCD
Cold!/ crack earth to scattering fragments. To a Shining Falcon. Nikolai Aseyev. RuPo
Cold, The/ with steely clutch. Winter. Adelaide Crapsey. MPB; PFE
Cold against the sky. Tanka, IV. Lewis Alexander. CDC
Cold air has scattered the people, A. Autumn. José Gorostiza. TwSpPo
Cold and brilliant streams the sunlight on the wintry banks of Seine. Funeral of Napoleon I. Sir John H. Hagarty. CaP; OCL
Cold and chill is de winter wind. Big Jim. *Unknown.* ABF
Cold and clear-cut face, why come you so cruelly meek. Tennyson. *Fr.* Maud, I. GEPC
Cold and holy oak. Rumba of the Three Lost Souls. Charles Madge. NeBP
Cold and raw. Winter Has Come. *Unknown.* CBPC
Cold and the colors of cold: mineral, shell. Cold. Robert Francis. NePoAm-2
Cold are the crabs that crawl on yonder hills. A Sonnet. Edward Lear. CenHV
Cold are the stones. War. Patric Dickinson. NeTW; SoV
Cold as a mountain in its star-pitched tent. Kinship with the Stars. George Meredith. *Fr.* Modern Love, IV. GTBS-W; LiA
Cold as the thin Marquis who bit when kissing. The Lucifer. Guy Glover. CaP
Cold blast at the casement beats, The. The Heart's Summer. Epes Sargent. AA
Cold Blast of Debt. Catullus, *tr. fr. Latin by* George Lamb. OnPM
Cold-blooded Creatures. Elinor Wylie. ChMo; ImOP
Cold Blows the Wind. John Hamilton. *See* Up in the Mornin' Early.
Cold blows the wind to my true love. The Unquiet Grave. *Unknown.* ViBoFo
Cold blows the winter wind: 'tis Love. Love at the Door. Meleager. AWP
Cold, clear, and blue, the morning heaven. The Morning Star. Emily Brontë. ChTr
Cold coiled line of mottled lead, A. The Massasauga. Hamlin Garland. AA
Cold, cold!/ Cold to-night is broad Moylurg. A Song of Winter. *Unknown.* AnIL; CH; OnYI
Cold. Cold. Cold winds and colder heart. A Knight of Ghosts and Shadows. Dunstan Thompson. NePA
Cold, cold is the north wind and rude is the blast. The Battle of Lovell's Pond. Longfellow. PAH
Cold, cold, the wind and the rain. The Wind and the Rain. *Unknown.* WhP
Cold, cold the year draws to its end. Old Chinese Poem [*or* Seventeen Old Poems, 15]. *Unknown.* AWP; BoFr; TrCh
Cold Colloquy. Patrick Anderson. Poem on Canada, V. CaP; PeCV
("What are you . .? they ask.") TwCaPo
"Cold coming we had of it, A." Journey of the Magi. T. S. Eliot. AmP; ChMo; CMP; CoBA; FaBoCh; FaBoMo; FaFP; GTBS-D; GTBS-W; InPo; LiTA; LiTM; LoGBV; MAP; MaPo; MoAB; MoAmPo; NePA; OAEP (2d ed.); OBMV; PoE; PoLFOT; PtOT; ReaPo; RiBV; ShBV-3; StJW; TrGrPo; TriL; TwCV; TwHP; TwP; UnPo (3d ed.)
Cold Confession. Vladimir Benediktov, *tr. fr. Russian by* C. M. Bowra. BoRS
Cold, deserted and silent. *Unknown.* *Fr.* Winter on Black Mingo. FiBHP
Cold earth slept below, The. Lines. Shelley. AnEnPo; ChER; EmBrPo; EnRP; LoBV
Cold eyelids that hide like a jewel. Dolores. Swinburne. EmBrPo; POTT; PoVP; ViPo; VLEP
Cold Fall. Richard Eberhart. FiMAP
Cold, gray light of the dawning, The. Ticonderoga. V. B. Wilson. IDAH; OTPC; PaA; PAP
Cold grew the foggy morn, the day was brief. The Patron. George Crabbe. *Fr.* Tales. EnSW
Cold grey hills they bind me around, The. The King on the Tower. Ludwig Uhland. OBVV
Cold has killed the corn off an' blighted all the wheat, The. A Country Philosopher. Frank L. Stanton. DDA
Cold Heaven, The. W. B. Yeats. AWP; InPo; JAWP; MoVE; NAMP; NP; OAEP (2d ed.); WBP
Cold heritique. *Unknown.* SeCSL
Cold hours pass, The. Night Piece. Edith Sitwell. NP
Cold ideal, The/ That mind selects. A Litany for Peace. Pearce Young. PtPa
Cold in the earth—and the deep snow piled above thee. Remembrance. Emily Brontë. AV; BMEP; CaAE; CH; CoEV; DiM; EmBrPo; EnLi-2; EnLit; EnLoPo; EtPaEn; EV-5; FaBoEn; FaFP; GTBS-D; GTBS-W; GTIV; GTML; GTSL; HBV; LiTB; LiTG; LiTL; LO; LoPo; LoPS; OAEP; OBEV (1st ed.); OxBI; PoD; PoEL-5; PoVP; RiBV; TrGrPo; ViP; VLEP
Cold Iron. Kipling. OS; VLEP
Cold is the night, and still, and strange. The House-Goblin. Viktor Rydberg. AnSL
Cold is the snow tonight. *Unknown.* *Fr.* Sweeney the Mad. SiB

Cold is the wind to-night, and rough the sea. In the Monastery. Norreys Jephson O'Conor. CAW; SBMV
Cold is the winter, the wind has arisen. Recollections of Caoilte. *Unknown.* SiB
Cold is wintertime, the wind. The Starkness of Earth. Frank O'Connor. TriL
Cold Kisses. Pierre de Ronsard, *tr. fr. French by* Alan Conder. TrFP
Cold limbs of the air, The. A Mountain Wind. "Æ." AWP; JAWP; WBP
Cold Mountain, The. Wang Wei, *tr. fr. Chinese.* WhP
Cold Night, A. Bernard Spencer. WaP
Cold Night, A. *Unknown, tr. fr. Old Irish by* Kuno Meyer. SiB
Cold north wind blows, The. The North Wind. *Unknown.* WhP
Cold Oxford unfamiliar now, around. Above the High. Geoffrey Grigson. EnLoPo
Cold rain falls on Dun-sur-Meuse to-night, The. Lest We Forget. Curtis Wheeler. AOAH
Cold rice mingled with sand. A Roadside Song. Lu Yu. WhP
Cold, Sharp Lamentation. Douglas Hyde, *tr. fr. Irish by* Lady Gregory. GTIV; OBMV
Cold shuttered loveless star, skulker in clouds. News of the World I. George Barker. FaBoMo; LiTB
Cold Spring, A. Elizabeth Bishop. FiMAP; Po
Cold steel may penetrate the flesh. Heart Wounds. Claire Richcreek Thomas. PoToHe (new ed.)
Cold, strange, withdrawn our friendly court and still. November 2 A.M. Conspiracy. Sara Bard Field. AnEnPo
Cold, the dull cold! What ails the Sun. A Seamark. Bliss Carman. PeCV
Cold till Doom! A Cold Night. *Unknown.* SiB
Cold transparent ham is on my fork, The. Sonnet to Vauxhall. Thomas Hood. PoEL-4
Cold, uncompassionate, bare. Across the Fens. Gilbert Thomas. HaMV
Cold was the day, when in a garden bare. The Child Jesus in the Garden. *Unknown.* ChrBoLe; CLS
Cold was the night wind, drifting fast the snows fell. The Widow. Robert Southey. OBEC
Cold was thy thought, O stricken son. To Giacomo Leopardi. T. Sturge Moore. PtP
Cold Water Flat. Philip Booth. NePoAm
Cold Wind Blows, A. Zoe Kincaid Brockman. NoCaPo
Cold wind of autumn, blowing loud. Autumn Daybreak. Edna St. Vincent Millay. LaNeLa
Cold winds swept the mountain-height, The. The Mother's Sacrifice. Seba Smith. *Fr.* The Snow Storm. LPS-1; MotAn
Cold winter now is in the wood. Elizabeth J. Coatsworth. TiPo
Cold winter's in the wood. In the Wood. Eileen Mathias. BoTP
Cold Winter's Night, A. *Unknown. See* Mary of the Wild Moor.
Cold Year, The. Tao Yuan-ming, *tr. fr. Chinese by* Yang Chi-sing. WhP
Colder the Air, The. Elizabeth Bishop. MiAP
Coldly, sadly descends. Rugby Chapel. Matthew Arnold. ATP (1935 ed.); BEL; BPN; EM-2; EmBrPo; EnL; EnLi-2; EnLit; EPN; EV-5; GEPC; GTBS; OAEP; OxBoCh; PIAE; PoE; PoEL-5; PoVP; TOP; TyEnPo; ViPo; ViPP; VLEP; WGRP
Coldness that falls upon the hours, The. Cold Fall. Richard Eberhart. FiMAP
Cold's the Wind. Thomas Dekker. *Fr.* The Shoemaker's Holiday, V, iv. ViBoPo
(Catch. A.) CBOV
("Cold's the wind, and wet's the rain.") ElSeCe; ReEn; TuPP
(Drinking Song.) TrGrPo
(Hey Derry Derry.) SeCePo
(Saint Hugh.) OBSC
(Second Three-Man's Song, The.) EV-2
(Second Three Men's Song, The.) EPP
(Troll the Bowl!) ElL
Cole, that unwearied prince of Colchester. Variations on an Air: After Lord Tennyson. G. K. Chesterton. InP
Cole Younger. *Unknown.* BeLS; CSF
Coleridge. Aubrey Thomas De Vere. GoBC
Coleridge. George Sidney Hellman. AA
Coleridge. Theodore Watts-Dunton. HBV; OBVV; PtP; VA
Coleridge and His Child. Samuel Taylor Coleridge. *Fr.* Frost at Midnight. RO
Coleridge, they say, lived in fantasy. A Plea for Alias. James Schevill. FiMAP
Colin. Anthony Munday. *See* To Colin Clout.
Colin and Lucy. Thomas Tickell. CEP; CG, *sl. abr.;* EiPP; EV-3; OBEC
(Lucy and Colin.) OTPC (1923 ed.)
Colin and Phebe—a Pastoral. John Byrom. *See* Pastoral, A: "My time, O ye Muses, was happily spent."
Colin Clout. John Skelton. *See* Colyn Cloute.
Colin Clout's Come Home Again, *sels.* Spenser.
Colin Clout at Court. OBSC
Her Heards Be Thousand Fishes. ChTr
"Shepheards boy, The (best knowen by that name)." ReIE
Colin, my dear and most entire beloved. To the Most Excellent and Learned Shepherd, Colin Clout. William Smith. *Fr.* Chloris. ReEn; TuPP
Colin, my deare, when shall it please thee sing. November. Spenser. *Fr.* The Shepheardes Calender. MaPo; PoEL-1
Colin, the Enamored Shepherd, Singeth This Passion of Love. George Peele. *See* O Gentle Love.
Colinetta, *sel.* Mary Leapor.
Autumn. BeR
Colin's Cattle. *Unknown, tr. fr. Gaelic by* Malcolm MacFarlane. EBSV
Colin's Complaint. Nicholas Rowe. OBEC
Colin's gone home, the glory of his clime. In Obitum Ed. Spenser Poetae Prestaniss. John Weever. ReIE
Colin's Passion of Love. George Peele. *See* O Gentle Love.
Coliseum, The ("Arches on arches"). Byron. *Fr.* Childe Harold's Pilgrimage, IV. BCEP; BEL; EPN; EV-4, *abr.;* LPS-2; TCEP, *abr.*
("Arches on arches! as it were that Rome," *abr.*) CoBE
Coliseum, The ("The stars are forth"). Byron. *Fr.* Manfred, III, iv. MCCG
(Coliseum by Moonlight, *sl. abr.*) LPS-2
(Manfred, *sl. abr.*) BCEP
Coliseum, The. Poe. AmPP (3d ed.); IAP; SPP; TCAP
Coliseum by Moonlight. Byron. *See* Coliseum, The ("The stars are forth").
Collar, The. George Herbert. AtBAP; ATP; AWP; BEL; BrBE; CaAE; CoBE; CoEV; ElSeCe; EM-1; EnL; EnLi-1; EnLit; EPP; EPS; EV-2; ExPo; FaBoEn; GTBS-W; HBV; InPo; JAWP; KN; LiTB; LiTG; LoBV; MaPo; MaRV; MeLP; MePo; NBE; OAEP; OBS; OuHeWo; OxBoCh; PC, *sl. abr.;* PoE; PoEL-2; PoFS; PoRA; PreP; ReEn; RiBV; SeCePo; SeCeV; SeCL; SeCV-1; SeEP; TCEP; TOP; TrGrPo; TwCrTr; TwHP; TyEnPo; UnPo (1st ed.); ViBoPo; WBP; WHA
Collar, The. *Unknown, tr. fr. Chinese.* WhP
Collar-Bone of a Hare, The. W. B. Yeats. AtBAP; EnL; NP
Collect the silver on a Sunday. The Lucky Coin. Austin Clarke. NeIP
Collection of Emblemes, Ancient and Moderne, A, *sel.* George Wither.
"Why, silly Man! so much admirest thou." SeCV-1
Collective Portrait, The. Robert Finch. BoCaPo (1948 ed.)
Colleen Oge Asthore. *Unknown.* OnYI
Colleen Rue. *Unknown.* OnYI
College Cat, The. Alfred Denis Godley. CenHV
College Colonel, The. Herman Melville. AA; RiBV
College of Surgeons, The. James Stephens. AnIL
College "Oil Cans." Will Victor McGuire. PTA-1
College Song. Ed Anthony. InMe
Collegian to His Bride, The. *Unknown.* LPS-3
Collegiate damsel named Breeze, A. *Unknown.* GoTP
Collen say why sittst thou soe. *Unknown.* SeCSL
Collie puppies in a dooryard. Wonder. Bernard Raymund. MW
Collier, The. Vernon Watkins. FaBoTw; MoVE; MoWP
Collier's Wife, The. D. H. Lawrence. HaMV
Collies, The. Edward Anthony. GoTP
Collige Rosas. W. E. Henley. *See* O Gather Me the Rose.
Collins. Lionel Johnson. EV-5
Colloque sentimental[e]. Paul Verlaine, *tr. fr. French.* EnLi-2, *tr. by* Ernest Dowson; MiFP, *tr. by* Arthur Symons
(Sentimental Colloquy, *tr. by* Alan Conder.) LO
(Sentimental Dialogue, *tr. by* Muriel Kittel.) AnFP
Colloquy. Al-Munsafi, *tr. fr. Arabic by* A. J. Arberry. MooP
Colloquy. Emily Dickinson. *See* I died for beauty.
Colloquy at Peniel. W. S. Merwin. NePoEA
Colloquy in Black Rock. Robert Lowell. AnNE; CoBMV; FiMAP; MiAP; MoAB; MoAmPo (1950 ed.); Po; ReMP
Colloquy of the Ancients, The, *sel. Unknown, tr. fr. Late Middle Irish by* Standish Hayes O'Grady *and* Kuno Meyer, *arr. by* Kathleen Hoagland.
"MacLugach! says Finn." OnYI
Colloquy with a King-Crab. John Peale Bishop. LiTA; MoPo
Colloquy with God, A. Sir Thomas Browne. *See* Evening Hymn.
Collusion between a Alegaiter and a Water-Snaik. J. W. Morris. LPS-3, *abr.;* NA
Collyn, I see, by thy new taken taske. To the Learned Shepheard. Gabriel Harvey. PtP
Colm had a cat. The Pets. Robert Farren. CoBE; OxBI
Cologne. John Bate. NeBP
Cologne. Samuel Taylor Coleridge. BoHiPo; BOHV; HBV; InMe; WhC
(Epigram: "In Köln [*or* Köhln], a town of monks and bones.") ALV; LPS-3
Cologne Cathedral. Frances Shaw. NP

Colombine. Hugh McCrae. BoAV; NeLNL
Colombine. Paul Verlaine, *tr. fr. French by* Arthur Symons. MiFP
(Columbine, *tr. by* Alan Conder.) TrFP
Colomen. Mary Webb. LoEn
Colonel B. Constance Carrier. NePoAm-2
Colonel B/ Drove from the tee. Afforestation. E. A. Wodehouse. FiBHP
Colonel Ellsworth. Richard Henry Stoddard. PAH
Colonel Fantock. Edith Sitwell. AnFE; MBP; MM; MoAB; MoBrPo; MoVE; OBMV
Colonel rode by his picket-line, The. The Two Wives. William Dean Howells. AA
Colonel Sharp. *Unknown.* BaBo
Colonia, you wish to have a long bridge built, I hear. Catullus, *tr. fr. Latin by* Jack Lindsay. LaP
Colonial Set. Alfred G. Bailey. BoCaPo
Colonial Song, A. Albert Durrant Watson. CPG
Colonist in His Garden, A. William Pember Reeves. AnNZ
Colonos. Henry Alford. VA
Colophon. Oliver St. John Gogarty. OBMV
Colophon, *in mod. Eng. Unknown.* TMEV
Color. Rowena Bennett. MPB (1956 ed.)
Color. W. W. Gibson. InP; NP
Color. Christina Rossetti. *Fr.* Sing-Song. GoBP; RAR
("What is pink? A rose is pink.") SUS; TiPo
Color Alone Can Speak. Louise Townsend Nicholl. NePoAm
Color gladdens all your heart, The. Sympathy. Althea Gyles. HBV; TIP
Color Guard, The. Charles W. Harwood. FOAH
Color in the Wheat. Hamlin Garland. HiLiAm; PTA-2
Color of my life, The. Chrysanthemums. *Unknown.* SoLD
Color of silence is the oyster's color, The. Earliness at the Cape. Babette Deutsch. NePoAm-2
Color of stone when leaves are yellow, The. Autumn. William Jay Smith. NePoAm
Color of the ground was in him, the red earth, The. Edwin Markham. *Fr.* Lincoln, the Man of the People. MaRV; PGD; PSO
Colorado. John D. Dillenback. PoOW
Colorado. Robert Fitzgerald. MoPo
Colorado Morton's Ride. Leonard Bacon *and* Rivers Browne. TCPD
Colorado Sand Storm, A. Eugene Field. PoOW
Colorado Trail, The, *with music. Unknown.* AS; CoSo
Colored Band, The. Paul Laurence Dunbar. MPB
Colored leaves, The. Kakinomoto no Hitomaro, *tr. fr. Japanese by* Kenneth Rexroth. OnPJ
Colored like fallen needles, the red squirrel goes. Squirrel. Frances Frost. BoChLi
Colored pictures. The Songs of Maximus. Charles Olson. NeAP
Colors. Phoebe Crosby Allnut. VOD
Colors, The. Nathalia Crane. MAP; NeMA; StaSt
(Standards.) GoTP
Colors. Weir Vernon. DDA
Colors in the sun, colors at night, the Army, Navy and Marines. The Lagoon. Ashton Greene. NePoAm
Colosseum. Harold Norse. TrJP
Colour. *Unknown.* BoTP
Colour. Adeline White. BoTP
Colour is a lovely thing. Colour. *Unknown.* BoTP
Colour of October. Lelia Jones. MuM
Coloured long-shore fishermen unfurl, The. The Gamblers. Anthony Delius. BoSA
Colours of Love, The. Denis Devlin. OxBI
Colours of the setting sun, The. The Sliprails and the Spur. Henry Lawson. BoAu
Colt, The. Raymond Knister. TwCaPo
Colt is tethered at the appointed gate, The. The Ride to Jerusalem. Norman Nicholson. StJW
Colubriad, The. William Cowper. BOHV; CG; CIV; OTPC (1923 ed.); PoC
Columbia. Timothy Dwight. BAV; HBV; IAP; IDAH; LPS-2; MC; PaA; PAH; TCAP
(Star of Columbia, *with music.*) TrAS
Columbia. Frederic Lawrence Knowles. IDAH
Columbia,/ If aught but loss of honor. Roosevelt. Peter Fandel. PEDC
Columbia, appear! To thy mountains ascend. Perry's Victory. *Unknown.* GA; PAH
Columbia, Columbia, to glory arise. Columbia [*or* Star of Columbia]. Timothy Dwight. BAV; HBV; IAP; IDAH; LPS-2; MC; PaA; PAH; TCAP; TrAS
Columbia, the Gem of the Ocean. David T. Shaw. FaBoBe; FOAH, *sl. diff.*; OIF
(Red, White, and Blue.) WBLP
Columbiad, The, *sels.* Joel Barlow.
Apparition of War, *fr.* V. APW
Creation, *fr.* IX. APW
League of Nations, A, *fr.* X. CoBA
(Union of the World, A.) IAP
Vision of Columbus, *fr.* IX. APW
Columbian Ode. Paul Laurence Dunbar. PoRL
Columbia's Emblem. Edna Dean Proctor. GN
Columbine. Paul Verlaine. *See* Colombine.
Columbus. Arthur Hugh Clough. BHV; DD; MC
Columbus. Florence Earle Coates. DD; MC
Columbus. Casimir Delavigne, *tr. fr. French by* Alan Conder. TrFP
Columbus. Charles Buxton Going. HH; VOD
(Great Master Dreamer.) PEDC (1931 ed.)
Columbus. Horace Gregory. *See* Homage to Columbus.
Columbus. Edward Everett Hale. DD; HH; MC; PAH
Columbus. Percy Hutchison. EtS
Columbus. Leroy F. Jackson. SiSoSe
Columbus. James Russell Lowell. BHV
"One day more/ These muttering shoalbrains leave the helm to me," *sel.* PGD
Columbus. Joaquin Miller. AA; AmPP (3d ed.); BAP; BBV; BeLS; BTP; CBPC; DD; DDA; EtS; FaBoBe; FaFP; FaPON; GN; HBV; HBVY; IAP; LBAP; LEAP; MC; MCCG; MPB; NeHB; NeMA; OBAV; OHFP; OnSP; OQP; OTPC (1946 ed.); PaA; PAH; PC, *sel.*; PCD; PECK; PEDC; PFY; PGD; PoeMoYo; PoRL; PTA-1; PYM; QP-1; StaSt; StVeCh; TiPo (1952 ed.); TreF; TSW; TSWC; WaKn; YaD; YeAr; YT
Columbus. James Montgomery. *Fr.* The West Indies. PEDC
(Inspiration, The.) PAH
Columbus. Lydia Huntley Sigourney. AA; DD; HBV; HH; MC; OTPC; PAH
Columbus. Helen L. Smith. PTA-2
Columbus. Annette Wynne. HH; MPB; TiPo
Columbus and the *Mayflower.* Richard Monckton Milnes. MC; PAH
Columbus at the Convent. John Townsend Trowbridge. BoHiPo; DD; MC; PAH
Columbus Day. Tennyson. HH; PEDC
Columbus Dying. Edna Dean Proctor. MC; PAH
Columbus Goes West. William Hart-Smith. BoAV; NeLNL
(Space.) MoAuPo
Columbus in Chains. Philip Freneau. MC; PAH
Columbus is remembered by young men. Homage to Columbus. Horace Gregory. ChMo
Columbus looked; and still around them spread. The First American Congress. Joel Barlow. PAH
Columbus looks towards the New World. Columbus Goes West [*or* Space]. William Hart-Smith. BoAV; MoAuPo; NeLNL
Columbus Never Knew. Gail Brook Burket. PGD
Columbus sailed over the ocean blue. Columbus. Leroy F. Jackson. SiSoSe
Columbus stands in the night alone, and, passing grave. The Triumph. Sidney Lanier. *Fr.* The Psalm of the West. PAH
Columbus the World-Giver. Maurice Francis Egan. OQP; PGD; QP-1
Columbus to Ferdinand. Philip Freneau, *wr. at. to* Jonathan Mason. PAH
Columbus turned; when rolling to the shore. Apparition of War. Joel Barlow. *Fr.* The Columbiad, V. APW
Columcile the Scribe. *At. to* St. Columcille. *See* St. Columcille the Scribe.
Colum-Cille's Farewell to Ireland. *At. to* St. Columcille. *See* Farewell to Ireland.
Columcille's Greeting to Ireland, *abr. At. to* St. Columcille, *but probably 12th cent., tr. fr. Middle Irish by* William Reeves *and* Kuno Meyer. OnYI
Columns and graven monuments, these can give. The Best Memorial. Agathias Scholasticus. OxBG
Colyn Cloute [*or* Colin Clout], *sels.* John Skelton.
"And if ye stand in doubt/ Who brought this rhyme about." ReEn
"My name is Colin Cloute." EPP
(Prelates, The.) BLV; TrGrPo
"What can it avail/ To drive forth a snail." SiCE; TuPP
Worldly Prelates. CoEV
Com, com sad turtle mateles moaninge. *Unknown.* SeCSL
Comarnad it is a very bonny place. Richie Story (B *vers.*). *Unknown.* ESPB
Comb out your golden hair and whisper, monkeys, monkeys. Flying Foxes and Others. Kay Boyle. AnAmPo
Combat, The. Matthew Arnold. *Fr.* Sohrab and Rustum. VA
Combat, The. Edwin Muir. ChMP; GTBS-D; LiTB
Combat, A. Shakespeare. King Henry IV, Pt. I, *fr.* V, iv. BHV
Combat, The. Thomas Stanley, *after the Greek of* Anacreon. AWP
Combat of Ferdiad and Cuchulain, The, *sels. Unknown, tr. fr. Middle Irish.*
"All was play, all was sport," *tr. by* Joseph Dunn. OnYI
(Cuchulainn's [*or* Cuchulain's] Lament for Ferdiad, *tr. by* George Sigerson.) AnIL; SiB
(Cuchullain's Lament over Fardiad, *tr. by* George Sigerson.) AnIV; BoFr
"Arise ye kings of Macha," *tr. by* Joseph Dunn. OnYI
"Ravens shall pick," *tr. by* Joseph Dunn. OnYI
"Roll of a chariot, The," *tr. by* Joseph Dunn. OnYI

Combat of Heracles and Cycnus. Hesiod, *tr. fr. Greek by* Sir William Marris. *Fr.* Shield of Heracles. OxBG
Combat raged not long, The; but ours the day. Captain Latané [*or* The Burial of Latané]. John Reuben Thompson. BIG; PAH
Combe, The ("The combe was ever dark"). Edward Thomas. EV-5; PrWP
Combed by the cold seas, Bering and Pacific. Love Letter from an Impossible Land. William Meredith. WaP
Combination of Wagner and burlesque. Job. E. W. Mandel. PeCV
Come. Anna Letitia Barbauld. *See* Come, Says Jesus' Voice.
Come! William Barnes. CH
Come. Sara Teasdale. ChMo; CMP; SBMV
"Come a little nearer, doctor—thank you—let me take the cup." Forceythe Willson. *Fr.* The Old Sergeant. AA; BeLS; PaA
Come about the meadow. What May Happen to a Thimble. "B." PRWS
Come again to the place. After the Visit. Thomas Hardy. FaBoEn; GTBS-D
Come, all brother sailors, I hope you'll draw nigh. The Beaver Island Boys. *At. to* Daniel Malloy. OuSiCo
Come all fair maids both far and near and listen unto me. Tragic Verses. *Unknown.* CoMu
Come all gallant [*or* you gallant] seamen that unite a meeting. The Death of Nelson [*or* A New Song Composed on the Death of Lord Nelson]. *Unknown.* CoMu; OxBoLi
Come all good people, I'd have you draw near. Naomi Wise. *Unknown.* ViBoFo
Come all kind friends and kindred dear. Harry Bale. *Unknown.* CSF
Come, all my boys and listen, a song I'll sing to you. The *Bigler* [*or* The *Bigler*'s Crew]. *Unknown.* IHA; OuSiCo
Come all my fair ones. Jack Tar. *Unknown.* ShS
Come all my friends and listen to me. Young McFee. *Unknown.* ABS
Come all of you bold shanty boys, and list while I relate. The Jam on Gerry's Rock. *Unknown.* BaBo
Come all of you, my brother scouts. The Old Scout's Lament. William F. Drannan. CoSo; CSF; PoOW
Come all of you people, I pray you draw near. The Arizona Boys and Girls. *Unknown.* CoSo; CSF
Come all of you young people who lives far and near. Poor Goins. *Unknown.* ABS
Come all that loves good company. The Merry Hoastess. *Unknown.* CoMu
Come, all ye bold Americans, to you the truth I tell. The Surrender of Cornwallis. *Unknown.* PAH
Come all ye bold sailors/ Who sail round Cape Horn. The Coast of Peru. *Unknown.* EtS
Come all ye [*or* you] bold sailors that follow the Lakes. Red Iron Ore. *Unknown.* ABF; AS; IHA; TiPo (1952 ed.)
Come all ye boys of Liverpool I'd have you to beware. Van Dieman's Land. *Unknown.* BaBo
Come all ye fine young fellows. Hunt the Buffalo. *Unknown.* TrAS, *with* Shoot the Buffalo
Come all ye good people, wherever you be. Polly Williams. *Unknown.* ABF
Come all ye Irish gentlemen, a story I would tell. How We Built a Church at Ashcroft. Jack Leahy. PoOW
Come all ye [*or* you] jolly fellows, wherever you may be. Gerry's Rocks. *Unknown.* ABF
Come all ye jolly good shanty boys, come listen to my song. Jim Porter's Shanty Song. *Unknown.* IHA
Come all ye jolly lumbermen, and listen to my song. Canaday I. O. Ephraim Braley. BaBo; ViBoFo, *with music*
Come all ye jolly lumbermen who lumbered on Gaspereaux. The Banks of the Gaspereaux. *Unknown.* ShS
Come, all ye jolly sailors bold. The *Arethusa.* Prince Hoare. LH; SG; TVSH
Come all ye jolly sailors bold. Captain Ward and the *Rainbow.* *Unknown.* ViBoFo
Come all ye jolly sailors, with courage stout and bold. Bob Sawyer. *Unknown.* SG
Come, all ye jolly shepherds. When the Kye Comes Hame. James Hogg. BLP; EBSV; EV-3; HBV; LPS-1
Come all ye lads and lassies and listen to me a while. The Maid of the Sweet Brown Knowe. *Unknown.* AnIV; OnYI
Come all ye lads who know no fear. Barney's Invitation. Philip Freneau. IAP; PAH
Come all ye maids of Simcoe, give ear to what I write. The Maids of Simcoe. *Unknown.* ShS
Come all ye pretty fair maids, O if ye did but know. Sailors' Come-All-Ye. *Unknown.* SoAmSa
Come all ye railroad section men an' listen to my song. Jerry, Go an' Ile That Car. *Unknown.* AS; CSF; IHA
Come all ye river-drivers, if a tale you wish to hear. How We Logged Katahdin Stream. Daniel G. Hoffman. MaC
Come, all ye seamen bold. Admiral Benbow. *Unknown.* EnSB
Come all ye sons of Brittany. Braddock's Fate, with an Incitement to Revenge. Stephen Tilden. PAH
Come, all ye sons of Canada, wherever you may dwell. The Hanging Limb. *Unknown.* IHA
Come all ye tender Christians and hearken unto me. The Death of Bendall. *Unknown.* ABS
Come all ye [*or* you] true-born shanty-boys, wherever you may be [*or* whoever that ye be]. The Jam on Gerry's Rock [*or* Young Monroe at Gerry's Rock]. *Unknown.* AmSS; AS; IHA; ViBoFo
Come all ye true-bred Irishmen. The *City of Baltimore.* *Unknown.* ShS
Come all ye who list to hear our noble England's praise. *See* Attend, all ye . . .
Come all ye Yankee sailors, with swords and pikes advance. The *Constellation* and the *Insurgente.* *Unknown.* PAH
Come all ye young fellows of Prince Edward Island. The Boys of the Island. Larry Gorman. ShS
Come all ye [*or* you] young fellows that [*or* who] follow the sea. Blow the Man Down [*or* The Black Ball Line]. *Unknown.* AmSS; ShS, *vers.* II; SoAmSa
Come all ye young females, I pray you'll attend. Sally Monroe. *Unknown.* ShS
Come all ye young people, come fathers and mothers, too. The Rowan County Crew. *Unknown.* OuSiCo
Come, all ye young sailormen, listen to me. The Boston Come-All-Ye; or, The Fishes. *Unknown.* ABF; SoAmSa; TrAS
Come all ye young tars who are cruising for sperm. Coast of Peru. *Unknown.* SoAmSa
Come, All Ye Youths. Thomas Otway. *Fr.* The Orphan. OAEP
Come all you blessed Christians dear. A Ballad from the Seven Dials Press. *Unknown.* CoMu
Come All You Bold Canadians, *with music.* *Unknown.* ShS
Come all you bold fishermen, listen to me. Song of the Fishes. *Unknown.* AmSS
Come all you bold ox teamsters. Teamster's Song. *Unknown.* TrAS
Come all you bold robbers and open your ears. Quantrell. *Unknown.* ABF; CoSo
Come all you bold sailors that follow the Lakes. *See* Come all ye bold sailors . . .
Come, all you bold undaunted men. Jack Donahoo [*or* Donahoe]. *Unknown.* ABF; CoSo; CSF
Come all you bold, undaunted ones. Fifteen Ships on George's Banks. *Unknown.* BaBo
Come all you brave Americans. Brave Paulding and the Spy. *Unknown.* GA; MC; PAH
Come all you brave Annapolis boys. Corbitt's Barkentine. *At. to* Tom Reynolds. ShS
Come, all you brave gallants, and listen awhile. Robin Hood and the Butcher. *Unknown.* ESPB (B *vers.*); OBB; REAL; RG
Come all you brave Sailors, that sails on the Main. The Famous Fight at Malago; or, The Englishmen's Victory over the Spaniards. *Unknown.* CoMu; SG
Come all you brave soldiers, both valiant and free. On Independence. Jonathan Mitchell Sewall. PAH
Come all you brave young shanty boys, and list while I relate. Foreman Monroe. *Unknown.* CSF
Come all you brave young shanty boys, I pray you. James Whaland. *Unknown.* AS; IHA
Come all you British hearts of oak, and listen unto me. The Glorious Victory of Navarino! *Unknown.* CoMu
Come, all you Californians, I pray ope wide your ears. Crossing the Plains. *Unknown.* ABF
Come all you fine young fellows with hearts so warm and true. Flat River Girl. *Unknown.* AS
Come all you gallant poachers, that ramble void of care. Van Diemans Land. *Unknown.* CoMu
Come all you gallant seamen that unite a meeting. *See* Come all gallant seamen . . .
Come all you good old boys and listen to my rhymes. Lackey Bill. *Unknown.* CoSo; CSF
Come all you hardy sons of toil, pray lend an ear to me. The History of Prince Edward Island. Larry Gorman. ShS
Come all you hearty roving blades, and listen to my song. The Frolicsome Parson Outwitted. *Unknown.* CoMu
Come all you humane countrymen, with pity lend an ear. Charles Gustavus Anderson, *vers.* II. *At. to* Joseph Keating, Sr. ShS
Come all you joky boys. Katy Dorey. *Unknown.* OuSiCo
Come all you jolly buffalo skinners and listen to my song. *See* Come all you jolly fellows . . .
Come all you jolly cowboys that follow the bronco steer. The Crooked Trail to Holbrook. *Unknown.* CoSo; CSF
Come all you jolly cowmen, don't you want to go. The Kansas Line. *Unknown.* CSF
Come all you jolly dogs, in the Grapes, and King's Head, and Green Man, and Bell Taps. Tom Tatter's Birthday Ode. Thomas Hood. LoBV; RO
Come all you jolly fellows [*or* buffalo skinners *or* skinners] and listen to my song. The Buffalo Skinners. *Unknown.* ABF; ABS; AS; CoSo; CSF; ViBoFo

Come, all you jolly fellows, wherever you may be. *See* Come, all ye jolly . . .
Come all you jolly freighters that has freighted on the road. Freighting from Wilcox to Globe. *Unknown.* CoSo; CSF
Come all you jolly lumbermen and listen to my song. The Jolly Lumbermen. *Unknown.* TrAS
Come all you jolly lumbermen, I'd have you for to know. The Banks of Gaspereaux. *Unknown.* BaBo
Come all you jolly railroad men, and I'll sing you if I can. Way Out in Idaho. *Unknown.* OuSiCo
Come all you jolly river boys, I'll have you all draw near. The Jam on Gerry's Rock, *vers.* I. *Unknown.* ShS
Come, all you jolly sailor lads, that love the cannon's roar. The Ballad of the *Rover.* Archibald MacMechan. CPG; OCL
Come all you jolly sailormen that follow the salt sea. The Schooner *Blizzard.* Henry Burke. ShS
Come all you jolly skinners and listen to my song. *See* Come all you jolly fellows . . .
Come all you jolly soldiers, I will sing to you a song. War Song. *Unknown.* ABF
Come, all you little runabouts. A Tract for Autos. Arthur Guiterman. MPB
Come all you Louisiana girls and listen to my noise. The Texian Boys. *Unknown.* CoSo
Come all you melancholy folks and listen unto me. The Melancholy Cowboy. *Unknown.* CoSo; CSF
Come all you melancholy folks wherever you may be. Old Time Cowboy. *Unknown.* CSF
Come all you men and maidens dear, to you I will relate. The Lexington Miller. *Unknown.* BaBo
Come all you men of Arkansas. Annie Breen. *Unknown.* CoSo
Come all you men of learning. Botany Bay. *Unknown.* ViBoFo
Come all you Milltown rowdies that drink and have no fear. Tomah Stream. Larry Gorman. ShS
Come, all you Mississippi girls, and listen to my noise. Mississippi Girls. *Unknown.* CSF
Come all you old cow-punchers, a story I will tell. A Man Named Hods. *Unknown.* CoSo; CSF
Come all you old-time cowboys and listen to my song. Boggy Creek. *Unknown.* CoSo
Come all you old-timers and listen to my song. John Garner's Trail Herd. *Unknown.* CoSo; CSF
Come all you pretty girls and listen to my noise. Cheyenne Boys. *Unknown.* ABS
Come all you pretty girls, to you these lines I'll write. The Buffalo Hunters. *Unknown.* CoSo; CSF; IHA
Come all you rambling sailor lads and listen unto me. The *Flying Cloud, vers.* I. *Unknown.* ShS
Come all you range riders and listen to me. The Range Riders. *Unknown.* CoSo; CSF
Come all you rounders if you want [*or* for I want you] to hear. Casey Jones. *Unknown.* ABF; ABS; AmPP; APW; AS; ATP; BeLS; IHA; KN; MaC. *arr. by* T. Lawrence Seibert; OxBoLi; TreF; TrGrPo; ViBoFo (A *and* B *vers.*)
Come all you sailors bold. The Death of Admiral Benbow. *Unknown.* CoMu; SG
Come, all you sailors of the southern waters. Phantoms All. Harriet Prescott Spofford. AA; PFY
Come all you sons of Erin, attention now I crave. Morrissey and the Russian Sailor. *Unknown.* AS
Come, all you sons of Liberty, that to the seas belong. The *General Armstrong.* *Unknown.* PAH
Come all you swaggering farmers, whoever you may be. The Times Have Altered. *Unknown.* CoMu
Come all you tender Christians. Charles Guiteau or James A. Garfield. *Unknown.* ABS; ViBoFo
Come all you Texas rangers, wherever you may be. The Texas Ranger[s]. *Unknown.* ABS; CoSo; CSF; OuSiCo
Come all you thoughtless young men, a warning take by me. The Murder of Maria Marten. W. Corder. CoMu
Come all you true-born shanty-boys, wherever you may be. *See* Come all ye true-born . . .
Come, all you true boys from the river. Johnny Stiles, or the Wild Mustard River. *Unknown.* OuSiCo
Come all you true lovers and the truth I'll unfold. The Jolly Young Sailor and the Beautiful Queen. *Unknown.* ShS
Come all you very merry London girls, that are disposed to travel. The Maydens of London's Brave Adventures. *Unknown.* SG
Come all you wild rovers. Wild Rovers. *Unknown.* CSF
Come, all you wild young people, and listen to my song. Young Edwin in the Lowlands Low (A *vers.*). *Unknown.* BaBo
Come all you woolly waddies. The Harrington Barn Dance. *Unknown.* CoSo
Come all you young Canadian boys, wherever that you be. The Jam on Jerry's Rock, *vers.* II. *Unknown.* ShS
Come, all you young companions. Young Companions. *Unknown.* CoSo; CSF
Come all you young fellows that [*or* who] follow the sea. *See* Come all ye young . . .
Come, all you young gallants that follow the gun. Young Molly Bawn. *Unknown.* OnYI
Come all you young ladies and make no delay. *Unknown.* OxNR
Come all you young men from the Nashwaak. Young Forbest. *Unknown.* ShS
Come all you young men [*or* people] who handle a [*or* the] gun. Molly Bawn [*or* Mollie Bond *or* Shooting of His Dear]. *Unknown.* ABS; BaBo; OxBoLi
Come all you young people, I pray you draw near. Naomi (Omie) Wise (A *vers.*). *Unknown.* BaBo
Come all you young people who handle the gun. *See* Come all you young men who handle a gun.
Come all you young sailors who cruise round Cape Horn. The Coast of Peru. *Unknown.* ShS
Come, all young girls, pay attention to my noise. Kansas Boys. *Unknown.* AS; IHA
Come all young men, please lend attention. Silver Dagger. *Unknown.* ABS
Come along boys, and listen to my tale. The Old Chisholm [*or* Chizzum] Trail. *Unknown.* ABF; ABS; BeLS; CoSo; CSF; FaBoBe; PreP
Come along, children, come along. Raise a Rukus Tonight. *Unknown.* ABF
Come along, get you ready. A Hot Time in the Old Town. Joe Hayden. YaD
Come along, girls, listen to my voice. Kansas Boys. *Unknown.* SoAF
Come along, 'tis the time, ten or more minutes past. Spectator ab Extra: Le Diner. Arthur Hugh Clough. OxBoLi
Come Always, Come. Vicente Aleixandre, *tr. fr. Spanish by* Eleanor L. Turnbull. CoSP
Come and buy—/ Have a try! Lemonade Stand. Dorothy Brown Thompson. SiSoSe
Come and get your quinine, and come and get your pills. Words for Army Bugle Calls: Sick Call. *Unknown.* TreF
Come and go a-berrying. Hey-Day. Witter Bynner. PoTo
Come and kiss me! Come and kiss me! The Blackbird Song. Marjory Christmas. ReTS
Come and kiss me, mistress Beauty. Refrain. Douglas Brooke Wheelton Sladen. *Fr.* Charles II. VA
Come and let me make thee glad. The Builder. Francis Sherman. CaP; OCL
Come, and let us drink of that new river. Easter Hymn. St. John of Damascus. BePJ
Come and let us live my Deare. Lesbia [*or* Counting Kisses]. Catullus. LiA; LiTW
Come, and pass, and go. Quiet. Yaha. WoL
"Come and see! Come and see!" What the Thrush Says. Queenie Scott-Hopper. BoTP
Come and see her as she stands. Fanny. Anne Reeve Aldrich. HBV
Come and see the chimney-pots, etched against the light! Paris; the Seine at Night. Charles Divine. HBMV
Come and smile into my eyes. Dawn. Kenton Kilmer. JKCP (1955 ed.)
Come and Welcome. Thomas Haweis. BePJ
"Come and you shall see." Shadow. Ann Mars. GoYe
Come, Anna! Come, the morning dawns. A Pastoral Song. Henry Kirke White. ERP
Come, Anthea, let us two. The Wake. Robert Herrick. ElSeCe; EPS; EV-2
Come, arm ye! Come, arm ye! The Garibaldi Hymn. Luigi Mercantini. WBLP
Come as artist, come as guest. A Welcome to "Boz." William Henry Venable. LPS-3
Come at dawn, my loved one. *Unknown, tr. fr. Spanish by* Eleanor L. Turnbull. TeCS
Come away, away, away. James Shirley. *Fr.* The Triumph of Peace. TuPP
Come Away, Come Away, Death. Shakespeare. *Fr.* Twelfth Night, II, iv. AnFE; AtBAP; CenL; CoEV; EG; EIL; ElSeCe; EM-1; EnLi-1 (1949 ed.); EPP; ExPo; InPo; KN; MaPo; OAEP; OBSC; SiCE; TCEP; TOP; TwHP; TwP; ViBoPo; WHA
(Come Away, Death.) BLV; PoRA; SeCeV
(Dirge.) OBEV
(Dirge for Love.) CBOV
(Dirge of Love.) GTBS; GTBS-D; GTBS-W; GTSE; GTSL
(Feste's Songs.) CoEV
(Lover's Lament, A.) EV-1
(Love's Despair.) TrGrPo
(Song.) CaAE; FiP; PoEL-2
(Two of Feste's Songs.) BoLiVe
Come away, come away from the straightness of the road Song of the Foot-Track. Elsie Cole. BoAu

Come away! come away! there's a frost along the marshes. The Wilderness. E. A. Robinson. BAV; POT; PoTo
Come Away, Come, Sweet Love. *Unknown.* BrBE; OAEP; OBSC; PoEL-2; ReEn; ReIE
(Come Away, Sweet Love.) LoBV
(To His Love.) ElL
Come Away Death. E. J. Pratt. BoCaPo; PeCV
Come Away, Death. Shakespeare. *See* Come Away, Come Away, Death.
Come away, elves, while the dew is sweet. Water-Lilies. Felicia Dorothea Hemans. OTPC
Come away, make no delay. Doom's-Day. George Herbert. NBE; SeCV-1
Come Away, Sweet Love. *Unknown. See* Come Away, Come, Sweet Love.
Come away to dreamin' town. Dreamin' Town. Paul Laurence Dunbar. VOD
Come, baby, and swing in the hammock with me. Hammock Lullaby. Charlotte Brewster Jordan. BOL
Come, Baby, come quick, for I want you to see. Baby Goes Out to Tea. *Unknown.* SAS
Come Back. Henry William Herbert. AA
Come back again, my olden heart! The Higher Courage. Arthur Hugh Clough. VLEP
Come back and bring my life again. Come Back. Henry William Herbert. AA
Come back and build my pyramids! Ján Ibn Ján. Rena Carey Sheffield. BAP
Come Back, Come Back, Behold with Straining Mast. Arthur Hugh Clough. Songs in Absence, V. BPN; EmBrPo; VLEP
"Come back! Come back!" he cried in Greek. Denny Misquotes. Edith Nesbit. *Fr.* The Would-be-Goods. BoN
Come back, come back, Jolly Jack Straw. Jack Overdue. John Pudney. AlDL
Come Back, Lincoln. Chauncey R. Piety. PGD
Come Back to Erin. Charlotte Alington Barnard. OlF; TreFS
Come back to me, little dancing feet that roam the wide world o'er. The Old Home Calls. L. M. Montgomery. CPG
"Come back to me, who wait and watch for you." Christina Rossetti. Monna Innominata, I. AV; EmBrPo; MBP; TCEP; ViPo
Come back, ye wandering Muses, come back home. On [*or* Proem to] the Hellenics. Walter Savage Landor. *Fr.* The Hellenics. BEL; BPN; EmBrPo; EnRP; EPN; ERP; ViBoPo
Come, bairns, come all to the frolic play. The Last Day of the Year. Alexander Smart. PCH
Come, be happy!—sit near me. Invocation to Misery. Shelley. EmBrPo
Come, be my valentine! Phyllis Inamorata. Francis Andrewes. ElSeCe; SeCL
"Come, before the summer passes." Travel Song. Anne Glenny Wilson. BoAu
Come, Blessèd Sleep. Christina Rossetti. PC
(Invitation to Sleep.) GTSE
Come, boy, and where the grass is thickest pied. Pierre de Ronsard. *Fr.* Amours de Cassandre. PrPoCR
Come, boy, to your dad. Let me tell you some things. A Talk to the Boy. Strickland Gillilan. FAOV
Come boyes, fill us a bumper, we'l make the Nation roare. The Courtier's Health; or, Merry Boys of the Times. *Unknown.* CoMu
Come Bravely On, My Masters. *Unknown.* AnEC
Come, Break with Time. Louise Bogan. ATP (1953 ed.); MAP; MoAmPo; NP
Come, break your heart, then, with the world's beauty. Sic Transit Gloria Mundi. James Wreford Watson. CaP
Come Bring with a Noise. Robert Herrick. *See* Ceremonies for Christmas.
Come, brother, come. Let's lift it. Cotton Song. Jean Toomer. CDC
Come, Brother—forward in the dark! To what? Dawn. Antoni Boguslawski. NeTW
Come, Brother, turn with me from pining thought. The Soul. Richard Henry Dana. LPS-2
Come, brothers, hail this great and twilight year. The Twilight of Liberty. Osip Emilyevich Mandelstamm. TrRV
Come, brothers! rally for the right! The Bonnie Blue Flag. Annie Chambers Ketchum. FOAH; PaA; PAH
"Come, Buck, come, Bouncer, my three bloodhounds." Johnie Cock (D *vers.*). *Unknown.* BaBo
Come, butter, come. Mother Goose. OxNR; PCH; StVeCh
Come Buy! Come Buy! Shakespeare. *See* Lawn as White as Driven Snow.
Come buy my fine wares. Apples. Swift. *Fr.* Verses for Fruitwomen. AnIV; OnYI
Come Buy My Nice Muffins. *Unknown.* PCH
Come, calf, now to mother. The Call. Björnstjerne Björnson. RAR
Come, Captain Age. Sarah N. Cleghorn. HBMV; TBM; VOD
Come, Celia, let's agree at last. Song. John Sheffield. HBV
Come, Charles, blow the trumpet. The Baby's Birthday. Eliza Lee Follen. PPL
Come, cheer up, my lads, like a true British band. A Song. *Unknown.* PAH
Come, cheer up, my lads! 'tis to glory we steer. Heart of Oak. David Garrick. BHV; HBV; OBEC; OxBoLi; SG
Come, Cheerful Day! Thomas Campion. BEL; ElL; ElSeCe
("Come cheerful day, part of my life to me.") EG; SiCE
(Sic Transit.) GTSL; TOP
Come, children, hear the joyful sound. The Big Bell in Zion. Theodore Henry Shackleford. BANP
Come, Children of Tomorrow, come! Children of Tomorrow. Zona Gale. OQP; QP-2
Come, Chloe, and Give Me Sweet Kisses. Sir Charles Hanbury Williams, *after the Latin of* Martial. HBV
(Epigram of Martial Imitated, An.) OBEC
Come, choose your road and away, my lad. The Call of the Spring. Alfred Noyes. SUS; VOD
Come, clear thy studious looks awhile. To Mr. Barbauld. Anna Letitia Barbauld. DiM
Come close to me, dear Annie, while I bind a lover's knot. Pot and Kettle. Robert Graves. HBMV
Come, come away. To His Tutor. John Hall. EG
"Come, come away, to the Tavern I say." *Unknown.* OBS
Come, come dear[e] night, Love's mart of kisses. Epithalamion Teratos [*or* Teratus]. George Chapman. *Fr.* Hero and Leander. AtBAP; ElL; EV-1; LoBV
Come, come fill up your glasses. The British Grenadier. *Unknown.* PAH
Come, come, lie down, and thou shalt see. *Unknown. Fr.* The Marriage of Wit and Science. TuPP
Come, come my hearts, a-hunting let us wend. The Hunting Song. *Unknown.* TuPP
Come, come, no time for lamentation now. A Brave Epitaph [*or* Death of Samson]. Milton. *Fr.* Samson Agonistes. BHV; ChTr; FiP
"Come, come," said Tom's father, "at your time of life." On Taking a Wife [*or* Epigram *or* A Joke Versified]. Thomas Moore. ALV; BOHV; HBV; LauV; LiTG; SiTL; TreF; WhC
Come come sweet Love why dost thou stay. *Unknown.* SeCSL
Come, Come Thou. Vicente Aleixandre, *tr. fr. Spanish by* Eleanor L. Turnbull. CoSP
Come, come, thou glorious object of my sight. Beauty Paramount. Sir William Killigrew. *Fr.* Selindra. SeCL
Come, Come, What Doe I Here? Henry Vaughan. MePo; SeCV-1
Come, comrades, come, your glasses clink. Down among the Dead Men. William Morris. EmBrPo; PoVP
Come, cool my wine till it surpass. To His Page. Pierre de Ronsard. TrFP
"Come!" cried Helen, eager Helen. Sisters. Eleanor Farjeon. FaPON
"Come!" cried my mind and by her might. The Wanderer: Clarity. William Carlos Williams. TwAmPo
Come cuddle close in daddy's coat. The Fairy Folk. Robert N. Bird. GFA; HBV; HBVY; OTPC; PRWS; RAR; TVC; TVSH
Come, cuddle your head on my shoulder, dear. Beautiful Land of Nod. Ella Wheeler Wilcox. BOL
Come dance a jig. *Unknown.* OxNR
Come, dance and song, in linkèd round! The Furies' Prayer. Aeschylus. *Fr.* Eumenides. OxBG
Come, dark-eyed Sleep, thou child of Night. And on My Eyes Dark Sleep by Night. "Michael Field." OBMV
Come, day, glad day, day running out of the night. Glad Day. Louis Untermeyer. TrJP
Come day, go day. Traveller's Ditty. Miriam Allen deFord. HBMV
Come, dear Amanda, quit the town. To Amanda. James Thomson. BSV
Come, dear children, let us away. The Forsaken Merman. Matthew Arnold. ATP (1935 ed.); BBV (1923 ed.); BEL; BeLS; BMEP; BoLiVe; BPN; CaAE; CBOV; CBPC; CG; EM-2; EmBrPo; EnL; EnLi-2; EnLit; EPN; EPP; EtS; EV-5; FaBoCh; FiP; GBV (1922 ed.); GEPC; GN; GTBS; GTBS-D; GTSL; HBV; HiLiEn; LoEn; LoGBV; LPS-3; MCCG; MotAn; MPB; OAEP; OBEV (1st ed.); OBVV; OnSP; OTPC; OuHeWo; PECK; PoVP; RG; SG; ShBV-1; TCEP; TOP; TVSH; VA; ViBoPo; ViPo; ViPP; VLEP; WHA; YT
Come, dear Heart! Corpus Christi. Evelyn Underhill. StJW
Come, dear old comrade, you and I. Bill and Joe. Oliver Wendell Holmes. AA; HBV; IAP; LPS-1; PCD
Come, Death, but free from pain. Song to Death. Juan Escrivá. LiTW
Come, doctor, use thy roughest art. The Cure. Abraham Cowley. PoP

Come, don't I know that, stumbling against shadows. To a Friend. Boris Pasternak. TrRV
Come Down. George Macdonald. TrPWD
Come down at dawn from windless hills. Sunrise on Rydal Water. John Drinkwater. GBV; HBV; LiTM; NP; NV; TCEP
Come down! Come down, balloon! In Soapsuds Street. Manuel Bandeira. AnCL
Come down, come down, my Lord, come down. My Lord's a-Writin' All de Time. *Unknown.* BoAN-1
"Come down, come down," said the farmer to his son. The Yorkshire Bite. *Unknown.* BaBo
Come down, come down to the Square. The Cat That Followed His Nose. John Kaye Kendall. CenHV
Come down from heaven to meet me when my breath. Invocation. Siegfried Sassoon. MBP; MoBrPo
Come down from the Cross, my soul, and save thyself—come down! Descent from the Cross. "Michael Field." MBP
Come down, O Christ, and help me! reach thy hand. E Tenebris. Oscar Wilde. CAW; ChIP; JKCP (1926 ed.); MaRV; MBP; MoBrPo; PoLi; StJW; TrPWD
Come Down, O Maid [from Yonder Mountain Height]. Tennyson. *Fr.* The Princess, Pt. VII. AnEnPo; AnFE; AtBAP; BrBE; EG; EmBrPo; EnL; EV-5; GTBS; MaPo; OBEV; OBVV; PIR; PoE; PoVP; RiBV; ShBV-3; TOP; ViBoPo; ViPo; ViPP; WHA
(From "The Princess.") LEAP
(Idyl, An.) TrGrPo
(Shepherd's Song.) LoBV
(Song.) FaBoEn
(Songs from "The Princess.") EnLi-2; MotAn; OAEP; SeCeV; VLEP
Come down, ye graybeard mariners. A Cry from the Shore. Ellen Mackay Hutchinson Cortissoz. AA
Come Down, You Bunch of Roses, Come Down, *with music.* *Unknown.* ShS
Come drawer some wine or wele pull downe your signe. *Unknown.* SeCSL
Come, drop your branches, strow the way. Palm-Sunday [*or* The Triumphant Entry]. Henry Vaughan. AtBAP; MaRV; StJW
Come, drunks and drug-takers: come, perverts unnerved! Several Voices Out of a Cloud. Louise Bogan. ExPo; MoVE
Come, each death-doing dog who dares venture his neck. Hot Stuff. Edward Botwood. PAH
Come, Evening, once again, season of peace. Winter Evening [*or* Evening] William Cowper. *Fr.* The Task, IV. CoBE; OBEC
Come exorcise the illness of this lovely girl. No Harm to Lovers [*or* Plea and Counsel]. Albius Tibullus. LaP; LiTW
Come, Faunus, lover of coy nymphs who flee. A Farmer's Prayer. Roselle Mercier Montgomery. LS
Come! fill a fresh bumper—for why should we go. Ode for a Social Meeting. Oliver Wendell Holmes. APW; BOHV; LPS-3; PIR
Come, fill the beaker, while we chaunt a pean of old days. Fort Duquesne. Florus B. Plimpton. PaA; PAH
"Come, Fill the Cup." *Unknown, tr. fr. Greek by* F. L. Lucas. *Fr.* Anacreontea. GrPE
Come, fill the cup, and in the fire of spring. The Bird of Time [*or* Fifteen Rubáiyát]. *Fr.* The Rubáiyát, *tr. by* Edward Fitzgerald. CBOV; InP; LiTW; OnPM; TreF; WGRP
Come fleetly, come fleetly, my hookabadar. Cossimbazar. Henry S. Leigh. BOHV; NA
Come Follow, Follow Me (*Christmas carol*). *Unknown.* AnEC
Come follow, follow me. The Fairy Queen [*or* The Queen of Fairies]. *Unknown.* BCEP; BoTP; EV-2; OTPC; PCD; PCH; PoRh; RG; ViBoPo
Come follow, heart upon your sleeve. A Maine Trail. Gertrude Huntington McGiffert. HBV; NLK
Come, Follow Me! Thomas Curtis Clark. ChIP
Come, follow me by the smell. Onions. Swift. *Fr.* Verses for Fruitwomen. AnIV; OnYI
Come Follow Me, You Country Lasses. John Fletcher *or* William Rowley. *Fr.* The Maid in the Mill. SeCL
Come for Arbutus. Sara Louisa Oberholtzer. SN
Come, forsake your city street! October. T. A. Daly. JKCP
Come forth, and let us through our hearts receive. Foliage. Felicia Dorothea Hemans. OBRV
Come Forth Come Forth! "Christopher North." OBRV
Come forth, come forth, the gentle spring. Song of Zephyrus and the Spring. Ben Jonson. *Fr.* Chloridia. EPS (1942 ed.)
Come forth, come forth, to the festal board. Thanksgiving. Hannah E. Garey. TOAH
Come forth; for Night is falling. The Invitation to the Gondola. John Addington Symonds. *Fr.* In Venice. PoVP
Come Forth! for Spring Is Singing in the Boughs. Arthur Davison Ficke. Sonnets of a Portrait Painter, XI. PFE; TBM
(April Moment.) HBMV
"Come forth!" my catbird calls to me. The Nightingale in the Study. James Russell Lowell. IAP
Come forth, you workers! Reveille. Lola Ridge. AnAmPo; HBMV; LA; PoFr; TCPD
Come forthe, sire sergeaunt, with your stately mace. The Dance. John Lydgate. *Fr.* The Dance of Death. PoEL-1
Come, Freemen of the land. Put It Through. Edward Everett Hale. MC; PAH
Come from my first, ay, come! Camp-Bell [*or* Charade]. Winthrop Mackworth Praed. GN; LPS-3
Come from your bed, my drowsy gentleman! The Cherry Tree. James Stephens. TCPD
Come Gather round Me, Parnellites. W. B. Yeats. PoFr
Come, Gaze with Me upon This Dome. E. E. Cummings. OxBA
Come, Gentle Death! Thomas Watson. *Fr.* Hecatompathia. ElL
("Come gentle Death. Who calls? One that's oppressed.") SiCE
Come, gentle death! come silently. Welcome Death. Juan Escrivá. AnSpL-1; OnPM
Come, gentle sleep! attend thy votary's prayer. Sleep. "Peter Pindar." LPS-3
Come, gentle Sleep, Death's image tho' thou art. A Translation from Michael Angelo. Michelangelo, *tr. by* Wordsworth. PC
Come, gentle Spring, ethereal mildness, come! The Seasons: Spring. James Thomson. TCEP
Come, gentle tripe, the hungry carter's joy. Tripe. J. B. Morton. InMe
Come, gentle Zephyr, tricked with those perfumes. George Peele. *Fr.* David and Bethsabe. ViBoPo
Come gentlemen all, and listen a while. Robin Hood and the Bishop of Hereford. *Unknown.* BaBo; CG; ESPB; OBB
Come, gentlemen Tories, firm, loyal and true. Sir Henry Clinton's Invitation to the Refugees. Philip Freneau. PAH
Come, Gently Stir. Hubbard Fulton Page. NoCaPo
Come, Georgia boy, come listen to my song. Georgia Boy. *Unknown.* OuSiCo
Come, gie's a sang, Montgomery cried [*or* cry'd]. Tullochgorum. John Skinner. BSV; EBSV; GoTS; OBEC
Come, great calm beautiful night. Litany of Night. Hugh Robert Orr. GrCo-2
Come, guard this night the Christmas pie. Christmas Eve—Another Ceremony. Robert Herrick. MuP; OHIP
Come, Harvey, let us sit awhile and talk about the times. Our Whippings. Eugene Field. FAOV
Come, Heavenly Child, and on this place. Two Inscriptions for the Christmas Candle. Anna Hempstead Branch. MaRV
Come heavy hart, whose sighs thy sorrowes shew. *Unknown.* SeCSL
Come, Heavy Sleep. *Unknown.* ReIE
Come, heavy souls, oppressed that are. Casting All Your Care upon God, for He Careth for You. Thomas Washbourne. OxBoCh
Come here and speak. What are you? Plaintiff or defendant? Lawyer Patelin. *Unknown.* LiA
Come, here are a slate, and a pencil, and string. Learning to Draw. Ann *or* Jane Taylor. SAS
Come here, come here, and dwell. Song of Wood-Nymphs. "Barry Cornwall." LPS-3
"Come here, come here, you freely feed." Kemp Owyne (B *vers.*). *Unknown.* ESPB
Come here, good people great and small, that wander far abroad. My Bath. John Stuart Blackie. VA
Come Here, Little Robin. *Unknown.* BoTP; OTPC (1923 ed.)
Come Here Lord! *with music.* *Unknown.* BoAN-2
Come here, my boy; hould up your head. The Irish Schoolmaster. James A. Sidney. BOHV; FiBHP
"Come here, my sweet Landlady, pray, how d'ye do?" Matthew Prior. *Fr.* Down Hall. MyFE
Come here, said my hostess, her face making room. Literary Dinner. Vladimir Nabokov. FiBHP
Come here, thou worthy of a world of praise. The Sirens' Song. Homer. *Fr.* The Odyssey, XII. EV-1
Come here to papa, and I'll tell my dear boy. Of What Are Your Clothes Made? Ann *and* Jane Taylor. OTPC (1923 ed.)
Come Hither. *Unknown.* *See* Come Hither, Little Puppy-Dog.
Come hither all sweet maidens soberly. On a Picture of Leander [*or* Sonnet]. Keats. BPN; EnRP; ERP; GEPC; PeBoSo; TOP
Come hither and behold this lady's face. Laura Sleeping. Louise Chandler Moulton. AA
Come hither, boy: if ever thou shalt love. Shakespeare. *Fr.* Twelfth Night, II, iv. LO

Come hither, child—who gifted thee. Lines. Emily Brontë. UnW

Come hither, Evan Cameron! Come, stand beside my knee. The Execution of Montrose. William Edmondstoune Aytoun. EV-5; GTBS; HBV; LPS-3; VA

Come hither, gallers of renown. To Some Reviewers Who Have Wilfully Abused Certain True Poets. Herbert Palmer FaBoTw

Come hither, lads, and harken [or hearken], for a tale there is to tell. The Day Is Coming. William Morris. BMEP; BPN; EmBrPo; EnLi-2; OAEP; POTT; PoVP; ViPo; VLEP; WGRP

Come hither, lads, and hearken, for a tale there is to tell. The Day Is Coming, parody. Sir Walter Besant. CenHV

Come hither, Little Puppy-Dog. Unknown. OTPC (1923 ed.); PPL
 (Come Hither.) FTB
 (Robin Knows Great A.) SAS

Come hither, my heart's darling. The Husband's Petition. William Edmondstoune Aytoun. BOHV

Come hither, Sir John, my picture is here. On a Lady Who Beat Her Husband. Unknown. FiBHP

Come hither, Sleep, from Chio's Isle! The Mother's Song. William P. M'Kenzie. BOL

Come hither, Sweet Robin, abr. Unknown. PPL
 (Feeding the Robin.) SAS

Come hither, womankind and all their worth. Kissing. Lord Herbert of Cherbury. EnLoPo; LiTL; ViBoPo

Come hither, ye mighty sons of Zeus. To Castor and Pollux. Alcaeus, tr. by Walter Petersen. GrR

Come, hoist the sail, the fast let go! The Pleasure-Boat. Richard Henry Dana. LPS-2

Come, Holy Babe! Mary Dickerson Bangham. ChIP; PGD

Come, Holy Dove,/ Descend on silent pinion. Hymn to the Holy Spirit. Richard Wilton. OxBoCh

Come Holy Ghost, Creator blest. Veni, Creator Spiritus. Unknown. WHL

Come Holy Ghost eternal God, and ease the woeful grief. For Whitsunday. Francis Kinwelmarsh. SiCE

Come, Holy Ghost! thou fire divine! Veni, Sancte Spiritus. Robert II of France. HBV; LPS-3

Come, Holy Spirit, heavenly Dove. Isaac Watts. OlF

Come Home, Come Home! And Where Is Home for Me. Arthur Hugh Clough. Songs in Absence, III. BPN; EmBrPo
 (Come Home, Come Home!) VLEP

Come Home, Father. Henry Clay Work. See Father, Dear Father, Come Home with Me Now.

Come home with me a little space. Christmas at Melrose. Leslie Pinckney Hill. BANP

Come home with white gulls waving across gray. Winter Landscape. Stephen Spender. MBP; MoAB; MoBrPo

Come, honest sexton, take thy spade. The Passing Bell. Unknown. ElSeCe; SeCL; SeEP

Come Hymen come, for here to thee we bring. A Wedding Hymn. Luis de Góngora. Fr. The Solitudes. TeCS

Come, I will make the continent indissoluble. For You O Democracy. Walt Whitman. APW; CoBA; IAP; PaA; PoFr; StaSt; TCAP; TrGrPo

Come I'll sing you a song, just for want of some other. Hop-o-My-Thumb. Unknown. Fr. Ballads on Napoleon. CoBE

Come In. Robert Frost. AmPP; AnNE; GTBS-W; LiTA; LiTM; MaPo; MoAB; MoAmPo; NeMA; ReMP; RiBV; TrGrPo; TwCV; UnPo (3d ed.)

Come in, come in, you little sparrow, tapping. The Snow-Sparrow. Elias Sehlstedt. AnSL

Come in from the veranda and the blaze. Michael. Val Vallis. NeLNL

"Come in out of the night," said the landlord. Number Five. John Crowe Ransom. TCPD

Come in the evening, or come in the morning. The Welcome. Thomas Osborne Davis. HBV; IrPN, 8 ll.; LPS-1; VA

Come in the garden. The Snowman. E. M. Adams. BoTP

Come! in this cool retreat. A New Zealand Regret. Eleanor Elizabeth Montgomery. VA

Come in this hour to set my spirit free. Before Day. Siegfried Sassoon. WGRP

Come into the garden, Kate. The Tryst. E. V. Knox. CenHV

Come Into the Garden, Maud. Tennyson. Maud, Pt. I, xxii. BEL; BPN; EM-2; EnLit; EPN; EPP; EV-5; ExPo; FiP; GEPC; GTBS; GTSE; GTSL; HBV; LEAP; LiTG; LiTL; LPS-1; MCCG; OBVV; PIAE; TreF; TyEnPo; UnPo (1st ed.); VA
 (Lyric from "Maud.") EnLi-2
 (Maud.) BMEP; GTBS-W; OBEV
 (Song [from "Maud"].) AWP; InPo; JAWP; TCEP; TOP; WBP

Come into the Whenceness Which. Whenceness of the Which. Unknown. BOHV

Come, John, sit thee down I have somewhat to say. An Amorous Dialogue between John and His Mistress. Unknown. CoMu

Come join hand in hand, brave Americans all. The Liberty Song [or A Song of American Freedom]. John Dickinson. AmPP; PoFr; TrAS

Come, keen iambics, with your badger's feet. The Rebel Scot. John Cleveland. EPS; OBS; ViBoPo

Come, Landlord, Fill the Flowing Bowl. Unknown. OxBoLi

Come lasses and lads, let me sing to-night. "Peg Away." Fred E. Weatherly. TVSH

Come lasses and lads, take leave of your dads. The Rural Dance about the Maypole. Unknown. OxBoLi; SeCL

"Come, Lazarus!" the Savior/ cried to him. Lazarus. José Asunción Silva. DaM

Come learn with me the fatal song. The Mighty Heart. Emerson. Fr. Woodnotes, II. AA

Come, leave the loathed stage. Ode to Himself. Ben Jonson. CoEV; EPS; EV-2; OBS; ReEn; SeEP

Come, leave this loathed country-life. Upon Himself. Robert Herrick. SeEP

Come! leave this sullen state, and let not wine. To His Retired Friend. Henry Vaughan. ViBoPo

Come, Lesbia, let us live and love. Catullus, tr. fr. Latin by Horace Gregory. RoL

Come, let me sing into your ear. Those Dancing Days Are Gone. W. B. Yeats. AtBAP

Come, let me write. And to what end? To ease. Astrophel and Stella, XXXIV. Sir Philip Sidney. ReIE; SiPS; TuPP

Come! let Mirth our hours employ. A Dithyrambic on Wine. Thomas Godfrey. TCAP

Come let us drink away the time. A Song of Sack. Unknown. OBS

Come, Let Us Eat and Drink Today. Juan del Encina, tr. fr. Spanish by Sir John Bowring. OnPM

Come, Let Us Find. W. H. Davies. HBMV

Come, let us go a-roaming! Travellers. Arthur St. John Adcock. BoTP

Come, Let Us Kiss and Part[e]. Michael Drayton. See Idea: "Since there's no help, come let us kiss and part."

Come, Let Us Make Love Deathless. Herbert Trench. EG; EtPaEn; GTIV; HBMV; LBBV; MBP; OBVV
 (Love, br. sel.) MaRV

Come, let us mount the breezy down. Harvest Home. Frederick Tennyson. OBVV

Come, let us now resolve at last. The Reconcilement. John Sheffield, Duke of Buckingham and Normanby. CEP; LiTL; LO; LoPo; LoPS; OBEV

Come let us pity those who are better off than we are. The Garret. Ezra Pound. BAP; MOAP; NP

Come, let us plant the apple tree. The Planting of the Apple Tree. Bryant. AA; ADAH; AnNE; DD; GN; HBV; HBVV; LaNeLa; LEAP; LPS-2; MPB (1956 ed.); OHIP; PECK; PTA-1; SN; StVeCh

Come let us rejoice. About Savannah. Unknown. PAH

"Come let us sigh a requiem over love." Robert Nichols. Sonnets to Aurelia, IV. OBMV

Come, let us sing! it is the time for summer. For an Eskimo. Annie Charlotte Dalton. CaP; OCL

Come, Let Us Sound with Melody the Praises. Thomas Campion. ReIE; SiCE; UnS

Come let's begin to revel 't out. Madrigal. Unknown. BoTP

Come, let's get out of here! Out of the din of it. City-weary. Edgar A. Guest. NLK

Come, let's to bed. Mother Goose. OnPM; OTPC; OxBoLi; OxNR; RIS; SiTL
 ("To bed, to bed, says sleepy-head.") SAS; WP

Come, life, my shining brother. Autumn. Hans Hartvig Seedorff Pedersen. BoDS

Come light and listen, you gentlemen all. Robin Hood and the Beggar, I. Unknown. BaBo; ESPB

Come, list and hark! the bell doth toll. The Passing Bell. Thomas Heywood. Fr. The Rape of Lucrece. SeCL

Come list to me, ye heroes, ye nobles, and ye braves. The Raging Can-all. Unknown. ABF

Come list ye landsmen, all to me. The Wonderful Crocodile. Unknown. ABF

Come listen a while and I'll sing you a song. Hard Times. Unknown. ABF; CSF

Come listen a while, you gentlemen all. Robin Hood Newly Revived. Unknown. BaBo; ESPB

Come, listen all unto [or listen to] my song. How Cyrus Laid the Cable. John Godfrey Saxe. MC; PaA; PAH; PTA-1

Come listen, and hear me tell/ the end of a tale so true. The Lass of Lynn's New Joy, for Finding a Father for Her Child. Unknown. CoMu

Come listen and I'll tell you. The Yankee Privateer. Arthur Hale. PaA; PAH

Come listen awhile, and I'll sing you a song. The Silly Old Man. Unknown. CoMu

Come, listen, good neighbors of every degree. Derry-Down [or The Liberty Pole]. Unknown. Fr. The Procession with the Standard of a Faction; a Cantata. APW; PAH

"Come, listen, my men, while I tell you again." How to

Recognize a Snark [*or* The Snark]. "Lewis Carroll." *Fr.* The Hunting of the Snark. BOHV; MPB; TSW; TSWC
Come listen, O Love, to the voice of the dove. The Voice of the Dove. Joaquin Miller. AA
Come listen to a ranger, you kind-hearted stranger. The Disheartened Ranger. *Unknown.* CoSo; CSF
Come listen to another song. The Old Scottish Cavalier. William Edmondstoune Aytoun. GN; HBV; PoVP
Come listen to me, you [*or* ye] gallants so free. Robin Hood and Allen [*or* Allan *or* Alan *or* Allin]-a-Dale. *Unknown.* BaBo; BoChLi; CG; EnLit; ESPB; EV-2; FaBoBe; GoTP; HBV; LoEn; LPS-2; MCCG; MoShBr; OBB; OnSP; PYM; StVeCh (1940 ed.); TyEnPo
Come listen to my ditty/ 'Twill not detain you long. Baldy Green. *Unknown.* PoOW
Come, listen to my song. *See* Come, listen all unto my song.
Come listen to my story, Molly Bawn. Molly Bawn and Brian Oge. *Unknown.* OnYI
Come, listen to my story, ye landsmen, one and all. Raging Canawl. *Unknown.* AS
Come, listen to my tragedy, good people, young and old. Henry Green. *Unknown.* BaBo
Come listen to the story of brave Lathrop and his Men. The Lamentable Ballad of the Bloody Brook. Edward Everett Hale. HBV; PAH
Come listen unto me a while. Old Sailor's Song. *Unknown.* SoAmSa
Come, little babe, come, silly soul. A Sweet Lullaby [*or* Cradle Song]. Nicholas Breton. BOL; ElL; EV-1; GTSL; HBV; LEAP; MotAn; OBEV; OBSC; SiCE; TOP; TuPP; ViBoPo
Come, little boy, to mother's knee. Christmas Dusk. Wilbur D. Nesbit. PEDC
Come, little children, gather round. The Shepherd's Madrigal. Geraldine Farrar. StJW
Come, little Drummer Boy, lay down your knapsack here. The Soldier's Friend. George Canning. OBEC
Come, little infant, love me now. Young Love. Andrew Marvell. EV-2
Come, Little Leaves. George Cooper. FaPON; MPB; OTPC; PCH; PPL; RIS
(Wind and the Leaves, The.) BoTP; RAR
Come, little one with drowsy eyes. A Winter Song. Pauline Frances Camp. BOL
Come live with me, and be my love. The Bait[e]. John Donne. AnEnPo; EnLP; EPS (1942 ed.); HoPM; LiTL; OAEP; PoRA; ReaPo; TuPP; WhC
Come live with me and be my love. That Strain Again. Ronald Hambleton. CaP
Come, Live with Me and Be My Love. C. Day Lewis. AtBAP; CoBMV; MaRV; OBMV
Come live with me and be my Love. The Passionate Shepherd to His Love [*or* The Shepherd to His Love *or* The Shepherd's Plea *or* The Milkmaid's Song]. Christopher Marlowe. AEV; AnEnPo; ATP; AWP; BEL; BLV; BoLiVe; BTP; CaAE; CBOV; CenL; CG; CoBE; EG; ElL; ElSeCe; EM-1; EnL; EnLi-1; EnLit; EPP; EV-1; ExPo; FaBoBe; FaBoEn; FaFP; GBV (1952 ed.); GN; GTBS; GTBS-D; GTBS-W; GTSE; GTSL; HBV; HoPM; InPo; JAWP; KN; LEAP; LiTB; LiTG; LiTL; LoBV; LoPo; LPS-1; NeHB; OAEP; OBEV; OBSC; OTPC (1923 ed.); OuHeWo; PG (1945 ed.); PIAE; PIR; Po; PoE; PoFS; PoRA; ReaPo; ReEn; ReIE; RG; RiBV; SeCePo; SeCeV; SiCE; SiPS; SiTL; TCEP; ThWaDe; TOP; TreF; TrGrPo; TuPP; TVSH; TwHP; UnPo (1st ed.); ViBoPo; WBP; WHA; WP
Come live with me and be my whore. The Wooing Rogue. *Unknown.* CoMu
Come, Lord Jesus. Charles Wesley. BePJ
Come, Love, Come, the Boat Lies Low, *with music.* *Unknown.* StDa
Come, love, help me move all the mirrors out of my workshop. Love, Give Me the Feel of To-Morrow. Ralph Cheyney. AOAH
Come, Love, Let's Walk. *Unknown.* ElL
Come Love or Death. Will Henry Thompson. AA
Come Lovely and Soothing Death. Walt Whitman. *See* Death Carol.
Come, Lovers, Bring Your Cares. John Jones. *Fr.* Adrasta. SeCL; TuPP
Come, loyal Britons all, rejoice, with joyful acclamation. Brave News from Admiral Vernon. *Unknown.* SG
Come lusty ladyes come come with pensive thoughte ye pyne. *Unknown.* SeCSL
Come, Mad Boys. *Unknown.* AnEC
Come, madam, come, all rest my powers defy. Going to Bed [*or* To His Mistress Going to Bed]. John Donne. Elegies, XIX. LiTB; LiTG; MePo; ReEn; SiTL
Come, master of the Rhodian art. To a Painter. *Unknown.* GrL
Come, May, and hang a white flag on each thorn. Thoughts at the Trysting Stile. Francis Ledwidge. TCEP
Come, men, stack arms! Pile on the rails. Stonewall Jackson's Way. John Williamson Palmer. AA; DD; GA; HBV; MC; PAH; SPP
Come, mete me out my loneliness, O wind. Mete Me Out My Loneliness. "Michael Field." MBP
Come Michaelmas. A. Newberry Choyce. HBMV
Come Micky and Molly and dainty Dolly. The Flitch of Dunmow. James Carnegie. HBV; VA
Come mighty Must! The Mighty Must. W. S. Gilbert. *Fr.* Princess Ida. BOHV
Come, mint me up the golden gorse. The Casual Man. Denis Glover. AnNZ
Come, Muse, migrate from Greece and Ionia. The Muse in the New World. Walt Whitman. Song of the Exposition, II, III, *abr.* APW; MAP; MoAmPo; OnAP
Come, Muses, come, and help me to lament. Deep Desire Sung This Song. George Gascoigne. TuPP
Come muster, my lads, your mechanical tools. The New Roof. Francis Hopkinson. PAH
Come, My Celia, Let Us Prove. Ben Jonson. *Fr.* Volpone, III, vii. AtBAP; ElL; ElSeCe; EnLi-1 (1949 ed.); MaPo; ReaPo; SiCE; WHA
(Come, My Celia.) TrGrPo
(Song to Celia.) EnL; OBS; SeCeV; SeCV-1; SiTL; TuPP
(To Celia.) FaBoEn; LoBV; ReEn; ReIE; TyEnPo
(Two Songs to Celia.) TwHP
(Vivamus Mea Lesbia atque Amemus.) EG
(Volpone's Song: To Celia.) PreP
Come, my dainty doxies. Thomas Middleton. *Fr.* More Dissemblers besides Women, IV, i. ElSeCe; TuPP
Come, my dearest, come, my fairest. The Saucy Sailor. *Unknown.* SaSa
Come my enemies, my friends. The Truth? John Cowper Powys. BAP
Come my friends and listen unto me. The Parson Grocer. *Unknown.* CoMu
Come, my little one, with me! The Shut-Eye Train. Eugene Field. PFE
Come, my little Robert, near. Cleanliness. Charles *and* Mary Lamb. OTPC (1923 ed.); PRWS
Come, my Lucasia, since we see. Friendship's Mystery. Katherine Philips. ViBoPo
Come, my *moo sarge,* let us go up that shining mountain. Wabanaki Song. *Unknown.* PeCV
Come my Oenone lett us doe. *Unknown.* SeCSL
Come, my songs, let us express our baser passions. Further Instructions. Ezra Pound. AnAmPo; BAP; CoV; LA; NP
Come, My Soul, Thy Suit Prepare. John Newton. PraP
Come, my sweet, whiles every strain. William Cartwright. EG
Come my tan-faced children. Pioneers! O Pioneers! Walt Whitman. AmPP; APW; ATP; CoBA; EV-5; FaBoBe; IAP; MOAP; MPB; PaA; PFE; PIAE; PoeMoYo; PYM; TCAP; TOP; UnPo (1st ed.); WHA
Come, my Way, my Truth, my Life. The Call. George Herbert. MeRV
Come, mysterious night. A Hymn to Night. Max Michelson. NP; TrJP
Come near me, for the night. Microcosmos, XL. Nigel Heseltine. NeBP
Come, Night. George Chapman. *See* Bridal Song ("O come . . .").
Come Night, Come Romeo. Shakespeare. *Fr.* Romeo and Juliet, III, ii. LiTL
Come, no more of grief and dying! Guadeamus Igitur. Margaret L. Woods. PoeT
Come not again! I dwell with you. The Flown Soul. George Parsons Lathrop. AA
Come not before me now, O visionary face! Seraphita. Ernest Dowson. VLEP
Come not in terrors clad, to claim. To Death. Caroline Anne Bowles. DiM; OBEV (1st ed.)
Come Not Near. Mary Elizabeth Osborn. NePoAm-2
Come Not near My Songs. *Tr. fr. Shoshone Indian by* Mary Austin. AWP; JAWP; LoPS; PG; WBP
Come not the earliest petal here. Quiet. Marjorie Pickthall. BoCaPo; PeCV; TwCaPo
Come Not the Seasons Here. E. J. Pratt. PeCV
Come Not, When I Am Dead. Tennyson. BPN; EmBrPo; PIR; PoVP; ViPo; VLEP
Come Nothing to My Comparable Soul. E. E. Cummings. MOAP
Come, now a roundel and a fairy song. The Fairies' Lullaby. Shakespeare. *Fr.* A Midsummer Night's Dream, II, ii. LPS-3
Come now, and let us wake them: time. Serenade. *Unknown.* AWP; JAWP; WBP
Come now behold. The Glory of and Grace in the Church. Edward Taylor. *Fr.* God's Determinations. AnNE
Come now each gen'rous feeling heart. The Framework-Knitters Lamentation. *Unknown.* CoMu

Come now, though Muses are not left to sing. Epithalamion. Donald Davidson. TBM
Come, O Come. Thomas Campion. *See* Come, Oh, Come, My Life's Delight.
Come, oh come in pious Laies. Hymne I: A Generall Invitation to Praise God. George Wither. *Fr.* Hallelujah; or, Britain's Second Remembrancer. SeCV-1
Come, Oh, Come, My Life's Delight. Thomas Campion. EG; ElL; InvP; LO; OBSC; SiCE
(Come, O Come.) AtBAP
(My Life's Delight.) TrGrPo
Come, O Friend, to Greet the Bride. Heine, *after the Hebrew of* Solomon Halevi Alkabez, *tr. fr. German by* Louis Untermeyer. *Fr.* Hebrew Melodies. MeRV; TrJP
Come, O Holy Spirit now. Veni, Sancte Spiritus. *Unknown.* LPS-2
Come, O Lord, like Morning Sunlight. Milton S. Littlefield. TrPWD
Come, O thou traveller unknown. Wrestling Jacob. Charles Wesley. CEP; EiPP; LPS-2; NBE; OBEC; OBEV (new ed.); OxBoCh; PoEL-3; SeCePo
Come, O Wind. James B. Kenyon. BOL
Come o'er the stream, Charlie. M'Lean's Welcome. James Hogg. EBSV
Come off to the stable, all you who are able. Words for Army Bugle Calls: Stable Call. *Unknown.* TreF
Come, oh, songs! Come, oh, dreams! The Wild Rose. Hermann Hagedorn, Jr. PFY
Come-on, come-on, come-on sir: give mee your hand, Sir. Mortality. Shakespeare. King Henry the Fourth, Pt. II, *fr.* III, ii. LiA
Come on! Come on! This hillock hides the spire. Sunday Afternoon Service in St. Enodoc Church, Cornwall. John Betjeman. MoVE
Come on, don't be afraid you'll spoil me. Serenade. Emanuel Carnevali. AnAmPo; LA
Come On, My Pink, an' Tell Me What You Think, *with music.* *Unknown.* StDa
Come on, sir; here's the place:—stand still. Dover Cliffs. Shakespeare. *Fr.* King Lear, IV, vi. LPS-2; SN
Come on, sir. Now, you set your foot on shore. Here's the Rich Peru. Ben Jonson. *Fr.* The Alchemist, II, i–ii. AtBAP; LiA; PoEL-2
Come on then, ye dwellers by nature in darkness. Chorus of Birds [*or* Grand Chorus of Birds *or* The Hymn of the Birds]. Aristophanes, *tr. by* Swinburne. *Fr.* The Birds. AWP; JAWP; OxBG; PoEL-5; WBP
Come, on thy swaying feet. The Spirit of the Fall. Danske Dandridge. AA; LBAP
Come, Ophrah, fill my cup—but not with wine. The Splendor of Thine Eyes. Moses ibn Ezra. TrJP
"Come out and hear the waters shoot, the owlet hoot, the owlet hoot." Apprenticed. Jean Ingelow. *Fr.* Songs of the Night Watches. AlDL; LiTL; OBVV
Come out and join the caroling. Join the Caroling. Rowena Bastin Bennett. SDH
Come out and join the revels! A Song for May Day. Frederick Herbert Adler. DD
Come out and walk. The last few drops of light. A Night Piece. Edward Shanks. HBMV
Come out, come out, this sunny day. Hay-Time. C. M. Lowe. BoTP
"Come out," he said. Tennyson. *Fr.* The Princess. EnSW
Come out o' door, 'tis Spring! 'tis May. May. William Barnes. GTBS-D; RO
Come out! oh, little comrade of the tresses flying free. Comrades. Arthur Guiterman. FAOV
Come out, O Little Moccasins, and frolic on the snow! Little Moccasins. Robert W. Service. CPG
Come Out of the Lily. Ruth Pitter. *See* O Come Out of the Lily.
Come out, old man, out from the tent to me! Watch before Dawn. Euripides. *Fr.* Iphigenia in Aulis. OxBG
Come out, 'tis now September. The Ripe and Bearded Barley. *Unknown.* ChTr
"Come out with me!" cried the little red sled. The Little Red Sled. Jocelyn Bush. PCH; TiPo
Come over, come over the river to me. Charlie Machree. William J. Hoppin. LPS-1
Come over the bourn [*or* born], Bessy. A Song[e] between the Queen's Majesty and England. William Birche. CoMu; TuPP
Come Pensive Nun. Milton. *Fr.* Il Penseroso. PraNu
Come, Phyllis, I've a cask of wine. To Phyllis. Eugene Field, *after* Horace. InMe
Come play with me. To a Squirrel at Kyle-na-no. W. B. Yeats. FaPON; ThWaDe
Come! pledge again thy heart and hand. Song for July 12th, 1843. John de Jean Frazer. TIP
Come, Poet, Come! Arthur Hugh Clough. BPN
Come, pretty lamb, do stay with me. The Lamb. *Unknown.* OTPC (1923 ed.)
Come pure in heart before this hallowed fane. A Pythian Oracle. *Unknown.* OxBG
Come, put off your gown of smooth lilac. Winter and Red Berries. Nicholas Moore. NeBP
Come, read to me some poem. Longfellow. *Fr.* The Day Is Done. YT
Come, rejoice, 'tis Easter Day. Christ Is Risen. Mrs. D. H. Dugan. BLRP
Come, rest beneath my pine-tree, murmuring sweet. Spoken by the God Pan. *Unknown.* OnPM
Come, Rest in This Bosom. Thomas Moore. EnRP; ERP; LPS-1
(Song: "Come, rest in this bosom, my own stricken deer.") PG
(Stricken Deer, The). GoBC
Come ride and ride to the garden. Lady Gregory. SUS
Come, Ride with Me to Toyland. Rowena Bennett. ChBR; SiSoSe
Come Roll Him Over. *Unknown.* SG
Come roll the cotton down, my boys. Roll the Cotton Down. *Unknown.* SG
Come, rosy angel, thy coronet donning. Evening. Robert Bridges, *after* William Blake. EPP
Come round me, little childer. The Ballad of Moll Magee. W. B. Yeats. TwP
Come, rouse up, ye bold-hearted Whigs of Kentucky. Old Tippecanoe. *Unknown.* GA; PAH
Come, said [*or* says] Jesus' sacred voice. Come, Says Jesus' Voice. Anna Letitia Barbauld. BePJ; BPP
Come, Said My Soul. Walt Whitman. IAP
"Come!" said Old Shellover. Old Shellover. Walter de la Mare. AtBAP; BoTP; UTS
Come Said the Muse. Walt Whitman. *Fr. various poems.* LiA
Come sail with me o'er the golden sea. The Lord of the World. G. A. Studdert-Kennedy. PGD; PSO
Come, sail-i-ors, landsmen, one and all. Erie Canal. *Unknown.* ABF
Come, Says Jesus' Voice. Anna Letitia Barbauld. BePJ
(Come.) BPP
Come Se Quando. Robert Bridges. MM
Come see the baby in her bath. The Baby's Bath. Sarah Jane S. Harrington. RAR
Come, see the *Dolphin*'s anchor forged—'tis at a white heat now. The Forging of the Anchor. Sir Samuel Ferguson. HBV; IrPN; LPS-2; PoVP; TVSH
Come, see thy friend, retir'd without regret. Nil Admirari. Congreve. *Fr.* Of Improving the Present Time. OBEC
Come sell your pony, cowboy. Sweetgrass Range [*or* Sweet Grass Range]. Edwin Ford Piper. CBOV; LEAP; MAP; PFY; TBM
Come, shall we come out of the listening season into the city. Entry. Josephine Miles. AnAmPo
Come sheathe your swords! my gallant boys. Sergeant Champe. *Unknown.* PAH
Come, Shepherds, Come! John Fletcher. *Fr.* The Faithful Shepherdess, I, iii. EG; ElL
Come shepherds, come! Your silent sheep. The Angel and the Shepherds. *Unknown.* ChrBoLe
Come, Silence, thou sweet reasoner. Silence. James Herbert Morse. AA
Come, Sirrah Jack, Ho! *Unknown.* OAEP
Come sit aneath this pinetree, whose lofty tressed crown. Country Music. Plato. LiTW; OxBG
Come, sit beneath/ The pine. A Statue of Pan. *Unknown.* OxBG
Come sit where elm twig scrapes on hazel shoot. Daphnis. Virgil. Eclogues, V. LaP
Come sit you down and give attention. Silver Dagger. *Unknown.* ABS
Come, Sleep. Beaumont *and* Fletcher. *Fr.* The Woman-Hater, III, i. ElL
("Come, sleep, and with thy sweet deceiving.") EG; SiCE
(Invocation to Sleep.) LPS-3
(Lullaby: "Come sleep, and with the sweet deceiving.") FaBoEn
(Sleep.) EV-2; HBV; OBEV (1st ed.); PC
"Come, Sleep . . ." Louise Bogan. OnAP
Come, Sleep. Sir Philip Sidney. *See* Come, sleep, O sleep, the certain knot of peace.
Come, Sleep! but mind ye! if ye come without. To Sleep. Walter Savage Landor. VA
Come, sleep, O sleep, the certain knot of peace. Astrophel and Stella, XXXIX. Sir Philip Sidney. AnFE; BCEP; BEL; BLV; BoLiVe; CaAE; CoBE; CoEV; ElL; ElSeCe; EnL; EnLi-1; EnLit; EPP; ES; EV-1; GTSL; HBV; InP; LEAP; LiTG; LoBV; LPS-3; MyFE; OAEP; OBEV; OBSC; PC; PeBoSo; PIAE; PoE; PoFS; PoRA; ReaPo; ReEn; ReIE; ShBV-4; SiCE; SiPS; TreFS; TrGrPo; TuPP; TwHP; ViBoPo; WHA
Come Slowly, Paradise. James Benjamin Kenyon. AA
Come, soft and soothing. Voice of Song. Steingrímur Thorsteinsson. IcP
Come, solace of the world, calm Night! The Hermit. Joseph von Eichendorff. AnGP

Come, soldiers, arouse ye! The Dead Comrade. Richard Watson Gilder. MDAH
Come solemn Muse and help me sing. A Sonet to the Tune of A Hone a Hone. Nicholas Breton. SiCE
Come, Sons of Mars, who thirst for Blood. A Drinking-Song, against All Sorts of Disputes in Drinking. William Wycherley. SeCV-2
Come, sons of summer, by whose toil. The Hock-Cart, or Harvest Home. Robert Herrick. EPS; EV-2; OAEP; OBS; OTPC (1923 ed.); PoE; ReEn; SeCV-1; SeEP; ViBoPo
Come, sons of Zeus, from Pelops' isle. Castor and Polydeuces. Alcaeus. OxBG
Come Sorrow wrap me in thy sable cloake. *Unknown.* SeCSL
Come, sound up your trumpets and beat up your drums. The Young Earl of Essex's Victory over the Emperor of Germany. *Unknown.* ESPB
Come, sprite, and dance! The sun is up. The Bacchante to Her Babe. Eunice Tietjens. HBMV; NP; NV
Come, spur [*or* spurre] away. An Ode to Mr. [*or* Master] Anthony Stafford to Hasten Him into the Country [*or* Ode on Leaving the Great Town]. Thomas Randolph. EG; ElSeCe; EV-2; FaBoEn; GoTL; HBV; LEAP; NLK; OBEV; OBS; SeCL; SeEP; ViBoPo
Come, stack arms, men; pile on the rails. Stonewall Jackson's Way. John Williamson Palmer. AA; BlG; DD; GA; HBV; MC; OTPC (1946 ed.); PaA; PAH; SPP
Come, stand we here within this cactus-brake. A Sicilian Night. Edward Cracroft Lefroy. Echoes from Theocritus, IV. VA
Come suddenly, O Lord, or slowly come. The Coming of the Lord. Jones Very. BePJ
"Come; sun and laughter wait us at the end!" Aut Caesar aut Nullus. Lilian White Spencer. CAW; TBM
Come! supper is ready. The Good Moolly Cow. Eliza Lee Follen. PPL
"Come, surly fellow, come! A song!" The Haunted House. Robert Graves. OxBI
Come, swallow your bumpers, ye Tories, and roar. Massachusetts Song of Liberty. Mercy Warren. PAH
Come, Sweet Lass. *Unknown.* SeCL
Come, sweeting, let us see if the rose. Spring. Pierre de Ronsard. TrFP
Come take a carouse. *Unknown.* SeCSL
Come take a woodland walk with me. The Oak. John Keble. EnSW
Come take up your hats and away let us haste. The Butterfly's Ball. William Roscoe. BoChLi; BoN; CBPC; GoTP; OTPC, *diff. vers.;* TVC; TVSH
"Come, tell me, dearest mother, what makes my father stay." Sorrowful Lamentation of Callaghan, Greally and Mullen. *Unknown.* TIP
"Come tell me, was it all for naught." Borodino. Mikhail Lermontov. BoRS
"Come tell us the name of the rebelly crew." The Patriot Mother. *Unknown.* MOAH
Come the little clouds out of the Ice-Caves. Indian Songs. Louis Mertins. StVeCh (1955 ed.)
Come, the wind may never again. Emily Brontë. EnLoPo
Come then, a song; a winding gentle song. In a Garden by Moonlight. Thomas Lovell Beddoes. *Fr.* Torrismond. VA
Come then, and like two doves with silv'ry [*or* silv'rie] wings. The Apparition of His Mistress Calling Him to Elysium [*or* Elizium]. Robert Herrick. ExPo; SeCV-1
Come then, as ever, like the wind at morning! Invocation to Youth. Laurence Binyon. OBEV; OBVV
Come then, my friend, and seize the flask. Archilochus, *tr. fr. Greek by* J. H. Merivale. GrPo
Come then, my friend, my genius! Come along! A Literary Poet to His Patron [*or* Henry St. John, Viscount Bolingbroke *or* The Poet's Friend]. Pope. *Fr.* An Essay on Man. CBE; LPS-3; OBEC
Come, then, my much-lov'd Prince. Evanthe's Invitation. Thomas Godfrey. *Fr.* The Prince of Parthia. NoCaPo
Come then, tell me, sage divine. Ode, on a Sermon against Glory. Mark Akenside. CEP
Come, thou almighty King. *Unknown, wr. at. to* Charles Wesley. OlF; WGRP
Come thou from the four winds, O breath. The Army of the Dead. William Rose Benét. QS
Come, Thou Holy Spirit, come. The Golden Sequence. Pope Innocent III. CAW
Come, Thou Monarch of the Vine. Shakespeare. *Fr.* Antony and Cleopatra, II, vii. BEL; OAEP; OnPM; ViBoPo
(Drinking Song, A.) OBSC
Come Thou My Light. Hugh Thomson Kerr. MaRV
Come thou, who art the wine and wit. His Winding Sheet. Robert Herrick. AnFE; EM-1; EPS (1942 ed.); HBV; OBEV
Come thro' the heather, around him gather. Wha'll Be King but Charlie? Lady Nairne. EBSV; EV-3
Come through the quiet fields; April again. April, 1940. Patrick Maybin. NeIP
Come to Bethlehem and ye shall see. A Carol of the Birth of Christ. *Unknown.* AnEC
Come to Birth. Abbie Huston Evans. NePoAm
Come to Britain; a Humble Contribution to the Movement. A. P. Herbert. WhC
Come to Calvary's Holy Mountain. James Montgomery. BePJ
Come to conquer. Cold Water Flat. Philip Booth. NePoAm
Come to Me. *Unknown, tr. fr. Japanese by* Ishii *and* Obata. *Fr.* Manyo Shu. OnPM
Come to me, angel of the weary-hearted! To Sleep. Frances Sargent Osgood. AA; LEAP
Come to Me, Beloved. Digby Mackworth Dolben. OxBoCh
(Homo Factus Est.) TrPWD
Come to Me, Dearest. Joseph Brenan. HBV; LPS-1
Come to me, Eros, if you needs must come. To the God of Love. Edmund G. V. Knox. ALV; HBMV
Come to Me, Gentle Sleep! Felicia Dorothea Hemans. ERP
Come to me, grief for ever. A Funeral[l] Song [*or* Lament over Sir Philip Sidney]. *Unknown.* BHV; CH; PoD; TriL
Come to me in my dreams, and then. Another Way. Andrew Lang. UnW
Come to me in my dreams, and then. Longing. Matthew Arnold. HBV; LO, *st.* 1; OAEP; VLEP
Come to me in the embalming hush of night. Folded Wings. Marian Osborne. CPG
Come to me in the silence of the night. Echo. Christina Rossetti. BLV; CH; EmBrPo; EPN; GTBS-D; LiTL; LO; LoBV; LoPo; LoPS; MBP; PoEL-5; POTT; SeCeV; TriL; ViBoPo; ViPo; VLEP
Come to me, my dearest. Come to Me. *Unknown. Fr.* Manyo Shu. OnPM
Come to me, my poems, all my far-flung armies. Catullus, *tr. fr. Latin by* Horace Gregory. LaP
Come to me, O my Mother! come to me. Homesick. David Gray. LPS-1; MOAH
Come to me, O ye children! Children. Longfellow. GTBS; IAP; PTA-2; TCAP
Come to me, O ye sorrowful and hungry! My Clarion Call. Alberto Ghiraldo. PoFr
Come to me out of the dark. Like a Cloud, like a Mist. Helen Hoyt. AV
Come to me, Pan, with your wind-wild laughter. Song for a Forgotten Shrine to Pan. John Farrar. BAP
Come to me when the swelling wind assails the wood with a sea-like roar. Late Light. Edmund Blunden. EnLoPo
Come to me, you with the laughing face, in the night as I lie. Pirates. Alfred Noyes. MCCG; VOD
Come to my bidding, gentle damsels fair. The Alhambra. Francisco Martínez de la Rosa. AnSpL-2
Come to my heart, cruel, sullen soul. Lethe. Baudelaire. AnFP
Come to my window in the evening twilight. Sunset. Hayyim Nahman Bialik. TrJP
Come to the Fair. Helen Taylor. OlF
Come to the festal board to-night. The Festal Board. *Unknown.* BLPA; TreFS
Come to the Park They Say Is Dead and See. Stefan George, *tr. fr. German by* Kenneth Gee. AnGP
Come to the terrace, May—the sun is low. A Sonnet in Dialogue. Austin Dobson. YT
"Come to the window, Mamma, and look out." Flying Flowers. Mrs. Motherly. SAS
Come to These Scenes of Peace. William Lisle Bowles. LPS-2
Come to this land of sunshine. Arizona. Margaret Rowe Clifford. PoRL
Come to Your Heaven, You Heavenly Choirs [*or* Quires]! Robert Southwell. EG; OxBoCh; PoLi
(New Heaven, New War [*or* Warre]. AlDL; LoBV; MePo; OBSC
Come tomorrow night. Young Man's Fancy. Ray Mathew. BoAV
Come, triumphe. enter Church, courte, citty, towne. A Gratulatory Elegy of the Peaceable Entry of King James. Sir John Harington. SiCE
"Come, try your skill, kind gentlemen." The Gipsy Girl. Ralph Hodgson. CMP; EnLit; GTML; MCCG; MoBrPo; PoeMoYo; POTE
Come Turn to Mee, Thou Pretty Little One. *Unknown.* CoMu
Come under My Plaidie. Hector MacNeill. EBSV
Come unto Me. Katharine Lee Bates. ChIP
Come unto Me. St. Matthew, XI: 28–30, Bible, *N.T.* MaRV
(My Yoke Is Easy.) TreFS
Come unto me. ye heroes. Saratoga Song. *Unknown.* PAH
Come unto me, ye weary. William C. Dix. OlF
Come unto these yellow sands. Ariel's Song. Shakespeare. *Fr.* The Tempest, I, ii. AEV; AnFE; AtBAP; BCEP; BEL; BoTP; CBE; CBPC; CG; CH; EG; ElL; EM-1; EV-1; FaBoCh; GN; GTSL; HBV; InPo; KN; LEAP; LoBV; LoGBV; MCCG; MPB (1956 ed.); OBEV; OBSC; OTPC (1923 ed.); PCH; PoEL-2; RAR; SiCE; ThWaDe; TOP; TwHP; ViBoPo
Come up, dear chosen morning, come. Marriage Song. Lascelles Abercrombie. BMEP, *abr.;* BrBE; LEAP, *abr.*

Come Up from the Fields, Father. Walt Whitman. AmPo; AmPP; APW; ATP (1935 ed.); CoBA; IAP; MAP; MCCG; MDAH; MoAmPo (1950 ed.); MOAP; NeMA; OuHeWo; OxBA; TCAP
Come up here, O dusty feet! Fairy Bread. Robert Louis Stevenson. GBV (1922 ed.); MeMeAg; OTPC (1946 ed.)
Come up in the orchard with grass to your knee. Apple Season. Frances Frost. BrR; SiSoSe
Come Up, Methuselah. C. Day Lewis. OBMV
Come up, my horse, to Budleigh Fair. *Unknown.* OxNR
Come up to me at early dawn. Invitation. Solomon ibn Gabirol. TrJP
Come Up to Umbria. Charles Phillips. SaFP
Come, virgin tapers of pure wax. Epithalamium. Richard Crashaw. ReEn; ViBoPo
Come Vyolle come lett me thy necke embrace. *Unknown.* SeCSL
Come walk with me. Walk on a Winter Day. Sara Van Alstyne Allen. YeAr
Come walk with me along this willowed lane. May. Henry Sylvester Cornwell. HBV
Come, Walter Savage Landor, come this way. Landor. John Albee. AA; LEAP
Come, Wandering Sheep. Edward Caswall. BePJ
Come, Wandering Sheep, O Come! Luis de Góngora, *tr. fr. Spanish by* Sir John Bowring. AnSpL-1
(Come, Wandering Sheep.) TeCS
Come Wary One. Ruth Manning-Sanders. CH
Come, we shepherds, whose blest sight. In the Holy Nativity of Our Lord God [*or* Holy Nativity of Our Lord God *or* Hymn of the Nativity *or* The Nativity *or* The Shepherd's Hymn]. Richard Crashaw. AtBAP; BEL; CoBE; ElSeCe; EnL; EPP, *sl. abr.;* EPS; EV-2, *sl. abr.;* MeLP; MePo; OBS, *sl. abr.;* OxBoCh; PoEL-2; PoLi; SeCeV; SeCV-1; SeEP; TCEP, *sl. abr.;* UnPo (1st ed.); WGRP, *sl. abr.*
Come, we who love the Lord. Isaac Watts. OlF
Come wench, are we almost at the well? The Song at the Well [*or* Fair Maiden]. George Peele. *Fr.* The Old Wives' Tale. AtBAP; PoEL-2
Come, when no graver cares employ. To the Rev. F. D. Maurice. Tennyson. CBE
Come When the Leaf Comes. Thomas Tod Stoddart. *See* Angler's Invitation, The.
Come, when the pale moon like a petal. Come. Sara Teasdale. ChMo; CMP; SBMV
Come when you're called. Rules of Behavior. Mother Goose. HBV; HBVY; OxNR; SAS
Come Where My Love Lies Dreaming. Stephen Collins Foster. OlF; TreFS
Come while the afternoon of May. Expectation. Theodore Wratislaw. VA
Come, white angels, to baby and me. A Baby Song. Elizabeth Stoddard. BOL
Come with me. The Train. Gerardo Diego. CoSP
Come with me, follow me, swift as a moth. The Pool. Marjorie Pickthall. CPG; MM; NLK (1947 ed.); OCL
Come with me then, my son. The Father. Sir Ronald Ross. FAOV; TCPD
Come with me, under my coat. The Coolin. James Stephens. POTE; TIP
Come with rain, O loud Southwester! To the Thawing Wind. Robert Frost. AlDL; OxBA; RIS
Come with the Spring-time, forth Fair Maid, and be. The Meddow Verse; or, Aniversary to Mistris Bridget Lowman. Robert Herrick. SeCV-1
Come with Thy Lute. J. P. Hullah. OlF
Come, workers! Poets, artists, dreamers, more and more. Angela Morgan. *Fr.* Let Us Declare! PGD
Come, worthy Greek! Ulysses, come. Ulysses and the Siren [*or* Syren]. Samuel Daniel. ElL; EV-1; LiA; LoBV; OBEV; OBSC; PoEL-2; ReaPo; ReEn; ReIE; SiCE; TuPP; TwCrTr; ViBoPo
Come, Ye Disconsolate. Thomas Moore. CAW; MaRV; WGRP
Come, ye faithful, raise the strain. St. John of Damascus, *tr. fr. Greek by* John Mason Neale. OlF
Come, ye heavy states of night. *Unknown.* OBSC
Come ye hither all, whose taste. The Invitation. George Herbert. TriL
Come, Ye Lads, Who wish to Shine. *Unknown.* PAH
Come, ye sinners, poor and needy. Joseph Hart. OlF
Come Ye Sons of Art. Henry Purcell. UnS
Come ye sons of Columbia, your attention I do crave. Fuller and Warren. *Unknown.* ABS; CSF, *with music, sl. diff. vers.*
Come ye, spirits three! The Conjurer. Lew Sarett. PFE
Come, ye students, sail with me. On First Looking into a Circular for a Student's Around-the-World Cruise. "B. A. D." CAG
Come, ye thankful people, come. Harvest Home [*or* Thanksgiving Day]. Henry Alford. MaRV; TOAH; WGRP
Come you gallants all, to you I do call. Robin Hood's Chase. *Unknown.* BaBo; ESPB
Come you ladies and you gentlemen and listen to my song. Hard Times in the Country. *Unknown.* OuSiCo
Come, you pretty false-eyed wanton. Thomas Campion. CoEV; ElSeCe; OBSC
Come, you seamen, deepwater mariners. A Nile Chantey. *Unknown.* OxBG
Come, You Whose Loves Are Dead. Beaumont *and* Fletcher. *Fr.* The Knight of the Burning Pestle, IV, iv. AtBAP; ElL; SiCE; TuPP
(Dirge: "Come, you whose loves are dead.") EV-2
Comedian. Louis Johnson. AnNZ
Comedian as the Letter C, The. Wallace Stevens. NePA; OxBA
Comedy. Thomas Bailey Aldrich. PR
Comedy. Mark Van Doren. NePoAm-2
Comedy of Patient and Meek Grissell, *sel.* John Phillip.
"Lulla by baby, lulla by baby." ReEn; TuPP
(Lullaby: "Lullaby baby, lullaby baby.") ElL; EM-1
Comely and capable one of our race. On the Portrait of a Woman about to Be Hanged. Thomas Hardy. ChMo; CMP
Comely Warrior, The. Ibn Sa'id of Alcala la Real, *tr. fr. Arabic by* A. J. Arberry. MooP
Comes a cry from Cuban water. Cuba Libre. Joaquin Miller. MC; PAH
Comes any good from Nazareth? From Nazareth. Margaret E. Sangster. ChIP
Comes Fall. Robert Nathan. HBMV
Comes not the springtime here. Come Not the Seasons Here. E. J. Pratt. PeCV
Comes something down with eventide. Eventide. Thomas Burbidge. VA
Comes the Charming Evening. Baudelaire, *tr. fr. French by* David Paul. MiFP
Comes the deer to my singing. Hunting-Song [*or* Navajo Hunting-Song]. *Unknown, tr. by* Natalie Curtis. APW; AWP; JAWP; WBP
Comes the lure of green things growing. Afoot. Sir Charles G. D. Roberts. CaP; HBV; NLK; OCL; VA
Comes the New Year; wailing the north winds blow. Thysia, XVI. Morton Luce. HBV
Comes with autumn the spent moment. Three Trees at Solstice. Mary Finnin. BoAV
Comet. Mary Fullerton. NeLNL
Comet, The. Charles Sangster. LPS-3
Comet at Yell'ham, The. Thomas Hardy. ExPo; ViP
Comet of Going-to-the-Sun, The. Vachel Lindsay. ChMo; CMP
Comet that my father saw, The. Comet. Mary Fullerton. NeLNL
Cometh the dawn: ye men who know. De Profundis. Brent Dow Allinson. *Fr.* Prayer in the Trenches. AOAH
Cometh the night. The wind falls low. The Night Cometh. John McCrae. CPG; PoP
Comets—On the Italian Duke Who Ran Away for Fear of the Comet of 1742. Samuel Johnson. BeR
Comfort. "Æ." ChMo
Comfort. Elizabeth Barrett Browning. HBV
Comfort. Mortimer Collins. LPS-3
Comfort. May Doney. HBMV
Comfort. Hafiz, *tr. fr. Persian by* Gertrude Bell. PeP
Comfort. Miyauchi, *tr. fr. Japanese by* Lois J. Erickson. SoLD
Comfort. Margaret French Patton. PC
Comfort. Margaret Widdemer. GoYe
Comfort for Poor Poets, A. Sir John Harington. SiCE
Comfort in Affliction. William E. Aytoun. BOHV; InMe
Comfort in Extremity. Christopher Harvey. OxBoCh
Comfort of the Fields. Archibald Lampman. CaP; OCL
Comfort of the Stars, The. Richard Burton. AnAmPo; LA; NLK
Comfort of the Trees, The. Richard Watson Gilder. PAH
Comfort thee, O thou mourner, yet awhile. To the Sister of Elia [*or* To Mary Lamb]. Walter Savage Landor. BPN; EmBrPo; HBV; TOP; TriL
Comfort thyself, my woful heart. Songs and Lyrics, XXXV. Sir Thomas Wyatt. SiPS
Comfort to a Youth That Had Lost His Love. Robert Herrick. EV-2; OBEV
Comfort ye, comfort ye my people. Comfort Ye My People. Isaiah. Bible. *O.T.* EM-1; LiA; TreFS; TrJP; WoL
Comfortable Song on the Poor Sailors, A. *Unknown.* SG
Comforter of sorrow and care, The. Work. Edwin L. Sabin. DD
Comforters, The. Dora Sigerson Shorter. BMEP; CH; DiM; GTIV; HBMV; LBBV
Comforts were few in eighteen-fifty-five. The Early Days. Basil Dowling. AnNZ
Comic Miseries. John Godfrey Saxe. BOHV
Comica Man, Da. T. A. Daly. StaSt
Comical Girl, The. M. Pelham. BOHV
Comical Revenge, The; or, Love in a Tub. *sels.* Sir George Etherege.

If She Be Not as Kind as Fair, *fr.* II, iii. SeCL
(Song: "If she be not as kind as fair.") CEP
Song: "Ladies, though to your conquering eyes," *fr.* V, iii. HBV; LO; OBEV (1st ed.); OBS
Comin' o' the Spring, The. Lady John Scott. EBSV
Comin' thro' [*or* through] the Rye (*diff. versions*). Burns. EBSV; ExPo; FaFP; HBV; LEAP; LiTB; LiTG; LiTL; OlF; TreF
(Coming through the Rye.) EV-3
Comin' through the craigs o' Kyle. Owre the Muir amang the Heather. Jean Glover. EBSV; HBV
Comin' through the Rye. *Unknown.* LPS-1; WBLP
Comin' through the Rye, poor body. Comin' thro' the Rye. Burns. EBSV; EV-3; HBV; LEAP. *See also* Gin a body meet a body.
Coming, The. Anthony Delius. BoSA
Coming American, The, *sel.* Sam Walter Foss.
Bring Me Men. OQP; QP-2
("Bring me men to match my mountains.") BBV (1951 ed.); BLPA; FaBoBe; MaRV; NeHB; PaA; WaKn
Coming and Going. Li Shang-yin, *tr. fr. Chinese.* WhP
Coming and Going. Grace Hyde Trine. BAP
Coming around a corner of the dark trail . . . what was wrong with the valley? The Inquisitors. Robinson Jeffers. MoAmPo (1950 ed.); PoLFOT
Coming around the Horn. *Unknown.* ABF
Coming Back to Mountains. Bianca Bradbury. MuM
Coming back to school again. Getting Back. Dorothy Brown Thompson. SiSoSe
Coming by evening through the wintry city. At a Bach Concert. Adrienne Cecile Rich. NePoEA
Coming Child, The. Richard Crashaw. MaRV
Coming Day, The. John Oxenham. *See* Morning Breaks, The.
Coming Day, The. John Addington Symonds. *See* Loftier Race, A.
Coming down the mountain road. The Mountain Road. Enid Derham. BoAu
Coming for to carry me home (*refrain*). Swing Low, Sweet Chariot. *Unknown.* GoSl
Coming Homeward Out of Spain. Barnabe Googe. ElL; MeRV; ReIE; SiCE; TuPP
Coming Huns, The. Valery Yakovlevich Bryusov, *tr. fr. Russian.* BoR, *tr. by* C. M. Bowra; TrRV, *tr. by* Babette Deutsch
Coming in splendor through the golden gate. This Is the Last. Gilbert Waterhouse. PGD; PSO
Coming is an empty word, going leaves no trace. Coming and Going. Li Shang-yin. WhP
Coming Night, The. Thomas Chatterton. *Fr.* Elegy to the Memory of Mr. Thomas Philips of Fairford. RO
Coming of Aphrodite, The. Hesiod, *tr. fr. Greek by* F. L. Lucas. *Fr.* Theogony. GrPE
Coming of Arthur, The. Tennyson. *Fr.* Idylls of the King. VLEP
Coming of Autumn, The. Ch'ien Lin, *tr. fr. Chinese by* Henry H. Hart. PoHN
Coming of Christ, The. *Unknown.* *See* Conquering and to Conquer.
Coming of Dawn, The. Grace Atherton Dennen. NLK
Coming of Dian, The. Keats. *Fr.* Endymion, I. BPN
Coming of Dusk upon a Village in Haiti, The. Henry Rago. HoPM
Coming of His Feet, The. Lyman W. Allen. BLPA; MaRV; NeHB
Coming of Jason to Iolcus, The. Pindar, *tr. fr. Greek by* F. L. Lucas. *Fr.* Pythian Odes, IV. GrPE
Coming of Love, The. James I, King of Scotland. *See* He Sees His Beloved.
Coming of Love, The, *sels.* Theodore Watts-Dunton.
"Beneath the loveliest dream." BMEP; LEAP
First Kiss, The. HBV; VA
Coming of Mary Louise, The. Gertrude Boughton Urquhart. PCH
Coming of Pharaoh, The. Cædmon(?). *See* Approach of Pharaoh, The.
Coming of Spring, The. Mary Howitt. RAR
(Spring Is Coming, *abr.*) PEDC
(Voice of Spring, The, *st.* 2.) OTPC (1923 ed.); PRWS
Coming of Spring, The. Wilhelm Müller, *tr. fr. German.* PEOR
Coming of Spring, The. Nora Perry. DD; HBVY; HH; PRWS
(Coming of the Spring, The.) YeAr
Coming of Spring, The. *Unknown.* PEDC
Coming of the End, The. Thomas Hardy. ChMo; CMP
Coming of the King, The. *Unknown.* *See* Yet if His Majesty, Our Sovereign Lord
Coming of the Lord, The. Jones Very. BePJ
Coming of the Rain, The. James Thomson. The Seasons: Spring. EPP
Coming of the Spring, The. Nora Perry. *See* Coming of Spring, The.
Coming of the Trees, The. Arthur Guiterman. PEDC
Coming of the White Man, The. Patrick Anderson. *Fr.* Poem on Canada. BoCaPo (1948 ed.); CaP
Coming of Theseus towards Athens, The. Bacchylides, *tr. fr. Greek by* F. L. Lucas. GrPE
Coming of War, The; Actaeon. Ezra Pound. NP; TwCV
Coming of War, 1889, The. Lionel Johnson. SoV
Coming of Winter. Boris Pasternak, *tr. fr. Russian by* Jack Lindsay. RuPo
Coming of Wisdom with Time, The. W. B. Yeats. TwP
Coming out from a movie. Catwise. Philip Booth. NePoAm-2
Coming out of the mountains of a summer evening. St. Gervais. Michael Roberts. FaBoCh; LoGBV
Coming through the Rye. Burns. *See* Comin' thro' the Rye.
Coming through the rye, poor body. *See* Comin' thro' the rye, poor body.
Coming [*or* Comming] to kiss[e] her lips [*or* lyps] (such grace I found). Amoretti, LXIV. Spenser. AtBAP; LoBV; PeBoSo
Coming to Port. Max Eastman. NV
Comma Caution. Harold Willard Gleason. DDA
Commandant's Isle. William Douw Lighthall. CPG
Commanders of the Faithful. Thackeray. ALV
Commandos Embarking. George Whalley. TwCaPo
Commemoration. Claude McKay. BANP
Commemoration. Sir Henry Newbolt. FaBoTw; OBVV
Commemoration Ode, The. James Russell Lowell. *See* Ode Recited at the Harvard Commemoration, July 21, 1865.
Commemoration Ode (World's Columbian Exposition, Chicago, 1892), *sels.* Harriet Monroe.
Democracy. AA
Lincoln. AA
Two Heroes. OHIP
Washington. AA; FaBoBe; MaRV; OQP; PoRL; QP-1; WOAH
Commencement. Margaret Elizabeth Sangster. PEDC
Commend me to the friend that comes. The Friend of My Heart. *Unknown.* PEOR
Commendation of Her Beauty, Stature, Behavior, and Wit. Francis Davison. *See* Her Commendation.
Commendation of Music, The. William Strode. *See* In Commendation of Music.
Commendations of Mistress Jane Scrope, The. John Skelton. *See* Maystress Jane Scroupe.
Comment. Dorothy Parker. ALV
(Some Beautiful Letters: Comment.) InMe
Commentary, *sel.* W. H. Auden.
"Some of our dead are famous, but they would not care." MoPo
Commercial Candour. G. K. Chesterton. ALV; WhC
Commination. Walter Savage Landor. ALV
Comming of Good Luck, The. Robert Herrick. AtBAP
Comming to kisse her lyps (such grace I found). *See* Coming to kiss her lips . . .
Commingling sky, A. Freely Espousing. James Schuyler. NeAP
Commissary Report. Stoddard King. ALV
Commission. Ezra Pound. MM
Commissioner, The, bet me a pony—I won. Song of the Squatter. Robert Lowe. VA
Committing wrong the chance may be that you elude men's eyes. Lucian, *tr. fr. Greek by* Lord Neaves. GrPo
Common Bill, *with music.* *Unknown.* AS
(I Will Tell You of a Fellow.) ABS
Common Blessings. Thomas Curtis Clark. TrPWD
Common Conditions, *sel.* *Unknown.*
"Lustily, lustily. lustily let us sail forth." ReEn; SiCE; TuPP
(Song of the Pirates.) MuP
Common Cormorant, The. *Unknown.* AlDL; FaBoCh; FiBHP; GoTP; LiL; LoGBV; SiTL; WhC
(Birds, Bags, Bears, and Buns.) OtMeF
(Common Cormorant or Shag, The.) ChTr
Common End, The. *Unknown, tr. fr. Greek by* F. L. Lucas. GrPE
Common Fires. Muriel Stuart. MBP
Common Form. Kipling. *Fr.* Epitaphs of the War. FaBoTw; LiA; PoVP
Common Inference, A. Charlotte Perkins Gilman. AA; AnAmPo; LA; WGRP
Common Lot, The. Adelbert Sumpter Coats. TrPWD
Common Lot, The. Menander, *tr. fr. Greek by* C. M. Bowra. OxBG
Common Lot, The. James Montgomery. BCEP; EBSV; LPS-1
Common Lot, The. Lizette Woodworth Reese. NP
Common Man, The. Goldsmith. *Fr.* The Deserted Village. MaRV
("Ill fares the land.") BHV
(Where Wealth Accumulates.) GrCo-1
Common practice is the reverse of Tessie's. Report. Robert Finch. TwCaPo

Common Problem, The. Robert Browning. *Fr.* Bishop Blougram's Apology. OQP; QP-1
Common Road, The. Silas H. Perkins. BLPA; FaBoBe; NeHB
Common Sense. James Thomas Fields. AA
Common Sense. Harry Graham. *See* Mr. Jones.
Common Street, The. Helen Gray Cone. AnAmPo; BAP; HBV; LA; NV; POT; PoTo
Common Tasks, The. Grace Noll Crowell. PoToHe (new ed.)
Common Things. Ann Hawkshaw. OTPC (1923 ed.)
Common Things, The. Barbara Young. OQP; QP-1
Commonplace, The. Walt Whitman. APW; MAP; MoAmPo; TrGrPo; TSW; TSWC
("Commonplace I sing, The.") YT
"Commonplace life, A," we say, and we sigh. Commonplaces. "Susan Coolidge." OQP; QP-2
Commonplaces. "Susan Coolidge." OQP; QP-2
God's Plan, *sel.* MaRV
Commonplaces. Kipling. BOHV; HBV; PA
Commonwealth of Birds, The. James Shirley. GoBC
Commonwealth of the Bees, The. Shakespeare. King Henry V, *fr.* I, ii. GN
(So Work the Honey-Bees.) BCEP
Communication. Elizabeth Jennings. NePoEA
Communication to Nancy Cunard, A. Kay Boyle. PoNe
Communion. Phoebe Smith Bachelder. ChIP
Communion. Loren W. Burch. ChIP
Communion. Edward Dowden. MaRV; TrPWD
Communion. Hildegarde Flanner. NP
Communion. Caroline Giltinan. CAW; JKCP
Communion. Wallace Gould. AnAmPo; LA
Communion. Sophie Jewett. PC
Communion. Jessie B. Rittenhouse. PR
Communion. P. M. Snider. PoToHe (new ed.)
Communion. J. L. Spicer. BLRP
Communion. John Banister Tabb. MaRV; WGRP
Communion. T. Turner. LO
Communion. Wordsworth. *Fr.* The Excursion, I. MaRV
("Such was the Boy—but for the growing Youth.") OBRV
Communion Hymn. William Gay. ChIP
Communion Hymn. Alice Freeman Palmer. MaRV; TrPWD
Communion Hymn of the Ancient Irish Church. *Unknown.* *See* May the Sweet Name of Jesus.
Communion with Nature. Byron. *See* Ocean, The.
Communion with Nature ("For I would walk alone"). Wordsworth. *Fr.* The Prelude, II. TOP
Communion with Nature ("Think you 'mid all this mighty sum"). Wordsworth. *Fr.* Expostulation and Reply. MaRV
Communion with the good is friendship's root. Indian Epigram. *Unknown.* BoFr
Communism? Aristophanes, *tr. fr. Greek by* Benjamin Bickley Rogers. *Fr.* The Ecclesiazusae. GrR
Community. John Donne. Po; TwP
Community. Iqbal, *tr. fr. Persian by* A. J. Arberry. PeP
Commuter. E. B. White. WhC
(Commuters.) BOHV
Companion of the highroad, hail! all hail! His Lady of the Sonnets, III. Robert Norwood. CPG
Companioned by long loneliness. En Route. George Dillon. NP
Companions. Charles Stuart Calverley. BOHV; HBV; NA; PoVP; TOP; TSW; VA
Companions of the Morass. Léonie Adams. MOAP
Company. Richard R. Kirk. *See* Thrice Blessed.
Company Commander. Guillaume Apollinaire, *tr. fr. French by* Dudley Fitts. AnFP
Company Cook, The. *Unknown.* ABF
Company Gone. Mark Van Doren. MOAP
Company of Lovers, The. Judith Wright. BoAV; MoAuPo
Compare me to the child that plays with fire. Fidessa, More Chaste than Kind, XIII. Bartholomew Griffin. SiCE; TuPP
Compared with Christ. Augustus Montague Toplady. BePJ
Comparison, The. Catullus, *tr. fr. Latin by* George Lamb. OnPM
Comparison, A. John Farrar. BrR; FaPON; MPB; TSW
Comparison, A. Addressed to a Young Lady. William Cowper. *See* To a Young Lady.
Comparison and Complaint, The. Isaac Watts. TrPWD
Comparison of His Love with the Faithful and Painful Love of Troilus to Cressid, A. *Unknown.* ReIE
Comparison of Life and Death. John Harington. *See* Elegy Wrote in the Tower, 1554.
Comparison of Love to a Streame Falling from the Alpes. Sir Thomas Wyatt. FaBoEn
Comparison of the Life of Man, A. Richard Barnfield. AEV; OBSC; SiCE
Comparison of the Sonnet and the Epigram. Sir John Harington. SiCE; TuPP
Comparisons. *Unknown.* *See* Similes.
Compassion. Sadi, *tr. fr. Persian by* Sir William Jones. PeP
Compassion So Divine. Anne Steele. BePJ
Compassionate eyes had our brave John Brown. John Brown; a Paradox. Louise Imogen Guiney. DD; GA
Compel Them to Come In. Leonard Dodd. BLRP
Compensate. Patrick D. Moreland. InP
Compensation. E. M. Brainard. PoToHe
Compensation. James Edwin Campbell. BANP
Compensation, *sl. abr.* Phoebe Cary. OQP; QP-1
Compensation. Thomas Stephens Collier. AA
Compensation. Paul Laurence Dunbar. BAP; HBV; LBAP; LEAP; PoNe
Compensation ("Why should I keep holiday"). Emerson. AnFE; AnNE; APA; CoAnAm; LiTA; RiBV; TCAP
Compensation ("The wings of Time"). Emerson. TCAP
("Wings of Time, The.") IAP
Compensation. Theodosia Garrison. PC
Compensation. Gerald Gould. HBMV
Compensation. Robinson Jeffers. MAP; MoAB; MoAmPo; NeMA
Compensation. William Ellery Leonard. SBMV
Compensation. Ruth Comfort Mitchell. PEDC
Compensation. Lizette Woodworth Reese. HBMV
Compensation. John Banister Tabb. SPP
Compensation. Celia Thaxter. HBV
Compensation. Ridgely Torrence. *Fr.* The House of a Hundred Lights. AA
Compensation ("The graves grow thicker"). *Unknown.* EOAH
Complacencies of the peignoir, and late. Sunday Morning. Wallace Stevens. AmP; AmPP (4th ed.); AnFE; AnNE; APA; CoAnAm; CoBA; CoBMV; CoV; CrMA; FaBoEn; InPo; LiTA; LiTG; LiTM; MAP; MAPA; MoAB; MoAmPo; MoVE; NePA; OxBA; ReMP; RiBV; SeCeV; TriL; TwAmPo
Complain we may, much is amiss. Totus Mundus in Maligno Positus. *Unknown.* SiCE; TuPP
"Complaine my lute, complaine on him." A Pleasant New Ballad of Two Lovers. *Unknown.* CoMu
Complains, Being Hindered the Sight of His Nymph. Philip Ayres. SeCL
Complaint, The. Mark Akenside. OBEV
Complaint. Evgeni Baratynsky, *tr. fr. Russian by* C. M. Bowra. BoRS
Complaint. Joseph Bennett. LiTA
Complaint, The. Catullus, *tr. fr. Latin by* Leigh Hunt. OnPM
Complaint, A. Lady Chwang Këang, *tr. fr. Chinese by* James Legge; *revised by* Helen Waddell. OuHeWo
Complaint. Samuel Taylor Coleridge. *See* Good, Great Man, The.
Complaint. John Gray. CaAE
Complaint. Vyacheslav Ivanov, *tr. fr. Russian by* C. M. Bowra. BoR
Complaint, The. Jacinto Fombona Pachano, *tr. fr. Spanish by* H. R. Hays. TwSpPo
Complaint. William Carlos Williams. PoP
Complaint, A. Wordsworth. ATP; OBRV; PoEL-4
Complaint, The; or, Night Thoughts. Edward Young. *See* Night Thoughts.
Complaint by Night of the Lover Not Beloved, A. Earl of Surrey, *after* Petrarch. AWP; CaAE; ElL; ElSeCe; FaBoEn; OuHeWo; SiCE; TuPP
("Alas, so all things now do hold their peace!") ReEn; SiPS
(Complaint by Night, A.) LoBV
(Night.) OBSC
Complaint for True Love Unrequited. Sir Thomas Wyatt. ReIE
Complaint of a Forsaken Indian Woman, The. Wordsworth. NBE
Complaint of a Lover Forsaken of His Love, The. *Unknown.* *See* Green Willow, The.
Complaint of a Lover Rebuked. Petrarch, *tr. fr. Italian by* the Earl of Surrey. *Fr.* Sonnets to Laura: To Laura in Life. AWP; BEL; CoBE; ElSeCe; EnLi-1 (1949 ed.); EnLit; EPP; LiTW; LyMA; OAEP; OnPM; ReIE; SiCE; TrGrPo; TuPP
("Love, that doth reign and live within my thought.") ReEn; SiPS
Complaint of a Lover That Defied Love and Was by Love After the More Tormented. Earl of Surrey. *See* Love's Rebel.
Complaint of Chaucer to His Empty Purse, The. Chaucer. *See* Compleint of Chaucer to His Empty Purse, The.
Complaint of Fantomas. Robert Desnos, *tr. fr. French by* Wallace Fowlie. MiCF
Complaint of Henrie Duke of Buckinghame, The. Thomas Sackville. *See* Mirror for Magistrates, A.
Complaint of Love. Sir Philip Sidney. *See* Loved I Am, and Yet Complaine of Love.
Complaint of New Amsterdam, The. Jacob Steendam. PAH
Complaint of Rosamund, The, *abr.* Samuel Daniel. OAEP; ReEn; ReIE; SiCE; TuPP
Sels.
Henry's Lament. OBSC

Lonely Beauty. OBSC
Rosamond's Appeal. OBSC
Complaint of Tarpeia's Door, The. Propertius, *tr. fr. Latin by* Frances Fletcher. LiTW
("I, entrance door to Tarpeia's house, swung open, once.") LaP
Complaint of the Absence of Her Lover Being upon the Sea. Earl of Surrey. ElL; ElSeCe; OBEV; SiCE
(Lady Complains of Her Lover's Absence, A.) SiPS
("O happy dames, that may embrace.") ReEn
(Seafarer, The.) CoEV; OBSC; RiBV
"When other lovers in arms across," *sel.* LO
Complaint of the Common Weill of Scotland. Sir David Lyndsay. GoTS
Complaint of the Fair Amoress, The. Villon. *See* Old Woman's Lamentations, An.
Complaint of the King of Thule. Jules Laforgue, *tr. fr. French by* William Jay Smith. AnFP
Complaint of the Lover Disdained. Earl of Surrey. BEL
Complaint of the Minstrel's Life. Colin Muset, *tr. fr. French by* J. G. Legge. LyMA
Complaint of the Moon in the Provinces. Jules Laforgue, *tr. fr. French by* Alan Conder. TrFP
Complaint of Troilus, The. Chaucer. *Fr.* Troilus and Criseyde, V. OBEV (new ed.)
Complaint on the Oblivion of the Dead. Jules Laforgue, *tr. fr. French by* William Jay Smith. AnFP; LiTW
(Lament of Forgetfulness of the Dead, *tr. by* Cecily Mackworth.) MiFP
Complaint That His Ladie after She Knew of His Love Kept Her Face Alway Hidden from Him. Earl of Surrey. *See* Cornet, The.
Complaint to His Empty Purse. Chaucer. *See* Compleint of Chaucer to His Empty Purse, The.
Complaint to the Moon. Henry Longan Stuart. GTIV
Complaint unto Pity, The. Chaucer. LyMA
Complaints. Bedros Tourian, *tr. fr. Armenian by* Zabelle C. Boyajian. ArmLP
Complaisant Swain, The. Ovid, *tr. fr. Latin by* F. A. Wright. AWP
Complaynt of Schir David Lindesay, The, *sel.* Sir David Lindsay.
Childhood of James V, The. AtBAP
Compleat Angler, The, *sel.* Izaak Walton.
Angler's Wish, The. HBV; LPS-2; SeCL
Compleint [*or* Compleinte *or* Compleynt] of Chaucer to His Empty Purse [*or* Purs] The. Chaucer. CoBE; EnLi-1; EnLit; EPP; LPS-3; TCEP; TyEnPo
(Chaucer's Complaint to His Empty Purse, *mod. vers. by* Louis Untermeyer.) TrGrPo
(Complaint of Chaucer to His Empty Purse, The.) BEL; EM-1; EnL; GoBC, *mod. vers. by* Belle Cooper; WHA
(Complaint of Chaucer to His Purse, The.) SiTL; ViBoPo
(Complaint to His Empty Purse.) LEAP
(To My Empty Purse.) BOHV
Complete Hen, The. Elizabeth J. Coatsworth. GoTP
Complete Lover, The. William Browne. HBV; LiTL
(Song: "For her gait, if she be walking.") BCEP; EPS (1942 ed.); LoPS; OBEV
(Sonnet: "For her gait if she be walking.") ElSeCe
Complete Misanthropist, The. Morris Bishop. FiBHP; SiTL
Completion. Eunice Tietjens. HBMV; LEAP; LoPS; NP
Complicated gentleman allow me to present, A. Sir Bailey Barre. W. S. Gilbert. *Fr.* Utopia, Limited. PCD
Compliment, The. Thomas Carew. LPS-1
Compliment, The. William Habington. ACP
Compliment. Ibn al-Haddad, *tr. fr. Arabic by* A. J. Arberry. MooP
Compliment to Mariners. George H. Dillon. TBM
Compliment to Queen Elizabeth. Shakespeare. *Fr.* A Midsummer-Night's Dream, II, ii. LPS-3
Compliments. Pope. *Fr.* Epistle to Dr. Arbuthnot. LiA
Compline. Patrick F. Kirby. GoBC
Compline. Duncan Campbell Scott. GoBC
Composed at Neidpath Castle, the Property of Lord Queensberry, 1803. Wordsworth. GTBS; GTBS-D; GTBS-W; GTSE; GTSL
Composed by the Sea-Side, near Calais, August, 1802. Wordsworth. ATP; BPN; CoBE; EM-2; EmBrPo; EnLi-2; EnRP; ERP; GEPC; OAEP; OuHeWo; PeBoSo; PoE; TOP; UnPo (1st ed.)
Composed by the Side of Grasmere Lake. Wordsworth. ERP
(Sonnet: Composed by the Side of Grasmere Lake.) ChER
Composed in One of the Catholic Cantons. Wordsworth. BPN
Composed in the Valley near Dover, on the Day of Landing. Wordsworth. BPN; EmBrPo; ERP
Composed on a May Morning, 1838. Wordsworth. ES
Composed upon an Evening of Extraordinary Splendor and Beauty. Wordsworth. BPN; EM-2; EmBrPo; EnRP; ERP; GEPC; PoE
Composed upon the Beach near Calais. Wordsworth. *See* It Is a Beauteous Evening, Calm and Free.
Composed upon Westminster Bridge, Sept. 3, 1802. Wordsworth. AnEnPo; AnFE; ATP; AWP; BEL; BoLiVe; BPN; CaAE; CBOV; ChTr; CoBE; EM-2; EmBrPo; EnL; EnLi-2; EnLit; EnLP; EnRP; EPN; EPP; ERP; ES; EV-3; ExPo; FaBoCh; FaFP; GEPC; HiLiEn; InP; InPo; InvP; JAWP; KN; LEAP; LoGBV; MaPo; OAEP; OBRV; OuHeWo; PeBoSo; PFE; PIAE; PoE; PoEL-4; PoeMoYo; PoFS; PoMa; PreP; ReaPo; RiBV; TCEP; TOP; TrGrPo; TwHP; TwP; TyEnPo; UnPo (1st ed.); WBP
(Earth Has Not Anything to Show More Fair.) EG; WHA
(Sonnet: Composed upon Westminster Bridge, September 3, 1802.) AEV; AlDL; FiP; HBV; LPS-2; OTPC
(Sonnet: "Earth has not anything to show more fair.") CoEV
(Upon Westminster Bridge.) BCEP; BLV; GTBS; GTBS-D; GTBS-W; GTSE; GTSL; LiTB; LiTG; MCCG; OBEV; PYM; SeCeV; ShBV-3; TreF; TVSH; WP
(Westminster Bridge.) CBE; EnSW; LoBV; PoRA; ViBoPo
Composed While under Arrest. Mikhail Yurevich Lermontov. *See* When the Yellow Rye-Field Billows.
Composer, The. W. H. Auden. UnS
Composer Liszt, The/ Banged the piano with his fist. Important People. Louis Untermeyer, *and others.* StaSt
Composing scales beside the rails. The Harmonious Heedlessness of Little Boy Blue [*or* Little Boy Blue]. Guy Wetmore Carryl. ALV; LauV; MPB; PFE; PIAE; YT
Composite whose body is of light, A. Wine. Dakiki. LiTW
Composition. George O'Neil. TBM
Composition for a Nativity. John Ciardi. MiAP
Composition in Late Spring. Irving Layton. PeCV
Composition of Distances, The. Pien Chih-lin, *tr. fr. Chinese by* Pien Chih-lin. LiTW
Compounded out of nothingness and all. This Sharpening Tension. Sister Mary St. Virginia. JKCP (1955 ed.)
Compressionist's Creed, A. Norman Bethune. PoP
Compromise. Laurence McKinney. InMe
Computation, The. John Donne. ATP (1935 ed.); ElSeCe; EPS (1942 ed.); OAEP; TuPP
Comrade, The. Lee Wilson Dodd. HBMV
Comrade Christ. Verne Bright. ChIP; OQP; QP-2
Comrade, Do Not Forget! Vasili Lebedev-Kumach, *tr. fr. Russian by* Dan Levin. PoFr
Comrade Jesus. Ralph Cheyney. ChIP; PGD
Comrade Jesus. Sarah N. Cleghorn. AnAmPo; BAP; BoFr; HBMV; LA; MaRV; NAMP; NV; OQP; PoFr; QP-1; StJW; WGRP
Comrade, Remember. Raymond Kresensky. PGD
Comrade Rides Ahead, A. Douglas Malloch. HBMV
Comrade to Comrade. Marguerite Wilkinson. BoFr
Comrade, why do you weep? The Somme Valley, 1917. Frank Prewett. MM
Comrade, within your tent of clay. Comrade, Remember. Raymond Kresensky. PGD
Comradery. Madison Cawein. AA; OBAV
Comrades. Henry Ames Blood. AA
Comrades. Fannie Stearns Davis. AV
Comrades. Henry R. Dorr. MC; PAH
Comrades. W. W. Gibson. BEL; ChMo; CMP
Comrades. Arthur Guiterman. FAOV
Comrades. Laurence Housman. BoFr; HBV
Comrades. Richard Hovey. BLV; LBMV; MAP; MoAmPo (1942 ed.); PC; PoeMoYo; POT
Comrades. Lionel Johnson. HBV
Comrades. George Edward Woodberry. BoFr; HBV; LBMV; PFY
Comrades as We Rest Within. Ronald Hambleton. CaP
Comrades, fill the banquet cup. Banquet Song. Edwin Osgood Grover. PR
Comrades, give me Homer's lyre. Give Me Homer's Lyre. *Unknown.* GrL
Comrades, I say this not to make you sad. Just One More Spring. Nicephorus Vrettakos. MoGP
Comrades in Death. Yiannis Griparis, *tr. fr. Modern Greek by* Rae Dalven. MoGP
Comrades Known in Marches Many. Charles G. Halpine. MDAH
(Song of the Soldier.) PAP
Comrades, leave me here a little, while as yet 'tis early morn. Locksley Hall. Tennyson. ATP (1935 ed.); BEL; BMEP; BPN; EM-2; EmBrPo; EnL; EnLi-2; EnLit; EPN; EPP; FaBoBe; FaFP; GEPC; HBV; LiTG; LPS-1; OAEP; PIAE; PIR; PoVP; REAL; TCEP; TOP; ViPo; ViPP; VLEP; WHA
Comrades of the Cross. Willard Wattles. *See* Acceptance.
Comrades of the Trail. Mary Carolyn Davies. NLK
Comrades, pour the wine tonight. Comrades. Richard Hovey. BLV; LBMV; MAP; MoAmPo (1942 ed.); PC; PoeMoYo; POT

Comrades, the Morning Breaks. Hafiz, *tr. fr. Persian by* Richard Le Gallienne. *Fr.* Odes. AWP
Comrades: the world is built upon our dead. Anonymous Speech. Jorge Carrera Andrade. TwSpPo
Comrades, when the air is sweet. At a Country Dance in Provence. Harold Monro. OBVV
Comrades, you may pass the rosy. The Lay of the Love-lorn [*or* The Cry of the Lovelorn]. William E. Aytoun *and* Sir Theodore Martin. BOHV; CenHV; PA
Comus; a Masque Presented at Ludlow Castle. Milton. EV-2; GEPC; OAEP
Sels.
"Before the starry threshold of Jove's Court."
(Prologue of the Attendant Spirit in Comus.) CBE
"By the rushy-fringèd bank." ElSeCe; TOP
Chastity ("A hidden strength"). OBS
"Goddess dear." ElSeCe
Haunt of the Sorcerer, The. BCEP; LPS-3
He That Has Light Within, 5 *ll.* MaRV
(Light Within.) BLP
Lady Lost in the Wood, The. LPS-3
Love Virtue. GrCo-1
"My sister is not so defenseless left." NBE
"O foolishness of men! that lend their ears." AtBAP; ViBoPo
(Comus Tempts the Lady.) CoEV
(Comus's Praise of Nature.) PoEL-3
Philosophy ("How charming is divine philosophy"). BCEP
Sabrina Fair. AtBAP; ATP (1935 ed.); EG; ElSeCe; FaBoCh; InPo; LoGBV; OBEV; PoEL-3; SeCeV; SeCL; TOP; ViBoPo
(Sabrina.) CH; HOAH; UnPo (1st ed.)
(Song: "Sabrina fair.") LoBV
"She that has that is clad in complete steel." InP
"Shepherd, 'tis my office best." ElSeCe
"Some say no evil thing that walks by night." LO
"Star that bids the shepherd fold, The." EG; FaBoCh; LoGBV; OBEV, *abr.*; SeCeV; TOP; ViBoPo; WHA
(Comus' Invocation to His Revelers.) BoLiVe; TrGrPo
(From "Comus.") LEAP
(Invocation of Comus, The.) OBS
(Mask, A.) FiP
(Night Mysteries.) BCEP
(Songs.) BLV
"Sweet Echo, sweetest nymph, that liv'st unseen." AtBAP; EG; ElSeCe; ExPo; KN; SeCeV; SeCL; TOP; ViBoPo
(Echo.) CoEV; OBEV; OBS
(Lady's Song.) BoLiVe; TrGrPo
(Song: "Sweet Echo, sweetest nymph that liv'st unseen.") BrBE; LoBV
(Songs.) BLV
Temperance and Virginity. OBS
"There is a gentle nymph not far from hence." MyFE; SeEP
(Nymph of the Severn, The.) LPS-3
(Sabrina.) OBS
"To the ocean now I fly." AtBAP; ElSeCe; OBEV; OBS; SeCeV; ViBoPo
(Farewell of the Attendant Spirit.) BoLiVe; TrGrPo
(From "Comus.") LEAP
(Songs.) BLV
"Virgin, daughter of Locrine." ElSeCe
Conall's Head. *Unknown, tr. fr. Old Irish by* George Sigerson. SiB
Conan of Fortingall. J. Corson Miller. TBM
Conceal not Time's misdeeds, but on my brow. To a Painter. Walter Savage Landor. EmBrPo; RiBV
Conceit Begotten by the Eyes. Sir Walter Ralegh. SiPS
(Affection and Desire.) OBSC
Conceits. Arlo Bates. AA
Concentred here th' united wisdom shines. The Federal Convention. *Unknown.* PAH
Conception. Waring Cuney. BANP; PoNe
Conception of Christ, The. *Unknown.* AnEC
Concerning a Storm. Richard Untermeyer *and* Louis Untermeyer. FAOV
(Storm, The.) RIS
Concerning brave Captains. Great-Heart [*or* Theodore Roosevelt]. Kipling. BoHiPo; HBV
Concerning Brownie. Nancy Byrd Turner. AlBD; PC
Concerning Cookies. Susan Adger Williams. DDA
Concerning Death. Hovhannes Tulkourantzi, *tr. fr. Armenian by* Zabelle C. Boyajian. ArmLP
Concerning Earth, the mother of all, shall I sing. To Earth, the Mother of All. *Unknown. Fr.* Homeric Hymns. GrL
Concerning Four Rural Sisters. Charles Cotton. *See* Resolution in Four Sonnets . . .
Concerning Geffray Teste Noire. William Morris. PoVP; ViPo; VLEP
Concerning Lawyers. Pero López de Ayala, *tr. fr. Spanish by* S. Griswold Morley. *Fr.* Palace Rhymes. AnSpL-1
Concerning Love. Josephine Preston Peabody. CIV; WhC
Concerning Mollberg's Parade to Corporal Boman's Grave. Karl Mikael Bellman, *tr. fr. Swedish by* Charles W. Stork. AnSL
Concerning Tabitha's Dancing of the Minuet. Arthur Colton. PR
Concerning the Honour of Books. John Florio. ES
(Of Books.) ElL
Concerning the Nature of Things. Lucretius. *See* De Rerum Natura.
Concerning the Rose and the Nightingale. Grigoris of Aghtamar, *tr. fr. Armenian by* Zabelle C. Boyajian. ArmLP
Concerning Virgil's Aeneids. Nicholas Grimald. ReIE
Concert, The. Phyllis McGinley. YeAr
Concert. Ibn Sharaf, *tr. fr. Arabic by* A. J. Arberry. MooP
Concert at Sea. Hubert Creekmore. WaP
Concert-hall creaked like a full-dress shirt, The. Unfamiliar Quartet. Stephen Vincent Benét. WhC
Concert Rehearsal, The. Wolstan Dixey. PEOR
Concert Party, A. Siegfried Sassoon. EnLit
Conclusion. Lord De Tabley. PoVP
Conclusion. Andrew Marvell. *See* Dialogue between the Soul and Body, A.
Conclusion, The. Sir Walter Ralegh. BCEP; BEL; BoHiPo; CBOV; EPP; HBV; LEAP; OBEV; OtMeF; PCD; TOP; WGRP
(Author's Epitaph, The.) EnLi-1 (1949 ed.)
(Author's Epitaph, The, Made by Himself [the Night before His Death].) ElSeCe; EnLit; EV-1; FaBoEn; OAEP; OxBoCh; SiCE
(Epitaph: "Even such is time.") OBSC
(Even Such Is Time.) ChTr; EG; ElL; ExPo; GTBS-W; LiTB; OnPM; PG (1955 ed.); PoE; PoRA; RiBV; SeCeV; SiPS; TreF; TVSH; WHA; WoL
(His Epitaph.) BLV; TrGrPo
(His Own Epitaph.) PIAE
(Last Lines.) ShBV-3
(Lines Found in His Bible.) LPS-3
(Lines Written the Night before His Execution.) EOAH
(Sir Walter Ralegh the Night before His Death.) PoFS
(Sir Walter Raleigh's Verses, Found in His Bible in the Gatehouse at Westminster.) MaRV
(Verses Found in His Bible in the Gate-House at Westminster.) EnL
(Verses Written in His Bible.) ViBoPo
Conclusion. Siegfried Sassoon. MPB; MoBrPo
Conclusion: "In vain, in vain—the all-composing hour." Pope. *Fr.* The Dunciad, IV. EnLi-1; RiBV; ViBoPo
(Chaos.) LoBV
(Finality.) ReTS
(Reign of Chaos, The.) FiP
(Triumph of Ignorance, The.) CoBE
Conclusion: "It was a close, warm, breezeless summer night." Wordsworth. *Fr.* The Prelude, XIV. PoEL-4
(Majestic Intellect, *shorter sel.*) RO
(Conclusion: "It was a summer's night, a close warm night," *sl. diff.*) FaBoEn
Conclusion: "Moon hung naked in a firmament, The." Wordsworth. *Fr.* The Prelude, XIV. ERP
Conclusion of the Whole Matter, The. Ridgely Torrence. *Fr.* The House of a Hundred Lights. AA; HBV
Conclusion; the Decision of the Gods. Keats. *Fr.* Endymion, IV. ERP
Conclusion to the May Queen and New Year's Eve. Tennyson. *Fr.* The May Queen. OTPC (1923 ed.)
Concord Hymn. Emerson. AA; AmP; AmPo; AmPP; AnAmPo; APW; AWP; BBV; BLPA; BTP; CBOV; CoBA; DD; DDA; ExPo; FaBoBe; FaBoEn; FaFP; FaPON; FOAH; GN; GTBS-W; HBV; HBVY; HH; IAP; InP; InPo; JAWP; LA; LEAP; LiTA; LiTG; MaRV; MC; MCCG; MOAP; MPB; MW; NeHB; NePA; OHFP; OlF; OnPM; OQP; OTPC; OuHeWo; OxBA; PaA; PAH; PEDC; PIR; Po; PoFr; PoFS; PoRL; PTA-1; PYM; QP-1; SeCeV; StVeCh; TOP; TreF; TrGrPo; TriL; TVSH; ViBoPo, *sts.* 1–2; WaaP; WBP; WoL; YaD; YT
(Concord Fight, The, *abr.*) PEOR
(Hymn: "By the rude bridge that arched the flood.") AnNE; IDAH; PG (1945 ed.)
(Hymn Sung at the Completion of the Concord Monument.) BAP; PAP; REAL; TCAP
Concubine, The (Sir Martyn), *sels.* William Julius Mickle.
Evening, *fr* II. RO
Flowers and Vegetables, *fr.* I. RO
Sunset, *fr.* II. OBEC
Wild [*or* Wyld] Romantic Dell, A, *fr.* II. OBEC; RO
Conde Niño all for love, The. Love than Death More Strong. *Unknown.* TeCS
Condemned, The. Edward Howland. AA
Condemned, The. Enrique González Martínez, *tr. fr. Spanish by* Samuel Beckett. AnMP
Condemned to Die, The. José de Espronceda, *tr. fr. Spanish by* James Kennedy. AnSpL-2
Condemned [*or* Condemn'd] to hope's delusive mine. On the Death of Mr. [*or* Dr.] Robert Levet. Samuel Johnson.

BCEP; BHV; CBOV; CEP; EiPP; EV-3; FaBoEn; HBV; LH; OBEC; OBEV; PoE; PoEL-3; PoFS; TriL
Conditional Surrender. Sir Philip Sidney. *See* Astrophel and Stella: Sonnets, LXIX.
Conditor Alme Siderum. *Unknown.* AnEC
Condor's Sleep, The. Leconte de Lisle, *tr. fr. French by* Alan Conder. TrFP
Conduct. Samuel Greenberg. CrMA; LiTA
Conductor Bradley. Whittier. TCAP
Conductor when he receives a fare, The. The Passenjare. Isaac H. Bromley. FiBHP
Conemaugh. Elizabeth Stuart Phelps Ward. PAH
Coney Island of the Mind, A, *sels.* Lawrence Ferlinghetti. NeAP
"Constantly risking absurdity."
"In Goya's greatest scenes we seem to see."
"Wounded wilderness of Morris Graves, The."
Confederacy, The. Jane T. H. Cross. BlG
Confederate Memorial Day. *Unknown.* BlG
Confederate Note, The. Samuel Alroy Jonas. *See* Lines on the Back of a Confederate Note.
Confederates in this white field. Meeting. Charles Eglington. BoSA
Conference, The, *sel.* Charles Churchill.
Conscience. OBEC
Conference-meeting through at last, The. The Doorstep. Edmund Clarence Stedman. HBV; LHV; PR
Conferences, adjournments, ultimatums. Autumn Journal, VII. Louis MacNeice. WaP
Confess Jehovah, *with music. Unknown.* TrAS
Confess'd from yonder slow-extinguish'd clouds. Summer Evening and Night. James Thomson. *Fr.* The Seasons: Summer. OBEC
Confessed. Josephine Miles. FiMAP
Confessio Amantis, *sels.* John Gower.
"Adieu, for now I've made an end," Conclusion, *fr.* VIII, *cond., mod. by* Muriel Bowden. MeEV
Alexander and the Pirate, *fr.* III. EV-1
"Flees he tok and goth to Bote, The," *fr.* V. AtBAP
Florent and the Loathly Hag, *fr.* I, *mod. by* Muriel Bowden. MeEV
House of Sleep, The, *fr.* IV. AtBAP
Jason and Medea, *fr.* V. ACP
"Jason, which sih his fader old," *fr.* V. EPP
Medea Goes to Gather Herbs for Her Incantations, *fr.* V. LiA
Parting of Venus and Old Age, The, *fr.* VIII. PoEL-1
Poet Meets Venus and Her Priest, The, *fr.* I, *cond., mod. by* Muriel Bowden. MeEV
Prolog: "Books composed before our day, The," *cond., mod. by* Muriel Bowden. MeEV
Story of Ulysses, The, *fr.* I, *mod. Eng.* SG
Tale of Rosiphelee, The, *fr.* IV. ArmLP
Confession. "Anna Akhmatova," *tr. fr. Russian by* Babette Deutsch. TrRV
Confession. Hervey Allen. TBM
Confession. Elsa Barker. *Fr.* The Spirit and the Bride. HBMV
Confession, *sel.* Carsten Hauch, *tr. fr. Danish by* Charles W. Stork.
"Happy the singer." BoDS
Confession. Donald Jeffrey Hayes. CDC
Confession. George Herbert. ReEn
Confession, The "Thomas Ingoldsby." BOHV; FiBHP
Confession. Kenneth Mackenzie. BOAV
Confession. Charles d'Orléans, *tr. fr. French.* ChTr
(Kiss, The, *mod. vers.*) ACP
("My gostly fader, I me confess.") EG; EnLoPo
Confession. D. S. Savage. NeBP
Confession, A. Paul Verlaine, *tr. fr. French by* Arthur Symons. CAW; WGRP
Confession, The. Wen Yi-tuo, *tr. fr. Chinese by* Ho Yung. ChTr; LiTW
Confession. Yüan Ti, *tr. fr. Chinese by* Henry H. Hart. PoHN
Confession in Holy Week. Christopher Morley. HBMV
Confession of a Glutton. Don Marquis. AlBD
Confession of a Hooligan. Sergei Yesenin, *tr. fr. Russian by* Jack Lindsay. RuPo
Confession of Bishop Golias, The. "The Archpoet of Cologne." *See* Confession of Golias, The.
Confession of Faith. Dryden. *See* Church's Testimony, The.
Confession of Faith. Elinor Wylie. AnAmPo; AnFE; APA; CoAnAm; LA; MAP; MoAmPo; TwAmPo
Confession of Colias, The. "The Archpoet of Cologne," *tr. fr. Latin by* George F. Whicher. LiTW, *abr.*; LyMA
(Confession of Bishop Golias, The, *abr.*, *tr. by* J. V. Cunningham.) LaP
Drinking Song, *sel.*, *tr. by* John Addington Symonds. LiA
Confession of the Deadly Sins, The. William Langland, *tr. fr. Middle English. Fr.* The Vision of Piers Plowman. MeEV
(Confessions of the Seven Deadly Sins, The, *shorter sel.*, *tr. by* W. A. Neilson *and* K. G. T. Webster.) EnLi-1 (1949 ed.)
("King and his knights went to church, The.") BEL
Confession Overheard in a Subway. Kenneth Fearing. LiTA; LiTM (rev. ed.); WaP
Confessional, The. Robert Browning. OtMeF; PoVP; ViBoPo
Confessional, The. Helen Parry Eden. JKCP
Confessions ("Face to face in my chamber"). Elizabeth Barrett Browning. OBVV; VLEP
Confessions ("What is he buzzing in my ears?"). Robert Browning. BPN; EmBrPo; EPN; GEPC; GTBS-D; GTML; PoVP; ViBoPo; ViPo; VLEP
Confessions of the Seven Deadly Sins, The. William Langland. *See* Confession of the Deadly Sins, The.
Confidants. William Alexander Percy. TBM
Confide in a Friend. *Unknown.* PoToHe (new ed.)
Confide ye aye in Providence. Its Ain Drap o' Dew. James Ballantine. HBV
Confidence. Marsden Hartley. AnFE; CoAnAm
Confidence. *Unknown.* BLRP
Confident Scientist, The. Alexis, *tr. fr. Greek by* T. F. Higham. OxBG
Confidential Data on the Loyalty Investigation of Herbert Ashenfoot. James Schevill. FiMAP
Configurations of time and singing. Beast in View. Muriel Rukeyser. FiMAP
Confined Love. John Donne. AnEnPo; EnLP; TuPP
Confinement, The. Mark Van Doren. MOAP
Confirmation, The. Edwin Muir. POTE
Confirmation for a Rumor. Phyllis McGinley. DDA
Confirmation of Faith, The. Addison. EV-3
Confiteor. *Unknown.* CoBE
Conflict. Caroline Clive. OBVV
Conflict. Lincoln Fitzell. AnAmPo; LA
Conflict, The. C. Day Lewis. AnEnPo; EnLit; FaBoMo; LiTB; LiTM; MBP; MoAB; MoBrPo
Conflict. F. R. Scott. BoCaPo; CaP; PeCV
Confluence, The. "John Crichton." CPG
Confluents. Christina Rossetti. BPN
Conformers, The. Thomas Hardy. EnLi-2 (1949 ed.); TyEnPo; ViBoPo
Confuse me not with impious things. A Caterpillar's Apology for Eating a Favorite Gladiolus. Charles Dalmon. TSW
Confused Dawn, The. William Douw Lighthall. VA
Congal, *sels.* Sir Samuel Ferguson.
"Land Is Ours, The." IrPN
"Princess with her women-train without the fort he found, The." TIP
Simile. IrPN
Conger Eel, The. Patrick MacGill. OnYI
Congo, The. Vachel Lindsay. AmP; AmPP; ChMo; CMP; CoBA; FaFP; GTBS-W; HoPM; LiTA; LiTG; MAP; MCCG; MoAB; MoAmPo; MOAP; NeMA; NP; OxBA; PFY; PoeMoYo; PoMa; PoNe; PoRA; PreP (I *and* III); PYM; ShBV-3; TCPD (I *and* III); TreF (I *and* III); WHA
Their Basic Savagery, I, *sel.* BAP
("Fat black bucks in a wine-barrel room.") LEAP
Congress, 1878. Victor Alexis de la Montagne, *tr. fr. Flemish by* Jethro Bithell. WoL
Conjecture. Florence Hamilton. *See* If a Man Die.
Conjecture, A. Charles Francis Richardson. AA
Conjectured to Be upon the Death of Sir Walter Raleigh. Henry King. EG
Conjugal Conjugations. A. W. Bellaw. BOHV
Conjugal Conundrum, A. *Unknown.* BOHV
Conjuh Man, De. James Edwin Campbell. BANP
Conjunction of Jupiter and Venus, The. Bryant. IAP
I Would Not Always Reason, *sel.* OQP; QP-2
Conjuration. Thomas Campion. *See* When Thou Must Home.
Conjuration, to Electra, A. Robert Herrick. AtBAP; PoEL-3
Conjurer, The. Lew Sarett. PFE
Conjuror, The. E. V. Lucas. BoChLi; PoMS
Connacht Caoine, A. *Unknown, tr. fr. Irish.* AnIV
Connachtman, A. Padraic Colum. LBBV
Connaught Lament, A. Nora Hopper. AV; LBBV
Connaught Rangers, The. Winifred M. Letts. HBMV; TCEP
Connecticut Peddler, The, *with music. Unknown.* ABF
Connecticut Road Song. Anna Hempstead Branch. OBAV
Connecticut Trilogy. Leila Jones. MuM
Connla's Well. "Æ." TIP
Connoisseur of Chaos. Wallace Stevens. LiTM (rev ed.); MoPo; Po
Connoisseurs. Dugald Sutherland MacColl. PoC
Connolly. Liam MacGowan. OnYI
Connubial Life. James Thomson. *Fr.* The Seasons: Spring. LPS-1
Conon in Alexandria. Lawrence Durrell. MoPo
Conopion. Callimachus, *tr. fr. Greek by* G. M. Young. GrL
Conor the king. The King of Ulster. *Unknown.* KiLC
"Conquer the gloomy night of thy sorrow." Defiance. Solomon ibn Gabirol. TrJP
Conquer the proud spirit in your breast, child. The Appeal of Phoenix. Homer. *Fr.* The Iliad, IX. OxBG

Conquered. Zoë Akins. HBMV
Conquered Banner, The. Abram Joseph Ryan. AA; BlG; DD, *abr.*; HBV; JKCP; LEAP; OBAV; PaA; PAH; PEDC; SPP; TCAP; TreF
Conquered King, The, *sel.* George Wither.
"Kings who without control the sceptre sway'd," 4 *ll.* PoFr
Conquering and to Conquer. *Unknown.* TMEV
(Coming of Christ, The, *shorter vers.*) ACP
Conquering Love of Jesus, The. Charles Wesley. BePJ
Conqueror, The. Ruth M. Williams. BePJ
Conqueror Renowned, The. Bernard of Clairvaux, *tr. fr. Latin.* BePJ
Conqueror Worm, The. Poe. *Fr.* Ligeia, *pr. tale.* AA; AmP; AnAmPo; AnFE; APA; AWP; BAV; CoAnAm; CoBA; HBV; IAP; InPo; LA; LiTA; MOAP; PIAE; SPP; TCAP
Conquerors, The. José Maria de Heredia, *tr. fr. French by* Alan Conder. TrFP
Conquerors, The. Harry Kemp. AnAmPo; BAP; ChIP; HBV; LA; LEAP; MaRV
Conqueror's Grave, The. Bryant. AA
Conquest. Leslie Savage Clark. ChIP
Conquest. Philippe Desportes. *See* Those Eyes Which Set My Fancy on Afire.
Conquest, The. Oliver St. John Gogarty. OBMV
Conquest, A. Walter Herries Pollock. OBVV; VA
Conquest of Canaan, The, *sel.* Timothy Dwight.
Battle of Ai, The. BAV
Conquest of Granada, The, *sels.* Dryden.
Epilogue: "They who have best succeeded on the stage," *fr.* Pt. II. CEP; EiPP; FiP; GEPC; SeCV-2; SeEP
How Unhappy a Lover Am I, *fr.* Pt. II, Act IV, sc. iii. SeCL
Love ("Love is that madness"), *fr.* Pt. II, Act III, sc. iii. FiP
Song of the Zambra Dance, *fr.* Pt. I, Act III, sc. i. AtBAP; OAEP; PoEL-3
(Zambra Dance, The.) CEP; SeCV-2
Bright Vision, The, *br. sel.* BeR
Stage Poets, *br. sel. fr.* Pt. I, Prologue. BeR
Wherever I Am, and Whatever I Do, *fr.* Pt. I, Act IV, sc. ii. MaPo
(Phyllis.) SeCL
(Song: "Wherever I am, and whatever I do.") EPS (1942 ed.)
Conquest of Love, The. Racine, *tr. fr. French by* Lacy Lockert. *Fr.* Phèdre. LiTW
Conquest of the Air, The. Harold T. Pulsifer. PFE
Conquests of Tamburlaine, The. Christopher Marlowe. *See* Tamburlaine the Great.
Conquistador. Elizabeth J. Coatsworth. GoTP
(Announcement.) MAP
Conquistador. A. D. Hope. MoAuPo
Conquistador, *sels.* Archibald MacLeish.
Ah How the Throat of a Girl, *fr.* Bk. 10. AtBAP
Argument, The. AtBAP
Bernál Díaz's Preface to His Book. AmPP (3d ed.)
Bernal Diaz' Preface: "We saw that city on the inland sea," *sel.* AtBAP
Dawn on the Wall-Head There, *fr.* Bk. 13. AtBAP
Conquistador, The. *Unknown.* DDA
Conrad in Twilight. John Crowe Ransom. OxBA
Conscience. Byron. MaRV
Conscience. Charles Churchill. *Fr.* The Conference. OBSC
Conscience. George Herbert. NBE
Conscience. Victor Hugo, *tr. fr. French by* Alan Conder. TrFP
Conscience. Shakespeare. *See* Sleep—Innocent Sleep.
Conscience. Sir Edward Sherburne. ACP
Conscience. Charles William Stubbs. *See* Conscience and Future Judgment.
Conscience. Henry David Thoreau. *Fr.* A Week on the Concord and Merrimack Rivers. AnNE; HBV; OnAP
Conscience and Future Judgment. Charles William Stubbs. MaRV; PTA-2
(Conscience.) BLPA
Conscience and Remorse. Paul Laurence Dunbar. MaRV
Conscience-Curst, The. "F. Anstey." CenHV
Conscience Doth Make Cowards of Us All. Menander, *tr. fr. Greek by* C. M. Bowra. OxBG
Conscience is instinct bred in the house. Conscience. Henry David Thoreau. *Fr.* A Week on the Concord and Merrimack Rivers. AnNE; HBV; OnAP
Conscience-Keeper, The. William Young. *Fr.* Wishmakers' Town. AA
Conscience's Song. Robert Wilson. *See* New Brooms.
Conscientious Objector, The. Karl Shapiro. AmPP (4th ed.); OxBA
Conscript, The. W. W. Gibson. ChMo; CMP; MaRV; PoeMoYo; POTT
Conscripts of the Dream, *sel.* Edwin Markham.
"Give thanks, O heart, for the high souls." PGD
Consecrate yourselves to God, all ye youths and maidens. Call to God's Service. Francis William Newman. GrCo-1
Consecration. "Marianne Farningham." MaRV
Consecration. Anna Hoppe. BePJ
Consecration. Patrick F. Kirby. GoBC
Consecration, A. John Masefield. BEL; BMEP; ChMo; CMP; CP; EnLit; GrCo-2; HBMV; HiLiEn; InP; MBP; MCCG; MoAB; MoBrPo; NeMA; NV; OtMeF; PCN; PoFr; POT; PoTo; POTT; PYM; VOD; WHA
Consecration. Murdoch O'Daly, *tr. fr. Irish by* Eleanor Hull. JKCP (1926 ed.)
Consecration. Benjamin Schmolck. *See* My Jesus, as Thou Wilt.
Consecration of the Common Way, The. Edwin Markham. SDH; StJW
Consecration of the House. W. S. Fairbridge. NeLNL
Conservative, A. Charlotte Perkins Gilman. AA; HBV; OBAV; PIAE
Conservative Shepherd to His Love, The, *parody.* Jack D'Arcy. InMe
"Conservatrix of Milésien." Ezra Pound. Hugh Selwyn Mauberley, XI. CoBMV; CoV; LiTA; LiTM (rev. ed.); MoPo
Consider. Giovanni Pico della Mirandola, *tr. fr. Italian by* Sir Thomas More. CAW
Consider. Christina Rossetti. GN
Consider, Friend, When We Together Spoke. Christian Morgenstern, *tr. fr. German by* Eileen Hutchins *and* Ursula Grahl. AnGP
Consider, if you can, the heads. On Viewing a Florist's Whimsy at Fifty-ninth and Madison. Margaret Fishback. WhC
Consider me a memory, a dream that passed away. Recessional. Georgia Douglas Johnson. CDC; PoNe
Consider, O my soul, what morn is this! A Meditation for Christmas. Selwyn Image. OBEV (new ed.)
Consider, please, the jacket blurb. The Blurb. Richard Armour. SiTL
Consider, pray, the artfulness. On a Christ in Jesuit Robes. Voltaire. LiA
Consider, reader, what fatigues I've known. John Gay. *Fr.* Trivia; or, The Art of Walking the Streets of London, III. EnLi-1 (1949 ed.)
Consider the auk. A Caution to Everybody. Ogden Nash. NePA
Consider the Lilies. William Channing Gannett. GrCo-1; MaRV; WGRP
Consider the lilies of the field, whose bloom is brief. Consider. Christina Rossetti. GN
Consider the lowering Lynx. Limerick. Langford Reed. CenHV
Consider the penguin. Enigma Sartorial. *Unknown.* DDA
Consider the ravens; for they neither sow nor reap. To His Disciples. St. Luke, Bible, *N.T.* CAW
Consider the sages who pulverize boulders. P Is for Paleontology. Milton Bracker. FiBHP; InMe; WhC
Consider the sea's listless chime. The Sea-Limits. Dante Gabriel Rossetti. AnEnPo; BMEP; BPN; EmBrPo; EPN; EtS; GrCo-2; PoVP; TOP; VA; VLEP
Consider, then, the flatterer's profession. The Profession of Flattery. Antiphanes. OxBG
Consider These, for We Have Condemned [Them]. C. Day Lewis. LiTB; LiTM; NAMP; SeCePo
Consider This and in Our Time. W. H. Auden. LiTB; LiTG; ReaPo; TwCV
Consider this man in the field beneath. Affinity. R. S. Thomas. HaMV; PoN
Consider [*or* Do but consider] this small dust, here in the glass. The Hour Glass. Ben Jonson. ElSeCe; EnLoPo; GTBS-W; LiTB; LiTG; SiTL
Consider Well. Sir Thomas More. ACP; CAW; GoBC
Consider when thou art movèd to be wroth. Consider. Giovanni Pico della Mirandola. CAW
Considerable Speck, A. Robert Frost. AmP; AmPP; MoAB; MoAmPo; WhC
Considerations of Murder. *Unknown, tr. fr. Sanskrit by* Swami Prabhavananda *and* Christopher Isherwood. *Fr.* Bhagavad-Gita. LiTW
(Debate between Arjuna and Sri Krishna.) WaaP
Considerations of Norfolk Island, *sel.* Kendrick Smithyman.
"High in the afternoon the dove." AnNZ
Considerations on Certain Music of J. S. Bach, *sel.* J. C. Beaglehole.
"Meditating in silence after the last note." AnNZ
Consigned for lading, marked for repairs. Chant of the Box Cars. Harry Kemp. PoMa
Consignee of silent storms and unseen lightning. Lynx. R. A. D. Ford. CaP
Consistent Anti to Her Son, A. Alice Duer Miller. FAOV
Consolation. Matthew Arnold. GEPC; ViPo
Consolation. Elizabeth Barrett Browning. OBEV (1st ed.); PoVP; VLEP
Consolation. George Darley. TriL
Consolation. Mary E. Wilkins Freeman. PR
Consolation. Rose Fyleman. GaP
Consolation. William Larminie. TIP

Consolation. John Frederick Nims. UnW
Consolation. James Larkin Pearson. NoCaPo
Consolation, A. Shakespeare. *See* Sonnets, XXIX.
Consolation. Earl of Surrey. OBSC
Consolation, The. Countess of Winchilsea. TriL
Consolation. W. B. Yeats. TwP
Consolation in July. Rayner Heppenstall. NeBP
Consolation of Philosophy, *sel.* Boethius, *tr. fr. Latin.*
Opening Poem, *tr. at. to* Alfred, King of England. LaP
Consolatory! St. John Emile Clavering Hankin. CenHV
Conspiracy. George Sterling. UnW
Conspiracy of Charles, Duke of Byron, The, *sels.* George Chapman.
"As when the moon hath comforted the night," *fr.* III, i. ViBoPo
"Give me a spirit that on this life's rough sea," *fr.* III, i. MyFE; ViBoPo
(Brave Spirit, A.) EV-1
(Invocation.) KN
(Master Spirit, The.) EtS
"Ile weare those golden spurres upon my heeles," *fr.* III, i. PoFr
"O that mine armes were wings, that I might flie," *fr.* III, i. NBE
"This hour by all rules of astrologie," *fr.* III, i. NBE
"To fear a violent good, abuseth goodness," *fr.* I, i. MyFE
"What place is this? what ayre? what rhegion?" *fr.* I, i. NBE
"Your Highness will excuse me; I will give you," *fr.* III, i. NBE
Conspirators, The. Frederic Prokosch. LiTM; NAMP; NePA; WaP
Constancy. Samuel Daniel. *Fr.* Hymen's Triumph. OBSC
Constancy. Charles Dibdin. LH
Constancy. George Herbert. CBE; EV-2
Constancy. John Boyle O'Reilly. BOHV; OnYI
Constancy. Coventry Patmore. The Angel in the House, II, xi, 4. OBVV
Constancy. Earl of Rochester. EPS; EV-3; GTSL; HBV; OBEV; OBS; SeCL; TOP
(I Cannot Change as Others Do.) EnLi-1 (1949 ed.)
(Song: "I cannot change . . .") CaAE; SeEP
Constancy. Sir John Suckling. *See* Constant Lover, The.
Constancy. *At. to* Joshua Sylvester. *See* Were I as Base as Is the Lowly Plain.
Constancy. Tzu Yeh, *tr. fr. Chinese by* Henry H. Hart. PoHN
Constancy ("My ornaments are arms"). *Unknown. See* Wandering Knight's Song, The.
Constancy ("One eve of beauty, when the sun"). *Unknown.* LPS-2
Constancy. Minor Watson. HBV
Constancy. Sir Thomas Wyatt. *See* Perdye I Saide Yt Not.
Constancye. Sidney Godolphin. MePo
Constant. Emily Dickinson. *See* Alter? When the hills do.
Constant. Frederic Thompson. JKCP (1926 ed.)
Constant Affection. *Unknown.* SeCL
Constant Bridegrooms, The. Kenneth Patchen. CrMA
Constant Cannibal Maiden, The. Wallace Irwin. BOHV
Constant Farmer's Son, The. *Unknown.* ABS
Constant Friend. Emilio Prados, *tr. fr. Spanish by* Eleanor L. Turnbull. CoSP
Constant Lover, The ("Out upon it"). Sir John Suckling. AEV; AWP; BLV; EM-1; EnLi-1; EPP; EV-2; FaFP; GTBS-W; HBV; InPo; JAWP; LiTB; LiTG; LiTL; MCCG; OBEV; OuHeWo; PG; PoMa; PreP; ReEn; SeCePo; TOP; TreFS; TrGrPo; WBP
(Constancy.) AnEnPo; BEL; CBOV; CoBE; EPS; LoBV; LPS-1; TyEnPo
(Out upon It [I Have Loved].) AnFE; BOHV; EG; ElSeCe; EnL; EnLit; LO; OBS; PoE; PoEL-3; PoRA; ReaPo; SeCeV; SeEP; SiTL; TwHP
(Poem, A: "Out upon it! I have loved.") ViBoPo
(Sir J.S.) SeCV-1
(Song: "Out upon it, I have loved.") CaAE; CoEV; MeLP; MePo; SeCL; WHA
Constant Lover, The ("Why so pale and wan"). Sir John Suckling. *See* Why So Pale and Wan?
Constant Lover, The. Aurelian Townsend. *See* Though Regions far Divided.
Constant North, The. J. F. Hendry. NeBP
Constant Penelope sends to thee, careless Ulysses! *Unknown.* EnLoPo; SiCE
Constant running up the path. Constant. Frederic Thompson. JKCP (1926 ed.)
Constant Service of the Antique World, The. Shakespeare. *Fr.* As You Like It, II, iii. EV-1
Constant Swain and Virtuous Maid, The. *Unknown.* HBV
Constantine's Vision of the Cross. Cynewulf, *tr. fr. Anglo-Saxon by* Charles W. Kennedy. *Fr.* Elene. AnOE
Constantly risking absurdity. A Coney Island of the Mind, 15. Lawrence Ferlinghetti. NeAP
Constellation. Merrill Moore. TrGrPo (1942 ed.)
Constellation, The. Henry Vaughan. SeCV-1
"Fair, order'd lights (whose motion without noise)," *sel.* NBE
Constellation and the *Insurgente*, The. *Unknown.* PAH
Constitution and *Guerrière*, The, *with music. Unknown.* ABF, *abr.*; SoAmSa
(*Constitution* and the *Guerrière*, The.) AmSS, *with music*; PAH; ViBoFo
Constitution for a League of Nations. Arthur Guiterman. InMe
Constitution of Athens, The. Solon, *tr. fr. Greek by* John Herman Merivale. GrR; PoFr
Constitution's Last Fight, The. James Jeffrey Roche. GA; MC; PAH
Constricted by my tortured thought. Prayer before Study. Theodore Roethke. TrPWD
Consuelo at the Country Club. Selden Rodman. NAMP
Consultation, The. William Green Brownson. *Fr.* The Country Doctor. PoP
Consummation. Elsa Barker. *Fr.* The Spirit and the Bride. HBMV
Consummation. Witter Bynner. *Fr.* To Celia. NP
Consummation. Thomas Traherne. SeCV-2
Consummation. James Terry White. OQP; QP-2
Contact. Dorothy Livesay. CaP
Contagion of Courage. Matthew Arnold. *Fr.* Rugby Chapel. MaRV
Contemplate all this work of Time. In Memoriam A. H. H., CXVIII. Tennyson. BEL; BPN; CoBE; EM-2; EmBrPo; EnL; EnLi-2; EPN; GEPC; MaPo; OAEP; PIAE; PoFS; SeCeV; TCEP; TOP; UnPo; ViPo; VLEP
Contemplation. Joachim du Bellay, *tr. fr. French by* Alan Conder. Les Amours, XXV. TrFP
Contemplation. John Alden Carpenter. RIS
Contemplation. Francis Thompson. EmBrPo; LoBV
"River has not any care, The," *sel.* FaBoEn
Contemplation; a Night Piece, *sel.* John Cunningham.
Moonrise. RO
Contemplation of Our State in Our Deathbed. John Donne. *Fr.* Of the Progresse of the Soule. OBS
Contemplation on Night, A. John Gay. CEP
Dawn and Night, *sel.* BeR
Contemplation upon Flowers, A. Henry King. ATP (1935 ed.); BLV, CaAE; CenL; ElSeCe; EV-2; HBV; LoBV; MeLP; MePo; OBEV; OBS; PG; PIAE; SeCL; SeEP; TrGrPo
("Brave flowers, that I could gallant it like you.") EG
Contemplation would make a good life, keep it strict. The Cruel Falcon. Robinson Jeffers. CoV
Contemplations. Anne Bradstreet. AmPP; AnFE; AnNE; APA; APW; CoAnAm; IAP; MOAP; PoEL-3, *abr.*
Sels.
Stanzas from "Contemplations" ("Some time now past in the autumnal tide"). Po
"When I behold the heavens as in their prime." BAV; MaRV
Contemplations, Les, *sel.* Victor Hugo, *tr. fr. French by* Sir George Young.
Bright Stars and Dark. LiA
Contemplative, The. Sister Mary Benvenuta. PraNu
Contemplative Quarry, The. Anna Wickham. BMEP; HBMV; NP
Contemplative Sentry, The. W. S. Gilbert. *Fr.* Iolanthe. ALV; EnLi-2; FiBHP; PoVP
Contemporaneity. Timotheus, *tr. fr. Greek by* F. L. Lucas. GrPE
Contemporaries. Richard Hovey. MAP; MoAmPo (1942 ed.)
Contemporary. Sara Bard Field. ChIP; QS
Contemporary Poets. Byron. *Fr.* Don Juan, XI. OBRV
Contemporary Song. Theodore Spencer. LiTA
Contemporary Suitor, The. Edward Sandford Martin. PR
Contempt for Dylan Thomas, A. Wilfred Watson. PeCV
Contempt of Poetry, The. Spenser. *See* October.
Contemptuous of kings, Empedocles. Empedocles. Thomas S. Jones, Jr. AnAmPo; LA
Contend in a sea which the land partly encloses. The Yachts. William Carlos Williams. AmPP; CoBMV; ExPo; InPo; LiTA; LiTM; MoAB; MoAmPo (1950 ed.); MoPo; MoVE; NAMP; NePA; OxBA; Po; PoFS; ReMP; SeCeV; ViBoPo (1958 ed.)
Contending with her streams, renascent stars. Aria for Flute and Oboe. Joseph Langland. NePoEA
Content. Barnabe Barnes. *See* Sonnet: "Ah, sweet Content."
Content. Elizabeth Barrett Browning. MaRV
Content. Thomas Campion. OBSC
Content. Stephen Crane. The Black Riders, XXVII. AA; LEAP
(Youth, A.) MoAmPo (1950 ed.)
("Youth in apparel that glittered, A") AnAmPo; LA; LiTA; NePA
Content. Thomas Dekker. *See* Happy Heart, The.
Content. Earl of Essex. *See* Happy Were He.
Content. Norman Gale. HBV; VA
Content. Robert Greene. *See* Sweet Are the Thoughts That Savor of Content.

Content. Dora Greenwell. PoToHe
Content ("My crown is in my heart"). Shakespeare. King Henry VI, Pt. III, *fr.* III, i. MaRV
("My crown is in my heart, not on my head.") PoToHe (new ed.)
Content. Thomas, Lord Vaux. *See* Of a Contented Mind.
Content. Geffrey Whitney. *See* In Crystal Towers.
Content and Resolute. William Drummond of Hawthornden. ES
Content and Rich. Robert Southwell. OBSC; SiCE
Content at Home. Pindar, *tr. fr. Greek by* F. L. Lucas. GrPE
Content, content! within a quiet room. Content. Dora Greenwell. PoToHe
Content in you. New Legends. Robert Graves. AtBAP
Content Thyself with Thy Estate. *Unknown.* EIL
Content within his wigwam warm. Canonicus and Roger Williams. *Unknown.* PAH
Contentation; Directed to My Dear Father, and Most Worthy Friend, Mr. Izaak Walton. Charles Cotton. EV-2; LPS-3
Contented at Forty. Sarah N. Cleghorn. HBMV
Contented Bachelor, The. John Kendall. InMe
Contented evening; comfortable joys. Week-End Sonnets, III. Harold Monro. CP; YT
Contented John. Jane Taylor. HBV; HBVY
Contented Lover, The. *Unknown.* SeCL
Contented Man, The. Pope. *See* Ode on Solitude.
Contented Mind, A. Joshua Sylvester. EV-1; HBV; PoToHe (1941 ed.); ReTS
(Contentment.) LPS-3
Contented river! in thy dreamy realm. To the Housatonic at Stockbridge. Robert Underwood Johnson. SN
Contented wi' Little [and Cantie wi' Mair]. Burns. BEL; BSV; TCEP
Contention between Four Maids Concerning That Which Addeth Most Perfection to That Sex. Sir John Davies. SiPS
Contention betwixt a Wife, a Widow, and a Maid, A. Sir John Davies. OBSC; SiPS
Contention of Ajax and Ulysses, The, *sel.* James Shirley.
"Glories of our blood and state, The," *fr.* sc. iii. AEV; CenL; ChTr; EG; ElSeCe; ExPo; InvP; LiTG; OBS; PG; PoRA; ReEn; SeEP; TrGrPo; TuPP; TVSH; ViBoPo; WaaP; WP; YT
(Calchas before the Body of Ajax.) CaAE
(Death the Conqueror.) LEAP
(Death the Level[l]er.) BCEP; CBE; CBOV; CoEV; GTBS; GTBS-D; GTBS-W; GTSE; GTSL; LiTB; LoBV; LPS-1; MaRV; OBEV; OtMeF; PoLi; RiBV; SeCeV; ShBV-4
(Death's Final Conquest.) EV-2; HBV
(Dirge, A.) ACP; AnFE; AWP; BEL; EnLit; InPo; JAWP; PoEL-2; TOP; WBP
(Equality.) AnEnPo
(King of Kings, The.) LH
(Levelling Dust, The.) BLV
(Of Death.) SeCL; WHA
(Our Blood and State.) GoBC
(Song.) FaBoEn
Contentions. *Unknown.* *See* It Was a Lording's Daughter.
Contentment. Al-Tutili, *tr. fr. Arabic by* A. J. Arberry. MooP
Contentment. Charles Stuart Calverley. ALV
Contentment. William Cowper.
(Olney Hymns.) CEP
Contentment. Sir Edward Dyer. *See* My Mind to Me a Kingdom Is.
Contentment ("Once on a time"). Eugene Field. CBPC
Contentment. Oliver Wendell Holmes. *Fr.* The Autocrat of the Breakfast Table, *ch.* 11. AmPP (4th ed.); AnNE; BOHV; HBV; HiLiAm; IAP; InMe; OnPP; OxBA; PIR; PR; REAL; TCAP; TOP; TreF
Contentment. Burges Johnson. AlBD
Contentment. Leonidas of Tarentum, *tr. fr. Greek by* F. A. Wright. GrR
Contentment. Olivier de Magny, *tr. fr. French by* Alan Conder. TrFP
Contentment. Sadi, *tr. fr. Persian by* L. S. Costello. LiTW
Contentment. Benjamin Schlipf. BLRP
Contentment. Sir Philip Sidney. *See* Get Hence Foule Griefe.
Contentment. Joshua Sylvester. *See* Contented Mind, A.
Contentment in the Dark. William Bell Scott. EBSV
Contentment Is a Sleepy Thing. Thomas Traherne. *Fr.* Christian Ethics. OxBoCh
Contentment of Willoughby, The. Frances Alexander. GoYe
Contentment; or, the Happy Workman's Song. John Byrom. CEP; OBEC
Contentment, parent of delight. A Cure for the Spleen. Matthew Green. *Fr.* The Spleen. OBEC
Contents of the Scedule Which Sir John of Bordeaux Gave to His Sons, The. Thomas Lodge. *Fr.* Rosalynde. ReIE; SiCE
Contessa to Her Judges, The. Cale Young Rice. SPP
Contest between Court and Country, A. *Unknown.* SeCL
Continence. Ibn Faraj, *tr. fr. Arabic by* A. J. Arberry. MooP
Continent's End. Robinson Jeffers. AnFE; AWP; CoAnAm; ImOP; InPo; JAWP; MOAP; ReMP; TwAmPo; WBP
Contingency. W. Wesley Trimpi. PtPa
Continual Conversation with a Silent Man. Wallace Stevens. LiTM (rev. ed.); NePA
Continual deprivation, now. Deprivation. H. A. Pinkerton. NePoAm
Continuance. A. Godwhen. TMEV
Continuation of Lucan, *br. sel.* Thomas May.
Death ("The wisest men are glad to die"). MaRV
Continued. Matthew Arnold. *See* To a Republican Friend, 1848, Continued.
Continued (King's College Chapel). Wordsworth. *See* They Dreamt Not of a Perishable Home.
Continuing Christ, The. W. Russell Bowie. ChIP; MaRV
Continuing City, The. Laurence Housman. WGRP
Continuing Love. Ibn Rashiq, *tr. fr. Arabic by* A. J. Arberry. MooP
Continuities. Walt Whitman. EOAH
Continuity. "Æ." ChMo; CMP; MBP; MoBrPo; NeMA; PoVP
Continuity, The. Paul Blackburn. NeAP
Continuity. H. P. Lovecraft. UnW
Contradiction. William Cowper. *Fr.* Conversation. LPS-3
Contrarimes, *sel.* Paul Jean Toulet, *tr. fr. French by* Cecily Mackworth.
"You who return from far Cathay." MiFP
Contrarious Passions in a Lover, The. Petrarch, *tr. by* Sir Thomas Wyatt. *See* Description of the Contrarious Passions . . .
Contrary Experience, The. Sir Herbert Read. FaBoMo
Contrary Joe. L. A. G. Strong. PoMa
Contrary Mary. Nancy Byrd Turner. HBMV; HBVY; TSW; TSWC
Contrary Theses, I. Wallace Stevens. OxBA
Contrast. Aubert Edgar Bruce. ChIP
Contrast, The. Helen Gray Cone. AA
Contrast. Eileen Duggan. AnNZ
Contrast. Charles Granville Hamilton. ChIP
Contrast. Issa, *tr. fr. Japanese by* Max Bickerton. PoFr
Contrast, A. James Russell Lowell. IAP; TCAP
Contrast, The. C. Morris. BOHV
Contrast in Styles, A. *See* Old Arm-Chair, The (*by* Eliza Cook), *and* On the Receipt of My Mother's Picture Out of Norfolk (*by* William Cowper).
Contretemps, The. Thomas Hardy. ChMo; CMP; LiTM (rev. ed.)
Contrite Heart, The. William Cowper. NBE; PoEL-3; TrPWD
(Lord Will Happiness Divine, The.) OxBoCh
"Thy Saints are comforted, I know," *sel.* MyFE
Contrition across the Waves. Caroline Giltinan. WHL
Contrivances, The, *sel.* Henry Carey.
Maiden's Ideal of a Husband, A. HBV; LPS-1
Contrive me, Vulcan, such a cup. The Bowl. Earl of Rochester. EV-3
Control of the Passes. W. H. Auden. ReaPo
Conundrum of the Workshops, The. Kipling. BMEP; HBV; MBP; MoBrPo; PoVP; VA
Convalescence, I–VIII. David McCord. WhC
Conveniently near to where. The Gastronomic Guile of Simple Simon. Guy Wetmore Carryl. GoTP; YT
Convent, The. Jeanne D'Orge. AnAmPo; LA
Convent Cemetery, Mount Carmel. Sister Mary St. Virginia. GoBC
Convent Echoes. Helen Louise Moriarty. JKCP
Convent Garden, The. Marie Kirkwood. PraNu
Convent Garden, The. Katharine Tynan. PraNu
Convent Morning. Sister Mary Eugene. PraNu
Convent of Pleasure, The, *sel.* Margaret Cavendish, Duchess of Newcastle.
Sea-Goddess, The. SeCL
Convent Threshold, The. Christina Rossetti. PoEL-5; PoVP
"For what is knowledge duly weighed?" *br. sel.* LO
Convention. Alfred Kreymborg. MAPA
Convention. Agnes Lee. BAP; HBMV; PoMa; SBMV
Convention Song. *Unknown.* PAH
Conventionality. Eloise Hackett. MaRV
Convergence of the Twain, The; Lines on the Loss of the *Titanic.* Thomas Hardy. CaAE; CoBMV; EnL; FaBoTw; InPo; LiTB; MaPo; MoAB; MoBrPo; MoPo; MoVE; OAEP (2d ed.); SeCeV; ShBV-3; ViP; ViPP
Conversation. John Berryman. LiTA; LiTM; NePA; WaP
Conversation, A. Sara Hamilton Birchall. NLK
Conversation. William Cowper. BCEP, *much abr.*
Sels.
Contradiction. LPS-3
Duelling. LPS-3
Conversation. Berenice C. Dewey. InMe
Conversation. Rose Fyleman. BoTP
Conversation. Louis MacNeice. FaBoMo
Conversation. Hannah More. *Fr.* Bas Bleu. OBEC
Conversation. Anne Robinson. SUS
Conversation. William F. Walsh. JKCP (1955 ed.)

Conversation at Midnight, *sel.* Edna St. Vincent Millay.
Anselmo Speaks ("There is no place on earth today save the peace in the heart"). TwCV
Conversation between Mr. and Mrs. Santa Claus. Rowena Bennett. ChBR; SiSoSe; TiPo (1959 ed.)
Conversation Galante. T. S. Eliot. HBMV; MAP; MoAmPo (1942 ed.)
Conversation in Black and White. May Sarton. GoYe
Conversation in Clichés. James Edward Tobin. JKCP (1955 ed.)
Conversation in the Forest. Joseph von Eichendorff, *tr. fr. German by* Herman Salinger. AnGP
Conversation in the Mountains. Li Po, *tr. fr. Chinese.* WhP
Conversation on an Autumn Night. Shimpei Kusano, *tr. fr. Japanese by* Takamichi Ninomiya *and* D. J. Enright. PoLJ
Conversation Piece. Smith Dawless. PreP
Conversation with an April Fool. Rowena Bennett. SiSoSe
Conversation with Rain. Louise D. Gunn. GoYe
Conversation with Three Women of New England. Wallace Stevens. NePA
Conversational. *Unknown.* ALV; BoHiPo; FiBHP
Conversational Neighbor, A. Richard Kirk. LS; PoMa
Conversational Reformer, The. Harry Graham. InMe; YaD
Conversion. Frances Angermayer. TreFS
(Last Thoughts of a Fighting Man.) PGD
Conversion ("Be vengeance wholly left to powers divine"). Dryden. *Fr.* The Hind and the Panther, III. ACP; CAW
(World Well Lost, The.) PoLi
(Worldly Vanity.) FiP
Conversion ("But, gracious God, how well dost Thou provide"). Dryden. *See* Church's Testimony, The.
Conversion. T. E. Hulme. FaBoMo; LoBV; MBP; MoBrPo (1942 ed.); ViBoPo
Conversion. Andrew Young. *Fr.* Nicodemus. MaRV
Conversion of the Magdalene, The, *sel.* Pedro Malon de Chaide, *tr. fr. Spanish by* Thomas Walsh.
"Encircling Thee Thy holy brides." CAW
Convert, The. G. K. Chesterton. GoBC; InP; JKCP (1926 ed.)
Converted Cannibals, The. G. E. Farrow. BOHV
Convict, The. Anthony Frisch. CaP
Convict, The. Beatrice Redpath. CPG
Convict, The. *Unknown.* CoSo; CSF
Convict of Clonmel [*or* Clonmala], The. *Unknown, tr. fr. Modern Irish by* Jeremiah Joseph Callanan. AnIL; AnIV; GTIV; IrPN; OxBI; OnYI; TIP
Convicts, The. Aleksey Konstantinovich Tolstoy, *tr. fr. Russian.* BoR, *tr. by* C. M. Bowra; WaL, *tr. by* Sir Cecil Kisch
Convinced by Sorrow. Elizabeth Barrett Browning. *Fr.* The Cry of the Human. BLRP; OQP; QP-2; WBLP
("'There is no God,' the foolish saith.") MaRV
Convinced of frailty, death. The Recoleta. Jorge Luis Borges. TwSpPo
Convoy. William Jay Smith. WaP
Coo-Coo, *with music.* *Unknown.* AS
"Coo, coo, coo." The Dove and the Wren. *Unknown.* RIS
Coo-coo, coo-oo-oo. Coo-Coo. *Unknown.* AS
Coogan's Wood. Francis Stuart. NeIP
Cogee. Henry Clarence Kendall. VA
Cook County. Archibald MacLeish. CrMA; NLK (1947 ed.)
(Weather.) MAP; MoAmPo; PIAE
Cook was a captain of the Admiralty. Five Visions of Captain Cook. Kenneth Slessor. BoAV
Cook we had upon the deck, The. The Erie Canal Ballad. *Unknown.* ABF
Cooking and Courting. *Unknown.* LPS-1
Cooking Egg, A. T. S. Eliot. CaAE
"Cooks shall be busied, by day and by night, The." Signs of the Season in the Kitchen. *Unknown.* SDH
Cooks who'd roast a sucking-pig. Recipes. *Unknown.* LPS-3
Cooky, every child agrees, A. Concerning Cookies. Susan Adger Williams. DDA
Cool, and palm-shaded from the torrid heat. The Pipe-Player. Sir Edmund Gosse. VA
Cool as a cucumber. Lily McQueen. Sara Jackson. DiM
Cool Gold Wines of Paradise, The. Robert Farren. AnIV; SeCePo
Cool is the autumn wind. Lines. Li Po. ChLP
Cool it is, and still. Crescent Moon. Basho. OnPM
Cool-matted silvery bed, A; but no dreams. She Sighs on Her Jade Lute. Wen T'ing-yun. ChLP
Cool of Evening, The. Lizette Woodworth Reese. LS
Cool perfume of bamboo pervades my room. Summer Night. Tu Fu. WhP
Cool shades and dews are round my way. A Scene on the Banks of the Hudson. Bryant. APW
Cool sky opens like a hand, The. William Blake Sees God. Roy McFadden. NeIP
Cool Tombs. Carl Sandburg. AmP; AmPP; AnFE; AtBAP; BAP; BLV; BoLiVe; CaAE; ChMo; CMP; CoAnAm; CoBA; CP; HBMV; IAP; MAP; MoAB; MoAmPo; MOAP; MoVE; NeMA; NV; TBM; TrGrPo; TwAmPo; TwCV; ViBoPo; WHA
Cool waters tumble, singing as they go. Garden of the Nymphs [*or* A Garden]. Sappho. GrL; OxBG
Cool Web, The. Robert Graves. AWP; ChMP; GTBS-D
Coole and Ballylee, 1931. W. B. Yeats. ChMo; CMP; OBMV
Coole Park, 1929. W. B. Yeats. OBMV; OxBI
Cooleen, The. Douglas Hyde. OBVV
Coolin, The. James Stephens. POTE; TIP
Cooling Fountain. *Unknown, tr. fr. Spanish by* Sir John Bowring. TeCS
Coolun, The. Maurice O'Dugan, *tr. fr. Late Middle Irish by* Sir Samuel Ferguson. AnIV; OnYI; OxBI
Coomb-Firtrees say that life is a moan. Yell'ham-Wood's Story. Thomas Hardy. TOP
Coon Can (Poor Boy), *with music.* *Unknown.* AS
Cooper. James Russell Lowell. *Fr.* A Fable for Critics. AnNE; OxBA
("Here's Cooper, who's written.") CoBA
Cooper o' Dundee, The. *Unknown.* CoMu
Cooper, whose name is with his country's woven. Red Jacket. Fitz-Greene Halleck. AA; IAP
Co-operation. J. Mason Knox. BLPA; YaD
Cooper's Hill. Sir John Denham. CEP; EPS; SeCV-1; SeEP
Sels.
"My eye, descending from the hill, surveys." EPP; ReEn; ViBoPo
(Praise of the Thames.) EV-2
(Thames from Cooper's Hill, The.) CoEV; OBS; SeCePo
Thames, The. BCEP; FaBoEn
Copa; the Barmaid. Virgil, *tr. fr. Latin by* Jack Lindsay. LaP
Cope sent a challenge frae Dunbar. Johnnie Cope [*or* Hey Johnnie Cope]. Adam Skirving. CBOV; EBSV; EV-3
Copernicus, *sel.* Robert D. Fitzgerald.
"Cock that crowed this dawn up, heard, The." BoAV
Cophetua was a merry King. King Cophetua and the Beggar Maid. Don Marquis. HBMV; InMe
Coplas de Manrique, *sel.* Longfellow.
"To One alone my thoughts arise." ChIP
Coplas on the Death of His Father. Jorge Manrique. *See* Ode on the Death of His Father.
Coppenter man said a wicked word, The. Sin of the Coppenter Man. Edmund Vance Cooke. PTA-2
Copper beech and holy thorn. The Thorn of Somerset. Elliott Coleman. NoCaPo (1941 ed.)
Copper concave of a sky, A. A Christ-Child Day in Australia. Ethel Turner. BoAu
Copper Song, The. Hermia Harris Fraser, *ad. fr. Haida Indian song.* CaP
Copper Song. Ethel Talbot Scheffauer. PoMS
Coptic Poem ("A Coptic deputation, going to Ethiopia"). Lawrence Durrell. FaBoMo
Copy of Verses sent by Cleone to Aspasia, A. Walter Savage Landor. *Fr.* Pericles and Aspasia. LoBV
Coquette, The. Aphra Behn. TrGrPo
(Coquet, The.) ViBoPo
Coquette, The. Witter Bynner. PR
Coquette, The. *At. to* Meleager *and to* Philodemus, *tr. fr. Greek by* F. L. Lucas. GrPE
Coquette, The. John Godfrey Saxe. PR
Coquette, The. Muriel Earley Sheppard. IHA
Coquette. Keith Stuart. NLK
Coquette Conquered, A. Paul Laurence Dunbar. MAP; MoAmPo (1942 ed.); NeMA
Cor Cordium. Swinburne. ATP (1935 ed.); BMEP; BPN; EmBrPo; EPN; PoVP; TOP; ViPo; VLEP
Cor Cordium. Wilbur Underwood. PraNu
Cor Mio. Christina Rossetti. BPN
Coracle, The. Lucan, *tr. fr. Latin by* Sir Walter Ralegh. ChTr
Coral. Christina Rossetti. *See* O Sailor, Come Ashore.
Coral Grove, The. James Gates Percival. AA; AnAmPo; AnNE; APW; EtS; GN; GoTP; LA; LPS-2; TVSH
Coral Insect, The. Lydia Huntley Sigourney. LPS-2
Coral Islands. Louis Ginsberg. OQP; QP-2
Coral Reef, The, *abr.* James Montgomery. *Fr.* The Pelican Island. LPS-2
Corbitt's Barkentine, *with music.* *At. to* Tom Reynolds. ShS
Corda Concordia, *sel.* Edmund Clarence Stedman.
Quest. AA
Cordage creaks and rattles in the wind, The. Columbus. James Russell Lowell. BHV
Cordial Soul. Sara Henderson Hay. BAP
Córdoba./ Distant and lonely. Rider's Song. Federico García Lorca. AnSpL-2; CoSP
Cordova. Ibn Zaydun, *tr. fr. Arabic by* H. A. R. Gibb. AWP; LiTW
Core, The. John Holmes. MiAP
Core. Jaime Torres Bodet, *tr. fr. Spanish by* Muna Lee. AnCL
Core of him is hate, The. Steel Mill [*or* Munitions Plant]. Louis Untermeyer. PIAE; TCPD

Coridon and Melampus' Song. George Peele. *See* Song of Coridon and Melampus.
Coridon and Phillis. Robert Greene. *Fr.* Perimedes. OBSC
(Phillis and Corydon.) HBV
Coridon's Song. John Chalkhill. EV-2; HBV; ViBoPo
Coridon's Supplication to Phillis. Nicholas Breton. *See* Corydon's Supplication to Phyllis.
Corinna. Thomas Campion. *See* When to Her Lute Corinna Sings.
Corinna Bathes. George Chapman. *Fr.* Ovid's Banquet of Sense. OBSC
(Natures Naked Jem.) FaBoEn
Corinna, from Athens, to Tanagra. Walter Savage Landor. *Fr.* Pericles and Aspasia. OBEV (new ed.); OBVV
(Corinna to Tanagra.) OBRV; ViBoPo, *abr.*
(Corinna to Tanagra from Athens.) BPN; TOP
Corinna Goes a-Maying. Robert Herrick. *See* Corinna's Going a-Maying.
Corinna Goes a-Singing. Frank Sidgwick. WhC
Corinna Is Divinely Fair. *Unknown.* ElSeCe; SeCL
Corinna, pride of Drury-Lane. A Beautiful Young Nymph Going to Bed. Swift. BeR
Corinna to Tanagra from Athens. Walter Savage Landor. *See* Corinna, from Athens, to Tanagra.
Corinna with a graceful air. Upon a Sickly Lady. *At. to* Charles Burnaby *and to* William Burnaby. *Fr.* The Reformed Wife. SeCL
Corinna's Going a-Maying. Robert Herrick. AIDL, *abr.*; AtBAP; ATP; BCEP; BEL; BoLiVe; CBOV; CoBE; DD, *abr.*; ElSeCe; EM-1; EnL; EnLi-1; EnLit; EPP; EPS; EV-2; ExPo; HBV; LEAP; LiA; MaPo; OAEP; OBEV; OBS; OuHeWo; Po; PoEL-3; PoFS; ReaPo; ReEn; RiBV; SeCeV; SeCV-1; SeEP; TCEP; TOP; TrGrPo; TyEnPo; UnPo (1st ed.); WHA
(Corinna Goes a-Maying.) PreP
(Corinna's Maying.) GTSL; PoRL, *sts.* 1–3
(Going a-Maying.) GN; LH; OTPC (1923 ed.)
"We shall grow old apace, and die," *sel.* PoD
Corinthian Lais received no such crowds in her home. Propertius. Elegies, II, 6. LaP
Corinthian of dogs, how word the grace. To an English Setter. Thomas Walsh. PFY
Corinthians I. *See* First Corinthians.
Coriolan, *sels.* T. S. Eliot.
Difficulties of a Statesman. OnAP
Triumphal March. KN; PoLFOT; ShBV-4; SoV; WaaP
Coriolanus, *sels.* Shakespeare.
"Let/ Thy mother rather feel thy pride," *fr.* III, ii. MotAn
Martial Friendship, *fr.* IV, v. LPS-1
Valour, *fr.* II, ii. BHV
Cork, The. Vladislav Felitsyanovich Khodasevich, *tr. fr. Russian by* Babette Deutsch. TrRV
Corliss Engine-Wheel. MacKnight Black. AnAmPo; LA
Corn. Esther Antin. *Fr.* On Our Farm. RIS
Corn. Sidney Lanier. CoBA; CoV; LaNeLa; TCAP
Corn-blossom maidens. Song after Rain. *Tr. by* Natalie Curtis. APW
Corn Cañon. Patric Stevenson. NeIP
Corn Crake, The. James H. Cousins. OnYI
Corn-Crake, The. David Gray. EBSV
Corn does not hurry, and the black grape swells. Second Wisdom. Henry Morton Robinson. GoYe
Corn-grinding Song. *Tr. fr. Laguna Indian by* Natalie Curtis. AWP; JAWP; SUS; WBP
Corn-grinding Song. *Tr. fr. Zuni Indian by* Natalie Curtis. SUS
Corn grows up, The. Incantation for Rain. *Unknown.* ExPo
Corn hangs from the rafters. Sierra. Jorge Carrera Andrade. AnCL
Corn Husker, The. Emily Pauline Johnson. CaP; OCL
Corn in the Wind. Iyad, *tr. fr. Arabic by* A. J. Arberry. MooP
Corn is down, The. Etched in Frost. James Stephens. ChMo; CMP
Corn-Law Hymn. Ebenezer Elliott. BCEP; LPS-2
Corn-planting. Peter McArthur. CPG
Corn Rigs. Burns. EBSV
Corn-shuckings and square dances, the fiddles, The. David Crockett. Donald Davidson. *Fr.* The Tall Men. SPP
Corn-Song, A. Paul Laurence Dunbar. AA; OBAV
Corn Song, The. John Wesley Holloway. BANP
Corn Song, The. Whittier. *Fr.* The Huskers. GN; OHIP; OTPC; TOAH, *abr.*
Cornelia, *sel.* Thomas Kyd.
Of Fortune, *abr.* EIL
Cornelia's Song. John Webster. *See* Call for the Robin Redbreast and the Wren.
Corner Boys. Bryan MacMahon. OnYI
Corner-Knot, The. Robert Graves. BLV
Corner Seat. Louis MacNeice. MoVE
Cornerstone, The. Edward A. Church. MaRV
Cornet, The. Rainer Maria Rilke, *tr. fr. German by* Constantine Fitz Gibbon. AnGP
Cornet, The. Earl of Surrey. ES; OBSC
(Complaint That His Ladie after She Knew of His Love Kept Her Face Alway Hidden from Him, *sl. diff.*) PoEL-1
("I never saw you, madam, lay apart.") SiPS
Cornfield. Leo Cox. CaP
Cornfield, The. Elizabeth Madox Roberts. SUS
Cornfield, The, *sel.* Muriel Rukeyser.
"For those given to voyages: these roads." FiMAP
Cornfield Holler, *with music. Unknown.* ABF
Cornfields, *abr.* Mary Howitt. OTPC (1923 ed.)
"When on the breath of autumn breeze," *sel.* PRWS; SN; VA
Cornish Magic. Ann Durell. FaPON
Cornish Miner, The. Walter F. Gries. IHA
Cornish Wind. Arthur Symons. LBBV
Cornucopia of Red and Green Comfits, The. Amy Lowell. NV
Cornwallis led a country dance. The Dance [*or* Cornwallis's Country Dance]. *Unknown.* PAH; TrAS, *with* Yankee Doodle
Cornwallis's Surrender. *Unknown.* PAH
Coromandel Fishers. Sarojini Naidu. BBV; EtS; MCCG; VOD
Corona Inutilis. James Lister Cuthbertson. BoAu
Coronach ("He is gone on the mountain"). Sir Walter Scott. *Fr.* The Lady of the Lake, III. AnFE; BEL; BHV; BPN; BSV; CaAE; CH; EBSV; EmBrPo; EnLi-2 (1949 ed.); EnLit; EnRP; ERP; EV-4; GTBS; GTBS-D; GTBS-W; GTSL; HBV; InP; LPS-1; MW; OAEP; OBRV; OHIP; PCD; PCN; PoRA; ShBV-1; TCEP; TOP; TreFS; TrGrPo; ViBoPo; WHA
("He is gone on the mountain.") EPN
Coronation. Helen Hunt Jackson. AA; BeLS; GN; HBV; LBAP; OBAV; PFY; TCAP
Coronation. Edward Perronet. HBV; MaRV; TreFS; WGRP
("All hail the power of Jesus' name!") OIF
Coronemus Nos Rosis Antequam Marcescant. Thomas Jordan. *See* Careless Gallant, The.
Coronet, The. Andrew Marvell. CenL; CoEV; ElSeCe; LoBV; MeLP; MePo; OBS; OxBoCh; SeCV-1; StJW
Coronet for His Mistress Philosophy, A, *sels.* George Chapman.
"Muses that Fame's loose feathers beautify," X. ReIE
"Muses that sing love's sensual empery," I. BrBE; CoBE; EIL; ElSeCe; LoBV; LPS-1; PoE; RiBV; TuPP
(Love and Philosophy.) OBSC; SeCePo
"Corporal Green!" the orderly cried. Roll-Call. Nathaniel Graham Shepherd. AA; BBV (1923 ed.); DD; HBV; MDAH; OHIP; PaA; PTA-2
Corpse, The. Salvador Díaz Mirón, *tr. fr. Spanish by* Samuel Beckett. AnMP
Corpse, clad with carefulness. Of Misery. Thomas Howell. EIL; TuPP
Corpse rotted from its exhibiting noose, The. The Example. Salvador Díaz Mirón. AnMP
Corpses in the Wood. Ernst Toller, *tr. fr. German by* E. Ellis Roberts. TrJP
Corpus Christi. Margery Mansfield. NV
Corpus Christi. Evelyn Underhill. StJW
Corpus Christi Carol. *Unknown. See* Falcon, The.
Correct Compassion, A. James Kirkup. ChMP; FaBoTw; ImOP; SeCePo
Correction, A. Robert Frost. WhC
Correlated Greatness. Francis Thompson. *See* Heart, The.
Correspondences. Baudelaire, *tr. fr. French.* AnFP, *tr. by* Kate Flores; AWP, *tr. by* Allen Tate; LiTW, *tr. by* Allen Tate; ReMP, *tr. by* R. G. Stern
(Affinities, *tr. by* Alan Conder.) TrFP
Correspondences. Christopher Pearse Cranch. IAP
Correspondent. Witter Bynner. AnFE; CoAnAm; TwAmPo
Corridor, The. Thom Gunn. NePoEA
Corridor, The. E. A. Robinson. BoFr
Corruption. Henry Vaughan. CAW; EPS; FaBoEn; MeRV; OBS; OxBoCh; SeCV-1
Corruption of Power, The. Walter Savage Landor. *Fr.* Antony and Octavius. RO
Corrymeela. "Moira O'Neill." AnIV; AWP; BMEP; HBV; JAWP; LBBV; TIP; WBP
Corsage Bouquet, A. Charles Henry Luders. HBV; PR
Corsair, The, *sels.* Byron.
Corsair's Life, The, *fr.* I. EV-4
(Song of the Corsairs.) EtS
(Song of the Rover.) LPS-2
Deep in My Soul, *fr.* I. EV-4
Summer, *fr.* III. OBRV
"Yet was not Conrad thus by Nature sent," *fr.* I. EV-4
"Cortayse Quen," thenne sayde that gaye. *Unknown. Fr.* The Pearl. NBE
Cortège. Leopoldo Marechal, *tr. fr. Spanish by* Dudley Fitts. AnCL
Cortège. Paul Verlaine, *tr. fr. French by* Arthur Symons. AWP; OnPM; WoL
Cortège for Rosenbloom. Wallace Stevens. TwAmPo

Corydon. Virgil, *pr. tr. fr. Latin by* Elizabeth Sommer. Eclogues, II. RoL
Corydon and Thyrsis. Virgil, *tr. fr. Latin by* Dryden. Eclogues, VII. AWP
Corydon and Tityrus. *Unknown, tr. fr. Dutch by* Montgomery Carmichael. CAW
Corydon, Arise, My Corydon! *Unknown. See* Phyllida's Love-Call.
Corydon to His Phyllis. Sir Edward Dyer. *See* Alas, My Heart.
Corydon's Song. Thomas Lodge. *See* Blith and Bonny Country Lass, A.
Corydon's Supplication to Phyllis. Nicholas Breton. ElSeCe (Coridon's Supplication to Phillis.) SiCE (Supplication, A.) OBSC
Corymbus for Autumn, A, *sel.* Francis Thompson.
"Or higher, holier, saintlier." VLEP
Corythos, *sel.* Walter Savage Landor.
Helen and Corythos. LoBV
Cosmic Egg, The. *Unknown.* BOHV; LPS-3
Cosmic Fabric, The. Yakov Petrovich Polonsky, *tr. fr. Russian by* Avrahm Yarmolinsky *and* Cecil Cowdery. TrRV
Cosmic Leviathan, that monstrous fish. Cosmogony. Edgell Rickword. FaBoTw
Cosmogony. David Daiches. LiTM
Cosmogony. Edgell Rickword. FaBoTw
Cosmopolitan Woman, A. Sam Walter Foss. BOHV
Cospatrick. *Unknown.* EBSV; OBB
Cossack Cradle-Song. Mikhail Lermontov, *tr. fr. Russian.* BOL, *tr. by* Elizabeth Champney; BoR, *tr. by* C. M. Bowra
Cossante: "Oh flowers, oh flowers of the tall green pine-tree." Dinis, King of Portugal, *tr. fr. Portuguese by* Seth G. Thornton. LyMA
Cossante: "Tell me, daughter, my lovely daughter." Pero Meogo, *tr. fr. Portuguese by* Seth G. Thornton. LyMA
Cossimbazar. Henry S. Leigh. BOHV; NA
Cost, The. Mary Elizabeth Colman. NeTW
Cost. Richard Watson Gilder. StJW
Cotswold Hills. Mary Colborne-Veel. MM
Cotswold Love. John Drinkwater. POT; PoTo
Cottage, The. Jones Very. OxBA
Cottage hidden in the wood, A. A Whittier Alphabet. *Comp. by* Caroline B. Le Row. PEOR
Cottage Hospital, The. John Betjeman. MoVE; UnPo (3d ed.)
Cottage Pictures, *sel.* Samuel Jackson Pratt.
"No village dames and maidens now are seen." EnSW
Cottage Song, A. Nikolai Alekseyevich Kluyev, *tr. fr. Russian by* Babette Deutsch. TrRV
Cottager, The, *sel.* John Clare.
"True as the church clock." OBRV
Cottager and His Landlord, The. Milton, *tr. fr. Latin by* William Cowper. OTPC (1923 ed.)
Cottager to Her Infant, The. Dorothy Wordsworth. BOL; CH; EV-3; HBV; OTPC (1923 ed.); PRWS (Cottager's Lullaby, The.) MOAH
Cottager's Hymn, The. Patrick Brontë. MaRV
Cottager's Lullaby, The. Dorothy Wordsworth. *See* Cottager to Her Infant, The.
Cotter's Saturday Night, The. Burns. BEL; BeLS; BoPo; BPP; CEP; EiPP; EM-1; EnL; EnLi-2; EnLit; EnRP; EPP; EV-3; FaBoBe; HBV; LPS-2; MCCG; OAEP; OBEC, *abr.*; TCEP; TOP
Sels.
"Cheerfu' supper done, The," *br. sel.* BHV; WGRP
November Evening. UnPo (1st ed.)
Prayer for My Native Land. MaRV
Cotter's Song. Johan Skjoldborg, *tr. fr. Danish by* Charles W. Stork. BoDS
Cottleston, Cottleston, Cottleston Pie! Hums of Pooh. A. A. Milne. *Fr.* Winnie the Pooh. BoN
Cotton blouse you wear, your mother said, The. McDonogh Day in New Orleans. Marcus B. Christian. PoNe
Cotton Boll, The. Henry Timrod. AA; AmPP; HiLiAm; IAP; SPP; TCAP
Cotton Cat, The. Mary Effie Lee Newsome. GoSl
Cotton Eye Joe ("Where did you come from"), *with music. Unknown.* OuSiCo
Cotton-eyed Joe ("If it had not 'a' been for Cotton-eyed Joe"), *with music. Unknown.* ABF
Cotton Field. Minnie Hite Moody. MuM
Cotton Field Song, *with music. Unknown.* ABF
Cotton-Mill Colic, *with music. Unknown.* OuSiCo
Cotton Mill Funeral. Stewart Atkins. NoCaPo
Cotton Song. Jean Toomer. CDC
Cotton-still spire cracks in chimes on the, The. Poem I. David Evans. MoWP
Cottonwood Leaves. Badger Clark. TiPo
Coughing in a shady grove. Ipecacuanha. George Canning. ChTr
Could all this be forgotten? Yes, a schism. Keats. *Fr.* Sleep and Poetry. ChER
Could but this be brought. Technique. Langdon Elwyn Mitchell. *Fr.* To a Writer of the Day. AA
Could every time-worn heart but see Thee once again. The Nativity. Henry van Dyke. *Fr.* To the Child Jesus. MaRV; TrPWD
Could he have made Priscilla share. Llewellyn and the Tree. E. A. Robinson. BeLS; HBMV; TwP
Could he return to us, how would we greet him? Woodrow Wilson. Robert Underwood Johnson. DD; GA
Could he, whose rules the rapid comet bind. Newton and Himself. Pope. *Fr.* An Essay on Man. BeR
Could I Believe. Ewart Milne. OxBI
Could I bring back lost youth again. Florine. Thomas Campbell. BSV
Could I but hear. Tanka, VIII. Lewis Alexander. CDC
Could I but retrace. Tanka, I. Lewis Alexander. CDC
Could I but teach man to believe. Adios. Joaquin Miller. OQP; QP-2
Could I change you, help you to love me sweet. Swinburne. *Fr.* Les Noyades. LoPS
Could I have said while he was here. In Memoriam A. H. H., LXXXI. Tennyson. EmBrPo; EnLi-2; EPN; GEPC; ViPo; VLEP
Could I have sung one song that should survive. Timor Mortis Conturbat Me. Sir Joseph Noel Paton. EBSV
Could I pass those lounging sentries, through. Death-Bed of Bomba, King of Naples. *Unknown.* LPS-3
Could I pluck down Aldebaran. The Unloved to His Beloved. William Alexander Percy. HBMV; LS
Could I take me to some cavern for mine hiding. O for the Wings of a Dove [*or* Longing *or* Escape]. Euripides. *Fr.* Hippolytus. AWP; GrR; JAWP; OxBG; PCD; ShBV-4; WBP
Could It Have Been a Shadow? Monica Shannon. FaPON; GAP; StVeCh (1955 ed.); TiPo
Could Juno's self more sovereign presence wear. Venus Victrix. Dante Gabriel Rossetti. The House of Life, XXXIII. BPN; PoVP; ViPo
Could love for ever. Stanzas. Byron. HBV; ViBoPo
Could Man Be Drunk Forever. A. E. Housman. Last Poems, X. EG; EmBrPo; EnLi-2 (1949 ed.); EnLit; InPo; LiTM; OBMV; OtMeF; PoE; TwP
Could my heart but see Creation as God sees it—from within. Immanence. Edmond G. A. Holmes. MaRV
Could not once blinding me, cruel, suffice? Samson to His Delilah. Richard Crashaw. TrGrPo
Could our first father, at his toilsome plough. Adam Posed. Countess of Winchilsea. Po
Could Poe walk again to-morrow, heavy with dyspeptic sorrow. What Troubled Poe's Raven. John Bennett. PA
Could she come back who has been dead so long. Separation. Alice Learned Bunner. *Fr.* Vingtaine. AA
Could then the babes from yon unshelter'd cot. Sonnet. Thomas Russell. OBEC
Could Time, his flight reversed, restore the hours. William Cowper. *Fr.* On the Receipt of My Mother's Picture. WHA
Could we but draw back the curtains. If We Understood. *Unknown.* PTA-2
Could we but see men as they are! A Window in the Breast. *Unknown.* OxBG
Could we float thus ever. Sunday up the River, XX. James Thomson. EmBrPo
Could we forget the widow'd hour. In Memoriam A. H. H., XL. Tennyson. BPN; EmBrPo; EPN; GEPC; ViPo; VLEP
Could ye come back to me, Douglas, Douglas. Douglas, Douglas, Tender and True [*or* Too Late]. Dinah Maria Mulock Craik. AV; BLPA; BMEP; HBV; LoPS; LPS-1; NeHB; OBVV; TreF; VA
"Could Ye Not Watch One Hour?" Godfrey Fox Bradby. MaRV
Could you bid an acorn. Lover's Reply to Good Advice. Richard Hughes. MBP; MoBrPo
Could you care for me, as I care for my cat? Plea for a Cat. Jewell Bothwell Tull. CIV
Could you not drink her gaze like wine? The Card-Dealer. Dante Gabriel Rossetti. BPN; EmBrPo; PoVP; ViP; ViPo; VLEP
Could You Not Watch with Me One Little Hour? Sara Bard Field. MuM
Could You Once Regain. Kendrick Smithyman. AnNZ
Could you tell me the way to Somewhere. Somewhere. Walter de la Mare. FaPON
Couldst thou, Great Fairy, give to me. The Pines. Harriet Prescott Spofford. AA
Couldst thou portray that face whose holy spell. Our Madonna at Home. Rafael Pombo. CAW
Council from a Poet, Middle-aged. John Holmes. CAG
Council Held by the Rats, The. La Fontaine, *tr. fr. French by* Elizur Wright. OuHeWo
("Old Rodilard, a certain cat," *tr. by* Elizur Wright.) CIV
("Tyrant Cat, by surname Nibbelard, A," *diff. tr.*) CIV

Council of Horses, The. John Gay. BoChLi; CG; GN
Council of Satan, The. Milton. *Fr.* Paradise Lost, I. PoEL-3
Councillor, The. Cullen Gouldsbury. BoSA
Counsel. Roselle Mercier Montgomery. HBMV
Counsel. Mollie E. Moore. HBV
Counsel of Moderation, A. Francis Thompson. MBP; MoBrPo
Counsel of Polonius, The. Shakespeare. *See* Polonius' Advice to Laertes.
Counsel to Girls. Robert Herrick. *See* To the Virgins, to Make Much of Time.
Counsel to Girls. Archibald Stodart-Walker. *Fr.* The Moxford Book of English Verse. CenHV
Counsel to Those That Eat, *sels.* E. V. Lucas.
  Chocolate-Cream, I. BOHV
  Potatoes. GaP
Counsel upon Marriage. Chaucer. PoLi
Counselor, The. Dorothy Parker. InMe
Counsels. Antonio Machado, *tr. fr. Spanish by* Thomas Walsh. AnSpL-2
Counsels of O'Riordan, the Rann Maker, The. T. D. O'Bolger. AnIV
Counsels of Sigrdrifa. *Unknown, tr. fr. Icelandic by* William Morris *and* Eiríkur Magnusson. *Fr.* The Elder Edda. AWP
Count Arnaldos. *Unknown, tr. fr. Spanish.* AnSpL-1, *tr. by* Nicholson B. Adams; LyMA, *tr. by* Richard Beaumont; TeCS, *tr. by* Sir John Bowring
Count each affliction, whether light or grave. Sorrow. Aubrey Thomas De Vere. BLPA; EPN; GoBC; HBV; JKCP; MaRV; NeHB; OBEV (1st ed.); OQP; QP-1; TIP; VA; WGAP
Count Filippo, *sels.* Charles Heavysege. PeCV
  "Now let the drums roll muffled; let the bells'."
  Song: "Who is lord of lordly fate."
Count Gismond. Robert Browning. BEL; BMEP; GEPC; PoVP; ViPP
Count me o'er earth's chosen heroes—they were souls that stood alone. James Russell Lowell. *Fr.* The Present Crisis. WGRP
Count me the stairs I climbed to your retreat. Pierre de Ronsard. *Fr.* Sonnets pour Hélène. PrPoCR
Count not thyself a starveling soul. The Kingdom Within. Percy Clough Ainsworth. MaRV
Count Orlo in England. Jon Manchip White. NePoEA
Count Ten. Bonaro Overstreet. PoToHe (new ed.)
Count That Day Lost. "George Eliot." MaRV; NeHB; OQP; QP-2
  (At Set of Sun.) PoToHe (new ed.)
  (Day Well Spent, A.) PTA-1
Count the flashes in the surf. Song for Music. Sir Edmund Gosse. VA
Count the sighs, and count the teares. The Broken Heart. Thomas Beedome. OBS
Count the white horses you meet on the way. White Horses. Eleanor Farjeon. PoRh
Count to Denmark took his way, The. Niels Ebbeson. *Unknown.* BoDaBa
Count up the dead by fever, shot and shell. Richard William Thomson. *Fr.* Peter Ottawa. CPG
Count up those books whose pages you have read. Indolence. Vernon Watkins. FaBoTw
Countenance like lightning, why do you stand. Colloquy at Peniel. W. S. Merwin. NePoEA
Counter-Attack. Siegfried Sassoon. EnLit; HiLiEn; MBP; MoBrPo; PIAE; PreP; TCEP; WaP
Counter-Serenade; She Invokes the Autumn Instant. Peter Viereck. CrMA
Counterfeit and choked up. Benares. Jorge Luis Borges. TwSpPo
Counterpoint. Mary H. Blodgett. CAG
Counterpoint, A. Robert Creeley. NeAP
Counterpoint. Owen Dodson. PoNe
Counters. Elizabeth J. Coatsworth. DDA; GaP; MW; PoRh; SUS
  (To Think.) MPB
Countersign. Arthur Ketchum. *Fr.* Legends for Trees. HBMV
Countersign, The. Charles J. Quirk. *Fr.* Quatrains. CAW
Countersign, The. *Unknown.* BIG; MDAH
Countersigns, The, *with music.* *Unknown.* SoAmSa
Countess, I see the flying year. To My Mistress. Frederick Locker-Lampson. VA
Countess Laura. George Henry Boker. BeLS; LPS-3
Countess of Montgomery's Urania, The, *sel.* Lady Mary Wroth.
  Love, What Art Thou? SeCL
Countess of Pembroke's Arcadia, The. Sir Philip Sidney. *See* Arcadia.
Countess Temple, Appointed Poet Laureate to the King of the Fairies. Horace Walpole. CEP
  (Anne Grenville, Countess Temple, Appointed Poet Laureate to the King of the Fairies.) OBEC
Countesse of Douglas out of her boure she came, The. The Knight of Liddesdale. *Unknown.* ESPB
Counting Kisses. Catullus. *See* Lesbia.
Counting Man, The. William Vaughn Moody. PoMS
Counting-out Rhyme. Edna St. Vincent Millay. MoShBr
Counting-out Rhyme. *Unknown.* ChTr
Counting-out Rhyme for March. Frances Frost. YeAr
Counting the Beats. Robert Graves. Po; ViBoPo (1958 ed.)
Counting the Days. James S. Tippett. ChBR
Counting the Mad. Donald Justice. NePoEA; UnPo (3d ed.)
Countless gold of a merry heart, The. Riches. Blake. BoLiVe; StaSt; TrGrPo
Countless stars, which to our human eye, The. The Starry Host. John Lancaster Spalding. *Fr.* God and the Soul. AA; HBV
Countless vagaries of maple leaves, The. Landscape. Maxwell Bodenheim. MOAP
Countrie men of England, who live at home with ease. *See* Countrymen of England . . .
Country Bedroom, The. Frances Cornford. MBP; MoBrPo
Country-Brook. Maxwell Bodenheim. MOAP
Country Carol, A. Margaret Widdemer. SDH
Country Cat. Elizabeth J. Coatsworth. GoTP
Country Child, The. Irene Thompson. BoTP
Country Church. Robert P. Tristram Coffin. MaRV; QS
Country Church, A. Violet Alleyn Storey. OQP; QP-2
Country Church, A. Pearce Young. PtPa
Country Churches. Maysie Tuley Klein. DDA
Country Clergyman's Trip to Cambridge, The. Macaulay. OxBoLi
Country Clown, The. John Trumbull. AnAmPo; LA
Country Club Sunday. Phyllis McGinley. CrMA
Country Cottage. Tu Fu, *tr. fr. Chinese by* Kenneth Rexroth. OnPC
Country curate, visiting his flock, A. The Lost Spectacles. *Unknown.* BOHV
Country Dance. Judith Wright. MoAuPo
Country Doctor, The, *sel.* William Green Brownson.
  Consultation, The. PoP
Country Doctor, The. Will M. Carleton. BLPA
Country ever has a lagging Spring, The. Spring in Town. Bryant. APW
Country Faith, The. Norman Gale. BoTP; CBPC; HBV; NLK; OBEV (new ed.); OBVV; OQP; OTPC; QP-1; VA; WGRP
Country farmer had a friend at court, A. Henry Parrot. SiCE
Country folk who pass have said to me, The. The Grave. John Lyle Donaghy. NeIP
Country Girl. Maxwell Bodenheim. MOAP
Country Girl, Don't Stay Away. Luis Carlos López, *tr. fr. Spanish by* Donald Devenish Walsh. AnCL; WoL
Country Girl's Policy, The; or, The Cockney Outwitted. *Unknown.* CoMu
Country Glee. Thomas Dekker *and* John Ford. *Fr.* The Sun's Darling. CoEV; OBSC
  ("Haymakers, rakers, reapers, and mowers.") CenL; ElSeCe; ViBoPo
  (Song: "Haymakers, rakers, reapers, and mowers.") EV-2
Country God, A. Edmund Blunden. MBP; MoBrPo
Country Gods. Cometas, *tr. fr. Greek by* T. F. Higham. FaBoCh; LoGBV; OxBG
Country Gods. Plato, *tr. fr. Greek by* Walter Leaf. OxBG
Country Graveyard. Charles F. Pressoir, *tr. fr. French by* Edna Worthley Underwood. PoNe
Country habit has me by the heart, The. Winter. V. Sackville-West. *Fr.* The Land. AIDL
Country House in the South, A. John Henry Boner. NoCaPo
Country Inn, The, *sel.* Joanna Baillie.
  Song: "Though richer swains thy love pursue." OBRV
Country Innocence. *Unknown.* *See* Happy Husbandman, The.
Country is no country I have seen, The. Civil War. Mark Van Doren. MoVE
Country, The, is still at war; no safety yet. Parting from My Old Wife. Tu Fu. WhP
Country Justice, The. John Langhorne. LaA
  Apology for Vagrants, I. OBEC
Country Kisses. Arthur Joseph Munby. *Fr.* Dorothy; a Country Story. VA
Country lad and bonny lass, A. Have-at a Venture. *Unknown.* CoMu
Country lanes are bright with bloom, The. Early Autumn. Dart Fairthorne. PEOR
Country Lasses Witty Invention, The. *Unknown.* *See* Unfortunate Miller, The.
Country Life, The. Robert Herrick. EPS; EV-2
Country Life. Horace, *tr. fr. Latin by* Dryden. AWP
  (Revery of a Business Man.) WoL
Country Life, A. Randall Jarrell. MiAP; MoAmPo (1950 ed.); NoCaPo (rev. ed.)
Country Life. Frank Kendon. POTE
Country Life. Lope de Vega, *tr. fr. Spanish by* Felicia Dorothea Hemans. AnSpL-1

Country life is sweet, A! The Useful Plough. *Unknown.* CG; DD; HBV; LPS-2; OTPC (1923 ed.); RIS; TVSH
Country Life, A; to His Brother, M. Tho. Herrick. Robert Herrick. SeCV-1
Country Lore. *Unknown, tr. fr. Greek by* T. F. Higham. OxBG
Country Lover's Complaint, The. *Unknown. See* Phillida Flouts Me.
Country men of England. *See* Countrymen of England . . .
Country Miracle. Abbie Huston Evans. LiTM
Country Music. Plato, *tr. fr. Greek by* Robert Bridges. LiTW; OxBG
Country-nurse once told her weeping boy, A. The Women and the Wolf. Avianus. LaP
Country of hunchbacks!—where the strong, straight spine. Sonnet to Gath. Edna St. Vincent Millay. CoBA; MAP; MoAB; MoAmPo
Country of No Lack. Jean Starr Untermeyer. MAP; MoAmPo
Country Parson, The. Goldsmith. *See* Village Preacher, The.
Country Pastor. Mitsuko Inoue, *tr. fr. Japanese by* Katue Kitasono. LiTW
Country Philosopher, A. Frank Lebby Stanton. DDA
Country Pleasures. Martial, *tr. fr. Latin by* F. A. Wright. AWP; OnPM
Country Proverbs. *Unknown.* StaSt
Country Reverie. Carol Coates. CaP
Country rings around with loud alarms, The. The Rude Militia. Dryden. *Fr.* Cymon and Iphigenia. CoEV
Country roads are yellow and brown. Street Lanterns. Mary Elizabeth Coleridge. BoTP; PoeT
Country Sabbath. Minnie Hite Moody. MuM
Country Sale. Edmund Blunden. NV
Country Saying. *Unknown. See* He That Would Thrive.
Country School. Allen Curnow. AnNZ
Country School, The. *Unknown.* APW
Country Song. Nicholas Breton. *See* Report Song, A.
Country Song. Shakespeare. *See* It Was a Lover and His Lass.
Country Song, A. Sir Philip Sidney. *Fr.* Arcadia. OBSC; SiPS
Country Song. Elinor Wylie. BAV
Country Store, The. *Unknown.* BLPA
Country Summer. Léonie Adams. AnEnPo; ATP (1953 ed.); BLV; BoLiVe (1939 ed.); LiTM; MAP; MoAB; MoAmPo; MoPo; MoVE; TCPD; TrGrPo; TwAmPo; ViBoPo (1958 ed.)
Country Summer Pastoral, A, *sl. abr.* Sam Walter Foss. BOHV
Country Thought. Sylvia Townsend Warner. MBP; MoBrPo; NeMA
Country Town, A. Philip James Bailey. *See* Aim of Life, The.
Country Towns. Kenneth Slessor. MoAuPo; NeLNL
Country Trucks. Monica Shannon. BrR; FaPON; TiPo (1950 ed.)
Country Tune. Elizabeth Riddell. BoAV; NeLNL
Country Vegetables. Eleanor Farjeon. *See* Vegetables.
Country Walk, The. John Dyer. PrWP
Yellow Barn, The, *sel.* RO
Country Walk. Geoffrey Taylor. OxBI
Country Ways. Marcia Masters. Impressions of My Father, I. GoYe
Country ways are full of mire, The. The Night before the Wedding; or, Ten Years After. Alexander Smith. LPS-1
Country Wedding. Francis Jammes, *tr. fr. French by* Alan Conder. TrFP
Country Wedding, The. *Unknown.* HBV
Country Witch, A. William Barnes. *See* Witch, A.
Country without a Mythology, A. Douglas Le Pan. BoCaPo (1948 ed.)
Countryman's God. Roger Winship Stuart. MaRV
Countrymen, The. John Masefield. *Fr.* Reynard the Fox, I. ChMo; CMP
Countrymen [*or* Countrie men] of England, who live at home with ease. Sailors [*or* Saylors] for My Money. Martin Parker. CoMu; SeCL; TuPP
Country's goin' fast to ruin, The. Old Canada; or, Gee Buck Gee. Alexander McLachlan. BoCaPo (1943 ed.)
Country's Greatness, A. Alcaeus, *tr. fr. Greek by* F. L. Lucas. GrPE
Countrywoman of Mine, A. Elaine Goodale Eastman. AA; OBAV
County Guy. Sir Walter Scott. *Fr.* Quentin Durward, *ch.* 4. BCEP; BEL; BPN; EBSV; EmBrPo; EPN; EtPaEn; EV-4; LPS-1; OAEP; OBRV; TCEP; TOP
(Serenade, A: "Ah! County Guy.") GTBS; GTBS-D; GTBS-W; GTSE; GTSL
(Song: "Ah! County Guy.") CH
County Mayo, The. Anthony Raftery, *tr. fr. Modern Irish by* James Stephens. AnIL; GTIV; KiLC, *tr. by* Frank O'Connor
County of Mayo, The. *At. to* Thomas Flavell [*or* Lavelle], *tr. fr. Modern Irish by* George Fox. AnIV; GTIV; IrPN; OBEV; OnYI; OxBI; TIP
County of squares and spires, in the middle of England. Canons Ashby. David Wright. PoN
County Sligo. Louis MacNeice. OnYI
Coup d'Etat. Ruth Herschberger. LiTA
Coup de Grace, The. Edward Rowland Sill. AA
Couple, A. Carl Sandburg. ReMP
Couplet· "God loves an idle rainbow." Ralph Hodgson. BMEP
Couplet: "Great things are done when men and mountains meet." Blake. *Fr.* Gnomic Verses. PC
(Gnomic Verses.) TrGrPo
Courage. Arthur Adams. BoAu
Courage. "Anna Akhmatova," *tr. fr. Russian by* Babette Deutsch. TrRV
Courage. Matthew Arnold. ReTS
Courage. Karle Wilson Baker. MaRV; PC; PoeMoYo
Courage. Stopford Brooke. WGRP
Courage. Ozora Stearns Davis. OQP; QP-1
Courage. Dorothy Dezouche. DDA
Courage. Amelia Earhart. BLP; MaRV; MoSiPe
Courage. Helen Frazee-Bower. HBMV
Courage ("Courage is but a word, and yet, of words"). John Galsworthy. HiLiEn
Courage ("If on a spring night I went by"). John Galsworthy. OtMeF
(Prayer, The.) QS
Courage. Paul Gerhardt, *tr. fr. German by* John Wesley. WGRP
Courage. George Herbert. *See* Dare to Be True.
Courage. Emyr Humphreys. NeTW
Courage. Virginia Moore. PC
Courage. Sadi, *tr. fr. Persian by* Sir Edwin Arnold. *Fr.* The Gulistan. AWP; JAWP; OnPM; WBP
Courage, All. Edwin Markham. HBMV
Courage and hope, true heart! The Message of the Snowdrop. *Unknown.* PEOR
Courage and Patience. Henry T. Tuckerman. APW
Courage, brother! do not stumble. Trust in God. Norman Macleod. BLRP
Courage Equal to Desire. W. B. Yeats. *Fr.* No Second Troy. LiA
Courage for the Pusillanimous. Paul Roche. GoYe
Courage Has a Crimson Coat. Nancy Byrd Turner. MoSiPe; PCD; PCH
"Courage!" he said, and pointed toward the land. The Lotos-Eaters. Tennyson. AtBAP; BEL; BMEP; BoLiVe; BPN; BrBE; ChTr; CoBE; EM-2; EmBrPo; EnL; EnLi-2; EnLit; EPN; EV-5; ExPo; FiP; GEPC; GoTL; HBV; LEAP; LiTB; MaPo; MCCG; OAEP; OBRV; OTPC; PECK; PoE; PoEL-5; PoFS; PoVP; ReaPo; RiBV; SeCeV; SG; ShBV-4; TCEP; TOP; TVSH; TwCrTr; TwHP; VA; ViPo; ViPP; VLEP
Courage in Exile. Pindar, *tr. fr. Greek by* F. L. Lucas. *Fr.* Pythian Odes, IV. GrPE
Courage is a fabric. To Archbishop Stepinac. Sister Mary Eulalia. JKCP (1955 ed.)
Courage is armor. Courage. Karle Wilson Baker. MaRV; PC; PoeMoYo
Courage is but a word, and yet, of words. Courage. John Galsworthy. HiLiEn
Courage is the price that life exacts for granting peace. Courage. Amelia Earhart. BLP; MaRV; MoSiPe
Courage Means Running. William Empson. LiTB
Courage, Mon Ami! Willard Wattles. PC
(Devil Is Dying, The.) PR
Courage my Soul, now learn to wield. A Dialogue between the Resolved Soul and Created Pleasure. Andrew Marvell. MeLP; OBS; MePo; SeCV-1
Courage, my Soul! now to the silent wood. Peace. Bhartrihari. AWP
Courage of man is one thing, but that of a maid is more, The. A Ballad of Emma Samson. John Trotwood Moore. BlG
Courage of the Lost, The. Edith M. Thomas. BAP
Courage to Live. Grace Noll Crowell. BPP; PoToHe
Courageous Cabot, brave Venetian born. The English Captains. Charles Fitzgeffrey. *Fr.* Sir Francis Drake. SG
Courageous Turk, The, *sel.* Thomas Goffe.
"Drop golden showers, gentle sleep." SeCL; SeEP
Coureurs de Bois. Douglas Le Pan. BoCaPo (1948 ed.); CaP
Couriers from Chihuahua go, The. The Bull Fight. L. Worthington Green. SCC
Course in pathless woods, The, which, without rein. Ariosto. *Fr.* Orlando Furioso, XXIII. PrPoCR
Course of each life must vary, The. Bread of Brotherhood. Lucia Trent. PGD
Course of my long life hath reached at last, The. On the Crucifix. Michelangelo. CAW
Course of Time, The, *sels.* Robert Pollok.
Byron, *fr.* IV. LPS-3

Course of Time, The *(continued)*
"Much of my native scenery appears," *fr.* V. EnSW
Ocean, *fr.* I. EtS; LPS-2
Course of True Love, The. Shakespeare. *Fr.* A Midsummer Night's Dream, I, i. LPS-1; TreFS; WHA
Courser and the Jennet, The. Shakespeare. *Fr.* Venus and Adonis. LoBV
(Courser, The.) OBSC
Court Historian, The. George Walter Thornbury. HBV; OBVV
Court is kept att leeue London, The. Hugh Spencer's Feats in France. *Unknown.* ESPB
Court Lady, A. Elizabeth Barrett Browning. BeLS; HBV; LPS-2; VA
Court of Charles II, The. Pope. *Fr.* To Augustus. OBEC
Court of Death, The. John Gay. EV-3
Court of Fairy, The. Michael Drayton. *See* Queen Mab's Chariot.
Court of Neptune, The. John Hughes. EtS
Court of Sapience, *sel.* John Lydgate.
Lament: "Farewell Mercy, farewell thy piteous grace." PoEL-1
Court Poet in Trouble, A. *Unknown, tr. fr. Old Irish by* Osborn Bergin. SiB
Courteous kind gallants all. Sir Walter Rauleigh His Lamentation. *Unknown.* CoMu
Courteous Pagan Shall Condemn, The. Roger Williams. *Fr.* A Key into the Language of America. AmPP (4th ed.)
(Brother Indian, The.) GrCo-1
Courtesan to Aphrodite, The. Poseidippus, *tr. fr. Greek by* F. L. Lucas. GrPE
Courtesies of good-morning and good-evening. On Dwelling. Robert Graves. MoPW; MoVE
Courtesy. Hilaire Belloc. ACP (1952 ed.); BMEP; HBMV; JKCP; LBBV; OtMeF; PoeT; SDH
Courtesy. Mary Mapes Dodge. BrR
Courtesy. Coventry Patmore. *Fr.* The Angel in the House, I, xi, 2. OBVV
Courtesy. Daniel Sargent. DDA; MW
Courtier, whose heart with pride so mighty grows. Upstart Courtier. Samuel Rowlands. SiCE
Courtier's a Riddle, A. Ralph Schomberg. *Fr.* The Judgment of Paris. TrJP
Courtier's Good-Morrow to His Mistress, The. *Unknown.* ElL
Courtier's Health, The; or, Merry Boys of the Times. *Unknown.* CoMu
Courtier's Life, The. Sir Thomas Wyatt. ReIE
Courtin', The. James Russell Lowell. *Fr.* The Biglow Papers, 2d series, Introduction. AA; AmPP; AnNE; APW; BeLS; BOHV; CoBA; EV-5; HBV; HiLiAm; IAP; IHA; InMe; LHV; LPS-3; MCCG; MOAP; MW; OBAV; OBVV; PTA-2; REAL; StVeCh (1940 ed.); TCAP; TreFS; YT
Courting in Kentucky. Florence E. Pratt. BOHV; PTA-2
Courting of Olga Karg, The. Watson Kirkconnell. TwCaPo
Courtling, I rather thou should'st utterly. To Censorious Courtling. Ben Jonson. ReIE
Courtship. Ibn Sa'id of Alcala la Real, *tr. fr. Arabic by* A. J. Arberry. MooP
Courtship, Merry Marriage, and Picnic Dinner of Cock Robin and Jenny Wren, The. *Unknown.* HBV; OTPC
("It was a merry time.") PPL
("It was on a merry time." Mother Goose *vers.*) BoChLi (1939 ed.)
Courtship of Billy Grimes, The. *Unknown.* ABS
Courtship of Miles Standish, The, *parody.* William F. Kirk. PoMa
Courtship of Miles Standish, The. Longfellow. BeLS; TreFS, *abr.*
Sels.
Expedition to Wessagusset, *fr.* V *and* VII. PAH
War-Token, The, *fr.* IV. PAH
Courtship of the Yonghy-Bonghy-Bo, The. Edward Lear. BoN; EnLoPo; GoTP; HBV; OTPC
(Yonghy-Bonghy-Bo, The.) BOHV; LBN; NA
Courtyard Pigeons, The. Caroline Giltinan. BLA
Cousin Lucrece. Edmund Clarence Stedman. OBAV
Cousin Nancy. T. S. Eliot. TwP
Covenant. Joseph Auslander. QS
Covenant, A. Frances Ridley Havergal. PraP
Covenant of His Grace, The. Charles Wesley. BePJ
Covenanter's Lament for Bothwell Brigg, The. Winthrop Mackworth Praed. OBRV
Coventry Carol, *with music.* *Unknown.* YaCaBo
(Carol at the Manger, A.) BOL
(Lullay, Lullay, Thou Little Tiny Child.) AnEC
Cover. Frances Frost. SUS
Cover Me Over. Richard Eberhart. FiMAP
Cover me over. Bringers. Carl Sandburg. NP
Cover mine eyes, O my love! Ecstasy. Sarojini Naidu. AV
Cover the embers. Longfellow. *Fr.* Curfew. WaKn
Cover Them Over with Beautiful Flowers. *Unknown.* MDAH
Cover your eyes with your hands. The Cripple. Robert P. Tristram Coffin. StVeCh (1955 ed.)
Covered Bridge, The. Madison Cawein. YT
Covered Bridge, The. Anderson M. Scruggs. DDA
Covered with snow, the herd, with none to guide. Without the Herdsman. Diotimus. AWP
Covering the Subject. Richard Armour. WaKn
Covertly under the line tree aspen. Epithalamium for Cavorting Ghosts. Dachine Rainer. NePoAm-2
Coves of Crail, The. "Fiona Macleod." VA
Cove's shining plate of blue and green, The. The Swimmers. Edward Shanks. PtOT
Covetousness. William Langland. *Fr.* The Vision of Piers Plowman, Passus V. CoEV
(Avarice, *mod. by* Henry W. Wells.) PoLi
Cow, The. Oliver Herford. *Fr.* More Animals. NA
Cow, The. Mrs. Motherly. PPL; SAS
Cow, The. Ogden Nash. CenHV
Cow, The. Bernard O'Dowd. BoAu
Cow, The. Theodore Roethke. FiBHP
Cow, The. Robert Louis Stevenson. BoChLi; FaPON; GFA; GoBP; MPB; OTPC (1946 ed.); PoVP; PPL; RAR; RIS; SAS; StVeCh; SUS; TiPo; UTS; VLEP
Cow, The. Ann *or* Jane Taylor. BoChLi; CBPC; HBV; HBVY; MPB; OTPC; RAR; UTS
(Pretty Cow.) PoRh; StVeCh; TVC; TVSH
(Thank You, Pretty Cow.) BoTP; PCH, *st.* 1; PRWS; SAS
Cow, The. Bert Leston Taylor. RIS
Cow and a calf, A. *Unknown.* OxNR
Cow and the Ass, The. Jane Taylor. BoTP; OTPC (1923 ed.)
Cow at Sullington, A. Charles Dalmon. TSW; TSWC
Cow-bosses are good-hearted chunks, The. Dogie Song. *Unknown.* CoSo; CSF
Cow Camp on the Range, A. *Unknown.* CoSo; CSF
Cow-Chace, The. John André. PAH
Cow eats green grass, The. Response to Rimbaud's Later Manner. T. Sturge Moore. HBMV
Cow-Feeders' Song, The. *Unknown, tr. fr. Chinese. Fr.* The Fountain of Old Poems. WhP
Cow has a cud, The. David McCord. TiPo (1959 ed.)
Cow Herd, The. Diotimus, *tr. fr. Greek by* R. A. Furness. OxBG
(Without the Herdsman, *tr. by* John William Burgon.) AWP
Cow in Apple-Time, The. Robert Frost. CV; MAP; MoAB; MoAmPo; NV; TwP
Cow is of the bovine ilk, The. The Cow. Ogden Nash. CenHV
Cow, The, is too well known, I fear. The Cow. Oliver Herford. *Fr.* More Animals. NA
Cow Time. Monica Shannon. SiSoSe
Cow Wandering in the Bare Field, The. Randall Jarrell. MoVE
Coward. Harold Lewis Cook. NP
Coward, The. Roland R. Greenwood. YT
Coward, The. Kipling. *Fr.* Epitaphs of the War. FaBoTw; GTBS; LiA; OAEP (2d ed.); PoVP
Coward, The. Eve Merriam. TrJP
Coward—of heroic size. Grizzly. Bret Harte. AA; AnAmPo; EV-5; LA; OBAV; SN
Cowardice. Emyr Humphreys. NeTW
Cowards ("Cowards die many times before their deaths"). Shakespeare. *Fr.* Julius Caesar, II, ii. BLP; MaRV
(Death of Cowards, The.) TreFS
(That Men Should Fear.) TrGrPo
Cowards fear to die: but courage stout. On the Snuff of a Candle. Sir Walter Ralegh. SiPS
Cowboy, The. John Antrobus. AA; FaBoBe; FaPON; OTPC (1946 ed.); PoRL
Cowboy, The ("All day on the prairie"), *with music. Unknown.* CoSo (A *and* B *vers.*); CSF
Cowboy, The ("He wears a big hat"). *Unknown.* MaC; SCC
Cowboy ("I'm wild and wooly"). Baird Boyd. *See* Drunken Desperado, The.
Cowboy, The ("It was only a few short years ago"). *Unknown.* CoSo
Cowboy, The ("Oh, a man there lives"). *Unknown.* CoSo
Cowboy Alone with His Conscience, A. James Barton Adams. SCC
Cowboy and His Love, The, *with music.* John Milton Hagen. CoSo
(Song of the Cattle Trail.) SCC
Cowboy and the Maid, The. *Unknown.* SCC
Cowboy at Church, The. *Unknown.* CoSo, *with music;* CSF
Cowboy at the Carnival, A. *Unknown.* SCC
Cowboy at Work, The. *Unknown.* CoSo; CSF
Cowboy Boasting Chants. *Unknown.* ABF
Cowboy Dance Song, A. *Unknown.* CoSo
Cow-Boy Fun. Wallace D. Coburn. PoOW
Cowboy Grace: "Eat your meat and save the skin." *Unknown.* CoSo

Cowboy Grace: "Thar's the bread, thar's the meat." *Unknown.* CoSo
Cowboy Grace: "Yes, we'll come to the table." *Unknown.* CoSo
Cowboy he lay on the prairie, A. The Dry-Landers. *Unknown.* CoSo
Cowboy Jack, *with music. Unknown.* CoSo
Cowboy Race, A. J. C. Davis. SCC
Cowboy Song ("I come from Salem County"). Charles Causley. NePoEA
Cowboy Song, A ("I could not be so well content"). *Unknown.* SCC
Cowboy Song ("One night as I lay on the prairie"). *Unknown.* ABS
Cowboy Songs ("Oh, slow up, dogies, quit your roving round"). *At. to* Harry Stephens. *See* Night-herding Song.
Cowboy stands beneath, The. Vaquero. Edward Dorn. NeAP
Cowboy Talks to a Pitching Horse. *Unknown. See* Cowboy to Pitching Bronco.
Cowboy to His Friends in Need. Burke Jenkins. SCC
Cowboy to Pitching Bronco, *with music. Unknown.* ABF
(Cowboy Talks to a Pitching Horse, *st.* 1.) CoSo
Cowboy Toast, A. James Barton Adams. SCC
Cowboy up to Date, The. Charles F. Thomas, Jr. CoSo
Cowboy versus Broncho. James Barton Adams. SCC
Cowboys' Ball, The. Henry Herbert Knibbs. SCC
(Cowboy's Ball, The.) PoOW
Cowboy's Christmas Ball, *with music.* Larry Chittenden. CoSo, *with music;* CSF; SCC; SoAF, *with music, abr.*
Cowboys, come and hear a story of Roy Bean in all his glory. Roy Bean. *Unknown, at. to* Charles J. Finger. ABF; BeLS; CoSo
Cowboy's Dance Song, The, *with music.* James Barton Adams. CoSo; SCC
Cowboy's Dream, The ("Last night as I lay on the prairie"). Charles J. Finger. CoSo, *with music;* CSF; IHA; MaC; YT
Cowboy's Dream, The ("When I think of the last great round-up"). *Unknown.* ABF
(Great Round-up, The.) CoSo; CSF
Cowboy's Fate, The. Wallace D. Coburn. PoOW
Cowboy's Gettin'-up Holler, *with music. Unknown.* ABF; CoSo; TrAS
Cowboy's Hopeless Love, A. James Barton Adams. SCC
Cowboy's Lament, The. *Unknown.* ChTr; CoSo, *with music;* CSF; FaFP; MaC; PoeMoYo, *abr.;* TreFS; ViBoFo (A *and* B *vers.*); WaKn
(As I Walked Out in the Streets of Laredo, *with music.*) AS
Cowboy's Life, The. *At. to* James Barton Adams. CoSo; CSF; MPB, *abr.;* POT; PoTo; TiPo
Cowboy's life is a dreary, dreary life, A. The Dreary, Dreary Life [*or* The Kansas Line]. *Unknown.* CoSo; CSF
Cowboy's Love Song, The. *Unknown.* SCC
Cowboy's Meditation, The. *Unknown.* CoSo; CSF
Cowboy's Prayer, The. Badger Clark. DDA
Cowboy's Salvation Song. Robert V. Carr. PoOW
Cowboy's Son, A. *Unknown.* SCC
Cow-Boy's Song, The. Anna Maria Wells. PRWS
Cowboy's Valentine, The. Charles Fletcher Lummis. SCC
Cowboy's Worrying Love, A. James Barton Adams. SCC
Cowdenknowes. Robert Crawford. EBSV
Cowgirl, The. *Unknown. See* Bucking Bronco.
Cowhorn-crowned, shockheaded, cornshuck-bearded. The Knight, Death, and the Devil. Randall Jarrell. CrMA
Cowley. Addison. EV-3
Cowman's Prayer, The. *Unknown.* CoSo, *with music;* CSF; SoAF, *with music*
Cowper. John Clare. PtP; TriL
Cowper at Olney. Sylvia Lynd. POTE
Cowper, the poet of the fields. Cowper. John Clare. PtP; TriL
Cowper's Grave. Elizabeth Barrett Browning. EmBrPo; EV-4; HBV; OBVV; PoVP; PtP; ViPo; VLEP
Cows. Judy Van der Veer. MuM
Cows are bawling in the mountains, The. First Snow. Charles E. S. Wood. TBM
Cows are milked, the horses fed, The. The Christmas Calf. Judy Van der Veer. BPP
Cows beneath a great oak tree. Communion. Jessie B. Rittenhouse. PR
Cows low in the pasture on the hill, The. The Song of the Robin. Beatrice Bergquist. SUS
Cowslips. Walter Savage Landor. *See* With Rosy Hand.
Coxcomb, A. Joseph Hall. *Fr.* Virgidemiarum. EV-2
Coxcomb Bird, The. Pope. *Fr.* Moral Essays. LiTB; RiBV; SiTL
Coy Clelia, veil those charming eyes. To Clelia. Matthew Coppinger. SeCL
Coy Lass Dress'd Up in Her Best, The. *Unknown.* LoPS
Coy Mistress, The. Anacreon, *tr. fr. Greek by* F. L. Lucas. GrPE
(Tell Me Why, *tr. by* J. M. Edmonds.) GrR
Coy Mistress, The. Asclepiades, *tr. fr. Greek by* F. L. Lucas. GrPE
Coy Nature (which remain'd, tho aged grown). Ode upon Doctor Harvey. Abraham Cowley. PoEL-2
Coy Polyphemus. Theocritus, *tr. fr. Greek by* R. C. Trevelyan. *Fr.* Idylls. OxBG
Coy Shepherdess, The; or, Phillis and Amintas. *Unknown.* CoMu
Coyote. George Sterling. DDA
(Father Coyote.) PoTo
Coyote and the Locust, The. *Tr. fr. Zuni Indian by* Frank Cushing. AWP; JAWP; WBP
(Locust, The.) FaPON; SUS
Cozy. T'ao Ch'ien, *tr. fr. Chinese by* C. W. Luh. OnPM
Cozzo Grillo. H. B. Mallalieu. WaP
Crab, The. Avianus, *tr. fr. Latin by* Jack Lindsay. LaP
Crab. John Blight. BoAV
Crab and the Snake, The. *Unknown, tr. fr. Greek by* Walter Headlam. OxBG
Crab-Apple. Ethel Talbot. PCH; TiPo
Crab once tried to turn and bumped instead, A. The Crab. Avianus. LaP
Crab, the bullace, and the sloe, The. Grave-Digger's Song [*or* Elegy]. Alfred Austin. *Fr.* Prince Lucifer. BMEP; VA
Crab Tree, The. Oliver St. John Gogarty. AnIL; OxBI
Crabbed Age and Youth. Shakespeare. The Passionate Pilgrim, XII. BCEP; BLV; CBOV; ElSeCe; EV-1; HBV; LEAP; LiA; LiTB; OBEV; ReEn; TreFS; ViBoPo
(Age and Youth.) EIL; FaBoEn
("Crabbed age and youth cannot live together.") SiCE
(Madrigal, A: "Crabbed age and youth.") GBV (1952 ed.); GTBS; GTBS-D; GTBS-W; GTSE; GTSL
(Youth and Age.) OBSC
"Crabbed Age and Youth." Theognis, *tr. fr. Greek by* J. M. Edmonds. GrR
"Crabbed Age and Youth." Theophilus, *tr. fr. Greek by* Gilbert Highet. OxBG
Crabbing. Norman Levine. CaP
Crabe dans Calalou, *with music. Unknown.* OuSiCo
Crabfish, The, *with music. Unknown.* SaSa
Crack, The. J. C. Hall. HaMV
Cracked Bell, The. Baudelaire, *tr. fr. French.* AnFP, *tr. by* Vernon Watkins; OnPM, *tr. by* Arthur Symons; TrFP, *tr. by* Alan Conder
Cracked by that accurate beak. Song of the Three Seeds in the Macaw's Beak. Elizabeth J. Coatsworth. TCPD
Crackle and blaze. A Winter Song. William Cox Bennett. PCH
Cradle, The. Austin Dobson. BPN; VA
Cradle-Boat, The. John Keynton. BOL
Cradle Carol. Eleanor Slater. MaRV
Cradle Hymn. Martin Luther, *tr. fr. German.* BoChLi; BOL; BoTP; ChBR; DD; FaPON; GaP; GFA; GoTP; HH; MeMeAg; MPB; MW; OHIP; OTPC (1946 ed.); PCH; PRWS; RAR; StVeCh; SUS; TiPo (1952 ed.)
(Away in a Manger.) ChrBoLe; MaRV; OIF; TreFS; YaCaBo, *with music*
Cradle Hymn, A. Isaac Watts. BOL; CEP; COAH; EiPP; HBV; LoBV; LPS-1; MOAH; MotAn; OBEC; OBEV; PoEL-3; PRWS; PTA-2; SUS; TreFS
(Cradle Song, A.) BoChLi; EV-2; OTPC; OxBoCh
(Hush My Dear, Lie Still and Slumber.) BPP
"See the kinder shepherds round him," *sel.* BeR
Cradle of Gold, The. Alfred Perceval Graves. BOL
Cradle of the Deep. Emma Hart Willard. *See* Rocked in the Cradle of the Deep.
Cradle Song: "All by the sides of the wide wild river." Alice Cary. BOL
Cradle Song, A: "Angels are stooping, The." W. B. Yeats. BOL; POTE; TSW
Cradle Song: "Baby, O baby, fain you are for bed." Louis Esson. BoAu
Cradle Song: "Baloo, baloo, my wee, wee thing." Richard Gall. BOL; EBSV
Cradle Song: "Christ by Thine own darkened hour." Padraic Colum. CAW; GTIV
Cradle Song: "Clock's untiring fingers wind the wool of darkness, The." Louis MacNeice. MBP; MoAB; MoBrPo
Cradle Song, A: "Come little babe, come silly soul." Nicholas Breton. *See* Sweet Lullaby, A.
Cradle Song: "Crickets in the corner sing, The." Rowan Stevens. BOL
Cradle Song: "Danaan children laugh, in cradles of wrought gold, The." W. B. Yeats. BOL
Cradle Song: "Ere the moon begins to rise." Thomas Bailey Aldrich. BOL; MOAH
(Sleepy Song.) GoTP
Cradle Song: "From groves of spice." Sarojini Naidu. BrR; FaPON; MoSiPe; MPB; RAR; VOD
(Hindu Cradle Song.) BoTP
Cradle Song: "Golden slumbers kiss your eyes." Thomas Dekker. *See* Golden Slumbers Kiss Your Eyes.

Cradle Song: "How do we know." Mariana Van Rensselaer. BOL
Cradle Song, A: "Hush, my dear, lie still and slumber." Isaac Watts. *See* Cradle Hymn.
Cradle Song: "In the darken'd alcove." Victor Hugo, *tr. fr. French* BOL
Cradle Song: "In the embers shining bright." Richard Watson Gilder. BOL
Cradle Song: "In the wingèd cradle of sleep I lay." Celia Thaxter. BOL
Cradle Song: "Light and rosy be thy slumbers." *Unknown, tr. fr. Swedish.* BOL
Cradle Song: "Lord Gabriel, wilt thou not rejoice." Josephine Preston Peabody. BOL; HBV; NP; SBMV
Cradle Song: "Low in the troubled west." *Unknown.* BOL
Cradle Song: "Lullaby, my little one." Karl Mikael Bellman, *tr. fr. Swedish.* FaPON
Cradle Song: "Lullaby, my pretty baby." *Unknown, tr. fr. Russian.* BOL
Cradle-Song: "Madonna, Madonna [*or* Madonnina]." Adelaide Crapsey. BOL; HBMV; ISi
Cradle Song: "Nightingale, oh, leave our garden." Raphael Patkanian, *tr. fr. Armenian by* Alice Stone Blackwell. ArmLP
Cradle Song: "O blue eyes close in slumber." Caris Brooke. BOL
Cradle Song: "O hush thee, my baby, thy sire was a knight." Sir Walter Scott. *See* Lullaby of an Infant Chief.
Cradle Song: "O lullaby, my baby. The bee has gone to sleep." Eben E. Rexford. BOL
Cradle Song, A: "O men from the fields." Padraic Colum. AS; BOL; CaAE; GoBC; ISi; MM; MP; OnYI; OxBI; PoeT; StJW; WHL
Cradle Song: "O my deir hert, young Jesus sweit." James, John, *and* Robert Wedderburn. *See* Balulalow.
Cradle Song: "Out in the dark something complains." F. R. Higgins. POTE
Cradle Song: "Sing it, Mother! sing it low." John Banister Tabb. BOL
Cradle Song: "Sleep, baby, sleep,/ Our cottage vale is deep." *Unknown.* BOL; CBPC
Cradle Song, A: "Sleep, baby, sleep,/ Thy father watches the sheep." *Unknown. See* Sleep, Baby, Sleep.
Cradle Song: "Sleep enfold thee,/ Jesukin." James L. Duff. ISi
Cradle Song: "Sleep, little baby of mine." *Unknown.* BOL; MOAH; LPS-1
Cradle Song: "Sleep my babe, your road of dreams." Laurence Housman. BOL
Cradle Song: "Sleep, my baby, sleep, my darling." *Unknown, tr. fr. Italian.* BOL
Cradle Song: "Sleep, my child, my little daughter." *Unknown, tr. fr. Yiddish by* Joseph Leftwich. TrJP
Cradle Song: "Sleep, my darling, sleep." Louis MacNeice. OxBI
Cradle Song: "Sleep, my eye, sleep, sleep a slumber hale." *Unknown, tr. fr. Arabic.* BOL
Cradle Song: "Sleep, my own baby, my darling thou art." *Unknown, tr. fr. German.* BOL
Cradle Song, A: "Sleep! sleep! beauty bright." Blake. BOL; CaAE; EnLi-2; EnRP; EV-3; GTSL; HBV; HBVY; MotAn; OBEC; OBEV; PoFS
(Sleep, Sleep, Beauty Bright.) OTPC
Cradle Song: "Slumber, slumber, dearest, sweetest treasure." *Unknown.* BOL
Cradlesong: "Softly, softly, softly, croon." Clemens Brentano, *tr. fr. German by* Herman Salinger. AnGP
Cradle Song: "Sweet and low, sweet and low." Tennyson. *See* Sweet and Low.
Cradle Song, A: "Sweet dreams, form a shade." Blake. *Fr.* Songs of Innocence. AnFE; BEL; BOL; EiPP; EM-1; EnLi-2: EnLit; EnRP; OAEP; RIS; ViBoPo
(Sweet Dreams Form a Shade.) OTPC
Cradle Song: "Sweet slumber now creeps o'er thee slow." Raphael Patkanian, *tr. fr. Armenian by* Zabelle C. Boyajian. ArmLP
Cradle Song: "There's a baby moon rocking far up in the sky." Pauline Frances Camp. BOL
Cradle Song: "Thy heart and mine are one, my dear." Florence Earle Coates. BOL
Cradle Song: "'Tis night on the mountain." Mary M. Bowen. BOL
Cradle Song: "To sleep the corn is sinking." Hoffmann von Fallersleben, *tr. fr. German.* BOL
Cradle Song: "What does little birdie say." Tennyson. *See* What Does Little Birdie Say?
Cradle Song: "What is the little one thinking about?" Josiah Gilbert Holland. *Fr.* Bitter-sweet. BOL; HBV; LPS-1; PCD
(Babyhood.) AA
Cradle Song: "Winds are whispering over the sea, The." Merle St. Croix Wright. BOL; MotAn
Cradle Song at Bethlehem. E. J. Falconer. BoTP
Cradle-Song at Twilight. Alice Meynell. BOL; TCPD
Cradle-Song for Summer. Roden Noel. BOL
Cradle Song of a Celtic Queen. James Edward Tobin. JKCP (1955 ed.)
Cradle Song of a Soldier's Wife. T. T. Barker. BOL
Cradle Song of Amy. Sydney Dobell. *Fr.* Balder. BOL
Cradle Song of the Elephants. Adriano del Valle, *tr. fr. Spanish by* Alida Malkus. FaPON
Cradle-Song of the Fisherman's Wife. Ella Higginson. BOL; MOAH
Cradle-Song of the Night Wind, A. Willis Boyd Allen. BOL
Cradle-Song of the Poor, The. Adelaide Anne Procter. BOL
Cradle Song of the Virgin ("Jesu, my sweet Son dear"). *Unknown.* ISi
(Christmas Night.) TMEV
Cradle-Song of the Virgin, A ("The Virgin stills the crying"). *Unknown, tr. fr. Latin by* H. R. Bramley. BOL
Cradle Song to Put a Negro Baby to Sleep. Ildefonso Pereda Valdés, *tr. fr. Spanish by* Muna Lee. AnCL
Cradle Songs. Swinburne. BOL
"Baby, baby bright," I.
"Baby, baby dear," II.
Cradle Will Rock, The, *sel.* Marc Blitzstein.
Art for Art's Sake. TrJP
Craft of a Keeper of Sheep, The. Moschus, *tr. fr. Greek by* Ernest Myers. AWP
Craft of Verse, The. Pope. *See* Sound and Sense.
Craftsman, The. Marcus B. Christian. PoNe
Craftsman, loving beauty, cut rare glass, A. Medallion of Saint Francis. Harry Elmore Hurd. SaFP
Craftsmanship. Nikolai Ushakov, *tr. fr. Russian by* Jack Lindsay. RuPo
Crafty Farmer, The. *Unknown.* BaBo; ESPB; TiPo (1952 ed.)
Crafty Fox. Toson Shimazaki, *tr. fr. Japanese by* Takamichi Ninomiya *and* D. J. Enright. PoLJ
Crafty Miss of London, The; or, The Fryar Well Fitted. *Unknown.* CoMu
Crafty Nix, more false than fair, The. The Nix. Richard Garnett. CG
Crag, The. Mikhail Lermontov, *tr. fr. Russian by* V. de S. Pinto. BoR
Crag, The. Joaquín Arcadio Pagaza, *tr. fr. Spanish by* Samuel Beckett. AnMP
Crags lay dark in strange eclipse, The. The Sea-Watcher. Aubrey Thomas De Vere. IrPN
Cragsman, The. Geoffrey Winthrop Young. PtOT
Craigbilly Fair. *Unknown.* ChTr
Cramped like sardines on the Queens, and sedated. Tourists. Howard Moss. FiBHP
Cranach. Sir Herbert Read. FaBoMo
Cranberry Road. Rachel Field. MoSiPe
Crane, The. J. Redwood Anderson. MM; TCPD
Crane, The. Hovhannes Toumanian, *tr. fr. Armenian by* Zabelle C. Boyajian. ArmLP
Crane Cries, The. *Unknown, tr. fr. Chinese.* WhP
Crane from the shore standing at the top of the steps, The. Going Alone to Spend a Night at the Hsien-yu Temple. Po Chü-i. TrCh
Crane has lost his way across the heaven, The. The Crane. Hovhannes Toumanian. ArmLP
Crane on the shore stood on a flight of stone steps, The. Sleeping Alone at the Hsien-yu Temple. Po Chü-i. WhP
Cranes, The. Po Chü-i, *tr. fr. Chinese by* Arthur Waley. MBP; MoBrPo (1942 ed.); TrCh
Crane's Flight, The. Hesiod, *tr. fr. Greek by* Arthur S. Way. *Fr.* Works and Days. GrR
Crane's Message, The. Theognis, *tr. fr. Greek by* Sir William Marris. GrL; OxBG
Cranes of Ibycus, The. Emma Lazarus. AA; PFY
Crankadox leaned o'er the edge of the moon, The. Spirk Troll-Derisive. James Whitcomb Riley. BOHV; LBN; NA
Cranmer's Prophecy of Queen Elizabeth. Shakespeare *and probably* John Fletcher. King Henry VIII, *fr.* V, v. WGRP
(England at Peace; a Vision.) EV-1
Crash along your echoing way. The Miner. Ibsen. AnNoLy
Crash at Leithfield. Allen Curnow. AnNZ
Crash of the crystal surf all night on the wind-wild beaches. Pescadero Pebbles. Charles Augustus Keeler. BAP
Crashed through the woods that lumbering coach. The Last Coachload. Walter de la Mare. SeCePo
Crashes made these ashes. Chelsea Crypt. Robert Herring. MoWP
Crashing sky has swept old paths aside, The. Make Way! Florence Crocker Comfort. PGD
Crass Times Redeemed by Dignity of Souls. Peter Viereck. MiAP
"Tenderness of dignity of souls, The," *sel.* HoPM
Crates robs Crates of his chattels. Forethought. Crates, *tr. by* J. M. Edmonds. GrR
Craven. Sir Henry Newbolt. BBV (1923 ed.); GA; HBV; HBVY; PAH; PoeMoYo
Crawdad Song, The. *Unknown. See* Sweet Thing.

Crawford Long and William Morton. Rosemary Benét *and* Stephen Vincent Benét. PoMa
Crawl, crawl, clock on the wall. Pendulum Rhyme. Selma Robinson. InMe
Crayfish, The. Robert Wallace. WaKn
Crazy bookcase, placed before, A. Epilogue to the Breakfast Table Series. Oliver Wendell Holmes. *Fr.* The Poet at the Breakfast Table. AA
Crazy Dixie, The, *with music. Unknown.* SoAF
Crazy Jane and Jack the Journeyman. W. B. Yeats. AtBAP
Crazy Jane and the Bishop. W. B. Yeats. AtBAP; TwP
Crazy Jane Grown Old Looks at the Dancers. W. B. Yeats. AtBAP
Crazy Jane on God. W. B. Yeats. AtBAP; MeRV; MoAB
Crazy Jane on the Day of Judgment. W. B. Yeats. AtBAP
Crazy Jane on the Mountain. W. B. Yeats. AtBAP
Crazy Jane Reproved. W. B. Yeats. AtBAP
Crazy Jane Talks with the Bishop. W. B. Yeats. AtBAP; CoBMV; CoEV; EnLP; ExPo; LiTG; LiTM (rev. ed.); OAEP (2d ed.); TwP
Crazy old vinegar man is dead, The. The Vinegar Man. Ruth Comfort Mitchell. MPB
Crazy Song to the Air of "Dixie." "Andy Lee." AS
Crazy Sweeney's Song of the Woods. *Unknown, tr. fr. Old Irish by* Owen Masters. *Fr.* Sweeney the Mad. LyMA
Crazy World, The. William Gay. BoAu; BoAV
Cream-cups, butter-cups. A Little Song of Spring. Mary Austin. YeAr
Cream of phosphorescent light, A. Jonah. Aldous Huxley. ChTr
Create Great Peace. James Oppenheim. *See* Would You End War?
Created, The. Jones Very. AmP
Created by the poet to sing my song. The Reaper. Robert Duncan. CrMA
Created Universe, The. Mark Akenside. *See* Nature's Influence on Man.
Creation, The. Cecil Frances Alexander. *See* All Things Bright and Beautiful.
Creation. Joel Barlow. *Fr.* The Columbiad, IX. APW
Creation, The. Genesis, Bible, *O.T.* TreF (I: 1–II: 3); WoL (I: 1–III: 24)
(Creator, The. I: 1–31.) GrCo-1
("In the beginning God created the heaven and the earth," I: 1–31.) ImOP
Creation. Ambrose Bierce. AA; BLP; LHV; PFY
Creation, *sel.* Sir Richard Blackmore.
"See colic, gout, and stone, a cruel train." PoP
Creation, The. Cædmon. *See* Hymn of the World's Creator, The.
Creation, The. Abraham Cowley. *Fr.* The Davideis, I. OBS
Creation. Mary Ballard Duryee. LauV
Creation, The [a Negro Sermon]. James Weldon Johnson. BANP; CDC; GoSl; MAP; MaRV; MoAmPo; NP; NV; PoNe; PreP; QS; TiPo (1952 ed.); YaD
Creation. Louise Townsend Nicholl. GoYe
Creation. Alfred Noyes. GoBC; OBVV; TCPD
Creation Hymn, The. *Unknown, tr. fr. Vedic by* R. T. H. Griffith. *Fr.* The Rig-Veda. OuHeWo
Creation of My Lady, The. Francesco Redi, *tr. fr. Italian by* Sir Edmund Gosse. AWP
Creation of Pandora. Hesiod, *tr. fr. Greek by* Arthur S. Way. *Fr.* Works and Days. GrR
Creation of the Infinite Universe, The; How It Is Maintained. Lucretius, *tr. fr. Latin by* Robie M. Macauley. *Fr.* De Rerum Natura, I. LaP
Creation of the World, The. Milton. *Fr.* Paradise Lost, VII. MaPo
Creation of the World, The. Ovid, *tr. fr. Latin by* John E. Hankins. *Fr.* Metamorphoses, I. LaP
Creation's and Creator's crowning good. To the Body. Coventry Patmore. *Fr.* The Unknown Eros. GoBC; OxBoCh; PoEL-5; PoLi; POTT; ViP
Creation's crust and crumb, breaking of bread. Bread. A. M. Klein. PeCV
Creation's Lord, We Give Thee Thanks. William De Witt Hyde. MaRV
Creative Force. Maude Miner Hadden. GoYe
Creativity. *Unknown, tr. fr. Chinese by* Y. S. Han. OQP; QP-1
Creator, The ("Creator of all men"). *Unknown, tr. fr. Egyptian.* PCH
Creator Spirit, by whose aid. Veni Creator Spiritus. *Unknown, paraphrased by* Dryden. AWP; CAG; CEP; CoBE; EV-3; GoBC; HBV; LPS-2; LyMA; MaRV; OuHeWo; SeCV-2; WBP; WGRP
Creatrix. Anna Wickham. BMEP; LBBV; MBP; MoBrPo; TrGrPo (1942 ed.)
Creature, begone, nor harrow me with horror! "Lo! I Am Saul." Charles Heavysege. *Fr.* Saul. BoCaPo
Crèche, The. Carol Ryrie Brink. ChrBoLe; SDH
Creçy. Francis Turner Palgrave. BeLS; HBV
Credences of Summer. Wallace Stevens. CoBMV
Creditor, The. Louis MacNeice. MoP; QS; ShBV-3
Credo. Zona Gale. TrPWD
Credo, *sel.* Richard Watson Gilder.
"Christ of Judea, look thou in my heart!" TrPWD
Credo. Robinson Jeffers. AnEnPo; MAP; MoAB; MoAmPo
Credo. Keats. *See* Thing of Beauty, A.
Credo. Alfred Kreymborg. AnAmPo; BAP; LA
Credo. "Seumas O'Sullivan." MBP; OnYI
Credo. John Oxenham. BLRP; ChIP; MaRV; OQP; QP-1; StJW
Credo. Lizette Woodworth Reese. QS
Credo. E. A. Robinson. AmPP; AnNE; ChMo; CMP; CoBA; GTBS-W; IAP; LiTM (rev. ed.); MaRV; MoAmPo; NeMA; NePA; OQP; OxBA; PoLFOT; QP-2; QS; WGRP
Credo. Siegfried Sassoon. QS
Credo. Arthur Symons. LBBV; OBVV; OQP; QP-2
Credo. Saul Tchernichowsky. *See* I Believe.
Credo, A. Thackeray. HBV
Credo. Vera Wheatly. NLK
Creed, A. Norman Gale. BMEP; LBBV, *abr.;* LEAP
Creed, A. Ellen Glasgow. OQP; QP-1
Creed, A. Edgar A. Guest. HH; PEDC
Creed, A. Norman Macleod. WGRP
Creed, A ("Here is the truth in a little creed"). Edwin Markham. *See* Quatrain: "Here is the truth . . ."
Creed, A ("There is a destiny that makes us brothers"). Edwin Markham. BLPA; FaBoBe; FaFP; MaRV; NeHB; PoRL; TreFS
Inbrothered, *sel.* GrCo-1
Creed, A. John Masefield. HBMV; WGRP
Creed. Anne Spencer. CDC
Creed. Mary Ashley Townsend. BLPA; FaBoBe; NeHB
Creed and Deed. Robert Loveman. MaRV; OQP; QP-1
Creed in a Garden, A. Newman Flower. MaRV
Creed of My Heart, The. Edmond Gore Alexander Holmes. UnW
Creed of the Wood, The. Katharine Lee Bates. PC
Creed thy father built, wherein his soul, The. Creeds. William O. Partridge. OQP; QP-2
Creede. Cy Warman. PoOW
Creedless Love, The. Sam Walter Foss. OQP; QP-2
Creeds. Karle Wilson Baker. HBMV; WGRP
Creeds. William O. Partridge. OQP; QP-2
Creeds. Willard Wattles. HBMV; InP; MaRV; OQP; PC; QP-1
Creek-Road, The. Madison Cawein. AA
Creep afore Ye Gang. James Ballantine. HBV
Creep into thy narrow bed. The Last Word. Matthew Arnold. BEL; BLV; BMEP; BoLiVe; BPN; BPP; EM-2; EnLi-2; EPP; FaBoEn; FiP; GTBS-D; HBV; MaRV; MCCG; NBE; OBVV; PG; PIAE; PoEL-5; PoFS; PoRA; PoVP; PreP; SoV; TCEP; TOP; TrGrPo; ViPo; VLEP
Creeping ivy clings against grey towers, The. Campus. Margaret E. Sangster. BPP
Creeping Vine, The. Aristotelis Valaoritis, *tr. fr. Modern Greek by* Rae Dalven. MoGP
Creeps in half wanton, half asleep. Wagner. Rupert Brooke. NAMP
Cremation. William Sawyer. BOHV
Cremation of Sam McGee, The. Robert W. Service. FaFP; MaC; StPo; TreF; TwCaPo; YT
Cremona. Sir Arthur Conan Doyle. HBV
Creole Girl. Leslie M. Collins. PoNe
Creole Girl, The. *Unknown.* ABS
Creole Slave-Song, A. Maurice Thompson. AA
Creon. Sophocles, *tr. fr. Greek by* F. Storr. *Fr.* Oedipus Rex. PoFr
Crept side by side beyond the thresh. Epithalamium. Vassar Miller. NePoEA
Crescent and the Cross, The. Thomas Bailey Aldrich. EOAH
Crescent Boat, The. Wordsworth. *Fr.* Peter Bell. ThWaDe (Among the Stars.) GoTP
Crescent Moon. Basho, *tr. fr. Japanese by* H. G. Henderson. OnPM
Crescent Moon, The. Mei Yao Ch'en, *tr. fr. Chinese by* Kenneth Rexroth. OnPC
Crescent Moon. Elizabeth Madox Roberts. SUS; TiPo (1952 ed.)
Crescent moon, again you're filling. Solomon's Hymn to the Moon. Oscar Levertin. AnSL
Crescent moon shines, The. The Crescent Moon. Mei Yao Ch'en. OnPC
Crescent-winged, sky-clean. To an Upland Plover. Percy MacKaye. BLA
Crescenzio, the Pope's Legate at the High Council, Trent. The Cardinal and the Dog. Robert Browning. AlBD
Cresseid's Lament. Robert Henryson. *Fr.* The Testament of Cresseid. CoEV
Cressid. Nora Perry. AA
Cressida, *sels.* James K. Baxter. AnNZ
Her Decision, XI.
Her First Song, V.
Her Second Song, IX.

Cressida (*continued*)
In the Lecture Room, I.
Lounge Bar, XII.
Parting, The, VI.
Sestina: "Swept clean of leaves, with stripped boughs, the garden," XV.
Cressida's Leprosy. Robert Henryson. *Fr.* The Testament of Cresseid. SeCePo
Cressid's Complaint. George Whetstone. ReIE
Crest and crowning of all good, The. Brotherhood. Edwin Markham. BBV (1951 ed.); MaRV; NeMA; OQP; PEDC; PGD; PoRL; POT; QP-1
Crest Jewel, The. James Stephens. AnIL; MBP; MoAB; MoBrPo
Crested heron flies over the lake, The. The Heron. Brian Vrepont. MoAuPo
Cretan, The. Dionysios Solomos, *tr. fr. Modern Greek by* Rae Dalven. MoGP
Cretan Merchant, A. Simonides, *tr. fr. Greek by* C. M. Bowra. GrL; OxBG
(Epitaph to a Merchant, *tr. by* F. L. Lucas.) GrR
(Unlooked-for Bargain, The, *tr. by* F. L. Lucas.) GrPE
Crethis. Callimachus, *tr. fr. Greek by* Richard Garnett. AWP
(Dead Playmate, The, *tr. by* F. L. Lucas.) GrPE
(On the Tomb of Crethis, *tr. by* Robert Allason Furness.) GrR
Creüsa cried for, through the tomb of Troy. Aeneid. Claire McAllister. NePA
Crew Poem, A. Edward Augustus Blount, Jr. AA; PC
Crib, The. Christopher Morley. FAOV
Cricket, The. Marjorie Barrows. BoChLi (1950 ed.)
Cricket, The. Vincent Bourne, *tr. fr. Latin by* William Cowper. HBV; HBVY; LPS-2; OTPC; SN
Cricket. Eleanor Alletta Chaffee. StaSt
Cricket ("'Twas later when the summer went"). Emily Dickinson. OnPM
Cricket, The. James B. Kenyon. LBAP
Cricket, The, *abr.* Sir Charles G. D. Roberts. LEAP
Cricket. Clinton Scollard. BAP; HBV; VOD
Cricket, The. Tu Fu, *tr. fr. Chinese by* Chi Hwang Chu *and* Edna Worthley Underwood. OnPM
Cricket and the Star, The. Mary Effie Lee Newsome. GoSl
Cricket Bowler, A. Edward Cracroft Lefroy. OBVV
Cricket, chirring in the autumn twilight. Cricket. Clinton Scollard. BAP; HBV; VOD
Cricket Cri du Coeur, A. *Unknown.* ShGoBo
Cricket cries, The. Fujiwara no Go-Kyogoku, *tr. fr. Japanese by* Kenneth Rexroth. OnPJ
Cricket does not sing, The. Pauses, II. José Gorostiza. OnPM; TwSpPo
Cricket is a slight creature, The. The Cricket. Tu Fu. OnPM
Cricket is chirring, The. Summer Song. Percy MacKaye. VOD
Cricket on his cymbal sounds, The. Cricket. Eleanor Alletta Chaffee. StaSt
Cricket sang, The. Evening. Emily Dickinson. GBV (1952 ed.); MAPA; TwAmPo
Cricket Singing in the Market-Place, A. Louella C. Poole. POT
Crickets, The. Harriet McEwan Kimball. SN
Crickets. Helen Wing. GFA
Crickets and Mice. Joseph Joel Keith. StVeCh (1955 ed.)
Crickets are making the merriest din. September [Is Here]. Edward Bliss Reed. DD; HBMV; HBVY; MPB; YeAr
Crickets at Dawn. Leonora Speyer. PFY
Cricket's Grave, The. Leonidas of Tarentum, *tr. fr. Greek by* F. L. Lucas. GrPE
Crickets in the corner sing, The. Cradle Song. Rowan Stevens. BOL
Crickets sing, and mans ore-labor'd sense, The. Shakespeare. *Fr.* Cymbeline, II, ii. AtBAP
Cricket's Story, The. Emma Huntington Nason. HBV; HBVY
Crier, The. Michael Drayton. CBOV; EIL; ElSeCe; InvP; OAEP; TuPP; WhC
(Cryer, The.) PoEL-2; SeEP
Cries of Birds, The. Lu Yu, *tr. fr. Chinese by* Pai Chwen-yu. WhP
Cries Out of Blindness. Tristan Corbière. *See* Blind Man's Cries.
Cries Sue to Will, in matrimonial strife. Epigram. *Unknown.* ALV
Cries Sylvia to a reverend Dean. Epigram. Robert Dodsley. ALV
Crime. Robert Penn Warren. AmP
Crime and Punishment. Kahlil Gibran. *Fr.* The Prophet. PoToHe (new ed.)
Crime Note. Hughes Mearns. *Fr.* Later Antigonishes. InMe
Crime of Orestes, The. Aeschylus, *tr. fr. Greek by* George Thomson. *Fr.* Choephoroe. LiA
Crime Took Place at Granada, The. Antonio Machado, *tr. fr. Spanish by* Rolfe Humphries. PoFr
Crimea Red. John Lehmann. MBP
Crimean Heroes, The. Walter Savage Landor. ALV; PIAE
Crimean war is over now, The. Sebastopol. *Unknown.* SG
Crimes of Lizzie Borden, The. *Unknown. See* Lizzie Borden.
Criminality of War, The. Edward Young. PGD
Crimson Cherry Tree, The. Henry Treece. LiTM (1946 ed.); MoWP; TriL; WaP
Crimson leafage fires the lawn, The. A Letter from Newport. Frederic William Henry Myers. VA
Crimson lute that comest in the dawn. Sister Juana Inés de la Cruz, *tr. fr. Spanish by* Samuel Beckett. AnMP
Crimson Pool. "Katharine Hale." CPG
Crimson rose was she, A. The Virgin. Ibn Sa'id of Alcala la Real. MooP
Crimson roses burn and glow, The. Vigil. Richard Dehmel. AWP; JAWP; LiTW; WBP
Crinog, melodious is your song. To Crinog. *Unknown.* AnIL; OnYI
Criole Candjo, *with music. Unknown, tr. fr. French.* ABF
Cripple, The. Robert P. Tristram Coffin. StVeCh (1955 ed.)
Cripple Dick upon a stick. *Unknown.* OxNR
Cripple in the wheelchair, The. Busy Day. James Laughlin. OnHM
Crisis. W. H. Auden. AtBAP; ReMP
(Where Do They Come From?) ReaPo
Crisis, The. Ethelyn Bryant Chapman. BPP
Crisis. G. S. Fraser. NeBP
Crisis. Mark Van Doren. NeTW
Crisis, The. Whittier. PAH
Crisp laconic words of wisdom. Don't Cut the String. George David Stewart. PoP
Crispus Attucks. John Boyle O'Reilly. PAH
Cristina. Robert Browning. BPN; EM-2; EmBrPo; EPN; GEPC; OAEP; PoVP; ViPo; VLEP
Critic, The. John Farrar. GaP
Critic, A. Walter Savage Landor. ChTr
Critical Fable, A, *sel.* Amy Lowell.
"'Expatriates, The/ Come next,' I began." PtP
Critical Fribble, A. Charles Churchill. *Fr.* The Rosciad. OBEC
(Criticaster, A.) FaBoEn
Criticism. Sir William Watson. BMEP
Critick Vermin, The. Swift. *Fr.* To Doctor Delany on the Libels Writ against Him. BeR
Critics. Sir John Harington, *after* Martial. *See* Critics and Cooks.
Critics. Swift. *Fr.* On Poetry; a Rhapsody. CoEV; OBEC; SeCePo
(Rhapsody on Poetry, A.) BCEP
Critics. Theognis, *tr. fr. Greek by* F. L. Lucas. GrPE
Critics all were jealous, The. Why My Poems Died. Bhartrihari. OnPM
Critics and Connoisseurs. Marianne Moore. AnAmPo; AnEnPo; LA; MoP; NePA; OxBA
Critics and Cooks. Sir John Harington, *after the Latin of* Martial. OnPM
(Against Writers That Carp at Other Men's Books.) TuPP
(Critics.) AWP
(Epigram: "Readers and the hearers like my books, The.") ALV
Critics avaunt! Tobacco is my theme. In Imitation of Young. Isaac Hawkins Browne. *Fr.* A Pipe of Tobacco. OBEC
Critic's heel is on ye, sure, Th'. To th' Minstrel Girl. T. A. Daly. BOHV
Critic's Rules, The. Robert Lloyd. *Fr.* Shakespeare; an Epistle to Mr. Garrick. OBEC
Critics sipping cups of tea. Obituary. Anthony Brode. FiBHP
Cro-Challain would gie me. Colin's Cattle. *Unknown.* EBSV
Croak of a raven hoar, The! Mammon Marriage. George Macdonald. OBVV
"Croak!" Said the Toad. *Unknown. See* Toad and the Frog, The.
Croaker Papers, The, *sels.* Fitz-Greene Halleck *and* Joseph Rodman Drake. AA
Man Who Frets at Worldly Strife, The.
National Paintings, The.
Ode to Fortune.
Crocodile, A. Thomas Lovell Beddoes. *Fr.* The Last Man. AnFE; NBE
Crocodile, The. "Lewis Carroll." *See* How Doth the Little Crocodile.
Crocodile, The. Laura E. Richards. UTS
Crocus, The. Walter Crane. OTPC (1946 ed.); PCH
Crocus. Sarah J. Day. MPB
Crocus, The. Mary Elliott. OTPC (1923 ed.)
Crocus, The. Harriet Eleanor Hamilton King. SN; VA
Crocus. Alfred Kreymborg. HBMV; MAP
Crocus ("Warm sunshine came down"). *Unknown.* GFA
Crocus. Marion Mitchell Walker. GFA
Crocus grows in any spot, The. To the Crocus—with My Love. Marion Sturges-Jones. BOHV
Crocus had slept in his little round house, The. Crocus. Sarah J. Day. MPB

Crocus, while the days are dark, The. The Year [*or* The Year's Round *or* Round the Year]. Coventry Patmore. BoTP; CaAE; GTSE; OTPC (1946 ed.); PoRL; ThWaDe
Crocuses. Josa, *tr. fr. Japanese by* William N. Porter. MPB; TiPo
Crocuses. Anna M. Platt. BoTP
Crocuses in [the] Grass. John Gray. CaAE; CAW
Crocuses in the Square, The. Extras. Richard Burton. AA
Croesus. Bacchylides, *tr. fr. Greek.* GrPE, *tr. by* F. L. Lucas; GrR, *tr. by* Arthur S. Way; OxBG, *tr. by* George Allen
Croesus. Chaucer. *Fr.* The Canterbury Tales: The Monk's Tale. MyFE
Croesus in Autumn. Robert Penn Warren. AnAmPo; LA
"Crom Cruach and his sub-gods twelve." The Burial of King Cormac. Sir Samuel Ferguson. AnIL; GTIV; IrPN; OnYI; TIP; TVSH
Cromek ("A pretty sneaking knave"). Blake. FiBHP; RO
Cromek Speaks. Blake. PIAE
Cromwell and Henrietta Maria. William Gorman Wills. *Fr.* Charles the First. VA
Cromwell Dead. Andrew Marvell. *Fr.* A Poem upon the Death of Oliver Cromwell. ChTr
("I saw him dead, a leaden slumber lies.") OBS; ViBoPo
Cromwell, I charge thee, fling away ambition. The Higher Loyalty [*or* Ambition]. Shakespeare, *and probably* John Fletcher. King Henry VIII, *fr.* III, ii. MaRV; TrGrPo
Cromwell, I did not think to shed a tear. Wolsey's Farewell [*or* Advice] to Cromwell [*or* Wolsey's Regrets]. Shakespeare, *and probably* John Fletcher. King Henry VIII, *fr.* III, ii. EV-1; InP; LPS-1; OTPC (1923 ed.); PIR; TreFS
Cromwell, our chief of men, who through a cloud. To the Lord General Cromwell [*or* To Oliver Cromwell]. Milton. AnEnPo; BEL; EM-1; EnLit; EPP; EPS; ES; LH; LPS-3; MaPo; OBS; OuHeWo; PeBoSo; PIR; SeCeV; TCEP; TrGrPo; TwCrTr; ViBoPo
Crooked are the thornwood spoons. The Greater East. *Unknown.* WhP
Crooked Footpath, The. Oliver Wendell Holmes. *Fr.* The Professor at the Breakfast Table. HBV; TreF
Crooked Gun, The, *with music. Unknown.* OuSiCo (Deer Hunt, A.) CSF
Crooked heels/ And scuffy toes. The Cobbler. Eleanor Alletta Chaffee. GaP; TiPo
Crooked paths go every way, The. The Goat Paths. James Stephens. AlDL; AnIV; AWP; CH; ChMo; CMP; GTIV; JAWP; LiTB; OxBI; PG; TwCV; UnPo (3d ed.); WBP; WHA
Crooked Trail to Holbrook, The. *Unknown.* CoSo; CSF
Croppy Boy, The. William B. McBurney. OnYI; TIP
Croppy Boy, The. *Unknown.* AnIL; AnIV; GTIV; OxBoLi; PoFr
Crops are all gathered, The. Harvest Sacrifice. Su T'ung-po. OnPC
Cross, The. Thomas Bancroft. StJW
Cross, The. Charles S. Braden. ChIP
Cross, The. Pedro Calderón de la Barca, *tr. fr. Spanish by* Richard Chenevix Trench. *Fr.* La Devocion de la Cruz. CAW; LiA; TeCS
(Dying Eusebio's Address to the Cross, The, *longer sel., tr. by* D. F. MacCarthy.) OuHeWo
Cross, The. Donald Earl Edwards. ChIP
Cross, The. Leon Gellert. BoAu
Cross, The. Eva Gore-Booth. ChIP; MaRV
Cross. Langston Hughes. AnAmPo; BANP; LA; PoNe; TBM
Cross, The. Sidney Lanier. *See* Ballad of Trees and the Master, A.
Cross, The. Charles N. Pace. BePJ; BLRP
Cross, The. Allen Tate. AWP; MAP; MoAmPo; MOAP; MoVE; OxBA; SPP
Cross, The. Ruby Weyburn Tobias. ChIP
Cross, The. Shirley Dillon Waite. ChIP; OQP; QP-2
Cross, The. Isaac Watts. TriL
Cross and Flag. Frederick L. Hosmer. FOAH
Cross and the Crown, The. Thomas Kelly. MaRV
Cross and the Tree, The. William L. Stidger. ChIP; PGD
Cross and Throne. Horatius Bonar. BePJ
Cross at the Crossways, The. John Oxenham. MaRV
Cross at the morning. Once and Upon. Madeline Gleason. NeAP
Cross between blackbird and crow, A. Purple Grackles. Frances Frost. BLA
Cross-fade of grief to nothingness. Zone Libre. Louis Aragon, MiFP
Cross I bore seemed heavy, and, The. Behold, My Cross Was Gone! Alice Mortenson. BePJ
Cross in God's own service I have ta'en, The. The Pilgrimage. Albrecht von Johannsdorf. LiTW
Cross is such a simple thing, The. The Cross. Charles N. Pace. BePJ; BLRP
Cross it standeth fast, The. Cross and Throne. Horatius Bonar. BePJ
Cross leaves marks the tree we fancy, A. An Owl Is an Only Bird of Poetry. Robert Duncan. NeAP
Cross Makers. Clyde McGee. MaRV
(Free Enterprise.) ChIP
Cross of Calvary, The. The Key. John Oxenham. BePJ
Cross of Gold, The. David Gray. AA
Cross of Snow, The. Longfellow. AmP; AmPP; AnAmPo; APW; CoBA; IAP; LA; LEAP; MaRV; OxBA; TriL
Cross of the angels, The. Prayer before Going to Sleep. *Unknown.* JKCP (1926 ed.)
Cross of the Dumb, The. "Fiona Macleod." ChrBoLe; CLS
Cross on a Hill, A. Carl S. Weist. BePJ
(Symbol of Hope.) ChIP
Cross, A.—One staggering beneath the weight. There was a Garden. Marie Barton. OQP; QP-1
Cross-patch,/ Draw the latch. Mother Goose. BrR; ChTr; OTPC; OxNR; PPL; SAS; SiTL
Cross Section of a Landscape. Donald Davidson. MAP; MoAmPo (1942 ed.)
Cross Speaks, The. *Unknown. Fr.* The Dream of the Rood. PoLi
Cross, The, stands firm; no blast of time. The Same Forever. Horatius Bonar. BePJ
Cross, A? That? The Cross. Charles S. Braden. ChIP
Cross that bears my Master slain, The. Interpretation. Sheldon Shepard. ChIP
Cross, the Cross, The. Tortoise Shell. D. H. Lawrence. ExPo
Cross they raised against the rain, The. The Suffering God. Raymond Kresensky. ChIP
Cross Was His Own, The. *Unknown.* BePJ; BLPA, *abr.*; MaRV
("Borrowed.") BLRP
Cross-bars and posts, the echo of distant bells. Football Field; Evening. J. A. R. McKellar. NeLNL
Crossed Apple, The. Louise Bogan. NP
Crossed Swords, The. Nathaniel Langdon Frothingham. AA
Crosses. Mabel Hicks. PEDC
Crossing a Creek. Herbert Clark Johnson. PoNe
Crossing Alone the Nighted Ferry. A. E. Housman. More Poems, XXIII. ChMP; PoD
Crossing at Fredericksburg, The. George Henry Boker. PAH
Crossing Boston Common. Louise Dyer Harris. WhC, *st.* 1
Crossing Brooklyn Ferry. Walt Whitman. AmPo; AmPP; ATP; CoBA; CoV; IAP; LiTA; TCAP
Sels.
"Ah, what can be more stately." AA
"It avails not, time nor place—distance avails not." NeMA; PIAE
Crossing the Alps ("The only track now visible was one"). Wordsworth. *Fr.* The Prelude, VI. CoBE
Crossing the Bar. Tennyson. BEL; BLRP; BLV; BMEP; BoLiVe; BPN; BTP; DD; EM-2; EmBrPo; EnL; EnLi-2; EnLit; EOAH; EPN; EPP; EtS; FaBoEn; FaFP; FiP; GEPC; GTBS-W; GTSL; HBV; HBVY; HiLiEn; InP; LEAP; LiTB; LiTG; MaRV; MCCG; NeHB; OAEP; OBEV (new ed.); OBVV; OHFP; OQP; OTPC (1946 ed.); OuHeWo; PECK; PFE; PG (1945 ed.); PIAE; PIR; PoE; PoeMoYo; PoRA; PoVP; PTA-1; PYM; QP-1; REAL; ReaPo; ShBV-3; StJW; TCEP; TOP; TreF; TrGrPo; TSW; TSWC; TwHP; TyEnPo; UnPo (1st ed.); VA; ViBoPo; ViPo; ViPP; VLEP; WBLP; WGRP; WHA
"Sunset and evening star," *sel., st.* 1. YT
Crossing the Blackwater. Robert Dwyer Joyce. VA
Crossing the border, the first city I came to. Three Cities. George Rostrevor Hamilton. POTE
Crossing the County Line. Elizabeth Randall-Mills. GoYe
Crossing the Mountain Alone. Princess Daihaku, *tr. fr. Japanese by* Arthur Waley. *Fr.* Manyo Shu. WoL
("How will you manage.") AWP; JAWP; WBP
Crossing the Plains. Joaquin Miller. AA; AnAmPo; AmPP (3d ed.); BAP; CBOV; GN; LA; LEAP; MAP; MoAmPo (1942 ed.); PaA
Crossing the Plains. *Unknown.* ABF
Crossing the river I pluck hibiscus-flowers. *Unknown, tr. fr. Chinese by* Arthur Waley. Seventeen Old Poems, 6. TrCh
Crossing the shallow holdings high above sea. The Hungry Grass. Donagh MacDonagh. NeIP; OxBI
Crossing the Straits. Charles Brasch. AnNZ
Crossing the Tropics. Herman Melville. AA
Crossing there under the trees with leaden pace. False Enchantment. Jean Starr Untermeyer. MoAmPo (1950 ed.)
Crossroads. Miguel Otero Silva, *tr. fr. Spanish by* Donald Devenish Walsh. WoL
Crossroads, The. Catherine Parmenter. PEDC
Crotalus. Bret Harte. AA; PFY
Crotalus, The. Bailey Millard. BAP
Crotalus Rex. Brewster Ghiselin. MoVE
Crotchet Castle, *sels.* Thomas Love Peacock.
"After careful meditation," *fr. ch.* 6. ALV

Crotchet Castle (*continued*)
Chorus: "If I drink water while this doth last, *fr. ch.* 6. ViBoPo
In the Days of Old, *fr. ch.* 18. HBV
Llyn-y-Dreiddiad-Vrawd; the Pool of the Diving Friar, *fr. ch.* 16. KN
Greatness ("He took castle and towns"). OtMeF
Priest and the Mulberry Tree, The, *fr. ch.* 18. BoTP; CG; EV-4; GN; OTPC; RIS; StPo; TVSH
Crouched [*or* Crouch'd] on the pavement, close by Belgrave Square. West London. Matthew Arnold. BMEP; BPN; EmBrPo; EPN; MCCG; OAEP; PeBoSo; PoFr; PoVP; VLEP
Crow, The. Mrs. Alexander. BoTP; OTPC (1946 ed.); PCH
Crow, A. Basho, *tr. fr. Japanese by* H. G. Henderson. OnPM
Crow, The. John Burroughs. BLA
Crow, The. William Canton. BMEP; GoTP; HBV
Crow. Mark Van Doren. BLA; WhBS
Crow, The. Ibn Sa'id of Alcala la Real, *tr. fr. Arabic by* A. J. Arberry. MooP
Crow, The. Albert Durrant Watson. CPG; OCL
Crow and Pie. *Unknown.* ESPB
Crow and the Fox, The. La Fontaine, *tr. fr. French by* Sir Edward Marsh. AWP; JAWP; MaC; WBP
Crow and the Nighthawk, The. Watson Kirkconnell. CaP
Crow Country. Kenneth Slessor. BoAV
Crow, in pulpit lone and tall. In the Pauper's Turnip-Field. Herman Melville. APW; PoEL-5
Crow lies over the cornfield, The. Ballad in Blonde Hair Foretold. Robert Bagg. NePoAm-2
Crow sat perched upon an oak, A. The Crow and the Fox. La Fontaine. AWP; JAWP; MaC; WBP
Crow, The—the crow! the great black crow! The Great Black Crow. Philip James Bailey. BOHV
Crow will tumble up and down, The. Crows in Spring. John Clare. EnRP
Crowd, The. Irene McKeighan. ChIP; MaRV
Crowd advances like a sounding sea, The. Song of the General Strike. Mario Bravo. PoFr
Crowd and Buckingham, The. Dryden. *See* Duke of Buckingham, The ("A numerous host").
Crowd at the Ball Game, The. William Carlos Williams. OxBA
(At the Ball Game.) ExPo
Crowd back the hills and give me room. Soul Lifted. Albert Durrant Watson. CaP; OCL
Crowd is thrilled to see a fighter downed, The. He Falls. William A. Donaghy. *Fr.* The Stations of the Cross. JKCP (1955 ed.)
Crowd makes way for them, The. Down Fifth Avenue. John Curtis Underwood. NV
Crowd of beauteous Quinta prate, The. The Comparison. Catullus. OnPM
Crowd was gathering beneath the tent, A. The Clown. Margaret E. Bruner. PoToHe
Crowd was thronging my doorstep, A. Christ the Carpenter. Leslie L. Haskin. BePJ
Crowded Ways of Life. Walter J. Gresham. BLPA
(Let Me Walk with the Men in the Road.) PTA-2
Crowing of the Red Cock, The. Emma Lazarus. AA; HBV; OBAV
Crown high the cup and pass it round. Hedylus, *tr. fr. Greek by* J. A. Pott. GrPo
Crown Him with Many Crowns. Matthew Bridges. MaRV; OlF
Crown His Bloodstained Pillow. Julia Ward Howe. LBAH
Crown imperials, peonies red. The Old Garden. Joseph von Eichendorff. AnGP
Crown of Days. *Unknown, tr. fr. Hebrew by* Herbert Loewe. TrJP
Crown of empire, The—must thou yield it now? I Have Overcome the World [*or* World Conqueror]. Laura Simmons. ChIP; MaRV
Crown of Power. The. John Charles McNeill. NoCaPo
Crown of thorns men gave to Christ, A. The Earth Worshiped! Catherine Cate Coblentz. ChIP
Crown Our Washington. Hezekiah Butterworth. DD; HH; PEDC; PEOR; PoRL; WOAH
Crown the Year. Frances Ridley Havergal. PraP
Crown we our heroes with a holier wreath. Lincoln. George Henry Boker. *Fr.* Our Heroic Times. DD; GA; LBAH; MC; OHIP
Crown'd with the sickle, and the wheaten sheaf. Autumn. James Thomson. *Fr.* The Seasons. CEP
Crowned. Amy Lowell. HBV; LoPS
Crowned Caprice is god of this world, A. A Prayer. Grant Allen. BMEP; LEAP
Crowned, girdled, garbed and shod with light and fire. Christopher Marlowe. Swinburne. *Fr.* Sonnets on English Dramatic Poets. BEL; PoVP; PtP; TOP; TrGrPo; VLEP
Crowned Poet, A. Anne Reeve Aldrich. AA
Crownèd with Flowers. *Unknown.* ElSeCe
("Crowned with flowers, I saw fair Amarillis.") EnLoPo; SiCE
(Love's Immortality.) CBOV
Crowning a bluff where gleams the lake below. The Lake. Herman Melville. APW
Crowning Gift, The. Gladys Cromwell. BAP; HBMV; MAP; NP
Crowning life so over-wise. Holy Poverty. Arthur Shearly Cripps. GTML
Crowning of Arthur, The. Charles Williams. FaBoMo
Crowning of Dreaming John, The. John Drinkwater. HBMV
Crowning Wonder, The. John Oxenham. StJW
Crowns. Louise Upham Brooks. ChIP
Crowns, The. John Freeman. CH
Crows, The. Louise Bogan. TBM; YT
Crows, The. David McCord. MAP; MoAmPo; TiPo (1959 ed.)
Crows. Lizette Woodworth Reese. MAP; MoAmPo (1942 ed.)
Crows, The. *Unknown.* RIS
("On the first of March.") OxNR
Crows are flying above the foyer of summer, The. The Novel. Wallace Stevens. ReMP
Crows at Nightfall, The. Li Po, *tr. fr. Chinese by* Shigeyoshi Obata. ChLP
Crows crowd croaking overhead. Summer Evening. John Clare. BoTP
Crows in Spring. John Clare. EnRP
Crows in the Garden, *with music.* *Unknown.* ABF
Crow's Nest. Richard F. Armknecht. GoYe
Crucified. Patrick Dacus Moreland. StJW
Crucifix, The. Alphonse de Lamartine, *tr. fr. French by* Henry Longan Stuart. CAW
Crucifix. Edith Lovejoy Pierce. ChIP
Crucifix, The. Pushkin. *See* Secular Power.
Crucifixion, The. Thomas Holley Chivers. SPP
Crucifixion, The, *sel.* Jean Cocteau, *tr. fr. French by* Wallace Fowlie.
"Accident happens, An." MiCF
Crucifixion. Waring Cuney. BANP; GoSl
Crucifixion. Eva Gore-Booth. MaRV; WGRP
Crucifixion. Hugh O. Isbell. ChIP; PGD
Crucifixion, The. John W. Lynch. JKCP (1955 ed.)
Crucifixion. Earl Marlatt. ChIP
Crucifixion, The. Alice Meynell. MeRV; OxBoCh; PoLi
Crucifixion, The. Henry Hart Milman. BePJ
Crucifixion. Frederick George Scott. ChIP; MaRV; OQP; QP-1
Crucifixion, The. G. A. Studdert-Kennedy. StJW
Crucifixion, The ("At the cry of the first bird"). *Unknown, tr. fr. Middle Irish by* Kuno Meyer. GTIV; OxBI; OnYI, *tr. by* Howard Mumford Jones
Crucifixion ("They [*or* Dey] crucified my Lord"). *Unknown.* APW; BoAN-1, *with music;* MaRV; TrGrPo
Crucifixion. Carl S. Weist. ChIP
Crucifixion and the Harrowing of Hell, The. William Langland, *tr. fr. Middle English. Fr.* The Vision of Piers Plowman. MeEV
Crucifixion of Noel, The. Marsden Hartley. AnAmPo; LA
Crucifixion of the Skyscraper. John Gould Fletcher. MM
Crucifixion to the World, by the Cross of Christ. Isaac Watts. *See* When I Survey the Wond'rous Cross.
Crucifixus pro Nobis. Patrick Carey. SeCL
(Hymn: Crucifixus pro Nobis.) OxBoCh
Cruciform. Winifred Welles. DiM; LO; POTE
Crucifying. John Donne. OBS
Crude Foyer. Wallace Stevens. LiTM (rev. ed.); **NePA**
Cruel Boy and the Kittens, The. *Unknown.* PoC
Cruel Brother, The, *sel.* Sir William Davenant.
What Is Past, *fr.* V, i. TrGrPo
Cruel Brother, The. *Unknown.* ABS; BaBo (A *and* B *vers.*); EM-1; EnLit; ESPB (A *and* B *vers.*); LoEn; OBB; PFE; TOP; ViBoFo
Cruel Clever Cat. Geoffrey Taylor. ChTr; LiTM; SiTL
Cruel Death, who can endure no sight of joy. On the Passing of My Little Daughter. Joost Van den Vondel. EBSV
Cruel disease, to grudge the soul of man. A Friend's Grave. Simonides. GrL; OxBG
Cruel Falcon, The. Robinson Jeffers. CoV
Cruel, farewell, since I do but annoy thee. Pierre de Ronsard. *Fr.* Sonnets pour Hélène. PrPoCR
Cruel flames have entirely devoured the house in which I was born, The. Prose Poem: House in the Heart. Judith Gautier. OnPM
Cruel Masters. Ibn Zaydun, *tr. fr. Arabic by* A. J. Arberry. MooP
Cruel Mistress, A. Thomas Carew. ElSeCe; EPS
Cruel Mistress, The. William Hammond. SeCL
Cruel Moon, The. Robert Graves. TSW; TSWC
Cruel Mother, The. *Unknown.* BaBo (A, B, *and* C *vers.*); ESPB (A, B, C, *and* P *vers.*); OBB; PIAE; ViBoFo
(Fine Flowers in the Valley, *diff. vers.*) CBOV; PIAE
Cruel Sister, The. *Unknown.* *See* Two Sisters, The.

Cruel Solstice, The. Sidney Keyes. POTE
Cruel Spite. Anne Boleyn. DiM
Cruel You Be. George Puttenham. ElL
Cruell Clarinda tell me why. *Unknown.* SeCSL
Cruelty. Margaret E. Bruner. CIV
Cruelty has a human heart. A Divine Image. Blake. AtBAP; ChTr
Cruise of the *Bigler*, The. *Unknown. See Bigler*, The.
Cruise of the *Fair American*, The. *Unknown.* PAH
(Bold Hathorne.) IAP
Cruise of the *Monitor*, The. George Henry Boker. MC; PAH
Cruise of the P. C., The. *Unknown.* NA
Cruisers, destroyers, carriers align. Victory Parade. George Edward Hoffman. PGD
Cruiskeen Lawn, The. *Unknown.* HBV; OnYI; TIP
Crumb for Robin. Emily Dickinson. *See* If I shouldn't be alive.
Crumbling [*or* Crumpling] a pyramid, humbling a rose. The Dust. Nathalia Crane. MAP; NeMA
Crumbling centuries are thrust, The. The Jewels. Austin Clarke. MoAB
Crumbs or the Loaf. Robinson Jeffers. ChMo; CMP
Crumbs to the Birds. Charles *and* Mary Lamb. OTPC
Crumpling a pyramid, humbling a rose. *See* Crumbling a pyramid . . .
Crusade. Hilaire Belloc. GoBC
Crusade, The. Rinaldo d'Aquino, *tr. fr. Italian by* "Moira O'Neill." CAW
Crusade, The. Thomas Warton, the Younger. EiPP
Crusader Chorus, The, *abr.* Charles Kingsley. *Fr.* The Saint's Tragedy. VA
Crusaders. Elizabeth Waddell. ChIP; OQP; QP-1
Crusaders Behold Jerusalem, The. Tasso. *See* Crusaders Reach Jerusalem, The.
Crusader's Hymn. *Unknown. See* Fairest Lord Jesus.
Crusaders Reach Jerusalem, The. Tasso, *tr. fr. Italian by* Edward Fairfax. *Fr.* Jerusalem Delivered, III. EnLi-1
(Crusaders Behold Jerusalem, The, *tr. by* J. H. Wiffen.) CAW
("Odorous air, morn's messenger, now spread, The," *tr. by* J. H. Wiffen.) PrPoCR
Crusaders' Song. *Unknown, tr. fr. French by* Walter Clifford Meller. CAW
Crush not yon ant, who stores the golden grain. Compassion. Sadi. PeP
Crushed by the waves upon the crag was I. Sea Dirge. Archias of Byzantium. AWP
Crushed Fender. Rosa Zagnoni Marinoni. MaRV; PoToHe (1941 ed.)
Crushing of a thousand petals, Lord, The. The Poet Prays. Grace Noll Crowell. TrPWD
Crusoe. Floris Clark McLaren. PeCV; TwCaPo
Crust of Bread, The. *Unknown.* HBV; HBVY; OTPC (1923 ed.)
Crust of bread and a corner to sleep in, A. Life. Paul Laurence Dunbar. CDC
Crustaceans. Roy Fuller. NeBP
Crusts. Walter Shea. ChIP
Crusty Critics. George Crabbe. *Fr.* The Library. OBEC
Cry, A. Herbert Edwin Clarke. VA
Cry, The. Federico Garcia Lorca, *tr. fr. Spanish by* Eleanor L. Turnbull. CoSP; OnPM
Cry, a greenish hollow undulation, A. High Dive. William Empson. AtBAP
Cry-baby, cry. *Unknown.* GoTP
Cry bravely, O town-crier. The Young Witch—1698. George Sterling. BAP
Cry Faugh! Robert Graves. CoBMV
Cry for Light, A. *Unknown.* BLRP
Cry from the Battlefield. Robert Menth. ISi
Cry from the Canadian Hills, A. Lilian Leveridge. BLPA
Cry from the Ghetto, A. Morris Rosenfeld, *tr. fr. Yiddish by* Charles Weber Linn. TrJP
Cry from the green-grained sticks of the fire, A. Surview. Thomas Hardy. ChMP; EmBrPo; LO
Cry from the Shore, A. Ellen Mackay Hutchinson Cortissoz. AA
Cry from the thicket my heart's bird! The Voice of Beauty Drowned. *Unknown.* PtOT
Cry has left in the wind, The. Lament. Federico García Lorca. CoSP
Cry in Distress, A ("My God, my God, why hast thou forsaken me?"). Psalms, XXII, Bible, *O.T.* TrGrPo
Cry, The, is: "Back to God!" Without respite. The Homeward Journey. L. Aaronson. FaBoTw; TrJP
Cry is up in England, which doth ring, A. Elizabeth Barrett Browning. *Fr.* Casa Guidi Windows, II. PoVP
Cry Kismet! and take heart. Eros is gone. Retractions, XII. James Branch Cabell. HBMV
Cry of a Dreamer, The. John Boyle O'Reilly. *See* Cry of the Dreamer, The.
Cry of man's anguish went up to God, The. Lord, Take Away Pain [*or* Pain]. *Unknown.* BPP; MaRV; OQP; QP-1
Cry of ruin strides the sky, A. The Traitors. Morton Dauwen Zabel. NP
Cry of the Age, The. Hamlin Garland. OQP; QP-2; WGRP
Cry of the Children, The. Elizabeth Barrett Browning. BCEP; BEL; BPN; BPP; EmBrPo; EnLi-2; EPP; EV-4; HBV; MaRV, *much abr.;* OAEP; PFE, *abr.;* PoFr, *sl. abr.;* PoVP; VA; ViBoPo; ViPo; VLEP
Cry of the cicada, The. Hokku. Basho. InP
Cry of the Daughter of My People, The. Jeremiah, VIII: 18–23, Bible, *O.T.* TrJP
Cry of the Dreamer, The. John Boyle O'Reilly. NLK; OnYI
(Cry of a Dreamer, The.) BLPA; NeHB; TreFS
Cry of the Hillborn, The. Bliss Carman. NLK
Cry of the Human, The. Elizabeth Barrett Browning. PoVP
Convinced by Sorrow, *sel.* BLRP; OQP; QP-2; WBLP
(" 'There is no God,' the foolish saith.") MaRV
Cry of the Lovelorn, The. William E. Aytoun *and* Sir Theodore Martin. *See* Lay of the Love-lorn, The.
Cry of the People. John G. Neihardt. BAP; CP; MAP; PoeMoYo; PoFr
Cry of the Peoples, The. Alter Brody. TrJP
Cry of the Song Children, The. Wilson MacDonald. CPG
Cry of the Stag. Emperor Jomei, *tr. fr. Japanese by* Ishii *and* Obata. OnPM
Cry of the stag, The. Otomo no Yakamochi, *tr. fr. Japanese by* Kenneth Rexroth. OnPJ
Cry on the Wind, A. "Fiona MacLeod." LBBV
Cry to Arms, A. Henry Timrod. MOAP; PAH; SPP
Cry unto the Lord to Stay His Hand, A, *sel.* Edward Johnson. *Fr.* The Wonder-working Providence of Sions Saviour in New England, 1628–1651.
"From silent night true register of moans." BAV
Cry what shall I cry? Difficulties of a Statesman. T. S. Eliot. *Fr.* Coriolan. OnAP
Cryderville Jail, The, *with music. Unknown, add. sts. by* C. E. Scoggins. ABF
(Po' Boy, *frag.*) ABF
Cryer, The. Michael Drayton. *See* Crier, The.
"Crying crane and wheeling crows." The Answer. Orrick Johns. NP
Crying, my little one, footsore and weary? Little One Weary. Christina Rossetti. BOL
Crying of Water, The. Arthur Symons. AnEnPo; BLV; MBP; MoBrPo
Cryptic Streets, The. Abu-l-Ala al-Maarri, *tr. fr. Arabic by* Ameen Rihani. LiTW
Crystal, The. George Barker. LiTM; OBMV; POTE
Crystal, The. Titus Munson Coan. AA
Crystal, The. Sidney Lanier. AmP; PtP; TCAP
Crystal Christ, The, *sel.* MaRV
("But Thee, but Thee, O sovereign Seer of Time.") BePJ; ChIP; TrPWD
Crystal and silver. The Islands of the Ever Living. *Tr. by* Padraic Colum. AnIV
Crystal Cabinet, The. Blake. CH; FaBoCh; LoGBV; OBRV; PoEL-4
Crystal Christ, The. Sidney Lanier. *Fr.* The Crystal. MaRV
("But Thee, but Thee, O sovereign Seer of Time.") BePJ; ChIP; TrPWD
Crystal flame, the ruby flame, The. Vinum Daemonum. Lionel Johnson. POTT
Crystal Gazer, The. Sara Teasdale. MAP; MoAmPo; NeMA
Crystal mirror, I, A. Submission. Jessie E. Williams. OQP; QP-1
Crystal Moment. Robert P. Tristram Coffin. PIAE; PoeMoYo
Crystal Palace, The. Thackeray. BOHV; InMe
Crystal parting the meads. The River in the Meadows. Léonie Adams. AnAmPo; LA; MAP; MoAB; MoAmPo; NP
Crystal Skull, The. Kathleen Raine. FaBoMo; NeBP
Crystal waters to a waiting world are gone. Winter 1939. George Ewart Evans. MoWP
Cuatro Palomitas Blancas, *with music. Unknown, tr. fr. Spanish.* ABF
Cuba. Harvey Rice. PAH
Cuba. Edmund Clarence Stedman. PAH
Cuba, disheveled, naked to the waist. On a Monument to Marti. Walter Adolphe Roberts. PoNe
Cuba Libre. Joaquin Miller. MC; PAH
Cuba to Columbia. Will Carleton. MC; PAH
Cuban Voyage. Paul Engle. ReMP
Cubbyhole I live in is a box, The. Out of Superstition. Boris Pasternak. LiTW; TrRV
Cubism. Hy Sobiloff. SiTL
Cubs of bears a living lump appear, The. The Phoenix Self-born. Ovid, *tr. by* Dryden. *Fr.* Metamorphoses, XV. ChTr
Cucaracha, La (The Cockroach), *with music. Unknown, tr. fr. Spanish.* AS; TrAS
Cuccu Song. *Unknown. See* Sumer Is Icumen In.
Cuchulain Comforted. W. B. Yeats. LiTG; LiTM (rev. ed.)

Cuchulain's Fight with the Sea. W. B. Yeats. AnIL; ChMo; CMP; PoVP
(Death of Cuchulain, The.) ChTr; GoTL
Cuchullain's Lament over Fardiad. *Tr. fr. Middle Irish by* George Sigerson. *Fr.* The Combat of Ferdiad and Cuchulain. AnIV; BoFr
(Cuchulain's [*or* Cuchulainn's] Lament for Ferdiad.) AnIL; SiB
Cuckoo! Hilaire Belloc. MoVE
Cuckoo, The. Francis Carlin. NV
Cuckoo, The. Patrick Reginald Chalmers. CenHV
Cuckoo, The. Rose Fyleman. UTS
Cuckoo, The. Gerard Manley Hopkins. MBP; MoAB; MoBrPo
(Fragment, A: "Repeat that, repeat.") AlDL
Cuckoo, The. Richard Le Gallienne. BLA; LBBV
Cuckoo, The. Frederick Locker-Lampson. HBV
Cuckoo. Katharine Tynan. BLA; TVSH
Cuckoo. *Unknown. See* Sumer Is Icumen In.
Cuckoo, The ("The cuckoo's a bonny [*or* fine] bird"). *Unknown.* CBPC, *sl. diff.*; ChTr; RIS
(Cuckoo Is a Fine Bird, The.) OTPC (1923 ed.)
Cuckoo, The ("In April/ Come he will"). *Unknown.* BoTP
("Cuckoo, cuckoo,/ What do you do?" *sl. diff.*) RIS
Cuckoo ("In former days my father and mother"). *Unknown, tr. fr. Anglo-Saxon by* Charles W. Kennedy. *Fr.* Riddles. AnOE
Cuckoo. Andrew Young. ChTr
Cuckoo and the Nightingale, The. Thomas Clanvowe, *tr. fr. Middle English by* Wordsworth. MeEV
Cuckoo at Laverna, The, *sel.* Wordsworth.
"Oft have I heard the nightingale and thrush." SaFP
Cuckoo calls, A. Fujiwara no Sanesada, *tr. fr. Japanese by* Kenneth Rexroth. OnPJ
Cuckoo! calls the cuckoo. The Captives. *Unknown.* PoFr
Cuckoo Clock, The. Caroline Anne Bowles. *Fr.* The Birthday. LPS-2
Cuckoo Clock, The. John Farrar. GFA
Cuckoo clock on the nursery wall, The. Ticking Clocks. Rachel Field. TiPo (1959 ed.)
Cuckoo comes in April, The. *Unknown.* OxNR
"Cuckoo! The," cried my child, the while I slept. The Oocuck. Justin Richardson. FiBHP
Cuckoo, cuckoo!/ In April skies were blue. Cuckoo Song. Katharine Tynan. OnYI
Cuckoo, cuckoo!/ Is it thy double note I hear. Cuckoo. Andrew Young. ChTr
Cuckoo, cuckoo,/ What do you do? *Unknown.* OxNR; RIS
Cuckoo, cuckoo, cherry tree. *Unknown.* OxNR
Cuckoo in the clock by day, The. The Cuckoo Clock. John Farrar. GFA
Cuckoo Is a Fine Bird, The. *Unknown. See* Cuckoo, The.
Cuckoo is a merry bird, The. *Unknown.* OxNR
Cuckoo is a tell-tale, The. The Cuckoo. Rose Fyleman. UTS
Cuckoo Sings, The. Wei Ying-wu, *tr. fr. Chinese.* WhP
Cuckoo Song. Hilda Doolittle ("H. D."). ChMo; CMP; TwCV
Cuckoo Song. Katharine Tynan. OnYI
Cuckoo Song. *Unknown. See* Sumer Is Icumen In.
Cuckoo-throb, the heartbeat of the Spring, The. Ardor and Memory. Dante Gabriel Rossetti. The House of Life, LXIV. PoVP; ViPo
Cuckoo Waltz, *with music. Unknown.* AS
Cuckoo, when the lambkins bleat, The. The Cuckoo. Patrick Reginald Chalmers. CenHV
Cuckoos. Andrew Young. ChTr; MoPW
Cuckoo's [*or* cuckoo is] a bonny [*or* fine] bird, The. The Cuckoo. *Unknown.* CBPC; ChTr; OTPC (1923 ed.); RIS
Cuckoo's double note, The. Wiltshire Downs. Andrew Young. AlDL; ChMP; GTBS-D
Cuckoo's Parting Cry, The. Matthew Arnold. *Fr.* Thyrsis. CBOV
(Departure of the Cuckoo, The.) SN
Cuckoo's Song, The. Josui, *tr. fr. Japanese by* William N. Porter. MPB
Cuddle Doon. Alexander Anderson. BOL; BTP; GN; HBV; OHFP; VA
Cuddle Down, Dolly. Kate Douglas Wiggin. PPL
Cuddy [*or* Cuddie], for shame hold up thy heavy head. October [*or* The Contempt of Poetry]. Spenser. *Fr.* The Shepheardes Calender. NBE; OBSC; ReEn; ReIE; SiCE
Cui Bono? Thomas Carlyle. HBV; OBRV; WGRP
Cuisine Bourgeoise. Wallace Stevens. LiTA
Cujus pulchritudinem. St. Agnes; a Responsory. Thomas Merton. MeRV
Cul-de-Sac, The. "Jan Struther." LO
Cullen ("Cullen renounced his cradle at fifteen"). P. K. Page. CaP
Culprit, The. A. E. Housman. PG (1955 ed.); TwP
Culprit Fay, The. Joseph Rodman Drake. LPS-3; TCAP
Sels.
Assembling of the Fays, The. GN
Elfin Song. AA; OBAV; PoMS
Fairy Dawn. GN
Fairy in Armor, A. FaPON; GaP; GFA; OTPC; PRWS; RAR
(Elfin Knight, An.) BoTP; TVSH
(Fay Arms Himself, The.) APW
Fay's Crime, The. GN
Fay's Sentence, The ("The monarch sat on his judgment-seat"). LEAP
Fay's Sentence, The ("Thou shalt seek the beach of sand"). GN
First Quest, The. AA
(Fay's Departure, The, *shorter sel.*) GN
Gathering of the Fairies, The. BAP
("'Tis the middle watch of a summer's night," *longer sel.*) BAV
Second Quest, The. AA
"Soft and pale is the moony beam." PFY
Throne of the Lily-King, The. GN
War under Water. APW
Cult of the Celtic, The. Anthony C. Deane. PA
Cultural Notes. Kenneth Fearing. ChMo
Cultural Presupposition, The. W. H. Auden. MaPo; TwHP
(Culture.) MoPW
Culture in the Slums. W. E. Henley. BOHV; CenHV; HBV; InMe; PA
Cultured Girl Again, The. Ben King. FiBHP
Cum Invocarem. Psalms, IV, Bible, *O.T., tr. by* Thomas Sternhold. SiCE
Cum, listen w'ile yore Unkel sings. 'Ittle Touzle Head. Ray Garfield Dandridge. BANP
Cumberbunce, The. Paul West. BOHV; NA
Cumberland, The. Longfellow. AA; AnNE; APW; BoHiPo; EtS; IAP; LH; MC; PaA; PAH; PAP
Cumberland, The. Herman Melville. PAH
Cumberland Gap, *with music. Unknown.* ABF
Cumberland's Crew, The, *with music. Unknown.* ShS
Cumbrous pollards that o'ershade, The. Modern Improvements. John Hookham Frere. EnSW
Cumha Mhic Leoid (Lament for the Son of Leod), *abr.* Mari Nighean Alisdair Ruaidh, *tr. fr. Gaelic by* Donald Campbell. BoFr
Cummerbund, The. Edward Lear. CenHV
Cumnor Hall. William Julius Mickle. BeLS; CEP; EV-3; OBEC
"Dews of summer night did fall, The," *sel.* ViBoPo
Cumulatives. Carl Sandburg. MOAP
Cun-ne-wa-bum—"one who looks on stars." Portrait of a Cree. "Katherine Hale." CaP; CPG
Cunning arts man, The/ Faltered not in a line. John Ford. *Fr.* The Lover's Melancholy. MyFE
Cunning Cobbler Done Over, The. *Unknown.* CoMu
Cunning fireflies, The. Ryoto, *tr. fr. Japanese by* Lois J. Erickson. SoLD
Cunning hand that carved this face, The. On an Intaglio Head of Minerva. Thomas Bailey Aldrich. HBV; LPS-3; PR
Cunning, wise, cautious, folly is, by which. Upon the Most Useful Knowledge, Craft or Cunning, Which Is More Wisdom, as 'Tis Less Wit. William Wycherley. SeCV-2
Cup, The. John Oldham, *after the Greek of* Anacreon. AWP
Cup, The. Frederick T. Roberts. ChIP
Cup, The. Theocritus, *tr. fr. Greek. Fr.* Idylls, I. GrR, *tr. by* R. C. Trevelyan; OxBG, *tr. by* Sir William Marris
Cup, The. John Townsend Trowbridge. HBV; SN
Cup-Bearer, The. Meleager. *See* Heliodore.
"Cup for hope, A!" she said. Three Seasons. Christina Rossetti. HBV; POTT; VLEP
Cup I sing is a cup of gold, The. The Cup. John Townsend Trowbridge. HBV; SN
Cup in hand, I can enjoy, A. Snow. Munetake. OnPM
Cup of Blessing, The. Charles Wesley. BePJ
Cup of Happiness, The. Gilbert Thomas. MaRV; TrPWD
Cup of Life, The. Mikhail Lermontov, *tr. fr. Russian by* C. M. Bowra. BoR
Cup of life is not so shallow, The. Good Hope. Emerson. OnPM
Cup of O'Hara, The. Turlough Carolan, *tr. fr. Modern Irish by* Sir Samuel Ferguson. OnYI
(When Kian O'Hara's Cup Was Passed to Turlough O'Carolan.) AnIV
Cup of wine, under the flowering trees, A. Drinking Alone by Moonlight, 1. Li Po. TrCh
Cup Reversed, The. Johan Sebastian Cammermeyer Welhaven, *tr. fr. Norwegian by* Charles W. Stork. AnNoLy
Cup, the ruby cup, The. To Peace. Katharine Lee Bates. AOAH
Cupboard, The. Walter de la Mare. BrR; FaPON; GoBP; PCH; PoRh; RAR; TiPo
Cupboard's bare, my child, The; oh bye. The Poor Poet's Lullaby. John H. Finley. BAP
Cupid. Blake. BOHV
Cupid. Emerson. *Fr.* The Initial Love. APW
Cupid. Ben Jonson. *See* Beauties, Have Ye Seen This Toy
Cupid. Sir Philip Sidney. *Fr.* Arcadia. SiPS

Cupid. *Unknown.* ElL
Cupid Abroad Was 'Lated in the Night. Robert Greene. *Fr.* Greene's Orpharion. ElSeCe; TuPP
Cupid and Campaspe. John Lyly. *See* Apelles' Song.
Cupid and Death, *sels.* James Shirley.
Love's Victories. GoBC
Victorious Men of Earth. EV-2; OBS; TrGrPo
(Death, the Conqueror.) GoBC
(Death's Emissaries.) LoBV
(Death's Subtle Ways.) HBV
(Last Conqueror, The.) GTBS; GTBS-D; GTBS-W; GTSE; GTSL
(More Ways to Kill.) BLV
(Song: "Victorious men of Earth, no more.") FaBoEn; SeCL
("Victorious men of earth, no more.") TuPP
Cupid and My Campaspe Played. John Lyly. *See* Apelles' Song.
Cupid and Venus. Mark Alexander Boyd. GoTS
Cupid, as he lay among. The Wounded Cupid. Robert Herrick. AWP; GrPo
Cupid at Court. Samuel Minturn Peck. PR
Cupid, because thou shin'st in Stella's eyes. Astrophel and Stella, XII. Sir Philip Sidney. ReEn; SiPS
Cupid blushes to behold. *Unknown.* SeCSL
Cupid did cry, his mother chid him so. The Compliment. William Habington. ACP
Cupid Drowned. Leigh Hunt. *See* Cupid Swallowed.
Cupid has woven the tresses. Anacreon. Gutierre de Cetina. AnSpL-1
Cupid, I hate thee, which I'd have thee know. Idea, XLVIII. Michael Drayton. LO
Cupid, I Scorn to Beg the Art. Sir Francis Fane. *Fr.* Love in the Dark. SeCL; SeEP
Cupid if thou tell-tale prove. *Unknown.* SeCSL
Cupid in a Bed of Roses. *Unknown.* ElL; ElSeCe
Cupid is my broker. Broker Cupid. Frank Dempster Sherman. PR
Cupid laid by his brand and fell asleep. Sonnets, CLIII. Shakespeare. PeBoSo
Cupid Mistaken. Matthew Prior. ALV; InMe
(Cupid's Mistaken.) ViBoPo
Cupid, My Little Boy, Come Home Again. Fulke Greville. Caelica, XXXV. AtBAP; PeBoSo
Cupid my mistriss hart assaild. *Unknown.* SeCSL
Cupid, my pretty boy, leave off thy crying. Fulke Greville. Caelica, XXV. AtBAP
Cupid once upon a bed. Cupid Stung. Thomas Moore. HBV; PECK
Cupid one day, in idle quest. Cupid's Failure. Carolyn Wells. PR
Cupid replied to him, "Phoebus, your shafts." Apollo and Daphne. Ovid. *Fr.* Metamorphoses. LaP
Cupid Stung. Thomas Moore. HBV; PECK
Cupid Swallowed. Leigh Hunt, *after the Greek of* Anacreon. BCEP; LPS-1
(Cupid Drowned.) HBV; PECK
Cupid tho' all his darts were lost. Swift. *Fr.* Cadenus and Vanessa. OxBI
Cupid thou art a sluggish boye. *Unknown.* SeCSL
Cupid, thou naughty boy, when thou wert loathed. To Cupid. Fulke Greville. Caelica, XII. ES; TuPP
Cupid Turned Plowman. Moschus, *tr. fr. Greek by* Matthew Prior. AWP; OnPM
Cupid Ungodded. James Shirley. GoBC
Cupid—Ungrateful Guest. *Unknown, tr. fr. Greek by* Thomas Girdlestone. GrR
Cupid, when you shoot your darts. Love the Archer. Rufinus. OxBG
Cupidon. William Jay Smith. NePoEA
Cupid's Curse. George Peele. *See* Fair and Fair.
Cupid's Darts. A. P. Herbert. BOHV; CenHV
Cupid's Failure. Carolyn Wells. PR
Cupids in vain around them hover. After the Wedding. Henry Luttrell. *Fr.* Advice to Julia. IrPN
Cupid's Indictment. John Lyly. *Fr.* Galathea. ElL
(Song of Diana's Nymph, A: "Oyes, Oyes! if any maid.") OBSC
Cupid's Mistaken. Matthew Prior. *See* Cupid Mistaken.
Cupid's Revenge, *sel.* Beaumont *and* Fletcher.
Lovers, Rejoice! ElL; FaBoEn
Cupids wearie of the Court. *Unknown.* SeCSL
Cupping her chin and lying there, the Bren. Defensive Position. John Manifold. MoBrPo (1950 ed.)
Cups are those a-flashing with wine. Mystic Cups. Iraqi. PeP
Cups of Illusion. Henry Bellamann. HBMV
Cups of Jade. Huang Pien, *tr. fr. Chinese by* Henry H. Hart. PoHN
Curate and the spinster sit, The. The Curate's Christmas Eve. Harold Monro. FaBoTw
Curate Thinks You Have No Soul, The. St. John Lucas. BLPA
Curate's Christmas Eve, The. Harold Monro. FaBoTw
Curate's Kindness, The. Thomas Hardy. CoBMV; PoVP
Curb for stubborn steed. Hymn to Christ the Saviour [*or* Earliest Christian Hymn]. Clement of Alexandria. CAW; WGRP
Curculio, *sels.* Plautus, *tr. fr. Latin by* F. A. Wright. LaP
"Bolt and bar, bolt and bar."
"To my nose there came a whiff."
Cure, The. Abraham Cowley. PoP
Cure-all. Edith M. Thomas. *See* Tell Me.
Cure for Fault-finding, A. Strickland W. Gillilan. *See* Watch Yourself Go By.
Cure for Poetry, A. *Unknown.* SiTL
Cure for the Spleen, A. Matthew Green. *Fr.* The Spleen. OBEC
Cure me with quietness. For Sleep or Death. Ruth Pitter. AlDL; TrPWD
Cure of Malaria, The. Sir Ronald Ross. PoP
Curé's Progress, The. Austin Dobson. HBV; MW; PoVP; VA
Curfew. Longfellow. AA; MCCG; MOAP; OxBA; PCD
"Cover the embers," *sel.* WaKn
Curfew. Sir Herbert Read. *Fr.* Eclogues. BrBE
Curfew Must Not Ring Tonight. Rose Hartwick Thorpe. BeLS; BLPA; FaBoBe; FaPON; HBV; LPS-1; NeHB; PTA-1; TreF; WBLP
Curfew tolls the knell of parting day, The. Elegy Written in a Country Churchyard. Thomas Gray. AEV; AnEnPo; AnFE; AtBAP; ATP; AWP; BCEP; BEL; BLV; BoLiVe; BrBE; BTP; CaAE; CBE; CBOV; CEP; CoBE; CoEV; EiPP; EM-1; EnL; EnLi-2; EnLit; EnRP; EPP; EV-3; ExPo; FaBoBe; FaBoEn; FaFP; GN; GoTL; GTBS; GTBS-D; GTBS-W; GTSE; GTSL; HBV; HBVY; HiLiEn; HoPM; InP; InPo; JAWP; LaA; LEAP; LiA; LiTB; LiTG; LoBV; LPS-1; MaRV; MCCG; MyFE; NeHB; OAEP; OBEC; OBEV; OHFP; OQP; OTPC; OuHeWo; PECK; PG (1945 ed.); PIAE; PIR; Po; PoE; PoEL-3; PoFS; PreP; PYM; QP-2; ReaPo; RiBV; SeCeV; ShBV-3; TBV; TCEP; TOP; TreF; TrGrPo; TriL; TVSH; TwHP; TyEnPo; UnPo; ViBoPo; WBLP; WBP; WHA; WoL; WP
Curfew tolls the knell of parting day, The. If Gray Had Had to Write His Elegy in the Cemetery of Spoon River Instead of in That of Stoke Poges, *parody.* J. C. Squire. WhC
Curio, aye [*or* ay] me! Thy mistress' monkey's dead. Satire VIII. John Marston. *Fr.* The Scourge of Villainy. ReEn; ReIE
Curiosity, *sels.* Charles Sprague. AA
Fiction.
News, The.
Curious child, who dwelt upon a tract, A. Wordsworth. *Fr.* The Excursion, IV. WGRP
Curious, curious Tiggady Rue. Tiggady Rue. David McCord. RIS; TiPo (1959 ed.)
Curious eyes of those blue skyey spaces. To the Stars That Have Gone Out. Afanasi Fet. BoR
Curious Something. Winifred Welles. TiPo
Curious, the ways of these folk of humble and hardy condition. Country Kisses. Arthur Joseph Munby. *Fr.* Dorothy; a Country Story. VA
Curious wits, seeing dull pensiveness, The. Astrophel and Stella, XXIII. Sir Philip Sidney. EV-1; ReEn; SiPS
Curiously enough/ I like. Festivals. Fuyuhiko Kitagawa. PoLJ
Curled in a maze of dolls and bricks. A Fairy Tale. Austin Dobson. POT
Curled up and sitting on her feet. L'Eau Dormante. Thomas Bailey Aldrich. HBV; PR
Curlew Calling. W. W. Gibson. ChMo; CMP
Curlew's Call, A. Jane Barlow. VA
Curliest Thing, The. *Unknown.* BoTP
Curls powdered with chalk like a black roman bust. Native Working on the Aerodrome. Roy Fuller. NeBP
Curly locks! Curly locks! wilt thou be mine? Mother Goose. CBPC; HBV; HBVY; OnHT; OTPC; OxNR; PCH; PPL; RIS; SAS
Currants and honey! The Cornucopia of Red and Green Comfits. Amy Lowell. NV
Currente Calamo. Arthur Hugh Clough. *Fr.* Mari Magno. LoBV
Curse, The. Elizabeth Barrett Browning. *Fr.* A Curse for a Nation. PoVP
Curse, The. John Donne. EnLP; OAEP
Curse, The. Edna St. Vincent Millay. NP
Curse, A. Rabi'a, Daughter of Ka'b, *tr. fr. Persian by* R. A. Nicholson. LiTW
Curse, The. Shelley. *Fr.* Prometheus Unbound, I. PoFr
Curse, The. J. M. Synge. ChTr; SiTL
Curse for a Nation, A. Elizabeth Barrett Browning. EPP
Sels.
Curse, The. PoVP
Prologue. PoVP
Curse for the Saxaphone, A. Vachel Lindsay. ATP (1935 ed.)

Curse of Cain was on the earth, The. The First Thanksgiving. Arthur Guiterman. DD; TOAH
Curse of Cromwell, The. W. B. Yeats. SeCePo
Curse of Doneraile, The. Patrick O'Kelly. OnYI
Curse of Faint Praise, The. Irwin Edman. InMe
Curse of Kehama, The, *sels.* Robert Southey.
"I charm thy life." LoBV; OBRV
(Malice.) BCEP
Immortality of Love. EV-4
("They sin who tell us.") OBRV
"Oh, when a mother meets on high." MotAn
"Stream descends on Meru Mountain, A." OBRV
"Two forms inseparable in unity." OBRV
Curse of the father, The. Comrades in Death. Yiannis Griparis. MoGP
Curse on a Closed Gate, A. James H. Cousins, *fr. the Irish.* AnIV
Curse the tongue in my head. Good Night! Good Night! John Holmes. PoToHe
Curse upon Edward, The. Thomas Gray. *Fr.* The Bard. BCEP; OBEV
"Cursed Be He Who First Taught Grecians War." Sophocles, *tr. fr. Greek by* Lewis Campbell. *Fr.* Ajax. GrR
Cursed Be the Day. Jeremiah, XX: 14–18, Bible, *O.T.* TrJP
Cursed be the verse, how well soe'er it flow. Scandal. Pope. *Fr.* Epistle to Dr. Arbuthnot. LPS-3
Cursed by the gods and crowned by shame. The Wife of Loki. Lady Charlotte Elliot. VA
Curses upon this land; till plague devours. Edmond Rostand. *Fr.* The Woman of Samaria. StJW
Cursor Mundi, *sel. Unknown.*
Flight into Egypt, The. CoBE; EPP, *Middle English and mod. vers.*
Curtain! Paul Laurence Dunbar. CenHV
Curtain, The (Old Tabor Grand Opera House). Jean Milne Gower. PoOW
Curtain, The. Tristan Klingsor, *tr. fr. French by* Alan Conder. TrFP
Curtain. Helen Spalding. NeTW; POTE
Curtain Curtain. André Breton, *tr. fr. French by* Wallace Fowlie. MiCF
Curtain Fell, The. Gulchin, *tr. fr. Persian by* A. J. Arberry. PeP
Curtain of the Wedding Bed, The. Wife of Liu Hsün, *tr. fr. Chinese by* Arthur Waley. TrCh
Curtain on the grouping dancers falls, The. The Music-Hall. Theodore Wratislaw. VA
Curtains are of lace, softening darkness, The. Curtains for a Spinster. Walter H. Kerr. NePoAm-2
Curtains Draw across the Brain, The. Robert Hillyer. MuM
Curtains for a Spinster. Walter H. Kerr. NePoAm-2
Curtains Now Are Drawn, The. Thomas Hardy. ChMo; CMP
Curtains of rock. Orpheus in the Underworld. David Gascoyne. FaBoTw; MoP
Curtains were half drawn, the floor was swept, The. After Death. Christina Rossetti. EnLi-2; POTT; PoVP; UnW; VA; VLEP
Curve, The. Bocho Yamamura, *tr. fr. Japanese by* Takamichi Ninomiya *and* D. J. Enright. PoLJ
Curve for the shore, A. A Japanese Print. Ruth Mason Rice. BAP
Curving, leaping line of light, A. Prairie Fires. Hamlin Garland. BAP
Curving shore was made to hold the sea, The. Design. Arthur Guiterman. FAOV
Cushla-Ma-Chree. John Philpot Curran. DD; HBV
Cushy Cow. Laura Benét. MPB; TSW
Cushy cow bonny, let down thy milk. Mother Goose. BoChLi; OxNR; PPL; SAS; StVeCh
Cushy Cow has curly horns. Cushy Cow. Laura Benét. MPB; TSW
Custer. Edmund Clarence Stedman. GA; PAH
Custer's Last Charge. Frederick Whittaker. BoHiPo; DD; GA; HBV; MC; PaA; PAH; PTA-1
Custom is lord of everything. The Power of Custom. Pindar. OxBG
Cut from the joints of this immense. The Night. Lawrence Durrell. *Fr.* Eight Aspects of Melissa. NeBP
Cut is the branch that might have grown full [*or* growne ful] straight. Chorus on the Death of Faustus. Christopher Marlowe. *Fr.* Dr. Faustus. LEAP; PoD; ViBoPo
Cut It Down. Mary Elizabeth Coleridge. MoVE
Cut out as if in porphyry against the sky. Cattle. Frederick Mortimer Clapp. LiTM (1946 ed.)
Cut out the deep design of life. Plan for a Novel. Frederic Thompson. JKCP (1955 ed.)
Cut the Cables. Robert Burns Wilson. PAH
Cut thistles in May. *Unknown.* OxNR
Cut your nails [*or* them] on Monday, cut them for news [*or* health]. Old Superstitions [*or* Old Wives' Sayings]. *Unknown.* HBV; OxNR; StaSt
Cutbert our cobbler can no more forbear. Henry Parrot. SiCE
Cuthullin sat by Tura's wall. James MacPherson. *Fr.* Fingal; an Ancient Epic Poem. EnLi-2
Cuttin' Rushes. "Moira O'Neill." AV
Cutty Sark. Hart Crane. *Fr.* The Bridge. AmPP; FaBoMo; LiTA; NP
Cutty Wren, The. *Unknown.* GTBS-W; LiTG; OxBoLi; SiTL
Cuvier Light. Pat Wilson. AnNZ
Cwa een like milk-wort and bog-cotton hair! Milk-Wort and Bog Cotton. "Hugh MacDiarmid." NeBP
Cwm Farm near Capel Curig. Huw Menai. MoWP
Cybele Drawn by Lions. Keats. *Fr.* Endymion. RO
Cyclamen, The. Arlo Bates. AA; HBV
Cycle. Langston Hughes. FaPON; GoSl
Cycle, The. Robinson Jeffers. TBM
Cycle; Seven War Poems. Seán Jennett. WaP
I Was a Labourer, *sel.* OnYI
Cycle was closed and rounded, A. Bennington. W. H. Babcock. PAH
Cycle's Rim, The, *sel.* Olive Tilford Dargan.
"Deep lies thy body." LEAP
Cycling to Dublin. Robert Greacen. OnYI
Cyclone at Sea, A. William Hamilton Hayne. AA
Cyclone Blues. *Unknown.* CoSo
Cyclops, The. Callimachus, *tr. fr. Greek by* G. M. Young. GrL
Cyclops, *sels.* Euripides, *tr. fr. Greek by* Shelley.
Chorus: Love Song. AWP; JAWP; WBP
("One with eyes the fairest.") GrPo
Chorus of Satyrs, Driving Their Goats. AWP; JAWP; WBP
("Where has he of race divine.") GrPo
Cyclops' Philosophy, A. OxBG
(Fair Exchange.) GrR
Cyclops' Views on Life, A. GrR
Cyclops, The. Theocritus, *tr. fr. Greek by* Elizabeth Barrett Browning. Idylls, XI. AWP; EnLi-1; JAWP; OuHeWo; WBP
(Cyclops in Love, The, *pr. tr. by* Andrew Lang.) GrL
(Giant's Wooing, The, *tr. by* C. S. Calverley.) GrR
Polyphemus to Galatea, *sel.* OxBG
Cyclops, The, now—where is he? Not at home? A Cyclops' Views on Life. Euripides, *tr. by* Shelley. *Fr.* Cyclops. GrR
Cyclops—terrific son of Ocean's God! Luis de Góngora. *Fr.* Polyphemus and Galatea. AnSpL-1
Cyclops' Philosophy, A. Euripides, *tr. fr. Greek by* Shelley. *Fr.* Cyclops. OxBG
(Fair Exchange.) GrR
Cyclops' Views on Life, A. Euripides, *tr. fr. Greek by* Shelley. *Fr.* Cyclops. GrR
Cydalises, The. Gérard de Nerval, *tr. fr. French by* Daisy Aldan. AnFP
Cydonian Spring with her attendant train. The Spring. Ezra Pound. MOAP; Po; TBM
Cygnet crested on the purple water, The. Similes. Edward Moxon. OBRV
Cygnet finds the water, but the man, The. Man. Elizabeth Barrett Browning. *Fr.* Aurora Leigh, I. BCEP
Cymbals crash, The. A Victory Ball. Alfred Noyes. EnLit
Cymbalum Mundi. Horace Gregory. ChMo
Cymbeline, *sels.* Shakespeare.
"Crickets sing, and mans ore-labor'd sense, The," *fr.* II, ii. AtBAP
Fear No More the Heat o' the Sun, *fr.* IV, ii. AnFE; ATP; BEL; CenL; ChTr; CoBE; EG; ElSeCe; EM-1; EnL; EnLi-1; EPP; ExPo; GTSL; LoBV; LPS-1; MaPo; OAEP; OuHeWo; PIR; PoE; PoRA; RiBV; SeCeV; TOP; TriL; TwHP; TyEnPo; WHA
(Dirge: "Fear no more the heat o' the sun.") CAW; CBOV; EnLit; EV-1; HBV
(Dirge from "Cymbeline.") WP
(Fear No More.) BLV; CH; ElL; FaFP; InPo; LiTB; LiTG; PoFS; ReaPo; TrGrPo; TwP; ViBoPo
("Feare no more the heate o' the sun.") AEV; AtBAP; BrBE; PoEL-2; SiCE
(Fidele.) BCEP; GTBS; GTBS-D; GTBS-W; GTSE; MCCG; OBEV; OQP; QP-2; ShBV-4
(Fidele's Dirge.) CoEV; FaBoCh; LoGBV; OBSC; PoD
(Funeral Song: "Fear no more the heat o' the sun.") CaAE; LiA
(Lament for Imogen.) TreF
(Lament of Guiderius and Arviragus.) FaBoEn
(Song: "Fear no more the heat o' the sun.") FiP; REAL
(Song of the Two Brothers.) BoLiVe
(Songs from "Cymbeline.") LEAP
(Songs from the Plays.) AWP; JAWP; WBP
(To Fidele.) TVSH
Hark! Hark! The lark, *fr.* II, iii. AnFE; ATP; BEL; BoTP; CBOV; CH; ChTr; CoBE; ElSeCe; EM-1; EnL; EnLi-1 (1949 ed.); EnLit; EPP; ExPo; FaBoCh; FaFP; FaPON; HBV; InP; InPo; KN; LiTB; LiTG; LoBV; LoGBV; LPS-2; OTPC; OuHeWo; PFE; PIR; PTA-2;

ReaPo; SeCeV; SiCE; TCEP; TOP; TreF; TrGrPo; TVSH; TyEnPo; ViBoPo; WHA
(Aubade.) BCEP; OBEV; ShBV-3
("Hearke, hearke, the larke at heavens gate sings.") AtBAP
(Morning Song, A.) BLV; EV-1; GN; PCH
(Morning Song for Imogen, A.) AnEnPo
(Morning Song from "Cymbeline.") PIAE
(Song: "Hark, hark, the lark at heaven's gate sings.") CaAE; ElL; FiP; REAL
(Song from "Cymbeline.") BLA; CBE
(Song of the Musicians.) BoLiVe
(Song to Imogen.) EG; OBSC
(Songs from "Cymbeline.") LEAP
(Songs from the Plays.) AWP; JAWP; WBP
(Three Songs.) UnPo (1st ed.)
Cymochles and Phaedria. Spenser. *Fr.* The Faerie Queene, II, 6. OBSC
Cymochles in the Bower of Bliss. Spenser. *Fr.* The Faerie Queene, II, 5. PreP
Cymon and Iphigenia, *sels.* Dryden.
"Deep recesses of the grove he gain'd, The." LiA
Power of Love, The. OBS
Rude Militia, The. CoEV
Cynara. Ernest Dowson. *See* Non Sum Qualis Eram Bonae sub Regno Cynarae.
Cynddylan's Hall. *Unknown, tr. fr. Welsh by* William Barnes. PrWP
Cynegetica, *sel.* Oppian, *tr. fr. Greek by* Gilbert Highet.
Ichneumon, The. OxBG
Cynic, The. Theodosia Garrison. AV; HBMV; PR
Cynic breaks stained windows, The. Destroyer. A. M. Sullivan. ALV; PFE
Cynic of the Woods, The. Arthur Patchett Martin. VA
Cynical Ode to an Ultra-cynical Public. Charles Mackay. BOHV
Cynical Portraits. Louis Paul. InMe
Cynics say that every rose, The. The Wisdom of Folly. Ellen Thorneycroft Fowler. BLP; HBV
Cynicus to W. Shakespeare [*or* Shakspere]. James Kenneth Stephen. *Fr.* Two Epigrams. BOHV; CenHV; WhC
Cynneddf, The. Rolfe Humphries. CrMA
Cynotaph, The, *sel.* "Thomas Ingoldsby."
Not a Sou Had He Got. HBV; PA
Cynthia, *sels.* Richard Barnfield.
"Now was the welkin all inveloped." ReIE
To His Mistress. SiCE; TuPP
Cynthia. Sir Edward Dyer. OBEC
Cynthia ("Away with these self-loving lads"). Fulke Greville. *See* Of His Cynthia.
Cynthia, because your horns look divers ways. Caelica, LV. Fulke Greville. ElSeCe; SiCE
Cynthia, Cynthia. Propertius, *tr. fr. Latin by* James Cranstoun. LiTW
Cynthia in the Snow. Gwendolyn Brooks. TiPo (1959 ed.)
Cynthia on Horseback. Philip Ayres. EnLoPo
Cynthia, Queen of seas and lands. The Mariner's Song. Sir John Dav'es. OBSC
Cynthia, to thy power and thee. Bridal Song. Beaumont *and* Fletcher. *Fr.* The Maid's Tragedy. OBEV; TuPP
Cynthia, whose glories are at full forever. Caelica, XVII. Fulke Greville. ElSeCe
Cynthia's Revels, *sels.* Ben Jonson.
Glove, The, *fr.* IV. ElL
"Queen and huntress, chaste, and fair," *fr.* V, vi. CBE; CenL; CH; EG; ElSeCe; OBEV; OBS; PoE; ReEn; SiCE
(From "Cynthia's Revels.") LEAP
(Hesperus' Hymn to Cynthia.) CaAE; LoBV; SeCV-1
(Hesperus' Song.) GN
(Hymn[e], The: "Queen[e] and huntress, chaste and fair[e].") AtBAP; EPS; PoEL-2; TwHP; ViBoPo
(Hymn to Cynthia.) SeCePo; SN
(Hymn to Diana.) AnFE; AWP; BCEP; BEL; BLV; BoLiVe; CBOV; ChTr; ElL; EM-1; EnLi-1 (1949 ed.); EnLit; EV-2; GTBS; GTBS-D; GTBS-W; GTSE; GTSL; InPo; JAWP; KN; PoRA; RG; ShBV-4; TOP; TrGrPo; TVSH; TyEnPo; WBP; WHA
(Moon Goddess.) CBPC
(Queen and Huntress.) EnL; OAEP; TuPP
(Song: To Cynthia.) HBV
(To Diana.) OTPC
"Slow, slow, fresh fount, keep time with my salt tears," *fr.* I, ii. AEV; CenL; CH; EG; ElSeCe; ExPo; NBE; OAEP; OBS; ReEn; SiCE
(Dirge for Narcissus.) BLV
(Echo's Dirge for Narcissus.) CBOV
(Echo's Lament of Narcissus.) AnEnPo; EV-2
(Echo's [*or* Eccho's] Song.) BoLiVe; LoBV; SeCV-1; TrGrPo
(Slow, Slow, Fresh Fount.) ChTr; ElL; EnLi-1 (1949 ed.); RiBV; TuPP; TyEnPo; UnPo; WHA
(Song: "Slow, slow, fresh fount.") AtBAP; FaBoEn; PoEL-2; ViBoPo
(Song of Echo.) GoBC
Song: "O, that joy so soon should waste," *fr.* IV, iii. LiTL; TuPP; ViBoPo
(Kiss, The.) HBV
(Song: Kiss, The.) EV-2
Cypress. John Peter. BoSA
Cypress-bough, and a rose-wreath sweet, A. Athulf's Death Song. Thomas Lovell Beddoes. *Fr.* Death's Jest Book, IV. VA
Cypress Curtain of the Night [Is Spread], The. Thomas Campion. LoBV; ReIE
(Cypresse Curtaine, The.) MeRV
Cypress stood up like a church, The. Bianca among the Nightingales. Elizabeth Barrett Browning. ViPo
Cypress swamp around me wraps its spell, The. Down the Bayou. Mary Ashley Townsend. AA; AnAmPo; LA; LEAP
Cypress Tree, The. Grace Blackburn. CPG
Cypress Wreath, The. Sir Walter Scott. *Fr.* Rokeby, V. ERP
Cyprian Woman, A; Greek Folk Song. Margaret Widdemer. AnAmPo; HBV; LA; NV
(Greek Folk Song.) NP
(Under Dusky Laurel Leaf.) AV
Cyrano de Bergerac, *sel.* Edmond Rostand, *tr. fr. French by* Brian Hooker.
Cyrano de Bergerac Discusses His Nose, *fr.* I. TreFS
Cyrene. Pindar. *See* Wooing of Cyrene, The.
Cyriack, this three years' day these eyes, though clear. To Cyriack Skinner. Milton. AnEnPo; ATP (1935 ed.); BEL; EM-1; EnLi-1; EPP; EPS; ES; GEPC; LPS-3; OBS; PeBoSo; RiBV; TCEP; TOP; TrGrPo
Cyriack, whose grandsire on the royal bench. To Cyriack Skinner [*or* Sonnet]. Milton. EM-1; ES; EV-2; GTBS; GTBS-D; GTBS-W; GTSE; GTSL; LoBV; OBEV; OBS; PC; SeEP
Cythère. Paul Verlaine, *tr. fr. French by* Arthur Symons. AWP
Cythere the Bithynian in prayer sets me before Thee. The Wife's Prayer. Antipater of Thessalonica. GrPE

D

D-Dawn. Margaret McGarvey. GoYe
D. L. and W.'s Phoebe Snow, The. *Unknown.* TreF
D Minor, The. E. L. Mayo. MiAP
D-9. James Schevill. FiMAP
"D. O. M." Sir Henry Wotton. *See* Hymn Made When He Was an Ambassador at Venice.
Da Capo. H. C. Bunner. HBV; PR
Da Silva Gives the Cue. Walter Hart Blumenthal. TrJP
Dabbing in the Dew. *Unknown.* CH
Daccus is all bedaubed with golden lace. Against Gaudy, Bragging, Undoughty Daccus. John Davies of Hereford. SiCE
Dachshund, The. Edward Anthony. GoTP
Dachshund, The. John E. Donovan. AlBD
Dacus, with some good color and pretense. In Dacum. Sir John Davies. TuPP
Dad, a Home Guard, when in liquor. *Unknown.* WhC
Dad 'n' Me. Stuart N. Lake. FAOV
Dada would have liked a day like this. Pictures of the Gone World, Sec. 23. Lawrence Ferlinghetti. NeAP
Daddy. Robert Freeman. FAOV
Daddy. Rose Fyleman. FAOV; SiSoSe
Daddy Fell into the Pond. Alfred Noyes. FaPON
Daddy goes a-riding in a motor painted grey. Differences. Rose Fyleman. GFA; GoBP; RAR
Daddy John. Jorge de Lima, *tr. fr. Portuguese by* Dudley Poore. AnCL
Daddy Knows. James William Foley. FAOV
Daddy like Mine, A. Douglas Malloch. FAOV
Daddy Neptune one day to Freedom did say. The Island. *Unknown.* BHV
Daddy Shot a Bear, *with music.* *Unknown.* OuSiCo
Dad's Birthday. Arthur Vine Hall. FAOV
Daedalus and Icarus. Ovid, *tr. fr. Latin by* Samuel Croxall. *Fr.* Metamorphoses, VIII. RoL
Daedalus in Crete, *sel.* Angelos Sikelianos, *tr. fr. Modern Greek by* Rae Dalven.
" 'In our darkness the sun is a lamp.' " MoGP
Daedalus Sings in the Dusk; Before the Skyline of New York. Virginia McCormick. LS
Daemon, The. Mikhail Lermontov. *See* Demon, The.
Daemon & Lectern & a Life-Size Mirror. Horace Gregory. PreP
Daemon Lover, The. *Unknown.* CG; EnLi-1; EnLit; OBB; SG

Daemon Lover, The (*continued*)
(Demon Lover, The.) EBSV; EnL; EnSB; LiTB; PoMS; TOP; UnPo
(House Carpenter, The, *diff. vers.*) ABS; AS, *with music*
(James Harris, *diff. vers.*) BaBo (A, B, C, *and* D *vers.*); ESPB (A, D, *and* F *vers.*); ViBoFo (A *vers.*; B *vers.*, *with music*)
Daemon of the World, The, *sel.* Shelley.
Trackless Deeps, The, *fr.* Pt. II. EtS
Daemones. Hesiod, *tr. fr. Greek by* F. L. Lucas. *Fr.* Works and Days. GrPE
Daffadowndilly/ Has come up to town. Mother Goose. *See* Daffy-down-dilly is new come up to town.
Daffodil. Michael Drayton. *See* Gorbo and Batte.
Daffodil. Katharine Tynan. TIP
Daffodil Time. Clinton Scollard. PR
Daffodils. Gina Ballantyne. BoAu
Daffodils. Ruth Guthrie Harding. HBMV; VOD
Daffodils. Robert Herrick. *See* To Daffodils.
Daffodils. Kikurio, *tr. fr. Japanese.* SUS; TiPo
Daffodils. Lizette Woodworth Reese. AA; OBAV; VOD
Daffodils. P. A. Ropes. BoTP
Daffodils. Shakespeare. *See* Flowers ("O Proserpina!").
Daffodils. Wordsworth. *See* I Wandered Lonely as a Cloud.
. . . daffodils/ That come before the swallow dares. Shakespeare. *Fr.* The Winter's Tale, IV, iii. TiPo (1959 ed.)
Daffodils dancing by moonlight in English meadows. On Broadway. W. W. Gibson. ChMo; CMP; CP
Daffodils over Night. David Morton. PCH; VOD
Daffodil's Return. Bliss Carman. CaP; OCL
Daffy-down-dilly. Anna B. Warner. MPB; OTPC; PRWS; TVC; TVSH
Daffy-down-dilly is new come [*or* Daffadowndilly/ Has come up] to town. Mother Goose. BoChLi; BrR; RIS; OxNR; TiPo
Daft Days, The. Robert Ferguson. BSV; CEP; EV-3
Dagger, The. Federico García Lorca, *tr. fr. Spanish by* Eleanor L. Turnbull. CoSP
Dagger. Mikhail Yurevich Lermontov, *tr. fr. Russian by* Max Eastman. AWP; JAWP; WBP
Dagger of the Mind, A. Shakespeare. *Fr.* Macbeth, II, i. LPS-3
("Is this a dagger which I see before me.") PIR
(Macbeth's Words before Murdering.) TreFS
(Night.) LiA
Dago shovelman sits by the railroad track, The. Child of the Romans. Carl Sandburg. LaNeLa
Dagonet, the fool, whom Gawain in his mood. The Last Tournament. Tennyson. *Fr.* Idylls of the King. ViPo
Dagonet's Canzonet. Ernest Rhys. BMEP; HBV; NV
Daguerreotype, The. William Vaughn Moody. AnAmPo; LA; LBMV; MOAH
Dahlia-red, the shadowed curtains. A Sister Lights the Candles. Sister Mary Jeremy. PraNu
Dahlias. Edith Agnew. GaP
Dahlias. Padraic Colum. NePoAm
Dai horse neighs against the bleak wind of Etsu, The. South-Folk in Cold Country. Ezra Pound. CrMA
Daily Bread. W. W. Gibson. *See* All Life Moving to One Measure.
Daily Bread. *Unknown.* BePJ
Daily Cross. Earl Bigelow Brown. ChIP
Daily Manna, The. Sara Henderson Hay. GoYe
Daily more zealous, through the tome I thumb. Dictionary. Samuel Marshak. RuPo
Daily Paradox. Sara Henderson Hay. InMe
Daily Prayer. Marion Strobel. NP
Daily Round, The. Ronald McCuaig. BoAV
Daily Task, The. "Marianne Farningham." PEOR
Daily the bending skies solicit man. Fragments on Nature and Life. Emerson. TOP
Daily the fishers' sails drift out. Beside the Sea. Ella Higginson. OTPC (1946 ed.)
Daily the yellow sun comes over the hill. The Sun. Georg Trakl. AnGP
Daily Trials. Oliver Wendell Holmes. PoEL-5
Daily walked the fair and lovely. The Azra. Heine. AWP; JAWP; WBP
Daily when I do seek and sue for peace. Amoretti, XI. Spenser. PeBoSo
Daily with You. Annie Johnson Flint. BLRP
Daily work in narrow space is bound, The. Escape. *Unknown.* MaRV
Dain do Eimhir, *sels.* Sorley Maclean. NeBP
"Bolshevik who never gave heed to queen or to king, A," XXX.
"I do not see the sense of my toil putting thoughts in a dying tongue," LV.
"I gave you immortality and what did you give me?" XIX.
"I walked with my reason out beside the sea," XXII.
(I Walked with My Reason.) LiTW
"Multitude of the skies, gold riddle of millions of stars," XVII.
"You were dawn on the Cuillin," LIV.
Dain Eile, *sel.* Sorley Maclean.
"My eye is not on Calvary, nor on Bethlehem the Blessed," NeBP
Dainty fairy lace-work, O so finely spun. Cobwebs. *Unknown.* GFA
Dainty Fine Bird. *Unknown.* TuPP
(Prisoners.) ElL
Dainty little cups of color. Crocus. Marion Mitchell Walker. GFA
Dainty little girl is what I'd wish for, A. Mother Fear. Tove Ditlevsen. BoDS
Dainty little maiden, whither would you wander? The City Child. Tennyson. BoTP; OTPC; PRWS
Dainty new ditty composed and penned, A. The Seaman's Compass. *Unknown.* SG
Dainty Sang, A. Allan Ramsay. *See* For the Love of Jean.
Dainty thing's the villanelle, A. Villanelle. W. E. Henley. InP; MBP; TOP
Daisies. Bliss Carman. BAP; HBV; MaRV; MoAmPo (1942 ed.); NeMA; NLK; PFY; PYM; TSW; TSWC
(Over the Shoulders and Slopes of the Dune.) BLP; PC
Daisies. Hilda Conkling. NV
Daisies, The. Kate Greenaway. MPB; RAR
Daisies. Christina Rossetti. *Fr.* Sing-Song. RIS
(Sing-Song.) MBP
Daisies. Frank Dempster Sherman. GoBP; RAR; TSW; TVC; TVSH
Daisies, The. James Stephens. AnIV; AWP; JAWP; PreP, *with music;* TIP; WBP
Daisies, The. George Edward Woodberry. LBAP
Daisies and Grasses. *Unknown.* BoTP
Daisies are at Delphi now, The. Delphi. Oliffe Richmond. NeTW
Daisies are broken. Love Song. William Carlos Williams. NP; TCPD
Daisies so bright,/ Grasses so green. Daisies and Grasses. *Unknown.* BoTP
Daisy, The. Chaucer. *Fr.* The Legend of Good Women: Prologue. LPS-2
("And as for me, thogh that I can but lyte.") CH
("And as for me, though that my wite be lite.") ViBoPo
("Of all the floures in the mede," *shorter sel.*) LO
Daisy, The. John Clare. PIAE
Daisy, The. John Mason Good. PEOR
Daisy, The. John Leyden. LPS-2
Daisy, The. James Montgomery. LPS-2; OTPC (1923 ed.); SN
(Field Flower, A.) HBV
"There is a flower, a little flower," *sel.* BoTP
Daisy, The. Sir Rennell Rodd. VA
Daisy, The. Virna Sheard. CPG
Daisy, The. Jane Taylor. *See* Field Daisy, The.
Daisy, The. Tennyson. EnLoPo; OBVV; PoEL-5; VA; VLEP
Daisy. Francis Thompson. AEV; AnEnPo; AWP; BeLS; BMEP; EnLit; GoBC; GTBS-D; GTML; HBV; LBBV; LEAP; MBP; MoAB; MoBrPo; NeMA; OBEV (new ed.); OBVV; PoeT; POTT; VA; VLEP; WHA
Tokens, The, *br. sel.* OtMeF
Daisy. William Carlos Williams. MAP; MoAB; MoAmPo
Daisy, The, *br. sel.* Wordsworth. *Fr.* So Fair, So Sweet, Withal So Sensitive. RO
Daisy, The. Marya Zaturenska. MoAmPo
Daisy and a buttercup, A. A Race. Mrs. Molesworth. BoN
"Daisy and Lily." Waltz. Edith Sitwell. OAEP (2d ed.)
Daisy and the Flood, The. Thomas Lovell Beddoes. *Fr.* The Second Brother. RO
Daisy Bell. Harry Dacre. TreF
Daisy Field, The. Margaret Widdemer. RAR
Daisy Fraser. Edgar Lee Masters. *Fr.* Spoon River Anthology. MoVE; NP
Daisy in an Alien Land, A. Nikolay Novosyolov, *tr. fr. Russian by* Babette Deutsch. TrRV
Daisy lives, and strikes its little root, The. The Daisy. John Clare. PIAE
Daisy's Song, A. Keats. ADAH; OTPC; PRWS
Dakota Land. *Unknown.* ABS; AS, *with music;* CoSo, *with music*
Dalecarlian March. Erik Axel Karlfeldt, *tr. fr. Swedish by* Charles W. Stork. AnSL
Dallas,/ A pompous-girthed merchant. Cities. Boyce House. HiLiAm
Dalliance of Leopards, The. *Unknown, tr. fr. Sanskrit by* E. Powys Mathers. OnPM
Dalliance of the Eagles, The. Walt Whitman. AA; APW; FaBoEn; MOAP
Dalmatian Nocturne. Aleksa Santic, *tr. fr. Serbo-Croatian by* Paul Selver. LiTW
Dalyaunce. *Unknown.* CH
"Welcome, fayre chylde, what is thy name?" AtBAP
Dam Neck, Virginia. Richard Eberhart. LiTA; MoAB; WaP
Damaetas' Jig. Sir John Wotton. *See* In Praise of His Love.
Damascus. Edna Holroyd Yelland. CIV

Damascus Nightingale, A. Stephen Crombie. BLA
Damascus Road, The. Daniel Hughes. ChIP
Damask meadows and the crawling streams, The. Dreams. Richard Corbet. EV-2
Dame, dame! the watch is set. The Witches' Charms. Ben Jonson. *Fr.* The Masque of Queens. ElL; PoMS; ThWaDe
Dame Duck's First Lecture on Education. Ann Hawkshaw. OTPC (1923 ed.)
(Dame Duck's Lecture, *abr.*) DDA
(Dame Duck's Lecture to Her Ducklings.) SAS
(Mother Duck.) BoTP
Dame, get up and bake your pies. *Unknown.* BoTP; OxNR
Dame Goose, the sun shines cheerfully. Fox and Goose. F. Hey. SAS
Dame Gundelil's Harping. *Unknown, tr. fr. Danish by* E. M. Smith-Dampier. BoDaBa
Dame Gunild, she dwells in Spire, The. Ravngard and Memering. *Unknown.* BaBo
"Dame, how the moments go." The Bride's Toilette. Ellen Mackay Hutchinson Cortissoz. AA
Dame Liberty Reports from Travel. Dorothy Cowles Pinkney. GoYe
Dame Music. Stephen Hawes. *Fr.* The Pastime of Pleasure. PoEL-1
Dame Nature. Spenser. *Fr.* The Faerie Queene, VII, 7. PoEL-1
Dame of Athelhall, The. Thomas Hardy. ChMo; CMP
Dame, said the Panther, times are mended well. Dryden. The Hind and the Panther, II. PoEL-3
Dame Trot and Her Cat. *Unknown.* BoTP; OxNR
Dame Trot and Her Comical Cat. *Unknown.* FTB
Dame Wiggins of Lee and Her [Seven] Wonderful Cats. *Unknown, at. to* Richard Scrafton Sharpe. BoN, *abr.;* CIV; FaBoBe
Damelus' Song to His Diaphenia. *At. to* Henry Constable *and to* Henry Chettle. *See* Diaphenia.
Dames of France are fond and free, The. The Girl I Left behind Me. Thomas Osborne Davis. AmSS; BoHiPo; FaBoBe; FaFP; HBV; OlF; OnYI; TreF
Damien lived with lepers. Contrition across the Waves. Caroline Giltinan. WHL
Damis, an author cold and weak. Epigram. *Unknown.* HBV
Damis the Nysaean of a little bark was master. Himself He Could Not Save. Antipater of Sidon. GrPE
Damn it all! all this our South stinks peace. Sestina: Altaforte. Ezra Pound. AmP; CoBMV; FaBoTw; LiTA; LiTG; LiTM (1946 ed.); MoAB; MoAmPo (1950 ed.); ReaPo
Damn the Filipinos, *with music. Unknown.* ABF
Damnation of Byron, The. A. D. Hope. MoAuPo
Damnation of the Infants. Michael Wigglesworth. *See* Infant's Petition, The.
Damned, The. Manuel Moreno Jimeno, *tr. fr. Spanish by* H. R. Hays. AnCL
Damned Minoan crevices, that I clog them up! Paranoia in Crete. Gregory Corso. NeAP
Damned ship lurched and slithered, The. Quiet and quick. A Channel Passage. Rupert Brooke. FaBoTw
Damoetas and the herdsman Daphnis had driven each his flock. A Lovesick Cyclops. Theocritus. *Fr.* Idylls. GrR
Damon and Celimena. Dryden. *Fr.* An Evening's Love. InvP; SeCL
Damon and Cupid. John Gay. EnLoPo; SeCeV
Damon died young; no bell was tolled for him. Toll the Bell for Damon. Maxwell Anderson. InMe
Damp clods with corn may thank the showers. The Snake. Roy Campbell. AtBAP
Damsel, The. Omar b. Abi Rabi'a, *tr. fr. Arabic by* W. G. Palgrave. AWP; LiTW
Damsel came in midnight rain, A. Over, Over. Thomas Love Peacock. *Fr.* Maid Marian. EV-4
Damsel donned her kirtle sheen, The. Christmas. Sir Walter Scott. *Fr.* Marmion. PCH
Damsels of Time [*wr.*]. *See* Daughters of Time . . .
Dan. Carl Sandburg. AlBD
Dan-Doodle-Dan. *Unknown. See* Wife Wrapt in Wether's Skin, The.
Dan Taylor. *Unknown.* CoSo, *with music;* CSF
Dana. "Æ." TIP
Danaan children laugh, in cradles of wrought gold, The. A Cradle Song. W. B. Yeats. BOL
Danaë. Simonides, *tr. fr. Greek.* GrL, *tr. by* T. F. Higham; GrR, *tr. by* John Addington Symonds; LiA, *tr. by* John Addington Symonds; LiTW, *tr. by* T. F. Higham; OxBG, *tr. by* T. F. Higham
(Danaë Adrift, *tr. by* F. L. Lucas.) GrPE
(Lamentation of Danaë, The, *tr. by* John Addington Symonds.) BOL
("When in the carven chest," *tr. by* John Addington Symonds.) GrPo
Danaë's Cradle-Song. *Unknown.* BOL
Danaë's Lullaby. Andrew Lang. BOL
Danaides, *sel.* Aeschylus, *tr. fr. Greek by* C. M. Bowra. Marriage of Heaven and Earth, The. OxBG
Dance, A. Francis Beaumont. *See* Shake Off Your Heavy Trance.
Dance, The. Hart Crane. *Fr.* The Bridge: Powhatan's Daughter. AnAmPo; AnFE; CoAnAm; LA; LiTA; LiTM; MoAB; MoAmPo; OxBA; SeCeV; TwAmPo
Dance, The. Robert Duncan. NeAP
Dance, The. Rudolph Chambers Lehmann. HBMV
Dance, The. John Lydgate. *Fr.* The Dance of Death. PoEL-1
Dance, The. Theodore Roethke. Four for Sir John Davies, I. CoBMV; CrMA; FiMAP; NePoAm; ReMP; UnS
Dance. Sadi, *tr. fr. Persian by* R. A. Nicholson. PeP
Dance, The. Spenser. *See* Dance of the Graces, The.
Dance. James Stephens. ChMo; CMP
Dance. Jaime Torres Bodet, *tr. fr. Spanish by* Rolfe Humphries. AnCL
Dance, The ("Cornwallis led a country dance"). *Unknown.* PAH
(Cornwallis's Country Dance, *abr., with* Yankee Doodle.) TrAS
Dance, The. *Unknown, at. to* Thomas Campion. ElL; ElSeCe; FaBoCh; LiTL; LoBV; LoGBV
Dance. Lula Lowe Weeden. CDC
Dance, The. William Carlos Williams. AmP; ExPo; LoGBV; OxBA
Dance a baby diddy. *Unknown.* OxNR
Dance at Silver Valley, The. William Maxwell. SCC
Dance at the Ranch, A. *Unknown.* SCC
Dance by the Roadside, The. Gustaf Fröding, *tr. fr. Swedish by* Charles W. Stork. AnSL; WoL
Dance Chant, A. *Tr. fr. Iroquois Indian by* E. S. Parker. WGRP
Dance Chant, A. *Tr. fr. Osage Indian by* D. G. Brinton. WGRP
Dance, dance in this museum case. Love Song to Eohippus. Peter Viereck. MoAmPo (1950 ed.)
Dance Figure (for the Marriage in Cana of Galilee). Ezra Pound. AnAmPo; ChMo; CMP; CoAnAm; CoV; LA; MAP; MoAB; MoAmPo; NP; ReMP; TwAmPo
Dance for Rain, A. Witter Bynner. HiLiAm; MuM; PoTo; TBM
Dance from its dancers circulates among the other, The. The Dance. Robert Duncan. NeAP
Dance in the township hall is nearly over, The. Country Dance. Judith Wright. MoAuPo
Dance is on the Bridge of Death, The. The Bridge of Death. *Unknown.* AWP
Dance Light. John Francis Waller. *See* Kitty Neil.
Dance, little baby, dance up high. The Baby's Dance. Mother Goose. GFA; OTPC; OxNR; PPL; RAR
Dance, little children, it is holy twilight. Snow-Dance for the Dead. Lola Ridge. AnAmPo; LA
Dance, lovely lady, dance and mask your face. Pierre de Ronsard. *Fr.* Sonnets pour Hélène. PrPoCR
Dance My Baby Diddy. *Unknown.* BOL; OTPC (1923 ed.)
Dance, my dearies, dance, my pretties. The Little Shepherdess to Her Lambs. Rose Fyleman. GoBP
Dance of blue-bells in the shady places, A. Sweet Surprises. S. Doudney. BoTP
Dance of Death. Aleksandr Blok, *tr. fr. Russian by* C. M. Bowra. BoRS
Dance of Death, The. Austin Dobson. HBV; TOP
Dance of Death. Kimball Flaccus. AnAmPo
Dance of Death, The, *sel.* John Lydgate. Dance, The. PoEL-1
Dance of Death, The, *sel. Unknown, tr. fr. Spanish.* "Lo! I am Death! With aim as sure as steady." AnSpL-1
Dance of Despair, The. Hayyim Nahman Bialik, *tr. fr. Hebrew by* A. M. Klein. TrJP
Dance of Love, The. Sir John Davies. *Fr.* Orchestra. ElL; SeCePo
Dance of Saul with the Prophets, The. Saul Tchernichowsky, *tr. fr. Hebrew by* I. M. Lask. TrJP
Dance of the Gnats. Marguerite Steffan. MuM
Dance of the Graces, The. Spenser. *Fr.* The Faerie Queene, VI, 10. OBSC; RiBV
(Dance, The, *shorter sel.*) TrGrPo
Dance of the Lost Key. Jacinto Fombona Pachano, *tr. fr. Spanish by* H. R. Hays. TwSpPo
Dance of the Macabre Mice. Wallace Stevens. NePA; OxBA; SeCeV
Dance of the Maskers. *Tr. fr. Apache Indian by* Mary Austin. APW
Dance of the Seven Deadly Sins [*or* Sevin Deidly Sinnis *or* Synnis], The. William Dunbar. BCEP, *abr., mod. by* Edwin Markham; BSV; EBSV; GoTS
Dance of the Sword, The. *Unknown, tr. fr. Breton by* Tom Taylor. WaaP
Dance Ring, The. Eleanor Farjeon. DiM
Dance Song, A. Burkhard von Hohenfels, *tr. fr. German by* Jethro Bithell. LiTW
Dance Song. Angelo Poliziano, *tr. fr. Italian by* John Heath-Stubbs. LyPI

Dance Song (*continued*)
(Three Ballate, III, *tr. by* John Addington Symonds.) AWP
Dance Song. *Unknown, tr. fr. Armenian by* Zabelle C. Boyajian. ArmLP
Dance Song. *Unknown, tr. fr. Chinese by* Arthur Waley. FaBoCh; LoGBV
(Unicorn's Hoofs, The.) WhP
Dance there upon the shore. To a Child Dancing in the Wind. W. B. Yeats. AlDL; GTIV
Dance, Thumbkin, dance. *Unknown.* OxNR
Dance to the beat of the rain, little Fern. Fern Song. John Banister Tabb. PRWS; RAR
Dance to your daddy [*or* daddie]. Mother Goose. OxNR; PPL; RIS; SAS; TiPo
Dance, wee maidens, dance your fill! A Grandfather's Ditty. Victor Hugo. TrFP
Dance with Banderillas. Richard Duerden. NeAP
Dancer, The. Joseph Campbell. GTIV; OBMV; OxBI; POTE
Dancer, The. Ednah Proctor Clarke. AA
Dancer, The. Ibn Kharuf, *tr. fr. Arabic by* A. J. Arberry. MooP
Dancer, The. Sadi, *tr. fr. Persian by* Sir Edwin Arnold. *Fr.* The Bustan. AWP; JAWP; OuHeWo; WBP
Dancer. Vincent Starrett. LEAP
Dancer, The. W. J. Turner. OBMV; POTE
Dancer, The. Edmund Waller. BLV; PoFS; TrGrPo
Dancer: O you translation. Rainer Maria Rilke. Sonnets to Orpheus, Pt. II, XVIII. OnPM
Dancer at Cruachan and Cro-Patrick, The. W. B. Yeats. UnS
Dancer of air. The Humming-Bird. Ednah Proctor Clarke. BLA; SN
Dancers, The. Babette Deutsch. HBMV
Dancers, The. "Michael Field." VA
Dancers with a Hop, The. James Schevill. FiMAP
Dances Inspired by Love. Ben Jonson. *Fr.* Love Restored. UnS
Dancing. Eleanor Farjeon. StVeCh (1955 ed.)
Dancing. Yang Kuei-fei, *tr. fr. Chinese by* Florence Ayscough *and* Amy Lowell. FaPON
Dancing Cabman, The. J. B. Morton. AlDL; MoShBr; ShBV-4
Dancing dancing down the street. Rain. Ella Young. TiPo (1952 ed.)
Dancing, drinking, gambling, fighting. Off Guard. *Unknown.* CoSo
Dancing Faun, The. Robert Cameron Rogers. AA
Dancing firefly, A! The Firefly. Taigi. OnPM
Dancing Girl, A. Frances Sargent Osgood. AA
(Celeste Dancing.) BAP
Dancing girl of Syria, her hair caught up with a fillet. Appendix Vergiliana. *Tr. by* Helen Waddell. DiM
Dancing lamely on a lacquered plain. The Tillaquils. Laura Riding. FaBoMo
Dancing Lesson, The. Eliza Grove. OTPC (1923 ed.)
Dancing of the Air, The. Sir John Davies. *Fr.* Orchestra. LPS-2
Dancing on the Shore. M. M. Hutchinson. BoTP
Dancing Partners. Philip Child. CaP
Dancing Sea, The. Sir John Davies. *Fr.* Orchestra. ChTr
(Sea Danceth, The.) EtS
Dancing Seal, The. W. W. Gibson. HBMV; WP; PoMS
Dancing through the air. Butterflies. Kageki. OnPM
Dandelion. Annie Rankin Annan. HBV
Dandelion. Kate L. Brown. TVC; TVSH
Dandelion, The. Richard Church. AlDL
Dandelion. Hilda Conkling. BoChLi; FaPON; GFA; MPB; PoRh; TiPo; TSW; TSWC; TVC; TVSH
Dandelion. Nellie M. Garabrant. GFA; PTA-2
Dandelion, The. Vachel Lindsay. BrR
Dandelion, The. Katharine Pyle. DD
Dandelion, The ("O dandelion, yellow as gold"). *Unknown.* PCH
Dandelion ("There was a pretty dandelion"). *Unknown.* GFA
Dandelion Puff, The. Mary K. Robinson. BoTP
Dandelion stares, The. The Little Dandelion. Lula Lowe Weeden. CDC
Dandelions. John Albee. AA
Dandelions, The. Helen Gray Cone. ADAH; DD; GFA; HBV; NLK; PRWS; SN
Dandelions. Frances M. Frost. TiPo
Dandelions. Howard Nemerov. NePA
Dandelions. Sacheverell Sitwell. RIS
Dandelions, The. *Unknown.* BoTP
Dandoo. *Unknown. See* Wife Wrapt in Wether's Skin, The.
Dandy Cat, The. Laura E. Richards. CIV
Dandy Dandelion. Christopher Morley. GFA
Dandy O, The. *Unknown.* CoMu
Danger, The. Norman Gale. LBBV
Danger. S. Frances Harrison. *Fr.* Down the River. CPG
Danger. Helen Hunt Jackson. AnFE; APA; CoAnAm
Danger. Theodora L. Paine. PGD
Danger is not in action, but in sloth. Tyrannicide. Walter Savage Landor. PoFr
Danger is silent in the bloodless square. Capital Square. Patrick Anderson. BoCaPo
Danger of Writing Defiant Verse, The. Dorothy Parker. InMe
Danger (the spurre of all great mindes) is ever. George Chapman. *Fr.* The Revenge of Bussy d'Ambois, V, i. NBE
Dangers of Football, The. John Gay. *Fr.* Trivia; or, The Art of Walking the Streets of London, II: Of Walking the Streets by Day. EnLi-1 (1949 ed.)
Daniel, *sel.* Bible, *O.T.*
Belshazzar's Feast, V. MuP, *abr.*; TreF
Daniel. Vachel Lindsay. ChMo; ChTr; CMP; PoE; ShBV-1
(Daniel Jazz, The.) MuP; TrGrPo
Daniel and Abigail. Epitaph. Miguel de Barrios. TrJP
Daniel, beside the subject of thy verse. Ad Samuelem Danielem. Thomas Bastard. SiCE
Daniel Boone. Stephen Vincent Benét. NAMP
Daniel Boone. Byron. *Fr.* Don Juan, VIII. LPS-3
Daniel Boone. Arthur Guiterman. FaPON; MaC; MoShBr; MPB; OnSP; PaA; PoFr
Daniel Boone. Cotton Noe. BoHiPo
Daniel Boone at twenty-one. Daniel Boone. Arthur Guiterman. FaPON; MaC; MoShBr; MPB; OnSP; PaA; PoFr
Daniel Boone's Last Look Westward. Cale Young Rice. LS; SPP
Daniel Gray. Josiah Gilbert Holland. AA; HBV; LEAP
Daniel Jazz, The. Vachel Lindsay. *See* Daniel.
Daniel Saw de Stone, *with music. Unknown.* BoAN-2
Daniel, thou in tragic note excels. Ad Samuelem Daniel. John Weever. ReIE
Daniel Webster. Oliver Wendell Holmes. LPS-3; PAH
Daniel Webster's Horses. Elizabeth J. Coatsworth. AnNE; MAP; MoAmPo; PoMS
Danish Barrow, A. Francis Turner Palgrave. VA
Danish Cradle Song, A. *Unknown.* BoTP
("Lullaby, sweet baby mine!/ Mother spins the threads so fine.") BOL
Dank, limber verses, stuft with lakeside sedges. Some of Wordsworth. Walter Savage Landor. ChTr
Dannebrog (The Danish Flag). Bernhard Severin Ingemann, *tr. fr. Danish by* Charles W. Stork. BoDS
Danny. J. M. Synge. AnEnPo
Danny Deever. Kipling. AnFE; BBV (1923 ed.); BEL; BPN; ChMo; CoEV; EnLi-2 (1949 ed.); EPP; ExPo; HBV; InP; LEAP; LiA; LiTB; LiTM (rev. ed.); MaC; MBP; MCCG; MoBrPo; NeMA; OAEP (2d ed.); OxBoLi; PFE; PoE; PoFS; PoVP; PYM; SeCePo; ShBV-3; TOP; TreFS; TrGrPo; TSW; TSWC; UnPo (3d ed.); VA; WaaP
Danny Murphy. James Stephens. BoTP; MW
Danny was a rascal. The Buccaneer. Nancy Byrd Turner. TiPo
Dans l'allée. Paul Verlaine, *tr. fr. French by* Arthur Symons. AWP
Danse Russe. William Carlos Williams. MOAP
Dante. Bryant. PtP; ViBoPo
Dante ("Oft have I seen"). Longfellow. *See* Oft Have I Seen . . .
Dante ("Tuscan, that wanderest"). Longfellow. AA; AnNE; BAV; CoBA; IAP; ReaPo; TCAP
Dante. Michelangelo, *tr. fr. Italian by* Longfellow. AWP; JAWP; WBP
(Sonnet: Dante.) LyPI
Dante, a sigh that rose from the heart's core. Sonnet: To Dante Alighieri (He Reports the Successful Issue of Lapo Gianni's Love). Guido Cavalcanti. AWP
Dante Alighieri, a dark oracle. Inscription for a Portrait of Dante [*or* A Tribute to Dante]. Boccaccio. AWP; GoBC; JAWP; OnPM; WBP
Dante Alighieri, Cecco, your good friend. Sonnet: To Dante Alighieri (On the Last Sonnet of the "Vita Nuova"). Cecco Angiolieri da Siena. AWP
Dante Alighieri, if I jest and die. Sonnet: To Dante Alighieri (He Writes to Dante). Cecco Angiolieri da Siena. AWP
Dante Alighieri in Becchina's praise. Sonnet: He Rails against Dante. Cecco Angiolieri da Siena. AWP; JAWP; WBP
Dante Enters the Gate of Hell. Dante, *tr. fr. Italian by* J. A. Carlyle. *Fr.* Divina Commedia: Inferno, III. LiA
Dante, if thou within the sphere of Love. Sonnets: To Dante in Paradise [*or* Fiammetta]. Boccaccio. AWP; GoBC
Dante saw the great white Rose. Slumber-Songs of the Madonna: Prelude. Alfred Noyes. BOL
Dante Sees Beatrice in Glory. Dante, *tr. fr. Italian by* Thomas Okey. *Fr.* Divina Commedia: Purgatorio, XXX. LiA
Dante, Shakespeare, Milton. Sydney Dobell. *Fr.* Balder. VA

Dante was naïf, although he had an inkling. Sonnets, II. Leonard Bacon. TBM
Dante, whenever this thing happeneth. Sonnet: To Dante Alighieri (He Conceives of Some Compensation in Death). Cino da Pistoia. AWP
Dante's Scourge. Sumako Fukao, *tr. fr. Japanese by* Takamichi Ninomiya *and* D. J. Enright. PoLJ
Danube River, The. Hamilton Aidé. VA
Danube to the Severn gave, The. In Memoriam A. H. H., XIX. Tennyson. BPN; EM-2; EmBrPo; EnL; EnLi-2; EPN; GEPC; LoBV; OAEP; TOP; ViPo; VLEP
Daphnaida, *sels.* Spenser.
"And ever as I see the starres to fall." PoD
"She fell away in her first ages spring." OBEV
Daphne. Bliss Carman. BoCaPo
Daphne. Hildegarde Flanner. HBMV; VOD (1935 ed.)
Daphne. Bernard le Bovier de Fontenelle, *tr. fr. French by* Alan Conder. TrFP
Daphne. Ann Louise Hayes. PtPa
Daphne. Thomas S. Jones, Jr. OHIP; VOD
Daphne. John Lyly. *Fr.* Midas. EIL
(Apollo's Song.) HBV
("My Daphne's hair is twisted gold.") SiCE
(Song of Daphne to the Lute, A.) OBSC
Daphne. Selden Rodman. PoNe
Daphne. Edith Sitwell. HBMV
Daphne and Apollo. George Macy. InMe
"Daphne with her thighs in bark." Ezra Pound. Hugh Selwyn Mauberley, XII. CoBMV; CoV; LiTA; LiTM (rev. ed.); MoPo
Daphne's Embarkation. James Russell Lowell. *Fr.* A Fable for Critics. APW
Daphnis. Theocritus, *tr. fr. Greek by* F. L. Lucas. Idylls, I. GrPE
Daphnis and Chloe, *sel.* Longus, *tr. fr. Greek.*
Daphnis, IV, 17, *pr. tr. by* F. A. Wright. LiA
Daphnis began the singing, for the challenge came from him. Coy Polyphemus. Theocritus. *Fr.* Idylls. OxBG
Daphnis Came on a Summer's [*or* Sommers] Day. *Unknown.* SeCSL; ViBoPo
Daphnis Song, The. Theocritus, *pr. tr. fr. Greek by* Andrew Lang. Idylls, I. GrL
Daphnis to Ganymede. Richard Barnfield. *Fr.* The Affectionate Shepherd. EIL; ThWaDe
Dappled Duck, A. Palmer Brown. LiL
Darby and Joan. St. John Honeywood. AA; LHV
Darby and Joan. Frederic Edward Weatherly. VA
Darby and Joan were dressed in black. *Unknown.* OxNR
D'Arcy Singer. Edgar Lee Masters. *Fr.* The New Spoon River. ChMo; CMP
Dare Quam Accipere. Mathilde Blind. OBVV
Dare to Be Free. Georg Herwegh, *tr. fr. German by* J. L. Joynes. PoFr
Dare to Be True. George Herbert. *Fr.* The Church Porch. GoTP
(Courage.) PCD; PCH
Dare we despair? Through all the nights and days. He Leads Us Still. Arthur Guiterman. OHIP; OQP; QP-1
Dare You? Edward Rowland Sill. AnNE
Dare you haunt our hallow'd green? The Fairies' Dance. *Unknown.* MPB
Darest Thou Now, O Soul. Walt Whitman. APW; ATP (1935 ed.); CBOV; CoBA; HBV; IAP; InP; LEAP; MaRV; NePA; OBAV; PoFS; TCAP; TOP; TrGrPo; ViBoPo; WGRP
Darien. Sir Edwin Arnold. MC; PAH
Daring young lady of Guam, A. *Unknown.* GoTP
Darius, *sel.* Sir William Alexander.
Illusion. EBSV
Darius Green and His Flying-Machine. John Townsend Trowbridge. BeLS; BoChLi; BOHV; FaBoBe; HBV; HBVY; IHA; InMe; MoShBr; MW; PTA-1; PYM; StVeCh (1940 ed.); YaD
Darius the Mede was a king and a wonder. Daniel [*or* The Daniel Jazz]. Vachel Lindsay. ChMo; ChTr; CMP; MuP; PoE; ShBV-1; TrGrPo
Dark, The "George Eliot." *Fr.* The Spanish Gypsy. VA
Dark all without it knits; within. In a Forest. Andrew Marvell. *Fr.* Upon Appleton House. EV-2
Dark, and death, and heat, The. Sisters. Olga Berggolts. Songs of the Spanish Children, I. RuPo
Dark and more dark the shades of evening fell. Sonnet: Composed after a Journey across the Hamilton Hills, Yorkshire. Wordsworth. ChER
Dark Angel. Elizabeth Bartlett. NePoAm-2
Dark Angel, The. Lionel Johnson. ACP; BLV; CAW; CoBE; GTBS-W; GTIV; JKCP; LBBV; LiTB; LiTG; LiTM (rev. ed.); MBP; MoBrPo; OBMV; PoLi; POTT; PoVP; TIP; ViP; ViPP; VLEP; WHA
"Ardour of red flame is thine, The," *sel.* LO
Dark Angel and I met as the long hand was vertical, The. Night Attack. Donald M. Woodruff. TwCaPo
Dark angel of the night, you come on folded wings. Dark Angel. Elizabeth Bartlett. NePoAm-2
Dark Angel, with thine aching lust. The Dark Angel. Lionel Johnson. ACP; BLV; CAW; CoBE; GTBS-W; GTIV; JKCP; LBBV; LiTB; LiTG; LiTM (rev. ed.); MBP; MoBrPo; OBMV; PoLi; POTT; PoVP; TIP; ViP; ViPP; VLEP; WHA
Dark Arabian woman of the dream, The. Don Juan's Dream. Edward Davison. MuM
Dark as a bell that, from the mist-hung tower. Bell-Birds. Benjamin F. Musser. SaFP
Dark as the clouds of even. The Black Regiment. George Henry Boker. GN; HBV; LPS-2; PAH; PAP
Dark Blot, The. Gérard de Nerval, *tr. fr. French by* Richmond Lattimore. AnFP
(Black Dot, The, *tr. by* Alan Conder.) TrFP
Dark blue crest in the azure skies, A. Mount Alvernia. H. E. G. Rope. SaFP
Dark Brother, The. Lewis Alexander. CDC
Dark brown is the river. Where Go the Boats? Robert Louis Stevenson. AlDL; BoChLi; FaBoBe; FaBoCh; GoBP; LoGBV; MPB; PRWS; RAR; StVeCh (1940 ed.); SUS; TiPo
Dark Cat, The. Audrey Alexandra Brown. CaP
Dark Cavalier, The. Margaret Widdemer. HBMV; NV; PFY; SBMV
Dark Chamber, The. Louis Untermeyer. LoPS; MAP; MoAmPo; TBM; TOP; WHA
Dark Château, The. Walter de la Mare. POTT
Dark cloud raged, The. Thunder Shower. Hilda Conkling. NP
Dark clouds gather around my path, The. Faith. John Gould Fletcher. ChMo; CMP
Dark-coated men with instruments. The Boston Symphony Orchestra. James Fenimore Cooper. POT; PoTo
Dark confusion now is done, The. Dawn. Paul Valéry. TrFP
Dark Cup, The, *sel.* Sara Teasdale.
May Day. CP; MM
Dark Danny. Ivy O. Eastwick. BrR; FaPON; TiPo
Dark, dark lay the drifters against the red West. Kilmeny. Alfred Noyes. EnLit; POT
Dark Day, A. Dante Gabriel Rossetti. The House of Life, LXVIII. PoVP; ViPo
Dark, deep and cold the current flows. Plaint [*or* The Land Which No One Knows]. Ebenezer Elliott. HBV; MeRV; OBEV; OBVV; TriL
Dark demon angel, by royal right. Black Cat in Prunus-Tree. Joseph Braddock. PoC
Dark, dim centuries at last shall cease, The. The Dead Earth. Arthur M. Sampley. *Fr.* Fragments of Eternity. MuM
Dark Eleanor and Henry sat at meat. The Rose of the World. John Masefield. PoRA
Dark, elusive shadow, A. Shadows. Arthur J. Peel. MoSiPe
Dark eyed,/ O woman of my dreams. Dance Figure. Ezra Pound. AnAmPo; ChMo; CMP; CoAnAm; CoV; LA; MAP; MoAB; MoAmPo; NP; ReMP; TwAmPo
Dark-eyed Canaller. *Unknown. See* Dark-eyed Sailor, The.
Dark-eyed Gentleman, The. Thomas Hardy. MBP; MoAB; MoBrPo
Dark-eyed Lad Columbus. Nancy Byrd Turner. SiSoSe
Dark-eyed Sailor, The, *with music. Unknown.* ShS
(Dark-eyed Canaller, *with music.*) OuSiCo
Dark eyes, wonderful, strange and dear they shone. The Half Door. "Seumas O'Sullivan." AnIV
Dark fell the night, the watch was set. Alfred the Harper. John Sterling. BeLS
Dark Flower. Louis Untermeyer. PIAE
Dark Flows the River. Arthur S. Bourinot. CaP
Dark Forest, The. W. W. Gibson. ChMo; CMP
Dark forests clothe the mountain-side. Ballad. Raffi. ArmLP
Dark-fringed eyelids slowly close, The. Tucking the Baby In. Curtis May. HBV
Dark frost was in the air without. Winter Dusk. Walter de la Mare. AnEnPo; UnW
Dark Girl. Arna Bontemps. GoSl
Dark Girl by the Holy Well, The. John Keegan. TIP
Dark Girl Dressed in Blue, The. *Unknown.* BeLS
Dark Girl's Rhyme, The. Dorothy Parker. InMe
Dark Glass, The. Dante Gabriel Rossetti. The House of Life. XXXIV. BMEP; BPN; EmBrPo; EPN; HBV; LEAP; PoVP; TOP; VA; ViPo; VLEP
Dark green and seaweed-cold, the snake-bright hair. The Mermaid. A. J. M. Smith. TwCaPo
Dark green summer, with its massive hues, The. Three Sonnets, III. Hartley Coleridge. RO
Dark green truck on the cement platform, The. Train Window. Robert Finch. BoCaPo; PeCV
Dark grey o' gloamin', The. Ae Happy Hour. Alexander Laing. EBSV
Dark Hills, The. E. A. Robinson. CoBMV; CP; FaFP; GTBS-W; InP; LiTA; LiTM; MAP; MM; MoAB; MoAmPo; MOAP; NeMA; NePA; OnPM; TBM; TOP; TwP
Dark house, by which once more I stand. In Memoriam A. H. H., VII. Tennyson. BEL; BoFr; BPN; CoBE;

Dark house, by which once more I stand (*continued*) EM-2; EmBrPo; EnL; EnLi-2; EnLit; EPN; FaBoEn; GEPC; LiTB; MaPo; OAEP; PoD; PoE; PoEL-5; ReaPo; SeCeV; TwHP; UnPo; ViPo; VLEP
Dark house, dark lonely grave. The Grave. T. Gwynn Jones. LiTW
Dark House, whose door denies. Beyond. John Richard Moreland. UnW
Dark Inanimate, The. Eric Wilson Barker. UnW
Dark is kind and cozy, The. God's Dark. John Martin. MaRV
Dark is shattered, The. New Things and Old. Sister Mary Madeleva. GoBC
Dark is the face of Harriet. Harriet Tubman. Margaret Walker. PoNe
Dark is the house, the hall, the mirror silent. Garden Party. Mary Mills. NePoAm
Dark is the light of prophecy—no heavenly dews distill. Sister Margaret Bourgeoys. Thomas D'Arcy McGee. PraNu
Dark is the morning with mist; in the narrow mouth of the harbour. Elegiac. Longfellow. BAV
Dark is the sapphire night. Half-Light. Jean Percival Waddell. CaP
Dark is the stair, and humid the old walls. The Belfry. Laurence Binyon. CH
Dark Lily without blame. A Scot to Jeanne d'Arc. Andrew Lang. VA
Dark Man, The. Nora Hopper. HBV; TIP
Dark Memory, The. John Hall Wheelock. LiTL
Dark mountain has grown black, The. The Three Pipes. *Unknown.* OnPM
Dark Night of the Soul, The. St. John of the Cross. *See* Obscure Night of the Soul, The.
Dark Night, the Wild Geese Fly High. Lu Lun, *tr. fr. Chinese.* WhP
Dark Palace, The. Alice Milligan. AnIV; TIP
Dark-prowed ship through surges cleft her way, The. Theseus. Bacchylides. GrL; GrPo
Dark Rapture. "Æ." SeCePo
Dark red roses in a honeyed wind swinging. June. Nora Hopper. YeAr
Dark-red Shadow-Spots, The. Yumei Kanbara, *tr. fr. Japanese by* Yone Noguchi. LiTW
Dark Road, The. Ethel Clifford. HBV
Dark rock angered to be blown by the blast, The. Tomb [of Paul Verlaine]. Stéphane Mallarmé. AnFP
Dark Rosaleen. *Unknown, at. to* Hugh O'Donnell, *tr. fr. Late Middle Irish by* James Clarence Mangan. ACP; AnFE; AnIL; AnIV; AWP; BCEP; CH; CoBE; EnRP; ERP; EV-4; GTIV; GTML; GTSL; HBV; IrPN; JAWP; JKCP; LEAP; LiTW; LO, *abr.*; OBEV; OBVV; OnYI; OxBI; PoFr, *abr.*; TIP; VA; ViBoPo; WBP
(Little Dark Rose, The, *tr. by* Padraic Pearse.) OnYI
(Roisin Dubh, *tr. by* Eleanor Hull.) OnYI
Dark shades of sunset, The. Riding to Tsan Shih. Wei Ying-wu. PoHN
Dark Song. Edith Sitwell. *Fr.* Façade. FaBoTw
Dark suffocates the world; but such. An Autumn Park. David Gascoyne. MoPo
Dark Symphony. Melvin B. Tolson. PoNe
Dark the halls, and cold the feast. The New Wife and the Old. Whittier. APW
Dark, thinned, beside the wall of stone. In Time of Grief. Lizette Woodworth Reese. AA; ATP (1935 ed.); LBAP; PFY; TCPD
Dark to me is the earth. Dark to me are the heavens. The Desolate City. *Unknown, tr. by* Wilfrid Scawen Blunt. AWP; JKCP; MBP; MoBrPo (1942 ed.); OBEV; OBVV
Dark under Froth. W. B. Yeats. *Fr.* The Fisherman. LiA
Dark war, exploding loud mephitic mines. Some Talk of Peace. Edmund Blunden. SoV
Dark was de night an' col' was de groun'. A Group of Negro Songs. *Unknown.* NAMP
Dark was the forest, dark was the mind. The Awakening. Conrad Aiken. The Kid, VII. MoVE
Dark was the sky, and not one friendly star. Death. Philip Freneau. *Fr.* The House of Night. OnAP
Dark was thick, The. A boy he seemed at that time. The Seven Times. Thomas Hardy. VLEP
Dark Way, The. Joseph Mary Plunkett. LBBV
Dark winds of the mountain. The Last Piper. Edward J. O'Brien. BAP; SBMV
Dark Wings. James Stephens. NP
Dark Winter Is Going. James Munro, *tr. fr. Gaelic by* Nigel MacNeill. EBSV
Dark Wood, The. John Hall Wheelock. PG (1955 ed.)
Dark World, A. E. J. Scovell. MoVE
Darkened hut outlined against the sky, A. The Sunrise of the Poor. Robert Burns Wilson. AA
Darkening Garden, The. *Unknown.* BoTP
Darkening hills loom yet more near, The. At Night. Sergei Smirnov. RuPo
Darkening the azure roof of Nero's world. Domine, Quo Vadis? Sir William Watson. WGRP
Darkling Thrush, The. Thomas Hardy. AnFE; ATP (1953 ed.); BLA; BLV; BoLiVe; ChMo; CMP; CoBE; CoBMV; EmBrPo; EnL; EnLi-2 (1949 ed.); EPN; EPP; ExPo; FaFP; GTBS-W; GTML; GTSL; HBMV; InP; KN; LiTB; LiTG; LiTM; MBP; MoAB; MoBrPo; MoPo; NeMA; OAEP; OBEV (new ed.); OBVV; PG (1955 ed.); PoFS; POTE; POTT; PoVP; ReaPo; ReMP; SeCeV; ShBV-4; TCEP; TCPD; TrGrPo; TwCV; TwHP; ViP; ViPo; ViPP; VLEP; WaP
Darkly, as by some gloomèd mirror glassed. History. Sir William Watson. BMEP
Darkly their glibs o'erhang. The Fate of King Dathi. Thomas Osborne Davis. OnYI
Darkness. Peggy Bacon. BrR
Darkness. Byron. BCEP; BPN; EmBrPo; EnRP; EPN; LiTB; OAEP; PoEL-4
Darkness. James Naumburg Rosenberg. AA
Darkness and death? Nay, Pioneer, for thee. Walt Whitman. Francis Howard Williams. AA; DD; GA
Darkness and stars i' the midday! They invite. A Rhapsody. Henry Vaughan. ReEn
Darkness brings no quiet here, the light, The. The Railway Station. Archibald Lampman. CPG
Darkness comes out of the earth. Twilight. D. H. Lawrence. OBMV
Darkness crumbles away, The. Break of Day in the Trenches. Isaac Rosenberg. CoEV; FaBoMo; MoBrPo; MoP; SeCePo; ViBoPo; WaaP; WaP
Darkness encloses the concert hall. Choral Symphony Conductor. Carol Coates. CaP
Darkness' Ethiop soldiery. Dawn. Ibn Billita. MooP
Darkness Gathers, The. Hjalmar Söderberg, *tr. fr. Swedish by* Charles W. Stork. AnSL; OnPM
Darkness has called to darkness, and disgrace. As a Plane Tree by the Water. Robert Lowell. CoBMV; CrMA; GTBS-W; LiTM (rev. ed.); MoAB; MoAmPo (1950 ed.); NePA; NePoEA; OxBA; TrGrPo (rev. ed.); UnPo (3d ed.)
Darkness has dawned in the East. Choruses from Hellas. Shelley. *Fr.* Hellas. BPN; EnRP
Darkness is in the hills, the eyes perish. Wir Sind Alle Verloren. Michael Roberts. *Fr.* Elegy for the Fallen Climbers. MoP
Darkness is not dark, nor sunlight the light of the sun. Foal. Vernon Watkins. FaBoMo
Darkness Is Thinning. St. Gregory the Great, *tr. fr. Latin by* John Mason Neale. LPS-2
Darkness o'er the world is creeping. Ancient Lullaby. Gerald Griffin. IrPN
Darkness passes, The; storms shall not abide. The Day Shall Yet Be Fair. Celia Thaxter. MaRV
Darkness rolls upward, The. The Blue Symphony. John Gould Fletcher. AnAmPo; ChMo; CMP; LA; MAPA; NP; TwAmPo
Darkness steals the forms of all the queens, The. Grief. D. H. Lawrence. NP
Darkness succeeds to twilight. Lines Suggested by the Fourteenth of February. Charles Stuart Calverley. ALV
Darkness: the rain sluiced down; the mire was deep. The Redeemer. Siegfried Sassoon. WGRP
Darkness was a richness in the room, The. From a Childhood. Rainer Maria Rilke. TrJP
Darky Sunday School. *Unknown.* ABF, *with music*; OxBoLi; SiTL
Darley Dale. Clinton Scollard. PR
Darlin', *with music. Unknown.* ABF
Darling, at last my tiny lute. Ad Persephonen. Franklin P. Adams. InMe
Darling, at the Beautician's you buy. A Valentine for a Lady. Lucilius. LiTW
Darling! Because My Blood Can Sing. E. E. Cummings. InvP; OxBA
Darling Birds, The. *Unknown.* PPL
Darling Cora, *with music. Unknown.* TrAS
(Darling Corey, *diff. vers., with music.*) OuSiCo
"Darling," he said, "I never meant." Two Truths. Helen Hunt Jackson. PR
Darling, I am growing old. Silver Threads among the Gold. Eben E. Rexford. FaFP; OlF; TreF
Darling, my darling!—It was mother singing low. At Bedtime. Mariana Griswold Van Rensselaer. HBMV
Darling, my heart I gave to thee. Good Night. Sana'i. PeP
Darling Nelly Gray. B. R. Hanby. OlF; TrAS, *with music*; TreFS
Darling of Gods and Men, beneath the gliding stars. Lucretius. *Fr.* De Rerum Natura, I. LaP
Darling, Tell Me Yes. John Godfrey Saxe. HBV
Darling, this is good-bye. The words are ordinary. Parting. Kathleen Raine. LiTL
Darlings of June and brides of summer sun. Easter Lilies. "Susan Coolidge." EOAH

Darned Mounseer, The. W. S. Gilbert. *Fr.* Ruddigore. TSW; TSWC
Dar's a lazy, sortah hazy. Sprin' Fevah. Ray Garfield Dandridge. BANP
Dar's a poe-ful rassle 'twixt de good and de bad. Time Goes by Turns. Joel Chandler Harris. *Fr.* Uncle Remus, His Songs and His Sayings. IHA
Dar's a shakin' an' er achin' amongst dese old bones. I Kilt er Cat. Virginia Frazer Boyle. CIV
D'Artagnan's Ride. Gouverneur Morris. AA
Dartmouth Winter-Song. Richard Hovey. AA
Dartsiae. Charles Kingsley. AlDL
Darweesh, The. Sadi, *tr. fr. Persian by* Sir Edwin Arnold. PeP
Darwin. Mortimer Collins. LPS-3
Darwin and Mendel laid on man the chains. Progress. David McCord. ImOP
Darwinian Ballad, A. *Unknown.* BOHV
Darwinism. Agnes Mary Frances Robinson. VA
Darwinism in the Kitchen. *Unknown.* FiBHP
Darwinity. Herman C. Merivale. BOHV; InMe; NA
Da's All Right, Baby, *with music.* *Unknown.* ABF
Das Ewig-Weibliche (The Eternal Feminine). James Russell Lowell. TCAP; TriL
Dash Back. Tennyson. LiTG; SiTL
Dash for the Colors, The. Frederick G. Webb. BeLS
Dash of rain on the pavement, A. Spring in Oxford Street. "John Presland." VOD
Dashing through [*or* thro'] the snow in a one-horse open sleigh. Jingle Bells. James S. Pierpont. FaFP; OlF; TreF; YaD
Dat Lonesome Stream, *with music.* *Unknown.* ABF
Dat nigger fum Shiloh. Pick a Bale o' Cotton. *Unknown.* ABF
Dat Ol' Mare o' Mine. Paul Laurence Dunbar. MW
Dat ol' Possum in de tree, he is waitin' jes to see. Dey Don' Know. Leigh Richmond Miner. BOL
Dat prodjeckin' son wuz de beatenest chap. De Prodjeckin' Son. Booth Lowrey. IHA
Dat Sunshine Special comin' around de bend. C. C. Rider. *Unknown.* AS
Data for Accreditation. Sister Mary Maura. JKCP (1955 ed.)
Dates. *Unknown, tr. fr. Arabic by* E. Powys Mathers. *Fr.* The Thousand and One Nights. AWP; FaPON; JAWP; LiTW; WBP
Dat's a mighty quare tale 'bout de appile tree. De Appile Tree. Joel Chandler Harris. IHA; TSW; TSWC
Dat's very cole an' stormy night on Village St. Mathieu. De Stove Pipe Hole. William Henry Drummond. IHA
Datur Hora Quieti. Robert Stephen Hawker. GoBC
Datur Hora Quieti. Sir Walter Scott. *See* Sun upon the Lake Is Low, The.
Dauber, *sels.* John Masefield.
"All through the windless night the clipper rolled," VI. AnFE; ChMo; CMP
Clipper Loitered South, The, *fr.* IV. EtS
Dauber Rounds Cape Horn, The, *fr.* VI. BBV
(Rounding the Horn.) EtS; MBP; MoAB; MoBrPo; NeMA; WHA
"Si talked with Dauber, standing by the side," *fr.* I. InP
Daughter at Evening, The. Robert Nathan. HBMV; TSW
Daughter, how the door is creaking. Evening Prayer. Arthur Fitger. AWP
Daughter of Admetus, A. T. Sturge Moore. FaBoTw
Daughter of Debate, The. Elizabeth, Queen of England. *See* Doubt of Future Foes, The.
Daughter of Egypt, veil thine eyes! Song. Bayard Taylor. AA; LBAP; LEAP
Daughter of Eve, A. Christina Rossetti. BPN; VLEP
Daughter of freedom-bearing Zeus. To Goddess Luck. Pindar. *Fr.* Olympian Odes, XII. GrR
Daughter of God! that sitt'st on high. Ode to Peace. William Tennant. LPS-2
Daughter of her whose face, and lofty name. Sonnets to Miranda, I. Sir William Watson. HBV
Daughter of Herodias, The. Henry Vaughan. MeRV
Daughter of Jove, relentless power. Hymn to [*or* of] Adversity. Thomas Gray. BrBE; CEP; EiPP; EnRP; EV-3; GTBS; GTBS-D; GTBS-W; GTSE; GTSL; OBEC
Daughter of Mendoza, The. Mirabeau B. Lamar. AA; HBV; HiLiAm
Daughter of Pelias, fare thee well. Praise of a Heroine. Euripides. *Fr.* Alcestis. GrR
Daughter of the ancient Eve. The After Woman. Francis Thompson. EmBrPo; ISi; TCPD
Daughter of the brightest. *Unknown.* *Fr.* Eulogistic Snatches. SiB
Daughter of the Farrier, The. *Unknown.* GoTP
Daughter of the Regiment, The. Clinton Scollard. BIG; PAH
Daughter of the Slava, The, *sel.* Jan Kollar, *tr. fr. Czech by* Edna Worthley Underwood.
"He only is worthy of freedom." PoFr
Daughter of the warrior Gileadite, The. Jephthah's Daughter. Tennyson. BHV
Daughter of Venice, fairer than the moon! To an Old Venetian Wine-Glass. Lloyd Mifflin. AA
"Daughter, thou art come to die." A Very Old Song. "William Laird." HBV
Daughter to that good Earl, once President. To the Lady Margaret Ley [*or* Two Sonnets]. Milton. ES; EV-2; GTBS; GTBS-D; GTBS-W; GTSE; GTSL; LiA; OBEV; OBS
Daughter! why roamest thou again so late. The Ancient Idyl; Europa and Her Mother. Walter Savage Landor. NBE
Daughters. William Rose Benét. FAOV
Daughters, daughters, do ye grieve? Thammuz. William Vaughn Moody. MOAP
Daughter's Love, A. William Dudley Foulke. FAOV
Daughters of Asopus, The. Corinna, *tr. fr. Greek by* C. M. Bowra. OxBG
Daughters of Atlas, The. Aeschylus, *tr. fr. Greek by* C. M. Bowra. OxBG
Daughters of Jove, whose voice is melody. Hymn to the Moon [*or* Hymn to Selene]. *Unknown.* *Fr.* Homeric Hymns. AWP; LiTW
Daughters of Philistia. Walter C. Smith. *Fr.* Olrig Grange. VA
Daughters of the Horseleech, The. Stanley Kunitz. CrMA
Daughters of the seraphim led round their sunny flocks, The. The Book of Thel [*or* The Lament of Thel]. Blake. BEL; CEP; ChER; EiPP; EnRP; Po; PoEL-4
Daughters of Time, the hypocritic Days. Days. Emerson. AA; AmPo; AmPP; AnAmPo; AnFE; AnNE; APA; APW; ATP; BAP; BLV; BoLiVe; CBOV; CoAnAm; CoBA; CoV; GTBS-W; IAP; LA; LBAP; LEAP; LiTA; MOAP; OBAV; OBVV; OnPM; OQP; OuHeWo; OxBA; PC; PFY; PIAE; Po; PoE; PoEL-4; PoeMoYo; PoFS; PoLFOT; QP-1; ReaPo; SeCeV; TrGrPo; UnPo (1st ed.); ViBoPo; WHA
Daughters of Troy, The. Euripides. *See* Trojan Women.
Daughter's Rebellion, The. Francis Hopkinson. PAH
Dauncing (bright Lady) then began to be[e]. Sir John Davies. *Fr.* Orchestra; or, A Poem of Dancing. AtBAP; FaBoEn; PoEL-2
D'Avalos' Prayer. John Masefield. *See* Prayer: "When the last sea is sailed."
Dave. J. Logie Robertson. EBSV
Dave Lilly. Joyce Kilmer. DaM; JKCP (1926 ed.); LEAP
David. Earle Birney. BoCaPo; CaP; TwCaPo; TwCV
David. Guy Butler. BoSA
David. Edmund Vance Cooke. TBM
David. Mary Carolyn Davies. HBMV
David. Walker Gibson. CrMA; NePoAm
David, Aged Four. Mildred Focht. DDA; MaRV
David and Bathsheba. Second Samuel, XI: 2–XII: 18, Bible, *O.T.* OuHeWo
(David and Uriah, the Hittite.) EM-1
David and Bethsabe, *sels.* George Peele.
"Come, gentle Zephyr, tricked with those perfumes," *fr.* sc. i. ViBoPo
"David. Bright Bethsabe shall wash in David's bower," *fr.* sc. i. LEAP
"Hot sun, cool fire, tempered with sweet air," *fr.* sc. i. ElSeCe; LO; PoEL-2; SiCE; TuPP
(Bathsheba's Song) InPo
(Bethsabe Bathing.) ElL; ExPo; LoBV; TrGrPo
(Bethsabe, Bathing, Sings.) BLV
(Bethsabe's Song.) AtBAP; ATP; CoEV; OBSC; OxBoLi; SeCeV
"Now comes my lover tripping like the roe," *fr.* sc. i. ViBoPo
"Now for the crown and throne of Israel," sc. xii. ViBoPo
David and Goliath. First Samuel, XVI, XVII: 1–51, Bible, *O.T.* TreFS
David and Goliath. John Banister Tabb. PoMa
David and I that summer cut trails on the Survey. David. Earle Birney. BoCaPo; CaP; TwCaPo; TwCV
David and Uriah, the Hittite. Second Samuel, Bible, *O.T.* *See* David and Bathsheba.
David ap Gwillam's Mass of the Birds. Padraic Colum. CAW
David. Bright Bethsabe shall wash in David's bower. George Peele. *Fr.* David and Bethsabe. LEAP
David Crockett. Donald Davidson. *Fr.* The Tall Men. SPP
David Drummond's destinie. The Coble o Cargill. *Unknown.* ESPB
David Exorcising Malzah, the Evil Spirit from the Lord. Charles Heavysege. *Fr.* Saul, a Drama. VA
David Garrick. Goldsmith. *Fr.* Retaliation. OBEC; SeCeV
David Gellatley's Song. Sir Walter Scott. *Fr.* Waverley, *ch.* 14. BSV
David Glasgow Farragut. Wallace Rice. GA
David Jazz, The. Edwin Meade Robinson. BAP; HBMV
David Livingstone. *Unknown.* MaRV
David Praiseth God for His Manifold and Marveilous Blessings. Psalms, XVIII, Bible, *O.T.* LiA

David sang to his hooknosed harp. King David. Stephen Vincent Benét. HBMV; TCPD
David Sings to Saul. Robert Browning. *See* Wild Joys of Living, The.
David, the king, was grieved and moved. David's Lamentation. William Billings. TrAS
David was a shepherd lad, beautiful as you. David. Mary Carolyn Davies. HBMV
David was a Young Blood, David was a striplin'. The David Jazz. Edwin Meade Robinson. BAP; HBMV
Davideis, *sels.* Abraham Cowley.
Annunciation, The, *fr.* II. OxBoCh
"Beneath the silent chambers of the earth," *fr.* I. SeEP
Creation, The, *fr.* I. OBS
Hell, *fr.* I. OxBoCh
"I sing the man who Judah's scepter bore," *fr.* I. SeEP
Invocation: "Awake, awake, my lyre." LPS-3
(Awake, Awake, My Lyre!) SeCL
(Music.) EV-2
(Supplication, A.) GTBS; GTBS-D; GTBS-W; GTSE; GTSL
Power of Numbers, The, *fr.* I. OBS
"Whilst thus his wrath with threats the tyrant fed," *fr.* I. SeEP
"With sober pace an heav'nly maid walks in," *fr.* II *and* III. SeCV-1
David's Epitaph on Jonathan. Francis Quarles. AEV
David's Lament. Second Samuel I: 19–27, Bible, *O.T.* ChTr (I: 17, 19–27); TrGrPo; TrJP
("Beauty of Israel is slain, The," I:19–26.) LO
(David's Lament for Saul and Jonathan.) AWP
(David's Lament over Saul and Jonathan.) ShBV-3
(How Are the Mighty Fallen.) LiTW; WaaP
(Lament over Saul.) BHV
David's Lament for Absalom, *abr.* Nathaniel P. Willis. PTA-2
David's Lament for Jonathan. Peter Abelard, *tr. fr. Latin by* Helen Waddell. LiTW
David's Lamentation, *with music.* William Billings. TrAS
David's Reconciliation with Absalom. "Michael Field." TwCV
David's Song. Robert Browning. *See* Wild Joys of Living, The.
David's Song to the Troubled King. Victor Starbuck. *Fr.* Saul, King of Israel. NoCaPo
Davis Matlock. Edgar Lee Masters. *Fr.* Spoon River Anthology. ChMo; CMP; LiTA; LiTM (rev. ed.)
Davy and the Goblin, *sels.* Charles Edward Carryl.
My Recollectest Thoughts, *fr. ch.* 7. HBV; HBVY; NA
Nautical Ballad, A, *fr. ch.* 8. FaPON; GFA; HBV; LauV; MPB; OTPC (1946 ed.); StVeCh
(Walloping Window-Blind, The.) GoTP; InMe; LBN; LiL; MoShBr; NA; TreFS; WhC
Robinson Crusoe's Story, *fr. ch.* 11. BeLS; BoChLi; BOHV; FiBHP; InMe; LEAP; MCCG; OnPP; OTPC (1946 ed.); PCD; PCN; PoRA; PoRh; TSW; TSWC
(Robinson Crusoe.) AA; HBV; HBVY; LHV; MPB
Davy Davy Dumpling. *Unknown.* OxNR
Davy Dicar's Dream. Thomas Churchyard. ReIE
Davy, the Dicer. Sir Thomas More. *Fr.* Two Short Ballettes . . . Made for His Pastime While He Was Prisoner in the Tower of London. TuPP
Dawn. "Æ." BEL
Dawn. Richard Aldington. NV
Dawn. Baudelaire, *tr. fr. French by* Edna St. Vincent Millay. WoL
Dawn. Ibn Billita, *tr. fr. Arabic by* A. J. Arberry. MooP
Dawn. Antoni Boguslawski, *tr. fr. Polish by* L. E. Gielgud. NeTW
Dawn Gordon Bottomley. *Fr.* Night and Morning Songs. BoTP; MBP; MoBrPo; NP
Dawn, The. Robert Buchanan. GTSE
Dawn. Isabel Butchart. PoMa; PoTo; VOD
Dawn. Chaucer. *See* Morning in May.
Dawn. Frances Cornford. AV; LoPS
Dawn. Miriam LeFevre Crouse. ChIP
Dawn. Louis Dudek. PeCV
Dawn. Paul Laurence Dunbar. GoSl; PoNe
Dawn. Euripides, *tr. fr. Greek. Fr.* Ion. GrR, *tr. by* A. W. Verrall; OxBG, *tr. by* C. M. Bowra
Dawn. Ernest Fewster. NeTW
Dawn. John Ford. *See* Fly Hence Shadows.
Dawn. Richard Watson Gilder. *Fr.* The New Day. LPS-2; SN
(Prelude: "Night was dark, though sometimes a faint star, The.") HBV
Dawn. Ibn Muqana, *tr. fr. Arabic by* A. J. Arberry. MooP
Dawn. Kenton Kilmer. JKCP (1955 ed.)
Dawn. George B. Logan, Jr. HBV
Dawn. "P. S. M." MCCG
Dawn, *sel.* Harold Monro.
God. WGRP
Dawn. Roselle Mercier Montgomery. LS
Dawn. "Rachel," *tr. fr. Hebrew by* Abraham M. Klein. TrJP
Dawn. Arthur Rimbaud, *tr. fr. French by* Angel Flores. AnFP
Dawn, The. W. W. E. Ross. BoCaPo
Dawn. Frederick George Scott. CaP; CPG; MaRV; OCL; UnW
Dawn. Frank Dempster Sherman. MAP
Dawn. Tanikado, *tr. fr. Japanese by* Lois J. Erickson. SoLD
Dawn ("By a bank as I lay"). *Unknown.* OBSC
Dawn, The ("One morning I rose and looked upon the world"). *Unknown.* PoToHe (new ed.)
Dawn. Paul Valéry, *tr. fr. French by* Alan Conder. TrFP
Dawn. William Carlos Williams. MAP; MoAB; MoAmPo; MOAP
Dawn, The. W. B. Yeats. MaPo; MoVE; NP
Dawn—and a magical stillness: on earth, quiescence profound. Dawn on the Headland. Sir William Watson. HBV
Dawn and Dark. Norman Gale. BMEP; HBV; TSW; TSWC; VA
Dawn: and foot on the cold stair treading. Aubade for Hope. Robert Penn Warren. MAP; MoAmPo
Dawn and Night. John Gay. *Fr.* A Contemplation on Night. BeR
Dawn—and one head-print on the pillow. Solitaire. John Zollie Howard. CAG
Dawn; and the jew's-harp's sawing seesaw song. Pilots, Man Your Planes. Randall Jarrell. MoAB; MoAmPo (1950 ed.)
Dawn—and the mist across the silent lane. A Hillside Farmer. John Farrar. HBMV
Dawn-Angels. Agnes Mary Frances Robinson. HBV; VA
Dawn at Flying-Fish Point. Clement B. Christesen. BoAu
Dawn at Liverpool. Archibald T. Strong. *Fr.* Sonnets of the Empire. BoAu
Dawn at the Rain's Edge. Joseph Auslander. MAP; MoAmPo (1942 ed.)
Dawn breeze, The. Sand Paintings. Alice Corbin. AnAmPo; LA; NP
Dawn came in through the bars of the blind, The. Triumph. H. C. Bunner. OBAV
Dawn came wild with rain, and all day long, The. Moonlight on Lake Sydenham. Wilson MacDonald. CaP
Dawn drives the dreams away, yet some abide. Omnia Somnia. Rosamund Marriott Watson. HBV
Dawn, first gleaming ashy gold, The. Rain in the Hills. Charles Buxton Going. VOD
Dawn from the foretop! Dawn from the barrel! The Ice-Floes. E. J. Pratt. CaP; OCL
Dawn has blossomed: the sun is nigh. Moods. Edward Rowland Sill. BTP
Dawn Has Yet to Ripple In. Melville Cane. MAP; MoAmPo
(Before Dawn.) PIAE
Dawn in Besieged Leningrad. Vera Inber, *tr. fr. Russian by* Jack Lindsay. RuPo
Dawn in Britain, The, *sels.* Charles M. Doughty.
Bladyn's Song of Cloten. PoEL-5
Druids' Hymn to the Sun. FaBoTw
Gauls Sacrifice Their Prisoners, The. FaBoTw
Roman Officer Writes Home, A. FaBoTw
Dawn in Inishtrahull. D. J. O'Sullivan. OnYI
Dawn in London. Nikolai Tikhonov, *tr. fr. Russian by* Jack Lindsay. RuPo
Dawn in the Cockloft. José Juan Tablada, *tr. fr. Spanish by* Samuel Beckett. AnMP
Dawn in the Desert. Clinton Scollard. POT; PoTo
Dawn in the Everglades. Halle W. Warlow. BLA
Dawn in the Town. *Unknown, tr. fr. Spanish by* R. Selden Rose *and* Leonard Bacon. *Fr.* The Cid. TeCS
Dawn is a/ slugger. Improvisation III. Harold Silverman. TwCaPo
Dawn is comin', callin', The. Forest Boat Song. Richard Clyde Ford. IHA
Dawn is dense with twitter. Wings at Dawn. Joseph Auslander. BAP; HBMV
Dawn is lonely for the sun, The. Chanson de Rosemonde. Richard Hovey. HBV
Dawn is rising bright and clear. Dawn. Ibn Muqana. MooP
Dawn is smiling on the dew that covers, The. The Genesis of Butterflies. Victor Hugo. AWP; JAWP; WBP
Dawn of a bright June morning. Mass of Love. *Unknown.* LiTW; TeCS
Dawn of a pleasant morning in May. Lee to the Rear. John Reuben Thompson. BlG; GA; MC; MDAH; PaA; PAH; SPP
Dawn of Day. William Browne. *Fr.* The Shepherd's Pipe. ElL
Dawn of Love, The. James I, King of Scotland. *Fr.* The Kingis Quare. EBSV
(Walking under the Tour.) SeCePo
Dawn of my intelligence, The. Wages. Ibn Kharuf. MooP
Dawn of Peace, The. Alfred Noyes. *Fr.* The Wine Press: Epilogue. MaRV; QS
Dawn of the Century. Anna H. Thorne. *See* Peace Universal.

Dawn of the everlasting day, The. Prayer. E. F. Benson. *Fr.* The Image in the Sand. PC
Dawn of the Golden Age. Virgil. *See* Fourth Eclogue, The.
Dawn of Womanhood. Harold Monro. HBV
Dawn of Woman's Day, The. Euripides, *tr. fr. Greek by* R. C. Trevelyan. *Fr.* Medea. GrR
(Chorus: "Upward and back to their fountains the sacred rivers are stealing," *tr. by* Arthur S. Way.) PoFr
(Shifting Fortune, *tr. by* F. L. Lucas.) OxBG
Dawn off the Foreland—the young flood making. Mine Sweepers. Kipling. ShBV-4
Dawn on Lake Katrine. Sir Walter Scott. *Fr.* The Lady of the Lake, III. EV-4
Dawn on Mid-Ocean. John Hall Wheelock. EtS
Dawn on the East Coast. Alun Lewis. FaBoMo
Dawn on the Headland. Sir William Watson. HBV
Dawn on the Lievre, The. Archibald Lampman. CaP; OCL
Dawn on the Somme. Robert Nichols. POTE
Dawn on the Wall-Head There. Archibald MacLeish. *Fr.* Conquistador, Bk. 13. AtBAP
Dawn over the Mountains. Tu Fu, *tr. fr. Chinese by* Kenneth Rexroth. OnPC
Dawn Patrol; Chicago. Richard V. Durham. GoSl
Dawn peered through the pines as we dashed at the ford. Riding with Kilpatrick. Clinton Scollard. PAH
Dawn shakes the candle, shoots a flame. May It Be. Boris Pasternak. BoRS; TrJP
Dawn Shall over Lethe Break. Hilaire Belloc. MM
(On a Sleeping Friend.) POTE
Dawn Song. Dietmar von Aist, *tr. fr. German by* O. L. Oliver. LyMA
Dawn Song. Ibn Sa'id of Alcala la Real, *tr. fr. Arabic by* A. J. Arberry. MooP
Dawn Song—Pachayachachi's Gate. A. S. Davis, Jr. CAG
Dawn Song—St. Patrick's Day. Violet Alleyn Storey. YeAr
Dawn-Song to Waken the Lovers. *Unknown, tr. fr. Latin by* Helen Waddell. LiTW
Dawn squall raking the harbour, an east wind's whistle. Trawlers. Hilton Brown. NeTW
Dawn talks to Day [*or* to-day]. The Day of Love. William Morris. *Fr.* Love Is Enough. AtBAP; BPN
Dawn that disheartens the desolate dunes. Quaeritur. Kipling. PA
Dawn, The; the birds'. The Dawn. W. W. E. Ross. BoCaPo
Dawn turned on her purple pillow. A December Day [*or* Winter Solstice]. Sara Teasdale. BoChLi; PoRL; YeAr; YT
Dawn upon dawn goes by,—one day there'll come. Omnes Eodem Cogimur. Ammianus. OxBG
Dawn was apple-green, The. Green. D. H. Lawrence. MBP; MoBrPo; MoP; NeMA; NP; TCEP
Dawn was on the mountains, The. Ballad of Coronado's Quest. Jessie Wilmore Murton. MuM
Dawn Wind, The. Kipling. POT; PoTo
Dawndrizzle ended, dampness steams. Anglosaxon Street. Earle Birney. BoCaPo
Dawne to darke. Lines for a Sundial. Thomas Herbert Warren. OBVV
Dawning, The. Henry Vaughan. CAW; EV-2; MePo; MeRV; OxBoCh; ReEn; TrPWD, *abr.*
Dawning o' the Year. The. Mary Elizabeth McGrath Blake. AA; LBAP
Dawning of the Day, The. James Clarence Mangan. GoBC; TIP
Dawning of the Day, The. *Unknown, tr. fr. Modern Irish by* Edward Walsh. OnYI; TIP
Dawns. Alfred Kreymborg. MAP
Dawn's Awake, The. Otto Leland Bohahan. BANP
Dawns leaden day: a grey. In Jerusalem. *Unknown.* StJW
Daw's Dinner. Joyce Kilmer. CAW
Dawson City mining man lay dying in the ice, A. Just from Dawson. *Unknown.* ABF
Day, The. George M. Brady. NeIP
Day, The. Witter Bynner. PGD; PoFr
Day, A. Emily Dickinson. *See* I'll tell you how the sun rose.
Day, A. Verner von Heidenstam, *tr. fr. Swedish by* Charles W. Stork. AnSL
Day. Sir Cecil Spring-Rice. BoTP
Day, A. William L. Stidger. PoToHe
Day. Jones Very. AnNE; APW
Day!/ Faster and more fast. Pippa Passes. Robert Browning. AlDL, *sel.*; BPN; EmBrPo; GEPC; GTSL, *sel.*; NLK, *sel.*; OQP, *sel.*; PoVP; QP-2, *sel*; SN, *sel.*; ViPP; VLEP
Day, a night, an hour of sweet content, A. Content. Thomas Campion. OBSC
Day; a Pastoral. John Cunningham. OBEC
Evening, *sel.* EnSW
Day After, A. Bedros Tourian, *tr. fr. Armenian by* Zabelle C. Boyajian. ArmLP
Day after Day. Rabindranath Tagore. Gitanjali; LXXV. OBMV
Day after day/ In vain we labor. Nature and Man. Wang Wei. PcP
Day after day/ The muffled shuttling of Her blood. Our Lady's Labor. John Duffy. ISi
Day after day/ I have climbed the hill. To My Mother. Hsing Ch'e. PoHN
Day after day and far into the night. Galatea to Pygmalion. Leonora Clawson Stryker. MuM
Day after day, for her, the sun. The Difference. Mark Van Doren. MOAP
Day after day her nest she moulded. The Swallow's Nest. Sir Edwin Arnold. OTPC (1946 ed.); PRWS
Day after day, O Lord of my life, shall I stand. Day after Day. Rabindranath Tagore. Gitanjali, LXXV. OBMV
Day after day of ceaseless rain. Flood. Tamiko Yamamuro. SoLD
Day after day of this azure May. Sunday at Hampstead, XI. James Thomson. EmBrPo
Day after day, thro' following night on night. The Ship and the Sea. B. E. Baughan. AnNZ
Day after day you who are as free as air. To a Blue Tit. V. H. Friedlaender. BLA
Day agone, as I rode sullenly, A. Dante. *Fr.* La Vita Nuova. AWP
Day and Dark. George Cabot Lodge. AnAmPo; AnFE; APA; CoAnAm; LA
Day and Night. Lewis Alexander. CDC
Day and Night. Helena Coleman. CPG
Day and Night. Victor Daley. BoAu
Day and Night. James Stephens. BoTP
Day and night are never weary. Greek Epigram. Ezra Pound. MAP; MoAB; MoAmPo; NeMA
Day and night I wander widely through the wilderness of thought. God. Gamaliel Bradford. MaRV; QS; WGRP
Day and Night My Thoughts Incline. Richard Henry Stoddard. *See* Jar, The.
Day and Night Songs. William Allingham. VA
("These little songs.") LEAP
Day and night, steeped in sterile study. Our Torah. Joseph Eliyia. MoGP
Day and the Work, The. Edwin Markham. OQP; PEDC; PSO; QP-1
Day and then a week passed by, A. The Cardinal Bird. William Davis Gallagher. AA; BLA; HiLiAm; SN
Day arrives of the autumn fair, The. The Sheep Fair. Thomas Hardy. NV
Day assembles through a broken sky, The. The Winter Flood. Pearce Young. PtPa
Day at the Farm, A. "L. J." BoTP
Day-Bed, The. Richard Eberhart. FiMAP
Day before April, The. Mary Carolyn Davies. BoTP; FaPON; GaP; LEAP; SBMV; SP; SUS; TiPo (1952 ed.)
Day before Christmas. Marchette Chute. ChBR
Day began with dismal doubt, The. *Unknown.* PoToHe (new ed.)
Day begins to droop, The. Winter Nightfall. Robert Bridges. GTBS-D; MBP; MM; MoAB; MoBrPo; NeMA; OBEV; PoVP
Day Breaks, The. Thomas Curtis Clark. ChIP
Day breaks on England down the Kentish hills. The Dying Patriot. James Elroy Flecker. EV-5; HBMV; LBBV; NV; POTT; ViBoPo; VOD (1931 ed.)
Day, brittle with ice, The. First Flight. Carol Coates. BoCaPo (1943 ed.)
Day by Day. Julia Harris May. BLRP; MaRV
Day by day,/ Dear Lord. Prayer for the New Year. Richard of Chichester. PraP
Day by day I float my paper boats one by one down the running stream. Paper Boats. Rabindranath Tagore. AlDL; FaPON; MCCG; PCH; RAR; SP
Day by day the manna fell. Daily Bread. *Unknown.* BePJ
Day by day the organ-builder in his lonely chamber wrought. The Legend of the Organ-Builder. Julia C. R. Dorr. BeLS; BLPA; FaBoBe; PTA-1
Day came slow, till five o'clock, The. Emily Dickinson. AmPo; AmPP
Day Closes, The. Carlton Talbott. ALV
Day Comes. Tu Fu, *tr. fr. Chinese by* Chi Hwang Chu *and* Edna Worthley Underwood. OnPM
Day comes. Perturbation at Dawn. Ibn Maatuk. LiTW
Day Dawn of the Heart. Mary T. Lathrop. ChIP; PGD
Day dawned. Bright tongues of scarlet flame. Morning. Harotune Toumanian. ArmLP
Day dawned; within a curtained room. History of a Life. "Barry Cornwall." LPS-3
Day departs this upper air. Song. Edward Coote Pinkney. MOAP; SPP
Day does not come with violence. Deer in Aspens. Kay De-Bard Hall. GoYe
Day Dream. *See* Daydream.
Day ends:/ Breasting the North. Day's End. Toyohiko Kagawa. GrCo-2; MaRV
Day for Wandering, A. Clinton Scollard. CP; NV
Day goeth bold in cloth of gold. Day and Night. Victor Daley. BoAu

Day grows brief, The; the afternoon is slanting. Life's Forest Trees. Ella Wheeler Wilcox. ADAH
Day grows hot, and darts his rays, The. Noon Quatrains. Charles Cotton. LoBV
Day had awakened all the things that be. Daybreak. Shelley. GN
Day had been a calm and sunny day, The. Winter. Bryant. LPS-2
Day hangs its light between two dusks, my heart. In the Dusk. Francis Ledwidge. VOD
Day has barred her windows close, and gangs wi' quiet feet. East Coast Lullaby. Lady Anne Lindsay. BOL; EtS
Day has her star, as well as Night. The Two Stars. W. H. Davies. ChMo; CMP; MBP; MoBrPo
Day has lengthened into eve, The. The Twilight of Thanksgiving. William D. Kelly. TOAH
Day! I lament that none can hymn thy praise. Day. Jones Very. AnNE; APW
Day I rode through Devonshire, The. Beneath Such Rains. James E. Warren, Jr. ChIP
Day in, day out. Corner Boys. Bryan MacMahon. OnYI
Day in Ireland, A. *Tr. fr. Irish by* Michael Cavanagh. AnIV; GTIV
Day in June, A. James Russell Lowell. *See* June.
Day, in Melting Purple Dying. Maria Gowen Brooks. *See* Song of Egla.
Day in Sussex, A. Wilfrid Scawen Blunt. PoeT
Day in the Pamfili Doria, A. Harriet Beecher Stowe. LPS-2
Day is a Negro, The. Day and Night. Lewis Alexander. CDC
Day is cold, and dark, and dreary, The. The Rainy Day. Longfellow. AnNE; AWP; BoPo; HBV; IAP; InPo; LPS-1; MaRV; MOAP; MW; NeHB; PTA-2
Day Is Coming, The. Sir Walter Besant. CenHV
Day Is Coming, The. William Morris. BMEP; BPN; EmBrPo; EnLi-2; OAEP; POTT; PoVP; ViPo; VLEP; WGRP
Day is coming near when trees, The. Christmas-Trees. Kenneth Grahame. CBPC
Day is curl'd about agen, The. An Anniversary. Richard Lovelace. LoBV
Day is dark, The. Sehnsucht; or, What You Will. "Corinna." FiBHP; InMe
Day is dark and the night, The. The Cloud Confines. Dante Gabriel Rossetti. BEL; EmBrPo; EnLi-2; TCEP; TOP; VLEP
Day Is Dead. Augusta Davies Webster. VA
Day Is Done, The, *parody.* Phoebe Cary. ALV; BOHV; PA
Day Is Done, The. Longfellow. AmPP (4th ed.); AnAmPo; AnNE; APW; BAP; BLPA; BLV; BTP; CaAE; CoBA; FaBoBe; FaFP; HBV; IAP; LA; LEAP; MaRV, *abr.;* MCCG; MOAP; NeHB; NLK (1947 ed.); OHFP; OuHeWo; OxBA; PCD; PG; PIR; PoRA; PreP; PYM; StaSt; TreF; TrGrPo; TSWC; TVSH
"Come, read to me some poem," *sel.* YT
Day is done, The. Evening Hymn. Elizabeth Madox Roberts. TiPo
Day is done, The. Returning. Ch'en Fu. PoHN
Day is done, night comes down, The. Run, Nigger, Run! *Unknown.* ABF
Day is done, the winter sun, The. At Castle Wood. Emily Brontë. ViBoPo; VLEP
Day is drawing to its fall, A. First Sight of Her and After. Thomas Hardy. PoEL-5
Day Is Dying. "George Eliot." *Fr.* The Spanish Gipsy. LPS-2
Day Is Dying in the West. Mary A. Lathbury. OIF; WGRP
Day is ended, The. Ere I sink to sleep. All's Well [*or* An Evening Prayer]. Harriet McEwen Kimball. AA; PraP
Day is ending; night is falling. Lullaby. John White Chadwick. BOL
Day Is Gone, The. Keats. EnRP; PeBoSo
Day is great and strong, The. World without Peculiarity. Wallace Stevens. CoV
Day is here! Day is here, is here! Daylight. *Tr. by* Natalie Barnes. MPB
Day is ours together, The. Full Moon. Galway Kinnell. NePoAm-2
Day is over, Mother, see, The. Compline. Patrick F. Kirby. GoBC
Day is quenched, and the sun is fled, The. A Song of Doubt. Josiah Gilbert Holland. WGRP
Day is set did earth adorn, The. Ode. Charles Cotton. ElSeCe
Day is stealing down the west. Lullaby. Florence Earle Coates. BOL
Day is the children's friend. The Prejudice against the Past. Wallace Stevens. LiTM (rev. ed.)
Day is tired with idleness and awe, The. Solstice. Charles Weekes. GTIV; OnYI
Day Lady Died, The. Frank O'Hara. NeAP
Day like a respectable woman went, The. Carnival. J. R. Hervey. AnNZ
Day like any Russian day, A. None Knew. "Demyan Bedny." RuPo
Day, like our souls, is fiercely dark. Battle Song. Ebenezer Elliot. BCEP; EV-4; LH; OBEV (1st ed.); OBRV
Day Lost, A. Gertrude Stein. AtBAP
Day of Atonement, The, *sel.* Joseph Leiser.
Kol Nidra. AA; TrJP
Day of Battle, The. A. E. Housman. A Shropshire Lad, LVI. ChMo; CMP; OHIP; PoVP; WaaP
Day of Christ, the day of God, The. Thy Glorious Face Above. Charles Wesley. BePJ
Day of Cold Food, The. Li Ch'ing-chao, *tr. fr. Chinese by* Kenneth Rexroth. OnPC
Day of Coming Days, The. Lionel Johnson. POTT
Day of Days, The. William Morris. BPN; PoVP
Day of Days, The. *Unknown.* PEOR
Day of Doom, The, *abr.* Michael Wigglesworth. TCAP
Sels.
Damnation of the Infants. APW
Heathen and the Infants, The. AmPP (3d ed.)
Infants' Petition, The. AnNE
Men of Good Works. AmPP
Sounding of the Last Trump. TCAP
(Summons, The.) APW
Day of glory! Welcome day! The Fourth of July. John Pierpont. AnNE; DD; HH; MC; OTPC (1946 ed.); PAH; PEOR; PoRL; YeAr
Day of golden beauty, A! A Day of the Indian Summer. Sarah Helen Whitman. TOAH
Day of Inverlochy, The. Iain Lom, *tr. fr. Gaelic.* GoTS
Day of Joy, The. Lucy Larcom. HH
Day of joy, A, a holiday! On Lincoln's Birthday. John Kendrick Bangs. HH
Day of Judgement [*or* Judgment], The. Swift. BeR; CEP; EiPP; FaBoEn
(On the Day of Judgement.) NBE
(On the World.) AnIV
Day of Judgement [*or* Judgment], The. Isaac Watts. BCEP; CEP; CoEV; EiPP; EV-3; LoBV; OBEV; SeCePo; TriL
Day of Judgement, The. Edward Young. OxBoCh
Day of Judgment, The. Dugald Buchanan, *tr. fr. Gaelic.* GoTS
Day of Judgment, The. Thomas of Celano. *See* Dies Irae.
Day of Liberty, The. Shelley. *Fr.* Prometheus Unbound, III, iv. EPN
Day of Love, The. William Morris. *Fr.* Love Is Enough. BPN
("Dawn talks to-day.") AtBAP
Day of Love, A. Dante Gabriel Rossetti. The House of Life, XVI. PoVP; ViPo
Day of Love, The, *abr.* Shelley. *Fr.* Prometheus Unbound, IV. EPN
("Snow upon my lifeless mountains, The.") NBE
Day of my life! Where can she get? Good-Night, Babette! Austin Dobson. BMEP; BPN; HBV; OBVV; POTT; PoVP; VA
Day of My Profession, The. Sister Mary Christina. PraNu
Day of Resurrection, The. St. John of Damascus, *tr. fr. Greek by* John Mason Neale. MaRV; OIF
(Resurrection, *st.* 1.) PGD
Day of sorrows, dreadful day. Dies Irae. Thomas of Celano. LaP
Day of Sunshine, A. Longfellow. TCAP
Day of tender memory, A. Memorial Day. Emma A. Lent. OQP; PSO; QP-1; WBLP
Day of the Circus Horse, The. T. A. Daly. RIS; TSWC; UTS
Day of the Indian Summer, A. Sarah Helen Whitman. TOAH
Day of the king most righteous. The Day of Wrath. St. Columcille. OxBI
Day of the Lord, The, *sel.* Charles Kingsley.
"Day of the Lord is at hand, The." BMEP
Day of the Slaves, The. Leonard Bacon. PoFr
Day of These Days. Laurie Lee. AtBAP; FaBoMo; MoVE
Day of vengeance, without morrow! Dies Irae. Thomas of Celano, *tr. by* John A. Dix. LPS-2
Day of Victory, The. Rachel Capen Schauffler. EOAH
Day of Wrath, The. St. Columcille, *tr. fr. Latin by* Helen Waddell. OxBI
Day of wrath, that day of burning. Dies Irae. Thomas of Celano, *tr. by* Abraham Coles. AA; CAW; HBV
Day [*or* That day] of wrath, that dreadful day, The. The Day of Judgment [*or* On the Day of Judgement]. Thomas of Celano, *tr. by* the Earl of Roscommon. BeR; TriL; WGRP
Day of wrath, the years are keeping. Dies Irae. Thomas of Celano, *tr. by Swinburne.* LiA; LiTW; LyMA
Day Returns, The. Burns. HBV
(Day Returns, My Bosom Burns, The.) LPS-1
Day Returns, My Natal Day, The. Walter Savage Landor. BPN; EmBrPo
(Lyrics and Epigrams, VII.) ERP
Day set on Norham's castled steep. Norham Castle. Sir Walter Scott. *Fr.* Marmion, I. LPS-2

Day Shall Yet Be Fair, The. Celia Thaxter. MaRV
Day she visited the dissecting room, The. Two Views of a Cadaver Room. Sylvia Plath. GoYe
Day slipped out of the web of her fog-wet gown. By Stubborn Stars. Kenneth Leslie. BoCaPo
Day-Star in the East, The. Helen Hunt Jackson. CV
Day-stars! that ope your eyes at morn to twinkle. Hymn to the Flowers. Horace Smith. LPS-2
Day that ends the world will be the one, The. Like a Whisper. Ethan Ayer. GoYe
Day That I Have Loved. Rupert Brooke. BEL; GTSL
Day that I was christened, The. Godmother. Dorothy Parker. PoRA
Day That Is Boundless as Youth, A. Laurence Binyon. PtOT
Day that my dear came to us, The. Early Mornings. *Unknown.* AS
Day That Was That Day, The. Amy Lowell. ChMo; CMP
Day that Youth had died, The. The Funeral of Youth: Threnody. Rupert Brooke. FaBoTw; SeCeV
Day the big tree went, The. The Tree. Pat Wilson. AnNZ
Day the Christ-child's tender eyes, The. His Birthday. May Riley Smith. SDH
Day the house and night the street. Through an Embrace. Paul Eluard. LiTW
Day the wind is white shall I be free, The. Apostasy. Mary Mills. NePoAm
Day the wind was hardly, A. Letter VI. W. S. Graham. ChMP
Day the Winds, The. Josephine Miles. FiMAP
Day Thou gavest, Lord, is ended, The. Evening. John Ellerton. PraP
Day to dream, A. Fishing. Edgar A. Guest. NLK
Day unfolds like a lotus bloom, The. Sunrise in the Hills of Satsuma. Mary McNeil Fenollosa. AA
Day was breaking. The Leper. Nathaniel Parker Willis. LPS-2; WGRP
Day was here when it was his to know, The. The New Tenants. E. A. Robinson. NP
Day was hot and the sun beat down, The. To a Nun Decorated with the Iron Cross. J. Corson Miller. PraNu
Day was hot, The. The forests were on fire. The Monkey. Vladislav Felitsyanovich Khodasevich. TrRV
Day was lingering in the pale northwest, The. Twilight. Charles Heavysege. VA
Day was long, the burden I had borne, The. Someone Had Prayed. Grace Noll Crowell. PraP
Day was nothing until this, A. A Letter. John Malcolm Brinnin. LoPS; TwAmPo
Day was one of weariness, The. The Beggar. Margaret E. Bruner. PoToHe
Day was set to a beautiful theme, The. The Dragon-Fly. Jessie B. Rittenhouse. POT; PoTo
Day Well Spent, A. "George Eliot." *See* Count That Day Lost.
Day when Charmus ran with five, The. A Mighty Runner. E. A. Robinson. Variations of Greek Themes, II. MOAP
Day Will Bring Some Lovely Thing, The. Grace Noll Crowell. TiPo (1952 ed.)
Day Will Come, The. Marion Strobel. TBM
Day will come, The: our sufferings will be. Ilya Ehrenburg, *tr. fr. Russian by* Y. Hornstein. BoRS
Day will dawn, when one of us shall harken, The. One of Us Two. Ella Wheeler Wilcox. PoToHe
Day Will Not Come, The. Aasmund Olafsson Vinje, *tr. fr. Norwegian by* Charles W. Stork. AnNoLy
Day will return with a fresher boon. A Song of Faith. Josiah Gilbert Holland. *Fr.* Bitter-sweet. WGRP
Day will soon be gone, The. Fujiwara no Michinobu. *Fr.* Hyaku-Nin-Isshu. AWP; JAWP; WBP
Day with sky so wide, A. The Motion of the Earth. Norman Nicholson. ImOP
Day with the Foreign Legion, A. Reed Whittemore. NePoEA
Day You Went, The. Beatrice Ravenel. BAP
Daybreak. Walter de la Mare. AlDL
Daybreak. John Donne. *See* Break of Day.
Daybreak. Ibn Burd, *tr. fr. Arabic by* A. J. Arberry. MooP
Daybreak. Longfellow. AnNE; APW; BoTP; HBV; LPS-2; MOAP; PIR; SN; WaKn
Daybreak. Shelley. GN
Daybreak. Samuel F. Smith. *See* Morning Light Is Breaking, The.
Daybreak. Stephen Spender. LiTL; POTE
Daybreak. Louis Untermeyer. NV
Daybreak Call, The. Gwendolen Haste. PFE
Daybreak in a Garden. Siegfried Sassoon. BoTP
Daybreak in the City. Callimachus, *tr. fr. Greek by* T. F. Higham. OxBG
Daybreak upon the hills. Peace. Adeline D. T. Whitney. PAH
Daybreakers, The. Arna Bontemps. CDC; GoSl; PoNe
Day Dream, A. Emily Brontë. UnW
Day-Dream, The, *sels.* Tennyson.
Departure, The. LPS-1; TriL
Revival, The. LPS-1
(Sleeping Beauty, The, II. The Fairy Prince's Arrival.) CG
Sleeping Beauty, The. LPS-1
(Sleeping Beauty, The, I. The Magic Sleep.) CG
Daydream. A. S. J. Tessimond. SeCePo
Day-Dreamer. *Unknown, ad. fr. German by* Louis Untermeyer. TiPo
(Proverbs.) RIS
Daydreams. Chang Chung Su, *tr. fr. Chinese by* Henry H. Hart. PoHN
Day Dreams. Tso Ssu, *tr. fr. Chinese by* Arthur Waley. TrCh
Day Dreams, or Ten Years Old. Margaret Johnson. BLPA
Daylight. *Tr. fr. Pawnee Indian by* Natalie Barnes. MPB
Daylight is waning, dewdrops are shining. At Sunset. Steingrimur Thorsteinsson. ICP
Daylight was down, and up the cool. Annus Mirabilis. Laurence Housman. LBBV; PoeT
Days. Karle Wilson Baker. GFA; OQP; QP-2; SBMV; SP; TiPo
Days. Emerson. AA; AmPo; AmPP; AnAmPo; AnFE; AnNE; APA; APW; ATP; BAP; BLV; BoLiVe; CBOV; CoAnAm; CoBA; CoV; GTBS-W; IAP; LA; LBAP; LEAP; LiTA; MOAP; OBAV; OBVV; OnPM; OQP; OuHeWo; OxBA; PC; PFY; PIAE; Po; PoE; PoEL-4; PoeMoYo; PoFS; PoLFOT; QP-1; ReaPo; SeCeV; TrGrPo; UnPo (1st ed.); ViBoPo; WHA
Days, The. Theodosia Garrison. BPP; HBMV
Days. Eliot Kays Stone. OQP; QP-2
Day's Affirmation. Sir Herbert Read. FaBoTw
(Inbetweentimes.) TwCV
Days after daffodils were up. Easter Snowfall. Harry Behn. TiPo (1959 ed.)
Days and Nights. T. Sturge Moore. HBMV
Days and years are the tools with which I fashion. The Secret Temple. Marjorie Allen Seiffert. BAP
Days are clear, The. Stay, June, Stay! Christina Rossetti. *Fr.* Sing-Song. RIS; TiPo; YeAr
Days are cold, the nights are long, The. The Cottager to Her Infant [*or* Cottager's Lullaby]. Dorothy Wordsworth. BOL; CH; EV-3; HBV; OTPC (1923 ed.); PRWS
Days are dead of bitter fray, of red despair and black distress, The. Memorial Day, 1898. Reginald Wright Kauffman. MDAH
Days are filled with duties, The. The Vesper Bells. Dwight Edwards Marvin. PraP
Days are sad, it is the Holy Tide, The. The Holy Tide. Frederick Tennyson. OBEV; OBVV
Day's at end and there's nowhere to go, The. More Sonnets at Christmas, II. Allen Tate. LiTA; LiTM; NePA; WaP
Days dawn on us that make amends for many. The Interpreters. Swinburne. BPN; PoEL-5
Days decay as flowers of grass, The. A Ballad of Antiquaries. Austin Dobson. POTT
Day's Demand, The. Josiah Gilbert Holland. *See* God Give Us Men.
Days drift by, The—as ships drift out to sea. In Summer. Charles Hanson Towne. HBMV
Day's End. Laurence Binyon. OBVV
Day's End. Hermann Hagedorn. *Fr.* Songs from the Rockies. VOD
Day's End. Toyohiko Kagawa, *tr. fr. Japanese by* Lois J. Erickson. GrCo-2; MaRV
Day's End. Sir Henry Newbolt. *See* End, The.
Day's Ending. Sara Teasdale. ChMo; CMP
Days go by, The. Time of Waiting. Vicente Huidobro. TwSpPo
Days Gone By, The. James Whitcomb Riley. TreF
Days grow long, the mountains, The. South Wind. Tu Fu. OnPC
Days grow short, The; but though the falling sun. The Husking [*or* The Pudding Prepared and Eaten]. Joel Barlow. *Fr.* The Hasty Pudding, III. AnNE; APW; BAV
Days grow shorter, the nights grow longer, The. Interlude [*or* Growing Old]. Ella Wheeler Wilcox. BLP; BLPA; HBV; LBAP
Day's grown old, the fainting sun, The. Evening Quatrains [*or* Evening *or* Summer Evening]. Charles Cotton. AEV; ChTr; EG; ExPo; LoBV; NBE; PoEL-3; TrGrPo
Days have slain the days, and the seasons have gone by, The. The Half of Life Gone. William Morris. EmBrPo
Days like These. Ella Elizabeth Egbert. NLK; PoMa
Day's March, The. Robert Nichols. LBBV
Day's No Rounder than Its Angles Are, The. Peter Viereck. AmP
Days of Birth. *Unknown.* MoShBr
Days of Bute and Grafton's fame, The. The Eight-Day Clock. Alfred Cochrane. HBV
Days of Forty-nine, The. *Unknown.* CoSo, *with music;* CSF, *with music;* IHA, MC; PAH

Days of My Youth. St. George Tucker. AA; HBV; LEAP
(Resignation.) SPP
Days of my youth left me long ago, The. The Chrysanthemums in the Eastern Garden. Po Chü-i. TrCh
Days of Our Youth, The. *Unknown, tr. fr. Arabic by* Wilfrid Scawen Blunt. AWP; JAWP; WBP
Days of Spring are here, The! the eglantine. Hafiz. *Fr.* Odes. AWP; JAWP; WBP
Days of the Leaders, 1925, *sel.* L. Lamprey.
Deaf, The. BBV (1951 ed.)
Days of the Week, The. John Farrar. GFA
Days pace by in weary seemliness, The. An Inhibited Persian. Richard Hart. CIV
Days pass like snaps of lightning. Earth. Brian Vrepont. NeLNL
Day's rain is done. The rainy mist of night. Pushkin, *tr. fr. Russian by* C. M. Bowra. BoR
Day's Ration, The. Emerson. BAV; IAP
Day's Run, A. Jorge Luis Borges, *tr. fr. Spanish by* H. R. Hays. TwSpPo
Days shorten, The, the south blows wide for showers now. Salmon-fishing. Robinson Jeffers. AnEnPo; PC
Day's swim done, we found some grass and flung, The. A Serendipity of Love. Richard Aldridge. NePoAm-2
Days That Are No More, The. Tennyson. *See* Tears, Idle Tears.
Days That Come and Go. John Vance Cheney. LBAP
Days That have been. W. H. Davies. PoeT; PrWP
Days That Were, The. William Morris. BPN
Days Too Short. W. H. Davies. MBP; MoBrPo; NeMA; NV; POTE; TCEP
Day's Work, The. Goethe. *See* Use Well the Moment.
Dayseye hugging the earth, The. Daisy. William Carlos Williams. MAP; MoAB; MoAmPo
Dayspring. Luis G. Urbina, *tr. fr. Spanish by* Samuel Beckett. AnMP
Dazel'd thus, with height of place. *See* Dazzled thus . . .
Dazzle on the sea, my darling, The. Leaving Barra. Louis MacNeice. ChMo; POTE; ReaPo
Dazzled by sun and drugged by space they wait. Calgary Station. Isabel Ecclestone Mackay. CPG
Dazzled [*or* Dazel'd] thus with height of place. Upon the Sudden Restraint of the Earl of Somerset, Then Falling from Favour. Sir Henry Wotton. MePo; OBS
Dazzling and Tremendous How Quick the Sun-Rise Would Kill Me. Walt Whitman. *Fr.* Song of Myself. AtBAP
De Amore, *sel.* Ernest Dowson.
"Lord over life and all the ways of breath." TrPWD
De Bombycibus, *sel.* Marco Girolamo Vida, *tr. fr. Latin by* Francis Sylvester Mahony.
Silkworm, The. CAW
De coenatione Micae. Martial, *tr. fr. Latin by* Robert Louis Stevenson. FaBoCh; LoGBV
("Look round: You see a little supper room.") LaP
De contemptu Mundi, *sels.* Bernard of Cluny, *tr. fr. Latin by* John Mason Neale.
Jerusalem, the Golden. CAW; MaRV; OlF, 4 *sts.*; WGRP
(Celestial Country, The.) GoBC, *abr.*; GrCo-1, *much abr.*; LPS-2
(Jerusalem, *abr.*) HBV; OBVV
"O land without guilt, strong city, safe built in a marvellous place," *tr. by* Swinburne. LaP
De! de! lambskin mine. Hush Rhymes—Albanian. *Unknown.* BOL
De Gelu Diutino, Anno Dom. 1607. John Heath. SiCE
De Guiana, Carmen Epicum. George Chapman. OBSC
"De Gustibus." Robert Browning. BPN; EmBrPo; EPN; GEPC; HBV; OAEP; PoeMoYo, *abr.*; PoVP; ReTS; VA; ViFo; VLEP; YT
De Gustibus. John Erskine. TBM
De Gustibus. St. John Emile Clavering Hankin. CenHV
De Ignoto. Everard Guilpin. *Fr.* Skialetheia. ReIE
De little black bull kem down de medder. Hoosen Johnny. *Unknown.* FaPON
De Lord he thought he'd make a man. Dese Bones Gwine to Rise Again. *Unknown.* SiTL
De Mense Ianuarii Quae Fuit An. Do. 1595. Thomas Bastard. SiCE
De Mexico ha venido, *with music. Unknown, tr. fr. Spanish.* TrAS
De Microcosmo. Thomas Bastard. SiCE
De Morte. *Unknown.* CenL
De Morte. *At. to* Sir Henry Wotton. OBS
"De Mortuis Nil Nisi Bonum." Richard Realf. HBV
De Naevo in Facie Faustinae. Thomas Bastard. LO
De Partu Virginis, *sel.* Jacopo Sannazaro, *tr. fr. Latin by* John C. Eustace.
Celestial Queen, *fr.* Bk. III. ISi
De Piscatione. Thomas Bastard. TuPP
De Poeta Martiali. Thomas Bastard. SiCE
De Profundis. Brent Dow Allinson. Prayer in the Trenches, II. AOAH
De Profundis. Psalms, CXXX, Bible, *O.T.* BLRP; MaRV; TreF; WGRP; WHL
(Out of the Depths.) TrJP
(Psalm CXXX.) EnLi-1; LiTW (*Book of Common Prayer*); OnPM
(Song of Supplication, A.) TrGrPo
De Profundis, *sel.* Elizabeth Barrett Browning.
"Whatever's lost, it first was won." TrPWD
De Profundis. David Gascoyne. *Fr.* Miserere. NeBP
De Profundis. "Hugh MacDiarmid." SeCePo
De Profundis. George Macdonald. EPN
De Profundis. Christina Rossetti. BPN; CoBE; OuHeWo; PoVP; VLEP
De Profundis. Tennyson. BPN; VLEP
De Profundis. Georg Trakl, *tr. fr. German by* Glauco Cambon. OnPM
De Profundis. Katharine Tynan. VA
De Profundis. Amos N. Wilder. TrPWD
De railroad bridge's. Homesick Blues. Langston Hughes. WaKn
De Ramis Cadunt Folia. *Unknown, tr. fr. Latin by* Helen Waddell. *Fr.* Carmina Burana. LaP
(Winter Love Song.) LiTW
De Regimine Principum, *sels.* Thomas Hoccleve.
Hoccleve's Lament for Chaucer and Gower, *abr.* OAEP
(On Chaucer, *longer sel., abr.*) EPP
Lament for Chaucer. OBEV; PtP
Prologue: "Musing upon the restles bisinesse." PoEL-1
To Chaucer. ACP
De Rerum Natura, *sels.* Lucretius, *tr. fr. Latin.*
Address to Venus, *tr. by* Spenser, *fr.* The Faerie Queene, IV, 10. AnEnPo; AWP
(Prayer to Venus.) EIL
Against the Fear of Death, *fr.* III, *tr. by* Dryden.
"As for the dog, the furies, and their snakes." PoD
Death ("So many monarchs with their mighty state"). BeR
Fear of Death, The ("The Sisiphus is he, whom noise and strife"). LoBV
"For thou shalt sleep, and never wake again." PoD
"What has this bugbear death to frighten man." AWP; JAWP; WBP
Creation of the Infinite Universe, The; How It Is Maintained, *fr.* I, *tr. by* Robie M. Macauley. LaP
"Darling of Gods and Men, beneath the gliding stars," *fr.* I, *tr. by* Basil Bunting. LaP
Earth, The, *fr.* V, *pr. tr. by* W. H. D. Rouse. LiA
Evolution of Life and Society, *fr.* V, *pr. tr. by* W. H. D. Rouse. RoL
Fear of Death, *fr.* III, *pr. tr. by* W. H. D. Rouse. RoL
From the Shore of Life, *fr.* II, *tr. by* Jeoffrey Johnson. LaP
Guileful Ocean, The, *fr.* II, *tr. by* H. S. Salt. LiA
Introduction; Combinations of Atoms; Creation and Destruction of Worlds, *fr.* II, *pr. tr. by* W. H. D. Rouse. RoL
Invocation; the Bondage of Religion, *fr.* I, *pr. tr. by* W. H. D. Rouse. RoL
Life of Primitive Man, The, *fr.* V, *tr. by* W. Taylor McLeod. LaP
No Single Thing Abides, *fr.* III, *tr. by* W. H. Mallock. AWP; ImOP, *abr.*; JAWP; PG (1945 ed.); WBP
Of the Nature of Things, *tr. by* William Ellery Leonard.
Beginnings of Civilization, *fr.* V. OuHeWo
Beyond Religion. AWP; PoFr, *shorter sel.*
Of Human Progress, *fr.* V. WoL
Origins and Savage Period of Mankind, *fr.* V. OuHeWo
Origins of Life, The. LiTW
Origins of Vegetable and Animal Life, *fr.* V. OuHeWo
Unpathed Haunts, *fr.* IV. LiA
When We Are No More, *fr.* III. LiA
On Human Ambitions, *fr.* III, *tr. by* Jack Lindsay. LaP
"Plague like this a tempest big with fate, A," *fr.* VI, *tr. by* John Mason Good. PoP
Sickness Which Is Love, The, *fr.* IV, *tr. by* Gilbert Highet. LaP
Suave Mari Magno, *tr. by* W. H. Mallock. AWP
De Roberval; a Drama, *sels.* John Hunter-Duvar.
Adieu to France. VA
Gallant Fleet, The. VA
"Here, then, we stand on the Canadian shore." CaP
La Belle Sauvage. BoCaPo (1948 ed.)
Ohnáwa. VA
Twilight Song. VA
De Rosis Hibernis. Sir Edmund Gosse. VA
De Se. John Weever. ReIE; TuPP
De Senectute. Franklin P. Adams. HBMV; TCAP
De Subiecto Operis Sui. Thomas Bastard. SiCE
De Tea Fabula. Sir Arthur Quiller-Couch. CenHV; PA
De Verdun of Darragh, *sel.* George Francis Savage-Armstrong.
Wicklow. TIP

Deacon Rogers he came to me. Value of Elemental Remedies. Charles Anson Ingraham. PoP
Deacon's Masterpiece, The; or, The Wonderful "One-Hoss Shay." Oliver Wendell Holmes. *Fr.* The Autocrat of the Breakfast Table, *ch.* II. AmP; AmPP; AnNE; APW; BBV (1923 ed.); BOHV; CoBA; DDA; EV-5; FaFP; HBV; HBVY; IAP; InMe; LHV; LiTA; LoGBV; MOAP; MoShBr; NePA; OBAV; OHFP; OnHT; OnSP; OTPC; OxBA; Po; PoRA; REAL; RIS; SiTL; StPo; StVeCh; TCAP; WBLP; YT
(Logical Story, A—The Deacon's Masterpiece; or, The Wonderful "One-Hoss Shay.") BAP; LEAP
(One-Hoss Shay, The; or, The Deacon's Masterpiece.) LPS-3; PIR; TreF
(Wonderful "One-Hoss Shay," The.) BeLS; FaBoBe; PYM; YaD
Dead, The. Mathilde Blind. DiM; EPN; ES; GTML; OBVV; VA; WGRP
Dead, The. John Le Gay Brereton. BoAu
Dead, The ("Blow out, you bugles"). Rupert Brooke. 1914, III. AOAH; BEL; GrCo-1; GTML; LBBV; LEAP; MCCG; OQP; PoFr; QP-1; TCEP; TreF; VOD; WGRP
(Dead, The, I.) NV
Dead, The ("These hearts were woven"). Rupert Brooke. 1914, IV. AnFE; ATP; CH; CP; EnLit; ES; GTSL; GTBS-W; HiLiEn; LiTB; LiTG; MCCG; OtMeF; PFE; PIAE; PoeMoYo; PoeT; PoRL; POTE; SeCeV; ShBV-4; TOP; TwCV; VOD; YT
(All This Is Ended.) AOAH
(Dead, The, II.) NV
Dead. Rhoda Coghill. OnYI
Dead, The. Robert J. Crot. MaRV
Dead, The. Charles Heavysege. *See* How Great unto the Living Seem the Dead.
Dead. Lionel Johnson. FaBoEn; GTBS-D; PoEL-5
Dead, The ("Think you the dead are lonely in that place"). David Morton. PAH
Dead, The. Selma Robinson. PIAE
Dead, The. Semonides, *tr. fr. Greek.* OxBG
Dead, The. Victor Starbuck. BLP; LS; NoCaPo
Dead, The. Jones Very. AA; AnNE; APW; IAP; LEAP; OxBA; TCAP
Dead, The. Isaac Watts. *Fr.* The Death and Burial of a Saint. BeR
Dead, The. John Williams. NePoAm-2
Dead abide with us, The. Though stark and cold. The Dead. Mathilde Blind. DiM; EPN; ES; GTML; OBVV; VA; WGRP
Dead Angels. Rafael Alberti, *tr. fr. Spanish by* Eleanor L. Turnbull. CoSP
Dead Antiquary O'Donovan. Thomas D'Arcy McGee. TIP
Dead are gone and with them we cannot converse, The. *Unknown, tr. fr. Chinese by* Arthur Waley. Seventeen Old Poems, 13. TrCh
Dead, The, are not to rise; their roll our grief. Aeschylus. *Fr.* Agamemnon. PoFr
Dead are silent, The. Passionless and still. The Dead. Robert J. Crot. MaRV
Dead as the Romans he adored. John Pattison Gibson. W. W. Gibson. MM
Dead Astronomer, A. Francis Thompson. VLEP
Dead at Clonmacnois, The. Angus O'Gillan, *tr. fr. Middle Irish by* T. W. Rolleston. AnIL; HBV; IrPN; OBEV; OBVV; OnYI; OxBI; PoD; TIP
(Clonmacnoise.) AnIV; GTIV; OBMV
Dead Aviator. Zoë Akins. LPS-1
Dead Aviator, The. Francis Hackett. JKCP (1926 ed.); LEAP
Dead Ballet-Dancer, The. Paulus Silentiarius, *tr. fr. Greek by* F. L. Lucas. GrPE
Dead Bee, The. Nathalia Crane. MAP; MoAmPo (1942 ed.)
Dead before Death. Christina Rossetti. EmBrPo
Dead Boy. Callimachus, *tr. fr. Greek by* Lord Neaves. OnPM
Dead Boy. John Crowe Ransom. LiTA; LS; MoPW; OxBA
Dead brood over Europe, the cloud and vision descends over cheerful France, The. Blake. The French Revolution, I. EiPP
Dead Brother, The. *Unknown.* EnSB
Dead Child, The. George Barlow. OBVV; VA
Dead Child [*or* Childe], A. Lucian, *tr. fr. Greek.* LiTW, *tr. by* Timothe Kendall; OnPM, *tr. by* Lord Neaves; OxBG, *tr. by* Timothe Kendall
("Frowning fates have taken hence, The," *tr. by* Timothe Kendall.) EnLi-1; GrPo
Dead Child, The. *Unknown, tr. fr. Greek by* F. L. Lucas. GrPE
Dead Church, The. Charles Kingsley. VA
Dead City, The. Clinch Calkins. AnAmPo; LA
Dead Cleopatra Lies in a Crystal Casket. Conrad Aiken. Discordants, IV [III]. ChMo; CMP; MOAP
Dead Coach, The. Katharine Tynan. HBV; VA
Dead Comrade, The. Richard Watson Gilder. MDAH
Dead Crab, The. Andrew Young. FaBoTw; LoBV
Dead Czar Nicholas, The. Dinah Maria Mulock Craik. LPS-3
Dead Dancer, The. Thyillus, *tr. fr. Greek by* F. L. Lucas. GrPE
Dead dancer, how is this?—the laurel here. Vernon Castle. Harriet Monroe. HBMV
Dead Days. Lloyd Roberts. BoCaPo (1943 ed.)
Dead do not specially depress me, The. At Morning an Iris. Patrick Evans. NeBP
Dead Eagle, The. Thomas Campbell. EnRP; ERP
Dead Earth, The. Arthur M. Sampley. *Fr.* Fragments of Eternity. MuM
Dead Enchantress. Harold Vinal. PR
Dead Faith, The. Fanny Heaslip Lea. HBV; WGRP
Dead Feast of the Kol-Folk, The. Whittier. PoEL-4
Dead Feel Not, The. Theognis, *tr. fr. Greek by* T. F. Higham. GrL; OxBG
Dead Fiddle, The. Humbert Wolfe. TrJP
Dead Fires. Jessie Redmond Fauset. BANP; PoNe
Dead Fowler, The. Mnasalcas, *tr. fr. Greek by* T. F. Higham. OxBG
Dead Fowler, The. *Unknown, tr. fr. Greek by* F. L. Lucas. GrPE
Dead Friend, A. Norman Gale. VA
Dead Gods. Erik Blomberg, *tr. fr. Swedish by* Charles W. Stork. AnSL
Dead Grenadier, The. Pedro Juan Vignale, *tr. fr. Spanish by* Donald Devenish Walsh. AnCL
"Dead hand of reaction now, The." Lines to a Future Historian. Kathleen Nott. PoN
Dead hangs the fruit on that tall tree. Burial of the Spirit. Richard Hughes. BLV; MBP; MoBrPo
Dead Harvest, A. Alice Meynell. MoVE; PoeT
Dead he lay among his books! Bayard Taylor. Longfellow. DD; GA; HBV
Dead heat and windless air. August Weather. Katharine Tynan. TIP
Dead here look upon the light from caves, The. Girod Street Cemetery; New Orleans. Harry Morris. GoYe
Dead Heroes, The. Isaac Rosenberg. MBP; MoBrPo; TrGrPo (1942 ed.); TriL
Dead Hind, The. *Unknown, tr. fr. Chinese by* E. D. Edwards. ChLP
Dead Horse, The, *with music. Unknown.* AmSS; AS
Dead Host's Welcome, The. John Fletcher. *Fr.* The Lovers' Progress, III, i. EV-2; SeCl; TrGrPo
('Tis Late and Cold.) ViBoPo
Dead in Europe, The. Robert Lowell. NePA; NePoEA; OxBA
Dead in Melanesia, The. Randall Jarrell. MiAP
Dead in the battle,—dead on the field. The Soldier's Dirge. Elizabeth Herman. DD; HH
Dead in the cold, a song-singing thrush, A. Christina Rossetti. *Fr.* Sing-Song. MBP
Dead in the Sierras. Joaquin Miller. AA; BAP; LEAP; PFY
Dead in Wars and in Revolutions. Mary Devenport O'Neill. NeIP
Dead! Is it possible? He, the bold rider. Custer's Last Charge. Frederick Whittaker. BoHiPo; DD; GA; HBV; MC; PaA; PAH; PTA-1
Dead Is Patroclus. Homer, *tr. fr. Greek by* Pope. *Fr.* The Iliad, XVIII. LiA
Dead is the roll of the drums. Abraham Lincoln. Henry Howard Brownell. GN; LBAH
Dead keep silence, The. All their stir. Interval. Dorothy E. Hanbury Rowe. MM
Dead Knight, The. John Masefield. CH
Dead leaves strew the forest walk, The. Stanzas. John G. C. Brainard. AnAmPo; BAV; LA
Dead leaves their rich mosaics, The. November. Samuel Longfellow. SN
Dead Letter, A. Austin Dobson. BPN; HBV; POTT; PoVP; VA
Dead Liar Speaks, A. Michael Lewis. GoTP
Dead lie drunk on heady rain, The. The Lufoten. Quentin Stevenson. POTE (1959 ed.)
Dead lie strewn about, The. Vultures. Al-Hajjam. MooP
Dead Locust, A. Aristodicus, *tr. fr. Greek by* Humbert Wolfe. OxBG
Dead, Long Dead. Tennyson. *Fr.* Maud. AtBAP
Dead Love. Mary Mathews Adams. AA
Dead Maiden's Complaint, A. Gerasimos Markoras, *tr. fr. Modern Greek by* Rae Dalven. MoGP
Dead Make Rules, The. Mary Carolyn Davies. HBMV; PoFr
Dead Man, A. *Unknown, tr. fr. Japanese by* Ishii *and* Obata. OnPM
Dead Man Ariseth and Singeth a Hymn to the Sun, The. *Unknown, tr. fr. Egyptian by* Robert Hillyer. *Fr.* Book of the Dead. AWP; JAWP; WBP

Dead man lay in front of our wire barricade, A. Brothers. Heinrich Lersch. BoFr
Deadman's Dirge. George Darley. *See* Sea-Ritual, The.
Dead Man's Dump. Isaac Rosenberg. FaBoMo; LiTM; MoPo; TrJP; WaP
Dead March, A. Cosmo Monkhouse. HBV; VA
"Play me a march," *sel.* OBVV
Dead Marine. Louis O. Coxe. WaP
Dead men are wisest, for they know. The Wise. Countee Cullen. PoNe
Dead men of 'ninety-two, also of 'ninety-three. Sonnet. Arthur Rimbaud. WaaP
Dead Men Tell No Tales. Haniel Long. HBMV; MCCG; NP; PC
"Dead men tell no tales!" they chuckled. The Singing Saviors. Clement Wood. BAP; MaRV; OQP; QP-1
Dead Men's Song, The. Young Ewing Allison. *See* Derelict.
Dead Moon, The. Danske Bedinger Dandridge. AA
Dead Morning. Raymond Holden. MAP; MoAmPo (1942 ed.)
Dead Musician, The. Charles L. O'Donnell. CAW; JKCP
Dead Nereid, The. Eugenio Florit, *tr. fr. Spanish by* H. R. Hays. TwSpPo
Dead Night. Nathaniel Lee. *Fr.* Theodosius; or, The Force of Love. BeR
Dead of Athens at Chalcis, The. Simonides. *See* Athenian Dead, The.
Dead of Night. Manuel Bandeira, *tr. fr. Portuguese by* Dudley Poore. AnCL
Dead of Sparta at Plataea, The. Simonides. *See* Spartan Monument, The.
Dead of Sparta at Thermopylae, The. Simonides. *See* Thermopylae.
Dead of the Wilderness, The. Hayyim Nahman Bialik, *tr. fr. Hebrew by* Maurice Samuel. AWP
"Yonder great shadow," *sel.* JAWP; WBP
Dead! one of them shot by the sea in the east. Mother and Poet. Elizabeth Barrett Browning. HBV; LPS-1; MOAH; MotAn; VA; VLEP
Dead Pan, The. Elizabeth Barrett Browning. BPN; EmBrPo; PoVP; ViPo
Dead Past, A. *At. to* C. C. Munson. BLRP; WBLP
Dead Player, The. Robert Burns Wilson. AA
Dead Playmate, The. Callimachus. *See* Crethis.
Dead Poet, The. Callimachus. *See* Heraclitus.
Dead Poet, The. Lord Alfred Douglas. BMEP; CaAE; HBMV; LEAP; MBP; MoBrPo (1942 ed.); PoVP; PtP; ViBoPo
Dead Poets. Enrique Peña Barrenechea, *tr. fr. Spanish by* Milton Ben Davis. AnCL; BoFr
Dead Ponies. Brenda Chamberlain. NeBP
Dead President, The. Edward Rowland Sill. PAH
Dead Pussy Cat, The. *Unknown, at. to* John Bennett *and to* Marion Short. CIV; PTA-1
Dead Quire, The. Thomas Hardy. OAEP; POTT
Dead return to us continually, The. Ghosts. Brian Hooker. PFY; UnW
Dead Ride Fast, The. R. P. Blackmur. MoPo
Dead Rose, A. Elizabeth Barrett Browning. EV-4
Dead roses and dying. Aleksandr Blok, *tr. fr. Russian by* C. M. Bowra. BoR
Dead Sea Scrolls, The, *sels. Unknown, tr. fr. Hebrew.* TrJP
Blessed Art Thou, O Lord, *tr. by* Theodor H. Gaster.
Lo, I Am Stricken Dumb, *tr. by* Theodor H. Gaster.
My Soul in the Bundle of Life, *tr. by* E. Margaret Rowley.
Though Mine Eye Sleep Not, *tr. by* Theodor H. Gaster.
Dead Shalt Thou Lie. Sappho, *tr. fr. Greek by* H. De Vere Stacpoole. GrR
(Forgotten, *tr. by* Thomas Hardy.) OxBG
Dead Shepherd, The. Leonidas of Tarentum, *tr. fr. Greek by* Walter Leaf. GrR
(Cleitagoras, *tr. by* William M. Hardinge.) AWP
(Shepherd, *tr. by* E. R. Bevan.) OxBG
(Shepherd's Last Sleep, The, *tr. by* F. L. Lucas.) GrPE
("Shepherds, ye that haunt these rocks," *tr. by* Walter Leaf.) GrPo
Dead Ship of Harpswell, The. Whittier. EtS; UnW
Dead Singer, A. John E. Logan. VA
Dead Singer, The. Mary Ashley Townsend. AA
Dead Snake. William Jay Smith. NePoAm-2
Dead Soldier. Nicolás Guillén, *tr. fr. Spanish by* Langston Hughes. AnCL; PoNe
Dead Soldier, A. George Edgar Montgomery. AA
Dead Solomon, The. John Aylmer Dorgan. AA
Dead Song-Writer, A. Lucilius, *tr. fr. Greek by* Humbert Wolfe. OxBG; WoL
Dead son's mother sat and wept, The. The Two Brothers. Theodosia Garrison. UnW
Dead soul lay in the light of day, A. Judgment. Grace Ellery Channing. AA
Dead Sparrow, The. William Cartwright. CH
("Tell me not of joy: there's none.") LO
Dead Sparrow, The. Catullus, *tr. fr. Latin by* Byron. EnLi-1; OuHeWo
Dead Starling, The. Catullus. *See* Death of Lesbia's Bird, The.
Dead Statesman, A. Kipling. *Fr.* Epitaphs of the War, 1914-18. LiA; OAEP (2d ed.); PoVP
Dead. The dead year is lying at my feet. New Year's Eve —Midnight. Frederika Richardson Macdonald. VA
Dead there are, who live, The. The Test. John Banister Tabb. LA
Dead, they'll burn you up with electricity. Marcus Argentarius. Kenneth Rexroth. CrMA
Dead to the Living, The. Laurence Binyon. POT
Dead Tree, The. Arthur Davison Ficke. MuM
Dead Tribune, The. Denis Florence MacCarthy. ACP
Dead Wasp. Kenneth Slade Alling. NePoAm
Dead Water, The. Wen Yi-tuo, *tr. fr. Chinese by* Harold Acton *and* Ch'en Shih-hsiang. LiTW; WhP
Dead Warrior, A. Laurence Housman. AOAH; HBMV
Dead Waters. Manuel Gutiérrez Nájera, *tr. fr. Spanish by* Samuel Beckett. AnMP
Dead Waters. Georges Rodenbach, *tr. fr. French by* Alan Conder. TrFP
Dead "Wessex," the Dog, to the Household. Thomas Hardy. CMP; ReaPo
Dead Wingman, The. Randall Jarrell. MiAP
Dead, with their eyes to the foe. Melville and Coghill. Andrew Lang. EBSV; VA
Dead wood with its load of stones. The Water-Wheel. Jack R. Clemo. ChMP
Dead Words, The. Vernon Watkins. LiTM (rev. ed.); MoWP
Dead you shall lie, for ever, a name that none recall. To a Rich Uncultured Woman. Sappho. GrPE
Dead young man stood up in his grave, The. Articles of War. Dunstan Thompson. WaP
Dead Youth, The. Kostes Palamas, *tr. fr. Modern Greek by* Rae Dalven. *Fr.* Life Immovable. MoGP
Deadfall. Martha Keller. GoYe
Deadly Kisses. Pierre de Ronsard, *tr. fr. French by* Andrew Lang. AWP
Deaf. H. C. Bunner. AA
Deaf, The. L. Lamprey. *Fr.* Days of the Leaders, 1925. BBV (1951 ed.)
Deaf and Dumb. "A." PRWS
Deaf and Dumb. Robert Browning. MaRV
Deaf, giddy, helpless, left alone. On His Own Deafness. Swift. BeR
Deaf Men. Merrill Moore. PoP
Deaf to God, who calls and walks. Doomsday Morning. Genevieve Taggard. MAP; MoAmPo
Deaf to the hurly-burly of the street. Israelite Graveyard. César Tiempo. AnCL
Deaf Woman's Courtship, The, *with music. Unknown.* SaSa
Deafening/ The first solitary note of day. Trumpet and Flute. Gunnar Hernaes. LiTW
Dean, The. Alan Porter. AnAmPo
Dean, if we believe Report, The. Swift. *Fr.* Verses on the Death of Dr. Swift. FaBoEn
Dean-bourn, a Rude River in Devon, by Which Sometimes He Lived ("Dean-bourn, farewell; I never look to see"). Robert Herrick. Po; SeCV-1
Dean's Consent, The. Coventry Patmore. *Fr.* The Angel in the House, I, vi. VA
Dean's Lady, The. George Crabbe. LoBV
Dear Agatha, I give you joy. The Doll's House. Anna Letitia Barbauld. OTPC (1923 ed.)
Dear Alice! you'll laugh when you know it. The Talented Man. Winthrop Mackworth Praed. ALV; CoBE; EnRP; ERP; FiBHP; HBV
Dear and great Angel, wouldst thou only leave. The Guardian-Angel. Robert Browning. BPN; EmBrPo; EV-5; GEPC; GoBC; HBV; PoVP
Dear Andrew, with the brindled hair. To Andrew Lang. Robert Louis Stevenson. PoVP; POTT
"Dear as remembered kisses after death." Constancy. Minor Watson. HBV
Dear Babe, that sleepest cradled by my side. Coleridge and His Child. Samuel Taylor Coleridge. *Fr.* Frost at Midnight. RO
Dear, back my wounded heart restore. The Divorce. Thomas Stanley. LO; MeLP
Dear Bargain, The. Richard Crashaw. *See* Charitas Nimia.
Dear, beauteous Death! the jewel of the just. Henry Vaughan. LO
Dear Betty, when an hour ago. Consolation. Mary E. Wilkins Freeman. PR
Dear Bill,/ When I search the past for you. A Letter to William Carlos Williams. Kenneth Rexroth. OnHM
Dear birds, that flutter happily. The Courtyard Pigeons. Caroline Giltinan. BLA
Dear black swallows and dear white birds. The Witch's Daughter. *Unknown.* MoGP

Dear boy, of thy race thou'rt the blossom and pride. Quarrel with Juventius. Catullus. OnPM

Dear boy unborn: the son but of my dream. To My Son. John Drinkwater. PtOT

Dear boy! whom, torn in early youth away. Memorial Trees. Juvenal. OnPM

Dear boy, you will not hear me speak. Pangloss' Song. Richard Wilbur. NePoAm-2

Dear boys, they've killed our woods: the ground. Ryton Firs. Lascelles Abercrombie. TCPD

Dear Brook, farewell! Tomorrow's noon again. Wordsworth. *Fr.* An Evening Walk. CoBE; EnRP

Dear brother, I have come these many miles, through. Catullus, *tr. fr. Latin by* Horace Gregory. RoL

Dear brother, would you know the life. A Letter. Emerson. OxBA

Dear charming nymph, neglected and decried. Farewell to Poetry. Goldsmith. *Fr.* The Deserted Village. OBEC

Dear Cherry Blossom. To a Japanese Girl Grieved over the War on China. Belle Chapman Morrill. MaRV

Dear child of Nature, let them rail! To a Young Lady. Wordsworth. BPN; EG; EmBrPo; EnRP; ERP

Dear child! whom sleep can hardly tame. To a Child. John Sterling. VA

Dear child, you in your native land unfold. Yesterday. Ethel Anderson. NeLNL

Dear Children: I write in great haste just to say. Santa Claus' Petition. Julie Matilde Lippmann. SDH

"Dear children," they asked in every town. The Kings from the East. Heine. ChTr

Dear Chloe [*or* Cloe], how blubbered is that pretty face! Answer to Chloe Jealous [*or* A Better Answer (to Cloe Jealous)]. Matthew Prior. ALV; AWP; CEP; EiPP; ElSeCe; EV-3; ExPo; FaBoEn; HBV; InPo; JAWP; LiTL; LO; NBE; OBEC; PoE; PoEL-3; SeCePo; SeCeV; SeCL; TCEP; TOP; ViBoPo; WBP

Dear Chloe, while the busy crowd. The Fireside. Nathaniel Cotton. LPS-1

Dear chorister, who from those shadows sends. *See* Dear quirister, who from those shadows sends.

Dear Citizens,/ I heard the newsboys shouting "Europe! Europe!" The True, the Good and the Beautiful. Delmore Schwartz. MiAP

Dear Cloe, how blubber'd is that pretty face. *See* Dear Chloe, how blubber'd is that pretty face.

Dear common flower, that grow'st beside the way. To the Dandelion. James Russell Lowell. ADAH; CoBA; DD; FaPON; GN; HBV; HBVY; IAP; MPB; OBAV; PEOR; SN; TCAP; TVSH; YT

Dear comrade, arise, from slumber awake. The Hoopoe's Call. Aristophanes. *Fr.* The Birds. OxBG

Dear Cosmopolitan, I know. A Familiar Epistle. Austin Dobson. VA

Dear creature by the fire a-purr. The Cat. Lytton Strachey. PoC

Dear Cynthia, though thou bear'st the name. To Cynthia, on Her Changing. Sir Francis Kynaston. EG; MePo; SeCL

Dear Cypris, if thou savest those at sea. Land and Sea. *Unknown.* OxBG

Dear damn'd, distracting town, farewell! A Farewell to London in the Year 1715. Pope. CEP

Dear Dark Head. William Rooney. JKCP (1926 ed.)

Dear Dark Head. *Unknown, tr. fr. Modern Irish by* Sir Samuel Ferguson. AnIV; GTIV; LoPS; OnYI; OxBI (Ceann Dubh Deelish.) IrPN; OBEV (1st ed.); SeCePo

Dear, dear, dear, is the rocky glen. The Thrush's Song. *Unknown, tr. by* William Macgillivray. CH; GoTP

Dear, dear! what can the matter be? Mother Goose. PPL

Dear, did you know how sweet to me. A Vain Desire. Theodore Wratislaw. VA

Dear, do not your fair beauty wrong. Love's Prime. Thomas May. *Fr.* The Old Couple, III, i. EG; ElSeCe; SeCL; TuPP: ViBoPo

Dear Doctor, I have read your play. A Publisher to His Client [*or* Epistle from Mr. Murray to Dr. Polidori]. Byron. CBE; EV-4

Dear Doctor, whose blandly invincible pen. To O. W. Holmes. Paul Hamilton Hayne. DD; GA

Dear Earth, within Thy bosom grant rest and long forgetting. Harvest Home. *Unknown.* GrPE

Dear Erin, how sweetly thy green bosom rises. Cushla-Ma-Chree. John Philpot Curran. DD; HBV

Dear Eustatio, I write that you may write me an answer. Amours de Voyage. Arthur Hugh Clough. EmBrPo

Dear eyes, set deep within the shade. The Protestation. Selwyn Image. VA

Dear Fanny. Thomas Moore. HBV; InMe

Dear father and dear mother: Let me crave. Erotion. Martial. AWP; JAWP; WBP

"Dear Father, tell me, Why are Worms?" Why? Walter de la Mare. FiBHP

Dear Father, whom we cannot see. A Prayer for Peace. John Oxenham. PraP

Dear fellow-artist, why so free. To a Young Beauty. W. B. Yeats. ChMo

Dear firstling of my little flock. To My Firstborn. Bernard Isaac Durward. JKCP (1926 ed.)

Dear friend, far off, my lost desire. In Memoriam A. H. H., CXXIX. Tennyson. BoFr; BPN; EmBrPo; EPN; GEPC; MaPo; MaRV; TOP; ViPo; VLEP

Dear friend, I know this world is kin. Death. George Frederick Cameron. BoCaPo

Dear friend, I pray thee, if thou wouldst be proving. Friendship. Ella Wheeler Wilcox. PoToHe

Dear Friend! whose presence in the house. Cana. James Freeman Clarke. LPS-2

Dear friends, there is no cause for so much sympathy. Illness. Po Chü-i. TrCh

Dear Friends and Patrons of the *Denver News!* Carrier's Address. *Unknown.* PoOW

"Dear friends, the wages of sin is death, indeed." The Prayer-Meeting. Gustaf Fröding. AnSL

Dear Fronto, famed alike in peace and war. Country Pleasures. Martial. AWP; OnPM

Dear George,/ At last the blowfly's buzz retreats. Letter to a Friend. John Thompson. BoAV

Dear gentle hands have stroked my hair. Mother's Hands. W. Dayton Wedgefarth. PoToHe

Dear Gill I ne'er thought till last night. The New Married Couple; or, A Friendly Debate between the Country Farmer and His Buxome Wife. *Unknown.* CoMu

Dear girl, I wish I knew her well. My Zoological Flame. Edna E. Linsley. CAG

Dear God, I humbly pray. Prayer of a Beginning Teacher. Ouida Smith Dunnam. TrPWD

Dear God, I stand with empty hands. Gifts. Mary Edgar Comstock. OQP; QP-1

Dear God, I wish I could have been. Finding You. Mary Dixon Thayer. CAW

Dear God, our country needs Thee. Our Country. *Unknown.* PraP

Dear God our Father, at Thy knee confessing. For Deeper Life. Katharine Lee Bates. TrPWD

Dear God, the light is come, our outgrown creeds. A Prayer. *Unknown.* OQP; QP-1

Dear God, they say my dog is dead. A Little Boy Prays for His Dog. *Unknown.* DDA

Dear God, Thou know'st how many tasks. A Prayer of Busy Hands. B. Y. Williams. MaRV

Dear God, though Thy all-powerful hand. Care Is Heavy. Conal O'Riordan. CAW

Dear God, 'way up there in the sky. A Prayer for Prince. Betsey Mann Collins. AlBD

Dear good angel of the spring, The. The Nightingale. Sappho. GrL; OxBG

Dear Grandmamma, with what we give. Grandmamma's Birthday. Hilaire Belloc. FiBHP

Dear gray-eyed Angel, wilt thou come to-night? Sleep. Sophie Jewett. PC

Dear, had the world in its caprice. Respectability. Robert Browning. BPN; EmBrPo; EnLoPo; EPN; PoVP; VA; ViBoPo; ViPP; VLEP

Dear Harp of My Country. Thomas Moore. AnIL; EnRP; ERP; OAEP

Dear heart. I shall not altogether die. Non Omnis Moriar. Manuel Gutiérrez Nájera. AnMP

Dear heart, I think the young impassioned priest. "Quia Multum Amavi." Oscar Wilde. ACP (1926 ed.)

Dear heart, when with a twofold mind. Insets. Laurence Housman. BMEP

Dear hearts, you were waiting a year ago. The Two Waitings. John White Chadwick. LPS-1

Dear, heaven-designing [*or* heavn-designed] soul! To a Young Gentle-Woman, Councel concerning Her Choice. Richard Crashaw. AtBAP; OBS

Dear holy Saint, you have given me loving counsel. The Wolf of Gubbio to Saint Francis. Anna McClure Sholl. SaFP

Dear, honored name, beloved for human ties. Name of Mary. John Boyle O'Reilly. JKCP

Dear hope! Earth's dowry and heaven's debt! For Hope [*or* Answer for Hope *or* Richard Crashaw's Answer; for Hope] Richard Crashaw. GTBS-W; LiTB; LiTG; MeLP: OBS: SeCV-1; ViBoPo

Dear, I could weep, but that my brain is dry. Thomas Lovell Beddoes. *Fr.* The Bride's Tragedy. LO

Dear, I do not count it flighty. To a Lady across the Way. E. B. White. InMe

Dear, I have lit a candle for your birthday. Candles. Sister Mary Eleanore. JKCP (1955 ed.)

Dear, I must be gone. Parting. W. B. Yeats. FaBoTw

Dear, if You Change. *Unknown.* ElL; ElSeCe ("Dear, if you change, I'll never choose again.") CoEV; EnLoPo: InvP; LO; OBSC; SiCE

Dear, if You Change (*continued*)
(Deare, if You Change.) AtBAP; PoEL-2

Dear, if you love me, hold me most your friend. **A Sonnet.** Alice Duer Miller. AA

Dear Is My Little Native Vale. Samuel Rogers. WP (Italian Song, An.) EV-3

Dear Islay! Thomas Pattison. EBSV

Dear Italy! The sound of thy soft name. Italian Rhapsody. Robert Underwood Johnson. HBV

"Dear Jack," said Kate, with eyes of blue. The Modest Poet. *Unknown.* CAG

Dear Jesus Christ, I'm Brother Gian. Brother Gian. Cale Young Rice. LS

Dear Jesus, Dear, may I come in? The Christ Child at Christmas. John Drinkwater. QS

Dear Jesus! ever at my side. The Nearest Friend. Frederick W. Faber. TreFS

Dear Jesus, I wish. A Small Boy's Prayer. Helen Gleaves Nunn. DDA

Dear Joseph—five-and-twenty years ago. An Epistle to Joseph Hill. William Cowper. CBOV

Dear Lady of the Cherries, cool, serene. Sonnet for the Madonna of the Cherries. A. P. Wavell. OtMeF

Dear Lady, When Thou Frownest. Robert Bridges. ChMo; CMP; HiLiEn; LiTL

Dear land, I greet you after many years. My Own, My Native Land. Menander. OxBG

Dear Land of All My Love. Sidney Lanier. *Fr.* The Centennial Meditation of Columbia. DD; GA; GN; HBVY; MPB; StVeCh
("Long as thine Art shall love true love.") PGD

Dear, let me dream of love. A Prayer. Selwyn Image. VA

Dear, let us two each other spy. Love's Vision. William Cavendish, Duke of Newcastle. LO; SeCL

Dear lilac-tree, a-spreaden wide. The Lilac. William Barnes. EV-4

Dear Lillian! (The "dear" one risks). To Lillian Russell. Bert Leston Taylor. WhC

Dear little child, this little book. With a First Reader. Rupert Hughes. HBMV

Dear little darkened way where we have climbed. The Trysting Path. Albert E. S. Smythe. CPG

Dear little Dorothy, she is no more! Dorothy. Rose Hawthorne Lathrop. AA

Dear little flag in the window there. The Service Flag. William Herschell. PEDC; PTA-2

Dear little house, dear shabby street. To the Little House. Christopher Morley. BAP; HBMV; TCAP

Dear little lady, three summers old, A. "As Busy as I Tan Be." A. B. Carroll. FAOV

Dear little one,/ I would still your cry. Issa, *tr. fr. Japanese by* Lois J. Erickson. SoLD

Dear little tree that we plant to-day. An Arbor Day Tree. *Unknown.* ADAH; DD; HH; MeMeAg; OHIP

Dear little Violet. Calling the Violet. Lucy Larcom. MPB

Dear Little Violets. John Moultrie. *See* Violets.

Dear Lizbie Browne. To Lizbie Browne. Thomas Hardy. EnLit; LO; ViP

Dear Lord,/ Let all the words. Radio Prayer. Lexie Dean Robertson. PraP

Dear Lord and Father of Mankind. Whittier. *Fr.* The Brewing of Soma. GrCo-1; MaRV; OIF; PreP, *with music;* TrPWD

Dear Lord, dear Lord. The Mother's Prayer. Elizabeth Barrett Browning. MotAn

Dear Lord, I do not ask. Let Me Guide a Little Child. *Unknown.* PraP

Dear Lord, I do not hesitate. A Business Man's Prayer. William Ludlum. BLRP

Dear Lord, I hold my hand to take. A Mother Understands. G. A. Studdert-Kennedy. OQP; QP-2

Dear Lord, I'm in the worstest trouble a little child could be. The Mother's Prayer. Cora A. McDermoth. DDA

Dear Lord, it's but a silver chain. Prayer for a Silver Jubilee. Sister Mary Colman. PraNu

Dear Lord! Kind Lord! The Prayer Perfect [*or* Love's Prayer]. James Whitcomb Riley. AA; MaRV; OQP; QP-2; PraP

Dear Lord, let me recount to Thee. It is Finished. Christina Rossetti. VA

Dear Lord of Life, if I will follow Thee. In the Longer Novitiate. Catharine McPartlin. PraNu

Dear Lord, on this day thy day of days. Thanksgiving. Jeanie Rogers Sherman. TOAH

Dear Lord, receive my son, whose winning love. Of His Dear Son Gervase. Sir John Beaumont. *Fr.* Of My Dear Son, Gervase Beaumont. GoBC; OBEV

Dear Lord, thy table is outspread. The Master's Invitation. Anson Davies Fitz Randolph. AA

Dear Lord, we are afraid. Prayer of the Homesteader. Gwendolen Haste. PoTo

Dear Lord we thank Thee for this day. A Child's Prayer. William L. Stidger. PraP

Dear Lord, Who Sought at Dawn. Harry Webb Farrington. MaRV

Dear Lord. Whose serving-maiden. Hymn. Josephine Preston Peabody. TrPWD

Dear Lord's best interpreters, The. In Earthern Vessels. Whittier. *Fr.* The Friend's Burial. BLRP

Dear loss! since thy untimely fate. Henry King. *Fr.* The Exequy. AEV; ATP; EV-2; LO; OBEV; OBS; WHA

Dear love, dost thou sleep fairly. Parting at Morning. Dietmar von Aist. AWP

Dear [*or* Deare] love, for nothing less [*or* lesse] than thee. The Dream [*or* Dreame]. John Donne. BrBE; CoEV; EG; EiL; ElSeCe; EnLP; GTBS-W; InvP; LEAP; LiTB; LiTG; LiTL; LO; LoBV; MeLP; MePo; OAEP; OBEV; OBS; RiBV; SeeP; TOP

Dear Love, it was so hard to say. Parting. Alice Freeman Palmer. AV

Dear Love, let me this evening die! The Dying Lover. Sir William Davenant. SeCL

Dear Love, remember how the saplings clung. Aliens. Phebe Ann Clarke. MuM

Dear love, when with a two-fold mind. Laurence Housman. *Fr.* All Fellows. WGRP

Dear Lucy, you know what my wish is. Ad Ministram [*or* Persicos Odi]. Thackeray. HBV; OBEV (new ed.)

Dear Madam, you have seen this play. At the Theater. A. P. Herbert. FiBHP

Dear maid, let me speak. Conjugal Conjugations. A. W. Bellaw. BOHV

Dear maid! put your head on my breast, you will hear. In Prison. Frederick Peterson. PR

Dear Maiden. Heine, *tr. fr. German by* John Todhunter. AWP

Dear maiden, when the sun is down. To My Promised Wife. John Walsh. TIP

Dear March, come in! Emily Dickinson. MW (March.) YeAr

Dear marshes, by no hand of man. Flood-Time on the Marshes. Evaleen Stein. AA

Dear Master, for this coming year. New Year. *Unknown.* PraP

Dear Master, in Whose life I see. Dreams and Deeds. John Hunter. ChIP; MaRV

"Dear me!" exclaimed Homer. E. C. Bentley. FiBHP

Dear me! what signifies a pin. The Pin. Ann Taylor. HBV; HBVY

Dear Miss Dix, I am a young man of half-past thirty-seven. Two and One Are a Problem. Ogden Nash. FiBHP

Dear Mr. Editor: I wish to say. A Grievance. James Kenneth Stephen. HBV; PA

Dear Mistress, do not grieve for me. Leo to His Mistress. Henry Dwight Sedgwick. BLPA; CIV

Dear Mrs. Spinks has had so very many. The Spinks. Don Marquis. LEAP

Dear Mother, dear Mother, the Church is cold. The Little Vagabond. Blake. BOHV; CEP; EM-1; SeCeV

Dear mother Earth, within your breast. A Gardener. *Unknown.* OxBG

Dear mother, how pretty. The New Moon. Eliza Lee Follen. BoChLi; PPL; RAR; TVC; TVSH

Dear mother, I remember well. Dear Mother, I've Come Home to Die. E. Bowers. BlG

Dear mother, in dreams I see her. Lullaby. Claxson Bellamy *and* Harry Paulton. *Fr.* Erminie. BOL

Dear Mother, I've Come Home to Die. E. Bowers. BlG

Dear mother! ne'er shall I forget. Ne'er Shall I Forget. William Goldsmith Brown. MotAn

Dear Mother of the Savior, yet remaining. Last Antiphon; To Mary. James J. Donohue. ISi

"Dear mother," said a little fish. The Little Fish That Would Not Do as It Was Bid. Ann *or* Jane Taylor. OHIP

Dear Mystery, The. John Hall Wheelock. TBM

Dear native brook! wild streamlet of the West! Sonnet: To the River Otter. Samuel Taylor Coleridge. ChER; EnSW

Dear Native Regions. Wordsworth. TCEP (At This Farewell.) PoRL (Extract from the Conclusion of a Poem Composed in Anticipation of Leaving School.) BPN; EmBrPo

Dear Nature's Child, he nestled close to her! Emerson. Elizabeth Clementine Kinney. PEOR

Dear, near and true—no truer Time himself. A Dedication. Tennyson. BPN; EmBrPo; EPN; PoVP; VLEP

Dear Ned, no doubt you'll be surprised. Cooking and Courting. *Unknown.* LPS-1

Dear night, the ease of care. Madrigal. William Drummond of Hawthornden. EV-2

Dear Night, This World's Defeat. Henry Vaughan. EG; MaRV (Night, The.) TrGrPo

Dear object of my love, whose manly charms. Pretty Maids Beware! *Unknown.* CoMu

Dear! of all happy in the hour, most blest. Safety. Rupert Brooke. *Fr.* 1914. EnLoPo; LoPo; PoFr; VOD

Dear old couple my grandparents were, A. The Child and the Mariner. W. H. Davies. CH; PCN; POTT
Dear Old Ireland. Timothy Daniel Sullivan. TIP
Dear old ladies whose cheeks are pink, The. Autumn Leaves. Janie Screven Heyward. HBMV; MPB
Dear Old Mothers. Charles S. Ross. OQP; PGD; PSO; QP-1
(Old Mothers.) MOAH; PoToHe (new ed.)
Dear Old Toiling One, The. David Gray. MOAH; VA
Dear old woman in the lane, The. Neighboring. Christina Rossetti. *Fr.* Sing-Song. GaP; PCH
Dear One, I cannot tell you in a word. Margot. George O'Neil. VOD
Dear one, I love thine eyes, amazed. Feodor Tyutchev, *tr. fr. Russian by* Maud F. Jerrold. BoR
Dear Perfection. Ruth Pitter. AlDL
Dear Possible. Laura Riding. LiTA
Dear President, The. John James Piatt. DD, *sl. abr.;* GA, *sl. abr.;* MC; PAH
Dear quirister [*or* chorister], who from those shadows sends. Sonnet [*or* To the Nightingale]. William Drummond of Hawthornden. ElSeCe; EV-2; HBV; LO; ViBoPo
Dear Refuge of my weary soul. Prayer. Anne Steele. PraP
Dear Saint Thomas. Air Mail, Special. Sister Mary Philip. JKCP (1955 ed.)
"Dear! Shall I see thy face," she said. The Dame of Athelhall. Thomas Hardy. ChMo; CMP
Dear singer of our fathers' day. To John Greenleaf Whittier. William Hayes Ward. AA; GA
Dear Sir,—You wish to know my notions. The Candidate's Letter. James Russell Lowell. *Fr.* The Biglow Papers, 1st Series, No. VII. AA
Dear Sir: Your astonishment's odd. Limerick. *Unknown.* LiBL
Dear Sir,—Your letter come to han'. Mr. Hosea Biglow to the Editor of the Atlantic Monthly. James Russell Lowell. *Fr.* The Biglow Papers, 2d Series, No. X. IAP
Dear Sirmio, that art the very eye. Home to Sirmio. Catullus, *tr. by* Sir Theodore Martin. OuHeWo
Dear Smith, the sleest, paukie thief. Epistle to James Smith. Burns. BSV; HoPM; MCCG; OBEC
Dear son of Aegeus, to the gods alone/ Comes never age nor death. Decay, Earth's Universal Law. Sophocles, *tr. by* Lewis Campbell. *Fr.* Oedipus at Colonus. GrR
Dear son of Aegeus, to the gods alone/ Belongs immunity from death and age. Everything Decays. Sophocles, *tr. by* C. M. Bowra. *Fr.* Oedipus at Colonus. OxBG
Dear son of Aegeus, to the gods alone/ Is given immunity from eld and death. The Triumph of Time. Sophocles, *tr. by* F. Storr. *Fr.* Oedipus at Colonus. LiA
Dear Son, when the warm multitudes cry. Alonso to Ferdinand. W. H. Auden. *Fr.* The Sea and the Mirror. MoPo
Dear Sons of God,—of Him whom Sinai saw. Jesus. Ramón Pimentel Coronel. CAW
Dear Stranger: Let me welcome you. To a Very Young Gentleman. Bliss Carman. FAOV
Dear stranger, reading this small, true book. Strength to War. Stephen Stepanchev. WaP
Dear, they are praising your beauty. Praise. "Seumas O'Sullivan." BMEP; HBV; LBBV; MBP
Dear, They Have Poached the Eyes You Loved So Well. Rupert Brooke. WhC
Dear Thomas, didst thou never pop. A Simile. Matthew Prior. BOHV; CEP; CoBE; EiPP; FaBoEn; TCEP
Dear, though the Night Is Gone. W. H. Auden. InvP
Dear, though your mind stand so averse. Hear Me Yet. *Unknown.* ElL
Dear tiger lily, fanged and striped! you are the bravest. The Return. Conrad Aiken. NePA
Dear to me always was this lonely hill. The Infinite. Giacomo Leopardi, *tr. by* R. C. Trevelyan. WoL
Dear to me ever was this lonely hill. The Infinite. Giacomo Leopardi, *tr. by* Romilda Rendel. LiA
Dear to me were the three sides. The Wife of Aed mac Ainmirech, King of Ireland, Laments Her Husband. *Unknown.* AnIL
Dear to my heart are the ancestral dwellings of America. The Ancestral Dwellings. Henry van Dyke. CV; HiLiAm; PoMa; VOD
Dear to my soul! then leave me not forsaken! Sonnet. Henry Constable. *Fr.* Diana. ElL; OBSC; ReEn; ReIE; SiCE; TuPP
Dear to the Loves, and to the Graces vowed. Mary Queen of Scots Landing at the Mouth of the Derwent, Workington. Wordsworth. ES
Dear Togetherness, The. William Channing Gannett. GrCo 1
Dear Tom, this brown jug that now foams with mild ale. The Brown Jug. Francis Fawkes. ViBoPo
Dear urge no more that killing cause. To One That Pleaded Her Own Want of Merit [*or* To Celia Pleading Want of Merit]. Thomas Stanley. MeLP; OBS
Dear victims, kindly bear with me a minute. Prologue for a Magician. Arthur Guiterman. PoMS
Dear Voyager, a lucky star be thine. Ageanax. Edward Cracroft Lefroy. Echoes from Theocritus, VI. OBVV
Dear, wakeful bird! I bid thine accents hail. The Landrail. Sir Aubrey De Vere. IrPN
Dear wanton, when the moon made light our bed. Mother of Men. Stephen Southwold. HBMV
Dear Was He. *Unknown, tr. fr. Late Middle Irish by* Standish Hayes O'Grady. *Fr.* The Life of St. Cellach of Killala. OnYI
Dear, when I did from you remove. Madrigal. Lord Herbert of Cherbury. ElL; ElSeCe
Dear, when I went with you. A Song of Two Wanderers. Marguerite Wilkinson. BAP; HBMV; PoTo; SBMV
Dear, when the sun is set. Give Me Not Tears: Joy. Rose Hawthorne Lathrop. AA
Dear, when we sit in that high, placid room. Touché. Jessie Fauset. CDC
Dear, when you see my grave. Give Me Not Tears: Despair. Rose Hawthorne Lathrop. AA
Dear, why make you more of a dog than me? Astrophel and Stella, LIX. Sir Philip Sidney. OAEP; SiPS
Dear [*or* Deare], why should you command me to my rest. Idea, XXXVII [*or* Night and Day *or* Sonnets to "Idea," 11]. Michael Drayton. EG; ElL; EPP; HBV; LiTB; LiTG; LiTL; LO; LoPo; OAEP; OBSC; PoEL-2; ReEn; TuPP; ViBoPo
Dear wife, last midnight, whilst I read. Dibdin's Ghost. Eugene Field. AA; OBAV
Dear wife, let me have a fire made. Sir T. J.'s Speech to His Wife and Children. *Unknown.* CoMu
Dear withered cheek—you know the hue. My Maiden Aunt. Charles Henry Luders. PR
Dear, you are old. Superannuation. Sister M. Eleanore. GrCo-2
Dear youth, too early lost, who now art laid. On the Death of a Young and Favorite Slave. Martial. AWP; JAWP; LiTW; WBP
Dear Zeus, at Thy ways I wonder. For all that live adore Thee. The Problem. Theognis. GrPE
Deare, if You Change. *Unknown. See* Dear, if You Change.
Deare love, for nothing lesse than thee. *See* Dear love, for nothing less than thee.
Deare Venus, if thou wilt bee kinde. *Unknown.* SeCSL
Dearest all faire is in your browne. *Unknown.* SeCSL
Dearest and nearest brother. Stephen Spender. Elegy for Margaret, VI. FaBoEn
Dearest, Do Not You Delay Me. *At. to* John Fletcher. *Fr.* The Spanish Curate. SeCL; ViBoPo
Dearest Friend, Thou Art in Love. Heine, *tr. fr. German by* Emma Lazarus. *Fr.* Homeward Bound. TrJP
Dearest, in that world so far away. Be near Me. Aleksandr Kovalenkov. BoRS
Dearest love [*or* one], do you remember. When This Cruel War Is Over [*or* Weeping, Sad and Lonely]. Charles Carroll Sawyer. BlG; TrAS
Dearest my wife who lies. Personal Poem. Kendrick Smithyman. AnNZ
Dearest of all the heroes! Peerles knight. Don Quixote. Arthur Davison Ficke. HBMV; PoeMoYo
"Dearest of men, for love of thee." Death in Bed. *Unknown.* *Fr.* The Life of Guthlac. PoLi
Dearest of thousands, now the time drawes neere. His Charge to Julia at His Death. Robert Herrick. SeCV-1
Dearest One ("Dearest one, can you not see"). Vladimir Soloviev, *tr. fr. Russian by* Oleg Maslenikov. BoFr
("Do you not see, Beloved?" *tr. by* R. M. Hewitt.) BoR
Dearest one, do you remember. *See* Dearest love, do you remember.
"Dearest papa," says my boy to me. The Legend of the Easter Eggs. Fitz-James O'Brien. BeLS
Dearest Poets, The. Leigh Hunt. BCEP; HBV; OTPC (1923 ed.)
(Poets, The.) ERP; PtP
Dearest Spot on Earth, The. W. T. Wrighton. FaBoBe; OlF
Dearest, these household cares remit. The Blackbird. Henry Charles Beeching. OBVV
Dearest, though dark was our fate, yet with joy have I sung of it. Love Rides the Lion. Karl Gjellerup. BoDS
Dearest, we are like two flowers. Frimaire. Amy Lowell. ChMo; CMP
Dearest, when your lovely head. But I Shall Weep. Beatrice Redpath. CaP; OCL
Dearly I love a friend; yet a foe I may turn to my profit. Friend and Foe. Schiller. BoFr
Death. Vicente Aleixandre, *tr. fr. Spanish by* Eleanor L. Turnbull. CoSP
Death. Maltbie D. Babcock. MaRV; OQP; QP-2; WGRP
(Emancipation.) BLRP; WBLP
Death. Evgeni Baratynsky, *tr. fr. Russian by* C. M. Bowra. BoR
Death. Maxwell Bodenheim. AnAmPo; BAP; LA; LiTM; MAP; MAPA; MoAmPo (1942 ed.); NP; PFY; TrJP

Death. *At. to* George Boleyn, *also to* Anne Boleyn. *See* O Death, Rock Me Asleep.
Death. Emily Brontë. AEV
Death. George Frederick Cameron. BoCaPo
Death. Agnes Lindsay Carnegie. EBSV
Death. Madison Cawein. AA
Death, *sel.* John Clare.
"Flowers shall hang upon the palls." PoD; RO
Death. Florence Earle Coates. HBV; OQP; QP-1
Death, *sel.* Mary Elizabeth Coleridge.
"Bid me remember, O my gracious Lord." TrPWD
Death. Grace Noll Crowell. PraP
Death ("The bustle in a house"). Emily Dickinson. *See* Bustle in a house, The.
Death ("Death is a dialogue"). Emily Dickinson. OQP; QP-1; WGRP
Death. William Croswell Doane. EOAH
Death. John Donne. *See* Death, Be Not Proud *and* Sonnet: "At the round earth's imagin'd corners, blow."
Death. Etna Doop-Smith. PSO
Death. Thomas Flatman. *See* Sad Day, The.
Death. Philip Freneau. *Fr.* The House of Night. OnAP
Death. George Herbert. MePo; OBS; PoFS; SeCL; SeCV-1
Death. Thomas Hood. ES; OBEV; PeBoSo
(It Is Not Death.) OBRV
("It is not death, that sometimes in a sigh.") EG
(Sonnet: "It is not death.") LoBV; ViBoPo
Death. Walter Savage Landor. *See* Death Stands above Me.
Death. Lucretius, *tr. fr. Latin by* Dryden. *Fr.* De Rerum Natura, III. BeR
Death. Lu Yu, *tr. fr. Chinese by* Pai Chwen-yu. WhP
Death. John Bruce MacCallum. PoP
Death. Arthur MacGillivray. JKCP (1955 ed.)
Death. Alan Mackintosh. LBBV
Death. Thomas May. *Fr.* Continuation of Lucan. MaRV
Death. Milton. *Fr.* Paradise Lost, II. LiA
(Challenge of Death, The.) BCEP
Death. James Oppenheim. WGRP
Death. George Pellew. AA
Death. Katherine Philips. AEV; WP
Death. Rainer Maria Rilke, *tr. fr. German by* Randall Jarrell. AnGP
Death, A. W. W. E. Ross. BoCaPo
Death ("Death is here, and death is there"). Shelley. UnPo (1st ed.)
Death ("They die—the dead return not"). Shelley. EmBrPo
Death ("What if some little paine the passage have"). Spenser. *See* What if Some Little Paine . . .
Death ("As when one layeth/ His worn-out robes away"). *Unknown, tr. fr. Sanskrit by* Sir Edwin Arnold. *Fr.* Bhagavad-Gita. MaRV
Death ("I am a stranger in the land"). *Unknown.* BLPA
Death ("Once he will miss, twice he will miss"). *Unknown. Fr.* The Thousand and One Nights. AWP; JAWP; WBP
Death ("Then shall he lie in the earth"). *Unknown, tr. fr. Greek by* C. M. Bowra. OxBG
Death. William Carlos Williams. OxBA; PoP
Death. W. B. Yeats. ChMP; GTBS-D; PoD; POTE; ShBV-4
Death./ The death of a million. Pastoral. Ron Loewinsohn. NeAP
Death; a Sonnet. William Walsh. SeCL
Death again has swooped and flown. Resurgence. John L. Bonn. JKCP (1955 ed.)
Death Alone. "Pablo Neruda," *tr. fr. Spanish by* Angel Flores. AnCL; OnHM
Death, Always Cruel. Dante, *tr. fr. Italian by* Dante Gabriel Rossetti. *Fr.* La Vita Nuova, III. LiTW
("Death, always cruel Pity's foe in chief.") AWP; JAWP; WBP
Death and Burial of a Saint, The, *br. sel.* Isaac Watts.
Dead, The. BeR
Death and Burial of Cock Robbin, The. *Unknown.* SiTL
Death and Cupid chanced to meet. Love and Death. *Unknown.* AnSpL-1
Death and darkness get you packing. Easter Hymn. Henry Vaughan. StJW; TriL
Death and Despair. W. J. Turner. PoD
Death and Doctor Hornbook. Burns. DaM; EBSV; PIR
Death and General Putnam. Arthur Guiterman. DDA; OnSP; PoMS
Death and Last Confession of Wandering Peter, The. Hilaire Belloc. OtMeF
Death and Life. Emily Dickinson. *See* Apparently with no surprise.
Death and Night. James Benjamin Kenyon. AA
Death and Resurrection. George Croly. WGRP
Death and the Fairies. Patrick MacGill. HBMV; LBBV
Death and the Lady. Léonie Adams. MAP; MoAB; MoAmPo; MOAP
Death and the Maiden, *sel.* W. H. Oliver.
"Mourn her in the valleys, you young lovers, and throughout your gloom." AnNZ
Death and the Maiden. *Unknown, tr. fr. Irish by* Frank O'Connor. KiLC
Death and the Resurrection of the Dead. First Corinthians, XV, Bible, *N.T.* EM-1
Death and the Ruffians. Chaucer. *See* Pardoner's Tale, The.
Death and the Youth. Letitia E. Landon. LPS-1
Death and Transfiguration. Marya Zaturenska. QS
Death-angel smote Alexander McGlue, The. Out of the Hurly-Burly. "Max Adeler." CenHV
Death as the Fool. Frank T. Marzials. VA
Death as the Teacher of Love-Lore. Frank T. Marzials. VA
Death at Daybreak. Anne Reeve Aldrich. AA; OQP; QP-2
Death at Sea. Coleman Rosenberger. DaM
Death at the headlands, Hesiod, long ago. Hesiod, 1908. Alexander Mair. GoTS
Death at the Thames Ice Fair. John Gay. *Fr.* Trivia; or, The Art of Walking the Streets of London. BeR
Death, Be Not Proud. John Donne. Holy Sonnets, X. BLV; BoLiVe; ChTr; CoBE; EPS; EV-2; FaFP; GoBC; GTBS-W; HBV; InvP; LiTB; LiTG; OnPM; PG (1955 ed.); PoE; PoFr; PoRA; ReaPo; RiBV; TreFS; TrGrPo; TwCrTr; TwP; WHA
(Death.) ATP; BEL; CBOV; EnLi-1; EnLit; EPP; ES; MaRV; OBEV; ShBV-4; TCEP; TOP; UnPo (1st ed.)
("Death be not proud, though some have called thee.") AnEnPo; AnFE; AtBAP; EiL; ElSeCe; EnL; EnLP; ExPo; FaBoEn; InPo; LoBV; MaPo; MeLP; MePo; MyFE; OAEP; OBS; PeBoSo; Po; PoEL-2; PoFS; PreP; ReEn; SeCeV; SeCV-1; SeEP; TuPP; TwHP; ViBoPo
(Holy Sonnet.) TyEnPo
Death beckons me—O that I could. Babylonian Sorrows. Heine. AnGP
Death Bed. *See* Deathbed.
Death before forty's no bar. Lo! Obit on Parnassus. F. Scott Fitzgerald. InMe; WhC
Death-blow is a life-blow to some, A. Emily Dickinson. AmPP
Death by Rarity. Marguerite Young. LiTA
Death by Water. T. S. Eliot. *Fr.* The Waste Land. CaAE
Death came to him so quickly. The Flies. Merrill Moore. AnAmPo; AnEnPo; LA; MOAP
Death came to me at twilight like a wraith. Since I Have Seen Death's Face. Fania Kruger. UnW
Death cannot surprise us who are driven. The People Has No Obituary. Eunice Clark. NAMP
Death cannot yet extinguish that entyre. *Unknown.* SeCSL
Death Carol: "Come, lovely and soothing Death." Walt Whitman. *Fr.* When Lilacs Last in the Dooryard Bloomed, XIV. AnFE; APA; CoAnAm; LBAP; LEAP; MaRV
(Come, Lovely and Soothing Death.) PoD
Death Chant Henri Michaux, *tr. fr. French by* Wallace Fowlie. MiCF
Death-Chant of the Centaurs, *sel.* Stephen Vincent Benét.
"Close his eyes with the coins." LEAP
Death-Child, The. "Fiona Macleod." VA
Death Come to My House He Didn't Stay Long, *with music. Unknown.* BoAN-2
Death comes like this, I know. Fog. John Reed. AnEnPo
Death Comes Riding. Einar Hjörleifsson Kvaran, *tr. fr. Icelandic by* Jakobina Johnson. *Fr.* Governor Lenhard. IcP
Death could not come between us two. Deep Waters. Van Tassel Sutphen. AA
Death, death:—O amiable lovely death! Shakespeare. *Fr.* King John, III. iv. PoD
Death Deposed. William Allingham. OnYI
Death devours all lovely things. Passer Mortuus Est. Edna St. Vincent Millay. MAP; MoAmPo; OxBA; TBM
Death—Divination. Charles Wharton Stork. NLK (1947 ed.); SBMV
Death done warn me right. Tokens. John Richard Moreland. IHA
Death Ends All Woe. Robert Herrick. EPS (1942 ed.)
Death Feast. Viktor Khlebnikov, *tr. fr. Russian by* C. M. Bowra. BoRS
Death from Cancer. Robert Lowell. FiMAP
(In Memory of Arthur Winslow.) MiAP
Death Fugue. Paul Celan, *tr. fr. German by* Clement Greenberg. TrJP
Death Goes before Me. Yvor Winters. NP
Death-Going of Scyld, The. *Unknown. Fr.* Beowulf. BCEP
Death-Grapple. Laura Bell Everett. OQP; QP-2
Death has come to visit us today. On the Acequia Madre. Alice Corbin. NP
Death hath two hands to slay with: with the one. Sonnets from "Two Lives." William Ellery Leonard. MOAP; TBM
Death hunted me for life, wherefor. The Double Crucifixion. John Malcolm Brinnin. LiTM (rev. ed.)

Death-Hymn, A. Felicia Dorothea Hemans. *See* Dirge: "Calm on the bosom of thy God."
Death I Can Understand. *Unknown.* BLP
Death, I denounce thy cruelty. Rondel. Villon. TrFP
Death I do not mind. The Still Search. Genevieve Taggard. NV
Death, I repent. Invocation of Death. Kathleen Raine. MoAB
Death, I say, my heart is bowed. The Shroud. Edna St. Vincent Millay. NP
Death, if thou wilt, fain would I plead with thee. A Dialogue. Swinburne. PoEL-5
Death in an ancient country was a simple passport. Elegy on the Pilot. Reuel Denney. PoF
Death in Battle. *Unknown. Fr.* The Battle of Maldon. PoLi
Death in Bed. *Unknown. Fr.* The Life of Guthlac. PoLi
Death in Boyhood. *Unknown, tr. fr. Greek by* F. L. Lucas. GrPE
Death in Carmel. Jessica Powers. PraNu
Death in Hospital, A. John Lehmann. AtBAP; ChMP
Death in Life. Thomas, Lord Vaux. *See* No Pleasure without Some Pain.
Death in Life. *Unknown.* OQP; QP-2
Death-in-Love. Dante Gabriel Rossetti. The House of Life, XLVIII. BPN; EmBrPo; PoVP; ViP; ViPo
Death in May. Muriel Newton. NeTW
Death in the Corn. Detlev von Liliencron, *tr. fr. German by* C. F. MacIntyre. WaaP
Death in the Desert, A. Robert Browning. GoTL; OxBoCh; PoVP; StJW
Sels.
"For life, with all it yields of joy and woe." OQP; QP-2
(Truth.) MaRV
"I say, the acknowledgment of God in Christ," 3 *ll.* ChIP
Illimitable God, The. MaRV
Death in the Sun. Eugenio Florit, *tr. fr. Spanish by* H. R. Hays. TwSpPo
Death in this tomb his weary limbs hath laid. Death's Epitaph. Philip Freneau. *Fr.* The House of Night. AA
Death Inevitable. Horace. *See* To Postumus.
Death Invoked. Philip Massinger. *See* Song: "Why art thou slow, thou rest of trouble, Death."
Death Is a Blessed Thing. "Angelus Silesius," *tr. fr. German by* Paul Carus. OnPM
Death is a dialogue. Death. Emily Dickinson. OQP; QP-1; WGRP
Death Is a Door. Nancy Byrd Turner. BLPA; NeHB
"Death is a voyage," I heard it lightly told. O Mariners! Archibald Rutledge. EtS
Death is all metaphors, shape in one history. Sonnet [*or* Two Sonnets]. Dylan Thomas. Sonnets, II. LiTM; MoAB; MoBrPo (1950 ed.)
Death is another milestone on their way. The Funeral. Stephen Spender. ChMo; MBP; MoAB; MoBrPo; NAMP; TwCV
Death Is at Hand. Heine, *tr. fr. German by* Herman Salinger. AnGP
Death Is before Me To-Day. *Unknown, tr. fr. Egyptian.* MaRV
Death Is but Death. Will Dyson. BoAV; MoAuPo
Death is but life's escape: a rung. Youth and Death. E. Merrill Root. OQP; PSO; QP-1
Death Is Dead. Paul Eluard, *tr. fr. French by* Patricia Terry. OnPM
Death Is Great. Rainer Maria Rilke, *tr. fr. German by* Herman Salinger. TwGV
Death is gwineter lay his cold icy hands on me. Death's Gwineter Lay His Cold Icy Hands on Me. *Unknown.* BoAN-2
Death is here, and death is there. Death. Shelley. UnPo (1st ed.)
Death is in the crows that flap their wings. Prevesa. Kostas Kariotakis. MoGP
Death is like moonlight in a lofty wood. Death—Divination. Charles Wharton Stork. NLK (1947 ed.); SBMV
Death is more than One X E. E. Cummings. FaBoMo
Death is no foeman, we were born together. Knights Errant. Sister M. Madeleva. CAW
Death is only an old door. Death Is a Door. Nancy Byrd Turner. BLPA; NeHB
Death is stronger than all the governments. Death Snips Proud Men. Carl Sandburg. ChMo; CMP; CoBA
Death Is the Chilly Night. Heine, *tr. fr. German by* Kate Flores. AnGP
Death is the strongest of all living things. Warning to One. Merrill Moore. MAP; MoAmPo; NP; PIAE; TrGrPo; YaD
Death it can bring. Issa, *tr. fr. Japanese by* Harold Gould Henderson. LiTW
Death, Life, Fear. Lilla Cabot Perry. PC
Death like a Rose. Sir Robert Howard *and* John Dryden. *Fr.* The Indian Queen. BeR
Death Lullaby, The. *Unknown.* BOL
Death May Be . . . Oliver St. John Gogarty. POTE
(Death May Be Very Gentle.) PoRA
Death of a Bird. Jon Silkin. NePoEA
Death of a Dove. The. James Schevill. FiMAP
Death of a Friar, The. Lascelles Abercrombie. MM
Death of a Friend. Mildred D. Ingalls. CAG
Death of a Hornet. D. G. Jones. PeCV
Death of a Jazz Musician. William Jay Smith. NePoAm-2
Death of a Queen, The. Congreve. *Fr.* The Mourning Muse of Alexis. BeR
Death of a Romish Lady, The. *Unknown. See* Romish Lady, The.
Death of a Soldier, The. Wallace Stevens. SoV
(Death of the Soldier.) AmPP
Death of a Son. Jon Silkin. NePoEA; PoN; POTE (1959 ed.)
Death of a Teacher. L. F. Gerlach. PtPa
Death of a Toad, The. Richard Wilbur. AmP; MiAP; MoVE
Death of a Zulu, The. William Plomer. BoSA
Death of Admiral Benbow, The. *Unknown.* CoMu; SG
Death of Admiral Blake, The. Sir Henry Newbolt. GTML
Death of Adonis, The. Shakespeare. *Fr.* Venus and Adonis. WHA
Death of Agamemnon, The. Aeschylus, *tr. fr. Greek by* George Thomson. *Fr.* Agamemnon. LiA
Death of Ailill, The. Francis Ledwidge. OnYI
Death of an Elephant. Bertram J. Warr. TwCaPo
Death of an Italian Beggar, The, *sel.* Brother Clement.
"Larks and the angels make a stir." SaFP
Death of an Old Man, The. Michael Hamburger. NePoEA
Death of Antony. Shakespeare. *Fr.* Antony and Cleopatra, IV, xiii. FiP
(Deaths of Antony and Cleopatra.) CBOV
("I am dying. Egypt, dying.") EtPaEn, *br. sel.;* LoPS
Death of Argus, The. Homer. *See* Ulysses and His Dog.
Death of Artemidora, The. Walter Savage Landor. *Fr.* Pericles and Aspasia, LXXXV. BEL; BPN; EnRP; EPN; ERP; InP; SeCeV; VA
("Artemidora! Gods invisible.") ViBoPo
Death of Artists, The. Baudelaire, *tr. fr. French by* Alan Conder. TrFP
Death of Astrophel, The. Spenser. *See* Astrophel.
Death of Azron, The. Alice Wellington Rollins. AA
Death of Bendall, The. *Unknown.* ABS
Death of Buckingham, The. Pope. *Fr.* Moral Essays, Epistle III: Of the Use of Riches. FiP
(Death of the Duke of Buckingham, The.) ExPo
(Duke of Buckingham.) OBEC
(Second Duke of Buckingham, The.) CoEV
Death of Chiron, The. J. P. McAuley. BoAV
Death of Christ. Arthur R. Macdougall, Jr. ChIP
Death of Chrysaor, The. Walter Savage Landor. *Fr.* The Hellenics. EmBrPo
Death of Cleopatra, The ("Nunc est bibendum"). Horace, *tr. fr. Latin by* Sir Stephen E. De Vere. Odes, I, 37. EnLi-1; OuHeWo
(Fall of Cleopatra, The, *tr. by* the Earl of Derby.) RoL
Death of Cleopatra. Shakespeare. *Fr.* Antony and Cleopatra, V, ii. FiP; TreFS
(Cleopatra's Death.) TrGrPo
(Deaths of Antony and Cleopatra.) CBOV
("Give me my robe, put on my crown.") AtBAP; LoPS; NBE
(I Am Fire, and Ayre.) LiA
Death of Colman, The. Thomas Frost. PAH
Death of Cowards, The. Shakespeare. *See* Cowards ("Cowards die many times before their deaths").
Death of Cuchulain. Eleanor Rogers Cox. JKCP
Death of Cuchulain, The. W. B. Yeats. *See* Cuchulain's Fight with the Sea.
Death of Custer. The. "Captain Jack" Crawford. PoOW
Death of Daphnis, The. Theocritus, *tr. fr. Greek by* Charles Stuart Calverley. Idylls, I. AWP; JAWP; WBP
Death of David, The. Hayyim Nahman Bialik, *tr. fr. Hebrew by* Herbert Danby. TrJP
Death of Death, The. Shakespeare. *See* Sonnets, CXLVI.
Death of Dermid, The. Sir Samuel Ferguson. IrPN
Death of Digenes Akritas, The. John Heath-Stubbs. NePoEA
Death of Don Pedro, The. *Unknown, tr. fr. Spanish by* John Gibson Lockhart. AnSpL-1; AWP
Death of Durandarte. *Unknown, tr. fr. Spanish by* Thomas Rodd. TeCS
(Montesinos and Durandarte.) LyMA
Death of Edward, The. Michael Drayton. *Fr.* Mortimeriados. ReIE
Death of Empedocles, The, *sel.* Friedrich Hölderlin, *pr. tr. fr. German.*
"You are permitted to live so long as you have breath." LiA
Death of Europe, The. Charles Olson. NeAP
Death of Eve, The, *sel.* William Vaughn Moody.
"Yea, Jubal?" Act I. WoL
Death of Falstaff, The. Shakespeare. King Henry V, *fr.* II, iii. LiA

Death of Friends, The. Adele Levi. GoYe
Death of Gaudentis. "Harriet Annie." WBLP
Death of General Pike, The. Laughton Osborn. PAH
Death of Goody Nurse, The. Rose Terry Cooke. PAH
Death of Gorguthion, The. Homer, *tr. fr. Greek by* F. L. Lucas. *Fr.* The Iliad, VIII. GrPE
(Death of Gorgythian, The, *tr. by* Pope.) GrR
Death of Grant, The. Ambrose Bierce. AA; BAP; GA; MDAH
Death of Grendel's Mother, The. *Unknown, tr. and ad. fr. Anglo-Saxon by* Chauncey Brewster Tinker. *Fr.* Beowulf. EPP
Death of Haidée, The. Byron. *Fr.* Don Juan, IV. FiP; WHA, *longer sel.*
Death of Hamlet. Shakespeare. *Fr.* Hamlet, V, ii. FiP
Death of Hampden, The. Pakenham Beatty. VA
Death of Harrison, The. Nathaniel Parker Willis. GA; PAH
Death of Hector, The. Homer. *See* Last Fight, The.
Death of Herminius, The. Macaulay. *Fr.* The Battle of the Lake Regillus. OtMeF
Death of Jack Hinton, The. *Unknown. See* Wreck on the C. & O., The.
Death of Jefferson, The. Hezekiah Butterworth. GA; PAH
Death of Jesse James. *Unknown. See* Jesse James.
Death of Jesus, The. St. Luke, XXIII: 1-46, Bible, *N.T.* TreF
Death of Jocasta, The. Sophocles. *See* Jocasta's Death.
Death of Kais, The. Nizami, *tr. fr. Persian by* James Atkinson. *Fr.* Laili and Majnún. PeP
Death of King Edward VII, The. *Unknown.* OxBoLi
Death of Kings, The ("Let's talk of graves"). Shakespeare. King Richard II, *fr.* III, ii. TrGrPo
(Kingship.) EV-1
(Richard II's Dejection.) TreFS
Death of Knight Stig, The. *Unknown, tr. fr. Danish by* E. M. Smith-Dampier. BoDaBa
Death of Laili, The. Nizami, *tr. fr. Persian by* James Atkinson. *Fr.* Laili and Majnún. PeP
Death of Leander, The. Thomas Hood. *Fr.* Hero and Leander. EnRP
Death of Lear. Shakespeare. *Fr.* King Lear, V, iii. FiP
("And my poor fool is hang'd!") PoD
(My Poore Foole.) LiA
Death of Lenin, The. Vladimir Mayakovsky, *tr. fr. Russian by* Jack Lindsay. *Fr.* Vladimir Ilyich-Lenin. RuPo
Death of Leonidas, The. George Croly. BeLS; LPS-2
Death of Lesbia's Bird, The. Catullus, *tr. fr. Latin by* Samuel Taylor Coleridge. AWP
(Dead Starling, The.) OnPM
Death of Lincoln, The. Bryant. *See* Abraham Lincoln.
Death of Little Boys. Allen Tate. LiTA; MAP; MoAB; MoAmPo; MOAP
Death of Llywelyn ap Gruffudd, The. Gruffudd ab yr Ynad Coch, *tr. fr. Welsh by* Gwyn Williams. LyMA
Death of Love. *Unknown, tr. fr. Chinese by* Henry H. Hart. ChLP; PoHN
Death of Lyon, The. Henry Peterson. BlG; GA; PAH
Death of Marlborough, The. George Walter Thornbury. VA
Death of Meleager, The. Swinburne. *Fr.* Atalanta in Calydon. BMEP; BPN; OBVV; PoVP; VLEP
Death of Master Tommy Rook, The. Eliza Cook. OTPC
Death of Minnehaha, The. Longfellow. The Song of Hiawatha, Pt. XX. AA
Death of Moses, The. *Unknown, tr. fr. Hebrew by* Alice Lucas. TrJP
Death of My Aunt. *Unknown.* OxBoLi; SiTL
Death of Napoleon, The. Isaac McLellan. BAP; PECK
Death of Nelson, The. *Unknown.* OxBoLi
(New Song Composed on the Death of Lord Nelson, A.) CoMu
Death of Nicou, The, *sel.* Thomas Chatterton.
Tygers. RO
Death of Oberon, The. George Walter Thornbury. HOAH
(Dirge on the Death of Oberon, the Fairy King.) CBPC
Death of Oenone, The. Quintus Smyrnaeus, *tr. fr. Greek by* F. L. Lucas. *Fr.* Posthomerica, X. GrPE
Death of Oenone, The. Tennyson. PreP
Death of Othello. Shakespeare. *See* Othello's Death.
Death of Parcy Reed, The. *Unknown.* BaBo (A *and* B *vers.*); ESPB; OBB
Death of Patroclus, The. Homer, *tr. fr. Greek by* Sir William Marris. *Fr.* The Iliad, XVI. OxBG
(Death of Patroklos, The, *pr. tr. by* Andrew Lang, Walter Leaf, *and* Ernest L. Myers.) GrR
("Now while the sun was going about mid-heaven," *longer sel., pr. tr. by* Lang, Leaf, *and* Myers.) GrPo
Death of Poetry, The, *sel.* Nathalia Crane.
Requiem. MoAmPo (1942 ed.)
Death of Polybius Jubb, The. Roy Campbell. *See* Limerick: "He died in attempting to swallow."
Death of Puck, The. Eugene Lee-Hamilton. HBMV; OBVV
Death of Queen Dagmar, The. *Unknown, tr. fr. Danish by* E. M. Smith-Dampier. BoDaBa
Death of Queen Jane, The. *Unknown.* BaBo (A, B, *and* D *vers.*); ESPB (A *and* B *vers.*); ViBoFo
(Jane Was a Neighbor, C *vers.*) BaBo
Death of Rhesus, The. Euripides, *tr. fr. Greek by* Gilbert Murray. *Fr.* Rhesus. OxBG
Death of Richard Wagner, The. Swinburne. LoBV
Death of Robert, Earl of Huntingdon, *sel.* Anthony Munday *and* Henry Chettle.
"Weep, weep, ye woodmen, wail." CH; EIL; ElSeCe; OBSC
(Dirge for Robin Hood.) TriL
(Song.) ThWaDe
Death of Robin Hood, The. William Rose Benét. OTPC (1946 ed.)
Death of Robin Hood, The. Eugene Field. StPo
Death of Robin Hood, The. *Unknown. See* Robin Hood's Death and Burial.
Death of Roland, The. *Unknown, tr. fr. Old French. Fr.* The Song of Roland. LiA, *tr. by* Henry Adams; MeRV, *tr. unknown*
Death of Saint Francis, The, *sel. Tr. fr. Spanish by* Marion O. Habig.
"His death began the day the stigmata." SaFP
Death of Saint Guthlac. Cynewulf, *tr. fr. Anglo-Saxon. Fr.* Guthlac. ACP
Death of Saint Therese of Lisieux. Jessica Powers. PraNu
Death of Samson. Milton. *See* Brave Epitaph, A.
Death of Schiller, The. Bryant. UnW
Death of Shelley, The. Donald Parson. MuM
Death of Sir Nihil, book the *n*th. Tywater. Richard Wilbur. GTBS-W; LiTA; LiTM (rev. ed.); MiAP; MoAB; NePA; ReMP
Death of Slavery, The. Bryant. AA; DD, *much abr.;* MDAH; PoFr, *abr.*
Death of Sohrab, The ("He spoke, and Sohrab kindled at his taunts"). Matthew Arnold. *Fr.* Sohrab and Rustum. LH
(Sohrab's Death.) WHA
Death of Sohrab, The ("He spoke; and Sohrab smiled on him, and took/ The spear"). Matthew Arnold. *Fr.* Sohrab and Rustum. FiP
Death of Talbot, The. Samuel Daniel. *Fr.* The Civil Wars. EV-1
Death of Tammuz, The. Saul Tchernichowsky, *tr. fr. Hebrew by* L. V. Snowman. TrJP
Death of the Ball Turret Gunner, The. Randall Jarrell. CoBMV; ExPo; FiMAP; MiAP; MoAmPo (1950 ed.); OxBA; ShBV-3; UnPo (3d ed.); WaaP; WaP
Death of the Beloved. Rainer Maria Rilke, *tr. fr. German by* Jessie Lemont. UnW
Death of the Bull. Roy Campbell. FaBoTw
Death of the Craneman, The. Alfred Hayes. LiTA; NAMP; WaP
Death of the Day. Walter Savage Landor. TriL
Death of the Dragon, The. Spenser. *Fr.* The Faerie Queene, I, 11. WHA
Death of the Duke of Buckingham, The. Pope. *See* Death of Buckingham, The.
Death of the Duke of Clarence and Avondale, The, *sel.* Tennyson.
Be Comforted. MaRV
Death of the Eagle, The. José Maria de Heredia, *tr. fr French by* John Hervey. *Fr.* Les Trophées. LiA
Death of the Flowers, The. Bryant. AA; AnAmPo; AnNE; APW; CoBA; DD, *abr.;* GN; HBV; IAP; LA; LBAP; LPS-2; OBAV; OTPC; PTA-2; PYM; TCAP; TreF; TVSH; WBLP
Death of the Hired Man, The. Robert Frost. AmPP; AnNE; ATP; BAV; CBOV; ChMo; CMP; CoBA; CoV; DDA; HoPM; MaC; MAP; MoAB; MoAmPo; MOAP; NeMA; OxBA; PCN; PFE; PIAE; PreP; SeCeV; TCAP; TCPD; TOP; TrGrPo; TwHP; UnPo (1st ed.)
Home, *br. sel.* MaRV
(Home Defined.) TreF
Death of the innocent by the innocent. On Reading Gene Derwood's "The Innocent." Willard Maas. NePA
Death of the King of Babylon. Isaiah, XIV: 7-12, Bible, *O.T.* PoD
Death of the Klepht, The. *Unknown, tr. fr. Modern Greek by* Rae Dalven. MoGP
Death of the Lincoln Despotism, The. *Unknown.* PAH
Death of the Old Year. Tennyson. DD; HBV; HH; LPS-3; OTPC; PECK; PIR
Death of the Poet. Rainer Maria Rilke, *tr. fr. German by* Vernon Watkins. AnGP
Death of the Sheriff, The. Robert Lowell. MoAB; MoAmPo (1950 ed.)
(Noli Me Tangere.) FiMAP
Death of the Soldier. Wallace Stevens. *See* Death of a Soldier, The.
Death of the White Fawn, The. Andrew Marvell. *See* Nymph Complaining for the Death of Her Fawn, The.

Death, of thee do I make my moan. To Death, of His Lady. Villon, *tr. by* Dante Gabriel Rossetti. AWP; OuHeWo
Death of Troilus, The. Chaucer. *Fr.* Troilus and Criseyde. PoD
Death of Turnus, The, *abr.* Virgil, *tr. fr. Latin by* Dryden. *Fr.* The Aeneid, XII. WoL
Death of Urgan, The. Swinburne. *Fr.* Tristram of Lyonesse. WHA
Death of Warren, The. Epes Sargent. GA; MC; PAH
Death of Wolfe, The. *Unknown.* PAH
Death of Wyatt, The. Earl of Surrey. SiPS
Death of Yeats, The. George Barker. LiTB
Death of Zenocrate, The. Christopher Marlowe. *See* Divine Zenocrate.
Death, on a solemn night of state. The Court of Death. John Gay. EV-3
Death on his mission sought my lady's side. George Henry Boker. Sonnets; a Sequence of Profane Love, XCV. MOAP
Death on the Rancherie. Emily Leavens. TwCaPo
Death over the Air. Jacinto Fombona Pachano, *tr. fr. Spanish by* Angel Flores. AnCL
Death Ray. Lola Ridge. TBM
Death, reaping the mad world, his crimson blade. The Foiled Reaper. William Kean Seymour. HBMV
Death-Scene, A. Emily Brontë. EmBrPo; EV-5
Death Sends Me the Flickering of Powdery Lids. Bilhana, *formerly at. to* Chauras, *tr. fr. Sanskrit by* E. Powys Mathers. *Fr.* Black Marigolds. OnPM
Death set his mark and left a mangled thing. Died of His Wounds. Sir Henry Head. PoP
Death shall be death forever unto thee. Forever Dead. Sappho, *tr. by* William Ellery Leonard. AWP; JAWP; LiA; LiTW; WBP
Death, since I find not one with whom to grieve. Canzone 17: He Beseeches Death for the Life of Beatrice. Dante. AWP; LyPI
Death Snips Proud Men. Carl Sandburg. ChMo; CMP; CoBA
Death Song, A. Paul Laurence Dunbar. AA; BANP; CDC; PoNe
Death Song. Robert Stephen Hawker. OBRV; OBVV
Death Song. Alonzo Lewis. PAH
Death-Song. Chief Long Lance. APW
Death Song, A. William Morris. EmBrPo; PoVP; VA; VLEP
Death Song in Taliesin. Richard Hovey. *Fr.* Taliesin. PC
Death Song of Egil the Son of Grim, The. Egil Skallagrimsson, *English vers. by* Henry Adams Bellows. PaOS
Death Song of Haakon the Good. Eyvindr Finsson, *tr. fr. Old Norse by* O. L. Oliver. LyMA
(Lay of Hakon, The, *tr. by* Lee M. Hollander.) PaOS
Death Speaks. Pedro Calderón de la Barca, *tr. fr. Spanish by* Gerald Brenan. TeCS
Death speaks:/ When men my scythe and darts supply. Thomas Parnell. *Fr.* Night Piece on Death. OnYI
Death Stands above Me [Whispering Low]. Walter Savage Landor. AEV; AnFE; BPN; CBOV; EmBrPo; EnRP; EPN; EV-4; LiTB; MaRV; OAEP; PoEL-4; TOP; WP
(Death.) HBV; PIAE
(Death Undreaded.) VA
(Lyrics and Epigrams, XII.) ERP
(No Word of Fear.) BPP
(On Death.) BoLiVe; EPP; InP; TrGrPo
(On His Own Death.) OBVV
Death stately came to a young man. Death Deposed. William Allingham. OnYI
Death stood beside us on your night of birth. To Duncan. Jessica Nelson North. NP
Death stretched down two hands. Casualty. Diana Witherby. ChMP
Death takes our loved ones. Selfishness. Margaret E. Bruner. MaRV; PoToHe
Death, that is small respecter of distinction. Trainwrecked Soldiers. John Frederick Nims. MiAP; ReMP
Death! that struck when I was most confiding. Death. Emily Brontë. AEV
Death the Conqueror ("The glories of our blood and state"). James Shirley. *See* Death the Leveller.
Death, the Conqueror ("Victorious men of earth! no more"). James Shirley. *See* Victorious Men of Earth.
Death the Enemy. Euripides, *tr. fr. Greek by* Robert Browning. *Fr.* Alcestis. OxBG
("O much-enduring heart and hand of mine!") GrPo
Death the Great. Elis Wyn o Lasynys, *tr. fr. Welsh by* George Borrow. LiTW
Death the Leveller. Anyte, *tr. fr. Greek by* F. L. Lucas. GrPE; GrR; OxBG, *tr. by* Sir William Marris
Death the Leveller [*or* Leveler]. James Shirley. *Fr.* The Contention of Ajax and Ulysses. BCEP; CBE; CBOV; CoEV; GTBS; GTBS-D; GTBS-W; GTSE; GTSL; LiTB; LoBV; LPS-1; MaRV; OBEV; OtMeF; PoLi; RiBV; SeCeV; ShBV-4
(Calchas before the Body of Ajax.) CaAE
(Death the Conqueror.) LEAP
(Death's Final Conquest.) EV-2; HBV
(Dirge, A: "Glories of our blood and state, The.") ACP; AnFE; AWP; BEL; EnLit; InPo; JAWP; PoEL-2; TOP; WBP
(Equality.) AnEnPo
(Glories of Our Blood and State, The.) AEV; ChTr; CenL; EG; ElSeCe; ExPo; InVP; LiTG; OBS; PG; PoRA; ReEn; SeEP; TrGrPo; TuPP; TVSH; ViBoPo; WaaP; WP; YT
(King of Kings, The.) LH
(Levelling Dust, The.) BLV
(Of Death.) SeCL; WHA
(Our Blood and State.) GoBC
(Song: "Glories of our blood and state, The.") FaBoEn
Death the Peacemaker. Ellen H. Flagg. BlG; MDAH
Death the Revealer. Albert E. S. Smythe. CPG
Death, tho I see him not, is near. Age. Walter Savage Landor. PoEL-4
Death, Thou Hast Seized Me. Isaac Luzzatto, *tr. fr. Hebrew by* Nina Davis Salaman. TrJP
Death, thou wast once an uncouth hideous thing. Death. George Herbert. MePo; OBS; PoFS; SeCL; SeCV-1
Death, though already in the world, as yet. The Legend of the Dead Lambs. "Owen Meredith." VA
Death, thou'rt a cordial old and rare. The Stirrup-Cup. Sidney Lanier. AA; AmP; BAP; CoBA; IAP; LBAP; MOAP; OBAV; OQP; PFY; QP-2; SPP; TCAP; TOP
Death thresholded old man hold. Double Ritual. Dachine Rainer. CrMA
Death to the Lady said. Death and the Lady. Léonie Adams. MAP; MoAB; MoAmPo; MOAP
Death to Us, A. Jon Silkin. NePoEA
Death Undreaded. Walter Savage Landor. *See* Death Stands above Me.
Death walks through the mind's dark woods. Poem. Henry Treece. NeBP
Death Warnings. Francisco de Quevedo y Villegas. *See* Sonnet: Death Warnings.
Death Was a Woman. Sydney King Russell. GoYe
Death Wedding. Pierre Emmanuel, *tr. fr. French by* Wallace Fowlie. MiCF
Death went up the hill. The Unseen. Sara Teasdale. TCAP
Death, what hast thou to do with one for whom. Swinburne. Sequence of Sonnets on the Death of Robert Browning, II. BPN
Death—What Is It? James Newton Matthews. PoP
Death, when I am ready, I. Pause en Route. Thomas Kinsella. OxBI
Death, who one day taketh all. Epitaph for a Kitten. Miriam Vedder. CIV
Death, why hast thou made life so hard to bear. Canzone: Of His Dead Lady. Giacomino Pugliesi. AWP; JAWP; WBP
Death, why so cruel? What! no other way. Bacon's Epitaph, Made by His Man. *Unknown.* AnAmPo; AWP; IAP; LA; PAH; SPP
Death-Wish, The. Louis MacNeice. AnFE
Death-Bed, A. James Aldrich. AA; HBV; LBAP
Death Bed, The. Waring Cuney. CDC; PoNe
Deathbed. Eric Robertson Dodds. MM
Death-Bed, The. Thomas Hood. BCEP; BEL; EnRP; EV-4; GTBS; GTBS-D; GTBS-W; GTSE; GTSL; HBV; MaRV; MCCG; OBEV; OBRV; OBVV; PG; TCEP; TreFS; VA
Death-Bed, The. Siegfried Sassoon. MoVE; POTE; TCEP
Death-Bed Hymn of Saint Anthony of Padua. St. Anthony of Padua, *tr. fr. Latin by* Thomas Walsh. CAW
Death-Bed, A, 1918. Kipling. ViP
Death-Bed of Bomba, King of Naples. *Unknown.* LPS-3
Deathless, The. Ednah Proctor Clarke. AA
Deathless Aphrodite, throned in flowers. Ode to Aphrodite. Sappho. AWP
Deathless Flower, A. Michelangelo. *See* Love's Justification.
Deathless Ones, The. Eleanor Glenn Wallis. NePoAm
Deathless Principle, Arise. Augustus Montague Toplady. OxBoCh
Deathless Tale, The. Charles Hanson Towne. ChIP; SDH; StJW
Deathless, though godheads be dying. In the Vastness, a God. *Unknown.* OQP; QP-2
Deathly Child, The. Stevie Smith. DiM
Deaths, The. Solveig von Schoultz, *tr. fr. Finnish by* Martin S. Allwood. LiTW
Death's a peculiar thing. The Coward. Roland R. Greenwood. YT
Death's Alchemy. William Sidney Walker. VA
Death's Apology. Francisco Manuel de Mello, *tr. fr. Spanish by* Edgar Prestage. CAW

Death's but one more to-morrow. Thou art gray. Of One Who Seemed to Have Failed. S. Weir Mitchell. AA; LBAP; OBAV
Death's Conqueror. First Corinthians, XV: 20, 21, 53, 55, Bible, *N.T.* MaRV
Death's Delight. Joseph von Eichendorff, *tr. fr. German by* Mabel Cotterell. AnGP
Death's Emissaries. James Shirley. *See* Victorious Men of Earth.
Death's Epitaph. Philip Freneau. *Fr.* The House of Night. AA
Death's Final Conquest. James Shirley. *See* Death the Leveller.
Death's first snows are drifting on my cheek. The Change-Song. Constance Lindsay Skinner. OCL
Death's Gwineter Lay His Cold Icy Hands on Me, *2 vers., with music. Unknown.* BoAN-2
Death's herd are we, and all the world a sty. Sentence of Death. Palladas. OxBG
Death's Jest Book, *sels.* Thomas Lovell Beddoes.
 Athulf's Death Song ("Cypress-bough, A, and a rose-wreath sweet"), *fr.* IV, iii. VA
 Bridal Song to Amala ("We have bathed"), *fr.* IV, iii. OBVV
 (Epithalamia.) PoEL-4
 (Song.) ChER; FaBoEn
 (Song[s] at Amala's Wedding.) LoBV; PoE
 Dirge: "If thou wilt ease thine heart," *fr.* II, ii. LiA; LiTB; LO; OBRV; PoEL-4; VA
 (Dirge for Wolfram.) PoE
 (If Thou Wilt Ease Thine Heart.) EG; EnRP; ERP; LPS-1
 (Wolfram's Dirge.) EV-4; OBEV
 Dirge: "Swallow leaves her nest, The," *fr.* I, iv. LoBV; OBVV; PoEL-4
 (Swallow Leaves Her Nest, The.) EPN; ERP
 (Voice from the Waters, A.) OBRV
 "Durst thou again say life and soul has lifted," *fr.* III, iii. LO
 "Hear'st thou, corpse, how I play thy part," *fr.* IV, iii. NBE
 "How strange it is that I can live to-day," *fr.* IV, i. NBE
 "I never knew before/ The meaning of this love," *fr.* II, iii. LO
 ". . . If man could see/ The perils and diseases that he elbows," *fr.* IV, i. PoP
 Isbrand's Song, *fr.* III, iii. PoE
 (Squats on a Toad-Stool under a Tree.) InvP
 L'Envoi: "Who findeth comfort in the stars and flowers." LO
 Mandrake's Song ("Folly hath now turned out of door"), *fr.* I, i. NBE
 "My will lies there, my hope, and all my life," *fr.* II, ii. LO; NBE
 Sibylla's Dirge ("We do lie beneath the grass"), *fr.* V, iv. GTBS-D; NBE; PoD; TriL
 (Second Dirge.) VA
 (We Do Lie beneath the Grass.) ERP
 Song: "Old Adam, the carrion crow," *fr.* V, iv. ChER; EPP; LiTB; OBRV; PoD; PoEL-4; TOP
 (Carrion Crow, The.) TrGrPo
 (Old Adam the Carrion Crow.) EnRP; ERP; PoMS
 (Song That Wolfram Heard in Hell, The.) NBE
 (Wolfram's Song.) BCEP; EV-4; GTBS-D; OBEV; OBVV; SiTL
 "Then all the minutes of my life to come," *fr.* II, iv. LO
 "Then listen, as I listened unto you," *fr.* III, iii. PoFr
 "Then no one hears me, O! the world's too loud," *fr.* IV, ii. ERP
 " 'Tis still and cold, and nothing in the air," *fr.* III, iii. NBE
 To Sea, To Sea, *fr.* I, i. EtS; OTPC; PCD; VA
 (Mariners' Song.) OBVV; YT
 (Sailors' Song.) EV-4; HBV
 (Sea, The.) CG
 (Sea Song.) GoTP
 (Song from the Ship.) GTBS-D; OBRV
 (To Sea.) CH; LPS-2; SG
Death's Jest Book ("In it Despair has married wildest mirth"), *br. sel.* Thomas Lovell Beddoes. *Fr.* Letters in Verse, to B. W. Procter, 1826. RO
Death's Men. W. J. Turner. TCPD
Death's nobility again. In Battle. Wallace Stevens. NP
Deaths of Antony and Cleopatra, The. Shakespeare. *See* Death of Antony *and* Death of Cleopatra.
Deaths of Myron and Klydone, The. Augusta Davies Webster. *Fr.* In a Day. VA
Death's pale cold orb has turned to an eclipse. Avalon. Thomas Holley Chivers. AnFE; CoAnAm; MOAP
Death's Ramble. Thomas Hood. BOHV
Death's Songsters. Dante Gabriel Rossetti. The House of Life, LXXXVII. PoVP; ViPo
Death's Subtle Ways. James Shirley. *See* Victorious Men of Earth.
Death's Summons ("Adieu, farewell, earth's bliss!"). Thomas Nashe. *See* Adieu, Farewell, Earth's Bliss!
Death's Summons ("Beauty is but a flower"). Thomas Nashe. *Fr.* Summer's Last Will and Testament. CBOV
 ("Beauty is but a flower.") LO
Death's Transfiguration. Israel Zangwill. TrJP
Death's Warning to Beauty. *Unknown, tr. fr. Early Modern Irish by* Robin Flower. AnIL
Debate between Arjuna and Sri Krishna. *Unknown. See* Considerations of Murder.
Debate in Ithaca, The. Homer, *tr. fr. Greek by* F. L. Lucas. *Fr.* The Odyssey, II. GrPE
Debate in the Sennit, The. James Russell Lowell. The Biglow Papers, 1st Series, No. V. GA, *abr.*; HBV; PAH
Debate of the Body and the Soul, The. *Unknown, ad. fr. Middle English.* BCEP, *abr., ad. by* Jessie L. Weston; CoBE, *abr., ad. by* Francis James Child; MeEV, *ad. by* Sir Theodore Martin
Debauch. Ibn Rashiq, *tr. fr. Arabic by* A. J. Arberry. MooP
Debonair. *Unknown, tr. fr. Chinese.* WhP
Deborah. William Weaver Christman. DDA
Deborah and Christopher brought me dandelions. Tribute. Aline Kilmer. TBM
Deborah danced, when she was two. Experience. Aline Kilmer. HBMV
Deborah Lee. William H. Burleigh. LPS-3
Débris. Lola Ridge. BAP; NP
Debt, The. Katharine Lee Bates. OQP; QP-1
Debt, The. Paul Laurence Dunbar. BANP; CDC; GrCo-1; MaRV
Debt, The. Theodosia Garrison. DD; PEDC
Debt, The. Jesse Edgar Middleton. NeTW
Debt. Jessie B. Rittenhouse. BAP; LEAP; LoPS
 (Debts.) AV; HBMV
Debt. Corinne Roosevelt Robinson. BoFr
Debt. Sara Teasdale. BAV; LEAP; LoPS; NP
Debt is paid, The. The Past. Emerson. AmP; FaBoCh; LiTA; LoGBV; PoEL-4; TCAP
Debts. Jessie B. Rittenhouse. *See* Debt.
Débutante, The. Guy Wetmore Carryl. POT; PoTo
Debutante was sitting in the parlor of her flat, A. Song: "Don't Tell Me What You Dreamt Last Night." Franklin P. Adams. FiBHP
Debutantrum. William Rose Benét. InMe; LHV
Decade, A. Amy Lowell. ChMo; CMP; LoPS; MAP; MoAmPo; NeMA; ReaPo
Decameron, The, *sel.* Boccaccio, *tr. fr. Italian by* Richard Aldington.
 Ballata: Flowers and Love. LyPI
Decanter of Madeira, Aged 86, to George Bancroft, Aged 86. Silas Weir Mitchell. AA; LEAP; OBAV; ViBoPo
Decay. George Herbert. EPS (1942 ed.); NBE; SeCV-1
Decay, Earth's Universal Law. Sophocles, *tr. fr. Greek by* Lewis Campbell. *Fr.* Oedipus at Colonus. GrR
 (Everything Decays, *tr. by* C. M. Bowra.) OxBG
 (Triumph of Time, The, *tr. by* F. Storr.) LiA
Decay of a People, The. William Gilmore Simms. AA; APW; SPP
Decay of Vanity, The. Ted Hughes. POTE (1959 ed.)
Decay pervades the rotting room. Amen. Georg Trakl. *Fr.* Rosary Songs. AnGP
Decayed Monastery, A. Thomas Dermody. OnYI
Decease, Release. Dum Morior, Orior. Robert Southwell. *See* At Fotheringay.
Deceased, The. Keith Douglas. FaBoTw
Deceased authors thou admir'st alone. Reactionary Critic. Martial. OnPM
Deceitful Hope. Julius Polyaenus, *tr. fr. Greek by* Hugh Macnaghten. OxBG
Deceitful snow, made of the gray sea. December Storm. John Hay. NePoAm
Deceiving world, that with alluring toys. A Palinode. Robert Greene. *Fr.* Greene's Groatsworth of Wit. OBSC; SiCE
December. Joel Benton. SN
December. Harriet F. Blodgett. COAH
December. Aileen Fisher. SiSoSe
December. Louisa Parsons Hopkins. PEOR
December. Victor Hugo, *tr. fr. French by* Alan Conder. TrFP
December. Thomas Caulfield Irwin. IrPN
December. Keats. *See* Stanzas: "In a drear-nighted December."
December. James Russell Lowell. *See* Winter Pictures.
December. Christina Rossetti. YeAr
December. Spenser. *Fr.* The Shepheardes Calender. BrBE
December, and the closing of the year. Christmas Eve in Whitneyville, 1955. Donald Hall. UnPo (3d ed.)
December Day, A. Robert Fuller Murray. EBSV
December Day, A. Sara Teasdale. PoRL; YeAr; YT
 (Winter Solstice.) BoChLi
December Daybreak. W. W. Gibson. NeTW
December Fugitive. Henry Morton Robinson. AnEnPo
 (November Fugitive.) GoYe

December is dying, her last minutes flying. The New Year. Donald E. Cooke. MPB (1956 ed.)
December, my dear, on the road to Nijmegen. The Road to Nijmegen. Earle Birney. BoCaPo (1948 ed.)
December: Of Aphrodite. W. S. Merwin. NePoEA
December Prayer, A. G. C. Wing. CAG
December Stillness, Teach Me [through Your Trees]. Siegfried Sassoon. ChMo; CMP
December Storm. John Hay. NePoAm
December Twenty-fourth. Eleanor Slater. ChIP; MaRV; OQP; QP-2
December 26. George Edward Hoffman. PGD
Decent Burial. Lois Seyster Montross. HBMV
Decent docent doesn't doze, The. History of Education. David McCord. WhC
Deceptions. Philip Larkin. NePoEA
Deciduous Branch. Stanley Kunitz. HoPM
Decision, The. Owen Dodson. PoNe
Decision, The. E. J. Pratt. TwCV
Decision. *Unknown.* PoToHe (new ed.)
Deck thyself, maiden. Esthonian Bridal Song. Johann Gottfried von Herder. AWP; JAWP; WBP
Deck us all with Boston Charlie. Boston Charlie. Walt Kelly. FiBHP
Declaration. Arthur Symons. ViBoPo
Declaration, The. Nathaniel Parker Willis. BOHV
Declare, my pretty maid. The Philanderer. Moses Mendes. *Fr.* The Chaplet. TrJP
Declare, ye bankis of Helicon. The Bankis of Helicon. Alexander Montgomerie. EBSV
Declivities of Heaven. George Darley. *Fr.* Nepenthe. RO
Decoration. Louise Bogan. MAP; MoAB; MoAmPo
Decoration. Thomas Wentworth Higginson. AA; OBAV
Decoration Day. Wallace Bruce. PEOR
Decoration Day. Richard Watson Gilder. MDAH
(Memorial Day.) OHIP
Decoration Day. Julia Ward Howe. DD
Decoration Day. Longfellow. DD; HH; MC; MDAH; MPB
(Sleep, Comrades, Sleep.) PEOR
Decoration Day at Charleston. Henry Timrod. *See* At Magnolia Cemetery.
Decoration Day Prayer. Arthur Roszelle Bemis, Jr. OQP; QP-1
Decoration Hymn. William H. Randall. PEOR
Decoy Partridge, A. Simmias, *tr. fr. Greek by* Walter Leaf. OxBG
Decrees of God, The. Chao Ying-tou, *tr. fr. Chinese by* William C. White. TrJP
Decrepit old gasman, named Peter, A. Limerick. *Unknown.* FaFP; LiBL; SiTL
Dedicated Spirit, A. Wordsworth. *Fr.* The Prelude. SeCePo
Dedicated to Dr. Harvey Cushing. Temple Fay. PoP
Dedication: "As years ago we carried to your knees." Kathleen Norris. *Fr.* Mother. MOAH
(Mother: "As long ago we carried . . .") PoToHe
Dedication: "Beyond the path of the outmost sun through utter darkness hurled." Kipling. *Fr.* Barrack-Room Ballads. ViPP
Dedication: "Bob Southey! You're a poet—Poet-laureate." Byron. *Fr.* Don Juan. BEL; BoLiVe; BPN; EnLi-2 (1949 ed.); EnLit; EnRP; ERP; EV-4; InP, 4 *sts.*; OAEP, 5 *sts.*; PoFS; PtP, *abr.*
(Dedication to the Poet Laureate, *abr.*) FiP
(Invocation.) LoBV
(Southey and Wordsworth.) TrGrPo
Dedication: "Child! do not throw this book about!" Hilaire Belloc. *See* Dedication on the Gift of a Book to a Child.
Dedication: "Christ and his Mother, heavenly maid." Robert Bridges. *Fr.* Founder's Day. MOAH
Dedication, A: "Dear, near and true—no truer Time himself." Tennyson. BPN; EmBrPo; EPN; PoVP; VLEP
Dedication: "Eugenius, thy son, who guards the Rock." Pope Eugenius III, *tr. fr. Latin by* Raymond F. Roseliep. ISi
Dedication: "From those condemned to labour." F. R. Scott. BoCaPo
Dedication: "From wounds and death they rest—this bow and quiver." *Unknown, tr. fr. Greek by* Robert Bland. OnPM
Dedication: "Had there been peace there never had been riven." Drummond Allison. FaBoTw
Dedication, A: "He was, through boyhood's storm and shower." G. K. Chesterton. FiBHP
Dedication: "Holy Jesus, Thou art born." Victoria Saffelle Johnson. GoBC; TrPWD
Dedication: "I speak with a proud tongue of the people who were." Patrick MacGill. OnYI
Dedication: "I would the gift I offer here." Whittier. *Fr.* Songs of Labor. AmPP (4th ed.); AnNE; CoBA; CoV; IAP; OxBA
Dedication: "If I were hanged on the highest hill." Kipling. *See* Mother o' Mine.
Dedication: "If the rose in meek duty." Francis Thompson. CoBE
Dedication: "I've gone about for years I find." Edward Salisbury Field. *Fr.* The Quest. MOAH
Dedication: "I've love songs of my springtime pride." Holger Drachmann, *tr. fr. Danish by* Charles W. Stork. BoDS
Dedication, A: "Life of my learning, fire of all my Art." Mary Elizabeth Coleridge. TrPWD
Dedication: "Long years you've kept the door ajar." Robert Bridges. *Fr.* Overheard in Arcady. MOAH
Dedication: "Lord, in the strength of grace." Charles Wesley. MaRV
Dedication, The: "Lord, my first-fruits present themselves to thee." George Herbert. OAEP
Dedication: "Mighty world's, The/ Eternity." Piet Hein, *tr. fr. Danish by* Charles W. Stork. BoDS
Dedication: "Mother to whose valiant will." Archibald Lampman. *Fr.* Lyrics of Earth. MOAH
Dedication, A: "My new-cut ashlar takes the light." Kipling. BMEP; GTSL; HBV; MaRV; OBEV (1st ed.); OBVV
(My New-cut Ashlar.) PoEL-5; POTT
Dedication: "O lyric Love, half angel and half bird." Robert Browning. *See* O Lyric Love.
Dedication: "O say not he is dead! What messenger." Marian Osborne. CPG
Dedication: "O thou whose gracious presence blest," *abr.* Louis F. Benson. MaRV; PraP
(Dedication for a Home [John Oxenham, *wr.*], *abr.*) ChIP
(O Thou Whose Gracious Presence Blest.) TrPWD
Dedication: Poems and Ballads. Swinburne. *See* Dedication to Poems and Ballads.
Dedication: "Sea gives her shells to the shingle, The." Swinburne. *See* Dedication to Poems and Ballads.
Dedication: "Sea of the years that endure not, The." Swinburne. EmBrPo
Dedication: "Since the external disorder, and extravagant lies." W. H. Auden. *Fr.* Look, Stranger! CaAE
Dedication: "Strongest and the noblest argument, The." Sir John Davies. *Fr.* Nosce Teipsum. SiPS
Dedication: "Stumbling, we see the future as a cup." Lilian Shuman Dreyfus. *Fr.* In Praise of Leaves. MOAH
Dedication: "Tall unpopular men." Oliver St. John Gogarty. OBMV
Dedication: "There was a time in boyhood, ere life ceased." Alfred Gordon. CPG
Dedication: "These to his Memory—since he held them dear." Tennyson. *Fr.* Idylls of the King. PoVP; ViPP
(To the Queen.) BHV
Albert the Good, *sel.* BMEP
Dedication, A: "They are rhymes rudely strung with intent less." Adam Lindsay Gordon. BoAu
Dedication: "They say my verse is sad: no wonder!" A. E. Housman. *See* They Say My Verse Is Sad.
Dedication: "'They shall not die in vain,' we said"). Ralph Gustafson. BoCaPo; CaP; TwCaPo; TwCV
Dedication: "Thou, whose unmeasured temple stands." Bryant. BLRP; PraP
(How Amiable Are Thy Tabernacles!) TrPWD
(Thou, Whose Unmeasured Temple Stands.) MaRV
Dedication: To Leigh Hunt. Keats. *See* To Leigh Hunt, Esq.
Dedication: "To that clear majesty which in the north." Sir John Davies. *Fr.* Nosce Teipsum. SiPS
(To My Most Gracious Dread Sovereign.) ReIE; SiCE
(To Queen Elizabeth.) OBSC
Dedication: "We dedicate a church today." Ethel Arnold Tilden. MaRV; OQP; PraP; QP-2
Dedication: "When I have ended, then I see." Laurence Housman. TrPWD
Dedication: "When imperturbable the gentle moon." John Erskine. PC
Dedication: "With favoring winds, o'er sunlit seas." Longfellow. *Fr.* Ultima Thule. CoV; ViBoPo
("With favouring winds, o'er the sunlit seas.") AlDL
Dedication for a Home. Louis F. Benson [John Oxenham, *wr.*]. *See* Dedication: "O thou whose gracious presence blest."
Dedication for a Spear. Simonides, *tr. fr. Greek by* T. F. Higham. OxBG
Dedication of a Home. Bertha Gerneaux Woods. PraP
Dedication of a Mirror. Plato, *tr. fr. Greek by* Dudley Fitts. LiTW
("Quand Vous serez bien Vieille," *tr. by* F. L. Lucas.) GrPE
Dedication of a Ship. Macedonius, *tr. fr. Greek by* Lord Neaves. OnPM
Dedication of the Chronicles of England and France. Robert Fabyan. ISi
Dedication of the Cook. Anna Wickham. MBP; MoBrPo
Dedication of the Illustrations to Blair's "Grave," *sel.* Blake.
Door of Death, The. ChTr
(To the Queen.) EnRP

Dedication of the Ring and the Book. Robert Browning. *See* O Lyric Love.
Dedication on the Gift of a Book to a Child. Hilaire Belloc. HBVY
(Dedication: "Child! do not throw this book about!") MOB
(Foreword, A.) TSW; TSWC
Dedication to a Book of Stories Selected from the Irish Novelists, The. W. B. Yeats. NAMP
Dedication to Aphrodite. Plato, *tr. fr. Greek by* J. M. Edmonds. GrR
Dedication to Athene, A. Archias, *tr. fr. Greek by* George Allen. OxBG
Dedication to My Gray Lady. Fra Jerome. SaFP
Dedication to Poems and Ballads [First Series]. Swinburne. PoVP; ViPo; VLEP
(Dedication: Poems and Ballads.) BPN
(Dedication: "Sea gives her shells to the shingle, The.") PIR
Dedication to the Duke of Bejar. Luis de Góngora, *tr. fr. Spanish by* Edward Meryon Wilson. *Fr.* The Solitudes. TeCS
Dedication to the Poet Laureate. Byron. *See* Dedication: "Bob Southey! You're a poet—Poet-laureate."
Dedications [*of* Orchestra]. Sir John Davies. SiPS
I. To His Very Friend, Master Richard Martin.
II. To the Prince.
Dedicatory. Mary Gilmore. BoAV
Dedicatory Ode, *sel.* Hilaire Belloc.
"I will not try the reach again." PoeT
Dedicatory Sonnet. Christina Rossetti. *See* To My First Love, My Mother.
Deduction. Mark Van Doren. BAP
Deduction. Reinmar von Hagenau, *tr. fr. German by* Margaret R. Richey. LyMA
Deed, The. T. Sturge Moore. PtOT
Deed, The. Shakespeare. *See* Murder, The.
Deed of Lieutenant Miles, The. Clinton Scollard. *See* Ballad of Lieutenant Miles.
Deed you evra see Joy. Da Pup een da Snow. T. A. Daly. AlBD; TSW
Deedle, deedle, dumpling, my son John. *See* Diddle, diddle, dumpling . . .
Deeds of Kindness. Epes Sargent, *sometimes at. to* Fanny Crosby. HBV; HBVY; OTPC; PPL
(Suppose.) TVC; TVSH
Deeds of Valor at Santiago. Clinton Scollard. HBV; MC; PAH
Deeds That Might Have Been, The. Wilfrid Scawen Blunt. *Fr.* In Vinculis. TrGrPo
Deem as ye list, upon good cause. Songs and Lyrics, XCIX. Sir Thomas Wyatt. SiPS
Deem Not [because You See Me]. George Santayana. Sonnets, XI. AnEnPo; TrGrPo
Deem not devoid of elegance the sage. Sonnet: Written in a Blank Leaf of Dugdale's "Monasticon." Thomas Warton, the Younger. Sonnets, III. EiPP; EV-3; OBEC; SeCePo
Deem not the days a breath of barren dust. Vita Magistra. Walter Stanley Senior. MM
Deep, The. John G. C. Brainard. AA; EtS
Deep, The, *sel.* Gladys Cromwell.
"Where floating shapes." PC
Deep affections of the breast, The. The Parrot. Thomas Campbell. OTPC
Deep and Dark Blue Ocean. Byron. *See* Ocean, The.
Deep asleep, deep asleep. The Ballad of Semmerwater. Sir William Watson. PoVP
Deep black against the dying glow. An Autumnal Evening. "Fiona Macleod." GBV
Deep-bosomed, stalwart-limbed, superbly made. Sonnet to a Plow-Woman of Norway. Margaret Tod Ritter. TBM
Deep cradled in the fringed mow to lie. Theophany. Evelyn Underhill. MaRV; WGRP
Deep Dark Night, The. Tennyson. *Fr.* The Devil and the Lady. SeCePo
Deep Dark River. Lloyd Roberts. CaP; OCL
Deep Desire Sung This Song. George Gascoigne. TuPP
Deep Discussion, A. Richard Moore. HoPM
Deep Down. James Stuart Montgomery. NLK
Deep down in the Siberian mine. *See* Deep in the Siberian mine.
Deep flows the flood. Underground. Ian Mudie. BoAV; MoAuPo
Deep green lies the grass along the river. Ancient Poem. *Unknown.* ChLP
Deep Honeysuckle! in the silent eve. To the Herald Honeysuckle. Emily Pfeiffer. VA
Deep in a distant bay, and deeply hidden. The Lonely Isle. Claudian. AWP; JAWP; WBP
Deep in a Rose's glowing heart. Sent with a Rose to a Young Lady. Margaret Deland. AA
Deep in a vale, a stranger now to arms. The American Soldier. Philip Freneau. MOAP
Deep in a vale where rocks on every side. Sonnets, I. Gustave Rosenhane, *tr. by* Sir Edmund Gosse. AWP; JAWP; WBP
Deep in Alabama earth. Alabama Earth (at Booker Washington's grave). Langston Hughes. GoSl
Deep in Canadian woods we've met. Dear Old Ireland. Timothy Daniel Sullivan. TIP
Deep in grey dusk the mill turns faltering. The Mill. Emile Verhaeren. WoL
Deep in my brain walks to and fro. My Cat. Baudelaire. CIV
Deep in my gathering garden. A Thrush Sings. W. E. Henley. YT
Deep in my heart I hear them, the gaunt hounds pacing. The Hounds of the Soul. Louis Ginsberg. TrJP
Deep in My Soul. Byron. *Fr.* The Corsair. EV-4
"Deep in the ages," you said, "Deep in the ages." In Memory of Vachel Lindsay. Sara Teasdale. PIAE
Deep in the fading leaves of night. Carol. W. R. Rodgers. ChMP; FaBoTw
Deep in the fastness of a Druid wood. Tree Woman. Dorothy Quick. DaM
Deep in the gold forests of that dream. Terror by Night. Leah Bodine Drake. UnW
Deep in the grass there lies a dead gazelle. Maytime. *Unknown. Fr.* Shi King. AWP
Deep in the greenwood of my heart. The Outlaw. Alfred Noyes. BMEP
Deep in the heart of a primal wood. Saint Francis. Gertrude Huntington McGiffert. SaFP
Deep in the heart of me. You. Ruth Guthrie Harding. SBMV
Deep in the heart of the forest the lily of Yorrow is growing. The Lily of Yorrow. Henry van Dyke. AA
Deep in the heart of the lake. Water Music. Alun Lewis. ChMP; GTBS-D
Deep in the Heavens. Ricarda Huch, *tr. fr. German by* Herman Salinger. TwGV
Deep in the man sits fast his fate. Fate. Emerson. BAV; RiBV
Deep in the mountain,/ Trampling the red maple leaves. The Priest Sarumaru, *tr. fr. Japanese by* Kenneth Rexroth. OnPJ
Deep in the night I woke: she, near me, held. Tennyson. *Fr.* The Princess. ReTS
Deep in the sea the sun's rays had been drowned. The Howlers. Leconte de Lisle. TrFP
Deep in the shady sadness of a vale. Hyperion. Keats. AnEnPo; ATP; BCEP; BEL; BPN; BrBE; CBE; ChER; EM-2; EmBrPo; EnRP; EPN; EPP; ERP; EV-4; ExPo; FaBoEn; FiP; GEPC; InP; LoBV; MyFE; OBRV; PoEL-4; ReaPo; TrGrPo; TwHP
Deep in the shelter of the cave. Neighbors of the Christ Night. Nora Archibald Smith. ChrBoLe; CLS; COAH; PRWS
Deep in [*or* down in] the Siberian mine. Message to Siberia. Pushkin. AWP; BoR; JAWP; PoFr; TrRV; WBP; WoL
Deep in the study. The Phoenix. Ogden Nash. CenHV; NePA
Deep in the wave is a coral grove. The Coral Grove. James Gates Percival. AA; AnAmPo; AnNE; APW; EtS; GN; GoTP; LA; LPS-2; TVSH
Deep in the winter plain, two armies. Two Armies. Stephen Spender. ChMP; CoBMV; SeCeV; WaP
Deep in the Woods. Mildred D. Shacklett. GFA
Deep in [*or* into] the woods we'll go. Heart of the Woods. Wesley Curtright. GoSl; PoNe
Deep in yon garden-shade. Easter. Genevieve M. J. Irons. EOAH
Deep into the woods we'll go. *See* Deep in the woods we'll go.
Deep lies thy body, jewel of the sea. Olive Tilford Dargan. *Fr.* The Cycle's Rim. LEAP
Deep lines of honour all can hit. The Portrait. Countess of Winchilsea. *Fr.* The Birthday of Catharine Tufton. OBEC
Deep loving, well knowing. Our Colonel. Arthur Guiterman. DD; GA; HH; PoRL
Deep mute midnight, skies pitch-black. Vestal Virgins. Yiannis Griparis. MoGP
Deep Night, Summer. Thad Stem, Jr. NoCaPo (rev. ed.)
Deep on the convent-roof the snows. St. Agnes' Eve [*or* St. Agnes]. Tennyson. BPN; CAW; CoBE; EM-2; EmBrPo; EnL; EnLit; EPP; EV-5; GEPC; GoBC; GTBS-W; GTSL; HBV; LiTB; LiTG; OAEP; OBEV; OBVV; OTPC; OxBoCh; PoVP; REAL; StJW; TCEP; TriL; ViPo; VLEP
Deep Peace. Josephine Royle. BAP
Deep peace, pure white of the moon to you. "Fiona Macleod." *Fr.* Invocation of Peace. BoTP

Deep recesses of the grove he gain'd, The. Dryden. *Fr.* Cymon and Iphigenia. LiA
Deep River ("Deep river, deep river, Lawd"), *with music.* *Unknown.* ABF
Deep River ("Deep river, my home is over Jordan"). *Unknown.* APW; BoAN-1, *with music;* OlF; TrAS, *with music*
Deep-Sea Fishing. "Hugh MacDiarmid." SeCePo
Deep-Sea Pearl, The. Edith M. Thomas. AV
Deep Sea Soundings. Sarah Williams. EtS; WGRP
Deep seclusion of this forest path, The. Enchantment. Madison Cawein. HBV
Deep Sleep. "Gabriela Mistral," *tr. fr. Spanish by* "K. G. C." AnCL
Deep Snow. Louise Morey Bowman. CPG
Deep Stuff. Keith Preston. WhC
Deep-sworn Vow, A. W. B. Yeats. GTIV; ReMP; TwP; UnPo
Deep the waters of the Black Pool, coloured like ink. The Dragon of the Black Pool. Po Chü-i. TrCh
Deep unto Deep. John Banister Tabb. PFE
Deep was the first draught, deep the next, no stint was there. After the Plague. *Unknown.* LiTW
Deep Water Man, The. James Stuart Montgomery. NLK
Deep Waters. Van Tassel Sutphen. AA
Deep well knows and knows it well, The. World Secret. Hugo von Hofmannsthal, *tr. by* Werner Heider. LiTW
Deep well knows it certainly, The. World-Secret. Hugo von Hofmannsthal, *tr. by* Charles Wharton Stork. TrJP
Deep well of my melancholy, The. Rondeau: The Well. Charles d'Orléans. LyMA
Deep Woods. Leslie Nelson Jennings. MuM
Deeper into the Forest. Roy Daniells. TwCaPo
Deeper Seas, The. Henry Bellamann. EtS
Deeper than sleep but not so deep as death. Night Feeding. Muriel Rukeyser. MiAP
Deeper than the narwhal sinketh. The Sea-Deeps. Thomas Miller. EtS
Deepest infamy man can attain, The. The Worst Treason. Victor Hugo. PoFr
Deepest thanksgiving I do give. A Thanksgiving. Carolyn Wells. PEDC
Deeply across the waves of our darkness fear. Dunkirk Pier. Alan Rook. SoV
Deeps of the wind-torn west. The Summons. Sir Charles G. D. Roberts. CPG
Deepstirred on Volga's banks I stare and listen. On Volga Banks. Bronislav Kezhyn. RuPo
Deer, The. Mary Austin. FaPON; PoTo
Deer. John Drinkwater. CH
Deer. Kenneth Rexroth. *Fr.* A Bestiary. HoPM
Deer, The. Tatsuji Miyoshi, *tr. fr. Japanese by* Takamichi Ninomiya *and* D. J. Enright. PoLJ
Deer and Bracken. Stella Gibbons. AlDL
Deer and Echo. Otomo Yakamochi, *tr. fr. Japanese by* Ishii *and* Obata. OnPM
Deer and the Snake, The. Kenneth Patchen. MoAmPo
Deer are gentle and graceful. Deer. Kenneth Rexroth. *Fr.* A Bestiary. HoPM
Deer are on the mountain, deer! Deer on the Mountain. Grace Fallow Norton. HBMV
Deer Come Down, The, *sels.* Edward Weismiller. MuM
"O cities, you have nudged at their velvet flanks," II.
"Softly, by night, the deer come down to drink," I.
Deer Hunt, A. *Unknown. See* Crooked Gun, The.
Deer in Aspens. Kay DeBard Hall. GoYe
Deer is humble, The, lovely as God made her. The Deer and the Snake. Kenneth Patchen. MoAmPo
Deer of Ireland, The. Padraic Colum. PoFr; TIP
(Old Man Said, An.) OxBI
(Stag, The.) GTIV
Deer on pine mountain, The. Onakatomi no Yoshinobu, *tr. fr. Japanese by* Kenneth Rexroth. *Fr.* Shui Shu. LiTW; OnPJ
Deer on the Mountain. Grace Fallow Norton. HBMV
Deer stand still now in the darkened forest, The. Love Song. Rudolf G. Binding. TwGV
Deer were bounding like blown leaves, The. Fire on the Hills. Robinson Jeffers. ChMo; CMP; CoV
Deer which lives, The. Onakatomi no Yoshinobu. *Fr.* Shui Shu. AWP
Deere my deere why are you cruell. *Unknown.* SeCSL
Deere turne awaye thyne eyes soe bright. *Unknown.* SeCSL
Deere, why should you commaund me to my rest. *See* Dear, why should . . .
Deer's Cry, The. *At. to* St. Patrick, *tr. fr. Old Irish by* Whitley Stokes, John Strachan, *and* Kuno Meyer. AnIL; CAW; OnYI; WGRP
(Breastplate of St. Patrick, The.) OxBI, *tr. by* Cecil Frances Alexander; WHL, *tr. by* Kuno Meyer
(St. Patrick's Breastplate, *tr. by* Cecil Frances Alexander.) FaBoCh; LoGBV; AnIV, *abr., tr. by* Kuno Meyer
St. Patrick's Breastplate: "I bind unto myself to-day," *sel.* MaRV
(Breastplate of St. Patrick, The.) BBV
Deevil's Waltz, The. Sidney Goodsir Smith. FaBoTw
Deface not with your sand. Sand. Ibn al-Arabi. MooP
Defeat. Witter Bynner. PoNe
Defeat and Victory. Wallace Rice. GA; MC; PAH
Defeat may serve as well as victory. Victory in Defeat. Edwin Markham. CV; MaRV; OQP; PC; PoeMoYo; QP-2; StaSt
Defeat o' the Hert. Sidney Goodsir Smith. AtBAP
Defeat of the Armada, The. *Unknown, at. to* William Warner. *See* Defeat of the Spanish Armada, The.
Defeat of the Rebels. Robert Graves. WaP
Defeat of the Spanish Armada, The. *Unknown, at. to* William Warner. SG
(Armada, The.) ShGoBo
(Defeat of the Armada, The.) CoBE
("Some years of late, in eighty-eight.") FaBoCh; LoGBV
(Spanish Armado, The.) EV-2; LiTG
Defeated, The, for Wales. Alun Lewis. MoWP; PrWP
Defeated Farmer. Mark Van Doren. AnAmPo; LA
Defeating oft the labours of the year. Storm in Harvest. James Thomson. *Fr.* The Seasons: Autumn. EPP
Defence [*or* Defense] of Guenevere, The. William Morris. BEL; BPN, *sl. abr.;* EmBrPo; EnL; EnLi-2; EnLit; OAEP; PoVP; ViP; ViPo; ViPP; VLEP
Defence of Lawrence, The. Richard Realf. MC; PAH
Defence of Lucknow, The. Tennyson. BeLS; BPN
Defence of Night, The. Michelangelo, *tr. fr. Italian.* CAW, *tr. by* Longfellow; OnPM, *tr. by* John Addington Symonds
Defence of the Alamo, The. Joaquin Miller. *See* Defense of the Alamo, The.
Defenceless Children, Your Great Enemy. Kendrick Smithyman. AnNZ
Defendant?/ Here he is. The Trial of the Dog. Aristophanes. *Fr.* The Wasps. OxBG
Defender, The. Arthur M. Sampley. GoYe
Defender of his country, The—the founder of liberty. Epitaph on Washington. *Unknown.* OHIP; PEDC
Defenders, The. John Drinkwater. PoeT
Defense against the Dark. Louis Ginsberg. UnW
Defense of Guenevere, The. William Morris. *See* Defence of Guenevere, The.
Defense [*or* Defence] of the Alamo, The. Joaquin Miller. BeLS; DD; FaBoBe; HBV; LEAP; MC; PaA; PAH
Defensive Position. John Manifold. MoBrPo (1950 ed.)
Defiance. Aeschylus, *tr. fr. Greek by* Lewis Campbell. *Fr.* Prometheus Bound. GrR
Defiance, The. Aphra Behn. EnLoPo
Defiance. Burns. *See* Macpherson's Farewell.
Defiance. Byron. *Fr.* Childe Harold's Pilgrimage, III. RO
("I have not loved the world, nor the world me.") OBRV
(Poet and the World, The.) SeCePo
Defiance, The. Thomas Flatman. AEV; CEP; OBS
Defiance. Solomon ibn Gabirol, *tr. fr. Hebrew by* Emma Lazarus. TrJP
Defiance. Walter Savage Landor. HBV
Defiance. Shelley. *Fr.* Prometheus Unbound, I. BHV
Defiance to False Gods. Bernice Kenyon. TBM
Deficient in the polite studies. Autumn Countryside. Tu Fu. WhP
Defilèd is my name full sore. Cruel Spite. Anne Boleyn. DiM
Defilement Cometh from Within. Menander, *tr. fr. Greek by* Francis G. Allinson. GrR
Definition. Grace Noll Crowell. MotAn; PoToHe (new ed.)
Definition. Edwin Rolfe. BoFr; NAMP
Definition of Beauty, The. Robert Herrick. NBE; Po
Definition of Creativeness. Boris Pasternak, *tr. fr. Russian by* Jack Lindsay. RuPo
Definition of Love, The. Andrew Marvell. AnFE; BLV; BoLiVe; CoEV; ElSeCe; EPS; FaBoEn; GTBS-W; LiTB; LiTG; LiTL; LoBV; MaPo; MeLP; MePo; NBE; OAEP; OBEV (new ed.); OBS; Po; PoE; PoEL-2; PoFS; ReEn; SeCL; SeCePo; SeCeV; SeCV-1; SeEP; TrGrPo; UnPo; WHA
Definition of My Brother. W. S. Graham. FaBoTw; NeBP
Definition of the Soul. Boris Pasternak, *tr. fr. Russian.* LiTW, *tr. by* J. M. Cohen; TrJP, *tr. by* Babette Deutsch; TrRV, *tr. by* Babette Deutsch
Definitions. Joseph Joel Keith. PoToHe (new ed.)
Definitions for a Tree. Anne Blackwell Payne. NoCaPo
Deflective rhythm under seas. Einstein among the Coffee-Cups. Louis Untermeyer. WhC
Deftly he crashed the hammer tipped with stone. The First Poem. Clifford Gessler. MuM
Degas called him "The Notary." Seurat. James Schevill. FiMAP
Degenerate Age, A. Solomon ibn Gabirol, *tr. fr. Hebrew by* Emma Lazarus. TrJP
Degenerate Douglas! O the unworthy lord! Composed at

Degenerate Douglas (*continued*)
Neidpath Castle, the Property of Lord Queensberry, 1803. Wordsworth. GTBS; GTBS-D; GTBS-W; GTSE; GTSL
Degrees of Shade. H. A. Pinkerton. NePoAm
Deh was a princess propose to be married. The Maid Freed from the Gallows (C *vers.*). *Unknown.* BaBo; ViBoFo
Dei Genitrix. Aubrey Thomas De Vere. IrPN
Deianira's Love Charm. Sophocles, *tr. fr. Greek by* Sir George Young. *Fr.* Trachiniae. GrR
Deianira's Wooing. Sophocles, *pr. tr. fr. Greek by* Gilbert Murray. *Fr.* Trachiniae. OxBG
Deid Folks' Ferry. Rosamund Marriott Watson. VA
Deid is now that divour and dollin in erd. The Widow Speaks. William Dunbar. *Fr.* The Tua Mariit Wemen and the Wedo. PoEL-1
Deidre's Lament for the Sons of Usnach. *Unknown. See* Deirdre's Lament for the Sons of Usnach.
Deigne at my hands this crown of prayer and praise. La Corona. John Donne. OBS
De'il's Awa wi' the Exciseman, The. Burns. CaAE; EV-3; OAEP; ViBoPo
(Exciseman, The.) GoTS
Deirdre, *sel.* Sir Samuel Ferguson.
Deirdre ("Give me my harp, and let me sing a song"). IrPN
Deirdre. James Stephens. AWP; ChMo; CMP; GTIV; GTSL; HBMV; JAWP; LBBV; LEAP; MM; NV; OBMV; OnPP; PG; PoRA; TwCV; ViBoPo; WBP
Deirdre, *sels.* W. B. Yeats.
"I will not make a bargain; I but ask." ReTS
" 'Why is it,' Queen Edain said." ViBoPo
Deirdre and Conchobar. *Unknown, tr. fr. Middle Irish by* Eugene O'Curry. SiB
Deirdre and the Poets. Ewart Milne. NeIP
Deirdre Is Dead. "Fiona Macleod." VLEP
Deirdre's Farewell to Alba. *Unknown, tr. fr. Middle Irish by* Sir Samuel Ferguson. IrPN; OnYI
(Deirdre Looks Back at Scotland, *tr. by* Seán O'Faoláin.) SiB
(Deirdre's Farewell to Scotland, *tr. by* Whitley Stokes *and* Kuno Meyer.) OnYI
Deirdre's Lament for the Sons of Usnach. *Unknown, tr. fr. Middle Irish by* Sir Samuel Ferguson. GTIV; IrPN; OnYI
(Deidre's Lament for the Sons of Usnach, *tr. by* Sir Samuel Ferguson.) SeCePo
(Deirdre's Lament, *tr. by* Whitley Stokes *and* Kuno Meyer.) LiTW; OnYI
(Deirdre's Lament over Naoisi, *tr. by* Whitley Stokes.) SiB
Deirdre's Song at Sunrise. Sister Maura. CaP
Deirin dé, Deirin dé! A Sleep Song. *Unknown.* BOL
Dejected Lover, The. George Crabbe. *Fr.* Tales of the Hall. FaBoEn
Dejection. Robert Bridges. TCPD
Dejection. Gaspar Núñez de Arce, *tr. fr. Spanish by* Ida Farnell. AnSpL-2
Dejection; an Ode. Samuel Taylor Coleridge. AnEnPo; BEL; BPN; EM-2; EmBrPo; EnL; EnLi-2; EnLit; EnRP; EPN; ERP; EV-4; FaBoEn; FiP; HBV; LiTB; LoBV; MaPo; NBE; OAEP; OBRV; PoE; PoFS; PoEL-4; ReaPo
Sels.
Life of Nature, The. RO
"Well! If the Bard was weather-wise, who made." SeCePo
Del Cascar. William Stanley Braithwaite. BANP; CDC
Delay. Charlotte Fiske Bates. AA
Delay. Elizabeth Jennings. NePoEA
Delay Has Danger. George Crabbe. *Fr.* Tales of the Hall. EnSW
Delay Not! Pierre de Ronsard, *tr. fr. French by* Alan Conder. TrFP
Delay your flight, delay your swift pursuit. Lone Swan. Rose Mills Powers. BLA
Delayed till she had ceased to know. Emily Dickinson. OBAV
(Too Late.) AA
Delectable Dream, A, *sel.* Humphrey Gifford.
"Woman's f·ce is full of wiles, A." ElL; ElSeCe; SiCE; TuPP
Delfica. Gérard de Nerval, *tr. fr. French by* Alan Conder. TrFP
Delia. Samuel Daniel *See* To Delia.
Delian Apollo, save! Delos. Pindar. OxBG
Deliberately chime/ The sounds that end a year. Take Up the Wings. Lawrence Lee. NeTW
Delicate Cluster! Flag of Teeming Life! Walt Whitman. IAP
Delicate differences. Elevation of Light. Jorge Guillén. CoSP
Delicate fabric of bird song, A. May Day. Sara Teasdale. *Fr.* The Dark Cup. CP; MM
Delicate silver gates are closed, the road ahead is paved with swords, The. Love Song. George Brandon Saul. TBM
Delicate white body will be buried today, The. The Lament for Urien, II. *Unknown. Fr.* The Red Book of Hergest. OBMV
Delicately chased, rare metal, pale as ice. The Wedding Ring. John Gould Fletcher. CMP
Deliciae Sapientiae de Amore. Coventry Patmore. The Unknown Eros. II, ix. OxBoCh; PoVP
Hail Virgin in Virginity a Spouse, *br. sel.* PraNu
Delicious beauty, that doth lie. Song. *At. to* John Marston. ElL
Délie, La, *sel.* Maurice Scève, *pr. tr. fr. French.*
"Bound to the Caucasus of my suffering." LiA
Delight in Disorder. Robert Herrick. ALV; BLP; BLV; BoLiVe; CaAE; CoBE; ElSeCe; EM-1; EnLi-1 (1949 ed.); EnLit; EnLoPo; EPS (1942 ed.); EV-2; FaBoEn; HBV; InMe; LEAP; LiTB; LiTG; LiTL; LoBV; LoPo; LPS-2; MaPo; OAEP; OBEV; OBS; PG (1945 ed.); PoE; PoFS; PoRA; ReaPo; ReEn; RiBV; SeCePo; SeCeV; SeCL; SeCV-1; SeEP; TreFS; TrGrPo; TwHP; TyEnPo; UnPo; ViBoPo; WHA
(Poetry of Dress, I.) GTBS; GTBS-D; GTBS-W; GTSE; GTSL
(Sweet Disorder [in the Dress], A.) AnFE; AWP; EG; InPo; JAWP; ShBV-4; TOP; WBP
Delight in God [Only]. Francis Quarles. *Fr.* Emblems. BCEP; LPS-2
("I love, and have some cause to love, the earth.") EPS (1942 ed.)
"In having all things, and not Thee, what have I?" *sel.* MaRV
Delight of Solitariness, The. Sir Philip Sidney. *See* O Sweet Woods.
Delight of thy face, and the sound of thy feet, and the wind of thy tresses, The. Swinburne. *Fr.* Hesperia. LoPS
Delightful, book, your trip. Aoibhinn, a leabhrain, do thriall. AnIV, *tr. by* Flann O'Brien; OxBI, *tr. by* Brian O'Nolan
Delightful I think it to be in the bosom of an isle. St. Columcille's Island Hermitage. *Unknown.* AnIL
Delightful to be on the Hill of Howth. Columcille's Greeting to Ireland. *At. to* St. Columcille. OnYI
Delights of Fancy. Mark Akenside. *Fr.* The Pleasures of Imagination, I. LPS-3
Delilah. Milton. *Fr.* Samson Agonistes. SeCePo
("But who is this, what thing on sea or land?") BoHiPo
Delilie was a woman, fine an' fair. Samson. *Unknown.* OuSiCo
Delit the Lombe for to devise. *Unknown. Fr.* The Pearl. NBE
Deliver Us From . . . Amelia Josephine Burr. OQP; QP-2
Deliverance. William James Dawson. OBVV
Deliverance of Jehovah, The. Psalms, XXVII, Bible, *O.T.* (*Moulton, Modern Reader's Bible*). WGRP
Deliverer, The. Milton. *Fr.* Samson Agonistes. OBS
(Choruses from "Samson Agonistes.") SeCeV
("Oh, how comely it is and how reviving.") OBEV
(Out of Adversity, *shorter sel.*) LH
Deliverer, Jove, The. *Unknown, tr. fr. Greek by* Lord Neaves. OnPM
Delivers papers to the doors of sleep. Herald. Josephine Miles. FiMAP
Dell, The. Samuel Taylor Coleridge. *Fr.* Fears in Solitude. EV-4
Dell of green through which a river sings, A. The Sleeper in the Valley. Arthur Rimbaud. TrFP
Della Cruscans The. William Gifford. *Fr.* The Baviad. OBEC
Delmonico's is where he dines. A Splendid Fellow. H. C. Dodge. BOHV
Delos. Callimachus. *See* To Delos.
Delos. Lawrence Durrell. NeBP
Delos. Pindar, *tr. fr. Greek.* GrPE, *tr. by* F. L. Lucas; OxBG, *tr. by* C. M. Bowra
Delos. Bernard Spencer. FaBoMo; PoN
Delphi. Oliffe Richmond. NeTW
Delphic and Theban and Corinthian. Four Legs, Two Legs, Three Legs. William Empson. MoPo
Delphica. Gérard de Nerval, *tr. fr. French by* Richmond Lattimore. AnFP
Delphinium is on my mantel. Eve of Revolution. Elliott Coleman. NoCaPo (1941 ed.)
Delphy. Alice Corbin. *Fr.* Echoes of Childhood. PoNe
Delta Autumn, The. William Alexander Percy. LS
Deluge, The, *sel. Unknown.*
Animals in the Ark, The. ChTr
Deluge, The. *Unknown, tr. fr. Lenape Indian by* C. S. Rafinesque. *Fr.* Wallam Olum. LiTA
Delusion of Reference, A. R. A. D. Ford. PeCV
Delusions IV ("Sometimes at evening travellers have heard"). Charles Madge. FaBoMo
Delusions VI ("Without surprise, on that not distant shore"). Charles Madge. NeBP
Delusions VIII ("Placed in a country on a desert verging"). Charles Madge. BoSA

Delusions of the days that once have been. Prologue. Longfellow. *Fr.* Giles Corey of the Salem Farms. PAH
Delve deep amongst the musty muniments. Nicolas Gatineau. Arthur S. Bourinot. CaP
Delve not so deep in the gloomy past. Ascent. Charles G. Blanden. OQP; QP-2
Dem Bones, *with music. Unknown.* OuSiCo
Demand no bay or laurel now. White Armour. Jean Starr Untermeyer. NLK (1947 ed.)
Deme as Ye List uppon Goode Cause. Sir Thomas Wyatt. PoEL-1
Demeter and Persephone. Tennyson. ViPP
Demeter at Eleusis. *Unknown, tr. fr. Greek by* W. M. W. Call *and* T. F. Higham. *Fr.* Homeric Hymns. OxBG
(Demeter Welcomed at Eleusis, *tr. by* Arthur S. Way.) GrR
Demeter devastated our good land. The Appeasement of Demeter. George Meredith. EnLi-2
Demeter, give us fruit and give us grain. Reapers' Song. Theocritus, *tr. by* Henry Harmon Chamberlin. *Fr.* Idylls. GrR
Demeter, rich in harvest of fruit and corn, to thee. Reapers' Song. Theocritus, *tr. by* T. F. Higham. *Fr.* Idylls. OxBG
Demeter Welcomed at Eleusis. *Unknown. See* Demeter at Eleusis.
Demetrios, go to the market. Asclepiades, *tr. fr. Greek by* William Wallace *and* Mary Wallace. GrPo
Demetrius Enters Athens. Hermocles, *tr. fr. Greek by* John Addington Symonds. OxBG
(Processional for Demetrius Poliorcetes.) GrPo
Demiurge's Laugh, The. Robert Frost. OxBA
Demobilized Soldier, The. Wordsworth. *Fr.* The Prelude, IV. RO
Democracy. Harriet Monroe. *Fr.* Commemoration Ode. AA
Democracy, *abr.* Whittier. PoFr; StaSt
Democratic Way, The; Pro and Con. Euripides, *tr. fr. Greek by* Arthur S. Way. *Fr.* Suppliants. GrR
Democritus. Robert Bridges. MeRV
Democritus Platonissans; or, An Essay upon the Infinity of Worlds out of Platonick Principles, *abr.* Henry More. SeCV-2
Demodocus Sings a Song of Troy. Homer, *tr. fr. Greek by* H. B. Cotterill. *Fr.* The Odyssey, VIII. GrR
(Phaeacian Nights—Demodocus, *pr. tr. by* T. E. Lawrence.) OxBG
Demogorgon's Last Words. Shelley. *Fr.* Prometheus Unbound. KN
(Demogorgon's Speech.) LoBV
(Epilogue of "Prometheus.") CBE
(Final Victory, The.) ShBV-3
(Ideal, The.) BHV
("This is the day which down the void abysm.") EnLit; OQP; QP-2; SeCeV
Demon. Aleksandr Blok, *tr. fr. Russian by* C. M. Bowra. BoR
Demon [*or* Daemon], The, *sel.* Mikhail Yurevich Lermontov, *tr. fr. Russian by* Babette Deutsch *and* Avrahm Yarmolinsky.
"On the sightless seas." AWP
("On the vast aerial ocean," *rev. tr. by* Babette Deutsch.) OnPM; TrRV
Demon bydes [*or* bides] in the breist in dern, A. Saagin. Sidney Goodsir Smith. AtBAP; PoN
Demon-Lover, The. James Abraham Hillhouse. AA
Demon Lover, The. *Unknown. See* Daemon Lover, The.
Demon Lovers. Elinor Wylie. OnAP
Demon of the Gibbet, The. Fitz-James O'Brien. DaM; PoMS
Demon of the Mirror, The. Bayard Taylor. BeLS
Demon on the Roof, The. Josephine Pollard. PEOR
Demon sought me out in my, The. In Her Entirety. Baudelaire. TrFP
Demon Speaks, The. Pedro Calderón de la Barca, *tr. fr. Spanish by* Shelley. *Fr.* El Magico prodigioso. CAW
Demonic Yankee who could taste. Emily Dickinson. Paul Engle. PtP
Demons of Opium, The. George Crabbe. *Fr.* Sir Eustace Grey. RO
Demophilus. Henry Wellesley, *after the Greek of* Nicarchus. ALV
Demos. E. A. Robinson. CoV; NP
Demos and His Flatterer. Aristophanes, *tr. fr. Greek by* T. Mitchell. *Fr.* The Knights. OxBG
(Political Cartoon, *tr. by* Benjamin Bickley Rogers.) GrR
Demos Rejuvenated. Aristophanes, *tr. fr. Greek by* Gilbert Murray. *Fr.* The Knights. OxBG
(Demus; a Return to His Better Self, *tr. by* Benjamin Bickley Rogers.) GrR
Demosthenes to the Radio Announcer. David Ross. PG (1945 ed.)
Demus Shriven. Aristophanes, *tr. fr. Greek by* Benjamin Bickley Rogers. *Fr.* The Knights. GrR
Den of the Titans, The. Keats. *Fr.* Hyperion, II. WHA
Denbigh Eisteddfod. Nigel Heseltine. MoWP
Denial, A. Elizabeth Barrett Browning. LEAP
Denial. George Herbert. EnL; EPS (1942 ed.); InPo; LoBV (1949 ed.)
(Deniall.) FaBoEn; MePo; PoEL-2
Denial. Lancaster Pollard. NLK
Denmark Song. Johannes V. Jensen, *tr. fr. Danish by* Charles W. Stork. BoDS
Denmark Speaks. Søren Hallar, *tr. fr. Danish by* Charles W. Stork. BoDS
Dennis was hearty when Dennis was young. The Grand Match. "Moira O'Neill." BMEP; HBMV
Denny Misquotes. Edith Nesbit. *Fr.* The Would-be-Goods. BoN
Denouement. Sister Mary Eulalia. JKCP (1955 ed.)
Denouement. Kenneth Fearing. OnHM
Dense darknesses, The. The Arrival. Kostes Palamas. *Fr.* The Twelve Songs of the Gypsy. MoGP
Dentist, The. Rose Fyleman. GaP; TiPo
Dentist, A. *Unknown.* See Epitaph on a Dentist.
Denuded Is the Land. Antonio Machado, *tr. fr. Spanish by* Philip Warnock Silver. TeCS
Denunciation: or, Unfrock'd Again. Philip Whalen. NeAP
Denver Jim. Sherman D. Richardson. SCC
Deny Yourself. Christopher Morley. LHV; YaD
Deo Gracias. *Unknown.* TMEV
Deo Opt. Max. George Sandys. Paraphrase on the Psalms of David, Psalm CIV. OBS
Deo Optimo Maximo. Louise Imogen Guiney. TrPWD
Deor's Lament. *Unknown, tr. fr. Anglo-Saxon.* TCEP
—*Tr. by* Francis B. Gummere. BEL
—*Tr. by* Charles W. Kennedy. AnOE
—*Tr. by* Harold S. Stine. EnLit
—*Tr. by* Stith Thompson. EnLi-1; OuHeWo
Depart, depart, depart! Lament of the Master of Erskine. Alexander Scott. BSV; CH; LO
Depart from Me. Mary Elizabeth Coleridge. TrPWD
Depart! The sentence of the damn'd I hear. The Parting. John Norris. NBE
Departed, The. John Banister Tabb. AA; LEAP; SPP
Departed Child! I could forget thee once. Maternal Grief. Wordsworth. MOAH
Departed Friend, A. Julia A. Moore. FiBHP
Departed Friend, The. Salvador Novo, *tr. fr. Spanish.* AnCL, *tr. by* Lloyd Mallan; WoL, *tr. by* Muna Lee
Departed Friends. Henry Vaughan. *See* They Are All Gone.
Departed out of parlement echone. The Despair of Troilus. Chaucer. *Fr.* Troilus and Criseyde, IV. LoBV
Departed to the judgment. Emily Dickinson. MaPo
(Soul Alone, The.) OnPM
Departing summer hath assumed. September, 1802 (Upon the Same Occasion). Wordsworth. BPN
Departmental. Robert Frost. AmP; AmPP; AnNE; GoYe; HoPM; MoAB; MoAmPo; OnAP; PoLFOT
Departs the glorious reign. Elegy for a Dead King. Al-Kutandi. MooP
Departure. Al-Hadrami, *tr. fr. Arabic by* A. J. Arberry. MooP
Departure. Kingsley Amis. NePoEA; PoN
Departure. Guillaume Apollinaire, *tr. fr. French by* Patricia Terry. OnPM
Departure, The. Carl Christian Bagger, *tr. fr. Danish by* Charles W. Stork. BoDS
Departure. Jorge Guillén, *tr. fr. Spanish by* Eleanor L. Turnbull. CoSP
Departure. Herman Hagedorn. LBMV; LEAP
Departure. Ibn Mujbar, *tr. fr. Arabic by* A. J. Arberry. MooP
Departure. Edna St. Vincent Millay. MAP; MoAmPo
Departure. Eduard Mörike, *tr. fr. German by* William R. Hughes. AnGP
Departure, The. Robert Pack. NePoEA
Departure. Coventry Patmore. The Unknown Eros, I, viii. ACP; BMEP; CoBE; GTBS-D; GTML; GTSL; HBV; JKCP; LEAP; LO; OBEV; OBVV; PG (1945 ed.); PoLi; POTT; PoVP; SeCePo; VLEP
Departure. Arthur Rimbaud, *tr. fr. French by* Francis Golffing. AnFP
Departure. Jalal ed-Din Rumi, *tr. fr. Persian by* R. A. Nicholson. PeP
Departure. May Riley Smith. AA
Departure. L. A. G. Strong. HaMV
Departure, The. Tennyson. *Fr.* The Day-Dream. LPS-1; TriL
Departure. Wang Wei, *tr. fr. Chinese.* WhP
Departure from Paradise, The. Milton. *Fr.* Paradise Lost, XII. OBS
Departure in the Dark. C. Day Lewis. ChMP; CoBMV; MoPo
Departure of Aeneas from Dido. Virgil, *tr. fr. Latin by* the Earl of Surrey. *Fr.* The Aeneid, IV. TCEP
Departure of Autumn. Li Ho, *tr. fr. Chinese by* Ho Chih-yuan. WhP

Departure of Martin Fierro, The, *abr.* José Hernández, *tr. fr. Spanish by* Walter Owen. PoFr
Departure of the Cuckoo, The. Matthew Arnold. *See* Cuckoo's Parting Cry, The.
Departure of the First-Born. Stefan George, *tr. fr. German by* Reginald H. Phelps. AnGP
Departure of the Good Daemon, The. Robert Herrick. NBE
Departure of the Swallow, The. William Howitt. LPS-2; VA
Departure Platform. Kenneth Allott. NeBP
Dependence on God. Francis Quarles. MaRV
Deportation. "M. J.," *tr. fr. Polish by* A. Glanz-Leyeless. TrJP
Deposition from Beauty, A. Thomas Stanley. EV-2; HBV
("Though when I lov'd thee thou wert fair.") EG
(When I Loved Thee.) LiTL
Deposition from Love, A. Thomas Carew. CoEV; ElSeCe; EV-2; MeLP; NBE; OAEP; OBS
Deprecating Parrots. Beulah May. EtS
Depreciating Her Beauty. Wilfrid Scawen Blunt. The Love Sonnets of Proteus, VI. OBMV
Deprivation. H. A. Pinkerton. NePoAm
Deprived of the green of that exclusive golf course, the scotch. Epistle to the Gentiles. Alfred Hayes. TrJP
Der Heilige Mantel von Aachen. Benjamin Francis Musser. ISi
Der lived a king inta da aste. King Orfeo. *Unknown.* ESPB; OBB; OxBoLi
Der Noble Ritter Hugo. *See* Noble Ritter Hugo, Der.
Deranged. Padraic Fiacc. NeIP
Derby Ram, The (*diff. vers.*). *Unknown.* SoAmSa, *with music*; ViBoFo, *with music*
("As I was going to Derby.") BoN; LiL; OxNR
(Ram, The.) SiTL
(Ram of Darby, The, *with music.*) OuSiCo
(Wonderful Derby Ram, The.) BoTP
Derbyshire Bluebells. Sacheverell Sitwell. ChMP
Dere now bemoany to de ouder air. Euripides. Aristophanes. *Fr.* The Thesmophoriazusae. GrR; OxBG
Dere was an old darkey [*or* nigger], dey called [him] Uncle Ned. Old Uncle Ned. Stephen Collins Foster. APW; OlF
Derelict. Young E. Allison. BBV; BLPA; EtS; FaBoBe; FaFP; HBMV; MCCG; NeHB; TreFS
(Buccaneers, The.) ABF
(Dead Men's Song, The.) AnAmPo; LA; LEAP
Derelict, The. Lucius Harwood Foote. AA
Derelict, The. Robert Munger. LEAP
Derelict. Elisabeth Cavazza Pullen. AA
Dereliction. Edward Shillito. ChIP
Dere's a Han'writin' on de Wall, *with music.* *Unknown.* BoAN-2
Dere's a li'l yaller cradle. Li'l Yaller Cradle. Louise Ayres Garnett. BOL
Dere's a star in de Eas' on Christmas morn. Rise Up Shepherd an' Foller. *Unknown.* BoAN-2; ChrBoLe
Dere's No Hidin' Place Down Dere, *with music.* *Unknown.* BoAN-1
Derricks and Rainbows. Joseph Auslander. PoMa
Derry-Down. *Unknown.* *Fr.* The Procession with the Standard of a Faction; a Cantata. APW
(Liberty Pole, The.) PAH
Dervorgilla's supremely lovely daughter. Portrait with Background. Oliver St. John Gogarty. OBMV
Des a little cabin. A Little Cabin. Charles Bertram Johnson. BANP
Descend, Fair Sun! George Chapman. *Fr.* The Masque of the Middle Temple and Lincoln's Inn. ElL; TuPP
Descend from heav'n Urania, by that name. Invocation to Urania. Milton. *Fr.* Paradise Lost, VII. BrBE; FiP; NBE; OBS; TCEP
Descend, O Dante. Florence Converse. NeTW
Descend, Ye Nine. Pope. *Fr.* Ode for Music on St. Cecilia's Day. GN
Descended, Adam to the bower where Eve. Banishment from Paradise. Milton. *Fr.* Paradise Lost, XII. TreFS
Descended of an ancient line. To Maecenas [*or* Horat. Ode 29. Book 3 *or* The Twenty-ninth Ode of the Third Book of Horace]. Horace, *paraphrased by* Dryden. *Fr.* Odes. AWP; CEP; JAWP; LiA; SeCV-2; WBP
Descending. Valentin Iremonger. *See* Going down the Mountain.
Descending from the great impassive Floods. Drunken Boat. Arthur Rimbaud. TrFP
Descent, The. Samuel Rogers. *Fr.* Italy. LPS-2
Descent. Jalal ed-Din Rumi, *tr. fr. Persian by* A. J. Arberry. PeP
Descent, The. William Carlos Williams. MoAB; ReMP
Descent for the Lost. Philip Child. CaP
Descent from the Cross. "Michael Field." MBP
Descent from the Cross, The, *sel.* Christina Rossetti.
Face of Jesus Christ, The. BePJ
("Is this the face that thrills with awe.") ChIP
Descent into Hell, The. William Langland. *Fr.* The Vision of Piers Plowman. PoEL-1
Descent of Odin, The; an Ode from the Norse Tongue. Thomas Gray. CEP; EiPP
Descent of the Child, The. Susan L. Mitchell. DiM; GTIV
Descent of the Holy Ghost. John Gilland Brunini. JKCP (1955 ed.)
Descent on Middlesex, The. Peter St. John. PAH
"Describe the Borough."—Though our idle tribe. General Description. George Crabbe. *Fr.* The Borough. AEV
Describes Rationally the Irrational Effects of Love. Sister Juana Inés de la Cruz, *tr. fr. Spanish by* Samuel Beckett. AnMP
Describes the Place where Cynthia Is Sporting Herself. Philip Ayres. EnLoPo
Description and Praise of His Love Geraldine. Earl of Surrey. EPP; OAEP; ReIE; SiCE; TuPP
("From Tuscan[e] came my lady's worthy race.") ReEn; SiPS; TwHP
Description is fine enough, The. Reply to the Apparition. Max Jacob. MiCF
Description of a City Shower, A. Swift. BrBE; CEP; EiPP; EnLi-1 (1949 ed.); ExPo; KN; LoBV; OnYI; PoE; PoFS; SeCePo; SeCeV
(City Shower, A.) UnPo (3d ed.)
Sels.
"Ah! where must needy poet seek for aid." ViBoPo
"Careful observers may foretell." CIV
Description of a Convent. Richard Crashaw. PraNu
Description of a Gun. Pandolphus, *tr. fr. Latin by* Sir Thomas Wyatt. ReIE; TuPP
Description of a Most Noble Lady, A. John Heywood. *See* Praise of His Lady, A.
Description of a Shepherd and His Wife, The. Robert Greene. *Fr.* Never Too Late. EV-1
Description of a Strange (and Miraculous) Fish, A. Martin Parker. CoMu
Description of a Summer's Eve. Henry Kirke White. ERP; OBRV
Description of an Envious and Naughty Neighbor, The. Thomas Tusser. SiCE
Description of an Irish Feast, The; or, O'Rourk's Frolic. Hugh MacGowran, *tr. fr. Modern Irish by* Swift. OnYI
(O'Rourk's Frolic.) LiTW
Description of Bath, The, *br. sel.* Mary Chandler.
Rocky Landscape. BeR
Description of Beauty, A. Samuel Daniel, *after the Italian of* Giambattista Marini. OBSC
(Fading Beauty.) AWP
Enjoy thy April Now, *sel.* ElL
Description of Cozeners. George Whetstone. TuPP
Description of Elysium. James Agee. CrMA
Description of Elysium, The. Michael Drayton. *Fr.* The Muses' Elysium. TuPP
Description of Hudibras and His Equipments. Samuel Butler. *See* Hudibras: "When civil dudgeon first grew high."
Description of Life and Riches, A. Thomas Tusser. SiCE
Description of Love, A. Sir Walter Ralegh. ALV; ElL; ElSeCe; LiTL; OBSC; PoFS; ReIE; TuPP
(Now What Is Love.) HBV
Description of Mercy. Giles Fletcher. *Fr.* Christ's Victory and Triumph, I. EV-2
Description of Sir Geoffrey Chaucer, The. Robert Greene. *Fr.* Greene's Vision. AnFE; OBSC
(Sir Geoffrey Chaucer.) FaBoCh; LoGBV
Description of Spring [Wherein Each Thing Renews, Save Only the Lover]. Earl of Surrey, *after* Petrarch. AnEnPo; AtBAP; BCEP; BEL; BrBE; CaAE; CoBE; ElL; ElSeCe; EnLi-1; EnLit; EPP; ES; LiTB; LoBV; OAEP; OBEV; PeBoSo; PoE; ReIE; SeCePo; SeCeV; SiCE; TCEP; TOP; TuPP; TyEnPo
("Soote season, that bud and bloom forth brings, The.") EG; ReEn; SiPS
(Spring.) OBSC
(Summer Comes.) OnPM
(Summer Is Come.) AWP; JAWP; LEAP; OuHeWo; WBP
Description of Such a One as He Would Love, A. Sir Thomas Wyatt. ElSeCe; EPP; TuPP
(Epigram: "Face that should content me, A.") OBSC
("Face that should content me wondrous well, A.") EnLoPo; ReEn; SiCE
Description of the Contrarious Passions in a Lover. Petrarch, *tr. fr. Italian by* Sir Thomas Wyatt. *Fr.* Sonnets to Laura: To Laura in Life. BLV; ElSeCe; EnLi-1 (1949 ed.); OAEP; PeBoSo; PoFS; ReIE; TrGrPo; TuPP
(Contrarious Passions in a Lover, The.) LiTL
(I Find No Peace.) LiTB
("I find no peace and all my war is done.") ReEn
(Love's Inconsistency.) AWP; JAWP; OuHeWo; PreP; WBP
(Sonnet: "I find no peace, and all my war is done.") SiPS

Description of the Lives of the Lasses of London, A. *Unknown. See* Innocent Country-Maid's Delight, The.
Description of the Morning, A, *sel.* Bernard Mandeville.
Another Dawn. BeR
Description of the Morning, A. Swift. BeR; CEP; EiPP; ExPo; FaBoEn; PoFS; SeCeV; ViBoPo
Description of the Properties of Winds All the [*or* at All] Times of the Year, A. Thomas Tusser. ReIE; SiCE; TuPP
Description of the Spring, A. Sir Henry Wotton. *See* On a Bank as I Sat a-Fishing.
Description of the Spring; Wherein Each Thing Renews, Save Only the Lover. Earl of Surrey. *See* Description of Spring.
Description of Time and the Year, A. Thomas Tusser. SiCE
Description of Virtue. Theodore Beza, *tr. fr. Latin by* Nicholas Grimald. CenL; SiCE; TuPP
(Virtue.) OBSC
Description of Wallace, A. Henry the Minstrel. *Fr.* The Wallace, IX. EBSV; GoTS
Descriptive Poem. Han Wu, *tr. fr. Chinese by* Arthur Christy. OnPM
Desdemona. Sister Mary Jeremy. JKCP (1955 ed.)
Desdemona's Song. Shakespeare. *Fr.* Othello, IV, iii. BCEP; KN; LoBV
Desdichado, El. Gérard de Nerval, *tr. fr. French.* AnFP, *tr. by* Richmond Lattimore; LO, *tr. by* Alan Conder; TrFP, *tr. by* Alan Conder
Dese Bones Gwine to Rise Again. *Unknown.* ABF, *with music;* APW; AS, *with music;* OxBoLi; SiTL; SoAF, *with music*
Desecration of the Han Tombs, The. Chang Tsai, *tr. fr. Chinese by* Arthur Waley. TrCh
Desert. Patrick Anderson. BoCaPo
Desert, The. Henry Herbert Knibbs. SCC
Desert, The ("Never have I found a place"). C. E. S. Wood. *Fr.* The Poet in the Desert. AnEnPo
Desert, The ("She is a nun"). C. E. S. Wood. *Fr.* The Poet in the Desert. AnAmPo; LA; MAP
Desert, The ("She is a queen"). C. E. S. Wood. *Fr.* The Poet in the Desert. BAP
Desert Burial. Glenn Ward Dresbach. MuM
Desert Dangers. Jakob Thorarensen, *tr. fr. Icelandic by* Watson Kirkconnell. IcP
Desert does not have to be, A. Deserts. Anne Hamilton. MaRV; OQP; QP-2
Desert Flowers. Keith Douglas. FaBoTw
Desert is mute, the tent is solitary, The. The Anger of Samson. Alfred de Vigny. LiA
Desert murmurs to the sun a strange murmur, The. C. E. S. Wood. *Fr.* The Poet in the Desert. PoFr
Desert Music, The, *sel.* William Carlos Williams.
"Music, The! the/ music! as when Casals struck." UnS
Desert of weed and water-darkened stone under my western windows, A. People and a Heron. Robinson Jeffers. ReMP
Desert Places. Robert Frost. AmPP (4th ed.); AnFE; AtBAP; ChMo; CoAnAm; CoBMV; MAP; MoAB; MoAmPo; MoVE; OxBA; ReMP; RiBV; TwAmPo; TwP; UnPo
Desert Remembers Her Reasons, The. Genevieve Taggard. TBM
Desert River. Patricia Benton. GoYe
Desert Shipwreck. Barbara Leslie Jordan. GoYe
Desert Travellers, The. L. D. Lerner. BoSA
Desert Wanderings. Thomas Curtis Clark. ChIP
Deserted. Madison Cawein. MAP; MCCG; PFE; SPP
Deserted Adobe, The. *Unknown.* CSF
Deserted by the waning moon. All's Well. Thomas Dibdin. *Fr.* The British Fleet. LPS-2
Deserted City, The. Sir Charles G. D. Roberts. BMEP; VA
Deserted City, The, *sel.* Francis Sherman.
House of Colour, The. CaP; OCL
Deserted Farm, A. George Sterling. LPS-1
Deserted Farms. Richard Burton. AnAmPo; LA
Deserted Garden, The. Elizabeth Barrett Browning. EmBrPo; EV-4; HBV; OBEV (1st ed.); VLEP
Deserted Garden, The. Li Po, *tr. fr. Chinese by* C. W. Luh. OnPM
Deserted Garden on the Road to Hua Chou, A. P'an I, *tr. fr. Chinese by* Henry H. Hart. PoHN
Deserted Hollow. Mark Van Doren. MM
Deserted Home, A. Sidney Royse Lysaght. CH
Deserted Home, The. *Tr. fr. Irish by* Kuno Meyer.
(Blackbird's Nest, The, *tr. by* George Sigerson.) SiB
(Ruined Nest, The.) OnYI, *tr. by* Kuno Meyer; TIP, *tr. by* George Sigerson
Deserted House, The. Mary Elizabeth Coleridge. BoTP; CH; MoVE; PCD; ThWaDe
Deserted House, The. Tennyson. VA
Deserted House, *sel.* Dorothy Wellesley.
Buried Child, The. Epilogue. GTBS-D; OBMV
Deserted Kingdom, The. Lord Dunsany. AnIV
Deserted Lover Consoleth Himself, The. Sir Thomas Wyatt. *See* Divers Doth Use, as I Have Heard and Know.
Deserted Maiden, The. Eduard Mörike, *tr. fr. German by* Norman Macleod. LiA
Deserted Pasture, The. Bliss Carman. HBV; NLK
Deserted Plantation, The. Paul Laurence Dunbar. IHA
Deserted Temple, A. Yüan Chen, *tr. fr. Chinese by* Henry H. Hart. PoHN
Deserted Village, The. Goldsmith. BEL; BeLS; CEP; CoBE; EiPP; EnL; EnLi-1; EnLit; EnRP; EPP; EV-3; FaFP; GoTL; HBV; HiLiEn; LaA; LoBV, *abr.;* LPS-2; MCCG; OAEP; OnYI; OuHeWo; OxBI; Po, *abr.;* PoE; PoEL-3; PYM, *abr.;* REAL; TCEP; TOP; TyEnPo; WP
Sels.
Blest Retirement. OBEC
Farewell to Poetry. OBEC
"Ill fares the land." BHV
(Common Man, The, 6 *ll.*) MaRV
(Where Wealth Accumulates, 6 *ll.*) GrCo-1
"Sweet Auburn! loveliest village of the plain." OTPC; TreFS; ViBoPo
(Auburn.) OBEC; SeCePo
(From "The Deserted Village.") LEAP
(Sweet Auburn.) LiTB
(Village, The.) TrGrPo
"Sweet smiling village, loveliest of the lawn." AnFE; PoFr, *abr.;* PreP
"Sweet was the sound, when oft at evening's close." BrBE; EnSW; FaBoEn
(Evening.) ShBV-2
(Village, The.) GTIV
Village Preacher, The. CBOV; GrCo-1; MaRV; TrGrPo, *shorter sel.*
(Country Parson, The.) OTPC (1923 ed.)
(Village Parson, The.) CoEV; OBEC; WGRP
Village Schoolmaster, The. BTP; OBEC; TrGrPo
(Schoolmaster, The.) CBOV; OTPC (1946 ed.); ShBV-2; TVSH
Still the Wonder Grew, 4 *ll.* TreF
"With louder plaints the mother spoke her woes," 6 *ll.* MotAn
Deserter, The. Joseph S. Cotter, Jr. CDC
Deserter, The. John Philpot Curran. EV-3; LH; ViBoPo
(Deserter's Lamentation, The.) IrPN; SeCePo
(Deserter's Meditation, The.) RO; TIP
(Let Us Be Merry [before We Go].) AnIV; BLV
Deserter, The. A. E. Housman. Last Poems, XIII. OBMV; POTT; SeCeV
Deserter, The. John Manifold. WaP
Deserter from the Cause, The. Gerald Massey. VA; YT
Deserter's Lamentation, The. John Philpot Curran. *See* Deserter, The.
Deserter's Meditation, The. John Philpot Curran. *See* Deserter, The.
Desertion of Beauty and Strength, The. *Unknown. Fr.* Everyman. ACP
Deserts. Anne Hamilton. MaRV; OQP; OP-2
Deserts ("Deserts are more than shimmering heat and sand"). Leigh Hanes. GoYe
Deservings. *Unknown.* HBV
Desideravi. Theodore Maynard. HBMV
Desideria. Lionel Johnson. VLEP
Desideria. Wordsworth. *See* Surprised by Joy—Impatient as the Wind.
Desiderium. John Byrom. *See* Desponding Soul's Wish, The.
Desiderium. Phineas Fletcher. *Fr.* The Purple Island, I. OBS
Desiderium Indesideratum. Francis Thompson. StJW; TriL
Design. Dryden. *Fr.* To My Honor'd Friend Sir Robert Howard. MaRV
Design. Robert Frost. CoBMV; CrMA; Po; SeCeV
Design. Arthur Guiterman. FAOV
Design for a List of Pictures. Arthur Symons. FaBoTw
Design for a Stream-lined Sunrise. Sister Mary Madeleva. GoBC; JKCP (1955 ed.)
Design for Mediaeval Tapestry. A. M. Klein. CaP
Job Reviles, *sel.* QS
Design for Peace. Janet Norris Bangs. PGD
Desire. "Æ." GTIV; OBMV; TrPWD
Desire. Matthew Arnold. LPS-2; WGRP
(Stagirius.) GEPC
Desire, A. Elizabeth Barrett Browning. *Fr.* Sonnets to George Sand. LPS-3
Desire. William Cornish. OBSC; SeCeV
("Knight knock'd at the castle gate, The.") EG
Desire. Nathalia Crane. MAP; MoAmPo (1942 ed.)
Desire. Hafiz. *See* I Cease Not from Desire.
Desire. "Fiona Macleod." OQP; QP-2
Desire. Kathleen Raine. MoPo
Desire. Sir Philip Sidney. *See* Thou Blind Man's Mark.
Desire. Thomas Traherne. EPS; OxBoCh
("For giving me desire.") LO
Desire, The. Katharine Tynan. BMEP; HBV; LEAP; TSW

Desire and Disillusion. Byron. *Fr.* Childe Harold's Pilgrimage, IV. EPN
Desire for Hermitage, The. *Unknown, tr. fr. Old Irish by* Seán O'Faoláin. AnIL; SiB
Desire in Spring. Francis Ledwidge. CP; NV; VOD
Desire Is a Witch. C. Day Lewis. ChMo
Desire Knows. Asclepiades, *tr. fr. Greek by* Charles Glenn Wallis. LiTW
Desire of love, Joy, The. Desire. "Fiona Macleod." OQP; QP-2
Desire of the Moth, The. Shelley. *See* One Word Is Too Often Profaned.
Desire of your light hands. Ancient Winter. Salvatore Quasimodo. OnPM
Desire, though thou my old [*or* olde] companion art. Astrophel and Stella, LXXII. Sir Philip Sidney. NBE; ReEn; SiPS
Desire We Past Illusions to Recall. Wordsworth. EmBrPo; EPN
Desired Swan-Song, The. Samuel Taylor Coleridge. *See* On a Bad Singer.
Desire's Government. "A. W." EIL
Desires of Men and Women. John Berryman. LiTM
Desk, The. Wen Yi-tuo, *tr. fr. Chinese.* WhP
Desk Motto, A. Don Marquis. DDA
Desolate. Claude McKay. CDC
Desolate and lone. Lost. Carl Sandburg. BrR; ChMo; CMP; MOAP; NP; ReaPo; TCAP; VOD; WHA
Desolate City, The. *Unknown, tr. fr. Arabic by* Wilfrid Scawen Blunt. AWP; JKCP; MBP; MoBrPo (1942 ed.); OBEV; OBVV
Desolate Field, The. William Carlos Williams. MOAP
Desolate is my station here on the height, O stranger. Hermes the Hermit. *Unknown.* GrPE
Desolate Lover, The. Eileen Shanahan. NeIP
Desolate Scythia. Edgar Lee Masters. ChMo; CMP; NP
Desolate shore, A. Rhymes and Rhythms, III. W. E. Henley. POTT
Desolate Valley, The, *sel.* Thomas Pringle.
"Then, couched at night in hunter's wattled shieling." BoSA
Desolate Wreath, The. Asclepiades, *tr. fr. Greek by* Robert Allason Furness. GrR
Desolation. Ann Louise Hayes. PtPa
Desolation. Tom Masson. PA
Desolation. Georg Trakl, *tr. fr. German by* Kate Flores. AnGP
Desolation. Henry T. Tuckerman. APW
Desolation. Wang Wei, *tr. fr. Chinese by* Li Fu-ning. WhP
Desolation in Zion. Lamentations, I: 12–17, Bible, *O.T.* TrJP
Desolation Is a Delicate Thing. Elinor Wylie. MAP; MoAmPo
Desolation of Berytus, The. Johannes Barbucallus. *See* Ruined Harbour, A.
Desolation of the Cyclades, The. Antipater of Thessalonica, *tr. fr. Greek by* F. L. Lucas. GrPE
Despair. Chu Shu Chen, *tr. fr. Chinese by* Henry H. Hart. PoHN
Despair. Fulke Greville. Caelica, LXXXIII [LXXXIV]. OBCS
("Who grace, for zenith had, from which no shadowes grow.") PoEL-1
Despair. Rose Hawthorne Lathrop. *Fr.* Give Me Not Tears. AA
Despair. Juan Meléndez Valdés, *tr. fr. Spanish by* Eleanor L. Turnbull. TeCS
Despair. Edward Bliss Reed. HBMV
Despair. Spenser. *Fr.* The Faerie Queene, I, 9. NBE; SeCePo, *shorter sel.*
(To Be or Not to Be.) FaBoEn
Despair. Theognis, *tr. fr. Greek by* F. L. Lucas. GrPE
(Better Part, The.) GrR
Despair and Hope. Israel Zangwill. TrJP
Despair of the Old Woman, The. Baudelaire, *tr. fr. French by* Arthur Symons. OnPM
Despair of Troilus, The. Chaucer. *Fr.* Troilus and Criseyde, IV. LoBV
Despairing beside a clear stream. Colin's Complaint. Nicholas Rowe. OBEC
Despairing Lover, The William Walsh. ALV; BCEP; CEP; EV-3; FaBoCh; LoGBV; OBEC; OxBoLi
Desperado, The. *Unknown.* CoSo; TreFS
(Boozer, The.) CSF
Desperate. Cino da Pistoia, *tr. fr. Italian by* L. R. Lind. LyMA; LyPI
Despise not any man that lives. Sam Walter Foss. *Fr.* Work for Small Men. PoToHe
Despised and Rejected. Katharine Lee Bates. OQP; QP-1
Despised and Rejected. Christina Rossetti. MaRV; StJW
Despite their boastful Margraves and their flags. Central Europe. Norman Cameron. MoPW
Despite Time. Shakespeare. *See* Sonnets, CXXIII.
Despondency. Matthew Arnold. PoVP; VLEP
Despondency Corrected. Wordsworth. *Fr.* The Excursion, IV. EnRP; ERP
Desponding Phillis was endu'd. Phillis; or, The Progress of Love. Swift. BeR; ExPo; PoEL-3
Desponding Soul's Wish, The. John Byrom. OBEC; TrPWD
(Desiderium.) EV-3
(My Spirit Longeth for Thee.) OxBoCh
Despot treads thy sacred sands, The. Carolina. Henry Timrod. BlG; MC; PAH; SPP
Despot's heel is on thy shore, The. My Maryland [*or* Maryland, My Maryland]. James Ryder Randall. AA; AnAmPo; APA; BAP; CoBA; FaBoBe; FaFP; HBV; IAP; JKCP; LA; LBAP; LEAP; MC; OBAV; PaA; PAH; PoFr; SPP; TreF
Dessert, The. Charles *and* Mary Lamb. OTPC (1923 ed.)
Destined to war from very infancy. Epitaphs, VI. Gabriello Chiabrera. AWP; JAWP; WBP
Destinie. Abraham Cowley. MeLP
Destiny. Sir Edwin Arnold. MaRV
(Somewhere.) PoToHe (new ed.)
Destiny. Nathalia Crane. GoTP; MAP; NeMA
Destiny. Emerson. IAP
Destiny. John Fletcher. *Fr.* Upon an Honest Man's Fortune. MaRV
Destiny. Harrison Smith Morris. AA
Destiny. Thomas Stanley. *See* Expectation.
Destiny. Whittier. MaRV
Destiny. Wordsworth. *See* It Is Not to Be Thought Of.
Destiny of Nations, The, *sels.* Samuel Taylor Coleridge.
"'Even so' (the exulting Maiden said)." ChER
"For what is Freedom, but the unfettered use." EnRP
Destroyer. A. M. Sullivan. ALV; PFE
Destroyer Life, *with music.* *Unknown.* ABF
Destroyer of Destroyers, The. Wallace Rice. PAH
Destroyers, The, *sel.* Archibald Fleming MacLiesh.
"Now all things melt and shift." NAMP
Destroyers in Collision. Kipling. *Fr.* Epitaphs of the War. PoVP
Destruction. Joachim du Bellay, *tr. fr. French by* Alan Conder. Antiquities of Rome, XIII. TrFP
Destruction of Jerusalem by the Babylonian Hordes, The. Isaac Rosenberg. MeRV
Destruction of Leire, The. *Unknown, tr. fr. Old Norse by* Lee M. Hollander. PaOS
Destruction of Letters. Babette Deutsch. HoPM
Destruction of Psara, The. Dionysios Solomos, *tr. fr. Modern Greek by* Rae Dalven. MoGP
Destruction of Sennacherib, The. Byron. ATP; BCEP; BEL; BeLS; BHV; BLPA; BLV; BoLiVe; BPN; BTP; CaAE; CBPC; CG; CoBE; EM-2; EmBrPo; EnLi-2; EnLit; EnRP; ERP; EV-4; FaBoBe; FaBoCh; FaFP; FaPON; GEPC; GN; GoTP; HBV; HiLiEn; InP; LiA; LiTG; LoGBV; LPS-2; MaRV; MCCG; MPB (1956 ed.); MuP; NeHB; OAEP; OTPC; OuHeWo; PCD; PECK; PIR; Po; PoE; PreP; REAL; RG; ShBV-1; TCEP; TOP; TreF; TVSH; TwCrTr; WBLP; WGRP
(Sennacherib.) LH
Destruction of Troy, The. Virgil, *tr. fr. Latin by* Sir John Denham. *Fr.* The Aeneid, II. SeCV-1
Desultory Poem, A, Written on the Christmas Eve of 1794, *sel.* Samuel Taylor Coleridge. *Fr.* Religious Musings.
"Lovely was the death." EmBrPo; EnRP; ERP
Detachment is a virtue, teachers say. Ballade on Eschatology. Sister Mary Madeleva. GoYe
Detail. Mary Ursula Bethell. AnNZ
Detail from an Annunciation by Crivelli. Rosemary Dobson. NeLNL
Determined with one sally to erase. Sonnet. Petrarch. Sonnets to Laura: To Laura in Life, II. LyPI
Deus Absconditus. Anne Ridler. FaBoMo
Detour—Gypsy Trail Closed. Sara Henderson Hay *and* Raymond Holden. StaSt
Deus Immensa Trinitas. *Unknown, tr. fr. Latin by* Alan G. McDougall. CAW
Deus Meus. Mael-Isu, *tr. fr. Irish by* George Sigerson. CAW
Deus Noster Ignis Consumens. Laurence Housman. HBMV
Deuteronomy, *sels.* Bible, *O.T.*
Blessed of the Lord Be His Land, XXXIII: 13–16. BrR
(Give Ear, O Ye Heavens, XXXIII: 13–16, 27.) PCH
Everlasting Arms, The, 2 *ll.*, XXXIII: 27. GrCo-1
Give Ear, Ye Heavens, XXXII: 1–43. TrJP
Lest We Forget: "Hear, O Israel," VI–VIII, *abr.* GrCo-1
Written in the Heart: "Hear, O Israel," VI: 4–7, XXX: 11–14, 19–20. GrCo-2
Development. Robert Browning. BPN; GEPC; PoVP; VLEP
Development of Man, The. Robert Browning. *Fr.* Paracelsus, V. EPN
Deviator, The. Bertram Warr. BoCaPo (1948 ed.)
Device. Sir Herbert Read. MBP; MoBrPo (1942 ed.)
Devil, *with music.* *Unknown.* StDa
Devil and the Angel, The, 1 ("Chancing upon the Devil in the doorway"). Rosemary Dobson. BoAV

Devil and the Angel, The, 6 ("The man was called Methusaleh"). Rosemary Dobson. BoAV
Devil and the Farmer's Wife, The, *with music. Unknown.* TrAS
Devil and the Lady, The, *sel.* Tennyson.
 Deep Dark Night, The. SeCePo
Devil at Home, The. Thomas Kibble Hervey. *Fr.* The Devil's Progress. LPS-3
Devil-Dancers, The. William Plomer. BoSA
Devil having nothing else to do, The. On Lady Poltagrue, a Public Peril. Hilaire Belloc. ALV; MBP; MoBrPo; WhC
Devil Is Dying, The. Willard Wattles. *See* Courage, Mon Ami!
Devil lef' Nine Hundud, wringin' wet with sweat. Devil. *Unknown.* StDa
Devil sits in his easy-chair, The. The Devil at Home. Thomas Kibble Hervey. *Fr.* The Devil's Progress. LPS-3
Devil sprang from box. Jack-in-the-Box. Elder Olson. NePA
Devil to Pay, The, *sels.* Dorothy L. Sayers. MaRV
 Choice of the Cross, The.
 Judgment and Mercy.
Devil up my attic stair, The. All, All. Baudelaire. WoL
Devil was given permission one day, The. Arizona. *Unknown.* ABF
Devil, we're told, in hell was chained, The. Hell in Texas. *Unknown.* ABF; BLPA; CSF
Devilish Mary, *with music. Unknown.* OuSiCo
Devils. Pushkin. *See* Evil Spirits.
Devil's Advice to Story-Tellers, The. Robert Graves. LiTM (rev. ed.)
Devil's Auction, The. Charles Erskine Scott Wood. BAP
Devil's Cauldron. Monk Gibbon. HaMV
Devil's Complaint, The. Sana'i, *tr. fr. Persian by* A. J. Arberry. PeP
Devil's Darning Needle. C. Lindsay McCoy. GFA
Devil's Dream. Kenneth Fearing. ChMo; PoLFOT
Devil's Law Case, The, *sels.* John Webster.
 All the Flowers of the Spring. AtBAP; BrBE; CaAE; EG; ElL; EV-2; ExPo; GTBS-W; LiTB; LiTG; OBS; PoEL-2; PoFS; PoRA; SiCE; ViBoPo
 (All Is Vanity.) CoEV
 (Burial, The.) CH; LoBV
 (Nets to Catch the Wind.) BLV; TrGrPo
 (Song: "All the flowers of the spring.") HBV
 (Vanitas Vanitatum.) BCEP; BEL; LEAP; OBEV
 "Vain the ambition of kings," 4 *ll.* PoFr
 "Oh heere's my mother: I ha strange newes for you." AtBAP
 "O, I shall run mad!" LO
Devil's Meditation, The. Michael Sweany. MaRV
Devil's Progress, The, *sel.* Thomas Kibble Hervey.
 Devil at Home, The. LPS-3
Devil's Swing, The. "Feodor Sologub," *tr. fr. Russian by* Babette Deutsch. TrRV
Devil's Tribute to Moling, The, *sel. Unknown, tr. fr. Old Irish by* Whitley Stokes *and* John Strachan.
 Holy Man, The. OnYI
Devil's Walk on Earth, The. Robert Southey *and* Samuel Taylor Coleridge. BOHV
 (Devil's Thoughts, The, *much abr.*) OxBoLi
 (Devil's Walk, The, *abr.*) LPS-3
 "From his brimstone bed at break of day," *sel.* PoMS
Devocion de la Cruz, La, *sel.* Pedro Calderón de la Barca, *tr. fr. Spanish.*
 Cross, The, *tr. by* Richard Chenevix Trench. CAW; LiA; TeCS
 (Dying Eusebio's Address to the Cross, The, *longer sel., tr. by* D. F. MacCarthy.) OuHeWo
Devoid of reason, thrall to foolish ire. Passion's Hounds. Thomas Lodge, *after* Pierre de Ronsard. Phyllis, XXXI. OnPM; ReEn: SiCE
Devon Maid, The. Keats. *See* Where Be You Going, You Devon Maid.
Devon to Me. John Galsworthy. HBMV
Devonshire Lane, The. John Marriott. BOHV
Devonshire Rhyme, A ("Walk fast in snow"). *Unknown.* BrR; MPB; SiSoSe
Devonshire Song, A ("Thou ne're wilt riddle"). *Unknown, at. to* William Strode. OBS; PoEL-2, *sl. diff.*
Devotion. Burns. *See* Mary Morison.
Devotion. Byron. *See* Ave Maria.
Devotion ("Follow thy fair sun, unhappy shadow"). Thomas Campion. *See* Follow Thy Fair Sun.
Devotion ("Follow your saint, follow with accents sweet!"). Thomas Campion. *See* Follow Your Saint.
Devotion. Pao Chao, *tr. fr. Chinese by* Henry H. Hart. PoHN
Devotion. *Unknown. See* Fain Would I Change That Note.
Devotion of the Flowers to Their Lady, The. Herman Melville. MeRV
Devotion to Duty. Siegfried Sassoon. MoPW
Devotional Incitements. Wordsworth. OxBoCh
Devotions. Ellinor L. Norcross. OQP; QP-2
Devourers, The. Rose Macaulay. PoeT
Devouring Time, blunt thou the lion's [*or* lyons] paws. Sonnets, XIX. Shakespeare. AtBAP; AWP; ChTr; CoEV; EG; GTBS-W; InPo; LiA; OBSC; PeBoSo; PoEL-2; ReIE; RiBV; SiCE; TrGrPo; TwP; WHA
Devout Angler, The. *Unknown.* DDA
Devout Fits. John Donne. *See* Sonnet: "Oh, to vex me . . ."
Devout Lover, A. Thomas Randolph. HBV; HoPM; LiTL; OBEV
 ("I have a mistress, for perfections rare.") EG
 (Love and Reverence.) BCEP
Devout thou wast as holy hermits are. Infant Roses in Their Bloom. John Oldham. *Fr.* To the Memory of Mr. Charles Morwent. BeR
Devoutly worshipping the oak. Canticle. William Griffith. BLA; CP; DD; HBMV; HBVY; NV
Dew. John Charles McNeill. NoCaPo
Dew. Frank S. Williamson. BoAu
Dew Each Trembling Leaf Inwreath'd, The. Mary Balfour. IrPN
Dew is gleaming in the grass, The. Among the Millet. Archibald Lampman. CaP; OCL
Dew is on the grasses, dear, The. Youth. Georgia Douglas Johnson. BANP; GoSl; PoNe
Dew is on the heather, The. The Captain's Feather. Samuel Minturn Peck. AA; LBAP
Dew it trembles on the thorn, The. Silent Love. John Clare. EnRP
Dew no more will weep, The. Richard Crashaw. *Fr.* The Weeper. EV-2
Dew on a Dusty Heart. Jean Starr Untermeyer. MAP; MoAmPo
Dew on her robe and on her tangled hair. My Lady April. Ernest Dowson. VLEP
Dew on the Garlic-Leaf, The. *Unknown, tr. fr. Chinese by* Arthur Waley. Burial Songs, I. TrCh
 (Burial Song.) WoL
Dew-Plants. Ernest G. Moll. NeLNL
Dew sat[e] on Julia's hair[e]. Upon Julia's Hair[e] Filled with Dew. Robert Herrick. AtBAP; EG
Dew, the rain and moonlight, The. A Net to Snare the Moonlight. Vachel Lindsay. ChMo; CMP
Dew upon the robin as he lilts there on the thorn. Dew. Frank S. Williamson. BoAu
Dew was falling fast, the stars began to blink, The. The Pet Lamb. Wordsworth. OTPC; PRWS; SAS
Dewdrop, A. Frank Dempster Sherman. PPL
Dewdrop, The. Joseph Skipsey. *See* Dewdrop, Wind and Sun.
Dew-drop came, with a spark of flame, A. Origin of the Opal. *Unknown.* LPS-3
Dewdrop of the darkness born, A. The Immaculate Conception. John Banister Tabb. ISi
Dewdrop, Wind and Sun. Skipsey. OBVV
 (Dewdrop, The.) VA
Dewdrops, The. Lydia Miller Mackay. GFA
Dewdrops. Soin, *tr. fr. Japanese by* H. G. Henderson. OnPM
Dewdrops cling, The. A Flute at Evening. Huang Wan Ch'iung. PoHN
Dewdrops, limpid, small. Dewdrops. Soin. OnPM
Dewdrops of shaded orchids. A Lady's Sepulcher. Li Ho. WhP
Dewey and His Men. Wallace Rice. PAH
Dewey at Manila. Robert Underwood Johnson. GA; HBV; MC; PAH
Dewey in Manila Bay. Richard Voorhees Risley. DD; GA; MC; PAH
Dews are all of one pale silvery white, The. Autumn Leaves. Toshiyuki. OnPM
Dews Disappear, The. Issa, *tr. fr. Japanese by* H. G. Henderson. OnPM
Dews drop slowly and dreams gather: unknown spears, The. The Valley of the Black Pig. W. B. Yeats. ChTr
Dews of summer night did fall, The. Cumnor Hall. William Julius Mickle. BeLS; CEP; EV-3; OBEC; ViBoPo
Dewy dawn from old Tithonus' bed, The. Jabberwocky. Julius Cooper. InMe
Dewy-eyed with shimmering hair. An Old Song by New Singers: Mr. Algernon C. Swinburne's Idea. A. C. Wilkie. BOHV; PA
Dewy, roseate morn had with her hairs, The. Phyllis, IX. Thomas Lodge. SiCE
Dexippos, *sel.* Victor Rydberg.
 Song of the Athenians. AnSL
Dey crucified my Lord. Crucifixion. *Unknown.* MaRV
Dey Don' Know. Leigh Richmond Miner. BOL
Dey is times in life when Nature. When de Co'n Pone's Hot. Paul Laurence Dunbar. BANP; MotAn
Dey tell me Joe Turner he done come [*or* Joe Turner's come and gone]. Joe Turner [Blues]. *Unknown.* AS; TrAS
Dey was hard times jes fo' Christmas. An Indignation Dinner. James David Corrothers. BANP; PoNe

Deze eatin' folks may tell me ub de gloriz ub spring lam'. Hog Meat. Daniel Webster Davis. BANP
Dharra and the Date-Stone, The. *Unknown, tr. fr. Arabic by* Sir Edwin Arnold. OnPM
Dhoon, The. Thomas Edward Brown. POTT
Dhows, The. Francis Brett Young. EtS
Diaduminius. Pierre Benoit, *tr. fr. French by* Joseph T. Shipley. CAW
Diagnosis of our hist'ry [*or* history] proves, A. The Rejected "National Hymns," III. "Orpheus C. Kerr." BOHV; InMe; LPS-3; PA
Diagonals. Aline Kilmer. AV
Diakos. Kostas Kariotakis, *tr. fr. Modern Greek by* Rae Dalven. MoGP
Dial faced the summer sun, The. The Song of the Dial. Peter Airey. OQP; QP-2
Dialectics of Flight. John Hall Wheelock. NePoAm-2
Dialogue. Walter Conrad Arensberg. SBMV
Dialogue, A. Austin Dobson. BPN; PoVP
Dialogue. John Erskine. HBMV
Dialogue. George Herbert. EV-2; MePo; OBEV; OBS; SeCV-1
Dialogue. Ibn Munakhkhal, *tr. fr. Arabic by* A. J. Arberry. MooP
Dialogue. Sister Mary Madeleva. CAW
Dialogue, A. Sir Philip Sidney. *See* Astrophel and Stella: Eleventh Song.
Dialogue, A. Swinburne. PoEL-5
Dialogue. Margaret Widdemer. MuM
Dialogue. Prince Yuhara, *tr. fr. Japanese by* Ishii *and* Obata. OnPM
Dialogue Anthem, A. George Herbert. StJW
Dialogue at the Cross. Frederick Spee, *tr. fr. German by* Mary E. Mannix. CAW
Dialogue between Mary and Gabriel. W. H. Auden. *Fr.* For the Time Being; a Christmas Oratorio. ISi
Dialogue between Poet and Patron. Taliesin, *tr. fr. Welsh by* D. S. Evans. LyMA
Dialogue between Strephon and Daphne, A. Earl of Rochester. SeCV-2
Dialogue between the Resolved Soul and Created Pleasure, A. Andrew Marvell. MeLP; MePo; OBS; SeCV-1
Dialogue between the Soul and Body, A. Andrew Marvell. CoEV; MeLP; MePo; NBE; OBS; OxBoCh; PoEL-2; PoFS; ReEn; SeCV-1; SeEP
Dialogue between Two Shepherds, Thenot and Piers, in Praise of Astrea, A. Countess of Pembroke. ReIE
Dialogue betwixt God and the Soul, A. *At. to* Sir Henry Wotton, *after* Horace. MeLP; OBS; OxBoCh
Dialogue betwixt Peace and War. Margaret Cavendish, Duchess of Newcastle. DiM
Dialogue betwixt Time and a Pilgrim[e], A. Aurelian Townsend. CoEV; MePo; NBE; OBS; PoEL-2; SeEP
Dialogue Containing the Number of the Effectual Proverbs in the English Tongue, A, *sels.* John Heywood. ReIE
"Among other things profiting in our tongue."
"Of mine acquaintance a certain young man."
Dialogue from Plato, A. Austin Dobson. BOHV; HBV
Dialogue from "The Dream Queen." Bhasa, *tr. fr. Sanskrit by* A. G. Shirreff *and* Panna Lall. *Fr.* The Dream Queen. LiTW
Dialogue I'll tell you as true as my life, A. The Coal-Owner and the Pitman's Wife. *Unknown.* CoMu
Dialogue: Lover and Lady. Ciullo d'Alcamo, *tr. fr. Italian by* Dante Gabriel Rossetti. AWP; LyPI
Dialogue of Self and Soul, A. W. B. Yeats. ExPo; FaBoMo; LiTB; LiTM; MoP; OAEP (2d ed.); Po; ReMP
Dialogue of the Body with the Soul [Which Is] Leading It to Judgment. Jacopone da Todi, *tr. fr. Italian by* Hubert Creekmore. LyMA; LyPI
Dialogue of the Way. Harold Stewart. BoAV
Dialogue—2 Dollmakers. Gregory Corso. NeAP
Dialogue with the Dead. Callimachus, *tr. fr. Greek by* G. M. Young. OxBG
Dialogue, without End. Isabel Harriss Barr. JKCP (1955 ed.)
Diamond, A. Robert Loveman. AA
Diamond Cut Diamond. Ewart Milne. FaBoCh; LoGBV; NeIP
Diamond Joe, *with music. Unknown.* CoSo; OuSiCo
Diamond, O gods, you create, The. Out of the Italian. Joel Elias Spingarn. BAP
Diamond you may draw, A. The Stubborn Fool. Bhartrihari. OnPM
Diamonds, Sparkling. Gifts that cannot ease. Dawn in Besieged Leningrad. Vera Inber. RuPo
Dian, that fain would cheer her friend the Night. Astrophel and Stella, XCVII. Sir Philip Sidney. ReEn; SiPS
Diana. Audrey Alexandra Brown. OCL
Diana, *sels.* Henry Constable.
"Dear to my soul, then leave me not forsaken!" OBSC; ReEn; ReIE; SiCE; TuPP
(Sonnet.) ElL
"Fair grace of graces, muse of muses all." TuPP
"Fair sun, if you would have me praise your light." OBSC; SiCE
"Grace full of grace, though in these verses here." OBSC
"Hope, like the hyena [*or* hyaena] coming to be old." EnLoPo; OBSC; SiCE
"If ever sorrow spoke from soul that loves." SiCE
(Sonnet.) ElL
"Mine eye with all the deadly sins is fraught." SiCE; TuPP
"Miracle of the world! I never will deny." OBSC; ReEn
(To His Mistress.) TuPP
"My lady's presence makes the roses red." CoBE; HBV; LEAP; OBSC; ReIE; SiCE
(Sonnet.) ElL
"My tears are true, though others be divine." OBSC
"Needs must I leave and yet needs must I love." InvP; OBSC; SiCE
"Not that thy hand is soft, is sweet, is white." OBSC
"Ready to seek out death in my disgrace." OBSC; SiCE
"Sun, his journey ending in the west, The." OBSC
"To live in hell, and heaven to behold." HBV; InvP; OBSC; ReEn; ReIE; SiCE; TuPP
(If This Be Love.) LiTL
"Uncivil sickness, hast thou no regard." ReIE
"When your perfections to my thoughts appear." SiCE
"Whilst echo cries, 'What shall become of me?'" OBSC; ReEn; ReIE; SiCE; TuPP
"You secret vales, you solitary fields." OBSC
Diana. Keats. *Fr.* Endymion, I. BCEP
Diana, *sels.* Jorge de Montemayor, *tr. fr. Spanish by* Bartholomew Young.
Melisea, Her Song in Scorn of Her Shepherd Narcissus. TuPP
Nymph Diana's Song, The. ReIE
"Shepherd, who can pass such wrong." SiCE
(Nymph Selvagia, The, Her Song.) ElSeCe; TuPP
(Song.) ElL
Diana. Sir Walter Ralegh. *See* Praised Be Diana's Fair and Harmless Light.
Diana. Ernest Rhys. OBVV; VA
Diana Fitzpatrick Mauleverer James. Miss James. A. A. Milne. MoShBr; MPB; TiPo
Diana guardeth our estate. Hymn to Diana. Catullus. AWP; LaP
Diana, mistress of the evening sky. From the Latin of Catullus. *Tr. by* Colgate Dorr. PtPa
Diana, naked in the shadowy pool. Madrigal 52. Petrarch. LyPI
Diana's Hunting-Song. Dryden. *Fr.* The Secular Masque. SeCePo; SeCL
(Songs from "The Secular Masque.") InPo
("With horns and with hounds I waken the day." ElSeCe
Diaphenia. *At. to* Henry Constable *and to* Henry Chettle. CH; EG; ElL; GoBC; GTBS; GTBS-D; GTBS-W; GTSE
(Damelus' Song to [*or* of] His Diaphenia.) ElSeCe; EPP; EV-1; FaBoEn; HBV; OBSC; PoEL-2; TuPP; ViBoPo
("Diaphenia, like the daffadowndilly.") LO
Diaphenia, drunk with sleep. Male and Female Created He Them. Aldous Huxley. ALV
Diaphenia, like the daffadowndilly. *At. to* Henry Constable *and to* Henry Chettle. *See* Diaphenia.
Diaries. Ethel Romig Fuller. PSO
Diary, *sel.* PGD
Diary of a Journey, *sel.* Vera Inber, *tr. fr. Russian by* Jack Lindsay.
Mayakovsky Memory. RuPo
Diary of a Raccoon. Gertrude Ryder Bennett. GoYe
Diaspora, The. W. H. Auden. *See* Jew Wrecked in the German Cell, The.
Diaulus now's a body snatcher. Un Médecin Malgré Eux. Martial. RoL
Diavolina. Fielding H. Garrison. PoP
Dibdin's Ghost. Eugene Field. AA; OBAV
Dicaeopolis and the Case for the Enemy. Aristophanes, *tr. fr. Greek by* Benjamin Bickley Rogers. *Fr.* The Acharnians. GrR
Dice Were Loaded, The. Mary Gilmore. BoAV; MoAuPo
Dicing. Agathias Scholasticus, *tr. fr. Greek by* Sir William Marris. OxBG
Dick and Will and Charles and I. Autumn. Elizabeth Madox Roberts. AnAmPo; LA; YaD
Dick Daring, the Poacher. *Unknown. See* Shining Night, A.
"Dick, I marvel much why in every plat." The "Gloria Patri." John Heywood. ACP
Dick Johnson Reel, The. "Jake Falstaff." WhC
Dick o' the Cow. *Unknown.* BaBo; ESPB; OBB
Dick Said. Louis Untermeyer. TSW; TSWC
Dick Turpin and the Lawyer. *Unknown. See* Turpin and the Lawyer.
Dick Turpin bold! Dick, hie away. My Bonny Black Bess. *Unknown.* CoMu
Dickens. Swinburne. PoVP
Dickens in Camp. Bret Harte. HBV; IAP; LBAP; LEAP; LPS-2; PoRL; TCAP

Dickery, dickery, dare! *Unknown.* BoN; OxNR
Dickey-Bird, The. Mrs. Motherly. SAS
Dickie found a broken spade. The Worm. Elizabeth Madox Roberts. BoChLi; GFA; PoeMoYo; UTS; VOD; YT
Dicky-Birds. Natalie Joan. BoTP
Dicky of Ballyman. *Unknown.* OTPC (1946 ed.)
Dictated by the Muse, these verses know. Dedication to the Duke of Bejar. Luis de Góngora. *Fr.* The Solitudes. TeCS
Dictator's Holiday. F. L. Lucas. NeTW
Dictionary. Samuel Marshak, *tr. fr. Russian by* Jack Lindsay. RuPo
Dictum Sapienti. Charles Henry Webb. ALV; PR
Did a fairy's fancy spin you. To a Kitten. Rena M. Manning. CIV
Did Adam love his Eve from first to last? Christina Rossetti. *Fr.* Later Life, XV. LO
Did all the lets and bars appear. The March into Virginia. Herman Melville. AmP; LiTA; LiTG; OnAP; TrGrPo; UnPo (3d ed.); ViBoPo; WaaP
Did any bird come flying. Bird or Beast? Christina Rossetti. BPN; EG
Did Bethlehem's stable loathe. Come, Holy Babe! Mary Dickerson Bangham. ChIP; PGD
Did Chaos form,—and water, air, and fire. Genesis. John Hall Ingham. AA
Did he say I said you said she said that? *Unknown.* SiTL
Did he steal away from the great Omphale for a night. Drunken Heracles. Wallace Gould. AnAmPo; LA
Did He who wrought the universe. This Little Earth. Leslie Savage Clark. ChIP
Did I aught else but utter. The Singer. Al-Buqaira. MooP
Did I ever think. Ono no Takamura. *Fr.* Kokin Shu. AWP
Did I follow Truth wherever she led. Herman Altman. Edgar Lee Masters. *Fr.* Spoon River Anthology. OxBA
Did I hear the news from Custer? The Death of Custer. "Captain Jack" Crawford. PoOW
Did I love thee? I only did desire. Rondo. George Moore. LoPS
Did I stand on the bald top of Nefin. The Brow of Nephin. *Unknown.* AnIL
Did love sojourn with you long. Black and White. Esther Lilian Duff. HBMV
Did Mary know when the Wise Men laid. Offering. Leslie Savage Clark. ChIP
Did my father curse his father for his lust I wonder. The Young Man Thinks of Sons. R. A. K. Mason. AnNZ
Did Not. Thomas Moore. ALV
(Quantum Est Quod Desit.) EnLoPo
Did not each poet amorous of old. Troubadours. Arthur Davison Ficke. Sonnets of a Portrait Painter, X. HBMV
Did Not the Heavenly Rhetoric of Thine Eye. Shakespeare. *Fr.* Love's Labour's Lost, IV, iii. LiTB; LiTG
(Heavenly Rhetoric, The.) GTBS-W
(Sonnet: "Did not the heavenly rhetoric . . .") ViBoPo
Did the love of adventure, the promise of gold. Diego's Bold Shores. *Unknown.* SoAmSa
Did the rose-bush or the oak. War. E. Merrill Root. OQP; QP-2
"Did they dare, did they dare, to slay Eoghan Ruadh [*or* Owen Roe] O'Neill?" Lament for the Death of Eoghan Ruadh [*or* Owen Roe] O'Neill. Thomas Osborne Davis. AnIV; GTIV; IrPN; OnYI; OxBI; TIP
Did times grow hard in Nazareth. Temple Offering. Leslie Savage Clark. ChIP
Did ye ever hear o guid Earl o Bran. Earl Brand. *Unknown.* BaBo (A *vers.*); ESPB
Did ye ever sleep at the foot o' the bed. Sleepin' at the Foot of the Bed. Luther Patrick. BLPA; BoHiPo
Did you ask dulcet rimes from me? To a Certain Civilian. Walt Whitman. CoBA; IAP; TCAP
Did you ask for the beaten brass of the moon? A House in Taos: Moon. Langston Hughes. CDC
Did you boys hear. Lord It's All, Almost Done. *Unknown.* OuSiCo
Did you deserve a quiet death? did you. Dream of a Decent Death. G. A. Borgese. NePoAm
Did you ever attempt to shampoo. Advice to Young Naturalists. Laura E. Richards. LiL
Did you ever come to the place. Mother's Love. Ross B. Clapp. WBLP
Did You Ever, Ever, Ever? *with music. Unknown.* AS
Did you ever go to meetin', Uncle Joe. Hop Up, My Ladies. *Unknown.* OuSiCo
Did you ever hear a rustling. Ghostries. Henry Cholmondeley-Pennell. CIV
Did you ever hear about Cocaine Lil? Cocaine Lil and Morphine Sue. *Unknown.* AS; OnAP; OxBoLi; SiTL; TrAS
Did You Ever Hear an English Sparrow Sing? Bertha Johnston. BLPA
Did you ever hear of Captain Wattle? Captain Wattle and Miss Roe. Charles Dibdin. OxBoLi
Did you ever hear of Editor Whedon. Daisy Fraser. Edgar Lee Masters. *Fr.* Spoon River Anthology. MoVE; NP
Did you ever hear of the Drummer Boy of Mission Ridge, who lay. The Drummer Boy of Mission Ridge. Kate B. Sherwood. PTA-1
Did you ever hear tell of sweet Betsy from Pike. Sweet Betsy from Pike. *Unknown.* ABF; CoSo
Did you ever hear the story 'bout Willy, the Weeper? Willy the Weeper. *Unknown.* AS
Did you ever hear the story of how one stormy night. The Stampede. Wallace D. Coburn. PoOW
Did you ever meet Miss Pixie of the Spruces? Miss Pixie. Lloyd Roberts. CPG
Did you ever note the beauty of the soft New England grasses. A Painter in New England. Charles Wharton Stork. HBMV
Did you ever see an alligator. Arlo Will. Edgar Lee Masters. *Fr.* Spoon River Anthology. ChMo; CMP; LiTA; NP
Did you ever see the nest. The Young Linnets. Ann Hawkshaw. OTPC
Did you ever think as the hearse rolls by. The Hearse Song. *Unknown.* ABF; AS
Did you ever think how queer. A Birthday. Rachel Field. SiSoSe; TiPo (1959 ed.)
Did you ever think you'd like to. Honest, Wouldn't You? *Unknown.* WBLP
Did you ever wait for daylight when the stars along the river. The Shallows of the Ford. Henry Herbert Knibbs. SCC
Did you ever want to take your two bare hands. The Struggle. Miriam Teichner. BLP
Did You Feed My Cow? *Unknown.* GoSl
Did you forget to bud in Spring. The Green Tree in the Fall. Jessie B. Rittenhouse. NLK
Did you hear of the curate who mounted his mare. The Priest and the Mulberry Tree. Thomas Love Peacock. *Fr.* Crotchet Castle. BoTP; CG; EV-4; GN; OTPC; RIS; StPo; TVSH
Did you hear of the fight at Corinth. The Eagle of Corinth. Henry Howard Brownell. PAH
Did you hear of the Widow Malone. The Widow Malone. Charles Lever. *Fr.* Charles O'Malley, the Irish Dragoon. BOHV; HBV; LPS-3; TIP; TreFS
Did you, in those few years before you died. A Poet to His Father. Mahlon Leonard Fisher. NV
Did you know, little child. The Welcome. Nettie Palmer. BoAu
Did you know Maureen O'Reilly? Maureen O'Reilly. Sister Mary Eugene. PraNu
Did you say you wished to see me, sir? step in; 'tis a cheerless place. Poor-House Nan. Lucy H. Blinn. PTA-1
Did you see my wife, did you see, did you see. *Unknown.* OxNR
Did you see Paidin. The Besom-Man. Joseph Campbell. OnYI
Did you tackle that trouble that came your way. How Did You Die? Edmund Vance Cooke. BLPA; MaRV; OHFP; PTA-2; TCPD
Didactic Poem, The. Richard Garnett. VA
Didactic Sonnet. Melvin Walker La Follette. NePoEA
Diddle, diddle [*or* Deedle, deedle], dumpling, my son John. Mother Goose. BoChLi; BoTP; BrR; OxNR; PCH; RIS; StVeCh
Diddledy, Diddledy, Dumpty. *Unknown.* OTPC (1923 ed.)
(Diddlety, diddlety, dumpty.") OxNR
Didn' [*or* Didn't] My Lord Deliver Daniel? *with music. Unknown.* BoAN-1; TrAS
Didn' Ol' John Cross the Water on His Knees, *with music. Unknown.* OuSiCo
Didn't It Rain. *Unknown.* APW
Didn't Old Pharaoh Get Los'? *Unknown.* BoAN-1, *with music;* OIF
Dido. Richard Porson. BOHV
(Note on the Latin Gerunds, A.) SiTL
(On the Latin Gerunds.) PIAE
Dido among the Shades. Virgil, *tr. fr. Latin by* Dryden. *Fr.* The Aeneid, VI. OBS
Dido My Dear, Alas, Is Dead. Spenser. *Fr.* The Shepheardes Calender: November. ChTr
("Up then Melpomene thou mournefulst Muse of nyne.") AtBAP
Dido of Tunisia. Phyllis McGinley. NeTW
Dido, on the Departure of Aeneas. Helen Pinkerton. PtPa
Dido to Aeneas. Virgil, *tr. fr. Latin by* Richard Stanyhurst. *Fr.* The Aeneid, IV. AnIV
Dido with the driven hair. The Beaten Path. Anne Goodwin Winslow. HBMV; TBM
Dido's Hunting. Virgil, *tr. fr. Latin by* the Earl of Surrey. *Fr.* The Aeneid, IV. OBSC
(Fourth Book of Virgil, The.) ReEn
Didyme. Asclepiades, *pr. tr. fr. Greek by* W. R. Paton. GrL
Didymus. Eileen Duggan. JKCP (1955 ed.)
Die, die my shriek, you will not be heard. Die My Shriek. Aaron Kushniroff. TrJP

Die Down, O Dismal Day. David Gray. LPS-2
Die for His Majesty. Li Ho, *tr. fr. Chinese by* Ho Chih-yuan. WhP
Die in de Fiel', *with music. Unknown.* BoAN-1
Die My Shriek. Aaron Kushniroff, *tr. fr. Yiddish by* Joseph Leftwich. TrJP
Die Not, Fond Man. *Unknown.* ElL
Die Pelzaffen. Charles Spear. AnNZ
Die, pussy, die. *Unknown.* OxNR
Died of His Wounds. Sir Henry Head. PoP
Diego's Bold Shores, *with music. Unknown.* SoAmSa
Diella, *sels.* Richard Lynche.
"End this enchantment, love, of my desires," XXXV. TuPP
"I know, within my mouth, for bashful fear," XIII. (Love's Despair.) ElL
"Soon as the azure-colored gates of th' east," II.
"Weary with serving where I nought could get," XXVIII.
"What sugared terms, what all-persuading art," IV. ElSeCe; ReEn; TuPP
"Dies Irae." Aeschylus, *tr. fr. Greek by* G. M. Cookson. *Fr.* Choephoroe. GrR
Dies Irae. James L. Duff. ChIP; JKCP; MaRV
Dies Irae. Inger Hagerup, *tr. fr. Norwegian by* Martin S. Allwood. LiTW
Dies Irae. Thomas of Celano, *tr. fr. Latin by* Abraham Coles. AA; CAW, *abr., sl. diff.*; HBV
——*Tr. by* Richard Crashaw. AWP; OuHeWo
——*Tr. by* John A. Dix. LPS-2
——*Tr. by* Howard Mumford Jones. LaP
——*Tr. by* the Earl of Roscommon. WGRP
(Day of Judgment, The.) TriL
(On the Day of Judgement.) BeR
——*Par. by* Sir Walter Scott. *Fr.* The Lay of the Last Minstrel, VI. GoBC; MaRV
(Hymn for the Dead: "That day of wrath.") BSV, *longer sel.*; EmBrPo; OBRV, *longer sel.*
——*Tr. by* Swinburne. LiA; LiTW; LyMA
——*Tr. by* Father Wingfield *and* Father Alward. WHL
Dies Irae—Dies Pacis. John Oxenham. MaRV
Dies Ultima. Frank Dempster Sherman. LBAP
Dieu Qu'il la Fait. Charles d'Orléans, *tr. fr. French by* Ezra Pound. AWP
Difference. Thomas Bailey Aldrich. TOP
Difference, The. Benjamin Franklin. WhC
Difference, The. Anne Blackwell Payne. NoCaPo
Difference, The. Laura E. Richards. HBV; HBVY ("Eight fingers.") PPL
Difference, The. Winfield Townley Scott. NePoAm
Difference, The. John Banister Tabb. BAP; BPP; PC
Difference, The. *Unknown.* GoTP
Difference, The. Mark Van Doren. MOAP
Difference between despair, The. Emily Dickinson. MOAP
Differences. Paul Laurence Dunbar. TreFS
Differences. Rose Fyleman. GFA; GoBP; RAR
Different Bicycles. Dorothy W. Baruch. FaPON; SUS; TiPo
Different Day, The. Grace Hazard Conkling. TCPD
Different Minds. Richard Chenevix Trench. *See* Some Murmur When Their Sky Is Clear.
Different Speech, A. Louise Townsend Nicholl. ImOP
Different Way, A. Esther Lloyd Hagg. ChIP
Different Winter. Louise Townsend Nicholl. NePoAm-2
Difficulties Arising from Uncharitable Cariages of Christians, *sel.* Edward Taylor. *Fr.* God's Determinations.
Stanzas: "When these assaults proove vain, the Enemy." OnAP
Difficulties of a Statesman. T. S. Eliot. *Fr.* Coriolan. OnAP
Difficulties of Translation, The, *abr.* Gawin Douglas. *Fr.* Prologues to the Aeneid: Prologue to Bk. I. GoTS
Difficulty to think at the end of the day, The. A Rabbit as King of the Ghosts. Wallace Stevens. ThWaDe
Difficulty with all, The. Knight, with Umbrella. Elder Olson. FiBHP
Diffidence. Wade Whipple. PTA-1
Diffugere Nives, 1917. Maurice Baring. HBMV; POTE
"Snows have fled, the hail, the lashing rain, The," *sel.* AlDL
Dig My Grave, *with music. Unknown.* OuSiCo
Digby, whence comes it that the world begins. To Master Everard Digby. Thomas Lodge. ReIE
Digdog. Ruth Pitter. AnFE
Digenis. *Unknown, tr. fr. Modern Greek by* Rae Dalven. MoGP
Digger's Grave, The. Sarah Welch. VA
Diggers' Song, The, *abr.* Gerard Winstanley. PoFr
Digging. Edward Thomas. MBP; MoAB; MoBrPo
Dighton Is Engaged! Gelett Burgess. BOHV; PR
Dignity. Bhartrihari, *tr. fr. Sanskrit by* Arthur W. Ryder. OnPM
Dignity of Labor, The. Robert Bersohn. WhC
Dignity of Labor, The. *Unknown.* PEOR
Dignity of Man—Lesson #1, The. Walter H. Kerr. NePoAm-2
Digression from Husbandry to a Point or Two of Huswifery, A. Thomas Tusser. ReIE
Digression to Hospitality, A. Thomas Tusser. SiCE
Dilemma. Bhartrihari, *tr. fr. Sanskrit by* Paul Elmer More. LiTW
Dilemma, The. Oliver Wendell Holmes. PR
Dilemma. Orrick Johns. LEAP; MAP; SBMV
Dilemma. Dorothy Parker. InMe
Dilemma of the Elm. Genevieve Taggard. MAP; MoAmPo
Diligently I hope. Circles. Miriam Waddington. BoCaPo (1948 ed.); PeCV
Dillar, a dollar, A,/ A ten o'clock scholar. Mother Goose. BoChLi; FaBoBe; FaFP; GaP; HBV; HBVY; OTPC; OxNR; RIS; SAS; SiTL; TiPo
Dim as the borrow'd beams of moon and stars. Reason and Revelation. Dryden. *Fr.* Religio Laici. BeR; CEP; CoEV; EiPP; FiP; LiA; LoBV; MeRV; OBS; OxBoCh; PoLi; SeCV-2; SeEP; ViBoPo
Dim-berried is the mistletoe. Before Dawn. Walter de la Mare. AlDL; ChrBoLe
Dim dawn behind the tamarisks—the sky is saffron-yellow. Christmas in India. Kipling. LPS-1
Dim eyes, deaf ears, cold stomach show. A New England Gentleman's Epitaph. Thomas Dudley. BAV
Dim Face of Beauty. "Fiona Macleod." PoVP
Dim, gradual thinning of the shapeless gloom. The Troops [*or* Prelude]. Siegfried Sassoon. ChMo; ChMP; CMP; GTBS-D; GTSL; POTE
"Dim grows your face, and in my ears." A Colonist in His Garden. William Pember Reeves. AnNZ
Dim Narrow Trail, The. *Unknown. See* Cowboy's Dream, The.
Dim sea glints chill, The. The Sign-Post. Edward Thomas. ViBoPo
Dim stars wheeled above the frontier post, The. The Gold Seekers. Marion Muir Richardson. PoOW
Dim the light in your faces: be passionless in the room. The Image. Richard Hughes. OBMV
Dim the mountains, far away the waters. To Hen Chu, Magistrate of Yangchow. Tu Mu. WhP
Dim vales, and shadowy floods. Fairy-Land. Poe. APW; IAP; OTPC
Dim wind pillared the hills: stiller than mist it seemed. Sunrise Trumpets. Joseph Auslander. AnAmPo; LA; TrJP
Dime I gave for sterling, A. Irony. Mabel Wing Castle. BLP
Dimidium Animae Meae. Charles A. Brady. GoYe
Diminuendo. Tom Kristensen, *tr. fr. Danish by* Charles W. Stork. BoDS
Diminutive, wandering bands of air. Infinity and Motor. José Moreno Villa. CoSP
Diminutivus Ululans. Francis MacNamara. OxBI
Dimmest and brightest month am I. December. Christina Rossetti. YeAr
Dimple Diggers. "Robin Christopher." RIS
Dimpled and flushed and dewy pink he lies. Baby. Elaine Goodale Eastman. AA
Dimpled of cheek and grave of gown. Hester. Lizette Woodworth Reese. VOD
Dimply damsel, sweetly smiling. To Miss Margaret Pulteney. Ambrose Philips. CEP; EV-3
Dinah. Norman Gale. MW; OTPC (1946 ed.)
Dinah Kneading Dough. Paul Laurence Dunbar. PR
Diner while dining at Crewe, A. Limerick [*or* New Limericks]. *Unknown.* RIS; StaSt
Ding dang, bell rang. *Unknown.* OxNR
Ding-Dong! Eliza Lee Follen. *See* Ding Dong! Ding Dong!
Ding Dong. *Unknown. Fr.* Swetnam, the Woman Hater. ElL
Ding, dong, bell,/ Pussy's in the well! Mother Goose. BoChLi; OTPC; OxNR; PoC; PPL; RIS; SAS; SiTL; StVeCh (1940 ed.); TiPo
Ding dong didero,/ Blow big bellows. Smith's Song. George Sigerson. OnYI
Ding Dong! Ding Dong! Eliza Lee Follen. SAS (Ding-Dong!) BoTP
Ding-dong, ding-dong, ding-dong. A Dirge for a Righteous Kitten. Vachel Lindsay. CIV; SUS; UTS
Ding-dong! ding-dong! Merry, merry. Song from Fragment of an Eccentric Drama. Henry Kirke White. OBRV
Dingdong! The Castle Bell! *Unknown.* ExPo
Ding! Dong! The moon is gleaming. The Enchanted Garden. Marjorie Barrows. GFA
Dingaan and Retief. Charles Barter. *Fr.* Stray Memories of Natal and Zululand. BoSA
Dingle dingle doosey. *Unknown.* OxNR
Dingty diddlety. *Unknown.* OxNR
Dining-Room Mirror. Jorge Carrera Andrade, *tr. fr. Spanish by* H. R. Hays. TwSpPo
Dining-Room Tea. Rupert Brooke. MBP; MoBrPo; POTE
Dinkey-Bird, The. Eugene Field. AA; BOHV; HBVY; HiLiAm; LBN; NA; PFY; TreFS; TSW; TSWC; UTS
Dink's Blues. *Unknown.* ABF

Dink's Song. *Unknown.* ABF, *with music;* OxBoLi; SiTL
Dinna Ask Me. John Dunlop. HBV; LPS-1
(Oh! Dinna Ask Me Gin I Lo'e Thee.) EBSV
Dinner at the Hotel de la Tigresse Verte. Donald Evans. AnAmPo; LA
Dinner Guest. Oscar Williams. TwAmPo
Dinner Hour, The. "Owen Meredith." *Fr.* Lucille. VA
Dinner-Party, The. Amy Lowell. ChMo; CMP; TCPD
Dinner party, coffee, tea, A. Breakfast. Mary Lamb. OTPC (1923 ed.)
Dinner Party, 1940. Phillip M. Sherlock. PoNe
Dinner with Ligurinus. Martial, *tr. fr. Latin by* James Elphinston. OnPM
Dinnshenchas, *sels. Unknown, tr. fr. Middle Irish.* OnYI
Enchanted Fawn, The, *tr. by* Edward Gwynn.
Story of Macha, The, *tr. by* Sir Samuel Ferguson.
Tara, *tr. by* Edward Gwynn.
Dinogad's Petticoat. *Unknown. See* For Little Dinogad.
Dinosaur, The. Bert Leston Taylor. ImOP; LHV; PoMa
Dinosaurs and violins played in the sky. Cubism. Hy Sobiloff. SiTL
Dinosaurs are not all dead, The. Steam Shovel. Charles Malam. PoMa
Diogenes. Max Eastman. HBV; OQP; QP-2
Dion. Wordsworth. GEPC
Dion of Syracuse. Plato, *tr. fr. Greek by* Charles Merivale. OxBG
("For Priam's queen and daughters at their birth.") GrPo
Dion of Tarsus. *Unknown, tr. fr. Greek by* Alma Strettell. AWP; JAWP; WBP
Dione; a Pastoral Tragedy, *sel.* John Gay.
Linnet on the Bough, The. BeR
Dionysiaca, *sels.* Nonnus, *tr. fr. Greek.*
Chalcomede Prays to Be Saved from Love, *tr. by* C. M. Bowra. OxBG
Chalcomede Wards Off Her Lover, *tr. by* Michael Balkwill. OxBG
"O daughter of Helios, Moon of many turnings, nurse of all!" *pr. tr. by* W. H. D. Rouse. GrPo
Tyre, *tr. by* F. L. Lucas. GrPE
Dionysius, of Tarsus, here doth rot. Better Unborn. *Unknown.* GrPE
Dionysus. Winthrop Palmer. SiTL
Dip, Boys, Dip the Oar. F. Sarona. OIF
Dip down upon the northern shore. In Memoriam A. H. H., LXXXIII [*or* April Days *or* Spring]. Tennyson. ADAH; BPN; EM-2; EmBrPo; EnLi-2; EPN; GEPC; HBV; LPS-2; MaPo; OAEP; SN; ViBoPo; ViPo; VLEP
Diplomatic Platypus, The. Patrick Barrington. *See* I Had a Duck-billed Platypus.
Diplomats, The. Alfred Noyes. MaRV
Dipped in the instincts of heaven. Woman. Thomas O'Hagan. CAW
Dipsychus, *abr.* Arthur Hugh Clough. EmBrPo
Sels.
"Afloat; we move. Delicious!" *fr.* Pt. II, sc. ii. PoVP; ViPP
As I Sat at the Café, I Said to Myself, *fr.* Pt. II, sc. ii, *also in* Spectator ab Extra. ViPP
(From "Spectator ab Extra.") ALV; FiBHP; LiTG
(So Pleasant It Is to Have Money.) SeCePo
Help, Sure Help, *fr.* Pt. II, sc. vii. VLEP
(At Torcello.) BHV
"I dreamt a dream; till morning light," *abr., fr.* Pt. I, sc. v. OAEP
"I had a vision; was it in my sleep?" *fr.* Pt. II, sc. vii. PoVP
"O let me love my love unto myself alone," *fr.* Pt. II, sc. ii. OAEP; ViPP
(Hidden Love, The, *diff. vers., individual poem.*) BPN
"Our gaieties, our luxuries," *fr.* Pt. II, sc. ii. BPN; EPN
"'There is no God!' the wicked saith," *fr.* Pt. I, sc. v. BHV; BMEP; BPN; EPN; PoVP; ViPP
(Spirit's Song, The.) LoBV
(There Is No God.) TreFS; VLEP
"What now? the Lido shall it be?" *fr.* Pt. I, sc. v. ViP
"When the enemy is near thee," *fr.* Pt. II, sc. vii. BPN
"Where are the great, whom thou would'st wish to praise thee?" *fr.* Pt. II, sc. ii. BPN; EPN
(Isolation.) OBVV
Dipsychus Continued, *sel.* Arthur Hugh Clough.
Pleasure and Guilt. VLEP
Dirce. Walter Savage Landor. *Fr.* Pericles and Aspasia. AnFE; AWP; BCEP; BLV; BoLiVe; BPN; CoEV; EnRP; EV-4; ExPo; FaBoEn; InPo; JAWP; LEAP; LiA; LiTB; LoBV; OAEP; OBEV; OBRV; PoEL-4; PoRA; SeCeV; TOP; TrGrPo; VA; ViBoPo; WBP; WHA; WhC
(Epigram: Stand Close Around, Ye Stygian Set.) AEV
(Lyrics and Epigrams, IV.) CBOV
(Stand Close Around.) ChTr
("Stand close around, ye Stygian set.") EG; GTBS-D
Dire Dilemma, A. Pope. *Fr.* Epistle to Dr. Arbuthnot. WHA
Dire is the violence of ocean waves. The Worst Horror. Euripides. OxBG
Dire rebel though he was. Philip Van Artevelde. Sir Henry Taylor. VA
Direct us, Lord, while our aerial saints. Domine, Dirige Nos. E. H. W. Meyerstein. NeTW
Direction to a Rebel. W. R. Rodgers. LiTM (rev. ed.)
Directive. Robert Frost. CoBMV; CrMA; LiTA; LiTM (rev. ed.); MaPo; MoAB; NePA; SeCeV
Diretro al Sol. Charles G. Bell. NePoAm
Dirge: "Call for the robin redbreast and the wren." John Webster. *See* Call for the Robin Redbreast.
Dirge: "Calm on the bosom of thy God." Felicia Dorothea Hemans. *Fr.* The Siege of Valencia. BCEP; EV-4; HBV, *longer vers.;* OBEV
(Death Hymn, A.) OBRV
Dirge: "Come away, come away, death." Shakespeare. *See* Come Away, Come Away, Death.
Dirge: "Come, you whose loves are dead." Beaumont *and* Fletcher. *See* Come, You Whose Loves Are Dead.
Dirge: "Fear no more the heat o' the sun." Shakespeare. *See* Fear No More the Heat o' the Sun.
Dirge: For One Who Fell in Battle. Thomas William Parsons. AA; APW; GN; HBV; LBAP; OBAV; PAH
Dirge, A: "Glories of our blood and state, The." James Shirley. *See* Death the Leveller.
Dirge: "Glories, pleasures, pomps, delights, and ease." John Ford. *See* Glories, Pleasures.
Dirge: "Hark, now everything is still." John Webster. *See* Hark! Now Everything . . .
Dirge: "Her house is become like a man dishonored." First Maccabees, II: 8–14, Bible, Apocrypha. TrJP
Dirge: "How should my lord come home to his lands." Maurice Hewlett. LBBV
Dirge: "How sleep the brave, who sink to rest." William Collins. *See* How Sleep the Brave.
Dirge: "I bring from funeral." Euripides, *tr. fr. Greek by* George Allen. *Fr.* Suppliants. OxBG
Dirge: "If thou wilt ease thine heart." Thomas Lovell Beddoes. *Fr.* Death's Jest Book, II, ii. LiA; LiTB; LO; OBRV; PoEL-4; VA
(Dirge for Wolfram.) PoE
(If Thou Wilt Ease Thine Heart.) EG; EnRP; ERP; LPS-1
(Wolfram's Dirge.) EV-4; OBEV
Dirge: "Knows he who tills this lonely field." Emerson. BoFr, *abr.;* OBAV
Dirge, A: "Lacewing has lighted upon the wall, A." Mokichi Saito, *tr. fr. Japanese by* Shio Sakanishi. PoP
Dirge: "Lay a garland on my hearse." Beaumont *and* Fletcher. *See* Aspatia's Song.
Dirge: "Let us keep him warm." Thomas Bailey Aldrich. OBAV
Dirge, A: "Looking on the peaceful face." Hisaki, *tr. fr. Japanese by* Asataro Miyamori. OnPM
Dirge: "Man born of desire." Robert Bridges. *Fr.* Ode to Music. TwCV
Dirge, A: "Naiad, hid beneath the bank." William Johnson Cory. *See* Anteros.
Dirge: "Never the nightingale." Adelaide Crapsey. AV; BAP; HBV; LEAP; NP; OBAV; VOD
Dirge: "O sad, sad world, O world that knows not love." Edith Lovejoy Pierce. MaRV; MuM
Dirge: "1-2-3 was the number he played." Kenneth Fearing. AmP; HoPM; LiTM; NAMP; PoRA; TrJP
Dirge: "Peerless yet hapless maid of Q." *Unknown.* BOHV
Dirge, A: "Rest on your battle-fields." Felicia Dorothea Hemans. BHV
Dirge: "Ring out your bells." Sir Philip Sidney. *See* Ring Out Your Bells.
Dirge: "Room for a soldier! lay him in the clover." Thomas William Parsons. PaA
Dirge, A: "Rough wind, that moanest loud." Shelley. BCEP; BEL; BoLiVe; BPN; CaAE; ChTr; EmBrPo; EnLi-2; EnLit; EnRP; EPN; ERP; GEPC; GTSL; MCCG; OAEP; PoFS; PoRA; PreP; RO; TCEP; TOP; TrGrPo; WHA
Dirge: "She came—." Alfred Kreymborg. NP
Dirge, The: "Sing from the chamber to the grave!" Robert Stephen Hawker. AEV
Dirge: "Softly! She is lying with her lips apart." Charles Gamage Eastman. AA
Dirge: "Sorrow, lie still and wear." Thomas Lovell Beddoes. TriL
Dirge: "Swallow leaves her nest, The." Thomas Lovell Beddoes. *Fr.* Death's Jest Book, I, iv. LoBV; OBVV; PoEL-4
(Swallow Leaves Her Nest, The.) EPN; ERP
(Voice from the Waters, A.) OBRV
Dirge: "Though you should whisper." Muna Lee. NP

Dirge: "To fair Fidele's grassy tomb." William Collins. *See* Song from Shakespeare's "Cymbeline," A.
Dirge: "To her couch of evening rest." Thomas Lovell Beddoes. ERP
Dirge: "Tuck the earth, fold the sod." William Alexander Percy. HBMV
Dirge: "Wail! wail ye o'er the dead!" George Darley. *Fr.* Sylvia; or, The May Queen. OBRV
Dirge: "We built our love up like a work of art." Louis Johnson. AnNZ
Dirge, A: "We enter our earthly bodies." *Unknown, tr. fr. Chinese by* Henry H. Hart. PoHN
Dirge: "Weep, weep, ye woodmen, wail." Anthony Munday *and* Henry Chettle. *See* Weep, Weep, Ye Woodmen.
Dirge: "Welladay, welladay, poor Colin." George Peele. *Fr.* The Arraignment of Paris. ElL
(Shepherd's Dirge, The.) OBSC
Dirge, The: "What is the existence of man's life." Henry King. EV-2
Dirge: "What shall her silence keep." Madison Cawein. AA; OBAV
Dirge: "Whose were they those voices? What footsteps came near me?" Aubrey Thomas De Vere. IrPN
Dirge, A: "Why were you born when the snow was falling?" Christina Rossetti. ChTr; LoBV; ViPo
Dirge, A, Concerning the Late Lamented King of the Cannibal Islands. William Augustus Croffut. BOHV; InMe
Dirge for a Righteous Kitten, A. Vachel Lindsay. CIV; SUS; UTS
Dirge for a Soldier. George Henry Boker. AA; AnFE; APA; CoAnAm; DD; GA; HBV; IAP; LBAP; LEAP; LPS-2; MC; OBAV; OBVV; PaA; PAH; PAP; TCAP; WaaP
Dirge for a Young Maiden. Thomas Lovell Beddoes. ERP
Dirge for an Infant. Leigh Hunt. ERP
Dirge for Ashby. Margaret Junkin Preston. GA; PAH
Dirge for Beauty. Marion Eells. CAG
Dirge for Fidele. William Collins. *See* Song from Shakespeare's "Cymbeline," A.
Dirge for Love. Shakespeare. *See* Come Away, Come Away, Death.
Dirge for McPherson, A. Herman Melville. BlG; GA; PAH; PoEL-5
Dirge for Narcissus. Ben Jonson. *See* Slow, Slow, Fresh Fount.
Dirge for Phyllip Sparowe. John Skelton. *Fr.* Phyllyp Sparrowe. EPP
Dirge for Robin Hood. Anthony Munday *and* Henry Chettle. *See* Weep, Weep, Ye Woodmen.
Dirge for Summer, A. Sebastian Evans. VA
Dirge for the Barrel-Organ of the New Barbarism. Louis Aragon, *tr. fr. French by* Selden Rodman. OnHM; WaaP
Dirge for the brave old pioneer, A! The Old Pioneer. Theodore O'Hara. SPP
Dirge for the New Sunrise. Edith Sitwell. *Fr.* Three Poems of the Atomic Age. AtBAP; MoAB; MoBrPo (1950 ed.); SeCePo
Dirge for the Ninth of Ab. *Unknown, tr. fr. Hebrew by* Nina Davis Salaman. TrJP
Dirge for the Year. Shelley. DD; HBV; HBVY
"Orphan hours, the year is dead!" *sel.* GN
Dirge for Two Clavichords and Bowler Hat. Kendrick Smithyman. AnNZ
Dirge for Two Veterans. Walt Whitman. BLV; BoLiVe; IAP; MoAmPo (1950 ed.); NeMA; PIAE; PoEL-5
(Two Veterans.) GN; LH; MDAH
Dirge for Wolfram. Thomas Lovell Beddoes. *See* Dirge: "If thou wilt ease thine heart."
Dirge from "Cymbeline." Shakespeare. *See* Fear No More the Heat o' the Sun.
Dirge in "Cymbeline." William Collins. *See* Song from Shakespeare's "Cymbeline," A.
Dirge in Woods. George Meredith. AEV; BLV; BMEP; BoLiVe; CaAE; CBOV; EmBrPo; EPN; EPP; GTML; LiA; OAEP; OBEV (new ed.); OBVV; POTT; PoVP; TOP; TwCV; VLEP; WHA
(Dirge in the Woods.) LoBV; SeCeV
("Wind sways the pines, A.") EG
Dirge is sung, the ritual said, The. I. H. B. William Winter. AA; OBAV
Dirge of Alaric the Visigoth. Edward Everett. BeLS; LPS-3
Dirge of Cael, The. *Unknown, tr. fr. Irish by* George Sigerson. TIP
Dirge of Jephthah's Daughter, The; Sung by the Virgins. Robert Herrick. MeRV
Dirge of Kildare, The. Aubrey Thomas De Vere. IrPN
Dirge of Love. Shakespeare. *See* Come Away, Come Away, Death.
Dirge of Lovely Rosabelle, The. Sir Walter Scott. *See* Rosabelle.
Dirge of O'Sullivan Bear. *Tr. by* Jeremiah Joseph Callanan. *See* Lament for O'Sullivan Beare, The.
Dirge of Rory O'More. Aubrey Thomas De Vere. IrPN; TIP
Dirge of the Lone Woman. Mary M. Colum. AnIV
Dirge of the Moolla of Kotal. George Thomas Lanigan. BOHV; NA
Dirge of the Munster Forest. Emily Lawless. DiM; GTIV; OBVV; OnYI
Dirge of the Three Queens. Fletcher *and* Shakespeare. *See* Funeral Song ("Urns and odors, bring away").
Dirge on the Death of Art O'Leary. *Tr. fr. Irish by* Eleanor Hull. AnIV
Dirge on the Death of Oberon, the Fairy King. George Walter Thornbury. *See* Death of Oberon, The.
Dirge upon the Death of the Right Valiant Lord, Bernard Stuart, A. Robert Herrick. SeCV-1
Dirge without Music. Edna St. Vincent Millay. AnNE; BLV; BoLiVe; GTBS-W; LiTA; LiTG; NePA; LO; NP; PG; TrGrPo
Dirge Written for a Drama. Thomas Lovell Beddoes. EnRP
Dirigible, The. Ralph Bergengren. FaPON
Dirt and Deity. Louis Ginsberg. OQP; QP-2
Dirty Jim. Jane Taylor. HBV; HBVY
Dirty Mistreatin' Women, *with music. Unknown.* ABF
Dirty Old Man, The. William Allingham. LPS-1; PCD
Dirty river by religious explorers, The. Mystic River. John Ciardi. AmP
Dirty Word, The. Karl Shapiro. MiAP
Dis Aliter Visum; or, Le Byron de Nos Jours. Robert Browning. ViPP
Dis is anudder Sunday when I done furgit my specks. Nigger Demus. John Charles McNeill. NoCaPo
Dis is gospel weathah sho'. Song of Summer. Paul Laurence Dunbar. MCCG; OTPC (1946 ed.); TSW; TSWC; VOD
Dis Mornin', Dis Evenin', So Soon. *Unknown. See* Old Bill.
Dis worl' was made in jiss six days. Dixie's Land. Daniel Decatur Emmett. APW
Disabled. Wilfred Owen. LiTM (rev. ed.); NAMP; WaP
"Disabled"—Armistice Day. Catherine Parmenter. PEDC
Disagreeable Feature, A. Edwin Meade Robinson. BAP; HBMV; PYM
Disagreeable Man, The. W. S. Gilbert. *Fr.* Princess Ida. ALV; FiBHP; MPB; PoVP
Disappointed Lover, The. Swinburne. *See* Sea, The.
Disappointed Shrimper, The. P. A. Ropes. BoTP
Disappointed Tenderfoot, The. Earl Alonzo Brininstool. SCC
Disappointment. Maria Gowen Brooks. *Fr.* Zophiel; or, The Bride of Seven. LPS-1
Disappointment. Thomas Stephens Collier. AA
Disappointment. John Boyle O'Reilly. ACP; OnYI
Disappointment. *Unknown.* WBLP
Disappointment—His Appointment. Edith Lillian Young. BLRP
Disarm the Hearts. Ethel Blair Jordan. PGD
Disarmament. Whittier. AOAH; BHV; ShGoBo
"'Put up the sword!' The voice of Christ once more," *sel.* PGD
Disarmed. Laura Catherine Redden Searing. AA
Disaster. Charles Stuart Calverley. BOHV; CenHV; HBV; LPS-3
Disaster. James Clarence Mangan. IrPN
Disaster, yea: and with disaster shame. The Death of Rhesus. Euripides. *Fr.* Rhesus. OxBG
Disasters on disasters grow. Human Frailty. Philip Freneau. AnAmPo; LA
Disavowal. Bertran de Born, *tr. fr. Provençal by* Edgar Taylor. LyMA
Discarded Christmas Tree. Elizabeth-Ellen Long. ChBR
Discarding even the bag of chocolates and the novel. La Belle Dame sans Merci. A. R. D. Fairburn. AnNZ
Discardment, The. Alan Paton. BoSA
Discharged. W. E. Henley. In Hospital, XXVIII. BPN; POTT; PoVP; VLEP
Disciple, The. Dwight Bradley. ChIP; OQP; QP-1
Disciple Speaks, The. W. F. Maxwell. CAG
Disciples, The, *sel.* Harriet Eleanor Hamilton King. Palermo. VA
Discipline. George Herbert. BLV; BoLiVe; CaAE; CoBE; EPS; EV-2; ExPo; HBV; LiTB; LoBV; MeLP; MePo; OBEV; OBS; OxBoCh; PG (1945 ed.); PIAE; PoFS; SeCePo; SeCeV; SeEP; TrGrPo; TwCrTr; TyEnPo; ViBoPo
"Throw away thy rod," *sel.* EG
Discipline in Education. William Cowper. *Fr.* The Task. CoBE
Discipline of Consequences, The. Eileen Duggan. JKCP (1955 ed.)
Discipline of Wisdom, The. George Meredith. EmBrPo; EPN; TyEnPo
Disconsolate and sad. Platonic Love. Edward Herbert. OBS; SeEP
Discontent. Sarah Orne Jewett. PRWS; TVC; TVSH

Discontented Colonel, The, *sel.* Sir John Suckling.
She's Pretty to Walk With. SeCL
Discontented Sugar Broker, A. W. S. Gilbert. PCD
Discontents in Devon. Robert Herrick. EM-1; EPS; OAEP; ReEn; SeCV-1; SeEP
Discord and darkness—but the song and the star. Pilgrimage. Elinor Lennen. PGD
Discord in Childhood. D. H. Lawrence. MoPW
Discordants, *sels.* Conrad Aiken.
Dead Cleopatra Lies in a Crystal Casket, IV [III]. ChMo; CMP; MOAP
"In the noisy street," V. MOAP
Music I Heard [with You], I. AWP; ChMo; CMP; FaFP; GTBS-W; HBV; LEAP; LiTA; LiTL; LiTM; LoPo; LoPS; MOAP; OxBA; PG; PoeMoYo; PoMa; PoRA; SBMV; TwCV
(Bread and Music.) MAP; MoAB; MoAmPo; NeMA; YT
"My heart has become as hard as a city street," II. MOAP
Discouraged Cherry Tree, The. Kathleen Millay. PEDC
". . . Discourse Heard One Day . . ." Donald C. Babcock. NePoAm-2
Discourse of the Adventures Passed by Master F. J., A. George Gascoigne. *See* Adventures of Master F. I., The.
Discourse of the Wanderer, and an Evening Visit to the Lake. Wordsworth. *Fr.* The Excursion, IX. EnRP
Discourse on the Real. Samuel Yellen. NePoAm
Discovered. Paul Laurence Dunbar. LEAP; MAP; MoAmPo (1942 ed.)
Discovered in Mid-Ocean. Stephen Spender. MBP; MoBrPo
(He Will Watch the Hawk.) ChMo; ReaPo
Discoverer, The. Nathalia Crane. PoMa; YT
Discoverer, The. Arthur Gordon Field. PGD
Discoverer, The. Edmund Clarence Stedman. AA; EOAH; HBV
Discoverer of the North Cape, The. Longfellow. AnNE; APW; AtBAP; DDA; LH; ShBV-1; StVeCh (1940 ed.) TCAP
Discoveries. Vernon Watkins. LiTM; WaP
Discovery. Hilaire Belloc. ViBoPo
Discovery, The. Charles Brasch. *Fr.* Genesis. AnNZ
Discovery, The. Mary Carolyn Davies. MOB
Discovery. Hildegarde Flanner. HBMV; TBM
Discovery. Philip Freneau. WoL
Discovery, The. Monk Gibbon. BMEP; OnYI
Discovery. Hermann Hagedorn. PC
Discovery. Benjamin Keech. PoToHe
Discovery, A. Arthur A. Knipe. GFA
Discovery. Raymond Kresensky. OQP; QP-2
Discovery. José Moreno Villa, *tr. fr. Spanish by* Eleanor L. Turnbull. CoSP
Discovery, The. Cardinal Newman. OBRV
Discovery. Catherine Parmenter. OQP; QP-2
Discovery. E. A. Robinson. ChMo; CMP
Discovery, The. Stanley Snaith. LO; POTE
Discovery, The. J. C. Squire. *See* There Was an Indian.
Discovery attends on every quest. The Confident Scientist. Alexis. OxBG
Discovery of No Importance, A. Willard Wattles. PR
Discovery of Pity. Shakespeare. *See* Take Physic, Pomp.
Discovery of San Francisco Bay, The. Richard Edward White. PAH
Discovery of This Time. Archibald MacLeish. LiTA; NeTW; WaP
Discreet householder exclaims on the grandsire, A. Old Man Playing with Children. John Crowe Ransom. MoPW
Disdain ("If in the world"). Sir Thomas Wyatt. *See* If in the World There Be More Woe.
Disdain Me Not without Desert. Sir Thomas Wyatt. ReIE; SiPS
Disdain Me Still. William Herbert, Earl of Pembroke. EIL
Disdain [*or* Disdaine] Returned. Thomas Carew. AWP; EnLit; EPS; EV-2; HBV; InPo; JAWP; LPS-1; OBS; OuHeWo; SeCL; SeCV-1; SeEP; TOP; TrGrPo; TyEnPo; ViBoPo, *2 sts.;* WBP
(He That Loves a Rosy Cheek.) BEL; EG; LiTB; LiTG, *2 sts;* WP
(Never-dying Fire.) BLV
(Steadfast Mind, The.) OnPM
(True Beauty, The.) GTBS; GTBS-D; GTBS-W; GTSE; GTSL; MCCG
(Unfading Beauty, The.) AtBAP, *2 sts.;* BCEP; CBOV; EnLi-1, *2 sts.;* HoPM, *2 sts.;* LiTL; OBEV
Disdaine me not sweet love though I be ould. *Unknown.* SeCSL
Disdainful Shepherdess, The. *Unknown. See* Phillada Flouts Me.
Disdains Zenocrate to live with me? Christopher Marlowe. *Fr.* Tamburlaine the Great, Pt. I. Marlowe. ViBoPo
Disembodied Spirit, The. Fernando de Herrera, *tr. fr. Spanish by* Longfellow. OnPM; TeCS
Disenchanted. Louis Untermeyer. GoTP
(Disenchantment.) TSWC
Disenchantment. Charles Leonard Moore. AA
Disentangle lush water-lily cables. Summer's End. Ethel Kirk Grayson. TwCaPo
Disgruntled Guest. *Unknown, tr. fr. German.* PIAE
Disguise upon disguise, and then disguise. Soul unto Soul Glooms Darkling. Charles Leonard Moore. AA
Disguised He stands without in the street. Holy Communion. Speer Strahan. JKCP
Disguises. Thomas Edward Brown. MBP; WGRP
Disgusted with the dreary hospital, and the rank fumes. Windows. Stéphane Mallarmé. AnFP
Dish for the bishop, a crushed and bitter dish, A. Almeria. "Pablo Neruda." LiTW; WaaP
Disheartened Ranger, The. *Unknown.* CSF; CoSo
Dishonored rock and ruin! that, by law. Eagles. Composed at Dunolly Castle. Wordsworth. PeBoSo
Disillusion. Byron. *Fr.* Don Juan, I *and* IV. GEPC
(My Days of Love Are Over.) FaBoEn
Disillusion. Bessie B. Decker. PoToHe (new ed.)
Disillusion. Sister Mary Edwardine. JKCP (1955 ed.)
Disillusion. William Wilkins. TIP
Disillusioned. "Lewis Carroll." CenHV
Disillusioned. Thomas Curtis Clark. ChIP
Disillusioned. Emily Dickinson. *See* It dropped so low in my regard.
Disillusionment of Ten o'Clock. Wallace Stevens. AmP; CrMA; OxBA
Disingenuous, The/ Charm of living. Limb and Mind. John Waller. NeBP
Disinherited. John Donne. PIAE
Dislike of a Governor. Issa. PoFr
Dismal and purposeless and gray. Pain. St. John Lucas. HBV
Dismal yew and cypress tall, The. The Wake of the Absent. Gerald Griffin. TIP
Dismantled Ship, The. Walt Whitman. AmPP (4th ed.); OxBA
Dismiss your apprehension, pseudo bard. At Shakespeare's Grave. Irving Browne. AA
Dismissal. Thomas Campion. *See* Hours of Sleepy Night, The.
Dismounting from my horse I enter the ruins of the old city. Visiting the Ruins. Chang Ch'ien. OnPM
Dismounting from my horse to drink with you. On Going Away. Wang Wei. WhP
Disobedient Child, The, *sel.* Thomas Ingelend.
Song, A: "Why doth the world study vain glory to attain." CaAE
Dispel, my fair, with smiles, the tim'rous cloud. The Rape of Helen. Thomas Gray. *Fr.* Agrippina. RO
Dispensary, The, *sels.* Sir Samuel Garth.
"Not far from that most famous theatre." CEP
"Speak, Goddess! since 'tis thou that best canst tell." PoP
Displeasure against Love, A. Nicholas Breton. CaAE; SiCE
Dispossessed Poet. Monk Gibbon. OnYI
Dispraise [*or* Disprayse] of a Courtly Life. Sir Philip Sidney. LoBV; OAEP; SiCE
Dispraise of Absalom, The. *Tr. fr. Irish by* Robin Flower. OxBI
Dispraise of Love, and Lovers' Follies. "A. W." EIL; HBV; OBSC
(Dispraise of Love.) BLV; TrGrPo
("If love be life, I long to die.") LO
Disprayse of a Courtly Life. Sir Philip Sidney. *See* Dispraise of a Courtly Life.
Disputation between the Greeks and the Romans, The. Juan Ruiz, Archpriest of Hita. *Fr.* The Book of Good Love. AnSpL-1
Dispute between Nose and Eyes. William Cowper. *See* Nose and the Eyes, The.
Dispute of the Heart and Body of François Villon, The. Villon, *tr. fr. French by* Swinburne. AWP
Disputes. Alonso Jerónimo de Salas Barbadillo, *tr. fr. Spanish by* Sir John Bowring. OnPM
Disquisition on Death, *sel.* A. R. D. Fairburn.
"I went through the market-place crying, There is no death." AnNZ
Dissecting Room. John Fallon. PoP
Dissembler. Charles Shaw. GoYe
Dissemblers, The. Thomas Hardy. VLEP
Dissent; a Fable. Donald Davie. PoN
Dissenter, The. Lillian M. Swenson. ChIP
Dissolution, The. John Donne. OAEP; SeCV-1
Dissolving in the chemic vat. Change. Stanley J. Kunitz. NP
Dissuasion. Evgeni Baratynsky, *tr. fr. Russian by* C. M. Bowra. BoRS
Distaff, A. Erinna, *tr. fr. Greek by* C. M. Bowra. OxBG
Distaff, the spinner's friend, gift of Athena. Lines Written to Accompany the Gift of a Distaff to Theugenis. Theocritus. *Fr.* Idylls. OxBG
Distance. Babette Deutsch. PoMa; VOD
Distance and Solitude. Petrarch, *tr. fr. Italian by* Barbarina

Distance and Solitude (*continued*)
Lady Dacre. Sonnets to Laura: To Laura in Life, Canzone XVII. LiA
Distance nor death shall part us, dear. Love Song. Henry Treece. MaRV
Distances, The. Charles Olson. NeAP
Distances to the Friend, The. Jonathan Williams. NeAP
Distant and long have I waited without going. To Mackinnon of Strath. Iain Lom. GoTS
Distant Footsteps. César Vallejo, *tr. fr. Spanish by* H. R. Hays. TwSpPo
Distant Prospect of the City of Armagh, A. James Stuart. *Fr.* Morna's Hill. IrPN
Distant Runners, The. Mark Van Doren. LiTA; LiTM; LoGBV; MAP; MoAmPo; NePA
Distant Sea. Pedro Salinas, *tr. fr. Spanish by* Eleanor L. Turnbull. CoSP
Distant View of England from the Sea. William Lisle Bowles. EnRP
Distant View of School. Kaoru Maruyama, *tr. fr. Japanese by* Takamichi Ninomiya *and* D. J. Enright. PoLJ
Distich. Shuraikh, *tr. fr. Arabic.* TrJP
Distiches. Barten Holyday. EV-2
Distichs. John Hay. BOHV
Distinction. Mark Antony De Wolfe Howe. AA
Distinction is in fire and division, The. Poem. José Garcia Villa. POTE (1959 ed.)
Distinguish god in your imaginings. The Power of God. *Unknown.* OxBG
Distracted Puritan, The. Richard Corbet. OxBoLi
Distracted with care. The Despairing Lover. William Walsh. ALV; BCEP; CEP; EV-3; FaBoCh; LoGBV; OBEC; OxBoLi
Distraction is the panacea, Sir! Modern Love, XXVII. George Meredith. ViPo
Distraught for Meropé. Richard Henry Horne. *Fr.* Orion. VA
Distressed Sailor's Garland, The. *Unknown.* SG
Distribution. Elsie B. Purcell. PoMa
District school not far away, A. The Smack in School. William P. Palmer. BOHV; HBV; LPS-1; PTA-1
District school-master was sitting behind his great bookladen desk, The. The School-Master's Guests. Will M. Carleton. IHA; PTA-2
Disturbing it is/ To take your stick sedately talking. The River Walk. Padraic Fallon. OxBI
Disused Temple, The. Norman Cameron. ChMP
Dithyramb in Retrospect. Peter Hopegood. BoAV
Dithyrambic on Wine, A. Thomas Godfrey. TCAP
Ditty: "Cock shall crow, The." Robert Louis Stevenson. TrGrPo; VLEP
Ditty: "Full fadom five thy father lies." Shakespeare. *See* Ariel's Song: "Full fathom five . . ."
Ditty: Heart Exchange. Sir Philip Sidney. *See* My True Love Hath My Heart.
Ditty: "If this town should tumble down." Audrey Beecham. PoD
Ditty, A: In Praise of Eliza, Queen of the Shepherds. Spenser. *See* Ditty, A: "See where she sits upon the grassie greene."
Ditty: "Moon will run all consciences to cover, The." Allen Tate. MOAP
Ditty, A: "My true love hath my heart and I have his." Sir Philip Sidney. *See* My True Love Hath My Heart.
Ditty: "O holy Love, religious saint!" Sir Robert Chester. *Fr.* Love's Martyr. EIL
Ditty, A: "Peace, peace, peace, make no noise." John Day. *Fr.* Humour Out of Breath. EIL
Ditty, A: "See where she sits upon the grassy [*or* grassie] green[e]." Spenser. *Fr.* The Shepheardes Calender: April. FaBoCh; OBEV
("See where she sits upon the grassy green," *2 sts.*) ViBoPo
Ditty: "Time was long and long ago, The." Ted Robinson. MaRV
Ditty, The: "Young Colin Clout." John Gay. *Fr.* The Shepherd's Week. LoBV
Ditty in Imitation of the Spanish, A ("Entre tanto que l'Avril"). Lord Herbert of Cherbury. EIL; OBS; SeEP
(Now That the April of Your Youth.) EV-2
Ditty of Saint Clare, A. Enid Dinnis. PraNu
Ditty of the Pen Inveighing against Usury and False Dealing, A. John Hall. ReIE
Ditty of the Six Virgins, The. Thomas Watson. *See* With Fragrant Flowers We Strew the Way.
Ditty of the White Clouds, The. *Unknown, tr. fr. Chinese by* James Legge. BoFr
Ditty the City Sang, The. Alfred Kreymborg. NeMA
Diuturnal infirmity of hope. Sister Juana Inés de la Cruz, *tr. fr. Spanish by* Samuel Beckett. AnMP
Divan, The. Richard Henry Stoddard. AA
Dive, The. Ted Robins. PreP
Diver, The. John Frederic Herbin. CaP
Diver, The. W. W. E. Ross. BoCaPo; PeCV
Diverging now (as if his quest had been). Wordsworth. *Fr.* The Excursion, II. OBRV
Divers, The. Peter Quennell. MBP; MoBrPo; MoVE; TCPD
Divers. Robert Haven Schauffler. TBM
Divers Doth Use, as I Have Heard and Know. Sir Thomas Wyatt. EnL; OAEP; ReEn; SiCE; TuPP
(Deserted Lover Consoleth Himself, The.) EPP
(Sonnet: "Divers doth use . . .") SiPS
Divers thy death do diversely bemoan. The Death of Wyatt. Earl of Surrey. SiPS
Diversions of the Re-echo Club. Carolyn Wells. BOHV
Diversity. Frank Ernest Hill. TBM
Diversity. Everard V. Thompson. BePJ
Diversity of Gifts Solon, *tr. fr. Greek by* T. F. Higham. OxBG
Diverting History of John Gilpin, The. William Cowper. BeLS; BoChLi; BOHV; BPP; CEP; CoBE; EiPP; FaBoBe; FiP; GN; HBV; HBVY; InMe; LPS-3; OBEC; OnSP; OTPC; RIS; TOP; TreFS
(John Gilpin.) CG; EV-3; InvP; MW; ViBoPo
(John Gilpin's Ride.) HiLiEn
Dives and Lazarus. *Unknown.* BaBo; ESPB; OBB
(Diverus and Lazarus.) ATP
(Dives and Laz'us.) ABF
(Lazarus, *with music.*) SaSa
Dives Asking a Drop. Richard Crashaw. AEV
(On Dives.) ACP
Dives, when you and I go down to Hell. To Dives. Hilaire Belloc. CAW; HBMV
Divided. David Gray. AA
Divided. Jean Ingelow. HBV
Divided Destinies. Kipling. BOHV
Divided Heart, The. George Wither. *See* I Wandered Out.
Divided Thought, A. *Unknown, tr. fr. Spanish by* Havelock Ellis. OnPM
Divided Thoughts. Dante, *tr. fr. Italian by* Dante Gabriel Rossetti. *Fr.* La Vita Nuova. OnPM
("All my thoughts always speak to me of Love.") AWP
Dividends. Hubert Creekmore. WaP
Divina Commedia. *sels.* Dante, *tr. fr. Italian.*
Inferno.
Dante Enters the Gate of Hell, *fr.* III, *tr. by* J. A. Carlyle. LiA
Francesca da Rimini, *fr.* V, *tr. by* Dante Gabriel Rossetti. EmBrPo; EPN; EPP
Inferno. EnLi-1 (*fr.* V *and* XIII), *tr. by* Frances Winwar; OuHeWo, *abr., tr. by* Henry F. Cary
Midway the Journey, *fr.* I, *tr. by* Laurence Binyon. ExPo
Paolo and Francesca, *fr.* V. ExPo, *tr. by* Laurence Binyon; LiA, *tr. by* Byron
Pier delle Vigne, *fr.* XIII, *tr. by* John Ciardi. HoPM
Ugolino, *fr.* XXXIII, *tr. by* Laurence Binyon. LiA
"While I was all absorbed," *fr.* XXVIII, *tr. by* Longfellow. CAW
Paradiso.
Affinity with the Stars, *tr. by* Wendell Phillips Stafford. GrCo-2
Being Underived, *fr.* I, *tr. by* Longfellow. CAW
"But not to deal/ Thus closely with thee longer," *fr.* XI, *tr. by* Henry F. Cary. SaFP
Freedom of the Will: Beatrice to Dante, *fr.* V, *tr. by* M. B. Anderson. GrCo-1
His Will Is Our Peace, *fr.* III, *tr. by* Wendell Phillips Stafford. GrCo-2
Incommunicable Glory, The, *fr.* I, *tr. by* Wendell Phillips Stafford. GrCo-2
"Into the justice of eternity," *fr.* XIX, *tr. by* Jefferson Butler Fletcher. PoFr
Love, *fr.* XXXIII, *tr. by* Philip Henry Wicksteed. LiA
"'Now say,' he said, 'were it not worse indeed,'" *fr.* VIII, *tr. by* Jefferson Butler Fletcher. PoFr
"O petty blood-nobility of ours!" *fr.* XVI, *tr. by* Jefferson Butler Fletcher. PoFr
One World, *4 ll.* MaRV
Paradise, *abr., tr. by* Henry F. Cary. OuHeWo
Paradise: Cacciaguida's Prophecy to Dante, *fr.* XVII, *tr. by* Frances Winwar. EnLi-1
Primal Cause, The, *fr.* XXVIII, *tr. by* Longfellow. CAW
St. Bernard's Prayer to the Virgin Mary, *fr.* XXXIII, *tr. by* Laurence Binyon. MeRV
(Saint Bernard's Prayer to Our Lady, *tr. by* Louis How.) ISi
("Thou Virgin Mother, daughter of thy Son," *tr. by* Longfellow.) CAW
Saints in Glory, The, *fr.* XXXI, *tr. by* Henry F. Cary. WGRP
Vision of God, The, *fr.* XXXIII, *tr. by* Laurence Binyon. ExPo
Vision of the Divine Mystery, *fr.* XXXIII, *tr. by* Laurence Binyon. LiTW

Purgatorio.
Buonconte Relates His Fate, *fr.* V, *pr. tr. by* Charles Eliot Norton. LiA
Celestial Pilot, The, *fr.* II, *tr. by* Longfellow. WGRP
Dante Sees Beatrice in Glory, *fr.* XXX, *tr. by* Thomas Okey. LiA
Freedom of the Will, *fr.* XVIII, *tr. by* M. B. Anderson. GrCo-1
"How haughty was thy mien," *fr.* VI, *tr. by* Jefferson Butler Fletcher. PoFr
Marvel Ye Not, *fr.* III, *tr. by* Thomas Okey. LiA
Moral Responsibility, *fr.* XVI, *tr. by* Jefferson Butler Fletcher. GrCo-2
Political Chaos in Italy, *fr.* VI, *tr. by* Longfellow. WoL
Purgatory, *abr., fr. tr. by* Henry F. Cary. OuHeWo
Purgatory: Dante's Dream, *fr.* IX, *tr. by* Frances Winwar. EnLi-1
Self-Guidance, *fr.* XXVII, *tr. by* Jefferson Butler Fletcher. GrCo-2
"'Twas now the hour that turneth," *fr.* VIII, *tr. by* Longfellow. CAW
"Veracious people, The," *fr.* XXX, *tr. by* Longfellow. CAW
Virgil's Farewell to Dante, *fr.* XXVII, *tr. by* Laurence Binyon. FaBoTw
Divina Commedia (*poems introductory to* Longfellow's *tr. of the* Divine Comedy, I–VI). Longfellow. AmP; AmPP; AnAmPo; AnFE; APA; APW; CoAnAm; CoBA; CoV; ES; IAP; LA; LPS-2; MOAP; NePA; OBAV; OxBA; PIAE; PtP; ReaPo; TCAP; TOP
Sels.
"How strange the sculptures that adorn these towers!" II. AnNE; GoBC; PoE; PoFS; REAL
"I enter, and I see thee in the gloom," III. AnNE; GoBC
"I lift mine eyes, and all the windows blaze," IV [V]. AnNE; GoBC; SeCeV; TriL
"O star of morning and of liberty!" V [VI]. AnNE; GoBC
"Oft have I seen at some cathedral door," I. AnNE; ATP; BPP; GoBC; HBV; LBAP; OQP; PoE; QP-1; TreF; TwCrTr; ViBoPo
(Dante.) OBEV (new ed.)
(On Dante's "Divine Comedy.") AnEnPo
(Peace through Prayer.) MaRV
(With the Ages.) GrCo-2
On Translating the "Divina Commedia," I, II, III, V. OuHeWo
Divination by a Daffodil. Robert Herrick. OBS; SeCV-1; SeEP
Divine Abundance. *Unknown.* BLRP
Divine Awe. George Edward Woodberry. Wild Eden, XVI. AA; LBAP
Divine Betrayal, The. Euripides, *tr. fr. Greek by* A. W. Verrall. *Fr.* Ion. GrR
Divine Call, The. Sister Mary Genevieve. PraNu
Divine Camenes, that with your sacred food. Of Edwards of the Chapel. Barnabe Googe. ReIE
Divine Care. Francis Quarles. MaRV
Divine Century of Spiritual Sonnets, A, *sels.* Barnabe Barnes.
"Fortress of hope, anchor of faithful zeal." MeRV; TuPP
"Gracious, Divine, and most omnipotent." SiCE
Life of Man, The. OBSC
(Blast of Wind, A, a Momentary Breath.) PeBoSo; SiCE; TuPP
"No more lewd lays of lighter loves I sing." TuPP
World's Bright Comforter, The. OxBoCh
(God's Virtue.) OBSC
(Sonnet.) EIL
("World's bright comforter, whose beamsome light, The.") SiCE
Divine Comedy, The. Dante. *See* Divina Commedia.
Divine Companion, The. Rabindranath Tagore. *Fr.* Gitanjali. GrCo-2
("Thou hast made me known to friends.") NP
(When One Knows Thee.) OQP; QP-2
Divine Compassion, The. Isaiah, Bible, *O.T.* *See* Ho, Every-one That Thirsteth.
Divine Compassion. Whittier. TriL
Divine Fantasy, The, *sel.* John Hall Wheelock.
"All afternoon the passion of heaven spent." LEAP
Divine Hand, The. William Williams. *See* Guide Me, O Thou Great Jehovah.
Divine Harmony, The. Shakespeare. *See* In Such a Night.
Divine Image, A ("Cruelty has a human heart"). Blake. AtBAP; ChTr
Divine Image, The ("To Mercy, Pity, Peace, and Love"). Blake. *Fr.* Songs of Innocence. BoTP; CEP; CoEV; EiPP; EM-1; EnL; EnLit; EnRP; FaBoEn; GrCo-2; LiTG; MaPo; MaRV; OAEP; OBEC; OnPM; OxBoCh; PoEL-4; ReaPo; TwCrTr; ViBoPo; WGRP
("To Mercy Pity Peace and Love.") LO
Divine Insect, The. John Hall Wheelock. GoYe
Divine Love. Richard Crashaw. *See* Song, A: "Lord, when the sense of thy sweet grace."
Divine Love. Charles Wesley. *See* Love Divine.
Divine Lover, The. Charles Wesley. *See* Jesus, Lover of My Soul.
Divine Name, brief and compendious. Song to the Most Holy Name of Jesus. Fernando de Córdova y Bocanegra. AnMP
Divine Narcissus, The. Sister Juana Inés de la Cruz, *tr. fr. Spanish by* Roderick Gill. CAW
Divine Office of the Kitchen, The. Cecily Hallack. BLRP
Divine Paradox, The. *Unknown.* MeEV
Divine Passion, The. Hortensio Félix Paravicino y Arteaga, *tr. fr. Spanish by* Thomas Walsh. CAW
Divine perfection, we have sinned, 'tis true. The Dean. Alan Porter. AnAmPo
Divine Philosopher, The. Empedocles, *tr. fr. Greek by* W. E. Leonard. OxBG
Divine Poems, *sels.* José Garcia Villa.
"Much, beauty, is, less, than, the, face, of," 102. POTE (1959 ed.)
"My most. My most, O my lost!" 57. BoW; POTE (1959 ed.)
Divine Presence, The. Aubrey Thomas De Vere. *Fr.* May Carols. BMEP; GoBC; MaRV
Divine Providence. Sadi, *tr. fr. Persian by* Ebenezer Pocock. PeP
Divine Rapture, A. Francis Quarles. *See* My Beloved Is Mine, and I Am His.
Divine Rebel, The. George Scheftel. ChIP
Divine rose, that in a pleasant garden. Sister Juana Inés de la Cruz, *tr. fr. Spanish by* Samuel Beckett. AnMP
Divine Songs to Ahura Mazda. Zoroaster, *tr. fr. Persian by* D. J. Irani. LiTW
Divine Sonnet. John Donne. *See* Sonnet: "At the round earth's imagin'd corners, blow."
Divine Wooer, The, *sel.* Phineas Fletcher.
"Me Lord? can'st Thou mispend." TrPWD
Divine Zenocrate. Christopher Marlowe. *Fr.* Tamburlaine the Great, Pt. II, Act II, sc. iii. WHA
"Black [*or* Blacke] is the beauty of the brightest day.") AtBAP; BoW; ViBoPo
(Death of Zenocrate, The.) PoD
(To Entertain Divine Zenocrate.) ChTr
Divinely shapen cup, thy lip. On a Greek Vase. Frank Dempster Sherman. AA; LBAP; OBAV
Divinely Superfluous Beauty. Robinson Jeffers. LiTL; MAP; MoAmPo
Divinest Sense. Emily Dickinson. *See* Much madness is divinest sense.
Divining Rod, The. Joseph von Eichendorff, *tr. fr. German by* Mabel Cotterell. AnGP
Divinity, The. Matthew Arnold. EPN
Divinity School Graduation Hymn. John White Chadwick. *See* Hymn: "Eternal Ruler of the ceaseless round."
Divisibility. Hyam Plutzik. FiMAP
Division, The. Thomas Hardy. PG (1945 ed.)
Divorce, The. Thomas Stanley. LO, *sts.* 1–2; MeLP
Divorce. Anna Wickham. MBP; MoBrPo
Divorce. Charles Williams. POTE
Divorce me now, good Death, from Love and ling'ring Life. A Libel of Divorce. George Gascoigne. ReEn
Dixie ("I wish I was in de land ob cotton"). Daniel Decatur Emmett. ABF; APW; BlG; BoHiPo; FaFP; FaPON; HBV; LEAP; OIF; PaA; PoFr; SPP; TrAS, *with music;* TreF; TrGrPo; YaD
Dixie ("Southrons, hear your country call you!"). Albert Pike. AA; APW; HBV; MC; MDAH; PaA; PAH; SPP; TCAP
Dixie Lullaby, A. T. A. Daly. BOL
Dixie Lullaby, A. Strickland W. Gillilan. LHV
Dixie's Land. Daniel Decatur Emmett. APW
Dixon, a Choctaw, twenty years of age. A Savage. John Boyle O'Reilly. AA; OBAV
Dizzy prairie spun, The. At Beecher's Island. John G. Neihardt. *Fr.* The Song of the Indian Wars. TCPD
Do all the good you can. John Wesley's Rule [*or* What to Do]. John Wesley. FaFP; HBVY; MeMeAg; PCH
Do but consider this small dust. *See* Consider this small dust.
Do but look on her eyes, they do light. Ben Jonson. *Fr.* A Celebration of Charis. LO
Do Come Back Again, *with music.* *Unknown.* OuSiCo
Do diddle di do. Jim Jay. Walter de la Mare. CenHV; CV; GaP; GoTP; HBMV; NV; RG; RIS; SiSoSe
Do Don't Touch-a My Garment, Good Lord, I'm Gwine Home, *with music.* *Unknown.* BoAN-2
Do fishes gleam with hope or flowers feel. Credo. Alfred Kreymborg. AnAmPo; BAP; LA
Do gold-tongued candles comfort Thee. Meditation in St. Mary's. Gertrude du Bois. ChIP
Do hearts forget the wonder-sweet delight. Query. Ann Louise Hayes. PtPa
Do I Love Thee? John Godfrey Saxe. HBV

Do I not see that fairest images. Amoretti, LI. Spenser. PeBoSo

Do I remember such and such an one? Pilate Remembers. Thomas Durley Landels. *Fr.* Pontius Pilate. MaRV

Do I sleep? Do I dream? De Tea Fabula. Sir Arthur Quiller-Couch. CenHV; PA

Do I sleep? do I dream? Truthful James. Bret Harte. CenHV

Do I venture away too far. Song. Keith Douglas. NePoEA

Do It Now. Berton Braley. BLPA; FaFP; WBLP

Do It Now! *Unknown.* BLPA; FaFP; WBLP

Do It Right. Samuel O. Buckner. WBLP

Do It Yrself. Larry Eigner. NeAP

Do Mercy before Thy Judgment, *in mod. Eng. Unknown.* TMEV

Do, my Johnny Boker. Johnny Boker. *Unknown.* ShS; SoAmSa

Do not ask: where? We Go. Karl Wolfskehl. TrJP

Do not be angry with me for the word. Sonnet. Phyllis Reid. DiM

Do not be astonished. Whisper in Agony. Jules Supervielle. MiCF

Do not be fretful of your old repose. Letter to the Dead in Spring. Mary Cecile Ions. MuM

Do not be offended because. An Excuse for Not Returning the Visit of a Friend. Mei Yao Ch'en. OnPC

Do not be surprised. Whisper in Agony. Jules Supervielle. MiFP

Do not buy precious scissors. Woodpeckers' Song. Po Chü-i. WhP

Do not come out in the broad daylight! Susaki Waterfront. Saisei Muro. PoLJ

Do not come when I am dead. My Hereafter. Juanita De Long. WGRP

Do not conceal thy [or those] radiant eyes. To Cynthia on Concealment of Her Beauty. Sir Francis Kynaston. CaAE; EG; HBV; LiTL; LO; MeLP; MePo; OBS; SeCL; SeEP; ViBoPo

Do not conceive that I shall here recount. A Virgin Declares Her Beauties. Francesco da Barberino, *tr.* by Dante Gabriel Rossetti. AWP; LyPI; MeRV

Do not crouch to-day and worship. The Present. Adelaide Anne Procter. WGRP

Do not despair. For Johnny. John Pudney. HaMV

Do not disdain, O straight up-raisèd pine. Graven Thoughts. Sir Philip Sidney. *Fr.* Arcadia. SiPS

Do not draw near. Your forehead, your passionate burning brow. Come Always, Come. Vicente Aleixandre. CoSP

Do not embrace a girl too thin. Rufinus, *tr. fr. Greek by* Elsie Spoerl. GrPo

Do Not Embrace Your Mind's New Negro Friend. William Meredith. WaP

Do not enforce the tired wolf. Prelude to an Evening. John Crowe Ransom. CoBMV; MAP; MoAB; MoAmPo; MoPo; MoVE; NePA; OxBA

Do Not Expect Again a Phoenix Hour. C. Day Lewis. LiTB; LiTM (rev. ed.); MBP; MoAB; MoBrPo; OxBI; PoRA

Do not fear. Release. Jean Grigsby Paxton. DDA; OQP; QP-2

Do not fear to put thy feet. The River God's Song [or The Song of the River God to Amoret]. John Fletcher. *Fr.* The Faithful Shepherdess, III, i. EIL; ElSeCe; EV-2; FaPON; MoShBr; OBS; PCH; ThWaDe; TuPP

Do not fear, my love; no danger. Fürchte Nichts, geliebte Seele. Heine, *tr. by* Louis Untermeyer. ALV

Do Not Follow the Great Chariot. *Unknown, tr. fr. Chinese.* WhP

Do not forget your cotton days. *Unknown, tr. fr. Chinese by* Herbert A. Giles. BoFr

Do Not Go Gentle into That Good Night. Dylan Thomas. ChMP; CoBMV; EnL; FaFP; MoAB; MoVE; PG (1955 ed.); Po; PoLFOT; SeCeV; ViBoPo (1958 ed.)

Do not hurry; have faith. Have Faith. Edward Carpenter. WGRP

Do not leave me, Lord, do not let the field lie fallow. Prayer for the Useless Days. Edith Lovejoy Pierce. TrPWD

Do not let any woman read this verse! Deirdre. James Stephens. AWP; ChMo; CMP; GTIV; GTSL; HBMV; JAWP; LBBV; LEAP; MM; NV; OBMV; OnPP; PG; PoRA; TwCV; ViBoPo; WBP

Do not look at my face. Sweet. *Unknown.* OnPM

Do Not Minute. Thomas Lovell Beddoes. LO; LoPS

Do Not, Oh, Do Not Prize. *Unknown.* EIL
("Do [or Doe] not, O do not prize thy beauty at too high a rate.") EG; NBE; OBSC
(O Do Not Prize Thy Beauty.) LiTL
(Pride Is the Canker.) TrGrPo

Do Not Open until Christmas. James S. Tippett. ChBR

Do not pay too much attention to the stupid old body. The Stupid Old Body. Edward Carpenter. WGRP

Do not pay too much attention to the wandering lunatic mind. The Wandering Lunatic Mind. Edward Carpenter. WGRP

Do not profane the work of doing well. Musophilus. Samuel Daniel. ReEn

Do not rumple my top-knot. The Coy Lass Dress'd Up in Her Best. *Unknown.* LoPS

Do not rustle, rye. Aleksey Koltsov, *tr. fr. Russian by* C. M. Bowra. BoR

Do not salute me, I am not your friend. The Ghost. Cú Chonnacht O Cléirigh. GTIV

Do not smile to yourself. Lady Otomo no Sakanoe, *tr. fr. Japanese by* Kenneth Rexroth. OnPJ

Do not suddenly break the branch. Usk. T. S. Eliot. Landscapes, III. CoBE; FaBoCh; KN; LoGBV

Do not suppose that I confess. The Contessa to Her Judges. Cale Young Rice. SPP

Do Not Torment Me, Woman ("Do not torment me, woman, for your honour's sake do not pursue me"). *Unknown, tr. fr. Late Middle Irish by* Kenneth Jackson. AnIL

Do not torment me, woman, let us set our minds at one. Reconciliation. *Unknown.* AnIL

Do Not Touch. Boris Pasternak, *tr. fr. Russian by* C. M. Bowra. BoRS

Do not trust black eyes, but fear them. Black Eyes. Avetis Isahakian. ArmLP

Do not trust him gentle lady. The Gipsy's Warning. *Unknown.* BeLS

Do not unjustly blame. To His Mistress. Samuel Butler. SeCL

Do not waste your pity, friend. A Wasted Sympathy. Winifred Howells. AA

Do not waste your time. To a Boy. *Unknown.* KiLC

Do not weep, maiden, for war is kind. War Is Kind, I [or If War Be Kind]. Stephen Crane. AmPP; AnAmPo; AnFE; APA; BAP; CoAnAm; CoBA; HBV; InPo; LA; LiTA; MOAP; OnAP; ViBoPo; WaaP

Do not worry if I scurry from the grill-room in a hurry. Cupid's Darts. A. P. Herbert. BOHV; CenHV

Do please show me, if it's not too much trouble. Catullus, *tr. fr. Latin by* Frances Fletcher. LaP

Do Right. *Unknown.* MeMeAg

Do skyscrapers ever grow tired. Skyscrapers. Rachel Field. FaPON; GFA; StVeCh

Do the boys and girls still go to Siever's. Hare Drummer. Edgar Lee Masters. *Fr.* Spoon River Anthology. TOP

Do the cranes wheel back to you again? And do the ships. The Archipelago. Friedrich Hölderlin. AnGP

Do the Dead Know What Time It Is? Kenneth Patchen. MoAmPo

"Do the fish still glitter in the waterpool?" Fisherman. Sacheverell Sitwell. AtBAP

Do the wife and baby travelling to see. The Sick Nought. Randall Jarrell. OxBA

Do the Work That's Nearest. Charles Kingsley. MaRV

Do They Miss Me at Home? Caroline Atherton Briggs Mason. TreFS

Do They Think of Me at Home. Joseph Edward Carpenter. FaBoBe; OlF; TreFS

Do They Whisper. Delmore Schwartz. FiMAP
(Do They Whisper behind My Back?) LiTA

Do Thy Day's Work. *Unknown.* PEDC

Do we indeed desire the dead. In Memoriam A. H. H., LI. Tennyson. AtBAP; BEL; BoFr; EM-2; EmBrPo; EnLi-2; EPN; GEPC; OAEP; PIAE; TOP; Vigy; VLEP

Do we presume too much upon God's mercy? The Zeal of Thy House. Dorothy L. Sayers. QS

Do what conscience says is right. Do Right. *Unknown.* MeMeAg

Do What Thy Manhood Bids Thee Do. Sir Richard Francis Burton. TreFS

Do What You Will. Dorothy Hobson. GoBC

Do write, my love, for but the sight. To a Neglectful Lover. Nancy Birckhead. PIAE

Do ye hear the children weeping, O my brothers. The Cry of the Children. Elizabeth Barrett Browning. BCEP; BEL; BPN; BPP; EmBrPo; EnLi-2; EPP; EV-4; HBV; OAEP; PFE; PoFr; PoVP; VA; ViBoPo; ViPo; VLEP

Do ye [or you] know the little wood-mouse. The Wood-Mouse. Mary Howitt. RAR; TVC

Do ye remember? . . . Surelye I remember. The Old Shepherds. Eleanor Farjeon. AIDL

Do you ask for a picture. Michihiko, *tr. fr. Japanese by* Lois J. Erickson. SoLD

Do you ask me how I prove. The Heart's Proof. James Buckham. BLRP; OQP; QP-2; WBLP

Do you ask [or know] what the birds say? Answer to a Child's Question [or The Birds or What the Birds Say]. Samuel Taylor Coleridge. BoTP; CBE; CBPC; CG; DD; EmBrPo; EnRP; ERP; EV-4; FaBoBe; HBV; HBVY; LPS-2; MeMeAg; NeHB; OTPC; PEDC; PRWS; RAR; ThWaDe; TVC; UTS

Do you carrot all for me? *Unknown.* SiTL

Do You Fear the Wind? Hamlin Garland. AA; BAP; DDA; HBV; HBVY; LBAP; MPB; NLK; OBAV; OQP; PC; PoeMoYo; PYM; QP-2; SP; TiPo; TSW; TSWC; YaD

(Do You Fear the Force of the Wind?) MCCG; PoMa
Do you feel your heart discouraged as you pass along the way? When Thou Passest through the Waters. Henry Crowell. BLRP
De you forget the shifting hole. To a Defeated Saviour. James Wright. NePoEA
Do you give yourself to me utterly. Sleep. Kenneth Slessor. BoAV; MoAuPo
Do You Guess It Is I? Eliza Lee Follen. OTPC (1946 ed.); PPL
Do you hear an ominous muttering as of thunder gath'ring round? It Is Coming. M. Florence Mosher. PEOR
Do you hear his whistle blowing. The Popcorn Man. Edith D. Osborne. GFA
Do you hear the cry as the pack goes by. Wind-Wolves. William D. Sargent. MPB; TiPo; UTS
Do you hear the noise of waters as they hiss along the sand? The Flowing Tide. Godfrey Fox Bradby. TVSH
"Do you herd sheep?" old gramma sighed. How Low Is the Lowing Herd. Walt Kelly. FiBHP
Do ye ken hoo to fush for the salmon? Master and Man. Sir Henry Newbolt. WhC
Do You Know? Christina Rossetti. *See* When the Cows Come Home.
Do You Know How Many Stars? *Unknown.* PPL
Do you know how the people of all the land. Potomac Side. Edward Everett Hale. From Potomac to Merrimac, I. PAH
Do you know, my Lesbia, how many of your kisses. Catullus, *tr. fr. Latin by* Horace Gregory. RoL
Do you know of the dreary land. The River Fight. Henry Howard Brownell. PaA; PAH; PAP
Do you know that your soul is of my soul such a part. Like Mother, Like Son [*or* To My Son]. Margaret Johnston Grafflin. BLPA; NeHB; PoToHe (new ed.)
Do you know the animal trainer's trick. Power of Memory. Ibsen. AnNoLy
Do you know the little wood-mouse. *See* Do ye know . . .
Do you know the neighbor who lives in your block. Your Neighbor. H. Howard Biggar. PoToHe
Do you know the old man who. The Wild Flower Man. Lu Yu. OnPC
Do you know there's lots of people. Get into the Boosting Business. *Unknown.* WBLP
Do you know those whom I so loved before. Aleksandr Odoevsky, *tr. fr. Russian by* C. M. Bowra. BoRS
Do you know what I could wish? Song for a Hot Day. Elizabeth J. Coatsworth. StVeCh (1955 ed.)
Do you know what the birds say? *See* Do you ask what the birds say?
Do you know what you are fighting against, fatuous mother. Son and Mother. Cale Young Rice. LS
Do you know what's in my pottet? A Little Boy's Pocket. *Unknown.* PPL
Do you know why the rabbits are caught in the snare. Why. H. P. Stevens. BOHV
Do you know you have asked for the costliest thing. A Woman's Question. Lena Lathrop. BLPA; PoToHe; PTA-1; WBLP
Do you like marigolds? Marigolds. Louise Driscoll. BoTP; LEAP
Do you long, my maiden. Papago Love-Songs, 2. *Tr. by* Mary Austin. APW
Do you love me. *Unknown.* SiTL
Do you 'member way last summer? You Kicked and Stomped and Beat Me. *Unknown.* OuSiCo
Do you mind the news while we eat? Dinner Party, 1940. Phillip M. Sherlock. PoNe
Do you ne'er think what wondrous beings these? Longfellow. *Fr.* The Birds of Killingworth. WBLP
"Do you not find something very strange about him?" The Assassination. Robert Hillyer. AnNE; MoAmPo; TrGrPo (1942 ed.)
Do You Not Hear? James Picot. BoAV
Do you not hear her song. Daphne. Thomas S. Jones, Jr. OHIP; VOD
Do you not hear how they ask for reality. Pedro Salinas, *tr. fr. Spanish by* Eleanor L. Turnbull. CoSP
Do you not hear me calling, white deer with no horns? He Mourns for the Change That Has Come upon Him and His Beloved, and Longs for the End of the World. W. B. Yeats. Po
Do you not see. To Him I Love. Tzu Yeh. PoHN
Do you not see, Beloved? Vladimir Soloviev. *See* Dearest One.
Do you not see the Christmas star. Song of the Wise Men. Edith Lovejoy Pierce. PGD
Do you not see the old flower-seller at the south gate of Hueichi. The Flower-Seller. Lu Yu. WhP
Do you not see the waters of the Yellow River flowing down from the sky? Song before Offering Wine. Li Po. WhP
"Do you not wish to renounce the Devil?" Epigram. Armand Lanusse. PoNe
Do you, now, as the news becomes known. Pay-off. Kenneth Fearing. ChMo
Do You Plan to Speak Bantu? or Abbreviation Is the Thief of Sanity. Ogden Nash. FiBHP
Do you recall that night in June. The Danube River. Hamilton Aïdé. VA
Do You Remember. Thomas Haynes Bayly. HBV
Do you remember/ Honey-melon moon. New Orleans. Lola Ridge. MAP; MoAmPo (1942 ed.); TBM
Do you remember/ How you won. To James [*or* More Letters Found near a Suicide]. Frank Horne. BANP; GoSl
Do you remember an inn. Tarantella. Hilaire Belloc. CH; FaBoCh; GoBC; LoGBV; MoBrPo; MoShBr; MoSiPe; MuP; NeMA; OBMV; OtMeF; PtOT; ShBV-2
Do you remember, Daphne, that archaic strain. Delphica. Gérard de Nerval. AnFP
Do you remember, father. The Whippoorwill. Henry van Dyke. WhBS
Do you remember, Heart's Desire. A Hallowe'en Memory. Christopher Morley. HOAH; LHV
Do you remember how the twilight stood. To Butterfly. William Alexander Percy. HBMV; LS
Do you remember how together. Mikhail Lermontov, *tr. fr. Russian by* C. M. Bowra. BoR
Do you remember how we came that day. Two Married: The Heights. Helen Frazee-Bower. HBMV
Do you remember, Joan (O vain to wonder). The Saint. Humbert Wolfe. *Fr.* Requiem. CAW; TwCV; VOD (1935 ed.)
Do you remember long ago. After Aughrim. Arthur Gerald Geoghegan. BoHiPo; OnYI; TIP
Do you remember, Mary. Aleksey Konstantinovich Tolstoy, *tr. fr. Russian.* BoR, *tr. by* Maurice Baring; WaL, *tr. by* Sir Cecil Kisch
Do You Remember Me? Walter Savage Landor. *Fr.* Ianthe. EnRP; GTBS-D; ViBoPo
(Ianthe's Question.) OBEV
(Lyrics to Ianthe.) BPN
(Years After.) EV-4
Do you remember Mr. Goodbeare, the carpenter. Elegy for Mr. Goodbeare. Sir Osbert Sitwell. AnFE; MBP; MoBrPo
Do you remember, my sweet, absent son. The Child's Wish Granted. George Parsons Lathrop. AA; HBV; JKCP
Do you remember now the autumn day. Innominata. Benjamin Sledd. NoCaPo
Do you remember, O Delphic Apollo. Webster Ford. Edgar Lee Masters. *Fr.* Spoon River Anthology. NP
Do you remember one immortal. To F. C. in Memoriam. Palestine. G. K. Chesterton. HBMV
Do you remember, passer-by, the path. James Garber. Edgar Lee Masters. *Fr.* Spoon River Anthology. ChMo; CMP
Do you remember that careless band. Fairyland. Anne Glenny Wilson. BoAu
Do You Remember That Night? *Unknown, tr. fr. Modern Irish by* Eugene O'Curry. AnIV; OnYI; OxBI
——*Tr. by* George Petrie. GTIV; IrPN
Do you remember that still summer evening. The Golden Room. W. W. Gibson. POTE
Do you remember the dark months you held the sector at Mametz. Aftermath. Siegfried Sassoon. AOAH; BMEP; GTSL; MBP; MCCG; TCEP
Do you remember the dark pool at Nimes. The Pool. Alice Corbin. NP
Do you remember, when we two were children. Over the Bridge. Li Kwang-t'ien. LiTW
Do you remember when you heard. Do You Remember. Thomas Haynes Bayly. HBV
Do you remember, when you were first a child. Message from Home. Kathleen Raine. ImOP
Do you see that bird in the sky? Bird-Song. Mary Dixon Thayer. CAW
Do you see that willow standing. The West Wind's Secret. Mary Jane Carr. BrR
Do you see them? I mean the Dead. Haunted Odysseus; the Last Testament. Horace Gregory. MoVE
Do you seek to bind me, ye gods. The Sword of Tethra. William Larminie. *Fr.* Moytura. OnYI
Do you still recall that evening? Shooting Stars. Otto C. Fønss. BoDS
Do you think I'd marry a woman. A Bachelor's Mono-Rhyme. Charles Mackay. BOHV
Do you think, my boy, when I put my arms around you. The Lonely Child. James Oppenheim. LEAP; NP
Do you think of me at all. Dead "Wessex," the Dog, to the Household. Thomas Hardy. CMP; ReaPo
Do you think that because I sing. The Swan's Singing. *Unknown.* OnPM
Do you think that odes and sermons. Sexsmith the Dentist. Edgar Lee Masters. *Fr.* Spoon River Anthology. NePA
Do you wilt and whine, if you fail to win. Playing the Game. *Unknown.* BLP
Do you wish the world were better? Better, Wiser and Happier. Ella Wheeler Wilcox. WBLP

Do you wish to give yourself to me until you lose colour. Exaltation of Elementary Materials. Xavier Abril. AnCL
Do you wonder to see him in chains? Columbus Day. Tennyson. HH; PEDC
Do you wonder what I am seeing. The Coast-Guard. Emily Huntington Miller. PEOR
Doan't You Be What You Ain't. Edwin Milton Royle. BLPA
Dobe Bill, he came a-riding. The Killer. *Unknown.* ABF; CoSo
Doc Hill. Edgar Lee Masters. *Fr.* Spoon River Anthology. BAP; NP
Dock Rats. Marianne Moore. AnAmPo; LA
Docks. Dorothy Wellesley. ShBV-3
Doctor, The, *sel.* George W. Caldwell.
"When one is wounded in the strife." PoP
Doctor, The. E. O. Laughlin. PoP
Doctor Bill Williams. Ernest Walsh. InvP
Dr. Birch and His Young Friends, *sel.* Thackeray.
End of the Play, The. BMEP, *much abr.;* COAH; FaFP; GN; LEAP; LPS-1; TreF; VA
Doctor Bottom was preparing to leave. Medical Aid. Walter Hard. WhC
Doctor came at half-past one, The. Little Billy. Sir Arthur Conan Doyle. FAOV
Dr. Clifford. E. C. Bentley. *Fr.* Biography for Beginners. CenHV
Dr. Coppelius. Wrey Gardiner. NeBP
Dr. Donne. Kenneth Slade Alling. NePoAm
Dr. Faustus. Christopher Marlowe. CoBE; EnLi-1; EnLit; TwCrTr, *abr.*
Sels.
"Ah Faustus,/ Now hast thou but one bare hour to live." AtBAP; BoLiVe; ChTr; MyFE; NBE; ViBoPo
(End of Dr. Faustus, The.) PoEL-2
(End of Faustus, The.) TrGrPo
(Finale.) WHA
(Last Hour of Faustus, The.) CBOV; ShBV-4
(O Lente, Lente, Curite Noctis Equi.) LiA
"But, leaving these vain trifles of men's souls." MyFE
"Cut is the branch that might have grown full [*or* growne ful] straight," *fr.* Epilogue. PoD, 3 *ll.;* ViBoPo, 8 *ll.*
(Chorus on the Death of Faustus, 4 *ll.*) LEAP
"Was this the face that launch'd a thousand ships?" AtBAP; BoHiPo; EtPaEn; InP; LEAP; LiTL; LoPS; PIAE; TreF, 3 *ll.;* TrGrPo; ViBoPo
(Faustus to Helen.) NeHB
(Faustus to the Apparition of Helen.) ReTS
(Helen.) BCEP; GTBS-W; LiTB; LiTG; WHA
(Helen of Troy.) CoEV; EV-1; LiA
Doctor Faustus was a good man. Mother Goose. GaP; OTPC (1946 ed.)
Doctor Fell. Thomas Brown. *See* I Do Not Love Thee, Doctor Fell.
Doctor fell in a deep well, A. *Unknown.* GoTP
Doctor Foster is a good man. *Unknown.* OxNR
Doctor Foster went to Gloucester [*or* Glos'ter]. Mother Goose. BoChLi; OxBoLi; OxNR; PCH; RIS; SiTL
Doctor Hilaire, *sel.* William Henry Drummond.
"Stranger might say it he see heem drink till he almos' fall, A." PoP
Dr. John Goodfellow—Office Upstairs. James Ball Naylor. DDA
Doctor Johnson. Blake. *Fr.* An Island in the Moon. RO
Dr. Johnson's Picture Cow. Edgar A. Guest. OnHT
Dr. Levett. Samuel Johnson. *See* On the Death of Mr. Robert Levet, a Practiser in Physic.
Doctor Meyers. Edgar Lee Masters. *Fr.* Spoon River Anthology. ChMo; CMP
Doctor of Billiards. E. A. Robinson. TwP
Doctor punched my vein, The. Scyros. Karl Shapiro. HoPM; LiTA; LiTM; MoVE; NePA; SeCeV; WaP
Dr. Syntax in Search of the Picturesque, *sel.* William Combe.
In Search of the Picturesque. OBRV
Dr. Unlikely, we love you so. Horror Movie. Howard Moss. SiTL
Doctors. *Unknown, tr. fr. German.* PIAE
Doctor's Dream, The, *sel.* William Snowden Battles.
"I had a dream, and in that dream." PoP
Doctor's Life, The, *sel.* Isaac N. Himes.
"Slowly, slowly, slowly we oxidize!" PoP
Doctors must die, too; all their knowledge of. Les Savants Ne Sont Pas Curieux. Merrill Moore. PoP
Doctor's Story, The. Will Carleton. BLPA
Doctrinal Point. William Empson. AtBAP
Doctrine. Heine, *tr. fr. German by* Lola Gruenthal. AnGP
Doctrine has wound of lovers' limbs. Chalk from Eden. Howard Moss. NePA
Documented union of these hands, The. The Wedding Ring. Donald F. Drummond. PtPa
Dodger, The, *with music. Unknown.* OuSiCo
Dodo, The. Hilaire Belloc. ChTr; LiL
Dodoism. W. J. Courthope. *Fr.* The Paradise of Birds. OtMeF
Dodona's Oaks Were Still. Patrick MacDonogh. NeIP
Doe, doe!/ I shall dever see her bore! Lay of the Deserted Influenzaed. Henry Cholmondeley-Pennell. BOHV; InMe
Doe you not wonder at the strange rare sound. *Unknown.* SeCSL
Doeg, though without knowing how or why. Dryden. *Fr.* Absalom and Achitophel, Pt. II. PoEL-3
Does a tear fall from the eye. Tragedy. Howard Moss. NePoEA
Does every proud and selfe-affecting dame. Cyril Tourneur. *Fr.* The Revenger's Tragedy. PoD
Does It Matter? Siegfried Sassoon. BMEP; HiLiEn; MBP; MoBrPo; NeMA; NP; PoeMoYo; SoV; WaP; YT
Does no one see that in your wood. Boy. Winifred Welles. NP
Does the eagle know what is in the pit? Thel's Motto. Blake. *Fr.* The Book of Thel. ChTr; LO
Does the elephant remember. Circus Elephant. Kathryn Worth. BrR
Does the heart grieve on. The Heart Recalcitrant. Leonora Speyer. PG
Does the Pearl Know? Helen Hay Whitney. AA
Does the road wind up-hill all the way? Up-Hill. Christina Rossetti. BLP; BLPA; BMEP; BrBE; CaAE; CBOV; CH; CoBE; EG; EmBrPo; EnLi-2; EV-5; FaBoBe; GTBS; HBV; LEAP; LoBV; LPS-2; MaRV; MCCG; NeHB; NLK; OAEP; OBEV; OBVV; OQP; OtMeF; OTPC (1946 ed.); PCD; Po; PoFS; PoMa; PoRA; POTT; PoVP; PreP; QP-1; ShBV-2; TCEP; TOP; TreFS; TrGrPo; TSW; TSWC; TyEnPo; VA; ViBoPo; ViP; ViPo; VLEP; WGRP; WHA
Does your heart go back to Galway, to The Blazers and stone walls. Blue Peter. Stanislaus Lynch. OnYI
Doesn't thou 'ear my 'erse's legs, as they canters awaäy? *See* Dosn't thou 'ear . . .
Dog, The. W. H. Davies. AlBD; MBP; MoBrPo
Dog, The ("I like a dog at my feet when I read"). Edgar A. Guest. AlBD
Dog, A ("Tis pity not to have a dog"). Edgar A. Guest. AlBD
Dog, The (As Seen by the Cat). Oliver Herford. AlBD; RIS
Dog, The. Valentin Iremonger. NeIP
Dog, The. Don Marquis. AlBD; PoeMoYo
Dog. Harold Monro. MBP; MoBrPo; TCEP
(Dogs.) GoTP
Dog. John Crowe Ransom. LiTA
Dog, The. *Unknown.* AlBD; WBLP
Dog Abandoned. Inez Clark Thorson. AlBD
Dog and a cat went out together, A. Mother Goose. PCH; SAS
Dog and the Cat, and the Duck and the Rat, The. Eliza Lee Follen. CIV
Dog and the Water-Lily, The. William Cowper. AlBD; CG; EV-3; OAEP
Dog Argos, The. Homer. *See* Ulysses and His Dog.
Dog Asleep. Margaret Mackprang Mackay. AlBD
Dog at Night. Louis Untermeyer. AlBD; GoTP; PoeMoYo; StaSt
Dog at the Schoolhouse Door. Goldie Capers Smith. AlBD
Dog barked, The; then the woman stood in the doorway. Roan Stallion. Robinson Jeffers. AmPP (4th ed.); BeLS; CoV; NAMP
Dog Barks, The. *Unknown.* RIS
Dog beneath the cherry-tree, The. The Ambiguous Dog. Arthur Guiterman. AlBD; PoMa
Dog beneath the Skin, The, *sel.* W. H. Auden.
"You with shooting-sticks." NAMP
Dog Day, A. Rachel Field. SiSoSe
Dog, Dog in My Manger. George Barker. LiTM
Dog Fiend, The. Frederick Marryat. *See* Snarleyyow, or, The Dog Fiend.
Dog fox rolls on his lolling tongue, The. The Hunt. Louis Kent. WaKn
Dog growing thinner, for want of a dinner, A. The Dog of Reflection. Jeffreys Taylor. OTPC
Dog in a Car. David McCord. AlBD
Dog in Chair. Margaret Mackprang Mackay. AlBD
Dog in the River, The. Phaedrus, *tr. fr. Latin by* Christopher Smart. AWP; JAWP; OnPM; WBP
Dog is black or white or brown, The. The Dog (As Seen by the Cat). Oliver Herford. AlBD; RIS
Dog is man's best friend, The. An Introduction to Dogs. Ogden Nash. AlBD; GoTP; MoShBr
Dog—Lost, A. Helen Brosi McLeod. AlBD
Dog lying near lifted his head and ears, A. Homer. *Fr.* The Odyssey, XVII. GrPo
Dog means dog. Blum. Dorothy Aldis. MoShBr
Dog Meets Cat. Margaret Mackprang Mackay. AlBD
Dog Named Ego [the Snowflakes as Kisses], A. Delmore Schwartz. The Repetitive Heart, X. AmP; LiTA; LiTM; MiAP
Dog of Reflection, The. Jeffreys Taylor. OTPC
Dog over Snow. Marion Strobel. NP

Dog Parade, The. Arthur Guiterman. AlBD
Dog Salesman, The. J. Harvey Haggard. AlBD
Dog Star now, negating all desires, The. Quatrains. John Heath-Stubbs. PoN
Dog That Howls at Night, The. Herbert J. Bryce. AlBD
Dog that is beat has a right to complain, The. On Sir Henry Clinton's Recall. *Unknown.* PAH
Dog that spoke, a monster born of sheep, A. Mongolian Idiot. Karl Shapiro. FiMAP
Dog Wanted. Margaret Mackprang Mackay. AlBD
Dog was there, outside her door, The. The Dog. W. H. Davies. AlBD; MBP; MoBrPo
Dog Who Ate a Pond Lily. Winifred Welles. NP
Dog will come when he is called, The. Beasts, Birds, and Fishes. Adelaide O'Keeffe. OTPC (1923 ed.)
Dog will often steal a bone, A. The Cat's Conscience. E. V. Lucas. The Nature of the Cat, IV. CIV
Dog will roll, and wag his tail, and fawn, The. Dignity. Bhartrihari. OnPM
Doggedly,/ Inch by bitter inch. Withdrawal from Crete. Audrey Alexandra Brown. NeTW
"Doggerel," he thought, "will do for churchwardens." Shakespeare's Grave. Robinson Jeffers. TriL
Doggies went to the mill, The. *Unknown.* BoTP; OxNR
Dogie Song. *Unknown.* CoSo; CSF
Dogrose. Patric Stevenson. NeIP
Dogs. Harold Monro. *See* Dog.
Dogs. Pope. *See* Epigram: "I am his Highness' dog at Kew."
Dogs and Dogs. *Unknown.* AlBD
Dogs and Weather. Winifred Welles. FaPON; StVeCh; TiPo
Dogs at the Homestead, The. Theocritus, *tr. fr. Greek by* Charles Stuart Calverley. *Fr.* Idylls. OxBG
Dogs barking, dust awhirling. Hail and Farewell. Anne Higginson Spicer. HBMV
Dog's Cold Nose, The. Arthur Guiterman. AlBD; StPo; TiPo (1959 ed.)
Dog's Death, A. J. C. Squire. TCEP
Dog's Eye View, A. Amelia Josephine Burr. AlBD
Dog's Howl, A. Lowe W. Wren. AlBD
Dog's Life, A. "Casual." AlBD
Dog's Life. A. Lew Sarett. AlBD
Dog's Life, A. Milly Walton. AlBD
Dogs of Bethlehem, The. Katharine Lee Bates. AlBD; ChrBoLe; CV
Dogs on a summer night. Serenade. Burges Johnson. AlBD
Dogs perceived their coming, yet far off, The. The Dogs at the Homestead. Theocritus. *Fr.* Idylls. OxBG
Dog's Vigil, A. Margaret E. Bruner. AlBD; PoToHe
Dogwood Blossoms. George Marion McClellan. BANP
Dogwood flakes. Variations Done for Gerald van de Wiele. Charles Olson. NeAP
Dogwood tree was once as broad, The. The Legend of the Dogwood Tree. Geraldine Farrar. StJW
Doing, a filthy pleasure is, and short. Keeping Endless Holiday [*or* Foeda Est in Coitu]. Petronius Arbiter, *tr. by* Ben Jonson LiA; LiTW
Doing Railroads for *The Rocky Mountain News.* Cy Warman. PoOW
Dolcino to Margaret. Charles Kingsley. HBV; LPS-1; PIR; PoVP
(Hey Nonny!) OBVV
Dole of the King's Daughter, The. *Unknown, tr. fr. French by* Oscar Wilde. AWP
Dolefull Passion, A. Nicholas Breton. CaAE
Doll ev'ry day had walk'd these treach'rous roads. Death at the Thames Ice Fair. John Gay. *Fr.* Trivia. BeR
Doll in the doll-maker's house, A. The Dolls. W. B. Yeats. TwHP
Dolladine. William Brighty Rands. PRWS
Dollar a day is a sailor's pay, A. Leave Her Johnny (C vers.) *Unknown.* SoAmSa
Dollar and a Half a Day, A, *with music. Unknown.* TrAS
Dollar Bill. John Frederick Nims. MiAP
Dollie, the night has come. A Lullaby. Louis C. Elson. BOL
Dolls, The. Frederic Prokosch. LiTM (1946 ed.)
Dolls, The. W. B. Yeats. TwHP
Doll's Cradle-Song. *Unknown, tr. fr. German.* BOL
Dolls' faces are rosier but these were children. Bombing Casualties in Spain. Sir Herbert Read. FaBoTw
Doll's House, The. Anna Letitia Barbauld. OTPC (1923 ed.)
Doll's Song. "Lewis Carroll." OTPC (1946 ed.)
Doll's Wooing, The. Eugene Field. RIS
Dolly's Dogs. "Lewis Carroll." BoN
Dolly's Lullaby. Juliana Horatia Ewing. BOL
Dolly's Lullaby. Mariana Griswold Van Rensselaer. BOL
Dolmens, The. Gonzalo Escudero, *tr. fr. Spanish by* Dudley Fitts. AnCL
Dolor. Theodore Roethke. AmP; CoBMV; FiMAP; MoVE
Dolor Oogo. Sir Arthur Quiller-Couch. SG
Doloras, *sels.* Ramón de Campoamor, *tr. fr. Spanish.*
After Twenty Years, *tr. by* J. D. M. Ford. AnSpL-2
Boredom. AnSpL-2, *tr. by* J. D. M. Ford; OnPM, *tr. by* Beatrice Gilman Proske
Great Banquet, The, *tr. by* J. D. M. Ford. AnSpL-2
If Only I Could Write! *tr. by* Ida Farnell. AnSpL-2
Dolores. Swinburne. EmBrPo; POTT, *abr.*; PoVP; ViPo; VLEP, *abr.*
Dolphin and Seal. Oppian, *tr. fr. Greek by* F. L. Lucas. *Fr.* Halieuticks. GrPE
Dolphins, The. Hamish Maclaren. EtS
Dolphins. Molly Michaels. RIS
Dolphin's Death, The. Oppian, *tr. fr. Greek by* F. L. Lucas. *Fr.* Halieuticks. GrPE
Dolphins in Blue Water. Amy Lowell. LaNeLa; TSW; TSWC
Dolphin's Tomb, The. Anyte, *tr. fr. Greek by* F. L. Lucas. GrPE
Dom Pedro, The, *with music. Unknown.* SoAmSa
Dombashawa. Peter Jackson. BoSA
Dome of Sunday, The [*or* A]. Karl Shapiro. CoBMV; LiTM; MoAB; MoAmPo (1950 ed.); MoPo; NePA; OxBA; WaP
Dome of the capitol looks to the Potomac river, The. Smoke Rose Gold. Carl Sandburg. NeMA; VOD; YT
Domed with the azure of heaven. Vapour and Blue. Wilfred Campbell. CaP; OCL
Domenic Darragh walked the land. The Mountainy Childer. Elizabeth Shane. HBMV
Domestic Asides; or, Truth in Parentheses. Thomas Hood. EnRP; ERP
Domestic Birds. James Thomson. *Fr.* The Seasons: Spring. BCEP; LPS-2
Domestic Didactics by an Old Servant. Thomas Hood. OBRV
Domestic Economy. Anna Wickham. BLV; NeMA
Domestic Scene. Theocritus, *tr. fr. Greek by* Henry Harmon Chamberlin. *Fr.* Idylls. GrR
Domestic Scenes. Miguel de Unamuno, *tr. fr. Spanish by* Thomas Walsh.
"Go, stir the brazier coals, my child." LiTW; WoL
(Brazier Coals, The.) OnPM
"Look not upon me with such eyes, my son." LiTW; WoL
"When shades of night have come." WoL
Domestic Science. *Unknown.* WBLP
Domicile of John, The. *Unknown, sometimes at. to* Pope. InMe; PA
(Modern House That Jack Built, The.) LPS-3
Domination of Black. Wallace Stevens. AmPP; AnFE; CoBMV; CoAnAm; MAP; MAPA; MoAB; MoAmPo; OxBA; TwAmPo
Domine, Cui Sunt Pleiades Curae. Sir Charles G. D. Roberts. *See* Child's Prayer at Evening, A.
Domine, Dirige Nos. E. H. W. Meyerstein. NeTW
Domine Jesu! John Duffy. JKCP (1955 ed.)
Domine Quid Multiplicati Sunt. Psalms, III, Bible, *O.T., tr. by* Thomas Sternhold. SiCE
Domine, Quo Vadis? *Unknown.* ACP; CAW
Domine, Quo Vadis? Sir William Watson. WGRP
Dominic came riding down, sworded, straight and splendid. The Lovers of Marchaid. Marjorie Pickthall. HBV
Dominie's daughter eloped with a suitor, The. A Question of Gender. Palladas. OxBG
Dominion of Australia, The (a Forecast, 1877). Brunton Stephens. BoAu; VA
Do mi nus,/ Help now, sweet Jesus! A Dirge for Phyllip Sparowe. John Skelton. *Fr.* Phyllyp Sparrowe. EPP
Dominus Illuminatio Mea. Richard Doddridge Blackmore. MaRV; OBEV; OBVV; TreFS
(At the Last.) TriL
(In the Hour of Death.) OQP; OP-1
Domungoirt! lump of a skewered gosling. *Unknown. Fr.* Abusive Snatches. SiB
Don. James T. Fields. AlBD
Don Carlos, *sel.* Schiller, *tr. fr. German by* R. D. Boylan.
"I understood thy hint, and thank thee for it," *fr.* I, ix. BoFr
Don Durk of Dowdee. Mildred Plew Meigs. *See* Pirate Don Durk of Dowdee.
Don Giovanni, *sel.* Lorenzo da Ponte, *tr. fr. Italian by* Natalie MacFarren.
"Giovinette, che fate all' amore." TrJP
Don Juan, *sels.* Byron.
"Alas! the love of women! it is known," *fr.* II. CoBE
(Love of Women, The.) BCEP
At Thirty Years, *fr.* I. FiP
(Labuntur Anni, *longer sel.*) BPN
Ave Maria, *fr.* III. ERP; ISi; MCCG
(Devotion.) GEPC
Canto I. ERP; OAEP, *sels.*, PreP, *sel.*
("I want a hero: an uncommon want.") EnL, *abr.*; EnLit, *sel.*; EnRP; Po, *sel.*
Canto II. EmBrPo; ERP; GEPC
Canto III. EnLi-2, *sels.*; OAEP, *sels.*; REAL
Canto IV. BEL, *abr.*; CoBE, *abr.*; EM-2, *abr.*; OAEP, *sel.*
Canto XI, *sels.* OAEP

Don Juan (*continued*)
Contemporary Poets, *fr.* XI. OBRV
Daniel Boone, *fr.* VIII. LPS-3
Death of Haidee, The, *fr.* IV. FiP; WHA, *longer sel.*
Dedication: "Bob Southey! You're a poet—Poet-laureate." BEL; BoLiVe; BPN; EnLi-2 (1949 ed.); EnLit; EnRP; ERP; EV-4; InP, 4 *sts.;* OAEP, 5 *sts.;* PoFS; PtP, *abr.*
(Dedication to the Poet Laureate, *abr.*) FiP
(Invocation.) LoBV
(Southey and Wordsworth.) TrGrPo
Disillusion, *fr.* I *and* IV. GEPC
(My Days of Love Are Over.) FaBoEn
Don Juan and Haidee, *fr.* II *and* IV. TOP
(Haidee, *fr.* II.) BPN
Don Juan's Education, *fr.* I. WHA
Donna Julia, *fr.* I. PoEL-4
Evening, *after* Sappho, *fr.* III. BLV; BoLiVe; LPS-2; OTPC; TrGrPo
(Hesperus.) CBOV; OnPM, 1 *st.*
(Hesperus the Bringer.) AWP; JAWP; OuHeWo; WBP
(Hymn to Hesperus.) TOP
Fame, *fr.* I *and* III. GEPC
"For me, I know nought," *fr.* XIV. OBRV
"Fourth day came, but not a breath of air, The," *fr.* II. ChER
Fragment: "I would to heaven that I were so much clay," *on the back of poet's MS of* I. ERP; FiP; OAEP
Gulbeyaz, *fr.* V. PoEL-4
Haidee ("One of the two, according to your choice"), *fr.* IV. SeCePo
His Politics, *fr.* IX. GEPC
"In the great world—which, being interpreted," *fr.* XI. OxBoLi
Isles of Greece, The, *fr.* III. AEV; AnFE; AWP; BCEP, *abr.;* BEL, *longer sel.;* BHV; BPN; BTP; ChTr; CoBE; EM-2, *longer sel.;* EmBrPo; EnLit; ERP; EV-4; FaBoEn; FiP; GEPC; HBV; InPo; LEAP; LiTB; OBEV; OBRV; OTPC, 3 *sts.;* PFE, *abr.;* PoFr; RiBV; SeCeV, *longer sel.;* TCEP, *longer sel.;* TOP; TreFS; TVSH; TwCrTr; ViBoPo; WHA; WP
(Glory That Was Greece, The.) CBPC; LH
(Isles of Greece: Ways of Poets, *longer sel.*) EPN
(Song of the Greek Bard.) LPS-2
(Song of the Greek Poet.) CBOV; PIR
"It was the cooling hour," *fr.* II. ViBoPo
(Haidee.) OBRV
(Juan and Haidee; Ways of Love.) EPN, *longer sel.;* MaPo
John Keats, *fr.* XI. BCEP
Juan in England *fr.* XI. FiP
Lady Adeline Amundeville, XIII. PoEL-4
Lake at Newstead, The, *fr.* XIII. GEPC
Lake Poets, The, *fr.* III. UnPo (1st ed.)
Lambro's Return, *fr.* III. OBRV
Learned Ladies, *fr.* IV. GEPC
Life ("Between two worlds life hovers like a star"), *fr.* XV. GEPC
London Literature and Society, *fr.* XI. BPN
London Town, *fr.* X. GEPC
Love and the Poets, *fr.* III. GEPC
"Man's love is of man's life a thing apart," *fr.* I. TreF
(Man's Love.) BCEP
"Mary," *fr.* V. GEPC
Money ("How beauteous are rouleaus!"), *fr.* XII. GEPC
Norman Abbey, *fr.* XIII. OBRV
"Nothing so difficult as a beginning," *fr.* IV. BPN; EnRP; PoFS
(Author's Purpose, The.) EPN
(Romantic to Burlesque, *shorter sel.*) FiP
"Oh ye! who teach the ingenuous youth of nations," *fr.* II. EnRP
"Old Lambro pass'd unseen a private gate," *fr.* III. EnRP
Poetical Commandments. *fr.* I. BPN; FiP; GEPC; OBRV
("If ever I should condescend to prose.") OxBoLi
(Poet's Credo.) SeCePo
Power of Money, The ("Why call the miser miserable?"), *fr.* XII. CoEV
Shipwreck, The, *fr.* II. BPN; LiA; MCCG, *much abr.;* OBRV; PoD, *much abr.;* TCEP, *longer sel.;* WHA
Siege of Ismail, The, VII *and* VIII, *abr.* WoL
"They tell me 'tis decided; you depart," *fr.* I. ViBoPo
(Julia's Letter.) EV-4
"Thus sung, or would, or could, or should have sung," *fr.* III. BPN
"Tis pleasing to be schooled in a strange tongue," *fr.* II. ViBoPo
'Tis Sweet [to Hear], *fr.* I. MaPo; MCCG; PIR; ViBoPo
(First Love.) LPS-1; OBRV
(Pleasant Things, *shorter sel.*) OTPC
Vanitas Vanitatum, *fr.* VII. GEPC
Wellington, *fr.* IX. GEPC; OBRV
("On, Wellington! or 'Villainton'—for fame.") FiP, *abr.;* OxBoLi
"When Juan woke he found some good things ready," *fr.* II. EnLit
"'Whom the gods love die young' was said of yore," *fr.* IV. EnLit
Don Juan. Callimachus, *tr. fr. Greek by* F. L. Lucas. GrPE
Don Juan. Lucius Harwood Foote. AA
Don Juan and Haidee. Byron. *Fr.* Don Juan, II *and* IV. TOP
(Haidee, *shorter sel., fr.* II.) BPN
Don Juan Declaims. James Elroy Flecker. OnPP
Don Juan had got out on Shooter's Hill. Juan in England. Byron. *Fr.* Don Juan, XI. FiP; OAEP
Don Juan has ever the grand old air. Don Juan. Lucius Harwood Foote. AA
Don Juan in Hell. Baudelaire, *tr. fr. French by* James Elroy Flecker. AWP; MiFP
Don Juan in Portugal. Florence Wilkinson Evans. TBM
Don Juan Muses. John Heath-Stubbs. MoPW
Don Juan's Address to the Sunset. Robert Nichols. AlDL; OBMV; POTE
Don Juan's Dream. Edward Davison. MuM
Don Juan's Education. Byron. *Fr.* Don Juan, I. WHA
Don' Let Yo' Watch Run Down, *with music. Unknown.* AS
Don Quixote. Craven Langstroth Betts. AA
Don Quixote. Austin Dobson. HBV; HBVY; PC
Don Quixote. Arthur Davison Ficke. HBMV; PoeMoYo
Don Quixote in England, *sels.* Henry Fielding.
A-Hunting We Will Go, *fr.* II. CBOV; HBV; LPS-2; OTPC (1923 ed.); ViBoPo
(Hunting Song.) CEP; OBEC; OxBoLi
(Song: A-Hunting We Will Go.) EV-3
Roast Beef of Old England, The, *fr.* I. CEP; LPS-2 (*with* 4 *add. sts. by* Richard Leveridge); OBEC
Don Sebastian, *br. sel.* Dryden.
Oak of State, The. BeR
Donal o' Dreams has no bed for his sleeping. The Fiddler. Edna Valentine Trapnell. HBMV
Donal Ogue. *Unknown. See* Donall Oge.
Donald. Henry Abbey. AA
Donald Caird. Sir Walter Scott. BSV
Donald, he's come to this town. Dugall Quin (B *vers.*). *Unknown.* ESPB
Donald Macdonald. James Hogg. PoFr
Donall Oge. *Unknown, tr. fr. Modern Irish by* Lady Gregory. DiM; GTIV
(Donal[l] Oge: Grief of a Girl's Heart, *longer vers., tr. by* Lady Gregory.) OnYI; OxBI
(Donal Ogue, *tr. by* Frank O'Connor.) KiLC
(Grief of a Girl's Heart, The, *tr. by* Lady Gregory.) ChTr
Done are the toils and the wearisome marches. Ode for Memorial Day. Paul Laurence Dunbar. MDAH
Done For. Rose Terry Cooke. AA
Done Foun' My Los' Sheep, *with music. Unknown.* BoAN-1
Done Is a Battle on the Dragon Black. William Dunbar. *See* Of the Resurrection of Christ.
Done is the work that saves! The Work That Saves! Horatius Bonar. BePJ
Done to death by slanderous tongues. Hero's Epitaph. Shakespeare. *Fr.* Much Ado about Nothing, V, iii. OBSC; TriL
Doney Gal, *with music. Unknown.* CoSo; OuSiCo
Dong with a Luminous Nose, The. Edward Lear. CenHV; ChTr; KN; LBN; PoEL-5; PoMS; SiTL; TOP
Donkey, The. G. K. Chesterton. ACP (1952 ed.); BLV; BMEP; CaAE; CBOV; GoBC; GTBS-D; MaRV; MBP; MM; MoBrPo; NeHB; NeMA; OBEV (new ed.); PIAE; PoMa; PoRL; POT; POTE; PoTo; QS; ShBV-1; StaSt; StJW; TCEP; TCPD; TOP; TwCV; WGRP; WP
"Tattered outlaw, The," *sel.* HBVY
Donkey, The. Rose Fyleman. BoTP
Donkey, A/ ascending a mountain. Proletarians. Luis Muñoz Marín. AnCL
Donkey, Donkey, do not bray. *Unknown.* OxNR
Donna Julia. Byron. *Fr.* Don Juan, I. PoEL-4
Donne, the delight of Phoebus, and each Muse. To John Donne. Ben Jonson. MaPo; OAEP; OBS; PtP; ReEn; SeCV-1; SeEP
Donnybrook Jig, The. Charles O'Flaherty. *See* Humours of Donnybrook Fair, The.
Donovans, The. Francis A. Fahy. TIP
Don't. James Jeffrey Roche. HBV
Don't Be Foolish Pray. *Unknown.* CoMu
Don't Be Sorrowful, Darling. Rembrandt Peale. HBV
(Faith and Hope.) LPS-1
"Don't Care" and "Never Mind" ("'Don't care' is no friend of mine"). John Kendrick Bangs. FaFP
Don't Cut the String. George David Stewart. PoP
Don't forget the crablike. The Hands. Denise Levertov. NeAP
Don't Give Up. Phoebe Cary. PCH; PTA-1
Don't Give Up. *Unknown.* FaFP; PoToHe (new ed.)

Don't give up hoping when the ship goes down. Hang to Your Grit! Louis E. Thayer. *Fr.* Keep Your Grit. WBLP
Don't Go In. Mrs. M. A. Kidder. PreP
Don't grow old too fast, my sweet! Mother's Song. *Unknown.* BOL
Don't Grow Weary, Boys. *Unknown.* CoSo
Don't Guess, Let Me Tell You. Ogden Nash. SiTL
Don't Kill the Birds. Daniel Clement Colesworthy. PTA-1
Don't Look Now but Mary Is Everybody. Peter Viereck. LiTA; LiTM (rev. ed.); ReMP
Don't neglect the quiet hour. Communion. J. L. Spicer. BLRP
Don't pay me for singing. Cantaliso in a Bar. Nicolás Guillén. AnCL
"Don't pick all the flowers!" cried Daisy one day. Meadow Talk. Nora Archibald Smith. PPL
Don't pull off my boots and pull off my hat. The Dying Desperado. *Unknown.* CoSo
Don't Quit. *Unknown.* BLPA
(You Mustn't Quit.) PoToHe
Don't Say You Like Tchaikowsky. Paul Rosner. FiBHP
Don't seek me where the myrtles bloom! My Camping Ground. Morris Rosenfeld. TrJP
Don't send my boy where your girl can't go. Sin Is Sin. *Unknown.* BLP
Don't shirk. Good Advice [*or* Old German Mottos *or* Proverbs]. *Unknown, ad. by* Louis Untermeyer. RIS; StaSt; TiPo (1952 ed.)
Don't stand at night by the gate, love. War Poem. Henry Treece. MaRV
Don't take on so, Hiram. Always Right. Eugene Field. TCAP
Don't Talk about It, *with music. Unknown.* OuSiCo
Don't talk of birth and family; all those. Menander, *tr. fr. Greek by* F. A. Paley. GrPo
Don't Tell All You Know. *Unknown.* PCH
Don't tell your friends about your indigestion. Of Tact [*or* How Are You?]. Arthur Guiterman. MoShBr; WhC
Don't throw your arms around me in that way. Footnote to John II: 4. R. A. K. Mason. AnNZ
"Don't touch. Fresh paint," the notice said. Do Not Touch. Boris Pasternak. BoRS
Don't Trouble Trouble. Mark Guy Pearse. MaRV; WBLP
Don't worry about growing old. Prayerwheel 2. David Meltzer. NeAP
Don't you hear the big spurs jingle? The Dance at Silver Valley. William Maxwell. SCC
Don't you hear the tramp of soldiers? One beneath Old Glory. *Unknown.* MDAH
Don't You Hurry Worry with Me, *with music. Unknown.* OuSiCo
Don't You Like It? *with music. Unknown.* OuSiCo
Don't [*or* Oh! don't] you remember sweet Alice, Ben Bolt. Ben Bolt. Thomas Dunn English. AA; FaBoBe; FaFP; HBV; LEAP; OBAV; OlF; TreF
"Don't you take no sail off 'er," the Ol' Man said. What the Old Man Said. Cicely Fox Smith. EtS
Don't you think it's probable. Little Talk. Aileen Fisher. FaPON
Don't you think the trees remember. Ambition. Anne Blackwell Payne. GFA
Don't you trouble trouble till trouble troubles you. Don't Trouble Trouble. Mark Guy Pearse. MaRV; WBLP
Don'tcha worry, honey chile. On Limited Warfare. *Unknown.* SiTL
Don'ts. D. H. Lawrence. LiTB; LiTM; OxBoLi
Donzella and the *Ceylon,* The, *with music. At. to* Daniel Smith. ShS
Doodledy, doodledy, doodledy, dan. *Unknown.* OxNR
Doom. Arthur O'Shaughnessy. MBP; MoBrPo (1942 ed.); OBVV
Doom-Bar, The. Alice E. Gillington. ReTS; VA
Doom-devoted. Louis Golding. HBMV
Doom in Bloom. Laura Riding. MoP
Doom Is Dark [and Deeper than Any Sea-Dingle]. W. H. Auden. ChMo; EnL; LiTB; ReaPo; TwCV; UnPo
(Chorus from a Play.) MBP; MoAB; MoBrPo
(Something Is Bound to Happen.) CoBMV; EnLit; OAEP (2d ed.); PoRA
Doom of Beauty, The. Michelangelo, *tr. fr. Italian by* John Addington Symonds. AWP; JAWP; LiTW; WBP
Doom of Devorgoil, The, *sels.* Sir Walter Scott.
Bonny Dundee, *fr.* II, ii. BEL; BHV; BPN; EBSV; EmBrPo; EnRP; ERP; EV-4; FaBoCh; HBV; LH; LoGBV; OBRV; OxBoLi; SeCeV; TCEP; TOP
(Bonnie Dundee.) OTPC (1923 ed.)
Song: When Friends Are Met o'er Merry Cheer, *fr.* II, ii. EmBrPo
Sun upon the Lake Is Low, The, I. EBSV
(Datur Hora Quieti.) GTBS; GTBS-D; GTBS-W; GTSE; GTSL
(Leonard: "Sun upon the lake is low, The.") EmBrPo
Doom of Hippolytus, The. Euripides, *tr. fr. Greek by* C. M. Bowra. *Fr.* Hippolytus. OxBG
Doom of the Titans, The. Hesiod, *tr. fr. Greek by* Arthur S. Way. *Fr.* Theogony. GrR
Doomed. *Unknown.* CIV
Doomed. Kostas Varnalis, *tr. fr. Modern Greek by* Rae Dalven. MoGP
Doomed as we are our native dust. Composed in One of the Catholic Cantons. Wordsworth. BPN
Doomed City, The. Poe. *See* City in the Sea, The.
Doomed in the depths to dwell. Thanksgiving. David Abenatar Melo. TrJP
Doomed Man, The. Joseph Addison Alexander. *Fr.* The Hidden Line. MaRV
Doomed to death bodies opposed in defiance. To the Dead of the Revolution. Ernst Toller. PoFr
Dooms-Day. George Herbert. NBE; SeCV-1
Doomsday. Elinor Wylie. CrMA
Doomsday Morning. Genevieve Taggard. MAP; MoAmPo
Dooms-Day [*or* Doomsday] Thought, A. Thomas Flatman. CEP
Hillocks of Mortality, *sel.* BeR
Door, The. Robert Creeley. NeAP
Door, The. Mary Carolyn Davies. HBMV; PC
Door, The. Robert Graves. LiTB
Door, The. Orrick Johns. LoPS; NP; TBM
Door, The. Leonard A. G. Strong. MBP; MoBrPo
Door and the Window, The. Henry Reed. NeBP
Door and Window Bolted Fast. Mani Leib, *tr. fr. Yiddish by* Joseph Leftwich. TrJP
Door at the End of Our Garden, The. Frederic E. Weatherly. OTPC (1946 ed.)
Door Between, The. Mary Ferguson Legler. UnW
Door can open, The/ the dog's howl can come in. Passage to the End. Eduardo Anguita. AnCL
Door closed against the splinters. Old Seawoman. Gordon LeClaire. CaP
Door creaks in the house, A. Outside the window. Scenario. D. S. Savage. NeBP
Door is locked, no foot is on the stair, The. Presence. Edith Willis Linn. UnW
Door is on the latch to-night, The. The Romance of a Christmas Card [*or* Christmas Eve]. Kate Douglas Wiggin. MaRV; OQP; QP-2
"Door is shut fast, The." Who's In? Elizabeth Fleming. BoTP; BrR; MoSiPe
Door-Mats. Mary Carolyn Davies. BAP; BPP; HBMV; YaD
Door of Death, The. Blake. *Fr.* Dedication of the Illustrations to Blair's "Grave." ChTr
(To the Queen.) EnRP
Door of Heaven is on the latch, The. All Souls. Katharine Tynan. BMEP; MBP
Door of Heaven open seemed, The. The Apple Tree. *Unknown.* ArmLP
Door of the temple is opposite to a door of the temple, A. A Small Girl. *Unknown.* ChLP
Door still swinging to, and girls revive, The. A Dream of Fair Women. Kingsley Amis. PoLFOT; PoN
Door was bolted and the windows of my porch, The. The Milkman. Isabella Gardner. NePA
Door was shut, as doors should be, The. Jack Frost. "Gabriel Setoun." BoTP; DD; GFA; HBV; HBVY; MPB; OnHT; OTPC; RAR
Door-Bell, The. Charlotte Becker. PoToHe (new ed.)
Doorbells. Rachel Field. FaPON; GaP; SteVCh (1955 ed.); TiPo
Doors. Hermann Hagedorn. AnAmPo; BAP; CBOV; LA; OBAV; PFY; SBMV
Doors, The. Lloyd Mifflin. AA; LEAP
Doors are shut, the windows fast, The. Canadian Folk Song. Wilfred Campbell. PCH; VA
Doors flapped open in Ulysses' house, The. The Return. Edwin Muir. MoPW
Doors in the Temple, The, *abr.* William Watson, *sometimes at. to* George Mathesen. OQP; QP-1
Doors of the Temple. Aldous Huxley. HBMV; QS
Doors that knew no shrill alarming bell, The. James Thomson. *Fr.* The Castle of Indolence. ViBoPo
Doors were cedar, The. Four Preludes on Playthings of the Wind, II. Carl Sandburg. AnAmPo; AnFE; BLV; CoBA; InP; LA; MAP; MoAB; MoAmPo; NePA; NP; SeCeV
Doors, where my heart was used to beat. In Memoriam A. H. H., CXIX. Tennyson. EmBrPo; EPN; GEPC; PoEL-5; ViPo; VLEP
Doorstep, The. Edmund Clarence Stedman. HBV; LHV; PR
Dora. Thomas Edward Brown. MBP; MotAn; OBEV (1st ed.); POTT; PoVP; ReaPo
Dora. Tennyson. BPN; CG; GEPC; PFE; VLEP
Dora Markus. Eugenio Montale, *tr. fr. Italian by* Maurice English. OnHM
Dora versus Rose. Austin Dobson. ALV; BOHV

Doralicia's Song. Robert Greene. *See* In Time We See That Silver Drops.
Doran's Ass. *Unknown.* OnYI
Dorcas. George Macdonald. OBVV
Dorchester Giant, The. Oliver Wendell Holmes. FaPON; MPB
Δώρια (Doria). Ezra Pound. LEAP; MAP; MoAB; MoAmPo; MoVE; NP; TBM; ViBoPo
Doric Reed, A, *sel.* Zitella Cocke.
  Greek Mother's Lullaby: "Sleep, my child, no care can cumber." BOL
Doricha. Poseidippus, *tr. fr. Greek by* E. A. Robinson. AWP; JAWP; WBP
  (For Doricha the Courtesan, *tr. by* J. M. Edmonds.) GrR
  (Variations of Greek Themes—V, *tr. by* E. A. Robinson.) MOAP
Doricha, 'tis but bone they now adorn. For Doricha the Courtesan. Poseidippus, *tr. by* J. M. Edmonds. GrR
Dorinda. Charles Sackville. *See* Song: "Dorinda's sparkling wit, and eyes."
Doris. Clarence S. Harper. CAG
Doris; a Pastoral. Arthur Joseph Munby. HBV; VA
Doris, see the amorous flame. *Unknown.* SeCSL
Dorlan's Home-Walk. Arthur Guiterman. PFE
Dormi, Jesu, mater ridet. Latin Lullaby. *Unknown.* CAW
Dormouse, The. Charlotte Druitt Cole. BoTP
Dormouse and the Doctor, The. A. A. Milne. WhC
Dormouse felt so sleepy, The. The Dormouse. Charlotte Druitt Cole. BoTP
Doron's Description of Samela. Robert Greene. *Fr.* Menaphon. AtBAP; ElSeCe; EV-1; LoBV; PoEL-2; ReIE; SiCE; TuPP
  (Samela.) ElL; HBV; OBEV; OBSC; ViBoPo
Doron's Jig [*or* Jigge]. Robert Greene. *Fr.* Menaphon. AtBAP; ElSeCe; PoEL-2; TuPP
  (Jig, A.) ElL
Dorothea. Sarah N. Cleghorn. HBMV
Dorothy. Alfred Kreymborg. AnAmPo; LA
  Her Body.
  Her Eyes.
  Her Hair.
  Her Hands.
Dorothy. Rose Hawthorne Lathrop. AA
Dorothy; a Country Story, *sels.* Arthur Joseph Munby. VA
  Beauty at the Plough.
  Country Kisses.
  Dorothy.
  Dorothy's Room.
Dorothy goes with her pails to the ancient well in the court-yard. Dorothy. Arthur Joseph Munby. *Fr.* Dorothy; a Country Story. VA
Dorothy in the Garret. John Townsend Trowbridge. LPS-1
Dorothy Q. Oliver Wendell Holmes. AA; AmPP (3d ed.); AnNE; APW; CoBA; DDA; HBV; HiLiAm; IAP; InMe; OBAV; OnPP; TCAP; TreFS
Dorothy's Room. Arthur Joseph Munby. *Fr.* Dorothy; a Country Story. VA
Dorus His Comparisons. Sir Philip Sidney. *See* My Sheep Are Thoughts.
Dorus's Song. Sir Philip Sidney. *See* O Sweet Woods.
Dose of Calomel, A. *Unknown.* *See* Calomel.
Dosn't [*or* Doesn't] thou 'ear my 'erse's legs, as they canters awaäy? Northern Farmer: New Style. Tennyson. BLP; BOHV; BoLiVe; BPN; EM-2; EmBrPo; EPN; EV-5; PoVP; ShBV-4; ViPo; VLEP
Dost ask (my dear) what service I will have? Robert Burton, *after the Latin of* Terence. *Fr.* The Anatomy of Melancholy. LO
Dost deem him weak that owns his strength is tried? The Strong. John Vance Cheney. AA; OBAV
Dost see how like the hyacinth is his hair. Daphnis. Longus. *Fr.* Daphnis and Chloe. LiA
Dost see how unregarded now. Sonnet. Sir John Suckling. ElSeCe; NBE
Dost thou deem that thyself. "Te Judice." Frederick George Scott. PeCV
Dost thou in conscience think—tell me, Emilia. Shakespeare. *Fr.* Othello, IV, iii. MyFE
Dost thou look back on what hath been. In Memoriam A. H. H., LXIV. Tennyson. BHV; BPN; EM-2; EmBrPo; EPN; GEPC; ViPo; VLEP
Dost thou not hear? Amid dun, lonely hills. An Aeolian Harp. "Michael Field." VA
Dost Thou not see about our feet. Edgar Lee Masters. *Fr.* Supplication. MaRV
Dost thou remember, friend of vanished days. In Tuscany. Eric Mackay. VA
Dost Thou Remember Me? Emily Dickinson. *See* Saviour, I've no one else to tell.
Dost thou still hope thou shalt be fair. The Fair Inconstant. Francis Thompson. GTSE
Dost thou weep, mourning mother. The Mourning Mother. Elizabeth Barrett Browning. MOAH
Dostoievsky to a Young Communist. Daniel J. Honan. JKCP (1955 ed.)
Doth it not thrill thee, Poet. The Passionate Reader to His Poet. Richard Le Gallienne. HBV; VA
Doth love live in beauty's eyes? A Solemn Conceit. Nicholas Breton. SiCE
Doth Not a Tenarif, or Higher Hill. John Donne. *Fr.* An Anatomy of the World: The First Anniversary. ChTr
Doth not our chiefest bliss then lie. Chorus. Sidney Godolphin. LO
Doth some one say that there be gods above? There Are No Gods. Euripides. *Fr.* Bellerophon. OxBG
Doth Then the World Go Thus. William Drummond of Hawthornden. BSV; EV-2; GTBS; GTSL
  ("Doth then the world go thus, doth all thus move?") GTBS-D; GTBS-W; GTSE
Double Ballad of Good Counsel, A. Villon, *tr. fr. French by* Swinburne. AWP
Double Ballade of Life and Fate. W. E. Henley. PoVP
Double Ballade of Primitive Man. Andrew Lang *and* Edward Burnett Tylor. BOHV; CenHV
  (Ballade of Primitive Man, 3 *sts.*) ATP
Double-Bear Dances. Lew Sarett. Thunderdrums, II. TCPD
Double Crucifixion, The. John Malcolm Brinnin. LiTM (rev. ed.)
Double-Dealer, The, *sel.* Congreve.
  Ancient Phyllis. SeCL
Double Duty. W. E. Farbstein. WhC
Double Fortress, The. Alfred Noyes. GoBC
Double Life. Norman MacCaig. PoN
Double Marriage, The, *sel.* John Fletcher *and* Philip Massinger.
  "'Tis a substantial thing, and not a word," *fr.* V, i. PoFr
Double Red Daisies. Robert Graves. PCH
Double Ritual. Dachine Rainer. CrMA
Double Rock, The. Henry King. AtBAP; BoW; NBE
Double Sestine. Sir Philip Sidney. *Fr.* Arcadia. AtBAP; LiTB; PoEL-1
  (Sestina.) LiTG
  (Strephon and Klaius.) CoEV
  ("Ye goat-herd gods that love the grassy mountains.") SiCE
Double Shame, The. Stephen Spender. GTBS-W; LiTB; LiTL; LiTM (rev. ed.)
Double Star, A. David McCord. MAP
Double Vision, The. C. Day Lewis. AtBAP
Doubt. Elinor Chipp. HBMV
Doubt. Margaret Deland. MaRV; PraP; TrPWD
Doubt, The. Elizabeth I, Queen of England. *See* Doubt of Future Woes, The.
Doubt. Fernand Gregh. WGRP
Doubt. Helen Hunt Jackson. WGRP
Doubt. Robert Cameron Rogers. AA
Doubt. Sara Teasdale. ChMo; CMP; LO
Doubt. Tennyson. *See* In Memoriam A. H. H.: "You say, but with no touch of scorn."
Doubt. Wang Chin Chu, *tr. fr. Chinese by* Henry H. Hart. PoHN
Doubt and Prayer. Tennyson. EPN
Doubt me, my dim companion! Emily Dickinson. ViBoPo
Doubt no longer miracles. Miracles. Arna Bontemps. GoSl; PoNe
Doubt Not a Dream. Sophocles. *See* Dreams Come True.
Doubt of Future Foes, The. Elizabeth I, Queen of England. TuPP
  (Daughter of Debate, The.) LiBL, 1 *st.*; OBSC
  (Doubt, The.) LEAP
  ("Doubt of future foes exiles my present joy, The.") ReEn; SiCE
Doubt of Martyrdom, A. Sir John Suckling. BEL; EnLi-1; EPS; HBV; OBEV; TyEnPo
  (Actuality.) LoBV
  (Sonnet: "Oh! for some honest lover's ghost.") ATP; BrBE; FaBoEn; MeLP; MePo; OBS; PoEL-3; ReEn; SeCV-1; SeEP
Doubt there hath been, when with his golden chain. Astrophel and Stella, LVIII. Sir Philip Sidney. ReEn; SiPS
Doubt which ye misdeem, fair love, is vain, The. Amoretti, LXV. Spenser. PeBoSo; SiCE
Doubt you to whom my Muse these notes entendeth. Astrophel and Stella: First Song. Sir Philip Sidney. AtBAP; ElL; ElSeCe; EV-1; HBV; LiTL; OBSC; PoFS; ReIE; SiCE; SiPS; TCEP; TuPP; WHA
Doubter, The. Richard Watson Gilder. TrPWD
  (Christ the Answer, *with add. st., at. to* George Macdonald.) MaRV
Doubter's Prayer, The. Anne Brontë. MaRV; TrPWD; WGRP
Doubtful Choice, A. Edward de Vere, Earl of Oxford. *See* Were I a King.
Doubting. Virginia McCormick. LS
Doubting Heart, A. Adelaide Anne Procter. HBV; LPS-1; VA

Doubting Thomas and loving John. Dare You? Edward Rowland Sill. AnNE
Doubtless the pleasure is as great. Samuel Butler. *Fr.* Hudibras, Pt. II. NBE
Doubts ("Our doubts are traitors"). Shakespeare. *Fr.* Measure for Measure, I, iv. MaRV
Douglas, *sel.* John Home.
  Norval, *fr.* II, i. LPS-2
Douglas, Douglas, Tender and True. Dinah Maria Mulock Craik. AV; BLPA; BMEP; LPS-1; NeHB; TreF
  (Douglas.) LoPS; OBVV
  (Too Late.) HBV; VA
Douglas Gordon. Frederic Edward Weatherly. VA
Douglas Tragedy, The. *Unknown.* BLV; BoLiVe; CaAE; EBSV; HBV; MaC; OBB; OnSP; PIAE, *sl. abr.*; TrGrPo
  Diff. vers.
  (Earl Brand.) BaBo (A *and* B *vers.*); ESPB (A, B, *and* F *vers.*); OBB (A *vers., sl. abr.*); ViBoFo (A *and* B *vers.*)
  (Fair Margaret and Sweet William.) BaBo; BLV; ESPB; OBB, *sl diff.*; TOP; ViBoFo
  (Sweet William.) ABS; BaBo; OuSiCo, *with music*
Dour thing in olive trees, The. Olive Trees. Bernard Spencer. FaBoMo
Douse thy weasand well in wine. Song of Thirst. Alcaeus. GrR
Dove, The. Abul Hasan of Seville, *tr. fr. Arabic by* A. J. Arberry. MooP
Dove, The. Judah Halevi, *tr. fr. Hebrew by* Amy Levy. TrJP
Dove, The. Keats. *See* I Had a Dove.
Dove and the Wren, The. *Unknown.* RIS
Dove-colored, the shadows melt and mingle. Twilight. Feodor Tyutchev. OnPM; TrRV
Dove did lend me wings, The. I fled away. A Day in Sussex. Wilfrid Scawen Blunt. PoeT
Dove of Dacca, The. Kipling. GN
Dove of New Snow, The. Vachel Lindsay. MAP; MoAmPo
Dove of rarest worth, A. The Dove. Judah Halevi. TrJP
Dove of Thought, The. Verner von Heidenstam, *tr. fr. Swedish by* Charles W. Stork. AnSL
Dove returns; it found no resting place, The. Where We Must Look for Help. Robert Bly. NePoEA
Dove, The, says, "Coo, coo, what shall I do?" Mother Goose. BoTP; OxNR; PCH
Dove walks with sticky feet, The. Pastoral. Kenneth Patchen. AtBAP
Dover Beach. Matthew Arnold. AEV; AnEnPo; ATP; AWP; BEL; BLV; BMEP; BoLiVe; BPN; CBOV; CoBE; CoEV; EM-2; EmBrPo; EnL; EnLi-2; EnLit; EPN; EtS; ExPo; FaBoBe; FaBoEn; FaFP; FiP; GBV; GEPC, GTBS-D; GTBS-W; GTSL; HBV; HoPM; InP; InPo; InvP; JAWP; KN; LEAP; LiTB; LiTG; LiTL; LoBV; LoPo; LoPS; LPS-2; MaPo; MaRV; MCCG; NBE; NeHB; OAEP; OBVV; OTPC (1946 ed.); OuHeWo; PFE; PG; PIAE; Po; PoE; PoEL-5; PoFS; PoLFOT; PoRA; PoVP; PreP; PYM; REAL; ReaPo; RiBV; SeCePo; SeCeV; SN; TCEP; TOP; TreFS; TrGrPo; TwCrTr; TwHP; TyEnPo; UnPo; VA; ViBoPo; ViPo; ViPP; VLEP; WBP; WHA
  Ah, Love, Let Us Be True, *sel.* OQP; QP-2
"Dover Beach"—a Note to That Poem. Archibald MacLeish. ReaPo
Dover Cliff. F. Wyville Home. VA
Dover Cliffs. William Lisle Bowles. EV-5; HBV
  (At Dover Cliffs.) EnRP; ViBoPo
  (Sonnet: At Dover Cliffs, July 20, 1787.) CEP; OBEC
Dover Cliffs. Shakespeare. *Fr.* King Lear, IV, vi. LPS-2; SN
Doves. E. J. Falconer. BoTP
Doves. Louise Imogen Guiney. BLA; PC
Doves, The. Katharine Tynan. AnIV; AWP; JAWP; WBP
Dove's Nest. Joseph Russell Taylor. HBV
Doves of Venice, The. Laurence Hutton. AA
Doves that coo in Colomen, The. Colomen. Mary Webb. LoEn
Dowie Dens o' Yarrow, The. Henry Scott Riddell. EBSV
Dowie Houms [*or* Dens] o' Yarrow, The. *Unknown.* BSV; CBOV; EBSV; GoTS; OBB; OBEV; OBS
  (Braes o' Yarrow, The.) BaBo; ESPB (A *and* E *vers.*); PCN; ViBoFo
Down, The Ibn Rashiq, *tr. fr. Arabic by* A. J. Arberry. MooP
Down/ a/ deep/ well. The Grasshopper. David McCord. LiL
"Down a down!" [*or* "Downe-a-downe"]. Phoebe's Sonnet. Thomas Lodge. ElSeCe; ViBoPo
Down a hill, then up a hill. An Autumn Road. Glenn Ward Dresbach. HBMV
Down a Sunny Easter Meadow. Nancy Byrd Turner. SiSoSe
Down a trail of the mountain. Burro Bells in the Moonlight. Glenn Ward Dresbach. PoTo
Down a Woodland Way. Mildred Howells. AA
Down among the Dead Men. William Morris. EmBrPo; PoVP
Down among the Wharves. Eleanore Myers Jewett. EtS
Down and Out. Clarence Leonard Hay. BeLS; BLPA
Down around the quay they lie, the ships that sail to sea. The Port o' Heart's Desire. John S. McGroarty. HBV; NLK
Down at the hall at midnight sometimes. Dance. Lula Lowe Weeden. CDC
Down below the combers drape. At Manly. Leonard Mann. MoAuPo
Down by a Drooping Willow. *Unknown.* *See* Jealous Lover, The.
Down by a shining water well. My Kingdom. Robert Louis Stevenson. OnHT
Down by the bridge/ They sit and wait. Water-Front. Cecil ffrench Salkeld. OnYI
Down by the flash of the restless water. Ballade of a Ship. E. A. Robinson. TSW; TSWC
Down by the Glenside. Peadar Kearney. AnIV
Down by the meadows, chasing butterflies. *Unknown.* BoTP
Down by the Old Mill Stream. John Read. TreFS
Down by the railroad in a green valley. Eye-Witness. Ridgely Torrence. BAP; CP; HBMV; NV; SBMV; TCPD
Down by the river. *Unknown.* OxNR
Down by the Salley Gardens. W. B. Yeats. ChMo; CMP; EnLi-2 (1949 ed.); EnLoPo; GTBS-D; GTIV; GTML; HBV; MM; OBEV (new ed.); OBVV; OnYI; OxBI; PG; PoEL-5; PoeT; POTE; POTT; ShBV-3; TCPD; TwCV; VLEP
  (Old Song Resung, An.) BLV; BMEP; BoLiVe; MBP; MoAB; MoBrPo; NeMA; PC; VA
  (Salley Gardens, The.) EG
Down by the stream dwelt the franklin free. Sir Bosmer in Elfland. *Unknown.* BoDaBa
Down by the Weeping Willow. *Unknown.* *See* Jealous Lover, The.
Down by yon garden green. The Laird of Wariston [*or* Waristoun] (A *vers.*). *Unknown.* BaBo; ESPB
Down by yon weeping willow. The Jealous Lover [*or* Fair Florella]. *Unknown.* BaBo (A *vers.*); ViBoFo
"Down cellar," said the cricket. The Potatoes' Dance. Vachel Lindsay. BoChLi; FaPON; MPB; SP; SUS
Down Channel. A. G. Prys-Jones. UnW
Down deep in a hollow, so damp and so cold. The Philosopher Toad. Rebecca S. Nichols. LPS-2
Down! Down! Eleanor Farjeon. SUS; TiPo
Down, down—born pioneers in time's despite. Hart Crane. *Fr.* The Bridge: The River. TrGrPo
Down, Down Derry Down, *with music.* *Unknown.* AS
Down, Down, Down, *with music.* William Keating. OuSiCo
Down, down, Ellen, my little one. Après. Arthur J. Munby. LPS-3
Down drop of the blackbird, The. Three Spring Notations on Bipeds. Carl Sandburg. AWP; InPo; JAWP; MOAP; WBP
Down East and Up Along. Edwin Osgood Grover. NLK
Down every passage of the cloister hung. Upon the Death of George Santayana. Anthony Hecht. NePA
Down Fifth Avenue. John Curtis Underwood. NV
Down from a sunken doorstep to the road. Romance. Mildred Howells. AA
Down from her dainty head. The Lily Princess. *Unknown.* MPB
Down from her head the earth has rolled. Nightfall. Feodor Tyutchev. LiTW
Down from the branches fall the leaves. De Ramis Cadunt Folia [*or* Winter Love Song]. *Unknown.* *Fr.* Carmina Burana. LaP; LiTW
Down from the neck unto that dainty breast. Robert Tofte. *Fr.* Laura. ReIE
Down from the rocky western steep. The Flock at Evening. Odell Shepard. HBMV; OBAV
Down from the sky on a sudden he drops. The Goldfinch. Odell Shepard. BLA
Down from the stately trees amain. A Visitation. Hesiod. *Fr.* Eoiae. OxBG
Down Hall. Matthew Prior. CEP
  "Come here, my sweet Landlady, pray, how d'ye do?" *sel.* MyFE
Down hill I came, hungry, and yet not starved. *See* Downhill I came . . .
Down in a bed, and on a bed of down. An Elegy. Giles Fletcher. *Fr.* Licia. ReIE
Down in a Coal Mine. J. B. Geoghegan. TreFS
Down in a dark dungeon I saw a brave knight. *Unknown.* PPL
Down in a deep dark ditch sat an old cow munching a beanstalk. Hexameter and Pentameter. *Unknown.* ChTr
Down in a field, one day in June. Discontent. Sarah Orne Jewett. PRWS; TVC; TVSH
Down in a Garden. *Unknown.* ALV; ElSeCe; SeCL; SeEP

Down in a garden golden. The Rose's Cup. Frank Dempster Sherman. AA
Down in a garden sat my dearest love. Down in a Garden. *Unknown.* ALV; ElSeCe; SeCL; SeEP
Down in a green and shady bed. The Violet. Jane Taylor. BoChLi; HBV; HBVY; OTPC; PECK; PRWS; RIS; TreF; TVC; TVSH
Down in a lonesome valley. Fair Florella; or, The Jealous Lover (B *vers.*). *Unknown.* BaBo
Down in a Valley [by a Forest's Side]. William Browne. Visions, VI. EPS (1942 ed.); PeBoSo (Visions.) ElSeCe
Down in a Wine Vault. Don Marquis. WhC, 4 *sts.*
Down in adoration falling. Tantum Ergo Sacramentum. *Unknown.* WHL
Down in Alabama I was born. Roll the Cotton Down, *vers.* II. *Unknown.* ShS
Down in Carlisle there lived a lady. The Lady of Carlisle. *Unknown.* OuSiCo
Down in Dumbarton there wonnd a rich merchant. Bonnie Annie (B *vers.*). *Unknown.* ESPB
Down in front of Casey's old brown wooden stoop. The Sidewalks of New York. James W. Blake. BLPA; BoHiPo; FaBoBe; LPS-1; TreFS; YaD
Down in Lehigh Valley. *Unknown.* TreF
Down in New Mexico, where the plains are brown and sere. Old Buck's Ghost. Frank Benton. PoOW
Down in old Kentucky. Ballad of the Lincoln Penny. Alfred Kreymborg. YaD
Down in our cellar on a Monday and a Tuesday. Old Ellen Sullivan. Winifred Welles. FaPON; GaP; MPB; TiPo
Down in St. Louis at 12th and Carr. Brady (A *vers.*). *Unknown.* AS
Down in the bleak December bay. The *Mayflower.* Erastus Wolcott Ellsworth. AA; DDA; FaBoBe; HH; MC; PAH
Down in the city's market-place. A Cricket Singing in the Market-Place. Louella C. Poole. POT
Down [*or* Downe] in the depth of mine iniquity. Caelica XCIX[C]. Fulke Greville. LiTG; LoBV (2d ed.); OBS; SiCE
Down in the grassy hollow. Merry Little Men. Kathleen M. Chaplin. BoTP
Down in the grassy lowland dells. Lilies of the Valley. Marion Mitchell Walker. GFA
Down in the Hollow. Aileen Fisher. SUS
Down in the land of the center-fire saddle. *Unknown. Fr.* Up the Trail. CoSo
Down in the Meadow. *Unknown. See* Springfield Mountain.
Down in the meadow, sprent with dew. Revelation. Alice Brown. *Fr.* The Road to Castaly. WGRP
Down in the mud I lay. The Assault Heroic. Robert Graves. NV
Down in the park the children play. Song at Summer's End. A. R. D. Fairburn. AnNZ
Down in the river the fishes are rising. In the Time of the Persecution. L. Aaronson. NeTW; QS
Down in the silent hallway. Unsatisfied Yearning. Richard Kendall Munkittrick. AlBD; BOHV; InMe; LauV; PoMa
Down in the South, by the waste without sail on it. Beyond Kerguelen. Henry C. Kendall. BoAu
Down in the Valley. *Unknown.* ABF, *with music;* AS, *with music;* FaFP; SiTL
Down in the valley were gathered, one day. The Trees' Choice. Grace B. Carter. PEOR
Down in the villages. The Murmuring of Pine Trees. Ryokwan. OnPM
Down in the west the shadows rest. Canoe Song at Twilight. Laura E. McCully. CaP; CPG; OCL
Down in yon garden sweet and gay. Willy Drowned in Yarrow. *Unknown.* EV-2; GTBS-D; GTBS-W
Down in Yonder Meadow. *Unknown.* CH
Down lay in a nook my lady's brach. Song. Sir Henry Taylor. *Fr.* Philip van Artevelde. VA
Down London Lanes, with swinging reins. Mosby at Hamilton. Madison Cawein. PAH
Down looked the moon, but looked no more. John Francis O'Donnell. *Fr.* Happy Christmases. IrPN
Down Newport Street, last Sunday night. Newport Street, E. Douglas Goldring. HBMV
Down on de Mississippi floating. Nelly Was a Lady. Stephen C. Foster. BAV
Down on My Luck. A. R. D. Fairburn. AnNZ
Down on the beach when the tide is out. Treasures. Mary Dixon Thayer. MPB
Down on the big ranch, down there where I lived. Allá en El Rancho Grande. *Unknown.* ABF
Down on the flat of the lake. Lake Harvest. Raymond Knister. AnCaPo; PeCV
Down on the Lumbee River. Sunburnt Boys. John Charles McNeill. NoCaPo
Down on the shadowed stream of time and tears. Christ and the Mourners. Katherine E. Conway. ChIP; OQP; QP-1
Down on the sunlit ebb with the wind in her sails and free. On the Embankment. W. W. Gibson. PoFr; POTT
Down on your knees, boys, holystone the decks. Cleaning Ship. Charles Keeler. EtS
Down some cold field in a world unspoken. The Soldier. Humbert Wolfe. *Fr.* Requiem. TCPD
Down South on the Rio Grande. *Unknown.* CoSo; CSF
Down stepped her old father dear. Lady Maisry (B *vers.*). *Unknown.* BaBo
Down, swelling thoughts, and do not press. His Despair. T. Beaumont. SeCL
Down swept the chill wind from the mountain peak. Winter Pictures [*or* The Brook in Winter *or* December]. James Russell Lowell. *Fr.* The Vision of Sir Launfal: Prelude to Part Second. BAP; GN; GoTP; LPS-2; OTPC; TreF
Down the ages comes a sound grown dark. Nirvana. Tom MacInnes. CPG
Down the Bayou. Mary Ashley Townsend. AA; AnAmPo; LA; LEAP
Down the black highway where no whisper stirs. Sonnets from a Sequence, XXIV. Shirley Barker. AnAmPo
Down the blue night the unending columns press. Clouds. Rupert Brooke. BrBE; GTSL; MoVE; OBEV (new ed.); OBMV; POTE
Down the bright stream the Fairies float. The Last Voyage of the Fairies. William H. Davenport Adams. HBVY; PRWS
Down the Burn, Davie. Robert Crawford. EBSV
Down the close, darkening lanes they sang their way. The Send-off. Wilfred Owen. CoEV; LiTB; MoAB; MoBrPo (1950 ed.); MoVE
Down the deep steps of stone, through iron doors. Judgment. William Rose Benét. AnAmPo; BAP; LA
Down the dimpled green-sward dancing. Gambols of Children [*or* Song]. George Darley. LPS-1; OnYI
Down the dripping pathway dancing through the rain. Rainy Song. Max Eastman. FaBoBe; HBMV
Down the Field. Rolfe Humphries. AnAmPo; LA
Down the glimmering staircase, past the pensive clock. Siegfried Sassoon. *Fr.* Vigils. AlDL
Down the glutted river's throat. The Floating Island. Ruth Miller. BoSA
Down the goldenest of streams. Mater Amabilis. Emma Lazarus. BOL; MOAH; OHIP
Down the green hillside fro' the castle window. Lady Jane. Sir Arthur Quiller-Couch. FiBHP; InMe; PA; WhC
Down the lane, and across the fields. Doris. Clarence S. Harper. CAG
Down the Little Big Horn. Francis Brooks. GA; PAH
Down the long hall she glistens like a star. Venus of the Louvre. Emma Lazarus. AA; AnAmPo; LA; LBAP; LEAP
Down the long path beneath the garden wall. A Dream. V. Sackville-West. MoVE
Down the market. *Unknown.* RIS
Down the Mississippi. John Gould Fletcher. ChMo; CMP; LiTA; MOAP; NP; SPP; TCAP
Sels.
Moon's Orchestra, The, IV. LaNeLa
Stevedores, The, V. HiLiAm; PoTo
Down the Ohio the flatboats go. Anthony Wayne. Arthur Guiterman. TiPo (1959 ed.)
Down the picket-guarded lane. "How Are You, Sanitary?" Bret Harte. MDAH; PaA; PAP
Down the quiet eve. Music. W. E. Henley. In Hospital, XXIII. BPN
Down the Rain Falls. Elizabeth J. Coatsworth. PoRh
Down the River, *sels.* S. Frances Harrison.
Benedict Brosse. CPG
Catharine Plouffe. CPG
Danger. CPG
Gatineau Point. CPG
Les Chantiers. CPG
Petite Ste. Rosalie. BoCaPo (1943 ed.); CPG
St. Jean B'ptiste. CPG
Voyageur, The. CPG
Down the Rivuh, Down, Boys, *with music. Unknown.* StDa
Down the road/ between the trees. The Pursuit. Struthers Burt. MuM
Down the road someone is practicing [*or* practising] scales. Sunday Morning. Louis MacNeice. CoBMV; FaBoMo; LiTB; MBP; MoAB; MoBrPo; MoVE; NeMA; PoE
Down the road to Llasa. The Pilgrims of Thibet. Cale Young Rice. PFY
Down the Savoy valleys sounding. The Church of Brou. Matthew Arnold. EmBrPo
Down the Simplon Pass. Wordsworth. *See* Simplon Pass, The.
Down the slide. Sliding. Marchette Chute. TiPo (1959 ed.)
Down the street, down the street, flying down the street. Jonathan Bing's Tea. Beatrice Curtis Brown. WaKn
Down the sultry arc of day. Description of a Summer's Eve. Henry Kirke White. ERP; OBRV
Down the valleys of Languedoc. At Carcassonne. Winfred Ernest Garrison. OQP; QP-2

Down the white steps of Heaven Christ came to meet him. Entrance into Heaven. Sara Henderson Hay. ChIP
Down the wintry mountain. Dinah Maria Mulock Craik. *Fr.* Highland Cattle. GN; OTPC
Down the Wolf river. Feasts of Death, Feasts of Love. Stuart Z. Perkoff. NeAP
Down the world with Marna! The Wander-Lovers. Richard Hovey. AA; HBV; LEAP; OBAV; TCAP
Down there, in the distance, the pine groves stretch. Vastness. Jorge Guillén. CoSP
Down through a valley that yucca clouded. The Last Cowboy. Glenn Ward Dresbach. HiLiAm
Down through the ancient Strand. Scherzando. W. E. Henley. London Voluntaries, III. AIDL; BPN; LEAP; POTT
Down through the rocks where the dark roots dry. The Grave of Arthur. G. K. Chesterton. JKCP (1955 ed.)
Down through the snow-drifts in the street. The Boy. Eugene Field. NA
Down through the spheres that chant the Name of One. The Path of the Stars. Thomas S. Jones, Jr. Four Sonnets, IV. ChIP; NV; SBMV; WGRP
Down to a bank where it was always evening. The Island. Giuseppe Ungaretti. LiTW
Down to earth's bosom deep below. Yearning for Death. "Novalis." Hymns to the Night, VI. AnGP
Down to Sleep. Helen Hunt Jackson. GN
Down to the pond came a pretty fawn. Life. Alice Brown. AA
Down to the Puritan marrow of my bones. Puritan Sonnet [*or* Sonnet]. Elinor Wylie. Wild Peaches, IV. InP; LiTA; MAP; MoAB; MoAmPo; NAMP; NeMA; OxBA; PIAE; PoeMoYo; TrGrPo
Down to the wharves, as the sun goes down. My Ship. Elizabeth Akers Allen. LPS-1
Down toward the deep-blue water, marching to throb of drum. Your Lad, and My Lad. Randall Parrish. MC; PAH
Down under the ground, deep leagues adown. In the Tenth Circle. *Unknown.* CAG
Down, Wanton, Down! Robert Graves. FaBoTw; LiTM; SiTL
Down Went McGinty. Joseph Flynn. TreF; YaD
Down went the gunner, a bullet was his fate. Praise the Lord and Pass the Ammunition. Frank Loesser. YaD
Down where the bed of ocean sinks profound. Mollusks. Henry Jerome Stockard. NoCaPo (1941 ed.)
Down with the lambs. *Unknown.* OxNR
Down with the rosemary and bayes [*or* bays]. Ceremonies for Candlemas Eve. Robert Herrick. EPS; EV-2; OAEP; OBS; OTPC; SeEP
Down with the rosemary and so. A Ceremony for Candlemas Day [*or* Ceremony upon Candlemas Eve]. Robert Herrick. EPS; OTPC; PoRL
Down, you mongrel, Death! The Poet and His Book. Edna St. Vincent Millay. MAP; MoAmPo; NePA; TCPD
Downcast, wretched sport am I, A. An Appeal to the Goddess A. Thomas Ybarra. CAG
"Downe-a-downe, downe-a-downe." *See* "Down a down."
Downe downe afflicted soule and paie thy due. *Unknown.* SeCSL
Downe downe proude minde, thou soarest farre aboue thy might. *Unknown.* NBE
Downe in a dale satt a nimph weeping. *Unknown.* SeCSL
Downe in a vale there satt a shepherdesse. *Unknown.* SeCSL
Downe in the depth of mine iniquity. *See* Down in the depth . . .
Downe too farre usurping day. *Unknown.* SeCSL
Downfall of Heathendom, The. *Unknown, tr. fr. Irish by* Frank O'Connor. KiLC
Downfall of Piracy, The. *At. to* Benjamin Franklin. PAH (Teach the Rover.) SG
Downfall of the Gael, The. Fearflatha O'Gnive, *tr. fr. Late Middle Irish by* Sir Samuel Ferguson. AnIV; AWP; JAWP; OnYI; WBP
Downfall of the Tyrant. Isaiah, XIV: 4-19, Bible, *O.T.* TrGrPo
Downhill I came, hungry, and yet not starved. The Owl. Edward Thomas. ChTr; FaBoTw; LiTB; MoP; UnPo (3d ed.)
Downing his drink to toasts of cut-rate jokes. 3 for 25. William Jay Smith. WaP
Downright Country-Man, The; or, The Faithful Dairy Maid. *Unknown.* CoMu
Downs, The. Robert Bridges. EPP; ReTS
Downs, The. John Galsworthy. MM
Downstairs I laugh, I sport and jest with all. L. E. L. Christina Rossetti. EmBrPo
Downward through the evening twilight. Hiawatha's Childhood. Longfellow. *Fr.* The Song of Hiawatha. AnNE; IAP
Downward was the wheeling Bear. At the Mid Hour of Night. *Unknown.* GrL; OxBG; WoL
. . . Downwards we hurried fast. Down the Simplon Pass [*or* Alpine Descent]. Wordsworth. *Fr.* The Prelude, VI. EPN; WHA
Downy came and dwelt with me. The Downy Woodpecker. John Burroughs. BLA
Downy Owl, The. Edith Willis Linn. BLA
Downy Woodpecker, The. John Burroughs. BLA
Dow's Flat—1856. Bret Harte. FaBoBe; HBV; IHA; LPS-3
Doxology. Thomas Ken. *See* Praise God, from whom all blessings flow! OlF
Doxology. Jessica Powers. JKCP (1955 ed.)
Doxology for Peace. R. B. Y. Scott. MaRV
Doxy, oh! thy glaziers shine. The Maunder's Praise of His Strowling Mort. *Unknown.* OxBoLi
Doze, The. James Reeves. GoTP
Dozen sandaled saints I see, A. So Runs Our Song. Mary Eva Kitchel. ChIP; PGD
Dozing on sand we make our fresh resolutions. Waiwera. Kendrick Smithyman. AnNZ
Dr. *See* Doctor.
Drab drugget paths protect these polished floors. Fantasia on a Wittelsbach Atmosphere. Siegfried Sassoon. MoVE
Drachma and Europa's yours, A. Antipater of Thessalonica, *tr. fr. Greek by* Elsie Spoerl. GrPo
Dracula of the Hills, A. Amy Lowell. DaM
Draft Riot, The. Charles De Kay. PAH
Drag your heart; go deep. Dragnet. Joseph Auslander. NV
Dragging an iron rake. Tractor. William Hart-Smith. AnNZ
Dragnet. Joseph Auslander. NV
Dragon, The. Mary Mullineaux. BoTP
Dragon, The. Spenser. *Fr.* The Faerie Queene, I, 11. SeCePo
Dragon, The. *Unknown, tr. fr. Danish by* E. M. Smith-Dampier. BoDaBa
Dragon Flies. W. J. Turner. GTBS-D
Dragon of our dreams roared in the hills, The. Y Ddraig Goch. Henry Treece. MoWP
Dragon of the Black Pool, The. Po Chü-i, *tr. fr. Chinese by* Arthur Waley. TrCh
Dragon of the Seas, The. Thomas Nelson Page. PAH
Dragon of Wantley, The. *Unknown.* CG
Dragon Sees His Advantage, The. Lyon Sharman. CPG
Dragon that our seas did raise his crest, The. Of the Great and Famous [Sir Francis Drake]. Robert Hayman. CH; FaBoCh
Dragon-Fly, A. Eleanor Farjeon. FaPON
Dragon-Fly, The. Walter Savage Landor. OBEV (new ed.); OBVV
(Lines to a Dragon Fly.) OBRV
Dragonfly, The Theodore Harding Rand. CaP; CPG; OCL
Dragon-Fly, The. Jessie Belle Rittenhouse. POT; PoTo
Dragon-Fly, The. Tennyson. *Fr.* The Two Voices. SN
Dragon-fly and I together, The. Two of a Trade. Samuel Willoughby Duffield. AA
Dragonfly who hurries by, The. The Elfin Plane. Rowena Bennett. MPB (1956 ed.)
Dragons. Edward Lovelle Stewart. PoP
Dragon's Warning, The. Lyon Sharman. CPG
Draherin O Machree. *Unknown.* AnIV
Drake. Charles Fitzgeffrey. *See* Sir Francis Drake.
Drake, *sels.* Alfred Noyes.
"Bring on the pomp and pride of old Castile," *fr.* XI. CAW
"Heart of England now is all on fire, The!" *fr.* X. ReTS
Song: "Now the purple night is past," *fr.* I. ChMo; CMP
Drake, who the world hast conquered like a scroll. To the Noble Sir Francis Drake. Thomas Beedome. SeEP
Drake's Drum ("Drake he's in his hammock an' a thousand miles away"). Sir Henry Newbolt. AnFE; BTP; CBE; CBOV; EPP; EtS; FaBoCh; GTBS; GTML; GTSL; HBV; HBVY; LBBV; LEAP; MBP; MCCG; MuP; OBMV; OBVV; OnSP; OtMeF; PoeT; PoRA; SG; ShBV-2; TCEP; TOP; TreF; TSW; TVSH; TwCV; WP
Drama. William Hart-Smith. BoAV; NeLNL
Drama of Exile, A, *sel.* Elizabeth Barrett Browning.
Live and Love. OQP; QP-2
Dramas of the Rose. James Schevill. FiMAP
Dramatic Fragment. Trumbull Stickney. OxBA
Dramatic Idyls, *sel.* Robert Browning.
Epilogue. BPN; PoVP
Dramatis Personae, *sel.* Robert Browning.
Epilogue. BPN
"That one Face, far from vanish, rather grows," 3 *ll.* ChIP; MaRV
Drank lonesome water. Lonesome Water. Roy Helton. DaM; DDA; MAP; MoAmPo; PoMS; WaKn
Draught of Life, The. Abu-l-Ala al-Maarri, *tr. fr. Arabic by* R. A. Nicholson. LiTW
Draught of Love, The. Meleager, *tr. fr. Greek by* Lord Neaves. OnPM
Draught-Ox, The. Addaeus. *See* Pensioned Ox, The.
Draw a circle round me thrice. In My End Is My Beginning. Rosemary Dobson. BoAV; NeLNL
Draw a Pail of Water. *Unknown.* BoTP; CBPC; MoShBr; OxNR

Draw back the cradle curtains, Kate. The King of the Cradle. Joseph Ashby-Sterry. HBV
Draw-Bridge Keeper, The. Henry Abbey. PEOR
Draw closer to me, God, than were I one. Prayer of an Unbeliever. Lizette Woodworth Reese. QS; TrPWD
Draw Me, Saviour, after Thee. Charles Wesley. BePJ
Draw near/ And list what with our council we have done. Richard II Banishes Bolingbroke. Shakespeare. King Richard II, *fr.* I, iii. PoFS
Draw near [*or* neer]/ You lovers that complain. The Exequies. Thomas Stanley. CaAE; MeLP; OBS; SeCL; SeEP
Draw near, and see. Song. *Unknown.* SeCL
Draw Near, O Son of God. Charles Wesley. BePJ
Draw near to the tables, ye that wear the cloaks. A Connacht Caoine. *Unknown.* AnIV
Draw near, ye gallant seamen, while I the truth unfold. A New Song on Lord Nelson's Victory of Copenhagen. *Unknown.* SG
Draw On, Sweet Night. *Unknown.* TuPP
Draw the Sword, O Republic. Edgar Lee Masters. AOAH; NV
Draw Thou my soul, O Christ. Thy Will Be Done. Lucy Larcom. PraP
Draw-to the curtains then, and let it rain. In Time of Suspense. Laurence Whistler. LoPS; NeTW; POTE
Drawing. Sergei Mikhalkov, *tr. fr. Russian by* Jack Lindsay. RuPo
Drawing near the Light. William Morris. BPN
Drawing-Room Ballad, A. Henry Duff Traill. CenHV
Drawn with th' attractive virtue of her eyes. To Delia, XLVIII. Samuel Daniel. ReIE
Drayman, The. Giovanni Pascoli, *tr. fr. Italian by* Glauco Cambon. OnPM
Drayman, The. Walt Whitman. *Fr.* Song of Myself. PoNe
Dread. J. M. Synge. MBP; MoBrPo
Dread are the death-pale kings. Still-Heart. Frank Pearce Sturm. OBMV
Dread episode sublime. Azrael. Gertrude Huntington McGiffert. BAP
Dread of Height, The. Francis Thompson. JKCP; VLEP
Dread Potter, in Thine hands we lay. A Pagan's Baptism. A. S. Cripps. BoSA
Dreaded Task, The. Margaret E. Bruner. PoToHe
Dreadful case of murder, A. Execution of Alice Holt. *Unknown.* OxBoLi
Dreadful hour with leaden pace approached, The. Lisy's Parting with Her Cat. James Thomson. CIV; PoC
Dreadful Story of Pauline and the Matches, The. Heinrich Hoffmann, *tr. fr. German.* CIV
(Dreadful Story about Harriet and the Matches, The, *sl. diff., tr. at. to* J. R. Planché.) BoN
(Harriet and the Matches, *sl. diff.*) RIS
Dreadnought, The, *with music. Unknown.* AmSS; ShS (2 *vers.*); SoAmSa
Dream, A. William Allingham. BMEP; CBOV; EV-5; GTIV; OxBI; UnW; VA
Dream, A. Matthew Arnold. SeCePo
Dream. Mary Austin. TBM
Dream, A. Thomas Lovell Beddoes. HoPM
Dream, The. John Peale Bishop. LiTA; LiTM (rev. ed.)
Dream, A. Blake. *Fr.* Songs of Innocence. CH; EnRP; EV-3; MPB; NBE; PECK; PoRh; RAR; TVC; TVSH
Dream, The. Louise Bogan. LiTA; LiTM; MoAB; MoAmPo (1950 ed.)
Dream. Anna Hempstead Branch. SBMV
Dream. Witter Bynner. NP
Dream, The. Byron. BCEP; BeLS; ChER; EmBrPo; GEPC; LPS-3
Dream, A, *sel.* Thomas Campbell.
"In a bark, methought, lone steering." UnW
Dream, The. Chaucer. *Fr.* The Book of the Duchesse. FiP
Dream, A. Hugh Connell. NeIP
Dream, The. Sir William Davenant. EV-2
Dream. Richard Watson Dixon. LoBV; NBE
Dream [*or* Dreame], The. John Donne. BrBE; CoEV; EIL; ElSeCe; EnLP; GTBS-W; InvP; LEAP, *abr.*; LiTB; LiTG; LiTL; LO; LoBV; MeLP; MePo; OAEP; OBEV; OBS; RiBV; SeEP; TOP
("Deare love, for nothing lesse than thee.") EG
Dream, A. Mary Fullerton. BoAV
Dream, A. William Gaston. NoCaPo
Dream. Marion Ethel Hamilton. MuM
Dream, A. Helen Hunt Jackson. AnFE; APA; CoAnAm
Dream! Jens Peter Jacobsen, *tr. fr. Danish by* Charles W. Stork. BoDS
Dream [*or* Dreame], The. Ben Jonson. ElSeCe; PoEL-2
Dream, A. Elizabeth Clementine Kinney. AA
Dream, A. Andrew Lang. BSV
Dream, A. William Langland. *Fr.* The Vision of Piers Plowman. CoEV
Dream. Mikhail Lermontov, *tr. fr. Russian.* BoR
Dream, The. Edwin Markham. OQP; QP-1
Dream, The. Francis Burdett Money-Coutts. OBVV
Dream, The, *sel.* Caroline Elizabeth Sarah Norton.
"Sweet is the image of the brooding dove." MOAH
Dream, A. Stephen Phillips. *See* Apparition, The.
Dream, A. Poe. IAP
Dream. Emilio Prados, *tr. fr. Spanish by* Eleanor L. Turnbull. CoSP
Dream, The. Theodore Roethke. AmP; MoVE
Dream, The. Christina Rossetti. EmBrPo
Dream, A. V. Sackville-West. MoVE
Dream, The. Smpad Shahaziz, *tr. fr. Armenian by* Zabelle C. Boyajian. ArmLP
Dream, A. Shen Yo, *tr. fr. Chinese by* Henry H. Hart. PoHN
Dream. William Jay Smith. MoVE
Dream, The, *sel.* Dionysios Solomos, *tr. fr. Modern Greek by* Rae Dalven.
"When the hands that scattered." MoGP
Dream, The. Helen Spalding. ChMP; DiM
Dream, The, *sel. Unknown, wr. at. to* Chaucer.
"And right anon as I the day espied." LEAP
Dream, A ("Benedicite, what dreamed I this night?") *Unknown.* OBSC
("Benedicite, what dreamed I this night?" *st.* 1.) LO
(Benedicite, What Dremid I This Night?) PoEL-1
Dream, The ("Last night I supped on lobster"). *Unknown.* OxBoLi
Dream, The. Georgios Vizinos, *tr. fr. Modern Greek by* Rae Dalven. MoGP
Dream, A. Charles Williams. OBEV (new ed.)
Dream across the Dark. Clifford J. Laube. JKCP (1955 ed.)
Dream, after Reading Dante's Episode of Paolo and Francesca, A. Keats. PtP
("As Hermes once took to his feathers light.") RO
(On a Dream.) EnRP; EV-4
Dream and Image. Heinrich von Morungen, *tr. fr. German by* Jethro Bithell. LiTW; LyMA
Dream and the Song. James David Corrothers. BANP
Dream as Reported, A. Virginia Earle. GoYe
Dream at Night, A. Mei Yao Ch'en, *tr. fr. Chinese by* Kenneth Rexroth. OnPC
Dream-Bearer, The. Mary Carolyn Davies. BAP
Dream Boat, The. Louise Ayres Garnett. BOL
Dream Called Life, The. Pedro Calderón de la Barca, *tr. fr. Spanish by* Edward Fitzgerald. AWP; CAW; JAWP; OuHeWo; WBP
Dream Carol, A. *Unknown. See* This Endernight I Saw a Sight.
Dream Data. Robert Duncan. NeAP
Dream, dream, thou flesh of me! Lullaby. "Patience Worth." BOL
Dream encounters. Otomo no Yakamochi, *tr. fr. Japanese by* I. W. Furukami. LiTW
Dream-fair, beside dream waters, it stands alone. The Shadow House of Lugh. "Ethna Carbery." AnIV
Dream Fairy, The. Thomas Hood. *Fr.* Queen Mab. BoTP
Dream Fantasy. "Fiona Macleod." WGRP
Dream Garden, A. Chaucer. *Fr.* The Parlement of Foules. CBOV
Dream has spilled its genial plenitude, The. Eurydice. Margaret Allonby. BoSA
Dream House. Catherine Parmenter Newell. PoToHe
Dream House, The. Marjorie Allen Seiffert. HBMV
Dream in a dream the heavy soul somewhere. Canto Amor. John Berryman. MoAmPo (1950 ed.); MoPo; MoVE; NePA
Dream in Early Spring, A. Fredegond Shove. MoVE; TwCV
Dream is a cocktail at Sloppy Joe's, The. Havana Dreams. Langston Hughes. GoSl; PoNe
Dream Is Not Enough, The. Zoe Kincaid Brockman. NoCaPo
Dream is the thought in the ghost, The. George Meredith. *Fr.* A Faith on Trial. WGRP
Dream it was in which I found myself, A. The Dream Called Life. Pedro Calderón de la Barca. AWP; CAW; JAWP; OuHeWo; WBP
Dream Land. Frances Anne Kemble. OBVV
Dreamland, *sel.* Charles Mair.
"We are not wholly blest who use the earth." CaP; OCL
Dream-Land. Poe. AmP; AmPo; AmPP; AnFE; APA; APW; CaAE; CoAnAm; CoBA; CoV; DaM; IAP; LiTA; MOAP; NePA; OxBA; PoFS; UnW
Dream Land. Christina Rossetti. EmBrPo; EnLi-2; GTML; MBP; POTT; PoVP; ViPo; VLEP
Dream-Love. Christina Rossetti. CH; GTBS-D; GTML; GTSL; MBP; PoEL-5
Dream Nocturne. Juan Ramón Jiménez, *tr. fr. Spanish.* AnSpL-2, *tr. by* Thomas McGreevy; TeCS, *tr. by* Eleanor L. Turnbull
Dream not of noble service elsewhere wrought. Life's Common Duties. Minot J. Savage. WBLP
Dream Observed, A. Anne Ridler. NeBP
Dream of a Blessed Spirit, A. W. B. Yeats. PoeT; TIP
Dream of a Boy Who Lived at Nine-Elms, The. William Brighty Rands. PPL; RIS
(Dream of a Little Boy Who Lived at Nine-Elms, The.) GaP

Dream of a Decent Death. G. A. Borgese. NePoAm
Dream of a Girl Who Lived at Seven-Oaks, The. William Brighty Rands. OTPC; PPL; RIS
(Dream of a Little Girl Who Lived at Seven-Oaks, The.) GaP
Dream of a Golden Catch. Theocritus, *tr. fr. Greek by* R. C. Trevelyan. *Fr.* Idylls. GrR
Dream of a Little Boy Who Lived at Nine-Elms, The. William Brighty Rands. *See* Dream of a Boy Who Lived at Nine-Elms, The.
Dream of a Little Girl Who Lived at Seven-Oaks, The. William Brighty Rands. *See* Dream of a Girl Who Lived at Seven-Oaks, The.
Dream of Ængus Og, The. Eleanor Rogers Cox. HBMV; SBMV
Dream of Artemis, A, *sel.* Francis Ledwidge.
"God, whose kindly hand doth sow." TrPWD
Dream of Beauty, A. Clark Ashton Smith. UnW
Dream of Chiangnan, A. Huang-fu Sung, *tr. fr. Chinese by* C. W. Luh. OnPM
Dream of Clarence, The. Shakespeare. King Richard III, *fr.* I, iv. UnW
("I saw a thousand fearful wrecks," *shorter sel.*) SG
(Methought I Saw a Thousand Fearful Wrecks, *shorter sel.*) EtS
Dream of Dakiki, The. Firdausi, *tr. fr. Persian by* A. V. Williams Jackson. WGRP
Dream of Death, A. "Owen Innsley." AA
Dream of Death, A. W. B. Yeats. PoeT; POTE
Dream of Dying. Thomas Lovell Beddoes. *Fr.* Fragments Intended for the Dramas. ERP; RO
Dream of Eugene Aram, The. Thomas Hood. BCEP; BeLS; CG; DaM; EnRP; ERP; EV-4; HBV; LPS-3; ShGoBo; StPo; UnW; VA
Dream of Fair Women, A. Kingsley Amis. PoLFOT; PoN
Dream of Fair Women, A. Tennyson. BEL; BPN; EmBrPo; EPP; EV-5; GEPC; OBRV, *orig. vers.*; ViPo; VLEP
Sels.
As When a Man, *first 4 sts. of orig. vers.* ChER
"I read before my eyelids dropt their shade." PtP
Iphigenia. BHV
(Helen and Iphigenia.) TwCrTr
Dream of Flowers, A. Titus Munson Coan. AA
Dream of Gerontius, The. Cardinal Newman. PoVP
Sels.
Angel ("My work is done"). GoBC
Angel ("Softly and gently, dearly-ransom'd soul"). OxBoCh
Angel of the Agony ("Jesu! by that shuddering dread which fell on Thee"). OxBoCh
"I went to sleep, and now I am refreshed." UnW
"Jesu, Maria—I am near to death." ACP; CoBE; EnLi-2
"Praise to the Holiest in the height." PoEL-5
(Fifth Choir of Angelicals.) GoBC
Soul before God, The ("Take me away, and in the lowest deep"). OxBoCh
Dream of His Lady. Giovanni Battista Guarini, *tr. fr. Italian by* Ronald Bottrall. LyPI
(Another Version, *tr. by* Philip Ayres.) LyPI
Dream of John Ball, A, *sel.* William Morris.
Sheriff, The. PoVP
Dream of Love. Bhai Vir Singh, *tr. fr. Punjabi by* Puran Singh. OnPM
Dream of Mountaineering, A. Po Chü-i, *tr. fr. Chinese by* Arthur Waley. TrCh
Dream of the future in blissful surrender. Hope. Andreas Munch. AnNoLy
Dream of the Romaunt of the Rose, The. Guillaume de Lorris, *tr. fr. French by* Chaucer. *Fr.* The Romance of the Rose. LoBV
Dream of the Rood, A. *Unknown, at. to* Cynewulf, *tr. fr. Anglo-Saxon.* AnOE, *tr. by* Charles W. Kennedy; CAW, *tr. by* Sister Mary Madeleva; EnLi-1, *tr. by* Stith Thompson; OuHeWo, *tr. by* Stith Thompson; StJW, *tr. by* LaMotte Iddings
Sels.
Cross Speaks, The. PoLi
"I am remembering in the long ago." ACP
Poet Prays to the Cross, The. PoLi
Dream of the Unknown, A. Shelley. *See* Question, The ("I dreamed that, as I wandered by the way").
Dream of the walls of a cave. The Fossil. John Lyle Donaghy. NeIP
Dream of the World without Death, The. Robert Buchanan. *Fr.* The Book of Orm. VA
Dream of Venus, A. Bion. *See* I Dreamt I Saw Great Venus.
Dream of Wrecks, A. Shakespeare. Richard III, *fr.* I, iv. ChTr
Dream of Youth, A. Lionel Johnson. VLEP
Dream-Pedlary. Thomas Lovell Beddoes. AlDL, *abr.*; AnFE; AtBAP, *sts.* 1-2; BCEP; BLV; BoTP; CaAE; CH; EnRP; EPN; EPP; ERP; EV-4; FaBoBe; GTBS-W, *sts.* 1-2; LEAP; LiA, *st.* 1; LiTB; LoBV; NeHB; OBEV; OBRV; OBVV; OQP; OtMeF; PCD; PFE; PG (1945 ed.), *sts.* 1-2; PoEL-4; PoP; QP-2; TCEP; TOP; TreFS; TrGrPo; VA; ViBoPo; WP; YT
(Dreams to Sell.) CBPC; OTPC (1946 ed.); *sts.* 1-2
("If there were dreams to sell.") EG
Dream People. Isabel Ecclestone Mackay. UnW
Dream Queen, The, *sel.* Bhasa, *tr. fr. Sanskrit by* A. G. Shirreff *and* Panna Lall.
Dialogue from "The Dream Queen" ("Look, look, my lord"). LiTW
Dream Ship, The. W. K. Holmes. BoTP
Dream Song. Lewis Alexander. PoNe
Dream-Song. Walter de la Mare. BOL
Dream Song. Richard Middleton. HBV
Dream-Teller, The. Padraic Gregory. HBMV; OnYI
Dream, the dream, where did it begin, The. Night in October. Miriam Waddington. BoCaPo (1948 ed.)
Dream the Great Dream. Florence Earle Coates. HBMV; PoMa; VOD
Dream Tryst. Richard Le Gallienne. HBMV
Dream-Tryst. Francis Thompson. AnFE; EmBrPo; EnLit; GTML; POTT; UnW; VA
Dream Variation. Langston Hughes. BAP; CDC; PoNe
Dream Verses. Edith Nesbit. BoN
Dream within a Dream, A. Poe. AmP; AmPP; AnFE; APA; APW; BLV; BoLiVe; ChTr; CoAnAm; CoBA; IAP; OxBA; TrGrPo; UnW
(To——: "Take this kiss upon thy brow!") LO
"I stand amid the roar," *sel.* RO
Dreame, The. John Donne. *See* Dream, The.
Dreame, The. Ben Jonson. *See* Dream, The.
Dreamed Realization, A. Gregory Corso. NeAP
Dreamer, The. Clifford Bax. TCPD
Dreamer, The. Walter de la Mare. ChMo; CMP; OTPC (1923 ed.)
Dreamer, The. Alice Furlong. TIP
Dreamer, The. Dorothy Gould. PGD
Dreamer, A. Arthur Guiterman. PoMa
Dreamer, The. Vachel Lindsay. LBMV
Dreamer, The. Christian Morgenstern, *tr. fr. German by* R. F. C. Hull. AnGP
Dreamer, The. Thomas Nunan. WBLP
Dreamer, The. Gunnar Mascoll Silfverstolpe, *tr. fr. Swedish by* Charles W. Stork. AnSL
Dreamer, The. *Unknown.* LPS-1
Dreamer in the Desert, The. Francis Flagg. DaM
Dreamer of Dreams. William Herbert Carruth. *See* Dreamers of Dreams.
Dreamer, to let my wing dive deep. Miss Mallarmé's Fan. Stéphane Mallarmé. TrFP
Dreamer turns, The. Street Cries. Josephine Pinckney. LS; SPP
Dreamer, waiting for darkness with sorrowful, drooping eyes. Forward. Edna Dean Proctor. HBV
Dreamers, The. Martha Haskell Clark. VOD (1931 ed.)
Dreamers, The. Theodosia Garrison. BLP; GaP; HBMV; OBAV; PoTo; TCAP; VOD
Dreamers. James Barron Hope. TCAP
Dreamers, The. Sydney Jephcott. BoAu
Dreamers. Siegfried Sassoon. CaAE; ChMo; CMP; HBMV; MCCG; MBP; MoBrPo; NeMA; PoeMoYo; PtOT; SoV; VOD
Dreamers and the Sea, The. Eithne Wilkins. *Fr.* Parzival. NeBP
Dreamers Cry Their Dream, The. Lucia Trent. PGD
Dreamers of Death, The. Julia Cooley Altrocchi. MuM
Dreamers of Dreams. William Herbert Carruth. MaRV; OQP; QP-2
(Dreamer of Dreams.) BTP
Dreamers turn, The. The Dreamers and the Sea. Eithne Wilkins. *Fr.* Parzival. NeBP
Dreamers upon the hilltops, The. The Dreamers Cry Their Dream. Lucia Trent. PGD
Dreamers, wake up! For you I beat the drum! I Beat the Drum. Jan Greshoff. PoFr
Dreamin' Town. Paul Laurence Dunbar. VOD
Dreaming along the haunted shore of time. Edgar Allan Poe. Clifford Lanier. PoRL
Dreaming in marble all the castle lay. Of Nicolette. E. E. Cummings. HBMV
Dreaming in the Trenches. William Gordon McCabe. AA; SPP
Dreaming of a Dead Lady. *Unknown, tr. fr. Chinese by* Arthur Waley. TrCh
Dreaming of a prince. After All and after All. Mary Carolyn Davies. GaP; MPB; SP; TiPo (1952 ed.)
Dreaming of Cities Dead. Eleanor Rogers Cox. CAW; JKCP
(On Broadway.) BAP
Dreaming of honeycombs to share. Waiting. Harry Behn. SiSoSe; TiPo
Dreaming of My Dead Wife. Su T'ung-po, *tr. fr. Chinese by* Yu Min-chuan. WhP
Dreaming of Wandering through the Tien-mu Mountain. Li Po, *tr. fr. Chinese.* WhP

Dreaming of Yüan Chen. Po Chü-i, *tr. fr. Chinese by* Arthur Waley. TrCh
Dreaming Spires. Roy Campbell. BoSA
Dreaming That I Went with Lu and Yu to Visit Yüan Chen. Po Chü-i, *tr. fr. Chinese by* Arthur Waley. BoFr; TrCh
Dreaming Trout, The. Charles Bruce. *Fr.* The Flowing Summer. CaP
Dreaming within a forest deep. At Easter Time. Charles G. Blanden. PSO
Dreamland. *See* Dream Land.
Dreams. Cecil Frances Alexander. OnYI; TIP
Dreams. Thomas Edward Brown. GTML; VLEP
Dreams. Chi Lan Yün, *tr. fr. Chinese by* Henry H. Hart. PoHN
Dreams. Richard Corbet. EV-2
Dreams, *sel.* Walter de la Mare.
"Ay, once I dreamed of an age-wide sea." UnW
Dreams. Robert Herrick. SeEP
Dreams. Langston Hughes. BoChLi (1950 ed.); GoSl
Dreams. Louise Labé, *tr. fr. French by* Alan Conder. TrFP
(Sonnet: "As soon as I begin to overtake," *tr. by* Ralph N. Currey.) FoS
Dreams. Andrew Lang. UnW
Dreams. Poe. AmPP (4th ed.); IAP; OxBA
Dreams. Philip M. Raskin. OQP; QP-2
Dreams. Thomas Traherne. MeRV
Dreams. Israel Zangwill. TrJP
Dreams Ahead, The. Edwin Carlile Litsey. PoToHe
Dreams and Deeds. John Hunter. ChIP; MaRV
Dreams and Life. Erik Axel Karlfeldt, *tr. fr. Swedish by* Charles W. Stork. AnSL
Dreams and Realities. Phoebe Cary. LPS-1
"Sometimes, I think, the things we see," *sel.* MaRV
Dreams are they—but they are God's dreams! God's Dreams. Thomas Curtis Clark. OQP; QP-1; QS
Dreams, books, are each a world; and books, we know. Books a Substantial World. Wordsworth. *Fr.* Personal Talk. MOB
Dreams! cheer the child with sights of joy. *Unknown, tr. fr. Greek by* C. B. Sheridan. BOL
Dreams Come True. Sophocles, *tr. fr. Greek by* J. T. Sheppard. *Fr.* Electra. OxBG
(Doubt Not a Dream, *tr. by* Robert Whitelaw.) GrR
Dreams come true, and everything. In the Haunts of Bass and Bream. Maurice Thompson. SN
Dreams cross his sleep, The. The Valley of Sleep. Hendrik Marsman. *Fr.* The Zodiac. LiTW
Dreams, dreams that mock us with their flitting shadows. Petronius Arbiter. *Tr. by* Helen Waddell. DiM
Dreams, Empty Dreams. William Cowper. *See* Stricken Deer, The.
Dreams in Hades. Gustaf Fröding, *tr. fr. Swedish by* Charles W. Stork. AnSL
Dreams of Flying. George Darley. UnW
Dreams of my Youth. Edward Kenealy. RO
Dreams of the Dreamer, The. Georgia Douglas Johnson. CDC
Dreams of the Sea. W. H. Davies. EtS; NLK; TCEP
Dreams of Yith. Duane W. Rimel. DaM
Dreams Old and Nascent. D. H. Lawrence. WGRP
Dreams out of a Wine-Cup. Bacchylides, *tr. fr. Greek by* Arthur S. Way. GrR
Dreams That Came True, The, *sel.* Jean Ingelow.
I Saw in a Vision. UnW
Dreams that delude with flying shade men's minds. We Are Such Stuff as Dreams. Petronius Arbiter. AWP
Dreams to Sell. Thomas Lovell Beddoes. *See* Dream-Pedlary.
Dreams within Dreams. "Fiona Macleod." PoVP
Dreamy crags with raucous voices croon, The. Hymn to the Sunrise. *Unknown.* NA
Dreamy rhymer's measur'd snore, The. Macaulay. Walter Savage Landor. LPS-3; VA
Dreary and brown the night comes down. Columbus at the Convent. John Townsend Trowbridge. BoHiPo; DD; MC; PAH
Dreary Black Hills, The, *diff. versions. Unknown.* ABF, *with music;* ABS; AS, *with music;* CoSo, *with music;* CSF, *with music;* IHA
Dreary, Dreary Life, The, *with music. Unknown.* CSF
(Kansas Line, The, *with music.*) CoSo
Dreary lay the long road, dreary lay the town. The Toy Band. Sir Henry Newbolt. BoTP
Dreary season to a tragic tale, A. The Testament of Cresseid. Robert Henryson. MeEV
Dreary Song, A. Shirley Brooks. PA
Drecker, the draw-bridge keeper, opened wide. The Draw-Bridge Keeper. Henry Abbey. PEOR
Dredged in a net the slender god. Archaic Apollo. William Plomer. ChMP
Dree Night, The. *Unknown.* ChTr
Dregs. Ernest Dowson. BMEP; HBV; LEAP; OBMV; POTT; SeCePo; ViPP; VLEP
Dregs. César Vallejo, *tr. fr. Spanish by* Muna Lee. AnCL
Dreidel Song. Efraim Rosenzweig. TiPo (1952 ed.)
Dreme, The, *sel.* Sir David Lindsay.
Prologue: "In-to the calendis of Januarie," *abr.* EBSV
Drenched earth has a warm, sweet radiance all her own, The. The Robin's Egg. Annie Charlotte Dalton. CaP; CPG; OCL
Drenched with purple. Simaetha. Hilda Doolittle ("H. D."). MAPA
Dresden shepherdess was one day, A. In a China Shop. George Sidney Hellman. AA
Dress. Henry Luttrell. *Fr.* Advice to Julia. OBRV
Dress now in sorrow, O all. Catullus, *tr. fr. Latin by* Horace Gregory. RoL
Dress of Spring, The. May Justus. YeAr
Dress that my brother has put on is thin, The. "The Lady of Sakanoye." *Fr.* Manyo Shu. AWP; JAWP; WBP
Dresscessional, A. Carolyn Wells. WBLP
Dressed and adorned as though for her wedding. Cortège. Leopoldo Marechal. AnCL
Dressed in a mantle of black. Soledad. Federico García Lorca. CoSP
Dressed Up. Langston Hughes. GoSl
Dressed up in my melancholy. Song. M. Carl Holman. PoNe
Dresser, The. Walt Whitman. *See* Wound-Dresser, The.
Dressing the Bride. Thomas Bailey Aldrich. BAV
Dressing the Doll. William Brighty Rands. PRWS; VA
Drevèn scud that auvercast, The. The Sky a-Clearèn. William Barnes. RO
Dribbling like a scribbled word to the seashore. Synthesis, above Swansea. Peter Hellings. MoWP
Dried Apple Pies. *Unknown.* BLPA
Dried-up Fountain, The. Robert Leighton. VA
Drift ("Drift drift upon the beach"). Denis Glover. AnNZ
Drifter, The. Dave Hughes. CoSo
Drifting. George Crabbe. CaAE
Drifting. John Francis O'Donnell. IrPN
Drifting. Thomas Buchanan Read. AA; GN; HBV; LBAP; LEAP; LPS-1; OBAV
Drifting Away. Charles Kingsley. OxBoCh
Drifting, groping. In the Night. William Alexander Percy. *Fr.* In New York. SPP
Drifting mist beyond the bar, A. Dawn. Isabel Butchart. PoMa; PoTo; VOD
Drifting Petal, A. Mary McNeil Fenollosa. AA
Drifting Sands and a Caravan. Yolande Langworthy. BLPA; NeHB
Drifting scent of the Georgia pines. O Daedalus Fly Away Home. Robert E. Hayden. PoNe
Driftwood, *abr.* Trumbull Stickney. HBV
Driftwood. Richard Wilbur. FiMAP
Driftwood Fires. John Richard Moreland. MuM
Drill, The. Harry Brown. NeTW; TwAmPo; WaaP
Drilling in Russell Square. Edward Shanks. OBMV
Drilling Missed Holes. Don Cameron. PoOW
Drimin Donn Dilis. John Walsh. TIP
Drink. Bertel Gripenberg, *tr. fr. Swedish by* Charles W. Stork. AnSL
Drink. William Carlos Williams. OxBA
Drink and Be Glad. *Unknown, tr. fr. Greek by* Bland *and* Wellesley. OnPM
Drink [*or* Drinke] and be merry, merry, merry boy[e]s. The Song[e]. Thomas Morton. *Fr.* New English Canaan. AmPP; IAP
Drink and be merry: there is no man knows. Quid Sit Futurum. *Unknown.* OxBG
Drink and sing, and eat and laugh. Song. Thomas Love Peacock. PoD
Drink by the pool. Water-Lilies. Ibn Hamdis. MooP
Drink, comrades, drink; give loose to mirth! The Death of Cleopatra. Horace. EnLi-1; OuHeWo
Drink, drink, Asclepiades. What use to wail your sorrows? "Fill the Can and Fill the Cup." Asclepiades. GrPE
Drink! drink! open your mouth! Sunday up the River, XIX. James Thomson. EmBrPo
Drink! drink! to whom shall we drink? The Old Man's Carousal. James Kirke Paulding. AA; LEAP
Drink freely when broached is the cask. Golden Mean of Thrift. Hesiod. *Fr.* Works and Days. GrR
Drink, Friends. Moses ibn Ezra, *tr. fr. Hebrew by* Solomon Solis-Cohen. *Fr.* Wine-Songs. TrJP
Drink full ones, tinker, methinks the monks are dry. The Tinker and the Monks. Nathaniel Whiting. *Fr.* Le Hore di Recreatione. SeCL
Drink, gossips mine! we drink no wine. Medieval Norman Songs, XVIII. *Unknown, tr. by* John Addington Symonds. AWP
Drink in moods. Tanka, III. Lewis Alexander. CDC
Drink (ingurgitate, engulph, engorge, gulp). A Thesaurus Nightmare. J. Willard Ridings. WhC
Drink, Melanippus, and be drunk with me. Immortalia Ne Speres. Alcaeus. GrL; OxBG

Drink on, love on, not always lover by love reposes. "Gather Ye Rosebuds." Strato. GrPE
Drink That Rot Gut. *Unknown.* ABF
(Drinking Song.) CoSo; CSF
Drink the Sweet Scent! Holger Drachmann, *tr. fr. Danish by* Charles W. Stork. BoDS
Drink! They dissolve, the faint-whispering. Champagne. Franz Mikael Franzén. AnSL
Drink to Me Only with Thine Eyes. Ben Jonson. *See* To Celia ("Drink to me only . . .").
Drink To-Day [and Drown All Sorrow]. John Fletcher, *and others. Fr.* The Bloody Brother, II, ii. ElSeCe; EnLit; HBV; OAEP; ViBoPo
(Drinking Song.) ElL; TuPP
(Song, The: "Drink to-day and drown all sorrow.") SeEP
Drink we now, and dancing round. The Fall of Cleopatra. Horace. *Fr.* Odes. RoL
Drink you with the lily white. Lilies and Roses. Ibn al-Qutiya. MooP
Drinke and be merry, merry, merry boyes. *See* Drink and be merry, merry, merry boys.
Drinker. Patrick Anderson. PeCV
Drinkers sprawl by night, The. Carousal. Ibn Safar. MooP
Drinking. Abraham Cowley, *after the Greek of* Anacreon. CEP; ElSeCe; EnLi-1 (1949 ed.); EPS; EV-2; HBV; LEAP; LoBV; MePo; OBEV; OtMeF; PG; PoFS; ReEn; SeCV-1; SeEP; ShBV-4; TrGrPo; WhC
(Anacreontic on Drinking.) SeCePo
(Of Drinking.) ALV
(On Drinking.) PoP
("Thirsty earth soaks up the rain, The.") EG
Drinking. Hsin Ch'i-chi, *tr. fr. Chinese by* Ching Ti. LiTW; WhP
Drinking Alone by Moonlight ("In the third month the town of Hsien-yang"). Li Po, *tr. fr. Chinese by* Arthur Waley. TrCh
Drinking Alone in Moonlight ("If Heaven had no love for wine"). Li Po, *tr. fr. Chinese.* WhP
(Drinking Alone by Moonlight: "If High Heaven had no love for wine," *tr. by* Arthur Waley.) TrCh
(Drinking Alone in the Moonlight: "If Heaven did not love wine," *tr. by* Amy Lowell *and* Florence Ayscough.) AWP
Drinking Alone under Moonlight ("Holding a jug of wine among the flowers"). Li Po, *tr. fr. Chinese by* Tsang Bing-ching. WhP
(Drinking Alone by Moonlight: "Cup of wine, under the flowering trees, A," *tr. by* Arthur Waley.) TrCh
(Drinking Alone in the Moonlight: "A pot of wine among flowers," *tr. by* Amy Lowell *and* Florence Ayscough.) AWP
(Drinking Alone with the Moon: "From a pot of wine among the flowers," *tr. by* Witter Bynner.) LiTW
Drinking at the Village. Lu Yu, *tr. fr. Chinese by* Pai Chwen-yu. WhP
Drinking Bout, A. Liu Chia, *tr. fr. Chinese by* Henry H. Hart. OnPM; PoHN
Drinking Fountain. Marchette Chute. TiPo (1959 ed.)
Drinking on East Slope at night. Listening to the River. Su T'ung-po. WhP
Drinking Song. "The Archpoet of Cologne," *tr. fr. Latin by* John Addington Symonds. *Fr.* The Confession of Golias. LiA
Drinking Song. Avenzoar, *tr. fr. Arabic by* A. J. Arberry. MooP
Drinking Song. Burns. *Fr.* The Jolly Beggars. PoFr; TrGrPo
Drinking-Song, A. Henry Carey. OBEV
Drinking Song. William Cartwright. *Fr.* The Royal Slave. SeCL
Drinking Song. Thomas Dekker. *See* Cold's the Wind.
Drinking Song. John Fletcher, *and others. See* Drink To-Day.
Drinking Song. Knud Lyhne Rahbek, *tr. fr. Danish by* Charles W. Stork. BoDS
Drinking Song. Thomas Randolph. *Fr.* Aristippus. SeCL
Drinking Song, A. Shakespeare. *See* Come, Thou Monarch of the Vine.
Drinking Song. Ubada, *tr. fr. Arabic by* A. J. Arberry. MooP
Drinking Song ("Drink that rot gut"). *Unknown. See* Drink That Rot Gut.
Drinking Song ("How happy's the prisoner that conquers his fate"). *Unknown.* SeCL
Drinking Song ("O night, O eyes of love!"). *Unknown, tr. fr. Arabic by* E. Powys Mathers. *Fr.* The Thousand and One Nights. LiTW
Drinking Song ("Tapster, fille another ale!"). *Unknown.* EnLit
Drinking Song, A. W. B. Yeats. TwP
Drinking-Song, A, against All Sorts of Disputes in Drinking; to One, Who Always Bawl'd to Have Reason Done Him, and Was Noisie, and Quarrelsom in His Cups. William Wycherley. SeCV-2
Drinking Song for Present-Day Gatherings. Morris Bishop. ALV
Drinking Songs. Alcaeus, *tr. fr. Greek by* C. M. Bowra. GrL; OxBG
(Two Drinking Songs.) LiTW
Drinking Time. D. J. O'Sullivan. OnYI
Drinking Vessels. Laura E. Richards. LiL
Dripping Sheet, The. *Unknown.* PA
Drive, A. Otto Gelsted, *tr. fr. Danish by* Charles W. Stork. BoDS
Drive It On, *with music. Unknown.* OuSiCo
Drive on, sharp wings, and cry above. The Redshanks. Julian Bell. LO; OBMV
Drive the orioles away. A Spring Sigh. Chin Ch'ang-hsü. ChLP
Driven by Desire to Set Affection. *Unknown.* ReIE
Driven from the soil of France, a female came. Sonnet: September 1, 1802. Wordsworth. ChER
Driven to achievement by youth and love. Haute Politique. Granville Trace. AWP
Driver rubbed at his nettly chin, The. To the Four Courts, Please. James Stephens. BLV; BMEP; EPP; HBMV; MBP; MoAB; MoBrPo; NeMA; TCEP
Driver Saying. Josephine Miles. FiMAP
Drivin' Steel, *with music. Unknown.* AS
Drivin' steel, drivin' steel. Hammer Man. *Unknown.* AS
Driving down from the turf bog in the rain. Merchandise. Seán Jennett. NeIP
Driving Home the Cows. Kate Putnam Osgood. AA; BeLS; BTP; HBV; LEAP; LPS-2; MDAH; PAH; PECK; PTA-2; TreFS
Driving in the Park. *Unknown.* OxBoLi
Driving Saw-Logs on the Plover. *Unknown.* AS, *with music;* IHA
Driving the Rafts. Moyshe Kulbak, *tr. fr. Yiddish by* Sarah Zweig Betsky. OnCuPl
Driving up the Mallerstang. The Mugger's Song. W. W. Gibson. ChMo; CMP
Drizzle from the mountain. Indian Rebellion. Jorge Carrera Andrade. TwSpPo
Drizzling murk of a March dawn, The. The Parting. James K. Baxter. Cressida, VI. AnNZ
Dromedary, The. Hilaire Belloc. WhC
Dromedary, The. Archibald Y. Campbell. HBMV; PFE; PoMa; PtOT; StaSt
Dromedary is a cheerful bird, The. The Dromedary. Hilaire Belloc. WhC
Droning a drowsy syncopated tune. The Weary Blues. Langston Hughes. PoNe; TCPD; UnS
Droning roar is quickened, and we lift, The. London to Paris, by Air. Lord Gorell. PoeMoYo
Droop, droop no more, or hang the head. Upon Julia's Recovery. Robert Herrick. AtBAP
Droop under doves' wings silent, breathing shapes. The Night Nurse Goes Her Round. John Gray. LoBV
Drooping and down at heel, I see them pass. The Pilgrimage. Louis Untermeyer. QS
Drop a Pebble in the Water. James W. Foley. BLPA; PoToHe
Drop a pebble in the water. Influence. Joseph Norris. MaRV
Drop down, drop down, white snowflakes! Winter [*or* Winter's] Song. *Unknown.* BoTP; PCH
Drop, Drop, Slow Tears. Phineas Fletcher. *See* Hymn, An: "Drop, drop, slow tears."
Drop Golden Showers, Gentle Sleep. Thomas Goffe. *Fr.* The Courageous Turk. SeCL; SeEP
Drop of Dew, A. Schmuel Halkin, *tr. fr. Yiddish by* Jacob Sonntag. TrJP
Drop of Dew, A. Andrew Marvell. *See* On a Drop of Dew.
Drop of Ink, A. Joseph Ernest Whitney. AA
Drop of sepia in the fragrant vase, The. Dusk. Abraham Z. Lopez-Penha. TrJP
Drop, one drop, how sweetly one fair drop, A. Dives Asking a Drop [*or* On Dives]. Richard Crashaw. ACP; AEV
Drop welled up, and then another, A. Elemental Rhythm. Elizabeth Selden. BoFr
Drop your offering in the box. Candles. *Unknown.* GoBC
Dropped feathers from the wings of God. Poet Songs, III. Karle Wilson Baker. HBMV
Dropping Corn. Maurice Thompson. PR
Dropping from bells a day draped in mourning. Return of Autumn. "Pablo Neruda." LiTW
Drought. David John Darlow. MM
Drought. Geoffrey Johnson. HaMV
Drought. Will H. Ogilvie. BoAu
Drought, *sels.* Francis Carey Slater. MM
"Powder is the grass."
"Softly and quietly."
Drought. Katharine Tynan. DiM; GTIV
Drouth. Mary Austin. NP
Drouth. *Unknown. See* Western Wind, When Wilt Thou Blow?

Drouth has taken the land, The! Drouth. Mary Austin. NP
Drove-Road, The. W. W. Gibson. EnLit
Drover, A. Padraic Colum. AnIL; AnIV; AWP; HBV; JAWP; LBBV; MBP; MoBrPo; NP; OBMV; OxBI; ViBoPo; WBP
Droves. Sergei Aleksandrovich Yesenin, *tr. fr. Russian by* Babette Deutsch. TrRV
Drowned descend with distance in their eyes, The. Elegy for the Drowned Men Who Return. Roberto Ibáñez. AnCL
Drowned in Harbour. Antipater of Thessalonica, *tr. fr. Greek by* Sir William Marris. OxBG
Drowned Lady, The. *Unknown.* ChTr
Drownèd Lover, The. Lady Margaret Sackville. AV
Drowned Mariner, The. Elizabeth Oakes Smith. AA
Drowned Sailor. Neufville Shaw. CaP
Drowned Seaman, The. Maude Goldring. HBMV
Drowned Soldier, A. Cyril Tourneur. *See* Walking Next Day upon the Fatal Shore.
Drowned Wife, The. Robert Horan. OnHM
Drowned Woman. Elinor Wylie. TBM
Drowning. John Ransom Palmer. PoP
Drowning is not so pitiful. Emily Dickinson. AnEnPo; ExPo
Drowning of Conaing, The. *Unknown, tr. fr. Old Irish by* Frank O'Connor. AnIL; SiB
Drowning of Pharaoh and His Army, The. Cædmon (?), *tr. fr. Anglo-Saxon by* Benjamin Thorpe. *Fr.* Exodus. TCEP
Drowsily come the sheep. Slumber Song. Louis V. Ledoux. FaPON; HBMV; MPB; SBMV; UTS; VOD
Drowsily hum, drowsily hum. The Love and Protection of Mother and Father—Italian. *Unknown.* BOL
Drowsy and dull with age the houses blink. Arkham. Robert Ervin Howard. DaM
Drowsy, friendly, comfortable creak, The. Dawn at the Rain's Edge. Joseph Auslander. MAP; MoAmPo (1942 ed.)
Drowsy Garden, The. Boris Pasternak, *tr. fr. Russian by* Babette Deutsch. TrRV
Drowsy Sleeper, The. *Unknown. See* Who's That at My Bedroom Window?
Drowsy sun went slowly to his rest, The. Evening. James Stephens. MoBrPo
Drowzy night hir wings has spred, The. *Unknown.* SeCSL
Drug Clerk, The. Eunice Tietjens. AnAmPo; HBMV; LA; TBM
Drug Store. Karl Shapiro. AmPP (4th ed.); FiMAP; MoVE; OxBA
Drug Store. John V. A. Weaver. HBMV; NP; PoeMoYo; YaD
Druid, The. John Banister Tabb. AA
Druid Song of Cathvah, The. John Todhunter. TIP
Druid Urien had daughters seven, The. A Ballad. Sir Walter Scott. BHV
Druidic Gums. T. I. Moore. MoAuPo
Druids' Hymn to the Sun. C. M. Doughty. *Fr.* The Dawn in Britain. FaBoTw
Drum, The. John Farrar. BrR; GFA
Drum. Langston Hughes. MAP; MoAmPo
Drum, The. John Scott of Amwell. OBEC; ViBoPo
(Retort on the Foregoing.) OBEV (new ed.)
Drum, The: The Narrative of the Demon of Tedworth. Edith Sitwell. *Fr.* Façade. BoW; FaBoTw
Drum for Ben Boyd, A, *sel.* Francis Webb.
Captain of the Oberon, The. NeLNL
Drum Majah, De. Ray Garfield Dandridge. BANP
Drum on your drums, batter on your banjos. Jazz Fantasia. Carl Sandburg. AnFE; CoAnAM; MAP; MoAB; MoAmPo; NeMA; PoNe; TwAmPo
Drumlin Woodchuck, A. Robert Frost. GoYe; PoLFOT; WaKn
Drummer, The. Anne Robinson. SUS
Drummer-Boy and the Shepherdess, The. William Brighty Rands. CBPC; MoShBr
Drummer Boy of Mission Ridge, The. Kate Brownlee Sherwood. PTA-1
Drummer-Boy's Burial, The. *Unknown.* LPS-2
Drummer Hodge. Thomas Hardy. AWP; CoBMV; EnL; InPo; JAWP; PoE; POTE; PoVP; RiBV; SeCeV; ViP; ViPo; WBP
Drums. Frances Angevine Gray. PoTo
Drum's a very quiet [*or* quiet little] fellow, The. The Drum. John Farrar. BrR; GFA
Drums are beat, the trumpets blow, The. The Stars and Stripes. Lucretia Gray Noble. FOAH
Drums, drums, and marching feet! Armistice Day. Mary Carolyn Davies. AOAH
Drums mutter for war and soon we must begin, The. Advice for a Journey. Sidney Keyes. SoV
Drums of Haiti. Marcus B. Christian. GoSl
Drums of Night, The. Tzu Yeh, *tr. fr. Chinese by* Henry H. Hart. PoHN
Drunk: On Crutches. Raymond Souster. PeCV
Drunk Again. Po Chü-i, *tr. fr. Chinese by* Henry H. Hart. PoHN
Drunk and senseless in [*or* on] his place. Ramon. Bret Harte. BeLS; LPS-3
Drunk and Sober. Tao Yuan-ming, *tr. fr. Chinese by* Yang Yeh-tzu. WhP
Drunkard, The. Proverbs, XXIII: 29-35, Bible, *O.T.* TrJP
Drunkard, The. Fenton Johnson. AnAmPo; LA
Drunkard, The. Mao Kuang Sheng, *tr. fr. Chinese by* Henry H. Hart. PoHN
Drunkard to His Bottle, A. Joseph Sheridan Le Fanu. OnYI
(Abhrain an Bhuideil.) TIP
Drunkard's Doom, The. *Unknown.* ABF, *with music;* AS
Drunkard's Hell, The. *Unknown.* CSF
Drunken Beauty. Ibn Billita, *tr. fr. Arabic by* A. J. Arberry. MooP
Drunken Boat, The. Arthur Rimbaud, *tr. fr. French.* AnFP, *tr. by* Stephen Stepanchev; LiA, *tr. by* Norman Cameron; LiTW, *tr. by* Norman Cameron; MiFP, *tr. by* Julian Bell and Charles Maurron; ReMP, *tr. by* Ben Belitt; TrFP, *tr. by* Alan Conder
Drunken Desperado, The. Baird Boyd. SCC
(Cowboy.) ChTr
(Cowboy Boasting Chants: "I'm wild and woolly," *st.* 1.) ABF
Drunken Fisherman, The. Robert Lowell. AmP; CrMA; FiMAP; LiTA; LiTM (rev. ed.); MoPo; MoVE; OxBA; SeCeV
Drunken Gunners. M. K. Joseph. AnNZ
Drunken Heracles (Metropolitan Museum). Wallace Gould. AnAmPo; LA
Drunken Man on Highgate Hill, A. Paul Hasluck. MoAuPo
Drunken Rose, The. Amarou, *tr. fr. Sanskrit by* E. Powys Mathers. AWP
Drunken Sailor, The; or, Early in the Morning, *with music. Unknown.* ShS; SoAmSa
Drunkenness of youth has passed like a fever, The. Inscription at the City of Brass. *Unknown. Fr.* The Thousand and One Nights. LiTW
Dry, and brown-withered and silent, they that remain. Winter Stalks. Bertram J. Warr. TwCaPo
Dry Be That Tear. Sheridan. OnYI; TIP
Dry Gap—a dingy general store. Western Town. David Wadsworth Cannon, Jr. PoNe
Dry-Landers, The, *with music. Unknown.* CoSo
Dry leaves are falling, The. Autumn. Nikolai Karamzin. BoRS
Dry leaves, soldier, dry leaves, dead leaves. The Wars. Conrad Aiken. *Fr.* The Soldier. WaaP
Dry lighted soul, the ray that shines in thee. To R. W. E. Ellen Hooper. AnAmPo; LA
Dry Loaf. Wallace Stevens. AtBAP; CrMA; OxBA; PoRA
Dry Salvages, The. T. S. Eliot. *Fr.* Four Quartets. LiTB; MaPo; OxBA; SeCePo; SeCeV
Sels.
"Lady, whose shrine stands on the promontory," IV. ISi
"To communicate with Mars, converse with spirits," V. AmPP; ATP (1953 ed.)
"Where is there an end of it, the soundless wailing," *fr.* II. FaBoTw
Dry Time. Norma Davis. NeLNL
Dryad, The. Alexander M. Stephen. CPG
Dryad Song. Margaret Fuller. AA; WGRP
Dryades; or, The Nymphs Prophecy, *sels.* William Diaper. BeR
Beginnings of Day, The.
Evening and Night and Meteors.
Dryad's home was once the tree, A. On Sivori's Violin. Frances Sargent Osgood. AA
Du Bartas: His First Week or Birth of the World, *sel.* Joshua Sylvester.
First Day of the First Week, The. Po
Du bist wie eine Blume. Heine, *tr. fr. German by* Kate Kroeker. *Fr.* Homeward Bound. AWP; JAWP; WBP; OuHeWo, *tr. by* Sir Theodore Martin
(Thou Seemest like a Flower, *tr. by* Emma Lazarus.) TrJP
(Translated Way, The, *tr. by* Franklin P. Adams.) BOHV
Du schönes Fischer-Mädchen. Heine. *See* Thou Lovely Fishermaiden.
Duality. Kenneth Slade Alling. AnAmPo; CAW
Duality. Arthur Sherburne Hardy. AA
Duality. Katherine Thayer Hobson. GoYe
Dubiety. Robert Browning. PoVP; ViPo
Dublin. Louis MacNeice. OxBI
Dublin Ballad, A; 1916. "Dermot O'Byrne." AnIV; OxBI
Dublin Bay. Ewart Milne. NeIP
Dublin Limerick, A. Ray Bradbury. SiTL
Dublin Made Me. Donagh MacDonagh. AnIV; NeIP; OxBI
Dublin; the Old Squares. Padraic Colum. NePoAm
"Ducats take, The! I'll sign the bond to-day." Two Argosies. Wallace Bruce. AA
Duchess. Lilian Bowes-Lyon. AlDL; HaMV; POTE

Duchess of Malfi, The, *sels.* John Webster.
"Farewell Cariola!" *fr.* IV, ii. LO
Hark, Now Everything Is Still, *fr.* IV, ii. BEL; EIL; EV-2; LoBV; OBS; SeCePo; TriL; ViBoPo
(General Mist of Error, A.) OnPM
(Hark.) CH
("Hark [*or* Hearke], now everything is still.") BrBE; CenL; EnLi-1; ReaPo; SiCE; TuPP
(Shrouding of the Duchess of Malfi, The.) BCEP; CoEV; OBEV
(Summons to Execution.) FaBoEn
Heart-Cry of the Duchess, The, *fr.* IV, ii. BCEP
("O that it were possible we might," *br. sel.*) PoD
"I am come to make thy tomb," *fr.* IV, ii. ChTr
"Is she dead?/ She is what you would have her," *fr.* IV, ii. AnFE
"It may be/ I'll join with thee in a most just revenge," 4 *ll. fr.* V, ii. PoFr
Oh, Let Us Howl Some Heavy Note, *fr.* IV, ii. InvP; SiCE
(Madman's Song, The.) EIL
"What hideous noyse was that?" *fr.* IV, ii. AtBAP; PoEL-2
"Yond's the Cardinall's window: This fortification," *fr.* V, iii. AtBAP; PoEL-2
Duchess's White Cats, The. Rafael Méndez Dorich, *tr. fr. Spanish by* Donald Devenish Walsh. AnCL
Duck. John Lyle Donaghy. OxBI
Duck, The. Edith King. BoTP; GFA; HBVY; StVeCh
Duck, The. Ogden Nash. MoShBr; WhC
Duck and a drake, A. *Unknown.* OxNR
Duck, and Mallard first, the falconers' only sport, The. Birds in the Fens. Michael Drayton. *Fr.* Polyolbion. ChTr
Duck and the Kangaroo, The. Edward Lear. BoChLi; GFA; MeMeAg, *st.* 2; OTPC (1946 ed.); PoRh; TiPo (1952 ed.)
Duck in Central Park. Frances Higginson Savage. GoYe
Duck is whiter than whey is, The. Quack! Walter de la Mare. TiPo
Duckle, Duckle, Daisy. Leroy F. Jackson. ChBR
Ducks. Norman Ault. BoTP
Ducks. Roy Daniells. TwCaPo
Ducks. Frederick William Harvey. HiLiEn; PtOT; YT
Sels.
"When God had finished the stars and whirl of coloured suns." PC; QS
"Yes, ducks are valiant things." BoTP
Ducks, The. Alice Wilkins. GFA; TiPo
Ducks at Dawn. James S. Tippett. SiSoSe; TiPo; UTS
Duck's [*or* Ducks'] Ditty. Kenneth Grahame. *Fr.* The Wind in the Willows, *ch.* 2. BoTP; FaPON; MoShBr; MPB; OTPC (1946 ed.); PCH; PoRh; RAR; SUS; TiPo; UTS; WaKn; WhBS
Ducks in the Millpond, *with music.* *Unknown.* OuSiCo
Ducks in the mill-pond eating up moss. Don't Grow Weary, Boys. *Unknown.* CoSo
Ducks require no ship and sail. What Ducks Require. John Crowe Ransom. FaBoMo
Dude, The. Martial, *tr. fr. Latin.* OnPM
Due Commendation of the Quipping Autor, A. Gabriel Harvey. *Fr.* Four Letters and Certain Sonnets. ReIE
Due North. Benjamin R. C. Low. EtS; HBMV
Duel, The. Eugene Field. BeLS; BoChLi; BTP; CenHV; FaBoBe; FaFP; FaPON; GFA; GoBP; HBV; HBVY; MoShBr; NeHB; OHFP; OnHT; OnSP; OTPC (1946 ed.); PECK; PoRA; RAR; StVeCh; TiPo; TreF; UTS; YT
Duel, The. Theodore Maynard. CAW
Duel, The. Harold Trowbridge Pulsifer. HBMV
Duel. Stepan Petrovich Shchipachev, *tr. fr. Russian.* RuPo, *tr. by* Jack Lindsay; TrRV, *tr. by* Babette Deutsch
Duel in the Park. Lisa Grenelle. GoYe
Duel with Verses over a Great Man, *sels. Unknown, tr. fr. Hebrew.* TrJP
"Against the guide of Truth," Epigram V.
"Forgive us, son of Amram, be not wroth," Epigram III.
"Here lies a man, and still no man," Epitaph I.
"Thou fool profane, be silent!" Epigram II.
"Thou Guide to doubt, be silent evermore," Epigram I.
"What thought ye to burn, when ye kindled the pyre," Epigram IV.
Duelling. William Cowper. *Fr.* Conversation. LPS-3
Duellist, The, *sels.* Charles Churchill.
Bishop among the Plotters, The. BeR
"Hail, Liberty! a glorious word." PoFr
Duenna, The, *sels.* Sheridan.
Air: "I ne'er could any luster see," *fr.* I, ii. HBV
"Bumper of good liquor, A," *fr.* II, iii. WhC
How Oft, Louisa, Hast Thou Told, *fr.* III, iii. EV-3
Oh, the Days When I Was Young, *fr.* III, i. EV-3
Song: "Had I a heart for falsehood framed," *fr.* I, v. CEP; HBV; OBEC; TIP
(Had I a Heart for Falsehood Framed.) EV-3
Song: "If a daughter you have, she's the plague of your life," *fr.* I, iii. CEP; NeHB
This Bottle's the Sun of Our Table, *fr.* III, v. EV-3
Duero, river Duero. Ballad of the River Duero. Gerardo Diego. CoSP
Duet. Erik Blomberg, *tr. fr. Swedish by* Charles W. Stork. AnSL
Duet. Charles Lotin Hildreth. PR
Duet, A. T. Sturge Moore. LEAP; MBP; OBEV; OBVV
Duet. Elizabeth Selden. BoFr
Duet. Leonora Speyer. BAP; HBMV; PC
Duff, The. David McKee Wright. AnNZ
Duffy's Hotel, *with music. Unknown.* ShS
Dugall Quin (A *and* B *vers.*). *Unknown.* ESPB
Dug-out, The. Siegfried Sassoon. AtBAP; CH; MBP; MCCG; MoBrPo; MoVE; NeMA; OHIP; POTE; WaaP; WaP
Duino Elegies, The, *sels.* Rainer Maria Rilke, *tr. fr. German.*
Ninth Duino Elegy, The, *tr. by* R. F. C. Hull. AnGP
Tenth Duino Elegy, The, *tr. by* Ruth Speirs. AnGP
Third Duino Elegy, The. AnGP, *tr. by* R. F. C. Hull; LiTW, *tr. by* Stephen Spender *and* J. B. Leishman
Duke di Broccoli and the Countess of Points, The. Pointillism. Joseph Bennett. SiTL
Duke Is the Lad, The. Thomas Moore. OnYI
Duke of Athole's Nurse, The. *Unknown.* BaBo; ESPB (A *and* B *vers.*)
Duke of Benevento, The. Sir John Henry Moore. CEP; OBEC
Duke of Buckingham, The ("A numerous host"). Dryden. *Fr.* Absalom and Achitophel, Pt. I. FaBoEn
(Crowd and Buckingham, The.) NBE
("Numerous host of dreaming saints succeed, A.") EPP
Duke of Buckingham, The ("In the first rank"). Dryden. *See* Zimri.
Duke of Buckingham, The. Pope. *See* Death of Buckingham, The.
Duke of Gordon's Daughter, The. *Unknown.* ESPB; OBB; *sl. diff.*
Duke of Grafton, The. *Unknown.* ChTr
Duke of Merchant's daughter walked out one summer's day, The. Six Questions. *Unknown.* BaBo
Duke of Plaza-Toro, The. W. S. Gilbert. *Fr.* The Gondoliers. ALV; FaPON; FiBHP; OnPP; PCD
Duke See the Tie Pile, *with music. Unknown.* StDa
"Dulce et Decorum." Tyrtaeus, *tr. fr. Greek by* F. L. Lucas. GrPE
Dulce et Decorum. T. P. Cameron Wilson. HBMV; VOD (1931 ed.)
Dulce et Decorum Est. Wilfred Owen. AnFE; CoBMV; FaBoTw; InP; InvP; LiTB; LiTM (rev. ed.); MBP; MoAB; MoBrPo; MoPW; OAEP (2d ed.); ShBV-3; TwCV; WaP
Dulce it is, and *decorum*, no doubt, for the country to fall. Arthur Hugh Clough. *Fr.* Amours de Voyage, II. OAEP; SoV
Dulce Mihi Quondam Studium Fuit. Politian, *tr. fr. Latin by* D. C. Allen. LaP
Dulcina. *At. to* Sir Walter Ralegh. ALV
(On Dulcina.) CoMu
(Shepherd's Wooing Dulcina, The.) TuPP
Dule's i' This Bonnet o' Mine, The. Edwin Waugh. HBV; LPS-1; VA
Dull and hard the low wind creaks. Suburb. Harold Monro. ChMo; CMP; HBV
Dull and muffled now the tumult of the city comes to me. Ola Hansson. *Fr.* Songs of Home. AnSL
Dull are the topics you want me to treat in my epigrams, Mister. Martial, *tr. fr. Latin by* Robert R. Schnorr. Epigrams, XI, 42. LaP
Dull August! Maiden of the sultry days. August. Charles Mair. BoCaPo; CPG
Dull Is My Verse. Walter Savage Landor. PoEL-4
(Lyrics and Epigrams, VI.) ERP
Dull masses of dense green. Embarkation. John Gould Fletcher. Down the Mississippi, I. ChMo; CMP; LiTA; MOAP; NP; SPP; TCAP
Dull, sick day, A; the sky opaque—a cloudy screen. The Clock. Jovan Ducic. LiTW
Dull soul aspire. To the Soul. John Collop. AEV; BCEP; TrGrPo
Dull, Sullen Prisoners. Pope. *Fr.* Elegy to the Memory of an Unfortunate Lady. BeR
("Most souls, 'tis true, but peep out once an age.") CH; PoD
Dull to myself[e], and almost dead to these. The Bad Season Makes the Poet Sad. Robert Herrick. LiTB; OAEP; SeCeV; UnPo (1st ed.)
Dulled by the slow glare of the yellow bulb. A Wartime Dawn. David Gascoyne. MoVE
Dullness. George Herbert. MeRV; TriL
Dulness Is Decent. Dryden. *Fr.* Troilus and Cressida: Prologue. BeR

Dum Diana Vitrea. *At. to* Peter Abelard, *tr. fr. Latin by* George F. Whicher. LyMA
(Dum Diane Vitrea, *tr. by* Helen Waddell.) LiA
Dum Librata Suis Haeret Radicibus Ilex. George Herbert, *tr. fr. Latin by* D. C. Allen. LaP
Dum Vivimus Vigilamus. [*or* Vigilemus]. Charles Henry Webb. AA; LEAP
Dum Vivimus, Vivamus. Philip Doddridge. *See* Live While You Live.
Dumain's Rhymes. Shakespeare. *See* On a Day—Alack the Day!
Dumb are the heavens: sphere controlling sphere. Thomas Caulfield Irwin. *Fr.* To a Skull. IrPN
Dumb are the trumpets, cymbals. Solomon. Heine. TrJP
Dumb, Dumb, Dumb. *Unknown.* OnYI
Dumb genius blows. From Another Room. Gregory Corso. NeAP
Dumb in June, *sel.* Richard Burton.
Summer, *fr.* II, III *and* IV. NLK
Dumb Maid, The. *Unknown.* CoBE
Dumb Mother of all maids, let me rest. Sonnet in a Garden. Josephine Preston Peabody. AA
Dumb Soldier, The. Robert Louis Stevenson. GoTP; OnHT
Dumb Wife Cured, The. *Unknown.* MaC
Dumbo rescue report: the weather was dirty. Time Zones for Forty-four. Donald A. Stauffer. WaP
Dummy Line, The, *with music. Unknown.* SoAF
Dun-Colour. Ruth Pitter. MoVE
Duna. Marjorie Pickthall. BMEP; HBV; MCCG; MLP; POT; PoTo; VOD
Dunbar. Anne Spencer. BANP; CDC
Duncan and Brady. *Unknown. See* Brady.
Duncan and his brother was playing pool. Brady (B *vers.*). *Unknown.* AS
Duncan, Duncan was a-tendin' the bar. Duncan and Brady. *Unknown.* OuSiCo
Duncan Gray. Burns. BEL; BSV; CBOV; CEP; CoMu; EBSV; EiPP; EM-1; EnLit; EPP; EV-3; GoTS; GTBS; GTBS-D; GTBS-W; GTSE; GTSL; LiTL; MCCG; OBEC; PoMa; TOP
(Duncan Gray Cam' Here to Woo.) ALV; LPS-1
Duncan, lad, blaw the cummers. Athol Cummers. James Hogg. EBSV
Duncan's Murder. Shakespeare. *Fr.* Macbeth, I, vii. EV-1
("If it were done when 'tis done, then 'twere well.") NBE; PIR
(Macbeth's Murder Meditation.) BCEP
(Murder Pact, The.) WHA
(Vaulting Ambition.) FiP
Dunce, The. Walter de la Mare. ImOP
Dunciad, The, *sels.* Pope.
"Books and the Man I sing," I (1729 ed.) CEP
Chaos on Her Throne, or the Triumph of Dullness, *fr.* IV. BeR
("She comes! She comes! The sable throne behold!") NBE
Conclusion: "In vain, in vain—the all-composing hour," *fr.* IV. EnLi-1; RiBV; ViBoPo
(Chaos.) LoBV
(Finality.) ReTS
(Reign of Chaos, The.) FiP
(Triumph of Ignorance, The.) CoBE
"High on a gorgeous seat, that far out-shone," *fr.* II. AtBAP
Last Lines of the Dunciad, *fr.* IV. GEPC
"Mighty mother, and her son, who brings, The," *fr.* I. AtBAP, *shorter sel.;* EiPP
"O muse! relate (for you can tell alone)," *fr.* IV. EPP; EV-3
(Triumph of Dulness, The.) CoEV; OBEC
"Yet, yet a moment, one dim ray of light," IV. AtBAP, *br. sel.;* EiPP; PoEL-3
Duncton Hill. Hilaire Belloc. GoBC; TwCV
Dunedin in the Gloaming. Jessie Mackay. BoAu
Dunedin Revisited. Denis Glover. AnNZ
Dungeon, The. Samuel Taylor Coleridge. *Fr.* Remorse (Osorio), V. MCCG
Dunkirk. Robert Nathan. MaC; NeTW; OnSP
Dunkirk, *sels.* E. J. Pratt.
In the Skies. BoCaPo
"So long as light shall shine upon a world." NeTW
Dunkirk Pier. Alan Rook. SoV
Dunna thee tell me it's his'n, mother. Whether or Not. D. H. Lawrence. MBP; MoBrPo
Dunno a heap about the what an' why. Vagabond. John Masefield. OtMeF
Duns Scotus's Oxford. Gerard Manley Hopkins. CoBE; MaPo; NAMP; OBMV; PoE; PoEL-5; TriL
Dunster Church. Margaret Willy. DiM
Duo. Olive Tilford Dargan. HBMV
Dupliciter Beatus. Henry Parrot. SiCE
Dupree. *Unknown.* OuSiCo, *with music;* ViBoFo (A *and* B *vers.*)
Dupree was a bandit; he was so brave and bol'. Dupree (B *vers.*) *Unknown.* ViBoFo
Durable Bon Mot, The. Keith Preston. HBMV
Duraluminum dove dives, The. Summary of the Distance between the Bomber and the Objective. Walter Benton. WaP
Durand of Blonden. Ludwig Uhland. *tr. fr. German by* James Clarence Mangan. AWP; JAWP; WBP
Durant Jail, The, *with music. Unknown.* CoSo
Durban Revisited. R. N. Currey. BoSA
Dürer would have seen a reason for living. The Steeple-Jack. Marianne Moore. *Fr.* Part of a Novel, Part of a Poem, Part of a Play. AmPP; CoBMV; CrMA; ExPo; FaBoMo; MoPo; OnHM; OxBA
Dürer's "Melancholia." Sir William Watson. CBOV
(On Dürer's "Melencolia.") VA
Durham Field. *Unknown.* ESPB; OBB, *sl. diff.*
Durham Lock-out, The. *Unknown.* CoMu
During a Chorale by César Franck. Witter Bynner. *Fr.* To Celia. AnAmPo; HBMV; LA; NP
During a lull in the Stygian Flames. An Outcast in Hell. *Unknown.* AlBD
During happy boyhood years. In Nazareth. Leslie Savage Clark. ChIP
During Lambing Season. Keidrych Rhys. MoWP
During Music. Arthur Symons. MBP; MoBrPo; VA
During the Storm. Théophile Gautier, *tr. fr. French by* Alan Conder. TrFP
During the strike, the ponies were brought up. The Ponies. W. W. Gibson. WaKn
During Wind and Rain. Thomas Hardy. ExPo; RiBV; SeCeV; ViPP
Durisdeer. Lady John Scott. EBSV
Durst thou again say life and soul has lifted. Thomas Lovell Beddoes. *Fr.* Death's Jest Book. LO
Duru, duru, duru, lia! The Love and Protection of Mother and Father—Sardinian. *Unknown.* BOL
Dusk. Guillaume Apollinaire, *tr. fr. French by* Dudley Fitts. AnFP
Dusk. Basho, *tr. fr. Japanese by* H. G. Henderson. OnPM; WoL
Dusk. Angelina Weld Grimké. CDC
Dusk. DuBose Heyward. HBMV; LS; SPP; TBM
Dusk. Abraham Z. Lopez-Penha, *tr. fr. Spanish by* Thomas Walsh. TrJP
Dusk. Archibald MacLeish. HBMV
Dusk. Clinton Scollard. BLP
Dusk. Helen Welshimer. PoToHe
Dusk at Sea. Thomas S. Jones, Jr. BAP; OBAV; SBMV
Dusk from a Train Window. Cale Young Rice. LS; MuM
Dusk-haired and gold-robed o'er the golden wine. For the "Wine of Circe"; a Picture by Edward Burne-Jones. Dante Gabriel Rossetti. ATP (1953 ed.); PoVP; VLEP
Dusk in the Low Country. DuBose Heyward. BAP; TCAP
Dusk is sudden with luminous music flooding, The. Arcum Conteret. Sister Mary Thérèse. PraNu
Dusk its ash-grey blossom sheds on violet skies. A Call. "Æ." NV
Dusk made a thrust at my heart. The Star. Grace Hazard Conkling. HBMV
Dusk of a lowering evening. Communion. Sophie Jewett. PC
Dusk of the Gods, *sel.* S. Funaroff.
"Of my deep hunger." NAMP
Dusk of this box wood, The. Hoof Dusk. Carl Sandburg. Po
Dusk on English Bay. Earle Birney. BoCaPo
Dusk on the convoy, still in ordered lines. The Bandage Is Red. John Ackerson. MuM
Dusk Song. William H. A. Moore. BANP
Dusky light—a purple flash, A. Opium Jottings. Samuel Taylor Coleridge. RO
Dusky night rides down the sky, The. A-Hunting We Will Go [*or* Hunting Song]. Henry Fielding. *Fr.* Don Quixote in England. CBOV; CEP; EV-3; HBV; LPS-2; OBEC; OTPC (1923 ed.); OxBoLi; ViBoPo
Dusky swallows will hang their nests, The. Rimas, LIII. Gustavo Adolfo Bécquer. AnSpL-2; TeCS
Dust. "Æ." BMEP; HBMV; LBBV; OQP; QP-1; WGRP
Dust. Sister Mary Angelita. JKCP (1926 ed.)
Dust. Rupert Brooke. ALV; HBV; MBP; MoBrPo; OBVV; TwCV
Dust, The. Nathalia Crane. MAP; NeMA
Dust. Waring Cuney. CDC
Dust, The. Gertrude Hall. AA; OBAV
Dust, The. Lizette Woodworth Reese. BAV; HBMV; PoMa; VOD
Dust. P. A. Ropes. BoTP
Dust. Stanley Snaith. POTE
Dust. André Spire, *tr. fr. French by* Jethro Bithell. TrJP
Dust always blowing about the town. A Peck of Gold. Robert Frost. LaNeLa
Dust and clay. Ascension-Hymn. Henry Vaughan. SeCV-1

Dust as we are, the immortal spirit grows. Wordsworth. *Fr.* The Prelude. CoEV
Dust blows up and down, The. The Dust. Lizette Woodworth Reese. BAV; HBMV; PoMa; VOD
Dust Bowl. Robert A. Davis. GoSl
Dust comes secretly day after day, The. Dusting. Viola Meynell. MoBrPo (1942 ed.)
Dust, Corpse of Time. Jorge Carrera Andrade, *tr. fr. Spanish by* H. R. Hays. TwSpPo
Dust Dethroned, The. George Sterling. *Fr.* Three Sonnets on Oblivion. BAP; LBMV
Dust-grey with tawny stripes on either side. The Yorktown Road. Virginia McCormick. LS
Dust hangs thick upon the trail, The. The Cowboy and His Love [*or* Song of the Cattle Trail]. John Milton Hagen. CoSo; SCC
Dust Hath Closed Helen's Eye. Thomas Nashe. *See* Adieu, Farewell, Earth's Bliss!
Dust in the Eyes. Robert Frost. CoV
Dust in the hour-glass which returns again and again, The. Of the Dust in an Hour-Glass. Girolamo Amaltheo. LaP
Dust is the end of all pursuit. Knell. George Chapman. MaRV
Dust of Snow. Robert Frost. AmPP; ChMo; CMP; InP; MoShBr; MoSiPe; OxBA; TiPo; TwP; UnPo
(Snow Dust.) BAP
Dust of the Overland Trail, The. James Barton Adams. PoOW
Dust of Timas, The. E. A. Robinson, *after the Greek of* Sappho. AWP; JAWP; WBP
(Variations of Greek Themes, VI.) MOAP
Dust on my mantle! dust. August. William D. Gallagher. APW; SN
Dust, through which. Dust. Waring Cuney. CDC
Dust to Dust. Walter de la Mare. TrPWD
Dust to Dust. Thomas Hood. *See* Epigram: "After such years of dissension and strife."
Dust to Dust. Theognis, *tr. fr. Greek by* F. L. Lucas. GrPE
Duster, dust away, my friend. Dust. André Spire. TrJP
Dusting. Viola Meynell. MoBrPo (1942 ed.)
Dusting of the Books, The. Dorothy Hughes. GoYe
Dustman, The. Clive Sansom. BoTP
Dustman, The. *Unknown.* BOL; BoTP
Dustman, The. Frederic Edward Weatherly. BOL; HBV; OTPC
Dusty Answer, A. George Meredith. *See* Modern Love: "Thus piteously Love closed what he begat."
Dusty Answer, *sel.* Florence Wilson Roper.
Sonnet: "There is a dream that comes to me by night." UnW
Dusty road is mine to tread, A. Pedlar Jim. Florence Hoare. BoTP
Dutch, The. George Canning. OxBoLi
Dutch Courtesan, The, *sel.* John Marston.
"O Love, How Strangely Sweet." AtBAP; ElSeCe; TuPP
(Song: "O Love, how strangely sweet.") ElL; LO
Dutch in the Medway, The. Andrew Marvell. *Fr.* Last Instructions to a Painter. OBS
Dutch Lover, The, *sel.* Aphra Behn.
Amyntas Led Me to a Grove. DiM
(Willing Mistress, The.) ViBoPo
Dutch Lullaby, A. Eugene Field. *See* Wynken, Blynken, and Nod.
Dutch Patrol, The. Edmund Clarence Stedman. OBAV
Dutch Picture, A. Longfellow. AmPP (4th ed.); CBPC; DDA; EtS; ExPo; HBVY; LH; MoShBr; MW; OBAV; OnPP; PCD; PFY; YT
(Simon Danz.) OBVV
Dutch Proverb, A. Matthew Prior. CEP
Dutch Seamen and New Holland, The. William Pember Reeves. AnNZ
Dutch Slumber Song. Viola Chittenden White. VOD
Dutchess of Monmouth's Lamentation for the Loss of Her Duke, The. *Unknown.* CoMu
Dutchesse of Malfy, The. John Webster. *See* Duchess of Malfi, The.
Dutchman, Dutchman, Won't You Marry Me? *Unknown.* ABS
Dutchman's Breeches. Arthur Guiterman. YT
Duties of Man, The. Romans, XII: 3–21, Bible, *N.T.* TreF
Duty. *At. to* Elizabeth Barrett Browning. *See* Reward of Service.
Duty. Arthur Hugh Clough. *See* Duty—That's to Say Complying.
Duty ("In an age of fops and toys"). Emerson. Voluntaries, III. AnNe; FaFP
(In an Age of Fops and Toys.) LiTA
(So Nigh Is Grandeur.) HBVY; TreFS; YT
(Voluntaries, III.) MaRV; PoeMoYo
Duty ("So nigh is grandeur to our dust"), *last 4 ll.* GN; HBV; TreF; YaD
(Heroism.) BAP; OQP; QP-2
(Quatrains, II.) CBOV
Duty. Ellen S. Hooper. BLPA; LPS-2; NeHB; OQP; QP-1; TreFS
(Beauty and Duty.) HBV
Duty. Edwin Markham. HBMV; HBVY; OQP; QP-1; TSW
Duty. *Unknown.* LPS-2
Duty is a path of pain and peril. Motherhood. William L. Stidger. PGD
Duty of Christian Folk, The, *in mod. Eng. Unknown.* TMEV
Duty of the Student. Edward Anthony. GoTP
Duty Our Ladder. Robert Leighton. OQP; QP-2
Duty—That's to Say Complying. Arthur Hugh Clough. ViPP
(Duty.) EmBrPo
Duty to Death, LD. Dick Roberts. WaP
Dwainie. James Whitcomb Riley. *Fr.* The Flying Islands of the Night. AA
Dwarf, The. W. Wesley Trimpi. PtPa
Dwarf barefooted, chanting, The. The Peasants. Alun Lewis. FaBoMo
Dwarf of Disintegration. Oscar Williams. LiTM (rev. ed.); MoPo; NePA; TwAmPo
Dwarf pines; the wild plum on the wind-grassed shore. Colloquy with a King-Crab. John Peale Bishop. LiTA; MoPo
Dwell, oh, dwell within your dream existence. Dream! Jens Peter Jacobsen. BoDS
Dwell with Me, Lovely Images. Theodore Maynard. GoBC
Dweller in yon dungeon dark. Ode, Sacred to the Memory of Mrs. Oswald of Auchencruive. Burns. EM-1
Dwellers, The/ In the old city. Temples Built with Hands. Su T'ung-po. PoHN
Dwelling Place, The. Henry Vaughan. MaRV; MeLP; OBS; OxBoCh; SeEP; TrPWD; WGRP
D'ye ken John Peel with his coat so gay? John Peel. John Woodcock Graves. CH; OxBoLi
Dyeing Prospector, The. Dan Foley. DDA
Dyer, The. *Unknown.* ChTr
("As I went by a dyer's door.") OxNR
Dying. Emily Dickinson. *See* I heard a fly buzz when I died.
Dying. Jessie Holt. ChIP; PGD
Dying. Roden Noel. *See* Old, The.
Dying Airman, The. *Unknown.* FaFP; LiTM; OxBoLi; SiTL
(Handsome Young Airman, The, *with music.*) AS
Dying Beauty, The, *sel.* Thomas Holly Chivers.
"She died in meekness, like the noiseless lamb." PoP
Dying Californian, The. *Unknown.* ABS; TrAS, *with music*
Dying Child, The. John Clare. EnRP; ERP; TrGrPo
Dying Christian to His Soul, The. Pope, *par. fr. the Latin of* Emperor Hadrian. AWP; CAW; EV-3; GoBC; HBV; JAWP; LEAP; LPS-2; MaRV; NeHB; OBEV; TreF; WBP
(Ode: Dying Christian to His Soul, The.) CEP
(Vital Spark of Heavenly Flame.) GTBS-W; LiTB; LiTG
Dying Cowboy, The ("As I walked through Tom Sherman's bar-room"). *Unknown.* ABS
Dying Cowboy, The ("Oh, bury me not on the lone prairie"). *Unknown.* CSF, *longer vers., with music;* CoSo, *longer vers., with music;* FaBoBe; OlF; PoeMoYo, *abr.;* PreP
(Bury Me Not on the Lone Prairie.) FaFP; TrAS, *with music*
(Lone Prairie, The.) APW; ViBoFo
(O, Bury Me Not on the Lone Prairie.) ABS; AS, *br. sel., with music;* ATP
Dying Cowboy of Rim Rock Ranch, The, *with music. Unknown.* CoSo
Dying Damsel's Doleful Destiny, The. *Unknown.* *See* Among the Violets, Fair Lilies and Roses.
Dying-Day of Death, The. Ronald Campbell Macfie. EBSV
Dying Desperado, The. *Unknown.* CoSo
Dying, dying. The Small Hours. Mary Ursula Bethell. OnPM
Dying Enthusiast, The. James Clarence Mangan. IrPN
Dying Eusebio's Address to the Cross, The. Pedro Calderón de la Barca. *See* Cross, The.
Dying figure against the sky, A. Calvary. Mary Hallet. ChIP; PGD
Dying Fireman, The. Walt Whitman. *See* Dying Heroes.
Dying Gipsy's Dirge, The. Sir Walter Scott. *See* Wasted, Weary, Wherefore Stay.
Dying Girl, The. Richard D'Alton Williams. OnYI; TIP
Dying Gladiator, The. Byron. *Fr.* Childe Harold's Pilgrimage, IV. CBE
Dying Heroes. Walt Whitman. *Fr.* Song of Myself, XXXIII. BHV
(Dying Fireman, The, *shorter sel.*) EV-5; LH
Dying Hogger, The. *Unknown.* AS, *with music;* IHA
Dying Hymn, A. Alice Cary. HBV; LPS-2
Dying is sweet. Mikhail Alekseyevich Kuzmin. *Fr.* Alexandrian Songs. TrRV
Dying Lover, The. Sir William Davenant. SeCL
Dying Lover, The. Richard Henry Stoddard. BAP; HBV

Dying Man in His Garden, The. George Sewell. GTBS; GTBS-D; GTBS-W; GTSE

Dying man to the Whitefriar gave, The. Mountain Liberty. Ernest Rhys. *Fr.* The Ballads of the Last Prince. PoFr

Dying Men. Shakespeare. King Richard II, *fr.* II, i. MaRV

Dying Newsboy, The. Emily Thornton. PTA-2

Dying of Père Pierre, The. John McCrae. BoCaPo

Dying Patriot, The. James Elroy Flecker. EV-5; HBMV; LBBV; NV; POTT; ViBoPo; VOD (1931 ed.)

Dying Ranger, The, *with music. Unknown.* CSF; CoSo (Dying Soldier, The, *diff. vers., with music.*) ShS

Dying Reservist, The. Maurice Baring. HBV

Dying Saviour, The. *Unknown. See* O Sacred Head, Now Wounded.

Dying Soldier, The. *Unknown. See* Dying Rangers, The.

Dying Soldier Boy, The. A. B. Cunningham. BIG

Dying Speech of an Old Philosopher. Walter Savage Landor. *See* On His Seventy-fifth Birthday.

Dying Spring. Lu Yu, *tr. fr. Chinese by* Pai Chwen-yu. WhP

Dying Stockman, The. *Unknown.* ViBoFo

Dying sun, shine warm a little longer! Lament for Pasiphae. Robert Graves. FaBoTw

Dying Swan, The. T. Sturge Moore. GTBS-D; MBP; OBMV; SeCePo

Dying Swan, The. Tennyson. EmBrPo; GTSE; OTPC

Dying Swan, The. *Unknown.* ChTr

Dying that I Might Live. Charles Wesley. BePJ

Dying, the seed will discover the self it finds in the losing. The Seeking of Self. Vyacheslav Ivanovich Ivanov. TrRV

Dying Thief, The. J. S. Phillimore. OQP; QP-1

Dying! To be afraid of thee. Emily Dickinson. MoPo

Dying Wife to Her Husband, A. Moses ibn Ezra, *tr. fr. Hebrew.* TrJP

Dying Words of Stonewall Jackson, The. Sidney Lanier. PAH

Dying Year, The. Clyde Walton Hill. PEDC

Dyke-Builder, The. Henry Treece. LiTB; LiTM; WaP

Dykes, The. Kipling. ChMo

Dynastic Tiff. Geoffrey Hellman. ALV

Dynasts, The, *sels.* Thomas Hardy.
After Jena, *fr.* Pt. II, Act I, sc. vii. WaaP
Albuera, *fr.* Pt. II, Act VI, sc. iv. WaaP
Chorus: "Yea, the coneys are scared by the thud of hoofs," *fr.* Pt. III, Act VI, sc. viii. LoBV
(Before Waterloo.) MoAB; PoVP; WaaP
(Field of Waterloo, The, *shorter sel.*) FaBoCh
"Eyelids of eve, The," *fr.* Pt. III, Act VI, sc. viii. EPP
Men Who March Away, *fr.* Pt. I, Act I, sc. i. CH
Night of Trafalgar, The, *fr.* Pt. I, Act V, sc. vii. AlDL; ChTr; FaBoCh; MBP; MoBrPo; OBMV; PoVP; ReTS; ShBV-1
(Boatman's Song, The.) WaaP
(Trafalgar.) CH
Overworld, The, Pt. III, After Scene. WoL
"When we lay where Budmouth Beach is," *fr.* Pt. III, Act II, sc. i. LO
(Budmouth Dears.) CH; MoVE; PoVP
(Hussar's Song.) TCPD

Dynasty, A. Witter Bynner. PtOT

Dynasty of Chimeras, *sel.* Kassaris Emmanuel, *tr. fr. Modern Greek by* Rae Dalven.
"Heavily-laden, snow-white, she departed from the shadow." MoGP

Dypsychus. Arthur Hugh Clough. *See* Dipsychus.

E

E. Phyllis McGinley. *Fr.* All Around the Town. LiL ("E is the Escalator.") TiPo

E. B. B. James Thomson. HBV; PtP; VLEP

$E = MC^2$. Morris Bishop. ImOP

E is the Escalator. E. Phyllis McGinley. *Fr.* All Around the Town. LiL; TiPo

E. P. Ode Pour l'Election de Son Sepulchre. Ezra Pound. *Fr.* Hugh Selwyn Mauberley. CoBMV; CoV; CrMA; FaBoEn; LiTA; LiTM (rev. ed.); MoPo; MoVE; NePA; OxBA; PreP; SeCeV; UnPo (3d ed.)
(Lyrics.) OnAP
(Ode pour l'Election de Son Sepulchre.) AmPP
(Pour l'Election de Son Sepulchre.) FaBoMo; LiTG

E Tenebris. Helen Spalding. NeTW

E Tenebris. Oscar Wilde. CAW; ChIP; JKCP (1926 ed.); MaRV; MBP; MoBrPo; PoLi; StJW; TrPWD

E to the X dy! dx! Engineer's Yell (University of California). *Unknown.* WhC

'E was sittin' on a door-step. The Road to Vagabondia. Dana Burnet. AlBD

Each a Part of All. Augustus Wright Bamberger. *See* Out of the Vast.

Each and All. Emerson. AA; AmP; AmPo; AmPP; AnNE; AWP; CoBA; CoV; HBV; HiLiAm; IAP; LPS-2; MCCG; MOAP; NePA; OBAV; OHFP; OQP; OxBA; PC; QP-2; REAL; TCAP; TOP; WGRP

Each beast can choose his fere according to his mind. Of a Lady That Refused to Dance with Him. Earl of Surrey. SiPS

Each blest drop, on each blest limn. On the Water of Our Lord's Baptism. Richard Crashaw. SeEP

Each care-worn face is but a book. The Strangers. Jones Very. APW; OxBA

Each day come to me tidings three. Three Sorry Things. *Unknown.* TMEV

Each day, dear love, my road leads far. The Homing Heart. Daniel Henderson. HBMV

Each day I walk with wonder. A Prayer. Clinton Scollard. TrPWD

Each day sees die the lonely leaf, sees die. Threnos. J. R. Hervey. AnNZ

Each day the same tree surrounded. Nothing Belongs to Us. Jorge Carrera Andrade. TwSpPo

Each day the string that joined their natural selves. The Cat and the Bird. Marvin Solomon. NePoAm-2

Each day to her a miracle. Mother. *Unknown.* PGD; PSO

Each day, when the glow of sunset. Are the Children at Home? Margaret Sangster. HBV; LPS-1; MotAn

Each day you live. Mother. Percy Waxman. PEDC

Each element to water yields. The First Olympionique to Hiero of Syracuse, Victorious in the Horse-Race. Pindar. *Fr.* Odes. ATP

Each eve earth falleth down the dark. The Day of Days. William Morris. BPN; PoVP

Each evening tulips close their eyes. The Sleepy Tulips. Marion Mitchell Walker. GFA

Each finite thing has definite boundary. Boundless. Leonora Clawson Stryker. MuM

Each flower of my wild wood-roses. Rosebush. Hermann Claudius. TwGV

Each for himself is still the rule. In the Great Metropolis. Arthur Hugh Clough. EmBrPo; PoVP; ViP; ViPP; VLEP

Each Found Himself at the End of . . . Ebbe Borregaard. NeAP

Each Friday morning, sharp at eight. Black Friday. Louella C. Poole. CIV

Each golden note of music greets. Moonlight Song of the Mocking-Bird. William Hamilton Hayne. AA

Each happy hour thou hast secure. Taylor's Song. Björnstjerne Björnson. *Fr.* Marie Stuart. AnNoLy

Each has his saint, and one may dream. St. Peter. Eileen Duggan. WHL

Each hath his drug for sorrow. To Each His Own. Margaret Root Garvin. HBV

Each hour until we meet is as a bird. Winged Hours. Dante Gabriel Rossetti. The House of Life, XXV. EmBrPo; EPN; PoVP; ViPo

Each, in himself, his hour to be and cease. Epilogue: Credo. Arthur Symons. LBBV; OBVV; OQP; PoVP; QP-2

Each in His Inmost Heart. John D. Sheridan. JKCP (1955 ed.)

Each in His Own Tongue. William Herbert Carruth. BAP; BBV; BLPA; BTP; CP; DDA; GrCo-1; HBV; LBAP; MaRV; NeHB; OHFP; OQP; PoeMoYo; POT; PoTo; PTA-1; QP-1; ReTS; WBLP; WGRP

Each in his proper gloom. Visions. Lionel Johnson. MeRV

Each lonely haunt where vanished tribes have dwelt. The Cathedral. Thomas S. Jones, Jr. MaRV

Each lover's longing leads him naturally. Sonnet: To Dante Alighieri (He Interprets Dante's Dream). Cino da Pistoia. AWP

Each man is captain of his soul. We Break New Seas Today. John Oxenham. OQP; QP-1

Each man is limited by inborn traits. Love Is Kind. Benjamin Keech. PoToHe

Each man me telleth I change most my devise. Sonnets, II. Sir Thomas Wyatt. SiPS

Each month hath praise in some degree. To the Month of September. Sir John Davies. *Fr.* Hymns of Astraea. CaAE; CenL

Each morning bees and butterflies. A Lovely Bed. Mattie Lee Hausgen. GFA

Each morning, from her childhood, she would come. No Child. Victor Hugo. TrFP

Each morning, in the eastern sky, I see. The Day-Star in the East. Helen Hunt Jackson. CV

Each morning there were lambs with bloody mouth. Foxes among the Lambs. Ernest G. Moll. BoAu

Each morning they sit down to their little bites of bread. Husbands over Seas. Lloyd Roberts. CPG

Each nation master at its own fireside. Nationality. John Kells Ingram. TIP

Each New Hour's Passage Is the Acolyte. Lord Alfred

Douglas. *Fr.* The City of the Soul. BMEP; MBP; MoBrPo (1942 ed.); WHA
Each night before I sleep. To My Terrier Rex. Agnes Kendrick Gray. TBM
Each of us is like Balboa: once in all our lives do we. Rare Moments. Charles Henry Phelps. AA
Each of us like you/ has died once. Adonis. Hilda Doolittle ("H. D."). AWP; BAV; InPo; JAWP; LiTA; MOAP; PFE; TBM; WBP
Each of us pursues his trade. The Scholar and the Cat. *Unknown.* KiLC
Each of us waking to the window's light. Exile. Donald Hall. NePA
Each one deserves great praise to have, but yet not like, I think. Fortitude; a Young Man of Egypt and Valerian. Richard Edwards. ReIE
Each other we meet but live grief rises early. Definition of My Brother. W. S. Graham. FaBoTw; NeBP
Each pale Christ stirring underground. Words for a Resurrection. Leo Kennedy. BoCaPo; OCL; PeCV
Each pregnant oak ten thousand acorns forms. Erasmus Darwin *Fr.* Of Good and Evil. PoP
Each ripple has been repeated before. Seine. Rhys Davies. MoWP
Each soldier as he passes looks at their breasts. Namkwin Pul. Bernard Gutteridge. WaP
Each star that rises and doth fade. Reminder. John Galsworthy. OQP; QP-1
Each storm-soaked flower has a beautiful eye. Rain. Vachel Lindsay. ChMo; CMP
Each the herald is who wrote. Astraea. Emerson. AnNE; TCAP
Each thin hand resting on a grave. The Blue and the Gray. *Unknown.* MDAH
Each thing must cede to time's prerogative. Salve. "H. T. R." CAG
Each Thought of Ours Is Like a Flower. Henri Frédéric Amiel, *tr. fr. French by* Alan Conder. TrFP
Each time I pass thru Holyoke Street. Ode to Lowell House. Frederick Bertolet. CAG
Each time I return to Johannesburg it is summer. Seven South African Poems. David Wright. BoSA
Each time we move, we break another plate. Sonnet from an Oil-Field. Dorothy McFarlane. DDA
Each to Each. Melville Cane. GoYe
Each tree did boast the wished spring-time's pride. Thomas Watson. *Fr.* The Tears of Fancy. TuPP
Each was honest after his way. The Diplomats. Alfred Noyes. MaRV
Each with each has borne in patience. To Edom. Heine. TrJP
Each year I have a birthday. A Giant's Cake. Evelina San Garde. BoTP
Eadem Mutato Resurgo. Selden Rodman. OnHM
Eadie, *with music. Unknown.* OuSiCo
Eager he looked: another train of years. A Union of the World [*or* A League of Nations]. Joel Barlow. *Fr.* The Columbiad, X. CoBA; IAP
Eager he wandered the streets of Scythopolis. A Stranger in Scythopolis. Katharine Lee Bates. StJW
Eager Spring. Gordon Bottomley. AlDL; BMEP; CP; MBP; MoBrPo; POTE
Eager to greet my task and have it done. Oxen. Ralph Mortimer Jones. BAP
Eagerly/ Like a woman hurrying to her lover. Four Glimpses of Night. Frank Marshall Davis. PoNe
Eagle, The (to Hiero of Syracuse). Bacchylides, *tr. fr. Greek by* F. L. Lucas. GrPE
Eagle, The. James Daly. AnAmPo; LA
Eagle, The. Arthur Guiterman. QS
Eagle, The. Khanlari, *tr. fr. Persian by* A. J. Arberry. PeP
Eagle, The. Tennyson. BEL; BLA; BLV; BMEP; BoLiVe; BoTP; BPN; CBE; CBOV; CH; CoEV; EG; EnL; ExPo; FaBoCh; FaPON; FiP; GN; GoTP; GTBS-D; GTML; GTSL; HBV; HiLiEn; LoGBV; LPS-2; MW; MyFE; OAEP; OTPC; PCD; PCH; PIAE; PIR; PoeMoYo; PoF; PoMa; PoVP; RIS; SeCePo; SeCeV; ShBV-1; ShGoBo; SN; StaSt; SUS; ThWaDe; TrGrPo; UnPo (3d ed.); UTS; ViPo; ViPP; VLEP; WhBS; YT
Eagle. James B. Thomas. BLA
Eagle and the Beetle, The. La Fontaine, *tr. fr. French by* Alan Conder. TrFP
Eagle and the Mole, The. Elinor Wylie. AnFE; APA; AWP; BLV; BoLiVe; CBOV; ChMo; CoAnAm; CoBA; GTBS-W; HBMV; LiTA; LiTM; MAP; MM; MoAB; MoAmPo; MOAP; NeMA; NP; NV; PG; PoE; PoeMoYo; TCPD; TSW; TwAmPo; ViBoPo; WHA
Eagle and Vulture, The. Thomas Buchanan Read. PAH
Eagle, The, did ye see him fall? The Eagle's Fall. Charles Goodrich Whiting. AA
Eagle, The, has passed on! . . . into the blue. Woodrow Wilson. Roselle Mercier Montgomery. GA
Eagle headed to the west, An. The Tall Axe-Man. Robert P. Tristram Coffin. PoFr
Eagle hunted Master Jackie Rabbit, The. The Eagle and the Beetle. La Fontaine. TrFP
Eagle Hunter, The. Rose O'Neill. TBM
Eagle of Corinth, The. Henry Howard Brownell. PAH
Eagle of Song, The. Bacchylides, *tr. fr. Greek by* T. F. Higham. OxBG
Eagle of the armies of the West, The. The Flight of the War-Eagle. Obadiah Cyrus Auringer. AA
Eagle of the Blue, The. Herman Melville. AA
Eagle on a Tombstone. Antipater of Sidon, *tr. fr. Greek by* John Leyden. OnPM
Eagle sat upon the fell, An. The Eagle's Love. Shushanik Gourghinian. ArmLP
Eagle Soars in the Summit of Heaven, The. T. S. Eliot. *Fr.* The Rock. NAMP; OBMV; OnHM; QS; TwCV (Knowledge without Wisdom.) MaRV
Eagle Song. Gordon Bottomley. *Fr.* Suilven and the Eagle. MBP; MoBrPo
Eagle Sonnets, *sels.* Clement Wood.
"Flower of the dust am I: for dust will flower," VII. HBMV
"How petty, then, the me above the you," X. NV
"I am a tongue for beauty," XIX. HBMV
"I have been sure of three things all my life," III. HBMV
"O bitter moon, O cold and bitter moon," IX. HBMV; NV
"We are the singing shadows beauty casts," XX. HBMV
"When down the windy vistas of the years," XI. HBMV
Eagle Swift, The. Adam of St. Victor, *tr. fr. Latin.* BePJ
Eagle That Is Forgotten, The. Vachel Lindsay. AmP; AnFE; APA; ATP; AWP; BAP; ChMo; CMP; CoAnAm; CP; HBV; IAP; InP; JAWP; LBMV; LEAP; LiTA; MAP; MoAB; MoAmPo; MOAP; NeMA; NePA; NP; OxBA; PFY; Po; PoeMoYo; PoFr; TCPD; TOP; TwAmPo; ViBoPo (1958 ed); WBP; WHA
Eagle Trail, The. Hamlin Garland. BAP
Eagle Valor, Chicken Mind. Robinson Jeffers. LiTA; OxBA; WaP
Eagle! why soarest thou above that tomb? Spirit of Plato [*or* Plato's Tomb]. *Unknown, tr. by* Shelley. AWP; EnLi-1; FaBoCh; JAWP; LiA; LoGBV; OxBG; UnW; WBP
Eagle Youth. Karle Wilson Baker. AOAH
Eagles. Vicente Aleixandre, *tr. fr. Spanish by* Eleanor L. Turnbull. CoSP
Eagles. Vasily Vaselyevich Bashkin, *tr. fr. Russian by* Babette Deutsch. TrRV
Eagles and Sparrows. José Santos Chocano, *tr. fr. Spanish by* Alice Stone Blackwell. PoFr
Eagles. Composed at Dunolly Castle in the Bay of Oban. Wordsworth. PeBoSo
Eagle's Fall, The. Charles Goodrich Whiting. AA
Eagles, leave your sky. Broadcast to the Scholars in the Eyrie. David Ross. PG (1945 ed.)
Eagle's Love, The. Shusanik Gourghinian, *tr. fr. Armenian by* Zabelle C. Boyajian. ArmLP
Eagle's Nature, The. *Unknown, tr. fr. Middle English. Fr.* The Bestiary. MeEV
Eagles over the Lambing Paddock. Ernest G. Moll. BoAu
Eagles, sea-dogs, and all the gristly race. How Sea-Calves Are Born. Oppian, *tr. by* William Diaper. *Fr.* Halieuticks. BeR
Eagle's Song, The. Mary Austin. NP
Eagle's Song, The. Richard Mansfield. DD; HBV; HBVY; MC; MDAH; PaA; PAH
Eagles, that wheel above our crests. The Cedars of Lebanon. Lamartine. AWP; JAWP; WBP
Eagles, you browless birds, who skim. Birds. Geoffrey Dearmer. PtOT
Eaper Weaper. *Unknown.* OxBoLi
Ear Is Not Deaf. Irene Dayton. GoYe
Ear the answer, The/ Hears the wrecked cry. The Hill of Intrusion. W. S. Graham. NePoEA
Eared flower blue yellow pricks. Gorse. Nigel Heseltine. MoWP
Earl Bothwell. *Unknown.* ESPB
Earl Brand. *Unknown. See* Douglas Tragedy, The.
Earl Crawford. *Unknown.* BaBo; ESPB
Earl March look'd on his dying child. The Maid of Neidpath [*or* Song]. Thomas Campbell. EBSV; GoTS; GTBS; GTBS-D; GTBS-W; GTSE; GTSL; HBV
Earl Mar's Daughter. *Unknown.* GN; HBV; OBB; OnSP (Earl of Mar's Daughter, The.) BaBo; CH, *abr.*; ESPB
Earl Mertoun's Song. Robert Browning. *See* There's a Woman like a Dewdrop.
Earl Norman and John Truman. Charles Mackay. VA
Earl o' Quarterdeck, The. George Macdonald. BeLS; EtS; LoEn; LPS-2
Earl of Aboyne, The. *Unknown.* BaBo; ESPB
Earl of Errol, The. *Unknown.* ESPB
Earl of Gawain wooed the Lady Barbara. Lady Barbara. Alexander Smith. LPS-1
Earl of Mar's Daughter, The. *Unknown. See* Earl Mar's Daughter.
Earl of Shaftesbury, The. Dryden. *See* Achitophel.

Earl of Surrey to Geraldine, The. Michael Drayton. *See* Henry Howard, Earl of Surrey, to the Lady Geraldine.
Earl of Westmoreland, The. *Unknown.* ESPB
Earl of Wigton had three daughters, The. Richie Story. *Unknown.* BaBo; ESPB
Earl Percie of Northumberland. Chevy Chase. *Unknown.* EnSB
Earl Richard had but ae daughter. The Kitchie-Boy. *Unknown.* BaBo
Earl Rothes. *Unknown.* BaBo; ESPB
Earl Sigurd's Christmas Eve. Hjalmar Hjorth Boyesen. CLS
Earle Douglasse for this day doth with the Percies stand, Th'. Michael Drayton. *Fr.* Polyolbion. OBS
Earliest Christian Hymn ("Curb for stubborn steed"). Clement of Alexandria, *tr. fr. Greek by* Edward H. Plumptre. WGRP
(Hymn to Christ the Saviour.) CAW
Earliest Christian Hymn, The ("Shepherd of tender youth"). Clement of Alexandria. *See* Shepherd of Eager Youth.
Earliest Spring. William Dean Howells. OBEV; OBVV
Earliest spring, and clouds at dawn are few. Dialogue of the Way. Harold Stewart. BoAV
Earliness at the Cape. Babette Deutsch. NePoAm-2
Early a-foot,/ On public roads. David Moir. *Fr.* The Angler. EnSW
Early and late the backdrop is for joy. This World. Abbie Huston Evans. NePoAm
Early April. Robert Frost. YeAr
Early Autumn. Dart Fairthorne. PEOR
Early Bacon. Archibald Stodart-Walker. *Fr.* The Moxford Book of English Verse. CenHV
Early before the day doth spring. Of Astraea [*or* The Virgin Queen; an Anagram]. Sir John Davies. *Fr.* Hymns of Astraea. BLV; SiCE; TrGrPo; TuPP
Early Bluebird, An. Maurice Thompson. AA
Early cheerful, mounting lark. To the Lark. Sir John Davies. *Fr.* Hymns of Astraea. SiCE
Early Christian, An. Robert Barnabas Brough. OBVV
Early Chronology. Siegfried Sassoon. FaBoTw; PtOT
Early Days, The. Basil Dowling. AnNZ
Early Death. Hartley Coleridge. HBV; MaRV; OBEV; TreFS
Early Death and Fame. Matthew Arnold. TriL
Early dew woos the half-opened flowers, An. Haroun's Favorite Song. *Unknown. Fr.* The Thousand and One Nights. AWP
Early Dutch. Jennie M. Palen. GoYe
Early, early, comes the dark. Witches' Song. Elizabeth J. Coatsworth. PoMS
Early, Early Easter Day. Aileen Fisher. SiSoSe
Early Evening Quarrel. Langston Hughes. HoPM
Early fire, An/ And ever-burning. "What Lack We?" Gudmundur Fridjónsson. IcP
Early for God ("It was too late for man"). Emily Dickinson. OnPM
Early Fragments, *sels.* Thomas Lovell Beddoes.
Grief-in-Idleness. AtBAP
Her Kisses. AtBAP
("Her kisses are/ Soft as a snow-tuft . . .") LO
I'll Be as True. AtBAP
Early Friendship. Stephen E. Spring Rice, *wr. at. to* Aubrey Thomas De Vere. BoFr; LPS-1
Early have a miser's insinuating rub, The. Timers. Flora J. Arnstein. GoYe
Early I rose/ In the blue morning. Love Song [*or* Papago Love Song]. *Tr. by* Mary Austin. APW; AWP; JAWP; LiTA
Early in the Mornin' ("Early in the mornin' "), *with music. Unknown.* StDa
Early in the Morning ("Way, hay, there she rises"). *Unknown.* AmSS
Early in the morning. A Watering Rhyme. P. A. Ropes. BoTP
Early in the morning, before the day began. The Angel in the Apple Tree. Winifred Welles. StVeCh
Early in the morning, when the dawn is on the roofs. The Milkman. Christopher Morley. GaP; MPB
Early in the spring when the snow is all gone. A Trip to the Grand Banks. *Unknown.* ShS
Early Influences. Mark Akenside. *Fr.* The Pleasures of Imagination, IV. OBEC
Early Levée, An. Po Chü-i, *tr. fr. Chinese by* Arthur Waley. TrCh
Early Light. Lilian Bowes-Lyon. AlDL
Early light of the rising sun shines on the beams of my house, The. Getting Up Early on a Spring Morning. Po Chü-i. TrCh
Early Love. V. Sackville-West. DiM
Early Lynching. Carl Sandburg. MAP; MoAmPo
Early May, after cold rain the sun. Dan. Carl Sandburg. AlBD
Early Moon. Carl Sandburg. LaNeLa; MOAP; PG
Early Morn. W. H. Davies. CH; PoeT
Early Morning, The. Hilaire Belloc. BMEP; BoTP; GTBS-D; HBMV; HBVY; JKCP; LEAP; POTE; RIS; WaKn
Early Morning at Bargis. Hermann Hagedorn. HBV; NLK
Early Morning in a Glade. Glenn Ward Dresbach. NP
Early Morning Meadow Song. Charles Dalmon. ALV; CH; HBMV
Early Mornings. *Unknown, tr. fr. Spanish by* Louis Untermeyer. AS
Early News. Anna Maria Pratt. AA
Early on a Monday morning. Kevin Barry. *Unknown.* AS
Early on a sunny morning, while the lark was singing sweet. Fetching Water from the Well. *Unknown.* LPS-1
Early once in Robledillo. Serranilla VIII. Marqués de Santillana. AnSpL-1
Early One Morning ("Early one morning in May I set out"). Edward Thomas. MoVE
Early One Morning ("Early one morning, just as the sun was rising"). *Unknown.* ChTr
Early one morning the bay will be full of pelicans. The Pelicans My Father Sees. Sister Maris Stella. GoBC
Early Pleasure. Ibn Hamdis, *tr. fr. Arabic by* A. J. Arberry. MooP
Early Primrose, The. Henry Kirke White. *See* To an Early Primrose.
Early rises the sun, summer draws nigh. His Delight. Meilir ap Gwalchmai. LiTW
Early Rising. Lady Flora Hastings. OTPC (1923 ed.)
Early Rising, *sel.* Ruth Pitter.
"I arose early, O my true love!" AlDL
Early Rising. John Godfrey Saxe. AnNE; APW; BOHV; HBV; InMe; LEAP; PR; WhC
Early Rising and Prayer. Henry Vaughan. EV-2
Early Snow. Ken Etheridge. MoWP
Early Spring. W. H. Davies. TVSH
Early Spring. Kalidasa. *Fr.* The Seasons. AWP
Early Spring. Sidney Keyes. FaBoMo
Early Spring. Helge Rode, *tr. fr. Danish by* Charles W. Stork. BoDS
Early Spring. Tennyson. DD; GTML; HBV; HBVY; LiA; NLK; SN
Early Spring Brook, The. Richard Henry Dana. BAV
Early Summer Night. Wen Yi-tuo, *tr. fr. Chinese by* Ho Yung. LiTW; WhP
Early sun on Beaulieu water. Youth and Age on Beaulieu River, Hants. John Betjeman. ChMP; FaBoTw
Early Thoughts. William Edward Hartpole Lecky. OnYI
Early to bed and early to rise. Early to Bed [*or* Rhymes to Remember *or* Some Proverbs in Verse]. *Unknown.* FaBoBe; PCH; StaSt
Early Waking. Léonie Adams. MoVE
Early, when first cocks crow. The Forsaken Maid. Eduard Mörike. AnGP
Early Willows. James Wreford Watson. BoCaPo
Earnest, earthless, equal, attuneable. Spelt from Sibyl's Leaves. Gerard Manley Hopkins. ChMo; CoBMV; CoEV; FaBoMo; LiTM; MaPo; MoPo; ViPP; VLEP
Earnest Suit to His Unkind Mistress Not to Forsake Him, An. Sir Thomas Wyatt. BEL; EnLit; GoBC; LiTL; LPS-1; TOP
("And wilt [*or* wylt] thou leave me thus?") AtBAP; EG; EIL; ElSeCe; EnLoPo; OAEP; ReEn; ReIE; SiCE; SiPS; TuPP
(Appeal, The.) OBEV; OBSC
(Lover's Appeal, The.) GTBS; GTBS-D; GTBS-W; GTSE; GTSL
(Say Nay.) LoBV
Ears in the Turrets Hear. Dylan Thomas. FaBoTw
Ears lack no food, for loaded time. Light Heart. T. Sturge Moore. POTE
Earth, The. "Æ." ChMo; CMP
Earth. Bryant. CoV
Earth, The. Emerson. AA
Earth. John Gould Fletcher. SPP
Earth. Alfonso Gutiérrez Hermosillo, *tr. fr. Spanish by* Dudley Fitts. AnCL
Earth. Oliver Herford. *Fr.* The Bashful Earthquake. BTP
(Proem: "If this little world tonight.") AA
Earth, The. Lucretius, *pr. tr. fr. Latin by* W. H. D. Rouse. *Fr.* De Rerum Natura, V. LiA
Earth, The. Leonard Mann. BoAV; MoAuPo; NeLNL
Earth. Laura Riding. MoP
Earth. William Caldwell Roscoe. VA
Earth. Sergei Smirnov, *tr. fr. Russian by* Jack Lindsay. RuPo
Earth, The. Jones Very. AmP; OxBA
Earth. Brian Vrepont. NeLNL
Earth. John Hall Wheelock. AnFE; APA; CoAnAm; CP; HBMV; InP; LiTA; MAP; MoAmPo; NV; PIAE; SBMV
Earth Abideth Forever, The. Ecclesiastes, I: 4-7, Bible, *O.T.* FaPON
Earth and Air. Frank Ernest Hill. MAP; MoAmPo (1942 ed.)

Earth and I are tired of Spring. A Poet at the Court of Pan. Lady Margaret Sackville. ReTS
Earth and Man, The. Stopford Brooke. HBV; OnYI; OTPC; TIP
Earth and Man. George Meredith. EmBrPo; EPN; ViPo
Earth and Sea. Pushkin, *tr. fr. Russian by* Sir Cecil Kisch. WaL
Earth and Sky. Euripides, *tr. fr. Greek by* C. M. Bowra. OxBG
Earth and Sky. Eleanor Farjeon. BoChLi; MeMeAg; SUS
Earth and Sky. Hovhannes Toumanian, *tr. by* Zabelle C. Boyajian. ArmLP
Earth and water, air and stars. Immortality. "Nikolai Maksimovich Minski." TrJP; TrRV
Earth Angel. Barbara Young. BAP
Earth at Night. Walt Whitman. *Fr.* Song of Myself, XXI. PIAE
(Bare-bosom'd Night.) SN
Earth awakes and takes, The. Morning. Mikhail Lukonin. RuPo
Earth bare the long-ridged mountains, within whose fair depths dwell. Mountains. Hesiod. *Fr.* Theogony. GrPE
Earth-bound. Theodore Maynard. QS
Earth Bows to the New Bomb. Aline Badger Carter. ChIP
Earth breaks up, time drops away. Robert Browning. *Fr.* Christmas-Eve and Easter-Day. ChIP
Earth Breath, The. "Æ." BEL
Earth-canonized. Henry Morton Robinson. CAW
Earth cries loud for blood, The; for never grew. Martyrdom. Leonard Van Noppen. BAP
Earth darkens and is beaded. Quod Tegit Omnia. Yvor Winters. MoVE
Earth dies to haze below, the cables sing. Clouds. Frank Ernest Hill. AnAmPo; LA; PoeMoYo; VOD (1935 ed.)
Earth does not lack. W. H. Davies Simplifies the Simplicities He Loves. Louis Untermeyer. WhC
Earth does not understand her child. The Return. Edna St. Vincent Millay. GTBS-W; InP; LiTA; MAP; MoAB; MoAmPo; MoPo; OxBA
Earth does not withhold, The, it is generous enough. The Great Mother. Walt Whitman. GrCo-2
Earth for Sale, The. Harold Monro. ChMo; CMP
Earth from heavenly light conceived heat, The. George Chapman. *Fr.* Ovid's Banquet of Sense. ReIE
Earth from her winter slumber breaks. Decoration Day. Julia Ward Howe. DD; OHIP
Earth gets its price for what Earth gives us. June. James Russell Lowell. *Fr.* The Vision of Sir Launfal, Pt. I, Prelude. LPS-2; PIR; TreF
Earth goes on, the earth glittering in gold, The. Inscription on Melrose Abbey. *Unknown.* LPS-1
Earth grows white with harvest; all day long, The. The Harvest of the Sea. John McCrae. EtS
Earth has borne a little son. The Aconite. A. M. Graham. BoTP
Earth has drunk the snow, The. The Fisherman. Li Po. ChLP
Earth has gone up from its Gethsemane. Earth's Easter. Robert Haven Schauffler. EOAH; SBMV
Earth has grown old with its burden of care, The. Christmas Carol. Phillips Brooks. COAH; HH; MaRV; PEDC; PSO; SDH
Earth has its rock: the body has its bone. Peasantry. Eileen Duggan. CoBE
Earth Has Not Anything to Show More Fair. Wordsworth. *See* Composed upon Westminster Bridge.
Earth has not anything to show more fair. On Mrs. W——. Nicolas Bentley. FiBHP
Earth holds you though your dreams run far. Council from a Poet, Middle-aged. John Holmes. CAG
Earth in Spring, The. Judah Halevi, *tr. fr. Hebrew by* Edward G. King. TrJP
Earth is a jealous mother; from her breast. Coelo et in Terra. Thomas Walsh. JKCP
Earth is a place on which England is found, The. Geography. G. K. Chesterton. *Fr.* Songs of Education. HBMV
Earth is awake and the birds have come, The. Corn-planting. Peter McArthur. CPG
Earth Is Enough. Edwin Markham. MaRV; OQP; PoTo; QP-1; TreFS
Earth Is Full of God's Goodness, The. James Montgomery. MaRV
Earth is gray no longer, The. Vicisti. Elliott Coleman. NoCaPo (1941 ed.)
Earth is green, the earth is wide, The. The Optimist. Sheila Kaye-Smith. ReTS
Earth is instinct with spirit everywhere. Immanence. Thomas Durley Landels. MaRV
Earth is like a spinning top, The. The Spinning Top. Sister Mary Angelita. WHL
Earth is raw with this one note. Crows. Lizette Woodworth Reese. MAP; MoAmPo (1942 ed.)
Earth Is So Lovely, The. Heine, *tr. fr. German by* Howard E. Hugo. AnGP
Earth is somnolent in the noon of its summer, The. Universalism. Kathleen Sutton. MuM
Earth is the Lord's, and the fullness thereof, The. Psalm XXIV, Bible, *O.T.* AWP; CBOV; EnLi-1; FaPON; JAWP; OHIP; OnPM; OuHeWo; PCD; PCH; PreP; TiPo (1952 ed.); TrGrPo; TrJP; WoL
Earth is the tower of granite, the floor of loam. Earth and Air. Frank Ernest Hill. MAP; MoAmPo (1942 ed.)
Earth is weary of our foolish wars, The. Let Us Have Peace. Nancy Byrd Turner. MaRV; OQP; PoToHe; QP-2
Earth keeps some vibration going, The. Fiddler Jones. Edgar Lee Masters. *Fr.* Spoon River Anthology. AMP; LiTA; LoGBV; NP; OxBA; TrGrPo; UnS
Earth, Late Choked with Showers, The. Thomas Lodge. *Fr.* Scillaes Metamorphosis. ElL; ElSeCe; SiCE; ViBoPo
(Melancholy.) OBSC
(Sonnet.) TuPP
Earth leads by the earth, The. Dream Nocturne. Juan Ramón Jiménez, *tr. by* Thomas McGreevy. AnSpL-2
Earth leads through the earth, The. Dream Nocturne. Juan Ramón Jiménez, *tr. by* Eleanor L. Turnbull. TeCS
Earth, let me speak to you. Earth. John Gould Fletcher. SPP
Earth, let thy softest mantle rest. Horace Greeley. Edmund Clarence Stedman. DD; GA
Earth Listens. Katharine Lee Bates. PGD; PSO
Earth Love. Beatrice Redpath. CPG
Earth-lover that I am, you say. Cloister. Mother Mary Campion. PraNu
Earth Melody. Christy MacKaye. PIAE
Earth, Mother Earth, do you feel light flowing. Peace Triumphant. Cale Young Rice. PEDC
Earth must breathe by hours, The! Funeral at High Tide. Hervey Allen. LS
Earth, My Likeness. Walt Whitman. NePA; OxBA
Earth now is green, and heaven is blue. To the Spring. Sir John Davies. *Fr.* Hymns of Astraea. ElL; SiCE; TuPP
Earth, Ocean, Air, belovèd brotherhood! Alastor. Shelley. BCEP; BEL; BPN; CBE; EmBrPo; EnLi-2 (1949 ed.); EnRP; EPN; ERP; EV-4; FiP; GEPC; MeRV; OAEP; TCEP; WHA
Earth of Greece, child of the Gods. The Ocean. Andreas Calvos. MoGP
Earth out of earth is worldly wrought. Earth upon Earth. *Unknown.* ChTr; TMEV
Earth puts her colours by. Envoi. P. H. B. Lyon. BoTP; PtOT
Earth raised up her head. Earth's Answer. Blake. *Fr.* Songs of Experience. EiPP; EnRP
Earth rebelled, The. And the Earth Rebelled. Yuri Suhl. TrJP
Earth, receive an honoured guest. W. H. Auden. *Fr.* In Memory of W. B. Yeats. ChMP; ChTr; FaBoTw; NeMA; PG (1955 ed.)
Earth, return to your place. A Prayer at Winter Thanksgiving. *Unknown.* *Fr.* The Fountain of Old Poems. WhP
Earth, sea, and sky expand the air. The Chart. Michael Lewis. StaSt
Earth seems a desolate mother, The. March. Charles Henry Webb. AA
Earth Song. David McKee Wright. AOAH
Earth-Spirit, The. William Ellery Channing. AnNE; APW; PFY
Earth, that gave body! Birth-Goddess, shelter in womb! Macedonius, *tr. fr. Greek by* William Stebbing. GrPo
Earth, that let us in, was soft as fern, The. En Route. E. L. Mayo. MiAP
Earth, that nourished thee, shall claim. Bryant. *Fr.* Thanatopsis. YT
Earth the Mother of All. *Unknown.* *See* Hymn to Earth the Mother of All.
Earth to Earth. Phoebe Cary. TVSH
Earth to Earth. "Michael Field." VA
Earth to Earth. *Unknown.* OnPM; WoL
Earth to earth, and dust to dust! Death and Resurrection. George Croly. WGRP
Earth took from earth with woe. Earth to Earth. *Unknown.* OnPM; WoL
Earth travails. At Harvest. Joseph Campbell. NP
Earth twitches its skin, The. Seismograph. A. M. Sullivan. JKCP (1955 ed.)
Earth, Universal Mother. *Unknown.* *See* Hymn to Earth the Mother of All.
Earth upon Earth, *in mod. Eng.* *Unknown.* ChTr; TMEV
Earth-Visitors. Kenneth Slessor. BoAV
Earth Voices, *sel.* Bliss Carman.
"I heard the spring light whisper," *fr.* II. OCL
Earth was green, the sky was blue, The. A Green Cornfield [*or* The Skylark]. Christina Rossetti. BoTP; GoTP; PFE

Earth was not Earth before her sons appeared. Appreciation. George Meredith. EmBrPo; ViBoPo
Earth, whereon his feet have pressed. Spiritus Intactus. Robert Germain Cole. CAG
Earth Will Stay the Same, The. Frank Ernest Hill. AnAmPo; LA
Earth, with all its fullness, is the Lord's, The. Poor for Our Sakes. Mary Brainerd Smith. BLRP
Earth with its dark and dreadful ills. A Dying Hymn. Alice Cary. HBV; LPS-2
Earth, with Thunder Torn, The. Fulke Greville. Caelica, LXXXVII. ElSeCe; PeBoSo; SiCE; TuPP
Earth with yellow pears, The. Halves of Life. Friedrich Hölderlin. AnGP
Earth Worshiped, The! Catherine Cate Coblentz. ChIP
Earth yields nothing more divine, The. Life's Purpose. "George Eliot." *Fr.* A Minor Prophet. MaRV
Earth, you have had great lovers in your hour. Poets. Hortense Flexner. BAP; HBMV
Earthborn. Peter McArthur. CaP; OCL
Earth-born. Odell Shepard. OBAV
Earthen Pot and the Iron Pot, The. La Fontaine, *tr. fr. French.* BoChLi
Earthfast. A. S. J. Tessimond. POTE
Earthly Illusion. Louise Leighton. GoYe
Earthly Love. Joseph Bennett. NePA
Earthly [*or* Eartly] nourris [*or* nourrice *or* nurrice] sits and sings, An. The [Great] Silkie of [*or* o'] Sule Skerry [*or* Skerrie]. *Unknown.* BaBo (B *vers.*); ChTr; ESPB; EtS; FaBoCh; OBB; SG; ViBoFo (A *vers.*)
Earthly Paradise, The, *sels.* William Morris.
Apology, An. AWP; BEL; BLPA; BPN; CoBE; EmBrPo; EnLi-2; EnLit; EPN; GTBS-W; GTSL; InP; OAEP; POTT; PoVP; TCEP; TOP; ViP; ViPP; VLEP
(Idle Singer, The, *abr.*) BMEP
("Of Heaven or Hell I have no power to sing.") EPP; LiTB; LoBV; ViBoPo, *abr.*; ViPo
(Prelude to "The Earthly Paradise.") LEAP
(Prologue: "Of Heaven or Hell I have no power to sing.") FaBoEn; OtMeF
(Prologue to "The Earthly Paradise.") BrBE
(Singer's Prelude, The.) HBV; VA
Atalanta's Race (*in* March). BEL; BMEP, *much abr.*; BPN; EV-5; LPS-1, *much abr.*; ViPo
Atalanta's Defeat. VA
Atalanta's Victory. VA
August. BPN
February, *abr.* ViPo
Golden Apples, The (*in* December). EPN
June. BPN; POTT; PoVP; ViPo, *abr.*; VLEP
("O June, O June, that we desired so," *abr.*) ViBoPo
King's Visit, The (*fr.* The Man Born to Be King, *in* March). VA
Lady of the Land, The (*in* June). EmBrPo; EPP; PoVP; TOP; VLEP, *abr.*
Land across the Sea. A. (*fr.* The Watching of the Falcon, *in* July). VA
L'Envoi: "Here are we for the last time face to face." BPN; EmBrPo; EnLi-2; PoVP; ViP; ViPo
March. HBV; LPS-2; OtMeF; POTT; VLEP
November, *abr.* EmBrPo; EPN; GTML; GTSL; ViPo; ViPP
"O love, this morn when the sweet nightingale" (*in* May). EG
October. EPN; POTT; ViPP; VLEP
("O love, turn from the unchanging sea, and gaze.") FaBoEn
Outlanders, Whence Come Ye Last? (Song from "The Land East of the Sun and West of the Moon," *in* September). AnEC; OxBoCh; StJW
(Minstrels and Maids.) COAH; GN
(Song from "The Land East of the Sun and West of the Moon.") POTT
Prologue: "Forget six counties overhung with smoke." BEL; EmBrPo, *abr.*; EPN, *abr.*; EPP, *abr.*; ViPo, *abr.*
(Introduction.) ViPP
Proud King, The (*in* April). EV-5
Song from "Ogier the Dane" (*in* August). BPN; OAEP; POTT; PoVP; VLEP
(Antiphony.) VA
("In the white-flowered hawthorn brake.") EG; ViBoPo
Song from "The Hill of Venus" ("Before our lady came on earth") (*in* February). POTT; PoVP; VLEP
Song from "The Story of Acontius and Cydippe" (*in* October). BPN; POTT; VLEP
(Song: "Fair is the night and fair the day.") HBV
Song from "The Story of Cupid and Psyche" ("O pensive maid") (*in* May). BPN; POTT; VLEP
(Song: To Psyche.) VA
Writing on the Image, The (*in* May). EmBrPo
Earthly roses at God's call have made, The. On the Death of a Pious Lady. Olof Wexionius. AWP; JAWP; WBP
Earthly tree a heavenly fruit it bare, An. A Carol for Christmas Day [*or* Cast Off All Doubtful Care]. *Unknown.* AnEC; TuPP
Earth's a virgin fair, The. Virgin Earth. Ibn al-Bain. MooP
Earth's Answer. Blake. *Fr.* Songs of Experience. EiPP; EnRP
Earth's Bondman. Betty Page Dabney. GoYe
Earth's Burdens. Ernest Charles Jones. VA
Earth's Common Things. Minot J. Savage. MaRV; OQP; QP-1
Earth's crammed with heaven. Glory in the Commonplace. Elizabeth Barrett Browning. *Fr.* Aurora Leigh, VII. MaRV
Earth's Easter. Robert Haven Schauffler. EOAH; SBMV
Earth's first Adam, he lay in the grass. Adam and Eve. Itzig Manger. TrJP
Earth's Immortalities. Robert Browning.
Fame. BPN; PoVP; VLEP
Love. BPN; EnLoPo; PIR; PoVP; VLEP
Earth's Night. William Allingham. GTBS-W; IrPN
Earth's Secret. George Meredith. EmBrPo; EPN; PoVP
Earth's Silences. Ethelwyn Wetherald. CPG
Earth's special mystery—volation blest. Life. Paul C. Boomer. PoP
Earth's Story. Thomas Curtis Clark. OQP; QP-2
Earthy Anecdote. Wallace Stevens. ThWaDe
Eartly nourris sits and sings, An. *See* Earthly nourris sits and sings, An.
Ease. Po Chü-i, *tr. fr. Chinese by* Arthur Waley. TrCh
Ease in Writing. Pope. *See* Sound and Sense.
Easily as a child that plays in his innocency. The Last Stand at the Ships. Homer. *Fr.* The Iliad, XV. GrPE
Easily, my dear, you move, easily your head. A Bride in the '30's. W. H. Auden. FaBoMo
Easily to the old. Exit. Wilson MacDonald. CaP; MM; OCL; TwCV; ViBoPo
East, The. Matthew Arnold. *Fr.* Obermann Once More. OtMeF
East a-Callin', The. Oscar Wilde. *Fr.* Ave Imperatrix! OtMeF
East and the South have ruled us long, The. Andrew Jackson. Stephen Vincent Benét. InMe
East and West. Matthew Arnold. BPN
East Anglian Bathe. John Betjeman. AlDL; GTBS-D
East bow'd low before the blast, The. The East. Matthew Arnold. *Fr.* Obermann Once More. OtMeF
East Coast—Canada. Elizabeth Brewster. CaP
East Coast Lullaby. Lady Anne Lindsay. BOL; EtS
East Coker. T. S. Eliot. *Fr.* Four Quartets. ChMP; FaBoMo; MoVE; NePA; PoLFOT
East in Gold. W. H. Davies. CBPC
East is a clear violet mass, The. A Street Scene. Lizette Woodworth Reese. PCH; TSW; VOD
East is yellow as a daffodil, The. Sunrise. Lizette Woodworth Reese. TSW; TSWC
East London. Matthew Arnold. BMEP; BPN; EM-2; EmBrPo; EPN; MaRV; OAEP; OHIP; PoVP; StJW; VLEP; WGRP
East-northeaster pounds the coast tonight, The. Euroclydon. Abbie Huston Evans. NePoAm
East of the City, Early Spring. Yang Ch'u-yuan, *tr. fr. Chinese.* WhP
East of the long Duck Mountain range. The Courting of Olga Karg. Watson Kirkconnell. TwCaPo
East unrolled a sheet of gold, The. As Helen Once. Muna Lee. HBMV; TBM
East Virginia, *with music. Unknown.* OuSiCo
East was crowned with snow-cold bloom. The." Oversoul [*or* Krishna]. "Æ." ChMo; CMP; MaRV; PoVP; VA
East Wind, The. Charles Buxton Going. LBAP
East Wind. Ou-yang Hsiu, *tr. fr. Chinese by* Kenneth Rexroth. OnPC
East wind blows gently, The. Begonias. Su T'ung-po. OnPC
East wind blows over the green rain mountains, The. On Seeing Ch'ang-an in Spring. Lu Lun. WhP
East wind is blowing in the north garden, The. The North Garden. Po Chü-i. WhP
Eastcoat, The. Christian Morgenstern, *tr. fr. German by* Herman Salinger. TwGV
Easter. Thomas Curtis Clark. OQP; QP-1
Easter. Elizabeth J. Coatsworth. YeAr
Easter. Hilda Conkling. HH; TiPo (1952 ed.)
Easter. Mary Carolyn Davies. OHIP
Easter. Richard Watson Gilder. DD
Easter. George Herbert. CaAE; EOAH; SeCV-1; SeEP; TriL
"I got me flowers to straw thy way," *sel.*, 3 *sts.* AtBAP; BoTP, 2 *sts.*; CH; EG; FaBoCh, 2 *sts.*, *diff. vers.*; FaBoEn; LEAP; LoGBV; OBEV, 2 *sts.*, *diff. vers.*; OBS; OHIP; PCH, 1 *st.*; TrGrPo
Easter. Genevieve M. J. Irons. EOAH
Easter. Joyce Kilmer. MPB; NP; TiPo
Easter. Martin Luther, *after the Latin of* John Huss, *tr. fr. German.* EOAH

Easter. Miyoshi, *tr. fr. Japanese by* Lois J. Erickson. SoLD
Easter. John G. Neihardt. *See* Easter, 1923.
Easter. John Oxenham. OQP; QP-2
Easter. Edwin L. Sabin. DD; HH; OHIP; PoRL
Easter. Spenser. *See* Amoretti, LXVIII.
Easter. Charles Hanson Towne. *See* Easter Prayer, An.
Easter. Katharine Tynan. YT
Easter ("Sing, soul of mine"). *Unknown.* OQP; QP-1
Easter ("This is the time man hath overcome"). *Unknown.* TMEV
Easter. John Van Brakle. ChIP
Easter. Paul Verlaine, *tr. fr. French by* Alan Conder. TrFP
Easter. Mary Hoge Wardlaw. PraP
Easter. Robert Whitaker. ChIP; PGD; PSO
Easter Advent. John Henry Boner. NoCaPo
Easter Airplane, The. Carolyn R. Freeman. GFA
Easter Beatitudes. Clarence M. Burkholder. BLRP
Easter Canticle, An: "In every trembling bud and bloom." Charles Hanson Towne. ChIP; MaRV, *abr.;* OHIP; QS; TrPWD
Easter Carol, An: "Flash forth, thou sun." Christina Rossetti. PCH; PoRL
Easter Carol: "O Earth! throughout thy borders." George Newell Lovejoy. ChIP; EOAH; DD; OHIP; OQP; PGD; PSO; QP-1
Easter Carol, An: "Spring bursts to-day." Christina Rossetti. DD; EAOH; HH; MaRV; MPB; OHIP; TriL
Easter Chick, An. Thirza Wakley. BoTP
Easter Chorus: "Christ is arisen." Goethe, *tr. fr. German by* Arthur Cleveland Coxe. *Fr.* Faust. MaRV
(Christ Is Arisen, *tr. by* Arthur Cleveland Coxe.) EOAH
(Easter Chorus from Faust, *abr., tr. by* Bayard Taylor.) WGRP
(Easter Hymn.) ChIP
Easter Dawn. Frances Ridley Havergal. EOAH
Easter Day. Arthur Hugh Clough. BMEP; BPN; EmBrPo; EPN; EPP; OAEP; PoVP; ViP; ViPP; VLEP
"Weep not beside his tomb," *sel., fr.* II. PGD
Easter Day. Richard Crashaw. MeRV; PoLi
Easter Day. Josephine Rice Creelman. EOAH
Easter Day. Jasper Heywood. ReIE
Easter Day. John Keble. EOAH
Easter Day. Juan Ruiz, Archpriest of Hita, *tr. fr. Spanish by* Ida Farnell. TeCS
Easter Day, *sel.* Christopher Smart.
"Ye that for psalmody contend." KN
Easter Day. Dionysios Solomos, *tr. fr. Modern Greek by* Rae Dalven. *Fr.* Lambros. MoGP
Easter Day. Charles Wesley. *See* Easter Hymn.
Easter day breaks! Rest Remaineth. Robert Browning. *Fr.* Christmas-Eve and Easter-Day. PoRL
Easter Day in Rome. Oscar Wilde. EOAH
Easter Day was a holiday. Sir Hugh (C *vers.*). *Unknown.* ViBoFo
Easter Day we got up early. Early, Early Easter Day. Aileen Fisher. SiSoSe
Easter duck and Easter chick. Some Things That Easter Brings. Elsie Parrish. MeMeAg; PCH
Easter Eggs. *Unknown.* GFA
Easter Eucharist. *Unknown.* MaRV
Easter Eve. James Branch Cabell. HBMV; MaRV
Easter Eve, 1945. Muriel Rukeyser. NePA; MiAP
Easter Even. Margaret French Patton. EOAH
Easter Even. Christina Rossetti. EOAH
Easter Evening, 1942. Leonard Bacon. NeTW
Easter Gloves. *Unknown.* PCH
("Rose is red, the violet blue, The.") SiTL
Easter-glow and Easter-gleam! A Madrigal. Clinton Scollard. EOAH
Easter has come around. W. D. Snodgrass. Heart's Needle, VI. NePoEA
Easter Hymn. Thomas Blackburn. HH
Easter Hymn. Goethe. *See* Easter Chorus.
Easter Hymn. A. E. Housman. More Poems, I. ChMP; MaRV; MoAB; ReaPo; SeCeV; TriL
Easter Hymn. St. John of Damascus, *tr. fr. Greek by* John Mason Neale. BePJ; CAW
Easter Hymn. Henry Vaughan. StJW; TriL
Easter Hymn. Charles Wesley. DD; HH; MaRV; OHIP
(Christ the Lord Is Risen Today.) BePJ; OlF
(Easter Day.) EOAH
(For Easter-Day.) CEP
Easter in the Woods. Frances Frost. BrR; SiSoSe
Easter is coming, and I without him. Mozarabic Songs, 4. *Unknown.* TeCS
Easter Island. Frederick George Scott. BoCaPo
Easter Island. Richard Leon Spain. MuM
Easter Joy. Daisy Conway Price. ChIP
Easter Joy. Nancy Byrd Turner. YeAr
Easter Light. Ida Norton Munson. ChIP
Easter Lilies. "Susan Coolidge." EOAH
Easter lilies! Can you hear. On Easter Day. Celia Thaxter. FaPON; YeAr
Easter lilies freshly bloom. Mary's Easter. Marie Mason. DD; EOAH
Easter Message. John Van Brakle. ChIP
Easter Monday. William Barnes. PoVP
Easter Morn. Giles Fletcher. *Fr.* Christ's Victory and Triumph. ElL
Easter Morning. St. Matthew, XXVIII: 1-10, Bible, *N.T.* TreF
Easter Morning. Phillips Brooks. MaRV
Easter Morning. Winfred Ernest Garrison. ChIP
Easter Morning. Frances Laughton Mace. EOAH
Easter Morning. Spenser. *See* Amoretti, LXVIII.
Easter Music. Margaret Wade Deland. ChIP; HH; OQP; PoRL; QP-1
Easter Must Be Reclaimed. George W. Wiseman. MaRV
Easter Night. Alice Meynell. ChIP; OHIP; StJW; WP
Easter 1916. W. B. Yeats. ChMP; CoBMV; CoEV; EnLP; FaBoMo; GTIV; LiTM; MoAB; OxBI; PoFS; SeCeV; ShBV-4
Easter, 1923. John G. Neihardt. AnAmPo; HBMV; LA
(Easter.) OHIP
Easter Parade. Marchette Chute. BrR; SiSoSe
Easter Poem, An. Herbert Edward Palmer. QS
Easter Poem. John Prichard. MoWP
Easter Poem. Kathleen Raine. LiTB
Easter Praise. Rodney Bennett. BoTP
Easter Prayer, An. Chester M. Davis. PraP
Easter Prayer. Frances Ridley Havergal. *See* For Easter.
Easter Prayer, An. Charles Hanson Towne. OQP; PSO; QP-1
(Easter.) ChIP
Easter Prayer. Nancy Byrd Turner. PraP
Easter Prayer, An. *Unknown.* PraP
Easter Reveille, An. John R. Slater. MaRV
Easter Robin, The. Geraldine Farrar. StJW
Easter Sacraments. Henry Park Schauffler. EOAH; OQP; QP-1
Easter Snowfall. Harry Behn. TiPo (1959 ed.)
Easter Song. Leo Alishan, *tr. fr. Armenian by* Alice Stone Blackwell. CAW
Easter Song. "Susan Coolidge." *See* Calvary and Easter.
Easter Song, An. T. W. Handford. MeMeAg
Easter Song. Mary A. Lathbury. OHIP
Easter Song. Caelius Sedulius. *See* Carmen Paschale.
Easter stars are shining, The. Flight to the City. William Carlos Williams. AnAmPo; LA
Easter Sunday, 1945. G. A. Borgese. NePoAm
Easter Surprise, An. Leona Covey. GFA
Easter thaws no overwintered mind. Autumn Love. John Crowe Ransom. SPP
Easter Thought. Leo Cox. CaP
Easter Tuesday. Christina Rossetti. MeRV
Easter Week. Charles Kingsley. DD; EOAH; OHIP
Easter Week. *Unknown.* OnYI
Easter Wings. George Herbert. ATP; ElSeCe; EOAH; EPS; ExPo; LiTB; MeLP; MePo; OAEP; OBS; PoEL-2; PoFS; PreP; SeEP; TwCrTr
Easter Wish, An. *Unknown.* OQP; QP-1
Easter Zunday. William Barnes. PoVP
Eastern Castle stands tall and high, The. *Unknown, tr. fr. Chinese by* Arthur Waley. Seventeen Old Poems, 11. TrCh
Eastern Evangelic Planet, *sel.* Carlos de Sigüenza y Góngora, *tr. fr. Spanish by* Samuel Beckett.
Invocation and Proposition. AnMP
Eastern Front. Georg Trakl, *tr. fr. German by* Christopher Middleton. AnGP
Eastern Gate, The. *Unknown, tr. fr. Chinese by* Arthur Waley. TrCh
Eastern Legend, An. Margaret L. Woods. UnW
Eastern Question, An. H. M. Paull. BOHV
Eastern Serenade. William E. Aytoun *and* Sir Theodore Martin. InMe
Eastern Shore. Charles Bruce. PeCV
Eastern Tempest. Edmund Blunden. MBP; MoBrPo; PtOT
Easter-Tide Deliverance, A.D. 430, An. Maria H. Bulfinch. EOAH
Eastmuir king, and Wastmuir king. Fause Foodrage (C *vers.*). *Unknown.* ESPB
Eastmure king, and the Westmure king, The. Fause Foodrage (B *vers.*). *Unknown.* ESPB
Eastward. Swinburne. *Fr.* Songs before Sunrise: Epilogue. CBOV
Eastward far anon. The Beacons. Henry Hart Milman. *Fr.* Samor. OBRV
Eastward lies the island. The Island. Audrey Alexandra Brown. BoCaPo
Eastward runs the Great River. Meditation at Red Cliff. Su T'ung-po. WhP
Easy Is the Triolet. W. E. Henley. PreP
(Triolet, The.) BOHV
Easy, Ned, easy, go soft, an it please 'ee. To Heaven on a Beetle. Aristophanes. *Fr.* The Peace. OxBG
Easy on your drums. Dark Girl. Arna Bontemps. GoSl

Easy the cry, while vengeance now is wrought. The Right of Asylum. Stephen Phillips. PoFr
Easy thing, O Power Divine, An. The Things I Miss. Thomas Wentworth Higginson. PraP; TrPWD
Easy, wind! Of a Small Daughter Walking Outdoors. Frances Frost. DDA; FAOV
Eat and drink, my comrades, rejoice and let us be gay. The Death of the Klepht. *Unknown.* MoGP
Eat and Walk. James Norman Hall. BLPA
Eat but simple food; go for early rising. Advice from an Expert. John Kieran. InMe
Eat no green apples or you'll droop. Advice to Small Children. Edward Anthony. GoTP
Eat thou and drink: to-morrow thou shalt die. The Choice, I. Dante Gabriel Rossetti. The House of Life, LXXI. ATP; BEL; BPN; EmBrPo; EnL; EnLi-2; EPP; HBV; MyFE; OBVV; PIAE; POTT; PoVP; PreP; TOP; ViBoPo; ViPo; VLEP; WHA
Eat your meat and save the skin. Cowboy Grace. *Unknown.* CoSo
Eaten Heart, The. *Unknown, tr. fr. Middle English by* Pearl London. *Fr.* The Knight of Curtesy. TrGrPo
Eating. Stephen Crane. *See* Heart, The.
Eating Bamboo-Shoots. Po Chü-i, *tr. fr. Chinese by* Arthur Waley. TrCh
Eating Nuts and Oranges. José Moreno Villa, *tr. fr. Spanish by* Eleanor L. Turnbull. CoSP
Eating of the Pudding, The. Joel Barlow. *Fr.* The Hasty Pudding, III. APW
Eating Song. Sir Walter Raleigh. WhC
Eau-forte. F. S. Flint. TwCV
Eavesdropper, The. Bliss Carman. BAP
Ebb. John Lyle Donaghy. NeIP
Ebb and Flow. George William Curtis. AA; HBV; LBAP; LEAP; OBAV
Ebb and Flow, The. Edward Taylor. AmP; AmPP; AnNE; CoV
Ebb slips from the rock, the sunken, The. Night. Robinson Jeffers. AmPP (3d ed.); AWP; CoBMV; InPo; JAWP; LiTA; MAP; MoAmPo; MOAP; MoPo; NP; OxBA; WBP; WHA
Ebb-Tide. John Gould Fletcher. ChMo; CMP
Ebb Tide. Robert Nathan. MuM
Ebb Tide. Marjorie Pickthall. CaP; OCL
Ebb-tide at ending of the sea. Ebb-Tide. John Gould Fletcher. ChMo; CMP
Ebbtide at Sundown. "Michael Field." CAW; GTML
Ebb tide to me as of the sea! The Old Woman of Beare. *Unknown, tr. by* Kuno Meyer. OnYI
Ebbtide with me, as with the sea. The Hag of Beare. *Unknown, tr. by* Seán O'Faoláin. SiB
Ebbé Skammelson. *Unknown, tr. fr. Danish.* BaBo; BoDaBa, *tr. by* E. M. Smith-Dampier
Ebbed and flowed the muddy Pei-ho by the gulf of Pechili. Blood Is Thicker than Water. Wallace Rice. PaA; PAH
Ebbing, the wave of the sea. The Woman of Beare. *Tr. by* Stephen Gwynn. AnIV; GTIV
Ebbs from soiled fields the last drab vestige of snow. February. D. S. Savage. NeBP
Ebenezer, The, *with music. Unknown.* ShS
Ebony and Ivory. Ibn Hamdin, *tr. fr. Arabic by* A. J. Arberry. MooP
Ebrius Dissimulans. Henry Parrot. TuPP
Ecce Autem Dulces Labris Pater Ingerit Uvas. Politian, *tr. fr. Latin by* D. C. Allen. LaP
Ecce Homo. John Ackerson. BoFr; MaRV
Ecce Homo. Witter Bynner. WGRP
Ecce Homo. David Gascoyne. *Fr.* Miserere. ChMP; FaBoTw; LiTM (rev. ed.); NeBP; OnHM
Ecce Homunculus. R. A. K. Mason. AnNZ
Ecce in Deserto. Henry Augustin Beers. AA; AnFE; APA; CoAnAm; OBAV
Ecce Puer. James Joyce. MeRV; ReaPo
"Ecce Quomodo Moritur Justus." Diogenes Laertius, *tr. fr. Greek by* Dudley Fitts. LiTW
Eccentric old person of Slough, An. Limerick. George Robey. CenHV
Eccho, The. Richard Leigh. MePo
Eccho's Song. Ben Jonson. *See* Slow, Slow, Fresh Fount.
Ecclesiastes. Bible *O.T.* WoL, *abr.*
Sels.
Cast Thy Bread upon the Waters, XI: 1-6. AWP; JAWP; TiPo (1952 ed.); WBP
(Life's Uncertainty, XI: 1-10.) TreFS
Earth Abideth Forever, The, I: 4-7. FaPON
"It Is Better . . . ," VII: 1-9. TrJP
(Better Path, The, VII: 1-5.) TreFS
Light Is Sweet, The, XI: 7. FaPON
Live Joyfully, IX: 7-11. TreFS
Remember Now Thy Creator, XII: 1-7. AWP; BLP; BrBE; CBOV; ChTr (XII: 1-8); HiLiEn; JAWP; LiTW; MaRV; NV; PoeMoYo; PYM; ShBV-1; TreF (1-14); WBP
(Remember Also Thy Creator.) ExPo
("Remember now thy Creator in the days of thy youth," XII: 1-8.) EnLi-1 (1949 ed.)
(Remember Then Thy Creator, XII: 1-8.) TrJP
Time for Everything, A, III: 1-8. TrGrPo
Vanity, I: 12-II: 26. OuHeWo
Words of the Preacher, The, I: 2-11. TreFS
(Vanity of Vanities, I: 2-9.) TrJP
Youth and Age. OuHeWo (XI: 1-XII: 7); TrGrPo (XII: 1-8)
Ecclesiastes. Morris Bishop. HBMV
Ecclesiastes. G. K. Chesterton. MoBrPo
Ecclesiastes. Joseph Langland. NePoEA
Ecclesiastical Sonnets, *sels.* Wordsworth.
Inside of King's College Chapel, Cambridge, Pt. III, Sonnet XLIII. BPN; EM-2; EmBrPo; EnLi-2; EnLP; EnRP; EPN; ES; GEPC; GoBC; MaRV; OAEP; OBRV; OxBoCh
(King's College Chapel, Cambridge.) CBE
(Within King's College Chapel, Cambridge.) GTBS; GTBS-D; GTBS-W; GTSE; GTSL
Mutability, Pt. III, Sonnet XXXIV. BPN; EmBrPo; EnLi-2; EnLP; EnRP; EPN; ExPo; GEPC; LiTB; OBRV; OQP; PC; PoE; PoEL-4; QP-2; REAL; RiBV; SeCeV
("From low to high doth dissolution climb." EG
(Sonnet: "From low to high doth dissolution climb.") CoEV
Persuasion, Pt. I, Sonnet XVI. MaRV
Same, The (King's College Chapel), Pt. III, Sonnet XLIV. GEPC
(Same, The: "What awful perspective! while from our sight"). EnLP
They Dreamt Not of a Perishable Home, Pt. III, Sonnet XLV. PeBoSo
(Continued [King's College Chapel].) GEPC
Walton's Book of Lives, Pt. III, Sonnet V. LPS-3
Ecclesiasticus, *sels,* Bible, Apocrypha.
"I am the mother of fair love," XXIV: 24-28, *Douay vers.* ISi
"Let us now praise famous men," XLIV: 1-14. BHV; ChTr
(Our Fathers, XLIV: 1-15.) TrJP
(Praise of Famous Men, XLIV: 10-14.) MaRV
Music, XXXII: 5-6. TrJP
O Death, XLI: 1-4. TrJP
On Death—a Sonnet, XLI (*Moulton, Modern Reader's Bible*). MaRV
Simon, Son of Onias, L: 5-14. BHV
Test of Men, The, XXVI: 5-8. TrJP
Ecclesiasticus. Donald Davidson. LS
Ecclesiazusae, The, *sels.* Aristophanes, *tr. fr. Greek by* Benjamin Bickley Rogers.
Communism? GrR
Praxagora Rehearses [Her Speech]. GrR; OxBG
Ecco il Santo. Katharine Lee Bates. QS
Ech, Sic a Pairish. *Unknown.* FiBHP
Echetlos. Robert Browning. BPN; ViPo
Echidna. Mary Elizabeth Counselman. DaM
Echo. Archias, *tr. fr. Greek by* Sir William Marris. OxBG
Echo. E. G. Bishop. CAG
Echo. Walter de la Mare. MoVE; OBMV; SeCeV; ShBV-4
Echo. Viscountess Grey of Fallodon. CH; GBV (1922 ed.)
Echo. Elizabeth Stanton Hardy. GoYe
Echo. Amory Hare. MuM
Echo. Milton. *See* Sweet Echo.
Echo. Thomas Moore. GoBC; GTIV; OxBI; TIP
(Echoes.) EV-4; GTBS; GTBS-D; GTBS-W; GTSE; GTSL
Echo. Pushkin, *tr. fr. Russian by* C. M. Bowra. BoRS
Echo. Christina Rossetti. BLV; CH; EmBrPo; EPN; GTBS-D; LiTL; LoBV; LoPo; LoPS; MBP; PoEL-5; POTT; SeCeV; TriL; ViBoPo; ViPo; VLEP
("Come to me in the silence of the night.") LO
Echo. John Godfrey Saxe. AnNe; BOHV; LPS-3; PTA-1; PTA-2
Echo. Sir Philip Sidney. *Fr.* Arcadia. SiPS
Echo, An. Grace Hyde Trine. BAP
Echo. *Unknown.* GFA
Echo. Mildred Weston. PoMa
Echo. Otomo Yakamochi, *tr. fr. Japanese by* Ishii *and* Obata. OnPM
Echo and Silence. Sir Samuel Egerton Brydges. LPS-3
Echo and the Ferry. Jean Ingelow. CBPC
Echo and the Lover. *Unknown.* LPS-3
Echo Club, The, *sel.* Bayard Taylor.
Palabras Grandiosas. BOHV
Echo from Willowwood, An. Christina Rossetti. VA
Echo [*or* Shepherd: Echo], I ween, will in the wood reply. A Gentle Echo on Woman. Swift. ALV; BOHV; FiBHP; LiTG; LiTL; OnYI; SiTL
Echo! mysterious nymph, declare. Echo and the Lover. *Unknown.* LPS-3
Echo of a Song, The. James W. Foley. PEDC

Echo Poem. M. Allan. FiBHP
Echo, tell me, while I wander. Song. Addison. BOHV
Echo to a Rock. Lord Herbert of Cherbury. AtBAP; PoEL-2
Echoes. W. E. Henley. *Poems indexed separately by titles and first lines.*
Echoes. Thomas Moore. *See* Echo.
Echoes. José Peón y Contreras, *tr. fr. Spanish by* Samuel Beckett. AnMP
Echoes from Theocritus, *sels.* Edward Cracroft Lefroy, *after* Theocritus.
Ageanax, VI. OBVV
Cleonicos, XXVII. AWP; JAWP; WBP
Epitaph of Eusthenes, The, XXVIII. AWP; OBVV
Flute of Daphnis, The, XXIII. AWP; ES; OBVV
Grave of Hipponax, The, XXX. AWP; JAWP; WBP
Monument of Cleita, The, XXIX. AWP; JAWP; WBP
Sacred Grove, A, XXIV. AWP
Shepherd Maiden, A, II. VA
Sicilian Night, A, IV. VA
Summer Day in Old Sicily, A, V. OBVV
Sylvan Revel, A, XXV. AWP; JAWP; WBP
Thyrsis, XXVI. AWP
Echoes of Childhood, *sels.* Alice Corbin. PoNe
Delphy.
Mandy's Religion.
Uncle Jim.
Echoes of Jesus. Lucile Coleman. ChIP
Echoes of Love's House. William Morris. GTML; GTSL
Echoing Chang Tzu-yeh's "Spring Daylight." Su T'ung-po, *tr. fr. Chinese by* Yu Min-chuan. WhP
Echoing Green, The. Blake. *Fr.* Songs of Innocence. BoTP; CBE; CEP; CH; EiPP; EV-3; GBV (1952 ed.); KN; OBEC; OTPC; PCH; PoRh
Echoing sounds of hammers, The. New Houses. Grace Noll Crowell. PEDC
Echo's Dirge for Narcissus. Ben Jonson. *See* Slow, Slow, Fresh Fount.
Echo's Lament of Narcissus. Ben Jonson. *See* Slow, Slow, Fresh Fount.
Echo's Song. Ben Jonson. *See* Slow, Slow, Fresh Fount.
Eclipse. Al-Ghassani, *tr. fr. Arabic by* A. J. Arberry. MooP
Eclipse, An. Pindar, *tr. fr. Greek by* C. M. Bowra. OxBG
Eclipse of Faith, The. Theodore Dwight Woolsey. AA
Ecliptic, The: Cancer, or, The Crab, *sel.* Joseph Gordon Macleod.
"Moonpoison, mullock of sacrifice." NeBP
Eclog. III: "Fisher-lad, A (no higher dares he look)." Phineas Fletcher. *Fr.* Piscatorie Eclogues. SeCV-1
Eclogue: "Late 'twas in June, the fleece when fully grown." Michael Drayton. The Shepherd's Garland, Eclogue IX. OBSC
Eclogue: "Lycon begin—begin the mournful tale." William Diaper. *Fr.* Nereides; or, Sea-Eclogues. SeCePo
Eclogue: Merchantman, The. John Davidson. *See* Merchantman, The.
Eclogue: "No one dies cleanly now." Frederic Prokosch. ViBoPo
Eclogue I: "Sweet lament of two Castilian swains, The." Garcilaso de la Vega, *tr. fr. Spanish by* Jeremiah Holmes Wiffen. AnSpL-1, *abr.;* TeCS
Eclogue: "When all the powers have fallen." Hal Summers. POTE
Eclogue: "Wouldst thou ken nature in her better part?" Thomas Chatterton. Eclogues, III. EV-3
Eclogue by a Five-barred Gate. Louis MacNeice. MoP; ReaPo
Eclogue for Christmas, An. Louis MacNeice. FaBoMo; MoPo; MoVE; OBMV; TwHP
Eclogue [*or* Eglogue] to Mr. Johnson, An. Thomas Randolph. SeEP
Poetry and Philosophy, *sel.* OBS
Eclogues. Michael Drayton. *See* Shepherd's Garland, The.
Eclogues. *sels.* Sir Herbert Read. BrBE
April.
Curfew.
Orchard, The.
Eclogues, *sels.* Virgil, *tr. fr. Latin.*
Corydon, II, *pr. tr. by* Elizabeth Sommer. RoL
("Burning with love, the shepherd Corydon," *tr. by* Mary Grant.) LaP
Corydon and Thyrsis, VII, *tr. by* Dryden. AWP
Daphnis, V, *tr. by* Anne Greet. LaP
Dawn of the Golden Age, IV, *tr. by* James Laughlin. RoL
(Fourth Eclogue, The.) LiTW
("Muses/ Muses of Sicily") LaP
Fatal Blindness, *fr.* VIII, *pr. tr. by* John Jackson. LiA
"From Jupiter the Muse begins, and Jupiter is everywhere," III, *tr. by* C. Day Lewis. LaP
Lycidas and Moeris, IX, *tr. by* Dryden. AWP
("Whither, Moeris, your haste? By the usual road to the city?" *tr. by* Geoffrey Johnson.) LaP
Messiah, The, IV, *tr. by* Dryden. AWP; JAWP; OuHeWo; WBP
Return of the Golden Age, with the Birth of Pollio, The, *fr.* IV, *tr. by* Dryden. BeR
Shepherd's Gratitude, The, I. AWP, *tr. by* Charles Stuart Calverley; RoL, *pr. tr. by* Minnie Jameson Smith.
Sibylline Prophecy, The, *fr.* IV, *tr. by* Roderick Gill. CAW
"What made thee then so keen to look on Rome?" *fr.* I, *tr. by* Charles Stuart Calverley. PoFr
"You to your beech tree, Tityrus, withdraw," I, *tr. by* John Thompson, Jr. LaP
Economy. Hipponax, *tr. fr. Greek by* F. L. Lucas. GrPE
Economy of Vegetation, The. Erasmus Darwin. *See* Botanic Garden, The.
Ecstacy, An. Richard Crashaw. *See* Song, A: "Lord, when the sense of thy sweet grace."
Ecstasie, rash production of the thoughts. George Darley. *Fr.* Errors of Ecstasie. OnYI
Ecstasies of Dialectic, The. Howard Nemerov. FiMAP
Ecstasy, The. Abraham Cowley. Po
Ecstasy, The. John Donne. ATP; BLV; CaAE; CoEV; EM-1; EPS; ExPo; LiTB; LiTG; LO, *abr.;* LoBV; MaPo; OBEV; PoFS; ReaPo; ReEn; RiBV; SeCePo; SeCeV; SeEP; TrGrPo; TuPP; TwP; TyEnPo; ViBoPo (Extasie, The.) AnFE; EnLoPo; EnLP; FaBoEn; MeLP; MePo; OBS; PoEL-2; ReIE; SeCV-1
Ecstasy. Eva Gore-Booth. DiM
Ecstasy. Victor Hugo, *tr. fr. French by* Alan Conder. TrFP
Ecstasy. Matthías Jochumsson, *tr. and ad. fr. Icelandic by* Charles W. Stork. IcP
Ecstasy. Vilhelm Krag, *tr. fr. Norwegian by* Charles W. Stork. AnNoLy
Ecstasy. Eric Mackay. VA
Ecstasy. Sarojini Naidu. AV
Ecstasy. Plato, *tr. fr. Greek by* F. L. Lucas. GrPE
Ecstasy. Harold Trowbridge Pulsifer. BAP; PC
Ecstasy. Duncan Campbell Scott. CaP; OCL
Ecstasy. Rachel Annand Taylor. CoTS
Ecstasy. W. J. Turner. CH; POTE; PtOT; TwCV
"I saw a frieze on whitest marble drawn," *sel.* AlDL
Ecstasy of Bliss. Jorge Guillén, *tr. fr. Spanish by* Eleanor L. Turnbull. CoSP
Ecstasy of thought upraised me where, An. Petrarch. *Fr.* Sonnets to Laura: To Laura in Death. PrPoCR
Ecstatic, The. C. Day Lewis. AlDL
Ecstatic bird songs pound. Dawn. William Carlos Williams. MAP; MoAB; MoAmPo; MOAP
Edda Sæmundar. *Unknown. See* Elder Edda, The.
Eddi, priest of St. Wilfrid. Eddi's Service. Kipling. OnSP; VLEP
Eddington's universe goes phut. Richard Tolman's Universe. Leonard Bacon. ImOP
Eddi's Service. Kipling. OnSP; VLEP
Eddystone Light, The. *Unknown.* StPo
Edelweiss. Carl Snoilsky, *tr. fr. Swedish by* Charles W. Stork. AnSL
Eden. Hilary Corke. PoN
Eden. Milton. *Fr.* Paradise Lost, IV. FaBoEn
("Thus was this place.") ATP
Eden. F. R. Scott. TwCaPo
Eden. Thomas Traherne. BLV; PoEL-2; ReaPo; SeCV-2; TrGrPc
Eden Bower. Dante Gabriel Rossetti. EmBrPo; PoVP
Eden-Gate. Sydney Dobell. OBVV
Eden: Or One View of It. Theodore Spencer. LiTM; NePA
Edgar, *sel.* Thomas Rymer.
Wit Predominant. SeCL
Edgar A. Guest Considers "The Old Woman Who Lived in a Shoe" and the Good Old Verities at the Same Time. Louis Untermeyer. FiBHP; WhC
(Edgar A. Guest Syndicates the Old Woman Who Lived in a Shoe.) PreP
Edgar Allan Poe. Clifford Lanier. PoRL
Edgar Guest/ Is never at his best. The Editor's Private Cocktail Party. Oscar Williams. SiTL
Edge, The. Lola Ridge. AnAmPo; LA; NP; OnYI
Edge of the Swamp, The. William Gilmore Simms. APW; SPP
Edge of the World, The. Sophocles, *tr. fr. Greek by* Gilbert Murray. OxBG
Edge of the World, The. Mary Fanny Youngs. BrR
Edges of the Sea. William Diaper. *Fr.* Nereides; or, Sea-Eclogues. BeR
Edges of the stones are sharp, The. The Builder. Caroline Giltinan. HBMV; LS; TBM
Edina, high in heaven wan. Edinburgh. Alexander Smith. EBSV
Edinburgh. Arthur Guiterman. WhC
Edinburgh. Alfred Noyes. HBV
Edinburgh. Alexander Smith. EBSV
Edison. Robinson Jeffers. AmPP (3d ed.)
Edith. William Ellery Channing. AA; HBV
Edith and Harold. Arthur Gray Butler. OBVV
Edith Cavell. George Edward Woodberry. HBMV
Edith, the silent stars are coldly gleaming. Edith. William Ellery Channing. AA; HBV

Editor sat in his easy chair, The. The Editor's Tragedy. St. John Emile Clavering Hankin. CenHV
Editor sat with his head in his hands, The. He Came to Pay. "Parmenas Mix." BOHV
Editor Whedon. Edgar Lee Masters. *Fr.* Spoon River Anthology. CrMA; NP; OxBA
Editor's Private Cocktail Party, The. Oscar Williams. SiTL
Editor's Tragedy, The. St. John Emile Clavering Hankin. CenHV
Editor's Wooing, The. "Orpheus C. Kerr." BOHV
Edlesborough. Anne Ridler. NeBP
Edmund Burke. Goldsmith. *Fr.* Retaliation. CoEV; InvP; OBEC; SeCeV
Edmund Campion. Sister Mary St. Virginia. JKCP (1955 ed.)
Edmund Pollard. Edgar Lee Masters. *Fr.* Spoon River Anthology. AnFE; APA; CoAnAm
Edmund's Song. Sir Walter Scott. *See* Brignall Banks.
Edom o' Gordon. *Unknown.* BSV; EBSV, *sl. diff.*; EV-2; HBV; OBB; OBEV (1st ed.)
(Captain Car; or, Edom o Gordon.) BaBo; EnLit; EPP; ESPB (A, B, F, *and* H *vers.*); OAEP; TOP; ViBoFo (A *and* B *vers.*)
Edoni, *sel.* Aeschylus, *tr. fr. Greek.*
Worship of Cotys, The. OxBG
Edouard. Ogden Nash. LiL; NePA; SiTL
Educated Love Bird, The. Peter Newell. FiBHP
Education. Arthur Guiterman. MaRV
Education. Josephine Miles. FiMAP
Education of Nature, The. Wordsworth. *See* Three Years She Grew.
Education vs. Fads. Aristophanes. *See* Old Education, The.
Edward. *Unknown.* ABS, *American vers.*; AnFE; AtBAP; ATP; BaBo (A, B, *and* C *vers.*); BEL; BoLiVe; BSV; CaAE; CBOV; CH; CoEV; EBSV; EM-1; EnLi-1; EnLit; ESPB; GoTS; HBV; HoPM (A *and* B *vers.*); OAEP; OBB; OBEV; OuHeWo; PCN; PoEL-1; TOP; TrGrPo; TwHP; UnPo (1st ed.); ViBoFo (A *and* B *vers.*)
(Edward, Edward.) BBV; BLV; EnRP; ExPo; LiTB; LiTG; MaC; OnSP; PG (1955 ed.); PIAE; PoRA; SeCeV; ShBV-3; TreFS; WHA
Edward, back from the Indian Sea. Neglectful Edward. Robert Graves. MBP; MoBrPo; NeMA
Edward, Edward. *Unknown.* *See* Edward.
Edward Edwards was a castaway sealer. Keith Sinclair. *Fr.* The Ballad of Halfmoon Bay. AnNZ
Edward Gray. Tennyson. OBVV
Edward Lear. W. H. Auden. InvP; PtP
Edward Millington. Richard Church. HaMV
Edward Plantagenet/ (Can you imagine it). Important People. Louis Untermeyer, *and others.* StaSt
Edward the Confessor,/ Slept under the dresser. Important People. Louis Untermeyer, *and others.* RIS; StaSt
Edward the Second, *sels.* Christopher Marlowe.
Edward's Death, *fr.* V, v. LiA
"I must have wanton poets, pleasant wits," *fr.* I, i. ViBoPo
"Look for rebellion, look to be depos'd," *fr.* II, ii. PoFr
Edward the Third, *sels.* *Unknown.* LO
"Thou hear'st me say that I do dote on thee."
"Whether is her beauty by her words divine?"
Edward's Death. Christopher Marlowe. *Fr.* Edward the Second, V, v. LiA
Edwin and Angelina. Goldsmith. *Fr.* The Vicar of Wakefield, *ch.* 8. CEP; EV-3; OTPC
(Hermit, The.) LPS-1
Edwin and Paulinus. *Unknown.* LPS-2
Edwin Booth. Alice Brown. HBV
Edwin Doe. *Unknown.* *See* Young Edwin in the Lowlands Low.
Edwin in the Lowlands Low. *Unknown.* *See* Young Edwin in the Lowlands Low.
Edwin the Fair, *sels.* Sir Henry Taylor.
Athulf and Ethilda. LPS-1
Scholar, The. LPS-3
Wind in the Pines, The. VA
Edwin, the Minstrel. James Beattie. *Fr.* The Minstrel, I. EV-3
Eeka, Neeka. Walter de la Mare. WaKn
Eel, The. Evan Morgan. CAW
Eel, The. Ogden Nash. FaPON
Eels, Tortoises, Soles, Lampreys. Oppian, *tr. fr. Greek by* William Diaper. *Fr.* Halieuticks. BeR
Eemis-Stane, The. "Hugh MacDiarmid." NeBP
E'en all-creating time could ne'er. Fortune's Tides. Pindar. *Fr.* Olympian Odes, II. GrR
E'en as a lovely flower. Du bist wie eine Blume. Heine, *tr. by* Kate Kroeker. AWP; JAWP; WBP
E'en as the Flowers Do Wither. *Unknown.* EG; OBSC; RiBV
E'en in thy native regions, how I blush. Praise of the Pudding. Joel Barlow. *Fr.* The Hasty Pudding. AnNE
E'en [*or* Even *or* Ev'n] like two little bank-dividing brooks. My Beloved Is Mine, and I Am His [*or* A Divine Rapture *or* A Mystical Ecstasy]. Francis Quarles. *Fr.* Emblems. CaAE; ElSeCe; GTSL; HBV; LiTL; LO; MeLP; OBEV; OBS; TrGrPo; TriL
Een Napoli. T. A. Daly. PoMa
E'en Such Is Time. Sir Walter Ralegh. *See* Conclusion, The.
E'en the Country Maid. Sappho, *tr. fr. Greek by* H. De Vere Stacpoole. GrR
E'en this, Lord, didst thou bless. Insomnia. John Banister Tabb. TrPWD
Eena, meena, mina, mo. *See* Eenie, meenie, minie, mo.
Eenie, meenie, mackeracka. *Unknown.* OxNR
Eenie meenie, minie [*or* miney], mo. *Unknown.* FaPON; RIS
(Eena, meena, mina, mo.) OxNR; SiTL
Eenity, feenity, fickety, feg. *Unknown.* OxNR
Eeny, meeny, miney, mo. The Counting Man. William Vaughn Moody. PoMS
Eeny, weeny, winey, wo. *Unknown.* OxNR
Eerily Sweet. Elizabeth J. Coatsworth. ChBR
Ees, twer at Liady-Day, ya know. Liady-Day an' Ridden House. William Barnes. OBRV
Ef I had 'bout—fo'ty-five dollahs. John Henry (D *vers.*). *Unknown.* ViBoFo
Ef I had wings like Noah's [*or* Norah's] dove. Dink's Song. *Unknown.* ABF; OxBoLi; SiTL
Ef I'd knowed dat my cap'n was blin'. Tie-tamping Chant. *Unknown.* ABF
Ef you strike a thorn or rose. Keep a-Goin'! Frank L. Stanton. OHFP; WBLP
Effect of Example, The. John Keble. HBV; HBVY; MaRV
(Example.) LPS-3
Effie. Sterling A. Brown. BANP
Effigy, The. Guido Cavalcanti, *tr. fr. Italian by* Hubert Creekmore. LiTW
(Sonnet: Effigy, The.) LyPI
Effigy of a Nun. Sara Teasdale. MAP; MoAmPo; NP
Effingham, Grenville, Raleigh, Drake. Admirals All. Sir Henry Newbolt. ShGoBo; TVSH
Effort at Speech between Two People. Muriel Rukeyser. MoAB; MoAmPo; TrGrPo (rev. ed.); TrJP
Effortlessly graceful. Country-Brook. Maxwell Bodenheim. MOAP
Eftsoons they heard a most melodious sound. The Bower of Bliss [*or* Gather the Rose]. Spenser. *Fr.* The Faerie Queene, II. CoEV; FaBoEn; LoBV; OBSC; UnS; ViBoPo; WHA
Eftsoons they saw an hideous host array'd. Sea Monsters. Spenser. *Fr.* The Faerie Queene, II. ChTr
Egan O Rahilly. *Unknown, tr. fr. Irish by* James Stephens. OBMV; SeCePo
Egeria, sweet creation of some heart. Byron. *Fr.* Childe Harold's Pilgrimage, IV. ViBoPo
Egg, The. Laura E. Richards. MPB; RAR; TiPo (1952 ed.)
Egg-and-Dart. Robert Finch. BoCaPo
Egg and the Machine, The. Robert Frost. MAP; MoAmPo
Egg for Easter, An. Irene F. Pawsey. BoTP
Egg is smooth and very pale, The. The Inefficacious Egg. Roy Bishop. HBMV
Eggleston was a taxi-driver. Cynical Portraits. Louis Paul. InMe
Eggs. Herbert Asquith. BrR
Eggs and the Horses, The. *Unknown.* LPS-3
Eggs for Breakfast. Irene F. Pawsey. BoTP
Eggs from a chain store grocery. One No. 7. John Frederick Frank. GoYe
Eggstravagance, An. Oliver Wendell Holmes. *See* Limerick: "Reverend Henry Ward Beecher, The."
Egidio of Coimbra (A.D. 1597). Thomas Walsh. JKCP
Egloga Quinta: "Some doleful thing there is at hand." Barnabe Googe. ReIE
Egloga Secunda: "My beasts, go feed upon the plain." Barnabe Googe. ReIE
Eglogs of the Poet B. Mantuan Carmelitan, The, *sel.* Mantuan, *tr. fr. Latin by* George Turberville.
Second Egloge Entituled Fortunatus, The. ReIE
Eglogue to Mr. Johnson, An. Thomas Randolph. *See* Eclogue to Mr. Johnson, An.
Ego Dominus Tuus. W. B. Yeats. ChMo; CMP; NP
Ego Sum. Gelett Burgess. *See* Bobby.
Egoism. W. Craddle. FiBHP; WhC
Egoist, The. Anna Wickham. FaBoTw
Egoist Dead, The. Elizabeth Brewster. CaP
Ego's Dream. Alfred Kreymborg. MAPA
Egotism. Edward Sandford Martin. AA
Egotist. John Bruce MacCallum. PoP
Egrets. Max Eastman. AnEnPo
Egypt. Hilda Doolittle ("H. D."). HBMV
Egypt, Jerusalem, Stamboul. Back Home. Harriet Monroe. PFE
Egyptian banks, an avenue of clay. Flighting for Duck. William Empson. MoPo

Egyptian Dead, The. Elizabeth Rowe. *Fr.* The History of Joseph, IV. BeR
Egyptian Lotus, The. Arthur Wentworth Hamilton Eaton. AA
Egyptian Serenade. George William Curtis. HBV
Egyptian tombs hold priceless things. Tombs. Louise Webster. ChIP
Egyptians, The, say, The Sun has twice. Samuel Butler. *Fr.* Hudibras, II, 3. ImOP
Egypt's Might Is Tumbled Down. Mary Elizabeth Coleridge. CH; POTE
Eheu Fugaces. R. H. Barham. OxBoLi
Eia Jesus Hodie. *Unknown.* AnEC
Eia, Martyr Stephane. *Unknown.* AnEC
Eiapopeia, my baby, sleep on. The Love and Protection of Mother and Father—Bohemian. *Unknown.* BOL
Eider Duck. The. Ibsen, *tr. fr. Norwegian by* Charles W. Stork. AnNoLy
Eidola. Samuel Daniel. *See* Are They Shadows?
Eidolon. Robert Penn Warren. FiMAP
Eidólons. Walt Whitman. APW
Eies look off theires no beeholdinge. *At. to* Francis Beaumont. SeCSL
Eight Aspects of Melissa. Lawrence Durrell. NeBP
Eight Bells, *with music. Unknown.* SaSa
Eight bells! Eight bells! their clear tone tells. All's Well! William Allen Butler. HBV
Eight-Day Clock, The. Alfred Cochrane. HBV
Eight days went by, eight days. The Wanderer: Soothsay. William Carlos Williams. TwAmPo
Eight fathoms from me stay, unquiet seas. A Tomb by the Sea [*or* Tomb of a Lost Mariner]. Asclepiades. GrR; OxBG
Eight fingers. The Difference. Laura E. Richards. HBV; HBVY; PPL
Eight Henry, heir indubitate of York and Lancaster. William Warner. *Fr.* Albion's England. TuPP
Eight hours' work, eight hours' play. Rhymes to Remember. *Unknown.* StaSt
Eight hundred years!—and still beneath your vine. To Omar Khayyám. Maud Ludington Cain. MuM
Eight lines of clergymen converged. Colonel B. Constance Carrier. NePoAm-2
Eight Melons. Malcolm Cowley. TwAmPo
Eight Months Old. Marion Strobel. NP
Eight o'Clock. Richard K. Arnold. PtPa
Eight o'Clock. A. E. Housman. Last Poems, XV. ExPo; InPo; LoBV; MBP; MoAB; MoBrPo; POTE; ReMP; ShBV-4; TrGrPo; TwP; ViP
Eight o'clock;/ The postman's knock! The Postman. Christina Rossetti. *Fr.* Sing-Song. EmBrPo; GaP; GFA; PCH; RIS; SAS; TiPo
Eight Volunteers. Lansing C. Bailey. PAH
Eight years old, crouched in a corner, eyeing the others askance. Party. Constance Carrier. NePoAm-2
Eighteen. Sister Mary Honora. NePoAm-2
1880. Christina Rossetti. *Fr.* Valentines to My Mother. DD; MOAH
1885. Christina Rossetti. *Fr.* Valentines to My Mother. BoChLi; DD; MOAH
1887. A. E. Housman. A Shropshire Lad, I. CoBMV; NAMP; PoVP; ReMP; RiBV; UnPo
1882. Christina Rossetti. *Fr.* Valentines to My Mother. MOAH
(Valentine to My Mother, A.) MotAn; OHIP
1811. Wordsworth. *See* Here Pause: The Poet Claims at Least This Praise.
1805. Robert Graves. ChMP; FaBoCh; HaMV; LoGBV
Eighteen hundred and ninety-one. Ain't Workin' Song. *Unknown.* OuSiCo
Eighteen-ninety. E. Richard Shipp. PoOW
1898–1899. Rupert Hughes. For Decoration Day, II. AA; MDAH
1894 in London. Charles Spear. AnNZ
Eighteen Sixty-one. Walt Whitman. CoV; IAP; TCAP
1861–1865. Rupert Hughes. For Decoration Day, I. AA; MDAH
Eighteenth-Century Vignettes, *sels.* Austin Dobson. BPN
Epilogue to Eighteenth Century Vignettes, 2d Series.
Prologue to Eighteenth Century Vignettes, 3d Series.
Eighteenth of October, The. The Fire of Frendraught. *Unknown.* ESPB; OBB; ViBoFo
Eighteenth Song, The: "New year hath come in sight, The." Hadewijch, *tr. fr. Dutch by* A. J. Barnouw. LiTW; LyMA
Eighth Air Force. Randall Jarrell. MiAP; MoVE; ReMP
Eighth Eclogue, The. Michael Drayton. *See* Cassamen and Dowsabel.
Eighth Elegy, *sel.* Muriel Rukeyser.
Children's Elegy. FiMAP
Eighth Sonnet, The. Sir Philip Sidney. *See* Astrophel and Stella: Eighth Song.
Eighth Street West. Rachel Field. ChBR; SiSoSe
Eighth Type of Ambiguity. John Wain. PoN
Eighty and nine with their captain. The Charge by the Ford. Thomas Dunn English. PAH
Eighty years ago a woman passed. Tomorrow Is a Birthday. Gwendolen Haste. GoYe
Eighty years have passed, and more. Under the Washington Elm, Cambridge. Oliver Wendell Holmes. PEOR
Eighty-four acre campus. Data for Accreditation. Sister Mary Maura. JKCP (1955 ed.)
Eileen Aroon. Gerald Griffin. AnIV; GoBC; HBV; OBEV (1st ed.); OBVV; PCD; TIP
(Aileen Aroon.) IrPN; OnYI
"When like the rising day," *sel.* OBEV (new ed.)
Eileen Aroon. Carrol O'Daly, *tr. fr. Middle Irish or fr. Late Middle Irish by* George Sigerson. OnYI
Eileen, Diarmuid and Teig. James Stephens, *after* Egan O'Rahilly. BoFr
Eileen of four. The Clock's Song. Rose Hawthorne Lathrop. AA; JKCP
Eilidh, Eilidh, Eilidh, dear to me, dear and sweet. Mo-Lennav-A-Chree. "Fiona Macleod." LEAP
Eily, Eily [*or* Eilidh, Eilidh],/ my bonnie wee lass. Hushing Song. "Fiona Macleod." BOL; MoSiPe
Einar Tamberskelver. Longfellow. Tales of a Wayside Inn: The Musician's Tale, Pt. I, xx. AmPP (4th ed.); YT
Eine Kleine Nachtmusik. Robert E. Hayden. PoNe
Eingang (Prelude). Rainer Maria Rilke. *See* Initiation.
Einstein. Archibald MacLeish. AnFE; APA; CMP; CoAnAm; MoPo; TwAmPo
"He lies upon his bed," *sel.* ImOP
Einstein among the Coffee-Cups. Louis Untermeyer. WhC
Eire. William Drennan. *See* Erin.
Eirich agus tiugainn O! Farewell to Fiunary. Norman Macleod. EBSV
Either a seer of dreams am I. Doubt Not a Dream. Sophocles. *Fr.* Electra. GrR
Either the sum of this sweet mutiny. Sonnets. George Henry Boker. MOAP
Either to keep the thinking in. Country Ways. Marcia Masters. *Fr.* Impressions of My Father. GoYe
"Ej Blot til Lyst." William Morton Payne. AA
El Aghir. Norman Cameron. FaBoTw
El Capitan-General. Charles Godfrey Leland. AA; HBV; YaD
El Emplazado. William Henry Venable. PAH
El Greco. E. L. Mayo. HoPM; MiAP
El Hombre. William Carlos Williams. LiTA
El Poniente. Ruth Comfort Mitchell. PoeMoYo; VOD
El Vaquero. Lucius Harwood Foote. AA
Elaine. Edna St. Vincent Millay. AV; BAV; LEAP; PoeMoYo; TBM
Elaine the fair, Elaine the loveable [*or* lovable]. Lancelot and Elaine. Tennyson. *Fr.* Idylls of the King. HeT; PoVP; ReTS; ViPo; ViPP; VLEP
Elaine's Song. Tennyson. *Fr.* Idylls of the King: Lancelot and Elaine. BPN; FaBoEn
El-a-noy, *with music. Unknown.* AS; TrAS
Elbowing its neighbours. The Minotaur. Eldon Grier. PeCV
Elder boy I do not know, The. Generation of Intention. Donald F. Drummond. PtPa
Elder Brother, The (Poem for All Good and Loyal Dogs). Elma Dean. NeMA
Elder Brother, The, *sel.* John Fletcher.
"Beauty clear and fair," *fr.* III, v. BEL; EPP; HoPM; LO; OAEP; OBEV; SeCL; SeEP; ViBoPo
(Beauty Cleere and Fair.) AtBAP
(Song: "Beauty clear and fair.") OBS
Elder Edda, The, *sels. Unknown, tr. fr. Icelandic.*
Attila the Hun, *tr. by* Henry Adams Bellows. PaOS
Beginning and the End, The, *abr., tr. by* Henry Adams Bellows. LiTW; LyMA
Counsels of Sigrdrifa, *tr. by* William Morris *and* Eiríkur Magnússon. AWP
First Lay of Gudrun, The, *tr. by* William Morris *and* Eiríkur Magnússon. AWP; JAWP; WBP
("Home They Brought Her Warrior Dead," *tr. by* Henry Adams Bellows.) PaOS
Freyr's Courtship, *tr. by* Henry Adams Bellows. PaOS
Helgi Thrice Born, *tr. by* Henry Adams Bellows. PaOS
Hell-Ride of Brynhild, The, *tr. by* William Morris *and* Eiríkur Magnússon. OuHeWo
Lay of Thrym, The, *tr. by* Henry Adams Bellows. LiTW; OuHeWo
(Thor Gets Back His Hammer, *tr. by* Bertha S. Phillpotts.) PaOS
(Thrymskvitha, *tr. by* Henry Adams Bellows.) LiA
Lay of Wayland, The, *tr. by* Henry Adams Bellows. PaOS
Sayings of the High One, The, *tr. by* Henry Adams Bellows. PaOS
Hava-Mal, The, *shorter sel.* BoFr
Short Lay of Sigurd, The, *tr. by* William Morris *and* Eiríkur Magnússon. EnLi-1
(Lay Called the Short Lay of Sigurd, The.) OuHeWo
(Lay of Sigurd, The.) AWP
Sigurth and I, *tr. by* Henry Adams Bellows. LiA

Elder Edda, The (*continued*)
  Voluspo, *tr. by* Henry Adams Bellows. AWP
    (Beginning and the End, The, *abr.*) PaOS
"Elder Father, though thine eyes." The Holy of Holies. G. K. Chesterton. WGRP
Elder folk shook hands at last, The. The Meeting. Whittier. AmPP (3d ed.); IAP; LPS-2
Elder Tree, The. *Unknown.* ChTr
Elderly Gentleman, The. George Canning. BOHV; NA; PA
Elderly Nun. Benjamin Francis Musser. PraNu
Elderly roué and the fantastic boy, The. Oscar Wilde and Aubrey Beardsley. John Waller. PoN
Elders and officers line the returning road. Good-bye to the People of Hang-chow. Po Chü-i. LiTW; TrCh
Elders at their services begin, The. Epigram [*or* Two Epigrams, I]. J. V. Cunningham. NePoAm; SiTL
Elders of Troy Behold Helen, The. Homer, *tr. fr. Greek by* the Earl of Derby. *Fr.* The Iliad, III. LiA
Eldorado. Poe. AmPP; AnFE; APA; AWP; BAV; CoAnAm; CoBA; DDA; FaBoBe; FaBoCh; HBV; IAP; InPo; LaNeLa; LoGBV; MOAP; NePA; OTPC (1946 ed.); OxBA; PoeMoYo; PoMa; RIS; SPP; StaSt; TCAP; WaKn; YT
Eldritch Dark, The. Clark Ashton Smith. DaM
Eleanor. Christina Rossetti. BPN
Eleazar Wheelock. Richard Hovey. LauV; WhC
Elected Kaiser, burgher and a knight. Charles the Fifth and the Peasant. Robert Lowell. MiAP
Elected Knight, The. *Unknown, tr. fr. Danish by* Longfellow. AWP; JAWP; LyMA; WBP
Elected Silence. Siegfried Sassoon. MBP; MoBrPo
Elected Silence, sing to me. The Habit of Perfection. Gerard Manley Hopkins. ACP; BLV; BoLiVe; CAW; ChMo; CoBMV; EnLit; JKCP; LiTB; LiTG; MBP; MoAB; MoBrPo; OAEP (2d ed.); OBEV (new ed.); OBMV; PoRA; PoVP; TrGrPo; UnS, 1 *st.*; ViBoPo; ViP; VLEP
Election Day. Patricia K. Page. BoCaPo (1948 ed.)
Election Handbill of Green. Jorge Carrera Andrade, *tr. fr. Spanish by* H. R. Hays. TwSpPo
Electra, *sels.* Euripides, *tr. fr. Greek.*
  "Blot as Black as Death, A," *tr. by* Gilbert Murray. GrR
  Electra and Orestes, *tr. by* George Allen. OxBG
  Guilt, *tr. by* Gilbert Murray. GrR
  Short Story, A, *tr. by* Gilbert Murray. GrR
  "Then in the corb Aegisthus set his hand," *tr. by* Gilbert Murray. ReTS
  What Makes the Man, *tr. by* R. Potter. GrR
Electra, *sels.* Sophocles, *tr. fr. Greek.*
  Burial Urn, The [*or* A]. GrR, *tr. by* Sir George Young; OxBG, *tr. by* J. T. Sheppard
  Chariot-Race, A. GrR, *tr. by* Robert Whitelaw; OxBG, *tr. by* J. T. Sheppard
  Dreams Come True, *tr. by* J. T. Sheppard. OxBG
    (Doubt Not a Dream, *tr. by* Robert Whitelaw.) GrR
  Electra ("Bethink you next what sort of days I pass"), *tr. by* Robert Whitelaw. GrR
  Light and Shadow, *tr. by* Sir George Young. GrR
  "O Zeus, I look upon this form laid low," *tr. by* F. Storr. LiA
  Plaint of the Nightingale, The, *tr. by* Robert Whitelaw. GrR
  "They took their stand where the appointed judges," *tr. by* Edward Bulwer-Lytton. GrPo
Electra. Francis Howard Williams. AA
Electra and Orestes. Euripides, *tr. fr. Greek by* George Allen. *Fr.* Electra. OxBG
Electric Poem, The, *sel.* Mikhail Prokofyevich Gerasimov, *tr. fr. Russian by* Babette Deutsch.
  First Bulb Lights Up, The. TrRV
Electric Sign Goes Dark, An. Carl Sandburg. HBMV
Electric stars/ Burn in the wind. Emigrant to America. Vicente Huidobro. TwSpPo
Electric Storm. Michael C. Martin. WaP
Electrocution. Lola Ridge. TCPD
Elegiac. Longfellow. BAV
Elegiac. Mimnermus, *tr. fr. Greek by* E. F. Watling. LiTW
Elegiac. James Gates Percival. AA; LBAP; LEAP; MDAH
  (It Is Great for Our Country to Die.) HBV
Elegiac Mood. Gordon Bottomley. *Fr.* Night and Morning Songs. LBBV; NP
Elegiac Sonnet. Charlotte Smith. *See* Sonnet: Written at the Close of Spring.
Elegiac Stanzas, Suggested by a Picture of Peele Castle, in a Storm. Wordsworth. BEL; BPN; ChER; EM-2; EmBrPo; EnRP; EPN; ERP; GEPC; HBV; MyFE; OAEP; OBRV; PoFS; TOP
  (Nature and the Poet.) GTBS; GTBS-D; GTBS-W; GTSE; GTSL
Elegie IX: Autumnall, The. John Donne. *See* Autumnal, The.
Elegie XI: Bracelet, The. John Donne. *Fr.* Elegies. EnLP
Elegie: Death, *sel.* John Donne.
  Of a Death in Winter, II. BoW
Elegie: Going to Bed. John Donne. *See* Going to Bed.
Elegie: His Picture. John Donne. *See* His Picture.
Elegie, An: "Let me be what I am, as Virgil cold." Ben Jonson. PoEL-2
Elegie, An: "Love, give me leave to serve thee, and be wise." Thomas Randolph. MePo
Elegie VI: "Oh, let mee not serve so, as those men serve." John Donne. *Fr.* Elegies. EnLP
Elegie: On His Mistris. John Donne. *See* On His Mistress.
Elegie, An: "Though beautie be the marke of praise." Ben Jonson. *See* Elegy, An: "Though beauty . . ."
Elegie on His Mistris. John Donne. *See* On His Mistress.
Elegie on the Death of a Mad Dog, An. Goldsmith. *See* Elegy on the Death of a Mad Dog, An.
Elegie on the Lady Marckham, *sel.* John Donne.
  "Man is the world, and death th' ocean." PoD
Elegie upon Anacreon. Abraham Cowley. PtP
Elegie [*or* Elegy] upon the death of the Dean[e] of Paul's, Dr. John Donne, An. Thomas Carew. EPS; MeLP; MePo; OBS; SeCV-1; SeEP
  (Elegy upon the Death of Doctor Donne, Dean of Paul's, An.) PtP
Elegie upon the Death of the Lord Hastings, An. Sir John Denham. SeCV-1
  ("Reader, preserve thy peace; those busy eyes.") ReEn
Elegies, *sels.* André Chénier, *tr. fr. French by* Arthur Symons.
  "Every man has his sorrows; yet each still." AWP; JAWP; WBP
  "Well, I would have it so. I should have known." AWP
  "White nymph wandering in the woods by night, A." AWP; JAWP; WBP
Elegies, *sels.* John Donne.
  Autumnal, The, IX. EPS (1942 ed.); ReEn; TuPP; ViBoPo
    (Autumnall, The.) NBE; PoEL-2; SeCV-1
    (Elegie [*or* Elegy] IX: Autumnal[l], The.) AtBAP; EnL; EnLP; OAEP; SeEP
  Change, III. LiTG; ViBoPo
  Elegie XI: Bracelet, The. EnLP
  Elegie VI: "Oh, let mee not serve so, as those men serve." EnLP
  Going to Bed, XIX. LiTB; LiTG
    (Elegie: Going to Bed.) MePo
    (To His Mistress Going to Bed.) ReEn; SiTL
  His Parting from Her, XII. OBS
    "O Fortune, thou'rt not worth my least exclaim," *sel.* CoBE
  His Picture, V. MeLP; NBE; OBS; ReEn
    (Elegie: His Picture.) FaBoEn; MePo
    (Elegy V: His Picture.) SeEP
  Love's Progress, XVIII. LiTB; LiTG; ViBoPo
  On His Mistress, XVI. EPS; LiTB; LiTG; MyFE; NBE; ReaPo; ReEn; TriL; TuPP; TwP; ViBoPo
    (Elegie on His Mistris.) MePo; SeCV-1
    (Elegy on His Mistress.) LoBV; SeCeV; SeEP
    (On His Mistris.) MeLP; PoEL-2
Elegies, *sels.* Ovid, *tr. fr. Latin by* Christopher Marlowe.
  "About my temples go triumphant bays," XII. ReIE
  "Envy, why carpest thou my time is spent so ill," XV. ReIE
    ("Envy, why twit'st thou me my time's spent ill," *tr. by* Ben Jonson.) ReIE
  To Verse Let Kings Give Place, *fr.* XV. ChTr
Elegies, *sels.* Propertius, *tr. fr. Latin.*
  Ah Woe Is Me, I, 1, *tr. by* F. A. Wright. AWP
  "All that you see here, stranger, where great Rome now stands," IV, 1, *tr. by* Frances Fletcher. LaP
  "And in that faroff age when Amphitryoniades," IV, 9, *tr. by* Frances Fletcher. LaP
  "Arethusa sends this message to her husband Lycotas," IV, 3, *tr. by* Frances Fletcher. LaP
  "Corinthian Lais received no such crowds in her home," II, 6, *tr. by* Frances Fletcher. LaP
  "Even now, mad girl, dost ape the painted Briton," *br. sel.* BoHiPo
  "Happiness, happiness! blessed night! and bless you," II, 15, *tr. by* Gilbert Highet. LaP
  Hylas, I, 20, *tr. by* F. A. Wright. AWP
  "I am compelled to make the long trip to classic Athens," III, 21, *tr. by* Frances Fletcher. LaP
  "I, entrance door to Tarpeia's house, swung open, once," I, 16, *tr. by* Frances Fletcher. LaP
    (Complaint of Tarpeia's Door, The.) LiTW
  "Is it true, Cynthia, that throughout Rome you are notorious," II, 5, *tr. by* Frances Fletcher. LaP
  "Jupiter Feretrius? His origin? I'll make a start: write," IV, 10, *tr. by* Frances Fletcher. LaP
  "Jupiter, have compassion, finally, on that sick girl, my sweetheart," II, 28 A *and* B, *tr. by* Frances Fletcher. LaP
  "Learn, you who wonder at my many forms," IV, 2, *tr. by* Frances Fletcher. LaP

"Let others write about you, or leave you all unknown," II, 11, *tr. by* John Angus Macnab. LaP
"Let us return, meantime, to the round of song," III, 2, *tr. by* Frances Fletcher. LaP
"Listen to what startled the neighbors, one night," IV, 8, *tr. by* Frances Fletcher. LaP
Love Is the God of Peace, III, 5, *tr. by* John Nott. RoL
Lover's Death, The, II, 13 A, *tr. by* John Nott. RoL
"May earth, O Acanthis, procuress, cover your grave," IV, 5, *tr. by* Frances Fletcher. LaP
"May your wellknown mercy, Persephone, remain steadfast," II, 28 C, *tr. by* Frances Fletcher. LaP
"Now, O Bacchus, I turn humbly to your shrine," III, 17, *tr. by* Frances Fletcher. LaP
"Priest performs rites, The: let there be silence during the rites," IV, 6, *tr. by* Frances Fletcher. LaP
Revenge to Come, III, 25, *tr. by* Kirby Flower Smith. AWP; JAWP; LiTW; WBP
("At the banquet tables of our social gatherings, I was ridiculed," *tr. by* Frances Fletcher.) LaP
Shade of Cornelia Consoles Her Husband, The, IV, 11, *pr. tr. by* H. E. Butler. LiA
("Cease, Paullus, to oppress my tomb with tears," *tr. by* Frances Fletcher.) LaP
(Roman Matron to Her Husband, A, *tr. by* James Cranstoun.) RoL
Plea of Cornelia, The ("Guard, Paullus, guard"), *br. sel., tr. by* E. D. A. Morshead. MOAH
"Shades are real, The. Death is not the end," IV, 7, *tr. by* Frances Fletcher. LaP
"Shades of Callimachus, and holy rites of Philetas," III, 1, *tr. by* Frances Fletcher. LaP
"She is gone whom I loved so long, my girl that I loved so dear," II, 8 A *and* B, 1–4, *tr. by* John Angus Macnab. LaP
"Tarpeia's grove; Tarpeia's traitor-tomb; capture of," IV, 4, *tr. by* Frances Fletcher. LaP
"This faith in your beauty, woman, is false," III, 24, *tr. by* Frances Fletcher. LaP
"What that man is, I often was: but in time, perhaps," II, 9, *tr. by* Frances Fletcher. LaP
"Who sees you, sins. Who has not seen you, therefore," II, 32, *tr. by* Frances Fletcher. LaP
"You who flee to escape a bloody death like mine," I, 21, *tr. by* Asa M. Hughes. LaP
Elegies, *sel.* Pierre de Ronsard, *tr. fr. French by* Curtis Hidden Page.
"Stay, woodsman, stay thy hand awhile, and hark." PrPoCR
Elegies, *sel.* Johannes Secundus, *tr. fr. Latin by* F. A. Wright.
Gather Ye Roses, I, 5. LaP
Elegies. Philippe Thoby-Marcelin, *tr. fr. French by* Edna Worthley Underwood. PoNe
Elegies, *sels.* Tibullus, *tr. fr. Latin.* LaP
"Hoards let others heap of tawny gold," I, 1, *tr. by* G. S. Fraser.
(Elegy, An: "Let others pile their yellow ingots high," *tr. by* Charles A. Elton.) LiTW
"How well I'd bear the break, my anger spoke it," I, 5, *tr. by* G. S. Fraser.
"Hush, all. Our crops, our lands we purify," II, 1, *tr. by* Jack Lindsay.
"I see enslavement to a mistress closing on me," II, 4, *tr. by* Hubert Creekmore.
"If you had already resolved to blight my joyless love," I, 9, *tr. by* Hubert Creekmore.
"Macer has joined the army, and what's to become of peaceable Cupid?" II, 6, *tr. by* Hubert Creekmore.
"What man first forged the terrifying blade?" I, 10, *tr. by* Jack Lindsay.
"You will sail the dancing Aegean, Messalla, without me," *fr.* I, 3, *tr. by* George Santayana.
Elegies for a Passing World. Edmund Wilson. *See* House of the Eighties, A, *and* Riverton.
Elegies over John Reed. Marya Zaturenska.
Elegy of the Kremlin Bells, The. BAP; NP
Song of the Scarlet Banners over John Reed. BAP
They Bury Him. BAP
Elegy: "Along the tangled path and in the red." Manuel José Othón, *tr. fr. Spanish by* Samuel Beckett. AnMP
Elegy: "April again and it is a year again." Sidney Keyes. FaBoMo; WaP
Elegy: "As leaden as the aftermath of wine." Pushkin, *tr. fr. Russian by* Maurice Baring. BoR
(Elegy: "Mirth, now dead, that once was madly bubbling, The," *tr. by* Babette Deutsch.) TrRV
Elegy: Autumnal[l], The. John Donne. *See* Autumnal, The.
Elegy: "Blest, who upon night's bed can lie." Nikolai Yazykov, *tr. fr. Russian by* C. M. Bowra. BoRS
Elegy: "Child, your white face is chanting memories." Karel van de Woestijne, *tr. fr. Flemish by* Jethro Bithell. LiTW
Elegy: "Clear and gentle stream!" Robert Bridges. *See* Clear and Gentle Stream.
Elegy: "Crab, the bullace and the sloe, The." Alfred Austin. *See* Grave-Digger's Song.
Elegy, An: "Down in a bed, and on a bed of down." Giles Fletcher. *Fr.* Licia. ReIE
Elegy: "End has come to all my yearning, An." Kondrati Ryleyev, *tr. fr. Russian by* C. M. Bowra. BoRS
Elegy: "Fled is the swiftness of all the white-footed ones." Joseph Auslander. MAP; MoAmPo (1942 ed.); NP; TrJP
Elegy: "Floods of tears well from my deepest heart, The." Immanuel di Roma, *tr. fr. Italian by* Joseph Chotzner. TrJP
Elegy: "Fond, frozen, first and only lover." Louis Johnson. AnNZ
Elegy: "Forgotten playground, grave." W. Wesley Trimpi. PtPa
Elegy, An: "Friend, whose unnatural early death." David Gascoyne. FaBoTw
Elegy: He Complains How Soon the Pleasing Novelty Is Over. William Shenstone. OBEC; RO
(Elegy XI.) CEP
Elegy: "Here, awaiting what hereafter." R. G. Howarth. MoAuPo
Elegy: His Parting from Her. John Donne. *See* His Parting from Her.
Elegy V: His Picture. John Donne. *See* His Picture.
Elegy: "I die for Your holy word without regret." Antonio Enríquez Gómez, *tr. fr. Spanish.* TrJP
Elegy: "I have lov'd flowers that fade." Robert Bridges. *See* I Have Loved Flowers That Fade.
Elegy: "I stood between two mirrors when you died." William Jay Smith. NePoEA
Elegy, An: "In early winter before the first snow." E. J. Scovell. ChMP
Elegy: "In pain she bore the son who her embrace." Moses ibn Ezra, *tr. fr. Hebrew by* Solomon Solis-Cohen. TrJP
Elegy: In Spring, *sel.* Michael Bruce.
"Now Spring returns: but not to me returns." BSV
Elegy: "Jackals prowl, the serpents hiss, The." Arthur Guiterman. BOHV; InMe
Elegy, An: "Let others pile their yellow ingots high." Albius Tibullus. *See* Pastoral Elegy, A.
Elegy: "Let them bury your big eyes." Edna St. Vincent Millay. Memorial to D. C., V. AnNE; BAP; HBMV; InP; MAP; MoAB; MoAmPo; NeMA; NePA; OxBA; PoRA
Elegy: "Mirth, now dead, that once was madly bubbling, The." Pushkin. *See* Elegy: "As leaden as the aftermath of wine."
Elegy: "My comrade is dead." Salomón de la Selva, *tr. fr. Spanish by* Donald Devenish Walsh. AnCL
Elegy IX: "My dear, observe the rose! though she desire it." William Bell. NePoEA
Elegy: "My prime of youth is but a frost of cares." Chidiock Tichborne. CenL; ChTr; ElSeCe; LoBV; OBSC; PoD
(Lament the Night before His Execution, A.) HBV
(Lines Written by One in the Tower.) LPS-3
(On the Eve of His Execution.) PG (1955 ed.); PoFS; TrGrPo
(Poem, Written on the Eve of Execution.) LiTG
(Retrospect.) ACP; GoBC
(Tichborne's Elegy, Written [with His Own Hand] in the Tower before His Execution, 1586.) ElL; EM-1; ReEn; TuPP
(Untimely End, The.) CoBE
(Verses Written in the Tower the Night before He Was Beheaded.) WP
(Written on the Eve of Execution.) AnFE; EG; GTBS-W; LiTB
(Written the Night before His Execution.) ViBoPo
Elegy: "My thoughts impelled me to the resting-place." Moses ibn Ezra, *tr. fr. Hebrew by* Emma Lazarus. TrJP
Elegy: "No more the white refulgent streets." Allen Tate. TriL
Elegy IX: "No spring nor summer beauty hath such grace" John Donne. EnL
Elegy X: "Now Christendom bids her cathedrals call." William Bell. NePoEA
Elegy, An: "O faithless world, and thy most faithless part." Sir Henry Wotton. ElSeCe
Elegy: "O snatch'd away in beauty's bloom!" Byron. *See* Oh! Snatched Away in Beauty's Bloom.
Elegy, An: "O youngest, best-loved daughter of Hsieh." Yüan Chen, *tr. fr. Chinese by* Witter Bynner. ChLP; LiTW
Elegy: On a Pet Dove. Alexander MacDonald, *tr. fr. Gaelic by* Alexander Stewart. EBSV
Elegy: On Delia's Being in the Country. James Hammond. Love Elegies, VII. CEP
Elegy: On His Mistress. John Donne. *See* On His Mistress.
Elegy: "Out on the roads of sky the moon stands poised." Roy McFadden. NeIP
Elegy: "Outlived are all my aspirations." Pushkin. *See* I've lived to bury my desires.

Elegy V: Separation of Man from God. George Barker. GTBS-W; LiTB
(Elegy V: "These errors loved no less than the saint loves arrows.") FaBoTw
(Sacred Elegy V.) MoPo
Elegy VIII: "Silent is Orpheus now, and silent now." William Bell. FaBoTw
Elegy, An: "Since you must go, and I must bid farewell." Ben Jonson. LoBV; TriL
Elegy, An: "So frail our life, perchance to-morrow's sun." Tsurayuki, *tr. fr. Japanese by* Basil Hall Chamberlain. OnPM
Elegy: Summer House on the Mound, The. Robert Bridges. GoTL
Elegy V: "These errors loved no less than the saint loves arrows." George Barker. *See* Elegy V: Separation of Man from God.
Elegy: "This winter eve how soft! how mild!" Richard Chenevix Trench. IrPN
Elegy: "Those reckless hosts rush to the wells." Baruch of Worms, *tr. fr. Hebrew.* TrJP
Elegy, An: "Though beauty be the mark of praise." Ben Jonson. OBEV
(Elegie, An: "Though beautie be the marke of praise.") SeCV-1
Elegy, An: "Though I see the white azaleas on the shore." *Unknown, tr. fr. Japanese by* Ishii *and* Obata. *Fr.* Manyo Shu. OnPM
Elegy: "Time makes an ending of the Pyramids," *sel.* Louise Labé, *tr. fr. French by* Ralph N. Currey. FoS
Elegy, An: To an Old Beauty. Thomas Parnell. CEP
Advice to an Old Beauty, *sel.* BeR
Elegy: To Delia. James Hammond. Love Elegies, XII. CEP
Elegy: To the Memory of an Unfortunate Lady. Pope. *See* Elegy to the Memory . . .
Elegy XII: "Tonight the moon is high, to summon all." William Bell. FaBoTw
Elegy: "Tumult of death, dizziness hath seized me, The." Moses Rimos of Majorca, *tr. fr. Hebrew by* Israel Abrahams. TrJP
Elegy: Unrewarded Lover, The. William Walsh. *See* Unrewarded Lover, The.
Elegy: "Waxen and the false grace of tulips, The." G. S. Fraser. NeBP
Elegy: "We knew that he was not a model cat." Margaret E. Bruner. CIV
Elegy: "What should you know at last when spirit's." Robert Fitzgerald. AnAmPo
Elegy: "When in the mirror of a permanent tear." Gene Derwood. LiTA
Elegy: "Whenever we touched, I thought of the Lying-in Hospital." Robert Layzer. NePoEA
Elegy: "Why blooms the radiance of the morning sky?" *sel.* Thomas Chatterton.
"Once, ere the gold-hair'd sun shot the new ray," 4 *sts.* RO
Elegy: "Wood is bare, The." Robert Bridges. CaAE; ChMo; CMP; OAEP; POTT; PoVP; VLEP
Elegy against a Latter Day. Kendrick Smithyman. AnNZ
Elegy before Death. Edna St. Vincent Millay. AnFE; APA; ChMo; CMP; CoAnAm; GTBS-W; LiTA; LiTM; MM; OBAV
Elegy by Green for Byles's Cat. Joseph Green. CIV
Elegy for a Countryman. Padraic Fallon. NeIP
Elegy for a Dead King. Al-Kutandi, *tr. fr. Arabic by* A. J. Arberry. MooP
Elegy for a Dead Soldier. Karl Shapiro. AmPP (4th ed.); CoBMV; MiAP; OnAP; OxBA; WaaP; WaP
Elegy for All Ages. "Pablo de Rokha," *tr. fr. Spanish by* H. R. Hays. TwSpPo
Elegy for an Estrangement. John Holloway. NePoEA
Elegy for an Unknown Soldier. James K. Baxter. AnNZ
Elegy for Bécquer. Enrique Peña Barrenechea, *tr. fr. Spanish by* Milton Ben Davis. AnCL
Elegy for D. H. Lawrence, An. William Carlos Williams. PtP; TriL
Elegy for Edward Thomas, *sel.* Charles Dalmon.
"Clods of battlefields are red, The." POTE
Elegy, for Father Anselm, of the Order of Reformed Cistercians, An. Helen Parry Eden. JKCP
Elegy for Garcilaso. Rafael Alberti, *tr. fr. Spanish by* Eleanor L. Turnbull. CoSP
Elegy for Jane. Theodore Roethke. AmP; FiMAP; GTBS-W; MoAB; NePA
Elegy for Lucy Lloyd. Llewelyn Goch, *tr. fr. Welsh by* Ernest Rhys. LiTW
Elegy for Margaret, *sel.* Stephen Spender.
"Dearest and nearest brother," VI. FaBoEn
Elegy for Margaret Howard, Lady Buckhurst. Robert Southwell. CoBE
Elegy for Minor Poets. Louis MacNeice. HaMV
Elegy for Mr. Goodbeare. Sir Osbert Sitwell. AnFE; MBP; MoBrPo
Elegy for My Father. Howard Moss. NePoEA
Elegy for Myself, An. Tao Yuan-ming, *tr. fr. Chinese by* Yang Chi-sing. WhP
Elegy for Our Dead. Edwin Rolfe. WaP
Elegy for the Drowned Men Who Return. Roberto Ibáñez, *tr. fr. Spanish by* Lloyd Mallan *and* Donald Devenish Walsh. AnCL
Elegy for the Fallen Climbers, *sel.* Michael Roberts.
Wir Sind Alle Verloren, III. MoP
Elegy for the Irish Poet Francis Ledwidge. Grace Hazard Conkling. *See* Francis Ledwidge.
Elegy for Two Banjos. Karl Shapiro. AtBAP; LiTA; TrJP; WaP
Elegy for William Soutar. William Montgomerie. NeBP
Elegy for Your Absence. Eugenio Florit, *tr. fr. Spanish by* H. R. Hays. TwSpPo
Elegy for Yueh, An. Li Po, *tr. fr. Chinese.* WhP
Elegy in a Country Churchyard. G. K. Chesterton. HBMV; LBBV; MBP; MoBrPo; NeMA; SoV; TCEP; TrGrPo; ViBoPo; WhC
Elegy in a Country Churchyard. Thomas Gray. *See* Elegy Written in a Country Churchyard.
Elegy in Memory of Joseph Rodman Drake. Fitz-Greene Halleck. *See* On the Death of Joseph Rodman Drake.
Elegy in the Orongorongo Valley. Hubert Witheford. AnNZ
Elegy Just in Case. John Ciardi. AtBAP; MiAP
Elegy, Montreal Morgue. Goodridge MacDonald. CaP
Elegy of His Lady's Not Coming to London. Michael Drayton. TriL
Elegy of the Duke of Marmalade. Luis Palés Matos, *tr. fr. Spanish by* Donald Devenish Walsh. AnCL; LiTW
Elegy of the Kremlin Bells, The. Marya Zaturenska. *Fr.* Elegies over John Reed. BAP; NP
Elegy on a Dead Mermaid Washed Ashore at Plymouth Rock. Robert Hillyer. EtS
Elegy on a Friend's Passion for His Astrophill, An. Matthew Royden. *See* Elegy, or Friend's Passion for His Astrophil, An.
Elegy on a Lady, Whom Grief for the Death of her Betrothed Killed. Robert Bridges. CoBMV; LEAP; OBEV (new ed.); OBVV; PoeT; POTT
Elegy on a Lap Dog, An. John Gay. HBV; PoE
Elegy on a Nordic White Protestant. John Gould Fletcher. PoNe
Elegy on Albert Edward the Peacemaker. *Unknown.* CoMu
Elegy on an Empty Skyscraper. John Gould Fletcher. AmP
Elegy on Ben Jonson, An. *At. to* John Cleveland, *also at. to* James Cleyton. ElSeCe; EPS; MeLP; OBS
(On Ben Jonson.) SeEP
Elegy on Captain Matthew Henderson. Burns. LPS-3
Elegy on Coleman. *Unknown.*
(Epigrams.) ALV
Elegy on Gordon Barber, Lamentably Drowned in His Eighteenth Year. Gene Derwood. FaFP; GTBS-W; LiTG; LiTM; NePA
Elegy on Herakleitos. Callimachus, *tr. fr. Greek by* Dudley Fitts. LiTW
Elegy on His Mistress. John Donne. *See* On His Mistress.
Elegy on Madam Blaize. Goldsmith. *See* Elegy on That Glory of Her Sex, Mrs. Mary Blaize.
Elegy on Mr. William Shakespeare. William Basse. *See* Elegy on Shakespeare.
Elegy on Mrs. Mary Blaize. Goldsmith. *See* Elegy on That Glory of Her Sex, Mrs. Mary Blaize.
Elegy on My Father. Allen Curnow. AnNZ
Elegy on Quintilia. Catullus, *pr. tr. fr. Latin by* F. W. Cornish. LiA
Elegy on Shakespeare. William Basse, *wr. at. to* Francis Beaumont. ElSeCe; OBS
(Elegy on Mr. William Shakespeare.) PtP
(Epitaph: "Renowned Spenser, lie a thought more nigh.") BCEP
(On Mr. Wm. Shakespeare.) ElL; SeEP; ViBoPo
(On William Shakespeare.) BoFr
("Renowned Spenser, lie a thought more nigh.") LEAP
Elegy, An, on That [*or* the] Glory of Her Sex, Mrs. Mary Blaize. Goldsmith. BOHV; CEP; HBV; InMe; MuP; NA; NeHB; OAEP; OBEC; OnYI
(Elegy on Madam Blaize.) BCEP; LPS-3
(Elegy on Mrs. Mary Blaize.) OnPP; WhC
(Mrs. Mary Blaize.) SiTL
Elegy, An, on That Most Orthodox and Pains-taking Divine, Mr. Sam Smith, Ordinary of Newgate, *sel.* Tom Brown.
Execution Chaplain, Mr. Sam Smith, Ordinary of Newgate, The. BeR
Elegy on the Death of a Mad Dog, An. Goldsmith. *Fr.* The Vicar of Wakefield, *ch.* 17. AlBD; BeLS; BLPA; BOHV; BTP; CEP; CG; EV-3; FaBoBe; FaBoCh; FaFP; GN; GTIV; HBV; HBVY; HiLiEn; LBN; LiTG; LoGBV; LPS-3; MaC; MCCG; NA; NeHB; OAEP; OBEC; OnSP; OTPC; PFE; PIR; PoeMoYo; RIS; SiTL; TreF; WaKn; WP
(Elegie on the Death of a Mad Dog.) ALV
Elegy on the Death of an Unfortunate Lady. Pope. *See* Elegy to the Memory of an Unfortunate Lady.

Elegy on the Death of Dr. Channing, *sels.* James Russell Lowell. MaRV
"Therefore I cannot think thee wholly gone."
Truth and Love Abide.
Elegy on the Death of Juliet's Owl. Maurice Baring. MM
Elegy on the Death of Mme Anna Pavlova, *sel.* E. H. W. Meyerstein.
"Glory and the ardour of the stage, The." UnS
Elegy on the Death of Mr. Oldham. Dryden. *See* To the Memory of Mr. Oldham.
Elegy on the Death of Peg Nicholson. Burns. RO
Elegy on the Death of Scots Music. Robert Fergusson. TCEP
Elegy on the Death of Thomas Shepard. Urian Oakes. EPS
"Oh, that I were a poet now in grain," *sel.* BAV
Elegy on the Death of Virginia Woolf. Ronald Hambleton. BoCaPo (1948 ed.)
Elegy on the Eve. George Barker. WaaP
Elegy, An, on the Glory of Her Sex, Mrs. Mary Blaize. Goldsmith. *See* Elegy, An, on That Glory of Her Sex, Mrs. Mary Blaize.
Elegy on the Grave of a Small Fighter. Nicephorus Vrettakos, *tr. fr. Modern Greek by* Rae Dalven. MoGP
Elegy on the L. C. John Donne. ATP (1953 ed.)
Elegy on the Late King of Patagonia, An. St. John Emile Clavering Hankin. CenHV
Elegy on the Loss of U.S. Submarine S4, *sel.* H. C. Canfield.
"Entrapped inside a submarine." FiBHP
Elegy on the Pilot. Reuel Denney. PoF
Elegy on the Times. John Trumbull. APW
Elegy on Thyrza. Byron. *See* And Thou Art Dead, as Young and Fair.
Elegy on William Cobbett. Ebenezer Elliott. VA
Elegy, or Friend's Passion for His Astrophil, An, *sel.* Matthew Royden.
On Sir Philip Sidney, 7 *sts.* EIL
(Sir Philip Sidney, 4 *sts.*) LPS-3
Elegy over a Tomb. Lord Herbert of Cherbury. AtBAP; EIL; FaBoEn; MeLP; MePo; OBEV (new ed.); OBS; PoEL-2; SeEP; TriL; ViBoPo
Elegy to the Invented Woman. Xavier Abril, *tr. fr. Spanish by* Muna Lee. AnCL
Elegy to the Lost and Already Blurred by Time. Xavier Abril, *tr. fr. Spanish by* Blanca López Castellón. AnCL
Elegy to the Memory of an Unfortunate Lady. Pope. ACP, *sl. abr.;* CoEV; EiPP; EV-3; FiP; HBV; LO; OBEC; OBEV; PoE; SeCeV; TriL
(Verses to the Memory of an Unfortunate Lady.) CEP
Sels.
"Most souls, 'tis true, but peep out once an age." CH; PoD, 6 *ll.*
(Dull, Sullen Prisoners, 6 *ll.*) BeR
"Poets themselves must fall like those they sung." PoD
Elegy to the Memory of Mr. Thomas Philips of Fairford, *sels.* Thomas Chatterton. RO
Autumn and Winter.
Coming Night, The.
Elegy to the Memory of My Beloved Friend, Mr. Thomas Godfrey. Nathaniel Evans. IAP
Elegy upon the Death of Doctor Donne, Dean of Paul's, An. Thomas Carew. *See* Elegie upon the Death of the Dean of Paul's, Dr. John Donne, An.
Elegy, An, upon the Death of That Holy Man of God Mr. John Allen, *sel.* Edward Taylor.
"How are our spirituall gamesters slipt away?" PoEL-3
Elegy upon the Most Incomparable King Charles the First, An, *sel.* Henry King.
"Thou from th' en'throned martyrs blood-stain'd line." OBS
Elegy Written in a Country Churchyard. Thomas Gray. AEV; AnEnPo; AnFE; AtBAP; ATP; AWP; BCEP; BEL; BLV; BoLiVe; BrBE; BTP; CaAE; CBOV; CEP; CoBE; CoEV; EiPP; EM-1; EnL; EnLi-2; EnLit; EnRP; EPP; EV-3; ExPo; FaBoBe; FaBoEn; FaFP; GN; GoTL; GTBS; GTBS-D; GTBS-W; GTSE; GTSL; HBV; HBVY; HiLiEn; HoPM; InP; InPo; JAWP; LaA; LEAP; LiA; LiTB; LiTG; LoBV; LPS-1; MaRV; MCCG; MyFE; NeHB; OAEP; OBEC; OBEV; OHFP; OTPC; OuHeWo; PECK; PG (1945 ed.); PIAE; PIR; Po; PoE; PoEL-3; PoFS; PreP; PYM, *abr.;* ReaPo; RiBV; SeCeV; ShBV-3; TCEP; TOP; TreF; TrGrPo; TriL; TVSH; TwHP; TyEnPo; UnPo; ViBoPo; WBLP; WBP; WHA; WoL; WP
(Elegy in a Country Churchyard.) CBE
Sels.
"Boast of heraldry, the pomp of power, The." LO
"Curfew tolls the knell of parting day, The." OQP; QP-2
Part of Gray's Elegy ("Beneath those rugged elms"). BHV
Stanzas Cancelled from the Elegy. ViBoPo
Elegy Written on a Frontporch. Karl Shapiro. MoPo
Elegy Wrote in the Tower, 1554. John Harington. EIL
(Comparison of Life and Death, *with add. sts.*) ReIE
Element, The. Struthers Burt. NoCaPo (1941 ed.)
Element. Patricia K. Page. BoCaPo (1948 ed.); PeCV
Element of air was out of hand, The. Interlude. Theodore Roethke. MiAP
Element that utters doves, angels and cleft flames. Air. Kathleen Raine. MoAB
Elemental. George Dillon. AnAmPo; LA
Elemental Rhythm. Elizabeth Selden. BoFr
Elementary School Classroom in a Slum, An. Stephen Spender. BoLiVe (1945 ed.); CoBMV; FaBoMo; LiTB; MBP; MoAB; MoBrPo; MoPo; OAEP (2d ed.); PoE; ReMP; TrGrPo
Elements, The. W. H. Davies. MBP; MoBrPo; OBVV; POTT; WaKn; YT
Elements. Carolyn Wilson Link. GoYe
Elements, The. Cardinal Newman. GoBC; OBRV; PoVP; VA
(Chorus of the Elements.) OBVV
Elements, The. Oscar Williams. NAMP
Elena's Song. Sir Henry Taylor. *Fr.* Philip van Artevelde, II. LEAP; OBEV; OBRV; OBVV
(Song: "Quoth tongue of neither maid nor wife.") VA
Elene, *sels.* Cynewulf, *tr. fr. Anglo-Saxon.*
Constantine's Vision of the Cross, *tr. by* Charles W. Kennedy. AnOE
"Forth then fared the folk-troop and a fighting-lay," *tr. by* Stopford Brooke. TCEP
Helena Embarks for Palestine, *tr. by* Charles W. Kennedy. AnOE
Eleonora, *sel.* Dryden.
"All offices of Heav'n so well she knew." NBE
Elephant, The. Herbert Asquith. BoTP; SUS; TiPo; UTS
Elephant, The. Hilaire Belloc. BoTP; LiL; RAR; TiPo; UTS
Elephant. N. H. Brettell. BoSA
Elephant, The. E. J. Falconer. BoTP
Elephant, The. Rachel Field. *Fr.* A Circus Garland. StVeCh
Elephant, An. Joseph G. Francis. MPB
Elephant! Tom Scherman. PCD
Elephant, The. Annette Wynne. GFA
Elephant always carries his trunk, The. The Elephant's Trunk. Alice Wilkins. GFA; TiPo
Elephant and the Bookseller, The. John Gay. LoBV
Elephant and the Flea, The, *with music. Unknown.* TrAS
Elephant Artist, The. Sergei Mikhalkov, *tr. fr. Russian by* Jack Lindsay. RuPo
Elephant in the Moon, The. Samuel Butler. BeR
Elephant is like a wall, The. The Elephant. E. J. Falconer. BoTP
Elephant Is Slow to Mate, The. D. H. Lawrence. LiTB; LiTM; NAMP
Elephant is very large, The. The Elephant. Annette Wynne. GFA
Elephant, The, or the Force of Habit. A. E. Housman. WhC
Elephant sat on some kegs, An. An Elephant. Joseph G. Francis. MPB
Elephant, the huge old beast, The. The Elephant Is Slow to Mate. D. H. Lawrence. LiTB; LiTM; NAMP
Elephants, The. Dorothy Aldis. *Fr.* At the Circus. UTS
Elephants, The. Leconte de Lisle, *tr. fr. French by* Alan Conder. TrFP
Elephants. Marianne Moore. FaBoMo
Elephants Are Different to Different People. Carl Sandburg. MAP; MoAmPo
Elephants Fought. Viktor Khlebnikov, *tr. fr. Russian by* Avrahm Yarmolinsky. TrRV
Elephant's Trunk, The. Alice Wilkins. GFA; TiPo
Elephants walking. Holding Hands. Lenore M. Link. FaPON; MoShBr; TiPo (1952 ed.); UTS
Eletelephony. Laura E. Richards. BoChLi; FaPON; LiL; MPB; TiPo; YaD
Elevated Train, The. James S. Tippett. SUS
Elevation. Baudelaire, *tr. fr. French by* Arthur Symons. AWP
Elevation of Light. Jorge Guillén, *tr. fr. Spanish by* Eleanor L. Turnbull. CoSP
Elevator car in the elevator shaft, The. A Modern Ballad. Caroline D. Emerson. BrR
Elevator rises, Negro men, The. Poem to Negro and Whites. Maxwell Bodenheim. PoNe
Eleven. Archibald MacLeish. ChMo; CMP; PoLFOT
Eleven men of England. The Red Thread of Honor. Sir Francis Hastings Doyle. BBV; LH; OtMeF; PoVP
Eleven, twelve, one. Lady Macbeth. Yu Min-chuan. WhP
Eleventh Song. Sir Philip Sidney. *See* Astrophel and Stella: Eleventh Song.
Elf, The. Marian Osborne. CPG
Elf and the Dormouse, The. Oliver Herford. AA; BoChLi; FaBoBe; FaPON; GFA; GoBP; GoTP; HBV; HBVY; MPB; OnHT; OTPC (1946 ed.); PCH; PoRh; PRWS; RAR; SP; TiPo; TSW; TSWC; TVC; TVSH; UTS
Elf Singing, The ("An elf sat on a twig"). William Allingham. GoTP; StVeCh
Elfer Hill. *Unknown, tr. fr. Danish by* Robert Jamieson. AWP

Elfin Artist, The. Alfred Noyes. CV
Elfin Knight, An. Joseph Rodman Drake. *See* Fairy in Armor, A.
Elfin Knight, The (*diff. versions*). *Unknown.* BaBo (A *vers.*); EBSV; ESPB; ViBoFo (A *and* B *vers.*)
(Cambric Shirt, The, B *vers.*) BaBo
("Can you make me a cambric shirt.") OxNR
(Lady Isabel and the Elf-Knight.) OBB
My Plaid Awa', *sel.* CH
Elfin Pedlar, The. George Darley. *See* Nephon's Song.
Elfin People Fill the Tubes, The. Winifred M. Letts. BoTP
Elfin Plane, The. Rowena Bennett. MPB (1956 ed.)
Elfin Shaft, The. *Unknown, tr. fr. Danish by* E. M. Smith-Dampier. BoDaBa
Elfin Skates. Eugene Lee-Hamilton. OBVV
Elfin Song. Joseph Rodman Drake. *Fr.* The Culprit Fay. AA; OBAV; PoMS
Elfland looms in the sea afar, An. Sunset Joy. Arne Garborg. AnNoLy
Eli, Eli, lama sabacthani? At the Ninth Hour. John Lancaster Spalding. *Fr.* God and the Soul. AA
Elijah in the House of Study. Mani Leib, *tr. fr. Yiddish by* Sarah Zweig Betsky. OnCuPl
Elijah's mantle fell upon. A Little Song of Work. Sarah Elizabeth Sprouse. BLRP
Elinda's Glove. Richard Lovelace. OBS
(Glove, The.) ALV; EG
Elinor Rumming [*or* Elynour Rummynge]. John Skelton. PoFS, *much abr.*
(Tunning of Elinour Rumming, The.) ReIE
Sels.
"And this comely dame." ViBoPo
"Tell you I chyll."
(Tunning of Elinour Rumming, The.) TrGrPo
(Tunnyng of Elynour Rummyng, The.) SiTL; TwHP
Eliot Cass was from Boston, Mass. The Old School Tie-up. Laurence McKinney. WhC
Elis. Georg Trakl, *tr. fr. German by* Kate Flores. AnGP
Elisa. Spenser. *Fr.* The Shepheardes Calender: April. CoEV; OBSC
(Aprill.) AtBAP
(Hobbinol's Lay of Fair Elisa.) ElSeCe
Elisa, or an Elegy upon the Unripe Decease of Sir Antony Irby, *sel.* Phineas Fletcher.
"My dearest Betty." ViBoPo
Elixir, The. George Herbert. AEV; BCEP; BLV; BoLiVe; BoTP; FaBoCh; GN; GrCo-1, *abr.;* LoGBV; MaRV; OHIP; PCH, *st.* 1; SeCV-1; TrGrPo; WGRP; WP
Eliza and Anne were extremely distress'd. The Bird's Nest. Elizabeth Turner. OHIP; OTPC (1923 ed.); RAR
Eliza Spaulding. Donald Burnie. PaA
Eliza Telefair. Jocelyn Macy Sloan. GoYe
Elizabeth. Valentin Iremonger. *See* Recollection in Autumn.
Elizabeth. George Brandon Saul. HBMV
Elizabeth. Sylvia Townsend Warner. MBP; MoAB; MoBrPo; NeMA
Elizabeth Ann Peabody. Ivy O. Eastwick. BrR
Elizabeth at the Piano. Horace Gregory. UnS
Elizabeth, frigidly stretched. Recollection in Autumn [*or* Elizabeth *or* This Houre Her Vigill]. Valentin Iremonger. NeIP; OnYI; OxBI
Elizabeth her frock has torn. Think Before You Act. Mary Elliott. HBVY
Elizabeth, Lizzy [*or* Elspeth], Betsy, and Bess. Mother Goose. HBV; HBVY; OTPC; OxNR; PPL; RIS
Elizabeth, my cousin, is the sweetest little girl. Mustard and Cress. Norman Gale. TVC; TVSH
Elizabeth of Bohemia. Sir Henry Wotton. *See* On His Mistress, the Queen of Bohemia.
"Elizabeth the Beloved." Elizabeth. Sylvia Townsend Warner. MBP; MoAB; MoBrPo; NeMA
Elizabethan Days, *sel.* Thomas Caulfield Irwin.
"'Tis pleasant, stretched on grassy lawn." IrPN
Elizabethan queen, not Dido now, The. Poem from "The Year of Loss." Nicholas Moore. TriL
Elizabethan Tragedy; a Footnote. Howard Moss. NePoEA
Elizabethans Called It Dying, The. James Schuyler. NeAP
Ella, fell a Maple tree. Picnic. Hugh Lofting. SUS
Ellen Bawn. *Unknown, tr. fr. Irish by* James Clarence Mangan. IrPN
Ellen Hanging Clothes. Lizette Woodworth Reese. PoeMoYo; VOD
Ellen McJones [*or* M'Jones] Aberdeen. W. S. Gilbert. HBV; InMe; PCD; TSW; TSWC
Ellen's Song. Sir Walter Scott. *See* Soldier, Rest!
Elliott Hawkins. Edgar Lee Masters. *Fr.* Spoon River Anthology. OxBA
Ellipse of a cry, The. The Cry. Federico García Lorca. CoSP; OnPM
Ellis Park. Helen Hoyt. HBMV; NLK; NP; PoMa; POT; PoTo; SBMV; SP; VOD; YT
Ellsworth. *Unknown.* PAH
Elm, The. Hilaire Belloc. GTML
Elm, The. Odell Shepard. HBMV
Elm Angel. Harold Monro. FaBoMo
Elm Beetle, The. Andrew Young. LoBV
Elm lets fall its leaves before the frost, The. The Pine. Augusta Davies Webster. DD; HBV; OHIP
Elms in the meadow springing. Trees and Waves. Al-Isra'ili. MooP
Elms of Protesilaus, The. Antiphilus of Byzantium, *tr. fr. Greek by* F. L. Lucas. GrPE
Elms of the Eastern Gate. *Unknown, tr. fr. Chinese by* Arthur Waley. *Fr.* Shi King. LiTW
Eloïsa to Abelard. Pope. CEP; EiPP; EnL; EnLi-1; GEPC; LoBV; OAEP; PoEL-3; ReaPo
Sels.
Eloisa. OBEC; SeCePo
Nun's Lot, The, *br. sel.* PraNu
(Vestal, The, *br. sel.*) ACP; CAW
Eloisa's Prayer for Abelard. GoBC
"How oft, when pressed to marriage." ViBoPo
Eloquent are the hills: their power speaks. The Green Lake. Michael Roberts. ChMP
Eloquent herald, An, this, a speech-crammed babbler! Euripides. *Fr.* Suppliants. PoFr
Elphin knight sits on yon hill, The. The Elfin Knight (A *vers.*). *Unknown.* BaBo
Elsa Wertman. Edgar Lee Masters. *Fr.* Spoon River Anthology. OxBA
Elsa's Eyes. Louis Aragon, *tr. fr. French by* W. J. Strachan. MiFP
Elsie. William Carlos Williams. *See* Pure Products of America, The.
Elsie Marley Is Grown So Fine. *Unknown.* OxNR; OTPC (1923 ed.)
("Elsie Marley's grown so fine.") SAS
Elusive Dove, The, 1946. Norman R. Jaffray. LauV
Elusive Maid, The. Abraham ibn Chasdai, *tr. fr. Hebrew by* Joseph Chotzner TrJP
Elusive Muse, The. Edward M. Freed. CAG
Elusive Nature. Henry Timrod. *See* Sonnet: At Last, Beloved Nature.
Elves, The. Leconte de Lisle, *tr. fr. French by* Alan Conder. TrFP
Elves' Dance, The. *Unknown, at. to* John Lyly *and to* Thomas Ravenscroft. *Fr.* The Mayde's Metamorphosis. CH; FaPON; HH; MPB; PoRh
(Fairy Dances, 2.) ElL
("Round about in a fair ring-a," *diff. vers.*) BoTP
Elves, with thyme and marjoram crowned, The. The Elves. Leconte de Lisle. TrFP
Elvira, *sel.* George Digby, Earl of Bristol.
Song: "See, O see!/ How every tree." SeCL
Elynour Rummynge. John Skelton. *See* Elinor Rumming.
Elyphants an' chariots a-ridin' in th' sky. Clouds. Charles R. Angell. LPS-1
Elysia. Antonio Beccadelli, *pr. tr. fr. Latin by* Richard Aldington. LaP
Elysium. Emily Dickinson. *See* Elysium is as far as to.
Elysium. Pindar, *tr. fr. Greek by* F. L. Lucas. GrPE
Elysium. Edward Coote Pinkney. MOAP
Elysium. Agnes Mary Frances Robinson. UnW
Elysium is as far as to. Emily Dickinson. AmPP (4th ed.); BoFr; CoBA; CoV; FaBoEn; InPo; MAP; MoAB; MoAmPo; MOAP; OxBA; PoLFOT
(Elysium.) WoL
(Suspense.) AWP; BAP; JAWP; LBAP; NeMA; OnPM; WBP
Emancipation. Maltbie D. Babcock. *See* Death.
Emancipation. *Unknown.* BLPA
Emancipation from British Dependence. Philip Freneau. IDAH; PAH
(Political Litany, A.) IAP
Emancipation Group, The. Whittier. LBAH
"Let man be free! The mighty word," *sel.* PGD
Emancipators, The. Randall Jarrell. WaP
Emaricdulfe, *sels.* "E. C."
"I am enchanted with thy snow-white hands." TuPP
"My heart is like a ship on Neptune's back," XXIX. ElSeCe; TuPP
"Within her hair Venus and Cupid sport them," VI. ElL; TuPP
Embalming is so intricate these days. And Dust to Dust. Charles David Webb. NePoAm-2
Embankment, The. T. E. Hulme. FaBoMo; MBP; MoBrPo (1942 ed.)
(Fantasia of a Fallen Gentleman on a Cold Bitter Night on the Embankment.) SeCePo
Embarcation. Thomas Hardy. EmBrPo
Embargo, The, *sel.* Bryant.
"But quit thy meaner game, indignant Muse." CoBA
Embark as joyfully you may; be gay. For a Young Idealist: "Godspeed!" John Gilland Brunini. JKCP (1955 ed.)
Embarkation. John Gould Fletcher. Down the Mississippi, I. ChMo; CMP; LiTA; MOAP; NP; SPP; TCAP
Embarkation. The, *abr.* Longfellow. *Fr.* Evangeline, I. PAH
Embarrassed Amorist, The. Louis Untermeyer. PR

Embarrassing Episode of Little Miss Muffet, The. Guy Wetmore Carryl. FaPON; MPB; StPo; TSW; TSWC
Embarrassment of Eyes. *Unknown, tr. fr. German.* PIAE
Embassy of Doves, An. Late. Helen Salz. GoYe
Ember Picture, An. James Russell Lowell. IAP
Embers. J. E. Cadden. CAG
Embers of the day are red, The. Evensong. Robert Louis Stevenson. BMEP; MaRV; PoVP; TCEP; TrPWD; VLEP
Embers sink to ashes, The. In the dusk. At the Fireside. Afanasi Afanasievich Fet. TrRV
Embittered Youth. Sophocles, *tr. fr. Greek by* Robert Whitelaw. *Fr.* Philoctetes. GrR
Emblazoned bleak in austral skies. Southern Cross. Herman Melville. AnFE; CoAnAm; LiTA
Emblem. Michael Hamburger. PoN
Emblem of England's ancient faith. To an Oak Tree. Sir Walter Scott. BHV
Emblems, *sels.* Francis Quarles.
Epigram: "Paul's midnight voice prevail'd; his music's thunder," V, 10. LoBV
"Flint-hearted Stoics, you whose marble eyes," II, 4. EPS (1936 ed.)
"Great All in All, that art my rest, my home," IV, 3. TrPWD
"I love, and have some cause to love, the earth," V, 6. EPS (1942 ed.)
(Delight in God Only.) BCEP; LPS-2; MaRV, *sel.*
"Like to the Arctic needle, that does guide," V, 4. SeEP
"Lord! Canst Thou see and suffer? Is Thy hand," I, 15. EPS
My Beloved Is Mine, and I Am His; He Feedeth among the Lilies, V, 3. CaAE; MePo; OBS; TrGrPo, *abr.*
(Canticle.) FaBoEn
(Divine Rapture, A, 3 *sts.*) HBV; LO; OBEV
(Even [*or* Ev'n] like Two Little Bank-dividing Brooks.) ElSeCe; MeLP; TriL
(He Is Mine, 3 *sts.*) LiTL
(Mystical Ecstasy, A, 3 *sts.*) GTSL
"'Tis but a foil at best, and that's the most," II, 14. LoBV
Vanity of the World, II, 5. BCEP; LEAP; LPS-3
(False World, Thou Ly'st.) ElSeCe; SeCePo; SeEP
(Wilt Thou Set Thine Eyes upon That Which Is Not?) OBS
(World's Fallacies.) EV-2
"Whene'er the old exchange of profit rings," IV, 3. EPS (1936 ed.)
"Why dost thou shade thy lovely face?" III, 7. SeCL; SeEP; TrPWD
(Wherefore Hidest Thou Thy Face, and Holdest Me for Thy Enemie?) MePo
Emblems. Allen Tate. AmPP (3d ed.); AWP; InPo; MOAP
Emblems of Conduct. Hart Crane, *after* Samuel Greenberg. LiTA; LiTM (rev. ed.); NAMP; NePA
Emblems of Evening. Robert Horan. CrMA
Emblems of Love, *sels.* Lascelles Abercrombie.
Epilogue: "What shall we do for Love these days?" AnFE; GTML; HBV; MBP; MV; OBVV; TCPD
Small Fountains. CH
Hymn to Love. OBEV (new ed.); OBVV
Judith, *fr.* Pt. III.
Balkis. BMEP; HBV; LEAP
(Song: "Balkis was in her marble town.") MBP; MoBrPo
Marriage Song. BMEP, *abr.*; BrBE
(From "Marriage Song," *abr.*) LEAP
Vashti, *fr.* Pt. I.
Woman's Beauty. MBP; MoBrPo; PG
Emblems of Love, *sel.* Philip Ayres.
"Her name is at my tongue whene'er I speak." LO
Embrace me then, ye hills, and close me in. Wordsworth. *Fr.* The Recluse. EnSW
Embroidery on the Kerchief, The. Kostas Krystallis, *tr. fr. Modern Greek by* Rae Dalven. MoGP
Embryo. Mary Ashley Townsend. AA; HBV
Emer, he is your man, now. Fand Yields Cuchulain to Emer. *Unknown.* AnIL; LyMA; SiB
Emerald April, September's gold. Song of the Seasons. Blanche De Good Lofton. YeAr
Emerald Is as Green as Grass, An. Christina Rossetti. *Fr.* Sing-Song. AlDL; TiPo
(Precious Stones.) GoTP
Emeralds are singing on the grasses, The. How Many Heavens. Edith Sitwell. MeRV; MoPW
Emergency. Isabel Fiske Conant. HBMV
Emerging at midnight. Day's Affirmation [*or* Inbetweentimes]. Sir Herbert Read. FaBoTw; TwCV
Emerson. Amos Bronson Alcott. AA; GA; OBAV
Emerson. Craven Langstroth Betts. GA
Emerson. Mary Mapes Dodge. AA; DD; GA; PoRL
Emerson. Elizabeth Clementine Kinney. PEOR
Emerson. James Russell Lowell. *Fr.* A Fable for Critics. AmPP (4th ed.); AnNE; APW; OnAP; OxBA
("There comes Emerson first, whose rich words, every one.") CoBA; OuHeWo; PtP; TCAP
Emerson Alphabet, An. *Comp. by* Caroline B. Le Row, *fr. various poems by* Emerson. PEOR
Emerson; Last Days at Concord. Horace Gregory. ChMo
Emigrant, The, *sels.* Alexander McLachlan. BoCaPo
In the Forest.
Song: "Old England is eaten by knaves."
Emigrant, The, *sels.* Standish O'Grady.
"And first Morency, far famed water, you." CaP
Old Nick in Sorel. BoCaPo
Winter in Lower Canada. BoCaPo
Emigrant Lassie, The. John Stuart Blackie. VA
Emigrant Mother, The. Wordsworth. BPN
Emigrant Song. "S. Ansky," *tr. fr. Yiddish by* Joseph Leftwich. TrJP
Emigrant to America. Vicente Huidobro, *tr. fr. Spanish by* H. R. Hays. TwSpPo
Emigrants, The; Introductory Stanzas. Thomas Pringle. BoSA
Emigrant's Child, The. Lyman H. Sproull. PoOW
Emigrant's Farewell, The. Thomas Pringle. EBSV
Emigration of the Fairies, The, *sels.* John Hunter-Duvar.
"Few days more they drifted, ever west, A." BoCaPo
"First halt. They heard within a sugar patch." CaP
Emigravit. Helen Hunt Jackson. AA; AnFE; APA; CoAnAm; OBAV
Emilia. Sarah N. Cleghorn. HBV; PFY
Emily Brontë. C. Day Lewis. ChMP
Emily Dickinson. Melville Cane. PoeMoYo
Emily Dickinson. Paul Engle. PtP
Emily Hardcastle, Spinster. John Crowe Ransom. ChMo; LS; NV
Emily Jane. Laura E. Richards. RIS
Emily, John, James, and I. W. S. Gilbert. InMe; WhC
Emily Sparks. Edgar Lee Masters. *Fr.* Spoon River Anthology. BoFr
Emily wandered through town and folks said that she saw. Old Emily. Hyacinthe Hill. GoYe
Emily's Prayer to Diana. Chaucer. *Fr.* The Canterbury Tales: The Knight's Tale. MyFE
Emma. Goldsmith. OnYI
Emmet's Epitaph. Robert Southey. *See* Written Immediately after Reading the Speech of Robert Emmet.
Emmonsail's Heath in Winter. John Clare. FaBoEn; PoEL-4
Emmy. Arthur Symons. HBV; OBVV; POTT; PoVP; TreF; VLEP
Emotion of Fiction, The. Roy Fuller. LiTM (1946 ed.)
Empedocles. Friedrich Hölderlin, *tr. fr. German by* R. F. C. Hull. AnGP
Empedocles. Thomas S. Jones, Jr. AnAmPo; LA
Empedocles on Etna. Matthew Arnold. ViPP
Sels.
"And you, ye stars," *fr.* II. VA
Empedocles' Song, *fr.* I, ii. EmBrPo; PIAE; TOP
(Lyric Stanzas of Empedocles.) BPN
"Far, far from here," *fr.* I, ii. NBE
(Cadmus and Harmonia.) OBVV; ViPo
(Song of Callicles, The.) FiP
"Fulness of life and power of feeling," *fr.* II. BrBE; OAEP
"Gods laugh in their sleeve, The," *abr., fr.* I, ii. BMEP
"Is it so small a thing," *fr.* I, ii. OBEV; OBVV
Life and Thought, *fr.* II. FiP
"Noon is hot, The. When we have crossed the stream," *fr.* I, ii. EPN; PoVP
"Oh, that fate had let me see," *fr.* II. NBE
"Through the black, rushing smoke-bursts," *fr.* II. PoVP
(Apollo.) LH; ViPo
(Callicles' Song.) BMEP; BPN; ChTr; EmBrPo; LoBV
(Last Song of Callicles.) VLEP
(Song for Apollo.) FiP
(Song of Callicles [on Etna], The.) GTBS; OBEV; OBVV; ShBV-3
"We would have inward peace," *fr.* I, ii. LEAP
Emperor, The. Tu Fu, *tr. fr. Chinese by* E. Powys Mathers. AWP
Emperor Nap he would set off, The. The March to Moscow. Robert Southey. BOHV; SiTL
Emperor of Ice-Cream, The. Wallace Stevens. AmP; AmPP (4th ed.); CoBMV; CoV; FaBoMo; LiTA; MoPo; MoVE; NePA; OxBA; PoFS; ViBoPo (1958 ed.)
Emperor of the East, The, *sel.* Philip Massinger.
Song: "Why art thou slow, thou rest of trouble, Death," *fr.* V, iii. ElSeCe; EV-2; SeEP; TuPP; ViBoPo
(Death Invoked.) ACP (1952 ed.)
(Sad Song, A.) OBS; SeCL
Emperor of the Moon, The, *sel.* Aphra Behn.
Serenade: "When maidens are young, and in their spring." SeCL
Emperor of the Threefold World. Christopher Marlowe. *Fr.* Tamburlaine the Great, Pt. II, Act IV, sc. iii. TrGrPo
(Bloody Conquests of Mighty Tamburlaine, The.) ChTr
Emperors and kings! in vain you strive. The Republican Genius of Europe. Philip Freneau. AmPP (3d ed.)

Emperor's Bird's Nest, The. Longfellow. MPB
Emperor's crown and peony red. The Old Garden. Joseph von Eichendorff. LiTW
Emperors of fourteen dynasties, The. The Middle Kingdom. Allen Upward. *Fr.* Scented Leaves from a Chinese Jar. NP
Empire Builder, The. John Jerome Rooney. JKCP
Empire Builders. Archibald MacLeish. Frescoes for Mr. Rockefeller's City, V. AmP; OxBA; Po; ReaPo; UnPo
Empire Is No More. Blake. *See* Morning Comes, The.
Empire (Persepolis). "Fiona Macleod." BMEP
"Empire to be lost or won, An!" Whitman's Ride for Oregon. Hezekiah Butterworth. GA; PAH
Empires. Francis Burdett Money-Coutts. OBVV
Employment ("He that is weary, let him sit"). George Herbert. EV-2; OxBoCh; OBS
Employment ("If as a flower doth spread and die"). George Herbert. AtBAP; ElSeCe; SeCV-1
Employment. Jane Taylor. OTPC (1923 ed.); PPL
Emptied and pearly skulls. The Statue and the Perturbed Burghers. Denis Devlin. OnYI
Empties Coming Back. Angelo de Ponciano. BLPA
(Emptys Cuming Back.) DDA
Emptiness. John Ransom Palmer. PoP
Empty all your quiver on me. Archias, *tr. fr. Greek by* F. A. Wright. GrPo
Empty are the ways. Ione, Dead the Long Year. Ezra Pound. TwCV
Empty Boat, The. Tao Yuan-ming, *tr. fr. Chinese by* Yang Yeh-tzu. WhP
Empty Cradle, The. José Selgas y Carrasco, *tr. fr. Spanish by* Thomas Walsh. CAW
Empty Houses. Mary Colborne-Veel. BoAu
Empty Jar, The. William Stenhouse. AnNZ
Empty Life, The. Shakespeare. *See* Tomorrow and Tomorrow and Tomorrow.
Empty Little House, The. Anne Sutherland. DDA
Empty my heart, Lord, of daily vices. Theodore Spencer. *Fr.* Invocation. TrPWD
Empty of heart we wait amid the snow. The Mountain Lake. Richard Church. AtBAP; POTE
Empty Purse, The. W. W. Gibson. ChMo; CMP
Empty Purse, The. Tu Fu, *tr. fr. Chinese.* OnPM, *tr. by* Chi Hwang Chu *and* Edna Worthley Underwood; WhP, *tr. by* Hsieh Wen Tung
Empty sky, a world of heather, An. Divided. Jean Ingelow. HBV
Empty Sleeve, The. J. R. Bagby. BlG
Empty Soul, The. Walter R. Bowie. MaRV
Empty the last drop. Plunger. Carl Sandburg. BLV; BoLiVe; NeMA
Empty Vessel. "Hugh MacDiarmid." FaBoTw
Empty your glass!—Behold where Death is waiting. To Old Movitz, Ill with Consumption. Karl Mikael Bellman. AnSL
Emptys Cuming Back. Angelo de Ponciano. *See* Empties Coming Back.
En bateau. Paul Verlaine, *tr. fr. French by* Arthur Symons. AWP
En Garde, Messieurs. William Lindsey. AA; BLP; LEAP; PFY
En Monocle. Donald Evans. AnAmPo; LA; NP
En roulant ma boule. *Unknown, tr. fr. French-Canadian folk song by* William McLennan. BoCaPo
En Route. Arthur Hugh Clough. Amours de Voyage, Canto I, *introd.* BPN
("Over the great windy waters.") EPN; ViPP
En Route. George Dillon. NP
En Route. E. L. Mayo. MiAP
En Voyage. Caroline Atherton Briggs Mason, *wr. at. to* Caroline Atwater Mason. HBV
(God Knows Best.) MaRV
(God's Will Is Best.) PTA-2
(That Wind Is Best, *abr.*) NLK
(Whichever Way the Wind Doth Blow.) OQP; QP-2; TreFS
Four Winds, The, *sel.* PCH
Enamel Girl, The. Genevieve Taggard. HBMV; MAP; MoAmPo; NP; TCPD
Enamored [*or* Enamoured] Architect of Airy Rhyme. Thomas Bailey Aldrich. AA; AnAmPo; AnFE; AnNE; APA; HBV; LA; LBAP; MAP; MCCG; OBAV; PC
Enamored so of form, of calculation. Of the Mathematician. Alice Clear Matthews. GoYe
Enchainment. Arthur O'Shaughnessy. HBV
Enchanted Book-Shelf, The. Josephine Thorp. MOB
Enchanted Castle, The. Jeanne D'Orge. AnAmPo; LA
Enchanted Fawn, The. *Unknown, tr. fr. Middle Irish by* Edward Gwynn. *Fr.* Dinnshenchas. OnYI
Enchanted Garden, The. Marjorie Barrows. GFA
Enchanted Ground. James Thomson. *See* Vale of Indolence.
Enchanted Heart, The. Edward Davison. BMEP; HBMV
Enchanted Island, The. Luke Aylmer Conolly. OBRV; TIP
Enchanted Knight, The. Edwin Muir. MoVE
Enchanted Mistress, The. Egan O'Rahilly, *tr. fr. Irish by* Lady Gregory. GTIV
Enchanted Orchard, The. Henry Mackenzie Green. MM
Enchanted Prince, The. Edwin Muir. MBP
Enchanted Sheep-Fold, The. Josephine Preston Peabody. AV; BAP; SBMV
Enchanted Shirt, The. John Hay. BBV; BLPA; BOHV; GN; GoTP; MaC; OnSP; PIAE; TiPo (1952 ed.); TSW; TSWC
Enchanted Spring, The. George Darley. RO
Enchanted Traveller, The. Bliss Carman. DDA
Enchanter, The. Emerson. HiLiAm; IAP
Enchanting night! Abode Divine. Al-Rusafi. MooP
Enchantment. Arthur S. Bourinot. CPG
Enchantment. Madison Cawein. HBV
Enchantment, The. Thomas Otway. EPP; EV-3; HBV; LiTL; LO; NeHB; OBEV; SeCL; ViBoPo
Enchantress. Al-Munfatil, *tr. fr. Arabic by* A. J. Arberry. MooP
Enchantress, The. Bliss Carman. VOD
Enchantress, touch no more that strain! Music and Memory. John Albee. AA
Encinctur'd with a twine of leaves. The Fruit Plucker [*or* Boy in the Wilderness *or* In a Moonlight Wilderness *or* Fragment]. Samuel Taylor Coleridge. *Fr.* The Wanderings of Cain. CH; FaBoCh; LoGBV; OTPC (1923 ed.); RO; SeCeV
Encircling Thee Thy holy brides. Pedro Malon de Chaide. *Fr.* The Conversion of the Magdalene. CAW
Enclosed the lacquered, coiling snake. The Zoo in the City. Sara Van Alstyne Allen. GoYe
Encompass me, my lover. The Constant North. J. F. Hendry. NeBP
Encompassed by a thousand nameless fears. As Day Begins to Wane. Helena Coleman. BoCaPo (1943 ed.); CaP; CPG
Encounter, The. Paul Blackburn. NeAP
Encounter. Denis Devlin. OnYI
Encounter, The. Lawrence Durrell. *Fr.* Eight Aspects of Melissa. NeBP
Encounter. William Griffith. BAP
Encounter. *Unknown, tr. fr. French by* Claude C. Abbott. LyMA
Encounter in the Field, An. Li Po, *tr. fr. Chinese by* Shigeyoshi Obata. ChLP
Encounter with Sleep. Keats. *Fr.* Endymion, IV. ERP
Encountering Sorrow. Chu Yuan, *tr. fr. Chinese.* WhP
Encouragement. Paul Laurence Dunbar. PTA-2; YT
Encouragement for Little Children, *sel.* Jane Taylor.
God Is So Good. MeMeAg; OTPC (1946 ed.)
(Little Hymn, A.) BOL
Encouragement to Exile. Petronius Arbiter, *tr. fr. Latin by* Howard Mumford Jones. AWP; JAWP; WBP
Encouragement to a Lover. Sir John Suckling. *See* Why So Pale and Wan?
End, The. Tristan Corbière, *tr. fr. French by* Kate Flores. AnFP
End, The. Walter de la Mare. OAEP (2d ed.)
End, The. Walter Savage Landor. *See* On His Seventy-fifth Birthday.
End, The. John Masefield. *See* There, on the Darkened Deathbed, Dies the Brain.
End, The. A. A. Milne. SiSoSe
End, The. Sir Henry Newbolt. MeMeAg
(Day's End.) RIS
(Finis.) GaP; TiPo
End, The. Wilfred Owen. CH; ES; HBMV; MeRV; MoVE; PeBoSo
End, The. Palladas, *tr. fr. Greek by* F. L. Lucas. GrPE
End, The. Wallace Rice. AA
End, An. Christina Rossetti. EmBrPo
End, The. Rabindranath Tagore. MOAH
End, An. Sara Teasdale. NV
End, The. Mark Van Doren. ViBoPo
End, The. Marguerite Wilkinson. *Fr.* Songs of an Empty House. HBMV; SBMV
End has come, as come it must, The. At School-Close. Whittier. PoRL
End has come to all my yearning, An. Elegy. Kondrati Ryleyev. BoRS
End of a Day in the Provinces, The. Jules Laforgue, *tr. fr. French by* Margaret Crosland. AnFP
End of a Leave, The. Roy Fuller. NeBP
End of a Venture, The. Zonas, *tr. fr. Greek by* F. L. Lucas. GrPE
End of a War, The. Sir Herbert Read. OBMV; WaP
End of Another Home Holiday. D. H. Lawrence. FaBoMo; MoVE
End of Aodh-of-the-Songs, The. "Fiona Macleod." LBBV
End of April, The. Robert Fuller Murray. CenHV
End of Being, The. Seneca, *tr. fr. Latin by* H. C. Leonard. MaRV; WGRP
End of Clonmacnois, The. *Unknown, tr. fr. Irish by* Frank O'Connor. KiLC

End of Day, The. W. B. Yeats. Upon a Dying Lady, IV. LiTB
End of Desire, The. Hugh McCrae. BoAV; MoAuPo
End of Dr. Faustus, The. Christopher Marlowe. *Fr.* Dr. Faustus. PoEL-2
("Ah, Faustus,/ Now hast thou but one bare hour to live.") BoLiVe; MyFE; NBE; ViBoPo
(End of Faustus, The.) TrGrPo
(Finale.) WHA
(Last Hour of Faustus.) CBOV
(O Lente. Lente, Curite Noctis Equi.) LiA
End of Elfintown, The, *sel.* Jane Barlow.
Flitting of the Fairies, The. TIP
End of everything approaches, The. Doomsday. Elinor Wylie. CrMA
End of Exploring, The. David Campbell. SeCePo
End of Faustus, The. Christopher Marlowe. *See* End of Dr. Faustus, The.
End of Fear, The. Ruth Pitter. POTE
End of Love, The. George Meredith. *See* Modern Love: "By this he knew she wept with waking eyes."
End of Man Is Death, The. Moses ibn Ezra, *tr. fr. Hebrew by* Solomon Solis-Cohen. TrJP
End of Season. Robert Penn Warren. TwAmPo
End of Sorrow, The. Edmond Fleg, *tr. fr. French by* Humbert Wolfe. *Fr.* The Wall of Weeping. TrJP
End of Steel. Thomas Saunders. CaP
End of Summer. Stanley Kunitz. CrMA
End of Summer. Jean Starr Untermeyer. YT
End-of-Summer Poem. Rowena Bastin Bennett. FaPON; SiSoSe
End of the Day, The. Duncan Campbell Scott. VA
End of the Drought, The. Peter McArthur. CPG
End of the Duel, The. Rachel Annand Taylor. CAW
End of the Episode, The. Thomas Hardy. LO; LoPS
End of the First Part, The. Christina Rossetti. *Fr.* Three Stages. EmBrPo
End of the Flower-World (A.D. 2300). Stanley Burnshaw. AnAmPo; LA; TrJP
End of the Last Fight of the *Revenge,* The. Gervase Markham. SG
End of the Play, The. Thackeray. *Fr.* Dr. Birch and His Young Friends. BMEP, *much abr.*; COAH; FaFP; GN; LEAP; LPS-1; TreF; VA
End of the Seers' Convention. Kenneth Fearing. LiTA
End of the Story, The. Terence Tiller. ChMP; NeBP
End of the Suitors, The. Homer, *tr. fr. Greek by* George Chapman. *Fr.* The Odyssey, XXII. OBS
End of the Trail. *Unknown.* SCC
End of the Way, The. Harriet Cole. BLRP
End of the World, The. Gordon Bottomley. CH; MBP; MoBrPo; MoVE; NV
End of the World, The. Raymond Kresensky. PSO
End of the World, The. Archibald MacLeish. AnEnPo; CoBMV; CoV; HoPM; LiTM; MAP; MoAB; MoAmPo; NeMA; NePA; NP; OxBA; PeBoSo; Po; TCPD; TrGrPo; TwHP
End of the World, The. Bertram Warr. BoCaPo (1948 ed.)
End of the Year, The. Su T'ung-po, *tr. fr. Chinese by* Kenneth Rexroth. OnPC
End of Travel, An. Robert Louis Stevenson. VLEP
End of Troy, The. Euripides, *tr. fr. Greek by* Gilbert Murray. *Fr.* Trojan Women. OxBG
End of Tyranny, The. Shelley. *Fr.* Prometheus Unbound. ShBV-3
End this enchantment, love, of my desires. Diella, XXXV. Richard Lynche. TuPP
End to all I've ever had to say, An. Endpiece. *Unknown.* KiLC
End Which Comes, The. Sir Edwin Arnold. *Fr.* The Light of Asia. LoBV
End will come swiftly in an early autumn. Final Autumn. Josephine W. Johnson. NAMP; NePA
Ended! Nikolaus Lenau, *tr. fr. German by* Dwight Durling. AnGP
Ended the watches of the night; oh, hear the bugles blow. Reveillé. Eden Phillpotts. POT
Endimion. John Lyly. *See* Endymion.
Endimion and Phoebe, *sels.* Michael Drayton.
Endymion's Convoy. OBSC
"In Ionia whence sprang old poets' fame." ReIE
(Phoebe on Latmus.) OBSC
Endimion Porter and Olivia. Sir William Davenant. *See* Song: "Before we shall again behold."
Endless, The. *Unknown, tr. fr. Japanese. Fr.* Manyo Shu. OnPM
Endless blue mountains disperse, The. On the Tower of Gathering Remoteness. Su T'ung-po. WhP
Endless Error, The. Donald F. Drummond. PtPa
Endless, foolish merriment of stars, The. Nodes. Alice Corbin. NP; WGRP
Endless lanes sunken in the clay. The Trenches. Frederic Manning. MCCG
Endless line of splendor, An. Foreign Missions in Battle Array. Vachel Lindsay. MaRV; OQP; QP-1; QS
Endless mime goes on, The; new faces come. The Play. James B. Kenyon. HBV
Endless part of disintegration, The. The Wisdom of Insecurity. Richard Eberhart. NePA
Endless Self. *Unknown, at. to* Lao-tzu, *tr. fr. Chinese by* Witter Bynner. *Fr.* Tao Teh King. OnPM
Endless snowfall, thick and damp, The. Christmas Eve. Olaf Bull. AnNoLy
Endless Song, The. Ruth McEnery Stuart. BOHV
Endless Yearning. Li Po, *tr. fr. Chinese by* Witter Bynner. ChLP
Endlessly, endlessly on the vast lake grow the water cresses. Rowing at Night on the West Lake. Su T'ung-po. WhP
Endlessly over the water. The Sweetness of Nature. *Unknown.* KiLC
Endow the fool with sun and moon. Fool and Wise. Coventry Patmore. PC
Endpiece. Olga Berggolts, *tr. fr. Russian by* Jack Lindsay. *Fr.* Parting. RuPo
Endpiece. *Unknown, tr. fr. Irish by* Frank O'Connor. KiLC
End-Piece for His Book, An. Robert Herrick. *See* To His Book's End.
Endrina and Trota-Conventos. Juan Ruiz, Archpriest of Hita, *tr. fr. Spanish by* Ida Farnell. TeCS
Endurance. Elizabeth Akers Allen. HBV; PoToHe, *abr.*
Endurance and Faithfulness ("Angustam amice"). Horace, *tr. fr. Latin by* Swift. Odes, III, 2. RoL
Endurance Test. Dacre Balsdon. FiBHP
Endure/ The farm? Lilacs for Remembrance. Irene Shirley Moran. PoMa
Endure friend-parting yet, old soldier. To a Friend Parting. Robert Penn Warren. BoFr
Endure, My Heart. Andrew Lang. BSV
Endure what life God gives and ask no longer span. Sophocles. *Fr.* Oedipus at Colonus. OBMV; PoD
Enduring, The. John Gould Fletcher. TBM; TSW; TSWC
Enduring Music, The. Harold Vinal. EtS
Enduring Word, The. Audrey Wurdemann. QS
Endymion [a Poetic Romance], *sels.* Keats.
Address to the Moon, *fr.* III. ERP
Adonis in Slumber, *fr.* II. ERP
(Cast Asleep.) BCEP
(Sleeping Youth, A.) SeCePo
"And, truly I would rather be struck dumb," *fr.* I. ViBoPo
Coming of Dian, The, *fr.* I. BPN
Conclusion; the Decision of the Gods, *fr.* IV. ERP
Cybele Drawn by Lions, *fr* II. RO
Diana, *fr.* I. BCEP
Encounter with Sleep, *fr.* IV. ERP
Endymion Chooses Mortal Love, *fr.* IV. ERP
Endymion's Vision, *fr.* I. ERP
Feast of Dian, The, *fr.* IV. BPN
Forest, The, *fr.* I. BCEP
He Saw Far in the Concave Green of the Sea, *fr.* III. EtS
Here Is Wine, *fr.* II. OBRV
Hymn to Pan, *fr.* I. AtBAP; BCEP; BPN; ChER; EPN; NBE; OBRV; PoEL-4
Indian Maid, The, *fr.* IV. ERP
Loss of the Mortal Maiden, *fr.* IV. ERP
Love and Friendship, *fr.* I. OBRV
"Muse of my native land! loftiest Muse!" IV. EnRP
"O Moon! the oldest shades 'mong oldest trees," *fr.* III. EnRP
"O sovereign power of love! O grief! O balm!" *fr.* II. EnRP; ViBoPo
(Induction.) ERP
(Invocation to the Power of Love.) BPN
Procession of Bacchus, *fr.* IV. TwCrTr
("Beneath my palm-trees, by the river side," *shorter sel.*) ViBoPo
Sacrifice to Pan, The, *fr.* I. BCEP
Sleep, *fr.* I BCEP
(Life Again.) SeCePo
Song of the Indian Maid, *fr.* IV. EV-4; OAEP; OBEV
(O Sorrow! *abr.*) CH
(Roundelay: "O Sorrow.") ATP (1935 ed.); BPN
(Song: "O Sorrow," *shorter sel.*) LoBV
"Thing of beauty is a joy forever, A," *fr.* I. ATP; BBV (1951 ed.), *br. sel.*; BEL; BLV; BoLiVe; BPN; CBE; CoBE; EM-2; EmBrPo; EnLi-2; EnLit; EnRP; EV-3; FiP; GrCo-2; HiLiEn, *br. sel.*; LiTB; LiTG; LPS-2; MaRV; MCCG; NeHB, *br. sel.*; OAEP; OBRV; OTPC; OuHeWo; PG; PreP; StVeCh, *br. sel.*; TCEP; TOP; TreF; TrGrPo; ViBoPo
(Beauty.) BCEP
(Credo.) ERP
(Endymion, Induction to.) TyEnPo
"To sorrow I bade good-morrow," *abr., fr.* IV. OBRV
Wherein Lies Happiness, *fr.* I. ERP
Endymion. Longfellow. AA; HBV; IAP; MOAP; TCAP
Endymion, *sel.* John Lyly.
Song by Fairies. OAEP; ReEn; TuPP

Endymion (*continued*)
(Fairy Revels.) EPP
(Fairy Song, A.) OBSC
Endymion. Edna St. Vincent Millay. *See* Oh, Sleep Forever in the Latmian Cave.
Endymion. Oscar Wilde. HBV; VLEP
Endymion. Humbert Wolfe. NP
Endymion and Diana. Philip Ayres. AEV
Endymion and Phoebe. Michael Drayton. *See* Endimion and Phoebe.
Endymion Chooses Mortal Love. Keats. *Fr.* Endymion, IV. ERP
Endymion's Convoy. Michael Drayton. *Fr.* Endimion and Phoebe. OBSC
Endymion's Vision. Keats. *Fr.* Endymion, I. ERP
Enemies, The. Elizabeth Jennings. MoPW
Enemies. Agnes Lee. NP
Enemies, The. Raymond Souster. BoCaPo (1948 ed.)
Enemies. R. D. N. Wilson. GTIV
Enemy, The. Baudelaire, *tr. fr. French.* AnFP, *tr. by* Vernon Watkins; OnPM, *tr. by* Arthur Symons
Enemy, The. John Waller. NeBP
Enemy forces are in wild flight, The. Defeat of the Rebels. Robert Graves. WaP
Enemy has forced an entry, The. Nikolai Tikhonov, *tr. fr. Russian by* C. M. Bowra. BoRS
Enemy I had, whose mien, An. My Enemy. Edwin L. Sabin. OQP; QP-2
Enemy of life, decayer of all kind, The. Epigram. Sir Thomas Wyatt. SiPS
Enemy who wears, The. Fourteenth Birthday. Phyllis McGinley. NePoAm-2
Energy of Light, The. John Hay. NePoAm-2
Enfant perdu. Heine, *tr. fr. German by* Richard Monckton Milnes. AWP; PoFr; WoL
(Lost Child.) OuHeWo
Enfidaville. Keith Douglas. HaMV
Engine. James S. Tippett. BoChLi; SUS
Engine Driver, The. "G. S. O." BoTP
Engine Driver's Story, The. William Wilkins. BeLS
Engine, engine, number nine. *Unknown.* RIS
Engine Failure. Timothy Corsellis. WaP
Engineers' Making Love, The. Robert J. Burdette. PTA-1
Engineer's Story, The. Eugene J. Hall. PTA-2
Engineer's Story, The. *Unknown.* BeLS
Engineer's Yell (University of California). *Unknown.* WhC
England. Laurence Binyon. PoeT
England. Elizabeth Barrett Browning. *Fr.* Aurora Leigh, I. VA
(Sweetness of England, The, *longer sel.*) EV-4
England. Wilfred Campbell. CPG
England. Grace Ellery Channing. AA
England. Samuel Taylor Coleridge. *Fr.* Fears in Solitude. ERP
England. William Cowper. *Fr.* The Task, II. BHV; CoEV; EV-3; FiP; LPS-2, *abr.*; OBEC; TOP
("England, with all thy faults, I love thee still.") BrBE
(Love of England.) LoBV
England. Richard Edwin Day. AA
England. W. E. Henley. *See* England, My England.
England. Kipling. *Fr.* The Return. OtMeF
England. Gerald Massey. HBV
England. George Edgar Montgomery. AA
England. Marianne Moore. CrMA; LiTA; MAP; MoAB; MoAmPo
England. Cardinal Newman. ACP; CAW; GoBC; JKCP; PoVP; VA
England ("This England never did"). Shakespeare. *Fr.* King John. *See* This England ("This England never did").
England ("This royal throne of kings"). Shakespeare. *Fr.* King Richard II. *See* This England ("This royal throne of kings").
England ("England, queen of the waves"). Swinburne. LH
England. Tennyson. Maud, Pt. III, v. BHV
England. *Unknown.* SeCL
England; an Ode ("Sea and strand"). Swinburne. ViPo
England and America, *sel.* Arthur Cleveland Coxe.
America. MC; PAH
England and America. James Kenneth Stephen. InMe
England and America in 1782. Tennyson. BPN; EPN; MC; OTPC (1946 ed.); PaA; PAH; PoFr; PoVP; VLEP
England and Switzerland, 1802. Wordsworth. *See* Thought of a Briton on the Subjugation of Switzerland.
England, Arise! Edward Carpenter. PoFr
England at Peace; a Vision. Shakespeare. *See* Cranmer's Prophecy of Queen Elizabeth.
England at War. Shakespeare. *See* King Henry before the Field of Saint Crispian.
England at War; Harfleur, England and St. George. Shakespeare. *See* Once More unto the Breach . . .
England! awake! awake! awake! Blake. *Fr.* Jerusalem, *ch.* 4. CBE; EnRP; OBRV
England, Awake Now. *Unknown.* PoFr
England, Be Glad. *Unknown.* ElSeCe; TuPP
England, 1802 ("Great men have been among us . . ."). Wordsworth. *See* Great Men Have Been among Us.
England, 1802 ("It is not to be thought of that the flood"). Wordsworth. *See* It Is Not to Be Thought Of.
England, 1802 ("Milton! thou should'st be living at this hour"). Wordsworth. *See* London, 1802.
England, 1802 ("O Friend! I know not which way I must look"). Wordsworth. *See* Written in London, September, 1802.
England, 1802 ("When I have borne in memory what has tamed"). Wordsworth. *See* When I Have Borne in Memory.
England, England, England,/ Girdled by ocean and skies. England. Wilfred Campbell. CPG
England, I stand on thy imperial ground. At Gibraltar. George Edward Woodberry. AA; AnAmPo; BAP; GN; HBV; LA; LBMV; LEAP
England in 1819. Shelley. CoEV; EM-2; EmBrPo; EnLi-2 (1949 ed.); EnRP; EPN; OBRV; PeBoSo; TrGrPo
(Sonnet: England in 1819.) BPN; EnL; FiP; OAEP; PoFS; PreP; SeCePo; SeCeV
England—June, 1940. Lord Gorell. NeTW
England, look up! Thy soil is stained with blood. The Martyrdom of Father Campion. Henry Walpole. ACP; GoBC
England may mourn, as many kingdoms may. Sorrowful Verses Made on the Death of Our Most Sovereign Lady Queen Elizabeth My Gracious Mistress. Thomas Churchyard. ReIE
England, My England. W. E. Henley. BMEP; EnLi-2 (1949 ed.); EV-5; HBV; MBP; MoBrPo; OBEV; OBVV; OTPC (1923 ed.); PoVP; TreF; YT
(England.) LBBV
(Pro Rege Nostro, *abr.*) VOD (1931 ed.)
(Rhymes and Rhythms, XXV.) BPN
England My Mother. Sir William Watson. PoVP
England! once Europs envye now her scorne. *Unknown.* SeCSL
England Reclaimed, *sel.* Sir Osbert Sitwell.
"Sound out, proud trumpets." ViBoPo
England! the time is come when thou shouldst wean. Sonnets. Wordsworth. ViBoPo
England, to whom we owe what we be and have. John Donne. *Fr.* The Storm. SG
England, unknown as yet, unpeopled lay. Defoe. *Fr.* The True-born Englishman, I. NBE
England, Unprepared for War. Mark Akenside. *Fr.* An Ode to the Country Gentlemen of England. OBEC
England, we love thee better than we know. Gibraltar. Richard Chenevix Trench. ES; OBRV; OBVV
England, with all thy faults, I love thee still. England [*or* Love of England]. William Cowper. *Fr.* The Task, II. BHV; BrBE; CoEV; EV-3; FiP; LoBV; LPS-2; OBEC; TOP
England with its baby rivers and little towns, each with its abbey or its cathedral. England. Marianne Moore. CrMA; LiTA; MoAB; MoAmPo
England's Darling; or, Great Britain's Joy and Hope on That Noble Prince James, Duke of Monmouth. *Unknown.* CoMu
England's Dead. Felicia Dorothea Hemans. HBV
England's Heroical Epistles, *sels.* Michael Drayton.
Henry Howard, Earl of Surrey, to the Lady Geraldine. ReEn; ReIE; TuPP
(Earl of Surrey to Geraldine, The.) OBSC
King Henry to Rosamond. OBSC
"Many there be excelling in this kind" (*also in* Idea). NBE; SiCE; TuPP
England's Prayer. William Blundell of Crosby. GoBC
England's Sovereigns in Verse. *Unknown.* BLPA
England's Standard. Macaulay. *Fr.* The Armada. OtMeF
England's sun was slowly setting. Curfew Must Not Ring Tonight. Rosa Hartwick Thorpe. BLPA; HBV; LPS-1; PTA-1; TreF; WBLP
England's Triumph; or, The Subjects' Joy. *Unknown.* CoMu
English, The. J. H. Goring. *See* Home.
English Ballad, An, on the Taking of Namur by the King of Great Britain, 1695. Matthew Prior. PoEL-3
English Bards and Scotch Reviewers, *sels.* Byron.
"Behold! in various throngs the scribbling crew." EnRP
"Illustrious Holland! hard would be his lot." OBRV
"Man must serve his time to every trade, A." EPP
"Next comes the dull disciple of thy school." OBRV
"Still must I hear?—shall hoarse Fitzgerald bawl." AtBAP; BCEP
"There be who say, in these enlighten'd days." PtP
"When vice triumphant holds her sov'reign sway." TCEP
English Captains, The. Charles Fitzgeffrey. *Fr.* Sir Francis Drake. SG
English Earth. Laurence Binyon. NeTW
English Easter, 7 A.M. Evelyn Underhill. MM
English Epitaph on Queen Elizabeth, Wife of Henry VII. *Unknown.* *See* Epitaph on Queen Elizabeth . . .

English Flag, The. Kipling. PECK
  (Flag of England, The.) LH
English Fog, The. John Dyer. *Fr.* The Fleece. TrGrPo
English Garden, The, *sels.* William Mason.
  "Happy art thou if thou can'st call thine own," *fr.* I.
  EnSW
  Landscape, *fr.* I. OBEC
  Making a Garden, *fr.* I. BeR
English Gentlewoman, The, *sel.* Richard Brathwaite.
  My Mistress. SeCL
English Girl, An. F. Wyville Home. VA
English Girl. *Unknown, tr. fr. Chinese by* Edward Powys
  Mathers. OBMV
English have a scornful insular way, The. Paris. Elizabeth
  Barrett Browning. *Fr.* Aurora Leigh, VI. ViP
English Hills. John Freeman. MM
English Horn. Laurence McKinney. WhC
English in Ireland, The. Swift. *Fr.* Verses Occasioned by
  the Sudden Drying Up of St. Patrick's Well. BeR
English in 1680, The. Dryden. *Fr.* Absalom and Achitophel,
  Pt. 1. NBE
English Irregular, '99–'02. Kipling. *See* Chant Pagan.
English lad, who, reading in a book, An. Keats. Lizette
  Woodworth Reese. AA; BAP
English Language, The, *abr.* William Wetmore Story. GN
English Liberal. Geoffrey Taylor. LiTM; SiTL
English Monsieur, The, *sel.* James Howard.
  Ladies, Farewell! SeCL
English Mother, An. Robert Underwood Johnson. HBV;
  MOAH
English Padlock, An. Matthew Prior. CEP; EiPP; FaBoEn;
  OBEC
English Poetry. Samuel Daniel. *Fr.* Musophilus; or, De-
  fence of All Learning. OBSC
  (Poetry of England, The.) CoBE
  (Treasure of Our Tongue, The, *abr.*) EV-1
English Race, The. Defoe. *Fr.* The True-born Englishman.
  OBEC
English Rider, The. "Robin Hyde." AnNZ
English Robin, The. Harrison Weir. LPS-2
English Schoolboy, The. John Heywood. *Fr.* The Play of
  the Weather. ACP
English Shell, An. A. C. Benson. VA
English Sparrow, The. Mary Isabella Forsyth. SN
English Sparrow, pert and free, An. A Card of Invitation
  to Mr. Gibbon, at Brighthelmstone. William Hayley.
  OBEC
English Thornton. Edgar Lee Masters. *Fr.* Spoon River
  Anthology. OxBA
English Weather. John Dyer. *Fr.* The Fleece, I. CoEV;
  OBEC
English Wood, An. Robert Graves. YT
Englishman, The. G. K. Chesterton. PtOT
Englishman, The. Walter de la Mare. PtOT
Englishman in Italy, The. Robert Browning. ExPo; PoEL-5;
  SeCePo; ViPo; ViPP; VLEP
Englishmen's Victory over the Spaniards, The. *Unknown.*
  See Famous Fight at Malago, The.
Englyn. Lynette Roberts. MoWP
Englyn. *Unknown, tr. fr. Welsh by* Gwyn Williams. *Fr.*
  The Black Book of Carmarthen. PrWP
Englynion. *Unknown.* PrWP
Englynion to His Love. David Jones. PrWP
Engraved on the Collar of a Dog, Which I Gave to His Royal
  Highness. Pope. *See* Epigram: "I am his Highness'
  dog at Kew."
Engraved on the Collar of His Highness' Dog. Pope. *See*
  Epigram: "I am his Highness' dog at Kew."
Engrossed, the abandoned crickets sing. At the Grave of
  Cecil Rhodes. Peter Jackson. BoSA
Enid's Song. Tennyson. *See* Turn, Fortune, Turn Thy
  Wheel.
Enigma. Joseph Auslander. NP
Enigma. Catherine M. Fanshawe. *See* Riddle, A: " 'Twas
  whispered in Heaven . . ."
Enigma. Jessie Redmond Fauset. PoNe
Enigma. Hugh McCrae. BoAV; MoAuPo
Enigma. Hugh Wilgus Ramsaur. MuM
Enigma. R. S. Thomas. ChMP
Enigma in Altman's. Phyllis McGinley. PoMa; WhC
Enigma of Sleep, An. James I, King of England. PeBoSo
Enigma on the Letter H. Catherine Fanshawe. *See* Riddle,
  A: " 'Twas whispered in Heaven . . ."
Enigma Sartorial. *Unknown.* DDA
Enitharmon's Song. Blake. *Fr.* Vala. ChTr
Enixa Est Puerpera. *Unknown.* AnEC
Enjoy the Hour. Horace, *par. fr. Latin by* Dryden. Odes,
  III, 29. BeR
Enjoy thy April Now. Samuel Daniel. *Fr.* A Description of
  Beauty. EiL
Enjoy today; this hour is best. Well-packed Wisdom. Ben-
  jamin Franklin. *Fr.* Poor Richard's Almanac. StaSt
Enjoy your goods as if your death were near. The Golden
  Mean. Lucian. GrPo; OnPM

Enjoyment. Theognis, *tr. fr. Greek by* John Hookham Frere.
  AWP
Enlargement. Helena Coleman. CPG
Enlightenment. Josephine Miles. FiMAP
Enlisted. "Eliza Calvert Hall." MDAH
Enlisted Today. *Unknown.* BlG
Enlistments, The. Stephen Vincent Benét. *Fr.* John Brown's
  Body. ATP
Ennerdale. Frederick William Faber. EnSW
Enobarbus' Description of Cleopatra. Shakespeare. *See* Cleo-
  patra.
Enoch, *sels.* Bible, Pseudepigrapha. TrJP
  Seven Metal Mountains, The, LII: 6–9.
  Wisdom's Plight, XLII: 1–3.
Enoch. Jones Very. APW
Enoch Arden. Tennyson. BeLS; VLEP
  Cast Your Cares on God, *br. sel.* MaRV
Enormous cloud-mountains that form over Point Lobos and into
  the sunset. Clouds of Evening. Robinson Jeffers. MAP;
  MoAB; MoAmPo
Enough. Charles G. Blanden. OQP; QP-1
Enough. Bunyan. *See* Shepherd Boy's Song, The.
Enough./ On you, who sit like one most miserable. Thou
  Shalt Not Die. Euripides. *Fr.* Heracles. OxBG
Enough; and leave the rest to fame! An Epitaph [*or* An
  Epitaph upon——]. Andrew Marvell. BCEP; LO;
  LoBV; OBEV; SeCL
Enough! enough! enough!/ Somehow I have been stunn'd.
  Song of Myself, XXXVIII. Walt Whitman. CoV
"Enough! for beauty is not needed." Temptation. Vladislav
  Khodasevich. BoR
"Enough, I am by promise tied." Fitz-James and Roderick
  Dhu. Sir Walter Scott. *Fr.* The Lady of the Lake, V.
  EPP; LPS-2
Enough is as good as a feast. Rhymes to Remember. *Un-
  known.* StaSt
Enough of Humble Arguments. Wordsworth. *Fr.* The Prel-
  ude. AtBAP
Enough of love; let's leave for something new. Song of the
  Vineyard Knife. Clément Marot. FoS
Enough of those who study the oblique. A Good Resolution.
  Roy Campbell. JKCP (1955 ed.)
Enough of thought, philosopher! The Philosopher. Emily
  Brontë. EmBrPo; VLEP
Enough seen. The vision has been met in all guises. De-
  parture. Arthur Rimbaud. AnFP
Enough that you must turn your days to discs. Quatrains for
  a Bank Cashier. Samuel A. De Witt. PG (1955 ed.)
Enough! we're tired, my heart and I. My Heart and I.
  Elizabeth Barrett Browning. HBV; VA
Enough! Why should a man bemoan. Per Iter Tenebricosum.
  Oliver St. John Gogarty. AnIL; OBMV; OxBI
Enough: you have the dream, the flame. Due North. Ben-
  jamin R. C. Low. EtS; HBMV
Enquiring Soul, The. Thomas Traherne. MaRV
Enquiry, The. John Dyer. OBEC
Ensamples of Our Saviour. Robert Southwell. PoEL-2
Ensanguined man. Plea for the Animals. James Thomson.
  Fr. The Seasons: Spring. LPS-3
Ensign Bearer, The. *Unknown.* PTA-2
Enslaved, *sel.* John Masefield.
  "Khalif's fury raged, The." ReTS
Enter America at Concord's bridge. Emerson; Last Days at
  Concord. Horace Gregory. ChMo
Enter and learn the story of the rulers. Inscriptions at the
  City of Brass. *Unknown. Fr.* The Thousand and One
  Nights. AWP; PoFr; WaaP
Enter General Brock and Lefroy. Charles Mair. *Fr.* Tecum-
  seh, IV, vi. CPG
Enter Patient. W. E. Henley. In Hospital, I. BPN; PoVP
Enter Saint Nicholas. *Unknown.* CAG
Enter the dream-house, brothers and sisters, leaving. News-
  reel. C. Day Lewis. MoAB; MoBrPo (1950 ed.);
  NeMA
Enter these enchanted woods. The Woods of Westermain.
  George Meredith. BEL; BMEP; EmBrPo; ShBV-3;
  ViPo; ViPP; WaKn
Enter with us, Lord, we pray. Dedication of a Home. Bertha
  Gerneaux Woods. PraP
Entered in the Minutes. Louis MacNeice. LiTB
Entering by His Door. Richard Baxter. *See* Lord, It Be-
  longs Not to My Care.
Entering casually the precincts of the cathedral. Alcestis in
  Ely. Nicholas Moore. NeBP
Entering the hall, she meets the new wife. The Rejected
  Wife. Yüan Ti. TrCh
Enterprise and *Boxer. Unknown.* PAH
Entertainment to James, *sel.* Thomas Dekker.
  Troynovant. ChTr; OBSC
Enthroned above the world although he sit. Immanence.
  Richard Hovey. OQP; QP-1; WGRP
Enthusiasm. James Clarence Mangan. IrPN
Enthusiast, The. Herman Melville. APW
Enthusiast, The; an Ode. William Whitehead. OBEC

Enthusiast, The; or, The Lover of Nature. Joseph Warton. CEP; EiPP; EnRP; Po; PoEL-3
Sels.
Charms of Nature, The. OBEC; SeCePo
"Ye green-rob'd Dryads, oft' at dusky eve." FaBoEn
Enticed by a beauty on a railway poster. Gay Summertime. Jun Yamamura. PoLJ
Entirely. Louis MacNeice. ChMo; LiTB; MoPW
Entrain airport: New York, Chicago, west. To My Generation (1919–1933) [*or* Valediction to My Contemporaries]. Horace Gregory. ChMo; MAP; MoAmPo
Entrance and exit wounds are silvered clean. Recalling War. Robert Graves. CoBMV; LiTM (rev. ed.); WaP
Entrance into Heaven. Sara Henderson Hay. ChIP
Entrance of Hyperion. Keats. *Fr.* Hyperion. ReTS
Entrance to Hell, The. Virgil, *tr. fr. Latin into Middle English by* Gawin Douglas. *Fr.* The Aeneid, VI. GoTS
Entrance to Tartarus, The. Virgil, *tr. fr. Latin into Middle English by* Gawin Douglas. *Fr.* The Aeneid, VI. BSV
Entranced, I saw a vision in the cloud. An Ode for the Fourth of July, 1876. James Russell Lowell. CoBA
Entrapped inside a submarine. H. C. Canfield. *Fr.* Elegy on the Loss of U.S. Submarine S4. FiBHP
Entre Paris et Saint-Denis. *Unknown, tr. fr. French-Canadian folk song by* William McLennan. BoCaPo (1948 ed.)
Entreat me not to leave thee. Ruth to Naomi. Ruth, Bible, *O.T.* TrGrPo
Entreaty. Nikolaus Lenau, *tr. fr. German by* Dwight Durling. AnGP
Entreaty to the Cloud. Amado Nervo, *tr. fr. Spanish by* Samuel Beckett. AnMP
Entropy. Roy G. Pearce. PoP
Entropy. Theodore Spencer. ImOP
Entry. Josephine Miles. AnAmPo
Entry April 28. Walter Benton. LoPS
Entry November 12. Walter Benton. LoPS
Entry to the Desert. James Rorty. MOAP; TBM
Enviable Isles, The. Herman Melville. AA; AnAmPo; APW; FaBoBe; LA; LEAP
Envied by us all. Maple Leaves. Shiko. OnPM
Envious neighbour is easy to find, An. The Description of an Envious and Naughty Neighbour. Thomas Tusser. SiCE
Envious wits, what hath been mine offence. Astrophel and Stella, CIV. Sir Philip Sidney. SiPS; TuPP
Environs. Larry Eigner. NeAP
Envoi: "Belovèd, till the day break." Josephine Preston Peabody. SBMV
Envoi: "Earth puts her colours by." P. H. B. Lyon. BoTP; PtOT
Envoi: "Fly, white butterflies, out to sea." Swinburne. *See* White Butterflies.
Envoi: "Go, dumb-born book." Ezra Pound. *See* Envoi (1919).
Envoi: "God, thou great symmetry." Anna Wickham. BLV; MBP; MoBrPo; NeMA; TrGrPo (1942 ed.)
Envoi: "How shall I say good-bye to you." Edward de Stein. BoFr
Envoi: "I strove with none, for none was worth my strife." Walter Savage Landor. *See* On His Seventy-fifth Birthday.
Envoi: "I warmed both hands before the fire of Life." D. B. Wyndham Lewis. FiBHP
Envoi: "O seek me not within a tomb." John G. Neihardt. HBV; NP; WGRP
(Envoy.) OQP; QP-1
(L'Envoi: "Seek not for me . . .") MaRV
Envoi: "O ye, who thoughtlessly repose." Nizami, *tr. fr. Persian by* James Atkinson. *Fr.* Laili and Majnún. PeP
Envoi: "So go forth to the world." Arthur Hugh Clough. *Fr.* Amours de Voyage. BPN
Envoi: "Take of me what is not my own." Kathleen Raine. NeBP
Envoi (1919). Ezra Pound. *Fr.* Hugh Selwyn Mauberley. APA; ChMo; CMP; CoAnAm; CoV; LiTA; LiTM (rev. ed.); MoP; MoPo; OnAP; TBM; UnPo (3d ed.)
(Envoi: "Go, dumb-born book.") GTBS-W; MAP; MoAB; MoAmPo; NePA; OxBA
Envoy: "All the songs here sung." Martin Armstrong. QS
Envoy: "Friends, sursum corda, soon or slow." Andrew Lang. SDH
Envoy, The: "Go litel book, go litel myn tregedie." Chaucer. *Fr.* Troilus and Criseyde, V. FiP
(From the Epilogue to "Troilus and Criseyde.") NBE
("Go, litel book . . .") MyFE; ViBoPo
Envoy: "Go, little book, and wish to all." Robert Louis Stevenson. *See* Go, Little Book.
Envoy: "Go, songs, for ended is our brief, sweet play." Francis Thompson. CoBE; EmBrPo; HBV; MBP; MoBrPo; POT; PoTo; POTT; PoVP; PreP; VLEP
Envoy: "God who made denial, The." Gerald Gould. QS
Envoy: "Have little care that life is brief." Bliss Carman. HBV; PC; VA
(On the Tomb of Bliss Carman.) MaRV
Envoy: "If homely virtues draw from me a tune." James Weldon Johnson. TrPWD
Envoy: "Legend of Felix is ended, the toiling of Felix is done, The." Henry van Dyke. *Fr.* The Toiling of Felix. BLPA
Envoy: "O seek me not within a tomb." John G. Neihardt. *See* Envoi: "O seek me not . . ."
Envoy: "On your altars I have spent my incense." Manuel José Othón, *tr. fr. Spanish by* Samuel Beckett. AnMP
Envoy: "So, at the last, I think that we must follow." Du Bose Heyward. NV
Envoy: "Sweet World, if you will hear me now." Sarah Morgan Bryan Piatt. AA
Envoy: "There's a whisper down the field where the year has shot her yield." Kipling. *See* Long Trail, The.
Envoy: "They are not long, the weeping and the laughter." Ernest Dowson. *See* Vitae Summa Brevis Spem Nos Vetat Incohare Longam.
Envoy: "When Earth's last picture is painted and the tubes are twisted and dried." Kipling. *See* L'Envoi: "When earth's last picture . . ."
Envoy: "When you and I have played the little hour." Sir Gilbert Parker. *See* Reunited.
Envoy: "Whose furthest footstep never strayed." Richard Hovey. *Fr.* More Songs from Vagabondia. AA; HBV; LEAP; OBAV
Envoy to an American Lady, An. Richard Monckton Milnes. *See* Our Mother Tongue.
Envoys, The. Clark Ashton Smith. DaM
Envy. Edgar Daniel Kramer. PoMa
Envy. Charles *and* Mary Lamb. OTPC (1923 ed.)
Envy. Charles Jeremiah Wells. BCEP
Envy-free. Anacreon, *tr. fr. Greek by* Judson France Davidson. GrR
Envy go weep; my muse and I. To Envy. Sir John Davies. *Fr.* Hymns of Astraea. SiCE
Envy Goes Groping. R. D. Fitzgerald. MoAuPo
Envy is pale, and pale is sad despair. Roses and Lilies. William Diaper. *Fr.* Nereides; or, Sea-Eclogues. BeR
Envy must own, I live among the great. The Mob. Pope. *Fr.* The First Satire of the Second Book of Horace Imitated. BeR
Envy the mad killer who lies in the ditch and grieves. Crime. Robert Penn Warren. AmP
Envy, why carpest thou my time is spent so ill. Ovid, *tr. by* Christopher Marlowe. *Fr.* Elegies. ReIE
Envy, why twit'st thou me my time's spent ill. Ovid, *tr. by* Ben Jonson. *Fr.* Elegies. ReIE
Envying a Little Bird. Sister Gregoria Francisca, *tr. fr. Spanish by* Thomas Walsh. CAW
Enzio's Kingdom, *sel.* William Alexander Percy.
Epilogue: "This wind upon my mouth, these stars I see." UnW
Eoiae, *sels.* Hesiod, *tr. fr. Greek by* Sir William Marris.
Light-footed Iphiclus. OxBG
Visitation, A. OxBG
Eolian Harp, The. Samuel Taylor Coleridge. EmBrPo; EnRP; ERP; RO
Eos. Richard Henry Horne. *Fr.* Orion. VA
Eph Kate was a cow-punchin' boy. Salty Dogs. *Unknown.* CoSo
Ephemera, The. *Unknown, tr. fr. Chinese by* E. D. Edwards. ChLP
Ephemerae for Bruska. Keidrych Rhys. MoWP
Ephesians, *sel.* Bible, *N.T.*
Forgiveness, IV: 26, 31–32. BoFr
Ephraim Cross drives up the trail. The Farm, 1750. Archibald MacLeish. ChMo; CMP
Epic. Patrick Kavanagh. OxBI
Epic. Virginia Moore. TSWC
Epic, The (Introduction to "Morte d'Arthur"). Tennyson. EmBrPo; PoVP; ViPP; VLEP
Epic characters, epic characters, executive or rounded. The Pale Conquerors. "Pablo de Rokha." TwSpPo
"Epic epigram, An," I heard you say. Martial, *tr. fr. Latin by* J. V. Cunningham. Epigrams, VI, 65. LaP
Epicede. Donald Evans. NP
Epicedium. J. Corson Miller. DD; HBMV; PAH
Epicedium. Horace L. Traubel. AA
Epicharis. Arthur Palmer. TIP
Epicoene; or, The Silent Woman, *sel.* Ben Jonson.
Simplex Munditiis, *fr.* I, i, *tr. fr. the Latin of* Jean Bonnefons. AWP; BCEP; CBOV; CoBE; EnLi-1; EnLit; EPS; GoBC; HBV; HoPM; InPo; JAWP; LEAP; OBEV; TOP; WBP
(Clerimont's Song.) BoLiVe; CaAE; LoBV; PreP; SeCV-1; TrGrPo
(Freedom in Dress.) LPS-2
(Simplicity and Sweet Neglect.) EV-2
(Song: "Still to be neat, still to be dressed.") AnEnPo; CoEV; ElSeCe; LiTL; NeHB; OBS; ViBoPo
(Still to Be Neat [Still to Be Dressed].) ALV; EG; EIL; EM-1; EnL; GTBS-W; LO; MaPo; OAEP;

OuHeWo; PoE; PoFS; ReaPo; ReEn; SeCePo; SiCE; TuPP; TyEnPo; WHA
(Sweet Neglect.) BLV
Epicure, The ("Fill the bowl with rosy wine"). Abraham Cowley, *after the Greek of* Anacreon. CaAE; EPS; HBV; OBS
(Today Is Ours.) TrGrPo
Epicure, The ("Underneath this myrtle shade"). Abraham Cowley, *after the Greek of* Anacreon. AWP; EV-2; OBEV; PG (1945 ed.); PoP; SiTL
("Underneath this myrtle shade." EG
Epicure. Ruth Lambert Jones. DDA
Epicure, dining at Crewe, An. Limerick. *Unknown.* CenHV; GoTP; LiBL; LiTG; LiTM (rev. ed.); SiTL; WhC
Epicure, The, Sung by One in the Habit of a Town Gallant. Thomas Jordan. *See* Careless Gallant, The.
Epicurean, The. Sir Francis Hastings Doyle. EPN; OBVV
Epicurean. William James Linton. VA
Epicurean Ode, An. John Hall. MeLP; MePo; SeEP
("Since that this thing we call the world.") EG
Epicurean Reminiscences of a Sentimentalist. Thomas Hood. ERP
Epicurean's Epitaph, An. Aubrey Thomas De Vere. VA
Epigram ("What is an epigram? A dwarfish whole"). Samuel Taylor Coleridge. HBV; InP
Epigram: "After such years of dissension and strife." Thomas Hood. HBV
(Dust to Dust.) GoTP
(Natural Tears.) FiBHP
Epigram V: "Against the guide of Truth." *Unknown, tr. fr. Hebrew. Fr.* Duel with Verses over a Great Man. TrJP
Epigram: "Alas, how soon the hours are over." Walter Savage Landor. *See* Plays.
Epigram: "Amid all triads let it be confest." Richard Garnett. OBVV
Epigram: "And what is love? Misunderstanding, pain." J. V. Cunningham. NePoAm
Epigram: Answer to the Parson, An. Blake. *See* Answer to the Parson, An.
Epigram: "Arms and the man I sing, and sing for joy." J. V. Cunningham. NePoAm
Epigram: "As in smooth oil the razor best is whet." *Unknown.* HBV
Epigram: "Avaro sick is seen to shiver." John Swanwick Drennan. IrPN
Epigram: "Beauty, a silver dew that falls in May." *Unknown.* OBSC
Epigram: "Because I am idolatrous and have besought." Ernest Dowson. ACP; BrBE
Epigram: "Bring hemlock, black as Cretan cheese." Robert Hillyer. WhC
Epigram: "Captains and conquerors leave a little dust." Sir William Watson. BPP
Epigram: Character, A. Blake. SiTL
(Character, A.) OxBoLi
Epigram: "Children romp within the graveyard's pale, The." Sir William Watson.
(Four Epigrams.) MBP; MoBrPo (1942 ed.)
Epigram: "'Come, come,' said Tom's father, 'at your time of life.'" Thomas Moore. *See* On Taking a Wife.
Epigram: "Cries Sue to Will, in matrimonial strife." *Unknown.* ALV
Epigram: "Cries Sylvia to a reverend Dean." Robert Dodsley. ALV
Epigram: "Damis, an author cold and weak." *Unknown.* HBV
Epigram: Diversity of Doctors. *Unknown.* ALV
Epigram: "'Do you not wish to renounce the Devil?'" Armand Lanusse, *tr. fr. French by* Langston Hughes. PoNe
Epigram: "Eagle! why soarest thou above that tomb?" *Unknown. See* Spirit of Plato.
Epigram: "Elders at their services begin, The." J. V. Cunningham. NePoAm
(Two Epigrams, I.) SiTL
Epigram: "Enemy of life, decayer of all kind, The." Sir Thomas Wyatt. SiPS
Epigram: Engraved on the Collar of a Dog, Which I Gave to His Royal Highness. *See* Epigram: "I am his Highness' dog at Kew."
Epigram: "Face that should content me wonders well, A." Sir Thomas Wyatt. *See* Description of Such a One as He Would Love.
Epigram: "Far happier are the dead, methinks, than they." *Unknown, tr. fr. Greek by* William Cowper. EnLi-1
(Expectation of Death.) OxBG
Epigram: Fatum Supremum. *Unknown.* OBS
(Fatum Supremum.) SeCL
Epigram: "Fool and knave with different views, A." Samuel Bishop. *See* Maiden's Choice, The.
Epigram: "For love is like a plant that clings." John Swanwick Drennan. IrPN
Epigram III: "Forgive us, son of Amram, be not wroth." *Unknown, tr. fr. Hebrew. Fr.* Duel with Verses over a Great Man. TrJP
Epigram: "Frank carves very ill, yet will palm all the meats." Matthew Prior. CEP
Epigram: "Friend, on this scaffold Thomas More lies dead." J. V. Cunningham. NePoAm
Epigram: "Fruit of all the service that I serve, The." Sir Thomas Wyatt. SiPS
Epigram: "God bless the King—I mean the faith's defender!" John Byrom. *See* Jacobite Toast, A.
Epigram: "Golden casket I designed, A." John Swanwick Drennan. IrPN
Epigram: "Grateful heart for all things blesses, The." Walter Savage Landor. ALV
Epigram: "Hail, ye indomitable heroes, hail!" Walter Savage Landor. *See* Crimean Heroes, The.
Epigram: "He is not drunk who, from the floor." Eugene Field. ALV
Epigram: "He who in his pocket hath no money." *Unknown.* HBV
Epigram: "Here at this solitary spring." "Lambros Porphyras," *tr. fr. Modern Greek by* Rae Dalven. MoGP
Epigram: "Here lie I, Martin Elginbrodde." *Unknown. See* Epitaph: "Here lie I . . ."
Epigram: "Here lies my wife. Eternal peace." J. V. Cunningham. NePoAm
Epigram: "Here lies my wife: here let her lie!" Dryden. *See* Epitaph Intended for His Wife.
Epigram: "Hoarse Maevius reads his hobbling verse." Samuel Taylor Coleridge. LPS-3
Epigram: "How odd/ Of God." W. N. Ewer. *See* Chosen People, The.
Epigram: "I am his Highness' dog at Kew." Pope. ALV; HBV; ShBV-4; TreFS
(Dogs.) GoTP
(Engraved on the Collar of a Dog, Which I Gave to His Royal Highness.) ChTr; LiTB; LiTG; OxBoLi; SeCeV; SiTL
(Engraved on the Collar of His Highness' Dog.) PIAE; WhC
(Epigram: Engraved on the Collar of a Dog, Which I Gave to His Royal Highness.) TOP
("I am his Highness' dog at Kew.") InP
(Inscribed on the Collar of a Dog.) PCH
(On the Collar of a Dog [Presented by Mr. Pope to the Prince of Wales].) ExPo; OnPM
Epigram: "I fish for minnows in the lake." Su T'ung-po, *tr. fr. Chinese by* Kenneth Rexroth. OnPC
Epigram: "I had gone broke, and got set to come back." J. V. Cunningham. NePoAm
Epigram: "'I hardly ever ope my lips,' one cries." Richard Garnett. HBV; OtMeF
(Silence and Speech.) ALV
Epigram: "I have lost my mistress, horse and wife." *Unknown.* ALV
Epigram: "I held her hand, the pledge of bliss." Walter Savage Landor. *See* I Held Her Hand.
Epigram: "I loved thee beautiful and kind." Robert, Earl Nugent. ALV
(I Loved Thee.) FiBHP
Epigram: "I owe, says Metius, much to Colon's care." Leonard Welsted. ALV
Epigram: "I wonder not that youth remains." Walter Savage Landor. *See* I Wonder Not That Youth Remains.
Epigram: "'I would,' says Fox, 'a tax devise.'" Sheridan. HBV
Epigram: "I'd like to be a bee." Tasso, *tr. fr. Italian by* L. R. Lind. LyPI
Epigram: "If a man who turnips cries." Samuel Johnson. *See* If the Man Who Turnips Cries.
Epigram: "If men be judged wise by their beards and their girth." Joseph Solomon del Medigo, *tr. fr. Hebrew.* TrJP
Epigram: "In Köln [*or* Köhln], a town of monks and bones." Samuel Taylor Coleridge. *See* Cologne.
Epigram: "Joe hates a sycophant. It shows." P. Dodd. ALV
(On Joe.) SiTL
Epigram: "Joy is the blossom, sorrow is the fruit." Walter Savage Landor. HBV
Epigram: "Justice walking o'er the frozen Thames, A." *Unknown.* ALV
Epigram: "King to Oxford sent a troop of horse, The." William Browne. ALV
Epigram: "Life is a jest, and all things show it." John Gay. *See* My Own Epitaph.
Epigram: "Loud brayed an ass. Quoth Kate, 'My dear.'" *Unknown.* ALV
Epigram: "Love, like a bird, hath perch'd upon a spray." Sir William Watson. ALV
(Four Epigrams.) MBP; MoBrPo (1942 ed.)
(Love.) TrGrPo
Epigram: "Love signed the contract blithe and leal." John Swanwick Drennan. IrPN

Epigram: "Lux my fair falcon, and your fellows all." Sir Thomas Wyatt. *See* Of Such as Had Forsaken Him.
Epigram: "Man who goes for Christian resignation, The." J. V. Cunningham. NePoAm
Epigram: "*Mayflower* once filled this shore, The." Robert Haven Schauffler. ADAH
Epigram: "Metaphysic Sphynx that preys on us, The." John Swanwick Drennan. IrPN
Epigram: "Momentous to himself as I to me." Sir William Watson. AnEnPo; BMEP; LEAP
Epigram: "No more of your titled acquaintances boast." Burns. ALV
Epigram: "No, my own love of other years." Walter Savage Landor. *See* In After Time.
Epigram: "No truer word, save God's, was ever spoken." Walter Savage Landor. HBV
(No Truer Word.) TreF
Epigram: "Nobles and heralds, by your leave." Matthew Prior. *See* Epitaph on Himself.
Epigram: "Of the divine and human thought." John Swanwick Drennan. IrPN
Epigram: "On parent knees, a naked new-born child." Sir William Jones. *See* Baby, The.
Epigram: On Sir Francis Drake. *Unknown.* CenL; OBS
(On Francis Drake.) TriL
Epigram: "Paul's midnight voice prevail'd; his music's thunder." Francis Quarles. Emblems, V, 10. LoBV
Epigram. "Philosopher, whom dost thou most affect." Richard Garnett. HBV
Epigram: "Poet gathers fruit from every tree, The." Sir William Watson. CaAE
(Four Epigrams.) MBP; MoBrPo (1942 ed.)
(Poet, The.) TrGrPo
Epigram: "Quoth Satan to Arnold." *Unknown.* PAH
Epigram: "Readers and the hearers like my books, The." Sir John Harington, *after* Martial. *See* Critics and Cooks.
Epigram: Respice Finem. Francis Quarles. OBEV
(Human Touch, The: "My soul, sit thou.") PoToHe
(Respice Finem.) MaRV
Epigram: "Rudely forced to drink tea, Massachusetts, in anger." *Unknown.* PAH
Epigram: "Scaurus hates Greek." *Unknown.* SPP
Epigram: "Should D——s print, how once you robb'd your brother." Pope. CEP
Epigram: "Sighs are my food, drink are my tears." Sir Thomas Wyatt. *See* Wyatt Being in Prison, to Bryan.
Epigram: "Sir, I admit your general rule." Pope, *also at. to* Matthew Prior *and to* Samuel Taylor Coleridge. FiBHP; HBV; LiTB; LiTG; SiTL; TreF
(Fool and the Poet, The.) BOHV
(Reply, A [*or* The].) GoTP; PIAE
Epigram: Sir Joshua Reynolds. Blake. *See* Sir Joshua Reynolds.
Epigram: "Sly Beelzebub took all occasions." Samuel Taylor Coleridge. *See* Job.
Epigram: Stand Close Around, Ye Stygian Set. Walter Savage Landor. *See* Dirce.
Epigram: "Statue, The—Buonarroti said—doth wait." Sir William Watson.
(Four Epigrams.) MBP; MoBrPo (1942 ed.)
(Sculpture and Song.) PIAE
Epigram: "They say your lady friends have no long life." Martial, *tr fr. Latin by* G. A. Pott *and* F. A. Wright. ALV
Epigram: "This house, where once a lawyer dwelt." William Erskine. HBV
Epigram: "Thou art in danger, Cincius, on my word." Marcus Argentarius, *tr. fr. Latin by* Richard Garnett. ALV
Epigram II: "Thou fool profane, be silent!" *Unknown, tr. fr. Hebrew. Fr.* Duel with Verses over a Great Man. TrJP
Epigram I: "Thou Guide to doubt, be silent evermore." *Unknown, tr. fr. Hebrew. Fr.* Duel with Verses over a Great Man. TrJP
Epigram: "Thou swearst thou'lt drink no more." *Unknown.* ALV
Epigram: "'Tis highly rational, we can't dispute." Richard Garnett. HBV
Epigram: "To all men thou dost slander me." Bernard de la Monnoye, *tr. fr. French by* Alan Conder. TrFP
Epigram: To English Connoisseurs. Blake. *See* To English Connoisseurs.
Epigram: To Flaxman. Blake. *See* To Flaxman.
Epigram: To Hunt. Blake. *See* To Hunt.
Epigram: "To John I owed great obligation." Matthew Prior. ALV; CEP; FaFP; LiA; LiTG; SiTL
(More than Quit.) OnPM
(Quits.) AWP
Epigram: "Tonight, grave Sir, both my poor house and I." Ben Jonson. *See* Inviting a Friend to Supper.
Epigram: "Translator who rhymed the Iliad, The." Jean Baptiste Rousseau, *pr. tr. fr. French.* LiA
Epigram: "Treason doth never prosper." Sir John Harington. *See* Of Treason.
Epigram: "Well, I remember how you smiled." Walter Savage Landor. *See* Well I Remember How You Smiled.
Epigram: "Were I a king, I could command content." Edward de Vere, Earl of Oxford. *See* Were I a King.
Epigram: "What is an epigram?" Samuel Taylor Coleridge. *See* What Is an Epigram.
Epigram: "'What? rise again with all one's bones.'" Samuel Taylor Coleridge. *See* Giles's Hope.
Epigram IV: "What thought ye to burn, when ye kindled the pyre." *Unknown, tr. fr. Hebrew. Fr.* Duel with Verses over a Great Man. TrJP
Epigram: "When doctrines meet with general approbation." David Garrick. HBV
Epigram: "When Eve upon the first of men." Thomas Moore. HBV
Epigram: "When I am dead, I hope it may be said." Hilaire Belloc. *See* On His Books.
Epigram: "When other ladies to the shades go down." Pope. PoEL-3
Epigram: "When Pontius wished an edict might be passed." Matthew Prior. ALV
Epigram: "When the devil was sick, the devil a monk would be." *Unknown.* ALV
Epigram: "When whelmed are altar, priest and creed." Sir William Watson. WGRP
Epigram: "While life was mine, the little hour." Thomas Moore, *after the Greek.* ALV
Epigram: "Whilst [*or* While] Adam slept, Eve from his side arose." *Unknown.* ALV; HBV
Epigram: "Who hath heard of such cruelty before?" Sir Thomas Wyatt. SiPS
Epigram: "Who killed Kildare? Who dared Kildare to kill?" Swift. HBV
Epigram: "With nought to hide or to betray." John Swanwick Drennan. IrPN
Epigram: "With women and apples both Paris and Adam." Thomas Moore. ALV
Epigram: "World of fools has such a store, The." *Unknown, tr. fr. French.* ALV
Epigram: "Years, many parti-coloured years." Walter Savage Landor. *See* Years, Many Parti-coloured Years.
Epigram: "Yes, every poet is a fool." Matthew Prior. CEP
(Another [Epigram].) LiA
Epigram: "You ask me how Contempt who claims to sleep." J. V. Cunningham. NePoAm
(Two Epigrams, II.) SiTL
Epigram: "You beat your pate, and fancy wit will come." Pope. *See* To a Blockhead.
Epigram: "You wonder why Drab sells her love for gold?" J. V. Cunningham. NePoAm
Epigram for the Dead at Tegea. *Unknown, tr. fr. Greek by* Richmond Lattimore. WaaP
Epigram of Inigo Jones, An. Ben Jonson. EPS (1942 ed.)
Epigram of Martial, Imitated. Sir Charles Hanbury Williams. *See* Come, Chloe, and Give Me Sweet Kisses.
Epigram on an Academic Visit to the Continent. Richard Porson. OxBoLi; WhC
(Academic Visit to the Continent, An.) OnPM
(On a German Tour, *sl. diff. vers.*) FiBHP
Epigram on Handel and Bononcini. John Byrom. OBEC; UnS
(Epigram on the Feuds between Handel and Bononcini.) CEP
Epigram on Marcus the Gnostic. St. Pothinus. CAW
Epigram on Milton. Dryden. *See* Lines Printed under the Engraved Portrait of Milton.
Epigram on Miltonicks. Samuel Wesley. OBEC
Epigram on the Death of Edward Forbes. Sydney Dobell. VA
Epigram on the Feuds between Handel and Bononcini. John Byrom. *See* Epigram on Handel and Bononcini.
Epigram on the Passing of Christmas. Edgar Bowers. PtPa
Epigram on the Poor of Boston Being Employed in Paving the Streets, 1774. *Unknown.* PAH
Epigram, An, on the Reverend Mr. Laurence Echard's, and Bishop Gilbert Burnet's Histories. Matthew Green. PoE
Epigram on the Toasts of the Kit-Kat Club, Anno 1716. Pope. CEP
Epigram on This Book of Epigrams, An. John Heywood. ReIE
Epigram on Two Ladies. Lady Burrell. DiM
Epigram to King Charles for an Hundred Pounds He Sent Me in My Sickness, An. Ben Jonson. OAEP
Epigram upon His Majestie's Great Ship (the *Sovereign of the Seas*) Lying in the Docks at Woolwich, An. Thomas Heywood. SG
Epigrammata Sacra, *sels.* Richard Crashaw, *tr. fr. Latin by* D. C. Allen. LaP
Ad Judaeos Mactatores Stephani, I, 38.
Aethiopus Lotus, I, 9.
Aquae in Vinum Versae, I, 96.
Beati Oculi Qui Vident, I, 76.
Christus Vitis ad Vinitorem Patrem, I, 61.
In Asinum Christi Vectorem, I, 2.
In Beatae Virginis Verecundiam, II, 11.

Piscatores Vocat, I, 84.
Pisces Multiplicati, II, 29.
Si Filius Dei Es, Dejice Te, I, 72.
Vincula Sponte Decidunt, I, 31.
Epigrams. Richard Aldington. PFE
Girl, A.
New Love.
October.
Epigrams. Ausonius, *tr. fr. Latin by* Richard Lovelace. LaP
Epigrams (I–VIII). John Swanwick Drennan. IrPN
Epigrams. Steingrimur Thorsteinsson, *tr. fr. Icelandic.* IcP
Generosity, *tr. by* Vilhjalmur Stefansson.
Lions and Swine, *tr. by* Vilhjalmur Stefansson.
Mountain and Hillock, *tr. by* Jakobina Johnson.
Epigrams. Sir Thomas Wyatt. SiPS
Epigrams on Castlereagh. Byron. ExPo
"So Castlereagh has cut his throat!—the worst," I.
"So He has cut his throat at last! He! Who?", II.
Epigrams should, I suppose, please their readers by saying it briefly. Martial, *tr. fr. Latin by* Robert R. Schnorr. Epigrams, VIII, 29. LaP
Epigraph for a Condemned Book. Baudelaire, *tr. fr. French by* Kate Flores. AnFP
Epilog: "Like the ears of the wheat." Heine. *Fr.* The North Sea. AWP; JAWP; WBP
Epilogue: "All is best, though we oft doubt." Milton. *See* All Is Best.
Epilogue: "And lo! it shines upon the cities." Margarita Aliger. *Fr.* Your Victory. TrRV
Epilogue: "At my casement I sat by night, while the wind remote in dark valleys." Aubrey Thomas De Vere. IrPN
Epilogue: "At the midnight in the silence of the sleep-time." Robert Browning. *Fr.* Asolando. AEV; BEL; BMEP; BoLiVe; BPN; CoBE; EM-2; EmBrPo; EnL; EnLi-2; EnLit; EPN; EPP; FaBoEn; FiP; GEPC; GTSL; HBV; HBVY; HiLiEn; InP; LEAP; MaRV; OAEP; OBVV; OHFP; OQP; OuHeWo; PC; PoeMoYo; PoVP; QP-1; TCEP; TOP; TrGrPo; VA; ViBoPo; ViPo; ViPP; VLEP
One Who Never Turned His Back, *sel.* GrCo-2
Epilogue: "Away, for we are ready to a man!" James Elroy Flecker. *Fr.* The Golden Journey to Samarkand (*also in* Hassan). CP; ShBV-3
Epilogue: "Carol, every violet has." Alfred Noyes. *Fr.* The Flower of Old Japan. MBP; MoBrPo
Epilogue: Credo. Arthur Symons. PoVP
Epilogue: "Giver of bliss and pain, of song and prayer," *sel.* William Alexander Percy. TrPWD
Epilogue: "Heaven, which man's generations draws." Francis Thompson. *Fr.* A Judgment in Heaven. MBP; MoAB; MoBrPo
Epilogue: "I am sure this Jesus will not do." Blake. *Fr.* The Everlasting Gospel. OBRV
Epilogue: "I, too, sing America." Langston Hughes. *See* I, Too.
Epilogue: "If Luther's day expand to Darwin's year." Herman Melville. *Fr.* Clarel. AnAmPo; AWP; ImOP; LA
Epilogue: "If thou disdain the sacred muse." Sir Edmund Gosse. TCEP
Epilogue: "Like the stalks of wheat in the fields." Heine, *tr. fr. German by* Emma Lazarus. *Fr.* The North Sea. TrJP
Epilogue: "Now my charms are all ore-throwne." Shakespeare. *See* Prospero's Epilogue.
Epilogue: "Now the hungry lion roars." Shakespeare. *See* Now the Hungry Lion Roars.
Epilogue: "O chansons foregoing." Ezra Pound. OxBA
Epilogue: "Oh, Love—no, Love! All the noise below, Love." Robert Browning. *Fr.* Ferishtah's Fancies. ViPP
Epilogue: "'O where are you going?' said reader to rider." W. H. Auden. *See* O Where Are You Going.
Epilogue: "On the first of the Feast of Feasts." Robert Browning. ViPo
Epilogue: "Pretty task, A; and so I told the Fool." Dryden. *Fr.* Aureng-Zebe. SeEP
Epilogue: "Said the voice of Evil to the ear of Good." Isabella Valancy Crawford. *Fr.* Gisli, the Chieftain. BoCaPo
Epilogue: "Savage I was sitting in my house, late, lone." Robert Browning. *Fr.* Fifine at the Fair. BPN
(Householder, The.) LO; NBE
Epilogue: "Terence [*or* Terrence], this is stupid stuff." A. E. Housman. *See* Terence, This Is Stupid Stuff.
Epilogue: "These, to you now." W. E. Henley. POTT
(Epilogue to Rhymes and Rhythms.) ViBoPo
Epilogue: "They who have best succeeded on the stage." Dryden. *Fr.* The Conquest of Granada, Pt. II. CEP; EiPP; FiP; GEPC; SeCV-2; SeEP
Epilogue: "This wind upon my mouth, these stars I see." William Alexander Percy. *Fr.* Enzio's Kingdom. LS; UnW
Epilogue: "Time is a thing." Stephen Spender. MBP; MoBrPo
Epilogue: "Tramp! Tonight the night is so fine." Tefcros Anthias, *tr. fr. Modern Greek by* Rae Dalven. MoGP
Epilogue: "Truly, My Satan, thou art but a Dunce." Blake. *See* To the Accuser Who Is the God of This World.
Epilogue: "Unmoved by all claims our times allow." Herman Melville. LA
Epilogue: "Virtue may unlock hell." Francis Thompson. *Fr.* A Judgment in Heaven. EmBrPo; PoLi
Epilogue: "Well, when all is said and done." "Æ." MoBrPo
Epilogue: "What a pretty tale you told me." Robert Browning. *Fr.* The Two Poets of Croisic. BPN
Epilogue: "What shall we do for Love these days?" Lascelles Abercrombie. *Fr.* Emblems of Love. AnFE; GTML; HBV; MBP; MoBrPo; OBVV; TCPD
Small Fountains, *sel.* CH
Epilogue: "With heart at rest I climbed the citadel's steep height." Baudelaire, *tr. fr. French by* Arthur Symons. AWP
(Epilogue to Prose Poetry.) OnPM
Epilogue: "With words as counters, talk of day and night." Edward Thompson. MM
Epilogue at Wallack's, An. John Elton Wayland. AA
Epilogue for a Masque of Purcell. Adrienne Cecile Rich. NePoEA
Epilogue of "Prometheus." Shelley. *See* Demogorgon's Last Words.
Epilogue of Schiller's "Song of the Bell," *sel.* Goethe, *tr. fr. German by* Edgar A. Bowring.
"He was our own!" BoFr
Epilogue of the Wandering Jew, The. Colin Newbury. AnNZ
Epilogue Spoken at Oxford by Mrs. Marshall. Dryden. ATP; CEP
(Epilogue Spoken by Mrs. Boutell.) SeCV-2
(To the University of Oxford, 1674.) FaBoEn
Epilogue to a Book of Verse. Arthur Guiterman. InMe
Epilogue to a Human Drama. Stephen Spender. EnLit
Epilogue to "A Midsummer Night's Dream." Shakespeare. *See* Now the Hungry Lion Roars.
Epilogue to Alun Mabon. John Ceiriog Hughes, *tr. fr. Welsh by* Sir Idris Bell. PrWP
Epilogue to "Dramatic Idyls." Robert Browning. BPN; PoVP
Epilogue to "Dramatis Personae." Robert Browning. BPN
"That one Face, far from vanish, rather grows," *sel., last st.* ChIP; MaRV
Epilogue to Eighteenth Century Vignettes. Austin Dobson. *Fr.* Eighteenth-Century Vignettes, 2d Series. BPN
Epilogue to "Fand." William Larminie. *See* Killarney.
Epilogue to "Fifine at the Fair." Robert Browning. *See* Epilogue: "Savage I was sitting in my house . . ."
Epilogue to Fratricidal Folly. Euripides, *tr. fr. Greek by* Arthur S. Way. *Fr.* Phoenician Maidens. GrR
Epilogue to "Mithridates, King of Pontus." Dryden. OAEP
Epilogue to Polycrates, An. Ibycus, *tr. fr. Greek by* C. M. Bowra. OxBG
Epilogue to Prose Poems. Baudelaire. *See* Epilogue: "With heart at rest I climbed the citadel's steep height."
Epilogue to the Accuser Who is the God of This World. Blake. *See* To the Accuser . . .
Epilogue to the Breakfast Table Series. Oliver Wendell Holmes. *Fr.* The Poet at the Breakfast Table. AA
Epilogue to "The Husband His Own Cuckold," *br. sel.* Dryden.
Fools in England. BeR
Epilogue to the Outrider. Dorothy Livesay. CaP
Epilogue to the Pacchiarotto Volume. Robert Browning. BPN
Epilogue to the Satires. Pope.
(One Thousand Seven Hundred and Thirty-eight, Dialogues I *and* II.) CEP
Sels.
Name No Names, *fr.* Dialogue II. BeR
Satire: "Ask you what provocation I have had?" *fr.* Dialogue II. OBEC
(In Defence of Satire.) CoBE
(Provocation to Satire.) BeR
Virtue and Vice, *fr.* Dialogue I. BeR
Epilogue to the Second Part of "The Conquest of Granada by the Spaniards." Dryden. *See* Epilogue: "They who have best succeeded on the stage."
Epilogue to "Troilus and Criseyde." Chaucer. *See* Envoy, The: "Go, litel book . ."
Epilogue to "Tyrannick Love." Dryden. OAEP; SeCV-2; ViBoPo
Epilogus: "Lo, ladies, here (if you can use it well)." George Whetstone. TuPP
Epilogus: "Thus have I waded through a worthless task." Henry Parrot. SiCE
Epiphany. Katherine Burton. PSO
Epiphany. Leconte de Lisle, *tr. fr. French by* Alan Conder. TrFP
Epiphany. Eileen Duggan. ISi
Epiphany. Reginald Heber. *See* Brightest and Best of the Sons of the Morning.
Epiphany. Eileen Shanahan. NeIP

Epiphany, The. George Strong. GoYe
Epiphany of Apollo, The. Callimachus, *tr. fr. Greek by* R. A. Furness. OxBG
Epipsychidion. Shelley. BPN; EmBrPo; EnRP; EPN; ERP
Sels.
Longest Journey, The. OtMeF
("I never was attached to that great sect.") NBE
Seraph of Heaven. ISi
"Ship is floating in the harbour now, A." OBRV
"Spouse! Sister! Angel! Pilot of the fate." BCEP; ChER; LoPS
"There was a Being whom my spirit oft." EnLi-2
"Thy wisdom speaks in me, and bids me dare." KN
True Love ("She met me, stranger"). LoBV
"True Love in this differs from gold and clay." LO
Episode, An. Muriel Earley Sheppard. IHA
Episode, An. John Addington Symonds. PoVP; VA
Episode of Adamastor off the Cape of Good Hope. Luís de Camões, *tr. fr. Portuguese by* Sir Richard Fanshawe. *Fr.* The Lusiads. LiA
(Cape of Tempests, The.) LiTW
Epistemology. Richard Wilbur. NePoEA
Epistemology of Poetry. Robert Conquest. PoLFOT
Epistle: "Christian, be up before the end of day." Robert Nathan. MaRV
Epistle, An: "Karshish, the picker-up of learning's crumbs." Robert Browning. *See* Epistle, An, Containing the Strange Medical Experience of Karshish, the Arab Physician.
Epistle I: "Meeting a monster of mourning wherever I go." George Barker. *See* Epistle to Dylan Thomas.
Epistle IV: "O Happiness! Our being's end." Pope. *Fr.* An Essay on Man. ATP
Epistle: To Charles Cowden Clarke. Keats. *See* Epistle to Charles Cowden Clarke.
Epistle: To George Felton Mathew. Keats. *See* Epistle to George Felton Mathew.
Epistle I: "Yes, you despise the man." Pope. *Fr.* Moral Essays. CEP
Epistle Answering to One That Asked to Be Sealed of the Tribe of Ben, An. Ben Jonson. OAEP; SeCV-1; TuPP
Epistle, An, Containing the Strange Medical Experience of Karshish, the Arab Physician. Robert Browning. EmBrPo; StJW; ViPo; ViPP
(Epistle, An: "Karshish, the picker-up of learning's crumbs.") PoVP; VLEP
(Epistle of Karshish, An.) EPN
(Karshish, the Arab Physician, *abr.*) WGRP
Sels.
All-loving, The. MaRV; OQP; QP-1
("So, the All-Great were the All-Loving too.") ChIP
Karshish and Lazarus. GoBC
Epistle Dedicatory to Chapman's Translation of the Iliad, The, *sels.* George Chapman.
"Princes statue, A, or in marble carv'd." AtBAP
(Poetry and Learning.) OBS
"Since perfect happiness, by princes sought." ReEn
(To the High-born Prince of Men, Henry.) ReIE
Epistle for Spring. R. Ellsworth Larsson. CAW
Epistle; from Dr. Franklin (Deceased) to His Poetical Panegyrists on Some of Their Absurd Compliments. Philip Freneau. MOAP; OnAP
Epistle from Mr. Murray to Dr. Polidori. Byron. EV-4
(Publisher to His Client, A.) CBE
Epistle from Mr. Pope, to Dr. Arbuthnot. Pope. *See* Epistle to Dr. Arbuthnot.
Epistle from Pontus, *sel.* Ovid, *tr. fr. Latin by* W. H. Alexander.
"Shall I complain or keep silence." BoFr
Epistle in Form of a Ballad to His Friends. Villon, *tr. fr. French by* Swinburne. AWP; LiTW; LyMA; OuHeWo
Epistle of Condolence. Thomas Moore. OnYI
Epistle of Karshish, An. Robert Browning. *See* Epistle, An, Containing the Strange Medical Experience of Karshish, the Arab Physician.
Epistle to a Famous Painter, *sel.* John Dyer.
To a Famous Painter. BeR
Epistle to a Friend. William Habington. EV-2
Epistle to a Lady, *sel.* Swift.
Satirist, The. BeR
Epistle to a Young Friend. Burns. BLP; MCCG
(Letter to a Young Friend.) OHFP
Epistle to Augusta. Byron. AnEnPo; BPN; EmBrPo; EnRP; EPN; ERP; GEPC
(To Augusta.) LPS-1
Epistle to Be Left in the Earth. Archibald MacLeish. BoLiVe (1945 ed.); ChMo; CMP; ImOP; MAP; MoAB; MoAmPo; PoLFOT; TrGrPo
Epistle to Boscán. Garcilaso de la Vega, *tr. fr. Spanish by* J. H. Wiffen. BoFr
Epistle to Burlington. Pope. *See* Moral Essays: Epistle IV.
Epistle to Charles Cowden Clarke. Keats. EmBrPo; GEPC
(To Charles Cowden Clarke.) EnRP
Epistle to Davie, a Brother Poet. Burns. EBSV; OBEC, *sts.* 1-5.
Epistle to Dr. Arbuthnot (Prologue to the Satires). Pope. BEL; CoBE; EiPP; EM-1; EnLi-1; EnLit; EV-3, *sl. abr.*; GEPC; LoBV, *abr.*; OAEP; PoE; PoEL-3; ReaPo; TOP, *abr.*; TyEnPo, *abr.*; WoL, *abr.*
(Epistle from Mr. Pope, to Dr. Arbuthnot.) CEP
(Prologue to the Satires, *abr.*) NBE
(To Dr. Arbuthnot, *abr.*) OxBoLi
Sels.
Atticus. AWP; JAWP; MaPo; OBEC; SeCePo; ShBV-4; WBP; WHA
(Addison.) BCEP; LPS-3
(Characters from the Satires: Atticus.) InPo
("Peace to all such! but were there one whose fires.") PoFS; ViBoPo
(Portrait of Atticus.) UnPo (1st ed.)
"Bless'd be the great! for those they take away." PtP
Bufo ("Proud as Apollo on his forked hill"). OBEC
Compliments ("But why then publish?"). LiA
Scandal ("Cursed be the verse, how well soe'er it flow"). LPS-3
"Shut, shut the door, good John! fatigu'd, I said." EPP, *abr.*; HoPM; LEAP, *shorter sel.*
(Author's Miseries, The, *abr., shorter sel.*) BCEP
(Dire Dilemma, A, *abr., shorter sel.*) WHA
Sporus. AWP; ChTr; JAWP; LPS-3; MaPo; WBP
(Characters from the Satires: Sporus.) InPo
("Let Sporus tremble—What? that thing of silk.") ViBoPo
(Lord Hervey.) CoEV
Verbal Critics ("Pains, reading, study, are their just pretence"). CoEV; OBEC
Why Did I Write ("Of all mad creatures if the learn'd are right"). OBEC
"Why did I write? what sin to me unknown." BeR; ChTr; FiP, *longer sel.*; ViBoPo
"Yet let me flap this bug with gilded wings." ExPo
Epistle to Dr. Blacklock, Ellisland, 21st Oct. 1789, *abr.* Burns. OBEC
Epistle to Dylan Thomas. George Barker. LiTM (1952 ed.)
(Epistle I.) LiTM (1946 ed.)
Epistle to Elizabeth, Countess of Rutland, *sels.* Ben Jonson.
"Beautie, I know, is good, and bloud is more." FaBoEn
Power of Poets, The. WHA
Epistle to Fabio. *At. to* Andrés Fernández de Andrada, *tr. fr. Spanish by* Eleanor L. Turnbull. TeCS
Epistle to George Felton Mathew. Keats. EmBrPo; GEPC
Epistle to George Keats. Keats. *See* Epistle to My Brother George.
Epistle to James Smith. Burns. BSV; MCCG; OBEC
(To James Smith, *sts.* 1-3.) HoPM
Epistle to John Lapraik [an Old Scottish Bard]. Burns. BEL; CEP; CoEV; EiPP; EM-1; EnLi-2; EnRP; MCCG, *first* 15 *sts.*; OAEP
(Epistle to J. Lapraik.) EnL; PIR
Spark o' Nature's Fire, A, *br. sel.* BLP
Epistle to Joseph Hill, Esq., An. William Cowper. CBOV
Epistle to Lady Rutland, An. Ben Jonson. *See* Epistle to Elizabeth, Countess of Rutland.
Epistle to [Miss *or* Mrs.] Martha Blount on Her Leaving Town after the Coronation. Pope. BrBE; CaAE; CEP
(Epistle to Miss Blount.) PoEL-3
(To a Young Lady.) OBEC
(To a Young Lady on Her Leaving the Town after the Coronation.) ExPo; SeCeV
Away from London, *sel.* BeR
Epistle to Mrs. Blount, with the Works of Voiture. Pope. CBOV
Epistle to Mr. Pope, An. George Lyttelton. Po
Epistle to My Brother George. Keats. EmBrPo; GEPC
(To My Brother George.) EnRP
"Should he upon an evening ramble fare," *sel.* ChER
Epistle to Pope, *sel.* Edward Young.
Fame and Envy. BCEP
Epistle to Reynolds, *sel.* Keats.
On Imagination. EPN
Epistle to Robert Lloyd, Esq., An. William Cowper. FiP
Epistle to the Gentiles. Alfred Hayes. TrJP
Epistle to the Lady Margaret. Samuel Daniel. *See* To the Lady Margaret, Countess of Cumberland.
Epistle to the Right Honourable the Earl of Burlington, An, *sel.* John Gay.
"Here sheep the pasture hide, there harvests bend." EnSW
Epistle to William Simpson, Ochiltree. Burns. *See* To William Simpson of Ochiltree.
Epistles to Mr. Pope Concerning the Authors of the Age, *sels.* Edward Young.
Black Militia of the Pen, The. BeR
Fame and Envy. BCEP
Epi-Strauss-ium. Arthur Hugh Clough. ViP; ViPP
Epitaph: "After long thirty years re-met." Sylvia Townsend Warner. BLV
Epitaph: "As I was, so be ye." *Unknown.* TreFS
Epitaph, An: "As shining sand-drift." Lady Margaret Sackville. *Fr.* Epitaphs. HBMV

Epitaph: "Bathsheba: To whom none ever said scat." Whittier. CIV
Epitaph, An: "Beneath this stone lies one good man; and when." W. H. Davies. ChMP
Epitaph: "By man came death." Antonia White. DiM
Epitaph: "Daniel and Abigail." Miguel de Barrios, *tr. fr. Spanish.* TrJP
Epitaph, An: "Enough; and leave the rest to fame." Andrew Marvell. BCEP; OBEV
("Enough: and leave the rest to fame.") LO
(Epitaph upon ——, An.) LoBV; SeCL
Epitaph, An: "Escaped the gloom of mortal life, a soul." James Beattie. *See* Epitaph, Intended for Himself.
Epitaph: "Even such is Time, which takes in trust." Sir Walter Ralegh. *See* Conclusion, The.
Epitaph: "Fate to beauty still must give." Claudian, *tr. fr. Latin by* Howard Mumford Jones. AWP; LaP
Epitaph: "For this she starred her eyes with salt." Elinor Wylie. ChMo; MAP; MoAmPo
Epitaph: "From out the stormy sea unto the shore." Azariah di Rossi, *tr. fr. Hebrew by* A. B. Rhine. TrJP
Epitaph, An: "Gaily I lived, as ease and nature taught." *Unknown.* ExPo
Epitaph: "He roamed half-round the world of woe." Aubrey Thomas De Vere. OBVV; PoVP
Epitaph: "Heap not on this mound." Edna St. Vincent Millay. *Fr.* Memorial to D. C. NP
Epitaph: "Her grieving parents cradled here." Sylvia Townsend Warner. BLV; MBP; MoBrPo; NeMA; PIAE
Epitaph, An: "Here dead lie we because we did not choose." A. E. Housman. *See* Here Dead Lie We.
Epitaph: "Here—for they could not help but die." Philip Freneau. *Fr.* The Fading Rose. AA
Epitaph: "Here lie [*or* lies] I, Martin Elginbrodde [*or* Elmrod]." *Unknown, at. to* George Macdonald. MaRV; WGRP
(At Aberdeen.) LiTG; SiTL
(Epigram.) HBV
(Gravestones, I.) OtMeF
(Here Lies . . .) GoTP
(Hic Jacet.) PIAE
(Martin Elginbrodde.) BMEP
Epitaph I: "Here lies a man, and still no man." *Unknown, tr. fr. Hebrew. Fr.* Duel with Verses over a Great Man. TrJP
Epitaph, An: "Here lies a most beautiful lady." Walter de la Mare. AnFE; BLV; BoLiVe; BrBE; CBOV; CoBMV; EPP; LBBV; LEAP; LiTB; LiTM; LoBV; MBP; MoAB; MoBrPo; MoVE; NeMA; NP; OAEP (2d ed.); OBEV (new ed.); OBVV; OnPP; PoeT; POTE; ShBV-3; SiTL; ViBoPo
Epitaph: "Here lies a piece of Christ; a star in dust." Robert Wild. *See* Epitaph For a Godly Man's Tomb, An.
Epitaph: "Here lies a poor woman who always was tired." *Unknown.* TreF
Epitaph: "Here lies a simple Jew." Sholom Aleichem, *tr. fr. Yiddish by* Joseph Leftwich. TrJP
Epitaph: "Here lies, in this small chamber." Villon, *tr. fr. French by* Ralph N. Currey. FoS
Epitaph, An: "Here lies Nachshon, a man of great renown." Isaac Benjacob, *tr. fr. Hebrew by* Joseph Chotzner. TrJP
Epitaph, An: "Here lies one who never drew." William Cowper. OTPC (1923 ed.)
Epitaph: "Here lies the body of Richard Hind." Francis Jeffrey. OxBoLi
Epitaph: "Here lies the body of William Jones." *Unknown.* PoD
Epitaph: "Here lies the flesh that tried." Louise Driscoll. HBMV; NV; WGRP
Epitaph: "Here lies the ideal of Saint Francis." Sister Mary Francis. SaFP
Epitaph: "Here lies the poet Wolker, lover of the world." Jiri Wolker, *tr. fr. Czech by* Karl W. Deutsch. WaaP
Epitaph: "Here rests a woman, good without pretence." Pope. *See* On Mrs. Corbet.
Epitaph, An: "Here sleeps, at last, in narrow bed." Austin Dobson. VLEP
Epitaph: "His fame the mock of shallow wits." Sir Charles G. D. Roberts. MM
Epitaph: "I, an unwedded wandering dame." Sylvia Townsend Warner. MBP; MoBrPo; NeMA
Epitaph: "I have lived through these times and for a thousand years." Robert Desnos, *tr. fr. French by* Wallace Fowlie. MiCF
Epitaph: "I never cared for life: life cared for me." Thomas Hardy. TriL
Epitaph: "I, Richard Kent, beneath these stones." Sylvia Townsend Warner. MBP; MoBrPo; NeMA
Epitaph: "Implacable angel, The." Leone da Modena, *tr. fr. Hebrew.* TrJP
Epitaph: "In this marble, buried lies." Thomas Jordan. SeCL
Epitaph: Inscription from Anticyra. *Unknown, tr. fr. Greek by* Richmond Lattimore. WaaP
Epitaph, An: "Interred [*or* Interr'd] beneath this marble stone." Matthew Prior. CEP; EiPP; OBEC; PoE; PoEL-3
Epitaph: "It seemed that he would rather hear." Edward Weismiller. PoMa
Epitaph: "It was for you that the mountains shook at Sinai." *Unknown.* TrJP
Epitaph: "John Bird, a laborer, lies here." Sylvia Townsend Warner. BLV; MBP; MoBrPo; NeMA; PIAE
Epitaph: "Know ye, fair folk who dwell on earth." Iraj, *tr. fr. Persian by* A. J. Arberry. PeP
Epitaph: "Lady Mary Villiers lies, The." Thomas Carew. *See* Epitaph on the Lady Mary Villiers.
Epitaph, An: "Let us not think of our departed dead." Edwin Markham. *See* Our Dead.
Epitaph, An: "Life is a jest, and all things show it." John Gay. *See* My Own Epitaph.
Epitaph: "Like silver dew." A. E. Coppard. OBMV
Epitaph, An: "Like thee I once have stemm'd the sea of life." James Beattie. *See* Epitaph, Intended for Himself.
Epitaph, An: "Lovely young lady I mourn in my rhymes, A." George John Cayley. BOHV; FiBHP; HBV
Epitaph: "Man, tak heed to me." *Unknown.* BSV
Epitaph: "Man who in his life trusts in this world, A." *Unknown.* TrJP
Epitaph: "May, be thou never graced with birds that sing." William Browne. EPP; OBEV; PCD
(Epitaph in Obitum M. S., X° Maij, 1614.) OBS
(In Obitum M. S., X Maii, 1614.) ElL; ElSeCe; SeCeV; SeEP
Epitaph: "Mr. Heath-Stubbs as you must understand." John Heath-Stubbs. NePoEA; PoN
Epitaph: "Napoleon took many captures and is dead." John Crowe Ransom. MOAP
Epitaph: "Nature and Nature's laws lay hid in night." Pope. *See* Epitaph Intended for Sir Isaac Newton.
Epitaph: "O mortal folk, you may behold and see." Stephen Hawes. *Fr.* The Pastime of Pleasure, *ch.* 42. ACP; BLV; OBEV; OtMeF; TrGrPo
(Epitaph of Graunde Amoure.) ChTr; OBSC; SeCeV
(His Epitaph.) BCEP; CBOV; GoBC; LEAP; TriL
("O mortal folk, you may behold and see.") MyFE
(Passetyme, The.) ViBoPo
Epitaph: "Of manners gentle, of affections mild." Pope. *See* On Mr. Gay . . .
Epitaph: On Sir Walter Rawleigh at His Execution. *Unknown.* OBS
Epitaph: "One whom I knew, a student and a poet." Alex Comfort. MoBrPo (1950 ed.)
(Poem.) SeCePo
Epitaph: "Renowned Spenser, lie a thought more nigh." William Basse. *See* Elegy on Shakespeare.
Epitaph: "Say he was sad, for there was none to love him." Robert Nathan. MuM
Epitaph: "Serene descent, as a red leaf's descending." Sara Teasdale. MM
Epitaph: "She was a high-class bitch and a dandy." Theodore Spencer. LiTA
Epitaph, An: "Shiftless and shy, gentle and kind and frail." J. C. Squire. BMEP; HBMV
Epitaph: "Sir, you should [*or* shall] notice me: I am the Man." Lascelles Abercrombie. MoBrPo; POTE; ViBoPo
Epitaph: "Spirit of death, so soft, so sweet." John Bruce MacCallum. PoP
Epitaph: "Stop, Christian passer-by!—Stop, child of God." Samuel Taylor Coleridge. EmBrPo; EnRP; EPN; ERP; EV-4; FiP; OAEP; OBRV; TriL
(Epitaph on Himself.) BCEP; LEAP; MaRV; OxBoCh
(O, Lift One Thought.) CH
Epitaph: "Stone cries from the wall, The." *Unknown.* TrJP
Epitaph: "These, who desired to live, went out to death." Lascelles Abercrombie. TCPD
(Epitaph Written for the Liverpool University Roll of Honour.) AEV
Epitaph: "This earthly tomb so low, and heaven so hie." *Unknown.* BSV
Epitaph: "This is the end of him, here he lies." Amy Levy. LBBV; TrJP
Epitaph, An: "This little vault, this narrow room." Thomas Carew. BEL; EnLi-1; UnPo (1st ed.)
(Epitaph on a Young Girl.) BLV; PIAE
(Epitaph on the Lady Villiers.) EPS (1942 ed.); LiTL
(Other, An.) SeCV-1; SeEP
("This little vault, this narrow room.") OBEV
Epitaph: "Thou whom these eyes saw never." Robert Browning. VA
Epitaph, An: "Under this sod and beneath these trees." *Unknown.* MoShBr
Epitaph: "Underneath this marble stone." Abraham Cowley. EnLoPo
Epitaph: "Underneath this sable hearse." William Browne. *See* On the Countess Dowager of Pembroke.
Epitaph: "We were not many, and no bronze asserts." Brooke Byrne. NeTW

Epitaph: "Weep with me, all you that read." Ben Jonson. *See* Epitaph on S. P.
Epitaph, The: "When from this good world I depart." John Alexander Bouquet. MaRV
Epitaph: "When you perceive these stones are wet." Sir William Davenant. ACP
Epitaph: "Where she fell swearing, hand to side." L. A. G. Strong. GTIV
Epitaph, An: "Wicked one lies buried here, A." *Unknown.* ShGoBo
Epitaph: "With death doomed to grapple." Byron. HBV
Epitaph, The: "Write on my grave when I am dead." Katharine Tynan. NLK; WGRP
Epitaph Acrostick on Robert Blake, The. George Harrison. SG
Epitaph and a Reply, An. *Unknown.* TreFS
Epitaph for a Bigot. Dorothy Vena Johnson. PoNe
Epitaph for a Cat. Margaret E. Bruner. CIV
Epitaph for a Concord Boy. Stanley Young. WaKn
Epitaph for a Funny Fellow. Morris Bishop. SiTL
Epitaph for a Godly Man's Tomb, An. Robert Wild. AEV; ChTr; OxBoCh; SeCL
(Epitaph: "Here lies a piece of Christ; a star in dust.") BCEP
Epitaph for a Judge. Benedict Jeitteles, *tr. fr. Hebrew by* Joseph Chotzner. TrJP
Epitaph for a Kitten. Miriam Vedder. CIV
Epitaph for a Man from Virginia City. Kenneth Porter. NePoAm-2
Epitaph for a Negro Woman. Owen Dodson. PoNe
Epitaph for a Poet. DuBose Heyward. LPS-1; PC
(Epitaph of a Poet.) LS; MuM
Epitaph for a Reno Woman. Donald F. Drummond. PtPa
Epitaph for a Sailor Buried Ashore. Sir Charles G. D. Roberts. EtS; VA
Epitaph for a Scotch Terrier. Rachel Field. AlBD
Epitaph for a Tyrannous Governor Who Choked on Wine. Adibi-i Sabir, *tr. fr. Persian by* R. A. Nicholson. LiTW
Epitaph for an American Bomber. James Bertram. AnNZ
Epitaph for Any New Yorker. Christopher Morley. PC; PIAE
Epitaph for Chaeroneia. *Unknown, tr. fr. Greek by* C. R. Kennedy. GrPo
Epitaph for Cimantha Proctor. Unknown. PreP
Epitaph for Elizabeth Ranquet. Corneille, *tr. fr. French.* CAW, *tr. by* Roderick Gill; TrFP, *tr. by* Alan Conder
Epitaph for Giotto, the Painter. Angelo Poliziano, *pr. tr. fr. Latin by* Richard Aldington. LaP
Epitaph for Himself, An. Aeschylus, *tr. fr. Greek by* Hugh Macnaghten. GrL
(Aeschylus. Simonides, *wr., tr. by* Lord Neaves.) OnPM
("Athenian Aeschylus, Euphorion's Son," *tr. by* Hugh Macnaghten.) GrPo
(His Own Epitaph, *tr. by* T. F. Higham.) OxBG
Epitaph; for Himself. Tristan Corbière, *tr. fr. French by* Joseph T. Shipley. AWP
(Epitaph for Tristan-Joachim-Edouard Corbière, Philosopher, Stray, Stillborn, *tr. by* Walter McElroy.) LiTW
(His Epitaph, *tr. by* Alan Conder.) TrFP
Epitaph for James Smith. Burns. *See* On a Wag in Mauchline.
Epitaph for John and Richard. Karl Shapiro. TwAmPo
Epitaph for Lincoln. Walt Whitman. *See* This Dust Was Once the Man.
Epitaph for Mr. Moses Levy. *Unknown.* TrJP
Epitaph for My Tomb. Alfonsina Storni, *tr. fr. Spanish by* Rolfe Humphries. AnCL
Epitaph for the Poet V., *sels.* Arthur Davison Ficke.
"Beauty—what is it? A perfume without name," III. HBMV
"For Beauty kissed your lips when they were young," II. HBMV
"It is ordained—or so Politian said," I. BAP; HBMV
"Peculiar ghost! great and immortal ghost," XVII. HBMV
Epitaph for the Race of Man, *sels.* Edna St. Vincent Millay.
"Before this coiling planet shall be cold," I. AmP
"Here lies, and none to mourn him but the sea," XVIII. MoPo; ReMP
(Sonnet XVIII.) AtBAP
"O Earth, unhappy planet born to die," IV. AmP
"Only the diamond and the diamond's dust," XVII. MoPo
See Where Capella with Her Golden Kids, VI. MAP; MoAmPo; MoAB
"When Death was young and bleaching bones were few," II. AmP
Epitaph for the Tombstone Erected over the Marquis of Anglesea's Leg, Lost at the Battle of Waterloo. George Canning. LPS-3
Epitaph for Tristan-Joachim-Edouard Corbière, Philosopher, Stray, Stillborn. Tristan Corbière. *See* Epitaph; for Himself.
Epitaph for the Unknown Soldier. Annette Kohn. DD
Epitaph for Us. Edgar Lee Masters. ChMo; CMP
Epitaph, Found Somewhere in Space. Hugh Wilgus Ramsaur. MaRV; MuM
Epitaph in Anticipation. Leonard Bacon. WhC
Epitaph; in Christ Church, Bristol, on Thomas Turner, Twice Master of the Company of Bakers. Francis Jeffrey. OxBoLi
Epitaph in Commendation of George Turberville, a Learned Gentleman, An. Sir John Harington. SiCE
Epitaph in Form of a Ballad, The, Which Villon Made for Himself and His Comrades, Expecting to Be Hanged Along with Them. Villon, *tr. fr. French by* Swinburne. EnLi-2; LiA; OuHeWo
(Ballad[e] of the Gibbet, *tr. by* Andrew Lang.) AWP; JAWP; WBP; WoL
(Ballade of the Hanged Men, *tr. by* Robert Fitzgerald.) LiTW; LyMA
(Epitaph in the Form of a Ballade, The, That Villon Made for Himself and His Fellows, Expecting to Be Hanged with Them, *tr. by* Alan Conder.) TrFP
(Villon's Epitaph in Ballade Form, *tr. by* Ralph N. Currey.) FoS
Epitaph in Obitum M. S., X° Maij, 1614. William Browne. *See* Epitaph: "May, be thou never graced with birds that sing."
Epitaph; in St. Olave's Church, Southwark, on Mr. Munday. Francis Jeffrey. OxBoLi
Epitaph in the Form of a Ballad, The. Villon. *See* Epitaph in Form of a Ballad, The.
Epitaph, Intended for Himself. James Beattie. EBSV; HBV, *2 sts.;* TriL
(Epitaph, An: "Escaped the gloom of mortal life, a soul.") BSV
(Epitaph: "Like thee I once have stemm'd the sea of life," *2 sts.*) OBEV
Epitaph Intended for His Wife. Dryden. BOHV; InMe; LauV; PreP
(Epigram: "Here lies my wife: here let her lie!") HBV
(Epitaph on His Wife.) PIAE; TrGrPo; WhC
("Here lies my wife; here let her lie!") TreF
Epitaph Intended for Sir Isaac Newton. Pope. CEP; FaBoEn; ImOP; SeCeV
(Epitaph: "Nature and Nature's laws lay hid in night.") InP
(Epitaph on Newton.) PIAE
(Epitaph on Sir Isaac Newton.) FiP; ViBoPo
(Intended for Sir Isaac Newton.) OAEP; TOP
("Nature and Nature's laws lay hid in night.") ExPo
(Science.) MaRV
Epitaph of a Courtesan. Asclepiades, *tr. fr. Greek by* Dudley Fitts. LiTW
Epitaph of a Poet. DuBose Heyward. *See* Epitaph for a Poet.
Epitaph of a Sailor. Leonidas of Tarentum, *tr. fr. Greek by* Dudley Fitts. LiTW
Epitaph of a Thessalian Hound. Simonides, *tr. fr. Greek by* Dudley Fitts. LiTW
Epitaph of a Young Man. *Unknown, tr. fr. Greek by* Dudley Fitts. LiTW
Epitaph of Bion. Moschus, *tr. fr. Greek by* Edmund Clarence Stedman. WoL
Epitaph of Dionysia. *Unknown.* HBV; OBEV (new ed.); OBVV; VA
Epitaph of Eusthenes, The. Edward Cracroft Lefroy. *Fr.* Echoes from Theocritus. AWP; OBVV
Epitaph of Graunde Amoure, The. Stephen Hawes. *See* Epitaph: "O mortal folk, you may behold and see."
Epitaph of Habbie Simpson, The. Robert Sempill. EBSV
(Life and Death of the Piper of Kilbarchan, The.) OBS
Epitaph of Robert Canynge. Thomas Chatterton. TCEP
Epitaph, An, of Sir Thomas Gravener, Knight. Sir Thomas Wyatt. OBSC; SiPS
Epitaph of the Countess Dowager of Pembroke. William Browne. *See* On the Countess Dowager of Pembroke.
Epitaph of the Death of Nicholas Grimald, An. Barnabe Googe. ReIE; SiCE; TriL; TuPP
Epitaph on a Bellows-Maker, An. John Hoskins. TuPP
Epitaph on a Bombing Victim. Roy Fuller. NeBP
Epitaph on a Dentist. *Unknown.* OxBoLi; TreFS
(Dentist, A.) LiTG; WhC
(On a Dentist.) GoTP
Epitaph on a Flute-Player. Diotimus of Athens, *tr. fr. Greek by* Charles Merivale. LiA
Epitaph on a Friend. Burns. MaRV
Epitaph on a Hare. William Cowper. CG; EV-3; FiP; HBV; HBVY; MW; PoEL-3; RG; SeCeV; ShBV-1; WP
Epitaph on a Husbandman, An. Sir Charles G. D. Roberts. LEAP
Epitaph on a Jacobite. Macaulay. *See* Jacobite's Epitaph, A.
Epitaph on a Madman's Grave. Morris Gilbert. YaD
Epitaph on a Man for Doing Nothing, An. John Hoskins. TuPP
Epitaph on a Pet Cat. Joachim du Bellay, *tr. fr. French by* Ralph N. Currey. FoS; PoC

Epitaph on a Pet Dog. Joachim du Bellay, *tr. fr. French by* Ralph N. Currey. FoS
Epitaph; on a Pet Mocking Bird. William Gaston. NoCaPo
Epitaph on a Robin Redbreast, An. Samuel Rogers. CG; OTPC (1923 ed.); PRWS
(Robin's Grave, The.) EV-3
Epitaph on a Sentry. L. A. G. Strong. NeMA
Epitaph on a Soldier. Cyril Tourneur. *Fr.* The Atheist's Tragedy, III, i. ElL
("His body lies interred within this mold.") SiCE
Epitaph on a Talkative Old Maid. Benjamin Franklin. WhC
Epitaph on a Vagabond. Alexander Gray. HBMV
Epitaph on a Virgin. Robert Herrick. *See* Epitaph upon a Virgin.
Epitaph on a Well-known Poet. Thomas Moore. *See* Epitaph on Robert Southey.
Epitaph on a Young Girl. Thomas Carew. *See* Epitaph, An: "This little vault."
Epitaph on Achilles. *Unknown, tr. fr. Greek by* William M. Hardinge. AWP
Epitaph on an Army of Mercenaries. A. E. Housman. Last Poems, XXXVII. BMEP; CoBMV; CoEV; GTBS; MM; MoAB; MoVE; OBEV (new ed.); OtMeF; PoFS; POTE; TwP; UnPo; ViBoPo; ViP; WaaP
Epitaph on an Infant. Samuel Taylor Coleridge. MotAn
Epitaph on an Infant. Crinagoras, *tr. fr. Greek by* John William Burgon. AWP
Epitaph on an Unfortunate Artist. Robert Graves. WhC
Epitaph on Charles II. Earl of Rochester. BLV; CoEV; EPP; EV-3; FiBHP; HBV; InP; OnPP; PreP; TOP; TreFS; TrGrPo; WhC; WP
(King Charles II.) OnPM; ViBoPo
(King's Epitaph, The.) EnLi-1 (1949 ed.); SeCePo; SeEP
(On Charles II.) ALV; BCEP; ExPo; GoTP; LEAP; PIAE
Epitaph on Claudy Phillips, a Musician, An. Samuel Johnson. TriL
(Epitaph upon the Celebrated Claudy Philips, Musician, Who Died Very Poor, An.) OBEC; UnS
Epitaph on Dr. Johnson. William Cowper. PtP
Epitaph on Dr. Parnell. Goldsmith. PtP
Epitaph on Elizabeth, L. H. Ben Jonson. ElL; EnL; EnLi-1 (1949 ed.); ElSeCe; EM-1; EPP; EPS; InPo; LPS-3; OBEV; OBS; PoE; ReEn; ReIE; RiBV; SeCV-1; SeEP; TuPP; ViBoPo; WHA
(On Elizabeth L. H.) HBV
Epitaph on Erotion. Martial. *See* Erotion.
Epitaph on Euripides. *At. to* Thucydides. *See* Euripides.
Epitaph on Himself. Callimachus, *tr. fr. Greek by* J. M. Edmonds. GrR
(Poet's Own Epitaph, The, *tr. by* R. A. Furness.) OxBG
Epitaph on Himself. Samuel Taylor Coleridge. *See* Epitaph: "Stop, Christian passer-by!"
Epitaph on Himself. Matthew Prior. LEAP; TreFS
(Epigram: "Nobles and heralds, by your leave.") HBV
(Prior's Epitaph.) TrGrPo
Epitaph on Himself. Mathurin Regnier, *tr. fr. French by* J. G. Legge. LiTW
Epitaph on His Deceased Friend, An. Robert Fletcher. SeCL
Epitaph on His Grandfather, An. Thomas Shipman. *See* Epitaph upon My Grandfather, An.
Epitaph on His Wife. Dryden. *See* Epitaph Intended for His Wife.
Epitaph on Husband and Wife Who Died and Were Buried Together, An. Richard Crashaw. *See* Epitaph upon Husband and Wife . . .
Epitaph on John Dove. Burns. InP
Epitaph on John Knott. *Unknown.* ChTr
Epitaph on King Charles I. James Graham, Marquess of Montrose. OBS
(His Metrical Vow.) ViBoPo
(Lines on the Execution of King Charles I.) GoTS
(On the Death of Charles I.) OnPM
(Upon the Death of King Charles I.) EV-2
Epitaph on Lady Ossory's Bullfinch. Horace Walpole. ChTr
Epitaph on Lady Salter. Thomas Carew. MeRV
Epitaph on Maria Wentworth. Thomas Carew. PoEL-3
Epitaph on Mrs. Corbet, Who Dyed of a Cancer in Her Breast. Pope. *See* On Mrs. Corbet.
Epitaph on Mrs. Margaret Paston of Barningham, in Norfolk. Dryden. CaAE
Epitaph on Mistress Mary Prideaux, An. *At. to* George Morley. SeCL
Epitaph on Mrs. William Mason. Thomas Gray. MeRV
Epitaph on My Dear and Ever Honoured Mother, An. Anne Bradstreet. AmPP (3d ed.)
Epitaph on My Father. Burns. FAOV; MaRV
Epitaph on Newton. Pope. *See* Epitaph Intended for Sir Isaac Newton.
Epitaph; on Peter Robinson. Francis Jeffrey. *See* On Peter Robinson.
Epitaph; on Prince Frederick. *Unknown. See* On Prince Frederick.
Epitaph on Queen Elizabeth, Wife of Henry VII. *Unknown.* AtBAP
(English Epitaph on Queen Elizabeth, Wife of Henry VII.) NBE
Epitaph on Rabelais. Pierre de Ronsard, *tr. fr. French by* Ralph N. Currey. FoS
Epitaph on Robert Southey. Thomas Moore. SiTL
(Epitaph on a Well-known Poet.) InMe
Epitaph on S. P. [Salamon *or* Salomon *or* Salathiel Pavy], a Child of Q. El.'s [Queen Elizabeth's] Chapel. Ben Jonson. BEL; BoFr; CBOV; CenL; CoBE; CoEV; ElL; ElSeCe; EM-1; EPP; EPS; FaBoEn; GoBC; InP; LoBV; MaPo; MePo; OAEP; OBEV; OBS; PIAE; PoE; PoEL-2; PoFS; ReEn; ReIE; SeCV-1; SeEP; TrGrPo; TuPP; TwHP; UnPo (1st ed.); ViBoPo
(Epitaph: "Weep with me, all you that read.") HBV
Epitaph on Sir Isaac Newton. Pope. *See* Epitaph Intended for Sir Isaac Newton.
Epitaph on Sir John Vanbrugh. Abel Evans. ViBoPo
(For Sir John Vanbrugh, Architect, 2 *ll.*) PIAE; WhC
(On Sir John Vanbrugh [Architect].) FiBHP; OBEC
Epitaph on Sir Philip Sidney. *At. to* Fulke Greville. AnFE; LiTB; LiTG; LoBV; OBSC; PtP; ReIE
(Another of the Same. Excellently Written by a Most Woorthy Gentleman.) SiCE, *at. to* Sir Edward Dyer
(Epitaph upon the Right Honorable Sir Philip Sidney, An.) TuPP
Epitaph on Sir Philip Sidney. Lord Herbert of Cherbury. SeEP
Epitaph on Sir Philip Sidney. *At. to* Sir Walter Ralegh. *See* Epitaph upon the Right Honorable Sir Philip Sidney . .
Epitaph on Sir William Williams. Thomas Gray. TriL
Epitaph, An, on the Admirable Dramatic Poet, William Shakespeare. Milton. *See* On Shakespeare.
Epitaph on the Countess [Dowager] of Pembroke. William Browne. *See* On the Countess Dowager of Pembroke.
Epitaph on the Duchess of Maine's Cat. François La Mothe le Vayer, *tr. fr. French by* Sir Edmund Gosse. PoC
Epitaph on the Earl of Leicester. *Unknown, at. to* Sir Walter Ralegh. SiPS
Epitaph on the Earl of Strafford. John Cleveland. MePo; OBS; PoD; SeCePo; TrGrPo
(Gravestones, II.) OtMeF
Epitaph on the Favourite Dog of a Politician. Hilaire Belloc. CoBE
Epitaph on the Lady Mary Villiers [*or* Villers] ("The Lady Mary Villiers lies"). Thomas Carew. EV-2; OAEP; OBEV; SeCL; SeCV-1; SeEP; ViBoPo
(Epitaph: "Lady Mary Villiers lies, The.") LEAP
Epitaph on the Lady Villiers. Thomas Carew. *See* Epitaph: "This little vault, this narrow room."
Epitaph on the Lap-Dog of Lady Frail. John Wilkes. ALV
Epitaph on the Late King of the Sandwich Isles. Winthrop Mackworth Praed. FiBHP
Epitaph on the Marchioness of Winchester, An. Milton. OBS; TriL
Epitaph on the Monument of Sir William Dyer at Colmworth, 1641. Lady Catherine Dyer. EnLoPo
Epitaph on the Politician. Hilaire Belloc. InP; MBP; MoBrPo; NeMA
(Epitaph on the Politician Himself.) CoBE
(On a Politician.) PIAE; WhC
Epitaph on the World. Henry David Thoreau. OnPM
Epitaph on Thomas Clere. Earl of Surrey. SiPS
Epitaph on Those Who Fell at the Battle of Chaeronea. Demosthenes, *tr. fr. Greek by* George Nathaniel Curzon. PoFr
Epitaph on Two Aged Priestesses. Diotimus of Miletus, *tr. fr. Greek by* Charles Merivale. LiA
Epitaph Placed on His Daughter's Tomb [by Mark Twain]. Robert Richardson, *ad. by* "Mark Twain." MaRV; TreF
(Requiem.) BMEP
Epitaph to a Dog. Byron. *See* Epitaph to a Newfoundland Dog.
Epitaph to a Merchant. Simonides. *See* Cretan Merchant, A.
Epitaph to a Newfoundland Dog. Byron. TreFS
(Epitaph to a Dog.) AlBD; BLPA
Epitaph to Baucis. Erinna. *See* Erinna to Her Friend.
Epitaph to the Liberty of America. José Joaquín Fernández de Lizardi, *tr. fr. Spanish by* Alice Stone Blackwell. PoFr
Epitaph upon ——, An. Andrew Marvell. *See* Epitaph, An: "Enough; and leave the rest to fame."
Epitaph upon a Child, An ("Virgins promised when I died"). Robert Herrick. SeCV-1
Epitaph upon a Child That Died ("Here she lies, a pretty bud"). Robert Herrick. EV-2; MaRV; OBEV
(Two Epitaphs on a Child That Died.) CBOV
(Upon a Child That Died.) EM-1; SeCV-1; SeEP
Epitaph upon a Virgin, An. Robert Herrick. OnPM; OxBoLi; PoEL-3; SeCV-1
(Epitaph on a Virgin.) EG
Epitaph upon Husband and Wife Which [*or* Who] Died and

Epitaph upon Husband and Wife (*continued*)
Were Buried Together, An. Richard Crashaw. ElSeCe; EV-2; LO; MaRV; OBEV; OBS; TreFS; TrGrPo
(Epitaph on Husband and Wife, An.) LiTL
(Epitaph upon a Young Married Couple, An.) OAEP; SeCePo; SeCL; SeEP; WHA
(Epitaph upon Husband and Wife.) BLV
(On a Young Married Couple.) FaBoEn
Epitaph upon Mr. Ashton a Conformable Citizen, An. Richard Crashaw. OBS
Epitaph upon My Grandfather, An. Thomas Shipman. ElSeCe
(Epitaph on His Grandfather, An.) SeCL
Epitaph upon the Celebrated Claudy Philips, Musician, Who Died Very Poor, An. Samuel Johnson. *See* Epitaph on Claudy Phillips, a Musician, An.
Epitaph upon the Death of Sir Philip Sidney, Knight, Lord-Governor of Vlissing, An. Richard Barnfield. ReIE
Epitaph upon the Death of Sir William Drury, An. Barnabe Rich. ReIE
Epitaph, An, upon the Death of the Right Reverent Father in God J. Jewel, Doctor of Divinity and Bishop of Sarisbury, Who Deceased the Twenty-second of September, 1571. Nicholas Bourman. ReIE
Epitaph upon the Right Honorable Sir Philip Sidney, An. *At. to* Fulke Greville. *See* Epitaph on Sir Philip Sidney.
Epitaph upon the Right Honorable Sir Philip Sidney, Knight, Lord Governor of Flushing, An. *At. to* Sir Walter Ralegh. ReIE; SiCE; TuPP
(Epitaph on Sir Philip Sidney.) SiPS
Epitaph Written for the Liverpool University Roll of Honour. Lascelles Abercrombie. *See* Epitaph: "These, who desired to live, went out to death."
Epitaphic Sonnets. *Unknown.* CAG
Epitaphium Citharistriae. Victor Plarr. AnEnPo; BMEP; EnLoPo; HBMV; LBBV; LEAP; MBP; ViBoPo
(Stand Not Uttering Sedately.) PoRA
Epitaphium Felis. John Jortin, *tr. fr. Latin by* "Seumas O'Sullivan." PoC
Epitaphs. Gabriello Chiabrera, *tr. fr. Italian by* Wordsworth.
"Destined to war from very infancy," VI. AWP; JAWP; WBP
"Not without heavy grief of heart did he," VIII. AWP; JAWP; WBP
"O flower of all that springs from gentle blood," VII. AWP
"O thou who movest onward with a mind," III. AWP; JAWP; WBP
"Pause, courteous spirit!—Balbi supplicates," IX. AWP
"Perhaps some needful service of the state," II. AWP
"There never breathed a man, who, when his life," IV. AWP; JAWP; WBP
"True is it that Ambrosio Salinero," V. AWP
"Weep not, beloved friends! nor let the air," I. AWP; JAWP; WBP
(Francesco Ceni.) OnPM
Epitaphs. Francis Jeffrey.
"Here lies the body of Richard Hind." OxBoLi
In Christ Church. OxBoLi
In St. Olave's Church. OxBoLi
On Peter Robinson. OxBoLi; WhC
Epitaphs. Lady Margaret Sackville.
"As shining sand-drift." HBMV
"How many generations." MM
"My days were lighter." MM
"My flesh was water." MM
"Myriad roots, The." MM
"Neither of earth." MM
"Why did you die?" MM
Epitaphs; for a Fickle Man. Mark Van Doren. ViBoPo
Epitaphs of the War, 1914–18, *sels.* Kipling.
Batteries Out of Ammunition. PoVP
Beginner, The. FaBoTw; LiA
Bombed in London. PoVP
Bridegroom, The. SoV
Common Form. FaBoTw; LiA; PoVP
Coward, The. FaBoTw; GTBS; LiA; OAEP (2d ed.); PoVP
Dead Statesman, A. LiA; OAEP (2d ed.); PoVP
Destroyers in Collision. PoVP
"Equality of Sacrifice." FaBoTw; OAEP (2d ed.)
Ex-Clerk. PoVP
Grave near Cairo, A. PoVP
Only Son, An. LiA
Refined Man, The. FaBoTw
Salonikan Grave. LiA; OAEP (2d ed.)
Servant, A. PoVP
Son, A. ChMP; PoVP
Wonder, The. PoVP
Epithalamia. Thomas Lovell Beddoes. *See* Bridal Song to Amala.
Epithalamion: "Come now, though Muses are not left to sing." Donald Davidson. TBM
Epithalamion, An: "Haile Bishop Valentine, whose day this is." John Donne. AtBAP
Hail, Bishop Valentine, *sel.* ChTr; EV-2
Epithalamion: "Hark, hearer, hear what I do." Gerard Manley Hopkins. AnEnPo
Epithalamion: "Smile then, children, hand in hand." James Elroy Flecker. POTT
Epithalamion: "So parc has a gate!" Nigel Heseltine. MoWP
Epithalamion: "Wind in the street, and sadness of unknown walkers." Terence Tiller. POTE
Epithalamion: "Ye learned sisters, which have oftentimes." Spenser. AEV; AtBAP, *abr.;* BCEP; BEL; BrBE; ElL; EM-1; EnL; EnLi-1 (1949 ed.); EPP, *much abr.;* EV-1; GEPC; HBV; LEAP; LiA; LiTL; OAEP; OBEV; OBSC; PeBoSo; PIAE; Po; PoEL-1; PoFS; ReEn; ReIE; SeCeV; SiCE; TOP; TyEnPo; ViBoPo; WoL
Sels.
"Ah! when will this long weary day have end." LO
Bride, The. LPS-1
"Hark how the minstrels gin to shrill aloud." WHA
"Now al is done; bring home the bride againe." FiP
Stanzas from Epithalamion ("Now cease, ye damsels, your delights forepast"). CoEV
Epithalamion for Amaryllis. John Farrar. PR
Epithalamion Made at Lincolnes Inne. John Donne. OBS
"Sunbeams in the east are spread, The," *sts.* 1–2. LEAP
Epithalamion Teratos [*or* Teratus]. George Chapman. *Fr.* Hero and Leander: Fifth Sestiad. AtBAP; ElL; EV-1; LoBV
(Wedding of Alcmane and Mya, The.) OBSC
Epithalamium, *sel.* Ben Jonson.
"Up, youths and virgins, up and praise." LEAP
Epithalamium, *sel.* W. J. Turner.
Song: "Can the lover share his soul." OBMV
Epithalamium: "Come, virgin tapers of pure wax." Richard Crashaw. ReEn; ViBoPo, *sts.* 1–6
Epithalamium: "Crept side by side beyond the thresh." Vassar Miller. NePoEA
Epithalamium: "He is here, Urania's son." A. E. Housman. Last Poems, XXIV. MM
Epithalamium: "High in the organ-loft with lilied hair." Sir Edmund Gosse. OBVV
Epithalamium: "I saw two clouds at morning." John Gardiner Calkins Brainard. *See* I Saw Two Clouds at Morning.
Epithalamium: "Let mother earth now deck[e] herself[e] in flowers." Sir Philip Sidney. *Fr.* Arcadia. EV-1; SiPS
Epithalamium: "No, she does not falter." Helene Mullins. PraNu
Epithalamium: "Rejoice,/ Ye woods and fountains." *Unknown.* SeCL
Epithalamium: "Sister, the bride-bed waits." Arthur Symons. FaBoTw
Epithalamium: "So you are married, girl. It makes me sad." Roy McFadden. NeIP
Epithalamium: "This body of my mother." Leo Kennedy. BoCaPo
Epithalamium: "We have found our peace." A. R. D. Fairburn. AnNZ
Epithalamium and Elegy. Witter Bynner. TBM
Epithalamium for Cavorting Ghosts. Dachine Rainer. NePoAm-2
Epithalamium for Mary Stuart and the Dauphin of France, *abr.* George Buchanan, *tr. fr. Latin.* GoTS
Epithalamium in Time of War. Ralph Gustafson. BoCaPo
Epithalamium on the Lady Elizabeth and Count Palatine Being Married on St. Valentine's Day, An. John Donne. *See* Epithalamion, An: "Haile Bishop Valentine."
Epitrepontes, *sel.* Menander, *tr. fr. Greek.*
Charisius Rebukes Himself, *tr. by* Gilbert Highet. OxBG
Guide Within, The, *tr. by* Francis G. Allinson. GrR
Epoch, The. Nikolai Tikhonov, *tr. fr. Russian by* Jack Lindsay. RuPo
Epode. Ben Jonson. SeCV-1
Epodes, *sels.* Horace, *tr. fr. Latin.*
Country Life, II, *tr. by* Dryden. AWP
(Revery of a Business Man.) WoL
"It was night with the shine of the moon amid the smaller stars shining," XV, *tr. by* G. S. Fraser. LaP
"Whither, curs'd rabble, do you rush? Why show," VII, *tr. by* Jack Lindsay. LaP
Epos. Julian Tuwim, *tr. fr. Polish by* Jack Lindsay. LiTW
Eppie Morrie. *Unknown.* ESPB
Epping Forest. John Davidson. *Fr.* November. CP; GTSL
Eppur Si Muove? Robert Hillyer. GoYe
Equal Troth. Dante Gabriel Rossetti. The House of Life, XXXII. BPN; PoVP; ViPo
Equality. James Shirley. *See* Death the Leveller.
"Equality of Sacrifice." Kipling. *Fr.* Epitaphs of the War. FaBoTw; OAEP (2d ed.)
Equanimity. Archilochus, *tr. fr. Greek by* H. Rushton Fairclough. GrR
("Tossed on a sea of troubles, Soul, my Soul," *tr. by* William Hay.) GrPo
Equation, An. Hyam Plutzik. FiMAP
Equilibrists, The. John Crowe Ransom. AmP; AnAmPo;

ChMo; CoBMV; LA; LiTM; LS; MoAB; MOAP; MoPo; MoVE; NePA; OxBA; UnPo (1st ed.)
Equinoctial. Adeline D. T. Whitney. HBV
Equinox, The. Du Bose Heyward. BAP
Equinox, The. Longfellow. *Fr.* Seaweed. EtS
Equipment. Paul Laurence Dunbar. TrPWD
Equipment. Edgar A. Guest. PoToHe (new ed.)
Equity with God. Omar Khayyám, *tr. fr. Persian by* Edward Fitzgerald. *Fr.* The Rubáiyát. OnPM
("Oh Thou, who Man of baser Earth didst make.") SeCeV
'Er looked at me bunnet (I knows 'e aint noo!). Her Allowance! Lillian Gard. VOD
'Er name's Doreen . . . Well, spare me bloomin' days! The Intro. C. J. Dennis. WhC
Erasers. *Unknown.* PoToHe
Erasistratus Forbear, *sel.* George L. Walton.
"Oh Erasistratus forbear." PoP
Erasmus. E. A. Robinson. TwP
Erat Hora. Ezra Pound. CoV; MOAP
Erce, Erce, Erce, Mother of earth. Charm for Unfruitful Land. *Unknown.* AnOE
Erd sould trymbill, the firmament sould schaik, The. Quod Dunbar to Kennedy. William Dunbar. OxBoLi
Ere daybreak Melanippus passed away. Brother and Sister. Callimachus. GrL
Ere five score years have run their tedious rounds. A Prophecy. *At. to* Arthur Lee. PAH
Ere, in the northern gale. Autumn Woods. Bryant. AnNE; PTA-1
Ere last year's moon had left the sky. My Bird. "Fannie Forester." AA; MOAH
Ere long the clouds were gone, the moon was set. Sights and Sounds of the Night [*or* Northern Lights]. Carlos Wilcox. AnAmPo; APW; LA
Ere long they come, where that same wicked wight. Despair [*or* To Be or Not to Be]. Spenser. *Fr.* The Faerie Queene, I. FaBoEn; NBE
Ere Love from barren Chaos drew the skies. Pierre de Ronsard. *Fr.* Amours de Cassandre. PrPoCR
Ere Mor the Peacock flutters, ere the Monkey People cry. The Song of the Little Hunter [*or* Fear]. Kipling. *Fr.* The Second Jungle Book. PtOT; ShBV-1
Ere Murfreesboro's thunders rent the air. The Battle of Murfreesboro. Kinahan Cornwallis. PAH
Ere my heart beats too coldly and faintly. The Truants. Walter de la Mare. ChMo; CMP; InP; MBP; MoBrPo
Ere on my bed my limbs I lay. The Pains of Sleep [*or* A Child's Evening Prayer]. Samuel Taylor Coleridge. BOL; BPN; EmBrPo; EnRP; EPN; ERP; OAEP; OBRV; OTPC (1923 ed.); SeCePo; TrPWD
Ere sin could blight or sorrow fade. Epitaph on an Infant. Samuel Taylor Coleridge. MotAn
Ere Sleep Comes Down to Soothe the Weary Eyes. Paul Laurence Dunbar. BANP; CDC; PoNe
Ere space exists, or earth, or sky. The Lord Is King. *Unknown.* TrJP
Ere the Golden Bowl Is Broken. Anna Hempstead Branch. AnAmPo; AnFE; APA; CoAnAm; LA; MAPA
Ere the long roll of the ages end. Fainne Gael an Lae. Alice Milligan. HBV
Ere the moon begins to rise. Cradle Song [*or* Sleepy Song]. Thomas Bailey Aldrich. BOL; GoTP; MOAH
Ere the morn the East has crimsoned. Lines Suggested by the Fourteenth of February. Charles Stuart Calverley. InMe
Ere the steamer bore him Eastward, Sleary was engaged to marry. The Post That Fitted. Kipling. CenHV; HBV
Ere this, had I abandoned holy house. William Ellery Leonard. *Fr.* Two Lives, Pt. III. LA; MOAP
Ere yellow Autumn from our plains retir'd. The Swallows; an Elegy. Richard Jago. CEP
Ere yet in Vergil I could scan or spell. "Hic Me, Pater Optime, Fessam Deseris." Lucy Catlin Robinson. AA
Ere yet my heart was sweet Love's tomb. Love, Pride, and Forgetfulness. Tennyson. BoFr
Ere yet the bands met Marmion's eye. The Battle. Sir Walter Scott. *Fr.* Marmion, VI. ERP
Ere yet the sun is high. The Iris. Gasetsu. MPB; TiPo
Erect in youthful grace and radiant. By the Sea of Galilee. Katharine Lee Bates. ChIP
Eremites, The. Robert Graves. LiTB
Eremites. Palladas, *tr. fr. Greek.* OxBG
Eremites of Old, The. Pushkin, *tr. fr. Russian by* Babette Deutsch. TrRV
(Prayer, A: "Hermits and blameless women full of grace," *tr. by* Maurice Baring.) BoR
Eretrian Dead, The ("Euboeans we, men of Eretria city"). Plato, *tr. fr. Greek by* T. F. Higham. OxBG
Eretrian Dead, The ("Far from the blue Aegean's boom and swell"). Plato, *tr. fr. Greek by* H. K. St. J. Sanderson. OxBG
(Farewell: "Far from the deep roar of the Aegean main," *tr. by* Charles Whibley.) AWP; WBP
Ere-while of musick, and ethereal mirth. Milton. *Fr.* The Passion. PoD
Eride, *sel.* Trumbull Stickney.
Now in the Palace Gardens, V. AnFE; CoAnAm; LiTA; TwAmPo
Erie, The ("We were forty miles from Albany"), *with music.* *Unknown.* ABF; AS
Erie Canal ("It was a long, long trip on the Erie"). *Unknown.* ABF
Erie Canal, The ("I've got a mule, her name is Sal"). William S. Allen. ABF; AS; IHA; TrAS, *with music*
(Low Bridge, Everybody Down, *longer vers., with music.*) ABF
Erie Canal Ballad, The. *Unknown.* ABF, *composite vers. of popular Erie Canal songs and choruses*
Erie's raging and the gin is going low, The. The Erie Canal Ballad. *Unknown.* ABF
Erik the prince came back from sea. The Slaying of the Witch. George Sterling. MOAP
Erin. Kenelm H. Digby. CAW
Erin. William Drennan. TIP
(Eire.) OnYI
Erinna. Antipater of Sidon, *tr. fr. Greek.* AWP, *tr. by* A. J. Butler; GrR, *tr. by* F. A. Wright; VA, *tr. by* Andrew Lang
(Preface to Erinna's Poems, *tr. by* A. J. Butler.) OxBG
Erinna, songstress of the honeyed lay. Leonidas of Tarentum, *tr. fr. Greek by* the Earl of Cromer. GrPo
Erinna to Her Friend. Erinna, *tr. fr. Greek by* Lord Neaves. OnPM
(Baucis.) AWP, *tr. by* Richard Garnett; OxBG, *tr. by* Sir William Marris
(Epitaph to Baucis, *tr. by* John Addington Symonds.) GrR
("Pillars of death! carved sirens! tearful urn!" *tr. by* C. A. Elton.) GrPo
Erinna's Poems. Asclepiades, *tr. fr. Greek by* Robert Allason Furness. GrR
(Preface to Erinna's Poems.) OxBG
Erl-King, The. Goethe, *tr. fr. German by* Sir Walter Scott. AWP; HOAH; JAWP; MaC; OTPC (1946 ed.); WBP; DaM, *tr. by* Frederic H. Hedge
Erlinton. *Unknown.* ESPB (A *and* B *vers.*); OBB
(Soldier, The, *diff. vers.*) ABS
Ermine or blazonry, he knew them not. Andrew. Thomas William Parsons. AA
Erminia Wanders in the Fields and Dreams of Love. Tasso, *tr. fr. Italian by* Edward Fairfax. *Fr.* Jerusalem Delivered, VII. LiA
Erminie, *sel.* Claxson Bellamy *and* Harry Paulton.
Lullaby: "Dear mother, in dreams I see her." BOL
Ernest Dowson. John Hall Wheelock. HBMV
Ernest Maltravers, *sel.* Sir Edward Bulwer-Lytton.
When Stars Are in the Quiet Skies. VA
(Night and Love.) HBV
Ernest was an elephant, a great big fellow. The Four Friends. A. A. Milne. GoTP; TiPo (1959 ed.)
Eroded beach on the bay, an empty scene. Unnatural, Unusual and Unfair. James Schevill. FiMAP
Ἔρως (Eros). Robert Bridges. ExPo; GTML; LiTB; LO; PoEL-5; RiBV; SeCeV; ViP
Eros. Emerson. AnNE; FaBoBe; HBV; IAP; TCAP
Eros. Coventry Patmore. GTSE
Eros and His Mother. Apollonius Rhodius, *tr. fr. Greek by* George Allen. *Fr.* Argonautica, III. OxBG
Eros and Psyche, *sels.* Lucius Apuleius, *tr. fr. Latin by* Robert Bridges.
"His skin is brilliant with the nimble flood." LO
"She took her then aside, and bade her heed." BrBE
Eros; Deus Catholicus. Euripides, *tr. fr. Greek by* F. W. Pember. *Fr.* Hippolytus. GrR
Eros Does Not Always Smite. "Michael Field." BoFr; LBBV
Eros thou yet behold'st me? Shakespeare. *Fr.* Antony and Cleopatra, IV, xii. PoD
Eros Turannos. E. A. Robinson. AnAmPo; AnFE; AnNE; APA; CoAnAm; CoBA; CoBMV; CrMA; LA; LiTA; LiTM (rev. ed.); MAP; MAPA; MoAB; MoAmPo; MOAP; MoPo; MoVE; NePA; NP; OnAP; OxBA; PoE; PoFS; RiBV; TwAmPo; TwP
Eros under his bluish dark lashes again. Autumn Love. Ibycus. LiTW
Erosion. James Larkin Pearson. NoCaPo
Erosion. E. J. Pratt. CaP; CoBE; OnPM; TwCaPo
Erotica Antiqua, *sel.* L. A. MacKay.
Propertian. PeCV
Erotion. Martial, *tr. fr. Latin by* Kirby Flower Smith. AWP; JAWP; WBP; OnPM, *tr. by* Leigh Hunt
(Epitaph on Erotion, *tr. by* Leigh Hunt.) OBRV
Erotion. Swinburne. EtPaEn; PoEL-5
Erotokritos, *sel.* Vincenzo Kornaros, *tr. fr. Modern Greek by* Rae Dalven.
"Aretousa much desires that the day turn to night," *fr.* III. MoGP

Errand Imperious, The. Edwin Markham. PGD
Erratic soul of some great purpose, doomed. The Comet. Charles Sangster. LPS-3
Erring in Company. Franklin P. Adams. BOHV; TCAP; TOP
Erris Coast, 1943. Hugh Connell. NeIP
Erris Fairy, An. Hal D'Arcy. BOL
Error and Loss. William Morris. BPN
Error Pursued. H. A. Pinkerton. NePoAm
Errors of Ecstasie, *sel.* George Darley.
"Ecstasie, rash production of the thoughts." OnYI
Errors of Observation. Gordon Wharton. PoN
Ersatz. Raymond Souster. BoCaPo (1948 ed.); PeCV
Erstwhile sinner knocked at Heaven's gate, An. The Countersign. Charles J. Quirk. CAW
Erubescent flax curls crisp and dry, The. Smoking Flax. Mary Josephine Benson. CaP
Erudite, solemn/ The pious bird. Rev Owl. A. M. Klein. TrJP
Eruption in Utopia. Genevieve Taggard. TCPD
Erysichthon. Callimachus, *tr. fr. Greek by* T. F. Higham. OxBG
'E's a bit of a vagabond, same as me. Laddie. Dana Burnet. AlBD
Es fällt ein Stern herunter. Heine, *tr. fr. German by* Richard Garnett. AWP; JAWP
Es stehen unbeweglich. Heine, *tr. fr. German by* James Thomson. AWP; JAWP; TrJP; WBP
Esbern Snare. *Unknown, tr. fr. Danish by* E. M. Smith-Dampier. BoDaBa
Escapade. Kenneth Leslie. EtS
Escape, The. Emily Rose Burt. GFA
Escape. Chaucer. *Fr.* Merciles Beaute. LoPS
(Merciles Beaute, III.) CaAE; LEAP; OBEV (1st ed.)
Escape. Emily Dickinson. NeMA
Escape, The. Lee Wilson Dodd. PC
Escape. Euripides. *See* O for the Wings of a Dove.
Escape. Robert Graves. MBP; MoBrPo
Escape. Daniel Whitehead Hicky. JKCP (1955 ed.)
Escape. Lionel Johnson. VLEP
Escape. Leonard Mann. NeLNL
Escape, The. Edwin Muir. WaP
Escape. James Rorty. PC
Escape. Dorothy Brown Thompson. DDA
Escape. *Unknown.* MaRV
Escape, The. Mark Van Doren. MAP; MoAmPo
Escape. Elinor Wylie. AnFE; APA; CoAnAm; GBV (1952 ed.); LiTA; MAP; MoAmPo; MOAP; PFY; TBM; ThWaDe; TwAmPo
Escape and Return. Elizabeth Jennings. NePoEA
Escape at Bedtime. Robert Louis Stevenson. AlDL; BrR; GoTP; HBVY; OTPC; PCH; PoRh; PoVP; RG; TiPo; TreFS; TrGrPo; TSW; TSWC; VLEP
Escape at Moonrise. Josephine Pinckney. LS
Escape from Cyclop, The. Homer, *tr. fr. Greek by* George Chapman. *Fr.* The Odyssey, IX. LiTW
Escape Me?—Never. Robert Browning. *See* Life in a Love.
Escaped the gloom of mortal life, a soul. An Epitaph [*or* Epitaph, Intended for Himself]. James Beattie. BSV; TriL
Escaping from the enemy's hand. The Escape. Edwin Muir. WaP
Eschatology. Morris Bishop. WhC
Escorial, The. Théophile Gautier, *tr. fr. French by* Alan Conder. TrFP
Escorted by two policemen, little doubting. Grief. Salvador Díaz Mirón. AnMP
Escorting Candidates to the Examination Hall. Po Chü-i, *tr. fr. Chinese by* Arthur Waley. TrCh
Eskimelodrama, An; or, The Eskapade of an Eskamaid. *Unknown.* CAG
Eskimo Baby, An. Lucy Diamond. BoTP
Eskimo baby, all dressed up in fur, An. Queer Habits. Corneille McCarn. GFA
Eskimo, explorers state, The. The Immoral Arctic. Morris Bishop. FiBHP; WhC
Eskimo Song: "There is fear in/ Turning the mind away." *Unknown, tr. fr. Cooper Eskimo song by* W. E. Calvert. PeCV
Eskimo String-Figure Chant. *Tr. fr. Eskimo song by* E. Hope Kerr. TwCaPo
Esope, my author, makis mentioun. The Taill of the Uponlandis Mous and the Burges Mous. Robert Henryson. BSV; EV-1
Esparsa. Gil Vicente, *tr. fr. Portuguese by* Seth G. Thornton. LyMA
Especially When the October Wind. Dylan Thomas. ChMP; LiTB; MaPo; MoAB; MoBrPo (1950 ed.); OAEP (2d ed.)
(Poem: "Especially when the October wind.") NeBP
(Poem in October.) MoWP
Esplanade Method, The. August Strindberg, *tr. fr. Swedish by* Charles W. Stork. AnSL
Essay in Defense of the Movies. Walker Gibson. NePoAm
Essay on Criticism, An. Pope. ATP; BEL; CEP; CoBE, Pts. I–II; EiPP; EM-1, *abr.;* EnLi-1; EnLit, Pts. I–II; GEPC; OAEP, *abr.;* OuHeWo, Pts. I–II; PIAE, *much abr.;* PoEL-3; TCEP, *abr.;* TOP, *abr.*
Sels.
Alps of Poetry, The ("Fir'd at first sight with what the muse imparts"), *fr.* Pt. II. BeR
(Heights of Arts, The.) LiA
Art of Writing, The, *fr.* Pt. II. BCEP
("But most by numbers judge a poet's song.") AnFE; EV-3; InP
(Poetical Numbers.) OBEC; SeCePo
"Avoid extreams; and shun the fault of such," *fr.* Pt. II. NBE
"But you who seek to give and merit fame," *fr.* Pt. I. EnL
Homer ("You then whose judgment the right course would steer"), *fr.* Pt. I. TwCrTr
"Horace still charms with graceful negligence," *fr.* Pt. III. PtP
Insects from the Nile ("Some have at first for wits, then poets passed"), *fr.* Pt. I. BeR
Little Learning, A, *fr.* Pt. II. ChTr; CoEV; LiTB; LiTG; OBEC; SeCePo
(Alps on Alps.) FaFP; GTBS-W
("Little learning is a dangerous thing, A.") BCEP; HoPM; PG (1955 ed.); TreF; TrGrPo
"Of all the causes which conspire to blind," *fr.* Pt. II. EnL; FaBoEn; NBE
"Others for language all their care express," *fr.* Pt. II. NBE
Sound and Sense ("True ease in writing comes from art, not chance," 14 *ll.*), *fr.* Pt. II. UnPo
(Craft of Verse, The, 12 *ll.*) BLV; BoLiVe
(Ease in Writing, 12 *ll.*) CBOV
(Sound and the Sense, The: "'Tis not enough . . .," 10 *ll.*) LiA
("True ease in writing comes from art, not chance.") ExPo, 12 *ll.;* TrGrPo, 22 *ll.*
"Those rules of old discover'd, not devis'd," *fr.* Pt. I. PoFS; PreP
"'Tis hard to say, if greater want of skill," *fr.* Pts. I–II. EPP; FaBoEn; FiP, *abr.;* TwP (Pt. I); TyEnPo (Pt. I); WHA
"'Tis with our judgments as our watches," *fr.* Pt. I. ViBoPo
Treatment for Old Jades and Janes, The ("'Tis best sometimes your censure to restrain"), *fr.* Pt. III. BeR
"True wit is Nature to advantage dress'd," *fr.* Pt. II. ShBV-3
Essay on Deity. Elder Olson. NP
Essay on Man, An. Pope. CEP; EiPP; GEPC; PoEL-3, Epistles I–III; TCEP, Epistles I–II
Sels.
"All are but parts of one stupendous whole," *fr.* Epistle I. WGRP
"Awake, my St. John! leave all meaner things," Epistle I. BEL; EnL; EnLi-1; EPP, *abr.;* OAEP; PIAE; PoEL-3; REAL; TCEP; TOP
Behold the Child, *fr.* Epistle II. BeR
"Far as creation's ample range extends," *fr.* Epistles I *and* II. ImOP
(Great Chain of Being, The.) ExPo
"For forms of government let fools contest," 8 *ll., fr.* Epistle III. ViBoPo
(Charity.) OBEC
"For modes of faith let graceless zealots fight," *fr.* Epistle III.
(Faith.) WGRP
"Force first made conquest, and that conquest, law," *fr.* Epistle III. PoFr
Fragments from "Essay on Man." BCEP
"Heav'n [*or* Heaven] from all creatures hides the book of fate," *fr.* Epistle I. EV-3; ViBoPo
(Future, The, *abr.*) BCEP
(Hope Springs Eternal.) CoEV; OBEC
Honest Man, An, 2 *ll., fr.* Epistle IV. TreF
"Honour and shame from no condition rise," *fr.* Epistle IV. PoFr; TrGrPo
(Greatness, *longer sel.*) LPS-3
(Man.) BLV; BoLiVe
(Pedigree, *longer sel.*) BeR
(True Worth.) CBE
(Worth Makes the Man.) CBOV; MaRV; PoeMoYo
"Hope humbly then; with trembling pinions soar," *fr.* Epistle I. TrGrPo
"Hope springs eternal in the human breast," *fr.* Epistle I.
(Hope.) MaRV, 2 *ll.;* TreF, 4 *ll.*
(Pleasure of Hope, The, 4 *ll.*) ACP
"Know, Nature's children all divide her care," *fr.* Epistle III. BeR
"Know then this truth, enough for man to know," *fr.* Epistle IV. EV-3

"Know then thyself, presume not God to scan," Epistle II. AnFE, *fr.* II *and* IV; EnLi-1 (1949 ed.); EnLit; EV-3; GoTL; LiTB; LiTG, *fr.* II *and* IV; MaPo; MaRV, 18 *ll.*; NBE, *abr.*; OBEC, 18 *ll.*; PG (1955 ed), 18 *ll.*; PoEL-3; SeCePo; TCEP; TOP, *abr.*; TrGrPo, 18 *ll.*; TWP; ViBoPo, 18 *ll.*
(Know Thyself, 18 *ll.*) TwCrTr
(Lines from "An Essay on Man," 18 *ll.*) GoBC
(Man, 18 *ll.*) BLV; BoLiVe; CBE, *longer sel., abr.*
(Paragon of Animals, The, 18 *ll.*) ACP
(Proper Study of Man, The, 18 *ll.*) TreFS
(Proper Study of Mankind, The, 30 *ll.*) FiP
(Riddle of the World, 18 *ll.*) GTBS-W
Life's Poor Play, *fr.* Epistle II. OBEC; SeCePo
Literary Poet to His Patron, A, *fr.* Epistle IV. CBE
(Henry St. John, Viscount Bolingbroke.) OBEC
(Poet's Friend, The.) LPS-3
Lo, the Poor Indian, *fr.* Epistle I. TreFS
Nature's Chain, *fr.* Epistle III. BCEP; LPS-2
Newton and Himself, *fr.* Epistle II. BeR
"Oh Happiness! our being's end and aim," Epistle IV. ATP; LEAP, 26 *ll.*
(Happiness, 34 *ll.*) LPS-3
Reason and Instinct, *fr.* Epistle III. LPS-3
Scale of Being, The, *fr.* Epistle I. BeR
Soul's Calm Sunshine, The, *fr.* Epistle IV. BeR
Unity of Nature, The, *abr., fr.* Epistle I. CBOV
Vice, 4 *ll., fr.* Epistle II. BLP
"Whate'er the passion—knowledge, fame, or pelf," *fr.* Epistle II. CBE; TrGrPo
(Human Folly.) FiP
(Man.) BLV; BoLiVe
Whatever Is, Is Right, *fr.* Epistle I. OBEC
"What's Fame? a fancied life in other's breath," *fr.* Epistle IV. ViBoPo
(Fame, *shorter sel.*) LPS-3
"Who sees with equal eye, as God of all," *fr.* Epistle I. FaBoEn
Essay on Man. *Unknown.* PoToHe (new ed.)
Essay on Memory. Robert D. Fitzgerald. BoAV; MoAuPo
Essay on Solitude. Abraham Cowley. *See* Of Solitude.
Essay on the Fine Arts, *sel.* John Trumbull.
Future of American Literature, The. AmPP (3d ed.)
Essay on the Fleet Riding in the Downes, An. "J. D." CoMu
Essay on the Genius of Pope, An, *sel.* Charles Lloyd.
"'Tis not so much, these men more forms survey." OBRV
Essay on Translated Verse, An, *sels.* Earl of Roscommon.
Advice. BeR
More Advice. BeR
Essence. Samuel Greenberg. MoPo; NePA
Essence of Existence, The. Chorus. Jack Kerouac. *Fr.* Mexico City Blues. NeAP
Essence of Opera, The. *Unknown, tr. fr. French by* Leigh Hunt. OnPM
Essentials. Samuel Greenberg. LiTA
Essex. Arthur Shearly Cripps. PoeT
Essex Junction. E. J. Phelps. DDA
Essex Regiment March. George Edward Woodberry. PAH
Established. Rose O'Neill. *See* I Made a House of Houselessness.
Estate, The, *sel.* Charles Brasch.
Waking by Night. AnNZ
Estella, Estella, they're cooking up Paella. Song in Praise of Paella. C. W. V. Wordsworth. FiBHP
Estevan, Saskatchewan. E. W. Mandel. PeCV
Esther. Wilfrid Scawen Blunt. *See* Esther; a Young Man's Tragedy.
Esther. Fray Angelico Chavez. GoBC
Esther; a Young Man's Tragedy, *sels.* Wilfrid Scawen Blunt.
"He who has once been happy is for aye," XL [L]. OBMV; TrGrPo; ViBoPo
(With Esther.) OBEV; OBVV
"Little honey! Ay, a little sweet, A," III. LEAP
"When I hear laughter from a tavern door," XLVI [LI]. MoBrPo (1942 ed.); OBMV; TrGrPo; ViBoPo
(From "Esther.") MBP
(With Esther.) OBEV; OBVV
Esther went early home that night. Young Girl. Einar Solstad. AnNoLy
Esthete in Harlem. Langston Hughes. BANP
Esthetic of Imitation, An. Donald Finkel. NePoEA
Esthétique du Mal. Wallace Stevens. LiTM (rev. ed.)
How Red the Rose That Is the Soldier's Wound, *sel.* FaBoMo; WaP
Esthonian Bridal Song. Johann Gottfried von Herder, *tr. fr. German by* W. Taylor. AWP; JAWP; WBP
Estranged. Walter de la Mare. FaBoEn
Estrangement. Wade Oliver. PoP
Estrangement. John Peter. BoSA
Estrangement. Sir William Watson. LBBV; MBP; MoBrPo (1942 ed.); PoeT
("So, without overt breach, we fall apart.") ES
Estrella de Sevilla, La, *sel.* Lope de Vega Carpio, *tr. fr. Spanish by* Henry Thomas.
Estrella Learns that Her Lover Has Killed Her Brother. LiA
Estuary, The. Ruth Pitter. MoVE
Estuary, The. Allen Upward. *Fr.* Scented Leaves from a Chinese Jar. NP
Estunt the Griff. Kipling. PA
Esyllt. Glyn Jones. MoWP
Et Cetera. Dee Walker. GoYe
Et Incarnatus, *in mod. Eng. Unknown.* TMEV
(Man, Be Joyful and Mirth Thou Make.) AnEC
(Three Christmas Carols, 2.) ACP
Et Mori Lucrum. John Lancaster Spalding. *Fr.* God and the Soul. AA
Et Sa Pauvre Chair. Alec Brock Stevenson. HBMV
Et Sunt Commercia Coeli. Herbert P. Horne. GTML
Etched in Frost. James Stephens. ChMo; CMP
Etchers of Eld. Donald Wing Hathaway. MuM
Etching, An. Sister Mary Imelda. CAW
Etching. Dennis Murphy. BAP
Etching at Dusk. Frederic Prokosch. BLA
Eteocles and Polynices. Euripides, *tr. fr. Greek by* George Allen. *Fr.* Phoenician Maidens. OxBG
Eteocles was I, whom hope of gain. Sea Trade. Isidorus. OxBG
Eternal. Agnes Foley Macdonald. CaP
Eternal, The. Esaias Tegnér, *tr. fr. Swedish by* Charles W. Stork. AnSL; LiTW
Eternal, The. Isaac Watts. GrCo-1
Eternal beauty smiled on me, The. The Perilous Light. Eva Gore-Booth. NLK
Eternal Christmas. Elizabeth Stuart Phelps Ward. ChIP; MaRV; PGD
Eternal Contour. Florida Watts Smyth. GoYe
Eternal Father, by whose might. Hymn for Those in the Air. Duncan Campbell Scott. NeTW; TwCV
Eternal Father, Strong to Save. William Whiting. MaRV; OIF; PraP; TreFS
Eternal Father, who hast given. God Bless Our Home. Robert Freeman. MaRV; PraP
Eternal Female groaned, The! It was heard over all the Earth. A Song of Liberty. Blake. EiPP; EnLi-2; EnRP
Eternal Feminine, The. Shakespeare. Antony and Cleopatra, II, v. LiA
Eternal Founder of the sky. Hymn. James J. Donohue. JKCP (1955 ed.)
Eternal God is thy dwelling place, The. The Everlasting Arms. Deuteronomy, Bible, *O.T.* GrCo-1
Eternal God! Maker of all. The Book. Henry Vaughan. EnL; EPS; EV-2; SeCV-1
Eternal God! Oh! Beatific Vision! *Unknown. Fr.* Everyman. CAW
Eternal God! O Thou that only art. Francis Quarles. *Fr.* Like to the Arctic Needle. MaRV
Eternal God omnipotent! The One. Invocation. Caelius Sedulius. *Fr.* Carmen Paschale [*or* Easter Song]. OnYI
Eternal God, our life is but. A Prayer. "Yehoash." TrJP
Eternal God. Whose Power Upholds. Henry Hallam Tweedy. MaRV
(Prayer: "Eternal God, whose power upholds.") PraP
Eternal God Whose Searching Eye Doth Scan. Edwin McNeill Poteat. MaRV; TrPWD
Eternal Good ("Eternal Good which overlies"). Whittier. *Fr.* Eventide. OQP; QP-2
Eternal Goodness, The ("O friends! with whom my feet have trod"). Whittier. AA; AmPP (3d ed.); AnAmPo; AnFE; AnNE; APA; APW; BLP; CoAnAm; CoBA; CoV; GrCo-1, *abr.*; IAP; LA; LBAP; LEAP; MaRV; OBAV; OHFP; PTA-1; TCAP; WGRP
Sels.
"And Thou, O Lord! by whom are seen." TrPWD
"I bow my forehead to the dust." OQP; QP-2
"I know not what the future hath." BLRP, *abr.*; OQP; QP-1; TreF
"I walk with bare, hushed feet the ground." BAP
Eternal hatred I have sworn against. Theseus and Hippolyta. Walter Savage Landor. BPN
Eternal Hope. *Unknown.* MaRV
Eternal Image, The. Ruth Pitter. MoBrPo
Eternal Jew, The. Jacob Cohen, *tr. fr. Hebrew by* I. M. Lask. TrJP
Eternal Justice, The. Anne Reeve Aldrich. AA
Eternal Justice made me seer, The. The Prophet. Mikhail Lermontov. BoR
Eternal Kinship, The. Maurice E. Peloubet. GoYe
Eternal Light! Thomas Binney. MaRV; WGRP
Eternal Lord! Eased of a Cumbrous Load. Michelangelo, *tr. fr. Italian by* Wordsworth. TrPWD
Eternal Masculine. William Rose Benét. AWP; InPo; MAP; MoAmPo; MOAP
Eternal Moment. "Katherine Hale." CaP; OCL

Eternal [*or* Eternall] Mover, whose diffusèd glory. Hymn Made When He Was an Ambassador at Venice [*or* "D. O. M."]. Sir Henry Wotton. EV-2; OxBoCh; TrPWD
Eternal people of the lower world. Thomas Lovell Beddoes. *Fr.* The Bride's Tragedy. NBE
Eternal Poem, An. Samuel Taylor Coleridge. BOHV
Eternal Power, of earth and air! The Doubter's Prayer. Anne Brontë. MaRV; TrPWD; WGRP
Eternal Quest, The. Job, XI: 7-8; Bible, *O.T.* (*Moulton, Modern Reader's Bible*). MaRV
(Job's Comforters.) WGRP
Eternal Question, The. D. B. Van Buren. CIV
Eternal Reward, Eternal Pain. Sir Thomas More. CoBE
Eternal Road, The, *sel.* Franz Werfel, *tr. fr. German by* Ludwig Lewisohn.
Ye Sorrowers. TrJP
Eternal Ruler of the ceaseless round. Hymn [*or* Divinity School Graduation Hymn]. John White Chadwick. GrCo-2; TrPWD
Eternal Sabbath. Isaac Leibush Peretz, *tr. fr. Yiddish by* Joseph Leftwich. TrJP
Eternal Search, The. Sir William Watson. PoVP
Eternal Self, The. *Unknown, tr. fr. Sanskrit by* Charles Johnston. *Fr.* The Bhagavad-Gita. WoL
Eternal Silence, The. Erinna, *tr. fr. Greek by* F. L. Lucas. GrPE
Eternal Spirit, Evermore Creating. Henry B. Robins. MaRV
Eternal Spirit of the chainless Mind! Sonnet on Chillon [*or* On the Castle of Chillon *or* Chillon]. Byron. The Prisoner of Chillon, *introd. sonnet.* AnEnPo; ATP; BCEP; BEL; BeLS; BLP; BoLiVe; BPN; EM-2; EmBrPo; EnLi-2; EnLit; EnRP; EPN; EPP; ExPo; FiP; GEPC; GTBS; GTBS-D; GTBS-W; GTSE; GTSL; HBV; HiLiEn; InP; LEAP; LiTB; LoBV; LPS-2; MaRV; MCCG; OAEP; OBRV; PFE; PoFr; PoFS; PYM; REAL; SeCeV; TCEP; TOP; TreFS; TrGrPo
Eternal Spirit, you/ Whose will maintains the world. A Prayer for My Son. Yvor Winters. CrMA; TrPWD
Eternal Spring, The. Milton. GN
Eternal Summer. Shakespeare. *See* Sonnets, XVIII.
Eternal Time, that wastest without waste. To Time. "A. W." ElL; TuPP
Eternal [*or* Eternall] Truth, almighty, infinite. Caelica, XCVII [XCVIII]. Fulke Greville. OBS; OxBoCh; SiCE
Eternal Values. Grace Noll Crowell. *See* Let Us Keep Christmas.
Eternal virgin, goddess true. To Astraea. Sir John Davies. *Fr.* Hymns of Astraea. SiCE
Eternal Way, The. Richard Le Gallienne. InP
Eternal Word, The. Longfellow. ChIP
Eternal word proceeding from. Verbum Supernum. *At. to* St. Ambrose. CAW
Eternal Young, The. Edgar A. Guest. OnHT
Eternall and all-working God, which wast. Michael Drayton. *Fr.* Noah's Floud. PoEL-2
Eternall Mover. Henry Wotton. *See* Hymn Made When He Was an Ambassador at Venice.
Eternity ("He who bends [*or* binds] to himself a joy"). Blake. AnFE; AWP; BLV; InPo; LoBV; TrGrPo
(He Who Bends to Himself.) ShBV-4
("He who binds to himself a joy.") EG; LO
(Liberty.) BoLiVe
(Unquestioning.) OQP; QP-2
Eternity. Emily Dickinson. AA; LEAP; TCAP
Eternity. Robert Herrick. SeCL; TriL; WHA
Eternity. Arthur Rimbaud, *tr. fr. French by* Francis Golffing. AnFP
Eternity. Arthur M. Sampley. *Fr.* Fragments of Eternity. MuM
Eternity. Henry Vaughan. *See* World, The.
Eternity and the Tooth. Christopher Morley. QS
Eternity encountered on the stair. Chez Madame. Sam Harrison. NeIP
Eternity is throned upon thy spires. Ode Written for the Completion and Opening of the New Buildings, Marischal College, Aberdeen. Ronald Campbell Macfie. EBSV
Eternity of Love Protested. Thomas Carew. ATP; MeLP; OBS
("How ill doth he deserve a lover's name.") EG
(Song: Eternity of Love Protested.) SeEP
Eternity of Nature. John Clare. MeRV
Eternity, when I think thee. Quoniam Ego in Flagella Paratus Sum. William Habington. ACP
Ethelstan, *sel.* George Darley.
O'er the Wild Gannet's Bath. ChTr; PoEL-4
Ethereal minstrel! pilgrim of the sky! To a [*or* the] Skylark. Wordsworth. BEL; BLA; BLV; BoLiVe; BPN; EM-2; EmBrPo; EnLi-2; EnLit; EnRP; EPN; EPP; ERP; EV-3; FaFP; GEPC; GTBS; GTBS-D; GTBS-W; GTSE; GTSL; HBV; HBVY; LPS-2; OAEP; PIAE; PIR; REAL; TCEP; TrGrPo
Etherealizing. Robert Frost. CoV
Ethics put it well, The. The Magnanimous. Ellen de Young Kay. NePoEA
Ethinthus, Queen of Waters. Blake. *Fr.* Europe. ChTr
Ethiopia Saluting the Colours [*or* Colors]. Walt Whitman. AmP; BAV; GTBS-D; IAP; PAH; PoNe; TCAP
Ethnic Anthem, The ("Ethnasia will last a thousand years"). Anthony Delius. The Great Divide. BoSA
Ethnogenesis; Written during the Meeting of the First Southern Congress, at Montgomery, February, 1861. Henry Timrod. AmPP (4th ed.); OxBA; SPP
Etiquette. W. S. Gilbert. BOHV; CenHV; EnLi-2; FaBoCh; FiBHP; MaC
Etiquette. Arthur Guiterman. PFE
'Ετώσιον ἄχθος ἀρούρης. Robert Bridges. FaBoTw
Etruscan Ring, An. John William Mackail. VA
Etruscan Tombs. Agnes Mary Frances Robinson. WHA
Etruscan Warrior's Head. Helen Rowe Henze. GoYe
Etsi Omnes, Ego Non. Ernest Myers. VA
Ettrick Banks. *Unknown.* EBSV
Ettrick [*or* Etrick] Forest is a fair foreste. The Outlaw Murray. *Unknown.* ESPB; OBB
Etude. Carlos Pellicer, *tr. fr. Spanish by* H. R. Hays. AnCL
Etude Géographique. Stoddard King. IHA; WhC
Etude Réaliste. Swinburne. BMEP; BPN; EPP; GN; HBV; OuHeWo; PoVP; VA
Sels.
Baby's Eyes, A, III. TSW
Baby's Feet, A, I. FaPON; InP; TSW; TSWC
Euboeans we, men of Eretria city. The Eretrian Dead. Plato. OxBG
Eucharist. E. Merrill Root. ChIP; OQP; QP-2
Euchenor Chorus. Arthur Upson. *Fr.* The City. LBMV
Euclid. Vachel Lindsay. ImOP; NAMP; TwAmPo; YaD
(Four Moon Poems.) TSW; TSWC
(Poems about the Moon.) MAPA
Euclid Alone Has Looked on Beauty Bare. Edna St. Vincent Millay. AmPP; ATP; ChMo; CMP; HBMV; ImOP; InP; InPo; LiTG; MAP; MoAB; MoAmPo; MOAP; MoVE; PFE; PreP; ReaPo; TBM
(Euclid.) BAP
(Euclid Alone.) CBOV; FaFP
(Sonnet: "Euclid alone has looked on beauty bare.") AWP; JAWP; NP; TCPD; WBP
(Two Sonnets.) CP
Euclid devised the trap. The Sextant. A. M. Sullivan. GoBC
Eugene Onegin, *sels.* Pushkin, *tr. fr. Russian.*
Girls' Song, *fr.* III, *tr. by* Oliver Elton. BoR
Tatyana's Letter, *fr.* III, *tr. by* Oliver Elton. BoR
(Tatyana's Letter to Onegin, *tr. by* Babette Deutsch.) TrRV
Eugenia, *sel.* George Chapman.
Presage of Storme. FaBoEn
Eugenia, young and fair and sweet. Old Tityrus to Eugenia. Charles Cotton. ViBoPo
Eugenics. Theognis, *tr. fr. Greek.* GrL, *tr. by* T. F. Higham; GrPE, *tr. by* F. L. Lucas; OxBG, *tr. by* T. F. Higham
(Advice to Kyrnos, *tr. by* T. F. Higham.) LiTW
Eugenio Pacelli. Francis Neilson. GoYe
Eugenius, thy son, who guards the Rock. Dedication. Pope Eugenius III. ISi
Eulalie; a Song. Poe. LaNeLa; MOAP
Eulogistic Snatches. *Unknown, tr. fr. Old Irish by* Kuno Meyer. SiB
Eulogium on Rum. Joseph Smith. LHV
Eulogy for Hasdai ibn Shaprut. *Unknown, tr. fr. Hebrew by* Israel Abrahams. TrJP
Eulogy of My House. Siegfried Sassoon. MoPW
Eumaeus Plays Host to His Master. Homer, *pr. tr. fr. Greek by* Samuel Butler. *Fr.* The Odyssey, XIV. GrR
Eumaeus the Swineherd. Homer, *pr. tr. fr. Greek by* Samuel Butler. *Fr.* The Odyssey, XIV *and* XV. OxBG
Eumaeus Tells the Story of His Life, *fr.* XV, *pr. tr. by* Samuel Butler. GrR
(Tale of Eumaeus, The, *tr. by* F. L. Lucas.) GrPE
Eumares. Asclepiades, *tr. fr. Greek by* Richard Garnett. AWP; JAWP; WBP
Eumenides, *sels.* Aeschylus, *tr. fr. Greek.*
Apollo Confounds the Furies, *tr. by* Gilbert Murray. GrR
Areiopagus, The; a Higher Justice Come to Dwell Among Men, *tr. by* Lewis Campbell. GrR
Athena's Faith, *tr. by* E. H. Plumptre. LiA
Chorus of the Furies ("Look, sisters, look!"), *tr. by* John Stuart Blackie. WoL
Eumenides, The ("'Pallas' home contenteth me"), *tr. by* G. M. Cookson. OxBG
Furies' Prayer, The, *tr. by* G. M. Cookson. OxBG
(Chorus of the Furies, The: "Weave the weird dance," *longer sel., tr. by* E. D. A. Morshead.) LiA
Golden Mean, The, *tr. by* Gilbert Murray. GrR
"Me, me suffer this!" *tr. by* J. F. Davies. GrPo
"O ye youngster gods!" *tr. by* J. F. Davies. GrPo
Transformation of the Furies, The, *tr. by* G. M. Cookson. GrR
Eunica laughed out at me when sweetly I would have kissed

her. The Neatherd's Lament. Theocritus. *Fr.* Idylls. GrL
Eunice in the Evening. Gwendolyn Brooks. TiPo (1959 ed.)
Eureka! Alfred Denis Godley. CenHV
"Euripidean" Chorus, A. Aristophanes, *tr. fr. Greek by* T. F. Higham. *Fr.* The Frogs. OxBG
Euripides. Alexander Aetolus, *tr. fr. Greek by* C. M. Bowra. OxBG
Euripides. Aristophanes, *tr. fr. Greek by* Benjamin Bickley Rogers. *Fr.* The Thesmophoriazusae. GrR; OxBG
Euripides. *At. to* Thucydides, *tr. fr. Greek by* Walter Leaf. OxBG
(Epitaph on Euripides.) GrR
Euripides Alexopoulos. Edgar Lee Masters. *Fr.* The New Spoon River. ChMo; CMP
Euroclydon. Abbie Huston Evans. NePoAm
Europa. Stephen Henry Thayer. AA
Europa. Terence Tiller. PoN
Europa and the Bull. Moschus, *tr. fr. Greek.* GrR, *tr. by* Henry Harmon Chamberlin; OxBG, *tr. by* George Allen
Europe, *sel.* Blake.
Ethinthus, Queen of Waters. ChTr
Europe, *sels.* Louis Dudek. PeCV
"Ignorant present has scribbled over the past, The."
"Sea retains such images, The."
Europe. Walt Whitman. IAP
Eurydice. Margaret Allonby. BoSA
Eurydice. Francis William Bourdillon. HBV; TVSH; VA
Eurydice to Orpheus. Robert Browning. EPN; TriL
Eurymachus's Fancy. Robert Greene. *Fr.* Francesco's Fortunes. OBSC
Eurystheus, trembling, called me to the throne. Heracles. Yvor Winters. TwAmPo
Eutaw Springs. Philip Freneau. *See* To the Memory of the Brave Americans.
Euterpe; a Symmetric. David McCord. *Fr.* New Chitons for Old Gods. UnS
Euthymiae Raptus; or, The Teares of Peace, *sels.* George Chapman.
"And, now gives time, her states description." PoEL-2
"But this is learning; to have skill to throwe." BrBE
(Learning.) SeCePo
Herculean Silence. EV-1
"Thus, by the way, to human loves interring." LoBV
Eutopia. Francis Turner Palgrave. OBVV; TOP
Eutychides. E. A. Robinson, *after* Lucilius. UnS
(Variations of Greek Themes, IV.) MOAP
Eutychides is dead, and what is worse. A Dead Song-Writer. Lucilius. OxBG; WoL
Eutychides, who wrote the songs. Eutychides. E. A. Robinson, *after* Lucilius. Variations of Greek Themes, IV. MOAP; UnS
Eutychus paints: and twenty sons he's got. The Portraitist. Lucilius. GrPE
Eva. Rainer Maria Rilke, *tr. fr. German by* Herman Salinger. TwGV
Evacuation of New York by the British. *Unknown.* PAH
Evadne. Hilda Doolittle ("H. D."). AV; LoPS; MAPA; MOAP
Evadne. Euripides, *tr. fr. Greek by* Arthur S. Way. *Fr.* Suppliants. GrR
Evadne and Her Son. Pindar, *tr. fr. Greek by* C. J. Billson. *Fr.* Olympian Odes, VI. OxBG
(Evadne, *br. sel.*) GrR
Evalina. *Unknown.* ABS
Evaluation. Elinor Lennen. OQP; QP-2
Evanescence. Frederic William Henry Myers. *See* I Saw, I Saw the Lovely Child.
Evanescence. Hugo von Hofmannsthal, *tr. fr. German by* Herman Salinger. AnGP
Evanescence. Harriet Prescott Spofford. AA; PR
Evangelical vicar in want. Limerick. Ronald Arbuthnott Knox. CenHV; LiBL
Evangeline. Longfellow. AnNE; BeLS
(Evangeline Trail, *ad. and abr. by* Otsie Vernona Betts.) HiLiAm
Sels.
Church Scene, The, *fr.* Pt. I. TreF
Embarkation, The, *fr.* Pt. I. PAH
Evangeline in Acadie ("Somewhat apart from the village"), *fr.* Pt. I. AA
Finding of Gabriel, The, *Fr.* Pt. II. AA
"In the Acadian land, on the shores of the Basin of Minas," *fr.* Pt. I. CoBA; IAP
"It was the month of May. Far down the Beautiful River," *fr.* Pt. II. BAV; IAP
Lakes of the Atchafalaya, The, *fr.* Pt. II. PoEL-5
Moonlight on the Prairie, *fr.* Pt. II. LPS-2
On the Atchafalaya, *abr., fr.* Pt. II. AA
"Pleasantly rose next morn the sun on the village of Grand-Pré," *fr.* Pt. I. IAP
"She was a woman now," Pt. I, *last* 5 *ll.* MotAn
"Still stands the forest primeval; but far away from its shadow," Conclusion. IAP
"Talk not of wasted affection! affection never was wasted," *fr.* Pt. II. PoToHe (new ed.)
"They were approaching the region where reigns perpetual summer," *fr.* Pt. II. FaBoEn
"This is the forest primeval," Prologue. AmPP (3d ed.), *with* Pt. I; CoBA; IAP; InP; LEAP; OBAV, *with sel. fr.* Pt. I; PIAE, *abr.;* TCAP, *with* Pt. I; TreF
(In the Forest.) PCD
(Primeval Forest, *abr.*) LPS-2; WBLP
(Prologue to "Evangeline.") CaAE
Evangeline. Norma E. Smith. CaP
Evangelist, The. Donald Davie. NePoEA
Evangelize! Henry Croker. BLRP
Evanthe's Invitation. Thomas Godfrey. *Fr.* The Prince of Parthia. NoCaPo
Evarra and His Gods. Kipling. MBP; MoBrPo
Eva's Lament, *sel. Unknown.*
"Alas! that ever [*or* evyr] that speche was spoken [*or* spokyn]." AtBAP; EnLoPo
Evasion. Blanaid Salkeld. NeIP
Eve. Manuel María Flores, *tr. fr. Spanish by* Samuel Beckett. AnMP
Eve. Oliver Herford. HBMV; YaD
Eve. Ralph Hodgson. AnEnPo; AnFE; AV; BLV; BMEP; BoLiVe; CBOV; CH; ChMo; CMP; EnLi-2 (1949 ed.); EPN; EPP; FaBoTw; GBV (1952 ed.); GTBS-D; HBV; HoPM; InP; LBBV; LiTB; LiTM; MBP; MoAB; MoBrPo; NeMA; NP; OtMeF; PoeMoYo; SeCeV; TCPD; TrGrPo
Eve, *sel.* Charles Péguy, *tr. fr. French by* Pansy Packenham.
"Happy are they who die for a temporal land." MiFP
(Happy Are Those Who Have Died, *shorter sel., tr. by* Jessie Degen *and* Richard Eberhart.) WaaP
Eve. Milton. *Fr* Paradise Lost, IX. OBS
Eve. Christina Rossetti. CH; NBE; OxBoCh; PoEL-5; SeCeV
Eve. Robert L. Wolf. HBMV
Eve and the Serpent. Milton. *Fr.* Paradise Lost, IX. BLV
(Satan Beholds Eve.) PoFS
Eve, as once I came upon her. Paul Valéry. *Fr.* The Serpent. MiFP
Eve of Agincourt, The. Shakespeare. *See* Now Entertain Conjecture of a Time.
Eve of Ascension Day, The. Derenik Demirjian, *tr. fr. Armenian by* Zabelle C. Boyajian. ArmLP
Eve of Bannockburn, The. John Barbour. *Fr.* The Bruce, XII. EBSV
Eve of Bunker Hill, The. Clinton Scollard. MC; PAH
(On the Eve of Bunker Hill.) DD; PEDC; PoRL
Eve of Crécy, The. William Morris. BPN; EmBrPo; EnLi-2 (1939 ed.); OBVV; POTT; PoVP; TVSH; ViPo; ViPP; VLEP
Eve of Election, *sel.* Whittier.
Indian Summer. PCH; PEOR
Eve of Revolution. Elliott Coleman. NoCaPo (1941 ed.)
Eve of Revolution, The, *sel.* Swinburne.
"O soul, O God, O glory of liberty." PoFr
Eve of St. Agnes, The. Keats. AEV; AtBAP; ATP; BCEP; BEL; BeLS; BLV; BoLiVe; BPN; CBOV; ChER; CoBE; EmBrPo; EnL; EnLi-2; EnLit; EnLP; EnRP; EPN; EPP; ERP; EV-4; ExPo; FiP, *abr;* GEPC; GoTL; HiLiEn; HoPM; LEAP; LiA; LiTL; LPS-1; MyFE; OAEP; OBRV; OnSP; PIAE; PIR; PoE; PoEL-4; PreP; REAL; ReaPo; RiBV; SeCeV; ShBV-4; TCEP; TOP; TreF; TrGrPo; TwCrTr; TwHP; TwP; TyEnPo; UnPo (1st ed.); WHA
Sels.
"Casement high and triple-arched there was, A," 2 *sts.* PC
"Out went the taper as she hurried in." ViBoPo
"Stol'n to this paradise, and so entranced." LO
Eve of Saint John, The. Sir Walter Scott. BPN; DaM; EmBrPo; EnRP; EPN; EV-4; PoEL-4
Eve of St. Mark, The. Keats. BPN; CH; EM-2; EmBrPo; EnRP; ERP; GEPC; NBE; OBRV
Eve of the Festival, The. Stefan George, *tr. fr. German by* Kenneth Gee. AnGP
Eve of [the Battle of] Waterloo, The. Byron. *See* Waterloo ("There was a sound . . .").
Eve Penitent. Milton. *Fr.* Paradise Lost, X. OBS
Eve, smiling, pluck'd the apple, then. The Apple. Lady Margaret Sackville. OBVV
Eve-Song. Mary Gilmore. MoAuPo
Eve to Adam ("With sorrow and heart's distress"). Milton. *Fr.* Paradise Lost, XII. LPS-1
Eve to Adam ("With thee conversing, I forget all time"). Milton. *Fr.* Paradise Lost, IV. CBE; FaBoEn; TreFS; TrGrPo
(Eve Speaks to Adam.) ChTr
Eve, with her basket, was. Eve. Ralph Hodgson. AnEnPo; AnFE; AV; BLV; BMEP; BoLiVe; CBOV; CH; ChMo; CMP; EnLi-2 (1949 ed.); EPN; EPP; FaBoTw; GBV (1952 ed.); GTBS-D; HBV; HoPM; InP; LBBV; LiTB; LiTM; MBP; MoAB; MoBrPo; NeMA; NP; OtMeF; PoeMoYo; SeCeV; TCPD; TrGrPo

Evelyn. Rossiter Johnson. AA
Evelyn Hope. Robert Browning. AEV; BLV; BMEP; BoLiVe; BPN; CaAE; EmBrPo; EPP; GEPC; HBV; LEAP; LPS-1; MaPo; OuHeWo; PIR; PoVP; PYM; TCEP; TrGrPo; VA; ViPo; VLEP
Evelyn Ray. Amy Lowell. MAP; MoAmPo; MOAP
Even a dirge, can Phoibus suit. Euripides. *Fr.* Hercules. GrPo
Even along the railway platform it was spring. We'll All Feel Gay. Winfield Townley Scott. MiAP
Even as a child, of sorrow that we give. Pride of Youth. Dante Gabriel Rossetti. The House of Life, XXIV. BPN; FaBoEn; PoVP; ViPo; ViPP
Even as a child whose eager fingers snatch. Sonnet of a Little Girl. Ernest Dowson. CaAE
Even as a nurse, whose child's imperfect pace. Divine Care. Francis Quarles. MaRV
Even as a young man/ I was out of tune with ordinary pleasures. Once More Fields and Gardens. Tao Yuan-ming. AWP
Even as gently from the slime we drew him. Antinous. Quentin Stevenson. POTE (1959 ed.)
Even as her fallen sons were leaving life. Epilogue to Fratricidal Folly. Euripides. *Fr.* Phoenician Maidens. GrR
Even as love grows more, I write the less. Sonnets, XVI. Robert Hillyer. HBMV
Even as my hand my pen on paper lays. To His Lady, Who Had Vowed Virginity. Walter Davison. OBSC
Even as tender parents lovingly. The Child in the Street. John James Piatt. AA
Even as the Bird. E. Merrill Root. ChIP
Even as the day when it is yet at dawning. Canzone; Of His Love. Prinzivalle Doria. AWP
Even as the moon grows queenlier in mid-space. Gracious Moonlight. Dante Gabriel Rossetti. The House of Life, XX. PoVP; ViPo
Even as the needle, that directs the hour. Dependence on God. Francis Quarles. MaRV
Even as the Others Mock. Dante, *tr. fr. Italian by* Dante Gabriel Rossetti. La Vita Nuova, VII. LiTW
("Even as the others mock, thou mockest me.") AWP
Even as the seed of the marigold. The Marigold. Allen Upward. *Fr.* Scented Leaves from a Chinese Jar. NP
Even as the shadows of the statues lengthen. Mrs. Southern's Enemy. Sir Osbert Sitwell. ViBoPo
Even as the sun with purple-colour'd face. Venus and Adonis. Shakespeare. BeLS
Even as water is most excellent. For Hieron of Syracuse. Pindar. *Fr.* Odes. LiA
Even as when the daughter of Pandareus. Wise Penelope. Homer. *Fr.* The Odyssey, XIX. LiA
Even at their fairest still I love the less. A Dream of Flowers. Titus Munson Coan. AA
Even during War. Muriel Rukeyser. *Fr.* Letter to the Front. TrJP
Even for the defeated life goes on. Poland, October. Charles Brasch. *Fr.* Nineteen Thirty-nine. AnNZ
Even for you I shall not weep. Finis. Rosamund Marriott Watson. AV
Even from themselves they are a secret. The Close Clan. Mark Van Doren. GoYe
Even horses cocked an eye upward, passers-by. Twitter of Swallows. Merrill Moore. PIAE
Even, I think, when you're bathing. A Bathing Girl. Johannes V. Jensen. BoDS
Even if wars to come sleep warm and small. That Day. Mark Van Doren. WaP
Even in a palace, life may be led well! Worldly Place. Matthew Arnold. BMEP; BPN; EmBrPo; EPN; GrCo-1; PoVP; VLEP
Even in death they prosper; even in the death. Necropolis. Karl Shapiro. MoAB
Even in July it is our winter corner. Frigidaire. A. M. Klein. TwCaPo
Even in the age. Ariwara no Narihira, *tr. fr. Japanese by* Kenneth Rexroth. OnPJ
Even in the Moment of Our Earliest Kiss. Edna St. Vincent Millay. ATP
Even in the Palace. Nago Okimaro, *tr. fr. Japanese by* Ishii *and* Obata. OnPM
Even in the time when as yet. The Wanderer. William Carlos Williams. MAPA; TwAmPo
Even is come; and from the dark park, hark. A Nocturnal Sketch. Thomas Hood. BOHV; FiBHP; SiTL
Even light itself, which every thing displays. Newton on Light. James Thomson. *Fr.* A Poem Sacred to the Memory of Sir Isaac Newton. BeR
Even like Two Little Bank-dividing Brooks. Francis Quarles. *See* My Beloved Is Mine and I Am His.
Even my tombstone gives the truth away. A Dead Liar Speaks. Michael Lewis. GoTP
Even now/ Death sends me the flickering of powdery lids. Death Sends Me the Flickering of Powdery Lids. Bilhana, *formerly at. to* Chauras. *Fr.* Black Marigolds. OnPM
Even now/ Her mouth carelessly scented as with lotus dust. Her Mouth Carelessly Scented. Bilhana, *formerly at. to* Chauras. *Fr.* Black Marigolds. OnPM
Even now/ I have a need to make up prayers, to speak. I Have a Need. Bilhana, *formerly at. to* Chauras. *Fr.* Black Marigolds. OnPM
Even now/ I have no surety that she is not Mahadevi. I Have No Surety. Bilhana, *formerly at. to* Chauras. *Fr.* Black Marigolds. OnPM
Even now/ I know my princess was happy. I Know My Princess. Bilhana, *formerly at. to* Chauras. *Fr.* Black Marigolds. OnPM
Even now/ I know that I have savoured the hot taste of life. I Know That I Have Savoured. Bilhana, *formerly at. to* Chauras. *Fr.* Black Marigolds. OnPM
Even now/ I love long black eyes that caress like silk. I Love Long Black Eyes. Bilhana, *formerly at. to* Chauras. *Fr.* Black Marigolds. OnPM
Even now/ I mind that I went round with men and women. I Mind That I Went Round with Men and Women. Bilhana, *formerly at. to* Chauras. *Fr.* Black Marigolds. OnPM
Even now/ I mind the coming and talking of wise men from towers. I Mind the Coming. Bilhana, *formerly at. to* Chauras. *Fr.* Black Marigolds. OnPM
Even now/ I mind the time of the falling of blossoms started my dream. I Mind the Time of the Falling of Blossoms. Bilhana, *formerly at. to* Chauras. *Fr.* Black Marigolds. OnPM
Even now/ I see her; far face blond like gold. I See Her. Bilhana, *formerly at. to* Chauras. *Fr.* Black Marigolds. OnPM
Even now/ I see the heavy startled hair of this reed-flute player. I See the Heavy Startled Hair. Bilhana, *formerly at. to* Chauras. *Fr.* Black Marigolds. OnPM
Even now/ I seem to see my prison walls come close. I Seem to See My Prison Walls. Bilhana, *formerly at. to* Chauras. *Fr.* Black Marigolds. OnPM
Even now/ If I see in my soul the citron-breasted fair one. If I See in My Soul. Bilhana, *formerly at. to* Chauras. *Fr.* Black Marigolds. OnPM
Even now/ If my girl with lotus eyes came to me again. If My Girl with Lotus Eyes. Bilhana, *formerly at. to* Chauras. *Fr.* Black Marigolds. OnPM
Even now/ Love is a god and Rati the dark his bride. Love Is a God. Bilhana, *formerly at. to* Chauras. *Fr.* Black Marigolds. OnPM
Even now/ My eyes that hurry to see no more are painting, painting. My Eyes That Hurry to See. Bilhana, *formerly at. to* Chauras. *Fr.* Black Marigolds. OnPM
Even now/ My thought is all of this gold-tinted king's daughter. Black Marigolds. Bilhana, *formerly at. to* Chauras. AWP; LiTW
Even now/ She swims back in the crowning hour of love. She Swims Back in the Crowning Hour. Bilhana, *formerly at. to* Chauras. *Fr.* Black Marigolds. OnPM
Even now/ She with young limbs as smooth as flower pollen. She with Young Limbs. Bilhana, *formerly at. to* Chauras. *Fr.* Black Marigolds. OnPM
Even now/ Spread we our nets beyond the farthest rims. Spread We Our Nets. Bilhana, *formerly at. to* Chauras. *Fr.* Black Marigolds. OnPM
Even now/ The pleased intimacy of rough love. The Pleased Intimacy. Bilhana, *formerly at. to* Chauras. *Fr.* Black Marigolds. OnPM
Even now/ The stainless fair appearance of the moon. The Stainless Fair Appearance. Bilhana, *formerly at. to* Chauras. *Fr.* Black Marigolds. OnPM
Even now/ The woodcutter and the fisherman turn home. The Woodcutter and the Fisherman Turn Home. Bilhana, *formerly at. to* Chauras. *Fr.* Black Marigolds. OnPM
Even now/ When all my heavy heart is broken up. When All My Heavy Heart. Bilhana, *formerly at. to* Chauras. *Fr.* Black Marigolds. OnPM
Even now, mad girl, dost ape the painted Briton. Propertius. *Fr.* Elegies. BoHiPo
Even on a Night like This. Ralph Friedrich. MuM
"Even on the cross a man will make a prayer." The Dying Thief. J. S. Phillimore. OQP; QP-1
Even So. Dante Gabriel Rossetti. EmBrPo
Even so distant, I can taste the grief. Deceptions. Philip Larkin. NePoEA
"Even so" (the exulting Maiden said). Samuel Taylor Coleridge. *Fr.* The Destiny of Nations. ChER
Even so to Ilion's city came by stealth. Human Responsibility. Aeschylus. *Fr.* Agamemnon. GrR
Even-Song. *See* Evensong.
Even Such Is Man. Henry King. *See* Sic Vita.
Even Such Is Time. Sir Walter Ralegh. *See* Conclusion, The.
Even the beauty of the rose doth cast. Shadow. Walter de la Mare. ChMo; CMP; MeRV
Even the bravest that are slain. The Trial by Existence. Robert Frost. CoBA

Even the dead laughter of the moon is beautiful. Cleansing. Heinrich Suso Waldeck. CAW
Even the gray Lenten season wraps carnival's domino. A Glimpse of Easter in the Azores. Henry Sandham. EOAH
Even the morning is formal. The Morning Porches. Donald Hall. NePoAm-2
Even the Rocks of Futami. Basho, *tr. fr. Japanese by* Lois J. Erickson. SoLD
Even the shrewd and bitter. Prologue to "Rhymes to Be Traded for Bread." Vachel Lindsay. ChMo; CMP; LaNeLa
Even the wild-ducks skimming. Not Alone. Princess Ki. OnPM
Even This Shall Pass Away. Theodore Tilton. BLPA; HBV; MaRV, *abr.*; NeHB; WGRP
(King's Ring, The.) PTA-2; TreFS
Even though it's raining. Others. Harry Behn. TiPo (1959 ed.)
Even thus, methinks, a city rear'd should be. Written in Edinburgh. Arthur Henry Hallam. VA
Even thy white bones in the tomb, I trow. On a Dog. Simonides. GrR
Even to the children. The Blade of Grass Sings to the River. Leah Goldberg. TrJP
Even to the Dead. Whitney Montgomery. UnW
Even you, dark pool. Crimson Pool. "Katherine Hale." CPG
Evenen in the Village. William Barnes. CaAE; GTSE
Evening. Richard Aldington. MBP; MoBrPo; SeCePo
Evening, An. William Allingham. EnLoPo; IrPN
Evening. Harry Behn. TiPo (1959 ed.)
Evening. Robert Bridges, *after* Blake. EPP
Evening. Byron, *after the Greek of* Sappho. *Fr.* Don Juan, III. BLV; BoLiVe; LPS-2; OTPC; TrGrPo
(Hesperus, 1 *st.*) CBOV; OnPM
(Hesperus the Bringer, 1 *st.*) AWP; JAWP; OuHeWo; WBP
(Hymn to Hesperus.) TOP
Evening. Ch'en Tzu-ang, *tr. fr. Chinese by* W. J. B. Fletcher. OnPM
Evening, *sel.* Mary Elizabeth Coleridge.
"Great rain is over, The." AlDL
Evening. Charles Cotton. *See* Evening Quatrains.
Evening. William Cowper. *See* Winter Evening ("Come, Evening").
Evening. Robert J. Craig. PraP
Evening. John Cunningham. *Fr.* Day; a Pastoral. EnSW
Evening. Emily Dickinson. *See* Cricket sang, The, *and* She sweeps with many-coloured brooms.
Evening. George Washington Doane. *See* Softly Now the Light of Day.
Evening. Hilda Doolittle ("H. D."). ChMo; CMP; FaBoMo; LoBV; OTPC (1946 ed.); Po; TwCV; YT
Evening. Joseph von Eichendorff, *tr. fr. German by* Edwin Morgan. AnGP
Evening. John Ellerton. PraP
Evening. John Fletcher. *See* Evening Song.
Evening. Wendell Phillips Garrison. *Fr.* Post-Meridian. AA
Evening, The. John Gay. *Fr.* Trivia; or, The Art of Walking the Streets of London, III: Of Walking the Streets by Night. EnLi-1 (1949 ed.)
Evening. Goldsmith. *See* Village, The ("Sweet was the sound").
Evening. Nikolai Stepanovich Gumilev, *tr. fr. Russian by* Babette Deutsch. TrRV
Evening, *sel.* John Keble.
"'Tis gone, that bright and orbed blaze." TrPWD
Evening. Archibald Lampman. MM; TwCV
Evening. William Julius Mickle. *Fr.* The Concubine, II. RO
Evening. Mary Matheson. CaP
Evening. S. Weir Mitchell. *See* Vespers.
Evening. Harold Monro. FaBoTw
Evening. Marjorie Pickthall. OCL
Evening. Rainer Maria Rilke, *tr. fr. German by* Randall Jarrell. AnGP
Evening. V. Sackville-West. DiM
Evening. Charles Sangster. CaP
Evening. Sappho, *tr. fr. Greek by* Sir Rennell Rodd. GrL; OxBG; WoL
(Evensong, *tr. by* F. L. Lucas.) GrPE
(Eventide, *tr. by* Edwin Marion Cox.) GrR
Evening. Edward Rowland Sill. AnAmPo; LA
Evening. Stephan G. Stephansson, *tr. fr. Icelandic by* Jakobina Johnson. IcP
Evening. James Stephens. MoBrPo
Evening. Georg Trakl, *tr. fr. German by* David Luke. AnGP
Evening. *Unknown.* BoTP
Evening. Victor van Vriesland, *tr. fr. Dutch by* Adrian J. Barnouw. TrJP
Evening. Whittier. *Fr.* Summer by the Lakeside. IAP
Evening. Charlotte Young. BOL
Evening! A flight of pigeons in clear sky. The Flute. José Maria de Heredia. AWP; EBSV
Evening, and Maidens. William Barnes. OBEV (new ed.); OBVV
Evening and Morning in June, An. Gawin Douglas. *Fr.* Prologues to the Aeneid, *prol. to* XIII. BSV
Evening and Morning in Winter, An. Gawin Douglas. *Fr.* Prologues to the Aeneid, *prol. to* VII. BSV
Evening and Night and Meteors. William Diaper. *Fr.* Dryades; or, The Nymphs Prophecy. BeR
Evening and quiet. Houses. F. S. Flint. PFE
Evening, and the slender sugar tongs of a bird's small voice. Dinner Guest. Oscar Williams. TwAmPo
Evening, as slow thy placid shades descend. Sonnet. William Lisle Bowles. CEP
Evening at Chung Shan. Wang An Shih, *tr. fr. Chinese by* Henry H. Hart. PoHN
Evening at the Abbey. William Julius Mickle. *Fr.* Pollio; an Elegy. RO
Evening at the Farm. John Townsend Trowbridge. BBV (1923 ed.); FaPON; GN; MPB; RIS; StVeCh (1940 ed.)
(Evening on the Farm.) MoShBr
(Farm-Yard Song.) BTP; PECK
Evening at the Inn of Yün Meng. Liu Tzu Hui, *tr. fr. Chinese by* Henry H. Hart. PoHN
Evening bends upon a stubborn day, The. Sonnet. Pearce Young. PtPa
Evening Blessing, An. James Edmeston. BePJ
Evening by the Sea, the Plovers Fly. Richard Leon Spain. MuM
Evening came, The; the golden vane. The Manichaean's Prayer. Longfellow. *Fr.* Tales of a Wayside Inn. APW
Evening Cloud, The. "Christopher North." HBV; LPS-2
Evening Clouds. Francis Ledwidge. MBP; VOD
Evening comes, the field is [*or* fields are] still, The. Bacchanalia; or, The New Age. Matthew Arnold. BPN; EmBrPo; GEPC; PoVP; VLEP
Evening Contemplation. George Washington Doane. *See* Softly Now the Light of Day.
Evening Darkens Over, The. Robert Bridges. ChMo; CMP; PoEL-5; POTT
Evening darkness shrouds, The. On Julia's Death. Vasili Kapnist. BoRS
Evening draws on apace now, The. The Old Mountain Troll. Gustaf Fröding. AnSL
Evening Ebb. Robinson Jeffers. AmPP (3d ed.); OTPC (1946 ed.)
Evening edition, The. The Clouds Have Already Told Me. Jacinto Fombona Pachano. TwSpPo
Evening Falls, An. James Stephens. SUS
Evening falls on the smoky walls. Ballad of the Londoner. J. E. Flecker. EnLoPo
Evening Fantasy. Friedrich Hölderlin, *tr. fr. German by* Frederic Prokosch. LiTW
Evening folds about itself the dark, The. Evening. Rainer Maria Rilke. AnGP
Evening Gleam, The. James Devaney. MoAuPo
Evening, grave, immense and clear. Gonzalo's Song. W. H. Auden. *Fr.* The Sea and the Mirror. MeRV
Evening has brought the glow-worm to the green. Shepherd. Edmund Blunden. HBMV
Evening hour is come; the sheep are folded, The. David's Song to the Troubled King. Victor Starbuck. *Fr.* Saul, King of Israel. NoCaPo
Evening Hymn. Cecil Frances Alexander. OTPC (1923 ed.)
Evening Hymn. Sabine Baring-Gould. *See* Now the Day Is Over.
Evening Hymn. Matilda Barbara Betham-Edwards. TVSH
Evening Hymn. Sir Thomas Browne. *Fr.* Religio Medici. EV-2; MaRV; OxBoCh
(Colloquy with God, A.) OBS; SeCL
Evening Hymn. George Washington Doane. *See* Softly Now the Light of Day.
Evening Hymn. William Henry Furness. AA; FaBoBe; HBV; TCAP
(Light of Stars, The.) TrPWD
Evening Hymn. Reginald Heber. BOL
Evening Hymn. John Keble. BePJ; MaRV
Evening Hymn, An, *abr.* Thomas Ken. OBS
Evening Hymn, *sel.* George Macdonald.
"O God, whose daylight leadeth down." TrPWD
Evening Hymn. Elizabeth Madox Roberts. TiPo
Evening Hymn, An. Ann *or* Jane Taylor. BOL
Evening Hymn ("I hear no voice, I feel no touch"). *Unknown.* BOL; RAR
(Evening Song.) OTPC (1946 ed.)
Evening Hymn ("Now the sun has passed away"). *Unknown* BOL
Evening Hymn. "R. W." BOL
Evening Hymn for a Child. John Pierpont. BOL
Evening Hymn for a Little Family, An. Ann *or* Jane Taylor. BOL; OTPC (1946 ed.)
Evening in Camp. Patricia Ledward. WaP

Evening in England, An. Francis Ledwidge. BMEP; MCCG; PIAE
Evening in February. Francis Ledwidge. AlDL; TCPD; VOD
Evening in Gloucester Harbor. Epes Sargent. EtS
Evening in May. Gabriele d'Annunzio, *tr. fr. Italian by* G. A. Greene. WoL
Evening in Paradise. Milton. *Fr.* Paradise Lost, IV. FaBoEn; GN; LoBV; LPS-2; TCEP
(Moon and the Nightingale.) ChTr
(Night Falls on Eden.) PoFS; TreFS
("Now came still evening on, and twilight gray.") BCEP; SeEP
Evening in Summer. Valentin Iremonger. NeIP
(Time, the Faithless.) OxBI
(While the Summer Trees Were Crying.) AnIV
Evening in the Capital. Pope. *Fr.* The Rape of the Lock, I. BeR
Evening in the Great Smokies. DuBose Heyward. LS
Evening in the Village. Lu Yu, *tr. fr. Chinese by* Kenneth Rexroth. OnPC
Evening in Tyringham Valley. Richard Watson Gilder. AA; NLK (1947 ed.)
Evening is coming, The. Bed-Time. *At. to* Thomas Hood. BOL; BoTP; OTPC (1946 ed.)
Evening is falling to sleep in the west. Falling to Sleep. *Unknown.* BOL
Evening is tawny on the old/ Deep-windowed farm. Gold. Martin Armstrong. BoTP
Evening Knell, The. John Fletcher. *See* Evening Song.
Evening Landscape. Pol de Mont, *tr. fr. Flemish by* Jethro Bithell. LiTW
Evening light has soaked with ancient gold, The. Cimmerian Twilight, I. Maximilian Aleksandrovich Voloshin. TrRV
Evening Meal in the Twentieth Century. John Holmes. MiAP; PreP
Evening Melody. Aubrey Thomas De Vere. GoBC; HBV
Evening mist, The. Shadows on the Wall. Tsun Tsao. PoHN
Evening mist on the land was lying. Aleksandr Blok, *tr. fr. Russian by* V. de S. Pinto. BoRS
Evening Music. Kendrick Smithyman. AnNZ
Evening of the ball was hushed, The. Summer Ball. Viktor Viktorovich Hofman. TrRV
Evening of the Feast-Day, The. Giacomo Leopardi, *tr. fr. Italian by* R. C. Trevelyan. LiTW
Evening of the Visitation, The. Thomas Merton. ISi
Evening on Calais Beach. Wordsworth. *See* It Is a Beauteous Evening, Calm and Free.
Evening on Howth Head. Eileen Brennan. NeIP
Evening on the Beach. Wordsworth. *See* It Is a Beauteous Evening, Calm and Free.
Evening on the Farm. John Townsend Trowbridge. *See* Evening at the Farm.
Evening on the Harbor. Virginia Lyne Tunstall. HBMV
Evening on the Moselle. Decimus Magnus Ausonius, *tr. fr. Latin by* Helen Waddell. AnEnPo; LiTW
Evening Out, The. Ogden Nash. MoAmPo (1950 ed.)
"Evening passes fast away, The." Self-Interrogation. Emily Brontë. EmBrPo
Evening; Ponte al Mare, Pisa. Shelley. KN
Evening Prayer, An. Bernard Barton. BOL
Evening Prayer. *At. to* C. Maud Battersby, *also to* Charles H. Gabriel. OQP; PraP; QP-1
(My Evening Prayer.) BLPA; FaBoBe; NeHB
Evening Prayer. Edward Benlowes. *Fr.* Theophila. FaBoEn
Evening Prayer, An. Mary Lundie Duncan. *See* Child's Evening Prayer, A.
Evening Prayer. Arthur Fitger, *tr. fr. German by* Jethro Bithell. AWP
Evening Prayer. Robert Freeman. PraP
Evening Prayer. Hermann Hagedorn. GoBC
Evening Prayer. Thomas Ken. *See* Glory to Thee This Night.
Evening Prayer, An. Laura E. Kendall. BLRP
Evening Prayer, An. Harriet McEwen Kimball. *See* All's Well.
Evening Prayer. Calvin W. Laufer. PraP
Evening Prayer, An ("Now I lay me down to sleep"). *Unknown. See* Now I Lay Me Down to Take My Sleep.
Evening Prayer ("Our Father, grant us to lie down in peace"). *Unknown, tr. fr. Hebrew by* Solomon Solis-Cohen. TrJP
Evening Prayer, An ("Upon my ryght syde y me leye"). *Unknown.* AtBAP
Evening Prayer, An. Isaac Watts. MeMeAg
Evening Primrose. John Clare, *wr. at. to* Emily Brontë. CH; RO; TrGrPo
("When once the sun sinks in the west.") EG
Evening Primrose, The. John Langhorne. CEP; OBEC
Evening Primrose, The. Dorothy Parker. ALV; InMe
Evening Quatrains. Charles Cotton. AEV; ChTr; ExPo; LoBV; NBE
("Day's grown old, The," *abr.*) EG
(Evening.) PoEL-3
(Summer Evening.) TrGrPo
Evening red and morning gray. Weather Signs [*or* Weather Wisdom *or* Rhymes about the Weather]. *Unknown.* FaBoBe; GoTP; HBV; HBVY; OTPC; OxNR; PPL; TreF
Evening Revery, An, *sel.* Bryant.
"Summer day is closed, the sun is set, The." AA; OBAV
Evening river is level and motionless, The. Flowers and Moonlight on the Spring River. Emperor Yang-ti. TrCh
Evening Sea. Shizuo Ito, *tr. fr. Japanese by* Takamichi Ninomiya *and* D. J. Enright. PoLJ
Evening Scene, An. Coventry Patmore. BLV
Evening Scene. E. J. Scovell. FaBoMo
Evening shades are falling. Lullaby. *Unknown.* BOL
Evening Sigh. Emil Aarestrup, *tr. fr. Danish by* Charles W. Stork. BoDS
Evening Sky. John Gould Fletcher. ChMo; CMP
Evening Sky, The. John Freeman. MM; TwCV
Evening Song. Cecil Frances Alexander. DD, *abr.*; OHIP, *abr.*; OTPC (1923 ed.); RAR, *abr.*; TVC, *abr.*
Evening Song. Sherwood Anderson. NP
Evening Song. Fannie Stearns Davis. BOL; GFA; SP; VOD
Evening Song. Kenneth Fearing. ChMo
Evening Song. John Fletcher. *Fr.* The Faithful Shepherdess, II, i. EV-2; GN; OTPC (1923 ed.); WP
(Evening.) CG
(Evening Knell, The.) ElL
(Folding the Flocks.) CH; LPS-2
(Invocation by the Priest of Pan.) CaAE
(Priest's Chant, The.) OBS
("Shepherds all, and maidens fair.") CenL
Evening Song. Edith King. BoTP
Evening Song. Sidney Lanier. AmPP (3d ed.); BAP; CoBA; IAP; LBAP; LEAP; LoPo; LoPS; MOAP; NeHB; OBAV; PG; PoeMoYo; PR; TCAP; TOP
Evening Song, An. Wilson MacDonald. OCL
Evening Song. Jean Toomer. CDC; PoNe
Evening Song. *Unknown. See* Evening Hymn ("I hear no voice . . .").
Evening Song of Senlin ("It is evening"). Conrad Aiken. *Fr.* Senlin; a Biography, II, ix. HBMV; MOAP
Evening Song of Senlin ("It is moonlight"). Conrad Aiken. *Fr.* Senlin; a Biography, II, x. SBMV
Evening Song of the Weary. Felicia Dorothea Hemans. ERP
Evening Songs. John Vance Cheney. AA
"Behind the hilltop drops the sun," IV.
"Birds have hid, the winds are low, The," I.
"It is that pale, delaying hour," II.
"Now is Light, sweet mother, down the west," III.
Evening spread its rags of melancholy, The. The Wild Swan. D. S. Savage. NeBP
Evening Star, The. Grace Blackburn. CPG
Evening Star, The. Thomas Campbell. *See* Song to the Evening Star.
Evening Star, The. John Clare. ChTr
Evening Star, The. Longfellow. AnNE
Evening Star, The. Alfred de Musset, *tr. fr. French by* Alan Conder. TrFP
Evening Star. Poe. AmP
Evening star that in the vaulted skies, The. Verse Written in the Album of Mademoiselle ——. Pierre Dalcour. PoNe
Evening star that softly sheds, The. Refracted Lights. Celia Parker Wooley. WGRP
Evening Sun, The. Emily Brontë. CH
Evening sun is shining bright, The. A Winter Shower. Harumi. OnPM
Evening takes them unawares, The. The Sisters Kastemaloff. Carlton Talbott. ALV
Evening, the sky coloured like a child's angel. Child's Poem. Kay Smith. TwCaPo
Evening Thought, An. Jupiter Hammon. PoNe
Evening traffic homeward burns. Before Disaster. Yvor Winters. HoPM
Evening Twilight. Heine. *Fr.* The North Sea. AWP; JAWP; WBP
Evening Voluntary. Wordsworth. CaAE
Evening Walk, The, *sel.* Caroline Anne Bowles.
"My lonely ramble yester-eve I took." EnSW
Evening Walk. David Einhorn, *tr. fr. Yiddish by* Sarah Zweig Betsky. OnCuPl
Evening Walk, An. Wordsworth. EmBrPo
Sels.
"But now the clear bright moon her zenith gains." RO
"Dear Brook, farewell! Tomorrow's noon again." CoBE; EnRP
Sunset in the Lake Country. EPN
Swans. OBEC
Evening Walk, An. Andrew Young. AlDL
Evening Walk in Spring. An. Arthur Hugh Clough. VLEP
Evening Watch, The; a Dialogue. Henry Vaughan. EOAH; MeRV

Evening Waterfall. Carl Sandburg. NP; OTPC (1946 ed.); TSW
Evening Wind, The. Bryant. AA; AnNE; APW; BAP; BAV; CoBA; IAP; LaNeLa; LPS-2; MOAP; PIR; REAL; TCAP
(To the Evening Wind.) MCCG
Evening wind, The. The Scholar. Ch'en Sheng Chi. PoHN
Evening Wind, The. Lu Yu, *tr. fr. Chinese by* Pai Chwen-yu. WhP
Evening without Angels. Wallace Stevens. MoPo
Evenings. Arthur Rimbaud, *tr. fr. French by* Vernon Watkins. AnFP
Evenings/ When the house is quiet. Setting the Table. Dorothy Aldis. FaPON; MPB; TiPo
Evenings in Greece, *sel.* Thomas Moore.
Two Streams, The. GoBC
Evening's Love, An, *sels.* Dryden.
Damon and Celimena, *fr.* V, i. InvP; SeCL
Song: "After the pangs of a desperate lover," *fr.* II, i. FaBoEn
(After the Pangs of a Desperate Lover.) OAEP; ViBoPo
Song: "Calm was the even, and clear [*or* cleer] was the sky," *fr.* IV, i. CEP; SeCV-2
(Calm Was the Even [and Clear Was the Sky].) MaPo; OAEP
Song: "You charm'd me not with that fair face," *fr.* II, i. BrBE; CEP; ElSeCe; SeCV-2
(You Charm'd Me Not.) ATP (1935 ed.)
Evenings of beatitude. Hours. Francisco González León. AnMP
Evensong. Conrad Aiken. HBMV; PG
Even-Song, An. Sydney Dobell. OBVV
Evensong. Carleton Drewry. GoYe
Even-Song. George Herbert. FaBoEn
Evensong. Sappho. *See* Evening.
Evensong. Ruth Schaumann, *tr. fr. German by* George N. Shuster. CAW
Evensong. Robert Louis Stevenson. BMEP; MaRV; PoVP; TCEP; TrPWD; VLEP
Evensong. Ridgely Torrence. HBV; LBMV; LEAP; OBAV
Even-Song. *Unknown, tr. fr. Polish.* BOL
Event, The. T. Sturge Moore. OBMV
Event stands clear of history, The. Against Time. Louis Untermeyer. MoAmPo (1942 ed.)
Eventide. Valery Yakovlevich Bryusov, *tr. fr. Russian by* Babette Deutsch. TrRV
Eventide. Thomas Burbidge. VA
Eventide. Caroline Atherton Briggs Mason. MaRV; TreFS
Eventide. Sappho. *See* Evening.
Eventide, *sel.* Whittier.
Eternal Good. OQP; QP-2
Eventide. Yang Kuei-fei, *tr. fr. Chinese by* Henry H. Hart. PoHN
Eventide is stillness bringing. The Gypsies. Pushkin. WaL
Events. George O'Neil. HBMV
Eventual Birth of Thought. B. J. Morse. MoWP
Ever after summer shower. Sunshine after a Shower. Thomas Warton, the Younger. *Fr.* On the Approach of Summer. OTPC
Ever and ever anon. The Road to the Bow. James David Corrothers. BANP
Ever as We Sailed. Shelley. *Fr.* The Revolt of Islam. SeCePo
Ever charming, ever new. John Dyer. *Fr.* Grongar Hill. SeCePo
Ever dead shalt thou lie under the earth. To an Uncultivated Woman. Sappho. GrL
"Ever, ever," the lady said. The Fool. Henry Baerlein. ReTS
Ever fainting with desire. Speak the Word. Charles Wesley. BePJ
Ever fresh the broad creation. The Immanent God. Emerson. *Fr.* Woodnotes. MaRV
Ever I wonder at what's to see. Over the Lofty Mountains. Björnstjerne Björnson. AnNoLy
Ever just over the top of the next brown rise. On the Road. Sir Charles G. D. Roberts. CPG
Ever let the fancy roam. Fancy [*or* The Realm of Fancy *or* To Fancy]. Keats. ATP (1935 ed.); BPN; EM-2; EmBrPo; EnLi-2; EnRP; EPN; EV-4; GEPC; GTBS; GTBS-D; GTBS-W; GTSE; GTSL; HBV; LoBV; LPS-3; OBEV; PC
Ever-present Spirit, The. Richard Realf. GrCo-1
(O Earth!) AnEnPo
Ever Since. Elizabeth J. Coatsworth. SiSoSe
Ever Since. Archibald MacLeish. NePA
Ever since the day. Absence. Chang Chiu-ling. PoHN
Ever since the day. Faith. Wan Yüan Chang. PoHN
Ever Since Uncle John Henry Been Dead, *with music. Unknown.* AS
Ever the loud-voiced waters, crying, calling. Heartbreak. Howard Mumford Jones. LS
Ever the words of the gods resound. The Words of the Gods. Emerson. *Fr.* My Garden. OQP; QP-2
Ever upon the blackboard of the night. Starry Classroom. E. Merrill Root. DDA
Ever upon this stage. The Annual Drama. Walt Whitman. GrCo-1
Ever Watchful. Ta' Abbata Sharra, *tr. fr. Arabic by* W. G. Palgrave. AWP; JAWP; WBP
Ever with grief and all too long. Sigurth and I. *Unknown. Fr.* The Elder Edda. LiA
Everest. Horace Shipp. HaMV
Everett. Thomas William Parsons. DD; GA
Evergreen. Ewart Milne. OxBI
Evergreen shadow and the pale magnolia, The. Souls Lake. Robert Fitzgerald. MoPo
Evergreens. Edward Coote Pinkney. BAV
Everlasting Arms, The. Deuteronomy, XXXIII: 27, Bible, *O.T.* GrCo-1
Everlasting Arms, The. Psalms, Bible, *O.T. See* God Our Refuge.
Everlasting Contenders, The. Kenneth Patchen. CrMA
Everlasting Gospel, The, *sels.* Blake.
Epilogue: "I am sure this Jesus will not do." OBRV
Humility and Doubt. RO
"Jesus was sitting in Moses' chair." EV-3; OxBoCh
"Vision of Christ that thou dost see, The." OBRV
"Was Jesus chaste?" OBRV
Everlasting Love, The. Annie Johnson Flint. BLRP
Everlasting Mercy, The. John Masefield. StJW
Sels.
Another Cross. MaRV
"By this the sun." GBV
"I did not think, I did not strive." QS
"I opened the window." WGRP
"O Christ who holds the open gate." TreFS
(Ploughman, The.) AtBAP
Open Gate, The. GrCo-2
"So up the road I wander slow." MM
Everlasting Rest. Shakespeare. *Fr.* Romeo and Juliet, V, iii. WHA
Everlasting Sorrow, The. Po Chü-1, *tr. fr. Chinese by* Ching Ti. WhP
Everlasting to Everlasting, *sel.* Namdev, *tr. by* R. T. Gribble.
"Before all Time, before all worlds." MaRV
Everlasting universe of things, The. Mont Blanc. Shelley. BPN; EmBrPo; EnRP; MaPo
Everlasting Voices, The. W. B. Yeats. AWP; BrBE; JAWP; WBP
Every branch big with it. Snow in the Suburbs. Thomas Hardy. AlDL; ChMo; CMP; MBP; MoAB; MoBrPo; OBMV; PoVP; ShBV-3; ThWaDe; ViPP; VLEP
Every Bush New Springing. *Unknown.* PoEL-2
Every button has a door. About Buttons. Dorothy Aldis. MoSiPe
Ev-er-y child who has the use. Geese [*or* Some Geese]. Oliver Herford. *Fr.* Child's Natural History. FiBHP; HBV; LEAP; NA
Every coin of earthly treasure. The Real Riches. John Godfrey Saxe. PTA-2
Every Day. *See also* Everyday.
Every Day. Elizabeth Haas. MeMeAg
Every Day. Felix Mendelssohn, *tr. fr. German.* PCD; PCH
(Love the Beautiful.) MeMeAg
Every Day. Mary I. Osborn. BoTP
Every day. Mariale. Bernard of Cluny. CAW
Every-Day Botany. Katherine H. Perry. PEOR
Every day brings a ship. Letters. Emerson. LPS-3; TCAP
Every-Day Characters, *sels.* Winthrop Mackworth Praed.
Belle of the Ball-Room, The, III. ALV; EnRP; EPP; ERP; HBV; InMe
(Belle of the Ball, The.) BOHV; LPS-3
("Our love was like most other loves," *2 sts.*) ViBoPo
Portrait of a Lady in the Exhibition of the Royal Academy, V. PoEL-4
Vicar, The, I. EnRP; InMe; OBEV (new ed.); PoEL-4
Every day, I'm glad to say. Every Day. Elizabeth Haas. MeMeAg
Every day is a fresh beginning. Begin Again [*or* New Every Morning]. "Susan Coolidge." BLP; MaRV
Every day on the way home from. By the Winding River, I. Tu Fu. OnPC
Every Day Thanksgiving Day. Harriet Prescott Spofford. DD; OHIP; PEDC
Every day will be fun for me. To Betty. "E. G. B." PCH
Every Earthly Creature. John Malcolm Brinnin. LiTA
Every evening Baby goes. Trot, Trot [to Town]. Mary Frances Butts. HBV; HBVY; PPL; SAS
Every eye must weep alone. To Chester Kallman. W. H. Auden. BoFr
Every hour and every minute. A Vow for New Year's. Mary Carolyn Davies. PoToHe
Every lady in this land. *Unknown.* BoN; OxNR
Every little while all day. Thirst. Ralph Bergengren. FAOV
Every Lover Is a Soldier. Ovid, *tr. fr. Latin by* Kirby Flower Smith. *Fr.* Amores, I, 9. RoL

Every Man. *See also* Everyman.
Every man for himself, and God for us all. How God Will Not Do for Us. John Heywood. SiCE
Every man has his sorrows; yet each still. Elegies, I. André Chénier. AWP; JAWP; WBP
Every mayor before me, far back as memory ran. Mayor Marston. Edgar Lee Masters. *Fr.* The New Spoon River. ChMo; CMP
Every morning at break of day. The Trains. "Seumas O'Sullivan." BoTP
Every morning at six o'clock, I go straight to my work. Everybody Works but Father. Charles W. McClintock. TreFS
Every morning bathing myself and shaving myself. Chandler Nicholas. Edgar Lee Masters. *Fr.* The New Spoon River. NAMP
Every morning from this home. The Heart to Carry On. Bertram Warr. PeCV
Every morning lean thine arms awhile. Begin the Day with God. *Unknown.* MaRV
Every morning the prisoner hears. The Prisoner. William Plomer. ChMP
Every morning when the sun. This Happy Day. Harry Behn. TiPo
Every night as I go to bed. Waltzing Mice. David McCord. RIS
Every night from eve [*or* even] till morn. To the Nightingale. Sir John Davies. *Fr.* Hymns of Astraea. OBSC; SiCE; TrGrPo
Every night I sleep. In the Trench. Leon Gellert. BoAV; MoAuPo
Every night my prayers I say. Reward. Bert Leston Taylor. RIS
Every night my prayers I say. System. Robert Louis Stevenson. PoVP; RIS; VLEP
Every Night When the Sun Goes In, *with music.* *Unknown.* ABF; TrAS
Every One. *See* Everyone.
Every rose on the little tree. The Little Rose Tree. Rachel Field. FaPON; SUS; TiPo
Every Soul Is a Circus, *sel.* Vachel Lindsay.
 Pontoon Bridge Miracle, The, IV. LiTM (rev. ed.); LoBV; NePA
Every soul that touches yours. Making Life Worth While. "George Eliot." MaRV
Every Sunday there's a throng. Westland Row. James Stephens. HBMV
Every Thing. *See also* Everything.
Every Thing. Harold Monro. AnEnPo; ChMo; CMP; EPP; MBP; MoBrPo; NeMA; NV
Every thought is public. Hush! Emerson. AnNE; APW
Every thread of summer is at last unwoven. Puella Parvula. Wallace Stevens. PoFS
Every Thursday morning. The Dustman. Clive Sansom. BoTP
Every Time I Climb a Tree. David McCord. GoTP; TiPo (1959 ed.)
Every time I come to town. *Unknown.* GoTP
Every time I write a letter. Writing Letters. Rodney Bennett. BoTP
Every time the bucks went clattering. Earthy Anecdote. Wallace Stevens. ThWaDe
Every tooth, ah me! has crumbled, dropped and fallen in decay! Lament in Old Age. Rudagi. PeP
Every towered city, every street. Exodus from a Renaissance Gallery. Ellen M. V. Acton. GoYe
Every votary of love. Love's Extremes. Antonio Villegas. OnPM
Every waiting moment is a fold of sorrow. Low Tide. Lynette Roberts. NeBP
Every wedding, says the proverb. The Groomsman to His Mistress. Thomas William Parsons. PR
Every week of every season out of English ports go forth. An English Mother. Robert Underwood Johnson. HBV; MOAH
Every winter the woods shrink back. Wood-Lot Hill. Frances Frost. BAP
Every year Emily Dickinson sent one friend. Accomplished Facts. Carl Sandburg. WHA
Every year they're marching slower. The Veterans. Denis A. McCarthy. PEDC
Everybody loved Chick Lorimer in our town. Gone. Carl Sandburg. AmP; AnFE; APA; CoAnAm; NP; OnPP; TCPD; TwAmPo
Everybody nowadays. Snail. C. Lindsay McCoy. GFA
Everybody Says. Dorothy Aldis. FaPON; MoSiPe
Everybody stands alone on the heart of the earth. And Suddenly It's Evening. Salvatore Quasimodo. OnPM
Everybody stop and listen to my ditty. Prince of Wales' Marriage. *Unknown.* CoMu
Everybody wants an intelligent son. At the Washing of My Son. Su T'ung-po. OnPC
Everybody Works but Father. Charles W. McClintock. TreFS
"Everybody Works but Father" as W. S. Gilbert Would Have Written It. Arthur G. Burgoyne. FiBHP
Everybody's Welcome, *with music.* *Unknown.* TrAS
Everyday Alchemy. Genevieve Taggard. PoeMoYo
Everyday Things. Jean Ayer. BoTP
Everyman. Siegfried Sassoon. BLV; BoLiVe; MBP; MoBrPo
Everyman (*Old English Morality Play*). *Unknown.* BEL, *mod.;* EnLi-1; MeEV, *abr., mod. in spelling;* PoEL-1; TCEP
 Sels.
 Desertion of Beauty and Strength, The. ACP (1952 ed.)
 "Eternal God! Oh! Beatific Vision!" *br. sel., paraphrased and mod. by* George Sterling. CAW
Everyone, Bacchus, goes your way! Sacrifice of the Bacchantes in Honor of Bacchus. Angelo Poliziano. *Fr.* Orfeo. LyPI
Every one, by instinct taught, performed its little task. The Coral Reef. James Montgomery. *Fr.* The Pelican Island. LPS-2
Everyone grumbled. The sky was grey. Daddy Fell into the Pond. Alfred Noyes. FaPON
Everyone knows he's blind as a bat. The Umpire. Walker Gibson. NePoAm
Every one of you won the war. You and You. Edith Wharton. PTA-1
Everyone [*or* Every One] Sang ("Everyone suddenly burst out singing"). Siegfried Sassoon. AlDL; AnFE; AOAH; BLV; BoLiVe; CBOV; CP; GTBS; GTML; GTSL; InvP; LBBV; MBP; MoBrPo; NeMA; NP; OBEV (new ed.); PtOT; TrJP; WaKn; WaP
Every One to His Own Way. John Vance Cheney. AA
Everything. *See also* Every Thing.
Everything Decays. Sophocles. *See* Decay, Earth's Universal Law.
Everything is black and gold. Black and Gold. Nancy Byrd Turner. MPB; TiPo; YeAr
Everything Is Dark. Pierre Reverdy, *tr. fr. French by* James Kirkup. MiFP
Everything is in flight now, trees and men. Flight. Babette Deutsch. NeTW
Everything is laughing, singing. It Is a Pleasant Day. *Unknown.* BoTP
Everything shall be erased. Villa Sciarra; Rome. Christine Turner Curtis. GoYe
Everything was wrong; the local slaves wore smiles. Harpers Ferry. Selden Rodman. PoNe
Everything's been different. The Birthday Child. Rose Fyleman. FaPON; SiSoSe
Everywhere. "A. Almi," *tr. fr. Yiddish by* Sarah Zweig Betsky. OnCuPl
Everywhere. Nancy Birckhead. RIS
Everywhere blood-red banners streaming. The Red Square. Nikolai Poletayev. BoRS
Everywhere, Everywhere, Christmas Tonight. Phillips Brooks. *See* Christmas Carol, A: "Everywhere, everywhere, Christmas tonight."
Everywhere, everywhere, following me. Camerados. Bayard Taylor. BOHV; PA
Everywhere I—hanh! Goin' Home. *Unknown.* ABF
Everywhere is far from somewhere else. Far from Somewhere. "Primus." WhC
Everywhere is our wilderness everywhere. George Barker. NeBP
Everywhere of silver, An. The Sea. Emily Dickinson. TCAP
Everywhere petals are flying. By the Winding River, II. Tu Fu. OnPC
Everywhere the wind blows. Spring Signs. Mildred Bowers Armstrong. GoBP
Eve's Cradle-Song. Walter Satterlee. BOL
Eve's Daughter. Edward Rowland Sill. PR
Eve's Lament. Milton. *Fr.* Paradise Lost, XI. LPS-1
Eve's Lament. *Unknown, tr. fr. Middle Irish.* OnYI, *tr. by* Kuno Meyer; SiB, *tr. by* Seán O'Faoláin (Gaelic Fragment, *tr. by* Kuno Meyer.) CAW
Eve's Sweet Pippin. Keats. *See* Sharing Eve's Apple.
Eviction. Elizabeth Brewster. CaP
Eviction. William James Linton. VA
Evidence. Thomas Curtis Clark. MaRV
Evidence. Arthur Kober. InMe
Evidence Read at the Trial of the Knave of Hearts. "Lewis Carroll." *Fr.* Alice's Adventures in Wonderland, *ch.* 12. FaFP; LiTG; OxBoLi; SiTL (Important Evidence.) ViP
Evil. Arthur Rimbaud, *tr. fr. French by* Norman Cameron. WaaP
Evil Designs. Shakespeare. *See* Winter of Our Discontent.
Evil Dragon. "Feodor Sologub," *tr. fr. Russian by* Babette Deutsch. TrRV
Evil Eye, The. John Ciardi. AtBAP
Evil Eye, the tiny night-bulb glowed, An. The Crisis. Ethelyn Bryant Chapman. BPP
Evil flees the earth. To the Nativity. Fernán González de Eslava. AnMP

Evil Genius, The. Timocreon, *tr. fr. Greek by* J. M. Edmonds. GrR
Evil in Women, The. *Unknown, tr. fr. Spanish by* Havelock Ellis. OnPM
Evil is generous, will not walk alone. Victus. Quentin Stevenson. POTE (1959 ed.)
Evil Landscape. Tristan Corbière, *tr. fr. French by* Kenneth Koch *and* Georges Guy. AnFP
(Landscape of Evil, *tr. by* A. J. Bull.) MiFP
"Evil Man, An!" Richard Beer-Hofmann, *tr. fr. German by* Ludwig Lewisohn. *Fr.* Der Graf von Charolais. TrJP
Evil sped the battle-play. The Swan-Neck. Charles Kingsley. EV-5
Evil spirit, your beauty haunts me still, An. Sonnet. Michael Drayton. Idea, XX. CoBE; ElL; ElSeCe; EPP; LoBV; OAEP; OBSC; ReEn; ReIE; SiCE; TuPP
Evil Spirits. Pushkin, *tr. fr. Russian by* Babette Deutsch. TrRV
(Devils, *tr. by* C. M. Bowra.) BoR
"Evil thing is honor, An," once of old. Ideal Passion, XXVIII. George Edward Woodberry. HBMV; MOAP
Evil to choose is easy, of her thou canst find thy fill. Worldly Wisdom. Hesiod. *Fr.* Works and Days. GrPE
Evil was dangled in front of him like an apple. A Man of Sense. Richard Eberhart. MiAP
Evil World, An. *Unknown, tr. fr. Middle Irish by* Standish Hayes O'Grady. OnYI
Evils of Money, The. Sophocles, *tr. fr. Greek by* Lewis Campbell. *Fr.* Antigone. GrR
Ev'n as a lovely swan before he dies. Néère. André Chénier. *Fr.* Bucoliques. LiA
Ev'n like Two Little Bank-dividing Brooks. Francis Quarles. *See* My Beloved Is Mine, and I Am His.
Evocation. Amado Nervo, *tr. fr. Spanish by* Samuel Beckett. AnMP
Evoe! Edith M. Thomas. BAP; HBV; LBAP; LEAP
Evolution. Langdon Smith. BAP; BeLS; BLPA; BoHiPo; DDA; FaBoBe; FaFP; HBV; TreF; YaD
Evolution. May Swenson. TrGrPo (rev. ed.)
Evolution. John Banister Tabb. AA; AmP; AnAmPo; BAP; InP; LA; LEAP; MaRV; OBAV; OQP; PFY; PoeMoYo; QP-1; QS; SPP; TreF; VOD
Evolution. *Unknown.* DDA
Evolution. Israel Zangwill. TrJP
Evolution of Life and Society. Lucretius, *tr. fr. Latin by* W. H. D Rouse. *Fr.* De Rerum Natura. RoL
Ev'ry night when the sun goes in. Every Night When the Sun Goes In. *Unknown.* ABF
Ev'ry singing bird that in the wood rejoices. Vezzosi Augelli. Thomas Watson. TuPP
Ev'ry Time I Feel de Spirit, *with music. Unknown.* BoAN-1
Ev'ry time I think about Jesus. Calvary. *Unknown.* BoAN-1
Evvie's Mother. Olive Tilford Dargan. LS; NoCaPo
"Ewa-yea! my little owlet!" Lullaby of Nokomis. Longfellow. *Fr.* The Song of Hiawatha. PCH
Ewe-Buchtin's Bonnie, The. Thomas Pringle. EBSV
Ewe-Bughts, Marion. *Unknown.* EBSV
Ewie wi' the Crookit Horn, The. John Skinner. EBSV
Ex and Squarey. *Unknown.* ChTr
Ex-Clerk. Kipling. *Fr.* Epitaphs of the War. PoVP
Ex Libris. Christian Morgenstern, *tr. fr. German by* R. F. C. Hull. AnGP
Ex Libris. Arthur Upson. HBV; LBMV; LEAP
Ex Maria Virgine. Norbert Engels. ISi
Ex Nihilo. David Gascoyne. *Fr.* Miserere. NeBP
Ex Ore Infantium. Francis Thompson. *See* Child's Prayer, A.
"Exactly So." Lady T. Hastings. BOHV
Exaggerator. Mark Van Doren. AnFE; CoAnAm
Exaltation. Franz Werfel, *tr. fr. German by* Edith Abercrombie Snow. TrJP
Exaltation of Elementary Materials. Xavier Abril, *tr. fr. Spanish by* H. R. Hays. AnCL
Exalted chief, in thy superior mind. To the Shade of Washington. Richard Alsop. WOAH
Examination of His Mistress' Perfections, The. Francis Beaumont. GoBC
Examination of Shakespeare, The. Walter Savage Landor. *See* Citation and Examination of William Shakespeare, The.
Examine the mirror closely, and your face. Sunday, July 14th; a Fine Day at the Baths. Julian Symons. WaP
Examiner. F. R. Scott. TwCaPo
Example, The. W. H. Davies. AnFE; BMEP; ChMo; CMP; GTML; HBMV; MBP; MoBrPo; PIAE; POTE; POTT; PtOT; TrGrPo; TSW; TSWC; WHA
Example, The. Salvador Díaz Mirón, *tr. fr. Spanish by* Samuel Beckett. AnMP
Example. Marty Hale. AlBD
Example. John Keble. *See* Effect of Example, The.
Example of the Praise of God for His Omnipotency, An, out of the CXIII Psalm. John Hall. ReIE
Example seekest of science springing in the heart? The Artists. Jalal ed-Din Rumi. PeP
Exasperated, worn, you conjure a mansion. Desires of Men and Women. John Berryman. LiTM
Excavation. Clifford Bax. PtOT
Excavation, The. Max Endicoff. PoMa
Excavator, explore rock from the great Ice Age. The Cave-Drawing. Vernon Watkins. LiTB
Exceeding sorrow. O Mors! Quam Amara Est Memoria Tua Homini Pacem Habenti in Substantiis Suis. Ernest Dowson. GTSL; LoPS; OBMV; PG; POTT; ViPP; VLEP
Exceeding tall, but built so well his height. House-Surgeon. W. E. Henley. *Fr.* In Hospital. PoVP
Excelente Balade of Charitie, An. Thomas Chatterton. CEP; EiPP; EnRP; EV-3; GoTL; LiTB; LiTG; OBEC; SeCePo; TCEP
(Excellent Ballad of Charity, An.) BCEP
Excellence. Amos Bronson Alcott. IAP
Excellency of Christ. Giles Fletcher. *Fr.* Christ's Victory and Triumph, I. BePJ; MaRV; StJW; WGRP
("He is a path, if any be misled.") ChIP
Excellency of Wine, The. Roger Boyle, Earl of Orrery. SeCL
("'Tis wine that inspires.") SeEP
Excellent Ballad of Charity, An. Thomas Chatterton. *See* Excelente Balade of Charitie, An.
Excellent mistresse fairer than the moone. *Unknown.* SeCSL
Excellent New Song on a Seditious Pamphlet, An. Swift. CoMu
Excellent New Song upon His Grace Our Good Lord Archbishop of Dublin, An. Swift. CoMu
Excellent ritual of oils, of anointing. Sarcophagi. Bernard Spencer. FaBoMo
Excellent Sonnet of a Nymph, An. Sir Philip Sidney. ReIE
Excellent work, my Hugh. The Beset Wife. Robert Farren. OxBI
Excelsior. Longfellow. FaPON; HBV; HBVY; IAP; LPS-3; MW; NeHB; OTPC; PoFS; PTA-2; TCAP; TreF; WBLP
Excelsior, *parody. Unknown.* PA
Except at lunch I cannot say. Our Village Eleven. W. L. Donaldson. ShGoBo
Except I Love. *At. to* Robert Parry. *Fr.* The Mirror of Knighthood. ElL
Except the Lord Build the House. Psalms, CXXVII, Bible, *O.T.* OnPM; TrJP
Except Ye Repent. J. Franklin Pineo. ChIP
Exception, The. Phocylides, *tr. fr. Greek by* T. F. Higham. OxBG
Exception That Proves the Rule, The. Phocylides, *tr. fr. Greek by* F. L. Lucas. GrPE
(Problem in Logic, *tr. by* Lord Neaves.) OnPM
Excerpt, An. Burns. BTP
Excerpts from a "Gothic Notebook." Mario Luzi, *tr. fr. Italian by* William Fense Weaver. *Fr.* Gothic Notebook. LiTW
Excesses of God, The. Robinson Jeffers. CoV; MaRV; OS
Exchange, The. Samuel Taylor Coleridge. EmBrPo; ERP; FiBHP; HBV; LPS-1; OAEP; WhC
Exchange. Sister Mary Dorothy Ann. GoBC; PraNu
Exchange. W. H. Gerry. CAG
Exchange. Hafsa, *tr. fr. Arabic by* A. J. Arberry. MooP
Exchange of Fortune, An. Statyllius Flaccus, *tr. fr. Greek by* T. F. Higham. OxBG
Exchanges. Ernest Dowson. OBMV
Exciseman, The. Burns. *See* De'il's Awa wi' the Exciseman, The.
Exclusion. Emily Dickinson. *See* Soul selects her own society, The.
Excursion, The. Tu Fu, *tr. fr. Chinese by* Florence Ayscough *and* Amy Lowell. AWP; JAWP; WBP
Excursion, The, *sels.* Wordsworth.
Churchyard among the Mountains, The, *fr.* VII. ERP
Despondency Corrected, *fr.* IV. EnRP; ERP
Discourse of the Wanderer, and an Evening Visit to the Lake, *fr.* IX. EnRP
"Diverging now (as if his quest had been)," *fr.* II. OBRV
"I have seen/ A curious child," *fr.* IV. OBRV
("Curious child, A," *shorter sel.*) WGRP
(Faith, *shorter sel.*) MaRV
(Tidings of Invisible Things, *shorter sel., abr.*) GrCo-1
"I see around me here," *fr.* I. OBRV
Margaret; or, The Ruined Cottage, *fr.* I. EnRP; ERP
Mist Opening in the Hills, *fr.* II. UnW
"Once more to distant ages of the world," *fr.* IV. InP
Parsonage, The, *fr.* VIII. ERP
Sky after Storm, *fr.* II. BLV; BoLiVe
Solitary, The, *fr.* II. EnRP; ERP
Springtime with One Love, *fr.* VI. LiA
"Such was the Boy," *fr.* I. OBRV
(Communion, *abr.*) MaRV
"Tenour which my life holds, The," *fr.* III. OBRV
These Helps Solicit, *fr.* IV. GrCo-2
"'Twas summer, and the sun had mounted high," *fr.* I. EnRP

Excursion, The (*continued*)
Unknown Poets, *fr.* I. LPS-3
Wanderer, The, *fr.* I. EnRP; GEPC
"Within the soul a faculty abides," *fr.* IV. OBRV
Excusation of the Auctor, The. Stephen Hawes. *Fr.* The Pastime of Pleasure. ReIE
Excuse, The. Robert Heath. SeCL
Excuse, The. Sir Walter Ralegh. SiPS
Excuse for Not Returning the Visit of a Friend, An. Mei Yao Ch'en, *tr. fr. Chinese by* Kenneth Rexroth. OnPC
Excuse me, reader, though I now and then. To the Reader. Everard Guilpin. *Fr.* Skialetheia. ReIE; SiCE
Excuse Us, Animals in the Zoo. Annette Wynne. TiPo; UTS
Excuses. Al-Asamm, *tr. fr. Arabic by* A. J. Arberry. MooP
Excuses, The. Ferid ed-Din Attar, *tr. fr. Persian by* Edward Fitzgerald. *Fr.* The Bird-Parliament. PeP
Execration upon Vulcan, An. Ben Jonson. ReEn
Execution Chaplain, Mr. Sam Smith, Ordinary of Newgate, The. Tom Brown. *Fr.* An Elegy on That Most Orthodox and Pains-taking Divine, Mr. Sam Smith, Ordinary of Newgate. BeR
Execution of Alice Holt. *Unknown.* OxBoLi
Execution of King Charles, The. Andrew Marvell. *Fr.* An Horation Ode upon Cromwell's Return from Ireland. AnEnPo; PoRA
Execution of Major André. Anna Seward. BoHiPo
Execution of Major André. Nathaniel P. Willis. BoHiPo
Execution of Montrose, The. William Edmondstoune Aytoun. EV-5; GTBS; HBV; LPS-3; VA
Execution of the Klepht, The. Julius Typaldos, *tr. fr. Modern Greek by* Rae Dalven. MoGP
Exequies, The. Thomas Stanley. CaAE; MeLP; OBS; SeCL; SeEP
Exequy, The. Henry King. AEV; AtBAP; ATP; BrBE, *abr.*; CoEV; EPS (1942 ed.); EV-2; FaBoEn; InvP; LoBV; MeLP; MePo; OBS; PoEL-2; ReEn; SeCePo; SeCL; ViBoPo, *much abr.*; WHA
(Exequy on His Wife.) KN; LiTL, *abr.*; OBEV, *abr.*
(Exequy, to His Matchless Never to Be Forgotten Friend, The.) SeEP
Sels.
"Dear loss! since thy untimely fate." LO
"Sleep on, my Love, in thy cold bed." BCEP; CH; LoPS; PoFS; TrGrPo
Exercise in a Meadow. Jean Elliot. GoYe
Exercise in Aesthetics. Winfield Townley Scott. FiMAP
Exert thy voice, sweet harbinger of spring! To the Nightingale. Countess of Winchilsea. CEP; EiPP
Exeunt. Richard Wilbur. FiMAP
Exhaustless, Nature, is thy patient mood. Vain Quest of Beauty. Viktor Rydberg. AnSL
Exhibit A; the edge of this long knife. Here Is Your Realism. Maxwell Bodenheim. AnAmPo; LA
Exhortation. Thomas Hastings. AA
Exhortation. Pearce Young. PtPa
Exhortation: Summer, 1919. Claude McKay. CDC
Exhortation to Learn by Others' Trouble. Earl of Surrey. SiCE; TuPP
(Lines to Ratclif.) SiPS
Exhortation to Prayer. Margaret Mercer. AA
Exhortation to the Artists. Hyam Plutzik. FiMAP
Exhortation to Youth. Chaucer. *Fr.* Troilus and Criseyde, V. PoLi
(Love Unfeigned, The.) OBEV
("O young freshe [*or* yonge fresshe] folkes, he or [*or* and] she"). CAW; ExPo; LO
Exiit Diluculo. *Unknown, tr. fr. Latin by* George F. Whicher. *Fr.* Carmina Burana. LaP
Exile. Audrey Beecham. NeBP
Exile. Rex Browne. DDA
Exile, The. Gerald Bullett. POTE
Exile, The. Katherine Burton. JKCP (1955 ed.)
Exile, The. John Clare. RO
Exile, The. Walter de la Mare. POTE
Exile, The. Robert Graves. MoP
Exile. Donald Hall. NePA
Exile. Heine, *tr. fr. German by* James Thomson. OnPM
Exile. Theodore Maynard. MBP; MoBrPo (1942 ed.)
Exile, The. Larry Rubin. GoYe
Exile. Kathryn White Ryan. TBM
Exile. Virna Sheard. PeCV
Exile. Sidney Goodsir Smith. PoN
Exile. Tu Fu, *tr. fr. Chinese by* Chi Hwang Chu *and* Edna Worthley Underwood. OnPM
Exile. *Unknown, tr. fr. Irish by* Frank O'Connor. KiLC
Exile. Paul Verlaine. *See* Oh Sad, Sad Was My Soul.
Exile. Jennette Yeatman. GoYe
Exile at Rest, The. John Pierpont. AA
Exile from God. John Hall Wheelock. GoBC; SBMV; WGRP
Exile has never a friend of loyal and steadfast will, The. Friendlessness. Theognis. GrPE
Exile in Rome. Joachim du Bellay, *tr. fr. French by* Alan Conder. Regrets, XXV. TrFP
Exile of Erin, The. Thomas Campbell. HBV; LPS-2
Exile Song. Morris Jacob Rosenfeld, *tr. fr. Yiddish by* Joseph Leftwich. LiTW
Exiled. Edna St. Vincent Millay. EtS; OBAV; PoRA
Exiled Mother, The. Dion Boucicault. TIP
(Peasant Woman's Song, A.) GTIV
Exiled to bowers of beauty. The Londoner in the Country. Richard Church. HaMV
Exiles. "Æ." MoBrPo
Exiles. William Hamilton Hayne. AA
Exile's Departure, The. Whittier. CoBA
Exile's Devotion, The. Thomas d'Arcy McGee. VA
Exile's Letter. Li Po, *tr. fr. Chinese by* Ezra Pound. FaBoMo; NP; OxBA; PoE; SeCeV
Exile's Return, The. Robert Lowell. MiAP; NePA; OxBA
Exile's Song, The. Robert Gilfillan. HBV; VA
(O Why Left I My Hame?) EBSV
Exile's Song, The. *Unknown, tr. fr. Armenian by* Zabelle C. Boyajian. ArmLP
Existentialism. Lloyd Frankenberg. FiBHP
Exit. William Stanley Braithwaite. Sandy Star and Willie Gee, III. BANP
Exit. John Gould Fletcher. InP; MOAP; PFE
Exit. Wilson MacDonald. CaP; MM; OCL; TwCV; ViBoPo
Exit. E. A. Robinson. MoAmPo
Exit. Sir William Watson. VA
Exit God. Gamaliel Bradford. HBMV; InMe; MaRV; QS
Exit the ribald clown. Colombine. Hugh McCrae. BoAV; NeLNL
Exodus. Roy Basler. SiTL
Exodus, *sels.* Bible, *O.T.*
Burning Bush, The, III: 1–14. GrCo-1
Child Moses, The, I: 7–II: 15. OuHeWo
Golden Calf, The, XXXII: 1–31, *abr.* GrCo-1
Ten Commandments, The. GrCo-1 (XIX: 1–XX: 21, *abr.*); OHFP (XX: 2–26); TreF (XX: 1–17); WBLP (XX: 2–26)
Song of Moses, The, XV: 1–18. LiTW
(Lord Is a Man of War, The, XV: 3–10.) WaaP
(Then Sang Moses, XV: 1–18.) TrJP
("Then sang Moses and the children of Israel this song," XV: 1–27.) PoFr
(Triumphal Chant, XV: 1–13, 18.) TrGrPo
(War Song of the Red Sea, XV: 1–10.) BHV
Exodus, *sels.* Cædmon(?), *tr. fr. Anglo-Saxon.*
Cloud by Day, The, *tr. by* Benjamin Thorpe. TCEP
Drowning of Pharaoh and His Army, The, *tr. by* Benjamin Thorpe. TCEP
Parting of the Red Sea, The, *tr. by* Charles W. Kennedy. AnOE
Exodus for Oregon. Joaquin Miller. AmPP (3d ed.); IAP; TCAP
"Tale half told and hardly understood, A," *sel.* BAP
Exodus from a Renaissance Gallery. Ellen M. V. Acton. GoYe
Exodus from Egypt, The. Ezekielos of Alexandria, *tr. fr. Greek by* E. H. Gifford. TrJP
Exorcism. Oliver St. John Gogarty. AnIL
Exordium. George Cabot Lodge. LBMV
Exortum Est in Love and Lysse. *Unknown.* AnEC
Exotic Perfume. Baudelaire, *tr. fr.* French. OnPM, *tr. by* Arthur Symons; TrFP, *tr. by* Alan Conder
(Parfum exotique, *tr. by* Arthur Symons.) AWP
Expanded waters gather on the plain, Th'. The Flood. Ovid. *Fr.* Metamorphoses, I. ChTr
Expansive puppets percolate self-unction. The Canadian Authors Meet. F. R. Scott. BoCaPo; WhC
Expatriate. Mary Brown Onstott. PoMa
"Expatriates, The/ Come next," I began. Amy Lowell. *Fr.* A Critical Fable. PtP
Expect! William Pierson Merrill. OQP; QP-2
Expect to-morrow to be fair. Afanasi Fet, *tr. fr. Russian by* Oliver Elton. BoRS
Expectans Expectavi. Charles Sorley. FaBoCh; HBMV; LoGBV; MaRV; QS; WGRP
Expectant at the country gate the lantern. III. Bernard Spencer. NeBP
Expectant Father, The. E. O. Laughlin. LauV
Expectation, The. Frederick William Faber. *Fr.* Our Lady's Expectation. ACP
Expectation. Thomas Stanley. ElSeCe; OBS; SeCL; SeEP
(Destiny.) LoBV
Expectation. Theodore Wratislaw. VA
Expectation of Death. *Unknown, tr. fr. Greek by* William Cowper. *See* Epigram: "Far happier are the dead, methinks, than they."
Expected Guest, The. Sidney Keyes. PoN
Expecting Him, my door was open wide. Praesto. Thomas Edward Brown. ChIP
Expedition to Wessagusset, The. Longfellow. *Fr.* The Courtship of Miles Standish, V *and* VII. PAH

Expense [*or* Expence] of spirit in a waste of shame, The [*or* Th']. Lust [*or* Past Reason Hunted]. Shakespeare. Sonnets, CXXIX. AnEnPo; AWP; BLV; BrBE; CaAE; CBE; CoBE; CoEV; ElSeCe; EnL; ES; ExPo; FaBoEn; GTBS-W; InPo; JAWP; KN; LiA; LiTB; LiTG; LiTL; LO; LoBV; MaPo; OBEV; OBSC; OtMeF; PeBoSo; PoE; PoEL-2; PoFS; ReaPo; ReEn; ReIE; RiBV; SeCePo; SeCeV; ShBV-4; TOP; TrGrPo; UnPo (3d ed.); ViBoPo; WBP
Expenses. Adelaide Crapsey. NP; TOP
Expensive Wife, The. Judah ibn Sabbatai. *Fr.* The Gift of Judah the Woman-Hater. TrJP
Experience. Emerson. AnAmPo; AnNE; IAP; LA; LiTA; MOAP; PoEL-4; TCAP
Experience. Lesbia Harford. BoAu
Experience. Hugo von Hofmannsthal, *tr. fr. German by* Alfred Schwarz. AnGP
Experience. Aline Kilmer. HBMV
Experience. Frederic W. H. Myers. *Fr.* Saint Paul. MaRV
Experience. John Boyle O'Reilly. ACP; OBVV
Experience. Dorothy Parker. InMe; WhC
Experience. Eden Phillpotts. LBBV
Experience, The. Edward Taylor. AmPP (4th ed.)
Experience. Tennyson. *See* Challenge of Life, The.
Experience. Edith Wharton. AA
Experience and a Moral, An. Frederick Swarthout Cozzens. LPS-1
Experience Evoked. Richard Eberhart. TwAmPo
Experience, The (Meditation Three). Edward Taylor. *Fr.* Sacramental Meditations. CoV
Experience now doth show what God us taught before. The Poor Estate to Be Holden for Best. *Unknown, at. to* Edward Seymour, Duke of Somerset. OBSC; SiCE; TuPP
"Experience, though all authority." The Wife of Bath's Prologue. Chaucer, *mod. by* Theodore Morrison. *Fr.* The Canterbury Tales. EnL
"Experience, though noon auctoritee." The Wife of Bath's Prologue. Chaucer. *Fr.* The Canterbury Tales. EnLi-1 (1949 ed.); OxBoLi; PoEL-1
Expert designing the long-range gun, The. Munitions Expert. W. H. Auden. MaRV
Experts on Woman. Arthur Guiterman. InMe
Expiation. Paul Verlaine, *tr. fr. French by* Alan Conder. TrFP
Expiatory chapel, chains. Jardin de la Chapelle Expiatoire. Robert Finch. PeCV
Expiration, The. John Donne. AtBAP; ATP; ElL; ElSeCe; EV-2; MeLP; MePo
("So, so, break off this last lamenting kiss.") EG
Explanation, An. Walter Learned. *See* In Explanation.
Explanation, An. Martial, *tr. fr. Latin by* Paul Nixon. RoL
Explanation of the Grasshopper, An. Vachel Lindsay. FaPON; GFA; OTPC (1946 ed.); PCH; PoRh; StVeCh (Grasshopper, The.) TSW; TSWC
Explanation, on Coming Home Late. Richard Hughes. ThWaDe
Explanations of Love. Carl Sandburg. ChMo; CMP; LiTL; LoPo
Exploiter of the shadows. Fox. Clifford Dyment. HaMV
Exploration by Air. A. Fleming MacLiesh. PoF
Explorations. Louis MacNeice. ChMP; CoBMV
Explorer, The. Anthony Delius. BoSA
Explorer, The. Kipling. PoTo; WHA
(Go, *2 sts.*) GrCo-2
Explorer, The. William Plomer. BoSA
Expostulation, An. Isaac Bickerstaffe. FiBHP
Expostulation, The. Thomas Shadwell. *Fr.* The Squire of Alsatia. OAEP
Expostulation. Whittier. IAP
Expostulation and Reply. Wordsworth. BEL; BPN; EM-2; EmBrPo; EnL; EnLi-2; EnLit; EnRP; EPN; EPP; ERP; GEPC; HBV; OAEP; OBRV; PoE; TwP; UnPo
Communion with Nature, *sel.* MaRV
Exposure. Ibn al-Zaqqaq, *tr. fr. Arabic by* A. J. Arberry. MooP
Exposure. Wilfred Owen. FaBoMo; LiTM (rev. ed.); MoVE; OnHM; WaP
Express. W. R. Rodgers. MoVE
Express, The. Stephen Spender. AlDL; AnFE; BBV (1951 ed.); EnL; EnLi-2 (1949 ed.); EnLit; ExPo; LiTM; MBP; MoAB; MoBrPo; MoVE; NAMP; NeMA; PoLFOT; ReaPo; SeCeV; ShBV-3
Express Train. Karl Kraus, *tr. fr. German by* Albert Bloch. TrJP
Express Trains. MacKnight Black. PoMa
Expression. Isaac Rosenberg. MoBrPo
Expulsion from Paradise. Milton. *Fr.* Paradise Lost, XII. BEL; ChTr
("He ended and they both descend the hill.") ATP; NBE; SeEP; TCEP
Exquisite face that agony must tear. The Boy Christ. Helene Mullins. StJW
Exquisite incompleteness, blossom foreshadowing fruit, An. Girlhood. *Unknown.* LPS-2
Exquisite invention this, An. Love-Letters Made in Flowers. Leigh Hunt. LPS-1
Exquisite Lady. Mary Elizabeth Osborn. NePoAm-2
Exquisite painter Ko-tsu was often reproached, The. The Windmill. Allen Upward. *Fr.* Scented Leaves from a Chinese Jar. NP
Exquisite reaper in a field of song. On a Favorite Poet. Sister Mary Thérèse. PraNu
Exquisite Sonnet, The. J. C. Squire. HBMV
Exquisite spirit, rudely caught and tangled. Psyche's Lamp. Ada Foster Murray. BAP
Exquisite stillness! What serenities. Don Juan's Address to the Sunset. Robert Nichols. AlDL; OBMV; POTE
Exquisite wines and comestibles. Martial in London. Mortimer Collins. ALV; BOHV; InMe
Exspecto Resurrectionem. Charlotte Mew. LO
Extasie, The. John Donne. *See* Ecstasy, The.
Extempore Effusion upon the Death of James Hogg. Wordsworth. BPN; EmBrPo; FiP; MyFE; OBRV; PoD, *6 sts.*; PtP; TriL
Extempore to Voltaire Criticising Milton. Edward Young. ViBoPo
Extempore Verses Intended to Allay the Violence of Party-Spirit. John Byrom. *See* Jacobite Toast, A.
Extempore Verses upon a Trial of Skill between the Two Great Masters of the Noble Science of Defence, Messrs. Figg and Sutton. John Byrom. OBEC
Exterior speech is oft a curse. Thomas Lake Harris. *Fr.* Silent Tongue. BAP
Extermination. Richard D'Alton Williams. OnYI
Extinguish My Eyes. Rainer Maria Rilke. *See* Put Out My Eyes, and I Can See You Still.
Extra at the House, The. Bud Cornish. AlBD
Extra Prayer, The. Annie Willis McCullough. PraP
Extract from Addresses to the Academy of Fine Ideas, An. Wallace Stevens. GTBS-W; LiTA; LiTM (rev. ed.)
Extract from the Conclusion of a Poem, Composed in Anticipation of Leaving School. Wordsworth. *See* Dear Native Regions.
Extracts from the Rubaiyat of Omar Cayenne. Gelett Burgess. BOHV
Extraordinary Dog, The. Nancy Byrd Turner. AlBD; TiPo
Extraordinary Visit. Vincent Starrett. DaM
Extras. Richard Burton. AA
Extreme Unction. Ernest Dowson. ACP; CAW; JKCP; LEAP; MBP; MoBrPo; OBMV; POTT; VLEP
Extremes. James Whitcomb Riley. FaPON; GoBP; HBVY; MPB; PCH; PPL
Extremum Tanain. Horace, *tr. fr. Latin by* Austin Dobson. Odes, III, 10. AWP; JAWP; WBP
Exultate Deo. Christina Rossetti. MeRV
Exultation. Emily Dickinson. *See* Exultation is the Going.
Exultation. Shaemus O'Sheel. PC
Exultation is the going. Exultation. Emily Dickinson. AmP; AmPP; CoBA
Eye, An. Karin Ek, *tr. fr. Swedish by* Charles W. Stork. AnSL
Eye, The. Robinson Jeffers. CoBMV; CrMA; FaBoEn; GTBS-W; LiTA; LiTM; OxBA; WaP
Eye, The. Allen Tate. LiTA
Eye, The. Eithne Wilkins. NeBP
Eye and Heart. Ibn al-Batti, *tr. fr. Arabic by* A. J. Arberry. MooP
Eye can hardly pick them out, The. At Grass. Philip Larkin. HaMV; NePoEA; PoN
Eye drags all of winter, The. News Reel. David Ross. GoYe
Eye-flattering [*or* Fie! flattering] fortune, look thou never so fair. Fortune [*or* Lewis, the Lost Lover]. Sir Thomas More. *Fr.* Two Short Ballettes. GoBC; OBSC; PoLi; TuPP
Eye for an Eye, An. Theognis, *tr. fr. Greek by* F. L. Lucas. GrPE
Eye of Humility, The. Kay Smith. BoCaPo (1948 ed.)
Eye of indifferent intent, The. He Is Shy. Theodore Colombo. CAG
Eye of stone./ Tear of bronze. Angelus. Carmen Alicia Cadilla. AnCL
Eye of the Beholder, The. James Lionel Michael. BoAu
Eye of the garden, queen of flowers. To the Rose. Sir John Davies. *Fr.* Hymns of Astraea. OBSC; SiCE; TuPP
Eye that mark'd thy flight with deadly aim, The. The Slain Eagle. William Gilmore Simms. APW
Eye whose magic wakes the hidden springs, An. Osler. William Sydney Thayer. PoP
Eye winker. *Unknown.* OxNR
Eye with the piercing eagle's fire, An. Thaddeus Stevens. Phoebe Cary. GA; MOAH; PAH
Eyelashes. Ibn al-Hammara, *tr. fr. Arabic by* A. J. Arberry. MooP
Eyeless and Limbless and Shattered. Cecil Roberts. *Fr.* Charing Cross. BMEP
Eyeless at Gaza. Milton. *Fr.* Samson Agonistes. LH
(Hero in Prison, A.) BHV

Eyeless at Gaza (*continued*)
(Samson Fallen.) OBS
Eyeless labourer in the night, The. Woman to Man. Judith Wright. BoAV; MoAuPo
Eyelids of eve fall together at last, The. Before Waterloo. Thomas Hardy. *Fr.* The Dynasts. EPP; MoAB; PoVP
Eyes, The. Ezra Pound. ChMo; CMP; PFE
Eyes and Tears. Andrew Marvell. EV-2; MePo
Eyes do not lie. Remainder. Frederika Blankner. GoYe
Eyes gaze no more as yet you may. *Unknown.* SeCSL
Eyes Have It, The. William Stephens. NAMP
Eyes, Hide My Love. Samuel Daniel. *Fr.* Hymen's Triumph. EIL
(Secrecy.) OBSC
Eyes I dare not meet in dreams. T. S. Eliot. *Fr.* The Hollow Men. GTBS-D
Eyes, lakes withal my simple drunkenness to be reborn. The Chastised Clown. Stéphane Mallarmé. AnFP
Eyes lie awake in hope of happy seinge. *Unknown.* SeCSL
Eyes like the morning star. The Colorado Trail. *Unknown.* AS; CoSo
Eyes of Children at the Brink of the Sea's Grasp, The. Josephine Jacobsen. NePoAm-2
Eyes of God, The. Hermann Hagedorn. HBMV; TBM
Eyes of God, The. "Gabriel Setoun." PPL
Eyes of Lincoln, The. Walt Mason. OQP; QP-1
Eyes of My Regret, The. Angelina Weld Grimké. CDC
Eyes of Night-Time. Muriel Rukeyser. MiAP; NePA
Eyes of twenty centuries, The. Judas Iscariot. Stephen Spender. MoAB; MoBrPo (1950 ed.)
Eyes of Wonder, The. Jessie Corrigan Pegis. JKCP (1955 ed.)
Eyes open to a cry of pulleys, The. Love Calls Us to the Things of This World. Richard Wilbur. FiMAP; NePA; NePoEA; PoLFOT; PoRA; TrGrPo (rev. ed.)
Eyes red, the lips blue, The. The Three Seamstresses. Isaac Leibush Peretz. TrJP
Eyes So Tristful. Diego de Saldaña, *tr. fr. Spanish by* Longfellow. AWP; JAWP; WBP
Eyes that are clear, serene. Madrigal. Gutierre de Cetina. LiTW
Eyes That Last I Saw in Tears. T. S. Eliot. InPo; ViBoPo
Eyes that weep for pity of the heart, The. Canzone. Dante, *tr. by* Dante Gabriel Rossetti. La Vita Nuova, XIX. AWP; LyMA; LyPI; OuHeWo; WGRP
Eyes that without a tongue can speak to me. Rispetto. Angelo Poliziano. LyPI
Eyes, the face, the limbs of heavenly mould, The. Petrarch. *Fr.* Sonnets to Laura: To Laura in Death. PrPoCR
Eyes which were first to gaze—my reckless eyes. Love's Assize [*or* Sonnet: Love's Assize]. Guido Cavalcanti. LiTW; LyPI
Eyesight and hearing flower, and the spirit flowers today. Uncle or Sun. Vladimir Kazin. RuPo
Eye-Witness. Ridgely Torrence. BAP; CP; HBMV; NV; SBMV; TCPD
Tramp Sings, The, *sel.* PFY
Ez fer war, I call it murder. War. James Russell Lowell. *Fr.* The Biglow Papers, 1st series, No. 1. MaRV
Ez for War. James Russell Lowell. *See* Letter from Mr. Ezekiel Biglow of Jaalam to the Hon. Joseph T. Buckingham, A.
Ezekiel. Laurence Binyon. ChMP
Ezekiel, *sels.* Bible, *O.T.*
Lamentation, XIX: 2–9. TrJP
Thy Mother Was like a Vine, XIX: 10–14. TrJP
Unfaithful Shepherds, XXXIV: 1–28. WoL
Ezekiel. Thomas S. Jones, Jr. QS
"Ezekiel he came out." Erie Canal. *Unknown.* ABF
Ezekiel in the valley of Dry Bones. Ezekiel. Laurence Binyon. ChMP
Ezekiel Saw de Wheel. *Unknown.* APW
(Ezekiel, You and Me, *with music, very diff. vers.*) AS
"Ezek'l saw de wheel, Ezek'l saw de wheel," *sel., sl. diff.* ExPo
Ezra Perrin's family, on his mother's side. A Health Note. Walter Hard. AnNE
Ezry. Archibald MacLeish. MoVE

F

F Is the Fighting Firetruck. Phyllis McGinley. *Fr.* All Around the Town. FaPON
Fa La La. *Unknown, at. to* John Hilton. CH
(Madrigal.) SiTL
("My mistress frowns when she should play.") OxBoLi
Fabius, this region desolate and drear. The Ruins of Itálica. Rodrigo Caro. AnSpL-1
Fable: "Bough will bend, the leaf will sometime fall, The." Mary Mills. NePoAm
Fable: "I led him on into the frosted wood." George O'Neil. NP
Fable, A: Mice and Felis, The. John Kendrick. CIV
Fable: "Mountain and the squirrel, The." Emerson. AmP; AmPP (3d ed.); AnNE; APW; BOHV; FaFP; HBV; HBVY; IAP; InMe; LiTA; LiTG; MPB; NePA; PG (1945 ed.); PRWS; PTA-1; RG; SiTL; StaSt; TCAP; TSW; TSWC; UTS; YaD
(Mountain and the Squirrel, The.) BeLS; BoChLi (1950 ed.); BoTP; CG; FaBoBe; FaPON; GoTP; LaNeLa; NeHB; OnHT; OTPC
Fable: "O the vines were golden, the birds were loud." Frederic Prokosch. LiTM (1946 ed.); WaP
Fable: "Oh, there once was a lady." Dorothy Parker. ALV
Fable: "Tale is every time the same, The." Maurice James Craig. NeIP
Fable: "Tin of corned beef, chained like a lorgnette, A." Alfred Jarry, *tr. fr. French by* A. L. Lloyd. MiFP
Fable for Critics, A. James Russell Lowell. IAP, *abr.*
Sels.
Bryant. AnNE
("There is Bryant, as quiet, as cool, and as dignified.") CoBA; PtP
Cooper. AnNE; OxBA
("Here's Cooper, who's written six volumes to show.") CoBA
Daphne's Embarkation. APW
Emerson. AmPP (4th ed.); AnNE; APW; OnAP; OxBA
("There comes Emerson first, whose rich words.") CoBA; OuHeWo; PtP; TCAP
Hawthorne. AmPP (4th ed.); AnNE; OxBA
("There is Hawthorne, with genius so shrinking and rare.") CoBA
Holmes. AnNE
("There's Holmes, who is matchless among you for wit.") CoBA
Irving. AnNE
("What! Irving? thrice welcome, warm heart and fine brain.") CoBA
Lowell. AmPP (4th ed.); OxBA
(On Himself.) AA
("There is Lowell, who's striving Parnassus to climb.") CoBA
Margaret Fuller. APW
Poe and Longfellow. AnNE; APW; OxBA
("There comes Poe, with his raven, like Barnaby Rudge.") CoBA; PtP
To His Countrymen. AA
Whittier. AmPP (4th ed.); AnNE; APW; OxBA
("There is Whittier, whose swelling and vehement heart.") CoBA; PtP
Fable of a Forgotten Woman. Louis Johnson. AnNZ
Fable of Acis, Polyphemus and Galatea, The, *sel.* Ovid, *tr. fr. Latin by* Dryden. *Fr.* Metamorphoses, XIII.
I Heard the Ruffian-Shepherd Rudely Blow. AtBAP
Fable of Belling the Cat, The. William Langland. *Fr.* The Vision of Piers Plowman: The Prologue (B *text*). EPP, *Middle English and mod. vers.*
Fable of Midas, The. Swift. EV-3
Fable of the Magnet and the Churn, The. W. S. Gilbert. *Fr.* Patience. FaPON; MPB
Fable of the War, A. Howard Nemerov. NePoEA
Fable of white sea, The. Coward. Harold Lewis Cook. NP
Fable which I now present, The. The Musical Ass. Tomaso de Yriarte. BOHV
Fables for the Ladies, *sel.* Edward Moore.
Poet and His Patron, The, V. CEP
Fables of Flora, The, *sels.* John Langhorne.
Evening Primrose, The. OBEC
Wall-Flower, The, *abr.* RO
Fabliau of Florida. Wallace Stevens. NP
Fabre, the Bughunter. James Schevill. FiMAP
Fabula. *Unknown.* CIV
Fabulists, The. Kipling. ChMP
Façade, *sels.* Edith Sitwell.
By the Lake. AV
Dark Song. FaBoTw
Drum, The; the Narrative of the Demon of Tedworth. BoW; FaBoTw
Fête Galante. CaAE
Madame Mouse Trots. FaBoCh
Satyr in the Periwig, The. AnEnPo
Sir Beelzebub. CoBMV; HoPM; MBP; MoAB; MoBrPo
(When Sir Beelzebub.) FaBoMo
Waltz. OAEP (2d ed.)
Face, A. Robert Browning. BPN; GEPC; PoVP; VA; VLEP
Face, The. Anthony Euwer. *See* Limerick: "As a beauty I'm not a great star."
Face, The. Ebenezer Jones. VA
Face, The. Edwin Muir. ChMP; FaBoMo
Face. Carl Sandburg. ReMP

Face, The. A. J. M. Smith. BoCaPo (1943 ed.)
Face. Jean Toomer. CDC
Face against the Pane, The. Thomas Bailey Aldrich. TreFS
Face at the latticed window. No More! Praxilla. GrR
Face of a Friend, The. Henry van Dyke. OQP; QP-2
Face of a gazelle, The. Gazelle. Ibn al-Qabila. MooP
Face of all the world is changed, I think, The. Sonnets from the Portuguese, VII. Elizabeth Barrett Browning. ATP; BEL; BPN; CoBE; EmBrPo; EnLi-2; EnLit; EPN; EPP; HBV; OAEP; OuHeWo; PFE; TOP; ViPo
Face of Jesus Christ, The. Christina Rossetti. *Fr.* The Descent from the Cross. BePJ
Face of the landscape is a mask, The. Mask. Stephen Spender. MoAB; MoBrPo; NeMA
Face of the precipice is black with lovers, The. In Defence of Humanism. David Gascoyne. LiTM (rev. ed.)
Face of the Waters, The. Robert D. Fitzgerald. BoAV; MoAuPo
Face on the Floor, The. Hugh D'Arcy. *See* Face upon the Floor, The.
Face that should content me wondrous [*or* wonders] well, A. A Description of Such a One As He Would Love [*or* Epigram]. Sir Thomas Wyatt. ElSeCe; EnLoPo; EPP; OBSC; ReEn; SiCE; TuPP
Face to Face. Frances Cochrane. HBV
Face to face in my chamber, my silent chamber, I saw her. Confessions. Elizabeth Barrett Browning. OBVV; VLEP
Face to Face with Reality. John Oxenham. WBLP
Face to face with the sunflower. The Secret Joy. Mary Webb. BoTP
Face to Face with Trouble, *sel.* Margaret E. Sangster.
"Oh, face to face with trouble," *st.* 6. PoToHe
Face upon [*or* on] the Floor, The. Hugh Antoine D'Arcy. BeLS; BLPA; FaBoBe; FaFP; HBV; NeHB; PTA-1; TreF; YaD
Face we choose to miss, The. Emily Dickinson. BoFr
Faces. Lola Ridge. MAP; MoAmPo (1942 ed.)
Faces. Walt Whitman. Po; PoEL-5
Whitman's Mother, *sel.* APW
(Justified Mother of Men, The.) OHIP
Faces I see, as through the street I go. In the Strand. Havelock Ellis. PoP
Faces in the Procession. Fuyuhiko Kitagawa, *tr. fr. Japanese by* Takamichi Ninomiya *and* D. J. Enright. PoLJ
Facets of the flesh require, The. Duality. Kenneth Slade Alling. AnAmPo; CAW
Facing Death. Chih Ming, *tr. fr. Chinese by* Henry H. Hart. OnPM; PoHN; WoL
Facing each other in drowsiness on the straw stool. The Guest Goes on His Way. Lu Yu. WhP
Facing My Portrait. Yolanda Bedregal de Cónitzer, *tr. fr. Spanish by* Donald Devenish Walsh. AnCL
Facing the Gulf. Margaret L. Woods. *Fr.* The Return. HBMV
Facing the New Year. Mark Guy Pearse. BLRP
Facing the New Year. *Unknown.* PGD; PSO
Facing the sudden gulf, the silent. Facing the Gulf. Margaret L. Woods. *Fr.* The Return. HBMV
Facing West from California's Shores. Walt Whitman. IAP; MoAmPo; MOAP; OnAP
Faction, that ever dwells. Love and Fortune. Fulke Greville. Caelica, XXIX. OBSC
Factories, The. Margaret Widdemer. BAP; CV; HBV; LEAP; MaRV; NeMA; PC; PFE; PoeMoYo; PoMa; POT; PoTo; PYM; TCAP
Factory, The, *sel.* Letitia E. Landon.
"There rests a shade above yon town." BCEP
Factory Children. Richard Burton. MaRV
Factory Girl. Maxwell Bodenheim. MAP; MoAmPo (1942 ed.)
Factory Girl, The, *with music. Unknown.* ABF
Factory Street in Daylight. Paul Zech, *tr. fr. German by* Thomas Riley. WoL
Factory Whistles. Aleksey Kapitonovich Gastev, *tr. fr. Russian by* Babette Deutsch. TrRV
Factory Windows Are Always Broken. Vachel Lindsay. CrMA; FaFP; LiTA; LiTM; NAMP; NePA; PoeMoYo; PoMa
Fade in the sound of summer music. Notes for a Movie Script. M. Carl Holman. PoNe
Fade, Then. Conrad Aiken. Priapus and the Pool, XX. MOAP
Faded boy in sallow clothes, A. Emily Dickinson. PoEL-5
Faded Coat of Blue, The. J. H. McNaughton. BlG
Faded Leaves. Alice Cary. PEOR
Faded Letter, A. William J. Fischer. CAW
Faded perfume of forgotten years, The. In a Volume of Austin Dobson. Mary Elizabeth Coleridge. PoVP
Faded Pictures. William Vaughn Moody. OBAV
Fades now the light where the sea mirrored the glory of heaven. Above the Dark. Jarl Hemmer. AnSL
Fadey had fought on every front. Vladimir Mayakovsky *and others. Fr.* The Tale of How Fadey Learned of the Law Protecting Workingmen. TrRV
Fading Autumn. Sir Walter Scott. *Fr.* The Lord of the Isles, I. EV-4
Fading Beauty. Samuel Daniel. *See* Description of Beauty, A.
Fading Beauty. *Unknown.* SeCL; SeEP
Fading-Leaf and Fallen-Leaf. Richard Garnett. OBVV; TOP
Fading light/ Dims the sight. Words for Army Bugle Calls: Taps. *Unknown.* TreF
Fading Rose, The, *sel.* Philip Freneau.
Epitaph: "Here—for they could not help but die." AA
Fading whistles outline our broken city, The. Poem from London, 1941. George Woodcock. NeBP
Faerie Fair, The. Florence Harrison. BoTP
Faerie Queen, The. Sir Walter Ralegh. *See* Vision upon This Conceit of the Faerie Queene, A.
Faerie Queene, The, *sels.* Spenser.
Address to Venus, *fr.* IV, 10, *tr. fr. the Latin of* Lucretius, *fr.* De Rerum Natura. AnEnPo; AWP
(Prayer to Venus.) ElL
"And as she backward cast her busy eye," *fr.* III, 11.
(Be Bold.) MyFE
"And fast beside there trickled softly downe," *fr.* II, 5. PC
"And him beside rides fierce revenging Wrath," *fr.* I, 4. MyFE
"And is there care in heaven? and is there love," *fr.* II, 8. OxBoCh
(Bright Squadrons, The.) GoBC
(Guardian Angels.) OBSC
(Heavenly Aid.) MaRV
(Ministering Angels.) CBE
(Ministering Spirits, The.) PC
(Ministry of Angels, The.) LPS-2
"And more to lulle him in his slumber soft," *fr.* I, 1. PC
Archimago's Hermitage, *mod. vers., fr.* I, 1. BCEP
Artegall and Radigund, *fr.* V, 5. OBSC
August, *fr.* VII, 7. GN
Autumn, *fr.* VII, 7. GN; HOAH, *abr.*
Balme, *fr.* I, 11. CH
Behold, O Man, *fr.* II, 6. ElL
"Both roof, and floor, and walls were all of gold," *fr.* II, 7.
(Mammon's House.) MyFE
Bower of Bliss, The, *fr.* II, 12. BCEP, *mod. vers., abr.*; CH; CoEV; FaBoEn; FiP; LoBV; LPS-3; OBSC; PoEL-1; UnS, *2 sts.*
("Eftsoons they heard a most melodious sound.") ViBoPo
(Gather the Rose.) ElL; WHA
("Thence passing forth, they shortly doe arryve.") ATP
Britomart in the House of Busirane, *fr.* III, 11-12. FiP
Cave of Despair, The, *fr.* I, 9. LoBV
Cave of Mammon, The, *fr.* II, 7. BCEP, *mod. vers.,* 29 *sts.*; FiP, 12 *sts.*; LiA, 3 *sts.*; PoEL-1
(House of Richesse, The, 3 *sts.*) CH
Cymochles and Phaedria, *fr.* II, 6. OBSC
Cymochles in the Bower of Bliss, *fr.* II, 5. PreP
Dame Nature, *fr.* VII, 7. PoEL-1
Dance, The: "It was an hill placed in an open plain," *fr.* VI, 10. TrGrPo
(Dance of the Graces, The.) OBSC; RiBV
Death of the Dragon, The, *abr., fr.* I, 11. WHA
Despair, *fr.* I, 9. NBE; SeCePo, *shorter sel.*
(To Be or Not to Be.) FaBoEn
Dragon, The, *fr.* I, 11. SeCePo
Garden of Adonis, The, *fr.* III, 6. NBE; PoEL-1
Garden of Proserpina, The, *fr.* II, 7. ChTr
"Gentle Knight was pricking on the plaine, A," I, 1. ATP; BoLiVe, *abr.*; CoBE; EPP (*fr.* 1 *and* 3); ExPo; PIAE (5 *sts.*); TyEnPo
(Red-Cross Knight, The, 2 *sts.*) GoBC
(Una and the Red Cross Knight.) LPS-3 (7 *sts.*)
Happy Isle, The, *fr.* IV, 10. OBSC
"He, making speedy way through 'spersèd air," *fr.* I, 1. InP
(Cave of Sleep. The.) LPS-3
(House of Morpheus, The.) UnPo (1st ed.)
"He there does now enjoy eternal[l] rest," *fr.* I, 9. MyFE; PoD
House of Ate, The, *fr.* IV, 1. OBSC
House of Pride, The, *fr.* I, 4. WHA
Idle Lake, The, *br. sel. fr.* II, 6. PC
"Joyous birds shrouded in cheerful shade, The," *fr.* II, 12.
(Music at the Bower of Bliss, The.) MyFE
Kinds of Trees to Plant, *fr.* I, 1. OHIP
Legend of Sir Guyon, or of Temperance, The, II, 12, *abr.* WHA
Legend of the Knight [*or* Knyght] of the Red Cross, or of Holiness, I, 1-12. BEL; EM-1 (1-3); EnLi-1 (1 *and* 2); GEPC; OAEP; TOP (1 *and* 4)
(Invocation to the Faerie Queene, *prol.*) FiP
("Lo! I, the man whose Muse whylome did maske.") EnLit, *prol.,* 1-2; REAL, *prol. and* 1; TCEP, *prol.,* 1, 3, 4, 5, *and* 12, *abr.*
(Story of the Red Cross Knight, or of Holiness, The, *sels. fr.* 1, 4, 9, 11, *and* 12.) EV-1
"Like as the tide that comes from th' Ocean main," *fr.* IV, 3. HoPM

Faerie Queene, The (*continued*)
Love, *introd. to* IV. OBSC
Malbecco and Hellenore, *fr.* III, 9 *and* 10. MaPo
"Mammon emovéd was with inward wrath," *fr.* II, 7. ViBoPo
Masque of Cupid, The, *fr.* III, 11 *and* 12. EV-1; PoEL-1 (*fr.* 12)
(Mask of Cupid, The, *fr.* 12.) OBSC
(Procession of Cupid, The, *fr.* 12.) NBE
May, *fr.* VII, 7. GN; PoRL
Mermaids, The, *fr.* II, 12. ChTr
Mutability [*or* Mutabilitie], *fr.* VII, 7 *and* 8. CoEV (*fr.* 8); FaBoEn (*fr.* 7); OxBoCh (*fr.* 8); PoEL-1 (*fr.* 7 *and* 8); TwCrTr (*fr.* 8)
Nature, *fr.* VII, 7. NBE
Next unto Him Was Neptune Pictured, *fr.* III, 11. EtS
"Noble heart that harbours virtuous thought, The," *fr.* I, 5. ViBoPo
(Fight of the Red Cross Knight and the Heathen Sansjoy, The.) FiP
Now Strike Your Sailes Ye Jolly Mariners, *fr.* I, 12, *and* II, 6. EtS
"Now when the rosy fingered Morning faire," *fr.* I, 2. BoLiVe
Nymphs and Graces Dancing to a Shepherd's Pipe, The, *mod. vers., fr.* VI, 10. BCEP
"One day, nigh wearie of the yrkesome way," *fr.* I, 3. BoLiVe
(Una and the Lion.) BCEP, *mod. vers.;* LPS-3
Pastoral, A: "From thence into the open fields he fled," *fr.* VI, 9. OBSC
Prayer to Venus, *fr.* IV, 10. ElL
Prince Arthur, *fr.* I, 7. OBSC
Prologue: "So oft as I with state of present time," *fr.* V. PoFS
Sea Monsters, *fr.* II, 12. ChTr; FaBoEn
("Waves come rolling, and the billowes rore, The.") AtBAP
Sleep after Toil, *fr.* I, 9. ChTr
"So, forth issew'd the Seasons of the yeare," *fr.* VII, 7.
(Mask of Mutability, The.) OBSC
(Pageant of the Seasons and the Months, The.) EV-1
(Procession of Times and Seasons, The.) NBE
(Seasons, *abr.*) GN
"So passeth, in the passing of a day," *fr.* II, 12.
(Song, The.) MyFE
Summer, *br. sel. fr.* VII, 7. GN
Temple of Venus, *fr.* IV, 10. WHA
"That celestial power, to whom the care," *fr.* II, 12. MyFE
Two Cantos of Mutabilitie, VII, 6, 7, *and* 8. ReEn; SiCE
Venus in Search of Cupid, Coming to Diana, *fr.* III, 6, *mod. vers.* BCEP
What if Some Little Paine the Passage Have, *br. sel., fr.* I, 9. CH
(Death.) MaRV
(Port after Stormie Seas.) EtS
"What man so wise, what earthly wit so ware," I, 7. CoBE
"Whylome, as antique stories tellen us," *fr.* IV, 2. PtP
Winter, *fr.* VII, 7. GN; OTPC
Faerie's Child, The. Thomas Caulfield Irwin. OnYI
Faeries' Song, The. Ben Jonson. *See* Gipsy Song.
Faeries' Song. W. B. Yeats. *See* Fairy Song.
Faery [*or* Faiery *or* Fairy] beam upon you, The. Gipsy Song [*or* Patrico's Song *or* The Faeries' Song]. Ben Jonson. *Fr.* The Gypsies Metamorphosed. AlDL; AtBAP; BoW; CenL; EPS (1942 ed.); FaBoCh; LoBV; LoGBV; PoRL; ReEn; SeCL; SeCV-1; TuPP
Faery Foster-Mother, The. Robert Buchanan. VA
Faery Queen, The. Sir Walter Ralegh. *See* Vision upon This Conceit of the Faerie Queene, A.
Faery Reaper, The. Robert Buchanan. OBVV
Faery Song. Keats. *See* Fairy Song.
Faery Song, A. Madeleine Nightingale. TVSH
Faery Song, A: "We who are old, old and gay." W. B. Yeats. CBE; POTE; ViBoPo
Faesulan Idyl. Walter Savage Landor. *See* Fiesolan Idyl, A.
Fagots blazed, the caldron's smoke, The. The Brewing of Soma. Whittier. PoEL-4
Faht's in there? What's in There. *Unknown.* CH
Failed. Phillips Thompson. PEOR
Failing blossoms, which a young plant bears, The. Upon Our Late Loss of the Duke of Cambridge. Edmund Waller. Po
Failure. Orrick Johns. PoMa
Failure. Mary Sinton Leitch. ChIP
Failure. Eithne Wilkins. NeBP
Failures. Arthur W. Upson. HBV; OQP; PoToHe (1941 ed.); OP-2; WGRP
Fain [*or* Faine] I would, but oh, I dare not. *Unknown.* ElL; SeCSL
Fain we ask Erinn. The Incantation. *At. to* Amergin. OnYI
Fain would I be sleeping, dreaming. The Plaint of the Wife. *Unknown.* AWP; JAWP; WBP
Fain Would I Change That Note. *Unknown, at. to* Tobias Hume. AtBAP; CenL; EG; ElL; ElSeCe; EtPaEn; EV-1; LiTL; LO; OBS; PoEL-2; TuPP; ViBoPo
(Devotion.) LiTB; OBEV
(Madrigal: "Fain would I change that note.") CBE
(No Other Choice.) TrGrPo
(Omnia Vincit.) GoBC; GTSL
(Song: "Fain would I change that note.") BrBE; CoEV; HBV
(To Love.) BCEP
(Where Truest Pleasure Is.) OnPM
Fain [*or* Faine] would I, Chloris, ere I die. A Lover's Legacy. *Unknown.* SeCL; SeCSL
Fain would I, Chloris, whom my heart adores. At Parting. *Unknown.* SeCL
Fain Would I Have a Pretty [*or* Prettie] Thing [to Give unto My Ladie]. *Unknown.* CoMu; ElL; InvP; ViBoPo
(Proper Song, A, Entitled: Fain Would I Have a Pretty Thing to Give unto My Lady.) ElSeCe; OAEP; ReEn; SiCE; TuPP
Fain would I have thee barter fates with me. To a Seabird. Sir William Watson. VA
Fain Would I Live in Safest Freedom. August, Graf von Platen, *tr. fr. German by* Edwin Morgan. AnGP
Fain would I ride with thee,/ Eivlin a rúin. Eileen Aroon. Carrol O'Daly. OnYI
Fain Would I Wed. Thomas Campion. ElSeCe; TuPP
("Fain would I wed a fair young man that night and day could please me.") ReEn
Fain would I write, my mind ashamèd is. The Song of Mary the Mother of Christ. *At. to* Henry Walpole. ISi
Fain would I write to thee, and great display. A Letter. Mu'tamid, King of Seville. LiTW
Fain Would My Thoughts. John Austin. OxBoCh
Faine I would but O I dare not. *See* Fain I would, but oh, I dare not.
Faine would I chang my maiden life. *Unknown.* SeCSL
Faine would I Cloris (ere I dye). *See* Fain would I, Chloris, ere I die.
Fainne Gael an Lae. Alice Milligan. HBV
Faint amorist, what! dost thou think. Wooing Stuff. Sir Philip Sidney. BCEP; ElSeCe
Faint as a climate-changing bird that flies. Demeter and Persephone. Tennyson. ViPP
Faint as the far-down tone. The Voice of Thought. Thomas Holley Chivers. AnAmPo; APW; LA; MOAP; SPP
Faint erroneous ray, A. Venus Shines Out. James Thomson. *Fr.* The Seasons: Summer. BeR
Faint, faint and clear. The Wind-swept Wheat. "Madeline Bridges." AA
Faint from our dear encounter, love, I lay. The Thirteenth Kiss: Love, Life and Death. Johannes Secundus. LaP
Faint grew the yellow buds of light. Om. "Æ." VA
Faint Heart. William James Linton. OBVV
Faint Heart Never Won Fair Lady. Vicente Espinel, *tr. fr. Spanish by* Sir John Bowring. AnSpL-1; OnPM
Faint Music. Walter de la Mare. FaBoCh; LoGBV
Faint not and falter not, nor plead. To Children of Girard, Pa. Whittier. PEOR
Faint now in the evening pallor. Silver Jubilee. Wyn Griffith. MoWP
Faint phoenix-tail gauze, fragrant and doubled, A. To One Unnamed. Li Shang-yin. ChLP
Faint shines the far moon. The Road. Nikolay Platonovich Ogarev. AWP
Faint white pillars that seem to fade. Fragment. E. A. Robinson. MAPA
Faint wind, blowing from World's End, A. Monition. Sir Charles G. D. Roberts. CPG
Faint wind sighs with autumn grief, The. The Wild Red Wine. Holger Drachmann. BoDS
Faint Yet Pursuing. Coventry Patmore. The Unknown Eros, I, xxi. OxBoCh; PoVP
Faintheart in a Railway Train. Thomas Hardy. EnLoPo
Faintly as tolls the evening chime. A Canadian Boat Song. Thomas Moore. CG; EV-4; GoBC; HBV; LPS-2; OBRV
Faintly at first, and low. Symphony: First Movement. John Hall Wheelock. UnS
Faintly the ne'er-do-well. The Flute of the Lonely. Vachel Lindsay. CrMA
Fair Agnete, The. Agnes Miegel, *tr. fr. German by* Margarete Münsterberg. CAW
Fair am I, mortals, as a stone-carved dream. La Beauté. Baudelaire. AWP; JAWP; WBP
Fair Amazon of Heaven who tookst in hand. To Saint Margaret. Henry Constable. ACP; GoBC
Fair Amoret is gone astray. Amoret [*or* A Hue and Cry after Fair Amoret]. Congreve. BCEP; CEP; ElSeCe; EV-3; GTIV; HBV; OBEC; OBEV; ViBoPo
Fair and Fair. George Peele. *Fr.* The Arraignment of Paris. ElL; EV-1; OBEV; ViBoPo
(Cupid's Curse.) BEL; LiA; TOP
(Fair and fair and twice so fair.") ElSeCe; ReaPo; ReEn; SiCE; TCEP; TuPP
(Song of Oenone and Paris.) OBSC

(Song of Paris and Oenone.) EPP
Fair and lovely maid, look from the shore. To Delia, XLII. Samuel Daniel. ReIE
Fair and purty the world is. Plants in the Earth. Paul Green. *Fr.* Shroud My Body Down. NoCaPo
Fair, and soft, and gay, and young. Song. Robert Gould. *Fr.* The Rival Sisters, III. CEP; SeCL
Fair Angels pass'd by next in seemly Bands. The Annunciation. Abraham Cowley. *Fr.* Davideis. OxBoCh
Fair Annie. *Unknown.* AnFE; BaBo (A *and* B vers.); BSV; CH; EBSV, *abr.;* ESPB (A, B, *and* E *vers.*); EV-2; HBV; OBB, *sl. abr.;* OBEV (1st ed.); ViBoFo (A, B, *and* C *vers.*)
Fair Annie an Sweet Willie. Lord Thomas and Fair Annet (I *vers.*). *Unknown.* ESPB
Fair Annie had a costly bower. The Holy Nunnery. *Unknown.* BaBo; ESPB
Fair Annie of Lochroyan. *Unknown.* *See* Lass of Lochroyan, The.
Fair are rill-bank and willow-foot. Full Fair. Hafiz. PeP
Fair are the flowers and the children, but their subtle suggestion is fairer. Indirection. Richard Realf. AA; AnAmPo; AnFE; BAP; CoAnAm; HBV; LA; LEAP; MaRV; OBAV; OQP; QP-1
Fair as the night—when all the astral fires. A Similitude. Charles Harpur. BoAu
Fair as the seven daughters of the sun. Pythagoras. Thomas S. Jones, Jr. AnAmPo; LA
Fair as unshaded light, or as the day. *See* Faire as unshaded light
Fair at Windgap, The. Austin Clarke. OnYI; SeCePo
Fair be thy speed, Sidonian ship! Euripides. *Fr.* Helen. GrPo
Fair Bersabe the bright, once bathing in a well. George Gascoigne. *Fr.* The Adventures of Master F. I. ReIE
Fair blue sky, A. Breeze and Billow. Albert Durrant Watson. CaP; CPG
Fair bosom! fraught with virtue's richest treasure. Amoretti, LXXVI. Spenser. PeBoSo
Fair brow in the strict cold shrine. The Nettle, the Flower. Morton Dauwen Zabel. NP
Fair by inheritance, whom born we see. Of the Nativity of the Lady Rich's Daughter. Henry Constable. OBSC
Fair Circassian, The. Richard Garnett. HBV; OBVV; VA
Fair copy of my Celia's face. To a Lady Resembling His Mistress. Thomas Carew. ElSeCe
Fair cousin mine! the golden days. Chivalry at a Discount. Edward Fitzgerald. HBV
Fair Cruel! why are ye so fierce and cruel? Amoretti, XLIX. Spenser. PeBoSo
Fair Cynthia mounted on her sprightly pad. Cynthia on Horseback. Philip Ayres. EnLoPo
Fair Daffodils [*or* Faire Daffadills], we weep to see. To Daffodils [*or* Daffadills]. Robert Herrick. AnEnPo; AtBAP; AWP; BCEP; BEL; BLV; BoLiVe; CaAE; CBOV; CBPC; CenL; CG; CoBE; CoEV; EG; ElSeCe; EM-1; EnL; EnLi-1; EnLit; EPP; EPS; EV-2; ExPo; FaBoCh; FaBoEn; GBV; GN; GTBS; GTBS-D; GTBS-W; GTSE; GTSL; HBV; HBVY; InPo; JAWP; LEAP; LiTB; LoBV; LPS-2; MaPo; OAEP; OBEV; OBS; OTPC; OuHeWo; PCN; PIAE; PoE; PoEL-3; PoFS; PoRA; ReaPo; ReEn; SeCeV; SeCL; SeCV-1; SeEP; ShBV-3; TrGrPo; TVSH; TwHP; TyEnPo; ViBoPo; WBP; WHA; WP
Fair Danubie is praised for being wide. Rivers. Thomas Storer. ElL; FaBoCh
Fair Days; or, Dawns Deceitful, *br. sel.* Robert Herrick. MyFE
Fair Dorothy, The. Baudelaire, *tr. fr. French by* Arthur Symons. MiFP
Fair earth smiled and turned herself and woke, The. The Feast of Harvest. Edmund Clarence Stedman. TOAH
Fair Eleanor. Blake. DaM
Fair Eleanor. *Unknown.* *See* Lord Thomas and Fair Annet.
Fair England. Helen Gray Cone. AA
Fair Erembor. *Unknown, tr. fr. French by* W. J. Linton. LyMA
Fair Eve devised a walking-suit. Fashion. Arthur Guiterman. PR
Fair Eve knelt close by the guarded gate. The Rose of Eden. Susan K. Phillips. BeLS
Fair Exchange. Euripides. *See* Cyclops' Philosophy, A.
Fair eyes, sweet lips, dear heart, that foolish I. Astrophel and Stella, XLIII. Sir Philip Sidney. SiPS
Fair [*or* Fayre] eyes! the mirror [*or* myrrour] of my mazèd heart [*or* hart]. Amoretti, VII. Spenser. PeBoSo; REAL
Fair eyes, ye mortal stars below. Dream of His Lady. Giovanni Battista Guarini. LyPI
Fair fa' your honest, sonsie face. Address to a Haggis. Burns. EBSV; ViBoPo
Fair Fannie Moore. *Unknown.* ABS; CSF
Fair Field for Satire, A. Juvenal, *tr. fr. Latin by* William Gifford. *Fr.* Satires, I. RoL
Fair fields, proud Flora's vaunt, why is't you smile. Menaphon's Ditty. Robert Greene. OBSC
Fair Florella; or, The Jealous Lover. *Unknown.* *See* Jealous Lover, The.
Fair flower of fifteen springs. To His Young Mistress. Pierre de Ronsard. *Fr.* Amours de Marie. AWP; OuHeWo; PrPoCR
Fair Flower of Northumberland, The. *Unknown.* BaBo; ESPB, *sl. diff.;* LoEn; OBB
Fair flower, that dost so comely grow. The Wild Honey Suckle. Philip Freneau. AA; AmP; AmPP; AnAmPo; APW; BAP; BAV; CoBA; CoV; HBV; HiLiAm; IAP; LA; LEAP; LiTA; MOAP; OxBA; PoEL-4; RiBV; TCAP; TrGrPo
"Fair, flowery Name! in none but Thee." The Holy Name of Jesus. Richard Crashaw. CAW
Fair Fools. Edward de Vere, Earl of Oxford. *See* If Women Could Be Fair.
Fair girl, I swore to stay apart from you. Paulus Silentiarius, *tr. fr. Greek by* Elsie Spoerl. GrPo
Fair girl was sitting in the greenwood shade, A. The Fairy Tempter. Samuel Lover. OTPC
Fair Golden Age! when milk was th' onely food. The Golden Age. Sir Richard Fanshawe, *after the Italian of* Giovanni Battista Guarini. *Fr.* Il Pastor Fido. LyPI
Fair golden thoughts and lovely words. About Women. H. Phelps Putnam. AnFE; CoAnAm; MAP; MoAmPo (1942 ed.); TwAmPo
Fair grace of graces, muse of muses all. Henry Constable. *Fr.* Diana. TuPP
Fair Greece! sad relic of departed worth! Greece. Byron. *Fr.* Childe Harold's Pilgrimage, II. EV-4; LPS-2; OBRV; PoFr
Fair-haired Girl, The. *Unknown, tr. fr. Modern Irish by* Sir Samuel Ferguson. OnYI
Fair Harvard. Samuel Gilman. InP
Fair Hebe. John West. HBV
Fair Helen. *Unknown.* *See* Helen of Kirconnell.
Fair Helen of Kirconnell. *Unknown.* *See* Helen of Kirconnell.
Fair Hermeline ask'd her father dear. The Lady and the Dwarf-King. *Unknown.* BaBo
Fair Hills of Eiré, The. Padraic Colum, *after the Irish.* CP
Fair Hills of Eiré, O, The! Donogh Mac-Con-Mara (Macnamara), *tr. fr. Irish by* James Clarence Mangan. IrPN; OBVV
Fair Hills of Ireland, The. *Unknown, tr. fr. Modern Irish by* Sir Samuel Ferguson. AnIV; GTIV; IrPN; OBEV; OBVV; OnYI
Fair hope! our earlyer heav'n by thee. Richard Crashaw. *Fr.* M. Crashaw's Answer for Hope. FaBoEn
Fair in a morn (O fairest morn). Song of Phillida and Coridon. Nicholas Breton. TuPP
Fair Inconstant, The. Francis Thompson. GTSE
Fair Indian Lass, The. *Unknown.* *See* Little Mohee, The.
Fair Ines. Thomas Hood. BCEP; EnRP; ERP; EV-4; HBV; LEAP; OBEV; OBRV; OBVV; PG (1945 ed.); TOP; UnPo (1st ed.); VA
Fair insect! that, with threadlike legs spread out. To a Mosquito. Bryant. AnNE; LPS-2
Fair Iris and Her Swain. Dryden. *Fr.* Amphitryon, IV, i. ViBoPo
Fair Iris I Love. Dryden. *See* Song: "Fair Iris I love, and hourly I die."
"Fair is Alexis," I no sooner said. On Alexis. Plato. AWP
Fair is each budding thing the garden shows. The Old-fashioned Garden. John Russell Hayes. AA
Fair is her body, bright her eye. Medieval Norman Song. *Unknown, tr. by* John Addington Symonds. AWP; JAWP; WBP; WoL
Fair is my dove, my loved one. Marriage Song. Judah Halevi. TrJP
Fair Is My Love. Samuel Daniel. *See* Fair is my love, and cruel as she's fair.
Fair Is My Love. Robert Greene. *See* Fair Is My Love for April in Her Face.
Fair Is My Love. Bartholomew Griffin. *See* Fair is my love that feeds among the lilies.
Fair Is My Love. *At. to* Shakespeare. The Passionate Pilgrim, VII. ElL
Fair is my love, and cruel as she's fair. To Delia, VI. Samuel Daniel. BCEP; CaAE; ElL; ES; GTBS-W; HBV; HoPM; LiTB; LiTG; LiTL; OAEP; OBEV; OBSC; PoEL-2; ReEn; ReIE; SiCE; TrGrPo; TuPP; TwHP; ViBoPo
Fair is my Love, but not so fair as fickle. Fair Is My Love. *At. to* Shakespeare. *Fr.* The Passionate Pilgrim. ElL
Fair Is My Love for April in [*or* Is *or* April's in] Her Face. Robert Greene. *Fr.* Perimedes. ElL; ElSeCe; HBV; ReIE; ViBoPo
Fair [*or* Faire] is my Love that feeds among the lilies. Bartholomew Griffin. Fidessa, More Chaste than Kind, XXXVII. BCEP; EG; ElL; LO; NBE; PeBoSo; PoEL-2; SiCE; TrGrPo; TuPP; ViBoPo

Fair is my love, when her fair golden hairs [*or* heares]. Amoretti, LXXXI. Spenser. ElL; ElSeCe; LiTL; LoPo; PeBoSo; PIAE; PoE
Fair Is My Yoke, though Grievous Be My Pains. William Drummond of Hawthornden. BSV
Fair is our lot—O goodly is our heritage! A Song of the English. Kipling. BPN
Fair is the hue of your mantle, Mary. The Mantle of Mary. Patrick O'Connor. ISi
Fair is the night and fair the day. Song from the Story of Acontius and Cydippe. William Morris. *Fr.* The Earthly Paradise: October. BPN; HBV; POTT; VLEP
Fair Is the Rose. *Unknown.* EG; ElL; ElSeCe
Fair is the Swan, whose majesty, prevailing. Dion. Wordsworth. GEPC
Fair is their fame who stand in earth's high places. Heroes. Laurence Housman. GrCo-2; POT; PoTo
Fair is thy face, Nantasket. Mary Clemmer Ames. *Fr.* Nantasket. SN
Fair Is Too Foul an Epithet. Christopher Marlowe. *Fr.* Tamburlaine the Great, Pt. I, Act V, sc. ii. LiTB
("Ah faire [*or* fair] Zenocrate, divine Zenocrate.") AtBAP; NBE; PoEL-2; ViBoPo
Fair Isabel, poor simple Isabel! Isabella; or, The Pot of Basil [*or* The Beginning of Love]. Keats. BPN; EmBrPo; EnRP; ERP; EV-4; GEPC; UnPo (1st ed.); ViBoPo
Fair Isabell of Rochroyall. The Lass of Roch Royal. *Unknown.* BaBo; EBSV (A *vers.*)
Fair islands of the silver fleece. Ballade of the Southern Cross. Andrew Lang. InP
Fair isle, that from the fairest of all flowers. Sonnet to Zante. Poe. IAP
Fair Janet. *Unknown.* BaBo; ESPB; OBB, *abr.*
Fair Japan. Bansui Tsuchii, *tr. fr. Japanese by* Takimichi Ninomiya *and* D. J. Enright. PoLJ
Fair Jesu, guide Thy straying sheep. The Straying Sheep. *Unknown.* JKCP (1926 ed.)
Fair Julia sitting by the fire. On a Spark of Fire Fixing on a Gentlewoman's Breast. Thomas Philipott. ElSeCe; SeCL
Fair ladies, weep, the while Love's own tears fall. Sonnet: On the Death of Cino da Pistoia. Petrarch. *Fr.* Sonnets to Laura: To Laura in Life. LyPI
Fair lady, I see you do complain. Cantiga de Amor. Dinis, King of Portugal. LyMA
Fair lady Isabel sits in her bower sewing. Lady Isabel and the Elf-Knight. *Unknown.* BaBo (A *vers.*); ESPB (A *vers.*); OAEP; ViBoFo (A *vers.*)
Fair lady, when you see the grace. To One Admiring Herself in a Looking Glass [*or* To a Lady Admiring Herself . . .]. Thomas Randolph. EV-2; LiTL; LPS-1; ViBoPo
Fair lady with the bandaged eye. Ode to Fortune. Fitz-Greene Halleck *and* Joseph Rodman Drake. *Fr.* The Croaker Papers. AA
Fair land of dear desire. To Italy. Corinne Roosevelt Robinson. AOAH
Fair liberty, our soul's most darling prize. To the Heirs of the Pilgrims. Benjamin Church. PoFr
Fair little girl sat under a tree, A. Good Night and Good Morning. Richard Monckton Milnes. BoTP; LPS-1; MeMeAg; OTPC; PRWS; PTA-1; RAR; SAS; TVC; TVSH
Fair Little Maiden, The. Dora Sigerson Shorter. DaM
Fair little scout, that when the iron year. The Song Sparrow. Archibald Lampman. BoCaPo
Fair little spirit of the woodland mazes. A Dead Singer. John E. Logan. VA
Fair Maid and the Sun, The. Arthur O'Shaughnessy. BeLS; VA
Fair Maid by the Seashore, The. *Unknown.* BaBo
Fair maid, had I not heard thy baby cries. To a Lofty Beauty, from Her Poor Kinsman. Hartley Coleridge. EV-4; OBVV
Fair maid in a garden walking, A. A Sweetheart in the Army (A *vers.*). *Unknown.* BaBo
Fair Maid of Amsterdam, The. *Unknown.* OxBoLi
(A-Roving, *with music.*) ShS (*vers.* I); SoAmSa
Fair Maid of the Exchange, The, *sel.* *At. to* Thomas Heywood.
Ye Little Birds That Sit and Sing. CBOV; ElL; ElSeCe; ViBoPo
(Go, Pretty Birds.) EPP
(Message, The.) HBV; OBEV (1st ed.)
(Ye Pretty Wantons, Warble.) EV-2
Fair Maid of the Inn, The. John Gay. *See* Molly Mog.
Fair Maid of the West, The. *Unknown.* CoMu
Fair maid sat in her bower [*or* front] door, A. The False Lover Won Back [*or* The Fause Lover *or* Young John]. *Unknown.* BaBo; CoBE; ESPB (A *vers.*); OBB
Fair maid who, [on] the first of May, The. Mother Goose. BoChLi; PCH
Fair maid, you need not take the hint. An Excerpt. Burns. BTP
Fair Maiden! Adam Oehlenschläger, *tr. fr. Danish by* Charles W. Stork. BoDS
Fair Maiden. George Peele. *See* Song at the Well, The.
Fair maiden, fair maiden. Invocation to the Muse. Richard Hughes. MBP; MoBrPo
Fair maiden, throw your window wide. Fair Maiden! Adam Oehlenschläger. BoDS
Fair maiden, white and red. A Voice Speaks from the Well. George Peele. *Fr.* The Old Wives' Tale. FaBoCh; LoGBV; OBSC; OxBoLi; RiBV; SiTL
Fair Maiden, Who Is This Bairn? *Unknown.* ISi
Fair Maidens' Beauty Will Soon Fade Away. Robert Dwyer Joyce. GTIV
Fair Maid's Choice or the Seaman's Renown, The. *Unknown.* SG
Fair Margaret and Sweet William. *Unknown.* *See* Douglas Tragedy, The.
Fair Margaret was a young [*or* proud] ladye. Proud Lady Margaret. *Unknown.* ESPB (E *vers.*); OBB
Fair Marjorie sat i her bower-door. Young Benjie. *Unknown.* ESPB
Fair Mary of Wallington. *Unknown.* ESPB (A *and* C *vers.*); OBB
Fair Millinger, The. Fred W. Loring. BOHV
Fair Moon, Who with Thy Cold and Silver Shine. William Drummond of Hawthornden. BSV
Fair Mother Earth lay on her back last night. Ode to the Spirit of Earth in Autumn. George Meredith. EmBrPo
Fair must that promised country be. The Promised Country. Speer Strahan. JKCP
Fair Naiads of the river, that reside. Sonnet. Garcilaso de la Vega. TeCS
Fair now is the spring-tide, now earth lies beholding. The Message of the March Wind. William Morris. EmBrPo; GTBS-D; OBVV
Fair of face, full of pride. A Lyke-Wake Song. Swinburne. PoVP; ViP
Fair of Kakava, The. Kostes Palamas, *tr. fr. Modern Greek by* Rae Dalven. *Fr.* The Twelve Songs of the Gypsy. MoGP
Fair, order'd light (whose motion without noise). The Constellation. Henry Vaughan. NBE; SeCV-1
Fair Oriana, Beauty's Queen. John Hilton. ReIE
Fair Oriana in the Morn. John Milton. ReIE
Fair our fleet at Castle Sweyn. Lay of Norse-Irish Sea-Kings. Arthur MacGurcaich. TIP
Fair Pamela came to town, The. Pamela in Town. Ellen M. H. Cortissoz. AA; HBV
Fair Penitent, The, *sel.* Nicholas Rowe.
Song: "Ah stay! ah turn! ah whither would you fly," *by* Congreve. AtBAP; LoBV; OBEC
Fair Phoebe and Her Dark-eyed Sailor. *Unknown.* *See* Dark-eyed Sailor, The.
Fair Phyllis. Ben Jonson. LiTL
Fair [*or* Faire] pledges of a fruitful tree. To Blossoms. Robert Herrick. CBOV; EG; EM-1; EPS; EV-2; GTBS; GTBS-D; GTBS-W; GTSE; GTSL; HBV; LoBV; LPS-2; OBEV; OBS; PYM; SeCV-1; SeCL; SeEP; UnPo (1st ed.)
Fair Portia's counterfeit? What demi-god. Portia's Picture. Shakespeare. *Fr.* The Merchant of Venice, III, ii. LPS-1
Fair *Princess Royal,* The. *Unknown.* *See* Bold *Princess Royal,* The.
Fair Proud! now tell me, why should fair be proud? Amoretti, XXVII. Spenser. ES; PeBoSo
Fair Quiet, have I found thee here. Andrew Marvell. *Fr.* Thoughts in a Garden. BCEP
Fair rebel to thyself and Time. The Revenge. Pierre de Ronsard. AWP
Fair, Rich, and Young. Sir John Harington, *after the Latin of* Martial. ElL; SeCePo
(Of a Fair Shrew.) SiCE
Fair rocks, goodly rivers, sweet woods, when shall I see peace? Echo. Sir Philip Sidney. *Fr.* Arcadia. SiPS
Fair room, the presence of sweet beauty's pride. Sonnet. Thomas Nashe. CaAE
Fair Rosamund. Thomas Deloney. CG
Fair Roslin Chapel, how divine. Roslin and Hawthornden. Henry van Dyke. AA
Fair sail shimmers, white and lonely, A. *See* Far sail shimmers . . .
Fair Salamis, the billow's roar. Chorus. Sophocles. *Fr.* Ajax. AWP; JAWP; WBP
Fair Seed-Time Had My Soul. Wordsworth. *Fr.* The Prelude, I. AtBAP; MaPo
(Childhood.) TCEP
(Childhood and School-Time.) FaBoEn
("Fair seed-time had my soul, and I grew up.") EnL; EnLi-2; EV-3; ExPo; NBE; OBRV; PoEL-4; TyEnPo
(Presences of Nature in Boyhood.) EPN
Fair ship, that from the Italian shore. In Memoriam A. H. H.,

IX. Tennyson. BoLiVe; BPN; EmBrPo; EnLi-2; EPN; GEPC; GTSL; LEAP; LPS-1; OAEP; OBEV (1st ed.); ReaPo; ViPo; VLEP

Fair-shoulder, Fionula fair. The Legend of the Glaive. J. Sheridan Le Fanu. DaM

Fair Singer, The. Andrew Marvell. EG; ElSeCe; EnLoPo; LiTL; LO, *2 sts.;* LoPo; MeLP; MePo; PoEL-2; ReEn; SeCL; UnPo (3d ed.)

Fair Sou-Chong-Tee, by a shimmering brook. Story of the Flowery Kingdom. James Branch Cabell. HBMV; PCD

Fair spoil I thought Him as I reached the well. Spoil. William E. Brooks. QS

Fair star, new-risen to our wondering eyes. Bacchylides. George Meason Whicher. AA

Fair Star of evening, Splendor of the west. Composed by the Sea-Side, near Calais, August, 1802. Wordsworth. ATP; BPN; CoBE; EM-2; EmBrPo; EnLi-2; EnRP; ERP; GEPC; OAEP; OuHeWo; PeBoSo; PoE; TOP; UnPo (1st ed.)

Fair stood the wind for France. Agincourt [*or* The Ballad (*or* Battle) of Agincourt *or* Ode to the Cambro-Britons]. Michael Drayton. AEV; AnFE; BCEP; BEL; BeLS; BHV; CaAE; ElL; ElSeCe; EnL; EnLi-1; EPP; EV-1; FaBoBe; FaBoCh; GN; GoTL; HBV; KN; LEAP; LH; LoGBV; LPS-2; MCCG; OAEP; OBEV; OBS; OnSP; PoRA; ReaPo; ReEn; ReIE; SeEP; ShBV-1; TCEP; TOP; TriL; TuPP; TVSH; TwHP; TyEnPo; WHA

Fair Summer Droops. Thomas Nashe. *Fr.* Summer's Last Will and Testament. ElL; LoBV; TuPP
(Waning Summer.) OBSC

Fair sun, if you would have me praise your light. Henry Constable. *Fr.* Diana. OBSC; SiCE

Fair, sweet and young, receive a prize. Song [*or* Fair, Sweet, and Young]. Dryden. BrBE; LiTL; OBS; SeCL; SeEP

Fair Sylvia. *Unknown.* OBS

Fair! that you may truly know. To Amoret. Edmund Waller. ElSeCe; SeCV-1

Fair the daughter known as Mary. An Old Song by New Singers (as Longfellow Might Have Done It). A. C. Wilkie. BOHV; PA

Fair the gift to Merlin given. Merlin's Apple-Trees. Thomas Love Peacock. *Fr.* The Misfortunes of Elphin. OBRV

Fair, the young acacia, thick with leaves. The Young Acacia. Hayyim Nahman Bialik. TrJP

Fair these broad meads—these hoary woods are grand. Canadian Boat Song. *Unknown, at. to* John Galt. BLPA; BSV; EBSV; GoTS; NBE; OBEV (new ed.); OBRV; OCL

Fair Thief, The. Charles Wyndham. HBV

Fair Thou Art. Mordecai ben Isaac, *tr. fr. Hebrew by* Herbert Loewe. TrJP

Fair-tinted cheeks, clear eyelids drawn. Cimabuella. Bayard Taylor. PA

Fair Tree! for thy delightful shade. The Tree. Countess of Winchilsea. CEP; CoBE; DiM; EiPP; OBEC; RiBV

Fair-tressed Pallas Athene, The. Pallas in Olympus. Charles Kingsley. *Fr.* Andromeda. CBOV

Fair Unknown, The. Poul Martin Møller, *tr. fr. Danish by* Charles W. Stork. BoDS

Fair varieties of earth, The. Life Is Love. William Johnson Fox. VA

Fair Verna! loveliest village of the west. Sweet Simplicity. Timothy Dwight. *Fr.* Greenfield Hill. AmPP

Fair Virgin,/ Vestured with the sun! Ode to the Virgin. Petrarch. *Fr.* Sonnets to Laura: To Laura in Death. ISi; PrPoCR

Fair Virtue, the Mistress of Philarete, *sels.* George Wither.
Farewell, Sweet Groves. BLV
Hence, Away, You Sirens, *also given in* Fidelia. ElL, *3 sts.*
(Sonnet: "Hence away, you sirens, leave me.") ElSeCe
Her Fairness, *abr.* EV-2
Her Virtue, *abr.* EV-2
I Wandered Out. SeCL
(Divided Heart, The.) TrGrPo
(Sonnet: "I wandered out a while agone.") ElSeCe
Shall I, Wasting in Despair, *also given in* Fidelia. ALV; AnFE; BEL; EG; ElL; EM-1; EnLi-1; EV-2; LiTB; LiTG; LoPo, *abr.;* OBS; OuHeWo; PreP; ReEn; WHA
(Author's Resolution [in a Sonnet], The.) BCEP; CaAE; EPS; ViBoPo
(Lover's Resolution, The.) AWP; EnLit; HBV; InMe; JAWP; LEAP; LiTL; OBEV; PG; TOP; TreFS; WBP
(Manly Heart, The.) GTBS; GTBS-D; GTBS-W; GTSE; GTSL; MCCG; TVSH
(Resolution, The.) ElSeCe
(Shepherd's Resolution.) LPS-1
(Sonnet: "Shall I, wasting in despair.") EPP; SeCV-1; SeEP
(What Care I?) BLV; CoEV; TrGrPo
Stolen Kiss, A. HBV; LiTL; PeBeSo; SeCL
(Sonnet upon a Stolen Kiss.) LPS-1

"Two pretty rills do meet." EPP; EPS

Fair was the dawn, and, but e'en now, the skies. Robert Herrick. *Fr.* Fair Days; or, Dawns Deceitful. MyFE

Fair was this yonge wyf, and ther-with-al. Alisoun. Chaucer. *Fr.* The Canterbury Tales: The Milleres Tale. CoEV

Fair were our visions! Oh, they were as grand [*or* Fair were our nation's visions and as grand]. In the Land Where We Were Dreaming [*or* Land Where We Were Dreaming]. Daniel B. Lucas. PAH; SPP

Fair Wildheart. Eduard Mörike, *tr. fr. German by* William R. Hughes. AnGP

Fair witch crept to a young man's side, A. The Witch Bride. William Allingham. DaM

Fair [*or* Fayre] ye be sure, but cruel and unkind. Amoretti, LVI. Spenser. EnLit; PeBoSo

Fair Young Virgin Is like the Rose Untainted, The. *Unknown.* ReIE

Faire and fayre and twise so faire. *See* Fair and Fair.

Faire and scornefull doe thy worst. *Unknown.* SeCSL

Faire Archibella to thine eyes. *Unknown.* SeCSL

Faire [*or* Fair] as unshaded light, or as the day. To the Queen, Entertain'd at Night by the Countess of Anglesey. Sir William Davenant. FaBoEn; MeLP; MePo; OBS; SeCL; SeEP

Faire Daffadills, we weep to see. *See* Fair Daffodils, we weep to see.

Faire eyes regard my love soe truelie tryed. *Unknown.* SeCSL

Faire Is My Love. Bartholomew Griffin. *See* Fair is my Love that feeds among the lilies.

Faire is the heaven where happy soules have place. Spenser. *Fr.* An Hymne of Heavenly Beautie. MeRV

Faire pledges of a fruitfull tree. *See* Fair pledges of a fruitful tree.

Faire will you then that I shall dy. *Unknown.* SeCSL

Fairer is the manuscript. The Pen. Al-Hajjam. MooP

Fairer is the sea. Paul Verlaine. *Fr.* Sagesse. AWP; JAWP; WBP

Fairer than Fairest. *Unknown.* SeCL
("Fairer than fairest, if your eyes.") SeEP

Fairer than the rosy east. To Chloris. John Cobbes. SeCL

Fairer than younger beauties, more beloved. Valentines to My Mother (1876–1886). Christina Rossetti. MOAH

Fairest action of our human life, The. Revenge of Injuries. Lady Elizabeth Carew. *Fr.* Mariam. LPS-3

Fairest eyes (O eyes in blackness fair!), The. Sonnet III: Upon His Absence from Her. Francis Davison. ReIE

Fairest He, The. Horatius Bonar. BePJ

Fairest, how poor is your lover today! The Flower. Henrik Wergeland. AnNoLy; LiTW

Fairest isle, all isles excelling. Song of Venus [*or* Song Sung by Venus in Honor of Britannia]. Dryden. *Fr.* King Arthur, V, i. EPS (1942 ed.); LoBV; OxBoLi; PoEL-3; SeCeV

Fairest Lord Jesus. *Unknown, tr. fr. German.* OlF; WGRP
(Crusader's Hymn.) MaRV, *tr. by* R. Storrs Willis
(Song of the Crusaders.) BePJ

Fairest Lord Jesus, serene You lay. God Incarnate. Ruth M. Williams. BePJ

Fairest of fair, O lady mine, Venus. Prayer to Venus. Chaucer. *Fr.* The Canterbury Tales: The Knight's Tale. LiTL

Fairest of Freedom's Daughters. Jeremiah Eames Rankin. PAH

Fairest of Her Days, The. *Unknown.* ElL

Fairest of morning lights, appear. Psalm for [*or* For] Christmas Day. Thomas Pestel. AnEC; OxBoCh

Fairest of the fairest, rival of the rose. Mabel, in New Hampshire. James T. Fields. HBV; PR

Fairest of valleys in this full-bloomed night. In Wiltshire. Edmund Blunden. POTE

Fairest Theina let me know. *Unknown.* SeCSL

Fairest Thing in Mortal Eyes, The. Charles d'Orléans, *tr. fr French by* Henry Francis Cary. LPS-1

Fairest thing that shines below. Clad All in White. Abraham Cowley. *Fr.* The Mistress. SeCV-1

Fairest things are those that silent come, The. He Leads. Elisabeth Scollard. MaRV

Fairest thing's uprightness, health the best, The. The Sampler. Theognis. GrR

Fairest, when by the rules of palmistry. Sonnet. William Browne. Caelia, III. ElSeCe

Fairfax, Whose Name in Arms through Europe Rings. Milton. MaPo
(On the Lord General Fairfax at the Siege of Colchester.) EM-1; OBS
(To the Lord General Fairfax.) PeBoSo

Fairford Nightingales. John Drinkwater. BLA

Fairies, The. William Allingham. AnEnPo; BMEP; BoChLi; BTP; CBPC; CG; CH; ChTr; DaM; DD, *abr.;* FaBoCh; FaPON; GBV; GFA, *abr.;* GTBS-D; HBV; HBVY; IrPN; LEAP; LiTG; LoGBV; LPS-3; OBEV; OBVV; OnYI; OTPC; OxBI; PCH; PoMS; PoRh; PTA-1;

Fairies, The (continued)
RAR; RG; SUS; TIP; TOP; TSW; TSWC; TVC; TVSH; VA; ViBoPo
(Fairy Folk, The.) GN; HOAH
(Up the Airy Mountain.) FaFP; StVeCh
Little Men, The, br. sel. OtMeF
Fairies. Marchette Chute. MoSiPe
Fairies. Hilda Conkling. GBV (1922 ed.); SP; TiPo
Fairies, The. Rose Fyleman. FaPON; HBMV; HBVY; HOAH; MPB; OTPC (1946 ed.); StVeCh; TSW; TSWC; TVC; TVSH
Fairies, The. John G. Herndon. MPB
Fairies, The. Robert Herrick. EPS; FaPON; MPB; OBS; OTPC (1946 ed.); SeEP
Fairies. Kikaku, tr. fr. Japanese. MPB
Fairies, The. Sybil Morford. OTPC (1946 ed.); PoRL; TVC; TVSH
Fairies. Thomas Tickell. Fr. Kensington Garden. OBEC
Fairies, The ("Come follow, follow me"). Unknown. See Fairy Queen, The.
Fairies. Louis Untermeyer. StaSt
Fairies are a charming folk, if all the tales be true, The. The Fairies. John G. Herndon. MPB
Fairies Break Their Dances, The. A. E. Housman. MoVE
Fairies' Dance, The ("Dare you haunt our hallow'd green?"). Unknown. MPB
Fairies dance the livelong night, The. In the Moonlight. Norreys Jephson O'Conor. HBMV; SUS
Fairies, fairies, come and be fed. Feeding the Fairies. Unknown. PPL
Fairies' Farewell, The. Richard Corbet. BLV; ElSeCe; LiTB; LiTG; LoGBV; OtMeF, abr.; PoFS; TrGrPo; UnPo (1st ed.); ViBoPo, abr.
(Farewell, Rewards and Fairies.) EV-2; FaBoCh, abr.; LoBV; SiTL
(Farewell to the Fairies.) CBPC; HBV; HBVY, abr.; LEAP; LPS-3; MoShBr
(Proper New Ballad, A, Intituled [or Entitled] The Fairies' Farewell or God-a-Mercy Will.) CenL; OBS; OxBoLi; PoE; ReEn; SeCL; SeEP
Fairies Feast, The. Charles M. Doughty. CH
Fairies Have Never a Penny to Spend, The. Rose Fyleman. BoChLi; FaPON; GBV (1922 ed.); HBMV; MPB; SP; TVSH
Fairies hold a fair, they say, The. The Faerie Fair. Florence Harrison. BoTP
Fairies in New Ross, The. Unknown. OnYI
Fairies, it is said, The. Fairies. Kikaku. MPB
Fairies' Lights. Alice Wilkins. GFA
Fairies' Lullaby, The ("Come, now a roundel"). Shakespeare. See You Spotted Snakes.
Fairies' Lullaby, The ("You spotted snakes"). Shakespeare. See You Spotted Snakes.
Fairies' Lullaby, The. Unknown, tr. fr. Irish by Eleanor Hull. BOL
Fairies of the Caldon Low, The. Mary Howitt. BeLS; HBV; HBVY; OTPC; PRWS; TVC; TVSH
Fairies' Recall. Felicia Dorothea Hemans. OTPC
Fairies' Shopping, The. Margaret Deland. HBVY; PRWS
Fairies' Siege, The. Kipling. OtMeF; VLEP
Fairies' Song. Thomas Randolph, tr. fr. Latin by Leigh Hunt. Fr. Amyntas. ALV; EPP; LPS-3; PoMS
(Fairy Song.) HBV
(Song of Fairies Robbing an Orchard.) OBRV
Fairies' Song, The. Shakespeare. See You Spotted Snakes.
Fairies, too, have aeroplanes, The. Fairy Aeroplanes. Anne Blackwell Payne. GFA; UTS
Fairness. St. Matthew, VII: 1-5, 12, Bible, N.T. BoFr
Fairy, The. Unknown. See Light-hearted Fairy, The.
Fairy Aeroplanes. Anne Blackwell Payne. GFA; UTS
Fairy and the soul proceeded, The. The Magic Car Moved On. Shelley. Fr. Queen Mab, I. GN
Fairy Artist, The. Nellie M. Garabrant. PCH
Fairy band are we, A. Song. Alfred Noyes. GBV (1922 ed.)
Fairy beam upon you, The. See Faery beam upon you, The.
Fairy Blessing, The. Shakespeare. See Now the Hungry Lion Roars.
Fairy Bombyca! thee do men report. Transfiguring Love. Theocritus. Fr. Idylls. GrR
Fairy Book, The. Abbie Farwell Brown. HBV; HBVY; MPB
Fairy Book, The. Norman Gale. HBV; HBVY; OHIP; OTPC (1946 ed.); RAR; TVC; TVSH
Fairy Boy, The. Samuel Lover. OTPC (1923 ed.)
Fairy Bread. Robert Louis Stevenson. GBV (1922 ed.); MeMeAg; OTPC (1946 ed.)
Fairy Carpets. Anne Blackwell Payne. GFA
Fairy Child, The. John Anster. LPS-3
Fairy Circus, The. Vachel Lindsay. HiLiAm
Fairy Cobbler, The. A. Neil Lyons. BoTP
Fairy Dances ("By the moon we sport and play"). Unknown. See By the Moon We Sport and Play.
Fairy Dances ("Round about, round about"). Unknown. See Elves' Dance, The.
Fairy Dawn. Joseph Rodman Drake. Fr. The Culprit Fay. GN
Fairy Days. Thackeray. GoTP; OTPC (1946 ed.)
Fairy Dream, A. Dorothy Gradon. BoTP
Fairy Faces. Unknown. COAH
Fairy! Fairy! list and mark. The Fay's Crime. Joseph Rodman Drake. Fr. The Culprit Fay. GN
Fairy Feet. Phyllis L. Garlick. BoTP
Fairy Fiddler, The. Nora Hopper. BMEP; GTIV; HBMV; TIP; ViBoPo
('Tis I Go Fiddling, Fiddling.) OxBI
Fairy Flute, The. Rose Fyleman. BoTP
Fairy Folk, The. William Allingham. See Fairies, The.
Fairy Folk, The. Robert Montgomery Bird. GFA; HBV; HBVY; OTPC; PRWS; RAR; TVC; TVSH
Fairy Frilly. Florence Hoatson. GFA; OTPC (1946 ed.)
Fairy Frock, The. Katharine Morse. UTS
Fairy Frolic. Annie Isobel Rentoul. GFA
Fairy Frolic, The. Unknown. See By the Moon We Sport and Play.
Fairy Godmothers. Eugene Lee-Hamilton. OBVV
Fairy Gold. John Todhunter. TIP
Fairy Harpers, The. James B. Dollard. CaP; CPG; OCL
Fairy has found a new fern, A! A New Fern. "A." PRWS
Fairy Host, The. Tr. fr. Irish by Alfred Perceval Graves. AnIV
Fairy in Armor, A. Joseph Rodman Drake. Fr. The Culprit Fay. FaPON; GaP; GFA; OTPC; PRWS; RAR
(Elfin Knight, An.) BoTP; TVSH
(Fay Arms Himself, The.) APW
Fairy King, The. William Allingham. IrPN; PoMS
Fairy Land. See Fairyland.
Fairy Life, The. Shakespeare. See Ariel's Song: "Come unto these yellow sands" and Ariel's Song: "Where the bee sucks . . ."
Fairy Lough, The. "Moira O'Neill." DiM; OBVV; TVSH; YT
Fairy Lover, The. Moireen Fox. AnIV
Fairy Lullaby ("Come, now a roundel"). Shakespeare. See You Spotted Snakes.
Fairy Lullaby ("You spotted snakes"). Shakespeare. See You Spotted Snakes.
Fairy Lullaby. Unknown, tr. fr. Irish by George Sigerson. BOL
Fairy Maimounè, The. John Moultrie. OBRV
Fairy Midir's Invitation to Etain, The. Unknown, tr. fr. Old Irish by Seán O'Faoláin. SiB
Fairy Music. Enid Blyton. BoTP
Fairy Music. Rose Fyleman. HH; TSW; TSWC
Fairy Music. Francis Ledwidge. YeAr
Fairy Nurse, The. Edward Walsh. BOL; OnYI
Fairy poet takes a sheet, The. In Fairyland. Joyce Kilmer. TSW
Fairy Queen, The. Shakespeare. See Over Hill, over Dale.
Fairy Queen, The ("Come follow, follow me"). Unknown. PCD; PCH, abr.; PoRh, abr.
(Fairies, The, abr.) BoTP
(Life of a Fairy, The, abr.) OTPC
(Old Song of Fairies, An.) RG
(Queen of Fairies, The.) BCEP; EV-2; ViBoPo
Fairy ran a circus, A. The Fairy Circus. Vachel Lindsay. HiLiAm
Fairy Revels. John Lyly. See Song by Fairies.
Fairy Ring, The. Unknown. BoTP
Fairy Ring, The. Andrew Young. ChTr
Fairy seed I planted, A. The Magic Vine. Unknown. GFA
Fairy Shoemaker, The. William Allingham. EV-5
(Leprecaun, The.) RG
(Leprecaun, or Fairy Shoemaker, The.) PCH
(Lupracaun, or Fairy Shoemaker, The.) OnYI
Fairy Shoemaker, The. Phyllis Garlick. BoTP
Fairy Shoes. Annette Wynne. MPB (1956 ed.)
Fairy Sleep and Little Bo-Peep, The. Unknown. BoTP
Fairy Song, A. Elizabeth T. Dillingham. OTPC (1946 ed.); PCH
Fairy Song. Felicia Dorothea Hemans. HBVY
Fairy Song. Keats. FaPON; HBV; HOAH; LPS-3; OTPC; PECK
(Faery Song.) CH; EV-4
Fairy Song, A. John Lyly. See Song by Fairies.
Fairy Song. Winthrop Mackworth Praed. EV-4; LEAP; OBEV (1st ed.); SeCePo
Fairy Song. Thomas Randolph. See Fairies' Song.
Fairy Song, A. Shakespeare. See Over Hill, over Dale.
Fairy Song. W. B. Yeats. Fr. The Land of Heart's Desire. MBP; MoBrPo; OnYI
(Faeries' Song, abr.) GBV
(Lyric from "The Land of Heart's Desire.") CP; NV
(Song: "Wind blows out of the gates of the day, The.") BEL; InP; TSW
(Song of the Faeries [or Fairies], The.) ChMo; CMP
(Voice, The.) PtOT

("Wind blows out of the gates of the day, The.") GTSL; ViBoPo
Fairy Songs ("Come unto these yellow sands"). Shakespeare. *See* Ariel's Song.
Fairy Songs ("Now the hungry lion roars"). Shakespeare. *See* Now the Hungry Lion Roars.
Fairy Songs ("Now, until the break of day"). Shakespeare. *Fr.* A Midsummer Night's Dream, V, ii. TrGrPo
Fairy Songs ("Over hill, over dale"). Shakespeare. *See* Over Hill, over Dale.
Fairy Songs ("Where the bee sucks"). Shakespeare. *See* Ariel's Song.
Fairy Songs ("You spotted snakes with double tongue"). Shakespeare. *See* You Spotted Snakes.
Fairy spirits of the breeze. Unwritten Poems. William Winter. AA
Fairy Tailor, The. Rose Fyleman. PoRh; TVC; TVSH
Fairy Tale, A. Austin Dobson. POT
Fairy Tale. John Frederick Nims. MiAP
Fairytales. Peter Hellings. MoWP
Fairy Tempter, The. Samuel Lover. OTPC
Fairy Thorn, The. Sir Samuel Ferguson. AnIV; CBOV; CH; GTIV; OnYI; PoVP; TIP; VA
Fairy Thorn-Tree, The. Dora Sigerson Shorter. DaM
Fairy Thrall, The. May Byron. HBV; HBVY; VA
Fairy to Puck, The. Shakespeare. *See* Over Hill, over Dale.
Fairy Tree, The. Temple Lane. StJW
Fairy Umbrellas. Lucy Diamond. GFA
Fairy Voyage, A. *Unknown.* OTPC (1946 ed.); PCH
Fairy was mending a daisy, A. The Wounded Daisy. *Unknown.* HOAH
Fairy Went a-Marketing, A. Rose Fyleman. BoTP; SUS; TVSH
Fairy Wings. Winifred Howard. SUS
Fairy-Land. Poe. APW; IAP; OTPC
Fairy Land. Shakespeare. *Fr.* A Midsummer Night's Dream. *See* Over Hill, over Dale *and* You Spotted Snakes.
Fairy Land. Shakespeare. *Fr.* The Tempest. *See* Ariel's Song.
Fairyland. Anne Glenny Wilson. BoAu
Fairy's Life, A. Shakespeare. *See* Ariel's Song: "Where the bee sucks."
Fairy's Song [*or* Wander-Song]. Shakespeare. *See* Over Hill, over Dale.
Fais dodo, mon fils (Go to sleep, my son). Crabe dans Calalou. *Unknown.* OuSiCo
Faith. Hebrews, XI: 1–XII: 2, *abr.*, Bible, *N.T.* GrCo-1
Faith. Sarah K. Bolton. PraP
Faith. Robert Browning. *Fr.* A Soul's Tragedy. OQP; QP-1
Faith. Emma Carleton. MaRV
Faith. Thomas Holley Chivers. MOAP; SPP
Faith. Preston Clark. HBMV; MaRV
Faith. Donald Earl Edwards. ChIP
Faith. Emerson. *See* Sacrifice.
Faith. John Gould Fletcher. ChMo; CMP
Faith. Hortense Flexner. PoMa; VOD
Faith. William Dean Howells. MaRV; OQP; QP-1; WGRP
(What Shall It Profit?) AA; LBAP
Faith. Hugh O. Isbell. ChIP
Faith. Maud Frazer Jackson. MaRV
Faith. Frances Anne Kemble. FaBoBe; HBV; LPS-3; OBVV; VA
(Trust.) MaRV; NeHB
Faith. Theodore Maynard. OQP; QP-2
Faith. F. B. Meyer. OQP; QP-2
Faith. John Richard Moreland. ChIP; LS; OHIP
Faith. John Oxenham. MaRV
Faith. Ray Palmer. *See* My Faith Looks Up to Thee.
Faith. Pope. *Fr.* An Essay on Man, Epistle III. WGRP
Faith. Edwin McNeill Poteat. ChIP; MaRV
Faith. George Santayana. *See* O World.
Faith. Louise Morgan Sill. CAW
Faith. G. A. Studdert-Kennedy. MaRV
Faith. John Banister Tabb. WGRP
Faith ("Thou canst not prove the Nameless"). Tennyson. *Fr.* The Ancient Sage. MaRV
Faith ("You say, but with no touch of scorn"). Tennyson. *See* In Memoriam A. H. H.: "You say . . ."
Faith ("I know not if the voice of man"). *Unknown, tr. fr. Pawnee Indian.* GrCo-1
Faith ("Keep this for me"). *Unknown.* PoToHe (new ed.)
Faith. Wan Yüan Chang, *tr. fr. Chinese by* Henry H. Hart. PoHN
Faith. Ella Wheeler Wilcox. BLRP; MaRV; OQP; PoToHe; QP-2
Faith. Wordsworth. *Fr.* The Excursion, IV. MaRV
("Curious child, A.") WGRP
("I have seen/ A curious child," *longer sel.*) OBRV
(Tidings of Invisible Things, *abr.*) GrCo-1
Faith and Despondency. Emily Brontë. EmBrPo
Faith and Freedom. Wordsworth. *Fr.* It Is Not to Be Thought Of. GN
Faith and Hope. Sir Robert Grant. *See* When Gathering Clouds.
Faith and Hope. Rembrandt Peale. *See* Don't Be Sorrowful, Darling.
Faith and Science. Thomas Curtis Clark. OQP; QP-2
Faith and Sight. Mary Gardiner Brainard. *Fr.* Not Knowing. MaRV
Faith and Sight. Anna M. King. BLRP
Faith be noe longer coy. *Unknown.* SeCSL
Faith for Tomorrow. Thomas Curtis Clark. PoToHe
Faith has no quarrel with science; she foreknows. Faith and Science. Thomas Curtis Clark. OQP; QP-2
Faith-Healer. *Unknown.* *See* Limerick: "There was a faith-healer of Deal."
Faith, Hope and Love. *Unknown.* BLRP
Faith, I Wish I Were a Leprechaun. Margaret Ritter. FaPON; TiPo
Faith in Time of Darkness. Whittier. *Fr.* Snow-bound. GrCo-2
Faith is a fine invention. Emily Dickinson. CoV; MoPW; OxBA; TwP
Faith is the assurance of things hoped for. Faith. Hebrews, Bible, *N.T.* GrCo-1
Faith is the flower that blooms unseen. Faith. Thomas Holley Chivers. MOAP; SPP
Faith is the wedding garment, lind within. The Wedding Garment. Rowland Watkyns. AEV
Faith, Love, and Death. Dowell O'Reilly. BoAu
Faith of a kind is what a man prefers. Comedian. Louis Johnson. AnNZ
Faith of Appearances. Mark Van Doren. TBM
Faith of Christ's Freemen, The. Thomas Curtis Clark. ChIP, *abr.*; OQP; QP-1
Faith of Our Fathers. Frederick William Faber. MaRV; OIF; TreFS
Faith of Our Mothers. Arthur B. Patten. MaRV; PSO
Faith on Trial, A, *sel.* George Meredith.
"Dream is the thought in the ghost." WGRP
Faith, peace and joy to-day brings: all has failed. There Are Still Kingfishers. A. Y. Campbell. BLA; GTML
Faith sees beyond the grave. Faith, Hope and Love. *Unknown.* BLRP
Faith Shall Build a Fairer Throne. Oliver Wendell Holmes. MaRV
Faith that life on earth is being shaped, The. The Tides of Faith. "George Eliot." GrCo-1
Faith to Each Other. *Unknown.* OQP; QP-1
Faith Trembling. "Madeline Bridges." AA
Faithful Angel, The. Milton. *Fr.* Paradise Lost, V. LPS-2
Faithful Bird, The, *abr.* William Cowper. CG
Faithful Dairy Maid, The. *Unknown.* *See* Downright Country-Man, The.
Faithful Dog, A. Richard Burton. POT
Faithful Friend, The. Margaret E. Bruner. AlBD
Faithful helm commands the keel, The. At Best. John Boyle O'Reilly. AA; LBAP
Faithful Lover, The. Robert Pack. NePoEA
Faithful Lovers, The. *Unknown, at. to* Sir Francis Cowley Burnand. LPS-1
Faithful reports of them have reached me oft. The Isles. Sir Charles G. D. Roberts. VA
Faithful Servant, A. Dioscorides, *tr. fr. Greek by* R. A. Furness. OxBG
("Lydian? Yes; to Timanthes foster father, and slave," *tr. by* William Stebbing.) GrPo
(Old Slave, The, *tr. by* F. L. Lucas.) GrPE
(Slave's Epitaph, A, *tr. by* R. A. Furness.) GrR
Faithful Servant, The. Richard R. Kirk. LS
Faithful Shepherd, The. Giovanni Battista Guarini. *See* Il Pastor Fido.
Faithful Shepherdess, The, *sels.* John Fletcher.
"Come, shepherds, come!" *fr.* I, iii. EG; ElL
Evening Song, *fr.* II, i. EV-2; GN; OTPC (1923 ed.); WP
(Evening.) CG
(Evening Knell, The.) ElL
(Folding the Flocks.) CH; LPS-2
(Invocation by the Priest of Pan.) CaAE
(Priest's Chant, The.) OBS
("Shepherds all, and maidens fair.") CenL
God of Sheep, The, *fr.* V, v. ElL; FaBoCh; LoGBV
("All ye woods, and trees, and bowers.") CenL
(Song to Pan.) EV-2
(To Pan.) BLV; TrGrPo
"Hail, holy earth, whose cold arms do embrace," I, i. MyFE
"Here be grapes, whose lusty blood," *fr.* I, i. ViBoPo
(Satyr, The.) EV-2
"Here be woods as green," *fr.* I, iii. ViBoPo
Hymn to Pan, *fr.* I, ii. BCEP; OBEV
(Pan.) WP
(Sing His Praises.) EG; ViBoPo
(Song: "Sing his praises.") OBS; SeEP
Morning Song ("Shepherds, rise"), *fr.* V, i. EV-2

Faithful Shepherdess, The (*continued*)
 River God, The ("I am this fountain's god"), *fr.* III, i. TrGrPo
 River God's Song, The, *fr.* III, i. FaPON; MoShBr; PCH
 ("Do not fear to put thy feet.") ElSeCe; TuPP
 (Song: "Do not fear to put thy feet.") ElL; OBS; ThWaDe
 (Song of the River God to Amoret, The.) EV-2
 Satyr's Song ("See, the day begins to break"), *fr.* IV, iv. OBS
 "Shall I stray/ In the middle air," *fr.* V, v. ViBoPo
 "Thou divinest, fairest, brightest," *fr.* V, v. LO
 (Satyr's Farewell, The.) OBS
 (Satyr's Leave-taking, The.) LoBV (2d ed.)
 "Who hath restored my sense, given me new breath," *fr.* III, i. LO
Faithful sky in lake and light repeats, The. On Lake Llanquihue. Wilberto L. Cantón. AnCL
Faithful unto Death. Richard Handfield Titherington. GA; PAH
Faithless and the Constant, The. Sir William Watson. CaAE
Faithless Flowers, The. Margaret Widdemer. MPB; SP
Faithless Friend, A. Theognis, *tr. fr. Greek by* T. F. Higham. GrL; OxBG
Faithless Generation Asked a Sign, A. Molly Anderson Haley. OQP; OP-2
Faithless Nelly [*or* Nellie] Gray. Thomas Hood. BOHV; EnRP; ERP; HBV; InMe; InP; LPS-3; NA; PIR; ShBV-2; SiTL; SoV; TOP; TreF; TSW
Faithless Sally Brown. Thomas Hood. BEL; BOHV; ERP; HBV; LPS-3; TreFS
Faithless Shepherdess, The. *Unknown.* EV-1; GTSL; OBEV
 (Adieu Love, Untrue Love.) ElL
 (Philon.) OBSC
 (Philon the Shepherd—His Song.) ALV
 (Unfaithful Shepherdess, The.) GTBS; GTBS-D; GTBS-W; GTSE
 (While That the Sun.) ElSeCe
 ("While that the sun with his beams hot.") SiCE
Faithless Wife, The. Federico García Lorca, *tr. fr. Spanish by* Rolfe Humphries. LiTW
Faith's Difficulty. Theodore Maynard. TrPWD
Faith's Vista. Henry Abbey. AA
Faiths washed away. Elegies, II. Philippe Thoby-Marcelin. PoNe
Fakenham Ghost, The. Robert Bloomfield. EV-3
Fala. Edward Anthony. AlBD
Falce love awaye, & all my sighes send back. *Unknown.* SeCSL
Falcon. William Rose Benét. MOAP
Falcon, The. Wilfrid Scawen Blunt. *See* To Manon, Comparing Her to a Falcon.
Falcon, The. "The Knight of Kürenberg," *tr. fr. German by* Margarete Münsterberg. LyMA
Falcon, The. Richard Henry Stoddard. AA
Falcon, The. *Unknown.* ACP; InPo; LiTB; OBB; OxBoCh; SeCeV; ViBoPo
 (Bereaved Maid, The.) TrGrPo
 (Corpus Christi Carol.) ChTr
 (Falcon Hath Borne My Mate Away, The.) CBOV
 (He Bare Him Up, He Bare Him Down.) MeEV
 (Knight of the Grail, The.) OBEV (new ed.)
 (Lully, Lulley [Lully, Lulley].) AnEC; AtBAP; BOL; CH; EG; EPP; ExPo; LoBV; NBE; OAEP
 (Over Yonder's a Park, A *vers.*) BaBo
Falcon and the Dove, The. Sir Herbert Read. FaBoMo; POTE
Falcon flew this morning from the East, A. Greeting. Jami. BoFr
Falcon Hath Borne My Mate Away, The. *Unknown. See* Falcon, The.
Falconer of God, The. William Rose Benét. BAP; CAW; CP; CV; GBV (1952 ed.); HBMV; LEAP; MaRV; NP; NV; PC; PG; PoeMoYo; POT; PoTo; QS; SBMV; TCAP; TCPD; WGRP
Fall, The. William Barnes. PoEL-4
Fall, The. Sir Richard Fanshawe, *after the Spanish of* Luis de Góngora. *Fr.* Il Pastor Fido. MePo; OBS
Fall. Aileen L. Fisher. TiPo (1952 ed.); YeAr
Fall, The. Milton. *Fr.* Paradise Lost, IX. PoEL-3
Fall, The. Kathleen Raine. MoPo
Fall, The. Nathaniel Wanley. SeEP
Fall, The. Earl of Rochester. EnLoPo
Fall Days. Marion Conger. SiSoSe
Fall flat upon your face. Not Made by Hands. Pyotr Vasilyevich Oreshin. RuPo
Fall Freshet. Thad Stem, Jr. NoCaPo (rev. ed.)
Fall gently, rain, on leaf and limb. Discarded Christmas Tree. Elizabeth-Ellen Long. ChBR
Fall in and prepare to march! Left March. Vladimir Mayakovsky. BoRS
Fall, Leaves, Fall. Emily Brontë. EmBrPo; EnLi-2 (1949 ed.); LoBV; OTPC (1946 ed.); PoEL-5; ShBV-4; TrGrPo
 ("Fall, leaves, fall; die, flowers, away.") FaBoCh; GTBS-D; LoGBV
Fall now, my cold thoughts, frozen fall. Lament. Laurence Binyon. MoVE
Fall of a Soul, The. John Addington Symonds. PoVP; VA
Fall of a Wall. John Donne. ReIE; TwP
Fall of Angels and of Man. *Unknown, at one time at. to* Cædmon, *mod. vers. Fr.* Genesis. PoLi
Fall of Cleopatra, The. Horace. *See* Death of Cleopatra, The.
Fall of Constantinople, The. *Unknown, tr. fr. Modern Greek by* Rae Dalven. MoGP
Fall of Hyperion, The, *sels.* Keats.
 "Fanatics have their dreams, wherewith they weave," *fr.* I. CoEV; EnRP
 "'High Prophetess,' said I, 'purge off,'" *fr.* I. CoEV
 ". . . Holy Power," *fr.* I. EV-4
 "Methought I stood where trees," *fr.* I. OBRV
 "None can usurp this height," *fr.* I. OBRV
 (Ars Gratia Artis, *shorter sel.*) LiA
 "Turning from these with awe, once more I raised," *fr.* I. CBE, *abr.*; NBE
Fall of Icarus, The. Ovid, *tr. fr. Latin by* Arthur Golding. PoF
Fall of J. W. Beane, The. Oliver Herford. StPo
Fall of Jerusalem, The, *sel.* Henry Hart Milman.
 Hebrew Wedding. LPS-1
Fall of Kings, The. Love of Nature. James Thomson. *Fr.* The Seasons: Autumn. OBEC
Fall of Man and the Early Ages of the Earth, The. Hesiod, *tr. fr. Greek by* F. L. Lucas. *Fr.* Works and Days. GrPE
Fall of Maubila, The. Thomas Dunn English. PAH
Fall of Niagara, The. John Gardiner Calkins Brainard. LPS-2
Fall of Princes, The, *sels.* John Lydgate.
 Like a Midsummer Rose. CoEV
 (Lat Noman Booste of Konnyng nor Vertu.) AtBAP; NBE
 "Sith of our language he was the lode-star," 3 *ll.* PtP
Fall of Richmond, The. Herman Melville. MC; PAH
Fall of Satan, The. Cædmon(?), *tr. fr. Anglo-Saxon by* Benjamin Thorpe. *Fr.* Genesis. TCEP
 (Fall of the Angels, The, *tr. by* C. W. Kennedy.) EPP
 (Satan's Presumption and Fall, *tr. by* Henry Morley.) BCEP
Fall of Satan, The. Roy Campbell. *Fr.* The Flaming Terrapin. BoSA
Fall of Siegfried, The, *abr. Unknown, pr. tr. fr. Middle High German by* Margaret Armour. *Fr.* The Song of the Nibelungs. WoL
Fall of Stars. George Dillon. NP
Fall of Tecumseh, The. *Unknown.* PAH
Fall of the Angels, The. Cædmon(?). *See* Fall of Satan, The.
Fall of the Angels, The. Milton. *Fr.* Paradise Lost, I. FiP
 ("Is this the region, this the soil, the clime.") MyFE; NBE
 (Satan Ponders His Fallen State.) TreFS
 (Satan's Kingdom.) CBE
Fall of the City, The; a Verse Play for Radio. Archibald MacLeish. MoAmPo
 Sels.
 Voice of the Announcer ("We are here on the central plaza"). HoPM
 Voice of the Studio Announcer ("Ladies and gentlemen:/ This broadcast comes to you from the city"). HoPM
Fall of the House of Usher, The, *sel.* Poe.
 Haunted Palace, The. AA; AmP; AnFE; APA; APW; BAP; BeLS; BoLiVe; CBOV; CH; ChTr; CoAnAm; DDA; EV-5; HBV; IAP; LiTA; LiTG; MCCG; MOAP; NePA; OBAV; OBVV; OnAP; OTPC; OxBA; PFE; PFY; Po; PoE; PoEL-4; PoeMoYo; SPP; TCAP; TOP; TreFS; TrGrPo; ViBoPo
 ("In the greenest of our valleys.") AmPP
Fall of the Leaf, The. Henry David Thoreau. AmP
Fall of the Nibelungs, The. *Unknown, pr. tr. fr. Middle High German by* Margaret Armour. *Fr.* The Song of the Nibelungs. LiA
Fall of the Oak, The. George Hill. APW
 (Oak, The.) HH
Fall of the Plum Blossoms, The. Ranko, *tr. fr. Japanese.* TiPo
Fall of the Year. Henry Ellison. OBVV
Fall of Troy, The. Virgil, *tr. fr. Latin by* Theodore C. Williams. The Aeneid, II. RoL
Fall on your face. Not By Hands Created. Piotr Vasilyevich Oreshin. TrRV
Fall, snow, and cease not! Flake by flake. Winter [*or* A Year of Sorrow]. Aubrey Thomas De Vere. *Fr.* The Year of Sorrow; Ireland, 1849. ACP; IrPN; TIP
Fallen, The. Duncan Campbell Scott. AOAH; TrPWD
Fallen ages fly away, we are tricked by the fugitive hours, The. To the Noble and Patrician Iovinus, Governor of Provence. Venantius Fortunatus. LaP
Fallen Angels, The ("Him the Almighty Power"). Milton. *See* Satan Defiant.

Fallen Angels, The ("Of Man's first disobedience, and the fruit"). Milton. *See* Invocation to the Heavenly Muse.
Fallen Angels, The ("Others apart sat on a hill retired"). Milton. *Fr.* Paradise Lost, II. CBE
Fallen as he is, this king of birds still seems. The Dead Eagle. Thomas Campbell. EnRP; ERP
Fallen cause still waits, The. The Cause of the South. Abram Joseph Ryan. LPS-2
Fallen Cities. Gerald Gould. PoeT; PtOT
Fallen Flowers. Li Shang-yin, *tr. fr. Chinese.* WhP
Fallen flowers seemed, The. Arakida Moritake, *tr. fr. Japanese by* I. W. Furukami. LiTW
Fallen Flyer Aged 19. David Ross. PG (1955 ed.)
Fallen? How fallen? States and empires fall. On the Defeat of a Great Man [*or* On the Defeat of Henry Clay]. William Wilberforce Lord. AA; GA; PAH
Fallen Leaves. Kathryn Munro. CaP; OCL
Fallen Leaves. *Unknown, tr. fr. Chinese by* Arthur Waley. *Fr.* Shi King. LiTW
Fallen Majesty. W. B. Yeats. InP; PoeMoYo
Fallen Olive-Tree, The. Homer, *tr. fr. Greek by* F. L. Lucas. *Fr.* The Iliad, XVII. GrPE
Fallen Poplar, The. Mary Webb. InP
Fallen Shrine, The. Delphic Oracle, *tr. fr. Greek by* Sir William Marris. OxBG
Fallen Star, The. George Darley. AnFE; BCEP; HBV; OBEV; TIP
Fallen that mighty form. Phillips Brooks. John Hall Ingham. GA
Fallen Tower of Siloam, The. Robert Graves. WaP
Fallen Tree. Helen Frazee-Bower. MuM
Fallen Tree, The. Patrick Maybin. NeIP
Fallen with autumn's falling leaf. On the Death of President Garfield. Oliver Wendell Holmes. GA; PAH
Fallen Yew, A. Francis Thompson. EmBrPo; MBP; MoAB; MoBrPo; VLEP
Falling Asleep. Siegfried Sassoon. MBP; MCCG; MoBrPo; MoVE
Falling Asleep over the Aeneid. Robert Lowell. CoBMV; CrMA; FiMAP; OxBA
Falling flowers! Translations from Modern Japanese Poetry. Akiko Yanagiwara. PFE
Falling from the ridge. Emperor Yozei, *tr. fr. Japanese by* Kenneth Rexroth. LiTW; OnPJ
Falling leaf and fading tree. Goodbye! George John Whyte-Melville. TreF
Falling leaf betrays the fawn, The. Late Autumn. A. M. Sullivan. GoBC
Falling Leaves. *Unknown, tr. fr. Chinese.* WhP
Falling of the night. Into the Darkness. Basho. OnPM
Falling of the Snow, The. Raymond Souster. CaP
Falling rain, The. Parting in the Rain. Ts'ui Shu. PoHN
Falling Snow. Amy Lowell. LA; NP
Falling Snow. *Unknown.* BoChLi; GFA; TiPo (1952 ed.)
Falling Star, The. Sara Teasdale. BrR; MoShBr; MoSiPe; PoRh; StVeCh; SUS; TiPo
Falling to Sleep. *Unknown.* BOL
Fall'n, fall'n, a silent heap; her heroes all. John Dyer. *Fr.* The Ruins of Rome. BeR; OBEC
Fall'n pile! I ask not what has been thy fate. Sonnet: Netley Abbey. William Lisle Bowles. CEP
Fallow Deer at the Lonely House, The. Thomas Hardy. AWP; CH; ChMo; CMP; InPo; MoVE
Fallow Field, The. Julia C. R. Dorr. AA
Fallow Land. Eunice Clark. NAMP
Fallow Land and Stubble Fields, *sel.* Vyacheslav Ivanovich Ivanov, *tr. fr. Russian by* Babette Deutsch.
"Sadness and stillness. What a bright transparency!" *fr.* III. TrRV
Fallow land, how low the crows fly! Fallow Land. Eunice Clark. NAMP
Falls from her heaven the Moon, and stars sink burning. Moon-Bathers. John Freeman. TCPD
Falls like a ripe pear in the storm. Definition of the Soul. Boris Pasternak. LiTW
Falltime. Carl Sandburg. NP
Falmouth. W. E. Henley. *See* O, Falmouth Is a Fine Town.
False Achitophel, The. Dryden. *See* Achitophel.
False Bay. F. T. Prince. BoSA
False diamond set in flint! hard heart in haughty breast! Fatima and Raduan. *Unknown.* LPS-1
False dreams, all false. Iliad. Humbert Wolfe. BLV; MBP; MoBrPo; PFE; PIAE; TCPD; TwCV
False Enchantment. Jean Starr Untermeyer. MoAmPo (1950 ed.)
False Fox, The. *Unknown.* ChTr
False Friend. Al-Hajjam, *tr. fr. Arabic by* A. J. Arberry. MooP
False Friends, The. Dorothy Parker. PR
False Friends—Like. William Barnes. CG
False Gallop of Analogies, A. W. St. Leger. CenHV; FiBHP; WhC
False Gods, The. E. A. Robinson. CP; NV
False Heart, The. Hilaire Belloc. *See* For False Heart.
False knave Flaccus once a bribe I gave, The. In Flaccum. Sir John Davies. TuPP
False Knight [*or* Fause Knicht] upon [*or* on] the Road, The. *Unknown* AtBAP; CH; EnSB; ESPB; OxBoLi
(False Knight, The, *diff. vers.*) ABS
(False Knight and the Wee Boy, The, *diff. vers.*) FaBoCh
False Lambkin was a mason. Lamkin (D *vers.*). *Unknown.* BaBo
False life! a foil and no more. Quickness. Henry Vaughan. LoBV; MaPo; MeLP; MePo; OBS; OxBoCh; ReEn; SeCePo; SeCV-1; TriL
False Linfinn. *Unknown. See* Lamkin.
False Love. Burns. *See* Banks o' Doon, The.
False Love. *At. to* John Lilliat. *See* Song: "When love on time and measure makes his ground."
False Love. Sir Walter Ralegh. OBSC; SiPS
("Farewell, false Love!") LO; ReEn
(Farewell to False Love, A.) ElL
False Love. Sir Walter Scott. *Fr.* Waverley, *ch.* 9. ViBoPo
False Love and True Logic. Laman Blanchard. BOHV
False Lover, The. *Unknown. See* Lady Isabel and the Elf-Knight.
False Lover Won Back, The. *Unknown.* BaBo; ESPB (A *and* B *vers.*)
(Fause Lover, The.) CoBE
(Young John.) OBB
False One, The. Theognis, *tr. fr. Greek by* F. L. Lucas. GrPE
False Poets and True. Thomas Hood. HBV
False Sir John a-wooing came. May Colvin. *Unknown.* BLV; EBSV; MaC; OBB; StPo; TrGrPo
False Step, A. Elizabeth Barrett Browning. BoFr; VLEP
False Summer, The. Marya Zaturenska. CrMA
"False," they said, "thy Pale-face lover, from the land of waking morn." The Pilot of the Plains. Emily Pauline Johnson. CPG; PCN
False Though She Be. Congreve. *See* Song: "False though she be to me and Love."
False world, good night! since thou hast brought. A Farewell to the World. Ben Jonson. OBEV (1st ed.)
False World, Thou Ly'st. Francis Quarles. *See* Vanity of the World, The.
Falsehood. William Cartwright. OBEV
Falsehood and hatred here. On Leaving Prison. Luis de León. AnSpL-1
Falsehood hath so corrupted all the world. Man's Natural Element. Abu-l-Ala al-Maarri. LiTW
Falstaff's Lament over Prince Hal Become Henry V. Herman Melville. ViBoPo
Falstaff's Song. Edmund Clarence Stedman. AA; BAP; DDA; HBV; LEAP; OBAV
Fame. Leonard Bacon. PoeMoYo
Fame. Clifford Bax. PtOT
Fame. Robert Browning. *Fr.* Earth's Immortalities. BPN; PoVP; VLEP
Fame ("From mighty wrongs to petty perfidy"). Byron. *Fr.* Childe Harold's Pilgrimage, IV. FiP
Fame ("What is the end of fame?"). Byron. *Fr.* Don Juan, I *and* III. GEPC
Fame. Eleanor Hollister Cantus. GoYe
Fame. Austin Dobson. *See* Fame Is a Food That Dead Men Eat.
Fame. Ben Jonson. LPS-3
Fame. Keats. *See* Two Sonnets on Fame.
Fame. James J. Montague. LPS-1
Fame. Pope. *Fr.* An Essay on Man, Epistle IV. LPS-3
("What's fame? a fancied life in others' breath.") ViBoPo
Fame. John Banister Tabb. AA; BAP
Fame and Envy. Edward Young. Fr. Epistle to Pope. BCEP
Fame and Fortune. Michael Drayton. *Fr.* The Legend of Robert, Duke of Normandy. OBSC
Fame and Friendship. Austin Dobson. *See* Fame Is a Food That Dead Men Eat.
Fame comes to the artist who paints all alone. Three Arts. Minerva Florence Swigert. LPS-1
Fame? I have never wished it . . . Ah! Fame. Clifford Bax. PtOT
Fame Is a Food That Dead Men Eat. Austin Dobson. BoFr; GTML; GTSL; HBV
(Fame.) MBP; MoBrPo (1942 ed.)
(Fame and Friendship.) OBEV (new ed.)
Fame, like a wayward girl, will still be coy. On Fame [*or* Fame *or* Two Sonnets on Fame, I]. Keats. BPN; EM-2; EmBrPo; EnLit; EnRP; ERP
Fame Makes Us Forward. Robert Herrick. EPS (1942 ed.)
Famed Hibernian, in this curious age, A. The Lion and the Terrapin. William Hill Brown. NoCaPo (rev. ed.)
Famed ship *California*, a ship of high renown, The. The Girls around Cape Horn. *Unknown.* SoAmSa
Fame's pillar here at last we set. The Pillar of Fame. Robert Herrick. EPS
Fames Plant takes Root from Vertue, grows thereby. Life and Death. Edward Benlowes. *Fr.* Theophila. FaBoEn

Familiar Daemon. Roy Campbell. JKCP (1955 ed.)
Familiar Epistle, A. Austin Dobson. VA
Familiar Friends. James S. Tippett. BoChLi; BoTP; SUS; UTS
Familiar Letter to Several Correspondents, A. Oliver Wendell Holmes. BOHV; InMe
Familiar Lines. *Unknown.* FiBHP
Familiarity Dangerous. Vincent Bourne, *tr. fr. Latin by* William Cowper. PoC
Families, when a child is born. On the Birth of His Son. Su T'ung-po. AWP; FAOV; JAWP; LiTW; OnPM; TrCh; WBP; WoL
Family, The. Donna R. Lydston. PoToHe (new ed.)
Family, The. *Unknown, tr. fr. German by* Rose Fyleman. TiPo (1959 ed.)
Family Court. Ogden Nash. FiBHP
Family Dinner-Party, The. Menander, *tr. fr. Greek by* C. M. Bowra. OxBG
Family Fool, The. W. S. Gilbert. *Fr.* Yeomen of the Guard. ALV; InMe; SiTL
Family Ghosts. W. H. Auden. *See* Strings' Excitement, The.
Family History. John Maher Murphy. JKCP (1955 ed.)
Family Life. Allan M. Laing. FiBHP
Family Man as a Poet, The. Joseph Schuyler Long. FAOV
Family Meeting, The. Charles Sprague. HBV
Family of Nations, The. Willard Wattles. PAH
Family Portrait. Leonard Feeney. ISi
Family Reunion. Hollis Summers. GoYe
Family Tree. Ibn al-Qaffun, *tr. fr. Arabic by* A. J. Arberry. MooP
Family Trees. Douglas Malloch. OHIP; PEDC
Famine. Georg Heym, *tr. fr. German by* Werner Heider. LiTW
Famine, The. Longfellow. The Song of Hiawatha, XX. BAV; IAP
Famine once we had. New England's Growth. William Bradford. PAH
Famine Year, The. Lady Wilde. OnYI; PoFr, *abr.*; TIP
Famous Ballad of the Jubilee Cup, The. Sir Arthur Quiller-Couch. InMe; NA; OnSP; WhC; YT, *cond.*
Famous Battle of Bumble-Bug and Bumble-Bee. *Unknown.* FTB
Famous city of Boston. Hubbub in Hub. Laurence McKinney. WhC
Famous Fight at Malago, The; or, The Englishmen's Victory over the Spaniards. *Unknown.* CoMu; SG
Famous Flower of Serving-Men, The. *Unknown.* *See* Lady Turned Serving Man, The.
Famous hen's my story's theme, A. The Hen. Matthias Claudius. BOHV; LPS-3
Famous kingdom of the birds, The. Somewhere Is Such a Kingdom. John Crowe Ransom. ChMo; LiTA
Famous Light Brigade, The, *with music.* *Unknown.* ShS
Famous poets with the muses nine, The. The Prologue. Alexander Barclay. *Fr.* Certain Eclogues. ReIE
Famous Sea-Fight, A. John Looke. CoMu
Famous Sea Fight between Captain Ward and the *Rainbow,* A. *Unknown.* *See* Captain Ward and the *Rainbow.*
Famous Toast, A. Sheridan. *See* Let the Toast Pass.
Famous warriors of the antique [*or* anticke] world, The. Amoretti, LXIX. Spenser. CoBE; PeBoSo; ReEn; SiCE
Famously she descended, her red hair. A Recollection. John Peale Bishop. LiTA; TwAmPo
Fan, The. Serafín Alvarez Quintero *and* Joaquín Alvarez Quintero, *tr. fr. Spanish by* Thomas Walsh. OnPM
Fan, The. Fan Tseng Hsiang, *tr. fr. Chinese by* Henry H. Hart. PoHN
Fan, The, *sel.* John Gay.
"Rise, happy youth, this bright machine survey." ViBoPo
Fan, The. Edith Sitwell. HBMV
Fan, The. Sokan, *tr. fr. Japanese.* GFA
Fan Fitzgerl. Alfred Perceval Graves. TIP
Fan, the Filly. Wilfrid Thorley. BoTP
Fanatics have their dreams, wherewith they weave. Keats. *Fr.* The Fall of Hyperion. CoEV; EnRP
Fancy. Keats. BPN; EM-2; EmBrPo; EnLi-2; EnRP; EPN; GEPC; LoBV; LPS-3; OBEV; PC
(Realm of Fancy, The.) ATP (1935 ed.); GTBS; GTBS-D; GTBS-W; GTSE; GTSL
(To Fancy.) EV-4; HBV
Fancy, A ("First shall the heavens want starry light"). Thomas Lodge. *Fr.* Rosalynde. ElL; LoBV; OBSC
("First shall the heavens want starry light.") SiCE
(Lover's Protestation, A.) GoBC
(Love's Protestation.) ACP
Fancy, A ("When I admire the rose"). Thomas Lodge. *Fr.* The Life and Death of William Longbeard. *See* Rose, The.
Fancy. Paul D. Page, Jr. CAG
Fancy. Shakespeare. *See* Tell Me Where Is Fancy Bred.
Fancy, and I, last evening walkt. To Amoret Gone from Him. Henry Vaughan. MeLP; OBS
Fancy from Fontenelle, A. Austin Dobson. BMEP; HBV; OBVV; POTT
(Rose and the Gardener, The.) BLP; MPB
Fancy halts my feet at the way-side well, A. The Way-Side Well. Joseph Seamon Cotter, Sr. CDC; PoNe
Fancy I had today, The. Prologue [*or* Amphibian]. Robert Browning. *Fr.* Fifine at the Fair. AlDL; BPN
Fancy in Nubibus. Samuel Taylor Coleridge. LPS-3
(Fancy in Nubibus, or the Poet in the Cloud.) ES
Fancy, which that I have servèd long, The. The Restless Heart. Earl of Surrey. SiPS
Fancy's Home. W. H. Davies. AtBAP; ChMo; CMP; POTT
Fancy's Knell. A. E. Housman. Last Poems, XLI. AnFE; BMEP; EG; FaBoCh; MM; MoPW; PoRA; POTT; ShBV-4; TwCV
Fand, *sels.* William Larminie.
Killarney. AnIV
(Epilogue to "Fand.") TIP
Speech of Emer, The. TIP
Fand Yields Cuchulain to Emer. *Unknown, tr. fr. Old Irish by* Seán O'Faoláin. AnIL; LyMA; SiB
Fandango. "Stanley Vestal." IHA
Fandango for Sorrow. Catherine Graham Miller. CAG
Fannia. Giovanni Pontano, *pr. tr. fr. Latin by* Richard Aldington. LaP
Fanny. Anne Reeve Aldrich. HBV
Fanny, *sels.* Fitz-Greene Halleck.
Fortune, *abr.* LPS-3
Weehawken and the New York Bay. LPS-2
(Weehawken.) BAV
Fanny Foo-Foo was a Japanese girl. The Japanese Lovers. *Unknown.* BeLS; BLPA
Fanny's Doves ("Fanny loves"). Christina Rossetti. SAS
Fantaisie d'Antan. Clark Ashton Smith. DaM
Fantasia. Carlos Drummond de Andrade, *tr. fr. Portuguese by* Dudley Poore. AnCL
Fantasia. G. K. Chesterton. HBMV
Fantasia. Dorothy Livesay. BoCaPo (1948 ed.); TwCV
Fantasia. Gérard de Nerval. *See* Old Tune, An.
Fantasia of a Fallen Gentleman on a Cold Bitter Night on the Embankment. T. E. Hulme. *See* Embankment, The.
Fantasia on a Wittelsbach Atmosphere. Siegfried Sassoon. MoVE
Fantasia under the Clear Sky. Kenji Miyazawa, *tr. fr. Japanese by* Takamichi Ninomiya *and* D. J. Enright. PoLJ
Fantastick Mind, The. Nicolas Boileau-Despréaux, *tr. fr. French by* Sir William Soames *and* John Dryden. *Fr.* L'Art poétique, III. BeR
Fantasy. Gwendolyn B. Bennett. CDC
Fantasy. Giosuè Carducci, *tr. fr. Italian by* Asa Hughes. LiTW
Fantasy, A. Crosbie Garstin. PFE
Fantasy. Ben Jonson. *Fr.* The Vision of Delight. LPS-3
Fantasy. Hugh McCrae. MM; MoAuPo
Fantasy. Gérard de Nerval. *See* Old Tune, An.
Fantasy. Ruth Mather Skidmore. PoMS
Fantasy. Louis Untermeyer. TSW
Fantasy for a Charming Friend. Arthur Davison Ficke. TCPD
Fantasy in a Forest. Leah Bodine Drake. MuM
Fantasy in Purple. Langston Hughes. BANP; CDC; TBM
Fantoches. Paul Verlaine, *tr. fr. French by* Arthur Symons. AWP; OBMV
Far above us where a jay. Morning on the Lièvre. Archibald Lampman. CPG; MM
Far across hill and dale. Plum Blossoms. Basho. SUS
Far and away in the Land of Nod. The Land of Nod. Elizabeth Hays Wilkinson. BOL
Far and near, and now, from never. Beauty. Isaac Rosenberg. TrJP
Far and Wide She Went. Cædmon(?), *tr. fr. Anglo-Saxon. Fr.* Genesis. EtS
Far are the Gaelic tribes and wide. The Dead Antiquary O'Donovan. Thomas D'Arcy McGee. TIP
Far are the shades of Arabia. Arabia. Walter de la Mare. GTBS; HBMV; POTE; PtOT; TCPD; WHA; WP
Far as Creation's ample range extends. The Scale of Being [*or* The Great Chain of Being]. Pope. *Fr.* An Essay on Man. BeR; ExPo; ImOP
Far as man can see. Song of the Rain Chant. *Tr. by* Natalie Curtis. AWP; JAWP; WBP
Far as the eye could reach, no tree was seen. Scotland. Charles Churchill. *Fr.* The Prophecy of Famine. BeR
Far as the utmost reach of heart's desire. The Way of Knowledge. Parmenides. OxBG
Far at sea and west of Spain. The Land of Cokaygne. *Unknown, at. to* Friar Michael of Kildare. OnYI
Far-away. George Sigerson. JKCP (1926 ed.); TIP
Far away and long ago. The Snare. Edward Davison. BMEP; PG (1955 ed.); ViBoPo (1941 ed.)
Far away arch-soul. Character and Talent. Jules Laforgue. OnPM
Far away beyond the glamor of the city and its strife. The

Picture That Is Turned toward the Wall. Charles Graham. TreF
Far Away from Flanders Field. L. S. Uphoff. PSO
Far away is one who now is sleeping. The Clock. Francis Scarfe. NeBP
Far away on the old city walls. Daydreams. Chang Chung Su. PoHN
Far away twinkles the Herd-boy star. *Unknown, tr. fr. Chinese by* Arthur Waley. Seventeen Old Poems, 9. TrCh
Far back, in my musings, my thoughts have been cast. The Old Kitchen Floor. *Unknown.* PTA-2
Far be the bookish Muses! Let them find. Invocation to the African Muse. Roy Campbell. *Fr.* The Flaming Terrapin. BoSA
Far behind him crept blackness and flickering glimmer. The Song of the Spirits. Joseph Sheridan Le Fanu. *Fr.* The Legend of the Glaive. OnYI
Far below Arles in those old days. The Aliscamp. Frédéric Mistral. CAW
Far better never to have heard the name. Wordsworth. *Fr.* The Prelude, I. GEPC
Far beyond/ White lilies. Kyoko, *tr. fr. Japanese by* Lois J. Erikson. SoLD
Far beyond the sky-line, where the steamers go. Hot Weather in the Plains—India. E. H. Tipple. HBV
Far beyond Us. *Unknown, tr. fr. Japanese by* Ishii *and* Obata. OnPM
Far Country, The. Robert Greacen. NeIP
Far Cry to Heaven, A. Edith M. Thomas. AA; PFY; WGRP
Far Distances. Henry W. Clark. OQP; QP-2
Far-distant concerts and opaline sparks of our first home in the burning heat of summer. The Hydra of Birds. Nikos Engonopoulos. LiTW
Far down in the meadow the wheat grows green. Alice's Supper. Laura E. Richards. MPB
Far down the purple wood. The Constant Bridegrooms. Kenneth Patchen. CrMA
Far East. Edmund Blunden. PtOT
Far—Far—Away. Tennyson. BPN; EmBrPo; EPN; GEPC; PoVP; ViPo; VLEP
Far, far away, beyond a hazy height. October in Tennessee. Walter Malone. AA
Far, far away is Bethlehem. The Continuing Christ. W. Russell Bowie. ChIP; MaRV
Far far from gusty waves, these children's faces. An Elementary School Classroom in a Slum. Stephen Spender. BoLiVe (1945 ed.); CoBMV; FaBoMo; LiTB; MBP; MoAB; MoBrPo; MoPo; OAEP (2d ed.); PoE; ReMP; TrGrPo
Far, far from here,/ The Adriatic breaks in a warm bay. Cadmus and Harmonia [*or* The Song of Callicles]. Matthew Arnold. *Fr.* Empedocles on Etna, I, ii. FiP; NBE; OBVV; ViPo
Far, far from here, I know not when, nor where. In the Arena. Antero de Quental. UnW
Far, far from here the church bells ring. In New York: On Sunday Morning. William Alexander Percy. QS; SPP
Far far the least of all, in want. The Prisoners. Stephen Spender. FaBoMo; GTBS-D; MBP; MoAB; MoBrPo
Far, far the mountain peak from me. The Christ of the Andes. Florence Earle Coates. BPP; StJW
Far, Far West, The. *Unknown.* CoSo
Far-Farers, The. Robert Louis Stevenson. BoTP
Far-fetched and dear-bought, as the proverb rehearses. A Singing Lesson. Swinburne. BPN; HBV; VLEP
Far from my dearest friend, 'tis mine to rove. An Evening Walk. Wordsworth. EmBrPo
Far from My Dearest Self. Tasso. *See* To His Mistress in Absence.
Far from shrewd companies. V. Sackville-West. *Fr.* The Land. AlDL
Far from Somewhere. "Primus." WhC
Far from the birds, the cattle herds, the village girls. Tear. Arthur Rimbaud. AnFP
Far from the blue Aegean's boom and swell. The Eretrian Dead. Plato, *tr. by* H. K. St. J. Sanderson. OxBG
Far from the churchyard dig his grave. A Gravestone. William Allingham. TIP
Far from the crowd they stood [*or* stand] apart. The V-a-s-e. James Jeffrey Roche. BOHV; HBV; LHV
Far from the deep roar of the Aegean main. Farewell. Plato, *tr. by* Charles Whibley. AWP; WBP
Far from the Heart of Culture. W. H. Auden. *Fr.* In Time of War. ChMo; WaaP
Far from the loud sea beaches. A Visit from the Sea. Robert Louis Stevenson. GN; YT
Far from the Madding Crowd. Nixon Waterman. BLPA; FaBoBe; MPB (1956 ed.); NeHB; NLK (Vacation.) WBLP
Far from the parlour have your kitchen placed. The Art of Cookery. William King. BeR
Far from the sea in his grey later days. "Cap'n." Arthur Wallace Peach. EtS
Far from the sun and summer-gale. Thomas Gray. *Fr.* The Progress of Poesy. LEAP; PtP
Far from the vulgar haunts of men. On the Same. Roy Campbell. BoSA
Far from the waves that soothed. The Lonely Shell. Martha Eugenie Perry. CaP
Far from the world, far from delight. Our Lady of the Snows. Lionel Johnson. JKCP
Far from thy dearest self, the scope. To His Mistress in Absence [*or* Far from My Dearest Self]. Tasso. AWP; JAWP; OnPM; WBP
Far from your native hills although you roam. To Claude McKay. Vivian L. Virtue. PoNe
Far had he hurled his bomber through the sky. Off Duty. George Herbert Clarke. NeTW
Far happier are the dead, methinks, than they. Epigram [*or* Expectation of Death]. *Unknown, tr. by* William Cowper. EnLi-1; OxBG
Far [*or* Farre] have I clamber'd [*or* clambred] in my mind. Hymn to Charity and Humility [*or* An Hymne in Honour of Those Two Despised Virtues]. Henry More. OBS; OxBoCh
Far I hear the bugle blow. The Day of Battle. A. E. Housman. A Shropshire Lad, LVI. ChMo; CMP; OHIP; PoVP; WaaP
Far in a Western Brookland. A. E. Housman. A Shropshire Lad, LII. AnFE; AWP; BEL; BPN; EnLi-2; EPN; GTBS-D; JAWP; LBBV; NLK (1947 ed.); OAEP; PoEL-5; POTT; PoVP; TOP; TwHP; ViP; ViPo; VOD (1935 ed.); WBP
Far in a wild, unknown to public view. The Hermit. Thomas Parnell. EV-3; GoTL
Far in sea, west of Spain. Cokaygne. *Unknown.* AnIL
Far in the bosom of the deep. The Lighthouse. Sir Walter Scott. OTPC (1946 ed.); PCH
Far in the country of Arden. Cassamen and Dowsabel [*or* The Ballad of Dowsabell *or* The Eighth Eclogue]. Michael Drayton. *Fr.* The Shepherd's Garland. LoBV; OBSC; ReEn; TuPP
Far in the east. The Green Corn Dance. Alice Corbin. BAP
Far in the heavens my God retires. The Incomprehensible. Isaac Watts. CEP; WGRP
Far in the sea and west of Spain. The Land of Cockayne. *Unknown.* MeEV; TMEV
Far Land, The. John Hall Wheelock. WGRP
Far lone amang the Highland hills. The Lass o' Arranteenie. Robert Tannahill. EBSV
Far look in absorbed eyes, unaware, A. Magnets. Laurence Binyon. HBMV
Far moon maketh lovers wise, The. Moonlight. Walter de la Mare. EnLoPo
Far more than I was wont myself I prize. The Amulet of Love. Michelangelo. OnPM
Far, oh, far is the Mango island. The Constant Cannibal Maiden. Wallace Irwin. BOHV
Far Off. Ruth Rutherford. LO
Far off a lonely hound. The Hounds. John Freeman. OBMV
Far-off a young state rises, full of might. Suggested Device of a New Western State [*or* Farther]. John James Piatt. AA; AnAMPo; LA
Far off, above the plain the summer dries. Second Air Force. Randall Jarrell. CoBMV; FiMAP; WaP
Far off, far off/ Those forests lie. Song of the Parrot. Elizabeth J. Coatsworth. StVeCh
Far off from these a slow and silent stream. *See* Farr off from these.
Far off I know not where you rest. Far Off. Ruth Rutherford. LO
Far off in Fu-chou she is watching the moonlight. On a Moonlight Night. Tu Fu. ChLP
Far off in the waste of desert sand. The Jim-Jam King of the Jou-Jous. Alaric Bertrand Stuart. BOHV
Far off is the sea, and the land is afar. Neap-Tide. Swinburne. EmBrPo; PoVP; ViPo
Far-off leafless forests slowly yield, The. Late November. Archibald Lampman. TwCV
Far off, most secret, and inviolate rose. The Secret Rose. W. B. Yeats. GTIV
Far off? Not far away. In the Twilight. George Cotterell. VA
Far-off Rose, A. Josephine Preston Peabody. AA
Far Off-Shore. Herman Melville. AmPP (4th ed.)
Far off the clocks are striking [*or* ticking]. On the Death of My Child. Joseph von Eichendorff. AnGP; UnW
Far off the sea is gray and still as the sky. Week-End by the Sea. Edgar Lee Masters. MoAmPo
Far on the desert ridges. Wind Song. *Tr. by* Natalie Curtis. SUS
Far on the moor some wild bird screams. Twilight. Margaret Ryan. GTIV
Far out at sea. White Horses. Irene F. Pawsey. BoTP
Far out at sea beneath rich Tyrian sails. May upon Ictis. Thomas S. Jones, Jr. TBM

Far out at sea—the sun was high. Genius. Richard Henry Horne. VA
Far out beyond our sheltered bay. Steering Home. Timothy Daniel Sullivan. TIP
Far out beyond the city's lights, away from din and roar. The Country Store. *Unknown.* BLPA
Far out in the hush of the mountain land. The Emigrant's Child. Lyman H. Sproull. PoOW
Far out in the wilds of Oregon. Jack Dempsey's Grave. —— MacMahon. SCC
Far over the billows unresting forever. Thalatta. Willis Boyd Allen. EtS
Far over yon hills of the heather sae green. The Lament of Flora Macdonald. James Hogg. BoHiPo; EBSV
Far over Yonder. Rafael Maya, *tr. fr. Spanish by* Rolfe Humphries. AnCL
Far peaks sleep, the great ravines, The. Night, [*or* Night and the Plain of Sparta]. Alcman. GrL; GrR; OxBG
Far [*or* Fair, *wr.*] sail shimmers, white and lonely, A. A Sail. Mikhail Lermontov. LiTW; OnPM; TrRV; WoL
Far spread, below. The Story of Vinland. Sidney Lanier. *Fr.* The Psalm of the West. PAH
Far Sweeter than Honey. Abraham ibn Ezra, *tr. fr. Hebrew by* Israel Abrahams. TrJP
Far the best time for the poet is early spring. East of the City, Early Spring. Yang Ch'u-yuan. WhP
Far, through the quiet night, my loved one came. The Return. Ethel Ashton Edwards. UnW
Far to the east I see them in my mind. The Wise Men. Edgar Bowers. NePoEA; PtPa
Far to the Northward there lies a land. By the Grey Gulf-Water. A. B. Paterson. TVSH
Far to the south, beyond the blue, there spreads. The Second Asgard. Matthew Arnold. *Fr.* Balder Dead. FiP
Far up in the Northern country. Christmas in the North. Margaret E. Sangster. PEDC
Far up in the wild and wintry hills in the heart of the cliff-broken woods. The Woodcutter's Hut. Archibald Lampman. BoCaPo (1948 ed.)
Far up the dim twilight fluttered. The Unknown God. "Æ." ChMo; CMP; EPP; GTSL; MBP; MoBrPo; NeMA; PFE; TOP; WGRP
Far up the lonely mountain-side. A Georgia Volunteer. Mary Ashley Townsend. AA; BIG; MDAH
Far Up the River. Tu Fu, *tr. fr. Chinese by* Kenneth Rexroth. OnPC
Far up yon river, opening to the sea. William Gilpin. *Fr.* Landscape Painting. EnSW
Far voices. Old Song. F. R. Scott. PeCV
Far West. A. J. M. Smith. BoCaPo (1948 ed.); PeCV
Fara Diddle Dyno. *Unknown.* ElL; FaBoCh; LoBV
("Ha ha! ha ha! this world doth pass.") LO; OxBoLi; ViBoPo
(Madrigal.) SiTL
Fare not abroad, O Soul, to win. Quo Vadis? Myles E. Connolly. JKCP (1926 ed.); MaRV
Fare thee, O babe, fare thee well. Fare Thee Well, Babe. *Unknown.* ABF
Fare Thee Well. Byron. BLPA; BPN; EM-2; EnLit; EnRP; ERP; FaFP; HBV; PoEL-4; TreFS
(Farewell to His Wife.) LPS-1
Fare Thee Well, Babe, *with music. Unknown.* ABF
Fare Well. Walter de la Mare. CoBMV; GTBS-D; MoVE; OBEV (new ed.); POTE
(Farewell: "When I lie where shades of darkness.") TwCV
Fare Ye Well, My Darlin', *with music. Unknown.* OuSiCo
Fare you well green fields. A Prisoner for Life. *Unknown.* CoSo; CSF
Fare you well, the Prince's Landing Stage. The Leaving of Liverpool. *Unknown.* ShS
. . . Farewel happy fields/ Where joy for ever dwells. Satan Greets Hell. Milton. *Fr.* Paradise Lost, I. LiA
Farewel the fields of Irwan's vale. A Farewell Hymn to the Valley of Irwan. John Langhorne. *Fr.* Solyman and Almena. CEP
Farewel, too little and too lately known. *See* Farewell, too little and too lately known.
Farewel ye guilded follies. pleasing troubles. *Unknown.* MeLP
Farewell, A: "And if I did, what then?" George Gascoigne. *See* And If I Did, What Then?
Farewell, The: "And now the prayer is over and the mass in its due course." *Unknown, tr. fr. Spanish by* R. Selden Rose *and* Leonard Bacon. *Fr.* The Cid. TeCS
Farewell, The: "And so, one day when the tide was away out." Pat Wilson. AnNZ
Farewell: "Boat two-oared, upon water, A." Euripides, *tr. fr. Greek by* Gilbert Murray. *Fr.* Alcestis. GrR
Farewell: "Far from the deep roar of the Aegean main." Plato. *See* Eretrian Dead, The ("Far from the blue Aegean's boom").
Farewell: "Farewell! Another gloomy word." Bert Leston Taylor. BOHV; TOP
Farewell: "Farewell! Farewell! the voice you hear." Sir Walter Scott. *See* Cleveland's Song: "Farewell! Farewell!"
Farewell: "Farewell! if ever fondest prayer." Byron. *See* Farewell! If Ever Fondest Prayer.
Farewell: "Farewell, then. It is finished." Wilfrid Scawen Blunt. The Love Sonnets of Proteus, LIII. MBP; MoBrPo (1942 ed.)
Farewell: "Farewell! Thou art too dear for my possessing." Shakespeare. *See* Sonnets LXXXVII.
Farewell: "Farewell to barn and stack and tree." A. E. Housman. *See* Farewell to Barn and Stack and Tree.
Farewell, The: "Farewell to Europe, and at once farewell." Charles Churchill. CEP
Farewell, A: "Flow down, cold rivulet, to the sea." Tennyson. BPN; EmBrPo; GTML; HBV; OTPC; PoVP; RIS; SN; TCEP
("Flow down, cold rivulet to the sea.") CBE
Farewell, A: "Go, fetch to me a pint o' wine." Burns. *See* My Bonnie Mary.
Farewell, The: "Gone, gone—sold and gone." Whittier. AA; AWP; InPo; LEAP; MOAH; MotAn; PoNe
Farewell, A: "Good-bye [*or* Good-by]—no [*or* nay], do not grieve that it is over." Harriet Monroe. AA; AV; BAP; HBMV; LBAP; LoPo; NP
Farewell, A: "Haue doone with care my harts, aborde amaine." George Peele. *See* Farewell to Sir John Norris and Sir Francis Drake, A.
Farewell, A: "I go down from the hill in gladness." "Æ." AnIV
Farewell: "I leave the world to-morrow." Enid Derham. BoAu
Farewell, A: "I put thy hand aside." "Madeline Bridges." AA
Farewell: "It is buried and done with." John Addington Symonds. OBVV; PG (1945 ed.); VA
Farewell, The: "It was a' for our rightfu' king." Burns. BSV; CBE; CH; EV-2; HBV; LiA; OBEV; ViBoPo
(It Was A' for Our Rightfu' King.) EBSV; EnRP; GoTS; PoEL-4
(True until Death.) LH
"He turn'd him right and round about," *sel.* PoD
Farewell: "Juliet, farewell. I would not be forgiven." Wilfrid Scawen Blunt. *Fr.* The Love Sonnets of Proteus. TrGrPo
Farewell, A: "Leave me, O love, which reachest but to dust." Sir Philip Sidney. *See* Leave Me, O Love . . .
Farewell: "Linden blossomed, the nightingale sang, The." Heine, *tr. fr. German by* John Todhunter. AWP
Farewell: "Look thy last on all things lovely." Walter de la Mare. CBE
Farewell, The: "Methinks I draw but sickly breath." *Unknown.* OxBoCh
Farewell, A: "My fairest child, I have no song to give you," 2 *sts.* Charles Kingsley. BLP; BLPA; BMEP; DD; FAOV, *sl. diff.*; GN; HBV, 3 *sts.*; HBVY, 3 *sts.*; LPS-1; NeHB; OTPC; PECK; PIR; PoVP; TreF; VA
Farewell, A: "My horse's feet beside the lake." Matthew Arnold. *Fr.* Switzerland. OAEP; ViPP
Farewell: "North wind sweeps over the land, The." Ts'en Ts'an, *tr. fr. Chinese by* Yuan Chia-hua. WhP
(Song of White Snow, A, *tr. by* Witter Bynner.) LiTW
Farewell: "Not soon shall I forget." Katharine Tynan. CH; LBBV; NLK; PoeT; VOD
Farewell, A: "Now most noble Brutus." Shakespeare. *Fr.* Julius Caesar. V, i. BHV
Farewell, The: "Oh, thou! in Hellas deem'd of heavenly birth." Byron. *Fr.* Childe Harold's Pilgrimage, I. EPP
Farewell, A: "Oft have I mused, but now at length I find." Sir Philip Sidney. ElL; EnLi-1; OBSC; ReIE; SiCE; SiPS
Farewell, A: "Only in my deep heart I love you, sweetest heart." "Æ." OBVV
Farewell: "Setting sun, The." Han Hung, *tr. fr. Chinese by* Henry H. Hart. PoHN
Farewell: "Shores of my native land." Isaac Toussaint-L'Ouverture, *tr. fr. French by* Edna Worthley Underwood. PoNe
Farewell: "Since there's no help, come let us kiss and part." Michael Drayton. *See* Idea: "Since there's no help . . ."
Farewell: "Smell of death was in the air, The." John Press. PoRA
Farewell: "Tell them, O Sky-born, when I die." Harry Kemp. HBMV; NLK
Farewell, A: "There lived a singer in France of old." Swinburne. *Fr.* The Triumph of Time. GTML; GTSL
Farewell: "Thou goest; to what distant place." John Addington Symonds. HBV
Farewell, A: "Thou wilt not look on me?" Alice Brown. HBV
Farewell, A: "Thus kiss I your fair hands, taking my leave." Henry King. LoPo
Farewell: "Tır'd with the noysom follies of the age." Earl of Rochester. *Fr.* Farewell to the Court. BeR
("Tired with the noisome follies of the age.") TrGrPo

Farewell, A: "Venus, take my votive glass." Matthew Prior. *See* Lady Who Offers Her Looking-Glass to Venus.
Farewell, A: "What is there left to be said?" A. R. D. Fairburn. AnNZ
Farewell: "What should I say." Sir Thomas Wyatt. CoEV; GoBC; LO; OBSC; UnPo (1st ed.)
(Farewell, Unkist.) LoBV
(Revocation, A.) LoPS; OBEV
("What should I say?") CaAE; ReEn; SiCE; SiPS
(What Shulde I Saye.) AtBAP; PoEL-1
Farewell: "When I lie where shades of darkness." Walter de la Mare. *See* Fare Well.
Farewell, A: "With all my will, but much against my heart." Coventry Patmore. The Unknown Eros, I, xvi. AnFE; ACP; BLV; EnLoPo; EtPaEn; FaBoEn; HBV; LiTL; LO; OBEV; OBVV; PoEL-5; POTT; PoVP; TrGrPo
Farewell!/ The hours of birth and death. A Soldier to His Wife. Liu Chi. OnPM; PoHN
Farewell! a long farewell, to all my greatness! Wolsey's Farewell to His Greatness [*or* Cardinal Wolsey's Farewell *or* Farewell to All My Greatness]. Shakespeare, *and probably* John Fletcher. King Henry VIII, *fr.* III, ii. BCEP; LiTB; LiTG; LPS-1; MaRV; OHFP; PIR; PTA-2; TreF; TrGrPo; TVSH
Farewell! A long farewell to all our school days! A Parody. Edith Putnam Painton. PEDC
Farewell, adieu, that courtly [*or* court-like] life! Song [*or* Haltersick's Song]. John Pickering. *Fr.* Horestes. ElL; ElSeCe; OBSC; ReEn; TuPP
Farewell all future hopes that guide the course. *Unknown.* SeCSL
Farewell, all my welfare! Sir Thomas Wyatt. SiPS
Farewell and adieu to you, gay [*or* fine] Spanish ladies. Spanish Ladies. *Unknown.* AmSS; FaBoCh; LoGBV; SG
Farewell and Hail! Thomas Curtis Clark. PGD
"Farewell!" Another gloomy word. Farewell. Bert Leston Taylor. BOHV; TOP
Farewell, Bristolia's dingy piles [*or* pile] of brick. Last Verses. Thomas Chatterton. BCEP; PoFS; TrGrPo
Farewell! but Whenever [You Welcome the Hour]. Thomas Moore. BCEP, *abr.*; FaBoBe; HBV; LPS-1; NeHB; OAEP
Farewell Cariola! John Webster. *Fr.* The Duchess of Malfi. LO
Farewell Content. Shakespeare. *Fr.* Othello, III, iii. TrGrPo
Farewell, Dear Love! Since Thou Wilt Needs Be Gone. *Unknown.* ElL; OAEP; OBSC
Farewell deere infante sucke from my pensive brest. *Unknown.* SeCSL
Farewell, Fair Armida. *At. to* Dryden. SeCL
Farewell, fair saint! let [*or* may] not the seas and wind. On His Mistress[e] Crossing the [*or* Going to] Sea. Thomas Cary. OBS; SeCL
Farewell, False Love! Beaumont *and* Fletcher. *See* Away, Delights!
Farewell, false Love, the oracle of lies. False Love [*or* Farewell to False Love]. Sir Walter Ralegh. ElL; LO; OBSC; ReEn; SiPS
Farewell! Farewell! Sir Walter Scott. *See* Cleveland's Song: "Farewell! Farewell! the voice you hear."
Farewell, farewell! but this I tell. He Prayeth Best. Samuel Taylor Coleridge. *Fr.* The Rime of the Ancient Mariner. BPP; PECK; YT
Farewell, Farewell! Her Vans the Vessel Tries. Arthur Hugh Clough. Songs in Absence, I. EmBrPo
"Farewell! farewell!" is often heard. Good By. Eliza Cook. LPS-1
"Farewell, farewell, my pretty maid." The True Lover's Farewell. *Unknown.* AS
Farewell, farewell, O brave and tender sage. In Salutation to My Father's Spirit. Sarojini Naidu. FAOV
Farewell, farewell, poor joys, let not my hearse. John Hall. LO
Farewell! Farewell! the voice you hear. Cleveland's Song. Sir Walter Scott. *Fr.* The Pirate, *ch.* 23. BSV; EBSV; LH
Farewell—farewell to thee, Araby's daughter! Farewell to Thee, Araby's Daughter. Thomas Moore. *Fr.* Lalla Rookh. LPS-1
Farewell! for now a stormy morn and dark. Outward Bound. Edward Sydney Tylee. GA; PAH
Farewell, friends! yet not farewell. Sir Edwin Arnold. *Fr.* Pearls of the Faith: After Death in Arabia. MaRV
Farewell has long been said; I have foregone thee. After a Parting. Alice Meynell. PoVP
"Farewell high mountains and crystalline springs." The Execution of the Klepht. Julius Typaldos. MoGP
Farewell Hymn to the Valley of Irwan, A. John Langhorne. *Fr.* Solyman and Almena. CEP
Farewell! I go to sleep; but when. The Evening Watch; a Dialogue. Henry Vaughan. EOAH; MeRV
"Farewell!" I murmur, and then hold my breath. Paulus Silentiarius, *tr. fr. Greek by* the Earl of Cromer. GrPo
Farewell! I tire thee; cruel one, farewell. No Other Slave. Pierre de Ronsard. *Fr.* Sonnets pour Hélène. TrFP
Farewell! If Ever Fondest Prayer. Byron. EmBrPo; EnRP; HBV; LPS-1; ViBoPo
(Farewell.) LoPS; TrGrPo
"Farewell, I'm fading!" cried. Indispensability. Arthur Guiterman. WaKn
Farewell in a Dream. Stephen Spender. MBP; MoAB; MoBrPo
Farewell in Memory of F. O. Haeller. Franz Staude, *tr. fr. German by* Elizabeth Selden. BoFr
Farewell in Secret. Po Chü-i, *tr. fr. Chinese.* ChLP
Farewell, incomparable element. Hymn to Earth. Elinor Wylie. BLV; BoLiVe; ChMo; LiTM; MAP; MoAB; MoAmPo; MoPo; MoVE; NePA; NP; PIAE; ReaPo; ReMP; TCPD; TwAmPo
Farewell, Life. Thomas Hood. BEL; EnRP; EPN; LPS-1
(Stanzas: "Farewell, Life! my senses swim.") ERP; VA
(Stanzas Written in Sickness.) EV-4
Farewell, love, and all thy laws for ever! A Renouncing of [*or* The Lover Renounceth] Love. Sir Thomas Wyatt. BEL; ElSeCe; EnLi-1 (1949 ed.); EnLit; FaBoEn; LiTB; LiTL; OAEP; ReEn; ReIE; SiCE; SiPS; TOP; TrGrPo; TuPP
Farewell Mercy, farewell thy piteous grace. Lament. John Lydgate. *Fr.* Court of Sapience. PoEL-1
Farewell, most charming of females. Passage On. Cedric Morris. PoC
Farewell! my adored country; region beloved of the sun. My Last Thought. José Rizal. PoFr
Farewell, my friends, I'm bound for Canaan. Parting Friends. *Unknown.* ABF
Farewell, my lyre! for now the course is run. Farewell to My Lyre. Esaias Tegnér. AnSL
Farewell, my more than fatherland! A Farewell to America. Richard Henry Wilde. AA; SPP
Farewell, my Muse! for, lo, there is no end. Ideal Passion, XLII. George Edward Woodberry. HBMV
Farewell, my sweet, until I come. To Chloris. Charles Cotton. EV-2
Farewell, my tender brother. Beatrice's Last Words. Shelley. *Fr.* The Cenci. FiP
Farewell, my youth! for now we needs must part. Ave atque Vale. Rosamund Marriott Watson. HBV; VA
Farewell now, Hope and Fortune. You get no more of me. "And in the Grave We're Safe, Surely." *Unknown.* GrPE
Farewell now my lady gaye. A Farewell to His Mistress. *Unknown.* AtBAP
Farewell, O Patrick Sarsfield. *Unknown, tr. fr. Modern Irish by* James Clarence Mangan. OnYI
(Farewell to Patrick Sarsfield [Earl of Lucan], A.) AnIV; OxBI
(Patrick Sarsfield, Lord Lucan, *tr. by* Frank O'Connor.) KiLC
Farewell, O Prince, farewell, O sorely tried! Theodor Herzl. Israel Zangwill. TrJP
Farewell of the Attendant Spirit. Milton. *See* To the Ocean Now Fly.
Farewell, old year! Old and New. *Unknown.* BLRP
Farewell Once More: To My Friend Yen at Feng Chi Station. Tu Fu, *tr. fr. Chinese by* Kenneth Rexroth. OnPC
Farewell Patrick Sarsfield wherever you may roam. Patrick Sarsfield, Lord Lucan. *Unknown, tr. by* Frank O'Connor. KiLC
Farewell, Peace. *Unknown.* MC
Farewell, Renown! Austin Dobson. MBP; MoBrPo (1942 ed.); TCEP
Farewell, Rewards and Fairies. Richard Corbet. *See* Fairies Farewell, The.
"Farewell, Romance!" the Cave-men said. The King. Kipling. BPN; InP; PoVP
Farewell Song of White Clouds, A. Li Po, *tr. fr. Chinese by* Shigeyoshi Obata. BoFr
Farewell, sweet boy, complain not of my truth. Farewell to Cupid. Fulke Greville. Caelica, LXXXV. OBSC
Farewell, Sweet Dust. Elinor Wylie. AnAmPo; LA; LiTA
Farewell, Sweet Groves. George Wither. *Fr.* Fair Virtue, the Mistress of Philarete. BLV
Farewell; the dark is falling on the wind. Farewell to Fields. Howard McKinley Corning. MAP; MoAmPo (1942 ed.)
Farewell! the doom is spoken. All is o'er. The Lost Tribune. George Sigerson. TIP
Farewell the heart [*or* reign] of cruelty. A Renouncing of Hardly Escaped Love. Sir Thomas Wyatt. ReIE; SiPS
Farewell, then. It is finished. Farewell. Wilfrid Scawen Blunt. The Love Sonnets of Proteus, LIII. MBP; MoBrPo (1942 ed.)
Farewell this company. Robert Chamberlain. *Fr.* The Swaggering Damsel. TuPP
Farewell, This World, *in mod. Eng.* *Unknown.* TMEV
Farewell! thou art too dear for my possessing. Sonnets, LXXXVII. Shakespeare. AnFE; BLV; BoLiVe; CaAE;

Farewell! thou art too dear (*continued*)
CoBE; ElL; EM-1; ES; EtPaEn; EV-1; GTBS; GTBS-D; GTBS-W; GTSE; GTSL; InvP; LiTB; LiTG; LPS-1; OAEP; OBEV; OBSC; PeBoSo; PG (1955 ed.); PIAE; PoEL-2; PoFS; ReIE; SiCE; TOP; TrGrPo; TwP; ViBoPo
Farewell, thou busy world. The Retirement [*or* To Mr. Izaak Walton]. Charles Cotton. CEP; HBV; LPS-3; NBE; OBS; SN; ViBoPo
Farewell, thou child of my right hand, and joy. On My [*or* His] First Son [*or* Sonne]. Ben Jonson. AtBAP; AWP; CoBE; ElL; ElSeCe; EnL; EPS; ExPo; FaBoEn; InPo; LiTB; LoBV; MaPo; OAEP; OBS; OnPM; PoD; PoE; PoEL-2; PoFS; ReEn; ReIE; SeCV-1; SeEP; TriL; TuPP; UnPo (3d ed.); WoL
Farewell, thou fertile soil that Brutus first found out. Going towards Spain. Barnabe Googe. ReIE; SiCE
Farewell, thou Sun, and Thou, O Power Divine. Complaints. Bedros Tourian. ArmLP
Farewell thou thing, time-past so knowne, so deare. His Fare-well to Sack. Robert Herrick. OAEP; SeCV-1
Farewell to a Fondling, A. Thomas Churchyard. *See* Lover Deceived by His Lady's Unconstancy Writeth unto Her as Followeth, The.
Farewell to Agassiz, A. Oliver Wendell Holmes. ImOP
Farewell to Alexandria, A. Emily Brontë. *See* Outcast Mother, The.
Farewell to All My Greatness. Shakespeare, *and probably* John Fletcher. *See* Wolsey's Farewell to His Greatness.
Farewell to America, A. Richard Henry Wilde. AA; SPP
Farewell to Anactoria. Sappho, *tr. fr. Greek by* Allen Tate. AWP; LiTW
Farewell to Arms, A. George Peele. *See* His Golden Locks.
Farewell to Barn and Stack and Tree. A. E. Housman. A Shropshire Lad, VIII. ChMo; CMP; EnLi-2 (1949 ed.); InPo; OAEP; PoVP; UnPo (3d ed.)
(Farewell.) MoAB; MoBrPo (1950 ed.)
Farewell to Bath. Lady Mary Wortley Montagu. CEP
Farewell to Bithynia. Catullus, *tr. fr. Latin by* Theodore Martin. OuHeWo
Farewell to Chao Ta-lin. Su T'ung-po, *tr. fr. Chinese by* L. Cranmer-Byng. BoFr
Farewell to Cuba. Maria Gowen Brooks. AA
Farewell to Cupid. Fulke Greville. Caelica, LXXXV. OBSC
Farewell to Europe, and at once farewell. The Farewell. Charles Churchill. CEP
Farewell to fair Alba, high house of the Sun. Deirdre's Farewell to Alba. *Unknown*. IrPN; OnYI
Farewell to Fál, A. Gerald Nugent, *tr. fr. Late Middle Irish by* Padraic Pearse. OnYI
Farewell to False Love, A. Sir Walter Ralegh. *See* False Love.
Farewell to Fields. Howard McKinley Corning. MAP; MoAmPo (1942 ed.)
Farewell to fields and butterflies. Garden-Song. James Branch Cabell. HBMV
Farewell to Fiunary. Norman Macleod, *tr. fr. Gaelic*. EBSV
Farewell to Folly, *sel*. Robert Greene.
Sweet Are the Thoughts That Savor of Content. BEL; CoBE; EG; EM-1; PoToHe; ReIE; SiCE; TuPP; TvEnPo
(Content.) EnLit; LPS-3; OnPM; WoL
(Maesia's Song.) ElSeCe; EV-1; HBV; OBSC; ReEn; WP
(Mind Content, A.) ElL; ViBoPo
(Poor Estate, The.) TrGrPo
(Song: "Sweet are the thoughts that savor of content.") CaAE; EnLi-1; EPP; OuHeWo; PoEL-2
Farewell to France. *At. to* Mary Queen of Scots, *tr. fr. French by* Ralph N. Currey. FoS
Farewell to Greatness. Shakespeare, *and probably* John Fletcher. *See* Wolsey's Farewell to His Greatness.
Farewell to Han So. Tu Fu, *tr. fr. Chinese by* Chi Hwang Chu *and* Edna Worthley Underwood. OnPM
Farewell to himself. The Bride. Ruth Comfort Mitchell. HBMV
Farewell to His Wife. Byron. *See* Fare Thee Well.
Farewell to His Mistress, A. *Unknown*. AtBAP
Farewell, A, to Ho Yung on His Leaving Min Valley for the Capital. Tu Fu, *tr. fr. Chinese by* Hsieh Wen Tung. WhP
Farewell to Ireland. *At. to* St. Columcille, *tr. fr. Middle Irish by* Douglas Hyde. AWP; JAWP; LiTW; WBP
(Colum-Cille's Farewell to Ireland.) AnIV
Farewell to Italy. Walter Savage Landor. BPN; VA
Farewell to Juliet ("I see you, Juliet, still, with your straw hat"). Wilfrid Scawen Blunt. The Love Sonnets of Proteus, XLVII. EnLoPo
Farewell to Juliet ("Juliet, farewell. I would not be forgiven"). Wilfrid Scawen Blunt. The Love Sonnets of Proteus, XXXIX. AnEnPo
(Farewell.) TrGrPo
Farewell to Juliet ("Lame, impotent conclusion to youth's dreams"). Wilfrid Scawen Blunt. The Love Sonnets of Proteus LII. ViBoPo
Farewell to Kind Hosts and a Godspeed. Homer, *tr. fr. Greek by* William Morris. *Fr.* The Odyssey, XIII. GrR
Farewell to Lesbia. Catullus, *tr. fr. Latin by* Robert Fitzgerald. LiTW
("Furius and Aurelius, Catullus's comrades.") LaP
Farewell to Lochaber, an' farewell my Jean. Lochaber No More. Allan Ramsay. EBSV; HBV; LPS-1
Farewell to London in the Year 1715, A. Pope. CEP
Farewell to Love, The. Beaumont *and* Fletcher. TriL
Farewell to Love. John Donne. BrBE; ReEn
Farewell to Maidenhood. Sappho. *See* Wedding Songs.
Farewell to My Love, A. Liu Yung, *tr. fr. Chinese*. ChLP
Farewell to My Lyre. Esaias Tegnér, *tr. fr. Swedish by* Charles W. Stork. AnSL
Farewell to My Mother. "Plácido." *See* Plácido's Sonnet to His Mother.
Farewell to Nancy. Burns. *See* Ae Fond Kiss.
Farewell to Nausicaa. Homer, *pr. tr. fr. Greek by* S. H. Butcher *and* Andrew Lang. *Fr.* The Odyssey, VIII. GrR
Farewell to one now silenced quite. Parted. Alice Meynell. PoeT
Farewell to Patrick Sarsfield, Earl of Lucan, A. *Unknown*. *See* Farewell, O Patrick Sarsfield.
Farewell to Po Chü I. Yüan Chen, *tr. fr. Chinese by* Henry H. Hart. PoHN
Farewell to Poetry. Goldsmith. *Fr.* The Deserted Village. OBEC
Farewell to Sir John Norris and Sir Francis Drake, A. George Peele. OBSC
(Farewell, A: "Haue doone with care my harts, aborde amaine.") EV-1
(Farewell to the Most Famous Generals, Sir John Norris and Sir Francis Drake, Knights, A.) SG
Farewell to Sliev Morna. Lay of the Forlorn. George Darley. OnYI; TriL
Farewell to slumber! Air that has been still. Night Shower. Milton. PoMa
Farewell to Sorrow, A, *Unknown*. *See* Careless Gallant, The.
Farewell to Spring. Hsü Ying Yü, *tr. fr. Chinese by* Henry H. Hart. PoHN
Farewell to Summer. George Arnold. AA; DD
Farewell to the Court. Sir Walter Ralegh. FaBoEn; OBSC; PeBoSo; SiPS
(Like Truthless Dreams.) SiCE; TuPP
(Sorrow Stays.) EG
"Like truthless dreams, so are my joys expired," *sel*. LO
Farewell to the Court, *sel*. Earl of Rochester.
Farewell: "Tir'd with the noysom follies of the age." BeR
("Tired with the noisome follies of the age.") TrGrPo
Farewell to the Fairies. Richard Corbet. *See* Fairies' Farewell, The.
Farewell to the Farm. Robert Louis Stevenson. BoChLi (1939 ed.); BoTP; FaPON; GaP; MPB; OTPC; TiPo
Farewell to the Glen. Dante Gabriel Rossetti. The House of Life, LXXXIV. BPN; PoVP; ViPo
Farewell to the Highlands, farewell to the North. My Heart's in the Highlands. Burns. AnEnPo; AWP; BBV; BEL; BHV; CBE; CEP; CoBE; EBSV; EM-1; EnRP; EV-3; FaFP; GN; HBV; InPo; JAWP; LiTG; LiTL; LPS-2; NeHB; OTPC; REAL; RIS; StaSt; TCEP; TOP; TVSH; WBP
Farewell to the land, where the gloom of my glory. Napoleon's Farewell. Byron. CBE
Farewell to the Most Famous Generals, Sir John Norris and Sir Francis Drake, Knights, A. George Peele. *See* Farewell to Sir John Norris and Sir Francis Drake, A.
Farewell to the Muses. John Hamilton Reynolds. OBRV
Farewell to the Old Year. Eleanor Farjeon. SiSoSe
Farewell to the Sea. Macedonius, *tr. fr. Greek by* F. L. Lucas. GrPE
Farewell to the World, A, *much abr*. Ben Jonson. OBEV (1st ed.)
Farewell to the World of Richard Bishop. *Unknown*. CoMu
Farewell to Thee, Araby's Daughter. Thomas Moore. *Fr.* Lalla Rookh. LPS-1
Farewell to Tobacco, A Charles Lamb. BOHV; LPS-2; NBE; OBRV; OxBoLi
Farewell to Town. Laurence Housman. HBMV
Farewell to Wives, A. *Unknown*. SeCL
Farewell [*or* Farewel], too little and too lately known. To the Memory of Mr. Oldham. Dryden. ATP; AWP; CEP; CoEV; EiPP; EV-3; ExPo; FaBoEn; FiP; InPo; JAWP; LiA; LoBV; NBE; OBS; PoD; PoEL-3; PtP; RiBV; SeCeV; SeCV-2; SeEP; UnPo (1st ed.); ViBoPo; WBP
Farewell, Ungrateful Traitor. Dryden. *Fr.* The Spanish Friar, V, i. InPo; LiTB; LiTG; SeCL; ViBoPo
("Farwell ungratfull traytor.") EnLoPo
(Love's Despair.) ACP
(Song: "Farewell, ungrateful traitor!") BCEP; EiPP; ElSeCe; FaBoEn; FiP; LEAP; OBS; SeCV-2; SeEP

Farewell, Unkind! Farewell! to me, no more a father! *Unknown.* EnLoPo
Farewell, Unkist. Sir Thomas Wyatt. LoBV
Farewell, whose like on earth I shall not find. Valedictory. Tennyson. GoBC
Farewell World. Sir Philip Sidney. *See* Leave Me, O Love.
Farewell, ye dungeons dark and strong. Macpherson's Farewell [*or* Defiance]. Burns. BSV; EBSV; LH; MCCG; OtMeF
Farewell, ye mountains, and ye much-loved paths. Schiller. *Fr.* The Maid of Orleans, *play.* PoFr
Farewell, you children that I might have borne. Sonnet. Eleanor Farjeon. DiM
Farewell, you water, leaping cool. Wayside Epigram. Leonidas of Tarentum. GrR
Farewells from Paradise. Elizabeth Barrett Browning. OBEV (new ed.); OBVV
Farm, The. Archibald MacLeish. ChMo; CMP
Farm, The. Jane Taylor. OTPC (1923 ed.)
Farm after farm, the schoolbus stops. Joy Meets Boy. Robert P. Tristram Coffin. OTPC (1946 ed.)
Farm Boy, The. Katharine Atherton Grimes. PoMa
Farm by the Lake, The. Chu Hsi, *tr. fr. Chinese by* Kenneth Rexroth. OnPC
Farm Cart. Eleanor Farjeon. BrR
Farm Child. R. S. Thomas. ChMP
Farm Died, The. Malcolm Cowley. *Fr.* Blue Juniata. MAP; MoAmPo (1942 ed.)
Farm Life. Ruth Edna Stanton. GFA
Farm on the Links, The. Rosamund Marriott Watson. OBVV; VA
Farm Picture, A. Walt Whitman. IAP; OnPM; MOAP; WoL
Farm Voices. Emilie Poulsson. MeMeAg
Farm was lonely, set so far, The. Finality. Winifred Virginia Jackson. BAP
Farm Wife. John Hanlon Mitchell. CaP; OCL
Farmwife coming in from outdoor tasks, The. Inarticulate. Mabel Ruggles Cobb. DDA
Farm Yard. *See* Farmyard.
Farmer. Liberty Hyde Bailey. YeAr
Farmer. Padraic Fallon. OxBI
Farmer, The. A. P. Herbert. CenHV
Farmer, The, *with music. Unknown.* AS
Farmer and Sailor. Plato, *tr. fr. Greek by* T. F. Higham. LiTW; OxBG
Farmer and the Farmer's Wife, The. P. G. Hiebert. FiBHP
Farmer Comes to Town, The, *with music. Unknown.* TrAS
Farmer in the dell, The. *Unknown.* RIS
Farmer is busy, so busy, to-day, The. Haymaking. E. M. Adams. BoTP
"Farmer, is the harvest ready." Bread. H. E. Wilkinson. BoTP
Farmer John's Thanksgiving. Isaac F. Eaton. TOAH
Farmer knew each time a friend went past, The. Hound on the Church Porch. Robert P. Tristram Coffin. AlBD; DDA
Farmer Lost at Sea, The. Isidorus. *See* Sea Trade.
Farmer, The, 1917. Fredegond Shove. TwCV
Farmer of Westerha', The. James Logie Robertson. *See* Ochil Farmer, An.
Farmer once planted some little brown seeds, A. A Growing Rhyme. J. M. Westrup. BoTP
Farmer ploughs into the ground, The. Seed. H. C. Bosman. BoSA
Farmer Remembers Lincoln, A. Witter Bynner. BAP; HH; MAP; MoAmPo (1942 ed.)
Farmer Remembers the Somme, The. Vance Palmer. MoAuPo
Farmer sat in his easy-chair, smoking his pipe, The. A Picture. Charles Gamage Eastman. LPS-1
Farmer took [*or* say to] de boll weevil, De [*or* The]. De Ballet [*or* Ballit] of de Boll Weevil. *Unknown.* ABF; AS; IHA
Farmer turns for home, The; his team's glad tread. Pastoral. Muriel Lewis. MoAuPo
Farmer was plowing his field one day, A. The Bad-tempered Wife. *Unknown.* MaC
Farmer went trotting [*or* riding] upon [*or* on] his grey mare, A. Mother Goose. BoTP; GFA; HBVY; OTPC; OxNR; PPL; RIS; StVeCh; TiPo
Farmer will never be happy again, The. The Farmer. A. P. Herbert. CenHV
Farmers. Helene Mullins. BPP; WGRP
Farmers. William Alexander Percy. MaRV; WGRP
Farmers. *Unknown.* OtMeF
Farmer's Advice to the Villagers, The. Timothy Dwight. *Fr.* Greenfield Hill, VI. IAP
Farmer's Boy, The, *sels.* Robert Bloomfield.
"Again the year's decline." OBRV
"Fled now the sullen murmurs of the north." LPS-2
"Live, trifling incidents." OBRV
Thrush and Blackthorn. RO
"Wide o'er the fields, in rising moisture strong." EnSW
Farmer's Boy, The ("The sun had set"). *Unknown.* ABS
Farmer's Boy, A ("They strolled down the lane"). *Unknown.* DDA
Farmer's Bride, The. Charlotte Mew. BMEP; HBMV; LBBV; MBP; MoAB; MoBrPo; NP; OnPP; PoRA; TCPD; TrGrPo
Farmer's Curst Wife, The. *Unknown.* BaBo (A *and* B *vers.*); ESPB (A *and* B *vers.*); ViBoFo
(Bad-tempered Wife, The.) MaC
(Tee Roo, *diff. vers., with music.*) OuSiCo
Farmer's daughter, The. Exiit Diluculo. *Unknown. Fr.* Carmina Burana. LaP
Farmer's goose, who in the stubble, The. The Progress of Poetry. Swift. BeR; InvP; OnYI
Farmer's heart with joy is filled when his crops are good and sound, The. The *Jamestown* Homeward Bound. *Unknown.* SoAmSa
Farmer's Ingle, The. Robert Fergusson. BSV; CEP
Farmer's Prayer, A. Roselle Mercier Montgomery. LS
Farmer's Rest, The. Leonidas of Tarentum, *tr. fr. Greek by* F. L. Lucas. GrPE
Farmer's Round, The. *Unknown.* OTPC (1923 ed.)
Farmer's Wife, The. Martha Ostenso. AV
Farmer's wife looked out of the dairy, The. The Rival. Sylvia Townsend Warner. BLV; BoLiVe (1939 ed.); MBP; MoAB; MoBrPo
Farmer's wife sat at the door, The. They Are Dear Fish to Me. *Unknown.* LPS-1
Farmer's Year, The. Hesiod, *tr. fr. Greek. Fr.* Works and Days. OxBG
Farmhands' Refrain. H. H. Lewis. LiTM
Farmhouse lingers, though averse to square, The [*or* A]. A Brook in the City. Robert Frost. OxBA; PIAE; TSW; TSWC
Farmhouse skyline, draped with trees, The. Pastoral. Alan Creighton. CaP
Farmhouses curl like horns of plenty. Blue Juniata. Malcolm Cowley. MAP; MoAmPo (1942 ed.)
Farming. *Unknown, tr. fr. Chinese by* Arthur Waley. *Fr.* Shi King. LiTW
Farms of Home Lie Lost in Even, The. A. E. Housman. More Poems, XIV. MaPo
Farmyard, The. A. A. Attwood. BoTP
Farmyard. Ruth Dallas. AnNZ
Farm Yard, The. Eliza Lee Follen. OTPC (1946 ed.)
Farm-Yard Song. John Townsend Trowbridge. *See* Evening at the Farm.
Farnese Hercules, The. Sacheverell Sitwell. FaBoMo; LiTM (rev. ed.)
Farr off from these a slow and silent stream. The Place of the Damned. Milton. *Fr.* Paradise Lost, II. FaBoEn
Farragut. William Tuckey Meredith. AA; DD; EtS; FaBoBe; GA; HBV; HBVY; MDAH; OnPP; PaA; PAH; TriL
Farre have I clambred in my mind. *See* Far have I clamber'd in my mind.
Farther. John James Piatt. *See* Suggested Device of a New Western State.
Farther and farther ran each wall. The Room. Louis Ginsberg. UnW
Farther in summer than the birds. Emily Dickinson. LiTA; PoEL-5
Farther up the gorge the sea's voice fainted and ceased. All the Little Hoofprints. Robinson Jeffers. Po
Farthest from any war, unique in time. Hollywood. Karl Shapiro. AmPP (4th ed.); OxBA
Farwell ungratfull traytor. *See* Farewell, Ungrateful Traitor.
Fascination of What's Difficult, The. W. B. Yeats. PoEL-5
Fashion. Arthur Guiterman. PR
Fashions in Dogs. E. B White. FiBHP
Fast Ball. Jonathan Williams. NeAP
Fast falls the snow, O lady mine. To F. C. Mortimer Collins. HBV; TreFS
Fast, fast, with heels wild spurning. The War-Horse. Macaulay. *Fr.* Lays of Ancient Rome. BHV
Fast this life of mine was dying. Life and Love. Elizabeth Barrett Browning. BPN; PoVP
Fasten the chamber! Bluebeard's Closet. Rose Terry Cooke. AA; OBAV
Fasten your hair with a golden pin. He Gives His Beloved Certain Rhymes. W. B. Yeats. EG
Fastened deep in firmest earth. Song of the Bell. Schiller, *tr. by* Longfellow. LiA
Faster. Geoffrey Scott. TwCV
Faster, Faster,/ O Circe, Goddess. The Strayed Reveller. Matthew Arnold. BPN; GEPC; LoBV; MyFE; ViPo; ViPP
Faster than fairies, faster than witches. From a Railway Carriage. Robert Louis Stevenson. AlDL; BoTP; FaPON; GFA; GoBP; TiPo
Fastidious! Callimachus, *tr. fr. Greek by* Robert Allason Furness. GrR
(Odi Profanum Vulgus.) OxBG
Fastidious Serpent, The. Henry Johnstone. BOHV; HBV; HBVY; LiL; OTPC (1946 ed.); PPL

Fastinge supper call you this, A. *Unknown.* SeCSL
Fat black bucks in a wine-barrel room. The Congo. Vachel Lindsay. AmP; AmPP; BAP; ChMo; CMP; CoBA; FaFP; GTBS-W; HoPM; LEAP; LiTA; LiTG; MAP; MCCG; MoAB; MoAmPo; MOAP; NeMA; NP; OxBA; PFY; PoeMoYo; PoMa; PoNe; PoRA; PreP; PYM; ShBV-3; TCPD; TreF; WHA
Fat-buttocked Bushmen, The. Ernest A. Hooton. WhC
Fat green frog sits by the pond. Grandfather Frog. Louise Seaman Bechtel. TiPo
Fat men go about the streets, The. Ballade of the Poetic Life. J. C. Squire. OBMV; WhC
Fat soil, full spring, sweet olive, grape of bliss. Christ's Bloody Sweat. Robert Southwell. ReIE
Fat torpedoes in bursting jackets. Fourth of July. Rachel Field. SiSoSe
Fata Morgana. Kathleen Raine. MoP
Fatal Blindness. Virgil, *pr. tr. fr. Latin by* John Jackson. *Fr.* Eclogues, VIII. LiA
Fatal Discovery. Sophocles, *tr. fr. Greek by* Gilbert Murray. *Fr.* Oedipus Rex. GrR
Fatal Oil-Flask, The. Aristophanes, *tr. fr. Greek by* Marshall MacGregor. *Fr.* The Frogs. OxBG
Fatal Sisters, The. Thomas Gray, *after the Icelandic.* BEL; CEP; CoBE; EiPP; EM-1; EnRP; EPP; OAEP; RO
Fatal Star, The. Thomas Lodge. TuPP
Fatal Vision, The. Shelley. *Fr.* The Two Spirits. RO
Fatal Wedding, The. *Unknown.* ABS
Fatal Wedding, The. W. H. Windom. TreFS
Fatalism. Omar Khayyám, *tr. fr. Persian by* Edward Fitzgerald. *Fr.* The Rubáiyát. MaRV
Fatalist, A. John W. Garvin. CPG
Fate. Louis James Block. AA
Fate. James Fenimore Cooper. HBMV
Fate. Emerson. BAV; RiBV
Fate. Bret Harte. BAP
Fate. Ibn Abdun, *tr. fr. Arabic by* A. J. Arberry. MooP
Fate. Henri Michaux, *tr. fr. French by* Wallace Fowlie. MiCF
Fate. Christian Morgenstern, *tr. fr. German by* R. F. C. Hull. AnGP
Fate. Susan Marr Spalding. AA; BBV (1951 ed.); BLPA; DDA; HBV; LEAP; NeHB; PoToHe
Fate. Swinburne. *See* Not as with Sundering of the Earth.
Fate and the Younger Generation. D. H. Lawrence. OxBoLi; SiTL; WhC
Fate Defied. Adelaide Crapsey. NP; NV; SBMV; VOD (1935 ed.); YT
Fate gave the word, the arrow sped. A Mother's Lament for the Death of Her Son. Burns. HoPM
Fate! I Have Asked. Walter Savage Landor. ViBoPo
Fate? I met her long ago. Mastery. Charles F. Lummis. BAP
Fate, I will not ask for wealth or fame. The Higher Good. Theodore Parker. FaBoBe
Fate of Astyanax, The. Euripides, *tr. fr. Greek by* Gilbert Murray. *Fr.* Trojan Women. GrR
Fate of John Burgoyne, The. *Unknown.* PAH
Fate of King Dathi, The. Thomas Osborne Davis. OnYI
Fate of Narcissus, The. William Warner. *Fr.* Albion's England. OBSC
Fate of the Cabbage Rose, The. Wallace Irwin. FiBHP
Fate of the Oak, The. "Barry Cornwall." OHIP; OTPC (1923 ed.)
Fate of the Prophets, The. Longfellow. *See* Prophets in Their Time.
Fate of the Sons of Usna, The. John Todhunter. *Fr.* The First Duan: The Coming of Deirdre. TIP
Fate struck the hour! Lincoln. Jane L. Hardy. OHIP
Fate to beauty still must give. Epitaph. Claudian. AWP; LaP
Fate wafts us from the pygmies' shore. Gods of War. "Æ." BEL
Fate with Devoted . . . Arthur Davison Ficke. AnEnPo
Fateful youngling of the dark and drift, A. Radium. Agnes Lee. PoMa
Fates, The. Stephen Spender. TwHP
Fates, The. Alfred de Vigny, *pr. tr. fr. French.* LiA
Fate's Malignity. Ibn Wahbun, *tr. fr. Arabic by* A. J. Arberry. MooP
Fates of Men. *Unknown, tr. fr. Anglo-Saxon by* Charles W. Kennedy. AnOE
Fates of the Apostles, *sel.* Cynewulf, *tr. fr. Anglo-Saxon* by Charles W. Kennedy.
"Now I pray the man who may love this lay." AnOE
Father, The. Dorothy Scott Ballard. ChIP
Father. Paul Carroll. NeAP
Father. Arthur Davison Ficke. OS; TrPWD
Father. Frances Frost. FaPON; SiSoSe; StVeCh (1955 ed.); TiPo (1959 ed.)
Father, The. W. W. Gibson. NV
Father. Arthur Vine Hall. FAOV
Father, The. Sara Henderson Hay. StaSt
Father, The. John Holmes. FAOV
Father, The. Richmond Lattimore. NePoAm-2
Father, The. Sir Ronald Ross. FAOV; TCPD
Father, The. George Francis Savage-Armstrong. VA
Father,/ Grant unto us true family love. A Prayer for Family Love [*or* For Family Love]. John S. Hoyland. GrCo-2; MaRV
Father Abbey's Will. John Seccomb. BHV
Father Abraham, *with music.* *Unknown.* BoAN-1
Father and founder of faith and felicity, The. Prologue. Sir David Lindsay. *Fr.* The Satire of the Three Estates. TMEV
Father and I went down to camp. Yankee Doodle [*or* The Yankee's (*or* Yankey's) Return from Camp]. *Unknown.* ABF; BoHiPo; FaFP; FaPON; HBV; IAP; MC; MW; OxBoLi; PaA; PAH; PoFr; PoRL; SiTL; TreF; YaD
Father and Son. F. R. Higgins. LiTM; OBMV; OxBI; PG (1955 ed.); POTE
Father and Son. Delmore Schwartz. LiTA
Father and Son. Shakespeare. King Henry VI, Pt. I, *fr.* IV, v *and* vii. BHV
Father, be praised for a white jasmine. Consolation in July. Rayner Heppenstall. NeBP
Father, between Thy strong hands Thou has bent. Prayer of a Teacher. Dorothy Littlewort. TrPWD
Father calls me William, sister calls me Will. Jest 'fore Christmas. Eugene Field. ChBR; DD; FaFP; FaPON; HBV; HBVY; HH; MPB; MW; OHFP; OTPC; SDH; TreF; YT
Father, chancing to chastise. Some Ruthless Rhymes, IV. Harry Graham. CenHV
Father Couture loves a fricassee. Petite Ste. Rosalie. S. Frances Harrison. *Fr.* Down the River. BoCaPo (1943 ed.); CPG
Father Coyote. George Sterling. *See* Coyote.
Father Damien. John Banister Tabb. ACP; AmP; JKCP
Father, Dear Father, Come Home with Me Now. Henry Clay Work. TreF
(Come Home, Father.) YaD
Father Dies. Abraham Sutskever, *tr. fr. Yiddish by* Sarah Zweig Betsky. OnCuPl
Father Does His Best, A. E. B. White. ALV; WhC
Father! father! where are you going? The Little Boy Lost. Blake. *Fr.* Songs of Innocence. EnRP; FAOV; TiPo (1952 ed.)
Father Francis. Walter Herries Pollock. VA
Father Gerard Hopkins, S.J. Joyce Kilmer. PtP
Father Gilligan. W. B. Yeats. *See* Ballad of Father Gilligan, The.
Father Grumble. *Unknown.* ABS; BaBo; ViBoFo
Father, Hear Thy Children. "A. G." BOL
Father heard his children scream. The Stern Parent [*or* Some Ruthless Rhymes]. Harry Graham. CenHV; ChTr
Father, here a temple in Thy name we build. Hymn of Dedication. Elizabeth E. Scantlebury. BLRP; PraP
Father, hold thou my hands. Make Thy Way Mine. "George Klingle." PraP
Father, How Wide Thy Glories Shine. Charles Wesley. TrPWD
Father! I bless thy name that I do live. In Him We Live. Jones Very. AmP; OxBA
Father, I fear your love. Filia Patri. Helen Pinkerton. PtPa
Father, I know that all my life. My Times Are in Thy Hand. Anna Laetitia Waring. PraP
Father, I lift my hands to Thee. Suppliant. Florence Earle Coates. TrPWD
Father! I now may lean upon your breast. The Shades of Agamemnon and Iphigeneia. Walter Savage Landor. BPN
Father, I scarcely dare to pray. A Last Prayer [*or* A Prayer]. Helen Hunt Jackson. AA; MaRV; OBAV; OQP; PCD; PraP; QP-2; TrPWD
Father, I will not ask for wealth or fame. The Higher Good [*or* A New Year Prayer]. Theodore Parker. AA; HBV; MaRV; PGD; PSO
Father in heaven! after the days misspent. Sonnet. Petrarch. *Fr.* Sonnets to Laura: To Laura in Life. CAW
Father in Heaven! from whom the simplest flower. A Prayer. Felicia Dorothea Hemans. TrPWD
Father in Heaven, give us bread. Prayer of the Unemployed. *Unknown.* MaRV
Father in Heaven! humbly before thee. A Prayer for Peace. Edward Rowland Sill. TrPWD
Father in Heaven, make me wise. A Mother's Prayer [*or* A Mother Speaks]. Margaret E. Sangster. MaRV; PraP; TrPWD
Father, in Thy mysterious presence kneeling. Prayer for Strength [*or* For Divine Strength]. Samuel Johnson. MaRV; PraP
Father, into Thy Hands. Thomas B. Pollock. BePJ
Father Is Coming. Mary Howitt. FAOV; OTPC
Father, it's your love that safely guides me. The Child to the Father. Robert Bridges. FAOV
Father John's bread was made of rye. Rye Bread. William Stanley Braithwaite. CDC
Father Knows, The. "F. L. H." BLRP

Father Land and Mother Tongue. Samuel Lover. HBV; LPS-3
Father, lead me, day by day. A Child's Prayer. *Unknown.* BLRP
Father lighted candles for me. For Hanukkah. Hayyim Nahman Bialik. TiPo (1952 ed.)
"Father, look up and see that flag." The American Boy. *Unknown.* PEDC
Father Malloy. Edgar Lee Masters. *Fr.* Spoon River Anthology. NP; OxBA
Father Mapple's Hymn. Herman Melville. *Fr.* Moby Dick, *ch.* 9. EtS; OnAP
(Ribs and Terrors, The.) ViBoPo
(Song: "Ribs and terrors in the whale, The.") MeRV
(Whale, The.) AtBAP; TrGrPo
Father Mat. Patrick Kavanagh. AnIL
"In a meadow/ Beside the chapel three boys were playing football," *sel.* MoAB
Father Missouri takes his own. Foreclosure. Sterling A. Brown. PoNe
Father Molloy. Samuel Lover. BOHV; HBV
Father, Now My Prayer Is Said. William Brighty Rands. OTPC (1946 ed.)
"Father of all—God!" Table Blessing. Lew Wallace. MeMeAg
Father of all! in Death's relentless claim. Oliver Wendell Holmes. *Fr.* A Poem: Dedication of the Pittsfield Cemetery, September 9, 1850. TrPWD
Father of all! in every age. The Universal Prayer. Pope. AEV; BCEP; BEL; CEP; EiPP; EnLit; EV-3; FaBoBe; GoBC; HBV; LPS-2; MaRV; OAEP; RiBV; TCEP; TOP; WGRP
Father of Energy,/ Pattern of Beauty, uncreated Light. Hymn to God. Arthur Symons. QS
Father of heaven! after the days all lost. Petrarch. *Fr.* Sonnets to Laura: To Laura in Life. PrPoCR
Father of heaven and earth! Evening Song of the Weary. Felicia Dorothea Hemans. ERP
Father of Heaven, and him, by whom. The Litanie. John Donne. AtBAP; PoEL-2
Father of heaven His own Son He Sent, The. A New Year, a New Year, a Child Was Yborn. *Unknown.* AnEC
"Father of Jealousy, be thou accursed from the earth!" Visions of the Daughters of Albion. Blake. ViBoPo
"Father of lakes!" thy waters bend. Lake Superior. Samuel Griswold Goodrich. AA
Father of life, with songs of wonder. Margaret L. Woods. *Fr.* The Return. TrPWD
Father of lights! what sunny [*or* sunnie] seed. Cock-crowing. Henry Vaughan. AtBAP; EPS; MaPo; MePo; NBE; SeCV-1
Father of mercies, in Thy Word. O How Sweet Are Thy Words! Anne Steele. BLRP
Father of the bare boughs, and the leaves that die. Sure. Ted Robinson. MaRV
Father of the Man. Elizabeth Mabel Bryan. GoYe
Father O'Flynn. Alfred Perceval Graves. BOHV; HBV; OnYI; TIP
Father, part of his double interest. Holy Sonnets, XVI. John Donne. OBS
Father Point in August. Leo Cox. TwCaPo
Father-Prayer. Margaret Widdemer. PraP
Father sees a son nearing manhood, A. Carl Sandburg. The People, Yes, 9. PoLFOT
Father, send us for this meal. Christmas Blessing. Franklin D. Elmer, Jr ChIP
Father Short came down the lane. *Unknown.* OxNR
Father, sitting on the side of your startled bed. D-Dawn. Margaret McGarvey. GoYe
Father! the little girl we see. Little Aglaë. Walter Savage Landor. *Fr.* Pericles and Aspasia, CXIII. BPN; VA
Father, this day,/ For our home we pray Thee. Prayer for Our Home. John S. Hoyland. MaRV
Father, thy hand. Bryant. *Fr.* A Forest Hymn. TrPWD
Father! thy wonders do not singly stand. The Spirit-Land [*or* The Present Heaven]. Jones Very. AnAmPo; IAP; LA; LPS-2
Father, thy word is past, man shall find grace. The Atonement. Milton. *Fr.* Paradise Lost, III. OBS
Father Time. Norman Ault. HBVY
Father to Daughter. Mary Ballard Duryee. FAOV
Father, to Thee. Frederick L. Hosmer. OQP; QP-1
(Prayer in Sorrow.) PraP
Father, today I bring to Thee. A Father's Prayer. Mouzon W. Brabham. PraP
Father too, The, does He not see and hear? A Voice. Samuel Valentine Cole. OQP; QP-1
Father, unto Thee I pray. Good-Night Prayer for a Little Child. Henry Johnstone. BOL; PPL
Father was and aye shall be, The. The Trinity. *Unknown.* ACP
Father, we come not as of old. Hymn. John W. Chadwick. TrPWD
Father, we thank Thee. We Thank Thee. Grenville Kleiser. PraP
Father, We Thank Thee ("For flowers that bloom about our feet"). *Unknown, sometimes at. to* Emerson. *See* We Thank Thee.
Father, We Thank Thee. *At. to* Rebecca J. Weston. *See* Prayer, A: "Father, we thank Thee for the night."
Father: We thank Thee for laughter. Thanks for Laughter. *Unknown.* OQP; QP-2
Father, we thank Thee for the night. A Prayer [*or* A Child's Prayer *or* Morning Prayer]. *At. to* Rebecca J. Weston. BoTP; MaRV; MeMeAg; OTPC (1946 ed.); PCH; PraP; RAR; TVC; TVSH
Father, where Do the Wild Swans Go? Ludvig Holstein, *tr. fr. Danish by* Charles W. Stork. BoDS; FAOV
Father, who keepest. Domine, Cui Sunt Pleiades Curae [*or* Child's Prayer at Evening]. Sir Charles G. D. Roberts. BOL; VA
Father, whom I murdered every night but one. Elegy for My Father. Howard Moss. NePoEA
Father! whose hard and cruel law. The Death of Grant. Ambrose Bierce. AA; BAP; GA; MDAH
Father, Whose Will Is Life and Good. Hardwicke Drummond Rawnsley. MaRV
Father William, *parody.* "Lewis Carroll." *Fr.* Alice's Adventures in Wonderland, *ch.* 5. BLV; BOHV; FaPON; FiBHP; GoTP; HBV; HoPM; InMe; LBN; LiL; LiTB; LiTG; MBP; MW; OnPP; OTPC (1946 ed.); PA; PC; PCD; PECK; PIR; PoRA; PoVP; PYM; RIS; SiTL; StaSt; TOP; TreF; TrGrPo; TSW; TSWC; WaKn
(You Are Old, Father William.) ALV; BoChLi; BTP; KN; PoeMoYo; ShBV-2; TiPo; WhC
Father William. Robert Southey. *See* Old Man's Comforts, The.
Father William. *Unknown.* BOHV; NA; SiTL
"Father, you seem to have been sleeping fair?" A Last Journey. Thomas Hardy. FAOV
Fathered by March, the daffodils are here. Daffodils. Lizette Woodworth Reese. AA; OBAV; VOD
Fatherhood. Henry Charles Beeching. PoeT
Fatherhood. Patterson Du Bois. FAOV
Fatherland, The. James Russell Lowell. BHV; GDAH; GN; HBV; HBVY; MaRV; OTPC; PGD; PoRL; TVSH
Fatherland. *At. to* Dmitry Vladimirovich Venevitinov, *tr. fr. Russian by* Babette Deutsch. TrRV
Fatherland Song (Norwegian National Hymn). Björnstjerne Björnson, *tr. fr. Norwegian by* William Ellery Leonard. AWP; PoFr
(National Song, *tr. by* Charles W. Stork.) AnNoLy
Fathers, The. Kostes Palamas, *tr. fr. Modern Greek by* Rae Dalven. *Fr.* The Altars. MoGP
Fathers and Sons. Arthur Davison Ficke. FAOV
Fathers and Sons. *Unknown, tr. fr. Irish by* Frank O'Connor. KiLC
"Fathers are in dust, yet live to God, The." Relics of Saints. Cardinal Newman. JKCP
Father's Birthday Cake. Ada Lorraine Jex. GFA
Father's Fury, A. Shakespeare. *See* Blow, Winds.
Father's gone a-flailing. *Unknown.* OxNR
Father's Heart Is Touched, A. Samuel Hoffenstein. FiBHP
Father's Hymn for the Mother to Sing, The. George Macdonald. BSV
Father's Journey. Sam Walter Foss.
He Comes. FAOV
He Goes. FAOV
Father's Letter. Eugene Field. IHA
Father's Prayer, A. Mouzon W. Brabham. PraP
Father's Prayer, A. T. A. Daly. *See* Man's Prayer, The.
Father's Prayer, A. Douglas Malloch. FAOV
Father's Story. Elizabeth Madox Roberts. FaPON; MPB
Father's Testament, A, *sel.* Phineas Fletcher.
Fond Soul. ElSeCe
Father's Testament, A. Judah ibn Tibbon, *tr. fr. Hebrew by* Israel Abrahams. TrJP
Fathom of earth shall be yours in death, A; no more thereafter. "For All the Saints and Sages." Marcus Argentarius. GrPE
Fathomless abyss is human pain, A. To Be. Manuel Gutiérrez Nájera. AnMP
Fathoms deep beneath the wave. Mermaids and Mermen. Sir Walter Scott. *Fr.* The Pirate. EtS
Fath'r and I went down to camp. Yankee Doodle. *Unknown.* TrAS
Fatigue. Hilaire Belloc. MoVE; SiTL
Fatigue Attacks the Nerves, the Brain. John Ransom Palmer. PoP
Fatima. Tennyson. LO; NBE; PIR; SeCePo
Fatima and Raduan. *Unknown, tr. fr. Spanish by* Bryant. LPS-1
Fatum Supremum. *Unknown. See* Epigram: Fatum Supremum.
Fault Is Mine, The. Edith M. Lee. PraP
Fault Is Not Mine, The. Walter Savage Landor. HBV
Faults. Sara Teasdale. BoFr; ChMo; CMP
Faun, The, *sels.* Richard Hovey.
"Hist! there's a stir in the brush." ADAH

Faun, The (*continued*)
"I will go out to grass with that old king." NLK
Faun, The. Haniel Long. HBMV
Faun, The. T. Sturge Moore. FaBoTw
Faun, The. Ezra Pound. FaBoCh; FaBoTw; LoGBV
Faun, The. Sara King Wiley. OBAV
Faun in Wall Street, A. John Myers O'Hara. LBMV
Faun Sees Snow for the First Time, The. Richard Aldington. MBP; MoBrPo; PFE
Faun-taken. Rose O'Neill. AnAmPo; HBMV; LA; LEAP
Faun Tells of the Rout of the Amazons, The. T. Sturge Moore. AnFE
Faunus, fleet-foot lover of flying wood-nymphs. To Faunus. Horace. *Fr.* Odes. LaP; LiTW
Faunus for feats of fencing bears the bell. Henry Parrot. SiCE
Faur oot i the sea-faem a wee bird keepit. Tuscan Folk Songs, 13. *Unknown, tr. into Scottish by* Edwin Morgan. LyPI
Fause Foodrage. *Unknown.* ESPB (A, B *and* C *vers.*); OBB, *sl. diff.*
Fause Knicht upon the Road, The. *Unknown. See* False Knight . . .
Fause Lover, The. *Unknown. See* False Lover Won Back, The.
Fause Sir John a-wooing came. May Colvin. *Unknown.* BLV; EBSV; OBB
Faust, *sels.* Goethe, *tr. fr. German.*
Christ Is Arisen, *tr. by* Arthur Cleveland Coxe. EOAH
(Easter Chorus: "Christ is arisen," *tr. by* Arthur Cleveland Coxe.) MaRV
(Easter Chorus from "Faust," *tr. by* Bayard Taylor, *abr.*) WGRP
(Easter Hymn.) ChIP
Faust Struggles with His Soul, *tr. by* C. F. MacIntyre. LiTW
"I'd open room for millions on the earth," *tr. by* F. Melian Stawell *and* Nora Purtscher-Wydenbruck. PoFr
King of Thule, The, *tr. by* James Clarence Mangan. AWP; JAWP; WBP; LPS-3, *tr. by* Bayard Taylor
Prayer: "Incline, O Maiden," *tr. by* Bayard Taylor. LiA
Prologue in Heaven, *tr. by* Shelley. AWP; JAWP; WBP
Soldier's Song, *tr. by* Bayard Taylor. AWP
Faust and the City, *sel.* Anatoli Vasilyevich Lunacharsky, *tr. fr. Russian by* L. A. Magnus *and* K. Walter.
Song of the Old Man in Chains. PoFr
Faustina hath a spot upon her face. De Naevo in Facie Faustinae. Thomas Bastard. LO
Faustina hath the fairer face. Madrigal. *Unknown.* ElSeCe; EV-1; OBSC
Faustine. Swinburne. BeLS; EmBrPo; PoVP; ViPo; ViPP; VLEP
Faustus. Christopher Marlowe. *See* Dr. Faustus.
Faustus. Hyam Plutzik. Horatio, III. FiMAP
Faustus to [the Apparition of] Helen. Christopher Marlowe. *See* Was This the Face.
Favonius. Hubert Church. AnNZ
Favored was he as that great Genoese. A Modern Columbus. Eleanor Robbins Wilson. PoMa
Favoritism. Meleager, *tr. fr. Greek by* Robert Allason Furness. GrR
Favour, The. Henry Vaughan. EV-2
"Favourite pleasure, A." Wordsworth. *Fr.* The Prelude, IV. OBRV
Favourites. Ibn Abd Rabbihi, *tr. fr. Arabic by* A. J. Arberry. MooP
Fawn, The. Edna St. Vincent Millay. LaNeLa
Fawn in the Snow, The. William Rose Benét. AnAmPo; LA; MAP; MoAmPo; MOAP
Fawn sleeps in the glade, A. Early Morning in a Glade. Glenn Ward Dresbach. NP
Fawnia. Robert Greene. *Fr.* Pandosto. HBV; OBEV; OBSC
("Ah, were she pitiful as she is fair.") EG; ElSeCe; ES; PeBoSo, *abr.*; TrGrPo, *abr.*; ViBoPo
(In Praise of His Loving and Best-beloved Fawnia.) AtBAP; PoEL-2
Fawn's First Snow, A. Glenn Ward Dresbach. PoTo
Fawn's Foster-Mother. Robinson Jeffers. AmPP (3d ed.); MOAP
Fay Arms Himself, The. Joseph Rodman Drake. *See* Fairy in Armor, A.
Fayned Fancye betweene the Spider and the Gowte, A, *sel.* Thomas Churchyard.
Old-Time Service. OBSC
Fayre eyes, the myrrour of my mazed hart. *See* Fair eyes! the mirror . . .
Fayre ye be sure, but cruell and unkind. *See* Fair ye be sure . . .
Fay's Crime, The. Joseph Rodman Drake. *Fr.* The Culprit Fay. GN
Fay's Departure, The. Joseph Rodman Drake. *See* First Quest, The.
Fay's Sentence, The ("The monarch sat on his judgment-seat"). Joseph Rodman Drake. *Fr.* The Culprit Fay. LEAP
Fay's Sentence, The ("Thou shalt seek the beach of sand"). Joseph Rodman Drake. *Fr.* The Culprit Fay. GN
Fe, fi, fo, fum. *See* Fee, fi, fo, fum.
Fealty. Wolfram von Eschenbach, *tr. fr. German by* Jethro Bithell. LiTW
Fear, The. Lascelles Abercrombie. OBMV
Fear, The. Robert Frost. ATP; BeLS; MAPA; NAMP; TwAmPo
Fear, The. W. W. Gibson. BEL; GTSL; NP
Fear. Kipling. *See* Song of the Little Hunter, The.
Fear, A. Ruth Messenger. BLP
Fear. Langdon Elwyn Mitchell. AA
Fear, The. Andrew Young. GTBS-D
Fear death?—to feel the fog in my throat. Prospice. Robert Browning. AEV; AnFE; BBV; BEL; BLP; BLV; BMEP; BoLiVe; BPN; CoBE; DD; EM-2; EmBrPo; EnL; EnLi-2; EnLit; EPN; EV-5; FaBoEn; FiP; GEPC; GTBS; GTBS-W; GTSL; HBV; HBVY; HiLiEn; InP; LEAP; LiTB; LiTL; MaRV; MCCG; NeHB; OAEP; OBEC; OBVV; OQP; OuHeWo; PC; PECK; PIAE; PoRA; PoVP; QP-1; REAL; RiBV; SeCeV; TCEP; TOP; TreFS; TrGrPo; TwP; TyEnPo; UnPo (1st ed.); VA; ViPo; ViPP; VLEP; WGRP; YT
Fear, facing the New Year. Facing the New Year. Mark Guy Pearse. BLRP
Fear is a wave. The Scene of War; Fear. Sir Herbert Read. TwCV
Fear it has faded and the night. Schoolgirls Hastening. John Shaw Neilson. BoAV
Fear made the superior sea. Stratagem. Allen Curnow. AnNZ
Fear me, virgin whosoever. After the Pleasure Party. Herman Melville. PoEL-5
Fear no longer for the lone grey birds. End of the Flower-World (A.D. 2300). Stanley Burnshaw. AnAmPo; LA; TrJP
Fear No More the Heat o' the Sun. Shakespeare. *Fr.* Cymbeline, IV, ii. AnFE; ATP; BEL; BLV; CenL; CH; ChTr; CoBE; EG; ElL; ElSeCe; EM-1; EnL; EnLi-1; EPP; ExPo; FaFP; InPo; LiTB; LiTG; LoBV; LPS-1; MaPo; OAEP; OuHeWo; PIR; PoE; PoFS; PoRA; ReaPo; RiBV; SeCeV; SiCE; TOP; TrGrPo; TriL; TwHP; TwP; TyEnPo; ViBoPo; WHA
(Dirge: "Fear no more the heat o' the sun.") CAW; CBOV; EnLit; EV-1; HBV
(Dirge from "Cymbeline.") WP
("Feare no more the heate o' th' sun.") AEV; AtBAP; BrBE; PoEL-2
(Fidele.) BCEP; GTBS; GTBS-D; GTBS-W; GTSE; MCCG; OBEV; OQP; QP-2; ShBV-4
(Fidele's Dirge.) CoEV; FaBoCh; LoGBV; OBSC; PoD
(Funeral Song.) CaAE; LiA
(Lament for Imogen.) TreF
(Lament of Guiderius and Arviragus.) FaBoEn
(Song: "Fear no more the heat o' the sun.") FiP; REAL
(Song of the Two Brothers.) BoLiVe
(Songs from "Cymbeline.") LEAP
(Songs from the Plays.) AWP; JAWP; WBP
(To Fidele.) TVSH
Fear Not, Dear Love. Thomas Carew. *See* Secrecy Protested.
Fear not, little flock. Poems by the Roadside. St. Luke, Bible, *N.T.* CAW
Fear not, O little flock! the foe. Battle Hymn. Michael Altenburg. WGRP
"Fear not, O maidens, shivering." The Little Ghost Who Died for Love. Edith Sitwell. CaAE; MoP
"Fear not to be alone," my lady said. Ideal Passion, XXII. George Edward Woodberry. MOAP
Fear of Death, The. Sir Edmund Gosse. *See* Last Night I Woke.
Fear of Death, The. Lucretius, *tr. fr. Latin. Fr.* De Rerum Natura. LoBV, *tr. by* Dryden; RoL, *pr. tr. by* W.H.D. Rouse
Fear of Death. Shakespeare. *Fr.* Measure for Measure, III, i. CoEV
(From "Measure for Measure.") NBE
(Life and Death.) KN; UnPo (1st ed.)
Fear of Dying, The. John Holmes. MiAP
Fear of Flowers, The. John Clare. OBRV; SeCeV
("Nodding oxeye bends before the wind, The.") AnFE; EG
Fear of poetry, The, is the/ fear. Reading Time: 1 Minute 26 Seconds. Muriel Rukeyser. MoPo; NePA
Fear of the Earth. Alex Comfort. MoBrPo (1950 ed.); NeBP
Fear of the Lord, The. Proverbs, I: 7, Bible, *O.T.* TrJP
Fear of Trembling, The. John Hollander. NePoEA
Fear the lights that cross the street. Suburban Lullaby. J. S. Manifold. BoAV

Fear thou no more, thou timid flower! The Snow-Drop. Samuel Taylor Coleridge. TriL
Fear? Yes . . . I heard you saying. Musing on a Great Soldier. Herbert Trench. PoeT
Feare No More the Heate o' the Sun. Shakespeare. *See* Fear No More the Heat o' the Sun.
Fearful "had the root of the matter," bringing. Courage Means Running. William Empson. LiTB
Fearful Joy. Michelangelo. *See* Joy May Kill.
Fearful of beauty, I always went. The Enamel Girl. Genevieve Taggard. HBMV; MAP; MoAmPo; NP; TCPD
Fearless follow, thou sad soul. Song. *Unknown.* SeCL
Fears and Scruples. Robert Browning. BPN
Fears in Solitude. Samuel Taylor Coleridge. EmBrPo; EnRP; ERP; SoV
Sels.
Dell, The. EV-4
England. EV-4
". . . Oh! my countrymen!/ We have offended very grievously." PreP
Feast, The. Nora B. Cunningham. OQP; QP-2
Feast. Edna St. Vincent Millay. BAP; NP; WHA
Feast being spread in spring-time, A. Her Birthday. Feng Yen-chi. ChLP
Feast by the Manzanares. Juan Ruiz de Alarcón, *tr. fr. Spanish by* Samuel Beckett. *Fr.* The Suspicious Truth, I. AnMP
Feast Day, The. Amy McDonall. PCH
Feast-day wore a frown, The. Rain at Festival. Ibn Rashiq. MooP
Feast is o'er, The. Now brimming wine. The Knight's Toast. *Unknown, at. to* Sir Walter Scott. MotAn; PCD; PTA-2
Feast o' St. Stephen. Ruth Sawyer. OHIP
Feast of Dian, The. Keats. *Fr.* Endymion, IV. BPN
Feast of Harvest, The. Edmund Clarence Stedman. TOAH
Feast of Padre Chala, The. Thomas Walsh. CAW
Feast of Saint Brigid of Kildare, The. *At. to* St. Bridget, *tr. fr. Middle Irish by* Eugene O'Curry. CAW; OnYI
(Heavenly Banquet, The, *sl. abr., tr. by* Seán O'Faoláin.) OnYI; SiB
(I Should Like to Have a Great Pool of Ale, *tr. by* Kenneth Jackson.) AnIL
Feast of the Doll, The. Nora Archibald Smith. PPL
Feast of the Snow, The. G. K. Chesterton. HBV
Feast on Wine or Fast on Water. G. K. Chesterton. ALV
(Song of Right and Wrong, The.) OtMeF
Feast Time of the Year, The. Dora Read Goodale. OHIP; PEDC
"Feast was over in Branksome tower, The." Sir Walter Scott. *Fr.* The Lay of the Last Minstrel, I. OBRV
Feast was over, the slaves gone, The. Ave Maria. Byron. *Fr.* Don Juan. ERP
Feast was spread, the wine was poured, The. The Sinner. Alcman. GrR
Feast's begun, The/ And the wine is done. Water Song. Solomon ibn Gabirol. TrJP
Feasts of Death, Feasts of Love. Stuart Z. Perkoff. NeAP
Feasts satiate; stars distress with height. The Amaranth. Coventry Patmore. *Fr.* The Angel in the House. LoBV (1949 ed.)
Feather, The. Lilian Bowes-Lyon. ChMP
Feather. Lew Sarett. NP
Feather, The. Vernon Watkins. FaBoTw; MoVE
Feather for My Cap, A. Ivy O. Eastwick. BoTP
Feather-footed and swift as a mouse. The Visitor. Rachel Field. TiPo (1952 ed.)
Feather or Fur. John Becker. FaPON; TiPo (1959 ed.)
"Feathered fowl's in your orchard, father, A." Brown Robin (B *vers.*). *Unknown.* ESPB
Feathered [*or* Featherd] songster chaunticleer, The. The Bristowe Tragedie; or, The Dethe of Syr Charles Bawdin. Thomas Chatterton. CEP; EiPP; EnRP; EPP; EV-3; OBEC
Feathered thing of silver-grey and jade, The. Dollar Bill. John Frederick Nims. MiAP
Feathers. Olive Hopegood. MoAuPo
Feathers in a fan, The. Man. Humbert Wolfe. *Fr.* Requiem. MBP; MoBrPo; POTE
Feathers of the Willow, The. Richard Watson Dixon. *See* Song: "Feathers of the willow, The."
Feathers on a robin's breast, The. Robin. Anne Blackwell Payne. GFA
Feathers or Lead? James Broughton. NeAP
Featherstone's Doom. Robert Stephen Hawker. VA
Feaver, A. John Donne. *See* Fever, A.
Februarie. Spenser. *Fr.* The Shepheardes Calender. EPP
(Oak and the Brere, The.) OBSC
February. James Berry Bensel. GoTP
February. Anna Neil Gilmore. *See* February, Tall and Trim.
February. Ann Louise Hayes. PtPa
February, *abr.* William Morris. *Fr.* The Earthly Paradise. ViPo
February. Dorothy Una Ratcliffe. BoTP
February. D. S. Savage. NeBP
February. James Schuyler. NeAP
February. Frank Dempster Sherman. PCH; YeAr
February. *Unknown.* PCH
("In the month of February.") BoTP
February. Adeline D. T. Whitney. YeAr
February. Francis Brett Young. HBMV; HBVY; LBBV; PoTo
February Afternoon. Edward Thomas. MoPW
February—February. Washington-Month. Will Carleton. WOAH
February—fortnights, two. February. Frank Dempster Sherman. PCH; YeAr
February 14, 22 B.C. Franklin P. Adams, *after the Latin of* Horace. InMe
February Morning on the Gulf. Nils Collett Vogt, *tr. fr. Norwegian by* Charles W. Stork. AnNoLY
February Night. Wyn Griffith. MoWP
February, Tall and Trim. Anna Neil Gilmore. YeAr
(February.) DD
February Twelfth. Mary F. Hepburn. PCH
February 12, 1809. Gail Brook Burket. PGD
February Twilight. Sara Teasdale. FaPON; MoSiPe; YeAr
Feckenham Men, The. John Drinkwater. CP; GBV; GTSL; TVSH
Feckless Dinner Party, The. Walter de la Mare. FaBoTw; MoPW
Fecundi Calices. Bacchylides, *tr. fr. Greek by* C. M. Bowra. OxBG
(Song and Wine.) LiTW
Fedele and Fortunio, *sels.* Anthony Munday, *ad. fr. the Italian of* Luigi Pasqualigo.
I Serve a Mistress. ElL; LO
(Fedele's Song.) ElSeCe; OBSC
"If love be like the flower that in the night." TuPP
Federal Constitution, The. William Milns. PAH
Federal Convention, The. *Unknown.* PAH
Federation of the World, The. Tennyson. *Fr.* Locksley Hall. *See* Prophecy.
Federico. Nicolás Guillén, *tr. fr. Spanish by* Ben F. Carruthers. PoNe
Fee, faw, fum! bubble and squeak! Holy-Cross Day. Robert Browning. OtMeF
Fee [*or* Fe], fi, fo, fum. *Unknown.* ExPo; OxNR
Feed. Raymond Knister. BoCaPo; PeCV
Feed/ Upon anticipation as you sow the seed. Harvest Time. Star Powers. GoYe
Feed, silly sheep, although your keeper pineth. Chloris, III. William Smith. TuPP
Feeding, The. Joel Oppenheimer. NeAP
Feeding the Fairies. *Unknown.* PPL
Feeding the Robin. *Unknown.* *See* Come Hither, Sweet Robin.
Feel like a Bird. May Swenson. TrGrPo (rev. ed.)
Feel of the friendly prairies, the softening shadows of night, The. Across Illinois. John Stoltze. PoMa; PoTo
Feel so low-down an' sad Lawd. Friendless Blues. Mercedes Gilbert. TrAS
Feel so sad and sorrowful runnin' over with the blues. Mountain Top Blues. Spencer Williams. APW
Feeling. Arthur Rimbaud, *tr. fr. French by* Alan Conder. TrFP
Feeling fretful toward evening. The Lo-yu Tombs. Li Shang-yin. WhP
Feeling hunger and cold, feeling. Sensuality. Kenneth Slessor. NeLNL
"Feeling inclined toward charity." Translations from Modern Japanese Poetry. Tabubokee Ishikawa. PFE
Feeling my face has the terrible shine of fish. Element. P. K. Page. BoCaPo (1948 ed.); PeCV
Feeling the useless arm. Hospital Observation. Julian Symons. WaP
Feelings are perceived as vague as limbs in my dismembered past. At Eighty-seven. Dachine Rainer. NePoAm
Feelings of a Republican on the Fall of Bonaparte. Shelley. AnEnPo
Feelings of the Tyrolese. Wordsworth. ERP
Feet. Dorothy Aldis. BoChLi; SUS
Feet. Mary Carolyn Davies. *See* Seeking.
Feet. "Harry." TiPo (1959 ed.)
Feet. Irene Thompson. BoTP
Feet o' Jesus. Langston Hughes. NP
Feet of Judas, The. George Marion McClellan. BANP; PoNe
Feet of people walking home, The. Emily Dickinson. MeRV
Feet of the rats, The. Four Preludes on Playthings of the Wind, IV. Carl Sandburg. AnAmPo; AnFE; BLV; BoLiVe; CoAnAm; CoBA; InP; LA; MAP; MoAB; MoAmPo; NePA; NP; SeCeV
Feet of the Young Men, The. Kipling. CBV; LBBV; OtMeF; PoRL
Feigned Courage. Charles *and* Mary Lamb. GN
Felicia Ropps. Gelett Burgess. FaPON; GaP; TiPo
Felicia's Song. Per Daniel Amadeus Atterbom, *tr. fr. Swedish by* Charles W. Stork. AnSL
Felicity. Isaac Watts. OxBoCh

Feline Anyway. Eden Phillpotts. BMEP
Felis sedit by a hole. A Fable: The Mice and Felis. John Kendrick. CIV
Félise. Swinburne. BeLS; EmBrPo
"What shall be said between us here," *sel.* LoPS
Felix Antonius. Sir Henry Newbolt. PtOT
Felix Infelix! Cat unfortunate. Ode to a Bobtailed Cat. *Unknown.* BOHV; CIV
Felix Randal. Gerard Manley Hopkins. EmBrPo; EnL; EnLi-2 (1949 ed.); EnLit; FaBoEn; FaBoMo; GTBS-D; GTBS-W; InPo; KN; LiTB; LiTM; MaPo; MBP; MoAB; MoBrPo; MoPo; NAMP; OAEP; OBEV (new ed.); PoRA; PoVP; ReMP; RiBV; TwCV; ViP; ViPo
Feller I Know, A. Mary Austin. FaPON; GaP; MW
Fellow be with kindly foemen, rather than with friends unkind. Proverbial Wisdom. *Unknown.* BoFr
Fellow-Citizens. Verner von Heidenstam, *tr. fr. Swedish by* Charles W. Stork. AnSL
"Fellow citizens, we cannot escape history." Lincoln Portrait. Aaron Copland. MaRV
Fellow in a market town, A. The Razor Seller. "Peter Pindar." BCEP; BOHV; HBV; InMe; LPS-3
Fellow near Kentucky's clime, A. John Thompson's Daughter. Phoebe Cary. BOHV; PA; PTA-2
Fellow-Passengers. Frank Wilmot. BoAu
Fellow topers fine and dandy. Potatores Exquisiti. *Unknown. Fr.* Carmina Burana. LaP
Fellows in Arms! whose Bliss, whose chiefest Good. Cato's Address to His Troops in Lybia. Lucan, *tr. by* Nicholas Rowe. *Fr.* Pharsalia, IX. OBEC
Fellows up in Personnel, The. The Perforated Spirit. Morris Bishop. FiBHP
Fellowship, The. Katharine Lee Bates. OQP; QP-2
Fellowship. Elinor Lennen. ChIP
Fellowship. *Unknown.* BLPA
Fellowship of Books. Edgar A. Guest. LPS-1
Fellowship of Prayer, The. Nancy Byrd Turner. BePJ; PraP
Felo-de-Se. James Elroy Flecker. LBBV
Felo de Se. Richard Hughes. OBMV
Felo de Se. Elinor Wylie. LoPS
Female Convict, The. Letitia Elizabeth Landon. LPS-1
Female Frailty, *sel.* Philip Freneau.
Song of Thyrsis. AA; AnFE; APA; APW; CoAnAm; HBV; LBAP; LEAP; LiTA; OnPM; PR; ViBoPo
Female Glory. Richard Lovelace. MyFE
Female God, The. Isaac Rosenberg. FaBoTw
Female Husband, Who Had Been Married to Another Female for Twenty-one Years, The. *Unknown.* CoMu
Female is fertile, and discipline, The. Praise for Sick Women. Gary Snyder. NeAP
Female Martyr, The. Whittier. PraNu
Female of the Species, The. Kipling. BLPA; BPN; HBV; OtMeF; TreFS; VLEP
Female Phaeton, The. Matthew Prior. HBV; NBE
Female Smuggler, The, *with music.* *Unknown.* AmSS
Female Warrior, The. *Unknown.* ShS
Feminine. H. C. Bunner. AA; PR
Feminine Arithmetic. Charles Graham Halpine. BOHV; PR
Femme et chatte. Paul Verlaine, *tr. fr. French by* Arthur Symons. AWP; JAWP; WBP; CIV, *tr. by* Ashmore Wingate
(Cat and Lady, *tr. by* Arthur Symons.) PoC
(Woman and Cat, *tr. by* Arthur Symons.) OnPM [*wr. at. to* Baudelaire]; WoL
Femmes Damnées, *sel.* Baudelaire, *tr. fr. French by* Aldous Huxley.
"Sunless your caverns are; the fever damps." MeRV
Fence, A. Carl Sandburg. AmP; InP
Fence or an Ambulance, A. Joseph Malins. BLPA; PTA-1
Fenceposts wear marshmallow hats, The. Snow. Dorothy Aldis. TiPo
Fences. Rebecca McCann. PoMa
Ferd Herold Blues, *with music.* *Unknown.* StDa
Ferdinand De Soto lies. The Distant Runners. Mark Van Doren. LiTA; LiTM; MAP; LoGBV; MoAmPo; NePA
Ferdinando and Elvira; or, The Gentle Pieman. W. S. Gilbert. BOHV; FiBHP; LBN; NA; PC
Ferdinando Ieronimi's Sonnet. George Gascoigne. ElSeCe
Fergus and the Druid. W. B. Yeats. CoBE
Ferishtah's Fancies, *sels.* Robert Browning.
"Ask not one least word of praise," *fr.* XI. BPN; VLEP
Epilogue: "Oh, Love—no, Love! All the noise below, Love." ViPP
"Fire is in the flint," *fr.* V. BPN; VLEP
"Man I am and man would be," *fr.* IV. VLEP
"Round us the wild creatures, overhead the trees," *fr.* I. BPN; VLEP
"Verse-making was least of my virtues," *fr.* IX. BPN
" 'Why from the world,' Ferishtah smiled, 'should thanks,' " *fr.* XII. BPN
"Wish no word unspoken, want no look away!" *fr.* II. BPN
Ferment of New Wine, The. Elizabeth Barrett Browning. *Fr.* Aurora Leigh, I. VA
Fern and flame had fought and died together, The. Common Fires. Muriel Stuart. MBP
Fern grows in the volcanic dust, The. The Goats of Juan Fernandez. Coleman Rosenberger. DaM
Fern Hill. Dylan Thomas. AtBAP; ChMP; CoBMV; EnL; FaBoEn; GTBS-D; LiTB; LiTM; LoGBV; MaPo; MoAB; MoBrPo (1950 ed.); MoPo; MoPW; MoVE; NeMA; OAEP (2d ed.); Po; PoRA; PrWP; ShBV-4; ThWaDe; TrGrPo (rev. ed.); ViBoPo (1958 ed.); WaKn
Fern House at Kew. Paul Dehn. ChMP
(Fern House, Kew.) PoN
Fern Song. John Banister Tabb. PRWS; RAR
Ferns. *Unknown.* PEOR
Ferrara! in thy wide and grass-grown streets. Byron. *Fr.* Childe Harold's Pilgrimage, IV. PtP
Ferries ply like shuttles in a loom, The. This Is My Hour. Zoë Akins. HBV; LEAP
Ferry, The. George Henry Boker. AA; OBAV
Ferry, The. Emperor Ch'ien Wen-ti, *tr. fr. Chinese by* Arthur Waley. ChLP; TrCh
Ferry Hinksey. Laurence Binyon. CBE; HBV
Ferry Me across the Water. Christina Rossetti. *Fr.* Sing-Song. ChTr; GaP; PoRh; SUS
(Boatman, The.) PCH
(Ferryman, The.) BoTP
Ferry Ride, *sel.* Selma Robinson.
Bus Ride. FaPON
Ferry-Boats. James S. Tippett. GFA; SUS; TiPo
Ferryman, The. Christina Rossetti. *See* Ferry Me across the Water.
Ferryman that rowest the barge the buried fare on. The Little Ghost. Zonas. GrPE
Ferryman, Venus, and Cupid, The. Michael Drayton. *Fr.* The Muses' Elysium. CG
Fertile and rank and rich the coastal rains. Advent. Brother Antoninus. NeAP
Fervent lover and the sage austere, The. Cats. Baudelaire. PoC
Fervid heat. Cornets sound harshly. Ardor. Jorge Guillén. CoSP
Fest. Puritatis. Aubrey Thomas De Vere. *Fr.* May Carols. PoVP
Festal Board, The. *Unknown.* BLPA; TreFS
Festal Song. William Pierson Merrill. *See* Rise Up, O Men of God!
Feste's Songs. Shakespeare. *Fr.* Twelfth Night. *See* Come Away, Come Away, Death *and* O Mistress Mine *and* When That I Was
Festival, The. Robert Eyres Landor. *Fr.* The Impious Feast, III. OBRV
Festival, The. Frederic Prokosch. LiTA; LiTM (1946 ed.); NeTW; WaP
Festival, The. Theocritus, *tr. fr. Greek by* F. L. Lucas. *Fr.* Idylls, VII. GrPE
Festival in Tuscany. William Force Stead. POTE
Festivals. Fuyuhiko Kitagawa, *tr. fr. Japanese by* Takamichi Ninomiya *and* D. J. Enright. PoLJ
Festivity. Jorge Guillén, *tr. fr. Spanish by* Eleanor L. Turnbull. CoSP
Festoons of Fishes. Alfred Kreymborg. HBMV; TCPD
Festum Nativitatis. Aubrey Thomas De Vere. *Fr.* May Carols. IrPN
Festus, *sels.* Philip James Bailey.
Aim of Life, The. LPS-3; OQP; QP-2
(Country Town, A, 4 *ll.*) PoToHe (new ed.)
(We Live in Deeds.) BMEP; MaRV
Helen's Song. VA
"I loved her for that she was beautiful." LO
(My Lady.) OBVV
Lucifer and Elissa. VA
Lucifer's Song. BMEP
Poet, The. VA
Poet of Nature, The. LPS-3
Youth, Love and Death. VA
Fetch, The. Dora Sigerson Shorter. DaM
Fetching Water from the Well. *Unknown.* LPS-1
Fete, A. Larry Eigner. NeAP
Fête Champêtre. Kenneth Allott. POTE
Fête Galante. Edith Sitwell. *Fr.* Façade. CaAE
Fêtes, Fates. John Malcolm Brinnin. LiTA
Fetish-woman crossed the stage, The. The Lady from Harlem. Malcolm Cowley. NP
Feud. Lew Sarett. AnAmPo; LA; MAP; TBM
Feud, The. Frederick George Scott. CPG; PCN
Feuerzauber. Louis Untermeyer. NP; SBMV; TrJP
Fever, A. John Donne. EPS; MyFE, *st.* 6
(Feaver, A.) EnLP
Fever. "Klabund," *tr. fr. German by* Babette Deutsch *and* Avrahm Yarmolinsky. OnPM
Fever, and crowds—and light that cuts your eyes. Hospital. John Allan Wyeth. PoP
Fever in My Blood Has Died, The. George Henry Boker. IAP

Fevered Sleep. Shan Ho Yü, *tr. fr. Chinese by* Henry H. Hart. PoHN
Few are my books, but my small few have told. Lovely Dames. W. H. Davies. PtOT
Few cities of the heroes still remain. Mycenae. Alphaeus. OnPM
Few Days, *with music. Unknown.* ABF
Few days after, A. Death of a Bird. Jon Silkin. NePoEA
Few days more they drifted, ever west, A. The Emigration of the Fairies. John Hunter-Duvar. BoCaPo
Few Days Off, A. John Charles McNeill. NoCaPo
Few footsteps stray when dusk droops o'er. The Tailor. Walter de la Mare. VOD
Few green islands in a sunny sea, A. Greece. William A. Breyfogle. CAG
Few hours remain. Darkness is big, is surly. New Words for an Old Song. Babette Deutsch. NePoAm
Few, in the days of early youth. The World I Am Passing Through. Lydia Maria Child. AA; HBV
Few lonely birds, A. Spring in New England. Carlos Wilcox. APW
Few long-hoarded pennies in his hand, A. Pennies. Joyce Kilmer. CAW
Few men of hero-mould. John Bright. Francis Barton Gummere. AA
Few minutes of a spring night, The. Spring Night. Su T'ung-po. OnPC
Few more days and snow will come, A. The Room. Francis Jammes. TrFP
Few more windy days, A. Song. Helen Dudley. NP
Few Old Proverbs, A. *Unknown.* ADAH
Few roads and far to grey Glencar. Glencar. Stephen Gwynn. LBBV
Few There Be. *Unknown, tr. fr. Greek by* Richard Garnett. OxBG
Few Things Can More Inflame. C. Day Lewis. OBMV
Few tricks there are a fox won't learn. Knowledge. Archilochus. OxBG
Few visitors come through this gate. The Heart in Autumn. Po Chü-i. WhP
Few were her words and all too short her songs. Erinna. Antipater of Sidon. GrR
Few Wholly Faithful. *Unknown.* BePJ
Few Words to Meng Hao-jan, A. Li Po, *tr. fr. Chinese.* WhP
Fewer Books, More Salad. Thomas Hood. *See* To Minerva.
Fey. *Unknown. Fr.* The Battle of Otterbourne. OtMeF
"Ffaith, master, whither you will." Captain Car, or Edom o Gordon (B *vers.*). *Unknown.* ESPB
"Ffor if your boone be askeable." Thomas Cromwell. *Unknown.* ESPB
"Ffor this same night att [Bucklesfeildberry]. Little Musgrave and Lady Barnard (B *vers.*). *Unknown.* ESPB
Fhairshon swore a feud. The Massacre of the Macpherson. William Edmondstoune Aytoun. CenHV; ChTr; OtMeF; VA
Fhir a bhata, na horo eile. The Boatman. *Unknown, tr. by* Thomas Pattison. EBSV
Fiametta. John Peale Bishop. LiTA; LiTL; TwAmPo
Fiammetta. Boccaccio, *tr. fr. Italian by* Dante Gabriel Rossetti. GoBC
(Sonnets.) AWP; JAWP; WBP
Fiammetta ("Behold Fiammetta, shown in vision here"). Dante Gabriel Rossetti. VLEP
Fiat Lux. Lloyd Mifflin. AA; AnAmPo; LA; LBMV; PFY
"Fiat!"—The flaming word. The Annunciation. John Banister Tabb. ISi
Fib Detected, A. Catullus, *tr. fr. Latin by* John Hookham Frere. AWP
Fichtenbaum steht einsam, Ein. Heine, *tr. fr. German by* James Thomson. AWP; JAWP; OuHeWo; WBP
(Lonely Pine Is Standing, A, *tr. by* Louis Untermeyer.) LiA
(Pine Tree, The, *st.* 1, *tr. by* Sidney Lanier.) PCH
Fickle Hope. Harrison Smith Morris. AA
Fickle Seat Whereon Proud Fortune Sits, The. Robert Greene. *Fr.* Morando, the Tritameron of Love. ReIE
Fickleness. Harry Kemp. PR
Fiction, A. "A. W." TuPP
Fiction. Charles Sprague. *Fr.* Curiosity. AA
Fiddle, The. Neil Munro. BoTP
Fiddle and the Bow, The. Humbert Wolfe. NV
Fiddle me away Little Man. Coaxing a Fairy Fiddler. Monica Shannon. BoChLi
Fiddlededee. Eliza Lee Follen. SAS
Fiddle-de-dee!/ Grasshoppers three. High June. Catherine A. Morin. BoTP
Fiddle-de-dee, fiddle-de-dee. *Unknown.* BoN; OTPC; RIS; SiTL
Fiddle-dee-dee. Eugene Field. DDA
Fiddler, A. Walter de la Mare. UnS
Fiddler, The. Edna Valentine Trapnell. HBMV
Fiddler and his wife, The. *Unknown.* OxNR
Fiddler Jones. Edgar Lee Masters. *Fr.* Spoon River Anthology. AmP; LiTA; LoGBV; NP; OxBA; TrGrPo; UnS
Fiddler of Dooney, The. W. B. Yeats. AlDL; BEL; FaBoCh; GTML; HBV; InP; LoGBV; MM; NeMA; OBVV; PoMa; TCPD; TiPo; TwCV; UnS; YT
Fiddler's Green. Theodore Goodridge Roberts. CaP; CPG; OCL
Fiddlers' Green. Margaret Widdemer. YT
Fiddles were playing and playing, The. Across the Door. Padraic Colum. HBV
Fiddling Lad, The. Adelaide Crapsey. MW; NLK (1947 ed.)
Fidele [*or* Fidele's Dirge]. William Collins. *See* Song from Shakespeare's "Cymbeline," A.
Fidele [*or* Fidele's Dirge]. Shakespeare. *See* Fear No More the Heat o' the Sun.
Fidelia, *sels.* George Wither.
Hence, Away, You Sirens! *also given in* Fair Virtue. ElL, 3 *sts.*
(Sonnet: "Hence away, you sirens, leave me," 10 *sts.*) ElSeCe
Shall I, Wasting in Despair, *also given in* Fair Virtue. ALV; AnFE; BEL; EG; ElL; EM-1; EnLi-1; EV-2; LiTB; LiTG; LoPo, *abr.*; OBS; OuHeWo; PreP; WHA
(Author's Resolution, The.) BCEP; ViBoPo
(Author's Resolution in a Sonnet, The.) CaAE; EPS
(Lover's Resolution, The.) AWP; HBV; InMe; JAWP; LEAP; LiTL; OBEV; PG; TOP; TreFS; WBP
(Manly Heart.) GTBS; GTBS-D; GTBS-W; GTSE; GTSL; MCCG; TVSH
(Resolution, The.) ElSeCe
(Shepherd's Resolution.) LPS-1
(Sonnet: "Shall I, wasting in despair.") EPP; SeCV-1
(What Care I.) BLV; CoEV; TrGrPo
Fidelis. Adelaide Anne Procter. BLPA; FaBoBe; NeHB
Fidelity. Ibn Zaydun, *tr. fr. Arabic by* A. J. Arberry. MooP
Fidelity. D. H. Lawrence. Po
Fidelity. Thomas Lodge. *See* Love Guards the Roses of Thy Lips.
Fidelity. Trumbull Stickney. AnFE; CoAnAm; LiTA; TwAmPo
Fidelity. Wordsworth. AlBD; CG; PECK
Fidelity and love are two different things, like a flower and a gem. Fidelity. D. H. Lawrence. Po
Fidessa, More Chaste than Kind, *sels.* Bartholomew Griffin.
"Arraign'd, poor captive at the bar I stand," V. ReIE; SiCE; TuPP
"Care-charmer sleep, sweet ease in restless misery," XV. ReEN; ReIE; SiCE; TuPP
(Sleep.) OBSC
"Compare me to the child that plays with fire," XIII. SiCE; TuPP
"Fair is my love that feeds among the lilies," XXXVII. BCEP; EG; LO; NBE; PeBoSo; SiCE; TuPP; ViBoPo
(Faire Is My Love.) PoEL-2
(My Love.) TrGrPo
(Sonnet: "Fair is my love that feeds among the lilies.") ElL
"Fly to her heart; hover about her heart," XXIII. PeBoSo; ReEn; ReIE; SiCE; TuPP
(Her Heart.) TrGrPo
"I have not spent the April of my time," XXXV. ElSeCe; ReEn; SiCE; TuPP
(Sonnet.) ElL
(Youth.) OBSC
"I see, I hear, I feel, I know, I rue," XLVII. ReIE
"If great Apollo offered as a dower," LIV. ReIE; TuPP
"Striving is past. Ah, I must sink and drown," XXIV. ReIE
"Tell me of love, sweet Love, who is thy sire?" XLIII. TuPP
"Venus and [*or* with] young Adonis sitting by her," III. PeBoSo; ReIE; ViBoPo, *sl. diff.*
"Work, work apace, you blessed sisters three," LI. SiCE; TuPP
Fie, Chloris! 'Tis silly to sigh thus in vain. To Chloris. *At. to* Dr. Waldren. SeCL
Fie, Fie on Blind Fancy! Robert Greene. *Fr.* Greene's Groatsworth of Wit. ElL
(Lamilia's Song.) OBSC
Fie, fie upon her! Portrait of Cressida. Shakespeare. *Fr.* Troilus and Cressida, IV, v. TrGrPo
Fie! flattering fortune, look thou never so fair. *See* Eye-flattering fortune, look thou never so fair.
Fie [*or* Fye] foolish Earth, think [*or* thinke] you the heaven wants glory. Love's Glory. Fulke Greville. Caelica, XVI. LO; OBSC; PoEL-1; ReIE; SiCE; TuPP
Fie! How doth gratitude when men are dead. Unpalatable Truths. Sophocles. *Fr.* Ajax. GrR
Fie on all courtesy, and unruly winds. The Coxcomb. Joseph Hall. *Fr.* Virgidemiarum, III. EV-2
Fie on Love. Francis Beaumont. AnEnPo
Fie on Sinful Fantasy! Shakespeare. *Fr.* The Merry Wives of Windsor, V, v. ViBoPo

Fie on these Lydian tunes which blunt our sprights. Everard Guilpin. *Fr.* Skialetheia. SiCE
Fie, Pleasure, Fie! George Gascoigne. ElL, *sl. abr.;* InvP
Fie, school of Patience, fie! Your lesson is. Astrophel and Stella, LVI. Sir Philip Sidney. ReEn; SiPS
Fie [*or* Fye], what a trouble 'tis to count this trash! Barabas in His Counting-House. Christopher Marlowe. *Fr.* The Jew of Malta. CoEV; NBE
Field and the stream nearby, The. The Rainbow. Konstantin Simonov. RuPo
Field cricket hammers: Go on, go on. Salvation. Aaron Zeitlin. OnCuPl
Field Daisy, The. Jane Taylor. BoTP
(Daisy, The.) PCH; PPL
Field Flower, A. James Montgomery. *See* Daisy, The.
Field-Flower. Francis Thompson. PoVP
Field Flowers. Thomas Campbell. OTPC (1923 ed.)
Field Full of Folk, The ("In a summer season"). William Langland. *See* Prologue: "In a somer sesun . . ."
Field Full of Folk, A ("What this mountain betokens"). William Langland. *See* Holy Church.
Field-Glasses. Andrew Young. ChMP
Field in June, A. Gerald Bullett. AlDL
Field-Mouse, The. Enid Blyton. BoTP
Field Mouse, The. "Fiona Macleod." FaPON; GBV; MoShBr
Field of Folk, The. William Langland. *See* Prologue: "In a somer sesun . . ."
Field of Glory, The. E. A. Robinson. ChMo; CMP; HBV; MAP; MoAmPo; TBM
Field of golden wheat there grows, A. Harvest Song. Richard Dehmel. AWP; JAWP; LiTW; WBP
Field of oats, field of rye, corn-field,—these the three. Three Fields. Adolf Heyduk. LiTW
Field of Tears. *Unknown, tr. fr. Russian by* W. R. S. Ralston. OnPM
Field of the Grounded Arms, The. Fitz-Greene Halleck. PoEL-4
Field of Waterloo, The. Thomas Hardy. *See* Before Waterloo.
Field of Waterloo, The, *sels.* Sir Walter Scott.
Charge at Waterloo, The, *ad.* PEOR
To Britain—after War: "Well hast thou stood, my country!" ShGoBo
Field-Path, The. Charles Swain. OBVV
Field Sports. Pope. *Fr.* Windsor Forest. OBEC; SeCePo
Fields. "Andrei Bely," *tr. fr. Russian by* Babette Deutsch. TrRV
Fields, The. Witter Bynner. SBMV
Fields Abroad with Spangled Flowers, The. *Unknown.* ChTr
Fields are bridal, flushed with dewy light, The. England—June, 1940. Lord Gorell. NeTW
Fields are chill; the sparse rain has stopped, The. Clearing at Dawn. Li Po. AWP; JAWP; TrCh; WBP
Fields Are Full, The. Edward Shanks. BMEP; POTE
Fields are full of poppies and the skies are very blue, The. In the Early, Pearly Morning. "Laurence Hope." LoPo
Fields are full of summer still, The. The Fields Are Full. Edward Shanks. BMEP; POTE
Fields are high with all the winter's snow, The. A Mess of Clams. Robert P. Tristram Coffin. DDA
Fields are in flower in the West, The. Narcissus Fields. Eleanor Farjeon. AlDL
Fields Are Spread, The. Elizabeth J. Coatsworth. PoRh
Fields are white still with the snow, The. Spring Waters. Feodor Tyutchev. BoRS
Fields at Evening. David Morton. AnAmPo; HBMV; LA
(These Fields at Evening.) BAP
Fields from Islington to Marybone, The. Blake. *Fr.* Jerusalem. ChTr; OBRV
(From Islington to Marybone.) TriL
Fields grow dim, The; the somber mills. Twilight. Gerald Gould. MBP; MoBrPo (1942 ed.)
Fields o' Ballyclare, The. Denis A. McCarthy. CV
Fields of Dawn, The, *sels.* Lloyd Mifflin.
April. ADAH; SN
Autumn. SN
Summer. SN
Fields of France are filled with weeping, The. To Becky in France. John Arey. LO
Fields of Soria, *sels.* Antonio Machado, *tr. fr. Spanish.*
"Lo, these are they that move 'twixt land and sky," IV, *tr. by* Ida Farnell. AnSpL-2; TeCS
"Silvered Hills," VII, *tr. by* Eleanor L. Turnbull. TeCS
"Undulating country, where the roads, An," III, *tr. by* Ida Farnell. AnSpL-2; TeCS
Fields were not black, nor skies of gloomy hue. Olympio's Sadness. Victor Hugo. TrFP
Fields were silent, and the woodland drear, The. In the Dark. Mary Potter Thacher Higginson. AA
Fiend's Weather. Louise Bogan. MoVE
Fierce and brooding holocaust of faith, The. Two Poems on the Catholic Bavarians, I. Edgar Bowers. PtPa
Fierce burns our fire of driftwood; overhead. Night in Camp. Herbert Bashford. AA
Fierce exulting worlds, the motes in rays, The. Love. Alexander Smith. OBEV (1st ed.)
Fierce from the stoking lech of spring. Europa. Terence Tiller. PoN
Fierce is the flame of the vengeance of Erin. O'Neill's War Song. Michael Hogan. OnYI
Fierce is the wind tonight. The Viking Terror. *Unknown.* AnIL; OnYI
Fierce Mars I bid a glad farewell. New Mexico and Arizona. George Canterbury. PoOW
Fierce musical cries of a couple of sparrow hawks hunting, The. Birds. Robinson Jeffers. BLA; CoBMV; MOAP; TwAmPo; TwCV
Fierce passions discompose the mind. Contentment. William Cowper. CEP
Fierce raged the tempest o'er the deep. Godfrey Thring. OlF
Fierce, round Achilles, rose the boiling wave. Scamander the River God. Homer. *Fr.* The Iliad, XXI. GrR
Fierce unrest seethes at the core, A. Unrest. Don Marquis. BAP; HBMV; MaRV; OQP; PC; PoeMoYo; PoFr; QP-1
Fierce Was the Wild Billow. Anatolius, *tr. fr. Greek by* John Mason Neale. MaRV
(Jesus, Deliverer.) BePJ
Fierce wrath of Solomon. The Burning of the Temple. Isaac Rosenberg. FaBoMo; TrJP
Fiercely, methinks, will he rage in his heart and loud will he bellow. The Rival Poets. Aristophanes. *Fr.* The Frogs. OxBG
Fiery bitter blue it burns. The Bird of Paradise. Laura Benét. BLA; PFY
Fiery Cross, The. Sir Walter Scott. *Fr.* The Lady of the Lake, III. ERP
Fiery cross against the night, A. Two Crosses. Addie M. Hedrick. ChIP
Fiesolan Idyl. Walter Savage Landor. BPN; EmBrPo; EnRP; EPP; ERP; OAEP; SeCePo; VA
(Faesulan Idyl.) EV-4; OBRV
Fife and Drum. Dryden. *See* Instruments, The.
Fife Tune. John Manifold. BoAV; ExPo; FaFP; GTBS-W; LiTB; LiTL; LiTM; LoGBV; ShBV-3; SiTL; WaaP; WaP
Fifine at the Fair, *sels.* Robert Browning.
Epilogue: "Savage I was sitting in my house, late, lone." BPN
(Householder, The.) LO; NBE
Prologue: "Fancy I had to-day, The." BPN
(Amphibian.) AlDL
Fifteen Acres, The. James Stephens. BoTP; GBV (1952 ed.); PtOT; ShBV-2
Fifteen day of July, The. *See* Fifteenth of July, The.
Fifteen foresters in the Braid alow. Johnie Cock (B *vers.*). *Unknown.* ESPB
"Fifteen men on the dead man's chest." Derelict [*or* The Buccaneers *or* The Dead Men's Song]. Young E. Allison. ABF; AnAmPo; BBV; BLPA; EtS; FaBoBe; FaFP; HBMV; LA; LEAP; MCCG; NeHB; TreFS
Fifteen or twenty feet below. The Anchorage. Pat Wilson. AnNZ
Fifteen Rubaiyat. Omar Khayyám, *tr. fr. Persian by* Edward Fitzgerald. *See* Bird of Time, The.
Fifteen Ships on George's Banks. *Unknown.* BaBo
1536–1936. Emyr Humphreys. MoWP
Fifteenth [*or* Fifteen day] of July, The. Lord Willoughby [*or* Brave Lord Willoughby]. *Unknown.* CoMu; EV-2; LH; TuPP
15th Raga: For Bela Lugosi. David Meltzer. NeAP
Fifteenth Volume, The. Po Chü-i, *tr. fr. Chinese by* Arthur Waley. TrCh
Fifth Choir of Angelicals. Cardinal Newman. *See* Praise to the Holiest in the Height.
Fifth Day. R. D. Fitzgerald. MoAuPo
Fifth Elegy. Alex Comfort. FaBoMo
Fifth from the north wall, The. The Cross of Gold. David Gray. AA
Fifth Ode of Horace, The ("Quis multa gracilis"). Horace. *See* To Pyrrha.
Fifth of May, The—Napoleon. Alessandro Manzoni, *tr. fr. Italian by* William Dean Howells. *Fr.* Ode. CAW
Fifth Philosopher's Song. Aldous Huxley. MBP; MoBrPo (1942 ed.); SiTL
Fifth Watch of the Night, The. Chien T'ang, *tr. fr. Chinese by* Henry H. Hart. ChLP; PoHN
Fifth Wheel. Dorothy Brown Thompson. DDA
Fiftieth Birthday of Agassiz, The. Longfellow. ImOP; LPS-3; OBAV
Manuscripts of God, The, *sel.* MaRV
Fifty Acres. James Larkin Pearson. DDA; NoCaPo
Fifty Faggots. Edward Thomas. EPP; MBP; MoAB; MoBrPo
Fifty leagues, fifty leagues—and I ride, and I ride. D'Artagnan's Ride. Gouverneur Morris, Jr. AA

Fifty, not having expected to arrive here. Journey toward Evening. Phyllis McGinley. GoYe
Fifty Quatrains. "Michael Field." TwCV
"Fifty stories more to fall." Rhyme of Rain. John Holmes. WaKn
Fifty Years, 1863–1913. James Weldon Johnson. BANP; PoFr; PoNe
Fifty Years Spent. Struthers Burt. HBMV; NoCaPo; SBMV
Fig for care, A, why should we spare? *Unknown.* SeCL
Fig for Momus, A, *sel.* Thomas Lodge.
To a Dear Friend Lately Given Over to Covetousness. SiCE
Fig for St. Denis of France, A. St. Patrick of Ireland, My Dear! William Maginn. BOHV; InMe
Fig for those by law protected, A. Drinking Song. Burns. *Fr.* The Jolly Beggars. PoFr; TrGrPo
Fig-tree log I used to be, A. Horace. Satires, I, 8. LaP
Fight, The. John Mitford. *Fr.* The Adventures of Johnny Newcome in the Navy. SG
Fight. *Unknown.* FaFP; LiTG; SiTL
Fight at Dajo, The. Alfred E. Wood. PAH
Fight at Fort Sumter, The. *Unknown.* BIG
(Fight at Sumter, The.) PAH
Fight at Nevadaville, The. *Unknown.* PoOW
Fight at San Jacinto, The. John Williamson Palmer. DD; PaA
(Fight at the San Jacinto, The.) AA; LEAP
Fight at Sumter, The. *Unknown. See* Fight at Fort Sumter, The.
Fight at the Bridge, The. Macaulay. *Fr.* Lays of Ancient Rome: Horatius. MaC; OtMeF
Fight at the San Jacinto, The. John Williamson Palmer. *See* Fight at the Jacinto, The.
Fight in the Centre, The. Macaulay. *Fr.* Lays of Ancient Rome: The Battle of the Lake Regillus. OtMeF
Fight of Faith, The. Anne Askewe. LPS-2
Fight of Paso Del Mar, The. Bayard Taylor. BeLS
Fight of the *Armstrong* Privateer, The. James Jeffrey Roche. PAH
Fight of the Forlorn, The, *sel.* George Darley.
"Bard! to no brave chief belonging." TIP
Fight of the Red Cross Knight and the Heathen Sansjoy, The. Spenser. *Fr.* The Faerie Queene, I, 5. FiP
("Noble heart that harbours virtuous thought, The.") ViBoPo
Fight over the Body of Keitt, The. *Unknown.* PAH
Fight that was no fight is over, The. The Bride. L. A. G. Strong. POTE
Fight the Good Fight. John S. B. Monsell. MaRV; OlF
Fight with a Water-Spirit. Norman Cameron. HaMV
Fight your little fight, my boy. Dont's. D. H. Lawrence. LiTB; LiTM; OxBoLi
Fighter, The. S. E. Kiser. BLPA
Fighting Failure, The. Everard Jack Appleton. HBV; YaD
Fighting-Man, A. Joseph Campbell. OnYI
Fighting McGuire. William Percy French. CenHV
Fighting on the South Frontier. Li Po, *tr. fr. Chinese.* WhP
(Nefarious War, The, *tr. by* Shigeyoshi Obata.) WoL
Fighting Parson, The. Henry Ames Blood. IDAH
Fighting Race, The. Joseph Ignatius Constantine Clarke. AA; BAP; BLPA; DD; DDA; HBV; LHV; MC; OBAV; OnYI; PaA; PAH; PFY; YaD
Fighting South of the Castle. *Unknown, tr. fr. Chinese by* Arthur Waley. AWP; JAWP; PreP; SoV; TrCh; WaaP; WBP
(Fighting South of the Ramparts.) LiTW
Fighting *Téméraire,* The. Sir Henry Newbolt. BBV (1923 ed.); HBV
Fighting Words. Dorothy Parker. InMe; LauV; NAMP
Figure for an Apocalypse. Thomas Merton. CrMA
Figure it out for yourself, my lad. Equipment. Edgar A. Guest. PoToHe (new ed.)
Figurehead, The. Léonie Adams. NP
Figure-Head, The. Crosbie Garstin. EtS; StPo
Figurehead. Dorothy Paul. EtS
Figures in a Nightmare. Leah Bodine Drake. UnW
Figures in the fields against the sky! Poems. Antonio Machado, *tr. by* John Dos Passos. AWP; JAWP; LiTW; WBP
Figurines. Manuel Machado, *tr. fr. Spanish by* Alice Jane McVan. AnSpL-2
Filia Patri. Helen Pinkerton. PtPa
Filial Love. Byron. *Fr.* Childe Harold's Pilgrimage, IV. LPS-1
Filing-cabinet of human lives, A. Apartment House. Gerald Raftery. PoMa
Filipino Hombre, A, *with music. Unknown.* AS
Filius Regis Mortuus Est et Resurexit, *in mod. Eng. Unknown.* TMEV
Fill a glass with golden wine. Echoes, VII. W. E. Henley. POTT; ViBoPo
Fill, comrades, fill the bowl right well. Ohnâwa. John Hunter-Duvar. *Fr.* De Roberval. VA
Fill fill the bowele the lusty wyne will dye. *Unknown.* SeCSL
Fill, fill the cup with sparkling wine. Love and Wine. Hafiz. PeP
Fill, fill the goblet full with sack! Song in a Siege. Robert Heath. OBS
Fill High the Bowl. John Keble. OxBoCh
Fill me a mighty bowl. A Bacchanalian Verse. Robert Herrick. BEL
Fill me, boy, as deep a draught. Temperate Drinking. Anacreon. OnPM
"Fill me this glass—it is antique Venetian." The Toast. Charles Warren Stoddard. CAW
Fill me with sassafras, nurse. Spring Ode. Don Marquis. PC
Fill the bowl with rosy [*or* rosie] wine. The Epicure [*or* To-day Is Ours]. Abraham Cowley. CaAE; EPS; HBV; OBS; TrGrPo
Fill the Bumper Fair. Thomas Moore. HBV
"Fill the Can and Fill the Cup." Asclepiades, *tr. fr. Greek by* F. L. Lucas. GrPE
Fill the cup, and again cry, again, again. To Heliodora. Meleager, *tr. by* Dudley Fitts. LiTW
Fill up, and say, "To Heliodore!" The Cup-Bearer [*or* A Toast to Heliodore]. Meleager, *tr. by* Robert A. Furness. GrR; OxBG
Fill up! fill up!/ The poison-cup. Anacreontic. Theophilus Hunter Hill. NoCaPo
Fill up your glass, O comrade true. The Pioneer. Eugene Field. PoOW
Fill your bowl with roses: the bowl, too, have of crystal. Chiaroscuro; Rose. Conrad Aiken. MAPA
Filled with coquettish art. Pierrot Makes a Song. William Griffith. *Fr.* Loves and Losses of Pierrot. PR
Filled with weariness and pain. Singing My Doubts Away. *Unknown.* BePJ
Filling Station. A. M. Klein. TwCaPo
Filling Station. E. Merrill Root. PoMa
Filling the mind. The Clouds. William Carlos Williams. MoPo
Filmy thread, tangled at either end, A. Life—What Is It? James Newton Matthews. PoP
Filostrato, Il, *abr.* Boccaccio, *tr. fr. Italian by* Hubertis Cummings. PrPoCR
Fin de Siècle. Edmund Vance Cooke. BLPA
Fin de Siècle. Newton Mackintosh. NA
Fin de Siècle. *Unknown.* BOHV
Final Armistice, The. Frank B. Cowgill. OQP; QP-2
Final Autumn. Josephine Winslow Johnson. NAMP; NePA
Final Chorus: "All is best, though we oft doubt." Milton. *See* All Is Best.
Final Chorus: "Bellies bitter with drinking." Archibald MacLeish. *Fr.* Panic. MAP; MoAmPo
Final Chorus: "Who shall contend." Swinburne. *Fr.* Atalanta in Calydon. BPN
Final Chorus from Hellas, The: "Victorious wrong, with vulture scream." Shelley. EnLi-2
Final Chorus from Hellas: "World's great age begins anew, The." Shelley. *See* Chorus: "World's great age begins anew, The."
Final Conflagration, The. *Unknown, tr. fr. Greek by* T. F. Higham. OxBG
Final Dirge. *Unknown. See* Lyke-Wake Dirge, A.
Final Faith, The. George Sterling. CAW
Final, finger-printed page is flipped, The. First Reader (Fifth Reading). Gladys McKee. JKCP (1955 ed.)
Final Green, The. Leah Bodine Drake. NePoAm
Final Inch, The. Emily Dickinson. *See* 'Twas like a maelstrom, with a notch.
Final Lesson, The. Arthur Stringer. MaRV
Final Man, The. Basil McFarlane. PoNe
Final Mystery, The. Sir Henry Newbolt. WGRP
Final Poem. Robert Bhain Campbell. MoPo; NePA
Final secret that two lovers shared, The. Speak This Kindly to Her. Robert Bagg. NePoAm-2
Final Soliloquy, The. Colin Thiele. *Fr.* Burke and Wills. NeLNL
Final Spring. Ralph Gustafson. BoCaPo
"Final Status Never Ascertained." Lloyds Registry. Merrill Moore. MAP; MoAmPo (1942 ed.)
Final Struggle, The. Louis James Block. *Fr.* The New World. PAH
Final Thoughts on the Weather in England during 1953. David Daiches. SiTL
Final Victory, The. Shelley. *See* Demogorgon's Last Words.
Finale. W. E. Henley. VOD
Finale. A. P. Herbert. *Fr.* Perseverance; or, Half a Coronet. InMe
Finale. Douglas Le Pan. TwCaPo
Finale. Christopher Marlowe. *See* End of Dr. Faustus, The.
Finale. James Picot. BoAV
Finale. Carl Sandburg. *Fr.* Slabs of the Sunburnt West. NeMA
Finale. Shakespeare. *See* Our Revels Now Are Ended.
Finality. Winifred Virginia Jackson. BAP

Finality. Pope. *See* Conclusion: "In vain, in vain . . ."
Finality broods upon the things that pass. A Walk by the Charles. Adrienne Cecile Rich. NePoEA
Finches, The. Philip Murray. NePoAm
Find, The. Francis Ledwidge. SP
Find a Way. John Godfrey Saxe. *See* Where There's a Will There's a Way.
Find me a lonely cave. Song. *Unknown.* SeCL
Finding Francesca full of tears, I said. Obituary. Thomas William Parsons. AA; HBV; HBVY
Finding is the first act. Emily Dickinson. MoVE
Finding of Gabriel, The. Longfellow. *Fr.* Evangeline, Pt. II. AA
Finding of Love, The. Robert Graves. TCPD
Finding of the Lyre, The. James Russell Lowell. PECK; PTA-2; TVSH
Finding of the Táin, The. Robert Farren. CoBE
Finding those beams (which I must ever love). Absence. Sir Philip Sidney. SiPS
Finding You. Mary Dixon Thayer. CAW
Fine Clay. Winifred Shaw. MoAuPo
Fine Day, A. Michael Drayton. *Fr.* The Muses' Elysium. BoTP; CG; GN; OTPC; PCH
(Lines: "Clear had the day been.") LoBV
(Sixth Nymphal [*or* Sixt Nimphall], The.) OBS; TuPP
Fine delight that fathers thought, The; the strong. To R. B. Gerard Manley Hopkins. CoBMV; InvP; POTT; PoVP; ViP; ViPP
Fine Flowers in the Valley. *Unknown.* *See* Cruel Mother, The.
Fine gold is here; yea, heavy yellow gold. The House of Colour. Francis Sherman. *Fr.* The Deserted City. CaP; OCL
Fine Knacks for Ladies. *Unknown.* CH; ElL; ElSeCe; LiTB; LoBV; TuPP; ViBoPo
("Fine knacks for ladies, cheap, choice, brave and new!") OBSC
(Honest Autolycus, An.) GTSL
(Pedlar, A.) CaAE; OBEV
Fine Nature, The. Edmund Blunden. BoFr; NeTW
Fine, neat, and curious Mistress Butterfly. Idle Housewife. Samuel Rowlands. SiCE
Fine New Ballad of Cawsand Bay. *Unknown.* *See* Cawsand Bay.
Fine new kirk is finished, wife—the old has had its day, The. In the Old Church. Jean Blewett. CPG
Fine Old English Gentleman, The. *Unknown.* CH; HBV; LPS-3; OnPP
Fine Old English Gentleman, The; New Version. Charles Dickens. CoMu
Fine Rain, The. Shinkichi Takahashi, *tr. fr. Japanese by* Takamichi Ninomiya *and* D. J. Enright. PoLJ
Fine rays of praise my asking rings from her. Bought. Francis Douglas Davison. NeBP
Fine, spruce young Pansa's grown a malcontent. Of Pansa. Everard Guilpin. *Fr.* Skialetheia. ReIE
Fine to taste they are. Aubergines. Ibn Sara. MooP
Fine Work with Pitch and Copper. William Carlos Williams. OxBA
Fine Young Folly. William Habington. *Fr.* The Queen of Aragon, IV, i. OBS
("Fine young folly, though you were.") ElSeCe
(Song: "Fine young folly, though you were.") FaBoEn; MePo
Fine youth Ciprius is more terse and neat, The. In Ciprium. Sir John Davies, *after the Latin of* Martial. ReIE; SiCE; TuPP
Fineen the Rover. Robert Dwyer Joyce. JKCP (1926 ed.); TIP
Finesse be first, whose elegance deplores. Six Poets in Search of a Lawyer. Donald Hall. SiTL
Finest, biggest fish you see, The. *Unknown.* GFA
Finest Fellowship, The. Edgar A. Guest. FAOV
Fingal; an Ancient Epic Poem, *sels.* James MacPherson.
"As a hundred winds on Morven," *fr.* III. BCEP
"As the dark shades of autumn fly," *fr.* II. BCEP
"Cuthullin sat by Tura's wall." EnLi-2
Finger Folk. H. M. Thorp. BoTP
Finger Play ("This little bunny said, 'Let's play' "). *Unknown.* BoTP
Finger Play for a Snowy Day, A. *Unknown.* BoTP
Fingers on the holes, Johnny. A Music Lesson. Alexander Hay Japp. VA
Finigan's Wake. *Unknown.* *See* Finnigan's Wake.
Finis. Waring Cuney. BANP; PoNe
Finis. *Tr. fr. Old Irish by* Robin Flower. GTIV; SiB; TriL
Finis. Walter Savage Landor. *See* On His Seventy-fifth Birthday.
Finis. John McClure. LS
Finis. Sir Henry Newbolt. *See* End, The.
Finis. Eden Phillpotts. LBBV
Finis. James Thomson. *See* Verses Occasioned by the Death of Dr. Aikman.
Finis. Rosamund Marriott Watson. AV
Finis to all the manuscripts I've penned. Finis. *Tr. by* Robin Flower. GTIV; SiB; TriL
Finished Course, The. St. Joseph of the Studium. WGRP
Finished, in Paestum's rose-embowering garden. Nameless and Immortal. Verner von Heidenstam. AnSL
Finite. Power Dalton. HBMV
Finite Reason. Dryden. *See* Reason and Revelation.
Finn on the mountain found the mangled man. The Death of Dermid. Sir Samuel Ferguson. IrPN
Finnegans Wake, *sel.* James Joyce.
Ballad of Persse O'Reilly, The. LiTB; SiTL
Finnigan to Flannigan. Strickland W. Gillilan. *See* Finnigin to Flannigan.
Finnigan's Wake. *Unknown.* OnAP; TrAS, *with music*
(Finigan's Wake.) BLPA
Finnigin to Flannigan. Strickland W. Gillilan. FaBoBe; StPo; TreF; YaD
(Finnigan to Flannigan.) BOHV; HBV
Fionnuala, *sel.* Edmund John Armstrong.
"With heaving breast the fair-haired Eileen sang." TIP
Fionula. Joseph Sheridan le Fanu. *Fr.* The Legend of the Glaive. TIP
Fiorentina. Ernest Myers. OBVV
Fir Forest. Ethel Romig Fuller. PGD
Fir-Tree, The. Edith M. Thomas. OHIP
Fir trees taper into twigs and wear, The. Firwood. John Clare. EG; TrGrPo
Fir'd at first sight with what the muse imparts. The Alps of Poetry [*or* The Heights of Arts]. Pope. *Fr.* An Essay on Criticism, Pt. II. BeR; LiA
Fire, The. William Burford. NePA
Fire, A. Rachel Field. GFA
Fire. Langston Hughes. NP
Fire. Ibn Sara, *tr. fr. Arabic by* A. J. Arberry. MooP
Fire. Merrill Moore. MOAP
Fire. José Moreno Villa, *tr. fr. Spanish by* Eleanor L. Turnbull. CoSP
Fire. Dorothy Wellesley. OBMV
Fire,/ Fire, Lord! Fire. Langston Hughes. NP
Fire, a hawser, bullets and an axe, A. Nikolai Tikhonov, *tr. fr. Russian by* C. M. Bowra. BoRS
Fire and Ice. Robert Frost. AmPP; AnFE; AnNE; APA; CaAE; ChMo; CMP; CoAnAm; CoBMV; CoV; FaFP; GTBS-W; HBMV; IAP; LiTA; LiTM; MAP; MoAB; MoAmPo; MOAP; MoVE; NePA; NP; OnPM; OxBA; PoLFOT; SiTL; TreFS; TrGrPo; TwAmPo; TwP; ViBoPo (1958 ed.); WHA; WoL
Fire and vinegar (fir-logs and vin ordinaire). Lugano, August 1937. H. L. R. Edwards. MoWP
Fire at Night, A. Robert P. Tristram Coffin. TwCV
Fire-Bringer, The, *sels.* William Vaughn Moody.
Pandora's Songs.
"Along the earth and up the sky." GBV; MOAP
"Because one creature of his breath." MOAP
"I stood within the heart of God." AnFE; APA; BAP; CBOV; CoAnAm; GBV; IAP; LBAP; MAP; MoAmPo (1942 ed.); MOAP; OQP; QP-1; QS; WGRP
"Of wounds and sore defeat." BAP; BBV; GBV; HBV; LBAP; MOAP; NV; PC; PFY; PoeMoYo; TCPD
(Lyric from "The Fire-Bringer.") BAV
"Thousand aeons, A, nailed in pain." MOAP
"Too far, too far, though hidden in thine arms." MOAP
Fire-Bringers, The. Lawrence Lee. NeTW
Fire Burial. Edgar McInnis. CaP; OCL
Fire Burns Down My Cottage, A. Tao Yuan-ming, *tr. fr. Chinese by* Yang Yeh-tzu. WhP
Fire burns—'tis chilly when it snows. The Philosophers. Schiller. PoP
Fire Down Below, *with music.* *Unknown.* SoAmSa
Fire! Fire! said the town crier. *Unknown.* OxNR
Fire i' the Flint, The. Lucy Catlin Robinson. AA
Fire in the Heavens [and Fire Along the Hills]. Christopher J. Brennan. CoBE; MM; MoAuPo; NeLNL; OnPM
Fire in the Snow, The. Vernon Watkins. GTBS-W; LiTM (rev. ed.); MoVE
Fire Is in the Flint. Robert Browning. *Fr.* Ferishtah's Fancies, III. VLEP
("Fire is in the flint: true, once a spark escapes.") BPN
Fire is out, and spent the warmth thereof, The. Dregs. Ernest Dowson. BMEP; HBV; LEAP; OBMV; POTT; SeCePo; ViPP; VLEP
Fire is what's precious now. Carol. Alison Boodson. NeBP
Fire-Logs. Carl Sandburg. BAP; NP
Fire-mist and a planet, A. Each in His Own Tongue. William Herbert Carruth. BAP; BBV; BLPA; BTP; CP; DDA; GrCo-1; HBV; LBAP; MaRV; NeHB; OHFP; OQP; PoeMoYo; POT; PoTo; PTA-1; QP-1; ReTS; WBLP; WGRP
Fire of Drift-Wood, The. Longfellow. AmPP (4th ed.); CoV; HBV; IAP; LBAP; OxBA
Fire of fierce and laughing light, A. Burns; an Ode. Swinburne. VLEP

Fire of Frendraught, The. *Unknown.* ESPB (A *and* C *vrs.*); OBB; ViBoFo
Fire of Heaven, The. Tennyson. *Fr.* Idylls of the King: Balin and Balan. EPN
Fire of heaven's eternal ray. Prayer to the Blessed Virgin. Rodriguez del Padrón. CAW
Fire of London, The. Dryden. *Fr.* Annus Mirabilis. BeR, 6 *sts.*; ChTr, *longer sel.*; EV-3, *longer sel.*; FaBoEn, 6 *sts.*
("But ah! how unsincere are all our joys!") SeEP
Fire of Love, The. Charles Sackville. *Fr.* The Amorous Bigot (*by* Thomas Shadwell). LiTL; LPS-1; SeCL
Fire of love was burning, yet so low, The. The Wind of Sorrow. Henry van Dyke. LBAP; PC
Fire on Belmont Street. Donald Davidson. The Tall Men: Epilogue. MAP; MoAmPo (1942 ed.); SPP
Fire on the Hills. Robinson Jeffers. ChMo; CMP; CoV
Fire Pictures. Emma Rounds. MPB
Fire rides calmly in the air. At War. Charles Madge. FaBoMo
Fire Shall Burn before Him, A. Benjamin Francis Musser. PraNu
Fire Ship, The, *with music.* *Unknown.* AmSS
Fire Tenders, The. Grace Noll Crowell. PEDC
Fire that cancels all that is. Burning Love Letters. Howard Moss. HoPM
Fire That Filled My Heart of Old, The. James Thomson. POTT; PoVP
Fire, the daughter of the flint. Fire. Ibn Sara. MooP
Fire, the Rope. Nikolai Tikhonov, *tr. fr. Russian by* Babette Deutsch. LiTW; TrRV
("Fire, a hawser, bullets and an axe, A," *tr. by* C. M. Bowra.) BoRS
(Fire the Noose, The, *tr. by* Jack Lindsay.) RuPo
Fire to see my wrongs for anger burneth, The. The Wronged Lover. Sir Philip Sidney. *Fr.* Arcadia. SiPS
Fire upon the hearth is low, The. In the Firelight [*or* My Mother's Faith]. Eugene Field. AA; MotAn
Fire was furry as a bear, The. Dark Song. Edith Sitwell. *Fr.* Façade. FaBoTw
Fire, water, woman, are man's ruin. A Dutch Proverb. Matthew Prior. CEP
Fire-Worshippers, The. Thomas Moore. *See* Linda to Hafed.
Fireborn Are at Home in Fire, The. Carl Sandburg. MoAmPo (1950 ed.)
Fired Pot, The. Anna Wickham. FaBoTw; TrGrPo (1942 ed.)
Fire-Dragon and the Treasure, The. *Unknown, tr. fr. Anglo-Saxon by* Charles W. Kennedy. *Fr.* Beowulf. AnOE
Fireflies. Grace Wilson Coplen. GFA; UTS
Fireflies. Edgar Fawcett. AnAmPo; BAP; HBV; LBAP
Fireflies. Carolyn Hall. FaPON; GFA; HBMV; HBVY; MPB; PCH; TSW; TSWC; UTS
Fireflies, The, *sel.* Charles Mair.
"How dreamy-dark it is!" BoCaPo
Fireflies, The. Tu Fu, *tr. fr. Chinese by* Henry H. Hart. OnPM; PoHN
Fireflies and the stars our only light, The. The Spinning Heart. John Berryman. LiTM (1946 ed.)
Fireflies are fairies' lights. Fairies' Lights. Alice Wilkins. GFA
Fireflies flitted in those dark spots. A Beautiful Night. Naoyoshi. OnPM
Fireflies in the Corn. D. H. Lawrence. NP; NV
Fireflies in the Garden. Robert Frost. AlDL; PoeMoYo
Fireflies massed upon the palm fronds, The. Buson, *tr. fr. Japanese by* Lois J. Erickson. SoLD
Fire-Flowers. José Maria de Heredia, *tr. fr. French by* Alan Conder. TrFP
Firefly, The. Ogden Nash. SiTL; WhC
Firefly. Elizabeth Madox Roberts. GFA; GoBP; LS; OTPC (1946 ed.); PoRh; SUS; TiPo; UTS
Firefly, The. Taigi, *tr. fr. Japanese by* H. G. Henderson. OnPM
Fire-Fly, The. John Banister Tabb. UTS
Firefly. Edna D. Wood. PCH
Firefly, A/ Flitted by. Ryoto, *tr. fr. Japanese by* Lois J. Erickson. SoLD
Firefly Lights His Lamp, The. *Unknown, tr. fr. Japanese by* William N. Porter. MPB
Firefly Song. Longfellow. *Fr.* The Song of Hiawatha, III. PCD
(Hiawatha's Childhood.) BoTP
Firefly's flame, The. The Firefly. Ogden Nash. SiTL; WhC
Firelight. Heine, *tr. fr. German by* Sir Theodore Martin. CIV
Firelight. E. A. Robinson. ChMo; CMP; InP; NP; PeBoSo
Firelight. Whittier. *Fr.* Snow-bound. AA
("Shut in from all the world without.") LaNeLa
Firelight flickered on the age-old beams, The. At the Ship. R. P. Lister. FiBHP
Fire-lit dining-room grew dark, and there, The. Sly-Boots. Arthur Rimbaud. TrFP
Fireman Save My Child. *Unknown.* *See* No More Booze.
Fireman's Story, The. *Unknown.* PTA-2
Fires. Elizabeth Fleming. BoTP
Fire's good companionable friend, A. The Winter Fire. Mary Howitt. OTPC (1923 ed.)
Fires of Driftwood. Isabel Ecclestone Mackay. CaP; CPG; OCL
Fires of war are quenched, The. Requiem. Thomas Curtis Clark. PEDC
Fireside, The. Nathaniel Cotton. LPS-1
Fireside, The. Whittier. *See* Winter Night.
Fire Side, The; a Pastoral Soliloquy. Isaac Hawkins Browne. *Fr.* The Foundling Hospital for Wit, IV. OBEC
Fireside Kitten, The. Elizabeth J. Coatsworth. CIV
Firetail's Nest, The. John Clare. EnRP
Firewood is bound and wound, The. Bound and Wound. *Unknown.* WhP
Fireworks. Phyllis Reid. DiM
Fireworks at the Redentore. Rob Lyle. PoN
Firing ceased and like a wounded foe, The. Hialmar. Roy Campbell. CoBE; SoV
Firm as young bones, fine as blown spume, still. Paradigm. Babette Deutsch. TrJP
Firm Belief. *Unknown.* PoToHe (new ed.)
Firm, familiar world, The. The Prairie Fire. John G. Neihardt. *Fr.* The Song of Three Friends. TCPD
Firm in the good brown earth. Planting a Tree. Nancy Byrd Turner. YeAr
Firm of Happiness Limited, The. Norman Cameron. FaBoTw
Firm-pillowed on the earth, with head to grass. Mountain Revery. Stanton A. Coblentz. MuM
Firm resolve of Silas Sharp, The. Patience. E. E. Nott-Bower. WhC
Firmament, a dense blue, The. Perfection. Jorge Guillén. AnSpL-2; CoSP
Firs' on table, nex' on de wall. Railroad Bill. *Unknown.* ABF
First a word was fuzzy, and was nothing. Words. Richard Eberhart. NePA
First Aid. Peter Hopegood. NeLNL
First Airing. John E. Donovan. AlBD
First American Congress, The. Joel Barlow. PAH
First American Sailors, The. Wallace Rice. PAH
First and riper world of men and skill, The. Thomas Bastard. TuPP
First and the Last, The. Horatius Bonar. BePJ
First Anniversary, The. John Donne. *See* Anatomy of the World, An.
First Anniversary of the Government under His Royal Highness the Lord Protector, The, *sel.* Andrew Marvell.
"'Tis not a freedom that, where all command." PoFr
First, April, she with mellow showers. The Succession of the Four Sweet Months [*or* The Four Sweet Months *or* July]. Robert Herrick. BoTP; CBPC; FaPON; OTPC (1946 ed.); PCH; YeAr
First Autumn, The. Marshall Schacht. CAG; YT
First Banjo, The. Irwin Russell. *See* Fust Banjo, De.
First Best Christmas Night, The. Margaret Deland. *See* While Shepherds Watched Their Flocks by Night.
First, Best Country, The. Goldsmith. *See* Home.
First Bluebird, The. James Whitcomb Riley. CV
Firstborn, The. Jean Blewett. CPG
First Born. Frances O'Connell Corridan. JKCP (1926 ed.)
Firstborn, The. John Arthur Goodchild. HBV
First Born, The. Oscar Williams. GTBS-W
First born of Chaos, who so fair didst come. Hymn to Light. Abraham Cowley. AtBAP; EPS; EV-2; MeLP; MePo; OBS; SeCV-1; SeEP
First Boston Thanksgiving—July, 1630, The. Hezekiah Butterworth. *See* Thanksgiving in Boston Harbor, The.
First Brutus, The, *sel.* Vittorio Alfieri, *tr. fr. Italian by* Edgar Alfred Bowring.
"What do we hear? What majesty, what force," *fr.* I, ii. PoFr
First Bulb Lights Up, The. Mikhail Prokofyevich Gerasimov, *tr. fr. Russian by* Babette Deutsch. *Fr.* The Electric Poem. TrRV
First Butterfly, The. Henrik Wergeland, *tr. fr. Norwegian by* Charles W. Stork. AnNoLy
First by Andromache the women's wail was led. The Wail for Hector. Homer. *Fr.* The Iliad, XXIV. GrPE
First came into being of speech-dowered men a race of gold. Five Ages of Man. Hesiod. *Fr.* Works and Days. GrR
First came the primrose. A Chanted Calendar [*or* Procession of the Flowers *or* Spring's Procession]. Sydney Dobell. *Fr.* Balder. BoTP; CBPC; DD; GBV; GN; GTSE; HBV; HBVY; OBEV; OTPC; RG; WP
First Cause. Joan Lamburn. DiM
First Chorus, The. George Gascoigne. *Fr.* The Glass of Government. Po
First Christmas, The. Norah M. Holland. ChrBoLe
First Christmas, The. St. Luke, Bible, *N.T.* *See* Adoration of the Shepherds, The.

First Christmas, The. Emilie Poulsson. MW; OHIP; PCH; SDH
First Christmas, The. Keith Preston. DDA
First Christmas, The. *Unknown.* HH; MeMeAg
(Hang Up the Baby's Stocking.) COAH
First Christmas Night of All. Nancy Byrd Turner. PEDC; SDH
First Citizen. James Jeffrey Roche. *See* Washington.
First come down was a raven white, The. Little Matthy Groves. *Unknown.* ABS
First come I. My name is Jowett. Henry Charles Beeching. *Fr.* The Masque of Balliol. CenHV
First comes January. The Farmer's Round. *Unknown.* OTPC (1923 ed.)
First Communion. José Asunción Silva, *tr. fr. Spanish by* Thomas Walsh. CAW
First Concerns. Abbie Huston Evans. NP
First concoction perfited, The. *Unknown.* SeCSL
First cool breeze of autumn, The. Afloat on the Lake. Shen Yü Ch'iu. PoHN
First Corinthians, *sels.* Bible, *N.T.*
Charity, XIII. BPP; EM-1; ShBV-4; StVeCh
(Gospel of Love, The.) OuHeWo
(Greatest of These Is Love.) GrCo-1; TrGrPo, *abr.*
(Greatness of Love, The, *tr. by* James Moffatt.) MaRV
(Love the Indispensable and Crowning Grace.) PG (1955 ed.)
(St. Paul on Charity.) TreF
("Though I speak with the tongues of men . . .") BoFr; BrBE; LO; PreP
Death and the Resurrection of the Dead, XV. EM-1
Death's Conqueror, XV: 20, 21, 53, 55. MaRV
Mystery of Death, The, XV: 51–58. BBV (1951 ed.)
Natural and Spiritual, XV: 44–49. GrCo-1
Many Parts, One Body, XI: 12–27. *Tr. by* Edgar J. Goodspeed. GrCo-1
Spiritual Gifts, XII: 1–XIII: 13. WoL
First Corncrake. John Hewitt. NeIP
First Cycle of Love Poems (I–V). George Barker. MoPo
Sels.
My Joy, My Jockey, My Gabriel, V. MoAB; MoBrPo (1950 ed.); MoPW
(Love Poem.) NeBP
"Then like the ship at rest in the bay," IV.
(Love Poem.) FaBoMo
First Dandelion, The. Walt Whitman. ADAH; APW; CBOV; NePA; TSW; TSWC
First Day, The. Christina Rossetti. Monna Innominata, II. EnLi-2; EPP; FaBoBe; HBV; LiTL; LO
("I wish I could remember that first day.") EmBrPo; TCEP; ViPo
First day he had gone, The. A Space in the Air. Jon Silkin. NePoEA; TrJP
First day in the month of May, The. The King of Triolets. Jacques Ranchin. LiA
First Day of Christmas, The. *Unknown.* *See* Twelve Days of Christmas, The.
First Day of Creation, The. Milton. *Fr.* Paradise Lost, VII. OxBoCh
First day of spring in the year ninety-three, The. Reynard the Fox. *Unknown.* OnYI
First Day of Teaching. Bonaro W. Overstreet. TrPWD
First Day of the First Week, The. Joshua Sylvester. *Fr.* Du Bartas: His First Week or Birth of the World. Po
First day of the month of May, The. Rondel. Charles d'Orléans. FoS
First day of Yule have we in mind, The. Make We Mirth for Christes Birth [*or* The Twelve Days of Christmas]. *Unknown.* AnEC; TMEV
First day she passed up and down through the Heavens, The. Laura Waits for Him in Heaven. Petrarch, *pr. tr. by* Synge. *Fr.* Sonnets to Laura: To Laura in Death. OBMV; TwCV
First-Day Thoughts. Whittier. AmPP; CoV; IAP; PreP
First day when Christ was born, The. Nowell, el, el, el, el. *Unknown.* AnEC
First day's night had come, The. Emily Dickinson. AmPP (4th ed.); LiTA; LiTM (rev. ed.); OxBA
First Departure. Frances Frost. SiSoSe
First did I fear, when first my love began. Licia, XX. Giles Fletcher. SiCE; TuPP
First Division Marches, The. Grantland Rice. DDA; PaA; YaD
First Dream, *sel.* Sister Juana Inés de la Cruz, *tr. fr. Spanish by* Samuel Beckett.
"But Venus first." AnMP
First drink a health, this solemn night. Hands All Round. Tennyson. PoFr
First Duan, The: The Coming of Deirdre, *sel.* John Todhunter.
Fate of the Sons of Usna, The. TIP
First Easter, The. St. Luke, XXIII: 54–56, XXIV, Bible, *N.T.* EOAH
First Elegy. Hamish Henderson. ChMP
First (entitled to the place), The. The Bishop among the Plotters. Charles Churchill. *Fr.* The Duellist. BeR
First Epistle of John, *sel.* Bible, *N.T.*
Love, Hate, Compassion, II: 9–IV: 20, *abr.* BoFr
First Epistle of the First Book of Horace Imitated, The, *sel.* Pope.
Ten Per Cent; Then as Now. BeR
First Epistle of the Second Book of Horace [Imitated], The. Pope. CEP; PtP
(To Augustus.) EiPP; GEPC
Sels.
Court of Charles II. OBEC
Ideals of Satire, The. FiP
Poet's Use, The. OBEC
("Of little use the man," *longer sel.*) EV-3
Pope on Dryden. BeR
First, erected ironworks in a spiry hollow. Charles Madge. *Fr.* Poem by Stages. BoSA
First faint dawn was flushing up the skies, The. Yellow Warblers. Katharine Lee Bates. NLK (1947 ed.); SBMV
First Fathers, The. Robert Stephen Hawker. OBVV
First Fig. Edna St. Vincent Millay. AmP; FaFP; InP; PC
(My Candle.) OtMeF
(My Candle Burns at Both Ends.) SiTL
First Flight. Carol Coates. BoCaPo (1943 ed.)
First Flight. Robert P. Tristram Coffin. PoMa
First Food, The. George Sterling. SBMV
First Footsteps. Swinburne. EmBrPo; GrCo-1; NeHB
First, for effusions due unto the dead. Upon His Sister in Law. Robert Herrick. SeEP
First Friend, The. Kipling. *Fr.* Just-so Stories. MPB
(Playing Robinson Crusoe.) PECK
First Frost. Edwin Curran. HBMV; TSW; TSWC
First Fruits in 1812. Wallace Rice. GA; MC
(Firstfruits in 1812.) PAH
First Garden, The. Frank Oliver Call. CPG
First Geography. Gladys McKee. JKCP (1955 ed.)
First get out the map and look at the country. The Subject of the Bishop's Miracle. John Philip. BoAV
First glad token of the Spring is here, The. Four Sonnets, II. Thomas S. Jones, Jr. SBMV
First good joy that [*or* our] Mary had, The. The Twelve Good Joys [*or* Joys Seven]. *Unknown.* OBB; SDH
First Grandchild. M. Whitcomb Hess. JKCP (1955 ed.)
First gray smoke of daylight blurs, The. Sunrise. Rowena Bennett. TiPo (1959 ed.)
First Grief, The. Felicia Dorothea Hemans. *See* Child's First Grief, The.
First halt. They heard within a sugar patch. John Hunter-Duvar. *Fr.* The Emigration of the Fairies. CaP
First he appeared in the realm inanimate. The Progress of Man. Jalal ed-Din Rumi. PeP
First he danced a solemn measure. Hiawatha's Wedding-Feast. Longfellow. *Fr.* Song of Hiawatha, XI. PEOR
First hour was a word the color of dawn, The. Spring Morning—Santa Fé. Lynn Riggs. TBM
First I am frosted. Mary Austin. *Fr.* Rhyming Riddles. TiPo
First, I detest the Spartans most extremely. Aristophanes. *Fr.* The Acharnians. GrPo
First I salute this soil of the blessed, river and rock! Pheidippides. Robert Browning. MW; PoVP
First, I saw a landscape fair. "Barry Cornwall." *Fr.* A Vision. OBRV
First I shall trace and show in argument. Primitive Man. Moschion. OxBG
First Impressions. Alfred Grant Walton. PoToHe (new ed.)
First in a carriage. *Unknown.* OxNR
First in the fight, and first in the arms. Zollicoffer. Henry Lynden Flash. BlG; PAH; SPP
First in the North. The black sea-tangle beaches. The Journey. Edwin Muir. MoVE
First in the World. Paul Eluard, *tr. fr. French by* Wallace Fowlie. MiCF
First it was a pretty flower, dressed in pink and white. *Unknown.* OTPC (1946 ed.)
First It Was Singing. Jon Silkin. NePoEA
First joy through eye and limb. First Joy. Vernon Watkins. ChMP
First king was Pharamond, The; after him came. Kings of France. Mary W. Lincoln. BLPA
First Kiss, The. Thomas Campbell. *See* Freedom and Love.
First Kiss, The. Norman Gale. VA
First Kiss, The. Theodore Watts-Dunton. *Fr.* The Coming of Love. HBV; VA
First Kiss of Love, The. Byron. HBV
First lambs have come, late snowfall to the hill. The Fox. Ian Serraillier. POTE
First Lamp, The. Pien Chih-lin, *tr. fr. Chinese.* WhP
First, last, and dearest. From Metastasio. Christina Rossetti. DiM
First Lay of Gudrun, The. *Unknown, tr. fr. Icelandic by*

William Morris *and* Eirikur Magnússon. *Fr.* The Elder Edda. AWP; JAWP; WBP
("Home They Brought Her Warrior Dead," *tr. by* Henry Adams Bellows.) PaOS
First Lord of the Admiralty [*or* First Lord's Song], The. W. S. Gilbert. *See* When I Was a Lad.
First Love. Byron. *See* 'Tis Sweet.
First Love. Charles Stuart Calverley. BOHV; FiBHP; InMe; LauV
First Love. Thomas Campion. OxBoLi
("Silly boy, 'tis full moon yet . . .") LO; SiCE
First Love. John Clare. ChTr; EnLoPo
First Love. Charles Gullans. NePoEA
First Love. Laurie Lee. ChMP
First Love. Toson Shimazaki, *tr. fr. Japanese by* Takamichi Ninomiya *and* D. J. Enright. PoLJ
First Love. W. B. Yeats. A Man Young and Old, I. TwP
First Love Remembered. Dante Gabriel Rossetti. BPN; POTT; PoVP; VLEP
First Maccabees, *sels.* Bible, Apocrypha.
Dirge: "Her house is become like a man dishonored," II: 8-14. TrJP
Great Mourning, I: 25-28. TrJP
Judas Maccabeus, III: 1-9. TrJP
First meridian, new with light, The. Academy. Sister Mary Jeremy. JKCP (1955 ed.)
First Miracle. Genevieve Taggard. HBMV
(Gladness.) NV
First month[s] of his absence, The. Song. Alun Lewis. ChMP; LiTM; WaaP
First Morning of the Second World, The. Delmore Schwartz. FiMAP
First Mother. Vivian Yeiser Laramore. MotAn
First mules in America, The. Ever Since. Elizabeth J. Coatsworth. SiSoSe
First Night, The. Isolde Kurz, *tr. fr. German by* Herman Salinger. TwGV
First Night, The. Jules Laforgue, *tr. fr. French by* William Jay Smith. AnFP
First Night Alone. Mark Van Doren. MOAP
First night when I come home, as drunk as I could be. Three Nights Drunk. *Unknown.* OuSiCo
First Note, Simple, The; the Second Note, Distinct. Conrad Aiken. Preludes to Attitude, X. LiTA; TwAmPo
First Nowell [the Angel Did Say], The. *Unknown.* AnEC; ChrBoLe; EV-2; LiTB; OlF; OTPC (1946 ed.); SDH; TreFS; ViBoPo; YaCaBo, *with music*
First O Songs for a Prelude. Walt Whitman. MDAH
(Manhattan Arming.) SoV
First o the second o the third o, The. An Autobiography. Bairam at Tunisie. LiTW
First of April, The. Mortimer Collins. ADAH
First of April, The. William Hone. PoRL
First of April, The. Geoffrey Johnson. PoRL
First of April, some do say, The. All Fools' Day [*or* April Fool's Day]. *Unknown.* BoTP; PCH; PoRL; SiSoSe
First of May, The. A. E. Housman. Last Poems, XXXIV. TCPD
First of the Emigrants, The, *with music. Unknown.* ShS
First, of the Heliconian Muses be my song. Religion. Hesiod. *Fr.* Theogony. GrPE
First Olympionique: To Hiero of Syracuse. Pindar. *See* For Hiero, Tyrant of Syracuse.
First on the list is Washington, Virginia's proudest name. Our Presidents—a Memory Rhyme. Isabel Ambler Gilman. PTA-2
First or Last. Thomas Hardy. ChMo; CMP; VLEP
First or Last? Margaret Veley. VA
First Pathways. Sidney Royse Lysaght. OBVV
First Philosopher's Song. Aldous Huxley. AWP; HBMV; InPo; JAWP; WBP
First pledge our queen this solemn night. Hands All Round. Tennyson. BPN
First Poem, The. Clifford Gessler. MuM
First Proclamation of Miles Standish, The. Margaret Junkin Preston. MC; PAH; YaD
First Pythian Ode of Pindar, The. Pindar, *tr. fr. Greek by* Arthur S. Way. Pythian Odes, I. WoL
First Quest, The. Joseph Rodman Drake. *Fr.* The Culprit Fay. AA
(Fay's Departure, The, *shorter sel.*) GN
First Rain. Zoë Akins. HBMV; PoeMoYo
First Reader (Fifth Reading). Gladys McKee. JKCP (1955 ed.)
First retainer, The. A Marriage. Robert Creeley. NeAP
First rise after a low. Rules of the Road. *Unknown.* SoAmSa
First Robin, The. Lilian Leveridge. CaP; OCL
First Samuel, *sels.* Bible, *O.T.*
"And when Saul saw David go forth against the Philistine," XVII: 55-XVIII: 5. LO
David and Goliath, XVI, XVII: 1-51. TreFS
Hannah's Song of Thanksgiving. II: 1-10. AWP
(Song of Hannah, The.) LiTW
Saul, David, and Jonathan, XVI: 15-XXIV: 20, *abr.* BoFr
First Satire of the Second Book of Horace Imitated, The, *sel.* Pope.
Mob, The. BeR
First scattering rain on the Polish cities, The. 1 September 1939. John Berryman. NeTW
1st September 1939. W. H. Auden. *See* September 1, 1939.
First Settler's Story, The. Will Carleton. IHA; PTA-1
First shall the heavens want starry light. A Fancy [*or* Love's Protestation]. Thomas Lodge. *Fr.* Rosalynde. ACP; EIL; GoBC; LoBV; OBSC; SiCE
First shot was fired to Wagnerian music, The. Laocoon. Don Gordon. WaaP
First Sight. Christopher Marlowe. *See* It Lies Not in Our Power to Love or Hate.
First Sight of Her and After. Thomas Hardy. PoEL-5
First Skylark of Spring, The. Sir William Watson. VA
First Smile of Spring. Théophile Gautier, *tr. fr. French by* Alan Conder. TrFP
First Snow. Marie Louise Allen. TiPo
First Snow. Ivy O. Eastwick. TiPo
First Snow. Charles Erskine Scott Wood. TBM
First snow fell on the hills last night, The. The Laurentians. Arthur S. Bourinot. OCL
First Snowfall. Giosuè Carducci, *tr. fr. Italian by* Asa Hughes. LiTW
First Snowfall [*or* Snow-Fall], The. James Russell Lowell. AA; AnNE; BLPA; BTP; FaBoBe; GFA; HBV; IAP; LPS-1; MCCG; NeHB; PCD; PEOR; PIR; PTA-1; REAL; TCAP; TreF; WBLP
"Snow had begun in the gloaming, The," *sel.* FaPON
First Snowfall, The. Charles Warren Stoddard. PraNu
First Song, The. Richard Burton. AA
First Song. Galway Kinnell. NePoAm
First Song: "Doubt you to whom my Muse these notes intended." Sir Philip Sidney. *See* Astrophel and Stella: First Song.
First Song-Sparrow, The. *Unknown.* PCH
First Song, Sung by Two Amazons, The. Jasper Mayne. *See* Time.
First Spousal, The. Coventry Patmore. The Unknown Eros, II, ii. OBVV
First Spring Day, The. Christina Rossetti. BPN
First Spring Flowers. Mary Woolsey Howland. LPS-1
First Spring Morning. Robert Bridges. BoTP; YeAr
First stands the lofty Washington. Our Presidents. *Unknown.* BLPA
First station off on a cold road to the country. The Chickadees. John Hay. NePoAm-2
First Step, The. Andrew Bice Saxton. AA
First Story, The. Nathalia Crane. TSWC
First streaks of dawn are faint, The. The Story of a Dream. Jun Yamamura. PoLJ
First Swallow, The. Charlotte Smith. CG; DD; HBV; OTPC
(Swallow, The.) LPS-2
First take a willow bough. How to Make a Whistle. *Unknown.* ADAH
First Temptation, The. Milton. *Fr.* Paradise Regained, I. OxBoCh
First Thanksgiving, The. Arthur Guiterman. DD; TOAH
First Thanksgiving, The. Clinton Scollard. MC; PAH
(First Thanksgiving Day.) DD
First Thanksgiving, The. Nancy Byrd Turner. *See* First Thanksgiving of All.
First Thanksgiving Day, The. Alice Williams Brotherton. DD; OHIP; TOAH
First Thanksgiving Day, The. Margaret Junkin Preston. HiLiAm; MC; PAH
First Thanksgiving Day. Clinton Scollard. *See* First Thanksgiving, The.
First Thanksgiving of All. Nancy Byrd Turner. FaPON; SiSoSe
(First Thanksgiving, The.) YeAr
First that we saw of the high-tone tramp, The. Broncho versus Bicycle. *Unknown.* SCC
First the artillery groaned beyond the Channel. My Sister Helen. Drummond Allison. FaBoTW
First, the middle, and the last, The. In Search of the Picturesque. William Combe. *Fr.* Dr. Syntax in Search of the Picturesque. OBRV
First the rain and then the wind. Rules of the Road. *Unknown.* SoAmSa
First, then, I ask thee that I fain would learn. Refugee. Euripides. *Fr.* Phoenician Maidens. GrR
First the two eyes, which have the seeing power. Sight. Sir John Davies. LoBV (2d ed.)
First the valley where the houses. Hydro Works. J. R. Hervey. AnNZ
First there was the lamb on knocking knees. Sonnets, III. Dylan Thomas. LiTM
First, there's the Bible. The Hundred Best Books. Mostyn T. Pigott. BOHV; InMe
First they dress in green. *Unknown.* OTPC (1946 ed.)

First thing, I think, is a keen sense, The. Juan Belmonte, Torero. Donald Finkel. NePoEA
First thing that I remember was Carlo tugging away, The. Asleep at the Switch. George Hoey. BeLS; PTA-1
First Things First. W. H. Auden. NePoAm-2
First Three, The. Clinton Scollard. MC; PAH
First Three-Man's Song, The. Thomas Dekker. *See* O, the Month of May.
First time he came to see me, The. Naomi (Omie) Wise (B *vers.*). *Unknown.* BaBo
First time he kissed me, he but only kissed. Sonnets from the Portuguese, XXXVIII. Elizabeth Barrett Browning. BLPA; BPN; DiM; FaBoBe; HBV; LPS-1; NeHB; RiBV; VA; ViBoPo; ViPo
First time I saw little Weevil he was on the western plain. The Ballet of the Boll Weevil (A *vers.*). *Unknown.* ViBoFo
First time I saw you, The. Peasant and Geisha Songs. *Unknown.* LiTW
First time I went to Frisco, I went upon a spree, The. Off to Sea Once More [*or* Jack Wrack]. *Unknown.* ABF; ShS, *vers.* I
First time that I dreamed, we were in flight, The. The Lesson. W. H. Auden. FaBoMo
First time that the sun rose on thine oath, The. Sonnets from the Portuguese, XXXII. Elizabeth Barrett Browning. BPN; LPS-1; ViBoPo; ViPo
First time the emperor Han, The. The Word. Allen Upward. *Fr.* Scented Leaves from a Chinese Jar. NP
First Tooth, The. Charles *and* Mary Lamb. OTPC (1923 ed.)
First Tooth, The. William Brighty Rands. HBV; HBVY
First train leaves at six P.M., The. The Poppy-Land Limited Express. Edgar W. Abbott. BOL
First Travels of Max. John Crowe Ransome. MAP; MoAmPo
First Trousers. Susie Dawson Brown. FAOV
First True Gentleman, The. Thomas Dekker. *Fr.* The Honest Whore. BCEP
("Patience [my lord], why 'tis the soul of peace.") LEAP; ViBoPo, *longer sel.*
First, two white arms that held him very close. Act V (Midnight). Thomas Bailey Aldrich. PFY
First Vision, The. Tadhg Dall O'Huiginn, *tr. fr. Late Middle Irish by* the Earl of Longford. AnIL
First Voyage of John Cabot, The. Katharine Lee Bates. CV; MC; PAH
First Warm Days. Edwin Denby. GTBS-W; LiTM; PeBoSo
First was a gray-beard Peter, The. The Three Peters. Molly Michaels. RIS
First was the world as one great cymbal made. Musick's Empire. Andrew Marvell. NBE
First went the holy poets, two on two. Francis Thompson. *Fr.* Ode for the Diamond Jubilee of Queen Victoria, 1897. PtP
First when Maggie was my care. Whistle o'er the Lave o't. Burns. BSV; CEP; EBSV; TCEP
First William the Norman, then William his son. History Lesson. *Unknown.* OxNR; RIS
First Woman's Lament. Brenda Chamberlain. NeIP
(Lament: "My man is a bone ringèd with weed.") NeBP
First Words before Spring. Louis Untermeyer. MAP
First world-sound that fell upon my ear, The. Sea Longings. Thomas Bailey Aldrich. SN
First World War. Kenneth Slade Alling. NePoAm
First Year, The, *sel.* E. J. Scovell.
"Before she first had smiled or looked with calm." FaBoMo
First you bite your fingernails. American Rhapsody (4). Kenneth Fearing. MoAmPo; PoLFOT; TrGrPo (1942 ed.)
First young lady all around in town. Swing on the Corner. *Unknown.* TrAS
First Zeppelin, The. James S. Tippett. GFA
Firstborn. *See* First born.
Firste stok, fader of gentilesse, The. Gentilesse. Chaucer. AWP; MaPo
Firwood. John Clare. TrGrPo
("Fir trees taper into twigs and wear, The.") EG
Fish, The. Elizabeth Bishop. ExPo; FiMAP; GoTP; LiTM (rev. ed.); MiAP; MoAB; MoAmPo (1950 ed.); NeMA; NePA; OnAP; Po; TrGrPo (rev. ed.); ViBoPo (1958 ed.)
Fish, The. Rupert Brooke. GTML; MM
Fish! Ch'en Te Chien, *tr. fr. Chinese by* Henry H. Hart. PoHN
Fish, The. Paul Eluard, *tr. fr. French by* Glauco Cambon. OnPM
Fish, The. Ralph Gustafson. BoCaPo (1948 ed.)
Fish, The. Marianne Moore. AnFE; APA; CoAnAm; MAP; MoAB; MoAmPo; MoVE; OnAP; OxBA; TwAmPo
Fish. W. W. E. Ross. BoCaPo (1948 ed.); PeCV
Fish;/ Nor art in this. Moron. S. G. Leonard. MoWP
Fish and Bird. Rosemary Brinckman. BoTP
Fish Answers, A. Leigh Hunt. *See* Fish, the Man, and the Spirit, The.
Fish are folded, The. The Root. Francis Maguire. JKCP (1926 ed.)
Fish-Cart, The. J. Redwood Anderson. PoTo; TCPD
Fish Crier. Carl Sandburg. MOAP; OxBA; WoL
Fish-Day. Mazie V. Caruthers. CIV
Fish dripping, A. Fish. W. W. E. Ross. BoCaPo (1948 ed.); PeCV
Fish (fly-replete, in depth of June). Heaven. Rupert Brooke. AlDL; AnFE; EPN; EV-5; ExPo; GTBS-D; GTBS-W; HoPM; LiTB; LiTM; MBP; MM; MoBrPo; PoE; PoRA; POTE; SeCeV; ShBV-4; SiTL; TOP; TwCV; WaKn; WGRP
Fish Food. John Wheelwright. AnFE; CoAnAm; LiTA; OnAP; TwAmPo
Fish has laid her succulent eggs. Vicissitudes of the Creator. Archibald MacLeish. NePA
Fish-Hawk, The. John Hall Wheelock. AnAmPo; BLA; BLV; EtS; HBMV; LA; NV; PoeMoYo
Fish in River. *Unknown, tr. fr. Anglo-Saxon by* Charles W. Kennedy. *Fr.* Riddles. AnOE
Fish in the Unruffled Lakes. W. H. Auden. AtBAP; ChMo; ChMP; GTBS-D; MaPo; NeMA
(Song: "Fish in the unruffled lakes.") MoAB; MoBrPo (1950 ed.)
Fish Peddler ("The fish man chats with the passers by"). Mei Yao Ch'en, *tr. fr. Chinese by* Kenneth Rexroth. OnPC
Fish Story, A. Henry A. Beers. BOHV
Fish, the Man, and the Spirit, The. Leigh Hunt. ATP; ChTr; EnRP; EPN; ES; OBEV (new ed.); PeBoSo; PoEL-4; RO; SeCePo; ViBoPo
Sels.
Fish to Man. MoShBr
(Fish Answers, A.) FiBHP
To Fish. PIAE
Fish took a notion, A. Tip-Toe Tale. Dixie Willson. GFA
Fish wade, The/ through black jade. The Fish. Marianne Moore. AnFE; APA; CoAnAm; MAP; MoAB; MoAmPo; MoVE; OnAP; OxBA; TwAmPo
Fish, when he's exposed to air, The. Autres Bêtes, Autres Mœurs. Ogden Nash. NAMP
Fisher, The. Goethe, *tr. fr. German by* Charles T. Brooks. LPS-3
Fisher, The. Roderic Quinn. BoAV
Fisher folk recount that in the south, The. The Lord of the Island. Stefan George. AnGP
Fisher, in your bright bark rowing. The Fisherman. *Unknown.* FaPON
Fisher was casting his flies in a brook, A. The Microscopic Trout and the Machiavelian Fisherman. Guy Wetmore Carryl. WhC
Fisher-lad, A (no higher dares he look). Eclog. III. Phineas Fletcher. *Fr.* Piscatorie Eclogues. SeCV-1
Fisher-Maiden, The. Heine. *See* Thou Lovely Fishermaiden.
Fisher-maids at Shika, The. No Spare Time. Ishikawa Kimiko. OnPM
Fisherman, The. Abbie Farwell Brown. EtS; FaPON; GaP
Fisherman, The. "Barry Cornwall." CG
Fisherman, The. Leonidas of Tarentum, *tr. fr. Greek by* Andrew Lang. AWP
Fisherman, The. Li Po, *tr. into English by* James Whitall *fr. the Chinese-to-French translation of* Judith Gautier. ChLP
Fisherman, The. David McCord. TiPo (1959 ed.)
Fisherman, The. Jay Macpherson. PeCV
Fisherman. Ou-yang Hsiu, *tr. fr. Chinese by* Kenneth Rexroth. OnPC
Fisherman. Sacheverell Sitwell. AtBAP
Fisherman, The. Su T'ung-po, *tr. fr. Chinese by* Yu Minchuan. WhP
Fisherman, The. *Unknown, tr. fr. Portuguese by* Anne Higginson Spicer. FaPON
Fisherman, The. W. B. Yeats. CoBMV; NP; ShBV-4
Dark under Froth, *sel.* LiA
Fisherman goes out at dawn, The. The Fisherman. Abbie Farwell Brown. EtS; FaPON; GaP
Fisherman Husband. Brenda Chamberlain. *See* Second Woman's Lament.
Fisherman lived on the shore, A. How a Fisherman Corked Up His Foe in a Jar. Guy Wetmore Carryl. PoMS
Fisherman of the Moon. José Gorostiza, *tr. fr. Spanish by* H. R. Hays. TwSpPo
Fisherman on Toast, The. Edward Abbott Parry. BoN
Fisherman Speaks, A. Scharmel Iris. ChIP
Fisherman's Blunder Off New Bedford, Massachusetts. Annemarie Ewing. NePoAm-2
Fisherman's Chant, The. Sir F. C. Burnand. BOHV
Fisherman's Hut, The. Theocritus. *See* Fishermen, The.
Fisherman's Hymn, The. Alexander Wilson. AA; EtS; LEAP
Fisherman's Light, The. Susanna Moodie. BoCaPo
Fisherman's Luck. W. W. Gibson. EtS
Fisherman's Prayer. Ethel Romig Fuller. DDA
Fisherman's Son. Charles Bruce. CaP
Fisherman's Song. Joanna Baillie. *Fr.* The Beacon. EBSV; EV-3
Fisherman's Song, The. Thomas D'Urfey. ALV

Fisherman's Song. Li Yu, *tr. fr. Chinese by* Hsiung Ting. WhP
Fishermen, The. Night at Yen Chou. Chou Shang Ju. PoHN
Fishermen, The. Theocritus, *tr. fr. Greek by* Charles Stuart Calverley. Idyll XXI. AWP
Fisherman's [*or* Fishermen's] Hut, *sel., tr. by* Henry Harmon Chamberlin. GrR; OxBG
Fishermen, The. Emile Verhaeren, *tr. fr. French by* Jethro Bithell. WoL
Fishermen, The. Whittier. EtS; TVSH, *abr.*
Fishermen say, when your catch is done, The. The Sea Wolf. Violet McDougal. FaPON; MPB
Fishermen will relate that in the South. The Lord of the Isle. Stefan George. AWP; JAWP; WBP
Fishermen's Hut, The. Theocritus. *See* Fishermen, The.
Fishermen's Weather. *Unknown. See* When the wind is in the east.
Fishers. Albert Reginald Gold. ChIP; OQP; QP-1
Fishers, The. Josephine Preston Peabody. StJW
Fishers. Edwin Meade Robinson. LHV
Fishers, The. Brian Vrepont. MoAuPo
Fisher's Apology, A. Arthur Johnstone, *tr. fr. Latin.* GoTS
Fisher's Boy, The. Henry David Thoreau. AA; AnAmPo; AnNE; ChTr; LA; MOAP; OBAV; TCAP
Fisher's Cottage, The. Heine. *See* Twilight.
Fishers in the Night. Beulah May. ChIP
Fisher's Life, The. *Unknown.* ChTr; EtS
Fisher's Widow, The. Arthur Symons. HBV; PoMa
Fisher-Wife's Song, The. Crofton Uniacke McLeod. BOL
Fishes, The. Mrs. Motherly. SAS
Fishes, The. *Unknown. See* Boston Come-All-Ye, The.
Fishes. Humbert Wolfe. *Fr.* Kensington Gardens. RIS; StaSt
Fishes and beasts and winged birds should devour each other. Hesiod. *Fr.* Works and Days. GrCo-1
Fishes' Heaven. Rupert Brooke. *See* Heaven.
Fishes, secure within the ocean, play! Piscatores Vocat. Richard Crashaw. Epigrammata Sacra, I, 84. LaP
Fishes swim in water clear. *Unknown.* OxNR
Fishes, swimmers, boats. The Fish. Paul Eluard. OnPM
Fishing. Edgar A. Guest. NLK
Fishing. Dorothy Wellesley. OBMV
Fishing boats out on the deep sea. Hopes and Memories. Giovanni Pascoli. OnPM
Fishing Fleet, The. Lincoln Colcord. HBMV; VOD
Fishing, if I, a fisher, may protest. De Piscatione. Thomas Bastard. TuPP
Fishing in the Australian Alps. Ernest G. Moll. WhC
Fishing in the Wei River. Po Chü-i, *tr. fr. Chinese by* Arthur Waley. TrCh
Fishing Pole, The. Mary Carolyn Davies. FaPON; GFA; OTPC (1946 ed.)
Fishing Song, A. William Brighty Rands. CenHV
Fishwife sits by the side, The. Ireland, Mother of Priests. Shane Leslie. JKCP
Fishy-fishy in the brook. *Unknown.* GoTP
Fishy pool, The/ With willow-herb was edged. Frederick William Faber. *Fr.* Sir Lancelot. EnSW
Fists in my holed pockets, I went along. Gipsying. Arthur Rimbaud, *tr. by* Alan Conder. TrFP
Fists in torn pockets I departed. My Bohemia. Arthur Rimbaud, *tr. by* Louise Varèse. AnFP
Fit of Rhyme [*or* Rime] against Rhyme [*or* Rime], A. Ben Jonson. InvP; NBE; PoEL-2; PoFS; SeCV-1; TuPP
Fit Only for Apollo. Francis Beaumont. *See* Shake Off Your Heavy Trance.
Fit theme for song, the sylvan maid. Madam Hickory. Wilbur Larremore. AA
Fitz-Greene Halleck. Whittier. LPS-3
Fitz-James and Roderick Dhu. Sir Walter Scott. *Fr.* The Lady of the Lake, V. EPP; LPS-2
(Roderick Dhu, *shorter sel.*) OBRV
(Roderick Dhu and Fitz-James; a Noble Action, *shorter sel.*) EV-4
Five, The. Swift. *See* Riddle, A: "We are little airy creatures."
Five Ages, The. Hesiod, *tr. fr. Greek by* Jack Lindsay. *Fr.* Works and Days. LiTW; OxBG
(Five Ages of Man, *tr. by* Arthur S. Way.) GrR
Five-and-thirty black slaves. The Key-Board. Sir William Watson. HBV
Five Arabic Verses in Praise of Wine. *Unknown, tr. fr. Arabic by* Hartwig Hirschfeld. TrJP
Five Bells. Kenneth Slessor. BoAV; MoAuPo; OnHM; PoRA; SeCePo
Five Best Doctors, The. O. S. Hoffman. PoToHe (new ed.)
Five Carols for Christmastide. Louise Imogen Guiney. ISi
Five colors lead to blindness, The. *Unknown, tr. fr. Chinese.* Tao Teh Ching, XVII. WhP
Five-Day Rain, The. Denise Levertov. NeAP
Five Days and Nights. Vera Inber, *tr. fr. Russian by* Jack Lindsay. RuPo
Five days we have been cruising, nor once have furled. Under Sail. Maximilian Alexsandrovich Voloshin. TrRV
Five Degrees South. Francis Brett Young. EtS
Five dollars a day is a white man's pay, way. A Dollar and a Half a Day. *Unknown.* TrAS
Five English Poets. Dante Gabriel Rossetti.
John Keats, 4. BPN; EmBrPo; EPN; PoVP; PtP
Percy Bysshe Shelley, 5. BPN; EmBrPo; PoVP; PtP
Samuel Taylor Coleridge, 3. BPN; EmBrPo; PoVP; PtP
Thomas Chatterton, 1. BPN; EmBrPo; PoVP; PtP
(Two English Poets.) BMEP
William Blake, 2. BPN; EmBrPo; PoVP; PtP
(Two English Poets.) BMEP
Five Epigrams. Donald Hall. NePoAm-2
Five Eyes. Walter de la Mare. PoC; UTS
Five fearless knights of the first renown. The First American Sailors. Wallace Rice. PAH
Five-fingered Maple, The. Kate Louise Brown. BoTP
Five geese deploy mysteriously. Bas-Relief. Carl Sandburg. CrMA; MOAP
Five Grand Odes, *sel.* Paul Claudel, *tr. fr. French by* John Hay.
"Blessed be your name, my God." OnHM
Five harsh black birds shining in bronze came crying. A Japanese Vase Wrought in Metals. Marjorie Allen Seiffert. NP
Five Joys, *in mod. Eng.* ("Hail to thee, Mary, maiden bright"). *Unknown.* TMEV
Five Joys, The ("I may sing of a may"). *Unknown.* AnEC
Five Kernels of Corn. Hezekiah Butterworth. DD; MC; PAH
Five kings rule o'er the Amorite. The Ballad of the Battle of Gibeon. G. K. Chesterton. YT
Five kittens in the haymow. Kittens. Catherine Parmenter. CIV
Five Little Brothers. Ella Wheeler Wilcox. BoTP
Five Little Chickens. *Unknown.* GFA; GoTP; MeMeAg; OTPC (1946 ed.); SAS
(Chickens, The.) FaPON; GoBP; MoShBr; RAR, *sl. abr.;* UTS
(Wishes.) BoTP
Five Little Fairies, The. Maud Burnham. HBVY; OTPC (1946 ed.); PCH; PPL
Five little monkeys. The Monkeys and the Crocodile. Laura E. Richards. BoChLi; FaPON; SUS; TiPo; UTS
Five Little Princesses, The. Laura E. Richards. GaP
Five [*or* Four] little pussy-cats invited out to tea. The Cats' Tea-Party. Frederic Edward Weatherly. MeMeAg; OTPC (1946 ed.); RAR; SAS; TiPo
Five Little Sisters Walking in a Row. Kate Greenaway. MoShBr
(Five Sisters.) BoTP
Five little squirrels. *Unknown.* RIS
Five Lives. Edward Rowland Sill. AnAmPo; AnFE; AnNE; APA; CoAnAm; LA; OnAP
Five long clangs from the house-clock nigh. The Shiver. Thomas Hardy. InPo
Five long years. A Lament. Ch'en Yü Hui. PoHN
Five men over the parapet, with a one-star loot in charge. The Patrol. J. H. Knight-Adkin. MCCG
Five minutes, five minutes more, please! Bedtime. Eleanor Farjeon. TiPo
Five mites of monads dwelt in a round drop. Five Lives. Edward Rowland Sill. AnAmPo; AnFE; AnNE; APA; CoAnAm; LA; OnAP
Five o'Clock. Richard K. Arnold. PtPa
Five oxen, grazing in a flowery mead. On a Seal. Plato. AWP; JAWP; WBP; WoL
Five Peas on a Barrelhead. Lew Sarett. PoMa
Five Pilgrims. Chaucer. *See* Canterbury Tales, The: Prologue.
Five Prayers. Blanche Edith Baughan. BoAu
Five Reasons [for Drinking], The. Henry Aldrich. *See* Reasons for Drinking.
Five Roses. Jacinto Verdaguer, *tr. fr. Spanish by* Thomas Walsh. CAW
Five score years the birds have flown. Failure. Orrick Johns. PoMa
Five Serpents. Charles Burgess. NePoAm-2
Five Sisters. Kate Greenaway. *See* Five Little Sisters Walking in a Row.
Five Smooth Stones. Stella Benson. MBP; MoBrPo (1942 ed.)
Five soldiers fixed by Mathew Brady's eye. Looking into History. Richard Wilbur. PoLFOT
Five Souls. W. N. Ewer. AOAH; MaRV; OQP; QP-2
Five Students, The. Thomas Hardy. ExPo; PoEL-5
Five summer days, five summer nights. The Blue-Fly. Robert Graves. MoVE
Five thousand followed him for fish and loaves. Calvary. Hugh Robert Orr. ChIP
Five thousand souls are here, and all are bounded. Troopship in the Tropics. Alun Lewis. WaP
Five thousand years have fled, let us suppose. The Archaeologist of the Future. Leonard Bacon. WhC
Five Times Zero. Donald F. Drummond. PtPa
Five Towns on the B. and O. Carl Sandburg. OnPM; WoL

Five Unmistakable Marks, The. David Jones. MoWP
Five Visions of Captain Cook. Kenneth Slessor. BoAV
"Two chronometers the captain had," *sel.* NeLNL
(Two Chronometers.) MoAuPo; SeCePo
Five War Epitaphs. Kipling. *See* Epitaphs of the War.
Five Wines. Robert Herrick. BOHV
Five workmen hired here to shovel dirt. Workmen. Herbert Morris. NePoAm-2
Five years ago (says story) I loved you. Inconstancy [*or* Love]. Abraham Cowley. EPS (1942 ed.); PoFS
Five years have passed; five summers, with the length. Lines Composed a Few Miles above Tintern Abbey [*or* Tintern Abbey]. Wordsworth. BCEP; BEL; BoLiVe; BPN; BrBE; CBOV; ChER; CoBE; EM-2; EmBrPo; EnL; EnLi-2; EnLit; EnLP; EnRP; EPN; EPP; ERP; EV-3; ExPo; FiP; GEPC; GoTL; HBV; InP; LiTB; LoBV; LPS-2; MaPo; MCCG; NBE; OAEP; OBRV; OuHeWo; PIAE; PoE; PoEL-4; PoFS; PreP; REAL; ReaPo; SeCePo; SeCeV; TCEP; TOP; TreFS; TrGrPo; TriL; TwHP; TwP; TyEnPo; UnPo (1st ed.); WHA
Five Years Old. Lysbeth Boyd Borie. SiSoSe
Fix'd were their habits; they arose betimes. Jonas Kindred's Household. George Crabbe. *Fr.* Tales. FaBoEn
Flag, The. George H. Boker. FOAH; HH
Flag, The. Henry Lynden Flash. FOAH; MC; PEOR
Flag, The. Edward A. Horton. HH
Flag, The. Julia Ward Howe. FOAH
Flag, The. Lucy Larcom. DD; FOAH; HH
Flag, The. Henry C. Potter. FOAH
Flag, The. James Jeffrey Roche. PaA; PAH
Flag, The. "M. W. S." FOAH
Flag and Cross. Alfred J. Hough. FOAH
Flag Goes By, The. Henry Holcomb Bennett. AA; BBV; DD; FaBoBe; FaFP; FaPON; FOAH; GN; HBV; HBVY; HH; LEAP; NeHB; OHFP; PaA; PCD; PECK; PEDC; PGD; PoRL; PSO; PTA-1; SiSoSe; TiPo (1952 ed.); TreF; TVSH; WBLP; YaD
Flag Mottoes. *Various authors.* FOAH
Flag o' My Land. T. A. Daly. HH
Flag of England, The. Rudyard Kipling. *See* English Flag, The.
Flag of Old England, The. Joseph Howe. BoCaPo
Flag of Our Union Forever, The. George Pope Morris. FOAH
Flag of Peace, The. Charlotte Perkins Gilman. NeHB; OQP; QP-2
Flag of Stars, The. Grace Ellery Channing. FOAH
Flag of the *Constellation,* The. Thomas Buchanan Read. EtS; FOAH; PaA
Flag of the fearless-hearted. Our Flag. Margaret E. Sangster. PEDC; PTA-2
Flag of the Free. Walter Taylor Field. HH
Flag of the Free. *Unknown.* OlF
Flag of the heroes who left us their glory. Union and Liberty. Oliver Wendell Holmes. FOAH; OHIP
Flag Play, *an exercise. Unknown.* FOAH
Flag Song, *an exercise.* Sarah F. Archer. FOAH
Flag Song. Harriet Prescott Spofford. FOAH
Flag Song. Lydia Avery Coonley Ward. MPB; OTPC (1946 ed.); PoRL; YeAr
(Song for Flag Day, A.) HH; PEDC
Flag Speaks, The. Emily Greene Balch. PGD
Flag We Fly, The. Aileen Fisher. YeAr
Flags. *Various authors.* FOAH
Flags of war like storm-birds fly, The. The Battle Autumn of 1862. Whittier. BlG; MC; PAH
Flags on Fifth Avenue, The. Christopher Morley. VOD (1931 ed.)
Flail. Power Dalton. HBMV
Flake of cloud was trembling cast, A. To a Texas Primrose. Olive Tilford Dargan. LS
Flakes of snow, with sails so white. Little Ships in the Air. Edward A. Rand. TVSH
Flame, The. Ezra Pound. CoAnAm
Flame/ rising the sooner to die. Dance. Jaime Torres Bodet. AnCL
Flame against the Wind. Florence Wilson Roper. MuM
Flame and Adventure, *sel.* Annie Charlotte Dalton.
"Ah, in the long procession of our life." CPG
Flame and Clarity. Georges Duhamel, *tr. fr. French by* Elizabeth Selden. BoFr
Flame and Snow. Mellin de Saint-Gelais. *See* Sonnet of the Mountain, The.
Flame at the core of the world. Song. Arthur Upson. HBV
Flame-flower, day-torch, Mauna Loa. Lines to a Nasturtium. Anne Spencer. CDC; PoNe
Flame-Heart. Claude McKay. BANP; CDC; PoNe
Flame in my heart is kindled by the might of the morn's pure breath, A. The Creed of My Heart. Edmond Gore Alexander Holmes. UnW
Flame is spent, I can no more, The. The Man. Helen Hay Whitney. AV
Flame of a man's imagination should be organic with his body, The. On Poetry. Louis Dudek. BoCaPo (1948 ed.)
Flame of the spirit, and dust of the earth. This Is the Making of Man [*or* The Making of Man]. Priscilla Leonard. MaRV; OQP; QP-2
Flame on the poppies and a gray mist weaves. Song of the Fire. Sister M. Maura. SaFP
Flame out, you glorious skies. The Dead Heroes. Isaac Rosenberg. MBP; MoBrPo; TrGrPo (1942 ed.); TriL
Flame Song. Nancy Byrd Turner. MW
Flame-throated robin on the topmost bough. A Robin. Robert Bridges. CMP
Flame went flitting through the wood, A. The Scarlet Tanager. Mary Augusta Mason. AA
Flame-wing'd seraph spake a word, The. Poeta Nascitur. Thomas Ashe. VA
Flames. E. Merrill Root. PoMa
Flames of Death, The. Pope. *See* Pheasant, The.
Flaming Banners. Bhartrihari, *tr. fr. Sanskrit by* Arthur W. Ryder. OnPM
Flaming Heart, The. Richard Crashaw. CAW; GoBC; LiTB; LoBV; MeRV; OxBoCh; PoEL-2; ReEn; SeCePo; SeCL; SeCV-1
Sels.
"Leave her that; and thou shalt leave her." PraNu
"Live here, great heart; and love and die [*or* dy] and kill." OBS; RiBV
(Upon the Book and Picture of the Seraphicall Saint Teresa.) AtBAP
"Live in these conquering leaves; live all the same." EV-2; LiA
"O heart! the equal poise of Love's both parts." EG; ElSeCe; KN; TrGrPo; TwHP
"O sweet incendiary! show here thy art." EPS; PoFS; SeEP
"O Thou undaunted daughter of desires!" CoBE; WHA
(Saint Teresa.) BLV
(Upon the Book and Picture of the Seraphical Saint Teresa.) BCEP; OBEV; PtP
Flaming Terrapin, The, *sels.* Roy Campbell.
Fall of Satan, The. BoSA
"For when the winds have ceased their ghostly speech." MM; TwCV
Invocation to the African Muse. BoSA
"Maternal Earth stirs redly from beneath." MBP; MoBrPo
Noah. BoSA
"Out of the Ark's grim hold." AlDL
Flaming Torches. Horace, *tr. fr. Latin by* Thomas Creech. *Fr.* Odes, IV, 11. BeR
Flamingo, The. Lewis Gaylord Clark. BOHV; NA
Flamingoes. Harriet Sennett. BLA
Flamingos, The. Rainer Maria Rilke, *tr. fr. German by* Jessie Lemont. OnPM
Flamingo's Egg, A. Terence Heywood. BoSA
Flammonde. E. A. Robinson. AmPP; AnAmPo; BLV; BoLiVe; ChMo; CMP; CoBA; IAP; InP; LA; LiTA; LiTM (rev. ed.); MAPA; NV; OBAV; PoLFOT; SBMV; SeCeV; TOP; TwP; UnPo (1st ed.)
Flanders Grave, A. Nathaniel Nathanson. POT
Flanders Poppies. Ian Colvin. AOAH
Flanders Roses. Nikolai Tikhonov, *tr. fr. Russian by* Jack Lindsay. RuPo
Flannan Isle. W. W. Gibson. CH; GoTL (1949 ed.); GTML; MoVE; OBVV; PCN; PoRA; ShBV-2; ShGoBo; StPo; TOP
Flap, flap, the captive bird in the cage. The Scholar in the Narrow Street. Tso Ssu. AWP; JAWP; TrCh; WBP
Flap, flap, you curtain in front of our bed! The Curtain of the Wedding Bed. Wife of Liu Hsün. TrCh
Flared down from broken cloud the calipered light. Winfield Townley Scott. Bermuda Suite, V. FiMAP
Flash. Hazel Hall. TBM
Flash Crimson. Carl Sandburg. MAP; MoAmPo
Flash forth, thou sun. An Easter Carol. Christina Rossetti. PCH
Flash Frigate, The, *with music. Unknown.* AmSS; SG
Flash in the Gulf. Jules Laforgue, *tr. fr. French by* Alan Conder. TrFP
Flash of harmless lightning, A. The Humming-Bird. John Banister Tabb. SN
Flash of light across the night, A. Ulric Dahlgren. Kate Brownlee Sherwood. BlG; PAH
Flash—The Fireman's Story. Will Carleton. BBV; PoRL
Flashing of an arc that bright and briefly, The. Flying Fish. Katherine Kelley Taylor. EtS
Flash-Lights. Mary Aldis. BAP; NP
Flat down I fell, and with all reverence. Thomas Sackville. *Fr.* Induction to "The Mirror for Magistrates." EPP
Flat Lands. Carl Sandburg. MOAP
Flat on the grey steel bulkhead arch her curves. Pin-up Girl. Louis O. Coxe. WaP
Flat River Girl. *Unknown. See* Jack Haggerty.
Flathouse Roof, The. Nathalia Crane. TCAP; YT
Flattered Lightning Bug, The. Don Marquis. *Fr.* Archy and Mehitabel. StPo

Flatterer, like a wrestler, stoopeth low, A. Of a Flatterer. John Davies of Hereford. SiCE
Flatterers are the worms who prey upon. Human Worms. Anaxilas. OxBG
Flattering Grandma. *Unknown.* PEOR
Flaunt of the sunshine I need not your bask. Song of Myself, XL. Walt Whitman. TrGrPo
Flavia the least and slightest toy. Written on [*or* in] the Leaves of a [White] Fan. Francis Atterbury. SeCL; SeEP
Flavia's a Wit, has too much sense to pray. Characters of Women: Flavia, Atossa, and Cloe. Pope. *Fr.* Moral Essays, *fr.* Epistle II. OBEC
Flavor the speaking of this one. Not to Forget Miss Dickinson. Marshall Schacht. LiTM
Flaw, A. "Michael Field." BLA
Flawless His Heart. James Russell Lowell. *Fr.* Ode for the Fourth of July, 1876. MC; PAH
Flax. Ivan Alekseyevich Bunin, *tr. fr. Russian by* Babette Deutsch *and* Avrahm Yarmolinsky. AWP; JAWP; WBP; TrRV, *rev. tr. by* Babette Deutsch
Flax Flower, The. Mary Howitt. PRWS
Flea, The. John Donne. ATP; EnLP; HoPM; LiTB; LiTG; LiTL; MePo; Po; ReaPo; ReEn; ReIE; SeCV-1; SiTL; TrGrPo; TuPP; TwP
Flea, The. Roland Young. WaKn; WhC
(Happy Bounding Flea, The.) SiTL
Flea and a fly flew up in a flue, A. *Unknown.* WhC
Flea and a fly got caught in a flue, A. The Flea and the Fly. *Unknown.* FaPON
Flea and a fly [*or* Fly and a flea] in a flue, A. Limerick. *Unknown.* GoTP; LiBL; LiL; LiTG; PoeMoYo; TiPo (1959 ed.); TSWC; WhC
Fleas, The. Augustus De Morgan. *See* Great Fleas.
Flecknо, an English Priest at Rome. Andrew Marvell. SeEP
Fled foam underneath us and round us, a wandering and milky smoke. The Island of Sleep. W. B. Yeats. *Fr.* The Wanderings of Oisin. TIP
Fled is the blasted verdure of the fields. James Thomson. *Fr.* The Seasons: Autumn. OAEP
Fled is the swiftness of all the white-footed ones. Elegy. Joseph Auslander. MAP; MoAmPo (1942 ed.); NP; TrJP
Fled now the sullen murmurs of the north. Robert Bloomfield. *Fr.* The Farmer's Boy. LPS-2
Fledgling Bard and the Poetry Society, The, *much abr.* George Reginald Margetson. BANP
Fledgling Robin, A. Leonard Feeney. JKCP (1926 ed.)
Fledglings. Thomas Lake Harris. AA
Flee fro the prees, and dwelle with sothfastnesse. Balade de Bon Conseyl [*or* Ballad of Good Counsel *or* Truth]. Chaucer. ACP; AWP; BCEP; BEL; BLV; CAW; CBOV; EM-1; EPP; EV-1; GoBC; GrCo-1; LEAP; LiTG; MaPo; MyFE; PoLi; TrGrPo; TyEnPo; ViBoPo
Flee fro' the Press. Matthew Arnold. *Fr.* The Scholar Gipsy. LH
"Flee from Love," you warn me? Lost labour! How should I. Labour Lost. Archias. GrPE
Flee from the crowd and dwell with truthfulness. Ballade of Good Counsel, *mod.* Chaucer. BLV; TrGrPo
Fleece, The, *sels.* John Dyer.
"Ah gentle shepherd, thine the lot to tend," *fr.* Bk. I. PoEL-3
British Commerce, *fr.* Bk. IV. OBEC
English Weather, *fr.* Bk. I. CoEV; OBEC
(English Fog, The.) TrGrPo
Nation's Wealth, A, *fr.* Bk. III. OBEC
Wool Trade, The, *fr.* Bk. III. OBEC; SeCePo
Fleecy mantle which of late conceal'd, The. Winter—Thaw. Thomas Gisborne. *Fr.* Walks in a Forest. EnSW
Fleecy white waters. Sea Music. Theodore Harding Rand. CPG
Fleeing I go from death. Song. Emilio Prados. CoSP
Flees he tok and goth to Bote, The. John Gower. *Fr.* Confessio Amantis: Jason and Medea. AtBAP
Fleet and fair. Gazelles and Unicorn. John Gray. *Fr.* The Long Road. ChTr
Fleet astronomer can bore, The. Vanity [*or* Vanitie]. George Herbert. EPS (1942 ed.); MePo; MeRV; ReEn; SeCV-1
Fleet at Santiago, The. Charles E. Russell. MC; PAH
Fleet, fleet and few, ay, fleet the moments fly. Two Sonnet-Songs, II. Frank T. Marzials. VA
Fleet Street. Arthur Adams. BoAu
Fleet Street. Shane Leslie. LBBV; OnYI; PoeT
Fleet Street Eclogues, *sels.* John Davidson.
"Patchwork sunshine nets the lea, The."
(From "Good Friday.") BSV
Prescription for a Spring Morning, A. CBPC
(From "Fleet Street Eclogues." LEAP
Fleet Street! Fleet Street! Fleet Street in the morning. A Song of Fleet Street. Alice Werner. HBV
Fleet with flags arrayed, A. A Ballad of the French Fleet. Longfellow. AA; HBV; MC; PAH
Fleeting Restlessness. Juana de Ibarbourou, *tr. fr. Spanish by* Elizabeth du Gué Trapier. LiTW
Fleeting Return. Juan Ramón Jiménez, *tr. fr. Spanish by* Eleanor L. Turnbull. TeCS
Fleeting Years, The. Wu Mou Ch'ien, *tr. fr. Chinese by* Henry H. Hart. PoHN
Fleetly hath pass'd the year. The seasons came. January 1, 1828. Nathaniel Parker Willis. BAV
Fleming Helphenstine. E. A. Robinson. TwP
Flemish Madonna, A. Charles Wharton Stork. BAP; HBMV
Flerida and Don Duardos. Gil Vicente, *tr. fr. Spanish by* Aubrey F. G. Bell. TeCS
Flesh, The. Tiroux Yamanaka, *tr. fr. Japanese by* Katue Kitasono. LiTW
Flesh and the Spirit, The. Anne Bradstreet. AmP; AmPP; AnAmPo; AnFE; APA; APW; CoAnAm; IAP; LA; LiTA; MOAP; NePA; OxBA
Flesh, I have knocked at many a dusty door. Sonnet. John Masefield. GTSL; LEAP; LiTM; MBP; MoBrPo; SeCePo
Flesh is sad, alas, The! and all the books are read. Sea-Wind. Stéphane Mallarmé, *tr. by* Arthur Symons. AWP; JAWP; VLEP; WBP
Flesh is sad, alas, The! and I have read all the books. Sea Breeze. Stéphane Mallarmé, *tr. by* Kate Flores. AnFP
Flesh is sad, The, alas, and I've read all the books. Sea Winds. Stéphane Mallarmé, *tr. by* Patricia Terry. OnPM
Flesh is sad but there are books unread, The. Charles Madge. *Fr.* Poem by Stages. BoSA
Flesh Is Weak, The. Stanton A. Coblentz. PoMa
"Flesh that hath life eat not," Pythagoras said. Alexis, *tr. fr. Greek by* F. A. Paley. GrPo
Flesh will heal and pain will fade. Claire Richcreek Thomas. PoToHe (new ed.)
Fletcher, though some call it thy fault, that wit. Upon the Dramatick Poems of Mr. John Fletcher. William Cartwright. OBS
Fletcher, to thee, wee doe not only owe. Upon Mr. John Fletcher's Playes. Edmund Waller. PtP
Fleur de Lys. Rayner Heppenstall. WaP
Flickering of incessant rain. Irradiations, V [VII]. John Gould Fletcher. AnFE; APA; MAP; MAPA; NePA; PFE; TwAmPo
Flies. Dorothy Aldis. UTS
Flies. Aleksey Nikolayevich Apukhtin, *tr. fr. Russian by* Sir Cecil Kisch. WaL
Flies, The. Merrill Moore. AnAmPo; AnEnPo; LA; MOAP
Flies in the buttermilk, skip to my Lou. Skip to My Lou. *Unknown.* TrAS
Flies, like the blackest of thoughts, through the day of all quiet deprive me. Flies. Aleksey Nikolayevich Apukhtin. WaL
Flies walk on ceilings. Flies. Dorothy Aldis. UTS
Flight. Madison Cawein. AA
Flight, The. C. Day Lewis. *Fr.* A Time to Dance. FaBoMo; MoVE, *longer sel.*
(Flight to Australia, *longer sel.*) ShBV-3
Flight. Babette Deutsch. NeTW
Flight. Edwin Wiley Fuller. *Fr.* The Angel in the Cloud. NoCaPo
Flight. Hazel Hall. AnAmPo; LA; MAP; MoAmPo (1942 ed.)
Flight, The. Lloyd Mifflin. AA; AnAmPo; HBV; LA; LBMV; LEAP
Flight, The. Theodore Roethke. *Fr.* The Lost Son. TrGrPo (rev. ed.)
Flight, The. Sara Teasdale. BAP; ChMo; CMP; HBMV; LEAP; MAP; MoAmPo; NP; TBM; WHA
Flight. Harold Vinal. FaPON; GA; MPB; WaKn
Flight. Lawrence Whistler. POTE
Flight, The. George Edward Woodberry. NV
Flight from Glory, A. Eugene Lee-Hamilton. BMEP; VA
Flight from Granada. *Unknown, tr. fr. Spanish by* John Gibson Lockhart. AnSpL-1
Flight from the Convent, The. Theodore Tilton. AA
Flight into Darkness. Ralph Gustafson. PeCV
Flight into Egypt, The. W. H. Auden. *Fr.* For the Time Being. OAEP (2d ed.); OxBA
Flight into Egypt, The. Longfellow. *Fr.* Christus; a Mystery, Pt. II. APW; OBVV
Flight into Egypt, The. Francis Sylvester Mahony. LPS-2
Flight into Egypt, The. Peter Quennell. LiTB; LiTM
Flight into Egypt, The. *Unknown.* *Fr.* Cursor Mundi. CoBE; EPP
Flight of Crows. William Ellery Leonard. FAOV
Flight of doves, with wanton wings, A. To Melvin Gardner: Suicide. John Charles McNeill. NoCaPo
Flight of Fondest Hopes, The. Thomas Moore. *Fr.* Lalla Rookh. BCEP
Flight of Love. Shelley. *See* Lines: "When the lamp is shattered."
Flight of Malzah, The. Charles Heavysege. *Fr.* Saul, a Drama. VA

Flight of Satan, The. Milton. *Fr.* Paradise Lost, II. PoF
Flight of Swans. Robinson Jeffers. CoV
Flight of the Arrow, The. Richard Henry Stoddard. AA
(Arrow, The.) MaRV
Flight of the Birds, The. Edmund Clarence Stedman. GN
Flight of the Bucket, The. Kipling. PA
Flight of the Duchess, The. Robert Browning. VLEP
Sels.
Gypsies. PCH
North Country, The. PCH
Flight of the Earls, The. *Unknown, tr. fr. Early Modern Irish by* Robin Flower. AnIL
Flight of the Geese, The. Sir Charles G. D. Roberts. *Fr.* Songs of the Common Day. BLA; PeCV; SN; VA
Flight of the Goddess, The. Thomas Bailey Aldrich. HBV; LBAP
Flight of the Heart, The. Dora Read Goodale. AA
Flight of the Roller-Coaster. Raymond Souster. PeCV
Flight of the Spirit. Felicia Dorothea Hemans. ES; UnW
Flight of the War-Eagle, The. Obadiah Cyrus Auringer. AA
Flight of the Wild Geese. William Ellery Channing. APW; PFY
Flight of Wild Geese, A. Harold Stewart. MoAuPo
Flight of Youth, The. Richard Henry Stoddard. AA; BAP; HBV; IAP; LBAP; LEAP; MaRV; OBAV; OQP; QP-2
(It Never Comes Again.) LPS-1
(There Are Gains for All Our Losses.) TCAP
Flight Shot, A. Maurice Thompson. AA; AnAmPo; LA; OBAV
Flight to Australia. C. Day Lewis. *See* Flight, The.
Flight to the City. William Carlos Williams. AnAmPo; LA
Flighting for Duck. William Empson. MoPo
Fling forth the triple-colored flag to dare. The Need of the Hour. Edwin Markham. PaA
Fling it from mast and steeple. Our Flag. Margaret Elizabeth Sangster. PEDC; PTA-2
Fling out the banner! let it float. The Banner of the Cross. George Washington Doane. BePJ
Fling yourself here, O traveller, in the lush meadow-grasses. Siesta. *Unknown.* GrPE
Flinging its arc of silver bubbles, quickly shifts the moon. Down the Mississippi, III: Full Moon. John Gould Fletcher. ChMo; CMP; LiTA; MOAP; NP; SPP; TCAP
Flint and the Steel, The. Tomás de Iriarte, *tr. fr. Spanish.* BoChLi
Flint-hearted Stoics, you whose marble eyes. Francis Quarles. *Fr.* Emblems. EPS (1936 ed.)
Flintlike, her feet struck. Hardcastle Crags. Sylvia Plath. GoYe
Flirt, The. Asclepiades, *tr. fr. Greek by* J. M. Edmonds. GrR
("Hermione/ was roguishly," *tr. by* William Wallace *and* Mary Wallace.) GrPo
Flirt, The. W. H. Davies. EnLoPo
Flirtation. Ibn Zaydun, *tr. fr. Arabic by* A. J. Arberry. MooP
Flit here from out the cold. The First Butterfly. Henrik Wergeland. AnNoLy
Flitch of Dunmow, The. James Carnegie, Earl of Southesk. HBV; VA
Flitting, The, *sels.* John Clare.
I Dwell on Trifles, *br. sel.* RO
"I've left my own old home of homes." EV-4; OBRV
Flitting arrow, speeding onward. Rima II. Gustavo Adolfo Bécquer. *Fr.* Rimas. AnSpL-2
Flitting of the Fairies, The. Jane Barlow. *Fr.* The End of Elfintown. TIP
Flo was fond of Ebenezer. The Tides of Love. T. A. Daly. InMe; LauV; WhC; YaD
Float aloft, thou stainless banner! Hymn to the National Flag. Margaret Junkin Preston. FOAH
Float, little bark, down yonder stream. Drifting. John Francis O'Donnell. IrPN
Floating, a floating, A. The Night Bird [*or* A Myth]. Charles Kingsley. GN; OTPC (1946 ed.); VA
Floating Barque, The. *Unknown, tr. fr. Urkrainian by* Florence Randal Livesay. CPG
Floating Island, The. Ruth Miller. BoSA
Floating Island, The, *sel.* William Strode.
Song: "My limbs I will fling," *fr.* I, iii. SeCL
("My limbs I will fling.") CenL
Floating on the gentle Yadkin in an olden-time canoe. Hunting Muscadines. John Henry Boner. NoCaPo
Flock at Evening, The. Odell Shepard. HBMV; OBAV
Flock of crows high from the Northland flies, A. Autumn. Detlev von Liliencron. AWP; JAWP; WBP
Flock of keys I had feeding out of my hand, A. Improvisation. Boris Pasternak. Po; TrRV
Flock of merry singing-birds were sporting in the grove, A. The O'Lincon [*or* O'Lincoln] Family. Wilson Flagg. HBV; HBVY; LPS-2; OTPC; SN
Flock of sheep that leisurely pass by, A. To Sleep [*or* Sleep]. Wordsworth. BLV; BoLiVe; BPN; EM-2; EnRP; EPN; EPP; ERP; GBV; GEPC; GTBS; GTBS-D; GTBS-W; GTSE; GTSL; HBV; InPo; LPS-3; MyFE; OBRV; PC; PeBoSo; PIAE; PoFS; ShBV-4; TrGrPo; ViBoPo
Flock of winds came winging from the North, A. The Roaring Frost. Alice Meynell. AlDL; NLK (1947 ed.)
Flodden. Sir Walter Scott. *Fr.* Marmion, VI. BHV; BSV; NBE, *shorter sel.;* PoFr, *abr.*
(Battle, The.) EnRP; ERP, *longer sel., abr.;* PoEL-4
(Flodden Field.) LiA, *shorter sel.;* LPS-2, *abr.*
(Flodden; the Attack.) LH
(Flodden; the March.) LH
(Flodden; the Last Stand.) EV-4, *abr.;* LH
Flodden Field. *Unknown.* ESPB
Floella. *Unknown. See* Jealous Lover, The.
Flood. Ethel Anderson. NeLNL
Flood. Mary Grant Charles. GoYe
Flood. James Joyce. MBP; MoBrPo
Flood, The. Ovid, *tr. fr. Latin by* Dryden. *Fr.* Metamorphoses, I. ChTr
Flood. Tamiko Yamamuro, *tr. fr. Japanese by* Lois J. Erickson. SoLD
Flood. T'ao Ch'ien, *tr. fr. Chinese by* Arthur Waley. AlDL
(Twelve Poems, 12.) TrCh
Flood, The. Andrew Young. ChMP
Flood of Years, The. Bryant. AA; IAP; LPS-3; MOAP
Flood Tide. Stephen Vincent Benét. PFY
Flood Tide. Hermann Hagedorn. PC
Flood Tide. Marjorie Alice Miller. NLK (1947 ed.)
Flood-tide below me! [*or* Flood-tide of the river, flow on!] I see [*or* watch] you face to face! Crossing Brooklyn Ferry. Walt Whitman. AmPo; AmPP; ATP; CoBA; CoV; IAP; LiTA; TCAP
Flooded fold of sarcenet, A. The End of Desire. Hugh McCrae. BoAV; MoAuPo
Floods and gales. Et Cetera. Dee Walker. GoYe
Floods Clap Their Hands, The. Psalms, XCVIII, Bible, *O.T.* TrGrPo
(O Sing unto the Lord a New Song.) TrJP
(Psalm XCVIII.) TriL
(Sing unto Jehovah.) BLRP
(Sing unto the Lord.) StaSt
Floods of tears well from my deepest heart, The. Elegy. Immanuel di Roma. TrJP
Flood-Time on the Marshes. Evaleen Stein. AA
Flooer o the cypress-tree. Tuscan Folk Songs, 5. *Unknown, tr. into Scottish by* Edwin Morgan. LyPI
Floor Is Dirty, The. Edward Field. NeAP
Floorless Room, The. Gelett Burgess. *See* I Wish That My Room Had a Floor.
Flora. *Unknown, tr. fr. Latin by* John Addington Symonds. LyMA
Flora hath been all about. Pastoral I. Nicholas Breton. *Fr.* The Passionate Shepherd. TuPP
Flora, take this flower; it means my love. Suscipe Flos Florem. *Unknown. Fr.* Carmina Burana. LaP
Flora's Lamentable Passion. *Unknown.* CoMu
Florence. Walter Savage Landor. SeCePo
Florence; Design for a City. Elizabeth Jennings. HaMV
Florence MacCarthy's Farewell to His English Love. Aubrey Thomas De Vere. IrPN
Florence Vane. Philip Pendleton Cooke. AA; HBV; SPP
Florent and the Loathly Hag. John Gower, *tr. fr. Middle English by* Muriel Bowden. *Fr.* Confessio Amantis. MeEV
Florida. Elizabeth Bishop. AmP
Florida Road Workers. Langston Hughes. GoSl; MAP; MoAmPo
Florin to the willing guard, A. The Rosy Bosom'd Hours. Coventry Patmore. EnLoPo
Florine. Thomas Campbell. BSV
Florist Rose, The. Robert Graves. AtBAP
Florist Shop, The. Rachel Field. MW
Flos Aevorum. Richard Le Gallienne. BMEP; LBAP
Flos Florum. Arthur Joseph Munby. VA
Flos Lunae. Ernest Dowson. OBMV; ViPP
Flos Virginum. Maurice Hewlett. BMEP; LEAP
Floss won't save you from an abyss. Emily Dickinson. LiTA; NePA
Flotsam and Jetsam. *Unknown.* LPS-2
Flour-barrels, cracker-boxes, cans, The. The Wolf. Donald Davidson. AnAmPo; LA; LS
Flour Fritters. *Unknown, tr. fr. Chinese by* Isaac Taylor Headland. PCH
Flour [*or* Flower] of England, fruit of Spain. Mother Goose. HBV; HBVY; OTPC; OxNR; PPL; RIS; SiTL
Flourishing and gaily-springing wight, The. His Admonition to Greene's Companions. Gabriel Harvey. *Fr.* Greene's Memorial; or, Certain Funeral Sonnets. ReIE
Flourishing vine, whose kindling clusters glow. Fragment: The Vine-Shroud. Shelley. RO
Flow and Ebb. Ibn Safar, *tr. fr. Arabic by* A. J. Arberry. MooP
Flow down, cold rivulet, to the sea. A Farewell. Tennyson.

BPN; CBE; EmBrPo; GTML; HBV; OTPC; PoVP; RIS; SN; TCEP
Flow Gently, Sweet Afton. Burns. AWP; BEL; EnLit; FaBoBe; FaFP; HBV; InPo; JAWP; OlF; REAL; TOP; WBP
(Afton Water.) Burns. CEP; EiPP; EV-3; InP; LPS-2; OAEP; PG; RO; SN; TCEP
(Sweet Afton.) BLV; BoLiVe; EM-1; EnLi-2; EnRP; GTBS-W; HiLiEn; LiTB; LiTG; LiTL; SiTL; TreF; TrGrPo; TyEnPo
Flow [*or* Flowe], my teares! fau [*or* falle] from your springs. Lachrimae. *Unknown.* AtBAP; SeCSL
Flow Not So Fast, Ye Fountains. *Unknown.* ReIE; ViBoPo
Flow, O My Tears! *Unknown.* ElL
Flowe, my teares! falle from your springes. *See* Flow, my teares! fau from your springs.
Flower, The. Lee Wilson Dodd. HBMV; TBM
Flower, The. George Herbert. AtBAP; AWP; EPS; EV-2; FaBoEn; InPo; LPS-3; MePo; NBE; OBS; OxBoCh; PoEL-2; ReEn; SeCV-1; TriL
"And now in age I bud again," *sel.* BCEP
Flower, The. John Holmes. LiTL
Flower, A? Po Chü-i, *tr. fr. Chinese by* Ching Ti. WhP
Flower, The. *At. to* Samuel Speed. OxBoCh; SeCL
Flower, The. Tennyson. BPN; EmBrPo; EPN; EV-2; HBV; InP; PoVP; VA; VLEP
Flower, The. Henry Vaughan. *See* I Walked the Other Day.
Flower, The. Henrik Wergeland, *tr. fr. Norwegian by* Charles W. Stork. AnNoLy; LiTW
Flower, A./ A willow. The Poem of Ten "Ones." Ho P'ei Yü. PoHN
Flower and the Leaf, The, *sel. Unknown.*
"And as I sat, the briddes herkning thus." DiM
Flower-born Blodueda, The. Song. Richard Hovey. *Fr.* The Marriage of Guenevere. OBAV
Flower-Cart Man, The. Rachel Field. SiSoSe
Flower Chorus. *Unknown, wr. at. to* Emerson. BoTP; NLK; PCH, *2 sts.*
(Laughing Chorus, A.) PTA-2
Flower-de-Luce. Longfellow. TCAP
Flower Dreams. *Unknown.* PEOR
Flower Factory, The. Florence Wilkinson Evans. CP; GrCo-1; HiLiAm; NV; PC; PFE
Flower-fed Buffaloes, The. Vachel Lindsay. ATP; ChTr; ExPo; FaPON; LoBV; LoGBV; MAP; MoAmPo; MPB; ShBV-1; ThWaDe; WaKn
Flower for a Professor's Garden of Verses. Irwin Edman. InMe
Flower Given to My Daughter, A. James Joyce. OBMV; ReMP; TwCV
Flower has opened in my heart, A. Siegfried Sassoon. *Fr.* The Heart's Journey. CoEV; TwCV
Flower—I never fancied; jewel—I profess you! Magical Nature. Robert Browning. BPN; PoVP; VLEP
Flower in the Crannied Wall. Tennyson. BBV (1951 ed.); BEL; BLP; BMEP; BoLiVe; BPN; EM-2; EmBrPo; EnLi-2 (1949 ed.); EnLit; FaFP; FaPON; GrCo-1; GTBS-W; HiLiEn; InP; LiTB; LiTG; MaRV; MC; MCCG; MPB; OQP; OTPC (1946 ed.); OuHeWo; PC; PIR; PoeMoYo; PoVP; PreP; QP-1; TCEP; TOP; TreFS; TrGrPo; VA; ViPo; VLEP; WGRP; YT
(Fragment.) BLPA; NeHB
Flower in the forest hidden. Mignonette. Erik Gustaf Geijer. AnSL
Flower in the Sea, The. Malcolm Cowley. NP
Flower Is Looking [through the Ground], A. Harold Monro. Strange Meetings, X. LBBV; MBP; MoBrPo; TCPD
Flower is the forest, The: behind the mountain. At First. Nigel Heseltine. MoWP
Flower Lullaby. Addie Litchfield. BOL
Flower Market, The. Po Chü-i, *tr. fr. Chinese by* Arthur Waley. TrCh; WoL
Flower o' Dumblane, The. Robert Tannahill. *See* Jessie, the Flower o' Dunblane.
Flower of Battle, The. Ralph Hale Mottram. MM
Flower of Beauty, The. George Darley. *See* Song: "Sweet in her green dell the flower of beauty slumbers."
Flower of drowsiness. The Menace of the Flower. Alfonso Reyes. AnMP
Flower of England, fruit of Spain. *See* Flour of England, fruit of Spain.
Flower of Exile. Max Dunn. BoAV
Flower of Flame, The, *sel.* Robert Nichols.
"Before I woke I knew her gone." OBMV
Flower of Hemp. Louise Ayres Garnett. NV
Flower of Jesse, The. *At. to* John Awdlay. *See* There Is a Flower.
Flower of Liberty, The. Oliver Wendell Holmes. DD; FOAH; HBVY; MC; PEOR; PoRL; PTA-2
Flower of Love, The. Thomas Love Peacock. *Fr.* Melincourt. EV-4
Flower of Mending, The. Vachel Lindsay. LEAP; OBAV; SBMV
Flower of Mullein, A. Lizette Woodworth Reese. MAP; MoAmPo; MOAP; NeMA
Flower of Old Japan, The, *sels.* Alfred Noyes.
Epilogue: "Carol, every violet has." MBP; MoBrPo
"When the firelight, red and clear." AlDL
Flower of Quince. Virginia Taylor McCormick. BAP
Flower of the dust am I: for dust will flower. Clement Wood. Eagle Sonnets, VII. HBMV
Flower of the medlar. A Pastoral. Théophile Marzials. HBV; VA
Flower of the moon! The Night-blooming Cereus. Harriet Monroe. AA
Flower of the pear-tree gathers and turns to fruit, The. At the End of Spring. Po Chü-i. TrCh
Flower of the shining Summer. The Pearly Everlasting. Ernest Fewster. CaP; OCL
Flower of Virtue is the heart's content, The. Sonnet: Of Virtue. Folgore da San Geminiano. AWP; JAWP; WBP
Flower of youth, in the ancient frame. Judith. William Young. AA
Flower petals fall. From Summer Hours. Albert Samain. AWP; JAWP; WBP
Flower-quiet in the Rush-strewn Sheiling. Austin Clarke. GTIV
Flower-Seller, The. Eleanor Farjeon. BoTP; PCH
Flower-Seller, The. Lu Yu, *tr. fr. Chinese by* Pai Chwen-yu. WhP
Flower-Seller, The. William Young. *Fr.* Wishmakers' Town. AA
Flower-seller's fat, The, and she wears a big shawl! The Flower-Seller. Eleanor Farjeon. BoTP; PCH
Flower-Songs, *sel.* Erik Axel Karlfeldt, *tr. fr. Swedish by* Charles W. Stork.
"As lily-blooms that quiver." AnSL
Flower-strewn Graves. Samuel Francis Smith. MaRV
Flower, that I hold in my hand. Tuberose. Louis James Block. AA
Flower that smiles to-day, The. Mutability. Shelley. BCEP; BEL; BPN; EM-2; EnLi-2; EnLit; EnRP; EPN; ERP; FaBoEn; HBV; TOP; ViBoPo
Flower Tokens. *Unknown. See* Hearts and Lace Paper.
Flower, Tree, and Bird. Hermann Hesse, *tr. fr. German by* Herman Salinger. TwGV
Flower unblown: a book unread, A. The New Year. Horatio Nelson Powers. OQP; PoRL; PoToHe; QP-1
Flowering Shrubs. William Cowper. *Fr.* The Task, VI. RO
Flowering Time. *Unknown, tr. fr. Latin by* George F. Whicher *Fr.* Carmina Burana. LyMA
(Tempus Instat Floridum.) LaP
Flowering Urn, The. Laura Riding. FaBoMo; LiTA
Flowering with trivial nets. Seafaring Towns. "Pablo de Rokha." TwSpPo
Flowering without End. Stefan Zweig, *tr. fr. German by* Eden Paul *and* Cedar Paul. *Fr.* Jeremiah. TrJP
Flowers. Harry Behn. FaPON
Flowers. Thomas Hood. HBV; LPS-2; OTPC; VA
Flowers, The. Kipling. OBVV; PoeT
Flowers. Longfellow. ADAH; DD, *abr.*; HBV
Flowers, *sel.* William Beans Magruder.
"Ye are God's messengers of love, O flowers!" PoP
Flowers. Stéphane Mallarmé, *tr. fr. French by* Alan Conder. TrFP
Flowers. Milton. *Fr.* Lycidas. ADAH
Flowers, The. William Brighty Rands. OBEV (1st ed.); OBVV
Flowers. Arthur Rimbaud, *tr. fr. French by* Angel Flores. AnFP
Flowers ("O Proserpina!"). Shakespeare. *Fr.* The Winter's Tale, IV, iii. ADAH; EV-1; SN
(Daffodils.) CBPC
("O Proserpina!/ For the flowers now.") LEAP
(Perdita's Garden.) WHA
(Spring Flowers.) BCEP
Flowers ("Out, alas!"). Shakespeare. *Fr.* The Winter's Tale, IV, iii. UnPo (1st ed.)
Flowers. Christopher Smart. *See* Flowers Are Great Blessings.
Flowers. The. Robert Louis Stevenson. FaPON; MPB
Flowers, The. *Unknown.* OTPC (1923 ed.)
Flowers all are sleeping, The. Little Sandman's Song. *Unknown.* RIS
Flowers along the palace, The. Waiting for Audience on a Spring Night. Tu Fu. OnPC
Flowers and Moonlight on the Spring River. Emperor Yang-ti, *tr. fr. Chinese by* Arthur Waley. TrCh
Flowers and Spice. Thomas Chatterton. *Fr.* Narva and Mored. RO
Flowers and Trees. Sir Walter Scott. *Fr.* The Lady of the Lake. EV-4
Flowers and Vegetables. William Julius Mickle. *Fr.* The Concubine, I. RO
Flowers are fresh, and bushes green. Blighted Love. Luís de Camoẽs. LPS-1

Flowers Are Great Blessings. Christopher Smart. *Fr.* Jubilate Agno. MeRV
(Flowers. *shorter sel.*) RO
Flowers are hidden as the shade of twilight emerges, The. Staying at the Official Residence on a Spring Night. Tu Fu. WhP
Flowers are shadowed, the palace darkens. A Night Vigil in the Left Court of the Palace. Tu Fu. LiTW
Flowers bright, the moon dim, and a light mist eddying about, The. The Tryst. Prince Li Yü. ChLP
Flowers by the Sea. William Carlos Williams. AnEnPo; ExPo; MoAB; MoAmPo; Po
Flowers dead, friends gone. Not Alone. Hayashi. SoLD
Flowers do better here than peas and beans. All Things Are a Flowing. R. P. Blackmur. TwAmPo
Flowers every night. Jalal ed-Din Rumi, *tr. fr. Persian by* A. J. Arberry. PeP
Flowers for Luis Bunuel. Stuart Z. Perkoff. NeAP
Flowers for our dead! For Our Dead [*or* Memorial Day]. Clinton Scollard. HH; MDAH; PEDC; PEOR
Flowers for the Altar. Digby Mackworth Dolben. GoBC
Flowers for the Brave. Celia Thaxter. OHIP; PEOR
Flowers for the Fallen Heroes. E. W. Chapman. PEOR
Flowers for the Graces. Sappho, *tr. fr. Greek by* C. M. Bowra. GrL; OxBG
Flowers for you, O Glory's son, war's prey! Unknown Soldier. Alta Booth Dunn. PGD; PSO
Flowers from clods of clay and mud? A Mystery. "Gabriel Setoun." PPL
Flowers from the earth have arisen, The. Nature's Easter Music. Lucy Larcom. EOAH; OHIP
Flowers hast thou in thyself, and foliage. Sonnet: To His Lady Joan, of Florence. Guido Cavalcanti. AWP; JAWP; WBP
Flowers have gone to bed, The. The Sandman. *Unknown.* BOL
Flowers have lost their withered red, The. Spring Scene. Su T'ung-po. WhP
Flowers I Would Bring. Aubrey Thomas De Vere. HBV; IrPN; VA
Flowers in a Library. Carrie Ward Lyon. MOB
Flowers in Ashes. James Matthew Legaré. SPP
Flowers in bud on the trees, The. On the Death of a New Born Child. Mei Yao Ch'en. OnPC
Flowers in the Valley. *Unknown.* AtBAP; OxBoLi
Flowers left thick at nightfall in the wood, The. In Memoriam; Easter 1915. Edward Thomas. SoV
Flower's Name, The. Robert Browning. Garden Fancies, I. EnLi-2 (1949 ed.); GEPC; GTBS-D; HBV; LPS-1; VLEP
"Flowers nodding gaily, scent in air." A Duet. T. Sturge Moore. LEAP; MBP; OBEV; OBVV
Flowers of Apollo, The. Hildegarde Flanner. HBMV; TBM
Flowers of Darkness. Frank Marshall Davis. PoNe
Flowers of Middle Summer. Shakespeare. *See* Flowers of Perdita, The.
Flowers of mist and silence. Yucca in the Moonlight. Glenn Ward Dresbach. HiLiAm
Flowers of Nazareth, The. Kaj Munk, *tr. fr. Danish by* Charles W. Stork. BoDS
Flowers of Perdita, The. Shakespeare. *Fr.* The Winter's Tale, IV, iii. FiP
(Flowers of Middle Summer.) YeAr
Flowers of Politics, The, I ("This is the huge dream of us that we are heroes"). Michael McClure. NeAP
Flowers of Politics, The, II ("Only what is heroic and courageious moves our blood"). Michael McClure. NeAP
Flowers of Sion, *sel.* William Drummond of Hawthornden. "New doth the sun appear." MeRV
(Change Should Breed Change.) BSV; EBSV; OBEV; OxBoCh
Flowers of Snow. Tsurayuki, *tr. fr. Japanese by* Basil Hall Chamberlain. OnPM
Flowers of the Bignonia, The. *Unknown, tr. fr. Chinese.* WhP
Flowers of the field, The. The Hawthorn Hath a Deathly Smell. Walter de la Mare. AtBAP
Flowers of the Forest, The. Alison Cockburn. BSV; EBSV; OBEC
Flowers of the Forest, The. Jane Elliot. BSV; CH; EBSV; EiPP; EPP; FaBoCh; GoTS; OBEC
(Lament for Flodden.) EV-3; GTBS; GTBS-D; GTBS-W; GTSE; GTSL; HBV; LiTG; OBEV; ShBV-3
Flowers of the Sea. *Unknown.* RO
Flowers of the Sea. Yasuhide, *tr. fr. Japanese by* Basil Hall Chamberlain. OnPM
Flowers of the wheat are in spike, The. Song of the Wheat in Flower. *Unknown. Fr.* The Fountain of Old Poems. WhP
Flowers of the willow-herb are wool. Seed-Time. George Meredith. BrBE
Flowers of the wood have lost their spring redness, The. To the Tune of "Meeting Happiness." Li Yu. WhP
Flowers rejoice when night is done. Matins. Henry van Dyke. MaRV
Flowers shall hang upon the palls. John Clare. *Fr.* Death. PoD; RO
Flowers take hold of hands, The. Flowers under the Lightning. Juan Ramón Jiménez. TeCS
Flowers—that have died upon my Sweet. A Song of Angiola in Heaven. Austin Dobson. HBV
Flowers that in thy garden rise, The. Song. Sir Henry Newbolt. FaBoTw
Flowers through the window. Nantucket. William Carlos Williams. OxBA
Flowers to the fair: To you these flowers I bring. To a Lady, with Some Painted Flowers. Anna Letitia Barbauld. DiM; LPS-1
Flowers under the Lightning. Juan Ramón Jiménez, *tr. fr. Spanish by* Eleanor L. Turnbull. TeCS
Flowers upon the rosemary spray, The. The Rosemary Spray. Luis de Góngora. AnSpL-1; AWP; LiTW
Flowers upon your lips and hands. Love Poem. Maurice James Craig. NeIP
Flowers whirl away, The. Prime Minister Kintsune, *tr. fr. Japanese by* Kenneth Rexroth. OnPJ
Flowers without Fruit. Cardinal Newman. EPN; LPS-3
Flowery Garments. Cypria, *tr. fr. Greek by* C. M. Bowra. OxBG
Flowery spring, The—I heard her, coming upon her way. The Footsteps of Spring. Alcaeus. GrPE
Flowing robe of words you weave, The. The Lethal Thought. Mary Boyd Wagner. GoYe
Flowing Stream. Ibn Hamdis, *tr. fr. Arabic by* A. J. Arberry. MooP
Flowing Summer, The, *sels.* Charles Bruce. CaP
Attic, The.
Dreaming Trout, The.
Hayfield, The.
Flowing Tide, The. Godfrey Fox Bradby. TVSH
Flown Soul, The. George Parsons Lathrop. AA
Flowry meadows, and the whispering trees, The. Submarine Landscape. William Diaper. *Fr.* Nereides; or, Sea-Eclogues. BeR
Fluid ebon masses, flow. Southerndown Beach. George Woodcock. MoWP
Fluid the world flowed under us. The Automobile. Percy MacKaye. AnAmPo; BAP; LA; LBMV; LEAP; PoeMoYo
Flung to the heedless winds. The Martyrs' Hymn. Martin Luther. LPS-2
Flush with the pond the lurid furnace burned. The Steam Threshing-Machine. Charles Tennyson Turner. CBOV; PoVP
Flushed with the hope of high desire. My Hero; to Robert Gould Shaw. Benjamin Brawley. BANP; PoNe
Flute, The. André Chénier, *tr. fr. French by* Alan Conder. TrFP
Flute, The. W. W. Gibson. ChMo; CMP; PCN
Flute, The. José Maria de Heredia, *tr. fr. French by* Herbert C. Grierson. EBSV
(Flute, The; a Pastoral.) AWP
Flute, The. Hilali, *tr. fr. Persian by* Emerson. OnPM
Flute, A. Nobutsuna, *tr. fr. Japanese by* Asataro Miyamori. OnPM
Flute, The. Joseph Russell Taylor. AA
Flute, The. Wang Mou Fang, *tr. fr. Chinese by* Henry H. Hart. PoHN
Flute at Evening, A. Huang Wan Ch'iung, *tr. fr. Chinese by* Henry H. Hart. PoHN
Flute begins to falter, to fidget, to fret, The. Evening Music. Kendrick Smithyman. AnNZ
Flute of Daphnis, The. Edward Cracroft Lefroy. Echoes from Theocritus, XXIII. AWP; ES; OBVV
Flute of God. John Daniel Logan. CPG
Flute of Krishna, The. James B. Thomas. BLA
Flute of May, The. Harry Woodbourne. GoYe
Flute of the Lonely, The. Vachel Lindsay. CrMA
Flute-Priest Song for Rain, *sel.* Amy Lowell.
"Whistle under the water." UnS
Flute-Song ("Hail, fathers, hail!"). *Unknown, tr. fr. Hopi Indian by* Natalie Curtis. APW
Flute Song ("Winter days and spring"). *Unknown, tr. fr. Greek by* T. F. Higham. OxBG
Flutesong willow winding weather. World War. Richard Eberhart. WaP
Flutes in the sunny air. Cleopatra Embarking on the Cydnus. Thomas Kibble Hervey. BCEP
Fluttered Wings. Christina Rossetti. VA
Fluttering Leaves. Rodney Bennett. BoTP
Fluttering [*or* Flutt'ring] spread thy purple pinions. Lines [*or* Song] by a Person of Quality [*or* A Love Song]. *At. to* Pope *and to* Swift. InMe; NA; PA; ReaPo
Fluttering swarm, A. Blossoms and Storm. Sadaiye. OnPM
Flux of night is power and will, slid, The. Nightflight and Sunrise. Geoffrey Dutton. BoAV
Fly, The. Blake. *Fr.* Songs of Experience. BLV; BoLiVe; EiPP; EM-1; EnL; GoTP; MaPo; OTPC (1923 ed.); TrGrPo

Fly, The. Walter de la Mare. CBPC
Fly, The. Barnabe Googe. *See* Once Musing as I Sat.
Fly, The. Ogden Nash. FaPON
Fly, The. William Oldys. *See* On a Fly Drinking Out of His Cup.
Fly, The. Karl Shapiro. CoBA; LiTM; MiAP; MoVE; NePA; TwAmPo
Fly, The. Theodore Tilton. RIS
Fly and a flea in a flue, A. *See* Flea and a fly in a flue.
Fly away, away, swallow. Full Valleys. F. R. Scott. CaP
Fly away, fly away over the sea. The Swallow. Christina Rossetti. *Fr.* Sing-Song. CoBE; GoTP; OTPC (1946 ed.); PoVP; StVeCh; SUS
Fly-away Horse, The. Eugene Field. GoTP
Fly Back to Christ. Charles Wesley. BePJ
Fly down, Death: Call me. Madboy's Song. Muriel Rukeyser. MoAmPo; TrJP
Fly envious Time, till thou run out thy race. On Time. Milton. BLV; GTBS-W; KN; LiTB; LiTG; LoBV; MaPo; MePo; MeRV; OBEV; OBS; OxBoCh; PoE; SeCeV; TyEnPo
Fly far from me. Iena's Song. Charles Mair. *Fr.* Tecumseh. VA
Fly, fly, my friends, I have my death wound; fly. Astrophel and Stella, XX. Sir Philip Sidney. MaPo; ReIE; SiPS; TuPP
Fly, fly! The foe advances fast. Henry Cotton. EG
Fly, fly, you happy shepherds, fly! Philira [*or* Song]. Sir John Vanbrugh. *Fr.* The Provoked Wife. SeCL; SeEP
Fly from the press and dwell with sothfastness. *See* Flee fro the prees . . .
Fly Hence Shadows. John Ford. *Fr.* The Lover's Melancholy, V, i. CenL; OnPM; SeCL; ViBoPo
(Dawn.) OBEV
(Matin Song.) EV-2
(Song: "Fly hence, shadows, that do keep.") LoBV
Fly in Church, The. Jocelyn C. Lea. DDA
Fly like an arrow, Night, O Night! Bard's Song. Nikolai Yazykov. BoRS
Fly, merry muse, unto that merry town. Ad Musam. Sir John Davies. ReIE; SiCE
Fly, Muse, thy wonted themes, nor longer seek. If Pope Had Written "Break, Break, Break." J. C. Squire. CenHV
Fly, Roadster, fly! Song for a Blue Roadster. Rachel Field. FaPON; TiPo (1950 ed.)
Fly Soft, Ye Gentle Hours. *Unknown.* SeCL
Fly to Her Heart. Bartholomew Griffin. Fidessa, More Chaste than Kind, XXIII. PeBoSo
("Fly to her heart, hover about her heart.") ReEn; ReIE; SiCE; TuPP
(Her Heart.) TrGrPo
Fly to Jesus. Charles Wesley. BePJ
Fly to the Desert, Fly with Me. Thomas Moore. *Fr.* Lalla Rookh. GTIV; LPS-1
"Fly to the mountain! Fly!" Conemaugh. Elizabeth Stuart Phelps Ward. PAH
Fly, white butterflies, out to sea. White Butterflies [*or* Envoi]. Swinburne. FaPON; MeMeAg; MPB; OTPC; PCD; PCH; RAR; StaSt; SUS; UTS
"Fly with me then to all's and the world's end." The World's End. William Empson. CoBMV; MoVE
Flycatchers. Robert Bridges. MoVE; POTE
Flyers, The. Frank Ernest Hill. PoeMoYo
Flyer's Fall. Wallace Stevens. MoAB
Flying. Florence Ripley Mastin. VOD (1935 ed.)
Flying. J. M. Westrup. BoTP
Flying birds,/ Beware! Shiko, *tr. fr. Japanese by* Lois J. Erickson. SoLD
Flying Charlie, *abr.* Louise Ayres Garnett. GA
Flying Cloud, The. *Unknown.* ABF, *with music;* AmSS, *with music;* BaBo; IHA; ShS (*2 vers.*), *with music;* SoAmSa, *with music;* ViBoFo, *with music*
Flying Crooked. Robert Graves. FaBoMo; LiTM (rev. ed.)
Flying Dead, The. Rose O'Neill. TBM
Flying Dutchman, The. Charles Godfrey Leland. DaM; PoMS
Flying Dutchman, The. A. M. Sullivan. EtS
Flying Dutchman, The, *with music. Unknown.* ShS
Flying Dutchman of the Tappan Zee, The. Arthur Guiterman. CP
Flying Fish. Mary McNeill Fenollosa. AA; OBAV
Flying Fish, The. John Gray. ChTr; LoBV; SG
Flying Fish. J. Corson Miller. EtS
Flying Fish. Katherine Kelley Taylor. EtS
Flying Flowers. Mrs. Motherly. SAS
Flying Fowl and Creeping Things, Praise Ye the Lord, *sel.* Isaac Watts.
Serpents. BeR
Flying Foxes and Others. Kay Boyle. AnAmPo
Flying in plane's rib. New York City. George Abbe. GoYe
Flying Inn, The, *sel.* G. K. Chesterton.
Wine and Water. ACP (1952 ed.); CenHV; FiBHP; GoBC; HBMV; InMe; LiTM; MBP; MoBrPo; ShBV-4; ViBoPo
Flying Islands of the Night, The, *sel.* James Whitcomb Riley.
Dwainie. AA
Flying Jim's Last Leap. Emma Dunning Banks. PTA-2
Flying Lesson, The. Petrarch, *tr. fr. Italian by* Agnes Tobin. Sonnets to Laura: To Laura in Death, LXXIV. CAW
Flying Mist, The. Edwin Markham. SN
Flying sea-bird mocked the floating dulse, The. The Sea-Weed. Elisabeth Cavazza Pullen. AA
Flying Squirrel, The. Mary E. Burt. PECK
Flying Trapeze, The. George Leybourne. *See* Man on the Flying Trapeze, The.
Flying Wheel, The. Katharine Tynan. WGRP
Flying word from here [there, *wr.*] and there, A. The Master. E. A. Robinson. AmP; BAP; GTBS-W; HBV; HH; InP; LBMV; LEAP; LiTA; LiTG; LiTM (rev. ed.); MAP; MoAB; MoAmPo; NeMA; NP; OHIP; OTPC (1946 ed.); PaA; PFY; PIAE; PoLFOT; PoRL; TCPD; TriL
Flyting of Dumbar and Kennedie, The, *sel.* William Dunbar.
"Iersch brybour baird, vyle beggar with thy brattis." AtBAP
Foal. Vernon Watkins. FaBoMo
Foam. *Unknown, tr. fr. Spanish by* Havelock Ellis. OnPM
Foam and Fangs. Walter Parke. BOHV; PA
Foam of Fancy. Mary Josephine Benson. CPG
Foam of leaves applauds the crimson signal, A. House Plant. Winthrop Palmer. SiTL
Foam resembling a thousand drifts of snow. Fisherman's Song. Li Yu. WhP
Focus of That Face, The. Edwin McNeill Poteat. ChIP
Foe at the Gates, The. John Dickson Bruns. PAH
Foe unconsecrated entered my courts, The. Lament to Nana of Erech. *Unknown.* LiTW
Foe Within, The. Longfellow. MaRV
Foeda Est in Coitu. Petronius Arbiter. *See* Keeping Endless Holiday.
Foes in plenty we shall meet. Hearts Courageous. John Oxenham. MaRV
Fog, The. Robert P. Tristram Coffin. CrMA; PreP
Fog, The. W. H. Davies. TiPo (1959 ed.); WaKn
Fog. Louis Ginsberg. NeMA
Fog. Robinson Jeffers. TBM
Fog, The. F. R. McCreary. BAP
Fog. Kenneth Patchen. TwAmPo
Fog. John Reed. AnEnPo
Fog ("Fog comes, The/ On little cat feet"). Carl Sandburg. AmPP; AnEnPo; BAP; BAV; BoChLi; CBOV; CoBA; CP; DDA; FaFP; FaPON; GFA; GoTP; HBMV; LaNeLa; MAP; MCCG; MoAmPo; MoAB; MOAP; MPB; NeMA; PFE; PoeMoYo; PoMa; PoRh; PYM; RAR; ReaPo; SP; StVeCh; SUS; TCAP; TiPo; TSW; TSWC; VOD; WoL; YT
Fog got him first. One, Two, Three. Samuel L. Albert. NePoAm-2
Fog has bandaged my eyes, The. I am blinded. The Dolmens. Gonzalo Escudero. AnCL
Fog is freezing on the trees and shrubs, The. White Dusk. Marion Margaret Boyd. HBMV
Fog rolls in across the fields of heather, The. New England Fog. Gertrude Callaghan. JKCP (1955 ed.)
Fog, the Magician. Melville Cane. MoSiPe
Foggy, Foggy Dew. *Unknown.* AS, *with music;* LiTB; LiTG; OxBoLi; SiTL
(Foggy Dew, The, *diff. vers.*) CoMu
(Weaver, The, *with music.*) AS
Fog-Horn. George Herbert Clarke. CaP; OCL
Foghorn in Horror. Muriel Rukeyser. FiMAP
Foil'd [*or* Foiled] by our fellow men, depress'd [*or* depressed], outworn. Immortality. Matthew Arnold. BPN; EmBrPo; EPN; FiP; MaRV; PoVP; PC; VLEP
Foiled Reaper, The. William Kean Seymour. HBMV
Fold away all your bright-tinted dresses. Hospital Duties. *Unknown.* BlG
Fold it up carefully, lay it aside. The Jacket of Gray. Caroline A. Ball. BlG
Fold the Banners. Will Henry Thompson. *Fr.* The High Tide at Gettysburg. BoHiPo
Fold thy hands, little one. Sleep, Darling, Sleep. Mary B. C. Slade. BOL
Fold up the banners! Smelt the guns! Fold the Banners. Will Thompson. BoHiPo
Fold up the gorgeous silken sun. Ashes of Glory. Augustus Julian Requier. BlG
Folded Flock, The. Wilfrid Meynell. CAW; GoBC; JKCP; TrPWD
Folded Power. Gladys Cromwell. HBMV; NP
Folded Skyscraper, A, *sel.* William Carlos Williams.
"Saloon is gone up the creek, The." AnAmPo; LA
(Hemmed-in Males.) MoVE
Folded Wings. Marian Osborne. CPG
Fol-de-rol and riddle-ma-ree. Spring Ring-Jingle. Michael Lewis. RIS
Folding a Shirt. Denise Levertov. NeBP
Folding the Flocks. John Fletcher. *See* Evening Song.

Foliage, *sel.* W. H. Davies.
Sweet Stay-at-Home. AtBAP; CH; GTBS; HBMV; POTE; POTT; PtOT; TCPD; TwCV
Foliage. Felicia Dorothea Hemans. OBRV
Foliage of Vision. James Merrill. MoPo
Folk of the Air, The. W. B. Yeats. *See* Host of the Air, The.
Folk rejoicing in labor, husbandmen busy and nimble, A. Singing on the Moselle. Ausonius. LaP
Folk-Song: "Back she came through the trembling dusk." Louis Untermeyer. HBV
Folk Song: "Hat you loved, the damask-trimmed reed-hat, The." *Unknown, tr. fr. Japanese by* Arthur Waley. LiTW
Folk Song: "Swallow, The, comes! She comes, she brings." *Unknown. See* Swallow Song.
Folk Songs. *Unknown, tr. fr. Spanish by* Havelock Ellis.
"Let the rich man fill his belly." LiTW; OnPM
"My father was a sailor." LiTW
(Sailors.) OnPM
(Spanish Folk Song.) AWP
Folk-Tune. Richard Wilbur. OnHM
Folk was affrighted, the flood-dread seized on, The. The Drowning of Pharaoh and His Army. Cædmon. *Fr.* Exodus. TCEP
Folk who lived in Shakespeare's day, The. Guilielmus Rex. Thomas Bailey Aldrich. AA; AnNE; TCAP
Folks ain't got no right to censuah othah folks about dey habits. Accountability. Paul Laurence Dunbar. AnAmPo; LA; YaD
Folks and Me. Lucile Crites. WBLP
Folks at home half the time are thinkin' about dirt, The. Soap, the Oppressor. Burges Johnson. DDA
Folks, I Give You Science! Al Graham. WhC
Folks Need a Lot of Loving. Strickland Gillilan. BLPA; MaRV; WBLP
(Need of Loving.) PoToHe
Folkways. Isabella Gardner. SiTL
Folkways of Sodom, The. "E. W." SiTL
Foller de Drinkin' Gou'd, *with music. Unknown.* ABF
Follow. Thomas Campion. *See* Follow Thy Fair Sun.
Follow a shadow [*or* shaddow], it still flies you. Song: That Women Are but Men's Shadows [*or* Follow a Shadow *or* The Shadow *or* Women Men's Shadows]. Ben Jonson. ALV; AtBAP; CaAE; ElL; ElSeCe; EnLit; FaBoEn; HBV; LiTL; OBEV; OBS; ReIE; ViBoPo; WBLP
Follow back from the gull's bright arc and the osprey's plunge. Water Ouzel. William H. Matchett. NePoEA
Follow, follow. Thomas Campion. EnLoPo
Follow, follow me into the South. Ballad. Marjorie Allen Seiffert. HBMV
Follow Me! Eliza Lee Follen. PPL
Follow Me. Longfellow. PGD
"Follow Me." Joseph Fort Newton. OQP; QP-1
Follow Me. John Oxenham. ChIP; MaRV
Follow Me! Sheldon Shepard. ChIP
Follow me, follow me. Will o' the Wisp. George Meredith. BMEP
"Follow Me 'Ome." Kipling. OAEP (2d ed.)
Follow my Bangalorey Man. *Unknown.* OxNR
Follow the Christ. Tennyson. *Fr.* Idylls of the King: Gareth and Lynette. ChIP; MaRV
Follow the crowds to where the turnstiles click. The Game. Dannie Abse. PrWP
Follow the Gleam. Tennyson. Merlin and the Gleam, IX. BBV; MaRV; OTPC (1946 ed.); PoRL
Follow the long snake. Desert River. Patricia Benton. GoYe
Follow the ribs of my thought, lines. Cactus. Terence Heywood. BoSA
Follow thee! follow thee! who wadna follow thee? Bonnie Prince Charlie. James Hogg. EBSV
Follow Thy Fair Sun [Unhappy Shadow]. Thomas Campion. ElL; EM-1; EnL1-1; EnLoPo; LiTB; LO; LoBV; OBSC; RiBV; UnPo; ViBoPo
(Devotion.) BCEP; OBEV
(Follow.) CH
(Followe Thy Faire Sunne.) AtBAP; PoEL-2; SiCE
(In Imagine Pertransit Homo.) GTSL
(Song: "Follow thy faire sunne, unhappy shadowe!") BrBE
(Song from a Booke of Ayres, A.) BoW
Follow Your Saint [Follow with Accents Sweet]. Thomas Campion. AEV; AtBAP; EG; ElL; ElSeCe; EnL; EnLoPo; EtPaEn; EV-2; ExPo; FaBoEn; InPo; LEAP; LO; OBSC; PoE; ReaPo; ReEn; ReIE; RiBV; SeCePo; TrGrPo; TuPP; TyEnPo; ViBoPo
(Devotion, 2.) OBEV
(It Shall Suffice.) BLV
(Songs from Lute Books.) CoEV
Follower, A. Daisy Conway Price. ChIP
Following across the moors a sound of bells. The Pansy and the Prayer-Book. Matilda Barbara Betham-Edwards. OBVV
Following forbidden streets. The Wraith-Friend. George Barker. OBMV
Following the Army to the Northern Expedition. Li I, *tr. fr. Chinese.* WhP
(Following the Army to the North.) OnPM
Followis How Dumbar Wes Desyr to Be ane Freir. William Dunbar. OAEP
Folly. Vivian Yeiser Laramore. NLK
Folly and Time have fashioned. Athassel Abbey. Louise Imogen Guiney. OBAV
Folly hath now turned out of door. Mandrake's Song. Thomas Lovell Beddoes. *Fr.* Death's Jest Book, I, i. NBE
Folly of Being Comforted, The. W. B. Yeats. AnIL; AnIV; GTBS; GTML; GTSL; LoPS; Po; PoE; PoeT
Folly of Brown, The. W. S. Gilbert. InMe
Folly of Obstinacy. Aeschylus, *tr. fr. Greek by* Lewis Campbell. *Fr.* Prometheus Bound. GrR
Fond Affection, *with music. Unknown.* AS
Fond affection, hence, and leave me! Song. *At. to* Robert Parry. *Fr.* The Mirror of Knighthood. ElL
Fond, frozen, first and only lover. Elegy. Louis Johnson. AnNZ
Fond Love, No More. Thomas Forde. *Fr.* Love's Labyrinth. SeCL
Fond man, Musophilus, that thus dost spend. Poet and Critic. Samuel Daniel. *Fr.* Musophilus. OBSC; ReIE; SiCE; TuPP
Fond maydes, take warninge while you may. *Unknown.* SeCSL
Fond men! whose wretched care the life soon ending. Song. Phineas Fletcher. *Fr.* Brittain's Ida. ElL
Fond muse surrender, weary as thou art. The Night. Ralph Hodgson. ChMo; CMP
Fond nymphs, from us true passion learn. In Derision of a Country Life. Edward Ravenscroft. *Fr.* The Italian Husband. SeCL
Fond scenes which delighted my youthful existence. The Exile's Departure. Whittier. CoBA
Fond Soul. Phineas Fletcher. *Fr.* A Father's Testament. ElSeCe
Fond Youth. Samuel Rogers. *Fr.* Human Life. OBRV
Fondly, too curious Nature, to adorn. On the Marriage of a Beauteous Young Gentlewoman with an Ancient Man. Francis Beaumont. LiTL; ViBoPo
Font in the Forest, The. Léonie Adams. CrMA
Fontainebleau. Sara Teasdale. TriL
Fontenoy. Thomas Osborne Davis. HBV; OnYI
Fontenoy, 1745. Emily Lawless. AnIV; PoFr
Food. Marchette Chute. BrR
Food. Ruby Weyburn Tobias. OQP; QP-2
Food and Drink. Louis Untermeyer. MAP; MoAmPo
"Let us give thanks before we turn," *sel.* PreP
Food for Fire, Food for Thought. Robert Duncan. NeAP
Food for Thought. Michael Lewis. RIS
Food of Love, The. Shakespeare. *See* If Music Be the Food of Love.
Fool, The. Henry Baerlein. ReTS
Fool, The. Padraic Pearse. OnYI
Fool. *Unknown, tr. fr. German.* PIAE
Fool, A, a fool! I met a fool i' the forest. Motley's the Only Wear. Shakespeare. *Fr.* As You Like It, II, vii. PIR; TrGrPo
Fool and False. *Unknown, tr. fr. Sanskrit by* Arthur W. Ryder. *Fr.* The Panchatantra. AWP; JAWP; WBP
Fool and knave with different views, A. The Maiden's Choice [*or* The Touch-Stone *or* Epigram]. Samuel Bishop. ALV; HBV; PIAE
Fool and the Poet, The. Pope. *See* Epigram: "Sir, I admit your general rule."
Fool and Wise. Coventry Patmore. PC
Fool by the Roadside, The. W. B. Yeats. MoVE
Fool Hath Said in His Heart, The. Psalms, XIV, Bible, *O.T.* OnPM; TrJP
Fool Hath Said in His Heart, The. Humbert Wolfe. QS
Fool I was to sleep at noon, A. Daughter of Eve. Christina Rossetti. BPN; VLEP
Fool Killer, The. Helen Bevington. NoCaPo (rev. ed.)
Fool of Nature, stood with stupid eyes, The. The Power of Love. Dryden. *Fr.* Cymon and Iphigenia. OBS
Fool, put your adventures. Hero. William Carlos Williams. MOAP
Fool Song. Cornel Lengyel. GoYe
Fool, take up thy shaft again. Song. Thomas Stanley. EnLoPo
"Fool, tender not ransom to me, neither make harangue." Achilles Refuses to Spare Lycaon's Life. Homer. *Fr.* The Iliad. LiA
Fool there was and he made his prayer, A. The Vampire [as Suggested by the Painting by Philip Burne-Jones]. Kipling. BLPA; BMEP; EnLit; HBV; LEAP; NeHB
Fool there was and he wrote a theme, A. The Literary Vampire. *Unknown.* CAG
Fool there was, and she lowered her pride, A. A Woman's

Answer to "The Vampire." Felicia Blake. BLPA; NeHB
Fool, who forgets a parent's piteous loss! The Plaint of the Nightingale. Sophocles. *Fr.* Ajax. GrR
Foolish about Windows. Carl Sandburg. MOAP
Foolish boy forbeare and flee. *Unknown.* SeCSL
Foolish Emily and Her Kitten. Adelaide O'Keeffe. OTPC (1923 ed.)
Foolish Flowers. Rupert Sargent Holland. GFA; MeMeAg; OTPC
Foolish Husband, The. Johannes Secundus, *tr. fr. Latin by* F. A. Wright. LaP
Foolish I, why should I grieve. Of Maids' Inconstancy [*or* The Wooer's Song]. Richard Brathwaite. *Fr.* A Strappado for the Devil. ElL; ElSeCe
Foolish Leander, The. Colombine. Paul Verlaine. MiFP
Foolish Leander. Mateo Vázquez de Leca, *tr. fr. Spanish by* Sir John Bowring. OnPM
Foolish little maiden bought a foolish little bonnet, A. What the Choir Sang about the New Bonnet. M. T. Morrison. BLPA; PTA-2
Foolish prater, what dost thou. The Swallow. Abraham Cowley. BCEP; BEL; CoBE; EV-2; OBEV; SeCL; TOP
Foolish Virgins, The. Tennyson. *Fr.* Idylls of the King: Guinevere. LPS-3
"Foolish wide Eyes! Lullaby!" *Unknown.* BOL
Foolish Woman, A. Proverbs, IX: 13–18, Bible, *O.T.* TrGrPo
Foolish young fellow named Hyde, A. *Unknown.* GoTP
Fools. Ben Jonson. *See* Nano's Song.
Fool's Adventure, The, *sel.* Lascelles Abercrombie.
Seeker, The. WGRP
Fools change in England, and new Fools arise. Fools in England. Dryden. *Fr.* Epilogue to "The Husband His Own Cuckold." BeR
Fools Gaze at Painted Courts. Michael Drayton. *Fr.* Polyolbion, Song 18. ChTr
Fools have said/ That knowledge drives out wonder. Alfred Noyes. *Fr.* The Torch Bearers: Watchers of the Sky: Newton. MaRV
Fools in England. Dryden. *Fr.* Epilogue to "The Husband His Own Cuckold." BeR
Fools in Love's College. John Lyly. *See* O Cupid! Monarch over Kings.
Fools laugh at dreamers, and the dreamers smile. Dreamers. James Barron Hope. TCAP
Fools may pine, and sots may swill. Double Ballade of Life and Fate. W. E. Henley. PoVP
Fools of Forty-nine, The. *Unknown.* CoSo; CSF
Fool's Prayer, The. Edward Rowland Sill. AA; AnNE; BAP; BeLS; FaBoBe; HBV; IAP; LBAP; LEAP; LHV; MAP; MaRV, *abr.;* MoAmPo (1942 ed.); NeHB; OBAV; OHFP; PFY; PG; TCAP; TreF; WBLP; WGRP
" 'Tis not by guilt the onward sweep," *sel.* TrPWD
Fool's Preferment, A, *sel.* Thomas D'Urfey.
I'll Sail upon the Dog-Star. FaBoCh; LoGBV; OxBoLi
Fool's Revenge, The, *sel.* Tom Taylor.
Jester and His Daughter, The. VA
Fools, they are the only nation. Nano's Song [*or* Fools *or* Fortunate Fool]. Ben Jonson. *Fr.* Volpone, I, ii. BLV; BoLiVe; CenL; ElL; InvP; LoBV; TrGrPo; TuPP
Fools, to ignore how much the more. Plain Living. Hesiod. *Fr.* Works and Days. OxBG
Fool's Tongue, A. John Heywood. SiCE
Foot Soldiers. John Banister Tabb. HBV; HBVY; PPL
Football and Rowing—an Eclogue. Alfred Denis Godley. CenHV
Football Field; Evening. J. A. R. McKellar. NeLNL
Football Is a Woman's Game. Al Graham. LauV
Football Player, A. Edward Cracroft Lefroy. VA
Footfall there, A/ Suffices to upturn to the warm air. At Ecelin. Robert Browning. *Fr.* Sordello. MyFE
Footfalls, footfalls/ coming clear,/ coming near. Stranger in the Night. August Derleth. DaM
Foot-hills called us, green and sweet, The. On the Height. Eunice Tietjens. HBMV; NP
Footnote, A. Stephen Spender. FaBoTw
Footnote to a Famous Lyric, A. Louise Imogen Guiney. AA
Footnote to History. Elizabeth J. Coatsworth. SiSoSe
Footnote to John II: 4. R. A. K. Mason. AnNZ
Footnote to Tennyson Gerald Bullett. FiBHP
Footpath Way, The. Shakespeare. *See* Jog On, Jog On.
Footpath Way, The. Katharine Tynan. HBV
Footprints. Ludvig Bødtcher, *tr. fr. Danish by* Charles W. Stork. BoDS
Footprints in the Snow. Frank Dempster Sherman. SN
Footprints now on bread or cake. To a Child with Eyes. Mark Van Doren. PCH
Footsloggers. Ford Madox Ford. LBBV; NP
Footstep struck her ear, A. James Fitz-James and Ellen. Sir Walter Scott. *Fr.* The Lady of the Lake, VI. LPS-2
Footsteps. Otto Freund. MuM
Footsteps. Hazel Hall. HBMV
Footsteps, The. Paul Valéry, *tr. fr. French.* LiTW, *tr. by* C. Day Lewis; TrFP, *tr. by* Alan Conder
Foosteps of a hundred years, The. The Founders of Ohio. William Henry Venable. MC; PaA; PAH
Footsteps of Angels. Longfellow. IAP; LPS-1
Footsteps of Spring, The. Alcaeus, *tr. fr. Greek by* F. L. Lucas. GrPE
Footwear. May Justus. YeAr
For a Blind Beggar's Sign. Clemente Biondi, *tr. fr. Italian by* Roderick Gill. CAW
For a cap and bells our lives we pay. June Weather [*or* June]. James Russell Lowell. *Fr.* The Vision of Sir Launfal: Prelude to Part First. AA; DD; GN; LEAP
For a Certain Dog. Catherine Parmenter. AlBD
For a Charity Annual. Austin Dobson. TCEP
For a Child. Fannie Stearns Davis. FaPON; MPB
For a Child. Denis Glover. AnNZ
For a Child Expected. Anne Ridler. LiTM; MoVE; NeBP; SeCePo
For a Child Named Katherine. Louise Townsend Nicholl. SP
For a Child Who Died. Joseph G. E. Hopkins. JKCP (1955 ed.)
For a Child's Drawing. Anton Vogt. AnNZ
For a Christening. Anne Ridler. DiM; MoPo
For a Cock. Eleanor Farjeon. *See* Cock, The.
For a Copy of Herrick. Austin Dobson. PtP; VLEP
For a Copy of "The Vicar of Wakefield." Austin Dobson. BPN
For a Copy of Theocritus. Austin Dobson. HBV; LPS-2; PtP; VA; VLEP
For a day and a night Love sang to us, played with us. At Parting. Swinburne. HBV; POTT; ViBoPo; VLEP
For a Dead Kitten. Sara Henderson Hay. BAP; CIV; StaSt
For a Dead Lady. E. A. Robinson. AmPP (4th ed.); AnFE; AnNE; APA; ChMo; CMP; CoAnAm; CoBMV; FaBoEn; GTBS-D; GTBS-W; IAP; InP; InvP; LiTA; LiTM; MAP; MAPA; MoAB; MoAmPo; MOAP; MotAn; OxBA; PoEL-5; PoeMoYo; PoRA; ReMP; RiBV; TCPD; TwAmPo; TwP; ViBoPo; WHA
For a Dewdrop. Eleanor Farjeon. HBVY; YT
For a Far-out Friend. Gary Snyder. NeAP
For a Fountain. "Barry Cornwall." OBEV (new ed.); OBVV
(Inscription for a Fountain.) OBRV
For a Friend Who Thinks Himself Urbane. Robert Penn Warren. BoFr
For a girl dark-eyed, pale-faced. To the Nun. Dafydd ap Gwilym. LyMA
For a Girl in Love. Florence Hynes Willette. GoBC
For a Good Dog. Arthur Guiterman. AlBD
For a Gravestone in Spain. Walter Savage Landor. TriL
For a Grotto. Mark Akenside. *See* Inscription for a Grotto.
For a Guest Book. S. Weir Mitchell. DDA
For a heavy long time on the long green bough. Apple and Mole. Donald Davidson. MAP; MoAmPo (1942 ed.)
For a hundred years I lived with coal in the mine. Ostrava. Petr Bezruc. LiTW
For a Lady I know. Countee Cullen. GoSl; PoNe
(Four Epitaphs, 4.) CDC
(Lady I Know, A.) MAP; MaRV; MoAmPo
For a Lamb. Richard Eberhart. FiMAP; MiAP
For a Library Door. Theda Kenyon. MOB
For a Little Bird That Blundered into Church. Sara Henderson Hay. BAP
For a Little Lady. Fred Saidy. InMe; LauV
For a Little Pupil. *Unknown.* WOAH
For a long time I have been staring at my long legs. Liturgy of My Legs. "Pablo Neruda." AnCL
For a long time we have not seen. The Shining Fool. Jacob Glatstein. OnCuPl
For a Marriage. Louise Bogan. MOAP
For a Materialist. Adelaide Love. MaRV; OQP; QP-2
For a Mocking Voice. Eleanor Farjeon. AlDL; CH; PoMS; TiPo (1959 ed.)
For a Modernist Sermon. Kenneth Burke. QS
For a Musician. George Wither. *Fr.* Hallelujah. OBS
(To a Musician, *wr. at. to* William Austin.) OxBoCh
For a name unknown. Why. Bliss Carman. LBMV; OBEV; OBVV
For a Nativity. Lisel Mueller. NePoAm-2
For a New Home. Rosa Zagnoni Marinoni. PoToHe
For A Novice. Sister Mary Edwardine. PraNu
For a Parting. Keith Sinclair. AnNZ
For a Patriot. Shakespeare. King Henry VIII, *fr.* III, ii PGD
For a Pessimist. Countee Cullen. PFE; PoeMoYo; PoMa
For a Poet. Countee Cullen. GoSl; PoNe
(I Have Wrapped My Dreams in a Silken Cloth.) MoSiPe
For a Poet Growing Old. Lawrence Lee. TBM
For a Second Marriage. James Merrill. NePoEA
For a Shakespearean Garden. Edna Davis Romig. PoTo
For a Siamese Cat. Mairi MacInnes. PoN

For a Statue of Chaucer at Woodstock. Mark Akenside. SeCePo

For A' That an' A' That ("The bonniest lass that ye meet neist"). *At. to* Robert Burns. CoMu

For A' That and A' That ("Is there for honest poverty"). Burns. *See* Man's a Man for A' That, A.

For a thing done, repentance is no good. Past Help [*or* Sonnet: He Is Past All Help]. Cecco Angiolieri da Siena. AWP; OnPM

For a Valentine. Mary Elizabeth Newell. PCH

For "A Venetian Pastoral" by Giorgione. Dante Gabriel Rossetti. Sonnets for Pictures, II. BPN; GTML; POTT; PoVP; ViBoPo; ViP; VLEP
(Venetian Pastoral, A.) ES; VA

For a Very Little Boy. Edmund Leamy. FAOV

For a Virgin Lady. Countee Cullen. MAP; MoAmPo

For a Warning. Caroline B. Le Row. PEOR

For a Young Idealist: "Godspeed!" John Gilland Brunini. JKCP (1955 ed.)

For a Young Musician. Marion Eells. CAG

For Adonis I am crying, for Adonis' beauty dead. Bion. *Fr.* Lament for Adonis. LiTW; OxBG

For adoration all the ranks. Christopher Smart. *Fr.* A Song to David. CoEV

For adoration, David's psalms. Christopher Smart. *Fr.* A Song to David. AnFE

For adoration seasons change. The Mermaid's Pap [*or* Adoration]. Christopher Smart. *Fr.* A Song to David. BeR; FaBoEn

For age is opportunity no less. Age Is Opportunity. Longfellow. *Fr.* Morituri Salutamus. PoToHe (new ed.); QP-2

For ages after Chaos gave it birth. Fire-Flowers. José Maria de Heredia. TrFP

For Alexidamus of Metapontum. Bacchylides, *tr. fr. Greek by* A. S. Way. GrL

For All Blasphemers. Stephen Vincent Benét. AtBAP; OxBA

For All Fanatics. Samuel Butler. *Fr.* Hudibras, I, 1. PoFr

For All Fathers. Stella Weston. FAOV

For all, for all, my thanks to Thee I offer. Gratitude. Mikhail Lermontov. BoR

For all her quiet life flowed on. Whittier. *Fr.* The Friend's Burial. MaRV

For all ill words that I have spoken. Last Confessional. John Drinkwater. LBBV

For All Ladies of Shalott. Aline Murray Kilmer. NP; TBM

For all life's beauties, and their beauteous growth. For Beauty, We Thank Thee [*or* We Thank Thee]. John Oxenham. BLRP; PGD

For All Our Loved Ones. *Unknown.* PraP

For All That Ever Has Been Ours. Ziche Landau, *tr. fr. Yiddish by* Marie Syrkin. LiTW

For, all that from her springs, and is ybredde. Mutability. Spenser. *Fr.* The Faerie Queene, VII. FaBoEn

For all that God, in mercy, sends. Give Thanks [*or* Thanks for Everything]. Helen Isabella Tupper. BLRP; PEOR; WBLP

For all the beauties of the day. Grace at Evening. Edgar A. Guest. TrPWD

For all the blessings of the year. A Hymn of Thanksgiving. Alice E. Sherwood. PraP

For all the faithful little dogs. A Poem for Little Dogs. Nancy Byrd Turner. AlBD

For all the gracious gifts in harvests fair. Thanksgiving Day. John Kendrick Bangs. TrPWD

For all the pains, my Lady, that I've borne. The Blameless Kiss. Joachim du Bellay. Les Amours, XV. TrFP

"For All the Saints and Sages." Marcus Argentarius, *tr. fr. Greek by* F. L. Lucas. GrPE

For all the saints who from their labors rest. Funeral Hymn [*or* For All the Saints]. William Walsham How. MaRV; WGRP

For all the vision that took fire this night. Burning Bush. Martin Feinstein. TrJP

For all the wonders of this wondrous world. John Oxenham. *Fr.* A Little Te Deum of the Commonplace. PGD; PSO

For all things beautiful, and good, and true. Thanksgiving. John Oxenham. BLRP; OQP; QP-2; WBLP

For all those beaten, for the broken heads. Litany for Dictatorships. Stephen Vincent Benét. AmPP; AnEnPo; NAMP; OxBA; PoFr

For all Thy ministries. We Thank Thee [Lord]. John Oxenham. PGD; WBLP

For all we sought and missed, or left unclaimed. The Road. Humbert Wolfe. QS

For All Who Need ("For all who watch tonight"). *Unknown.* MaRV
(Tonight.) PraP

For all your days prepare. Preparedness. Edwin Markham. FaFP; MAP; MoAmPo; NeMA; OQP; PoeMoYo; PYM; QP-1; YT

For Ammonis Who Died at 29 in 610. C. P. Cavafy, *tr. fr. Modern Greek by* Rae Dalven. MoGP

For an Argonaut, Age Seven. Ted Olson. FAOV

For an Autograph. James Russell Lowell. InP
Sels.
"Greatly begin! though thou have time." MCCG
"Life is a leaf of paper white." MaRV

For an Autumn Festival, *sel.* Whittier.
Harvest Hymn, *sts.* 5–12. OHIP, *abr.*; PoRL; PSO, *abr.*; TOAH
("Once more the liberal year laughs out," *abr.*) PGD
(Thanksgiving Ode.) PEOR

For an Emigrant. Randall Jarrell. OxBA

For an Epicurean Club Dinner. Poseidippus, *tr. fr. Greek by* J. M. Edmonds. GrR

For an Epitaph at Fiesole. Walter Savage Landor. BPN; OBRV; TOP; VA
(His Epitaph.) OBVV

For an Eskimo. Annie Charlotte Dalton. CaP; OCL

For an Hour. Winfred Ernest Garrison. OQP; QP-1

For an hour on Christmas eve. Two Christmas-Cards, II. Robinson Jeffers. MeRV; NeTW

For an Old Man. Norbert Engels. JKCP (1955 ed.)

For Anne Gregory. W. B. Yeats. EnLP; ExPo; FaBoMo; FaFP; GTBS-W; InPo; LiTL; LiTM; LoBV; LoPo; RiBV; SeCeV; SiTL

For Annie. Poe. AmP; AmPP; AnFE; APA; APW; BAV; CoAnAm; EV-5; HBV; IAP; LiTA; LO; LPS-1; MOAP; OBEV; OBVV; NePA; OxBA; TreFS

For Any Beachhead. M. K. Joseph. AnNZ

For any golfer of resource. The Crow and the Nighthawk. Watson Kirkconnell. CaP

For Any Lady's Birthday. Lawrence Lee. TBM

For Any Member of the Security Police. Josephine Jacobsen. NePoAm

For April Showers. Emily Rose Burt. GFA

For Arkesilas of Kyrene. Pindar, *tr. fr. Greek by* H. T. Wade-Gery *and* C. M. Bowra. Pythian Odes, IV. GrL

For Artaud. Michael McClure. NeAP

For Arvia. E. A. Robinson. TSW; TSWC

For Asopichus of Orchomenus. Pindar, *pr. tr. fr. Greek by* Sir John Sandys. Olympian Odes, XIV. LiA

For at the window of my house. She of the Impudent Face. Proverbs, Bible, *O.T.* TrJP

For aught that ever I could read. The Course of True Love. Shakespeare. *Fr.* A Midsummer Night's Dream, I, i. LPS-1; WHA

For August, be your dwelling thirty towers. Sonnets of the Months: August. Folgore da San Gemignano. AWP; LyPI

For auld lang syne, my dear. *See* Should auld acquaintance be forgot.

For authorities whose hopes. The Paper Nautilus. Marianne Moore. FaBoMo

For beauty being the best of all we know. The Growth of Love, VIII. Robert Bridges. PoVP

For beauty I am not a star. *See* As a beauty I'm not a great star.

For Beauty kissed your lips when they were young. Epitaph for the Poet V., II. Arthur Davison Ficke. HBMV

For Beauty, We Thank Thee. John Oxenham. PGD
(We Thank Thee.) BLRP

For breakfast we have coffee. Grandma's Tea. Dorothy Bregg. DDA

For Brian Priestman. F. R. Scott. TwCaPo

For bringing us this fair New Year. Prayer at New Year's. Nancy Byrd Turner. PraP

For Britons, chief. British Commerce. James Thomson. *Fr.* Liberty, IV. OBEC

For C. Philip Whalen. NeAP

For C. K. at His Christening. Daniel Lawrence Kelleher. NeIP

For captious fashion and capricious fad. Questions on a Nun's Habit: Of Crowns. Sister Mary Madeleva. PraNu

For certain he hath seen all perfectness. Dante. La Vita Nuova, XVII. AWP

For certain soldiers lately dead. A Martial Elegy for Some Lead Soldiers. Robert Louis Stevenson. SoV

For Charlie's Sake. John Williamson Palmer. HBV; LPS-1

For Charlotte Brontë. Emily Dickinson. CoBA

For Chloris long I sigh'd in vain. Pastoral. Thomas Godfrey. NoCaPo

For Choice. Anacreon, *tr. fr. Greek by* J. M. Edmonds. GrR

For Christmas. Dorothy Aldis. ChBR; GoBP; UTS

For Christmas. Rachel Field. ChBR; GaP

For Christmas Day. Eleanor Farjeon. ChBR; TiPo (1952 ed.)

For Christmas Day. Joseph Hall. AnEC

For Christmas Day. Francis Kinwelmersh. AnEC; ReIE

For Christmas Day. Thomas Pestel. *See* Psalm for Christmas Day.

For Christmas-Day. Charles Wesley. CEP

For Christmas Eve—a Prayer. *Unknown.* PraP

"For Christ's sweet sake, I beg an alms." James Russell Lowell. *Fr.* The Vision of Sir Launfal, Pt. II. WGRP

For close designs and crooked councils fit. Character of the Earl of Shaftesbury. Dryden. *Fr.* Absalom and Achitophel, I. LPS-3

For Communion with God, *sel.* Thomas Shepherd.
"Alas, my God, that we should be." TrPWD
(Alas, My God, *longer sel.*) OxBoCh
For Crethis' store of tales and pleasant chat. Crethis. Callimachus, *tr. by* Richard Garnett. AWP
For Crethis the teller of stories, for that sweet head so clever. The Dead Playmate. Callimachus, *tr. by* F. L. Lucas. GrPE
For Danny whistling slowly. Feed. Raymond Knister. BoCaPo; PeCV
For days and days I've climbed a tree. Contemplation. John Alden Carpenter. RIS
For days gold-bright. Song of Thanksgiving. John Richard Moreland. PGD
For death must come, and change, and, though the loss. Immutabilis. Alice Learned Bunner. Vingtaine, II. AA
For death we all are nurtured, the greatest and the least. The Slaughter-House. Palladas. GrPE
For Decoration Day. Rupert Hughes. AA; MDAH
For Deeper Life. Katharine Lee Bates. TrPWD
For Demerara bound with cod she flies. Escapade. Kenneth Leslie. EtS
For Dinah, the Adeneys' Cat. Anne Wilkinson. PeCV
For Dissection. Jerome Meyers. PoP
For Divine Strength. Samuel Johnson. *See* Prayer for Strength.
For do but note a wild and wanton herd. The Power of Music. Shakespeare. *Fr.* The Merchant of Venice, V, i. GN
For Dominion Day. Jesse Edgar Middleton. CPG
For Doricha the Courtesan. Poseidippus. *See* Doricha.
For down this path has April come again. Old April. Virginia Lyne Tunstall. Sonnets of an Old Town, II. LS
For each and every joyful thing. For Joy. Florence Earle Coates. VOD
For each new morning with its light. Thanksgiving. Emerson. MeMeAg; PCH
For each of us a different path to God. Pilgrimage. Blanche Shoemaker Wagstaff. MaRV; MuM
For each true deed is worship; it is prayer. True Work Is Worship. Edwin Markham. *Fr.* The Angelus. MaRV
For Eager Lovers. Genevieve Taggard. AnAmPo; LA; NP
For ease and for dispatch the morning's best. On Walking the Streets by Day [*or* The Morning]. John Gay. *Fr.* Trivia; or, The Art of Walking the Streets of London, II. EnLi-1 (1949 ed.); TOP
For Easter. Frances Ridley Havergal. OQP; QP-1
(Easter Prayer.) PraP
For Easter-Day. Charles Wesley. *See* Easter Hymn.
For Emily Dickinson. Hortense Landauer. PIAE
For England. J.D. Burns. BoAu
For England, in Grateful Appreciation, *sel.* Anton Vogt.
"I was five when we moved to England, and the strange voices." AnNZ
For England, when with fav'ring gale. Heaving [of] the Lead [*or* The Leadsman's Song *or* By the Deep Nine]. *At. to* J. [*or* W.] Pearce *and to* Charles Dibdin. ChTr; EtS; HBV; LPS-2; SG
For England's Sake Men Give Their Lives. Winifred M. Letts. LEAP
For Ever. *See* Forever.
For Every Day. Frances Ridley Havergal. *See* Lord, Speak to Me.
For every evil under [*or* ill beneath] the sun. Mother Goose. GoTP; HBV; HBVY; OTPC; OxNR; PPL
For every hill I've had to climb. Friendly Obstacles. *Unknown.* MaRV
For every hour that thou wilt spare me now. Love's Usury. John Donne. SeEP
For every parcel I stoop down to seize. The Armful. Robert Frost. ChMo; CMP
For everything is sacred, poetry. Islwyn. *Fr.* The Storm. PrWP
For Exmoor. Jean Ingelow. DiM; OBEV (new ed.); OBVV
For eyes he waves greentipped. Slug in Woods. Earle Birney. BoCaPo; CaP; PeCV
For False Heart. Hilaire Belloc. MBP; MoBrPo
(False Heart, The.) FaBoCh; HBMV; LoGBV
For Family Love. John S. Hoyland. *See* Prayer for Family Love, A.
For February Twelfth. Muriel M. Gessner. YeAr
For Federico García Lorca. Dorothy Livesay. BoCaPo
For fifteen long years. The Almond Blossoms of Chao Village. Po Chü-i. PoHN
For fifteen years we've never been. A Wife to a Husband. Hsi P'ei Lan. PoHN
For Fifty Years. Arthur C. Coe. CAG
For flowers so beautiful and sweet. We Thank Thee. Mattie M. Renwick. HH; MeMeAg; OTPC (1946 ed.); PEDC
For flowers that bloom about our feet. We Thank Thee [*or* Father, We Thank Thee *or* Spring Prayer]. *Unknown, at. to* Emerson. BoTP; HH, *abr.*; PraP; PSO, *sl. abr.*; TOAH, *abr.*
For Fog and Fate no charm is found. Destroyers in Collision. Kipling. *Fr.* Epitaphs of the War. PoVP
For Forgiveness. John Donne. *See* Hymn to God the Father, A.
For Forms of Government let fools contest. Charity. Pope. *Fr.* An Essay on Man. OBEC; ViBoPo
For forty years, for forty-one. This Dim and Ptolemaic Man. John Peale Bishop. CrMA; ImOP; LiTA; LiTM (rev. ed.); NePA
For forty years I shunned the lust. For a Virgin Lady. Countee Cullen. MAP; MoAmPo
For forty years my country and my home. To the Tune of "Breaking through Battle." Li Yu. WhP
For France two grenadiers held their way. The Grenadiers. Heine. OuHeWo
For Francis Ledwidge. Norreys Jephson O'Conor. PtP
For Futures. Josephine Miles. FiMAP
For G. W. W. Gibson. LO; LoPS
For gainful hours of pain and loss. We Thank Thee. *Unknown.* TOAH
For giving me desire. Desire. Thomas Traherne. EPS; LO; OxBoCh
For glowing autumn's brimming yield. We Thank Thee! Thomas Curtis Clark. PGD
For God hath not given us the spirit of fear. Second Timothy, Bible, *N.T.* TiPo (1952 ed.)
For God, our God is a gallant foe. Ballad for Gloom. Ezra Pound. LiTM (rev. ed.); MAP; MoAmPo; NeMA; NePA; OBVV
For God So Loved the World. Georgia Harkness. ChIP
"For God So Loved the World." Robert Whitaker. OQP; QP-1
For God so loved the world, that he gave his only begotten Son. St. John, Bible, *N.T.* LO
For God's sake, do not explain that picture. Daemon & Lectern & a Life-Size Mirror. Horace Gregory. PreP
For God's sake [*or* Godsake] hold your tongue, and let me love. The Canonization. John Donne. ATP; BEL; BLV; BoLiVe; CoBE; EIL; EM-1; EnL; EnLi-1 (1949 ed.); EnLoPo; EnLP; EPS; EV-2; GTBS-W; GTSE; LiTB; LiTG; LiTL; LoBV; MaPo; MePo; OBS; Po; PoE; PoEL-2; PoFS; ReEn; ReIE; RiBV; SeCePo; SeCeV; SeCV-1; SeEP; TOP; TrGrPo; TuPP; TwP; ViBoPo
For God's sake, let us be men. Let Us Be Men. D. H. Lawrence. MoPW
For God's sake, let us sit upon the ground. *See* For heaven's sake . . .
For God's sake mark that fly. Nulla Fides. Patrick Carey. SeEP
For Good Luck. Juliana Horatia Ewing. FaPON; OTPC (1946 ed.); PRWS
(Little Kings and Queens of the May.) BoTP
For government, though high, and low, and lower. The Commonwealth of the Bees [*or* So Work the Honey-Bees]. Shakespeare. King Henry V, *fr.* I, ii. BCEP; GN
For gray Folk in the falling leaves. On the Eve of All Hallows. Arthur L. Phelps. CPG
For Gwenhwyfar and Blodeuwedd. Davies Aberpennar. MoWP
For half a month it has rained without cease. On a Puppy. Feng Chih. LiTW
For Hanukkah. Hayyim Nahman Bialik. TiPo (1952 ed.)
For happiness or for grief we felt no shame. Meeting. Olga Berggolts. *Fr.* Songs of the Spanish Children. RuPo
For Haroun Al Raschid. Abu'l-Atahija, *tr. fr. Arabic by* Herbert Howarth *and* Ibrahim Shukrallah. LiTW
For Harry and June. Ray Mathew. NeLNL
For Having Thee. Francis X. Connolly. JKCP (1955 ed.)
For he five days/ 'Mong shrubs and pathless briars and rushes green. Pathless Briars. Pindar. *Fr.* Odes. LiA
For He Had Great Possessions. Richard Middleton. HBV
For he was of that stubborn crew. For All Fanatics. Samuel Butler. *Fr.* Hudibras. PoFr
For He Was Scotch and So Was She. Jean Blewett. CPG
For heaven's [*or* God's] sake, let us sit upon the ground. Of the Death of Kings. Shakespeare. King Richard II, *fr.* III, ii. ChTr; HoPM; PoFr
For heaven's sake, what d'you mean to do? Resolved to Be Beloved. Abraham Cowley. CaAE
For Hectors glorie still he stood; and ever went about. Homer, *tr. by* George Chapman. *Fr.* The Iliad, XV. LiA
For Hecuba, for Troy's daughters, a doom of tears and sorrow. "Passing the Love of Women." Plato. GrPE
For Hellas! Euripides, *tr. fr. Greek by* Arthur S. Way. *Fr.* Iphigenia in Aulis. GrR
For her gait, if she be walking. The Complete Lover [*or* Song *or* Sonnet]. William Browne. BCEP; ElSeCe; EPS (1942 ed.); HBV; LiTL; LoPS; OBEV
For Her Heart Only. *Unknown.* EIL
("Only, sweet Love, afford me but thy heart.") LO
For Her on the First Day Out. Robert Bagg. NePoAm-2
For here lies Juliet, and her beauty makes. Thus with a Kiss I Die [*or* Here Lies Juliet]. Shakespeare. *Fr.* Romeo and Juliet, V, iii. FaFP; TreFS; TrGrPo
For He's a Jolly Good Fellow! *Unknown.* OlF
For Hettie. LeRoi Jones. NeAP

For Hiero of Syracuse. Bacchylides, *tr. fr. Greek by* Arthur S. Way. GrL
For Hiero, Tyrant of Syracuse. Pindar, *tr. fr. Greek by* Arthur S. Way. Olympian Odes, I. GrL
("Best of all things is water; but gold, like a gleaming fire," *tr. by* Richmond Lattimore.) GrPo
(First Olympionique: To Hiero of Syracuse, *tr. by* Ambrose Philips.) ATP
(For Hieron of Syracuse, *pr. tr. by* Sir John Sandys.) LiA
(Olympian Ode I: To Hiero the Syracusan, *tr. by* Abraham Moore.) EnLi-2; OuHeWo
For him cease in such frenzy to cry. Nikolai Alekseyevich Nekrasov, *tr. fr. Russian by* Sir Cecil Kisch. WaL
For him, it seems, everything was molten. The Laughing Hyena, by Hokusai. D. J. Enright. PoN
For him what countless tears I must have shed. Six Sonnets. Mary Queen of Scots. DiM
For Him, who, lost to ev'ry Hope of Life. Apology for Vagrants. John Langhorne. *Fr.* The Country Justice. OBEC
For him who must see many years. Early Death and Fame. Matthew Arnold. TriL
For him who sought his country's good. Washington's Monument. *Unknown.* OHIP; PAH
For Hire. Morris Jacob Rosenfeld, *tr. fr. Yiddish by* Rose Pastor Stokes *and* Helena Franks. LiTW
For His love that bought us all dear. Christ, the Fleur-de-Lis [*or* Sing We All, for Time It Is]. *Unknown.* AnEC; MeRV
For His Own Epitaph. W. B. Yeats. *Fr.* Under Ben Bulben. AnFE
For His Own Tomb-Stone. Matthew Prior. TOP
For his religion it was fit. The Religion of Hudibras. Samuel Butler. *Fr.* Hudibras, I, I. BOHV; InMe; FaBoEn; LoBV; LPS-2; ViBoPo
For His Sake. Annie Denman. BePJ
For home and friends and loved ones dear. Our Thanks. Nan F. Weeks. PraP
For Hope. Richard Crashaw. GTBS-W; LiTB; ViBoPo
(Answer for Hope.) MeLP
(M. Crashaw's Answer for Hope.) OBS; SeCV-I
(Richard Crashaw's Answer; for Hope.) LiTG
"Fair hope! our earlyer heav'n by thee," *sel.* FaBoEn
For hours the princess would not play or sleep. The Yak. Virna Sheard. CaP; PeCV
For hours without stopping. The Shopper [*or* Unchanged]. Martial. RoL; WoL
For how long known this boundless wash of light. Summer Beach. Frances Cornford. ChMP
For human nature Hope remains alone. Hope. Theognis. AWP; JAWP; WBP
For I am not without authority in my jeopardy, which I derive inevitably from the glory of the name of the Lord. Christopher Smart. *Fr.* Jubilate Agno. EiPP
For I am rightful fellow of their band. Mentors. Gwendolyn Brooks. PoNe
For I Am Sad. Don Marquis. BOHV
For I dipt [*or* dipped] into the future, far as human eye could see. Prophecy [*or* A Poet's Prophecy *or* A Vision]. Tennyson. *Fr.* Locksley Hall. AOAH; BoHiPo; CBE; GTBS-W; PGD; PTA-I; PYM; TreF; WBLP. *See also* I dipt into the future . . .
For I have been, ere now, a girl and a boy. Transmigration. Empedocles. OxBG
For I Have Done a Good and Kindly Deed. Franz Werfel, *tr. fr. German by* Edith Abercrombie Snow. TrJP
For I have dreamed a dream where Fate and God. Sonnet. Arthur Davison Ficke. MuM
For I have learned/ To look on Nature. I Have Felt a Presence [*or* Lines Written above Tintern Abbey]. Wordsworth. *Fr.* Lines Composed a Few Miles above Tintern Abbey. BBV; MaRV; OQP; PC; QP-2
For I have learnt, though late. Bitterness. Sophocles. *Fr.* Ajax. LiA
For I have loved [*or* lov'd] the rural walk through lanes. The Rural Walk. William Cowper. *Fr.* The Task, I. EnRP; TOP
For I have seen this light. I did not dream. Sonnet. Leonora Speyer. *Fr.* Sonnets for the Beloved. UnW
For I have taken to my house a maid. Deianira's Love Charm. Sophocles. *Fr.* Trachiniae. GrR
For I learn as the years roll onward. Lessons of the Year. *Unknown.* BLRP
For I Must Sing of All I Feel and Know. James Thomson. PoVP
For I, my mother, I. *Unknown, tr. fr. Spanish by* Eleanor L. Turnbull. TeCS
For I pray God to bless improvements in gardening till London be a city of palm-trees. The Search for Pearls. Christopher Smart. *Fr.* Jubilate Agno. RO
For I saw the field full of folk that before I described. The Confession of the Deadly Sins. William Langland. *Fr.* The Vision of Piers Plowman. MeEV
For I say, through the grace given unto me. The Duties of Man. Romans, Bible, *N.T.* TreF
For I the Ballad Will Repeat. Shakespeare. *Fr.* All's Well That Ends Well, I, iii. ViBoPo
For I was a gaunt grave councillor. La Fraisne. Ezra Pound. NP; PG
For I Will Consider My Cat Jeoffry. Christopher Smart. *See* My Cat Jeoffry.
For I would walk alone. Communion with Nature. Wordsworth. *Fr.* The Prelude, II. OBRV; TOP
For if the shaft of destiny hath quit. The Great Poet. Mu'tamid, King of Seville. LiTW
For I'm called Little Buttercup—dear Little Buttercup. Little Buttercup. W. S. Gilbert. *Fr.* H. M. S. Pinafore. TreFS
For in the warm blue summer weather. Alfred Noyes. Slumber-Songs of the Madonna, IV. BOL
For infants time is like a humming shell. O Dreams, O Destinations. C. Day Lewis. MoPo
For Inspiration. Michelangelo, *tr. fr. Italian by* Wordsworth. CAW; GoBC; WGRP
(Prayer for Inspiration, A.) OQP; QP-I
(Supplication, A.) GrCo-I
(To the Supreme Being.) AWP; JAWP; LiTW; TrPWD; WBP
For it is the Archer Apollo, and the Muses, that inspire. Poetry. Hesiod. *Fr.* Theogony. GrPE
For James Dean. Frank O'Hara. NeAP
For January I give you vests of skins. Sonnets of the Months: January. Folgore da San Geminiano. AWP; LyPI
For Jillian of Berry she dwells on a hill. Jillian of Berry [*or* Merrythought's Song]. *At. to* Francis Beaumont. *Fr.* The Knight of the Burning Pestle (*by* Beaumont *and* Fletcher). EIL; OBS
For Jim, Easter Eve. Anne Spencer. PoNe
For John Keats, Apostle of Beauty. Countee Cullen. PFE
(Four Epitaphs, 2.) CDC
For Johnny. John Pudney. HaMV
For Joy. Florence Earle Coates. VOD
For July in Siena, by the willow-tree. Of the Months: July. Folgore da San Geminiano. AWP
For just a brief while every day. Rendezvous. Mary Scott Fitzgerald. PoToHe (new ed.)
For knighthood is not in the feats of war. The True Knight [*or* True Knighthood]. Stephen Hawes. *Fr.* The Pastime of Pleasure. ACP; AnEnPo; OBEV; TrGrPo
For know, my girl, there is always the axe. Les Chantiers. S. Frances Harrison. *Fr.* Down the River. CPG
For Knowledge must make shift by narrow ways. The Limitations of Knowledge. Empedocles. OxBG
For Lack of Gold. Adam Austin. EBSV
For lack of rain. Rakuten, *tr. fr. Japanese by* Lois J. Erickson. SoLD
For Life I Had Never Cared Greatly. Thomas Hardy. BEL; ChMo; CMP; EnLit; HBMV; LiTM (rev. ed.); PoVP
For life, with all it yields of joy and woe. Truth. Robert Browning. *Fr.* A Death in the Desert. MaRV; OQP; QP-2
For Little Dinogad. *Unknown, tr. fr. Welsh by* H. Idris Bell. LyMA
(Dinogad's Petticoat, *tr. by* Gwyne Williams.) PrWP
For lo! the board with cups and spoons is crowned. Pope. *Fr.* The Rape of the Lock. ViBoPo
For lo! the living God doth bare his arm. Democracy. Harriet Monroe. *Fr.* Commemoration Ode. AA
For [*or* And] lo! the sea that fleets about the land. The Dancing Sea [*or* The Sea Danceth]. Sir John Davies. *Fr.* Orchestra. ChTr; EtS
For, Lo, the Winter Is Past. Song of Solomon, II: 10–13, Bible, *O.T.* TreF
("For, lo, the winter is past," II: 11–12.) SUS; TiPo
(Lo, the Winter Is Past.) FaPON (11–13); ShBV-3 (11–12)
(Spring, 11–12.) PCD; PCH
(Winter Is Past, The, 11–12.) YeAr
For long at the foot of the steps I stood. Rosamunde. Guillaume Apollinaire. TrFP
For long he did not think of shells as fair. A Boy. Hugo von Hofmannsthal. AnGP
For long I stood motionless, watching. Afanasi Fet, *tr. fr. Russian by* V. de S. Pinto. BoR
For, Lord, the Crowded Cities Be. Rainer Maria Rilke, *tr. fr. German by* Ludwig Lewisohn. AWP; JAWP; TrJP; WBP
For Louise, Age 17. Irving Layton. PeCV
For love he offered me his perfect world. Gift to a Jade. Anna Wickham. NP
For love—I would. The Warning. Robert Creeley. NeAP
For Love is like a plant that clings. Love. John Swanwick Drennan. IrPN
For Love of Appin. Jessie Mackay. AnNZ
For love of lovely words, and for the sake. Skerryvore. Robert Louis Stevenson. VLEP

For love's sake, kiss me once again. Begging Another, on Colour of Mending the Former [*or* The Kiss]. Ben Jonson. *Fr.* A Celebration of Charis. AtBAP; LO; LoPS; OAEP; PoEL-2; TuPP
For Love's Sake Only. Elizabeth Barrett Browning. *See* Sonnets from the Portuguese: "If thou must love me, let it be for naught."
For M——. Bruce Williamson. NeIP
For M. S. Singing Frühlingsglaube in 1945. Frances Cornford. UnS
For Madame Chiang Kai-shek. Amanda Benjamin Hall. NeTW
For Maister Geoffrey Chaucer. Robert Hillyer. PtP
For Man to Act. Thomas Traherne. *Fr.* Christian Ethics. OxBoCh
For man to tell how human life began. Adam, First Man of Men. Milton. *Fr.* Paradise Lost, VIII. MaPo
For man's unceasing quest for God. The Quest Eternal. Alice M. Pullen. MaRV
For many a mile the tawny mountains heaved. A Wicklow Scene. George Francis Savage-Armstrong. *Fr.* Lugnaquillia. TIP
For many a year I've watched the ships a-sailing to and fro. The Ships. J. J. Bell. BoTP; TVSH
For many and many a year. Enemies. Agnes Lee. NP
For many blessings I to God upraise. Nature and the Child. John Lancaster Spalding. *Fr.* God and the Soul. AA
For many, many days together. Riding Together. William Morris. BPN; LPS-3; PCN; ViPo; ViPP; VLEP; WaKn
For many thousand ages. Es stehen unbeweglich. Heine. AWP; JAWP; TrJP; WBP
For Martha's Kitchen. Fay Inchfawn. OQP; QP-2
For Mary McLeod Bethune. Margaret Walker. PoNe
For Me. *Unknown.* ChIP; OQP; QP-1
For me all the world is glowing. The Young Girl's Song. Vilhelm Krag. AnNoLy
For me, for me, two horses wait. The Wizard's Funeral. Richard Watson Dixon. GTBS-D; LoBV
For me, I know nought; nothing I deny. Byron. *Fr.* Don Juan, XIV. OBRV
For me my spear is kneaded bread; wine from the Thracian land. The Freelance. Archilochus. GrPE
For me one silly task is like another. Cassandra. Louise Bogan. LA; MAP; MOAP; NP
For me the balm shall bleed, and amber flow. Glitter. Pope. *Fr.* Windsor Forest. BeR
For me the jasmine buds unfold. Song [*or* The World Is Mine]. Florence Earle Coates. AA; HBV; LBMV; NV; PoMa; VOD
For me, the naked and the nude. The Naked and the Nude. Robert Graves. SiTL
For me there is no dismay. The Poet. C. Day Lewis. OxBI
For Mercy, Courage, Kindness, Mirth. Laurence Binyon. *See* Song, A: "For Mercy, Courage, Kindness, Mirth."
For metaphors of man we search the skies. Sir William Watson. InP
For modes of faith let graceless Zealots fight. Faith. Pope. *Fr.* An Essay on Man. WGRP
For mony lang year I ha'e heard frae my grannie. The Hazlewood Witch. Richard Gall. EBSV
For more than twenty years. Mirrors. Toyohiko Kagawa. SoLD
For Morn, my dome of blue. A Child's Prayer. Siegfried Sassoon. BoTP
For mother-love and father-care. We Thank Thee. *Unknown.* FaPON; MPB; OTPC (1946 ed.)
For much imaginary work was there. Shakespeare. *Fr.* The Rape of Lucrece. MyFE
For Music. Byron. *See* Stanzas for Music: "There be none of beauty's daughters."
For My Brother. Thomas Merton. InPo; TreFS
For My Brother. Su T'ung-po, *tr. fr. Chinese by* Yang Chising. WhP
For My Father. Rachel Field. InMe
For My Father. Paul Potts. FaBoTw
For My Fireplace. Henry Noyes Pratt. DDA
For my first twenty years, since yesterday. *See* For the first twenty years, since yesterday.
For My Funeral. A. E. Housman. More Poems, XLVII. ChMo; ReaPo; TrPWD; ViBoPo
For My Grandfather. Francis Webb. BoAV
For My Grandmother. Countee Cullen. GoSl; MAP; MoAmPo (Four Epitaphs, 1.) CDC
For My Own Monument. Matthew Prior. CEP; HBV; LoBV; OBEC; OBEV
For My Own Tomb-Stone. Matthew Prior. LiA
For My People. Margaret Walker. PoFr; PoNe
For my sister's sake. Hitomaro. *Fr.* Manyo Shu. AWP; LiTW
For My Son Antoni Boguslawski, *tr. fr. Polish by* L. E. Gielgud. PoFr
For My Son. John Frederick Nims. MiAP
For my soul engaged in far matters. Three Sections from "Anabasis." "St.-J. Perse." *Fr.* Anabasis. LiTW
For My Students, Returning to College. John Williams. NePoAm-2
For My thoughts are not your thoughts. My Thoughts Are Not Your Thoughts. Isaiah, Bible, *O.T.* TrJP
For My Twenty-fifth Birthday in Nineteen Forty-one. John Ciardi. WaP
For My Wife. Julian Symons. NeBP; WaP
For Nature ever faithful is. Emerson. *Fr.* Woodnotes. OBAV
For Nijinsky's Tomb. Frances Cornford. UnS
"For nine days then we were driven by the tempest's ruinous blast." Lotus-Land and the Cyclops' Cave. Homer. *Fr.* The Odyssey, IX. GrPE
For no man wist who was best. The Round Table. Robert Mannyng. ACP
For noble minds, the worst of miseries. Poverty. Theognis. AWP; JAWP; OnPM; WBP
For nought hath grown. The Evils of Money. Sophocles. *Fr.* Antigone. GrR
For now, and since first break of dawne the Fiend. Milton. *Fr.* Paradise Lost, IX. BrBE
For now, and then a hollow murmuring sound. Tydes-Well, the Third Wonder of the Peak. Charles Cotton. *Fr.* The Wonders of the Peake. BeR
For now are wider ways, profounder tides. The Deeper Seas. Henry Bellamann. EtS
For now, love thou, I rede, Christ, as I thee tell. Love. Richard Rolle. *Fr.* Love Is Life. ACP; BCEP; CAW
For now should I have lain still and been quiet. Job Longeth for Death. Job, Bible, *O.T.* PoD
. . . For now too nigh/ Th' Archangel stood. Their Banishment. Milton. *Fr.* Paradise Lost, XII. BrBE; SeCePo
For, O America, our country!—land. America. Arlo Bates. *Fr.* The Torch-Bearers. AA; PaA
For Old Lovers. T. A. Daly. OBAV
For Omar. Humbert Wolfe. PtP
For on that night they killed him. *Unknown, tr. fr. Spanish by* Eleanor L. Turnbull. TeCS
For Once, Then, Something. Robert Frost. AnFE; CoAnAm; IAP; PoFS
For one carved instant as they flew. Sea Gulls. E. J. Pratt. EtS; TwCaPo
For one copper. Another [Beggar Poem]. Issa. PoFr
For One Last Time. Pushkin, *tr. fr. Russian by* Babette Deutsch. TrRV
("For the last time I risk caresses," *tr. by* C. M. Bowra.) BoR
For One Lately Bereft. Margaret E. Bruner. PoToHe
For one month afterwards the eye stays true. Departure. Kingsley Amis. NePoEA; PoN
For one New England pinewood on a hill. Proposed Barter. Grace Hazard Conkling. TBM
For One of Low Degree. Walther von der Vogelweide, *tr. fr. German by* Margaret R. Richey. LyMA
For One Retired into the Country. Charles Wesley. SN
For One Who Died. Jessica Powers. BPP
For One Who Is Serene. Margaret E. Bruner. PoToHe (new ed.)
For One Who Would Not Be Buried in Westminster Abbey. Pope. ACP (1926 ed.); PIAE
For One Who Would Not Take His Life in His Hands. Delmore Schwartz. NAMP
For Orford and for Waldegrave. Impromptus. Byron. BPN
For others she may not be fair. Mother. Thomas Curtis Clark. PGD
For Our Dead. Clinton Scollard. HH; MDAH; PEOR (Memorial Day.) PEDC
For "Our Lady of the Rocks." Dante Gabriel Rossetti. MeRV; NBE
(Our Lady of the Rocks.) OxBoCh
"For our martyr'd Charles I pawn'd my plate." The Old Cavalier. Sir Francis Hastings Doyle. VA
For Our Sakes. Oscar Wilde. PGD
For our sore-shattered Jewish life. For All That Ever Has Been Ours. Ziche Landau. LiTW
For pacing to and fro before the loom. The Wooing of Cyrene. Pindar. *Fr.* Pythian Odes, IX. GrR
For Palm Sunday. Henry Hart Milman. OQP; QP-1
(Ride On in Majesty.) VA
("Ride on, ride on in majesty.") OIF
For pastime, often those who sail the deep. The Albatross. Baudelaire. OnPM
For Paul Laurence Dunbar. Countee Cullen. GoSl
(Four Epitaphs, 3.) CDC
For people/ on trial. Perambulator Poems, II. David McCord. WhC
For Perfect Peace. Charles Wesley. BePJ
For Pity, Pretty Eyes, Surcease. Thomas Lodge. EIL; ElSeCe; ReIE; SiCE
(Armistice.) OBSC
For pleasing Arts behold her matchless charms. The Future

For pleasing Arts behold her matchless charms (*continued*) of American Literature. John Trumbull. *Fr.* Essay on the Fine Arts. AmPP (3d ed.)
For Poets Slain in War. Walter Adolphe Roberts. BAP
For Posterity. Kathleen Raine. NeBP
For Posterity. Alexander Smith. ADAH
For Priam's queen and daughters at their birth. Dion of Syracuse. Plato. GrPo; OxBG
For raiment and for daily bread. Thanksgiving. Odell Shepard. PEDC
For Randolph Bourne. James Oppenheim. AnAmPo; LA
For Religion's Sake. Walt Whitman. *See* Necessity of Religion, The.
For Remembrance. Basil Ebers. DD; HH
For Remembrance. Niu Hsi-chi, *tr. fr. Chinese by* Ch'u Ta'kao. ChLP
For Remembrance. Edward Shanks. LBBV
For Rhoda. Delmore Schwartz. *See* Time Is the Fire.
For right is right, since God is God. Right Is Right. Frederick William Faber. WBLP
For Righteousness' Sake. Whittier. CoV; PoEL-4
For rigorous teachers seized my youth. Matthew Arnold. *Fr.* Stanzas from the Grande Chartreuse. ViBoPo
For road-mates and companions he chose twelve. On the Road. John Oxenham. StJW
For round about, the wals yclothed were. The Masque of Cupid. Spenser. *Fr.* The Faerie Queene, III. EV-1
For St. Bartholomew's Eve. Malcolm Cowley. NAMP
For St. Felix' Day. Paulinus of Nola, *tr. fr. Latin by* Helen Waddell. LaP
For Sale, a Horse. Charles Edward Taylor. AA
For Sale or Rent. *Unknown.* PoToHe (new ed.)
For Scotland. Robert Fuller Murray. BSV
For Scotland's and for freedom's right. Bruce and the Spider. Bernard Barton. BeLS; LPS-2
For seven long years I courted Nancy. The Wild Miz-Zou-Rye. *Unknown.* ABF
For Shame! Kaj Munk, *tr. fr. Danish by* Charles W. Stork. BoDS
For shame deny that thou bear'st love to any. Sonnets, X. Shakespeare. PeBoSo
For shame, thou everlasting wooer. The Antiplatonick. John Cleveland. MePo
For she is a vapour/ of the power of God. Wisdom, Bible, Apocrypha (*Douay vers.*). ISi
For sheer urbanity, I deem. Song of Fairly Utter Despair. Samuel Hoffenstein. CIV
For Sheila. Margaret Allonby. BoSA
For, Singing Till His Heaven Fills. George Meredith. *Fr.* The Lark Ascending. BLA; VA, *shorter sel.*
For Sir John Vanbrugh, Architect. Abel Evans. *See* Epitaph on Sir John Vanbrugh.
For sixty days and upwards. Vicksburg—a Ballad. Paul Hamilton Hayne. AA; BlG; MC; MDAH; PAH; SPP; TCAP
For Sleep or Death. Ruth Pitter. AlDL; TrPWD
For Sleep When Overtired. Sarah N. Cleghorn. OQP; OQ-2 (For Sleep When Overtired or Worried.) PC
For Snow. Eleanor Farjeon. CH; RAR; TiPo
For Soldiers. Humphrey Gifford. CH; ElL; ElSeCe; SiCE; TriL; TuPP
For Steve. Earle Birney. BoCaPo (1948 ed.); WaP
For stock and stone. In Praise of Common Things. Lizette Woodworth Reese. LS
For such as you, I do believe. The Mother in the House. Hermann Hagedorn. DD; HBMV; MotAn; OHIP; PoRL; PoToHe
For summer rain, and winter's sun. A Thanksgiving. John Kendrick Bangs. MaRV
For summer's bloom and autumn's blight. Hymn. Josiah Gilbert Holland. *Fr.* Bitter-sweet. TrPWD
For sunlit hours and visions clear. Gratitude. Clyde McGee. BLRP; OQP; QP-1
For T. S. E. Only. Hyam Plutzik. FiMAP
For ten days now they have done no work. The walls. Maxwell Anderson. *Fr.* Journey to Jerusalem. QS
For ten miles the mountains rise. The Farm by the Lake. Chu Hsi. OnPC
For ten years I never left my books. After Passing the Examination. Po Chü-i. AlDL; Po; TrCh
For that He Looked Not upon Her. George Gascoigne. ElL
For that lovely face will fail. Persuasions to Love. Thomas Carew. LiTL; ViBoPo
For That Pale God of Silence Men Call Death. Lois Carver. CAG
For the Baptist[e]. William Drummond of Hawthornden. BSV; EBSV; GoTS; HBV; LoBV; OBS; OxBoCh; SeEP
(Baptist, The.) TrGrPo
(Baptist's Sonnet, The.) EPS (1942 ed.)
(John the Baptist.) PIAE
(Saint John Baptist.) CBOV; ES; EV-2; GTBS-D; GTBS-W; GTSE; GTSL; OBEV; OnPP; PeBoSo
For the Bath of Pallas. Callimachus, *tr. fr. Greek by* Robert Allason Furness. GrR
For the Beauty of the Earth. Folliott Sandford Pierpoint. MaRV
For the Bed at Kelmscott. William Morris. *See* Inscription for an Old Bed.
For the Birthday of a Middle-aged Child. Aline Kilmer. FAOV
For the Blinded Soldiers. Austin Dobson. BPN
For the Book of Love. Jules Laforgue, *tr. fr. French by* Jethro Bithell. AWP; LiTW; AnFP, *tr. by* Vernon Watkins
For the brother who slumbers the city wails. Hymn to Tammuz. *Unknown.* LiTW
For the Burial of the Dead. Prudentius, *tr. fr. Latin by* Basil Blackett. LaP
For the Candle Light. Angelina W. Grimké. CDG; PoNe
For the child, fascinated by prints and maps. The Voyage. Baudelaire. LiTW
For the Conjunction of Two Planets. Adrienne Cecile Rich. ImOP
For the Dancer of the King of Wu, When She Is Half Drunk. Li Po, *tr. fr. Chinese.* WhP
For the days when nothing happens. Thanksgiving. Margaret E. Sangster. BLRP
For the Dead Gregorians. Ignacio Ramírez, *tr. fr. Spanish by* Samuel Beckett. AnMP
For the Depressed. Julian Symons. WaP
For the discipline of sorrow. Let Us Give Thanks. "Marianne Farningham." PEDC
For the dream unfinished. Plain Chant for America. Katherine Garrison Chapin. PoFr
For the Eightieth Birthday of a Great Singer. Edward Shanks. UnS
For the Fallen. Laurence Binyon. AnFE; CaAE; GTBS; InP; MaRV; MM; MuP; OBEV (new ed.); PoeT; PoFr; POTE; ShBV-3; TVSH; TwCV
"They went with songs to the battle," *sel.* ViBoPo
For the Feast of Giordano Bruno. Swinburne. PoFr; ViPo
For the feast of trumpets should be kept up. Christopher Smart. *Fr.* Jubilate Agno. UnS
For the few hours of life allotted me. Prayer. *Tr. fr. Latin by* Abraham Cowley. PoFr
For the first man to climb the hill. Pioneers. *Unknown.* MaRV
For the first Monday of my week. In the Cemetery of the Sun. Wilfred Watson. PeCV
For the [*or* my] first twenty years [*or* yeares], since yesterday. The Computation. John Donne. ATP (1935 ed.); ElSeCe; EPS (1942 ed.); OAEP; TuPP
For the fount of life eternal. The Joys of Paradise. St. Augustine. CAW
For the Gifts of the Spirit. Edward Rowland Sill. TrPWD
For the gladness here where the sun is shining. Our Prayer of Thanks. Carl Sandburg. NP
For the gods keep hidden from men the means of life. Pandora. Hesiod. *Fr.* Works and Days. LiA
For the happy/ there is song of angels. Heaven. Cynewulf. *Fr.* Christ. PoLi
For the hay and the corn and the wheat that is reaped. Giving Thanks. *Unknown.* PEDC; TOAH
For the heart, willing and not willing. The Clovers. Jean Garrigue. MoPo
For the Holy Family by Michelangelo. Dante Gabriel Rossetti. GoBC
For the kingdom of heaven is as a man traveling into a far country. The Parable of the Talents. St. Matthew, Bible, *N.T.* EnLi-1
For the Lady Olivia Porter; a Present upon a New-Years Day. Sir William Davenant. MeLP; MePo; OBS
For the last time Beowulf uttered his boast. Beowulf and Wiglaf Slay the Dragon. *Unknown.* *Fr.* Beowulf. AnOE
For the last time I risk caresses. Pushkin. *See* For One Last Time.
For the Letter ל Which Signifies God. Christopher Smart. *Fr.* Jubilate Agno. AtBAP
For the lifting up of mountains. Mountains. Lucy Larcom. WBLP
For the long nights you lay awake. To Alison Cunningham. Robert Louis Stevenson. PoVP
For the Lord made a Nosegay in the meadow. Flowers Are Great Blessings. Christopher Smart. *Fr.* Jubilate Agno. MeRV
For the Lost Generation. Galway Kinnell. NePoAm
For the Love of Jean. Allan Ramsay. *Fr.* The Gentle Shepherd. EBSV
(Dainty Sang, A.) OBEC
For the Magdalene. William Drummond of Hawthornden. AtBAP; ElSeCe; LoBV; PoEL-2
For the Magi. J. Patrick Walsh. JKCP (1955 ed.)
For the Marriage of Faustus and Helen (I–III). Hart Crane. NePA
"Capped arbiter of beauty in this street," III. FaBoMo; LiTM

For the Master's Use. *Unknown.* BLRP
(Watered Lilies, The.) BLPA
For the Nativity of Our Lord ("O than the fairest day"). William Drummond of Hawthornden. *See* Shepherds, The.
For the New Railway Station in Rome. Richard Wilbur. NePoEA
For the New Year. Edwin Markham. OQP; QP-1
For the New Year. Norman Nicholson. NeBP
For the Old Year. Raymond Kresensky. PSO
For the One Who Would Take Man's Life in His Hands. Delmore Schwartz. FiMAP; LiTA; LiTM; MiAP; MoAB; MoAmPo; MoVE; NePA; WaP
For the outside leagues of liberty. Sidney Lanier. *Fr.* The Symphony. PoFr
For the palace that lies desolate. We Sit Solitary. *Unknown.* TrJP
For the past three days she had been wandering, and following. Charles Péguy. *Fr.* The Passion of Our Lady. ISi
For the Peace of Jerusalem. Charles Wesley. BeJP
For the Picture, "The Last of England." Ford Madox Brown. VA
For the Poor Blind Man. Francisco A. de Icaza, *tr. fr. Spanish by* Samuel Beckett. AnMP
For the poor body that I own. Garadh. Padraic Colum. OnYI; PG (1955 ed.)
For the precision that dares hardly look. To the Precision. Richard Brathwaite. *Fr.* A Strappado for the Devil. SiCE
For the Quakers. Bianca Bradbury. BoFr; NeTW
For the Records. Joseph Easton McDougall. MM
For the Right Honorable Lucy, Countess of Huntingdon, 1649. Thomas Pestel. ReEn
For the rosebud's break of beauty. Lucy Larcom. *Fr.* A Thanksgiving. TrPWD
For the sake of a night. The Stewardess of the Empress Koka, *tr. fr. Japanese by* Kenneth Rexroth. OnPJ
For the Sake o' Somebody. Burns. *See* For the Sake of Somebody.
For the sake of a weathered gray city set high on a hill. Perugia. Amelia Josephine Burr. HBV
For the Sake of [*or* o'] Somebody. Burns. AtBAP; EV-3
(Somebody.) BSV
For the Sexes: the Gates of Paradise. Blake. LiTB; PoEL-4
For the Signboards. Vladimir Mayakovsky, *tr. fr. Russian by* Jack Lindsay. RuPo
For the Sin. *Unknown, tr. fr. Hebrew.* TrJP
For the Sisters of the Hôtel Dieu. A. M. Klein. BoCaPo (1948 ed.)
For the Slender Beech and the Sapling Oak. Thomas Love Peacock. *See* Song: "For the tender beech and the sapling oak."
For the sole edification. A Credo. Thackeray. HBV
For the springs of living waters pants my parched soul athirst. The Glory of Paradise. St. Peter Damian. LaP
For the Sun Declined, *sel.* Yitzhak Lamdan, *tr. fr. Hebrew by* Simon Halkin.
"Where am I, O awesome friend?" TrJP
For the sun that shone at the dawn of spring. A Song of Thanks. Edward Smyth Jones. BANP
For the tender beech and the sapling oak. Song [*or* For the Slender Beech and the Sapling Oak *or* The Greenwood Tree *or* The Oak and the Beech]. Thomas Love Peacock. *Fr.* Maid Marian. ADAH; ERP; GTSE; OHIP; OTPC; PRWS
For the Time Being; a Christmas Oratorio, *sels.* W. H. Auden.
Advent. OAEP (2d ed.)
Dialogue between Mary and Gabriel. ISi
Flight into Egypt, The, I-IV. OAEP (2d ed.); OxBA
After Christmas, III. MoAB; MoBrPo (1950 ed.)
(Well, So That Is That.) LiTA
Chorus: "He is the Way," IV. AnFE
(He Is the Way.) MaRV
Fugal-Chorus from "For the Time Being" ("Great is Caesar"). LiTM (rev. ed.); NePA; SeCeV
Herod. OnHM
If, on Account of the Political Situation. LiTA; WaP
"Our Father, whose creative Will." TrPWD
(Chorale.) QS
For the Undefeated. Eleanor Wells. NeTW
For the wealth of pathless forests. A Thanksgiving. Lucy Larcom. OHIP
For "The Wine of Circe"; a Picture by Edward Burne-Jones. Dante Gabriel Rossetti. Sonnets for Pictures, III. ATP (1953 ed.); PoVP
(For "The Wine of Circe" by Edward Burne-Jones.) VLEP
For the Word Is Flesh. Stanley J. Kunitz. AnAmPo; LA; NP
For the youth they gave and the blood they gave. The Debt. Theodosia Garrison. DD; PEDC
For thee a crown of thorns I wear. Any Father to Any Son. Francis Burdett Money-Coutts. OBVV
For thee a stead was builded. The Grave. *Unknown.* ACP
For thee I shall not die. I Shall Not Die for Thee. *Unknown, tr. by* Douglas Hyde. AnIL; GTIV; MBP; OxBI
For thee, O dear dear Country! Jerusalem [the Golden]. Bernard of Cluny, *tr. by* John Mason Neale. *Fr.* De Contemptu Mundi. HBV; OBVV; WGRP
For Thee They Died ("For thee their pilgrim swords"). John Drinkwater. AOAH
For thee this woven garland have I braided. The Garland. Euripides. *Fr.* Hippolytus. OxBG
For thee was a house built. The Grave. *Unknown.* BCEP
For Them. Eleanor Farjeon. ChBR
For Them All. John Hall Wheelock. HBMV; TSW; TSWC
For them no stately canopy is spread. The Indian Massacre. Joseph Howe. *Fr.* Acadia. BoCaPo
For them, O God, who only worship Thee. Worship. William Wilberforce Lord. AA
For Them That Died in Battle. William Alexander Percy. LS
For them the Ceylon diver held his breath. The Proud Florentines. Keats. *Fr.* Isabella; or, The Pot of Basil. PoFr
For them the sun shines ever in full might. Life after Death [*or* After-Life]. Pindar. GrR; OxBG
For there are two heavens, sweet. Two Heavens. Leigh Hunt. GN
For there is no height in which there are not flowers. Flowers. Christopher Smart. *Fr.* Jubilate Agno. RO
For Theron, Tyrant of Akragas. Pindar, *tr. fr. Greek by* A. S. Way. *Fr.* Olympian Odes, II. GrL
For These. Edward Thomas. TCPD
For they are dead. Respect for the Dead. Laura Riding. LiTA
For They Are England. Walter O'Hearn. NeTW
For thirty year, come herrin'-time. The Skipper-Hermit. Hiram Rich. EtS
For thirty years what madness I have known. The Masters of the Heart Touched the Unknown. Delmore Schwartz. FiMAP
For thirty years you sat facing the wall. On the Fasting Monk Chu Chuan. Po Chü-i. WhP
For this agility chance found. The Age Demanded. Ezra Pound. *Fr.* Hugh Selwyn Mauberley. CoBMV; CoV; LiTA; LiTM (rev. ed.); MoPo
For this is Wisdom; to love, to live. Wisdom? "Laurence Hope." OtMeF
For this one thing above all I would be praised as a man. Chorus from "King Oedipus." Sophocles. *Fr.* Oedipus Rex. LiTW
For this peculiar tint that paints my house. My House. Claude McKay. CDC
For this present, hard. Woodnotes, I. Emerson. AnNE; BAV; IAP; MOAP
For this shall never prevail, that the things which are not. Parmenides, *tr. fr. Greek by* Charles H. Kahn. GrPo
For this she starred her eyes with salt. Epitaph. Elinor Wylie. ChMo; MAP; MoAmPo
For this the ancient stars were hurled. Evolution. Israel Zangwill. TrJP
For This, the Tide. Val Vallis. BoAV
For This True Nobleness. James Russell Lowell. IAP
(Sonnet: "For this true nobleness I seek in vain.") CoBA
For This World, *sel.* Walter Rauschenbusch.
For This Universe. OQP; QP-2
For this your mother sweated in the cold. To Jesus on His Birthday. Edna St. Vincent Millay. ChMo; CMP; LiTG; MaRV; ReaPo; StJW; TrGrPo
For those given to voyages: these roads. Muriel Rukeyser. *Fr.* The Cornfield. FiMAP
For those my unbaptizèd rhymes. His Prayer for Absolution. Robert Herrick. BCEP; ElSeCe; EM-1; EnL; EnLi-1 (1949 ed.); EPS; MaRV; MeRV; OxBoCh; ReEn; SeCV-1; TOP; TrPWD
For those Sabbath lights that flame. Jewishness. Jacob Glatstein. OnCuPl
For those that never know the light. The Children of the Night. E. A. Robinson. AmPP (4th ed.); NePA; OxBA; QS
For Those Who Died. Thomas Curtis Clark. PGD
For Those Who Died in Battle. Louis Mercier, *tr. fr. French by* Alan Conder. TrFP
For Those Who Fail. Joaquin Miller. BTP; CBPC; MaRV; OQP; PC; PoToHe; QP-2; TSW; TSWC
For those who fell at Thermopylae. The Thermopylae Ode. Simonides. WaaP
For Those Who Fly. Alice B. Joynes. PraP
For those who had the power. C. Day Lewis. *Fr.* A Time to Dance. FaBoMo; MoP; POTE; TwCV
For those who place their blooms on new-made graves. Time's Hand Is Kind. Margaret E. Bruner. PoToHe

For thou art founded in the eternal fact. George Edward Woodberry. *Fr.* My Country. PoFr
For thou shalt sleep, and never wake again. Against the Fear of Death. Lucretius, *tr. by* Dryden. *Fr.* De Rerum Natura. PoD
For though the Caves Were Rabitted. Henry David Thoreau. FaBoEn; PoEL-4
For though, with men of high degree. Leaders, Old Style. Sir Walter Scott. *Fr.* Marmion. OtMeF
For thoughts that curve like winging birds. I Yield Thee Praise. Philip Jerome Cleveland. TrPWD
For thousands of miles the nightingale sings. The Nightingales. Tu Mu. WhP
For three whole days across the sky. After Rain. Archibald Lampman. CPG
For three years, diabolus in the scale. Mauberley, II. Ezra Pound. *Fr.* Hugh Selwyn Mauberley. CoBMV; CoV; LiTA; LiTM (rev. ed.); MoPo; NP
For three years, out of key with his time. E. P. Ode pour l'Election de Son Sepulchre [*or* Lyrics]. Ezra Pound. *Fr.* Hugh Selwyn Mauberley. AmPP; CoBMV; CoV; CrMA; FaBoEn; FaBoMo; LiTA; LiTG; LiTM (rev. ed.); MoPo; MoVE; NePA; OnAP; OxBA; PreP; SeCeV; UnPo (3d ed.)
For thy love's sake, O maiden, I will cross the tumbling sea. Musaeus. *Fr.* Hero and Leander. GrPo
For Thy Sweet Love. Shakespeare. *See* Sonnets, XXIX.
For to Admire. Kipling. MBP; MoBrPo
For Transient Things. James A. S. McPeek. OQP; QP-2
For trewthe [*or* treuthe] telleth that love is triacle of hevene [*or* to abate sinne] The Incarnation. William Langland. *Fr.* The Vision of Piers Plowman. OBEV (new ed.); PoEL-1
For Tu Fu. Feng Chih, *tr. fr. Chinese by* Chu K'an. LiTW
For twenty days and twenty nights he lay. The Heart. Boris Lebedev. TrRV
For twenty minutes between the end of storm. Green and Red and Darkness. Winfield Townley Scott. FiMAP
For twenty years and more surviving. Widows. Edgar Lee Masters. MoAmPo
For Two Girls Setting Out in Life. Peter Viereck. MiAP
For Us. Charlotte Perkins Gilman. OQP; PSO; QP-1
For us, born into a world. Overtures to Death. C. Day Lewis. ChMo
For us like any other fugitive. Another Time. W. H. Auden. OxBA
For us, the dead, though young. The Unreturning. Clinton Scollard. DD; PAH
For Virginia Dare. Lucy Cherry Crisp. NoCaPo (rev. ed.)
For W. A. Mozart. Edgar Bowers. PtPa
For want I will in woe I plain. Sir Thomas Wyatt. SiPS
For want of a nail, the shoe was lost. Mother Goose. FaBoBe; GoTP; HBV; OTPC; OxNR; PPL; SiTL
For wars his life and half a world away. A Lullaby. Randall Jarrell. FiMAP
For we are all Christ's creatures, and by his coffer are we wealthy. Love We as Brothers. William Langland. *Fr.* The Vision of Piers Plowman. PoLi
For We Are Thy People. *Unknown.* TrJP
For we the mighty mountain plains have trod. The Sacraments of Nature. Aubrey Thomas De Vere. ACP; CAW
For weeks and weeks the autumn world stood still. How One Winter Came in the Lake Region. Wilfred Campbell. BoCaPo; CaP; OCL; PeCV
For weeks the clouds had raked the hills. Whittier. *Fr.* Among the Hills. SN
For wha ere had a lealer luve. Brown Adam. *Unknown.* ESPB (B *vers.*)
For what are we, my brother? What Are We? Thomas Wolfe. QS
For what emperor. Bowl. Wallace Stevens. NP
For what is Freedom, but the unfettered use. Samuel Taylor Coleridge. *Fr.* The Destiny of Nations. EnRP
For what is knowledge duly weighed? Christina Rossetti. *Fr.* The Convent Threshold. LO
For What Is Life? Ben Jonson. BHV
For what is old you nothing care. New and Old. Austin Dobson. VLEP
For what the World admires I'll wish no more. The Resolve. Mary, Lady Chudleigh. OBEC
For what we owe to other days. Exit. E. A. Robinson. MoAmPo
For when it dawn'd—they dropp'd their arms. Samuel Taylor Coleridge. *Fr.* The Rime of the Ancient Mariner. UnS
For when the One Great Scorer comes. Grantland Rice. *Fr.* Alumnus Football. MaRV
For when the winds have ceased their ghostly speech. Roy Campbell. *Fr.* The Flaming Terrapin. MM; TwCV
For when they meet, the tensile air. The Paradigm. Allen Tate. MOAP
For whether earth already to its doom. John Davidson. *Fr.* The Testament of a Prime Minister, I. BSV
For whiles I mark this weak and wretched world. George Gascoigne. *Fr.* The Steel Glass. ReIE; SiCE; TuPP
For Whitsunday. Francis Kinwelmersh. SiCE
For who can longer hold? when every Press. Prologue. John Oldham. *Fr.* Satires upon the Jesuits. CEP; SeCV-2
For who shall change with prayers or thanksgivings. Swinburne. *Fr.* Anactoria. AtBAP
For whom, consumed/ With anguish, do you keep the unseen splendor. Stéphane Mallarmé. *Fr.* Hérodiade. AnFP
For Whom, Pyrrha? Horace. *See* To Pyrrha.
For whom, sweet Muse, this harvest do you ravish. His Anthology. Meleager. OxBG
"For Whom the Bell Tolls." Gavin Ewart. WaP
For whom this pretty pamphlet, polished new. Catullus, *tr. fr. Latin by* James Elroy Flecker. LaP
For why should we the busy soul believe. Sir John Davies. *Fr.* The Immortality of the Soul. ViBoPo
For why, who writes such histories as these. Books. John Higgins. LPS-3
For William Edward Burghardt DuBois on His Eightieth Birthday. Bette Darcie Latimer. PoNe
For winter's rains and ruins are over. Spring Song. Swinburne. PCD
For X. Louis MacNeice. EnLoPo
For years he pried among the strata. A Geologist's Epitaph. Jane W. Stedman. WhC
For years I sought the Many in the One. The Quest. Eva Gore-Booth. MaRV; OQP; QP-1
For years I thought I knew, at the bottom of the dream. The Meeting. Louise Bogan. NePoAm-2
For years I've heard. Poem. Robin Blaser. NeAP
For years I've prayed, and yet I see no change. Shall I Pray On? Edith L. Mapes. PraP
For years I've read the books on how to. A Little Bow to Books on How To. Irwin Edman. WhC
For years we live solitary in the soul's hermitage. From Desert to Metropolis. Sister Mary Estelle. JKCP (1955 ed.)
For years you lived between life and death. Sonnets, III. Feng Chih *Fr.* Twenty-seven Sonnets. WhP
For You. Carl Sandburg. ChMo; CMP; MAP; MoAmPo; WaKn
For you—ancestral acres. Nomads of Beauty. Vyacheslav Ivanovich Ivanov. TrRV
For You, Mother. Hilda Conkling. HH
For You, My Son. Horace Gregory. MAP; MoAmPo
For You O Democracy. Walt Whitman. APW; CoBA; IAP; PaA; PoFr; StaSt; TCAP; TrGrPo
For you Sulpicia is decked, mighty Mars, on your festal day. The Matronalia, March 1. Tibullus. LaP
For you the lilac and the apple blossom. In a British Cemetery Overseas, May, 1940. Richard Elwes. NeTW
For you the white-wracked Waste—yet not for me. From the Hills. Thomas S. Jones, Jr. LEAP
For you there is no song. Song for a Lute, II. Edna St. Vincent Millay. BoFr
For you was a house built before you were born. The Grave. *Unknown.* LyMA
For Youth, who goes to War. Age Intercedes for Youth. Rachel Annand Taylor. EBSV
For Zion's sake will I not hold my peace. Isaiah, Bible, *O.T.* PoFr; TrJP
Foray, The. Sir Walter Scott. EmBrPo; EPN
Foray of Con O'Donnell [A.D. 1495], The, *sels.* Denis Florence MacCarthy.
  Irish Wolf Hound, The. SN; VA
  "'Now, by Columba!' Con exclaimed.' OnYI
Forbear, bold youth; all's heaven here. To One Persuading a Lady to Marriage. Katherine Philips. EV-2; OBEV
Forbear, my love. Excuses. Al-Asamm. MooP
Forbear to ask me why I weep. Cloe Jealous. Matthew Prior. CEP; EiPP
Forbearance. William Cowper. MaRV
Forbearance. Emerson. AA; AmPP (3d ed.); AnAmPo; AnNE; APW; BAP; BBV (1923 ed.); BoLiVe; CoBA; GN; HBV; HBVY; IAP; LA; LaNeLa; LEAP; LiTA; MCCG; MOAP; MPB; OnPM; OQP; OTPC; PCD; PoRL; PreP; QP-2; TCAP; TrGrPo; ViBoPo; WGRP; YT
Forbeare fond swaine I cannot love. *Unknown.* SeCSL
Forbidden Drink. Robert Lovett. WhC
Forbidden Fire, The. Tristan Tzara, *tr. fr. French by* Cecily Mackworth. MiFP
Forbidden Fruit, I ("Forbidden fruit a flavor has"). Emily Dickinson. AnNE; TCAP
Forbidden Fruit, II ("Heaven is what I cannot reach!"). Emily Dickinson. AnNE; TCAP
Forbidden Lure, The. Fannie Stearns Davis. HBV
Forby Sutherland. George Gordon M'Crae. VA
Force. "Nikolai Maksimovich Minski," *tr. fr. Russian by* Babette Deutsch. LiTW; TrRV
Force. Edward Rowland Sill. AA
Force first made conquest, and that conquest, law. Pope. *Fr.* An Essay on Man, Epistle III. PoFr
Force of Prayer, The, *sel.* Wordsworth.

"Oh! there is never sorrow of heart." MaRV
Force of snow and furious hail is sent, The. The Constitution of Athens. Solon. GrR; PoFr
Force That through the Green Fuse [Drives the Flower], The. Dylan Thomas. ATP (1953 ed.); CaAE; CoBMV; ExPo; ImOP; InPo; LiTB; LiTM; MaPo; MoAB; MoBrPo; MoPo; MoVE; NeMA; OAEP (2d ed.); PG (1945 ed.); Po; PoE; ReMP; UnPo (3d ed.); ViBoPo
(Poem.) NeBP
(Poem Five.) CoEV
Forced Music, A. Robert Graves. MBP; MoBrPo
Forced Recruit, The. Elizabeth Barrett Browning. PoVP
Forcing a Way. *Unknown.* NA
Forcing House. Theodore Roethke. AtBAP
Ford o' Kabul River. Kipling. FaBoTw; POTT
Fore-royal furled, I pause and I stand, The. Making Land. Thomas Fleming Day. EtS
Forebearance. "Owen Meredith." PCD
Forebears. Monk Gibbon. NeIP
Forebears. Elizabeth Riddell. BoAV
Foreboding, A. "Violet Fane." DiM; VA
Foreboding, The. Robert Graves. ChMP; GTBS-D
Foreboding. Hazel Hall. HBMV
Foreboding. Pushkin, *tr. fr. Russian by* C. M. Bowra. BoR
Foreboding. *Unknown, tr. fr. Japanese by* Ishii *and* Obata. *Fr.* Manyo Shu. OnPM
Foreboding sudden of untoward change. By the Conemaugh. Florence Earle Coates. PAH
Forecast, A. Archibald Lampman. VA
Forecast. Josephine Miles. CrMA
Forecast. Elspeth MacDuffie O'Halloran. PR
Foreclosure. Sterling A. Brown. PoNe
Foreclosure. Mark Van Doren. CrMA
Forefather, The. Richard Burton. AA; OBAV
Forefathers. Edmund Blunden. ChMP; OBEV (new ed.); OBMV; POTE
Forefathers' Song. *Unknown. See* New England's Annoyances.
Foreground and Background. Albert Teodor Gellerstedt, *tr. fr. Swedish by* Charles W. Stork. AnSL
Foreign Children. Robert Louis Stevenson. BoChLi; BoTP; GaP; GFA; MPB; OTPC (1946 ed.); RIS; SUS; TVSH
Foreign Gate, The, *sel.* Sidney Keyes.
Were I to Mount beyond the Field, V. MoPo
Foreign Land, The. Coventry Patmore. The Angel in the House, II, ix, 2. HBV
(Woman.) OBVV
Foreign Lands. Robert Louis Stevenson. ADAH; BoTP; GFA; HBV; HBVY; MPB; OTPC; PCH; PoVP; RIS; TiPo (1952 ed.); TVC; VA
Foreign Missions in Battle Array. Vachel Lindsay. MaRV; OQP; QP-2; QS
Foreign Ruler, A. Walter Savage Landor. PoFr; SoV; ViBoPo
Foreigner, The. Francis Sherman. BoCaPo (1943 ed.); OCL
Foreknown. Doris Kenyon. UnW
Foreman Monroe. *Unknown.* CSF
Foremost and first I would wish to inquire of them. A Woman's Antidote for War. Aristophanes. *Fr.* Lysistrata. GrR
Foremost of false philosophies. Sea, False Philosophy. Laura Riding. TCPD
Forenoon and afternoon and night—forenoon. Life. Edward Rowland Sill. BLP; BLRP; LBAP; MaRV; OQP; QP-1
Forensic Jocularities; the History of a Case Shortly Reported by a Master in Chancery. *Unknown.* OxBoLi
Forepledged. John Lancaster Spalding. AA
Forerunners. Emerson. AA; AnNE; IAP; MOAP; OBAV; OBEV (new ed.); OBVV; OxBA; TCAP
Forerunners, The. George Herbert. MePo; MeRV; ReEn
Forerunners. Alexander Smith. *Fr.* A Life-Drama. VA
Foreseen for so many years: these evils, this monstrous violence. May–June, 1940 [*or* Battle]. Robinson Jeffers. AmPP; LiTA; LiTM (rev. ed.); MoAB; MoAmPo; NePA; WaP
Foreseen in the vision of sages. America. Bayard Taylor. *Fr.* National Ode . . July 4, 1876. AA; FOAH; HiLiAm; PoFr
Foreshore, The. George Crabbe. *Fr.* The Borough, Letter XXII. CoEV
(Peter Grimes.) FaBoEn; SeCePo
Forest. Harriet Gray Blackwell. GoYe
Forest. Jean Garrigue. LiTM
Forest, The. Nikolai Gumilev, *tr. fr. Russian by* Y. Hornstein. BoRS
Forest, The. Keats. *Fr.* Endymion, I. BCEP
Forest, The. Miltiades Malakassis, *tr. fr. Modern Greek by* Rae Dalven. MoGP
Forest, The. Paul Zech, *tr. fr. German by* Glauco Cambon. OnPM
Forest-Bird, The. W. J. Turner. POTE
Forest Boat Song. Richard Clyde Ford. IHA
Forest falls asleep and dreams, The. Nocturne. Conrado Nalé Roxlo. AnCL
Forest Fire, The. Arthur W. Monroe. PoOW
Forest Glade, The. Charles Tennyson Turner. VA
Forest God. Dorothy Quick. DaM
Forest has three hundred and sixty-five trees, The. Serenade of Laughing Life. Vicente Huidobro. TwSpPo
Forest Hymn, A. Bryant. AA; ADAH; AmP; AmPP; AnNE; BPP; CoBA; CoV; HiLiAm; IAP; LPS-2; MOAP; OBAV; TCAP; TOP
Sels.
"Father, thy hand." TrPWD
"Groves were God's first temples, The." BAP
Forest Idyll. Eduard Mörike, *tr. fr. German by* Charles E. Passage. AnGP
Forest Maid, The. Bryant. OBVV
Forest Meditation, A. Bernice Hall Legg. PGD
Forest of Arden, The. Michael Drayton. *Fr.* Polyolbion: The Thirteenth Song. SeEP
Forest of Arden, The. Shakespeare. *See* Uses of Adversity, The.
Forest of Tiveden, The, *sel.* Verner von Heidenstam, *tr. fr. Swedish by* Charles W. Stork.
"Hark how the fir-trees in dismal tones." AnSL
Forest Ranger, The. Mary Austin. MW
Forest so much fallen from what she was before, The. The Thirteenth Song. Michael Drayton. *Fr.* Polyolbion. SeCePo
Forest Song. A. W. Page. CAG
Forest Song. William Henry Venable. PEDC
Forest Trees, The. Eliza Cook. PEOR
Forest Wedding, The. Christian Richardt, *tr. fr. Danish by* Charles W. Stork. BoDS
Forest you dreaded, The/ to walk through. The Forest. Miltiades Malakassis. MoGP
Foresters, The, *sel.* Tennyson.
Song: "There is no land like England," *fr.* II, i. VA
Forester's Song. A. E. Coppard. FaPON; MPB
Forests. Walter de la Mare. ChMo; CMP
Forest's afire, The! October's Song. Eleanor Farjeon. AlDL
Forests are made for weary men. Leading. Mary Carolyn Davies. MaRV
Forest's Queen, The. Philip Massinger. GoBC
Foretelling of Cathbad the Druid at Deirdre's Birth, The. *Unknown, tr. fr. Middle Irish by* Lady Augusta Gregory. LiTW
Forethought. Crates, *tr. fr. Greek by* J. M. Edmonds. GrR
Forethought. Josephine Preston Peabody. PR
"Forever." Charles Stuart Calverley. ALV; InMe; WhC
Forever. Halper Leivick, *tr. fr. Yiddish by* Sarah Zweig Betsky. OnCuPl
Forever. John Boyle O'Reilly. BoFr; CAW; HBV; MaRV; OnYI; OQP; QP-2; WGRP, *abr.*
For Ever. William Caldwell Roscoe. *See* Parting.
Forever am I conscious, moving here. The Undiscovered Country. Thomas Bailey Aldrich. AA
Forever and a Day. Thomas Bailey Aldrich. HBV; LHV
Forever at his side to walk. Emily Dickinson. CoBA
Forever Dead. Sappho, *tr. fr. Greek by* William Ellery Leonard. AWP; JAWP; LiA; LiTW; WBP
Forever dear, forever dreaded Prince. The Author to Queen Elizabeth, in Praise of Her Reading. Sir John Harington. SiCE
For Ever, Fortune. James Thomson. EV-3
("For ever, Fortune, wilt thou prove.") GTBS; GTBS-D; GTBS-W; GTSE; GTSL
(To Fortune.) BSV; EBSV
Forever in Advent. Motif from the Second Shepherd's Play. Sister Mary Maura. JKCP (1955 ed.)
Forever in My Dream and in My Morning Thought. Henry David Thoreau. PoEL-4
Forever is composed of Nows. Emily Dickinson. TwP
Forever Mexicans 'tis prostrate here. Epitaph to the Liberty of America. José Joaquín Fernández de Lizardi. PoFr
For-ever Morning. Laura Riding. LiTA
Forever on Thanksgiving Day. Wilbur D. Nesbit. PEDC
Forever over now, forever, forever gone. The Cameo. Edna St. Vincent Millay. LiTA; MAP; MoAmPo
Forever; 'tis a single word! "Forever." Charles Stuart Calverley. ALV; InMe; WhC
Forever we are eating up Thy bread. Refreshment. George Edward Hoffman. ChIP
Forever with the Lord. James Montgomery. *See* At Home in Heaven.
Forewarned. Alice Brown. PR
Foreword, A: "Child! do not throw this book about." Hilaire Belloc. *See* Dedication on the Gift of a Book to a Child.
Forfairn's My Hert. August, Graf von Platen, *tr. fr. German into Scottish by* Edwin Morgan. AnGP
Forge, The. Oliver St. John Gogarty. AnIV
Forget. John Donne. *See* If Poisonous Minerals, and If That Tree.
Forget It, *abr. Unknown.* WBLP

Forget Me Not. Alfred de Musset, *tr. fr. French by* Alan Conder. TrFP
Forget not bees in winter, though they sleep. Bee-Master. V. Sackville-West. HaMV
Forget Not Yet [the Tried Intent]. Sir Thomas Wyatt. AnFE; AtBAP; ElL; ElSeCe; EnLi-1 (1949 ed.); EnLit; GoBC; GTSE; HBV; LoPS; MaPo; OAEP; OBEV; Po; PoE; ReEn; ReIE; ShBV-3; SiCE; SiPS; TuPP; TyEnPo
(Lover Beseecheth His Mistress Not to Forget His Steadfast Faith and True Intent, The.) LO; TOP; ViBoPo
(Steadfastness.) CoEV; OBSC
(Supplication, A.) GTBS; GTBS-D; GTBS-W; GTSL; WoL
Forget six counties overhung with smoke. The Earthly Paradise: Prologue. William Morris. BEL; EmBrPo; EPN; EPP; ViPo; ViPP
Forget the dead, this time. There Are Children in the Dusk. Bertram Warr. PeCV
Forget the past and live the present hour. Live in the Present [*or* Live Today]. Sarah Knowles Bolton. MaRV; OQP; QP-1
Forget the slander you have heard. Just Forget. Myrtle May Dryden. WBLP
Forget the tube of bark. Very Tree. Stanley J. Kunitz. NP
Forget Thee? John Moultrie. BLPA; FaBoBe; LPS-1; NeHB
"'Forget thee?'—If to dream by night and muse on thee by day," *sel.* PoToHe (new ed.)
Forget them not, O Christ, who stand. Our Missionaries. Margaret E. Sangster. MaRV; PraP
Forget thine anguish. Meditations. Solomon ibn Gabirol. TrJP
Forget this rotten world; and unto thee. John Donne. *Fr.* The Second Anniversarie: Of the Progresse of the Soule. FaBoEn
Forget, with me, this babbling, scented room. Mongol. Dana Kneeland Akers. UnW
Forgetful Hour. Yetza Gillespie. DaM
Forgetful Pa. Edgar A. Guest. IHA; PoRL
Forgetfulness. Maxwell Bodenheim. MAPA
Forgetfulness. Sosei, *tr. fr. Japanese by* Basil Hall Chamberlain. OnPM
Forget-me-not, The. *Unknown.* BoTP
Forget-me-not Day. Nan Terrell Reed. HH
Forgettin'. "Moira O'Neill." HBV
Forging boldly ahead. The Bay Fight. Henry Howard Brownell. GA; PAH; PAP
Forging of the Anchor, The. Sir Samuel Ferguson. HBV; IrPN; LPS-2; PoVP; TVSH
Forgive. Lalia Mitchell Thornton. BePJ
Forgive. Whittier. MaRV; OQP; QP-1
Forgive!/ And tell me that sweet tale. Francis Burdett Money-Coutts. *Fr.* A Little Sequence. OBVV
Forgive Me. *Unknown.* PraP
Forgive me! forgive me! Matthew Arnold. *Fr.* Switzerland, II: Parting. VLEP
Forgive me, heart, that of my own free will. Lonely Tryst. Kathleen Sutton. MuM
Forgive me if I speak possessively of him. To a New Daughter-in-Law. *Unknown.* PoToHe (new ed.)
Forgive me, Lord, for careless words. Forgive Me. *Unknown.* PraP
Forgive me, Lord, the callow things I say. Finale. James Picot. BoAV
Forgive me that I love you as I do. Incompatibility. Aubrey Thomas De Vere. IrPN
Forgive, O Lord, our severing ways. Forgive. Whittier. MaRV; OQP; QP-1
"Forgive them, for they know not what they do!" Abraham Lincoln. Edmund Clarence Stedman. GA; PAH
Forgive us, son of Amram, be not wroth. Epigram III. *Unknown.* *Fr.* Duel with Verses over a Great Man. TrJP
Forgive what I, adventuring highest themes. The Author's Last Words to His Students. Edmund Blunden. PtOT
Forgive your faithful friend. Apology. Ibn al-Haddad. MooP
"Forgive yourself" is part of the command. Insubordination. Margaret Evelyn Singleton. ChIP
Forgiven? Jeannette Bliss Gillespy. Cameos, II. AA
Forgiven. Margaret E. Sangster. PoToHe
Forgiveness. Al-Jaziri, *tr. fr. Arabic by* A. J. Arberry. MooP
Forgiveness. Ephesians, IV: 26, 31-32, Bible, *N.T.* BoFr
Forgiveness. St. Matthew, XVIII: 15, 21-22, Bible, *N.T.* BoFr
Forgiveness, A, *sel.* Robert Browning.
"'Stay!' she said. 'Keep at least one soul unspecked.'" ReTS
Forgiveness. W. H. Davies. ChMo; CMP
Forgiveness. Henry Francis Lyte. BePJ; PraP
Forgiveness. Charles L. O'Donnell. LEAP; TBM
Forgiveness. Sadi, *tr. fr. Persian by* Sir Edwin Arnold. PeP
Forgiveness. Whittier. AmPP (3d ed.); IAP; MaRV
Forgiveness Lane. Martha Dickinson Bianchi. AA; PCD
Forgiveness of Sins a Joy Unknown to Angels. Augustus Lucas Hillhouse. AA
Forgotten. "Æ." ChMo; CMP
Forgotten. Sappho. *See* Dead Shalt Thou Lie.
Forgotten City, The. William Carlos Williams. LiTA; NePA
Forgotten Countersign, The. Corinne Roosevelt Robinson. OQP; QP-2
Forgotten Dreams. Edward Silvera. PoNe
Forgotten Grave, The. Austin Dobson. VA
Forgotten Objects on a Beach. Patricia Excell. BoAV
Forgotten People, *sel.* Rex Ingamells.
"No more the smoke-wisp signal climbs; no more." BoAu
Forgotten playground, grave. Elegy. W. Wesley Trimpi. PtPa
Forgotten Rock, The. Richard Eberhart. NePA
Forgotten soldier, in the winter grass. Trooper Temple Pulvermacher. William Branford. BoSA
Forgotten Star, The. Thomas Curtis Clark. PGD
Forgotten Wars. Grantland Rice. DDA
Forked Radish, A. Jonathan Price. PoN
Forlorn. Ma Yüeh Lo, *tr. fr. Chinese by* Henry H. Hart. PoHN
Forlorn and white. White Symphony. John Gould Fletcher. AnFE; APA; ChMo; CMP; CoAnAm; MAPA; SPP; TwAmPo
Forlorn, he waits beside the schoolhouse door. Dog at the Schoolhouse Door. Goldie Capers Smith. AlBD
Forlorn One, The. "Thomas Ingoldsby." BOHV
Forlornly. Heine. *See* Mein Liebchen, wir sassen zusammen.
Form. Polly Chase Boyden. NP
Form. Eva Gore-Booth. MaRV; TriL
"Form Fours." Frank Sidgwick. WhC
Form Is Delight. Ernst Stadler, *tr. fr. German by* Glauco Cambon. OnPM
Form of Flight, A. Emilio Prados, *tr. fr. Spanish by* Eleanor L. Turnbull. CoSP
Form 1040A. Phyllis Eleanor Armstrong. SiTL
Formal Lyric. W. J. Turner. FaBoTw
Formation Flight ("Part more wise"). Milton. *Br sel. fr.* Paradise Lost, VII. PoF
Forme of Prayer, A. Francis Quarles. MePo
Formed long ago, yet made today. Riddles [*or* A Bed]. Mother Goose. HBV; HBVY; OTPC; OxNR; RIS
Former Barn Lot. Mark Van Doren. MAP; MoAmPo; MOAP
Former Beauties. Thomas Hardy. At Casterbridge Fair, II. BEL; EmBrPo; EnLi-2 (1949 ed.); EnLit; OBMV; PoVP
Former Life, The. Baudelaire, *tr. fr. French by* Dwight Durling. AnFP
Former one could chide his lord, The. In Asinum Christi Vectorem. Richard Crashaw. Epigrammata Sacra, I, 2. LaP
"Formerly a Slave." Herman Melville. PoNe
Formosae Puellae. Herbert P. Horne. VA
Forms of the Human. Richard Eberhart. FiMAP
Fornication is a filthy business. Petronius, *tr. fr. Latin by* Kenneth Rexroth. LaP
Forsake me not thus, Adam, witness heav'n. Eve Penitent. Milton. *Fr.* Paradise Lost, X. OBS
Forsaken, The. Hamilton Aïdé. VA
Forsaken. Kao Shuang, *tr. fr. Chinese by* Henry H. Hart. PoHN
Forsaken. Sappho. *See* Night.
Forsaken, The. Siegfried Sassoon. TwCV
Forsaken. Zalman Schneour, *tr. fr. Yiddish by* Joseph Leftwich. TrJP
Forsaken, The. Duncan Campbell Scott. CaP; MM; OCL; TwCaPo
Forsaken [*or* Forsaken Bride]. *Unknown. See* Waly, Waly.
Forsaken Garden, A. Po Chü-i, *tr. fr. Chinese by* Henry H. Hart. PoHN
Forsaken Garden, A. Swinburne. BoLiVe; BPN; EmBrPo; EPN; FaBoEn; GTBS; GTBS-D; GTML; GTSL; HBV; InP; LiTB; LiTG; LoBV; MBP; OBVV; PIAE; PoE; PoFS; PoVP; ShBV-4; TCEP; TOP; VA; ViP; ViPo; VLEP; WHA
Forsaken Maid, The. Eduard Mörike, *tr. fr. German by* Vernon Watkins. AnGP
Forsaken Maiden's Lament, A. *Unknown.* SeCePo
Forsaken Merman, The. Matthew Arnold. ATP (1935 ed.); BBV (1923 ed.); BEL; BeLS; BMEP; BoLiVe; BPN; CaAE; CBOV; CBPC; CG; EM-2; EmBrPo; EnL; EnLi-2; EnLit; EPN; EPP; EtS; EV-5; FaBoCh; FiP; GBV (1922 ed.); GEPC; GN; GTBS; GTBS-D; GTSL; HBV; HiLiEn; LoEn; LoGBV; LPS-3; MCCG; MotAn; MPB; OAEP; OBEV (1st ed.); OBVV; OnSP; OTPC; OuHeWo; PECK; PoVP; RG; SG; ShBV-1; TCEP; TOP; TVSH; VA; ViBoPo; ViPo; ViPP; VLEP; WHA; YT
"Children dear, was it yesterday," *sel.* BoTP
Forsaken of all comforts but these two. My Faggot and My Pipe. Sir Robert Aytoun. PeBoSo
Forsworn. *Unknown, tr. fr. Chinese by* Bernhard Karlgren. *Fr.* Shi King. ChLP
Fort Bowyer. Charles L. S. Jones. PAH

Fort by the oak trees there, The. The Fort of Rathangan. *At. to* Berchan. ChTr
Fort Duquesne. Florus B. Plimpton. PaA; PAH
Fort McHenry. *Unknown.* MC, *abr.*, PAH
Fort of Fathnangan, The. *Unknown, at. to* Berchan, *tr. fr. Irish by* Kuno Meyer. CH; FaBoCh; GTIV; LoGBV; OxBI; SoV; ChTr, *tr. unknown*
Forth by the light of day I dare not ride. Sir Laurens Steals a Bride. *Unknown.* BoDaBa
Forth from a rugged arch, in the dusk below. Cybele Drawn by Lions. Keats. *Fr.* Endymion. RO
Forth from Calais, at dawn of night, when sunset summer on autumn shone. A Channel Passage. Swinburne. VLEP
Forth from earth's opened side. The Magnolia Tree. Hubert Witheford. AnNZ
Forth from its scabbard, pure and bright. The Sword of Robert Lee. Abram Joseph Ryan. BlG; GA; JKCP; PaA; PoRL; SPP
Forth from the dust and din. London Voluntary. W. E. Henley. London Voluntaries, II. PIAE
Forth, from the glittering spirit's peace. Love in Action. Coventry Patmore. *Fr.* The Angel in the House, II, x. EG
Forth from the purple battlements he fared. Sir Eggnogg. Bayard Taylor. PA
Forth from the wolds where the west winds are blowing. A Song of the Thames. Ernest Myers. TVSH
Forth he fared at the fateful moment. The Death-going of Scyld. *Unknown. Fr.* Beowulf. BCEP
Forth in shining phalanx marching from the shrouding mists of time. Gods and Heroes of the Gael. Eleanor Rogers Cox. JKCP
Forth into the warm darkness faring wide. Wings in the Dark. John Gray. SG
Forth, My Gallant Honey-Bees! Ludvig Holstein, *tr. fr. Danish by* Charles W. Stork. BoDS
Forth of this hut we set our faces clear. A Short Story. Euripides. *Fr.* Electra. GrR
Forth rushed from envy sprung and self-conceit. Protest against the Ballot. Wordsworth. EPN
Forth sped thy gallant sailors, blithe and free. Gloriana's England. Archibald T. Strong. *Fr.* Sonnets of the Empire. BoAu
Forth then fared the folk-troop, and a fighting-lay. Cynewulf. *Fr.* Elene. TCEP
Forth they go/ In endless procession. The Burial of Gustaf Fröding. Verner von Heidenstam. AnSL
Forth welling from the breast of sapphire lakes. Easter Song. Leo Alishan. CAW
Forth went the candid man. The Candid Man. Stephen Crane. War Is Kind, IX. MAP; MoAmPo
Forthfaring. Winifred Howells. AA
Fortitude. Reinmar von Zweter, *tr. fr. German by* Jethro Bithell. LiTW; LyMA
Fortitude; a Young Man of Egypt and Valerian. Richard Edwards. ReIE
Fortress of Hope. Barnabe Barnes. *Fr.* A Divine Century of Spiritual Sonnets. MeRV
("Fortress of hope, anchor of faithful zeal.") TuPP
Fortù, Fortù, my beloved one. The Englishman in Italy. Robert Browning. ExPo; PoEL-5; ViPo; ViPP; VLEP
Fortunate are the feet of the swallow. Song. W. J. Turner. LO
Fortunate Being. Juan Ramón Jiménez, *tr. fr. Spanish by* Eleanor L. Turnbull. TeCS
Fortunate Dead, The. Swinburne. *Fr.* Atalanta in Calydon. EmBrPo
Fortunate Fool. Ben Jonson. *See* Nano's Song.
Fortunate Isles, The. Joaquin Miller. PTA-2; WGRP
Fortunate Isles and Their Union, The, *sel.* Ben Jonson.
Chorus: "Spring all the Graces of the age," *also in* Neptune's Triumph. OBS; SeCL
Fortunate One, The. Harriet Monroe. AA
Fortunati Nimium. Thomas Campion. *See* Jack and Joan.
Fortunatus Nimium. Robert Bridges. ChMo; CMP; PoP
(Nimium Fortunatus.) MBP; MoAB; MoBrPo
Fortunatus the R. A. ("Fortunatus the portrait-painter got twenty sons"). Nicarchus, *tr. fr. Greek by* Dudley Fitts. LiTW
Fortune. Thomas Dekker. *See* Fortune and Virtue.
Fortune, *abr.* Fitz-Greene Halleck. *Fr.* Fanny. LPS-3
Fortune. Charles Madge. MoPW
Fortune. Sir Thomas More. *Fr.* Two Short Ballettes. GoBC; PoLi
(Lewis, the Lost Lover.) OBSC; TuPP
Fortune. Tennyson. *See* Turn, Fortune, Turn Thy Wheel.
Fortune ("The Lady Fortune is both friend and foe"). *Unknown.* ACP
Fortune ("Weal, thou art a crooked thing"), *in mod. Eng. Unknown.* TMEV
Fortune. Sir Thomas Wyatt. OBSC
Fortune and Men's Eyes. Shakespeare. *See* Sonnets, XXIX.
Fortune and Virtue. Thomas Dekker. *Fr.* Old Fortunatus. GoTL
(Fortune.) OBSC
(Fortune Smiles.) AtBAP
(Song: "Fortune smiles: cry holiday.") EPP
Fortune for Mirabel. Horace Gregory. TwAmPo
Fortune has brought me down—her wonted way. His Children [*or* He Thinks of His Children]. Hittan of Tayyi. *Fr.* Hamasah. AWP; FAOV; JAWP; LiTW; WBP
Fortune, in power imperious. Of Fortune. Thomas Kyd. *Fr.* Cornelia. ElL
Fortune Is like the Moon. Sophocles, *tr. fr. Greek by* Gilbert Murray. OxBG
Fortune is stately, solemn, proud, and high. Of Fortune. Sir Thomas More. CoBE
Fortune, not reason, rules the state of things. Virtue the Safest Guide. George Chapman. *Fr.* Bussy d'Ambois, I, i. CoEV
Fortune Smiles. Thomas Dekker. *See* Fortune and Virtue.
Fortune-Teller, A. Witter Bynner. HBMV; TCAP
Fortune Teller, The. John Holmes. NePoAm-2
Fortune-Teller, The. Matthew Prior. CEP
Fortune with big wings. Death Chant. Henri Michaux. MiCF
Fortune's Finger. Shakespeare. *Fr.* Hamlet, III, ii. BLP
Fortune's Freehold. *Unknown, tr. fr. Greek by* F. L. Lucas. GrPE
Fortune's Tides. Pindar, *tr. fr. Greek by* C. J. Billson. *Fr.* Olympian Odes, II. GrR
Fortune's Treachery. Judah Halevi, *tr. fr. Hebrew by* Solomon Solis-Cohen. TrJP
Fortune's Wheel. Lord De Tabley. OBVV; PoVP; VA
Fortune's Wheel. Euripides, *tr. fr. Greek by* M. Wodhull. *Fr.* Children of Heracles. GrR
Fortune's worst shafts could ne'er have reached me more. To an Ungrateful Friend. Tasso. BoFr
Fortunio's Song. Alfred de Musset, *tr. fr. French. Fr.* Le Chandelier, II. LiA, *tr. by* William Frederic Giese; TrFP, *tr. by* Alan Conder
Forty days and forty nights. George Hunt Smyttan. OlF
Forty-five artisans and sixty apprentices. The Bridge of Arta. *Unknown.* MoGP
Forty-five Years since the Fall of the Ch'ing Dynasty. Philip Whalen. NeAP
Forty full-grown products of the old hand-in-hands. Psychology Class. Elizabeth K. Campbell. TwCaPo
Forty-gun frigate from Baltimore came, A. Paul Jones. *Unknown.* ViBoFo
'49. Joaquin Miller. BAV
Forty-Niner Tells His Story, A. *Unknown.* IHA
Forty Singing Seamen. Alfred Noyes. AnFE; BBV; BEL; BMEP; BoChLi; ChMo; CMP; CV; GBV; GDAH; NV; PCN; PYM; ShBV-1; StPo; TOP
Forty teeth have I complete. The Strange Teeth. Nancy Birckhead. RIS
Forty times I meant to dig. Spades. Cale Young Rice. PR
Forty Viziers saw I go. The Fair Circassian. Richard Garnett. HBV; OBVV; VA
Forty Years After. H. H. Porter. BOHV
Forty Years Ago. *Unknown, at. to* Francis Huston, *to* Dill Amor Smith, *and to* A. J. Gault. HBV
(Twenty Years Ago.) BLPA
Forty years back, when much had place. George Meredith. Thomas Hardy. EmBrPo; EPN
Forty years he has pursued his love. Professor of Medieval Balladry. Sister Mary Maura. JKCP (1955 ed.)
Forty Years On. Edward Ernest Bowen. HBV
Forward. "Susan Coolidge." PEOR
Forward. Edna Dean Proctor. HBV
Forward rush by the lamp in the gloom, A. The Contretemps. Thomas Hardy. ChMo; CMP; LiTM (rev. ed.)
Forward, then, ye jades! Christopher Marlowe. *Fr.* Tamburlaine the Great. ViBoPo
Forward through the Ages. Frederick Lucian Hosmer. GrCo-1
Forward violet thus did I chide, The. Sonnets, XCIX. Shakespeare. EG; EnLi-1; EPP; ES; LPS-1; OAEP; OBSC; PeBoSo; PIAE
Forward young woman, Miss Chaos, A. The Trumpeter. *Unknown.* CoMu
Forward youth that would appear[e], The. An Horatian Ode upon Cromwell's Return from Ireland [*or* Two Kings]. Andrew Marvell. AEV; BEL; BrBE; CoEV; EPS; EV-2; GTBS; GTBS-D; GTBS-W; GTSE; GTSL; HBV; LEAP; LH; LiA; LoBV; MaPo; MePo; OBEV; OBS; PoEL-2; SeCV-1; SeEP; TOP; UnPo (1st ed.)
Foscari, The. *sel.* Byron.
Swimming. LPS-2
Fossil, The. John Lyle Donaghy. NeIP
Fossil. Paul Engle. ReMP
Fossils. James Stephens. OnYI
Fo'ty acres jes' fo' me! Freedom in Mah Soul. David Wadsworth Cannon, Jr. PoNe
Fo'ty days, fo'ty nights, de rain it kep'-a fallin'. Didn't It Rain. *Unknown.* APW
Foul canker of fair virtuous action. To Detraction [I Present

Foul canker of fair virtuous action (*continued*)
My Poesie]. John Marston. *Fr.* The Scourge of Villany. LoBV; OBSC; ReIE; SiCE; TuPP
Foul fa [*or* 'a] the breast first treason bred in! Hobie Noble. *Unknown.* BaBo; ESPB; OBB; ViBoFo
Foules Rondel. Chaucer. *See* Roundel, A: "Now welcom, somer . . ."
Found. Josephine Preston Peabody. AV
"Found." Dante Gabriel Rossetti. EmBrPo; PoVP; VLEP
Found a family, build a state. Fragments of a Lost Gnostic Poem of the Twelfth Century. Herman Melville. PoEL-5; ViBoPo
Found in the garden dead in his beauty. The Burial of the Linnet. Juliana Horatia Ewing. PRWS
Found in the Woods. Irene F. Pawsey. BoTP
Found on an English Sun Dial. *Unknown.* *See* Love over All.
Founder's Day. Robert Bridges. OBVV
Dedication: "Christ and his Mother, heavenly maid," *sel.* MOAH
Founders of Ohio, The. William Henry Venable. MC; PaA; PAH
Founding of Bolton Priory, The. Wordsworth. OTPC
Foundling Hospital for Wit, The, *sel.* Isaac Hawkins Browne.
Fire Side, The; a Pastoral Soliloquy, *fr.* IV. OBEC
Fount of Freshness. *Unknown, tr. fr. Spanish by* Sir John Bowring. AnSpL-1
Fount of Mary's Joy, The. The Son of God. Charles L. O'Donnell. JKCP
Fount That Freely Flows, The. St. John of the Cross, *tr. fr. Spanish by* E. Allison Peers. TeCS
Fount there is, doth overfling, A. At the Fountain. Marcabrun. AWP; JAWP; WBP
Fountain, The. Luis Cernuda, *tr. fr. Spanish by* Eleanor L. Turnbull. CoSP
Fountain, The. Rose Fyleman. GFA
Fountain, The. Herbert S. Gorman. NV
Fountain, The. Ibn al-Ra'i'a, *tr. fr. Arabic by* A. J. Arberry. MooP
Fountain, The. James Russell Lowell. BAV; BoTP; CG; GoTP; MW; OTPC; PCH; PRWS; PTA-1; RG; TVSH
Fountain, The. Mu'tamid, King of Seville, *tr. fr. Arabic by* Dulcie L. Smith. AWP; JAWP; WBP
Fountain, The. Sir Edward Sherburne. ElSeCe
Fountain, The. A. J. M. Smith. CaP
Fountain, The. Henry Longan Stuart. GTIV
Fountain, The. Sara Teasdale. ChMo; CMP; TwCV; VOD
Fountain, The. Wordsworth. BPN; EmBrPo; EnRP; ERP; EV-3; GEPC; GTBS; GTBS-D; GTBS-W; GTSE; GTSL; OBRV; SeCePo
Fountain at the Tomb, The. Nicias, *tr. fr. Greek by* Charles Merivale. AWP; JAWP; WBP
Fountain blows its breathless spray, The. Irradiations, VI [VIII]. John Gould Fletcher. AnFE; APA; MAPA; TwAmPo
Fountain falls from laughing mouth of stone, The. The Fountain. Henry Longan Stuart. GTIV
Fountain, fountain, what do you say. The Fountain. Sara Teasdale. ChMo; CMP; TwCV; VOD
Fountain murmuring of sleep, The. In Fountain Court. Arthur Symons. PoeT; POTT; VLEP
Fountain of Bandusia, The. Horace. *See* To the Fountain of Bandusia.
Fountain of fire whom all divide. I Seek Thee in the Heart Alone. Herbert Trench. WGRP
Fountain of Old Poems, The, *sels.* *Unknown, tr. fr. Chinese.* WhP
Fountain of sorrow, inn of cursed ire. Sonnet. Petrarch. Sonnets to Laura: To Laura in Life, CVII. PoFr
Fountain of Sweets! Eternal Dove! Whit Sunday. Joseph Beaumont. OxBoCh
Fountain of Tears, The. Arthur O'Shaughnessy. OBEV (1st ed.); OBVV; PoVP; VLEP
Fountain of the Fairies, The. Robert Southey. OTPC
Fountain of Youth, The. Hezekiah Butterworth. PAH
Fountains, The. W. R. Rodgers. MoVE
Fountains ("Proud fountains, wave your plumes"). Sir Osbert Sitwell. MBP; MoBrPo
Fountains ("This night is pure and clear as thrice refinèd silver"). Sacheverell Sitwell. LBBV; MBP; MoBrPo
Fountains and the garden, The. Song for Music. G. S. Fraser. ChMP
Fountains mingle with the river, The. Love's Philosophy. Shelley. AEV; AtBAP; BLPA; BPN; CoBE; EM-2; EmBrPo; EnLi-2 (1949 ed.); EnLit; EnRP; EPN; ERP; EV-4; FaBoBe; GTBS; GTBS-D; GTBS-W; GTSE; GTSL; HBV; HoPM; LiA; LiTG; LiTL; LoPo; LPS-1; NeHB; OAEP; OBRV; PG; PoFS; PoToHe (new ed.); TOP; TrGrPo; TyEnPo; ViBoPo; WP
Fountains that frisk and sprinkle. Ballade Made in the Hot Weather [*or* Made in the Hot Weather]. W. E. Henley. AnFE; GN; MBP; MoBrPo; POTT
Founts of Song, The. "Fiona Macleod." WGRP
Four, The. Geoffrey Grigson. WaP
Four an twenty noblemen they rode thro Banchory fair. Glenlogie; or, Jean o Bethelnie. *Unknown.* ESPB
Four and Eight. ffrida Wolfe. BoTP; SiSoSe
Four-and-eighty years are o'er me; great-grandchildren sit before me. The Battle of Monmouth. Thomas Dunn English. PAH
Four and twenty bonny boys. Sir Hugh; or, The Jew's Daughter. *Unknown.* BaBo (A *and* B *vers.*); CH; EM-1; EnSB; ESPB (A *and* C *vers.*); ViBoFo (A *vers.*)
Four and Twenty Drummers. *Unknown.* MuP
Four-and-twenty Highland men. Eppie Morrie. *Unknown.* ESPB
Four-and-twenty ladies fair/ Was playing at the ba. Bonny Baby Livingston (C *vers.*). *Unknown.* ESPB
Four and twenty laides fair, all being at a ball. Lord Banner. *Unknown.* BaBo
Four-and-twenty nobles rade to the King's ha'. Glenlogie. *Unknown.* OBB
Four and twenty nobles sits in the king's ha. Glenlogie, or, Jean o Bethelnie (B *vers.*). Unknown. ESPB
Four and twenty tailors went to kill a snail. Mother Goose. OTPC (1923 ed.); OxNR
Four are the names of the seasons—spring, summer, autumn, and winter. Three Children Sliding. *Unknown.* PA
Four Arms Have I. *Unknown.* OTPC (1946 ed.)
Four arms, two necks, one wreathing. Song. *Unknown.* ElL
Four be the things I am wiser to know. Inventory. Dorothy Parker. AnAmPo; LA
Four Best Things, The. *Unknown, tr. fr. Greek by* Robert Herrick. OxBG
Four Birds. *Unknown.* *See* Robin and the Wren, The.
Four Blessings, The. *Unknown, tr. fr. Greek by* Thomas Moore. OnPM
Four blue stones in this thrush's nest. The Nest. Andrew Young. AlDL
Four boards of the coffin lid, The. After Death. Swinburne. ViP
Four Bridges, The, *sel.* Jean Ingelow.
"But those old bridges claim another look." EnSW
Four bright pennies in a purse of brown. Penny Problem. John Farrar. GaP
Four Brothers, The, *sel.* Carl Sandburg.
Man-Hunt, The. OQP; QP-2
Four children on a rumbling cart. Tinker's Moon. Ewart Milne. OnYI
Four-cornered Tower, The; Llanybri. Nigel Heseltine. MoWP
Four deadly years we fought. Heroes of the South. Paul Hamilton Hayne. MDAH
Four Deer, The. Mary Hoxie Jones. GoYe
Four Ducks on a Pond. William Allingham. BMEP; EV-5; GTIV; IrPN; OTPC (1946 ed.); OxBI; ThWaDe (Memory, A.) HBVY; LiA; OBVV; PIAE; YT
Four Epigrams. John Owen, *tr. fr. Latin by* Thomas Harvey. PrWP
Bed, The.
King Arthur's Round Table.
Of Labienus.
To Polla.
Four Folk-Songs in Hokku Form. *Unknown, tr. fr. Japanese by* Lafcadio Hearn. LiTW
"All things change, we are told," 3.
"If with my sleeve I hide the faint color of the dawning sun," 4.
"Things never changed since the Time of the Gods," 1.
"Thinking tomorrow remains," 2.
Four Footprints. Thomas Hardy. BMEP
Four for Sir John Davies. Theodore Roethke. CoBMV; FiMAP; ReMP
Sels.
Dance, The, I. CrMA; NePoAm; UnS
Partner, The, II. NePA; NePoAm
Four Friends. Leo Ward. GoBC
Four Friends, The. A. A. Milne. GoTP; TiPo (1959 ed.)
Four gallant ships from England came. The Battle of Stonington on the Seaboard of Connecticut. Philip Freneau. PAH
Four Glimpses of Night. Frank Marshall Davis. PoNe
Four great gates has the city of Damascus. Gates of Damascus. James Elroy Flecker. AnFE; GTML; HBMV; LBBV; POTT
Four great walls have hemmed me in. Four Walls. Blanche Taylor Dickinson. CDC
Four hooves rang out and now are still. Early Waking. Léonie Adams. MoVE
Four horizons cozen me. Shooting the Sun. Amy Lowell. MoAmPo (1950 ed.)
Four hundred thousand men. The Nation's Dead. *Unknown.* MDAH
Four hundred urgent springs and ripened summers. Ronsard. Miriam Allen DeFord. HBMV
Four hundred years ago a tangled waste. Columbian Ode. Paul Laurence Dunbar. PoRL
Four Kinds of Wading. Mildred D. Shacklett. GFA
Four-Leaf Clover. Wesley Curtright. GoSl

Four-Leaf Clover. Ella Higginson. AA; ADAH; FaPON; HBV; OTPC (1946 ed.); POT; PoTo; PTA-1
Four-Leaf Clover, The. Monica Shannon. BrR
Four-legg'd Elder, The; or, A Horrible Relation of a Dog and an Elder's Maid. Sir John Birkenhead. CoMu
Four-legg'd Quaker, The. *Unknown.* CoMu
Four Legs, Two Legs, Three Legs. William Empson. MoPo
Four Letters and Certain Sonnets, *sel.* Gabriel Harvey.
Due Commendation of the Quipping Autor, A. ReIE
Four Little Foxes. Lew Sarett. BAP; FaPON; GoTP; NP; NV; PCD; PoeMoYo; PoMa; PoTo; PYM; TBM; TCPD; WaKn; YeAr
Four little pussy-cats, invited out to tea. *See* Five little pussy-cats . . .
Four little sunbeams came earthward one day. The Four Sunbeams. "M. K. B." TVC
Four little white doves. Cuatro Palomitas Blancas. *Unknown.* ABF
Four Men. Jennette Yeatman. UnW
Four Men of God. Edgar A. Guest. OHFP (1958 ed.)
Four men stood by the grave of a man. Alexander the Great. *Unknown.* CH
Four miles at a leap, over the dark hollow land. Health. Edward Thomas. SeCePo
Four o'clock, four o'clock, four o'clock. Cow Time. Monica Shannon. SiSoSe
Four of us went to the woods one day. Jack-in-the-Pulpit. Rupert Sargent Holland. OTPC; StVeCh (1940 ed.)
Four or five coppers in his box! The Misery of the Beggars at the Gate of Zenkoji. Issa. PoFr
4 Part Geometry Lesson, A. Robin Blaser. NeAP
Four-Paws. Helen Parry Eden. BoTP; HBMV
Four pelicans went over the house. Pelicans. Robinson Jeffers. MAP; MoAmPo; TCPD
Four Pets. Christina Rossetti. *Fr.* Sing-Song. PPL
("Pussy has a whiskered face.") TiPo
Four Poems for April. Louis Adeane. NeBP
Four Prayers. *Unknown, tr. fr. Modern Irish by* Eleanor Hull. OnYI
Sels.
I Lie Down with God. AnIV; GTIV
I Rest With Thee, O Jesus. JKCP (1926 ed.)
Sacred Trinity, The ("Three folds of the cloth"). JKCP (1926 ed.)
Four Preludes on Playthings of the Wind. Carl Sandburg. AnAmPo; AnFE; BLV; BoLiVe; CoAnAm; CoBA; InP; LA; MAP; MoAB; MoAmPo; NePA; NP; SeCeV
Four P's, The, *sel.* John Heywood.
Palmer, The. ACP; CAW
Four Quartets, *sels.* T. S. Eliot.
Burnt Norton. AnFE; AtBAP; CoAnAm; LiTG; LiTM (rev. ed.); MoAB; MoAmPo (1950 ed.); MoPo; PoE; TwAmPo; TwHP
"Garlic and sapphires in the mud," II. GTBS-W
"Words move, music moves," V. UnS (12 *ll.*); ViBoPo (1958 ed.)
Dry Salvages, The. LiTB; MaPo; OxBA; SeCePo; SeCeV
"Lady, whose shrine stands on the promontory," IV. ISi
"To communicate with Mars, converse with spirits," V. AmPP; ATP (1953 ed.)
"Where is there an end of it, the soundless wailing," II. FaBoTw
East Coker. ChMP; FaBoMo; MoVE; NePA; PoLFOT
Little Gidding. AmPo; ExPo; FaBoEn; OAEP (2d ed.)
"Ash on an old man's sleeve," II. FaBoTw; GTBS-W; PoFS
"We shall not cease from exploration," V. ImOP
Four Quartz Crystal Clocks. Marianne Moore. ImOP
Four rows of jaw teeth. Cowboy Boasting Chants. *Unknown.* ABF
Four sails of the mill, The. Lubber Breeze. T. Sturge Moore. CH
Four Saints in Three Acts, *sel.* Gertrude Stein.
"Pigeons on the grass alas." CrMA
Four Scarlet Berries. Mary Vivian. BoTP
Four Seasons. Rowena Bennett. SiSoSe; TiPo (1959 ed.)
Four seasons fill the measure of the year. The Human Seasons. Keats. BPN; CBE; CoBE; EnRP; EV-4; FaFP; GTBS; GTBS-D; GTBS-W; GTSE; GTSL; HBV; OBRV; PeBoSo; PG (1955 ed.); PoP
Four Seasons of the Year, *sel.* Anne Bradstreet.
Spring. AnNE; TCAP
Four sharp scythes sweeping—in concert keeping. A Day in Ireland. *Tr. by* Michael Cavanagh. AnIV; GTIV
Four Short Poems. *Unknown, tr. fr. Old Irish by* Owen Masters. LyMA
"I don't know with exactly whom."
"I've heard many times."
"Trip to Rome, A—great pains and little gain!"
"Winter has come with pinching dearth."
Four Sides to a House. Amy Lowell. ChMo; CMP; MOAP; NP; PoRA
Four Songs. *Unknown, tr. fr. Spanish by* Seth G. Thornton. LyMA
"If the night's so full of darkness."
"These pains of mine, oh mother."
"Under the oak tree, oak tree."
"Unhappily married beauty."
Four Sonnets. Thomas S. Jones, Jr.
Garden, The, III. SBMV
Last Spring, The, II. SBMV
Path of the Stars, The, IV. ChIP; NV; SBMV; WGRP
Sanctuary, I. SBMV
Four Sonnets to Helen. Pierre de Ronsard. *See* Sonnets pour Hélène.
Four Sonnets to Orpheus. Rainer Maria Rilke. *See* Sonnets to Orpheus.
Four stiff-standers. A Riddle. *Unknown.* ChTr; OxNR
Four straight brick walls, severely plain. The Quaker Graveyard. Silas Weir Mitchell. AA; OBAV
Four Sunbeams, The. "M. K. B." TVC
Four Sweet Months, The. Robert Herrick. *See* Succession of the Four Sweet Months, The.
Four Things. Proverbs, XXX: 24–28, Bible, *O.T.* FaPON; GoTP
Four Things. *Unknown.* MaRV
Four Things. Henry van Dyke. AA; BBV; BTP; GoTP; HBV; HBVY; MaRV; PCD; PoToHe (new ed.); TreF
(Four Things to Do.) OQP; QP-2; WBLP
Four things in any land must dwell. Four Things. *Unknown.* MaRV
Four Things to Do. Henry van Dyke. *See* Four Things.
Four III. E. E. Cummings. MoP
Four times the sun had risen and set; and now on the fifth day. Embarkation. Longfellow. *Fr.* Evangeline. PAH
Four tiny folk. Less Lonely. Alfred Kreymborg. AnAmPo; LA
Four trees upon a solitary acre. Emily Dickinson. PoEL-5
Four Walls. Blanche Taylor Dickinson. CDC
Four waters out of Eden flow. Eden. Hilary Corke. PoN
Four-way winds of the world have blown, The. Strike the blow. "F. McK." PAH
Four white birches. Quadrille. Fiona Stewart. DiM
Four Winds, The. Shane Leslie. OnYI
Four Winds, The. Longfellow. *Fr.* The Song of Hiawatha. AnNE
Four Winds, The. Charles Henry Luders. AA; HBV; LBAP; OBAV
Four Winds, The. Caroline Atherton Briggs Mason. *Fr.* En Voyage. PCH
Four Winds, The. Frank Dempster Sherman. TVC; TVSH
Four Winds. Sara Teasdale. HBV; LBMV; LEAP; PR
Four Wonders, The. *Unknown.* TuPP
Four Years. Dinah Maria Mulock Craik. HBV
Four Years. Nicholas Pappas, *tr. fr. Modern Greek by* Rae Dalven. MoGP
Four Years!—and didst thou stay above. Geist's Grave. Matthew Arnold. HBV; PoVP; VA
Four years of night and nightmare, years of black. Daybreak. Louis Untermeyer. NV
Four Years Only. *Unknown, tr. fr. Greek by* Robert Guthrie MacGregor. OnPM
Four years passed and all of us did not die. Four Years. Nicholas Pappas. MoGP
Four Years Were Mine at Princeton. John Peale Bishop. CAG
Four young men, of a Monday morn. The Prize of the *Margaretta.* Will Carleton. PAH
Four Zoas, The. Blake. *See* Vala; or, The Four Zoas.
Foure horses fierce, as red as flaming fire. The Lunar Valley of Lost Things. Ariosto. *Fr.* Orlando Furioso, XXXIV. LiTW
14 July 1956. L. D. Lerner. BoSA
Fourteen small broidered berries on the hem. What the Sonnet Is. Eugene Lee Hamilton. HoPM; OBVV; VA
Fourteenth Birthday. Phyllis McGinley. NePoAm-2
Fourteenth of July had come, The. La Tricoteuse. George Walter Thornbury. BeLS; BMEP
Fourth Act. Robinson Jeffers. LiTA; WaP
Fourth Book of Sibylline Oracles, The, *sel. At. to* "The Jewish Sibyl," *tr. fr. Greek by* Bohn.
There Is a City. TrJP
Fourth Cycle of Love Poems, *sel.* George Barker.
Love Poem: "Less the dog begged to die in the sky." NeBP
Fourth day came, but not a breath of air, The. Byron. *Fr.* Don Juan, II. ChER
Fourth Day's Battle, The. Dryden. *Fr.* Annus Mirabilis. OBS
Fourth Dimensional. "Katherine Hale." OCL
Fourth Eclogue, The. Virgil. *tr. fr. Latin by* James Laughlin. *Fr.* Eclogues. LiTW
(Dawn of the Golden Age.) RoL
("Muses/ Muses of Sicily.") LaP
Sibylline Prophecy, The, *sel., tr. by* Roderick Gill. CAW; ISi, *tr wr. at. to* Thomas Walsh
Fourth Eglogue of Alexander Barclay, The, Entituled Codrus and Minalcas, Treating of the Behavior of Rich Men against Poets. Alexander Barclay. ReIE

Fourth Eglogue, The, *abr.* George Wither. *Fr.* The Shepheards Hunting. SeCV-1
Fourth of July. Marchette Chute. MeMeAg; SiSoSe
Fourth of July. Rachel Field. SiSoSe
Fourth of July, The. Charles Leonard Moore. IDAH
Fourth of July, The. John Pierpont. AnNE; DD; HH; MC; OTPC (1946 ed.); PAH; PEOR; PoRL; YeAr
Fourth of July, The. Charles Sprague. IDAH
Fourth of July Night. Dorothy Aldis. SiSoSe; TiPo
Fourth of July Ode. James Russell Lowell. HH; PoRL; TSW; TSWC
Fourth of July Song. Lois Lenski. SiSoSe
Fourth of July, they say, sir. Young America. Carolyn Wells. DD
Fourth Song, The, *sel.* Michael Drayton. *Fr.* Polyolbion.
"Mongst whom, some there were bards, that in their sacred rage." PrWP
Fourth Song: "Only [*or* Onely] joy, now here you are." Sir Philip Sidney. *Fr.* Astrophel and Stella. AtBAP; ElL; InvP; LEAP; OBSC; ReEn; ReIE; SiCE; SiPS; TuPP
Fourth Station. Paul Claudel, *tr. fr. French by* Sister Mary David. ISi
Fourth Station. Padraic Colum. ISi
Fourth Station. William A. Donaghy. ISi
Fourth Station. Ruth Schaumann, *tr. fr. German by* William J. Brell. ISi
Fowler, The. "Eduard Bagritsky," *tr. fr. Russian by* C. M. Bowra. BoRS
Fowler, The. W. W. Gibson. BMEP; HBMV; PoTo
Fox. Clifford Dyment. HaMV
Fox, The. Phoebe Hesketh. HaMV
Fox, The. R. Williams Parry, *tr. fr. Welsh by* Gwyn Williams. PrWP
Fox, The. Kenneth Patchen. AnAmPo
Fox, The. Marjorie Somers Scheuer. GoYe
Fox, The. Ian Serraillier. POTE
Fox, The (*diff. versions*). *Unknown.* BaBo; GFA; StPo
(Ballad of the Fox.) GoTP; OTPC (1946 ed.)
(Fox Jumped Up on a Moonlight Night, The.) OTPC (1923 ed.)
("Fox jumped up one winter's night, A.") OxNR
(Fox Went Out One Frosty Night, The.) BLPA
(Fox, The, Went through the Town, Oh! *with music.*) SoAF
(Hungry Fox, The, *with music.*) FTB
(Visit from Mr. Fox, A.) StVeCh
Fox, The. *Unknown, tr. fr. Armenian by* Zabelle C. Boyajian. ArmLP
Fox, almost with hunger dying, A. The Fox and the Grapes. La Fontaine. OnPM
Fox and Goose. F. Hey. SAS
Fox and the Bust, The. La Fontaine, *tr. fr. French by* Elizur Wright. OnPM
Fox and the Cat, The. J. Cunningham. CG
Fox and the Grapes, The. La Fontaine, *tr. fr. French by* Elizur Wright. OnPM
Fox and the Grapes, The. Joseph Lauren. GoTP; RIS
Fox at the Point of Death, The. John Gay. BrBE; CG; EnLi-1 (1949 ed.); OBEC; OTPC (1923 ed.)
Fox Awakes, The. John Masefield. *Fr.* Reynard the Fox. MoVE
Fox came lolloping, lolloping, The. Hunting Song. Donald Finkel. NePoEA
Fox Hunt, The. John Masefield. *Fr.* Reynard the Fox, II. CoEV
("From the Gallows Hill to the Tineton Copse.") NAMP
Fox Hunters of Hell. Byron Herbert Reece. DaM
Fox, in heaven's trap that gleams, A. The Stars Go By. Lilian Bowes-Lyon. ChMP
Fox, in life's extreme [*or* extream] decay, A. The Fox at the Point of Death. John Gay. BrBE; CG; EnLi-1 (1949 ed.); OBEC; OTPC (1923 ed.)
Fox in the pasture, bronze and beautiful. Lost Fox. Frances Frost. PoTo
Fox Jumped Up on a Moonlight Night, The. *Unknown. See* Fox, The.
Fox jumped up one winter's night, A. *Unknown.* OxNR
Fox knew well that, before they tore him, The. John Masefield. *Fr.* Reynard the Fox. OtMeF
Fox may steal your hens, Sir, A. John Gay. *Fr.* The Beggar's Opera. CEP
Fox ran up into the mill, The. The Fox. *Unknown.* ArmLP
Fox set [*or* went] out in [a] hungry plight, The. The Fox [*or* A Visit from Mr. Fox *or* The Hungry Fox]. *Unknown.* FTB; GFA; StVeCh
Fox Sparrow, The. W. W. Christman. BLA
Fox, the Wolf, and the Bear, The. *Unknown, tr. fr. Armenian by* Zabelle C. Boyajian. ArmLP
Fox went out on a [*or* one] chilly night, A. The Fox [*or* Ballad of the Fox]. *Unknown.* GoTP; StPo
Fox Went Out One Frosty Night, The. *Unknown. See* Fox, The.
Fox, The, Went through the Town, Oh! *Unknown. See* Fox, The.
Foxes among the Lambs. Ernest G. Moll. BoAu
Foxes can talk if you know how to listen. My Paw Said So. Edgar A. Guest. OnHT
Foxes have holes in the ground, The. Hard Trials. *Unknown.* ABF
Foxglove bells, with lolling tongue, The. Foxgloves. Mary Webb. BoTP
Foxglove by the cottage door, The. Four and Eight. ffrida Wolfe. BoTP; SiSoSe
Foxgloves. Mary Webb. BoTP
Foxhole for the Night, A. John Quinn. BoAV
Foxtrot from a Play. W. H. Auden. LiTM
Fra Bank to Bank. Mark Alexander Boyd. *See* Sonnet: "Fra bank to bank, fra wood to wood I rin."
Fra Carmelo's Morning Sacrifice. Gervase Toelle. JKCP (1955 ed.)
Fra Giacomo. Robert Buchanan. LPS-3
Fra Lippo Lippi. Robert Browning. BEL; BoLiVe; BPN; EM-2; EnL; EnLi-2; EnLit; EmBrPo; EPN; EPP; GEPC; OAEP; OtMeF; PoVP; ReaPo; TCEP; TwCrTr; ViBoPo; ViPo; ViPP; VLEP
Fra Pandolf, have you tried to reproduce. Technique. Burnham Eaton. GoYe
Fra whaur in fragrant wuds ye bide. Spring on the Ochils. J. Logie Robertson. EBSV; OBVV
Frae great Apollo, poet, say. The Poet's Wish; an Ode. Allan Ramsay. CEP; EiPP
Frae the Second Canzone o Dante's "Vita Nuova." Dante, *tr. fr. Italian into Scottish by* Douglas Young. *Fr.* La Vita Nuova. LyPI
Fragile affirmations of the springtime, The. April. Francis Sweeney. JKCP (1955 ed.)
Fragment: Abyss of War, The. Wilfred Owen. POTE
Fragment: "All night a wind of music." Thomas Lovell Beddoes. CaAE
Fragment: "Amid the shining swords and lances." Sharaf al-Din, *tr. fr. Arabic by* A. J. Arberry. MooP
Fragment: "As balmy as the breath of her you love." Dante Gabriel Rossetti. RO
Fragment: "As if stone Caesar shook." Hugh McCrae. BoAV
Fragment: "Breath of life imbued those few dim days, The." Jessie Redmond Fauset. CDC
Fragment: "Encinctur'd with a twine of leaves." Samuel Taylor Coleridge. *See* Fruit Plucker, The.
Fragment: "Faint white pillars that seem to fade." E. A. Robinson. MAPA
Fragment: "Flower in the crannied wall." Tennyson. *See* Flower in the Crannied Wall.
Fragment: Furl of Fresh-leaved Dog-Rose Down, The. Gerard Manley Hopkins. AtBAP
Fragment: "Give me your hands, and let your strange wild eyes." Edmund John. BMEP
Fragment: "Hedgerow hips to glossy scarlet turn, The." John Clare. RO
Fragment, A: "His eye was stern and wild—his cheek was pale and cold as clay." *Unknown.* BOHV
Fragment, A: "I am fur from my sweetheart." *Unknown. See* I Am Fur from My Sweetheart.
Fragment: "I know not what to do." Hilda Doolittle ("H. D."). *See* Fragment Thirty-six.
Fragment: "I walk'd [*or* walked] along a stream for pureness rare." Gervase Markham, *at. to* Christopher Marlowe. CaAE; LoBV; OBSC
Fragment: "I went into the deserts of dim sleep." Shelley. RO
Fragment: "I would to heaven that I were so much clay." Byron. Don Juan, *on the back of poet's MS of* I. ERP; FiP; OAEP
Fragment, A: "I'd rather hear a rattler rattle." *Unknown.* CSF
Fragment: "Language has not the power to speak what love indites." John Clare. PoEL-4
Fragment: "Mountain summits sleep, The." Alcman, *tr. fr. Greek by* Thomas Campbell. AWP; JAWP; RO; WBP
(Sleep upon the World.) ChTr
Fragment: Music. Shelley. *See* Music ("I pant for the music which is divine").
Fragment: "Near where the riotous Atlantic surge." William Allingham. IrPN
Fragment: "Not honey." Hilda Doolittle ("H. D."). *See* Not Honey.
Fragment: "O pale art thou, my lamp, and faint." Henry Kirke White. ERP
Fragment: "Or I will burst/ Damnation's iron egg, my tomb." Thomas Lovell Beddoes. *Fr.* The Last Man. RO
Fragment: "Pity, religion has so seldom found." William Cowper. *Fr.* Table Talk. WGRP
Fragment: "Praise not the avaricious man." Ibn al-Missisi, *tr. fr. Arabic by* A. J. Arberry. MooP
Fragment: Rain. Shelley. ChER
Fragment, A: "Repeat that, repeat." Gerard Manley Hopkins. *See* Cuckoo, The.
Fragment: "So here confin'd, and but to female clay." Countess of Winchilsea. TriL

Fragment: "Spirit, who lov'st Britannia's Isle." Blake. RO
Fragment: "Strike, churl; hurl, cheerless wind, then; heltering hail." Gerard Manley Hopkins. NAMP
Fragment: "There is a river clear and fair." Catherine Fanshawe. *See* Fragment in Imitation of Wordsworth.
Fragment, A: "They say that poison-sprinkled flowers." Adam Lindsay Gordon. CaAE
Fragment: "This I remember clearly: from stone to stepping-stone." Clark Ashton Smith. UnW
Fragment: "Though decked the tray." Jami. *Fr.* Baharistan. CIV
Fragment, A: To Music. Shelley. BoLiVe; ERP
(Music.) TrGrPo
Fragment: To the Moon. Shelley. *See* Moon, The ("Art thou pale . . .").
Fragment: "To thirst and find no fill—to wail and wander." Shelley. BLV
Fragment: "Ukraina is sad for that she has no place to dwell in." *Unknown, tr. fr. Ukrainian by* Florence Randal Livesay. PoFr
Fragment: Vine-Shroud, The. Shelley. RO
Fragment: "Virtue to an upgrowing life lends grace." Bacchylides, *tr. fr. Greek by* J. M. Edmonds. GrR
Fragment: "Walk with thy fellow-creatures: note the hush." Henry Vaughan. WGRP
Fragment, A: "What are the falling rills, the pendent shades." Pope. CaAE
Fragment: "What is poetry? Is it a mosaic." Amy Lowell. WGRP
Fragment: "When soft winds and sunny skies." Shelley. EmBrPo; ERP
Fragment, A: "When the hornet hangs in the hollyhock." Madison Cawein. BAP
Fragment: "Wing'd seeds with decaying wings, The." William Allingham. IrPN
Fragment, A: Woodman and the Nightingale, The. Shelley. EmBrPo
Fragment: "You see/ Nestled into a hollow of the downs." William Allingham. *Fr.* By the Way. EnSW; IrPN
Fragment from a Ballad, A. Alexander Smith. BMEP
Fragment from "Clemo Uti—the Water Lilies." Ring Lardner. FiBHP
Fragment from Saint Gregory Nazianzen, A. Cardinal Newman. *See* Married and the Single, The.
Fragment from Sappho. Sappho. *See* To a Bride.
Fragment in Imitation of Wordsworth. Catherine Fanshawe. HBV; PA
(Fragment: "There is a river clear and fair.") ALV
(Imitation of Wordsworth, An.) BOHV; NA
Fragment of a Greek Tragedy. A. E. Housman. CenHV
Chorus: "In speculation," *sel.* BMEP
Fragment of a rainbow bright, A. The Rainbow. John Keble. CG
Fragment of a Sleep-Song. Sydney Dobell. BOL; VA
(Fragment of a Sleepy Song.) RAR
Fragment of a Sonnet. Pierre de Ronsard, *tr. fr. French by* Keats. AWP; JAWP; OuHeWo; WBP
Fragment of an Agon. T. S. Eliot. LiTB
Fragment of an Anti-Papist Ballad. *Unknown.* CoMu
Fragment of an Ode to Maia [Written on May Day, 1818]. Keats. BCEP; EM-2; EmBrPo; EnRP; LEAP; OAEP; OBEV; OBRV; PoEL-4
(To Maia.) EPN; TwCrTr
Fragment of Chorus of a "Dejaneira." Matthew Arnold. ViPP
Fragment of Death. Villon. *See* Fragment on Death.
Fragment of moon that shines, A. Vespers. Luis Carlos López. AnCL
Fragment of Sappho. Sappho. *See* To a Bride.
Fragment on [*or* of] Death. Villon, *tr. fr. French by* Swinburne. AWP; OuHeWo
Fragment 113: "Not honey." Hilda Doolittle ("H. D."). *See* Not Honey.
Fragment Thirty-six: "I know not what to do." Hilda Doolittle ("H. D."). ChMo; CMP; OxBA; TwCV
(Hesperides—Fragment Thirty-six.) NP
Fragments. Emerson. *See* Music.
Fragments. John Masefield. PoeT
Fragments Intended for the Dramas, *sels.* Thomas Lovell Beddoes.
Beautiful Night, A. ChER; ERP; LoBV
Dream of Dying. ERP; RO
Insignificance of the World. ERP
Lofty Mind, A. ERP
Subterranean City. ERP
Fragments of a Lost Gnostic Poem of the Twelfth Century. Herman Melville. PoEL-5; ViBoPo
Fragments of Eternity, *sels.* Arthur M. Sampley. MuM
Dead Earth, The.
Eternity.
Fragments on a Theme. Samuel Taylor Coleridge. AlDL
Fragments on Nature and Life. Emerson. TOP
Atom from Atom, *2 ll.* ImOP
("Atom from atom yawns as far.") TiPo (1959 ed.)

Fragments on the Poet and the Poetic Gift, *sels.* Emerson.
"Pale genius roves alone." TOP
"Teach me your mood, O patient stars!"
(Quatrains, I.) CBOV
Fragoletta, blessed one! Songs for Fragoletta, I. Richard Le Gallienne. HBV
Fragrance drifts through our thoughts of Him. Incense. Leslie Savage Clark. ChIP
Fragrance, The, fades from the lotoses, emerald leaves wither. To the Tune of "Mountain Flowers." Li Yu. WhP
Fragrance, The, of the pink lotos fails, the jade mat hints of autumn. To the Tune of "A Sprig of Plum Blossom." Li Ch'ing-chao. WhP
Fragrance of the south wind, The. Song of the South Wind. *Unknown. Fr.* The Fountain of Old Poems. WhP
Fragrance of the trees, The. The Goodness of God. Nagata. SoLD
Fragrance silver-gray of twilight filled, A. Experience. Hugo von Hofmannsthal. AnGP
Fragrant Blossoms, The. Tzu Yeh, *tr. fr. Chinese by* Henry H. Hart. PoHN
Fragrant prayer upon the air, A. A Poem to Be Said on Hearing the Birds Sing. *Tr. fr. Irish by* Douglas Hyde. AnIV; AWP; JAWP; WBP
Fragrant silence filled the purple air, A. The Rosary. Sister Maura. ISi
Fragrant Thy Memories. "Judah," *tr. fr. Hebrew by* Herbert Loewe. TrJP
Frail Beauty. Earl of Surrey. *See* Brittle Beauty.
Frail beauty, green, gold and incandescent whiteness. Lunch. F. S. Flint. PFE
Frail branches of the arbor, The. When the Moon Is in the River of Heaven. Ou-yang Hsiu. OnPC
Frail children of sorrow, dethroned by a hue. Hope. Georgia Douglas Johnson. CDC
Frail is the bamboo that thrives in solitude. The Nineteen Han Poems, VIII. *Unknown, tr. fr. Chinese.* WhP
Frail Life! in which, through mists of human breath. Life and Death. Sir William Davenant. *Fr.* The Christian's Reply to the Philosopher. OBS
Frail lilies that beneath the dust so long. Hath Hope Kept Vigil? Sir Charles G. D. Roberts. MM; TwCV
Frail little body, A. The Little Servant. Sophia Mavroidi Papadaky. MoGP
Frail Sleep, that blowest by fresh banks. To Sleep. Percy MacKaye. HBMV
Frail Sound of a Tunic Trailing, A. Antonio Machado, *tr. fr. Spanish by* John Dos Passos. TeCS
(Four Poems, 1.) LiTW
(Poems, 1.) AWP; JAWP; WBP
Frail the white rose and frail are. A Flower Given to My Daughter. James Joyce. OBMV; ReMP; TwCV
Frail, wistful guardian of the broom. The Sweeper. Agnes Lee. BAP; HBMV; NP
Frailty. George Herbert. ElSeCe; OxBoCh
Frailty and Hurtfulness of Beauty, The. Earl of Surrey. *See* Brittle Beauty.
Frailty of Beauty, The. "J. C." *Fr.* Alcilia. ElL
Frailty, Thy Name Is Woman. Shakespeare. *See* O! That This Too, Too Solid Flesh Would Melt.
Frainchman he don't lak to die in de fall. On Meesh-e-gan. *Unknown.* ABF; TrAS
Framed by a silken fringe, in strange accord. The Tapestry. Stefan George. LiTW
Framed in its shadow-rectangle. Facing My Portrait. Yolanda Bedregal de Cónitzer. AnCL
Framed in the cavernous fire-place sits a boy. An Old Thought. Charles Henry Luders. AA
Framed in the front of forlorn hope past all recovery. His Good Name Being Blemished, He Bewaileth. Edward de Vere, Earl of Oxford. ReIE
Framed in the sedan windows, the tall triangular faces. Giraffes. N. H. Brettell. BoSA
Framework-Knitters Lamentation, The. *Unknown.* CoMu
Framework-Knitters Petition, The. C. Briggs. CoMu
France. Goldsmith. *Fr.* The Traveller. OBEC
France. Percy MacKaye. BAP; LEAP
France. Elliott Napier. BoAu
France. Wordsworth. *Fr.* The Prelude, XI. ERP
France; an Ode. Samuel Taylor Coleridge. ATP; BEL; BPN; EM-2; EmBrPo; EnLi-2 (1949 ed.); EnRP; EPN; ERP; LiA; OAEP; PoFr, *abr.*; TCEP; TOP
Rebellion, *sel.* RO
France! It is I answering. Republic to Republic. Witter Bynner. PAH
France (June, 1938; June, 1941). Charles Schiff. NeTW
Franceline rose in the dawning gray. Vive La France. Charlotte Holmes Crawford. BoHiPo; POT
Francesca. Ezra Pound. MOAP
Francesca da Rimini. Dante, *tr. fr. Italian by* Dante Gabriel Rossetti. *Fr.* Divina Commedia: Inferno. EmBrPo; EPN; EPP
Francesca da Rimini/ Lived in a chiminey. Important People. Louis Untermeyer, *and others.* StaSt

Francesco Ceni. Gabriello Chiabrera, *tr. fr. Italian by* Wordsworth. OnPM
(Epitaph, I.) AWP; JAWP; WBP
Francesco's Fortunes, *sels.* Robert Greene.
Eurymachus's Fancy. OBSC
Penitent Palmer's Ode, The. LoBV; OBSC
Francis Ledwidge. Grace Hazard Conkling. SBMV
(Elegy for the Irish Poet Francis Ledwidge.) VOD
Francis, my brother, in the clear, wide morning. Boy Playing an Organ. Francis Sweeney. GoBC
Francis' New Jig. George Attowell. ReIE
Francis of Assisi. Bertha Gerneaux Woods. SaFP
Francis rode to battle in the armor of a knight. Stigmata. A. M. Sullivan. SaFP
Francis spoke to the birds. Saint Francis. Dorothy Bennett. SaFP
Francis, thou wast lonely plying. Saint Francis of Assisi. Shane Leslie. SaFP
Francis was preaching in the lazarhouse courtyard. St. Clare Hears St. Francis. Sarah N. Cleghorn. AV; NV
Franciscan. Katherine Brégy. SaFP
Franciscan Aspiration. Vachel Lindsay. *See* St. Francis.
Franciscan Dream, A. Enid Dinnis. CAW; SaFP
Franciscan Prayer, A. Enid Dinnis. SaFP
Franciscans. Hyacinth Blocker. SaFP
Francisco Coronado rode forth with all his train. Quivira. Arthur Guiterman. PAH; PFY; PoeMoYo
Franciscus Christificatus. Francis Thompson. SaFP
Franciscus de Verulamio Sic Cogitavit. James Russell Lowell. TCAP
Frangipanni. *Unknown.* NA
Frank Baker's my name, and a bachelor I am. Starving to Death on a Government Claim. *Unknown.* ABS
Frank carves very ill, yet will palm all the meats. Epigram. Matthew Prior. CEP
Frank Courtship, The. George Crabbe. *Fr.* Tales. OBRV
Frank Sylvan, *sel.* Thomas Aird.
"O! now the summer woods! and O! the joy." EnSW
Frankie and Johnny [*or* Johnnie]. *Unknown.* AmPP (3d ed.); APW; AS, *with music;* ATP; BeLS; FaFP; LiTG; LiTL; NeHB; OxBoLi; SiTL; TrAS, *with music;* TreF; TrGrPo; UnPo; YaD
(Frankie and Albert, *with music.*) ABF (A *and* B *vers.*); AS; BaBo (A *and* B *vers.*); ViBoFo (A *and* B *vers.*)
(Frankie Blues, *with music.*) AS
(Josie, *diff. vers., with music.*) AS
(Sadie, *diff. vers., with music.*) AS
Frankie's Trade. Kipling. ETS
Frankincense. Ibn al-Zaqqaq, *tr. fr. Arabic by* A. J. Arberry. MooP
Franklin! our Franklin! America's loved son! Benjamin Franklin. Florence Earle Coates. GA
Franklin's Crew, *with music. Unknown.* SoAmSa
Franklin's Prologue, The. Chaucer. *Fr.* The Canterbury Tales. OAEP
Franklin's Tale, The. Chaucer. *Fr.* The Canterbury Tales. OAEP
Frankly, I do not greatly care. Change Is Sweetest of All. Clove Bell. DDA
Frankly, I prefer the blue. Sentimental Lines to a Young Man Who Favors Pink Wallpaper, While I Personally Lean to the Blue. Margaret Fishback. FiBHP
Franklyn's dogge leped over a style, A. Verses Prefixed to the "Lay of St. Gengulphus." "Thomas Ingoldsby." EV-4
Frascati's. Aldous Huxley. InPo; ViBoPo
"Frater Ave atque Vale." Tennyson. BPN; ChTr; EM-2; EmBrPo; EPN; GEPC; GTML; PoVP; PtP; TCEP; ViPo; VLEP
Fraternity. Anne Reeve Aldrich. AA
Fraternity. John Banister Tabb. HBV
Fratri Dilectissimo. John Buchan. OtMeF
Frau Bauman, Frau Schmidt, and Frau Schwartze. Theodore Roethke. MoAB; NePoAm
Fraud of Men, The. William Shakespeare. *See* Sigh No More.
Fraudulent perhaps in that they gave. Swans. Lawrence Durrell. FaBoMo; SeCePo
Fraught with stars the dark nights come and go. And Thou, Expectant . . . Amado Nervo. AnMP
Fray began at the middle gate, The. A Ballad of Orleans. Agnes Mary Frances Robinson. HBV; VA
Fray Serra. Lilian White Spencer. BAP
Freckles; a fragment. *Unknown.* CSF
Freckles numberless as stars on my forehead. My Portrait. Moishe-Leib Halpern. TrJP
Fred. Eleanor Farjeon. OnPP
Fred. David McCord. TiPo (1959 ed.)
Fred Apollus at Fava's. Nicholas Moore. NeBP
Fred likes creatures. Fred. Eleanor Farjeon. OnPP
"Fred, where is north?" West-running Brook. Robert Frost. AmP; MAP; MoAB; MoAmPo; PoLFOT; ReaPo
Freddie [*or* Freddy] and the Cherry Tree ("Freddie saw some fine [*or* nice] ripe cherries"). Ann Hawkshaw. OTPC (1923 ed.); SAS
Frederick Douglass. Robert E. Hayden. PoNe
Frederick Knieps, Physician of the Bed-Chamber to the Empress Theresa. The Big Mystical Circus. Jorge de Lima. AnCL
Fredericksburg. Thomas Bailey Aldrich. BAP; MDAH; PaA; PAH; PAP; PFY
Free. Mary Carolyn Davies. *Fr.* A Girl's Songs. SBMV
Free America. *At. to* Joseph Warren. PAP; PoFr
Free are the Muses, and where freedom is. Breath on the Oat. Joseph Russell Taylor. HBV; PAH
Free at las'—free at las'. I Thank God I'm Free at Las'. *Unknown.* BoAN-2
Free Besieged, The, *sels.* Dionysios Solomos, *tr. fr. Modern Greek by* Rae Dalven. MoGP
I Walked the Road of the Dawn.
Temptation.
Free Enterprise. Clyde McGee. *See* Cross Makers.
Free Fantasia on Japanese Themes. Amy Lowell. MAP; MoAmPo
Free Flag, The. *Unknown.* FOAH
Free Love. Henry David Thoreau. MOAP
Free Martin. Peter Hopegood. BoAV
Free Men. Struthers Burt. PoFr
Free Nation, A. Edwin Markham. MaRV
Free Parliament Litany, A. *Unknown.* OxBoLi
Free Thoughts on Several Eminent Composers. Charles Lamb. OBRV; OxBoLi
Free to all souls the hidden beauty calls. Walls. Eva Gore-Booth. MBP
Free to look at fact. To the New Women. John Davidson. PoVP
Free to Serve. Milton. *Fr.* Paradise Lost, V. GrCo-2
("To whom the angel; Son of Heav'n and Earth.") NBE
Free us, safe God. Libera Nos a Malo. Eric Bruno. JKCP (1955 ed.)
Free Will and God's Foreknowledge. Milton. *Fr.* Paradise Lost, III. ExPo
Free, with white muscles touching stars. Grasses. Scudder Middleton. NV
Free Woman, The. Theodosia Garrison. BAP; HBMV
Freebooters' lair, old corsairs' nest. To Old Roscoff. Tristan Corbière. TrFP
Freed dove flew to the Rajah's tower, The. The Dove of Dacca. Kipling. GN
Freedom. Joan Agnew. BoTP
Freedom. John Barbour. *Fr.* The Bruce, I. BSV; EBSV; EV-1; FaBoCh; GoTS; LoGBV; OBEV; TrGrPo
("A! fredome is a noble thing!") PoFr; ViBoPo
Freedom. Joel Barlow. *See* To Freedom.
Freedom. Emerson. PoFr
Freedom. Abraham ibn Ezra, *tr. fr. Hebrew by* Solomon Solis-Cohen. TrJP
Freedom ("Are we, then, wholly fallen? Can it be"). James Russell Lowell. PaA
"We are not free: Freedom doth not consist," *sel., 2 sts.* BHV
Freedom ("Men! whose boast it is that ye"). James Russell Lowell. *See* Stanzas on Freedom.
Freedom ("They are slaves who fear to speak"). James Russell Lowell. *See* Stanzas on Freedom: Slaves.
Freedom. Leonard Mann. NeLNL
Freedom. Georgi Efimovich Nechayev, *tr. fr. Russian by* George Z. Patrick. PoFr
Freedom. Nikolai Alekseyevich Nekrasov, *tr. fr. Russian by* Babette Deutsch. TrRV
Freedom. Palladas, *tr. fr. Greek by* George Allen. OxBG
Freedom, *sel.* Charles Péguy, *tr. fr. French by* Julian Green.
"Such is the mystery of man's freedom, says God." PoFr
Freedom. "Jan Struther." LoPS; POTE
Freedom. Rabindranath Tagore. PoFr
Freedom ("O thou so fair in summers gone"). Tennyson. PoVP; VLEP
Freedom ("Of old sat Freedom"). Tennyson. *See* Of Old Sat Freedom at the Heights.
Freedom ("I am not strong"). *Unknown.* PGD
Freedom all winged expands. Emerson. Voluntaries, II. PoFr
Freedom and Faith went wooing for a soul. The Rivals. Robert Whitaker. OQP; QP-1
Freedom and Love. Thomas Campbell. BSV; GTBS; GTBS-D; GTBS-W; GTSE
(First Kiss, The.) LPS-1
(How Delicious Is the Winning.) EBSV
(Song: "How delicious is the winning.") HBV
Freedom called them—up they rose. The Gallant Fifty-one. Henry Lynden Flash. PAH
Freedom, farewell! Or so the soldiers say. Port of Embarkation. Randall Jarrell. MiAP
Freedom for the Mind. William Lloyd Garrison. AA; FaBoBe
(Sonnet Written While in Prison for Denouncing the Domestic Slave-Trade.) LPS-2

Freedom from fear is the freedom I claim for you, my Motherland! Freedom. Rabindranath Tagore. PoFr
Freedom has a thousand charms to show. William Cowper. *Fr.* Table Talk. PoFr
Freedom has called us and we've come across the wave. The Patriotic Band. *Unknown. Fr.* Washington, Lincoln and the American Flag. FOAH
Freedom I never saw in words. After Bombardment. John Pudney. WaP
Freedom in Dress. Ben Jonson. *See* Simplex Munditiis.
Freedom in Mah Soul. David Wadsworth Cannon, Jr. PoNe
Freedom is a hard-bought thing. Song of the Settlers. Jessamyn West. FaPON
Freedom is more than a word, more than the base coinage. The *Nabara.* C. Day Lewis. HaMV
Freedom is the finest gold. Ode to Freedom. Thomas of Strengnaes. PoFr
Freedom, not won by the vain. To Freedom. James Russell Lowell. PSO
Freedom of the Moon, The. Robert Frost. PFE
Freedom of the Press, The. Henrik Arnold Wergeland, *tr. fr. Norwegian by* Elias Gordon. PoFr
Freedom of the Will. Dante, *tr. fr. Italian by* M. B. Anderson. *Fr.* Divina Commedia: Purgatorio, XVIII. GrCo-1
Freedom, one of the greatest blessings of Heaven. Battle Hymn of the Chinese Revolution (1912). *Unknown.* PoFr
Freedom, Our Queen. Oliver Wendell Holmes. PEDC
Freedom the Goddess. Arthur Wilberforce Jose. BoAu; PoFr
Freedom's first champion in our fettered land! Garrison. Amos Bronson Alcott. AA; GA; OBAV; PoFr
Freedom's Hero. Byron. *See* Sonnet on Chillon.
Freedom's Natal Day. Elizabeth M. Griswold. PEOR
Freedom's War Song. Thomas Chatterton. *Fr.* Goddwyn. BLV; PoFr
(Ode to Liberty.) TrGrPo
Freelance, The. Archilochus, *tr. fr. Greek by* F. L. Lucas. GrPE
Freelance, The. Hybrias, *tr. fr. Greek by* F. L. Lucas. GrPE
Freely Espousing. James Schuyler. NeAP
Freely, with glorious harp in hand, of old men rode away. The Mercenary Muse. Pindar. *Fr.* Isthmian Odes, II. GrPE
Freeman, The. William Cowper. *Fr.* The Task, VI. LPS-2
Freeman once of London made a Knight, A. Dupliciter Beatus. Henry Parrot. SiCE
Freight Boats. James S. Tippett. BrR; FaPON; GFA; MPB; StVeCh (1955 ed.)
Freighter. Bruce Ruddick. CaP
Freighter, gay with rust, The. Jews at Haifa. Randall Jarrell. MoAmPo (1950 ed.)
Freighting from Wilcox to Globe. *Unknown.* CoSo; CSF
French and English. Thomas Hood. ERP
French and Russian they matter not. A Chant [*or* Hymn] of Hate against England. Ernst Lissauer. HBV; OtMeF
French and [the] Spanish Guerrillas, The. Wordsworth. SoV; WaaP
(Sonnet: French and Spanish Guerrillas, The.) ChER
French Clock. Hortense Flexner. HBMV
French Cookery. Thomas Moore. *Fr.* The Fudge Family in Paris. OBRV
French guns roll continuously, The. The Iron Music. Ford Madox Ford. HBMV; VOD (1931 ed.)
French Lisette; Ballad of Maida Vale. William Plomer. LiTM (rev. ed.); SiTL
French Nun, A. Dinah Maria Mulock Craik. PraNu
French Peasants. Monk Gibbon. HaMV; NeIP; OxBI; POTE
French Polisher, The. Constance Davies. MoWP
French Princess, The. *Unknown, tr. fr. Spanish by* George Borrow. AnSpL-1
French Revolution, The, *sels.* Blake.
"Dead brood over Europe, the cloud and vision descends over cheerful France, The," *fr.* I. EiPP
"Noise of trampling, the wind of trumpets, The." *fr.* I. ChER
French Revolution, The. Erasmus Darwin. PoFr
French Revolution, The. Wordsworth. *Fr.* The Prelude, XI. BPN; ERP; FiP; RO; TOP
("Oh! pleasant exercise of hope and joy!") EnLi-2; EV-3; OBRV
(Residence in France, Continued.) PoEL-4
French with a Master. Theodore Tilton. PR
Frenchie. Frank C. McCarthy. AIBD
Frenchman's Ball, The, *with music. Unknown.* OuSiCo
Frend, farly nocht; na caus is to complene. Gawin Douglas. *Fr.* Prologues to the Aeneid, X. OxBoCh
Freres Tale, The. Chaucer. *See* Friar's Tale, The.
Fresco-Sonnets to Christian Sethe. Heine, *tr. fr. German by* John Todhunter. AWP; JAWP; WBP
"Give me a mask, I'll join the masquerade," 2.
"I laugh at each dull bore, taste's parasite," 1.
Frescoes for Mr. Rockefeller's City. Archibald MacLeish.
I. Landscape as a Nude. AmPP (4th ed.); ReaPo; UnPo
II. Wildwest. ReaPo; ReMP; UnPo
III. Burying Ground by the Ties. AmPP (4th ed.); MAP; MoAmPo; NAMP; ReaPo; UnPo; WoL
IV. Oil Painting of the Artist as the Artist. NAMP; OnHM; ReaPo; UnPo
V. Empire Builders. AmP; OxBA; Po; ReaPo; UnPo
VI. Background with Revolutionaries. ReaPo; TwHP; UnPo
Fresh Air. Kenneth Koch. NeAP
Fresh Air, The. Harold Monro. CH
Fresh are the dews, come brothers and sing. Mowers in the Line of Fire. Valery Bryusov. RuPo
Fresh blows the wind, the sun is gliding. Afternoon on the Water. Johann Sebastian Cammermeyer Welhaven. AnNoLy
Fresh, bright bloom of the daffodils, The. April Fantasie. Helen Mackay Hutchinson Cortissoz. AA
Fresh clad from heaven in robes of white. In My Own Album [*or* Lines Written in My Album]. Charles Lamb. EV-4; OBRV
Fresh fields and woods! the earth's fair face! Retirement. Henry Vaughan. EPS (1942 ed.)
Fresh flower of womanly nature. To My Lady Dear. *Unknown.* TMEV
Fresh from His Fastnesses. W. E. Henley. PoVP
Fresh from the dewy hill, the merry year. Song. Blake. CoBE; EiPP; EnLit; EnRP
Fresh from the fountains of the wood. The Valley Brook. John Howard Bryant. LPS-2
Fresh in the flush light gleam. The Sorrow of Unicume. Sir Herbert Read. ChMP
Fresh in wild holiness over. Hermits. Frederick Robert Higgins. MM
Fresh light from a morning sky blocked through clouds. Light. Carol Coates. CaP
Fresh Morning, A. J. C. Squire. MBP; WhC
Fresh morning gusts have blown away all fear. Sonnet to a Young Lady Who Sent Me a Laurel Crown. Keats. EmBrPo; EnRP
Fresh Paint. Boris Pasternak, *tr. fr. Russian by* Babette Deutsch. TrJP; TrRV
Fresh palms for the Old Dominion! The Battle of Charlestown. Henry Howard Brownell. PAH
Fresh spring gust blew down upon us, A. The New Church. Ivan Alekseyevich Bunin. TrRV
Fresh spring, the herald of love's mighty king. Spenser. Amoretti, LXX. AWP; BEL; CaAE; ChTr; EIL; ElSeCe; EnLit; ES; FaBoEn; HBV; JAWP; LEAP; LiTB; LiTL; OBEV; OBSC; OnPM; PeBoSo; PoFS; ReEn; ReIE; SeCeV; SiCE; TOP; ViBoPo; WBP
Fresh Start, The. Anna Wickham. ViBoPo
Fresh with all airs of woodland brooks. With a Copy of Herrick. Sir Edmund Gosse. PtP; TCEP; TCPD; VA; WP
Freshet, A. Antiphilus of Byzantium, *tr. fr. Greek by* Sir William Marris. LiTW; OxBG
Freshly the cool breath of the coming eve. The Healing of the Daughter of Jairus. Nathaniel Parker Willis. StJW
Fret not thyself because of evil doers. Psalm XXXVII, Bible, *O.T.* BLRP, *par. by* Charles Frederic Sheldon; TiPo (1952 ed.); WoL
Fret of Father Carty, The. Joseph I. C. Clarke. JKCP (1926 ed.)
Fret on fond Cupid, curse thy feeble bow. *Unknown.* SeCSL
Frétillon. Pierre Jean de Béranger, *pr. tr. fr. French.* LiA
Freya's Spinning Wheel. Adam Oehlenschläger, *tr. fr. Danish by* Charles W. Stork. BoDS; LiTW
Freya's Star. Christian K. F. Molbech, *tr. fr. Danish by* Charles W. Stork. BoDS
Freyr's Courtship. *Unknown, tr. fr. Old Norse by* Henry Adams Bellows. *Fr.* The Elder Edda. PaOS
Friar, The. Julian del Casal, *tr. fr. Spanish by* Thomas Walsh. CAW; SaFP; WHL
Friar had said his paternosters duly, The. Necrological. John Crowe Ransom. MOAP
Friar in the Well, The. *Unknown. See* As I Lay Musing.
Friar Laurence's Cell. Shakespeare. Romeo and Juliet, II, vi. GoBC
Friar Lubin. Clément Marot, *tr. fr. French by* Longfellow. AWP; WoL
(Ballade of a Friar, *tr. by* Andrew Lang.) HBV
Friar of Genoa, The. Scharmel Iris. JKCP
Friar of Orders Gray, The. John O'Keeffe. *Fr.* Merry Sherwood. BOHV; OnYI; OxBI
(I Am a Friar of Orders Gray.) LPS-3
Friar of Orders Gray [*or* Grey], The. *Unknown.* ACP, *abr.*; BCEP; CAW; CEP; EV-3; GoBC; HBV; LPS-1; OBEC; WHL, *abr.*
Friar of Orders Grey, The. Dante Gabriel Rossetti. GoBC
(Old Song Ended, An.) PoVP
Friar of Orders Grey, The. Shakespeare. *See* How Should I Your True Love Know?

Friar's Hunting Song. Thomas Love Peacock. *See* Though I Be Now a Gray, Gray Friar.
Friar's Tale, The. Chaucer. *Fr.* The Canterbury Tales. BCEP, *mod. by* Edwin Markham; EnLi-1 (1949 ed.), *mod. by* Edwin M. Everett
(Freres Tale, The, *sl. abr., orig. and mod. vers. by* Frank E. Hill.) BLV
Friction. Esther Pinch. PoMa
Friday. Sir Walter Scott. BoTP
Friday came and the circus was there. The Circus. Elizabeth Madox Roberts. FaPON; GFA; MPB; UTS
Friday Night. Evelyn Underhill. PraNu
Friday night's dream on a Saturday told. Old Superstitions. Mother Goose. HBVY; TreF
Friday; or, The Dirge. John Gay. *Fr.* The Shepherd's Week. CEP; EiPP
Blouzelinda's Funeral, *sel.* OBEC
Fridolin dances free. Song after Harvest. Erik Axel Karlfeldt. AnSL
Fridolin's Pleasure-Garden, *sel.* Erik Axel Karlfeldt, *tr. fr. Swedish by* Charles W. Stork.
Prelude: "My muse dwelleth not on Parnassus." AnSL
Friend, A. Esther Birdsall Darling. AlBD
Friend, A. Lionel Johnson. BoFr; CaAE; HBV; JKCP; PoeT; VLEP
Friend, A. Marguerite Power. FaFP; SiTL
Friend, A. Santob de Carrion. TrJP
Friend, A. Sir Thomas Noon Talfourd. *See* Sympathy.
Friend, A. *Unknown.* PoToHe (new ed.)
Friend Advises Me to Stop Drinking, A. Mei Yao Ch'en, *tr. fr. Chinese by* Kenneth Rexroth. HoPM; OnPC
Friend after friend departs. Parted Friends. James Montgomery. LPS-1
Friend and Foe. Schiller, *tr. fr. German by* Edgar A. Bowring. BoFr
Friend and Lover. "Madeline Bridges." AA; HBV
Friend and lover mine. Song. Dinis, King of Portugal. CAW
Friend Cato. Anna Wickham. MBP; MoBrPo
Friend Cheng is too proud to serve the world. To Cheng on His Deposal. Tu Fu. OnPM
Friend, for your epitaphs I'm griev'd. On One Who Made Long Epitaphs. Pope. ALV
Friend, I have watched you down the mountain. A Parting. Wang Wei. LiTW
Friend, if the mute and shrouded dead. Love and Death. Catullus. AWP; JAWP; WBP
Friend, in my mountain-side demesne. To a Gardener. Robert Louis Stevenson. AnEnPo
Friend! in our land of conquering steeds thou art come. Lovely Colonus! Sophocles, *tr. by* Lewis Campbell. *Fr.* Oedipus at Colonus. GrR
Friend in the Garden, A. Juliana Horatia Ewing. BoTP; FaPON; GFA; MPB; OTPC (1946 ed.); RAR; StVeCh; TVC; TVSH; UTS
Friend of Humanity and the Knife Grinder, The. George Canning *and* John Hookham Frere. CEP; HBV; LPS-3; OBEC; TOP
(Knife-Grinder, The.) BCEP; BOHV; InMe
Friend of mine, a St. Bernard, A. Fala. Edward Anthony. AlBD
Friend of mine was married to a scold, A. All's Well that Ends Well. *Unknown.* BOHV; FaFP; SiTL
Friend of My Heart, The. *Unknown.* PEOR
Friend of my many years! A Legacy. Whittier. BoFr
Friend of Ronsard, Nashe, and Beaumont. On a Birthday. J. M. Synge. ChTr; OBMV
Friend of Sinners. Richard Burnham. BePJ
Friend of Souls. *Unknown.* BePJ
Friend of the Changeless Love. Prayer for a Friend. Annie Johnson Flint. PraP
Friend of the humblest man, peer of the highest. Theodore Roosevelt. Edna Dean Proctor. BoHiPo
Friend of the thoughtful mind and gentle heart! Sea-Weeds. Annie Chambers Ketchum. BIG
Friend of the Wise! and Teacher of the Good! To William Wordsworth. Samuel Taylor Coleridge. BPN; EmBrPo; EnRP; ERP; PtP
Friend, on this scaffold Thomas More lies dead. Epigram. J. V. Cunningham. NePoAm
Friend or Stranger. Bhartrihari, *tr. fr. Sanskrit by* Paul Elmer More. OnPM
Friend! Poor, foolish blossom. Beauty. Peter Hille. AWP
Friend sparrow, do not eat, I pray. Basho, *tr. fr. Japanese by* Curtis Hidden Page. AWP
Friend!—the Great Ruler, easily content. Friendship. Schiller. BoFr
Friend, there be they on whom mishap. Contentment. Charles Stuart Calverley. ALV
Friend, though thy soul should burn thee, yet be still. The Truth. Archibald Lampman. CaP; OCL
Friend, when I think of your delicate feminine face. On the Death of an Acquaintance. Oscar Williams. *Fr.* Variations on a Theme. LiTA; NePA
"Friend, whereto art thou come?" Thus Verity. Whereto Art Thou Come? Francis Thompson. VLEP
Friend Who Just Stands By, The. B. Y. Williams. PoToHe
Friend, whose unnatural early death. An Elegy. David Gascoyne. FaBoTw
Friend, why so solemn and so cranky-eyed? "Hence Loathèd Melancholy . . ." Euripides. *Fr.* Alcestis. GrR
Friend writes me from the temperate zone, A. Termites. Charles G. Bell. NePoAm-2
Friend, you are grieved that I should go. Creeds. Karle Wilson Baker. HBMV; WGRP
Friend, you have come from the world's end home. Antimenidas. Alcaeus. OxBG
Friend, you seem thoughtful. I not wonder much. A Sea Dialogue. Oliver Wendell Holmes. EtS
Friendless and faint, with martyred steps and slow. Calvary. E. A. Robinson. AnNE; ChIP; CoBA; LBMV; MaRV; MoAmPo; MOAP; NeMA; QS; StJW; TreFS; TwP
Friendless Blues, *with music.* Mercedes Gilbert. TrAS
Friendlessness. Theognis, *tr. fr. Greek by* F. L. Lucas. GrPE
Friendly Address, A. Thomas Hood. PoEL-4
Friendly Beasts, The. *Unknown.* ChBR; ChrBoLe; FaPON; SiSoSe
Friendly Blight, The. Aubrey Thomas De Vere. IrPN
Friendly cow all red and white, The. The Cow. Robert Louis Stevenson. BoChLi; FaPON; GFA; GoBP; MPB; OTPC (1946 ed.); PoVP; PPL; RAR; RIS; SAS; StVeCh; SUS; TiPo; UTS; VLEP
Friendly Debate between the Country Farmer and His Buxome Wife, A. *Unknown.* *See* New Married Couple, The.
Friendly Faces of Old Sorrows, The. Karle Wilson Baker. OQP; QP-2
Friendly Obstacles. *Unknown.* MaRV
Friendly People. John G. Herndon. MPB
Friendly Wood, The. Paul Valéry, *tr. fr. French by* Vernon Watkins. AnFP
Friendly Zephyr. Hafiz, *tr. fr. Persian by* John Nott. PeP
Friends. Abbie Farwell Brown. HBV; HBVY
Friends. Thomas Curtis Clark. PoToHe
Friends. A. E. Housman. A Shropshire Lad, LVIII. SeCePo
("When I came last to Ludlow.") EmBrPo; PoVP
Friends. Lionel Johnson. GoBC
Friends. E. V. Lucas. BoFr; HBV
Friends, The. *Unknown.* BoFr
Friends. L. G. Warner. OTPC (1946 ed.)
Friends. W. B. Yeats. BoFr
So Great a Sweetness, *sel.* LiA
Friends!/I come [*or* came] not here to talk. Rienzi to the Romans. Mary Russell Mitford. *Fr.* Rienzi. BCEP; LPS-2; PoFr; TreFS
Friends and Enemies. *At. to* Ali Ben Abu Taleb, *tr. fr. Persian by* Emerson. OQP; QP-2
(Friends and Foes.) OnPM
(From the Persian.) AnNE
(Make Friends.) MaRV
Friends and loves we have none, nor wealth nor blessed abode. The Seekers. John Masefield. HBV; MaRV; OQP; QP-1; QS; TVSH; WGRP
Friends are many o'er cup and platter. Café Society. Theognis. GrR
Friends, are ye sad for the troubled Friar. The Troubled Friar. *Unknown.* GTIV
Friends Beyond. Thomas Hardy. CoBMV; MaPo; OBEV (new ed.); OBVV; PoD; POTT; PoVP; TCPD; ViP
Friends Beyond. Frederick L. Hosmer. MaRV
Friend's Burial, The. Whittier. OBVV
Sels.
"For all her quiet life flowed on." MaRV
In Earthen Vessels, *last 2 sts.* BLRP
Friends Departed. Henry Vaughan. *See* They Are All Gone.
Friends Drinking Together. Lady Otomo of Sakanoe, *tr. fr. Japanese by* Ishii *and* Obata. OnPM
Friend's Grave, A. Simonides, *tr. fr. Greek by* Sir William Marris. GrL; OxBG
Friend's Greeting, A. Edgar A. Guest. BLPA
Friends, hear the story of. Enchantress. Al-Munfatil. MooP
Friends! hear the words my wandering thoughts would say. On Southey's Death [*or* Lyrics and Epigrams]. Walter Savage Landor. BPN; CBOV; EmBrPo; TOP
Friends: I come not here to talk. *See* Friends!/ I come not here to talk.
Friends in Paradise. Henry Vaughan. *See* They Are All Gone.
Friends, my heart is half aweary. The Old Times Were the Best. James Whitcomb Riley. FaFP
Friends of His Youth, The. W. B. Yeats. *Fr.* A Man Young and Old. AtBAP
Friends of my heart: O worker at the frieze. Words for Artificers. Claude F. Koch. JKCP (1955 ed.)
Friends of the Muse, to you of right belong. The Strong Heroic Line. Oliver Wendell Holmes. AA
Friends Old and New. Joseph Parry. OQP; QP-2; PoToHe
(New Friends and Old Friends.) BLPA; NeHB

Friend's Prayer, A. *Unknown.* PraP
Friends, push round the bottle, and let us be drinking. Song for a Venison Dinner at Mr. Bunyan's, New York, 1781. Joseph Stansbury. BoCaPo (1948 ed.)
Friends, Romans, countrymen, lend me your ears. Antony's Oration [*or* Mark Antony's Oration]. Shakespeare. *Fr.* Julius Caesar. BCEP; EV-1; LiTB; LPS-3; PIR; PYM; TreF; TrGrPo
Friend's Song for Simoisius, A. Louise Imogen Guiney. PFY; TCPD
Friends, sursum corda, soon or slow. Envoy. Andrew Lang. SDH
Friends that are, and friends that were, The. J. D. R. Oliver Wendell Holmes. IAP
Friends whom one fine day life gave me. Dead Poets. Enrique Peña Barrenechea. AnCL; BoFr
Friends, whom she lookt at blandly from her couch. Myrtis. Walter Savage Landor. *Fr.* Pericles and Aspasia. OBRV; VA
Friends—with a Difference. Mary Elizabeth Coleridge. BoFr
Friendship. Robert Blair. *Fr.* The Grave. OBEC
Friendship. Robert Bridges. *Fr.* The Testament of Beauty. MaRV
Friendship. Byron. *See* To Thomas Moore.
Friendship. Cervantes, *tr. fr. Spanish by* Peter Motteux. OnPM
Friendship. Hartley Coleridge. ES; OBEV; PeBoSo
(To a Friend.) BoFr; HBV; OBRV
Friendship. Samuel Taylor Coleridge. *See* Quarrel of Friends, The.
Friendship. Florence Converse. BoFr
Friendship. Dinah Maria Mulock Craik. BLPA; NeHB; PoToHe (new ed.)
Friendship. Simon Dach, *tr. fr. German by* Elizabeth Selden. BoFr
Friendship ("A ruddy drop of manly blood"). Emerson. AmPP (3d ed.); IAP; LPS-1; MOAP
Friendship. Marty Hale. AIBD
Friendship. Jami, *tr. fr. Persian.* BoFr
Friendship. Meng Chia, *tr. fr. Chinese.* BoFr
Friendship. Corinne Roosevelt Robinson. BoFr
Friendship. Sadi, *tr. fr. Persian by* L. Cranmer-Byng. *Fr.* The Gulistan. AWP; BoFr; JAWP; WBP
Friendship. Schiller, *tr. fr. German by* Edward Bulwer-Lytton. BoFr
Friendship ("Horatio, thou art e'en as just a man"). Shakespeare. *Fr.* Hamlet, III, ii. LPS-1
("Nay, do not think I flatter.") PIR
(Noble Friendship, A; Hamlet and Horatio.) EV-1
Friendship ("When to the sessions of sweet silent thought"). Shakespeare. Sonnets, XXX. PoeMoYo
Friendship. Sir Philip Sidney. *See* My True Love Hath My Heart.
Friendship. Tao Yuan-ming, *tr. fr. Chinese by* Yang Yeh-tzu. WhP
Friendship. *Unknown.* PoToHe
Friendship, The. Mark Van Doren. MOAP
Friendship after Love. Ella Wheeler Wilcox. AV; ReaPo (Friendship.) PoToHe
Friendship in Absence, *sel.* Abraham Cowley.
"'Twere an ill world, I'll swear, for every friend." EPS (1942 ed.)
Friendship in Fashion, *sel.* Thomas Otway.
Song: "How blest he appears." SeCL
Friendship is constant in all other things. Beauty Is a Witch. Shakespeare. *Fr.* Much Ado about Nothing, II, i. TrGrPo
Friendship is in loving rather than in being lov'd. Friendship. Robert Bridges. *Fr.* The Testament of Beauty. MaRV
Friendship, like love, is but a name. The Hare with [*or* and] Many Friends. John Gay. ATP (1935 ed.); EnLi-1 (1949 ed.); EPP; EV-3; HBV
Friendship needs no studied phrases. Friendship. *Unknown.* PoToHe
Friendship of the rogue or saint, The. Indian Epigrams. *Unknown, tr. fr. Sanskrit.* BoFr
Friendship Veers with Fortune. *Unknown, tr. fr. Chinese by* William Jennings. BoFr
Friendship's an inn the roads of life afford. The Inn. "John Presland." VOD
Friendship's Mystery. Katherine Philips. ViBoPo
Friendship's Servitude. Euripides, *tr. fr. Greek by* Gilbert Murray. *Fr.* Hippolytus. GrR
Frieze, A. John Peale Bishop. MoPo
Frieze of warm bronze that glides with catlike movements. The Stevedores. John Gould Fletcher. *Fr.* Down the Mississippi. ChMo; CMP; HiLiAm; LiTA; MOAP; NP; PoTo; SPP; TCAP
Frigate Pelican, The. Marianne Moore. InvP; PoF
Frightened Face. Marion Strobel. HBMV
Frightened Man, The. Louise Bogan. MOAP
Frightened Ploughman, The. John Clare. PoEL-4
Frightening Death. Charles Anson Ingraham. PoP
"'Frightful face, A?' Wal, yes, yer correct." The Fireman's Story. *Unknown.* PTA-2
Frigidaire. A. M. Klein. TwCaPo
Frimaire. Amy Lowell. ChMo; CMP
Fringed Gentian. Emily Dickinson. *See* God made a little gentian.
Fringed Gentians. Amy Lowell. BrR; FaPON; MPB; SP
Fringèd vallance of your eyes advance, The. Song [*or* A Good-Morrow]. Thomas Shadwell. *Fr.* Timon of Athens. SeCL; ViBoPo
Fringed with coral, floored with lava. Christmas Island. Katharine Lee Bates. HBMV; HBVY; TSW
Fringilla Melodia, The. Henry Beck Hirst. AA
Fringing cypress forests dim. Sassafras. Samuel Minturn Peck. AA
Frippery. Horace. *See* Persian Fopperies.
Frisky as a lambkin. The Lovable Child. Emilie Poulsson. HBV; MPB
Frisky Lamb, A. Christina Rossetti. *Fr.* Sing-Song. BoTP
Frithiof's Saga, *sels.* Esaias Tegnér, *tr. fr. Swedish by* Longfellow.
Frithiof's Farewell. AWP; JAWP; WBP
Frithiof's Homestead. AWP
Frog, The. Hilaire Belloc. BMEP; BoChLi; BOHV; FaBoBe; FaPON; FiBHP; GoBP; HBV; InMe; LiL; MoShBr; MPB; NA; PoeMoYo; TSW
Frog, The. Rose Fyleman. BoTP
Frog, The. Shimpei Kusano, *tr. fr. Japanese by* Takamichi Ninomiya *and* D. J. Enright. PoLJ
Frog, The. *Unknown.* DDA; MoShBr; SiTL; WhC; YaD
Frog and the Bird, The. Vera Hessey. BoTP
Frog and the Mouse, The. *Unknown. See* Frog Went a-Courting.
Frog beneath the juniper, The. The Question in the Cobweb. Alastair Reid. WaKn
Frog half fearful jumps across the path, The. Summer Evening. John Clare. GTML
Frog He Would a-Wooing Go, A. *Unknown.* OnHT; OTPC, *abr.*; OxNR; RIS; WP
Frog Went a-Courting [*or* Courtin']. *Unknown.* ABF, *with music;* BLPA; FTB, *with music;* GoTP; IHA; TrAS, *with music*
(Frog and the Mouse, The, *with music*). SoAF
(Frog's Courtin', The.) APW; RIS
(Mister Frog Went a-Courting, *with music.*) AS
Frogs, The, *sels.* Aristophanes, *tr. fr. Greek.*
Aeschylean Chorus, An, *tr. by* T. F. Higham. OxBG
As between Gentlemen's Gentlemen, *tr. by* Benjamin Bickley Rogers. GrR
"Euripidean" Chorus, A, *tr. by* T. F. Higham. OxBG
("O gloom of night," *tr. by* A. D. Cope.) GrPo
Fatal Oil-Flask, The, *tr. by* Marshall MacGregor. OxBG
(Tell-Tale Tag, The, *tr. by* Benjamin Bickley Rogers.) GrR
Frogs' Song, The. GrR, *tr. by* Benjamin Bickley Rogers; OxBG, *tr. by* T. F. Higham
(Chorus: "Brekeke-kesh, koash, koash," *tr. by* J. Hookham Frere.) PreP
Hymn of the Initiates. OxBG
(Initiates, *tr. by* Benjamin Bickley Rogers.) GrR
"Let us hasten—let us fly." MaRV
Rival Poets, The, *tr. by* Marshall MacGregor. OxBG
(Rivals, The, *tr. by* Benjamin Bickley Rogers.) GrR
Rogue, The, *tr. by* Arthur S. Way. LiA
Symptoms of an Ailing Democracy, *tr. by* Benjamin Bickley Rogers. GrR
Frog's a very funny thing, A. Spring Wish. John Farrar. GFA
Frogs are croakin'. Dialogue. Ibn Munakhkhal. MooP
Frogs at School. George Cooper. BoChLi; GFA; StVeCh (1940 ed.); UTS
(Twenty Froggies.) OTPC; PCH; PPL
Frog's Courtin', The. *Unknown. See* Frog Went a-Courting.
Frogs jump. Jump or Jiggle. Evelyn Beyer. TiPo
Frogs' Song, The. Aristophanes, *tr. fr. Greek. Fr.* The Frogs. GrR, *tr. by* Benjamin Bickley Rogers; OxBG, *tr. by* T. F. Higham
(Chorus: "Brekeke-kesh, koash, koash," *tr. by* J. Hookham Frere.) PreP
Frogs Who Wanted a King, The ("The frogs were living happy as could be"). Aesop, *ad. fr. Greek by* Joseph Lauren. GoTP; MaC; RIS; StaSt
Frolic. "Æ." BoTP; FaPON; GTML; GTSL; MBP; MoBrPo; OTPC (1946 ed.); TwCV
Frolic Mariners of Devon, The. William Browne. *See* Hail Thou My Native Soil.
Frolicksome Farmer, The. *Unknown.* CoMu
Frolicsome Duke, or the Tinker's Good Fortune, The. *Unknown.* EV-2
Frolicsome Parson Outwitted, The. *Unknown.* CoMu
From a branch the bird called. The Bird. Max Michelson. NP; TrJP
From a Car-Window. Ruth Guthrie Harding. AV; HBMV; VOD

From a Childhood. Rainer Maria Rilke, *tr. fr. German by* C. F. MacIntyre. TrJP
From a Chinese Vase. Winifred Welles. MAP
From a Church Tower. Eduard Mörike, *tr. fr. German by* Edwin Morgan. AnGP
From a Churchyard in Wales. *Unknown.* FiBHP
("This spot is the sweetest I've seen in my life.") WhC
From a city window, 'way up high. Motor Cars. Rowena Bastin Bennett. FaPON; GFA; PoMa; TiPo
From a Cypress Grove, 1623. William Drummond of Hawthornden. *See* To Sir William Alexander.
From a Downtown Skyscraper. Wilfred J. Funk. DDA
From a Felucca. Cale Young Rice. LS; SPP
From a Full Heart. A. A. Milne. BOHV; InMe
From a golden stadium—amid silken cords. Flowers. Arthur Rimbaud. AnFP
From a High Place. *Unknown. Fr.* The Poems of West Ham. UnW
("From a high place I saw the city.") BMEP
From a Hint in the Minor Poets. Samuel Wesley. OBEC
From a junto that labor with absolute power. Emancipation from British Dependence [*or* A Political Litany]. Philip Freneau. IAP; IDAH; PAH
From a land of milk and honey. Weeping and Singing. César Tiempo. AnCL
From a little seed/ A flower grows. Little Things. Eileen Mathias. BoTP
From a lover's trysting came the maiden. Johan Ludvig Runeberg. *Fr.* Idylls and Epigrams. AnSL
From a magician's midnight sleeve. Late Air. Elizabeth Bishop. FiMAP
From a mountain top a poet looked down. The Poet. Seumas O'Brien. JKCP (1926 ed.)
From a Munster vale they brought her. The Dying Girl. Richard D'Alton Williams. OnYI; TIP
From a Pet-Shop Window. Margaret E. Sangster. AlBD
From a pot of wine among the flowers. Drinking Alone with the Moon. Li Po. LiTW
From a poverty-shadowed life. Imagined Happiness. Erik Axel Karlfeldt. AnSL; LiTW
From a Prison. Paul Verlaine, *tr. fr. French by* Alan Conder. TrFP
From a Railway Carriage. Robert Louis Stevenson. AlDL; BoTP; FaPON; GFA; GoBP; TiPo
From a Street Corner. Eleanor Hammond. HBMV
From "A Vigo-Street Eclogue." Sir Owen Seaman. WhC
From a village up the Hudson. The Dark Girl Dressed in Blue. *Unknown.* BeLS
From a vision red with war I awoke and saw the Prince. The New Day. Fenton Johnson. BANP
From a Window in Princes Street. W. E. Henley. BPN; POTT
From a Winnower of Corn to the Winds. Joachim du Bellay. *See* Hymn to the Winds.
From a Woman to a Greedy Lover. Norman Cameron. Three Love Poems, I. FaBoTw
From a wreck of tree in the wash of night. Speak with the Sun. David Campbell. NeLNL; SeCePo
From Aesculapius escaping. To N. N. Pushkin. TrRV
From afar so lov'd and near, so cloudless fair. Sonnet. Stéphane Mallarmé. LiA
From age to age, they gather, all the brave of heart and strong. Cross and Flag. Frederick L. Hosmer. FOAH
From all division let our land be free. Australian Federation. William Gay. BoAu; PoFr
From all eternity the Beloved unveiled His beauty in the solitude of the unseen. The Song of Mystic Unity. Jami. LiTW
From All Peoples, *sel.* Nathan Alterman, *tr. fr. Hebrew by* Simon Halkin.
"When our children cried in the shadow of the gallows." TrJP
From all that dwell below the skies. The Eternal. Isaac Watts. GrCo-1
From all that terror teaches. Litany. G. K. Chesterton. OtMeF
From all the blasts of heaven thou hast descended. Shelley. *Fr.* Prometheus Unbound. NBE
From All the Fools Who Went Before. Margaret Root Garvin. TBM
From All the Queens. Iwan Goll, *tr. fr. French by* Iwan Goll. OnPM
From All These Events. Stephen Spender. LiTB; NAMP
From All Uneasy Passions Free. John Sheffield, Duke of Buckingham. SeCL
From all vain pomps and shows. He That Doeth the Will. Longfellow. ChIP
From Ammanford to Fleur-de-Lys. Idris Davies. MoWP
From an Irish-Latin Macaronic. Geoffrey Taylor. NeIP
From an Old House. Harold Monro. TCEP
From an Upland Valley. Richard Church. MBP; MoBrPo (1942 ed.)
From ancient Edens long forgot. A White-Throat Sings. Walter Prichard Eaton. DD; HBMV
From Ancient Fangs. Peter Viereck. LiTA; MiAP
From Another Room. Gregory Corso. NeAP
From Arranmore the weary miles I've come. Mavrone. Arthur Guiterman. BOHV; FiBHP; InMe
From art, from nature, from the schools. In Memoriam A. H. H., XLIX. Tennyson. EmBrPo; EnLi-2; EPN; GEPC; ViPo; VLEP
From Battle Clamour. Samuele Romanelli, *tr. fr. Hebrew by* Nina Davis Salaman. TrJP
From Beaulieu down to Brixham town. Sailors. Patric Dickinson. NeTW
From being anxious or secure. John Donne. *Fr.* The Litany. EnLit; NBE; OxBoCh
From bending always over bars, his glance. The Panther. Rainer Maria Rilke. ReMP
From Bethlehem Blown. Mary Sinton Leitch. PGD
From Bethlehem to Calvary. Meredith Nicholson. ChIP; PGD
From Bethlehem to Calvary. Christ and the Winds. John Banister Tabb. StJW
From Bethlehem to Calvary the Savior's journey lay. From Bethlehem to Calvary. Meredith Nicholson. PGD
From Beyond. Lucia Trent. PGD
From birth to age, and in between. To Patricia, Eleven. Robert Underwood Johnson. PYM
From blackhearted water colder. Castles and Distances. Richard Wilbur. FiMAP
From blue to dusk and the lights came. A Window, a Table, on the North. Ralph Gustafson. PeCV
From body's self the body. Body's Freedom. Helen Neville. NePA
From Boston Harbor we set sail. Boston. *Unknown.* SoAmSa
From Break of Day. *Unknown, tr. fr. Chinese by* Henry H. Hart. WoL
(Hundred Names, The.) PoHN
(Workman.) OnPM
From breakfast on through all the day. The Land of Nod. Robert Louis Stevenson. GoTP; MPB (1956 ed.); PoVP; VA; VLEP
From Brescia swiftly o're the bord'ring Plain. Sir William Davenant. *Fr.* Gondibert. CEP
From British novels a thrill I get. Britannia Rules of Orthography. "Firth." InMe; WhC
From Brooklyn, over the Brooklyn Bridge, on this fine morning. Invitation to Miss Marianne Moore. Elizabeth Bishop. MoVE
From Burton the Anatomist. Maurice James Craig. NeIP
From Calatrava as I took my way. Serranilla. Marquis of Santillana. TeCS
From Calvary a cry was heard. Calvary's Cry. John William Cunningham. BePJ
From camp to camp, through the foul womb of night. Before Agincourt. Shakespeare. *Fr.* King Henry V, *prologue to* Act IV. ChTr
From Casco Bay. The Song of the Hermit Thrush. James B. Thomas. BLA
From child to youth; from youth to arduous man. The Heart of the Night. Dante Gabriel Rossetti. The House of Life, LXVI. BPN; EmBrPo; EPN; PoVP; TCEP; TOP; ViPo; VLEP
From Childhood's Hour. Poe. NePA; PoEL-4
(Alone.) APW; CoV; LaNeLa
From church to Boule's hop on Sunday they'll away. *See* Boule's Hop. *Unknown.* IHA
From cities' pyramids, untrammelled saint. Prayer to Saint Francis for Poverty. Liam Brophy. SaFP
From Clee to heaven the beacon burns. 1887. A. E. Housman. A Shropshire Lad, I. CoBMV; EmBrPo; NAMP; PoVP; ReMP; RiBV; UnPo; ViPo
From Country to Town. Hartley Coleridge. OBRV
From cunning fingers comes this limning; see. On a Portrait. Erinna. GrR
From dark the striped muscles sprang. "God's First Creature Was Light." Winifred Welles. ImOP
From Dark to Light. S. Weir Mitchell. *See* Vespers.
From darkened eyes no tears are falling. The Weavers. Heine. PoFr
From darkening embers in the gloaming. At the Fireside. Afanasi Afanasievich Fet. WaL
From Dawn to cedars of the Sacred Story. Paris Two-banked Galley. Charles Péguy. TrFP
From dawn to dark they stood. "Our Left." Francis Orrery Ticknor. MC; PAH
From Dawn to Evensong. C. Austin Miles. PraP
From Dawn to Noon. Dante Gabriel Rossetti. The House of Life, LXXX. PoVP; ViPo
. . . From day to day/ The calcium in our cells grows less and less. Leningrad: 1943. Vera Inber. *Fr.* The Pulkovo Meridian. WaaP
From day to day lamenting, lingering on. Mortal Grief. Francisco de Figueroa. OnPM
From day to day we are born, as each night wanes. We Are Born Every Day. Palladas. OxBG

From death, Christ on the Sabbath morn. Sabbath Morn. Nicolai Grundtvig. EOAH
From Death then is there no relief? Death the Great. Elis Wyn o Lasynys. LiTW
From deep within the garden. The Child. Vaughtie Carroll. CAG
From Desert to Metropolis. Sister Mary Estelle. JKCP (1955 ed.)
From Disciple to Master. Monk Gibbon. AnIV
From Distant Lands. Peter Hellings. MoWP
From "Divine Poems." Edmund Waller. *See* Old Age.
From Dover. L. C. Nielsen, *tr. fr. Danish by* Charles W. Stork. BoDS
From Drogheda all along the coast, the Irish Sea. Back to Dublin. R. A. D. Ford. CaP
From Dublin soon to London spread. Swift. *Fr.* Verses on the Death of Dr. Swift. ViBoPo; WHA
From dusk till dawn the livelong night. Betsy's Battle Flag. Minna Irving. DD; GA; MC; PAH; PEDC; PoRL
From dust I rise. Thomas Traherne. *Fr.* The Salutation. FaBoEn
From east and south the holy clan. The Bishop of Rum-Ti-Foo. W. S. Gilbert. CenHV; PoVP
From Eastertide to Eastertide. A Ballad of a Nun. John Davidson. BeLS; BMEP; EnLit; HBMV; LBBV; LEAP; MBP; MoBrPo; PoVP; VLEP
From England to California I went. Roll, *Julia,* Roll. *Unknown.* ShS
From eve to morn, from morn to parting night. On His Own Agamemnon and Iphigeneia [*or* On His Own Iphegeneia and Agamemnon]. Walter Savage Landor. BPN; EmBrPo; OBRV
From every point they gaily come. A Dance at the Ranch. *Unknown.* SCC
From every quarter came the night confounding. Burial at Sea. E. J. Pratt. *Fr.* The *Roosevelt* and the *Antinoe.* CaP; OCL
From Exile. Hsü Chu, *tr. fr. Chinese by* Henry H. Hart. ChLP; PoHN
From fairest creatures we desire increase. Sonnets, I. Shakespeare. AtBAP; EG; FaBoEn; LiTB; LiTL; OAEP; OBSC; PeBoSo; SiCE; TrGrPo
From fall to spring, the russet acorn. Holidays. Emerson. IAP
From falling leaf to falling leaf. October. Dollie Radford. VA
From false astrologies with somewhat lugubrious manners. Savor. "Pablo Neruda." TwSpPo
From falsehood and error. A Prayer. Digby Mackworth Dolben. GoBC
From Far Away. William Morris. OHIP, *st.* 1; SDH
From far away, from far away. My Letter. Grace Denio Litchfield. AA
From far away we come to you. From Far Away. William Morris. OHIP; SDH
From Far, from Eve and Morning. A. E. Housman. A Shropshire Lad, XXXII. AnEnPo; MoBrPo; NeMA; PoEL-5; PoVP; ViPo
From far she watched his wanderings, and sighed. Seven Sad Sonnets, IV. Mary Aldis. HBMV
From far she's come, and very old. Age in Youth. Trumbull Stickney. MAP; MoAmPo (1942 ed.); MOAP
From feast and song the simple cowherd crept. Cædmon. Thomas S Jones, Jr. InP
From Feathers to Iron, *sels.* C. Day Lewis.
Now She Is like the White Tree-Rose. ChMo; FaBoTw; MBP; MoBrPo
"Now the full throated daffodils." ViBoPo
"Suppose that we, to-morrow or the next day." CoEV; TwCV
From food when it is hash. Prayer. Edward Shippen. LauV
From Fortune's frowns and change removed. Old Damon's Pastoral. Thomas Lodge. OBSC; SiCE
From Four Lakes' Days. Richard Eberhart. MiAP
From France, desponding and betray'd. On the British Invasion. Philip Freneau. PAH
From frozen climes, and endless traks [*or* tracts] of snow. To the Earl of Dorset. Ambrose Philips. CEP; LoBV; OBEC
From Generation to Generation. William Dean Howells. AA; PFY
From Generation to Generation. Sir Henry Newbolt. FaBoTw
From Gestures to the Dead. John Wheelwright. MoVE
From Ghoulies and Ghosties. Litany for Halloween. *Unknown.* PoRL; SiSoSe
From giant oaks, that wave their branches dark. Vegetable Loves. Erasmus Darwin. *Fr.* The Botanic Gardens: The Loves of the Plants. OBEC; SeCePo
From Glowing Purple Spoke the Wrath of Heaven. Stefan George, *tr. fr. German by* R. F. C. Hull. AnGP
(From out the Glow the Wrath of Heaven Spoke, *tr. by* Babette Deutsch *and* Avrahm Yarmolinsky.) OnPM
From God to God. Virgil, *tr. fr. Latin by* F. W. H. Myers. MaRV
From God's lofty City/ my Lady looks down. Lady of Lidice. Fray Angelico Chavez. ISi; JKCP (1955 ed.)
From gold to gray. Indian Summer. Whittier. *Fr.* Eve of Election. PCH; PEOR
From golden dawn to purple dusk. The March of Humanity. J. Corson Miller. HBMV
From Gombor. Nikolai Tikhonov, *tr. fr. Russian by* Jack Lindsay. RuPo
From gossamer illusion. Middle-aged Quixote. Louise Crenshaw Ray. JKCP (1955 ed.)
From Greenland to Iceland. *Unknown.* FaFP; SiTL
From Greenland's Icy Mountains. Reginald Heber. HBV; OIF; OTPC; TreF; WGRP
From groves of spice. Cradle-Song [*or* Hindu Cradle Song]. Sarojini Naidu. BoTP; BrR; FaPON; MoSiPe; MPB; RAR; VOD
From Gumiel de Hizán to Gumiel del Mercado. Rafael Alberti, *tr. fr. Spanish by* Eleanor L. Turnbull. CoSP
From Halifax station a bully there came. Halifax Station. *Unknown.* PAH
From harmony, from heavenly [*or* heav'nly] harmony. A Song for St. Cecilia's Day. Dryden. AtBAP; ATP; AWP; BCEP; BEL; BoLiVe; CBOV; CEP; CoEV; EiPP; ElSeCe; EnL; EnLi-1 (1949 ed.); EnLit; EV-3; ExPo; FaBoEn; GEPC; GoBC; GTBS; GTBS-D; GTBS-W; GTSE; GTSL; HBV; InPo; JAWP; LiTB; LiTG; LPS-3; MaPo; OAEP; OBEV; Po; PoEL-3; PoLi; PreP; RiBV; SeCV-2; SeEP; TCEP; TOP; TrGrPo; TriL; TwCrTr; UnS; WBP
From heart to heart, from creed to creed. The Stream of Faith. William Channing Gannett. OQP; QP-1; WGRP
From Heaven High I Come to You, *with music.* John Sterling. YaCaBo
From heaven his spirit came, and robed in clay. The Soul of Dante [*or* On Dante Alighieri]. Michelangelo. GoBC; OnPM
From Heaven I fall, though from earth I begin. Whiter than White. Swift. RIS
From heaven was sent an angel of light. Now We Should Sing and Say Nowell. *Unknown.* AnEC
From Heaven's Gate to Hampstead Heath. The Ballad of Hampstead Heath. James Elroy Flecker. MoBrPo
From heavy dreams fair Helen rose. William and Helen. Sir Walter Scott, *after* Bürger. BPN; EmBrPo; EnRP; ERP; OAEP
From hence the critick vermin sprung. The Critick Vermin. Swift. *Fr.* To Doctor Delany on the Libels Writ against Him. BeR
From her grave the dead young woman spoke. Ghost. Agnes Miegel. TwGV
From her willing heart He hewed Him a Cross. Impress of the Crucifix. Mother Mary Alphonsa. PraNu
From here through tunnelled gloom the track. The Railway Junction. Walter de la Mare. ChMP
From here to there,/ To Washington Square. *Unknown.* OxNR
From hill to hill he harried me. War. Arthur Stringer. BoCaPo (1943 ed.); OCL; TwCaPo
From hill to hill I roam, from thought to thought. Distance and Solitude. Petrarch. *Fr.* Sonnets to Laura. LiA
From hills that echo strangely clear. Reincarnation. Lloyd Frank Merrell. ChIP
From his brimstone bed at break of day. The Devil's Thoughts [*or* The Devil's Walk on Earth]. Robert Southey *and* Samuel Taylor Coleridge. BOHV; LPS-3; OxBoLi; PoMS
From His Canadian Home. *Unknown.* IHA
From his cradle in the glamourie. Peak and Puke. Walter de la Mare. BOL
From his flock stray'd Coridon. Robert Greene. EG
From his garden bed our Lord. The Harvesting of the Roses. Menahem ben Jacob. TrJP
From his shoulder Hiawatha. Hiawatha's Photographing. "Lewis Carroll." CenHV; FiBHP
From holy flower to holy flower. The Study of a Spider. Lord De Tabley. BMEP
From Holy, Holy, Holy ones. The Lancashire Puritane. *Unknown.* CoMu
From House to Home, *sel.* Christina Rossetti.
"I have no words to tell what way we walked." MBP
From house to house he goes. A Lane [*or* An Irish Riddle]. *Unknown.* BoTP; OTPC (1946 ed.); PCH; RIS
From hunger and cold who lives more free. Song of the Beggars. Richard Brome. *Fr.* A Jovial Crew. CenL; SeCL
From Ida's top Hephaestus, lord of fire. The Beacons. Aeschylus. *Fr.* Agamemnon. GrR
From ignominious sleep, where age on age. To Italy. Giovanni Guidiccioni. PoFr
From Illinois and Indiana came a later myth. Carl Sandburg. The People, Yes, Sec. 2. CoV
From inland ledges I had dreamed this bay. At the Battery Sea-Wall. Clifford James Laube. GoYe

From Islington to Marybone. Blake. *See* Fields from Islington to Marybone, The.
From its blue vase the rose of evening drops [*or* droops]. An Evening in England. Francis Ledwidge. BMEP; MCCG; PIAE
From its thin branch high in the autumn wind. Leaf-Movement. Arthur Davison Ficke. MAP; NP
From J. Haydn to Constanze Mozart (1791). Edgar Bowers. PtPa
From Java, Sumatra, and old Cathay. A Ship Comes In. Oliver Jenkins. DDA; EtS; PCH
From Jupiter the Muse begins, and Jupiter is everywhere. Virgil. Eclogues, III. LaP
From keel to fighting top, I love. Manila Bay. Arthur Hale. PAH
From Killybegs to Ardara is seven Irish miles. A Road of Ireland. Charles L. O'Donnell. HBMV
From Knees Up, Muvver Brown, *sels.* H. L. R. Edwards. MoWP
"Between my thighs an extraordinary," I.
"It is true the haggard has nested," IV.
From Le Havre. Charles G. Bell. NePoAm
From learned Florence, long time rich in fame. Henry Howard, Earl of Surrey, to [the Lady] Geraldine. Michael Drayton. *Fr.* England's Heroical Epistles. OBSC; ReEn; ReIE; TuPP
From Lewis, Monsieur Gérard came. Yankee Doodle's Expedition to Rhode Island. *Unknown.* PAH
From Life. Brian Hooker. HBV; OnPP
From little signs, like little stars. Honoria's Surrender. Coventry Patmore. *Fr.* The Angel in the House. VA
From Liverpool to Frisco a-rovin' I went. Row, Bullies, Row. *Unknown.* SoAmSa
From loftiest turret to foundation-stone. Macedonius, *tr. fr. Greek by* W. C. Lawton. GrPo
From loud sound and still chance. Baroque Comment. Louise Bogan. CrMA
From low to high doth dissolution climb. Mutability [*or* Sonnet]. Wordsworth. *Fr.* Ecclesiastical Sonnets. BPN; CoEV; EG; EmBrPo; EnLi-2; EnLP; EnRP; EPN; ExPo; GEPC; LiTB; OBRV; OQP; PC; PoE; PoEL-4; QP-2; REAL; RiBV; SeCeV
From magistrate was bought. Algebra of Divorce. L. F. Gerlach. PtPa
From many a field with patriot blood imbued. Decoration Day. George Hurlbut Barbour. OHIP
From me, my Dear, O seek not to receive. What Was a Cure for Love? Thomas Godfrey. AnAmPo; LA
From meadows with the sheep so shorn. The Ruined Chapel. Andrew Young. POTE
From men the source of life has been hidden well. Pandora. Hesiod. *Fr.* Works and Days. OxBG
From Men Who Died Deluded. May Sarton. NeTW
From mental mists to purge a nation's eyes. New Morality. George Canning, J. H. Frere, *and others.* CEP
From Metastasio. Christina Rossetti. DiM
From Mexico there's just come a strange new decree. De Mexico ha venido. *Unknown.* TrAS
From middle March to April. Alisoun. *Unknown.* BLV
From mighty wrongs to petty perfidy. Fame. Byron. *Fr.* Childe Harold's Pilgrimage. FiP
From morn to midnight, all day through. Expectans Expectavi. Charles Sorley. FaBoCh; HBMV; LoGBV; MaRV; QS; WGRP
From mountains covered deep with snow. Chipeta's Ride. John W. Taylor. PoOW
From My Arm-Chair. Longfellow. BLPA
From My Diary, July 1914. Wilfred Owen. CoBMV; FaBoMo; LiTM (rev. ed.); MBP; MoAB; MoBrPo
From my farm, from her farm. Saturn. Sir Arthur T. Quiller-Couch. BMEP; LBBV
From My Father. Michael Earls. FAOV
From my grief on Fál's proud plain I sleep. Geoffrey Keating. *Fr.* My Grief on Fál's Proud Plain. OnYI
From my high castle I look at the town below. After Collecting the Autumn Taxes. Po Chü-i. TrCh
From My High Love. Kenneth Patchen. MoAmPo (1950 ed.)
From My Loitering. Vernon Watkins. MoWP
From my mother's sleep I fell into the State. The Death of the Ball Turret Gunner. Randall Jarrell. CoBMV; ExPo; FiMAP; MoAmPo (1950 ed.); MiAP; OxBA; ShBV-3; UnPo (3d ed.); WaaP; WaP
From my room I look upon the little plaza. Rubbish. Luis Carlos López. TwSpPo
From My Rural Pen. T. S. Watt. FiBHP
From my sonorous city. Women. José Gorostiza. AnCL
From My Thought. Daniel Smythe. GoYe
From my wind-blown book I look. Spring. W. R. Rodgers. AnIL
From My Window. Mother M. Columba. WHL
From my window, facing South. The Autumn House. George M. Brady. OnYI
From my window I can see. The Open Sea. Dorothea Mackellar. BoAu
From mysteries of the Past. To the Modern Man. John Hall Wheelock. HBMV
From naked stones of agony. Spirit's House. Sara Teasdale. *Fr.* Interlude: Songs Out of Sorrow. OQP; QP-1; QS
From Nature doth emotion come, and moods. Imagination and Taste, How Impaired and Restored. Wordsworth. *Fr.* The Prelude, XII *and* XIII. ERP
From Nazareth. Margaret E. Sangster. ChIP
From Nazareth to Bethlehem. The Nativity. Louisa Parsons Hopkins. PEOR
From near the sea, like Whitman my great predecessor, I call. Ode: Salute to the French Negro Poets. Frank O'Hara. NeAP
From Nether Dark the Seed. Stefan George, *tr. fr. German by* Babette Deutsch *and* Avrahm Yarmolinsky. OnPM
From Nevada's hoary ridges, from stormy coasts of Maine. Benny Havens, Oh! O'Brien. ABF
From never-vanquished Hercules ye boast. Tyrtaeus, *tr. fr. Greek.* GrPo
From noise of Scare-fires rest ye free. The Bell-Man. Robert Herrick. CH; HOAH; OBS; PCD
From noiseful arms, and acts of prowess done. The Holy Grail. Tennyson. *Fr.* Idylls of the King. PoVP; ViPo; ViPP; VLEP
From Nowhere to the North Pole, *sel.* Tom Hood.
Quadrupedremian Song, A. BoN
From now on kill America out of your mind. Millions Are Learning How. James Agee. NAMP
From Oberon, in fairy land. Robin Goodfellow. *Unknown.* EV-2; FaBoCh; HOAH; SeCL; SeEP; ViBoPo
From one shaft at Cleator Moor. Cleator Moor. Norman Nicholson. FaBoTw; NeBP
From one unused in pomp of words to raise. To Benjamin West. Washington Allston. AnAmPo; LA
From Orford Ness to Shingle Street. Dawn on the East Coast. Alun Lewis. FaBoMo
From our hidden places. The Others. "Seumas O'Sullivan." AnIV; GBV; GTIV; HBMV; NP; OxBI; TIP
From our low seat beside the fire. The Call. Charlotte Mew. ChMP; MoP
From out a book into my lap. A Withered Rose. "Yehoash." TrJP
From out a bright cloud's purple band. The Swan. Johan Ludvig Runeberg. AnSL
From out Cologne there came three kings. The Three Kings of Cologne. Eugene Field. CLS; SDH; StJW
From out his castle on the sand. The Sea-King. L. Frank Tooker. EtS
From out its womb it weaves with care. Vowel Englyn to the Spider. *Unknown.* LiTW
From out my deep, wide-bosomed West. Rejoice. Joaquin Miller. PAH
From out of a wood did a cuckoo fly. The Birds. *Unknown.* ChrBoLe
From out of the dreamland ere glow of the dawn. The Morning Sprite. Clinton H. Collester. CAG
From out of the North-land his leaguer he led. Saint Leger. Clinton Scollard. PAH
From out our crowded calendar. Memorial Day. McLandburgh Wilson. DD; MaRV
From out the dark of sleep I rose, on the wings of desire. The Secret Gate. "Fiona Macleod." ReTS
From out the earth I dig this plant, an herb of most effectual power. Charm to Quell a Rival. *Unknown. Fr.* The Rigveda. LiTW
From out the Glow the Wrath of Heaven Spoke. Stefan George. *See* From Glowing Purple Spoke the Wrath of Heaven.
From out the grave of one whose budding years. The Lachrymatory. Charles Tennyson Turner. VA
From out the kitchen window. Belinda's Window. Margaret Widdemer. PEDC
From out the South the genial breezes sigh. The Mother. *Tr. by* George Barrow. MOAH; OHIP
From out the stormy sea unto the shore. Epitaph. Azariah di Rossi. TrJP
From pastoral meads, from tasks of field and fold. The Aeneid. John William Mackail. PtP
From Paumanok Starting I Fly Like a Bird. Walt Whitman. CoBA; IAP
From Pembroke's princely dome, where mimic Art. Sonnet: Written after Seeing Wilton-House. Thomas Warton the Younger. Sonnets, V. OBEC
From Pent-up Aching Rivers. Walt Whitman. ViBoPo
From plains that reel to southward, dim. Heat. Archibald Lampman. BoCaPo; CaP; CPG; OCL; PeCV; VA
From Plane to Plane. Robert Frost. MoAmPo (1950 ed.)
From point to point there leaped across the gulf. Before the Storm. Albert Samuel Davis. CAG
From Potomac to Merrimac. Edward Everett Hale. PAH
Merimac Side, and Agiochook, III.

Potomac Side, I.
Signal Fires, II.
From prehistoric distance, beyond clocks. Street Fight. Harold Monro. FaBoTw
From Prison. Richard Lovelace. *See* To Althea from Prison.
From pure white silk winds and frost arise. The Painting of an Eagle. Tu Fu. WhP
From purest wells of English undefiled. James Russell Lowell. Whittier. DD; GA
From rock-built nest. The Eagle Trail. Hamlin Garland. BAP
From Romany to Rome. Wallace Irwin. HBV
From Santiago, spurning the morrow. The Destroyer of Destroyers. Wallace Rice. PAH
From shadows of rich oaks outpeer. The Pike. Edmund Blunden. AnFE; MoVE; ShBV-3
From shores of Senegal, from Lake Omandaba. O My Swallows! Ernst Toller. TrJP
From shuddering trees and painted leaves. Chickamauga. G. T. Ferris. MDAH
From silent night true register of moans. A Cry unto the Lord to Stay His Hand. Edward Johnson. BAV
From Slavery to Slavery. Sadi, *pr. tr. fr. Persian by* Sir Edwin Arnold. *Fr.* The Gulistan. OuHeWo
From sluggish sleep and slumber. The Bellman's Good-Morrow. *Unknown.* PoLi
From Solitude to Solitude towards Life. Paul Eluard, *tr. fr. French by* Stephen Spender *and* Frances Cornford. LiTW
From some far-off unknown island. A Coco-nut. Toson Shimazaki. PoLJ
From some sweet home, the morning train. The School Girl. William Henry Venable. AA
From Somerset and Devon. Names. Abbie Farwell Brown. POT; PoTo
From song and dream forever gone. Elegiac Mood. Gordon Bottomley. *Fr.* Night and Morning Songs. LBBV; NP
From sound to stone and from the voice to the dream. Second Dream. Bernardo Ortiz de Montellano. AnCL
From Sparta to Apollo we. Lost at Sea. Simonides. GrL; OxBG
From Stirling [*or* Sterling] castle we had seen. Yarrow Unvisited. Wordsworth. BEL; BPN; EM-2; EmBrPo; EnLi-2; EnRP; ERP; GEPC; GTBS; GTBS-D; GTBS-W; GTSE; GTSL; HBV; PoRA
From Stone to Steel ("From stone to bronze, from bronze to steel"). E. J. Pratt. PeCV
From summer and the wheel-shaped city. Washington Cathedral. Karl Shapiro. MiAP
From Summer Hours. Albert Samain, *tr. fr. French by* Jethro Bithell. AWP; JAWP; WBP
From Sunset to Star Rise. Christina Rossetti. PeBoSo
From Susquehanna's farthest springs. The Indian Student; or, Force of Nature. Philip Freneau. AmPP (4th ed.); APW; OxBA
From tangled vines along the rows. Shelling Peas. Elizabeth Fleming. DDA
From tempting Satan to tempt us. A Litanie from "Holy Sonnets." John Donne. *Fr.* The Litany. MeRV
From Texas to Maine. George Henry Preble. FOAH
From that blest earth, on which her body lies. The Death of a Queen. Congreve. *Fr.* The Mourning Muse of Alexis. BeR
From that last acre on oblivion's heap. Mother Goose Up-to-Date: Edna St. Vincent Millay Exhorts Little Boy Blue. Louis Untermeyer. MoAmPo
From the age of the gods. Separation. Empress Kogyoku. OnPM
From the ageless garden plot of Time he came. Christmas Rose. Margaret Evelyn Singleton. ChIP
From the Antique. Christina Rossetti. EnLoPo
From the Arabic. Shelley. HBV
("My faint spirit was sitting in the light.") OBEV
From the besieged Ardea all in post. The Rape of Lucrece. Shakespeare. BeLS
From the Blue's gold avalanches and the snow. Flowers. Stéphane Mallarmé. TrFP
From the bonny bells of heather. Heather Ale. Robert Louis Stevenson. AnEnPo; PCN; ShBV-1; VA
From the borders of the swamp I sang. To C. T. C. Joseph Bennett. LiTM (rev. ed.)
From the Bridge. Keats. *Fr.* I Stood Tip-Toe. PCH
From the Bridge. Don Marquis. OBAV
From the bright Vision's head. The Bright Vision. Dryden. *Fr.* The Conquest of Granada. BeR
From the bustle of liveried soldiers. Café Scene. Saunders Lewis. PrWP
From the cassowary's beak come streaks of light. Morning at Arnheim. William Jay Smith. NePoEA
From the Chuck Wagon. *Unknown.* ABF
(Tail Piece.) CSF
From the Cliffs at Puye, New Mexico. Katharine Shepard Hayden. MuM
From the commandant's quarters on Westchester height. Aaron Burr's Wooing. Edmund Clarence Stedman. GA; PAH
From the Conflict of Convictions. Herman Melville. APW
From the cool and dark-lipped furrows. The Earth Breath. "Æ." BEL
From the Country to the City. Elizabeth Bishop. CrMA
From the cross uplifted high. Come and Welcome. Thomas Haweis. BePJ
From the crow of the cock to the shut of the day. Before the Fair. Anna Hempstead Branch. PR
From the crowded belfry calling. Bega. Marjorie Pickthall. CaP; OCL
From the Crystal. Sidney Lanier. BePJ
From the dark mood's control. The Recovery. Edmund Blunden. MBP; MoBrPo; MoPW
From the dark of the ages gliding. Cantata for the Graduation Festival at Upsala, the Sixth of September, 1877. Viktor Rydberg. AnSL
From the Dark Tower. Countee Cullen. BANP; CDC; NeMA; PoNe
From the dark tower which is a ship's mast. Stroke of One. Jorge Carrera Andrade. AnCL; OnPM
From the dark woods that breathe of fallen showers. The Zebras. Roy Campbell. AnFE; BoSA; CTBS-D; LiTB; LiTM; MBP; MoBrPo; MoPW; ReMP; ShBV-4; ViBoPo
From the Day-Book of a Forgotten Prince. Jean Starr Untermeyer. HBMV; TSW; TSWC
From the dead and lichened tree. The Dark Inanimate. Eric Wilson Barker. UnW
From the dead hand I take the bow he wielded. Funeral Hymn. *Unknown.* *Fr.* The Rigveda. LiTW
From the deep mystery of the past I called her. Evocation. Amado Nervo. AnMP
From the depth of the dreamy decline of the dawn. Nephelidia. Swinburne. *Fr.* The Heptalogia. ALV; BOHV; EnLi-2 (1941 ed.); HBV; HoPM; InMe; NA; OAEP; PA; PoFS; PoVP; ViP; ViPo; VLEP
From the desert I come to thee. Bedouin Song. Bayard Taylor. AA; AmP; AnAmPo; BAP; BBV; FaBoBe; GBV; HBV; IAP; LA; LBAP; LoPo; LPS-1; MCCG; NeHB; OBAV; PFY; PIR; TCAP
From the drear North, a cold and cheerless land. The Heritage. Edward Bliss Reed. EtS
From the drear wastes of unfulfilled desire. Disappointment. Thomas Stephens Collier. AA
From the Duck-Pond to the Carousel. Muriel Rukeyser. FiMAP
From the dull confines of the drooping west. His Return to London. Robert Herrick. EnLit; EPS; SeEP
From the dusk forest or the dark'ning strand. Perdita. John Swanwick Drennan. IrPN
From the elm-tree's topmost bough. Robin's Come. William Warner Caldwell. DD; HBVY; SN
From the ends of the earth thou art come. A Terrible Man. Alcaeus. GrR
From the far horizon, and breaking in triumph towards him. Henry Reed. *Fr.* The Place and the Person. GTBS-D
From the far-off Rocky Mountains, where they meet the eastern hills. The Gathering on the Plains. William T. Butler. PoOW
From the first circle I made my descent. Inferno. Dante. *Fr.* Divina Commedia. EnLi-1
From the first cry. First It Was Singing. Jon Silkin. NePoEA
From the Flats. Sidney Lanier. AmP; CoBA; IAP; NePA; OxBA; TCAP
From the flotsam of a city street we built the Swinging Stair. The Swinging Stair. Nathalia Crane. YT
From the Foothills. Robert Hillyer. MuM
From the forests and highlands. Hymn of Pan. Shelley. AtBAP; BCEP; BPN; EmBrPo; EnRP; ERP; ExPo; FaBoCh; HBV; LoGBV; MyFE; OAEP; OBEV; OBRV; PoEL-4; RG; SeCeV; TVSH
From the four corners of the earth. Carl Sandburg. The People, Yes, Sec. 1. CoV
From the Gallows Hill to the Tineton Copse. The Fox Hunt. John Masefield. *Fr.* Reynard the Fox. CoEV; NAMP
From the Garden of Heaven. Hafiz, *tr. fr. Persian by* Gertrude L. Bell. LiTW
From the gathered nations thrust. Prayer for Faith in Peace. Bertha Gerneaux Woods. PraP
From the gray woods they come, on silent feet. The Dancers. Babette Deutsch. HBMV
From the Greek Anthology ("Bill Jupp lies 'ere"). L. A. G. Strong. WhC
From the Greek Anthology ("I saw no doctor"). *Unknown, tr. fr. Greek by* Humbert Wolfe. PIAE; WhC
From the grey wicket of the morn. John Francis O'Donnell. *Fr.* To Spring. IrPN
From the Gulf. Will H. Ogilvie. BoAu
From the hag [*or* hagg] and hungry [*or* hungrie] goblin.

From the hag and hungry goblin (*continued*)
Tom o' Bedlam's Song [*or* Tom o' Bedlam]. *Unknown.* AnFE; AtBAP; BCEP; BLV; BoW; ChTr; CoEV; EG; EnSB; HBV; HoPM; InvP; KN; LiTB; LiTG; NBE; OtMeF; OxBoLi; PoEL-2; PoFS; RiBV; SeCeV; SeEP; SiTL; TrGrPo; ViBoPo
From the halls of Montezuma. The Marines' Hymn. *Unknown, at. to* L. Z. Phillips. OlF; PoRL; TreF; YaD
From the Harbor Hill. Gustav Kobbé. HBV
From the heart of the mighty mountains strong-souled for my fate I came. The Song of the Colorado. Sharlot Mabridth Hall. HBV
From the heart to the heart. Address to Tragedy. Olga Berggolts. RuPo
From the heights the Sire of gods. The Thunder of Zeus. Homer. *Fr.* The Iliad. LiA
From the Hills. Thomas S. Jones, Jr. LEAP
From the Hills of Dream. "Fiona Macleod." MoSiPe
From the hills of home forth looking, far beneath the tent-like span. The Garrison of Cape Ann. Whittier. IAP
From the Kei to Umzimkulu. Jim. Perceval Gibbon. BoSA
From the Latin of Catullus ("Diana, mistress of the evening sky"). *Tr. by* Colgate Dorr. PtPa
From the laurel's fairest bough. The Battle of Valparaiso. *Unknown.* PAH
From the lone sheiling of the misty island. Scotland Yet. *Unknown, at. to* John Galt. *Fr.* Canadian Boat Song. OtMeF
From the low palace of old Father Ocean. Nereids Rise Out of the Sea and Sing, Tritons Dance. Dryden. *Fr.* Albion and Albanius. BeR
From the madding crowd they stand apart. The v-a-s-e. James Jeffrey Roche. BOHV; HBV; LHV; PreP
From the misty shores of midnight, touched with splendors of the moon. Tennyson [*or* In Lucem Transitus, October, 1892]. Henry van Dyke. AA; BTP; InP
From the moors and the tors of old England. Americans All. Minna Irving. PEDC
From the mountains to the sea. Georgia. Robert Loveman. PoRL
From the Night of Forebeing, *abr.* Francis Thompson. OBVV
Sels.
"Cast wide the folding doorways of the East." OtMeF
"Higher and a solemn voice, A." VLEP
"Not without fortitude I wait." VLEP
"Shade within shade! for deeper in the glass." VLEP
From the North the populated breeze. A Book for Christmas. Margaret Allonby. BoSA
From the ocean half a rood. Among the Sand-Hills. William Alexander. TIP
From the oracular archives and the parchment. Sonnets, IX. Dylan Thomas. LiTM
From the oriels one by one. In the Library. Clinton Scollard. *Fr.* Lyrics from a Library. MOB
From the Parthenon I Learn. Willard Wattles. BAP; HBMV
From the Past and Unavailing. The Pilot. E. A. Robinson. ChMo; CMP
From the peaks a vulture of the mountains cries. Morning. Konstantin Balmont. BoRS
From the Persian. *At. to* Ali Ben Abu Taleb, *tr. by* Emerson. *See* Friends and Enemies.
From the plane,/ the panoramic orchestra of Rio de Janeiro. Third Time. Carlos Pellicer. AnCL
From the Pope's Speech. Robert Browning. *Fr.* The Ring and the Book, X. EV-5
From the Rain Down. Rhina P. Espaillat. GoYe
From the Recesses of a Lowly Spirit. Sir John Bowring. LPS-2
(From the Recesses.) VA
From the Rio Grande's waters to the icy lakes of Maine. Buena Vista. Albert Pike. PAH
From the sea of heaven the waves of cloud arise. The Moon's Ship. Hitomaro. OnPM
From the sharp-scented cupboards bring to-night. Autumn Song. Nyleen Newton. CAG
From the shieling that stands by the lone mountain river. War Song of O'Driscol. Gerald Griffin. OnYI
From the Shore of Life. Lucretius, *tr. fr. Latin by* Geoffrey Johnson. *Fr.* Rerum Natura, II. LaP
From the silver sands of a gleaming shore. The Tree, the Serpent, and the Star. A. P. Gray. BlG
From the soft dyke-road, crooked and waggon-worn. Haying. John Frederic Herbin. CaP; PeCV
From the solitary desert. The Simple [*or* Bewildered] Arab. Jami, *tr. by* Edward Fitzgerald. *Fr.* Salámán and Absál. PeP; WoL
From the south they came, Birds of War. Ojibwa War Songs. *Unknown.* AWP; JAWP; WBP
From the starry heav'ns descending. Christmas Carol. J. R. Newell. BLRP
From the start of Life. The Solar Road. Francis Carlin. JKCP
From the sun-touched hills the mists begin to withdraw. For Remembrance. Niu Hsi-chi. ChLP
From the tall hill-top some great star. Riding by Moonlight. *Unknown.* RAR
From the tattered banana tree after months of waiting. Banana. Charles G. Bell. NePoAm-2
From the Temple torn asunder. The Crucifixion. Thomas Holley Chivers. SPP
From the thin slats of the Venetian blinds. Underwood. Howard Moss. NePA
From the Threshold of a Dream. Antonio Machado, *tr. fr. Spanish by* Eleanor T. Turnbull. TeCS
From the time of our old Revolution. That Things Are No Worse, Sire. Helen Hunt Jackson. OHIP; PEOR
From the time when Nature in her furious fancy. The Giantess. Baudelaire. OnPM
From the top of high Caucasus. Tom of Bedlam. *Unknown.* SiTL
From the top of the bluff, where the wind blows free. The Edge of the World. Mary Fanny Youngs. BrR
From the tragic-est novels at Mudie's. Dora versus Rose. Austin Dobson. ALV; BOHV
From the Train. Marjorie Wilson. BoTP
From the Turkish ("The chain I gave was fair to view"). Byron. HBV
From the unseen world descends. In the Secret Rose Garden. Sa'd ud-din Mahmud Shabistari. LiTW
From the uttermost part of the earth. I Waste Away. Isaiah, Bible, *O.T.* TrJP
From the vast caverns of old ocean's bed. Philip Freneau. *Fr.* The Beauties of Santa Cruz. AmPP (4th ed.); IAP
From the Virgins. Katherine Mann. EBSV
From the West. Martial, *tr. fr. Latin by* Paul Nixon. RoL
From the winter's gray despair. Ave, Caesar! W. E. Henley. In Hospital, XIV. POTT
From Thee all skill and science flow. The Great Physician. Charles Kingsley. MaRV
"From Thee to Thee." Solomon ibn Gabirol, *tr. fr. Hebrew by* Israel Abrahams. TrJP
From their folded mates they wander far. Black Sheep. Richard Burton. AA; BPP; HBV; LBMV; OBAV
From their high pillared halls the guests have flown. Fallen Flowers. Li Shang-yin. WhP
From them no words come. The White Chrysanthemum. Ryota. OnPM
From thence into the open fields he fled. A Pastoral. Spenser. *Fr.* The Faerie Queene, VI, 9. OBSC
From these hie hilles as when a spring doth fall. Comparison of Love to a Streame Falling from the Alpes. Sir Thomas Wyatt. FaBoEn
From thick clouds over the black Warrumbungles. Flood. Ethel Anderson. NeLNL
From this carved chair wherein I sit to-night. The Voice of D. G. R. Sir Edmund Gosse. VA
From this high quarried ledge I see. The Mountain over Aberdare. Alun Lewis. MoWP
From this hundred-terraced height. The Centennial Meditation of Columbia. Sidney Lanier. PAH
From this low-lying valley, oh, how sweet. Two Points of View. Lucian B. Watkins. BANP
From this proud eminence on all sides round. William Crowe. *Fr.* Lewesdon Hill. EnSW
From this quaint cabin window I can see. By the Pacific. Herbert Bashford. AA; BAP
From this small humble village hidden in a valley. The Highway. Ai Ching. WhP
From this tower room above the wall. Cups of Illusion. Henry Bellamann. HBMV
From this valley they say you are going. Red River Valley. *Unknown.* AS; CoSo; FaBoBe; FaFP; OlF; TrAS; TreFS
From thorax of storm the voices of verbs. Three Memorial Sonnets, II. George Barker. WaP
From those blessed regions where the sun displays. The Hymn of the Three Eastern Magi. Elizabeth Rowe. BeR
From those condemned to labour. Dedication. F. R. Scott. BoCaPo
From thought to thought, from mountain-peak to mountain. Canzone 129. Petrarch. Sonnets to Laura: To Laura in Life, Canzone XVII. LyPI
From thy fair face I learn, O my loved lord. Sonnet LIV. Michelangelo. BoFr
From time of swamp to perfumed Lebanon. Paris Twin-Galleys. Charles Péguy. MiFP
From Tomorrow On. *Unknown, tr. fr. Yiddish by* Joseph Leftwich. TrJP
From troubles of the world. Ducks. Frederick William Harvey. HiLiEn; PtOT; YT
From trough to tip the gap is thick with laurel. Sal's Gap. Olive Tilford Dargan. LS
From Tuscan[e] came my lady's worthy race. Description and Praise of His Love Geraldine. Earl of Surrey. EPP; OAEP; ReEn; ReIE; SiCE; SiPS; TuPP; TwHP

From twig to twig the spider weaves. Outer and Inner. George Meredith. PrWP
From twigs of visionary boughs. Prophet and Fool. Louis Golding. HBMV
From unremembered ages we. Chorus of Spirits. Shelley. *Fr.* Prometheus Unbound. LoBV
From upland slopes I see the cows file by. Evening. Archibald Lampman. MM; TwCV
From Venice Was That Afternoon. Jean Garrigue. LiTA
From Virgin's womb this day to us did spring. For Christmas Day. Francis Kinwelmersh. ReIE
From wars and plagues come no such harms. To a Coquet Beauty. John Sheffield, Duke of Buckingham and Normanby. CEP
From way down south on the Rio Grande. Down South on the Rio Grande. *Unknown.* CoSo; CSF
From what a far antiquity, my soul. George Edward Woodberry. Ideal Passion, XXXI. MOAP
From what dark wine, with what disastrous gall. Lidice. Mary Sinton Leitch. NeTW
From what dripping cell, through what fairy glen. A Drunkard to His Bottle [*or* Abhrain an Bhuideil]. Joseph Sheridan Le Fanu. OnYI; TIP
From what nebula. The First Bulb Lights Up. Mikhail Prokofyevich Gerasimov. *Fr.* The Electric Poem. TrRV
From what old ballad, or from what rich frame. Wealth. Joyce Kilmer. LEAP; LoPo; VOD
From what proud star I know not, but I found. The Giant Puffball. Edmund Blunden. FaBoTw; LBBV
From where I paused, intent and still. Pilgrimage. Sydney King Russell. UnW
From where I sit, I see the stars. Midnight. Archibald Lampman. BoCaPo; PeCV; TwCV
From White's and Will's. Song. Ambrose Philips. CEP
From Whitsuntide to Whitsuntide. A Ballad of a Bun. Sir Owen Seaman. CenHV
From whose flute, playing in some hidden place, come those flying notes. Hearing a Flute on a Spring Night. Li Po. ChLP
From whose white summits was this wind released. The Storm at Nightfall. Morton Dauwen Zabel. NP
From Wibbleton to Wobbleton is fifteen miles. *Unknown.* OxNR
From Wicklow to the throb of dawn. Sea Dawn. Francis Hackett. AnIV
From William Tyndale to John Frith. Edgar Bowers. NePoEA
From within/ Slight rain seems to purr. Rain on a Cottage Roof. Freda Laughton. OnYI
From witty men and mad. Poetry Defined. Thomas Randolph. EV-2
From women's eyes this doctrine I derive. Love and the Poet. Shakespeare. *Fr.* Love's Labour's Lost, IV, iii. CoEV
From wounds and death they rest—this bow and quiver. Dedication. *Unknown.* OnPM
From Wynyard's Gap the livelong day. A Trampwoman's Tragedy. Thomas Hardy. AtBAP; BeLS; HBMV; MoVE
From yonder wood mark blue-eyed Eve proceed. Walter Savage Landor. *Fr.* Progress of Evening. EnSW
From Yorktown on the fourth of May. The Gallant Fighting "Joe." James Stevenson. PAH
From Yoshino. Fujiwara no Masatsune, *tr. fr. Japanese by* Kenneth Rexroth. OnPJ
From you have I [*or* I have] been absent in the spring. Sonnets, XCVIII. Shakespeare. AWP; BEL; ChTr; EIL; EM-1; EnLi-1; InPo; JAWP; LiTB; LiTG; LoPo; PeBoSo; ReEn; ReIE; SiCE; TOP; TwP; ViBoPo; WBP
From you, Ianthe, little troubles pass. Walter Savage Landor. *Fr.* Ianthe. BLV; BoLiVe; CaAE; EV-4; OBEV; OnPM; PIAE; TrGrPo; TyEnPo; ViBoPo
From Zeus begin we, never nameless we. Proem. Aratus. *Fr.* Phaenomena. OxBG
Front Line. William Rose Benét. AOAH
Frontier, The. John Masefield. NP
Fronting amazed Cythera grows. Pushkin, *tr. fr. Russian by* R. M. Hewitt. BoR
Frontispiece. Max Jacob, *tr. fr. French by* Wallace Fowlie. MiCF
Frontispiece. May Swenson. NePoEA
Frost, The. Emily Dickinson. *See* Apparently with no surprise.
Frost. Yevgeny Aronovich Dolmatovsky, *tr. fr. Russian by* Babette Deutsch. TrRV
Frost. Ethel Romig Fuller. GFA
Frost, The. Hannah Flagg Gould. BLPA; HBV; HBVY; LPS-1; NeHB; PECK; PTA-1; RIS; TVC; TVSH
(Jack Frost.) DD; OTPC; PRWS
Frost. John Hewitt. NeIP
Frost. Edith M. Thomas. AA; BAP
Frost, The. Tzu Yeh, *tr. fr. Chinese by* Henry H. Hart. PoHN
Frost and snow, frost and snow. Ariel. David Campbell. NeLNL
Frost at Midnight. Samuel Taylor Coleridge. BEL; BPN; EM-2; EmBrPo; EnLi-2; EnRP; EPN; ERP; EV-4; FaBoEn; FiP; KN; LoBV; MeRV; NBE; OAEP; OBRV; PoE; PoEL-4; ShBV-4; TyEnPo
Sels.
Coleridge and His Child. RO
"I was reared/ In the great city, pent 'mid cloisters dim." AlDL
"Therefore all seasons shall be sweet to thee." EnSW
(All Seasons Shall Be Sweet.) BoTP
Frost at Night. James Thomson. *Fr.* The Seasons: Winter. CoEV; OBEC
Frost at Sea. William Diaper. *Fr.* Nereides; or, Sea-Eclogues. BeR
Frost called to water "Halt!" Hard Frost. Andrew Young. MoVE
Frost came in the night and stole my world, A. A Hard Frost. C. Day Lewis. HaMV
Frost Elves, The. Archibald Lampman. UnW
Frost Fancy, A. Richard Le Gallienne. OTPC (1946 ed.)
Frost flowers on the window glass. A Valentine. Eleanor Hammond. GFA; TiPo; YeAr
Frost has sealed/ The still December field. Tree in December. Melville Cane. MAP; MoAmPo
Frost in Spring. Jessie B. Rittenhouse. NV
Frost in the air and music in the air. The Waits. John Freeman. BoTP
Frost is an elf. Frost. Ethel Romig Fuller. GFA
Frost is here, The. Winter. Tennyson. PCH
Frost is out, and in the open fields, The. October. Jones Very. AnNE
Frost is tight upon the land. Now in the Time of This Mortal Life. Norman Nicholson. NeBP
Frost-King, The. Mary Mapes Dodge. DD
Frost lies white, The. Otomo no Yakamochi, *tr. fr. Japanese by* Kenneth Rexroth. OnPJ
Frost-locked all the winter. Spring. Christina Rossetti. BPN
Frost looked forth one still, clear night, The. The Frost [*or* Jack Frost]. Hannah Flagg Gould. BLPA; DD; HBV; HBVY; LPS-1; NeHB; OTPC; PECK; PRWS; PTA-1; RIS; TVC; TVSH
Frost-Morning. William Alexander, Archbishop of Armagh. IrPN
Frost of the moon stood over my floor, The. Six Green Singers. Eleanor Farjeon. SDH
Frost Pane, The. David McCord. BrR; RIS; StaSt; StVeCh
Frost performs its secret ministry, The. Frost at Midnight. Samuel Taylor Coleridge. BEL; BPN; EM-2; EmBrPo; EnLi-2; EnRP; EPN; ERP; EV-4; FaBoEn; FiP; KN; LoBV; MeRV; NBE; OAEP; OBRV; PoE; PoEL-4; ShBV-4; TyEnPo
Frost shall freeze; fire melt wood. Maxims [*or* Gnomic Lines]. *Unknown.* AnOE; LiTW
Frost Spirit, The. Whittier. BAV; HBV; PCH
Frost To-Night. Edith M. Thomas. BLP; CP; LBMV; MCCG; NV; PCD; POT; PoTo
Frost will bite us soon, The. Harvest-Home Song. John Davidson. VA
Frost Work. Mary Emily Bradley. PEOR
Frostbite. Conrad Aiken. SiTL
Frosted Pane, The. Sir Charles G. D. Roberts. HBV; LEAP; SN
Frosty chill was in the air, A. I Will Help You. Wolstan Dixey. PEOR
Frosty Christmas Eve, A. Noel: Christmas Eve, 1913. Robert Bridges. CAW; GTML; LiTB; MeRV; MoVE; OxBoCh; PoEL-5
Frosty Day, A. Lord De Tabley. LoBV
Frosty Night, A. Robert Graves. CH; MoAB; MoBrPo; MPB
Frosty region ringis of the year, The. The Winter. Gawin Douglas. *Fr.* Prologues to the Aeneid, Bk. VII. EBSV
Frosty, the bite of the autumn air. Blessing the Hounds. Mary Winter. GoYe
Froth on the lip of a crescent sea. At the Seaside. George Ewart Evans. MoWP
Frothi's Meal, *sel. Unknown, tr. fr. Icelandic by* Arthur Gilchrist Brodeur. *Fr.* The Younger [*or* Snorra *or* Prose] Edda *by* Snorri Sturluson.
"They to the flour-mill." PaOS
Froude informs the Scottish youth. William Stubbs. CenHV
Froward Gull, The. Donald F. Drummond. PtPa
Frowned the Laird on the Lord: "So, red-handed I catch thee?" Muckle-Mouth Meg. Robert Browning. BPN; HBV; OtMeF; PoVP; VA; VLEP
Frowning Cliff, The. Herbert Asquith. BrR
Frowning fates have taken hence, The. A Dead Child[e]. Lucian. EnLi-1; GrPo; LiTW; OxBG
Frowning, the mountain stronghold stood. The Lost Colors. Elizabeth Stuart Phelps Ward. AA; HBV; HBVY

Frowning, the owl in the oak complained him. Owl against Robin. Sidney Lanier. LaNeLa
Frozen City, The. Howard Nemerov. FiMAP
Frozen Fire. Floris Clarke McLaren. CaP
Frozen Grail, The. Elsa Barker. LBMV; LEAP
Frozen ground is broken, The. In February. P. A. Ropes. BoTP
Frozen Ocean, The. Viola Meynell. CH
Frozen river is drifted deep with snow, The. In the Evening I Walk by the River. Ou-yang Hsiu. OnPC
Frozen territory surrounds me, A. The Stranger. Jorge Carrera Andrade. BoFr; TwSpPo
Frugal crone, whom praying priests attend, The. The Ruling Passion. Pope. *Fr.* Moral Essays, Epistle I. BOHV
Frugal snail, with forecast of repose, The. The Housekeeper [*or* The Snail]. Vincent Bourne, *tr. by* Charles Lamb. GN; GoTP; HBV; LPS-2; MoShBr; MW; OTPC; SN; TVSH
Fruit. Ruth Miller. BoSA
Fruit. *Unknown, tr. fr. Spanish by* Havelock Ellis. OnPM
Fruit breaks on the summer mouth. The Garden. George M. Brady. NeIP
Fruit-gathering, *sels.* Rabindranath Tagore. NV
" 'Sire,' announced the servant to the King."
"Sudas, the gardner, plucked from his tank."
Fruit of all the service that I serve, The. Epigram. Sir Thomas Wyatt. SiPS
Fruit of the Flower. Countee Cullen. PoNe
Fruit of the goodly tree, leaves of the palm tree. The Hut. Avigdor Hammeiri. LiTW
Fruit of the orchard is over-ripe, Elaine, The. Lancelot. Arna Bontemps. CDC
Fruit Piece, A. Eden Phillpotts. PtOT
Fruit Plucker, The. Samuel Taylor Coleridge. *Fr.* The Wanderings of Cain. CH; SeCeV
(Boy in the Wilderness.) OTPC (1923 ed.)
(Fragment: "Encinctur'd with a twine of leaves.") RO
(In a Moonlight Wilderness.) FaBoCh; LoGBV
Fruit Rancher, The. Lloyd Roberts. CaP; CPG
Fruit Tree. Ibn Qadi Mila, *tr. fr. Arabic by* A. J. Arberry. MooP
Fruit-tree's branch by very wealth, The. The Penalty of Virtue. *Unknown. Fr.* The Panchatantra. AWP; PoFr
Fruit-vender church. Sunday. Jorge Carrera Andrade. AnCL
Fruit Vendor, The. Frances Beatrice Taylor. CPG; MW
Fruit white and lustrous as a pearl. The Lychee. Wang I. FaBoCh
Fruitful Earth Drinks Up the Rain. Thomas Stanley, *after the Greek of* Anacreon. OnPM
(All Things Drink.) AWP
Fruitful was the land, rich its pastures, flowing with milk and honey. Psalm of the Singing Grave. Alexander Janta. LiTW
Fruitionless. Ina Donna Coolbrith. AA; LBAP
Fruits of Experience. James Broughton. SiTL
Fruits of Friendship, The ("Know'st thou, Lorenzo, what a friend contains?"). Edward Young. *Fr.* Night Thoughts, II. GrCo-1
Fruits of War, The. George Gascoigne. ReIE
Fruits of Warre Is Beggery, The. *Unknown. See* Maunding Souldier, The.
Frustra. Shakespeare. *See* Take, O Take Those Lips Away.
Frustrate. Louis Untermeyer. HBMV; InMe; YaD
Frustrated Male. Hughes Mearns. *Fr.* Later Antigonishes. InMe; SiTL
Frutta di Mare. Geoffrey Scott. ChTr; EtS; OBMV
Fryar was walking in Exeter-street, A. The Crafty Miss of London; or, The Fryar Well Fitted. *Unknown.* CoMu
Fryar Well Fitted, The. *Unknown. See* Crafty Miss of London, The.
Fuchsia Hedges in Connacht. Padraic Colum. GoBC
Fudge Family in Paris, The, *sel.* Thomas Moore.
French Cookery. OBRV
Fufidia (Lady Mary Wortley Montagu). Pope. *Fr.* Sober Advice from Horace to the Young Gentlemen about Town. BeR
Fugal-Chorus from "For the Time Being" ("Great is Caesar"). W. H. Auden. *Fr.* For the Time Being. LiTM (rev. ed.); NePA; SeCeV
Fugitive, The. William Rose Benét. MOAP
Fugitive, The. John Freeman. MBP
Fugitive Beauty. John Gould Fletcher. ChMo; CMP
Fugitive Slave's Apostrophe to the North Star, The. John Pierpont. AA
Fugitives, The. Florence Wilkinson Evans. LBMV; NV; OQP; QP-2
Fugitives, The, *st.* 1. Shelley. PCH
Fugue. Constance Carrier. GoYe
Fugue, A, *sel.* Hubert Church.
"There was a music throbbed athwart the street." AnNZ
Fugue. Harold Lewis Cook. NP
Fugue. Alfonso Gutiérrez Hermosillo, *tr. fr. Spanish by* Dudley Fitts. AnCL
Fugue. R. A. K. Mason. OnPM
Fuimus Troes, *sels.* Jasper Fisher.
Morisco, A. SeCL; TuPP
(Song: Morisko, A.) SeEP
Song to a Viol. LO; LoPS; SeCL
("So the silver-feathered swan.") SeEP; TuPP
Fujiyama—on sale! Japan for Sightseeing. Iku Takenaka. PoLJ
Fulfil Thy Will. Christina Rossetti. PraP
Fulfill, O gracious God, to-day. Pentecost. Adelbert Sumpter Coats. TrPWD
Fulfillment. Helene Johnson. CDC; PoNe
Fulfillment. Cathleen Keegan. UnW
Fulfillment. William A. Muhlenberg. WGRP
Fulfillment. Charlotte Newton. OQP; QP-2
Fulfillment, The. Delmore Schwartz. FiMAP
Fulfillment. Eunice Tietjens. *See* Psalm to My Belovèd.
Fulfilment. Elsa Barker. *Fr.* The Spirit and the Bride HBMV
Fulfilment. Louis V. Ledoux. HBMV
Fulfilment. Robert Nichols. BMEP; HBMV; MBP; PtOT
Full-berried the elderbush; tranquilly childhood lived. Childhood. Georg Trakl. AnGP
Full-Circle. Maxwell Anderson. QS
Full clear and bright this Christmas night range fields of Heaven fire-sown. Christmas Rede. Jane Barlow. OBVV
Full Cycle. John White Chadwick. PAH
Full dozen times, Zoilus, during a meal, A. Thermometrical. Martial. RoL
Full early in the morning. *Unknown.* BoTP
Full Edition, A. Joseph Lilienthal. CAG
Full facing their swift flight, from ebon streak. Loss of the Mortal Maiden. Keats. *Fr.* Endymion, IV. ERP
Full fadom five thy father lies. *See* Full fathom five . . .
Full Fair. Hafiz, *tr. fr. Persian by* John Payne. PeP
Full faith I have she holds that rarest gift. Modern Love, XXXII. George Meredith. ViPo
Full Fathom Five. A. R. D. Fairburn. AnNZ
Full fathom [*or* fadom] five thy father lies. Ariel's Song [*or* A Sea Dirge]. Shakespeare. *Fr.* The Tempest, I, ii. AnEnPo; AnFE; AtBAP; ATP; AWP; BCEP; BEL; BLV; BoLiVe; BrBE; CaAE; CBOV; CBPC; CenL; CG; ChTr; CoEV; EG; ElL; ElSeCe; EM-1; EnLi-1; EPP; EtS; EV-1; ExPo; FaBoCh; FaBoEn; GN; GTBS; GTBS-D; GTBS-W; GTSE; GTSL; HBV; HoPM; InPo; JAWP; KN; LEAP; LiA; LiTB; LiTG; LoBV; LoGBV; MaPo; MCCG; NeHB; OAEP; OBEV; OBSC; OTPC; OuHeWo; PFE; PIR; PoEL-2; PoRA; ReaPo; SeCePo; SeCeV; SG; ShBV-1; SiCE; ThWaDe; TOP; TrGrPo; TwHP; TwP; TyEnPo; ViBoPo; WBP; WHA
Full forty days he pass'd, whether on hill. The First Temptation. Milton. *Fr.* Paradise Regained, I. OxBoCh
Full gently then Love laid me on his breast. Ideal Passion, XV. George E. Woodberry. MOAP
Full happy is the man who comes at last. The Year's End. Timothy Cole. HBV
Full Heart, The. Robert Nichols. HBMV; LEAP; NLK (1947 ed.)
Full in her glory, she as Tirzah fair. The Prophet Jeremiah and the Personification of Israel. *At. to* Eleazar ben Kalir. TrJP
Full in the middle of this pleasantness. The Sacrifice to Pan. Keats. *Fr.* Endymion, I. BCEP
Full is Dinogad's petticoat, see! For Little Dinogad. *Unknown.* LyMA
Full is my sorrow now that you are dead. The Atheist Buries His Son. Abu'l-Atahija. LiTW
Full knee-deep lies the winter snow. Death of the Old Year. Tennyson. DD; HBV; HH; LPS-3; OTPC; PECK; PIR
Full Life, A. Carphyllides, *tr. fr. Greek by* Lord Neaves. OnPM
Full life, sweet rest, great love that cannot cease. Four Friends. Leo Ward. GoBC
Full little knowest thou, that hast not tried. At Court. Spenser. *Fr.* Mother Hubberds Tale. PoFr
Full many a century it crept, the child. The Silkworm. Marco Girolamo Vida. *Fr.* De Bombycibus. CAW
Full many a dreary hour have I past. Epistle to My Brother George. Keats. EmBrPo; EnRP; GEPC
Full many a glorious morning have I seen. Sonnets, XXXIII. Shakespeare. AEV; ATP; AWP; BCEP; BEL; BLV; BoLiVe; CoBE; CoEV; EG; ElL; ElSeCe; EM-1; EnL; EnLi-1; ES; EV-1; FaBoEn; FaFP; HBV; InPo; JAWP; KN; LEAP; LiTB; LiTG; LoBV; OAEP; OBSC; OtMeF; OuHeWo; PeBoSo; PIAE; PoRA; ReaPo; ReEn; ReIE; RiBV; SeCePo; SeCeV; SiCE; SN; TOP; TreFS; TrGrPo; TwHP; TwP; TyEnPo; UnPo (1st ed.); ViBoPo; WBP
Full many a project that never was hatched. Humpty Dumpty. Adeline D. T. Whitney. *Fr.* Mother Goose for Grown Folks. HBV

Full many a quiet, modest man. The Junior's Foxy Friends. Raymond W. Walker. CAG
Full many a sinful notion. Apple-Pie and Cheese. Eugene Field. LHV
Full many a year in the village church. What the Village Bell Said. John G. M'Lemore. BlG
Full many are the centuries since the days. Assurance. Ida Norton Munson. PGD
Full many lift and sing. Negro Poets. Charles Bertram Johnson. BANP
Full merrily rings the millstone round. Song of the Elfin Miller. Allan Cunningham. OTPC (1946 ed.); TVSH
Full Moon. Clifford Bax. POTE
Full Moon. Walter de la Mare. AtBAP; TiPo
Full Moon. John Gould Fletcher. Down the Mississippi, III. ChMo; CMP; LiTA; MOAP; NP; SPP; TCAP
Full Moon. Robert Graves. FaBoEn; POTE
Full Moon. Galway Kinnell. NePoAm-2
Full Moon. V. Sackville-West. AlDL; DiM; MBP; MoBrPo (1942 ed.); MoShBr; PtOT; TwCV
Full Moon. Sappho, *tr. fr. Greek by* William Ellery Leonard. AWP; JAWP; WBP
Full Moon. Sara Teasdale. *See* Full Moon; Santa Barbara.
Full Moon. Tu Fu, *tr. fr. Chinese by* Kenneth Rexroth. OnPC
Full Moon. Elinor Wylie. CrMA; MAP; MoAB; MoAmPo
Full moon easterly rising, furious, The. A Love Story. Robert Graves. AtBAP; FaBoTw; LiTB; MoVE
Full moon floods the vast Pacific tides. Dawn at Flying-Fish Point. Clement B. Christesen. BoAu
Full Moon from Her Cloudless Skies, The. Robert Bridges. VLEP
Full moon is partly hidden by cloud, The. A Fable of the War. Howard Nemerov. NePoEA
Full Moon; New Guinea. Karl Shapiro. MiAP
Full Moon on the Colosseum, The. Colosseum. Harold Norse. TrJP
Full moon rising on the waters of my heart. Evening Song. Jean Toomer. CDC; PoNe
Full Moon; Santa Barbara. Sara Teasdale. BrR
(Full Moon.) TSW; TSWC
Full nineteen centuries have passed since then. A Call to Pentecost. Inez M. Tyler. BLRP
Full of dread/ Must be that fortune thou canst name. Out of Suffering, Tolerance. Sophocles. *Fr.* Oedipus at Colonus. GrR
Full of Grace exceedingly. Hymn of the Angels and Sibyls. Gil Vicente. CAW
Full of her long white arms and milky skin. The Equilibrists. John Crowe Ransom. AmP; AnAmPo; ChMo; CoBMV; LA; LiTM; LS; MoAB; MoAP; MoPo; MoVE; NePA; OxBA; UnPo (1st ed.)
Full of Life Now. Walt Whitman. BoFr; IAP
Full of proud hopes, upon the pass of war. The Trojan Camp-Fires. Homer. *Fr.* The Iliad, VIII. GrR
Full of rebellion, I would die. Nature. George Herbert. OAEP
Full of wrath was Hiawatha. The Hunting of Pau-Puk-Keewis. Longfellow. *Fr.* The Song of Hiawatha. CoBA
Full oft beside some gorgeous fane. The Mother. Sara Coleridge. DiM; OBVV
Full oft of old the islands changed their names. Epitaph on an Infant. Crinagoras. AWP
Full often I think in my trim swallow-tail. An Old Beau. Richard Kendall Munkittrick. PR
Full River Red. Yo Fei, *tr. fr. Chinese by* Wang Sheng-chih. WhP
Full Sea Rolls and Thunders, The. W. E. Henley. EtS
(Echoes.) POTT
Full Sky. Jules Supervielle, *tr. fr. French by* Wallace Fowlie. MiCF
Full soon the Queen this crafty sleight 'gan smell. Virgil, *tr. by* the Earl of Surrey. *Fr.* The Aeneid, IV. EnLit
Full-spread the pointed leaf, bright-tipped the stalk. In Description. Ann Louise Hayes. PtPa
Full Valleys. F. R. Scott. CaP
Full well I know that you are gone—and yet. For a Certain Dog. Catherine Parmenter. AlBD
Full well it may be seen. Sir Thomas Wyatt. SiPS
Full well, my gentle sir, I know. To an Artful Theatre Manager. Lorenzo da Ponte. *Fr.* Il Capriccio Dramatico. TrJP
Full winter; and the lusty woodman brings. Midwinter. Oscar Wilde. *Fr.* Humanitad. PCH
Full woods overflow, The. Bounty. Mary Webb. AlDL
Fuller and Warren. *Unknown.* ABS; BeLS; CoSo, *with music;* CSF, *with music;* ViBoFo
Fullness. Thomas Traherne. CaAE
Fulness of life and power of feeling. Matthew Arnold. *Fr.* Empedocles on Etna. BrBE; OAEP
Fult Faithorne. William Aspenwall Bradley. BAP
Fume-bitten no-grassness of mountains. Landore. George Woodcock. MoWP
Fun. Douglas Malloch. OnHT
Fun in a Garret. Emma C. Dowd. GFA; SUS; TiPo
Fun on the Beach. Alice Wilkins. GFA
Fun with Fishing. Eunice Tietjens. FaPON; GaP
Fundisi. Ruth Miller. BoSA
Funebrial Reflections. Ogden Nash. ImOP
("Among the anthropophagi.") CenHV
Funeral. Murray Bennett. GoYe
Funeral, The. Walter de la Mare. MoVE
Funeral[l], The. John Donne. ATP; AWP; BrBE; CoBE; ElSeCe; EM-1; EnLi-1 (1949 ed.); EnLoPo; EPP; EPS; EV-2; InPo; JAWP; KN; LEAP; LiTL; LO; MeLP; OBEV; OBS; PoE; PoEL-2; PoRA; ReaPo; ReEn; SeCV-1; SeEP; TCEP; TOP; TuPP; TwHP; TwP; WBP
Funeral. Vyacheslav Ivanov, *tr. fr. Russian by* Babette Deutsch. OnPM; TrRV
(Funerals, *tr. by* C. M. Bowra.) BoRS
Funeral, The. "M. J.," *tr. fr. Polish by* A. Glanz-Leyeless. TrJP
Funeral, The. Stephen Spender. ChMo; MBP; MoAB; MoBrPo; NAMP; TwCV
Funeral at High Tide. Hervey Allen. LS
Funeral Dirge for Marcello. John Webster. *See* Call for the Robin Redbreast.
Funeral Elegy on the Death of His Very Good Friend, Mr. Michael Drayton. Sir Aston Cokayne. OBS
Funeral Hymn. William Walsham How. WGRP
(For All the Saints.) MaRV
Funeral Hymn. *Unknown, tr. fr. Sanskrit by* Arthur A. Macdonnell. *Fr.* The Rigveda. LiTW
Funeral in Hungary. Kay Boyle. AnEnPo
Funeral of a Poor Girl, The. Auguste Brizeux, *tr. fr. French by* Alan Conder. TrFP
Funeral of Napoleon I. Sir John H. Hagarty. CaP; OCL
Funeral of Philip Sparrow, The. John Skelton. *Fr.* Phyllyp Sparowe. ACP
Funeral of Time, The. Henry Beck Hirst. AA; APW
Funeral of Youth, The: Threnody. Rupert Brooke. FaBoTw; SeCeV
Funeral Pyre, The. *Unknown, tr. fr. Anglo-Saxon by* Charles W. Kennedy. *Fr.* Beowulf. AnOE
Funeral Rites of the Rose, The. Robert Herrick. EV-2; OBEV
Funeral Song ("Urns and odors, bring away"). Fletcher *and* Shakespeare. *Fr.* The Two Noble Kinsmen, I, v. AtBAP; ChTr; UnPo (1st ed.)
(Dirge of the Three Queens.) OBEV
(Song.) BoW
(Urns and Odours Bring Away!) ElL; SiCE
Funeral Song ("Fear no more . . ."). Shakespeare. *See* Fear No More the Heat o' the Sun.
Funeral Song, A ("Come to me, grief, for ever"). *Unknown. See* Funerall Song, A.
Funeral Song upon the Decease of Annes, His Mother, A. Nicholas Grimald. ReIE; TuPP
Funeral [*or* Funerall] stone, A. To Laurels. Robert Herrick. ElSeCe; ExPo; SeCV-1
Funeral Toast. Stéphane Mallarmé, *tr. fr. French by* Hubert Creekmore. LiTW
Funerall, The. John Donne. *See* Funeral, The.
Funerall [*or* Funeral] Song, A: "Come to me, grief, for ever." *Unknown.* CH; PoD; TriL
(Lament over Sir Philip Sidney, *abr.*) BHV
Funerall stone, A. *See* Funeral stone, A.
Funerals. Vyacheslav Ivanov. *See* Funeral.
Funerals. *Unknown.* DDA
Fungi from Yuggoth. H. P. Lovecraft. DaM
Funniest sight that ever I saw, The. *Unknown.* GoTP
Funniest Thing in the World, The. James Whitcomb Riley. PPL
Funny and Wise. Jack Lowell. DDA
Funny Face, *sel.* Ira Gershwin.
Babbitt and the Bromide, The. ALV
Funny, how Felicia Ropps. Felicia Ropps. Gelett Burgess. FaPON; GaP; TiPo
Funny how it come about! The Cowboy and the Maid. *Unknown.* SCC
Funny old lady named Borgia, A. *Unknown.* WhC
Funny Old Man and His Wife, The. *Unknown.* SUS
Funny old person of Slough, A. Limerick. *Unknown.* RIS
Funny, solemn, little old grey owl. Yearning. Alfred Kreymborg. MAPA
Funny the Way Different Cars Start. Dorothy W. Baruch. FaPON
Fur and Feather. Christina Rossetti. CBPC
Fur Coat, The. James Stephens. BMEP
Fürchte Nichts, geliebte Seele. Heine, *tr. fr. German by* Louis Untermeyer. ALV
Furies, The. Aeschylus. *See* Eumenides.
Furies, The. Euripides. *See* Powers of Darkness.
Furies' Prayer. The. Aeschylus. *See* Chorus of the Furies, The ("Weave the weird dance").
Furious gun, in his most raging ire, The. The Lover Com-

Furious gun (*continued*)
pareth His Heart to the Overcharged Gun. Sir Thomas Wyatt. ReIE
Furious prisoner of the womb, The. An Argument—Of the Passion of Christ. Thomas Merton. CrMA
Furius and Aurelius, Catullus's comrades. Farewell to Lesbia. Catullus. LaP; LiTW
Furius, my small estate, my charming villa. Cataclysm. Catullus. LiTW
Furius, you've no slaves, no box to hold your money. Catullus, *tr. fr. Latin by* Horace Gregory. LaP
Furl of fresh-leaved dog-rose down, The. Fragment. Gerard Manley Hopkins. AtBAP
Furl that Banner, for 'tis weary. The Conquered Banner. Abram Joseph Ryan. AA; BlG; DD; HBV; JKCP; LEAP; OBAV; PaA; PAH; PEDC; SPP; TCAP; TreF
Furl your sail, my little boatie. Little Boatie. Henry van Dyke. BOL
Furlough. Ann Louise Hayes. PtPa
Furlough in heart and hand, the soldier at last walks. No Furlough. Stephen Stepanchev. WaP
Furnished room beyond the stinging of, A. Good-bye for a Long Time. Roy Fuller. NeBP
Furniture of a Woman's Mind, The. Swift. CEP
Furred from the farmhouse. Winter Saturday. Earle Birney. TwCaPo
Furrow and the Hearth, The. Padraic Colum. NV
"Stride the hill, sower," *sel.* TwCV
Furry Bear. A. A. Milne. StVeCh (1955 ed.); TiPo (1959 ed.)
Furry coat has the bear to wear, A. The Pig's Tail. Norman Ault. BoTP
Furry Home, The. J. M. Westrup. BoTP
Further Bank, The. Rabindranath Tagore. AlDL
Further Instructions. Ezra Pound. AnAmPo; BAP; CoV; LA; NP
Furtive wind of winter, The. Alas, Alas, the Winter. Edith Lovejoy Pierce. MuM
Fury of a creature when it drips, The. David's Renconciliation with Absalom. "Michael Field." TwCV
Fury of Aerial Bombardment, The. Richard Eberhart. AmP; ExPo; HoPM; LiTA; MiAP; Po; UnPo (3d ed.); WaP
Fury of taunt was followed by fury of blow, The. E. J. Pratt. *Fr.* Brébeuf and His Brethren, XII. PeCV; TwCaPo
"Fury said to/ a mouse." A Long and a Sad Tale. "Lewis Carroll." *Fr.* Alice's Adventures in Wonderland. ViP
Fuscara; or, The Bee Errant. John Cleveland. EPS
Fuscus, the man of life upright [*or* upright life] and pure. Integer Vitae [*or* To Aristius Fuscus *or* Purity]. Horace, *tr. by* Sir Theodore Martin. *Fr.* Odes. EnLi-1; OuHeWo; RoL
Fuseli's "Nightmare." Erasmus Darwin. *Fr.* The Botanic Garden: The Loves of the Plants, III. RO
Fussy. Laura E. Richards. MPB
Fust Banjo, De. Irwin Russell. *Fr.* Christmas-Night in the Quarters. AA; BAP; BLPA; HBV; IHA; LEAP; PFY
(First Banjo, The.) BOHV; LHV; SPP
Futile Sacrifice. Murray Skinner. ChIP
Futility. Louise Driscoll. DDA
Futility. Glycon, *tr. fr. Greek by* J. A. Pott. OxBG
Futility. Mary S. Hawling. DDA; PoMa; VOD (1935 ed.)
Futility. Robert Ervin Howard. DaM
Futility. Wilfred Owen. AtBAP; ChMP; CoBMV; FaBoMo; GTBS-D; HiLiEn; LiTM; LO; MBP; MoAB; MoBrPo; MoP; MoPW; NeMA; OAEP (2d ed.); PoE; SeCePo; SoV; TrGrPo
Future, The. Matthew Arnold. BPN; EM-2; EmBrPo; EOAH; EPP; EV-5; GTBS; OAEP; PoVP; ViPo; VLEP
Future, The. George Frederick Cameron. BoCaPo
Future, The. James Oppenheim. TrJP
Future, The. Pope. *See* Hope Springs Eternal.
Future, The. Edward Rowland Sill. AnNE; HBV
Future Is Not for Us, The. Ronald Bottrall. MoP
Future lies, The/ With those whose eyes. The Goal and the Way. John Oxenham. PGD
Future Life, The. Bryant. LPS-1
Future of American Literature, The. John Trumbull. *Fr.* Essay on the Fine Arts. AmPP (3d ed.)
Future of the Classics, The. *Unknown.* BOHV
Future Peace and Glory of the Church, The. William Cowper. TriL
Fuzzy fellow without feet, A. The Secret. Emily Dickinson. RIS
Fuzzy-Wuzzy. Kipling. BEL; CV; EnLi-2 (1949 ed.); EnLit; HBV; MBP; MCCG; MoBrPo; PoVP; PYM; StaSt; TrGrPo; VA; ViPP; VLEP; YT
Fuzzy wuzzy, creepy crawly. Lillian Schulz Vanada. SUS; TiPo
Fuzzy Wuzzy Leaves Us, *parody.* "E. P. C." PA
Fuzzy Wuzzy was a bear. *Unknown.* GoTP
Fy let us a' to the bridal. The Blythsome Bridal. *Unknown.* EBSV
Fye awaye fye what meane you by this. *Unknown.* SeCSL
Fye foolish Earth, thinke you the heaven wants glory. *See* Fie! foolish earth, think you . . .
Fye; what a trouble tis to count this trash. *See* Fie, what a trouble . . .
Fyll the cuppe, Phylyppe. *Unknown.* EPP

G

G. Hilaire Belloc. FiBHP
G. K. Chesterton. Humbert Wolfe. TrJP
G stands for Gnu, whose weapons of defense. G. Hilaire Belloc. FiBHP
Gaberlunzie Man, The. *Unknown, at. to* James IV, King of Scotland. BSV; EBSV; EnSB; GoTS
Gabriel. Willard Wattles. HBMV
Gabriel, brighter than the sun. Make We Merry This New Year. *Unknown.* AnEC
Gabriel, Gabriel, come blow your horn! Trumpet for Yuletide. Louis J. Sanker. JKCP (1955 ed.)
Gabriel had gathered moss. The Crèche. Carol Ryrie Brink. ChrBoLe; SDH
Gabriel Meets Satan. Milton. *Fr.* Paradise Lost, IV. LoBV
Gabriel of high degree. Nova, Nova: Ave Fit ex Eva. *Unknown.* AnEC
Gabriel, that angel bright. Regina Celi, Letare. *Unknown.* AnEC
Gabriel's Trumpet, *with music.* *Unknown.* StDa
Gae bring my guid auld harp ance mair. Scotland Yet. Henry Scott Riddell. EBSV; HBV
Gaelic, The. Blanche Mary Kelly. CAW
Gaelic Christmas, A. Liam P. Clancy. ISi
Gaelic Fragment: "I am Eve." *Unknown.* *See* Eve's Lament.
Gaelic Litany to Our Lady, The. *Unknown, tr. fr. Old Irish by* Eugene O'Curry. CAW; ISi
Gaelic Lullaby. *Unknown.* GFA; RAR
(Lullaby: "Hush! the waves are rolling in.") SAS
(Old Gaelic Cradle-Song, An.) BOL
(Old Gaelic Lullaby.) PRWS
Gaelic Rune of Hospitality. *Unknown.* *See* Rune of Hospitality, The.
Gaelic Speech; or, "Auld Lang Syne" Done Up in Tartan. *Unknown.* PA
Gaffer Gray. Thomas Holcroft. EV-3; HBV
Gaffers, gammers, huzzies, louts. Holiday at Hampton Court. John Davidson. BMEP
Gaffer's Song, The. Eden Phillpotts. *See* Man's Days.
Gage d'Amour, A. Austin Dobson. VA
Gai lon la, gai le rosier. *Unknown, tr. fr. French-Canadian folk song by* George T. Lanigan. BoCaPo (1948 ed.)
Gaiety of Descendants. Douglas Newton. NeBP
Gaiety of three winds is a game of green, The. White Goat, White Ram. W. S. Merwin. NePoEA
Gaily and greenly let my seasons run. Wishes of Youth. Samuel Laman Blanchard. ES
Gaily [*or* Gayly] bedight/ A gallant knight. Eldorado. Poe. AmPP; AnFE; APA; AWP; BAV; CoAnAm; CoBA; DDA; FaBoBe; FaBoCh; HBV; IAP; InPo; LaNeLa; LoGBV; MOAP; NePA; OTPC (1946 ed.); OxBA; PoeMoYo; PoMa; RIS; SPP; StaSt; TCAP; WaKn; YT
Gaily I lived, as ease and nature taught. An Epitaph. *Unknown.* ExPo
Gain without gladness. Liadain. *Unknown.* KiLC
Gaius was so very thin. Old Greek Nonsense Rhymes. Lucilius. BoN
Gal I Left Behind Me, The ("I struck the trail in seventy-nine"), *with music.* *Unknown.* ABF; CoSo; CSF
Gal I Left Behind Me, The ("If ever I travel"). *Unknown.* ABF
Galatea Again. Genevieve Taggard. WHA
Galatea to Pygmalion. Leonora Clawson Stryker. MuM
Galathea [*or* Gallathea], *sel.* John Lyly.
Song of Diana's Nymphs, A. OBSC
(Cupid's Indictment.) ElL
Gale, The. John Gould Fletcher. *Fr.* Sand and Spray; a Sea Symphony. PIAE
Gale. John Holloway. PoN
Gale day where the straight masts perform, A. The Wind Harbour. Norman Levine. PeCV
Gale from the north comes rushing apace, A. In the Storm. Peter Andreas Jensen. AnNoLy
Gale had passed, but chilling was the air, The. Circumstance without Pomp. John Kendall. WhC
Gale in April. Robinson Jeffers. AmPP; ChMo; CMP; MAP; MoAB; MoAmPo; NeMA
Gale of August, '27, The, *with music.* George Swinamer. ShS

Gale of Wind, A. John Mitford. *Fr.* The Adventures of Johnny Newcome in the Navy. SG
Gale that wrecked you on the sand, The. Northman. Emerson. APW
Gale Warning. Michael Roberts. AlDL
Galilean. Margielea Stonestreet. ChIP
Galileo. Albert Durrant Watson. CPG
Gall is the taste of life when we. Good Friday. Vincent Holme. ChIP
Gallant and gay in their doublets gray. The Swallows. Sir Edwin Arnold. DD; PoRL; WhBS
Gallant Château. Wallace Stevens. MAP; MoAB; MoAmPo
Gallant Fifty-one, The. Henry Lynden Flash. PAH
Gallant Fighting "Joe," The. James Stevenson. PAH
Gallant Fleet, The. John Hunter-Duvar. *Fr.* De Roberval. VA
Gallant foeman in the fight, A. Robert E. Lee. Julia Ward Howe. BIG; DD; GA; HiLiAm; MC; PAH; PoRL
Gallant good Timocritus lies here, The. A Soldier's Grave. Anacreon. GrR
Gallant gray-beard, can't you see. Old and Blind. Josiah Gilbert Holland. PoP
Gallant laird of Lamington, The. Katharine Jaffray. (B *vers.*). *Unknown.* ESPB
Gallant Seaman's Resolution, The. *Unknown.* SG
Gallant Seaman's Return from the Indies, The. *Unknown.* SG
Gallant Seaman's Song at His Meeting of Betty, The. *Unknown.* SG
Gallant Ship, The. Sir Walter Scott. BoTP
Gallant youth at Gravesend lived, a seaman neither rich nor poor, A. The Gallant Seaman's Resolution. *Unknown.* SG
Gallant Youth, who may have gained, The. Yarrow Revisited. Wordsworth. BPN; EM-2; EmBrPo; EnLi-2; EnRP; GEPC
Gallants attend and hear a friend. The Battle of the Kegs [*or* British Valor Displayed]. Francis Hopkinson. BAV; HiLiAm; IAP; OnAP; PaA; PAH; TCAP
Gallants strum their serenades, The. Mandolines. Paul Verlaine. TrFP
Gallathea. John Lyly. *See* Galathea.
Galleons in sea-pomp sails. An Armada of Thirty Whales. Daniel G. Hoffman. NePA
Gallery, The. Andrew Marvell. MeLP; OBS; ReEn; SeEP
Galley, The. Ibn Hariq, *tr. fr. Arabic by* A. J. Arberry. MooP
Galley, The. Sir Thomas Wyatt. *See* Lover Compareth His State to a Ship in Perilous Storm Tossed on the Sea, The.
Galley of Count Arnaldos, The. Longfellow. *See* Secret of the Sea, The.
Galley-Slave, The. Kipling. BEL
Galleys of Spain. *Unknown, tr. fr. Spanish by* Sir John Bowring. TeCS
Galliass, The. Walter de la Mare. FaBoTw
Gallop, Gallop to a Rhyme. Monica Shannon. SiSoSe
Galloping Randy Dandy O! *with music. Unknown.* SoAmSa
Gallows, The. Edward Thomas. BMEP; ChMP; GTBS-D; HaMV; LiTB; MBP; MoAB; MoBrPo; PoE; UnPo (3d ed.)
Gallows and Cross. J. E. H. MacDonald. CaP
Gallows' Brother's Song. Christian Morgenstern, *tr. fr. German by* R. F. C. Hull. AnGP
Gallows in my garden, The, people say. A Ballade of Suicide. G. K. Chesterton. ALV; BOHV; FiBHP; HBV; InMe; JKCP (1955 ed.)
Gallows Tree, The. F. R. Higgins. OnYI
Gallows Tree, The. *Unknown. See* Maid Freed from the Gallows, The.
Gallows tree is straight and tall, The. Changeling. Vincent Starrett. DaM
Galoshes. Rhoda W. Bacmeister. BrR; TiPo
Galway. Donagh MacDonagh. NeIP
Galway. Louis MacNeice. OxBI
Galway. Mary Davenport O'Neill. NeIP; OxBI
Galway Bay. George Barker. FaBoMo
Galway Races. *Unknown.* GTIV; OxBoLi
Galymaufery, A. William Turner. *See* Turners Dish of Lentten Stuffe.
Gamarra is a dainty steed. The Blood Horse. "Barry Cornwall." BCEP; GN; HBV; LPS-2; OTPC; VA
Gamble. Iraqi, *tr. fr. Persian by* A. J. Arberry. PeP
Gambler. G. A. Studdert-Kennedy. ChIP; MaRV
(He Was a Gambler Too.) QS
Gambler, The. *Unknown.* ABS; ViBoFo
Gamblers, The. Anthony Delius. BoSA
Gamblers, The. Vachel Lindsay. ChMo; CMP
Gambler's Blues (St. James Infirmary Blues), *with music. Unknown.* TrAS
(Those Gambler's Blues, A *and* B *vers., with music.*) AS
Gambler's Repentance, The. Gerald, Baron of Offaly. AnIV
Gamboling Man, The. *See* Roving Gambler, The.
Gambols of Children, The. George Darley. LPS-1
(Song: "Down the Dimpled Greensward Dancing.") OnYI
Game, The. Dannie Abse. PrWP
Game, The. Walker Gibson. NePoAm-2
Game, The. Conrado Nalé Roxlo, *tr. fr. Spanish by* Milton Ben Davis. AnCL; OnPM
Game, The. Winfield Townley Scott. AnAmPo
Game at Salzburg, A. Randall Jarrell. MiAP
Game of Chess, A. T. S. Eliot. *Fr.* The Waste Land. PreP
Game of Chess, The. David Skaats Foster. PR
Game of Consequences, A. Paul Dehn. FiBHP
Game of Cricket, The. Hilaire Belloc. FiBHP
Game of Dice, The. *Unknown, tr. fr. Danish by* E. M. Smith-Dampier. BoDaBa
Game of Glass, A. Alastair Reid. NePoEA
Game of Life, The. John Godfrey Saxe. BLPA; NeHB
Game of Tag, A. *Unknown.* PCH
(Playful Crickets, The.) RIS
Game Out of Hand. Allison Ross. GoYe
Gamesters All. DuBose Heyward. HBMV; InP; LS
Gammer Gurton's Needle, *sel. At. to* William Stevenson.
Back and Side Go Bare, Go Bare. BEL; EG; ElSeCe; EM-1; EnLi-1; InvP; LiTB; OAEP; PoRA; ReEn; RiBV; SiCE; TOP; TuPP; ViBoPo
(Good Ale.) LPS-3
(I Cannot Eat but Little Meat.) ExPo
(In Praise of Ale.) TrGrPo
(Jolly Good Ale [and Old].) EV-1; HBV; LEAP; OBEV; SeCeV; SiTL
(Of Jolly Good Ale and Old.) ElL
(Song of Ale, A.) AnFE; OBSC; UnPo (1st ed.)
Gandhi. Angela Morgan. BAP
Gane Were But the Winter-Cauld. Allan Cunningham. *See* Spring of the Year, The.
Gang of labourers on the piled wet timber, A. Morning Work. D. H. Lawrence. MoAB; MoBrPo (1950 ed.)
Gangan my lane amang the caulkstane alps. Ice-Flumes Owregie Their Lades. Douglas Young. SeCePo
Ganymede. Witter Bynner. AnFE; CoAnAm; TwAmPo
Ganymede. Johan Sebastian Cammermeyer Welhaven, *tr. fr. Norwegian by* Charles W. Stork. AnNoLy
Gaps of blue shrank fast in span, The. Coventry Patmore. *Fr.* Tamerton Church Tower. EnSW
Garadh. Padraic Colum. OnYI; PG (1955 ed.)
García Lorca. Louis Dudek. BoCaPo (1948 ed.)
García Lorca. In Memory of García Lorca. Eldon Grier. PeCV
Garçon! You—you. The Hero of the Commune. Margaret Junkin Preston. AA; OBAV
Garden, The. Al-Nashshar, *tr. fr. Arabic by* A. J. Arberry. MooP
Garden, The. Esther Antin. *Fr.* On Our Farm. RIS
Garden, The. Joseph Beaumont. OBS; OxBoCh; SeCL; SeEP
Garden, The. George M. Brady. NeIP
Garden, A. Thomas Edward Brown. *See* My Garden.
Garden, The. Roy Campbell. TriL
Garden, The, *sel.* Abraham Cowley.
Great Diocletian. ChTr
Garden, The. William Cowper. The Task, III. CEP; EiPP
Garden, The. Digby Mackworth Dolben. GoBC
Garden, The. Hilda Doolittle ("H. D."). AnFE; APA; AtBAP; CoAnAm; CoBA; LiTA; MAPA; NP; TwAmPo
Heat, *sel.* BAP; BLV; MAP; MoAmPo; NeMA; OxBA; PIAE; SBMV; TSW; UnPo; WHA
Garden, The. Caroline Giltinan. HBMV
Garden, The. Nicholas Grimald. PoLi; ReIE
Garden, The. Thomas S. Jones, Jr. Four Sonnets, III. SBMV
Garden, The. Gertrude Huntington McGiffert. VOD
Garden, The ("How vainly men themselves amaze"). Andrew Marvell. AEV: AnEnPo; AtBAP; ATP; AWP; BEL; BLV; BoLiVe; BrBE; CaAE; CoBE; CoEV; ElSeCe; EnL; EnLi-1; EPP; EPS; ExPo; FaBoEn; HBV; InPo; InvP; JAWP; LEAP; LiA; LiTB; LoBV; MaPo; MeLP; MePo; OAEP; OBS; OuHeWo; Po; PoE; PoEL-2; PoFS; PoRA; ReEn; RiBV; SeCePo; SeCeV; SeCL; SeCV-1; SeEP; TOP; TrGrPo; TwHP; TyEnPo; UnPo (1st ed.); ViBoPo; WBP; WHA; WP
(Thoughts in a Garden.) EV-2; GTBS; GTBS-D; GTBS-W; GTSE; GTSL; LiTG; OBEV; PIAE; SN
Sels.
"Fair Quiet, have I found thee here?"
(Thoughts in a Garden, 5 *sts.*) BCEP
"Here at the fountain's sliding foot," 1 *st.* YT
"What wondrous life is this I lead." CH, 4 *sts.*; ChTr, 3 *sts.*
(From "Thoughts in a Garden," 3 *sts.*) CBOV
Garden, A ("See how the flowers, as at parade"). Andrew Marvell. *Fr.* Upon Appleton House. CEP; EPS (1942 ed.); HBV; OBEV; ShGoBo
(Upon Appleton House.) TrGrPo
Garden, The. Edgar Lee Masters. NP
Garden, The. Belle F. Owens. ChIP

Garden, The. Rose Parkwood. WGRP
Garden, The. Ezra Pound. AWP; CoV; InPo; JAWP; LiTA; MoAB; MoAmPo (1950 ed.); NP; WBP
Garden, A. Sappho. *See* Garden of the Nymphs.
Garden, A. Shelley. *See* Sensitive Plant, The.
Garden, The. James Shirley. OBS
Garden, The. Marvin Solomon. NePoAm
Garden, The. Jones Very. AmP; OxBA
Garden, The. Oscar Wilde. *See* Le Jardin.
Garden and Cradle. Eugene Field. AA
Garden at St. John's, The. May Swenson. NePoEA
Garden at Sunset. Marj Kuhl, *tr. fr. Arabic by* A. J. Arberry. MooP
Garden beds I wandered by, The. A Conservative. Charlotte Perkins Gilman. AA; HBV; OBAV; PIAE
Garden bower in bower, A. God's Mother. Laurence Housman. ISi
Garden bright, A. Jessamine. Ibn al-Abbar. MooP
Garden by Moonlight, The. Amy Lowell. NP; PFY; TOP; YT
Garden by the Sea, A. William Morris. *See* I Know a Little Garden-Close.
Garden called Gethsemane, The. Gethsemane. Kipling. FaBoTw
Garden cannot move, The. Mortally. James Kirkup. NeBP
Garden Fairies. Philip Bourke Marston. VA
Garden Fancies. Robert Browning.
  I. The Flower's Name. EnLi-2 (1949 ed.); GEPC; GTBS-D; HBV; LPS-1; VLEP
  II. Sibrandus Schafnaburgensis. EnLi-2 (1949 ed.); VLEP
Garden flew round with the angel, The. The Pleasures of Merely Circulating. Wallace Stevens. LiTA; OnHM
Garden gives good food, and ayd for leaches cure, The. The Garden. Nicholas Grimald. PoLi
Garden in Liberty Square. Carlos Drummond de Andrade, *tr. fr. Portuguese by* Dudley Poore. AnCL
Garden Incident. George O'Neil. TCPD
Garden, A, is a lovesome thing, God wot! My Garden. Thomas Edward Brown. BMEP; DD; DDA; EnLit; GBV; GoTP; GTML; GTSL; HBV; HBVY; LEAP; MaRV; MBP; NeHB; NLK; OBEV; OBVV; OQP; OTPC (1946 ed.); PC; PIR; PoFS; POTT; PoVP; QP-1; TOP; TreF; VLEP; VOD; WBLP; WGRP; YT
Garden is a royal court, The. Jester Bee. Frank Dempster Sherman. UTS
Garden Is My Soul, A. Gerald Gould. TCPD
Garden is very quiet tonight, The. Dusk Song. William H. A. Moore. BANP
Garden lies spattered with the wet green moonlight, The. Green Apples. Louise Morey Bowman. CPG
Garden like a chalice-cup, A. Mary. Eleanor Downing. JKCP
Garden-Lion. "Evelyn Hayes." ChTr
Garden Lyric, A. Frederick Locker-Lampson. HBV
Garden Muse, The, *sel.* William Aspenwall Bradley.
  "To you who've lived your life elate."
  (Dedications.) MOAH
Garden now is sealed and dead, The. The Garden. Belle F. Owens. ChIP
Garden of Adonis, The. Spenser. *Fr.* The Faerie Queene, III, 6. NBE; PoEL-1
Garden of Amour, The. Guillaume de Lorris, *tr. fr. French by* Chaucer. *Fr.* The Romance of the Rose. PoEL-1
Garden of Boccaccio, The. Samuel Taylor Coleridge. BPN; EmBrPo; EPN
Garden of Eden, The. Genesis. II: 4–III: 24, Bible, *O.T.* EnLi-1; OuHeWo
Garden of Eden, The. Cædmon, *tr. fr. Anglo-Saxon by* Benjamin Thorpe. *Fr.* Genesis. TCEP
Garden of Eden, The. Milton. *Fr.* Paradise Lost, IV. EV-2
  (Satan Discovers Eden.) ExPo
  ("So on he fares, and to the border comes.") PreP
Garden of Epicurus, The. George Meredith. ATP (1953 ed.); EPN
Garden of God, The. "Æ." WGRP
Garden of Love, The. Blake. *Fr.* Songs of Experience. AWP; EM-1; EnLi-2 (1949 ed.); EnLoPo; EnRP; ExPo; InPo; JAWP; LEAP; LiTB; LiTG; LiTL; LO; LoBV; OAEP; PoE; PoFS; SeCeV; TOP; TyEnPo; ViBoPo; WBP
Garden of Proserpina, The. Spenser. *Fr.* The Faerie Queene, II, 7. ChTr
Garden of Proserpine, The. Swinburne. AnFE; AWP; BMEP; BoLiVe; CaAE; CoBE; CoEV; EmBrPo; EnL; EnLi-2; EnLit; EPP; ExPo; HBV; InP; InPo; LEAP; LiTB; LiTG; MBP; OuHeWo; PG (1945 ed.); PIAE; PIR; PoE; PoEL-5; PoFS; PoRA; PoVP; PreP; REAL; ReaPo; RiBV; SeCePo; SeCeV; TrGrPo; TVSH; TwCrTr; TwHP; ViBoPo; ViP; ViPo; ViPP
  Sels.
  Proserpine. ChTr
  ("Pale, beyond porch and portal.") FaBoEn
  Swan Song. OtMeF
Garden of Regrets, The. Andrew Lang. BoN
Garden of Shadow, The. Ernest Dowson. BrBE; FaBoEn; HBV
Garden of Shushan! Before the Feast of Shushan. Anne Spencer. BANP
Garden of the Golden Valley, The. Tu Mu, *tr. fr. Chinese by* Witter Bynner. ChLP
  (Garden of the Gold Valley, The.) WhP
Garden of the Holy Souls, The. Harriet Eleanor Hamilton King. *Fr.* Hours of the Passion. ACP; JKCP (1926 ed.)
Garden of the Nymphs. Sappho, *tr. fr. Greek by* T. F. Higham. GrL
  (Garden, A.) OxBG
Garden Party, The. Hilaire Belloc. MoVE
Garden Party, The. Donald Davie. NePoEA
Garden Party. Mary Mills. NePoAm
Garden Path, The. Charlotte Druitt Cole. GFA
Garden Path, A. May Justus. PCH
Garden Prayer, A. Thomas Walsh. OQP; QP-2
Garden rose I paid no honour to, The. Jean Moréas. *Fr.* Stances. MiFP
Garden saw I, full of blosmy bowes, A. A Dream Garden. Chaucer. *Fr.* The Parlement of Foules. CBOV
Garden Seat, The. Thomas Hardy. TriL
Garden-Song. James Branch Cabell. HBMV
Garden Song, A. Austin Dobson. GTSE; HBV; LEAP; LoBV; OBEV; OBVV; POTT; TOP; VLEP
Garden Song. Arthur Guiterman. MoSiPe
Garden Song: "I wonder where I may gather some sweet pretty flowers." *Unknown, ad. fr. Maya Indian.* PCH
Garden That I Love, The. Florence L. Henderson. HBV
Garden under Lightning. Leonora Speyer. PFY
Garden Visitor. Betsey Mann Collins. DDA
Garden was pleasant with old-fashioned flowers, The. The Lavender Beds. William Brighty Rands. CBPC
Garden Where There Is No Winter, The. Louis James Block. AA
Garden within was shaded, The. Thisbe. Helen Gray Cone. AA; PR
Garden Year, The. Sara Coleridge. FaBoBe; HBV; HBVY; MPB; PCH; PPL; RAR; StVeCh; TSW
  (Calendar, A.) GoTP
  ("January brings the snow.") TiPo
  (Months, The.) CBPC; DD; MeMeAg; OTPC; RIS; StaSt
Gardener, The. Evelyn Eaton. GoYe
Gardener. Emerson. *Fr.* Quatrains. APW; OxBA
Gardener, The. Laurence Housman. TrPWD
Gardener, The. Sidney Keyes. ChMP; MoAB
Gardener, The. Louis MacNeice. *Fr.* Novelettes. AlDL
Gardener, The. Lucy Fitch Perkins. PCH
Gardener, The. Robert Louis Stevenson. HBV; HBVY; MPB; OTPC; TreFS
Gardener, The, *sels.* Rabindranath Tagore.
  In the Dusky Path of a Dream, LXII. OBMV
  "Over the green and yellow rice fields," LXXXIV. AlDL
  (From "The Gardener.") NP
  Yellow Bird Sings, The, XVII. OBMV
Gardener, The. *Unknown.* BaBo, *sl. abr.*; ESPB, *sl. abr.*; OBB
Gardener, A. *Unknown, tr. fr. Greek by* R. A. Furness. OxBG
Gardener and the Hog, The. John Gay. BeR
Gardener does not love to talk, The. The Gardener. Robert Louis Stevenson. HBV; HBVY; MPB; OTPC; TreFS
Gardener has pretty blooms, The. Stanzas for the Harp. *Unknown.* PrWP
Gardener Janus Catches a Naiad. Edith Sitwell. MBP; MoAB; MoBrPo
Gardener of Eden and Gethsemane. Unearth. Alfred Barrett. GoBC
Gardener standing by, The. *Unknown.* LO
Gardener stands in his bower-door, The. The Gardener. *Unknown.* BaBo; ESPB; OBB
Gardener to the Magdalene, A. Diversity. Everard V. Thompson. BePJ
Gardener's Cat, The. Patrick R. Chalmers. CIV; HBMV; HBVY; VOD
Gardener's Daughter, The, *sel.* Tennyson.
  "Lightly he laugh'd, as one that read my thoughts." EnSW
Gardener's Song, The. "Lewis Carroll." *Fr.* Sylvie and Bruno. HBV; OTPC
  (He Thought He Saw.) GBV (1952 ed.), 7 *sts.*; HBVY, 6 *sts.*
  (He Thought He Saw a Banker's Clerk.) LBN; NA, 5 *sts.*
  ("He thought he saw an elephant," 5 *sts.*) EnLi-2
  (Mad Gardener's Song, The, 9 *sts.*) BoN; FiBHP, 7 *sts.*; PoRh; SiTL; TreFS, 6 *sts.*
  (Metamorphoses, 7 *sts.*) MBP
  (Some Hallucinations, 7 *sts.*) BOHV
  (Strange Wild Song, A, 7 *sts.*) StVeCh
Gardeners were at work setting their beds, The. The Youth in the Landscape. Hugo von Hofmannsthal. AnGP

Gardening. John Keble. OTPC
Gardens. Jorge Guillén, *tr. fr. Spanish by* Eleanor L. Turnbull. CoSP
Gardens. *Unknown.* OQP; QP-1
Gardens Are All My Heart. Eve Triem. GoYe
Gardens delightful to her, you must fade. Horti, Deliciae Dominae, Marcescite Tandem. George Herbert. LaP
Gardens of the Sea, The. George Sterling. EtS
Garden's Queen, The. John Reynolds. *See* Nosegay.
Garden's quit with me. The: as yesterday. The Garden. Joseph Beaumont. OBS; OxBoCh; SeCL; SeEP
Gardin was, by mesuring, The. The Garden of Amour. Guillaume de Lorris, *tr. by* Chaucer. *Fr.* The Romance of the Rose. PoEL-1
Gard'ner of peculiar taste, A. The Gardener and the Hog. John Gay. BeR
Gareth and Lynette. Tennyson. *Fr.* Idylls of the King. HeT
Follow the Christ, 4 *ll.* MaRV
("Man am I grown, a man's work must I do.") ChIP
Garfield's Ride at Chickamauga. Hezekiah Butterworth. BlG; GA, *abr.*; PAH
Gargantua. Hervey Allen. BAP; MAP; PFY; PoeMoYo
Gargantua. Hugh Wilgus Ramsaur. MuM
Gargantuan ranges of blue-dappled hills. Gargantua. Hervey Allen. BAP; MAP; PFY; PoeMoYo
Gargoyle in the Snow, The. Kathleen Millay. PoMa
Gargoyles at Oxford. Margaret Willy. DiM
Garibaldi Hymn, The. Luigi Mercantini, *tr. fr. Italian.* WBLP
Garland, The. Euripides. *See* Votary to His Goddess, A.
Garland, The. Matthew Prior. SeCL
Garland, The. Henry Vaughan. AnEnPo; MeRV
Garland and the Girdle, The. Michelangelo, *tr. fr. Italian by* John Addington Symonds. AWP
Garland fades on Heliodora's brow, The. Heliodora's Garland. Meleager, *tr. by* Robert Guthrie MacGregor. OnPM
Garland for a Storyteller. Jessie Farnham. GoYe
Garland for Heliodora, A. Meleager, *tr. fr. Greek by* "Christopher North." AWP; EnLi-1; JAWP; OuHeWo; WBP
(Wreath for Heliodora.) OnPM
Garland of Recital Programs, A. Franklin P. Adams. InMe
Garland of the Blessed Virgin Marie, The. "B. I." *See* Ghyrlond of the Blessed Virgin Marie, The. Ben Jonson.
Garland Sunday. Padraic Colum. GoYe
Garlande of Laurell, The, *sels.* John Skelton.
House of Fame, The. NBE
"O noble Chaucer whos pullisshyd eloquence." PtP
To Mistress Gertrude Statham. OAEP
To Mistress [*or* Maystres] Isabel[l] Pennell. AtBAP; KN; LiTG; LiTL; LO; OAEP; OBEV (new ed.); OBSC; OxBoLi; PoEL-1; PoFS; SeCeV; TrGrPo; TuPP; ViBoPo
("By Saint Mary, my lady.") EG
(In Praise of Isabel Pennell.) CH
To Mistress Margaret Hussey. ACP; AnFE; AtBAP; CoEV; EnLoPo; EV-1; GN; GoBC; HBV; HoPM; InPo; KN; LiTL; LoBV; LPS-1; OAEP; OBEV; OBSC; OTPC (1923 ed.); PG (1955 ed.); PoEL-1; PoRA; ReEn; SeCeV; SiCE; ThWaDe; TrGrPo; TuPP; ViBoPo
(Merry Margaret.) GoTP; RIS
(Mistress Margaret Hussey.) FaBoCh; LoGBV
(To Mistress Margery Wentworth, *wr. title.*) LEAP
To Mistress Margery Wentworth. CoEV; EnLoPo; EV-1; LoBV; OBEV; OBSC; TrGrPo; ViBoPo
("With margerain gentle.") EG
To My Lady Mirriel Howard. LoBV
Garlands fade that Spring so lately wove, The. Sonnet Written at the Close of Spring [*or* Elegiac Sonnet]. Charlotte Smith. FaBoEn; OBEC
Garlands upon his grave. Charles Sumner. Longfellow. GA; PEOR
Garlic and sapphires in the mud. T. S. Eliot. *Fr.* Four Quartets: Burnt Norton. GTBS-W
Garment. Langston Hughes. GoSl
Garment of Good Ladies, The. Robert Henryson. ACP, *mod. and abr.*
(Garmont of Gude Ladies, The.) EBSV; GoTS
Garment of Mortality, The. Shih Ling Yü, *tr. fr. Chinese by* Henry H. Hart. PoHN
Garnyvillo. Edward Lysaght. IrPN
Garret, The. Pierre Jean de Béranger, *tr. fr. French by* Thackeray. HBV
Garret, The. Ezra Pound. BAP; MOAP; NP
Garrison. Amos Bronson Alcott. AA; GA; OBAV; PoFr
Garrison ("The storm and peril"). Whittier. GA
Garrison of Cape Ann, The. Whittier. IAP
Garrison Town. Emanuel Litvinoff. WaP
Garrisons pent up in a little fort. Sonnet of Brotherhood. R. A. K. Mason. AnNZ
Garryowen. *Unknown.* OnYI
Gas flaring on the yellow platform; voices running up and down. The Night-Ride. Kenneth Slessor. NeLNL
Gas was on in the Institute, The. A Shropshire Lad. John Betjeman. ShBV-4
Gascoigne's Arraignment. George Gascoigne. *See* Arraignment of a Lover, The.
Gascoigne's De Profundis. George Gascoigne. TuPP
Gascoigne's Good Morrow. George Gascoigne. SiCE; TriL; TuPP
Gascoigne's Good-Night. George Gascoigne. ReEn; ReIE; SiCE
Gascoigne's Lullaby [*or* Lullabie]. George Gascoigne. *See* Lullaby of a Lover, The.
Gaspar Becerra. Longfellow. AnNE
Gaspara Stampa. William Rose Benét. HBMV
Gastronomic Guile of Simple Simon, The. Guy Wetmore Carryl. GoTP; YT
Gate, The. Edwin Muir. LiTM (rev. ed.)
Gate at the End of Things, The. *Unknown.* BLPA
Gate of the Armies, The. Henri de Regnier, *tr. fr. French by* James Elroy Flecker. MiFP
Gate of the Year, The, *sel.* M. Louise Haskins.
"And I said to the man who stood at the gate of the yea ." MaRV; TreFS
Gate was thrown open, I rode out alone, The. How Salvator Won. Ella Wheeler Wilcox. PTA-2
Gates. Sister Mary Madeleva. GoBC
Gates and Doors. Joyce Kilmer. ChrBoLe; CV; GBV (1952 ed.); HBV; HBVY; QS; SDH
Gates are open on the road, The. The Seekers. Charles Hamilton Sorley. WGRP
Gates clanged and they walked you into jail, The. The Conscientious Objector. Karl Shapiro. AmPP (4th ed.); OxBA
Gates of Damascus. James Elroy Flecker. AnFE; GTML; HBMV; LBBV; POTT
Gates of Dreamland, The. "Æ." *See* Carrowmore.
Gates of Paradise, The, *sels.* Blake.
"I rent the veil where the Dead dwell." PoD
In Weary Night. LiA
To the Accuser Who Is the God of This World. TrGrPo; UnPo; ViBoPo
(Epilogue: "Truly, my Satan, thou art but a Dunce.") FaBoEn
(Epilogue to the Accuser . . .) NBE
Gates to England, The. Marjorie Wilson. BoTP
Gates were triple adamant, The. For Emily Dickinson. Hortense Landauer. PIAE
Gathas, *sel. At. to* Zoroaster, *tr. fr. Persian. Fr.* The Avesta.
Zoroaster Devoutly Questions Ormazd, *tr. by* A. V. Williams Jackson. WGRP
(O Great Creator, *tr. by* L. H. Mills.) GrCo-1
(Sacred Book, The, *tr. by* A. V. Williams Jackson.) AWP
Gather all kindreds of this boundless realm. The Poet. Cornelius Mathews. AA
Gather all the sweet of May. Song for Youth. Dana Burnett. MPB
Gather for festival. Hilda Doolittle ("H. D."). *Fr.* Songs from Cyprus. MAP; MoAmPo; TwCV
Gather Kittens while you may. Song. Oliver Herford. PA
Gather the garlands rare to-day. Memorial Day. Cy Warman. DD; HH
Gather the people, for the battle breaks. The Coming of War, 1889. Lionel Johnson. SoV
Gather the Rose. Spenser. *See* Bower of Bliss, The.
Gather the stars if you wish it so. Stars, Songs, Faces. Carl Sandburg. ChMo; CMP
Gather up the ribbons, give the 'orn a toot! The Phantom Mail Coach. L. O. Welcome. BoHiPo; PoMS
Gather Us In. George Matheson. OQP; QP-1
"Gather Ye Rosebuds." Mimnermus, *tr. fr. Greek by* F. L. Lucas. GrPE
"Gather Ye Rosebuds." Strato, *tr. fr. Greek by* F. L. Lucas. GrPE
Gather Ye Rose-Buds While Ye May. Robert Herrick. *See* To the Virgins, to Make Much of Time.
Gather Ye Roses. Johannes Secundus, *tr. fr. Latin by* F. A. Wright. Elegies, I, 5. LaP
Gather ye soap-suds while ye may. Counsel to Girls. Archibald Stodart-Walker. *Fr.* The Moxford Book of English Verse. CenHV
Gathering, The. Herbert B. Swett. PAH
Gathering Bamboo. Ku Jo P'u, *tr. fr. Chinese by* Henry H. Hart. PoHN
Gathering Dolichos. *Unknown, tr. fr. Chinese.* WhP
Gathering of the Fairies, The. Joseph Rodman Drake. *Fr.* The Culprit Fay. BAP
(" 'Tis the middle watch of a summer's night," *longer sel.*) BAV
Gathering on the Plains, The. William T. Butler. PoOW
Gathering Song of Donald the Black [*or* Donald Dhu *or* Donuil Dhu]. Sir Walter Scott. *See* Pibroch of Donuil Dhu.

Gathering, tall. a wave in a vicious sea. Heart's Desire. John Peter. BoSA
Gathering the echoes of forgotten wisdom. Odes, III. George Santayana. AnAmPo; AnFE; APA; CoAnAm; LA; TwAmPo
Gathering War Clouds. Aeschylus, *tr. fr. Greek by* Gilbert Murray. *Fr.* Seven against Thebes. GrR
(News of War, *tr. by* E. R. Bevan.) OxBG
Gatineau Point. S. Frances Harrison. *Fr.* Down the River. CPG
Gatineaus, The. James Wreford Watson. CaP
Gaudeamus Igitur. *Unknown, tr. fr. Latin by* John Addington Symonds. *Fr.* Carmina Burana. HBV; LaP; WoL
Gaudeamus Igitur. Margaret L. Woods. PoeT
Gauger walked with willing foot, The. A Song of the Road. Robert Louis Stevenson. OTPC (1946 ed.); POTT; PoVP; YT
Gauguin. Marion Ethel Hamilton. MuM
Gauley Bridge is a good town for Negroes, they let us stand around. George Robinson: Blues. Muriel Rukeyser. FiMAP
Gauls Sacrifice Their Prisoners, The. C. M. Doughty. *Fr.* The Dawn in Britain. FaBoTw
Gaunt and relentless wolf, possessed, A. The Inhuman Wolf and the Lamb sans Gene. Guy Wetmore Carryl. ALV
Gaunt-built woman and her son-in-law, A. Polonius and the Ballad-Singers. Padraic Colum. NP
Gaunt in the midst of the prairie. Chicago. John Boyle O'Reilly. PAH
Gaunt, rueful knight, on raw-boned, shambling hack. Don Quixote. Craven Langstroth Betts. AA
Gautama. Thomas S. Jones, Jr. AnAmPo; LA
Gautatyr sent forth Gondul and Skogul. The Lay of Hakon. Eyvindr Finsson. PaOS
Gave My Life for Thee. Frances Ridley Havergal. VA
Gay, The. "Æ." OBMV; POTE
Gay and audacious crime glints in his eyes. In the Vices. Donald Evans. HBMV; NP
Gay belles of fashion may boast of excelling, The. The Needle. Samuel Woodworth. APW; GN; HBV
Gay citizen, myself, and thoughtful friend. Allen Tate. More Sonnets at Christmas, IV. LiTA; NePA
Gay Crimson Leaves. Elizabeth Pickett. CAG
Gay day flames, The. The grass is still. Poppies. Innokenti Annensky. BoRS
Gay Feast. Pushkin, *tr. fr. Russian by* Babette Deutsch. OnPM; TrRV
Gay go up and gay go down. The Bells of London [*or* London Bells]. *Unknown.* BoTP; BrR; ChTr; HBV; HBVY; LiTB; LiTG; OTPC; OxBoLi; OxNR; PCH; PoRA; PPL; SiTL; WP
Gay Goshawk [*or* Goss-Hawk], The. *Unknown.* BaBo; EBSV; EnLit; ESPB (A *and* E *vers.*); EV-2, *abr.;* GN; HBV; OBB; RG; TOP
Gay, guiltless pair. The Winged Worshippers. Charles Sprague. AA; HBV; LPS-2; SN
Gay Jemmie, the Miller, *with music. Unknown.* SoAF
Gay jolly cowboy is up with the sun. Up the Trail. *Unknown.* CoSo
Gay little Dandelion. Little Dandelion. Helen Barron Bostwick. DD; HBV; HBVY; OTPC (1923 ed.); PRWS
Gay little Girl-of-the-Diving-Tank. At the Carnival. Anne Spencer. BANP; CDC; PoNe
Gay Old Hag, The. *Unknown.* IrPN
Gay on the wold at eventide. The Stolen Bride. *Unknown.* BoDaBa
Gay Provence. George Francis Savage-Armstrong. TIP
Gay Robin Is Seen No More. Robert Bridges. BoTP
Gay sea-plants familiar were to her, The. Sea-nurtured. Jean Ingelow. EtS
Gay Summertime. Jun Yamamura, *tr. fr. Japanese by* Takamichi Ninomiya *and* D. J. Enright. PoLJ
Gay the little plover flew. The Golden Plover. Jónas Hallgrímsson. IcP
Gay Wag, The. Berton Braley. AlBD
Gay went the dance in King Valdemar's hall. Valdemar and Tove. *Unknown.* BoDaBa (B *vers.*); PaOS
Gay went the dance in the kirkyard there. The Knavish Merman. *Unknown.* BoDaBa
Gayetez. Pierre de Ronsard, *tr. fr. French by* Curtis Hidden Page. PrPoCR
Gayly bedight, a gallant knight. Poe. *See* Gaily bedight.
Gaze not at me, my poor unhappy bird. Ode to Mother Carey's Chicken. Theodore Watts-Dunton. VA
Gaze not on swans, in whose soft breast. Beauty Extoll'd [*or* On His Mistress]. *Unknown, at. to* Henry Noel *and to* William Strode. ChTr; CoEV; LO; OBS; PoEL-2
Gaze not on thy beauties pride. Good Counsell to a Young Maid. Thomas Carew. OBS
Gaze on me, thou eye of darkness. Entreaty. Nikolaus Lenau. AnGP
Gazelle. Ibn al-Qabila, *tr. fr. Arabic by* A. J. Arberry. MooP
Gazelle, A. Richard Henry Stoddard. AA
Gazelles. Heine, *tr. fr. German by* Sir Theodore Martin. LiA
Gazelles, The. T. Sturge Moore. OBMV; PtOT
Gazelles and Unicorn. John Gray. *Fr.* The Long Road. ChTr
Gazelles come bounding from the brake. Gazelles. Heine. LiA
Gazeteer of Newfoundland. Michael Harrington. CaP
Gazing after Her Husband. Lu Yu, *tr. fr. Chinese by* Pai Chwen-yu. WhP
Gazing at the Moon while Journeying Homewards. Otomo Yakamochi, *tr. fr. Japanese by* Ishii *and* Obata. OnPM
Gazing upon the distant land of France. Ballade Written during Captivity in England. Charles d'Orléans. LyMA; TrFP
Gean trees drive me to love, The. The Name Like a River. W. S. Graham. FaBoTw
Gebir, *sels.* Walter Savage Landor.
"But Gebir when he heard of her approach," *fr.* I. OBRV
Charoba at Her Bath. RO
"I sing the fates of Gebir," I. BPN
"Long awaited day at last approached, The," *fr.* VII. OBRV
Masar, *fr.* V. LoBV
("Once a fair city, courted then by kings," *shorter sel.*) OBRV
Nymph, The, *fr.* I. RO
(Tamar and the Nymph.) VA
(Tamar's Wrestling.) EnRP
("'Twas evening, though not sunset, and the tide.") NBE
Sea-Nymph's Parting, The. FaBoEn
Shells, The, *fr.* I. BCEP
Gee Ho, Dobin. *Unknown.* CoMu
Gee I Like to Think of Dead. E. E. Cummings. HoPM
Gee-up Dar, Mules. Edwin Ford Piper. YaD
Gee up, Neddy, to the fair. *Unknown.* OxNR
Geese. Oliver Herford. *Fr.* Child's Natural History. HBV; LEAP
(Some Geese.) FiBHP; NA
Geese drive northward, The. The Fox Sparrow. W. W. Christman. BLA
Geese Flying over England. Kathleen Sutton. MuM
Geese, geese,/ Very white geese. Goosegirl's Song. *Unknown, tr. fr. Czech.* PCH
Geese in Autumn. *Unknown, tr. fr. Japanese by* Basil Hall Chamberlain. OnPM
Geese in lofty flight recross, The. The Spring. Chang Chung-sur. OnPM
Geese in the Running Water. Raymond Holden. MAP; MoAmPo (1942 ed.)
Geese, soaring arrow-sharp through thickening fog. Geese Flying over England. Kathleen Sutton. MuM
Gehazi. Kipling. OtMeF
Geist's Grave. Matthew Arnold. HBV; PoVP; VA
Gellatley's Song to the Deerhounds. Sir Walter Scott. *See* Hie Away.
Gem and the Flower, The. Pope. *Fr.* Moral Essays, Epistle I. OBEC
Gem of all isthmuses and isles that lie. Sirmio. Catullus. AWP; JAWP; WBP
Gem of the crimson-colour'd even. To the Evening Star. Thomas Campbell. GTBS; GTBS-D; GTBS-W; GTSE; GTSL
Gemini and Virgo. Charles Stuart Calverley. WhC
"And, if you asked of him to say," *sel.* FiBHP
Gemlike Flame, The. R. P. Lister. FiBHP
Genau'r Glyn, Tywyn, each day from these to Rhys's halls. Ode to Rhys ap Maredudd of Tywyn. Dafydd Nanmor. PrWP
Genealogical Reflection. Ogden Nash. ALV
Genealogy. Sister Mary Francis. SaFP
General, A. Archilochus. *See* Ideal General, The.
General, The. Siegfried Sassoon. FiBHP; MoVE; OxBoLi
(Leaders, New Style.) OtMeF
General Albert Sidney Johnston. Mary Jervey. GA
General Armstrong, The. *Unknown.* PAH
General Communion, A. Alice Meynell. JKCP
General Dabney H. Maury. Rosewell Page. BlG
General dashed along the road, The. The General's Death. Joseph O'Connor. AA
General Description. George Crabbe. *Fr.* The Borough, Letter I. TCEP
General Galliéni. Robert Hillyer. PG (1955 ed.)
General Howe's Letter. *Unknown.* PAH
General John. W. S. Gilbert. GoTP; NA
General Joseph Warren's Address. John Pierpont. *See* Warren's Address.
General Mist of Error, A. John Webster. *See* Hark, Now Everything Is Still.
General Paresis. Louis J. Karnosh. PoP
General Prologue, The. Chaucer. *See* Canterbury Tales, The: Prologue.

General Quiroga Rides to Death in a Carriage. Jorge Luis Borges, *tr. fr. Spanish by* H. R. Hays. TwSpPo
General silence fell; and all gave ear, A. The Fall of Troy. Virgil. The Aeneid, II. RoL
General Store. Rachel Field. BoChLi; GaP; GoBP; MPB (1956 ed.); StVeCh (1955 ed.); SUS
General Summary, A. Kipling. HBV
General William Booth Enters into Heaven. Vachel Lindsay. AmPP; ATP; BAP; BAV; CBOV; ChMo; CMP; CoBA; DDA; FaBoMo; HBV; IAP; InPo; LEAP; LiTA; LiTM; MAP; MaRV; MM; MoAB; MoAmPo; MOAP; MoP; MoPo; NP; OBAV; OnAP; OxBA; PoeMoYo; PYM; ReMP; SBMV; SeCeV; TCPD; TOP; TreFS; TrGrPo; TwCV; WGRP
General's Death, The. Joseph O'Connor. AA
Generation of Intention. Donald F. Drummond. PtPa
Generations, The. George M. Brady. OnYI
Generations as they rise, The. A Charge to Youth. "Æ." GrCo-2
Generations of the virgin are tattooed on her unblemished belly, The. Poem of Any Virgin. Jorge de Lima. AnCL
Generosity. Al-Liss, *tr. fr. Arabic by* A. J. Arberry. MooP
Generosity. Virginia Brasier. StVeCh (1955 ed.)
Generosity. Steingrímur Thorsteinsson, *tr. fr. Icelandic by* Vilhjalmur Stefansson. *Fr.* Epigrams. IcP
Generosity. *Unknown, tr. fr. Irish by* Frank O'Connor. KiLC
Generous and jealous, soft and hard of heart. Martial, *tr. fr. Latin by* Richard A. Bell. Epigrams, XII, 47. LaP
Generous Creed, A. Elizabeth Stuart Phelps Ward. WGRP
Generous man will not deny, The. An Elegy on the Late King of Patagonia. St. John Emile Clavering Hankin. CenHV
Genesis, *sels.* Bible, *O.T.*
Abraham and Isaac, XXII: 1–13. EnLi-1 (1949 ed.); OuHeWo
"And when Joseph came home," XLIII: 26–31. LO
Creation, The. TreF (I: 1–II: 3); WoL (I: 1–III: 24)
(Creator, The, I: 1–31.) GrCo-1
("In the beginning God created the heaven and the earth," I: 1–31.) ImOP
Garden of Eden, The, II: 4–III: 24. EnLi-1; OuHeWo
"I will put enmities," III: 15, *Douay vers.* ISi
Joseph and His Brethren, XXXVII: 3–36, XXXIX: 1–XLVI: 30. OuHeWo
Noah and the Flood, VI: 5–VIII: 22. OuHeWo
"Thus the heavens and the earth were finished," II: 1–III: 13. LO
Wrestling with God, XXXII: 22–30. GrCo-1
Genesis. Ronald Bottrall. CoEV
Genesis, *sel.* Charles Brasch.
Discovery, The. AnNZ
Genesis, *sels.* Cædmon(?), *tr. fr. Anglo-Saxon.*
Approach of Pharaoh, The, *tr. by* C. W. Kennedy. ACP; WaaP
(Coming of Pharaoh, The.) CAW
Beginning of Creation, The, *tr. by* F. B. Gummere. BCEP
Fall of Angels and of Man, *mod. vers.* PoLi
Fall of Satan, The, *tr. by* Benjamin Thorpe. TCEP
(Fall of the Angels, The, *tr. by* C. W. Kennedy.) EPP
(Satan's Presumption and Fall, *tr. by* Henry Morley.) BCEP
Far and Wide She Went. EtS
Garden of Eden, The, *tr. by* Benjamin Thorpe. TCEP
Noah's Flood, *tr. by* C. W. Kennedy. AnOE; BEL
Temptation and Fall of Man, The, *tr. by* C. W. Kennedy. AnOE
Genesis. Geoffrey Hill. NePoEA; PoLFOT; PoN
Genesis. John Hall Ingham. AA
Genesis. Ray Mathew. NeLNL
Genesis. Arthur Wallace Peach. LPS-1
Genesis, *sel.* Delmore Schwartz.
You Are a Jew! TrJP
Genesis. A. M Sullivan. JKCP (1955 ed.)
Genesis. Swinburne. ViP
Genesis. Jules Alan Wein. TrJP
Genesis of Butterflies, The. Victor Hugo, *tr. fr. French by* Andrew Lang. AWP; JAWP; WBP
Genesis of Vowels. James Broughton. CrMA
Genevieve. Samuel Taylor Coleridge. *See* Love.
Genius. R. J. P. Hewison. FaFP; SiTL
Genius. Richard Henry Horne. VA
Genius. Gertrude MacGregor Moffat. CPG
Genius. Edward Lucas White. AA; WGRP
Genius in Beauty. Dante Gabriel Rossetti. The House of Life, XVIII. BPN; EmBrPo; EnLit; InP; OAEP; POTT; PoVP; TOP; ViP; ViPo; VLEP
Genius Loci Margaret L. Woods ES; HBV; OBEV; OBVV
Genius of ancient Greece! whose faithful steps. Invocation to the Genius of Greece. Mark Akenside. *Fr.* The Pleasures of Imagination, I. OBEC
Genius of Death, The. George Croly. HBV; LPS-3
Genius of Greece, The. Walter Savage Landor. EmBrPo
Genius, that power which dazzles mortal eyes. Success. C. C. Cameron. PoToHe (new ed.)
Gen'ral, The! one of those brave old commanders. The Old General. Sir Charles Hanbury Williams. *Fr.* Isabella. OBEC
Genseric. "Owen Meredith." CBPC; MeRV
Genteel in personage. A Maiden's Ideal of a Husband. Henry Carey. *Fr.* The Contrivances. HBV; LPS-1
Gentian. Elizabeth Green Crane. AA
Gentian sleeps in waters, The. Symphony in Blue. Raymond F. Roseliep. ISi
Gentian weaves her fringes, The. Emily Dickinson. MaPo; PoRA
Gentilesse. Chaucer. AWP; MaPo
Gentle Air, thou breath of lovers. A Sigh. Countess of Winchilsea. CEP
Gentle Alice Brown. W. S. Gilbert. BHP; BOHV; FiBHP; InMe; MBP; NA; OnSP; PIAE
Gentle and generous, brave-hearted, kind. The Comfort of the Trees. Richard Watson Gilder. PAH
Gentle and grave, in simple dress. Wordsworth. Francis Turner Palgrave. PtP; VA
Gentle Beasts, The. *Unknown, tr. fr. Slovakian by* Leclaire Alger. ChrBoLe
Gentle breeze with a whispered cry, The. Rimas, IX. Gustavo Adolfo Bécquer. TeCS
Gentle Check, The. Joseph Beaumont. SeCL
Gentle, cheerful ticking of a clock, The. Quiet Days. Mildred T. Mey. PoToHe (new ed.)
Gentle Cock, The. *Unknown. See* I Have a Gentil Cok.
Gentle Craft, The, *sels.* Thomas Deloney.
Song: "Primrose in the green forest, The." AlDL; TiPo (1959 ed.); ViBoPo
Would God That It Were Holiday! ElL
Gentle dove the icicle is now, A. Winter 1939–1940. Laurie Lee. PoN
Gentle East wind is blowing, A. On the Siu Cheng Road. Su T'ung-po. OnPC
Gentle Echo on Woman, A. Swift. ALV; BOHV; FiBHP; LiTG; LiTL; OnYI; SiTL
Gentle Fatherland. Ramón López Velarde, *tr. fr. Spanish by* H. R. Hays. TwSpPo
Gentle Herdsman, Tell to Me. *Unknown.* EV-2
Gentle Jesus [Meek and Mild]. Charles Wesley. BOL; MaRV; MeMeAg; OTPC; OxBoCh; TreFS
Gentle Knight was pricking on the plaine, A. Una and the Red Cross Knight [*or* The Red Cross Knight]. Spenser *Fr.* The Faerie Queene, I. ATP; BoLiVe; CoBE; EPP; ExPo; GoBC; LPS-3; PIAE; TyEnPo
Gentle Mary, noble maiden, give us help! Prayer to the Virgin. *Unknown.* OnYI
Gentle milk jug blue and white, The. The Milk Jug. Oliver Herford. HBMV; HBVY; PCH; RAR; TSW; TSWC; UTS
"Gentle, modest little flower." To Phoebe. W. S. Gilbert. BOHV; InMe; InP; PFE
Gentle Name. Selma Robinson. MoShBr; MoSiPe
Gentle Nymphs, Be Not Refusing. William Browne. *Fr.* Britannia's Pastorals, I. ElL; ViBoPo
Gentle Park, A. Moss Herbert. GoYe
Gentle Reminders, *abr.* Goethe, *tr. fr. German by* F. Melian Stawell *and* Nora Purtscher-Wydenbruck. PoFr
Gentle Richard. Shakespeare. King Richard II, *fr.* V, ii. LiA
Gentle River, Gentle River. *Unknown, tr. fr. Spanish by* Thomas Percy. AWP; JAWP; LiTW; WBP
Gentle shepheard satte beside a springe, The. December. Spenser. *Fr.* The Shepheardes Calender. BrBE
Gentle Shepherd, The, *sels.* Allan Ramsay.
Dainty Sang, A. OBEC
(For the Love of Jean.) EBSV
My Peggy. BSV; CoBE; GN, *abr.;* HBV; OTPC (1923 ed.), *abr.*
(Peggy.) EV-3; OBEV; ViBoPo
(Sang: "My Peggy is a young thing.") CEP; LoBV; OBEC
(Waukin' o' the Fauld, The.) EBSV
"Gentle Sleep, if you will take him." The North Wind and the Child. *Unknown.* PCH
Gentle Snorer, The. Mona Van Duyn. NePA
Gentle, soft-voiced herringdove, The. The Herringdove. Kenyon Cox. RIS
Gentle squire would gladly entertain [*or* intertain], A. The Trencher Chaplain [*or* Satire]. Joseph Hall. *Fr.* Virgidemiarum. EV-2; ReIE; SiCE; TuPP; ViBoPo
Gentle Storm. Martha Banning Thomas. PoMa
Gentle Swallow, thou we know. To the Swallow. *Unknown.* GrL; OxBG
Gentle thought there is will often start, A. La Vita Nuova, XXVI. Dante. AWP; JAWP; OuHeWo; WBP
Gentle Touch, A. *Unknown, at. to* Lao-tzu. *tr. fr. Chinese by* Witter Bynner. *Fr.* Tao Teh King. OnPM
Gentle Wind, A. Fu Hsüan, *tr. fr. Chinese by* Arthur Waley. AWP; TrCh

Gentle Word, A. *Unknown.* PoToHe (new ed.)
Gentlefolks, in my time, I've made many a rhyme. Sir Sidney Smith. Thomas Dibdin. CG
Gentleman, The. Menahem ben Judah Lonzano, *tr. fr. Hebrew by* A. B. Rhine. TrJP
Gentleman cam oure the sea, A. The Cruel Brother (B *vers.*). *Unknown.* ESPB
Gentleman of City fame, A. A Discontented Sugar Broker. W. S. Gilbert. PCD
Gentleman of Fifty Soliloquizes, A. Don Marquis. HBMV; LEAP
Gentleman of the Old School, A. Austin Dobson. BPN; EnLit; HBV; POTT
Gentleman who lives next door, The. My Neighbor. Seigniora Laune. DDA
Gentleman young and carefully reared, A. The Young Philosopher and His Friends. Félix María de Samaniego. AnSpL-2
Gentlemen and ladies, I pray you lend an ear. Colonel Sharp. *Unknown.* BaBo
Gentlemen of the High Command. Ogden Nash. *Fr.* Heil, Heilige Nacht! MaRV
Gentlemen of the jury, 'tis not birth. Herodas, *tr. fr. Greek by* Hugo Sharpley. GrPo
Gentlemen Topers. Anacreon, *tr. fr. Greek by* J. M. Edmonds. GrR
Gentlemen who boss the age. Ballade in a Bad Temper. Louis MacNeice. PoFr
Gentleness of rain was in the wind, The. Fragment: Rain. Shelley. ChER
Gentlest Lady, The. Dorothy Parker. ISi
Gentlewoman Forsweareth Hereafter to Be Won with Flattering Promises, A. George Whetstone. *See* Give Me My Work.
Gentlie, gently prethee tyme. *Unknown.* SeCSL
Gently a little breeze begins to creep. Arques—Afternoon. Arthur Symons. PoVP
Gently Death came to him and bent to him asleep. Close Up the Ranks. Edward S. Van Zile. PEDC
Gently dip, but not too deep. The Song at the Well [*or* The Voice from the Well *or* Celanta at the Well of Life]. George Peele. *Fr.* The Old Wives' Tale. ChTr; ExPo; FaBoEn; LoBV; SeCeV; ThWaDe
Gently dream, my darling child. Song of the Indian Mother. James Gowdy Clark. BOL
Gently!—gently!—down!—down! Chorus of Spirits. George Darley. *Fr.* Sylvia; or, The May Queen. OnYI; VA
Gently He Draweth. *Unknown.* BePJ
Gently I stir a white feather fan. In the Mountains on a Summer Day. Li Po. AWP; TrCh
Gently I wave the visible world away. The Absinthe-Drinker. Arthur Symons. FaBoTw
Gently illumined by the April sun. In a Sunny Nook. Hans Vilhelm Kaalund. BoDS
Gently, Lord, O gently lead us. Thomas Hastings. AA; HBV; OIF
Gently o gently without fright. *Unknown.* SeCSL
Gently with delicate mindless fingers. The Old Man's Dream after He Died. Robinson Jeffers. *Fr.* Cawdor. CoV
Geographers. Sebastian Brant, *tr. fr. German by* Alexander Barclay. *Fr.* The Ship of Fools. ACP
Geographers, The. Karl Shapiro. OxBA
Geography. G. K. Chesterton. *Fr.* Songs of Education. HBMV
Geography. Eleanor Farjeon. BrR; FaPON
Geography of This Time. Archibald MacLeish. CoV; PG (1945 ed.); PoLFOT
Geologist's Epitaph, A. Jane W. Stedman. WhC
Geometry. Alfred Kreymborg. AnAmPo; LA
Geordie. *Unknown.* BaBo (A, B, *and* C *vers.*); ESPB (A *and* D *vers.*)
George. Hilaire Belloc. FiBHP; YT
(George Who Played with a Dangerous Toy . . .) GoTP
George Aloe and the *Sweepstake,* The. *Unknown.* BaBo; ESPB; ViBoFo
(*George-Aloe,* The.) OBB
(Sailor's Onely Delight, The.) SG
George and Martha Washington/ Are smiling in our hall. Picture People. Rowena Bennett. MPB (1956 ed.); YeAr
George and the Chimney-Sweeper. Adelaide O'Keeffe. OTPC (1923 ed.)
George Britton, *with music.* *Unknown.* CoSo
George Crabbe. E. A. Robinson. AmPP (4th ed.); CoBA; CoBMV; LiTA; LiTM (rev. ed.); MAP; MoAB; MoAmPo; MoVE; NAMP; NePA; OxBA; PoEL-5; PtP
George Gray. Edgar Lee Masters. *Fr.* Spoon River Anthology. TOP
George Herbert. Thomas S. Jones, Jr. PtP
George, it is thy genius innated. To George Chapman. Thomas Freeman. SiCE
George Levison. William Allingham. IrPN
George lives in an apartment. Radiator Lions. Dorothy Aldis. GoBP; MPB: UTS
George loved the cause of freedom, but reproved. George Crabbe. *Fr.* Tales of the Hall. PoFr
George Meredith. Thomas Hardy. EmBrPo; EPN
George Moses Horton, Myself. George Moses Horton. NoCaPo
George Robinson; Blues. Muriel Rukeyser. FiMAP
George Sand. Dorothy Parker. FiBHP
George the First was always reckoned. The Georges. Walter Savage Landor. ChTr; FiBHP
George the Fourth in Ireland. Byron. OBRV
George III. E. C. Bentley. OxBoLi
("George the Third.") FiBHP
George the Third. Byron. *Fr.* The Vision of Judgment. FiP
George Turbervile in Praise of the Translator of This Book. George Turberville. ReIE
George Washington. Rosemary Benét *and* Stephen Vincent Benét. FaPON; MaC
George Washington ("Only a baby, fair"). *At. to* Eliza Cook. GA: MPB; OHIP; PEDC; PEOR
George Washington. John Hall Ingham. AA; HH; OHIP; PAH; WOAH
George Washington ("Soldier and statesman, rarest union"). James Russell Lowell. *See* Washington ("Soldier and statesman . . .").
George Washington. Francesca Falk Miller. PEDC
George Washington. James S. Tippett. YeAr
George Washington ("By broad Potomac's silent shore"). *Unknown.* LPS-3
George Washington ("In seventeen hundred thirty-two"). *Unknown, at. to* M. Alice Bryant. HH
George Whalen. *Unknown.* *See* Whalen's Fate.
George Who Played with a Dangerous Toy, and Suffered a Catastrophe of Considerable Dimensions. Hilaire Belloc. *See* George.
Georges, The. Walter Savage Landor. ChTr; FiBHP
Georgey Porgey [*or* Georgie Porgie], pudding and pie. Mother Goose. BoChLi; OxNR; RIS; SiTL
Georgia. Robert Loveman. PoRL
Georgia Boy, *with music.* *Unknown.* OuSiCo
Georgia Dusk. Jean Toomer. AnAmPo; CDC; LA; MAP; PoNe
Georgia Land, *with music.* *Unknown.* OuSiCo
Georgia Volunteer, A. Mary Ashley Townsend. AA; BIG; MDAH
Georgia Waters. Thomas Holley Chivers. SPP
(Song: "On thy waters thy sweet valley waters.") MOAP
Georgiad, The, *sel.* Roy Campbell.
"Hail, Mediocrity, beneath whose spell." MoBrPo
Georgian Dublin. Maurice James Craig. PoN
Georgics, *sels.* Virgil, *tr. fr. Latin.*
After the Rain, *fr.* I, *tr. by* Dryden. BeR
Honey-Farm, The, *abr., fr.* IV, *tr. by* Dryden. WoL
"My heart's desire is that the Muses fair," *fr.* II, *tr. by* Zechariah Chafee, Jr. LaP
Prelude: "What makes a plenteous harvest," *tr. by* Dryden. AWP
Sex among Lions, *br. sel. fr.* III, *tr. by* Dryden. BeR
Snake, The, *fr.* III, *tr. by* Dryden. LiA
Stateliest Measure, The, *fr.* III, *tr. by* H. R. Fairclough. LiA
"Until Jove let it be, no colonist," I, *tr. by* Robert Fitzgerald. LaP
(Georgic I.) LiTW
We Have Paid Enough Long Since in Our Own Blood, *tr. by* Richmond Lattimore. WaaP
"What makes the cornfields happy, under what constellation," I, *tr. by* C. Day Lewis. RoL
Georgie Porgie. Franklin P. Adams. HBMV
Georgie Porgie, pudding and pie. Mother Goose. *See* Georgey Porgey . . .
Géorgiques Chrétiennes, *sel.* Francis Jammes, *tr. fr. French by* George N. Shuster.
"This day, O Father, give us daily bread." CAW
Geraint and Enid. Tennyson. *See* Idylls of the King.
Gerald kissed me when he left. Another Cynical Variation. "Helen." InMe
Geraldines, The, *sel.* Thomas Osborne Davis.
"Geraldines, The! the Geraldines!—'tis full a thousand years." IrPN
Geraldine's Daughter, The. Egan O'Rahilly, *tr. fr. Modern Irish by* James Clarence Mangan. AnIL; OnYI
"Beauty all stainless, a pearl of a maiden, A," *sel.* IrPN
Geraldine's Garden. John Francis O'Donnell. IrPN
Geraldines, The! the Geraldines!—'tis full a thousand years. Thomas Osborne Davis. *Fr.* The Geraldines. IrPN
Geraniums. W. W. Gibson. AEV; POTT; TCPD
Germ, The. Ogden Nash. CenHV; MoShBr
German Fatherland, The. Ernst Moritz Arndt, *tr. fr. German.* HBV
German Prisoners. Joseph Johnston Lee. BLP; MaRV

German singers! sing and praise. The Tendency. Heine. PoFr
German Slumber Song. Karl Simrock. *See* Go to Sleep.
Germand Gladensvend. *Unknown, tr. fr. Danish by* E. M. Smith-Dampier. BoDaBa
Germans live in Germany, The. Home [*or* The English]. J. H. Goring. MoShBr; SiTL
Germinal. "Æ." MoBrPo; OBEV (new ed.); OBMV; TwCV
Geron and Histor. Sir Philip Sidney. *Fr.* Arcadia. SiPS
Geron, whose moldy memory corrects. In Gerontem. Sir John Davies. ReIE
Geronimo. Ernest McGaffey. AA; PAH
Gerontion. T. S. Eliot. AmPP; AnAmPo; AnFE; APA; BrBE; ChMo; ChMP; CMP; CoAnAm; CoBA; CoBMV; CoEV; ExPo; FaBoEn; GTBS-W; LA; LiTA; LiTM; LoBV; MAP; MAPA; MaPo; MoAmPo (1942 ed.); MOAP; MoPo; NAMP; NePA; OAEP (2d ed.); OxBA; PoE; PoFS; POTE; ReMP; RiBV; SeCePo; SeCeV; TwAmPo
Gerry's Rocks. *Unknown. See* Jam on Gerry's Rock, The.
Gert Swasey. Winfield Townley Scott. FiMAP
Gertrude's Prayer. Kipling. FaBoEn
Gest Hystoriale of the Destruction of Troy, *sel. Unknown.* Medea. NBE
Gest of Robyn Hode, A. *Unknown.* ESPB
(Little Geste of Robin Hood and His Meiny, A.) OBB
Robin Hood's End, Fytte VIII. GoTL
Gesture. Winifred Welles. BAP; HBMV; MaRV
Gesture in space, A. The Triolet. Michael Lewis. PIAE
Gesture of a gift is adequate, The. If You Have Nothing. Jessica Powers. JKCP (1955 ed.)
Gesture the gesture the gesture the gesture, The. Michael McClure. Hymn to St. Geryon, I. NeAP
Get a Transfer. *Unknown.* BLPA; WBLP
"Get down, get down, loving Henry," she said. Loving Henry. *Unknown.* BaBo
Get Hence Foule Griefe. Sir Philip Sidney. *Fr.* Arcadia. AtBAP; PoEL-1
(Contentment.) SiPS
Get into the Boosting Business. *Unknown.* WBLP
Get ivy and hull, woman, deck up thine house. Christmas. Thomas Tusser. AnEC
Get on board, little chillun. The Gospel Train. *Unknown.* TrAS
Get ready your money and come to me. *Unknown.* OxNR
Get Somebody Else. *At. to* Paul Laurence Dunbar. BLRP; MaRV
(Too Busy.) WBLP
Get thee a ship well rigged and tight. In Praise of Fidelia. Mildmay Fane, Earl of Westmorland. ElSeCe; SeCL
Get thee behind me. Even as, heavy-curled. The House of Life, XC: "Retro Me, Sathana!" Dante Gabriel Rossetti. BPN; EmBrPo; PoVP; ViPo
Get There If You Can and See the Land You Once Were Proud to Own. W. H. Auden. NAMP
Get Up. Nikolai Rylenkov, *tr. fr. Russian by* Babette Deutsch. TrRV
Get Up and Bar the Door. *Unknown.* ATP; BaBo; BEL; BLV; BoChLi; BoLiVe; BSV; EBSV; EnL; EnLi-1; EnLit; EnSB; ESPB (A *and* B *vers.*); GoTP; GoTS; MaC; OBB; StPo; TiPo (1952 ed.); TrGrPo; TyEnPo; ViBoPo
Get up at once, now, Margaret May! Eggs for Breakfast. Irene F. Pawsey. BoTP
Get Up, Get Up. *Unknown.* FiBHP
Get up, get up for shame, the blooming morn. Corinna's Going a-Maying. Robert Herrick. AlDL; AtBAP; ATP; BCEP; BEL; BoLiVe; CBOV; CoBE; DD; ElSeCe; EM-1; EnL; EnLi-1; EnLit; EPP; EPS; EV-2; ExPo; GN; GTSL; HBV; LEAP; LH; LiA; MaPo; OAEP; OBEV; OBS; OTPC (1923 ed.); OuHeWo; Po; PoEL-3; PoFS; PoRL; PreP; ReaPo; ReEn; RiBV; SeCeV; SeCV-1; SeEP; TCEP; TOP; TrGrPo; TyEnPo; UnPo (1st ed.); WHA
Get up, get up, you lazy-head. Get Up, Get Up. *Unknown.* FiBHP
Get Up, Jack! John, Sit Down! *Unknown.* ABF
Get up, little boy, you are sleeping too long. Sleepy Harry. *Unknown.* OTPC (1923 ed.)
Get up, little sister, the morning is bright. Early Rising. Lady Flora Hastings. OTPC (1923 ed.)
"Get up, our Anna dear, from the weary spinning-wheel." The Fairy Thorn. Sir Samuel Ferguson. AnIV; CBOV; CH; GTIV; OnYI; PoVP; TIP; VA
Get you a lass that's young and tight. Bachelor's Maid. John Gay. *Fr.* Work for a Cooper. BeR
Gethsemane. M. Betham-Edwards. BePJ
Gethsemane. Arna Bontemps. CDC
Gethsemane. Annette von Droste-Hülshoff, *tr. fr. German by* George N. Shuster. CAW
Gethsemane. Kipling. FaBoTw
Gethsemane. Edmund Leamy. JKCP; OQP; PSO; QP-1
Gethsemane. *Unknown, tr. fr. Japanese by* Lois J. Erickson. SoLD
Gethsemane. Charles Russell Wakeley. OQP; QP-1
Gethsemane. Ella Wheeler Wilcox. MaRV; OQP; PSO; QP-1
Gethsemane, Illinois. Martin S. Allwood, *tr. fr. Swedish by* Martin S. Allwood. LiTW
Gethsemane Now. Bobb Hamilton. MeRV
Gethsemane's Gift. Katherine Brégy. MaRV; StJW
Gettin' Born. Anthony Euwer. WhC
Getting Back. Dorothy Brown Thompson. SiSoSe
Getting Gray. William Green Brownson. PoP
Getting Information Out of Pa. *Unknown.* FAOV
Getting Out of Bed. Eleanor Farjeon. SiSoSe
Getting Ready for Town. Robert P. Tristram Coffin. DDA
Getting Through. Robert P. Tristram Coffin. AnNE
Getting Up. Lilian McCrea. BoTP
Getting Up Early on a Spring Morning. Po Chü-i, *tr. fr. Chinese by* Arthur Waley. TrCh
Gettown fro their you. Sona Dialect. David Evans. MoWP
Gettysburg. James Jeffrey Roche. BlG; MC; PaA; PAH
Gettysburg. Edmund Clarence Stedman. PAH
Gettysburg Ode, The, *sel.* Bayard Taylor.
Lincoln at Gettysburg. BlG; PAH
("After the eyes that looked.") LBAH; OHIP
Ghaisties. Robert Garioch. NeBP
Ghastly, ghoulish, grinning skull. To a Skull. Joshua Henry Jones. BANP
Ghazal of Isa Akhun Zada. *Unknown, tr. fr. Pushtu by* E. Powys Mathers. PG (1945 ed.)
Ghazel on the Letter Kiaf. Jalal ed-Din Rumi, *tr. fr. Persian.* BoFr
Ghetto, The, *sels.* Lola Ridge.
"Lights go out." LEAP; MAP; MoAmPo (1942 ed.); TCPD
"Old Sodos no longer makes saddles." MAP; MoAmPo (1942 ed.)
"Sallow dawn is in the sky, A." MAP; MoAmPo (1942 ed.); TCPD
Ghetto Cradle-Song, A. Philip M. Raskin. BOL
Ghetto Song. Jacob Glatstein, *tr. fr. Yiddish by* Sarah Zweig Betsky. OnCuPl
Ghost, The. Baudelaire, *tr. fr. French by* Alan Conder. TrFP
Ghost. Witter Bynner. AnFE; CoAnAm; TwAmPo
Ghost, The. Walter de la Mare. CaAE; ChMo; ChMP; CoEV; DaM; EnLoPo; HaMV; HBMV; MBP; MoAB; MoBrPo; MoP; MoVE; OAEP (2d ed.); POTE; POTT
Ghost, The. Hermann Hagedorn. UnW
Ghost, The. Thomas Hood. DaM
Ghost. Alexa Lane. MuM; UnW
Ghost, The. Robert Lowell, *after the Latin of* Sextus Propertius. AtBAP; MoVE; POTE (1959 ed.)
Ghost. Agnes Miegel, *tr. fr. German by* Herman Salinger. TwGV
Ghost. Joseph Corson Miller. UnW
Ghost, The. Cú Chonnacht O Cléirigh, *tr. fr. Irish by* James Stephens. GTIV
Ghost, The. Stevie Smith. DiM
Ghost. John V. A. Weaver. BAP; HBMV
Ghost-/ Bird of the Louis'. White Peacock. Brenham McKay. BLA
Ghost-Flowers. Mary Potter Thacher Higginson. AA
Ghost-grey the fall of night. A Robin. Walter de la Mare. ChMo; ChTr; CMP
Ghost in the Cellarage, The. John Heath-Stubbs. NeBP
Ghost is someone, A: death has left a hole. The Ghost. Robert Lowell. AtBAP; MoVE; POTE (1959 ed.)
Ghost Kings, The. Robert Ervin Howard. DaM
Ghost Lake's a dark lake, a deep lake and cold. The Skater of Ghost Lake. William Rose Benét. TBM
Ghost Night. Lizette Woodworth Reese. HBMV; HOAH
Ghost of a little white kitten, The. The Little Cat Angel. Leontine Stanfield. BLPA; CIV
Ghost, The, of a sergeant growls—"Fall In." Back Home Again. Grantland Rice. BoHiPo
Ghost of Dareius [*or* Darius], The. Aeschylus, *tr. fr. Greek. Fr.* Persians. GrR, *tr. by* Lewis Campbell; LiA, *tr. by* Herbert Weir Smyth
Ghost of Ninon would be sorry now, The. Veteran Sirens. E. A. Robinson. AnAmPo; AnNE; BLV; BoLiVe; LA; OnHM; TwP
Ghost of Patroclus, The. Homer, *tr. fr. Greek by* William Cowper. *Fr.* The Iliad, XXIII. OxBG
(Shade of Patroclus, The, *shorter sel., tr. by* the Earl of Derby.) LiA
Ghost of the Beautiful Past. Wilfrid Scawen Blunt. VLEP
Ghost of the Buffaloes, The. Vachel Lindsay. *See* Ghosts of the Buffaloes, The.
Ghost of the Past, The. Thomas Hardy. BrBE
Ghost Pet. Horatio Colony. GoYe
Ghost shall come gloating in its grief, The. The Soul to the Body. *Unknown.* PoLi
Ghost That Jim Saw, The. Bret Harte. PoMS

Ghost, that loved a lady fair, A. The Phantom-Wooer [*or* The Phantom-Lover]. Thomas Lovell Beddoes. DaM; EnRP; LO; NBE; OBRV; TrGrPo; ViBoPo
Ghost-Wolf Dances. Lew Sarett. Thunderdrums, IV. TCPD
Ghost-Yard of the Goldenrod, The. Bliss Carman. TwCaPo
Ghostesses. *Unknown.* ChTr
Ghostly Battles. Glenn Ward Dresbach. TBM
Ghostly Crew, The, *2 vers., with music. Unknown.* ShS
Ghostly Galley, The. Jessie B. Rittenhouse. TBM
Ghostly Reaper. Harold Vinal. TBM; UnW
Ghostly through the drifting mist the lingering snow-wreaths glimmer. Angus Armstrong. W. W. Gibson. *Fr.* Casualties. VOD
Ghostly rogue and vagabond, A. The Mendicant. Enid Dinnis. SaFP
Ghostly Tree. Léonie Adams. MAP; MoAB; MoAmPo; MOAP
Ghostries. Henry Cholmondeley-Pennell. CIV
Ghosts. J. R. Ackerley. POTE
Ghosts. Robert Bridges. FaBoTw
Ghosts. Brian Hooker. PFY; UnW
Ghosts, The. Longfellow. *Fr.* The Song of Hiawatha, XIX. DaM; HOAH; LoBV
Ghosts. Ethna MacCarthy. NeIP
Ghosts. R. K. Munkittrick. AA; YT
Ghosts. Henri Charles Read, *tr. fr. French by* Alan Conder. LO
Ghosts. Marguerite Wilkinson. CP
Ghosts. Margaret L. Woods. UnW
Ghost's Complaint, The. *Unknown.* BoHiPo
Ghost's Confession, The. "Lewis Carroll." *Fr.* Phantasmagoria, IV. HOAH
Ghosts' Moonshine, The. Thomas Lovell Beddoes. DaM; LO; NBE
Ghosts of flowers went sailing, The. Changelings. Mary Potter Thacher Higginson. AA
Ghosts of Indians. Witter Bynner. OBAV; PoeMoYo; PoTo; VOD
Ghosts of the Buffaloes, The. Vachel Lindsay. AnAmPo; AnEnPo; LA; MAP; MoAmPo; NePA; PreP; RG; TCPD
(Ghost of the Buffaloes, The.) CoBA
Ghosts of the early earth! Hopi Ghosts. William Haskell Simpson. *Fr.* In Arizona. NP
Ghost's Petition, The. Christina Rossetti. DaM
Ghost's Promenade, The. Thomas Caulfield Irwin. IrPN
Ghost's Song, The. *Unknown. See* Cauld Lad of Hilton, The.
Ghosts there must be with me in this old house. Solitude. Walter de la Mare. ChMo; FaBoEn
Ghoul Care. Ralph Hodgson. AnEnPo; MoBrPo
Ghyrlond of the Blessed Virgin Marie, The. Ben Jonson. ISi; MeRV
(Garland of the Blessed Virgin Marie, The. "B. I.") SeCL
Giacobbe Finelli so funny, O! My! Da Comica Man. T. A. Daly. StaSt
Giant, The. Esaias Tegnér, *tr. fr. Swedish by* Charles W. Stork. AnSL
Giant came to me when I was young, A. The Lost Genius. John James Piatt. AA; OBAV
Giant flagons in a row—flashing in the sun. Filling Station. E. Merrill Root. PoMa
Giant Puffball, The. Edmund Blunden. FaBoTw; LBBV
Giantess. Baudelaire, *tr. fr. French.* MiFP, *tr. by* Karl Shapiro; OnPM, *tr. by* Arthur Symons
Giant's Cake, A. Evelina San Garde. BoTP
Giant's Tomb in Georgian Bay. "Katherine Hale." CaP
Giant's Wooing, The. Theocritus. *See* Polyphemus to Galatea.
Giaour, The, *sels.* Byron.
Greece. LPS-2
("Clime of the unforgotten brave!") PoFr
Picture of Death, A. LPS-1
Transient Beauty. LPS-1
Giardino Pubblico. Sir Osbert Sitwell. ChMP
Gibberish. Mary Elizabeth Coleridge. MoVE; PoeT
Gibbet Dance. Arthur Rimbaud, *tr. fr. French by* Alan Conder. TrFP
Gibbs, *sel.* Muriel Rukeyser.
"It was much later in his life he rose." ImOP
Gibraltar. Wilfrid Scawen Blunt. ACP; ES; GTML; GTSL; HBV; OBEV; OBVV; OTPC (1923 ed.); SoV; VA
Gibraltar. Richard Chenevix Trench. ES; OBRV; OBVV
Gideon at the Well. Geoffrey Hill. NePoEA
"Gie corn to my horse, mither." The Mother's Malison; or, Clyde's Water (B *vers.*). *Unknown.* ESPB
Gi'e me a lass with a lump of land. Give Me a Lass. Allan Ramsay. CEP; CoBE
Gie the Lass Her Fairin'. Burns. CoMu
Giffen's Debt. Kipling. ViP
Gift, The. Abu Aiyub, *tr. fr. Arabic by* A. J. Arberry. MooP
Gift, The. Abul Arab, *tr. fr. Arabic by* A. J. Arberry. MooP
Gift, The. "Æ." ChMo; CMP; HBMV; LEAP; LoPo; LoPS; TCPD
Gift, The. Elizabeth Barrett Browning. *See* Sonnets from the Portuguese: "What can I give thee back."
Gift, The. Margaret E. Bruner. PoToHe
Gift, The. Aline Kilmer. CP; NV
Gift, The. Louis V. Ledoux. SBMV
Gift, The. George Newell Lovejoy. *See* Mother, The.
Gift, A. Amy Lowell. BAP; ChMo; CMP; LEAP; NP
Gift, The. Rose O'Neill. BAP
Gift, The. Laura Spencer Portor. PEDC; StJW
Gift, The. Rabindranath Tagore. MOAH
Gift, The. *Unknown, tr. fr. German.* SAS
Gift, The. William Carlos Williams. NePoAm-2
Gift-Card Enclosed. Theocritus. *See* Lines Written to Accompany the Gift of a Distaff.
Gift from the cold and silent Past! The Norsemen. Whittier. PAH
Gift haphazard, unavailing. May 26, 1828. Pushkin. BoR
Gift most precious to Creative Thought, The. Freedom of the Will: Beatrice to Dante. Dante. *Fr.* Divina Commedia. GrCo-1
Gift of a Mirror to a Lady. David Wagoner. NePoAm-2
Gift of a Skull, The. John Skelton. *See* Upon a Dead Man's Head.
Gift of Flowers, A. Leonard Feeney. WHL
Gift of God, The. E. A. Robinson. AnAmPo; CoBMV; CP; MAP; MAPA; MoAB; MoAmPo; OxBA; TCPD; TwAmPo
Gift of Judah the Woman-Hater, The, *sel.* Judah ibn Sabbatai.
Expensive Wife, The. TrJP
Gift of Poets, The. Alice Hunt Bartlett. BAP
Gift of Song, The. Horace. *See* This Is Thy Gift, O Muse.
Gift of Speech, The. Sadi, *tr. fr. Persian by* L. Cranmer-Byng. *Fr.* The Gulistan. AWP; LiTW
Gift of the living God to mortal man. Peace Universal [*or* Dawn of the Century]. Anna H. Thorne. PEDC; PEOR; PoRL
Gift of the Muses. Hesiod, *tr. fr. Greek by* Arthur S. Way. *See* Muses' Gift, The.
Gift of Tritemius, The. Whittier. TVSH
Gift of Water, The. Hamlin Garland. AA; AnAmPo; LA
Gift of Work, The. Edwin Markham. DD
Gift Outright, The. Robert Frost. AmP; AmPP (4th ed.); CoBMV; CrMA; FaBoEn; InPo; LiTM; LoGBV; MaPo; MoAB; MoAmPo (1950 ed.); NeTW; OxBA; WaKn; WaP
Gift to a Jade. Anna Wickham. NP
Gift to Be Simple, The. Howard Moss. ImOP
Gifts. Helen Wieand Cole. ChIP; OQP; QP-1
Gifts. Mary Elizabeth Coleridge. PoVP
Gifts. Mary Edgar Comstock. OQP; QP-2
Gifts. Emerson. APW
Gifts. Juliana Horatia Ewing. AV
Gifts. Viola Gerard Garvin. AlDL
Gifts. Huang Pien, *tr. fr. Chinese by* Henry H. Hart. PoHN
Gifts. Emma Lazarus. TrJP; WGRP
Gifts. Muna Lee. BAP
Gifts. Sister Mary of the Visitation. WHL
Gifts. Chauncey R. Piety. PGD
Gifts, The. Odell Shepard. ChrBoLe
Gifts. James Thomson. *See* Give a Man a Horse He Can Ride.
Gifts for the New Year. Ruby E. Weyburn. PSO
Gifts of God, The. George Herbert. *See* Pulley, The.
Gifts of God, The. Jones Very. AA
Gifts of heav'n my foll'wing song pursues, The. The Honey-Farm. Virgil, *tr. by* Dryden. *Fr.* Georgics. WoL
Gifts of one who loved me. Gifts. Emerson. APW
Gifts of Poverty, The. Aristophanes, *pr. tr. fr. Greek by* Henry Fielding *and* William Young. *Fr.* The Plutus. OxBG
Gifts Returned [*or* Return'd] The. Walter Savage Landor. BOHV; OBVV
Gifts that to our breasts we fold, The. Recompense. Nixon Waterman. HBV
Gifts without Season. Joseph Auslander. MaRV
Gigha. W. S. Graham. FaBoMo; NeBP
Gil Brenton. *Unknown.* BaBo; ESPB
Gil Morice. *Unknown. See* Childe Maurice.
Gil, the Toreador. Charles Henry Webb. AA
Gila Monster Route, The. L. F. Post *and* Glenn Norton. ABF; APW; OnAP; SCC
Gilboa. Victor Starbuck. *Fr.* Saul, King of Israel. MuM
Gilderoy was a bonnie boy. My Handsome Gilderoy. *Unknown.* AtBAP; CH
Gile Machree. Gerald Griffin. TIP
Gilead. Mary Brennan Clapp. OQP; QP-2
Giles Collin he said to his mother one day. Lady Alice (C *vers.*). *Unknown.* ESPB
Giles Collins he said to his old mother. Lady Alice (B *vers.*). *Unknown.* ESPB
Giles Corey. *Unknown.* PAH

Giles Corey of the Salem Farms, *sels.* Longfellow.
  Prologue: "Delusions of the days that once have been." PAH
  Trial, The. PAH
Giles Corey was a wizard strong. Giles Corey. *Unknown.* PAH
Giles's Hope. Samuel Taylor Coleridge. BOHV
  (Epigram: " 'What? rise again with all one's bones.' ") HBV
Gilgamesh, *abr. Tr. fr. Babylonian tablets by* William Ellery Leonard. WoL
  Gilgamesh Laments the Death of Engidu, *sel., tr. by* Hermann Ranke *and* William Ellery Leonard. LiTW
Gill Morice stood in stable-door. Childe Maurice. *Unknown.* ESPB (D *vers.*); ViBoFo
Gillespie. Sir Henry Newbolt. ShBV-1; TCPD
Gillian, *parody. Unknown.* BOHV; PA
Gilliflower. Ibn al-Abbar, *tr. fr. Arabic by* A. J. Arberry. MooP
Gilliflower [*or* Gillyflower] of Gold, The. William Morris. AnFE; BPN; CBOV; EmBrPo; MBP; POTT; PoVP; ReaPo; TCEP; TOP; TVSH; VA; ViPo; VLEP; WHA
Gilly of Christ, The. Joseph Campbell. *See* I Am the Gilly of Christ.
Gilly Silly Jarter. *Unknown.* OxNR
Gillyflower, before you fade. To My Gillyflower. Henrik Wergeland. AnNoLy
Gillyflower of Gold, The. William Morris. *See* Gilliflower of Gold, The.
Gil's history appears to me. An Epigram, on the Reverend Mr. Laurence Echard's, and Bishop Gilbert Burnet's Histories. Matthew Green. PoE
Gimli. Miriam Waddington. BoCaPo (1948 ed.)
Gimme Dat Ol'-Time Religion, *with music. Unknown.* BoAN-1
Gimme de Banjo, *with music. Unknown.* ShS
"Gimme my scarlet tie." Bangkolidye. Barry Pain. BOHV
Gimme Yo' Han', *with music. Unknown.* BoAN-2
Gin a body meet a body. Comin' thro' the Rye. Burns. FaFP; LiTB; LiTG; LiTL; OlF; TreF. *See also* Comin' through the rye, poor body.
Gin a body meet a body. Comin' through the Rye. *Unknown.* LPS-1; WBLP
Gin a body meet a body. Rigid Body Sings [*or* In Memory of Edward Wilson]. James Clerk Maxwell. BOHV; PA; WhC
Gin by Pailfuls. Sir Walter Scott. ChTr
Gin ye but kent the wecht o dule in prief. Tuscan Folk Songs, 9. *Unknown, tr. into Scottish by* Edwin Morgan. LyPI
Gineral B. is a sensible man. *See* Guvener B. is a sensible man.
Gineral C. is a dreffle smart man. What Mr. Robinson Thinks. James Russell Lowell. *Fr.* The Biglow Papers. APW; BAP
Ginevra. Samuel Rogers. *Fr.* Italy. BeLS; EV-3; LPS-3
Ginevra, *sel.* Shelley.
  "She is still she is cold." ChER
Gingerbread Man, The. Eva Rowland. GFA
Gingham dog and the calico cat, The. The Duel. Eugene Field. BeLS; BoChLi; BTP; CenHV; FaBoBe; FaFP; FaPON; GFA; GoBP; HBV; HBVY; MoShBr; NeHB; OHFP; OnHT; OnSP; OTPC (1946 ed.); PECK; PoRA; RAR; StVeCh; TiPo; TreF; UTS; YT
Gingilee. Moishe-Leib Halpern, *tr. fr. Yiddish by* Joseph Leftwich. TrJP
Gingo Biloba. Goethe, *tr. fr. German by* Edward Dowden. *Fr.* West-Eastern Divan. BoFr
Gioconda. Thomas McGreevy. OnYI
Giorno dei Morti. D. H. Lawrence. MeRV; POTE; SeCePo; ShBV-4; TriL
Giostra, La, *sel.* Angelo Poliziano, *tr. fr. Italian by* Iain Fletcher.
  Simonetta. LyPI
Giotto, I have not found. To Giotto. Wesley Trimpi. NePoEA
Giotto's Campanile. Thomas O'Hagan. JKCP
Giotto's Tower. Longfellow. APW; CoBA; IAP; LBAP; TCAP
Giovinette, che fate all' amore. Lorenzo da Ponte, *tr. fr. Italian by* Natalie MacFarren. *Fr.* Don Giovanni. TrJP
Gipsies. *See also* Gypsies.
Gipsies ("The gipsies seek wide sheltering woods again"). John Clare. ChTr
Gipsies ("The snow falls deep; the forest lies alone"). John Clare. CH; PoEL-4; ShBV-2
  (Gipsy Camp, The.) ChTr
Gipsies, The, *sel.* Pushkin, *tr. fr. Russian by* C. M. Bowra.
  Gipsy's Song. BoRS
Gipsies, The. "Richard Scrace." *See* Gypsies, The.
Gipsies came to lord Cassilis' gate, The. Johnny Faa, the Lord of Little Egypt. *Unknown.* EnSB
Gipsies came to our good lord's gate, The. *See* Gypsies came to our good lord's gate, The.
Gipsies came to the good Squire's gate, The. *Unknown.* LO
Gipsies lit their fires by the chalk-pit anew, The. The Idlers. Edmund Blunden. BoTP; CH
Gipsies Metamorphosed, The. Ben Jonson. *See* Gypsies Metamorphosed, The.
Gipsies passed her little gate, The. *See* Gypsies passed her little gate, The.
Gipsies seek wide sheltering woods again, The. Gipsies. John Clare. ChTr
Gipsy Camp, The. John Clare. *See* Gipsies ("The snow falls deep").
Gipsy feet. Fannie Stearns Davis. NLK
Gipsy, gipsy, gipsy girl! Gipsy Song. Sara Hamilton Birchall. NLK
Gipsy Girl, The. Ralph Hodgson. CMP; EnLit; GTML; MCCG; MoBrPo
  (Gypsy Girl, The.) PoeMoYo; POTE
Gipsy-Heart. Katharine Lee Bates. *See* Gypsy-Heart.
Gipsy Jane. William Brighty Rands. BoTP; FaPON
  (Gypsy Jane.) TiPo
Gipsy Laddie, The. *Unknown. See* Wraggle Taggle Gipsies, The.
Gipsy Love. Arthur Symons. VLEP
Gipsy Man. Dorothy King. BoTP
Gipsy Queen. John Alexander Chapman. OBEV (new ed.)
Gipsy Song. Sara Hamilton Birchall. NLK
Gipsy Song ("The faery beam upon you"). Ben Jonson. *Fr.* The Gypsies Metamorphosed. AlDL; EPS (1942 ed.); FaBoCh; LoGBV; SeCL
  (Faeries' Song, The.) SeCV-1
  ("Faery beam upon you, The.") CenL
  ("Fairy beam upon you, The.") ReEn; TuPP
  (Jackman's Song, The.) AtBAP
  (Patrico's Song.) BoW; LoBV
  (Wish, A.) PoRL
Gipsy Song ("To the old, long life and treasure"). Ben Jonson. *Fr.* The Gypsies Metamorphosed. EPS (1942 ed.); SeCL
Gipsy tents are on the down, The. Gipsy Love. Arthur Symons. VLEP
Gipsy Trail, The. Kipling. HBV; InP; NLK; PoeMoYo; PoRA
Gipsy Vans. Kipling. OtMeF; VLEP
Gipsy Wedding, The. Sara Hamilton Birchall. NLK
Gipsying. Arthur Rimbaud. *See* My Bohemia.
Gipsy's Dirge, The. Sir Walter Scott. *See* Wasted, Weary, Wherefore Stay.
Gipsy's Song. Pushkin, *tr. fr. Russian by* C. M. Bowra. *Fr.* The Gipsies. BoRS
Gipsy's Warning, The. *Unknown.* BeLS
Giraffe, The. Geoffrey Dearmer. AlDL
Giraffe, The. Nikolai Gumilev, *tr. fr. Russian by* Y. Hornstein. BoRS; LiTW
  "Listen:/ There roams, far away, by the waters of Clead," *sel.* FaPON
Giraffe, The. Marvin Solomon. NePoAm-2
Giraffe and Tree. W. J. Turner. CH
Giraffes. N. H. Brettell. BoSA
Giraffes, The. Roy Fuller. ChMP; NeBP
Giraffes and bears grow big and tall. A Little Boy Speaks. E. V. Emans. DDA
Gird on thy Sword. Robert Bridges. GTBS
Gird up thy loins now like a man; I will demand of thee. Out of the Whirlwind. Job, Bible, *O.T.* AWP; JAWP; WBP
Girdle, The. Paul Valéry, *tr. fr. French by* Alan Conder. TrFP
Girdled by Huron's throbbing and thunder. Manitou. Wilfred Campbell. OCL
Girl, A. Richard Aldington. *Fr.* Epigrams. PFE
Girl, A. Archilochus. *See* Miniature.
Girl, A. Babette Deutsch. BAP; HBMV
Girl, A. Viola Meynell. MBP; MoBrPo (1942 ed.)
Girl, A. Ezra Pound. MAP; MoAB; MoAmPo; MoPW; NeMA
Girl, A. Sappho, *tr. fr. Greek by* C. M. Bowra. GrL; OxBG
Girl am I and gladly do rejoice in the new season of the year, A. Ballata: Flowers and Love. Boccaccio. *Fr.* The Decameron. LyPI
Girl and Butterfly. Edith Sitwell. MoPW
Girl and Her Fawn, The. Andrew Marvell. *Fr.* The Nymph Complaining for the Death of Her Fawn. BoTP; OTPC (1923 ed.)
  (Girl Describes Her Fawn, The.) GTSL
  (Nymph and Her Fawn, The.) FaBoCh; LoGBV
Girl and the Cuckoo, The. *Unknown, tr. fr. Russian by* W. R. S. Ralston. OnPM
Girl arose so lovely, The. Alvorada. Dinis, King of Portugal. LyMA
Girl Asleep. Raymond Souster. TwCaPo
Girl Athletes. Haniel Long. HBMV
Girl awaiting her lover is not more still with fear, A. Night Alert. Alison Boodson. NeBP
Girl Betrayed. Hedylos, *tr. fr. Greek by* Dudley Fitts. LiTW

Girl, could you once regain. Could You Once Regain. Kendrick Smithyman. AnNZ
Girl Describes Her Fawn, The. Andrew Marvell. *See* Girl and Her Fawn, The.
Girl from Roumely. Alexandros Pallis, *tr. fr. Modern Greek by* Rae Dalven. MoGP
Girl from Tarentum, The. Naevius, *tr. fr. Latin by* Jack Lindsay. LaP
Girl I Left behind Me, The ("The dames of France"). Thomas Osborne Davis. AmSS, *with music;* BoHiPo; FaBoBe; FaFP; HBV; OlF; OnYI; TreF
Girl I Love, The. *Unknown, tr. fr. Modern Irish by* Jeremiah Joseph Callanan. IrPN; OnYI
Girl I Took to the Cocktail Party, The. Trevor Williams. FiBHP
Girl in a Library, A. Randall Jarrell. FiMAP
Girl in a Nightgown. Wallace Stevens. OxBA
Girl in a Tree. Frances Frost. NLK (1947 ed.)
Girl in the Carriage, The. *Unknown, tr. fr. Chinese by* Arthur Waley. *Fr.* Shi King. LiTW
Girl in the lane, The. *Unknown.* OxNR
Girl in the Snow, A. Robert Conquest. PoLFOT
Girl in the Subway. Sydney King Russell. StaSt
Girl Is Dead, The. Paul Fort, *tr. fr. French by* Alan Conder. TrFP
Girl, more beautiful than a soft rose. Fannia. Giovanni Pontano. LaP
Girl of All Periods, The. Coventry Patmore. VA
Girl of Dunbwy, The. Thomas Osborne Davis. TIP
Girl of Pompeii, A. Edward Sandford Martin. AA; HBV; OBAV
Girl of the Cottage, The. Johan Ludvig Runeberg, *tr. fr. Swedish by* Charles W. Stork. AnSL
Girl of the Future, feared of all. A "Dresscessional." Carolyn Wells. WBLP
Girl of the musing mouth. Statuette: Late Minoan. C. Day Lewis. EnLit; OxBI
Girl of the Red Mouth. Martin MacDermott. HBV; JKCP (1926 ed.); OnYI; TIP
Girl of three cows don't crow! Showing Off. *Unknown.* KiLC
Girl of whom in olden days, The. A Maiden. Kageki. OnPM
Girl of Yueh, The ("She is gathering lotos seed in the river of Yueh"). Li Po, *tr. fr. Chinese.* WhP
Girl of Yueh, A ("The waters of Mirror Lake are white like the moon"). Li Po, *tr. fr. Chinese.* WhP
Girl on the Milk-white Horse, The. Rachel Field. *Fr.* A Circus Garland. StVeCh
Girl said to her sister, late, when their friends had gone, A. A Girl to her Sister. E. J. Scovell. DiM
Girl Takes Her Place among the Mothers, The. Marya Zaturenska. HBMV
Girl to Her Sister, A. E. J. Scovell. DiM
Girl today, dreaming, A. Auf dem Wasser zu Singen. Stephen Spender. EnLoPo
Girl Walking. Charles G. Bell. NePoAm-2
Girl, who has so many wilful ways, A. Her Likeness. Dinah Maria Mulock Craik. LPS-1
Girl who sells melons beside the stream, The. Melon Girl. Mei Yao Ch'en. OnPC
Girl who weighed many an oz., A. *Unknown.* GoTP
Girl with eyes like dying flowers. Lullaby. Max Harris. BoAV; MoAuPo
Girl with the Blue Lamp, The. José María Eguren, *tr. fr. Spanish by* Donald Devenish Walsh. AnCL
Girl with the Cows, The, *sel.* Alfred Perceval Graves.
"So he trassed away dreamin' of Nora na Mo." TIP
Girlhood. Archilochus. *See* Miniature.
Girlhood. *Unknown.* LPS-2
Girlish face is what appears through the lattice-slot, A. Praxilla, *tr. fr. Greek by* Moses Hadas. GrPo
Girls, The. Siasconset Song. Philip Booth. NePoAm
Girls and boys come out to play. Mother Goose. BoTP; BrR; MPB (1956 ed.); OTPC; PPL; StVeCh; TiPo
Girls and Soldiers Singing. Leonard Mann. BoAu
Girls are laughing with the boys and gaming by the fire, The. Hallows' E'en. Winifred M. Letts. DD
Girls around Cape Horn, The, *with music. Unknown.* SoAmSa
Girl's far treble, muted to the heat, The. Milkmaid. Laurie Lee. ChMP; FaBoTw
Girls Going to the Fair. William Allingham. IrPN
Girls in Spring. Owari, *tr. fr. Japanese by* Ishii *and* Obata. OnPM
Girl's Lamentation, The. William Allingham. IrPN; SeCePo, *sl. abr.*
Girls, look you, Kupris is not Kupris only. Sophocles, *tr. fr. Greek by* John Addington Symonds. GrPo
Girls' Lot, The. Agathias Scholasticus, *tr. fr. Greek by* Sir William Marris. OxBG
Girl's Love Song. Eduard Mörike, *tr. fr. German by* R. F. C. Hull. AnGP
Girl's Mood, A. Lizette Woodworth Reese. HBMV
Girls' Names. Eleanor Farjeon. SUS; TiPo
Girls of Samos often ask, The. On the Tomb of Crethis. Callimachus. GrR
Girls of Yueh, The. Li Po, *tr. fr. Chinese.* WhP
(Girls on the Yueh River.) ChTr
Girls scream,/ Boys shout. School's Out. W. H. Davies. MuP; OBMV; POTE
Girl's Song, A. Aubrey De Vere. GTBS-D
Girl's Song. W. W. Gibson. ChMo; CMP
Girl's Song, A. Thomas Moore. *See* By Bendemeer's Stream.
Girls' Song. Pushkin. *tr. fr. Russian by* Oliver Elton. *Fr.* Eugene Onegin, III. BoR
Girl's Song. Aleksey Surkov, *tr. fr. Russian by* Jack Lindsay. RuPo
Girl's Song, A. Katharine Tynan. OnYI
Girl's Songs, A. Mary Carolyn Davies. SBMV
Borrower.
Free.
Kiss, The.
Vintage, The.
Girl's Treasures, A. *Unknown. See* Young Bride, The.
Girl's voice in the night troubled my heart, A. Going Over. Sir Charles G. D. Roberts. TwCaPo
Girls, when I am gone away. Song. Edward Dowden. GTIV
Girls who made that fighting body love, The. A Boxer Called Panther. Reuel Denney. PreP
Girl's Yearning, A. Li Yu. *See* Meditation.
Girod Street Cemetery; New Orleans. Harry Morris. GoYe
Girondins, The. Alexandre Dumas, *tr. fr. French by* John Oxenford. *Fr.* Le Chevalier de maison rouge. PoFr
Girt in dark growths, yet glimmering with one star. Sleepless Dreams. Dante Gabriel Rossetti. The House of Life, XXXIX. OAEP; PoVP; ViPo
Girt in my guiltless gown, as I sit here and sew. A Woman's Answer. *At. to* the Earl of Surrey. SiPS
Girt round with rugged mountains the fair Lake Constance lies. A Legend of Bregenz. Adelaide Anne Procter. PTA-1
Girt Woak Tree That's in the Dell, The. William Barnes. HBV; PoVP
(Oak Tree, The.) OBVV
Girt wold house o' mossy stoune, The. The Old House. William Barnes. OBVV
Gisli, the Chieftain, *sels.* Isabella Valancy Crawford. BoCaPo
Epilogue: "Said the voice of Evil to the ear of Good."
Song of the Arrow, The.
Git Along, Little Dogies. *Unknown. See* Whoopee Ti Yi Yo, Git Along, Little Dogies.
Git on Board, Little Chillen. *Unknown. See* Gospel Train, The.
Git yer [*or* yo] little sage hens ready. At a Cowboy Dance [*or* Idaho Cowboy Dance]. James Barton Adams. ABF; HBV; IHA; PoOW; SCC
Gita Govinda, The, *sels.* Jayadeva, *tr. fr. Sanskrit by* Sir Edwin Arnold.
Hymn to Vishnu. AWP
Song: "Low whispers the wind from Malaya." LiTW
Gitanjali, *sels.* Rabindranath Tagore.
"Day after day," LXXVI. OBMV
"Early in the day," XLII.
"Have you not heard his silent steps?" XLV. WGRP
"Here is thy footstool," X. MaRV; WGRP (X–XI)
"I have got my leave," XCIII. OBMV
"I was not aware of the moment," XCV. NP
"If it is not my portion," LXXIX. OBMV
"Life of my life, I shall ever try," IV.
(Because of Thee.) GrCo-1
"On the day when the lotus bloomed," XX. NP; NV
"On the slope of the desolate river," LXIV. OBMV
"This is my prayer to Thee," XXXVI.
(Prayer for Strength.) MaRV
"Thou art the sky and thou art the nest," LXVII. OBMV
"Thou hast made me known to friends," LXIII. NP
(Divine Companion, The.) GrCo-2
(When One Knows Thee.) OOP; QP-2
"Thy gifts to us mortals fulfil all our needs," LXXV. InP
"Where the mind is without fear," XXXV. MM; PoFr
(My Free Country.) GrCo-2
Gittin'-up Hollers. *Unknown.* CoSo
Giuseppe Caponsacchi. Robert Browning. *Fr.* The Ring and the Book. PoVP; VLEP
Giuseppe, da barber, ees greata for "mash." Mia Carlotta. T. A. Daly. BAP; InMe; LEAP; MAP; MoAmPo (1942 ed.); NeMA; PCN; PoeMoYo; PYM; ShBV-3; TreFS; WhC
Giv but to things their tru Esteem. Right Apprehension. Thomas Traherne. PoEL-2
Give a Boy a Dawg. Douglas Malloch. AlBD
Give a Man a Horse He Can Ride. James Thomson. Sunday up the River, XV. CaAE; EBSV; EmBrPo; EnLi-2; EnLit; EPP; GTSL; LEAP; POTT; PoVP; VLEP
(Gifts.) BBV; HBV; OBEV; OBVV; TOP; TreF

Give a Rouse. Robert Browning. Cavalier Tunes, II. EmBrPo; EnLi-2; EnLit; EPP; PC; PoVP; PreP; ShBV-1; ViPo
(Cavalier Tune, A.) BLV; BoLiVe
Give a rouse, then, in the Maytime. A Stein Song. Richard Hovey. *Fr.* Spring. AnAmPo; CP; HBV; LA; MAP; MoAmPo (1942 ed.); NeMA; PFY
Give All to Love. Emerson. AmP; AmPo; AmPP (4th ed.); AnAmPo; AnEnPo; AnFE; AnNE; APA; APW; AWP; BAP; CoAnAm; CoV; EV-4; FaBoEn; FaFP; HBV; IAP; InPo; JAWP; LA; LEAP; LiTA; LiTL; LO; LoPo; MOAP; NePA; OBEV; OBVV; OxBA; PCD; PFY; PG (1955 ed.); PIR; PoE; PoEL-4; PoeMoYo; PoLFOT; TCAP; TOP; TreFS; TrGrPo; ViBoPo; WaKn, *abr.*; WBP
Give as you would if an angel. How to Give. *Unknown.* BLRP
Give away, give away, ye gates, and win. The Wassail. Robert Herrick. EPS
Give away her gowns. Chorus. Edna St. Vincent Millay. *Fr.* Memorial to D.C. NP
Give Beauty All Her Right. Thomas Campion. OBSC; ReEn; SiCE; TuPP; ViBoPo
(Beauty Is Not Bound.) TrGrPo
(Beauty Unbound.) BLV
Give but the happiness our tongue. Grant that We Die Young. Verner von Heidenstam. AnSL
Give Ear, O Ye Heavens. Deuteronomy, Bible, *O.T.* *See* Blessed of the Lord Be His Land.
Give ear to my prayer, O God; and hide not thy self. Psalm LV, Bible, *O.T.* AWP
Give Ear to the Very Faint Song. Paul Verlaine, *tr. fr. French by* Vernon Watkins. AnFP
Give ear, ye British hearts of gold. Rodney's Glory. Owen Roe O'Sullivan. OnYI
Give Ear, Ye Heavens. Deuteronomy, XXXII: 1-43, Bible, *O.T.* TrJP
Give ear you lusty gallants. A Famous Sea-Fight. John Looke. CoMu
Give freely to the friend thou hast. Κοινὰ τὰ τῶν Φίλων (Koina ta ton Philon). John Addington Symonds. OBVV
Give Heed to the Old. Helene Mullins. MuM
Give her but a least excuse to love me! Song. Robert Browning. *Fr.* Pippa Passes. EPN; GTBS; GTSL; ViBoPo
Give him, Lord, eyes to behold the truth. Prayer for a Priest. *Unknown.* WHL
Give him the darkest inch your shelf allows. George Crabbe. E. A. Robinson. AmPP (4th ed.); CoBA; CoBMV; LiTA; LiTM (rev. ed.); MAP; MoAB; MoAmPo; MoVE; NAMP; NePA; OxBA; PoEL-5; PtP
Give honor and love forever more. Peter Cooper. Joaquin Miller. AA
Give honour unto Luke Evangelist. Old and New Art: St. Luke the Painter. Dante Gabriel Rossetti. The House of Life, LXXIV. BPN; GoBC; PoVP; ViPo
Give, if thou canst, an alms; if not, afford. Robert Herrick. *Fr.* Alms. MyFE
Give life its full domain and feed the soul. Of Wonder. Mary Gilmore. BoAV; NeLNL
Give Love To-Day. Ethel Talbot. HBV
Give me a battle to fight. A Battle Cry. Lee Shippey. MaRV
"Give me a fillet, Love," quoth I. Love and Life. Julie Mathilde Lippmann. AA; HBV
Give Me a Gentle Heart. Percy Thomas. OQP; QP-2
Give me a good digestion, Lord. A Prayer [*or* An Ancient Prayer], *after* A Prayer Found in Chester Cathedral. Thomas Harry Basil Webb. BBV (1951 ed.); BLPA; DDA; FaBoBe; NeHB; PoMa; PoToHe (new ed.); TreFS
Give me a harsh land to ring music from. This Land. Ian Mudie. BoAu
Give me a home in the far, far West. The Far, Far West. *Unknown.* CoSo
Give me a kiss from those sweet lips of thine. An Incomparable Kiss. *Unknown.* InvP; SeCL; SeEP
Give Me a Lass [with a Lump of Land]. Allan Ramsay. CEP; CoBE
Give me a light that I may see her. Lyric. John Masefield. CaAE
Give me a man that is not dull. His Desire. Robert Herrick. EV-2; OAEP
Give me a mask, I'll join the masquerade. Heine. Fresco-Sonnets to Christian Sethe, 2. AWP; JAWP; WBP
Give me a mattress aft and a good tarpaulin's shelter. Simple Pleasures. Antiphilus of Byzantium. GrPE
"Give me a motto," said a youth. The Old Man's Motto. John Godfrey Saxe. BPP
Give me a night in June that's clear and quiet. Bewitched. W. H. Davies. AlDL
Give me a nobler, wider sphere. Anno 1829. Heine. LiTW
Give me a race that is run in a breath. The Hundred-Yard Dash. William Lindsey. AA
"Give me a son." The blessing sent. Mother, Nurse, and Fairy. John Gay. MOAH
Give me a spirit that on [this] life's rough sea. The Master Spirit [*or* A Brave Spirit *or* Invocation]. George Chapman. *Fr.* The Conspiracy of Charles, Duke of Byron. EtS; EV-1; KN; MyFE; ViBoPo
Give me a spoon of oleo, Ma. Domestic Science. *Unknown.* WBLP
Give me ae spark o' Nature's fire. Spark o' Nature's Fire. Burns. *Fr.* Epistle to John Lapraik. BLP
Give Me Ale. *Unknown. See* In Praise of Ale.
Give me an ebbing sunset of the fall. The Delta Autumn. William Alexander Percy. LS
"Give me but two brigades," said Hooker. The Battle of Lookout Mountain. George Henry Boker. MC; PAH
Give me courage, Lord, to sail. A Prayer for Courage. Joseph Morris. PraP
Give me fortune, give me health. Thomas Middleton. *Fr.* The Widow. TuPP
Give me, full-handed, lilies, give me the rose. Sonnet. Matteo Maria Boiardo. LyPI
Give me, give me Buriano. Bacchus's Opinion of Wine, and Other Beverages. Francesco Redi. *Fr.* Bacchus in Tuscany. AWP
Give Me Homer's Lyre. *Unknown, tr. fr. Greek by* J. M. Edmonds. GrL
Give me hunger. At a Window. Carl Sandburg. ChMo; CMP; FaBoBe; HBMV; LEAP; NP; PCD; PoToHe; TrPWD
Give me, in this inconstant ebb and flow. Seaward Bound. Alice Brown. TrPWD
Give Me Jesus, *with music. Unknown.* BoAN-1
Give me kisses! Do not stay. To Lesbia. John Godfrey Saxe. HBV
Give Me Leave. "A. W." *See* Petition to Have Her Leave to Die.
Give me leave to rail at you. A Song. Earl of Rochester. EG; EPS
Give me, Love, kisses unnumbered. Kisses. Cristóbal de Castillejo. AnSpL-1
Give Me More Love, or More Disdain. Thomas Carew. *See* Mediocrity in Love Rejected.
"Give me my bow," said Robin Hood. The Death of Robin Hood. Eugene Field. StPo
Give me my harp, and let me sing a song. Deirdre. Sir Samuel Ferguson. *Fr.* Deirdre. IrPN
Give me, my love, that billing kiss. The Kiss. Thomas Moore. EnLoPo
Give me my robe, put on my crown. Death of Cleopatra. Shakespeare. *Fr.* Antony and Cleopatra, V, ii. AtBAP; CBOV; FiP; LiA; LoPS; NBE; TreFS; TrGrPo
Give me my scallop shell of quiet. The Passionate Man's Pilgrimage [*or* His Pilgrimage *or* The Pilgrimage]. Sir Walter Ralegh. AnFE; AtBAP; BBV (1951 ed.); BCEP; BEL; BLV; CaAE; CAW; CBE; CenL; ChTr; CoBE; CoEV; EG; ElL; ElSeCe; EnLit; EV-1; HBV; KN; LEAP; LiTB; LoBV; LPS-2; MePo; OAEP; OBEV; OBSC; OxBoCh; PC; PoE; PoEL-2; PoFS; PoRA; ReEn; SeCePo; SiCE; SiPS; TOP; TreFS; TrGrPo; TriL; TuPP; TyEnPo; ViBoPo; WGRP
Give Me My Self. Michael Drayton. *See* Idea: "You're not alone when you are still alone."
Give me my sword./ Who's there? Shakespeare. *Fr.* Macbeth, II, i. MyFE
Give Me My Work. George Whetstone. ElL
(Gentlewoman Forsweareth, A.) ElSeCe
Give me no gift! Less than thyself were nought. Broken Friendship. Mary E. Coleridge. BoFr
Give me no hard white pavements, no house of brick or stone. Wander-Lure. Hermann Ford Martin. DDA
Give Me No Lover Young with Love. Lucia Trent. TBM
Give me no mansions ivory white. The Desire. Katharine Tynan. BMEP; HBV; LEAP; TSW
Give Me Not Tears. Rose Hawthorne Lathrop. AA
Despair.
Joy.
Give me, O friend, the secret of thy heart. Rosa Rosarum. Agnes Mary Frances Robinson. HBMV; VA
Give me, O God, the understanding heart. The Understanding Heart. Georgia Harkness. MaRV
Give me, O indulgent Fate! The Petition for an Absolute Retreat. Countess of Winchilsea. BLV; OBEC; PoEL-3; TrGrPo
Give me of every language, first my vigorous English. The English Language. William Wetmore Story. GN
Give me of love my love to prove. H. G. Andrews. LO
"Give me of your bark, O Birch-Tree!" Hiawatha's Sailing [*or* Hiawatha's Canoe]. Longfellow. *Fr.* The Song of Hiawatha. BBV; IAP; PCH; StVeCh (1940 ed.); TVSH
Give me one kiss. To Dianeme. Robert Herrick. FaBoBe; LiTL; NeHB
Give me purple asters in a flaming bowl. The Blind Girl. Marjorie Cole. CAG

Give me some music.—Now, good morrow, friends. Shakespeare. Twelfth Night, II, iv. MyFE
Give me some musicke: musicke, moody foode. The Eternal Feminine. Shakespeare. Antony and Cleopatra, II, v. LiA
Give me that grand old Volume, the gift of a mother's love. The Bible My Mother Gave Me. *Unknown.* PTA-2
Give me that man that dares bestride. Herrick's Cavalier. Robert Herrick. PoFr
Give me the avowed, the erect, the manly foe. George Canning. TreFS
Give me the clear blue sky overhead, and the long road to my feet. Road Song. W. G. Tinckom-Fernandez. NLK
Give me the dance of your boughs, O Tree. Song to a Tree. Edwin Markham. FaPON; MPB
Give me the darkest corner of a cloud. Sonnet. R. W. Dixon. LO
Give Me the Eyes. Walter Savage Landor. EmBrPo; EPN ("Give me the eyes that look on mine.") BPN
Give me the faith that asks not "Why?" A Prayer. *Unknown.* PraP
Give me the harp of epic song. Odes of Anacreon, *tr. by* Thomas Moore. OuHeWo
Give me the hills and wide water. The Hills and the Sea. Wilfred Campbell. CaP; OCL
Give me the hills, that echo silence back. The Silent Ranges. Stephan Moylan Bird. HBMV
Give me the lowest place: not that I dare. The Lowest Place. Christina Rossetti. EnLi-2; EPP; MaRV; TrPWD; ViPo
Give me the merchants of the Indian mines. Mine Argosy from Alexandria. Christopher Marlowe. *Fr.* The Jew of Malta, I, i. ChTr; LO
Give me the murmur of men. In the City. T. P. Cameron Wilson. *Fr.* The City Tramp. MW
Give Me the Old. Robert Hinckley Messinger. *See* Winter Wish, A.
Give me the pay I have served for. Walt Whitman. *Fr.* By Blue Ontario's Shore, XIV. LEAP
Give me the room whose every nook. The Library. Frank Dempster Sherman. AA; OBAV
Give me the scorn of the stars and a peak defiant. The Song of the Soldier-born. Robert W. Service. LEAP
Give me the sky. Ilo Orleans. RIS
Give Me the Splendid Silent Sun. Walt Whitman. AA; AmPP (3d ed.); BLV; BoLiVe; FaPON; LBAP; MaPo; MoAmPo (1950 ed.); OBAV; PG (1945 ed.); TCAP; TSW
"Give me the splendid silent sun with all his beams full-dazzling," *sel.* PIAE
Give Me the Sun. Sister Miriam. JKCP (1955 ed.)
Give me the thoughts of long dead years. A December Prayer. G. C. Wing, Jr. CAG
Give me this day a faith not personal. Allen Tate. More Sonnets at Christmas, III. LiTA; LiTM; NePA; WaP
Give me those flowers there, Dorcas. Flowers. Shakespeare. *Fr.* The Winter's Tale, IV, ii. ADAH; EV-1; SN
Give Me Three Grains of Corn, Mother. Amelia Blanford Edwards. AS, *abr. and arr. with music;* BLPA; LPS-1
Give me thyself! It were as well to cry. Thyself. John Addington Symonds. *Fr.* Stella Maris. PoVP; VA
Give me thy hand, pretty, pretty. *Unknown.* The Baby's Charms—Sardinian. BOL
Give Me Thy Heart. Adelaide Anne Procter. ACP; CAW; GoBC
Give me thy joy in sorrow, gracious Lord. Thy Joy in Sorrow. Chauncey Hare Townshend. VA
Give me Thy strength for my day, Lord. Thy Strength and My Day. Annie Johnson Flint. PraP
Give me to die unwitting of the day. Mors Benefica. Edmund Clarence Stedman. AA; BLP; LEAP
Give me to live and love in the old, bold fashion. The Song of the Soldier-Born. Robert W. Service. LEAP
Give me truths. Blight. Emerson. BAV; CDC; IAP
Give me white paper! Columbus. Edward Everett Hale. DD; HH; MC; PAH
Give me wide walls to build my house of life. Wide Walls. *Unknown.* PoToHe (new ed.)
Give me work to do. A Prayer. *Unknown.* PGD; PSO
Give me your hands, and let your strange wild eyes. Fragment. Edmund John. BMEP
Give me your poppies. Choros. Hilda Doolittle ("H. D."). *Fr.* Morpheus. FaBoMo
Give me your tired, your poor. Inscription on the Statue of Liberty. Emma Lazarus. *Fr.* The New Colossus. PaA; PoFr; PoRL
Give Me Your Whole Heart. *Unknown, tr. fr. Sanskrit by* Swami Prabhavananda *and* Christopher Isherwood. *Fr.* The Bhagavad-Gita. MaRV
Give me yourself one hour; I do not crave. Request. "Laurence Hope." BMEP
Give money me; take friendship whoso list! Of Money. Barnabe Googe. EIL
Give no pity because my feet. Blind. Fanny Crosby. MaRV
Give No White Flower. Brenda Chamberlain. NeIP
Give Our Conscience Light. Aline Badger Carter. ChIP; TrPWD
Give over to high things the fervent thought. To Lovers of Earth: Fair Warning. Countee Cullen. CDC
Give pardon, blessèd soul, to my bold cries. On the Death of Sir Philip Sidney [*or* To Sir Philip Sidney's Soul]. Henry Constable. EIL; ES; GoBC; OBEV; OBSC; PtP; SeCePo
Give place all ye that doth rejoice. Sir Thomas Wyatt. SiPS
Give place, ye ladies, and be gone. John Heywood. *See* Give place, you ladies . . .
Give Place, Ye Lovers. Earl of Surrey. *See* Praise of His Love, A.
Give place, you [*or* ye] ladies, and be gone. A Praise of His Lady [*or* A Description of a Most Noble Lady]. John Heywood, *wr. at. to* Thomas Heywood. BCEP; CoBE; EIL; ElSeCe; HBV; LPS-1; OBEV; OBSC; SiCE; TuPP; ViBoPo
Give proof, oh! stranger, as thou passest by. Peace to the Tomb. *At. to* Theocritus *and to* Leonidas of Tarentum. LiA
Give Thanks. Helen Isabella Tupper. BLRP; PEOR; (Thanks for Everything.) WBLP
Give Thanks fer What? W. F. Croffut. TOAH
Give thanks, O heart, for the high souls. Edwin Markham. *Fr.* Conscripts of the Dream. PGD
Give them eternal rest, for they are tired. For Those Who Died in Battle. Louis Mercier. TrFP
Give Them the Flowers Now. Leigh M. Hodges. PTA-2; WBLP
Give thy thoughts no tongue. Polonius's Advice to Laertes. Shakespeare. *Fr.* Hamlet, I, iii. PYM
Give to barrows, trays and pans. Art. Emerson. PEOR
Give to imagination some pure light. Modern Love, XXXVIII. George Meredith. ViPo
Give to me the life I love. The Vagabond. Robert Louis Stevenson. AlDL; AnFE; BBV; BMEP; CBE; EV-5; GTSL; HBV; HBVY; HiLiEn; MCCG; OnPP; OTPC (1946 ed.); PCN; PoeMoYo; PoeT; PoMa; PoRL; POTT; PYM; ShBV-1; TCEP; ViBoPo; VLEP
Give to Pa a horse to drive. Give a Boy a Dawg. Douglas Malloch. AlBD
Give to the Living. Ida Goldsmith Morris. WBLP
Give to the winds thy fears. Courage. Paul Gerhardt. WGRP
Give unto the Lord, O ye mighty. Psalm XXIX, Bible, *O.T.* AWP; OnPM; PFE
"Give us a song!" the soldiers cried. The Song of the Camp. Bayard Taylor. AA; BeLS; BTP; GN; HBV; HBVY; LPS-1; OBAV; OTPC; PTA-1; TCAP; WBLP (Song in Camp, The.) BBV (1923 ed.); PECK
Give us a virile Christ for these rough days! A Virile Christ. Rex Boundy. ChIP; MaRV; OQP; QP-1; WGRP
Give us a watchword for the hour. Evangelize! Henry Croker. BLRP
Give us a wrack or two, Good Lard. The Wreckers' Prayer. Theodore Goodridge Roberts. BoCaPo (1948 ed.); PeCV
Give us from dawn to dark. The Bush. James Lister Cuthbertson. BoAu
Give Us Great Dreams. Marie LeNart. OQP; QP-1
Give us Jesus Christ, the Carpenter. Comrade Christ. Verne Bright. ChIP; OQP; QP-2
Give Us Men! Edward Henry Bickersteth. BLPA; MaRV
Give Us Men. Josiah Gilbert Holland. *See* God Give Us Men.
Give us men!/ men from every rank. Give Us Men. Edward Henry Bickersteth. BLPA; MaRV
Give us our daily bread. Our Daily Bread. Adelaide Anne Procter. JKCP
Give Us This Day. Josephine Royle. BAP
"Give Us This Day Our Daily Bread." Maltbie D. Babcock. *See* Our Daily Bread.
Give Way! Charlotte Perkins Gilman. WGRP
Give way, give way, ye gates, and win. The Wassail[e]. Robert Herrick. AnEC; EPS
Give Way, Ye Gates. Theodore Roethke. FiMAP
Give ye good-den. Wait's Carol. Barbara Young. MoSiPe
Giveaway, The. Phyllis McGinley. PoRA
Given a roof, and a taste for rations. Life in Laconics. Mary Mapes Dodge. BOHV
Given, not lent. Unto Us a Son Is Given. Alice Meynell. ChIP; GTBS; JKCP; OQP; PoRL; QP-1; SDH; StJW
Given Over. Thomas Woolner. VA
Given the "Cat," it was not only that he ran. The Cat-o'-Nine-Tails. John Blight. BoAV; NeLNL
Given this light. Ostia Antica. Anthony Hecht. NePA
Givenchy village lies a wreck, Givenchy church is bare. A Song of the Old Days. Patrick MacGill. MaRV
Giver of All. Christopher Wordsworth. MaRV (Giving to God.) VA
Giver of bliss and pain, of song and prayer. William Alexander Percy. *Fr.* Epilogue: "O God, author of song." TrPWD

Giver of good and perfect gifts. Prayer at a Wedding. Charles Carroll Albertson. PraP
Giving. William F. Kirk. MaRV
Giving. *Unknown.* PoToHe
Giving a Heart. *Unknown. See* Popular Songs of Tuscany.
Giving and Forgiving. Thomas Grant Springer. PoToHe
Giving and Taking. Hesiod, *tr. fr. Greek by* Sir William Marris. *Fr.* Works and Days. OxBG
Giving oneself to the dentist or doctor who is a good one. The Kind of Act of. Robert Creeley. NeAP
Giving Thanks. *Unknown.* PEDC; TOAH
Giving to God. Christopher Wordsworth. *See* Giver of All.
Glabrous girl and hispid boy, The. ♂ and ♀. W. Craddle. WhC
Glacier. Mary Sinton Leitch. BAP
Glacier, The. Louis MacNeice. AnFE
Glad April smiled. April. Florence Hamilton. BAP; PYM
Glad, but not flush'd with gladness. Swinburne. *Fr.* Before the Mirror. OBEV (new ed.)
Glad Day. W. Graham Robertson. CBPC; HBV
Glad Day. Louis Untermeyer. TrJP
Glad Earth. Ella C. Forbes. YeAr
Glad Flow'ring Time. Mimnermus, *tr. fr. Greek by* J. M. Edmonds. GrR
Glad harvest greets us, The; brave toiler for bread. Song of the Harvest. Henry Stevenson Washburn. OHIP
Glad, mad wind went singing by, The. A Morning. Theodosia Garrison. NLK
Glad message of the voice of Zeus. In Time of Pestilence. Sophocles. *Fr.* Oedipus Rex. OxBG
Glad steers the sailor home to the quiet stream. Home. Friedrich Hölderlin. AnGP
Glad that I live am I. A Little Song of Life. Lizette Woodworth Reese. BrR; FaPON; HBMV; MPB; MW; PC; PoMa; TiPo (1959 ed.)
Glad Tidings from the King of Kings. Charles Coffin, *tr. fr. Latin by* John Chandler. BePJ
Glad Young Chamois, The. Burges Johnson. TSW; TSWC
Gladde Things. *Unknown.* TiPo (1952 ed.)
Glade, The. Edward Shanks. LO
Gladly they saw me sleeping on the shore. Philoctetes Deserted. Sophocles. *Fr.* Philoctetes. OxBG
Gladness. Anna Hempstead Branch. PC
Gladness. Genevieve Taggard. *See* First Miracle.
Gladness of Nature, The. Bryant. ADAH; DD; HBV; HBVY; OTPC; SN
Gladness of the May, The. Wordsworth. YeAr
Gladstone. Julian Symons. WaP
Gladstone was still respected. Yeux Glauques. Ezra Pound. *Fr.* Hugh Selwyn Mauberley. CoBMV; CoV; LiTA; LiTM (rev. ed.); MoPo
Glamor of regret is on the brown, A. The Captains. Walter Adolphe Roberts. PoNe
Glamour on the phantom shore, A. At Les Eboulements. Duncan Campbell Scott. SG; VA
Glance, The. George Herbert. EPS
Glance, The. Ibn Iyad, *tr. fr. Arabic by* A. J. Arberry. MooP
Glance behind the Curtain, A, *sel.* James Russell Lowell. Labor. MaRV
Glasgerion. *Unknown.* BaBo (A *and* B *vers.*); BLV; ESPB (A *and* B *vers.*); OBB; ViBoFo
(Glenkindie.) EBSV
Glasgow. Alexander Smith. BSV; EBSV
Glasgow Chap's Story, The; or, Confessions over a Bottle. Alexander McLachlan. BoCaPo (1948 ed.)
Glasgow Peggie. *Unknown.* BaBo; ESPB
Glass antique, 'twixt thee and Nell. Nell Gwynne's Looking Glass. Laman Blanchard. HBV; VA
Glass Blower, The. Eleanor Jordan Houston. MuM
Glass Bubbles, The. Samuel Greenberg. LiTA; NePA
Glass Dialectic. Howard Nemerov. WaP
Glass falls lower, The. Sad Green. Sylvia Townsend Warner. MBP; MoBrPo
Glass of Beer, A. James Stephens, *after the Irish of* David O'Bruaidar. AnFE; ExPo; FiBHP; LiTM; OBMV; SeCePo; ShBV-4; SiTL; WhC
(Righteous Anger.) AnIV; LiTW; MBP; MoAB; MoBrPo
Glass of Government, The, *sel.* George Gascoigne.
First Chorus, The. Po
Glass of Water, The. Wallace Stevens. AtBAP; CoBMV; MoAB; MoAmPo (1950 ed.); MoPo; OxBA
Glass Swan, The. W. Wesley Trimpi. PtPa
Glass was the street, in tinsel peril. Emily Dickinson. OxBA
Glasses are raised, the voices drift into laughter, The. Pub. Julian Symons. LiTB; LiTM; WaP
Glauce. Aubrey Thomas De Vere. IrPN
Glaucopis. Richard Hughes. OBMV
Glaucous-Gull's Death, The. Daniel James O'Sullivan. NeIP
Glaucus. Sidney Keyes. FaBoMo
Glaucus, look! at sea already splashing waves. Rough Sea. Archilochus. OxBG
Glaucus, the islander, whose ferry crossing. The Old Ferryman. Antiphilus of Byzantium. OxBG
Glaukos and Diomedes. Homer, *pr. tr. fr. Greek by* Andrew Lang, Walter Leaf, *and* Ernest Myers. *Fr.* The Iliad, VI. GrR
(Story of Bellerophon, The, *shorter sel., pr. tr. by* Hallam Tennyson *and* Alfred Tennyson. OxBG
Glaukos, why is it you and I are honored beyond all men. Sarpedon to Glaukos. Homer, *tr. by* Richmond Lattimore. *Fr.* The Iliad, XII. WaaP
Glazed silk, newly cut, smooth, glittering, white. A Song of Grief. Pan Chieh-yu. ChLP
Gleam of gold in gloom and grey, A. Allegra Agonistes. Grace Fallow Norton. NP
Gleam of sunlight crowned her, A. A Spring-Time Sweetheart (If I Had Had One). Gustaf Fröding. AnSL
Gleaming, gleaming are the white clouds. Song of the Emperor Yu on the Making of the Nine Tripods. *Unknown. Fr.* The Fountain of Old Poems. WhP
Gleaming Sea, The. Moschus, *tr. by* Shelley. *See* Ocean, The.
Gleaner, The. Vivian L. Virtue. PoNe
Glee for King Charles. Sir Walter Scott. *See* Here's a Health to King Charles.
Glee for Winter, A. Alfred Domett. DD; HBV; SN; VA
Glee—The Ghosts. Thomas Love Peacock. *Fr.* Melincourt. ViBoPo
Glen-Almain, the Narrow Glen. Wordsworth. GTSL
Glen of Silence, The. "Hugh MacDiarmid." NeBP
Glenara. Thomas Campbell. HBV; UnW
Glenaradale. Walter Chalmers Smith. EBSV; OBEV (new ed.); OBVV
Glenarm. John Lyle Donaghy. NeIP
Glencar. Stephen Gwynn. LBBV
Glencoe. G. K. Chesterton. LEAP
Glenfinlas; or, Lord Ronald's Coronach. Sir Walter Scott. EmBrPo; GoTL
Glenkindie. William Bell Scott. HBV; VA
Glenkindie. *Unknown. See* Glasgerion.
Glenlogie (*sl. diff. versions*). *Unknown.* GN; HBV; OBB
(Glenlogie; or, Jean o' Bethelnie, A *and* B *vers.*). ESPB
Glenn Miller and I were heroes. Chorus. Jack Kerouac. *Fr.* Mexico City Blues. NeAP
Glens, The. John Hewitt. NeIP
Glide gently, thus for ever glide. Remembrance of Collins. Wordsworth. PtP
Glide on, my life! I love thee not so much. My Life. Verner von Heidenstam. AnSL
Glide Soft, Ye Silver Floods. William Browne. *Fr.* Britannia's Pastorals. AEV; ElL
(Shepherd's Moan, A.) ElSeCe
Glimmers gray the leafless thicket. The Song-Sparrow. George Parsons Lathrop. SN
Glimpse, A. Frances Cornford. OBMV
Glimpse, A. Walt Whitman. AmPP (4th ed.); NePA; OxBA
Glimpse in Autumn. Jean Starr Untermeyer. StVeCh (1940 ed.); TSW; TSWC
Glimpse into a Courtyard, A. P'eng Chien P'u, *tr. fr. Chinese by* Henry H. Hart. PoHN
Glimpse of a Plain Cap, The. *Unknown, tr. fr. Chinese by* Arthur Waley. *Fr.* Shi King. LiTW
Glimpse of Beauty, A. Chien Liang Tse, *tr. fr. Chinese by* Henry H. Hart. OnPM
Glimpse of Pan, A. James Whitcomb Riley. DaM
Glimpse of Time, A. Laurence Binyon. AnFE
Glimpse through an interstice caught, A. A Glimpse. Walt Whitman. AmPP (4th ed.); NePA; OxBA
Glimpses. Roy Helton. HBMV
Glint of a Raindrop, The. Austin Dobson. BPN
Glints of the Year—from a Window. Thomas Caulfield Irwin. IrPN
Glion?—Ah, twenty years, it cuts. Obermann Once More. Matthew Arnold. BPN; EPN; GEPC; PoEL-5; PoVP; VLEP
Glisk o the burn. Tuscan Folk Songs, 7. *Unknown, tr. into Scottish by* Edwin Morgan. LyPI
Glistening riders, beautiful bright lords. Leonardo da Vinci, I. Thomas S. Jones, Jr. MuM
Glistering high in the midnight sky the starry rockets soar. Dewey and His Men. Wallace Rice. PAH
Glist'ning with dew the green-hair'd Spring. The Seasons. William Julius Mickle. *Fr.* Ode on Vicissitude. RO
Glitter. Pope. *Fr.* Windsor Forest. BeR
Glittering Frost. Ambrose Philips. *Fr.* A Winter Piece. BeR
Glittering leaves of the rhododendrons, The. Green Symphony. John Gould Fletcher. AnFE; APA; CoAnAm; MAP; MAPA; MoAmPo; MoVE
Glittering roofs are still with frost, The. A January Morning. Archibald Lampman. CPG; MW; TwCV
Glittering shows of Flora's dames, The. A Proper Ditty. *Unknown.* ReIE
Glittering-throned, undying Aphrodite. Hymn [*or* Ode] to Aphrodite. Sappho, *tr. by* John Addington Symonds. GrR; LiA

Glitters with brass my mansion wide. Alcaeus, *tr. fr. Greek by* J. H. Merivale. GrPo
Gloaming. Robert Adger Bowen. HBV
Gloire de Dijon. D. H. Lawrence. EnLoPo; LBBV; OAEP (2d ed.)
Gloom of death is on the raven's wing, The. The Raven. E. A. Robinson. AWP; JAWP; LiTW; MOAP; UnS; WBP
Gloom of the night, gloom of the night. A "Euripidean" Chorus. Aristophanes. *Fr.* The Frogs. OxBG
Gloom of the sea-fronting cliffs, The. Aboard the *Sea-Swallow.* Edward Dowden. TIP
Gloom that breathes upon me with these airs, The. A Dark Day. Dante Gabriel Rossetti. The House of Life, LXVIII. PoVP; ViPo
Glooms of the live-oaks, beautiful-braided and woven. The Marshes of Glynn. Sidney Lanier. AA; ADAH; AmPP; AnFE; ATP; CoAnAm; CoBA; HBV; IAP; LEAP; LiTA; LiTG; MAP; MCCG; NeMA; NePA; OxBA; PC; PG (1933 ed.); PoMa; SPP; TCAP; TOP; WGRP; WHA
Gloomy and dark art thou, O chief of the mighty Omahas. To the Driving Cloud. Longfellow. ChTr; FaBoEn; Po; PoEL-5
Gloomy grammarians in golden gowns. Of the Manner of Addressing Clouds. Wallace Stevens. AnFE; APA; CoAnAm
Gloomy hulls, in armour grim, The. The *Temeraire.* Herman Melville. APW; WaaP
Gloomy night before us flies, The. Jefferson and Liberty. *Unknown.* TrAS
Gloomy night embraced the place. A Hymn of the Nativity. Richard Crashaw. *Fr.* In the Holy Nativity. ViBoPo
Gloomy Night Is Gathering Fast, The. Burns. EBSV; MCCG
Gloomy Winter's Now Awa'. Robert Tannahill. EBSV
Gloomy with wind and driving cloud, the night. Leaving Troy. Thomas Caulfield Irwin. IrPN
Gloria in Excelsis. *Unknown.* WGRP
Gloria, Laus, et Honor. *Unknown.* WHL
Gloria Mundi. Siegfried Sassoon. MoPW
"Gloria Patri," The. John Heywood. ACP
Gloria, Tibi, Domine. *Unknown.* BOL
Gloria Tibi, Domine. A Little Child There Is Yborn. *Unknown.* AnEC
Gloriana's England. Archibald T. Strong. *Fr.* Sonnets of the Empire. BoAu
Glories. Lionel Johnson. TriL
Glories of Athens, The. Sophocles. *See* Grove of Colonus, The.
Glories of Our Blood and State, The. James Shirley. *See* Death the Leveller.
Glories of the world sink down in gloom, The. Sic Transit. Joseph Mary Plunkett. ACP
Glories, Pleasures. John Ford. *Fr.* The Broken Heart, V, iii. ElSeCe; ViBoPo
(Broken Heart, A.) OnPM
(Dirge: "Glories, pleasures, pomps, delights, and ease.") EPP; EV-2; LoBV
("Glories, pleasures, pomps, delights, and ease.") TuPP
(Song: "Glories, pleasures, pomps, delights, and ease.") OBS
Glorified, The. Gérard de Nerval, *tr. fr. French by* Alan Conder. TrFP
Glorious armies of the sky, The. Hymn. Elizabeth Rowe. BeR
Glorious day, A! The Curtain. Tristan Klingsor. TrFP
Glorious Game, The. Richard Burton. HBMV
Glorious Gift of God, The. Benjamin Beddome. BePJ
Glorious God, The. Jami, *tr. fr. Persian by* F. Hadland Davis. OnPM
Glorious God had great pity. Sing We with Mirth, Joy and Solace. *Unknown.* AnEC
Glorious God in Trinity. Jesu, Fili Dei. *At. to* John Trouluffe *and* Richard Smert. AnEC
Glorious God, whose bounty, mercy, grace, The. The Glorious God. Jami. OnPM
Glorious goddess in her eyes, A. An Absent Friend. Sappho. GrL; OxBG
Glorious image of the Maker's beauty, The. Amoretti, LXI. Spenser. PeBoSo; SiCE; TCEP
Glorious is death, when thou in the first line gallantly fallest. Song of the Athenians. Viktor Rydberg. *Fr.* Dexippos. AnSL
Glorious King. Giraut de Bornelh, *tr. fr. Provençal by* Elio Gianturco. LiA
Glorious Name, The. Amos R. Wells. BePJ
Glorious people vibrated again, A. Ode to Liberty. Shelley. BEL; GEPC
Glorious portrait of that angel's face, The. Amoretti, XVII. Spenser. PeBoSo
Glorious Song of Old, The. Edmund H. Sears. *See* It Came Upon the Midnight Clear.
Glorious sun went blushing to his bed, The. Sonnets to Idea, IV. Michael Drayton. Idea's Mirrour, XXV. OBSC
Glorious Survivors, The. A. E. Coppard. FaBoTw
Glorious the day when in arms at Assunpink. Assunpink and Princeton. Thomas Dunn English. MC; PAH
Glorious the Sun in Mid Career. Christopher Smart. *Fr.* A Song to David. FaBoCh; LiTG; LoGBV
Glorious Things of Thee Are Spoken. John Newton. MaRV; OlF; WGRP
Glorious tree is the gray old oak, A. The Fall of the Oak [*or* The Oak]. George Hill. APW; HH
Glorious Twelfth, The. Robert Greacen. NeIP
Glorious Victory of Navarino, The! *Unknown.* CoMu
Glorious with scars and rents the battle-banners rise. The Great Cross of Mercy. Theodosia Garrison. PEDC
Glory. D. H. Lawrence. POTE
Glory, The. Edward Thomas. POTE
Glory and Danger ever are allied. James Kirke Paulding. *Fr.* The Backwoodsman. BAV
Glory and gallant deeds and fame forgetting. Aleksandr Blok, *tr. fr. Russian by* C. M. Bowra. BoRS
Glory and honor and fame and everlasting laudation. Sherman. Richard Watson Gilder. AA; CA; MDAH; OBAV
Glory and loveliness have passed away. To Leigh Hunt, Esq. [*or* Dedication to Leigh Hunt]. Keats. BPN; EmBrPo; EnRP; ERP; ViBoPo
Glory and the ardour of the stage, The. E. H. W. Meyerstein. *Fr.* Elegy on the Death of Mme Anna Pavlova. UnS
Glory be to God for dappled things. Pied Beauty. Gerard Manley Hopkins. AlDL; AnEnPo; AnFE; ATP (1953 ed.); AWP; BLV; BoLiVe; BrBE; CaAE; ChMo; CoBE; CoBMV; CoEV; EnL; EnLi-2 (1949 ed.); EnLit; FaBoEn; FaBoMo; FaFP; GoTP; GTBS; GTBS-D; GTBS-W; GTML; InPo; InvP; KN; LiTB; LiTG; LiTM; MaPo; MaRV; MBP; MoAB; MoBrPo; MoVE; MuP; NAMP; NeMA; OAEP (2d ed.); OBEV (new ed.); OBMV; PG (1955 ed.); PoRA; POTT; PoVP; ReaPo; ReMP; ShBV-3; ThWaDe; TreFS; TrGrPo; TriL; TwHP; ViBoPo; ViP; ViPo; ViPP; VLEP; VOD (1935 ed.); WaKn
Glory be to God on high, and on earth peace, good-will towards men. Gloria in Excelsis. *Unknown.* WGRP
Glory be to thee, Word: Glory be to thee Grace. Amen. Hymn of Our Lord at the Last Supper. Apocryphal Acts of St. John. MeRV
Glory, Glory to the Sun. John Alford. HBMV
Glory Hallelujah! or, John Brown's Body. *Unknown, at. to* Charles Sprague Hall. *See* John Brown's Body.
Glory in the Commonplace. Elizabeth Barrett Browning. *Fr.* Aurora Leigh, VII. MaRV
Glory is of the sun, too, and the sun of suns. Glory. D. H. Lawrence. POTE
Glory of and Grace in the Church, The. Edward Taylor. *Fr.* God's Determinations. AnNE
Glory of clouds in her raiment, the flowers shine like her face, The. A Song of Ching-ping. Li Po. WhP
Glory of Early Rising, The. Frank Sidgwick. WhC
Glory of God, The. Psalms, XIX, Bible, *O.T.* *See* Heavens Declare the Glory of God, The.
Glory of God in Creation, The. Thomas Moore. MaRV; OHIP
(Thou Art, O God, *sl. abr.*) TrPWD
Glory of God Revealed in Jesus, The. Second Corinthians, IV: 6, Bible, *N.T.* MaRV
Glory of him from whom all things have motion, The. The Incommunicable Glory. Dante. *Fr.* Divina Commedia: Paradiso, I. GrCo-2
Glory of Lincoln, The. Thomas Curtis Clark. PGD
Glory of Love is brightest when the glory of self is dim, The. The True Apostolate. Ruby T. Weyburn. BLRP
Glory of Motion, The. R. St. John Tyrwhitt. VA
Glory of Paradise, The. St. Peter Damian, *tr. fr. Latin by* Basil Blackett. LaP
Glory of soundless heaven, wheel of stars. Valediction. John Hall Wheelock. NePoAm
Glory of sunrise and sunset. Enchantment. Arthur S. Bourinot. CPG
Glory of the beauty of the morning, The. The Glory. Edward Thomas. POTE
Glory of the Day Was in Her Face, The. James Weldon Johnson. BANP; CaAE; CDC; PoNe
Glory of the Garden, The. Kipling. VLEP
Glory of the Grass, The. Claire Wallace Flynn. StJW
Glory of the sunset and the night, The. Youth. Preston Clark. HBMV
Glory of Toil, The. Edna Dean Proctor. PGD
Glory of warrior, glory of orator, glory of song. Wages. Tennyson. BPN; EmBrPo; EPN; EPP; OAEP; OQP; PoVP; QP-2; TCEP; VLEP
Glory of Women, The. Siegfried Sassoon. TwCV
Glory, praise, and honor. Gloria, Laus, et Honor. *Unknown.* WHL
Glory Road, De. Clement Wood. BAP; HBMV; IHA; PFY; YaD

Glory That Was Greece, The. Byron. *See* Isles of Greece, The.
Glory to Cypris. Asclepiades, *tr. fr. Greek by* Walter Leaf. GrR
Glory to God and to God's Mother chaste. Sonnet: To Dante Alighieri. Giovanni Quirino. AWP; OnPM
Glory to God in Heaven, Glory! Glory to the Corn! *Unknown.* OnPM
Glory to God on high, and jolly mirth. A Christmas Carol. Francis Quarles. *Fr.* The Shepherd's Oracles. AnEC
Glory to God who made a man like this! To a Happy Warrior. Wilfrid Scawen Blunt. AnEnPo
Glory to Osiris, the Prince of Everlastingness. He Singeth a Hymn to Osiris, the Lord of Eternity. *Unknown. Fr.* Book of the Dead. AWP
Glory to the Corn! *Unknown, tr. fr. Russian by* W. R. S. Ralston. OnPM
Glory to the Name of Jesus! A. B. Simpson. BePJ
Glory to Thee, Father of All the Immortal. Canticle de Profundis. Lucy Larcom. MDAH
Glory to Thee [My God] This Night. Thomas Ken. BePJ
(Evening Prayer.) MaRV
Glory to Them. Anderson M. Scruggs. MaRV; MuM; OQP; QP-2
Glory Trail, The. Badger Clark. CP; IHA; PoeMoYo; SCC; SoAF, *with music;* StPo
Glorying. Miyauchi, *tr. fr. Japanese by* Lois J. Erickson. SoLD
Glo'ster girls they have no combs. The Codfish Shanty. *Unknown.* SoAmSa
Gloucester Harbor. Elizabeth Stuart Phelps Ward. AA
Gloucester Moors. William Vaughn Moody. AmPP; ATP; HBV; IAP; LBMV; MAP; MoAmPo (1942 ed.); OBAV; OxBA; PFY; PIAE; TCPD; TOP; WHA
Sels.
"Mile behind is Gloucester, A." BAP
"This earth is not the steadfast place." PoFr; WGRP
Glove, The. Robert Browning. EmBrPo; PCN; PIAE; PoVP; PreP; VLEP
Glove, The. Ben Jonson. *Fr.* Cynthia's Revels, IV, i. ElL
Glove, The. Richard Lovelace. *See* Elinda's Glove.
Glove and the Lions, The. Leigh Hunt. BeLS; BHV; EnLit; EV-4; FaPON; GN; HBV; HBVY; HoPM; LPS-2; MaC; OnSP; OTPC; PCD; PCN; PECK; PoMa; PreP; TreF; WBLP
Glove of Black in White Hand Bare. *Unknown, tr. fr. Spanish by* Longfellow. AnSpL-1
Glow and the glory are plighted, The. A Nice Correspondent. Frederick Locker-Lampson. HBV
Glow, lonely heart. Flower, Tree, and Bird. Hermann Hesse. TwGV
Glow of the restaurant is faked, the dream, The. Reality. Raymond Souster. CaP
Glow-Worm, The. William Lisle Bowles. EnSW
Glow-Worm, The. Edward Shanks. WHA
Glow-Worm, The ("Among all lovely things"). Wordsworth. LO
(Among All Lovely Things My Love Had Been.) MyFE
Glow-Worm, The ("I heard/ After the hour of sunset yester-even"). Wordsworth. *Fr.* The Prelude, VII. RO
Glowworm in a garden prayed, A. A Very Minor Poet Speaks. Isabel Valle. BLPA
Glow-worm-like the daisies peer. John Davidson. *Fr.* Summer. VLEP
Glow-Worms, The. Ann Hawkshaw. OTPC (1923 ed.)
Glow-Worms. P. A. Ropes. BoTP
Gluggity Glug. George Colman. *Fr.* The Myrtle and the Vine. HBV; LPS-3
Glugs abide in a far, far land, The. Joi, the Glug. C. J. Dennis. NeLNL
Glut on the Market, A. Patrick Kavanagh. *See* Pegasus.
Glutton, The. Al-Sumaisir, *tr. fr. Arabic by* A. J. Arberry. MooP
Glutton, The. La Fontaine, *tr. fr. French by* Elizur Wright. LiA
Glutton, The. William Langland. *See* Glutton and Bat the Brewer.
Glutton. Samuel Rowlands. SiCE
Glutton and Bat the Brewer. William Langland. *Fr.* The Vision of Piers Plowman, Passus 5. CoBE
(Glutton, The.) ACP
(Gluttony.) CoEV
Glycine's Song. Samuel Taylor Coleridge. *Fr.* Zapolya, Pt. II, Act II, sc. i. EmBrPo; ERP; OBEV; OTPC (1946 ed.)
(Song: "Sunny shaft did I behold, A.") BoTP; BPN; LO; TCEP; TwHP
(Sunny Shaft, A.) CEP
Glyph. *Unknown, tr. fr. Washoe-Paiute by* Mary Austin. LiTA
Gnarled arms. Wisteria. M. Kathleen Ahern. CAG
Gnarly and bent and deaf's a pos'. Zeke. L. A. G. Strong. MBP; MoBrPo
Gnat, The. Joseph Beaumont. LoBV; OBS
Gnat. Rosalie Moore. GoTP
Gnome, The. Harry Behn. FaPON; TiPo (1959 ed.)
Gnomic Lines. *Unknown. See* Maxims (Exeter Book).
Gnomic Verses, *sels.* Blake.
"Abstinence sows sand all over." ExPo; TrGrPo
(Abstinence and Desire.) OnPM
(Poems from MSS.) ViBoPo
"Angel that presided o'er my birth, The." OBRV; TrGrPo
(Injunction.) BLV; BoLiVe
"Great things are done when men and mountains meet." PC; TrGrPo
"He that has observed the golden rule." TrGrPo
Riches. BoLiVe; StaSt; TrGrPo
"Sword sang on the barren heath, The." TrGrPo
(Sword, The, and the Sickle.) BoLiVe; ChTr
"They said this mystery shall never cease." TrGrPo
Gnosis. Christopher Pearse Cranch. AnAmPo; HBV; IAP; LA; LBAP
(Thought.) BAP; LPS-3; UnW; WGRP
Stanza from an Early Poem, *sel.* AA
Γνῶθι σεαυτόν—and is this the prime. Self-Knowledge. Samuel Taylor Coleridge. SeCePo
Gnu, The. Hilaire Belloc. BMEP
Gnu Wooing, The. Burges Johnson. HBVY
Go! Kipling. *Fr.* The Explorer. GrCo-2
Go and ask Robin to bring the girls over. Vision by Sweetwater. John Crowe Ransom. CoBMV; CrMA; FaBoMo; MoAB; OxBA
Go and Catch a Falling Star. John Donne. *See* Song: "Go and catch a falling star."
Go & choose what sport you will. *Unknown.* SeCSL
Go and dig my grave both long and narrow. Dig My Grave. *Unknown.* OuSiCo
Go and lightly tread. Hermes of the Ways. *Unknown.* OnPM
Go and spy on the sheep. The Good Shepherd. Keidrych Rhys. NeBP
Go and tell Aunt Nancy. The Old Grey Goose. *Unknown.* ChTr
"Go ask Papa," the maiden said. Proposal. *Unknown.* TreFS
Go back now; pause to mark. Horizon Thong. George Abbe. GoYe
Go bow thy head in gentle spite. To a Lily. James Matthew Legaré. AA; AnAmPo; LA; SPP
"Go break to the needy sweet charity's bread." How Long Shall I Give? *Unknown.* BLRP
Go Bring Me Back My Blue-eyed Boy, *with music. Unknown.* AS
(London City, *diff. vers.*) AS
"Go bring the captive, he shall die." Ortiz. Hezekiah Butterworth. PAH
Go, burning sighs, unto the frozen heart. The Lover Sendeth Sighs to Move His Suit. Sir Thomas Wyatt. LiTL
Go, Crystal Tears. *Unknown.* ReIE
Go, Cupid, and my sweetheart tell. A Valentine. Eugene Field. PoRL
Go, daughters of Zion. The Death of Tammuz. Saul Tchernichowsky. TrJP
Go dig a hole in the meadow. Darling Cora. *Unknown.* TrAS
Go Down Death. James Weldon Johnson. AnAmPo; LA; MaRV; PoeMoYo; TCPD
Go Down, Moses. *Unknown.* AmPP; APW; BoAN-1, *with music;* OlF; PreP, *with music;* SPP; TrAS, *with music;* TreF
Go down, O ruddy sun! Help Us, Moon! *Unknown.* OnPM
Go Down, Ol' Hannah, *with music. Unknown.* OuSiCo
Go Down to Kew in Lilac-Time. Alfred Noyes. *Fr.* The Barrel Organ. BoTP
(At Kew.) TVSH
Go Down, You Little Red Rising Sun, *with music. Unknown.* OuSiCo
Go, dumb-born book. Envoi (1919). Ezra Pound. *Fr.* Hugh Selwyn Mauberley. APA; ChMo; CMP; CoAnAm; CoBMV; CoV; GTBS-W; LiTA; LiTM (rev. ed.); MAP; MoAB; MoAmPo; MoP; MoPo; NePA; OnAP; OxBA; TBM; UnPo (3d ed.)
Go, empty joys. Lately Written by Thomas, Earl of Strafford. *Unknown.* EV-2
("Goe empty joyes.") SeCSL
Go Far; Come Near. Walter de la Mare. CoBMV
Go, Feel What I Have Felt. *Unknown.* LPS-2
Go Fetch to Me a Pint o' Wine. Burns. *See* My Bonnie Mary.
Go, flaunting Rose. Aesthete to the Rose. *Unknown.* PA
Go Fly a Saucer. David McCord. ImOP
"I've seen one flying saucer," *sel.* FaPON
Go, for they call you, shepherd, from the hill. The Scholar-Gipsy. Matthew Arnold. AEV; AnFE; BEL; BPN; CaAE; ChTr; CoEV; EM-2; EmBrPo; EnL; EnLi-2; EnLit; EnSW; EPN; EPP; EV-5; FaBoEn; FiP; GEPC; GoTL; GTBS; GTML; HBV; LEAP; LoBV; MaPo; OAEP; OBEV; OBVV; Po; PoE; PoEL-5; PoFS;

Go, for they call you (*continued*) PoVP; REAL; ReaPo; SeCeV; ShBV-4; TOP; TyEnPo; UnPo (1st ed.); ViBoPo; ViPo; ViPP; VLEP; WP

Go, Forget Me. Charles Wolfe. HBV

Go forth, my son. Benediction. Georgia Douglas Johnson. GoSl

"Go Forward." "A. R. G." BLRP

Go, friendly Zephyr! whisp'ring greet. Friendly Zephyr. Hafiz. PeP

Go from me: I am one of those who fall. Mystic and Cavalier. Lionel Johnson. CaAE; GTIV; MBP; MoBrPo; SeCePo; ViPP

Go from me, summer friends, and tarry not. From Sunset to Star Rise. Christina Rossetti. PeBoSo

Go from me. Yet I feel that I shall stand. Nevermore Alone [*or* Go from Me]. Elizabeth Barrett Browning. Sonnets from the Portuguese, VI. AV; BCEP; BPN; CaAE; EmBrPo; EPN; ES; EV-4; GBV; GTSL; HBV; LEAP; LoPo; LoPS; LPS-1; MaRV; OBEV; OBVV; PG (1955 ed.); PIAE; PIR; TreFS; TrGrPo; VA; ViBoPo; ViPo

Go from the east to the west, as the sun and the stars direct thee. Arthur Hugh Clough. *Fr.* Hope Evermore and Believe! MaRV

"Go get me some of your father's gold." Pretty Polly. *Unknown.* AS

Go Get the Axe, *with music. Unknown.* AS; TrAS

Go get the third johnny head and touch it north. Sis Joe. *Unknown.* OuSiCo

Go get water, water is good to drink. Hymn for Water. Merrill Moore. TrGrPo (1942 ed.)

Go Get You Gone, Begone, Begone. Charles d'Orléans, *tr. fr. French by* Alan Conder. TrFP

Go, glorious sun. To The Sun. Patterické Jenkyn. SeCL

Go, go, complete the overthrow! Love-Ending. Rose O'Neill. BAP; LEAP

Go, go, quaint follies, sugared [*or* queint folies, sugred] sin. Idle Verse. Henry Vaughan. AtBAP; ElSeCe; NBE; OAEP

Go, happy book, and let my Candia see. To His Mistress; Sending Her the Arcadia. Thomas Beaumont. ElSeCe; SeCL

Go [*or* Goe], happy Rose, and, interwove [*or* enterwove]. To the Rose: A Song [*or* To the Rose]. Robert Herrick. EPS; HBV; OBS

Go, Heart, unto the Lamp of Licht. *Unknown.* BSV; GoTS

Go I must; when I am gone. To His Tomb-Maker. Robert Herrick. SeCV-1

Go, I will shut the windows. Alienation. Harry Kemp. BAP; HBMV

Go, intercept some fountain in the vein. Andrew Marvell. ReEn

"Go into the highways." Compel Them to Come In. Leonard Dodd. BLRP

Go learn, O green-eyed monster's fatal brood. The Battle of the Books. Callimachus. OxBG

Go, let the fatted calf be kill'd. The Welcome. Abraham Cowley. *Fr.* The Mistress. SeCV-1

Go, litel book [*or* bok], go litel my tragedie [*or* myn tregedie]. The Envoy. Chaucer. *Fr.* Troilus and Criseyde. FiP; MyFE; NBE; ViBoPo

Go, Little Book. Robert Louis Stevenson. InP; MBP; MoBrPo; NeMA; PoRA
(Envoy: "Go, little book, and wish to all.") HBV; MOB; PoRL; YT
(Wishes.) OBEV (new ed.); OBVV

Go, little book, and leave me still in doubt. Epilogue to a Book of Verse. Arthur Guiterman. InMe

Go, little book, and to the world impart. To His Book. William Walsh. CEP; EV-3

Go, little book, and wish to all. Go, Little Book [*or* Envoy *or* Wishes]. Robert Louis Stevenson. HBV; InP; MOB; MBP; MoBrPo; NeMA; OBEV (new ed.); OBVV; PoRA; PoRL; YT

Go little book: thyself present. To His Book. Spenser. *Fr.* The Shepheardes Calender. CaAE; ReIE; SiCE

Go, lovely boy! to yonder tow'r. Verses Written during the War 1756–1763. Thomas Osbert Mordaunt. OBEC

Go, Lovely Rose. Edmund Waller. AEV; ALV; ATP; AWP; BCEP; BEL; BLV; BTP; CenL; CoBE; EG; ElSeCe; EM-1; EnLi-1; EnLit; EnLoPo; EPP; EV-2; GTBS; GTBS-D; GTBS-W; GTSE; GTSL; HBV; InPo; JAWP; LEAP; LiTL; LO; LoPo; LPS-1, *add. st. by* Henry Kirke White; OAEP; OBEV; OuHeWo; PG (1945 ed.); PIAE; PoE; PoFS; PoRA; ReEn; RiBV; SeCeV; SeCL; TCEP; TOP; TreFS; TrGrPo; TyEnPo; ViBoPo; WBP; WHA
(Song: "Go lovely rose.") AtBAP; CaAE; CEP; CoEV; EPS; EtPaEn; ExPo; LoBV; NeHB; OBS; PoEL-3; SeCV-1; SeEP; UnPo (3d ed.)
(Song: "Goe lovely rose.") FaBoEn; MePo

Go, loving [*or* lovely] woodbine, clip with lovely grace. On a Pair of Garters. Sir John Davis. EG; SiPS

Go, Magi, on Your Way. *Unknown, tr. fr. French by* Edward Bliss Reed. ChrBoLe

Go make thy garden fair as thou canst. Gardens. *Unknown.* OQP; QP-1

Go Michael, of Celestial Armies Prince. War in Heaven (The First Battle). Milton. *Fr.* Paradise Lost, VI. ExPo

Go, Muse, unto the Bower. Nicholas Breton. ReIE

Go, My Flock. Sir Philip Sidney. Astrophel and Stella: Ninth Song. SiPS

Go, my songs, seek your praise from the young and from the intolerant. Ité. Ezra Pound. MAP; MoAB; MoAmPo; TwAmPo

Go, my songs, to the lonely and the unsatisfied. Commission. Ezra Pound. MM

Go Not, Happy Day. Tennyson. Maud, Pt. I, xvii. BPN; LiTL; OBVV; TOP
(Song: "Go not, happy day.") ATP

Go not into the lofty house. The Lofty House. John Gould Fletcher. MAP; MoAmPo

Go not, my soul, in search of Him. The Indwelling God. Frederick Lucian Hosmer. MaRV; OQP; QP-2; WGRP

Go not to marts of costly show. Ballade of Queen's Lace. Richard Le Gallienne. CV

Go not to the hills of Erin. The Wind on the Hills. Dora Sigerson Shorter. HBMV; JKCP; TIP

Go not too frequently thy friends to see. Advice to Bores. Abraham ibn Chasdai. TrJP

Go not too near a house of rose. Emily Dickinson. BLV; BoLiVe; MAP; MoAB; MoAmPo
(Joy in Insecurity.) NeMA

Go now! and with some daring drug. Temperance, or The Cheap Physician. Richard Crashaw. LPS-2; SeCV-1

Go Now, My Song. Andrew Young. ChTr

"Go now, Skirnir! and seek to gain." Freyr's Courtship. *Unknown. Fr.* The Elder Edda. PaOS

Go on your way. Meeting. Robert Desnos. MiCF

Go, one of you, find out the forester. The Music of Hounds [*or* Theseus and Hippolyta]. Shakespeare. *Fr.* A Midsummer Night's Dream. AlBD; EV-1

Go Out. Eileen Mathias. BoTP

Go out, good ships, across the tide. Ships. Nancy Byrd Turner. SUS

Go patter to lubbers and swabs, do ye see. Poor Jack. Charles Dibdin. BeLS; EV-3; HBV; LPS-2

Go, Ploughman, Plough. Joseph Campbell. HBMV; MPB

Go, Pretty Birds! *At. to* Thomas Heywood. *See* Ye Little Birds That Sit and Sing.

Go, Pretty Child. Robert Herrick. *See* To His Saviour, a Child; a Present by a Child.

Go, pretty page, with the dimpled chin. The Age of Wisdom. Thackeray. *Fr.* Rebecca and Rowena. ALV; BMEP; HBV; LEAP; LPS-1; VA

Go, pytyous hart, rasyd with dedly wo. At the Instance of a Noble Lady. John Skelton. CaAE

Go, roads, to the four quarters of our quiet distance. The Evening of the Visitation. Thomas Merton. ISi

Go roll a prairie up like cloth. The Merry Miner. *Unknown.* IHA; StVeCh

Go, Rose, and in her golden hair. To a Rose. Frank Dempster Sherman. AA; LEAP; OBAV

Go saddle up my milk-white steed. Geordie (C *vers.*). *Unknown.* BaBo

Go, seek Cassandra, men! Make your best speed. Cassandra. Euripides. *Fr.* Trojan Women. GrR

Go, silly worm, drudge, trudge, and travel. Go, Silly Worm [*or* Omnia Somnia]. Joshua Sylvester. ElL; OBS

Go, simple Book of Ballads, go. To Mary Sinclair, with a Volume of His Poems. Thomas Campbell. ERP

Go Sleep, Ma Honey. Edward D. Barker. AA; BOL; MOAH

Go, songs, for ended is our brief, sweet play. Envoy. Francis Thompson. CoBE; EmBrPo; HBV; MBP; MoBrPo; POT; PoTo; POTT; PoVP; PreP; VLEP

Go, soul [*or* Goe, soule], the body's [*or* bodies] guest. The Lie [*or* The Soul's Errand]. Sir Walter Ralegh. AtBAP; BCEP; BHV; BLV; ChTr; CoEV; ElSeCe; EnLi-1 (1949 ed.); ExPo; HBV; InvP; LiTB; LPS-3; OAEP; OBSC; PECK; PoEL-2; PoFr; PoFS; ReEn; RiBV; SeCeV; SiCE; SiPS; SiTL; TrGrPo; TuPP; ViBoPo; WGRP; WoL

Go, speed the stars of thought. Intellect. Emerson. OnPM

Go spend your penny, Beauty, when you will. Sonnet. John Masefield. *Fr.* Sonnets ("Long, long ago"). AEV; TCPD

"Go steal your father's weight in gold." Lady Isabel and the Elf-Knight (B *vers.*). *Unknown.* ViBoFo

Go, stir the brazier coals, my child. The Brazier Coals. Miguel de Unamuno. *Fr.* Domestic Scenes. LiTW; OnPM; WoL

Go, stranger, tell the Spartans that we rest. On the Spartans Who Fell at Thermopylae. Simonides, *tr. by* Walter Leaf. GrR

Go study to disdain. Minotaur. Elinor Wylie. TwAmPo

Go t' sleep, li'l honey, white chile. Black Mammy's Lullaby, 1855. Wightman F. Melton. BOL
Go, teach our sturdy youth the trade of war. Endurance and Faithfulness. Horace. Odes, III, 2. RoL
Go tell Aunt Rhody [*or* Aunt Nancy *or* old Nancy]. The Old Gray Goose. *Unknown.* ABF; FTB; LaNeLa
Go tell the Spartans, thou that passest by. Thermopylae [*or* Inscription to Spartans Dead at Thermopylae]. Simonides, *tr. by* William L. Bowles. AWP; GrPo; JAWP; TreF; WBP
Go Tell Them that Jesus Is Living. *Unknown.* BePJ
Go ter sleep, go ter sleep. Go to Sleepy. *Unknown.* TrAS
Go, Thames, and tell the busy town. Written at Mr. Pope's House at Twickenham. George Lyttelton. CEP
Go, the rich Chariot instantly prepare. The Muse. Abraham Cowley. BEL; Po
Go thou and seek the House of Prayer! Written on a Sunday Morning. Robert Southey. BEL
Go Thou, That Vainly Dost Mine Eyes Invite. Henry King. SeCL
Go thou thy way, and I go mine. Mizpah. Julia A. Baker. BLPA; FaBoBe; NeHB; OQP; PTA-2; QP-2
Go Thou to Rome. Shelley. *Fr.* Adonais. ChTr
(Grave of Keats.) TCEP
Go through the gates with closed eyes. Close Your Eyes! Arna Bontemps. CDC; PoNe
Go thy waies since thou wilt goe. *Unknown.* SeCSL
Go thy way, eat thy bread with joy, and drink thy wine with a merry heart. Live Joyfully. Ecclesiastes, Bible, *O.T.* TreFS
Go to Bed. *Unknown.* ChTr
("Go to bed first.") OxNR; PPL; RIS
Go to bed early—wake up with joy. *Unknown.* BoTP
Go to bed late. *Unknown.* OxNR
Go to bed, Tom. *Unknown.* OxNR
Go to Dark Gethsemane. James Montgomery. ChIP
(Christ Our Example in Suffering.) HBV
Go to him, ah, go to him, and lift your eyes aglow to him. To Her—Unspoken. Amelia Josephine Burr. HBV
Go to Sleep. Karl Simrock, *tr. fr. German by* Louis Untermeyer. RIS
(German Slumber Song.) GoTP
Go to sleep, McKade. Evening Song. Kenneth Fearing. ChMo
Go to sleep, my son. *See* Fais dodo, mon fils.
Go to sleep—though of course you will not. A Goodnight. William Carlos Williams. MoAB; MoAmPo; MOAP
Go to sleep, you poor little darling. *Unknown.* BOL
Go to Sleepy, *with music. Unknown.* AS, *longer vers.;* TrAS
Go to the Ant. Proverbs, Bible, *O.T. See* Reproof, A.
Go to the dull church-yard and see. Hillocks of Mortality. Thomas Flatman. *Fr.* A Dooms-Day Thought. BeR
Go to the end of the void. *Unknown, tr. fr. Chinese.* Tao Teh Ching, I. WhP
Go to the Shine That's on a Tree. Richard Eberhart. FiMAP; UnS
Go to the sick man's bedside—mark how dim. Samuel Bartlett Parris. *Fr.* Anticipations and Recollections. PoP
Go to the western gate, Luke Havergal. Luke Havergal. E. A. Robinson. AA; AmP; AmPP; AWP; CoBA; CoBMV; CoV; CrMA; DaM; InPo; JAWP; LEAP; LiTA; LiTM (rev. ed.); MAP; MoAB; MoAmPo; MOAP; MoPo; MoVE; NePA; PFY; Po; PoEL-5; PoRA; TriL; TwP; UnPo (3d ed.)
Go to Thy Rest. Lydia Huntley Sigourney. LPS-1
Go, topless Geraneia, and gaze, foul precipice. Lost at Sea. Simonides. GrL; OxBG
Go, Valentine, and tell that lovely Maid. Sonnet. Robert Southey. ERP
"Go, wash thyself in Jordan—go, wash thee and be clean!" Naaman's Song. Kipling. OtMeF
Go way, Eadie, you dirty dog. Eadie. *Unknown.* OuSiCo
Go 'way, fiddle! folks is tired o' hearin' you a-squawkin'. De Fust [*or* The First] Banjo. Irwin Russell. *Fr.* Christmas Night in the Quarters. AA; BAP; BLPA; BOHV; HBV; IHA; LEAP; LHV; PFY; SPP
Go 'Way f'om Mah Window. *Unknown.* ABF; AS
Go! What does it matter? Go! Black Frost. May Folwell Hoisington. LPS-1
Go Where Glory Waits Thee. Thomas Moore. LPS-1; TreFS
Go with me, Master, by the way. By the Way. Annie Johnson Flint. PraP
Go with your tauntings, go. Song. John Clare. OBRV
Go wretch, resign thy presidential chair. On Jefferson. Bryant. BoHiPo
"Go ye into the highways." Compel Them to Come In. Leonard Dodd. BLRP
Go you, O winds that blow from north to south. To Pandora [*or* Sonnet]. Alexander Craig. EIL; TuPP
Goal, The. Frank W. Gunsaulus. MaRV
Goal, The. Ella Wheeler Wilcox. BLP; MaRV; OQP; QP-1
Goal and the Way, The. John Oxenham. PGD
Goal of Intellectual Man, The. Richard Eberhart. MoPo
Goal of Life, The. Burns. *See* Auld Lang Syne.
Goat, The. Anyte, *tr. fr. Greek by* W. H. D. Rouse. OxBG
Goat, The. Roland Young. WhC
Goat Paths, The. James Stephens. AlDL; AnIV; AWP; CH; ChMo; CMP; GTIV; JAWP; LiTB; OxBI; PG; TwCV; UnPo (3d ed.); WBP; WHA
Goat-Pen. Luis L. Franco, *tr. fr. Spanish by* Muna Lee. AnCL
Goat was nibbling on a vine, A. The Vine and the Goat. Aesop. AWP
Goatherd, The. Grace Hazard Conkling. GaP; TiPo
Goat-herd follows his flock, The. Juan Quintana. Alice Corbin. BAP; HBMV; NP
Goatherds' Thank-Offering, The. Leonidas of Tarentum, *tr. fr. Greek by* F. L. Lucas. GrPE
Goats. C. E. S. Wood. AnEnPo; PoTo
Goats of Juan Fernandez, The. Coleman Rosenberger. DaM
Goats with strutting dugs shall homeward speed, The. The Return of the Golden Age, with the Birth of Pollio. Virgil, *tr. by* Dryden. *Fr.* Eclogues. BeR
Goblin, The. Rose Fyleman. BoTP; TiPo
Goblin Feet. J. R. R. Tolkien. FaPON; PoMS
Goblin Goose, The. *Unknown.* PA
Goblin has a wider mouth, The. How to Tell Goblins from Elves. Monica Shannon. FaPON; TiPo
Goblin, A, lives in our house, in our house, in our house. The Goblin. Rose Fyleman. BoTP; TiPo
Goblin marked his monarch well, The. The First Quest [*or* The Fay's Departure]. Joseph Rodman Drake. *Fr.* The Culprit Fay. AA; GN
Goblin Market. Christina Rossetti. AnFE; AtBAP; DaM; EmBrPo; EV-5; GoTL; OAEP; OnSP; PCN; PoVP; TCEP; ViP; ViPo; VLEP
"Morning and evening," *sel.* BoTP
Goblin Tower, The. Frank Belknap Long. DaM
Goblinade, A. Florence Page Jaques. GoBP; TiPo
Goblins came, on mischief bent. The Temptation of St. Anthony. R. L. Gales. WP
Goblins on the doorstep. This Is Halloween. Dorothy Brown Thompson. BrR; TiPo; YeAr
Goblin's Song, The. James Telfer. ChTr
Go-cart trundles on the road, A. The Hard Journey. Jules Supervielle. TrFP
God. Gamaliel Bradford. MaRV; QS; WGRP
God. Catherine Cate Coblentz. OQP; QP-1
God. Gavril Romanovich Derzhavin, *tr. fr. Russian by* Sir John Bowring. PTA-2
(O Thou Eternal One!) WGRP
God. Emerson. *Fr.* Woodnotes, Pt. II. OQP; QP-2
God. Gonzalo Escudero, *tr. fr. Spanish by* Dudley Fitts. AnCL
God, *sel.* Alexander MacLachlan.
"Hail, Thou great mysterious Being!" CaP
God. Harold Monro. *Fr.* Dawn. WGRP
God. Isaac Rosenberg. MoPo
God. John Banister Tabb. MaRV
God. *Unknown, tr. fr. Sanskrit by* Dhan Ghopal Mukerji. *Fr.* The Upanishads. MW
God. James Cowden Wallace. *See* God the Omniscient.
God, a man at Yale, adopted a monkey. Monkey. Josephine Miles. FiMAP
God above, for man's delight, The. A New Ballade of the Marigolde [*or* The Marigold]. William Forrest. CoMu; PoLi
God, although this life is but a wraith. *See* God, though this life is but a wraith.
God and His Creation. Elizabeth Rowe. DiM
God and I in space alone. Illusion. Ella Wheeler Wilcox. WGRP
God and Man. S. A. Nagel. MaRV
God and Man. Pindar, *tr. fr. Greek by* F. L. Lucas. *Fr.* Nemean Odes, VI. GrPE
God and Man. Sophocles, *tr. fr. Greek by* Robert Whitelaw. *Fr.* Oedipus Rex. OxBG
(Chorus: "Oh, may my constant feet not fail.") WGRP
(People Pray, The.) GrR
God and Man. Albert Durrant Watson. CPG
God and the devil in these letters. The Postman's Bell Is Answered Everywhere. Horace Gregory. MoAmPo; MoVE
God and the Fairies, be true, be true! For a Child Named Katherine. Louise Townsend Nicholl. SP
God and the Soldier. *Unknown.* TreFS
God and the Soul, *sels.* John Lancaster Spalding.
At the Ninth Hour. AA
Et Mori Lucrum. AA
Nature and the Child. AA
Starry Host, The. AA; HBV
Void Between, The. AA
God and the Strong Ones. Margaret Widdemer. CP; HBMV; HiLiAm; PoFr; QS
God and yet a man, A. The Divine Paradox. *Unknown.* MeEV

God answers prayer; sometimes when hearts are weak. Answered Prayer. Myra Goodwin Plantz. PraP
God approached dissolves into the air, The. Doctrinal Point. William Empson. AtBAP
God! ask me not to record your wonders. Scholfield Huxley. Edgar Lee Masters. *Fr.* Spoon River Anthology. ChMo; CMP; LiTA; MoPo; TrPWD
God bade the birds break not the silent spell. The Thrush. Laura Benét. BLA; HBMV
God be here, God be there. *Unknown.* OxNR
God Be in My Head. *Unknown. Fr.* Sarum Primer. MaRV; OxBoCh; PoLi
(Hymnus.) ChTr
(Knight's Prayer, The.) BoTP
(Mihi Adhaerere Deo Bonum Est.) PG (1955 ed.)
God be merciful unto us, and bless us. Let the Nations Be Glad. Psalm LXVII, Bible, *O.T.* FaPON; OnPM
God be praised/ Antonio Stradivari has an eye. Working with God. "George Eliot." *Fr.* Stradivarius. MaRV
God be thanked the place is here. Joseph and the Shopkeeper. *Unknown.* ChrBoLe
God be with the night that's gone! The Vanished Night. Niall MacMurray. KiLC
God be with thee, my belovèd—God be with thee! A Valediction. Elizabeth Barrett Browning. HBV
God Be with You. *Unknown.* PoToHe (new ed.)
God be with you in the Springtime. Through the Year. Julian S. Cutler. BLPA
God be with you in your need! Resurgat. A. S. Cripps. BoSA
God Be with You till We Meet Again. J. E. Rankin. OlF; TreFS
God behind the Veil. Jami, *tr. fr. Persian by* F. Hadland Davis. OnPM
God, bless all little boys who look like Puck. Blessing on Little Boys. Arthur Guiterman. DDA; TBM; TrPWD
God bless our country's emblem. Our Country's Emblem. *Unknown.* WBLP
God bless our dear United States. The People's Prayer. Amos R. Wells. PraP
God bless our Fathers' Land. International Ode. Oliver Wendell Holmes. PEOR; TCAP
God Bless Our Home. Robert Freeman. MaRV; PraP
God bless our home, and help us. Prayer for Help. *Unknown.* PraP
God bless our meat. *Unknown.* OxNR
God Bless Our Native Land! *Sts.* 1-2, Siegfried A. Mahlmann, *tr. fr. German by* Charles Timothy Brooks *and* John S. Dwight; *st.* 3, William E. Hickson. MaRV; OlF, *sts.* 1-2
(Our Native Land, *sts.* 1-2.) PEDC
God bless pawnbrokers! Pawnbrokers. Marguerite Wilkinson. HBMV
God bless the craft of Clanranald. Birlinn Chlann-Raghnaill. Alexander MacDonald. GoTS
God bless the field and bless the furrow. The Robin's Song. *Unknown, at. to* C. Lovat Fraser. BoTP; MoShBr
God Bless the Flag. *Unknown.* PoRL
God bless the King—I mean the Faith's defender. A Jacobite Toast [*or* Extempore Verses *or* A Toast *or* Which Is Which?]. John Byrom. BOHV; EV-3; HBV; OBEC; OtMeF; PIAE; ViBoPo
"God bless the man who first invented sleep!" Early Rising. John Godfrey Saxe. AnNE; APW; BOHV; HBV; InMe; LEAP; PR; WhC
God bless the master of this house,/ The mistress also. Christmas Carol [*or* Good-bye *or* A Grace]. *Unknown.* BoTP; BrR; ChBR; MeMeAg; MoShBr; OHIP; OxNR; SiSoSe; StVeCh; TiPo; YaCaBo
God bless the master of this house, and all that are therein. The Singers in the Snow. *Unknown.* OHIP; SDH
God bless thee and keep thee thro' the coming days. A New Year's Wish. "J. H. S." BLRP
God bless this food, and bless us all. Table Graces, or Prayers. *Unknown.* BLRP
God bless this house and all within it. Lines for a Friend's House. Edgar A. Guest. PraP
God bless this house from thatch to floor. *Unknown.* OxNR
God Bless Us Every One. James Whitcomb Riley. COAH
God Bless You. *Unknown.* PoToHe
God Bless You, Dear, To-Day! John Bennett. AA; HBV
God bless your house this holy night. This Holy Night. Eleanor Farjeon. ChBR
God braced me with His firm hand. The Tool of Fate. "Yehoash." TrJP
God breathe a blessing on. Bestiary. A. M. Klein. BoCaPo
God broke the years to hours and days. As Thy Days So Shall Thy Strength Be. "George Klingle." BLRP
God built the earth. Honeymoon. Mary Carolyn Davies. PR
God! but this rain-sweet greenness shakes the heart. Soon with the Lilac Fades Another Spring. Patrick MacDonogh. OxBI
God by land and sea defend you. Take Thought. Plato. OxBG
God, by the sea, by the resounding sea. Hymn for the Victorious Dead. Herman Hagedorn. AOAH
God called the nearest angels who dwell with Him above. The Two Angels. Whittier. AA
God can wake light/ Out of black night. Lord of Nature. Pindar. GrR
God Cares. Helen Annis Casterline. BLRP
God Cares. "Marianne Farningham." BLRP
(He Careth.) WBLP
God cares! How sweet the strain. God Cares. Helen Annis Casterline. BLRP
God Chose a Star. *Unknown.* BPP
God counts time not by minutes nor by days. In His Sight. Anna R. Baker. OQP; QP-2
God Dawg My Lousy Soul, *with music. Unknown.* StDa
God Don't Like It, *with music. Unknown.* OuSiCo
God don't want no coward soldiers. God's Goin' to Set This World on Fire (B *vers.*). *Unknown.* AS
God dreamed a man. The Bugler. F. W. Harvey. BMEP
God dreamed—the suns sprang flaming into place. Creation. Ambrose Bierce. AA; BLP; LHV; PFY
God ever bless the earth. The Lute. Ibn Qadi Mila. MooP
God ever guard the memory. Exchange. Hafsa. MooP
God Everywhere. Abraham ibn Ezra, *tr. fr. Hebrew by* "D. E. de L." TrJP
God Everywhere in Nature. Carlos Wilcox. LPS-2
God favored England on that April day. Shakespeare. Agnes MacCarthy Hickey. PFE
God fills my being to the brim. Doxology. Jessica Powers. JKCP (1955 ed.)
God flings/ In air His box of things. Faster. Geoffrey Scott. TwCV
God for You, A. Marion Strobel. NP
God-forgotten. Thomas Hardy. BEL; PoVP; TOP; ViP; VLEP
God Forsakes Anthony. C. P. Cavafy, *tr. fr. Modern Greek by* Rae Dalven. MoGP
God from the first created diversely. Women. Semonides. GrPE
God gave all men all earth to love. Sussex. Kipling. GTML; PoeT; POTT; TCPD; ViPP; VLEP
God gave His children memory. Roses in December. G. A. Studdert-Kennedy. BLPA
God gave my son in trust to me. My Son. James D. Hughes. BLPA
God gave my world to me. My World. Chauncey R. Piety. MaRV; OQP; QP-1
God gave the pig. Ode of Lament. Randolph Jeck. WhC
God girt her about with the surges. New Zealand. William Pember Reeves. BoAu
God, give me a song for the world that's glad. A Christmas Song. Ruth Winant Wheeler. PraP
God, give me back the simple faith. A Prayer for Faith. Margaret E. Sangster. PoToHe
God Give Me Joy. Thomas Curtis Clark. OQP; QP-2
God, give me love! I do not only pray. A Prayer for Love. Elsa Barker. OQP; QP-1
God, give me speech, in mercy touch my lips. The Unutterable Beauty. G. A. Studdert-Kennedy. TrPWD
God Give to Men ("God give the yellow man"). Arna Bontemps. BANP; CDC
God Give Us Men! Josiah Gilbert Holland. BLPA; NeHB; OQP; PaA; PoRL; QP-1; TreF; WBLP
(Day's Demand, The.) MaRV
(Give Us Men.) PTA-1
(Wanted.) BoPo; PoMa; PoP; TrPWD
God give us Mothers, this we plead. A Prayer for Mothers. John F. Todd. PraP
"God give you peace!" Your happy lay. Joculator Domini. Sister Mary John Frederick. GoBC
God give us joy that we may give. Giving. *Unknown.* PoToHe
God, God, be lenient her first night there. Prayer for a Very New Angel. Violet Alleyn Storey. BLPA; DDA; MotAn; TreFS
God grant that all who watch today. A Shining Hope. Julia H. Thayer. OQP; QP-1
God grant that I may never be. Prayer in April. Sara Henderson Hay. MaRV; OQP; QP-2; TrPWD
God, grant thy peace in perfect measure. July, 1850. Feodor Ivanovich Tyutchev. WaL
God, grant to us Thy blessed Gift again. Bartimeus. Laura Simmons. ChIP
God grant us wisdom in these coming days. A New Earth. John Oxenham. MaRV
God 'graves His cryptic script with inexorable pen. Palimpsest. Hyman Edelstein. CaP
God guard me from those thoughts men think. A Prayer for Old Age. W. B. Yeats. BrBE
God guard you, and greet you well. Odes, IV, 21. Pierre de Ronsard. PrPoCR
God had called us, and we came. The Blue-Flag in the Bog. Edna St. Vincent Millay. AnAmPo; LA

God had hardly time to plan it. Creation. Mary Ballard Duryee. LauV
God has a special place for still-born things. A Special Place. Dorothy Quick. MuM; QS
God has a way of making flowers grow. In Desert Places. Sister Mary Madeleva. GoTP
God has builded a house with a low lintel. Sanctuary. Aline Kilmer. LEAP
God has power, A. But can a mere man follow. The Poet. Rainer Maria Rilke. OnHM
God Has Put It Away. Jörgen Moe, *tr. fr. Norwegian by* Charles W. Stork. AnNoLy
"God has so many singing birds." The Last Song. Eileen Duggan. CAW
God has spoken: Love me, son, thou must; oh, see. My God Has Spoken. Paul Verlaine. CAW
God hath been patient long. In eons past. The Harvest Waits. Lloyd Mifflin. BPP; HBV
God hath not promised. What God Hath [*or* Has] Promised. Annie Johnson Flint. BLRP; MaRV; WBLP
God hath two wings, which He doth ever move. Mercy and Love. Robert Herrick. SeCV-1
God, He called John while he was a-writin'. John Was a-Writin'. *Unknown.* OuSiCo
God He rejects all prayers that are sleight. Prayers Must Have Poise. Robert Herrick. LiTB
God Hears Prayer. Ethel Romig Fuller. *See* Proof.
God, He's Gwine to Set Dis World on Fire. *Unknown. See* God's Goin' to Set This World on Fire.
God Hide the Whole World in Thy Heart. Emerson. *Fr.* Woodnotes, II. OQP; QP-2
God, how I envy you these great oak roots. A Jew Walks in Westminster Abbey. Aubrey Hodes. TrJP
God, I am traveling out to death's sea. Valley of the Shadow. John Galsworthy. HiLiEn; MaRV; OHIP; QS; TrPWD
God, I fain would pray with fervor. Prayer. Joseph von Eichendorff. AnGP
God I love thee in Thy robe of roses. Zebaoth. Else Lasker-Schüler. TrJP
God, I return to you on April days. Mockery. Louis Untermeyer. LBMV; QS
God, if this were enough. If This Were Faith [*or* If This Were Enough]. Robert Louis Stevenson. BLP; BMEP; EPP; MaRV; OQP; PC; PoeT; POTT; QP-2; TrPWD; WGRP
God, if thou livest, Thine eye on me bend. Plaint of Friendship by Death Broken. Robert M. Nichols. TCPD
God, in His ages past the dawn of days. Niagara. Edward F. Garesché. JKCP
God in His Goodness Sent the Grapes. *Unknown.* DDA
God, in His infinite wisdom. Acceptance. Langston Hughes. NePoAm-2
God in the Nation's Life. *Unknown.* BLRP; WBLP
God, in Thy Heaven hast Thou ever known. Earth Love. Beatrice Redpath. CPG
God Incarnate. Ruth M. Williams. BePJ
God is a proposition. C. Day Lewis. *Fr.* The Magnetic Mountain. QS
God Is at the Anvil. Lew Sarett. HBMV; MaRV; NLK; WGRP
God Is at the Organ. Egbert Sandford. MaRV; OQP; QP-1
God is beauty. God. Catherine Cate Coblentz. OQP; QP-1
God is eternity, the sky, the sea. God and Man. Albert Durrant Watson. CPG
God Is Faithful. Frances Ridley Havergal. BLRP
God is great and God is good. Table Graces for Prayers. *Unknown.* BLRP
God is grown ancient. He no longer hears. Job Reviles. A. M. Klein. *Fr.* Design for Mediaeval Tapestry. QS
God Is Here. Madeleine Aaron. MaRV; OQP; QP-2
God Is in Every Tomorrow. Laura A. Barter Snow. BLRP
God, is it sinful if I feel. A Prayer. Mary Dixon Thayer. HBMV; TrPWD
God Is Love. Sir John Bowring. FaBoBe; MaRV; NeHB; OIF
God is my sheepherd; therefore I can lack nothing. Psalm XXIII, Bible, *O.T. Fr.* The Bishops' Bible. ReIE
God Is My Strong Salvation. James Montgomery. MaRV
God Is Near. Elizabeth McE. Shields. PraP
God Is Not Dumb. James Russell Lowell. *Fr.* Bibliolatres. MaRV; OQP; QP-1; WGRP
God Is One. Panatattu. MaRV
(Unity of God, The.) WGRP
God is One and Alone, and there is none other with him. The One God. *Unknown, tr. fr. Egyptian by* E. A. Wallis Budge. MaRV
God is our refuge and strength. Psalm XLVI, Bible, *O.T.* AWP; MaRV; OnPM; TrGrPo; WGRP
God is praise and glory. Psalm of Battle. *Unknown. Fr.* The Thousand and One Nights. AWP; JAWP; WBP
God is seen God/ In the star, in the stone, in the flesh. God with Us. Robert Browning. *Fr.* Saul. GrCo-2
God is shaping the great future of the Islands of the Sea. The Islands of the Sea. George Edward Woodberry. MC; PAH
God Is So Good. Jane Taylor. *Fr.* Encouragement for Little Children. MeMeAg; OTPC (1946 ed.)
(Little Hymn, A.) BOL
God is still glorified. Building in Stone. Sylvia Townsend Warner. MBP; MoBrPo
God is the Oneness. God the Life of Nature. Mordecai Kaplan. QS
God is too high to measure out each thing. Credo. Lizette Woodworth Reese. QS
God is very near to me. Presence. Mary E. McCullough. MaRV
God Is Working His Purpose Out. A. C. Ainger. BLRP
God keep my heart attuned to laughter. As I Grow Old. *Unknown.* MaRV; OQP; PraP; QP-2
God Keep You. "Madeline Bridges." AA; MaRV
God keep you safe, my little love. My Little Love. Charles B. Hawley. HBV
God keep you, swallows heralding. Spring Song. Pierre de Ronsard. TrFP
God Kneph, trembling, rocked the universe, The. Horus. Gérard de Nerval. AnFP
God Knoweth Best. *Unknown.* WBLP
(Your Father Knoweth.) BLRP
God Knows Best. Caroline Atherton Briggs Mason. *See* En Voyage.
God knows how many nights upon her bed. *See* Old Maid. J. U. Nicholson. HBMV
God knows it, I am with you. To a Republican Friend, 1848. Matthew Arnold. EmBrPo; EPN; PoFr; PoVP; ViPP; VLEP
God knows there's plenty of earth for all of us! If I Must. Lloyd Roberts. CPG
God Leads the Way. Cleanthes, *tr. fr. Greek by* C. C. Martindale. OxBG
(Stoic's Resignation, The, *tr. by* F. L. Lucas.) GrPE
God, let me be a giver. Let Me Be a Giver. Mary Carolyn Davies. PoToHe
God—let me be aware. Awareness. Miriam Teichner. BLP; MaRV; OQP; QP-1
God let me find the lonely ones. Prayer for a Day's Walk. Grace Noll Crowell. PoToHe
God, let me flower as I will! Let Me Flower as I Will. Lew Sarett. TrPWD
God, let me live each lovely day. My Prayer. Elsie Janis. BLP
God! let never soe old a man. Old Robin of Portingale. *Unknown.* ESPB; OBB
God, let our sons this Holy Night. This Holy Night. Gertrude Hanson. ChIP
God, listen through my words to the beating of my heart. Prayer. Margueritte Harmon Bro. TrPWD
God love you. A Poem for the Old Man. John Wieners. NeAP
God love you now, if no one else will ever. Ode for the American Dead in Korea. Thomas McGrath. NePoEA
God loves an idle rainbow. Couplet. Ralph Hodgson. BMEP
God Lyaeus. John Fletcher. *Fr.* The Tragedy of Valentinian, V, viii. LEAP; OBEV
("God Lyaeus, ever young.") ElSeCe; OnPM; TuPP; ViBoPo
(Song to Bacchus.) BEL; EPP; EV-2; TOP
God made a garden when the world was young. The First Garden. Frank Oliver Call. CPG
God made a little gentian. Emily Dickinson. OBAV
(Fringed Gentian.) AA
God made Him birds in a pleasant humour. The Making of Birds. Katharine Tynan. BMEP; DD; GTIV; HBMV; JKCP; OxBI
God made my cathedral. Worship. Ruth Furbee. MaRV
God made my lady lovely to behold. How My Song of Her Began. Philip Bourke Marston. HBV; VA
God made my mother on an April day. My Mother. Francis Ledwidge. HBMV; OHIP
God made seas to play beside. Pete's Theology. Don Marquis. AIBD
God made the bees. *Unknown.* GoTP
God Made the Country. William Cowper. *Fr.* The Task, I. FiP; PoEL-3
("God made the country, and man made the town.") AnFE; NBE
(Town and Country.) FaBoEn
God made the wicked Grocer. The Song against Grocers. G. K. Chesterton. CenHV
God made thee perfet, not immutable. Milton. *Fr.* Paradise Lost, V. PoFr
God made, they say, the country. City Lights. Karle Wilson Baker. PCD
God Made This Day for Me. Edgar A. Guest. NLK
God made trees. *Unknown.* LO
God make me brave for life. A Prayer for Courage. Grace Noll Crowell. PraP
God make me kind! Make Me Kind. Duncan McNeil. PraP

God make my life a little light. A Child's Prayer [or A Child's Hymn]. M. Betham-Edwards. BOL; MeMeAg; OTPC; PRWS; TVC; TVSH
God-Maker, Man, The. Don Marquis. HBV; OBAV; QS; WGRP
Sels.
"As the skull of man." OQP; QP-1
"Yes, nothing seems changeless, but Change." MaRV
God Makes a Path. Roger Williams. BPP; MaRV; PAH; WGRP
(Shelter, Food, and Company.) GrCo-1
God makes not good men wantons, but doth bring. Good Men Afflicted Most. Robert Herrick. LiTB
God makes sech nights, all white an' still. The Courtin'. James Russell Lowell. *Fr.* The Biglow Papers. AA; AmPP; AnNE; APW; BeLS; BOHV; CoBA; EV-5; HBV; HiLiAm; IAP; IHA; InMe; LHV; LPS-3; MCCG; MOAP; MW; OBAV; OBVV; PTA-2; REAL; StVeCh (1940 ed.); TCAP; TreFS; YT
God meant me to be hungry. God's Will. Mildred Howells. HBV
God Meets Me in the Mountains. Badger Clark. OQP; QP-1
God might have made the earth bring forth. The Use of Flowers. Mary Howitt. LPS-2
God Moves in a Mysterious Way. William Cowper. *See* Light Shining Out of Darkness.
God Moves on the Water, *with music. Unknown.* OuSiCo
God must have loved the silence, for he laid. Silence. Mavis Clare Barnett. BLP; OQP; QP-2
God, must I pass clumsily back to you in the end? How Shall I Go? Muriel Strode. BAP
God Needs Antonio. "George Eliot." *Fr.* Stradivarius. GrCo-2
God of a Universe within Whose Bounds. Katharine L. Aller. MaRV
God of Abraham, of Isaac, and of Jacob. *Unknown, tr. fr. Yiddish by* Olga Marx. TrJP
God of all power and might. Cecil Arthur Spring-Rice. *Fr.* In Memoriam, A. C. M. L. TrPWD
God of Fair Beginnings, The. The Song of Diego Valdez. Kipling. OtMeF
God of Galaxies, The. Mark Van Doren. ImOP
God of gods stood up, stood up to try, The. The Lord and Judge. Mikhail Lomonosov. BoRS
God of Grace and God of Glory. Harry Emerson Fosdick. MaRV
God of grave nights. A Chant Out of Doors. Marguerite Wilkinson. CP; POT; PoTo; SP; TrPWD
God of light and blossom. Prayer. James P. Mousley. GoYe
God of Love, The. Wen Yi-tuo, *tr. fr. Chinese.* WhP
God of Love, The—ah, benedicite! The Cuckoo and the Nightingale. Thomas Clanvowe, *tr. by* Wordsworth. MeEV
God of love among the silent flowers, A. The Moment of the Rose. Dunstan Thompson. LiTA
God of love my shepperd is, The. *Unknown.* SeCSL
God of Mercy. Evening Prayer. Robert Freeman. PraP
God of Might, God of Right. *Unknown.* TrJP
God of Music, The. Edith M. Thomas. PECK
(Music.) HBV
God of our boyhood, whom we yield. Boy's Prayer. A. B. Ponsonby. MaRV
God of our fathers, known of old. Recessional [or Lest We Forget]. Kipling. AWP; BBV; BEL; BLPA; BLRP; BLV; BMEP; BoLiVe; BPN; BTP; CaAE; ChMo; CP; CV; EnLi-2; EnLit; EPN; FaFP; GN; GrCo-1; GTBS; GTBS-W; GTSL; HBV; HBVY; InP; InPo; JAWP; LBBV; LEAP; LiA; LiTB; LiTM; LPS-1; MaRV; MBP; MCCG; MoBrPo; NeHB; NeMA; OAEP (2d ed); OBEV; OBVV; OHFP; OIF; OQP; PECK; PFE; PIR; PoE; PoMa; POT; PoTo; PoVP; PraP; PTA-1; PYM; QP-1; TCEP; TCPD; TOP; TreF; TrGrPo; TSW; TSWC; TVSH; TwCV; ViBoPo; ViP; ViPP; VLEP; VOD; WBLP; WBP; WGRP; WHA; YT
God of our fathers, whose almighty hand. National Hymn. Daniel C. Roberts. PaA
God of our fathers, with bowed heads we come. The War at Home. Willard Wattles. OQP; QP-2
God of Our Life through All the Circling Years. Hugh Thomson Kerr. BPP; MaRV
God of our lives, O hear our prayer. Reconsecration. Dorothy Gould. PGD
God of pity and love, return to this earth. Sonnet XIII. Robert Nathan. QS
God of Sheep, The. John Fletcher. *Fr.* The Faithful Shepherdess, V, v. EIL; FaBoCh; LoGBV
("All ye woods, and trees, and bowers.") CenL
(Song to Pan.) EV-2
(To Pan.) BLV; TrGrPo
God of Summer—I have seen. Touring. David Morton. TrPWD
God of the Earth, the Sky, the Sea. Samuel Longfellow. MaRV
(God, through All and in You All.) TrPWD
God of the glowing love, making men brothers. A World-Nation. Earl B. Marlatt. MaRV
God of the Granite and the Rose. A Prayer. Elizabeth Doten. *Fr.* Reconciliation. OQP; QP-1; TrPWD
God of the harvest, thanks to Thee. Harvest Prayer. Rowena Bennett. MeMeAg
God of the Harvest, Thou, whose sun. Harvest Hymn. Charles Sangster. CPG
God of the Living, The. John Ellerton. *See* Living unto Thee.
God of the Lowly, The. Perses, *tr. fr. Greek by* F. L. Lucas. GrPE
God of the Nations. Walter Russell Bowie. MaRV; TrPWD
God of the Nations. John Haynes Holmes. MaRV
God of the Open Air, *sels.* Henry van Dyke.
These Are the Gifts I Ask. FaBoBe; NeHB; OQP; QP-1
"While the tremulous leafy haze." ADAH
God of the Prophets. Denis Wortman. MaRV
God of the River, The. Chu Yuan, *tr. fr. Chinese by* Shen Yu-ting. *Fr.* The Nine Songs. WhP
God of the seasons, hear my parting prayer. The Old Year's Prayer. Minna Irving. PGD; PSO
God of the sky, enthroned in azure blue. A Prayer for Aviators. Norman E. Richardson. MaRV; PraP
God of the Strong, God of the Weak. Richard Watson Gilder. *See* Hymn: "God of the strong . . ."
God of the sunlight, God of the sea. Prayer. Grenville Kleiser. PraP
God of the thunder! from whose cloudy seat. Jewish Hymn in Babylon. Henry Hart Milman. LPS-2
God of the vineyard's royal store. The Husbandman. Frances Beatrice Taylor. CaP; OCL
God of the World. Israel Najara, *tr. fr. Hebrew by* Israel Abrahams. TrJP
God of things that are, The. Altruism. David Starr Jordan. OQP; QP-2
God of us who kill our kind! A Prayer of the Peoples. Percy MacKaye. TrPWD, 3 *sts.;* WGRP
God of Visions. Emily Brontë. *See* Plead for Me.
God of War, The. Sophocles, *tr. fr. Greek by* C. M. Bowra. OxBG
God of War, Money Changer of Dead Bodies, The. Aeschylus, *tr. fr. Greek by* Richmond Lattimore. *Fr.* Agamemnon. WaaP
God of war resigns his room to me, The. The Vaunts of Tamburlaine. Christopher Marlowe. *Fr.* Tamburlaine the Great, Pt. I, Act V, sc. ii. BCEP
God of Wealth, The. Timocreon, *tr. fr. Greek by* T. F. Higham. OxBG
God of winds, when thou art growne. *Unknown.* SeCSL
God of Years, Thy Love Hath Led Us. Jay Glover Eldridge. PraP
God, Our Dwelling Place. Psalms, XC, Bible, *O.T.* MaRV (*Moulton, Modern Reader's Bible*).
(Psalm XC.) AWP
(Span of Man, The.) EM-1
(Thou Art God, *abr.*) BPP
God Our Father. Frederick William Faber. WGRP
There's a Wideness in God's Mercy, *sel.* OIF; WBLP, *abr.*
(All-embracing, The.) BLRP
(God's Mercy.) MaRV
(Heart of the Eternal, The.) BPP; OQP; QP-1
God Our Help. *Unknown.* OxBoCh
God Our Refuge. Psalms, XCI, Bible, *O.T.* MaRV (*Moulton, Modern Reader's Bible*).
(Everlasting Arms, The, *Moulton, Modern Reader's Bible.*) WGRP
("He that dwelleth in the secret place of the Most High.") AWP; PC; WoL
(Mighty Fortress, A.) TrGrPo
(Protection of the Lord.) EM-1
God Our Refuge. Richard Chenevix Trench. MaRV; OxBoCh
(If There Had Anywhere Appeared.) TrPWD
God, patient of beginnings. A Prayer for the New Year. Violet Alleyn Storey. TrPWD
God pity all the brave who go. God's Pity. Louise Driscoll. MaRV; PC; WGRP
God, pity broken little families. A Prayer for Broken Little Families. Violet Alleyn Storey. PoToHe
God pity eyes that have not seen the dawn. This Is the Tragedy. Helen Frazee-Bower. MaRV; MuM
God planned/ The little grain of sand. God's Plan. Miyoshi. SoLD
God pours for me His draught divine. Thanks from Earth to Heaven. John Hall Wheelock. HBMV
God Prays. Angela Morgan. GrCo-2, *abr.;* MaRV; WGRP
"And the Lord God whispered and said to me," *sel.* OQP; QP-1

God proclaims a paean, earth and the heavens resound. The Fall of Constantinople. *Unknown.* MoGP
God prosper long our gracious King. An Ode for the New Year. *At. to* John Gay. OxBoLi
God prosper long our noble king. Chevy Chase [*or* The Hunting of the Cheviot]. *Unknown.* BaBo (B *and* C *vers.*); BHV; EnLi-1 (1949 ed.); ESPB (B *vers.*); EV-2; GN; HBV; LEAP; LH; LPS-2; OAEP; PFE; TOP; ViBoFo
God Provides. St. Matthew, VI: 26-34, *abr.*, Bible, *N.T.* BLRP
God Punish You. Knut Hamsun, *tr. fr. Norwegian by* Charles W. Stork. AnNoLy
God Punishes. Archilochus, *tr. fr. Greek by* C. M. Bowra. OxBG
God Replies. Job, XXXVIII: 2-41, Bible, *O.T.* TrGrPo
God rest that Jewy woman. Song for the Clatter-Bones. F. R. Higgins. AnIL; LiTB; LiTM; OBMV; OnYI; OxBI; SiTL
God Rest Ye Merry, Gentlemen. Dinah Maria Mulock Craik. BPP; COAH; GN; HH; OHIP; OTPC; PCH, *2 sts.*; SDH
(Christmas Carol, A.) MeMeAg, *2 sts.*
God Rest You Merry, Gentlemen. *Unknown.* AnEC; COAH; DD; EV-2; FaFP; HBV; HBVY; LiTB; MaRV, *4 sts.*; OlF; TreFS; ViBoPo; YaCaBo, *with music*
God rest you, merry gentlemen!/ May nothing you dismay;/ Not even the dyspeptic. The Newest Thing in Christmas Carols. *Unknown.* COAH; PA
God rest you, rest you, rest you, Ireland's dead! To the Dead of '98. Lionel Johnson. HBV
God rules above in Heaven. Rulers. *Unknown.* OnPM
God Said. Paul Verlaine, *tr. fr. French by* Muriel Kittel. AnFP
God said, "I am tired of kings." God's Message to Men. Henry van Dyke. PTA-2
God Said, "I Made a Man." José Garcia Villa. AnFE; CoAnAm; TwAmPo
God said, Let there be light! and there was light. At the Sunrise in 1848. Dante Gabriel Rossetti. BPN; PoVP
God Said: Let There Be Sky. James J. Donohue. JKCP (1955 ed.)
God said: "My son you must love me. You see." God Said. Paul Verlaine. AnFP
God Save Elizabeth. Francis Turner Palgrave. HBV
God save great George our King. God Save the King. *Unknown, at. to* Henry Carey. OBEC
God Save Ireland. Timothy Daniel Sullivan. OnYI
God save our gracious King,/ Long live our noble King. God Save the King. *Unknown, at. to* Henry Carey. HBV; MaRV; TreFS; WBLP
God, save our land from that unblessed sedateness. Of Greatness in Teaching. Leslie Pinckney Hill. MaRV
God Save Our President. Francis de Haes Janvier. PaA; PAH
God Save the Flag. Oliver Wendell Holmes. FaFP; OHFP
God Save the King. Joseph Stansbury. BoCaPo (1948 ed.)
God Save the King. *Unknown, at. to* Henry Carey. HBV; MaRV, *st. 2 by* William E. Hickson; OBEC, *sl. diff.*; TreFS; WBLP, *sl. diff.*
God Save the Nation. Theodore Tilton. AA
God Save the People. Ebenezer Elliott. *See* When Wilt Thou Save the People?
God save the Rights of Man! Ode. Philip Freneau. AmPP (3d ed.); CoBA; HiLiAm; IAP; PoFr
God save this tree we plant! A Hymn for Arbor Day. Henry Hanby Hay. ADAH
God save us all from creeds, and keep. A Prayer for Singleness of Vision. Sherard Vines. QS
God Scatters Beauty. Walter Savage Landor. CBOV; EmBrPo; EnRP; EPN; ERP
God-seeking. Sir William Watson. WGRP
God send the Devil is a gentleman. The Knight Fallen on Evil Days. Elinor Wylie. MAP; MoAmPo
God send the land deliverance. The Death of Parcy Reed. *Unknown.* BaBo (B *vers.*); ESPB; OBB
God send us a little home. A Prayer for a Little Home. Florence Bone. BLPA; FaBoBe; FaFP; MaRV; MW; NeHB; OQP; PCH; PraP; PTA-2; QP-2
God Send Us Men. Frederick J. Gillman. MaRV
God send us peace, and keep red strife away. At Fredericksburg. John Boyle O'Reilly. BIG; MC; PAH
God send us wit to banish far. Peace in the World. John Galsworthy. MaRV
God sends his teachers unto every age. Rhoecus. James Russell Lowell. IAP; MCCG; TCAP
God sends no message by me. I am mute. A Creed. Norman Gale. BMEP; LBBV; LEAP
God sent us here to make mistakes. Mistakes. Ella Wheeler Wilcox. PoToHe
God shield ye, comrades of the road! The Blooming of the White Thorn. Edith M. Thomas. ChrBoLe; CLS
God shield ye, heralds of spring! Return of Spring. Pierre de Ronsard. LPS-2
God spake three times and saved Van Elsen's soul. Van Elsen. Frederick George Scott. HBV; VA
God Speaks in All Religions. Thomas Lake Harris. BAP; MaRV
God Speaks to the Man in Despair. Stevie Smith. DiM
God speed the year of jubilee. The Triumph of Freedom. William Lloyd Garrison. PoFr
God spoke! and from the arid scene. The Birth of the Flowers. Mary McNeil Fenollosa. OQP; QP-1
God spoke once that made your girdle fall, The. Daphne. Selden Rodman. PoNe
God spreads a book before my eyes. God's Book. Edgar Daniel Kramer. OQP; QP-2
God spreads a carpet soft and green. The Welcome. Arthur Powell. NLK; OQP; POT; QP-1
God strengthen me to bear myself. Who Shall Deliver Me? [*or* The Battle Within]. Christina Rossetti. MaRV; OxBoCh
God Suffers. Georgia Harkness. QS
God That Doest Wondrously. Moses ibn Ezra, *tr. fr. Hebrew by* Solomon Solis-Cohen. TrJP
God, that harnesseth the winds. For a Little Bird That Blundered into Church. Sara Henderson Hay. BAP
God, that madest Earth and Heaven. Evening Hymn. Reginald Heber. BOL
God, that mad'st her well regard her. Dieu Qu'il la Fait. Charles d'Orléans. AWP
God the Architect. Harry Kemp. HBMV; MaRV; WGRP
(To God, the Architect.) TrPWD
God, the Artist. *At. to* Angela Morgan. *See* God, When You Thought of a Pine Tree.
God the Father, God the Son, and God the Holy Ghost. The Archpriest's Prayer. Juan Ruiz, Archpriest of Hita. *Fr.* The Book of Good Love. AnSpL-1
God the Life of Nature. Mordecai Kaplan. QS
God, the Omnipotent. Henry F. Chorley *and* John Ellerton. MaRV
God the Omniscient. James Cowden Wallace. BLRP
(God.) WGRP
God Thinks of Man. Jules Supervielle, *tr. fr. French by* Wallace Fowlie. MiCF
God, thou great symmetry. Envoi. Anna Wickham. BLV; MBP; MoBrPo; NeMA; TrGrPo (1942 ed.)
God, though [*or* although] this life is but a wraith. Prayer. Louis Untermeyer. BAP; GoTP; MAP; MaRV; MoAmPo; NeMA; OQP; PC; PoFr; PoMa; PYM; QP-2; StaSt; TOP; TrJP; VOD; WGRP; YT
God thought to give the sweetest thing. The Mother [*or* The Gift]. George Newell Lovejoy. DD; PGD
God, through All and in You All. Samuel Longfellow. *See* God of the Earth, the Sky, the Sea.
God to Man. *Fr.* The Talmud. TrJP
God, to whom we look up blindly. Bayard Taylor. *Fr.* The Poet's Journal. TrPWD
God took a fit of Paradise-wind. Field-Flower. Francis Thompson. PoVP
God Wants a Man. *Unknown.* BLRP
God wants not Man to humble himself. Humility and Doubt. Blake. *Fr.* The Everlasting Gospel. RO
God wants our best. He in the far-off ages. What Shall We Render. *Unknown.* BLRP
God watches o'er us all the day. The Eyes of God. "Gabriel Setoun." PPL
God, we don't like to complain. Caliban in the Coal Mines. Louis Untermeyer. BAP; CP; HBV; LEAP; MAP; MaRV; MMV; MoAmPo; NeMA; NV; PoeMoYo; PoMa; TreFS; TrJP
God, what a day it is to be abroad! Out-of-doors. Robert Whitaker. TrPWD
God, what a world, if men in street and mart. True Brotherhood. Ella Wheeler Wilcox. OQP; QP-1; WBLP
God, When You Thought of a Pine Tree. *At. to* Angela Morgan. NLK
(God, the Artist.) BLPA; PoToHe (new ed.)
God, who commanded the light to shine out of darkness. The Glory of God Revealed in Jesus. Second Corinthians, Bible, *N.T.* MaRV
God who created me. Prayers [*or* A Boy's Prayer]. Henry Charles Beeching. BoTP; CP; GN; LH; MaRV; OBEV; OBVV; OTPC (1946 ed.); PoeT; PoRL; TVSH; VA
God, who created me from sodden clay. "Feodor Sologub," *tr. fr. Russian by* C. M. Bowra. BoR
God, who devisedst man who then devised. Prayer for the Age. Myron H. Broomell. TrPWD
God who formed the mountains great, The. All Nature Has a Voice to Tell. J. Gilchrist Lawson. BLRP
God, who had made you valiant, strong and swift. Maurice Baring. *Fr.* In Memoriam, A. H. CAW
God who had such heart for us, The. The Cool Gold Wines of Paradise. Robert Farren. AnIV; SeCePo
God, Who Hath Made the Daisies. E. P. Hood. OHIP
God Who Hides, The. Francis Quarles. *See* Why Dost Thou Shade Thy Lovely Face?
God who made denial, The. Envoy. Gerald Gould. QS

God, who made man out of dust. The Continuing City. Laurence Housman. WGRP
God who made New Hampshire, The. Ode Inscribed to W. H. Channing. Emerson. ViBoPo
God, who through ages past. New Dreams for Old. Thomas Curtis Clark. OQP; QP-2
God, who touchest earth with beauty. A Youth's Prayer [or A Prayer-Poem]. Mary S. Edgar. BLRP; MaRV
God who, whatever frenzy of our fretting. Frederic William Henry Myers. *Fr.* Saint Paul. PC
God, Whom Shall I Compare to Thee? Judah Halevi, *tr. fr. Hebrew by* Alice Lucas. TrJP
God whose goodness filleth every clime, The. Chorus. Racine. *Fr.* Athalie. CAW; WGRP
God, whose kindly hand doth sow. Francis Ledwidge. *Fr.* A Dream of Artemis. TrPWD
God will have all, or none; serve Him, or fall. Neutrality Loathsome [or "Ye Cannot Serve God and Mammon"]. Robert Herrick. LiTB; PoFr
God will never fail us. God Is Faithful. Frances Ridley Havergal. BLRP
God will not change; the restless years may bring. Changeless [or In Whom Is No Variableness]. Edith Hickman Divall. MaRV; OQP; QP-2
God will not let my field lie fallow. The Ploughman. Karle Wilson Baker. WGRP
God Wills It. Richard F. Grady. JKCP (1955 ed.)
God Wills It. "Gabriela Mistral," *tr. fr. Spanish by* "K. G. C." AnCL
God wills no man a slave. The man most meek. Washington. James Jeffrey Roche. GA; MC; PAH
God with His million cares. Dawn and Dark. Norman Gale. BMEP; HBV; TSW; TSWC; VA
God with honour hang your head. At the Wedding March. Gerard Manley Hopkins. PoLi; ViP
God with Us. Robert Browning. *Fr.* Saul, XVII. GrCo-2
God with Us. Nancy Byrd Turner. ChIP; OQP; QP-1
God Within Yet Above. Sir Lewis Morris. MaRV
God wrote His loveliest poem on the day. Silver Poplars. Grace Noll Crowell. LS
God ye hear not, how shall ye hear me? John Knox's Indictment of the Queen. Swinburne. *Fr.* Bothwell. VA
God, You Have Been Too Good to Me. Charles Wharton Stork. MaRV; NV; TrPWD; WGRP
God, you have given me a son. A Father's Prayer. Douglas Malloch. FAOV
God, You need not make for me. Sunsets. Florence Boyce Davis. OQP; QP-2
God, you've so much to do. Idleness. Andrew Young. POTE
Godamighty Drag, *with music. Unknown.* OuSiCo
Goddess, The. Théodore de Banville, *tr. fr. French by* Stuart Merrill. OnPM
Goddess. Amir Khusrau, *tr. fr. Persian by* J. H. Hindley. PeP
Goddess, The. Denise Levertov. NeAP
Goddess, The. Kathleen Raine. FaBoTw
Goddess azure-mantled and aureoled. Our Lady. Robert Bridges. ISi; QS
Goddess ceased, and with the soft embrace, The. On Some Verses of Virgil. Virgil. *Fr.* The Aeneid, VIII. LiA
Goddess dear. Milton. *Fr.* Comus. ElSeCe
Goddess! hear these tuneless numbers. To Psyche. Keats. TwCrTr
Goddess of Cyprus come. Invocation. Sappho. GrR
Goddess of Liberty! O thou. An Invocation: Read at the Celebration of Independence Day in San Francisco in 1888. Ambrose Bierce. BAP
Goddess of the Hearth, The. *Unknown, tr. fr. Greek by* Jack Lindsay. *Fr.* Homeric Hymns. OxBG
Goddesses' Glory, The. *Unknown.* SeCL
Goddwyn, *sel.* Thomas Chatterton.
Freedom's War Song. BLV; PoFr
(Ode to Liberty.) TrGrPo
Godës Son for the love of man. Make We Merry in This Feast. *Unknown.* AnEC
Godfrey Gordon Gustavus Gore. William Brighty Rands. BoChLi; BoTP; FaPON; GaP; HBVY; MPB; TiPo; TSW; TSWC
(Reformation of Godfrey Gore, The.) HBV; OnPP; OTPC
Godfrey of Bulloigne. Tasso. *See* Jerusalem Delivered.
Godhead here in hiding, whom I do adore. Rhythmus ad SS. Sacramentum. St. Thomas Aquinas. LaP
Godiva. Oliver Herford. PA
Godiva. Tennyson. BeLS, *sl. abr.*; BPN; HBV; LPS-2, *sl. abr.*; PoVP; VLEP
Godlike, The. Goethe, *tr. fr. German by* Edgar A. Bowring. LiA
Godlike beneath his grave divinities. The Druid. John Banister Tabb. AA
Godlike Brute, The. John Arbuthnot. *Fr.* Know Yourself. BeR
Godlike Heart. Goethe, *tr. fr. German by* John S. Dwight. OnPM
Godly and the Ungodly, The. Psalms, I, Bible, *O.T.* TreF
(Blessed Is the Man.) EnLi-1; HiLiEn
(Psalm I.) AWP; JAWP; WoL
(Tree and the Chaff, The, *Moulton, Modern Reader's Bible.*) WGRP
Godly Casuistry. Samuel Butler. *Fr.* Hudibras, II, 2. OBS
Godly Girzie. Burns. CoMu
Godmother. Phyllis B. Morden. BrR; MoSiPe
Godmother. Dorothy Parker. PoRA
Gododdin, *sel.* Aneirin, *tr. fr. Welsh by* Thomas Gray.
"To Cattraeth's vale in glittering row." PrWP
Godolphin Horne. Hilaire Belloc. CenHV; RIS; StaSt
Gods. Walt Whitman. AnAmPo; LA
God's Acre. Blanche Edith Baughan. BoAu
God's Acre. Witter Bynner. AnEnPo; SBMV
God's-Acre. Longfellow. HBV; LPS-1; PoRL
God's a-Gwineter Trouble de Water, *with music. Unknown.* BoAN-2
(Wade in de Water.) APW
God's Aid implored; the sum of all proposed. The First Day of the First Week. Joshua Sylvester. *Fr.* Du Bartas: His First Week or Birth of the World. Po
God's Altar. Emerson. MaRV
Gods and furies now depart. On Reading the *Metamorphoses*. George Garrett. NePoAm-2
Gods and Heroes of the Gael. Eleanor Rogers Cox. JKCP
Gods are dead, The. The earth has covered them. Sonnet. Frank Belknap Long. DaM
Gods are happy, The. The Strayed Reveller to Ulysses. Matthew Arnold. *Fr.* The Strayed Reveller. BrBE; OBEV (new ed.)
Gods are strong, Odysseus, The. Musings on Man's Sad Estate. Sophocles. *Fr.* Ajax. GrR
God's blessing lead us, help us! *At. to* St. Colman. *Fr.* Hymn against Pestilence. OnYI
God's Blessing on Munster. *At. to* St. Patrick, *tr. fr. Old Irish by* Whitley Stokes. OnYI
God's blessing rest upon you. An Easter Prayer. *Unknown.* PraP
God's Blessings. William Cornish. *See* Pleasure It Is.
God's body is all space. Essay on Deity. Elder Olson. NP
God's Book. Edgar Daniel Kramer. OQP; QP-2
God's child in Christ adopted—Christ my all. On His Baptismal Birthday. Samuel Taylor Coleridge. MaRV
Gods' Children, The. Aeschylus, *tr. fr. Greek by* C. M. Bowra. *Fr.* Niobe. OxBG
God's Concern. Palladas, *tr. fr. Greek by* A. J. Butler. OxBG
God's Creatures. Christopher Smart. RO
God's Dark. John Martin. MaRV
God's deathless plaything rolls an eye. Leviathan. Louis Untermeyer. GoTP
God's Determinations, *sels.* Edward Taylor.
Accusation of the Inward Man, The. LiTA
Christ's Reply. PoEL-3
Difficulties Arising from Uncharitable Cariages of Christians. Stanzas: "When these assaults proove vain, the Enemy." OnAP
Glory of and Grace in the Church, The. AnNE
God's Selecting Love in the Decree. PoEL-3
Joy of Church Fellowship [Rightly Attended], The. AmP; AmPP; CoV; OxBA
Our Insufficiency to Praise God Suitably for His Mercy. LiTA
Outward Man Accused, The. LiTA
Preface: "Infinity, when all things it beheld." AmPP; CoV; OxBA
Souls Groan to Christ for Succour, The. PoEL-3
God's Dominion and Decrees. Isaac Watts. CEP; OBEC
God's Dream. William Norris Burr. OQP; QP-1
God's Dreams. Thomas Curtis Clark. OQP; QP-1; QS
God's-Eye View. Robert Haven Schauffler. TCAP
God's Ferns. John Henry Jowett. CBOV
"God's First Creature Was Light." Winifred Welles. ImOP
Gods Forget, The. Diodorus, *tr. fr. Greek by* F. L. Lucas. GrPE
God's Funeral. Thomas Hardy. QS; WGRP
God's Garden. Richard Burton. OQP; QP-1
God's Garden. Dorothy Frances Gurney. *See* Lord God Planted a Garden, The.
God's Gift. Alfred Noyes. POT; PoTo
God's Glory. Psalms, XIX, Bible, *O.T.* *See* Heavens Declare the Glory of God, The.
God's Goin' to Set This World on Fire (A *and* B *vers., with music*). *Unknown.* AS
(God, He's Gwine to Set Dis World on Fire, *sl. diff., with music.*) SoAF
God's Goodness. C. D. Martin. WBLP
God's Grandeur. Gerard Manley Hopkins. AnFE; AWP; CaAE; ChMo; CoBE; EmBrPo; EnLi-2; EnLit; ExPo; FaFP; GTBS-D; GTBS-W; InPo; InvP; LiTB; LiTG; LiTM; LoBV; MaPo; MBP; MoAB; MoBrPo; MoPo;

MoVE; OxBoCh; PG (1955 ed.); PIAE; Po; PoE; PoLi; PoVP; ReMP; RiBV; SeCeV; TrGrPo; TwCV; ViP; ViPP; VLEP
God's Green Inn. Robert Louis Stevenson. *See* Camp, A.
God's Handmaid. Hugh F. Blunt. PraNu
God's Harp. Gustav Falke, *tr. fr. German by* Ludwig Lewisohn. AWP; JAWP; WBP
Gods have heard me, Lyce, The. Revenge. Horace. Odes, IV, 13. AWP; WoL
Gods have not ordained hunger to be our death, The. To Liberality. *Unknown. Fr.* Vedic Hymns: Rig-Veda. PoFr
Gods have taken alien shapes upon them, The. Exiles. "Æ." MoBrPo
"Gods held me in Egypt, longing to sail for home, The." The Old Man of the Sea. Homer. *Fr.* The Odyssey, IV. GrPE
Gods held talk together, group'd in knots, The. Matthew Arnold. *Fr.* Balder Dead. BPN
God's house is heaven and it is here within. A Carmelite Breaks Silence. Sister Miriam. PraNu
Gods I am pent in a cockroach. The Wail of Archy. Don Marquis. *Fr.* Archy and Mehitabel. FiBHP
God's in His Heaven: He never issues. Ninth Philosopher's Song. Aldous Huxley. ViBoPo
God's Judgment [*or* Judgement] on a Wicked Bishop. Robert Southey. EnRP; HBV; HBVY; LPS-3; OBRV; OTPC (1923 ed.); PCN; PTA-1
(Bishop Hatto.) CG; ChTr; StPo; TVSH
(Bishop Hatto and the Rats.) EV-4
(Legend of Bishop Hatto.) PECK
God's Justice. Nagata, *tr. fr. Japanese by* Lois J. Erickson. SoLD
God's lark at morning I would be! A Little Page's Song. William Alexander Percy. HBV
Gods laugh in their sleeve, The. Matthew Arnold. *Fr.* Empedocles on Etna, I, ii. BMEP
God's Little Creatures: Foreword. Joaquin Antonio Peñalosa, *tr. fr. Spanish by* Arthur Train, Jr. SaFP
God's Little Epigrams. Richard Kirk. PIAE
God's Little Mountain. Geoffrey Hill. NePoEA
God's Love. *Unknown.* BLRP
God's love and peace be with thee, where. Benedicite. Whittier. IAP; LPS-1; MOAP
God's Mercy. Frederick William Faber. *See* There's a Wideness in God's Mercy.
God's Message to Men. Henry van Dyke. PTA-2
God's Mother. Laurence Housman. ISi
God's Mothers. Douglas Malloch. PEDC
Gods of Hellas, gods of Hellas. The Dead Pan. Elizabeth Barrett Browning. BPN; EmBrPo; PoVP; ViPo
Gods of the Nile, should this stout fellow here. A Grave near Cairo. Kipling. *Fr.* Epitaphs of the War. PoVP
Gods of War. "Æ." BEL
God's Pity. Louise Driscoll. MaRV; PC; WGRP
God's pity on poor kings. Poor Kings. W. H. Davies. HBV
God's Plan. "Susan Coolidge." *Fr.* Commonplaces. MaRV
God's Plan. Miyoshi, *tr. fr. Japanese by* Lois J. Erickson. SoLD
God's plan made a hopeful beginning. Limerick. *Unknown.* LiBL
God's Plans. May Riley Smith. BLRP; MaRV
God's Plans. *Unknown.* BLRP
God's Precepts Perfect. Psalms, XIX: 7-9, Bible, *O.T.* BLRP
God's Promises. *Unknown.* BLRP
God's Remembrance. Francis Ledwidge. GTIV
God's revelation of Himself may be. The Revelation. Leslie Clare Manchester. OQP; QP-2
God's Riding. Vincent Starrett. LPS-1
God's Road is all uphill. A Poet's Proverb. Arthur Guiterman. MaRV
God's rod doth watch while men do sleep; and then. The Rod. Robert Herrick. LiTB
God's Selecting Love in the Decree. Edward Taylor. *Fr.* God's Determinations. PoEL-3
God's Son is born, His mother is a maid. Blessed Be That Lady Bright. *Unknown.* AnEC
God's Speech to Job. Robert Frost. *Fr.* A Masque of Reason. OnHM
God's spice I was, and pounding was my due. The Martyrdom of Mary, Queen of Scots. Robert Southwell. *Fr.* At Fotheringay. ACP
God's Sunshine. John Oxenham. WBLP
God's Trails Lead Home. John R. Clements. BLRP
God's Two Dwellings, *sel.* Thomas Washbourne.
Humility ("Though Heaven be high"). MaRV
God's Unspeakable Gift. Mrs. Macey P. Sealey. BePJ
God's Virtue. Barnabe Barnes. *See* World's Bright Comforter, The.
God's Voice. Charles Augustin Sainte-Beuve, *tr. fr. French by* Alan Conder. TrFP
God's Way. Horatius Bonar. MaRV; PraP
(Thy Way, Not Mine.) OxBoCh; TrPWD; VA
("Thy way, not mine, O Lord.") OlF
God's Way. Dorothy Clarke Wilson. MaRV
God's Ways. *Unknown.* MaRV
God's Ways Are Strange. Margaret E. Bruner. PoToHe
God's Ways to Man. Archilochus, *tr. fr. Greek by* H. Rushton Fairclough. GrR
Gods, what a sun! I think the world's aglow. A Summer Day in Old Sicily. Edward Cracroft Lefroy. Echoes from Theocritus, V. OBVV
Gods who own Olympus as dwelling-place, The. The Five Ages. Hesiod. *Fr.* Works and Days. LiTW; OxBG
God's Will. Charles E. Guthrie. BLRP
God's Will. Mildred Howells. HBV
God's Will. Robert Munger. AA
God's Will. Alice Nevin. BLRP
God's Will for Us. *Unknown.* BLRP; WBLP
God's will in me. God's Will. Alice Nevin. BLRP
God's Will Is Best. Caroline Atherton Briggs Mason. *See* En Voyage.
God's Word. John Clifford. *See* Anvil, The—God's Word.
God's Word. Takayoshi Matsuyama, *tr. fr. Japanese by* Lois J. Erickson. SoLD
God's works are good. The Acorn and the Pumpkin. La Fontaine. BoChLi
God's World. Mildred Keeling. BLRP
God's World. Edna St. Vincent Millay. BAP; BTP; ChMo; CMP; CoBA; FaBoBe; GoTP; HBV; MAP; MCCG; MoAmPo; NLK; NP; PoTo; PYM; SBMV; TCAP; TSW; TSWC; YT
God's Youth. Louis Untermeyer. PFY
Godspeed. Harriet Prescott Spofford. EtS
Goe, and catche a falling starre. John Donne. *See* Song: "Go and catch a falling star."
Goe & seeke some other love. *Unknown.* SeCSL
Goe bidd the swan in silence dye. *Unknown.* SeCSL
Goe empty joyes. *See* Go empty joys.
Goe happy Rose, and enterwove. *See* Go, happy Rose, and, interwove.
Goe! hunt the whiter ermine! and present. For the Lady Olivia Porter; a Present upon a New-Years Day. Sir William Davenant. MeLP; MePo; OBS
Goe hurtles soules, whom mischiefe hath oppresst. The Angry Kynges. Seneca, *tr. by* Thomas Heywood. *Fr.* Hercules Furens. LiA
Goe little booke: thy selfe present. *See* Go little book . . .
Goe lovely Rose. *See* Go, Lovely Rose.
Goe now; and with some daring drugg. *See* Go now! and with some daring drug.
Goe smiling soules, your new built cages breake. To the Infant Martyrs. Richard Crashaw. SeCV-1
Goe soule the bodies guest. *See* Go, soul, the body's guest.
Goe thow my soule to thy desired rest. *Unknown.* SeCSL
Goe thy waies and turne no more. *Unknown.* SeCSL
Goes in and out with its gigantic tread. The Tide. Harry Kemp. TBM
Goes through the mud. *Unknown.* OxNR
Goethals, the Prophet Engineer. Percy MacKaye. PoeMoYo; PoRL; StVeCh
(Goethals.) BAP
Goethe and Frederika. Henry Sidgwick. HBV
Goethe in Weimar sleeps, and Greece. Memorial Verses. Matthew Arnold. BMEP; BPN; EM-2; EmBrPo; EPN; FiP; GEPC; HBV; OAEP; PoVP; PtP; TCEP; TriL; TwHP; VA; ViPo; ViPP; VLEP
Goin' Down to Town, *with music. Unknown.* AS; SoAF
Goin' Home, *with music. Unknown.* ABF
Goin' to Walk All ovah God's Heb'n. *Unknown. See* All God's Chillun Got Wings.
Goin' up the River, *with music. Unknown.* TrAS
Going, The. W. W. Gibson. CBOV; HiLiEn; NP
(Rupert Brooke.) BoFr
(To Rupert Brooke.) GTSL
(To the Memory of Rupert Brooke.) CP
Going, The. Thomas Hardy. EtPaEn; LiTB; MaPo; UnPo (3d ed.); ViPP
Going about our business day by day. War. J. C. Hall. HaMV; PoN
Going abruptly into a starry night. Starlight. William Meredith. NePoEA
Going Alone to Spend a Night at the Hsien-yu Temple. Po Chü-i. *See* Sleeping Alone at the Hsien-yu Temple.
Going a-Maying. Robert Herrick. *See* Corinna's Going a-Maying.
Going and Coming. Edward A. Jenks. LPS-3
Going and Staying. Thomas Hardy. ChMo; CMP; EPP
Going a-Nutting. Edmund Clarence Stedman. *See* Autumn Song.
Going Back Again. "Owen Meredith." FiBHP
Going Back to School. Stephen Vincent Benét. LaNeLa
Going beyond the Jade Gate Pass. Wang Chi-wen, *tr. fr. Chinese.* WhP
Going Blind. Ella Higginson. MOAH
Going Blind. Rainer Maria Rilke, *tr. fr. German by* Herman Salinger. TwGV
Going Blind. John Banister Tabb. SPP

Going down Hill on a Bicycle. Henry Charles Beeching. BBV (1951 ed.); CP; HBV; HBVY; OBEV; OBVV; OTPC (1923 ed.)
(Bicycling Song.) GN
Going Down in Ships. Harry Kemp. NLK
Going down the Mountain. Valentin Iremonger. NeIP
(Descending.) EnLoPo
Going down the old way. Song. Margaret Widdemer. HBMV
Going down to sea in ships. Going Down in Ships. Harry Kemp. NLK
Going down to town. Lynchburg Town. *Unknown.* OuSiCo
Going for Water. Robert Frost. HBMV; NP
Going from us at last. The Escape. Mark Van Doren. MAP; MoAmPo
Going Home. Mark Van Doren. MOAP
Going home one night through the frozen fall. Winter in Montreal. Patrick Anderson. BoCaPo (1948 ed.)
Going In to Dinner. Edward Shanks. OBMV
Going in trains up north against the north. Ski Train. Patrick Anderson. TwCaPo
Going into Breeches. Charles *and* Mary Lamb. EV-4; OTPC; PRWS
Going my way of old. Marriage. W. W. Gibson. HBV; MaRV
Going of His Feet, The. Harry Kemp. NLK; QS
Going of the glade-boat, The. The Load of Sugar-Cane. Wallace Stevens. NP
Going on six thousand years. After Six Thousand Years. Victor Hugo. WaaP
Going out, those bold days. Autumn. W. R. Rodgers. NeBP
Going Over. Sir Charles G. D. Roberts. TwCaPo
Going—the great round Sun. Going and Coming. Edward A. Jenks. LPS-3
Going, the wild things of our land. The Passing of the Buffalo. Hamlin Garland. StVeCh
Going to Bed. Marchette Chute. BoChLi (1950 ed.)
Going to Bed. John Donne. Elegies, XIX. LiTB; LiTG
(Elegie: Going to Bed.) MePo
(To His Mistress Going to Bed.) ReEn; SiTL
Going to Bed at Night. Adelaide O'Keeffe. BOL; OTPC (1923 ed.)
Going to Boston, *with music. Unknown.* ABF
Going to Church. Coventry Patmore. *Fr.* The Angel in the House, I, x. LoBV
Going to him! Happy letter! Tell him. Emily Dickinson. CoBA
Going to Mass by the heavenly mercy. Mary Hynes. Anthony Raftery. KiLC
Going to Mass Last Sunday. Donagh MacDonagh. NeIP; OxBI
Going to School. Karl Shapiro. TrJP
Going to sing about Emily. Microcosmos, XXV. Nigel Heseltine. NeBP
Going to the Dogs. *Unknown.* DDA; TreFS
Going to the Fair. James Whitcomb Riley. IHA
Going to the Mountains with a Little Dancing Girl, Aged Fifteen. Po Chü-i, *tr. fr. Chinese by* Arthur Waley. TrCh
Going to the Warres [*or* Wars]. Richard Lovelace. *See* To Lucasta, on Going to the Wars.
Going Too Far. Mildred Howells. TiPo
Going towards Spain. Barnabe Googe. ReIE; SiCE
Going up to London. Nancy Byrd Turner. GaP; HBMV; MW; PC
Going Upstairs. Arnold Wall. MM
Gol-darned Wheel, The. *Unknown.* CoSo, *with music;* CSF; IHA; PoMa
Gold. Martin Armstrong. BoTP
Gold. John Drinkwater. TCPD
Gold. "Michael Field." LBBV
(Gold Is the Son of Zeus: Neither Moth nor Worm May Gnaw It.) OBMV
(More Gold than Gold.) MBP
Gold. Thomas Hood. *Fr.* Miss Kilmansegg and Her Precious Leg. MaRV; OQP; QP-2; WBLP
(Her Moral.) VA
Gold. Glyn Jones. NeBP
Gold,/ Silver. *Unknown.* OxNR
Gold and black regent-bird, The. Regent-Bird and Girl. Clem Christesen. MoAuPo
Gold and flashing chariot along the Appian Way. Vehicles. Alba Zizzamia. CaG
Gold and frankincense and myrrh. Three Gifts. Edward Judson Hanna. ChIP; OQP; QP-1
Gold are the staircases, and like a kingfisher's wings. To His Wife on His Departure. Li Po. ChLP
Gold-armoured ghost from the Roman road, The. The Youth with Red-gold Hair. Edith Sitwell. FaBoTw; MoVE
Gold as the hair of fairy-story queens. Lincolnshire Remembered. Frances Cornford. HaMV
Gold China Tree. *Unknown. See* Golden Vanity, The.
Gold Coast Customs, *sel.* Edith Sitwell.
"One fantee wave." OBMV
Gold crocus reaches up, The. The Crocus. Walter Crane. PCH
Gold Dust Fire, The, *with music. Unknown.* StDa
Gold for the crown of Mary. A Song of Colours. Theodore Maynard. JKCP
Gold fringe on the purpling hem, A. Sunset on the Bearcamp. Whittier. TCAP
Gold! gold! gold! gold! Gold [*or* Her Moral]. Thomas Hood. MaRV; OQP; QP-2; VA; WBLP
Gold Hair. William Morris. BPN
Gold in the hills, gold in the rocks. Arrowtown. Denis Glover. AnNZ
Gold in the Mountain. Herman Melville. APW
"Gold is for the mistress—silver for the maid." Cold Iron. Kipling. QS; VLEP
Gold Is the Son of Zeus: Neither Moth nor Worm May Gnaw It. "Michael Field." *See* Gold.
Gold I've none, for use or show. Lyrick for Legacies. Robert Herrick. OBS
Gold locks, and black locks. The Barber's. Walter de la Mare. GaP; MPB; PCH; RAR; SUS
Gold of a ripe oat straw, gold of a southwest moon. Falltime. Carl Sandburg. NP
Gold-of-Ophir Roses. Grace Atherton Dennen. AA
Gold of the tangled wilderness of wattle. Wattle and Myrtle. James Lister Cuthbertson. BoAu
Gold on her head, and gold on her feet. The Eve of Crécy. William Morris. BPN; EmBrPo; EnLi-2 (1939 ed.); OBVV; POTT; PoVP; TVSH; ViPo; ViPP; VLEP
Gold, red and green flies. Near Dusk. Joseph Auslander. FaPON; OTPC (1946 ed.)
Gold Rivers and Jade Gates. Tu Mu, *tr. fr. Chinese.* WhP
Gold-Seekers, The. Hamlin Garland. AA; FaBoBe; MC; OBAV; YaD
Gold Seekers, The. Marion Muir Richardson. PoOW
Gold Seeker's Song, The. *Unknown.* PoOW
Gold tane from the king's harbengers. Robin Hood and Queen Katherine. *Unknown.* BaBo; ESPB (A *and* B *vers.*)
Gold Wings across the Sea. William Morris. *Fr.* Golden Wings. AtBAP
(Song: "Gold wings across the sea!") KN; LoBV
(Song of Jehane du Castel Beau, The.) ChTr
Goldbrown upon the sated flood. Flood. James Joyce. MBP; MoBrPo
Golden. Francisco A. de Icaza, *tr. fr. Spanish by* Samuel Beckett. AnMP
Golden Age, The. Ernest Francisco Fenollosa. AA
Golden Age, The, *sel.* Thomas Heywood.
Hymn to Diana. EIL
("Hail, beauteous Dian, queen of shades.") SiCE
Golden Age, The. Tasso, *tr. fr. Italian. Fr.* Aminta. AWP; WoL, *tr. by* Leigh Hunt; LyPI, *tr. by* Henry Reynolds (John Reynolds, *wr.*)
Golden Apples, The. William Morris. *Fr.* The Earthly Paradise: December. EPN
Golden as your singing-note. Amber Beads. Audrey Alexandra Brown. CaP
Golden Ball, The. *Unknown. See* Maid Freed from the Gallows, The.
Golden bee a-cometh, A. A Merry Bee. Joseph Skipsey. OBVV
Golden Bells. Po Chü-i, *tr. fr. Chinese by* Arthur Waley. TrCh
Golden Bough. Helen Hoyt. HBMV
Golden Bough. Elinor Wylie. MAP; MoAmPo
Golden bowl, A. Yearning. Huang Pien. PoHN
Golden Calf, The. Exodus, XXXII: 1-31, *abr.,* Bible, *O.T.* GrCo-1
Golden Carol, The. *Unknown.* OHIP
(Golden Carol of Melchior, Balthazar and Gaspar, the Three Kings, The.) SDH
Golden casket I designed, A. Epigram. John Swanwick Drennan. IrPN
Golden City, *with music. Unknown.* StDa
Golden City of St. Mary, The. John Masefield. GTSL; MCCG
Golden cloud slept for her pleasure, A. The Mountain. Mikhail Lermontov. AWP; JAWP; WBP
Golden Cobwebs. Rowena Bennett. ChBR
Golden Corpse, The. Stephen Vincent Benét. TCPD
Golden cradle under you, and you young, A. He Meditates on the Life of a Rich Man. Douglas Hyde. OBMV
Golden crocus reaches up, The. The Crocus. Walter Crane. OTPC (1946 ed.)
Golden Crown Sparrow of Alaska. John Burroughs. SN
Golden Day, The. Arthur Wallace Peach. PEDC
Golden day, A. Sea-Stretch. Rena Cary Sheffield. BLA
Golden dreamboat's ready, all her silken sails are spread, The. Lullaby. Edgar A. Guest. OnHT
Golden dreams of youth, The. Hope's Song. Helen Maria Winslow. PEOR
Golden eagle swooped out of the sky, The. Salmon Drowns Eagle. Malcolm Lowry. BoCaPo (1948 ed.); TwCaPo

Golden Echo, The. Gerard Manley Hopkins. *See* Leaden Echo and the Golden Echo, The.
Golden Elegy, The. Leopold Staff, *tr. fr. Polish by* Watson Kirkconnell. LiTW
Golden eve is all astir, The. Theme. James Stephens. POTE
Golden Eyes. Rufinus, *tr. fr. Greek by* Andrew Lang. GrL
Golden Falcon. Robert P. Tristram Coffin. BLA; CAW; TBM
Golden Fish, The. George Arnold. HBV; LPS-1; PR
Golden Fish. Titanomachia, *tr. fr. Greek by* T. F. Higham. OxBG
Golden Flower, The. Oliver Wendell Holmes. PEOR
Golden gates of Sleep unbar, The. A Bridal Song. Shelley. EV-4; OBRV
Golden Gift, The. Earl of Surrey. Po
("Golden gift that Nature did thee give, The.") SiPS
Golden gilliflower [*or* gillyflower] today, A. The Gilliflower [*or* Gillyflower] of Gold. William Morris. AnFE; BPN; CBOV; EmBrPo; MBP; POTT; PoVP; ReaPo; TCEP; TOP; TVSH; VA; ViPo; VLEP; WHA
Golden Girl, A. "Barry Cornwall." LPS-1
Golden Glove, The. *Unknown.* MaC
Golden Glow. Abul Hasan of Seville, *tr. fr. Arabic by* A. J. Arberry. MooP
Golden goats on a hillside black. Futility. Robert Ervin Howard. DaM
Golden Hair. James Joyce. *See* Goldenhair.
Golden hair that Gulla wears, The. Bought Locks. Martial. AWP; JAWP; LiTW; OuHeWo; WBP; WoL
Golden Hands. *Unknown.* PC
Golden harps are sounding. Frances Ridley Havergal. OlF
Golden Heart, The. Witter Bynner. HBMV
Golden Hook, The. Spenser. *See* Amoretti, XLVII.
Golden is my steed. A Yellow Horse with a Blaze. Ibn Sa'id of Alcala la Real. MooP
Golden Journey, The. William Vaughn Moody. MOAP
Golden Journey to Samarkand, The. James Elroy Flecker. AlDL; HBMV; POTT; TCPD
Sels.
"Away, for we are ready to a man," Epilogue; *also given in* Hassan, V, ii. CP; ShBV-3
Golden Road, The ("We are the Pilgrims, master"). OtMeF
"We who with songs beguile your pilgrimage," Prologue. GTBS; MM; OBMV; ReTS; TwCV
Golden Keys. *Unknown.* PTA-1
Golden Legend, The, *sel.* Longfellow.
This Is Indeed the Blessed Mary's Land. ISi
Golden lemon is not made, The. A Song for the Spanish Anarchists. Sir Herbert Read. ChMP
Golden Mean, The. Aeschylus, *tr. fr. Greek by* Gilbert Murray. *Fr.* Eumenides. GrR
Golden Mean, The. Anacreon, *tr. fr. Greek by* T. F. Higham. GrL; OxBG
Golden Mean, The. Horace. *See* To Licinius.
Golden Mean, The. Lucian, *tr. fr. Greek by* William Hay. OnPM
("Enjoy your goods as if your death were near.") GrPo
Golden Mean, The. Earl of Surrey. SiPS
Golden Mean of Thrift. Hesiod. *See* Spending and Sparing.
Golden Mile-Stone, The. Longfellow. PoEL-5
Golden Month, The. Marion Doyle. YeAr
Golden New York night. Alternating Nocturne. José Juan Tablada. AnMP
Golden Outline. Winifred Welles. MuM
Golden Palace, The. *Unknown, tr. fr. Chinese by* Arthur Waley. TrCh
Golden pallor of voluptuous light, A. The Mocking-Bird. Paul Hamilton Hayne. AmPP (3d ed.); BAV
Golden Plover, The. Jónas Hallgrímsson, *tr. fr. Icelandic by* Watson Kirkconnell. IcP
Golden Pulse. John Myers O'Hara. LBMV
"Golden rain! Golden rain! Out of the sky!" Summer Rain. Apollon Nikolayevich Maikov. TrRV
Golden Road, The. James Elroy Flecker. *Fr.* Hassan. OtMeF
Golden-Robin's Nest, The. John White Chadwick. AA
Golden-rod is yellow, The. September. Helen Hunt Jackson. GoTP
Golden Room, The. W. W. Gibson. POTE
Golden rose the house, in the portal I saw. Apparuit. Ezra Pound. APA; CoAnAm; TwAmPo
Golden Rowan. Bliss Carman. VA
Golden Sequence, The. Pope Innocent III, *tr. fr. Latin.* CAW
Golden Sestina, The. Giovanni Pico della Mirandola, *tr. fr. Italian by* Ezra Pound. LiTW
Golden Slumbers [Kiss Your Eyes]. Thomas Dekker, *and others. Fr.* The Pleasant Comedy of Patient Grissell. CenL; CH; EV-2; HBV; OTPC; PoE; ReEn; ShBV-4; SiCE; TuPP; ViBoPo
(Cradle Song.) OBSC; TrGrPo
(Lullaby: "Golden slumbers kiss your eyes.") BLV; BOL; ElL; LoBV
Golden Sorrow, A. Martial, *tr. fr. Latin by* Paul Nixon. LiTW
Golden spider of the sky, The. Solar Myth. Genevieve Taggard. MAP; MoAmPo
Golden spring redeems the withered year, The. Robert Hillyer. Sonnets, II. HBMV
Golden Spurs. Virginia Scott Miner. PoRL; SiSoSe; StaSt
Golden stag is dead, The. The Stag. Harold Lewis Cook. MM
Golden stars give warmthless fire, The. Christmas and Ireland. Lionel Johnson. JKCP
Golden Stockings. Oliver St. John Gogarty. GTIV; OxBI
Golden sun is garish, The. Rain. Frances Shaw. HBMV
Golden sun that brings the day, The. In Praise of the Sun. "A. W." OBSC; SiCE
Golden Tacks. Mildred D. Shacklett. GFA
Golden [*or* Goldyn] Targe, The. William Dunbar. BSV; EBSV; SiCE
Sels.
"And as I did awake." NBE
Poet's Dream, The. PoEL-1
Golden Text, The. George Frederick Cameron. VA
Golden through the golden morning. The Return. Eleanor Rogers Cox. PAH
Golden trees of England, The. The Jungle Trees. Marjorie Wilson. BoTP
Golden-tressed Adelaide. "Barry Cornwall." VA
Golden upon the wind her loose hair streaming. Petrarch. *Fr.* Sonnets to Laura: To Laura in Life. PrPoCR
Golden Vanity, The. *Unknown.* BaBo (C *vers.*); CH; FaBoCh; OBB, *mod.*; OnSP; SG, *mod.*; ShBV-1; SoAmSa, *with music;* ViBoFo
(Golden Vanitie, The.) EnSB
(Goulden Vanitee [*or* Vanitie], The.) AtBAP; SG
(Low-down, Lonesome Low, The, *with music, diff. vers.*) OuSiCo
(Sir Walter Raleigh Sailing in the Low-Lands, *diff. vers.*) OxBoLi; SG
(Sweet Trinity, The, A *and* B *vers.*) BaBo; ESPB
Golden Verses. Gérard de Nerval, *tr. fr. French by* Daisy Aldan. AnFP
Golden Wedding, The. David Gray. FaBoBe; HBV
Golden Wedding. William W. Pratt. MaRV
Golden Whales of California, The, *sel.* Vachel Lindsay.
"Yes, I have walked in California." AtBAP
Golden Willow Tree, The, *with music. Unknown.* SoAF
Golden Wings. William Morris. WHA
Sels.
Gold Wings across the Sea. AtBAP
(Song: "Gold wings across the sea!") KN; LoBV
(Song of Jehane du Castel Beau, The.) ChTr
Ladies' Gard. BMEP
(Ancient Castle, An.) SeCePo
("Midways of a walled garden.") ChTr; LiA
Golden world is past, saith some, The. Of the Golden World. Thomas Howell. SiCE; TuPP
Golden Year, The. Tennyson. PSO
Goldenhair. James Joyce. Chamber Music, V. BoTP; ChTr; HBMV; MoSiPe
(Golden Hair.) LEAP
("Lean out of the window.") TwCV
(Song: "Lean out of the window.") POTE
Goldenhair climbed up on grandpapa's knee. Little Goldenhair. F. Burge Smith. LPS-1
Goldenrod. Elaine Goodale Eastman. HBV
Golden-Rod. Lucy Larcom. PEOR
Golden Rod, The. Frank Dempster Sherman. BoChLi; FaPON
Goldenrod [*or* Golden rod] is yellow, The. September [Days Are Here]. Helen Hunt Jackson. BoChLi; FaPON; MPB; OnHT; OTPC (1946 ed.); PEDC; PoRL; PRWS; RAR; TiPo (1959 ed.); YeAr
Goldfinch, The. Odell Shepard. BLA
Goldfinches. Keats. GN
Goldfinches. Elisabeth Scollard. BLA; WhBS
Goldfish, The. Audrey Alexandra Brown. CaP
Goldfish, The. William F. Kirk. LHV
Goldfish on the Writing Desk. Max Brod, *tr. fr. German by* Babette Deutsch *and* Avrahm Yarmolinsky. LiTW; TrJP
Goldfish play, The. Aquarium. José Gorostiza. AnCL
Goldsmith, The. Rainer Maria Rilke, *tr. fr. German by* Herman Salinger. TwGV
Goldsmith's Wife, The. *Unknown, tr. fr. Irish by* Frank O'Connor. KiLC
Goldyn Targe, The. William Dunbar. *See* Golden Targe, The.
Golf Links, The. Sarah N. Cleghorn. DDA; FaFP; InMe; LiTM; PoeMoYo; SiTL
(Golf Links Lie So Near the Mill, The.) BAP; HBMV; PoTo
(Quatrain.) MaRV; NAMP
Golfer's Rubaiyat, The. H. W. Boynton. PA
Golgotha. Frederic L. Knowles. OQP; OQ-1
Golgotha. Katherine Greenleaf Pedley. ChIP

Golgotha Is a Mountain. Arna Bontemps. CDC; PoNe
Golgotha's Cross. Raymond Kresensky. ChIP; OQP; QP-2
Golgotha's Journey is an ancient way. Crucifixion. Hugh O. Isbell. ChIP; PGD
Goliath and David. Louis Untermeyer. *See* Apocryphal Soliloquies.
Goliathus goliathus, the one banana. The Zoo. Gilbert Sorrentino. NeAP
Goll's Parting with His Wife. *Unknown, tr. fr. Early Modern Irish by* Eoin MacNeill. AnIL
Golly, How Truth Will Out. Ogden Nash. LiTA; LiTM; MoAmPo
Gondibert, *sels.* Sir William Davenant.
"By what bold passion am I rudely led," *fr.* I, 3. FaBoEn; OBS
"From Brescia swiftly," II, 5. CEP
"Of all the Lombards, by their trophies knowne," *fr.* I, 1. SeCV-1
Praise and Prayer, *fr.* I, 6. GoBC; OBEV
"To streets (the people's region) early fame," II, ii. SeEP
Gondoliers, The, *sels.* W. S. Gilbert.
Duke of Plaza-Toro, The. ALV; FaPON; FiBHP; OnPP; PCD
There Lived a King. FiBHP; StPo; WhC
(King Goodheart.) ALV; InMe
Gondul and Skogul the great god sent. Death Song of Haakon the Good. Eyvindr Finsson. LyMA
Gone. Mary Elizabeth Coleridge. HBV; MBP; OBEV (new ed.); OBVV; OQP; QP-2; TOP
Gone, A. Larry Eigner. NeAP
Gone. Adam Lindsay Gordon. BoAu
Gone! Ethel Runyon Knott. BPP
Gone. Carl Sandburg. AmP; AnFE; APA; CoAnAm; NP; OnPP; TCPD; TwAmPo
Gone Are Ilium's Kings. Euripides, *tr. fr. Greek by* Arthur S. Way. *Fr.* Andromache. GrR
Gone are the coloured princes, gone echo, gone laughter. The Ruin. Richard Hughes. OBMV; POTE
Gone are the days when my heart was young and gay. Old Black Joe. Stephen Collins Foster. FaFP; IHA; OlF; TreFS
Gone are the sensuous stars, and manifold. Chaucer. Benjamin Brawley. BANP
Gone are the tales that once we read! Ballade of Dime Novels. Arthur Guiterman. PFE
Gone are those resolute trekkers—pilgrims who passed through the desert. Francis Carey Slater. *Fr.* The Karroo. MM
Gone are those three, those sisters rare. The Three Sisters. Arthur Davison Ficke. HBV; LEAP; MAP; SBMV
Gone art thou? gone, and is the light of day. To the Dead. William Bell Scott. VA
Gone at last. The Old Admiral. Edmund Clarence Stedman. GA; LPS-3
Gone Boy. Langston Hughes. NePoAm-2
Gone down in the flood, and gone out in the flame! The Sinking of the *Merrimac[k]*. Lucy Larcom. MC; PAH
Gone—faded out of the story, the sea-faring friend I remember? Pasa Thalassa Thalassa. E. A. Robinson. EtS; LaNeLa
Gone Forward. Margaret Junkin Preston. DD; GA
Gone! Gone! Forever Gone. Gerald Griffin. OnYI
Gone, gone—sold and gone. The Farewell. Whittier. AA; AWP; InPo; LEAP; MOAH; MotAn; PoNe
Gone in the Wind. James Clarence Mangan, *after the German of* Friedrich Rückert. ACP, *abr.*; BCEP, *abr.*; CAW, *abr.*; GoBC; GTIV, *abr.*; IrPN; MaRV; OBVV; OnYI; OxBI; PoLi; SeCePo; TIP
Gone is the city, gone the day. The Right Kind of People. Edwin Markham. BLPA; PoToHe; StaSt
Gone Is Youth. Salamah, Son of Jandal. *Fr.* The Mufaddaliyat. AWP
Gone, my white tangible angel falling. Four Poems for April, IV. Louis Adeane. NeBP
Gone the three ancient ladies. Frau Bauman, Frau Schmidt, and Frau Schwartze. Theodore Roethke. MoAB; NePoAm
Gone to the Dogs. William Hankins Chitwood. AlBD
Gone was all hope of life. The night was dark. The Return from Troy. Quintus Smyrnaeus. *Fr.* Posthomerica. OxBG
Gone were but the Winter. Spring Quiet. Christina Rossetti. BoTP; CH; EG; LoBV; PoEL-5; ThWaDe
Gone Were But the Winter Cold. Allan Cunningham. *See* Spring of the Year, The.
"Gone West." Geoffrey Anketell Studdert-Kennedy. OQP; QP-1
"Goneys an' gullies an' all o' the birds o' the sea." Sea-Change. John Masefield. AtBAP; FaBoTw; OBMV
Gonzalo's Song. W. H. Auden. *Fr.* The Sea and the Mirror. MeRV
Good! *sel.* Vladimir Mayakovsky, *tr. fr. Russian by* Jack Lindsay.
Hungry Winter. RuPo
Good Advice. Christina Rossetti. *See* Seldom "can't."
Good Advice. *Unknown, ad. fr. German by* Louis Untermeyer. TiPo (1952 ed.)
(Old German Mottos.) StaSt
(Proverbs.) RIS
Good, aged Bale, that, with thy hoary hears. To Doctor Bale. Barnabe Googe. ReIE; TuPP
Good Ale. *At. to* William Stevenson. *See* Back and Side Go Bare, Go Bare.
Good and Bad. James Stephens. MBP; MoBrPo; NeMA
Good and Bad. *Unknown. See* Charity.
Good and bad and right and wrong. Good and Bad. James Stephens. MBP; MoBrPo; NeMA
Good and Bad Children. Robert Louis Stevenson. FaBoCh; FaFP; HBV; HBVY; LoGBV; OTPC (1923 ed.); PoVP; TreF; VLEP
Good and Bad Luck. John Hay, *after* Heine. ALV; BOHV; InMe
Good & Bad Wives. *Unknown.* CoMu
Good and Great God! Ben Jonson. *See* To Heaven.
Good and great God! How should I fear. No Coming to God without Christ. Robert Herrick. OxBoCh
Good Angel, The. Rafael Alberti, *tr. fr. Spanish by* Eleanor L. Turnbull. CoSP
Good, better, best. *Unknown.* OxNR
Good Bishop, The. *Unknown, tr. fr. German by* William Taylor. CAW; WGRP
Good Boy, The, *with music. Unknown.* AS
Good bread,/ Good meat. Grace. *Unknown.* SiTL
Good brother Philip, I have borne you long. To a Sparrow. Sir Philip Sidney. Astrophel and Stella, LXXXIII. SiPS
Good-by. Margaret E. Bruner. PoToHe
Good-by, A. Ednah Proctor Clarke. AA
Good By. Eliza Cook. LPS-1
Good By. Emerson. *See* Good-bye.
Good-by. Grace Denio Litchfield. PoToHe
Good-by. Christina Rossetti. VA
Good-by can be a happy word. Good-by. Margaret E. Bruner. PoToHe
Good-by [*or* Good-bye], good-by to summer! Robin Redbreast [*or* A Child's Song]. William Allingham. BoChLi; CBPC; CG; DD; EV-5; FaBoBe; HBV; HBVY; MoShBr; MPB; OTPC; PEDC; PRWS; TVC; TVSH; UTS
"Good-by," I said to my conscience. Conscience and Remorse. Paul Laurence Dunbar. MaRV
"Good-by in fear, good-by in sorrow." Good-by. Christina Rossetti. VA
Good-by Liza Jane, *with music. Unknown.* AS
Good-by, Mother, *with music. Unknown.* ABF
Good-by: nay, do not grieve that it is over. *See* Good-bye—no, do not grieve . . .
Good-by [*or* Good-bye], Old Paint, *with music. Unknown.* ABF; CoSo; TrAS
(Old Paint.) CSF
Good-by. Pretty Mama, *with music. Unknown.* ABF
Good-by, Proud World. Emerson. *See* Good-bye.
Good-by, schoolhouse! Good-by, books! Camp Chums. Rose Waldo. MPB
Good-by, the tears are in my eyes. Rondel. Villon. AWP; JAWP; WBP
Good-by—to My Mother. Margaret Larkin. BLP
Good-by to my pals of the prairie. The Dying Cowboy of Rim Rock Ranch. *Unknown.* CoSo
Goodby was not an easy word to voice. Resignation. Julia Claire O'Connor. PraNu
Good-by, Young Man, Good-by. A. E. Housman. *See* Oh, See How Thick the Goldcup Flowers.
Goodbye, The. Guillaume Apollinaire, *tr. fr. French by* Glauco Cambon. OnPM
Good-bye. Fannie Stearns Davis. BAP
Good-bye. Walter de la Mare. FaBoEn
Good-bye. Emerson. AnAmPo; AnNE; APW; BAP; CoBA; FaFP; HBV; IAP; LA; LEAP; LiTA; MaRV; NLK (1947 ed.); OBAV; PG (1945 ed.); PoeMoYo; PoToHe (new ed.); TreF; YT
(Good By.) LPS-3
(Good-by, Proud World.) PYM
(Good-bye, Proud World.) WGRP
In the Woods, *sel.* OQP; QP-2
Goodbye. Nordahl Grieg, *tr. fr. Norwegian by* Charles W. Stork. AnNoLy
Good-bye. Norreys Jephson O'Conor. SBMV
Good-bye. Pierre de Ronsard, *tr. fr. French by* Alan Conder. TrFP
Good-bye ("God bless the master of this house"). *Unknown. See* Christmas Carol: "God bless the master . . ."
Goodbye! George John Whyte-Melville. TreF
Goodbye./ Incredulously the laced fingers loosen. Curtain. Helen Spalding. NeTW; POTE
Good-bye and Keep Cold. Robert Frost. ChMo; GoTP; NV; OBAV
Good-bye, Brother, *with music. Unknown.* AS

Good-bye Cassandra, and Marie good-bye. Good-bye. Pierre de Ronsard. TrFP
Good-bye, Fare You Well, *with music. Unknown.* AmSS; SoAmSa
Good-bye for a Long Time. Roy Fuller. NeBP
Good-bye! Forget the days of wane. Nikolai Nekrasov, *tr. fr. Russian by* Maurice Baring. BoR
Good-bye, good-bye to summer! *See* Good-by, good-by to summer!
Goodbye, little Bonny, goodbye. Little Bonny. *Unknown.* OuSiCo
Good-bye, little desk at school, good-bye. Vacation Time. Frank Hutt. BoTP
Good-bye, My Fancy. Walt Whitman. AnFE; APA; CoAnAm; CoBA; FaFP; IAP; LEAP; LiTA; MOAP; OBAV; PG (1945 ed.)
Goodbye, My Love, Goodbye, *with music. Unknown.* SoAmSa
Good-bye [*or* Good-by]—no [*or* nay], do not grieve that it is over. A Farewell. Harriet Monroe. AA; AV; BAP; HBMV; LBAP; LoPo; NP
Good-bye; no tears nor cries. On the Death of Arnold Toynbee. John William Mackail. PoeT
Goodbye Now; or, Pardon My Gauntlet. Ogden Nash. FiBHP
Good-bye Now, Plato and Hegel. Louis MacNeice. *Fr.* Autumn Journal. OnHM
Good-bye now to the streets and the clash of wheels and locking hubs. A Teamster's Farewell. Carl Sandburg. CoBA
Good-bye, Old Paint. *Unknown. See* Good-by, Old Paint.
Good-bye, Proud World. Emerson. *See* Good-bye.
Goodbye to Mr. Pope. Thomas Warton, the Younger. *Fr.* The Pleasures of Melancholy. BeR
Good-bye to pleasant France. Farewell to France. *At. to* Mary Queen of Scots. FoS
Goodbye to the Aegean. Plato, *tr. fr. Greek by* Ralph Gladstone. GrPo
Good-bye to the People of Hang-chow. Po Chü-i, *tr. fr. Chinese by* Arthur Waley. LiTW; TrCh
Good-bye to tree and tower. Good-bye. Norreys Jephson O'Conor. SBMV
Good-bye, Winter. Prognosis. Louis MacNeice. ChMo; OxBI
Goodbyes and griefs come here to join the world. Railway Station. John Hay. WaP
Good Christian Men, Rejoice, *with music. Unknown, tr. fr. Latin by* John Mason Neale. YaCaBo
Good Christians. Robert Herrick. LiTB
Good Christians all attend unto my ditty. A Ballad of the Strange and Wonderful Storm of Hail. *Unknown.* CoMu
Good Christians all, both great and small. The Avondale Mine Disaster. *Unknown.* BaBo; ViBoFo
Good citizens, our Argive seigniory. Clytemnestra. Aeschylus. *Fr.* Agamemnon. GrR
Good Companion, The. Belle F. Owens. ChIP
Good Company. Karle Wilson Baker. FaPON; HBV; HiLiAm; NLK; NV; OQP; POT; PoTo; QP-1; SBMV; VOD; WGRP
Good Company. Henry VIII, King of England. *See* Pastime with Good Company.
Good Comrade, A. Djivan, *tr. fr. Armenian by* Alice Stone Blackwell. BoFr
Good Comrade, The. Ludwig Uhland, *tr. fr. German.* BoFr, *tr. by* Bayard Q. Morgan; LiA, *tr. by* Norman Macleod
Good comrade, beautiful and virtuous, A. A Good Comrade. Djivan. BoFr
Good Counseil of Chaucer. Chaucer. *See* Balade de Bon Conseyl.
Good Counsel. James I, King of Scotland. ACP; EBSV
Good Counsel of Chaucer. Chaucer. *See* Balade de Bon Conseyl.
Good Counsell to a Young Maid. Thomas Carew. OBS
Good Creatures, Do You Love Your Lives. A. E. Housman. More Poems, XXVI. EmBrPo; TwP
Good Creed, A. *Unknown.* PoToHe
(New Year Prayer, A, *sl. diff.*) PraP
Good dame looked from her cottage, The. The Leak in the Dike. Phoebe Cary. FaFP; FaPON; OnSP; OTPC; PTA-1; StVeCh (1940 ed.); TreF
Good dame Mercy with dame Charite, The. The Seven Deadly Sins. Stephen Hawes. *Fr.* The Pastime of Pleasure. PoEL-1
Good Day, The. Henry Howarth Bashford. HBV
Good Day, Good Day. *Unknown.* AnEC
Good day my heart, my sweetest life good day. Song. Pierre de Ronsard. TrFP
Good days/ I'm out. Perambulator Poems, VII. David McCord. WhC
Good Days and Bad. Hesiod, *tr. fr. Greek by* Sir William Marris. *Fr.* Works and Days. OxBG
Good Deacon Roland—"May his tribe increase!" Inasmuch. S. V. R. Ford. PTA-2
Good Deeds. Shakespeare. *Fr.* The Merchant of Venice, V, i. BLP
Good Deeds Past. Shakespeare. *Fr.* Troilus and Cressida. *See* Time ("Time hath, my lord").
Good Dobbin. Ann *or* Jane Taylor. SAS
Good Earth, The. Sir Charles G. D. Roberts. CPG
Good Earth, The. *Unknown, tr. fr. Greek by* William Hay. OnPM
Good Eating Song, A. William Cartwright. *Fr.* The Ordinary. SeCL
Good English Hospitality. Blake. *Fr.* An Island in the Moon. CoMu
(Mayors, The.) CH
Good Expectations. *Unknown, tr. fr. Greek by* Lord Neaves. OnPM
Good Farmer, The. *Unknown, tr. fr. Greek by* Hodgson *and* Bland. OnPM
Good Fates, The. Mark Van Doren. MuM
Good Father John O'Hart. The Priest of Coloony. W. B. Yeats. OnYI
Good Fight, The. Bryant. *Fr.* The Battlefield. BPP
Good flat earth . . . and not so very high, The. Two Mountains Men Have Climbed. Pauline Starkweather. GoYe
Good folk [*or* folke], for gold or hire [*or* hyre]. The Crier [*or* Cryer]. Michael Drayton. CBOV; ElL; ElSeCe; InvP; OAEP; PoEL-2; SeEP; TuPP; WhC
Good folks ever will have their way. The Doctor's Story. Will M. Carleton. BLPA
Good Fortune. Heine, *tr. fr. German by* Louis Untermeyer. BLPA
Good frend for Jesus sake forbeare. Inscription on Stone over Shakespeare's Grave. *Unknown.* TreFS
Good Friday. Peter Abelard, *tr. fr. Latin by* Jack Lindsay. LyMA
(Good Friday; the Third Nocturn, *tr. by* Helen Waddell.) LiTW
Good Friday. Vincent Holme. ChIP
Good Friday. Hugh O. Isbell. PSO
Good Friday. Alice B. Jurica. ChIP
Good Friday. Edgar Daniel Kramer. OQP; QP-1
Good Friday. Lizette Woodworth Reese. OQP; QP-1; QP-2
Good Friday. Christina Rossetti. ChIP; MaRV; MeRV; PoEL-5; StJW; TriL; ViP
Good Friday. Girolamo Savonarola. ChIP; OQP; QP-1
Good Friday. A. J. M. Smith. CaP; MaRV; StJW; TwCV
Good Friday. Martha Provine Leach Turner. MaRV; OQP; QP-2
Good Friday. *Unknown.* ChTr
Good Friday. A. J. Young. MM
Good Friday Evening. Christina Rossetti. PGD
Good Friday in My Heart. Mary Elizabeth Coleridge. PGD
Good Friday Night. William Vaughn Moody. APA; CBOV; StJW; TCAP
Good Friday; Rex Tragicus, or Christ Going to His Cross. Robert Herrick. TriL
Good Friday Rhapsody. Pierre Emmanuel, *tr. fr. French by* Wallace Fowlie. MiCF
Good Friday [*or* Goodfriday], 1613. Riding Westward. John Donne. AtBAP; ATP (1953 ed.); ExPo; MeLP; MePo; OBS; OxBoCh; Po; PoEL-2; ReaPo; ReEn; SeCV-1; SeEP; TriL; TuPP
Good Friday Song. Robert P. Tristram Coffin. QS
Good Friday; the Third Nocturn. Peter Abelard. *See* Good Friday.
Good Friday was the day. The Martyr. Herman Melville. PoEL-5; PoFr; TrGrPo
Good Friday's Hoopoe. Douglas Ainslie. EBSV
Good friends. On Being Stricken with Paralysis. Po Chü-i. PoHN
"Good from a Book." Elizabeth Barrett Browning. *See* Reading.
Good Girl, The. Elizabeth Turner. Mrs. Turner's Object-Lessons, VIII. OTPC
Good God of scholar, simpleton, and sage! Grace; before Reading Emily Brontë's Poems. Johnstone G. Patrick. TrPWD
Good God, what a night that was. Three Lyrics. Petronius Arbiter, *tr. fr. Latin by* Kenneth Rexroth. LaP; LiTW
Good, Great Man, The. Samuel Taylor Coleridge. BPN; EmBrPo; EPN; HBV; LPS-3
(Complaint.) WhC
Good Green Bus. Rachel Field. BrR
Good grey guardians of art, The. Museum Piece. Richard Wilbur. MiAP; NePA
Good Ground, The. Virginia Moore. YT
Good Hamlet, cast thy nighted color off. Grief. Shakespeare. *Fr.* Hamlet, I, ii. LPS-1
Good heaven, I thank thee since it was designed. On Myself. Countess of Winchilsea. TrGrPo
Good Hope. Emerson. OnPM
Good Hour, The. Louise Driscoll. HBMV
Good Hours. Robert Frost. RG
Good house, and ground whereon, A. The Salt Garden. Howard Nemerov. FiMAP; NePoEA
Good Housewife, The. Proverbs, XXXI: 10-29, Bible, *O.T.* GrCo-2
(Good Wife, The, XXXI: 10-31.) TrGrPo
(Virtuous Wife, The, XXXI: 10-31). MaRV

Good Housewife, The (*continued*)
(Virtuous Woman, The, XXXI: 10–31.) TrJP
Good Humor Man, The. Phyllis McGinley. MoShBr
Good husband and housewife, now chiefly be glad. Christmas Husbandly Fare. Thomas Tusser. SiCE; TuPP
Good in Everything. Shakespeare. *See* Uses of Adversity, The.
Good in graves as heavenly seed are sown, The. The Christians Reply to the Phylosopher. Sir William Davenant. MeLP
Good Inn, The. Herman Knickerbocker Viele. *Fr.* The Inn of the Silver Moon. HBV
Good Joan, The. Lizette Woodworth Reese. FaPON; MoShBr; MPB; SP; TiPo (1952 ed.); VOD; WHL
Good Junipero the Padre slowly read the king's commands. The Discovery of San Francisco Bay. Richard Edward White. PAH
Good King Wenceslas. *Unknown, tr. fr. Latin by* John Mason Neale. BBV (1923 ed.); ChrBoLe; CLS; HBV; HBVY; OHIP; OIF; OTPC; PoRL; SDH; TreFS; TVSH; YaCaBo, *with music*
Good King Wenceslas Look'd Out. "Sagittarius." NeTW
Good Kosciusko! thy great name alone. To Kosciusko. Keats. PoFr
Good ladies, ye that have your pleasure in exile. The Lady Again Complains. Earl of Surrey. SiPS
Good Lawd Know My Name, De. Frank L. Stanton. WBLP
Good Life, Long Life. Ben Jonson. *See* It Is Not Growing like a Tree.
Good little boys should never say. Politeness. Elizabeth Turner. HBV; HBVY
Good Live for Ever, The. Callimachus. *See* Saon of Acanthus.
Good-looking Boy, The. *Unknown, tr. fr. Chinese.* WhP
Good Lord, behold this dreadfull enemy. The Souls Groan to Christ for Succour. Edward Taylor. *Fr.* God's Determinations. PoEL-3
Good Lord Douglas paced the deck, The. The Heart of the Bruce. William E. Aytoun. LPS-2
Good Lord gave, the Lord has taken from me, The. The Mother's Prayer. Dora Sigerson Shorter. HBV
Good Lord Graeme is to Carlisle gane. Graeme and Bewick. *Unknown.* EnSB
Good Lord! I can't understand your taste. Wild Flowers and Potted Plants. Ibsen. AnNoLy
Good Lord Nelson had a swollen gland, The. A Ballad of the Good Lord Nelson. Lawrence Durrell. LiTM; OnHM; PoN; SiTL
"Good lord of the land, will you stay thane." Lord Maxwell's Last Goodnight. *Unknown.* BaBo; ESPB
Good Lord saves us from disease, The. Doctors. *Unknown.* PIAE
Good Lord Scroope to the hills is gane. Hughie the Graeme. *Unknown.* LH
Good Luck. Oliver St. John Gogarty. JKCP (1926 ed.)
Good luck is the gayest of all gay girls. Good and Bad Luck. John Hay. ALV; BOHV; InMe
Good luck to the milkman. The Milkman. "Seumas O'Sullivan." GaP; SUS
"Good Luck to Your Fishing!" Austin Dobson. BPN
Good Man, The. *Fr.* The Talmud. TrJP
Good man was ther of religioun, A. The Parson [*or* The Good Parson *or* The Poor Parson]. Chaucer. *Fr.* The Canterbury Tales: Prologue. ACP; CAW; CBOV; GoBC; GrCo-1; MaRV; PoLi; WGRP
Good manners may in seven words be found. Of Courtesy. Arthur Guiterman. TiPo
Good Master, bless each dog that no one owns. A Prayer for Dogs. Goldie Capers Smith. AIBD
Good master, you and I were born. A Decanter of Madeira, Aged 86, to George Bancroft, Aged 86. S. Weir Mitchell. AA; LEAP; OBAV; ViBoPo
Good Men Afflicted Most. Robert Herrick. LiTB
"Good men and true! in this house who dwell." The Croppy Boy. William B. McBurney. OnYI; TIP
Good Mr. Peeps or Peps or Pips. The Gospel of Mr. Pepys. Christopher Morley. InMe
Good Moolly Cow, The. Eliza Lee Follen. PPL
Good Morning. Joanna Baillie. OTPC (1923 ed.)
(Morning Song.) LPS-2
(Wake, Lady!) HBV
Good Morning. Robert Browning. *See* Year's at the Spring, The.
Good Morning. Rose Fyleman. BoTP
Good Morning. Muriel Sipe. SUS; TiPo
Good-Morning. *Unknown.* SAS
Good morning, Algernon: Good morning, Percy. On Mundane Acquaintances. Hilaire Belloc. FiBHP; MoVE
Good Morning, America! Harry Kemp. PEDC; PoTo
Good Morning, America, *sel.* Carl Sandburg.
"Code arrives. A; language; lingo; slang." ReMP
Good morning, Father Francis. *Unknown.* OxNR
"Good morning; good morning!" the General said. The General. Siegfried Sassoon. FiBHP; MoVE; OtMeF; OxBoLi
Good is an orchard, the saint saith. Of an Orchard. Katharine Tynan. GoBC; HBV; OBVV; WGRP
Good is the Saxon speech! clear, short, and strong. Our Anglo-Saxon Tongue. James Barron Hope. SPP; TCAP
Good morning, Life—and all. A Greeting. W. H. Davies. BMEP; MBP; MoBrPo; NeMA; WaKn
Good morning, Lords and Ladies, it is the first of May. May Day. *Unknown.* MeMeAg; RIS
"Good morning, Merry Sunshine." Merry Sunshine. *Unknown.* MPB; RAR
Good morning, Mistress and Master. *Unknown.* OxNR
Good morning to the day; and, next, my gold. Ben Jonson. *Fr.* Volpone, I, i. AtBAP; NBE
Good morning, to You, Almighty God. Kaddish. Levi-Yitzhok of Berditchev. TrJP
Good morning to you and good morning to you. Good Morning. Rose Fyleman. BoTP
Goodmorning with Light. John Ciardi. WaP
Good-Morrow, The. John Donne. AnFE; AtBAP; AWP; BLV; BoLiVe; CoEV; EIL; EnL; EnLoPo; EnLP; EPS; EV-2; ExPo; FaBoBe; FaBoEn; GTBS-W; HBV; HoPM; InPo; InvP; LEAP; LiTB; LiTG; LiTL; LoBV; LoPo; LoPS; MaPo; MeLP; MePo; NBE; OBS; Po; PoE; PoEL-2; PoFS; PoRA; ReaPo; ReEn; SeCeV; SeCV-1; SeEP; TrGrPo; TuPP; TwHP; TwP; ViBoPo
("I wonder, by my troth, what thou and I.") EG
Good-Morrow. Thomas Heywood. *See* Pack, Clouds, Away.
Good-Morrow, A. Thomas Shadwell. *See* Song: "Fringéd vallance of your eyes advance, The."
"Good-morrow, friend," so spoke, upon a day. The Caterpillar and the Butterfly. José Rosas Moreno. OnPM
"Good morrow, my lord!" in the sky alone. Sir Lark and King Sun. George Macdonald. *Fr.* Adela Cathcart. HBV; HBVY; OTPC
Good morrow neighbor! Hast thou heard the prate? Gossip (A.D. 1585). Mildred Plew Meigs. VOD (1935 ed.)
Good Morrow, 'Tis Saint Valentine's Day. Shakespeare. *See* Tomorrow Is Saint Valentine's Day.
Good morrow to the day so fair. The Mad Maid's Song. Robert Herrick. AWP; BLV; BoLiVe; CaAE; CH; EG; EnLoPo; EPS (1942 ed.); EV-2; InPo; LoBV; OBEV; PoFS; SeCL; SeCV-1; SeEP; TrGrPo; ViBoPo; WP
Good morrow to thy sable beak. The Heath-Cock. Joanna Baillie. LPS-2
Good morrow to you both. O Foole, I shall Go Mad. Shakespeare. *Fr.* King Lear, II, iv. AtBAP; LiA
Good Morrow to You, Valentine. *Unknown.* OxNR; PCH
Good Muse, rock me asleep. A Sweet Pastoral [*or* To His Muse]. Nicholas Breton. LO; OBSC; SiCE
Good my King, in your garden close. The King's Ballad. Joyce Kilmer. HBV
Good Name, A. Shakespeare. *Fr.* Othello, III, iii. BCEP; BTP; FaFP; OTPC (1946 ed.); TreFS
Good name is better than precious oil [*or* ointment], A. The Better Path. Ecclesiastes, Bible, *O.T.* TreFS; TrJP
Good-natur'd Man, The, *sel.* Goldsmith.
Prologue: "Prest by the load of life, the weary mind," *by* Samuel Johnson. LoBV
Good neighbor, tell me why that sound. The Neighbors of Bethlehem. *Unknown.* OHIP; SDH
Good neighbors, dear, be cautious. Allalu Mo Wauleen. *Unknown.* AnIV
Good News. Lin I Ning, *tr. fr. Chinese by* Henry H. Hart. ChLP; PoHN
Good news from heaven the angels bring. A Christmas Carol for Children. Martin Luther. COAH; SDH
Good Night. Ruth Ainsworth. BoTP
Good-Night. Joanna Baillie. OTPC (1923 ed.)
Good Night. William Barnes. RO
Good-Night. Hester A. Benedict. HBV
Good Night. Bernard Isaac Durward. JKCP (1926 ed.)
Good-Night. George Hill. BOL
Good Night. Thomas Hood. GaP; MPB (1956 ed.); SiSoSe
Good Night. Victor Hugo, *tr. fr. French.* BoTP; FaPON; GFA; MeMeAg; OQP; OTPC (1946 ed.); PCH; QP-1; SiSoSe; SUS; TiPo
Good Night. Karl Theodor Körner, *tr. fr. German by* Charles T. Brooks. LPS-2
Good Night. S. Weir Mitchell. HBV; MaRV
Good-Night. Harrison S. Morris. BOL
Good Night. John Nichol. OBVV
Good Night. Dorothy Mason Pierce. BrR; SiSoSe; TiPo (1952 ed.)
Good-Night, A. Francis Quarles. EPS (1942 ed.); OBS; SeCL; SeEP; TrGrPo; TriL
Good Night. Sana'i, *tr. fr. Persian by* E. G. Browne. PeP
Good-Night. Shelley. HBV; LiTL; ViBoPo
Good Night. Jane Taylor. BoChLi; BOL; CBPC; HBV; HBVY; OTPC; PPL; RAR; SAS, *st.* 1
Good-Night. Nancy Byrd Turner. BLP; OQP; QP-1
Good-Night ("Good-night! Be thy cares forgotten quite"). *Unknown, tr. fr. German.* BOL
Good Night. Mark Van Doren. BAP

Good-Night. Elizabeth Hays Wilkinson. BOL
Goodnight, A. William Carlos Williams. MoAB; MoAmPo; MOAP
Good night,/ Sleep tight. Night Blessing [or Hush Rhymes]. *Unknown.* BOL; HBVY; PCH; SAS
Good-Night? ah! no; the hour is ill. Good-Night. Shelley. HBV; LiTL; ViBoPo
Good Night and Good Morning. Richard Monckton Milnes. BoTP; CPN; LPS-1; MeMeAg; OTPC (1923 ed.); PRWS; PTA-1; RAR; SAS; TVC; TVSH
Good-Night, Babette! Austin Dobson. BMEP; BPN; HBV; OBVV; POTT; PoVP; VA
Good-night! Be thy cares forgotten quite. Good-Night. *Unknown.* BOL
Good night, big world. Back to the Ghetto. Jacob Glatstein. TrJP
Good-night, dear friend! I say good-night to thee. Good-Night. Hester A. Benedict. HBV
Good night. Ensured release. Parta Quies [or Alta Quies]. A. E. Housman. More Poems, XLVIII. EmBrPo; ReaPo; SeCeV; TriL; TwP
Good night, God bless you. *Unknown.* OxNR
Good Night! Good Night! John Holmes. PoToHe
Good night! Good night!/ Far flies the light. Good Night. Victor Hugo. BoTP; FaPON; GFA; MeMeAg; OTPC (1946 ed.); PCH; SiSoSe; SUS; TiPo
Good-night! Good-night!/ Far from us day takes its flight. Good Night. Victor Hugo. OQP; QP-1
Good-night, good-night,/ The stars are bright. *Unknown.* BOL
Good-night. Good-night. Ah, good the night. Good Night. S. Weir Mitchell. HBV; MaRV
Good-night, good-night, the day is done. Good-Night. Harrison S. Morris. BOL
Good night, good rest. Ah! neither be my share. A Night Watch. *Unknown.* OBSC
"Good-night!" he sang out cheerily. The Flute. W. W. Gibson. ChMo; CMP; PCN
Good-night! I have to say good-night. Palabras Cariñosas. Thomas Bailey Aldrich. AA; HBV; InP; LBAP; OBAV; PR
Good night: it is scribbled on the panels. Finale. Carl Sandburg. *Fr.* Slabs of the Sunburnt West. NeMA
Goodnight, Ladies. *Unknown.* OlF
Good night, my Love, may gentle rest. Ode. Charles Cotton. ViBoPo
Good-Night, or Blessing, The. Robert Herrick. ALV
Good-Night Prayer for a Little Child. Henry Johnstone. BOL; PPL
"Good Night," Says the Owl. Lady Erskine-Crum. BoTP
"Good night, Sir Rook," said a little lark. The Lark and the Rook. *Unknown.* OTPC (1923 ed.); PRWS
"Good-night, sleep well!" we say to those we love. Good-Night. Nancy Byrd Turner. BLP; OQP; QP-1
Good night, sweet repose. *Unknown.* OxNR
Good night, to each weary, toil-worn wight! Good Night. Karl Theodor Körner. LPS-2
Goodnight to the Season. Winthrop Mackworth Praed. ALV; InvP; OxBoLi; PoEL-4
Good night! which put the candle out? Emily Dickinson. BoFr
Good oars, for Arnold's sake. Pax Paganica. Louise Imogen Guiney. AA
Good of the Chaplain to enter Lone Bay. Billy in the Darbies. Herman Melville. *Fr.* Billy Budd. AmPP (4th ed.); AtBAP; FxPo: KN; LoBV; OxBoLi; PoEL-5
Good Ol' Mountain Dew, *with music.* *Unknown.* ABF
Good Old Finn. *Unknown, tr. fr. Old Irish by* Owen Masters. LyMA
Good old Mother Fairie. To Mother Fairie. Alice Cary. OTPC (1946 ed.); PCH
Good old mountain ridges there, The. The Old Mountains. Ivar Aasen. AnNoLy
Good old negro in the slums of the town, A. The Congo, III. Vachel Lindsay. AmPP; ChMo; CMP; CoBA; LiTA; LiTG; MAP; MCCG; MoAmPo; MOAP; NeMA; NP; OxBA; PFY; PoeMoYo; PoMa; PoNe; PreP; PYM; TCPD; TreF; WHA
Good old priest, The! Real Miracles. Max Jacob. MiCF
Good Old Rebel. Innes Randolph. *See* Rebel, The.
Good Parson, The. Chaucer. *See* Parson, The.
Good pastry is vended. LouLou and Her Cat. Frederick Locker-Lampson. ALV
"Good" People, The. Kostas Varnalis, *tr. fr. Modern Greek by* Rae Dalven. MoGP
Good people all, of every sort. An Elegy on the Death of a Mad Dog. Goldsmith. *Fr.* The Vicar of Wakefield. AlBD; ALV; BeLS; BLPA; BOHV; BTP; CEP; CG; EV-3; FaBoBe; FaBoCh; FaFP; GN; GTIV; HBV; HBVY; HiLiEn; LBN; LiTG; LoGBV; LPS-3; MaC; MCCG; NA; NeHB; OAEP; OBEC; OnSP; OTPC; PFE; PIR; PoeMoYo; RIS; SiTL; TreF; WaKn; WP
Good people all, with one accord. An Elegy on That [or the] Glory of Her Sex, Mrs. Mary Blaize. Goldsmith. BCEP; BOHV; CEP; HBV; InMe; LPS-3; MuP; NA; NeHB; OAEP; OBEC; OnPP; OnYI; SiTL; WhC
Good people attend now, and I will declare. Man's Amazement. *Unknown.* CoMu
Good people, come and listen, a sad story I will tell. The Gale of August, '27. George Swinamer. ShS
Good people come buy/ The fruit that I cry. A New Song of an Orange. *Unknown.* CoMu
Good people draw near as you pass along. Alphabetical Song on the Corn Law Bill. *Unknown.* OxBoLi
Good people, give attention, a story you shall hear. Lord Delamere. *Unknown.* ESPB
Good people, I pray now attend to my muse. The Lord Chancellours Villanies Discovered; or, His Rise and Fall in the Four Last Years. *Unknown.* CoMu
Good people, what, will you of all be bereft. A Ballad on the Taxes. Edward Ward. OxBoLi; SiTL
Good Play, A. Robert Louis Stevenson. FaPON; GFA; MoShBr; MPB; OTPC; StVeCh (1940 ed.); TiPo; VLEP
Good poets, who so full of pain. Epistle; from Dr. Franklin (Deceased) to His Poetical Panegyrists on Some of Their Absurd Compliments. Philip Freneau. MOAP; OnAP
Good rain knows when to fall, The. The Rain at Night. Tu Fu. WhP
Good reader! if you e'er have seen. Nonsense. Thomas Moore. BOHV; InMe; NA
Good Reasons. Keith Preston. WhC
Good Resolution, A. Roy Campbell. JKCP (1955 ed.)
Good Samaritan, The. St. Luke, X: 25–37, Bible, *N.T.* TreF
Good Shepherd, The. St. John, X, Bible, *N.T.* TreFS (7–18); WoL (1–30)
Good Shepherd, The. J. Harold Gwynne. BePJ
Good Shepherd, The. H. P. Hawkins. BOL
Good Shepherd, The. D. N. Howe. PTA-2
Good Shepherd, The. Lope de Vega, *tr. fr. Spanish by* Longfellow. BePJ; CAW; TeCS
Good Shepherd, The. Keidrych Rhys. NeBP
Good Shepherd, The. Christina Rossetti. ChIP
Good Shepherd, The. Clyde Edwin Tuck. BePJ
Good shepherd, tell this youth what 'tis to love. Shakespeare. *Fr.* As You Like It, V, ii. LO
Good Shepherd with the Kid, The. Matthew Arnold. BMEP; MeRV; PoVP
Good Ship *Castle Down,* The. William B. McBurney. TIP
Good sir, beleeve that no perticular torture. George Chapman. *Fr.* The Revenge of Bussy d'Ambois. NBE
Good sir, not Croesus' monument you see. A Poor Man's Epitaph. Simonides. GrR
Good Sir, Whose Powers Are These? Shakespeare. *Fr.* Hamlet, IV, iv. WaaP
Good sir, your words we don't gainsay. From the Virgins. Katherine Mann. EBSV
Good speed, for I this day. To the Lark. Robert Herrick. BLA; WP
Good stay-at-home season is Autumn, A. Autumn Song. *Unknown.* SiB
Good stout tankard at a Rhineland inn, A. Der Heilige Mantel von Aachen. Benjamin Francis Musser. ISi
Good struggles with evil, youth with age. The Maker Alone Knows. *Unknown.* PoLi
Good Susan be as secrett as you can. *Unknown.* SeCSL
Good sword and a trusty hand, A. The Song of the Western Men [or And Shall Trelawney Die?]. Robert Stephen Hawker. ACP (1926 ed.); AEV; BCEP; CBE; EnRP; ERP; EV-4; GoBC; GTBS; GTSL; HBV; LH; OBRV; OBVV; OtMeF; PoFr; ShBV-1; TCEP; TVSH; VA; WP
Good Thanksgiving, A. "Marian Douglas." TVC
Good Thoughts. Katherine Maurine Haaff. PoToHe (new ed.)
Good Tidings. Luke, IV: 18–19, Bible, *N.T.* MaRV
Good Tidings. *Unknown.* PCH
Good Tidings of Great Joy to All People. James Montgomery. *See* Angels, from the Realms of Glory.
Good Time Coming, The. Charles Mackay. PEOR
Good time is coming, I wish it were here, A. When Santa Claus Comes. *Unknown.* ChBR
Good time will never come back again, The. Li Ling. *Unknown.* TrCh
Good, to forgive. La Saisiaz: Prologue. Robert Browning. BPN; EmBrPo; PoVP
Good toll-gate keeper, kindle a light! Halt and Parley. George Herbert Clarke. BoCaPo (1943 ed.); CaP; OCL
Good Tradition, The. *Unknown, tr. fr. Early Modern Irish by* Robin Flower. AnIL
Good we must love, and must hate ill. Community. John Donne. Po; TwP
Good-wif [or Good Wyf] was ther of biside [or bisyde] Bathe, A. A Wife of Bath [or Seven Pilgrims]. Chaucer. *Fr.* The Canterbury Tales: Prologue. ATP; CBOV; NBE; TrGrPo
Good Wife, The. Proverbs, Bible, *O.T.* *See* Good Housewife, The.

Good Wife, The. Sadi, *tr. fr. Persian by* G. S. Davie. PeP
Goodwife Relents, The. Gwen Clear. MM
Good wife rose from her bed one morn, A. Love Lightens Labor. *Unknown.* LPS-1
"Good-will and peace! peace and good-will!" Our Christmas Hymn. John Dickson Bruns [Burns, *wr.*]. BlG
Good wine of Lanling smells of apple seed, The. On a Journey. Li Po. WhP
Good Wish. *Unknown, tr. fr. Gaelic by* Alexander Carmichael. FaBoCh; LoGBV
Good woman, don't love the man. Parasite. Alfred Kreymborg. NP
Good Woman Made Welcome in Heaven, The. Richard Crashaw. CBPC
Good wood. Food for Fire, Food for Thought. Robert Duncan. NeAP
Good Wyf was ther of bisyde Bathe, A. *See* Good-wif was ther of biside Bathe, A.
Good Year, A. Alejandro Carrión, *tr. fr. Spanish by* Dudley Fitts. AnCL
Good, your worship, cast your eyes. The Maunding Souldier; or, The Fruits of Warre Is Beggery. Martin Parker. CoMu; WaaP
Goodby. *See* Good-by.
Goodbye. *See* Good-bye.
Goode friend for Iesus sake forbeare. Inscription in a Library. W. G. Wendell. WhC
Goodfriday, 1613. Riding Westward. John Donne. *See* Good Friday, 1613. Riding Westward.
Goodly host one day was mine, A. Mine Host of "The Golden Apple." Thomas Westwood. DD; GN; OHIP; OTPC
Goodlye Doctrine and Instruction, *sel.* John Halle.
"When thou arte callde at anye time." PoP
Goodness in Things Evil. Shakespeare. King Henry V, *fr.* IV, i. EV-1
Goodness of Age. *Unknown, tr. fr. Japanese by* Ishii *and* Obata. OnPM
Goodness of God, The. Nagata, *tr. fr. Japanese by* Lois J. Erickson. SoLD
Goody Blake and Harry Gill. Wordsworth. BEL; CG; EmBrPo; GEPC
Goody Bull and her daughter together fell out. World Turned Upside Down, The. *Unknown.* PAH
Goody O'Grumpity. Carol Ryrie Brink. FaPON; GaP
Goose. The. Tennyson. BOHV; EV-5; GBV (1952 ed.); PIR
Goose à la Mode. Elisabeth Cavazza Pullen. PA
Goose and Gander. *Unknown. See* Gray Goose and Gander.
Goose Fish, The. Howard Nemerov. FiMAP; NePoEA
Gooseflesh. Vincent Starrett. DaM
Goose Girl, The. Dorothy Roberts. CaP; OCL
Goosegirl's Song. *Unknown, tr. fr. Czech.* PCH
Goosey, goosey gander,/ Who stands yonder? *Unknown.* OxNR
Goosey Goosey Gander—by Various Authors. William Percy French. CenHV
Goosey, goosey, gander, where [*or* whither] shall I [*or* we] wander? Mother Goose. BoChLi; HBV; OTPC; OxNR; PPL; RIS; SiTL
Gorbo and Batte. Michael Drayton. *Fr.* The Shepherd's Garland, Eclogue IX. LoBV
(Daffodil.) EV-1; WP
("Gorbo. as thou camest this way.") CenL; ViBoPo
(Ninth Eclogue, The.) OAEP; TuPP
(Roundelay, The.) ElSeCe
(Sheepheards Daffadill, The.) FaBoEn
(Shepherd's Daffodil, The.) ElL
Gordian Knot, The. *At. to* Thomas Tomkis. *Fr.* Lingua. ElL
Gordon. Ernest Myers. VA
Gorgio Lad. Amelia Josephine Burr. BAP; HBMV
Gorgo and Praxinoa. Theocritus. *See* Syracusan Women, The.
Gorse. Helen Foley. POTE
Gorse, The. W. W. Gibson. AtBAP; TCPD
Gorse. Nigel Heseltine. MoWP
Gorse is on the granite, The. Sung in Spring. Oliver St. John Gogarty. AlDL
Gorse is yellow on the heath. The. The First Swallow. Charlotte Smith. CG; DD; HBV; LPS-2; OTPC
Goshen! Edgar Frank. MaRV; OQP; QP-2
Gospel According to St. John, The. Bible, *N.T. See* St. John.
Gospel According to St. Luke, The. Bible, *N.T. See* St. Luke.
Gospel According to St. Mark, The. Bible, *N.T. See* St. Mark.
Gospel According to St. Matthew, The. Bible, *N.T. See* St. Matthew.
Gospel according to You, The. *Unknown.* BLRP
Gospel of Consolation, The. Havelock Ellis. PoP
Gospel of Labor, The, *sels.* Henry van Dyke.
"But I think the king of that country comes out from his tireless host." WGRP
"This is the gospel of labor, ring it, ye bells of the kirk!" OQP; PSO; QP-1; WBLP
Gospel of Love, The. First Corinthians, Bible, *N.T. See* Charity.
Gospel of Mr. Pepys, The. Christopher Morley. InMe
Gospel of Peace, The. James Jeffrey Roche. PAH
Gospel of the Fields, The. Arthur Upson. NLK
Gospel Train, The. *Unknown.* GoSl; PCH; TrAS, *with music*
(Git on Board, Little Chillen, *with music.*) BoAN-1
Gosport Tragedy, The (A *and* B *vers.*). *Unknown.* BaBo
Gossamer, The. Charlotte Smith. ViBoPo
Gossip, The. John Richard Moreland. PR
Gossip. Lexie Dean Robertson. MoSiPe
Gossip (A.D. 1585). Mildred Plew Meigs. VOD (1935 ed.)
Gossip grows like weeds. Kakinomoto no Hitomaro, *tr. fr. Japanese by* Kenneth Rexroth. OnPJ
Gossips, The. Nathalia Crane. MAP
Gossips tell a story of the Sparrow and the Cat, The. Etiquette. Arthur Guiterman. PFE
Got a sliver in my hand. Dr. Johnson's Picture Cow. Edgar A. Guest. OnHT
"Got any boys?" the marshal said. The Puzzled Census-Taker. John Godfrey Saxe. HBV
Got Dem Blues, *with music. Unknown.* AS
Got my hands on the gospel plow. Keep Your Hands on That Plow. *Unknown.* OuSiCo
Got up and dressed up. Chorus. Jack Kerouac. *Fr.* Mexico City Blues. NeAP
Got up one morning, went out to plow. Tee Roo. *Unknown.* OuSiCo
Gotham, *sel.* Charles Churchill.
"Happy, thrice happy now the savage race." PoFr
Gothic. Jean Starr Untermeyer. AnAmPo; LA
Gothic Landscape. Irving Layton. TrJP
Gothic Notebook, *sel.* Mario Luzi, *tr. fr. Italian by* William Fense Weaver.
Excerpts from a "Gothic Notebook" ("Once more the stars of love cross"). LiTW
Gougane Barra. Sir Aubrey De Vere. TIP
Gougaune Barra. Jeremiah Joseph Callanan. LPS-2
Goulden Vanitee, The. *Unknown. See* Golden Vanity, The.
Gourd and the Palm, The. *Unknown, tr. fr. Persian by* Charles Mackay. OTPC
Gourd Has Bitter Leaves, The. *Unknown, tr. fr. Chinese.* WhP
(I Wait My Lord, *tr. by* Helen Waddell.) AWP; JAWP; WBP
Gouty-footed Colonel J. Martial, *tr. fr. Latin by* "T. W. M." Epigrams, I, 98. LaP
Gouty Merchant and the Stranger, The. Horace Smith. BeLS; BOHV; LPS-3
Government building, not my own home, A. Written when Governor of Soochow. Po Chü-i. TrCh
Government-bull yoked to a Government-cart, A! The Chancellor's Gravel-Drive. Po Chü-i. TrCh
Government gave Simeon Clay, The. And/Or. Clarence Day. WhC
Government Injunction [Restraining Harlem Cosmetic Co.]. Josephine Miles. FiMAP; PoNe
Government Official. Paul Dehn. WaP
Governor B. is a sensible man. *See* Guvener B. is a sensible man.
Governor Lenhard, *sels.* Einar Hjörleifsson Kvaran, *tr. fr. Icelandic by* Jakobina Johnson. IcP
Death Comes Riding.
My Country Lies Wounded.
Governor your husband lived so long, The. John Berryman. *Fr.* Homage to Mistress Bradstreet. AmP; MoVE
Gowan glitters on the sward, The. The Shepherd's Song. Joanna Baillie. EBSV; EV-3
Gowk, The. William Soutar. GoTS; NeBP
Gown, The. Mary Carolyn Davies. HBMV
Gown which I do use to wear, The. The Image of Death. Robert Southwell. ViBoPo
Grace. Emerson. AmPo; AmPP; CoBA; IAP; TrPWD
Grace. George Herbert. SeCV-1
Grace ("Here a litle child I stand"). Robert Herrick. *See* Grace for a Child.
Grace. Johnstone G. Patrick. TrPWD
Grace, A. Thomas Tiplady. *See* Prayer for the Presence of Christ, A.
Grace, A ("God bless the master of this house"). *Unknown. See* Christmas Carol: "God bless the master of this house."
Grace ("Good bread/ Good meat"). *Unknown.* SiTL
Grace. Richard Wilbur. LiTA
Grace after Meals. *Unknown, tr. fr. Hebrew by* Alice Lucas. TrJP
Grace and Beauty Has the Maid. Gil Vicente, *tr. fr. Spanish by* Alice Jane McVan. AnSpL-1
(Song.) LiTW; TeCS
Grace and Her Friends. Lucy Larcom. TVSH

Grace and Love. George Meredith. EmBrPo
Grace and peace in Christ to my heartily dear little son. Martin Luther to His Son, Hans. Martin Luther. FAOV
Grace and Thanksgiving. Elizabeth Gould. BoTP
Grace at Evening. Edgar A. Guest. TrPWD
Grace at Evening. Edwin McNeill Poteat. ChIP; TrPWD
Grace before Meat. Robert Herrick. *See* Grace for a Child.
Grace before Sleep. Sara Teasdale. TrPWD
Grace for a Child. Robert Herrick. AWP; BEL; CaAE; ElSeCe; EnLi-1; FaPON; InPo; JAWP; LoBV; MoShBr; OAEP; PoRA; RIS; ThWaDe; TOP; TrGrPo; TyEnPo; ViBoPo; WBP
(Another Grace for a Child.) EM-1; EPS; InvP; OBS; OxBoCh; ReEn; SeCV-1; SeEP; TwHP
(Child's Grace, A.) BoTP; EV-2; FaBoCh; LiTB; LoGBV; MeMeAg; OBEV; OTPC; SeCeV; TreFS
(Grace.) OtMeF
(Grace before Meat.) ChTr
("Here a little child I stand.") EG
Grace for a Spring Morning in the Mountains. Esther Davis Langdon. RoKL
Grace for Children ("What God gives, and what we take"). Robert Herrick. OxBoCh
(Another Grace for a Child.) EV-2
Grace for Gardens. Louise Driscoll. NLK; TrPWD
Grace for Grace. Mark Guy Pearse. OQP; QP-2
Grace for Light. "Moira O'Neill." CP; PoRh; SP; WHL
Grace for Theology. William Langland. *See* Theology.
Grace full of grace, though in these verses here. Henry Constable. *Fr.* Diana. OBSC
Grace of the Way. Francis Thompson. EmBrPo
"Now of that vision I, bereaven," *sel.* MBP; MoAB; MoBrPo
Grace that never can be told. All Needs Met. J. H. Sammis. BLRP
Graceful Acacia. Walter Savage Landor. PoEL-4
Graceful and sure with youth, the skaters glide. The Skaters. John Williams. NePoAm-2
Graceful son of Pan! About your forehead. Antique. Arthur Rimbaud. AnFP
Gracefullest leaper, the dappled fox-cub. Young Reynard. George Meredith. HoPM
Gracefully he turns, to pass. Exposure. Ibn al-Zaqqaq. MooP
Graces are four, The. A Statue of Berenice. Callimachus. GrL
Graces, seeking everlasting peace, The. To Aristophanes. Plato, *tr. by* Humbert Wolfe. GrR
Graces, seeking for a shrine, The. Plato, *tr. by* Charles Merivale. GrPo
Graces sought some holy ground, The. On Aristophanes. Plato, *tr. by* Lord Neaves. OnPM
Gracious, Divine, and most omnipotent. Barnabe Barnes. *Fr.* A Divine Century of Spiritual Sonnets. SiCE
Gracious God, our Heavenly Father. Our Airmen. Gertrude Robinson Dugan. PraP
Gracious Lady:/ Simple as when I asked your aid before. Prayer to the Virgin of Chartres. Henry Adams. CAW; GoBC; ISi
Gracious Lady, pity! Nobilis, Precor. *Unknown. Fr.* Carmina Burana. LaP
Gracious Moonlight. Dante Gabriel Rossetti. The House of Life, XX. PoVP; ViPo
Gracious Mother of our Redeemer, for ever abiding. Alma Redemptoris Mater. *At. to* Hermanus Contractus. ISi
Gracious Saviour Born of Mary. Edmund Hamilton Sears. SDH
Gracious Spirit, dwell with me! Holy Spirit, Dwell with Me. Thomas Toke Lynch. MaRV
Gracious Spirit o'er this earth presides, A. Wordsworth. *Fr.* The Prelude, V. OBRV
Gracious Time, The ("Some say that ever 'gainst that season comes"). Shakespeare. *Fr.* Hamlet, I, i. ChrBoLe; GN
(Christmas.) EV-1; ChTr
(Hallowed Season, The.) MaRV
("It faded on the crowing of the cock.") MyFE
("Some say that ever 'gainst that season comes.") ChIP; TiPo (1952 ed.)
Gracius and Gay. *Unknown.* SeCePo
Grackles have come, The. Purple Grackles. Amy Lowell. BLA; ChMo; CMP; CP; CV; IAP
Gradatim. Josiah Gilbert Holland. BLP; FaFP; DD; HBV; HBVY; LBAP; MaRV; OHFP; OQP; PTA-1; QP-1; TreFS; WGRP
(Heaven Is Not Reached at a Single Bound.) PECK
Graduate Leaving College, The. George Moses Horton. NoCaPo
Graduates are going forth, The. At Graduating Time. *Unknown.* DD; PEDC; PEOR; PoRL
Graduating Class, The. Eunice Tietjens. FAOV
Graecinus (well I wot) thou touldst me once. Ovid, *tr. by* Christopher Marlowe. Amores, II, 10. LaP
Graeme and Bewick. *Unknown.* EnSB
Graf von Charolais, Der, *sel.* Richard Beer-Hofmann, *tr. fr. German by* Ludwig Lewisohn.
"Evil Man, An!" TrJP
Grail, The. Sidney Keyes. FaBoTw
Grain Elevator. A. M. Klein. CaP; TwCaPo
Grain is gathered in, The. Indian Summer. Eudora Bumstead. TOAH
Grain of corn within the earth, The. Birth. E. Merrill Root. TBM
Grain of Rice, A. Francis Reginald Scott. PeCV
Grain of Salt, A. Wallace Irwin. BOHV; HBV; WhC
Grain-Tribute, The. Po Chü-i, *tr. fr. Chinese by* Arthur Waley. TrCh
Grains of corn were planted, The. Story of the Corn. K. Fisher. BoTP
Gramercy, Death, as you've my love to win. Sonnet: He Argues His Case with Death. Cecco Angiolieri. AWP
Grammar in a Nutshell. *Unknown.* HBVY; MeMeAg; TreFS
(Grammar in Rhyme.) HBV; OTPC
(Parts of Speech, The.) PTA-2
Grammar of Love, The. Martial, *tr. fr. Latin by* J. A. Pott *and* F. A. Wright. ALV
Grammarian's Funeral, A. Robert Browning. AnFE; BEL; BMEP; BoLiVe; BPN; CoBE; EM-2; EmBrPo; EnLit; EPN; EPP; EV-5; GEPC; GTBS; HBV; LEAP; LoBV; MaRV, *sl. abr.*; OAEP; PoE; PoVP; TOP; TyEnPo; ViPo; ViPP; VLEP; WGRP
Grammars and the spellers, The. Vacation Time. Margaret E. Sangster. DD
Gramophone, The. James Reaney. CaP; TwCaPo
Grampa Schuler. Ruth Suckow. HBMV
Grampy Sings a Song. Holman F. Day. BOHV
Granada. Mikhail Svetlov, *tr. fr. Russian by* Jack Lindsay. RuPo
Grand attempt some Amazonian Dames, A. On a Fortification [at Boston Begun by Women]. Benjamin Tompson. PAH; TCAP
Grand Ballet. Frances Cornford. MoP
Grand Canal, The. Wang Chih Huan, *tr. fr. Chinese by* Henry H. Hart. PoHN
Grand Canyon, The. Adelaide Crapsey. PoeMoYo
Grand Canyon of the Colorado, The. John Gould Fletcher. ChMo; CMP; TwCV
Clouds across the Canyon, IV. TCPD
Grand Chorus of Birds. Aristophanes. *See* Chorus of Birds.
Grand conglomerate hills of Araby, The. Hadramaut. Bayard Taylor. PA
Grand Cortège, The. Christopher Brennan. MoAuPo
Grand Duke, The, *sel.* W. S. Gilbert.
Out of Sorts. ALV
Grand Houses at Lo-yang, The. Po Chü-i, *tr. fr. Chinese by* Arthur Waley. TrCh
Grand Match, The. "Moira O'Neill." BMEP; HBMV
Grand old Duke of York, The. Mother Goose. BoTP; TiPo
Grand Opening of the People's Theatre. O. J. Goldrick. PoOW
Grand red sun has glistened in, The. Morning. Hugh McCrae. BoAV
Grand road from the mountain goes shining to the sea, The. The Little Waves of Breffny. Eva Gore-Booth. AnIV; BMEP; CP; HBV; HBVY; LBBV; MBP; NLK; OnYI; POT; PoTo; StaSt; TSW; TSWC; TVSH; YT
Grand Ronde Valley, The. Ella Higginson. AA
Grand State of Maine. State of Maine Song. Roger Vinton Snow. PoRL
Grand Style, The. Shakespeare. *See* Our Revels Now Are Ended.
Grandeur. Winifred M. Letts. BMEP
Grandeur of Ghosts. Siegfried Sassoon. AnFE; HaMV; MBP; MM; MoBrPo; OBMV; PtOT; TwCV
Grandeur of this earthly round, The. Plato to Theon. Philip Freneau. AA
Grandeurs of Mary, The. Frederick William Faber. JKCP
Grandeza Mexicana, *sel.* Bernardo de Balbuena, *tr. fr. Spanish by* Samuel Beckett.
Immortal Springtime and Its Tokens. AnMP
Grandfa' Grig/ Had a pig. *Unknown.* OxNR; SiTL
Grandfather Frog. Louise Seaman Bechtel. TiPo
Grandfather Gabriel. Robert Penn Warren. AnAmPo; LA
Grandfather Watts's Private Fourth ("Grandfather Watts used to tell us boys"). H. C. Bunner. StPo; TiPo (1959 ed.)
Grandfather's Clock. Henry Clay Work. FaFP; NeHB; PTA-2; TreF
Grandfather's Ditty, A. Victor Hugo, *tr fr. French by* Alan Conder. TrFP
Grandiloquent Goat, The. Carolyn Wells. LiL; MoShBr
Grandma. Moyshe Kulbak, *tr. fr. Yiddish by* Sarah Zweig Betsky. OnCuPl
Grandma, May She Rest in Peace, Died. Moyshe Kulbak, *tr. fr. Yiddish by* Sarah Zweig Betsky. OnCuPl

Grandma told me all about it. The Minuet. Mary Mapes Dodge. BAP; OHFP; PTA-2
Grandma was a Jewess of modest piety. Grandma. Moyshe Kulbak. OnCuPl
Grandmamma's Birthday. Hilaire Belloc. FiBHP
Grandma's Advice. *Unknown.* APW
Grandma's Mistake. *Unknown, sometimes at. to* Margaret Johnson. DDA
Grandma's Tea. Dorothy Bregg. DDA
Grandmither, Think Not I Forget. Willa Cather. AV; HBV; LBMV; NV
Grandmother, The. Elizabeth Madox Roberts. GaP; MPB
Grandmother and Child. Ruth Dallas. AnNZ
Grandmother and Grandson. Hugo von Hofmannsthal, *tr. fr. German by* Herman Salinger. TwGV
Grandmother's Garden. Miriam Ott Munson. GFA
Grandmother's mother: her age, I guess. Dorothy Q. Oliver Wendell Holmes. AA; AmPP (3d ed.); AnNE; APW; CoBA; DDA: HBV; HiLiAm; IAP; InMe; OBAV; OnPP; TCAP; TreFS
Grandmother's Old Armchair. *Unknown.* BLPA
Grandmother's Quilt. *Unknown.* PTA-2
Grandmother's Story of Bunker Hill Battle. Oliver Wendell Holmes. GoTP; IAP; PAH; PAP
Grandpa. Edgar A. Guest. OnHT
Grandpa and Bess. Emily Huntington Miller. PEOR
Grandpa Dropped His Glasses. Leroy F. Jackson. GaP
Grandpapa. Harry Graham. WhC
Grandser. Abbie Farwell Brown. BAP; HBMV
Granduncle used to beau, he said. A Modern Lochinvar. George S. Bryan. PR
Grania. *Unknown, tr. fr. Irish by* Frank O'Connor. KiLC
Granite. John C. Frohlicher. DDA
Granite. Lew Sarett. BAP
Granite and Cypress. Robinson Jeffers. AnAmPo; LA
Granite cliff on either shore, A. The Brooklyn Bridge. Edna Dean Proctor. MC; PAH
Granite Mountain, The. Lew Sarett. HBMV
Gran'ma said, "It's a very queer thing." Whistling Girls. *Unknown.* APW
"Granny, I saw a witch go by," Halloween. Marie A. Lawson. SiSoSe; TiPo (1959 ed.)
Granny Tassia. "Markos Avgeris," *tr. fr. Modern Greek by* Rae Dalven. MoGP
Granny's gone a-visitin'. Opportunity. Paul Laurence Dunbar. MW
Granny's Nodding. Victor Hugo, *tr. fr. French by* Alan Conder. TrFP
Granny's Story. Emily Huntington Miller. TOAH
Grant at Appomattox. Gertrude Claytor. GoYe
Grant at Rest. John James Meehan. GA
Grant him eternal rest, poor wight! Rondel. Villon. TrFP
Grant, in good sooth, our great dead, all the same. The Greatest Tribute. Philemon. OxBG
Grant it, Father. Petition. Eleanor Slater. TrPWD
Grant me, dear Lord, the alchemy of toil. Suppliant. Alan Sullivan. CaP; CPG; OCL
Grant me for celebration on my pipe of seven reeds. Ruris Opes Saturi, Gnavoque Agitanda Colono. Politian. LaP
Grant me, O Lord, this day to see. A Prayer. Edgar A. Guest. PraP
Grant Me Peace. Catullus, *tr. fr. Latin by* William Walsh. LiA
Grant me sweet Christ the grace to find. The Hermitage. *Unknown, at. to* St. Manchan of Lemanaghan in Offaly. KiLC
Grant me the great and solemn breath withdrawn. Invocation and Prelude. Stefan George. AWP
Grant me to share the common, human lot. The Common Lot. Adelbert Sumpter Coats. TrPWD
Grant, O regal in bounty, a subtle and delicate largess. Hymn to the Sea. Sir William Watson. EtS; LiA
Grant that We Die Young. Verner von Heidenstam, *tr. fr. Swedish by* Charles W. Stork. AnSL
Grant us the knowledge that we need. Henry van Dyke. *Fr.* The Builders. TrPWD
Grant us the will to fashion as we feel. A Prayer. John Drinkwater. BMEP
Grape Hill, The. Endre Ady, *tr. fr. Hungarian by* Cornell Lengyel. OnPM
Grape-gathering. Abraham Shlonsky, *tr. fr. Hebrew by* I. M. Lask. TrJP
Grapes. Sister Maris Stella. GoBC
Grapes. Pushkin, *tr. fr. Russian by* Babette Deutsch. OnPM; TrRV
Grapes. *Unknown, tr. fr. Greek by* Alma Strettell. AWP
Grapes Making. Léonie Adams. MoVE; NePA; UnPo (3d ed.)
Grapes of Wrath, The. Christopher Morley. WhC
Grapevine, The. Zoe Kincaid Brockman. GoYe
Grapevine Swing, The. Samuel Minturn Peck. POT
Grape-Vine Swing, The. William Gilmore Simms. AnAmPo; HBV; LA; LPS-2; SPP
Grasp. Jules Supervielle, *tr. fr. French by* Glauco Cambon. OnPM
Grasped by a mighty power and, fearless, hurled. The Prophet. George Matthews Perkins. CAG
Grass, The. Emily Dickinson. *See* Grass so little has to do, The.
Grass. John Holmes. MiAP
Grass. Edwin Muir. MBP
Grass. Po Chü-i, *tr. fr. Chinese by* Ching Ti. WhP
Grass. Carl Sandburg. AmPP; AWP; BBV (1951 ed.); BAV; BLV; BoLiVe; CV; JAWP; MAP; MaRV; MCCG; MoAB; MoAmPo; MOAP; MoVE; NeMA; NP; OHFP; OxBA; PoeMoYo; PoMa; PSO; ReaPo; TBM; TCAP; TrGrPo; WaaP; WBP; WHA
Grass. Walt Whitman. Song of Myself, VI. GTBS-W; LiTG; NePA; NLK, *sel.;* PIAE
("Child, A, said, *What is the grass?*") AtBAP; BBV (1951 ed.); BoLiVe; CoV; InP; MaPo; PG (1955 ed.); TrGrPo
(From "Walt Whitman.") PFY
(Leaves of Grass, *fr.* VI *and* XX.) AA; ADAH
(What Is the Grass?) PCD, *abr.;* PCH; TSW, *sel.;* TSWC, *sel.*
Grass afield wears silver thatch. A Frosty Day. Lord De Tabley. LoBV
Grass again is spread upon the ground, The. Stephen Duck. *Fr.* The Thresher's Labour. EnSW
Grass and Milk. Alfonso Gatto, *tr. fr. Italian by* Glauco Cambon. OnPM
Grass creeps everywhere, The. Enough. Charles G. Blanden. OQP; QP-1
Grass Fingers. Angelina Weld Grimké. CDC
Grass grows long in the meadow, The. July Meadow. Louise Driscoll. YeAr
Grass grows profusely in the temple courts. Old Temple in Mountains. Chang Chi. OnPM
Grass grows slowly up the hill, The. The Undiscouraged God. *Unknown.* MaRV
Grass hung wet on Rydal banks, The. With Wordsworth at Rydal. James Thomas Fields. AA
Grass is beneath my head, The. In the Garden. F. S. Flint. NP
Grass is green on Bunker Hill, The. The People's Song of Peace. Joaquin Miller. *Fr.* The Song of the Centennial. LPS-2
Grass is green, the sky is blue, The. Spring Song of a Super-Blake. Louis Untermeyer. HBMV
Grass is taller, greener, The. Morning Song. Lancaster Pollard. NLK
Grass is tougher than steel. Pilgrim. A. M. Sullivan. JKCP (1955 ed.)
Grass is very green, my friend, The. A Unison. William Carlos Williams. SeCeV
Grass of fifty Aprils hath waved green, The. On the Proposal to Erect a Monument in England to Lord Byron. Emma Lazarus. AA; LBAP
Grass of levity. An Inscription. *Unknown.* ElL
Grass of Yen grows green and fine as silk, The. Spring Thoughts. Li Po. ChLP
Grass on the Mountain, The. *Tr. fr. Paiute Indian by* Mary Austin. AWP; FaPON; JAWP; WBP
Grass shall never forget this grave, The. The Mound by the Lake. Herman Melville. APW; MotAn
Grass singed and low. Chickory. Zerubavel Gal'ed. TrJP
Grass so little has to do, The. The Grass. Emily Dickinson. ADAH; FaPON; GFA; GN; HBVY; OTPC; YT
Grass still is pale, and spring is yet only a wind stirring, The. Only the Wind Says Spring. Helen Janet Miller. GoTP
Grass that is under me now, The. The Dying Lover. Richard Henry Stoddard. BAP; HBV
Grass there doth not. Night on the Fields of Enna. Louis Golding. MBP
Grass-Tops. Witter Bynner. MAP; MoAmPo (1942 ed.); NP
Grasse-Hopper, The. Richard Lovelace. *See* Grasshopper, The.
Grasses/ Rippling in green waves before the breeze. Forlorn. Ma Yüeh Lo. PoHN
Grasses. Scudder Middleton. NV
Grasses are clothed, The. Divine Abundance. *Unknown.* BLRP
Grasshopper, The. *At. to* Anacreon, *tr. fr. Greek by* Abraham Cowley. AWP; CG; EnLi-1; EPS; EV-2; GoTP; HBV; HBVY; JAWP; LPS-2; OTPC (1923 ed.); SeCV-1; WBP
("Happy insect! what can be.") GrPo
Grasshopper, The. Remy Belleau, *tr. fr. French by* Alan Conder. TrFP
Grasshopper, The. Vachel Lindsay. *See* Explanation of the Grasshopper, The.
Grasshopper, The. Richard Lovelace. AtBAP; EPP, *sts.* 1–3; EPS; FaBoEn; LoBV; MeLP; MePo; OBEV, *sts.* 1–3; OBS; PIAE; Po; SeCePo; SeCL; SeCV-1; SeEP
(Ode: Grasshopper, The.) ReEn

(To the Grasshopper.) EV-2
Grasshopper, The. David McCord. LiL
Grasshopper, The. Edith M. Thomas. SN
Grasshopper and the Ant, The. La Fontaine, *tr. fr. French by* Alan Conder. TrFP
Grasshopper and the Cricket, The. Leigh Hunt. *See* To the Grasshopper and the Cricket.
Grasshopper and the Cricket, The. Keats. *See* On the Grasshopper and the Cricket.
Grasshopper, charm for sleepless night. To a Caged Grasshopper. Meleager, *tr. by* Walter Leaf. GrR
Grasshopper Green. *Unknown.* BoChLi (1950 ed.); BoTP; FaPON; GFA; GoBP; HBVY; MeMeAg; MPB; OTPC (1946 ed.); PCH; RAR; TVSH; UTS
Grasshopper had blithely sung, The. The Grasshopper and the Ant. La Fontaine. TrFP
Grasshopper once had a game of tag, A. A Game of Tag [*or* The Playful Crickets]. *Unknown.* PCH; RIS
Grasshopper, the grasshopper, The. An Explanation of the Grasshopper [*or* The Grasshopper]. Vachel Lindsay. FaPON; GFA; OTPC (1946 ed.); PCH; PoRh; StVeCh; TSW; TSWC; UTS
Grasshopper, your fairy song. Earth. John Hall Wheelock. AnFE; APA; CoAnAm; CP; HBMV; InP; LiTA; MAP; MoAmPo; NV; PIAE; SBMV
Grasshoppers, The. Dorothy Aldis. UTS
Grasshoppers four a-fiddling went. Rilloby-Rill. Sir Henry Newbolt. HBVY
Grasshopper's Song, The. Hayyim Nahman Bialik, *tr. fr. Hebrew by* Jessie Sampter. FaPON; YeAr
Grateful heart for all things blesses, The. Epigram. Walter Savage Landor. ALV
Gratiana Dancing [*or* Dauncing] and Singing. Richard Lovelace ElSeCe; EPS; EV-2; LiTL; LoBV; MeLP; MePo; OAEP; OBS; ReEn; SeCL; SeCV-1; SeEP
Gratias Age. Geoffrey Howard. NLK
Gratitude. William Cornish. *See* Pleasure It Is.
Gratitude. Mikhail Lermontov, *tr. fr. Russian by* Babette Deutsch. LiTW; OnPM; TrRV; BoR, *tr. by* C. M. Bowra
Gratitude. Clyde McGee. BLRP; OQP; QP-1
Gratitude. Margaret E. Sangster. MaRV; PraP
Gratitude. Shakespeare. King Henry VI, Pt. II, *fr.* II, i. MaRV
Gratitude for Work. John Oxenham. *See* Sacrament of Work, The.
Gratitude to the Unknown Instructors. W. B. Yeats. TwP
Gratulatory Elegy of the Peaceable Entry of King James, A. Sir John Harington. SiCE
Gratulatory to Mr. Ben Johnson for His Adopting of Him to Be His Son, A. Thomas Randolph. OBS
Grave, The. Robert Blair. BEL; CEP, *abr.;* EiPP; EnRP, *abr.;* EPP
Sels.
All Impelled Onward Alike. EV-3
Church of Graves, The. BeR
Friendship. OBEC
Peace the End of the Good Man. EV-3
"See yonder hallow'd fane! the pious work." EnSW; ViBoPo
(Church and Church-yard at Night.) OBEC
"While some affect the sun, and some the shade." CoBE
Grave. Waring Cuney. PoNe
Grave, The. John Lyle Donaghy. NeIP
Grave, The. T. Gwynn Jones, *tr. fr. Welsh by* Ernest Rhys. LiTW
Grave, A. Marianne Moore. AnAmPo; CrMA; ExPo; FaBoEn; LA; LiTA; MoPo; MoVE; PoFS; SeCeV; UnPo (3d ed.)
(Graveyard, A.) NP
Grave, A. John Richard Moreland. HBMV; OQP; QP-1
Grave, The, *sel.* Kostes Palamas, *tr. fr. Modern Greek by* Rae Dalven.
"On the voyage where/ the Black Horseman leads you." MoGP
Grave, A. Simonides, *tr. fr. Greek by* T. F. Higham. GrL; OxBG
Grave, The. *Unknown, tr. fr. Anglo-Saxon.* ACP, *tr. unknown;* BCEP, *tr. by* Longfellow; LyMA, *tr. by* Charles W. Kennedy
Grave, The ("When the turf is thy tower"). *Unknown. See* When the Turf Is Thy Tower.
Grave, The. Yvor Winters. MoVE
Grave and the Rose, The. Victor Hugo, *tr. fr. French by* Andrew Lang. AWP; JAWP; WBP
Grave and reverend divine, The. A Saki Refusing to Drink Wine. Ibn al-Tarawa. MooP
Grave came to him, at his wish, before, The. Dr. Donne. Kenneth Slade Alling. NePoAm
Grave Charge in Mayfair Bathroom Case. Headline History. William Plomer. SiTL
Grave fops my envy now beget. Love's Slavery. John Sheffield. CEP
Grave Gentleman, The. Andrew Hewitt. NoCaPo
Grave in Hollywood Cemetery, Richmond, A. Margaret Junkin Preston. AA
Grave in the Busento, The. August, Graf von Platen, *tr. fr. German by* Dwight Durling. AnGP
Grave in Ukraine, A. Saul Tchernichowsky, *tr. fr. Hebrew by* L. V. Snowman. TrJP
Grave is open, soon to close, The. An Open Grave. Walter Savage Landor. TriL
Grave Jonas Kindred, Sybil Kindred's sire. The Frank Courtship. George Crabbe. *Fr.* Tales. OBRV
Grave near Cairo, A. Kipling. *Fr.* Epitaphs of the War. PoVP
Grave of Albert Sidney Johnston. J. B. Synnott. BlG
Grave of Arthur, The. G. K. Chesterton. JKCP (1955 ed.)
Grave of Hector, The. Ausonius, *tr. fr. Latin.* LaP
Grave of Hipponax, The. Edward Cracroft Lefroy. Echoes from Theocritus, XXX. AWP; JAWP; WBP
Grave of Keats, The ("Go thou to Rome . . ."). Shelley. *See* Go Thou to Rome.
Grave of Keats, The. Oscar Wilde. PoVP
Grave of King Arthur, The. Thomas Warton, the Younger. CEP; EnRP; GoTL
Grave of Lawrence, The. Clinton Scollard. GA
Grave of Love, The. Thomas Love Peacock. BCEP; CH; ERP; EV-4; GTBS; GTBS-D; HBV; OBEV
(Beneath the Cypress Shade.) EnRP; OBRV
Grave of Rury, The. Thomas W. H. Rolleston. AnIL; AnIV; GTIV; IrPN; OnYI
Grave of the Hundred Head, The. Kipling. PIR
Grave on Ossa, A. Aeschylus, *tr. fr. Greek by* T. F. Higham. OxBG
Grave Piece. Richard Eberhart. ReMP
Grave said to the Rose, The. The Grave and the Rose. Victor Hugo. AWP; JAWP; WBP
Grave seems only six feet deep, A. A Grave. John Richard Moreland. HBMV; OQP; QP-1
Grave Teacher, stern Preceptress! Wordsworth. *Fr.* The Prelude, VIII. NBE
Grave-Tree, The. Bliss Carman. CaP; CPG; OCL
Gravedigger, The. Bliss Carman. CP; LBAP; MAP; MoAmPo (1942 ed.); OCL
Grave-Digger's Song. Alfred Austin. *Fr.* Prince Lucifer. VA
(Elegy: "Crab, the bullace, and the sloe, The.") BMEP
Gravel Path, The. Laurence Alma-Tadema. PPL; RAR
Gravel-Pit Field, The. David Gascoyne. NeBP; PoN
Gravel shone with streaks of gold, The. The River. Alan Porter. MoP
Graven on the Palms of His Hands. Charles Wesley. BePJ
Graven Thoughts. Sir Philip Sidney. *Fr.* Arcadia. SiPS
Graves. Carl Sandburg. AnEnPo
Graves grow thicker, and life's ways more bare, The. Compensation. *Unknown.* EOAH
Graves of a Household, The. Felicia Dorothea Hemans. CG; HBV; PTA-2; WBLP
Graves of Infants. John Clare. OBVV
Graves of the Patriots, The. James Gates Percival. MDAH
Gravestone, A. William Allingham. TIP
Gravestones, I ("Here lie I, Martin Elginbrodde"). *Unknown, at. to* George Macdonald. *See* Epitaph: "Here lie I . . ."
Gravestones, II ("Here lies wise and valiant dust"). John Cleveland. *See* Epitaph on the Earl of Strafford.
Gravestones, III ("Betwixt the stirrop and the ground"). *Unknown.* OtMeF
Gravestones. Vernon Watkins. ChMP
Graveyard, The. Hayyim Nahman Bialik, *tr. fr. Hebrew by* Bertha Beinkinstadt. TrJP
Graveyard, A. Marianne Moore. *See* Grave, A.
Graveyard, The. *Unknown, tr. fr. Chinese by* Arthur Waley. Burial Songs, II. TrCh
Graveyard by the Sea, The. Paul Valéry. *See* Cemetery by the Sea, The.
Graveyard in the City. Luis Cernuda, *tr. fr. Spanish by* Eleanor L. Turnbull. CoSP
Graveyard Rabbit, The. Frank Lebby Stanton. AA; LHV
Gray. *See also* Grey.
Gray. Frederick R. McCreary. TBM
Gray. Oscar Williams. NLK
Gray and blue, the boy ghosts with guns are in the spring woods. Codicil for Pvt. John Hogg's Will. Winfield Townley Scott. FiMAP
Gray battalions were driving down, The. The Man of the Marne. Bliss Carman. AOAH
Gray cat, very willful, took a notion once to wander, A. The Resolute Cat. Nancy Byrd Turner. RIS
Gray clouds against a leaden sky. Easter Morning. Winfred Ernest Garrison. ChIP
Gray-cowled wind of the east! The East Wind. Charles Buxton Going. LBAP
Gray despair/ Was on the old mare. The Old Mare. Elizabeth J. Coatsworth. MAP; MoAmPo
Gray distance hid each shining sail. Jubilate. George Arnold. EtS

Gray Dove's Answer, The. Frederic Edward Weatherly. TVC; TVSH
Gray financier in a thin black auto, A. Dead Snake. William Jay Smith. NePoAm-2
Gray Geese Flying. Frederic Prokosch. BLA
Gray [or Grey] Goose and Gander. *Unknown.* OxBoLi; OxNR
(Goose and Gander.) ChTr
Gray grassy hill, A. Prairie Spring. Edwina Fallis. SUS
Gray, gray [or Grey, grey] is Abbey Asaroe, by Ballyshanny [or Belashanny] town. Abbey Asaroe. William Allingham. GTIV; OnYI; OxBI
Gray hulk of the granary uplooms against the sky, The. A Harvest Song. Edwin Markham. PEDC
Gray is the morn with a morning mist blended. On the Road. Ivan Sergeyevich Turgenev. WaL
Gray Matter. Ford Madox Ford. MBP; MoBrPo (1942 ed.)
(Grey Matter.) ReTS
Gray Nights. Ernest Dowson. PoVP
Gray [or Grey] o'er the pallid links, haggard and forsaken. The Farm on the Links. Rosamund Marriott Watson. OBVV; VA
Gray owl sings f'um de chimbly top, De. A Plantation Ditty. Frank Lebby Stanton. AA; BAP; HBV; LHV; OBAV
Gray Plume, The. Francis Carlin. HBMV
(Grey Plume, The.) TBM
Gray-robed wanderer in sleep. Meeting. Arthur Davison Ficke. NP
Gray Rocks and Grayer Sea. Sir Charles G. D. Roberts. NLK
(Grey Rocks and Greyer Sea.) LBMV
Gray sea and the long black land, The. *See* Grey sea . . .
Gray Shore. James Rorty. EtS; MOAP
Gray Squirrel, The. Humbert Wolfe. BLV; MBP; MoBrPo; NeMA
(Grey Squirrel, The.) PIAE
Gray steel, cloud-shadow-stained. Watch the Lights Fade. Robinson Jeffers. ChMo
Gray Swan, The. Alice Cary. BeLS; BLPA; GN; PTA-2
Gray swept the angry waves. How the *Cumberland* Went Down. S. Weir Mitchell. BIG; MC; PAH
Gray the vacant circle of the sea, The. Bermuda Suite. Winfield Townley Scott. MiAP
Gray tide flows and flounders in the rocks, The. At Sainte-Marguerite. Trumbull Stickney. LiTA; MoVE; OxBA; TwAmPo
Gray waves rock against the gray sky-line, The. When Nature Hath Betrayed the Heart That Loved Her. Sophie Jewett. AA
Gray Weather. Robinson Jeffers. ChMo
Gray whales are going south, The: I see their fountains. Ocean. Robinson Jeffers. CoBMV; CoV
Gray [or Grey] Winter hath gone, like a wearisome guest. September in Australia. Henry C. Kendall. BoAu; OBVV; VA
Grayport Legend, A. Bret Harte. *See* Greyport Legend.
Greasy sky-line where the grey, A. The Sailor. Goodridge MacDonald. CaP
Great A, little a. Mother Goose. OxNR; RIS
Great A was alarmed at B's bad behaviour. *Unknown.* OxNR
Great Adventure, The. Henry David Thoreau. HBV; OBVV
Great Adventurer, The. *Unknown. See* Love Will Find Out the Way.
Great Ali, the Sultan, I've heard. The Poem on Spring. Arthur Guiterman. LHV
Great All in All, that art my rest, my home. Francis Quarles. *Fr.* Emblems. TrPWD
Great Amazon of God behold your bread. For Mary McLeod Bethune. Margaret Walker. PoNe
Great American, The. Lyman Whitney Allen. *Fr.* The Star of Sangamon. PSO
Great and Mighty Wonder, A, *with music.* St. Germanus, *tr. fr. Greek by* John Mason Neale. YaCaBo
Great and mighty wonder, A! Peace on Earth. Anatolius. BePJ; CAW
Great and Small. Charles Mackay. BSV
Great and strong is the Cyprian alway to win. Deianira's Wooing. Sophocles. *Fr.* Trachiniae. OxBG
Great are like the maskers of the stage, The. The Fox and the Bust. La Fontaine. OnPM
Great are the fallen of Thermopylae. The Greek Dead at Thermopylae. Simonides. GrL; OxBG
Great Argument. Omar Khayyám. *See* Worldly Wisdom.
Great Armistice, The. Robert Haven Schauffler. AOAH
(Worlds at War.) GDAH
Great Art Thou, O Lord. St. Augustine, *tr. fr. Latin.* MaRV
Great Auk's Ghost, The. Ralph Hodgson. MoShBr; WhC
Great Author of a world, of sky, of sea. Prayer before Poems. Anne Blackwell Payne. NLK
Great Banquet, The. Ramón de Campoamor, *tr. fr. Spanish by* J. D. M. Ford. *Fr.* Doloras. AnSpL-2
Great Bell Roland, The. Theodore Tilton. PAH
Great big, black bull came tearin' down the mountain. Tearin' Out-a Wilderness. *Unknown.* ABF
Great big dog. The Tale of a Dog and a Bee. *Unknown.* BoTP
Great black bird like to a great black cloud, A. The Song of the Vulture. Elia Demirjibashian. ArmLP
Great Black Crow, The. Philip James Bailey. BOHV
Great blue ceremony of the air, The. Mary and the Bramble. Lascelles Abercrombie. OBMV
Great Breath, The. "Æ." CBOV; CMP; EPN; EPP; GTIV; LBBV; MBP; MoBrPo; OBEV; OBMV; OxBI; PFE; VA; WGRP; WHA
Great Britain's Joy and Hope on That Noble Prince James, Duke of Monmouth. *Unknown. See* England's Darling.
Great brother to the lofty and the low. Master, Make Us One! Hermann Hagedorn. *Fr.* Lincoln; an Ode. PSO
Great Brown Owl, The. Ann Hawkshaw. OTPC (1923 ed.)
Great Captain, Glorious in our Wars. Thomas Bailey Aldrich. GA
Great Ceres, now that the seed is sown. To Demeter. Andrea Navagero. LaP
Great Chain of Being, The. Pope. *See* Scale of Being, The.
Great Charles, among the holy gifts of grace. An Epigram to King Charles for an Hundred Pounds He Sent Me in My Sickness. Ben Jonson. OAEP
Great City. Harold Monro. NP
Great City, The. Walt Whitman. *Fr.* Song of the Broad-Axe, IV *and* V. BAP, *fr.* V; GrCo-1, *fr.* IV *and* V
(What Endures? *shorter sel., fr.* IV.) BHV
Great collector was the Saxon king, A. Old China. Carl Snoilsky. AnSL
Great Cowley then (a mighty genius) wrote. Cowley. Addison. EV-3
Great, creaking worm. The Elevated Train. James S. Tippett. SUS
Great Cross of Mercy, The. Theodosia Garrison. PEDC
Great cup tumbled, ringing like a bell, The. The Grail. Sidney Keyes. FaBoTw
Great Dark Sleep, A. Paul Verlaine, *tr. fr. French by* Kate Flores. AnFP
Great Day. *Unknown.* APW; BoAN-2, *with music;* OlF
Great deeds I sing! my guide recording time! Kiumers. Firdausi. *Fr.* Shah Namah. PeP
Great Destiny the Commissary of God. The Progress of the Soul. John Donne. OxBoCh
Great Diocletian. Abraham Cowley. *Fr.* The Garden. ChTr
Great Divide, The, *sels.* Anthony Delius. BoSA
"And round these men spread the sub-tropic latitudes," II, 33.
"But stricken with the high cafard, the town," II, 7.
Ethnic Anthem, The, II, 11.
"Let's say, the Opposition knows the ring," II, 29.
"Oh, Jack St James can always cut a dash," II, 31.
"Ocean, with a calm sardonic titter, The," II, 3.
Great Divide, The. Lew Sarett. BAP; HBMV
Great Duke of Wellington, The. E. C. Bentley. *Fr.* Biography for Beginners. CenHV
Great earth itself, The. The Endless. *Unknown. Fr.* Manyo Shu. OnPM
Great-enough both accepts and subdues. Phenomena. Robinson Jeffers. OxBA
Great eucalypti, black amid the flame. The Grave. Yvor Winters. MoVE
Great fabric of oppression. Protestant Ascendency. John O'Hagan. TIP
Great fame can be obtained. Autumn Thoughts. Lu Yu. OnPC
Great Farewells, The. Amanda Benjamin Hall. GoYe
"Great father Alighier, if from the skies." To Dante. Vittorio Alfieri. AWP; JAWP; WBP
Great Father, hear our earnest prayer. For Those Who Fly. Alice B. Joynes. PraP
"Great Father, you know clearly beforehand." *Unknown. Fr.* Homeric Hymns. GrPo
Great fear is expected to flash, The. Shrouds and Away. Alfred G. Bailey. PeCV
Great Fight, A. Robert Henry Newell. BOHV
Great Fire, The. Dryden. *Fr.* Annus Mirabilis. FiP
Great fish devour the smaller ones. Stalker of Dreams. Lilith Lorraine. UnW
Great Fleas ("Great fleas have little fleas"). Augustus De Morgan. ALV; LauV; WaKn; WhC
(Fleas, The.) LiTG; SiTL
(On Fleas.) TreFS
Great Fortune is an hungry thing. Chorus. Aeschylus. *Fr.* Agamemnon. AWP; JAWP; WBP
Great Friend. Henry David Thoreau. CoV; PoEL-4
Great Frost, The. John Gay. *Fr.* Trivia; or, The Art of Walking the Streets of London. OBEC; SeCePo
Great Gawd, I'm Feelin' Bad, *with music. Unknown.* AS
Great Giver of the open hand. Four Prayers. *Unknown.* OnYI
Great God-a'mighty, *with music. Unknown.* ABF

Great God, I Ask Thee for No Meaner Pelf. Henry David Thoreau. *See* My Prayer.
Great God! I'd rather be/ A Pagan suckled in a creed outworn. The World. Wordsworth. *Fr.* The World Is Too Much with Us. LiA
Great God of Nations, now to Thee. Hymn of Gratitude. *Unknown.* BLRP
Great God! snow, hail! make darkness! thunder! burn! Zeus Too Is a Victim. Asclepiades. OxBG
Great God, that bowest sky and star. Hymn for the Church Militant. G. K. Chesterton. OxBoCh
Great God, Thou giver of all good. Table Graces, or Prayer. *Unknown.* BLRP
Great god whom I shall carve from this gray stone. The Idol-Maker Prays. Arthur Guiterman. SBMV
Great God: within whose simple essence. To God the Father. Henry Constable. GoBC; PoLi
Great Goddesse to whose throne in Cynthian fires. Hymnus in Noctem. George Chapman. *Fr.* The Shadow of Night. AtBAP; PoEL-2; ReIE
Great gold apples of light, The. People. D. H. Lawrence. EPP
Great, good, and just, could I but rate. Epitaph on King Charles I [*or* Lines on the Execution of King Charles I *or* Upon the Death of King Charles I]. James Graham, Marquess of Montrose. EV-2; GoTS; OBS; OnPM; ViBoPo
Great good fortune ere it is had. The Nineteenth Song. Hadewijch. LyMA
Great-Granddad, *with music.* *Unknown.* CoSo; SoAF
Great-Grandmother, The. Robert Graves. MoPW
Great-grandmother talks by the hour to me. Irish Grandmother. Katherine Edelman. SiSoSe
Great, grey caravans moving in the night. Caravans. Hal Borland. MoSiPe
Great Grey Plain, The. Henry Lawson. BoAu
Great Grey Water, The. E. J. Brady. BoAu
Great Guest Comes, The. Edwin Markham. *See* How the Great Guest Came.
Great-Heart. Kipling. HBV (Theodore Roosevelt.) BoHiPo
Great Heart. John Oxenham. *See* Where Are You Going, Great-Heart?
Great Heart. Pindar, *tr. fr. Greek by* C. J. Billson. *Fr.* Pythian Odes, IV. GrR
Great Heart is dead, they say. Promotion. John Oxenham. MaRV
Great heart, who taught thee so to die. Epitaph: On Sir Walter Raleigh [*or* Rawleigh] at His Execution. *Unknown.* OBS
Great Heav'n! how frail thy Creature Man is made! Love and Reason. Matthew Prior. *Fr.* Solomon, II. OBEC
Great Herod on his golden throne. The Little Christmas Donkey. Geraldine Farrar. StJW
Great Hunger, The, *sel.* Patrick Kavanagh.
"Health and wealth and love he too dreamed of in May." MoAB
Great Hunt, The. Carl Sandburg. NP; SBMV
Great Idealist, The. Jami, *tr. fr. Persian.* LiTW, *tr. by* E. H. Whinfield; OnPM, *tr. by* F. Hadland Davis
Great is Caesar: He has conquered Seven Kingdoms. Fugal-Chorus W. H. Auden. *Fr.* For the Time Being. LiTM (rev. ed.); NePA; SeCeV
Great is my beauty, like a dream of stone. To Beauty. Baudelaire. EnLi-2
Great is she, born in serfdom. The Revolution. Filip Stepanovich Shkulev. PoFr
Great is the folly of a feeble braine. The Love-Sicke Poet [*or* Satire]. Joseph Hall. *Fr.* Virgidemiarum. FaBoEn; ReIE
Great is the rose. Tadmor: Song. Nathalia Crane. MAP; MoAmPo (1942 ed.)
Great is the sun, and wide he goes. Summer Sun. Robert Louis Stevenson. MBP; MoBrPo
Great is the tumult of men's anger grown. From Bethlehem Blown. Mary Sinton Leitch. PGD
Great Jehovah speaks to us, The. The Old Testament [*or* Names and Order of the Books of the Old Testament]. Thomas Russell. BLPA; TreFS
Great jewels glitter like a wizard's rain. On Broadway. George Sylvester Viereck. OQP; QP-2
Great Journey, The. *Unknown, tr. fr. Sanskrit by* Sir Edwin Arnold. *Fr.* Mahabharata. BoFr
Great Julius was a cuckold & may I. *Unknown.* SeCSL
Great King Sun is out in the cold. Snowdrops. W. Graham Robertson. OTPC; PPL
Great King, the Sovereign [*or* Sov'raigne] Ruler of this land. To His Late Majesty, Concerning the True Form of English Poetry. Sir John Beaumont. OBS; SeEP
"Great lady, were you Helen long ago?" Helen—Old. Isabel Ecclestone Mackay. CaP; OCL
Great lamps of silver light his last retreat. Richard Crashaw. Thomas S. Jones, Jr. PtP
Great Land, The. William Rose Benét. NeTW
Great Lords, that keep the dignities of Thebes. Jocasta's Death. Sophocles. *Fr.* Oedipus Rex. LiA; OxBG
Great love doth keep a Royal state. To My Dearest Son. Helen Selina Sheridan. DiM
Great love is ever sorrow. In some way. Love's Shadow. George Sterling. MuM
Great Lover, The. Rupert Brooke. BEL; BLV; BoLiVe; CaAE; EnLit; EPP; FaFP; HoPM; LiTB; LiTM; MBP; MCCG; MoBrPo; NeMA; PIAE; PoeMoYo; PoMa; POT; PoTo; POTT; TCEP; TCPD; TreF; TrGrPo; TwCV; VOD; WaP
"These I have loved," *sel.* BMEP; NAMP; ShBV-2
Great Macedon, that out of Persia chased, The. In Praise of Wyatt's Psalms. Earl of Surrey. SiPS
Great Man, A. Goldsmith. NA
Great Man, The. Eunice Tietjens. AV; NP; VOD; WGRP
Great master! Boyish, sympathetic man! To John Keats. Amy Lowell. PtP
Great Master Dreamer. Charles Buxton Going. *See* Columbus.
Great master of the poet's art! John Greenleaf Whittier. Phoebe Cary. DD; GA
Great masters of the commonplace, The. *See* Great masters of the commonplace, The.
Great Men Have Been among Us. Wordsworth. BPN; EM-2; EmBrPo; EnRP; ES; GEPC; PoEL-4 (England, 1802, III.) HBV; OBEV
Great men have lived. There Lived a Man. Thomas Curtis Clark. ChIP
Great Michelangelo, with age grown bleak. Michelangelo's Kiss. Dante Gabriel Rossetti. The House of Life, XCIV. BPN; PoVP; ViPo
Great Misgiving, The. Sir William Watson. HBV; OBEV (1st ed.); OBVV
Great mistress, from an unpolluted mead. A Votary to His Goddess. Euripides. *Fr.* Hippolytus. GrR
Great Mother, The. Walt Whitman. *Fr.* A Song of the Rolling Earth. GrCo-2
Great Mother Nature! teach me, like thee. George Meredith. *Fr.* Ode to the Spirit of Earth in Autumn. EPN
Great Mourning. First Maccabees, I: 25–28, Bible, Apocrypha. TrJP
Great names of the great captains gone before. Canada to England. Marjorie Pickthall. PoFr
Great Nature clothes the soul, which is but thin. The Soul's Garment. Margaret Cavendish, Duchess of Newcastle. MeRV; OxBoCh; SeCePo; SeCL
Great Nature Is an Army Gay. Richard Watson Gilder. HBV; SN
Great Night, The. Rainer Maria Rilke, *tr. fr. German by* Randall Jarrell. AnGP
Great Oak. Bennett Chapple. HH
Great Ocean! strongest of creation's sons. Ocean. Robert Pollok. *Fr.* The Course of Time. EtS; LPS-2
Great Offence, The. Abu Nuwas, *tr. fr. Arabic by* E. Powys Mathers. LiTW
Great Osmond knows not how he shall be known. Satire. Joseph Hall. *Fr.* Virgidemiarum. ReIE
Great Outdoors, The. Maud Russell. NLK
Great Overdog, The,/ That heavenly beast. Canis Major. Robert Frost. *Fr.* A Sky Pair. AlBD; AlDL; MAP; MoAB; MoAmPo
Great Pacific Railway, The. The Railroad Cars are Coming. *Unknown.* AS; BrR; FaPON; MPB
Great paire of authors, whom one equall star. To the Memory of the Incomparable Paire of Authors Beaumont and Fletcher. *Unknown.* BoFr
"Great Pan is dead!" so cried an airy tongue. O, Tempora! O Mores! John Dickson Bruns [Burns, *wr.*]. BIG
Great Panjandrum [Himself], The. Samuel Foote. FaBoCh; LiL; LoGBV; MoShBr; RIS; WhC
Great Physician, The. Charles Kingsley. MaRV
Great Physician, The. Sadi, *tr. fr. Persian by* Sir Edwin Arnold. *Fr.* The Bustan. AWP; OuHeWo
Great Poet, The. Mu'tamid, King of Seville, *tr. fr. Arabic by* Dulcie L. Smith. LiTW
Great poets must be always. Point of View. Virginia Lyne Tunstall. BAP
Great Powers Conference. Edith Lovejoy Pierce. PGD
Great Prince of heaven, begotten of that King. To God the Son. Henry Constable. OBSC
Great princes have great playthings. Playthings. William Cowper. WaaP
Great rain is over, The. Mary Elizabeth Coleridge. *Fr.* Evening. AlDL
Great Redeemer Lives, The. Anne Steele. BePJ
Great Refusal, The. Thomas S. Jones, Jr. QS
Great Republic goes to war, The. War. Grace Ellery Channing. AA
Great Rhea,/ Pregnant, to high Parrhasia's cliffs retired. Callimachus. *Fr.* Hymn to Zeus. GrPo
Great River, The. Henry van Dyke. TrPWD
Great river flowing broad and free. To the Ottawa. Arthur S. Bourinot. CPG

Great Roads the Romans built that men might meet. What Shall Endure? Ethelyn M. Hartwich. OQP; QP-2
Great Round-up, The. *Unknown.* *See* Cowboy's Dream, The.
Great Sassacus fled from the eastern shores. Death Song. Alonzo Lewis. PAH
Great Sea, The. Man and the Sea. Tu Hsün Hao. OnPM
Great sea-dog, fighter in the great old way! Hawke. Archibald T. Strong. *Fr.* Sonnets of the Empire. BoAu
Great sea-roads to England, The. The Gates to England. Marjorie Wilson. BoTP
Great Seducer, The. Cale Young Rice. TBM
Great Shepherd of the Sheep. Charles Wesley. BePJ
Great ship lantern-girdled, The. The Landing. Padraic Colum. TIP
Great ship spreads her wings, her plumes are flying, The. Godspeed. Harriet Prescott Spofford. EtS
Great Silence. Sister Mary St. Virginia. JKCP (1955 ed.)
Great Silkie of Sule Skerry [*or* Skerrie], The. *Unknown.* BaBo (A *and* B *vers.*); ChTr; ESPB; FaBoCh; OBB; ViBoFo (A *vers.*; B *vers., with music*)
(Silkie o' Sule Skerrie, The.) EtS
Great soft downy snow storm like a cloak, The. The Snow Storm. Ethelwyn Wetherald. VA
Great son of night! come from thine ebon cell. On Morpheus. *Unknown.* SeCL
Great Song, A. Li Ho, *tr. fr. Chinese by* Ho Chih-yuan. WhP
Great soul, thou sittest with me in my room. To the Spirit of Keats. Amy Lowell. BAV; IAP
Great soul, to all brave souls akin. The Star. Marion Couthouy Smith. DD; PAH
Great Sovereign of the earth and sea. Europa. Stephen Henry Thayer. AA
Great Spirit of the speeding spheres. Hymn. John Haynes Holmes. TrPWD
Great Spirit, when I soar away. A Tramp's Prayer. Harry Kemp. QS
Great Spirits Now on Earth Are Sojourning. Keats. *See* Addressed to Haydon.
Great star stooped from heaven and loved a flower, A. Shelley and Harriet Westbrook. Sir William Watson. BMEP; LEAP
Great Statue of the General Du Puy, The. Wallace Stevens. LiTA
Great, still shape, alone, A. Ireland. John James Piatt. AA; LBAP
Great stone hearth is gone, The. Fire. Dorothy Wellesley. OBMV
Great storm has arisen on the plain of Ler, A. The Song of the Sea. *Unknown, at. to* Rumann MacColmain. SiB
Great Strafford! worthy of that name, though all. On the Earl of Strafford's Trial and Death. John Denham. LoBV
Great stream grows not muddy by one stone, A. Forgiveness. Sadi. PeP
Great streets of silence led away. Emily Dickinson. AtBAP
Great Summons, The. Chu Yuan, *tr. fr. Chinese by* Arthur Waley. AWP; LiTW; TrCh
Great sun sinks behind the town, The. To an Ungentle Critic. Robert Graves. HBMV; InMe
Great Swamp Fight, The. Caroline Hazard. PAH
Great swart cheek and the gleam of tears, A. The Washer-Woman. Otto Leland Bohanan. BANP
Great Sword Bearer, The, only knows just when he'll wound my heart—not I. The Conclusion of the Whole Matter. Ridgely Torrence. *Fr.* The House of a Hundred Lights. AA; HBV
Great Tao, The, is unanchored: goes left and right. Tao Teh Ching, XXVI. *Unknown, tr. fr. Chinese.* WhP
Great tempest rages on the plain of Ler, A. Song of the Sea. *Unknown, at. to* Rumann MacColmain. OnYI
Great Things. Thomas Hardy. GTML; GTSL; MoVE
Great things are done when men and mountains meet. Gnomic Verses [*or* Couplet]. Blake. PC; TrGrPo
Great thoughts in crude, unshapely verse set forth. On Reading. Thomas Bailey Aldrich. AA
Great Tides, The. Lyon Sharman. CPG
Great Time, A. W. H. Davies. AlDL; AnFE; BLV; BMEP; ExPo; LBBV; LiTB; MoBrPo; MoVE; MPB; POTE; WHA; YT
Great Tom. Richard Corbet. OxBoLi
Great Towers of Steel. Eleanor Foote Soderbeck. PoMa
Great toy-maker, light-bringer, patient, A. Edison. Robinson Jeffers AmPP (3d ed.)
Great trees in the south. Home. *Unknown.* OuHeWo
Great truths are dearly bought. The common truth. How We Learn. Horatius Bonar. HBV
Great unequal conflict past, The. Occasioned by General Washington's Arrival in Philadelphia, on His Way to His Residence in Virginia. Philip Freneau. GA; PAH
Great Unity, the Sovereign of the East, The. Chu Yuan, *tr. fr. Chinese by* Shen Yu-ting. *Fr.* The Nine Songs. WhP
Great, unknown spirit, living with us still. Armenia's Love to Shakespeare. Zabelle C. Boyajian. ArmLP
Great Venus, Queene of Beautie and of grace. Address to Venus. Lucretius, *tr. by* Spenser. *Fr.* De Rerum Natura *and fr.* The Faerie Queene. AnEnPo; AWP; EIL
Great Victory, The. R. V. Gilbert. BLRP
Great Virginian, The. James Russell Lowell. *Fr.* Under the Old Elm, VII. PGD; PSO
Great Voice, The. Clinton Scollard. BLP; MaRV
Great Voices, The. Charles Timothy Brooks. HBV
Great Wager, The. G. A. Studdert-Kennedy. ChIP
Great War had begun: but masters' scrutiny, The. W. H. Auden. *Fr.* Letter to Lord Byron. PoLFOT
Great was Chuang in the kingdom of Ku. A Ballad of a Famous Fisherman. Lyon Sharman. CPG
Great was his soul and high his aim. Mind and Matter. Sir Arthur Conan Doyle. PoP
Great wave of youth, ere you be spent. Sew the Flags Together. Vachel Lindsay. AOAH
Great waves, crashing on desert shores. Rimas, LII. Gustavo Adolfo Bécquer. TeCS
Great were the hearts and strong the minds. Washington. Bryant. PTA-2
Great whale is a fish, The. The Whale's Nature. *Unknown.* *Fr.* The Bestiary. MeEV
Great while ago, there was a school-boy, A. Old Grey [*or* Gray] Squirrel. Alfred Noyes. PoMa; POT; PoTo
Great, wide, beautiful, wonderful world. The Wonderful World [*or* The World *or* The Child's World]. William Brighty Rands. BoChLi; BoTP; DD; FaPON; GFA; HBV; HBVY; MPB; OBVV; OHIP; OnHT; OTPC; PCH; PRWS; PTA-1; RAR; StVeCh (1940 ed.); TiPo (1959 ed.); TVC; TVSH
Great Wind, The. Liu Pang, *tr. fr. Chinese.* WhP
Great wind sweeps, A. Wild Weather. Katharine Lee Bates. PGD
Great winds may blow now. Knocking at the Door. John Freeman. HBMV
Great without pomp, without ambition brave. Tribute to Washington. *Unknown.* OHIP
Great woods gird me now around. The Blackbird's Song. *Unknown.* TIP
Great Word, The. Estelle Duclo. BAP
Great words like solemn music sweep my heart. Strange Promise. Inez Barclay Kirby. UnW
Great wrong I do, I can it not deny. Amoretti, XXXIII. Spenser. PeBoSo; ReEn; ReIE
Great you call Demosthenes. Self-Portrait. Moses Mendelssohn. TrJP
Great Zimbabwe. Peter Jackson. BoSA
Greata Basaball, Da. T. A. Daly. TSWC
Greata Stronga Man, Da. T. A. Daly. PYM; YT
Greater and taller than our minds can figure them. Prose Poem: The Angels. Théodore de Banville. OnPM
Greater Birth, The. Hermann Hagedorn. UnW
Greater Cats, The. V. Sackville-West. *Fr.* King's Daughter. DiM; GTBS-D; MoP; OBMV; PoC; POTE; ShBV-4
("Greater cats with golden eyes, The.") LO
Greater East, The. *Unknown, tr. fr. Chinese.* WhP
Greater Gift, The. Margaret E. Bruner. PoToHe (new ed.)
Greater Glory, The. Myra Brooks Welch. MaRV
Greater Guilt, The. John Richard Moreland. ChIP
Greater Love. Antipater of Sidon, *tr. fr. Greek by* T. F. Higham. OxBG
Greater Love. Wilfred Owen. AtBAP; BLV; BoLiVe; EnLi-2 (1949 ed.); EnLoPo; FaBoMo; FaFP; GTBS-W; LiTB; LiTG; LiTM; LO; MBP; MoAB; MoBrPo; NAMP; OAEP (2d ed.); SeCeV; ViBoPo; WaaP; WaP
Greater [*or* Great] masters of the commonplace, The. Staff-Nurse: Old Style. W. E. Henley. *Fr.* In Hospital. BPN; InP; PIAE; PoVP
Greater Music, The. Theodore Weiss. NePoAm-2
Greater Mystery, The. John Myers O'Hara. TBM
Greater sweetness on these lips there grows, A. Death like a Rose. Sir Robert Howard *and* John Dryden. *Fr.* The Indian Queen. BeR
Greater Trial, The. Countess of Winchilsea. BLV; TrGrPo
Greater world is water, The. The Tower. Mark Van Doren. MoPo
Greatest, The. Marion Brown Shelton. MaRV
Greatest Battle That Ever Was Fought, The. Joaquin Miller. MaRV; NeHB; OQP; PSO; QP-2; TreF
Greatest bore is boredom, The. *Unknown.* CenHV
Greatest Commandments, The. St. Matthew, XXII: 35–40, Bible, *N.T.* GrCo-2
("Then one of them, which was a lawyer.") PoFr
Greatest Gift, The. Blanche Edith Baughan. BoAu
Greatest kings do least command content, The. Another, of Another Mind. *Unknown.* TuPP
Greatest Loss, The. Frances Brown. MaRV
(Losses.) LPS-1
Greatest man who ever was, The. Some Youngster's Dad. Douglas Malloch. FAOV

Greatest of These Is Love, The. First Corinthians, Bible, *N.T. See* Charity.
Greatest of virtues is humility. Against Women's Fashions. John Lydgate. ACP
Greatest Person in the Universe, The. Daniel L. Marsh. BLRP
Greatest poem ever known, The. To a Child. Christopher Morley. BAP; HBMV
Greatest Tribute, The. Philemon, *tr. fr. Greek by* Robert Browning. OxBG
Greatest Work, The. Ray M. Johnson. MaRV; OQP; QP-2
Greatly begin! though thou have time. James Russell Lowell. *Fr.* For an Autograph. MCCG
Greatly instructed I shall hence depart. The Sum of Wisdom. Milton. *Fr.* Paradise Lost, XII. MaPo
Greatly shining,/ The autumn moon floats in the thin sky. Wind and Silver. Amy Lowell. MAP; MoAmPo; NeMA; ReaPo
Greatness ("He took castle and towns"). Thomas Love Peacock. *Fr.* Crotchet Castle: Llyn-y-Dreiddiad-Vrawd, *ch.* 16. OtMeF
Greatness. Pope. *See* Worth Makes the Man.
Greatness. *Unknown.* OBS
Greatness in Littleness. Ben Jonson. *See* It Is Not Growing like a Tree.
Greatness of Love, The. First Corinthians, Bible, *N.T. See* Charity.
Greatness Passing By. John Drinkwater. MaRV
Greatness. Warmth, and human insight. A Chromium-plated Hat; Inlaid with Scenes from Siegfried. Howard Nemerov. FiMAP
Greaty-great Grannie. Lysbeth Boyd Borie. GaP
Grecian Muse, to earth who bore, The. California. Thomas Lake Harris. AA
Grecian tulip and the gothic rose, The. Poem. Terence Tiller. POTE
Greco, El. *See* El Greco.
Greece. William A. Breyfogle. CAG
Greece. Robert Browning. *Fr.* Cleon. OtMeF
(Cleon.) TwCrTr; ViPo
Greece ("Clime of the unforgotten brave"). Byron. *Fr.* The Giaour. LPS-2
("Clime of the unforgotten brave!") PoFr
Greece ("Fair Greece! sad relic"). Byron. *Fr.* Childe Harold's Pilgrimage, II. EV-4, *abr.;* LPS-2, *abr.;* OBRV; PoFr
Greece/ For this one crime, aye for this one, shall weep. Lycophron. *Fr.* Alexandra. GrPo
Greece. Lord Vansittart. NeTW
Greece was; Greece is no more. "The White City." Richard Watson Gilder. PAH
Greed is dumb at sight of so much gold. A Field in June. Gerald Bullett. AlDL
Greedy Fox and the Elusive Grapes, The. Aesop, *ad. fr. Greek by* Louis Untermeyer. MaC
Greedy Jane. *Unknown.* HBVY
Greedy Little Pig, The. Irene F. Pawsey. BoTP
Greedy Lover, Pause Awhile. Sir Albertus Morton. TuPP
Greedy Piggy That Ate Too Fast, The. Eliza Grove. OTPC (1923 ed.)
Greek Children's Song. *Unknown.* See Swallow Song.
Greek Dead at Thermopylae, The. Simonides, *tr. fr. Greek by* T. F. Higham. GrL; OxBG
("Of those who at Thermopylae were slain," *tr. by* John Sterling.) GrPo
(On Those Who Fell at Thermopylae, *tr. by* Robert Bland.) GrR; PoFr
(Thermopylae, *tr. by* Lord Neaves.) OnPM
(Thermopylae Ode, The, *tr. by* Richmond Lattimore.) WaaP
Greek Earth. Georgios Drossinis, *tr. fr. Modern Greek by* Rae Dalven. MoGP
Greek Epigram. Ezra Pound. MAP; MoAB; MoAmPo; NeMA
Greek Excavations. Bernard Spencer. ChMP
Greek Fathers, The. Cardinal Newman. JKCP
Greek Folk Song; a Cyprian Woman. Margaret Widdemer. *See* Cyprian Woman, A; Greek Folk Song.
Greek Folk Song; Remembrance. Margaret Widdemer. *See* Remembrance; a Greek Folk Song.
Greek, Four Credits. James L. MacKavanaugh. CAG
Greek Gift, A. Austin Dobson. *Fr.* Rose-Leaves. BPN; MBP; MoBrPo (1942 ed.)
Greek Idyl, A. Mortimer Collins. VA
Greek Mother's Lullaby. Zitella Cocke. *Fr.* A Doric Reed. BOL
Greek Vase. Margaret R. Richter. MuM
Greek War-Song ("Sons of the Greeks, arise!"). *Unknown, tr. fr. Greek by* Byron. PoFr
Greeks were wrong who said our eyes have rays, The. Lamarck Elaborated. Richard Wilbur. NePoEA
Green. Juan Ramón Jiménez, *tr. fr. Spanish by* J. B. Trend. AnSpL-2
Green. D. H. Lawrence. MBP; MoBrPo; MoP; NeMA; NP; TCEP
Green. Paul Verlaine, *tr. fr. French by* C. F. MacIntyre. LiTW
Green afternoon serene and bright, along my street you sail away. A City Afternoon. Edith Wyatt. LiTM (1946 ed.); NP
Green and Black. Sir Charles Scott Sherrington. PoP
Green and Red and Darkness. Winfield Townley Scott. FiMAP
Green and silent spot, amid the hills, A. Fears in Solitude. Samuel Taylor Coleridge. EmBrPo; EnRP; ERP; SoV
Green Apples. Louise Morey Bowman. CPG
Green are the tussocks of the marsh-grass springing. Yellow. Kenton Kilmer. GoYe
Green arsenic smeared on an egg-white cloth. L'Art, 1910. Ezra Pound. OxBA
Green Autumn Stubble, The. *Tr. fr. Irish by* Patrick Browne. OxBI
Green be the turf above thee. On the Death [*or* Elegy in Memory] of Joseph Rodman Drake. Fitz-Greene Halleck. AA; AnAmPo; BAP; BAV; BLPA; BoHiPo; DD; DDA; GA; HBV; IAP; LA; LBAP; LPS-2; MaRV; OBAV; OBVV; PAH; PoEL-4; TCAP; TreFS
Green bird, A. A Glimpse into a Courtyard. P'eng Chien P'u. PoHN
Green blood fresh pulsing through the trees. April—and Dying. Anne Reeve Aldrich. AA
Green-blue ground, The. On Gay Wallpaper. William Carlos Williams. MAP; MoAB; MoAmPo
Green Branches. "Joan Ramsay." MaRV
Green Broom. *Unknown.* ALV; CH; LoEn; OnSP; StPo
(Broom, Green Broom.) KN; LiTB; LiTG; OxBoLi; SiTL
Green Bus, The. James S. Tippett. GFA
Green Candles. Humbert Wolfe. HBMV; MBP; MoBrPo; NeMA; NV; PoMS
Green catalpa tree has turned, The. April Inventory. W. D. Snodgrass. NePoEA
Green cheese, yellow laces. *Unknown.* OxNR
Green Coat, The. *Unknown, tr. fr. Chinese.* WhP
Green Coconuts. Lawrence Durrell. FaBoMo
Green Corn Dance, The. Alice Corbin. BAP
Green corn waving in the dale, The. The Windmill. Robert Bridges. ChMo; CMP; PoTo; TCPD; WP
Green Cornfield, A. Christina Rossetti. BoTP; PFE
(Skylark, The.) GoTP
Green Councillors. Howard McKinley Corning. NP
Green Crosses. Abbie Farwell Brown. CV
Green elm with the one great bough of gold, The. October. Edward Thomas. BrBE; ChMP; MoVE; POTE
Green enravishment of human life. Sister Juana Inés de la Cruz, *tr. fr. Spanish by* Samuel Beckett. AnMP
Green Estaminet, The. A. P. Herbert. HBMV
Green eye—and a red—in the dark, A. The Train. Mary Elizabeth Coleridge. BoTP
Green Eye of the Yellow God, The. J. Milton Hayes. BLPA
Green-eyed Care. Old Cat Care. Richard Hughes. AlDL; OBMV; ShBV-1; ThWaDe
Green Fiddler, The. Rachel Field. BoChLi; StPo
Green Fields of England! Arthur Hugh Clough. Songs in Absence, IV. BPN; EmBrPo; EV-5; OAEP; VLEP
(Song in Absence.) CBE
Green for April, pink for June. The Best Time of All. Nancy Byrd Turner. GFA
Green gardens in Laventie! Home Thoughts in Laventie. Edward Wyndham Tennant. DaBS; HBMV
Green Gnome, The. Robert Buchanan. MW; StPo
Green-Gown, The. *Unknown.* CoMu
Green grape, and you refused me. Brief Autumnal. *Unknown.* LiTW
Green Grass. *Unknown.* CH; OxBoLi
("A dis, a dis, a green grass.") BoTP; LO; OxNR
Green Grass and White Milk. Winifred Welles. TiPo
Green Grass Growing. Patrick Evans. NeBP
Green Grass Growing All Around, The. *Unknown.* HBVY; MoShBr; MPB
Green grass growing upward splits the concrete pavement. Green Grass Growing. Patrick Evans. NeBP
Green grass is bowing, The. To Ellen at the South [*or* The Wind in the Grass]. Emerson. BoTP; LaNeLa
Green, green,/ The cypress on the mound. *Unknown, tr. fr. Chinese by* Arthur Waley. Seventeen Old Poems, 3. TrCh
Green, green,/ The grass by the river-bank. *Unknown, tr. fr. Chinese by* Arthur Waley. Seventeen Old Poems, 2. TrCh
Green, green are the rush leaves. The Rush Leaves. *Unknown.* WhP
Green, green, I want you green. Somnambulistic Ballad. Federico García Lorca, *tr. by* Roy Campbell *and* Mary Campbell. LiTW; OnHM
Green, green is my love. Somnambulant Ballad. Federico García Lorca, *tr. by* Warren Carrier. ReMP

Green grew the reeds and pale they were. Symbols. Vance Thompson. AA
Green Grow the Rashes. Burns. BEL; CEP; EiPP; EnLi-2 (1949 ed.); EV-3; FaFP; LiTG; LiTL; PoE; REAL; TCEP; ViBoPo; WHA
(Green Grow the Rashes, O.) ALV; EBSV; EM-1; EnLit; EnRP; HBV; LEAP; LiTB; LPS-1; OBEC; SeCePo; SiTL
(Song: "Green grow the rashes.") AWP; EnLi-2 (1939 ed.); EPP; InPo; JAWP; TOP; WBP
Green Grow the Rashes ("Green grow the rashes, O"). *Unknown.* CoMu
Green Grow the Rushes, O ("I'll sing you twelve O"). *Unknown.* OxBoLi; SiTL
Green Groweth the Holly. Henry VIII, King of England. ElSeCe; TrGrPo; TuPP
(As the Holly Groweth Green.) ViBoPo
(Holly.) OBSC
Green Growing Bush. Helen Pinkerton. PtPa
Green Hills of Africa, The. Roy Fuller. BoSA
Green hobgoblin, A. A Goblinade. Florence Page Jaques. GoBP; TiPo
Green, how I want you green. Somnambule Ballad. Federico García Lorca, *tr. by* J. L. Gili *and* Stephen Spender. AnSpL-2
Green, humped, wrinkled hills, The: with such a look. The Green Hills of Africa. Roy Fuller. BoSA
Green Hunters, The. Florence M. Wilson. AnIV
Green, in the wizard arms. The Banshee. John Todhunter. OnYI; VA
Green Inn, The. Theodosia Garrison. HBMV; NLK
Green is on the grass and the blue is in the sky, The. In Exile. Mary Elizabeth Blake. LBAP
Green is the night, green kindled and apparelled. The Candle a Saint. Wallace Stevens. PoRA
Green is the plane-tree in the square. A London Plane-Tree [*or* A Plane-Tree]. Amy Levy. DiM; MW; OBVV; VA
Green Isle of Lovers, The. Robert Charles Sands. AA
Green Jade Plum Trees in Spring. Ou-yang Hsiu, *tr. fr. Chinese by* Kenneth Rexroth. OnPC
Green Lady, The. Charlotte Druitt Cole. BoTP
Green Lake, The. Michael Roberts. ChMP
Green lane now I traverse, where it goes, The. John Clare. *Fr.* Summer Images. OBRV
Green Leaves All Turn Yellow, The. James Kenney. IrPN
Green leaves panting for joy with the great wind rushing through. A Summer Day. Henry Charles Beeching. VA
"Green leaves, what are you doing." The Five-fingered Maple. Kate Louise Brown. BoTP
Green light floods the city square, The. Sunken Evening. Laurie Lee. PoN
Green light from the moon. Conrad Aiken. Variations, II. NV
Green Linnet, The. Wordsworth. AEV; AtBAP; BPN; EmBrPo; EnRP; EPN; ERP; EV-3; GEPC; GTBS; GTBS-D; GTBS-W; GTSE; GTSL; HBV; OTPC
Green Lions. Douglas Stewart. AnNZ
Green Little Shamrock of Ireland, The. Andrew Cherry. DD; HBV; MPB; PoRL
(Shamrock, The.) HH
Green little vaulter in the sunny grass. To the Grasshopper and the Cricket [*or* The Grasshopper and the Cricket]. Leigh Hunt. BCEP; EnLi-2; EnRP; EPN; ERP; ES; EV-4; GBV (1922 ed.); GN; GoTP; HBV; LEAP; LPS-2; OTPC (1946 ed.); PCD; TCEP; TVSH
Green marsh-mallows, The. The Place of His Rest. Sir Charles G. D. Roberts. CPG; OCL
Green Mistletoe! Winter. Walter de la Mare. ChTr; OBMV; MoVE; YeAr
Green morning of indolence one hedge beyond, A. Morning in the Park. John Ciardi. MiAP
Green Moth. Winifred Welles. BoChLi (1950 ed.); FaPON; StVeCh; TiPo; UTS
Green Mountain Boy. Florida Watts Smyth. GoYe
Green Mountain Boys, The. Bryant. AnNE; GA; MC; PAH
Green Mountain Justice, The. Henry Reeves. PTA-1
Green mountain lies beyond the north wall of the city, The. Saying Farewell to a Friend. Li Po. WhP
Green mwold on zummer bars do show. Tokens. William Barnes. PoEL-4
Green Navies, The. John Prichard. MoWP
Green, oh I want you green. Ballad Walking in Sleep. Federico García Lorca. CoSP
Green o' the Spring, The. Denis A. McCarthy. POT; PoTo
Green of earth, and the gold of sun, The. My Love for You, Mother. Eva Ingersoll Swasey. BAP
Green Parrot, The. Humbert Wolfe. TwCV
Green points on the shrub. An Elegy for D. H. Lawrence. William Carlos Williams. PtP; TriL
Green Rain. Mary Webb. CH; FaPON
Green River. Bryant. AmPP (4th ed.); CoBA; IAP; OxBA; PEOR; TCAP
Green River, The. Lord Alfred Douglas. BMC; HBMV; MBP; MoBrPo (1942 ed.); OBEV (new ed.); OBVV; PIAE; PoVP
Green Roads, The. Edward Thomas. POTE
Green rushes with red shoots. Plucking the Rushes. *Unknown.* ChLP; OnPM; ShBV-4; TrCh; WoL
Green rustlings, more-than-regal charities. Royal Palm. Hart Crane. ChMo; MAP; MoAB; MoAmPo; TrGrPo
Green sea and grey sky and blue sky. The Best That I Have. Juan Ramón Jiménez. TeCS
Green Shawl. Helen Bayley Davis. PoTo
Green Shepherd, The. Louis Simpson. NePoEA
Green Singer, The. Shaw Neilson. BoAu
Green spider wine, just mellowed. Cozy. T'ao Ch'ien. OnPM
Green spires of the forest, The. A Forest Meditation. Bernice Hall Legg. PGD
Green Spring. Chang Shou, *tr. fr. Chinese by* Henry H. Hart. PoHN
Green Spring receiveth. The Great Summons. Chu Yuan. AWP; LiTW; TrCh
Green spring tide has risen, until its crest, The. Spring in England. Charles Buxton Going. HBMV; VOD
Green Sunday. Katue Kitasono, *tr. fr. Japanese by* Katue Kitasono. LiTW
Green-sweatered mother walks and walks the street, The. The Mother. Kadie Molodowsky. OnCuPl
Green Symphony. John Gould Fletcher. AnFE; APA; CoAnAm; MAP; MAPA; MoAmPo; MoVE
Green Things Growing. Dinah Maria Mulock Craik. ADAH, 3 *sts.;* DD; FaFP; GN; HBV; HBVY; OHIP; OTPC; SN
Green Thistles, The. *Unknown, tr. fr. Chinese.* WhP
Green Tree in the Fall, The. Jessie B. Rittenhouse. NLK
Green triangles have come on the ground. March. Camilla Doyle. MBP
Green Valley. Dorothy Vena Johnson. PoNe
Green Valley, The. Sylvia Townsend Warner. MoBrPo (1950 ed.)
Green Wall My Grave. Martin Seymour-Smith. MoPW
Green was the maiden, green, green! Green. Juan Ramón Jiménez. AnSpL-2
Green were the meadows with last summer's store. The Merry Christmas Time. George Arnold. PEOR
Green were the willows. Returning Spring. Joseph von Eichendorff. CAW
Green! What a world of green! My startled soul. June Rapture. Angela Morgan. HBMV
Green Willow, The. *Unknown.* OBSC
(Complaint of a Lover Forsaken of His Love, The.) CoMu
Green Willow Is My Garland, A. John Heywood. CoBE
("All a green willow, willow, willow.") EIL
Green willows are for girls to study under. Heresy for a Classroom. Rolfe Humphries. PoMa; PreP
Green Yule, A. Charles Murray. EBSV
Greene, garlanded with February's few flowers. The Many. Swinburne. *Fr.* Sonnets on English Dramatic Poets (1590–1650). PoVP
Greene the Cony-catcher, of this dream the autor. A Due Commendation of the Quipping Autor. Gabriel Harvey. *Fr.* Four Letters and Certain Sonnets. ReIE
Greene's Farewell to Folly. Robert Greene. *See* Farewell to Folly.
Greene's Groatsworth of Wit, *sels.* Robert Greene.
"Deceiving world, that with alluring toys." SiCE
Fie, Fie on Blind Fancy! EIL
(Lamilia's Song.) OBSC
Palinode, A. OBSC
"What meant the Poets in invective verse." LO
Greene's Memorial; or, Certain Funeral Sonnets, *sels.* Gabriel Harvey.
His Admonition to Greene's Companions. ReIE
His Apology of His Good Father. ReIE
Greene's Mourning Garment, *sels.* Robert Greene.
Hexametra Alexis in Laudem Rosamundi. EIL; PoEL-2; TuPP
In Praise of Rosamund. AtBAP
Shepherd's Wife's Song, The. CoEV; EIL; ElSeCe; EnLit; EPP; EV-1; HBV; LoBV; OBSC; PG; ReEn; SiCE; TOP; TuPP; ViBoPo
("Ah what is love? It is a pretty thing.") EG
(Shepherd and the King, The.) LPS-1
Greene's Never Too Late. Robert Greene. *See* Never Too Late.
Greene's Orpharion, *sel.* Robert Greene.
Cupid Abroad Was Lated [in the Night]. ElSeCe; TuPP
Greene's Vision, *sel.* Robert Greene.
Description of Sir Geoffrey Chaucer, The. AnFE; OBSC
(Sir Geoffrey Chaucer.) FaBoCh; LoGBV
Greenest of grass in the long meadow grows, The. June. Jane G. Stewart. BoTP
Greenfield Hill, *sels.* Timothy Dwight.

"And when new regions prompt their feet to roam." Po
Church and School. AmPP (3d ed.)
Farmer's Advice to the Villagers. IAP
Sweet Simplicity. AmPP
Two Ways of Visiting. AmPP (4th ed.)
Greenfields, *with music.* *Unknown.* AS
Greenland Fishery, The. *Unknown.* OBB; SoAmSa, *with music*
(Greenland Whale Fishery, The.) BaBo; OuSiCo, *with music;* ViBoFo, *with music*
(Whale, The.) AmSS, *with music;* ChTr; SG
Greenland Winter, A. Lucy Diamond. BoTP
Greenness. Angelina Weld Grimké. CDC
Greenock. John Davidson. *Fr.* A Ballad in Blank Verse of the Making of a Poet. BSV
Greens, *with music.* *Unknown.* AS
Greensleeves and pudding pies. *Unknown.* LO
Greensleeves was all my joy. A New Courtly Sonnet of the Lady Greensleeves. *Unknown.* CenL; ElL; FaBoCh; NBE; OAEP; OBSC; ReEn; ReIE; SiCE; TuPP. *See also* Alas, my Love! you do me wrong.
Greenwich Observatory. Sidney Keyes. MoAB
Greenwich Pensioner, The. *Unknown.* CBPC; SG
Greenwood, The. William Lisle Bowles. LPS-2
Greenwood, The. Shakespeare. *See* Under the Greenwood Tree.
Greenwood Cemetery. Crammond Kennedy. LPS-1
Greenwood fawn at the hidden brook, The. Song for the Greenwood Fawn. I. L. Salomon. GoYe
Greenwood Shrift, The. Robert Southey *and* Caroline Anne Southey. LPS-2
Greenwood Tree, The. Thomas Love Peacock. *See* Song: "For the tender beech and the sapling oak."
Greenwood Tree, The. Shakespeare. *See* Under the Greenwood Tree.
Greer County. *Unknown.* ABF; CSF; CoSo, *with music*
Greet All Equally. Macedonius, *tr. fr. Greek by* Lord Neaves. OnPM
Greet all the company for me. Rondel. Charles d'Orléans. FoS
Greeting, A. W. H. Davies. [Charles Kingsley, *wr.*] BMEP; MBP; MoBrPo; NeMA; WaKn
Greeting, A. Austin Dobson. BPN; GTML
(Greeting, A; to W. C.) BoFr
Greeting, The. W. W. Gibson. POTE
Greeting, A. Jónas Hallgrímsson, *tr. fr. Icelandic by* Jakobina Johnson. IcP
Greeting. Jami, *tr. fr. Persian.* BoFr
Greeting, A. Philip Bourke Marston. VA
Greeting. Ella Young. AnIV
Greeting from England. *Unknown.* PAH
Greeting of the Roses, The. Hamlin Garland. AA
Greeting on New Year's Morning, A, *mod. Eng.* *Unknown.* TMEV
Greeting, A; to W. C. Austin Dobson. *See* Greeting, A.
Greetings! Clare Hough Babbitt. MeMeAg
Greetings! Wang An Shih, *tr. fr. Chinese by* Henry H. Hart. PoHN
Greetings for Two. James W. Foley. IHA
Greetings, friends, we welcome you! Greetings! Clare Hough Babbitt. MeMeAg
Greetings of the Season. Hilaire Belloc. SiTL
Greetings to Norway. Jóhann Sigurjónsson, *tr. fr. Icelandic by* Jakobina Johnson. IcP
Gregory Griggs, Gregory Griggs. *Unknown.* OxNR
"Gregory," his dam would chide. Little Gregory. Theodore Botrel. CAW
Greife com away and doe not thou refuse. *Unknown.* SeCSL
Grenada. Mikhail Svetlov, *tr. fr. Russian by* Alexander Kaun. WaaP
Grenadier. A. E. Housman. Last Poems, V. EG; OBMV
Grenadiers, The. Heine, *tr. fr. German by* Sir Theodore Martin. OuHeWo
Grenadiers of Austria are proper men and tall, The. Cremona. Sir Arthur Conan Doyle. HBV
Grenstone Elm, A. Witter Bynner. VOD
Grenstone River. Witter Bynner. PFY; PoeMoYo
Gret big church wuz crowded full uv broadcloth an' of silk, The. The Volunteer Organist. Sam Walter Foss. PTA-2
Grey. *See also* Gray.
Grey. Karle Wilson Baker. LS
Grey. Archibald T. Strong. BoAu
Grey brick upon brick. Dublin. Louis MacNeice. OxBI
Grey Brother. U. M. Montgomery. BoTP
Grey Cock, The (A *and* B *vers.*). *Unknown.* BaBo
(Grey Cock, The; or, Saw You My Father?) ESPB
Grey Company, The. Jessie Mackay. BoAu
Grey countries and grim empires pass away. Morning in the North-West. Arthur Stringer. CaP; OCL
Grey dawn—and lucent star that slowly paled. Faith, Love, and Death. Dowell O'Reilly. BoAu
Grey Day, A ("Grey drizzling mists . . ."). William Vaughn Moody. AnFE; APA; CoAnAm; OBAV
Grey daylight, loathed of lovers, how listless-slow your crawling. "O Lente, Lente." Meleager. GrPE
Grey dust runs on the ground like a mouse, The. Dust. P. A. Ropes. BoTP
Grey Eye Weeping, A. Egan O'Rahilly, *tr. fr. Modern Irish by* Frank O'Connor. AnIL; KiLC; OBMV; OxBI
Grey-eyed morn was saddened with a shower, The. At Hooker's Tomb. John Keble. ES
Grey Eyes, *in mod. Eng.* *Unknown.* TMEV
Grey-faced Spirit! let us sit. Thomas Caulfield Irwin. *Fr.* Antique Glimpses. IrPN
Grey Friar, The. Thomas Love Peacock. ALV
Grey gaunt days dividing us in twain, The. The Minute before Meeting. Thomas Hardy. NBE
Grey goat grazed on the hill, The. Grey Brother. U. M. Montgomery. BoTP
Grey Goose, The. *Unknown.* ABF, *with music;* WaKn
Grey goose and gander. *See* Gray Goose and Gander.
Grey, grey is Abbey Asaroe, by Belashanny town. *See* Gray, gray is Abbey Asaroe, by Ballyshanny town.
Grey Hair, The. Judah Halevi, *tr. fr. Hebrew by* Joseph Chotzner. TrJP
Grey Hair. Rufinus, *tr. fr. Greek by* Sir William Marris. OxBG
"Grey Horse Troop," The. Robert William Chambers. HBV; PAH
Grey in the sky and blue against the trees. Journey. Sam Harrison. NeIP
Grey Linnet, The. James McCarroll. CaP; OCL
Grey, low ceiling, sough of sea wind along forest. The Lairdless Place. Kate Rennie Archer. GoYe
Grey Matter. Ford Madox Ford. *See* Gray Matter.
Grey Monk, The, *sel.* Blake.
Tear Is an Intellectual Thing, A. BCEP
("But vain the sword and vain the bow.") LEAP
Grey o'er the pallid links. *See* Gray o'er
Grey old man, savage man. Gipsy's Song. Pushkin. *Fr.* The Gipsies. BoRS
Grey Plume, The. Francis Carlin. *See* Gray Plume, The.
Grey pussy-willows. Slumber in Spring. Elizabeth Gould. BoTP
Grey road whereupon we trod became as holy ground, The. The Winds of Angus. "Æ." ChMo; CMP
Grey Rocks and Greyer Sea. Sir Charles G. D. Roberts. *See* Gray Rocks and Grayer Sea.
Grey [*or* Gray] sea and the long black land, The. Meeting at Night. Robert Browning. AWP; BEL; BLV; BMEP; BoLiVe; BPN; CaAE; EM-2; EmBrPo; EnL; EnLi-2; EnLit; EPN; EtPaEn; FaBoEn; FiP; GBV (1952 ed.); GEPC; GTBS-D; GTBS-W; GTML; GTSL; HBV; InPo; InvP; JAWP; LiTL; LoPo; LoPS; LPS-1; MCCG; OAEP; OBEV; PCD; PFE; PG (1955 ed.); PIAE; PIR; PoeMoYo; PoFS; PoRA; PoVP; PreP; PYM; SeCePo; ShBV-3; TOP; TrGrPo; TwP; TyEnPo; UnPo (3d ed.); VA; ViBoPo; ViPo; ViPP; VLEP; WBP
Grey Spring, The. Alfred Noyes. BMEP
Grey Squirrel, The. Humbert Wolfe. *See* Gray Squirrel, The.
Grey Squirrels, The. William Howitt. TVC; TVSH
Grey Uncles. Ephraim Auerbach, *tr. fr. Yiddish by* Sarah Zweig Betsky. OnCuPl
Grey was the morn, all things were grey. A Bit of Colour. Horace Smith. BoTP
Grey Washer by the Ford, The. Sean Jennett. MeRV
Grey wind weeps, the grey wind weeps, the grey wind weeps, The. Deirdre Is Dead. "Fiona Macleod." VLEP
Grey Winter hath gone, like a wearisome guest. *See* Gray Winter . . .
Grey Wolf, The. Arthur Symons. FaBoTw
Greyer than the tide below, the tower. Homage to Jack Yeats. Thomas McGreevy. OBMV
Greyhound skims the boulevard, The. Dog over Snow. Marion Strobel. NP
Greyhound Speaks, The. Edward Anthony. AlBD
Greyport Legend. Bret Harte. EtS
(Grayport Legend, A.) GN
Grief. Elizabeth Barrett Browning. AnFE; BLV; BPN; ES; GTBS-D; GTML; GTSL; HBV; LoBV; OBEV; OBVV; PoVP; TrGrPo; ViPo
Grief. Byron. *Fr.* And Thou Art Dead, as Young and Fair. LiA
Grief. Salvador Díaz Mirón, *tr. fr. Spanish by* Samuel Beckett. AnMP
Grief. Albert Ehrenstein, *tr. fr. German by* Glauco Cambon. OnPM
Grief. D. H. Lawrence. NP
Grief. Angela Morgan. PC
Grief ("Good Hamlet, cast thy nighted color off"). Shakespeare. *Fr.* Hamlet, I, ii. LPS-1
Grief Ago, A. Dylan Thomas. AtBAP
Grief and God. Stephen Phillips. WGRP
Grief fills the room up of my absent child. Shakespeare. *Fr.* King John, III, iii. MotAn

Grief, find the words; for thou hast made my brain. Astrophel and Stella, XCIV. Sir Philip Sidney. ReEn; SiPS
Grief for the Dead. *Unknown.* LPS-1
Grief hath been known to turn the young head gray. The Young Gray Head. Caroline Anne Bowles. BeLS; LPS-3
Grief-in-Idleness. Thomas Lovell Beddoes. *Fr.* Early Fragments. AtBAP
Grief is a mouse. Emily Dickinson. OnAP
Grief may have thought it was grief. They Were Welcome to Their Belief. Robert Frost. AtBAP
Grief Must Go. Jane Barton. DiM
Grief of a Girl's Heart, The. *Unknown. See* Donall Oge.
Grief of Joy, The, *sel.* George Gascoigne.
"Grief of joy in worthy wise to write, The." ReEn
Grief of Love, The. *Unknown, tr. fr. Arabic by* Wilfrid Scawen Blunt. AWP
Grief struck me. I so shook in heart and wit. The Outlet. Eleanor Farjeon. DiM
Grief that is but feigning, The. The Valley of Vain Verses. Henry van Dyke. HBV
Griefs of Hillelille, The. *Unknown, tr. fr. Danish by* E. M. Smith-Dampier. BoDaBa
Grief's Ship. *Unknown. Fr.* The Phoenix Nest. CoEV
Griesly Wife, The. John Manifold. ATP (1953 ed.); MoBrPo (1950 ed.)
Grievance. Amy Lowell. ViBoPo (1941 ed.)
Grievance, A. James Kenneth Stephen. HBV; PA
Grieve Not, Dear Love. John Digby, Earl of Bristol. SeCL
Grieve Not for Beauty ("Almost the body leads the laggard soul"). Witter Bynner. *Fr.* The New World. NP
"Grieve not for the invisible, transported brow," *sel.* LEAP; NV
Grieve Not, Ladies. Anna Hempstead Branch. AnAmPo; BAP; FaFP; HBV; LA; LBMV; LEAP; PR
Grieve not too much for April, lost and forgotten. Winter's Tree. Marjorie Allen Seiffert. BAP
Grieved though I am to see the man depart. Conditions in Rome. Juvenal, *tr. by* William Gifford. Satires, III. EnLi-1
Grieving mother stood in the square, The. Stabat Mater. Jozef Wittlin. PoFr
Grievous folly shames my sixtieth year, A. Hafiz. *Fr.* Odes. AWP
Grievous is the hermit's plight. Boredom. Ramón de Campoamor. *Fr.* Doloras. AnSpL-2
Grievous Peril of a Gallant in Moth Metaphor. Luis de Sandoval y Zapata, *tr. fr. Spanish by* Samuel Beckett. AnMP
"Grill me some bones," said the Cobbler. At the Keyhole. Walter de la Mare. MBP; MoAB; MoBrPo
Grim dawn lightens thin bleak clouds, The. Dawn. Richard Aldington. NV
Grim death took little Jerry. *Unknown.* WhC
Grim eagle, The. Eagle. James B. Thomas. BLA
Grim in my little black coat as the sleazy beetle. Tom, Tom, the Piper's Son. John Crowe Ransom. ViBoPo
Grim old king, The. The King Dying on the Battle-Field. Alexander Smith. BMEP
Grinder, who serenely grindest. Lines on Hearing the Organ. Charles Stuart Calverley. CenHV; FiBHP; InMe
Grinding machinery of a throbbing world stands still, The. Christmas Today. E. G. Reith. PSO
Grinding yoke from Israel's neck he tore, The. Eulogy for Hasdai ibn Shaprut. *Unknown.* TrJP
Grindstone, The. Robert Frost. PoE
Gripsholm Stone, The. *Unknown, tr. fr. runic inscription by* Henry Goddard Leach. PaOS
Grisaille. Terence Heywood. BoSA
Grisaille with a Spot of Red. Samuel Yellen. NePoAm-2
Griselda. Chaucer. *See* Chaucer's Envoy to the Story of Patient Griselda.
Griselda ("Griselda is greedy, I'm sorry to say"). Eleanor Farjeon. GoTP
Griselda's dead, and so's her patience. Patient Griselda. Chaucer, *mod. by* Edward Hodnett. *Fr.* The Canterbury Tales: The Clerk's Tale. PoRA
Grisette Dines. Antoinette Deshoulières, *tr. fr. French.* CIV
Grizzled trapper of the log stockade, The. The Oregon Trail. William Rose Benét. PaA
Grizzly. Bret Harte. AA; AnAmPo; EV-5; LA; OBAV; SN
Grizzly Bear. Mary Austin. FaPON; TiPo
Grizzly Bear is huge and wild, The. Infant Innocence. A. E. Housman. CenHV; ChTr; FaBoCh; FaFP; LiTB; LiTM; LoGBV; OxBoLi; SiTL
Groaning Board, The. "Pink." InMe
Groatsworth of Wit. Robert Greene. *See* Greene's Groatsworth of Wit.
Grocer and the Gold-Fish, The. Wilfrid Thorley. BrR
Grocery Store Cat, The. Margaret E. Bruner. CIV
Grodek. Georg Trakl, *tr. fr. German by* Kate Flores. AnGP
Groined by deep glens and walled along the west. The Glens. John Hewitt. NeIP
Grongar Hill. John Dyer. CEP; ChTr; EiPP; EnRP; EPP, *abr.;* EV-3; GoTL; LoBV; LPS-2; OBEC; PIAE; PoE; PoEL-3; TOP
Sels.
"Below me trees unnumber'd rise." FaBoEn
"Ever charming, ever new." SeCePo
"O may I with myself agree." TrGrPo
"Old castles on the hill arise." ViBoPo
"See on the mountain's southern side." CoEV
"Wide and wider spreads the vale." EnSW
Groomsman to His Mistress, The. Thomas William Parsons. PR
Groping along the tunnel, step by step. The Rear-Guard. Siegfried Sassoon. BLV; BMEP; BoLiVe; MBP; MCCG; MoBrPo; NeMA; TCEP; WaP
Grotesque! Otomo Tabito, *tr. fr. Japanese by* Ishii *and* Obata. OnPM
Grotesque patterns of blue-gray mould. The Orchard. Sir Herbert Read. *Fr.* Eclogues. BrBE
Grotesques, *sels.* Don Marquis. FiBHP
"I sometimes think that I will," III.
"Was it fancy, sweet nurse," I.
Grotto, The. Francis Scarfe. NeBP
Grotto of Egeria, The. Thomas Kibble Hervey. BCEP
Groun' Hog. *Unknown. See* Ground Hog.
Groundhog, The. Richard Eberhart. AmP; AnFE; CoAnAm; ExPo; FaBoMo; FaFP; GTBS-W; LiTA; LiTG; LiTM; MiAP; MoAB; MoPo; MoVE; NePA; OnAP; PG (1955 ed.); ReMP; SeCeV; TwAmPo; UnPo (3d ed.); WaP
Ground Hog. *Unknown.* APW; SoAF, *with music;* TrAS, *with music*
(Groun' Hog, *longer vers., with music.*) ABF
Ground I walk'd on felt like air, The. The Secret of the Nightingale. Roden Noel. VA
Ground of contradictions, where motif, A. The Cemetery Is. Audrey McGaffin. NePoAm-2
Groundswell, The. John Gould Fletcher. ChMo; CMP; TBM
Ground Swell. G. Stanley Koehler. NePoAm-2
Ground-Swell, The. E. J. Pratt. CaP; CPG; OCL
Ground was all covered with snow one day, The. The Snow-bird's Song. Francis C. Woodworth. PPL; SAS
Groundflame of the crocus breaks the mould, The. Tennyson. *Fr.* The Progress of Spring. EnSW
Group of jolly cowboys, discussing plans at ease, A. When the Work's All Done This Fall. *Unknown, at. to* D. J. O'Malley *or* D. J. White. AS; CoSo; IHA
Group of Verse, A. Charles Reznikoff. NP
Grouped nightly at the cold, accepted wall. The Cocky Walkers. Mervyn Peake. POTE; ShBV-4
Grove, The. Edwin Muir. LiTM (rev. ed.); MoPo
Grove, A,/ A swamp. Tortoise. Sakutaro Hagiwara. PoLJ
Grove and Building. Edgar Bowers. NePoEA
Grove of Colonus, The. Sophocles, *tr. fr. Greek by* Walter Headlam. *Fr.* Oedipus at Colonus. OxBG; WoL
(Glories of Athens, The, *pr. tr. by* R. C. Jebb.) LiA
(Lovely Colonus, *tr. by* Lewis Campbell.) GrR
Grover Cleveland. Joel Benton. DD; GA; PAH
Groves of Blarney, The. Richard Alfred Millikin. GTIV; HBV; IrPN; OnYI, *with add. verse by* Francis Sylvester Mahony; OxBI; OxBoLi
Groves of Eden, vanish'd now so long, The. Pope. *Fr.* Windsor Forest. BEL; OBEC
Groves were God's first temples, The. A Forest Hymn. Bryant. AA; ADAH; AmP; AmPP; AnNE; BAP; BPP; CoBA; CoV; HiLiAm; IAP; LPS-2; MOAP; OBAV; TCAP; TOP
Grow, grow, thou little tree. Agamede's Song. Arthur Upson. *Fr.* The City. LBMV; LEAP
Grow no older than your fears. Exhortation. Pearce Young. PtPa
Grow Not Too High, Grow Not Too Far from Home. Edna St. Vincent Millay. MOAP
Grow old along with me! Rabbi Ben Ezra [*or* Youth and Age]. Robert Browning. ATP (1935 ed.); BBV (1951 ed.); BEL; BMEP; BPN; CoBE; EM-2; EmBrPo; EnLi-2; EnLit; EPN; EPP; EV-5; FaFP; FiP; GEPC; GrCo-2; GTBS; GTBS-W; GTSL; HBV; HiLiEn; LiTG; MaRV; MCCG; OAEP; OBVV; OQP; OuHeWo; PECK; PIAE; PoFS; PoToHe; PoVP; PreP; QP-1; REAL; TCEP; TOP; TwP; TyEnPo; UnPo (1st ed.); ViPo; ViPP; VLEP; WGRP; YT
Grow old and die, rich day. A Lyke-Wake Carol. Arthur Shearly Cripps. PoeT
Grow weary if you will, let me be sad. Lesbia. Richard Aldington. NP
Growing. *Unknown.* MaRV
Growing Gray. Austin Dobson. HBV; LPS-3
Growing in the Vale. Christina Rossetti. *Fr.* Sing-Song. BrR; GFA; RAR; RIS; TiPo
(Sweet Daffadowndilly.) BoChLi
Growing need to be moving around it to see it, The. A View of the Brooklyn Bridge. William Meredith. MoVE
Growing Old. Matthew Arnold. BPN; EmBrPo; EnLi-2;

EnLit; FaFP; FiP; GEPC; HBV; OuHeWo; PoEL-5; PoVP; VLEP
Growing Old. Karle Wilson Baker. *See* Let Me Grow Lovely.
Growing Old. "Vandyke Brown." PR
Growing Old. Rose Henderson. BoChLi (1950 ed.)
Growing Old. Walter Learned. HBV
Growing Old. Francis Ledwidge. LEAP
Growing Old. *Unknown, tr. fr. Irish by* Frank O'Connor. KiLC
(Autumn.) OBMV
Growing Old [*or* Older]. Rollin J. Wells. *See* As We Grow Older.
Growing Old. Ella Wheeler Wilcox. *See* Interlude.
Growing Rhyme, A. J. M. Westrup. BoTP
Growing River, The. Rodney Bennett. BoTP
Growing Up. Harry Behn. SiSoSe
Growing Up. Marchette Chute. GoBP
Growing Up. Edna Kingsley Wallace. MoSiPe
Growltiger's Last Stand. T. S. Eliot. FaBoCh; LoGBV; OnSP
Grown sick of war, and war's alarms. On the British King's Speech. Philip Freneau. PAH
Grownup, The. Rainer Maria Rilke, *tr. fr. German by* Randall Jarrell. AnGP
Grown-ups. Rose Fyleman. HH
Grown-ups, The. César Vallejo, *tr. fr. Spanish by* Donald Devenish Walsh. AnCL
Grownups. William Wise. TiPo (1959 ed.)
Growth of Lorraine, The. E. A. Robinson. NP
Growth of Love, *sels.* Robert Bridges.
"All earthly beauty hath one cause and proof," XXXV. ChMo; CMP; PoVP; ViP
"For beauty being the best of all we know," VIII. PoVP
"I heard great Hector sounding war's alarms," LIII. (Hector in Hades.) CBOV
"I will be what God made me, nor protest," LXII. PoVP
"I would be a bird, and straight on wings I arise," CXXXIX [XXII]. GTML
"O weary pilgrims, chanting of your woe," XXIII. ChMo; CMP; MBP; MoAB; MoBrPo; PoVP
"This world is unto God a work of art," XVI. PoVP
"Very names of things beloved are dear, The," IV. ChMo; CMP; PoVP
"When I see childhood on the threshold seize," CXLIII [XLII]. GTML
World Comes Not to an End, The, L. ChMo; CMP
"World still goeth about to show and hide, The," XX. PoVP
Growth of Perseus, The. W. Wesley Trimpi. PtPa
Gr-r-r—there go, my heart's abhorrence. Soliloquy of the Spanish Cloister. Robert Browning. ATP; BEL; BLV; BMEP; BoLiVe; CBOV; EM-2; EmBrPo; EnL; EnLi-2; EnLit; EPN; ExPo; LiTB; OAEP; OtMeF; PIAE; PoE; PoVP; PreP; RiBV; SeCeV; ShBV-4; TOP; TrGrPo; TwCrTr; TwP; UnPo (1st ed.); ViPo; ViPP; VLEP
Gruach. Gordon Bottomley. TCPD
Grub Street Recessional, A. Christopher Morley. InMe
Grubber's Day. Jay G. Sigmund. AnAmPo; LA
Grumble Family, The. *Unknown.* WBLP
Grumbling Hive, The; or, Knaves Turn'd Honest. Bernard Mandeville. CEP; EiPP
Moral to "The Grumbling Hive," The, *sel.* BeR
Grumbling Truck, The. Rowena Bennett. MPB (1956 ed.)
Grunto lies groaning of a grievous gout. Olim Haec Meminisse Juvabit. Henry Parrot. SiCE
Gryll Grange, *sel.* Thomas Love Peacock.
Love and Age. EV-4; HBV; OBEV; ViBoPo
Guadalupe. Grace Hazard Conkling. NP
Guard. Michael C. Martin. WaP
Guard of the Sepulcher, A. Edwin Markham. StJW; WGRP
Guard, Paullus, guard the pledges of our love. The Plea of Cornelia. Propertius. *Fr.* Elegies. MOAH
Guard well these little things; they are. Children of the Poor. Victor Hugo. TrFP
Guarded within the old red wall's embrace. A Tulip Garden. Amy Lowell. VOD
Guarded Wound, The. Adelaide Crapsey. AnAmPo; LA; NP; NV
Guardian-Angel, The. Robert Browning. BPN; EmBrPo; EV-5; GEPC; GoBC; HBV; PoVP
Guardian Angel, The. Thomas S. Jones, Jr. UnW
Guardian Angel. Cardinal Newman. GoBC
Guardian Angels. Spenser. *See* Ministering Angels.
Guardian of All. *Unknown, tr. fr. Arabic by* Sir Edwin Arnold. OnPM
Guardian of Hill and Woodland. Horace, *tr. fr. Latin by* John Conington. OnPM
Guardian of the gate/ Of Suma. Minamoto no Kanemasa, *tr. fr. Japanese by* Kenneth Rexroth. OnPJ
Guardians, The. Ibn Sa'id of Alcala la Real, *tr. fr. Arabic by* A. J. Arberry. MooP
Guardians. Sadi, *tr. fr. Persian by* E. B. Eastwick. PeP
Guardianship. Georgia Douglas Johnson. GoSl
Guarding the cattle on my native hill. The Sling. Roy Campbell. BoSA
Guards Came Through, The. Sir Arthur Conan Doyle. BoHiPo
Gude auld Kirk o' Scotland, The. The Auld Kirk o' Scotland. George Murray. EBSV
Gude Lord Scroope's to the hunting [*or* huntin] gane. Hughie Grame [*or* Hughie the Graeme]. *Unknown.* ESPB (C *vers.*); OBB
Gude Wallace. *Unknown.* BaBo; ESPB (A *and* G *vers.*)
Gudrun of old days. The First Lay of Gudrun. *Unknown. Fr.* The Elder Edda. AWP; JAWP; WBP
Guenevere at Almesbury. Margaret Potts. CAG
Guerdon, The. John James Piatt. AA
Guerdon of the Sun, The. George Sterling. HBMV
Guess who is this creature. A Song to the Wind. Taliesin. FaBoCh
Guessing Song. Henry Johnstone. OTPC (1946 ed.); PRWS
Guest, The. Jorge Carrera Andrade, *tr. fr. Spanish by* Muna Lee. AnCL
Guest, The. Michael Drayton. Idea, XXIII. ES
Guest, The. Harriet McEwen Kimball. AA; LEAP
Guest, The. Harold Monro. NeMA
Guest. Beresford Richards. ReTS
Guest, The. *Unknown. See* Yet If His Majesty, Our Sovereign Lord.
Guest Goes on His Way, The. Lu Yu, *tr. fr. Chinese by* Pai Chwen-yu. WhP
Guest resides in me, A. Drunk and Sober. Tao Yuan-ming. WhP
Guests. *Unknown. See* Yet If His Majesty, Our Sovereign Lord.
Guid-by, auld ba'! Fu' mony a year. A Scot's Farewell to His Golf Ball. James J. Montague. LHV; PoMa
Guidance. Robert Browning. *See* In His Good Time.
Guidance. Harriet B. Williams. PraP
Guide, The. Emerson. *Fr.* Woodnotes, II. APW
(Heart of All the Scene, The.) AA
Guide and Friend. *Unknown.* BLRP
Guide Me. *Unknown.* PraP
Guide Me, O Thou Great Jehovah. William Williams, *tr. fr. Welsh by* Peter Williams, *ad. by* John Keble. BPP, *abr.*; OlF
(Arglwydd Arwain.) PrWP
(Christian Pilgrim's Hymn, The.) WGRP
(Divine Hand, The, *much abr.*) BLRP
Guide Within, The. Menander, *tr. fr. Greek by* Francis G. Allinson. *Fr.* Epitrepontes. GrR
Guided Missiles Experimental Range. Robert Conquest. PoLFOT; PoN
Guides at Cabul, 1879, The. Sir Henry Newbolt. MBP
Guido. Robert Browning. The Ring and the Book, XI. VLEP
"You never know what life means till you die," *sel.* OAEP
Guido, I would that Lapo, thou, and I. Sonnet: To Guido Cavalcanti. Dante. AWP; JAWP; LyMA; LyPI; WBP
Guileful Ocean, The. Lucretius, *tr. fr. Latin by* H. S. Salt. *Fr.* De Rerum Natura, II. LiA
Guilielmus Rex. Thomas Bailey Aldrich. AA; AnNE; TCAP
Guilt! Euripides, *tr. fr. Greek by* Gilbert Murray. *Fr.* Electra. GrR
Guilt and Sorrow, *sel.* Wordsworth.
"All, all was cheerless to the horizon's bound." EnSW
Guilt unavowed is guilt in its extreme. Error Pursued. H. A. Pinkerton. NePoAm
Guilty. Marguerite Wilkinson. MaRV; OQP; QP-1
Guilty Father to His Daughter, A. James Schevill. FiMAP; Po
"Guilty or Not Guilty?" *Unknown.* BeLS; BLPA; PTA-1
Guinea. Jacques Roumain, *tr. fr. French by* Langston Hughes. AnCL; PoNe
Guinea Pig, The. *Unknown. See* There Was a Guinea-Pig.
Guinevere. Tennyson. *Fr.* Idylls of the King. BPN; EnLit; EPN; GEPC; VLEP
(Queen Becomes an Abbess, A, *abr.*) PraNu
Guitar, The. Federico García Lorca, *tr. fr. Spanish by* Elizabeth du Gué Trapier. AnSpL-2
Guitar. Iosif Utkin, *tr. fr. Russian by* Jack Lindsay. RuPo
Guitar, The/ makes the dreams weep. Six Strings. Federico García Lorca. AnSpL-2; CoSP
Guitar Song. Martha Barris. CAG
Gulbeyaz. Byron. *Fr.* Don Juan, V. PoEL-4
Gulf, The. Baudelaire, *tr. fr. French by* Kate Flores. AnFP
Gulf, The. Katherine Mansfield. DiM
Gulf between us and the brutes, The. Jigsaw III. Louis MacNeice. HaMV
Gulf of Mexico. Alfonso Reyes, *tr. fr. Spanish.* AnCL, *tr. by* Dudley Fitts; OnHM, *tr. by* J. B. Trend
Gulf of silence separates us from each other, A. The Gulf. Katherine Mansfield. DiM
Gulf of Tartary and a Butterfly, The. Fuyue Anzai, *tr. fr. Japanese by* Takamichi Ninomiya *and* D. J. Enright. PoLJ

Gulf Stream, The. Henry Bellamann. EtS
Gulf Stream. "Susan Coolidge." AA; EtS
Gulf-Weed. Cornelius George Fenner. EtS; LPS-2
Gulistan, The, *sels.* Sadi, *tr. fr. Persian.*
Alas! *tr. by* L. Cranmer-Byng. AWP; WoL
Courage, *tr. by* Sir Edwin Arnold. AWP; JAWP; OnPM; WBP
Friendship, *tr. by* L. Cranmer-Byng. AWP; BoFr; JAWP; WBP
From Slavery to Slavery, *pr. tr. by* Sir Edwin Arnold. OuHeWo
Gift of Speech, The, *tr. by* L. Cranmer-Byng. AWP; LiTW
He Hath No Parallel, *tr. by* L. Cranmer-Byng. AWP; LiTW
Help, *tr. by* Sir Edwin Arnold. AWP; JAWP; OnPM; WBP
Hyacinths to Feed Thy Soul. BLPA; FaBoBe; MaRV; NeHB
Love's Last Resource, *tr. by* L. Cranmer-Byng. AWP; LiTW
Mesnevi, *tr. by* L. Cranmer-Byng. AWP; JAWP; LiTW; WBP
On the Deception of Appearances, *tr. by* L. Cranmer-Byng. AWP; LiTW
Purgatory May Be Paradise, *pr. tr. by* Sir Edwin Arnold. OuHeWo
Sooth-Sayer, The, *tr. by* Sir Edwin Arnold. AWP
Take the Crust, *tr. by* L. Cranmer-Byng. AWP
Wealth, *tr. by* Sir Edwin Arnold. AWP; OuHeWo
Wrestler, The, *pr. tr. by* Sir Edwin Arnold. OuHeWo
Gull. Glyn Jones. MoWP
Gull. William Jay Smith. TiPo (1959 ed.)
Gull Decoy, The, *with music.* Larry Gorman. ShS
Gull Goes up, A. Léonie Adams. MOAP; WHA
Gull Lake set in the rolling prairie. At Gull Lake. Duncan Campbell Scott. BoCaPo
Gull shall whistle in his wake, the blind wave break in fire, The. The Voortrekker. Kipling. HBV
Gulling Sonnets, *sels.* Sir John Davies.
"Hardness of her heart and truth of mine, The," IV. ElSeCe; TuPP
"Lover under burthen of his love, The," I. ElL; TuPP
"My case is this: I love Zepheria bright," VIII. TuPP
"Sacred muse that first made love divine, The," VI. TuPP
To His Good Friend, Sir Anthony Cooke, *introduction.* TuPP
Gulliver. Kenneth Slessor. BoAV
Gulls. Stanley Snaith. POTE
Gulls. William Carlos Williams. FaBoEn; MOAP; OxBA
Gulls and Dreams. Lionel Stevenson. CaP; OCL
Gull's image and the gull, The. Before March. Archibald MacLeish. PIAE
Gulls in an Aëry Morrice. W. E. Henley. VLEP
(Rhymes and Rhythms.) BPN
Gulls over Great Salt Lake. Ross Sutphen. BLA
Gulls, The. Provincetown Harbor. Benjamin Albert Botkin. CAG
Gulls, that live by the water and hang around docks. Random Reflections on a Cloudless Sunday. John Hall Wheelock. NePoAm
Gulls when they fly move in a liquid arc. A Gull Goes Up. Léonie Adams. MOAP; WHA
Gully, The, *sels.* Frank Wilmot.
"If I could take your mountains in my heart," X. BoAV; NeLNL
"Looking from the hut door one dawn in June," II. BoAV; NeLNL
"Now I have touched your soil I will go back," XIII. NeLNL
"There breaks upon my sight," VII. BoAV; NeLNL
Gum-Gatherer. The. Robert Frost. NV
Gunga Din. Kipling. BBV; BEL; BPN; ChMo; CV; EnLi-2 (1949 ed.); EnLit; FaFP; HBV; HiLiEn; LiTB; LiTM (rev. ed.); MBP; MCCG; MoBrPo; NeMA; PoMa; PoVP; PTA-2; PYM; ShBV-2; TreF
Gunnar in the Pit of Adders. William Morris. *Fr.* The Story of Sigurd the Volsung, IV. PoVP; ViPo
Gunner, The. Francis Webb. BoAV
Gunners move like figures in a dance, The. Drunken Gunners. M. K. Joseph. AnNZ
Guns are hushed, The. On every field once flowing. The Rear Guard. Irene Fowler Brown. BlG; PAH
Guns in the Grass, The. Thomas Frost. MC; PAH
Guns know what is what, but underneath, The. Memories of a Lost War. Louis Simpson. NePoAm
Guns of war are silent, The. The Golden Day. Arthur Wallace Peach. PEDC
Guns spell money's ultimate reason, The. Ultima Ratio Regum. Stephen Spender. BBV (1951 ed.); EnLi-2 (1949 ed.); FaFP; LiTB; LiTM; MaRV; PoLFOT; SeCePo; SoV; WaaP; WaP
Gup, Scot! John Skelton. OxBoLi
Gus; the Theatre Cat. T. S. Eliot. CenHV
Gush of waters, A! faint and sweet and wild. The Grotto of Egeria. Thomas Kibble Hervey. BCEP
Gustavo Adolfo Bécquer, who in the garden of slumber. Elegy for Bécquer. Enrique Peña Barrenechea. AnCL
Gusts of the sun race on the approaching sea. Of Thomas Traherne and the Pebble Outside. Sydney Clouts. BoSA
Gusts of winter are gone, the sky no longer lowers, The. Meleager, *tr. fr. Greek by* L. P. Chamberlayne. GrPo
Gusty and raw was the morning, a fog hung over the sea. The Fight of Paso Del Mar. Bayard Taylor. BeLS
Gusty morns are here, The. To a Dog's Memory. Louise Imogen Guiney. AnAmPo; LA; OBAV
Guta's Song. Charles Kingsley. *Fr.* The Saint's Tragedy, II, ii. ReTS
Guthlac, *sel.* Cynewulf, *tr. fr. Anglo-Saxon.*
Death of Saint Guthlac. ACP
Gutted of station, noise alone. Crow Country. Kenneth Slessor. BoAV
Guvener [*or* Gineral] B. is a sensible man. What Mr. Robinson Thinks. James Russell Lowell. *Fr.* The Biglow Papers. AA; AmPP; AnNE; APW; BAP; BOHV; DDA; HBV; IAP; IHA; InMe; LEAP; LHV; LPS-3; PAH; TOP; YaD
Guy Fawkes. *Unknown.* ABS
Guy Mannering, *sels.* Sir Walter Scott.
Nativity Chant, The. ChTr; FaBoCh; LoGBV
Twist Ye, Twine Ye! Even So, *fr. ch.* 3. BPN; EmBrPo; EnRP; TOP
Wasted, Weary, Wherefore Stay, *fr. ch.* 27. BPN; EmBrPo; EnRP
(Dying Gipsy's Dirge, The.) BHV
(Gipsy's Dirge, The.) BSV
Gwalia Deserta, *sel.* Idris Davies.
"O what can you give me?" MoWP
G'way an' quit dat noise, Miss Lucy. When Malindy Sings. Paul Laurence Dunbar. MCCG; PoNe; VOD
Gwel uwchlaw cymylau amser. Islwyn, *tr. fr. Welsh by* Gwyn Williams. PrWP
Gwendoline. Bayard Taylor. PA
Gwenwynwyn withdrew from the feasts of his hall. Llyn-y-Dreiddiad-Vrawd; the Pool of the Diving Friar. Thomas Love Peacock. *Fr.* Crotchet Castle. KN
Gwine down to mah shack. Nobody's but Mine. *Unknown.* SoAF
Gwine to Alabamy, *with music. Unknown.* TrAS
Gwine to harness in the morning soon, soon. Gwineter Harness in de Mornin' Soon. *Unknown.* ABF
Gwine to lay my head right on de railroad track. Railroad Blues. *Unknown.* APW
Gwine Up, *with music. Unknown.* BoAN-1
Gwineter Harness in de Mornin' Soon, *with music. Unknown.* ABF
Gwineter Ride Up in de Chariot Soon-a in de Mornin', *with music. Unknown.* BoAN-2
Gwineter Sing All along de Way, *with music. Unknown.* BoAN-1
Gyges ring they bear[e] about them still, A. Lovers How They Come and Part. Robert Herrick. ATBAP; LO; OxBoLi; PoEL-3
Gymnastic Clock, The. Mary Carolyn Davies. TVC; TVSH
Gypsies. *See also* Gipsies.
Gypsies. Robert Browning. *Fr.* The Flight of the Duchess. PCH
Gypsies. Rachel Field. BoTP; GoBP; PoRh
Gypsies, The. Pushkin, *tr. fr. Russian by* Sir Cecil Kisch. WaL
Gypsies, The. "Richard Scrace." OCL
(Gipsies, The.) CaP
Gypsies [*or* Gipsies] came to our good lord's gate. The Gypsy Laddie [*or* Johnnie Faa]. *Unknown.* BaBo (A *vers.*); EBSV; ESPB
Gypsies came wearing/ gaudy holiday costumes. The Fair of Kakava. Kostes Palamas. *Fr.* The Twelve Songs of the Gypsy. MoGP
Gypsies in the Wood. *Unknown.* OxBoLi
("My mother said that I never should.") BoTP; FaBoCh; LoGBV; OxNR; SiTL
Gypsies Metamorphosed, The, *sels.* Ben Jonson.
All Your Fortunes We Can Tell Ye. ChTr
Gipsy Song ("The faery beam upon you"). AlDL; EPS (1942 ed.); FaBoCh; LoGBV; SeCL
(Faeries' Song, The.) SeCV-1
("Faery [*or* Fairy] beam upon you, The.") CenL; ReEn; TuPP
(Jackman's Song, The.) AtBAP
(Patrico's Song.) BoW; LoBV
(Wish, A.) PoRL
Gipsy song ("To the old, long life and treasure"). EPS (1942 ed.); SeCL
Gypsies on the March. Baudelaire, *tr. fr. French by* Arthur Symons. OnPM
Gypsies [*or* Gipsies] passed her little gate, The. The Dreamers. Theodosia Garrison. BLP; GaP; HBMV; OBAV; PoTo; TCAP; VOD

Gypsies' Road, The. Dora Sigerson Shorter. OBVV
Gypsies they came to [my] lord Cassilis' yett [*or* gate], The. The Gypsy Laddie [*or* Johnny Faa *or* Jackie Faa]. *Unknown.* AtBAP; BaBo (B *vers.*); ChTr; ESPB (B *vers.*); ViBoFo (A *vers.*)
Gypsy, The. Eleanor Farjeon. GBV (1952 ed.)
Gypsy, The. Ezra Pound. ThWaDe
Gypsy, a gypsy, A/ Is what I'd like to be. Being a Gypsy. Barbara Young. BrR; TiPo (1952 ed.)
Gypsy Children. Rachel Field. GaP
Gypsy Countess, The. *Unknown.* OBB
Gypsy Daisy [*or* Davy], The. *Unknown. See* Wraggle Taggle Gipsies, The.
Gypsy Daisy came riding o'er the plain, The. The Gypsy Laddie (C *vers.*). *Unknown.* BaBo
Gypsy Girl, The. Henry Alford. HBV; OTPC
Gypsy Girl, The. Ralph Hodgson. *See* Gipsy Girl, The.
Gypsy-Heart. Katharine Lee Bates. HBMV; POT; PoTo (Gipsy-Heart.) NLK
Gypsy Heart, The. Harry Noyes Pratt. BAP; PoMa; POT; PoTo
Gypsy Jane. William Brighty Rands. *See* Gipsy Jane.
Gypsy Laddie, The. *Unknown. See* Wraggle Taggle Gipsies, The.
Gypsy lives on Kithurst, A. The Gypsy. Eleanor Farjeon. GBV (1952 ed.)
Gypsy Man. Langston Hughes. TCPD
Gypsy passed me with a song, A. Songs of the Plains, III. Glenn Ward Dresbach. NP
Gypsy standing at my door. To a Passing Gypsy. Elizabeth Ruhnka. CAG
Gypsy Women. Anne O'Brien. CAG
Gypsying, The. Theodosia Garrison. NLK; VOD
Gyroscopic Lamp, A. Kaoru Maruyama, *tr. fr. Japanese by* Takamichi Ninomiya *and* D. J. Enright. PoLJ

H

H. Baptisme. George Herbert. *See* Holy Baptism.
"H. H." John H. Finley. BAP
H. L. A. L.; with penknife deep embedded. The Happy Hour. Sylvia Lynd. LO
H.M.S. Pinafore, *sels.* W. S. Gilbert.
British Tar, The. ALV
I'm Called Little Buttercup. OlF (Little Buttercup.) TreFS
It Was the Cat. CIV
When I Was a Lad, *with music.* PreP (First Lord of the Admiralty, The.) LiA (First Lord's Song, The.) TreFS (Ruler of the Queen's Navee, The.) OlF (Sir Joseph's Song.) CoBE; LiTB; SiTL
H——, thou return'st from Thames, whose naiads long. Ode on the Popular Superstitions of the Highlands of Scotland. William Collins. EiPP
H: W: In Hiber: Belligeranti. John Donne. BoFr
H. W. L. John Nichol. VA
H was an indigent hen. Limerick. Bruce Porter. NA
Ha! are there wood-ghosts in this solitude. La Belle Sauvage. John Hunter-Duvar. *Fr.* De Roberval; a Drama. BoCaPo (1948 ed.)
Ha! bully for me again, when my turn for picket is over. The Brier-Wood Pipe. Charles Dawson Shanly. LPS-2
Ha ha! ha ha! this world doth pass. Fara Diddle Dyno. *Unknown.* ElL; FaBoCh; LO; LoBV; OxBoLi; SiTL; ViBoPo
Ha! now you think you've cheated me. Oh, no! John Dancer. LO
Ha! Posanes, by my loss of peace tis shee! *Unknown.* SeCSL
Ha! sir, I have seen you sniffing and snoozling. The Faun. Ezra Pound. FaBoCh; FaBoTw; LoGBV
Ha' we lost the goodliest fere o' all. Ballad of the Goodly Fere. Ezra Pound. BAP; BLV; CAW; ChMo; CMP; CoV; HBV; LEAP; LiTA; LiTM; MAP; MoAB; MoAmPo; NePA; NP; PoRA; PreP; ReaPo; TCPD; TrGrPo
Ha! whare [*or* whaur *or* where] ye gaun, ye crowlin [*or* crawlin'] ferlie? To a Louse. Burns. BLPA; CEP; CoBE; EM-1; EnL; EnLit; EnRP; FaFP; HiLiEn; InvP; LiTB; LiTG; LPS-2; OAEP; PIR; Po; PoE; SeCeV; SiTL; TCEP; TreF; ViBoPo; WoL
Haarlem Heights. Arthur Guiterman. PAH
Habakkuk, *sels.* Bible, *O.T.*
O Lord, How Long Shall I Cry, I: 2–II: 20. LiTW
Prayer of Habakkuk, The, III. BHV
Habeas Corpus. Helen Hunt Jackson. AA; AnAmPo; BAP; LA; LEAP; OBAV; WGRP
"Ah, well, Friend Death," *sel.* OHIP
Habit, The. *At. to* Berton Braley. CSF; SCC (Once You Git the Habit.) CoSo
Habit of Perfection, The. Gerard Manley Hopkins. ACP; BLV; BoLiVe; CAW; ChMo; CoBMV; EnLit; JKCP; LiTB; LiTG; MBP; MoAB; MoBrPo; OAEP (2d ed.); OBEV (new ed.); OBMV; PoRA; PoVP; TrGrPo; ViBoPo; ViP; VLEP
"Elected Silence, sing to me," *sel.* UnS
Habit of these years is constant choice, The. The World, the Times. Donald Hall. PoLFOT
Habits of the Hippopotamus. Arthur Guiterman. FiBHP; TiPo (1959 ed.)
Habitué. Helen Frith Stickney. GoYe
Hack and Hew. Bliss Carman. CaP; HBV; OCL; VA
Had a great ride boss. Artists Shouldn't Have Offspring. Don Marquis. *Fr.* Archys Life of Mehitabel. CrMA
Had a Little Fight in Mexico, *with music. Unknown.* OuSiCo
Had Cain been Scot, God would have changed his doom. On Scotland. John Cleveland. BOHV
Had Christ rebuffed me as he did that mother. The Syro-Phoenician Woman. *Unknown.* StJW
Had Gadya—a Kid, a Kid. *Unknown, tr. fr. Hebrew.* TrJP
Had God no other heart but this. The Jelly Fish. Robert P. Tristram Coffin. CAW
"Had he and I but met." The Man He Killed. Thomas Hardy. BMEP; ChMo; CMP; CoBE; CoBMV; EnL; FaFP; GTBS-W; InP; LEAP; LiTB; LiTM; MBP; MoAB; MoBrPo; NP; OQP; PoeMoYo; QP-1; SoV; TCEP; TreF; UnPo; VLEP; WaaP; WHA
Had he been at home, he would have slept. On Seeing a Dead Man. Prince Shotoku. OnPM
Had he but spar'd his tongue and pen. Swift. *Fr.* Verses on the Death of Dr. Swift. FaBoEn
Had he not breathed his breath. The Deathless Tale. Charles Hanson Towne. ChIP; SDH; StJW
Had I a Golden Pound. Francis Ledwidge. AnIV; EnLit; JKCP; LoPS; TCPD; VOD; WP
Had I a Heart for Falsehood Framed. Sheridan. *See* Song: "Had I a heart for falsehood framed."
Had I a rood of earth—hill, vale or plain. Ambitious Dreams. Joseph Marie Soulary. TrFP
"Had I a thousand hearts, I'd raise." Love to My Lord. Louisa Van Plattenhaus. BePJ
Had I a thousand lives to live. Consecration. Anna Hoppe. BePJ
Had I a thousand souls with which to love thee. Infinity of Wishes. *Unknown.* OnPM
Had I a trumpet, and that trumpet fames. *Unknown.* SeCSL
Had I a voice of steel to tune my song. Giles Fletcher. *Fr.* Christ's Victory and Triumph: Christ's Triumph after Death. LoBV
Had I an hundred mouths, as many tongues. O Tempora! O Mores! Thomas Freeman. SiCE
Had I been there that cruel day. Crucifixion. Carl S. Weist. ChIP
Had I been worthy of the love you gave. Troilus and Cressida. Aubrey Thomas De Vere. IrPN
Had I but lived a hundred years ago. At Lulworth Cove a Century Back. Thomas Hardy. ChMP
Had I but plenty of money, money enough and to spare. Up at a Villa—Down in the City. Robert Browning. BEL; BPN; EM-2; EmBrPo; EnLi-2 (1949 ed.); EnLit; EPN; GEPC; HBV; InP; PoRA; PoVP; SeCeV; TCEP; TOP; ViPo; ViPP; VLEP; WoL
Had I had an inn at Bethlehem. Lineage. Robert Farren. CoBE
Had I, my father, Orpheus' gift of speech. Euripides, *tr. by* G. M. A. Grube. *Fr.* Iphigenia in Aulis. GrPo
Had I, my father, the persuasive voice. Euripides, *tr. fr. Greek. Fr.* Iphigenia in Aulis. EnLi-2
Had I Not Loved Before. Ralph Cheyney. PR
Had I not seen him by a swerve of eye. Heron in Swamp. Frances Minturn Howard. GoYe
Had I pen ink and paper. In a Garden. Stephen Spender. TwHP
Had I plantation of this isle, my lord. Shakespeare. *Fr.* The Tempest, II, i. PoFr
Had I plenty of money, money enough and to spare. *See* Had I but plenty of money . . .
Had I Some Magic Power. Christian Winther, *tr. fr. Danish by* Charles W. Stork. BoDS
Had I that haze of streaming blue. In Phaeacia. James Elroy Flecker. HBMV; ReTS
Had I the Choice. Walt Whitman. NLK
Had I the heavens' embroidered cloths. Aedh [*or* He] Wishes for the Cloths of Heaven. W. B. Yeats. ChMo; CMP; EPP; MBP; MoBrPo; NeMA; OBEV (new ed.); OBVV; PoeT; PtOT; SP; TwCV
Had I the power to cast a bell. A Bell. Clinton Scollard. AA; SDH; VOD
Had I the power to Midas given of old. The Queen's Song. James Elroy Flecker. HBV; POTT

Had I the tongue of Orpheus, O my sire. The Prayer of Iphigenia. Euripides. *Fr.* Iphigenia in Aulis. GrR

Had it pleas'd Heaven. Shakespeare. *Fr.* Othello, IV, ii. NBE

Had Life remained one whole. Unit. Mary Fullerton. BoAV

Had Lucan hid the truth to please the time. To the Translator of Lucan's Pharsalia (1614). Sir Walter Ralegh. SiPS

Had Sacharissa lived when mortals made. At Penshurst. Edmund Waller. EPS; OAEP; PoFS; ReEn; SeCV-1

Had she come all the way for this. The Haystack in the Floods. William Morris. AEV; AnEnPo; ATP (1935 ed.); BEL; BeLS; BMEP; BPN; CaAE; EmBrPo; EnL; EnLi-2; EnLit; EPN; ExPo; GTBS; HoPM; LiTL; LoBV; MBP; OAEP; OuHeWo; PoE; PoEL-5; PoRA; POTT; PoVP; ReaPo; SeCeV; ShBV-3; ViP; ViPo; ViPP; VLEP; WHA

Had Sorrow Ever Fitter Place. Samuel Daniel. *Fr.* Hymen's Triumph. AtBAP; ElL
(Sorrow.) OBSC

Had the cloud, in its wide embrace. The Cloud by Day. Cædmon(?). *Fr.* Exodus. TCEP

Had the gods pity? Passed he with no pain. Oedipus' Last Hour. Sophocles. *Fr.* Oedipus at Colonus. GrR

Had There Been Peace. Edith Lovejoy Pierce. ChIP

Had there been peace there never had been riven. Dedication. Drummond Allison. FaBoTw

Had this effulgence disappeared. Composed upon an Evening of Extraordinary Splendor and Beauty. Wordsworth. BPN; EM-2; EmBrPo; EnRP; EPN; ERP; GEPC; PoE

Had Those That Dwell in Error Foul. Ben Jonson. *Fr.* The Second Mask, Which Was of Beauty. TuPP

Had two little cottages out on the green. Larrie O'Dee. William O. Fink. BOHV; HBV

Had we a difference with some petty isle. John Fletcher. *Fr.* Bonduca. PoFr

"Had we a king," said Wallace then. Gude Wallace. *Unknown.* BaBo; ESPB

Had we but world enough, and time. To His Coy Mistress. Andrew Marvell. AnFE; AtBAP; ATP; AWP; BCEP; BLV; BoLiVe; BrBE; CaAE; CBOV; CEP; CoBE; CoEV; EG; ElSeCe; EnL; EnLi-1 (1949 ed.); EnLit; EnLoPo; EPP; EPS; EtPaEn; EV-2; ExPo; FaBoEn; FaFP; GTBS-W; HBV; HoPM; InPo; InvP; JAWP; KN; LiTB; LiTG; LiTL; LO; LoBV; LoPo; LoPS; MaPo; MeLP; MePo; NeHB; OAEP; OBEV; OBS; OtMeF; PoE; PoEL-2; PoFS; PoRA; ReaPo; ReEn; RiBV; SeCePo; SeCeV; SeCL; SeCV-1; SeEP; ShBV-4; SiTL; TrGrPo; TwHP; TyEnPo; UnPo; ViBoPo; WBP; WHA

Had we two gone down the world together. Virgilia. Edwin Markham. BAP

Had you been strong I would have dared. Award. Gertrude Callaghan. JKCP (1955 ed.)

Had you but herd her sing. *Unknown.* SeCSL

Hadad, *sel.* James Abraham Hillhouse.
Demon-Lover, The. AA

Hades laid hand upon me while yet my years were blooming. "The Whole World Kin." *Unknown.* GrPE

Hades of Science, The. Edward Willard Watson. PoP

Hadn't we better rise and go. The Last Night. Orrick Johns. PR; TBM

Hadramaut. Bayard Taylor. PA

"Hadst thou stayed, I must have fled!" The Legend Beautiful. Longfellow. *Fr.* Tales of a Wayside Inn. CBPC; PTA-2

"Haec Est Domus Dei et Porta Coeli." Sister Maria del Rey. JKCP (1955 ed.)

"Haec Olim Meminisse Iuvabit." Deems Taylor. InMe

Hag, The. Robert Herrick. BEL; EnL; EPS; FaBoCh; GoTP; LoGBV; MuP; OTPC; SeEP
(Witch, The.) ReTS

Hag and the Slavies, The. La Fontaine, *tr. fr. French by* Edward Marsh. AWP

Hag is astride, The. The Hag. Robert Herrick. BEL; EnL; EPS; FaBoCh; GoTP; LoGBV; MuP; OTPC; SeEP

Hag of Beare, The. *Unknown. See* Woman of Beare, The.

Hagar's Last Night at Abraham's. Itzik Manger, *tr. fr. Yiddish by* Sarah Zweig Betsky. OnCuPl

Hagen of Trony went to Kriemhild. The Fall of Siegfried. *Unknown. Fr.* The Song of the Nibelungs. WoL

Hagesichora. Alcman, *tr. fr. Greek by* Gilbert Highet. GrL; OxBG

Haggadah. Abraham M. Klein. TrJP

Hagiograph. Rayner Heppenstall. NeBP

Haidee ("How long in his damp trance"). Byron. *Fr.* Don Juan, II. *See* Don Juan and Haidee.

Haidee ("It was the cooling hour"). Byron. *Fr.* Don Juan, II. *See* Juan and Haidee; Ways of Love.

Haidee ("One of the two, according to your choice"). Byron. *Fr.* Don Juan, IV. SeCePo

Haikai. Issa, *tr. fr. Japanese by* Max Bickerton. PoFr

Haiku: "Autumn cicada, The." Joso, *tr. fr. Japanese by* Kenneth Rexroth. OnPJ

Haiku: "Autumn evening." Basho, *tr. fr. Japanese by* Kenneth Rexroth. OnPJ

Haiku: "Blind child, A." Kikaku, *tr. fr. Japanese by* Kenneth Rexroth. OnPJ

Haiku: "In my life." Issa, *tr. fr. Japanese by* Kenneth Rexroth. LiTW; OnPJ

Haiku: "Long, long river, The." Boncho, *tr. fr. Japanese by* Kenneth Rexroth. LiTW; OnPJ

Haiku: "New moon in the sky." Basho, *tr. fr. Japanese by* Nobuyuki Yuasa. Po

Haiku: "No one spoke." Ryota, *tr. fr. Japanese by* Kenneth Rexroth. LiTW; OnPJ

Haiku: "Old pond, An." Basho, *tr. fr. Japanese by* Kenneth Rexroth. LiTW; OnPJ

Haiku: "On this road." Basho, *tr. fr. Japanese by* Kenneth Rexroth. LiTW; OnPJ

Haiku: "Over the vast field of mustard flowers." Buson, *tr. fr. Japanese by* Kenneth Rexroth. OnPJ

Haiku: "Summer grass." Basho, *tr. fr. Japanese by* Kenneth Rexroth. *See* Afterglow, The.

Haiku: "Wild goose, wild goose." Issa, *tr. fr. Japanese by* Kenneth Rexroth. OnPJ

Haiku: "Wild sea, A." Basho, *tr. fr. Japanese by* Kenneth Rexroth. OnPJ

Haiku of a Day. José Juan Tablada, *tr. fr. Spanish by* Samuel Beckett. AnMP

Haiku of the Flowerpot. José Juan Tablada, *tr. fr. Spanish by* Samuel Beckett. AnMP

Hail, aged God who lookest on thy Father. He Prayeth for Ink and Palette That He May Write. *Unknown. Fr.* Book of the Dead. AWP

Hail, America. Frederic Lawrence Knowles. FOAH

Hail and beware the dead who will talk life until you are blue. A Newly Discovered "Homeric" Hymn. Charles Olson. NeAP

Hail and Farewell. Byron. *See* On This Day I Complete My Thirty-sixth Year.

Hail and Farewell. Catullus. *See* On the Burial of His Brother.

Hail and Farewell. Anne Higginson Spicer. HBMV

Hail and farewell! Lo, I am the last of a glorious fleet of sail. The Last Gloucesterman. Gordon Grant. EtS

Hail and farewell to those who fought and died. The Dead. John Le Gay Brereton. BoAu

Hail, Bandusian spring, clearer than crystal pure. Horace. Odes, III, 13. LaP

Hail, banner of glory! Hail, banner of light! From Texas to Maine. George Henry Preble. FOAH

Hail be thou, holie hearbe. Old English Charm Song. *Unknown.* CAW

Hail, beauteous Dian, queen of shades. Hymn to Diana. Thomas Heywood. *Fr.* The Golden Age. EIL; SiCE

Hail! beauteous lands that crown the Southern Seas. Canto Twenty-third. George Canning *and* John Hookham Frere. *Fr.* The Progress of Man. CEP

Hail, beauteous stranger of the grove [*or* wood]! To the Cuckoo [*or* Ode: To the Cuckoo]. Michael Bruce, *revised by* John Logan. BCEP; BSV; CG; DD; EBSV; EiPP; EV-3; HBV; LEAP; LPS-2; OBEC; OBEV; OTPC; SN; TVSH; ViBoPo

Hail, Bishop Valentine, whose day this is. *See* Haile Bishop Valentine

Hail, blessed virgin, full of heavenly grace. On the Infancy of our Saviour [*or* The Child Jesus]. Francis Quarles. AnEC; ElSeCe; OBS; OxBoCh; SeCePo; SeCL; StJW

Hail, blissfulest maiden. On the Annunciation. *Unknown.* ISi

Hail, blushing goddess, beauteous Spring! Esther Vanhomrigh. LO

Hail, bright morning beam! The Dream. Francis Burdett Money-Coutts. OBVV

Hail, Camerados! The Poets at a House-Party. Carolyn Wells. PA

Hail! Christ's pure Body—born of the Holy Virgin. To Our Lord in the Sacrament. St. Anselm. CAW

Hail, Columbia! Joseph Hopkinson. AA; APW; BAV; FaBoBe; FaFP; HBV; LEAP; MC; OlF; PaA; PAH; PEDC; PoFr; TCAP; TreFS; YaD

Hail, Comely and Clean. *Unknown. See* Haylle, Comly and Clene.

Hail, Day of Days! In Peals of Praise. Fortunatus, *tr. fr. Latin.* BePJ

Hail, Fair Morning. *Unknown, tr. fr. Late Middle Irish by* Standish Hayes O'Grady. *Fr.* The Life of St. Cellach of Kallala. OnYI

Hail falls pitterpat, The. Hail on the Pine Trees. Basho. MPB

Hail, Father! whose creating call. Hymn to God the Father. Samuel Wesley. OxBoCh

Hail, fathers, hail! Flute-Song. *Tr. by* Natalie Curtis. APW

Hail, favour'd casement!—where the sight. In Search of the

Picturesque. William Combe. *Fr.* Dr. Syntax in Search of the Picturesque. OBRV

Hail, Freedom! thy bright crest. A New National Hymn. F. Marion Crawford. HH; IDAH; PAH; PEOR

Hail, gentle Evening, that bringest back. Eventide. Sappho. GrR

Hail, gladdening Light, of his pure glory poured. Hymn for the Lighting of the Lamps. *Unknown, at. to* St. Athenogenes. CAW

Hail, glorious edifice, stupendous work! Loyal Effusion. Horatio *and* James Smith. OBRV

Hail, God revived in glory. Hymn to Horus. Mathilde Blind. OBVV

Hail, great Apollo! guide my feeble pen. The British Lyon Roused. Stephen Tilden. PAH

Hail, guest! We ask not what thou art. America Greets an Alien [*or* Welcome over the Door of an Old Inn]. *Unknown.* PGD; PoToHe (new ed.); PSO

Hail! Hail! Hail! A Dance Chant. *Tr. by* E. S. Parker. WGRP

Hail, hail to thy blessed name, O Mary. Hymn to Mary [*or* Salutation]. Zerea Jacob. CAW; ISi

Hail, happy Britain, Freedom's blest retreat. Prophecy. Gulian Verplanck. MC

Hail, happy day, when, smiling like the morn. To the Right Honorable William, Earl of Dartmouth. Phillis Wheatley. PoFr; TCAP

Hail! Ho!/ Sail! Ho! A Sea Song from the Shore. James Whitcomb Riley. BoTP; GaP; PRWS; TiPo; TVC; TVSH

Hail, holy earth, whose cold arms do embrace. John Fletcher. The Faithful Shepherdess, I, i. MyFE

Hail, Holy Light. Milton. *Fr.* Paradise Lost, III. ExPo; FiP; GTBS-W; LiA; LoBV; ShBV-4; WHA
("Hail holy light! offspring of Heav'n first-born.") AtBAP; ATP; BrBE; EM-1; InP; OAEP; SeEP; ViBoPo
(Hymn to Light.) FaBoEn; GrCo-2
(Invocation to Light.) CoEV; EV-2; LPS-2
(Light.) LiTB; OBEV; OBS; RiBV

Hail, holy Queen. Salve Regina. *Unknown.* WHL

Hail, Jesus' Virgin-Mother ever Blest. Votive Ode. Erasmus. ISi

Hail, Liberty! a glorious word. Charles Churchill. *Fr.* The Duellist. PoFr

Hail, lovely, sleepful night, sombre and sparkling! Hymn to Night. André Chénier. TrFP

Hail, Maiden Root. Caelius Sedulius, *tr. fr. Latin by* Raymond F. Roseliep. *Fr.* Carmen Paschale. ISi

Hail Man! Angela Morgan. WGRP

Hail Mary full of grace! Prelude of the New Testament. St. Luke, Bible, *N.T.* (*Douay vers.*). CAW

Hail Mary, Full of Grace, Mother in Virginity. *Unknown.* AnEC

Hail, Master Mariner of Sainte Malo! Cartier; Dauntless Discoverer. John Daniel Logan. CPG

Hail me Diogenes underground, O Stranger, and pass by. Epitaph of a Young Man. *Unknown.* LiTW

Hail, Mediocrity, beneath whose spell. Roy Campbell. *Fr.* The Georgiad. MoBrPo

Hail, meek-eyed [*or* meek-ey'd] maiden, clad in sober gray. Ode to Evening. Joseph Warton. ATP; UnPo (1st ed.)

Hail, Mighty Rum! how wondrous is thy pow'r! Eulogium on Rum. Joseph Smith. LHV

Hail, mildly pleasing Solitude. Hymn on Solitude. James Thomson. CEP; EiPP; OBEC

Hail! Minnesota! Truman E. Rickard *and* Arthur Upson. PoRL

Hail, most holy Queen and Lady. Saint Francis' Salute to Our Lady. St. Francis of Assisi. SaFP

Hail! Mother-Maid, unmatched since time was born. Salutations: To Mary, Virgin. *Unknown.* ISi

Hail, Mother most pure! Salve, Virgo Florens. *Unknown. Fr.* The Little Office of the Immaculate Conception. WHL

Hail, Mother of the Savior. Adam of Saint Victor, *tr. fr. Latin by* Digby S. Wrangham. ISi

Hail, Muse! *et cetera.* We left Juan sleeping. Byron. Don Juan, III. REAL

Hail, native Language, that by sinews weak. At a Vacation Exercise. Milton. OBS

Hail, O most worthy in all the world! Advent Lyrics, IX. *Unknown. Fr.* Christ, I. AnOE

Hail, O Queen of heaven enthroned! Ave Regina. *Unknown.* WHL

Hail, old October, bright and chill. Old October. Thomas Constable. HBV

Hail, old patrician trees, so great and good! Of Solitude [*or* On Solitude *or* Essay on Solitude]. Abraham Cowley. EPS; EV-2; OBS; SeCL; SeEP; ViBoPo

Hail on the Pine Trees. Basho, *tr. fr. Japanese.* MPB

Hail, sacred Peace, who claim'st thy bright abode. Hymn to Peace. Joel Barlow. APW

Hail, sacred shades! cool, leafy house! Upon the Priory Grove, His Usual Retirement. Henry Vaughan. TriL

Hail Saint Mary! Cantiga de Santa Maria. Alfonso X, King of Castile and Leon. LyMA

Hail, St. Michael with the long spear! A Satire on the People of Kildare. *Unknown, at. to* Friar Michael of Kildare. OnYI

Hail [*or* Haile], sister springs! The Weeper [*or* Saint Mary Magdalene]. Richard Crashaw. AtBAP; MeLP; MePo; OBEV; PoFS; ReEn; SeCV-1; SeEP; ViBoPo

Hail, son of peak and prairie. Hail, America. Frederic Lawrence Knowles. FOAH

Hail, sons of generous valor. To the Defenders of New Orleans. Joseph Rodman Drake. DD; PAH

Hail! South Dakota. Deecort Hammitt. PoRL

Hail Sovereign Queen of secrets who hast power. *At. to* Shakespeare. *Fr.* The Two Noble Kinsmen. PoEL-2

Hail, Star of the Sea. Star of the Sea. Richard Webb Sullivan. ISi

Hail sterne superne! Hail in eterne. Ane Ballat of Our Lady [*or* Ballad of Our Lady]. William Dunbar. ACP; CAW; EBSV

Hail, sword of Carroll! Oft hast thou been in the great woof of war. The Song of Carroll's Sword. *At. to* Dallan MacMore. OnYI

Hail! the Glorious Golden City. Felix Adler. WGRP
(City of Light, The, *sl. diff.*) GrCo-1
(City of Our Hopes, The.) MaRV

Hail, thou great God in thy Boat. He Embarketh in the Boat of Ra. *Unknown. Fr.* Book of the Dead. AWP

Hail, Thou great mysterious Being! Alexander McLachlan. *Fr.* God. CaP

Hail, Thou Head! Bernard of Clairvaux, *tr. fr. Latin.* BePJ

Hail thou most sacred venerable thing. Hymn to Darkness. John Norris. GTSL; MePo; OBS; OxBoCh; SN

Hail Thou My Native Soil. William Browne. *Fr.* Britannia's Pastorals, II, Song 3. EPS; EV-2
(Frolic Mariners of Devon, The.) ChTr

Hail, Thou Once Despised Jesus! John Bakewell. BePJ

Hail, Thou star of ocean. Ave, Maris Stella. *Unknown.* WHL

Hail, thou who shinest from the Moon. He Establisheth His Triumph. *Unknown. Fr.* Book of the Dead. AWP; JAWP; WBP

Hail to Hobson! Hail to Hobson! hail to all the valiant set. The Men of the *Merrimac.* Clinton Scollard. PAH

Hail to our Keltic brethren, wherever they may be. Salutation to the Kelts. Thomas D'Arcy McGee. TIP

Hail to the brightness of Zion's glad morning. The Latter Day. Thomas Hastings. AA

Hail to the Chief, Who in Triumph Advances! Sir Walter Scott. *See* Boat Song.

Hail to the Headlong! the Headlong Ap-Headlong! Chorus. Thomas Love Peacock. *Fr.* Headlong Hall. OBRV

Hail to the land whereon we tread. New England. James Gates Percival. AA; APW

Hail to the Lord's Anointed. The King Eternal. James Montgomery. MaRV

Hail to the planting of Liberty's tree. American Independence. Alfred Billings Street. PEDC

Hail to the springtime of deathless creation. Psalm II. Björnstjerne Björnson. AnNoLy

Hail to thee, beautiful, mighty, and golden! Deirdre's Song at Sunrise. Sister Maura. CaP

Hail to Thee, Blithe Spirit. Laura Simmons. BAP

Hail to thee, blithe spirit. To a Skylark [*or* Ode to a Skylark *or* To the Skylark]. Shelley. AnFE; AtBAP; ATP; BCEP; BEL; BLA; BLV; BoLiVe; BPN; BTP; CBOV; CBPC; CoBE; DD; EM-2; EmBrPo; EnL; EnLi-2; EnLit; EnRP; EPN; EPP; ERP; EV-4; FaBoBe; FaFP; FaPON; GBV; GEPC; GN; GTBS; GTBS-D; GTBS-W; GTSE; GTSL; HBV; HH; HiLiEn; InP; InvP; LEAP; LiTB; LiTG; LoBV; LPS-2; MCCG; MPB; MyFE; NP; OAEP; OBEV; OBRV; OHFP; OTPC; OuHeWo; PECK; PFE; PIAE; PIR; PoFS; PTA-1; PYM; REAL; ReaPo; ShBV-4; TCEP; TOP; TreFS; TrGrPo; TVSH; TwHP; TyEnPo; WHA

Hail to thee, Boy, Mighty One! Hymn of the Curetes. *Unknown.* OxBG

Hail to thee, gallant foe. Cervera. Bertrand Shadwell. PAH

Hail to thee, Mary, maiden bright! A Song of the Five Joys. *Unknown.* TMEV

Hail to thee, Mary, thou Mother of Christ. Ave Maria! *Unknown.* TMEV

Hail to thee, monarch of African mountains. Kilimandjaro. Bayard Taylor. AmP

Hail to thee, our Savior's mother! Hail, Mother of the Savior. Adam of Saint Victor. ISi

Hail to thee Sun! Oh, list and stay thy course! Hymn to the Sun. José de Espronceda. TeCS

Hail to Thee, true Body, sprung. Ave Verum Corpus Natum. *Unknown.* WHL

Hail to you, green hymn, that in superb. To an Araucaria. Salvador Díaz Mirón. AnMP

Hail, Vermont! Josephine Hovey Perry. PoRL

Hail Virgin, if you be, as these cheek-roses. A Novice. Shakespeare. *Fr.* Measure for Measure, I, v. PraNu
Hail Virgin in Virginity a Spouse. Coventry Patmore. *Fr.* Deliciae Sapientiae de Amore. PraNu
Hail, water-nymphs, to whom Hermocreon paid. Water-Nymphs. Hermocreon. OxBG
Hail [*or* Haile] wedded love, mysterious law, true source. Wedded Love [*or* Their Wedded Love]. Milton. *Fr.* Paradise Lost, IV. OBS; SeCePo
Hail, ye indomitable heroes, hail! The Crimean Heroes. Walter Savage Landor. ALV; PIAE
Haile [*or* Hail] Bishop Valentine, whose day this is. An Epithalamion [*or* Hail, Bishop Valentine]. John Donne. AtBAP; ChTr; EV-2
Haile great Redeemer, man, and God, all haile. A Hymne to Our Saviour on the Crosse. George Chapman. PoEL-2
Haile, sister springs. *See* Hail, sister springs!
Haile wedded love, mysterious law, true source. *See* Hail wedded love, mysterious law, true source.
Hair. Gelett Burgess. *See* I'd Rather Have Fingers than Toes.
Hair. Remy de Gourmont, *tr. fr. French by* Jethro Bithell. AWP
Hair—silver-gray. Face. Jean Toomer. CDC
Haircut. Karl Shapiro. FiMAP; MoPo; MoVE
Hairless beast in old clothes. Citizen. Louis Grudin. NePA
Hair's Breadth, The. Nicholas Moore. NeBP
Hairy Dog, The. Herbert Asquith. AlBD; BoChLi; FaPON; StVeCh; SUS; TiPo; UTS
Haitches! Edwina May. SiTL
Hakluyt Unpurchased. Franklin McDuffee. EtS
Halcyon, *sel.* Hilda Doolittle ("H. D.").
"I'm not here,/ everything's vague." MAP; MoAmPo
Halcyon Days. Walt Whitman. NePA; OxBA
Halcyon, that from the wave-swept reef. Euripides. *Fr.* Iphigenia in Tauris. GrPo
Halcyons, The. Alcman, *tr. fr. Greek by* H. T. Wade-Gery. GrL; OxBG
(No More, O Maidens, *tr. by* Olga Marx *and* Ernst Morwitz.) LiTW
(Old Poet to His Maiden Choir, The, *tr. by* F. L. Lucas.) GrPE
(To His Maiden Quire, *tr. by* H. T. Wade-Gery.) GrR
Hale, and though sixty, without a stoop. Benedict Brosse. S. Frances Harrison. *Fr.* Down the River. CPG
Hale in the Bush. *Unknown.* *See* Nathan Hale.
Hale John Spratt, The—oft called for shortness Jack. An Idyll of Phatte and Leene. *Unknown.* BOHV; PA
Haleluiah, or Britan's Second Remembrancer. George Wither. *See* Hallelujah; or, Britain's Second Remembrancer.
Half a bar, half a bar. Village Choir. *Unknown.* BOHV; PA
Half a league, half a league. The Charge of the Light Brigade. Tennyson. BBV; BEL; BeLS; BHV; BLPA; BPN; CG; EM-2; EmBrPo; EPN; EV-5; FaBoBe; FaFP; FaPON; GEPC; GN; HBV; HBVY; HiLiEn; HoPM; LEAP; LPS-2; MaC; MCCG; NeHB; OHFP; OnHT; OnSP; OTPC; PC; PCD; PECK; PFE; PIR; PoVP; PTA-1; PYM; ShBV-1; TCEP; TOP; TreF; TSWC; TVSH; VA; VLEP; WBLP
Half artist and half anchorite. France. Percy MacKaye. BAP; LEAP
Half-asleep. Thelma Harrington Bell. RAR
Half-asleep, The. Thomas Wade. OBEV (1st ed.)
Half-awake and half-dozing. At Memphis Station. Johannes V. Jensen. WoL
Half baked potato named Sue, A. Limerick. George Libaire. LiBL
Half-blown Rose, The. Samuel Daniel. *See* To Delia: "Look, Delia, how we esteem the half-blown rose."
Half-Breed Girl, The. Duncan Campbell Scott. CaP; CPG; OCL
Half-breed, slim, and sallow of face, A. Gatineau Point. S. Frances Harrison. *Fr.* Down the River. CPG
Half-burned tree-trunks stretched like praying hands, The. Burned Forests. Frank Oliver Call. OCL
Half-dead with fever, here in bed I sprawl. Sick-Bed. Edmund Blunden. PtOT
Half Door, The. "Seumas O'Sullivan." AnIV
Half doun the hill, whaur [*or* where] fa's the linn. The Gowk. William Soutar. GoTS; NeBP
Half-dream crumbles and falls through, The. Verification. Christopher Morley. PC
Half fish, half fallen angel, none of you. The Mermaid at Zennor. John Heath-Stubbs. FaBoMo
Half hero and half ignoramus. On Count M. S. Vorontzov. Pushkin. TrRV
Half hidden by trees, the sheer roof of the barn. The Barn. Stephen Spender. HaMV
Half-hidden in a graveyard. The Stranger. Walter de la Mare. MoVE
Half Holiday. Olive Enoch. BoTP
Half Horse and Half Alligator. Samuel Woodworth. *See* Hunters of Kentucky, The.
Half Hours with the Classics. H. J. DeBurgh. BOHV; InMe
Half I belong with those who toil and half with those who sing. Status. Alberta Robison. MuM
Half kneeling yet, and half reclining. The Queen's Vespers. Aubrey Thomas De Vere. VA
Half-Light. Jean Percival Waddell. CaP
Half loving-kindliness, and half disdain. To My Cat. Rosamund Marriott Watson. PoC; POT; PoTo; VA
Half masonry, half pain; her head. London, 1941. Mervyn Peake. NeTW
Half-Mast. Lloyd Mifflin. PAH
Half-mast the flag, and let the bell be tolled. Theodore Roosevelt. Samuel Valentine Cole. PEDC
Half-Moon Westers Low, My Love, The. A. E. Housman. PoLFOT
Half of Life, The. Friedrich Hölderlin, *tr. fr. German by* Frederic Prokosch. LiTW
(Halves of Life, *tr. by* Kate Flores.) AnGP
(Life Half Lived, *tr. unknown.*) ChTr
Half of Life Gone, The. William Morris. EmBrPo
Half of my life is gone, and I have let. Mezzo Cammin. Longfellow. AmPP (3d ed.); CoBA; IAP; TCAP
Half past nine—high time for supper. In Praise of Cocoa, Cupid's Nightcap. Stanley J. Sharpless. FiBHP
Half past seven in the morning. His Majesty the Letter-Carrier. Emanuel Carnevali. AnAmPo; LA
Half Past Tears. Edith Ogden. AlBD
Half past twelve. The time has passed quickly. Since Nine o'Clock. C. P. Cavafy. MoGP
Half-satyr and half-saint, you walk alone. The Celibate. Joan Lamburn. DiM
Half-seen memories of childish days, The. Early Friendship. Stephen E. Spring Rice, *wr. at. to* Aubrey Thomas De Vere. BoFr; LPS-1
Half Stun'd I Look Around. Sir Ronald Ross. PoP
Half the horizon is the sea. Sunrise; Maine Coast. Robert P. Tristram Coffin. CAG
Half through the night at a deep clock-stroke. A Child Cried at Night. Ernst Wiechert. TwGV
Half-Tide Ledge. R. P. Blackmur. AnFE; CoAnAm; TwAmPo
Half-waking. William Allingham. MOAH; VA
Halfway. Maxine W. Kumin. GoYe
Half way along the sloping earth. Socrates Prays a Day and a Night. George O'Neil. AnAmPo; LA
Halfway Down. A. A. Milne. FaPON; TiPo (1959 ed.)
Half-Way Knowledge. Bhartrihari, *tr. fr. Sanskrit by* Paul Elmer More. OnPM
Halfway up the Hemlock valley turnpike. Emilia. Sarah N. Cleghorn. HBV; PFY
Halfway Up the Mountain. Liu Tzu Hui, *tr. fr. Chinese by* Henry H. Hart. PoHN
Half-world's width divides us, The; where she sits. Divided. David Gray. AA
Halibut Cove Harvest. Kenneth Leslie. CaP
Halieuticks [*or* Halieutica], *sels.* Oppian, *tr. fr. Greek.*
"As when abroad some celebrated Fair," *tr. by* John Jones. GrPo
Dolphin and Seal, *tr. by* F. L. Lucas. GrPE
Dolphin's Death, The, *tr. by* F. L. Lucas. GrPE
Eels, Tortoises, Soles, Lampreys, *tr. by* William Diaper. BeR
How Sea-Calves Are Born, *tr. by* William Diaper. BeR
Lions and Dragons, *tr. by* William Diaper. BeR
Mullet and the Hook, The, *tr. by* F. L. Lucas. GrPE
Shoal of Slime-Fish, The, *tr. by* William Diaper. BeR
Temptation, *tr. by* Gilbert Highet. OxBG
Halifax Station. *Unknown.* PAH
Hallelu-u-u, Hallelu, O, my Lord. Death Come to My House He Didn't Stay Long. *Unknown.* BoAN-2
Halleluja!/ What sound is this across the dark. A Christmas Eve Choral. Bliss Carman. ISi
Hallelujah. Psalms, CXLVI, Bible, *O.T.* TrJP
Hallelujah! A. E. Housman. FiBHP
Hallelujah! *Unknown.* BoAN-1, *with music;* OlF
Hallelujah. George Wither. *See* Hallelujah; or, Britain's Second Remembrancer.
Hallelujah!/Praise God in His Sanctuary. The Closing Doxology. Psalm CL, Bible, *O.T.* (Smith-Goodspeed *tr.*) MaRV
Hallelujah!/ Praise the Lord from the Heavens. A Hallelujah Chorus. Psalm CXLVIII, Bible, *O.T.* (Smith-Goodspeed *tr.*). MaRV
Hallelujah./ Praise the Lord, O my soul. Hallelujah. Psalm CXLVI, Bible, *O.T.* TrJP
Hallelujah./ Praise ye the Lord from the heavens. Praise Ye the Lord. Psalm CXLVIII, Bible, *O.T.* TrJP
Hallelujah! an' a hallelujah! Hallelujah! *Unknown.* BoAN-1; OlF
Hallelujah, Bum Again. *Unknown.* *See* Hallelujah, I'm a Bum.
Hallelujah Chorus, A. Psalms, CXLVIII, Bible, *O.T.* (Smith-Goodspeed *tr.*). MaRV

Hallelujah, I'm a Bum. *Unknown.* APW; AS, *sl. abr., with music;* TrAS, *with music*
(Hallelujah, Bum Again, *with music.*) ABF
Hallelujah; or, Britain's Second Remembrancer, *sels.* George Wither.
For a Musician. OBS
(To a Musician, *wr. at to* William Austin.) OxBoCh
Hymne I: General Invitation to Praise God, A. SeCV-1
Rocking Hymn, A. AnEC; BOL
(Hymn L: Rocking Hymn, A.) SeCV-1
(Lullaby, A: "Sweet baby, sleep; what ails my dear.") EV-1, *abr.;* OxBoCh, *abr.* [*wr. at. to* William Austin]
When We Are upon the Seas. BEL
"Hallelujah!" was the only observation. Hallelujah! A. E. Housman. FiBHP
Halley's Comet appeared in 1910. Chance Encounter. Katsumi Tanaka. PoLJ
Hallo My Fancy. William Cleland, *and others.* CH; LPS-3; OxBoLi
(Hallow My Fancie, *sl. diff.*) NBE
(Hollo, My Fancy! *sl. diff.*) SeCL
Halloo to man, the pleasuring, lording creature. So, Man? Gene Derwood. NePA
Hallow days o' Yule are come, The. The Wife of Usher's Well (B *vers.*). *Unknown.* ESPB
Hallow Even. Carrie Ward Lyon. HOAH
Hallow My Fancie. William Cleland, *and others. See* Hallo My Fancy.
Hallow the threshold, crown the posts anew! On the Queen's Return from the Low Countries. William Cartwright. MePo; OBEV
Hallowed be the Ordainer of/ the world! A Little Prayer. Paul Goodman. LiTA
Hallowed be the Sabbaoth. Epitaphs. Francis Jeffrey. OxBoLi
Hallowed Ground. Thomas Campbell. BLPA; HBV; LPS-3; MaRV, *abr.*
Hallowed Places. Alice Freeman Palmer. HBV
Hallowed Season, The. Shakespeare. *See* Gracious Time, The.
Hallowe'en. Harry Behn. FaPON; GBV (1952 ed.); SiSoSe; StVeCh (1955 ed.); TiPo; YeAr
Hallowe'en. Joel Benton. DD; HOAH; OTPC (1946 ed.); PoRL
Hallowe'en. Burns. HOAH; OBEC, *abr.*
Hallowe'en. Molly Capes. HOAH; MoSiPe
Hallowe'en. Arthur Cleveland Coxe. DD
Hallowe'en. Frances Frost. TiPo (1959 ed.)
Halloween. Marie A. Lawson. SiSoSe; TiPo (1959 ed.)
Halloween. Carrie Ward Lyon. HOAH
Hallowe'en. John Mayne. HBV
Hallowe'en. Anna Medary. GFA
Hallowe'en. Virna Sheard. DD
Hallowe'en. *Unknown.* MeMeAg; OTPC (1946 ed.)
("Hey-how for Hallowe'en!") FaBoCh; LoGBV
(Witches, The.) ChTr
Hallowe'en. Helen Wing. GFA
Halloween Concert. Aileen Fisher. SiSoSe
Hallowe'en Meeting, A. George Butler. MeMeAg
Hallowe'en Memory, A. Christopher Morley. HOAH; LHV
Hallowe'en's the time for nuts. Hallowe'en. Anna Medary. GFA
Hallows' E'en. Winifred M. Letts. DD
Hallucination, I. Arthur Symons. VLEP
Hallucinations? Beverley Randolph Tucker. PoP
Haloes. Idella Purnell. DDA
Halt, The. Josephine Miles. FiMAP
Halt and Parley. George Herbert Clarke. BoCaPo (1943 ed.); CaP; OCL
Halt looks into the eyes of the halt and looks away, The. The Halt. Josephine Miles. FiMAP
Halt! Shoulder arms! Recover! As you were! Sonnet to Britain. W. E. Aytoun. SoV
Halted against the shade of a last hill. Spring Offensive. Wilfred Owen. LiTB; MoVE
Haltersick's Song. John Pickering. *Fr.* Horestes. OBSC
("Farewell, adieu, that courtly life.") ElSeCe; ReEn; TuPP
(Song: "Farewell, adieu, that court-like life!") ElL
Halves of Life. Friedrich Hölderlin. *See* Half of Life, The.
Halways sound your Haitches. Haitches! *Unknown.* SiTL
Ham and eggs, Lord, pork and beans. I Got to Roll. *Unknown.* OuSiCo
Hamadan is my native place. A Blessed Spot. Abulfadhel Ahmed. OnPM
Hamadryad, The. Walter Savage Landor. *Fr.* The Hellenics. BPN; CBOV; EmBrPo; EnRP; EPN; ERP; TOP; VA
Hamadryad, The. Theodore Goodridge Roberts. CPG
Hamasah, *sel.* Hittan of Tayyi, *tr. fr. Arabic by* Sir Charles Lyall.
His Children. AWP; JAWP; LiTW; WBP
(He Thinks of His Children.) FAOV
Hamatreya. Emerson. AmP; AmPo; AmPP; AnNE; BAV; CoBA; CoV; FaBoEn; IAP; MOAP; OnAP; OxBA; PoE; PoEL-4; SeCeV; WoL
Hambone and the Heart, The. Edith Sitwell. OBMV
Hame came our goodman. Our Goodman. *Unknown.* BaBo; EnLi-1; ESPB; ViBoFo (A *vers.*)
Hame, Hame, Hame. Allan Cunningham. BSV; CH; EBSV; HBV; OBEV; OBRV; OTPC
("Hame, hame, hame, hame fain wad I be," *first* 6 *ll.*) LO
(Loyalty, *abr.*) GN; LH
Hamelin Town's in Brunswick. The Pied Piper of Hamelin. Robert Browning. BBV; BeLS; BMEP; BoChLi; BOHV; BPN; CG; EmBrPo; EV-5; FaBoBe; FaBoCh; FaFP; GEPC; GN; GoTP; HBV; HBVY; HiLiEn; LoGBV; LPS-3; OnHT; OnSP; OtMeF; OTPC; PoE; PoVP; RG; RIS; ShBV-1; StVeCh; TCEP; TiPo (1952 ed.); TVSH; WP
Hamilcar Barca. Roger Casement. JKCP (1926 ed.)
Hamilton. Marie E. J. Pitt. BoAu
Hamilton Greene. Edgar Lee Masters. *Fr.* Spoon River Anthology. OxBA
Hamlet, *sels.* Shakespeare.
"But looke where sadly the poore wretch comes reading," *fr.* II, ii. AtBAP
Christmas, *fr.* I, i. ChTr
Death of Hamlet, *fr.* V, ii. FiP
Fortune's Finger, *fr.* III, ii. BLP
Friendship ("Horatio, thou art e'en as just a man"), *fr.* III, ii. LPS-1
("Nay, do not think I flatter.") PIR
(Noble Friendship, A; Hamlet and Horatio.) EV-1
Good Sir, Whose Powers Are These? *fr.* IV, iv, *abr.* WaaP
Gracious Time, The ("Some say that ever 'gainst that season comes"), 7 *ll., fr.* I, i. ChrBoLe; GN
(Christmas.) EV-1
(Hallowed Season, The.) MaRV
("It faded on the crowing of the cock," 8 *ll.*) MyFE
("Some say that ever 'gainst that season comes.") ChIP, 7 *ll.;* TiPo (1952 ed.), 4 *ll.*
Grief ("Good Hamlet, cast thy nighted colour off"), *fr.* I, ii. LPS-1
Hamlet's Instructions to the Players, *fr.* III, ii. TreFS
"How all occasions do inform against me," *fr.* IV, iv. HoPM
"How now? what noise is that?" *fr.* IV, v. AtBAP
"I am thy Father's Spirit," *fr.* I, v. AtBAP
"Is she to bee buried in Christian buriall," *fr.* V, i. AtBAP
"Let four captains/ Bear Hamlet, like a soldier, to the stage," *fr.* V, ii. MyFE
"Looke heere upon this picture, and on this," *fr.* III, iv, *abr.* NBE
"Mother, for love of grace," *fr.* III, iv. MotAn
"Now Hamlet, where's Polonius?" *fr.* IV, iii. AtBAP
O That This Too Too Solid Flesh Would Melt, *fr.* I, ii. BCEP; PIR
(Frailty, Thy Name Is Woman.) LiA; TrGrPo
(Hamlet Broods over the Death of His Father.) TreFS
"O what a noble mind is here o'erthrown," *fr.* III, i.
(Shakespeare Gallery, A: Hamlet.) MaC
"O, what a rogue and peasant slave am I," *fr.* II, ii. PIR; PreP
Ophelia's Death, *fr.* V, i. ChTr
Ophelia's Songs, *fr.* IV, v.
And Will He [*or* A'] Not Come Again? EG; InPo; PoEL-2; ViBoPo
(Ophelia's Songs, 2.) AnFE; TrGrPo
"He is dead and gone, lady." LO
How Should I Your True Love Know. CBOV; EG; EnLoPo; EPP; EV-1; InPo; LiTB; LiTG; LiTL; PoRA; TCEP; ViBoPo
(Friar of Orders Grey, The.) GoBC
(Ophelia's Song.) CBE; ChTr; OBSC
(Ophelia's Songs, 1.) AnFE; TrGrPo
(Song: "How should I your true love know.") CH
(Song from "Hamlet.") LEAP
Tomorrow Is [*or* Good Morrow, 'Tis] Saint Valentine's Day. EnLoPo; InPo; ViBoPo
(Saint Valentine's Day.) LiTB; LiTG
(Song: "Tomorrow [*or* Good morrow] is Saint Valentine's day.") FaPON; HH; MPB; SiSoSe (4 *ll.*)
Polonius' Advice to Laertes, *fr.* I, iii. BBV; FAOV; OHFP; OQP; PoeMoYo; PTA-1; PYM; QP-1
(Be True, 3 *ll.*) PCD; PCH
(Counsel of Polonius, The.) TVSH
(Polonius' Advice to His Son.) BTP; MaRV; PECK; TreF
(Polonius Advises His Son.) BCEP
(Polonius to Laertes.) GN
(". . . There; my blessing with thee.") PIR
(These Few Precepts.) EV-1
(This above All.) TrGrPo
(To Thine Own Self Be True.) FaFP; LiTB; LiTG
"To be, or not to be, that is the question," *fr.* III, i.

Hamlet (*continued*)
AtBAP; EV-1; FaFP; FiP; GTBS-W; HoPM; LiA; LiTB; LiTG; PIR; TrGrPo; WHA
(From "Hamlet.") LEAP
(Hamlet Contemplates Death.) MaRV
(Hamlet Contemplates Suicide.) TreF
(Hamlet's Soliloquy.) BCEP; NeHB; PYM; WBLP
(Soliloquy from "Hamlet.") OHFP; OQP; QP-1
(Soliloquy on Death.) LPS-1
"What a piece of work is man!" *fr.* II, ii. InP
(Man.) TreF
"Where is the beauteous Majesty of Denmark?" *fr.* IV, v. AtBAP
"Who's there?" *fr.* I, i, iv, *and* v. ExPo
"Why, let the stricken deer go weep," 4 *ll.*, *fr.* III, ii. CoBE
Hamlet Ballytullagh, small and old, The. Ballytullagh. William Allingham. *Fr.* Laurence Bloomfield in Ireland. IrPN
Hamlet of A. MacLeish, The, *sel.* Archibald MacLeish.
"Night after night I lie like this listening." AnAmPo; LA; PoLFOT; PreP
Hamlet's Instructions to the Players. Shakespeare. *Fr.* Hamlet, III, ii. TreFS
Hamlet's Soliloquy. Shakespeare. *See* To Be or Not to Be.
Hamlet's Soliloquy Imitated. Richard Jago. SiTL
Hammam Name, The. James Elroy Flecker. FaBoTw
Hammer Man, *with music.* *Unknown.* AS
Hammer Song, The. *Unknown.* ABF
Hammer-Throw, The. Reuel Denney. PreP
Hammers, The. Ralph Hodgson. CMP; MBP; MoBrPo; PoMa; POTE; YT
Hammers and Anvil. John Clifford. *See* Anvil, The—God's Word.
Hammock Lullaby. Charlotte Brewster Jordan. BOL
Hampton Beach. Whittier. LPS-2; MOAP
Han Poem, IX. *Unknown, tr. fr. Chinese.* ChLP
Ha'nacker Mill. Hilaire Belloc. HBMV; MPB; MM; MoBrPo
Hand, The. Ebenezer Jones. OBVV
Hand, A. Bernard Spencer. NeBP
Hand and Foot, The. Jones Very. NePA; OxBA; PoEL-4
Hand in hand they dance in a row. The Clothes-Line. Charlotte Druitt Cole. BoTP
Hand is to the plough an' the e'e is to the trail, The. For Love of Appin. Jessie Mackay. AnNZ
Hand me the comet lashing with. For Gwenhwyfar and Blodeuwedd. Davies Aberpennar. MoWP
Hand me the sweet cup fashioned from that clay. "The Lip of This Poor Earthen Urn." Zonas. GrPE
Hand-Mirror, A. Walt Whitman. OxBA
Hand of Douglas is his own, The. Marmion and Douglas. Sir Walter Scott. *Fr.* Marmion. OtMeF
Hand of Glory, The. "Thomas Ingoldsby." *Fr.* The Ingoldsby Legends. DaM
Hand of Labor. Lilburn H. Townsend. PEDC
Hand of Lincoln, The. Edmund Clarence Stedman. AA; OHIP; PGD
Hand of Nature, The. Mark Akenside. EV-3
Hand over Hand. *Unknown.* SG
Hand That Rocks the Cradle, The. William Croswell Doane. *See* Modern Baby, The.
Hand That Rules the World, The. William Ross Wallace. PTA-1
(Hand That Rocks the Cradle Is the Hand That Rules the World, The, *abr.*) FaFP; TreF; WBLP
(What Rules the World.) DD; MotAn, 8 *ll.*; OHIP; OTPC (1946 ed.), 8 *ll.*; PoRL, 8 *ll.*
Hand That Signed the Paper Felled a City, The. Dylan Thomas. GTBS-W; HaMV; InPo; LiTM; MoAB; MoBrPo; MoP; MoPo; PoLFOT; POTE; SeCePo; SoV; TrGrPo (rev. ed.); WaP
Hand that swept the sounding lyre, The. On a Dead Poet. Frances Sargent Osgood. AA
Handel, Bendel, Mendelssohn. A Rhyme for Musicians. E. Lemke. BOHV
Handful came to Seicheprey, A. Seicheprey. *Unknown.* PAH
Handful here, that once was Mary's earth, The. Her Epitaph. Thomas William Parsons. AA; APW; HBV
Handful of Dust, A. James Oppenheim. BAP; LEAP; TrJP
Handful of moss from the woodside, A. The Pine Tree. *Unknown.* PEOR
Handful of old men walking down the village street, A. Memorial Day. Theodosia Garrison. DD; MPB; OHIP; PEDC
Handfuls. Carl Sandburg. NP
Handle a large kingdom with as gentle a touch as if you were cooking a small fish. A Gentle Touch. *Unknown, at. to* Lao-tzu. *Fr.* Tao Teh King. OnPM
Hands. Dorothy Aldis. SUS
Hands. Earle Birney. BoCaPo (1943 ed.); TwCV
Hands. Frederick Cloud. LaNeLa
Hands. Geoffrey Dearmer. AlDL
Hands, The. Anthony Euwer. *Fr.* The Limeratomy. HBMV; TSWC
Hands. W. W. Gibson. PFE; PoMa; VOD
Hands. Margaret Lathrop Law. PoMa
Hands, The. Denise Levertov. NeAP
Hands. William Morris. BPN
Hands. Louis Untermeyer. AnAmPo; LA
Hands-across-the-Sea Poem, The. J. C. Squire. HBMV
Hands All Round. Tennyson. BPN; PoFr, *orig. vers.*
Hands of beggars peddle cigarets, The. Cante Hondo. Ellen de Young Kay. NePoEA
Hands of Christ, The. Leslie Savage Clark. ChIP; MaRV
Hands of Christ. Francisco E. Estrello, *tr. fr. Spanish by* H. M. Sein. ChIP
Hands of Christ, The. His Hands. John Richard Moreland. ChIP; DDA; MaRV; OQP; QP-1
Hands of the King are soft and fair, The. The Way of the World. James Jeffrey Roche. CAW; ChIP; JKCP; WBLP
Hands on a Card-Table. Polly Chase Boyden. NP
Hands they were made to assist, The. The Hands. Anthony Euwer. *Fr.* The Limeratomy. HBMV; TSWC
Hands Thrust in Pockets. Tefcros Anthias, *tr. fr. Modern Greek by* Rae Dalven. MoGP
Handsel Ring, The. George Houghton. AA
Handsome? I hardly know. Her profile's fine. A Countrywoman of Mine. Elaine Goodale Eastman. AA; OBAV
Handsome Knight, The. Mu'tamid, King of Seville, *tr. fr. Arabic by* A. J. Arberry. MooP
Handsome Young Airman, The. *Unknown.* *See* Dying Airman, The.
Handsome young gent down in Fla., A. *Unknown.* SiTL
Handsome young noble of Spain, A. *Unknown.* GoTP
Handwriting on the Wall, The. Knowles Shaw. BLPA
Handy Andy, *sel.* Samuel Lover.
Widow Machree. HBV; LPS-1; TIP; VA
Handy dandy. *Unknown.* OxNR
Handy high and handy low. So Handy. *Unknown.* ShS
Handy ship, and a handy crew, A. Hand over Hand. *Unknown.* SG
Handy Spandy, Jack-a-dandy. Mother Goose. GaP; OTPC; PCH; RIS
Hang a small bugle cap on, as big as a crown. The Beau's Receipt for a Lady's Dress. *Unknown.* CoMu
Hang at my hand as I write now. Verses for a First Birthday. George Barker. *Fr.* Second Cycle of Love Poems. MoAB; MoBrPo (1950 ed.)
Hang it all, Ezra Pound, there is only the one sestina! Sestina. Donald Hall. NePoEA
Hang it all, Robert Browning. Canto II. Ezra Pound. AmPP (4th ed.); AtBAP; CoBMV; MoAB; NePA; OxBA
Hang Me among Your Winds. Lew Sarett. MaRV
Hang Out the Flags. James S. Tippett. SiSoSe
Hang sorrow, cast away care. Song. *Unknown.* OBS
Hang to Your Grit! Louis E. Thayer. *Fr.* Keep Your Grit. WBLP
Hang Up His Harp; He'll Wake No More. Eliza Cook. BMEP
Hang Up the Baby's Stocking. *Unknown.* *See* First Christmas, The.
Hang up those dull and envious fools. In Defense of Their Inconstancy. Ben Jonson. ReEn
Hange golden sleepe uppon hir eye-lids faire. *Unknown.* SeCSL
Hanging, The. J. E. H. MacDonald. BoCaPo (1943 ed.)
Hanging bridge is lost in wandering mist, The. The Ravine of the Flowering Peach Tree. Chang Hsu. WhP
Hanging from the beam. The Portent. Herman Melville. AmPP; ExPo; OxBA; PoEL-5; PoFS
Hanging Johnny. *Unknown.* AmSS, *with music;* SG; ShS, *with music;* SoAmSa, *with music*
Hanging Limb, The. *Unknown.* IHA
Hanging of the Crane, The. Longfellow. IAP
Sels.
Household Sovereign, *fr.* Pt. III. LPS-1
New Household, A, *fr.* Pt. I. GN
Hanging Out the Linen Clothes, *with music.* *Unknown.* AS
Hanging raindrops, The. The Monk Jakuren, *tr. fr. Japanese by* Kenneth Rexroth. OnPJ
Hangman, *with music.* *Unknown.* AS
Hangman at Home, The. Carl Sandburg. ChMo; CMP
Hangman, hangman, slack up on your rope. Sweetheart, sweetheart can you give me any hope. Hangman. *Unknown.* AS
"Hangman, hangman, slack up your rope, O slack it for a while." The Hangman's Song. *Unknown.* ABS
Hangman's Tree [*or* Song], The. *Unknown.* *See* Maid Freed from the Gallows, The.
Hangover. Philip H. Rhinelander. WhC
Hangsaman. *Unknown.* *See* Maid Freed from the Gallows, The.
Hannah Bantry, in the pantry. *Unknown.* OxNR; RIS; SiTL

Hannah Binding Shoes. Lucy Larcom. GN; HBV
Hannah offering her first-born. Lycosa the Spider. Annie Charlotte Dalton. BoCaPo (1943 ed.)
Hannah's Song of Thanksgiving. First Samuel, Bible, *O.T.* *See* Song of Hannah, The.
Hannibal and Scipio, *sel.* Thomas Nabbes.
"Beauty no more the subject be." TuPP
(Song.) SeCL
Hanrahan and Cathleen the Daughter of Hoolihan, *sel.* W. B. Yeats.
Red Hanrahan's Song about Ireland. BEL; ChMo; CMP; FaBoCh; FaBoMo; GTIV; LoGBV; OnYI; OxBI
Hans Breitmann's Party [*or* Barty]. Charles Godfrey Leland. BOHV; CenHV; HBV; LEAP; LHV; LPS-3
Hans Christian Andersen. Sir Edmund Gosse. VA
Hansel and Gretel, *sel.* Adelheid Wette, *tr. fr. German.*
Witch's Ride, The. PCH
Hansom Cabbies. Wilfrid Thorley. HBMV
Han'som stranger? Yes, she's purty an' ez peart ez she kin be. The Engineer's Story. Eugene J. Hall. PTA-2
Han'some night, with the trees snow-white, A. The Second Settler's Story. Will Carleton. IHA
Hap. Thomas Hardy. AWP; ChMo; CMP; CoBMV; EmBrPo; EnLi-2 (1949 ed.); InPo; JAWP; MoBrPo; OAEP (2d ed.); PeBoSo; PoE; PoLFOT; ViPo; ViPP; WBP
Hapless Doom of Woman. Tennyson. *Fr.* Queen Mary. VLEP
(Low, Lute, Low!) BPN
Hapless lover's heart is of his wooing weary, The. The Mock Caliph. *Unknown. Fr.* The Thousand and One Nights. EnLi-1
Haply you dally. Compliment. Ibn al-Haddad. MooP
Happened like this: it was hot as hell. The Death of the Craneman. Alfred Hayes. LiTA; NAMP; WaP
Happened that the moon was up before I went to bed. Mockery. Katherine Dixon Riggs. BrR; MPB; RAR; SP
Happening. Edwin Honig. NePA
Happier, I would surely be. The Unfortunate Male. Kalonymos ben Kalonymos. *Fr.* The Touchstone. TrJP
Happier than green-kirtled apple-trees. Forgetfulness. Maxwell Bodenheim. MAPA
Happiest Day, the Happiest Hour, The. Poe. AmPP (4th ed.); NePA; OxBA
(Happiest Day, The.) GTBS-W; LiTA
Happiest Heart, The. John Vance Cheney. AA; AnAmPo; AnFE; APA; BAP; CoAnAm; HBV; HBVY; LA; LBMV; LEAP; MaRV; OBAV; OQP; PoMa; POT; QP-1; TreFS; WGRP
Happiest life that here we have, The. To Master Henry Cobham of the Most Blessed State of Life. Barnabe Googe. SiCE
Happiest Mortals Once Were We, The. George Granville. SeCL
(Song: "Happiest mortals once were we, The.") ElSeCe
(Song: To Myra.) CEP
Happiness. Katherine Beeman. BLP
Happiness. Grethe Heltberg, *tr. fr. Danish by* Charles W. Stork. BoDS
Happiness. Horace, *par. by* Dryden. *See* Happy the Man.
Happiness. Priscilla Leonard. BLPA; NeHB; PoToHe (new ed.)
Happiness. Mikhail Lvovich Matusovsky, *tr. fr. Russian by* Babette Deutsch. TrRV
Happiness. A. A. Milne. TiPo
Happiness. Pope. *Fr.* An Essay on Man, Epistle IV. LPS-3
("Oh Happiness! our being's end and aim.") ATP; LEAP
Happiness. Carl Sandburg. OxBA; WoL
Happiness. Arschag Tchobanian, *tr. fr. Armenian by* Zabelle C. Boyajian. ArmLP
Happiness amidst Troubles. Immanuel di Roma, *tr. fr. Italian by* Joseph Chotzner. TrJP
Happiness an Art. Edward Young. *Fr.* Night Thoughts, VIII. OBEC
Happiness Betrays Me. Helen Hoyt. NP
Happiness Dependent on Ourselves. Goldsmith. *Fr.* The Traveller. OBEC
Happiness Found, *sel.* Augustus M. Toplady.
"Lord, it is not Life to live." MaRV; OxBoCh; TrPWD
Happiness, happiness! blessed night! and bless you. Propertius. Elegies, II, 15. LaP
Happiness is like a crystal. Happiness. Priscilla Leonard. BLPA; NeHB; PoToHe (new ed.)
Happiness Makes Up in Height for What It Lacks in Length. Robert Frost. MoAB; MoAmPo; MoPo
Happy are men who yet before they are killed. Insensibility. Wilfred Owen. BrBE; ChMP; CoEV; ExPo; FaBoTw; GTBS-W; LiTB; LiTM; MoAB; OAEP (2d ed.); SeCeV; WaP
Happy are they and charmed in life. Memorials on [*or* On] the Slain at Chickamauga. Herman Melville. AA; APW; MDAH
Happy are they who die for a temporal land. Charles Péguy. *Fr.* Eve. MiFP
Happy are those who can relieve. Sir Herbert Read. *Fr.* Ode: Written during the Battle of Dunkirk, May, 1940. MaRV; QS
Happy Are Those Who Have Died. Charles Péguy, *tr. fr. French by* Jessie Degen *and* Richard Eberhart. *Fr.* Eve. WaaP
("Happy are they who die for a temporal land," *longer sel., tr. by* Pansy Packenham.) MiFP
Happy art thou if thou can'st call thine own. William Mason. *Fr.* The English Garden. EnSW
Happy as a King. "Gabriel Setoun." TVSH
Happy as Ulysses, his voyage done. Sonnet. Joachim du Bellay. *Fr.* Regrets. FoS
Happy Beggarman, The. *Unknown.* OnYI
Happy Birds. Sarah Jane S. Harrington. RAR
Happy bit hame this auld world would be, A. We Are Brethren A'. Robert Nicoll. HBV; LPS-1
Happy Bounding Flea, The. Roland Young. *See* Flea, The.
Happy boy, happy boy. Youth in Arms. Harold Monro. BMEP; LEAP; NP
Happy Britannia. James Thomson. *Fr.* The Seasons: Summer. OBEC; SeCePo
Happy Change, The. William Cowper. EiPP
(Olney Hymns.) CEP
Happy Child, The. W. H. Davies. AtBAP; POTE
Happy Child, A. Kate Greenaway. BoTP; OTPC; PPL
Happy choristers of air [*or* aire]. A Pastoral[l] Hymn[e]. John Hall. EG; MeLP; NBE; OBS; OxBoCh; SeCL; TriL; TrPWD
Happy Christmas, A. Frances Ridley Havergal. BLRP
Happy Christmases, *sels.* John Francis O'Donnell. IrPN
"Down looked the moon, but looked no more."
"In the December weather, grey and grim."
" 'Twas summer time, the radiant world of June."
Happy Countryman, The. Nicholas Breton. *See* Merry Country Lad, The.
Happy creature is your snail indeed, A! Philemon, *tr. fr. Greek by* F. A. Paley. GrPo
Happy day at Whitsuntide, A. The Castle Ruins. William Barnes. VA
Happy Death. John Freeman. HBMV
Happy Ending. W. H. Auden. TwHP
(Silly Fool, The.) OBMV
Happy Ending. Harry Silleck Grannatt. StaSt
Happy eve, happy eve! A Mother's Song. Sydney Dobell. BOL
Happy Farmer, The. Tse Nan, *tr. fr. Chinese by* Henry H. Hart. OnPM; PoHN
Happy Farmer, The. *Unknown.* GoTP
Happy father thou, when sturdy sons, A. A Daughter's Love. William Dudley Foulke. FAOV
Happy grave, thou dost enshrine. An Epitaph on Mistress Mary Prideaux. *At. to* George Morley. SeCL
Happy, Happy Country Swains. *Unknown.* SeCL
Happy, happy little birds. Happy Birds. Sarah Jane S. Harrington. RAR
Happy Harvesters, The, *sels.* Charles Sangster.
Autumn Change, An. BoCaPo
Soldiers of the Plough, The. BoCaPo (1943 ed.)
Happy He. *Unknown.* ElL
Happy, he heard the crass brass band. Willy Smith at the Ball Game. George Sterling. BAP
Happy he who, in his home at night. The Love of Books. James R. Clemens. PIAE
Happy He with Such a Mother. Tennyson. *Fr.* The Princess, Pt. VII. PSO
("I loved her, one/ Not learned, save in gracious household ways.") PGD
Happy Heart, The. Thomas Dekker, *and others. Fr.* The Pleasant Comedy of Patient Grissell, I, i. GTBS; GTBS-D; GTBS-W; GTSE; GTSL; HBV; LEAP; LPS-2; WoL
(Art Thou Poor?) TOP; ViBoPo
("Art thou poor, yet hast thou golden slumbers?") EG; ElSeCe; OAEP; SiCE; TCEP; TuPP
(Basket-Maker's Song, The.) CenL; OBSC; ThWaDe; TrGrPo
(Content.) BBV (1923 ed.); CBE; EnLi-1; EPP
(O Sweet Content.) AtBAP; BEL; BLV; CBOV; EV-2; ShBV-2
(Sweet Content.) CH; ElL; EnLit; LoBV; OBEV; OtMeF; PG; TVSH; WHA
Happy Hour, The. Mary Frances Butts. DD; MOAH
Happy Hour. The. Sylvia Lynd. LO
Happy Husbandman, The; or, Country Innocence. *Unknown.* CoMu
Happy Hyena, The. Carolyn Wells. *See* Limerick: "There once was a happy hyena."
Happy insect! ever blest. A Soliloquy. Walter Harte. LPS-2
Happy Insect! what can be. The Grasshopper. Abraham Cowley, *after* Anacreon. AWP; CG; EnLi-1; EPS;

Happy Insect (*continued*)
EV-2; GoTP; GrPo; HBV; HBVY; JAWP; LPS-2; OTPC (1923 ed.); SeCV-1; WBP
Happy Insensibility. Keats. *See* Stanzas: "In a drear-nighted December."
Happy Is England! I Could Be Content. Keats. ERP; EV-4
Happy Is He. Leonora Speyer. BLA
Happy is he/ Who for himself winneth. *Unknown. Fr.* The Elder Edda: The Hava-Mal. BoFr
Happy is he returning from abroad. The Artificer. Ewart Milne. PoN
Happy is he that owns ancestral lands. The Old Man near Verona Who Never Left His Farm. Ausonius. LaP
Happy is he who journeys everywhere. Returning Home. Joachim du Bellay. LiTW
Happy is he who lies awake. Happy Is He. Leonora Speyer. BLA
"Happy is he who lives to understand." Despondency Corrected. Wordsworth. *Fr.* The Excursion, IV. ERP
Happy Is the Country Life. *Unknown.* OBS
Happy Is the Man. Psalms, I, Bible, *O.T.* TrJP
Happy Is the Man That Findeth Wisdom. Proverbs, III, Bible, *O.T.* TreF (11–18); TrJP (13–18)
Happy is the man who loves the woods and waters. Beatus Vir. Richard Le Gallienne. HBMV; OHIP; PoTo
Happy is the man whom Thou hast set apart. Psalm. "Yehoash." TrJP
Happy Islands, The. Isabel Maud Peacocke. BoAu
Happy Isle, The. Spenser. *Fr.* The Faerie Queene, IV, 10. OBSC
Happy Life, The. Martial. *See* Means to Attain a Happy Life, The.
Happy Life, The, *sel.* William Thompson.
"Book, A, a friend, a song, a glass." ViBoPo
Happy Life, The. Sir Henry Wotton. *See* Character of a Happy Life, The.
Happy Lifetime to You. Franklin P. Adams. InMe
Happy lover who has come, A. In Memoriam A. H. H., VIII. Tennyson. EmBrPo; EnLi-2; EPN; GEPC; ViPo; VLEP
Happy Man, The. William Cowper. *Fr.* The Task, VI. LPS-3
("He is the happy man, whose life ev'n now.") BrBE
Happy Man, The. Gilles Ménage. BOHV
Happy Man, A. E. A. Robinson, *after the Greek of* Carphyllides. AWP; JAWP; LiTW; WBP
(Variations of Greek Themes, 1.) MOAP
Happy Martyrdom. Pierre de Ronsard, *tr. fr. French by* Alan Conder. TrFP
Happy Mean, The. Rufinus, *tr. fr. Greek by* F. L. Lucas. GrPE
Happy men that lose their heads, The. Fantasia. G. K. Chesterton. HBMV
Happy Miner, The. *Unknown.* CoSo; CSF; IHA, *abr.*
Happy mortal, who these treasures share, The. The Island of the Blest. Pindar. *Fr.* Olympic Odes, II. OBEC
Happy mother stalk of corn, A. Baby Corn. Lydia Avery Coonley Ward. GFA; PRWS
Happy Myrtillo. Henry Carey. SeCePo
Happy Night, The. J. C. Squire. BMEP; HBMV
Happy night and happy silence downward softly stealing. Hymn for the Nativity. Edward Thring. COAH
Happy Old Man, A. Liu Tzu Hui, *tr. fr. Chinese by* Henry H. Hart. PoHN
Happy on earth he was—the happiest. An Old Gentleman of Seventy-seven. *Unknown. Fr.* Carmina Epigraphica. LaP
Happy Oxen in a Stall. Annette Wynne. ChrBoLe
Happy Pair, The, *sel.* Sir Charles Sedley.
"Man, like the sordid earth, from which he sprung." BeR
Happy people die whole, they are all dissolved in a moment. Post Mortem. Robinson Jeffers. MAP; MoAmPo; MoPo; TrGrPo
Happy Piper, The. Blake. *See* Piping down the Valleys Wild.
Happy Regret. Tu Mu, *tr. fr. Chinese.* WhP
Happy road that brought me here, The Shankill. Eileen Shanahan. NeIP
Happy Sheep, The. Wilfrid Thorley. GFA; PCH
Happy Song-sparrow, that on woodland side. The Fringilla Melodia. Henry Beck Hirst. AA
Happy Songs. Blake. *See* Piping down the Valleys Wild.
Happy Swain, The. Ambrose Philips. EnLoPo
Happy that company who are intoxicated with each other's speech. Cliques and Critics. Sa'ib of Isfahan. LiTW
Happy that easy-tempered bard I call. Nikolai Nekrasov, *tr. fr. Russian by* J. S. Phillimore. BoRS
Happy that first white age when we. Metrum V. Henry Vaughan. EPS
Happy the animals! they do not bother. Philemon, *tr. fr. Greek by* F. A. Paley. GrPo
Happy the feeling from the bosom thrown. Sonnet: To ——. Wordsworth. ChER
Happy the hare at morning, for she cannot read. The Cultural Presupposition [*or* Culture]. W. H. Auden. MaPo; MoPW; TwHP
Happy the Man. Horace, *par. fr. Latin by* Dryden. *Fr.* Odes, III, 29. MaRV
(Happiness, 4 *ll.*) TreF
(To Maecenas, *longer sel.*) PoFr
(Today and Tomorrow, 4 *ll.*) GoTP
Happy the Man. Pope. *See* Ode on Solitude.
Happy the man, and happy he alone. Happy the Man [*or* Imitation of Horace *or* To Maecenas]. Horace, *par. by* Dryden. *Fr.* Odes, III, 29. GoTP; MaRV; PoFr; TreF
Happy the man, who his whole time doth bound. The Old Man of Verona. Claudian, *tr. by* Abraham Cowley. AWP; JAWP; LyMA; WBP; WoL
Happy the man, who on the mountain-side. After Reading Homer. Digby Mackworth Dolben. GoBC
Happy the man who, safe on shore. The Hurricane. Philip Freneau. AmPP (4th ed.); CoBA
Happy the man who so hath Fortune tried. Of Temperance in Fortune. Richard Watson Dixon. *Fr.* Mano; a Poetical History. VA
Happy the man who, void of cares and strife. The Splendid Shilling; an Imitation of Milton. John Philips. BOHV; CEP; EiPP; LPS-3
Happy the man, whose wish and care. Ode on Solitude [*or* Ode to Solitude *or* Solitude *or* The Quiet Life *or* The Contented Man *or* Happy the Man]. Pope. ALV; ATP; AWP; BLV; BoLiVe; BPP; CEP; EG; EV-3; ExPo; FaFP; FiP; GoBC; GTBS; GTBS-D; GTBS-W; GTSE; GTSL; HBV; HBVY; InMe; InPo; InvP; JAWP; LPS-1; MaRV; MCCG; NeHB; OAEP; OBEC; OnPP; OTPC (1923 ed.); PECK; PG (1955 ed.); PoE; PoFS; PoRA; PoToHe; SeCeV; SeCL; SN; TreFS; TrGrPo; ViBoPo; WBP; WP
Happy the moment when we are seated in the palace, thou and I. Thou and I. Jalal ed-Din Rumi. BoFr
Happy the nations of the moral North! Donna Julia. Byron. Fr. Don Juan. PoEL-4
Happy the poets who fell in magnificent ways! For Poets Slain in War. Walter Adolphe Roberts. BAP
Happy the singer. Carsten Hauch. *Fr.* Confession. BoDS
Happy the stark bare wood on the hill of Bree! The Triad of Things Not Decreed. Alice Furlong. AnIV
Happy they who die for the earth which also dies. Happy Are Those Who Have Died. Charles Péguy. WaaP
Happy think a lifetime a short stage, The. Time as Variable. Lucian. OnPM
Happy those early days [*or* dayes], when I. The Retreat[e]. Henry Vaughan. AtBAP; ATP; AWP; BCEP; BEL; BLV; BoLiVe; CaAE; CAW; CBOV; CenL; CoBE; CoEV; EG; EM-1; EnL; EnLi-1; EnLit; EOAH; EPP; EPS; EV-2; ExPo; FaBoEn; GTBS; GTBS-D; GTBS-W; GTSE; GTSL; HBV; InPo; InvP; JAWP; LEAP; LiTB; LiTG; LO; LoBV; MaPo; MeLP; MePo; OAEP; OBEV; OBS; PoEL-2; PoFS; PoP; PoRA; PreP; ReEn; RiBV; SeCePo; SeCeV; SeCL; SeCV-1; SeEP; TCEP; TOP; TrGrPo; TwCrTr; TwHP; TyEnPo; UnPo (1st ed.); UnW; ViBoPo; WBP; WHA
Happy Thought. Gertrude Pahlow. DDA
Happy Thought. Robert Louis Stevenson. BoTP; FaBoBe; HBV; HBVY; InP; LEAP; MeMeAg; OTPC; PoVP; RIS; SAS; TiPo; TreFS; VLEP
Happy Thought. Bert Leston Taylor. RIS
Happy Thought for Some Struggling Nation. Morrie Ryskind. PIAE
Happy, thrice happy now the savage race. Charles Churchill. *Fr.* Gotham. PoFr
Happy, thrice happy times in silver age! Desiderium. Phineas Fletcher. *Fr.* The Purple Island, I. OBS
Happy Time, A. *Unknown. See* Limerick: "There was a young fellow named Hall."
Happy Townland, The. W. B. Yeats. ThWaDe
Happy Tree, The. Gerald Gould. MBP; MoBrPo (1942 ed.); WGRP
Happy Ulysses, The. Joachim du Bellay, *tr. by* G. K. Chesterton. *See* Heureux qui, comme Ulysse, a fait un beau voyage.
Happy Vale of Tormes. *Unknown, tr. fr. Spanish by* James Young Gibson. TeCS
Happy Valley, The. Páll Ólafsson, *tr. fr. Icelandic by* Watson Kirkconnell. IcP
Happy View, A. C. Day Lewis. ChMo
Happy Wanderer, The. Percy Addleshaw. OBVV; VA
Happy Warrior, The. Wordsworth. *See* Character of the Happy Warrior.
Happy was I. Jalal ed-Din Rumi, *tr. fr. Persian by* A. J. Arberry. PeP
Happy Were He. Earl of Essex. ElL
(Content.) OBSC; RiBV
("Happy were he could finish forth his fate.") CenL
(Passion, A.) ElSeCe; TuPP
(Wish, A.) GTSL
Happy, who like Ulysses or that lord. Heureux qui, comme Ulysse, a fait un beau voyage [*or* The Happy Ulysses *or*

Translation from Du Bellay]. Joachim du Bellay, *tr. by* G. K. Chesterton. *Fr.* Regrets. AWP; InP; WoL
Happy Wind. W. H. Davies. NLK; OTPC (1946 ed.); PCH; RIS; StaSt; TSW; TSWC
Happy Woman, A. Agathias, *tr. fr. Greek by* Lord Neaves. OnPM
Happy World, The. William Brighty Rands. MeMeAg; OTPC (1946 ed.); PCH; PPL
(Brown Bee.) StVeCh (1940 ed.)
Happy ye leaves! when as those lily [*or* lilly] hands. Amoretti, I. Spenser. ATP; BEL; CoBE; EnLi-1; EnLit; ES; LoBV; PeBoSo; Po; ReEn; ReIE; SiCE
Happy: yea, happy for ever and aye! Fulfilment. Louis V. Ledoux. HBMV
Harangue on the Death of Hayyim Nahman [*or* Chayim Nachman] Bialik. César Tiempo, *tr. fr. Spanish by* Donald Devenish Walsh. AnCL; TrJP
Harbingers are come, The. See, see their mark. The Forerunners. George Herbert. MePo; MeRV; ReEn
Harbor [*or* Harbour], The. Winifred M. Letts. PoMa; VOD
Harbor, The. Carl Sandburg. CoBA; NP; PreP
Harbor Dawn, The. Hart Crane. *Fr.* The Bridge: Powhatan's Daughter. AmP; CoV; LiTA; MoPo; NePA; OxBA
Harbor in a sunny, southern city, A. Columbus. Helen L. Smith. PTA-2
Harbor Music. Edward Thompson. MM
Harbor View. Frances Taylor Patterson. NeTW
Harbor Water. Beatrice Ravenel. Tidewater, II. LS
Harbury. Louise Driscoll. BAP; LEAP; POT; PoTo; SBMV
Hard above all things mortal is. Love's Fragility. Alan Porter. POTE
Hard aport! Now close to shore sail! Adrian Block's Song. Edward Everett Hale. PAH
Hard as hurdle arms, with a broth of goldish flue. Harry Ploughman. Gerard Manley Hopkins. BrBE; EmBrPo; FaBoMo
Hard blue winds of March, The. The Three Winds. Laurie Lee. FaBoMo
Hard by a Crystal Fountain. Thomas Morley. ReIE
Hard by the Indian lodges, where the bush. The Corn Husker. Pauline Johnson. CaP; OCL
Hard by the lilied Nile I saw. A Crocodile. Thomas Lovell Beddoes. *Fr.* The Last Man. AnFE; NBE
Hard Daddy. Langston Hughes. BANP
Hard from the southeast blows the wind. Elizabeth J. Coatsworth. TiPo (1952 ed.)
Hard Frost, A. C. Day Lewis. HaMV
Hard Frost. Andrew Young. MoVE
Hard harted faire, if thou wilt not consent. *Unknown.* SeCSL
Hard is the stone, but harder still. The Image-Maker. Oliver St. John Gogarty. OBEV (new ed.); OBMV; PoRA
Hard is yon rock, around whose head. Sonnet. Fernando de Herrera. AnSpL-1
Hard it is that impious men, of base forebears. Sophocles, *tr. fr. Greek by* Moses Hadas. GrPo
Hard it is to be a fowler. The Fowler. "Eduard Bagritsky." BoRS
Hard it is, very hard. The Choice of the Cross. Dorothy L. Sayers. *Fr.* The Devil to Pay. MaRV
Hard it is wholly to win worthy manhood. Human Imperfection. Simonides. GrL; OxBG
Hard jailor who chains Peter, you shall know. Vincula Sponte Decidunt. Richard Crashaw. Epigrammata Sacra, I, 31. LaP
Hard Journey, The. Jules Supervielle, *tr. fr. French by* Alan Conder. TrFP
Hard Lovers, The. George Dillon. AnAmPo; LA; TCPD
Hard Luck. Langston Hughes. NP
Hard north-easter fifty winters long, A. In Fisherrow. W. E. Henley. VOD
Hard on a high flower comes the sun. The Energy of Light. John Hay. NePoAm-2
Hard on the high road side, midway between. Thomas Francis. *Fr.* The Offspring. EnSW
Hard pomegranate wide-open now. Pomegranates. Paul Valéry, *tr. by* Alan Conder. TrFP
Hard pomegranates split wide. Pomegranates. Paul Valéry, *tr. by* Herman Salinger. LiTW
Hard pomegranates sundered. Pomegranates. Paul Valéry, *tr. by* Kate Flores. AnFP
Hard Rows to Hoe. Daniel Henderson. PaA
Hard sand breaks, The. Hermes of the Ways. Hilda Doolittle ("H. D."). LiTA; MM; MOAP; NP
Hard Times ("Come listen awhile"). *Unknown.* ABF; CSF
Hard Times in the Country, *with music.* *Unknown.* OuSiCo
Hard tin bird was my lover, A. Weathercock. Elizabeth Jennings. NePoEA
Hard to Be a Nigger. *Unknown.* ABF
Hard Trials, *with music.* *Unknown.* ABF
Hard Weather. George Meredith. EmBrPo; EPN; Po; POTT; TyEnPo; ViP; ViPP
Hard were the task, and shrewd the intent. Politics and Perquisites. Aristophanes. *Fr.* The Wasps. GrR
Hard Winter melts; the welcome Spring again. Spring. Horace. Odes, I, 4. RoL
Hard-working Miner, The, *with music.* *Unknown.* ABF
Hardcastle Crags. Sylvia Plath. CoYe
Harder Task, The. *Unknown.* BLRP; MaRV
Hardest headlands, The/ Gravel down. La Rose des Vents. Richard Wilbur. MiAP
Hardest It Is. F. R. Scott. BoCaPo (1943 ed.)
Harding Hill. Clinton Scollard. MuM
Hardly a shot from the gate we storm'd. Badminton. Sir Alfred Comyn Lyall. *Fr.* Studies at Delhi. OBVV
Hardly Think I Will, *with music.* *Unknown.* ABF
Hardness of her heart and truth of mine, The. Sir John Davies. Gulling Sonnets, IV. ElSeCe; TuPP
Hardship of Accounting, The. Robert Frost. FaBoCh; FaFP; LoGBV; WhC
Hare, The. Walter de la Mare. TiPo
Hare, The. Stanley Snaith. HaMV
Hare and Many Friends, The. John Gay. *See* Hare with Many Friends, The.
Hare Drummer. Edgar Lee Masters. *Fr.* Spoon River Anthology. TOP
Hare has only the hound to fear, The. Death. Arthur MacGillivray. JKCP (1955 ed.)
Hare-hunting. William Somervile. *Fr.* The Chace, II. OBEC
Hare with Many Friends, The. John Gay. EPP; HBV
(Hare and Many Friends, The.) ATP (1935 ed.); EnLi-1 (1949 ed.); EV-3
Harebells in June. Annette Wynne. SUS
Hark. John Webster. *See* Hark, Now Everything Is Still.
Hark! ah, the nightingale. Philomela. Matthew Arnold. AtBAP; BEL; BLA; BLV; BMEP; BoLiVe; BPN; CBOV; EM-2; EmBrPo; EnL; EnLi-2; EnLit; EPP; GEPC; GTBS; GTBS-D; GTSE; GTSL; HBV; InP; LPS-2; MaPo; MCCG; OAEP; OBEV; PIR; PoFS; PoVP; PreP; ReaPo; SeCeV; SN; TCEP; TOP; TwCrTr; TyEnPo; UnPo (1st ed.); VA; ViPo; ViPP; VLEP; WHA
Hark, All You Ladies That Do Sleep! Thomas Campion. OAEP; PoE; ReIE
(Hark, All You Ladies.) ElL; TuPP
(Harke, Al You Ladies That Do Sleep.) PoEL-2
(Proserpina.) OBSC
Hark, already the winter crows. Lament of the Organist of Notre-Dame de Nice. Jules Laforgue. AnFP
Hark, already you can hear the working song. Sonnets to Orpheus, Pt. II, XXV. Rainer Maria Rilke. OnPM
Hark at the lips of this pink whorl of shell. A Quatrain. Frank Dempster Sherman. AA
Hark, Celia, hark! but lay thou close thine ear. The Secret. *Unknown.* SeCL
Hark! do I hear again the roar. Columbus Dying. Edna Dean Proctor. MC; PAH
Hark! even here, into the chambers of the Palace. Even in the Palace. Nago Okimaro. OnPM
Hark! for the message cometh from the King! The Modern Rubaiyat. Kate Masterson. PA
Hark! from the dizzy heart of the forest come. A Little Music. Victor Hugo. TrFP
Hark! from yon covert, where those tow'ring oaks. Hare-hunting. William Somervile. *Fr.* The Chace, II. OBEC
Hark, girl! There's some one knocking at the door. Herodas, *tr. fr. Greek by* Hugo Sharpley. GrPo
Hark, happy lovers, hark! A Kiss. William Drummond of Hawthornden. ElL
Hark! Hark! Leonora Speyer. BAP; NLK (1947 ed.)
Hark Hark. *Unknown.* Po
Hark! hark! down the century's long reaching slope. Yorktown Centennial Lyric. Paul Hamilton Hayne. PAH
Hark hark how Bellona thunders. *Unknown.* SeCSL
Hark, hark, I hear the North Wind roar. Winter. Charles Cotton. BrBE
Hark, hark, I hear the trumpet sound; it calleth me to come away. The Seaman's Reply. *Unknown.* SG
Hark, hark! the advent cry again. The Prince of Peace. Edward Henry Bickersteth. BePJ
Hark! hark! The dogs do bark. Mother Goose. BoChLi; GaP; HBVY; OTPC; OxNR; PCH; Po; RIS; SiTL; TiPo
Hark! Hark! the Lark. Shakespeare. *Fr.* Cymbeline, II, iii. AnFE; AtBAP; ATP; BEL; BoTP; CBOV; CH; ChTr; CoBE; ElSeCe; EM-1; EnL; EnLi-1 (1949 ed.); EnLit; EPP; ExPo; FaBoCh; FaFP; FaPON; HBV; InP; InPo; KN; LiTB; LiTG; LoBV; LoGBV; LPS-2; OTPC; OuHeWo; PFE; PIR; PTA-2; ReaPo; SeCeV; SiCE; TCEP; TOP; TreF; TrGrPo; TVSH; TyEnPo; ViBoPo; WHA
(Aubade.) BCEP; OBEV; ShBV-3
(Morning Song, A.) BLV; EV-1; GN; PCH
(Morning Song for Imogen, A.) AnEnPo
(Morning Song from "Cymbeline.") PIAE
(Song: "Hark, hark, the lark at heaven's gate sings.")

Hark! Hark! the Lark (*continued*)
CaAE; ElL; FiP; REAL
(Song from "Cymbeline.") BLA; CBE
(Song of the Musicians.) BoLiVe
(Song to Imogen.) EG; OBSC
(Songs from "Cymbeline.") LEAP
(Songs from the Plays.) AWP; JAWP; WBP
(Three Songs.) UnPo (1st ed.)
Hark! hark! the merry warder's horn. A Hawking Party in the Olden Time. Mary Howitt. OTPC (1923 ed.)
Hark! hark! to the wind! 'Tis the night, they say. Hallowe'en. Virna Sheard. DD
Hark, hearer, hear what I do. Epithalamion. Gerard Manley Hopkins. AnEnPo
Hark! how all the welkin rings. For Christmas-Day. Charles Wesley. CEP
Hark, how chimes the Passing Bell. The Passing Bell. James Shirley. ACP
Hark, how my Celia, with the choice. Celia Singing. Thomas Carew. OAEP
Hark, how the birds do sing. Man's Medley. George Herbert. ViBoPo
Hark how the Duke of Lorraine comes. The Victory in Hungary. Thomas Shadwell. *Fr.* The Squire of Alsatia. SeCL
Hark how the fir-trees in dismal tones. Verner von Heidenstam. *Fr.* The Forest of Tiveden. AnSL
Hark how the Lyrick Choristers o' th' wood. To Clarestella on St. Valentines Day Morning. Robert Heath. OBS
Hark how the minstrels gin to shrill aloud. Spenser. *Fr.* Epithalamion. WHA
Hark how the passing bell. Upon a Passing Bell. Thomas Washbourne. SeCL
Hark, I hear the bells of Westgate. Westgate-on-Sea. John Betjeman. OxBoLi
Hark I hear the cannons roar. A Carrouse to the Emperor, the Royal Pole, and the Much-wronged Duke of Lorrain. *Unknown.* CoMu
Hark! I hear the tramp of thousands. The Reveille. Bret Harte. BlG; EV-5; GN; HBV; LH; MC; OHIP; OtMeF; OTPC (1946 ed.); PaA; PAH; PoRL; TVSH
Hark! in the still night. Who goes there? Sixteen Dead Men. Dora Sigerson Shorter. ACP; OnYI
Hark! My Beloved! The Song of Solomon, II: 8–13, Bible, *O.T.* TrJP
Hark, My Soul. John Austin. OxBoCh
Hark, My Soul! It Is the Lord. William Cowper. *See* Lovest Thou Me?
Hark [*or* Hearke], Now Everything Is Still. John Webster. *Fr.* The Duchess of Malfi, IV, ii. BEL; BrBE; CenL; ElL; EV-2; LoBV; OBS; ReaPo; SeCePo; SiCE; TriL; TuPP; ViBoPo
(Dirge: "Hark, now everything is still.") EnLi-1
(General Mist of Error, A.) OnPM
(Hark.) CH
(Shrouding of the Duchess of Malfi, The.) BCEP; CoEV; OBEV
(Summons to Execution.) FaBoEn
Hark! of a matchless vision would I speak. The Dream of the Rood. *Unknown.* StJW
Hark! on the wind that whistles from the West. Clouds in the West. Augustus Julian Requier. BlG
Hark! one saith: "Proclaim!" All Flesh Is Grass. Isaiah, Bible, *O.T.* TrJP
Hark, Reader! wilt be learn'd i' th' wars? To My Truly Valiant, Learned Friend, Who in His Book Resolv'd the Art Gladiatory into the Mathematics. Richard Lovelace. PoEL-3
Hark! she is called [*or* call'd], the parting hour [*or* houre] is come. On [*or* In] the Glorious Assumption of Our Blessed Lady [*or* On the Assumption of the Virgin Mary]. Richard Crashaw. AEV; ElSeCe; ISi; LoBV; OBS; PoLi
Hark! She is calling to her cat. The Cat. Richard Church. AlDL
Hark, some wild trumpeter, some strange musician. The Mystic Trumpeter. Walt Whitman. IAP; TCAP
Hark! 't is our Northern Nightingale that sings. The White-throated Sparrow. A. West. SN
Hark! 't is the voice of the mountain. The Battle of Eutaw. William Gilmore Simms. PAH
Hark, that quick darting snort! The Haunt of the Deer. Duncan MacIntyre. *Fr.* Ben Dorain. EBSV
Hark! the cock crows, and yon bright star. The New Year. Charles Cotton. CEP; GoTL; OBS
Hark! the faint bells of the sunken city. The Sunken City. Wilhelm Müller. LPS-3
Hark! the flow of the four rivers. Farewells from Paradise. Elizabeth Barrett Browning. OBEV (new ed.); OBVV
Hark! the glad sound! the Saviour comes. The Prince of Peace. Philip Doddridge. MaRV
Hark! the Herald Angels Sing. Charles Wesley. MaRV; OBEV; OlF; OTPC (1946 ed.), *st.* 1; PCH, *st.* 1; SDH; TreFS; YaCaBo, *with music*
(Christmas Day.) COAH
(Nativity, The.) BLRP
Hark the herald angels sing. On Dean Inge. Humbert Wolfe. ChTr
Hark! the Hoopoe's Call. Aristophanes. *See* Hoopoe's Call, The.
Hark! the Lambeth Guardians sing. Christmas Hymn for Lambeth. J. C. Squire. TCPD
Hark! the Mavis. Burns. *See* Ca' the Yowes to the Knowes.
Hark! the shrill cock, the rising morn proclaims. Moses Browne. *Fr.* The Nocturnal Eclogue. EnSW
Hark! the tiny cowslip bell. Spring Has Come. *Unknown.* BoTP
Hark! the Vesper Hymn Is Stealing. Thomas Moore. EnRP; ERP
Hark! the voice of love and mercy. It Is Finished. Jonathan Evans. BePJ
Hark! They cry! I hear by that. Yolp, Yolp, Yolp, Yolp. *Unknown.* ElL
Hark! 'tis Freedom that calls, come, patriots, awake! A Song. *Unknown.* PAH
Hark 'tis the bluebird's venturous strain. The Bluebird. Thomas Bailey Aldrich. *Fr.* Spring in New England. BLA; SN
Hark! 'tis the twanging horn! O'er yonder bridge. The Winter Evening [*or* The Postman]. William Cowper. The Task, IV. CoBE; CoEV; EiPP; EnLi-2; EnLit; EV-3; FiP; OAEP; SeCePo; TOP
Hark to a poor soul, all you who pass by. Lament at the Day's End. Jules Laforgue. MiFP
Hark to the cowbells, hark how the singing. Pastoral. Gustaf Fröding. AnSL
Hark to the merry birds, hark how they sing! Last Week of February (1890). Robert Bridges. POTT
Hark to the Roaring Sheep. *Unknown. See* Derby Ram, The.
Hark to the Shouting Wind. Henry Timrod. NLK
Hark to the shrill trumpet calling. The Soldier's Burial. Caroline Elizabeth Sarah Norton. PEOR
Hark to the story of poor Romeo! Romeo and Juliet. Fred Newton Scott. InMe
Hark to the story of Willie the Weeper. Willie the Weeper. *Unknown.* TrAS
Hark to the whimper of the sea-gull. The Sea-Gull. Ogden Nash. FaFP; LiTM; NePA; SiTL
Hark! . . What booming. Arcana Sylvarum. Charles De Kay. AA
Hark! what mean those holy voices. John Cawood. OlF
Hark what, now loud, now low, the pining flute complains. The Flute. Hilali. OnPM
Hark you such sound as quivers? Kings will hear. November. Mahlon Leonard Fisher. BAP; HBV; PFY
Hark! Young Democracy from sleep. Young Democracy. Bernard O'Dowd. BoAu
Harke, Al You Ladies That Do Sleep. Thomas Campion. *See* Hark, All You Ladies That Do Sleep!
Harke, harke, me thinkes I heer love saye. *Unknown.* SeCSL
Harke how the nightingale displayes. *Unknown.* SeCSL
Harke this lesson. *Unknown.* SeCSL
Harken all good men. A Little Sooth Sermon. *Unknown.* TMEV
Harken how the flute complains. Serenade. Clemens Brentano. AnGP
Harlaw. Sir Walter Scott. *Fr.* The Antiquary, *ch.* 40. BSV; EnLi-2
(Herring, The, *st.* 1.) BOHV
("Herring loves the merry moonlight, The.") FaBoCh; LoGBV
(Oyster, The, *st.* 1.) RIS
(Red Harlaw, The.) LH
Harlem. Jean Brierre, *tr. fr. French by* John F. Matheus. PoNe
Harlem Dancer, The. Claude McKay. BANP; MAP
Harlem Shadows. Claude McKay. BANP; PoNe
Harlem Sweeties. Langston Hughes. PoNe
Harlequin of Dreams, The. Sidney Lanier. AA; CoV; TCAP
Harley, the nation's great support. Horace, Epistle VII, Book I, Imitated. Swift. CEP
Harlots' Catch. Robert Nichols. FaBoTw
Harlot's House, The. Oscar Wilde. LEAP; MBP; MoBrPo; PIR; PoVP; ViPP
Harmless rabbit gambols with its young, The. Oscar Wilde. *Fr.* The Burden of Itys. VLEP
Harmodius and Aristogeiton. *Unknown, tr. fr. Greek by* Gilbert Highet *and* T. F. Higham. GrL; OxBG
Harmodius Song, The. Callistratus, *tr. fr. Greek by* J. M. Edmonds. GrR
Harmon Whitney. Edgar Lee Masters. *Fr.* Spoon River Anthology. SBMV
Harmonie du soir. Baudelaire, *tr. fr. French by* Lord Alfred Douglas. AWP; JAWP; WBP
Harmonious Heedlessness of Little Boy Blue, The. Guy Wetmore Carryl. MPB; PIAE; YT

(Little Boy Blue.) ALV; LauV; PFE
Harmonious Vision of the Earth, The. Paul Fort, *tr. fr. French by* Vernon Watkins. MiFP
Harmony. Thomas Grant Springer. PoToHe
Harmony of colours, features, grace, The. Epitaph on Lady Salter. Thomas Carew. MeRV
Harmony of the Church, The, *sels.* Michael Drayton. ReIE
Most Excellent Song Which Was Salomon's, The.
Song of Jonah in the Whale's Belly, The.
Harmosan. Richard Chenevix Trench. TVSH
Harness me down with your iron bands. The Song of Steam. George W. Cutter. LPS-2
Harnet and the Bittle, a Wiltshire Tale, The ("A harnet zet in a hollur tree"). J. Y. Akerman. ChTr
Harold at Two Years Old. Frederic W. H. Myers. HBMV
Harold Bates, who lives next door. Neighbors. "Lennox." InMe
Harold the Dauntless, *sel.* Sir Walter Scott.
'Tis Merry in Greenwood. ADAH; FaPON; MPB; OHIP
Harold the Valiant. Mary Elizabeth Hewitt Stebbins. AA
Harold's Song [to Rosabelle]. Sir Walter Scott. *See* Rosabelle.
Haroun Al-Rachid for Heart's-Life. *Unknown, tr. fr. Arabic by* E. Powys Mathers. *Fr.* The Thousand and One Nights. AWP
Haroun, the Caliph, through the sunlit street. Power. Thomas Stephens Collier. AA
Haroun's Favorite Song. *Unknown, tr. fr. Arabic by* E. Powys Mathers. *Fr.* The Thousand and One Nights. AWP
Harp, The. Thomas Moore. *See* Harp That Once through Tara's Halls, The.
Harp, The. Po Chü-i, *tr. fr. Chinese by* Ching Ti. WhP
Harp, The. Jakob Jóhannesson Smári, *tr. fr. Icelandic by* Watson Kirkconnell. IcP
"Harp and carp, Thomas!" she said. *Unknown. Fr.* Thomas the Rhymer. LO; LoPS
Harp at Nature's advent strung, The. The Worship of Nature. Whittier. GrCo-1
Harp in the Rigging. Hamish Maclaren. EtS
Harp Music. Rolfe Humphries. UnS
Harp of Alfred, The. G. K. Chesterton. *Fr.* The Ballad of the White Horse. MoVE
Harp of Alfred, The. Robert Ervin Howard. DaM
Harp of David, The. Jacob Cohen, *tr. fr. Hebrew by* Sholom J. Kahn. TrJP
Harp of David, The. "Yehoash," *tr. fr. Yiddish by* Alter Brody. TrJP
Harp of Sorrow, The. Ethel Clifford. HBV; WGRP
Harp of the land I love! forgive this hand. An Apology to the Harp. Thomas D'Arcy McGee. GTIV
Harp of the North. Sir Walter Scott. The Lady of the Lake: Prologue. BHV; EmBrPo; EnLi-2 (1949 ed.); ERP
(Chase, The.) EnRP
("Harp of the North! that mouldering long hast hung.") OAEP; ViBoPo
Harp of the North, Farewell. Sir Walter Scott. The Lady of the Lake: Epilogue. BPN; CoBE; EV-4
(Harp of the North.) BEL; EPN
("Harp of the North, farewell! The hills grow dark.") ViBoPo
Harp of the Wind, The. Frances Shaw. NP
Harp of Wild and Dream-Like Strain. Emily Brontë. VLEP
Harp Song of the Dane Women. Kipling. AtBAP; FaBoEn; OAEP (2d ed.); OtMeF; PoRA; POTE; SeCePo; ShBV-3; TwCV
Harp That Once through Tara's Halls, The. Thomas Moore. ACP; AnFE; AnIL; ATP (1935 ed.); BCEP; BEL; CaAE; CoBE; EnLi-2; EnLit; EnRP; EPN; EPP; ERP; EV-4; GN; GTIV; LiTG; LPS-2; NeHB; OAEP; OIF; OnYI; OxBI; PECK; PG; PIR; PoFr; PTA-2; TCEP; TreF; ViBoPo
(Harp, The.) BTP
(Tara.) LEAP
Harp You Play So Well, The. Marianne Moore. *See* That Harp You Play So Well.
Harpalus' Complaint [of Phillida's Love]. *Unknown.* OBSC; TuPP; ViBoPo
Harper, The. Thomas Campbell. ERP
(Irish Harper and His Dog, The.) CH; MPB
(My Dog Tray.) GoTP
(Poor Dog Tray.) AlBD; CG
Harper, The. Helene Mullins. TBM
Harper, The. *Unknown, tr. fr. Early Modern Irish by* Frank O'Connor. AnIL; KiLC
Harper draws his golden string, The. An Etching. Sister Mary Imelda. CAW
Harper of Chao, The. Po Chü-i, *tr. fr. Chinese by* Arthur Waley. MoPW; TrCh; UnS
Harpers' Farm, The. Dorothy Aldis. RIS
Harpers Ferry. Selden Rodman. PoNe
Harps Hung Up in Babylon. Arthur Colton. BAP; LBMV; WGRP
(Harps in Babylon.) PFY
Harried we were, and spent. The Waradgery Tribe. Mary Gilmore. BoAV; NeLNL
Harriet and the Matches. Heinrich Hoffmann. *See* Dreadful Story of Pauline and the Matches, The.
Harriet Beecher Stowe. Paul Laurence Dunbar. AA; DD
Harriet Hutch. Nonsense Verses. Laura E. Richards. RIS
Harriet Simper Has Her Day. John Trumbull. *Fr.* The Progress of Dulness. AmPP (4th ed.)
Harriet Tubman. Margaret Walker. PoNe
Harrington Barn Dance, The. *Unknown.* CoSo
Harrow Grave in Flanders, A. Marquess of Crewe. HBV
(Harrow and Flanders.) MM
Harrowing of Hell, The. *Unknown.* ACP; CAW
Harry Bale. *Unknown.* CSF
Harry Carey's General Reply, to the Libelling Gentry, Who Are Angry at His Welfare. Henry Carey. HBV
Harry Dunne, *2 vers., with music. Unknown.* ShS
Harry, Harry, hobbillschowe! The Manere of the Crying of ane Playe. William Dunbar. AtBAP
Harry Lorrequer, *sel.* Charles Lever.
Pope, The. BOHV
(Pope He Leads a Happy Life, The.) HBV
Harry, our King in England, from London town is gone. King Henry VII and the Shipwrights. Kipling. PCN
Harry Pearce. David Campbell. NeLNL
Harry Ploughman. Gerard Manley Hopkins. BrBE; EmBrPo; FaBoMo
H——y P——tt. *Unknown.* CoMu
Harry whose tuneful and well measur'd [*or* well-measured] song. To Mr. H. Lawes on His Airs [*or* Sonnet]. Milton. AWP; EM-1; ES; InPo; JAWP; LoBV; OBS; WBP
Harsh cry the crows. The Solitary. Nietzsche. AWP
Harsh frost hugs and mauls, The. Blue Hussars. Nikolai Aseyev. RuPo
Harsh winter is here, The. *Unknown. Fr.* Sea Snatches. SiB
Harshness of gorse darkens the yellow cliff-edge. A view of Rangitoto. Charles Brasch. AnNZ
Hart Crane. Julian Symons. LiTM (1946 ed.)
Hart he loves the high wood, The. *Unknown.* FaBoCh; LoGBV; OxNR
Hart-Leap Well. Wordsworth. BeLS; CG; LPS-2; MyFE
Hart's Castle. Gawin Douglas. *Fr.* King Hart. AtBAP; PoEL-1
Harvard Commemoration Ode, The. James Russell Lowell. *See* Ode Recited at the Harvard Commemoration, July 21, 1865.
Harvest, The. Alice Corbin. BoTP
Harvest. Ellen Mackay Hutchinson Cortissoz. AA; HBV
Harvest. Eva Gore-Booth. CP; HBMV; OQP; QP-1; WGRP
Harvest. Hafiz, *tr. fr. Persian by* Richard Le Gallienne. PeP
Harvest. M. M. Hutchinson. BoTP
Harvest. Aleksey Koltsov, *tr. fr. Russian by* C. M. Bowra. BoRS
Harvest. Thomas Nashe. *Fr.* Summer's Last Will and Testament. OBSC
Harvest. Robert Haven Schauffler. PC
Harvest. Gene Shuford. GoYe
Harvest. Edith Sitwell. OAEP (2d ed.)
Harvest. John Addington Symonds. PoVP
Harvest Dust. Winifred Welles. MAP
Harvest Elves, The. Wilfrid Thorley. BrR
Harvest Home. Henry Alford. MaRV; WGRP
(Thanksgiving Day.) TOAH
Harvest Home, *br. sel.* George Darley.
Sunset. RO
Harvest Home. Arthur Guiterman. YeAr
Harvest Home. Frederick Tennyson. OBVV
Harvest Home. Theocritus, *tr. fr. Greek by* Charles Stuart Calverley. Idylls, VII. AWP; GrR, *sel.;* GrL, *pr. tr. by* Andrew Lang.
("Once on a time did Eucritus and I," *tr. by* Charles Stuart Calverley.) GrPo
Bound for the Harvest-Home, *sel., tr. by* Walter Headlam. OxBG
Harvest Home. *Unknown, tr. fr. Greek by* F. L. Lucas. GrPE
Harvest-Home. Zonas, *tr. fr. Greek by* F. L. Lucas. GrPE
Harvest-Home Song. John Davidson. VA
Harvest Hymn. Charles Sangster. CPG
Harvest Hymn. Whittier. *Fr.* For an Autumn Festival. OHIP, *abr.;* PoRL; PSO, *abr.;* TOAH
("Once more the liberal year laughs out," *abr.*) PGD
(Thanksgiving Ode.) PEOR
Harvest is over in mist and moist moonlight. A Song of Apple Gathering. Gordon Bottomley. ReTS
Harvest Moon, The. Longfellow. GN
Harvest Moon. Josephine Miles. FiMAP
Harvest of Dust. Carol M. Ritchie. MuM
Harvest of the Sea, The. John McCrae. EtS
Harvest of Time, The. Harold Trowbridge Pulsifer. HBMV

Harvest Overflowing. *Unknown, tr. fr. Chinese.* WhP
Harvest Prayer. Rowena Bennett. MeMeAg
Harvest Sacrifice. Su T'ung-po, *tr. fr. Chinese by* Kenneth Rexroth. OnPC
Harvest Slumber Song. Wilfred Campbell. BOL
Harvest Song. Richard Dehmel, *tr. fr. German by* Ludwig Lewisohn. AWP; JAWP; LiTW; WBP
Harvest Song. Dryden. *Fr.* King Arthur, V, i. BeR
(Song: "Your hay it is mowed and your corn is reap'd.") CEP; SeCV-2
Harvest Song. Ludwig Hölty, *tr. fr. German by* Charles T. Brooks. AWP; JAWP; WBP; WoL
Harvest Song, A. Edwin Markham. PEDC
Harvest Song. *Unknown.* BoTP
("Boughs do shake and the bells do ring, The.") OxNR
Harvest sun lay hot and strong, The. The Firstborn. Jean Blewett. CPG
Harvest Sunset. Carl Sandburg. TSW; TSWC
Harvest Time. Star Powers. GoYe
Harvest to Seduce, A. Melville Cane. PG (1955 ed.)
Harvest Waits, The. Lloyd Mifflin. BPP; HBV
Harvester's Song ("All ye that lovely lovers be"). George Peele. *Fr.* The Old Wives' Tale. BLV; TrGrPo
(Harvestmen a-Singing.) EPP
Harvesters—they say themselves, The. The Harvest Elves. Wilfrid Thorley. BrR
Harvesting. Selma Robinson. InMe
Harvesting of the Roses, The. Menahem ben Jacob, *tr. fr. Hebrew.* TrJP
Harvestmen a-Singing. George Peele. *See* Harvester's Song.
Harvests. Marie de L. Welch. PoFr
Harvey Logan, *with music. Unknown.* OuSiCo
Harvey, the happy above happiest men. To the Right Worshipful, My Singular Good Friend, Master Gabriel Harvey, Doctor of the Laws. Spenser. ReIE
Has a love of adventure, a promise of gold. The Whaleman's Song. *Unknown.* EtS
Has any old fellow got mixed with the boys? *See* Has there any old fellow got mixed with the boys.
Has any one seen my fair. Cressid. Nora Perry. AA
Has anybody seen my Mopser? The Bandog. Walter de la Mare. TiPo
Has anybody seen my mouse? Missing. A. A. Milne. MoShBr
Has auld Kilmarnock seen the deil? Tam Samson's Elegy. Burns. PoEL-4
Has he forsaken heaven quite. To the Schooner *Casco.* Grace Hazard Conkling. PoeMoYo; VOD
Has Life No Sourness? Pope. *Fr.* The Second Epistle of the Second Book of Horace. BeR
Has no one said those daring. Two Years Later. W. B. Yeats. GTIV
Has no one seen my heart of you? Thomas Lovell Beddoes. EG
Has not altered. Spenser's Ireland. Marianne Moore. GTBS-W; LiTA; LiTG; LiTM (rev. ed.); NePA; OxBA
Has not the night been as a drunken rose. The Drunken Rose. Amarou. AWP
Has Sorrow Thy Young Days Shaded? Thomas Moore. GTIV; OxBI
Has Summer Come without the Rose? Arthur O'Shaughnessy. *See* Song: "Has summer come without the rose?"
"Has the Marquis La Fayette." A New Song. Joseph Stansbury. PAH
Has the sun's chariot halted up in heaven. At the Rendezvous. A. W. Schack von Staffeldt. BoDS
Has there any old fellow got mixed with the boys? The Boys. Oliver Wendell Holmes. BAP; BLP; CoBA; GDAH; HBV; HiLiAm; IAP; LPS-3; PTA-2; PYM; TCAP; WBLP
Has winter brought you to the Sabine fire. Persius. Satires, VI. LaP
Has your dinner lost its savor? Camping Song. Bliss Carman. NLK
Hasbrouck and the Rose. H. Phelps Putnam. AnFE; CoAnAm; MOAP; MoVE; OxBA; TwAmPo; ViBoPo
Hasheesh. Victor Robinson. PoP
Hashish-Eater, The. Clark Ashton Smith. DaM
Hassan, *sels.* James Elroy Flecker.
"Away, for we are ready to a man," V, ii, *also a sel. fr.* Golden Journey to Samarkand.
(Epilogue.) ShBV-3
(Golden Journey to Samarkand: Epilogue.) CP; HBMV; POTT; TCPD
Golden Road, The, *fr.* V, ii. OtMeF
"Thy dawn, O Master of the world, thy dawn," *fr.* II, ii. OtMeF
War Song of the Saracens, The, *fr.* III, iii. GTML; MBP; MM; MoBrPo; MuP; OBVV; OtMeF; ShBV-2; WHA
Yasmin, *fr.* I, ii. LoPS; TCPD; TwCV
(Hassan's Serenade.) OBEV (new ed.)
Hassan Bedriddin, clad in rags, ill-shod. Religion. Ambrose Bierce. BAP
Hassan Ben Khaled, *sel.* Bayard Taylor.
Rose, The. LPS-2
Hassan; or, The Camel Driver. William Collins. Persian Eclogues, II. EV-3
Hassan's Serenade. James Elroy Flecker. *See* Hassan.
Hast heard the voices of the fen. Warning. Clark Ashton Smith. DaM
Hast seen on highest rock a maid. The Storm. Pushkin. WaL
Hast thou a charm to stay the morning-star. Hymn before Sunrise, in the Vale of Chamouni. Samuel Taylor Coleridge. BCEP; BEL; BPN; EmBrPo; EnRP; ERP; HBV; LPS-2; MaRV; MCCG; OAEP; OxBoCh; PIAE; REAL; TCEP; TOP; WGRP
Hast thou a cunning instrument of play. Preparation. Thomas Edward Brown. OBEV (new ed.); OBVV; TOP; VLEP
Hast thou a friend? Thou hast indeed. On a True Friend. William Cowper. BoFr
Hast thou a heritage. In Shadow. Caroline Hazard. GoBC
Hast thou a lamp, a little lamp. The Lamp. Sarah Pratt Greene. AA
Hast thou entered into the treasures of the snow? The Treasures. Job, Bible, *O.T.* BoW
Hast thou explor'd the secrets of the deep. The Chambers of Death. Edward Young. *Fr.* A Paraphrase on Part of the Book of Job. BeR
Hast thou given the horse strength [*or* his might]? The Horse [*or* The War-Horse]. Job, Bible, *O.T.* BHV; ChTr; FaPON; GoTP; InP; ShBV-2; TrGrPo
Hast Thou Heard the Nightingale? Richard Watson Gilder. AA
Hast thou heard what wise men say. Old Tom's Song. Paul Green. *Fr.* The Lost Colony. NoCaPo
Hast thou named all the birds without a gun? Forbearance. Emerson. AA; AmPP (3d ed.); AnAmPo; AnNE; APW; BAP; BBV (1923 ed.); BoLiVe; CoBA; GN; HBV; HBVY; LA; LaNeLa; LEAP; LiTA; MCCG; MOAP; MPB; OnPM; OQP; OTPC; PCD; PoRL; PreP; QP-2; TCAP; TrGrPo; ViBoPo; WGRP; YT
Hast thou no right to joy. Ode on Conflicting Claims. Richard Watson Dixon. VA
Hast thou not known? Power to the Faint. Isaiah, Bible, *O.T.* GrCo-1
Hast thou not marked, when o'er thy startled head. A Tempest. Sir Walter Scott. *Fr.* The Lord of the Isles. EV-4
Hast Thou Not Seen an Aged Rifted Tower. Hartley Coleridge. EnRP
(Three Sonnets, I.) RO
"Hast thou ony greencloth." Robin Hood's End. *Unknown.* A Gest of Robyn Hode, Fytte VIII. GoTL
Hast thou seen. Song. Heinrich von Morungen. LyMA
"Hast thou seen that lordly castle." The Castle by the Sea. Ludwig Uhland. AWP; JAWP; UnW; WBP
Hast Thou Seen the Down in the Air. Sir John Suckling. *See* Song to a Lute.
Hast Thou Seen with Flash Incessant. Wordsworth. BPN
"Hast thou then nought wiser to bring." The Catechism. Walter de la Mare. ChMo
Hast thou, which art but aire, a touch, a feeling. Shakespeare. *Fr.* The Tempest, V, i. NBE
Haste my Nannette, my lovely maid. Nannette. Matthew Prior. AEV
Haste Not, Rest Not. Goethe, *tr. fr. German.* MaRV; OQP, *abr.*; QP-1, *abr.*
Haste, Sylvia, haste, my charming maid! The Invitation. Thomas Godfrey. AnFE; APA; CoAnAm; IAP; TCAP
Haste thee, Nymph, and bring with thee. Milton. *Fr.* L'Allegro. OTPC (1946 ed.); PC; YT
Haste thee, Nymph, and bring with thee. L'Allegsho—Invitation au Bal. *Unknown.* CAG
Haste thee, Winter, haste away. Old Song. *Unknown.* PCH
Haste, ye purple gleams of light. An African Song. Thomas Chatterton. LoBV; RO
Hasten hither, saki mine. Drinking Song. Ubada. MooP
Hasten. The countenance of the year is hardened, the face wan, drawn. After Tschaikowsky. Wallace Gould. AnAmPo
Hasten to your duty. Mist. Ibn Bassam. MooP
Hastening on, the wanderer strode. The Wanderer. "Yehoash." TrJP
Hastening to Granada's gates. The Christian Lady and the Moor. José Zorrilla. AnSpL-2
Hastings Mill. Cicely Fox Smith. HBV; WaKn
Hasty Pudding, The. Joel Barlow. AmPP; CoBA; IAP; MOAP; TCAP
Sels.
"Days grow short, The; but though the falling sun," III. BAV
Choice in Spoons, A, *fr.* III. OnAP
Eating of the Pudding, The, *fr.* III. APW
Husking, *fr.* III. APW
Pudding Prepared and Eaten, The, *fr.* III. AnNE
"Let the green succatash with thee contend," *fr.* I. LoGBV

"Ye Alps audacious, thro' the Heavens that rise," I. OxBA (Hasty Pudding Described, The, *abr.*) APW
Praise of the Pudding, *fr.* I. AnNE
Hat Bar. Mildred Weston. FiBHP
Hat Given to the Poet by Li Chien, The. Po Chü-i, *tr. fr. Chinese* by Arthur Waley. AtBAP; BoW; TrCh
Hat you loved, the damask-trimmed reed-hat, The. Folk Song. *Unknown.* LiTW
Hatched in a rasping darkness of dry sand. Letter IV. William Empson. LiTB
Hate! Pavel Antokolsky. *tr. fr. Russian* by Babette Deutsch. TrJP; TrRV
Hate. Herbert E. Palmer. POTE
Hate. James Stephens. BMEP; BoFr; ChMo; CMP; MBP; MoAB; MoBrPo; NP; OBVV; PoeMoYo; PtOT; TCEP; TSW; TSWC; TwCV
Hate and the Love of the World, The. Max Ehrmann. PoToHe (new ed.)
Hate, be a faithful prop, and find. Hate! Pavel Antokolsky. TrJP; TrRV
Hate in the world's hand. A Proud Lady. Elinor Wylie. ChMo
Hate is only one of many responses. Poem. Frank O'Hara. NeAP
Hate me or love, I care not, as I pass. The Unicorn. Ruth Pitter. LO; MoBrPo; MoVE
Hate me, or love, my Helen, as you list. Four Sonnets to Helen, 2. Pierre de Ronsard. *Fr.* Sonnets pour Hélène. LiTW
Hate only will I love. Love and Hate. *Unknown.* KiLC
Hate-Song, A. Shelley. EnLoPo
Hate the Idle Pleasures. Shakespeare. *See* Winter of Our Discontent.
Hate Whom Ye List. Sir Thomas Wyatt. TuPP
("Hate whom ye list, for I care not.") SiCE; SiPS
Hated of dwellers around, by the gods immortal belovèd. Neutral Argos. Delphic Oracle. OxBG
Hater he came and sat by a ditch, A. A Hate-Song. Shelley. EnLoPo
Hath any loved you well, down there. Song from "Chartivel" [*or* Sarrazine's Song]. Marie de France, *tr.* by Arthur O'Shaughnessy. *Fr.* Chartivel. AWP; EnLoPo; GTIV; HBV; JAWP; LEAP; LiTW; LyMA; PoVP; WBP
Hath Hope Kept Vigil. Sir Charles G. D. Roberts. MM; TwCV
Hath not the dark stream closed above thy head. The Tears of the Poplars. Edith M. Thomas. AA; AnAmPo; LA; LEAP
Hath not the morning dawned with added light? Ethnogenesis; Written during the Meeting of the First Southern Congress . . . 1861. Henry Timrod. AmPP (4th ed.); OxBA; SPP
Hath the rude laugh of Boreas frighted thee. To a Mayflower. William E. Marshall. CaP
Hath this world, without me wrought. Questionings. Frederic Henry Hedge. HBV
Hatikvah—a Song of Hope. Naphtali Herz Imber, *tr. fr. Hebrew* by Henry Snowman. TrJP
Hatred. Gwendolyn Bennett. BANP; CDC
Hatred. Arthur C. Coe. CAG
Hatred and greed and pride shall die. He Shall Speak Peace. Thomas Curtis Clark. OQP; QP-1; WBLP
Hatred and vengeance, my eternal portion. Lines Written during a Period of Insanity [*or* Lines Written under the Influence of Delirium]. William Cowper. AtBAP; FiP; InPo; NBE; PoEL-3
Hatred, furious revenging. Sapphics upon the Passion of Christ. *Unknown.* ReIE
Hats. F. S. Flint. TwCV
Hats off!/ Along the street there comes. The Flag Goes By. Henry Holcomb Bennett. AA; BBV; DD; FaBoBe; FaFP; FaPON; FOAH; GN; HBV; HBVY; HH; LEAP; NeHB; OHFP; PaA; PCD; PECK; PEDC; PGD; PoRL; PSO; PTA-1; SiSoSe; TiPo (1952 ed.); TreF; TVSH; WBLP; YaD
Hattage. A. P. Herbert. FiBHP
Hatteras. Philip Freneau. CoV
Hatteras. Joseph William Holden. NoCaPo
Haug-eye Man, The. Opie Read. BoHiPo
Haughty Aspen, The; a German Legend. Nora Archibald Smith. ChrBoLe; CLS; SDH
Haughty herons circling low. Carolina Herons. Zoe Kincaid Brockman. NoCaPo
Haughty lady, discard that look. The Cactus. *Unknown.* APW
Haughty they said he was, at first, severe. Whom We Revere. James Russell Lowell. *Fr.* Under the Old Elm. PGD
Haul Away, Joe, *with music. Unknown.* AmSS; ShS, 2 *vers.;* SoAmSa
(Haul Away, My Rosy, *with music.*) OuSiCo
(Haul Away O.) SG
Haul on the Bowline, *with music. Unknown.* AmSS; ShS; SoAmSa

(Haul the Bowline.) SG
Haul on the rope. Make the high bell lean. To the Bell-Ringer. Robert Farren. OnYI
Haul up the flag, you mourners. Elegy for Two Banjos. Karl Shapiro. AtBAP; LiTA; TrJP; WaP
Haulage. E. E. Nott-Bower. WhC
Haulms burn/ in distant fields. September Fires. Sir Herbert Read. TwCV
Haunch of Venison, The. Goldsmith. CEP; EV-3; TCEP
Haunt of Grendel, The. *Unknown, tr. fr. Anglo-Saxon* by Francis B. Gummere. *Fr.* Beowulf. BCEP
Haunt of the Deer, The. Duncan MacIntyre, *tr. fr. Gaelic* by John Campbell Shairp. *Fr.* The Praise of Ben Dorain. EBSV
Haunt of the Sorcerer, The. Milton. *Fr.* Comus. BCEP; LPS-3
Haunted. Walter de la Mare. TwCV
Haunted. Helen Lanyon. GTIV
Haunted. Amy Lowell. DaM
Haunted Country. Robinson Jeffers. MOAP; OxBA
Haunted Garden, The. Henry Treece. NeBP
Haunted Hazel, The. James B. Dollard. CPG; OCL
Haunted Heart, The. Jessie B. Rittenhouse. AV
Haunted House, The. Wilfrid Scawen Blunt. UnW
Haunted House, The. Robert Graves. OxBI
Haunted House, The. Thomas Hood. AnEnPo, *abr.;* BCEP, *abr.;* DaM; LiA; SeCePo; UnW, *abr.*
Sels.
"Beds were all untouch'd by hand or tool, The." RO
"No human figure stirr'd, to go or come." MyFE
Haunted House, The. George Sylvester Viereck. AnAmPo; LA
Haunted Houses. Longfellow. AnNE; UnW
Haunted in Old Japan. Alfred Noyes. LEAP
Haunted Oak, The. Paul Laurence Dunbar. BANP
Haunted Odysseus; the Last Testament. Horace Gregory. MoVE
Haunted Palace, The. Poe. *Fr.* The Fall of the House of Usher. AA; AmP; AnFE; APA; APW; BAP; BeLS; BoLiVe; CBOV; CH; ChTr; CoAnAm; DDA; EV-5; HBV; IAP; LiTA; LiTG; MCCG; MOAP; NePA; OBAV; OBVV; OnAP; OTPC; OxBA; PFE; PFY; Po; PoE; PoEL-4; PoeMoYo; SPP; TCAP; TOP; TreFS; TrGrPo; ViBoPo
("In the greenest of our valleys.") AmPP
Haunted Room, A. John Myers O'Hara. BAP
Haunted Ship, The. Kassaris Emmanuel, *tr. fr. Modern Greek* by Rae Dalven. MoGP
Haunted Stairs, The. Yetza Gillespie. DaM
Haunter, The. Thomas Hardy. AtBAP; ChMP; GTBS-D
Haunting Fingers. Thomas Hardy. MaPo
Haunts of the Halcyon, The. Charles Henry Luders. AA
Hava-Mal, The. *Unknown. See* Sayings of the High One.
Havana Dreams. Langston Hughes. GoSl; PoNe
Havbor and Signelil. *Unknown, tr. fr. Danish* by E. M. Smith-Dampier. BoDaBa
Have angleworms attractive homes? An Alphabet. Charles E. Carryl. LBN
Have-at a Venture. *Unknown.* CoMu
Have carved upon thine arch, proud Emperor. To a Triumpher. José Maria de Heredia. TrFP
Have courage, O my comradry of dreamers! The Dreamers. Sydney Jephcott. BoAu
Have dark Egyptians stolen thee away. Mimma Bella, I. Eugene Lee-Hamilton. ViPP
Have done with care, my hearts! aboard amain. A Farewell to Sir John Norris and Sir Francis Drake [*or* A Farewell to the Most Famous Generals . . .]. George Peele. EV-1; OBSC; SG
Have done, you men and women all! The Animals in the Ark. *Unknown. Fr.* The Deluge. ChTr
Have fair fallen, O fair, fair have fallen, so dear. Henry Purcell. Gerard Manley Hopkins. UnS; ViPP
Have Faith. Edward Carpenter. WGRP
Have, have ye no regard, all ye. His Saviour's Words Going to the Cross. Robert Herrick. StJW
Have I a hundred years since or. John Landless Leads the Caravan. Iwan Goll. TrJP
Have I a wife? Bedam I have! The Brewer's Man. L. A. G. Strong. FiBHP; WhC
Have I caught my heavenly jewel. Stella Sleeping. Sir Philip Sidney. Astrophel and Stella: Second Song. SiPS
Have I Found Her? *Unknown.* EIL
("Have I found her? O rich finding!") CaAE
Have I nocht made ane honest shift. Sir David Lindsay. *Fr.* The Satire of the Three Estates. GoTS
Have I not known the sky and sea. The Mystic. Don Marquis. UnW
Have I not seen your face before. An Angel of Perugino. Arthur Symons. VLEP
Have I watcht the winters nyght. *Unknown.* SeCSL
Have little care that life is brief. Envoy [*or* On the Tomb of Bliss Carman]. Bliss Carman. HBV; MaRV; PC; VA

Have mercy upon me, O God, after thy great goodness. Psalm LI, Bible, *O.T.* LiTW
Have no wide fears for Earth. Earth. Laura Riding. MoP
"Have other lovers—say, my love." Unsatisfactory. *Unknown.* LPS-1
Have patience; it is fit that in this wise. Sonnets, IX. George Santayana. MOAP; WGRP
Have Pity, Grief. Peter Hausted. *Fr.* The Rival Friends. EG; SeCL
("Have pity, grief, I cannot pay.") TuPP
(Song, The: "Have pity (Grief) I can not pay.") SeEP
Have pity, O harsh lamb upon these last two. The Two Witnesses. Pierre Jean Jouve. MiFP
Have pity on us, Power just and severe. Prayer. John Hall Wheelock. NePoAm
Have pity, pity, friends, have pity on me. Epistle in Form of a Ballad to His Friends. Villon. AWP; LiTW; LyMA; OuHeWo
Have the rocks on the hillside voices. In Palestine. George W. Carlin. ChIP
Have the swallows come? The Swallows. Patric Dickinson. ChMP
"Have, then, thy wish!" He whistled shrill. Roderick Dhu and Fitz-James; a Noble Action. Sir Walter Scott. *Fr.* The Lady of the Lake, V. EV-4
Have we not all, amid life's petty strife. No Star Is Ever Lost. Adelaide Anne Procter. MaRV
Have we seen her, The New City, O my brothers, where she stands. The New City. Marguerite Wilkinson. MaRV; OQP; PEDC; QP-2
Have we, then lost the war. "Separate Peace." Harrison S. Morris. MC
Have ye beheld (with much delight). Upon the Nipples of Julia's Breast. Robert Herrick. LiTL; ViBoPo
"Have ye founded your thrones and altars, then." A Parable. James Russell Lowell. PGD
Have ye heard of our hunting, o'er mountain and glen. The Hunters of Men. Whittier. AnAmPo; LA
Have ye seen the morning sky. The Happy Swain. Ambrose Philips. EnLoPo
Have You? Harry M. Dean. NLK
Have you a desire to see. Of His Mistress. Peter Hausted. *Fr.* The Rival Friends. EG; SeCL; TuPP
Have you a gold cup. The Question. Robert Duncan. NeAP
Have You an Eye? Edwin Ford Piper. SBMV
Have you any gooseberry wine. Mazilla and Mazura. *Unknown.* ChTr
Have you any idea. The Mother of the Commander Michitsuna, *tr. fr. Japanese by* Kenneth Rexroth. OnPJ
Have you any work for a tinker, Mistris. *Unknown.* OBS
Have You Been at Carrick? *Tr. fr. Irish by* Edward Walsh. AnIV; TIP
Have you been at Garnyvillo? Garnyvillo. Edward Lysaght. IrPN
Have you been at sea on a windy day. A Windy Day. Winifred Howard. FaPON
Have you been catching of fish, Tom Noddy? Tit for Tat. Walter de la Mare. UTS
"Have you been with the king to Rome." The Palatine. Willa Cather. BAP; HBMV; InP; LEAP; NP
Have you come then, O my darling!—with the third night's end, at last! Lovers' Meeting. Theocritus. *Fr.* Idylls, XII. GrPE
Have you come to the Red Sea place in your life. At the Place of the Sea [*or* Red Sea Place in Your Life]. Annie Johnson Flint. BLPA; BLRP; OQP; QP-2
"Have you cut the wheat in the glowing field." Thanksgiving [*or* Poetic Responses]. Amelia E. Barr. PEDC; TOAH
Have you dug the spill. Harlem Sweeties. Langston Hughes. PoNe
"Have you e'er a new song." The Limerick Lasses. Alfred Perceval Graves. TIP
Have you ever asked yourselves—ladies, ladies. Gert Swasey. Winfield Townley Scott. FiMAP
Have you ever been down to my countree. The Land Where I Was Born. Shaw Neilson. BoAu
Have you ever built a camp-fire at the closing of the day? Have You? Harry M. Dean. NLK
Have you ever felt the beating of the rain upon your face. The Silent Wooded Place. Rachel E. Miller. CAG
Have you ever heard of the Sugar-Plum Tree? The Sugar-Plum Tree. Eugene Field. FaFP; GoBP; HBV; HBVY; MPB; OTPC (1946 ed.); PCH; TreF
Have you ever heard that a tailor was ill? The Tailor. Joseph Leftwich. TrJP
Have you ever heard the tapping of the fairy cobbler men. The Fairies. Sybil Morford. OTPC (1946 ed.); PoRL; TVC; TVSH
Have you ever heard the wind go "Yooooo"? The Night Wind. Eugene Field. FaPON
Have you ever in your life seen a Possum play possum? Opossum. William Jay Smith. GoTP; TiPo (1959 ed.)
Have you ever noticed the mill pond in the dog days? Henry Zoll, the Miller. Edgar Lee Masters. *Fr.* The New Spoon River. TCAP
Have you ever sat by the r. r. track. Emptys Cuming Back [*or* Empties Coming Back]. Angelo de Ponciano. BLPA; DDA
Have you ever seen that wondrous building. The Chragan Palace. Thomas Terzyan. ArmLP
Have you ever seen the dawn. Ballad of Hope and Fear. Charles Madge. FaBoMo
Have you ever seen the moon. Have You Seen It. Lula Lowe Weeden. CDC
Have you ever thought, my friend. The Gospel of the Fields. Arthur Upson. NLK
Have you forgotten yet? Aftermath. Siegfried Sassoon. AnFE; AOAH; GTSL; HiLiEn; MaRV; MBP; MCCG; MoBrPo; NeMA; PoeMoYo; TCEP; TrJP; ViBoPo; WaP
Have you found your life distasteful? My Sun Sets to Rise Again. Robert Browning. *Fr.* At the Mermaid. MaRV
Have you gazed on naked grandeur, where there's nothing else to gaze on. The Call of the Wild. Robert W. Service. CaP; NLK; OCL
Have you got a brook in your little heart. Emily Dickinson. OBAV
(Brook of the Heart, The.) LiTL
Have you had a kindness shown? Pass It On. Henry Burton. BLRP; MaRV
Have you had your tonsils out? The New Neighbor. Rose Fyleman. GaP; TiPo
Have you hastened and aspired. The Poetry Cure. Robert Haven Schauffler. MOB
Have you heard how a girl saved the lightning express. Kate Shelly. Eugene J. Hall. PTA-1
Have you heard of Millington? Edward Millington. Richard Church. HaMV
Have you heard of one Humpty Dumpty. The Ballad of Persse O'Reilly. James Joyce. *Fr.* Finnegans Wake. LiTB; SiTL
Have you heard of our fighting Twenty-first. The Dash for the Colors. Frederick G. Webb. BeLS
Have you heard of the manly turning taken. The Day of Inverlochy. Iain Lom. GoTS
Have you heard of the Sugar-Plum Tree? *See* Have you ever heard of the Sugar-Plum Tree?
Have you heard of the terrible family They. "They Say." Ella Wheeler Wilcox. WBLP
Have you heard of the wonderful one-hoss-shay. The Deacon's Masterpiece; or, The Wonderful "One-Hoss-Shay." Oliver Wendell Holmes. *Fr.* The Autocrat of the Breakfast-Table. AmP; AmPP; AnNE; APW; BAP; BBV (1923 ed.); BeLS; BOHV; CoBA; DDA; EV-5; FaBoBe; FaFP; HBV; HBVY; IAP; InMe; LEAP; LHV; LiTA; LoGBV; LPS-3; MOAP; MoShBr; NePA; OBAV; OHFP; OnHT; OnSP; OTPC; OxBA; PIR; Po; PoRA; PYM; REAL; RIS; SiTL; StPo; StVeCh; TCAP; TreF; WBLP; YaD; YT
Have you heard the blinking toad. The Song of the Toad. John Burroughs. DDA; FaPON
Have you heard the calling, calling, of the distance? The Call. Cora D. Fenton. NLK
Have you heard the golden city. The City of Light. Felix Adler. GrCo-1
Have you heard the secret voices go whispering in your blood. The Secret Voices. Ethel Mannin. NLK
Have you heard the story that gossips tell. John Burns of Gettysburg. Bret Harte. DDA; GA; HBV; LHV; MC; OHIP; PaA; PAH; PAP
Have you heard the tale of the Aloe plant. The Aloe Plant. Henry Harbaugh. BLPA
Have you hearkened the eagle scream over the sea? The Irish Hurrah. Thomas Osborne Davis. OnYI
Have You Learned Lessons Only of Those Who Admired You? Walt Whitman. *See* Stronger Lessons.
Have You Lost Faith? *Unknown.* WBLP
Have you mark'd but the fall of the snow. The Triumph. Ben Jonson. *Fr.* The Celebration of Charis. PG
"Have you news of my boy Jack?" My Boy Jack. Kipling. OtMeF
Have you no tender thoughts, Cerinthus, for your sweetheart. To Cerinthus. Sulpicia. LaP
Have you not fallen asleep to strong men's rowing. The Rowers. Laura Benét. GoYe
Have you not heard his silent steps? Rabindranath Tagore. *Fr.* Gitanjali. WGRP
Have you not heard of Monsieur Maximus. Henry Parrot. SiCE
Have you not heard the poets tell. Baby Bell. Thomas Bailey Aldrich. HBV; LPS-1
Have you not noted, in some family. The Birth-Bond. Dante Gabriel Rossetti. The House of Life, XV. BPN; EmBrPo; HBV; OAEP; POTT; PoVP; ViPo
Have You Not Oft, in the Still Wind. George Darley. UnW

Have you noticed the docile appeal. Letter from a State Hospital. Frank Mundorf. GoYe
Have you observ'd the wench in the street. *Unknown.* OBS
Have you read in the Talmud of old. Sandalphon. Longfellow. AmPP (3d ed.); AnNE; APW; IAP; OBAV; TCAP
Have You Seen a Bright Lily Grow. Ben Jonson. *Fr.* A Celebration of Charis. OTPC (1923 ed.)
(From "Love's Chariot.") LEAP
("Have you seen but a bright lily grow.") EG; FaBoCh; LoGBV; ReEn
(She.) BCEP
(So Sweet Is She.) GN
(So White, So Soft, So Sweet.) TrGrPo
(Triumph, The.) LoPS; PG, 8 *ll.*
Have you seen a witch to-day. The Enchantress. Bliss Carman. VOD
Have you seen an apple orchard in the spring? Apple Blossoms [*or* The Apple Orchard in the Spring]. William Martin. GN; OTPC
"Have you seen Hugh." The King of Connacht. *Unknown.* KiLC
Have You Seen It. Lula Lowe Weeden. CDC
Have you seen the lights of London, how they twinkle, twinkle, twinkle. Parliament Hill. H. H. Bashford. BrR; MPB; SP; VOD
Have you seen walking through the village. Mollie McGee. Edgar Lee Masters. *Fr.* Spoon River Anthology. BAP; NP
Have you sometimes, calm, silent let your tread aspirant rise. Heard on the Mountain. Victor Hugo. AWP
"Have you the face to utter such a threat, most grasping Atrides?" Homer. *Fr.* The Iliad, I. GrPo
Have You Watched the Fairies? Rose Fyleman. SP; TiPo
Haven. Donald Jeffrey Hayes. PoNe
Haven and last refuge of my pain, The. Last Refuge. Michelangelo. AWP; LiTW
Haven roars, and O, the haven roars, The. Lament for Cael. *Unknown.* SiB
Haven't got no special likin' fur the toney sorts o' play. Cowboy versus Broncho. James Barton Adams. SCC
Havildar Ganga Singh, V. C. Stanley Gerald Dunn. MM
Having a wheel and four legs of its own. The Grindstone. Robert Frost. PoE
Having a Wonderful Time. D. B. Wyndham Lewis. FiBHP
Having attained success in business. Robert Whitmore. Frank Marshall Davis. PoNe
Having been tenant long to a rich Lord. Redemption. George Herbert. ElSeCe; ExPo; GTBS-W; LiTB; LiTG; MeLP; MePo; OBS; PeBoSo; PoE; SeCeV; SeCV-1; SeEP; StJW
Having bitten on life like a sharp apple. Aubade. Louis MacNeice. ViBoPo
Having Climbed to the Topmost Peak of the Incense-Burner Mountain. Po Chü-i, *tr. fr. Chinese by* Arthur Waley. TrCh
Having come to this place. This Place in the Ways. Muriel Rukeyser. MiAP
Having finished the Blue-plate Special. In Schrafft's. W. H. Auden. MaPo
Having inherited a vigorous mind. My Descendants. W. B. Yeats. Meditations in Time of Civil War, IV. LiTB
Having interr'd her infant-birth. An Ode upon a Question Moved, Whether Love Should Continue for Ever? Lord Herbert of Cherbury. CoEV; MeLP; MePo; OBS; SeEP
Having little else to do. The Gossip. John Richard Moreland. PR
Having loved is my heart not nobler now. Public Acclaim. Friedrich Hölderlin. AnGP
Having New England Fathers. John Holmes. PG (1955 ed.)
Having passed over the world. The Last Frontier. John Gould Fletcher. InPo; MOAP
Having scrubbed away the gray sweat. Old Michael. George M. Brady. NeIP
Having so rich a treasury, so fine a hoard. The Daisy. Marya Zaturenska. MoAmPo
Having taken offence with the society of my friends at Damascus. From Slavery to Slavery. Sadi. *Fr.* The Gulistan. OuHeWo
Having this day my horse, my hand, my lance. Astrophel and Stella, XLI. Sir Philip Sidney. AnFE; ATP; BEL; CBOV; CoBE; EG; ElSeCe; EnL; EnLit; EPP; ES; OAEP; OBSC; PeBoSo; PoFS; ReEn; ReIE; SiCE; SiPS; TOP; TuPP
Having thus fulfilled her purpose Athene went away to Olympus. Nausicaa [*or* Olympus]. Homer. *Fr.* The Odyssey. LiA; OxBG
Having to travel back now from this far place. On Leaving the Tomb of Premier Fang. Tu Fu. BoFr
Haw-Blossoms. James Matthew Legaré. SPP
Hawaii! sea-girt land! Our Native Land. Kalakaua, King of the Hawaiian Islands. PoRL
Hawaiian Hilltop. Genevieve Taggard. PoMa
Hawk, The. A. C. Benson. BLA
Hawk, The. Aleksandr Aleksandrovich Blok, *tr. fr. Russian by* Frances Cornford *and* Esther Polianowsky Salaman. TrRV
Hawk, The. Sydney Clouts. BoSA
Hawk, The. W. H. Davies. BLA; GTML
Hawk, The. Ibn al-Qabturnu, *tr. fr. Arabic by* A. J. Arberry. MooP
Hawk, The. Raymond Knister. BoCaPo
Hawk. Clinton Scollard. BLA
Hawk, The. W. B. Yeats. AtBAP
Hawk Afield. Evelyn Scott. BLA
Hawk and the Dove, The. *Unknown, tr. fr. Armenian by* Zabelle C. Boyajian. ArmLP
Hawk broods earthward, The. The Hawk. Sydney Clouts. BoSA
Hawk from Cuckoo Tavern, A, *abr.* Lawrence Lee. GA
Hawk hovers in air, A. Loneliness. Tu Fu. OnPC
Hawk or shrike has done this deed. Whimper of Sympathy. George Meredith. EPN
Hawk, The, said to the Dove, "My dear." The Hawk and the Dove. *Unknown.* ArmLP
Hawk Shadow. Florence Wilkinson Evans. TBM
Hawk slipped out of the pine, and rose in the sunlit air, The. The Hawk. A. C. Benson. BLA
Hawkbit, The. Sir Charles G. D. Roberts. HBV; SN
Hawke. Sir Henry Newbolt. BBV
Hawke. Archibald T. Strong. *Fr.* Sonnets of the Empire. BoAu
Hawkesyard. Sister Mary Benvenuta. JKCP (1926 ed.)
Hawking for the Partridge. Thomas Ravenscroft. OxBoLi
Hawking Party in the Olden Time, A. Mary Howitt. OTPC (1923 ed.)
Hawks. James Stephens. BMEP; HBMV; NP; PYM
Hawk's Nest, The. Bret Harte. BAV
Hawks stir the blood like fiercely ringing bells. The Swan. Elizabeth J. Coatsworth. BLA; WhBS
Hawk's Thoughts, A. Aleksey Koltsov, *tr. fr. Russian.* BoR
Hawk's Way. Ted Olson. HoPM
Haworth Churchyard. Matthew Arnold. VLEP
Haws cling to the thorn, The. Dead Days. Lloyd Roberts. BoCaPo (1943 ed.)
Hawthorn, The. *Unknown.* ChTr
Hawthorn fair, whose burgeoning. Odes, IV, 22. Pierre de Ronsard. PrPoCR
Hawthorn Hath a Deathly Smell, The. Walter de la Mare. AtBAP
Hawthorn [*or* Hawthorne] Tree, The. Willa Cather. AV; HBMV
Hawthorn Tree, The. Roberta Teale Swartz. TBM
Hawthorne. Amos Bronson Alcott. AA; DD
Hawthorne. Longfellow. CoBA; GA; IAP; PoEL-5; TCAP; TriL
Hawthorne. James Russell Lowell. *Fr.* A Fable for Critics. AmPP (4th ed.); AnNE; OxBA
("There is Hawthorne, with genius so shrinking and rare.") CoBA
Hawthorne Tree, The. Willa Cather. *See* Hawthorn Tree, The.
Hawthorne Tree, The. *Unknown.* *See* Katie's Secret.
Hay Appeareth, The. Proverbs, XXVII: 25, Bible, *O.T.* FaPON
Hay Harvest. Patrick R. Chalmers. BoTP
Hay Harvest, The. Apollon Nikolayevich Maikov, *tr. fr. Russian by* Frances Cornford *and* Esther Polianowsky Salaman. TrRV
(Haymaking, *tr. by* Sir Cecil Kisch.) WaL
Hay, house-dust, or the fur from cats. Allergy. Walker Gibson. NePoAm
Hay is for horses. *Unknown.* OxNR
Hay Mowing. Moyshe Kulbak, *tr. fr. Yiddish by* Sarah Zweig Betsky. OnCuPl
Hay nonny no! *See* Hey Nonny No!
Hay! Now the Day Dawis. Alexander Montgomerie. *See* Night Is Near Gone, The.
Hay-Time. C. M. Lowe. BoTP
Haytime. Irene F. Pawsey. BoTP
Hay Wagon. Helen Frith Stickney. DDA
Hay with scent the meadow drenches. Haymaking. Apollon Nikolayevich Maikov. WaL
Haycocks stand along the fence, The. Peggy Considers Her Grandmothers. Josephine Pinckney. NP
Hayfield, The. Charles Bruce. *Fr.* The Flowing Summer. CaP
Hay Field, The. Ethelwyn Wetherald. CPG
Hayfoot; strawfoot; the illiterate seasons. Wessex Guidebook. Louis MacNeice. HaMV
Haying. John Frederic Herbin. CaP; PeCV
Hayley, thy tenderness fraternal shown. Sonnet to William Hayley. William Cowper. BoFr
Hayll [*or* Haylle], Comly and Clene. *Unknown.* *Fr.* The Second Shepherds' Play. AtBAP; BoW; OBEV (new ed.); OxBoLi
(Hail, Comely and Clean.) AnEC
(Shepherds at Bethlehem, The.) ChTr; CoEV

Hayloft, The. Robert Louis Stevenson. GFA; OnHT; PCH; TSW
Haymaker's Lullaby, The. Francis Carlin. BOL
Haymakers, rakers, reapers and mowers. Country Glee [*or* Song]. Thomas Dekker *and* John Ford. *Fr.* The Sun's Darling. CenL; CoEV; ElSeCe; EV-2; OBSC; ViBoPo
Haymakers' Song, The. Alfred Austin. VA
Haymaking. E. M. Adams. BoTP
Hay Making. Joanna Baillie. EV-3
Hay-Making. Karl Erik Forsslund, *tr. fr. Swedish by* Charles W. Stork. AnSL
Haymaking. A. P. Graves. BoTP
Haymaking. Apollon Nikolayevich Maikov. *See* Hay Harvest, The.
Haymaking. Edward Thomas. AnFE; MBP; MoAB; MoBrPo; SeCePo
Haymow, The. Luella Markley Mockett. BrR
Hay's Wharf. Richard Church. HaMV
Hayseed, *with music.* *Unknown.* AS
Haystack in the Floods, The. William Morris. AEV; AnEnPo; ATP (1935 ed.); BEL; BeLS; BMEP; BPN; CaAE; EmBrPo; EnL; EnLi-2; EnLit; EPN; ExPo; GTBS; HoPM; LiTL; LoBV; MBP; OAEP; OuHeWo; PoE; PoEL-5; PoRA; POTT; PoVP; ReaPo; SeCeV; ShBV-3; ViP; ViPo; ViPP; VLEP; WHA
Hazard, The. John Kendrick Bangs. PR
Hazard. Nils Petersen, *tr. fr. Danish by* R. P. Keigwin. LiTW
Hazard of Loving the Creatures, The. Isaac Watts. CEP; EiPP
(Where-e'er My Flatt'ring Passions Rove.) OxBoCh
Haze. Carl Sandburg. OnHM
Haze. Henry David Thoreau. *Fr.* A Week on the Concord and Merrimack Rivers. AmPP (3d ed.); CoBA; InPo; MOAP; OnAP
(Woof of the Sun [Ethereal Gauze].) AnNE; OnPM; ViBoPo
Haze, char, and the weather of All Souls'. In the Elegy Season. Richard Wilbur. FiMAP; MoAB; NePoEA
Haze on the far horizon, A. Autumn. William Herbert Carruth. MPB
Haze upon the meadow, The. What Is Winter? Edmund Blunden. ChMP; GTBS-D
Hazel Buds. Mary Webb. AIDL
Hazel Dorn. Bernard Sleigh. HOAH
Hazeleye's Lullaby. Simon Pokagon. BOL
Hazlewood Witch, The. Richard Gall. EBSV
Hazlitt Sups. Katharine Day Little. GoYe
He. Lawrence Ferlinghetti. NeAP
He. Stanley Kunitz. CrMA
He Abjures Love. Thomas Hardy. NBE
He, above the rest/ In shape and gesture proudly eminent. Milton. *Fr.* Paradise Lost, I. InP; LiA
He adds each day grace unto grace. My All. Takamoto. SoLD
He ain't much of a dog to look at. Jack. *Unknown.* AIBD
He also fix'd the wandering Queen of Night. Newton Fixes the Moon. James Thomson. *Fr.* A Poem Sacred to the Memory of Sir Isaac Newton. BeR
He always comes on market days. The Balloon Man. Rose Fyleman. BoTP; SUS
He always has something to grumble about. A Chip on His Shoulder. *Unknown.* BLPA; WBLP
He always said he would retire. Retired Business Man. Anderson M. Scruggs. DDA
He always was one for a jeer and a jest. Epitaph for a Funny Fellow. Morris Bishop. SiTL
He and His Family. Laura E. Richards. DDA
He and I. Dante Gabriel Rossetti. The House of Life, XCVIII. PoVP; ViPo
He and I sought together. Heliodora. Hilda Doolittle ("H. D."). ChMo; CMP
He and She. Sir Edwin Arnold. BLPA; BMEP
(Secret of Death, The.) LPS-1
(She and He.) HBV; UnW
He and She. Christina Rossetti. VLEP
He and She. Eugene Fitch Ware. BOHV; YaD
He Approacheth the Hall of Judgment. *Unknown, tr. fr. Egyptian by* Robert Hillyer. *Fr.* Book of the Dead. AWP; JAWP; WBP
He arose from the dead. New Crucifixion. Thomas Curtis Clark. ChIP
He arrived back at the sacred peak of Kyllene at dawn. *Unknown.* *Fr.* Homeric Hymns. GrPo
He Asketh Absolution of God. *Unknown, tr. fr. Egyptian by* Robert Hillyer. *Fr.* Book of the Dead. AWP
He ate and drank the precious words. Emily Dickinson. AmPo; AmPP; InP; OBAV; PoFr
(Book, A.) AA; MOB
(Precious Words.) BBV (1951 ed.); NeMA; PIAE
He Bare Him Up, He Bare Him Down. *Unknown.* *See* Falcon, The.
He bathes among orchids, washes his hair in the scented streams. The Lord Who Dwells in the Clouds. Chu Yuan. *Fr.* The Nine Songs. WhP
He beats us out upon the anvil of the days. The Master Blacksmith. Arnold Andrews. OQP; QP-1
He, before the captain, still and silent stood. Ballad. Ivan Sergeyevich Turgenev. WaL
He, behind the straight plough [*or* plow], stands. Ploughman [*or* Plowman] at the Plough [*or* Plow]. Louis Golding. HBMV; MBP; OHIP
He, being one, rules over all and everything. *Unknown.* *Fr.* The Upanishads. PoFr
He Biddeth Osiris to Arise from the Dead. *Unknown, tr. fr. Egyptian by* Robert Hillyer. *Fr.* Book of the Dead. AWP
He Bids Adieu to His Mistress. Alexander Montgomerie. *See* Adieu to His Mistress.
He Bids His Beloved Be at Peace. W. B. Yeats. Po
He blinks upon the hearth-rug. On a Cat Aging. Alexander Gray. PoC
He Bloomed among Eagles. David Ross. PG (1955 ed.)
He blows his dream into the sea-blue glass. The Glass Blower. Eleanor Jordan Houston. MuM
He boasts nor wealth nor high descent, yet he may claim to be. Nature's Gentleman. W. James Linton. BHV
He bore the brunt of it so long. His Deaths. Haniel Long. BAP; LEAP; NP
He brandished the two pillars like a spear. Who'll Toll the Knell? Alfred Alvarez. PoN
He breaks and gives his finger ring. The Passing of Richard Somers. Wallace Rice. GA
"He Bringeth Them unto Their Desired Haven." Lewis Frank Tooker. HBV
He brought a Grecian queen, whose youth and freshness. Portrait of Helen. Shakespeare. *Fr.* Troilus and Cressida, II, ii *and* IV, i. TrGrPo
He brought a lily white. To His Mother. John Banister Tabb. *Fr.* The Child. AA
He brought them from the muddy creek. Boy and Tadpoles. Louis Untermeyer. YT
He built a house; time laid it in the dust. The Greatest Work. Ray M. Johnson. MaRV; OQP; QP-2
He built a kingdom with his heart and brain. Resurrection and Ascension. Earl D. Todd. ChIP
He built no temple, yet the farthest sea. The Man Christ. Therese Lindsey. BePJ; BPP; ChIP; MaRV
He built of his dawn-bright dreaming. Shipwreck. Viktor Rydberg. AnSL
He burned no fiery cross. His Cross. Marguerite Wilkinson. OQP; QP-1
He calleth to me out of Seir, Watchman, what of the night? Watchman, What of the Night. Isaiah, Bible, *O.T.* AWP
He came,/ striding. Paul Bunyan. Arthur S. Bourinot. FaPON; TwCaPo
He came, a youth, singing in the dawn. Paul Laurence Dunbar. James David Corrothers. BANP; PoNe; PtP
He came across the meadow-pass. The Old Story. John O'Hagan. TIP
He came all so still. Carol [*or* An Ancient Christmas Carol]. *Unknown.* BoTP; DD; HBV; HBVY; OHIP; PCH; RG
He came and took me by the hand. The Mystery. Ralph Hodgson. BLV; BMEP; BoLiVe; CAW; CH; ChMo; CMP; HBV; LEAP; MaRV; MBP; MoAB; MoBrPo; NeMA; NP; OQP; QP-1; QS; WGRP
He came arrayed. Blue and Gold. Ibn Burd. MooP
He came from Ballyvourney and we called him "Ballyvourney." Ballyvourney. Thomas Boyd. GTIV
He came from hills to comfortable plains. The Mountaineer. Robert Nathan. BAP; TrJP
He came from Malta; and Eumelus says. A Maltese Dog. Tymnes. FaBoCh; LoGBV; OxBG; TiPo (1959 ed.)
He came from out eternal years. *See* He came to her from out eternal years.
He came from out the void. *See* He came out the void.
He came from the North, and his words were few. The Man of the North Countrie. Thomas D'Arcy McGee. OnYI
He came in from the damp. The Misjudged Fiddler. Erik Axel Karlfeldt. AnSL
He came in silvern armour, trimmed with black. Sonnets, I. Gwendolyn B. Bennett. CDC; PoNe
He came not as the princes born to rule. Lincoln. Clyde Walton Hill. PEDC; PGD
He came not in the red dawn. The Adventurer. Odell Shepard. HBMV; OBAV
He came out [*or* from out] the void. Roosevelt. Robert H. Davis. GA; HH; PEDC
He came—the infant Christ of God. The Christ of God. Russell E. Kauffman. BePJ
He came to be The Light. It Was Not Strange. Esther Lloyd Hagg. PGD
He came to call me back from death. Eurydice. Francis William Bourdillon. HBV; TVSH; VA
He came to earth one blue-skied day. Christ in the Street. Jay G. Sigmund. ChIP

He came to her [*or* He came] from out eternal years. The Spouse of Christ. D. A. Casey. JKCP; PraNu

He came to me. Saint Ite. Robin Flower. MM; PraNu

He came to me in his swift course. *Unknown. Fr.* Sweeney the Mad. OnYI

He came to my desk with quivering lip. The [*or* A] New Leaf. Kathleen Wheeler. BLRP; MaRV; OQP; PGD; PoToHe; PSO; QP-1; WBLP

He Came to Pay. "Parmenas Mix." BOHV

He came to the desert of London town. William Blake. James Thomson. EmBrPo; HBV; OAEP; OBVV; POTT; PoVP; PtP; VLEP

He Came Too Late. Elizabeth Bogart. AA

He Came Unlook'd For. Sara Coleridge. *Fr.* Phantasmion. OBRV; VA

(Song: "He came unlook'd for, undesir'd.") OBVV

He came with roses in his mouth. Joy o' Living. Amanda Benjamin Hall. HBMV

He cannot as he came depart. Influence. John Banister Tabb. PoMa

He cannot be complete in aught. On a Sense of Humor. Frederick Locker-Lampson. BOHV; InP

He cannot forfeit it. Not any power. The Poet and His Song. Anna Hempstead Branch. MuM

He cannot heal who has not suffered much. Stigmata. Edwin McNeill Poteat. MaRV

He captured light and caged it in a glass. And Yet Fools Say. George S. Holmes. PoeMoYo; VOD (1935 ed.)

He Cares. "Susan Coolidge." MaRV

He Cares. Kabir, *tr. fr. Hindi.* MaRV

He Careth. "Marianne Farningham." *See* God Cares.

He carried endless failure. Sketch. Donald Jeffrey Hayes. DDA

He carved the red deer and the bull. In the Caves of Auvergne. W. J. Turner. HBMV; POTE; TCPD

He cast his robe away. At Beecher's Island. John G. Neihardt. *Fr.* The Song of the Indian Wars. TCPD

He casts a sheep's eye at her: a strange eye-spread. Of a Sheep's Eye. John Heywood. SiCE; TuPP

He caught from silver stars, each one, a note. Beethoven. Florence Ellenwood Allen. CAG

He caught his chisel, hastened to his bench. The Death of Azron. Alice Wellington Rollins. AA

He ceas'd, but while he spake, Rustum had risen. The Combat. Matthew Arnold. *Fr.* Sohrab and Rustum. VA

He ceased; and Satan stayed not to reply. Satan Views the World. Milton. *Fr.* Paradise Lost, II. WHA

He Charges Her To Lay Aside Her Weapons. Pierce Ferriter, *tr. fr. Late Middle Irish by* the Earl of Longford. AnIL; LiTW; OnYI

"He chases shadows," sneered the British [*or* Bristol] tars. The First Voyage of John Cabot. Katharine Lee Bates. CV; MC; PAH

He cherished a girl who was pure as snow. A Man's Love. Tove Ditlevsen. LiTW

He chose the sea, mother, emancipator. The Man Who Wanted to Be a Seagull. J. R. Hervey. AnNZ

He circles about his master's knees. Old Dogs. William Sydney Thayer. PoP

He clasps the crag with crooked [*or* hooked] hands. The Eagle. Tennyson. BEL; BLA; BLV; BMEP; BoLiVe; BoTP; BPN; CBE; CBOV; CH; CoEV; EG; EnL; ExPo; FaBoCh; FaPON; FiP; GN; GoTP; GTBS-D; GTML; GTSL; HBV; HiLiEn; LoGBV; LPS-2; MW; MyFE; OAEP; OTPC; PCD; PCH; PIAE; PIR; PoeMoYo; PoF; PoMa; PoVP; RIS; SeCePo; SeCeV; ShBV-1; ShGoBo; SN; StaSt; SUS; ThWaDe; TrGrPo; UnPo (3d ed.); UTS; ViPo; ViPP; VLEP; WhBS; YT

He climbed up the candlestick. The Mouse. *Unknown.* PCH

He Climbs a Hill and Turns His Face. Lionel Wiggam. PoMa

He closed the Bible carefully, putting it down. The Slaver. Stephen Vincent Benét. *Fr.* John Brown's Body. AmPP; TwCV

He Comes. Sam Walter Foss. *Fr.* Father's Journey. FAOV

He Comes. Jalal ed-Din Rumi, *tr. fr. Persian by* R. A. Nicholson. PeP

He comes again! Madrigal. Sir Edmund Gosse. PtP

He Comes Among. George Barker. OBMV

He comes; and fawn and branch and moon delight. *Unknown. Fr.* The Mock Caliph. EnLi-1

He comes—he comes—the Frost Spirit comes! The Frost Spirit. Whittier. BAV; HBV; PCH

He comes in the night! He comes in the night! Santa Claus. *Unknown.* BoTP; ChBR; COAH; HBVY; HH; MeMeAg; PEDC; PRWS; TVC

He comes on chosen evenings. The Blackbird. John Drinkwater. BLA; TVSH; WP

He comes, the happy warrior. Sinfonia Eroica. Alice Archer James. AA

He comes, the old one, his shabby cap askew. Old Man with a Mowing Machine. May Carleton Lord. GoYe

He comes to the oat-field each night to feed. In the Elk Season. Erik Axel Karlfeldt. AnSL

He comes with herald clouds of dust. Superior Nonsense Verses. *Unknown.* NA

"He comes with western winds, with evening's wandering airs." Emily Brontë. *Fr.* The Prisoner. GTBS-D

He comes! Yohewah! the Great Spirit, comes. Charles Mair. *Fr.* Tecumseh. PeCV

He Cometh. Judah Halevi, *tr. fr. Hebrew by* Emma Lazarus. TrJP

He Cometh Forth into the Day. *Unknown, tr. fr. Egyptian by* Robert Hillyer. *Fr.* Book of the Dead. AWP; JAWP; WBP

He Cometh Late. *Unknown.* OQP; QP-1

He cometh, O bliss! He Cometh. Judah Halevi. TrJP

He Commandeth a Fair Wind. *Unknown, tr. fr. Egyptian by* Robert Hillyer. *Fr.* Book of the Dead. AWP

He compares his beloved to a snake. Microcosmos, VII. Nigel Heseltine. NeBP

He Complains How Soon the Pleasing Novelty of Life Is Over. William Shenstone. *See* Elegy: He Complains . . .

He could not die when trees were green. The Dying Child. John Clare. EnRP; ERP; TrGrPo

He could not separate the thought. Country Church. Robert P. Tristram Coffin. MaRV; QS

He could not tell the way he came. The Way. William Stanley Braithwaite. Sandy Star and Willie Gee, IV. BANP

He could not win you easily, your death. In Memory of Robin Hyde, 1906–39. Charles Brasch. AnNZ

He could raise scruples dark and nice. Sir Hudibras. Samuel Butler. *Fr.* Hudibras. UnPo (1st ed.)

He could see the little lake. The Lake. James Stephens. AnEnPo; MoBrPo

He could sing sweetly on a string. Orpheus. Elizabeth Madox Roberts. MAP; MoAmPo

He couldn't hear their roar. Drowned Sailor. Neufville Shaw. CaP

He crawls along the mountain walls. On the Heights. Lucius Harwood Foote. AA

He crawls to the cliff and plays on the brink. The Sea-Child. Eliza Cook. VA

He cried aloud to God: "The men below." Genius. Edward Lucas White. AA; WGRP

He crouches, and buries his face on his knees. The Last of His Tribe. Henry Clarence Kendall. VA

He crouches in the chapel, on his knees. Alien. Mary Brent Whiteside. SaFP

He cut a sappy sucker from the muckle rodden-tree. The Whistle. Charles Murray. EBSV; GoTS; ShBV-1

He dared not ask a kiss. The Hazard. John Kendrick Bangs. PR

He Declares That Albeit He Were Imprisoned in Russia, Yet His Mind Was at Liberty and Did Daily Repair to His Friend. George Turberville. TuPP

He deemed his task a solemn one. Priest and Pagan. Albert Durrant Watson. CaP; CPG; OCL

He Defendeth His Heart against the Destroyer. *Unknown, tr. fr. Egyptian by* Robert Hillyer. *Fr.* Book of the Dead. AWP

He Desires Her Husband's Death. Dafydd ap Gwilym, *tr. fr. Welsh by* David Bell. LyMA

He did not come to judge the world, he did not come to blame. His Name. Dora Greenwell. ChIP

He did not come to woo U Nu. Just Dropped In. William Cole. FiBHP

He did not kill. Ballad. Jacob Glatstein. OnCuPl

He Did Not Know. Harry Kemp. WGRP

He did not wear his scarlet coat. The Ballad of Reading Gaol. Oscar Wilde. AnFE; BeLS; BMEP; EnLi-2; EnLit; HBV; LEAP; LiTG; MBP; MoBrPo; OBMV; OnYI; OtMeF; PIR; PoVP; TCEP; TreF; VLEP

He didn't know much music. The Mocking-Bird. Frank L. Stanton. AA; POT; PoTo

He Didn't Oughter. A. P. Herbert. ALV; FiBHP

He died—a hero in the fight. Judgment. Eleanor Graham. DDA

He died alone; in all this mighty city. The Army of Despair. John Chalmers DaCosta. PoP

He died! and with him perished all that men hold dear. Hope. *Unknown.* ChIP; OQP; QP-1

He Died for Me. George Washington Bethune. BePJ

He died for me: what can I offer him? Not Yours but You. Christina Rossetti. ChIP; MaRV

He died in attempting to swallow. The Death of Polybius Jubb [*or* Limerick]. Roy Campbell. LiBL; LiTG; SiTL; WhC

He disappeared in the dead of winter. In Memory of W. B. Yeats. W. H. Auden. ATP (1953 ed.); BoLiVe (1945 ed.); ChMo; CoBMV; EnL; FaFP; GTBS-W; HoPM; InPo; LiTB; LiTM; MaPo; MoAB; MoBrPo; MoVE; NePA; OAEP (2d ed.); OnHM; Po; PoFS; PreP;

He disappeared in the dead of winter (*continued*) PtP; ReMP; TrGrPo; TwHP; UnPo (3d ed.); ViBoPo (1958 ed.)

He does not die that can bequeath[e]. Duncton Hill. Hilaire Belloc. GoBC; TwCV

He does not hear the struck string. Music God. Mark Van Doren. UnS

He does not think that I haunt here nightly. The Haunter. Thomas Hardy. AtBAP; ChMP; GTBS-D

He doesn't know when it was that the last door closed. After Some Day of Decision. Reed Whittemore. NePoEA

He Doeth All Things Well. Anne Brontë. MaRV

He doeth well who doeth good. Best of All. *Unknown.* WBLP

He dowelles ther al that day, and dresses on the morn. *Unknown. Fr.* Sir Gawain and the Green Knight. NBE

He dreamt that he saw the Buffalant. A Quadrupedremian Song. Tom Hood. *Fr.* From Nowhere to the North Pole. BoN

He drew a circle that shut me out. Outwitted. Edwin Markham. AnAmPo; BAP; BLPA; BLV; CV; DDA; GrCo-1; LA; MAP; MaRV; MCCG; MoAmPo; NeMA; OQP; PC; PIAE; PoeMoYo; PoToHe; PreP; PYM; QP-1

He drew a straight line. Within the Alamo. Karle Wilson Baker. HiLiAm

He dropt a tear on Susan's bier. Susan. Frederick Locker-Lampson. BOHV

He drowsed and was aware of silence heaped. The Death-Bed. Siegfried Sassoon. MoVE; POTE; TCEP

He dumped her in the wheelbarrow. Wheelbarrow. Eleanor Farjeon. FiBHP

He dwelt among "Apartments let." Jacob. Phoebe Cary. BOHV; InMe; PA

He earns the oblivion of book and shelf. Without Sleep. Glenway Wescott. NP

He either fears his fate too much. The Touch. James Graham *Fr.* My Dear and Only Love. OtMeF

He Embarketh in the Boat of Ra. *Unknown, tr. fr. Egyptian by* Robert Hillyer. *Fr.* Book of the Dead. AWP

He ended, and they both descend the hill. The Expulsion from Paradise. Milton. *Fr.* Paradise Lost, XII. ATP; BEL; NBE; SeEP; TCEP

He ended; and thus Adam last replied [*or* reply'd]. The Retreat from Paradise. Milton. *Fr.* Paradise Lost, XII. CoBE; MyFE; PoEL-3

He entered the shop/ To buy some toy. Birthday Gift. Ethel Barnett de Vito. AlBD

He entered with the authority of politeness. The Southerner. Karl Shapiro. FiMAP; PoNe

He Entereth the House of the Goddess Hathor. *Unknown, tr. fr. Egyptian by* Robert Hillyer. *Fr.* Book of the Dead. AWP

He enters my mind and laughs. We talk thought-talk. Meditation on Jesus Christ. Johanna Rachel Branigan. QS

He Establisheth His Triumph. *Unknown, tr. fr. Egyptian by* Robert Hillyer. *Fr.* Book of the Dead. AWP; JAWP; WBP

He ever warred with freedom and the free. Byron. *Fr.* The Vision of Judgment. PoFr

He Falls. William A. Donaghy. *Fr.* The Stations of the Cross. JKCP (1955 ed.)

He feels small as he awakens. The Awakening. Robert Creeley. NeAP

He fell, a slave of tinsel honour. On the Death of Pushkin. Mikhail Yurevich Lermontov. PoFr

He Fell among Thieves. Sir Henry Newbolt. BBV; CP; HBV; HBVY; OBEV; OBVV; PCN; PoeT; PoMa; ShBV-3; ShGoBo; TCEP; TwCV

"He Fell among Thieves." *Unknown, tr. fr. Greek by* F. L. Lucas. GrPE

He fell at Loos: and when she heard. Katherine Veitch. W. W. Gibson. CV

He felt the wild beast in him between whiles. Modern Love, IX. George Meredith. EmBrPo; POTT; ViPo

He finds that talk of music, books and art is. A Man of Culture. A. S. J. Tessimond. HaMV

He first deceas'd: she for a little tried [*or* tri'd]. Upon [*or* On] the Death of Sir Albert Morton's Wife. Sir Henry Wotton. BLV; CaAE; CBOV; EnLoPo; EV-2; OBEV; OBS; OnPM; PIAE; SeEP; TrGrPo; ViBoPo; WoL

He fixed his hat Kildare-side on. Light Shoes. Patrick Kelly. JKCP (1926 ed.)

He followed the pair to Pawtucket. Limerick. *Unknown.* HBV (8th ed.)

He fought for his soul. His Ally [*or* The Last Ally]. William Rose Benét. PC; PoeMoYo

He found a formula for drawing comic rabbits. Epitaph on an Unfortunate Artist. Robert Graves. WhC

He found a woman in the cave. Thalaba and the Magic Thread. Robert Southey. *Fr.* Thalaba the Destroyer. EV-4; SeCePo

He found her by the ocean's moaning verge. Modern Love, XLIX. George Meredith. BEL; BMEP; EmBrPo; EnLi-2; HBV; OAEP; PoE; POTT; ViP; ViPo

He found life a pattern. Paul. Earl B. Marlatt. OQP; QP-1

He found me sitting among flowers. Song. Aubrey Thomas De Vere. IrPN

He gathered cherry-stones, and carved them quaintly. An Art Master. John Boyle O'Reilly. AA

He gathered for His own delight. Ere the Golden Bowl Is Broken. Anna Hempstead Branch. AnAmPo; AnFE; APA; CoAnAm; LA; MAPA

He gathers data. The Statistician. Charles Wharton Stork. PoMa

He gave a last pull at his pipe and then. The Ballad of Nails. Nikolai Tikhonov. RuPo

He gave his card. How many times have I. Contact. Dorothy Livesay. CaP

He gave his life for those he loved. Woodrow Wilson. Edward Parker Davis. LPS-1

He gave his life upon a [*or* the] cross. His Garments. Esther Lloyd Hagg. ChIP; PGD

He gave me a quince. The Quince. *Unknown.* ChLP; WhP

"He gave the little wealth he had." Swift. *Fr.* Verses on the Death of Dr. Swift. ViBoPo

He gave the solid rail a hateful kick. The Egg and the Machine. Robert Frost. MAP; MoAmPo

He gave the world, in darkness pent. The Tragedy. Thomas Curtis Clark. ChIP

He gave us all a good-bye cheerily. Messmates. Sir Henry Newbolt. CH; HBV; LEAP; MCCG; SG; ShBV-2; TVSH

He girded on his shining sword. The Quest of the Purple Cow. Hilda Johnson. BOHV

He Gives His Beloved Certain Rhymes. W. B. Yeats. EG

He Gives Nothing. James Russell Lowell. *Fr.* The Vision of Sir Launfal, Pt. I. MaRV

He Giveth More. Annie Johnson Flint. BLRP; WBLP

He Goes. Sam Walter Foss. *Fr.* Father's Journey. FAOV

He goes out with his dreams. A Boy of the Ghetto. Margaret Widdemer. CV

He grasped his ponderous hammer; he could not stand it more. The Blacksmith of Limerick. Robert Dwyer Joyce. TIP

He greets you with a smile from friendly eyes. Solway Ford. W. W. Gibson. TCPD

He grew!/ From tiny babe to sturdy boy and vigorous man. The Son of Man. Dorothy J. Langford. BePJ

He grew where waves ride nine feet high. In Memoriam: Roy Campbell. R. N. Currey. BoSA

He grins a little as they drive him by. Dog in a Car. David McCord. AlBD

He had a coat of Christendom as Holy Church teaches. The Average Man. William Langland. *Fr.* The Vision of Piers Plowman. PoLi

He had a whim and laughed it out. Laughing It Out. William Stanley Braithwaite. Sandy Star and Willie Gee, II. BANP

He had been long t'wards mathematicks. Portrait of Sidrophel [*or* Sir Sidrophel, the Conjuror]. Samuel Butler. *Fr.* Hudibras. FaBoEn; PoEL-3

He had been singing—but I had not heard his voice. The Quiet Singer. Charles Hanson Towne. HBV; LBMV; VOD

He had been to the far places. Strange. Dorothy Quick. DaM

He had his beer. *Unknown.* WhC

He Had His Dream. Paul Laurence Dunbar. MaRV

He had in his hand a red plant. Meeting by the Gjulika Meadow. Geoffrey Grigson. WaP

He had no royal palace. A Christmas Verse. "Kay." BoTP

He had no times of study, and no place. The Poet of Nature. Philip James Bailey. *Fr.* Festus. LPS-3

He had not reckoned on a visitor. Death Was a Woman. Sydney King Russell. GoYe

He had played by the cottage fire. The Ballad of the Fiddler. "Seumas O'Sullivan." MPB

He had the plowman's strength. Lost in France; Jo's Requiem. Ernest Rhys. POTE; SoV

He harried lions up the peaks. A Rhyme for All Zionists. Vachel Lindsay. MeRV

He has a drooping winged moustache. Texas Types—"The Bad Man." William Lawrence Chittenden. PoOW

He has a giant's frame. Locomotive. Shigeharu Nakano. PoLJ

He has come the way of the fighting men and fought by the rules of the game. The Fighting Failure. Everard Jack Appleton. HBV; YaD

He has conned the lesson now. Fairy Song. Winthrop Mackworth Praed. EV-4; LEAP; OBEV (1st ed.); SeCePo

He has dust in his eye, a fan for a wing. My What-Is-It. Robert Frost. RIS

He Has Fallen from the Height of His Love. Wilfrid Scawen Blunt. The Love Sonnets of Proteus, XIV. ViBoPo
He Has Fine Eyes. Alma Ellis Hoernecke. MuM
He has gone/ the silent road. Last Journey. Enrique González Martínez. AnMP
He has no soul, who dares to doubt. With a Nosegay. Henrik Wergeland. AnNoLy
He has observed the golden rule. Blake. *Fr.* Gnomic Verses. TrGrPo
He has outsoared the shadow of our night. Shelley. *Fr.* Adonais. CoEV
He has soared to the crest. The Champion. Ibn Baqi. MooP
He has solved it—Life's wonderful problem. Laurels and Immortelles. *Unknown.* BLPA
He has stolen from the cat his agile grace. Prose Poem: Harlequin. Théodore de Banville. OnPM
He has taken away the things that I love [*or* loved] best. The Gift. Aline Kilmer. CP; NV
He has th' enjoyment of a flower's birth. The Poet's Portion. Thomas Hood. RO
He has told me more than once. Forecast. Elspeth MacDuffie O'Halloran. PR
He Hath No Parallel. Sadi, *tr. fr. Persian by* L. Cranmer-Byng. *Fr.* The Gulistan. AWP; LiTW
He hath no place to rest his head. Judaeus Errans. Louis Golding. TrJP
He heard, and madly at the motion pleased. Homer. *Fr.* The Iliad, IV. GrPo
He Heard Her Sing, *sel.* James Thomson.
"And thus all-expectant abiding I waited not long." VA
He heard the Voice that spake and, unafraid. Shakespeare. Henry Jerome Stockard. NoCaPo
He hears me pray to Him upon the deep. In All Things, Victory. Nagata. PraP; SoLD
He held no dream worth waking; so he said. On the Death of Robert Browning. Swinburne. A Sequence of Sonnets on the Death of Robert Browning, VII. BPN; EmBrPo; EnLit; EPN; PoVP; VLEP
He hides within the lily. Consider the Lilies. William Channing Gannett. GrCo-1; MaRV; WGRP
He Holdeth Fast to the Memory of His Identity. *Unknown, tr. fr. Egyptian by* Robert Hillyer. *Fr.* Book of the Dead. AWP; JAWP; WBP
He holds the universe in his grasp. God. *Unknown, tr. by* Mukerji. *Fr.* The Upanishads. MW
He Hopes That Time Will Render Her More Merciful. Petrarch, *tr. fr. Italian by* Robert Guthrie MacGregor. Sonnets to Laura: To Laura in Life, XI. EnLi-1; OuHeWo
He huffs from the north. March Wind. Maud E. Uschold. YeAr
He Inadvertently Cures His Love-Pains. Thomas Hardy. ChMo; CMP
He Inspects His Armory. Hyam Plutzik. FiMAP
He invented a rainbow but lightning struck it. Bushed. Earle Birney. PeCV
He is a bird round which a trap closes. The Holy Man. *Unknown. Fr.* The Devil's Tribute to Moling. OnYI
He is a friend, who, although meeting with enmity. Friendship. Jami. BoFr
He is a hat and coat. Neighbour. J. R. Hervey. AnNZ
He is a heart. A Love Song. *Unknown.* AnIL
He is a leopard that changed each spot. Two. Ralph Cheyney. PR
He is a man—magnanimous broad brow. Christ before Pilate. George Herbert Clarke. StJW
He is a path, if any be misled. Excellency of Christ. Giles Fletcher. *Fr.* Christ's Victory and Triumph. BePJ; ChIP; MaRV; StJW; WGRP
He is a roguish little elf. Dandelion. Kate L. Brown. TVC; TVSH
"He is a sinner," you are pleased to say. Self-Righteousness. John Byrom. MaRV
He is a tower unleaning. But how will he not break. Vaunting Oak. John Crowe Ransom. OxBA
He is alive with pain: His body lifts. The Crucifixion. John W. Lynch. JKCP (1955 ed.)
He is always standing there. My Policeman. Rose Fyleman. BoChLi; TiPo
He is an alien to all grief whose heart. Song for Dark Days. Anderson M. Scruggs. MuM
He is an old man. Stooped and tired. Very Seldom. C. P. Cavafy. MoGP
He is as old as I. The Old Apothecary. Lu Yu. WhP
He is away gathering dolichos. Gathering Dolichos. *Unknown.* WhP
He Is Buried. William A. Donaghy. *Fr.* The Stations of the Cross. JKCP (1955 ed.)
He is carved in alabaster, he is called the Reading Boy. The Reading Boy. Nathalia Crane. PoTo
He is changed to a god [he] who looks on her. Catullus, *tr. fr. Latin by* Horace Gregory. LaP; RoL
He is coming, my long-desired lord. The River of Heaven. *Unknown. Fr.* Manyo Shu. AWP; LiTW
He Is Condemned. William A. Donaghy. *Fr.* The Stations of the Cross. QS
He is daily with us, loving, loving, loving. "Daily with You." Annie Johnson Flint. BLRP
He is dead and gone—a flower. Dirge for an Infant. Leigh Hunt. ERP
He is dead and gone, lady. Ophelia's Songs. Shakespeare. *Fr.* Hamlet, IV, v. LO
He is dead, the beautiful youth. Killed at the Ford. Longfellow. BBV; IAP; OHIP; TCAP
He Is Declared True of Word. *Unknown, tr. fr. Egyptian by* Robert Hillyer. *Fr.* Book of the Dead. AWP; JAWP; WBP
He is dying. The Vanishing Boat. Sir Edmund Gosse. TCPD
He is gone: better so. We should know who stand under. The Deserter from the Cause. Gerald Massey. VA; YT
He is gone on the mountain. Coronach. Sir Walter Scott. *Fr.* The Lady of the Lake, III. AnFE; BEL; BHV; BPN; BSV; CaAE; CH; EBSV; EmBrPo; EnLi-2 (1949 ed.); EnLit; EnRP; EPN; ERP; EV-4; GTBS; GTBS-D; GTBS-W; GTSL; HBV; InP; LPS-1; MW; OAEP; OBRV; OHIP; PCD; PCN; PoRA; ShBV-1; TCEP; TOP; TreFS; TrGrPo; ViBoPo; WHA
He is here, Urania's son. Epithalamium. A. E. Housman. MM
He Is Jealous of the Heavens and Earth. Petrarch, *pr. tr. fr. Italian by* J. M. Synge. *See* Translation from Petrarch, A ("What a grudge I am bearing . . .").
He Is like the Lotus. *Unknown, tr. fr. Egyptian by* Robert Hillyer. *Fr.* Book of the Dead. AWP; JAWP; WBP
He Is like the Serpent Saka. *Unknown, tr. fr. Egyptian by* Robert Hillyer. *Fr.* Book of the Dead. AWP
He is made one with Nature: there is heard. Shelley. *Fr.* Adonais. WGRP
He Is Mine. Francis Quarles. *See* My Beloved Is Mine, and I Am His.
He is murdered upright in the day/ his flesh is opened and displayed. Vaticide. Myron O'Higgins. OnHM
He Is My Countryman. Antoni Slonimski, *tr. fr. Polish by* Frances Notley. TrJP
He is no friend who in thine hour of pride. Friendship. Sadi. *Fr.* The Gulistan. AWP; BoFr; JAWP; WBP
He is not a brother to me. The Brother. Semyon Yakovlevich Nadson. TrJP
He Is Not Dead. James Whitcomb Riley. *See* Away.
He Is Not Dead. Shelley. *Fr.* Adonais. MaRV
(Against Oblivion.) TreFS
("Peace, peace! he is not dead, he doth not sleep.") BoFr; FaBoEn; LEAP; LO; UnW
He Is Not Dead. Maurice Thompson. *Fr.* Lincoln's Grave. PSO
(Lincoln's Grave.) LBAH
(Prophecy, A.) AA
He is not dead,/ Your son, your dear beloved son. Joseph Auslander. *Fr.* He Is Risen. MaRV
He is not dead nor liveth. The Buried Child. Dorothy Wellesley. Deserted House: Epilogue. GTBS-D; OBMV
He is not desolate whose ship is sailing. In Solitude. Virna Sheard. CPG
He is not drunk who, from the floor. Epigram. Eugene Field. ALV
He is not greatest who with pick and spade. Sir Walter Raleigh. Henry Jerome Stockard. NoCaPo
He is not here, the old sun. No Possum, No Sop, No Taters. Wallace Stevens. AmP; MoVE; OxBA; PoFS
He is not John, the gardener. A Friend in the Garden. Juliana Horatia Ewing. BoTP; FaPON; GFA; MPB; OTPC (1946 ed.); RAR; StVeCh; TVC; TVSH; UTS
He Is Not Risen. W. S. Handley Jones. MaRV
He is not seen. His Triumph. Pedro Salinas. CoSP
He is one of the prophets come back. He. Lawrence Ferlinghetti. NeAP
He is our great High Priest today. Our High Priest. Annie Johnson Flint. PraP
"He Is Our Peace." Molly Anderson Haley. PGD
He is quick, thinking in clear images. In Broken Images. Robert Graves. CoEV; MoP
He Is Risen. Cecil Frances Alexander. EOAH
He Is Risen, *sel.* Joseph Auslander.
"He is not dead,/ Your son, your dear beloved son." MaRV
He Is Risen. John Oxenham. ChIP
He Is Shy. Theodore Colombo. CAG
He is sleeping, soundly sleeping. A Departed Friend. Julia A. Moore. FiBHP
He is so little, and the way is dim. Okura, *tr. fr. Japanese by* Lois J. Erickson. SoLD
He is stark[e] mad, who ever say[e]s. The Broken Heart. John Donne. AtBAP; ElSeCe; LiTL; LoPo; PoFS; ReEn; TuPP

He is that fallen lance that lies as hurled. A Soldier. Robert Frost. MoPo; NePA; SeCeV; SoV; TriL; TwP; WaaP; WaP
He is the Ancient Wisdom of the World. The Holy Child. Charles Carroll Albertson. ChIP; MaRV; StJW
He is the despots' despot. All must bide. The Dance of Death. Austin Dobson. HBV; TOP
He is the freeman whom the truth makes free. The Freeman. William Cowper. *Fr.* The Task, VI. LPS-2
He is the happy man, whose life ev'n [*or* even] now. The Happy Man. William Cowper. *Fr.* The Task, VI. BrBE; LPS-3
He is the happy wanderer who goes. The Happy Wanderer. Percy Addleshaw. OBVV; VA
He Is the Lonely Greatness. Madeleine Caron Rock. CAW; CH; ChIP
He is the Star of the Morning. Star of the Morning. D. V. Johnstone. BePJ
He Is the Way. W. H. Auden. *See* Chorus: "He is the Way."
He is to weet a melancholy carle. Spenserian Stanzas on Charles [Armitage] Brown [*or* A Portrait]. Keats. BOHV; InMe; PA
He is truly the only One. The Only One. Jo Gardner. BePJ
He isn't all Indian. Our Hired Man (and His Daughter, Too). Monica Shannon. FaPON
He isn't woolly, he isn't sweet. Lower Animals. Alan Anderson. PCD
He Jests at Scars [That Never Felt a Wound]. Shakespeare. *Fr.* Romeo and Juliet, II, ii. LiTB; LiTG; LiTL
(Balcony Scene, The.) TreF
(Living Juliet, The.) TrGrPo
He jumped, seeing an island like a hand. Hart Crane. Julian Symons. LiTM (1946 ed.)
He kept them pointed straight ahead. The Caravels of Columbus. Elias Lieberman. PEDC (1949 ed.)
He killed and kept. The Thoroughgoing. Josephine Miles. FiMAP
He killed the noble Mudjokovis. The Modern Hiawatha. George A. Strong. *Fr.* The Song of Milkanwatha. BOHV; FaPON; FiBHP; HBV; InMe; LiTG; MoShBr; NA; PA; PIAE; TreFS; WhC; YaD
He Kindleth a Fire. *Unknown, tr. fr. Egyptian by* Robert Hillyer. *Fr.* Book of the Dead. AWP
He kissed her on the face and the crew began to roar. Up She Goes. *Unknown.* SoAmSa
He knelt beside her pillow, in the dead watch of the night. Asleep. William Winter. AA; OBAV
He knew death only from what all men say. Death of the Beloved. Rainer Maria Rilke. UnW
He knew how Roman legions looked, for he. The Fog. Robert P. Tristram Coffin. CrMA; PreP
He knew not that the trumpet he had blown. David Livingstone. *Unknown.* MaRV
He knew what hunger a man can feel. Bread. Leslie Savage Clark. ChIP
He knocks upon your door. Boy at the Door. Louis J. Sanker. JKCP (1955 ed.)
He Knoweth Not That the Dead Are Thine. Mary Elizabeth Coleridge. *See* Unpunished.
He Knoweth the Souls of the East. *Unknown, tr. fr. Egyptian by* Robert Hillyer. *Fr.* Book of the Dead. AWP
He Knoweth the Souls of the West. *Unknown, tr. fr. Egyptian by* Robert Hillyer. *Fr.* Book of the Dead. AWP; JAWP; WBP
He knows celebrities . . . or else he lies. Savage Portraits. Don Marquis. HBMV
He knows not bit nor bridle, his nostrils are flaming. The Neighing North. Annie Charlotte Dalton. CaP
He knows the safeways and unsafe. Pan. Francis Ledwidge. TCPD
He knows why certain sycophants adore him. Portrait. Sydney King Russell. PoMa
He labored in a lonely field. Lincoln. Laura Simmons. LPS-1; PSO
He Laughed Last. Francis Whiting Hatch. WhC
He lay, and those who watched him were amazed. The Sprig of Lime. Robert Nichols. MM; POTE; TwCV
He lay. His propped-up countenance was clear. Death of the Poet. Rainer Maria Rilke. AnGP
He lay in's armour; as if that had been. A Soldier's Death. Cyril Tourneur. *Fr.* The Atheist's Tragedy. SeCePo
He lay upon his dying bed. The Sword of Bunker Hill. William Ross Wallace. PEDC
He Leadeth Me. Joseph H. Gilmore. BLRP; MaRV; WBLP; WGRP
("He leadeth me! O blessèd thought!") OIF
He Leadeth Me. *Unknown, at. to* H. H. Barry. BLRP
(On the Twenty-third Psalm, *abr.*) MaRV; OQP; QP-1
He Leads. Elisabeth Scollard. MaRV
He leads us on. Through the Maze. *Unknown.* BLRP
He Leads Us Still. Arthur Guiterman. OHIP; OQP; QP-1
He leans far out and watches: down below. The Moonshiner. Madison Cawein. The Mountain Still, I. SPP
He leant at the door. The Unfrocked Priest. Joseph Campbell. AnIL; OnYI
He leapt to arms unbidden. The Volunteer. Sir Henry Newbolt. CBE; PoeT
He leaves the end of the world to the accordion. Nature vive. Vicente Huidobro. TwSpPo
He leaves unplowed his furrow. Here's to the Ranger! *Unknown.* CSF; CoSo
He led me out to water, as you may understand. The Messenger Song. *At. to* John Calhoun. ShS
He left his horses standing. Boy with a Silver Plow. Dennis Murphy. BAP
He left his hose, his Hannah, and his love. To the Memory of a Young Man. *Unknown.* WhC
He left his office for the street. Home. Hermann Ford Martin. BLP
He left his pants upon a chair. The Mistake. Theodore Roethke. NePoAm-2
"He left no relatives," they said. Only a Dog. Marty Hale. AlBD
He left the land of youth, he left the young. Herodotus in Egypt. Andrew Lang. PoVP
He left two children, who for virtue, wit. Of Sir Philip Sidney. Sir John Beaumont. GoBC
He lies here. See the bush. His Epitaph. Frederick William Ophel. BoAu
He lies low in the levelled sand. At the Grave of Walker. Joaquin Miller. AA; AnAmPo; AnFE; APA; CoAnAm; LA; OBAV
He lies on the grass, looking up at the sky. Deaf and Dumb. "A." PRWS
He lies unloosened of his white clothes. A Dead Man. *Unknown.* OnPM
He lies upon his bed. Archibald MacLeish. *Fr.* Einstein. ImOP
He Lifted from the Dust. Helen Rogers Smith. BePJ
He lifted up her hand from off her breast. Thomas Holly Chivers. *Fr.* The Raising of Tabitha. PoP
He lifts his hopeful eyes at each new tread. Lost Dog. Frances Rodman. AlBD; PoRL
He Lived a Life. H. N. Fifer. BPP
"What was his creed?" *sel.* PoToHe (new ed.)
He Lived amidst th' Untrodden Ways. Hartley Coleridge. *See* On Wordsworth.
He lived at Dingle Bank—he did. At Dingle Bank. Edward Lear. WhC
He lived in a cave by the seas. Double Ballade of Primitive Man [*or* Ballade of Primitive Man]. Andrew Lang *and* Edward Burnett Tylor. ATP; BOHV; CenHV
He lived in that past Georgian day. A Gentleman of the Old School. Austin Dobson. BPN; EnLit; HBV; POTT
He lived one hundred and five. *Unknown.* WhC
He lives acrost the street from us. Chums. James William Foley. PTA-2
He Lives at Last. Lucile Lippitt. MaRV
He Lives! He Lives! Irene Rutherford McLeod. VOD
He lives, he wakes—'tis Death is dead, not he. One with Nature. Shelley. *Fr.* Adonais. MaRV
He Lives Long Who Lives Well. Thomas Randolph. WBLP
He lives, the great Redeemer lives. The Great Redeemer Lives. Anne Steele. BePJ
He lives within the hollow wood. The Charcoal-Burner. Sir Edmund Gosse. OBVV
He Liveth Long Who Liveth Well. Horatius Bonar. HBV; HBVY
(Who Liveth Well.) MaRV
He loathed his bond, but could not stir. Maurice Hewlett. *Fr.* The Song of the Plow, V. PoFr
He locked the window. First Night Alone. Mark Van Doren. MOAP
He loiters down the avenues of time. The Anthologist. Anderson M. Scruggs. DDA
He longs with a tireless yearning. Longing. Viktor Rydberg. AnSL
He Looked at Me with Eyes I Thought. A. E. Housman. More Poems, XLI. BoFr
He looked up and saw the rich men. The Widow's Mites. St. Luke, Bible, *N.T.* GrCo-1
He looks not holy; simple in his belief. The Modern Saint. Richard Burton. OQP; QP-1
He look't and saw what numbers numberless. The Parthians. Milton. *Fr.* Paradise Regained, III. OBS
"He lost his life"—yet was the reach. For Any Beachhead. M. K. Joseph. AnNZ
He loved her, having felt his love begin. The Contrast. Helen Gray Cone. AA
He loved the brook's soft sound. The Peasant Poet. John Clare. WGRP
He loves me. *Unknown.* OxNR
He loves not well whose love is bold! The Queen. William Winter. HBV

He lying spilt like water from a bowl. Poem. Alison Boodson. NeBP

He made a place in his dream for the pines to grow. Farmyard. Ruth Dallas. AnNZ

He made honest doors. Integrity. William L. Stidger. ChIP; OQP; QP-2

He made no history, even. Elegy for a Countryman. Padraic Fallon. NeIP

He Made the Night. Lloyd Mifflin. HBV

He made them and He called them good. Address to the Crown. Charles L. O'Donnell. GoBC

He Made This Screen. Marianne Moore. TCPD

He Made Us Free. Maurice Francis Egan. AA; JKCP

He Maketh Himself One with Osiris. *Unknown, tr. fr. Egyptian by* Robert Hillyer. *Fr.* Book of the Dead. AWP

He Maketh Himself One with the God Ra. *Unknown, tr. fr. Egyptian by* Robert Hillyer. *Fr.* Book of the Dead. AWP

He Maketh Himself One with the Only God, Whose Limbs Are the Many Gods. *Unknown, tr. fr. Egyptian by* Robert Hillyer. *Fr.* Book of the Dead. AWP; JAWP; WBP

He, making speedy way through 'spersèd air [*or* ayre]. The House of Morpheus [*or* The Cave of Sleep]. Spenser. *Fr.* The Faerie Queene, I. InP; LPS-3; UnPo (1st ed.)

He many a creature did anatomize. The Virtuoso. Mark Akenside. BCEP; LPS-3

He may be six kinds of a liar. Loyalty. Berton Braley. BLPA

He Meditates on the Life of a Rich Man. Douglas Hyde, *tr. fr. Modern Irish by* Lady Gregory. OBMV

He meets, by heavenly chance express. The Lover. Coventry Patmore. *Fr.* The Angel in the House, I. EPP; EV-5; PoVP

He Meets His Mother. William A. Donaghy. *Fr.* The Stations of the Cross. QS (Fourth Station.) ISi

He mends the shoes. Cobbler. Peggy Bacon. PoMa

He might have won the highest guerdon that heaven to earth can give. Saturninus. Katherine Eleanor Conway. AA; JKCP

He mightn't have had wherewith to buy. Last Mathematician. Hyman Edelstein. CaP

He Mourns for the Change That Has Come upon Him and His Beloved, and Longs for the End of the World. W. B. Yeats. Po

He must needs go through Samaria. Living Water. Ruth M. Williams. BePJ

He must not laugh at his own wheeze. The Humorist. Keith Preston. ALV; HBMV; WhC

He myghte neither steppe ne stonde til he his staffe hadde. Gluttony. William Langland. *Fr.* The Vision of Piers Plowman. CoEV

He Need Speak No Longer in Behalf of Sulpicia and Cerinthus. Tibullus, *tr. fr. Latin by* Hubert Creekmore. LaP

He needs must work, though time's onrushing wings. My Neighbor. Virginia Eaton. BPP

He ne'er had seen one earthly sight. The Blind Highland Boy. Wordsworth. OTPC

He never completed his History of Ephesus. On a Certain Scholar. W. Craddle. SiTL; WhC

He never found that far look. Estrangement. Wade Oliver. PoP

He never gave me a chance to speak. After the Quarrel. Adam Lindsay Gordon. OBVV

He never heard of Newton's law. The Rigger. Washington Jay McCormick. WhC

He never made parade of tooth or claw. A Ranger. Badger Clark. SCC

He never made the dive—not while I watched. The Springboard. Louis MacNeice. ChMP

He Never Smiled Again. Felicia Dorothea Hemans. HBV

He never spoke a word to me. Simon the Cyrenian Speaks. Countee Cullen. BBV (1951 ed); MAP; MaRV; MoAmPo; NeMA; OQP; PoNe; QP-1; QS; StJW

He never thought an honour done him. Swift. *Fr.* Verses on the Death of Dr. Swift. PoFr

He never used to notice me. The Policeman. Marjorie Seymour Watts. PCH; TiPo

He nothing common did or mean. King Charles upon the Scaffold. Andrew Marvell. *Fr.* An Horatian Ode upon Cromwell's Return from Ireland. ChTr

He, of his gentleness. In the Wilderness. Robert Graves. OxBI

He often came and stood outside my door. The Lonely Dog. Margaret E. Bruner. AlBD; PoToHe

He often crept out late at night. The Clown. Beatrice Redpath. CPG

He often spoke of things of home. Son of Man. Leslie Savage Clark. ChIP

He on a lean, ill-favored beast is set. The Death of Edward. Michael Drayton. *Fr.* Mortimeriados. ReIE

He, on whose natal hour you glance. This Is Thy Gift, O Muse [*or* The Gift of Song]. Horace, *tr. by* Christopher Smart. Odes, IV, 3. LiA; LiTW

He only is worthy of freedom who honors the freedom of others. Jan Kollar. *Fr.* The Daughter of the Slava. PoFr

He or she that hopes to gain. Song. *Unknown.* SeCL

He Overcometh the Serpent of Evil in the Name of Ra. *Unknown, tr. fr. Egyptian by* Robert Hillyer. *Fr.* Book of the Dead. AWP

He past; a soul of nobler tone. In Memoriam A. H. H., LX. Tennyson. EmBrPo; EPN; GEPC; ViPo; VLEP

He paused on the sill of a door ajar. The Newcomer's Wife. Thomas Hardy. PoFS

He paused: the listening dames again. Sir Walter Scott. *Fr.* The Lay of the Last Minstrel, IV. OBRV

He paweth in the valley and rejoiceth in his strength. The Horse. Job, Bible, *O.T.* StaSt

He peeps in through the key-hole. The Sand-Man. George Cooper. BOL

He Persuadeth His Friend from the Fond Affects of Love. Thomas Churchyard. ReIE

He placed a prayer wheel where the wild winds dance. Orisons. Edwin McNeill Poteat. NoCaPo (rev. ed.); OQP; QP-2

He planked down sixpence and he took his drink. Henry Turnbull. W. W. Gibson. FaBoTw

He planted an oak in his father's park. The Sower and His Seed. W. E. H. Lecky. TIP

He played by the river when he was young. Washington. Nancy Byrd Turner. FaPON; MPB; TiPo; YeAr

He plays across the centuries. Master Musician. Margaret Evelyn Singleton. ChIP

He plays for all the little side-streets, while. The Street Musician. *Unknown.* TSW; TSWC

He plays the deuce with my writing time. In New York. William Vaughn Moody. *Fr.* Song-Flower and Poppy. LEAP

He Plays the Piano with a Razor. Malcolm Lowry. BoCaPo (1948 ed.)

He poises a moment and looks at the earth far under. Parachute. Stanley Snaith. HaMV

He polished snubs till they were regnant art. In the Gentlemanly Interest. Donald Evans. NP

He praised the greatness of the child I bore. Thetis. Aeschylus. OxBG

He Praises Her Hair. *Unknown, tr. fr. Late Middle Irish by* the Earl of Longford. AnIL

He Praises His Wife When She Has Left [*or* Had Gone from] Him. *Unknown, tr. fr. Late Middle Irish by* Robin Flower. AnIL; OxBI

He prayed by the stone. Resignation. William L. Stidger. ChIP

He prayed for strength that he might achieve. Blessed [*or* How God Answers]. *Unknown.* MaRV; OQP; PraP; QP-2

He Prayeth Best. Samuel Taylor Coleridge. *Fr.* The Rime of the Ancient Mariner, VII. BPP; FaPON, 1 *st.;* GoTP, 1 *st.;* GrCo-1, 4 *sts.;* MaRV, 4 *sts.;* MeMeAg, 1 *st.,* PCH, 1 *st.,* PECK; StVeCh, 1 *st.* ("He prayeth best, who loveth best," 1 *st.*) LO; YT (He Prayeth Well, 6 *ll.*) BoTP

He Prayeth for Ink and Palette That He May Write. *Unknown, tr. fr. Egyptian by* Robert Hillyer. *Fr.* Book of the Dead. AWP

He Prayeth Well. Samuel Taylor Coleridge. *See* He Prayeth Best.

He preached upon "breadth" till it argued him narrow. Emily Dickinson. AmP; AmPo; AmPP; PoE

He protested all his life long. Mrs. Meyers. Edgar Lee Masters. *Fr.* Spoon River Anthology. ChMo; CMP

He pulled a flower. Ballad. Leonard Cohen. PeCV

He put away his tiny pipe. Spring Cricket. Frances Rodman. FaPON; SiSoSe

He put his acorn helmet on. A Fairy in Armor [*or* The Fay Arms Himself *or* An Elfin Knight]. Joseph Rodman Drake. *Fr.* The Culprit Fay. APW; BoTP; FaPON; GaP; GFA; OTPC; PRWS; RAR; TVSH

He quickly [*or* Pigwiggen] arms him for the field. The Arming of Pigwiggen [*or* Pigwiggen Prepares for the Fight with King Oberon]. Michael Drayton. *Fr.* Nymphidia. BoTP; EV-1; GN; MoShBr; OTPC

He ran right out of the woods to me. The Story of the Baby Squirrel. Dorothy Aldis. TiPo

He ran up the candlestick. A Chinese Nursery Rhyme. *Tr. by* Isaac Taylor Headland. RAR; TVC; TVSH

He reached the West in a palace car where the writers tell us the cowboys are. The Disappointed Tenderfoot. Earl Alonzo Brinninstool. SCC

He reaches Weymouth—treads the Esplanade. The Royal Tour. "Peter Pindar." OxBoLi

He reeled, intoxicated. Drunken Beauty. Ibn Billita. MooP

He Remembers Forgotten Beauty. W. B. Yeats. *See* Michael Robartes Remembers Forgotten Beauty.
He Remembers the Vista of a Towering Peak. Wordsworth. *Fr.* The Prelude, I. LiA
He rides at their head. The College Colonel. Herman Melville. AA; RiBV
He rides his white charger by the Fortalice of Gold. By the Great Wall. Li Po. ChLP
He rides no dashing charger in the tournament of life. The Knight. Sister Maryanna. WHL
He rises and begins to round. The Lark Ascending. George Meredith. CoBE; EmBrPo; EnLi-2; EPN; LoBV; OAEP; PoeT; POTT; PoVP
He rises from his guests, abruptly leaves. Ghost. Witter Bynner. AnFE; CoAnAm; TwAmPo
He riseth from supper, and laid aside his garments. The New Commandment. St. John, Bible, *N.T.* BoFr
He roamed half-round the world of woe. Epitaph. Aubrey Thomas De Vere. OBVV; PoVP
He roars in the swamp. The Alligator. Beatrice Ravenel. LS; TCPD
He rode at dusk down woodlands strange. The Knight Errant. Arthur Stringer. BoCaPo (1943 ed.)
He rose at dawn and, fired with hope. The Sailor Boy. Tennyson. BHV; BLP; BPN
He rubbed his eyes and wound the silver horn. Little Boy Blue. John Crowe Ransom. LiTM; TwAmPo
He Ruleth Not though He Reign [*or* Raigne] over Realms That Is Subject to His Own Lusts. Sir Thomas Wyatt. BrBE; ReIE; SiCE
("If thou wilt mighty be, flee from the rage.") SiPS
He runs before the wise men. He. Stanley Kunitz. CrMA
He said: and on his horses' shoulder-point. Apollo Destroys the Wall. Homer. *Fr.* The Iliad. OxBG
He said, and twang'd the string. The Death of Gorgythian. Homer. *Fr.* The Iliad. GrR
He said, and urged him forth, who binding on. Reunion of Ulysses and Telemachus [*or* Telemachus Finds His Father]. Homer. *Fr.* The Odyssey. GrR; OxBG
He said, "Awake my soul, and with the sun." Barthélémon at Vauxhall. Thomas Hardy. UnS
He said his legs were stiff and sore. Autumn Fields. Elizabeth Madox Roberts. BrR
He said: I am a parson, but I take. Fishing in the Australian Alps. Ernest G. Moll. WhC
He said, "I will forget the dying faces." In Acceptance Lieth Peace. Amy Carmichael. MaRV
He Said: "If in His Image I Was Made." Trumbull Stickney. AnFE; APA; CoAnAm; LiTA; TwAmPo
He Said That He Was Not Our Brother. John Banim. OnYI; TIP
He Said the Facts. Merrill Moore. CrMA
He said: "The shadows darken down." Ballad. May Kendall. HBV
He sang above the vineyards of the world. The Singing Man. Josephine Preston Peabody. HBV; LEAP; PoFr
He sang an old song. The Kilkenny Boy. Eileen Shanahan. NeIP
He sang at his bench in Nazareth. Carpenter. Leslie Savage Clark. ChIP
He sang of God—the mighty source. The Catholic Amen. Christopher Smart. *Fr.* A Song to David. BLV; GBV; GoBC; GTBS-W; GTSL; LiTG
He sang of joy; whate'er he knew of sadness. A Hero. Florence Earle Coates. BLP; GA; OHIP
He sang one song and died—no more but that. The Singer of One Song. Henry Augustin Beers. AA
He sang so wildly, did the boy. Mother's Love. Thomas Burbidge. MOAH; VA
He sang the airs of olden times. The Blind Psalmist. Elizabeth Clementine Kinney. AA
He sang, too. Crucifixion. Earl Marlatt. ChIP
He sat among the woods; he heard. Aesop. Andrew Lang. VA
He sat at the dinner table. Just like a Man. *Unknown, at. to* Lizzie M. Hadley. BoTP
He sat by a fire of seven-fold heat. The Refiner's Fire. *Unknown.* BLRP
He sat down opposite his wife on the seat he had left. Penelope Makes Trial of Odysseus. Homer. *Fr.* The Odyssey. OxBG
He sat in a wheeled chair, waiting for dark. Disabled. Wilfred Owen. LiTM (rev. ed.); NAMP; WaP
He sat one winter 'neath a linden tree. A Minor Poet. Alexander Smith. *Fr.* A Life-Drama. VA
He sat the quiet stream beside. A Greek Idyl. Mortimer Collins. VA
He sat upon a car (and the large pearl). Maria Gowen Brooks. *Fr.* Zophiel. BAP
He sat upon the rolling deck. Sailor. Langston Hughes. GoSl
He Satisfies. Frederick William Faber. BePJ
He saves the sheep, the goats he doth not save. The Good Shepherd with the Kid. Matthew Arnold. BMEP; MeRV: PoVP
He Saw Far in the Concave Green of the Sea. Keats. *Fr.* Endymion. EtS
He saw her from the bottom of the stairs. Home Burial. Robert Frost. AmPP; AnFE; AnNE; APA; BLV; BoLiVe; CoAnAm; CoBMV; MAPA; MaPo; MotAn; TwAmPo
He Saw Her Home. Mikhail Isakovsky, *tr. fr. Russian by* Jack Lindsay. RuPo
He saw his white walls shining in the sun. Lambro's Return. Byron. *Fr.* Don Juan, III. OBRV
He saw it clearly and clairvoyant bright. Blueprint. D. B. Steinman. GoYe
He saw it last of all before they herded in the steerage. Teresina's Face. Margaret Widdemer. HBMV; NP
He Saw My Heart's Woe. Charlotte Brontë. TriL
He saw not the two maidens, nor their smiles. Conclusion: The Decision of the Gods. Keats. *Fr.* Endymion. ERP
He saw the wind diffuse soft dust. Alien. Ann Louise Hayes. PtPa
He saw the Word that spake it. This Is My Body. John Donne. ChIP
He sayde and, on his Son with rayes direct. Milton. *Fr.* Paradise Lost, VI. NBE
He says, *My reign is peace,* so slays. A Foreign Ruler. Walter Savage Landor. PoFr; SoV; ViBoPo
He scanned it, staggered, dropped the loop. Emily Dickinson. PoEL-5
He scans the world with calm and fearless eyes. The New Negro. James Edward McCall. CDC
He scarce had ceas'd [*or* ceas't] when the superior Fiend. Satan and the Fallen Angels [*or* Satan Rallies the Fallen Angels *or* The Superior Fiend]. Milton. *Fr.* Paradise Lost, I. BCEP; CoEV; LiTB; MaPo; OBS; SeCePo
He scarce had finished, when such murmur filled. Beelzebub Rises to Speak. Milton. *Fr.* Paradise Lost, II. UnPo (1st ed.)
He seeks the mountains where the olives grow. The Transfiguration. James M. Hayes. JKCP
He Sees His Beloved. James I, King of Scotland. *Fr.* The Kingis Quair. PoEL-1
("Bewailling [*or* Bewailing] in my chamber thus allone," *shorter sel.*) BSV; LEAP, *abr.*
(Coming of Love, The, *shorter sel.*) GoTS
He sees the circle of the world. Golden Falcon. Robert P. Tristram Coffin. BLA; CAW; TBM
He sees the rosy apples cling like flowers to the bough. The Fruit Rancher. Lloyd Roberts. CaP; CPG
He sees them pass. Once. Eric N. Batterham. CH
He sent men out to preach the living Word. The Teacher. Hildegarde Hoyt Swift. ChIP; MaRV; OQP; QP-1
He set the world aflame. Jalal ed-Din Rumi, *tr. fr. Persian by* A. J. Arberry. PeP
He shall be my jailer. Drowned Woman. Elinor Wylie. TBM
He shall not hear the bittern cry. Thomas MacDonagh [*or* Lament for Thomas MacDonagh]. Francis Ledwidge. AnIV; GTIV; OnYI; OxBI; TCPD
He Shall Speak Peace. Thomas Curtis Clark. OQP; QP-1; WBLP
He Shall Speak Peace unto the Nations. Lila V. Walters. BePJ; WBLP
He should be walking in the clear moonlight. Drowning. John Ransom Palmer. PoP
He shudders . . . feeling on the shaven spot. Electrocution. Lola Ridge. TCPD
He Singeth a Hymn to Osiris the Lord of Eternity. *Unknown, tr. fr. Egyptian by* Robert Hillyer. *Fr.* Book of the Dead. AWP
He Singeth in the Underworld. *Unknown, tr. fr. Egyptian by* Robert Hillyer. *Fr.* Book of the Dead. AWP; JAWP; WBP
He Sins Not Who Sins Unwittingly. Sophocles, *tr. fr. Greek by* Robert Whitelaw. *Fr.* Oedipus at Colonus. GrR
He sipped a weak hock and seltzer. The Arrest of Oscar Wilde at the Cadogan Hotel. John Betjeman. InvP; LiTM (rev. ed.); SiTL
He sits above the clang and dust of Time. The Sovereign Poet. Sir William Watson. BMEP; LBBV; PoVP; WGRP
He sits at the foot of Golgotha. Lament for a Poor Poet. Myles Connolly. CAW
He sits in a stall at South Ferry. The Clam Man. Burke Boyce. DDA
He sits in silence on his porch at night. An Old Habitant. Frank Oliver Call. *Fr.* A Sonnet Series of French Canada. CaP; CPG; OCL
He sits over the glimmering coal. The Old Age Pensioner. Joseph Campbell. AnIL
He sits there on the low, rude backless bench. One of Our Presidents. Wendell Phillips Stafford. GrCo-2

He sits upon gold that glows—the Son of Heaven. The Love of a King. Tu Fu. ChLP
He sits upon his perch in the far evening. The Caged Eagle. John Gould Fletcher. ChMo; CMP
He sits upon the wharf. Ports Astern. Joseph Singer. DDA
He sleeps as a lamb sleeps. Lambs. Katharine Tynan. GTIV
He sleeps at last—a hero of his race. A Dead Soldier. George Edgar Montgomery. AA
He sleeps, he slumbers. Pan. Apollon Maikov. BoR
He sleeps in his last sleep, long time. The Veteran's Grave. Mikhail Lermontov. BoR
He sleeps on the top of a mast. The Unbeliever. Elizabeth Bishop. FiMAP; LiTA
He sleeps somewhere beneath the sod in France. For One Who Died. Jessica Powers. BPP
He sleeps, the "little general" sleeps. General Dabney H. Maury. Rosewell Page. BlG
He snuggles his fingers. After Winter. Sterling A. Brown. GoSl; PoNe
He sought Australia's far-famed isle. The Digger's Grave. Sarah Welch. VA
He sought the mountain and the loneliest height. Jesus Praying. Hartley Coleridge. MaRV; StJW
He sought the old scenes with eager feet. The Return. John Burroughs. MaRV
He sought the sea; His footsteps press the dry. Christ Quiets the Tempest. Caelius Sedulius. *Fr.* Carmen Paschale. OnYI
He spake; he swung up in his mighty hand. Quintus Smyrnaeus. *Fr.* Posthomerica, I. GrPo
He spake not truth, however wise, who said. Dreams. Andrew Lang. UnW
He spake, to whom I, answ'ring, thus replied. Of the Shade of Achilles. Homer. *Fr.* The Odyssey, XI. GrPo; OxBG
He Speaks for the Girl, on Cerinthus' Birthday. Tibullus, *tr. fr. Latin by* Hubert Creekmore. LaP
He speaks not well who doth his time deplore. The Heroic Age. Richard Watson Gilder. AA; OHIP
He spoke, and death and beauty stooped together. Franklin McDuffee. *Fr.* Michelangelo. BAP
He spoke; and Sohrab kindled at his taunts. The Death of Sohrab. Matthew Arnold. *Fr.* Sohrab and Rustum. LH; WHA
He spoke; and Sohrab smiled on him, and took/ The spear. The Death of Sohrab. Matthew Arnold. *Fr.* Sohrab and Rustum. FiP
He spoke, and what he spoke was all fulfilled. Moschus, *tr. fr. Greek by* H. H. Chamberlin. GrPo
He spoke of undying love. The Talker. Benjamin Appel. TrJP
He sported round the watery world. Jonah and the Whale. Viola Meynell. EtS; MBP; MoBrPo (1942 ed.)
He squats by the fire. Lob Lie-by-the-Fire. Walter de la Mare. CV
He Standeth at the Door. Arthur Cleveland Coxe. HBV
He stands against a window. Street Hawker. Allen Dow. CAG
He stands and walks as if his knees were tensed. Eastern Shore. Charles Bruce. PeCV
He stands around. The Wandering Void. *Unknown.* CAG
He stands big-shouldered and august. The Iron Horse. Israel Newman. PoMa
He stands in the porch of the world. The Red Patrol. Sir Gilbert Parker. CPG
He stands, the symbol of the things that were. The Blockader. DuBose Heyward. LS
He stands there in his glory. Bismarck. K. C. Ossian-Nilsson. AnSL
He stands where the white light showers. In the Art Museum. Gertrude Hall. OBAV
He started out to sing of labor. Portrait of a Poet. Edgar Lee Masters. *Fr.* Jack Kelso. ATP
He stayed: and was imprisoned in possession. W. H. Auden. *Fr.* In Time of War. ChMo; EnLit
He steps down from the dark train, blinking; stares. Ten Days Leave. W. D. Snodgrass. UnPo (3d ed.)
He stood a moment at the edge. Life or Death. Glenn Ward Dresbach. *Fr* In Western Mountains. HBMV
He stood a soldier to the last right end. Ben Jonson. *Fr.* A Pindaric Ode. CoBE
He stood, a worn-out City clerk. Peace. Charles Stuart Calverley. ViP; WhC
He stood alone within the spacious square. James Thomson. *Fr.* The City of Dreadful Night, IV. AnFE; EnLi-2; POTT
He stood among a crowd at Dromahair [*or* Drumahair]. The Man Who Dreamed of Faeryland. W. B. Yeats. GTIV; OAEP (2d ed.)
He stood and call'd his legions, angel forms. The Summons. Milton. *Fr.* Paradise Lost, I. WHA
He stood, and heard the steeple. Eight o'clock. A. E. Housman. Last Poems, XV. ExPo; InPo; LoBV; MBP; MoAB; MoBrPo; POTE; ReMP; ShBV-4; TrGrPo; TwP; ViP
He stood before the Sanhedrim. Religion and Doctrine. John Hay MaRV; OBAV; StJW; WGRP
He stood on his head by the wild seashore. His Mother-in-Law. Walter Parke. BOHV; FiBHP
He stood up in our khaki with the poise. Gee-up Dar, Mules. Edwin Ford Piper. YaD
He stood upon a slope of Olivet. And Thou Would'st Not! Winifred Stoddard LeBar. ChIP
He stood upon the world's broad threshold; wide. Wendell Phillips. James Russell Lowell. IAP; PEOR
He stooped down suddenly and thrust his hand. The Puffin. W. W. Gibson. ChMo; CMP
He stoops above the clumsy snare. The Snare. Patrick MacDonogh. NeIP
He stoopt Pierea, and thence. Calypso's Island. Homer. *Fr.* The Odyssey. OxBG
He strangely gazes up. Vessels. Francis Carlin. JKCP (1955 ed.)
He stretched his arms, and would embrace the knight. Ariosto. *Fr.* Orlando Furioso, XXXIX. PrPoCR
He strides across the grassy corn. The Scarecrow. Andrew Young. FaBoTw
He strode along the chapel aisle. Sabbath Reflection. Denis Wrafter. NeIP
He stroked the cats on account of a specific cause. Why He Stroked the Cats. Merrill Moore. MOAP
He struggled to kiss her. She struggled the same. Old-fashioned Love. *Unknown.* MaC
He stumbled home from Clifden fair. High and Low. James H. Cousins. HBMV; OnYI; OxBI
He surely is not built for speed. The Rhinocerostrich. *Fr.* Mixed Beasts. Kenyon Cox. RIS
He tasted love with half his mind. In Memoriam A. H. H., XC. Tennyson. EmBrPo; EPN; GEPC; ViPo; VLEP
He taught me all the mercy, for he show'd me all the sin. Tennyson. *Fr.* The May Queen. ChIP
He that believeth on me, believeth not on me. The Light of the World. St. John, Bible, *N.T.* WoL
He that could so well express those frantic fits. In Ariostum Orlandi Furiosi Autorem. John Heath. SiCE
He That Doeth the Will. Longfellow. ChIP
He that dwelleth in the secret place of the Most High. God Our Refuge [*or* The Everlasting Arms *or* A Mighty Fortress *or* Protection of the Lord]. Psalm XCI, Bible, *O.T.* AWP; EM-1; MaRV; PC; TrGrPo; WGRP; WoL
He that fights and runs away. *Unknown.* TreF
He that for fear his Master did deny. To St. Peter and St. Paul. Henry Constable. ReEn; TuPP
He that from dust of worldly tumults flies. Of True Liberty. Sir John Beaumont. OBS; PoFr
He that had come that morning. Ballad of John Cable and Three Gentlemen. W. S. Merwin. NePoEA
He That Has and a Little Tiny Wit. Shakespeare. *Fr.* King Lear, III, ii. ViBoPo
He That Has Light Within. Milton. *Fr.* Comus. MaRV (Light Within.) BLP
He that hath such acuteness, and such wit. On Mr. Francis Beaumont (Then Newly Dead). Richard Corbet. OBS
He that holds fast the golden mean. Moderation. Horace. *Fr.* Odes. PoToHe (new ed.)
He that intends to take a wife. The Wife-Hater. *Unknown.* CoMu
He that is by Mooni now. Mooni. Henry Clarence Kendall. OBEV; OBVV
He that is down needs fear no fall. The Shepherd Boy's Song [*or* The Shepherd Boy Sings in the Valley of Humiliation]. Bunyan. *Fr.* The Pilgrim's Progress. BCEP; BLRP; BOL; BoTP; CaAE; EG; EV-2; GBV; GN; GoTP; HBV; HBVY; LEAP; MaRV; OBEV; OBS; OQP; OTPC (1923 ed.); OxBoCh; PCH; QP-2; SeEP; TVSH; WGRP
He that is grown to wisdom hurries not. Sonnet: Of Moderation and Tolerance. Guido Guinicelli. AWP; JAWP; WBP
He that is in the battle slain. Fight. *Unknown.* FaFP; LiTG; SiTL
He that is Joy through meadows of joyance hath led me. Profession Song. Sister Mary of the Visitation. PraNu
He that is my soul's repose. Jalal ed-Din Rumi, *tr. fr. Persian by* A. J. Arberry. PeP
He That Is Slow to Anger. Proverbs, XVI: 32, Bible, *O.T.* FaPON; TiPo (1952 ed.)
He that is weary, let him sit. Employment. George Herbert. EV-2; OBS; OxBoCh
He that leadeth men must be just. The Leader. Second Samuel, Bible, *O.T.* PCH
He that lies at the stock. Rock, Ball, Fiddle. *Unknown.* CH; OxBoLi; OxNR; SiTL
He That Loves a Rosy Cheek. Thomas Carew. *See* Disdain Returned.
He That Loves a Rosy Cheek. Heinrich von Rugge, *tr. fr. German by* Jethro Bithell. AWP; JAWP; WBP

He that many bokes redys. Books. *Unknown.* LPS-3
He That Marries a Merry Lass. *Unknown.* ALV; SiTL
He that meddleth with all thing may shoe the gosling. Of Common Meddlers. John Heywood. SiCE
He That Never Read a Line. *Unknown, tr. fr. Old Irish by* Robin Flower. AnIL
He that of such a height hath built his mind. To the Lady Margaret, Countess of Cumberland [*or* Epistle to the Lady Margaret *or* The High Mind]. Samuel Daniel. AnEnPo; EPP; EV-1; LoBV; OBSC; ReIE; SiCE; TuPP
He that only rules by terror. The Captain. Tennyson. TCEP
He that owns wealth, in mountain, wold, or waste. Wealth. Sadi. *Fr.* The Gulistan. AWP; OuHeWo
He That Regards the Precious Things of Earth. Moses ibn Ezra, *tr. fr. Hebrew by* Solomon Solis-Cohen. *Fr.* The World's Illusion. TrJP
He that ruleth over men must be just. The Leader. Second Samuel, Bible, *O.T.* PCD
He that saith he is in the light, and hateth his brother. Love, Hate, Compassion. First Epistle of John, Bible, *N.T.* BoFr
He that seeth on the rood. Christ on the Cross. *Unknown.* TMEV
He that sleeps here, did little ere he went. In Memoriam. F. L. Lucas. CaAE
He that sweareth. Advice. Hugh Rhodes. GoTP
He that to God's law doth cling. Freedom. Abraham ibn Ezra. TrJP
He that will not love, must be. Not to Love. Robert Herrick. OAEP
He that will not reason is a bigot. Reason. *Unknown.* TreF
He that would catch and catching hold. *Unknown.* SeCSL
He That Would Thrive. *Unknown.* OTPC; OxNR; PPL
(Country Saying.) RIS
(Proverbs.) HBV
(Rules of Behavior.) HBVY
He the Wind that's ever moving. Hymn to the Wind God. *Unknown.* *Fr.* Song of Quetzalcoatl. LiTW
He there does now enjoy eternal[l] rest. Sleep after Toil. Spenser. *Fr.* The Faerie Queene, I, 9. ChTr; MyFE; PoD
He—They—We. John Oxenham. ChIP
He Thinks of His Children. Hittan of Tayyi. *See* His Children.
He Thinks of His Past Greatness When a Part of the Constellations of Heaven. W. B. Yeats. OAEP (2d ed.); PoEL-5
He Thinks of the Friend of His Youth, and of His Rooms at College. Robert Nathan. *Fr.* Youth Grows Old. BoFr
He thinks that he is then most blessed. Wine's Sting. Alcaeus. GrR
He thought he kept the universe alone. The Most Of It. Robert Frost. CoV; CrMA; MaPo; MoPo; NePA
He thought he saw an elephant [*or* a buffalo]. The [Mad] Gardener's Song. "Lewis Carroll." *Fr.* Sylvie and Bruno. BOHV; BoN; EnLi-2; FiBHP; GBV (1952 ed.); HBV; HBVY; LBN; MBP; NA; OTPC; PoRh; SiTL; StVeCh; TreFS
He thought the world was wrong. The Elusive Music. Edward M. Freed. CAG
He thought to quell the stubborn hearts of oak. Buonaparte. Tennyson. PoVP; VLEP
He thunders from the cherubs' glowing wheels. Ezekiel. Thomas S. Jones, Jr. QS
He toiled and saved his earnings every day. Life's Illusion. Alexander Louis Fraser. OQP; QP-1
He told himself and he told his wife. The Riddle. Ralph Hodgson. WhC
He told the barmaid he had things to do. Dodona's Oaks Were Still. Patrick MacDonogh. NeIP
He, Too, Loved Beauty. Edwin McNeill Poteat. ChIP
He took a thousand islands and he didn't lose a man. Dewey in Manila Bay. Richard Voorhees Risley. DD; GA; MC; PAH
He took castle and towns; he cut short limbs and lives. Greatness. Thomas Love Peacock. *Fr.* Crotchet Castle, *ch.* 16. OtMeF
He took her fancy when he came. Takings [*or* What He Took]. Tom Hood. BOHV; CoMu
He took me out to see the stars. Applied Astronomy. Esther B. Tiffany. PR
He Took My Place. Horatius Bonar. BePJ
He took the great harp wearily. The Songs of Guthrum and Alfred. G. K. Chesterton. *Fr.* The Ballad of the White Horse. HBV
He took the quaint cup in unpractised hands. Poor Fool. Evan V. Shute. CaP
He tore the curtains yesterday. The Pup. Edgar A. Guest. AIBD
He treads no more the paths of Galilee. The Christ of the World's Highway. Dorothy Clarke Wilson. MaRV
He trembled for us. O Theophilus. Margaret Allonby. BoSA
He Tries Out the Concords Gently. "Eduard Bagritsky," *tr. fr. Russian by* C. M. Bowra. TrJP
He tripp'd up the steps with a bow and a smile. The Jacobite on Tower Hill. George Walter Thornbury. VA
He truly adored the sun, as, crimson, it sank from the hilltop. Caspar Hauser Song. Georg Trakl. AnGP
He turn'd him right and round about. Burns. *Fr.* The Farewell. PoD
He turned and looked upon them, and he wept very sore. The Banishment of the Cid. *Unknown.* *Fr.* The Cid. AnSpL-1; TeCS
He turned his pale face to the wall. Barbara Ellen. *Unknown.* IHA
He turned his prow to/ The southern seas. Burnt Ships. Ibsen. AnNoLy
He Understands the Great Cruelty of Death. Petrarch, *pr. tr. fr. Italian by* J. M. Synge. *Fr.* Sonnets to Laura: To Laura in Death. OBMV; TwCV
He understood what it is that we are trying to work out. The Sky-Goer. Zona Gale. LEAP
He unlocked an apple first, then lifted the latch. Summer's Joe. Patrick Anderson. BoCaPo
He unto whom thou art so partial. Post-Obits and the Poets. Martial, *tr. by* Byron. AWP; JAWP; OuHeWo; WBP
He used me today. The Gardener. Evelyn Eaton. GoYe
He used to dream of things he'd do. The Dreamer. Thomas Nunan. WBLP
He used to write in the air with his forefinger. Pedro Rojas. César Vallejo. TwSpPo
He Visits a Hospital. Rolfe Humphries. AnAmPo; LA; TBM
He walked by me with open eyes. The Foreigner. Francis Sherman. BoCaPo (1943 ed.); OCL
He walked in glory on the hills. Heights and Depths. William Canton. PoeT
He walked those mountains wild, and lived within that nook. Gonzalo de Berceo. *Fr.* The Life of San Millan. AnSpL-1; CAW
He walked through the woods. The Walk. W. W. E. Ross. PeCV
He walked up and down the street 'till the shoes fell off his feet. Tramp, Tramp, Tramp, Keep on a-Tramping. *Unknown.* AS
He Walketh by Day. *Unknown, tr. fr. Egyptian by* Robert Hillyer. *Fr.* Book of the Dead. AWP; JAWP; WBP
He walks amid the worldly, yet in his heart afar. The Poet. William Rooney. JKCP (1926 ed.)
He walks beside me every day. My Companion. Joyce Ramage. BePJ
He walks still upright from the root. The Hewel, or Woodpecker. Andrew Marvell. *Fr.* Upon Appleton House. ChTr
He walks with God upon the hills! The Poet. Ina Donna Coolbrith. POT; PoTo
He was a big two-fisted brute. Bucko-Mate. Samuel Schierloh. GoYe
He Was a Gambler Too. G. A. Studdert-Kennedy. *See* Gambler.
He was a gentle lobster. The Lobster and the Maid. Frederic Edward Weatherly. OTPC
He was a good man. Wake Cry. Waring Cuney. BANP
He was a man as hot as whiskey. Andrew Jackson. Martha Keller. GoTP; MaC
He was a man of rare redoubted might. Cymochles in the Bower of Bliss. Spenser. *Fr.* The Faerie Queene, II, 5. PreP
He was a man who, with his hand. To a Mate. Roland Robinson. NeLNL
He was a rat, and she was a rat. An Old Rat's Tale [*or* What Became of Them?]. *Unknown.* BoTP; GFA
He was a reprobate I grant. The Deceased. Keith Douglas. FaBoTw
He was a wizard's son. A Love Story. Oliver Herford. PoMS
He was a worthy citizen of the town. Fire on Belmont Street. Donald Davidson. *Fr.* The Tall Men. MAP; MoAmPo (1942 ed.); SPP
He was an arrogant cat, My Lord. My Lord's Motoring. Vincent Starrett. CIV
He was as old as old could be. Danny Murphy. James Stephens. BoTP; MW
He was at Naples writing letters home. Esthétique du Mal. Wallace Stevens. LiTM (rev. ed.)
He was born in Alabama. Of DeWitt Williams on His Way to Lincoln Cemetery. Gwendolyn Brooks. PoNe
He was born in Ballytearim, where there's little work to do. The Boy from Ballytearim. "Moira O'Neill." CP; NV
He was born in Deutschland, as you would suspect. The Progress of Faust. Karl Shapiro. MoAB; OnHM
He was brought up out of the sea. Lifesaver. Elizabeth Riddell. NeLNL
He was caught in the whirlpool of dismay. The Whirlpool. *Unknown.* PoToHe (new ed.)
He was found by the Bureau of Statistics to be. The Un-

known Citizen. W. H. Auden. ChMP; LiTA; LiTM; MoAB; NePA; PoRA; ShBV-4; SiTL
He was her husband then, this stranger. Penelope. Persis Greely Anderson. DDA
He was in Cincinnati, she in Burlington. A Couple. Carl Sandburg. ReMP
He was in logic a great critic. The Presbyterian Knight [*or* Logic of Hudibras *or* The Metaphysical Sectarian]. Samuel Butler. *Fr.* Hudibras, I. AtBAP; CoEV; LPS-3; MeLP; OBS; OxBoLi; PoEL-3; SiTL
He was in love with Truth and knew her near. Walt Whitman. Harrison Smith Morris. AA; DD; GA
He was just a lonely cowboy. Cowboy Jack. *Unknown.* CoSo
He was little an' peaked an' thin, an' narry a no account horse. Freckles; a Fragment. *Unknown.* CSF
He was lost!—not a shade of doubt of that. Little Lost Pup. Arthur Guiterman. AlBD; BBV (1951 ed.); PCD; TreFS
He was lovelier than the white birch. The Mad Lover. Speer Strahan. CAW
He was master of self, master of nothing. Manuel Altolaguirre, *tr. fr. Spanish by* Eleanor L. Turnbull. CoSP
He was my only passion. The Devil's Complaint. Sana'i. PeP
He was no dreamer, dwelling in a cloud. The Man of Galilee. Hildegarde Hoyt Swift. ChIP
He was no stranger to salty tears, he. The World's Lone Lover. J. R. Perkins. ChIP
He was not able to read or write. The Gardener. Louis MacNeice. *Fr.* Novelettes. AlDL
He was not armed like those of eastern clime. The Soldier. Jones Very. IAP; TCAP
He was not helped by knowing well. The Bore. Mark Van Doren. MOAP
He was not only my friend and my lover. Second Woman's Lament [*or* Fisherman Husband]. Brenda Chamberlain. NeIP; PrWP
He was not sworn of the priesthood. Taliessin's Song of Lancelot's Mass. Charles Williams. ReTS
He was of that stubborn crew. The Religion of Hudibras. Samuel Butler. *Fr.* Hudibras, Pt. I. BPP; LPS-2
He was one who followed. Sailor Man. H. Sewall Bailey. EtS
He was only a common puncher, such as the punchers were. Panhandle Cob. *At. to* H. D. Maclachlan. CoSo
He was only a lavender cowboy. The Lavender Cowboy. *Unknown.* CoSo
He was our own! How social, yet how great. Goethe. *Fr.* Epilogue of Schiller's "Song of the Bell." BoFr
He was put out of Eden. The Exile. Katherine Burton. JKCP (1955 ed.)
He was sitting on the doorstep as I went strolling by. The Road to Vagabondia. Dana Burnet. DDA; NLK; POT; PoTo
He was six years old, just six that day. A Little Boy's Vain Regret. Edith M. Thomas. AA
He was straight and strong, and his eyes were blue. A Lynmouth Widow. Amelia Josephine Burr. AV; BAP; NV; SBMV
He was such a curious lover of shells. Full Fathom Five. A. R. D. Fairburn. AnNZ
He was such a little puppy, in a window of a shop. In a Shop Window. Margaret E. Sangster. AlBD
He was the boy of the house you know. The Boy of the House. Jean Blewett. CPG
He was the Chairman of the Guild. The Meeting of the Clabberhuses. Sam Walter Foss. BOHV
He was the half-wit of that prairie town. Village Portrait. Thomas W. Duncan. MoSiPe
He was the North, the South, the East, the West. Lincoln. Maurice Thompson. PEDC
He was the player and the played upon. The Dead Musician. Charles L. O'Donnell. CAW; JKCP
He was the slave of ambition. The Mills of the Gods. *Unknown.* BLPA
He was the Word that spake it. This Is My Body. John Donne. OQP; QP-1
He was their servant—some say he was blind. W. H. Auden. *Fr.* In Time of War. ChMo
He was, through boyhood's storm and shower. A Dedication. G. K. Chesterton. FiBHP
He wasn't, well, a fancy kind o' dog. Jim-Dog. Margaret E. Sangster. AlBD
He watched the spring come like a gentle maid. To One Who Died in Autumn. Virginia McCormick. HBMV
He watched the stars and noted birds in flight. W. H. Auden. *Fr.* In Time of War. ChMo
He wears a big hat, big spurs, and all that. The Cowboy. *Unknown.* MaC; SCC
He wears a red rose in his buttonhole. In a Restaurant. W. W. Gibson. PoeMoYo; VOD
He wears a tattered coat of dreams. Love's Growing Pains. James Gallagher. JKCP (1955 ed.)
He weeps, who never knew the weight of tears. Nightingale. Eleanor Alletta Chaffee. MuM
He went, and he was gay to go. The Return. W. W. Gibson. BMEP; ChMo; CMP; TwCV
He went his way, leftward bent towards Pyxa. Late Summer in the Country. Theocritus. *Fr.* Idylls. OxBG
He went into the bush, and passed. The Waif. A. C. Smith. VA
He went out to their glorious/ war. The Summons. James Laughlin. ExPo; LiTA
He went so blithely on the way. The Blithe Mask. Dollett Fuguet. MaRV
He went to meet death singing. Jane C. Crowell. *Fr.* Saint Francis of Assisi. SaFP
He went to the wood and caught it. *Unknown.* OxNR
He whistled soft whistlings I knew were for me. In the Park. Helen Hoyt. AV; HBMV
He Who Ascends to Mountain-Tops. Byron. *Fr.* Childe Harold's Pilgrimage, III. OQP; QP-2 (Isolation of Genius, The.) WBLP
He who binds [*or* bends] to himself a joy. Eternity [*or* Liberty *or* Unquestioning]. Blake. AnFE; AWP; BLV; BoLiVe; EG; InPo; LO; LoBV; OQP; QP-2; ShBV-4; TrGrPo
He who but yesterday would roam. Epitaph for a Sailor Buried Ashore. Sir Charles G. D. Roberts. EtS; VA
He who by a mother's love. Christmas Meditation. George Macdonald. BSV
He who checks the child with terror. Reprove Gently. *Unknown.* FAOV
He, who could sack a gated town. Heracles and Meleager. Bacchylides. OxBG
He who created time, and out of nothing. Sonnet. Michelangelo. LyPI
He who died at Azan sends. After Death in Arabia. Sir Edwin Arnold. *Fr.* Pearls of the Faith. BMEP; EOAH; HBV; VA; WGRP
He who directs the sparrowes tender flight. Prayer for an Airman. Richard Zouche. ShGoBo
He who does not wear love's colour. Ghazel on the Letter Kiaf. Jalal ed-Din Rumi. BoFr
He who ever gazed upon true beauty. Tristan. August, Graf von Platen. AnGP
He Who Feels Punctured. *Unknown, at. to* Lao-tzu, *tr. fr. Chinese by* Witter Bynner. *Fr.* Tao Teh King. OnPM
He who first met the Highlands' swelling blue. The Highlands' Swelling Blue. Byron. *Fr.* The Island. OBRV
He Who Forsakes the Clerkly Life. *Unknown, tr. fr. Late Middle Irish by* Standish Hayes O'Grady. *Fr.* The Life of St. Cellach of Killala. OnYI
He who gives a child a book. The Child and the Book. William L. Stidger. BAP
He who has a thousand friends has not a friend to spare. Friends and Enemies [*or* From the Persian *or* Make Friends]. *At. to* Ali Ben Abu Taleb, *tr. by* Emerson. AnNE; MaRV; OnPM; OQP; QP-2
He who has gazed against the sun sees everywhere. The Dark Blot. Gérard de Nerval. AnFP
He Who Has Known a River. Mary Sinton Leitch. TBM
He who has lost soul's liberty. Soul's Liberty. Anna Wickham. MBP; MoBrPo
He who has never known hunger. Elizabeth J. Coatsworth. TiPo
He who has no hands. Orator. Emerson. AnNE; OxBA
He who has once been happy is for aye. With Esther. Wilfrid Scawen Blunt. *Fr.* Esther. OBEV; OBMV; OBVV; TrGrPo; ViBoPo
He who has rolled his pants up to his knee. Crossing a Creek. Herbert Clark Johnson. PoNe
He who has toiled and bought for himself books. Proverbs. Samuel ha-Nagid. TrJP
He Who Has Vision. Folger McKinsey. PTA-2
He who hath bent him o'er the dead. A Picture of Death. Byron. *Fr.* The Giaour. LPS-1
He who hath led will lead. Guide and Friend. *Unknown.* BLRP
He Who Hath Loved. Walter Malone. AA
He who in his pocket hath no money. Epigram. *Unknown.* HBV
He, who in his youth. Wordsworth. *Fr.* The Prelude, V. NBE
He who is both brave and bold. Faint Heart Never Won Fair Lady. Vicente Espinel. AnSpL-1; OnPM
He who is fair is good to look upon. Though Youth Be Gone. Sappho. GrR
He who is innocent and pure. Horace. Odes, I, 22. LaP
He who knows not, and knows not that he knows not. Arabian Proverb [*or* He Who Knows *or* Philosophic Advice]. *Unknown.* BLPA; GoTP; NeHB; PFE; TreF
He who knows not what thing is Paradise. Ballata of Myrrha's Eyes [*or* Three Ballate]. Angelo Poliziano. AWP; LiTW
He who learns to love his wrath. In the Mood of Blake. William Soutar. HaMV

He who looks from the outside into an open window. Prose Poem: The Windows. Baudelaire. OnPM
He who loves life, and has the winging thought. Sonnet. Arthur Davison Ficke. MuM
He Who Loves the Ocean. Mary Sinton Leitch. PoMa
He who mangold-patch doth hoe. A Purpose of Amendment. Helen Parry Eden. JKCP
He who plants a tree. Plant a Tree. Lucy Larcom. ADAH; DD; HBVY; OHFP; OnHT; PEOR; PGD; WBLP
He who prefers to grant only half of the total which Linus. Martial, *tr. fr. Latin by* Robert R. Schnorr. Epigrams, I, 75. LaP
He who said suddenly, "Let there be light!" To Milton—Blind. Stephen Phillips. MBP
He who seeks God has yet no need of wings. Ecstasy. Eva Gore-Booth. DiM
He who sees. The Wise. *Unknown, tr. by* Sir Edwin Arnold. *Fr.* Bhagavad-Gita. OQP; QP-2
He who sits from day to day. Lines on a Bill of Mortality, 1790. William Cowper. OxBoCh
He who walks through the meadows of Champagne. The Cathedral of Rheims. Emile Verhaeren. CAW
He Who was bodiless, having heard the bidding secretly in his soul. The Akathistos Hymn. *Unknown.* ISi
He who would be reborn must seek. Frances Crawford. PtPa
He who would climb the heights of tone. Behold This Dreamer. Elizabeth Bartlett. NePoAm-2
He who would do good to another, must do it in minute particulars. Blake. *Fr.* Jerusalem, *ch.* 2. NBE
He who would echo Horace' lays. Horace. John Osborne Sargent. AA
He who would like to see what art and nature. Sonnet. Joachim du Bellay. FoS
He who would start and rise. An Epitaph on a Husbandman. Sir Charles G. D. Roberts. LEAP
He who would Tao in the service of a king. Tao Teh Ching, XXVII. *Unknown, tr. fr. Chinese.* WhP
He who would valiant be. Bunyan. *Fr.* The Pilgrim's Progress. OIF
He who writ this, not without pains and thought. Prologue to "Secret Love; or, The Maiden-Queen." Dryden. SeCV-2; SeEP
He Whom a Dream Hath Possessed. Shaemas O'Sheel. AnIV; BAP; BLP; HBV; HBVY; JKCP; LBMV; MaRV; OQP; POT; PoTo; QP-1; WGRP
He whom you could correct. On Friendship. Marqués de Santillana. BoFr
He whom you see to walk in so much state. The Dude. Martial. OnPM
He will come;/ I know not when or how. The Superman. Albert Bigelow Paine. MaRV
He will come, the gallant, flying boy. The Ongoing. Mary Siegrist. BAP
He Will Give Them Back. "George Klingle." BLRP
He will have to resemble me. God Thinks of Man. Jules Supervielle. MiCF
He will insist on. The Bath. Joel Oppenheimer. NeAP
He will not come, and still I wait. A Little Boy in the Morning. Francis Ledwidge. MCCG; OnYI; POT; TIP
He will not hear the cuckoo call. The Farmer's Wife. Martha Ostenso. AV
He will silently plan for thee. God's Plans. *Unknown.* BLRP
He Will Watch the Hawk. Stephen Spender. *See* Discovered in Mid-Ocean.
He willed, and Heaven's blue arch vaulted the air. The Shadows Worship. *Unknown.* OnPM
He willed to lack; He willed to bear. Mater Christi. Aubrey Thomas De Vere. *Fr.* May Carols. PoVP
He, willing to justify himself, said unto Jesus. On Compassion. St. Luke, Bible, *N.T.* BoFr
He winks at twinklings of the frost. His Christmas Sled. James Whitcomb Riley. FAOV
He Wishes for the Cloths of Heaven. W. B. Yeats. *See* Aedh Wishes for the Cloths of Heaven.
He Wishes He Might Die and Follow Laura. Petrarch, *pr. tr. fr. Italian by* J. M. Synge. *Fr.* Sonnets to Laura: To Laura in Death. OBMV; TwCV
He without noyse still travell'd to his end. Andrew Marvell. *Fr.* A Poem upon the Death of His Late Highness the Lord Protector. PoD
He Wore a Crown of Thorns. Alice Mortenson. BePJ
He wore a frock coat. Possibly. Elspeth MacDuffie O'Halloran. PR
He wore his [*or* a] coffin for a hat. For a Pessimist. Countee Cullen. PFE; PoeMoYo; PoMa
He wore the day in his belt. Responsory for García Lorca. Oscar Castro Z. AnCL
He Worked. J. N. Scholes. ChIP
He Worried about It. Sam Walter Foss. PTA-2
He would burn his books and gladly die. An Aged Writer. Roy McFadden. NeIP
He would declare and could himself believe. Never Again Would Birds' Song Be the Same. Robert Frost. CrMA
He Would Have His Lady Sing. Digby Mackworth Dolben. CAW; GoBC; GTML
He wrapped himself in wool. Beauty in Rags. Ibn al-Arabi. MooP
He wrote in the sand . . . the wind-blown sands. Men Have Forged. Jay G. Sigmund. OQP; QP-2
He Wrote to the Same Friend from Excester This Sonnet Following. George Gascoigne. ReIE
He Wrote untc a Scottish Dame Whom He Chose for His Mistress in the French Court as Followeth. George Gascoigne. ReIE
He wrote upon his heart. Inscription. Donald Jeffrey Hayes. CDC
He wrought at one great work for years. A Ballad of Heaven. John Davidson. BeLS; EnLit; MeRV; PoVP; TCEP; UnW; VA; VLEP
He wrought with patience long and weary years. The Artist. Arthur Grissom. AA
Head and Heart. C. D. B. Ellis. LiTM; SiTL
Head bumper. *Unknown.* OxNR
Head-downward hung the bat. Viewpoints. Arthur Guiterman. UTS
Head I bear, The—the Eagle of Gal. The Lament for Urien. *Unknown. Fr.* The Red Book of Hergest. OBMV
Head of a Faun. Arthur Rimbaud, *tr. fr. French by* Alan Conder. TrFP
Head of Bran, The. George Meredith. LH
Head of Medusa. Marya Zaturenska. MoAmPo
Head-Stone, The. William Barnes. *See* Readen ov a Head-Stwone.
Head that once was crowned with thorns, The. The Cross and the Crown. Thomas Kelly. MaRV
Head the ship for England! Homeward Bound. William Allingham. FaBoBe; HBV; HBVY
Head thrusts in as for the view, A. All Revelation. Robert Frost. MoPo; NePA
Head to the East I lie. Mother Church. Walter Freeman. PoP
Headaches Jes' 'fore School. Maurice C. Johnson. FAOV
Headin' Home. E. W. Patten. BTP
Headless Phantoms, The. *Unknown, tr. fr. Early Modern Irish by* Eoin MacNeill. AnIL
Headless, without an arm, a figure leans. On a Cast from an Antique. George Pellew. AA
Headline History. William Plomer. SiTL
Headlong Hall, *sels.* Thomas Love Peacock.
Chorus: "Hail to the Headlong!" OBRV
In His Last Binn Sir Peter Lies. EnRP (Song.) OBRV; ViBoPo
Heads and Tails. "Claudia Lars," *tr. fr. Spanish by* Donald Devenish Walsh. AnCL
Heads and Tails of Love, The. James Wreford Watson. BoCaPo (1948 ed.)
Heads of strong old age are beautiful, The. Promise of Peace. Robinson Jeffers. BLV; BoLiVe; CoBMV; GTBS-W; LiTA; LiTM (rev. ed.); MAP; MoAB; MoAmPo; NePA
Headsong. Joseph Bennett. LiTM (rev. ed.); NePA
Headwaiter says, The. In This Hotel. Emanuel Carnevali. AnAmPo; LA; NP
Healer, The. Whittier. MaRV
"So stood the holy Christ," *sel.* PGD
Healin' Waters, *with music.* *Unknown.* ABF
Healing. William Lisle Bowles. *See* Time and Grief.
Healing. Abraham Reisen, *tr. fr. Yiddish by* Joseph Leftwich. LiTW; TrJP
Healing Hands, The. Victor Robinson. PoP
Healing of the Daughter of Jairus, The. Nathaniel Parker Willis. StJW
Healing of the Leper, The. Vernon Watkins. FaBoTw
Health, *sel.* Nathaniel Cotton.
"Would you extend your narrow span." PoP
Health, A. Edward Coote Pinkney. AA; AnAmPo; APW; BAP; HBV; IAP; InP; LA; LBAP; LPS-1; MOAP; PR; SeCePo; SPP; TCAP; TreFS
Health and Wealth. *Unknown.* PTA-2
Health and wealth and love he too dreamed of in May. Patrick Kavanagh. *Fr.* The Great Hunger. MoAB
Health at the Ford, A. Robert Cameron Rogers. AA; FaBoBe
Health from the lover of the country, me. To Fuscus Aristus. Horace. AWP; JAWP; WBP
Health is a jewel, true; which when we buy. John Heath. SiCE
Health is the best that Heaven sends. Life's Best. Simonides. GrPE
Health is the first good lent to men. The Four Best Things. *Unknown.* OxBG
Health Note, A. Walter Hard. AnNE
Health of Body Dependent on Soul. Jones Very. WGRP
Health to the Birds, A. Seumas MacManus. BLA
Health unto His Majesty, A. *Unknown, at. to* Jeremy Savile. *See* Song: "Here's a health unto His Majesty!"
Healthy Spot, A. W. H. Auden. EnLit

Heap Cassia, Sandal-Buds and Stripes. Robert Browning. *Fr.* Paracelsus, Pt. IV. BPN; EmBrPo; EV-5; GTML; GTSL; MyFE; OBRV; PoVP
(Song: "Heap cassia, sandal-buds, and stripes."). AnFE; OBEV; WHA
Heap high the board with plenteous cheer and gather to the feast. Thanksgiving. Alice Williams Brotherton. PGD
Heap not on this mound. Epitaph. Edna St. Vincent Millay. *Fr.* Memorial to D.C. NP
Heap of Rags, The. W. H. Davies. EPP
Heap of stones lay at his command, A. His Passion. George Conrad Pullman. ChIP
Heap on more wood!—the wind is chill. Christmas in the Olden Time [*or* Old Christmas-Tide]. Sir Walter Scott. *Fr.* Marmion. ChBR; DD; EPP; GN; GoBC; LPS-2; MPB; OTPC; PCH; PEOR; PoRL; SDH; SiSoSe; TiPo
Heaped be the fagots high. Twelfth Night Song. Stephen Sennett. SDH
Hear a voice announcing Irving in the Bells—sledge's Bells! The Bells. "Judy." PA
Hear, Epicydes' son: 'twere much to thy present advantage. The Power of an Oath. Delphic Oracle. OxBG
Hear, Father, hear thy faint afflicted flock. Hymn of the Waldenses. Bryant. AnNE
Hear! hear! hear! The Mocking Bird. Richard Hovey. BLA; TSW; TSWC
Hear how my friend the robin sings! In the Snow. W. H. Davies. POTE
Hear how the nightingales on ev'ry spray. A Turkish Ode of Mesihi. Sir William Jones. RO
Hear, how yon reed in sadly pleasing tales. The Song of the Reed. Jalal ed-Din Rumi. PeP
Hear, Lord, hear. The Leper Cleansed. John Collop. BCEP; TrGrPo
Hear me as if thy eares had palate, Jack. An Ode in the Praise of Sack. *Unknown.* OBS
Hear me, brother! The Temple. Lee Wilson Dodd. BAP
Hear me, hear me. Byron. *Fr.* Manfred. ReTS
Hear me, hear me. Hermit Thrush. Kathleen Millay. BAP
Hear me, my warriors: my heart is sick and sad. War. Chief Joseph. PGD
Hear me [*or* Heare mee], O God! A Hymn [*or* Hymne] to God the Father. Ben Jonson. EV-2; GoBC; MaRV; MePo; OBS; OxBoCh; ReEn; RiBV; SeCV-1; TrPWD
Hear me, therefore; mark me well. Man, the Feeblest of Earth's Creatures. Homer, *tr. by* William Cowper. *Fr.* The Odyssey. GrR
"Hear me. ye elders, look upon me!" Gilgamesh Laments the Death of Engidu. *Unknown.* LiTW
Hear Me Yet *Unknown.* ElL
Hear, my beloved, an old Milesian story! Catullian Hendecasyllables. Samuel Taylor Coleridge. EtPaEn
Hear my voice, Birds of War. Ojibwa War Songs. *Unknown.* AWP; JAWP; WBP
"Hear, noble suitors! ye who throng these halls." The Return of Ulysses. Homer. *Fr.* The Odyssey, XXI. BBV (1923 ed.); OBS
Hear now, O Soul, the last command of all. The Final Mystery. Sir Henry Newbolt. WGRP
Hear now this fairy legend of old Greece. James Russell Lowell. *Fr.* Rhoecus. AA
Hear, O Israel! André Spire, *tr. fr. French by* Stanley Burnshaw. TrJP
Hear, O Israel. Shema Yisrael. *Unknown.* TrJP
Hear, O Israel, Jehovah, the Lord our God is one. Israel. Israel Zangwill. TrJP
Hear, O Israel, the commandments of life. The Path of Wisdom. Baruch, Bible, Apocrypha. TrJP
Hear, O Israel, the Lord our God is one Lord. Lest We Forget [*or* Written in the Heart]. Deuteronomy, Bible, *O.T.* GrCo-1: GrCo-2
Hear, O Self-Giver, infinite as good. Morton Luce. Thysia, XXXVII. AA
Hear! O Trees that gird our camp! Taking of the Name. *Unknown, tr. fr. Omaha Indian.* PCH
Hear, Sweet Spirit. Samuel Taylor Coleridge. *See* Invocation, An: "Hear, sweet spirit."
Hear that crickley, crackley static. Static. Gertrude Van Winkle. GFA
Hear the blessings now we pour. Litany for Argos. Aeschylus. *Fr.* Suppliants. GrR
Hear the boat a-whistlin'. The Macombrey Queen. *Unknown.* StDa
Hear the fierce dispute and strife which passed between the Night and Day. Night and Day. Asadi. PeP
Hear the geysers in the highlands. Iceland's Song. Grímur Thomsen. IcP; LiTW
Hear the legend of the Admen. The Legend of the Admen. Everett W. Lord. BLPA
Hear the robin in the rain. The Robin in the Rain. Charles Coke Woods. POT
Hear the sledges with the bells—/ Silver bells! The Bells. Poe. AA; AmPo; AmPP (3d ed.); APW; BBV; CoBA; CoV; FaFP; FaPON; GN; HBV; HiLiAm; IAP; LiTA; LPS-2; NeHB; NePA; OBAV; OHFP; OTPC; PCD; PCH; PFE; PG (1945 ed.); PIAE; PIR; PoeMoYo; PYM; ShBV-1; TCAP; TreF; TVSH; WBLP
Hear the Voice of the Bard (*Introd. to* Songs of Experience). Blake. GTBS-D; OBEC
(Ancient Trees, The.) LiA
(Bard, The.) WGRP
(Hear the Voice.) OBEV
(Introduction: "Hear the voice of the Bard!") EiPP; EnRP; LoBV; OAEP; PoEL-4
(Introduction to "Songs of Experience.") ExPo
(Poet's Voice, The.) ChTr
(Voice of the Bard, The.) LEAP
Hear the Word of the Lord. Isaiah, I: 10-23, Bible, *O.T.* TrJP
Hear the word that Jesus spake. A Lost Word of Jesus. Henry van Dyke. WGRP
Hear then what to my mind/ Deliberate thought presents. Euripides. *Fr.* Iphigenia in Aulis. EnLi-2
Hear this, O ye that would swallow the needy. O Ye That Would Swallow the Needy. Amos, Bible, *O.T.* TrJP
Hear through the morning drums and trumpets sounding. Jackson at New Orleans. Wallace Rice. DD; GA; PAH
Hear Us, in This Thy House. Philip Doddridge. BePJ
Hear what God the Lord hath spoken. The Future Peace and Glory of the Church. William Cowper. TriL
Hear what Highland Nora said. Nora's Vow. Sir Walter Scott. BOHV; EmBrPo; EV-4
Hear what the mournful linnets say. Christina Rossetti. *Fr.* Sing-Song. EmBrPo
Hear, Ye Ladies [That Despise]. John Fletcher. *Fr.* The Tragedy of Valentinian. BCEP; ElL; LiTG; OBEV; ViBoPo
("Hear ye ladies that despise.") OAEP
(Mighty Love.) TrGrPo
(Power of Love.) HBV
(Song: "Heare ye Ladies that despise.") PoEL-2
Hear, ye sullen Pow'rs below. Song. Dryden. *Fr.* Oedipus. PoD
Hear ye virgins, and I'll teach. To Virgins. Robert Herrick. ViBoPo
"Hear your sovereign's proclamation." Soliloquy of a Water-Wagtail. James Montgomery. OTPC (1923 ed.)
. . heard him gladly. Waldere I. *Unknown.* AnOE
"Heard melodies are sweet, but those unheard." Of Melodies Unheard. Mahlon Leonard Fisher. MuM
Heard on Leaving the Opera. Phyllis Merrill. CAG
Heard on the Mountain. Victor Hugo, *tr. fr. French by* Francis Thompson. AWP
Heard on the Roof at Midnight. Leah Bodine Drake. DaM
"Heard say that four times four is eight." A Footnote. Stephen Spender. FaBoTw
Heard ye eer of the silly blind harper. The Lochmaben Harper. *Unknown.* ESPB; OBB
Heard ye how the bold McClellan. How McClellan Took Manassas. *Unknown.* PAH
Heard ye not yet of Captain Ferdinand? Henry Parrot. SiCE
Heard ye of Nimrud? Cities fell before him. Nimrud and the Gnat. *Unknown.* OnPM
Heard ye that thrilling word. Dirge for Ashby. Margaret Junkin Preston. GA; PAH
Heard ye the thunder of battle. Trafalgar. Francis Turner Palgrave. BeLS; FaBoBe
"Heard'st thou over the fortress wild geese flying and crying?" The Ban-Shee. William Allingham. TIP
Heäre, The. William Barnes. VA
Heare Mee, O God! *See* Hear me, O God!
Heare Nature, heare deere Goddesse, heare. Shakespeare. *Fr.* King Lear, I, iv. NBE
Heares non but onelie I. *Unknown.* SeCSL
Hearing a Flute on a Spring Night. Li Po, *tr. fr. Chinese by* Arthur Christy. ChLP
Hearing: hearing: hearing. Spring Poem. Colleen Thibaudeau. TwCaPo
Hearing him, the birds came in a crowd. Saint Francis and the Birds. Roy McFadden. OxBI
Hearing his courtesies/ Blissfully smiling did she her eyes abash. Amor Omnipotens. Apollonius Rhodius. *Fr.* Argonautica. OxBG
Hearing his son and daughter. The Father. John Holmes. FAOV
Hearing I ask from the holy races. The Beginning and the End [*or* Voluspo]. *Unknown.* *Fr.* The Elder Edda. AWP; LiTW; LyMA; PaOS
Hearing of Harvests Rotting in the Valleys. W. H. Auden. MoAB; MoBrPo; ReaPo; TriL
(Paysage Moralisé.) LiTB
Hearing one saga, we enact the next. Remembering the 'Thirties. Donald Davie. NePoEA
Hearing that His Friend Was Coming Back from the War. Wang Chien, *tr. fr. Chinese by* Arthur Waley. BoFr; LiTW; TrCh

Hearing the Early Oriole. Po Chü-i, *tr. fr. Chinese by* Arthur Waley. TrCh; UnS
Hearing the strange night-piercing sound. The Screech-Owl. Ethelwyn Wetherald. CPG; OCL
Heark how she laughs aloud. Lucasta Laughing. Richard Lovelace. PoEL-3
Heark, my Flora! Love doth call us. A Song of Dalliance. William Cartwright. ALV; NBE
Hearke, hearke, the larke at heaven's gate sings. *See* Hark, Hark, the Lark.
Hearke, Now Everything Is Still. John Webster. *See* Hark, Now Everything Is Still.
Hearken!—now the hermit bee. The Quiet Enemy. Walter de la Mare. ChMo; CMP
Hearken! O Eileithyia. Pindar, *tr. fr. Greek by* C. J. Billson. *Fr.* Nemean Odes, VII. GrR
Hearken the stirring story. The Fall of Maubila. Thomas Dunn English. PAH
Hearken, thou craggy ocean pyramid! To Ailsa Rock. Keats. BPN; EnRP; ES
Hearken to me, both old and ying. Of a Rose, a Lovely Rose. *Unknown.* AnEC
Hearken to me, gentlemen. King Estmere. *Unknown.* ESBP; OBB
Hearken to my tale that I shall show to you. Mirabile Dictu. *Unknown.* TMEV
Hears Not My Phyllis. Sir Charles Sedley. ElSeCe
(Knotting Song, The.) SeCL
(Phillis Knotting.) NBE; OBS
(Song: "Hears not my Phillis [*or* Phyllis] how the birds.") EnLoPo; EPS (1942 ed.); SeCV-2; SeEP
Hears the heavy rising hay. Beach. Glyn Jones. MoWP
Hearse Song, The. *Unknown.* ABF, *with music;* AS (A *and* B *vers.*); OxBoLi
Hearse was the oven of the crematory, The. The Funeral. "M. J." TrJP
Hear'st thou, corpse, how I play thy part? Thomas Lovell Beddoes. *Fr.* Death's Jest Book, IV, iii. NBE
Hear'st thou, Daphne, the song they sang of yore. Delfica. Gérard de Nerval. TrFP
Hear'st thou, my soul, what serious things. Dies Irae. Thomas of Celano, *tr. by* Richard Crashaw. AWP; OuHeWo
Heart. MacKnight Black. AnAmPo; LA
Heart, The. Stephen Crane. The Black Riders, III. HoPM; MAP; MoAmPo; NeMA
(Eating.) BAP
Heart, The. Michael Drayton. SeEP
Heart, The. Elizabeth Fergusson. ReTS
Heart, The. Boris Lebedev, *tr. fr. Russian by* Babette Deutsch. TrRV
Heart, The. Harvey Shapiro. HoPM
Heart, The. Jacob Steinberg, *tr. fr. Hebrew by* Harry H. Fein. TrJP
Heart. Jules Supervielle, *tr. fr. French by* Wallace Fowlie. MiCF
Heart, The. Francis Thompson.
"Heart you hold too small, The," I. OBMV; PeBoSo
"O nothing, in this corporal earth of man." II. AnFE; BLV; BoLiVe; OBMV; PeBoSo; PIAE; VLEP
(All's Vast.) MBP; MoAB; MoBrPo
(Correlated Greatness.) GTML
Heart, The. *Unknown, ad. fr. French by* Louis Untermeyer. MaC
Heart-affluence in discursive talk. In Memoriam A. H. H., CIX. Tennyson. EmBrPo; EPN; GEPC; ViPo; VLEP
Heart and Mind. Edith Sitwell. AtBAP; ChMP; CoEV; FaBoTw; GTBS-D; MoPo; OAEP (2d ed.); Po
Heart and Nature, The. "Owen Meredith." GTML
Heart and service to you proffer'd, The. Sir Thomas Wyatt. SiPS
Heart and Will. William James Linton. VA
Heart asks pleasure first, The. Emily Dickinson. AnNE; IAP; InPo; MAP; MoAB; MoAmPo; MOAP; OnPM; OxBA; TrGrPo; TwP
Heart can set its boundaries, The. Boundaries. Jessica Powers. JKCP (1955 ed.)
Heart-Cry, The. Francis W. Bourdillon. POT
Heart-Cry of the Duchess, The. John Webster. *Fr.* The Duchess of Malfi, IV, ii. BCEP
("O that it were possible we might," 4 *ll.*) PoD
Heart Exchange. Sir Philip Sidney. *See* My True Love Hath My Heart.
Heart for All Her Children. Albert J. Hebert, Jr. ISi
Heart free, hand free. Sic Vita. William Stanley Braithwaite. BANP; CP; LBMV; NLK; OOP; QP-2
Heart Has Its Reasons, The. *Unknown.* GoBC
Heart, Have No Pity on This House of Bone. Edna St. Vincent Millay. AmPP
Heart in Autumn, The. Po Chü-i, *tr. fr Chinese by* Ching Ti. WhP
Heart in Brahma, The. Bhartrihari, *tr. fr. Sanskrit by* Paul Elmer More. OnPM
Heart in Wonder, The. Robert Nathan. MuM
(Sonnet: "Heart in wonder, like a lonely wren, The.") BoFr
Heart Is a Strange Thing, The. Minnie Case Hopkins. OQP; QP-2
Heart Is Bethlehem, The. Gertrude Hanson. ChIP
Heart is but a narrow space, The. At the Heart. Mark Antony De Wolfe Howe. PC
Heart is cold that has not chilled, The. Gilead. Mary Brennan Clapp. OQP; QP-2
Heart is cold under a breast of pitiful fear, The. The Death of Llywelyn ap Gruffudd. Gruffudd ab yr Ynad Coch. LyMA
Heart, it is time. The fruitful summer yields. Autumn. Rainer Maria Rilke, *tr. by* James McAuley. MoAuPo
Heart Knoweth Its Own Bitterness, The. Aline Kilmer. CBOV; LEAP; NP
Heart Knoweth Its Own Bitterness, The. Christina Rossetti. EmBrPo
Heart leaps with the pride of their story, The. The Fleet at Santiago. Charles E. Russell. MC; PAH
Heart Looks On, The. Leonora Speyer. NP
Heart must always come again to home. The Heart's Wild Geese. Henry Treece. WaP
Heart, my heart, with cares past curing thou that liest sore oppressed. Sursum Corda. Archilochus, *tr. by* F. L. Lucas. GrPE
Heart, my heart with griefs confounded. Be Still, My Soul. Archilochus, *tr. by* C. M. Bowra. GrL; OxBG
Heart of a bird! Heart of a bird! Persephone (Singing). Louis V. Ledoux. BAP
Heart of a Girl Is a Wonderful Thing, The. *Unknown.* BLPA
Heart of a Woman, The. Georgia Douglas Johnson. BANP; CDC; PoNe
Heart of All the Scene, The. Emerson. *See* Guide, The.
Heart of Earth, let us be gone. Song of the Wulfshaw Larches. Ernest Rhys. VA
Heart of England now is all on fire, The! Alfred Noyes. *Fr.* Drake. ReTS
Heart of flaming sulphur, flesh of tow, A. Beauty and the Artist. Michelangelo. PoFr
Heart of God, The. W. E. Littlewood. BePJ
Heart of hearts—I whisper this for name. Cor Cordium. Wilbur Underwood. PraNu
Heart of Light. David Campbell. BoAV
Heart of Light, The. Winifred Welles. NP
Heart of man, walk it which way it will, The. Heart-Rest. Sir Henry Taylor. *Fr.* Philip van Artevelde. LPS-1
Heart of Midlothian, The, *sels.* Sir Walter Scott.
Proud Maisie, *fr. ch.* 38. AtBAP; BCEP; BLV; BPN; BSV; CaAE; CBOV; CH; ChTr; CoBE; CoEV; EBSV; EmBrPo; EnLi-2; EnLit; EnRP; EPN; ERP; EtPaEn; EV-4; GoTS; GTSL; HBV; InP; LEAP; LoBV; OAEP; OBEV; OBRV; OTPC (1923 ed.); PIAE; PoE; PoEL-4; SeCePo; SeCeV; ShBV-1; TCEP; TrGrPo; TyEnPo; UnPo
(Pride of Youth.) CG; GTBS; GTBS-D; GTBS-W
("Proud Maisie is in the wood.") EG; FaBoCh; LoGBV
Heart of My Heart. *Unknown.* HBV
Heart of my heart. Awake! Awake! Serenade. H. W. Bell. CAG
Heart of my heart, the world is young. Unity. Alfred Noyes. HBV; InP; VOD
Heart of my nights. Nocturne. Eugenio Florit. TwSpPo
Heart of Oak. David Garrick. BHV; HBV; OBEC; OxBoLi; SG
Heart of Oak. Charles Henry Luders. AA
Heart of the bird, The. In. Vicente Huidobro. TwSpPo
Heart of the Bruce, The. William Edmondstoune Aytoun. LPS-2
Heart of the Eternal, The. Frederick W. Faber. *See* There's a Wideness in God's Mercy.
Heart of the heartless world. Huesca [*or* Poem *or* To Margot Heinemann]. John Cornford. ChMP; LoPS; POTE
Heart of the Night, The. Dante Gabriel Rossetti. The House of Life, LXVI. BPN; EmBrPo; EPN; PoVP; TCEP; TOP; ViPo; VLEP
Heart of the Tree, The. H. C. Bunner. ADAH; DD; HH; OHFP; OHIP; OQP; PGD; QP-2
Heart of the Woman, The. W. B. Yeats. GTML; GTSL; LoPo; LoPS; POTE
Heart of the Woods. Wesley Curtright. GoSl; PoNe
Heart of the World, The. Nahman of Bratzlav, *tr. fr. Yiddish by* Joseph Leftwich. TrJP
Heart of Youth, The, *sel.* Hermann Hagedorn.
Lift Up the Curtain. QS
Heart of Youth, The. *Unknown.* BLA
Heart on the Hill, The. Petrarch, *tr. fr. Italian by* C. B. Cayley. Sonnets to Laura: To Laura in Life, CCV. AWP
Heart oppress'd with desperate thought. Sir Thomas Wyatt. SiPS
Heart Recalcitrant, The. Leonora Speyer. PG

Heart-Rest. Sir Henry Taylor. *Fr.* Philip van Artevelde. LPS-1
Heart-Searchings of Medea, The. Apollonius Rhodius, *tr. fr. Greek by* F. L. Lucas. *Fr.* Argonautica, III. GrPE
Heart soars up like a bird, The. The Flight of the Heart. Dora Read Goodale. AA
Heart Specialist. Elias Lieberman. ImOP
Heart-stealing Homer, marrow of the Muses. Charles Fitzgeffrey. *Fr.* Sir Francis Drake. PtP
Heart, Steel Thyself! Euripides, *tr. fr. Greek by* Gilbert Murray. *Fr.* Medea. GrR
Heart-summoned. Jesse Stuart. GoYe
Heart that loves with patience—a stone 'tis, not a heart, The. Wantoning. Sadi. PeP
Heart, thou must learn to do without. Rondel. George Macdonald. BSV
Heart to Carry On, The. Bertram Warr. PeCV
Heart, we will forget him! Emily Dickinson. AA; LEAP; LiTL; LoPS; OBAV; ViBoPo
Heart Wound. Otto Freund. MuM
Heart Wounds. Claire Richcreek Thomas. PoToHe (new ed.)
Heart you hold too small and local thing, The. The Heart. Francis Thompson. OBMV; PeBoSo
Heartbeat of Democracy. Virginia Brasier. StVeCh (1955 ed.)
Heartbreak. Howard Mumford Jones. LS
Heartbreak fall of sound recurs, The. The Seasons' Fool. Goronwy Rees. MoWP
Heartbreak Road. Helen Gray Cone. BAP; HBMV
Heartbreak that is too new. The Vintage. Mary Carolyn Davies. *Fr.* A Girl's Songs. SBMV
Heartbroken that I could not reach your bed side. Arielle Grierson. Edgar Lee Masters. *Fr.* The New Spoon River. ChMo; CMP
Heartening, The. Winifred Webb. PTA-2
Hearth. Peggy Bacon. FaPON; MPB
Hearth of Urien, The. Llywarch the Aged, *tr. fr. Welsh by* William Barnes. ChTr
Hearth Song. Robert Underwood Johnson. YeAr
Hearthstone. Harold Monro. OBMV
Heart's Anchor, The. William Winter. PoToHe
Hearts and darts and maids and men. Valentine to One's Wife. John Erskine. BAP; PR; TBM
Hearts and Lace Paper. *Unknown.* PCH
(Flower Tokens.) RIS
("Lilies are white,/ Rosemary's green.") BoTP; OxNR
Hearts, beat no more! Earth's Sleep has come. Requiem of Archangels for the World. Herbert Trench. MM
Heart's Chill Between. Christina Rossetti. BPN
Heart's Compass. Dante Gabriel Rossetti. The House of Life, XXVII. BPN; EmBrPo; EPN; Po; PoVP; ViPo; VLEP; WHA
Heart's Content. *Unknown.* HBV; OTPC (1923 ed.)
Heart's Country, The. Florence Wilkinson Evans. AV; LBMV
Hearts Courageous. John Oxenham. MaRV
Heart's Desire. John Peter. BoSA
Heart's-Ease. Walter Savage Landor. BPN; EnRP; VA
Heart's-ease, an herb that sometimes hath been seen. On His Mistress' Garden of Herbs. *Unknown.* SeCL
Heart's Flower, The. Karl Jonas Love Almquist, *tr. fr. Swedish by* Charles W. Stork. AnSL
Hearts good and true. Written in a Little Lady's Little Album. Frederick William Faber. HBV; HBVY
Heart's Haven. Kendall Banning. MaRV; MuM
Heart's Haven. Dante Gabriel Rossetti. The House of Life, XXII. EmBrPo; EPN; OAEP; PoVP; ViPo; VLEP
Heart's Hope. Dante Gabriel Rossetti. The House of Life, V. BMEP; BPN; EmBrPo; EnLit; EPN; HBV; LEAP; PoVP; ViP; ViPo; VLEP
Heart's Journey, The, *sels.* Siegfried Sassoon.
"Flower has opened in my heart, A," XXXIV. CoEV; TwCV
"What you are I cannot say," IV. LoPS
"You were glad to-night," V. CaAE; TwCV
Hearts, like Doors. *Unknown.* OTPC; PPL
("Hearts, like doors, will ope with ease.") OxNR
(Politeness.) MeMeAg; PCH
(Rules of Behavior.) HBV; HBVY
Heart's Low Door, The. Susan Mitchell. HBMV
Heart's Music. *Unknown.* OBEV (new ed.)
Heart's Needle, *sels.* W. D. Snodgrass. NePoEA
"Easter has come around," VI.
"Here in the scuffled dust," VII.
"I thumped on you the best I could," VIII.
"Late April and you are three; today," II.
"No one can tell you why," IV.
"Vicious winter finally yields, The," X.
Heart's Not Yet a Neighbour, The. Mary Fullerton. NeLNL
Hearts of the everlasting-flowers, The. By Momba Tracks. Roderic Quinn. NeLNL
Heart's Poverty. Gloria T. Stein. JKCP (1955 ed.)
Hearts Proof, The. James Buckham. BLRP; OQP; QP-2; WBLP
Heart's Summer, The. Epes Sargent. AA
Hearts Were Made to Give Away. Annette Wynne. PoRL; TiPo (1959 ed.)
Heart's Wild-Flower. William Vaughn Moody. LEAP; TOP
Heart's Wild Geese, The. Henry Treece. WaP
Hearty friend of good girls, you know Frétillon! Frétillon. Pierre Jean de Béranger. LiA
Heat. J. Redwood Anderson. TCPD
Heat. Hilda Doolittle ("H. D."). The Garden, II. BAP; BLV; MAP; MoAmPo; NeMA; OxBA; PIAE; SBMV; TSW; UnPo; WHA
Heat. John Gould Fletcher. *Fr.* Down the Mississippi, II. ChMo; LiTA
Heat. Gilberto González y Contreras, *tr. fr. Spanish by* Dudley Fitts. AnCL
Heat. Archibald Lampman. BoCaPo; CaP; CPG; OCL; PeCV; VA
Heat, The. Gertrude Stein. AtBAP
Heat and burden of the day. Prayer on Entering Church. Bertha Gerneaux Woods. PraP
Heat and cold, dusk and dawn have crowded one upon the other. The Spring River. Po Chü-i. TrCh
Heat, and light, and glitter of the sun, The. France (June, 1938; June, 1941). Charles Schiff. NeTW
Heat is past that did me fret, The. The Lover Deceived by His Lady's Unconstancy Writeth unto Her as Followeth [*or* A Farewell to a Fondling]. Thomas Churchyard. EIL; ReIE; TuPP
Heat me these irons hot. Hubert and Arthur [*or* Prince Arthur]. Shakespeare. King John, IV, i. ShGoBo
Heat the furnace hot. To the New Men. John Davidson. EPN; PoVP; TOP
Heat was like a solid thing, The. Heat. J. Redwood Anderson. TCPD
Heath, The. Thomas Boyd. OnYI
Heath-Cock, The. Joanna Baillie. LPS-2
Heath This Night Must Be My Bed, The. Sir Walter Scott. *Fr.* The Lady of the Lake, III. ERP
(Song: "Heath this night must be my bed, The.") EV-4; LPS-1
Heathcliffe Mourns for Cathy. Margaret Willy. DiM
Heathen and the Infants, The. Michael Wigglesworth. *Fr.* The Day of Doom. AmPP (3d ed.)
Heathen Are Come into Thine Inheritance, The. Psalms, LXXIX, Bible, *O.T.* TrJP
Heathen Chinee, The. Bret Harte. *See* Plain Language from Truthful James.
Heathen Hymn, A. Sir Lewis Morris. MaRV
"I praise Thee not, with impious pride," *sel.* TrPWD
Heathen Pass-ee, The. A. C. Hilton. CenHV; PA
Heather, The. Steen Steensen Blicher, *tr. fr. Danish by* Charles W. Stork. BoDS; LiTW
Heather, The. Neil Munro. EBSV; OBVV
Heather Ale. Robert Louis Stevenson. AnEnPo; PCN; ShBV 1; VA
Heautontimoroumenos. Baudelaire, *tr. fr. French by* Bert M-P. Leefmans. AnFP
(Heauton Timoroumenos, *tr. by* Alan Conder.) TrFP
Heave at the windlass!—Heave O, cheerly, men! Windlass Song. William Allingham. BBV (1923 ed.); GN; OTPC
Heave Away, *2 vers., with music.* *Unknown.* ShS
Heave Away ("Heave away, heave away, I'd rather court a yellow gal") *with music.* *Unknown.* ABF; AS; TrAS
Heave Away (We're All Bound to Go), *with music.* *Unknown.* SoAmSa
(We're All Bound to Go.) AmSS, *diff. vers.*
Heave away, Rio! Rio Grande, *vers.* I. *Unknown.* ShS
Heave of mighty shoulders to the yoke, A. A Yoke of Steers. DuBose Heyward. LS; NP; TBM
Heaven. Martha Dickinson Bianchi. AA; HBV
Heaven. Rupert Brooke. AlDL; AnFE; EPN; EV-5; ExPo; GTBS-D; GTBS-W; HoPM; LiTB; LiTM; MBP; MM; MoBrPo; PoE; PoRA; POTE; SeCeV; SiTL; TOP; TwCV; WaKn; WGRP
(Fishes' Heaven.) ShBV-4
Heaven. Cynewulf. *Fr.* Christ. PoLi
Heaven. Edwin Hatch. MaRV
Heaven. George Herbert. BLV; BoLiVe; TrGrPo
Heaven. Langston Hughes. *See* Heaven; the City Called Heaven.
Heaven. Milton. *Fr.* Paradise Lost, III. OBS
Heaven. Nancy Woodbury Priest. LPS-2
Heaven. Takamoto, *tr. fr. Japanese by* Lois J. Erickson. SoLD
Heaven. Jeremy Taylor. LPS-2
Heaven. Clarence A. Vincent. OQP; QP-1
Heaven. Isaac Watts. WGRP
(Prospect of Heaven Makes Death Easy, A.) EiPP; OBEC
("There is a land of pure delight.") OIF
Heaven, The/ Darkens and thunder rolls. Aeneas and Dido. Virgil. *Fr.* The Aeneid, IV. LaP

Heaven above is softer blue. Possession. *Unknown.* BLRP
Heaven and Earth. Annabel Ledlie Berry. DDA
Heaven and Earth. James I, King of England. ChTr
(Sonnet: "Azured vault, the crystal circles bright, The.") ElL; SeCePo
Heaven and Earth. Frederic Thompson. CAW
Heaven and earth, and all that hear me plain. A Protest. Sir Thomas Wyatt. OBSC; SiPS
Heaven and Earth are without benevolence. *Unknown, tr. fr. Chinese.* Tao Teh Ching, XXI. WhP
Heaven and earth, cloud and water. Translations from Modern Japanese Poetry. Akiko Yanagiwara. PFE
Heaven and Earth endure eternally. Substance, Shadow, and Spirit. Tao Yuan-ming. WhP
Heaven and Hell. Blake. *Fr.* The Marriage of Heaven and Hell. RO
Heaven and Hell. Omar Khayyám. *See* Soul Is All, The.
Heaven and Hell. James Kenneth Stephen. CenHV
Heaven and Hell. Sir William Watson. QS
Heaven for which I wait has neither guard nor gate, The. Credo. Siegfried Sassoon. QS
Heaven from all creatures hides the book of fate. *See* Heav'n from all creatures hides . . .
Heaven hath no rage like love to hatred turned. William Congreve. *Fr.* The Mourning Bride, III, viii. TreF
Heaven-Haven. Gerard Manley Hopkins. ACP; BLV; BoLiVe; CAW; ChMo; CoBE; EmBrPo; EnL; EnLi-2; FaBoEn; GoBC; LoBV; MBP; MoAB; MoBrPo; MoP; NeMA; OAEP; OBEV (new ed.); POTT; PoVP; TrGrPo; ViBoPo; ViP; VLEP; WaKn
(I Have Desired to Go.) CBOV
Heaven, I think, would not be great or strange. Prophecy. *Unknown.* DDA
Heaven in My Hand. Raymond Kresensky. OQP; QP-2
Heaven is/ The place where. Heaven; the City Called Heaven. Langston Hughes. GoSl; TiPo
Heaven is a fine place, a fine place entirely. In a Low Rocking-Chair. Helen Coale Crew. BOL; HBMV
Heaven is bright, The. Infant Woe—Chinese. *Unknown.* BOL
Heaven is eternal, Earth enduring. *Unknown, tr. fr. Chinese.* Tao Teh Ching, XV. WhP
Heaven Is Heaven. Christina Rossetti. *See* Skylark and Nightingale.
Heaven is in my hand, and I. A Blackbird Suddenly. Joseph Auslander. BAP; BLA; MaRV; MPB; NLK; PC; PIAE; PoRL; TiPo; VOD
Heaven is lovelier than the stars. Driftwood. Trumbull Stickney. HBV
Heaven is mirrored, Love, deep in thine eyes. Aidenn. Katrina Trask. AA
Heaven Is Not Far. Christina Rossetti. OxBoCh
Heaven is not reached at a single bound. Gradatim. Josiah Gilbert Holland. BLP; DD; FaFP; HBV; HBVY; LBAP; MaRV; OHFP; OQP; PECK; PTA-1; QP-1; TreFS; WGRP
Heaven is open every day. The Way to Heaven. Charles Goodrich Whiting. AA
Heaven is what I cannot reach! Forbidden Fruit, II. Emily Dickinson. AnNE; TCAP
Heaven, O Lord, I Cannot Lose. Edna Dean Proctor. AA
Heaven o'erbrimming with life, O eye beloved and glorious. An Eye. Karin Ek. AnSL
Heaven Overarches [Earth and Sea]. Christina Rossetti. HBV; MeRV; POTT
(If So Tomorrow Saves.) PC
Heaven shall forgive you bridge at dawn. Ballade d'une Grande Dame. G. K. Chesterton. OxBoLi
Heaven-shrieking gale harries the earth this depth of winter, A. To the Tune of "Pusa Barbarian." Nalan Hsinteh. WhP
Heaven sinc thou art the only place of rest. *Unknown.* SeCSL
Heaven Soaring Lark, The. Mary Eleanor Roberts. BAP
Heaven; the City Called Heaven. Langston Hughes. GoSl
(Heaven.) TiPo
Heaven took my wife. Now it. Sorrow. Mei Yao Ch'en. OnPC
Heaven Tree. Henry Morton Robinson. JKCP (1955 ed.)
Heaven [*or* Heav'n], what an age is this! what race. Contentation, Directed to My Dear Father, and Most Worthy Friend, Mr. Izaak Walton. Charles Cotton. EV-2; LPS-3
Heaven, which man's generations draws. Epilogue. Francis Thompson. *Fr.* A Judgment in Heaven. MBP; MoAB; MoBrPo
Heaven Will Protect the Working Girl. Edgar Smith. FaFP; TreF
"You may tempt the upper classes," *sel.* FiBHP
Heaven, You Say, Will Be a Field in April. Conrad Aiken. MM; TBM; TwCV
Heavenborn Helen, Sparta's queen. Troy Town. Dante Gabriel Rossetti. EmBrPo; PoVP; ViP; ViPo; ViPP
Heavenlie Visitor, A. *Unknown.* *See* Yet If His Majesty, Our Sovereign Lord.
Heavenly Aid. Spenser. *See* Ministering Angels.
Heavenly Archer, bend thy bow. Dust to Dust. Walter de la Mare. TrPWD
Heavenly Banquet, The. *At. to* St. Bridget. *See* Feast of Saint Brigid of Kildare, The.
Heavenly bay, ringed round with cliffs and moors, The. In Guernsey. Swinburne. ATP (1935 ed.); BPN; PoVP; VLEP
Heavenly Breeze, The. George Burgess. BePJ
Heavenly City, The. Stevie Smith. FaBoTw
Heavenly City, The. *Unknown.* *See* New Jerusalem, The.
Heavenly Father, bless this food. Table Graces, or Prayers. *Unknown.* BLRP
Heavenly Father, hear our prayer. *Unknown.* PraP
"Heavenly Father," take to thee. Emily Dickinson. PoEL-5
Heavenly Friend, A. Paul Tucker. BePJ
Heavenly Home, The. Luis de León. *See* Life of the Blessed, The.
Heavenly Jerusalem, The. Giles Fletcher. *Fr.* Christ's Victory and Triumph. OxBoCh
Heavenly Pilot, The. Cormac, *tr. fr. Old Irish by* George Sigerson. *Fr.* Book of Leinster. CAW; OnYI
Heavenly Rhetoric, The. Shakespeare. *See* Did Not the Heavenly Rhetoric of Thine Eye.
Heavenly rider passed, The. Jalal ed-Din Rumi, *tr. fr. Persian by* A. J. Arberry PeP
Heavenly Runaway, The. John Daniel Logan. CPG
Heavenly song, I dare well say, An. This Day. *Unknown.* AnEC
Heavenly Stranger, The. Ada Blenkhorn. BLRP
Heavenly thing is fire, A. Fire. José Moreno Villa. CoSP
Heavens, The. Psalms, XIX, Bible, *O.T.* *See* Heavens Declare the Glory of God, The.
Heavens Above and the Law Within, The. Psalms, XIX, Bible, *O.T.* *See* Heavens Declare the Glory of God, The.
Heaven's angry face is scowling, The. Winter Evening. Pushkin. WoL
Heavens are more vast at evening tide. Wanderers. Rose Myra Phillips. BPP
Heavens Are Our Riddle, The. Herbert Bates. AA
Heavens are the mind of God, the systems are His word, The. Omnipresence. Stanton A. Coblentz. MaRV
Heavens are wroth; the thunder's rattling peal, The. Written in a Thunderstorm, 15 July 1841. John Clare. RO
Heavens Declare the Glory of God, The. Psalms, XIX, Bible, *O.T.* FaPON (1–3); HiLiEn; MaRV (1–6); TreF
(Glory of God, The.) TrJP
(God's Glory.) TrGrPo
(Heavens, The, 1–4.) ChTr
(Heavens Above and the Law Within, The, *Moulton, Modern Reader's Bible.*) WGRP
(Heavens Declare, The.) ShBV-1
(Nineteenth Psalm.) WBLP
(Psalm XIX.) AWP; InP (1–4); JAWP; OuHeWo; PC; WoL
Heavens first in tune I'll set, The. Love Sets Order in the Elements. Thomas Nabbes. *Fr.* Microcosmus. UnS
Heaven's Glory Shone. Emily Brontë. EmBrPo
Heaven's Hour. William Winter. LEAP
Heaven's Last Best Work. Pope. *Fr.* Moral Essays, Epistle II. OBEC
Heaven's Magnificence. William Augustus Muhlenberg. AA
Heaven's Mould, The. William Cavendish, Duke of Newcastle. LO; SeCL
Heaven's power [*or* Heav'n's pow'r] is infinite: earth, air, and sea. Baucis and Philemon. Ovid, *tr. by* Dryden. *Fr.* Metamorphoses. RoL; WoL
Heavens themselves, the planets and this center [*or* centre], The. On Degree [*or* Ulysses; on Degree]. Shakespeare. *Fr.* Troilus and Cressida, I, iii. ExPo; ImOP
Heavens! what a goodly prospect spreads around. Happy Britannia. James Thomson. *Fr.* The Seasons: Summer. OBEC; SeCePo
Heavenward. Lady Nairne. HBV
Heavier the Cross. Benjamin Schmolke, *tr. fr. German.* BePJ
Heaviest Cross of All, The. Katherine Eleanor Conway. AA; JKCP
Heavily-laden, snow-white, she departed from the shadow. Kassaris Emmanuel. *Fr.* Dynasty of Chimeras. MoGP
Heaving Roses of the Hedge Are Stirred, The. Richard Watson Dixon. CH
(Winter Will Follow.) GTBS-D
Heaving the Lead. *At. to* J. [*or* W.] Pearce *and to* Charles Dibdin. EtS
(By the Deep Nine.) ChTr
(Heaving of the Lead, The.) LPS-2
(Leadsman's Song, The.) HBV; SG
Heav'n & beautye are aly'de. *Unknown.* SeCSL
Heav'n Boun' Soldier, *with music.* *Unknown.* BoAN-1
Heav'n [*or* Heaven] from all creatures hides the book of fate. Hope Springs Eternal [*or* The Future]. Pope. *Fr.* An

Essay on Man, Epistle I. BCEP; CoEV; EV-3; OBEC; ViBoPo
Heav'n's pow'r is infinite: earth, air, and sea. *See* Heaven's power is infinite . . .
Heavy and glittering goblet, The. Bright Death. "Andrei Bely." BoRS
Heavy Bear, The. Delmore Schwartz. The Repetitive Heart, IX. AnAmPo; CrMA; FiMAP; LiTA; LiTG; LiTM; ReMP
(Heavy Bear Who Goes with Me, The.) MiAP; MoPo; MoVE; NePA; TrJP; UnPo (3d ed.)
Heavy Brigade, The. Tennyson. *See* Charge of the Heavy Brigade at Balaclava, The.
Heavy, broad,/ large and widely scattered. Spring Storm. Miltiades Malakassis. MoGP
Heavy clouds at length are scattering, The. Pushkin, *tr. fr. Russian by* Maud F. Jerrold. BoR
Heavy Dragoon The. W. S. Gilbert. *Fr.* Patience. PC
Heavy hangs the raindrop. The Two Children. Emily Brontë. PoEL-5
Heavy-hearted. Judah Al-Harizi, *tr. fr. Hebrew.* TrJP
Heavy heavy lies over our head. Game Out of Hand. Allison Ross. GoYe
Heavy-hipted Woman, The, *with music. Unknown.* ABF
Heavy is the grief that absorbed. Cumha Mhic Leoid. Mari Nighean Alisdair Ruaidh. BoFr
Heavy mists have crept away, The. Mark. Ernest McGaffey. AA
Heavy sky, and a drizzling rain, A. A London Idyll. "John Presland." VOD
Heavy smells of Spring, The. Jack. Louis Golding. TrJP
Heavy snow is falling, A. A Visit with Yang Chi. Cheng Hsieh. PoHN
Heavy sounds are over-sweet, The. City-Storm. Harold Monro. MBP; MoBrPo
Heavy Taxes. Po Chü-i, *tr. fr. Chinese by* Ching Ti. WhP
Heavy train through the dim country went rolling, rolling, The. Late Snow. J. C. Squire. PtOT
Heavy were the glasses, though. Wings of Wine. Ibn al-Yamani. MooP
Heavy with salt, and warm. The Equinox. DuBose Heyward. BAP
Heavy with unshed tears—weary with pain. A Sea Change. Dorothy Peace. NLK
Heavy with years and far, he heard the call. Fray Serra. Lillian White Spencer. BAP
Heavy yellow spider, The. Street. Alan Brown. TwCaPo
Hebe. James Russell Lowell. AA; AnFE; AnNE; APA; CoAnAm; HBV; IAP; MOAP; TCAP
Hebrew girl, with flaming brow, The. Magdalen. James Ryder Randall. JKCP
Hebrew Melodies, *sels.* Heine, *tr. fr. German.*
By the waters of Babylon, *tr. by* Charles Godfrey Leland. TrJP
Come, O Friend, to Greet the Bride, *after the Hebrew of* Solomon Halevi Alkabez, *tr. by* Louis Untermeyer. MeRV; TrJP
Hebrew Melody. Mikhail Yurevich Lermontov, *tr. fr. Russian by* Sir Cecil Kisch. WaL
Hebrew Wedding. Henry Hart Milman. *Fr.* The Fall of Jerusalem. LPS-1
Hebrews, *sel.* Bible, *N.T.*
Faith, XI: 1–XII: 2, *abr.* GrCo-1
Hebrews. James Oppenheim. MAP; MoAmPo (1942 ed.); TBM; TCPD; TrJP
Hebrides, The. Louis MacNeice. ReaPo
Hecate. Sophocles, *tr. fr. Greek by* C. M. Bowra. OxBG
Hecatompathia; or, Passionate Century of Love, *sels.* Thomas Watson.
Come, Gentle Death! ElL; SiCE
If Cupid Were a Child. TuPP
"If Jove himself be subject unto love." ElSeCe
"Love is a sour delight, a sug'red grief." ReIE
"My heart is set him down, twixt hope and fears." ReIE
"Resolved to dust, entombed here lieth Love."
(Here Lieth Love.) ElL
(Love's Grave.) OBSC
(My Love Is Past.) ElSeCe; ReIE; TuPP
Some That Report. TuPP
"Time wasteth years, and months, and hours." SiCE
(Time.) OBSC
To the Author. *By* George Peele. ReIE
"When first these eyes beheld with great delight." ReIE
"Where tender love had laid him down to sleep." ReIE
"Ye stately dames, whose beauties far excel." ReIE
Heccar and Gaira, *sel.* Thomas Chatterton.
Cawna. RO
Hector. Valentin Iremonger. NeIP; OxBI
Hector and Andromache. Homer. *See* Parting of Hector and Andromache, The.
Hector and his men bring the girl, her eyes gleaming. Andromache's Wedding. Sappho. GrL; OxBG
Hector in Hades. Robert Bridges. The Growth of Love, LIII. CBOV
Hector Protector was dressed all in green. Mother Goose. HBV; HBVY; MoShBr; OTPC; OxNR; RIS
Hector to Andromache. Homer. *See* Parting of Hector and Andromache, The.
Hector, the captain bronzed, from simple fight. Geoffrey Scott. *Fr.* The Skaian Gate. OBMV
Hector's wife had as yet heard nothing. Andromache. Homer, *pr. tr. by* Samuel Butler. *Fr.* The Iliad, XXII. OxBG
Hecuba, *sels.* Euripides, *tr. fr. Greek.*
"I Shame to Wear a Heart So White," *tr. by* Hugh Owen Meredith. GrR
Ilion Overthrown, *tr. by* Hugh Owen Meredith. GrR
(Troy, *tr. by* J. T. Sheppard.) OxBG
Polyxena. GrR, *tr. by* Hugh Owen Meredith; OxBG, *tr. by* George Allen
Sacrifice of Polyxena, The, *tr. by* Hugh Owen Meredith. GrR
Whither Away, *tr. by* T. F. Higham. OxBG
"Whole vast concourse of the Achaean host, The," *tr. by* John Addington Symonds. GrPo
He'd Nothing but His Violin. Mary Kyle Dallas. AA, *abr.;* DDA; HBV
He'd roamed so long and roamed so far. Song of the Mountebank. Jules Supervielle. TrFP
He'd take a human life as soon as he would take a drink. A Tough Cuss from Bitter Creek. James Barton Adams. PoOW
Hedge between, A/ Keeps friendship green. Country Proverbs. *Unknown.* StaSt
Hedge of trees surrounds me, A. The Scribe. *Unknown.* AnIL; OnYI
Hedge Schoolmasters, The. Seumas MacManus. CAW
Hedgehog, The. Laura Benét. PoeMoYo
Hedgehog, The. John Clare. SeCeV
Hedgehog, The. Edith King. BoTP
Hedgehog and His Coat, The. Elizabeth Fleming. BoTP
Hedgehog, hail the happy day. The Hedgehog. Laura Benét. PoeMoYo
Hedgehog hides beneath the rotten hedge, The. The Hedgehog. John Clare. SeCeV
Hedgehog is a little beast, The. The Hedgehog. Edith King. BoTP
Hedgerow hips to glossy scarlet turn, The. Fragment. John Clare. RO
Hedge-Row Story, The. Lilian Bowes-Lyon. POTE
Hedgerows are wiser than I, The. Easter Thought. Leo Cox. CaP
Hee balou, my sweet wee Donald. The Highland Balou. Burns. BOL
Hee that loves a rosie cheeke. Thomas Carew. *See* Disdain Returned.
Heed her not, O Cuhoolin, husband mine. The Speech of Emer. William Larminie. *Fr.* Fand. TIP
Heed not the folk who sing or say. The Optimist. Rosamund Marriot Watson. PC
Heed the old oracles. The Undersong. Emerson. *Fr.* Woodnotes, II. AA
Heedless Cruelty. William Cowper. *Fr.* The Task, VI. BCEP
(Humanity.) LPS-3
Heedless o' My Love. William Barnes. RO
Heedless she strayed from note to note. The Waiting Chords. Stephen Henry Thayer. AA
Heedless that now the mists of spring arise. Wild Geese. Ise. OnPM
Heere is better then the open ayre, take it thankfully. Shakespeare. *Fr.* King Lear, III, vi. AtBAP
Heh! Walk her round. Heave, ah, heave her short again! Anchor Song. Kipling. PIR
Heia, men, our shout goes out and echoes back, heia! Boating Song. *At. to* St. Columban. LaP
Heigh! brother mine, art a-waking or a-sleeping? Les Belles Roses sans Mercie. Arthur Shearly Cripps. OBVV
Heigh Ho! Jean Ingelow. *See* Seven Times Four.
Heigh-ho, April! Eleanor Farjeon. PoRh
Heigh ho! daisies and buttercups. Seven Times Four [*or* Maternity *or* Heigh Ho!]. Jean Ingelow. *Fr.* Songs of Seven. BoTP; GBV (1922 ed.); HBV; LPS-1; MOAH; OHIP; PTA-1
Heigh ho! my heart is low. *Unknown.* OxNR
Heigh-ho! my thoughts are far away. The Love of a Boy. Richard Hovey. PR
"Heigho, my precious!" sings the little brown Mary. Sleep Fairy. Annie E. Tynan. BOL
"Heigho," yawned one day King Francis. The Glove. Robert Browning. EmBrPo; PCN; PIAE; PoVP; PreP; VLEP
Height. Anne Morrow Lindbergh. BAP
Height of the Ridiculous, The. Oliver Wendell Holmes. AA; ALV; AnNE; APW; BAP; BBV (1951 ed.); BOHV; DDA; FaFP; FiBHP; HBV; HiLiAm; IAP; LauV; LEAP; LHV; LPS-3; MCCG; MOAP; MoShBr; MPB; NeHB; OTPC (1946 ed.); PFE; PIR; PoeMoYo; PTA-2; SiTL; StVeCh; WhC; YaD

Heights, The. Longfellow. *Fr.* The Ladder of St. Augustine. TreF
Heights and Depths. William Canton. PoeT
Heights by great men reached and kept, The. The Heights. Longfellow. *Fr.* The Ladder of St. Augustine. TreF
Heights of Arts, The. Pope. *See* Alps of Poetry, The.
Heiho, my coat is green. The Green Coat. *Unknown.* WhP
Heiho, my husband is brave. My Husband. *Unknown.* WhP
Heiho, the sun in the east! The Sun in the East. *Unknown.* WhP
Heilige Nacht. Joseph Mohr. *See* Silent Night.
Heimkehr, Die, *sels.* Heine, *tr. fr. German by* Ezra Pound.
"Mutilated choir boys, The." AWP
(Choir Boys, The.) LiTW
"Tell me where thy lovely love is." AWP
"This delightful young man." AWP
Heine's Grave. Matthew Arnold. EmBrPo; LPS-3, *abr.;* PoVP; PtP; VLEP
Heine ("The spirit of the world"), *sel.* BPN
Heinesque. Vladimir Mayakovsky, *tr. fr. Russian by* Babette Deutsch. TrRV
Heinrich Heine. Ludwig Lewisohn. TrJP
Heir and Serf. Don Marquis. HBMV
Heir of Linne, The. *Unknown.* BaBo; ESPB (A *and* B *vers.*); EV-2; OBB
Heir of Vironi, The, *sel.* Isaac Pocock.
Song: "Oh! say not woman's love [*or* heart] is bought." HBV (8th ed.)
Heiress and Architect. Thomas Hardy. PoVP; ViP
Heirloom. A. M. Klein. BoCaPo; PeCV; TrJP
Heirs of great yesterdays, be proud with me. To My Countrymen. Robert Underwood Johnson. OQP; QP-2
Heivenly leddy, earthly sovereign. The Prayer, Made in Ballat Form bi Villon for His Mither. Villon, *tr. by* Tom Scott. PoN
Hekatompathia. Thomas Watson. *See* Hecatompathia.
Hektor and Andromache. Homer. *See* Parting of Hector and Andromache, The.
Hektor to Andromache. Homer. *See* Parting of Hector and Andromache, The.
Hektor turn'd/ Back from his house with speed. Hektor and Andromache. Homer, *tr. by* Maurice Hewlett. *Fr.* The Iliad, VI. OxBG
Hélas. Oscar Wilde. AnIV; BMEP; GTIV; GTSL; LBBV; LEAP; MBP; MoBrPo; PoVP; ViPP; VLEP
Held and thrilled by the vision. From the Bridge. Don Marquis. OBAV
Held by a federal bond from pole to pole. Joaquín de Olmedo. *Fr.* Ode to Bolivar. BoFr
Held Fast. Sadi, *tr. fr. Persian by* A. J. Arberry. PeP
Held on the slightest of bamboo poles. Ode to the Chinese Paper Snake. Richard Eberhart. CrMA
Helen. Aeschylus, *tr. fr. Greek by* Jack Lindsay. *Fr.* Agamemnon. OxBG
(Helen; and the Wages of War, *tr. by* E. D. A. Morshead.) GrR
Helen. "Susan Coolidge." AA
Helen. Hilda Doolittle ("H. D."). BAV; CBOV; FaBoTw; MAP; MoAmPo; MoVE; PreP
Helen. "Odysseus Elytis," *tr. fr. Modern Greek by* Rae Dalven. MoGP
Helen, *sels.* Euripides, *tr. fr. Greek.*
"Fair be thy speed, Sidonian ship!" *tr. by* A. W. Verrall. GrPo
Hymn to the Sirens, *tr. by* Arthur S. Way. GrR
(Siren-Spirits, *tr. by* J. T. Sheppard.) OxBG
Pater Noster, *tr. by* Arthur S. Way. GrR
Prophets Exposed, *tr. by* M. Wodhull. GrR
"Soul of the deceased, although it live, The." MaRV
Helen. Homer, *tr. fr. Greek. Fr.* The Iliad, III. GrR, *tr. by* Maurice Hewlett; OxBG, *tr. by* William Cowper
Helen. Mary Lamb. *Fr.* John Woodvil; a Tragedy (*by* Charles Lamb). OBRV
Helen. Cecil Francis Lloyd. OCL
Helen. Christopher Marlowe. *See* Was This the Face.
Helen. Edward A. U. Valentine. AA
Helen. Paul Valéry. *See* Helen, the Sad Queen.
Helen and Corythos. Walter Savage Landor. *Fr.* Corythos. LoBV
Helen and Hermia. Shakespeare. *Fr.* A Midsummer Night's Dream, III, ii. GN
Helen and Iphigenia. Tennyson. *See* Iphigenia.
Helen; and the Wages of War. Aeschylus. *See* Helen.
Helen and Thetis. Alcaeus, *tr. fr. Greek by* Sir William Marris. GrL; OxBG
Helen Hunt Jackson. Ina Donna Coolbrith. AA
Helen Keller. Edmund Clarence Stedman. AA
Helen, Menelaos, and Memories of Troy. Homer, *tr. fr. Greek by* George Chapman. *Fr.* The Odyssey, IV. GrR
(At Sparta; Helen and Menelaus, *pr. tr. by* Samuel Butler.) OxBG
Helen of Kirconnell [*or* Kirkconnel]. *Unknown.* AnFE; AWP; BBV (1923 ed.); BCEP; BSV; CBE; CBOV; CH; EtPaEn; GoTS; HBV; InPo; LEAP; LH; LiTB; LiTG; LoBV; OBB; OBEV; SeCeV; UnPo (1st ed.); WP
(Fair Helen.) EV-2; FaFP; GBV (1922 ed.); GTBS; GTBS-D; GTBS-W; GTSE; GTSL; InP; LiTL; ViBoPo
(Fair Helen of Kirconnel.) *Unknown.* BrBE; EBSV; OTPC
Helen of Laughing Ledge. Robert Haven Schauffler. TCAP
Helen of Troy. Christopher Marlowe. *See* Was This the Face.
Helen of Tyre. Longfellow. MeRV
Helen—Old. Isabel Ecclestone Mackay. CaP; OCL
Helen on the Walls of Troy Looking for Her Brothers. Homer, *tr. fr. Greek by* Edward Craven Hawtrey. *Fr.* The Iliad, III. LiA
(Helen Seeks for Her Brothers among the Army of the Greeks before Troy.) CBOV
Helen out of Helas came. The Incendiary Sex. Don Marquis. LPS-1
Helen; the Penitent. Homer, *tr. fr. Greek by* the Earl of Derby. *Fr.* The Iliad, VI. GrR
Helen, the Sad Queen. Paul Valéry, *tr. fr. French by* Joseph T. Shipley. AWP; CAW; JAWP; WBP
(Helen.) AnFP, *tr. by* Andrew Chiappe; TrFP, *tr. by* Alan Conder
(Hélène, *tr. by* Janet Lewis.) Po
Helen the wise did Paris, another neatherd, ravish! The Wooing of Daphnis. Theocritus. *Fr.* Idylls. GrL
Helen, this age, by your exceeding worth. Pierre de Ronsard. *Fr.* Sonnets pour Hélène. PrPoCR
Helen, thy beauty is to me. To Helen. Poe. AA; AmP; AmPo; AmPP; AnAmPo; AnFE; APA; APW; AtBAP; ATP; AWP; BAP; BAV; BLV; BoLiVe; BTP; CaAE; CBE; CH; ChTr; CoAnAm; CoBA; CoV; DD; DDA; EG; EtPaEn; EV-5; ExPo; FaBoBe; FaBoEn; FaFP; GA; GTBS-D; GTBS-W; GTSE; HBV; HBVY; HoPM; InP; InPo; InvP; JAWP; KN; LA; LaNeLa; LBAP; LEAP; LiA; LiTA; LiTG; LiTL; LoBV; LoPo; MCCG; MOAP; NeHB; NePA; OBAV; OBEV; OBRV; OtMeF; OTPC; OuHeWo; OxBA; PC; PFE; PFY; PG (1945 ed.); PIAE; PIR; Po; PoEL-4; PoFS; PoRA; REAL; ReaPo; RiBV; SeCeV; SPP; TCAP; TOP; TreF; TrGrPo; TSW; TSWC; TwCrTr; UnPo (1st ed.); ViBoPo; WBP; WHA; YT
Helen Unreproached by Hector. Homer, *tr. fr. Greek by* William Cowper. *Fr.* The Iliad, XXIV. LiA
Helena Embarks for Palestine. Cynewulf, *tr. fr. Anglo-Saxon by* Charles W. Kennedy. *Fr.* Elene. AnOE
Hélène. Paul Valéry. *See* Helen, the Sad Queen.
Helen's Birthday. Pierre de Ronsard, *tr. fr. French by* Alan Conder. TrFP
Helen's Bosom. Pierre de Ronsard, *tr. fr. French by* Alan Conder. TrFP
Helen's lips are drifting dust. Love Triumphant. Frederic Lawrence Knowles. BAP; HBV; LBMV; PR
Helen's Rape. Thom Gunn. PoN
Helen's Song. Philip James Bailey. *Fr.* Festus. VA
Helga. Carl Sandburg. ChMo; CMP; NP; TSW; TSWC
Helgi Thrice Born. *Unknown, tr. fr. Old Norse by* Henry Adams Bellows. *Fr.* The Elder Edda. PaOS
Heliades, *sel.* Aeschylus, *tr. fr. Greek by* C. M. Bowra.
Zeus. OxBG
Helicon and Cithaeron. Corinna, *tr. fr. Greek by* C. M. Bowra. OxBG
Helicopter bee fines down, The. Honey. Ruth Miller. BoSA
Heliodora. Hilda Doolittle ("H. D."). ChMo; CMP
Heliodora ("Tears for my lady dead"). Meleager, *tr. fr. Greek by* Andrew Lang. OxBG
(Heliodore Dead, *tr. by* Andrew Lang.) VA
(Irreparable Rose, *tr. by* Humbert Wolfe.) GrR
Heliodora and the Bee. Meleager, *tr. fr. Greek by* Humbert Wolfe. GrR
Heliodora, this last offering. Irreparable Rose. Meleager, *tr. by* Humbert Wolfe. GrR
Heliodora's Garland. Meleager, *tr. fr. Greek by* Robert Guthrie MacGregor. OnPM
Heliodora's Wreath. Meleager, *tr. fr. Greek by* Robert Allason Furness. OxBG
(Spring Garland, A.) GrR
Heliodore. John Daniel Logan. CaP; OCL
Heliodore ("Pour wine"). Meleager, *tr. fr. Greek by* Andrew Lang. OBVV; POTT
(Cup-Bearer, The, *tr. by* Robert Allason Furness.) OxBG
(To Heliodora, *tr. by* Dudley Fitts.) LiTW
(Toast to Heliodore, A, *tr. by* Robert Furness.) GrR
Heliodore Dead. Meleager. *See* Heliodora.
Helios. Joel Elias Spingarn. AA
Heliotrope. Harry Thurston Peck. AA; HBV; LEAP; PR
Hell. Abraham Cowley. *Fr.* Davideis, I. OxBoCh
("Beneath the silent chambers of the earth.") SeEP
Hell. Milton. *Fr.* Paradise Lost, II. OBS
Hell and Heaven. *Unknown.* ABF, *with music;* OxBoLi; SiTL

Hell-bound Train, The. *Unknown, at. to* J. W. Pruitte. BeLS; BLPA; CoSo, *with music*
Hell Gate. A. E. Housman. Last Poems, XXXI. ReaPo; UnPo
Hell in Texas. *At. to* John R. Steele. ABF, *with music;* BLPA; CoSo, *with music;* CSF
Hell-Ride of Brynhild, The. *Unknown, tr. fr. Icelandic by* William Morris *and* Eirikur Magnússon. *Fr.* The Elder Edda. OuHeWo
He'll See It When He Wakes. Frank Lee. MDAH
Hellas, *sels.* Shelley.
Chorus: "Darkness has dawned in the East." BPN; EnRP
Chorus: "Life may change, but it may fly not." BPN; EmBrPo; EnRP; EPN
Chorus: "O Slavery! thou frost of the world's prime." PoFr
Chorus: "Victorious wrong, with vulture scream." (Final Chorus from "Hellas.") EnLi-2
Chorus: "World's great age begins anew, The." AtBAP; CoEV; EnRP; ERP; ExPo; FaBoEn; HBV; LoBV; MyFE; OAEP; PoE; PoEL-4; RiBV; SeCeV; TCEP; TOP; WoL
(Final Chorus.) BEL; BoLiVe; BPN; EmBrPo; EnLit; EPP; OBRV; PoFS; SeCePo
(Hellas.) ChTr; EM-2; EPN; InPo; OBEV; ShBV-4
(New World, A.) BLV; TrGrPo
(World's Great Age Begins Anew, The.) AWP; BCEP; FiP; GEPC; JAWP; LEAP; SoV; TreFS; TwCrTr; WBP
Chorus: "Worlds on worlds are rolling ever." BPN; EmBrPo; EnRP; OAEP
(Worlds on Worlds Are Rolling Ever.) PoFS
"Power from the unknown God, A." StJW
Hellenics, The, *sels.* Walter Savage Landor.
Death of Chrysaor, The. EmBrPo
Hamadryad, The. BPN; CBOV; EmBrPo; EnRP; EPN; ERP; TOP; VA
Iphigeneia and Agamemnon. BeLS; EmBrPo
(Iphigeneia.) EnRP
Proem. ViBoPo
(On the Hellenics.) BEL; BPN; EmBrPo; EnRP; EPN; ERP
Ternissa! You Are Fled! ExPo; GTSE; LoBV; PoEL-4; SeCeV
(Ternissa.) FaBoEn; TriL
Thrasymedes and Eunoe. EmBrPo
Hellenistics. Robinson Jeffers. OnAP
Hello! Louise Ayres Garnett. SiSoSe
Hello, Central, what's the matter with this line? The Hesitating Blues. W. C. Handy. GoSl
Hello dar, Miss Melerlee! Miss Melerlee. John Wesley Holloway. BANP; PoNe
Hello, Girls. *Unknown. See* Kansas Boys.
Hello, Somebody, *with music. Unknown.* ShS
Hello there, Walt! To Walt Whitman. Tom MacInnes. BoCaPo; CaP; OCL
Hell's Road. Charles Heavysege. *Fr.* Saul, a Drama. BMEP
Helmet of the legion, this, A. On a Roman Helmet. Will H. Ogilvie. EBSV
Helmet Orchid. Douglas Stewart. BoAV
Helmsman, The. Hilda Doolittle ("H. D."). AnAmPo; LA; MOAP; OxBA
Helmsman, The. Mark Antony De Wolfe Howe. PC
Helmsman, The; an Ode. J. V. Cunningham. MoVE
Heloise and Abelard, *wr. title.* Pope. *See* Eloisa to Abelard.
Helot, The, *sel.* Isabella Valancy Crawford.
"Who may quench the god-born fire." CPG; PeCV
Help. Sadi, *tr. fr. Persian by* Sir Edwin Arnold. *Fr.* The Gulistan. AWP; JAWP; OnPM; WBP
Help-Givers, The. Laurence Housman. MaRV
Help, Good Shepherd. Ruth Pitter. OxBoCh
Help! Help!/ What's to do? Trouble at the Farm. Ivy O. Eastwick. BoTP
Help me to bear Thy spring, dear Lord; to bless. May. Laura Simmons. LPS-1
Help me to hold the vision undefiled. The Scribe's Prayer. Arthur Guiterman. TrPWD
Help me to make this working day. Invocation. Francesca Falk Miller. PEDC
Help Me to Seek. Sir Thomas Wyatt. InvP; ReIE; SiCE; TuPP
(Rondeau: "Help me to seek, for I lost it there.") Po; SiPS
Help me to suffer when I most would spare. Remembering Calvary. Ethel Fanning Young. OQP; QP-2
Help Me Today. Elsie Robinson. PoToHe
Help One Another. G. F. Hunting. PCH
Help, Sure Help. Arthur Hugh Clough. *Fr.* Dipsychus, II. VLEP
(At Torcello.) BHV
("I had a vision; was it in my sleep?") PoVP
Help Us, Moon! *Unknown, tr. fr. Russian by* W. R. S. Ralston. OnPM
Help Wanted. Franklin Waldheim. BLPA
Helpe O helpe kinde Abraham & send. *Unknown.* SeCSL
Helping the Handicapped. Emily Dickinson. *See* If I can stop one heart from breaking.
Helpless am I indeed. "Labourers Together with God." Lucy Alice Perkins. BLRP
Helpless, condemned, yet still for mercy croaking. Mazeppa. Roy Campbell. AnFE
Helpless is God in struggling with that star. The Birth of Lucifer. John Gould Fletcher. MAP; MoAmPo
Helvellyn. Sir Walter Scott. BHV; LPS-2
Hem and Haw. Bliss Carman. HBV; LA; MAP; MaRV; MoAmPo (1942 ed.); NeMA; PCN
Hem of His Garment, The. Anna Elizabeth Hamilton. TrPWD
Hemisphere could float upon, A. History Class. Robert Finch. TwCaPo
Hemlock, The ("I think the hemlock likes to stand"). Emily Dickinson. OnPM
Hemlock Mountain. Sarah N. Cleghorn. HBV
Hemmed-in Males. William Carlos Williams. *Fr.* A Folded Skyscraper. MoVE
("Saloon is gone up the creek, The.") AnAmPo; LA
Hemorrhage, The. Stanley Kunitz. WaP
Hen, The. Matthias Claudius, *tr. fr. German.* BOHV; LPS-3
Hen, The. Oliver Herford. LBN; NA
Hen and the Carp, The. Ian Serraillier. AlDL
Hen and the Oriole, The. Don Marquis. *Fr.* Archy and Mehitabel. FiBHP; TwCV
Hen remarked to the mooley cow, The. Art. *Unknown.* BLPA
Hen-Roost Man, The. Ruth McEnery Stuart. BOHV
Hen to herself said one beautiful day, "Cluck, cluck," The. Cluck, Cluck. *Unknown.* FTB
Hen with the Golden Eggs, The. La Fontaine, *tr. fr. French by* Elizur Wright. OnPM
Hence All You Vain Delights. John Fletcher. *See* Melancholy.
Hence away, nor dare intrude! Inscription on a Grot. Samuel Rogers. *Fr.* The Pleasures of Memory. OBEC
Hence, Away, You Sirens! George Wither. *Fr.* Fidelia *and also* Fair Virtue. ElL, 3 *sts.*
(Sonnet: "Hence away, you sirens, leave me," 10 *sts.*) ElSeCe
Hence childish boy too long have I. *Unknown.* SeCSL
Hence, flames and darts! ye amorous sighs, hence! The Honeymoon. Henry Luttrell. *Fr.* Advice to Julia. OBRV
Hence flattring hopes. Cease longing and give ore. *Unknown.* SeCSL
Hence, Hairt. Alexander Scott. AEV; EBSV
(Bequest of His Heart, A.) OBEV
(Hence, Heart, with Her That Must Depart.) BSV
Hence, hence, profane; soft silence let us have. A Dirge upon the Death of the Right Valiant Lord, Bernard Stuart. Robert Herrick. SeCV-1
Hence, hence unhallowed ears and hearts more hard. Democritus Platonissans; or, An Essay upon the Infinity of Worlds out of Platonick Principles. Henry More. SeCV-2
"Hence Loathèd Melancholy . . ." Euripides. *See* Hospitality.
Hence, loathèd Melancholy. L'Allegro. Milton. AnFE; AWP; BCEP; BEL; BLV; BoLiVe; BrBE; CBE; CBOV; CoBE; EM-1; EnL; EnLi-1; EnLit; EPP; EV-2; FaFP; FiP; GEPC; GN; GTBS; GTBS-D; GTBS-W; GTSE; GTSL; HBV; HiLiEn; HoPM; InPo; LEAP; LiA; LiTB; LiTG; LoBV; LPS-3; MaPo; MCCG; MyFE; OBEV; OBS; OuHeWo; PIAE; PIR; PoE; ReaPo; SeCePo; SeCeV; ShBV-3; TCEP; TOP; TreFS; TrGrPo; TVSH; TwCrTr; ViBoPo; WHA; WoL
Hence loathèd Melody, whose name recalls. Ode to Discord. *Unknown.* PC
Hence, lying world, with all thy care. For One Retired into the Country. Charles Wesley. SN
Hence, rude Winter! crabbed old fellow. A Glee for Winter. Alfred Domett. DD; HBV; SN; VA
Hence, stern, grim, puritanic days. To November. G. W. Adams. TOAH
Hence These Rimes. Bert Leston Taylor. FiBHP
Hence through the continent Ten Thousand Greeks. The Ten Thousand. James Thomson. BHV
Hence, vain deluding Joy[e]s. Il Penseroso. Milton. AEV; AWP; BCEP; BLV; BoLiVe; BrBE; CBE; CBOV; CEP; EM-1; EnL; EnLi-1; EnLit; EPP; EV-2; FiP; GEPC; GTBS; GTBS-D; GTBS-W; GTSE; GTSL; HBV; HoPM; HiLiEn; InPo; LEAP; LiA; LiTB; LiTG; LPS-3; MaPo; MyFE; OBEV; OBS; OuHeWo; PIAE; PIR; Po; PoE; ReaPo; SeCeV; ShBV-3; TCEP; TOP; TrGrPo; TVSH; TwCrTr; UnPo (1st ed.); ViBoPo; WHA
Hence vaine delights beegone, tempte mee noe more. *Unknown.* SeCSL

Hence with Passion, Sighs and Tears. Thomas Heywood. *Fr.* A Maidenhead Well Lost. SeCL
Hence, ye profane! I hate you all. The Profane. Abraham Cowley. AWP
Hence, ye profane; mell not with holy things. Joseph Hall. *Fr.* Virgidemiarum. SiCE
Henceforth, from the Mind. Louise Bogan. LiTA; MoPo; MoVE; NePA
Henchman, The. Whittier. HBV; OBEV (new ed.); OBVV; PR
Henchman sworn of Ares, Lord God of War, I live, A. Life and Art. Archilochus. GrPE
Henchman's Speech, The ("So we made our way"). Euripides, *tr. fr. Greek by* Gilbert Murray. *Fr.* Hippolytus. ReTS
Henley on Taieri. Charles Brasch. AnNZ
"Henri Heine"—'tis here! Heine's Grave. Matthew Arnold. EmBrPo; LPS-3; PoVP; PtP; VLEP
Henry and King Pedro clasping. The Death of Don Pedro. *Unknown.* AnSpL-1; AWP
Henry before Agincourt: October 25, 1415. John Lydgate. CH
Henry Blake's father goes fishing with him. An Unusual Chum. James W. Foley. FAOV
Henry C. Calhoun. Edgar Lee Masters. *Fr.* Spoon River Anthology. AmP; LiTA; LiTM (rev. ed.); NP
Henry Cogdal. Edgar Lee Masters. *Fr.* The New Spoon River. ChMo; CMP; TCAP
Henry Ditch. Edgar Lee Masters. The New Spoon River. LEAP
Henry VIII. Eleanor *and* Herbert Farjeon. OnPP; StPo
Henry VIII. Shakespeare *and probably* John Fletcher. *See* King Henry VIII.
Henry Fielding. Austin Dobson. BPN
Henry V. Shakespeare. *See* King Henry V.
Henry V at [*or* before] Harfleur. Shakespeare. *See* Once More unto the Breach . . .
Henry V to His Soldiers. Shakespeare. *See* Once More unto the Breach.
Henry Fifth's Address to His Soldiers. Shakespeare. *See* Once More unto the Breach . . .
Henry IV, Pt. I. Shakespeare. *See* King Henry IV, Pt. I.
Henry IV, Pt. II. Shakespeare. *See* King Henry IV, Pt. II.
Henry IV's Soliloquy on Sleep. Shakespeare. King Henry IV, Pt. II, *fr.* III, i. TVSH
(Cares of Majesty, The.) LiTB; TreF
(Sleep.) BCEP; EV-1; LPS-3
(Soliloquy on Sleep.) FiP
(Uneasy Lies the Head.) BLP
Henry Green. *Unknown.* BaBo
Henry Howard, Earl of Surrey, to [the Lady] Geraldine. Michael Drayton. *Fr.* England's Heroical Epistles. ReEn; ReIE; TuPP
(Earl of Surrey to Geraldine.) OBSC
Henry Hudson's Quest. Burton Egbert Stevenson. HBV; MC; PAH
Henry James/ (Whatever his other claims). Jacobean. Clifton Fadiman. FiBHP
Henry King. Hilaire Belloc. CenHV; HBMV; TSW; TSWC
Henry Martin [*or* Martyn]. *Unknown.* BaBo; ESPB (A *and* E *vers.*); SG (A *vers.*); ViBoFo (A *vers.*; B *vers., with music*)
Henry Purcell. Gerard Manley Hopkins. UnS; ViPP
Henry St. John, Viscount Bolingbroke. Pope. *See* Literary Poet to His Patron, A.
Henry VI, Pt. I. Shakespeare. *See* King Henry VI, Pt. I.
Henry VI, Pt. II Shakespeare *See* King Henry VI, Pt. II.
Henry VI, Pt. III. Shakespeare. *See* King Henry VI, Pt. III.
Henry Spaulding. Donald Burnie. PaA
Henry the Eighth. Shakespeare. *See* King Henry VIII.
Henry the Fifth. Shakespeare. *See* King Henry V.
Henry the Fourth, Pt. I. Shakespeare. *See* King Henry IV, Pt. I.
Henry the Fourth, Pt. II. Shakespeare. *See* King Henry IV, Pt. II.
Henry the Sixth, Pt. I. Shakespeare. *See* King Henry VI, Pt. I.
Henry the Sixth, Pt. II. Shakespeare. *See* King Henry VI, Pt. II.
Henry the Sixth, Pt. III. Shakespeare. *See* King Henry VI, Pt. III.
Henry Turnbull. W. W. Gibson. FaBoTw
Henry Vaughan. Thomas S. Jones, Jr. PtP
Henry Wadsworth Longfellow. Austin Dobson. DD; GA; HBV
Henry Wadsworth Longfellow. William Wetmore Story. GA; PEOR
Henry Ward Beecher. *At. to* Oliver Wendell Holmes. *See* Limerick: "Reverend Henry Ward Beecher, The."
Henry Ward Beecher. Charles Henry Phelps. AA
Henry Was a Worthy King. *Unknown.* MoShBr
Henry Zoll, the Miller. Edgar Lee Masters. The New Spoon River. TCAP
Henry's Lament. Samuel Daniel. *Fr.* The Complaint of Rosamond. OBSC
Hens, The. Elizabeth Madox Roberts. FaPON; GoTP; HBMV; MPB; PoeMoYo; PoRh; SP; StVeCh; SUS; TiPo; TSW; TSWC; UTS; VOD
Heptalogia, The, *sels.* Swinburne.
Higher Pantheism in a Nutshell, The, *parody.* ALV; BOHV; EmBrPo; HBV, *abr.;* NA; PA; ViPo; VLEP
John Jones. NA; OAEP
Nephelidia. ALV; BOHV; EnLi-2 (1949 ed.); HBV; HoPM; InMe; NA; OAEP; PA; PoFS; PoVP; ViP; ViPo; VLEP
Sonnet for a Picture. OAEP
Hepzibah of the Cent Shop. Virginia McCormick. LS; VOD (1935 ed.)
Her Absent Lord, *sel.* Ugga Byan, *tr. fr. Arakanese by* Maurice Collis.
"This is a colder winter than last year." LiTW
Her aged hands are worn with works of love. To One Being Old. Langdon Elwyn Mitchell. AA; OBAV
Her Allowance! Lillian Gard. VOD
Her angel looked upon God's face. The Eternal Image. Ruth Pitter. MoBrPo
Her Answer. John Bennett. AA; BLPA; NeHB
Her Apotheosis. Thomas Hardy. ViPP
Her arms across her breast she laid. The Beggar Maid. Tennyson. BeLS; BoTP; BPN; CG; EmBrPo; HBV; OTPC; PoVP; TCEP; WP
Her arms first cradled me with mother love and care. My Mother. Samuel N. Wilson. PEDC
Her Beauty. Max Plowman. HBMV
Her Beauty. Shakespeare. *See* Sonnets, CVI.
Her beauty smoothed earth's furrowed face. The Tokens. Francis Thompson. *Fr.* Daisy. OtMeF
Her Birthday. Feng Yen-chi, *tr. fr. Chinese by* Ch'u Ta'kao. ChLP
Her black eyes are made of beads. The Old Doll. Wilhelmina Seegmiller. MPB
Her blue eyes they beam and they twinkle. Winny. William Allingham. OTPC
Her Body. Alfred Kreymborg. *Fr.* Dorothy. AnAmPo; LA
Her body is not so white as. Queen-Ann's-Lace. William Carlos Williams. MAP; MoAB; MoAmPo
Her Bright Smile, *with music.* J. C. Carpenter. SoAmSa
Her casement like a watchful eye. Balder's Wife. Alice Cary. AA; AnAmPo; LA
Her chariot of a snail's fine shell. The Court of Fairy. Michael Drayton. *Fr.* Nymphidia. EPP
Her chariot ready straight is made. Queen Mab's Chariot [*or* Queen Mab Visits Pigwiggen]. Michael Drayton. *Fr.* Nymphidia. EV-1; OBS; OTPC; PCH
Her cheek was pale, her form was gaunt. The Leper of London. Herman Scheffauer. BAP
Her Choice. Mattie Lee Hausgen. GFA
Her Commendation. Francis Davison. OBSC
(Madrigal: "Some there are as fair to see to.") EIL
(Commendation of Her Beauty, Stature, Behavior, and Wit.) TuPP
Her Confirmation. Selwyn Image. VA
Her constant gesture spanned the air. Venus. Edgar Bowers. PtPa
Her Courage. W. B. Yeats. Upon a Dying Lady, VI. LiTB
Her Courtesy. W. B. Yeats. Upon a Dying Lady, I. LiTB
Her curving bosom images. Bodily Beauty. George Rostrevor Hamilton. HBMV
Her Dairy. Peter Newell. NA; PCH
Her day out from the workhouse-ward, she stands. The Ice. W. W. Gibson. EPN
Her Dead Brother. Robert Lowell. NePoEA
Her Death. W. W. Gibson. ChMo; CMP
Her Death. Thomas Hood. *Fr.* Miss Kilmansegg and Her Precious Leg. VA
Her Death and After. Thomas Hardy. PoVP
Her Decision. James K. Baxter. Cressida, XI. AnNZ
Her deed and her name will be lost. On a Dead Teacher. Gerald Raftery. JKCP (1926 ed.)
Her Dilemma. Thomas Hardy. EmBrPo; Po
Her Dilemma. Paul B. McVey. CAG
Her dimpled cheeks are pale. A Southern Girl. Samuel Minturn Peck. AA
Her door opened on the white water. The Little Lady of Ch'ing-hsi. *Unknown.* ChLP; TrCh
Her drooping flowers dabble upon. Betty by the Sea. Ronald McCuaig. BoAV
Her drooping wrist, her arm. Piano Recital. Babette Deutsch. NePoAm
Her Dwelling-Place. Ada Foster Murray. HBV; LEAP
Her Epitaph. Thomas William Parsons. AA; APW; HBV
Her Explanation. Edward Rowland Sill. OBAV
Her eye is blue and so modest as well. What She Is. Ludvig Bødtcher. BoDS
Her eye that glances piercingly. The Old-Clothes Woman. Stéphane Mallarmé. MiFP

Her Eyes. Alfred Kreymborg. *Fr.* Dorothy. AnAmPo; LA
Her Eyes. John Crowe Ransom. LiTM (rev. ed.); NePA
Her eyes are deepest wells of hidden thought. Sister. Marian Osborne. CPG
Her eyes are gold, her cheek is hyalite. Grey Hair. Rufinus. OxBG
Her eyes are homes of silent prayer. In Memoriam A. H. H. XXXII. Tennyson. BPN; EmBrPo; EPN; EPP; GEPC; TOP; ViPo; VLEP
Her eyes are like forget-me-nots. To a Little Girl. Gustav Kobbé. HBV
Her eyes are sunlit hazel. Portrait of a Lady. Sarah N. Cleghorn. CP
Her eyes are two magicians' fires, molten and black and round. Nephree-ti-ta. Stanton A. Coblentz. UnW
Her eyes be like the violets. Anne. Lizette Woodworth Reese. AA; PR
Her eyes? Dark pools of deepest shade. Portrait. George Leonard Allen. CDC
Her eyes flashed lightning. Heinesque. Vladimir Mayakovsky. TrRV
Her eyes have seen the monoliths of kings. Three Sonnets on Oblivion. George Sterling. HBV
Her eyes hold black whips. Her Eyes. Alfred Kreymborg. *Fr.* Dorothy. AnAmPo; LA
Her eyes that might be filled with wishes. Thenot Protests. "C. N. S." InMe
Her eyes the glow-worm lend thee. Night Piece, to Julia [*or* On a Dark Road]. Robert Herrick. AnFE; AtBAP; ATP; BCEP; BEL; BoTP; CaAE; CBOV; CenL; CoBE; CoEV; EG; ElSeCe; EM-1; EnLi-1 (1949 ed.); EnLit; EPS; EV-2; HBV; InvP; LEAP; LiTB; LiTL; LoBV; MaPo; NeHB; OAEP; OBEV; OBS; OTPC; PCD; PoEL-3; PoFS; PoRA; ReEn; RiBV; SeCeV; SeCL; SeCV-1; SeEP; ShBV-2; TOP; TwHP; TyEnPo; WHA
Her face has made my life most proud and glad. Of His Lady's Face [*or* Sonnet]. Jacopo da Lentino. AWP; OnPM
Her Face, Her Tongue, Her Wit. *At. to* Sir Walter Ralegh. ReIE
(Sonet, A.) SiCE
Her face is hushed in perfect calm. A Child's Portrait. William James Dawson. VA
Her face was very fair to see. Our Sister. Horatio Nelson Powers. HBV
Her failing spirits with derisive glee. Helen and Corythos. Walter Savage Landor. *Fr.* Corythos. LoBV
Her Fair Inflaming Eyes. Thomas Campion. LiTL
Her Fairness, *abr.* George Wither. *Fr.* Fair Virtue, the Mistress of Philarete. EV-2
Her Fairness, Wedded to a Star. Edward J. O'Brien. FaBoBe; HBMV; JKCP (1926 ed.)
Her Faith. Hilaire Belloc. GoBC
Her Fame. Michael Drayton. *See* Idea: "How many paltry . . ."
Her father loved me; oft invited me. Othello's Defense. Shakespeare. *Fr.* Othello, I, iii. TreF
Her Faults. Harry B. Smith. PR
Her Favorites. Mattie Lee Hausgen. PCH
Her feet along the dewy hills. Dusk. Clinton Scollard. BLP
Her feet beneath her petticoat. The Bride. Sir John Suckling. *Fr.* A Ballad upon a Wedding. BLV; LPS-1; TrGrPo
Her feet press down the velvet ways. Society Woman. Lucia Trent. PR
Her fingers shame the ivory keys. Amy Wentworth. Whittier. BeLS; IAP; MOAP
Her First-born. Charles Tennyson Turner. MOAH; VA
Her First Song. James K. Baxter. Cressida, V. AnNZ
Her floating life vanished like a bubble. After Seeing Her in a Dream. Nalan Hsinteh. ChLP
Her Friends Bring Her a Christmas Tree. W. B. Yeats. Upon a Dying Lady, VII. LiTB
Her gait detached her from the moving throng. The Beautiful Negress. Ruth Pitter. MoVE
Her gally down the silver Cydnow row'd. Cleopatra. Dryden. *Fr.* All for Love, III. BeR
Her Gifts. Dante Gabriel Rossetti. The House of Life, XXXI. BPN; EmBrPo; HBV; PoVP; VA; ViPo
Her glance denied to me. The Glance. Ibn Iyad. MooP
Her glance swung my body. Meeting. William Saphier. AnAmPo; LA
Her Great Secret. Strickland Gillilan. PEDC
Her grieving parents cradled here. Epitaph. Sylvia Townsend Warner. BLV; MBP; MoBrPo; NeMA; PIAE
Her Hair. Sir Robert Chester. *Fr.* Love's Martyr. ElL
Her Hair. Alfred Kreymborg. *Fr.* Dorothy. AnAmPo; LA
Her Hair the Net. *Unknown.* ElSeCe
(Her Hair.) LiTL
("Her hair the net of golden wire.") EG
(So Fast Entangled.) TrGrPo
Her hair was a waving bronze and her eyes. Disappointment. John Boyle O'Reilly. ACP; OnYI
Her hair was tawny with gold, her eyes with purple were dark. A Court Lady. Elizabeth Barrett Browning. BeLS; HBV; LPS-2; VA
Her hand a goblet bore for him. The Two. Hugo von Hofmannsthal. AWP; JAWP; WBP
Her Hands. Anna Hempstead Branch. *Fr.* Songs for My Mother. MPB; PoTo
(My Mother's Hands.) DD; MW, *abr.*
(Song for My Mother, A: Her Hands.) OHIP; RG
(Songs for My Mother: Her Hands.) HH; LBMV; MOAH; OBAV; POT; YT
Her Hands. Alfred Kreymborg. *Fr.* Dorothy. AnAmPo; LA
Her hands are cold; her face is white. Under the Violets. Oliver Wendell Holmes. *Fr.* The Professor at the Breakfast Table. AA; IAP
Her hands have much/ Of Christlike touch. Mother—a Portrait. Ethel Romig Fuller. PGD; PSO
Her hands of white jade by a window of snow. On Hearing Her Play the Harp. Li Tüan. ChLP
Her hands were wrinkled like an autumn leaf. Gypsy Woman. Anne O'Brien. CAG
Her head is bowed downwards; so pensive her air. Bowing Her Head. *Unknown.* BlG
Her Heards Be Thousand Fishes. Spenser. *Fr.* Colin Clout's Come Home Again. ChTr
Her Heart. Bartholomew Griffin. *See* Fly to Her Heart.
Her Heart. John Masefield. BMEP
Her heart is like her garden. My Mother's Garden. Alice E. Allen. BLPA; FaBoBe; NeHB
Her heart she locked fast in her breast. The Secret Combination. Ellis Parker Butler. BOHV
Her heart that loved me once is rottenness. Two Thoughts of Death. Christina Rossetti. DiM
Her Heaven. Dante Gabriel Rossetti. The House of Life: True Woman. LVIII. BMEP; BPN; EmBrPo; EPN; GTML; ViPo
Her high freeboard towering above the pier. The *Roosevelt* and the *Antinoe*. E. J. Pratt. HeT
Her hips, so wide-distended. Hips. Abu Hafs. MooP
Her Horoscope. Mary Ashley Townsend. AA
Her house is all of Echo made. Fame. Ben Jonson. LPS-3
Her house is become like a man dishonored. Dirge. First Maccabees, Bible, Apocrypha. TrJP
Her husband present, Lesbia lashes me with words. Catullus, *tr. fr. Latin by* Frances Fletcher. LaP
Her Immortality. Thomas Hardy. VLEP
Her Infinite Variety. Shakespeare. *Fr.* Antony and Cleopatra, II, ii. EV-1
(Shakespeare Gallery, A: Cleopatra.) MaC
Her Initials. Thomas Hardy. EmBrPo; InP
Her Irish maids could never spoon out mush. Mary Winslow. Robert Lowell. AnNE; MiAP; MoVE
Her ivory face, quivering but trembling not. Child of War. Lionel Johnson. SoV
Her ivory hands on the ivory keys. In the Gold Room. Oscar Wilde. CaAE
Her jade-white staircase is cold with dew. A Sigh from a Staircase of Jade. Li Po. ChLP
Her Kisses. Thomas Lovell Beddoes. *Fr.* Early Fragments. AtBAP
("Her kisses are/ Soft as a snow-tuft in the dewless cup.") LO
Her Last Lines. Emily Brontë. *See* Last Lines: "No coward soul is mine."
Her "Last Poems." Emily Dickinson. PtP
Her laughter was infectious: so, some found. The Ecstasies of Dialectic. Howard Nemerov. FiMAP
Her legs were long. Girl in a Tree. Frances Frost. NLK (1947 ed.)
Her Letter. Bret Harte. CoBA; HBV; InP; LPS-1; PR; YT
Her life-path winds through shadowed ways. Sister Veronica. Margaret Holmes. PraNu
Her life was like a swiftly rushing stream. A Life. John Gould Fletcher. ChMo; CMP
Her Likeness. Dinah Maria Mulock Craik. LPS-1
Her Lips. Walter Savage Landor. NeHB
(Song: "Often I have heard it said.") HBV
Her Lips ("Her lips they are redder than coral"). *Unknown.* LiTG
Her Lips ("Lady, when I behold the roses sprouting"). *Unknown.* EG; ElSeCe; LiTL
Her lips' remark was: "Oh, you kid!" Servant Girl and [the] Grocer's Boy. Joyce Kilmer. LHV; YaD
Her lips they are redder than coral. Her Lips. *Unknown.* LiTG
Her lips were so near. In [*or* An] Explanation. Walter Learned. AA; ALV; HBV; LBAP; PR
Her Little Boy. *Unknown.* PEDC
Her little face is like a walnut shell. Visitor. W. E. Henley. In Hospital, XX. PIAE
Her Little Feet. W. E. Henley. BOHV
Her little feet in scarlet shoon. Anne Boleyn. Barbara Bingley. ReTS

Her little hot room looked over the bay. Sanary. Katherine Mansfield. AnNZ
Her Love. Dante Gabriel Rossetti. The House of Life, LVII. BPN; EmBrPo; EPN; ViPo
Her love is like an island. Mother's Love. *Unknown.* OQP; PSO; QP-1
Her love is true I know. True Love. Waring Cuney. CDC
Her loved I most,/ By thee that's lost. To His Rival. Michael Drayton. ReEn
Her loveliness stirred my circumstances. Moved by Her Music. Richard Gillman. NePoAm-2
Her Man Described by Her Own Dictamen. Ben Jonson. *Fr.* A Celebration of Charis. AtBAP; NBE
Her master gave the signal, with a look. Sweet Nature's Voice. Arthur Joseph Munby. *Fr.* Susan; a Poem of Degrees. VA
Her Matchless Person. Ariosto, *tr. fr. Italian by* John Hoole. Orlando Furioso, VII. LiA
Her Merriment. W. H. Davies. EnLoPo
Her Milking Pail. "Madeline Bridges." PR
Her mind is a library, where Dickens, Scott. Mother. Ethel Barnett de Vito. MotAn
Her mission accomplished is o'er. The Mission of Sister Seraphine, a Sister of Charity. "Owen Meredith." *Fr.* Lucile. PraNu
Her mist of primrose within her breast. A Summer Night. "Æ." TCEP; TCPD
Her Mood around Me. Brewster Ghiselin. LiTL
Her Moral. Thomas Hood. *See* Gold.
Her Mother. Alice Cary. OHIP
Her mother died when she was young. Kemp Owyne. *Unknown.* BaBo; BEL; BoLiVe; CoBE; EM-1; EnLi-1 (1949 ed.); EnSB; ESPB; OBB; SeCeV; TOP; ViBoFo
Her Mouth Carelessly Scented. Bilhana, *formerly at. to* Chauras, *tr. fr. Sanskrit by* E. Powys Mathers. *Fr.* Black Marigolds. OnPM
Her mouth is fragrant as a vine. Cleopatra. Swinburne. BeLS
Her Music. Martha Dickinson Bianchi. AA
Her Name. Walter Savage Landor. *See* Well I Remember How You Smiled.
Her Name. Paul Verlaine, *tr. fr. French by* Alan Conder. TrFP
Her name is at my tongue whene'er I speak. Philip Ayres. *Fr.* Emblems of Love. LO
Her Name upon the Strand. Spenser. *See* Amoretti, LXXV.
Her name was Abba-labba-lá. Abba-labba-lá. Davíd Stefánsson. IcP
Her name was Ate, mother of debate. The House of Ate. Spenser. *Fr.* The Faerie Queene, IV. OBSC
Her name was Marian Claribel Lee. The Ballad of Sir Brian and the Three Wishes. Newman Levy. FiBHP
Her noblest poem was a life that bore. Sister Ann Raphael. E. Mary. PraNu
Her Only Flaw. Rufinus, *tr. fr. Greek by* T. F. Higham. OxBG
Her Passing. William Drummond of Hawthornden. *See* Madrigal: "Beauty, and the life, The."
Her Pedigree. Arthur Davison Ficke. Sonnets of a Portrait Painter, IX. HBMV
Her Picture. Ellen Mackay Hutchinson Cortissoz. AA; LBAP
Her Picture. Julianus, *tr. fr. Greek by* F. L. Lucas. GrPE
Her Pity. Philip Bourke Marston. VA
Her Polka Dots. Peter Newell. NA
Her Praise. W. B. Yeats. Po
Her Praises. Anthony Scoloker. ElL
Her pretty feet. Upon Mistress Susanna Southwell, Her Feet [*or* Upon Her Feet]. Robert Herrick. EnLi-1; PoFS; ViBoPo
Her price is far above rubies. The Good Housewife. Proverbs, Bible, *O.T.* GrCo-2
Her printed breath should be a flower. The Mistress. S. G. Leonard. MoWP
Her Race. W. B. Yeats. Upon a Dying Lady, V. LiTB
Her Rambling. Thomas Lodge. *See* My Mistress When She Goes.
Her Reply. Sir Walter Ralegh. *See* Nymph's Reply to the Shepherd, The.
Her rising cheeks set round with flowing hair. Two Sea Nymphs. William Diaper. *Fr.* Nereides; or, Sea-Eclogues. BeR
Her Rival for Aziza. *Unknown, tr. fr. Arabic by* E. Powys Mathers. *Fr.* The Thousand and One Nights. AWP
Her Sacred Bower. Thomas Campion. *See* Where She Her Sacred Bower Adorns.
Her sails are strong and yellow as the sand. The Clipper. Thomas Fleming Day. EtS
Her Second Song. James K. Baxter. Cressida, IX. AnNZ
Her Shadow. Elisabeth Cavazza Pullen. AA
Her sight is short, she comes quite near. Jenny Wren. W. H. Davies. CMP; MBP; MoBrPo; PIAE; StaSt
Her significance lies. Portrait. Jeanne D'Orge. AnAmPo; LA
Her skin is so white as a lily, an' each. Padraic Colum. LO
Her smock was of the holland fine. A Ballet Song of Mary. Elizabeth Madox Roberts. MAP; MoAmPo; NP
Her son—albeit the Muse's livery. An Orson of the Muse. George Meredith. EPN
Her Strong Enchantments Failing. A. E. Housman. Last Poems, III. CBE; CoEV; FaBoTw; MoPW; ShBV-4
Her suffering ended with the day. A Death-Bed. James Aldrich. AA; HBV; LBAP
Her Sweet Voice. Thomas Carew. *See* Celia Singing ("You that think . . .").
Her tale was told, the other's listening done. Daybreak in the City. Callimachus. OxBG
Her talk was all of woodland things. The Wife from Fairyland. Richard Le Gallienne. HBV; LBMV
Her tears fell with the dews at even. Tennyson. *Fr.* Mariana. LO
Her temper so extravagant we find. Woman. Earl of Rochester. *Fr.* The Nature of Women. BeR
Her thoughts are like a flock of butterflies. From Life. Brian Hooker. HBV; OnPP
Her Triumph. Ben Jonson. *See* Triumph of Charis, The.
Her veil was artificial flowers and leaves. Christopher Marlow. *Fr.* Hero and Leander. HoPM
Her Virtue, *abr.* George Wither. *Fr.* Fair Virtue, the Mistress of Philarete. EV-2
Her voice did quiver as we parted. On Fanny Godwin. Shelley. ChER; FaBoEn; LoPS
Her voice is low and gives a hollow sound. Mirth and Melancholy. Margaret Cavendish, Duchess of Newcastle. DiM
Her voice was like the song of birds. A Child. Richard Watson Gilder. AA
Her voice was so charming, so heart-felt and clear. The Snow-Bunting. Thorsteinn Erlingsson. IcP
Her washing ended with the day. The Wife. Phoebe Cary. BOHV
Her Way. William Rose Benét. HBMV
Her ways were gentle while a babe. Elizabeth Oakes Smith. *Fr.* The Sinless Child. AA
Her White Bosom Bare. *Unknown.* CSF
Her whole life is an epigram, smart, smooth, and neatly penned. Epigram: A Character [*or* A Character]. Blake. OxBoLi; SiTL
Her Window. Richard Leigh. SeCL; SeEP
Her window opens to the bay. To Her Absent Sailor. Whittier. *Fr.* The Tent on the Beach. LPS-1
Her Words. Anna Hempstead Branch. *Fr.* Songs for My Mother. FaPON; NV; PoTo
(My Mother's Words.) CV
(Song for My Mother, A: Her Words.) BoChLi; OHIP; SiSoSe; TiPo (1959 ed.); YeAr
(Songs for My Mother: Her Words.) HH; LBMV; MOAH; OBAV; POT; YT
Heracles [*or* Hercules Furens], *sels.* Euripides, *tr. fr. Greek.*
"Even a dirge, can Phoibos suit," *tr. by* Robert Browning. GrPo
Madness of Heracles, The, *tr. by* Hugh Owen Meredith. GrR
New Theology, A, *tr. by* Hugh Owen Meredith. GrR
Thou Shalt Not Die, *tr. by* C. M. Bowra. OxBG
Youth, *tr. by* George Allen. OxBG
(Youth of All Blessings Best, *shorter sel., tr. by* Arthur S. Way.) GrR
Heracles. Sophocles. *See* Heracles' Errant Love.
Heracles. Yvor Winters. TwAmPo
Heracles and the Wraith of Meleager. Bacchylides, *tr. fr. Greek by* F. L. Lucas. GrPE
(Heracles and Meleager, *tr. by* C. M. Bowra.) OxBG
Heracles' Errant Love. Sophocles, *tr. fr. Greek by* Robert Whitelaw. *Fr.* Trachiniae. GrR
(Heracles.) OxBG
Heraclidae. Euripides. *See* Children of Heracles.
Heraclitus. Callimachus, *tr. fr. Greek by* G. M. Young. GrL
(Dead Poet, The, *tr. by* F. L. Lucas.) GrPE
Heraclitus. William Johnson Cory, *paraphrased fr. the Greek of* Callimachus. AWP; EnLi-1; EV-5; GrL; GTBS; GTBS-D; GTSE; GTSL; HBV; JAWP; LEAP; LiA; OBEV; OBVV; OuHeWo; OxBG; PCD; PIAE; PoRA; SeCePo; ShBV-4; TOP; TreF; TVSH; VA; ViBoPo; WBP; WoL; WP
("They told me, Heraclitus, they told me you were dead.") GrPo
(To Heracleitus.) GrR
Heraclitus in the West. Charles G. Bell. NePoAm
Heraclitus to His Popular Critics. *Unknown, tr. fr. Greek by* F. L. Lucas. GrPE
Herakles Archer. Morton Dauwen Zabel. NP
Herald. Josephine Miles. FiMAP
Herald am I from the Land of Dreams, A. The Land of Dreams. H. F. Sargent. BOL
Herald Crane, The. Hamlin Garland. BLA; HBV; SN
Heraldic siren puts away. Sheffield Dawn. D. G. Bridson. MuP

Heralds of dawn are blowing at the last star, The. The Masked Ball. Wilson MacDonald. MaRV
Herb-Leech, The. Joseph Campbell. AnIL; OnYI
Herbs. Lizette Woodworth Reese. TBM
Herculean Silence. George Chapman. *Fr.* Euthymiae Raptus; or, The Tears of Peace. EV-1
Hercules Furens. Euripides. *See* Heracles.
Hercules Furens, *sels.* Seneca, *tr. fr. Latin.*
Angry Kynges, The, *tr. by* Thomas Heywood, *fr.* IV. LiA
Chorus: "Let th' ayre complayne, and eke the parent great," *tr. by* Thomas Newton. LaP
Herd Boy. *See* Herdboy.
Herd Laddie, The. Alexander Smart. EBSV
Herd of Horses, The. Sergei Yesenin, *tr. fr. Russian by* C. M. Bowra. BoR
Herdbell—meek evening remote, The. Grass and Milk. Alfonso Gatto. OnPM
Herd Boy, The. Haniel Long. HBMV
Herd Boy, The. Lu Yu, *tr. fr. Chinese by* Arthur Waley. ChTr; TrCh
Herdboys shout unseen among the rocks, The. The Death of Chiron. J. P. McAuley. BoAV
Herdmen, The. *Unknown. See* Quiet Life, The.
Herds are gathered in from plain and hill, The. Who's That Calling So Sweet? ———Deveen. SCC
Herdsman, The. "Seumas O'Sullivan." TIP
Herdsman, The. Theocritus, *tr. fr. Greek by* C. S. Calverley. Idylls, IV. AWP
Here/ High on the hill. Song of the Hill. Edith Lodge. GoYe
Here/ We Quench/ Our thirst. Hat Bar. Mildred Weston. FiBHP
Here a little child I stand. Grace for a Child [*or* Another Grace for a Child *or* A Child's Grace *or* Grace]. Robert Herrick. AWP; BEL; BoTP; CaAE; ChTr; EG; ElSeCe; EM-1; EnLi-1; EPS; EV-2; FaBoCh; FaPON; InPo; InvP; JAWP; LiTB; LoBV; LoGBV; MeMeAg; MoShBr; OAEP; OBEV; OBS; OtMeF; OTPC; OxBoCh; PoRA; ReEn; RIS; SeCeV; SeCV-1; SeEP; ThWaDe; TOP; TreFS; TrGrPo; TwHP; TyEnPo; ViBoPo; WBP
Here, a maiden of bronze, I stand on Midas' grave. Midas' Tomb. *At. to* Cleobulus of Lindus. GrPE
Here a Nit-Wit Lies. Patrick Barrington. WhC
Here a perfect people set—on red rock. Broken Voices. Lynette Roberts. MoWP
Here a pretty baby lies. Upon a Child. Robert Herrick. CBOV; LoBV; OBEV; OBS; PIAE; SeCV-1; TrGrPo
Here, a sheer hulk, lies poor Tom Bowling. Tom Bowling [*or* Poor Tom Bowling *or* The Perfect Sailor]. Charles Dibdin. AmSS; CBOV; EtS; EV-3; HBV; LH; LPS-2; OBEC; OxBoLi; SG; TVSH
Here a solemn [*or* solemne] fast we keep[e]. An Epitaph upon [*or* on] a Virgin. Robert Herrick. EG; OnPM; OxBoLi; PoEL-3; SeCV-1
Here, above,/ cracks in the buildings are filled with battered moonlight. The Man-Moth. Elizabeth Bishop. LiTA; MiAP; MoAB; MoAmPo (1950 ed.)
Here Æthelstan the king, of earls the lord. The Battle of Brunanburh. *Unknown.* EnLi-1 (1949 ed.)
Here all is sunny, and when the truant gull. Skerryvore: The Parallel. Robert Louis Stevenson. VLEP
Here Am I. *Unknown.* PraP
Here am I,/ Little jumping Joan. Mother Goose. BoN; MeMeAg; OxNR; TiPo
Here am I among elms again—ah, look. Riverton. Edmund Wilson. *Fr.* Elegies for a Passing World. AnFE; CoAnAm; TwAmPo
Here am I, for what end God knows, not I. Columbus. James Russell Lowell. BHV
Here am I now cast down. Ex Nihilo. David Gascoyne. *Fr.* Miserere. NeBP
Here Am I—Send Me. Isaiah, VI: 1-8, Bible, *O.T.* GrCo-2
Here am I, this carrot eating. In Common. Gene Derwood. NePA
Here am I yet, another twelvemonth spent. "Blank Misgivings of a Creature Moving About in Worlds Not Realized," I. Arthur Hugh Clough. EmBrPo; VLEP
Here an immortal river had its rise. On the Skull of Shakespeare. George Sterling. BAP; PFE
Here Ananias lies because he lied. F. W. MacVeagh. WhC
Here and Now, *sel.* Bliss Carman.
Where Is Heaven? GoTP; MaRV; OQP; QP-2
Here and Now. Catharine Cater. PoNe
Here and there by country ways. Butterfly Weed—Indian Fire. Florence Randal Livesay. CPG
Here and there, Freedom is an empty name. Svatopluk Cech. *Fr.* Songs of the Slave. PoFr
Here are cakes for thy body. The Other World. *Unknown. Fr.* Book of the Dead. AWP; JAWP; WBP
Here are crocuses, white, gold, grey! O Dear Me! Walter de la Mare. TiPo
Here, are five letters in this blessed Name. The Ghyrlond of the Blessed Virgin Marie. Ben Jonson. ISi; MeRV; SeCL
Here are green tiles and scarlet balustrades. Tien-ho Temple. Su T'ung-po. WhP
Here are old trees, tall oaks and gnarled pines. The Antiquity of Freedom. Bryant. AA; AnNE; APW; CoBA; CoV; IAP; IDAH; TOP
Here Are Sands, Ignoble Things. Menander, *tr. fr. Greek by* T. F. Higham. OxBG
Here are sweet peas, on tiptoe for a flight. Sweet Peas. Keats. *Fr.* I Stood Tip-Toe upon a Little Hill. ADAH; GN; MPB (1956 ed.); PCH
Here are the lady's knives and forks. *Unknown.* OxNR
Here are the needs of manhood satisfied. On the Heights. Edward Dowden. TIP
Here are the ragged towers of vines. The Labourer in the Vineyard. Stephen Spender. NeBP
Here are the Schubert Lieder. Now begin. For M. S. Singing Frühlingsglaube in 1945. Frances Cornford. UnS
Here are the tiny lads, the grave, the dream-lit faces. Sleepers. J. Corson Miller. TBM
Here are the tracks upon the sand. Four Footprints. Thomas Hardy. BMEP
Here are three ways to get your answer to me. Answer. Merrill Moore. NeMA
Here are we for the last time face to face. L'Envoi. William Morris. *Fr.* The Earthly Paradise. BPN; EmBrPo; EnLi-2; PoVP; ViP; ViPo
Here, as a bare, unlichened wall, the Castle front goes up. At Ferns Castle. Padraic Colum. NePoAm
Here as I sit by the Jumna bank. The Hindu Ascetic. Sir Alfred Comyn Lyall. *Fr.* Studies at Delhi. OBVV
Here, as it were, in the heart of roaring Rome. Wild Cats. Vachel Lindsay. MAP; MoAmPo
Here, as where the measured sun. Poems of the Machine Age. MacKnight Black. PoeMoYo
Here at my earthly station set. The Stationary Journey. Edwin Muir. POTE
Here at my hand here at my heart lie still. First Cycle of Love Poems, II. George Barker. MoPo
Here at right of the entrance this bronze head. A Bronze Head. W. B. Yeats. LiTB
Here, at the airport, waiting. At the Airport. John Malcolm Brinnan. MoAB
Here at the center of the turning year. New Year. Stephen Spender. AWP
Here at the country inn. The Forefather. Richard Burton. AA; OBAV
Here at the crossroads is the night so black. The Lynching Bee. William Ellery Leonard. PoNe
Here at the fountain's sliding foot. Andrew Marvell. *Fr.* The Garden. YT
Here at the frozen crossroads of the city. Waiting. Alan Hodge. LO; MoP
Here at the gate of the Northland we welcome you. A Welcome to Bliss Carman. Dorothy Choate Herriman. CPG
Here at the inn, become anonymous! Secret Service. Richard Church. MoP
Here at the roots of the mountains. Rapids at Night. Duncan Campbell Scott. CaP; OCL
Here at the Stable Door. Sister Mary Paulinus. JKCP (1955 ed.)
Here at the tribal rendezvous. Afternoon Call. Donald Davidson. LS
Here at the village crossing. The Call. Daniel Corkery. OnYI
Here at the wayside station, as many a morning. The Wayside Station. Edwin Muir. FaBoTw; MoVE
Here at the wharves is payment for a loathing. Matthew. Sister Margaret Teresa. JKCP (1955 ed.)
Here at this solitary spring. Epigram. "Lambros Porphyras." MoGP
Here at this sudden age of mine. An Autumn Walk. Witter Bynner. GoYe
Here Awa', There Awa'. *Unknown.* EBSV; OBS
Here awa', there awa', wandering Willie. Wandering Willie. Burns. EBSV
Here, awaiting what hereafter. Elegy. R. G. Howarth. MoAuPo
Here be grapes, whose lusty blood. The Satyr. John Fletcher. *Fr.* The Faithful Shepherdess, I, i. EV-2; ViBoPo
Here be woods as green. John Fletcher. *Fr.* The Faithful Shepherdess, I, iii. ViBoPo
Here, before the better streets begin. Cherry Way. Ruth Comfort Mitchell. NV
Here Beginneth the Pastime of Pleasure. Stephen Hawes. *Fr.* The Pastime of Pleasure. SiCE
Here begins the sea that ends not till the world's end. On the Verge. Swinburne. *Fr.* A Midsummer Holiday, III. BPN; PoVP; VLEP
Here behind the huddled houses. The Blackbird in the Town. Oliver St. John Gogarty. PoP

Here beside my Paris fire, I sit alone and ponder. Retrospect. Agnes Mary Frances Robinson. OBVV

Here between lunch and teatime, and days and hours between. Lines to Dr. Ditmars. Kenneth Allan Robinson. ImOP; PoMa

Here betwixt Ass and Oxen Mild, *with music. Tr. fr. French by* Winifred Douglas. YaCaBo

Here blew winter once with the snowstorms spurning. The Enchanted Heart. Edward Davison. BMEP; HBMV

Here blooms the flower. Sir Philip Sidney. Eleanor *and* Herbert Farjeon. OnPP

Here bring your purple and gold. Flowers for the Brave. Celia Thaxter. OHIP; PEOR

Here Brotachus from Cretan Gortyn lies. A Cretan Merchant. Simonides, *tr. by* C. M. Bowra. GrL; OxBG

Here Brotachus of Gortyna, a Cretan born, is laid. Epitaph to a Merchant [*or* The Unlooked-for Bargain]. Simonides, *tr. by* F. L. Lucas. GrPE; GrR

Here busy and yet innocent lyes dead. On the Death of a Monkey. Thomas Heyrick. MePo

Here by the baring bough. Autumn in King's Hintock Park. Thomas Hardy. PoVP

Here by the gray north sea. A Northern Vigil. Bliss Carman. BoCaPo; OBEV (new ed.); OBVV; PeCV; TwCV

Here by the rose-tree. Love in Jeopardy. Humbert Wolfe. NeMA

Here, by this brook, we parted; I to the East. The Brook; an Idyl. Tennyson. EV-5

Here by this calm backwater, where the tides. The Maker of Toy Boats. Frank Oliver Call. CPG

Here by this midland lake, the sand-shored water. Paul Engle. *Fr.* America Remembers. NAMP

Here by this well at noon He sat. Samaritan Woman. Mother Francis d'Assisi. JKCP (1955 ed.)

Here, by your leave, upon this pitiful star. Spilled Flame. Joseph Auslander. BAP

Here, Charmian, take my bracelets. Cleopatra. William Wetmore Story. AA; BAP; BAV; OBAV

Here Cleita sleeps. You ask her life and race? The Monument of Cleita. Edward Cracroft Lefroy. Echoes from Theocritus, XXIX. AWP; JAWP; WBP

Here clove the keels of centuries ago. The Salt Flats. Sir Charles G. D. Roberts. CaP; OCL

Here come real stars to fill the upper skies. Fireflies in the Garden. Robert Frost. AlDL; PoeMoYo

Here Come Three Merchants a-Riding, *with music. Unknown.* TrAS

Here comes a candle to light you to bed. Mother Goose. OTPC (1946 ed.)

Here comes a girl so damned shapely. Girl Walking. Charles G. Bell. NePoAm-2

Here Comes a Lusty Wooer. *Unknown.* CH; OxNR
(Lily Bright and Shine-a.) AtBAP
(Old Rhyme.) LO

Here comes holly that is so gent. Alleluia, Alleluia, Alleluia, Now Sing We. *Unknown.* AnEC

Here comes Kate Summers who, for gold. The Bird of Paradise. W. H. Davies. AtBAP; MoVE

Here comes my lady with her little baby. *Unknown.* OxNR

Here comes old Father Christmas. Christmas. Rose Terry Cooke. COAH

Here comes the elephant. The Elephant. Herbert Asquith. BoTP; SUS; TiPo; UTS

Here comes the Marshall. The Proclamation. Longfellow. *Fr.* John Endicott. PAH

Here Comes the Thief. Hazel Hall. MAP; MoAmPo (1942 ed.)

Here comes the wind, with a noise and a whirr. Wind Song. *Unknown.* GFA

Here, Cyprian, is my jeweled looking-glass. To Aphrodite; with a Mirror. Aline Kilmer. HBMV

Here Cypris dwells. Always it was her will. A Statue of Cypris. Anyte. OxBG

Here Dead Lie We. A. E. Housman. More Poems, XXXVI. InPo; OtMeF
(Epitaph: "Here dead lie we because we did not choose.") MoVE

Here dear [*or* deare] Iölas lies. Iölas' Epitaph. William Drummond of Hawthornden. AtBAP; PoEL-2; TriL

Here Dicon's son, Acanthian Saon lies. Callimachus, *tr. fr. Greek by* Lord Neaves. GrPo

Here dock and tare. In the Grave No Flower. Edna St. Vincent Millay. CrMA

Here doth Dionysia lie. Epitaph of Dionysia. *Unknown.* HBV; OBEV (new ed.); OBVV; VA

Here down my wearied limbs I'll lay. On Himself. Robert Herrick. TriL

Here dwell together still two men of note. 221B. Vincent Starrett. DaM

Here een Noo Yorka, where am I. Een Napoli. T. A. Daly. PoMa

Here enter not vile bigots, hypocrites. The Inscription Set upon the Great Gate of Theleme. Rabelais. *Fr.* Gargantua. PoFr

Here, ever since you went abroad. Absence. Walter Savage Landor. OBEV (1st ed.); TOP

Here falls no light of sun nor stars. Richard Hovey. *Fr.* Taliesin. AA; OBAV

Here first the day does break. Her Window. Richard Leigh. SeCL; SeEP

Here Followeth the Songe of the Death of Mr. Thewlis. *Unknown.* CoMu

Here Folowith Divers Balettis and Dities Solacious, Devised by Master Skelton, Laureate. John Skelton. *See* Lullay, Lullay.

Here—for they could not help but die. Epitaph. Philip Freneau. *Fr.* The Fading Rose. AA

Here, foremost in the dangerous paths of fame. Epitaph on Sir William Williams. Thomas Gray. TriL

Here Freedom stood, by slaughtered friend and foe. Princeton. Alfred Noyes. POT; POTT

Here friends come, sorrowing, to say farewell. Lao-lao Ting, a Tavern. Li Po. BoFr

Here from the brow of the hill I look. The Old Mill. Thomas Dunn English. AA

Here further up the mountain slope. The Birthplace. Robert Frost. LoGBV

Here, gladden'd by pure air and savour sweet. To the Rt. Hon. John Hookham Frere in Malta. William Stewart Rose. EnSW

Here goes a man of seventy-four. Seventy-four and Twenty. Thomas Hardy. WhC

Here goes my lord. Mother Goose. SAS

Here halt, I pray you, make a little stay. His Epitaph. Alcuin, *tr. by* Helen Waddell. TriL

Here halt we our march, and pitch our tent. The Green Mountain Boys. Bryant. AnNE; GA; MC; PAH

Here has my salient faith annealed me. Key West. Hart Crane. ChMo

Here hath been dawning. To-Day. Thomas Carlyle. BCEP; EBSV; HBV; HBVY; MW; OQP; PTA-1; QP-2; TVSH; WGRP

Here Have I Dwelt. *Unknown.* MeEV
(Now Have Good Day, Now Have Good Day!) AnEC

Here he can sleep, far inland from the sea. No Gull's Wings. Paul Engle. PoMa

Here he lets go the struggling imp, to clutch. Shakespeare. Thomas Hood. *Fr.* The Plea of the Midsummer Fairies. OBRV

Here helms and swords are made of chalices. On Rome in the Pontificate of Julius II. Michelangelo. PoFr

Here, here I live with what my board. His Content in the Country. Robert Herrick. EnLit; EPS; SeCV-1; SeEP

Here, I admit, there are no green fields to see. Venetian Sonnets, VI. August, Graf von Platen. AnGP

Here I Am. Nancy Birckhead. RIS

Here I Am. Abraham Sutzkever, *tr. fr. Yiddish by* Joseph Leftwich. TrJP

Here I am, an old man in a dry month. Gerontion. T. S. Eliot. AmPP; AnAmPo; AnFE; APA; BrBE; ChMo; ChMP; CMP; CoAnAm; CoBA; CoBMV; CoEV; ExPo; FaBoEn; GTBS-W; LA; LiTA; LiTM; LoBV; MAP; MAPA: MaPo; MoAmPo (1942 ed.); MOAP; MoPo; NAMP; NePA; OAEP (2d ed.); OxBA; PoE; PoFS; POTE; ReMP; RiBV; SeCePo; SeCeV; TwAmPo

Here I am before all a man of sense. The Pretty Redhead. Guillaume Apollinaire. AnFP

Here I am, sprouted to my full height. Here I Am. Abraham Sutzkever. TrJP

Here I am with my rabbits. *Unknown.* OxNR

Here I come creeping, creeping everywhere. The Voice [*or* Song] of the Grass. Sarah Roberts Boyle. AA; BoTP, *wr. at. to* Leigh Hunt; DD; HBV; HBVY; LPS-2; PCH; PRWS; SN

Here I drone in this human hive. The Landlubber's Chantey. James Stuart Montgomery. HBMV

Here I have [*or* have I] dwelt [*or* dwelled] with more and less. Here Have I Dwelt [*or* Now Have Good Day . . .]. *Unknown.* AnEC; MeEV

Here I have waited, none with me. "Anna Akhmatova," *tr. fr. Russian by* C. M. Bowra. BoRS

Here I lie at the chancel door. Four Country Epitaphs. *Unknown.* GoTP

Here I lie dead, and here I wait for thee. Waiting. *Unknown.* OxBG

Here I make oath. "By Reason of Thy Law." Francis Thompson. VLEP

Here I rest, says Alfonsina, here I lie. Epitaph for My Tomb. Alfonsina Storni. AnCL

Here I Sit Alone. *Unknown.* OxBoCh

Here I stand, the gravestone that tells where you are lying. "The Hunter Home from the Hill." *Unknown.* GrPE

Here I'd come when weariest! Ballade of His Choice of a Sepulcher [*or* Of His Choice of a Sepulcher]. Andrew Lang. BSV; POTT; PoVP; VA

Here, if you please, is a Whirligig. Whirligig Beetle. C. Lindsay McCoy. GFA
Here in a distant place I hold my tongue. Egan O Rahilly. *Tr. by* James Stephens. OBMV; SeCePo
Here in a garden sung for two. Youth Autumnal. Raymond Roseliep. JKCP (1955 ed.)
Here in a quiet and dusty room they lie. The Seed Shop. Muriel Stuart. DiM; GoTP; GoTS; MBP; MW; NP; POTE
Here in a world whose heaven is powder-white. Unreasoning Heart. Louis Untermeyer. MAP; MoAmPo (1942 ed.)
Here in Ch'ang An. On Hearing a Blackbird at Ch'ang An. Wei Ting. PoHN
Here, in cool grot and mossy cell. Inscription: On a Tablet against a Root-House. William Shenstone. EiPP
Here in life's chaos make no foolish boast. The Nail-torn God. Edwin Markham. MaRV; QS
Here in my curving hands I cup. This Quiet Dust. John Hall Wheelock. AnEnPo; MAP; MM; MoAmPo; QS; WHA
Here in my head, the home that is left for you. Burning the Letters. Randall Jarrell. MiAP; MoAB; MoAmPo (1950 ed.)
Here, in my rude log cabin, few poorer men there be. The Battle of New Orleans. Thomas Dunn English. GA; PAH; PAP
Here, in my snug little fire-lit chamber. Alone by the Hearth. George Arnold. HBV
Here in the Cloisters a fourth dimension evolves. The Cloisters. Samuel Yellen. NePoAm
Here in the country's heart. The Country Faith. Norman Gale. BoTP; CBPC; HBV; NLK; OBEV (new ed.); OBVV; OQP; OTPC; QP-1; VA; WGRP
Here in the dark, O heart. Second Best. Rupert Brooke. MBP; MoBrPo; OBVV
Here in the dark what ghostly figures press! In Tesla's Laboratory. Robert Underwood Johnson. AA
Here, in the dusk to-night, the dying Sun. Sunset on an English Hill. Marion Acton-Bond. ReTS
Here, in the field, last year. Compensation. Gerald Gould. HBMV
Here in the German. *See* Here is the German.
Here in the green scooped valley I walk to and fro. The Green Valley. Sylvia Townsend Warner. MoBrPo (1950 ed.)
Here in the grove it is evening, whether of time or mood. A House of the South. Charles Edward Eaton. NoCaPo (rev. ed.)
Here in the hindered freshet cloaked with slime. Ode to a Frog. George O'Neil. PFE
Here in the leafy place quiet he lies. *See* Here in this leafy place.
Here in the level country, where the creeks run straight and wide. Men of Harlan. William Aspenwall Bradley. POT; SBMV
Here in the lonely chapel I will wait. Ash Wednesday. John Erskine. NV
Here in the marshland, past the battered bridge. A Harrow Grave in Flanders [*or* Harrow and Flanders]. Marquess of Crewe. HBV; MM
Here, in the midnight of the solemn wood. Marquette on the Shores of the Mississippi. John Jerome Rooney. CAW; JKCP
Here in the midnight, where the dark mainland and island. Night Hymns on Lake Nipigon. Duncan Campbell Scott. CoBE; MM
Here in the minster tower. Tudor Church Music. Sylvia Townsend Warner. UnS
Here in the mountain village. Evening in the Village. Lu Yu. OnPC
Here in the orchard's breezy nook. Anyte, *tr. fr. Greek by* Walter Leaf. GrPo
Here, in the palace gardens, where the stately fountains play. Versailles. Godfrey Fox Bradby. TVSH
Here in the quiet of my room. Prayer of an Unemployed Man. W. C. Ackerly. MaRV; PoToHe
Here, in the sand, where some one laid him down. Cruciform. Winifred Welles. DiM; LO; POTE
Here in the scuffled dust. W. D. Snodgrass. Heart's Needle, VII. NePoEA
Here in the self is all that man can know. Sonnet. John Masefield. AWP; JAWP; WBP
Here, in the slow-edged evenings of May. Spring Poem. Nikolai Ushakov. RuPo
Here in the soil a cistern is rooted. The Cistern. George Seferis. MoGP
Here in the uplands. Scotland. Alexander Gray. GoTS
Here in the warm sunshine. Sonnets, V. Feng Chih. *Fr.* Twenty-seven Sonnets. WhP
Here, in the withered arbor, like the arrested wind. Statue and Birds. Louise Bogan. MAP; MoAB; MoAmPo
Here in these hills the Spring comes slow. Arctic Agrarian. Louis Untermeyer. PIAE
Here in this ancient garden. Sorrow in a Garden. May Riley Smith. NLK
"Here in this corner, ladies and gentlemen." The Wrestling Match. Robert Penn Warren. AnAmPo; LA; PreP
Here in this darkened room, as daylight goes. To a Little Girl. Amory Hare. MuM
Here in this glowing hall of treasures. Aphrodite and the Knife-Grinder. Carl Snoilsky. AnSL
Here in this great house in the barrack's square. The Hambone and the Heart. Edith Sitwell. OBMV
Here in this inland garden. Alien. Archibald MacLeish. EtS
Here in this [*or* the] leafy place. Before Sedan. Austin Dobson. BPN; LPS-2; MBP; MoBrPo (1942 ed.); NeMA; TreFS
Here, in this little Bay. Magna Est Veritas [*or* Truth]. Coventry Patmore. *Fr.* The Unknown Eros. AnFE; BLV; BMEP; CaAE; CAW; CoBE; GoBC; GTML; MaRV; OBEV (new ed.); OBVV; OnPM; OQP; PC; PG (1945 ed.); POTT; PoVP; QP-2; TrGrPo; ViP; VLEP
Here in this narrow room there is no light. Prothalamium. A. J. M. Smith. CaP
Here in this room where first we met. As She Feared It Would Be. Lilla Cabot Perry. Meeting after Long Absence, I. AA; OBAV
Here, in this sequestered [*or* sequester'd] close. A Garden Song. Austin Dobson. GTSE; HBV; LEAP; LoBV; OBEV; OBVV; POTT; TOP; VLEP
Here in this simple house his presence clings. House in Springfield. Gail Brook Burket. PGD
Here in this wild, primeval dell. The Pipe of Pan. Elizabeth Akers Allen. SN
Here in this windy place. Green Councillors. Howard McKinley Corning. NP
Here in this world of fog like amethyst. Fog. Louis Ginsberg. NeMA
Here in thy home we await thy tread. Hymn of the Initiates. Aristophanes. *Fr.* The Frogs. OxBG
Here is a coast; here is a harbor. Arrival at Santos. Elizabeth Bishop. FiMAP
Here is a ditch of dead and hopeless water. The Dead Water. Wen Yi-tuo. LiTW; WhP
Here is a face that says half-past seven. Clocks. Carl Sandburg. CrMA
Here is a house with a pointed door. A Little Finger Game. E. J. Falconer. BoTP
Here is a little girl. Translations from Modern Japanese Poetry. Akiko Yosano. PFE
Here is a poem. Gertrude Stein. *Fr.* Land of Nations. AtBAP
Here is a quiet room! Meditation. Donald Cox. MaRV
Here is a riddle most abstruse. Riddle. *Unknown.* SiTL
Here is a room with heavy-footed chairs. The Nature of an Action. Thom Gunn. NePoEA
Here is a sack, a gunny sack. The Metal Checks. Louise Driscoll. NP
Here is a ship you made. The Ship. J. F. Hendry. NeBP
Here is a story shall stir you! Stand up, Greeks dead and gone. Echetlos. Robert Browning. BPN; ViPo
Here is a symbol in which. Rock and Hawk. Robinson Jeffers. MoVE; OxBA
Here is a theme that is worthy of our cognizance. The Poets at a House-Party. Carolyn Wells. PA
Here is a woman whom a man can greet. Charioteer. Witter Bynner. AnFE; CoAnAm; TwAmPo
Here Is a Wound That Never Will Heal. Edna St. Vincent Millay. TOP
Here is another dream, another forgetting, another doorway. Radio. A. S. J. Tessimond. HaMV
Here is cruel Frederick, see! The Story of Cruel Frederick. Heinrich Hoffmann. BoN
Here is cruel Psamtek, see. The Story of Cruel Psamtek. *Unknown.* NA
Here is dominion for peace. Country Reverie. Carol Coates. CaP
"Here is Honor, the dying knight." The Soul Speaks. Edward H. Pfeiffer. HBMV; LPS-1
Here is Israel. Pictures at an Exhibition. Nathan Rosenbaum. GoYe
Here is Kit Logan with her love-child come. Kit Logan and Lady Helen. Robert Graves. HBMV
Here is little Effie's head. Portrait. E. E. Cummings. AnAmPo; LA
Here is Martin's round house. Free Martin. Peter Hopegood. BoAV
"Here is my heart; it's clean." Refusal. Raymond Kresensky. OQP; QP-2
Here is my last good-bye. Before Exile. Louise Mack. BoAu
Here is my love to you, flag of the free, and flag of the tried and true. A Song for the Flag. Denis A. McCarthy, PEDC

Here is my relief at last. Catullus, *tr. fr. Latin by* Horace Gregory. RoL
Here is no easy fate, nor may you find. The House to the Man. John Gould Fletcher. SPP
Here is no golden-crowned, celestial queen. A Flemish Madonna. Charles Wharton Stork. BAP; HBMV
Here is no peace, although the air has fainted. Innocent Landscape. Elinor Wylie. OxBA
Here is no shadow but cloudshadow and nightshadow. Hide in the Heart. Lloyd Frankenberg. AnFE; CoAnAm; LiTA; TwAmPo
Here is no tragedy. Christopher La Farge. *Fr.* Prologue, Each to the Other. AnAmPo
Here is nothing, and nothing there. Nothing and the Soul. Bhartrihari. OnPM
Here is one leaf reserved for me. Verses Written in an Album. Thomas Moore. LPS-1
Here is refinement's start. Rice Fields. Basho. OnPM
Here is the ancient floor. The Self-Unseeing. Thomas Hardy. FaBoEn; GTBS-D; MoBrPo; MoPW; ViPP
Here is the church, and here is the steeple. *Unknown.* OxNR
Here is the crab tree. The Crab Tree. Oliver St. John Gogarty. AnIL; OxBI
Here is the foreign cliff and the fabled sea. On a Picture by Michele da Verona. Anne Ridler. PoN
Here is [*or* in] the German. Disenchanted [*or* Disenchantment]. Louis Untermeyer. GoTP; TSWC
Here is the haven: pain touched with soft magic. Hospital. Wilfred Funk. PoToHe
Here is the high arena of the winds. At Timberline. Richard Leon Spain. MuM
Here is the hinge of history—the hour. The Nativity. E. Merrill Root. ChIP
Here is the house from which the tenant fled. To an Egyptian Mummy. Donald Parson. MuM
Here is the house, in readiness for you. To the New Owner. Lucile Hargrove Reynolds. PoToHe
Here is the ice that girdles joyless ocean. Cross Section of a Landscape. Donald Davidson. MAP; MoAmPo (1942 ed.)
Here is the island but I do not know. Crusoe. Floris Clark McLaren. PeCV; TwCaPo
Here is the long-looked-for [*or* long-bided] hour: the labor of years is accomplished. Work. Pushkin. AWP; JAWP; TrRV; WBP
Here is the place my Lord, good my Lord enter. Shakespeare. *Fr.* King Lear, III, iv. AtBAP
Here is the place; right over the hill. Telling the Bees. Whittier. AmPP (3d ed.); AnNE; APW; AWP; BAV; CoBA; GBV (1952 ed.); HBV; HiLiAm; IAP; InP; InPo; LaNeLa; MOAP; PFY; PTA-1; TCAP; TOP
Here Is the Place Where Loveliness Keeps House. Madison Cawein. HBV; LBMV; LEAP; PFY
Here is the rose you planted long ago. For an Old Man. Norbert Engels. JKCP (1955 ed.)
Here is the same familiar land. Thoughts upon a Walk with Natalie, My Niece, at Houghton Farm. Harold Trowbridge Pulsifer. HBMV
Here is the soundless cypress on the lawn. The Nightingale near the House. Harold Monro. BMEP; EPP; HBMV; MBP; MM; MoBrPo; TwCV; VOD
Here Is the Tale, *parody.* Anthony C. Deane. BOHV; InMe; NA
(Ballad of Jack and Jill, The.) YT
(Jack and Jill.) PA
(Jack and Jill—as Kipling Might Have Written It.) CenHV
Here is the train!/ Here is the train! The Holiday Train. Irene Thompson. BoTP
Here is the Truth in a little creed. Quatrain [*or* A Creed]. Edwin Markham. ChIP; MaRV; OQP; QP-1
Here is the way the white man's heaven felt. On a Picture by Pippin, Called "The Den." Selden Rodman. PoNe
Here is the Will of Cathaeir Mor. The Testament of Cathaeir Mor. *Unknown. Fr.* Book of Rights. OnYI
Here is the yoke, with arrow and share nearby. The Laborer. José Maria de Heredia. AWP; JAWP; WBP
Here is this frail, phantom ship again! The Haunted Ship. Kassaris Emmanuel. MoGP
Here is thy footstool and there rest thy feet where live the poorest. Rabindranath Tagore. *Fr.* Gitanjali. MaRV; WGRP
Here Is Wine. Keats. *Fr.* Endymion, II. OBRV
Here Is Your Realism. Maxwell Bodenheim. AnAmPo; LA
Here it comes! Here it comes! Circus Parade. James S. Tippett. UTS
Here it comes sparkling. The Cataract of Lodore. Robert Southey. BOHV; GN; HBV; LPS-2; OTPC; PEOR; PYM; WBLP
Here it is night: I stay at the Summit Temple. The Summit Temple. Li Po. WhP
Here it was once Leander crossed; here beats the swelling. Hero's Tower. Antipater of Thessalonica. GrPE
Here I've got you, Philip Desmond, standing in the market-place. John Francis O'Donnell. *Fr.* Limerick Town. IrPN
Here Jack and Tom Are Paired with Moll and Meg. George Meredith. Modern Love, XVIII. InvP; PoEL-5; ViPo
Here Johnson is laid. Have a care how you walk. A Postscript to "Retaliation." Austin Dobson. POTT; PoVP
Here Johnson lies, a sage by all allowed. Epitaph on Dr. Johnson. William Cowper. PtP
Here Keats and Shelley heard. Piazza di Spagna. Willard M. Grimes. GoYe
Here lapped in hallowed slumber Saon lies. Saon of Acanthus. Callimachus. AWP
Here let my Lord hang up his conquering lance. The Celestial City. Giles Fletcher. *Fr.* Christ's Victory and Triumph. OBS
Here let the brows be bared. At the Tomb of Washington. Clinton Scollard. DD; GA; MC; OHIP; PEDC
Here let them lie, remembered well. A Grave. Simonides. GrL; OxBG
Here let us leave him; for his shroud the snow. On a Grave at Grindelwald. Frederic William Henry Myers. VA
Here lie Ciardi's pearly bones. Elegy Just in Case. John Ciardi. AtBAP; MiAP
Here lie [*or* lies] I, Martin Elginbrodde [*or* Elmrod]. Epitaph [*or* At Aberdeen *or* Epigram *or* Gravestones *or* Hic Jacet *or* Martin Elginbrodde]. *Unknown, at. to* George Macdonald. BMEP; GoTP; HBV; LiTG; MaRV; OtMeF; PIAE; SiTL; WGRP
Here lie, I, Timon; who, alive, all living men did hate. Timon's Epitaph. Callimachus, *tr. by* Shakespeare. AWP; GrPo; JAWP; WBP
Here lie the remains of Thomas Wood*hen.* On Thomas Woodcock. *Unknown.* WhC
Here Lies . . . Michael Lewis. YT
Here Lies . . . *Unknown, at. to* George Macdonald. *See* Epitaph: "Here lie I, Martin Elginbrodde."
Here lies/ A worthy matron of unspotted life. Epitaph on My Dear and Ever Honoured Mother, An. Anne Bradstreet. AmPP (3d ed.)
Here lies a bard, Hippònax—honored name! The Grave of Hippònax. Edward Cracroft Lefroy. Echoes from Theocritus, XXX. AWP; JAWP; WBP
Here lies a clerk who half his life had spent. *See* Here lies the clerk . .
Here lies a common man. His horny hands. Mortis Dignitas. Richard Burton. BAP
Here lies a Dog: may every Dog that dies. Epitaph on the Favourite Dog of a Politician. Hilaire Belloc. CoBE
Here lies a frigid man whom men deplore. A Man Whom Men Deplore [*or* Call Him High Shelley Now]. Alfred Kreymborg. HBMV; TBM
Here lies a great and mighty King. The King's Epitaph. Earl of Rochester. SeCePo; SeEP. *See also* Here lies our Sovereign Lord the King.
Here Lies a Lady. John Crowe Ransom. AnAmPo; AnFE; AWP; ChMo; CoAnAm; CoBMV; HBMV; InPo; InvP; LA; LiTM; MAP; MoAB; MoAmPo; MOAP; NAMP; NeMA; PoRA; ReaPo; SPP; TBM; TwAmPo
Here lies a little bird. On a Little Bird [*or* A Bird's Epitaph]. Martin Armstrong. CH; POTE
Here lies a little boy who made believe. A Dreamer. Arthur Guiterman. PoMa
Here lies a man, and still no man. Epitaph I. *Unknown. Fr.* Duel with Verses over a Great Man. TrJP
Here lies a man who was killed by lightning. At Great Torrington, Devon. *Unknown.* SiTL
"Here Lies a Most Beautiful Lady." Agathias Scholasticus, *tr. fr. Greek by* F. L. Lucas. GrPE
Here lies a most beautiful lady. An Epitaph. Walter de la Mare. AnFE; BLV; BoLiVe; BrBE; CBOV; CoBMV; EPP; LEAP; LiTB; LiTM; LoBV; MBP; MoAB; MoBrPo; MoVE; NeMA; NP; OAEP (2d ed.); OBEV (new ed.); OBVV; OnPP; PoeT; POTE; ShBV-3; SiTL; ViBoPo
Here lies a piece of Christ; a star in dust. An Epitaph for a Godly Man's Tomb. Robert Wild. AEV; BCEP; ChTr; OxBoCh; SeCL
Here lies a poor woman who always was tired. Epitaph. *Unknown.* TreF
Here Lies a Prisoner. Charlotte Mew. MoBrPo
Here lies a simple Jew. Epitaph. Sholom Aleichem. TrJP
Here lies a spendthrift who believed. Epitaph for [*or* of] a Poet. DuBose Heyward. LPS-1; LS; MuM; PC
Here lies a woman—known to me, and you. R. I. P. "Jan Struther." InMe
Here lies a wretched corse. Shakespeare. *Fr.* Timon of Athens. MyFE
Here lies an agèd corpse, which late. An Epitaph upon [*or* on] His [*or* My] Grandfather. Thomas Shipman. ElSeCe; SeCL
Here lies, and none to mourn him but the sea. Sonnet XVIII. Edna St. Vincent Millay. *Fr.* Epitaph for the Race of Man. AtBAP; MoPo; ReMP

Here lies Archeanassa of Kolophon, whose face. Epitaph of a Courtesan. Asclepiades. LiTW
Here lies at rest, unknown to fame. A Mongrel Pup. Nancy Byrd Turner. PoMa
Here Lies Bill. Oliver Herford. WhC
Here lies Callimachus, who could both sing. Epitaph on Himself. Callimachus. GrR
Here lies Cock Robbin dead and cold. The Death and Burial of Cock Robbin. *Unknown.* OxBoLi; SiTL
Here lies David Garrick—describe me who can. David Garrick. Goldsmith. *Fr.* Retaliation. OBEC; SeCeV
Here lies Eunikides. The tomb. Sepulchral Imprecation. Crinagoras. LiTW
Here lies father, mother, sister, and I. In a Staffordshire Churchyard [*or* Four Country Epitaphs]. *Unknown.* GoTP; WhC
Here lies Fred. On Prince Frederick. *Unknown.* GoTP; OxBoLi; TreFS; WhC
Here lies I [*or* me] and my three daughters. *Unknown.* GoTP; SiTL; WhC
Here lies, in this small chamber. Epitaph. Villon. FoS
Here lies John Auricular. *Unknown.* WhC
Here lies John Bun. On John Bun [*or* John Bun]. *Unknown.* GoTP; WhC
Here lies John Goddard, maker of bellows. An Epitaph on a Bellows-Maker. John Hoskins. TuPP
Here lies John Hill, a man of skill. *Unknown.* WhC
Here lies John Knott. Epitaph on John Knott. *Unknown.* ChTr
Here lies Johnny Cuncapod. *Unknown.* WhC
Here lies Johnny Pidgeon. Epitaph on John Dove. Burns. InP
Here lies [*or* lyes] Jonson [*or* Johnson] with the rest. Upon Ben Jonson. Robert Herrick. BEL; BoFr; OAEP; OBS; PtP; SeCV-1
Here lies Judge A——, he's done with legal tort. Epitaph for a Judge. Benedict Jeitteles. TrJP
Here Lies Juliet. Shakespeare. *See* Thus with a Kiss I Die.
Here lies magnanimous humility. Upon the Tomb of John Cotton. Benjamin Woodbridge. BAV
Here lies me and my three daughters. *See* Here lies I and my three daughters.
Here lies Mr. Chesterton. G. K. Chesterton. Humbert Wolfe. TrJP
Here lies my gude and gracious Auntie. *Unknown.* WhC
Here lies my wife. At Leeds. *Unknown.* WhC
Here lies my wife. Eternal peace. Epigram. J. V. Cunningham. NePoAm
Here lies my wife: here let her lie! Epitaph Intended for [*or* on] His Wife [*or* Epigram]. Dryden. BOHV; HBV; InMe; LauV; PIAE; PreP; TreF; TrGrPo; WhC
Here lies Nachshon, a man of great renown. An Epitaph. Isaac Benjacob. TrJP
Here lies Nolly Goldsmith. David Garrick. BEL; EPP
Here lies old Hobson, Death hath broke his girt. On the University Carrier [Who Sickn'd in the Time of His Vacancy]. Milton. FaBoCh; LoGBV; MePo
Here lies old Jones. *Unknown.* WhC
Here lies old Theris: death has set him free. Leonidas of Tarentum, *tr. fr. Greek by* F. A. Wright. GrPo
Here lies one blown out of breath. Merideth [*or* On a Man Named Merideth]. *Unknown.* GoTP; WhC
Here lies one Box within another. *Unknown.* WhC
Here lies one that made shipwreck. But thou, sail on. On a Shipwrecked Sailor. Theodoridas. GrPE
Here lies one who for medicine would not give. *Unknown.* WhC
Here lies one who never drew. An Epitaph. William Cowper. OTPC (1923 ed.)
Here lies our good Edmund, whose genius was such. Edmund Burke. Goldsmith. *Fr.* Retaliation. CoEV; InvP; OBEC; SeCeV
Here lies our Sovereign Lord the King. Epitaph on Charles II [*or* King Charles II *or* On Charles II *or* Epigram *or* The King's Epitaph]. Earl of Rochester. ALV; BCEP; BLV; CoEV; EnLi-1 (1949 ed.); EPP; EV-3; ExPo; FiBHP; GoTP; HBV; InP; LEAP; OnPM; OnPP; PIAE; PreP; TOP; TreFS; TrGrPo; ViBoPo; WhC; WP. *See also* Here lies a great and mighty King.
Here lies poor Burton. A Brewer. *Unknown.* WhC
Here lies poor stingy Timmy Wyatt. *Unknown.* SiTL; WhC
Here lies returned to clay. *Unknown.* WhC
Here lies Richard Dent. On Richard Dent, Landlord. *Unknown.* GoTP
Here lies Robert Trollope. On a Newcastle Architect. *Unknown.* WhC
Here lies the body of Ann Mann. *Unknown.* WhC
Here lies the body of Henry Round. *Unknown.* WhC
Here lies the body of Jonathan Near. *Unknown.* WhC
Here lies the body of Jonathan Pound. Four Country Epitaphs. *Unknown.* GoTP
Here lies the body of Jonathan Stout. *Unknown.* WhC
Here lies the body of Mary Anne Lowder. Mary Anne Lowder. *Unknown.* WhC
Here lies the body of Michael Shay. On Stubborn Michael Shay. *Unknown.* GoTP
Here lies the body of Richard Hind. Epitaph. Francis Jeffrey. OxBoLi
Here lies the body of Sarah Sexton. *Unknown.* WhC
Here lies the body of this world. Epitaph on the World. Henry David Thoreau. OnPM
Here lies the body of William Jones. Epitaph. *Unknown.* PoD
Here lies the [*or* a] clerk who half his life had spent. The Volunteer. Herbert Asquith. LBBV; MM; OtMeF
Here lies the Devil—ask no other name. On a Lord. Samuel Taylor Coleridge. FiBHP
Here lies the flesh that tried. Epitaph. Louise Driscoll. HBMV; NV; WGRP
Here lies the ideal of Saint Francis. Epitaph. Sister Mary Francis. SaFP
Here lies the late Cimantha Proctor. Epitaph for Cimantha Proctor. *Unknown.* PreP
Here lies the man Richard. *Unknown.* WhC
Here lies the man was born, and cried. An Epitaph on a Man for Doing Nothing. John Hoskins. TuPP
Here lies the mother of children seven. *Unknown.* WhC
Here lies the noble warrior, that never blunted sword. Epitaph on the Earl of Leicester. *Unknown, at. to* Sir Walter Ralegh. SiPS
Here lies the peerless paper lord, Lord Peter. On Peter Robertson. John Gibson Lockhart. SiTL
Here lies the poet Wolker, lover of the world. Epitaph. Jiri Wolker. WaaP
Here lies the preacher, judge, and poet, Peter. Epitaph; on Peter Robinson. Francis Jeffrey. *Fr.* Epitaphs. OxBoLi; WhC
Here lies the purple sleeping and here lie. To a Dead Actress. Luis Sandoval y Zapata. AnMP
Here lies the Reverend Jonathan Doe. On the Reverend Jonathan Doe. *Unknown.* ChTr
Here lies the ruined cabinet. An Epitaph on His Deceased Friend. Robert Fletcher. SeCL
Here lies the shipwrecked Theris. Landward the rollers threw me. A Seaside Grave. Archias of Byzantium. GrPE
Here lies the son of Battus. The Poet's Own Epitaph. Callimachus. OxBG
Here lies the street of the three balls. To an Avenue Sport. Helen Johnson Collins. PoNe
Here lies the woven garb he wore. The Robe of Grass. John Le Gay Brereton. BoAu; MM
Here lies [*or* lyes] to each her parents' ruth. On My First Daughter. Ben Jonson. EPS; LoBV; OBS; PoFS; ReIE; SeCV-1; SeEP
Here lies what's left. On Leslie Moore. *Unknown.* GoTP
Here lies, whom hound did ne'er pursue. Epitaph on a Hare. William Cowper. CG; EV-3; FiP; HBV; HBVY; MW; PoEL-3; RG; SeCeV; ShBV-1; WP
Here lies Will Smith—and, what's something rarish. On Will Smith. *Unknown.* SiTL
Here lies wise and valiant dust. Epitaph on the Earl of Strafford [*or* Gravestones]. John Cleveland. MePo; OBS; OtMeF; PoD; SeCePo; TrGrPo
Here lieth he who never aught. In Tumulum Avari. John Weever. SiCE
Here lieth Hercules the Second. John Baynham's Epitaph. Thomas Dermody. OnYI
Here Lieth Love. Thomas Watson. *See* My Love Is Past.
Here lieth one, who did most truly prove. On the Oxford Carrier. Milton. BOHV; NA
Here lith the fresshe flowr of Plantagenet. Epitaph on Queen Elizabeth, Wife of Henry VII. *Unknown.* AtBAP; NBE
Here lived the soul enchanted. Poe's Cottage at Fordham. John Henry Boner. AA; GA; LBAP; NoCaPo; OBAV; PtP
Here love the slain with love the slayer lies. The Play of "King Lear." Sir William Watson. VA
Here lyes Charles the first the Great. *Unknown.* SeCSL
Here lyes Jonson with the rest. *See* Here lies Jonson with the rest.
Here lyes the fairest Flowre, that stood. David's Epitaph on Jonathan. Francis Quarles. AEV
Here lyes, to each her parents' ruth. *See* Here lies . . .
Here lying on the ancient mount. The Enchanted Prince. Edwin Muir. MBP
Here malice, rapine, accident, conspire. London Delights. Samuel Johnson. *Fr.* London. BeR
Here may the band, that now in triumph shines. The Heavenly Jerusalem. Giles Fletcher. *Fr.* Christ's Victory and Triumph. OxBoCh
Here meet together the prefiguring day. The Passover in the Holy Family. Dante Gabriel Rossetti. GoBC
Here 'mid these leafy walls. Woodland Worship. Ethelwyn Wetherald. CaP; OCL
Here Miranda came up and said, "Phoebus, you know."

Here Miranda came up and said (*continued*)
Margaret Fuller. James Russell Lowell. *Fr.* A Fable for Critics. APW
Here Morris, on the plains that we have loved. Duncan Campbell Scott. *Fr.* Lines in Memory of Edmund Morris. CPG
Here my chameleon muse herself doth change. To His Good Friend, Sir Anthony Cooke. Sir John Davies. TuPP
Here, Nancy, let me take your hand. To a Child. Norreys Jephson O'Conor. HBMV
Here Nature holds as in a hollowed hand. The Skylark's Nest. R. H. Long. BoAu
Here! No sweetness trips so well as here. Bird Song. John Hay. NePoAm-2
Here, no woman, nor man besides. Man in a Room. William Carlos Williams. NP
Here not the flags, the rhythmic. Neutrality. Sidney Keyes. MoAB
Here, now, in this huddled time. Madam Rumour. Wyn Griffith. MoWP
Here now once more I lie. Tenth Reunion. Edward Steese. GoYe
Here, O lily-white lady mine. The Handsel Ring. George Houghton. AA
Here, O my Lord, I see Thee face to face. Horatius Bonar. *Fr.* This Do in Remembrance of Me. OlF; TrPWD
Here of a truth the world's extremes are met. At the Grave of Dante Gabriel Rossetti. Mackenzie Bell. VA
Here on Ecbatana's midland plain lie we. To the Eretrian Dead. Plato. GrR
Here on my breast have I bled! Ojibwa War Songs. *Unknown.* AWP; JAWP; WBP
Here on my lap an open volume lies. Ballade of Remembered Roses. George Macy. PIAE
Here, on our native soil, we breathe once more. Composed in the Valley near Dover, on the Day of Landing. Wordsworth. BPN; EmBrPo; ERP
Here on our rock-away horse we go. Johnny's By-low Song. Laura E. Richards. BoChLi; BOL
Here on the arid shoulder. The Broom. Giacomo Leopardi. WoL
Here on the Cropped Grass. W. H. Auden. ChMo
Here on the flyleaf of the garish day. I Would Define My Love. Jessica Powers. JKCP (1955 ed.)
Here on the hill. Sir Charles G. D. Roberts. Hill-Top Songs, I. CP; CPG
Here on the mountain lie the carlin's blackened bones. A Witch of King Charles's Time. Karl Jonas Love Almquist. AnSL
Here on the mountain-pass. On the Heights. Basho. OnPM
Here on the ridge where the shrill north-easter trails. The Ridge, 1919. W. W. Gibson. POTE
Here on the valley's slope is the olive grove. Old Olives at Bordighera. Duncan Campbell Scott. TwCV
Here, on these hills, no sense of loneliness. Whence Cometh My Help. P. L. Montgomery. OQP; QP-2
Here on this open, ancient book. Diary of a Raccoon. Gertrude Ryder Bennett. GoYe
Here, on this rock, and on this sterile soil. The Pilgrim Fathers. John Boyle O'Reilly. PEDC
Here, on this sunny shore, in simpler days. By an Ancient Sea. Thomas Curtis Clark. ChIP; QS
Here once the evenings sobbed. The Pear-Tree. Iwan Goll. TrJP
Here, Osmyn, we may reason unobserv'd. Racine. *Fr.* Bajazet. LiA
Here our murdered brother lies. Wake of William Orr. William Drennan. GTIV; TIP
Here part we, love, beneath the world's broad eye. George Henry Boker. *Fr.* Sonnets. MOAP
Here Pause: The Poet Claims at Least This Praise. Wordsworth. BPN; EM-2; EmBrPo; EnRP; EPN
(1811.) PoFr
Here pause: these graves are all too young as yet. Shelley. *Fr.* Adonais. MyFE
Here penned within the human fold. The Human Fold. Edwin Muir. LiTM (rev. ed.)
Here Philip laid Nicoteles, who died. Nicoteles. Callimachus. GrL
Here Pilate's Court is. The Stations of the Cross. Padraic Colum. GoBC
Here ploughshares rot and farmers. Garrison Town. Emanuel Litvinoff. WaP
Here poise, like flowers on flowers, the butterflies. At the Grave of Champernowne. John Albee. HBV
Here poppies move beneath the sun. Poem. Ann Louise Hayes. PtPa
Here rage the furies that have shaped the world. Land's End (Point Lobos, California). Stanton A. Coblentz. EtS
Here rest in peace the bones of Henry Reece. A History of Peace. Robert Graves. HBMV
Here rest no homes, here grow no seeds. Where No Seeds Grow. "Dorothy Dow." TBM
Here rest the great and good. Here they repose. The Graves of the Patriots. James Gates Percival. MDAH
Here rest the relics of a friend below. Tray's Epitaph. "Peter Pindar." TreFS
Here rests a lad. Sleeping Now in Coventry. Arthur Stanley Bourinot. NeTW
Here rests a woman, good without pretence. On Mrs. Corbet [*or* Epitaph V]. Pope. BCEP; CEP
Here rests, and let no saucy knave. Epitaph for the Tombstone Erected over the Marquis of Anglesea's Leg, Lost at the Battle of Waterloo. George Canning. LPS-3
Here Reynolds is laid, and to tell you my mind. Sir Joshua Reynolds. Goldsmith. *Fr.* Retaliation. OBEC; SeCePo
Here richly, with ridiculous display. Epitaph on the Politician [*or* On a Politician]. Hilaire Belloc. CoBE; InP; MBP; MoBrPo; NeMA; PIAE; WhC
Here room and kingly silence keep. By the Pacific Ocean. Joaquin Miller. AA; AnAmPo; LA; MAP; MoAmPo (1942 ed.)
Here Rules Love. Petrarch, *tr. fr. Italian by* Anna Maria Armi. Sonnets to Laura: To Laura in Life, Canzone XIV. LiA
Here sank Icarus, boldest youth of all. Icarus. Philippe Desportes. TrFP
Here Saon of Acanthus. Saon. Callimachus. BoFr
Here shall remain all tears for lovely things. To Song. Thomas S. Jones, Jr. HBV; VOD
Here She Goes and There She Goes. James Nack. BOHV
Here She Is. Mary Britton Miller. TiPo (1959 ed.)
Here she is, in the gaze now empty of landscapes and clouds. On Someone's Death. Eugenio Florit. AnCL
Here she lies, a pretty bud. Epitaph upon a Child That Died [*or* Upon a Child That Died]. Robert Herrick. CBOV; EM-1; EV-2; MaRV; OBEV; SeCV-1; SeEP
Here she lies, in bed of spice. Upon a Maid. Robert Herrick. ChTr; ElSeCe; FaBoCh; KN; LoGBV; OxBoLi; SeEP
Here, she says, we have only one sun a month. I Am Writing You from a Distant Land. Henri Michaux. MiCF
Here She Was Wont to Go. Ben Jonson. *Fr.* The Sad Shepherd. ElSeCe; EPS; TuPP
(Aeglamour's Lament.) CH
(Aeglamour Seeks His Shepherdess.) CoEV
Here sheep the pasture hide, there harvests bend. John Gay. *Fr.* An Epistle to the Right Honourable the Earl of Burlington. EnSW
Here, Shock, the pride of all his kind, is laid. On His Dog. John Gay. ALV
Here silent art, yet wise and watchful-eyed. The Cathedral in Trondheim. Jakob Thorarensen. IcP
Here sit a shepherd and a shepherdess. The Green Shepherd. Louis Simpson. NePoEA
"Here sits the Lord Mayor." The City Show. Eleanor Farjeon. GaP
Here sits the Lord Mayor. Mother Goose. ExPo; HBV; HBVY; OTPC (1923 ed.); OxNR; PPL; SAS
Here Skugg Lies Snug. Benjamin Franklin. SiTL; WhC
(On Skugg.) GoTP
Here sleeps, at last, in narrow bed. An Epitaph. Austin Dobson. VLEP
Here slow suns burned down stifling afternoons. Summer Bayou. John T. Westbrook. MuM
Here "solitaries," two-a-penny. Eremites. Palladas. OxBG
Here Sorrow Had No Limit. Stepan Petrovich Shchipachev, *tr. fr. Russian by* Babette Deutsch. TrRV
Here sown to dust lies one that drave. A Dead Warrior. Laurence Housman. AOAH; HBMV
Here sparrows build upon the trees. My Early Home. John Clare. BoTP; HBV; OTPC (1923 ed.)
Here spread the waters dark and deep. Alone by the Lake. Verner von Heidenstam. AnSL
Here stands a good apple tree. Apple-howling Songs. *Unknown.* OTPC (1923 ed.); PCH
Here stillness sounds like echoes in a tomb. In a Museum. Babette Deutsch. HBMV
Here stood a sacred forest. Cimmerian Twilight, II. Maximilian Aleksandrovich Voloshin. TrRV
Here, stretch'd upon this heav'n ascending hill. The Coming Night. Thomas Chatterton. *Fr.* Elegy to the Memory of Mr. Thomas Philips of Fairford. RO
Here! sweep these foolish leaves away. Midsummer. Oliver Wendell Holmes. SN
Here take my picture; though I bid farewell. His Picture. John Donne. Elegies, V. FaBoEn; MeLP; MePo; NBE; OBS; ReEn; SeEP
Here the big stars roll down. Spoken through Glass. Eithne Wilkins. NeBP
Here the crow starves, here the patient stag. Rannoch by Glencoe. T. S. Eliot. Landscapes, IV. FaBoEn; KN; LoGBV
Here the gallows, there the cord. Among Foes. Nietzsche. PoFr
"Here the hangman stops his cart." The Carpenter's Son. A. E. Housman. A Shropshire Lad, XLVII. BLV;

BoLiVe; BPN; CoBMV; EmBrPo; MoAB; MoBrPo; NeMA; PoVP; ReaPo
Here the hills are earth's bones. Asian Desert. Dorothy Wellesley. OBMV
Here the horse-mushrooms make a fairy ring. The Fairy Ring. Andrew Young. ChTr
Here the human past is dim and feeble and alien to us. Haunted Country. Robinson Jeffers. MOAP; OxBA
Here the jack-hammer jabs into the ocean. Colloquy in Black Rock. Robert Lowell. AnNE; CoBMV; FiMAP; MiAP; MoAB; MoAmPo (1950 ed.); Po; ReMP
Here the oceans twain have waited. Panama. James Jeffrey Roche. MC; PAH; PoRL
Here the river's body flows. Body and Soul. Abul Fadl. MooP
Here the spirit of Beauty keepeth. Lyric to the Isles. Charles Sangster. CPG
Here the sudden iron sound. Song. Arthur G. Coe. CAG
Here the tides flow. Newfoundland. E. J. Pratt. TwCaPo
Here the Trace. Boris Pasternak, *tr. fr. Russian by* Babette Deutsch. LiTW; TrRV
Here the tram crashes to a stop. La Perouse. William Hart-Smith. BoAu
Here the white-ray'd anemone is born. In a Spring Grove. William Allingham. IrPN
Here, then, we stand on the Canadian shore. John Hunter-Duvar. *Fr.* De Roberval. CaP
Here there are men who vomit words. Seminary. Meurig Walters. MoWP
Here they give me greeting. A Changeling Grateful. Josephine Preston Peabody. AA
Here they went with smock and crook. Forefathers. Edmund Blunden. ChMP; OBEV (new ed.); OBMV; POTE
Here those whom stern Love has consumed with cruel wasting. With Wound Still Fresh. Virgil. *Fr.* The Aeneid, VI. LiA
Here through our little world of outward sense. Eternal Moment. "Katherine Hale." CaP; OCL
Here Time is God: his shadow on this land. Point Lobos, California. Eric Wilson Barker. MuM
Here to the leisured side of life. The Lamplighter. "Seumas O'Sullivan." OxBI
Here to this ancient garden. Sorrow in a Garden. May Riley Smith. NLK
Here to this wide black earth, which, aeons past. Peat-Cutters. Geoffrey Johnson. HaMV
Here to your testing, polished in the sun. Exploration by Air, III: Airman's Certificate—No. 39289—U. S. Civil Aeronautics Authority. A. Fleming MacLiesh. PoF
Here toil the striplings, who should be a-swarm. Factory Children. Richard Burton. MaRV
Here too the birds, god's children. The Dead Fowler. Mnasalcas. OxBG
Here too were steadfast men and brave. A Grave on Ossa. Aeschylus. OxBG
Here under Heaven ringed. Northern Light. L. A. G. Strong. POTE
Here under leafy bowers. Under Leafy Bowers. Judah Al-Harizi. TrJP
Here, under sacred ground. The Unknown. Harry Kemp. AOAH
Here under this sod and under these trees. Solomon Pease. *Unknown.* WhC
Here upon earth eternity is won. Quatrain XI. Thomas S. Jones, Jr. PFE
Here, wand'ring long, amid these frowning fields. George Crabbe. *Fr.* The Village. NBE
Here war is simple like a monument. W. H. Auden. *Fr.* In Time of War. EnLit
Here was gold. The Bridge. Geoffrey Scott. TwCV
Here was I with my arm and heart. Too Late. Robert Browning EmBrPo; PoVP
Here was love's parting; that regretful hour. A Haunted Room. John Myers O'Hara. BAP
Here was no shivering winter, nipped and sere. An Old Labourer. Margaret Willy. DiM
Here was old Rome that stretched her empire far. On Old Rome. Philip Ayres. AEV
Here was she wont to go! *See* Here She Was Wont to Go.
Here was the sound of water falling only. The Owl. Robert Penn Warren. MAP; MoAmPo
Here we are all, by day; by night we are hurled. Dreams. Robert Herrick. SeEP
Here we are, gentlemen; here's the whole gang of us. At Your Service; the Panama Gang. Berton Braley. BLPA
Here we are, if you have any more. Thomas Middleton. *Fr.* The Changeling, V, iii. AtBAP; PoEL-2
Here we are on this afternoon of mid-November. Remembrance Sunday, Coombe Church, 1940. A. L. Rowse. NeTW
Here we bring new water. A New Year Carol. *Unknown.* AtBAP; BoTP; CH; MeRV; OxBoLi; ThWaDe
Here we broached the Christmas barrel. The House of Hospitalities. Thomas Hardy. MoPW
Here We Come a-Caroling. *Unknown.* FaPON; MPB; TiPo (1952 ed.)
Here We Come a-Haying. Eunice Close. BoTP
Here We Come a-Piping. *Unknown.* BoTP; CH; ExPo; HH; OTPC (1946 ed.); PoRh; SiSoSe; TiPo (1959 ed.)
Here We Come a-Wassailing, *with music.* *Unknown.* YaCaBo (Wassail Song, The.) OHIP (Wassailers' Carol, The.) AnEC
Here We Come a-Whistling. *Unknown.* AnEC; SDH (Twelfth Night Carol.) PCD; PCH; PoRL
Here we go a-walking, so softly, so softly. Walking Song. Charles Williams. AIDL; BoTP; TCPD
Here we go dancing jingo-ring. *Unknown.* OxNR
Here we go in a flung festoon. Road-Song of the Bandar-Log. Kipling. *Fr.* The Jungle Book. NV; OAEP (2d ed.); VLEP
Here we go round ring by ring. *Unknown.* OxNR
Here we go up, up, up. *Unknown.* BoTP; OTPC; SAS
Here We Have Idaho. Harry A. Powell. PoRL
Here we part. Farewell Once More: To My Friend Yen at Feng Chi Station. Tu Fu. OnPC
"Here we stan' on the Constitution, by thunder!" The Debate in the Sennit. James Russell Lowell. *Fr.* The Biglow Papers. GA; HBV; PAH
Here were planes. But everything else was gone. Wendling. Coman Leavenworth. *Fr.* Norfolk Memorials. LiTA
Here, west of winter, lies the ample flower. Prayer for This Day. Hildegarde Flanner. TrPWD
Here, when precipitate Spring with one light bound. *See* Here, where precipitate Spring . . .
Here, when the Greeks, by strength of heart and hand. The Deliverer, Jove. *Unknown.* OnPM
Here where a new life stirs and broods. Ode. Elise Aylen. BoCaPo (1943 ed.)
Here, where aspiring arch or pillar raises. To a Medieval Workman; Winchester. Margaret Willy. DiM
Here where each road-worn one. The Stirrup Cup. Aline Kilmer. CAW
Here, where fecundity of Babel frames. Babylon and Sion (Goa and Lisbon). Luís de Camões. AWP; WoL
Here, where my father lies under the ornamental plum. Churchyard of St. Mary Magdalene, Old Milton. John Heath-Stubbs. NePoEA
Here, where my soul doth trust and dare in thee. To Don Angelo Grillo. Tasso. BoFr
Here where no increase is. Supplication. Josephine Johnson. QS; TrPWD
Here, where [*or* when] precipitate Spring with one light bound. A Fiesolan [*or* Faesulan] Idyl. Walter Savage Landor. BPN; EmBrPo; EnRP; EPP; ERP; EV-4; OAEP; OBRV; SeCePo; VA
Here, where the baby paddles in the gutter. Lean Street. G. S. Fraser. NeBP
Here where the cold pure air is filled with darkness. Of Silence and the Air. Ruth Pitter. MeRV
Here where the curfew. Cousin Lucrece. Edmund Clarence Stedman. OBAV
Here where the fields lie lonely and untended. A Deserted Home. Sidney Royse Lysaght. CH
Here where the gulls and the pilots fly. Harbor View. Frances Taylor Patterson. NeTW
Here where the moonlight gleams like a fountain falling. Salt Tides. Lucia Trent. MuM
Here, where the night is clear as sea-water. Lament for a Sailor. Paul Dehn. WaP
Here, where the pale grass struggles with each wind. A Decayed Monastery. Thomas Dermody. OnYI
Here where the pirate chieftains sailed. The Caribbean. Stephanie Ormsby. PoNe
Here, where the road goes winding on its way. Hay Wagon. Helen Frith Stickney. DDA
Here where the season swiftly turns. Exile. Theodore Maynard. MBP; MoBrPo (1942 ed.)
Here where the sunlight. The White Peacock. "Fiona Macleod." PoVP; VA
Here where the taut wave hangs. Life's Circumnavigators. W. R. Rodgers. AnIV; FaBoMo; OxBI
Here where the wind is always north-north-east. New England. E. A. Robinson. AmP; CoV; FaBoEn; InPo; MAP; MoAB; MoAmPo; MOAP; MoVE; OxBA; PoeMoYo; WhC
Here, where the world is quiet. The Garden of Proserpine. Swinburne. AnFE; AWP; BMEP; BoLiVe; CaAE; CoBE; CoEV; EmBrPo; EnL; EnLi-2; EnLit; EPP; ExPo; HBV; InP; InPo; LEAP; LiTB; LiTG; MBP; OuHeWo; PG (1945 ed.); PIAE; PIR; PoE; PoEL-5; PoFS; PoRA; PoVP; PreP; REAL; ReaPo; RiBV; SeCePo; SeCeV; TrGrPo; TVSH; TwCrTr; TwHP; ViBoPo; ViP; ViPo; ViPP
Here where tumultuous vines. The Song Sparrow's Nest. Ethelwyn Wetherald. CPG

Here where under earth is head. Etsi Omnes, Ego Non. Ernest Myers. VA
Here, where Vespasian's legions struck the sands. Embarcation. Thomas Hardy. EmBrPo
Here where Virginia's storied river runs. Statue Inscribed "Lee," Richmond [*or* "Lee"]. Mary Sinton Leitch. BoHiPo; LS
Here where we found him sleeping let him lie. Desert Burial. Glenn Ward Dresbach. MuM
Here will we rest us, under these. The Flight into Egypt. Longfellow. *Fr.* Christus; a Mystery. APW; OBVV
Here, with my beer I sit. Beer. George Arnold. AA; LEAP
Here would seem a mastery of time. Swansea Bay. John Prichard. MoWP
Here ye sit, lords and dames, intertwining. At the Manor House. Christian Winther. BoDS
Here you have sky high one wall. Moonrise in City Park. Josephine Miles. FiMAP
Here! You sons of the men. English Thornton. Edgar Lee Masters. *Fr.* Spoon River Anthology. OxBA
Hereabouts is desert, it's a bad country. Desert. Patrick Anderson. BoCaPo
Hereafter. Harriet Prescott Spofford. HBV
Hereafter. Rosamund Marriott Watson. VA
Heredity. Thomas Bailey Aldrich. AA; AnAmPo; LA; LEAP; MAP; PFY
Heredity. Thomas Hardy. EPP; ImOP; MoPW
Heredity. William Dean Howells. BAP
Heredity. Theda Kenyon. DDA
Heredity. Frederick Peterson. PoP
Heredity. Lydia Avery Coonley Ward. HBV
Heredity and Ego. Mary Josephine Benson. CPG
Here's a body—there's a bed! Good Night. Thomas Hood. GaP; MPB (1956 ed.); SiSoSe
Here's a clean year. A New Year. Mary Carolyn Davies. OQP; QP-2; YeAr
Here's a guessing story. What Is It? H. E. Wilkinson. BoTP
Here's a hand to the boy who has courage. Our Heroes. Phoebe Cary. BLPA
Here's a Health to King Charles. Sir Walter Scott. *Fr.* Woodstock, *ch.* 20. BPN; EmBrPo; TCEP
(Glee for King Charles.) CoBE; EPN
Here's a health to the birds one and all! A Health to the Birds. Seumas MacManus. BLA
Here's a health to thee, Tom: a bright bumper we drain. A Toast. Joseph Howe. BoCaPo (1948 ed.)
Here's a Health to Them That's Awa'. Burns. HBV; PoFr
Here's a health to them that's away. *Unknown.* CBE
Here's a health unto His Majesty. Song [*or* His Majesty's Health *or* A Health unto His Majesty]. *Unknown, at. to* Jeremy Savile. ChTr; EV-2; SeCL
Heres a jolly couple O the jolly jolly couple. *Unknown.* SeCSL
Here's a knocking indeede. Shakespeare. *Fr.* Macbeth, II, iii. AtBAP
Here's a land where all are equal. Creede. Cy Warman. PoOW
Here's a large one for the lady. *Unknown.* OxNR
Here's a moccasin track in the drifts. The Chase. *Unknown.* SCC
Here's a Poor Widow from Babylon. *Unknown.* OTPC; OxNR
("Here's to the poor widow from Babylon.") BoTP
Here's a present for Rose. A Greek Gift. Austin Dobson. *Fr.* Rose-Leaves. BPN; MBP; MoBrPo (1942 ed.)
Here's a reward for who'll find Love! A Lost Child. H. C. Bunner. PR
Here's a song. Scel Lem Duib. *Tr. fr. Irish by* Brian O Nolan. OxBI
Here's a song of praise for a beautiful world. The Beautiful World. W. L. Childress. OHIP
Here's a summer, heavy and hard. Elegy for Lucy Lloyd. Llewelyn Goch. LiTW
Here's Abbey Way: here are the rooms. The Chrysanthemum Show. C. Day Lewis. MoVE
Here's an adventure! What awaits. On Opening a New Book. Abbie Farwell Brown. YeAr
Here's an example from/ A butterfly. The Example. W. H. Davies. AnFE; BMEP; ChMo; CMP; GTML; HBMV; MBP; MoBrPo; PIAE; POTE; POTT; PtOT; TrGrPo; TSW; TSWC; WHA
Here's another day, dear. Glad Day. W. Graham Robertson. CBPC; HBV
Here's Christianity again! On the Reported New Outbreak of Christianity. James H. McCabe. JKCP (1955 ed.)
Here's Cooper, who's written six volumes to show. Cooper. James Russell Lowell. *Fr.* A Fable for Critics. AnNE; CoBA; OxBA
Here's Finiky Hawkes. Black Your Shoes, Your Honour? *Unknown.* OxNR; PCH
Here's flowers for you. The Flowers of Perdita [*or* Flowers of Middle Summer]. Shakespeare. *Fr.* The Winter's Tale, IV, iii. FiP; YeAr
Here's good wind, here's sweet wind. Song of the Full Catch. Constance Lindsay Skinner. *Fr.* Songs of the Coast Dwellers. BoCaPo; CaP; NV; OCL; TBM
Here's my baby's bread and milk. Breakfast and Puss. Ann *or* Jane Taylor. PoC
Here's my case. Of old I used to love him. Fears and Scruples. Robert Browning. BPN
Here's no more news than virtue: I may as well. To Sir Henry Wotton. John Donne. TuPP
Here's Pericles, our own squill-headed Zeus. Pericles. Cratinus. OxBG
Here's pretty conduct, Hugh O'Rourke. To Tomas [*or* Tomaus] Costello at the Wars. *At. to* Tomas O'Higgins, *tr. by* Frank O'Connor. AnIV; KiLC
Here's shade and comfort by this towering tree. Christmas 1942. Eric Irvin. BoAV
Here's Sulky Sue. *Unknown.* OxNR
Here's the drover with his cattle. Farm Voices. Emilie Poulsson. MeMeAg
Here's the garden she walked across. The Flower's Name. Robert Browning. Garden Fancies, I. EnLi-2 (1949 ed.); GEPC; GTBS-D; HBV; LPS-1; VLEP
Here's the golden cup all bossy with satyrs and saints. Melting of the Earl's Plate. George Walter Thornbury. VA
Here's the mail, sort it quick. A Sure Sign. Nancy Byrd Turner. PCH; TiPo
Here's the mistress that I choose. The Sort of Girl He Prefers. Ausonius. LaP
Here's the mould of a musical bird long passed from light. In a Museum. Thomas Hardy. UnS
Here's the Rich Peru. Ben Jonson. The Alchemist, II, i–ii. LiA
("Come on, sir. Now, you set your foot on shore.") AtBAP; PoEl-2
Here's the spot. Look around you. Above on the height. Caldwell of Springfield. Bret Harte. PAH
Here's the tender coming. The Press-Gang. *Unknown.* CBPC; ChTr; SG
Here's the way to Slumber Town. To Slumber Town. "M. E. W." BOL
Here's to good old Boston. *See* And this is good old Boston.
Here's to him that grows it. The Haymakers' Song. Alfred Austin. VA
Here's to Nelson's Memory. Robert Browning. ViPo
Here's to New Haven and Boston. To New Haven and Boston. Walter Foster Angell. TreFS
Here's to the end of the century, lads. Last Party. *Unknown.* CAG
Here's to the home that was never, never ours! Song of the Drift Weed. Jessie Mackay. BoAu
Here's to the Maiden. Sheridan. *See* Let the Toast Pass.
Here's to the man who invented stairs. Stairs. Oliver Herford. FiBHP; InMe; WhC
Here's to the man with the leather lung. My Candidate. Norman H. Crowell. YaD
Here's to the men who lose! To the Men Who Lose. George L. Scarborough. BLPA
Here's to the passing cowboy, the plowman's pioneer. A Cowboy Toast. James Barton Adams. SCC
Here's to the poor widow from Babylon. *See* Here's a Poor Widow from Babylon.
Here's to the Ranger! *Unknown.* CoSo; CSF
Here's to the RED of it. A Toast to the Flag. John Daly. BAP; POT
Here's to the town of New Haven. On the Democracy of Yale [*or* New Haven]. Frederick Scheetz Jones. BoHiPo; BOHV; HBV; TreFS; WhC; YaD
Here's to the white carnation. The White Carnation. Margaret E. Sangster. PEDC
Here's to the year that's awa'! The Year That's Awa'. John Dunlop. HBV
Here's to thee, old apple tree. Apple-howling Songs. *Unknown.* OTPC (1923 ed.); OxNR; PCH
Here's to those who love us. Toast. *Unknown.* SiTL
Here's to ye absent lords, may they. A Toast. *Unknown.* ALV; WhC
Here's to you, belov'd Rhode Island. Rhode Island. T. Clarke Brown. PoRL
Here's to your eyes. Toast. Frank Horne. BANP; PoNe
Here's tropic flora. Hotel Lobby. Mildred Weston. WhC
Here's two or three jolly boys. *Unknown.* OxNR
Here's Winter. Pushkin, *tr. fr. Russian by* Babette Deutsch. TrRV
Heresy for a Classroom. Rolfe Humphries. PoMa; PreP
Heresy Indeed. Sara Henderson Hay. QS
Heretic, The. Bliss Carman. WGRP
Heretics All. Hilaire Belloc. ACP (1952 ed.)
Heretic's Tragedy, The. Robert Browning. NBE
Hereto I come to view a voiceless ghost. After a Journey. Thomas Hardy. AtBAP; ChMP; CoEV; EnLoPo; FaBoEn; GTBS-D; MoPW; MoVE; PoEL-5
Heriot's Ford. Kipling. PoRA

Heritage. Gwendolyn Bennett. BANP
Heritage. Stanton A. Coblentz. AlBD
Heritage. Countee Cullen. BANP; MAP; MoAmPo; PoNe; TBM; TCPD
Heritage, The. James Russell Lowell. HBV; HBVY; OTPC; PTA-2
Heritage. Claude McKay. PoNe
Heritage. Dorothy Paul. VOD
Heritage, The. Edward Bliss Reed. EtS
Heritage. A. M. Sullivan. JKCP (1955 ed.)
Heritage of hopes and fears, An. The Soul. Madison Cawein. AA
Herman Altman. Edgar Lee Masters. *Fr.* Spoon River Anthology. OxBA
Herman Melville. W. H. Auden. GTBS-W; LiTA; LiTM (rev. ed.); NePA; OAEP (2d ed.); OxBA
Hermann and Dorothea, *sel.* Goethe, *tr. fr. German.*
"All is changing now—it seems as though all must be parted," *sel., tr. by* F. Melian Stawell *and* Nora Purtscher-Wydenbruck. PoFr
Hermatic Poems. Elias Ashmole. LO
Hermes of the Lonely Hill. *Unknown, tr. fr. Greek by* T. F. Higham. OxBG
Hermes of the Playground. Nicias, *tr. fr. Greek by* J. A. Pott. OxBG
Hermes of the Ways. Hilda Doolittle ("H. D."). LiTA; MM; MOAP; NP
Hermes of the Ways. *Unknown, tr. fr. Greek by* Anne Hyde Greet. OnPM
Hermes the Hermit. *Unknown, tr. fr. Greek by* F. L. Lucas. GrPE
Hermes the Philosopher. William Dunbar. EBSV
Hermes Trismegistus. Hilda Doolittle ("H. D."). *Fr.* A Tribute to the Angels. FaBoTw
Hermes Trismegistus. Longfellow. OBAV
"Herminius! Aulus greets thee." The Death of Herminius. Macaulay. *Fr.* Lays of Ancient Rome. OtMeF
Hermione. "Barry Cornwall." OBVV
Hermione/ was roguishly. Asclepiades, *tr. fr. Greek by* William Wallace *and* Mary Wallace. GrPo
Hermione once play'd with me. The Flirt. Asclepiades, *tr. by* J. M. Edmonds. GrR
Hermit, The. "Æ." BEL; CaAE; PoVP
Hermit, The. James K. Baxter. AnNZ
Hermit, The, *sel.* James Beattie.
"At the close of the day." EV-3; LPS-3
Hermit, The. W. H. Davies. MBP; MoBrPo
Hermit, The. Joseph von Eichendorff, *tr. fr. German by* Mabel Cotterell. AnGP
Hermit, The. Goldsmith. *See* Edwin and Angelina.
Hermit, The. Hsü Pen, *tr. fr. Chinese by* Henry H. Hart. PoHN
Hermit, The. Howard Moss. NePoAm
Hermit, The. Thomas Parnell. EV-3; GoTL
Hermit, The. *At. to* Sir Walter Ralegh. *See* Like to a Hermit.
Hermit, The. Tao Yuan-ming, *tr. fr. Chinese by* Yang Yeh-tzu. WhP
Hermit and the King, The. *Unknown, tr. fr. Old Irish by* Seán O'Faoláin. SiB
Hermit Hoar. Samuel Johnson. *Fr.* Boswell's Life of Johnson. ViBoPo
Hermit Thrush. Kathleen Millay. BAP
Hermit Thrush, The. Nelly Hart Woodworth. SN
Hermit Thrush in the Catskills, A. William Griffith. BLA
Hermitage, The. *Unknown, at. to* St. Manchan of Lemanaghan in Offaly, *tr. fr. Irish by* Frank O'Connor. KiLC
Hermits. F. R. Higgins. MM
Hermits and blameless women full of grace. A Prayer. Pushkin. BoR
Hermit's house beside a stream, A. On Retirement [*or* Retirement]. Philip Freneau. CoV; IAP; OBAV
Hermit's Song, The. *Unknown. See* Wish of Manchin of Liath, The.
Hermotimus. William Edmondstoune Aytoun. OBVV
Hern flew east, the hern flew west, The. *See* Heron flew east . . .
Hernani, *sel.* Victor Hugo, *tr. fr. French by* Mrs. Newton Crosland.
Oh, Thou, My Lover, *fr.* V, iii. LiA
Herndon. S. Weir Mitchell. PAH
Hero, The. Ambrose Bierce. OQP; PoRL; QP-2
Hero, A. Florence Earle Coates. BLP; GA; OHIP
Hero, The. Roy Fuller. FaBoMo
Hero, The. Leroy F. Jackson. SiSoSe
Hero, The. Marianne Moore. *Fr.* Part of a Novel, Part of a Poem, Part of a Play. OnHM; OxBA
Hero, The. Robert Nicoll. HBV; VA
Hero, The. Sir Henry Taylor. VA
Hero, The. W. J. Turner. SoV
Hero. William Carlos Williams. MOAP
Hero, The. George Woodcock. TwCaPo
Hero and Leander. John Donne. ReIE
Hero and Leander, *sels.* Thomas Hood.
Death of Leander, The. EnRP
"O poppy death!" ERP
Scylla's Lament. EnRP
Hero and Leander. Christopher Marlowe (First *and* Second Sestiads), *completed by* George Chapman. OBSC (First *and* Second Sestiads); ReaPo (First *and* Second Sestiads); ReEn (First *and* Second Sestiads); ReIE (First *and* Second Sestiads); TuPP (First *and* Second Sestiads)
Sels.
Bridal Song, *fr.* Fifth Sestiad. Chapman. BCEP; OBEV ("O come, soft rest of cares! come, Night!") EG
(Song: "O come, soft rest of cares, come, Night!") ViBoPo
"But as he shook with passionate desire," *fr.* Third Sestiad. Chapman. NBE
Epithalamion Teratus, *fr.* Fifth Sestiad. Chapman. AtBAP; ElL; EV-1; LoBV
(Wedding of Alcmane and Mya, The.) OBSC
"Her veil was artificial flowers and leaves," *fr.* First Sestiad. Marlowe. HoPM
Hero the Faire, *fr.* First Sestiad. Marlowe. FaBoEn; WHA
It Lies Not in Our Power to Love or Hate, *fr.* First Sestiad. Marlowe. BoLiVe; TrGrPo; WHA
(First Sight.) BLV; CoEV
(Love at First Sight.) EV-1; FaBoEn
(Who Ever Loved, That Loved Not at First Sight?) BCEP; FaFP; LiTB; LiTG; LiTL
"Men of wealthie Sestos, everie yeare, The," *fr.* First Sestiad. Marlowe. BrBE
"O Hero, Hero, thus he cry'de full oft," *fr.* Second Sestiad. Marlowe. AtBAP
"On Hellespont, guilty of true love's blood," First Sestiad. Marlowe. AnFE, *sel.;* AtBAP; BCEP, *sel.;* EPP, *abr.;* LoBV, *sel.;* OAEP; OBSC; PoEL-2; ReaPo; SeCePo; SiCE
"On this feast day, O curséd day and hour," *fr.* First Sestiad. Marlowe. ViBoPo
Repentance, *fr.* Third Sestiad. Chapman. OBSC
Hero and Leander. Musaeus, *tr. fr. Greek by* F. L. Lucas. GrPE
Sels.
"And now the maiden Hero walked to Aphrodite's temple," *tr. by* L. P. Chamberlayne. GrPo
"For thy love's sake, O maiden, I will cross the tumbling sea," *tr. by* L. P. Chamberlayne. GrPo
"In gladness past all words her white arms flung," *tr. by* Sir Edwin Arnold. GrPo
Leander's Death, *tr. by* Michael Balkwill. OxBG
"Lightly he touched her soft and rosy hand," *tr. by* Sir Edwin Arnold. GrPo
"Sing, Muse, the beacon gleaming bright above," *tr. by* Sir Edwin Arnold. GrPo
"Tir'd with vain toil, scar'd with each dreadful blast," *tr. by* John Sterling. GrPo
Hero and Leander. Joseph S. Newman. FiBHP
Hero Cockroach, The. Don Marquis. *See* Archy Experiences a Seizure.
Hero Entombed, I. Peter Quennell. FaBoMo; LiTB
Hero first thought it, The. Truth. "Æ." AnIL; BMEP; GTML; GTSL; MoBrPo; TOP
Hero in Despair, A, *abr.* Milton. *Fr.* Samson Agonistes. BHV
Hero in Prison, A. Milton. *See* Eyeless at Gaza.
Hero in the Land of Dough, A. Robert Clairmont. WaKn; WhC
Hero of Bridgewater, The. Charles L. S. Jones. PAH
Hero of His Village. Nigel Heseltine. MoWP
Hero of the Commune, The. Margaret Junkin Preston. AA; OBAV
Hero of Vimy, The. Brent Dow Allinson. AOAH
Hero Song. Robert Duncan. CrMA
Hero the Fair[e]. Christopher Marlowe. *Fr.* Hero and Leander, First Sestiad. FaBoEn; WHA
Hero to Leander. Tennyson. LPS-1
Hero Wanted. Berton Braley. FAOV
Hero-Worship. William Bell Scott. VA
Herod. W. H. Auden. *Fr.* For the Time Being. OnHM
Herod, *sels.* Stephen Phillips.
Benediction: "Now unto Him who brought His people forth." MaRV
"I dreamed last night of a dome of beaten gold." PC
"Pour out those pearls."
(From "Herod.") LEAP
Herod by his great cruelty. Christ Brought Home. *Unknown.* PoLi
Herod sitting on his throne. The Children's Ghosts. Winifred M. Letts. BMEP; HBMV
Herod that was both wild and wode. Worship We This Holy Day. *Unknown.* AnEC
Herod the King came sounding through. In Galilee. Jessie Mackay. AnNZ
Hérodiade, *sels.* Stéphane Mallarmé, *tr. fr. French.*
"For whom, consumed/ With anguish, do you keep the un-

Hérodiade (*continued*)
seen splendor," *tr. by* Kate Flores. AnFP
"To mine own self I am a wilderness," *tr. by* Arthur Symons. LiA
Herodotus in Egypt. Andrew Lang. PoVP
Herod's Suspicions. Richard Crashaw. StJW
Heroes. Laurence Housman. GrCo-2; POT; PoTo
Heroes. Edna Dean Proctor. GA; HBV; TVSH
Heroes. Kathleen Raine. DiM
Heroes, The. Louis Simpson. NePoAm
Heroes. Walt Whitman. *Fr.* Song of Myself. AA
Heroes, and kings! your distance keep. For One Who Would Not Be Buried in Westminster Abbey. Pope. ACP (1926 ed.); PIAE
Heroes' Day, The. *Unknown.* PEOR
Heroes of the South. Paul Hamilton Hayne. MDAH
Heroes out of music born. The Farnese Hercules. Sacheverell Sitwell. FaBoMo; LiTM (rev. ed.)
Heroic Age, The. Richard Watson Gilder. AA; OHIP
Heroic Answer to the Servant Problem, An. Homer, *pr. tr. fr. Greek by* Samuel Butler. *Fr.* The Odyssey. GrR
Heroic good, target for which the young. Faint yet Pursuing. Coventry Patmore. OxBoCh; PoVP
Heroic Love James Graham, Marquess of Montrose. *Fr.* My Dear and Only Love. EV-2; LH, *abr.*
Heroic Poem, A, *sel.* Lynette Roberts.
"We must uprise O my people." MoWP
Heroic soul, in homely garb half hid. Lincoln. John Townsend Trowbridge. LBAH; PGD
Heroic [*or* Heroique] Stanzas, Consecrated to the Glorious Memory of His Most Serene and Renowned Highnesse, Oliver, Late Lord Protector of This Common-Wealth. Dryden. CEP; SeCV-2
Stanzas on Oliver Cromwell, *sel.* EPP
Heroic Vengeance. Milton. *Fr.* Samson Agonistes. OBS
("O dearly-bought revenge, yet glorious!") TwHP
Heroics. Elinor Wylie. CoBA
Heroism ("Ruby wine is drunk"). Emerson. AtBAP; OnAP; ViBoPo
Heroism ("So nigh is grandeur to our dust"). Emerson. *See* Duty.
Heroism. Lizette Woodworth Reese. LS; MaRV; PC
Heron. Philip Booth. NePoEA
Heron, The. John Lyle Donaghy. NeIP
Heron, The. La Fontaine, *tr. fr. French by* Alan Conder. TrFP
Heron, The. Edward Hovell-Thurlow. BLA; HBV
(To a Bird.) LPS-2
Heron, The. Mary Howitt. TVSH
Heron, The. Theodore Roethke. MiAP
Heron, The. *Unknown.* EnSB
(Knight in the Bower, The, *sl. diff.*) ChTr
Heron, The. Brian Vrepont. MoAuPo
Heron, The. Vernon Watkins. ChMP; UnPo (3d ed.)
Heron cries in sorrow, The. Ki no Tsurayuki, *tr. fr. Japanese by* I. W. Furukami. LiTW
Heron [*or* Hern] flew east, the heron [*or* hern] flew west, The. The Heron [*or* The Knight in the Bower]. *Unknown.* ChTr; EnSB
Heron in Swamp. Frances Minturn Howard. GoYe
Heron is harsh with despair. Song. Brenda Chamberlain. NeBP; NeIP
Heron stands in water where the swamp, The. The Heron. Theodore Roethke. MiAP
Heron That Liked Crab-Meat, The. *Unknown, tr. fr. Sanskrit by* Arthur W. Ryder. *Fr.* The Panchatantra. OuHeWo
Herons. Robin Blaser. NeAP
Herons, The. Francis Ledwidge. *See* Ardan Mór.
Herons. *Unknown, tr. fr. Japanese.* SUS
Herons on Bo Island, The. Elizabeth Shane. BLA
Hero's daughter, Leinster's loveliest! All Gold. *Unknown.* KiLC
Hero's Epitaph. Shakespeare. *Fr.* Much Ado about Nothing, V, iii. TriL
("Done to death by slanderous tongues.") OBSC
Hero's Invocation to Death. Margaret Tod Ritter. TBM
Hero's Lamp. Dante Gabriel Rossetti. The House of Life, LXXXVIII. PoVP; ViPo
Hero's Tower. Antipater of Thessalonica, *tr. fr. Greek by* F. L. Lucas. GrPE
Herrick's Cavalier. Robert Herrick. PoFr
Herring. Kenneth Rexroth. *Fr.* A Bestiary. HoPM
Herring, The. Sir Walter Scott. *See* Harlaw.
Herring Is King. Alfred Perceval Graves. TIP
Herring is prolific, The. Herring. Kenneth Rexroth. *Fr.* A Bestiary. HoPM
Herring loves the merry moonlight, The. Harlaw [*or* The Herring *or* The Red Harlaw]. Sir Walter Scott. *Fr.* The Antiquary. BOHV; BSV; FaBoCh; LH; LoGBV; RIS
Herring-run was over, The. The long days. The Hayfield. Charles Bruce. *Fr.* The Flowing Summer. CaP
Herring Weir, The. Sir Charles G. D. Roberts. *Fr.* Songs of the Common Day. PeCV
Herringdove, The. Kenyon Cox. *Fr.* Mixed Beasts. RIS
Herrings. Swift. *Fr.* Verses for Fruitwomen. AnIV; OnYI
Hers was the last authentic rape. Helen's Rape. Thom Gunn. PoN
Hersel pe Highland shentleman. The Turnimspike. Dougal Graham. EBSV
Herself. John Holmes. HoPM; MiAP
Herself. Dante Gabriel Rossetti. The House of Life, LVI. BPN; EmBrPo; EPN; POTT; ViPo
Herself a Rose Who Bore the Rose. Christina Rossetti. ISi
Herself and Myself. Patrick Joseph McCall. TIP
Herself hath given back my life to me. Love Song. *Unknown.* LiTW
Herself listening to herself, having no name. Herself. John Holmes. HoPM; MiAP
Hertha. Swinburne. BEL; BMEP; BPN; EmBrPo; EnLi-2; EPN; HBVY; MBP; MW; OAEP; OBEV (1st ed.); POTT; PoVP; REAL; TOP; VA; ViP; ViPo; ViPP; VLEP
"I am that which began," *sel.* PIAE
Hervarar Saga, *sel. Unknown, tr. fr. Danish by* E. M. Smith-Dampier.
Alf of Odderskerry. BoDaBa
Hervé Riel. Robert Browning. BEL; BeLS; BPN; FaBoBe; GN; HBV; LH; LPS-2; MCCG; OtMeF, OTPC (1946 ed.); PECK; PIR, *first 7 sts.*; PoVP; TCEP; TOP
Herz und Mund, *sel.* Johann Sebastian Bach, *tr. fr. German.*
"Jesu, joy of man's desiring." OlF
He's a little dog, with a stubby tail. Bum. W. Dayton Wedgefarth. AlBD; BLPA; LPS-1
He's a-choppin' in de new groun'. Great God-a'mighty. *Unknown.* ABF
He's Come! The Saviour Has Come! Alice Mortenson. BePJ
He's dead/ the dog won't have to. Death. William Carlos Williams. OxBA; PoP
He's gone./ I do not understand. The Going [*or* To Rupert Brooke]. W. W. Gibson. BoFr; CBOV; CP; GTSL; HiLiEn; NP
He's Gone Away, *with music. Unknown.* APW; AS; TrAS
He's gone to school, wee Hughie. Wee Hughie. Elizabeth Shane. HBMV
He's helping me now—this moment. This Moment. Annie Johnson Flint. BLRP
He's Jus' de Same Today, *with music. Unknown.* BoAN-1
He's Just Away. James Whitcomb Riley. *See* Away.
He's my doll! A Kiss. *Unknown.* KiLC
He's not so fine nor is he proud. Ode to a Dawg. Eloise Burtis. AlBD
He's nothing much, but fur. A Kitten. Eleanor Farjeon. TiPo
He's run his little legs orff, and at last he's gone to sleep. The Nipper's Lullaby. M. B. Spurr. BOL
He's sentenced, 'tis too late. Man New Made. Shakespeare. *Fr.* Measure for Measure, II, ii. GoBC
He's slight and old and sits up timidly. Old Man of Tennessee. John Hay. NePoAm-2
He's something in the city. Who shall say. Impressions. Harold Monro. BMEP
He's struttin' sho ernuff. De Drum Majah. Roy Garfield Dandridge. BANP
He's such a wanderer in his thoughts. The Wanderer. Amanda Benjamin Hall. HBMV
Hesiod, 1908. Alexander Mair. GoTS
Hesiod's the theme, and style. To Aratus. Callimachus. OxBG
Hesitant Heart, The. Winifred Welles. VOD
Hesitating Blues, The. W. C. Handy. GoSl
Hesper, thou golden light of Love's Queen sprung from the sea. Love's Tryst. Bion. GrPE
Hesperia. Swinburne. EmBrPo; OBVV; VA
"Delight of thy face, and the sound of thy feet, The," *sel.* LoPS
Hesperia, *sel.* Richard Henry Wilde.
"New world hath its wonders, The." BAV
Hesperides. Thomas Bailey Aldrich. BAV
Hesperides ("I sing of brooks, of blossoms, birds and bowers"). Robert Herrick. *See* Argument of His Book, The.
Hesperides. Harry Kemp. NLK
Hesperides, The. Tennyson. ViPP
Hesperides—Fragment Thirty-six. Hilda Doolittle ("H. D."). *See* Fragment Thirty-six: "I know not what to do."
Hesperus. Byron. *See* Evening.
Hesperus. James Stephens, *after* Sappho. GTIV
Hesperus' Hymn [*or* Song] to Cynthia. Ben Jonson. *See* Hymn to Diana.
Hesperus Sings. Thomas Lovell Beddoes. *See* Poor Old Pilgrim Misery.
Hesperus the Bringer. Byron. *See* Evening.

Hesperus! the day is gone. The Evening Star. John Clare. ChTr
Hesperus with the host of heaven came. Joseph Blanco White. *Fr.* Night and Death. MyFE
Hester. Charles Lamb. EnRP; ERP; EV-4; GTBS; GTBS-D; GTBS-W; GTSE; GTSL; HBV; LEAP; LoBV; LPS-1; OBEV; OBRV; OTPC (1923 ed.); PoE; TriL
"Springy motion in her gait, A," *sel.* LO
Hester. Lizette Woodworth Reese. VOD
Hester MacDonagh. Jeannette Slocomb Edwards. GoYe
Hestia, wherever homes shelter, raised to the sky. The Goddess of the Hearth. *Unknown.* *Fr.* Homeric Hymns. OxBG
Heterodoxy, A. Lord Dunsany. OnYI; UnW
"Heureux Qui Comme Ulysse." John Manifold. WaaP; WaP
Heureux qui, comme Ulysse, a fait un beau voyage. Joachim du Bellay, *tr. fr. French by* G. K. Chesterton. *Fr.* Regrets. AWP
(Happy Ulysses, The, *tr. by* G. K. Chesterton.) WoL
(My House, *tr. by* Alan Conder.) TrFP
(Returning Home, *tr. by* William Stirling.) LiTW
(Sonnet: "Happy as Ulysses, his voyage done," *tr. by* Ralph N. Currey.) FoS
(Translation from Du Bellay: "Happy, who like Ulysses or that lord," *tr. by* G. K. Chesterton.) InP
Hewel, or Woodpecker, The. Andrew Marvell. *Fr.* Upon Appleton House. ChTr
Hex on the Mexican X, A. David McCord. FiBHP
Hexameter and Pentameter. *Unknown.* ChTr
Hexametra Alexis in Laudem Rosamundi. Robert Greene. *Fr.* Greene's Mourning Garment. ElL; PoEL-2; TuPP
(In Praise of Rosamund.) AtBAP
Hey, Betty Martin! *Unknown.* AS, *with music;* ExPo
Hey! Crackerjack—jump! Dolphins in Blue Water. Amy Lowell. LaNeLa; TSW; TSWC
Hey-Day. Witter Bynner. PoTo
Hey Derry Derry. Thomas Dekker. *See* Cold's the Wind.
Hey diddle diddle,/ And hey diddle dan! *Unknown.* OxNR
Hey diddle diddle,/ The physicists fiddle. Paul Dehn. *Fr.* Rhymes for a Modern Nursery. FiBHP
Hey [*or* Hi *or* High *or* Sing hey], diddle, diddle, the cat and the fiddle. Mother Goose. BoChLi; BoN; FaBoBe; FaFP; HBV; HBVY; HoPM; LiTG; OTPC; OxBoLi; OxNR; PCH; PPL; RIS; SAS; SiTL; StVeCh; TiPo
Hey diddle diddle, the cat and the fiddle,/ Bombers come with the moon. Maturity. J. Elgar Owen. WaP
Hey diddle, dinkety, poppety, pet. Mother Goose. BoTP; OTPC (1923 ed.); OxNR; PPL
Hey, diddle doubt,/ My fire is out. *Unknown.* BoN
Hey diddle dout,/ My candle's out. *Unknown.* OxNR
Hey ding a ding. *Unknown.* OxNR
Hey, dorolot, dorolot! *Unknown.* OxNR
"Hey, down a down!" did Dian sing. A Nymph's Disdain of Love. *Unknown.* ElL; EPP; SiCE; TuPP
Hey, Hey, Hey, Hey,/ The Boar's Head Is Armed Gay. *Unknown.* AnEC
Hey ho, care away, let the world pass. *Unknown.* *Fr.* The Trial of Treasure. TuPP
"Hey, I've found some moneywort." Kids. Witter Bynner. MPB
Hey, Joe! Cigarette! Cioccolat'! Cigarette for the Bambino. Gavin Ewart. WaP
Hey Johnnie Cope. Adam Skirving. *See* Johnnie Cope.
Hey, laddie, hark, to the merry, merry lark. The Sky-Lark's Song. John Bennett. *Fr.* Master Sky-Lark. AA
Hey, Lads. Viktor Khlebnikov, *tr. fr. Russian by* Jack Lindsay. RuPo
Hey! little evergreens. The Little Fir-Trees. Evaleen Stein. PTA-2
Hey, my kitten, my kitten. Mother Goose. OTPC; OxNR; PPL; SAS
Hey, my lad, ho, my lad! Welcome to the New Year. Eleanor Farjeon. MoSiPe; YeAr
Hey! My Pony! Eleanor Farjeon. FaPON
Hey, Nonny! Charles Kingsley. *Fr.* Dolcino to Margaret. OBVV
Hey Nonny No. Marguerite Merington. AA
Hey Nonny No! *Unknown.* BLV; CH; ChTr; EG; ElL; ElSeCe; EnLi-1; EV-1; LoBV; OBEV; TrGrPo; ViBoPo
(Carpe Diem.) PoFr
(Round, A.) FaBoCh; LoGBV
Hey! Now the Day Dawns! Alexander Montgomerie. *See* Night Is Near Gone, The.
Hey rub-a-dub, three maids in a tub. *Unknown.* SAS
Hey, rub-a-dub-dub [ho! rub-a-dub], three men in a tub. Mother Goose. GaP; SiTL
Hey! the little postman. The Postman. Laura E. Richards. TiPo
"Hey, troly, loly lo, maid, whither go you?" Pastourelle. *Unknown.* LO; OBSC
Hey, Wully Wine. *Unknown.* CH
Heyhow for Hallowe'en. Hallowe'en [*or* The Witches]. *Unknown.* ChTr; FaBoCh; LoGBV; MeMeAg; OTPC (1946 ed.)
Heyst-sur-Mer. Richard Middleton. BMEP; LEAP
Heywood goes down, saith Davie, sickerly. Thomas Bastard. SiCE
Heywood, th' old English epigrammatist. Ad Modernos Epigrammatistas. John Heath. SiCE; TuPP
Heywood was held for epigrams the best. Tempus Edax Rerum. Henry Parrot. SiCE
Heywood, which did in epigrams excel. In Haywodum. Sir John Davies. ReIE; SiCE; TuPP
Hi! diddle diddle. *See* Hey, diddle, diddle.
"Hi! Harry Holly! Halt—and tell." Our Folks. Ethel Lynn Beers. PTA-1
Hi! Hi! Hi!/ My wild feet fly. Thunderdrums, II. Lew Sarett. TCPD
Hi! Hi! Hi! Hi! The Blue Duck. Lew Sarett. NP
Hi! hi! hi! hi! The Witch's Ride. Adelheid Wette. *Fr.* Hansel and Gretel. PCH
Hi! Just you drop that! Stop, I say. Up the Spout. Swinburne. BOHV; PA
"Hi!" said the blackbird, sitting on a chair [*or* swinging on the air]. The Birds' Courting Song. *Unknown.* APW; TrAS
Hi! we shout with voice ecstatic. Roundel in the Rain. *Unknown.* FiBHP
Hi-yo, the boatsmen row. *Unknown.* LaNeLa
Hialmar. Roy Campbell. CoBE; SoV
Hialmar's Heart. Leconte de Lisle, *tr. fr. French by* Alan Conder. TrFP
(Hialmar Speaks to the Raven, *tr. by* James Elroy Flecker.) AWP
Hiawatha. Longfellow. *See* Song of Hiawatha, The.
Hiawatha and Mudjekeewis. Longfellow. The Song of Hiawatha, IV. AnNE; EV-1; IAP; TCAP
Hiawatha's Brothers. Longfellow. *Fr.* The Song of Hiawatha, III. BoTP; PCH
(Hiawatha's Chickens, *br. sel.*) PCH
Hiawatha's Canoe. Longfellow. *See* Hiawatha's Sailing.
Hiawatha's Childhood. Longfellow. The Song of Hiawatha, III. AnNE; BoChLi, *sel.;* BoTP, *sel.;* FaPON, *sel.;* GFA, *sel.;* IAP; MPB, *sel.;* OHFP, *sel.;* PECK, *sel.;* PoRh, *sel.;* RAR, *sel.;* RIS *abr.;* ShBV-1, *sel.;* StVeCh, *sel.;* TiPo, *sel.;* TreF, *sel.;* TVSH, *sel.;* WBLP, *sel.*
Hiawatha's Departure. Longfellow. The Song of Hiawatha, XXII. IAP
Hiawatha's Mittens. *Unknown.* ShBV-1
Hiawatha's Photographing. "Lewis Carroll." CenHV; FiBHP
Hiawatha's Sailing. Longfellow. The Song of Hiawatha, VII. BBV; IAP; PCH, *sel.;* TVSH
(Hiawatha's Canoe.) OHIP, *sel.;* StVeCh (1940 ed.), *abr.*
Hiawatha's Wedding-Feast. Longfellow. *Fr.* The Song of Hiawatha, XI. PEOR
Hiawatha's Wooing. Longfellow. The Song of Hiawatha, X. BeLS; IAP; TreFS
Hibernalia. Jessica Nelson North. NP
Hibiscus on the Sleeping Shores. Wallace Stevens. NP
Hibiscus was red. Red. Charles Ould. MM
Hiboux, Les. Baudelaire. AWP; JAWP; WBP
Hic, Hoc, the Carrion Crow. *Unknown.* OxBoLi
Hic Jacet. Louise Chandler Moulton. AA; AnAmPo; AnFE; APA; CoAnAm; LA; LBAP; LEAP; OBAV
Hic Jacet. *Unknown, at. to* George Macdonald. *See* Epitaph: "Here lie I, Martin Elginbrodde."
"Hic Me, Pater Optime, Fessam Deseris," Lucy Catlin Robinson. AA
"Hic Vir, Hic Est." Charles Stuart Calverley. OxBoLi
Hiccup, sniccup. *Unknown.* RIS
Hick-a-more, hack-a-more. Mother Goose. BoChLi; OxNR; TiPo (1952 ed.)
Hickety, pickety, i-silicity. *Unknown.* OxNR
Hickety, pickety, my black hen. *See* Higgledy, piggledy . . .
Hickok rests by Calamity Jane. Lay of the Last Frontier. Harold Hersey. PoOW
Hickory, dickory, dock. Mother Goose. BoChLi; FaBoBe; FaFP; HBV; HBVY; OTPC; OxNR; PCH; PPL; RIS; SAS; SiTL; StVeCh (1940 ed.); TiPo
Hid by the august foliage and fruit. To a Chameleon. Marianne Moore. GoYe
Hid in a maze of quaintly-fashioned things. A Wedgwood Bowl. Frances Beatrice Taylor. CaP; OCL
Hidden. ffrida Wolfe. TVC; TVSH
Hidden Fires. *Unknown, tr. fr. Japanese by* Basil Hall Chamberlain. OnPM
Hidden Flame, The. Dryden. *See* Song: "I feed a flame within . . ."
Hidden Flower, The. Henry Vaughan. *See* I Walked the Other Day.
Hidden Joys. Laman Blanchard. VA
Hidden Line, The. Joseph Addison Alexander. BLPA; NeHB
Doomed Man, The, *2 sts.* MaRV

Hidden Love, The. Arthur Hugh Clough. *See* O Let Me Love My Love unto Myself Alone.
Hidden lovers' woes. His Own True Wife. Wolfram von Eschenbach. AWP; JAWP; WBP; WoL
Hidden Mermaids, The. Walter de la Mare. OTPC
Hidden no longer. St. Valentine's Day. Theophilus Hunter Hill. NoCaPo
Hidden Rose-Tree, A. Marguerite A. Power. TIP
Hidden senses of the universe. Manuel Altolaguirre, *tr. fr. Spanish by* Eleanor L. Turnbull. CoSP
Hidden Sorrow, The. Georgios Vizinos, *tr. fr. Modern Greek by* Rae Dalven. MoGP
Hidden strength, A. Chastity. Milton. *Fr.* Comus. OBS
Hidden Tide, The. Roderic Quinn. BoAu
Hidden Truth, The. Jami, *tr. fr. Persian.* LiTW, *tr. by* E. H. Whinfield; OnPM, *tr. by* F. Hadland Davis
Hidden Weaver, The. Odell Shepard. WGRP
Hidden Years [at Nazareth], The. Allen Eastman Cross. BPP; ChIP
Hide and Seek. "Robin Christopher." RIS; StaSt
Hide and Seek. Phyllis Drayson. BoTP
Hide and Seek. Sister Mary Philip. PraNu
Hide from me all lovely things. All Lovely Things. Richard Aldington. NeMA
Hide, happy damask, from the stars. Serenade. Henry Timrod. HBV; PR
Hide in the Heart. Lloyd Frankenberg. AnFE; CoAnAm; LiTA; TwAmPo
Hide not, hide not. The Rousing Canoe Song. Hermia Harris Fraser. BoCaPo; CaP
Hide, Oh, Hide Those Hills. John Fletcher, *and others. Fr.* The Bloody Brother, V, ii. ViBoPo
Hide of a leopard and hide of a deer. The Giraffe. Geoffrey Dearmer. AlDL
Hide of My Mother, The. Edward Dorn. NeAP
Hide this one night thy crescent, kindly Moon. To the Moon. Pierre de Ronsard. *Fr.* Amours de Marie. AWP; PrPoCR
Hiding. Dorothy Aldis. BoChLi; FaPON; MPB; RIS; SUS; TiPo
Hiding the Skeleton. George Meredith. *See* Modern Love: "At dinner she is hostess, I am host."
Hiding tuft, a green-barked yew-tree, A. The Hermit's Song. *Unknown.* KiLC
Hie Away! Sir Walter Scott. *Fr.* Waverley, *ch.* 12. BoTP; MoShBr; MPB; OTPC; PCD; PCH; PRWS; RAR; ViBoPo
(Gellatley's Song to the Deerhounds.) AlDL; OBRV
(Hie Away, Hie Away.) BPN; EmBrPo; EnRP; EV-4; TiPo
Hie, hie, says Anthony. Mother Goose. OxNR; RIS
Hie sits oor king in Dumfermline. Sir Patrick Spens (C *vers.*) *Unknown.* BaBo
Hie to the market, Jenny come trot. *Unknown.* OxNR
Hie upon Hielands [*or* High upon Highlands]. Bonnie [*or* Bonny] George [*or* James] Campbell [*or* Ballad]. *Unknown.* AWP; BaBo (B *vers.*); BEL; BLV; BoLiVe; BSV; CBOV; CH; EBSV; EnLit; EnRP; ERP; ESPB; GoTS; HBV; InPo; OBB; OxBoLi; PCD; TCEP; ViBoPo
Hiems. Shakespeare. *See* When Icicles Hang by the Wall.
Hierarchie of the Blessed Angels, *sels.* Thomas Heywood.
Search for God, The ("I asked myself . . ."), 1 *st.* QS
Search for God, The ("I sought Thee . . ."), *abr.* MaRV; OxBoCh
("I sought Thee round about, O Thou my God.") WGRP
Hierusalem, My Happy Home. *Unknown. See* New Jerusalem, The.
Higgledy-piggledy here we lie. *Unknown.* OxNR
Higgledy, piggledy [*or* Higgleby, piggleby *or* Hickety, pickety], my black [*or* fat] hen. Mother Goose. BoChLi; BoTP; FaBoBe; HBV; OTPC; OxNR; PCH; RIS; StVeCh; TiPo
Higgledy, piggledy! see how they run! Kate Greenaway. TiPo
Higglety, Pigglety, Pop! Samuel Goodrich. LiL; OxNR
(Nonsense!) BoN
High/ Up/ Over the top. The Grasshoppers. Dorothy Aldis. UTS
High above all a cloth of state was spred. The House of Pride. Spenser. *Fr.* The Faerie Queene, I, 4. WHA
High above hate I dwell. Sanctuary. Louise Imogen Guiney. AA
High adventure/ And bright dream. Maps. Dorothy Brown Thompson. BrR; TiPo
High among the lonely hills. Guta's Song. Charles Kingsley. *Fr.* The Saint's Tragedy, II, ii. ReTS
High and General Cause, The. George Chapman. *Fr.* The Revenge of Bussy d'Ambois. EV-1
("Good sir, believe that no particular torture.") NBE
High and inscrutable the old man stood. The Death of Haidee. Byron. *Fr.* Don Juan, IV. WHA
High and Low. James H. Cousins. HBMV; OnYI; OxBI
High and Low. Dora Read Goodale. PRWS
High and Low. John Banister Tabb. BrR
High and low, wise and simple, all busily hoard up the moments of life. Substance, Shadow, and Spirit. T'ao Ch'ien. Twelve Poems, 7. TrCh
High and mighty lord of Glendare, The. The Cricket's Story. Emma Huntington Nason. HBV; HBVY
High and proud on the barnyard fence. Chanticleer. John Farrar. GFA; PCH; TiPo; UTS
High and solemn mountains guard Rioupéroux. Rioupéroux. James Elroy Flecker. OBEV (new ed.); OBVV
High at the window in her cage. A Caged Bird. Sarah Orne Jewett. BLA; SN
High Barbaree, The. Laura E. Richards. CIV; SUS
High Barbaree, The, *with music. Unknown.* AmSS; OuSiCo; SoAmSa; ViBoFo
(High Barbary.) BaBo
High bare field, A, brown from the plough. The Potato Harvest. Sir Charles G. D. Roberts. CaP; OCL
High-born child, your brothers twain. Family Tree. Ibn al-Quaffun. MooP
High-born Helen, round your dwelling. Helen. Mary Lamb. OBRV
High Chin Bob. *Unknown.* SCC
High Country Weather. James K. Baxter. AnNZ
High diddle diddle. *See* Hey diddle diddle.
High diddle ding, did you hear the bells ring? *Unknown.* OxNR
High Dive. William Empson. AtBAP
High Diver. Robert Francis. NePoAm
High Flight. John Gillespie Magee, Jr. BBV (1951 ed.); FaFP; FaPON; MaC; MaRV; NeTW; PGD; POTE; PreP; QS; TreFS; TwCV; WaKn
High Germany. Edward Shanks. OBMV
High Germany. *Unknown.* WaaP
High grace, the dower of queens. Her Gifts. Dante Gabriel Rossetti. The House of Life, XXXI. BPN; EmBrPo; HBV; PoVP; VA; ViPo
High grew the snow beneath the low-hung sky. The Axe [*or* The Axe of the Pioneer]. Isabella Valency Crawford. CaP; OCL; VA
High Hill, The. Clinton Scollard. MaRV
High hills that meet, and one beyond still higher. Hills Take Command. Anne Hopkins. CAG
High hopes that burned like stars-sublime. To-Day and To-Morrow. Gerald Massey. BMEP
High in the afternoon the dove. Kendrick Smithyman. *Fr.* Considerations of Norfolk Island. AnNZ
High in the air. Wishes. Semyon Kirsanov. RuPo
High in the breathless hall the minstrel sate. Song at the Feast of Brougham Castle. Wordsworth. EmBrPo; EnRP; ERP; GEPC
High in the dark the moon rides white. Serenade. Paul Fearon. CIV
High in the heavens a single star. The Christmas Star. Nancy Byrd Turner. MaRV
High in the heaven's azure hemisphere. The Kingis Quair. James I, King of Scotland. MeEV
High in the mountains. Song of the Hawk. Maxim Gorki. BoRS
High in the noon's bright bowl of blue. Feather. Lew Sarett. NP
High in the organ-loft with lilied hair. Epithalamium. Sir Edmund Gosse. OBVV
High in the pine-tree. The Turtle-Dove's Nest. *Unknown.* BoTP; HBVY; OTPC (1923 ed.); SAS
High in [*or* on] the top of an old pine-tree. The Little Doves. *Unknown.* PPL; SAS
High is our calling, friend! To B. R. Haydon. Wordsworth. BPN; EM-2; EmBrPo
High June. Catherine A. Morin. BoTP
High-lying, sea-blown stretches of green turf. The Beds of Fleur-de-Lys. Charlotte Perkins Gilman. AA
High Mass/ Under the new/ Bronze baldachino. September 17. Sister M. Margaret Patricia. SaFP
High Midnight was garlanding her head, The. Moonlight. Jacques Tahureau. AWP
High Mind, The. Samuel Daniel. *See* To the Lady Margaret, Countess of Cumberland.
High noon,/ And from the purple-veiled hills. High Noon at Midsummer on the Campagna. "Fiona Macleod." PoVP
High noon;/ And on the clouds above. Shiki, *tr. fr. Japanese by* Lois J. Erickson. SoLD
High Noon at Midsummer on the Campagna. "Fiona Macleod." PoVP
High noon draws near, the hour is meet. A Road to Firenze. Agnes Kendrick Gray. TBM
High Noon; Galveston Beach. Stanley E. Babb. HiLiAm
High o'er his moldering castle walls. A Voice from the Invisible World. Goethe. AWP; JAWP; WBP
High o'er the black-backed Skerries, and far. The Light-House. *Unknown.* PEOR
High o'er the dales with their verdant pride. Norway's Highlands. Johan Sebastian Cammermeyer Welhaven. AnNoLy

High o'er the Poop the Audacious Seas Aspire. William Falconer. EtS
High on a banyan tree in a row. Monkey. William Jay Smith. TiPo (1959 ed.)
High on a bright and sunny bed. The Poppy. Jane Taylor. OTPC; TVC; TVSH
High on a gorgeous seat, that far out-shone. Pope. *Fr.* The Dunciad, II. AtBAP
High on a leaf-carv'd ancient oaken chair. The Old Baron. Thomas Miller. VA
High on a pole, he labors in the sky. Lineman. Gerald Raftery. PoMa
High on a Ridge of Tiles. Maurice James Craig. PoC
(Poem: "High on a ridge of tiles.") NeIP
High on a shelf we keep the books you had. For a Child Who Died. Joseph G. E. Hopkins. JKCP (1955 ed.)
High on a throne of royal state, which far. Milton. *Fr.* Paradise Lost, II. AtBAP; CoBE; EnL; EnLi-1; EnLit; REAL; SeEP; TCEP
High on the bold, gray granite shelf. The Stationed Scout. Lyman H. Sproull. PoOW
High on the dove-cot. Doves. E. J. Falconer. BoTP
High on the Mountain of Sunrise where standeth the Temple of Sebek. He Knoweth the Souls of the West. *Unknown. Fr.* Book of the Dead. AWP; JAWP; WBP
High on the rim edge of the Argentine. Christ in the Andes. Carl John Bostelmann. ChIP
High on the top of an old pine-tree. *See* High in the top . . .
High on the top of Ararat alone. Noah. Roy Campbell. *Fr.* The Flaming Terrapin. BoSA
High on the world did our fathers of old. Under the Stars and Stripes. Madison Cawein. FOAH
High on this point of rock, this mighty needle. Paul Engle. *Fr.* The Troubadour of Eze. PoeMoYo
High over us belated clouds are flying. May Night. Afanasi Afanasievich Fet. WaL
High, pale, imperial places of slow cloud. Upper Air. Frank Ernest Hill. AnAmPo; LA; MAP; MoAmPo (1942 ed.)
High Place, A. Eithne Wilkins. NeBP
High poplars, with their stealthy rustling leaves. Landscape. Henri de Régnier. TrFP
High Prairie neighborhood could not afford. Salary. Billy B. Cooper. DDA
High Priest, The. *Unknown, tr. fr. Hebrew by* Arthur Davis. TrJP
High Priz'd Harlot, The. *Unknown. See* Penurious Quaker, The.
"High Prophetess," said I, "purge off." Keats. *Fr.* The Fall of Hyperion. CoEV
High Resolve. *Unknown.* PoToHe
High rises the Eastern Peak. Climbing a Mountain. Tao-yün. TrCh
High Road, The. *Unknown.* BPP
High Road, The. *Unknown, tr. fr. Chinese.* WhP
High Sailboat, The. Salvatore Quasimodo, *tr. fr. Italian by* Creighton Gilbert. LiTW
High seriousness is not for seventeen years. Novel. Arthur Rimbaud. TrFP
High sheriff tol' de deputy, "Go out an' bring me Laz'us." Po' Laz'us. *Unknown.* ABF
High Song, The. Humbert Wolfe. *Fr.* Requiem. MM; ReTS; TCPD
High Spanish galleons, carven, silken-sailed. Ships. Margaret Barrington. MW
High-spirited friend. An Ode [*or* True Balm *or* Noble Balm]. Ben Jonson. EV-2; LH; OBEV
High steward of thy vines. John Day. *Fr.* The Parliament of Bees. ViBoPo
High stretched upon the swinging yard. Disguises. Thomas Edward Brown. MBP; WGRP
High Summer. Shuzo Hishiyama, *tr. fr. Japanese by* Takamichi Ninomiya *and* D. J. Enright. PoLJ
High sun, having halted, The. Canticle of Saint John. Stéphane Mallarmé. TrFP
High the vanes of Shrewsbury gleam. The Welsh Marches. A. E. Housman. A Shropshire Lad, XXVIII. FaBoTw; POTT; PoVP; TCPD; ViPo; VLEP
High thoughts and noble in all lands. The Human Touch. Richard Burton. BLP; BLPA; LBAP; OQP; QP-2
High Tide, The. Jean Ingelow. *See* High Tide on the Coast of Lincolnshire, The.
High Tide. Jean Starr Untermeyer. MAP; MCCG; MoAmPo; NeMA; TSW; TSWC
High Tide at Gettysburg, The. Will Henry Thompson. AA; BeLS; BlG; BLPA; FaBoBe; HBV; LBAP; LEAP; MC; MDAH; PaA; PAH; PFY; PoFr; TreFS
Fold the Banners, *sel.* BoHiPo
High Tide on the Coast of Lincolnshire, The (1571). Jean Ingelow. BeLS; BMEP; EV-5; GBV; GN; GTBS; GTBS-D; GTSL; HBV; LPS-1; OBVV; OtMeF; PIR; ShBV-3; TOP; VA
(Brides of Enderby, The; or, The High Tide.) PECK
(High Tide, The.) PTA-2
High-toned Old Christian Woman, A. Wallace Stevens. CoBMV; CoV; MoVE; PoFS
High towered the palace and its massive pile. Palace of the Gnomes. Maria Gowen Brooks. *Fr.* Zophiel. AA; BAP
High trees grieve like the sea's water, The. In Wicklow. Rhoda Coghill. NeIP
High up among the mountains, through a lovely grove of cedars. Bears. Arthur Guiterman. PoRA
High up are the angels with best quality wings. Cosmogony. David Daiches. LiTM
High up in the courts of Heaven to-day. The Little Dog-Angel. Norah M. Holland. CPG
High up on the lonely mountains. A Night with a Wolf. Bayard Taylor. GoTP
High up on the mountain the wind bloweth wild. *Unknown.* BOL
High up the mountain-meadow, Echo with never a tongue. The Voice of the Hills. Satyrus. GrPE
High upon Highlands. *See* Hie upon Hielands.
High upon the gallows tree swung the noble-hearted three. God Save Ireland. Timothy Daniel Sullivan. OnYI
High upon the hillside where the shadows play. Skippets, the Bad One. Christine E. Bradley. BoTP
High walls and huge the body may confine. Freedom for the Mind [*or* Sonnet Written While in Prison . . .]. William Lloyd Garrison. AA; FaBoBe; LPS-2
High Way and a Low, A. John Oxenham. *See* Ways, The.
High Wind, The. *Unknown. See* Wind, The.
High wisdom holds my wisdom less. In Memoriam A. H. H., CXII. Tennyson. EmBrPo; EPN; GEPC; ViPo; VLEP
High with the clouds migrating birds forgather. Old Age. Joseph von Eichendorff. AnGP
High-yellow of my heart, with breasts like tangerines. The Peasant Declares His Love. Emile Roumer. AnCL; LiTW; PoNe
Highbridge, *with music. Unknown.* AS
Higher ("The shadows of night were a-comin' down swift"). *Unknown.* FiBHP; PA
Higher and a solemn voice, A. Francis Thompson. *Fr.* From the Night of Forebeing. VLEP
Higher Catechism, The. Sam Walter Foss. WGRP
Sels.
"And what is faith? OQP; QP-1
Nature and Religion. OQP; QP-2
True Bible, The. BPP
Higher Command, The. Sophocles. *See* State versus Conscience, The.
Higher Courage, The. Arthur Hugh Clough. VLEP
Higher Good, The. Theodore Parker. AA; FaBoBe; HBV; MaRV
(New Year Prayer, A.) PGD; PSO
Higher Kinship, The. Wilfred Campbell. OCL
Higher Loyalty, The. Shakespeare, *and probably* John Fletcher. King Henry VIII, *fr.* III, ii. MaRV
(Ambition, *abr.*) TrGrPo
Higher Pantheism, The. Tennyson. BEL; BMEP; BPN; EM-2; EmBrPo; EnLi-2; EPN; EPP; GrCo-1; HBV; MaRV; PoVP; ViPo; ViPP; VLEP; WGRP
Higher Pantheism in a Nutshell, The, *parody.* Swinburne. *Fr.* The Heptalogia. ALV; BOHV; EmBrPo; HBV; NA; PA; PoVP; SiTL; ViP; ViPo; ViPP; VLEP
Higher than a house, higher than a tree. Mother Goose. OxNR; PPL; TiPo
Higher than hate, and the abused. Above the Battle. Mark Van Doren. MOAP
Higher than heaven they sit. The Hope of the World. Sir William Watson. WGRP
Higher than the slim eucalyptus. A Song for My Mate. Marguerite Wilkinson. AV
Higher that the cedar tree under the heavens do grow, The. Of the Mean Estate. Thomas, Lord Vaux. SiCE
Highest apple swinging in the treetop, The. To Sappho, about Her Apple. Aline Kilmer. BAP; LEAP
Highest Divinity. *Unknown, tr. fr. Hebrew by* Israel Zangwill. TrJP
Highest form of goodness is like water, The. Tao Teh Ching, XIV. *Unknown, tr. fr. Chinese.* WhP
Highest Fruit, The. Sappho, *tr. fr. Greek by* Ralph Marcus. OnPM
Highest of Immortals bright. Indra, the Supreme God. *Unknown. Fr.* The Rigveda. AWP
Highest Wisdom, The. Jacopone da Todi, *tr. fr. Italian by* Mrs. Theodore Beck. CAW
Highland Balou, The. Burns. BOL
Highland Call, The, *sel.* Paul Green.
Hymn to Democracy, A. NoCaPo
Highland Cattle, *sel.* Dinah Maria Mulock Craik.
"Down the wintry mountain." GN; OTPC
Highland Croon, A. *Unknown.* BOL
("Hush-a-ba, birdie, croon, croon.") OxNR
Highland Laddie, *with music. Unknown.* ShS; SoAmSa
Highland Mary. Burns. AEV; AnFE; ATP (1935 ed.); AWP; BCEP; BEL; BoLiVe; BTP; CaAE; CEP;

Highland Mary (*continued*)
EBSV; EiPP; EM-1; EnLi-2; EnLit; EnRP; EPP; EV-3; GTBS; GTBS-D; GTBS-W; GTSE; GTSL; HBV; InP; InPo; JAWP; LEAP; OAEP; OBEC; OBEV; OuHeWo; PTA-2; PYM; TCEP; TOP; TreFS; TrGrPo; TyEnPo; ViBoPo; WBLP; WBP
Highland Tinker, The. *Unknown.* CoMu
Highlandmen hae a' come down, The. The Lady of Arngosk. *Unknown.* ESPB
Highlands of Hudson! ye saw them pass. The Storming of Stony Point. Arthur Guiterman. MC; PAH
Highlands' Swelling Blue, The. Byron. *Fr.* The Island. OBRV
Highly Educated Man, The, *with music.* *Unknown.* ABF
Highmindedness, a jealousy for good. Addressed to Haydon. Keats. EmBrPo
Highroad's barren scar, A. Autumn Dawn. Antonio Machado. TeCS
Highway, The. Ai Ching, *tr. fr. Chinese.* WhP
Highway, The. Manuel Bandeira, *tr. fr. Portuguese by* Dudley Poore. AnCL
Highway, The. Louise Driscoll. HBV
Highway, The. William Channing Gannett. WGRP
Highway since you my chief Parnassus be. Astrophel and Stella, LXXXIV. Sir Philip Sidney. CaAE; ElL; ES; EV-1; GTBS-W; GTSL; LiTB; LiTG; OAEP; OBEV; OBSC; ReEn; SiPS
Highwayman, The. Alfred Noyes. ATP; BBV; BEL; BeLS; BMEP; ChMo; CMP; CP; CV; EnLit; FaFP; FaPON; GoTP; GTSL; HBV; HBVY; HiLiEn; InP; LBBV; LoEn; MaC; MCCG; MW; OHFP; OnSP; PCD; PFE; PoeMoYo; PoMa; POT; PoTo; PYM; ShBV-2; TCEP; TOP; TreFS; TSW; TSWC; TwCV; YT
Highwayman's Ghost, The. Richard Garnett. DaM; StPo
Highways. Leslie Nelson Jennings. NLK
Highways and Byways. John Vanderbilt. PCD
Highways and the byways, The, the kind sky folding all. Wanderlust. Isabel Ecclestone Mackay. NLK
Highways run in figure of the rood, The. November. Emile Verhaeren. WoL
Highty, tighty, paradighty, clothed in green. Riddle. *Unknown.* ChTr; OxNR
Hilas, o Hilas, why sit we mute. *See* Hylas, O Hylas! why sit we mute.
Hilda and Sophie and Belle-Marie. The Three Princesses. Cecilia MacKinnon. CPG
Hildebrand. Hilaire Belloc. BoN
Hildina. *Unknown, tr. fr. Norse by* N. Kershaw. PaOS
Hill, The. Rupert Brooke. CBOV; EnLit; GTML; GTSL; HBV; LEAP; LiTL; LoPo; LoPS; MBP; MoBrPo; POTE; POTT; ViBoPo
Hill, The. Horace Holley. WGRP
Hill, The. Edgar Lee Masters. *Fr.* Spoon River Anthology. AmP; ExPo; LiTA; LiTM; NePA; NP; OxBA; ReMP; SeCeV; ViBoPo
Hill above the Mine, The. Malcolm Cowley. NAMP
Hill and Dell. William Barnes. EnSW
Hill-born, The. Struthers Burt. MaRV; PC
Hill-born. W. W. Gibson. NP
Hill cedars and piñons, The. In the Desert. Alice Corbin. NP
Hill Farmer Speaks, The. R. S. Thomas. HaMV
Hill flank overlooking the Axe valley, A. Watching Post. C. Day Lewis. AlDL
Hill full, a hole full, A. Mother Goose. TiPo
Hill Hunger. Joseph Auslander. NLK; VOD
Hill in Picardy, A. Clinton Scollard. VOD (1931 ed.)
Hill of Intrusion, The. W. S. Graham. NePoEA
Hill people turn to their hills. The Heart's Country. Florence Wilkinson Evans. AV; LBMV
Hill Pines Were Sighing, The. Robert Bridges. EG; ExPo; OAEP; PoeT; POTT
Hill Song, A. Helen Merrill Egerton. CPG
Hill Summit, The. Dante Gabriel Rossetti. The House of Life, LXX. BPN; CaAE; EmBrPo; PoVP; REAL; TCEP; ViPo
Hill Top. *See* Hilltop.
Hill was flowing with sheep, The. Pastoral. Marion Strobel. NP
Hill Wife, The. Robert Frost. AmPo; ChMo; CMP; IAP; MOAP; NP; TwP
Sels.
House Fear. BAP; SBMV
Impulse, The. AWP; LiTM; LO; NePA; SBMV
Loneliness. BAP; FaBoEn; SBMV
Oft-repeated Dream, The. PG (1945 ed.); SBMV
Hill-Woman, A. John Farrar. OnPP; TBM
Hillcrest. E. A. Robinson. CoBMV; CoV; FaBoEn; MoAB; MOAP; OxBA
Hillocks of Mortality. Thomas Flatman. *Fr.* A Dooms-Day Thought. BeR
Hilloo, hilloo, hilloo, hilloo! Snowshoeing Song. Arthur Weir. POT; PoTo; VA
Hills. Guillaume Apollinaire, *tr. fr. French by* Dudley Fitts. AnFP
Hills, The. Berton Braley. MCCG; POT; PoTo
Hills. Hilda Conkling. GBV; PCH; StaSt; StVeCh
Hills, The. Frances Cornford. MBP; MoBrPo; TwCV
Hills, The. Rachel Field. GFA
Hills, The. Theodosia Garrison. NLK
Hills. Arthur Guiterman. BAP; HBVY; MaRV; NLK; PoeMoYo; PoMa; POT; PoTo; VOD; YT
Hills and rivers of the lowland country, The. A Protest in the Sixth Year of Ch'ien Fu (A.D. 879). Ts'ao Sung. LiTW; MoPW; OnPM; PoFr; TrCh
Hills and the Sea, The. Wilfred Campbell. CaP; OCL
Hills and valleys where April rallies his radiant squadron of flowers and birds. On the South Coast. Swinburne. EmBrPo
Hills are bright with maples yet, The. Faded Leaves. Alice Cary. PEOR
Hills are calling me from care and reason, The. Bright Abandon. Tessa Sweazy Webb. GoYe
Hills are going somewhere, The. Hills. Hilda Conkling. GBV; PCH; StaSt; StVeCh
Hills are high in Caribou, The. The Yellow Witch of Caribou. Clyde Robertson. PoOW
Hills are Tipped with Sunshine, The. Christina Rossetti. PoVP
Hills are verdigris and sallow, The. Bi-focal. Hal Porter. BoAV
Hills are white, but not with snow, The. An Orchard at Avignon. Agnes Mary Frances Robinson. HBV
Hills are wroth, The; the stones have scored you bitterly. To a Young Girl Leaving the Hill Country. Arna Bontemps. CDC
Hills far-off were blue, blue, The. The Enchanted Sheep-Fold. Josephine Preston Peabody. AV; BAP; SBMV
Hills have vanished in dark air, The. The Forgotten. "Æ." ChMo; CMP
Hills Keep Holy Ground, The. Hellene Seaman. MaRV
Hills lie white and silent sleeping in the snow, The. Canadian Ski Song. Arthur S. Bourinot. CPG
Hills o' My Heart. "Ethna Carbery." HBV
Hills of autumn drop, The. Kakinomoto no Asomi Hitomaro, *tr. fr. Japanese by* I. W. Furukami. LiTW
Hills of Cualann, The. Joseph Campbell. AnIV
Hills of God, The. Takamoto. SoLD
Hills of Home. Witter Bynner. BAP; OBAV; SBMV
Hills of Pomeroy, The. Ewart Milne. NeIP
Hills of Rest, The. Albert Bigelow Paine. HBV; MaRV; OQP; POT; PoTo; QP-2; WGRP
Hills of Sewanee, The. George Marion McClellan. BANP
Hill's Summit, The. Dante Gabriel Rossetti. *See* Hill Summit, The.
Hills Take Command. Anne Hopkins. CAG
Hills that had been lone and lean, The. The Consecration of the Common Way. Edwin Markham. SDH; StJW
Hills, The, the Blue Hills, what say the Blue Hills? The Blue Hills. Philip Francis Little. GTIV
Hills turn hugely in their sleep, The. Prothalamion: Second Section. Robert Hillyer. MAP; MoAmPo
Hills Were Made for Freedom, The. William Goldsmith Brown. PoFr
Hills, wrapped in gray, standing along the west. Sundown. John Charles McNeill. NoCaPo
Hillside Farmer, A. John Farrar. HBMV
Hillside Pause. Catharine Morris Wright. GoYe
Hillside Thaw, A. Robert Frost. ExPo; IAP; TSW; TSWC
Hill-Side Tree. Maxwell Bodenheim. MAP; MAPA; MoAmPo (1942 ed.)
Hillsides were of rushing, silvered water, The. Gioconda. Thomas McGreevy. OnYI
Hill-Top, The. Clark Ashton Smith. MuM
Hill Top Songs. Sir Charles G. D. Roberts. CP; CPG
Hilltops. Leslie Savage Clark. ChIP
Him Arsinoa, his nurse. Orestes. Pindar. *Fr.* Pythian Odes. OxBG
Him I Follow. "Clemence Dane." *Fr.* Will Shakespeare. QS
Him I hold as happy as God in Heaven. The Beloved. Sappho. GrPE
Him not the golden fang of furious heaven. Sonnet XIV. Edna St. Vincent Millay. AtBAP
Him on his throne and glorious. The Fifth of May—Napoleon. Alessandro Manzoni. *Fr.* Ode. CAW
. . . Him the Almighty Power/ Hurl'd headlong flaming. Satan Defiant [*or* The Fallen Angels]. Milton. *Fr.* Paradise Lost, I. AnFE; FaBoEn; MyFE; WHA
Himself, *sel.* Edwin John Ellis.
"At Golgotha I stood alone." OBMV
Himself He Could Not Save. Antipater of Sidon, *tr. fr. Greek by* F. L. Lucas. GrPE
Himself is least afraid. The Poet. Mildred I. McNeal Sweeney. LBMV
Himself let no one spare nor flatter. The Glutton. La Fontaine. LiA

Himself, the sire of men, of gods the sire. Zeus Dances. Titanomachia. OxBG
Hind, The. Sir Thomas Wyatt, *after the Italian of* Petrarch. ES; OBSC; SeCeV; TrGrPo
(Sonnet: "Whoso list to hunt, I know where is an hind.") SiPS
(Who So List to Hount.) AtBAP; PoEL-1
(Whoso List to Hunt [I Know Where Is an Hind].) ElSeCe; InvP; MaPo; ReEn; RiBV; TuPP
Hind and the Panther, The, *sels.* Dryden.
"But, gratious God, how well dost thou provide," *fr.* I. TrPWD
(Church's Testimony, The.) ACP; CAW
(Confession of Faith.) UnPo (1st ed.)
(Conversion: "But, gracious God, how well dost thou provide.") PoLi
Church of England, The, *fr.* I. OBS
Conversion ("Be vengeance wholly left to pow'rs divine"), *fr.* III. ACP; CAW
(World Well Lost, The.) PoLi
(Worldly Vanity.) FiP
"Dame, said the Panther, times are mended well," II. PoEL-3
King James II, *fr.* III. ACP
"Milk-white Hind, immortal and unchanged, A," I. CEP; CoBE; EiPP; GEPC, *shorter sel.*; NBE, *br. sel.*; SeCV-2; SeEP
(Churches of Rome and of England, *much abr.*) ACP
"Of all the tyrannies of human kind," *fr.* I. PoFr
"One evening, while the cooler shade she sought," *fr.* I. PoEL-3
"One in herself not rent by schism, but sound," *fr.* II. SeEP
(Catholic Church, The.) OBS
Presbyterians, The, *fr.* I. OBS
Private Judgment Condemned, *fr.* I. OBS
(Prayer, A: "What weight of ancient witness can prevail.") FiP
"To this the Panther, with a scornfull smile," *fr.* III. SeCV-2; SeEP
Hind Etin. *Unknown.* BaBo (A *vers.*); ESPB (A *and* B *vers.*)
(Hynd Etin.) OBB
(Lady and the Dwarf-King, The, B *vers.*) BaBo
Hind Horn. *Unknown. See* Hynd Horn.
Hindoo died—a happy thing to do, A. Paradise; a Hindoo Legend. George Birdseye. BOHV; HBV
Hinds of Kerry, The. William S. Wabnitz. GoYe
Hindu Ascetic, The. Sir Alfred Comyn Lyall. Studies at Delhi. OBVV
Hindu Cradle Song. Sarojini Naidu. *See* Cradle Song: "From groves of spice."
Hinged in the brooding west a black sun hung. The Last Hour. Robert Ervin Howard. DaM
Hinklemedunk, Ohio. *Unknown.* DDA
Hinky Dinky [Parlee-Voo]. *Unknown. See* Mademoiselle from Armentières.
Hint from Herrick, A. Thomas Bailey Aldrich. HBV
Hint from Voiture. William Shenstone. EnLoPo
Hint o' Hairst, The. Charles Murray. EBSV
Hint to the Wise, A. Pringle Barret. HBVY; PCH
Hinted Wish, A. Martial, *tr. fr. Latin by* Samuel Johnson. AWP; JAWP; OuHeWo; WBP; LiTW, *tr. by* Francis Lewis
(Legacy, A, *tr. by* Samuel Johnson.) OnPM
Hints on Writing Verse. Jack Mitchell. *See* Ballad of the Sailor Ben.
Hinty, minty, cuty, corn. Counting-out Rhymes. *Unknown.* FaPON
Hinx, minx, the old witch winks. *Unknown.* OxNR
Hipe, The. Patrick MacGill. VOD
Hippety hop to the barber shop. Mother Goose. TiPo
Hippity Hop to Bed. Leroy F. Jackson. GFA; TiPo
Hippolytus, *sels.* Euripides, *tr. fr. Greek.*
Chorus: "Could I take me to some cavern for mine hiding," *tr. by* Gilbert Murray. ShBV-4
(Birds of God, The.) OxBG
(Escape.) GrR
(Longing.) PCD
(O For the Wings of a Dove.) AWP; JAWP; WBP
Eros: Deus Catholicus, *tr. by* F. W. Pember. GrR
Friendship's Servitude, *tr. by* Gilbert Murray. GrR
Henchman's Speech, The: "So we made our way," *tr. by* Gilbert Murray. ReTS
His Death, *tr. by* George Allen. OxBG
Leave-taking of Artemis, The, *tr. by* Gilbert Murray. GrR
"Love distills desire upon the eyes," *tr. by* David Grene. GrPo
No More, O My Spirit, *tr. by* Hilda Doolittle ("H. D."). AWP
Precarious Life of Man, *tr. by* F. W. Pember. GrR
Ride to Doom, The, *tr. by* Gilbert Murray. GrR
(Doom of Hippolytus, The, *tr. by* C. M. Bowra.) OxBG
Votary to His Goddess, A, *tr. by* F. W. Pember. GrR
(Garland, The, *tr. by* C. M. Bowra.) OxBG
"Would that I were under the cliffs, in the secret hiding-places of the rocks," *tr. by* David Grene. GrPo
Hippolytus Temporizes. Hilda Doolittle ("H. D."). MOAP
Hippopotamothalamion. John Hall Wheelock. FiBHP; NePoAm-2
Hippopotamus, The. Hilaire Belloc. FiBHP; CenHV; ShBV-2; UTS; WhC
("I shoot the Hippopotamus.") CenHV
Hippopotamus, The. Georgia Roberts Durston. GFA; TiPo; UTS
Hippopotamus, The. T. S. Eliot. AmPP; AnAmPo; AWP; ChMo; CMP; HoPM; LA; LiTB; LiTM (1946 ed.); MOAP; NAMP; OBMV; TwP
Hippopotamus, The. Oliver Herford. NA
Hippopotamus had a bride, A. Hippopotamothalamion. John Hall Wheelock. FiBHP; NePoAm-2
Hippopotamus is strong, The. Habits of the Hippopotamus. Arthur Guiterman. FiBHP; TiPo (1959 ed.)
Hips. Abu Hafs, *tr. fr. Arabic by* A. J. Arberry. MooP
Hiram Hover. Bayard Taylor. BOHV; PA
"Hiram, I think the sump is backing up." Mending Sump. Kenneth Koch. NeAP
Hiram Power's Greek Slave. Elizabeth Barrett Browning. BCEP
His Admonition to Greene's Companions. Gabriel Harvey. *Fr.* Greene's Memorial; or, Certain Funeral Sonnets. ReIE
His Ally. William Rose Benét. PC
(Last Ally, The.) PoeMoYo
His Answer to a Question. Robert Herrick. EPS; ReEn
His Anthology. Meleager, *tr. fr. Greek by* George Allen. OxBG
His Apology of His Good Father. Gabriel Harvey. *Fr.* Greene's Memorial; or, Certain Funeral Sonnets. ReIE
His Are the Thousand Sparkling Rills. Cecil Frances Alexander. GTIV; OxBI
His are the whitenesses of soul. A Friend. Lionel Johnson. HBV; JKCP; VLEP
His arm—a wonder and an admiration. The Wrestler. Stefan George. AnGP
His art is eccentricity, his aim. Pitcher. Robert Francis. NePoAm
His Ballad of Agincourt. Michael Drayton. *See* Agincourt.
His Banner over Me. Gerald Massey. HBV; VA; WGRP
His bark/ The daring mariner shall urge far o'er. Prophecy. Luigi Pulci. *Fr.* Il Morgante maggiore. BoHiPo; PAH
His Bedchamber. Oliver Goldsmith. RO
His bees went very far that night. Bees before Winter. Merrill Moore. RIS
His Birthday. May Riley Smith. SDH
His body doubled/ under the pack. On the Swag. R. A. K. Mason. AnNZ
His body lies interred within this mould. Epitaph on a Soldier. Cyril Tourneur. *Fr.* The Atheist's Tragedy. ElL; SiCE
His body lies upon the shore. Richard Somers. Barrett Eastman. AA
His Books. Robert Southey. *See* My Days among the Dead Are Past.
His boy had stolen some money from a booth. North Star. Zona Gale. BAP; LEAP
His bridle hung around the post. Horse. Elizabeth Madox Roberts. PoeMoYo; TiPo (1959 ed.); UTS
His broad-brimmed hat pushed back with careless air. Vaquero. Joaquin Miller. AA; BAP; PFY
His Camel. Alqamah, *tr. fr. Arabic by* Sir Charles Lyall. *Fr.* The Mufaddaliyat. AWP; JAWP; WBP
His car was worth a thousand pounds and more. One Poet Visits Another. W. H. Davies. FaBoTw
His cedar paddle, scented, red. The Lily Bed. Isabella Valancy Crawford. PeCV
His Charge to Julia at His Death. Robert Herrick. SeCV-1
His cheeks grow red from the candle heat. The Altar Boy. Leonard Feeney. WHL
His cherished woods are mute. The stream glides down. At Chappaqua. Joel Benton. AA
His Children. Hittan of Tayyi, *tr. fr. Arabic by* Sir Charles Lyall. *Fr.* Hamasah. AWP; JAWP; LiTW; WBP
(He Thinks of His Children.) FAOV
His chosen comrades thought at school. What Then? W. B. Yeats. ChMo; POTE
His Christmas Sled. James Whitcomb Riley. FAOV
His classic studies made a little puzzle. Don Juan's Education. Byron. *Fr.* Don Juan. WHA
His claw against the world, he prowls athwart. Othello: Tomcat. Laura Simmons. CIV; DDA
His collar is frayed, and his trousers unpressed. Shabby Old Dad. Anne Campbell. PoToHe (new ed.)
His Complaint against Love and Fortune. Nicholas Breton. ReIE
His Content in the Country. Robert Herrick. EnLit; EPS; SeCV-1; SeEP
His Country. Thomas Hardy. BoFr

His country cowered under the mailed fist. The Poltroon. Sarah N. Cleghorn. QS
His Creed. Robert Herrick. ElSeCe; SeCeV; TriL
His Cross. Marguerite Wilkinson. OQP; QP-1
His Death. Euripides, *tr. fr. Greek by* George Allen. *Fr.* Hippolytus. OxBG
His death began the day the stigmata. *Tr. by* Marion A. Habig. *Fr.* The Death of Saint Francis. SaFP
His Deaths. Haniel Long. BAP; LEAP; NP
His Defense against the Idle Critic. Michael Drayton. ReIE
His Delight. Meilir ap Gwalchmai, *tr. fr. Welsh by* H. Idris Bell. LiTW
His Desire. Robert Herrick. EV-2; OAEP
His Despair. Thomas Beaumont. SeCL
His Dog. Ethel M. Kelley. AlBD
His echoing axe the settler swung. The Settler. Alfred Billings Street. AA; BAP; FaBoBe; LPS-2; MC; PAH
His Ejaculation to God. Robert Herrick. SeCV-1
His Epitaph. Alcuin, *tr. fr. Latin by* Helen Waddell. TriL
His Epitaph. Tristan Corbière. *See* Epitaph; for Himself.
His Epitaph. John Gay. *See* My Own Epitaph.
His Epitaph. Stephen Hawes. *See* Epitaph: "O mortal folk, you may behold and see."
His Epitaph. Walter Savage Landor. *See* For an Epitaph at Fiesole.
His Epitaph. Frederick William Ophel. BoAu
His Epitaph. Sir Walter Ralegh. *See* Conclusion, The.
His Excellency, *sels.* W. S. Gilbert.
Played-out Humorist, The. BOHV
Practical Joker, The. BOHV
His Excellency General Washington. Phillis Wheatley. APW; PoNe; TCAP
His Excuse for Loving. Ben Jonson. *Fr.* A Celebration of Charis. PoEL-2; SeCV-1; SeEP; TuPP
His eye was stern and wild,—his cheek was pale and cold as clay. Fragment. *Unknown.* BOHV
His eyes are closed. They are closed. His eyes are closed. The Mummy. Vernon Watkins. MoPo; NeBP
His eyes are quickened so with grief. Lost Love. Robert Graves. AWP; CH; ChMP; FaBoCh; JAWP; LoGBV; MBP; MoAB; MoBrPo; POTE; WBP
His eyes grow hot, his words grow wild. The Wise Woman. Louis Untermeyer. ALV; HBMV; PR; TBM
His eyes said, "Come and buy me." From a Pet-Shop Window. Margaret E. Sangster. AlBD
His eyes saw all things in the symmetry. Coleridge. Aubrey Thomas De Vere. GoBC
His Face. Florence Earle Coates. GA; OHIP
His face? I know not whether it be fair. The Surgeon's Hands. Ida Norton Munson. OQP; QP-1
His Face Is Forever. *Unknown, tr. fr. Arabic by* Sir Edwin Arnold. OnPM
His face is smooth as sculptured faces are. Plastic Airman. Wrenne Jarman. DiM
His face is truly of the Roman mould. A Character. Charlotte Fiske Bates. AA
His face like parchment skin with many a scar. An Old Collier. Ken Etheridge. MoWP
His face was glad as dawn to me. Shule, Shule, Shule, Agrah! "Fiona Macleod." OBVV; PoVP
His face was the oddest that ever was seen. The Strange Man. *Unknown.* FaPON; MPB; OTPC (1946 ed.); StVeCh (1940 ed.)
His falchion flashed along the Nile. The Exile at Rest. John Pierpont. AA
His fame the mock of shallow wits. Epitaph. Sir Charles G. D. Roberts. MM
His Farewell to His Unkind and Unconstant Mistress. Francis Davison. ElL; OBSC
(Sweet, If You Like and Love Me Still.) ElSeCe
His Farewell to Sack. Robert Herrick. OAEP; SeCV-1
His father, once a sergeant, was poor and old and gray. Sven Duva. Johan Ludvig Runeberg. AnSL
His father was a whale. He and His Family. Laura E. Richards. DDA
His father's steel, piercing the wholesome fruit. King Honor's Eldest Son. Elinor Wylie. CoBA
His feet went here and there. The Going of His Feet. Harry Kemp. NLK; QS
His feet were shod with music and had wings. Milton. Lloyd Mifflin. AA
His First Love. Lizette Woodworth Reese. AV
His flaggy wings when forth he did display. The Dragon. Spenser. *Fr.* The Faerie Queene. SeCePo
His followers had fled like frightened sheep. The Crowning Wonder. John Oxenham. StJW
His footprints have failed us. Dead in the Sierras. Joaquin Miller. AA; BAP; LEAP; PFY
His form upon the ground reclined. The Condemned to Die. José de Espronceda. AnSpL-2
His fourscore years and five. Whittier. Margaret E. Sangster. AA; DD; GA
His friend the watchman was still awake. A Leave-taking. Arno Holz. AWP; JAWP; WBP
His friends he loved. His direst earthly foes. Sir William Watson. InP
His friends went off and left Him dead. The Resurrection. Jonathan Henderson Brooks. CDC; PoNe
His Further Resolution. *Unknown.* HBV
His Garments. Esther Lloyd Hagg. ChIP; PGD
His generous bearing was a new invention. W. H. Auden. *Fr.* In Time of War. ChMo
His Gift and Mine. Edith B. Gurley. BLRP
His glory, by whose might all things are moved. Paradise. Dante, *tr. by* Henry F. Cary. *Fr.* Divina Commedia. OuHeWo
His Glory Tell. Horatius Bonar. BePJ
His Golden Lock[e]s [Time Hath to Silver Turned]. George Peele. *Fr.* Polyhymnia. AtBAP; ElL; ElSeCe; EM-1; LoBV; PoE; ReEn; ReIE; TuPP; ViBoPo; WHA
(Farewell to Arms, A.) AnFE; CBOV; CoBE; CoEV; EG; EnLi-1; EPP; EV-1; HBV; LEAP; OBEV; PoRA
("My golden locks time hath to silver turned.") BrBE; CenL
(Old Knight, The.) ChTr; OBSC; TrGrPo
(Sonet, A.) FaBoEn; PoEL-2; SiCE
(Sonnet: "His golden locks . . .") CaAE
His Good Name Being Blemished, He Bewaileth. Edward de Vere, Earl of Oxford. ReIE
His gospel sounds in every wind that sings. Communion Hymn. William Gay. ChIP
His Grace. Ishii, *tr. fr. Japanese by* Lois J. Erickson. SoLD
His Grace! impossible! what dead! A Satirical [*or* Satyrical] Elegy on the Death of a Late Famous General. Swift. BeR; ExPo; HoPM; PoEL-3; SeCeV
His Grace of Marlborough, legends say. Tradition of Conquest. Sara Morgan Bryan Piatt. AA
His grace the Abbot and his servynge ladde. Of the Abbot and His Valet. Clément Marot. LiA
His grandmother. The Mother. Tsung Wan Sheng. PoHN
His Grange, or Private Wealth. Robert Herrick. EPS; OAEP; OTPC (1923 ed.); SeCV-1; SeEP
(His Grange, His Private Wealth.) EnLit
("Though clock/ To tell how night.") EG
His Great Love on High. Michelangelo. *See* On the Brink of Death.
His haire was blacke, and in small curls did twine. Christ's Victorie on Earth. Giles Fletcher. *Fr.* Christ's Victory and Triumph. SeCV-1
His hammer falls with rhythmic, Titan grace. The Riveter. Margaret E. Sangster. PEDC
His Hand Shall Cover Us. Isaac ben Samuel of Dampière, *tr. fr. Hebrew by* Nina Davis Salaman. TrJP
His Hands. John Richard Moreland. ChIP; DDA; MaRV; OQP; QP-1
His hands with earthly work are done. Earth to Earth. Phoebe Cary. TVSH
His harp, whereon was al his gle. *Unknown.* *Fr.* Sir Orfeo. AtBAP
His head split in four parts. Promenade. David Ignatow. TrJP
His hearing left him twenty years ago. Old Farmer Alone. Robert P. Tristram Coffin. PoTo
His heart, to me, was a place of palaces. I Have Been through the Gates. Charlotte Mew. AV; BLV; CBOV; GTML; MBP; MoAB; MoBrPo; TrGrPo; TwCV
His heart was light, and all the living day. Canadian Farmer. Genevieve Bartole. CaP
His Heart Was True to Poll. F. C. Burnand. HBV
(True to Poll.) BOHV
His Hirsute Suit. Frank Sidgwick. WhC
His holly hair, his berry eye are here. Nativity. W. R. Rodgers. NeBP
His home a speck in a vast universe. Microcosm. Bertram Dobell. OBVV
His home is on the heights; to him. The Poet. Edwin Markham. WGRP
His hooves kicked up the saffron dust. A Tartar Horse. Herbert S. Gorman. TBM
His hope undone, now raves the impious king. The Slaughter of the Innocents by Order of King Herod. Caelius Sedulius. *Fr.* Carmen Paschale [*or* Easter Song]. OnYI
His house is a haven where fingers dare. Heart Specialist. Elias Lieberman. ImOP
His Immortality. Thomas Hardy. ChMo; CMP
His Incomparable Lady. Earl of Surrey. *See* Praise of His Love, A.
His iron arm had spent its force. Death and General Putnam. Arthur Guiterman. DDA; OnSP; PoMS
His Is the Way. Thomas Curtis Clark. ChIP
His kiss is sweet, his word is kind. The Boatman of Kinsale. Thomas Osborne Davis. VA
His Lachrimae or Mirth, Turned to Mourning. Robert Herrick. SeCV-1; SeEP
His Lady of the Sonnets, *sels.* Robert Norwood. CPG
"Companion of the highroad, hail," III.
"I meet you in the mystery of the night," II.

His Lady's Cruelty. Sir Philip Sidney. *See* Astrophel and Stella: Sonnets, XXXI.
His Lady's Death. Pierre de Ronsard, *tr. fr. French by* Andrew Lang. *Fr.* Amours de Marie. AWP
("Twain that were foes, while Mary lived, are fled.") PrPoCR
His Lady's Eyes. Fulke Greville. *See* You Little Stars That Live in Skies.
His Lady's Hand. Sir Thomas Wyatt. *See* O Goodly Hand.
His Lady's Might. Philippe Desportes. *See* Those Eyes Which Set My Fancy on Afire.
His Lady's Tomb. Pierre de Ronsard, *tr. fr. French by* Andrew Lang. *Fr.* Amours de Marie. AWP; JAWP; WBP
("As in the gardens, all through May, the rose," *tr. by* Andrew Lang.) PrPoCR
(As When the Rose, *tr. by* Alan Conder.) TrFP
His lamp, his bow, and quiver laid aside. Cupid Turned Plowman. Moschus. AWP; OnPM
His landlocked dreams were rainbow-tides that ran. Old Voyager. Walter Blackstock. GoYe
His last days linger in that low attic. The Old Jockey. F. R. Higgins. AnIV; GTBS-D; OBMV; OxBI
His Last Sonnet. Keats. *See* Bright Star! Would I Were Steadfast As Thou Art.
His Last Week. Elinor Lennen. PGD
His Laureate. Joyce Kilmer. StJW
His laurels fresh from song and lay. Our Autocrat. Whittier. PEOR
His learning such, no author, old or new. Ben Jonson's Commonplace Book. Lucius Cary. LPS-3
His left hand held the lyre, and in his right. Music's Mastery. *Unknown. Fr.* Homeric Hymns. GrR
His Letanie, to the Holy Spirit. Robert Herrick. *See* His Litany to the Holy Spirit.
His life is in the body of the living. The Soul and Body of John Brown. Muriel Rukeyser. MoAmPo
His life was gentle, and the elements. The Perfect Tribute. Shakespeare. *Fr.* Julius Caesar, V, v. MaRV
His life was private; safely led, aloof. A Characterization. Sir Henry Taylor. VA
His light still shines in Bethlehem Town. In Bethlehem, Today. Madeleine Sweeny Miller. PSO
His Litany to the Holy Spirit. Robert Herrick. BCEP; EM-1; EnLi-1; EPS; EV-2; HBV; InPo; MaPo; OAEP; OxBoCh; PoE; SeCePo; SeCL; SeEP; TyEnPo; UnPo (1st ed.)
(His Letanie, to the Holy Spirit.) OBS; SeCV-1
(Holy Spirit, The.) LPS-2
(In the Hour of My Distress.) MaRV
(Litany to the Holy Spirit.) CoBE; EnLit; OBEV; PoFS; TriL
His little son of twelve years old Philippus here has laid. Dead Boy. Callimachus. OnPM
His Living Monument. Minna Irving. PGD
His locks are whitened with the snows of nigh a hundred years. Myles O'Hea. Charles J. Kickham. TIP
His locks were wild, and wild his eye. Taking Long Views. May Kendall. CenHV
His Lover's Triumphs. Thomas Campion. *See* When Thou Must Home.
His Love's Riches. Spenser. *See* Amoretti, XV.
His Lullaby. Robert Healy. BOL
His lustrous brow is fair to see. The Comely Warrior. Ibn Sa'id of Alcala la Real. MooP
His Majesty's Health. *Unknown, at. to* Jeremy Savile. *See* Song: "Here's a health unto His Majesty!"
His massive frame once held so proudly straight. Stricken. *Unknown.* BPP
His Metrical Vow; on the Death of King Charles I. James Graham. *See* Epitaph on King Charles I.
His mind dove down from the stars and curled in his head. Old Talk. Winfield Townley Scott. FiMAP
His Mistress. Earl of Rochester. *See* Mistress, The; a Song.
His most kind sister all his secrets knew. Repentance. George Chapman. *Fr.* Hero and Leander, Third Sestiad. OBSC
His mother dear, Cupid offended late. Astrophel and Stella, XVII. Sir Philip Sidney. SiPS
His Mother in Her Hood of Blue. Lizette Woodworth Reese. ISi; OHIP
His Mother-in-Law. Walter Parke. BOHV; FiBHP
His Mother's Joy. John White Chadwick. AA
His Mother's Service to Our Lady. Villon, *tr. fr. French by* Dante Gabriel Rossetti. AWP; CAW; ISi; LiTW; LyMA; MeRV
(Ballad: "Lady of Heaven, Regent of the earth," *tr. by* John Payne.) LiA
(Ballade That Villon Made at the Request of His Mother to Intercede with Our Lady, *tr. by* Alan Conder.) TrFP
(Prayer, Made in Ballat Form bi Villon for His Mither, The, *tr. into Scots by* Tom Scott.) PoN
His Mother's Song. *Unknown.* PTA-2
His murderers met. Their consciences were free. Easter Eve. James Branch Cabell. HBMV; MaRV
His naked skin clothed in the torrid mist. The Serf. Roy Campbell. BoSA; LiTB; LiTM; MoBrPo; NAMP; OBMV; ReMP; TrGrPo (1942 ed.)
His Name. Charles Poole Cleaves. OQP; QP-1
His Name. Dora Greenwell. ChIP
His name it is Pedro-Pablo-Ignacio-Juan-/ Francesco García y Gabaldon. A Feller I Know. Mary Austin. FaPON; GaP; MW
"His name shall be Wonderful." This Babe for whom. And His Name Shall Be Called Wonderful. Martha Snell Nicholson. BePJ
His name was Chance, Jack Chance, he said. Ballad of a Strange Thing. Phelps Putnam. MAP; MoAmPo (1942 ed.); MOAP; MoVE; OxBA; TCPD
His name, when uttered, thrills the world. Theodore Roosevelt. William W. Peavyhouse. HH
His name yields the richest perfume. Nothing to Wish or to Fear. John Newton. BePJ
His New Suit. Samuel Ellsworth Kiser. MDAH
His nose is short and scrubby. My Dog. Marchette Chute. FaPON; MoSiPe; TiPo
His overalls hung on the hook by his hat, and I noticed his pockets were bulging out fat. Treasures. *Unknown.* PoToHe (new ed.)
His Own Epitaph. Aeschylus. *See* Epitaph for Himself, An.
His Own Epitaph. John Gay. *See* My Own Epitaph.
His Own Epitaph. Naevius, *tr. fr. Latin by* Geoffrey Johnson. LaP
His Own Epitaph. Pacuvius, *tr. fr. Latin by* Geoffrey Johnson. LaP
His Own Epitaph. Sir Walter Ralegh. *See* Conclusion, The.
His Own True Wife. Wolfram von Eschenbach, *tr. fr. German by* Jethro Bithell. AWP; JAWP; WBP; WoL
His pads furring the scarp's rime. The Snow-Leopard. Randall Jarrell. MoPo
His Parting from Her. John Donne. Elegies, XII. OBS
"O Fortune, thou'rt not worth my least exclaim," *sel.* CoBE
His Parting with Mrs. Dorothy Kennedy, *sel.* Robert Herrick.
"Prithee (lest maids should censure thee)." MyFE
His Passion. George Conrad Pullman. ChIP
His Peace. William Alexander Percy. QS
His pedigree—from a Dogdom tree. The Extra at the House. Bud Cornish. AlBD
His Petition to Queen Anne of Denmark (1618). Sir Walter Ralegh. SiPS
His petticoats now George cast off. George and the Chimney-Sweeper. Adelaide O'Keeffe. OTPC (1923 ed.)
His Picture. John Donne. Elegies, V. MeLP; NBE; OBS; ReEn
(Elegie: His Picture.) FaBoEn; MePo
(Elegy V: His Picture.) SeEP
His Pilgrimage. Sir Walter Ralegh. *See* Passionate Man's Pilgrimage, The.
His Poetry His Pillar. Robert Herrick. CenL; CoEV; EM-1; EnL; EnLit; LoBV; MyFE, *abr.*; SeCL; SeEP
(His Poetrie His Pillar.) FaBoEn; OBS
("Only a little more.") EG
"His policy," do you say? Mr. Johnson's Policy of Reconstruction. Charles Graham Halpine. PAH
His Politics. Byron. *Fr.* Don Juan, IX. GEPC
His Prayer for Absolution. Robert Herrick. BCEP; ElSeCe; EM-1; EnL; EnLi-1 (1949 ed.); EPS; MaRV; MeRV; OxBoCh; ReEn; SeCV-1; TOP; TrPWD
His Prayer to Ben Jonson [*or* Johnson]. Robert Herrick. BLV; BoLiVe; ElSeCe; EM-1; EnL; EnLit; EPS; OAEP; OBS; OxBoLi; PtP; ReEn; SeCeV; SeCV-1; SeEP; TrGrPo; UnPo; WP
(Prayer to Ben Jonson.) AEV
His Presence Came like Sunrise. Ralph S. Cushman. *See* Secret, The.
His pride/ Had cast him out from Heaven. Satan. Milton. *Fr.* Paradise Lost, I. BLV; TrGrPo
His Promises. Martha Snell Nicholson. BePJ
His puissant sword unto his side. Hudibras' Sword and Dagger. Samuel Butler. *Fr.* Hudibras, Pt. I, 1. LPS-2
His Quest. Lewis Frank Tooker. AA
His radiant fingers so adorning. Dawn. George B. Logan, Jr. HBV
His Request to Julia. Robert Herrick. EM-1; EPS (1942 ed.); OBS; SeEP
His Return to London. Robert Herrick. EnLit; EPS; SeEP
His Reward. Sir Thomas Wyatt. *See* With Serving Still.
His Rise and Fall in the Four Last Years. *Unknown. See* Lord Chancellours Villanies Discovered, The
His Sailing from Julia. Robert Herrick. PoEL-3
His Saviour's Words Going to the Cross. Robert Herrick. StJW
His seat was by a window. So he dreamed. School. Winifred Welles. BAP; PoeMoYo; VOD

His sense of Dignity [or worth] is strong. My Pompous Friend. Lawrence Emerson Nelson. DDA; PoMa
His shadow monstrous on the palace wall. Oedipus. Thomas Blackburn. FaBoTw
His Shield. Marianne Moore. LiTM; NePA; TwAmPo
His shoulder did I hold. Any Saint. Francis Thompson. EmBrPo; MBP; MoBrPo
His sight from ever gazing through the bars. The Panther. Rainer Maria Rilke. LiTW
His skin is brilliant with the nimble flood. Lucius Apuleius. *Fr.* Eros and Psyche. LO
His softest feathers winter thither sent. The Snow. Joseph Beaumont. StJW
His Son. Callimachus. *See* Nicoteles.
His son of twelve, a father's hope most dear. Nicoteles. Callimachus. GrR
His songs were a little phrase. Of [or On] a Poet Patriot. Thomas MacDonagh. AnIV; CAW; HBMV; LBBV; MBP; OnYI; OxBI; PoFr; TSW
His soul extracted from the public sink. The Scurrilous Scribe. Philip Freneau. AA
His soul fared forth (as from the deep home-grove). Samuel Taylor Coleridge. Dante Gabriel Rossetti. Five English Poets, 3. BPN; EmBrPo; PoVP; PtP
His soul stretched tight across the skies. Preludes, IV. T. S. Eliot. AnAmPo; BAV; BoLiVe (1945 ed.); CoBA; InP; LA; LiTA; OBMV; ReMP; UnPo
His Majesty. Theron Brown. AA
His Majesty the Letter-Carrier. Emanuel Carnevali. AnAmPo; LA
His soul to god! on a battle-psalm! Albert Sidney Johnston. Francis Orrery Ticknor. PAH
His Sovereignty. Kalonymos ben Moses of Lucca, *tr. fr. Hebrew by* Nina Davis Salaman. TrJP
His speckled pastures dipped to meet the beach. Biography. Charles Bruce. CaP; PeCV
His spirit in smoke ascended to high heaven. The Lynching. Claude McKay. BANP
His spirit lives; he died and is alive. Alive for Evermore. Amos Niven Wilder. MaRV
His Statement of the Case. James Herbert Morse. AA
His stature was not very tall. The Description of Sir Geoffrey Chaucer. Robert Greene. *Fr.* Greene's Vision. AnFE; FaBoCh; LoGBV; OBSC
His tail is remarkably long. The Kangarooster. Kenyon Cox. *Fr.* Mixed Beasts. RIS; TiPo
His Task—and Ours. Dorothy Gould. PGD
His Tears to Thamasis. Robert Herrick. OAEP
His the pardon, ours the sin. It Is Finished. Horatius Bonar. BePJ
His Theme. Robert Herrick. *See* Argument of His Book, The.
His thought of it was like a button pressed. Going Home. Mark Van Doren. MOAP
His thoughts are so much higher than his state. A Lofty Mind. Thomas Lovell Beddoes. *Fr.* Fragments Intended for the Dramas. ERP
His Throne Is with the Outcast. James Russell Lowell. ChIP
His tongue was touched with sacred fire. Henry Ward Beecher. Charles Henry Phelps. AA
His Trees. Mark Van Doren. AnFE; CoAnAm; TwAmPo
His Triumph. Pedro Salinas, *tr. fr. Spanish by* Eleanor L. Turnbull. CoSP
His triumphs of a moment done. On the Departure of the British from Charleston. Philip Freneau. PAH
His unregarded grave here Piron has. Epitaph. Alexis Piron. PAH
His valour passed beyond the Andes. Sepulchral Inscription. Jorge Luis Borges. AnCL
His verse that soars on smooth, swift wing. A Poet. Daniel Henderson. PFE
His vigil was the stars; his eyes were bright. Nox Ignatiana. James J. Daly. CAW; JKCP
His voice runs before me; I follow, it flies. Cuckoo. Katharine Tynan. BLA; TVSH
His wage of rest at nightfall still. The Defenders. John Drinkwater. PoeT
His way in farming all men knew. At Marshfield. William Cleaver Wilkinson. *Fr.* Webster, an Ode. AA
His weary glance, from passing by the bars. The Panther. Rainer Maria Rilke. OnPM
His well shaped ears were chestnut brown and they. The Huckster's Horse. Julia Hurd Strong. GoYe
His whims are threads of starshine woven in a chain. Reason. Marjory E. Cole. CAG
His whole life through. By Candlelight. Jules Supervielle. MiFP
His Widow. Cale Young Rice. PR
His Wife and Daughters Come to the Exiled One. *Unknown, tr. fr. Spanish by* R. Selden Rose *and* Leonard Bacon. *Fr.* The Cid. TeCS
"His wife not dead a month—and there he sits." William Ellery Leonard. *Fr.* Two Lives, Pt. III. MOAP
His Wife's Wedding Ring. George Crabbe. *See* Marriage Ring, A.
His wild heart beats with painful sobs. The Scene of War; the Happy Warrior. Sir Herbert Read. TwCV
His Will. Kanda, *tr. fr. Japanese by* Lois J. Erickson. SoLD
His Will Be Done. Annie Johnson Flint. BLRP
His Will Is Our Peace. Dante, *tr. fr. Italian by* Wendell Phillips Stafford. *Fr.* Divina Commedia: Paradiso, III. GrCo-2
His Winding Sheet. Robert Herrick. AnFE; EM-1; EPS (1942 ed.); HBV; OBEV
His window is over the factory flume. Widow Brown's Christmas. John Townsend Trowbridge. BeLS
His Wisdom. Nicholas Breton. *Fr.* The Strange Fortunes of Two Excellent Princes. ALV; OBSC
(I Would Thou Wert Not Fair [or I Were Wise].) ElL; InvP
His Wish to God. Robert Herrick. OxBoCh
His words were magic and his heart was true. Uncle Ananias. E. A. Robinson. AnNE; BAV; BoLiVe (1945 ed.); IAP; LaNeLa; MaPo; MoAmPo (1950 ed.); NePA; PoeMoYo; TwP
His work all done, two of my soldiers more. The Escape from Cyclop. Homer. *Fr.* The Odyssey, IX. LiTW
His work is done; his toil is o'er. Faithful unto Death. Richard Handfield Titherington. GA; PAH
His work well done, the leader stepped aside. First Citizen. James Jeffrey Roche. PGD
His yoke-ox, growing feeble with age and years of ploughing. The Pensioned Ox. Addaeus. GrPE
His young bride stood beside his bed. Hang Up His Harp; He'll Wake No More! Eliza Cook. BMEP
His Youth. John Oxenham. StJW
"Hiss! Hiss!" said the Goose, "They've taken us three." Thanksgiving Philosophy. Charlotte W. Thurston. TOAH
Hist, hist, ye winds, ye whispering wavelets hist. Two Sonnet-Songs, I. Frank T. Marzials. VA
Hist, oh hist! Thomas Lovell Beddoes. EG
Hist! there's a stir in the brush. Richard Hovey. *Fr.* The Faun. ADAH
Hist? Through the corridor's echoes. Clinical. W. E. Henley. In Hospital, XI. TCEP
Historians say that in the ancient days. Jesus and the Sinner. Sadi. PeP
Historic be the survey of our kind. Society. George Meredith. EPN
Historic Time. Robert Eyres Landor. *Fr.* The Impious Feast, VIII. OBRV
Historical Incidents. Clarence Day. InMe
History. Laurence Binyon. POTE
History. Babette Deutsch. NeTW
History, *sel.* Emerson.
Informing Spirit, The. AWP; IAP; InPo; MOAP; WGRP
(History.) BBV (1951 ed.)
(No Great, No Small.) MaRV
History. Robert Fitzgerald. MoVE
History. "Paul Tanaquil." HBMV
History. Sir William Watson. BMEP
History A. John Williams. NePoAm-2
History among the Rocks. Robert Penn Warren. Kentucky Mountain Farm, III. MAP; MoAmPo; MoVE; SPP
History, and nature, too, repeat themselves, they say. Same Old Story. Harry B. Smith. BOHV
History Class. Robert Finch. TwCaPo
History Lesson. *Unknown.* RIS
("First William the Norman.") OxNR
History of a Life. "Barry Cornwall." LPS-3
History of a Literary Movement. Howard Nemerov. NePoEA
History of Communications and a Running Account, The. Pien Chih-lin, *tr. fr. Chinese by* Pien Chih-lin. LiTW
History of Education. David McCord. WhC
History of Honey, The. Nathalia Crane. PoTo
History of Horestes, The. John Pickering. *See* Horestes.
History of Joseph, The, *sel.* Elizabeth Rowe.
Egyptian Dead, The, *fr.* IV. BeR
History of King Richard II, *sel.* Nahum Tate.
Love's Delights. SeCL
History of Peace, A. Robert Graves. HBMV
History of Prince Edward Island, The. Larry Gorman. ShS
History of Sir Francis Drake, The, *sel.* Sir William Davenant.
Sir Francis Drake Reviv'd. SG
History of the Modern World. Stanton A. Coblentz. PGD
History of the U.S., The. Winifred Sackville Stoner. BLPA; TreF; YaD
Histrion. Ezra Pound. ChMo; CMP
Hit. W. W. Gibson. MCCG; NP; TCEP
(Battle: Hit.) HiLiEn
Hit at the Times, A. A. O. McGrew. PoOW
Hit wes upon a Scere-thorsday that ure loverd aros. Judas. *Unknown.* BaBo; ESPB; OBB; ViBoFo
Hitch up my buggy, saddle up my black mare. I'm a Stranger Here. *Unknown.* OuSiCo
Hitchen May-Day Song. *Unknown.* *See* Song of the Mayers.

Hither haste, and gently strew. Song. Thomas Lovell Beddoes. EG
Hither she comes; she comes to me; she lingers. George Meredith. *Fr.* Love in the Valley. EtPaEn
Hither, Sleep! A mother wants thee! An Invocation to Sleep. Josiah Gilbert Holland. BOL
Hither, Strephon, Chloe, Phyllis. A Woodland Revel. Clarence Urmy. HBMV
Hither, thither, little feet. Behind the Door. Bert Leston Taylor. LHV
Hither thou com'st: the busy [*or* busie] wind all night. The Bird. Henry Vaughan. AtBAP; EPS; LoBV; OBEV (new ed.); PoEL-2; SeCL; SeCV-1
Hither, where tangled thickets of the acacia. The Babiaantje. F. T. Prince. BoSA; ChMP
Hitherto and Henceforth. Annie Johnson Flint. BLRP
Hitherto Hath the Lord Helped. *Unknown.* BLRP
Hitherto, in progress through this Verse, my mind hath looked. Wordsworth. *Fr.* The Prelude, V. NBE
Hitherto the Lord hath helped us. Hitherto and Henceforth. Annie Johnson Flint. BLRP
Hit's a mighty fur ways up de Far'well Lane. My Honey, My Love. Joel Chandler Harris. *Fr.* Uncle Remus and His Friends. AA; FaBoBe
Hit's agittin' mighty late, w'en de guinny-hins squall. Plantation Play-Song. Joel Chandler Harris. *Fr.* Uncle Remus, His Songs and His Sayings. MCCG
Hitty Pitty within the wall. *Unknown.* OxNR
Hive at Gettysburg, The. Whittier. APW
Hm Hm my Lord! Hm. Po' Mourner's Got a Home at Las'. *Unknown.* BoAN-2
Hm Mos' done toilin' here. Mos' Done Toilin' Here. *Unknown.* BoAN-2
Ho, a song by the fire! Dartmouth Winter-Song. Richard Hovey. AA
Ho, all you cats in all the street. Cat's Meat. Harold Monro. MoP; OBMV; PoC; TSW; TSWC
Ho! are you there, Bill Hawkins. Bloody Bill. D. M. Ross. AnNZ
Ho, boys, ho! for California, O! The Banks of Sacramento. *Unknown.* AS; SG
Ho, boys, is you right? Tie-Shuffling Chant. *Unknown.* ABF
Ho, bring her hither, happy boy. Wine, My Love. Abu Jaafar. MooP
Ho! broder [*or* brother] Teague, dost hear de decree. Lilli Burlero [*or* Lilliburlero *or* A New Song]. Thomas, Lord Wharton. CoMu; OxBoLi; ViBoFo
Ho, brother! Art thou prisoned too? To a Captive Crane. Hamlin Garland. BAP
Ho! brother Teague, dost hear de decree? *See* Ho! broder Teague . .
Ho! burnish well, ye cunning hands. Song of the Mariner's Needle. C. R. Clarke. EtS
Ho! City of the gay! The Return of Napoleon from St. Helena. Lydia Huntley Sigourney. AA
Ho, Everyone That Thirsteth. Isaiah LV: 1-3, 6-7, Bible, *O.T.* MaRV
(Divine Compassion, The, LV: 1-3, 6-13.) GrCo-2
Ho, Everyone That Thirsteth. A. E. Housman. More Poems, XXII. ChMo
Ho! For Carolina! William Bernard Harrell. NoCaPo
Ho, for Lubberland! *Unknown.* SG
(Invitation to Lubberland, An.) CoBE
Ho! for Pike's Peak, where gold is found. Song for the Pike's Peaker. *Unknown.* PoOW
Ho, for taxis green or blue. Taxis. Rachel Field. FaPON; GFA; GoBP; MPB; PoRh; StVeCh (1940 ed.); TiPo
Ho! for the blades of Harden! The Blades of Harden. Will H. Ogilvie. *Fr.* Whaup o' the Rede. GoTS
Ho, for the Pirate Don Durk of Dowdee! Pirate Don Durk of Dowdee. Mildred Plew Meigs. BoChLi; GaP; PCD; PoRh; TiPo
Ho! he exclaim'd, King George of England standeth in judgement! The Absolvers. Robert Southey. *Fr.* A Vision of Judgement. EnRP; ERP
Ho! hear me shout. Thunderdrums, III. Lew Sarett. TCPD
Ho! Ho! Ho!/ In the winds that blow. Thunderdrums, IV. Lew Sarett. TCPD
Ho! Ho! Yes! Yes! It's very all well. Ballade of Soporific Absorption. J. C. Squire. InMe
Ho! is there any will ride with me. Sir Giles' War-Song. William Morris. BPN; EmBrPo; PoVP; ViPo
"Ho!" laughs the Winter. March. Arthur Guiterman. YeAr
Ho, let her rip—with her royal clew a-quiver. In the Trades. Cicely Fox Smith. EtS
Ho, Moeris! whether on thy way so fast. Lycidas and Moeris. Virgil. Eclogues, IX. AWP
Ho! pony. Down the lonely road. Army Correspondent's Last Ride. George Alfred Townsend. AA; MDAH
Ho, pretty page, with the dimpled chin. The Age of Wisdom [*or* Love at Two Score]. Thackeray. *Fr.* Rebecca and Rowena. ALV; BMEP; HBV; LEAP; LPS-1; PoVP; VA; WhC
"Ho, Rose!" quoth the stout Miles Standish. The First Proclamation of Miles Standish. Margaret Junkin Preston. MC; PAH; YaD
Ho, Russians. Sergei Aleksandrovich Yesenin. *Fr.* Transfiguration. TrRV
"Ho, sailor of the sea!" "How's My Boy?" Sydney Dobell. BMEP; CG; CH; EtS; GN; HBV; LPS-2; MOAH; OHIP; VA
Ho! the sky of living black. Dance of the Maskers. *Unknown.* APW
"Ho There, Death!" *Unknown, tr. fr. Russian by* W. R. S. Ralston. OnPM
"Ho, there! Fisherman, hold your hand!" The Lost Steamship [*or* The Second Mate]. Fitz-James O'Brien. AA; DaM
Ho! who comes here along with bagpiping and drumming? *Unknown.* SiCE
"Ho! why dost thou shiver and shake." Gaffer Gray. Thomas Holcroft. EV-3; HBV
Ho! wind of the far, far prairies! The Call of the Plains. Ethel MacDiarmid. SCC
Ho! woodsmen of the mountainside! A Cry to Arms. Henry Timrod. MOAP; PAH; SPP
Ho! workers of the old time styled. The Shoemakers. Whittier. AmPP (4th ed.); AnNE; CoBA; IAP; MOAP
Hoar-Frost. Amy Lowell. LA; NP
Hoarded Joy. Dante Gabriel Rossetti. The House of Life, LXXXII. BPN; PoVP; ViPo
Hoards let others heap of tawny gold. Tibullus. Elegies, I, 1. LaP
Hoarse Maevius reads his hobbling verse. Epigram. Samuel Taylor Coleridge. LPS-3
Hoary mountains seem gray and cold, The. At Timber Line. Frank H. Mayer. PoOW
Hob, shoe, hob; hob, shoe, hob. *Unknown.* OxNR
Hob the Elf. Norman M. Johnson. BoTP
Hobbes clearly proves that every creature. Critics [*or* A Rhapsody on Poetry]. Swift. *Fr.* On Poetry; a Rhapsody. BCEP; CoEV; OBEC; SeCePo
Hobbie Noble. *Unknown.* *See* Hobie Noble.
Hobbinol's Lay of Fair Elisa. Spenser. *See* Elisa.
Hobbledy Hops. *Unknown.* MeMeAg; OTPC (1946 ed.)
Hobby Horse, The. *Unknown, tr. fr. French.* PCH
Hobie [*or* Hobbie] Noble. *Unknown.* BaBo; ESPB; OBB; ViBoFo
Hobnelia, seated in a dreary vale. Thursday; or, The Spell. John Gay. *Fr.* The Shepherd's Week. CEP; EiPP; PoEL-3
Hobo's Dog, The. Margaret E. Bruner. AlBD
Hobson and His Men. Robert Loveman. PAH
Hoc Cygno Vinces. Henry Hawkins. ACP
Hoc Est Corpus. Alex Comfort. LiTB; LiTM; POTE
Hoc, Genitrix, Scriptum Proles Tibi Sedula Mittit. George Herbert, *tr. fr. Latin by* D. C. Allen. LaP
Hoccleve's Humorous Praise of His Lady. Thomas Hoccleve. OAEP
Hoccleve's Lament for Chaucer and Gower, *abr.* Thomas Hoccleve. *Fr.* De Regimine Principum. OAEP
(On Chaucer, *longer sel., abr.*) EPP
Hoch! Der Kaiser. Alexander Macgregor Rose. *See* Kaiser & Co.
Hock Cart, or Harvest Home, The. Robert Herrick. EPS; EV-2; OAEP; OBS; OTPC (1923 ed.); PoE; ReEn; SeCV-1; SeEP
"Come sons of Summer, by whose toil," *sel.* ViBoPo
Hoddley, poddley, puddle and fogs. *Unknown.* BoN; OxNR
Hoddy doddy. *Unknown.* OxNR
Hodge the Cat. "Susan Coolidge." CIV
Hog Butcher for the World. Chicago. Carl Sandburg. AmPP; BAP; ChMo; CMP; CoBA; CoV; HBMV; IAP; InP; LEAP; LiTM (rev. ed.); LoGBV; MAP; MoAB; MoAmPo; MOAP; MoVE; NePA; NP; OxBA; PFE; PoeMoYo; PreP; PYM; TCAP; TCPD; TOP; TreF; TwCV; ViBoPo (1958 ed.); YaD
Hog-Eye, *with music.* *Unknown.* AS
Hog-Eye Man, The, *with music.* *Unknown.* AS; SoAmSa
Hog Meat. Daniel Webster Davis. BANP
Hog Rogues on the Harricane, *with music.* *Unknown.* OuSiCo
Hogger on his death-bed lay, A. The Dying Hogger. *Unknown.* AS; IHA
Hohenlinden. Thomas Campbell. BCEP; BeLS; BHV; BTP; CBOV; CH; ChTr; EBSV; EnRP; ERP; EV-4; FaBoCh; GN; GTBS; GTBS-D; GTBS-W; GTSE; GTSL; HBV; LiA; LPS-2; OBRV; PECK; TCEP; TreF; TVSH; WaaP; WBLP; WHA
(Battle of Hohenlinden.) OTPC (1923 ed.)
Hoist the Flag! Oscar II, King of Sweden, *tr. fr. Swedish by* Charles W. Stork. AnSL
Hokey, pokey, whisky, thum. *Unknown.* OxNR
Hokey-pokey, winky, wang. *Unknown.* BoN
Hokku: "Bits of song—what else?" Yone Noguchi. NP
Hokku: "Cry of the cicada, The." Basho, *tr. fr. Japanese by* W. G. Aston. InP

Hokku: "I thought I saw the fallen leaves." Arakida Moritake, *tr. fr. Japanese by* Yone Noguchi. InP
Hokku: "Wayside cherry tree, A." Basho, *tr. fr. Japanese by* William N. Porter. InP
Hol' de Win' Don't Let It Blow, *with music*. *Unknown*. BoAN-2
"Hold." Patrick R. Chalmers. HBV
Hold, are you mad? you damn'd confounded dog. Tyrannic Love: Epilogue. Dryden. OAEP; SeCV-2; ViBoPo
Hold Back Thy Hours. Beaumont *and* Fletcher. *See* Bridal Song ("Hold back thy hours").
Hold cruell love oh hold I yield. *Unknown*. SeCSL
Hold fast to dreams. Dreams. Langston Hughes. BoChLi (1950 ed.); GoSl
Hold Fast Your Dreams. Louise Driscoll. BLPA; FaBoBe; FaPON; HBMV; MPB; NeHB; TiPo
Hold hard, Ned! Lift me down once more, and lay me in the shade. The Sick Stockrider. Adam Lindsay Gordon. BoAu; OBVV; VA
Hold Hard, These Ancient Minutes. Dylan Thomas. CoBE
Hold High the Torch. *Unknown*. MaRV
Hold high the woof, dear friends, that we may see. On a Piece of Tapestry. George Santayana. AA; OBAV
Hold how you may what masks to hide your dreaming. Music. Anne Ryan. CAW
Hold it up sternly—see this it sends back. A Hand-Mirror. Walt Whitman. OxBA
Hold, Men, Hold! *Unknown*. ChBR
Hold my rooster, hold my hen. Precious Things. *Unknown*. GoSl
Hold not thy life too dear because of death. Life and Death. Herbert E. Clarke. PSO
Hold On, Abraham. *Unknown*. ABF
Hold on, hold on, while yet ye can. Spring Song. Aubrey Thomas De Vere. IrPN
Hold out yo' light you heav'n boun' soldier. Heav'n Boun' Soldier. *Unknown*. BoAN-1
Hold Thou Me Fast. Christina Rossetti. BePJ
Hold up your head. *Unknown*. OxNR
"Hold your hand, Lord Judge," she says. The Maid Freed from the Gallows. *Unknown*. ESPB (I *vers.*)
Hölderlin's Journey. Edwin Muir. PtP; TriL
Holding a beggar's child. Meditation. Toyohiko Kagawa. MaRV
Holding a jug of wine among the flowers. Drinking Alone under Moonlight. Li Po. WhP
Holding a myrtle rod she blithely moved. Miniature [*or* A Girl]. Archilochus. GrR; OxBG
Holding a stone which has no voice. Sad Love and Sad Song. Homei Iwano. LiTW
Holding apoise in air. The Links of Chance. Edward Rowland Sill. PFY
Holding Hands. Lenore M. Link. FaPON; MoShBr; TiPo (1952 ed.); UTS
Holding his body steady, the three upper parts erect. Yoga. *Unknown*. *Fr.* The Upanishads. OnPM
Holding-Paddock. William Hart-Smith. AnNZ
Holding the distance up before his face. The Traveller. W. H. Auden. ReMP
Holding the naked body I had bought. A Bought Embrace. G. S. Fraser. WaP
Hole in the head where the bullet, The. On a Very Young, Very Dead Soldier. Richard Gillman. NePoAm
Holger Danske and Stout Didrik. *Unknown, tr. fr. Danish by* E. M. Smith-Dampier. BoDaBa
Holiday. John Davidson. OBVV
Holiday ("Festo quid potius die"). Horace, *tr. fr. Latin by* Louis Untermeyer. Odes, III, 28. AWP; JAWP; WBP (Celebration for Neptune, *tr. by* Roselle M. Montgomery.) LiA
Holiday. Henry Dawson Lowry. OBVV
Holiday, A. Lizette Woodworth Reese. AA; OBAV
Holiday. Edith Sitwell. CoEV
Holiday. Ella Young. TiPo (1952 ed.)
Holiday at Hampton Court. John Davidson. BMEP
Holiday, holiday, on the very first day of the year, year. Little Mathie Grove. *Unknown*. BaBo
Holiday in Reality. Wallace Stevens. NePA; OxBA
Holiday Romance, *sel.* Charles Dickens. Cannibal Song. BoN
Holiday Task, A. Gilbert Abbott à Beckett, *also at. to* Barclay Philips. NA (Polka Lyric, A.) BOHV
Holiday Train, The. Irene Thompson. BoTP
Holidays. Emerson. IAP
Holidays. Longfellow. MPB (1956 ed.); PoToHe (new ed.), 3 *ll.*
Holier Night. Leslie Savage Clark. ChIP
Holiest of all holidays are those, The. Holidays. Longfellow. MPB (1956 ed.); PoToHe (new ed.)
Holiness. John Drinkwater. BMEP; CP
Holiness[e] on the head. Aaron. George Herbert. MeLP; MePo; OAEP; OBS; PoFS; TwCrTr

Holla, ye pampered jades of Asia. The Vaunts of Tamburlaine. Christopher Marlowe. *Fr.* Tamburlaine the Great, Pt. I, V, ii. BCEP
Holland. Barbara Jane Provost. PCH
Holland, that scarce deserves the name of land. Andrew Marvell. *Fr.* The Character of Holland. ChTr
Hollo, My Fancy! William Cleland, *and others. See* Hallo My Fancy.
Holloa! the Good Ship of Delight. Lope de Vega, *tr. fr. Spanish by* George Ticknor. TeCS
Hollow Land, The, *sel.* William Morris. "Christ keep the Hollow Land." AtBAP; ChTr (Song.) PoD; PoEL-5; ThWaDe
Hollow Men, The. T. S. Eliot. APA; BAV; BoLiVe (1945 ed.); ChMo; CoAnAm; CoBE; CoBMV; EnL; LiTA; LiTM; MAP; MAPA; MoAB; MoAmPo; MoP; NAMP; NeMA; OBMV; Po; PoLFOT; POTE; PreP; TwAmPo; TwCV; TwHP; TwP
"Eyes I dare not meet in dreams," *sel.* GTBS-D
Hollow moon, and up between, The. Charles Warren Stoddard. *Fr.* Tamalpais. BAP
Hollow reed against his lips, A. The Reed-Player. Archibald MacLeish. HBMV
Hollow sea-shell which for years hath stood, The. Sea-Shell Murmurs. Eugene Lee-Hamilton. VA
Hollow shell of a house, The. The House. Henry Treece. MaRV
Hollow sound of your hard felt hat, The. Hats. F. S. Flint. TwCV
Hollow winds begin to blow, The. Signs of Rain. Edward Jenner. BLPA; CG; LPS-2; OTPC; PoP; PRWS; RIS
Holly. Helen Bevington. NoCaPo (rev. ed.)
Holly, The. Walter de la Mare. ChMo; CMP
Holly, The. Henry VIII, King of England. *See* Green Groweth the Holly.
Holly, The. Edith King. ChBR
Holly and Ivy ("Holly bereth beris"). *Unknown*. CoEV (Nay, Nay, Ivy!) AnEC
Holly and Ivy Made a Great Party. *Unknown*. AnEC (Carol in Praise of the Holly and Ivy.) OHIP (Holly and Ivy.) TMEV
Holly and the Ivy, The ("The holly and the ivy,/ When they are both full grown"). *Unknown*. AnEC; CH; ChTr; OxBoCh; PoLi; SDH; TriL; YaCaBo, *with music*
Holly Bough, The. Charles Mackay. *See* Under the Holly Bough.
Holly Carol. Margaret Widdemer. SDH
Holly Fairies. Aileen Fisher. ChBR
Holly stands in the hall, fair to behold. A Song on the Ivy and the Holly. *Unknown*. AnEC
Holly! the holly! oh, twine it with bay, The. The Christmas Holly. Eliza Cook. COAH; OTPC (1946 ed.); PRWS
Holly Tree, The. Robert Southey. ADAH; EnRP; ERP; HBV; LPS-2; TVSH
Hollyhock, A. Frank Dempster Sherman. AA; ADAH; BAP
Hollyhock with crimson bells, The. Proud Hollyhock. Marguerite Buller. BrR
Hollyhocks, The. Craven Langstroth Betts. AA
Hollyhocks, The. Ray Laurence. NLK
Hollyhocks are ten feet tall, The. Wet Summer. May Williams Ward. GoYe
Hollywood. Don Blanding. YaD
Hollywood. Karl Shapiro. AmPP (4th ed.); OxBA
Hollywood . . . Hollywood . . ./ Fabulous Follywood. Hollywood. Don Blanding. YaD
Holmes. James Russell Lowell. *Fr.* A Fable for Critics. AnNE ("There's Holmes, who is matchless among you for wit.") CoBA
Holmes Alphabet, A. *Comp. by* Caroline B. Le Row, *fr. various poems by* Holmes. PEOR
Holstenwall. Sidney Keyes. FaBoTw
Holy Angels, The, *abr. Unknown*. WHL
Holy angels and blest. The Madonna, to Her Sleeping Child [*or* A Christmas Cradlesong *or* Lullaby of the Virgin]. Lope de Vega. AnSpL-1; BOL; ChrBoLe; TeCS
Holy Balshemtov, The. Zisha Landau, *tr. fr. Yiddish by* Sarah Zweig Betsky. OnCuPl
Holy Baptism. George Herbert. HBV (H. Baptisme.) SeCV-1 (Holy Baptisme.) PoEL-2
Holy Bible, Book Divine. John Burton. BLRP; WBLP
Holy boy, The/ Went from his mother. Children of Love. Harold Monro. CMP; MBP; MM; MoBrPo; TwCV
Holy Child, The. Charles Carroll Albertson. ChIP; MaRV; StJW
Holy Children boldly stand, The. Nativity Ode. St. Cosmas. CAW
Holy Church. William Langland, *tr. fr. Middle English. Fr.* The Vision of Piers Plowman, Passus I. MeEV (Field Full of Folk, A, *mod. by* Grover Cronin, Jr.) CoBE (Holy Church Speaks, *mod. by* Henry W. Wells.) PoLi

Holy City, A. Maxwell Anderson. *Fr.* The Star Wagon. QS
Holy City, The. W. Russell Bowie. MaRV
Holy City, The. Frederic Edward Weatherly. BLRP; WBLP
Holy Communion. Speer Strahan. JKCP
Holy Confessor, blessed in the merit. Sancte Confessor. Rhabanus Maurus. CAW
Holy Cross. *Unknown.* ACP; CAW
(Steadfast Cross!) TMEV
Holy-Cross Day. Robert Browning. OtMeF
Holy Eclogue, The. Sister Francisca Josefa del Castillo, *tr. fr. Spanish by* Thomas Walsh. CAW
Holy Eucharist, The. Pedro Calderón de la Barca, *tr. fr. Spanish by* Richard Chenevix Trench. CAW
Holy Fair, The. Burns. BEL; CEP; EiPP; EnRP; OAEP
Holy Family. Muriel Rukeyser. MoAmPo
Holy Father, bless us. Evening Prayer. Calvin W. Laufer. PraP
Holy Father, cheer our way. Light at Evening Time. R. H. Robinson. PraP
Holy Field, The. Henry Hart Milman. OxBoCh
Holy Fire. Henry Vaughan. MeRV
Holy Ghost, *with music. Unknown.* OuSiCo
Holy Ghost is to thee sent, The. Hail Mary, Full of Grace, Mother in Virginity. *Unknown.* AnEC
Holy God, we praise Thy name! Hymn of Thanksgiving. *Unknown.* WHL
Holy Grail, The. Tennyson. *Fr.* Idylls of the King. PoVP; ViPo; ViPP; VLEP
Holy Heaven longs to thrust the Earth, The. The Marriage of Heaven and Earth. Aeschylus. *Fr.* Danaides. OxBG
Holy Hill, A. "Æ." AWP; JAWP; WBP
Holy, Holy, Holy. Reginald Heber. BPP; HBV; MaRV; OHIP; OlF; OTPC
(Thrice Holy.) WGRP
Holy Innocents, The. Robert Lowell. ATP (1953 ed.); InPo; InvP; MoAB; MoAmPo (1950 ed.); NePoEA
Holy Innocents, The. Prudentius, *tr. fr. Latin by* H. T. Henry. CAW
Holy Innocents. Christina Rossetti. BOL; BPN; HBV; HBVY
Holy Jesus, Thou art born. Dedication. Victoria Saffelle Johnson. GoBC; TrPWD
Holy Lady Poverty, The. A Ditty of Saint Clare. Enid Dinnis. PraNu
Holy Land. Richard Watson Gilder. StJW
Holy Land of Walsingham, The. Benjamin Francis Musser. ISi
Holy Land of Walsinghame, The. *Unknown, at. to* Sir Walter Ralegh. *See* As You Came from the Holy Land.
Holy Light. John Hall Wheelock. LiTM (1946 ed.); PG (1955 ed.)
Holy Lullaby. *Unknown.* GoTP
Holy maiden, blessed thou be. Singē We, Singē We. *Unknown.* AnEC
Holy Man, The. *Unknown, tr. fr. Old Irish by* Whitley Stokes *and* John Strachan. *Fr.* The Devil's Tribute to Moling. OnYI
Holy Matrimony. John Keble. HBV; MaRV; VA
Holy Matrimony. Harold Monro. ChMo; CMP
Holy monks, concealed from men, The. St. Philip in Himself. Cardinal Newman. GoBC
Holy Mother at the Cross, The. Richard Watson Dixon. ViP
Holy Name of Jesus, The. Richard Crashaw. CAW
Holy Nation, A. Richard Realf. *Fr.* Of Liberty and Charity. PoFr
Holy Nativity of Our Lord God. Richard Crashaw. *See* In the Holy Nativity of Our Lord God.
Holy Night. Nathaniel A. Benson. CaP
Holy Night, The. Elizabeth Barrett Browning. CLS
Holy Night!/ How long is the road of thy horses. Euripides. *Fr.* Andromeda. OxBG
Holy night that Christ was born, The. The Ox. John Gray. GBV (1952 ed.)
Holy Nunnery, The. *Unknown.* BaBo; ESPB
Holy of England! since my light is short. On First Entering Westminster Abbey. Louise Imogen Guiney. AA
Holy of Holies, The. G. K. Chesterton. WGRP
Holy Office, The. James Joyce. FaBoTw; SiTL
Holy Ones, the Young Ones, The. Chayyim Zeldis. TrJP
Holy Order. J. B. Boothroyd. FiBHP
Holy Places. Herbert D. Gallaudet. MaRV
Holy Poems (I–III). George Barker. MoPo
Holy Poet, I have heard. John Hall Wheelock. *Fr.* Thanks from Earth to Heaven. TrPWD
Holy Poverty. Arthur Shearly Cripps. GTML
. . . "Holy Power." Keats. *Fr.* The Fall of Hyperion. EV-4
Holy Ramadan. Ramadan. Al-Qalami. MooP
Holy-Rood come forth and shield. The Old Wives Prayer. Robert Herrick. SeCV-1
Holy Rose, The. Vyacheslav Ivanovich Ivanov, *tr. fr. Russian by* Babette Deutsch *and* Avrahm Yarmolinsky. AWP; JAWP; TrRV; WBP
Holy Saturday. John Banister Tabb. MaRV; StJW
Holy Satyr. Hilda Doolittle ("H. D."). MAP; MoAmPo
Holy Song. *Unknown, tr. fr. Winnebago Indian by* Natalie Curtis. APW
Holy Sonnets, *sels.* John Donne.
"As due by many titles I resign[e]," II. EPS; MePo; NBE; OBS; SeEP
(Resignation to God.) EV-2
"At the round earth's imagin'd [*or* imagined] corners, blow," VII. AnEnPo; AtBAP; ATP (1953 ed.); CoBE; CoEV; ElSeCe; EnLP; EPS; ExPo; FaBoEn; InPo; LiTB; LiTG; LoBV; MaPo; MeLP; MePo; MyFE; NBE; OAEP; OBS; OxBoCh; PeBoSo; Po; PoD; PoEL-2; PoFS; ReaPo; ReEn; SeCeV; SeCV-1; SeEP; ShBV-4; TuPP; TwCrTr; TwHP; TwP; ViBoPo
(Blow Your Trumpets, Angels.) ChTr
(Death.) EV-2
(Divine Sonnet.) TriL
"Batter my heart, three-person'd God; for, you," XIV. AnEnPo; AnFE; BoLiVe; CaAE; CoEV; EnL; EnLP; EPS; ExPo; FaFP; GoBC; GTBS-W; LiTB; LiTG; MaPo; MaRV; MeLP; MePo; NBE; OAEP; OBS; OxBoCh; PeBoSo; Po; PoE; PoEL-2; PoFS; ReEn; RiBV; SeCePo; SeCeV; SeCV-1; SeEP; TrGrPo; TrPWD; TuPP; TwCrTr; TwP
(Prayer for Violence.) BLV
"Death, be not proud, though some have called thee," X. AnEnPo; AnFE; AtBAP; BLV; BoLiVe; ChTr; CoBE; EIL; ElSeCe; EnL; EnLP; EPS; EV-2; ExPo; FaBoEn; FaFP; GoBC; GTBS-W; HBV; InPo; InvP; LiTB; LiTG; LoBV; MaPo; MeLP; MePo; MyFE; OAEP; OBS; OnPM; PeBoSo; PG (1955 ed.); Po; PoE; PoEL-2; PoFr; PoFS; PoRA; PreP; ReaPo; ReEn; RiBV; SeCeV; SeCV-1; SeEP; TreFS; TrGrPo; TuPP; TwCrTr; TwHP; TwP; TyEnPo; ViBoPo; WHA
(Death.) ATP; BEL; CBOV; EnLi-1; EnLit; EPP; ES; MaRV; OBEV; ShBV-4; TCEP; TOP; UnPo (1st ed.)
"Father, part of his double interest," XVI. OBS
"I am a little world made cunningly," V. EnL; EPS; MyFE; OBS; OxBoCh; PeBoSo; ReEn; SeEP; TwP
"If faithful soules be alike glorifi'd," VIII. OBS; SeEP
"If poisonous [*or* poysonous] mineral[l]s, and if that tree," IX. AnEnPo; AtBAP; ATP (1953 ed.); EnLP; ExPo; GTBS-W; LiTB; MaPo; MePo; OBS; PeBoSo; PoEL-2; ReEn; RiBV; TuPP; TwP; UnPo
(Forget.) EPP; WHA
"O might those sighs and tears return again," III. AnEnPo; OBS; PeBoSo; SeEP
"Oh my black[e] soul[e]! now thou art summoned," IV. MePo; MyFE; OBS
"Oh, to vex me, contraries [*or* contraryes] meet in one," XIX. EPS (1942 ed.); NBE; PeBoSo; PoEL-2
(Devout Fits.) SeCePo
(Inconstancy.) MaRV
"Show me dear[e] Christ, thy spouse, so bright and clear," XVIII. EnLP; EPS; ExPo; MeLP; OAEP; OBS; SeEP; TuPP
"Since she whom I lov'd hath payd [*or* paid] her last debt," XVII. EnLP; MePo; NBE; OAEP; PeBoSo; PoD; SeEP; TwP
"Spit in my face you Jews, and pierce my side," XI. EPS; OBS; OxBoCh; SeEP
"This is my play's [*or* playes] last scene, here heavens appoint," VI. AnEnPo; EPS; LoBV; MeLP; MePo; MyFE; OAEP; OBS; OxBoCh; PeBoSo; PoFS; SeEP; TuPP
"Thou hast made me, and shall Thy work decay?" I. AnEnPo; EG; EPS; FaBoEn; MaPo; MeLP; NBE; OAEP; OBS; OxBoCh; PeBoSo; Po; PoEL-2; PoFS; SeEP; TwCrTr
"What if this present were the world's last night?" XIII. ElSeCe; ExPo; GTBS-W; LiTB; MeLP; MeRV; OAEP; OBS; SeCeV; SeEP; TuPP
"Why are we by all creatures waited on?" XII. MaPo; OBS; PeBoSo; PoEL-2; TuPP
"Wilt thou love God, as he thee? then digest," XV. EnLP; OBS
Holy Spirit, The. Harriet Auber. MaRV
Holy Spirit, The. Robert Herrick. *See* His Litany to the Holy Spirit.
Holy Spirit, Dwell with Me. Thomas Toke Lynch. MaRV
Holy Spirit, I worship thee. Prayer amid Flames. Verner von Heidenstam. AnSL
Holy Spring. Dylan Thomas. MeRV; WaP
Holy Star, The. Bryant. *See* Christmas.
Holy stillness, beautiful and deep, A. A Summer Noon at Sea. Epes Sargent. EtS
Holy Thorn, The. Thomas S. Jones, Jr. PSO
Holy Thursday ("Is this a holy thing to see"). Blake. *Fr.* Songs of Experience. CEP; CoBE; EiPP; EM-1; EnL; EnLi-2 (1949 ed.); EnRP; OAEP; PoE; ReaPo

Holy Thursday ("'Twas on a Holy Thursday"). Blake. *Fr.* Songs of Innocence. AnFE; CEP; CH; CoBE; EiPP; EnL; EnRP; EV-3; HBV; OAEP; OBEC; OTPC; PoE; PoFS
Holy Thursday. Leonard McCarthy. JKCP (1955 ed.)
Holy Tide, The. Frederick Tennyson. OBEV; OBVV
Holy Transportations, *sel.* Charles Fitzgeffrey.
Take Frankincense, O God. ChTr
Holy Viaticum Comes to Me, The. Giovanni Prati, *tr. fr. Italian by* Florence Trail. CAW
Holy War, The. Kipling. TCPD
Holy Week. Phoebe Smith Bachelder. ChIP
Holy Week. Robert Whitaker. ChIP; MaRV
Holy Well, The. *Unknown.* AnEC; BaBo; FaBoCh; LoGBV; OBB; OxBoCh
Holy Willie's Prayer. Burns. BEL; BOHV; CEP, *sl. abr.*; EBSV; EiPP; EM-1; EnL; EnRP; GoTS; KN; LiA; OxBoLi; PIAE, *abr.*; PIR; PoE; PoEL-4; TOP, *abr.*; TyEnPo; ViBoPo
Holy Women, The. William Alexander Percy. LS
Holy Writ saith no thing soother. "Amend Me and Punish Me Not." *Unknown.* TMEV
Homage. Kenneth Fearing. ChMo
Homage. Helen Hoyt. AnAmPo; AV; LA; NV
Homage. Gustave Kahn, *tr. fr. French by* Jethro Bithell. TrJP
Homage. George O'Neil. AnAmPo; LA
Homage (Diptych, 2). R. J. Schoeck. GoYe
Homage of War. Bruce Williamson. NeIP
Homage to change that scatters the poppy seed. Rondeau. Ronald Bottrall. MoVE
Homage to Circe. Horace Gregory. MoAmPo (1950 ed.)
Homage to Columbus. Horace Gregory. ChMo
Homage to Hieronymus Bosch. Thomas McGreevy. OnYI
Homage to Jack Yeats. Thomas McGreevy. OBMV
Homage to Literature. Muriel Rukeyser. NAMP
Homage to Mistress Bradstreet, *sels.* John Berryman.
"Governor your husband lived so long, The." AmP; MoVE
"When by me in the dusk my child sits down." CrMA; ReMP
Homage to Mürren. Morton Dauwen Zabel. NP
Homage to Our Leaders. Julian Symons. NeBP
Homage to Sextus Propertius, *sels.* Ezra Pound.
Me Happy, Night, Night Full of Brightness. InvP
"Now if ever it is time to cleanse Helicon." CrMA
"Shades of Callimachus, Coan Ghosts of Philetas." MoAB; MoVE; OxBA
"When, when, and whenever death closes our eyelids." MoAB; OBMV
"Who, who will be the next man to entrust his girl to a friend?" FaBoMo
Homage to Texas. Robert Graves. LiTB
Homage to the British Museum. William Empson. FaBoMo; LiTM (rev. ed.); MoAB
Homage to the Empress of the Blues. Robert E. Hayden. PoNe
Homage to the Philosopher. Babette Deutsch. ImOP; TrJP
Homage to thee, O Ra, at thy tremendous rising. The Dead Man Ariseth and Singeth a Hymn to the Sun. *Unknown. Fr.* Book of the Dead. AWP; JAWP; WBP
Homage to Vaslav Nijinsky. James Kirkup. UnS
Homage to William Cowper. Donald Davie. NePoEA
Home. Joseph Beaumont. *See* House and Home.
Home, The, *sel.* Fredrika Bremer.
Song of the Dove. BOL
(Swedish Mother's Lullaby.) MOAH
Home. Stephen Chalmers. HBMV
Home. Joachim du Bellay. *See* Sonnet to Heavenly Beauty.
Home. Léon Paul Fargue, *tr. fr. French by* Wallace Fowlie. MiCF
Home. Robert Frost. *Br. sel. fr.* The Death of the Hired Man. MaRV
(Home Defined.) TreF
Home. W. W. Gibson. *See* So Long Had I Travelled.
Home. Goldsmith. *Fr.* The Traveller. LPS-1
(First, Best Country, The.) GN
Home. J. H. Goring. MoShBr
(English, The.) SiTL
Home. Dora Greenwell. HBV
Home. Edgar A. Guest. BLPA; FaBoBe; OHFP; PTA-2; TreF; YaD
Home. June Brown Harris. PoToHe (new ed.)
Home. Verner von Heidenstam, *tr. fr. Swedish by* Charles W. Stork. AnSL
Home. W. E. Henley. *See* O, Falmouth Is a Fine Town.
Home. Nellie Womack Hines. PoToHe
Home. Friedrich Hölderlin, *tr. fr. German by* Vernon Watkins. AnGP
Home. Homer C. House. MuM
Home. Leonidas of Alexandria, *tr. fr. Greek by* Robert Bland. LPS-1
Home. Liu Ping, *tr. fr. Chinese by* Henry H. Hart. PoHN
Home. Sidney Royse Lysaght. *Fr.* Old Landmarks. GrCo-2
Home. Hermann Ford Martin. BLP
Home! *sel.* Vladimir Mayakovsky, *tr. fr. Russian by* Babette Deutsch.
"I don't want/ to be plucked like a flower." TrRV
Home. Nikolai Nekrasov, *tr. fr. Russian by* Oliver Elton. BoR
Home. William Alexander Percy. In New York, V. LS
(In New York.) SPP; TBM
Home. Edward Rowland Sill. AnNE; HBV
Home. Ivan Swift. BAP
Home ("A melancholy little man"). *Unknown.* HBV
Home ("Great trees"). *Unknown, tr. fr. Chinese by* Witter Bynner *and* Kiang Kang-hu. OuHeWo
Home!/ My very heart's desire is safe. Home. Nellie Womack Hines. PoToHe
Home and Mother. Mary Mapes Dodge. BOHV
Home at Last. G. K. Chesterton. OQP; QP-1; WGRP
Home! at the word, what blissful visions rise. Home, Sweet Home, with Variations, IV [V]. H. C. Bunner. BOHV; CenHV; InMe; PA
Home-bound ship stood out to sea, The. The Mystery of Cro-a-tàn. Margaret Junkin Preston. PAH
Home Brunt, The. Kay Riley. AlBD
Home Burial. Robert Frost. AmPP; AnFE; AnNE; APA; BLV; BoLiVe; CoAnAm; CoBMV; MAPA; MaPo; MotAn; TwAmPo
Home came the old man. Our Goodman (B *vers.*) *Unknown.* ViBoFo
Home comes a lad with the bonnie hair. The Pipes o' Gordon's Men. J. Scott Glasgow. HBV
Home-coming. Léonie Adams. HBMV; MAP; MoAmPo; MOAP; NeMA; NV; PoeMoYo; TSW; TSWC
Homecoming, The. James K. Baxter. AnNZ
Home-coming. Albert Ehrenstein, *tr. fr. German by* Babette Deutsch *and* Avram Yarmolinsky. TrJP
Home-coming. Gustaf Fröding, *tr. fr. Swedish by* Charles W. Stork. AnSL
Home-coming. Homer, *tr. fr. Greek by* J. W. Mackail. *Fr.* The Odyssey, XIII. OxBG
Home-coming. "Isobel Hume." HBMV
Homecoming. Karl Shapiro. MiAP
Homecoming. *Unknown.* AnIV
Homecoming in Storm. Bernice L. Kenyon. EtS
Homecoming—late at Night. Tu Fu, *tr. fr. Chinese by* Kenneth Rexroth. OnPC
Homecoming of the Sheep, The. Francis Ledwidge. EnLit; HBMV; LBBV; TIP; VOD; YT
Homecoming of Ulysses, The. Stephen Phillips. *Fr.* Ulysses. MW
Home, Dearie, Home, *with music. Unknown.* AmSS; SoAmSa
Home Defined. Robert Frost. *See* Home.
Home did I say, ye homeless? Not to ye. Lyttelton Harbour, VIII. D'Arcy Cresswell. AnNZ
Home Field, The; Evening. Charles Tennyson Turner. EnSW
Home Fire, The. Orrick Johns. HBMV
Home Folks. *Unknown.* LPS-1
Home for Love. John Freeman. TCPD
Home from the observatory. Stella. Charles Henry Crandall. AA
Home from the Wars. Hsüeh T'ao, *tr. fr. Chinese by* Henry H. Hart. OnPM; PoHN
Home from the wars trudged a poor sailor. The Sailor's Return. *Unknown.* SaSa
Home furthest off grows dearer from the way. The Soldier. John Clare. SoV
Home, home from the horizon, far and clear. At Night [*or* To W. M.]. Alice Meynell. CH; EV-5; GoBC; HBV; LBBV; LiTL; LoPo; NV; OBVV; PoeT; POTT
Home, home—where's my baby's home? Anne Hutchinson's Exile. Edward Everett Hale. PAH
Home, in War-Time. Sydney Dobell. VA
Home is the place where, when you have to go there. Home [*or* Home Defined]. Robert Frost. *Fr.* The Death of the Hired Man. MaRV; TreF
Home Is Where There's [*or* There Is] One to Love Us. Charles Swain. BLPA; FaBoBe; MaRV; NeHB; PoToHe
Home Means Nevada. Bertha Raffetto. PoRL
Home Mission Prayer, A. Bryant. *See* Other Sheep I Have, Which Are Not of This Fold.
Home No More Home to Me. Robert Louis Stevenson. CH
(Wandering Willie.) POTT
Home of Aphrodite, The. Euripides. *See* Song of the Bacchanals.
Home of Helen, The. T. Sturge Moore. LBBV
Home of my heart, I sing of thee! Michigan, My Michigan. Mrs. Henry F. Lyster. PoRL
Home of My Thoughts. Marie Barton. PraP
Home of the Naiads, The. John Armstrong. *Fr.* The Art of Preserving Health, II. OBEC
Home of the Percy's high-born race. Alnwick Castle. Fitz-Greene Halleck. AA; IAP; LPS-3

Home of the Soul. Ellen M. Huntington Gates. BLRP
Home on the Range, A. *Unknown.* CoSo (A *and* B *vers., with music*); CSF; FaBoBe; MPB; OlF; PIAE; PoRL; PoTo; TreFS
(Oh, Give Me a Home Where the Buffalo Roam.) FaFP; SiTL
Home, Rose, and Home, Provence and La Palie. Arthur Hugh Clough. *See* Ite Domum Saturae, Venit Hesperus.
Home Song. Longfellow. GN; OTPC
(Song: "Stay, stay at home, my heart, and rest.") CBE; HBV
(Stay, Stay at Home, My Heart, and Rest.) BPP
Home, Sweet Home. John Howard Payne. *Fr.* Clari, the Maid of Milan. AA; APW; BAV; BLPA; BoHiPo; FaBoBe; FaFP; HBV; LEAP; LPS-1; MaRV; NeHB; OBAV; OlF; OnHT; OTPC; PECK; TCAP; TreF; WBLP
Home, Sweet Home: "We were lying on a prairie on Slaughter's ranch one night." *Unknown.* CoSo
Home, Sweet Home, with Variations, *parody.* H. C. Bunner. BOHV; CenHV; InMe; PA
Home they brought her sailor son. The Recognition. William Sawyer. HBV; PA
Home They Brought Her Warrior Dead. Tennyson. *Fr.* The Princess, Pt. V. BEL; BPN; EM-2; EnLi-2; EPN; EV-5; HBV; LEAP; LPS-1; MaRV; OTPC; PoVP; PTA-2; TreFS; TrGrPo; ViPP
(Home They Brought.) BHV; BoLiVe
(Lyrics from "The Princess.") OuHeWo
(Songs from "The Princess.") EmBrPo; OAEP; ViPo; VLEP
(Widow and Child.) MOAH
"Home They Brought Her Warrior Dead." *Unknown.* *See* First Lay of Gudrun, The.
Home, thou return'st from Thames. Ode on the Popular Superstitions of the Highlands of Scotland. William Collins. CEP; EnRP; EV-3; OAEP; OBEC
Home Thoughts. Guy Butler. BoSA
Home Thoughts. Denis Glover. AnNZ
Home Thoughts. Claude McKay. GoSl
Home Thoughts. Odell Shepard. HBMV
Home Thoughts. Kyukin Susukida, *tr. fr. Japanese by* Takamichi Ninomiya *and* D. J. Enright. PoLJ
Home Thoughts from Abroad. Robert Browning. ADAH; AnEnPo; AnFE; AWP; BBV; BEL; BLV; BMEP; BoLiVe; BoTP; BPN; BTP; CaAE; CBE; CBOV; CBPC; CG; CoBE; EG; EM-2; EmBrPo; EnLi-2 (1949 ed.); EnLit; EPN; EPP; EV-5; FaBoBe; FaBoEn; FaFP; FaPON; FiP; GBV (1922 ed.); GEPC; GTBS; GTBS-W; GTML; GTSL; HBV; HBVY; HiLiEn; InPo; JAWP; LEAP; LiTB; LiTG; MCCG; NeHB; OAEP; OBEV; OBVV; OtMeF; OTPC; PCH, *st.* 1; PFE; PIAE; PIR; PoeMoYo; PoFS; PoRA; PoVP; PYM; SeCeV; ShBV-2; SN; TCEP; TOP; TreF; TrGrPo; TyEnPo; VA; ViPo; ViPP; VLEP; WBP; WHA; WP; YT
(April in England.) GN
Wise Thrush, The, *sel.* BLA; WhBS
Home Thoughts from Europe. Henry van Dyke. *See* America for Me.
Home Thoughts, from the Sea. Robert Browning. AWP; BEL; BPN; CBPC; EM-2; EnLi-2 (1949 ed.); EV-5; FaBoCh; FiP; GEPC; GTBS; GTSL; InP; InPo; JAWP; LH; OAEP; OBEV; OBVV; OTPC; PoVP; ShBV-2; TOP; ViPo; ViPP; VLEP; WBP
Home Thoughts in Laventie. Edward Wyndham Tennant. HBMV
Home to me is laughter. Home. June Brown Harris. PoToHe (new ed.)
Home to Sermio. Catullus, *tr. fr. Latin by* Leigh Hunt. OnPM
(Home to Sirmio, *tr. by* Sir Theodore Martin.) OuHeWo
("O my little almost island, little island Sirmio," *tr. by* Horace Gregory.) LaP; RoL
(Return to Sirmio, *tr. by* Horace Gregory.) LiTW
Home Travell. John Hall. AEV
("What need I travel, since I may.") EG
Home Truths from Abroad, *parody.* *Unknown.* PA
Home Winner, The. Gene Lindberg. PoOW
Home without a Bible, A. Charles D. Meigs. WBLP
Home, Wounded. Sydney Dobell. LPS-1
Homecoming. *See* Home Coming.
Homeland, The. Dana Burnet. BLP; SBMV
Homeland, The. Emile Cammaerts, *tr. fr. French by* Witter Bynner. PoFr
Homeland, The. Hugh Reginald Haweis. BLRP
Home-Land. Verner von Heidenstam, *tr. fr. Swedish by* Charles W. Stork. AnSL
Homeland, The. Sir Cecil Spring-Rice. *See* I Vow to Thee, My Country.
Homeland, The! Oh, the Homeland! The Homeland. Hugh Reginald Haweis. BLRP
Homeless! Despised and Rejected. Katharine Lee Bates. OQP; QP-1
Homeless. Ts'ao Chih, *tr. fr. Chinese by* Henry H. Hart. PoHN
Homeless beggar, A. Izan, *tr. fr. Japanese by* Lois J. Erickson. SoLD
Homeless man goes, even on life's sunniest slope. Lines. William Hurrell Mallock. ACP (1926 ed.); JKCP (1926 ed.)
Homely, forgotten flower. Marigold. Bayard Taylor. BAV
Homely Meats. John Davies. *See* Author Loving These Homely Meats, The.
Homer. Alpheus, *tr. fr. Greek by* F. L. Lucas. GrPE
Homer. Albert Ehrenstein, *tr. fr. German by* Babette Deutsch *and* Avrahm Yarmolinsky. TrJP
Homer ("You then whose judgment the right course would steer"). Pope. *Fr.* An Essay on Criticism, Pt. I. TwCrTr
Homer and Hesiod and Virgil knew. Ploughing. V. Sackville-West. *Fr.* The Land. TCPD
Homer and Hesiod fathered on the Gods' divinity. Wickedness of Poets. Xenophanes. GrPE
Homer in a Garden. James Larkin Pearson. NoCaPo
Homer of moly and nepenthe sings. Of Tabacco. Sir John Davies. ReIE
Homer was a vinous Greek who loved the flowing bottle. Chantey of Notorious Bibbers. Henry Morton Robinson. InMe
Homeric Epigram; Midas' Tomb. *Unknown, tr. fr. Greek by* Sir William Marris. OxBG
Homeric Hymns, *sels.* *Unknown, tr. fr. Greek.*
Goddess of the Hearth, The, *tr. by* Jack Lindsay. OxBG
Homeric Hymn to Neptune, *tr. by* George Chapman. EtS
Hymn to Aphrodite. GrPE, *tr. by* F. L. Lucas; GrR, *tr. by* John Addington Symonds; LiTW, *abr., tr. by* Jack Lindsay
Afterthoughts, *tr. by* Jack Lindsay. OxBG
Aphrodite on Ida, *tr. by* Jack Lindsay. OxBG
"More to instruct thee, when five years shall end," *tr. by* Congreve. GrPo
"Sing, Muse! the force and all-informing fire," *tr. by* Congreve. GrPo
Vesting of Aphrodite, The, *tr. by* Arthur S. Way. GrR
Hymn to Ares, *tr. by* F. L. Lucas. GrPE
(Hymn to Mars, *tr. by* George Chapman.) KN
(To Mars, *tr. by* George Chapman.) LoBV
Hymn to Athena, *tr. by* Shelley. AWP
Hymn to Castor and Pollux, *tr. by* Shelley. AWP
Hymn to Demeter ("Ceres! to thee belongs the votive lay"), *tr. by* Richard Hole. GrPo
Demeter at Eleusis, *tr. by* W. M. W. Call *and* T. F. Higham. OxBG
Demeter Welcomed at Eleusis, *tr. by* Arthur S. Way. GrR
Rape of Persephone, The. GrR, *tr. by* Arthur S. Way; OxBG, *tr. by* W. M. W. Call *and* T. F. Higham
"Thrice happy he among the favoured few," *tr. by* Richard Hole. GrPo
Hymn to Dionysus, *tr. by* F. L. Lucas. GrPE
(To Dionysus, *tr. by* T. F. Higham.) OxBG
Hymn to Earth the Mother of All, *tr. by* Shelley. AWP; JAWP; WBP
(Earth the Mother of All, *tr. by* Shelley.) OxBG
(Earth, Universal Mother, *tr. by* Shelley.) GrR
("O universal Mother, who dost keep," *tr. by* Shelley.) GrPo
(To Earth, the Mother of All.) GrCo-1, *pr. tr. by* H. A. Evelyn White; GrL, *pr. tr. by* Andrew Lang; OuHeWo, *tr. by* Shelley
Hymn to Hermes [*or* Mercury], *abr., tr. by* Shelley. LiTW
"And Phoebus stooped under the craggy roof," *tr. by* Shelley. GrPo
Birth of Hermes, The, *br. sel., tr. by* Shelley. GrR
Cattle-Thief, The, *tr. by* Shelley. OxBG
"Great Father, you know clearly beforehand," *tr. by* Shelley. GrPo
"He arrived back at the sacred peak of Kyllene at dawn," *pr. tr. by* N. O. Brown. GrPo
Music's Mastery, *tr. by* Shelley. GrR
Pocket-Cattle-Thief, *tr. by* Shelley. GrR
Power of Music, The, *tr. by* Shelley. OxBG
"Seized with a sudden fancy for fresh meat," *tr. by* Shelley. GrPo
"Sing, Muse, the son of Maia and of Jove," *tr. by* Shelley. GrPo
Singing Tortoise, The, *tr. by* Shelley. GrR
To Hermes, *pr. tr. by* Andrew Lang. GrL
Tortoise-Shell, The, *abr., tr. by* Shelley. OxBG
"You butcher of cattle, cunning schemer, hard worker," *pr. tr. by* N. O. Brown. GrPo
Hymn to Pan, *tr. by* F. L. Lucas. GrPE
(To Pan.) GrR, *tr. by* Arthur S. Way; OxBG, *longer sel., tr. by* Jack Lindsay
Hymn to the Delian Apollo, *tr. by* F. L. Lucas. GrPE
Blind Old Man, The, *tr. by* T. F. Higham. OxBG

Homeric Hymns (*continued*)
  Choirs of Heaven, The, *tr. by* T. F. Higham. OxBG
   (Immortal Choirs, The, *tr. by* Arthur S. Way.) GrR
  Ionian Holiday, *tr. by* T. F. Higham. OxBG
   To Apollo, *tr. by* Jack Lindsay. OxBG
 Hymn to the Moon, *tr. by* Shelley. LiTW
   (Hymn to Selene, *tr. by* Shelley.) AWP
   To the Moon, *shorter sel., pr. tr. by* Andrew Lang. GrL
Homeric Moonlight, A. Homer, *tr. fr. Greek by* Pope. *Fr.* The Iliad, VIII. BeR
Homeric Unity. Andrew Lang. HBV
Homer's Iliad. Homer. *See* Iliad, The.
Homer's Odyssey. Homer. *See* Odyssey, The.
Home's not merely four square walls. Home Is Where There Is One to Love Us. Charles Swain. BLPA; FaBoBe; MaRV; NeHB; PoToHe
Homes of England, The. Felicia Dorothea Hemans. CG; DiM; LPS-1; PECK
 ("Stately homes of England, The," *st.* 1.) WhC
Homes of the Cliff Dwellers. Stanley Wood. PoOW
Homesick. Julia C. R. Dorr. NLK
Homesick. David Gray. LPS-1; MOAH
Homesick. Dorothy Frances McCrae. BoAu
Homesick. Ts'en Ts'an, *tr. fr. Chinese by* Henry H. Hart. PoHN
Homesick Blues. Langston Hughes. CDC; MAP; MoAmPo; NeMA; WaKn
Homesick in England. Robert Haven Schauffler. PC
Home-Sickness. Justinus Kerner, *tr. fr. German by* James Clarence Mangan. AWP; JAWP; UnW; WBP
Home-Sickness. Hedwig Lachmann, *tr. fr. German by* Jethro Bithell. TrJP
Homestead—Winter Morning. Mary Ballard Duryee. GoYe
Homesteader, The. Isabel Ecclestone Mackay. CPG
Homeward. Li Pin, *tr. fr. Chinese by* Herbert A. Giles. OuHeWo
Homeward Bound, The. Bill Adams. EtS
Homeward Bound. William Allingham. FaBoBe; HBV; HBVY
Homeward Bound, *sels.* Heine, *tr. fr. German.*
 And When I Lamented, *tr. by* Emma Lazarus. TrJP
 Dearest Friend, Thou Art in Love, *tr. by* Emma Lazarus. TrJP
 Du bist wie eine Blume, *tr. by* Kate Kroeker. AWP; JAWP; WBP; OuHeWo, *tr. by* Sir Theodore Martin
  (Thou Seemest like a Flower, *tr. by* Emma Lazarus.) TrJP
  (Translated Way, The, *tr. by* Franklin P. Adams.) BOHV
 I, a Most Wretched Atlas, *tr. by* Emma Lazarus. TrJP
 Mortal, Sneer Not at the Devil, *tr. by* Emma Lazarus. TrJP
 Thou Hast Diamonds, *tr. by* Emma Lazarus. TrJP
Homeward Bound. D. H. Rogers. AnNZ; BoAu; EtS
Homeward Bound. Robert Southey. EtS
Homeward Bound. L. Frank Tooker. EtS
Homeward Bound, 3 *vers., with music. Unknown.* ShS
 Homeward Bound ("To Pensacola town we'll bid adieu"), *sl. diff., with music.* AmSS
Homeward Bound. George Edward Woodberry. Wild Eden, XXV. AA
Homeward bound and ready for sea. Canso Strait. *Unknown.* ShS
Homeward from earth's far ends thou art returned. To His Brother in the Service of Nebuchadnezzar. Alcaeus. GrPE
Homeward Journey, The. L. Aaronson. FaBoTw; TrJP
Homing. Arna Bontemps. CDC
Homing, The. John Jerome Rooney. AA
Homing Heart, The. Daniel Henderson. HBMV
Homing Song. Rebecca Cushman. NoCaPo
Homing Swallows. Claude McKay. TSW
Homo Factus Est. Digby Mackworth Dolben. *See* Come to Me, Beloved.
Homoeopathic Soup. *Unknown.* BOHV
Homosexual young men and the amorous girls, The. The Lone Gentleman. "Pablo Neruda." AnCL
Homunculus et la Belle Etoile. Wallace Stevens. MAP; MoAB; MoAmPo
Honest and a perfect man, An. Destiny. John Fletcher. *Fr.* Upon an Honest Man's Fortune. MaRV
Honest Autolycus, An. *Unknown. See* Fine Knacks for Ladies.
Honest Doubt. Robert Weston. MaRV
Honest Fame. Pope. *Fr.* The Temple of Fame. OBEC
Honest lover whosoever [*or* whatsoever]. Song [*or* The Art of Love]. Sir John Suckling. ElSeCe; EPS; LO
Honest Man, An. Pope. *Br. sel. fr.* An Essay on Man, Epistle IV. TreF
Honest man here lies at rest, An. Epitaph on a Friend. Burns. MaRV
Honest Man's Fortune, The. John Fletcher. *See* Upon an Honest Man's Fortune.
Honest Mr. Robin. Eleanor Hammond. GFA
Honest, Mom, I didn't coax him. A Kid and His Dog. Leroy J. Fleury. AlBD
Honest regular work Dick Daring gave up. A Shining Night; or, Dick Daring, the Poacher. *Unknown.* CoMu
Honest Stradivari made me. The Violin's Complaint. William Roscoe Thayer. AA
Honest Whore, The, *sels.* Thomas Dekker.
 First True Gentleman, The, *fr.* Pt. I. BCEP
  ("Patience [my lord], why, 'tis the soul of peace.") LEAP; ViBoPo, *longer sel.*
 "Like an ill husband, though I knew the same," *fr.* Pt. II. LO
Honest, Wouldn't You? *Unknown.* WBLP
Honesty. Horatius Bonar. *See* Be True.
Honesty. Sir Thomas Wyatt. OBSC
 (Of Dissembling Words.) SiCE
Honesty at a Fire. J. C. Squire. FiBHP
Honey. Ruth Miller. BoSA
Honey/ When de man. Sister Lou. Sterling A. Brown. GoSl; PoNe
Honey Baby take yo' time. Take Yo' Time. *Unknown.* StDa
Honey Bear. Elizabeth Lang. BoTP
Honey Bee, The. Philip Freneau. *See* On a Honey Bee.
Honey Bee. C. Lindsay McCoy. GFA
Honey Bee, The. Don Marquis. SiTL; WhC
Honey-Bee. Lucy Fitch Perkins. SUS
Honey bee is sad and cross, The. The Honey Bee. Don Marquis. SiTL; WhC
"Honey Bee," its habitat, The. Honey Bee. C. Lindsay McCoy. GFA
Honey Dew Falls from the Tree. John Clare. AtBAP
Honey Dripping from the Comb. James Whitcomb Riley. AA
Honey-Farm, The, *abr.* Virgil, *tr. fr. Latin by* Dryden. *Fr.* Georgics, IV. WoL
Honey for the Heart. Louis J. Sanker. JKCP (1955 ed.)
Honey from silkworms who can gather. Lines to a Critic. Shelley. EPN
Honey from the Lion. Leah Bodine Drake. NePoAm
Honey Harvest. Martin Armstrong. MM; TwCV
Honey in the horn! I brought my horse from the water. The Valley Harvest. Harold Lenoir Davis. NP
Honey in the lion's mouth. The Holy Eucharist. Pedro Calderón de la Barca. CAW
Honey-Mead. *Unknown, tr. fr. Anglo-Saxon by* Charles W. Kennedy. *Fr.* Riddles. AnOE
Honey mist on a day of frost in a dark oak wood, A. The Cooleen. Douglas Hyde. OBVV
Honey, pepper, leaf-green limes. Jamaica Market. Agnes Maxwell-Hall. PoNe
Honey, see dat jay-bird dah. Settin' on de Fence. *Unknown.* WBLP
Honey-sweet, sweet as honey smell the lilies. Summer-sweet. Katharine Tynan. TIP
Honey, Take a Whiff on Me. *Unknown.* ABF, *with music;* LiTM; OxBoLi; SiTL
Honey-tongued [*or* -tong'd] Shakespeare, when I saw thine issue. Ad Gulielmum Shakespeare. John Weever. ReIE; SiCE; TuPP
Honey, trus' der Lawd a bit, an' doan fohgit to smile. Trus' an' Smile. B. Y. Williams. BLRP
Honeymoon. Samuel L. Albert. GoYe
Honeymoon. Mary Carolyn Davies. PR
Honey-Moon, The. Walter Savage Landor. BOHV
Honeymoon, The. Henry Luttrell. *Fr.* Advice to Julia. OBRV
Honey-moon is very strange, The. The Honey-Moon. Walter Savage Landor. BOHV
Honeysuckle, The. Dante Gabriel Rossetti. BPN; EmBrPo; PoVP
Honour. Ada Cambridge. BoAu
Honour. Bernard Mandeville. *Fr.* On Honour. BeR
Honor and Desert. Coventry Patmore. The Angel in the House, II. iv, 1. HBV
Honor [*or* Honour] and shame from no condition rise. Worth Makes the Man [*or* Man]. Pope. *Fr.* An Essay on Man, Epistle IV. BeR; BLV; BoLiVe; CBE; CBOV; LPS-3; MaRV; PoeMoYo; PoFr; TrGrPo
Honor and truth and manhood. Things That Endure. Ted Olson. WBLP
"Honor be to Mudjekeewis!" The Four Winds. Longfellow. *Fr.* The Song of Hiawatha. AnNE
Honour corruption villainy holiness. Chaucer. E. E. Cummings. MeRV
Honour Dishonoured. Wilfrid Scawen Blunt. *See* Prison Sonnet.
Honor, honor, is the town. Barbara Allen (B *vers.*). *Unknown.* ABS
Honour in Bud. Ben Jonson. *See* It Is Not Growing like a Tree.
Honor in chief, our oath is to uphold. Chorus Primus. Fulke Greville. *Fr.* Mustapha. OBS
Honor invoked, no man may save his hide. As Always. James Gallagher. JKCP (1955 ed.)

Honour is so sublime perfection. To the Countesse of Bedford. John Donne. MeLP
Honour of Bristol, The. *Unknown.* EV-2; LH, *sl. abr.*; SG
"Honor," said the man. Definitions. Joseph Joel Keith. PoToHe (new ed.)
Honour the leaves, and the leaves of life. The Holy Well. *Unknown.* BaBo
Honour the salutation of the unknown! Goethe. *Fr.* West-eastern Divan. BoFr
Honourable Entertainment Given to the Queen's Majesty in Progress at Elvetham, 1591, *sels.* Nicholas Breton, *and others.*
 Phillida and Corydon [*or* Coridon]. Nicholas Breton. BCEP; BLV; EV-1; HBV; LPS-1; OBEV; ReEn; TuPP; ViBoPo
 ("In the merry month of May.") EG
 (Pastoral, A.) TrGrPo
 (Phyllida and Corydon.) ElL; ElSeCe; EM-1; EPP; OAEP; OBSC; ReIE; SeCePo
 (Ploughman's Song, The.) ALV; CenL; LiTL; OBSC
 (Plowman's Song, The.) FaBoEn; SiCE
 With Fragrant Flowers We Strew the Way. Thomas Watson. ElL
 (Ditty of the Six Virgins, The.) OBSC; SiCE
Hon. Mr. Sucklethumbkin's Story. "Thomas Ingoldsby." *Fr.* Ingoldsby Legends. OBRV
Honorable the City Clerk, The: Dear Sir. Letter to the City Clerk. Frederick A. Wright. FaFP
"Honored [*or* Honoured] I lived erewhile with honored men." Prison Sonnet [*or* Honour Dishonoured]. Wilfrid Scawen Blunt. CAW; OBMV
Honoria's Surrender. Coventry Patmore. *Fr.* The Angel in the House, I, xii. VA
Honors. Jean Ingelow. OQP; QP-2
Honors of War. John James Piatt. BlG
Honours that the people give always, The. The Thespians at Thermopylae. Norman Cameron. ChMP
Hoo the Warld Wags. Heine, *tr. fr. German into Scottish by* Edwin Morgan. AnGP
Hooded figure followed me, A. A Masque of Life and Death. Witter Bynner. AnAmPo; LA
Hooded in angry mist, the sun goes down. Nightfall. Herbert Asquith. MoP
Hoof-beat on the early air. Indictment. Margaret Tod Ritter. AnAmPo; LA
Hoof Dusk. Carl Sandburg. Po
Hoofs of the Horses, The. Will H. Ogilvie. EBSV
Hoofs of thunder, fetlocks splashed with sunrise. March-Patrol of the Naked Heroes. Herbert S. Gorman. TCPD
Hook for Leviathan, A. Norman Cameron. ChMP
Hooker's Across. George Henry Boker. PAH
Hoopoe's Call, The. Aristophanes, *tr. fr. Greek by* T. F. Higham. *Fr.* The Birds. OxBG
 (Hark! the Hoopoe's Call, *tr. by* Benjamin Bickley Rogers.) GrR
Hoopskirt, The. John Gould Fletcher. LaNeLa
Hoosen Johnny. *Unknown.* AS, *with music*; FaPON
Hop, a skip, and off you go, A! Dancing. Eleanor Farjeon. StVeCh (1955 ed.)
Hop, hop, hop, nimble as a top. My Little Pony. *Unknown.* SAS
Hop-o-My-Thumb. *Unknown.* *Fr.* Ballads on Napoleon. CoBE
Hop-poles stand in cones, The. The Midnight Skaters. Edmund Blunden. CoEV; ExPo; FaBoTw; GTBS-D; MBP; MoBrPo; PoD; POTE
Hop Up, My Ladies, *with music.* *Unknown.* OuSiCo
Hope. William Lisle Bowles. EnRP
Hope. Gamaliel Bradford. HBMV
Hope, A. Anne Brontë. MaRV
Hope ("Unfading hope!"). Thomas Campbell. *Fr.* The Pleasures of Hope. LPS-3
Hope. Arthur Hugh Clough. *See* Say Not the Struggle Naught Availeth.
Hope, *sel.* William Cowper.
 "Though clasp'd and cradled in his nurse's arms." PoEL-3
Hope. Sir Richard Fanshawe. *Fr.* Il Pastor Fido. OBS
Hope. Goldsmith. *Fr.* The Captivity; an Oratorio, II. OBEC
 "Hope, like a gleaming taper's light," *sel.* MaRV
Hope. George Herbert. PoEL-2
Hope. William Dean Howells. AA; OBAV
Hope. Randall Jarrell. MoAB; MoAmPo (1950 ed.)
Hope. Georgia Douglas Johnson. CDC
Hope. Mikhail Lermontov, *tr. fr. Russian by* C. M. Bowra. BoR
Hope. Anna Blake Mezquida. MaRV
Hope. Andreas Munch, *tr. fr. Norwegian by* Charles W. Stork. AnNoLy
Hope ("Hope springs eternal in the human breast"). Pope. *Fr.* An Essay on Man, Epistle I. MaRV, *2 ll.*; TreF, *4 ll.*
 (Pleasure of Hope, The, *4 ll.*) ACP
Hope. William Shenstone. *Fr.* A Pastoral Ballad. KN; OBEC; RO
 (Shepherd's Home, The.) CG; GN
Hope. Phillips Stewart. CaP; OCL
Hope. Sarah Wingate Taylor. JKCP (1955 ed.)
Hope. Theognis, *tr. fr. Greek by* John Hookham Frere. AWP; JAWP; WBP
Hope ("He died!"). *Unknown.* ChIP; OQP; QP-1
Hope ("Life has conquered"). *Unknown, tr. fr. Irish by* Frank O'Connor. KiLC
Hope ("Soft as the voice"). *Unknown.* MaRV
Hope. Oscar Wilde. *Fr.* The Ballad of Reading Gaol. MaRV
Hope. Countess of Winchilsea. TriL
Hope and Despair. Lascelles Abercrombie. HBV; OBMV
Hope and Faith. Isaac Leibush Peretz, *tr. fr. Yiddish by* Henry Goodman. TrJP
Hope and Fear. Thomas Campion. PoP
Hope and Fear. Swinburne. BPN; EmBrPo; EPN; EPP; EV-5; FaBoBe; HBV; PoVP; VA
Hope, art thou true, or dost thou flatter me? Astrophel and Stella, LXVII. Sir Philip Sidney. ReEn; SiPS
Hope Evermore and Believe. Arthur Hugh Clough. BEL; BPN; EmBrPo; EPN; GrCo-2; PoVP; WGRP
 (Hope Evermore.) BHV
 "Go from the east to the west," *sel.* MaRV
Hope for Miracles. Wolfram von Eschenbach, *tr. fr. German by* Jethro Bithell. LiTW; LyMA
Hope for Those Separated by War, A. Sidney Keyes. LoPS
Hope humbly then; with trembling pinions soar. Pope. *Fr.* An Essay on Man, Epistle I. TrGrPo
Hope I dreamed of was a dream, The. Mirage. Christina Rossetti. BLV; BrBE; EnLi-2; KN; MBP; PoRA
Hope in Failure. "Æ." PC
Hope in Him While Thou Livest. Kabir, *tr. fr. Hindi.* MaRV
Hope is a subtle glutton. Emily Dickinson. MOAP
Hope Is a Tattered Flag. Carl Sandburg. *Fr.* The People, Yes. NAMP
Hope is like a harebell trembling from its birth. Christina Rossetti. *Fr.* Sing-Song. MBP
Hope is the thing with feathers. Emily Dickinson. AmP; AmPP (4th ed.); GBV (1952 ed.); GTBS-D; MoAB; MoAmPo (1950 ed.); MoShBr; NeMA; OxBA; PG
Hope, is this thy hand. Fickle Hope. Harrison Smith Morris. AA
Hope, like a gleaming taper's light. Hope. Goldsmith. *Fr.* The Captivity; an Oratorio. MaRV
Hope, like the hyena [*or* hyaena], coming to be old. Henry Constable. *Fr.* Diana. EnLoPo; OBSC; SiCE
Hope! Not distant is the Springtime. Hope and Faith. Isaac Leibush Peretz. TrJP
Hope, of all ills that men endure. In Praise of Hope. Abraham Cowley. EV-2
Hope of my heart, in thy cradle reposing. The Love and Protection of Mother and Father—Venetian. *Unknown.* BOL
Hope of Our Hearts. Sir Edward Denny. BePJ
Hope of the Resurrection, The. Frances Brown. EOAH
Hope of the World, The. Sir William Watson. WGRP
Hope of Truth grows stronger, day by day, The. Sub Pondere Crescit. James Russell Lowell. MaRV
Hope Overtaken. Dante Gabriel Rossetti. The House of Life, XLII. PoVP; ViPo
Hope Springing Up. John Wesley. BePJ
Hope Springs Eternal ("Heav'n from all creatures hides the book of fate"). Pope. *Fr.* An Essay on Man, Epistle I. CoEV; OBEC
 (Essay on Man, An.) EV-3; ViBoPo
 (Future, The, *abr.*) BCEP
Hope springs eternal in the human breast. Hope [*or* The Pleasure of Hope]. Pope. *Fr.* An Essay on Man, Epistle I. ACP; MaRV; TreF
Hope we not in this life only. Not in Vain. *Unknown.* BLRP
Hope, whose weak being ruined is. Against Hope. Abraham Cowley. *Fr.* The Mistress. GTBS-W; LiTB; LiTG; LoBV; MeLP; MePo; OBS; SeCV-1
Hopefully Waiting. Anson D. F. Randolph. LPS-2
Hopeless Desire Soon Withers and Dies. "A. W." OBSC; ReIE
Hopeless Love. *Unknown, tr. fr. Irish by* Sir Samuel Ferguson. IrPN
Hopes. Ibn al-Imam, *tr. fr. Arabic by* A. J. Arberry. MooP
Hopes and Memories. Giovanni Pascoli, *tr. fr. Italian by* Glauco Cambon. OnPM
Hopes grimly banished from the heart. Exiles. William Hamilton Hayne. AA
Hopes, on which our spirits live. George Henry Boker. *Fr.* The Book of the Dead. MOAP
Hopes, Painted. Sergei Aleksandrovich Yesenin, *tr. fr. Russian by* Babette Deutsch. TrRV
Hope's Song. Francis Carlin. HBMV
Hope's Song. Helen Maria Winslow. PEOR
Hopi Ghosts William Haskell Simpson. *Fr.* In Arizona. NP
Hoping all the time. *Unknown.* *Fr.* Kokin Shu. AWP

Hopped upon the *Richmond*, an' then upon the *Lee*. Oh, Annie, Oh! *Unknown*. StDa
Hopping Frog. Christina Rossetti. UTS
Hoppity. A. A. Milne. TiPo
Hops, The. Ivan Alekseyevich Bunin, *tr. fr. Russian by* Babette Deutsch. TrRV
Hora Christi. Alice Brown. HBV; LBMV; MaRV; QS; SDH; TrPWD; WGRP
Horace. John Osborne Sargent. AA
Horace à la Mode. "J. C. C. H., Jr." CAG
Horace, Book V, Ode III. Charles Larcom Graves. CenHV
Horace, Epistle VII, Book I, Imitated and Addressed to the Earl of Oxford. Swift. CEP
Horace, for whom I entertain. Two Garden Scenes. Charles Burgess. NePoAm-2
Horace Greeley. Edmund Clarence Stedman. DD; GA
Horace Paraphrased. Isaac Watts. *See* Insignificant Existence.
Horace still charms with graceful negligence. Pope. *Fr.* An Essay on Criticism, Pt. III. PtP
Horace the Wise. Morrie Ryskind. HBMV
Horace to Pyrrha. Horace. *See* To Pyrrha.
Horas Tempestatis Quoque Enumero; the Sundial. John Hollander. NePoEA
Horat. Ode 29. Book 3. Paraphras'd in Pindarique Verse. Horace. *See* To Maecenas.
Horatian Epode to the Duchess of Malfi. Allen Tate. FaBoMo
Horatian Ode, An. Richard Henry Stoddard. *See* Abraham Lincoln ("Not as when some great captain").
Horatian Ode upon Cromwell's Return from Ireland, An. Andrew Marvell. AEV; BEL; BrBE; CoEV; EPS; EV-2; GTBS; GTBS-D; GTBS-W; GTSE; GTSL; HBV; LEAP; LiA; LoBV; MaPo; MePo; OBEV; OBS; PoEL-2; SeCV-1; SeEP; TOP; UnPo (1st ed.)
(Two Kings.) LH
Sels.
Execution of King Charles, The. AnEnPo; PoRA
King Charles upon the Scaffold, *sl. shorter.* ChTr
"So restless Cromwell could not cease." ViBoPo
Horatio. *sels.* Hyam Plutzik. FiMAP
Faustus, III.
Ostler, The, II.
Horatio, of ideal courage vain. Feigned Courage. Charles *and* Mary Lamb. GN
Horatius [at the Bridge]. Macaulay. *Fr.* Lays of Ancient Rome. BBV, *abr.*; BCEP, *abr.*; BeLS; BHV; CBPC; EV-4; FaBoCh, *abr.*; FaFP; HBV; HBVY; LH; LoGBV, *abr.*; LPS-2; MCCG; OHFP, *abr.*; OnSP; PECK; PIR, *abr.*; ShBV-1; TreF
Sels.
"And in the nights of winter." AlDL
Fight at the Bridge, The. MaC; OtMeF
"Then out spake brave Horatius." LEAP, 6 *sts.*; PoFr, 5 *sts.*
"Horatius Flaccus, B.C. 8." To Q. H. F. Austin Dobson. PtP
Horch, horch, die Bell am Backdoor ringt! Morning Song. Kurt M. Stein. FiBHP
Horestes, *sel.* John Pickering.
"Farewell, adieu, that courtly life." ElSeCe; ReEn; TuPP
(Haltersick's Song.) OBSC
(Song: "Farewell, adieu, that court-like life!") ElL
Horizon. *Unknown. See* 'Tis Life Beyond.
Horizon Thong. George Abbe. GoYe
Horizons. Struthers Burt. NoCaPo (1941 ed.); TBM
Horizons. Gwendolen Haste. BAP
Horizons. Rebecca McCann. PoMa
Horizons. Clinton Scollard. OQP; QP-2
Horizons cannot nourish me. Derricks and Rainbows. Joseph Auslander. PoMa
Horizon's hatred smites Magellan. Magellan. Allen Curnow. AnNZ
Horizontal World. Thomas Saunders. CaP
Horn, The. Léonie Adams. AnAmPo; InPo; LA; MAP; MoAB; MoAmPo
Horn. James Hayford. NePoAm-2
Horn, The. James Reaney. PeCV
Horn, A. *Unknown, tr. fr. Anglo-Saxon. Fr.* Riddles. AnOE, *tr by* Charles W. Kennedy; EPP, *tr. by* Herbert B. Brougham; OuHeWo, *tr. by* Stith Thompson
Horn, The. Alfred de Vigny. *See* Sound of the Horn, The.
Horned Owl, The. "Barry Cornwall." *See* Owl, The.
Horner, aroused, looks up again. Variations on a Theme. Joseph G. E. Hopkins JKCP (1955 ed.)
Hornets. C. Lindsay McCoy. GFA
Hornets build in plaster-dropping rooms, The. Abandoned. Madison Cawein. YT
Hornpipe. Edith Sitwell. MoVE; SeCePo
Horns of Elfland, The. Tennyson. *See* Bugle Song.
Horns to Bulls Wise Nature Lends. Thomas Stanley, *after* Anacreon. *See* Beauty.
Horny-Goloch Is an Awesome Beast, The. *Unknown*. FaBoCh; LiL
Horologium, *sel. Unknown, tr. fr. Greek by* G. R. Woodward.
Mother of God, The. ISi
Horoscope. J. V. Cunningham. NePoAm
Horror. Peter Baum, *tr. fr. German by* Jethro Bithell. AWP
Horror Movie. Howard Moss. SiTL
Horror on Dagoth Wold, The. Frank Belknap Long. DaM
Horrors of Civil War, The. Horace, *tr. fr. Latin by* Stephen Edward De Vere. WoL
Horse, The. Job, XXXIX, Bible, *O.T.* FaPON (19–21, 24–25); GoTP (19–25); StaSt (21–25); TrGrPo (19–25)
("Hast thou given the horse his might?" XXXIX: 19–XL: 2.) InP
(Hast Thou Given the Horse Strength? XXXIX: 19–25.) ChTr
(War Horse, The, XXXIX: 19–25.) BHV; ShBV-2
Horse. Elizabeth Madox Roberts. PoeMoYo; TiPo (1959 ed.); UTS
Horse, The. Naomi Royde-Smith. FiBHP; LiTM; SiTL
("I know two things about the horse.") CenHV
Horse, The. Shakespeare. King Henry V, *fr.* III, vii. GoTP
Horse, A. Shakespeare. *Fr.* Venus and Adonis. ExPo
Horse and a flea and three blind mice, A. *Unknown*. FaFP; SiTL
Horse and hattock. The Witch's Broomstick Spell. *Unknown*. ChTr
Horse and His Master, The. Philip F. Allen. PA
Horse and mule live 30 years, The. Liquor & Longevity. *Unknown*. LiTG; SiTL; WhC
Horse & Rider. Wey Robinson. WhC
Horse can't pull while kicking, A. Horse Sense. *Unknown*. BLPA; NeHB; WBLP
Horse-Chestnut Tree. Witter Bynner. DDA
Horse Chestnut Tree, The. Richard Eberhart. AtBAP; CrMA; FiMAP; MoAB; NePA; NePoAm; Po
Horse from Cleres and Valery, The. Hilaire Belloc. *Fr.* The Ballad of Val-ès-Dunes. AlDL
Horse in a Field. Walter de la Mare. HBMV
Horse Named Bill, The, *with music. Unknown*. AS
Horse of poetry nibbles, The. The Invitation. Donagh MacDonagh. OnYI
Horse Sense. *Unknown*. BLPA; NeHB; WBLP
Horse Thief, The. William Rose Benét. BBV (1951 ed.); CP; HBMV; MAP; MoAmPo; TCAP; TSW; TSWC
Horse-Trough, The. Richard Hughes. AlDL
Horse would tire, A. Elizabeth J. Coatsworth. TiPo
Horse Wrangler, The. D. J. O'Malley. CoSo, *with music*; CSF
(Tenderfoot, The, *with music.*) AS
Horse Xanthus Warns Achilles, The. Homer, *tr. fr. Greek by* F. L. Lucas. *Fr.* The Iliad, XIX. GrPE
Horseback Ride, The. "Grace Greenwood." LPS-2
Horseman, The. Walter de la Mare. AlDL; SUS; TiPo (1959 ed.)
Horseman high alone as an eagle on the spur, A. The Coast-Road. Robinson Jeffers. PreP
Horseman resorts to the city, A. Dialogue between Poet and Patron. Taliesin. LyMA
Horseman riding, A. Woodcut. R. N. D. Wilson. OxBI
Horseman Springing from the Dark; a Dream. Lilla Cabot Perry. PC
Horsemen of the sleepless night, cavalry. Insomnia. Jules Supervielle. MiCF
Horsemen on the Great Szechuan Road. Ts'en Ts'an, *tr. fr. Chinese by* Wang Sheng-chih. WhP
Horses. Richard Armour. WhC
Horses. Edwin Muir. AlDL; FaBoCh; HaMV; LoGBV; MoVE; SeCePo
Horses. Dorothy Wellesley. AlDL; ChMP; OBMV; ShBV-4
Horses and Men in Rain. Carl Sandburg. MOAP
Horses bore me as far as my desire, The. Parmenides, *tr. fr. Greek by* Charles H. Kahn. GrPo
Horses Chawin' Hay. Hamlin Garland. StVeCh
Horses of Achilles, The. Homer. *See* Immortal Steeds of Achilles, The.
Horses of the Sea, The. Christina Rossetti. *Fr.* Sing-Song. FaPON; GFA; PCD; PoRh; RAR; SUS; UTS
Horses on the Camargue. Roy Campbell. AtBAP; POTE; SeCePo; ShBV-3
Horses, resigned to their black plague of flies. Drought. Geoffrey Johnson. HaMV
Horses, the pigs, The. Familiar Friends. James S. Tippett. BoChLi; BoTP; SUS; UTS
Horseshoe, The. Edna St. Vincent Millay. *See* Wonder Where This Horseshoe Went.
Horseshoes they hammer which turn on a swivel. Gypsies. Robert Browning. *Fr.* The Flight of the Duchess. PCH
Horti, Deliciae Dominae, Marcescite Tandem. George Herbert, *tr. fr. Latin by* D. C. Allen. LaP
Horus. Gérard de Nerval, *tr. fr. French*. AnFP, *tr. by* Barbara Howes; TrFP, *tr. by* Alan Conder
Hos Ego Versiculos. Francis Quarles. *Fr.* Argalus and

Parthenia. CaAE; CenL; OBS; SeEP. *See also* Man's Mortality, *sl. diff. vers. at. to* Simon Wastell, *fr.* Microbiblion.
(Like as the Damask Rose.) LoBV
Hosanna. Thomas Traherne. PoEL-2; SeCV-2
Hosanna to the King. Psalm CXLVIII. Christopher Smart. RO
Hosea Biglow's Lament. James Russell Lowell. *See* Mr. Hosea Biglow to the Editor of the Atlantic Monthly.
Hospital. Wilfred Funk. PoToHe
Hospital. John Allan Wyeth. PoP
Hospital Duties. *Unknown.* BlG
Hospital for sick and needy Jews, A. The New Jewish Hospital at Hamburg. Heine. TrJP
Hospital Observation. Julian Symons. WaP
Hospital Prison Ship, The. Philip Freneau. *Fr.* The British Prison Ship, III. IAP
Hospital Train. John Allan Wyeth. PoP
Hospital Verses. Mokichi Saito, *tr. fr. Japanese by* Shio Sakanishi. PoP
Hospital Ward (of this Generation). George Rostrevor Hamilton. POTE
Hospitality. Euripides, *tr. fr. Greek by* Robert Browning. *Fr.* Alcestis. OxBG
("Hence Loathèd Melancholy . . . ," *tr. by* Gilbert Murray.) GrR
("Why look'st so solemn and so thought-absorbed?" *tr. by* Robert Browning.) GrPo
Hospitality. John Banister Tabb. PPL
Hospitality in Ancient Ireland. *Unknown, tr. fr. Middle Irish by* Kuno Meyer. OnYI
Host and Guest. Henry W. Clark. OQP; PSO; QP-1
Host is riding from Knocknarea, The. The Hosting of the Sidhe. W. B. Yeats. TIP
Host lifts high the candlelight, The. The Young Mother. Lizette Woodworth Reese. LS; MOAP
Host of the Air, The. W. B. Yeats. CBOV; CH; GTIV; LoEn; OnYI; PoVP; SeCeV
(Folk of the Air, The.) VA
Host set forth, The; and pour'd his steele waues, farre out of the fleete. Achilles Goes Forth to Battle. Homer. *Fr.* The Iliad, XIX. EV-1
Host was set, The. The Sacrifice of Polyxena. Euripides. *Fr.* Hecuba. GrR
Hostess, The. Wang Mou Fang, *tr. fr. Chinese by* Henry H. Hart. PoHN
Hostess' Daughter, The. Ludwig Uhland, *tr. fr. German by* Margarete Münsterberg. AWP; JAWP; WBP
(From the German of Uhland, *tr. by* James Weldon Johnson.) CDC
(Landlady's Daughter, The, *tr. by* J. S. Dwight.) LPS-1
Hostile Sun, The. D. H. Lawrence. CaAE
Hosting, The. Brooke Byrne. NeTW
Hosting of the Sidhe, The. W. B. Yeats. TIP
Hostlers and shepherds hailed His birth. Not Kings. Kenneth W. Porter. PSO
Hosts, The. George M. Brady. NeIP
Hosts of Don Rodrigo were scattered in dismay, The. The Lamentation of Don Roderick. *Unknown.* AnSpL-1; TeCS
Hosts of Faery. The. *Unknown, tr. fr. Middle Irish by* Kuno Meyer. OnYI
Hot Cake. Shu Hsi, *tr. fr. Chinese by* Arthur Waley. AlDL; AtBAP; BoW; MBP; MoBrPo (1942 ed.)
Hot cross buns, hot cross buns;/ One a penny poker. *Unknown.* OxNR
Hot-cross buns! Hot-cross buns!/ One a penny, two a penny. Mother Goose. BoTP; GaP; OTPC; OxNR; PCH
Hot Flame of My Grief, The. Moses ibn Ezra, *tr. fr. Hebrew by* Solomon Solis-Cohen. TrJP
Hot Ir'n! S. Omar Barker. PoOW
Hot muffins and crumpets too. Come Buy My Nice Muffins. *Unknown.* PCH
Hot September sun shone down on the wide and peaceful bay, The. The Wide Open Spaces. Oscar H. Lear. InMe
Hot Stuff. Edward Botwood. PAH
Hot Sun at its zenith weeps ingots, The. Summer Landscape. Jules Laforgue. AnFP
Hot sun [*or* sunne], cool fire, tempered with sweet air. Bethsabe's Song [*or* Bethsabe Bathing]. George Peele. *Fr.* David and Bethsabe. AtBAP; ATP; BLV; CoEV; ElL; ElSeCe; ExPo; InPo; LO; LoBV; OBSC; OxBoLi; PoEL-2; SeCeV; SiCE; TrGrPo; TuPP
Hot Stagnant Evening, A. Jules Laforgue, *tr. fr. French by* William Jay Smith. AnFP
Hot Tamale Man, The. Hazel Harper Harris. HiLiAm
Hot through Troy's ruin Menelaus broke. Menelaus and Helen. Rupert Brooke. SeCePo
Hot Time in the Old Town, A. Joe Hayden. YaD
Hot Weather. Dorothy Aldis. GFA
Hot Weather in the Plains—India. E. H. Tipple. HBV
Hot-Weather Song, A. Don Marquis. HBMV; StVeCh; WhC; YaD
Hot with sorrow or with joy. Inspiration. Per Hallström. AnSL
Hotel, The. Harriet Monroe. AnAmPo; LA; NP
Hotel Continental. William Jay Smith. WaP
Hotel de l'Univers et Portugal. James Merrill. MoAB; NePoAm
Hotel Lobby. C. R. Holmes. PtPa
Hotel Lobby. Mildred Weston. WhC
Hotel of Sparks. André Breton, *tr. fr. French by* Wallace Fowlie. MiCF
Hotel Transylvanie. Frank O'Hara. NeAP
Hotspur. Shakespeare. *See* My Liege, I Did Deny No Prisoners.
Hostpur's Description of a Fop. Shakespeare. *See* My Liege, I Did Deny No Prisoners.
Hottentot, The. Thomas Pringle. OBRV
Hottentot Cradle-Song. Fanny Raymond Ritter. BOL
Hottentot Tot, The. Newman Levy. RIS
Hould lingell hould the coblers silken twyne. *Unknown.* SeCSL
Hound, The. Babette Deutsch. HBMV; NLK
Hound, The. Sidney Lanier. *Fr.* The Jacquerie. AA; AlBD; PFY; PoMS
(Song for "The Jacquerie.") MAP; MoAmPo (1942 ed.); MOAP; SPP
Hound, A. Simonides, *tr. fr. Greek by* F. L. Lucas. GrL; OxBG; WoL
(Hound's Grave, The.) GrPE
Hound and the Huntsman, The. John Gay. TCEP
Hound at Night. Louise Ayres Garnett. TBM
Hound of Heaven, The. Francis Thompson. ACP; AnFE; ATP; BEL; BLV; BMEP; BoLiVe; CaAE; CAW; CBPC; CoBE; CP; EmBrPo; EnL; EnLi-2; EnLit; EPN; EPP; EV-5; FaFP; GoBC; GoTL; GrCo-2, *much abr.;* GTBS-W; GTSL; HBV; JKCP; LBBV; LEAP; LiA; LiTB; LiTM; LoBV; MaRV; MBP; MCCG; MM; MoAB; MoBrPo; OAEP; OBMV; OtMeF; OxBoCh; PIAE; PIR; PoE; PoEL-5; PoLi, *abr.;* POTT; PoVP; PreP; SeCePo; SeCeV; TCEP; TCPD; TOP; TreF, *br. sel.;* TrGrPo; TwCrTr; TyEnPo; UnPo (1st ed.); ViBoPo; ViP; ViPP; VLEP; WGRP; WHA
Hound on the Church Porch. Robert P. Tristram Coffin. AlBD; DDA
Hound Voice. W. B. Yeats. POTE
Hound was cuffed, the hound was kicked, The. The Hound [*or* Song for "The Jacquerie"]. Sidney Lanier. AA; AlBD; MAP; MoAmPo (1942 ed.); MOAP; PFY; PoMS; SPP
Hounded Lovers, The. William Carlos Williams. LoPS; TrGrPo
Hounded slave that flags in the race, The. The Wounded Person. Walt Whitman. *Fr.* Song of Myself. PoNe
Hounds, The. Patric Dickinson. ChMP
Hounds, The. John Freeman. OBMV
Hounds are all out, and the morning does peep, The. The Huntsman's Rouse. Henry Carey. SeCePo
Hound's Grave, The. Simonides. *See* Hound, A.
Hounds of Spring, The. Swinburne. *See* When the Hounds of Spring.
Hounds of the Soul, The. Louis Ginsberg. TrJP
Hounds, The. The great man's dream. The stone. The Hounds. Patric Dickinson. ChMP
Hour, The. Jessie B. Rittenhouse. BAP
Hour after hour the cards were fairly shuffled. Whist. Eugene Fitch Ware. DDA
Hour before Dawn, The. John Cowper Powys. BAP
Hour by Hour. "George Klingle." OQP; QP-1
Hour ere sudden sunset fired the west, An. Beaumont and Fletcher. Swinburne. *Fr.* Sonnets on English Dramatic Poets (1590–1650). PoVP
Hour Glass, The. Ben Jonson. EnLoPo; GTBS-W; LiTB; LiTG; SiTL
(On a Lover's Dust, Made Sand for an Hour-Glass.) ElSeCe
Hour Glass, The. Edward Quillinan. OBRV
Hour-Glass Whispers, The. W. H. Auden. ChMo
(Our Bias.) AtBAP
Hour-hand and the minute-hand upon a polished dial, The. The Speed Track. "Peter." BoTP
Hour I saw my dear ones part, The. The Raven. Kuthaiyir. MooP
Hour Is Late, The. Ida Norton Munson. ChIP
Hour Is Late, The. Winfield Townley Scott. FiMAP
"Hour is late, The," the shepherds said. The Shepherd Left Behind. Mildred Plew Meigs. ChBR
Hour is starry, and the airs that stray, The. Lines Written at Geneva; July, 1824. Thomas Lovell Beddoes. ERP
Hour is sweet, The. Lovely Athens stretches out. Athens. Kostas Kariotakis. MoGP
Hour of Autumn. Myrtle Alice McCarey. DDA
Hour of Death, The. Felicia Dorothea Hemans. HBV; LoBV
Hour of Death, The. *Unknown. Fr.* The Seafarer. PoLi

Hour of Good, a day of Ill, An. Three Proverbs. James Clarence Mangan, *after the Ottoman.* IrPN
Hour of Magic, The. W. H. Davies. MBP; MoBrPo; NeMA
Hour of National Emergency. Aeschylus, *tr. fr. Greek by* Lewis Campbell. *Fr.* Seven against Thebes. GrR
Hour of Peaceful Rest, The. William Bingham Tappan. AA; HBV
Hour of sight, The. Still Life. Kathleen Raine. NeBP
Hour of the Morning-Star, The. John Hall Wheelock. PR
Hour was late, was lost, The. Before the Aragva at Night. Nikolai Tikhonov. RuPo
Hour was on us, The; where the man? Lincoln. John Vance Cheney. DD; GA; LBAH; OHIP; PEDC
Hour which might have been yet might not be, The. Stillborn Life. Dante Gabriel Rossetti. The House of Life, LV. BPN; EmBrPo; EnLi-2; EPN; PoVP; ViPo
Hour with Thee, An. Richard Chenevix Trench. *See* Prayer: "Lord, what a change within us."
Hours, The. John Peale Bishop. MoVE; OxBA
Hours. Tristan Corbière, *tr. fr. French by* Kenneth Koch *and* Georges Guy. AnFP
Hours. Francisco González León, *tr. fr. Spanish by* Samuel Beckett. AnMP
Hours. *Unknown, tr. fr. Greek by* Gilbert Highet. OxBG
Hours and days and years are fleeting, The. Aleksandr Blok, *tr. fr. Russian by* C. M. Bowra. BoRS
Hours before dawn we were woken by the quake. Aubade. William Empson. FaBoTw; LiTB
Hours drag, The. Tears. Huang Pien. PoHN
Hours Grey. Francis Viélé-Griffin, *tr. fr. French by* Jethro Bithell. MiFP
Hours I have known when color, song or friendship. Peace. Marguerite Wilkinson. BAP
Hours I Remember Lonely and Lovely to Me. Thomas Caulfield Irwin. IrPN
Hours I spent with thee, dear heart, The. The Rosary. Robert Cameron Rogers. AA; BPP; FaBoBe; HBV; LBMV; LEAP; TreF; WBLP
Hours of Sleep. *Unknown.* GoTP; PFE, *sl. diff.*
Hours of Sleepy Night, The. Thomas Campion. *Fr.* The Mountebank's Mask. EIL
(Dismissal.) OBSC
Hours of the Day, The. George Dillon. NP
Hours of the Passion, *sel.* Harriet Eleanor Hamilton King.
Garden of the Holy Souls, The. ACP; JKCP (1926 ed.)
Hours of the Prime Passion, *sel.* William of Shoreham.
"At Prime Jesus was y-led." ACP; CAW
Hours of the Planets, The. Charles Madge. FaBoMo
"Now English eyes the cancerous sun behold!" *sel.* BoSA
Hours reel off the golden spool of time, The. Timeless Island. Clifford Gessler. MuM
Hours Rise Up [Putting Off Stars], The. E. E. Cummings. *See* Impression—IV.
Hous of Fame, The, *sels.* Chaucer.
"There saugh I stonden, out of drede," *fr.* III. PtP
"This egle, of which I have you told," *fr.* II. NBE
"With this worde he, right anoon," *fr.* III. NBE
House. Robert Browning. BPN; OAEP; PoVP; PreP; ViPo; VLEP
House, A, *sel.* Ford Madox Ford.
"I am the House," Pt. I. MBP; MoBrPo (1942 ed.)
House, The. Ibn al-Hammara, *tr. fr. Arabic by* A. J. Arberry. MooP
House, The. Paula Nelson. GoYe
House. Carl Sandburg. ChMo; CMP
House, The. Winfield Townley Scott. MiAP
House, A. J. C. Squire. MBP; NV
House, The. Henry Treece. MaRV
House and a road and a train reel in air, A. The Singer. Kadie Molodowsky. OnCuPl
House and Grounds, A. Leigh Hunt. OBRV
House and Home. Joseph Beaumont. OBS
(Home) GoTL
House and Home. Victor Hugo, *tr. fr. French.* MaRV
House and Land. Allen Curnow. AnNZ
House and the Road, The. Josephine Preston Peabody. CP; CV; LBMV; NV
House at Evening, The. William Rose Benét. TBM
House Beautiful, The. Robert Louis Stevenson. BSV; CaAE; CBE; EV-5; GTML; PoeT; PoVP
House Blessing, A. William Cartwright. ChTr
House Blessing. Arthur Guiterman. BrR; MaRV; PraP; TiPo; TrPWD
House by the Side of the Road, The. Sam Walter Foss. BAP; BLPA; BTP; CV; DDA; FaBoBe; FaFP; HBV; HBVY; MaRV; NeHB; OHFP; OQP; POT; PoTo; PTA-1; QP-1; TreF; WBLP; WGRP
House Carpenter. *Unknown. See* Daemon Lover, The.
House Cat, The. Annette Wynne. StVeCh
House Demolished. Charles Malam. PoMa
House Dog. George Boas. AlBD
House Fear. Robert Frost. *Fr.* The Hill Wife. BAP; ChMo; CMP; IAP; MOAP; NP; SBMV
House full, a hole full, A. *Unknown.* OxNR
House-Goblin, The. Viktor Rydberg, *tr. fr. Swedish by* Charles W. Stork. AnSL
House had gone to bring again, The. The Need of Being Versed in Country Things. Robert Frost. FaBoEn; OxBA
House in Springfield. Gail Brook Burket. PGD
House in Taos, A. Langston Hughes. CDC
House in the Heath, The. Annette von Droste-Hülshoff, *tr. fr. German by* James Edward Tobin. AnGP
House in Wartime, A. Richard Church. NeTW; POTE
House is built of logs and stone, A. House and Home. Victor Hugo. MaRV
House is crammed, The: tier beyond tier they grin. "Blighters." Siegfried Sassoon. FaBoTw; MoVE
House is in disorder, The. Valse des Fleurs. Denis Hudson. NeTW
House is so quiet now, The. The Vacuum. Howard Nemerov. NePoEA
House lies vacant now, forbear to knock, The. Miser. Gordon LeClaire. CaP
House my earthly parent left, The. The Cottage. Jones Very. OxBA
House of a Hundred Lights, The, *sels.* Ridgely Torrence.
Carpe Diem. AA
Compensation. AA
Conclusion of the Whole Matter, The. AA; HBV
"What! doubt the Master Workman's hand." PC
Young Lovers, The. AA
Youth and Age. AA
House of Ate, The. Spenser. *Fr.* The Faerie Queene, IV, I. OBSC
House of Broken Swords, The, *sel.* William Hervey Woods.
Prayer of Beaten Men, The. HBV
House of Calvin. Leonora Speyer. QS
House of Cards, A. Christina Rossetti. *Fr.* Sing-Song. PCH
House of Christmas, The. G. K. Chesterton. GoBC; HBV; HBVY; MaRV; MBP; MoBrPo; QS; TSW; TwCV
House of Chung, The. Han Shan, *tr. fr. Chinese by* Henry H. Hart. PoHN
House of Colour, The. Francis Sherman. *Fr.* The Deserted City. CaP; OCL
House of Death, The. Louise Chandler Moulton. BAP; OBAV
House of Dust, The, *sels.* Conrad Aiken.
Palimpsest; a Deceitful Portrait, Pt. IV, iii. ChMo; CMP
Portrait of One Dead, Pt. III, vi. ChMo; CMP; HBMV; NP; WHA
House of Falling Leaves, The. William Stanley Braithwaite. PoNe
House of Fame, The. John Skelton. *Fr.* Garlande of Laurell. NBE
House of God and Gate of Heaven. "Haec Est Domus Dei et Porta Coeli." Sister Maria del Rey. JKCP (1955 ed.)
House of Hospitalities, The. Thomas Hardy. MoPW
House of Life, The. Dante Gabriel Rossetti. PoVP; ViPo
Sels.
Ardour and Memory, LXIV. PoVP; ViPo
Autumn Idleness, LXIX. PoVP; ViPo; ViPP; VLEP
Barren Spring, LXXXIII. BPN; FaBoEn; NBE; PoEL-5; PoVP; ViPo; VLEP
Beauty's Pageant, XVII. BPN; PoVP; ViPo
Birth-Bond, The, XV. BPN; EmBrPo; HBV; OAEP; POTT; PoVP; ViPo
Body's Beauty, LXXVIII. ATP (1953 ed.); BMEP; BPN; EmBrPo; EnL; HBV; LEAP; POTT; PoVP; TrGrPo; ViP; ViPo; ViPP; VLEP
Bridal Birth, II. BMEP; BPN; EmBrPo; OAEP; POTT; PoVP; RiBV; ViPo; VLEP
Broken Music, XLVII. PoVP; VA; ViPo; VLEP
Choice, The, LXXI–LXXIII. ATP; BEL; BPN; EmBrPo; EnL; EnLi-2; EPP; HBV; MyFE; OBVV; PIAE; POTT; PoVP; PreP; TOP; ViBoPo; ViPo; VLEP
"Eat thou and drink," LXXI. WHA
"Think thou and act," LXXIII. GTML; OBEV (new ed.); OHIP; WHA
Cloud and Wind, XLIV. PoVP; ViPo
Dark Day, A, LXVIII. PoVP; ViPo
Dark Glass, The, XXXIV. BMEP; BPN; EmBrPo; EPN; HBV; LEAP; PoVP; TOP; VA; ViPo; VLEP
Day of Love, A, XVI. PoVP; ViPo
Death-in-Love, XLVIII. BPN; EmBrPo; PoVP; ViP; ViPo
Death's Songsters, LXXXVII. PoVP; ViPo
Equal Troth, XXXII. BPN; PoVP; ViPo
Farewell to the Glen, LXXXIV. BPN; PoVP; ViPo
From Dawn to Noon, LXXX. PoVP; ViPo
Genius in Beauty, XVIII. BPN; EmBrPo; EnLit; InP; OAEP; POTT; PoVP; TOP; ViP; ViPo; VLEP
Gracious Moonlight, XX. PoVP; ViPo
He and I, XCVIII. PoVP; ViPo
Heart of the Night, The, LXVI. BPN; EmBrPo; EPN; PoVP; TCEP; TOP; ViPo; VLEP

Heart's Compass, XXVII. BPN; EmBrPo; EPN; Po; PoVP; ViPo; VLEP; WHA
Heart's Haven, XXII. EmBrPo; EPN; OAEP; PoVP; ViPo; VLEP
Heart's Hope, V. BMEP; BPN; EmBrPo; EnLit; EPN; HBV; LEAP; PoVP; ViP; ViPo; VLEP
Her Gifts, XXXI. BPN; EmBrPo; HBV; PoVP; VA; ViPo
Hero's Lamp, LXXXVIII. PoVP; ViPo
Hill Summit, The, LXX. BPN; CaAE; EmBrPo; PoVP; REAL; TCEP; ViPo
Hoarded Joy, LXXXII. BPN; PoVP; ViPo
Hope Overtaken, XLII. PoVP; ViPo
Inclusiveness, LXIII. EmBrPo; EnLi-2; PoVP; VA; ViPo
Known in Vain, LXV. BPN; EmBrPo; EnLi-2; EPP; PoVP; TCEP; ViPo
Lamp's Shrine, The, XXXV. PoVP; ViPo
Landmark, The, LXVII. BPN; EmBrPo; EPN; EPP; PoVP; TCEP; ViPo
Last Fire, XXX. PoVP; ViPo
Life-in-Love, XXXVI. PoVP; ViPo; VLEP
Life the Beloved, XCVI. BPN; PoVP; ViPo
Lost Days, LXXXVI. BPN; EmBrPo; EnL; EnLi-2; EnLit; EPN; EPP; ES; GoBC; GTML; MaRV; NBE; OAEP; PIAE; POTT; PoVP; TOP; ViPo; ViPP; WHA
Lost on Both Sides, XCI. BPN; GTML (XCVII); GTSL; PoVP; SeCePo; ViPo; ViPP
Love and Hope, XLIII. PoVP; ViPo
Love Enthroned, I. BMEP; BPN; CoBE; EmBrPo; PIAE; PoVP; ViPo; VLEP
Love-Letter, The, XI. BPN; EmBrPo; PoVP; REAL; ViPo; VLEP
Love-Moon, The, XXXVII. PoVP; ViPo
Love-Sweetness, XXI. BEL; BPN; EmBrPo; EnLit; EPN; EPP; EtPaEn; EV-5; OAEP; POTT; PoVP; TOP; ViPo; VLEP
Lovers' Walk, The, XII. BPN; OAEP; PoVP; TOP; ViPo
Love's Baubles, XXIII. PoVP; ViPo
Love's Fatality, LIV. PoVP; ViPo
Love's Last Gift, LIX. BPN; PoVP; ViPo
Love's Lovers, VIII. BPN; EmBrPo; PoVP; ViPo
Love's Testament, III. BPN; PoVP
("O thou who at Love's hour.") ViPo
Lovesight, IV. BEL; BLV; BMEP; BoLiVe; BPN; CaAE; CoBE; EmBrPo; EnLi-2; EnLit; EPN; EPP; ES; EV-5; FaBoEn; GTBS-D; GTSL; HBV; LEAP; OAEP; OBVV; PIAE; POTT; PoVP; ReaPo; TCEP; TOP; TrGrPo; TyEnPo; VA; ViBoPo; ViPo; ViPP; VLEP; WHA
Memorial Thresholds, LXXXI. BPN; EmBrPo; PoVP; ReaPo; ViPo
Michelangelo's Kiss, XCIV. BPN; PoVP; ViPo
Mid-Rapture, XXVI. BEL; BPN; EPP; FaBoBe; HBV; LEAP; OAEP; PoE; PoVP; TOP; TyEnPo; ViPo
Monochord, The, LXXIX. CaAE; PoVP; TCEP; ViPo
Moonstar, The, XXIX. PoVP; ViPo
Morrow's Message, The, XXXVIII. GTSE; PoVP; ViPo; VLEP
Newborn Death, XCIX–C. BPN; EmBrPo; PoVP; ViPo
Nuptial Sleep, VI (A). BrBE; LoBV; PeBoSo; PoVP; ViPo; ViPP
Old and New Art, LXXIV–LXXVI.
Husbandman, The. BPN; PoVP; ViPo
Not as These. BPN; PoVP; ViPo
St. Luke the Painter. BPN; GoBC; PoVP; ViPo
One Hope, The, CI. BEL; BPN; EmBrPo; EnLi-2; EnLit; EPN; EPP; HBV; NBE; POTT; PoVP; REAL; ViPo; ViPP
Parted Love, XLVI. PoVP; ViPo
Passion and Worship, IX. BPN; EmBrPo; PoVP; ViPo
Portrait, The, X. BPN; EmBrPo; OAEP; PoVP; ViPo; VLEP
Pride of Youth, XXIV. BPN; FaBoEn; PoVP; ViPo; ViPP
"Retro Me, Sathana!" XC. BPN; EmBrPo; PoVP; ViPo
Secret Parting, XLV. EtPaEn; PoVP; ViPo
Severed Selves, XL. BPN; EmBrPo; PoVP; ViPo
Silent Noon, XIX. BEL; BLV; BoLiVe; BPN; EmBrPo; EnLi-2; EnLit; EPN; GTBS-D; HBV; LiTL; LO; LoPo; LoPS; OAEP; PIAE; PoEL-5; POTT; PoVP; RiBV; TCEP; TrGrPo; TwHP; TyEnPo; ViP; ViPo; ViPP; VLEP; WHA
Sleepless Dreams, XXXIX. OAEP; PoVP; ViPo
Song-Throe, The, LXI. BPN; PoVP; ViPo
Sonnet, The ("A sonnet is a moment's monument"), *introd.* BEL; BMEP; BPN; CoBE; EmBrPo; EnL; EnLi-2; EnLit; EPN; EPP; ES; GTBS-W; HBV; InP; LEAP; OAEP; PFE; PoVP; TCEP; TOP; ViBoPo; ViP; ViPo; ViPP; VLEP
(Introductory.) VA
Soul-Light, XXVIII. CoBE; EPP; PoVP; ViPo; VLEP
Soul's Beauty, LXXVII. BMEP; BPN; CoBE; EmBrPo; EnLit; OAEP; OBEV (new ed.); OBVV; POTT; PoVP; ViP; ViPo; ViPP; VLEP
(Sibylla Palmifera.) EV-5; GTML
Soul's Sphere, The, LXII. PoVP; ViPo
Stillborn Love, LV. BPN; EmBrPo; EnLi-2; EPN; PoVP; ViPo
Sun's Shame, The, XCII–XCIII. PoVP; ViPo
Superscription, A, XCVII. BEL; BMEP; BPN; EmBrPo; EnL; EnLi-2; EnLit; EPP; FaBoEn; HBV; LEAP; LO; NBE; PoEL-5; PoVP; SeCePo; TOP; VA; ViPo; ViPP; VLEP; WHA
(Nevermore, The.) LPS-3
Supreme Surrender, VII. EtPaEn; POTT; PoVP; ViPo
Through Death to Love, XLI. BPN; PoVP; ViPo; VLEP
Transfigured Life, LX. BPN; PoVP; ViPo
Trees of the Garden, The, LXXXIX. BPN; PoVP; ViPo
True Woman, LVI–LVIII.
Her Heaven. BMEP; BPN; EmBrPo; EPN; GTML; PoVP; ViPo
Her Love. BPN; EmBrPo; EPN; PoVP; ViPo
Herself. BPN; EmBrPo; EPN; POTT; PoVP; ViPo; ViPP
Vain Virtues, LXXXV. EmBrPo; EnLi-2; EPP; HBV; PoVP; ViPo; ViPP
Vase of Life, The, XCV. PoVP; ViPo
Venus Victrix, XXXIII. BPN; PoVP; ViPo
"What smouldering senses in death's sick delay," VI. PoVP; ViPo
Willowwood, XLIX–LII. BPN; EmBrPo; OAEP; POTT; PoVP; ReaPo; TCEP; ViP; ViPo; VLEP
"I sat with Love," XLIX. HBV; PoEL-5; TyEnPo; WHA
"O ye, all ye that walk in Willowwood," LI. BrBE; ViPP
Winged Hours, XXV. EmBrPo; EPN; PoVP; ViPo
Without Her, LIII. BPN; CoBE; EmBrPo; GTBS-W; PoEL-5; PoVP; ReaPo; VA; ViBoPo; ViP; ViPo; VLEP
Youth's Antiphony, XIII. BPN; PoVP; TOP; ViPo
Youth's Spring Tribute, XIV. BPN; PoVP; REAL; ViPo; VLEP
House of Lords, The. W. S. Gilbert. *See* House of Peers, The.
House of Morpheus, The. Spenser. *Fr.* The Faerie Queene, I, 1. UnPo (1st ed.)
(Cave of Sleep, The.) LPS-3
("He, making speedy way through 'spersèd air.") InP
House of Night, The, *sels.* Philip Freneau.
"By some sad means, when Reason holds no sway." AmPP; PoEL-4
Death. OnAP
Death's Epitaph, *br. sel.* AA
"O'er a dark field I held my dubious way." APW
"Trembling I write my dream, and recollect." AnFE; APA; CoAnAm
(Vision, A, *abr.*) IAP; TCAP
House of Pain, The. Florence Earle Coates. BPP; HBV; LBAP; OQP; QP-1
House of Peers, The. W. S. Gilbert. *Fr.* Iolanthe. InMe; MBP
(House of Lords, The.) TrGrPo
(Song: "When Britain really ruled the waves.") InP
House of Pride, The. William J. Dawson. MaRV; PoToHe
House of Pride, The. Spenser. *Fr.* The Faerie Queene, I, 4. WHA
House of Richesse, The. Spenser. *See* Cave of Mammon, The.
House of Sleep, The. John Gower. *Fr.* Confessio Amantis: Ceix and Alceone. AtBAP
House of sleepers—I, alone unblest, A. Insomnia. Edith M. Thomas. AA
House of Sorrows, The. Francis Thompson. MeRV
House of Splendour, The. Ezra Pound. InPo; MOAP
House of the Dawn! And of the evening Light. Hymn to the Sun. Edgar Lee Masters. *Fr.* Acoma. ChMo; CMP
House of the Eighties, A. Edmund Wilson. AnFE; CoAnAm; TwAmPo
House of the Heart, The. Siraj, *tr. fr. Arabic by* A. J. Arberry. MooP
House of the Mouse, The. Lucy Sprague Mitchell. TiPo
House of the Silent Years, The. Lizette Woodworth Reese. MOAP
House of the South, A. Charles Edward Eaton. NoCaPo (rev. ed.)
House of the Trees, The. Ethelwyn Wetherald. CaP; CPG; NLK; OCL; OQP; QP-2; VA
House of Wisdom, The ("Wisdom hath builded her house"). Proverbs, IX: 1–6, Bible, *O.T.* TrGrPo
House on the Hill, The. E. A. Robinson. AA; AnNE; BAP; CoBA; CV; FaPON; HBMV; InP; LaNeLa; MAP; MoAmPo; MOAP; MPB; PCD; PFE; PG; PIAE; TCAP; TrGrPo; TSW; TSWC; TwP; WHA; YT
House Plant. Winthrop Palmer. SiTL

House ringed round with trees and in the trees, A. Asylum. John Freeman. OBMV
House Sonnet. Elinor Wylie. *See* I Hereby Swear That to Uphold Your House.
House-Surgeon. W. E. Henley. *Fr.* In Hospital. PoVP
House That Jack Built, The. Samuel Taylor Coleridge. BOHV; PA
House That Was, The. Laurence Binyon. MBP; MoBrPo
House, though you've harboured grave-yards full of lives. Eulogy of My House. Siegfried Sassoon. MoPW
House to the Man, The. John Gould Fletcher. SPP
House-Top, The. Herman Melville. APW; LiTA
House was crammed from roof to floor, The. At the Pantomime. Oliver Wendell Holmes. AnNE
House was lost to the weather, The. Old Cellar. Robert P. Tristram Coffin. DDA
House-weary. Ian Drag. OQP; QP-2
House well supplied, A. Drinking Song. Avenzoar. MooP
House where I was born, The. The Doves. Katharine Tynan. AnIV; AWP; JAWP; WBP
House where white hands are longer, A. A Court Poet in Trouble. *Unknown.* SiB
House with Nobody in It, The. Joyce Kilmer. BLPA; DDA; MPB; MW; PTA-2; SP; StVeCh
House with Two Doors. Enrique González Martínez, *tr. fr. Spanish by* Samuel Beckett. AnMP
House, you are done. Consecration of the House. W. S. Fairbridge. NeLNL
Houseful, a roomful, A. *Unknown.* RIS
Household Art. Austin Dobson. VLEP
Household Gods. J. H. Macnair. DDA; PoMa; POT; PoTo
Household Sovereign, The. Longfellow. *Fr.* The Hanging of the Crane, III. LPS-1
Householder, The. Robert Browning. *See* Epilogue: "Savage I was sitting . . ."
Householder is Goathooves, A. The Faun. T. Sturge Moore. FaBoTw
Housekeeper, The. Vincent Bourne, *tr. fr. Latin by* Charles Lamb. GN; HBV; LPS-2; MW; OTPC; SN; TVSH
(Snail, The.) GoTP; MoShBr
House-Mates. Leon Gellert. MoAuPo
Houses. F. S. Flint. PFE
Houses, The, *sels.* "Robin Hyde."
"Adolicus; that's a creeper rug, its small," III. AnNZ
"Section and brick and grass," VI. AnNZ
Houses and rooms are full of perfumes, the shelves are crowded with perfumes. Song of Myself, II. Walt Whitman. CoV; TrGrPo
Houses are haunted, The. Disillusionment of Ten o'Clock. Wallace Stevens. AmP; CrMA; OxBA
Houses Have Open Eyes. Paul Zech, *tr. fr. German by* Glauco Cambon. OnPM
Houses I love with scaffoldings. New Day. Mikhail Lukonin. RuPo
Houses like Angels. Jorge Luis Borges, *tr. fr. Spanish by* Robert Stuart Fitzgerald. AnCL
Houses Should Have Homes to Live In. David Ross. PG (1933 ed.)
Housewife, The. Catherine Cate Coblentz. BLRP; ChIP; StJW; TrPWD
Housewife, The. W. W. Gibson. NP
Housewife. Josephine Miles. FiMAP
Housewife called out with a frown, A. *Unknown.* GoTP
Housewife, The; Winter Afternoon. Karle Wilson Baker. LS
Housewifery. Edward Taylor. AmP; AmPP; AnNE; GTBS-W; LiTA; NePA
(Huswifery.) OnAP; OxBA
Housewife's Prayer, The. Blanche Mary Kelly. DDA; GoBC; JKCP; WHL
Hovering and huge, dark, formless sway, The. The Virgin Mary. Edgar Bowers. NePoEA; PtPa
How? Franklin P. Adams. PFE
How? Abraham Sutskever, *tr. fr. Yiddish by* Sarah Zweig Betsky. OnCuPl
How a Cat Was Annoyed and a Poet Was Booted. Guy Wetmore Carryl. CIV; MAP; MoAmPo (1942 ed.)
How a Fisherman Corked Up His Foe in a Jar. Guy Wetmore Carryl. PoMS
How a Girl Was Too Reckless of Grammar by Far. Guy Wetmore Carryl. BOHV; FiBHP
How a Poet's Soul Comes into Play. Robert Browning. *Fr.* Sordello. MyFE
How about this lot? said the auctioneer. In an Auction Room. Christopher Morley. OBAV
How, after all, the ways that lie between. After All. Thomas S. Jones, Jr. VOD
How all is changed with the years! A Deserted Garden on the Road to Hua Chou. P'an I. PoHN
How all men wrongly death to dignify. Sonnet. A. J. M. Smith. PeCV
How all occasions do inform against me. Shakespeare. *Fr.* Hamlet, IV, iv. HoPM
How all's to one thing wrought! On a Piece of Music. Gerard Manley Hopkins. UnS
How am I hitched. Suffering. Albert Ehrenstein. TrJP
How Am I like Her? Winthrop Mackworth Praed. ERP
How am I to withhold my soul. Love Song. Rainer Maria Rilke. AnGP
How Amiable Are Thy Tabernacles! Bryant. *See* Dedication: "Thou, whose unmeasured temple stands."
How and with what will you fill. How? Abraham Sutskever. OnCuPl
How Annandale Went Out. E. A. Robinson. AmP; CoBMV; HBMV; MAP; MoAB; MoAmPo; TwP
How are our Spirituall Gamesters slipt away? Edward Taylor. *Fr.* An Elegy upon the Death of That Holy Man of God Mr. John Allen. PoEL-3
How Are the Mighty Fallen. Second Samuel, Bible, *O.T.* *See* David's Lament.
How Are Thy Servants Blest. Addison. OxBoCh
(Ode: "How are thy servants blest, O Lord!") OBEC; TrPWD
(Thanksgiving after Travel.) EV-3
How Are You? Arthur Guiterman. *See* Of Tact.
How Are You, Dear World, This Morning? Horace Traubel. TrJP
"How Are You, Sanitary?" Bret Harte. MDAH; PaA; PAP
How, as a spider's web is spun. To Jessie's Dancing Feet. William De Lancey Ellwanger. AA
How avarice loseth all. The Hen with the Golden Eggs. La Fontaine. OnPM
How Bateese Came Home. William Henry Drummond. IHA
How Beastly the Bourgeois Is. D. H. Lawrence. ChTr; LiTM; SiTL
How beauteous are rouleaus! how charming chests. Money. Byron. *Fr.* Don Juan, XII. GEPC
How beautiful are the bodies of men. Canticle of the Race: Song of Men. Edgar Lee Masters. ChMo; CMP
How beautiful are those eyes! The God of Love. Wen Yi-tuo. WhP
How beautiful are thy feet with shoes, O prince's daughter! Song of Solomon, Bible, *O.T.* LoPS
How beautiful Death is! Exuberant. Surgical Art Versus Beauty. Rodulfo Figueroa. PoP
How beautiful! from his blue throne on high. The Ocean. George D. Prentice. EtS
How beautiful is a woman whose avarice is over. Woman without Fear. George Dillon. AnEnPo
How beautiful is genius when combined. Sacred Poetry. John Wilson. WBLP
How beautiful is night! Night [*or* Night in the Desert]. Robert Southey. *Fr.* Thalaba the Destroyer. GN; OTPC
How beautiful is the flesh of women. Canticle of the Race: Song of Women. Edgar Lee Masters. ChMo; CMP
How beautiful is the human spirit. Canticle of the Race: Song of the Human Spirit. Edgar Lee Masters. ChMo; CMP
How beautiful is the rain! Rain in Summer. Longfellow. BAV; BBV (1923 ed.); BoChLi; BoTP; CG; GN; LPS-2; MW; OTPC; PCH; RIS; SN
How beautiful is the world. Rano Raraku. André Breton. MiCF
How beautiful it is to wake at night. Night Rhapsody. Robert Nichols. PtOT
How beautiful it was, that one bright day. Hawthorne. Longfellow. CoBA; DD; GA; IAP; PoEL-5; TCAP; TriL
How beautiful she looks, opening the pearly casement. A Bitter Love. Li Po. ChLP
How beautiful this night! the balmiest sigh. Night. Shelley. *Fr.* Queen Mab, IV. LPS-2
How beautiful to live as thou didst live! Tennyson. Florence Earle Coates. AA
How Beautiful upon the Mountains. Isaiah, LII: 7-10, Bible, *O.T.* TrJP
How beautiful, white and hard, are the teeth of this dead man. Don Juan Muses. John Heath-Stubbs. MoPW
How, best of kings, dost thou a scepter beare! To King James. Ben Jonson. OAEP
How Big Was Alexander? Elijah Jones. BLPA
How bleak and drear the earth would seem. No Flowers. *Unknown.* PEOR
How blessed is he, who leads a country life. To My Honour'd Kinsman, John Dryden [*or* Driden], of Chesterton. Dryden. OBS; SeEP
How blessed Sophocles, who, dying old. Sophocles. Phrynichus. OxBG
How blessed [*or* blest] thy creature is, O God. The Happy Change. William Cowper. CEP; EiPP
How blessèd were Judean hills. Noel. Gail Brook Burket. PGD
How blest are lovers in disguise! Song. George Farquhar. *Fr.* Love and a Bottle. SeCL
How blest art thou, canst love the countrey, Wroth. To Sir Robert Wroth. Ben Jonson. SeCV-1

How blest he appears. Song. Thomas Otway. *Fr.* Friendship in Fashion. SeCL
How blest the Maid whose heart—yet free. The Three Cottage Girls. Wordsworth. HBV
How blest thy creature is, O God. *See* How blessed thy creature is, O God.
How blest was the created state. The Fall. Earl of Rochester. EnLoPo
How blind men are! We surely cannot know. Understanding. H. W. Bliss. PoToHe
How blossomy must be the halls of Death. For Them That Died in Battle. William Alexander Percy. LS
"How brent is your brow, my Lady Elspat!" Lady Elspat. *Unknown.* ESPB
How Brer Tarrypin Learned to Fly. Joel Chandler Harris. TSW; TSWC
How brief that holy hour they knew. Magi. Leslie Savage Clark. ChIP
How bright are the honors which await those who. A Tribute to Our Honored Dead. Henry Ward Beecher. AOAH; MDAH
How bright on the blue. The Kite. Harry Behn. FaPON; TiPo (1959 ed.)
How brim-full of nothing's the life of a Beau! The Life of a Beau. James Miller. OBEC
How burn the stars unchanging in the midnight skies. New Year. John J. Moment. MaRV
How, Butler, How! *Unknown.* ViBoPo
How calm and proud that lady, Nefertiti, walked. Lady and Crocodile. Charles Burgess. NePoAm-2
How calm that little lake! no breath of wind. The Wild Duck and Her Brood. James Grahame. EnSW
How calm the sky above the roof. From a Prison. Paul Verlaine. TrFP
How calm they sleep beneath the shade. Greenwood Cemetery. Crammond Kennedy. LPS-1
"How came that blood on thy coat-lap?" The Dead Brother. *Unknown.* EnSB
How came the noble Timon to this change? Shakespeare. *Fr.* Timon of Athens, IV, iii. MyFE
How came this troubled one to stray. Boy in the Wind. George Dillon. MAP; MoAmPo (1942 ed.); TBM
"How camest thou by thy roses, Child?" Paper Roses. Dana Burnet. NV
How can a girl with such a big belly be so desirable? Mrs. Loewinsohn &c. Ron Loewinsohn. NeAP
How can a man's life keep its course. Lao-Tzu. *Fr.* Tao Teh King. WaKn
How can I cease to pray for thee? Prayer for One Dead. Julia C. R. Dorr. OQP; QP-1
How can I dread you, O portentous wise. The Woman with the Baby to the Philosopher. Frances Cornford. PoMa
How can I keep silence, soul? Apollo the Betrayer. Euripides. *Fr.* Ion. OxBG
How Can I Leave Thee. Friedrich Kücken, *tr. fr. German.* OlF
How Can I Sing? *Unknown.* MaRV
How can I sing light-souled and fancy-free. Two Lyrics, 2. Lorenzo de' Medici, *tr. fr. Italian by* John Addington Symonds. AWP; JAWP; WBP
How Can I Smile. Florence B. Hodgson. BLRP
How can I tell which days have yielded fruit? Days. Eliot Kays Stone. OQP; QP-2
How can I tell you, dear. Soseki, *tr. fr. Japanese by* Lois J. Erickson. SoLD
How can I, that girl standing there. Politics. W. B. Yeats. ChMo; POTE
How can I then return in happy plight. Sonnets, XXVIII. Shakespeare. OBSC; PeBoSo
How can I work when you play the piano. How? Franklin P. Adams. PFE
How can it be that I forget. Recollection. Anne Reeve Aldrich. AA; BAP; LEAP
How Can Man Die Better. Tyrtaeus, *tr. fr. Greek by* T. F. Higham. GrL; OxBG; WaaP
How can my Muse want subject to invent. Sonnets, XXXVIII. Shakespeare. EnLit; PeBoSo; ReEn
How can new Aprils come, when one was lost. Lost—an April. Mary Brent Whiteside. TBM
"How can one e'er be sure." Lady Horikawa. *Fr.* Hyaku-Nin-Isshu. AWP; JAWP; PFE; WBP
How can our minds and bodies be. Grace before Sleep. Sara Teasdale. TrPWD
How can she catch the sunlight. Questions. Lord Thomson of Cardington. OtMeF
How can that tree but withered be. Song. *Unknown.* ElL
How can the cripple get, in running race, the game? The Lover in Distress Exclaimeth against Fortune. *Unknown.* ReIE
How can the heart for sea and stone. On a Memory of Beauty. G. S. Fraser. FaBoMo; NeBP
How Can the Heart Forget Her. Walter Davison. HBV; OBEV; PG
(At Her Fair Hands.) ElL; LiTL; LO; WHA
(Ode: "At her fair hands.") OBSC
(Ode II: Dialogue between Him and His Heart, A.) SiCE
How can the tree but waste and wither away. Death in Life [*or* No Pleasure without Some Pain]. Thomas, Lord Vaux. ElL; OBSC; SiCE; TuPP
How Can They Honor Him? Anderson M. Scruggs. *See* Christmas, 1930.
"How can you, friend?" the Swedish say. How Do You Do? H. Bedford-Jones. WBLP
"How can you live in Goshen?" Goshen! Edgar Frank. MaRV; OQP; QP-2
How can you smile when pain is everywhere. Beauty. Mary Craig Sinclair. OQP; QP-2
How careful was I, when I took my way. Sonnets, XLVIII. Shakespeare. PeBoSo
How carefully she does her mouth. Artist. Ernestine Mercer. InMe
How certain the mule's step in the abyss. Rhapsody for the Mule. José Lezama Lima. AnCL
How changed is here each spot man makes or fills! Thyrsis. Matthew Arnold. BMEP; BPN; CP; EM-2; EmBrPo; EnLi-2; EnLit; EnSW; EV-5; FiP; GEPC; GTML; GTSL; LEAP; LiA; OAEP; OBEV (new ed.); OBVV; PoE; PoVP; ReaPo; TOP; TyEnPo; ViPo; ViPP; VLEP
"How changed is here each spot," *sel.* NBE
How charming is divine philosophy! Philosophy. Milton. *Fr.* Comus. BCEP
How clean this holy black comes from the pool! Aethiopus Lotus. Richard Crashaw. Epigrammata Sacra, I, 9. LaP
How clear, how keen, how marvellously bright. November 1. Wordsworth. BPN; EPN
How Clear, How Lovely Bright. A. E. Housman. More Poems, XVI. MaPo
How Clear She Shines! Emily Brontë. VLEP
How close the white-ranked crosses stand. Armistice. Charles Buxton Going. AOAH; DD; HBMV; PEDC
How cold are thy baths, Apollo! Jugurtha. Longfellow. AA; CoBA; CoV; IAP
"How come that blood on your shirt sleeve." Edward. *Unknown.* ABS
"How comes that blood all over your shirt?" Edward (B *vers.*). *Unknown.* HoPM; ViBoFo
How cool beneath this stone the soft moss lies. Epitaph for a Negro Woman. Owen Dodson. PoNe
How could she know, that child who thought. Innocence. "Æ." ChMo
How could the love between Thee and me sever? Two Songs, 2. Kabir. LiTW
How Could We, Beforehand, Live in Quiet. Nikolai Gumilev, *tr. fr. Russian by* Jeannette Eyre. WaaP
How could we do without you. Mr. Nigger. John Charles McNeill. NoCaPo
How Could You Know? Ben Ray Redman. PoMa
How courteous is the Japanese. The Japanese. Ogden Nash. InMe; WhC
How cracked and poor his laughter rings! The Old Beau. Edgar Fawcett. OBAV; PR
How Creatures Move. *Unknown.* GFA
How crowded is the heavenly House of Light. For Those Who Died. Thomas Curtis Clark. PGD
How cruel they! the cause of all. Crusts. Walter Shea. ChIP
How cruels love when shees too kinde. *Unknown.* SeCSL
How Cyrus Laid the Cable. John Godfrey Saxe. MC; PaA; PAH; PTA-1
How D.D. swaggers, M.D. rolls! Epigram: Diversity of Doctors. *Unknown.* ALV
How dare one say it? The Unexpress'd. Walt Whitman. NePA
How dare we deem that in this age. Empires. Francis Burdett Money-Coutts. OBVV
How dare we look askance at these two men. Simon and Judas. Kenneth W. Porter. OQP; QP-2
How dare you be so far, whose arms surrounded. Dialogue. Margaret Widdemer. MuM
How dare you sing such cheerful notes? To the Birds. Peter McArthur. CPG
How dazzling are the heavens to-day! Lovers' Wine. Baudelaire. TrFP
How dear to hearts by hurtful noises scarred. Earth's Silences. Ethelwyn Wetherald. CPG
How Dear to Me the Hour. Thomas Moore. CoBE; ERP
How dear to my heart are the grand politicians. The Old Hokum Buncombe. Robert E. Sherwood. InMe
How dear to my [*or* this] heart are the scenes of my childhood. The Old Oaken Bucket [*or* The Bucket]. Samuel Woodworth. AA; APW; BAV; BLPA; FaBoBe; FaFP; FaPON; HBV; LEAP; LPS-1; NeHB; OBAV; OlF; OTPC (1946 ed.); PECK; PIR; PYM; TCAP; TreF; WBLP

How deep is his duplicity who in a flash. High Diver. Robert Francis. NePoAm

How deep yon azure dyes the sky! Thomas Parnell. *Fr.* A Night Piece on Death. EV-3

How delicate a thing it is! Query. Virginia Lawrence. PR

How delicately they are wild. Egrets. Max Eastman. AnEnPo

How Delicious Is the Winning. Thomas Campbell. *See* Freedom and Love.

How delightful, at sunset, to loosen the boat. The Excursion. Tu Fu. AWP; JAWP; WBP

How desolate!/ Ah! how forlorn. Solitude. Thomas Traherne. OBS; SeEP

How desolate were nature, and how void. God Everywhere in Nature. Carlos Wilcox. LPS-2

How did he know, the young sky-rover. Wings. Blanche W. Schoonmaker. DD; GA

How Did He Live? Ernest Crosby. OQP; QP-1
(Life and Death.) MaRV

"How did he look, the Lord of Light." Corpus Christi, II. Margery Mansfield. NV

How did it happen that we quarreled? Words! Words! Jessie Fauset. CDC

How did the Devil come? When first attack? Norfolk. John Betjeman. ChMP

How did the party go in Portman Square? Juliet. Hilaire Belloc. EnLoPo

How did you come to me, my sweet? To a Child Who Inquires. Olga Petrova. BLPA

How Did You Die? Edmund Vance Cooke. BLPA; MaRV; OHFP; PTA-2; TCPD

How did you feel, you libertarians. Jacob Godbey. Edgar Lee Masters. *Fr.* Spoon River Anthology. ChMo; CMP; LiTA

How disagreeable it is. Translations from Modern Japanese Poetry. Takeko Kujo. PFE

How do I know that God is good? I don't. Faith. G. A. Studdert-Kennedy. MaRV

How do I know that you will come again? Surety. Lizette Woodworth Reese. MAP; MoAmPo

How do I love thee? Let me count the ways. Sonnets from the Portuguese, XLIII. Elizabeth Barrett Browning. AnFE; ATP; AV; BBV (1951 ed.); BCEP; BEL; BLV; BPN; CoBE; DiM; EmBrPo; EnLi-2; EnLit; EPN; EPP; EV-4; FaBoBe; FaFP; GTBS; GTBS-W; GTML; GTSL; HBV; HiLiEn; HoPM; InP; LEAP; LiTB; LiTG; LiTL; LO; LoPo; MaRV; OAEP; OQP; OuHeWo; PFE; PG; PIAE; PIR; Po; PoeMoYo; PoFS; PoMa; PoRA; PoRL; PoToHe (new ed.); PreP; PYM; QP-2; ReaPo; ShBV-4; TCEP; TreF; TrGrPo; TyEnPo; UnPo; VA; ViBoPo; ViP; ViPo; WHA; YT

How do I love you? I do not know. Song. Irene Rutherford McLeod. HBV; VOD

How do robins build their nests? What Robin Told. George Cooper. FaPON; GFA; MPB; TiPo

How do the daughters. How the Daughters Come Down at Dunoon. Henry Cholmondeley-Pennell. BOHV

How do the pussy-willows grow? Spring Questions. Clara Doty Bates. PPL

How do we know how the seasons go? Cradle-Song. Mariana Van Rensselaer. BOL

How Do You Do? H. Bedford-Jones. WBLP

How Do You Do? *Unknown.* ChTr

How do you do, little Frankie Pankie? Baby on Her Travels. *Unknown.* SAS

How do you know it is time to bloom. Creative Force. Maude Miner Hadden. GoYe

How do you know that May has come. May-Day at Sea. John F. Finerty. EtS

How do you know that the pilgrim track. The Year's Awakening. Thomas Hardy. ChMo; NLK

How do you like to go up in a swing. The Swing. Robert Louis Stevenson. BoChLi; FaBoBe; FaFP; GFA; GoBP; MeMeAg; MPB; NeHB; OTPC; PCH; StVeCh; SUS; TiPo; TreF; VLEP

How does a person get to be a capable liar? Golly, How Truth Will Out. Ogden Nash. LiTA; LiTM; MoAmPo

How does a spider ever weave. The Spider Web. Mattie Lee Haussgen. GFA

How does it seem, for one who stood alone. Fallen Tree. Helen Frazee-Bower. MuM

How does my Royall Lord? How fares your Majesty? Lear and Cordelia. Shakespeare. *Fr.* King Lear, IV, vii. LiA

How Does the Soul Grow? "Susan Coolidge." MaRV

"How does the water come down at Lodore?" The Cataract of Lodore. Robert Southey. BOHV; GN; HBV; HiLiEn; LPS-2; OTPC; PEOR; PoeMoYo; PYM; TreFS; WBLP

How do's your Grace? The Vision. Shakespeare. King Henry the Eighth, IV, ii. LiA

How dost thou wear and weary out thy days. Chorus. Samuel Daniel. *Fr.* The Tragedie of Philotas. OBSC

How doth the city sit solitary, that was full of people. The Misery of Jerusalem. Lamentations, Bible, *O.T.* AWP; LiTW

How doth the jolly little spider. The Spider. A.P. Herbert. RIS

How Doth the Little Busy Bee. Isaac Watts. FaPON; HBV; HBVY; HoPM; OTPC; PPL; TreF; TVC; TVSH
(Against Idleness and Mischief.) CEP; NeHB; OBEC; PoFS
(Bee, The.) GoTP
(Busy Bee, The.) PCH
(Little Busy Bee.) StVeCh

How Doth the Little Crocodile, *parody.* "Lewis Carroll." *Fr.* Alice's Adventures in Wonderland, *ch. 2.* BoChLi; FaBoCh; FaFP; FaPON; LiL; LoGBV; MoShBr; MPB; OTPC (1946 ed.); PreP; PYM; TiPo; TreFS; WaKn; WhC; YT
(Crocodile, The.) EnLi-2 (1949 ed.); GFA; GoTP; HoPM; MBP; PA; PoFS; TrGrPo

How dreamy-dark it is! Charles Mair. *Fr.* The Fireflies. BoCaPo

How Dreary Looks the Ivied Cot. Gertrude Hall. OBAV

How dull and heavy sank the sun. Sleepless Night. Annette von Droste-Hülshoff. AnGP

How dumb the vanished billions who have died! Omnia Exeunt in Mysterium. George Sterling. BAP; LA; LEAP; NP; SBMV; TBM; WGRP

How D'-y'-do and Good-by. William Robert Spencer. OTPC (1923 ed.)

How Each Thing save the Lover in Spring Reviveth to Pleasure. Earl of Surrey. ReIE
("When Windsor walls sustain'd my wearied arm.") SiPS

How Easily Men's Cheeks Are Hot with Wrath! Verner von Heidenstam, *tr. fr. Swedish by* Charles W. Stork. AnSL; LiTW

How erring oft the judgment in its hate. English Weather [or The English Fog]. John Dyer. *Fr.* The Fleece. CoEV; OBEC; TrGrPo

How excellent an antidote for love's inoculation. The Cyclops. Callimachus. GrL

How fades that native breath. Sweets That Die. Langdon Elwyn Mitchell. AA

How fair is youth that flies so fast! Carnival Song: Triumph of Bacchus and Ariadne. Lorenzo de' Medici. LyPI

How fair the smile of the Danish coast. Denmark Song. Johannes V. Jensen. BoDS

How fair you are, my mother! To My Mother. Eugene Field. MOAH

How falls it, oriole, thou hast [or has] come to fly. To an Oriole [or Oriole]. Edgar Fawcett. BLA; GoTP; HBV; LBAP; LEAP; OTPC; SN; WhBS

How far away the nights when I could sleep. Thoughts of a Briton in the Fourth Year of War. E. H. W. Meyerstein. *Fr.* Two War Sonnets. NeTW

How Far Is It Called to the Grave? *Unknown.* BLPA

"How far is it to Babylon?" The Road to Babylon. Margaret A. Wilson. HBMV

How Far Is It to Bethlehem? Frances Chesterton. BoTP; DD; HBMV; HBVY; MaRV; SDH; YaCaBo, *with music*
(Children's Song of the Nativity.) AIDL

"How far is it to Bethlehem Town?" How Far to Bethlehem. Madeleine Sweeny Miller. BLPA; MaRV; NeHB; OQP; PSO; QP-1

How far is it to peace, the piper sighed. Our Lady Peace. Mark Van Doren. WaP

"How far is St. Helena from a little child at play?" A St. Helena Lullaby. Kipling. AtBAP; FaBoCh; MoVE; OAEP (2d ed.); OBMV; OtMeF; PoEL-5; POTE; ShBV-2; ViPP

How far that little candle throws his beams! Good Deeds. Shakespeare. *Fr.* The Merchant of Venice, V, i. BLP

How far they throw their cheer, their gracious glow. At Christmastide. Laura Simmons. PGD

How Far to Bethlehem? Madeleine Sweeny Miller. BLPA; MaRV; NeHB; OQP; PSO; QP-1

"How fared you when you mortal were?" After. Ralph Hodgson. ChMo; CMP; MBP; MoBrPo

How fares it with the happy dead? In Memoriam A. H. H., XLIV. Tennyson. EmBrPo; EnLi-2; EPN; GEPC; OBEV (1st ed.); ViPo; VLEP

How fares my lord? Norval. John Holmes. *Fr.* Douglas, II, i. LPS-2

How fearful/ And dizzy 'tis to cast one's eyes so low! On Dover Cliffs. Shakespeare. *Fr.* King Lear, IV, vi. LPS-2; SN

How felt the land in every part. Washington's Vow. Whittier. OHIP

How fevered is the man, who cannot look. On Fame [or Fame *or* Two Sonnets on Fame]. Keats. BPN; EM-2; EmBrPo; EnL; EnLit; EnRP; EPN; ERP; ES

How few, of all the hearts that loved. The Wanderer from the Fold. Emily Brontë. EmBrPo; EnLit

How fickle's health! when sickness thus. Upon a Friend's Pet Cat, Being Sick. John Winstanley. PoC
How fine has the day been! how bright was the sun! A Summer Evening. Isaac Watts. LPS-2
How Firm a Foundation. "K.," *perhaps* Robert Keene, *sometimes at. to* George Keith. MaRV; OlF; WGRP
How first began their voyage? The Quest of the Golden Fleece [*or* The Argonauts]. Pindar. *Fr.* Pythian Odes, IV. GrR; OxBG
How fond are men of rule and place. The Lion and the Cub. John Gay. CG; GN; HBV; OTPC (1923 ed.)
How foolishly I loved. Poema Morale. Charles Gullans. NePoEA
How, forsooth,/ Shall any man, by curses or by groans. E. A. Robinson. *Fr.* Captain Craig. BoFr
How frail/ Above the bulk. Niagara. Adelaide Crapsey. BAV; MAP; MoAmPo (1942 ed.)
How frail is mortal love. Mortal Love. Basil Dowling. AnNZ
How Fraught with Struggle. Minnie Hite Moody. MuM
How fresh, O Lord, how sweet and clean. The Flower. George Herbert. AtBAP; AWP; EPS; EV-2; FaBoEn; InPo; LPS-3; MePo; NBE; OBS; OxBoCh; PoEL-2; ReEn; SeCV-1; TriL
How fruitless is each human hope, how vain. Sonnet. Lorenzo de' Medici. LyPI
How full the glittering shops are now. Through a Shop Window. Eleanor Farjeon. ChBR; GaP
How gaily laughs the morn at roses' tears! In Early Spring. Victor Hugo. TrFP
How gay those bulks that tattered. Ship Bottom. Richmond Lattimore. NePoAm-2
How gentle and how friendly seem. Gulls. Stanley Snaith. POTE
How gently sings my soul and whets its wings. Laurence Dakin. *Fr.* Tancred, III, i. CaP
How Gently You Rock My Child to Sleep. Pedro Salinas, *tr. fr. Spanish by* Eleanor L. Turnbull. AnSpL-2; CoSP
How glorious fall the valiant, sword in hand. Pro Patria [*or* The Young Hero]. Tyrtaeus, *tr. by* Thomas Campbell. BHV; GrR
How Glorious Is Thy Name. Psalms, VIII, Bible, *O.T.* *See* What Is Man?
How glows each patriot bosom that boasts a Yankee heart. The *United States* and *Macedonian*. *Unknown.* PAH
How God Answers. *Unknown.* *See* Blessed.
How God Will Not Do for Us. John Heywood. SiCE
How Goes the Night? *Unknown, tr. fr. Chinese by* Helen Waddell. *Fr.* Shi King. AWP; JAWP; WBP
How good that you found me. Marriage. Ina Seidel. TwGV
How good to hear your voice again. The Priest Rediscovers His Psalm-Book. *Unknown.* KiLC
How good to lie a little while. Friends. Abby Farwell Brown. HBV; HBVY
How goodly are thy tents, O Jacob. Balaam's Blessing. Numbers, Bible, *O.T.* TrGrPo
How grace this hallowed day? Christmas. Henry Timrod. MOAP; SPP
How gracious. how benign, is Solitude. Wordsworth. *Fr.* The Prelude, IV. NBE
How Grand Amour Walked in a Meadow and Met with Fame Environed with Tongues of Fire. Stephen Hawes. *Fr.* The Pastime of Pleasure. ReIE
How grand beneath the feet that company. The Mendip Hills over Wells. Henry Alford. EnSW
How grandly glow the bays. On the Death of Francis Thompson. Alfred Noyes. OBVV
How gray the rain. Elizabeth J. Coatsworth. TiPo
How great the tale, that there should be. Consecration. Murdoch O'Daly. JKPC (1926 ed.)
How Great unto the Living Seem the Dead! Charles Heavysege. CaP
(Dead, The.) BoCaPo
How green the earth, how blue the sky. The Settlers. Laurence Housman. HBV; OBVV
How happy a thing were a wedding. On Marriage [*or* The Bachelor's Song]. Thomas Flatman. EnLoPo; FiBHP; WhC
How happy are we now the wind is abaft. Sailor's Delight. *Unknown.* SG
How happy art thou & I. *Unknown.* SeCSL
How happy could I be with either. John Gay. *Fr.* The Beggar's Opera, II, xiii. ViBoPo
How happy had he been, if Destiny. Dryden. *Fr.* Absalom and Achitophel. BrBE
How happy I can be with my love away! The Absence. Sylvia Townsend Warner. MBP; MoBrPo
How happy I was on my father's farm. Sweet Fields of Violo. *Unknown.* ABS
How happy in his low degree. Country Life [*or* Revery of a Business Man]. Horace, *tr. by* Dryden. AWP; WoL
How Happy Is He Born. Sir Henry Wotton. *See* Character of a Happy Life, The.
How happy is the blameless vestal's lot! The Nun's Lot. Pope. *Fr.* Eloisa to Abelard. ACP; CAW; PraNu
How happy is the little stone. Emily Dickinson. AlDL; AmP; AmPP; NePA
(Simplicity.) AnNE; APW; TCAP; TSW; TSWC
(Stone, The.) NeMA
How happy now would I be. Street Cry under Sea. Rafael Alberti. AnSpL-2; CoSP
How happy the holly-tree looks, and how strong. The Holly. Edith King. ChBR
How Happy the Little Birds. *Unknown, tr. fr. Modern Irish by* Padraic Pearse. OnYI
How Happy the Lover. Dryden. *Fr.* King Arthur, IV, i. ElSeCe; LoBV; OnPM; ViBoPo
(Song.) SeEP
(Song to a Minuet.) EPS (1942 ed.); SeCL
How Happy the Soldier. *Unknown.* LoGBV
How happy to be a fish. Fish and Bird. Rosemary Brinckman. BoTP
How happy were my days, till now. Song. Isaac Bickerstaffe. *Fr.* Love in a Village, I. OBEC
How Happy's That Lover. *Unknown.* SeCL
How happy's the prisoner that conquers his fate. Drinking Song. *Unknown.* SeCL
How hard for unaccustomed feet. In the Time of Trouble. Leslie Savage Clark. TrPWD
How hard is my fortune. The Convict of Clonmel [*or* Clonmala]. *Unknown, tr. by* Jeremiah Joseph Callanan. AnIL; AnIV; GTIV; IrPN; OnYI; OxBI; TIP
How hard the year dies: no frost yet. Intercession in Late October. Robert Graves. MoAB
How hard, when those who do not wish. The Art of Book-Keeping. Thomas Hood. LPS-3; MOB
How has kind Heav'n adorn'd the happy Land. Italy and Britain. Addison. *Fr.* A Letter from Italy. OBEC
How hath the oppressor ceased! Downfall of the Tyrant. Isaiah, Bible, *O.T.* TrGrPo
How haughty was thy mien. Dante. *Fr.* Divina Commedia: Purgatorio. PoFr
How have I been [*or* bin] religious? what strange good. To Fletcher Reviv'd. Richard Lovelace. OBS; PtP
How have I labored? Ortus. Ezra Pound. LEAP; LiTA; NePA; NP
How have we fallen from our high estate. The Offering. Olive Cecilia Jacks. MaRV
How have you managed to enter so, like a mist. Nocturne. Xavier Abril. AnCL
How he departed hence, you who stood by. The Passing of Oedipus. Sophocles. *Fr.* Oedipus at Colonus. OxBG
How He Saved St. Michael's. Mary A. P. Stansbury. BLPA; PTA-1, *sl. abr.*
How He Saw Her. Ben Jonson. *Fr.* A Celebration of Charis. OAEP; SeCV-1
"I beheld her, on a day," *br. sel.* AtBAP
How he survived them they could never understand. The Diaspora [*or* The Jew Wrecked in the German Cell]. W. H. Auden. LiTA; PeBoSo; QS; WaP
How He Turned Out. Edwin Meade Robinson. PCN
How healthily their feet upon the floor. Two Sonnets, 2. Edna St. Vincent Millay. CP
How Heavy. Jules Supervielle, *tr. fr. French by* Wallace Fowlie. MiCF
How heavy do I journey on the way. Sonnets, L. Shakespeare. EtPaEn; PeBoSo; ReEn; ReIE; SiCE
How heavy the earth is to bear! you might say. How Heavy. Jules Supervielle. MiCF
How Hellas' youth,/ liegemen Achaean of brothers embattled. An Aeschylean Chorus. Aristophanes. *Fr.* The Frogs. OxBG
How high Thou art! our songs can own. The Mediator. Elizabeth Barrett Browning. TrPWD
How history repeats itself. Can't. Harriet Prescott Spofford. DD; GA; MC; PAH
How Holy Church Is Underfoot, *in mod. Eng. Unknown.* TMEV
How Homer Should Have Written the Iliad. Edwin Meade Robinson. *Fr.* Limericised Classics. HBMV
"How, how," he said. "Friend Chang," I said. The Chinese Nightingale. Vachel Lindsay. AmPP (3d ed.); ChMo; CMP; HBMV; IAP; LiTM (rev. ed.); MAP; MAPA; MoAmPo; NePA; NP; OnSP; SBMV; TCPD
How I am harnessed. Grief. Albert Ehrenstein. OnPM
How I am held within a tranquil shell. The Woman with Child. Freda Laughton. OnYI
How I Brought the Good News from Aix to Ghent (or Vice Versa). R. J. Yeatman *and* W. C. Sellar. FiBHP; WhC
How I do [*or* doe] love thee, Beaumont, and thy Muse. To Francis Beaumont. Ben Jonson. OAEP; OBS; PtP; SeEP; TuPP
How I forsook/ Elias and Pisa after, and betook. Giovanni Battista Guarini, *tr. by* Sir Richard Fanshawe. *Fr.* Il Pastor Fido. AWP

How I lived, ere my human life began. Rephan. Robert Browning. VLEP
How I love the world in all its beauty. Mikhail Alekseyevich Kuzmin. *Fr.* Alexandrian Songs. TrRV
How I Love You. John Godfrey Saxe. *See* My Eyes! How I Love You.
How I loved/ Witness, ye days and nights. Dryden. *Fr.* All for Love, II. LO
How I Sailed on the Lake till I Came to the Eastern Stream. Lu Yu, *tr. fr. Chinese by* Arthur Waley. TrCh
"How I should like a birthday!" said the child. Stevenson's Birthday. Katherine Miller. AA; PECK
How I should love. Peonies. Liu Yü Shih. PoHN
How I was caught. The Missed Train. Thomas Hardy. MaPo
How ill doth he deserve a lover's name. Eternity of Love Protested [*or* Song]. Thomas Carew. ATP; EG; MeLP; OBS; SeEP
How in Heaven's name did Columbus get over. Columbus. Arthur Hugh Clough. BHV; DD; MC
How Infinite Are Thy Ways. William Force Stead. *Fr.* Uriel. OBMV
("I thought the night without a sound was falling.") TrPWD
How insane was Majnun. Self-Love. Shams Tabrez. OnPM
How is it I can eat bread here and cut meat. Evening Meal in the Twentieth Century. John Holmes. MiAP; PreP
How is it proved? The Great Wager. G. A. Studdert-Kennedy. ChIP
How is it, when death comes, the simple things. Remembrance. John Bunker. JKCP (1955 ed.)
How is King Ringang's daughter named? Fair Wildheart. Eduard Mörike. AnGP
How is 't, my Soul, that thou giv'st eyes their sight. To My Soul in Its Blindness. Phineas Fletcher. OxBoCh; SeCL
How Is the Gold Become Dim. Lamentations, IV: 1–5, Bible, *O.T.* ChTr
How it came to an end! The Coming of the End. Thomas Hardy. ChMo; CMP
How It Strikes a Contemporary. Robert Browning. EmBrPo; GEPC; PoVP; ViPo; ViPP
How Jack Found That Beans May Go Back on a Chap. Guy Wetmore Carryl. ALV; HoPM; MAP; MoAmPo (1942 ed.)
How Jacke Cade Traiterously Rebelling agaynst His Kyng, Was for His Treasons and Cruell Doinges Wurthely Punyshed. *At. to* William Baldwin. *Fr.* A Mirror for Magistrates. SiCE
How joyous his neigh. Song of the Horse. *Unknown, tr. fr. Navajo Indian.* APW; AWP; JAWP; WBP
How joyously the young sea-mew. The Sea-Mew. Elizabeth Barrett Browning. HBV; OTPC
How keep beauty? is there any way? The Leaden Echo and the Golden Echo. T. Sturge Moore. ReaPo
How kind is night/ After the fierceness of the summer day. Nox Benigna. William Pember Reeves. AnNZ
How King Edward and His Menge Met with the Spaniards in the Sea. Laurence Minot. NBE
How languid is the dreaming moon to-night! Sadness of the Moon. Baudelaire. TrFP
How large unto the tiny fly. The Fly. Walter de la Mare. CBPC
How large was Alexander, father. Lawyer and Child. James Whitcomb Riley. FAOV
How larger is remembrance than desire! Ebbtide at Sundown. "Michael Field." CAW; GTML
How late the assassins ply their trade tonight. Nausea. E. L. Mayo. MiAP
How leapt our hearts, when from an airy height. "Christopher North." *Fr.* The Angler's Tent. EnSW
How life and death in Thee. Upon the Savior's Tomb [*or* To Our Blessed Lord upon the Choice of His Sepulchre]. Richard Crashaw. ACP; StJW
How lightly leaps the youthful chamois. The Glad Young Chamois. Burges Johnson. TSW; TSWC
How like a beckoning finger shows. The Moon. Camilla Doyle. MBP
How like a marriage is the season of clouds. Cloud Country. James Merrill. NePoEA
How like a mighty picture, tint by tint. To W. H. H. Paul Hamilton Hayne. SPP
How like a tender mother. Evening. Charlotte Young. BOL
How like a winter hath my absence been. Sonnets, XCVII. Shakespeare. ATP; AWP; BEL; CaAE; EIL; EM-1; EnLi-1; EnLoPo; EPP; ES; EV-1; FaBoEn; GTBS; GTBS-D; GTBS-W; GTSL; JAWP; LiTG; LoPo; LoPS; OBEV; OBSC; PeBoSo; PIAE; PoFS; PoRA; REAL; ReIE; ReaPo; TOP; TrGrPo; WBP
How like a Woman. Caroline Duer *and* Alice Duer Miller. PR
How like an angel came I down! Wonder. Thomas Traherne. AtBAP; CH; EPS; LiTB; LiTG; LoBV; PoE; ReaPo; SeCePo; SeCeV; SeCL; SeCV-2; SeEP; TrGrPo; TriL; TwHP; WHA
How like her! But 'tis she herself. In the Mile End Road. Amy Levy. VA
How like the consummation and despair. A Photograph of Isadora Duncan. Robert E. Hayden. PoNe
How like the leper, with his own sad cry. The Buoy-Bell. Charles Tennyson Turner. EtS; VA
How like the sky she bends above her child. Niobe. Alfred Noyes. MOAH
How like the stars are these white nameless faces. Broadway. Hermann Hagedorn. DDA; NV
How Like You This? Sir Thomas Wyatt. *See* Lover Showeth How He Is Forsaken of Such as He Sometime Enjoyed, The.
How little curious is man. Travelling. Henry David Thoreau. CoV
How little do the landmen know. A Comfortable Song on the Poor Sailors. *Unknown.* SG
How little do they know of sorrow. Sonnet. William Ellery Leonard. *Fr.* Two Lives. MOAP; MuM
How little fades from earth when sink to rest. Shakespeare. John Sterling. PtP; VA
How living are the dead! Immortal. Florence Earle Coates. MaRV
How Lonely, How Drear. Mikhail Yurevich Lermontov, *tr. fr. Russian by* Sir Cecil Kisch. WaL
How long, dear sleeper, must I wait. The Vigil. T. Sturge Moore. POTE
How long false hope, wilt thou mislead myne eyes. *Unknown.* SeCSL
How long, great God, how long must I. The Aspiration. John Norris. BeR; LoBV; MeRV; OxBoCh
How long have I been lying asleep. A Drinking Bout. Liu Chia. OnPM; PoHN
How long have standing men—by such a stone. Now the Sky. Mark Van Doren. MOAP
How long in his damp trance young Juan lay. Don Juan and Haidée [*or* Haidee]. Byron. *Fr.* Don Juan. BPN; TOP
How long in stealthy silence must we watch with glances hidden? Stronger than Death. Paulus Silentiarius. GrPE
How long it seems to me since that mild April night. Seaward. Celia Thaxter. AA
How long I've loved thee, and how well. Love's Wisdom. Margaret Deland. AA
How long must we two hide the burning gaze. United. Paulus Silentiarius. AWP
How long, my heroes, shall we live in bondage. War Hymn. Rhigas Pheraios. MoGP
How long, O lion, hast thou fleshless lain? The Lion's Skeleton. Charles Tennyson Turner. VA
How long, O Lord, to wait. The Old Pastor. John Banister Tabb. AmP
How long, O sister, how long. The Bells at Midnight. Thomas Bailey Aldrich. PAH
"How long shall fortune faile me now." The Earl of Westmoreland. *Unknown.* ESPB
How Long Shall I Give? *Unknown.* BLRP
How long shall this like-dying life endure. Amoretti, XXV. Spenser. PeBoSo
How long she waited for her executioner! Head of Medusa. Marya Zaturenska. MoAmPo
How long this giant hugged and spanned. Windmill on the Cape. William Vincent Sieller. GoYe
How long this way: that everywhere. Two Songs on the Economy of Abundance. James Agee. MAP; MoAmPo
How Long till April? Maurice C. Fields. JKCP (1955 ed.)
How long, upon vain hopes intent. Crinagoras, *tr. fr. Greek by* W. C. Lawton. GrPo
How long will ye slumber? when will ye take heart. Rallying Song. Callinus, *tr. by* H. N. Coleridge. GrPo; GrR; PoFr
How Long Will You Remain? Emily Brontë. VLEP
How long with vain complaining. Questo di Verde. Thomas Watson. TuPP
How long, young men, unsoldiered, disregarding. A Call to Action. Callinus, *tr. by* T. F. Higham. GrL; OxBG; WaaP
How look'd your love, sweet Shepherd, yestereven. The Orchard by the Shore; a Pastoral. Elinor Sweetman. OBVV
How Looked She When She Breathed Good-bye? Marjorie Pickthall. BoCaPo (1948 ed.)
How lost is the little fox at the borders of night. Night of Wind. Frances M. Frost. FaPON; TiPo
How loud the storm blew all that bitter night! The Haunted House. Wilfrid Scawen Blunt. UnW
How loudly and how surely the musician plays! The Musician. R. P. Lister. UnS
How Love came in, I do not know. Of Love. Robert Herrick. EV-2
How lovely are the tombs of the dead nymphs. Panope. Edith Sitwell. MBP; MoAB; MoBrPo; NP

How lovely are the waters of Babylon. R. N. Currey. *Fr.* Ultimate Exile. BoSA
How lovely are these swans. The Swans. Andrew Young. MoBrPo (1942 ed.); POTE
How lovely are thy dwellings fair! Psalm LXXXIV. Milton. TrPWD
How Lovely Are Thy Tabernacles. Psalms, LXXXIV: 1–5, Bible, *O.T.* TrJP
How lovely is the heaven of this night. A Beautiful Night. Thomas Lovell Beddoes. ChER; ERP; LoBV
How lovely is the silence of green, growing things. Let All the Earth Keep Silence. Lucy A. K. Adee. OQP; QP-2
How lovely is the sound of oars at night. Boats at Night. Edward Shanks. CH; MCCG; POTE
How lovely the elder brother's. Brothers. Gerard Manley Hopkins. OAEP; POTT
How Low Is the Lowing Herd. Walt Kelly. FiBHP
"How low the world beneath me lies." The Metaphysician. Schiller. RO
How low when angels fall their black descent. George Meredith. Modern Love: Prologue. ViPo
How luxuriant the grass in the meadow! Grass. Po Chü-i. WhP
How McClellan Took Manassas. *Unknown.* PAH
How many a father have I seen. In Memoriam A. H. H., LIII. Tennyson. BEL; EmBrPo; EnLi-2; EPN; GEPC; OAEP; TOP; ViPo; VLEP
How many a supple bough. Changes. Ibn Sa'id of Alcala la Real. MooP
How many a thing which we cast to the ground. Modern Love, XLI. George Meredith. EnLit; HBV; LEAP; ViPo
How many a time have I. Swimming. Byron. *Fr.* The Two Foscari. GN; LPS-2
How many an acorn falls to die. Compensation. John Banister Tabb. SPP
How Many Bards Gild the Lapses of Time! Keats. BPN; EM-2; EmBrPo; EnRP; EPN; ERP
(Sonnet: "How many bards gild the lapses of time.") GEPC
How many blessèd groups this hour are bending. Sabbath Sonnet. Felicia Dorothea Hemans. EnSW
How many buds, how many sticky butts. Spring. Boris Pasternak. LiTW; TrRV
How many buds in this warm light. Wasted Hours. W. H. Davies. PoTo
How many buttons are missing today? Nobody Knows but Mother. Mary Morrison. BLPA
How many colors here do we see set. The Spectrum. Cosmo Monkhouse. VA
How many dawns, chill from his rippling rest. To Brooklyn Bridge [*or* Proem]. Hart Crane. *Fr.* The Bridge. AmP; AmPP; ChMo; CoBMV; CoV; CrMA; ExPo; FaBoEn; GTBS-W; LiTA; LiTM; MoAB; MoAmPo (1950 ed.); MoPo; NePA; OxBA; PoE; ReMP; SeCeV
How many days has my [*or* the] baby to play? Mother Goose. BoTP; OTPC (1946 ed.); OxNR; PPL; TiPo
How many days now is it we have lain. A Barge Wife. John Farrar. TBM
How many days to Christmas? Counting the Days. James S. Tippett. ChBR
How many dear companions who enlivened for us. Remembrance. Vasily Zhukovsky. TrRV
How many equal with the Argive queen. The Power of Poets. Ben Jonson. *Fr.* Epistle to Elizabeth, Countess of Rutland. WHA
How Many Faults. Elinor Wylie. ChMo
How many generations yet shall pass. Lady Margaret Sackville. Epitaphs, VII. MM
How Many Heavens. Edith Sitwell. MeRV; MoPW
How many human loves swarm to my arms. Ideal Passion, VI. George Edward Woodberry. MOAP
How many humble hearts have dipped. To a Post-Office Inkwell. Christopher Morley. InP; LEAP; PoeMoYo
How many kisses do I ask. To Anne. Sir William Stirling-Maxwell. HBV
How many kisses, Lesbia, you ask. Ad Lesbiam. Catullus, *tr. by* Niall Sheridan. OxBI
How many lives, made beautiful and sweet. Giotto's Tower. Longfellow. APW; CoBA; IAP; LBAP; TCAP
How many lost things there were. Pedro Salinas, *tr. fr. Spanish by* Eleanor L. Turnbull. CoSP
How many miles [is it] to Babylon [*or* Barley Bridge]? Mother Goose. BoN; BoTP; ExPo; FaBoCh; LoGBV; MoShBr; OxBoLi; OxNR; PCH; SiTL; WP
How many million Aprils came. Blue Squills. Sara Teasdale. ChMo; CMP; HBMV; SBMV; TCAP; TwCV; VOD
How many million stars must shine. A Song of Content. Frederic Lawrence Knowles. PR
How Many New Years Have Grown Old. *Unknown.* ElL; ElSeCe
How many of us ever stop to think. Music. *Unknown.* MaRV
How many paltry, foolish, painted things. Sonnet. Michael Drayton. Idea, VI. BCEP; ElL; EnLoPo; ES; HBV; InP; LoBV; NBE; OBSC; ReEn; ReIE; RiBV; SiCE; TuPP
How many pipes have dittied unto thee. April. John Francis O'Donnell. IrPN
How many pounds does the baby weigh. Weighing the Baby. Ethel Lynn Beers. HBV; PoToHe (new ed.)
How many rivers swerved aside. The Desert Remembers Her Reasons. Genevieve Taggard. TBM
"How many?" said our good Captain. Sea Ballad. Sydney Dobell. *Fr.* Balder. VA
How Many Seconds in a Minute? Christina Rossetti. PTA-1; SiSoSe
How many sons, how many generations. Rizpah. Swinburne. EmBrPo
How many Springs have we been apart? You do not come home. After Being Separated for a Long Time. Li Po. ChLP
How many strive to force a way. Forcing a Way. *Unknown.* NA
How many summers, love. The Poet's Song to His Wife. "Barry Cornwall." HBV; LPS-1; VA
How many thousand of my poorest subjects. Henry IV's Soliloquy on Sleep [*or* The Cares of Majesty *or* Sleep *or* Soliloquy on Sleep *or* Uneasy Lies the Head]. Shakespeare. King Henry IV, Pt. II, *fr.* III, i. BCEP; BLP; EV-1; FiP; LiTB; LPS-3; TreF; TVSH
How Many Times Do I Love Thee, Dear? Thomas Lovell Beddoes. *See* Song: "How many times do I love thee, dear?"
How Many Times Night's Silent Queen Her Face. William Drummond of Hawthornden. BSV
How many times these low feet staggered. Emily Dickinson. MaPo; PoEL-5; ReMP
How many times upon your hill. To Silver Birches. Charles G. Blanden. PoTo
How many verses have I thrown. Verses Why Burnt. Walter Savage Landor. VA
How Many Voices Gaily Sing. Walter Savage Landor. BPN; EmBrPo; LEAP
(How Many Voices.) EPN
How Many Ways. John Masefield. *Fr.* Sonnets ("Long long ago"). LiTB
("How many ways, how many times.") WGRP
How many ways can you bring me ten? Making Tens. M. M. Hutchinson. BoTP
How Marigolds Came Yellow. Robert Herrick. ChTr
How marvellous and fair a thing. Springtime in Cookham Dean. Cecil Roberts. HBMV; VOD
How may I sing, unworthy I. Maria Immaculata. Condé Benoist Pallen. JKCP
How may one hold these days of wonderment. Four Sonnets, I. Thomas S. Jones, Jr. SBMV
How may the beauty of bright birds atone. Terror in Beauty. M. Eugenie Perry. TwCaPo
How memory cuts away the years. Autumn. Jean Starr Untermeyer. HBMV; MAP; MCCG; MoAmPo; NeMA; PFY; SBMV
How Men Write. Samuel Butler. BeR
How Miracles Abound. Clinton Scollard. NLK
How monarchs die is easily explained. On a Royal Demise. Thomas Hood. FiBHP
How more than blind the hooded fates to weave. Renunciation. Cathleen Keegan. *Fr.* Three Sonnets. MuM
How most unnatural-seeming, yet how proper. Sirocco at Deyá. Robert Graves. MoVE
How mournful seems, in broken dreams. Not Lost, but Gone Before. Caroline Elizabeth Sarah Norton. BLRP; WBLP
How Much Longer Will I Be Able to Inhabit the Divine Sepulcher. John Ashbery. NeAP
How Much of Godhood. Louis Untermeyer. BAP; NV; SBMV
How much, preventing God, how much I owe. Grace. Emerson. AmPo; AmPP; CoBA; IAP; TrPWD
How much the heart may bear and yet not break! Endurance. Elizabeth Akers Allen. HBV; PoToHe
How much we have forgotten that we knew. Old Meadows. Hervey Allen. TBM
How much we pay to say, *"Je suis."* Samuel Hoffenstein. *Fr.* As the Crow Flies. WhC
How much wood would a woodchuck chuck. If a Woodchuck Would Chuck. *Unknown.* FaPON; StVeCh (1955 ed.); TiPo
How, my dear Mary, are you critic-bitten. The Witch of Atlas. Shelley. EmBrPo
How My Songs of Her Began. Philip Bourke Marston. HBV; VA
How my thoughts betray me! A Prayer for Recollection. *Unknown.* KiLC
How Narrow Is the Circle. Aleksandr Aleksandrovich Blok, *tr. fr. Russian by* Babette Deutsch. TrRV
How natural the way that they have greeted each other. The Inner Significance of the Statues Seated outside the

How natural the way (*continued*)
Boston Public Library. Walter Conrad Arensberg. AnAmPo; LA
How near am I now to a happiness. Thomas Middleton. *Fr.* Women Beware of Women. LO; LoPS
How near me came the hand of death. Hymn for a Widower or a Widow Deprived of a Loving Yoke-Fellow [*or* A Widow's Hymn]. George Wither. ElSeCe; LO; OBEV
How near to good is what is fair. Love Freed from Ignorance and Folly. Ben Jonson. LPS-2
How Nice. Mary Dixon Thayer. GFA
How nice it is to eat! Beautiful Meals. T. Sturge Moore. BoTP; TCPD; WP
How No Age Is Content. Earl of Surrey. ElL, *shorter vers.;* FAOV, *abr.;* LiTB; LoBV; SiCE; TuPP
(Age of Children Happiest, The.) CG
(Laid in My Quiet Bed [in Study as I Were].) CH; InvP
How now could body-soul's symbol be this. The White Rat. Marguerite Young. MoPo
How now my noble cossin—what in blacke! John Webster. *Fr.* The White Devil, III, ii. AtBAP
How now, spirit? whither [*or* whether] wander you? Puck and the Fairy. Shakespeare. *Fr.* A Midsummer Night's Dream, II, i. AtBAP; GN
How now? what noise is that? Shakespeare. *Fr.* Hamlet, IV, v. AtBAP
How odd/ Of God. Epigrams, III [*or* The Chosen People]. W. N. Ewer. ALV; OtMeF; SiTL
How of the Virgin Mother Shall I Sing? Ennodius, *tr. fr. Latin. Fr.* Hymnus Sanctae Mariae. ISi
How oft against the sunset sky or moon. Wild Geese. Frederick Peterson. BLA; DDA; HBV; HBVY; OBAV; OTPC (1923 ed.)
How oft amid the heaped and bedded hay. Written in July, 1824. Mary Russell Mitford. OBRV
How oft do they their silver bowers leave. The Ministering Angels. Spenser. *Fr.* The Faerie Queene, II, iii. CBE; LPS-2; OBSC; PC
How Oft Has the Banshee Cried. Thomas Moore. AnIV; AWP; JAWP; WBP
How oft I dream of childhood days, of tricks we used to play. Rosie Nell. *Unknown.* AS
How oft I've watch'd thee from the garden croft. Orion. Charles Tennyson Turner. VA
How Oft, Louisa, Hast Thou Told. Sheridan. *Fr.* The Duenna. EV-3
How oft some passing word will tend. Our Mother. *Unknown.* PEDC
How oft when men are at the point of death. Romeo's Last Words. Shakespeare. *Fr.* Romeo and Juliet, V, iii. AtBAP; FiP; NBE
"How oft, when pressed to marriage." Pope. *Fr.* Eloisa to Abelard. ViBoPo
How oft, when thou, my music, music play'st. Sonnets, CXXVIII. Shakespeare. ElL; EM-1; EnLi-1 (1949 ed.); EnLit; PeBoSo; ReEn; ReIE
How Often. Ben King. BOHV; HBV; PA
How often does a man need to see a woman? The Word Made Flesh. W. J. Turner. OBMV
How often, for some trivial wrong. Retaliation. Margaret E. Bruner. PoToHe
How often have I now outwatched the night. John Addington Symonds. *Fr.* Stella Maris. PoVP
How often have I peered. Good Friday. A. J. Young. MM
How often have we known a dog to be. Beyond the Grave. Margaret E. Bruner. AlBD; PoToHe
How often I turn round. The Fear. Andrew Young. GTBS-D
How often in our chamber, O adored one. Lionel Grierson. Edgar Lee Masters. ChMo; CMP
How often in the summer-tide. Across the Fields to Anne. Richard Burton. HBV; LBMV; POT; PoTo; PR
How often must I pass the moonlight nights alone? Ai Ai Thinks of the Man She Loves. Ting Liu Niang. ChLP
How often must I shake my bells and kiss. The Death of Artists. Baudelaire. TrFP
How Often Sit I. Arthur Hugh Clough. *Fr.* Blank Misgivings of a Creature Moving About in Worlds Not Realized. EPN
(Blank Misgivings.) BPN
("How often sit I, poring o'er.") GTBS-D; VLEP
How often was my spirit wrung. Endpiece. Olga Berggolts. *Fr.* Parting. RuPo
How often we neglect a friend. Atonement. Margaret E. Bruner. MaRV; PoToHe
How Often, When Life's Summer Day. Walter Savage Landor. EmBrPo
How Old Are You? *At. to* Edward Tuck *and to* H. S. Fritsch. PoToHe
(Age.) DDA; PoRL
"How old art thou?" said the garrulous gourd. The Gourd and the Palm. *Unknown.* OTPC
How Old Brown Took Harper's Ferry. Edmund Clarence Stedman. GA; HBV; MC; OBAV; PaA; PAH; PAP; PoNe
(John Brown of Osawatomie.) PFY; PoFr
How Old Is My Heart? Christopher Brennan. BoAV
How old may Phillis [*or* Phyllis] be, you ask. Phillis's [*or* Phyllis's] Age. Matthew Prior. BOHV; CEP; EnLoPo
How old was Mary out of whom you cast. Charlotte Mew. *Fr.* Madeleine in Church. LO; MBP; MoAB; MoBrPo
How One Winter Came in the Lake Region. Wilfred Campbell. BoCaPo; CaP; OCL; PeCV
How Oswald Dined with God. Edwin Markham. CV
How Paddy Stole the Rope. *Unknown.* BLPA
How peaceful in the afterglow. The House in the Heath. Annette von Droste-Hülshoff. AnGP
How peacefully he sleeps out there. The Unknown Soldier. Virginia Eaton. BoHiPo
How perilous life will become on earth. The Earth for Sale. Harold Monro. ChMo; CMP
How petty, then, the me above the you. Clement Wood. Eagle Sonnets, X. NV
How picturesque/ The slender group of airy elm. John Scott of Amwell. *Fr.* Amwell; a Descriptive Poem. EnSW
How pitiful are little folk. Creeds. Willard Wattles. HBMV; InP; MaRV; OQP; PC; QP-1
How pitiful is her sleep. In Memory of Kathleen. Kenneth Patchen. MoAmPo
How plain soe'er the house or poor the guests. The King. Mary Frances Butts. OQP; QP-2
How pleasant, as the sun declines, to view. Sunset in the Lake Country. Wordsworth. *Fr.* An Evening Walk. EPN
How pleasant is Saturday night. Saturday Night. *Unknown.* SAS
How Pleasant Is This Flowery Plain. *Unknown.* OBS
How pleasant it is that always. Song. Florence Smith. BLPA
How pleasant the life of a bird must be. Birds in Summer. Mary Howitt. HH; MPB; OTPC; PRWS
How Pleasant to Know Mr. Lear. Edward Lear. ChTr; FiBHP; GoTP; WhC
(Author of the "Pobble," The.) OTPC
(By Way of Preface.) InvP; KN; OnPP; OxBoLi; PoEL-5; ViP
(Lines to a Young Lady.) InMe; NA
(Mr. Lear.) RIS
(Self Portrait.) ShBV-4
(Self-Portrait of the Laureate of Nonsense.) FaBoCh; SiTL
How pleased within my native bowers. Song: The Landskip [*or* The Landscape]. William Shenstone. CEP; OBEC; SeCePo
How poor, how rich, how abject, how august. Man. Edward Young. *Fr.* Night Thoughts. BCEP; EPP; LPS-3; MaRV
How populous, how vital is the grave! Edward Young. *Fr.* Night Thoughts. PoD
How pretty the prints of the birds in the snow. Hunter's Song. Eduard Mörike. AnGP
How proud a fall, an end how sweet. Secret Ode. Paul Valéry. TrFP
How, Providence? and yet a Scottish crew? The Rebel Scot. John Cleveland. EPS
How provoked you get. Names (For Mother). Elwyn Chauncey West. DD
How pure and bright is the moon. *Unknown, tr. fr. Chinese.* The Nineteen Han Poems, XIII. WhP
How pure, and frail, and white. The Annunciation. Adelaide Anne Procter. JKCP
How pure at heart and sound in head. In Memoriam A. H. H., XCIV. Tennyson. CoBE; EmBrPo; EPN; GEPC; LPS-1; ViPo; VLEP
How pure the hearts of lovers as they walk. Prothalamium. May Sarton. NePoAm
How quickly doth the reader pass away. Ad Lectorem. Thomas Bastard. SiCE; TuPP
How quiet the day is. The Leaf. John Williams. NePoAm-2
How quietly in ruined state. Aix-la-Chappelle, 1945. Edgar Bowers. NePoEA
How ran lithe monkeys through the leaves! Monkeys. Joaquin Miller. *Fr.* With Walker in Nicaragua. PCH
How Red the Rose That Is the Soldier's Wound. Wallace Stevens. *Fr.* Esthétique du Mal. FaBoMo; WaP
(Soldier's Wound, The.) WaaP
How rewarding to know Mr. Smith. Mr. Smith. William Jay Smith. FiBHP
How rich, O Lord! how fresh thy visits are! Unprofitableness. Henry Vaughan. AtBAP; EPS; SeCV-1
How rich the wave, in front, imprest. Lines Written near Richmond, upon the Thames, at Evening. Wordsworth. OBEC
How Robin Hood Rescued the Widow's Sons. *Unknown. See* Robin Hood and the Widow's Three Sons.
How Roses Came Red. Robert Herrick. BEL; ChTr; EnL; EPS (1942 ed.); TCEP; TyEnPo

How rough the sea! On Izumo Cliff. Basho. OnPM
How sad if, by some strange new law. Suppose. Anne Reeve Aldrich. HBV
How sad it is to be a woman! Woman. Fu Hsüan. TrCh; WoL
How sad the note of that funeral drum. On the Death of Commodore Oliver Hazard Perry. John G. C. Brainard. GA; PAH
How sad's a scorch'd lovers fate. *Unknown.* SeCSL
How Salvator Won. Ella Wheeler Wilcox. PTA-2
How Samson Bore Away the Gates of Gaza. Vachel Lindsay. NP
How, save only by death, from thee, O life, can I flee? The Way of Life. Aesopus. OxBG
How Sea-Calves Are Born. Oppian, *tr. fr. Greek by* William Diaper. *Fr.* Halieuticks. BeR
How see you Echo? When she calls I see. Echo. Viscountess Grey of Fallodon. CH; GBV (1922 ed.)
"How seldom, friend! a good great man inherits." The Good Great Man [*or* Complaint]. Samuel Taylor Coleridge. BPN; EmBrPo; EPN; HBV; LPS-3; WhC
How shall a man fore-doom'd to lone estate. Three Sonnets, II. Hartley Coleridge. RO
How shall a Writer change his ways? Prologue to Eighteenth Century Vignettes. Austin Dobson. *Fr.* Eighteenth Century Vignettes. BPN
How shall come the kingdom holy. An Affirmation. Minot Judson Savage. MaRV
How shall I a habit break? John Boyle O'Reilly. *Fr.* A Builder's Lesson. PoToHe (new ed.)
How shall I address Thee, O God? how shall I praise thee? *Unknown.* *Fr.* Nanak and the Sikhs. WGRP
"How shall I be a poet?" Poeta Fit, Non Nascitur. "Lewis Carroll." PC
How Shall I Build. Wilfrid Scawen Blunt. CAW; JKCP
How Shall I Ever Come to Any Good? Winfield Townley Scott. FiMAP
"How shall I find it, and which way lies?" The Pathway to Paradise. Ozora Stearns Davis. OQP; QP-2
How shall I forsake wisdom? In Praise of Wisdom. Solomon ibn Gabirol. TrJP
How Shall I Go? Muriel Strode. BAP
How shall I guard my soul so that it be. The Song of Love. Rainer Maria Rilke. AWP
How shall I keep April. Foreboding. Hazel Hall. HBMV
How shall I know thee in the sphere which keeps. The Future Life. Bryant. LPS-1
How shall I know, unless I go. To the Not Impossible Him. Edna St. Vincent Millay. PR
How shall I lament thine end? Elegie upon Anacreon. Abraham Cowley. PtP
How shall I plead my cause, when you, my judge. Cleopatra and Antony. Dryden. *Fr.* All For Love, II. FiP
How shall I report. *See* Howe shall I report.
How shall I say good-bye to you, wonderful, terrible days. Envoi. Edward de Stein. BoFr
How shall I sing for you. The Promised Landscape. Sidney Keyes. LoPS
How shall I sing whose harp-strings rot upon. Bough of Babylon. Joseph Auslander. TBM
How shall I tell the measure of my love? Thysia, XLV. Morton Luce. HBV
How shall it be said that you have no clothes? Ode I/XI/8. *Unknown.* BoFr
How shall the bayonet and bomb. Design for Peace. Janet Norris Bangs. PGD
How shall the river learn. Max Schmitt in a Single Scull. Richmond Lattimore. NePoAm-2
"How shall the stone be rolled away?" The Stone of the Sepulcher. "Susan Coolidge." EOAH
How shall the wine be drunk, or the woman known? A Voice from under the Table. Richard Wilbur. NePoEA
How shall unsainted John. Apollyon. George Rostrevor Hamilton. SoV
How shall we answer? And rest in a Flame. Francis Maguire. JKCP (1955 ed.)
How Shall We Honor Lincoln. Thomas Curtis Clark. PoToHe (1941 ed.)
How Shall We Honor Them? Edwin Markham. OQP; PGD; QP-2
How shall we keep it. Nineteen Twenty-six. Wilson MacDonald. MaRV
How shall we know it is the last good-bye? The Last Good-by. Louise Chandler Moulton. AA; LBAP
How shall we praise the magnificence of the dead. Tetélestai. Conrad Aiken. ChMo; CMP; LiTA; LiTM (rev. ed.); MAP; MAPA; MoAB; MoAmPo; MOAP
How Shall We Rise to Greet the Dawn? Sir Osbert Sitwell. WGRP
How shall we summon you? Hymn to Chance. Phelps Putnam. MOAP; TwAmPo; WoL
How Shall We Tell an Angel. Gertrude Hall. OBAV
(Angels.) AA
How she grew old happened in fine-darned places. The People, II. "Robin Hyde." AnNZ
How She Resolved to Act. Merrill Moore. MAP; MoAmPo; MOAP; NeMA; PIAE
How short a time suffices to estrange. The Sadness of Olympio. Victor Hugo. *Fr.* Les Rayons et les ombres. LiA
How short a while ago you eagerly bent. To Comrade Intellectuals. Valery Bryusov. RuPo
How Should I Be So Pleasant? Sir Thomas Wyatt. LoBV; SiPS
(Betrayal.) OBSC
How should I be to Love unjust. Vision. Robert Bridges. ChMo; CMP
How should I love my best. Madrigal. Lord Herbert of Cherbury. PoEL-2; ViBoPo
How should I praise thee, Lord! how should my rhymes. The Temper. George Herbert. AtBAP; EPS (1942 ed.); MePo; OBS; OxBoCh; PoEL-2; PoFS; SeCL; WHA
How should I praise theise sug'red plenties. *Unknown.* SeCSL
"How should I your true love know." The Friar of Orders Grey, 3 [*or* An Old Song Ended]. Dante Gabriel Rossetti. GoBC; PoVP
How Should I Your True Love Know. Shakespeare. *Fr.* Hamlet, IV, v. CBOV; EG; EnLoPo; EPP; EV-1; InPo; LiTB; LiTG; LiTL; PoRA; TCEP; ViBoPo
(Friar of Orders Grey, The.) GoBC
(Ophelia's Song.) CBE; ChTr; OBSC
(Ophelia's Songs, 1.) AnFE; TrGrPo
(Song.) CH
(Song from "Hamlet.") LEAP
How should my lord come home to his lands? Dirge. Maurice Hewlett. LBBV
How sick I get. Father. Paul Carroll. NeAP
How silent comes the water round that bend. Minnows [*or* From the Bridge]. Keats. *Fr.* I Stood Tiptoe. GN; MyFE; PCH
How Sleep the Brave. William Collins. BCEP; BLV; CBPC; DD; EV-3; GN; HBV; HBVY; HH; LEAP; LPS-2; MDAH; OBEV; OtMeF; OTPC; PECK; TreF
(Dirge: "How sleep the brave, who sink to rest.") CBE
(Ode: "How sleep the brave, who sink to rest.") LoBV; NeHB; PoFr; TCEP; ViBoPo; WP
(Ode Written in 1746.) GTBS; GTBS-D; GTBS-W; GTSE; ShBV-3; TrGrPo; TVSH; WHA
(Ode Written in the Beginning of the Year 1746.) ATP; AWP; BEL; BrBE; CaAE; CEP; CoBE; CoEV; EiPP; EM-1; EnL; EnLi-2; EnRP; EPP; ExPo; InPo; JAWP; OAEP; OBEC; OuHeWo; PoE; PoEL-3; PoFS; PreP; SeCeV; TOP; TriL; TyEnPo; WBP
(Sleep of the Brave, The.) OHIP
How Sleep the Brave. Donald F. Drummond. PtPa
"How Sleep the Brave." Walter de la Mare. TOP
How sleep the brave who sink to rest. On a Watchman Asleep at Midnight. James Thomas Fields. CenHV
How slight a thing may set one's fancy drifting. Honey Dripping from the Comb. James Whitcomb Riley. AA
How slowly creeps the hand of Time. The Churchyard. Robert Buchanan. HBV; VA
How slowly learns the child at school. Citizenship; Form 8889512, Sub-Section Q. G. K. Chesterton. OxBoLi
How slowly the hours pass. You Will Grieve. Guillaume Apollinaire. OnPM
How small a tooth hath mined the season's heart! Frost. Edith M. Thomas. AA; BAP
How solitary gleams the lamplit street. The Roadmenders. Laurence Binyon. PoeT
How soon a mighty throne can fall. Sovereignty. Leslie Savage Clark. ChIP
How soon, alas, the hours are over. Plays. Walter Savage Landor. BCEP; BLP; HBV; VA
How soon doth man decay! Mortification. George Herbert. MePo; OAEP; PoD; PoFS; ViBoPo
How Soon Hath Time, the Subtle Thief of Youth. Milton. *See* On His Having Arrived at the Age of Twenty-three.
How soon the prophet stars decree. The Danger. Norman Gale. LBBV
How soothing sound the gentle airs that move. Avenue in Savernake Forest. William Lisle Bowles. EnSW
How sound are ye sleeping, comrades. Bitter Question. Arthur R. Macdougall, Jr. PGD
How splendid in the morning glows the lily. Yasmin [*or* Hassan's Serenade]. James Elroy Flecker. *Fr.* Hassan. LoPS; OBEV (new ed.); TCPD; TwCV
How spoke the King, in his crucial hour victorious? King of the Belgians. Marion Couthouy Smith. PAH
How Stands the Glass Around? James Wolfe. BoHiPo; PAH
How stately stand yon pines upon the hill. Spring to Winter. George Crabbe. *Fr.* The Ancient Mansion. ChTr
How stately yon palace uplifts its proud head. Joseph Rodman Drake. *Fr.* The King of the Doctors. PoP

How steadfastly she worked at it! The Cradle. Austin Dobson. BPN; VA
How still and silent. Midnight. Chao Tz'u. PoHN
How still Earth lies!—behind the pines. The Reaper. James Matthew Legaré. SPP
How still, how very still the air is. The Unwilling Guest; an Urban Dialogue. Horace Gregory. CrMA
How still it is among the junipers! Autumn. Sergei Aleksandrovich Yesenin. TrRV
How still it is here in the woods. Solitude. Archibald Lampman. BoCaPo; ExPo; PeCV
How still the day is, and the air how bright! By the Wood. Robert Nichols. ChMP; HBBV; LBBV; NP
How still the morning of the hallow'd day! Sunday Morning. James Grahame. *Fr.* The Sabbath. EnSW; LPS-2; OBRV
How still the room is! But a while ago. In Death. Mary Emily Bradley. AA
How still the sea! behold; how calm the sky! The Sixth Pastoral [*or* Pastoral Landscape]. Ambrose Philips. *Fr.* Pastorals. CEP; OBEC
How still they sleep within the city moil. In Trinity Churchyard. Thomas S. Jones, Jr. VOD
How still this quiet cornfield is to-night! August, 1914. John Masefield. HBV
How strange and pitiful that man. Values. Leslie Savage Clark. ChIP
How strange are the freaks of memory! An Ember Picture. James Russell Lowell. IAP
How strange it is that I can live to-day. Thomas Lovell Beddoes. *Fr.* Death's Jest Book. NBE
How strange it is that, in the after age. Praeterita ex Instantibus. William Douw Lighthall. VA
How strange it is to wake. The Shadow of Night. Coventry Patmore. CH
How strange it seems! These Hebrews in their graves. The Jewish Cemetery at Newport. Longfellow. AmP; AmPP; AnNE; APW; CoV; OnAP; OxBA; PoE; RiBV
How strange that grass should sing. Quatrains. Gwendolyn B. Bennett. CDC
How strange the sculptures that adorn these towers! Divina Commedia, II. Longfellow. AmP; AmPP; AnAmPo; AnFE; AnNE; APA; APW; CoAnAm; CoBA; CoV; ES; GoBC; IAP; LA; LPS-2; MOAP; NePA; OBAV; OuHeWo; OxBA; PIAE; PoE; PoFS; PtP; REAL; ReaPo; SeCeV; TCAP; TOP
How Strange You Are. William Carlos Williams. *Fr.* Paterson. OnAP
How strongly does my passion flow. Song. Aphra Behn. EV-3
How subtle-secret is your smile! Oscar Wilde. *Fr.* The Sphinx. MBP; MoBrPo
How sure the soul is that if truth destroy. The Torch Bearers: Wotton to Kepler. Alfred Noyes. GrCo-1
How sweet and lovely dost thou make the shame. Sonnets, XCV. Shakespeare. PeBoSo; ReEn; TrGrPo
How sweet and silent is the place. Communion Hymn. Alice Freeman Palmer. MaRV; TrPWD
How sweet, how sweet to hear those tales again. Snow. Alfred de Vigny. TrFP
How Sweet I Roamed from Field to Field. Blake. *See* Song: "How sweet I roamed from field to field."
How sweet is Life, how beautiful. The Joy of Life. W. H. Davies. ChMo; CMP; TriL
How sweet is the season, the sky how serene. Song for a Fishing Party near Burlington, on the Delaware, in 1776. Jonathan Odell. BoCaPo (1948 ed.)
How sweet is the shepherd's sweet lot! The Shepherd. Blake. *Fr.* Songs of Innocence. BoTP; BrBE; EiPP; EnRP; ExPo; GaP; GoTP; HBV; KN; LoBV; OBEC; OTPC; PoRh; ThWaDe; TiPo (1959 ed.); TOP; TVC; TVSH
How sweet it is, when mother Fancy rocks. Sonnet. Wordsworth. EnSW
How sweet it was to breathe that cooler air. The Soldier's Return. Robert Bloomfield. LPS-2
How sweet only to delight in lambs and laugh by streams. Sonnet. Rex Warner. LO
How sweet the answer Echo makes. Echo [*or* Echoes]. Thomas Moore. EV-4; GoBC; GTBS; GTBS-D; GTBS-W; GTIV; GTSL; OxBI; TIP
How sweet the gale of morning breathes! Morning Air. Jami. PeP
How sweet the harmonies of afternoon! The Blackbird. Frederick Tennyson. HBV; LPS-2; VA
How sweet the moon is climbing heaven's hill! Moonlight. Edward Moxon. OBRV
How Sweet the Moonlight Sleeps upon This Bank! Shakespeare. *Fr.* The Merchant of Venice, V, i. CBE; MeRV; PIR; TreFS; TrGrPo
(From "The Merchant of Venice.") LEAP
(In Tune with the Infinite.) MaRV
(Moonlight.) OHFP; SN
(Moonlight and Music.) BCEP
(Moonlight Music.) EV-1
(Music.) LPS-3
How Sweet the Name of Jesus Sounds. John Newton. *See* Name of Jesus, The.
How sweet the sacred legend—if unblamed. The Mother's Secret. Oliver Wendell Holmes. MotAn
How sweet the tuneful bells' responsive peal! Sonnet: At Ostend [*or* The Bells of Ostend *or* Ostend on Hearing the Bells]. William Lisle Bowles. EnRP; ES; OBEC; PTA-2
How Sweet This Lone Vale. Andrew Erskine. EBSV
How sweet this morning air in spring. Early Spring. W. H. Davies. TVSH
How Sweet Thy Precious Gift of Rest. Menahem ben Makhir of Ratisbon, *tr. fr. Hebrew by* Herbert Loewe. TrJP
How sweet to wear a shape of snow. Duck in Central Park. Frances Higginson Savage. GoYe
How sweet you were . . . how young and soft you were. Ponto the Fool. Beatrice Redpath. CPG
How sweetly doth My Master sound! My Master! The Odour. George Herbert. EV-2; OBS
How sweetly keen, how stirred the air! An Anniversary. William Knox Johnson. TIP
How sweetly on the autumn scene. The Hawkbit. Sir Charles G. D. Roberts. HBV; SN
How sweetly on the wood-girt town. Pentucket. Whittier. MC; PAH
"How sweetly," said the trembling maid. The Fire Worshippers. Thomas Moore. *Fr.* Lalla Rookh. EV-4; LPS-1
How sweetly sings this stream. Laurence Dakin. *Fr.* Pyramus and Thisbe, III, iii. CaP
How swift was your departure. Welcome Home! Su Ch'an I. PoHN
How swiftly it dries. The Dew on the Garlic-Leaf. *Unknown.* Burial Songs, I. TrCh; WoL
How swiftly, once, on silvery feet. So I May Feel the Hands of God. Anna Hempstead Branch. PC
How tedious and tasteless the hours. Greenfields. *Unknown.* AS
How tender the heart grows. Nightfall. Una Marson. PoNe
How tenderly, how superstitiously. Last Love. Feodor Ivanovich Tyutchev. TrRV
How tenderly it goes, this farewell day. Last Leave. Gilean Douglas. MuM
How terrible their trust, the little leaves. April, 1942. Mark Van Doren. WaP
How that vast heaven intitled First is rolled. Sonnet. William Drummond of Hawthornden. EIL
How the Babes in the Wood Showed They Couldn't Be Beaten. Guy Wetmore Carryl. RIS
How the blithe Lark runs up the golden stair. The Skylark. Frederick Tennyson. GN; HBV; SN
How the branch trembles of Apollo's bay! The Epiphany of Apollo. Callimachus. OxBG
How the British Fleet Bombarded New York. Philip Freneau. LauV
How the Crow-Hen Killed the Black Snake. *Unknown, tr. fr. Sanskrit by* Arthur W. Ryder. *Fr.* The Panchatantra. OuHeWo
How the *Cumberland* Went Down. Silas Weir Mitchell. BlG; MC; PAH
How the Daughters Come Down at Dunoon. Henry Cholmondeley-Pennell. BOHV
How the Feud Started. Arthur Guiterman. AlBD
How the Flowers Grow. "Gabriel Setoun." MPB
How the Froggies Go to Sleep, *sel.* J. K. Nutting. Little, Wee Froggies, The. SAS
How the Grain Grows. *Unknown, tr. fr. Russian by* W. R. S. Ralston. OnPM
How the Great Guest Came. Edwin Markham. BeLS; BLPA
(Great Guest Comes, The.) WBLP
How the greenest of wheat rang gold at his birth! For My Son. John Frederick Nims. MiAP
How the ground escapes me! Manuel Altolaguirre, *tr. fr. Spanish by* Eleanor L. Turnbull. CoSP
How the heart pulls at its tether. May-Lure. Richard Burton. NLK
How the Helpmate of Blue-Beard Made Free with a Door. Guy Wetmore Carryl. InMe
How the Kite Learned to Fly. *Unknown.* *See* How the Little Kite Learned to Fly.
How the Leaves Came Down. "Susan Coolidge." DD; HBV; HBVY; MPB; OTPC; PECK; PRWS; TVC; TVSH
How the leaves sing to the wind! In the Golden Birch. Jane Elizabeth Gostwycke Roberts. VA
How the Little Kite Learned to Fly. *Unknown, at. to* Katharine Pyle. HBV; HBVY; OnHT; OTPC; TVC; TVSH
(How the Kite Learned to Fly.) GFA
How the moon triumphs through the endless nights. James Thomson. *Fr.* The City of Dreadful Night. BMEP; GTML; GTSL

How the mountains talked together. A Farewell to Agassiz. Oliver Wendell Holmes. ImOP
How the Old Horse Won the Bet. Oliver Wendell Holmes. AnNE; IAP; TCAP
How the people held their breath. Jesse James [*or* Death of Jesse James]. *Unknown.* ABS; ATP; BoHiPo
How the Ransom Was Paid. *Unknown.* PEOR
How the streets smell sweetly strewn with palms. The Mother of Christ. Kostas Varnalis. MoGP
How the swift river runs bright to its doom. At the Leap of the Waters. Edward F. Garesché. JKCP
How the Wallflower Came First and Why So Called. Robert Herrick. EV-2
How the waters closed above him. Emily Dickinson. PoEL-5
How the Women Will Stop War. Aristophanes, *tr. fr. Greek by* B. B. Rogers. *Fr.* Lysistrata. OxBG; WaaP
How they are provided for upon the earth. Beginners. Walt Whitman. AA; IAP
How they begrudged him yet. Departure. Al-Hadrami. MooP
How They Brought the Good News from Ghent to Aix. Robert Browning. BBV (1923 ed.); BEL; BeLS; BMEP; BoChLi; BPN; CG; EM-2; EmBrPo; EnLi-2 (1949 ed.); EPP; EV-5; FaBoBe; FaFP; GEPC; GN; GoTP; HBV; HBVY; HoPM; LPS-2; MCCG; MW; OnHT; OnSP; OTPC; PC; PCD; PECK; PFE; PoVP; PYM; ShBV-1; StVeCh; TCEP; TiPo (1952 ed.); TOP; TreF; TSWC; TVSH; VA; ViPo; ViPP; VLEP
How They Do It. J. C. Squire. *See* Poor Old Man, The.
How they have learned the secrets of the ether! The Patient Scientists. Bertha Gerneaux Woods. MaRV; OQP; QP-2
How They Sleep. *Unknown.* PPL
How they walled the sea and felled the woods. The Seven Cities of America. Edgar Lee Masters. ChMo; CMP
How thickly the far fields of heaven are strewn with stars! Come Se Quando. Robert Bridges. MM
How Thomas Wolsey Did Arise unto Great Authority and Government, His Maner of Life, Pompe, and Dignity, and How Hee Fell Downe into Great Disgrace, and Was Arested of High Treason. Thomas Churchyard. *Fr.* A Mirror for Magistrates. SiCE
How thou art like the daisy in Noah's meadow. The Daisy and the Flood. Thomas Lovell Beddoes. *Fr.* The Second Brother. RO
How through Green-grassed Fields. Zisha Landau, *tr. fr. Yiddish by* Sarah Zweig Betsky. OnCuPl
How Time Consumeth All Earthly Things. *Unknown. See* Proper Sonnet, A, How Time Consumeth . . .
How to Ask and Have. Samuel Lover. *See* Ask and Have.
How to Be Happy. *Unknown.* BLPA
How to Catch a Trolley. *Unknown.* DDA
How to Catch Unicorns. William Rose Benét. CV; HBMV; TSW
How to Eat Watermelons. Frank L. Stanton. BOHV
How to Forget. Rebecca Foresman. PoToHe (new ed.) (If.) WBLP
How to Give. *Unknown.* BLRP
How to Go and Forget. Edwin Markham. HBMV
How to kéep—is there ány any, is there none such. The Leaden Echo and the Golden Echo. Gerard Manley Hopkins. CaAE; ChMo; CoBMV; EnLi-2 (1949 ed.); FaFP; GTBS-D; GTBS-W; LiA; LiTB; LiTM; LoBV; MBP; MoAB; MoBrPo; MoVE; OAEP (2d ed.); OBMV; PreP; ReaPo; TwCV; ViPo; VLEP
How to Kill. Keith Douglas. ChMP
How to Know the Wild Animals. Carolyn Wells. *See* How to Tell the Wild Animals.
How to Make a Man of Consequence. Mark Lemon. BOHV
How to Make a Whistle. *Unknown.* ADAH
How to Raise a Son. Martial, *tr. fr. Latin by* L. R. Lind. LiTW
("Lupus, you question carefully.") LaP
How to Read Me. Walter Savage Landor. VA
How to Recognize a Snark. "Lewis Carroll." *Fr.* The Hunting of the Snark, II. MPB
("Come, listen, my men, while I tell you again.") BOHV
(Snark, The.) TSW; TSWC
How to Tell Goblins from Elves. Monica Shannon. FaPON; TiPo
How to Tell Juan Don from Another. Gardner E. Lewis. FiBHP
How to Tell the Wild Animals. Carolyn Wells. FaFP; FaPON; FiBHP; HBVY; MaC; MPB; TiPo; TSW; UTS
(How to Know the Wild Animals.) GoTP
How to the Singer Comes the Song? Richard Watson Gilder. WGRP
How to Treat Elves. Morris Bishop. FiBHP
How to Write a Letter. Elizabeth Turner. MoShBr; OTPC (1923 ed.)
How tranquil is the life. The Life Removed. Luis de León. TeCS; WoL
How true it is when I am sad. Work. John W. Thompson. PoToHe (new ed.)
How ugly nature is here, truly. Fatherland. *At. to* Dmitri Vladimirovich Venevitinov. TrRV
How uneasy is his life. The Joys of Marriage. Charles Cotton. BOHV; InMe
How Unhappy a Lover Am I. Dryden. *Fr.* The Conquest of Granada, Pt. II. SeCL
How unhappy (though unmarried) is an uncle who, bereft. Horace, Book V, Ode III. Charles Larcom Graves. CenHV
How unpleasant to meet Mr. Eliot! Lines for Cuscuscaraway and Mirza Murad Ali Beg. T. S. Eliot. FiBHP
How vain! he cried. A God? a mole, a worm! Man as God. John Davidson. *Fr.* A Ballad in Blank Verse of the Making of a Poet. BMEP
How vainly men themselves amaze. The Garden [*or* Thoughts in a Garden]. Andrew Marvell. AEV; AnEnPo; AtBAP; ATP; AWP; BEL; BLV; BoLiVe; BrBE; CaAE; CoBE; CoEV; ElSeCe; EnL; EnLi-1; EPP; EPS; EV-2; ExPo; FaBoEn; GTBS; GTBS-D; GTBS-W; GTSE; GTSL; HBV; InPo; InvP; JAWP; LEAP; LiA; LiTB; LiTG; LoBV; MaPo; MeLP; MePo; OAEP; OBEV; OBS; OuHeWo; PIAE; Po; PoE; PoEL-2; PoFS; PoRA; ReEn; RiBV; SeCePo; SeCeV; SeCL; SeCV-1; SeEP; SN; TOP; TrGrPo; TwHP; TyEnPo; UnPo (1st ed.); ViBoPo; WBP; WHA; WP
How vastly pleasing is my tale. Blessings on Doneraile. Patrick O'Kelly. OnYI
How very modern once they were. The Modernists. Tom MacInnes. CaP
How very sad it is to think. Poor Brother. *Unknown.* NA
How Violets Came Blue. Robert Herrick. EnL; EPS (1942 ed.)
How warm this woodland wild Recess! Recollections of Love Samuel Taylor Coleridge. ChER
How was he honoured in the midst of the people. Simon, Son of Onias. Ecclesiasticus, Bible, Apocrypha. BHV
How was I worthy so divine a loss. Das Ewig-Weibliche (The Eternal Feminine). James Russell Lowell. TCAP; TriL
How was November's melancholy endear'd to me. Robert Bridges. *Fr.* The Testament of Beauty. MoVE
How was thy mother a lioness. Lamentation. Ezekiel, Bible, *O.T.* TrJP
How wasteful, as they say, is Nature. Love. Walker Gibson. NePoAm-2
How We Beat the Favo[u]rite. Adam Lindsay Gordon. OtMeF; VA
How We Became a Nation. Harriet Prescott Spofford. MC; PAH
How We Built a Church at Ashcroft. Jack Leahy. PoOW
How We Burned the *Philadelphia.* Barrett Eastman. GA, *abr.;* PaA; PAH
How we dally out our days! Upon our Vain Flattery of Ourselves that the Succeeding Times Will Be Better than the Former. Robert Gomersal. SeCL
How We Learn. Horatius Bonar. HBV
How We Logged Katahdin Stream. Daniel G. Hoffman. MaC
How weak a star doth rule mankind. Death. Katherine Philips. AEV; WP
How weak those dear, uncertain hands. To Doris. Lee Wilson Dodd. FAOV
How Well for the Birds. *Unknown, tr. fr. Irish by* Frank O'Connor. KiLC
How well I know the fount that freely flows. The Fount That Freely Flows. St. John of the Cross. TeCS
How well I know what I mean to do. By the Fireside. Robert Browning. BMEP; EmBrPo; EV-5; SN; VLEP
How well I'd bear the break, my anger spoke it. Tibullus. Elegies, I, 5. LaP
How well my eyes remember the dim path! Elegy: The Summer House on the Mound. Robert Bridges. GoTL
How well we loved, in Summer solitude. Summer. Lloyd Mifflin. *Fr.* The Fields of Dawn. SN
How—When—Where. John Oxenham. MaRV
How wild, how witch-like weird that life should be! The Wonder of It. Harriet Monroe. NP
"How will death come?" he asked his visitor. Guest. Beresford Richards. ReTS
How will it dawn, the coming Christmas Day? Christmas Day. Charles Kingsley. EnSW
How Will It Seem? Charles Hanson Towne. VOD (1931 ed.)
How will you manage. Crossing the Mountain Alone. Princess Daihaku. *Fr.* Manyo Shu. AWP; JAWP; WBP; WoL
How Will You Remember Me? Joan Lamburn. DiM
How wisely nature did decree. Eyes and Tears. Andrew Marvell. EV-2; MePo
How witty's ruin! how importunate. John Donne. *Fr.* The First Anniversary. ReEn
How wonderful and unspeakable. The Moon. Edith Södergran. LiTW
How wonderful is Death. Shelley. *Fr.* Queen Mab. EmBrPo

How would the centuries long asunder. Hero-Worship. William Bell Scott. VA
How wretched is he borne or taught. *Unknown.* SeCSL
How wretched is the state wee all are in. *Unknown.* SeCSL
How you gwine ter git ter de Promise Lan'. De Promise Lan'. John Richard Moreland. IHA
How your eyes dazzle down into my soul! James Thomson. Sunday at Hampstead, II. EmBrPo
Howard Lamson. Edgar Lee Masters. *Fr.* The New Spoon River. LEAP; NAMP; ViBoPo
Howdy, Mister Hop-Toad! Glad to see you out! Mister Hop-Toad. James Whitcomb Riley. CV
Howdy, Mr. Winter! Wilbur D. Nesbit. OnHT
Howe [*or* How] shall I report. Maystress Jane Scroupe [*or* The Commendations of Mistress Jane Scrope]. John Skelton. *Fr.* Phyllyp Sparowe. EG; NBE; OBSC; ViBoPo
Hower is come in which I must resigne, The. *Unknown.* SeCSL
Howe'er it be, it seems to me. Nobility. Tennyson. *Fr.* Lady Clara Vere de Vere. OTPC (1946 ed.)
However fine and mortal be. The Bee. Paul Valéry. TrFP
However gracefully/ the spare leaves of the fig tree. Casa d'Amunt. Alastair Reid. NePoEA
However the battle is ended. An Inspiration. Ella Wheeler Wilcox. WGRP
However they talk, whatever they say. Motto. *Unknown.* *Fr.* Proverbs. RIS; TiPo
However we wrangled with Britain awhile. Literary Importation. Philip Freneau. IAP
However well a man may plan his days. Soliloquy of Cicero. Colgate Dorr. PtPa
Howl. Allen Ginsberg. AmP; NeAP (I–II)
Howle, howle, howle, howle: O you are men of stones. Shakespeare. *Fr.* King Lear, V, iii. AtBAP
Howlers, The. Leconte de Lisle, *tr. fr. French by* Alan Conder. TrFP
Howling storm is brewing, A. The Storm. Heine. AWP; JAWP; WBP
"How's My Boy?" Sydney Dobell. BMEP; CG; CH; EtS; GN; HBV; LPS-2; MOAH; OHIP; VA
"How's your father?" came the whisper. Conversational. *Unknown.* ALV; BoHiPo; FiBHP
Hoyda, hoyda, jolly rutterkin. Rutterkin. William Cornish. PoMS
Hrolf's Thrall, His Song. Willard Wattles. SBMV
Hrothgar spoke, the defence of the Scyldings. The Death of Grendel's Mother. *Unknown.* *Fr.* Beowulf. EPP
Hrothwulf and Hrothgar held the longest. The Anglian Tradition. *Unknown.* *Fr.* Widsith. PaOS
Hu Chiu Shan. Hsüeh Lan Ying, *tr. fr. Chinese by* Henry H. Hart. PoHN
Hub, The. Oscar Williams. MaRV
Hub for the Universe, A. Walt Whitman. *See* Letters from God.
Hubbub in Hub. Laurence McKinney. WhC
Hubbubing down the dale. A Royal Pickle. Carlton Talbott. ALV
Hubert and Arthur ("Heat me these irons hot"). Shakespeare. *Fr.* King John, IV, i. ShGoBo
Huckleberry Hunting, *with music.* *Unknown.* ShS; SoAmSa
Huckster's Horse, The. Julia Hurd Strong. GoYe
Hudibras, *sels.* Samuel Butler.
 Astral Fates, The, *fr.* II, 3. BeR
 Calf's Head Meeting, A, 4 *ll.*, *fr.* III, 2. BeR
 "Doubtless the pleasure is as great," *fr.* II, 3. NBE
 "Egyptians, The, say, The Sun has twice," *fr.* II, 3. ImOP
 Godly Casuistry, *fr.* II, 2. OBS
 Hudibras the Sectarian ("Beside he was a shrewd philosopher"), *fr.* I, i. SeCePo
 Hudibras' Sword and Dagger, *abr.*, *fr.* I, 1. LPS-2
 "In Mathematicks he was greater," *fr.* I, 1. ImOP
 Lady's Answer, The, *fr.* III, 3. BeR
 "Learning, that cobweb of the brain," *fr.* I, 3. NBE
 Love, *fr.* III, 1. BeR
 Presbyterian Church Government, *fr.* I, 3. OBS
 Presbyterian Knight [and Independent Squire] ("He was in logic a great critic"), *abr.*, *fr.* I, 1. CoEV; OBS
  (Hudibras, the Presbyterian Knight, *abr.*) OxBoLi; SiTL
  (Logic of Hudibras.) LPS-3
  (Metaphysical Sectarian, The.) MeLP
  (Portrait of Hudibras.) AtBAP; PoEL-3
   Sir Hudibras ("He could raise scruples dark and nice"). UnPo (1st ed.)
 "Quoth she, 'The matter's not so far gone,'" *fr.* II, 1. NBE
 Religion of Hudibras, The, *fr.* I, 1. BOHV; InMe; LPS-2
  (Art of Love, The.) FaBoEn
  (For All Fanatics.) PoFr
  ("For his religion it was fit.") LoBV; ViBoPo
  ("He was of that stubborn crew.") BPP
  (Sir Hudibras's Religion.) FaBoEn
 Saintship versus Conscience, *fr.* III, 1. BCEP
  (Rules of Life.) BeR
 Sidrophel, the Rosicrucian Conjurer, *fr.* II, 3. OxBoLi
  ("This said, he turned about his steed.") NBE
 Sir Sidrophel, the Conjuror ("He had been long t'wards mathematicks"). FaBoEn
  (Portrait of Sidrophel.) PoEL-3
 "This sturdy squire, he had, as well," *fr.* I, 1. ViBoPo
 Tyranny and Law, *fr.* II, 2. BeR
 "We grant, altho' he had much wit [*or* evil]," *abr.*, *fr.* I, 1. EPP
 "When civil fury [*or* dudgeon] first grew high," *fr.* I, 1. CEP; EiPP; EPS, *abr.*; EV-2; SeCV-2; SeEP; TOP; ViBoPo
  (Description of Hudibras and His Equipments, *abr.*) BCEP
Hudibras Redivivus, *sel.* Edward Ward.
 In a London Street. BeR
Hudson, The. George Sidney Hellman. AA
Hudson, The. Harriet Plimpton. VOD (1935 ed.)
Hue and Cry after Cupid, The, *sel.* Ben Jonson.
 Beauties, Have Ye Seen This Toy. OAEP; TuPP
  (Cupid.) BOHV, *abr.*; InMe
  (Venus' Runaway.) HBV; ReEn
Hue and Cry after Fair Amoret, A. Congreve. *See* Amoret.
Hue and Cry after Love. Meleager, *tr. fr. Greek by* F. L. Lucas. GrPE
Hues of the rich unfolding morn. Morning. John Keble. OBRV
Huesca. John Cornford. ChMP
 (Poem.) POTE
 (To Margot Heinemann.) LoPS
Hug Me Tight. John Kendall. WhC
Huge and alert, irascible yet strong. A Toast to Our Native Land. Robert Bridges. HiLiAm; MC; PAH
Huge elm, with rifted trunk all notched and scarred. The Shepherd's Tree. John Clare. GTML
Huge Leviathan, The. Spenser. *Fr.* Visions of the World's Vanity. ChTr
Huge red-buttressed mesa over yonder, The. Rain in the Desert [*or* Rain in the Street]. John Gould Fletcher. Arizona Poems, VI. NP; TCPD
Huge wound in my head began to heal, The. The Wound. Thom Gunn. NePoEA
Hugest mammal in the land, The. Ant-ology. Christian Morgenstern. AnGP
Hugh Maguire. *At. to* Eochadh O'Hussey. *See* O'Hussey's Ode to the Maguire.
Hugh of Lincoln. *Unknown.* *See* Sir Hugh; or, The Jew's Daughter.
Hugh Selwyn Mauberley (Life and Contacts). Ezra Pound. CoBMV; CoV; LiTA; LiTM (rev. ed.); MoPo
 Sels.
 E. P. Ode pour L'Élection de son Sépulcre, I–V. CrMA; FaBoEn; MoVE; NePA; OxBA; PreP (I *only*); SeCeV; UnPo (3d ed.)
  (Lyrics.) OnAP
  (Ode pour l'Election de Son Sepulchre.) AmPP
  (Pour L'Election de Son Sepulchre.) FaBoMo; LiTG
   Age Demanded an Image, The, II. InPo; MOAP
   These Fought in Any Case, IV–V. NP; WaaP
 Envoi (1919). APA; ChMo; CMP; CoAnAm; MoP; OnAP; TBM; UnPo (3d ed.)
  (Envoi: "Go, dumb-born book.") GTBS-W; MAP; MoAB; MoAmPo; NePA; OxBA
 "For three years, diabolus in the scale," Mauberley, II.
  (Mauberley, 1920.) NP
Hugh Spencer's Feats in France (A *and* B *vers.*). *Unknown.* ESPB
Hugh, the Carter, Tarries. Willard Wattles. PR
Hugh was a cabbage. Vegetable Fantasies. Helen Hoyt. RIS
Hughie Grame (A *and* C *vers.*). *Unknown.* ESPB
 (Hughie the Graeme.) LH; OBB
Hughie Seeks to Console a Brother Shepherd. Over-grieving for the Loss of His Son. James Logie Robertson. BSV
Hughie the Graeme. *Unknown.* *See* Hughie Grame.
Hughie's Advice to Dauvit to Enjoy the Fine Weather. James Logie Robertson. BSV
Hughley Steeple. A. E. Housman. A Shropshire Lad, LXI. PoVP; ViPo; VLEP
Huguenot, A. Mary Elizabeth Coleridge. OBVV; PoeT; PoVP; TVSH
Huh! All the other fellers went. The Anonymous Valentine. Wilbur D. Nesbit. OnHT
Hulking glooms of looming houses, The. Kirov Is with Us. Nikolai Tikhonov. RuPo
Hullo! Sam Walter Foss. PTA-2
 ("W'en you see a man in woe.") CenHV
Hull's Surrender. *Unknown.* PAH
Hum: ha? Is this a vision? Is this a dreame? doe I sleepe? What I Am, I Cannot Avoide. Shakespeare. *Fr.* The Merry Wives of Windsor. LiA
Humaine Cares. Nathaniel Wanley. *See* Human Cares.
Human Abstract, The. Blake. *Fr.* Songs of Experience. EiPP; EnRP; MaPo; PoEL-4

Human affairs are dreams. Midautumn at Huang-chou. Su T'ung-po. WhP
Human Being Is a Lonely Creature, The. Richard Eberhart. FiMAP; NePoAm
Human Cares. Nathaniel Wanley. SeCL
(Humaine Cares.) OBS
Human Cylinders. Mina Loy. AnAmPo; LA
Human Dignity. W. B. Yeats. A Man Young and Old, II. TwP
Human Fold, The. Edwin Muir. LiTM (rev. ed.)
Human Folly. Pope. *Fr.* An Essay on Man, Epistle II. FiP
(Man.) BLV; BoLiVe
("Whate'er the passion—knowledge, fame, or pelf.") CBE; TrGrPo
Human Frailty. William Cowper. HBV
Human Frailty. Philip Freneau. AnAmPo; LA
Human hand lying on my hand, The. A Hand. Bernard Spencer. NeBP
Human Happiness. Dryden. *Fr.* The Indian Emperor, IV, i. FiP
Human Heart, The. Frank Carleton Nelson. PoToHe (new ed.)
Human hopes are ever. Hopes. Ibn al-Imam. MooP
Human Image, The, *sel.* Blake.
London ("There souls of men are bought and sold"). ChTr
Human Imperfection. Simonides, *tr. fr. Greek by* Gilbert Highet. GrL; OxBG
Human Life. Matthew Arnold. EmBrPo; EPN
Human Life. Aubrey Thomas De Vere. HBV; JKCP; OnYI; VA
(Sad Is Our Youth [—for It Is Ever Going].) LPS-1; MaRV
Human Life. W. H. Malloch. ACP (1926 ed.); JKCP (1926 ed.); OQP; QP-2
Human Life. Pindar. *See* Only a Dream-Shadow.
Human Life, *sels.* Samuel Rogers.
Fond Youth. OBRV
Marriage. LPS-1
Human Life; on the Denial of Immortality. Samuel Taylor Coleridge. ChER
Human Mind, The. Ai Shih-te, *tr. fr. Chinese by* William C. White. TrJP
Human Outlook, The. John Addington Symonds. *See* Loftier Race, A.
Human Plan, The. Charles Henry Crandall. AA
Human Progress. Walt Whitman. *Fr.* Song of the Open Road. GrCo-1
Human race, The/ To you, means such a child or such a man. "Where There is no Vision." Elizabeth Barrett Browning. *Fr.* Aurora Leigh, II. MaRV
Human Race Comes to Be Judged, The. Cynewulf. *See* Last Judgment, The.
Human Races, The. R. P. Lister. FiBHP
Human Responsibility. Aeschylus, *tr. fr. Greek by* E. D. A. Morshead. *Fr.* Agamemnon. GrR
Human Seasons, The. Keats. BPN; CBE; CoBE; EnRP; EV-4; FaFP; GTBS; GTBS-D; GTBS-W; GTSE; GTSL; HBV; OBRV; PeBoSo; PoP
(Four Seasons Fill the Measure.) PG (1955 ed.)
Human Soul Speaks, The. William Langland, *mod. by* Henry W. Wells. *Fr.* The Vision of Piers Plowman. PoLi
Human spirits saw I on a day, The. The Questioning Spirit. Arthur Hugh Clough. BPN; EmBrPo; PoVP; VLEP
Human Touch, The. Richard Burton. BLP; BLPA; LBAP; OQP; QP-2
Human Touch, The. Spencer Michael Free. FaBoBe; MaRV; NeHB; PoP; PoToHe
Human Touch, The. Helen King. PoToHe
Human Touch, The. Francis Quarles. *See* Epigram: Respice Finem.
Human will, that force unseen, The. Will. Ella Wheeler Wilcox. BLPA
Human Worms. Anaxilas, *tr. fr. Greek by* T. F. Higham. OxBG
Humane Mikado, The. W. S. Gilbert. *Fr.* The Mikado. ALV; SiTL
(Let the Punishment Fit the Crime.) PoVP
(Mikado's Song, The.) LiTB
Humane Thought. Rebecca McCann. DDA; YaD
Humanitad, *sels.* Oscar Wilde.
Joy. PCH
Midwinter. PCH
Humanitarian, The, *sel.* Angela Morgan.
"Seeing how the world suffered and bled." OQP; QP-2
Humanities. Robert Conquest. PoLFOT
Humanity. William Cowper. *See* Heedless Cruelty.
Humanity. Richard Watson Dixon. EPN; OBVV; OQP; QP-2; VA
Humanity, in whom the best. Summum Bonum. Abu-l-Ala al-Maarri. LiTW
Humanity struggles on and is blind. Lore. Edna Ethel Davis. ChIP
Humble-Bee, The. Emerson. AA; AmPP; AnNE; APW; BAP; CBOV; EV-4; GN; HBV; HBVY; HiLiAm; IAP; LaNeLa; LHV; MOAP; OBAV; OTPC; OxBA; PIAE; PYM, *abr.*; REAL; SN; TCAP
(To the Humblebee.) LPS-2
"Burly dozing humble-bee," *sel.* FaPON
Humble boon was soon obtain'd, The. Sir Walter Scott. *Fr.* The Lay of the Last Minstrel. OBRV
Humble Bumble Bee, The. Vachel Lindsay. UTS
Humble Petition of Frances Harris, The. Swift. *See* To Their Excellencies the Lords Justices of Ireland, the Humble Petition of Frances Harris.
Humble poet looked upon a maiden, A. To Francesca Frazer. Dionysios Solomos. MoGP
Humble Pomp. Robert Southwell. *See* New Prince, New Pomp.
Humble room appears to smile, The. An Alcove at Sunrise. Victor Hugo. TrFP
Humble we must be, if to heaven we go. Humility. Robert Herrick. GoTP
Humble Yo'self de Bell Done Ring, *with music.* *Unknown.* BoAN-2
Humblest of herte, highest of reverence. The Bill of Complaint. Chaucer. LyMA
Humbling of Sparta, The. *Unknown.* *See* Lacedaemon.
Humbly. Ramón López Velarde, *tr. fr. Spanish by* Samuel Beckett. AnMP
Humbly Sheweth./ That I went to warm my self in Lady Betty's Chamber. *See* That I went to warm my self . . .
Humbug Steamship Companies. *Unknown.* IHA
Humility. Robert Browning. PoVP
Humility. Robert Herrick. GoTP
Humility. Thomas Washbourne. *Fr.* God's Two Dwellings. MaRV
Humility and Doubt. Blake. *Fr.* The Everlasting Gospel. RO
Humming Bird, The. Ednah Proctor Clarke. BLA; SN
Humming Bird. Robert P. Tristram Coffin. BLA
Hummingbird, The. Emily Dickinson. *See* Route of evanescence, A.
Humming Bird, A. Edgar Fawcett. BLA
Humming Bird, The. Mary Howitt. OTPC; PCH
Humming Bird, The. Harry Hibbard Kemp. FaPON; HBMV; MPB
Humming-Bird. D. H. Lawrence. AIDL; GTBS-D; LiTB; LiTM; MoPW; SeCePo; TwCV
Hummingbird. Elizabeth Palmer. WhBS
Hummingbird. Violet Alleyn Storey. PoMa
Humming Bird, The. Ivan Swift. BLA
Humming-Bird, The. John Banister Tabb. SN
Humming Bird, The. Maurice Thompson. BLA
Humming-bird, The! the humming-bird! The Humming Bird. Mary Howitt. OTPC; PCH
Humor of Tobacco and the Rest, The. Henry Parrot. SiCE
Humoradas, *sel.* Ramón de Campoamor, *tr. fr. Spanish by* Arthur Symons.
"You wave your fan with such a graceful art." AnSpL-2
Humoresque. Alice Corbin. NP
Humorist, The. Keith Preston. ALV; HBMV; WhC
Humour Out of Breath, *sel.* John Day.
Ditty, A: "Peace, peace, peace, make no noise." EIL
Humours of Donnybrook Fair, The. Charles O'Flaherty, *wr. at. to* Viscount Dillon. OnYI
(Donnybrook Jig, The.) BOHV
Humours of Donnybrook Fair, The. *Unknown.* OnYI
Hump-backed and rugged, blue on blue. For My Father. Rachel Field. InMe
Hump, the Escalator. Dorothy Faubion. BrR
Humpty Dumpty. Adeline D. T. Whitney. *Fr.* Mother Goose for Grown Folks. HBV
Humpty Dumpty Dickery Dan. The Gingerbread Man. Eva Rowland. GFA
Humpty, dumpty, diddle-dum-dee! *Unknown.* SAS
Humpty Dumpty has country cousins. Easter Eggs. *Unknown.* GFA
Humpty Dumpty sat on a wall. Mother Goose. BoChLi; ExPo; FaBoBe; HBV; HBVY; OTPC; OxBoLi; OxNR; PCH; PPL; RIS; SiTL; StVeCh
Humpty Dumpty sat on the wall. Mother Goose (circa 2054). Irene Sekula. SiTL
Humpty Dumpty's Recitation. "Lewis Carroll." *Fr.* Through the Looking-Glass. BOHV; ChTr; FiBHP; GoTP; SiTL
(Humpty Dumpty's Song.) OxBoLi; SAS
Hums of Pooh. A. A. Milne. *Fr.* Winnie the Pooh. BoN
"Cottleston, Cottleston, Cottleston Pie!" 2.
"On Monday, when the sun is hot," 1.
Hunc, Said He. *Unknown.* ChTr
Hunchback, The. Edward A. Blount, Jr. PoP
Hunchback in the Park, The. Dylan Thomas. FaBoTw; LiTM; MoAB; MoBrPo (1950 ed.); MoPW; NeMA
Hunchback on the corner, with gum and shoelaces, The. Pursuit. Robert Penn Warren. CrMA; FiMAP; LiTA; MoPo; NePA; PoFS; ReMP; TwAmPo
Hunchèd camels of the night, The. An Arab Love Song. Francis Thompson. AWP; BMEP; EG; LBBV; LEAP; LoPo; LoPS; MBP; MoAB; MoBrPo; OtMeF; POTE; POTT; VLEP; VOD (1935 ed.); YT

Hundred, A, a thousand to one; even so. In the Round Tower at Jhansi. Christina Rossetti. EmBrPo
Hundred autumns he has wheeled, A. Crow. Mark Van Doren. BLA; WhBS
Hundred Best Books, The. Mostyn T. Pigott. BOHV; InMe
Hundred Collars, A. Robert Frost. YaD
Hundred mares, all white! their manes, A. The Mares of the Camargue. Frédéric Mistral. AWP
Hundred Names, The. *Unknown. See* From Break of Day.
Hundred Noble Wishes, A. Charles Francis Richardson. MaRV
Hundred Pipers, The. Lady Carolina Nairne. CBOV; EBSV
Hundred strange things, A. Ghost Night. Lizette Woodworth Reese. HBMV; HOAH
Hundred Tartars shall attend on thee, A. Tamburlaine's Love. Christopher Marlowe. *Fr.* Tamburlaine the Great. ShBV-4
Hundred Thousand Northmen, A. Wait for the Wagon. *Unknown.* PAH
Hundred trains, a hundred ships, A. At Dawn. José Moreno Villa. CoSP
Hundred warblers in the nearest aching gap, An. Warblers. Marsden Hartley. AnFE; CoAnAm; TwAmPo
Hundred women's eyes with love-light shone, A. The Hunchback.. Edward A. Blount, Jr. PoP
Hundred-Yard Dash, The. William Lindsey. AA
Hundred Years Ago, A, *with music. Unknown.* AS
Hundred Years from Now. Mary A. Ford. BLPA
Hundred years from now, dear heart, A. In a Rose Garden. John Bennett. BLPA; FaBoBe; HBV; NeHB
Hundred years is a very long time, A. A Hundred Years Ago. *Unknown.* AS
Hundred Years on the Eastern Shore, A (D *vers. of* A Long Time Ago). *Unknown.* SoAmSa
Hundred Years to Come, A. Hiram Ladd Spencer, *wr. at. to* William Goldsmith Brown. HBV
Hundreds of birds are singing in the square. Marché aux Oiseaux. Richard Wilbur. FiMAP
Hundreds of houses, thousands of houses,—like a chessboard. Climbing the Terrace of Kuan-yin and Looking at the City. Po Chü-i. TrCh
Hundreds of stars in the pretty [*or* deep blue] sky. Our Mother [*or* Only One Mother *or* Mother]. George Cooper. AA; BoTP; BTP; FaPON; HH; MeMeAg; MPB; OHIP; OTPC; PCH; PPL; SiSoSe
Hundreds there have been, loftier than their kind. Abraham Lincoln. Rose Terry Cooke. LBAH
Hundredth Psalm, The (Metrical Version). William Kethe. OtMeF
(Old Hundredth.) MaRV
(Scotch Te Deum.) WGRP
Hundredth good points of good husbandry, A. Thomas Tusser. ReIE
Hundredth suns—in course but not in kind, A. He Wrote to the Same Friend from Excester This Sonnet Following. George Gascoigne. ReIE
Hung be the heavens with black, yield day to night! A King Is Dead. Shakespeare. King Henry VI, Pt. I, *fr.* I, i. ChTr
Hunger. Laurence Binyon. MM; POTE; TwCV
Hunger. Mary Carolyn Davies. AnAmPo
Hunger. Emily Dickinson. *See* I had been hungry all the years.
Hunger. Hazel Hall. NP
Hunger. Arthur Rimbaud, *tr. fr. French by* Edgell Rickword. AWP
Hunger, and sultry heat, and nipping blast. The French and the Spanish Guerrillas [*or* Sonnet]. Wordsworth. ChER; SoV; WaaP
Hunger and Thirst. Louis Ginsberg. PFE
Hunger drives me along my road. The Beggar. Tao Yuan-ming. WhP
Hunger is a/ Poet's Bread. Poet's Bread. Sister Mary Philip. GoBC
Hungering Hearts. *Unknown.* PoToHe
Hungry, The. Caroline Giltinan. OQP; QP-2
Hungry and cold we stand below the city. Below the City of P'ing. Li Ho. WhP
Hungry China, *sel.* Cha Liang-cheng, *tr. fr. Chinese by* Cha Liang-cheng.
"I see Hunger watching at every house door." LiTW
Hungry Fox, The. *Unknown. See* Fox, The.
Hungry Grass, The. Donagh MacDonagh. NeIP; OxBI
Hungry Heart, The. Edna St. Vincent Millay. TSW; TSWC
Hungry Heart, Hungry Heart, where have you been? The Ballad of a Lost House. Leonora Speyer. TBM
Hungry Master and Hungry Cat. Abu Shamaqmaq, *tr. fr. Arabic by* A. S. Tritton. PoC
Hungry old man from the Rhine, A. New Limericks. *Unknown.* StaSt
Hungry One, The. Nikolai Nekrasov, *tr. fr. Russian by* Juliet M. Soskice. *Fr.* Who Can Be Happy and Free in Russia? BoR
Hungry unnumbered since the birth of time. Answer. Mary Elizabeth Colman. BoCaPo (1943 ed.)
Hungry Winter. Vladimir Mayakovsky, *tr. fr. Russian by* Jack Lindsay. *Fr.* Good! RuPo
"Hungry winter, this winter." To Hell with It. Frank O'Hara. NeAP
Hunt, The. Sheldon Christian. CAG
Hunt, The. Babette Deutsch. AnAmPo; LA
Hunt, The. Louis Kent. WaKn
Hunt. Melvin Walker La Follette. NePoEA
Hunt, The. Pierre de Ronsard, *tr. fr. French by* Alan Conder. TrFP
Hunt, The. Harriet Prescott Spofford. AA
Hunt, The. *Unknown.* CoMu
Hunt Is Up, The. William Gray. CBOV; CH; OTPC (1923 ed.)
(King's Hunt Is Up, The.) TuPP
Hunt is up, the hunt is up, The. The Song of the Hunt. John Bennett. *Fr.* Master Sky-Lark. AA
Hunt of Sliabh Truim, The, *sel. Unknown, tr. fr. Late Middle Irish.*
'"One day that we mustered on Sliabh Truim."' OnYI
Hunt the Buffalo. *Unknown. See* Shoot the Buffalo.
Hunted ("Hunted hare seeks out some dark retreat, The"). Una Marson. PoNe
Hunter, A. Ray Ellis. CAG
Hunter, The. Raymond Souster. BoCaPo (1948 ed.)
Hunter, The. Walter James Turner. HBMV; PtOT
Hunter, The. Eleanor Glenn Wallis. NePoAm-2
Hunter by his lonely fire, The. The Vision of the Milk-white Doe. Benjamin Sledd. NoCaPo
"Hunter Home from the Hill, The." *Unknown, tr. fr. Greek by* F. L. Lucas. GrPE
Hunter Hunted, The. Theocritus, *tr. fr. Greek by* F. L. Lucas. GrPE
Hunter learns a soldier's trade, The. In Praise of Hunting. *Unknown.* OxBG
Hunter of huntsmen bred, The. The Lament of Quarry. Léonie Adams. NP
Hunter of the Prairies, The. Bryant. AA
Hunter once built him a cabin, A. The Aged Indian. *Unknown.* ABS
Hunter Trials. John Betjeman. FiBHP
Hunters, The. Ruth Temple Lindsay. JKCP
Hunter's e'e grows bright as the fox frae covert steals, The. The Bonny Tweed for Me. William A. Foster. EBSV
Hunters, Epicydes, go, The. Love's Capriciousness [*or* Hunting Code]. Callimachus. GrR; OxBG
Hunters in the Snow: Brueghel. Joseph Langland. NePoEA
Hunters of Kentucky, The. Samuel Woodworth. PAH; TrAS, *abr., with music*
(Hunters of Kentucky, The; or Half Horse and Half Alligator, *with music.*) AS
Hunters of Men, The. Whittier. AnAmPo; LA
Hunter's Song, The. William Basse. SeCL
Hunter's Song, The. "Barry Cornwall." BBV (1923 ed.); GN; OTPC, *abr.*; VA
Hunter's Song. Eduard Mörike, *tr. fr. German by* Kate Flores. AnGP
Hunter's Thanksgiving. Crinagoras, *tr. fr. Greek by* F. L. Lucas. GrPE
Hunter's Vision, The. Bryant. UnW
Hunting, The. Eden Phillpotts. MBP
Hunting. "Yehoash," *tr. fr. Yiddish by* Isidore Goldstick. TrJP
Hunting Code. Callimachus. *See* Love's Capriciousness.
Hunting Horns. Guillaume Apollinaire, *tr. fr. French.* AnFP, *tr. by* Dudley Fitts; MiFP, *tr. by* W. J. Strachan
Hunting-hound of Midas, Lampon, perished thirsting, The. The Vengeance of the Nymphs. Antipater of Sidon. GrPE
Hunting Muscadines. John Henry Boner. NoCaPo
Hunting of Cupid, The, *sels.* George Peele.
Coridon and Melampus' Song.. TuPP
(Song of Coridon and Melampus.) OBSC
What Thing Is Love? EIL; OAEP; ReEn; RiBV; SeCePo; TuPP
(Love.) OBSC
Hunting of Pau-Puk-Keewis, The. Longfellow. *Fr.* The Song of Hiawatha. CoBA
Hunting of the Cheviot, The. *Unknown. See* Chevy Chase.
Hunting of the Gods, The. Walter Wasse. OxBoLi; SeCL
Hunting of the Snark, The. "Lewis Carroll." BoN; FiBHP, *much abr.*; NA, *much abr.*; PoEL-5; SiTL
Sels.
Baker's Tale, The, III. BoChLi; MBP; PoVP
How to Recognize a Snark, *fr.* II. MPB
("Come, listen, my men, while I tell you again.") BOHV
(Snark, The.) TSW; TSWC
("We have sailed many months," *abr.*) NA
Landing, The, I. WhC
Hunting Song. Samuel Taylor Coleridge. *Fr.* Zapolya, Pt. II, Act IV, sc. i. PRWS; ThWaDe
(Choral Song of Illyrian Peasants.) CG

(Up, Up! Ye Dames and Lasses Gay!) BoTP; OTPC
Hunting Song. Thomas D'Urfey. *Fr.* The Marriage-Hater Match'd, II, i. SeCL
(Solon's Song.) CEP; SeEP
Hunting Song. Henry Fielding. *See* A-Hunting We Will Go.
Hunting Song. Donald Finkel. NePoEA
Hunting Song. Richard Hovey. *Fr.* King Arthur. HBV; NLK
Hunting Song. Sir Walter Scott. BLV; BPN; CBE; CBPC; CoBE; EBSV; EmBrPo; EnLi-2; EnLit; EnRP; EPN; EV-4; GN; GTBS; GTBS-D; GTBS-W; GTSE; GTSL; InP; LEAP; LiTG; OAEP; OTPC; RG; TOP; TrGrPo; TyEnPo
(Waken, Lords and Ladies Gay.) LPS-2
Hunting-Song. *Unknown, tr. fr. Navaho Indian song by* Natalie Curtis. AWP; JAWP; WBP
(Navajo Hunting-Song.) APW
Hunting Song, The. *Unknown.* TuPP
Hunting Song. Paul Whitehead. *Fr.* Apollo and Daphne. OBEC; OxBoLi
Hunting-Song of the Seeonee Pack. Kipling. AlDL
Hunting tribes of air and earth, The. Man the Enemy of Man. Sir Walter Scott. *Fr.* Rokeby. WBLP
Huntress, The. José Joaquín Pesado, *tr. fr. Spanish by* Samuel Beckett. AnMP
Huntsman, The. John Wheelwright. CrMA
Huntsman, Epicydes, across the mountains follows, The. Don Juan. Callimachus. GrPE
Huntsman, That on the Hills Above. Avetis Isahakian, *tr. fr. Armenian by* Zabelle C. Boyajian. ArmLP
Huntsman's Rouse, The. Henry Carey. SeCePo
Huntsmen, The. Walter de la Mare. CenHV; HBMV; InP; PreP; SiSoSe; StVeCh; TiPo
Huntsmen's Chorus, The. Swinburne. *See* When the Hounds of Spring.
Huntswoman-moon was my mother, The. The Singing Huntsman. Witter Bynner. MAP; MoAmPo (1942 ed.)
Hurdy-Gurdy Days. Martha Haskell Clark. MPB
Hurdy-Gurdy Man, The. Elizabeth Fleming. BoTP
Hurdy-gurdy, public piano of the past, The. The Road from Election to Christmas. Oscar Williams. NAMP
Hurled back, defeated, like a child I sought. Earthborn. Peter McArthur. CaP; OCL
"Hurler avec les Loups." Theognis, *tr. fr. Greek by* F. L. Lucas. GrPE
Hurly, hurly, roon the table. Two Graces. *Unknown.* FaBoCh; LoGBV
Hurrah! for a day with the farmer. A Day at the Farm. "L. J." BoTP
Hurrah for the buffalo hunters! The "Metis" Song of the Buffalo Hunters. —— Robindeau. CSF
Hurrah for the choice of the nation! Lincoln and Liberty. F. A. Simpson. AS; TrAS
Hurrah for the great white way! The Song of the "Metis" Trapper. *Unknown.* CSF
Hurrah! the seaward breezes. The Fishermen. Whittier. EtS; TVSH
Hurrahing in Harvest. Gerard Manley Hopkins. ChTr; InvP; LO; MBP; MoAB; MoBrPo; MoP; MoPo; MoVE; PoVP
Hurray, hurray, the jade's away. The Witch o' Fife. James Hogg. *Fr.* The Queen's Wake. BCEP; BSV
Hurricane, The. Bryant. LPS-2; PEOR
Hurricane, The. Hart Crane. AmP; ChMo; CoBMV; MoAB; MoAmPo; OxBA
Hurricane, The. Philip Freneau. AmPP (4th ed.); CoBA
Hurricane, The. Luis Palés Matos, *tr. fr. Spanish by* Alida Malkus. FaPON
Hurrier, The. Harold Monro. MBP; MoBrPo
Hurry me Nymphs! O, hurry me. The Sea [*or* Lines]. George Darley. *Fr.* Nepenthe. BLV; HoPM
"Hurry!" said the leaves. A Summer Shower. *Unknown.* BoTP
Hurry the baby as fast as you can. Making a Man. Nixon Waterman. BLPA
Hurry to bless the hands that play. The Players Ask for a Blessing on the Psalteries and on Themselves. W. B. Yeats. UnS
Hurrying on my trip. Waiting for Dawn. Toyohiko Kagawa. SoLD
Hurt Hawks. Robinson Jeffers. AmP; AmPP; AtBAP; BAV; BLV; BoLiVe; ChMo; CMP; CoBA; CoBMV; LiTA; MAP; MoAB; MoAmPo; MOAP; MoVE; NeMA; NP; OxBA; PoLFOT
Hurt No Living Thing. Christina Rossetti. *Fr.* Sing-Song. FaPON; PCH; PoRL; RIS; SiSoSe
Hurt of strife they knew not in their day, The. When Justice Dwelt on Earth. Aratus. *Fr.* Phaenomena. OxBG
Hurt was the Nation with a mighty wound. Lincoln. Paul Laurence Dunbar. LBAH; OQP; QP-1
Husband, The. Leon Gellert. BoAu
Husband and Heathen. Sam Walter Foss. BOHV
Husband and Wife. Arthur Guiterman. PoToHe (new ed.)
Husband and Wife. Edward Harry William Meyerstein. LO; LoPS
Husband and Wife's Grave. Richard Henry Dana. LPS-1
Husband Betrayed. John Crowe Ransom. TwAmPo
Husband is not lost without a mort of sighing, A. The Young Widow. La Fontaine. TrFP
Husband of Poverty, The, *sel.* Henry Neville Maugham.
Knight of Bethlehem, A. CBPC; ChIP; MaRV; OQP; QP-2
(Song: "There was a Knight of Bethlehem.") BoTP
Husbandman, The. Dante Gabriel Rossetti. The House of Life, LXXVI. BPN; ViPo
Husbandman, The. Frances Beatrice Taylor. CaP; OCL
Husbandry. William Hammond. SeCL
Husband's Message, The. *Unknown, tr. fr. Anglo-Saxon.* AnOE, *tr. by* Charles W. Kennedy; EnLit, *tr. by* Harold S. Stine
Husbands over Seas. Lloyd Roberts. CPG
Husband's Petition, The. William E. Aytoun. BOHV
Hush! Emerson. AnNE; APW
Hush a while, my darling, for the long day closes. Ring o' Roses. W. Graham Robertson. CBPC
Hush, all. Our crops, our lands we purify. Tibullus. Elegies, II, 1. LaP
Hush, All Ye Sounds of War. William H. Draper. ChIP; MaRV
Hush and balou, babie. Hush Rhymes—English and Scotch. *Unknown.* BOL
Hush, baby, hush, sweet robin's in the bush. The Warm Cradle. Laurence Alma-Tadema. BOL
Hush, baby, hush, while the shadows are falling. The Fisher-Wife's Song. Crofton Uniacke McLeod. BOL
Hush, A. Beneath the fence the breeze. Accordionist. Vladimir Kazin. RuPo
Hush! Did you hear. Chopin Prelude. Eleanour Norton. HBMV
Hush dove the summer. Lullaby. Miriam Waddington. CaP
Hush! for the shadow of a flower. To One Who Spoke of Eternal Things. John Cowper Powys. BAP
Hush had fallen on the birds, A. The Young Calves. Robert P. Tristram Coffin. StVeCh (1955 ed.); TiPo
Hush harlequin brain, wild brain! a tale I'd tell. An Easter Poem. Herbert Edward Palmer. QS
Hush! hear you how the night wind keens around the craggy reek? A Lay of the Famine. *Unknown, at. to* Rosa Mulholland. OnYI; TIP
Hush, Hush. Mani Leib, *tr. fr. Yiddish by* Joseph Leftwich. TrJP
Hush, hush! Baby grows quiet. Norwegian Cradle-Song. Natanael Fransen. BOL
Hush, hush, baby mine. Hush Rhymes—Swedish. *Unknown.* BOL
Hush, hush, do not speak. Hush, Hush. Mani Leib. TrJP
Hush, hush, hush! Hush Rhymes—English and Scotch. Thomas Dekker. BOL
Hush, hush, little baby. Evening. *Unknown.* BoTP
Hush, hush, my little babe! *Unknown, tr. fr. Greek by* C. B. Sheridan. BOL
Hush, hush, rest my sweet. A Lullaby. Mary Newmarch Prescott. BOL
Hush! I cannot bear to see thee. The Cradle-Song of the Poor. Adelaide Anne Procter. BOL
Hush, Li'l Baby, *with music.* *Unknown.* OuSiCo
Hush, little baby, don't say a word. *Unknown.* OxNR
Hush! lulla, lullaby! So mother sings. The Baby's Charms—Venetian. *Unknown.* BOL
Hush, lullay,/ Your treasures all. Lullaby. Léonie Adams. BLV; BoLiVe (1939 ed.); MAP; MoAB; MoAmPo; NeMA
Hush, my baby, do not cry. *Unknown.* OxNR
Hush! my baby, or soon you will hear. Weeng; an Indian Slumber Song. Lew Sarett. GaP
Hush, my baby, sleep. *Unknown.* BOL
Hush, my darling; hush, my darling. *Unknown.* BOL
Hush, my darling, sleep quickly. *Unknown.* BOL
Hush, My Dear, Lie Still and Slumber. Isaac Watts. *See* Cradle Hymn.
Hush, my little one! Hush! Lie Down! Slumber Fairies. Katharine Lee Bates. BOL
Hush, my little round-faced daughter; thou art like the stormy sea. The Baby's Charms—Sicilian. *Unknown.* BOL
Hush now, my little one, and sleep. Christmas Lullaby. Ulrich Troubetzkoy. YeAr
Hush now, O wooded hill of the Dryads! Hush your leaping. Pan's Piping. Plato. GrPE
Hush! oh ye billows. Hymn. Joseph Sheridan Le Fanu. *Fr.* Beatrice. OnYI
Hush Song, A. Paul Gregan. BOL
Hush Song. Mary Anne O'Reilly. BOL
Hush Song. Elizabeth Shane. BOL; LBBV; MoSiPe
Hush, the waves are rolling in. Gaelic Lullaby [*or* An Old Gaelic Cradle-Song]. *Unknown.* BOL; GFA; PRWS; RAR; SAS

Hush thee, hush: one bright star. Lullaby. "R. D. H." CAG
Hush Thee, hush Thee, little Son. The Virgin's Lullaby. Nora Hopper. BOL
Hush thee, my babby [*or* baby], lie still with thy daddy. Hush Rhymes—English and Scotch. *Unknown.* BOL; OTPC; OxNR; PPL
Hush thee, my baby boy, hush thee to sleep. A Lullaby. *Tr. by* Alexander Stewart. BOL; EBSV
Hush thee, my baby, oh hush thee to sleep. Bohemian Cradle-Song. *Unknown.* BOL
Hush thee, my baby, O! never thee cry. Lullaby of the Pict Mother. Louise Lamprey. BOL
Hush thee, my baby, thy mother's over the mountain gone. Hush Rhymes—Zulu. *Unknown.* BOL
Hush thee, sweet baby. Lullaby. Thomas Davidson. BOL
Hush! 'tis the gap between two lightnings. Non Pax—Expectatio. Francis Thompson. PeBoSo; PreP
Hush, true Love, as we sit and think. Candle Light. John Cowper Powys. LEAP
Hush! With a sudden gush. Overflow. John Banister Tabb. CAW; HBV
Hush, woman, do not speak to me! The Tryst after Death. *Unknown.* LiTW; OnYI, *abr.*
Hush ye, hush ye, little pet ye. Rewards and Punishments—Scotch. *Unknown.* BOL
Hush ye! Hush ye! My babe is sleeping. At Even. Frederic Manning. NP
Hush your prayers, 'tis no saintly soul. Requiem. Conal O'Riordan. HBV
Husha, oh, husha. Jewish Lullaby. Louis Untermeyer. RIS
Hush-a-ba, birdie, croon, croon. A Highland Croon. *Unknown.* BOL; OxNR
Hush-a-baa, baby, dinna mak' a din. Rewards and Punishments—English. *Unknown.* BOL; OxNR
Hushaby. Thomas Hastings. BOL
Hushaby. McLandburgh Wilson. BOL
Hush-a-by, baby,/ Your name is so lovely. Italian Lullaby. *Unknown.* FaPON
Hush-a-by, baby! your baby, mamma. Dolly's Lullaby. Juliana Horatia Ewing. BOL
Hushaby, Darling. Lachlan Macbean. BOL
Hushaby, don't you cry. All the Pretty Little Horses. *Unknown.* ABF; OxBoLi
Hushaby, hushaby, Baby, do not weep. Hushaby. Thomas Hastings. BOL
Hushaby! Hushaby! Sheep-Bells are tinkling. A Romany Lullaby. Edith De Charms. BOL
Hush-a-by, hush-a-by! Sleepily nod. Hush Rhymes—Corsican. *Unknown.* BOL
Hushaby, lullaby, rockaby, dear. A Winter Lullaby. Madeleine Sweeny Miller BOL
Hushaby, my darling boy. *Unknown.* BOL
Hush-a-bye a baa lamb. *Unknown.* OxNR
Hush-a-bye, baby,/ The beggar shan't have 'ee. *Unknown.* OxNR
Hush-a-bye, baby, daddy is near. Hush Rhymes—English and Scotch. *Unknown.* BOL
Hush-a-bye [*or* Rock-a-bye], baby, on [*or* in] the tree top. Mother Goose. HBVY; OTPC (1923 ed.); OxNR; PPL; RIS; SAS; StVeCh; TiPo (1959 ed.)
Hush-a-bye, baby, sleep like a lady. *Unknown, tr. fr. Welsh.* BOL
Hush-a-bye, baby, they're gone to milk. *Unknown.* OxNR
Hush-a-bye, baby, thy cradle is green. *See* Rock-a-bye, baby, thy cradle is green.
Hush-a-bye, lie still and sleep. *Unknown.* BOL
Hushabye Sea. Harry Noyes Pratt. BOL
Hush'd Be the Camps To-Day. Walt Whitman. *Fr.* Memories of President Lincoln. CaAE; DD; GA; LBAH; MC; OHIP; TCAP
Hush'd is each [busy] shout. Prelude. A. C. Benson. LEAP; OBVV
Hushed are the pigeons cooing low. The Christmas Silence. Margaret Deland. ChrBoLe; CLS; COAH; OHIP; PRWS; SDH
Hushed be sighing, near the string. Dirge for a Young Maiden. Thomas Lovell Beddoes. ERP
Hushed by the Hands of Sleep. Angelina W. Grimké. CDC
Hushed, cruel, amber-eyed. Pumas. George Sterling. BAP
Hushed in the smoky haze of summer sunset. Sunset; St. Louis. Sara Teasdale. PoMa; VOD
Hushed is the harp: the Minstrel gone. The Minstrel's Lowly Bower. Sir Walter Scott. *Fr.* The Lay of the Last Minstrel. EV-4
Hushed is the storm, but the sea is like lead and it threatens. The Swell. Apollon Nikolayevich Maikov. TrRV
Hushed the storm that raged at night. Of Madame Bergström's Portrait at the Inn of Lilya in Torshälla. Karl Mikael Bellman. AnSL
Hushed to inaudible sound the deepening rain. The Tea-Tree and the Lyrebird. Roland Robinson. NeLNL
Hushed was the courtyard of the temple. The Cicada. Ouyang Hsiu. AWP
Hushed with broad sunlight lies the hill. Beaver Brook. James Russell Lowell. CoBA; IAP; TCAP
Husheen the herons are crying. Lullaby. "Seumas O'Sullivan." BOL; GBV; OnYI; TVSH
Hushie ba, burdie beeton. *Unknown.* OxNR
Hushing Song. "Fiona Macleod." BOL; MoSiPe
Hushoo! hushoo! tiny King. St. Bridget's Lullaby. Dorothy Una Ratcliffe. CAW
Husht gardens. Flickering clouds. On the Road to the Sovkoz. Stepan Shchipachev. RuPo
Hushy baby, my doll, I pray you don't cry. A Nursery Rhyme. *Unknown.* BOL
Huskers, The. Whittier. HOAH; IAP; MOAP; PTA-1, *abr.*; REAL
Corn Song, The, *sel.* GN; OHIP; OTPC; TOAH, *abr.*
Husking, The. Joel Barlow. *Fr.* The Hasty Pudding, III. APW
("Days grow short, The; but though the falling sun.") BAV
(Pudding Prepared and Eaten, The.) AnNE
Husky Hi. Rose Fyleman. TiPo
Hussar's Song. Thomas Hardy. *See* Budmouth Dears.
Hustle and Grin. *Unknown.* WBLP
Huswifery. Edward Taylor. *See* Housewifery.
Hut, The. Avigdor Hammeiri, *tr. fr. Hebrew by* Jacob Sloan. LiTW
Hut, The. Ruth Pitter. AlDL
Hut, The. Hilda Van Stockum. BrR
Hut, and a tree, A. Diogenes. Max Eastman. HBV; OQP; QP-2
Hut near Desolated Pines. Alistair Campbell. AnNZ
Hut of straw in Paraguay, A. The Wait for Death. Jules Supervielle. TrFP
Huts that stand like plaited baskets. Village and Factory. Alexander Ilyich Bezymensky. TrJP; TrRV
Huzza for our liberty, boys. Terrapin War. *Unknown.* PAH
Huzza! Hodgson, we are going. Lines to Mr. Hodgson. Byron. PoE
Huzza Huzza for Admiral Byrd. Admiral Byrd. Ogden Nash. InMe; YaD
Huzza, my Jo Bunkers! no taxes we'll pay. A Radical Song of 1786. St. John Honeywood. PAH
Hy-Brasail, the Isle of the Blest. Gerald Griffin. *See* O Brazil, the Isle of the Blest.
Hyacinth. Louise Morey Bowman. CPG
Hyacinth for Edith, A. A. J. M. Smith. BoCaPo; TwCaPo
Hyacinths to Feed Thy Soul. Sadi, *tr. fr. Persian. Fr.* The Gulistan. BLPA; FaBoBe; MaRV; NeHB
Hyah dar, Mistah Robin. Robin on da Fence. Edith Himstedt. CAG
Hyaku-Nin-Isshu, *sels. Tr. fr. Japanese by* Curtis Hidden Page.
"Day will soon be gone, The." Fujiwara no Michinobu. AWP; JAWP; WBP
"How can one e'er be sure." Lady Horikawa. AWP; JAWP; PFE; WBP
"I would that even now." Princess Shoku. AWP; JAWP; WBP
"Like a great rock, far out at sea." Lady Sanuki. AWP; JAWP; WBP
H'yar, Pot-liquor! What you at? You heah me callin' you? Selling a Dog. Irwin Russell. AlBD
Hyd [*or* Hyde], Absolon, thy gilte tresses clere. Balade [*or* Of His Lady]. Chaucer. *Fr.* The Legend of Good Women. AtBAP; AWP; BrBE; ChTr; EG; ExPo; FiP; InPo; JAWP; LiTG; LoBV; LyMA; OBEV; SeCeV; WBP
Hyder Iddle. *Unknown.* BOHV; NA; OxNR
Hydra of Birds, The. Nikos Engonopoulos, *tr. fr. Modern Greek by* Kimon Friar. LiTW
Hydro Works. J. R. Hervey. AnNZ
Hydrographic Poem. Jorge Carrera Andrade, *tr. fr. Spanish by* H. R. Hays. TwSpPo
Hydrographic Report. Frances Frost. EtS
Hygienist, in your dental chair. Ode to a Dental Hygienist. Earnest A. Hooton. FiBHP; WhC
Hyla Brook. Robert Frost. AnFE; AnNE; APA; CoAnAm; MAPA; MOAP; TwAmPo
Hylas. Apollonius Rhodius, *tr. fr. Greek by* George Allen. *Fr.* Argonautica, I. OxBG
Hylas. L. A. Mackay. BoCaPo
Hylas. Propertius, *tr. fr. Latin by* F. A. Wright. Elegies I, 20. AWP
Hylas. Theocritus, *tr. fr. Greek by* Charles Stuart Calverley. *Fr.* Idylls. GrR; OxBG; GrPE, *tr. by* F. L. Lucas
Hylas, O Hylas [*or* Hilas, o Hilas]! why sit we mute. Chloris and Hylas [*or* Hilas]. Edmund Waller. SeCL; SeCV-1
Hymen, *sels.* Hilda Doolittle ("H. D.").
Never More Will the Wind. TrGrPo
(Hymen.) ViBoPo
Where Love Is King. BAP; ChMo; CMP; HBMV
Hymen ("Hymen, god of marriage-bed"). Joseph Rutter. *Fr.* The Shepherd's Holiday. SeCL

Hymen hath together tyed. *Unknown.* SeCSL
Hymenaei, *sel.* Ben Jonson.
  Angel Describes Truth, An, II. OBS
Hymeneal Chant of an Algonquin Maiden. *Unknown, tr. fr. French pr. vers. by* William T. Allison. CPG
Hymen's Triumph, *sels.* Samuel Daniel.
  Constancy. OBSC
  Eyes, Hide My Love. ElL
  (Secrecy.) OBSC
  Had Sorrow Ever Fitter Place. AtBAP; ElL
  (Sorrow.) OBSC
  Love Is a Sickness. AtBAP; BEL; EV-1; LiTG; LiTL; LO; LoBV; LPS-1; OAEP; OBEV; PG; PoEL-2; SiCE; TreFS; TuPP; ViBoPo
  (Love.) ElL; OBSC
  (Song: "Love is a sickness.") HBV
  Reminiscence of Early Love, A. EV-1
Hymettus' bees are out on filmy wing. The Sunflower to the Sun. Mary Elizabeth Hewitt Stebbins. AA
Hymn: "Ah, what are strength and beauty?" Synesius, *tr. fr. Greek by* Roderick Gill. CAW
Hymn: "All this night shrill chanticler." William Austin. *See* Chanticleer.
Hymn: "At morn, at noon, at twilight dim." Poe. IAP; ISi
  (Hymn of the Angelus.) CAW
Hymn: "Britannia's sons, though slaves ye be." John Bramwich. PoFr
Hymn: "By the rude bridge that arched the flood." Emerson. *See* Concord Hymn.
Hymn: "Christ, whose glory fills the skies." Charles Wesley. *See* Morning Hymn, A.
Hymn: Confirmation of Faith, The. Addison. *See* Spacious Firmament on High, The.
Hymn: Crucifixus pro Nobis. Patrick Carey. *See* Crucifixus pro Nobis.
Hymn: "Dear Lord, Whose serving-maiden." Josephine Preston Peabody. TrPWD
Hymn, An: "Drop, drop, slow tears." Phineas Fletcher. CoEV; ElL; ElSeCe; LoBV; MeRV; SeEP
  (Drop, Drop, Slow Tears.) EV-2; LPS-2
  (Hymne, An: "Drop, drop, slow tears.") OBS
  (Litany, A.) AtBAP; BoW; OBEV; OxBoCh
Hymn: "Eternal Founder of the sky." James J. Donahue. JKCP (1955 ed.)
Hymn: "Eternal Ruler of the ceaseless round." John White Chadwick. TrPWD
  (Divinity School Graduation Hymn.) GrCo-2
Hymn: "Father, we come not as of old." John White Chadwick. TrPWD
Hymn: "For Summer's bloom and Autumn's blight." Josiah Gilbert Holland. *Fr.* Bitter-sweet. TrPWD
Hymn, A: "From all that terror teaches," *br. sel.* G. K. Chesterton.
  Litany. OtMeF
Hymn: "Glorious armies of the sky, The." Elizabeth Rowe. BeR
Hymn: "God moves in a mysterious way." William Cowper. *See* Light Shining Out of Darkness.
Hymn: "God of the strong, God of the weak," *abr.* Richard Watson Gilder. TrPWD
  (God of the Strong, God of the Weak, *abr.*) MaRV
Hymn: "Great Spirit of the speeding spheres." John Haynes Holmes. TrPWD
Hymn: "He sendeth sun, he sendeth shower." Sarah Flower Adams. VA
Hymn: "How sweet the name of Jesus sounds." John Newton. *See* Name of Jesus, The.
Hymn: "Hush! oh ye billows." Joseph Sheridan Le Fanu. *Fr.* Beatrice. OnYI
Hymn, A: "Hymn of glory let us sing, A." The Venerable Bede. *See* Hymn of Glory Let Us Sing, A.
Hymn, A: "I sing the Name which none can say." Richard Crashaw. *See* Hymn to the Name of Jesus.
Hymn: "It was the winter wild." Milton. *Fr.* On the Morning of Christ's Nativity. WHA, *sts.* 1-23
  (Christmas Hymn, *sts.* 1-13, *abr.*) BCEP
Hymn, A: "Lead gently, Lord, and slow." Paul Laurence Dunbar. MaRV; TrPWD
Hymn: "Lead us, heavenly Father, lead us." James Edmeston. *See* Prayer to the Trinity.
Hymn, A: "Lord, give them freedom who are weak." Nikolai Alekseyevich Nekrasov, *tr. fr. Russian by* Frances Cornford *and* E. P. Salaman. LiTW
Hymn: "Lord the people of the land." *Unknown.* IDAH
Hymn: "Lord when the wise men came from farr." Sidney Godolphin. *See* Lord, When the Wise Men Came from Far.
Hymn: "Lord, with glowing heart I'd praise thee." Francis Scott Key. TrPWD
Hymn: "Mighty fortress is our God, A." Martin Luther. *See* Mighty Fortress Is Our God, A.
Hymn: "My God, I love thee, not because." St. Francis Xavier. *See* My God, I Love Thee.
Hymn: "O Christ, the glorious crown." Philip Howard. ACP; CAW
Hymn, A: "O fly, my soul! What hangs upon." James Shirley. *See* O Fly My Soul.
Hymn, A: "O God of earth and altar." G. K. Chesterton. HBMV; InP; QS; TrPWD
  (O God of Earth and Altar.) MaRV
  (Prayer: "O God of earth and altar.") WGRP
Hymn: "O God, Who guid'st the fate of nations." Gunnar Wennerberg, *tr. fr. Swedish by* Charles W. Stork. AnSL; PoFr
Hymn: "O li'l' lamb out in de col'." Paul Laurence Dunbar. AA; BAP; VOD
Hymn: "O Lord, with good the people dower!" Nikolai Alekseyevich Nekrasov, *tr. fr. Russian by* Sir Cecil Kisch. WaL
Hymn: "O Thou of soul and sense and breath." Oliver Wendell Holmes. LBAH
Hymn: "O Thou who camest from above." Charles Wesley. OBEC; SeCePo
  (Oh Thou Who Camest from Above.) TrPWD
Hymn: "O world of love and beauty." George Edward Hoffman. MaRV
Hymn: On Opening a Place for Social Prayer. William Cowper. BrBE
Hymn: "Once again thou flamest heavenward, once again we see thee rise." Tennyson. *Fr.* Akbar's Dream. PoVP
Hymn: "Our God, our help in ages past." Isaac Watts. *See* O God, Our Help in Ages Past.
Hymn: "Queen and huntress chaste and fair." Ben Jonson. *See* Hymn to Diana.
Hymn: "Rise, crowned with light, imperial Salem, rise!" Pope. *See* Rise, Crowned with Light.
Hymn L: Rocking Hymn, A. George Wither. *See* Rocking Hymn, A.
Hymn: "Since without Thee we do no good." Elizabeth Barrett Browning. TrPWD
Hymn: "Sing, my tongue, the Saviour's glory." St. Thomas Aquinas. *See* Hymn for Corpus Christi Day.
Hymn: "Slant of sun on dull brown walls, A." Stephen Crane. War Is Kind, XIV. BAP; MAP; MoAmPo
  (Slant of Sun, A.) AmP; AmPP; TCAP
Hymn: "Spacious firmament on high, The." Addison. *See* Spacious Firmament on High, The.
Hymn: "These, as they change, Almighty Father, these." James Thomson. *See* Hymn on the Seasons, A.
Hymn: "Thou God of all, whose presence dwells." John Haynes Holmes. TrPWD
Hymn: "Thou hidden love of God, whose height." John Wesley. CEP; OBEC
  (Love of God Supreme, The.) LPS-2
Hymn: "To the Dearest One, to the beauty divine." Baudelaire, *tr. fr. French by* Alan Conder. TrFP
Hymn: "When all thy mercies, O my God." Addison. *See* When All Thy Mercies.
Hymn: "When by the marbled lake I lie and listen." Wathen Mark Wilks Call. OBVV
Hymn: "When storms arise." Paul Laurence Dunbar. TrPWD
Hymn: "When winds are raging o'er the upper ocean." Harriet Beecher Stowe. PoToHe
Hymn: "Whilst I beheld the neck o' the dove." Patrick Carey. SeCL
Hymn: "Ye golden Lamps of Heav'n, farewel." Philip Doddridge. CEP; OBEC
  (Ye Golden Lamps of Heaven.) OxBoCh; RO, 3 *sts.*
Hymn against Pestilence, *sel. At. to* St. Colman, *tr. fr. Old Irish by* Whitley Stokes *and* John Strachan.
  "God's blessing lead us, help us!" OnYI
Hymn before Sunrise, in the Vale of Chamouni. Samuel Taylor Coleridge. BCEP; BEL; BPN; EmBrPo; EnRP; ERP; HBV; LPS-2; MaRV; MCCG; OAEP; OxBoCh; PIAE; REAL; TCEP; TOP; WGRP
Hymn for a Household. Daniel Henderson. ChIP; HBMV; MaRV; OQP; PraP; QP-1; StJW
Hymn for a Widower or a Widow Deprived of a Loving Yoke-Fellow. George Wither. ElSeCe
  (Widow's Hymn, A.) LO; OBEV
Hymn for Arbor Day, A. Henry Hanby Hay. ADAH
Hymn for Atonement Day. Judah Halevi, *tr. fr. Hebrew by* Solomon Solis-Cohen. TrJP
Hymn for Canada, A. Albert Durrant Watson. CaP; CPG; OCL
Hymn for Christmas. Felicia Dorothea Hemans. COAH; GN; OTPC, *sts.* 1-2
Hymn for Christmas Day. John Byrom. MaRV; OBEC; PoEL 3
  (Christians, Awake, Salute the Happy Morn, *with music.*) YaCaBo
Hymn for Christmas Day, A. Thomas Chatterton. MaRV; OTPC (1923 ed.)
Hymn for Christmas Day, A ("Awake, my soul, and come away"). Jeremy Taylor. AnEC

Hymn for Christmas Day ("Where is this blessed Babe"). Jeremy Taylor. AnEC
Hymn for conquering Martyrs raise, The. Hymnum Canentes Martyrum. The Venerable Bede. CAW
Hymn for Corpus Christi Day. St. Thomas Aquinas, *tr. fr. Latin by* J. M. Neale, E. Caswall, *and others.* LiA
(Hymn: "Sing, my tongue, the Saviour's glory," *tr. by* Edward Caswall.) CAW; WGRP
(Pange Lingua Gloriosa, *abr., tr. by* Edward Caswall.) WHL
Hymn for Grief. Margaret Widdemer. QS
Hymn for Laudes; Feast of Our Lady, Help of Christians. *Unknown, tr. fr. Latin by* Sister Maura. ISi
Hymn for Laudes; Feast of Our Lady of Good Counsel. *Unknown, tr. fr. Latin by* Sister Maura. ISi
Hymn for Memorial Day. Henry Timrod. *See* At Magnolia Cemetery.
Hymn for Morning. Prudentius, *tr. fr. Latin by* Basil Blackett. *Fr.* Cathemerinon. LaP
Hymn for Pentecost. James Clarence Mangan. CAW; JKCP
Hymn for St. John's Eve. *Unknown, tr. fr. Latin at. to* Dryden. AWP
Hymn for Second Vespers; Feast of the Apparition of Our Lady of Lourdes. *Unknown, tr. fr. Latin by* Raymond F. Roseliep. ISi
Hymn for the Church Militant. G. K. Chesterton. OxBoCh
Hymn for the Day. "Gabriela Mistral," *tr. fr. Spanish by* James H. McLean. MaRV
Hymn for the Dead. Sir Walter Scott. *Fr.* The Lay of the Last Minstrel, VI. BSV, *longer sel.*; EmBrPo
(Dies Irae.) GoBC, *longer sel.*; MaRV
("Nought of the bridal will I tell," *longer sel.*) OBRV
Hymn for the Dedication of a Church. Andrews Norton. AA
Hymn for the Eve of the New Year. Abraham Gerondi, *tr. fr. Hebrew by* Solomon Solis-Cohen. TrJP
Hymn for the Feast of the Annunciation. Aubrey Thomas De Vere. ISi
Hymn for the Lighting of the Lamps. *Unknown, at. to* St. Athenogenes, *tr. fr. Greek by* John Keble. CAW
Hymn for the Nativity. Edward Thring. COAH
Hymn for the Nativity of My Savior, A. Ben Jonson. *See* Hymn on the Nativity of My Saviour, A.
Hymn for the New Age, A. William Steward Gordon. MaRV; OQP; QP-1
Hymn for the Sixteenth Sunday after Trinity. Henry Hart Milman. VA
Hymn for the Victorious Dead. Hermann Hagedorn. AOAH
Hymn for Those in the Air. Duncan Campbell Scott. NeTW; TwCV
Hymn for Water. Merrill Moore. TrGrPo (1942 ed.)
Hymn from the French of Lamartine, *sel.* Whittier.
"O Thou who bidst the torrent flow." TrPWD
Hymn in Adoration of the Blessed Sacrament. Richard Crashaw. *See* Hymn of Saint Thomas in Adoration of the Blessed Sacrament, The.
Hymn in Contemplation of Sudden Death. Dorothy L. Sayers. QS
Hymn in Honor of Love, An. Spenser. ReIE
Hymn, A, in Honor of Saint Teresa. Richard Crashaw. *See* Hymn, A, to the Name and Honor of the Admirable Saint Teresa.
Hymn in Honour of Beauty, An. Spenser. *See* Hymne in Honour of Beautie, An.
Hymn in Praise of Neptune, A. Thomas Campion. GTSL; OBEV; TVSH
(Hymne in Prayse of Neptune, A.) EtS
(Neptune.) OBSC
Hymn Made When He Was an Ambassador at Venice, in the Time of a Great Sickness There. Sir Henry Wotton. EV-2
("D. O. M.") OxBoCh
(Eternall Mover, *abr.*) TrPWD
Hymn Not in Favor of Evolution, A. Catherine Graham Miller. CAG
Hymn of a Virgin of Delphi at the Tomb of Her Mother. Thomas Moore. MOAH
Hymn of Adam, The. Joost van den Vondel. *See* Adam's Hymn in Paradise.
Hymn of Adversity. Thomas Gray. *See* Hymn to Adversity.
Hymn of Apollo. Shelley. EmBrPo; EnL; EnLit; EnRP; HBV; OAEP; OBRV
Hymn of Armageddon, The. George Sylvester Viereck. LPS-1
Hymn of At-One-Ment. John Haynes Holmes. MaRV
Hymn of Being, The. Ralph Hodgson. *See* Song of Honour, The.
Hymn of Cleanthes, The. Cleanthes. *See* Hymn to Zeus.
Hymn of Creation. *Unknown, tr. fr. Sanskrit by* Arthur A. Macdonnell. *Fr.* The Rigveda. LiTW
Hymn of Dedication. Elizabeth E. Scantlebury. BLRP; PraP
Hymn of Freedom, A. Mary Perry King. OBAV
Hymn of Glory Let Us Sing, A. The Venerable Bede, *tr. fr. Latin by* Elizabeth Charles. BePJ
(Ascension Hymn.) MaRV
(Hymn, A.) WGRP
Hymn of Gratitude. *Unknown.* BLRP
Hymn of Hate, The. Joseph Dana Miller. PGD; PSO
Hymn of Hate against England, A. Ernst Lissauer. *See* Chant of Hate against England, A.
Hymn [*or* Hymne] of Heavenly Love, An. Spenser. EV-1; ReIE; StJW
Hymn of Joy. Henry van Dyke. MaRV
Hymn of Love. St. Francis Xavier. WHL
Hymn of Man. Swinburne. EmBrPo; PoVP; VLEP
"Thou and I and he are not gods made men for a span," *sel.* WGRP
Hymn of Marriage. Burns. *See* John Anderson, My Jo.
Hymn of Nature, A. Robert Bridges. YeAr
Hymn of Our Lord at the Last Supper. Apocryphal Acts of St. John. MeRV
Hymn of Pan. Shelley. AtBAP; BCEP; BPN; EmBrPo; EnRP; ERP; ExPo; FaBoCh; HBV; LoGBV; MyFE; OAEP; OBEV; OBRV; PoEL-4; RG; SeCeV; TVSH
Hymn of Peace, A. Ernest Bourner Allen. MaRV
Hymn of Peace. Aristophanes, *tr. fr. Greek by* B. B. Rogers. *Fr.* Lysistrata. OxBG
(Rejoicings for Peace.) GrR
Hymn of praise to Ra, A, when he riseth in the Eastern part of heaven. Hymn to Ra. *Unknown.* OuHeWo
Hymn of Saint Thomas in Adoration of the Blessed Sacrament, The. Richard Crashaw. OBS; PoLi
(Hymn in Adoration of the Blessed Sacrament.) MeLP
Hymn of Sivaite Puritans. *Unknown.* WGRP
Hymn of Thanksgiving, A. Wilbur D. Nesbit. OHIP
Hymn of Thanksgiving, A. Alice E. Sherwood. PraP
Hymn of Thanksgiving. *Unknown.* WHL
Hymn of the Angels and Sibyls. Gil Vicente, *tr. fr. Spanish by* Thomas Walsh. CAW
Hymn of the Angelus. Poe. *See* Hymn: "At morn, at noon, at twilight dim."
Hymn [*or* Hymne] of the Ascension, An. William Drummond of Hawthornden. EPS; OBS
(Song of the Ascension, *abr.*) SeCL
Hymn of the Birds, The. Aristophanes. *See* Chorus of Birds.
Hymn of the Blessed Virgin, The. St. Luke, Bible, *N.T.* *See* Magnificat, The.
Hymn of the City. Bryant. BAV; IAP; MOAP
Hymn of the Curetes. *Unknown, tr. fr. Greek by* C. M. Bowra. OxBG
Hymn of the Earth. William Ellery Channing. AA; AnNE; APW; IAP
Hymn of the Holy Cross, The. Richard Crashaw. StJW
Hymn of the Initiates. Aristophanes, *tr. fr. Greek.* *Fr.* The Frogs. OxBG
Hymn of the Moravian Nuns of Bethlehem. Longfellow. PAH
Hymn of the Nativity. Richard Crashaw. *See* In the Holy Nativity of Our Lord God.
Hymn of the Nativity [of My Savior], A. Ben Jonson. *See* Hymn on the Nativity of My Saviour, A.
Hymn of the New World. Percy MacKaye. PEDC; PoRL
Hymn of the Soviet Union. Sergei Mikhalkov *and* El-Registan, *tr. fr. Russian by* Louis Untermeyer. PoFr
Hymn of the Three Eastern Magi, Adoring Our Saviour at His Nativity, The. Elizabeth Rowe. BeR
Hymn of the Unemployed. Thomas Tiplady. MaRV
Hymn of the Waldenses. Bryant. AnNE
Hymn of the West. Edmund Clarence Stedman. HBV; PaA; PAH
(Hymn to the West.) TrPWD
Hymn of the World Within, The. Psalms, CIII, Bible, *O.T.* (Moulton, *Modern Reader's Bible*). WGRP
(Psalm CIII.) AWP; JAWP; PC, *abr.*
Hymn of the World Without. Psalms. CIV, Bible, *O.T.* (Moulton, *Modern Reader's Bible*). WGRP
(Psalm CIV.) OHIP, *sel.*
Hymn of the World's Creator, The. Cædmon, *tr. fr. Anglo-Saxon.* CAW
(Creation, The.) PoLi
Hymn of Trust. Oliver Wendell Holmes. *Fr.* The Professor at the Breakfast Table, *ch.* 11. AA; IAP; MaRV; NeHB; PraP; TrPWD
("O love divine, that stooped to share.") OlF
Hymn of Trust, A. Nettie M. Sargent. BLRP
Hymn of Unity, A. Robert Freeman. OQP; QP-1
Hymn of Unity. *Unknown, tr. fr. Hebrew by* H. M. Adler. TrJP
Hymn of Victory: Thutmose III. Amon-Re, *tr. fr. Egyptian by* James Henry Breasted. WaaP
Hymn of Weeping. Amittai ben Shefatiah, *tr. fr. Hebrew by* Nina Davis Salaman. TrJP
Hymn on Solitude. James Thomson. CEP; EiPP; OBEC
Solitude, *sel.* BeR
Hymn on the Ascension. Luis de León, *tr. fr. Spanish by* George Ticknor. AnSpL-1
Hymn on the Morning of Christ's Nativity. Milton. *Fr.* On the Morning of Christ's Nativity. CBE; CBOV;

EV-2; MotAn; OBEV; OtMeF, *abr.*; StJW
(Hymn on the Nativity.) COAH
(On the Morning of Christ's Nativity.) FiP; KN
Sels.
Hymn: "It was the winter wild," *sts.* 1-23. WHA
(Christmas Hymn, *sts.* 1-13, *abr.*) BCEP
Peaceful Night, The, *sts.* 5-7. ChrBoLe; CLS
Hymn on the Nativity of My Saviour, A. Ben Jonson. AnEC; EV-2
(Hymn for the Nativity of My Savior, A.) StJW
(Hymn of the Nativity [of My Savior], A.) COAH; SDH
(Hymne on the Nativitie of My Saviour, A.) SeCV-1
Hymn on the Omnipresence, An. John Byrom. CEP; TrPWD
Hymn on the Seasons. Anna Maria Porter. DiM
Hymn on the Seasons, A. James Thomson. *Fr.* The Seasons. EnRP; EV-3; OxBoCh; PoE
(Hymn: "These, as they change, Almighty Father, these.") CEP; EiPP; LPS-2
Hymn Sung as by the Shepherds, A. Richard Crashaw. *Fr.* In the Holy Nativity of Our Lord God. GoBC
(Shepherds' Hymn: "We saw thee in thy balmy nest.") ACP; CAW; TrGrPo, 3 *sts.*
(Shepherds Hymn Their Saviour, 2 *sts.*) EG
(Verses from the Shepherds' Hymn.) OBEV
Hymn Sung at the Completion of the Concord Monument. Emerson. *See* Concord Hymn.
Hymn the Finders! Hymn the bold. Laurence Binyon. *Fr.* The Sirens. TCPD
Hymn to Adversity. Thomas Gray. BrBE; CEP; EiPP; EnRP; GTBS; GTBS-D; GTBS-W; GTSE; GTSL; OBEC
(Hymn of Adversity.) EV-3
Hymn to Amen Ra, the Sun God. *Unknown, tr. fr. Egyptian by* Frank Lloyd Griffith. WGRP
Hymn to America. Walt Whitman. *See* Thou Mother With Thy Equal Brood.
Hymn to Aphrodite. Sappho. *See* Ode to Aphrodite.
Hymn to Aphrodite. *Unknown, tr. fr. Greek. Fr.* Homeric Hymns. GrPE, *tr. by* F. L. Lucas; LiTW, *abr., tr. by* Jack Lindsay
Hymn to Apollo. Callimachus, *tr. fr. Greek by* H. W. Tytler. GrPo
Hymn to Apollo. Sir Philip Sidney. EPP
Hymn to Ares. *Unknown, tr. fr. Greek by* F. L. Lucas. *Fr.* Homeric Hymns. GrPE
(Hymn to Mars, *tr. by* George Chapman.) KN
(To Mars, *tr. by* George Chapman.) LoBV
Hymn to Astarte, *sel.* Lord De Tabley.
From "Hymn to Astarte": "What foreland fledged with myrrh." LEAP
Hymn to Athena. *Unknown. Fr.* Homeric Hymns. AWP
Hymn to Beauty. Baudelaire, *tr. fr. French by* Alan Conder. TrFP
Hymn to Castor and Pollux. *Unknown. Fr.* Homeric Hymns. AWP
Hymn to Chance. H. Phelps Putnam. MOAP; TwAmPo; WoL
Hymn to Charity and Humility. Henry More. OxBoCh
(Hymne in Honour of Those Two Despised Virtues, Charitie and Humilitie, An.) OBS
Hymn [*or* Hymne] to Christ, at the Author's Last Going into Germany, A. John Donne. AnEnPo; EPS (1942 ed.); EV-2; FaBoEn; LiTB; LiTG; MeLP; MePo; MeRV; OAEP; OBS; OxBoCh; Po; SeCV-1; SeEP; TuPP; ViBoPo; WoL
Hymn to Christ the Saviour. Clement of Alexandria. *See* Earliest Christian Hymn ("Curb for stubborn steed.")
Hymn to Color. George Meredith. EmBrPo; PoVP
Hymn to Comus. Ben Jonson. *Fr.* Pleasure Reconciled to Virtue. ElL; OAEP
(Hymn to the Belly.) SeCePo; SiTL
(Song: To Comus.) SeEP
Hymn to Contentment, A. Thomas Parnell. CEP; EiPP; OBEC
Hymn to Cynthia. Ben Jonson. *See* Hymn to Diana.
Hymn to Darkness. John Norris. GTSL; MePo; OBS; OxBoCh; SN
Hymn to Death. Bryant. IAP
Hymn to Demeter. Louis V. Ledoux. *Fr.* The Story of Eleusis. LEAP
Hymn to Democracy, A. Paul Green. *Fr.* The Highland Call. NoCaPo
Hymn to Diana. Catullus, *tr. fr. Latin.* AWP, *tr. by* Sir Richard Jebb; LiA, *tr. by* Sir William Marris
("Diana guardeth our estate," *tr. by* Sir Richard Jebb.) LaP
Hymn to Diana. Thomas Heywood. *Fr.* The Golden Age. ElL
("Hail, beauteous Dian, queen of shades.") SiCE
Hymn to Diana. Ben Jonson. *Fr.* Cynthia's Revels, V, vi. AnFE; AWP; BCEP; BEL; BLV; BoLiVe; CBOV; ChTr; ElL; EM-1; EnLi-1 (1949 ed.); EnLit; EV-2; GTBS; GTBS-D; GTBS-W; GTSE; GTSL; InPo; JAWP; KN; PoRA; RG; ShBV-4; TOP; TrGrPo; TVSH; TyEnPo; WBP; WHA
(From "Cynthia's Revels.") LEAP
(Hesperus' Hymn to Cynthia.) CaAE; LoBV; SeCV-1
(Hesperus' Song.) GN
(Hymn [*or* Hymne], The: "Queen, and huntress, chaste, and fair.") AtBAP; EPS; PoEL-2; TwHP; ViBoPo
(Hymn to Cynthia.) SeCePo; SN
(Moon Goddess.) CBPC
(Queen and Huntress, Chaste and Fair.) CBE; CenL; CH; EG; ElSeCe; OBEV; OBS; PoE; ReEn; SiCE
(Queene and Huntresse.) EnL; OAEP; TuPP
(Song: To Cynthia.) HBV
(To Diana.) OTPC
Hymn to Dionysus. *Unknown, tr. fr. Greek by* F. L. Lucas. *Fr.* Homeric Hymns. GrPE
(To Dionysus, *tr. by* T. F. Higham.) OxBG
Hymn to Earth. Elinor Wylie. BLV; BoLiVe; ChMo; LiTM; MAP; MoAB; MoAmPo; MoPo; MoVE; NePA; NP; PIAE; ReaPo; ReMP; TCPD; TwAmPo
Hymn to Earth the Mother of All. *Unknown, tr. fr. Greek by* Shelley. *Fr.* Homeric Hymns. AWP; JAWP; WBP
(Earth the Mother of All, *tr. by* Shelley.) OxBG
(Earth, Universal Mother, *tr. by* Shelley.) GrR
("O universal Mother, who dost keep," *tr. by* Shelley.) GrPo
(To Earth, the Mother of All.) GrCo-1, *pr. tr. by* H. A. Evelyn White; GrL, *pr. tr. by* Andrew Lang; OuHeWo, *tr. by* Shelley
Hymn to God. Arthur Symons. QS
Hymn to God in Time of Stress, A. Max Eastman. QS; TrPWD
Hymn [*or* Hymne] to God, My God, in My Sickness[e]. John Donne. AtBAP; CaAE; ChTr; CoEV; ElSeCe; EnL; EnLP; FaBoEn; GoBC; LoBV; MaPo; MeLP; MePo; NBE; OAEP; OBS; OxBoCh; PoEL-2; ReEn; SeCL; SeCV-1; SeEP; TrPWD, *abr.*; TuPP
"Since I am comming to that Holy roome," *sel.* UnS
Hymn [*or* Hymne] to God the Father, A. John Donne. AnFE; AtBAP; AWP; BEL; CenL; CoBE; ElSeCe; EnLi-1; EnLit; EnLP; EPS; EV-2; GoBC; GTSE; HBV; InPo; JAWP; LiTB; LiTG; LoBV; MaRV; MeLP; MePo; OBEV (1st ed.); OBS; OxBoCh; PG (1945 ed.); Po; PoE; PoEL-2; PoFS; PoRA; PreP; ReEn; RiBV; SeCeV; SeCL; SeCV-1; SeEP; ShBV-4; TOP; TrGrPo; TrPWD; TuPP; TwCrTr; TwHP; TyEnPo; ViBoPo; WBP
(For Forgiveness.) WGRP
(To Christ.) CaAE
("Wilt thou forgive that sin where I begun.") EG
Hymn [*or* Hymne] to God the Father, A. Ben Jonson. EV-2; GoBC; MaRV; MePo; OBS; OxBoCh; ReEn; RiBV; SeCV-1; TrPWD
Hymn to God the Father. Samuel Wesley. OxBoCh
Hymn to Her Unknown. Walter James Turner. LiTL; LiTM; OBMV
Hymn to Hesperus. Byron. *See* Evening.
Hymn to Horus. Mathilde Blind. OBVV
Hymn to Intellectual Beauty. Shelley. AnEnPo; AnFE; BCEP; BEL; BoLiVe; BPN; CoBE; EM-2; EmBrPo; EnL; EnLi-2; EnLit; EnRP; EPN; EPP; ERP; GEPC; OAEP; OBRV; OuHeWo; Po; PoE; PoFS; REAL; ReTS; TOP; TwCrTr; TyEnPo; UnPo (1st ed.)
Hymn to Joy. Schiller. *See* Ode to Joy.
Hymn to Labor. Angela Morgan. MaRV
Hymn to Liberty, *sel.* Dionysios Solomos, *tr. fr. Modern Greek by* Rae Dalven.
"I know you by the blade." MoGP
Hymn to Light. Abraham Cowley. AtBAP; EPS; EV-2; MeLP; MePo; OBS; SeCV-1; SeEP
"Say, from what golden quivers of the sky," *sel.* LPS-2
Hymn to Light. Milton. *See* Hail, Holy Light.
Hymn to Love. Lascelles Abercrombie. *Fr.* Emblems of Love. OBEV (new ed.); OBVV
Hymn to Marduk, *sels. Unknown, tr. fr. Assyrian.*
"O Marduk, lord of countries, terrible one." WGRP
"O mighty, powerful, strong one of Ashur." WGRP
Hymn to Mars. *Unknown. See* Hymn to Ares.
Hymn to Mary. Zerea Jacob, *tr. fr. Abyssinian* [*or Amharic*] *by* Father Baetman. CAW
(Salutation.) ISi
Hymn to Mercury, *abr. Unknown, tr. fr. Greek by* Shelley. *Fr.* Homeric Hymns. LiTW
("And Phoebus stooped under the craggy roof.") GrPo
(Pocket-Cattle-Thief.) GrR
Hymn to Moloch. Ralph Hodgson. HBMV
Hymn to My God in a Night of My Late Sicknesse, A. Sir Henry Wotton. MeLP; MePo; OBS
(It Is Finished.) BePJ
Hymn to Night. George Washington Bethune. LPS-3
Hymn to Night. Melville Cane. MAP; MoAmPo
Hymn to Night. André Chénier, *tr. fr. French by* Alan Conder. TrFP

Hymn to Night, A. Max Michelson. NP; TrJP
Hymn to Night. *Unknown, tr. fr. Sanskrit by* R. T. H. Griffith. *Fr.* The Rigveda. LiTW
Hymn to No One Body, A. James Palmer Wade. NAMP
Hymn to Pan. John Fletcher. *Fr.* The Faithful Shepherdess, I, ii. BCEP; OBEV
(Pan.) WP
(Sing His Praises.) EG; ViBoPo
(Song: "Sing his praises that doth keep.") OBS; SeEP
Hymn to Pan. Keats. *Fr.* Endymion, I. AtBAP; BCEP; BPN; ChER; EPN; NBE; OBRV; PoEL-4
Hymn to Pan. *Unknown. See* To Pan ("Sing me of Hermes' beloved son").
Hymn to Passion. Kostes Palamas, *tr. fr. Modern Greek by* Rae Dalven. MoGP
Hymn to Peace. Joel Barlow. APW
Hymn to Poseidon. *At. to* Arion, *tr. fr. Greek by* Herbert Kynaston. OxBG
("Mighty master of the ocean!" *tr. by* Sir Edwin Arnold.) GrPo
Hymn to Priapus. D. H. Lawrence. CoBMV; MoAB; OBMV
Hymn to Proserpine. Swinburne. BEL; BPN; EmBrPo; EnL; EnLi-2; EPN; OAEP; OBVV; PoEL-5; POTT; PoVP; SeCeV; TCEP; ViP; ViPo; ViPP; VLEP
Sels.
"Thou hast conquered, O pale Galilean." MBP; WHA
Wilt Thou Yet Take All. UnPo (1st ed.)
Hymn to Ra. *Unknown, pr. tr. fr. Egyptian by* E. A. Wallis Budge. *Fr.* Book of the Dead. OuHeWo
Hymn to St. Geryon, *sel.* Michael McClure.
"Gesture the gesture the gesture the gesture, The," I. NeAP
Hymn to Saint Teresa. Richard Crashaw. *See* Hymn, A, to the Name and Honor of the Admirable Saint Teresa.
Hymn to Satan, *abr.* Giosuè Carducci, *tr. fr. Italian by* Leonard Bacon. PoFr
Hymn to Science. Mark Akenside. CEP; PoEL-3; PoP
Hymn to Selene. *Unknown. See* Hymn to the Moon.
Hymn to Sophia; the Wisdom of God. "Hugh MacDiarmid." TriL
Hymn to Sorrow. Luis Cernuda, *tr. fr. Spanish by* Eleanor L. Turnbull. CoSP
Hymn to Sorrow. Alphonse de Lamartine, *pr. tr. fr. French.* LiA
Hymn to Spring. Theodor Caspari, *tr. fr. Norwegian by* Charles W. Stork. AnNoLy
Hymn to Tammuz. *Unknown, tr. fr. Babylonian by* Stephen Langdon. LiTW
Hymn to the Belly. Ben Jonson. *See* Hymn to Comus.
Hymn to the Blessed Virgin. *Unknown. See* Hymn to the Virgin, A.
Hymn to the Creation. Addison. *See* Spacious Firmament on High, The.
Hymn to the Delian Apollo. *Unknown, tr. fr. Greek by* F. L. Lucas. *Fr.* Homeric Hymns. GrPE
Hymn to the Evening, An. Phillis Wheatley. BAV
Hymn to the Flowers, The. Horace Smith. LPS-2
Hymn to the Guardian Angel. J. Corson Miller. JKCP (1926 ed.)
Hymn to the Harvest Moon. Erik Axel Karlfeldt, *tr. fr. Swedish by* Charles W. Stork. AnSL
Hymn to the Holy Cross. Venantius Fortunatus. *See* Vexilla Regis.
Hymn to the Holy Spirit. Richard Wilton. OxBoCh
Hymn to the Moon. *Unknown, tr. fr. Greek by* Shelley. *Fr.* Homeric Hymns. LiTW
(Hymn to Selene, *tr. by* Shelley.) AWP
(To the Moon, *shorter sel., pr. tr. by* Andrew Lang.) GrL
Hymn to the Morning. Phillis Wheatley. BAV
Hymn, A, to the Name and Honor [*or* Honour] of the Admirable Saint [*or* Sainte] Teresa. Richard Crashaw. CaAE; CoEV; EPS; EV-2, *abr.;* FaBoEn; KN, *abr.;* LiA; LoBV; OAEP; OBEV, *abr.;* OBS; PoEL-2; PoFS; ReEn; SeCL; SeCV-1, *abr.;* SeEP; TriL
(Hymn, A, in Honor of Saint Teresa, a Carmelite Nun.) PraNu
(Hymn to Saint Teresa.) ACP; MeLP; MePo; OxBoCh; WGRP
"O how oft shalt thou complain," *sel.* PoLi
Hymn to the Name of Jesus. Richard Crashaw. LEAP
(Hymn, A: "I sing the Name which none can say.") NBE
(To the Name above Every Name, the Name of Jesus, a Hymn.) SeCV-1
Hymn to the National Flag. Margaret Junkin Preston. FOAH
Hymn to the Night. Longfellow. AA; AmP; AmPP; AnAmPo; AnEnPo; AnFE; AnNE; APA; APW; BAP; BAV; CoAnAm; ExPo; HBV; HBVY; IAP; LA; LaNeLa; LEAP; LoBV; LPS-2; MOAP; NePA; OBAV; OTPC; OuHeWo; OxBA; PoFS; StVeCh (1940 ed.); TCAP; TOP; TreFS; TrGrPo; ViBoPo; WHA
Hymn to the Night, II. "Novalis," *tr. fr. German by* Mabel Cotterell. *Fr.* Hymns to the Night. LiTW
Hymn to the North Star. Bryant. OTPC
Hymn to the Perfect. Edith Lovejoy Pierce. ChIP
Hymn to the Sea, A. Richard Henry Stoddard. EtS
Hymn to the Sea. Sir William Watson. EtS; LiA
Hymn to the Spirit of Nature. Shelley. *See* Life of Life.
Hymn to the Sirens. Euripides, *tr. fr. Greek by* Arthur S. Way. *Fr.* Helen. GrR
(Siren-Spirits, *tr. by* J. T. Sheppard.) OxBG
Hymn to the Sun. George Darley. TIP
Hymn to the Sun. José de Espronceda, *tr. fr. Spanish by* Ida Farnell. TeCS
Hymn to the Sun. Ikhnaton (Amenhotep IV), *tr. fr. Egyptian.* GrCo-1, *tr. by* J. H. Breasted; LiTW, *tr. by* T. Eric Peet; WoL, *tr. by* J. H. Breasted
Hymn to the Sun. Edgar Lee Masters. *Fr.* Acoma. ChMo; CMP
Hymn to the Sun. William Alexander Percy. TrPWD
Hymn to the Sun. Michael Roberts. FaBoCh; LoGBV
Hymn to the Sunrise. *Unknown.* NA
Hymn to the Victorious Dead. Hermann Hagedorn. PEDC
Hymn to the Virgin. Juan Ruiz, Archpriest of Hita, *tr. fr. Spanish by* Longfellow. *Fr.* The Book of Good Love. AnSpL-1; TeCS
Hymn to the Virgin. Sir Walter Scott. *Fr.* The Lady of the Lake, III. EnRP; GoBC
(Ave Maria.) ISi
Hymn to the Virgin, A. *Unknown.* OBEV
(Hymn to the Blessed Virgin.) CAW
(Of On That Is So Fayr and Bright.) BEL
(Of One That Is So Fair and Bright.) CoBe; ISi
(Prayer to the Virgin.) EnLit
(Song to Our Lady.) PoLi
(Song to the Virgin, A.) SeCePo
Hymn to the Virgin Mary. Conal O'Riordan, *tr. fr. Irish by* Eleanor Hull. ISi
Hymn to the Volunteers of the Republic, *sel.* César Vallejo, *tr. fr. Spanish.*
"Battles? No! Agonies! And before the agonies." PoFr
Hymn to the West. Edmund Clarence Stedman. *See* Hymn of the West.
Hymn to the Wind God. *Unknown, tr. fr. Aztec by* John Hubert Cornyn. *Fr.* Song of Quetzalcoatl. LiTW
Hymn to the Winds. Joachim du Bellay, *tr. fr. French by* Andrew Lang. AWP; WoL
(From a Winnower of Corn to the Winds, *tr. by* Alan Conder.) TrFP
(Winnower of Wheat to the Winds, A, *tr. by* Ralph N. Currey.) FoS
Hymn to Truth. James Byers Colton, 2d. CAG
Hymn to Varuna, God of Fire and Light. *Unknown, tr. fr. Sanskrit by* R. T. H. Griffith. *Fr.* The Rigveda. LiTW
Hymn to Venus. Edith Sitwell. FaBoMo
Hymn to Vishnu. Jayadeva. *Fr.* The Gitã Gõvinda. AWP
Hymn to Zeus. Aeschylus. *Fr.* Agamemnon. WGRP
Hymn to Zeus, *sel.* Callimachus, *tr. fr. Greek by* Matthew Prior.
"Great Rhea,/ Pregnant, to high Parrhasia's cliffs retired." GrPo
Hymn to Zeus. Cleanthes, *tr. fr. Greek.* GrCo-2, *tr. by* James G. Frazer; GrL, *tr. by* James Adam; OxBG, *tr. by* Michael Balkwill; WGRP, *tr. by* Edward Hayes Plumptre
(Hymn of Cleanthes, The, *tr. by* James Adam.) MaRV
("O God most glorious, called by many a name," *tr. by* James Adam.) GrPo
Hymn Unsung, The. Arthur Hugh Clough. *See* Hymnos Ahymnos.
Hymn Written for the Two Hundredth Anniversary of the Old South Church, Beverly, Massachusetts. Lucy Larcom. OHIP
Hymnal: "Bringer of sun, arrower of evening, star-begetter and moon-riser." Harold Vinal. TrPWD
Hymne, An: "Drop, drop, slow tears." Phineas Fletcher. *See* Hymn, An: "Drop, drop, slow tears."
Hymne I: Generall Invitation to Praise God, A. George Wither. *Fr.* Hallelujah; or Britain's Second Remembrancer. SeCV-1
Hymne, The: "Queene, and Huntresse, chaste, and faire." Ben Jonson. *See* Hymn to Diana.
Hymne [*or* Hymn] in Honour of Beautie [*or* Beautee *or* Beauty], An. Spenser. GEPC; SiCE
Sels.
"Ah whither, Love, wilt thou now carrie mee?" ReEn
Beauty ("So every spirit, as it is most pure"). LPS-3
Beauty ("What time this world's great workmaster did cast"). OBSC
(Soul Is Form, *abr.*) GoBC
("What time this world's great workmaster," *abr.*) EPP
Hymne in Honour of Those Two Despised Virtues, Charitie and Humilitie, An. Henry More. *See* Hymn to Charity and Humility.

Hymne in Prayse of Neptune, A. Thomas Campion. *See* Hymn in Praise of Neptune, A.
Hymne of Heavenly Beautie [*or* Beauty], An. Spenser. TwCrTr
Sels.
"But whoso may, thrice happy man him hold." WGRP
"Faire is the heaven where happy soules have place." MeRV
"Means, therefore, which unto us is lent, The." EPP
Hymne of Heavenly Love, An. Spenser. *See* Hymn of Heavenly Love, An.
Hymne of the Ascension, An. William Drummond of Hawthornden. *See* Hymn of the Ascension, An.
Hymne on the Nativitie of My Saviour, A. Ben Jonson. *See* Hymn on the Nativity of My Saviour, A.
Hymne to Christ, at the Authors Last Going into Germany, A. John Donne. *See* Hymn to Christ . . .
Hymne to God My God, in My Sicknesse. John Donne. *See* Hymn to God, My God, in My Sickness.
Hymne to God the Father, A. John Donne. *See* Hymn to God the Father, A.
Hymne to God the Father, A. Ben Jonson. *See* Hymn to God the Father, A.
Hymne to Our Saviour on the Crosse, A. George Chapman. PoEL-2
Ὕμνος Ἄυμνος (Hymnos Ahymnos). Arthur Hugh Clough. BPN; EPN; PoVP; ViPP; VLEP
(Hymn Unsung, The.) EmBrPo
(O Thou Whose Image.) TrPWD
Hymns and Spiritual Songs, *sel.* Christopher Smart.
Christmas Day, Hymn XXXII. ChTr
Hymns for the Amusement of Children, *sel.* Christopher Smart.
Lark's Nest, A. FaBoCh; LoGBV
Hymns of [*or* to] Astraea, *sels.* Sir John Davies.
Of Astraea. SiCE; TrGrPo; TuPP
(Virgin Queen, The; an Anagram.) BLV
To Astraea. SiCE
To Envy. SiCE
To the Lark. SiCE
To the Month of September. CaAE; CenL
To the Nightingale. OBSC; SiCE; TrGrPo
To the Rose. OBSC; SiCE; TuPP
To the Spring. ElL; SiCE; TuPP
Hymns of Praise. Psalms, VIII, XV, XIX, XXIII, XXIV, XCV, CXXI. Bible, *O.T.* OuHeWo
Hymns of the Marshes, *sel.* Sidney Lanier.
Sunrise. AA; ADAH; HiLiAm; PoEL-5; SPP; TCAP
"Tide's at full, The: the marsh with flooded streams," *shorter sel.* FaBoEn
Hymns to Astraea. Sir John Davies. *See* Hymns of Astraea.
Hymns to the Night, I–VI. "Novalis," *tr. fr. German by* Mabel Cotterell. AnGP
Hymn to the Night, II. LiTW
Hymnum Canentes Martyrum. The Venerable Bede, *tr. fr. Latin by* John Mason Neale. CAW
Hymnus: "God be in my hede." *Unknown. See* God Be in My Head.
Hymnus in Noctem. George Chapman. *Fr.* The Shadow of Night. PoEL-2; ReIE, *abr.*
Sels.
"All you possessed with indepressed spirits." TuPP
"Great Goddesse to whose throne in Cynthian fires." AtBAP
Hymnus Sanctae Mariae, *sel.* Ennodius, *tr. fr. Latin.*
How of the Virgin Mother Shall I Sing? ISi
Hynd Etin. *Unknown. See* Hind Etin.
Hynd [*or* Hynde] Horn. *Unknown.* GN; LoEn; OBB
(Hind Horn.) ATP; BaBo (A *and* B *vers.*); EP, *sl. abr.*; ESPB (A *and* G *vers.*); TOP; ViBoFo
Hyperboreans, The. Pindar, *tr. fr. Greek by* C. J. Billson. *Fr.* Pythian Odes, X. GrR; OxBG
Hyperion; a Fragment. Keats. BCEP, *abr.*; BPN; BrBE, *abr.*; EmBrPo; EnRP; EPN; ERP; GEPC; ReaPo; TwHP
Sels.
"Apollo then, with sudden scrutiny and gloomless eyes," *fr.* III. NBE; OBRV
"As when upon a trancèd summer-night," *fr.* I. ViBoPo
"But one of the whole mammoth-brood," *fr.* I. OBRV
"Deep in the shady sadness of a vale," I. ATP, *sel.*; BEL; CBE, *sel.*; ChER; EM-2; EPP, *sel.*, EV-4, *sel.*; ExPo, *sel.*; FaBoEn, *sel.*; FiP; InP; *br. sel.*; MyFE, *fr.* I *and* II; OAEP; OBRV, *sel.*; PoEL-4
(Saturn, *sel.*) LoBV; TrGrPo
(Saturn Fallen, *sel.*) AnEnPo
Den of the Titans, The, *fr.* II. WHA
Hyperion's Arrival, *fr.* II. OBRV
("All eyes were on Enceladus's face.") BrBE
(Entrance of Hyperion.) ReTS
(Hyperion and Saturn.) SeCePo
"Just at the self-same beat of Time's wide wings," *fr.* II. OBRV
"Meanwhile in other realms big tears were shed," *fr.* I. NBE
"O leave them, Muse," *fr.* III. ViBoPo
Hyperion; a Vision. Keats. *See* Fall of Hyperion, The.
Hyperion's Arrival. Keats. *Fr.* Hyperion, II. OBRV
("All eyes were on Enceladus's face.") BrBE
(Entrance of Hyperion.) ReTS
(Hyperion and Saturn.) SeCePo
Hyperion's clear star is not yet risen. Dawn-Song to Waken the Lovers. *Unknown.* LiTW
Hyperion's Song. Friedrich Hölderlin. *See* Song of Fate.
Hypnotized and told they're seeing red. Humanities. Robert Conquest. PoLFOT
Hypocrisy. Samuel Butler. BOHV
Hypocrite, The. Kalonymos ben Kalonymos, *tr. fr. Hebrew by* Joseph Chotzner. *Fr.* The Touchstone. TrJP
Hypocrite Auteur. Archibald MacLeish. CoV; MoVE; NePA
Hypocrite is strange of race, A. The Hypocrite. Kalonymos ben Kalonymos. *Fr.* The Touchstone. TrJP
Hypocrites, The. Ibn al-Batti, *tr. fr. Arabic by* A. J. Arberry. MooP
Hyssop from a grave's edge. Bitters. Lizette Woodworth Reese. DaM
Hysteria. Chu Shu Chen, *tr. fr. Chinese by* Kenneth Rexroth. OnPC
Hywel and Blodwen. Idris Davies. MoWP

I

"I." Louis Golding. TrJP
"I/ Through/ Blue/ Sky/ Fly." The Aeronaut to His Lady. Frank Sidgwick. WhC
I/ Why? The Shortest Poem in the World [*or* Lines (2) on the Questionable Importance of the Individual]. Eli Siegel. PIAE; SiTL
I, a Most Wretched Atlas. Heine, *tr. fr. German by* Emma Lazarus. *Fr.* Homeward Bound. TrJP
I a tender young maid have been courted by many. My Thing Is My Own. *Unknown.* CoMu
I a weaponed warrior was! Now in pride bedecks me. Riddle. *Unknown.* TCEP
I abide and abide and better abide. Sonnets, VI. Sir Thomas Wyatt. EnLoPo; SiPS
I Accept. Harold Trowbridge Pulsifer. HBMV; OQP; QP-2
I 'ad no education, and my pile. A Ballade of Any Father to Any Son. J. C. Squire. PIAE; WhC
I adjure you, O daughters of Jerusalem. The Song of Solomon, Bible, *O.T.* LiTW
I admire the artificial art of the East. Where the Grizzly Dwells. James Fox. SCC
I adore Thee humbly, O Thou hidden God. Adoro Te Devote. St. Thomas Aquinas. WHL
I adventured fearlessly. Immunity. Ibn Maimun. MooP
I advocate a semi-revolution. A Semi-Revolution. Robert Frost. LiTM; SiTL
I advocate a total revolution. A Total Revolution. Oscar Williams. LiTM; SiTL
I affirm. Perambulator Poems, III. David McCord. WhC
I agree that I'm no beauty. The Bulldog Speaks. Edward Anthony. AlBD
I ain't afeard [*or* afraid] uv snakes, or toads, or bugs, or worms, or mice. Seein' Things. Eugene Field. BoChLi; DDA; HBV; HBVY; HOAH; MAP; MoAmPo (1942 ed.); MPB; NeMA; OTPC; PoMa; PTA-1; RIS; TCAP; TreF
I ain't been long in this here army. A Rookie's Lament. *Unknown.* ABF
I ain't got no father. Poor Lonesome Cowboy. *Unknown.* ABF; AS; CoSo; CSF; TiPo
I ain't gwine a work till my dyin' day. A Few Days Off. John Charles McNeill. NoCaPo
I ain't no wagon, ain't no dray. I'm a Round-Town Gent. *Unknown.* GoSl
I Almost Had Forgotten. Christopher Morley. TBM
I almost never say my prayers. Devotions. Elinor L. Norcross. OQP; QP-2
I almost thought the silent door. The Door Between. Mary Ferguson Legler. UnW
I always eat peas with honey. Peas. *Unknown.* SiTL
I always knew that sometime I must go. The Sudden Call. Narihira. PFE
I always knew the Ural Mountains glowed. The Mineral Collection. Abbie Huston Evans. NP
I always liked to go to bed. A Song for My Mother—Her Stories. Anna Hempstead Branch. MotAn; OHIP
I always loved this solitary hill. L'Infinito. Giacomo Leopardi. AWP; JAWP; WBP
I always loved to call my lady Rose. Madrigal. *Unknown.* ElL

I always said, shall say, and now do say. Lope de Vega Carpio, *tr. fr. Spanish by* Elizabeth Selden. BoFr
I always say I won't go back to the mountains. Sourdough Mountain Lookout. Philip Whalen. NeAP
I always see—I don't know why. The Knowledgeable Child. L. A. G. Strong. OBMV
I always shout when Grandma comes. Afternoon with Grandmother. Barbara A. Huff. FaPON
I always take my judgment from a fool. Cromek Speaks. Blake. PIAE
I always think of garden phlox. Phlox. Louise Driscoll. MW
I always thought, old witch. A Hallowe'en Meeting. George O. Butler. MeMeAg
I always wanted/ A little carved bowl. The Little Carved Bowl. Margaret Widdemer. BrR; YT
I always wanted a red balloon. Tragedy. Jill Spargur. BLPA; DDA
I always was afraid of Somes's Pond. Atavism. Elinor Wylie. AnEnPo; HBMV; NP; TCAP
I Am. John Clare. *See* Written in Northampton County Asylum.
I Am. Hilda Conkling. FaPON; NP; TiPo
I am/ A clam! Nirvana [*or* A Clam]. *Unknown.* BOHV; StaSt
I am a boatman by trade. Jack Williams. *Unknown.* ABS
I am a bold cowboy, from Midland I came. The Lovesick Cowboy. Charles A. Bobston. CoSo
I am a bold fellow. The Young Dandelion. Dinah Maria Mulock Craik. DD; GoTP; MPB; NLK
I Am a Brisk and Sprightly Lad. *Unknown.* AmSS
I am a broken-hearted milkman, in grief I'm arrayed. Polly Perkins. *Unknown.* OxBoLi
I am a cloud in the dome of space. The Dreamer. Gunnar Mascoll Silfverstolpe. AnSL
I am a cloud in the heaven's height. The Cloud. Sara Teasdale. POT; PoTo
I am a composite being of all the people of America. I Am the Flag. Lawrence M. Jones. PGD; PSO
I am a confidant of dawn. Dawn. Roselle Mercier Montgomery. LS
I am a copper wire slung in the air. Under a Telephone Pole. Carl Sandburg. PoeMoYo; PoTo; VOD (1935 ed.)
I am a cowboy by my trade. A Wild Rattling Cowboy. *Unknown.* CoSo
I am a distant descendant of Kao Yang Ti. Encountering Sorrow. Chu Yuan. WhP
I am a downright country-man, both faithful (aye) and true. The Downright Country-Man; or, The Faithful Dairy Maid. *Unknown.* CoMu
I am a faire maide, if my glasse doe not flatter. The Wooing Maid. Martin Parker. CoMu
I Am a Friar of Orders Gray. John O'Keeffe. *See* Friar of Orders Gray, The.
I am a garden of red tulips. Prayer. Richard Aldington. PFE
I am a gentleman in a dustcoat trying. Piazza Piece. John Crowe Ransom. BLV; CoBMV; InPo; MAP; MoAB; MoAmPo; MOAP; MoPW; MoVE; NeMA; OxBA; PG (1955 ed.); Po; TBM; TrGrPo
I am a goddess of the ambrosial courts. Artemis Prologizes. Robert Browning. AnEnPo; LoBV (2d ed.)
I am a gold lock. Mother Goose. PPL
I Am a Grown Man. Franz Werfel, *tr. fr. German by* Herman Salinger. TwGV
I am a happy Christmas wind. Ballad of the Happy Christmas Wind. Sister Mary Madeleva. ChrBoLe
I am a happy miner. The Happy Miner. *Unknown.* CSF; IHA
I am a hearthrug. Midsummer Madness. *Unknown.* BOHV
I am a jolly shanty boy. Bung Yer Eye [*or* The Shanty Boy]. *Unknown.* ABF; CSF; IHA
I am a jolly young fellow. The Jolly Driver. *Unknown.* CoMu
I am a jovial collier lad, and blithe as blithe can be. Down in a Coal Mine. J. B. Geoghegan. TreFS
I am a jovial marriner, our calling is well known. The Jovial Marriner; or, The Sea-Man's Renown. John Playford. CoMu
I am a kind of farthing dip. A Portrait. Robert Louis Stevenson. SeCePo
I am a lamp, a lamp that is out. She Warns Him. Frances Cornford. Two Poems, I. EnLoPo
I am a little boy. Feet. "Harry." TiPo (1959 ed.)
I Am a Little Church (No Great Cathedral). E. E. Cummings. NePoAm-2
I am a little music box. A Music Box. Abbie Farwell Brown. PPL
I am a little thing. Do You Guess It Is I? Eliza Lee Follen. OTPC (1946 ed.); PPL
I am a little world made cunningly. Holy Sonnets, V. John Donne. EnL; EPS; MyFE; OBS; OxBoCh; PeBoSo; ReEn; SeEP; TwP
I am a lone, unfathered chick. Orphan Born. Robert J. Burdette. BOHV
I am a lonely woodland lake. The Lake. John Banister Tabb. AmP
I am a lover yet was never loved. *Unknown.* SeCSL
I am a man defeated in his loins. Beggar to Burgher. A. R. D. Fairburn. AnNZ
I am a man of war and might. A Soldier. Sir John Suckling. SeCV-1
I am a man who knew Abe Lincoln well. The Man from Sangamon, at Gettysburg. Eleanor G. R. Young. OQP; QP-2
I am a Mormon bishop and I will tell you what I know. The Mormon Bishop's Lament. *Unknown.* CoSo; CSF
I am a most superior person. Henry Charles Beeching. *Fr.* The Masque of Balliol. CenHV
I am a Negro:/ Black as the night is black. Proem [*or* The Negro]. Langston Hughes. BAP; PreP
I Am a Parcel [of Vain Strivings Tied]. Henry David Thoreau. AnNE; CoV; FaBoEn; GTBS-W; PoEL-4 (Sic Vita.) AmPP (4th ed.); MOAP; NePA; OxBA
I am a part of all that I have met. The Challenge of Life [*or* Experience]. Tennyson. *Fr.* Ulysses. MaRV; OQP; QP-2
I am a part of all you see. Penetralia. Madison Cawein. CP; NV
"I am a passion; I am a flame." Song. Gustavo Adolfo Bécquer. Rimas, XI. OnPM; TeCS
I am a peevish student, I. Melancholia. *Unknown.* NA
I am a poetaster. Apology. John McClure. LS; TBM
"I am a poor girl, and my fortune is bad." The Wagoner's Lad (A *vers.*). *Unknown.* BaBo
"I am a poor unhappy boy." Whittington and His Cat. *Unknown.* CIV
I am [*or* I'm just] a poor wayfaring stranger. Poor Wayfaring Stranger [*or* Over Jordan]. *Unknown.* OuSiCo; TrAS
I am a poor workman as rich as a Jew. Contentment; or, The Happy Workman's Song. John Byrom. CEP; OBEC
I am a poore & harmless mayde. *Unknown.* SeCSL
I am a pretty wench. *Unknown.* OxNR
I am a priest upon whose head. After the Order of Melchisedec. Robert Norwood. CPG
I am a prisoner in the hands of the enemy. The Other Side of the Valley. *Unknown.* TrCh
I am a puny opinion-moulder. A Ballade of 1933. Franklin P. Adams. PIAE
I am a quiet gentleman. The Tired Man. Anna Wickham. BMEP; HBMV; LBBV; NP; ViBoPo (1941 ed.); YT
I am a reek and a rambling one. The Reek and the Rambling Blade. *Unknown.* OuSiCo
I am a robber from over the seas. The Robber in England. Marguerite Wilkinson. OBAV
I am a roving cowboy off from the Western plains. The Black Tail Range. *Unknown.* CoSo
I am a roving gambler, I've gambled all around. The Roving Gambler. *Unknown.* ABF; AS; TrAS
I am a roving traveler and go from town to town. The Gamboling Man. *Unknown.* AS
I am a sea-shell flung. Frutta di Mare. Geoffrey Scott. ChTr; EtS; OBMV
I am a shepherd—I have hated. The Sheep Herd. Sister Mariella. ChrBoLe; WHL
I am a shipwrecked sailor's tomb; a peasant's there doth stand. One to All Men. Plato. OnPM
I am a shoemaker by my trade. The Shoemaker. *Unknown.* TrAS
I am a sinful man of men. The Joyce's Repentance. *Unknown, tr. by* Douglas Hyde. GTIV; MeRV
I am a spruce tree tall and strong. The Spruce Tree. Dorothy Choate Herriman. CPG
I am a stern old bachelor. The Old Bachelor. *Unknown.* ABF
I am a strange contradiction; I'm new and I'm old. *See* I'm a strange contradiction
I am a stranger in the land. Death. *Unknown.* BLPA
I am a Texas cowboy, light-hearted, gay and free. The Texas Cowboy. Mrs. Robert Thomson. CSF
I am a tongue for beauty. Not a day. Eagle Sonnets, XIX. Clement Wood. HBMV
I am a tramp by the long trail's border. Vachel Lindsay. *Fr.* The Santa-Fé Trail. LaNeLa
I am a vaquero by trade. Pinto. *Unknown.* CoSo; CSF
I am a very personable man. A New Shakespeare. Andrew Lang. CenHV
I am a wandering, bitter shade. What's in a Name? Helen F. More. GA; PAH
I am a wandering cowboy, from ranch to ranch I roam. The Wandering Cowboy. *Unknown.* CoSo
I am a weakling. God, who made. The Weakling. Arthur Adams. BoAu
I am a weaver by my trade. Wil the Merry Weaver, and Charity the Chamber-Maid; or, A Brisk Encounter between a Youngman and His Love. *Unknown.* CoMu
I am a white falcon, hurrah! The Falcon. Richard Henry Stoddard. AA

I am a wild and roving lad. Rambling Boy. *Unknown.* CSF
I Am a Wild Young Irish Boy, *with music.* *Unknown.* ShS
I am a willow-wren. Netted Strawberries. Gordon Bottomley. AtBAP; WP
I am a witch, and a kind old witch. The Old Witch in the Copse. Frances Cornford. TCPD
I am a woman, sick for passion. Appuldurcombe Park. Amy Lowell. ChMo; CMP
I am a woman—therefore I may not. A Woman's Thought. Richard Watson Gilder. BAP; HBV
I am a young jolly brisk sailor. Tarpauling Jacket. *Unknown.* OxBoLi
I am a youth as passionate. Love's Code. Mutarrif. MooP
I am a youthful lady, my troubles they are great. Victory. *Unknown.* CoMu
I am adrift in a desert where too much sun. Desert Shipwreck. Barbara Leslie Jordan. GoYe
I am afraid of drums. Drums. Frances Angevine Gray. PoTo
I am afraid of silence. The Voice. Sister Maris Stella. GoBC
I am afraid to own a body. Emily Dickinson. LiTA
I Am Aladdin. Robert Carlton Brown. AnAmPo; LA
I am all alone in the room. Ancient Beautiful Things. Fannie Stearns Davis. AV; BAP; SBMV
I am all alone, with the iron wounded. Riddle. Cynewulf. TCEP
I am all bent to glean the golden ore. Madrigal: To His Lady Selvaggia Vergiolesi. Cino da Pistoia. AWP; JAWP; WBP
I am all the way from Buffalo. Ballad of the Erie Canal. *Unknown.* ABF; IHA
I am all Thine, Beloved. Exchange. Sister Mary Dorothy Ann. GoBC; PraNu
I Am an Acme of Things Accomplished. Walt Whitman. *Fr.* Song of Myself, XLIV. SN
I Am an American. Elias Lieberman. FaPON; GrCo-1; HiLiAm; MaRV; PaA; PoeMoYo; PSO
I am an ancient jest! Ballad [*or* Ballade] of the Primitive Jest. Andrew Lang. BOHV; HBV
I am an ancient reluctant conscript. Old Timers. Carl Sandburg. AnAmPo; BAP; CoV; LA; NP; TBM; YaD
I am an elf. The Elf. Marian Osborne. CPG
I am an old man some sixty years old. The Old Gray Mule. *Unknown.* CSF
I am an old woman. The Old Patient. Jerome Meyers. PoP
I am an old woman, comfortable, calm and wise. The Old Nurse. Frances Cornford. TCPD
I am an unadventurous man. De Gustibus. St. John Emile Clavering Hankin. CenHV
"I am an urn of anger," cried the bull. The Bull. Freda Laughton. NeIP
I am Andrew Cecil Bradley. Cecil Arthur Spring-Rice. *Fr.* The Masque of Balliol. CenHV
I am anxious after praise. Egoism. W. Craddle. FiBHP; WhC
"I am," Apollo cried to Daphne, panting. Daphne. Bernard le Bovier de Fontenelle. TrFP
I am ardorous, I am dark. Rimas. Gustavo Adolfo Bécquer. CAW
I am as brave as Caesar in this war. War and Wine. Jean Le Houx, *formerly at. to* Olivier Basselin. FoS
"I am as brown as brown can be." The Brown Girl. *Unknown.* BaBo (A *vers.*); ESPB; OBB
I am as I am and so will I be. Sir Thomas Wyatt. SiPS
I Am as Light as Any Roe. *Unknown.* ViBoPo
(Praising of Women, A, *in mod. Eng.*) TMEV
("To onpreise womene it were a shame.") LO
I am ashamed before the earth. Therefore I Must Tell the Truth. Torlino. ExPo
I am ashamed of all my former faults. Demus Shriven. Aristophanes. *Fr.* The Knights. GrR
I am awake. . . . A coffin-lid. . . . I strain. Never. Afanasi Fet. BoR
I am aware. Kinship. Angela Morgan. BPP
I am beautiful as a dream of stone, but not maternal. Beauty. Baudelaire. OnPM
I am Ben Ammar: my repute. Poet's Pride. Ibn Ammar. MooP
I am bereavement, gloom and desolation. El Desdichado. Gérard de Nerval. LO; TrFP
I am bewildered still and teased by elves. Tricksters. William Rose Benét. HBMV
I am black and comely; my lips are glowing. Rima XI. Gustavo Adolfo Bécquer. *Fr.* Rimas. AnSpL-2
I am black and I have seen black hands. I Have Seen Black Hands. Richard Wright. PoNc
I am bringing you, my sweet beloved. Cervantes. *Fr.* The Siege of Numancia. BoFr
I am broken by the tumult of the years. Old Joyce. Seán Jennett. NeIP
"I am busy," said the sea. Day. Sir Cecil Spring-Rice. BoTP
I am but clay in thy hands; but thou art the all-loving artist. I in Thee, and Thou in Me. Christopher Pearse Cranch. HBV; IAP
"I am by promise tied." Fitz-James and Roderick Dhu. Sir Walter Scott. *Fr.* The Lady of the Lake, V. EPP; LPS-2
I am called Childhood: in play is all my mind. Childhood. Sir Thomas More. TuPP
I am caught in an iridescent spider-web. The Web. Witter Bynner. *Fr.* Chapala Poems. NP
I am cold and alone. The Boy Fishing. E. J. Scovell. HaMV; ThWaDe
I am come home again. Home-coming. "Isobel Hume." HBMV
I am come into my garden, my sister, my spouse. Song of Solomon, Bible, *O.T.* LoPS
I am come of the seed of the people, the people that sorrow. The Rebel. Padraic Pearse. PoFr
I am come to make thy tomb. John Webster. *Fr.* The Duchess of Malfi. ChTr
I am coming, I am coming! The Voice of Spring. Mary Howitt. OTPC (1923 ed.); PRWS
I am coming, little maiden. The Coming of Spring [*or* Spring Is Coming]. Mary Howitt. PEDC; RAR
I am compelled to make the long trip to classic Athens. Propertius. Elegies, III, 21. LaP
I am concerned because my mind. Ballade to My Psychoanalyst. Kenneth Lillington. FiBHP
I am constantly wounded. Rumor Laetalis [*or* Letalis]. *At. to* Peter Abelard. LaP; LiTW; LyMA
I am content, for I am told. The Islands; Puget Sound. James Rorty. MOAP
I am content, I do not care. Careless Content. John Byrom. CEP; EV-3; HBV; LO, *2 sts.;* OBEC
I am content with latticed sights. Late Winter. Hazel Hall. HBMV
I Am Content with Life and at Peace with the World. Lo Yin, *tr. fr. Chinese by* Henry H. Hart. PoHN
I am contented by remembrances. Retractions, II. James Branch Cabell. HBMV
I am Count Orlo come to say farewell. Orlo's Valediction. Jon Manchip White. NePoEA
I Am Dark and Fair to See. *Unknown.* LO; LoPS
I am dead, but I wait your coming. For another you shall wait. The Common End. *Unknown.* GrPE
I am dead, Horatio. Wretched queen, adieu! Death of Hamlet. Shakespeare. *Fr.* Hamlet, V, ii. FiP
I am desolate,/ Bereft by bitter fate. Love's Despair. Diarmad O'Curnain. GTIV; OnYI; OxBI; TIP
I am Don Juan, curst from age to age. Don Juan Declaims. James Elroy Flecker. OnPP
I am dying, Egypt, dying. Antony to [*or* and] Cleopatra. William Haines Lytle. AA; BeLS; BLPA; HBV; LPS-1; NeHB; OBAV; OnPP; TreF
I am dying, Egypt, dying. Death of Antony. Shakespeare. *Fr.* Antony and Cleopatra, IV, xiii. CBOV; EtPaEn; FiP; LoPS
I am enamoured, and yet not so much. Sonnet: He Will Not Be Too Deeply in Love [*or* Not Too Deeply in Love]. Cecco Angiolieri da Siena. AWP; OnPM
I am enchanted with thy snow-white hands. "E. C." *Fr.* Emaricdulfe. TuPP
I am endlessly yearning. Endless Yearning. Li Po. ChLP
I am engag'd, both in my words, and hand. George Chapman. *Fr.* The Revenge of Bussy d'Ambois. NBE
I am Ethell, the son of Conn. Aubrey Thomas De Vere. *Fr.* The Bard Ethell. TIP
I am Eve, great Adam's wife. Eve's Lament [*or* Gaelic Fragment]. *Unknown.* CAW; OnYI; SiB
I am exceedingly rich. Cat. "Jan Struther." GoTP
I am far frae my hame, an' I'm weary often whiles. My Ain Countree. Mary Augusta Demarest. HBV; WGRP
I am featly-tripping Lee. Henry Charles Beeching. *Fr.* The Masque of Balliol. CenHV
I am fevered with the sunset. The Sea Gypsy [*or* Gipsy]. Richard Hovey. AlDL; BAP; BBV; BTP; CBPC; EtS; FaPON; GBV; GoTP; HBV; HBVY; LBMV; LEAP; MCCG; OBAV; OQP; PIAE; POT; PoTo; PYM; QP-2; StaSt; TCAP; TreFS; TSW; TSWC; YT
I Am Fire, and Ayre. Shakespeare. *See* Death of Cleopatra.
I am for ever bathed in tears, I rend. Sonnet. Garcilaso de la Vega. TeCS
I am forever haunted by one dread. Vale. Maurice Baring. JKCP (1955 ed.)
I am Forgetfulness. I am that shadow. Another Altar. Edmund Blunden. MoPW
I am four monkeys. The Tree. Alfred Kreymborg. BAP; HBMV; TSW; TSWC
I am fourteen years. Childhood. Boris Pasternak. *Fr.* 1905. RuPo
I Am Frightened. Gerald Gould. MoBrPo (1942 ed.)
I am from Ireland. Dispossessed Poet. Monk Gibbon. OnYI
I am full of grief, and the tear runs from my eye. Five Arabic Verses in Praise of Wine, IV. *Unknown.* TrJP

I Am Fur from My Sweetheart. *Unknown.* CoSo (Fragment, A: "I am fur from my sweetheart.") CSF

I am gai. I am poet. I dwell. Vers Nonsensiques. George Du Maurier. HBV; NA

I am gentle with the strong. From Solitude to Solitude towards Life. Paul Eluard. LiTW

I Am Glad Daylong. William Stanley Braithwaite. GoSl (Rhapsody.) BANP

I am glad I met you on the edge. A Childhood. Stephen Spender. NeBP

I am glad, I think, my happy mother died. Memory of England. Edna St. Vincent Millay. NeTW

I am glad that I am not to-day. Something to Be Thankful For. Clara J. Denton. HH; TOAH

I am glad to think/ I am not bound to make the world go right. I Will Trust. Jean Ingelow. MaRV

I am going out West, partner. Po' Laz'us. *Unknown.* OuSiCo

I am going to market. Marketing. E. J. Falconer. BoTP

I am grown haggard and forlorn, from dreams. The Making of the Soul of Man. Upton Sinclair. OQP; QP-2

I Am Ham Melanite. William Millett. GoYe

I Am He That Walks [with the Tender and Growing Night]. Walt Whitman. *Fr.* Song of Myself, XXI. AtBAP; ChTr; ExPo; MCCG; TSW

I am he through whom dead painting lived again. Epitaph for Giotto, the Painter. Angelo Poliziano. LaP

I am He who howls in the night. Psychopompos. Howard Phillips Lovecraft. DaM

I am he who knows not where to set his feet. While I Sang My Song. Jacinto Fombona Pachano. AnCL

I am here. And if this is what they call the world, I don't think much of it. A Baby's Soliloquy. *Unknown.* PA

I am here for thee. To Fancy. Richard Watson Dixon. GTML

I am here, I have traversed the tomb, I behold thee. He Cometh Forth into the Day. *Unknown. Fr.* Book of the Dead. AWP; JAWP; WBP

I am here, the other elsewhere, the silence seems to live. Shadows. Paul Claudel. CAW

I am His Highness' dog at Kew. Epigram [or Engraved on the Collar of a Dog]. Pope. ALV; ChTr; ExPo; GoTP; HBV; InP; LiTB; LiTG; OnPM; OxBoLi; PCH; PIAE; SeCeV; ShBV-4; SiTL; TOP; TreFS; WhC

"I am Holy Church," she said, "and you should know me." Holy Church Speaks. William Langland. *Fr.* The Vision of Piers Plowman. PoLi

I am homesick for the mountains. The Cry of the Hillborn. Bliss Carman. NLK

I am Huxley, blond and merry. John Bowyer Buchanan Nichols. *Fr.* The Masque of Balliol. CenHV

I am immortal! I know it! I feel it! Dryad Song. Margaret Fuller. AA; WGRP

I am in love, I am in love: I have drunk a good dizzying gulp. Thunderbolt. Jules Laforgue. AnFP

I Am in Love with High Far-seeing Places. Arthur Davison Ficke. Sonnets of a Portrait Painter, XIII. LEAP; LoPo; LoPS; NP; NV; OQP; QP-2 (View from Heights.) HBMV

I am in love with life. I Shall Live On. Ralph S. Cushman. PSO

I am in love with the laughing sickness. Zizi's Lamanet. Gregory Corso. NeAP

I am in love with the sea, but I do not trust her yet. The Sea-Captain. Gerald Gould. EtS

I Am Ireland. Padraic Pearse, *tr. fr. Irish by* Lady Gregory. GTIV; OBMV

I am i'th way to study a long silence. John Webster. *Fr.* The White Devil. PoD

I am jealous: I am true. My Share of the World. Alice Furlong. HBV; OBVV

I am Juniper and I am wicked. Juniper. Eileen Duggan. CAW

I am just a mad scholar. Song of the Golden Pavilion for Liang Fen. Nalan Hsinteh. WhP

I am just on my way tomb. Oracle. E. L. Mayo. MiAP

I am just seventeen years and five months old. Pompilia. Robert Browning. *Fr.* The Ring and the Book, VII. EM-2; OAEP; PoVP; ViPo; ViPP; VLEP

I am just two and two, I am warm, I am cold. A Riddle. William Cowper. HBV

I am kindred to those people who made this land their own. Adelphos. Manuel Machado. AnSpL-2

I am less of myself and more of the sun. Flash. Hazel Hall. TBM

I am less patient than this horse. Man and Beast. Francis Meynell. MBP; MoBrPo (1942 ed.)

I am like a flag unfurled in space. Presaging. Rainer Maria Rilke. AWP; JAWP; TrJP; WBP

I am like a scrub oak tree. Scrub Oak. E. Merrill Root. MAP

I am like bound because of Abraham's knife. Microcosmos, LVI. Nigel Heseltine. NeBP

I am like thee, O Night, dark and naked. Night and the Madman. Kahlil Gibran. BAP

I am living more alone now than I did. The Last Chapter. Walter de la Mare. ChMo; MoBrPo

I Am Lonely. "George Eliot." *Fr.* The Spanish Gypsy. GN; HBV

I am looking rather seedy now while holding down my claim. The Little Old Sod Shanty. *Unknown.* ABS; AS; CoSo; CSF; IHA

I am lying in a white-lined coat while the spring approaches. Spring Rain. Li Shang-yin. ChLP

I am lying in thy tomb, love. Lament. Roden Noel. MOAH; VA

"I am made to sow the thistle for wheat, the nettle for a nourishing dainty." The Price of Experience. Blake. *Fr.* Vala; or, The Four Zoas. EnRP; RO

I am making songs for you. A God for You. Marion Strobel. NP

I am mature, a man child. Chicago. Sherwood Anderson. NP

I am minded to sing of bodies to new forms changing. The Creation of the World. Ovid. *Fr.* Metamorphoses. LaP

"I am Miss Catherine's book" (the album speaks). The Pen and the Album. Thackeray. VA

I Am Monarch of All I Survey. William Cowper. *See* Verses Supposed to Be Written by Alexander Selkirk . . .

I am more tall today than ever before. The Love-Song. Bernice Lesbia Kenyon. AV

I am my ancient self. The Pilgrim. Richard Wightman. WGRP

I Am My Beloved's. The Song of Solomon, VII: 11–14, Bible, O.T. TrJP

I Am My Beloved's, and His Desire Is towards Me. Francis Quarles. *See* Like to the Arctic Needle.

I am my mammie's ae bairn. I'm O'er [or Owre] Young to Marry Yet. Burns. EBSV; LO; LoPS; ViBoPo

I am naked, and naked Lucia holds me in her arms. Lucia. Francesco Franchini. LaP

I am no brazen face to hale the Lord. Rabbi Yom-Tob of Mayence Petitions His God. A. M. Klein. TrJP

I am no gentleman, not I! The Working Man's Song. John Stuart Blackie. VA

I am no poet who can set. Patric Dickinson. LO

I Am No Subject unto Fate. *Unknown.* OBS

I am not a painter, I am a poet. Why I Am Not a Painter. Frank O'Hara. NeAP

I am not afraid in April. White Fear. Winifred Welles. BAP; HBMV; MW; TBM

"I am not as these are," the poet saith. Not as These. Dante Gabriel Rossetti. The House of Life, LXXV. BPN; PoVP; ViPo

I am not bred and born New Englander. Late Comer. Fanny de Groot Hastings. GoYe

I am not concern'd to know. True Riches. Isaac Watts. OBEC

I am not moved, my God, to love Thee so. To Christ Crucified. *Unknown, tr. by* James Young Gibson. AnSpL-1

I am not moved to love thee, my Lord God. To Christ Crucified. *Unknown, tr. by* Samuel Beckett. AnMP

I am not moved to love Thee, O my Lord. To Christ Crucified. *Unknown, tr. by* Thomas Walsh. CAW; OnPM

I am not of the saints, O Lord, to wear. Psalm IX. A. M. Klein. QS

I am not of those fierce, wild wills. My Political Faith. George Frederick Cameron. BoCaPo; PeCV

I am not of those miserable males. Modern Love, XX. George Meredith. EmBrPo; EnLit; ViPo

I am not old, but old enough. Interlude. Scudder Middleton. BAP; NV; SBMV

I am not one who much or oft delight. Personal Talk. Wordsworth. BEL; BPN; EM-2; EmBrPo; EnRP; EPN; EPP; ERP; GEPC; InPo; MyFE; PeBoSo

I am not poor, but I am proud. Thought. Emerson. AmPP (3d ed.); CoBA; IAP; MOAP

I am not resigned to the shutting away of loving hearts. Dirge without Music. Edna St. Vincent Millay. AnNE; BLV; BoLiVe; GTBS-W; LiTA; LiTG; LO; NePA; NP; PG; TrGrPo

I am not sorry for my soul. Longing. Sara Teasdale. ChMo; CMP

I am not strong till Thou hast clasped my hand. Freedom. *Unknown.* PGD

I am not sure that earth is round. Certainty Enough. Amelia Josephine Burr. HBMV

I am not two and twenty, yet aweary of the sun. Plaything. Asclepiades. GrR

I am not what I was yesterday. The Butterfly. Alice Archer James. AA

I am not what my lips explain. Utterance. Donald Davidson. TBM

I am not wholly yours, for I can face. The Haunted Heart. Jessie B. Rittenhouse. AV

I am not yet born; O hear me. Prayer before Birth. Louis MacNeice. LiTB; OAEP (2d ed.)
I Am Not Yours. Sara Teasdale. ChMo; CMP
I am nothing, so for me. First Cause. Joan Lamburn. DiM
I am numb from world-pain. A Little Swirl of Vers Libre. Thomas R. Ybarra. BOHV
I Am of Ireland. *Unknown. See* Irish Dancer, The.
"I Am of Ireland." W. B. Yeats. LiTB; NAMP; OnYI
I am of little worth and poor, apart. Song of Loneliness. Judah Halevi. TrJP
I am of old and young, of the foolish as much as the wise. Walt Whitman. Song of Myself, XVI. CoBA
I am of Shropshire, my shins be sharp. A Shropshire Lad. *Unknown.* ChTr
I am of value to men, variously am found. *Unknown. Fr.* Riddles. EnLit
I am off down the road. Goblin Feet. J. R. R. Tolkien. FaPON; PoMS
I am old and blind! Milton's Prayer. Elizabeth Lloyd Howell. AA; MaRV; WGRP
I am old Euphron, with no broad array. The Poor Farmer's Offering. Apollonides. OxBG
I am old, sick, and lonely. Verses. Su T'ung-po. WhP
I am older than I was in winters and in lore. *Unknown. Fr.* Poema Morale. EPP
I am one of a band of outlaws [*or* highwaymen], Cole Younger is my name. Cole Younger. *Unknown.* BeLS; CSF
I am one of the wind's stories. Man and His Makers. Muriel Stuart. NP
I am out on the wind. Changeling. Leah Bodine Drake. DaM; PoMS
I am part of the seas and stars. Kinship. Edward H. S. Terry. MaRV; OQP; QP-2
I Am Partly Moon. Vicente Huidobro, *tr. fr. Spanish by* Joseph Staples. AnCL; LiTW
I am persuaded now; there is no victory. Portrait of Several Selves. Charles Davies. MoWP
I am poor and old and blind. Belisarius. Longfellow. BAV; PoEL-5; TBM
I am poor brother Lippo, by your leave! Fra Lippo Lippi. Robert Browning. BEL; BoLiVe; BPN; EM-2; EmBrPo; EnL; EnLi-2; EnLit; EPN; EPP; GEPC; OAEP; OtMeF; PoVP; ReaPo; TCEP; TwCrTr; ViBoPo; ViPo; ViPP; VLEP
I am put high over all others in the city today. Killers. Carl Sandburg. MoVE
I am Queen Anne, of whom 'tis said. Queen Anne. *Unknown.* ChTr
I am quite sure He thinks that I am God. Bishop Doane on His Dog "Cluny." William Croswell Doane, *wr. at. to* George Washington Doane. AlBD; BBV (1951 ed.); BLPA; FaBoBe; NeHB
I Am Raftery [*or* Rafterty]. Anthony Raftery, *tr. fr. Modern Irish by* Douglas Hyde. AnIV; AWP; GTIV; JAWP; LiTW; OnYI (*incl. tr. by* James Stephens); SeCePo; WBP; AnIL, *tr. by* James Stephens
I am remembering in the long ago. *Unknown. Fr.* The Dream of the Rood. ACP
I am reproached for drinking. The Old Toper. Ibn Sa'id of Alcala la Real. MooP
I am resolved, when April comes once more. Resolutions for April. Anne Blackwell Payne. NoCaPo
I am returned, my fair, but see. The Retreat. Charles Cotton. SeCL
I am riding on a limited express, one of the crack trains of the nation. Limited. Carl Sandburg. AmP; LoGBV; MAP; MoAB; MoAmPo; NeMA; OxBA
I am riding, riding, riding, on the hard dirt road. Cadences. Samuel T. Clover. POT; PoTo
I am rooted in the wall. Snapdragon. Cardinal Newman. GoBC
I Am Rose. Gertrude Stein. LiTM; NePA; SiTL; TrJP
I am round and very small. Pablo. Grace Hazard Conkling. GaP
I am sailing to the leeward. In the Shadows. E. Pauline Johnson. CPG
I am Saint John on Patmos of my heart. Holy Poems, I. George Barker. MoPo
I am Shmuel-Itse Chimneysweep. The Jew. Moyshe Kulbak. *Fr.* The Secret Saint. OnCuPl
I am sick of war, said the captain. Said the Captain. Alan Pryce Jones. MoWP
I am sicke of this false world, and will love nought. Shakespeare. *Fr.* Timon of Athens, IV, iii. NBE
I am singing to you. Killers. Carl Sandburg. NP
I am sitting alone by a fire. Our Departed Comrades. J. Marion Shirer. BlC
I am sitting here. The Poor Girl's Meditation, *tr. by* Padraic Colum. GTIV; OBMV
I am six years old. The New George Washington. *Unknown.* WOAH
I am sleepless in the glow and shadow of the lamplight. Visiting Tsan, Abbot of Ta-yun. Tu Fu. OnPC
I am sleepy, I'm tired, and I'm hungry and dry. Qu'avec vous, oui, belle blonde. *Unknown.* OuSiCo
I am so empty and so incomplete. Fulfilment. Elsa Barker. *Fr.* The Spirit and the Bride. HBMV
I Am So Glad. E. E. Cummings. ChMo
I am so glad of the colors of things. Colors. Phoebe Crosby Allnut. VOD
I am so little that the gods go by. The Common Lot. Lizette Woodworth Reese. NP
I am so lost. Narihira, *tr. fr. Japanese by* Kenneth Rexroth. LiTW
I am so old a king that I remember. The Old King. John Heath-Stubbs. NePoEA
I am so out of love through poverty. Sonnet: Of Why He Would Be a Scullion. Cecco Angiolieri da Siena. AWP
I am so passing rich in poverty. Sonnet: He Jests concerning His Poverty. Bartolomeo di Sant' Angelo. AWP
I am so sure that your presence. Pedro Salinas, *tr. fr. Spanish by* Eleanor L. Turnbull. CoSP
I am so tired and weary. Supplication. Joseph Seamon Cotter, Jr. BANP; CDC; PoNe
I am sorry, my little cat, I am sorry. War Cat. Dorothy L. Sayers. PoC
I am standing on the threshold of eternity at last. On the Threshold. *Unknown.* BLPA
I Am Still Rich. Thomas Curtis Clark. PoToHe
I am supported against your breast. Hymn to Sorrow. Luis Cernuda. CoSP
I am sure this Jesus will not do. Epilogue. Blake. *Fr.* The Everlasting Gospel. OBRV
I am telling you a number of half-conditioned ideas. Sunday Evening. Barbara Guest. NeAP
I am that Adam who, with snake for guest. The Exile. Walter de la Mare. POTE
I am that king, that olden king. Royalty. Stuart Merrill. TrFP
I am that man who with a luminous look. Brevities. Siegfried Sassoon. MoPW
I am that serpent-haunted cave. The Pythoness. Kathleen Raine. FaBoMo; ViBoPo (1958 ed.)
I am that which began. Hertha. Swinburne. BEL; BMEP; BPN; EmBrPo; EnLi-2; EPN; HBVY; MBP; MW; OAEP; OBEV (1st ed.); PIAE; POTT; PoVP; REAL; TOP; VA; ViP; ViPo; ViPP; VLEP
I am that witness through whom the whole. Spiritual Explorations, VI. Stephen Spender. PoLFOT
I am that woman who would wait the dawn. Could You Not Watch with Me One Little Hour? Sara Bard Field. MuM
I Am the Autumn. Itzig Manger, *tr. fr. Yiddish by* Joseph Leftwich. TrJP
I am the baby. The Baby. Mary Raymond Shipman Andrews. DDA
I Am the Blood. Isaac Rosenberg. MoBrPo
I Am the Bread of Life. St. John VI: 35-40, Bible, *N.T.* TreFS
I am the breath of Tethra, voice of Tethra. The Sword of Tethra. William Larminie. *Fr.* Moytura. TIP
I am the bride of Christ, she said. A Sister. "A. Page." PraNu
I am the broken arrow. Lucifer Sings in Secret. Elinor Wylie. MM
I am the captain of my soul. An Awful Responsibility. Keith Preston. WhC
I Am the Cat. Leila Usher. BLPA
I am the cat of cats. I am. The Cat of Cats [*or* The Kitten Speaks *or* Kitty: What She Thinks of Herself]. William Brighty Rands. *Fr.* The White Princess. CBPC; CIV; MoShBr; RIS
I am the chaunt-rann of a Singer. The Poet. Padraic Fiacc. NeIP
I am the Child. The Child's Appeal. Mamie Gene Cole. MaRV; OQP; QP-2
I am the child by the Yangtse running. Child of the World. Edna L. S. Barker. GoYe
I Am the Cross. William L. Stidger. ChIP
I Am the Cry. Muriel Strode. BAP
I am the dancer of the wood. The Spirit of the Birch. Arthur Ketchum. *Fr.* Legends for Trees. MPB; MW; OHIP; SP
I am the dark cavalier; I am the last lover. The Dark Cavalier. Margaret Widdemer. HBMV; NV; PFY; SBMV
I am the dark, the widowed, the disconsolate. El Desdichado. Gérard de Nerval. AnFP
I am the daughter of Earth and Water. Shelley. *Fr.* The Cloud. PoF
I am the Dean of Christ Church, Sir. Cecil Arthur Spring-Rice. *Fr.* The Masque of Balliol. CenHV
I am the death who am come to you. The Address of Death to Tomas de Roiste. *Unknown.* TIP
I am the dog world's best detective. The Bloodhound Speaks. Edward Anthony. AlBD; GoTP
I Am the Door. Richard Crashaw. OAEP

I Am the Door. *Unknown.* BLP; OQP; QP-1
I am the Empire at the end of its decadence. Apathy. Paul Verlaine. AnFP
I am the family face. Heredity. Thomas Hardy. EPP; ImOP; MoPW
I am the farmer, stripped of love. The Hill Farmer Speaks. R. S. Thomas. HaMV
I am the first, of all the rancorous men. The Tree at Post 4. Kenneth Mackenzie. MoAuPo
I Am the Flag. Lawrence M. Jones. PGD; PSO
I am the flower of the field. Canticle of Canticles (The Song of Solomon), Bible, *O.T.* (*Douay vers.*). ISi
I am the flute of Daphnis. On this wall. The Flute of Daphnis. Edward Cracroft Lefroy. Echoes from Theocritus, XXIII. AWP; ES; OBVV
I am the gay Nasturtium. The Nasturtiums. *Unknown.* GFA
I am the ghost of Shadwell Stair. Shadwell Stair. Wilfred Owen. FaBoTw; PoD
I Am the Gilly of Christ. Joseph Campbell. AnIL; LBBV; OnYI
(Gilly of Christ.) GTIV
I am the God Thor. The Challenge of Thor. Longfellow. *Fr.* Tales of a Wayside Inn: The Saga of King Olaf. AmPP (4th ed.)
I am the great Professor Jowett. *Unknown.* FiBHP
I am the house! Ford Madox Ford. *Fr.* A House. MBP; MoBrPo (1942 ed.)
I am the key that parts the gates of Fame. Death. Florence Earle Coates. HBV; OQP; QP-1
I am the land of their fathers. The Recall. Kipling. POTE; PoVP
I Am the Last. Edward Shillito. OQP; QP-1
(One Love.) MaRV
I am the last village-poet. Sergei Yesenin, *tr. fr. Russian by* C. M. Bowra. BoRS
I am the leaf. Spiritus Sanctus. Sara Jackson. DiM
I am the learned ass who stumps professors. The Learned Ass. Francis Jammes. TrFP
I am the little ass of Christ. The Ass Speaks. Katharine Tynan. MaRV
I am the little New Year, ho, ho! The New Year. *Unknown.* BoTP
I am the Lord of Light, the self-begotten youth. He Maketh Himself One with the God Ra. *Unknown.* *Fr.* Book of the Dead. AWP
I am the Lord thy God. The Ten Commandments. Exodus, Bible, *O.T.* OHFP; WBLP
I am the luring Vivien. Woman. Zora Cross. BoAu
I am the lute. If you wish to write. The Lute. Rainer Maria Rilke. OnPM
I am the man, I suffer'd, I was there. Come Said the Muse. Walt Whitman. *Fr. various poems.* LiA
I am the man in the middle, the rare achievement. The Sandwich Man. Louis Johnson. AnNZ
I am the man that hath seen affliction. Affliction. Lamentations, Bible, *O.T.* TrJP
I am the mashed fireman with breast-bone broken. Dying Heroes [*or* The Dying Fireman]. Walt Whitman. *Fr.* Song of Myself, XXXIII. BHV; EV-5; LH
I am the mother of fair love. Ecclesiasticus, Apocrypha, Bible (*Douay vers.*). ISi
I Am the Mountainy Singer. Joseph Campbell. AnIL; BMEP; EPP; GoBC; HBMV; JKCP; MBP; MCCG; MoBrPo
I am the mown grass, dying at your feet. Moritura. Margaret Gilman Davidson. AA
I Am the New Year. *Unknown.* PSO
I am the New Year, and I come to you pure and unstained. The New Year. J. D. Templeton. OQP; PGD; PSO; QP-1
I am the New Year, I am the one unspoiled bit. I Am the New Year. *Unknown.* PSO
I am the nor'west air nosing among the pines. Time. Allen Curnow. AnNZ
I am the old woman of Beare. The Old Woman of Beare. *Unknown.* AnIL
I am the one who loved her as my life. The Legend of Qu'Apelle Valley. Emily Pauline Johnson. UnW
I Am the Only Being. Emily Brontë. VLEP
Sels.
"I am the only being whose doom." ViBoPo
"Where wilt thou go my harassed heart?" LO
I am the other—I who come. The Other. "Ethna Carbery." AV
I am the past and the present, and I bear. *Unknown.* *Fr.* Book of the Dead. LiTW
I Am the People, the Mob. Carl Sandburg. AmPP; CoV; OxBA
I am the Poet Davies, William. W. H. Davies. MoPW
I am the poet of the body and I am the poet of the soul. Walt Whitman. Song of Myself, XXI. BAV; CoBA; CoV; RiBV; SeCeV; TrGrPo
I am the prince in the field. He Maketh Himself One with Osiris. *Unknown.* *Fr.* Book of the Dead. AWP
I am the pure lotus. He Is like the Lotus. *Unknown.* *Fr.* Book of the Dead. AWP; JAWP; WBP
I am the pure, the true of word, triumphant. He Defendeth His Heart against the Destroyer. *Unknown.* *Fr.* Book of the Dead. AWP
I am the pure traveler. He Entereth the House of the Goddess Hathor. *Unknown.* *Fr.* Book of the Dead. AWP
I am the queen Herodias. Swinburne. *Fr.* The Masque of Queen Bersabe. AtBAP
I am the Rabbi Ben Israel. The Village School. Longfellow. *Fr.* Christus; a Mystery. APW
I am the reality of things that seem. Poetry. Ella Heath. HBV; WGRP
I Am the Reaper. W. E. Henley. OQP; QP-1
"I Am the Resurrection and the Life," Saith the Lord! Robert Stephen Hawker. GoBC
I am the river, I have been immense. Lifetime. Winifred Welles. VOD
I am the rooftree and the keel. Tapestry Trees. William Morris. FaPON; MPB; OHIP
I Am the Rose of Sharon. Song of Solomon, Bible, *O.T.* *See* Love Idyll, A.
I Am the Rose of Sharon. Catherine Winkworth. BePJ
I am the serpent, fat with years. He Is like the Serpent Saka. *Unknown.* *Fr.* Book of the Dead. AWP
I am the singer who, of late, put by. Portico. Rubén Darío. CAW
I am the sister of him. Little. Dorothy Aldis. FaPON; SUS; TiPo
I am the small gray memory-mother. The Quest. Agnes Lee. VOD
I am the sombre wake. I Am the Wake. Iwan Goll. OnPM
I am the son of the mountain. Son of the Mountain. Eifion Wyn. PrWP
I am the spirit astir. Autochthon. Sir Charles G. D. Roberts. CaP; OCL; SN; VA
I am the spirit of the morning sea. Ode. Richard Watson Gilder. AA; OBAV
I am the spouse. She took her necklace off. It Must Be Abstract. Wallace Stevens. OnAP
I am the stage, impassive, mute and cold. Nature. Alfred de Vigny. AWP; JAWP; WBP
I am the still rain falling. Moods. Sara Teasdale. SBMV
I am the strong one, and I have power. Johan Olof Wallin. *Fr.* The Angel of Death. AnSL
I am the sun's remembrancer, the boy. The Dandelion. Richard Church. AlDL
I am the teacher of athletes. Walt Whitman. Song of Myself, XLVII. CoBA; PreP
I am the tender voice calling "Away." Dana. "Æ." TIP
I am the tomb of Crethon; here you read. The Tomb of Crethon. Leonidas of Tarentum. AWP; JAWP; WBP
I am the torch, she saith, and what to me. Modern Beauty. Arthur Symons. EnLit; HBV; MBP; MoBrPo; POTT; PoVP
I am the true vine, and my Father is the husbandman. The True Vine. St. John, Bible, *N.T.* WoL
I am the trumpet blown by time. The Trumpet. Ilya Ehrenburg. BoRS; TrJP
I am the Turquoise Woman's son. The War God's Horse Song. *Unknown.* LiTA; LoGBV
I am the unnoticed, the unnoticeable man. The Man in the Bowler Hat. A. S. J. Tessimond. HaMV; POTE
I am the very model of a modern college president. The Very Model of a Modern College President, *parody.* Harold A. Larrabee. WhC
I am the very model [*or* pattern] of a modern Major General. The Modern Major-General [*or* Major-General's Song]. W. S. Gilbert. *Fr.* The Pirates of Penzance. CoBE; InMe; OnPP; PCD; SoV
I am the Virgin; from this granite ledge. The Wayside Virgin. Langdon Elwyn Mitchell. AA; OBAV; PoTo
I am the voice of mere opinion. Rhaiadr. Constance Davies. MoWP
I am the voice of the uplands ringing from hill to hill. The Peace Call. Edgar Lloyd Hampton. PEDC
I Am the Wake. Iwan Goll, *tr. fr. French by* Claire Goll. OnPM
"I Am the Way." Alice Meynell. ACP; CAW; GoBC; JKCP; LBBV; MaRV; OBMV; OQP; POTT; PoVP; QP-1
I Am the Wind. Zoë Akins. AV; BAP; HBV; NP; TOP
I am the Wind. The Wind. Victor Starbuck. NoCaPo
I am the wind that wavers. I Am the Wind. Zoë Akins. AV; BAP; HBV; NP; TOP
I am the wind which breathes upon the sea. The Mystery. *At. to* Amergin. OnYI; OxBI
I am the worm. Butterfly. Mary White Slater. PSO
I am thine harp between thine hands, O mother! Swinburne. *Fr.* Mater Triumphalis. BMEP; BPN

I am thinking tonight in sadness. A Christmas of Long Ago. Morton Bryan Wharton. BIG
I am thinking tonight of the days that are gone. The Plain Golden Band. *At. to* Joe Scott. ShS
I am this fountain's god. The River God. John Fletcher. *Fr.* The Faithful Shepherdess, III, i. TrGrPo
I am thy fathers spirit. Shakespeare. *Fr.* Hamlet, I, v. AtBAP
I am thy fugitive, thy votary. To the Lord Love. "Michael Field." OBMV
I am Thy grass, O Lord! Trust. Lizette Woodworth Reese. AA; OBAV
"I am thy soul, Nikoptis. I have watched." The Tomb at [*or* of] Akr Çaar. Ezra Pound. APA; CoAnAm; TwAmPo
I am tired of city sounds. Discovery. Catherine Parmenter. OQP; QP-2
I am tired of cursing the Bishop. Crazy Jane on the Mountain. W. B. Yeats. AtBAP
I am tired of echoes in the old house. It Is Time to Build. Elias Lieberman. MaRV
I am tired of planning and toiling. The Cry of the [*or* a] Dreamer. John Boyle O'Reilly. BLPA; NeHB; NLK; OnYI; TreFS
I Am Tired of the Wind. Gordon Bottomley. POTE
"I am tired of this barn!" said the colt. The Barn. Elizabeth J. Coatsworth. AnNE; ChBR; GoTP; UTS
I am tired of work; I am tired of building up somebody else's civilization. Tired. Fenton Johnson. BANP; PoNe
I am to follow her. There is much grace. Modern Love, XLII. George Meredith. ViBoPo; ViPo
I am told, sir, you're keeping an eye on your wife. The Careful Husband. *Unknown, tr. by* the Earl of Longford. OnYI; OxBI
I am too near, too clear a thing for you. A Flower of Mullein. Lizette Woodworth Reese. MAP; MoAmPo; MOAP; NeMA
I am two fools [*or* fooles], I know. The Triple Fool. John Donne. CenL; CoBE; ElSeCe; EPS (1942 ed.); OAEP; Po
I am unable, yonder beggar cries. A Lame Beggar. John Donne. TuPP
I Am Undone. Virginia Moore. TBM
I am undone: there is no living, none. Love's Memory. Shakespeare. *Fr.* All's Well That Ends Well, I, i. LPS-1
I am unhappy. Prince Motoyoshi, *tr. fr. Japanese by* Kenneth Rexroth. OnPJ
I am valued by men, fetched from afar. Honey-Mead. *Unknown. Fr.* Riddles. AnOE
I Am Waitin' on the Levee, *with music. Unknown.* StDa
I am waiting for the dawning. Waiting for the Dawning. *Unknown.* BLRP
I am War. The upturned eyeballs of piled dead men greet my eye. War. Sam Walter Foss. MDAH
I am watching for the early buds to wake. First Spring Flowers. Mary Woolsey Howland. LPS-1
I am wearied with insatiable longing. Coquette. Keith Stuart. NLK
I Am Weary of Being Bitter. Arthur Davison Ficke. NLK (1947 ed.); NP
I am weary of disbelieving: why should I wound my love. The Old Sceptic. Alfred Noyes. QS
I am weary of lying within the chase. Ballade de Marguerite. *Unknown.* AWP; JAWP; WBP
I am weary of the frequent blob. A Cricket Cri du Coeur. *Unknown.* ShGoBo
I am weary of the garden. Said the Rose. George H. Miles. BLPA
I am weary of waiting in sorrow. I Cannot Wait Longer. Jay Paul. CAG
I am what is around me. Theory. Wallace Stevens. CoV
I Am What You Make Me. Franklin K. Lane. PGD
I am willowy boughs. I Am. Hilda Conkling. FaPON; NP; TiPo
"I Am with Thee." Ernest Bourner Allen. BLRP
I Am with You Alway. Edwin Henry Nevin. BePJ
I am within as white as snow. Riddle. *Unknown.* ChTr
I am without a single doubt. The Perfect Child. Molly Michaels. RIS
I am worn out with dreams. Men Improve with the Years. W. B. Yeats. CoEV
I am writing near the lamp. It's fine weather. Pleasant stillness. Promenades and Interiors. François Coppée. CAW
I Am Writing You from a Distant Land. Henri Michaux, *tr. fr. French by* Wallace Fowlie. MiCF
I am yesterday. I am gone from you forever. Yesterday. Frank Crane. OQP; QP-1
I am yesterday, today and to-morrow. He Walketh by Day. *Unknown. Fr.* Book of the Dead. AWP; JAWP; WBP
I am: yet what I am none [*or* who] cares or knows. Written in Northampton County Asylum [*or* I Am]. John Clare. CaAE; CBE; EnRP; EV-4; FaBoEn; GTBS-W; GTSE; GTSL; InvP; LiTB; OBEV; OBVV; PG; PoE; PoEL-4; TrGrPo; TriL; ViBoPo; WHA
I Am Young. George Frederick Cameron. CPG
I Am Your Brook. Iwan Goll, *tr. fr. French by* Claire Goll. OnPM
I am your colony where you have dispatched. Child to Parents. Viola Meynell. PtOT
I am your conscience, I the voice that pierces. Poem for This Age. Stefan George. AnGP
I Am Your Loaf, Lord. David Ross. GoYe
I Am Your Wife. *Unknown.* PoToHe (new ed.)
I, an old man. Girl and Butterfly. Edith Sitwell. MoPW
I, an old woman in the light of the sun. An Old Woman. Edith Sitwell. CoBMV; MoPo
I, an old woman whose heart is like the Sun. Harvest. Edith Sitwell. OAEP (2d ed.)
I, an unwedded wandering dame. Epitaph [*or* Four Epitaphs]. Sylvia Townsend Warner. MBP; MoBrPo; NeMA
I and my cousin Wildair met. Praise-God Barebones. Ellen Mackay Hutchinson Cortissoz. AA
I and my sisters three. Victorian Song. John Farrar. GoYe
I and my white Pangur. The Monk and His Pet Cat. *Unknown, tr. by* W. Stokes, J. Strachan, *and* K. Meyer. CH; OnYI
I and Pangur Bán my cat. Pangur Bán [*or* The White Cat and the Student]. *Unknown, tr. by* Robin Flower. AnIL; FaBoCh; LoGBV; LyMA; OnYI; OxBI; PoC; RIS
I and You. Nikolai Gumilev, *tr. fr. Russian by* V. de S. Pinto. BoR
I, Angelo, obese, black-garmented. Angelo Orders His Dinner. Bayard Taylor. BOHV; PA
I Announce the Kingdom of the Star. Jacinto Fombona Pachano, *tr. fr. Spanish by* H. R. Hays. TwSpPo
I appeal to you, therefore, brothers. A Living Sacrifice. Romans, Bible, *N.T.* GrCo-1
I Arise from Dreams of Thee. Shelley. *See* Indian Serenade, The.
I arise in the east in all my immensity. The Lord of the East. Chu Yuan. *Fr.* The Nine Songs. LiTW; WhP
I arise to-day. The Deer's Cry [*or* St. Patrick's Breastplate]. *At. to* St. Patrick. AnIL; AnIV; CAW; OnYI; WGRP; WHL
I arose early, O my true love! Ruth Pitter. *Fr.* Early Rising. AIDL
I arose swiftly that night, for I heard a knock at my door. The Future. James Oppenheim. TrJP
I, as all the parish knows. The Satirist. Swift. *Fr.* Epistle to a Lady. BeR
I ask good things that I detest. Prayer. Robert Louis Stevenson. TrPWD
I ask, in truth, what right was given to me. Words. Sir Thomas Herbert Parry-Williams. PrWP
I ask my love to take a walk. The Old Shawnee. *Unknown.* ABS
I ask myself forever, "Who am I?" The Stranger. Amanda Benjamin Hall. MuM
I ask no heaven till earth be Thine. Here Am I. *Unknown.* PraP
I ask no kind return of [*or* in] love. Prayer for Indifference. Fanny Greville. DiM; LO; OBEC; OBEV
I ask no other vengeance, Love, from you. Rispetto. Angelo Poliziano. LyPI
I ask not Gyges' riches. Vive Hodie. *Unknown. Fr.* Anacreontea. GrPE
I ask not how thy suffering came. Fraternity. Anne Reeve Aldrich. AA
I ask not that my bed of death. A Wish. Matthew Arnold. BPN; EmBrPo; EPN; HBV; PoVP; VLEP
I ask thee, whence those ashes were. A Question. *Unknown.* SeCL
I ask, who will buy a poem? Who Will Buy a Poem? Mahon O'Heffernan. AnIL
I ask you, my friend. Success. Wang Chi. PoHN; WoL
I ask you this. Prayer. Langston Hughes. CDC
I Asked a Thief. Blake. ExPo; SeCeV
(Angel, The.) LiTB; LiTG; SiTL
("I asked a thief to steal me a peach.") ViBoPo
I asked an aged man, with hoary hairs. What Is Time? William Marsden. BCEP; LPS-3
I asked for bread; God gave a stone instead. Prayer. *Unknown.* OQP; QP-1
I asked for bread! Life led me to a plain. The Quest. Chester B. Emerson. OQP; QP-1
I asked for grace to lift me high. God's Ways. *Unknown.* MaRV
I asked for just a crumb of bread. More than We Ask. Faith Wells. BLRP
I Asked for Peace. Digby Mackworth Dolben. OxBoCh
(Requests.) MaRV; TrPWD

I asked if I got sick and died, would you. A Question. J. M. Synge. GTIV; MBP; MoBrPo; OBMV; OBVV; OxBI
I Asked My Fair, One Happy Day. Gotthold Ephraim Lessing, *tr. fr. German by* Samuel Taylor Coleridge. HBV
I asked my love to take a walk. On the Banks of the Old Pedee. *Unknown.* ABS
I Asked My Mother. *Unknown.* MoShBr
("I asked my mother for fifty [*or* fifteen] cents.") FaFP; GoTP; SiTL; TiPo
(Nursery Rhymes.) OxBoLi
I asked my soul where springs the ill-omened seed. Forgetfulness. Sosei. OnPM
I asked myself what this great God might be. The Search for God. Thomas Heywood. *Fr.* Hierarchie of the Blessed Angels. QS
I asked no other thing. Emily Dickinson. MaPo; OxBA
I asked of Echo, t' other day. Echo. John Godfrey Saxe. AnNE; BOHV; LPS-3; PTA-1; PTA-2
I asked of Night, that she would take me. Morning Dreams. Mary Coleridge. AlDL
I asked philosophy how I should. Hermatic Poems. Elias Ashmole. LO
I asked professors who teach the meaning of life. Happiness. Carl Sandburg. OxBA; WoL
I asked the heaven of stars. Night Song at Amalfi. Sara Teasdale. ChMo; CMP; MAP; MoAmPo; NeMA; SBMV
I asked the Master for a motto sweet. God's Will. Charles E. Guthrie. BLRP
I asked the New Year for some message sweet. The Message of the New Year. *Unknown.* OQP; QP-1
I asked the New Year, "What am I to do." Questioning. Grace Noll Crowell. DD
I asked the wind who painted the clouds. Quester. Elizabeth Griswold King. CAG
I ate a yellow violet. Interview. Lila Terry. DDA
I ate at Ostendorff's, and saw a dame. Traümerei at Ostendorff's. "William Laird." HBMV
I ate my fill and drank my fill and many a man cursed I. A Mock Epitaph. Simonides. GrR
I ate my fill of army bread. The Air Sentry. Patrick Barrington. CenHV
I attended school and I liked the place. Values in Use. Marianne Moore. NePoAm-2
I await God greedily. . . . Now I am accursed. Ill Will. Arthur Rimbaud. AnFP
I awoke in the Midsummer not to call night. Moonrise. Gerard Manley Hopkins. MBP; MoAB; MoBrPo; SeCePo
I awoke with a start. Dreams. Chi Lan Yün. PoHN
I axed de chillun fer de joke. Spring. John Charles McNeill. NoCaPo
I bade my Lady think what she might mean. Modern Love, XL. George Meredith. ViPo
I bargained with Life for a penny. My Wage. Jessie Belle Rittenhouse. BLP; BLPA; NeHB; PC; PoMa; PoToHe (new ed.)
I bear an unseen burden constantly. The Burden of Love. "Owen Innsley." AA
I bear the lyre, and marry voice and song. Ideal Passion, V. George Edward Woodberry. MOAP
I bear the scourge of just Rhamnusia. Proemium in Librum Primum. John Marston. *Fr.* The Scourge of Villainy. ReIE
I Beat the Drum. Jan Greshoff, *tr. fr. Dutch by* A. J. Barnouw. PoFr
I Been a Bad, Bad Girl, *with music.* *Unknown.* OuSiCo
I been 'buked an' I been scorned. Hell and Heaven. *Unknown.* SiTL
I beg of you calm souls—whose wondering pity. Pray for Me! Adelaide Anne Procter. PraP
I beg the pardon of these flowers. With Lilacs. Charles Henry Crandall. AA
I beg you, Chung Tzu. Chung Tzu. *Unknown.* WhP
I beg you come to-night and dine. The Menu. Thomas Bailey Aldrich. HBV
I begin through the grass once again to be bound to the Lord. Reconciliation. "Æ." ChMo; CMP; LBBV; OBMV; OxBI; PoVP
I beheld her, on a day. How He Saw Her. Ben Jonson. *Fr.* A Celebration of Charis. AtBAP; OAEP; SeCV-1
I Beheld My Love This Morning. Sayat Nova, *tr. fr. Armenian by* Zabelle C. Boyajian. ArmLP
I, Being Born a Woman. Edna St. Vincent Millay. ALV
I, being Protestant, can never bow. To Mary, Mother of Christ. Una W. Harsen. ChIP
I Believe. J. B. Lawrence. BLRP
I Believe. Saul Tchernichowsky, *tr. fr. Hebrew by* Reginald V. Feldman. TrJP
(Credo, *tr. by* Maurice Samuel.) LiTW
I believe/ In the whispering of the peacock-plumaged sea. Credo. Vera Wheatley. NLK
I believe a leaf of grass is no less than the journey-work of the stars. Miracles [*or* The Microcosm]. Walt Whitman. Song of Myself, XXXI. AmPP; AnFE; CBOV; CoAnAm; CoBA; CoV; LiTA; MAP; MaRV; MoAmPo; NeMA; OQP; OxBA; PG (1955 ed.); PoeMoYo; QP-2; SeCeV; SN; TiPo; TrGrPo; YT
I believe if I should die. Creed. Mary Ashley Townsend. BLPA; FaBoBe; NeHB
I believe in human kindness. A Creed. Norman Macleod. WGRP
I believe in the brook as it wanders. Nature's Creed. *Unknown.* MaRV; OHIP
I believe in the God of my garden, the God of the trees. A Creed in a Garden. Newman Flower. MaRV
I believe in the omnipotent idea which bestows. Thirsting Amphora. Rafael Heliodoro Valle. AnCL
I believe in Trudeau. A Compressionist's Creed. Norman Bethune. PoP
I believe in you my soul, the other I am must not abase itself to you. Song of Myself, V. Walt Whitman. CoV
I believe it! 'Tis thou, God, that givest, 'tis I who receive. Robert Browning. *Fr.* Saul. ChIP; StJW
"I believe" sang the guns and the squares. Viktor Khlebnikov, *tr. fr. Russian by* C. M. Bowra. BoRS
I believe. That is to say. I Believe. J. B. Lawrence. BLRP
I Believe Thy Precious Blood. John Wesley. BePJ
I belong to the tide. Deep Peace. Josephine Royle. BAP
"I belt the morn with ribboned mist." Under Arcturus. Madison Cawein. LBMV
I bend above the moving stream. Solitude and the Lily. Richard Henry Horne. OBVV; VA
I Bended unto Me. Thomas Edward Brown. BLV; MBP; PoVP
I bent in the deep of night. The Pedigree. Thomas Hardy. CoBMV
I bent my ears to a lily's cup. Mother Love. Janie Alford. PGD; PSO
I bent to lift a comrade from the water. Ecce Homo. John Ackerson. BoFr; MaRV
I bent unto the ground. The Voice of God. James Stephens. WGRP
I bequeath my turtle dove. *Unknown.* EG
I Bid You Keep Some Few Small Dreams. Helen Frazee-Bower. MoSiPe
I bid you, mock not Eros. Of a Child That Had Fever. Christopher Morley. PFY; PoeMoYo; PR; TBM
I Bind My Heart. Lauchlan MacLean Watt. MaRV
I bind myself [*or* unto myself] to-day. St. Patrick's Breastplate [*or* The Breastplate of Saint Patrick]. *At. to* St. Patrick. *Fr.* The Deer's Cry. BBV; FaBoCh; LoGBV; MaRV; OxBI
I bind the Soul that fathered me. The Hanging. J. E. H. MacDonald. BoCaPo (1943 ed.)
I bleed Sebastian's brother on the ground. Holy Poems, II. George Barker. MoPo
I bless the fates that I may toil. Blessing of Toil. Samuel Ellsworth Kiser. PEDC
I bless Thee for the devious ways. At All Times. Alice Reynolds Flower. PraP
I bless Thee, Lord, because I grow. Paradise. George Herbert. BLV; BoLiVe; TrGrPo
I blew, I blew, the trumpet loudly sounding. The Trumpeter. Thomas Wentworth Higginson. BLP; LBAP
I bloom but once, and then I perish. Il Fior degli Eroici Furori. John Addington Symonds. VA
I boiled hot water in an urn. Old Greek Nonsense Rhymes. *Unknown, after* Nicarchus. BoN
I Bore with Thee, Long, Weary Days. Christina Rossetti. *See* "Love of Christ Which Passeth Knowledge, The."
I bought a gay-roofed house upon a sunny hill. Only Heaven Is Given Away. Rose Darrough. MaRV
I Bought Me a Wife. *Unknown.* ABS
I bow, I scrape, I doff my hat. Unrequited Love on the Back Piazza. Margaret Fishback. CIV
I bow my forehead to the dust. Whittier. *Fr.* The Eternal Goodness. OQP; QP-2
I break my smooth, full loaf of warm white bread. Whatsoever I Do. Mary Louise Hector. GoBC
I break up cypress and make a book-box. On a Box Containing His Own Works. Po Chü-i. TrCh
I breathe but, "Oh!" Moritake, *tr. fr. Japanese by* Lois J. Erickson. SoLD
I Breathed into the Ash. Roland Robinson. BoAV
I breathed the blowing breeze. The Breeze. Al-Husri. MooP
I bring fresh showers for the thirsting flowers. The Cloud. Shelley. ATP; BCEP; BEL; BLV; BoLiVe; BPN; CBOV; ChER; EM-2; EmBrPo; EnL; EnLi-2; EnLit; EnRP; EPN; EPP; ERP; EV-4; FaPON; GBOV; GEPC; GN; GTBS-W; HBV; ImOP; InP; KN; LiTB; LiTG; LPS-3; MCCG; MPB; MW; OAEP; OBAV; OBRV; OHFP; OTPC; OuHeWo; PCH; PIAE; PoE; PoEL-4; PTA-1; PYM; ReaPo; RG; RIS; SeCeV; SN; StaSt; TCEP; TOP; TreF; TrGrPo; TVSH; TyEnPo; ViBoPo

I bring from funeral. Dirge. Euripides. *Fr.* Suppliants. OxBG
"I bring good news," said Spring. Translations from Modern Japanese Poetry. Takeko Kujo. PFE
I bring my sins to Thee. To Thee. *Unknown.* BePJ
I bring to the waiting fields the snow. Winter. Meta E. B. Thorne. *Fr.* Songs of the Seasons. PEOR
I Bring to You as Offering Tonight. Emile Verhaeren, *tr. fr. French by* Jethro Bithell. AnEnPo
I bring ye love. What will love do? Upon Love, by Way of Question and Answer. Robert Herrick. Po
I bring you all my olden days. To-Day. Benjamin R. C. Low. HBV
I bring you the infant of Idumaean night! Bestowal of the Poem. Stéphane Mallarmé. AnFP
I bring you the scent of the earth on my body. The Faun. Haniel Long. HBMV
I broider the world upon a loom. The Loom of Dreams. Arthur Symons. PoVP
I broke my heart because of you, my dear. Literary Love. Harry Kemp. HBMV
I broke one day a slender stem. A Spray of Honeysuckle. Mary Emily Bradley. AA
I Broke the Spell that Held Me Long. Bryant. AmPP (3d ed.); IAP; OBAV
I, Brotachus, came not hither. Man of Crete. J. R. Hervey. AnNZ
I built a chimney for a comrade old. Two at a Fireside. Edwin Markham. OQP; QP-2
I built a hut in a little wood. My Hut. E. Mathias. BoTP
I built for myself a lodge in a fringe of the forest. Smoke, II. Bernard Freeman Trotter. CPG
I Built My Hut. Tao Yuan-ming, *tr. fr. Chinese by* Arthur Waley. AWP
(Chrysanthemums: "I built my cottage," *tr. by* Yang Yeh-tzu.) WhP
(Twelve Poems, 4, *tr. by* Arthur Waley.) TrCh
I built my soul a lordly pleasure-house. The Palace of Art. Tennyson. BEL; BPN; EM-2; EmBrPo; EnLi-2; GEPC; NBE; OAEP; PoVP; UnPo (1st ed.); ViPo; ViPP; VLEP
I buried my head in my thick arms. Paul Valéry. *Fr.* La Jeune Parque. LiA
I buried you deeper last night. To a Persistent Phantom. Frank Horne. BANP; CDC
I Burn for England with a Living Flame. Gervase Stewart. WaaP
(Poem: "I burn for England with a living flame.") WaP
I burn no incense, hang no wreath. Votive Song [*or* The Widow's Song]. Edward Coote Pinkney. AA; AnFE; APA; APW; BAV; CoAnAm; IAP; LEAP; MOAP; OBAV; SPP
"I burned, I wept, I sang; I burn, sing, weep again." Gaspara Stampa. William Rose Benét. HBMV
I Burned My Candle at Both Ends. Samuel Hoffenstein. FiBHP
I burned my life that I might find. The Alchemist. Louise Bogan. AWP; MAP; MoAmPo; MOAP
I Call and I Call. Robert Herrick. ChTr
I call my years back, I, grown old. The Days. Theodosia Garrison. BPP; HBMV
I call no fight a losing fight. Victory. Miriam Teichner. BLP
I call not death the child of darkness. Death. Evgeni Baratynsky. BoR
I call on Zeus, whoever Zeus may be. The Sacrifice of Iphigenia. Aeschylus. *Fr.* Agamemnon. OxBG
I Call the Old Time Back. Whittier. Mabel Martin: Proem. ViBoPo
(Mabel Martin.) BAV
I Call the Swallows. Toyohiko Kagawa, *tr. fr. Japanese by* Lois J. Erickson. SoLD
I call thee from the changing land. The Sea. Nora Hopper. NLK
I call to mind a moment's glory. To A. P. Kern. Pushkin. BoR
I call to the eye of the mind. Salt Sea Wind. W. B. Yeats. *Fr.* At the Hawk's Well. LiA
I called out of mine affliction. Jonah's Prayer. Jonah, Bible, *O.T.* TrJP
I called to gray squirrel. Conversation. Anne Robinson. SUS
I called upon God, and there came to me a spirit of wisdom. Wisdom. The Wisdom of Solomon, Bible, Apocrypha. GrCo-1
I called you. You called me. Dream. Emilio Prados. CoSP
I Came a-Riding. Reinmar von Zweter, *tr. fr. German by* Jethro Bithell. AWP
I came as a shadow. Nocturne Varial. Lewis Alexander. PoNe
I came. Cool are the meadows here. "Feodor Sologub," *tr. fr. Russian by* C. M. Bowra. BoRS
I came [*or* I come] from Alabama. Oh! Susanna. Stephen Collins Foster. FaFP; OIF; PaA; RIS; StaSt; TrAS; TreF
I came from England into France. The Journey into France. *Unknown.* CoMu
I came from Salem City. I Come from Salem City. *Unknown.* AmSS
I came from the village. The "Good" People. Kostas Varnalis. MoGP
I came from Tigris' sandy plain. The Three Wise Men. John Finley. ChIP; OQP; QP-1
I came home from the library. The Revelation. Max Jacob. MiCF
I came, I saw, and was undone. The Thraldome. Abraham Cowley. *Fr.* The Mistress. SeCV-1
I came in light that I might behold. A Parable of the Spirit. John Arthur Goodchild. VA
I came into the city and none knew me. An Upper Chamber. Frances Bannerman. HBV; OBEV
I came into this world to see the sunlight. Konstantin Dmitreyevich Balmont. BoR
I came into your room and spoke. Menace. Katharine Tynan. AV
I came on them yesterday (merely by chance). Pussy Willows. Rowena Bastin Bennett. GFA
I came the Womack Road from Sandy Bridge. Young Kentucky. Jesse Stuart. SPP
I came to an orchard—blossoms blowing. Afternoon. George Dillon. PFE
I came to look, and lo! The Fall of the Plum Blossoms. Ranko. TiPo
I came to Oxford in the light. Oxford. Gerald Gould. PoeT
I came to the crowded Inn of Earth. The Inn of Earth. Sara Teasdale. ChMo; CMP; LiTA
I came to the door of the House of Love. Song. Alfred Noyes. HBV
I Came to This Country in 1865, *with music. Unknown.* OuSiCo
I came [*or* come] to town de udder night. Old Dan Tucker. Daniel Decatur Emmett. ABF; APW; TrAS
I came to you with a greeting. Morning Song. Afanasi Afanasievich Fet. AWP
I came upon it unaware. Honey from the Lion. Leah Bodine Drake. NePoAm
I came upon the children at their play. The Lonely Child. Ernest Briggs. NeLNL
I came upon them by a strip of sea. The Net-Menders. Brian Vrepont. BoAV
I can but name thee, and methinks I call. To His Honoured Kinsman Sir William Soame. Robert Herrick. AtBAP; BoW
I can die tomorrow and I have not loved. For the Book of Love. Jules Laforgue. AnFP
I can feel the loneliness. Minamoto no Muneyuki, *tr. fr. Japanese by* Kenneth Rexroth. OnPJ
I can have no speech with them. War Widow. Bertram Warr. BoCaPo (1948 ed.)
I can hear banjos. Slave Quarter. Carl Carmer. MoSiPe
I can imagine, in some other world. Humming-Bird. D. H. Lawrence. AlDL; GTBS-D; LiTB; LiTM; MoPW; SeCePo; TwCV
I can imagine quite easily ending up. Plains. W. H. Auden. NePA
I can love both fair and brown. The Indifferent. John Donne. ATP (1935 ed.); BEL; EG; ElSeCe; EM-1; EnL; EnLit; EnLP; EPP; EPS; OAEP; OuHeWo; ReEn; ReIE; SeCV-1; TOP; TuPP; TwP
"I" Can Never Be a Great Man, An. Stephen Spender. OBMV
I can never remake the thing I have destroyed. Shards. Aline Kilmer. PFY
I can preserve your letters, not your love. Ceremony. Vassar Miller. NePoEA
I can recall an orchard gnarled and old. A Visit with a Woodpecker. Charles Commerford. BLA
I can remember flowers at your hand. Ad Matrem, in Caelis. Charles L. O'Donnell. WHL
I can remember how the autumn came. Autumn in Wartime. Gilean Douglas. MuM
I can remember our first meeting. To Madame A. P. Kern. Pushkin. LiTW
I can remember our tears, I can remember our laughter. Memory. Helen Hoyt. NP
I can see a picture. Pictures. F. Ann Elliott. BoTP
I can see from the window a little brown house. The Sunset Garden. Marion St. John Webb. TVC; TVSH
I can seldom see anyone without beating him up. My Occupation. Henri Michaux. MiCF
I can still see that homely, grass-grown trail. A Road and a Memory. Jim Thompson. CAG
I can survive on ears the huskers leave. Hibernalia. Jessica Nelson North. NP
I can take the wildest bronco in the tough old woolly West. The Gol-darned Wheel. *Unknown.* CoSo; CSF; IHA; PoMa

I can tell just how it happened, though it's fifty years ago. For a Warning. Caroline B. Le Row. PEOR
I can wade grief. The Test. Emily Dickinson. TCAP
I canna tell what has come ower me. Ich weiss nicht, was soll es bedeuten. Heine, *tr. by* Alexander MacMillan. AWP; PreP
I cannot always feel his greatness. The Great Man. Eunice Tietjens. AV; NP; VOD; WGRP
I cannot be a Washington. Something Better. Clara J. Denton. WOAH
I cannot bear the beauty of one rose. One Rose. Mary Sinton Leitch. PR
I cannot bear the spring this year. Doubting. Virginia McCormick. LS
I Cannot Believe That I Am of Wind. Samuel Greenberg. LiTA
I cannot brook thy gaze, belovèd bird. Mother Carey's Chicken. Theodore Watts-Dunton. OBVV
I cannot but ask, in the park and the streets. Spectator ab Extra, III. Arthur Hugh Clough. OxBoLi
I cannot but remember. When the Year Grows Old. Edna St. Vincent Millay. SBMV; YT
I cannot call my mistress fayre. *Unknown.* SeCSL
I Cannot Change as Others Do. Earl of Rochester. *See* Constancy.
I cannot choose between them now. The Embarrassed Amorist. Louis Untermeyer. PR
I cannot choose but think upon the time. Brother and Sister. "George Eliot." GN
I cannot dance upon my toes. Emily Dickinson. UnS
I cannot do it alone. Jesus and I. Dan Crawford. BLRP
I cannot do the big things. Big and Little Things. Alfred H. Miles. OTPC (1923 ed.)
I cannot dry my eyes when I think of the distant time. Microcosmos, LVII. Nigel Heseltine. NeBP
I Cannot Eat but Little Meat. *At. to* William Stevenson. *See* Back and Side Go Bare, Go Bare.
I cannot find my way: there is no star. Credo. E. A. Robinson. AmPP; AnNE; ChMo; CMP; CoBA; GTBS-W; IAP; LiTM (rev. ed.); MaRV; MoAmPo; NeMA; NePA; OQP; OxBA; PoLFOT; QP-2; QS; WGRP
I cannot find thee! Still on restless pinion. The Quest [*or* Who by Searching Can Find Out God?]. Eliza Scudder. GrCo-1; MaRV; TrPWD; WGRP
I cannot follow them into their world of death. Chrysothemis. Henry Reed. MoVE
I cannot forget/ The sight of that straight young neck. Kevin Barry. Terence Ward. OnYI
I cannot forget my Joe. A Poor French Sailor's Scottish Sweetheart. William Johnson Cory. VA
I Cannot Forget with What Fervid Devotion. Bryant. AmPP (3d ed.); CoBA; IAP
I cannot give you the Metropolitan Tower. Parting Gift. Elinor Wylie. BAP; OxBA
I cannot guess her face or form. Mater Desiderata. Winthrop Mackworth Praed. OBVV
I cannot hide from thee how much I fear. Disavowal. Bertran de Born. LyMA
I cannot hold, I cannot, I, indure. Satire II. John Marston. *Fr.* The Scourge of Villainy. ReIE
I cannot hold my peace, John Keats. To John Keats, Poet. At Springtime. Countee Cullen. BANP; CDC
I Cannot Know That Other Men Exist. Clement Wood. TBM
I cannot live with you. Emily Dickinson. AmP; AmPP (4th ed.); AnNE; CoV; MoAB; MoAmPo; OnAP; OxBA; PoEL-5
(In Vain.) TCAP
I cannot look above and see. The Clouds. William Croswell. AA
I cannot look upon thy grave. To a Lost Love. Stephen Phillips. GTML
I cannot love thee as I ought. In Memoriam A. H. H., LII. Tennyson. BEL; EmBrPo; EnLi-2; EnLit; EPN; GEPC; OAEP; RiBV; ViPo; VLEP
I cannot make him dead! My Child. John Pierpont. AA; BAV; LBAP; LPS-1; OBAV
I cannot ope mine eyes. Matins [*or* Mattens]. George Herbert. CBE; TrPWD
I cannot praise the Doctor's eyes. On Hearing a Lady Praise a Certain Rev. Doctor's Eyes. George Outram. BOHV; LauV
I cannot pray, as Christians use [*or* used] to pray. Credo. "Seumas O'Sullivan." MBP; OnYI
I cannot put the Presence by, of Him, the Crucified. The Voice of Christmas. Harry Kemp. HBV; MaRV; OQP; POT; PoTo; QP-1
"I cannot quite remember . . . There were five." The Messages. W. W. Gibson. ChMo; CMP; InP; MCCG; NV; OHIP
I cannot reach it; and my striving eye. Childhood. Henry Vaughan. EPS; EV-2; OxBoCh; SeEP
I cannot say, and I will not say. Away [*or* He's Just Away *or* He Is Not Dead]. James Whitcomb Riley. BLP; BLRP; LPS-1; MaRV; NeHB; WGRP
I cannot say, beneath the pressure of life's care. Amen. Frederick G. Browning. BLRP
I cannot say why. The Queen in Parliament, 1941. A. P. Herbert. OnPP
I Cannot See. Iraqi, *tr. fr. Persian by* Sir Denison Rose. PeP
I cannot see/ Why men should turn from Thee. My Lord. Martha Snell Nicholson. BePJ
I cannot see fairies. Fairies. Hilda Conkling. GBV (1922 ed.); SP; TiPo
I cannot see the bright sun's glow. Canso. Bernard de Ventadorn. LyMA
I cannot see the clouds from where I stand. Written in an Old Cemetery. Mary Newton Baldwin. UnW
I cannot see the features right. In Memoriam A. H. H., LXX. Tennyson. EmBrPo; EnL; EPN; GEPC; LiTB; PoEL-5; UnW; ViPo; VLEP
I cannot see the stars and flowers. St. George's Day. John Davidson. BMEP
I Cannot Sing the Old Songs. Charlotte Alington Barnard. OlF; TreF
I cannot sing the old songs. Songs without Words, *parody.* Robert J. Burdette. BOHV; PA
I cannot sing to thee as I would sing. Ecstasy. Eric Mackay. VA
I cannot sleep or take the air. A Snowy Day. Dafydd ap Gwilym. LyMA
I cannot sleep; the beautiful Lynnhaven. The River. Mary Sinton Leitch. HBMV
I cannot sleep. The long, long/ Night. Night Thoughts. Lu Yu. OnPC
I cannot sleepe, my eyes ill neighbouring lids. John Marston. *Fr.* The Malcontent. PoEL-2
I cannot spare water or wine. Mithridates. Emerson. OnAP; TCAP
I cannot stay, I cannot stay! Song to the Wanderer. Hermia Harris Fraser. BoCaPo
I cannot, sweetest mother. Lost Heart. Sappho. GrPE
I cannot tell, not I, why she. Poem. Walter Savage Landor. ERP; RO
I cannot tell their wonder nor make known. Ships. John Masefield. CP; LEAP; NP; NV
I cannot tell what you say, green leaves. Dartsiae. Charles Kingsley. AlDL
I cannot tell what's coming o'er me. Loreley. Heine. OuHeWo
I cannot tell who loves the skeleton. La Bella Bona Roba. Richard Lovelace. AtBAP; PoEL-3
I cannot tell why there should come to me. Pray One for Another. "Marianne Farningham" *and* James M. Gray. PraP
I cannot tell why this imagined. The Loreley. Heine. GoTP
I cannot tell you how I love. Post-Impressionism. Bert Leston Taylor. BAP; BOHV; HBMV; InMe; PoeMoYo; PYM
I cannot tell you how it was. May. Christina Rossetti. BPN; EG; EmBrPo; VLEP
I cannot tell you now. The Great Hunt. Carl Sandburg. NP; SBMV
I cannot thank you, Lord—because. Ode II. Gerald Gould. QS
I cannot think of any word. Old Saul. Lizette Woodworth Reese. LS; MAP; MoAmPo; SPP; TCAP
I cannot think of Paradise a place. Paradise. Charles G. Blanden. OQP; QP-1
I cannot think of them as dead. My Dead [*or* Their Silent Ministry]. Frederick Lucian Hosmer. GrCo-1; GrCo-2; MaRV; WGRP
I cannot think or [*or* nor] reason. Acceptance [*or* Comrades of the Cross]. Willard Wattles. HBMV; OQP; QP-1; SBMV
I cannot think that God could be content. God Suffers. Georgia Harkness. QS
I cannot think that thou shouldst pass away. Sonnet. James Russell Lowell. LPS-1
I cannot think that you have gone away. To My Father. Iris Tree. FAOV; HBMV
I cannot think the glorious world of mind. Books. Robert Leighton. MOB
I cannot understand how the winds are set. Alcaeus, *tr. fr. Greek by* Richmond Lattimore. GrPo
I cannot view the bloom upon the rose. Blind. Norman V. Pearce. MaRV; PoToHe
I cannot vouch my tale is true. The Romance of Nick Van Stann. John Godfrey Saxe. PTA-2
I Cannot Wait Longer. Jay Paul. CAG
"I cannot wash my dog," she said. An Insectarian. John Banister Tabb. UTS
I cannot wax ecstatic with the throng. Holy Week. Robert Whitaker. ChIP; MaRV
I can't be talkin' of love, dear. Song. Esther Mathews. FaFP; LiTL; LiTM; NePA; SiTL

I can't blow bubbles. Boredom. Mildred Bowers Armstrong. GoBP
I can't buy a toga, a slave, or some books. Nor a Lender Be. Martial. RoL
I can't get 'em up, I can't get 'em up. Words for Army Bugle Calls: Reveille. *Unknown.* TreF
I can't sleep, and there's no light. Night Piece. Pushkin. BoR
I can't tell much about the thing, 'twas done so powerful quick. The Railroad Crossing. Hezekiah Strong. PTA-2
I Can't Think What He Sees in Her. A. P. Herbert. FiBHP
I care not for Spring; on his fickle wing. A Christmas Carol. Charles Dickens. *Fr.* The Pickwick Papers. COAH
I care not for the idle state. Odes of Anacreon. *Tr. by* Thomas Moore. OuHeWo
I Care Not for These Ladies. Thomas Campion. LiTL; OAEP; OBSC; ReIE; TyEnPo; ViBoPo
(Amarillis.) HBV; LEAP
(Amaryllis.) EG; EIL
I care not, Fortune, what you me deny. Indifference to Fortune. James Thomson. *Fr.* The Castle of Indolence. OBEC
I care not that the storm sways all the trees. The Goal. Frank W. Gunsaulus. MaRV
I care not, though it be. My Little Saint. John Norris. LPS-1
I care not what the sailors say. Crazy Jane Reproved. W. B. Yeats. AtBAP
I care not who the man may be. Fellowship of Books. Edgar A. Guest. LPS-1
I carried a burden of bitterness. Japanese Cherries. Katherine Brégy. JKCP (1926 ed.)
I carry my sheepish life about in the teeth of a wolf. In Wolfen Teeth. Chaim Grade. OnCuPl
I carry the great Singing-Book. The Illuminated Canticle. Florence Wilkinson Evans. PFY
I carry the groundhog along by the tail. The Hunter. Raymond Souster. BoCaPo (1948 ed.)
I cast from me the medications. Loneliness. Franz Werfel. TrJP
I cast my care on Him. The Peace of Prayer. Nagata. PraP
I cast my cloud off, and appear myself. John Fletcher. *Fr.* Rule a Wife and Have a Wife. MyFE
I cast my nets in many streams. Poet Songs, II. Karle Wilson Baker. HBMV
I cast these lyric offerings at your feet. Sonnets to Miranda, V. Sir William Watson. HBV
I Catcha da Plenty of Feesh, *with music. Unknown.* AS; TrAS
I Catherine am a Douglas born. The King's Tragedy. Dante Gabriel Rossetti. BPN; EmBrPo; EPN; PoVP; TOP; ViPo; VLEP
"I caught a fella last night in the South Pacific." Radio. Harriet Monroe. PoeMoYo
I caught a tremendous fish. The Fish. Elizabeth Bishop. ExPo; FiMAP; GoTP; LiTM (rev. ed.); MiAP; MoAB; MoAmPo (1950 ed.); NeMA; NePA; OnAP; Po; TrGrPo (rev. ed.); ViBoPo (1958 ed.)
I caught but a glimpse of him. Summer was here. A Glimpse of Pan. James Whitcomb Riley. DaM
I caught this morning morning's minion. The Windhover. Gerard Manley Hopkins. ACP; AnFE; AtBAP; ATP (1953 ed.); BrBE; CAW; ChMo; CoBE; CoBMV; CoEV; EmBrPo; EnL; EnLi-2 (1949 ed.); EnLit; ExPo; FaBoEn; FaBoMo; InvP; LiTB; LiTM; LoBV; MaPo; MoAB; MoBrPo; MoP; MoPo; MoPW; MoVE; OAEP; Po; PoE; PoEL-5; PoF; PoRA; POTT; PoVP; PreP; ReaPo; ReMP; SeCeV; ShBV-4; TwHP; UnPo (3d ed.); ViP; ViPo; ViPP; VLEP
I Cease Not from Desire. Hafiz, *tr. fr. Persian by* Gertrude Lowthian Bell. *Fr.* Odes. AWP; WoL
(Desire.) PeP
I celebrate myself, and sing myself. Song of Myself. Walt Whitman. AA; AmP; AmPo; AmPP; AnFE; APA; APW; ATP (1935 ed.); CoAnAm; CoBA; CoV; FaBoBe; IAP; LEAP; LiTA; MAP; MoAmPo; NeMA; NePA; OBAV; OnAP; OxBA; PoFS; PoLFOT; REAL; TCAP; TrGrPo; ViBoPo; WHA
I celebrate the personality of Jack. Jack and Jill (As Walt Whitman Might Have Written It). Charles Battell Loomis. PA
I certainly intend. Red Wine in a Black Glass. Ibn Mujbar. MooP
I challenge not the oracle. Sundered. Sidney Henry Morse. LBAP
I challenge you to find. The Wind. Ibn Sa'id of Alcala la Real. MooP
I, Chang P'ing-tzu, had traversed the Nine Wilds and seen their wonders. The Bones of Chuang Tzu. Chang Heng. AtBAP; AWP
I Change. Witter Bynner. HBMV
I change, and so do women too. Written on a Looking-Glass. *Unknown.* HBV; LauV
I charge you, lady young and fair. He Charges Her To Lay Aside Her Weapons. Pierce Ferriter. AnIL; LiTW; OnYI
I charge you, O winds of the West. Mathilde Blind. *Fr.* Love in Exile. TrJP; VA
I charm thy life. Malice. Robert Southey. *Fr.* The Curse of Kehama. BCEP; LoBV; OBRV
I chatter, chatter, as I flow. Tennyson. *Fr.* The Brook. PECK
I chatter over stony ways. Tennyson. *Fr.* The Brook. GFA
"I choosed my love at the bonny yates of Gight." Geordie (B *vers.*). *Unknown.* BaBo
I claim the right of knowing whom I serve. Manhood. Oliver Wendell Holmes. *Fr.* The Poet at the Breakfast Table. APW
I climb the hill: from end to end. In Memoriam A. H. H., C. Tennyson. EmBrPo; EnLi-2; EPN; GEPC; PoEL-5; TOP; ViPo; VLEP
I climb the tower of Ste. Anne des Monts. The Bells of Ste. Anne des Monts. Leo Cox. CaP
I climb to the ridge of Pei Mang Mountain. The Ruins of Lo-yang. Ts'ao Chih. TrCh
I climb to the tower-top and lean upon broken stone. I See Phantoms of Hatred and of the Heart's Fullness and of the Coming Emptiness. W. B. Yeats. Meditations in Time of Civil War, VII. LiTB
I climb'd a hill, whose summit crown'd with wood. An Essay on the Fleet Riding in the Downes. "J. D." CoMu
I climbed a hill as light fell short. The Song of Honour [*or* The Hymn of Being]. Ralph Hodgson. AtBAP; CAW; CBE; ChMo; CMP; CP; GrCo-2; GTML; GTSL; LiTB; MBP; MCCG; MM; MoBrPo; OtMeF; TSW; TSWC
I climbed the dark brow of the mighty Helvellyn. Helvellyn. Sir Walter Scott. BHV; LPS-2
I climbed the hill when the first wild swans were thrown. Dry Time. Norma Davis. NeLNL
I climbed up on the merry-go-round. Merry-go-round. Dorothy Walter Baruch. BrR; MPB (1956 ed.); StVeCh; SUS; TiPo
I cling and swing. The Fifteen Acres. James Stephens. BoTP; GBV (1952 ed.); PtOT; ShBV-2
I clink my castanet. A Starling's Spring Rondel. James Cousins. HBV; HBVY
I close your Marlowe's page, my Shakespeare's ope. After Reading "Tamberlaine the Great." Sir William Watson. BMEP; LEAP. *See also* Yon page being closed . . .
I Closed My Door to the World. Emilio Prados, *tr. fr. Spanish by* Eleanor L. Turnbull. CoSP; OnPM
I Closed My Eyes To-Day and Saw. William Force Stead. OBMV; POTE
I closed my hands upon a moth. Beware. Dora Sigerson Shorter. GTML; GTSL
I Closed My Shutters Fast Last Night. Georgia Douglas Johnson. PoNe
I Come Again. Afanasi Afanasievich Fet, *tr. fr. Russian by* Frances Cornford *and* Esther Polianowsky Salaman. LiTW; TrRV
I come among the peoples like a shadow. Hunger. Laurence Binyon. MM; POTE; TwCV
I come dis night to sing an' pray. Oh, Yes! Oh Yes! Wait 'til I Git on My Robe. *Unknown.* BoAN-2
I come from Alabama. *See* I came from Alabama.
I come from busy haunts of men. The Cynic of the Woods. Arthur Patchett Martin. VA
I come from Castlepatrick, and me heart is on me sleeve. Me Heart. G. K. Chesterton. OtMeF
I come from good olde Boston. On the Aristocracy of Harvard. *At. to* Samuel C. Bushnell. BOHV. *See also* Boston Toast, A.
I come from haunts of coot and hern. The Brook [*or* The Song of the Brook *or* The Brook's Song]. Tennyson. BoChLi; BoTP; BPN; CBPC; CG; EmBrPo; EPN; FaBoBe; FaFP; FaPON; GEPC; GN; GTBS; HBV; HBVY; HiLiEn; LPS-2; MCCG; MPB; MW; OnHT; OTPC; PC; PCH; PIR; PoVP; PTA-1; PYM; RIS; ShBV-2; SN; TreF; TVSH; VLEP; WP
I come from heaven to tell. Ane Sang of the Birth of Christ, with the Tune of Baw Lulalaw. *Unknown.* AnEC
I come from Ireland. The Irish Dancer. *Unknown.* TMEV
I come from mountains under other stars. A Voice from the Nile. James Thomson. EmBrPo
I come from nothing, but from where. A Song of Derivations [*or* The Modern Poet]. Alice Meynell. GTML; MaRV; PoVP; TCPD; VA; WGRP
I Come from Salem City, *with music. Unknown.* AmSS
I come from Salem County. Cowboy Song. Charles Causley. NePoEA
I come from the city of Boston. Boston. *At. to* Samuel C. Bushnell. LiTM; OxBoLi; SiTL. *See also* Boston Toast, A.
I Come from the Rose Garden, Mother. Gil Vicente, *tr. fr. Spanish by* Eleanor L. Turnbull. TeCS
(Rose Song, The, *tr. by* Sir John Bowring.) OnPM

I come from woods enchaunted. Dream Song. Richard Middleton. HBV
I come! I come! ye have called me long. The Voice of Spring. Felicia Dorothea Hemans. OTPC (1946 ed.); PECK; PEOR; PTA-2
I come in the little things. Immanence. Evelyn Underhill. GrCo-2; MaRV; QS; StJW
I come like a comet ablaze, like the sun when the dawn is awaking. Revolution. "Basil Dahl." PoFr
I come more softly than a bird. Mary Austin. *Fr.* Rhyming Riddles. TiPo
I come not here to talk. You know too well. Rienzi to the Romans. Mary Russell Mitford. *Fr.* Rienzi. BCEP; LPS-2
I come not to conquer your body tonight, O creature. Anguish. Stéphane Mallarmé. AnFP
I come of a mighty race. Hebrews. James Oppenheim. MAP; MoAmPo (1942 ed.); TBM; TCPD; TrJP
I come of the seed of the people, the people that sorrow. The Rebel. Padraic Pearse. OnYI
I Come Singing. Joseph Auslander. POT; PoTo
I Come to Bury Caesar. Shakespeare. *See* Antony's Oration.
I Come to Supplicate. Simeon ben Isaac ben Abun of Mainz, *tr. fr. Hebrew by* Nina Davis Salaman. TrJP
I come to the garden alone. C. Austin Miles. OIF
I come to thee, O God long since forgot. Before the Statue of Apollo. Saul Tchernichowsky. TrJP
I come to town de udder night. *See* I came to town de udder night.
I come to visit thee agen. To a Cyclamen. Walter Savage Landor. BPN; VA
I come to work as well as play. The March Wind. *Unknown.* GFA
I come today to high Pichencha's brow. Words of the Last Inca. José Eusebio Caro. PoFr
I come unto you, forgotten god of the ages. Before a Statue of Apollo. Saul Tchernichowsky. LiTW
I Come Up Out uv Egypt, *with music.* *Unknown.* StDa
I come with chaplet woven new. Memorial Day. Wallace Bruce. MDAH
"I come your sin-rid souls to shrive." Father Francis. Walter Herries Pollock. VA
I command all ye rattens that here be about. Rats Away. *Unknown.* TMEV
I conceived. And sorrow/ Stirred. Maria Minor. Margaret Avison. BoCaPo
I condemn all luxury Oriental. Horace. Odes, I, 38. LaP
I consecrate this fountain Helen's, praying. Pierre de Ronsard. *Fr.* Sonnets pour Hélène. PrPoCR
I could bear grief, if it were only thorough. I Am Undone. Virginia Moore. TBM
I could believe that I am here alone. Solipsism. George Santayana. AnFE; APA; CoAnAm; TwAmPo
I could have painted pictures like that youth's. Pictor Ignotus. Robert Browning. BPN; EmBrPo; PoVP; ViPo; ViPP; VLEP
I could have stemmed misfortune's tide. The Wife. Anna Peyre Dinnies. AA
I could know. Childhood. Louis Ginsberg. RIS
I could make you songs. Song. Dorothy Dow. HBMV
I could never have the power. Beaumont *and* Fletcher. *Fr.* The Maid's Tragedy. TuPP
I could not be so well content. A Cowboy Song. *Unknown.* SCC
I could not bear to see those eyes. The Protest. James Russell Lowell. PR
I could not choose but gaze; a fascination. Shelley. *Fr.* The Revolt of Islam. ChER
I could not dig: I dared not rob. A Dead Statesman. Kipling. *Fr.* Epitaphs of the War. LiA; OAEP (2d ed.); PoVP
I could not even think. Rapunzel. William Morris. EmBrPo; PoVP
I could not, ever and anon, forbear. The Solitary. Wordsworth. *Fr.* The Excursion, II. EnRP
I could not have beat back my way to life. William Ellery Leonard. *Fr.* Two Lives, Pt. III. MOAP
I could not keep love down. The Power of Love. *Unknown.* *Fr.* The Thousand and One Nights. LiTW
I could not know/ if it was your heaven or mine. Man's Road. Enrique Peña Barrenechea. AnCL
I could not leave Thee, Christ! For when I tried. The Disciple. Dwight Bradley. ChIP; OQP; QP-1
I could not look on Death, which being known. The Coward. Kipling. *Fr.* Epitaphs of the War. FaBoTw; GTBS; LiA; OAEP (2d ed.); PoVP
I could not love you, dear, so much. Had I Not Loved Before. Ralph Cheyney. PR
I could not see You with my eyes. Sight and Insight. Eleanor Slater. TrPWD
I Could Not Sleep for Thinking of the Sky. John Masefield. Lollingdon Downs, V. ChMP; GTBS-W; LiTM (rev. ed.) (Sonnet.) LiTG; NV
I Could Not Though I Would. George Gascoigne. PoEL-1
I could not through the burning day. Dollie Radford. LEAP
I could not understand the sudden quiet. The Quiet. W. W. Gibson. BEL
I could not welcome you, oh! longed-for peace. To Peace, with Victory. Corinne Roosevelt Robinson. AOAH
I could praise you once with beautiful words ere you came. The Silence of Love. "Æ." ChMo; CMP
I could resign that eye of blue. To Cloe. Thomas Moore, *after* Martial. AWP; OuHeWo
I could wish to be dead! The Tragic Mary Queen of Scots. "Michael Field." GTML; MBP; OBMV; TCPD
I couldn't find you in the church, God. Religion. Hildegarde Dolson. CAG
I Couldn't Hear Nobody Pray. *Unknown.* APW; BoAN-1, *with music*
I couldn't help weeping with delight. Styx River Anthology. Carolyn Wells. BOHV
I couldn't touch a stop and turn a screw. Thirty Bob a Week. John Davidson. FaBoTw; FaFP; LiTB; LiTG; LiTM (rev. ed.); PoFr; PoVP
I count it always a joy to be young. Youth. Euripides. *Fr.* Heracles. OxBG
I count it happiness. This World Is All a Fleeting Show. Menander. OxBG
I count it true which sages teach. In Memoriam Technicam. Tom Hood. BOHV
I Count My Time by Times That I Meet Thee. Richard Watson Gilder. AA; LBAP; OBAV
I count my treasures o'er with care. Christmas Treasures. Eugene Field. SDH
I count this thing to be grandly true. Only in Dreams. Josiah Gilbert Holland. PEOR
I count up in this song of cheer. A Thanksgiving Rosary [*or* A Rhyme for Thanksgiving Day]. Edwin Markham. BLP; PEDC
I, country-born an' bred, know where to find. James Russell Lowell. *Fr.* The Biglow Papers, 2d Series, No. VI. SN
I courted pretty Polly the live-long night. Pretty Polly. *Unknown.* OuSiCo
I crave an ampler, worthier sphere. Anno 1829. Heine. AWP; JAWP; WBP; WoL
I crave, dear Lord. Ike Walton's Prayer. James Whitcomb Riley. AA
I crave not Amalthaea's horn. Envy-free. Anacreon. GrR
I craved for flash of eye and sword. Dreams. Israel Zangwill. TrJP
I creature being mad. A Poem of Margery Kempe. Howard Nemerov. FiMAP
I crept into being as faintly. Otsuta. Toson Shimazaki. PoLJ
I cried over beautiful things knowing no beautiful thing lasts. Autumn Movement. Carl Sandburg. NP; SBMV
I cried unto God with my voice, even unto God with my voice. Psalm LXXVII, Bible, *O.T.* AWP
I cross a weedy meadow. Thistle, Yarrow, Clover. Kenneth Porter. NePoAm
I crossed over the county line. Crossing the County Line. Elizabeth Randall-Mills. GoYe
I crossed the gangway in the winter's raining. Stowaway. Bill Adams. EtS
I Cry: Love, Love! Blake. *Fr.* Visions of the Daughters of Albion. RO
I Cry, Love! Love! Theodore Roethke. MoVE
I cry to the mountains! I cry to the sea. We [He, *wr.*] Whom the Dead Have Not Forgiven. Sara Bard Field. MuM; PGD
I cry you mercy, sir, I knew you not. Henry Parrot. SiCE
I cry your mercy—pity—love!—aye, love! To Fanny. Keats. EmBrPo; EnRP; ERP; LoPo; LoPS; TrGrPo; TwP
I cultivate a white rose. José Martí. *Fr.* Simple Verses. BoFr
I curse the time, wherein these lips of mine. Thomas Watson. LO
I cursed the puddle when I found. The Puddle. Eden Phillpotts. BMEV; HBMV
I curst thee oft, I pity now thy case. Astrophel and Stella, XLVI. Sir Philip Sidney. SiPS
I cut a branch from the cherry-tree and take to the road again. Road Song. Louis Untermeyer. StaSt
I dance and dance! Another faun. The Dancers. "Michael Field." VA
I dance and dance [*or* sing] without any feet. Spells. James Reeves. AlDL; PoMS
I dance on your paper. Jack o' the Inkpot. Algernon Blackwood. BoTP
I Danced before I Had Two Feet. Max Dunn. BoAV
I Dare Believe. Rose Mills Powers. BAP
I dare but sing of you in such a strain. Sonnets to Miranda, III. Sir William Watson. HBV
I dare not ask a kiss. To Electra. Robert Herrick. ALV; BEL; EG; EM-1; EnLit; EV-2; HBV; HoPM; LoBV; OBEV; OBS; PG (1945 ed.); RiBV; SeCV-1; TCEP

I dare not ask your very all. Your Tears. Edwin Markham. BoFr; HBMV; TBM
I dare not! Look! the road is very dark. The Lion Path. Charlotte Perkins Gilman. BLP
I Dare Not Pray to Thee. Maurice Baring. TrPWD
I dare not say how fond I am. The Virtuous Clam. Winifred Fry Webster. DDA
I dare not sing my lady's praise. Reticent Lover. Clinton Scollard. PR
I dare not slight the stranger at my door. The Trimmed Lamp [*or* Vigil]. Laura Simmons. ChIP; LPS-1; MaRV
I dare not think that thou art by, to stand. Infinity. Philip Henry Savage. AA; LBAP
I dared to rest, or wander—like a rest. Elizabeth Barrett Browning. *Fr.* Aurora Leigh, I. EnSW
I, dark in light, exposed. Milton. *Fr.* Samson Agonistes. TrGrPo
I deemed it not the voice of Zeus that spake. The State versus Conscience. Sophocles. *Fr.* Antigone. GrR
I deemed thy garments, O my Hope, were gray. Hope Overtaken. Dante Gabriel Rossetti. The House of Life, XLII. PoVP; ViPo
I delight in this naethingness. De Profundis. "Hugh MacDiarmid." SeCePo
I demanded beauty, tasking. Answer. Isabel Fiske Conant. TBM
I, Denys of Tarsus, lie dead. An Unhappy Man. *Unknown.* OxBG
I descend through the forest alone. Song of the Search. Constance Lindsay Skinner. *Fr.* Songs of the Coast-Dwellers. CPG
I desire/ Words that are as sweet as dawn. The Nuns. Edward F. Garesché. PraNu
I despise my friends more than you. To an Enemy. Maxwell Bodenheim. NP; TrJP
I devise to end my days—in a tavern drinking. The Jovial Priest's Confession. Leigh Hunt. BOHV
I did but crave that I might kiss. The Slight. Thomas Flatman. LO; SeCL
I did [*or* do] but look and love awhile. The Enchantment. Thomas Otway. EPP; EV-3; HBV; LiTL; LO; NeHB; OBEV; SeCL; ViBoPo
I did but prompt the age to quit their clogs. On the Detraction Which Followed upon My Writing Certain Treatises [*or* On the Same *or* Second Sonnet on "Tetrachordon"]. Milton. ATP; CaAE; EM-1; ExPo; MaPo; PeBoSo; PoFr; SeCeV; TOP
I did not chide him, though I knew. Heart's Chill Between. Christina Rossetti. BPN
I did not choose thee, dearest. It was Love. To Manon, on His Fortune in Loving Her. Wilfrid Scawen Blunt. The Love Sonnets of Proteus, III. CaAE; GTSL; LEAP; OBEV (1st ed.)
I did not come to kiss her for she was kiss herself. All of Her. Samuel L. Albert. NePoAm-2
I did not cut myself this hollow reed. It Is the Reed. Sister Maris Stella. GoBC
I Did Not Heed That Spring Was Here. John Richard Moreland. LS
I did not keep the rose he brought. Forethought. Josephine Preston Peabody. PR
I did not know; child, child, I did not know. Asking Forgiveness. Arthur Symons. BMEP; LEAP
I did not know how brittle. Hound at Night. Louise Ayres Garnett. TBM
I did not know she'd take it so. Under the Mistletoe. Countee Cullen. GoSl
I did not know, the day I nailed. Resurrection. Lloyd Frank Merrell. ChIP
I did not live until this time. To My Excellent Lucasia, on Our Friendship. Katherine Philips. EG; ElSeCe; LO; MeLP; OBS; SeCL; SeEP
I did not look upon her eyes. Penumbra. Dante Gabriel Rossetti. PoVP; VLEP
I Did Not Lose My Heart [in Summer's Even]. A. E. Housman. More Poems, XXXVII. BoFr; LiTM; MaPo; TwP
I did not make the conditions of my life whereby. Desire. Kathleen Raine. MoPo
I did not question anything. Finite. Power Dalton. HBMV
I did not raise mine eyes to hers. Et Sunt Commercia Coeli. Herbert P. Horne. GTML
I did not see the crown. Faith. Donald Earl Edwards. ChIP
I did not see the pachyderms. The Circus. E. B. White. InMe
I did not see you even when I went. Two Sonnets; to a Spiritual Entity, I. Helen Pinkerton. PtPa
I did not sleep; 'twas noon of day. Lines by Claudia. Emily Brontë. UnW
I did not think, I did not strive. John Masefield. *Fr.* The Everlasting Mercy. QS
I did not think that I should find them there. The Clerks. E. A. Robinson. AA; AnNE; MAP; MoAB; MoAmPo; MoVE; NeMA; PoEL-5; TwP
I did not think to find You there. Christ in Woolworth's. Teresa Hooley. ChIP; DDA; QS; StJW
I did not wish eternity. Longing. Clement Wood. TBM
I did . . . was't worth the pain? . . . for pain was long. William Ellery Leonard. *Fr.* Two Lives, Pt. III. MOAP
I Didn't Like Him. Harry B. Smith. BOHV
I didn't like the way he went away. The Smile. Robert Frost. *Fr.* The Hill Wife. ChMo; CMP; IAP; MOAP; NP
I didn't make you know how glad I was. A Servant to Servants. Robert Frost. AmPo
I didn't mean to hurt you, firefly. Firefly. Edna D. Wood. PCH
I Die [*or* Dye] Alive. Robert Southwell. MeRV; ReIE; SiCE
I Die because I Do Not Die. St. Theresa of Avila, *tr. fr. Spanish by* E. Allison Peers. AnSpL-1
I Die, Being Young. David Gray. VA (In the Shadows.) BMEP
"I Die Daily." Phil. J. Fisher. MaRV
I die for Your holy word without regret. Elegy. Antonio Enríquez Gómez. TrJP
I die, no matter what I do I die. Sestina. Richard Eberhart. FiMAP
I die of thirst beside the fountain's brim. Ballade. Villon. FoS
I die with too transporting joy. Sonnet. *Unknown, tr. by* John Hughes. AEV
I died, and they looked in my head: 2 plus 2. Natural Causes. Winfield Townley Scott. LiTL
I died for beauty, but was scarce/ Adjusted in the tomb. Emily Dickinson. AmPo; AnFE; AnNE; APA; AWP; CoAnAm; FaFP; GTBS-W; InPo; LiTA; LiTM; MAP; MAPA; MoAB; MoAmPo; MOAP; MoVE; OnPM; PreP; ReaPo; TwAmPo; TwP; WHA (Beauty and Truth.) NeMA (Colloquy.) BAP
I died from mineral and plant became. Resurgence. Jalal ed-Din Rumi. LiTW
I died last night. . . . Upon a narrow bed. November 24, 1918. Vincent Starrett. MuM
I died; they wrapped me in a shroud. A Dream of Death. "Owen Innsley." AA
I Died True. Beaumont *and* Fletcher. *See* Aspatia's Song.
I dined with a friend in the East, one day. The Sunbeam. *Unknown.* NA
I dipt [*or* dipped] into the future, far as human eye could see. The Vision of the World [*or* Federation of the World]. Tennyson. *Fr.* Locksley Hall. GrCo-1; PoRL *See also* For I dipt . . .
I dismount from my horse at the Hsi-lin Temple. Visiting the Hsi-lin Temple. Po Chü-i. TrCh
I Dive Down into the Depth. Rabindranath Tagore. MM
I do affirm that thou hast saved the race. Delay. Charlotte Fiske Bates. AA
I do be thinking God must laugh. Boys. Winifred M. Letts. HBMV
I do be thinking, lassie, of the old days now. The Shoogy-Shoo. Winthrop Packard. HBV
I do believ. Thomas Traherne. *Fr.* Solitude. FaBoEn
I do believe that die I must. His Creed. Robert Herrick. ElSeCe; SeCeV; TriL
"I do believe the world is swinging toward the light." Swinging toward the Light. Georgia Harkness. MaRV
I do but look and love awhile. *See* I did but look and love awhile.
I do come about the copse. The Fairy Frolic. John Lyly. PCH
"I do complain and can find no release." Love Dialogue. *Unknown.* CoBE
I do confess, in many a sigh. Lying. Thomas Moore. BOHV; FiBHP
I do confess my fault. Traitors. Shakespeare. King Henry V, *fr.* II, ii. BHV
I do confess thou'rt smooth and fair. To His Forsaken Mistress [*or* Inconstancy Reproved]. *At. to* Sir Robert Ayton. BCEP; BSV; EBSV; ElL; EV-2; HBV; LiTL; LO; OBEV; OBS; SeCePo
I Do Know God Don't Lie. *Unknown.* APW
I do not ask/ That crowds may throng the temple. The Parson's Prayer. Ralph Spaulding Cushman. MaRV; PraP
I do not ask a truce. Prayer. Peter Gething. OQP; QP-2
I do not ask for any crown. My Kingdom. Louisa May Alcott. MaRV
I do not ask for love, ah! no. Lethe. Georgia Douglas Johnson. CDC
I do not ask—for you are fair. The Complaisant Swain. Ovid. AWP
I do not ask God's purpose. He gave me the sword. The Soldier. Humbert Wolfe. *Fr.* Requiem. TCPD
I do not ask, O Lord, that life may be. Per Pacem ad Lucem. Adelaide Anne Procter. MaRV; TrPWD; VA

I do not ask that God will keep all storms away. The All-sufficient Christ. Bernice W. Lubke. BLRP
I do not ask that you repay. A Mother's Reward. Ona Freeman Lathrop. MaRV
I Do Not Ask Thee, Lord. *Unknown.* BLRP
I do not ask Thee, Lord, for outward sign. Jesus Himself. Henry Burton. BLRP
I do not ask Thee, Lord, that all my life may be. I Do Not Ask Thee, Lord. *Unknown.* BLRP
I do not ask Thee straightway to appear. Supplication. Edith Lovejoy Pierce. TrPWD
I do not believe this room. A Game of Glass. Alastair Reid. NePoEA
I do not care for Gyges' store of gold. Simple Tastes. Archilochus. OxBG
I do not care for kisses. 'Tis a debt. The Pleasures of Love. Wilfrid Scawen Blunt. HBV
"I do not care for noise and flags," I said. The Parade. Mary Esther Badley. PEDC
I do not count the hours I spend. Waldeinsamkeit. Emerson. AmPP (3d ed.); APW; HBV; IAP; OBAV; SN; WGRP
I do not despise you priests, all time, the world over. Walt Whitman. Song of Myself, XLIII. CoBA
I do not dread an alter'd heart. A Foreboding. "Violet Fane." DiM; VA
I Do Not Fear. Robert Louis Stevenson. POTT
I do not fear/ To walk the lonely road. Apprehension. James Anderson Fraser. MaRV; OQP; QP-2
I do not fear to die. The Fear. W. W. Gibson. BEL; GTSL; NP
I do not fear to lay my body down. Exile from God. John Hall Wheelock. GoBC; SBMV; WGRP
I do not fear to own me kin. I Do Not Fear. Robert Louis Stevenson. POTT
I do not fear to tread the path. Leading. Nagata. SoLD
I do not fear to tread the path that those I love long since have trod. My Creed. Jeannette L. Gilder. BPP; WGRP
I do not go, my dear, to storm. On Going to the Wars. Earle Birney. NeTW; WaP
I do not grudge them; Lord, I do not grudge. The Mother. Padraic Pearse. OnYI
I do not here, upon this humorous stage. To the Right Worthy and Judicious Favorer of Virtue, Maister Fulke Greville. Samuel Daniel. *Fr.* Musophilus. ReIE; SiCE
I do not hold with him who thinks. Thoughts on the Cosmos. Franklin P. Adams. HBMV
I do not know how I shall look. More Letters Found near a Suicide. Frank Horne. BANP
I do not know how wide the spaces are. This Only Do I Know. *Unknown.* BePJ
I do not know, I cannot see. Confidence. *Unknown.* BLRP
I do not know if you will know, XV. Frances Crawford. PtPa
I do not know much about gods; but I think that the river. The Dry Salvages. T. S. Eliot. *Fr.* Four Quartets. LiTB; MaPo; OxBA; SeCePo; SeCeV
I do not know of anything under the sky. A Lament for Ireland. Shemus Cartan. GTIV
I do not know what. Antique Carved Figures. Raymond E. F. Larsson. JKCP (1955 ed.)
I do not know what death may bring. Voyage. Vincent Starrett. LPS-1
I do not know what I can bring. Panegyric. Abu Bakr Muhammad. MooP
I do not know why at times. Traces. Rafael Estrada. AnCL
I do not know why this confronts me. Ich weiss nicht, was soll es bedeuten. Heine, *tr. by* Louis Untermeyer. PreP
I do not lack for Jack or Joan. Me. Hughes Mearns. *Fr.* Later Antigonishes. InMe
I Do Not Like a Roof Tonight. Grace Noll Crowell. SDH
I do not like a swagger captain. Archilochus, *tr. fr. Greek by* N. H. Dole. GrPo
I do not like my garden, but I love. The Garden. Edgar Lee Masters. NP
I do not like the other sort. An Ulsterman. "Lynn Doyle." OnYI
I do not like thee, Doctor Fell. Thomas Brown. *See* I Do Not Love Thee, Doctor Fell.
"I do not like to go to bed." Sleepy Harry. Ann *or* Jane Taylor. SAS
I do not love a wanton, I do not love a prude. The Happy Mean. Rufinus. GrPE
I Do Not Love Thee. Caroline E. S. Norton. DiM; EV-5; GTBS; GTSL; HBV; LoP; LoPS; OBEV
I Do Not Love Thee, Doctor Fell. Thomas Brown, *after the Latin of* Martial. GoTP; MoShBr; RIS; WhC (Doctor Fell.) ChTr; FaFP; LiTG; PoeMoYo; SiTL ("I do not like thee, Doctor Fell.") OxNR (No Reason Why.) OnPM (Non Amo Te.) AWP; ImOP; JAWP; WBP (Written While a Student at Christ Church, Oxford.) PreP
I do not love thee for that fair. The Compliment. Thomas Carew. LPS-1
I do not love thee! No! I do not love thee! I Do Not Love Thee. Caroline E. S. Norton. DiM; EV-5; GTBS; GTSL; HBV; LoP; LoPS; OBEV
I Do Not Love to See Your Beauty Fire. John Hall Wheelock. HBMV
I do not love to wed. The Poet Loves a Mistress, but Not to Marry. Robert Herrick. ALV
I do not need the skies'/ Pomp. All Flesh. Francis Thompson. PoeT
I do not own an inch of land. A Strip of Blue. Lucy Larcom. AA; HBV; LBAP; MaRV; NLK; OBAV; OQP; OTPC; QP-2; SN; WGRP
I do not pity the old men, fumbling after. Pity. Babette Deutsch. TBM; WHA
I do not pray for peace nor ease. Prayer for Pain. John G. Neihardt. HBV; NP; PFY; TBM; TrPWD; WGRP
I do not see the sense of my toil putting thoughts in a dying tongue. Dain do Eimhir, LV. Sorley Maclean. NeBP
I do not thank Thee, Lord. Thanks Be to God. Janie Alford. MaRV; PGD; PoToHe
I do not think that skies and meadows are. Reciprocity. John Drinkwater. EPP; NeMA; NP
I do not think the rearing of her brood. "Brother." Virginia Lyne Tunstall. LS
I do not understand. The Unknown. E. O. Laughlin. AOAH; BLPA; BoHiPo
I do not want to be reflective any more. Wolves. Louis MacNeice. BrBE
I do not want to be your weeping woman. Poem. Alison Boodson. NeBP
I do not weep for Aprils. Compensate. Patrick D. Moreland. InP
I do not wish to know. After the Persian. Louise Bogan. NePoAm
I do not wish to see my sins more plain. The True Need. Thomas Curtis Clark. OQP; QP-1
I do not wish you joy without a sorrow. A Birthday Wish. Dorothy Nell McDonald. PoToHe (new ed.)
I do not wonder that God chose a star. God Chose a Star. *Unknown.* BPP
I Do Remember You. Roberta Teale Swartz. AV
I do your will, yet cherish still the wish. Two Lovers in the Toils of Honor. Corneille. *Fr.* The Cid. LiTW
I doe confess I love thee. *Unknown.* SeCSL
I doe confesse that thou art faire. *Unknown.* SeCSL
I Done Done What Ya' Tol' Me to Do, *with music.* *Unknown.* BoAN-1
I don't appwove this hawid waw. Swell's Soliloquy. *Unknown.* FiBHP; LPS-3
I don't believe in telling fibs. Her Dilemma. Paul B. McVey. CAG
I don't go much on religion. Little Breeches. John Hay. AA; AmPP (3d ed.); BeLS; BOHV; CoBA; DDA; FaBoBe; GoTP; HBV; LPS-3; OBAV; StaSt; TreFS; TSW; TSWC
I don't know any greatest treat. The Parterre. E. H. Palmer. BOHV; NA
I don't know how he came. Ossawatomie. Carl Sandburg. OxBA; PFY; TCPD
I doant know how it was. Mystery. "Yehoash." TrJP
I don't know what it is. Roofs. Witter Bynner. TCAP
I don't know where I'd get another one. The Faithful Servant. Richard R. Kirk. LS
I don't know who they are. The Pointed People. Rachel Field. FaPON; MPB
I don't know with exactly whom. *Unknown.* *Fr.* Four Short Poems. LyMA
I don't like bees. Bees. Marchette Chute. BoChLi (1950 ed.)
I Don't Like No Railroad Man, *with music.* *Unknown.* AS (Railroaders and Hobos.) OuSiCo
"I don't like the look of little Fan, mother." Little Fan. James Reeves. PoMS
I don't look back; God knows the fruitless efforts. We See Jesus. Annie Johnson Flint. BLRP
I Don't Mean to Tell You Her Name. *Unknown.* *See* Lovely Village Fair, The.
I don't mind eels. The Eel. Ogden Nash. FaPON
I don't remember anything of then, down there around the magnolias. Ode to Michael Goldberg's Birth and Other Births. Frank O'Hara. NeAP
I don't say that the Fates were actuated. The Poet. H. C. Bosman. BoSA
I don't want/ to be plucked like a flower. Vladimir Mayakovsky. *Fr.* Home! TrRV
I don't want a dog that is wee and effeminate. Dog Wanted. Margaret Mackprang Mackay. AlBD
I don't want none of your weevily wheat. Weevily Wheat. *Unknown.* TrAS
I Don't Want to Be a Gambler, *with music.* *Unknown.* AS
I Dote upon Myself. Walt Whitman. *Fr.* Song of Myself, XXIV. AnEnPo

I Doubt a Lovely Thing Is Dead. Neil Tracy. BoCaPo; CaP
I doubt if ten men in all Tilbury Town. E. A. Robinson. *Fr.* Captain Craig. PoEL-5
I doubt not God is good, well-meaning, kind. Yet Do I Marvel. Countee Cullen. AnAmPo; BANP; CDC; LA; NP; PoNe
I dragged my body to the pool of sleep. The Pool of Sleep. Arlo Bates. LBAP; PC
I dragged my feet [*or* flesh] through desert gloom. The Prophet. Pushkin. AWP; JAWP; WBP; WGRP
I dragged my life along with sullen sighs. Pierre de Ronsard. *Fr.* Amours de Cassandre. PrPoCR
I drank at a spring, time was, where dark the water bubbled. "Cherchez Fortune Ailleurs." Theognis. GrPE
I drank at every vine. Feast. Edna St. Vincent Millay. BAP; NP; WHA
I dreaded that first robin so. Emily Dickinson. AnAmPo; CoV; IAP; LA; MAP; MoAmPo
I dream now of green places. In the Third Year of War. Henry Treece. WaP
I dream of Jeanie with the light brown hair. Jeanie with the Light Brown Hair. Stephen Collins Foster. FaFP; OlF; TrAS; TreF
I dream of a red-rose tree. Women and Roses. Robert Browning. EmBrPo; EPN; ViBoPo
I dream of you, to wake: would that I might. Monna Innominata, III. Christina Rossetti. EmBrPo; ViPo
I dream'd before the altar that I led. Zempoalla's Dream. Sir Robert Howard *and* John Dryden. *Fr.* The Indian Queen. BeR
I dream'd I saw a little brook. A Vision of Children. Thomas Ashe. VA
I Dream'd in a Dream. Walt Whitman. APW; BoFr; IAP; MaRV
I dream'd that, as I wander'd by the way. *See* I dreamed that, as I wandered by the way.
I dream'd that I walk'd in Italy. Going Back Again. "Owen Meredith." FiBHP
I dream'd that I woke from a dream. Song. George Macdonald. VA
I dream'd there would be Spring no more. In Memoriam A. H. H., LXIX. Tennyson. EmBrPo; EPN; GEPC; OAEP; UnW; ViPo; VLEP
I dream'd we both were in a bed. The Vision to Electra. Robert Herrick. ALV
I dreamed a dream last night, when all was still. Reality. Angela Morgan. WGRP
I dreamed a dream next Tuesday week. My Dream. *Unknown.* BOHV; GoTP; LauV; NA; SiTL
I dreamed a dream the other night. *See* I dreamt a dream . . .
I dreamed a dream! what can it mean? *See* I dreamt a dream . . .
I dreamed a dream within a dream. "Again I Saw Another Angel." Margaret L. Woods. UnW
"I dreamed a dreary dream this night." The Braes o' Yarrow. *Unknown.* ESPB; ViBoFo
I dreamed all my fortitude screamed. Letter across Doubt and Distance. M. Carl Holman. PoNe
I dreamed and I awoke, the morning light. Foreknown. Doris Kenyon. UnW
I dreamed I held/ A sword against my flesh. Lady Kasa, *tr. fr. Japanese by* Kenneth Rexroth. LiTW; OnPJ
I Dreamed I Moved among the Elysian Fields. Edna St. Vincent Millay. MOAP
I dreamed I passed a doorway. The Unknown Belovèd. John Hall Wheelock. HBMV; SBMV
I dreamed I saw that ancient Irish queen. Chivalry. "Æ." ViBoPo
I dreamed I was a cave-boy. The Cave-Boy. Laura E. Richards. FaPON
I Dreamed Last Night. Snow Longley. UnW
(Sonnet: "I dreamed last night I stood with God on high.") PC
I dreamed last night. A Dream. Shen Yo. PoHN
I dreamed last night a deathly dream. Iphigenia's Dream. Euripides. *Fr.* Iphigenia in Tauris. GrR
I dreamed last night I stood with God on high. I Dreamed Last Night [*or* Sonnet]. Snow Longley. PC; UnW
I dreamed last night of a dome of beaten gold. Stephen Phillips. *Fr.* Herod. PC
I Dreamed Last Night of My True Love. *Unknown.* *See* Locks and Bolts.
I dreamed my love came in my sleep. Lowlands, *vers.* I. *Unknown.* AmSS
I dreamed of him last night, I saw his face. The Dead Poet. Lord Alfred Douglas. BMEP; CaAE; HBMV; LEAP; MBP; MoBrPo (1942 ed.); PoVP; PtP; ViBoPo
I dreamed of paradise—and still. The Dear Togetherness. William Channing Gannett. GrCo-1
I dreamed of war-heroes, of wounded war-heroes. The Heroes. Louis Simpson. NePoAm
I dreamed one man stood against a thousand. Graves. Carl Sandburg. AnEnPo
I dreamed one night I came. A Heterodoxy. Lord Dunsany. OnYI; UnW
I dreamed [*or* dream'd] that, as I wandered by the way. The Question [*or* A Dream of the Unknown]. Shelley. BPN; CBE; CH; EmBrPo; EnRP; EPN; EV-4; FiP; GTBS; GTBS-D; GTBS-W; GTSE; GTSL; HBV; MyFE; OBEV; OBRV; RO
I dreamed that dead, and meditating. The Weed. Elizabeth Bishop. MoPo
I dreamed that each most lovely, perfect thing. A Dream of Beauty. Clark Ashton Smith. UnW
I dreamed that I. Slings. Rubén Darío. PoFr
I dreamed that I was dead and crossed heavens. A Dream. Helen Hunt Jackson. AnFE; APA; CoAnAm
I dreamed that I was thrown from a crag. Sonnet. Francisco de Terrazas. AnMP
I Dreamed That in a City Dark as Paris. Louis Simpson. NePoEA
I dreamed that one had died in a strange place. A Dream of Death. W. B. Yeats. PoeT; POTE
I dreamed that somewhere in the shadowy place. Lost in Hades. Andrew Lang. UnW
I dreamed that stone by stone. The Temple. Tennyson. OQP; QP-2
I dreamed that when I died a jukebox played. Death of a Jazz Musician. William Jay Smith. NePoAm-2
I dreamed the fairies wanted me. Crab-Apple. Ethel Talbot. PCH; TiPo
I dreamed the Saviour came to be. Interceding. Opal Leonore Gibbs. BePJ; PraP
I dreamed there was an Emperor Antony. Cleopatra's Lament. Shakespeare. *Fr.* Antony and Cleopatra, V, ii. UnPo
I dreamed two spirits came—one dusk as night. The Two Spirits. James Benjamin Kenyon. AA
I dreamt [*or* dreamed] a dream the other night. Lowlands [Away]. *Unknown.* ChTr; LO; MuP; OxBoLi; SG; SoAmSa
I dreamt a dream; till morning light. Arthur Hugh Clough. *Fr.* Dipsychus, Pt. I, sc. v. OAEP
I dreamt [*or* dreamed] a dream! what can it mean? The Angel. Blake. *Fr.* Songs of Experience. CH; EiPP; EnRP
I dreamt I came to a kind inn. A Kind Inn. George Dillon. GoYe
I dreamt I climbed to a high, high plain. The Pitcher. Yüan Chen. AWP; JAWP; TrCh; WBP
I Dreamt I Dwelt in Marble Halls. Alfred Bunn. *See* I Dreamt That I Dwelt in Marble Halls.
I Dreamt I Saw Great Venus. Bion, *at. also to* Moschus, *tr. fr. Greek by* Leigh Hunt. OnPM
(Dream of Venus, A.) AWP
I dreamt. I saw three ladies in a tree. The Three Ladies. Robert Creeley. NeAP
I dreamt I was in love again. The One before the Last. Rupert Brooke. OBVV
I dreamt it! such a funny thing. What the Prince of I Dreamt. Henry Cholmondeley-Pennell. NA
I dreamt last night of you, John-John. John-John. Thomas MacDonagh. AnIV; AWP; HBMV; JAWP; LBBV; OnYI; OxBI; TIP; WBP
I dreamt not that love's way. W. W. Gibson. *Fr.* Marriage. LO
I Dreamt She Came. Vaughn Francis Meisling. MuM
I Dreamt That I Dwelt in Marble Halls. Alfred Bunn. *Fr.* The Bohemian Girl. OlF
(I Dreamt I Dwelt in Marble Halls.) TreFS
I dreamt that suddenly the metropolitan sky. Metropolis. John Hall. NeTW
I dreamt that with a bullet in my side. The Triple Dream. Mikhail Lermontov. LiTW
I Dreamt the Old, Old Dream Anew. Heine, *tr. fr. German by* Herman Salinger. AnGP
I drew it from its china tomb. A Dead Letter. Austin Dobson. BPN; HBV; POTT; PoVP; VA
I drew the blind on Christmas Morn. Red Sky at Morning. Gilbert Thomas. LO; TreFS
I drink of the ale of Southwark, I drink of the ale of Chepe. The Maltworm's Madrigal. Austin Dobson. HBV
I drive my chariot down through the East Gate. The Nineteen Han Poems, XIV. *Unknown, tr. fr. Chinese.* WhP
I drive my chariot up to the Eastern Gate. *Unknown, tr. fr. Chinese by* Arthur Waley. Seventeen Old Poems, 12. TrCh
I drive through the radiant peace that dwells. My Troop. Björnstjerne Björnson. AnNoLy
I, driven, deeper driven in the glade. Tree Purge. George Rostrevor Hamilton. POTE
I dropped my pen—and listened to the wind. Sonnet: Composed While the Author Was Engaged in Writing a Tract Occasioned by the Convention of Cintra. Wordsworth. ChER

I dropped my wad. Limericised Classics, V: Spoon River Anthology. Edwin Meade Robinson. HBMV
I drove up to the graveyard, which. The Soul Longs to Return Whence It Came. Richard Eberhart. AmP; ExPo; LiTM; TriL
I du believe in Freedom's cause. The Pious Editor's [*or* The Candidate's] Creed. James Russell Lowell. *Fr.* The Biglow Papers. AnNE; BOHV; IAP; MOAP; PIAE; REAL; TOP; YaD
I dug and dug amongst the snow. Christina Rossetti. *Fr.* Sing-Song. EmBrPo
I dug, beneath the cypress shade. The Grave of Love [*or* Beneath the Cypress Shade]. Thomas Love Peacock. BCEP; CH; EnRP; ERP; EV-4; GTBS; GTBS-D; HBV; OBEV (1st ed.); OBRV
I dwell alone—I dwell alone, alone. Autumn. Christina Rossetti. EmBrPo
I dwell apart. The Hermit. Hsü Pen. PoHN
I dwell for a short space in a lofty tower. Through Arched Windows. Frank Oliver Call. CPG
I dwell in grace's court. Content and Rich. Robert Southwell. OBSC; SiCE
I dwell in groves that gilt are with the sun. Mirth and Melancholy. Margaret Cavendish, Duchess of Newcastle. DiM
I dwell in mountain caverns. The Giant. Esaias Tegnér. AnSL
I dwell in possibility. Emily Dickinson. OxBA
I dwell in the sea that is wild and deep. The Sea by the Wood. Duncan Campbell Scott. CPG
I dwell in the wood that is dark and kind. The Wood by the Sea. Duncan Campbell Scott. CPG
I Dwell on Trifles. John Clare. *Fr.* The Flitting. RO
I dwells in the herth and I breathes in the hair. Cockney Enigma on the Letter H [*or* Travesty of Miss Fanshawe's Enigma]. Horace Mayhew. BOHV; PA
I dwelt alone. Eulalie; a Song. Poe. LaNeLa; MOAP
I dwelt in a city enchanted. The City of Prague. William Jeffery Prowse. CenHV
I Dye Alive. Robert Southwell. *See* I Die Alive.
I dyed my rooms in candle glow. The Heart Is Bethlehem. Gertrude Hanson. ChIP
I eagerly await your miniature, wish the artist would hurry. Letter to My Wife. Keidrych Rhys. WaP
I eat my peas with honey. Peas. *Unknown.* BoN; CenHV; FaPON
I edged back against the night. High Tide. Jean Starr Untermeyer. MAP; MCCG; MoAmPo; NeMA; TSW; TSWC
I, Egill, rover of the North, am cast. The Death Song of Egil the Son of Grim. Henry Adams Bellows. PaOS
I encountered the crowd returning from amusements. Resolution of Dependence. George Barker. FaBoTw; LiTB; LiTM (rev. ed.)
I end as I began. L'Envoi. Robert Buchanan. TVSH
I enter and as I enter all is abandoned. Microcosmos, I. Nigel Heseltine. NeBP
I enter, and I see thee in the gloom. Divina Commedia, III. Longfellow. AmP; AmPP; AnAmPo; AnFE; AnNE; APA; APW; CoAnAm; CoBA; CoV; ES; GoBC; IAP; LA; LPS-2; MOAP; NePA; OBAV; OuHeWo; OxBA; PIAE; PtP; ReaPo; TCAP; TOP
I enter the court. A Forsaken Garden. Po Chü-i. PoHN
I enter'd in—I knew not where. Verses Written upon an Ecstasy of High Contemplation. St. John of the Cross, *tr. by* E. Allison Peers. TeCS
I entered a vast cathedral. Worship. Bob Jones, Jr. BePJ
I entered an ancient temple at the dawn. Sanctuary in Po-shan Temple. Chang Ch'ien. WhP
I entered in, I know not where. Verses Written after an Ecstasy of High Exaltation. St. John of the Cross, *tr. by* Roy Campbell. AnSpL-1
I, entrance door to Tarpeia's house, swung open, once. The Complaint of Tarpeia's Door. Propertius. Elegies, I, 16. LaP; LiTW
I Entreat You, Alfred Tennyson. Walter Savage Landor. OAEP
I envy every flower that blows. A Lover's Envy. Henry van Dyke. HBV
I envy no mans rest. *Unknown.* SeCSL
I envy not Endymion now no more. Sonnet. Earl of Stirling. Aurora, XXIX. ElL
I envy not in any moods. In Memoriam A. H. H., XXVII [*or* Lost Love]. Tennyson. BEL; BPN; CoBE; EM-2; EmBrPo; EnL; EnLi-2; EnLit; EPN; EPP; FaBoEn; GEPC; GTSL; HBV; LEAP; LiTB; LiTG; LiTL; MaRV; OAEP; OuHeWo; PIAE; TCEP; TOP; TreFS; TyEnPo; ViPo; VLEP
I envy not the lark his song divine. Invention. Sir William Watson. HBV
I envy not the sun. Aspiration. John Banister Tabb. LO
I envy that village. Girl from Roumely. Alexandros Pallis. MoGP
I envy the feeble old man. The Lover Envies an Old Man. Shaemas O'Sheel. SBMV
I, Epictetus, was a slave; a cripple, I. The Sage. *Unknown.* GrPE
I even I know the Eastern Gate of Heaven. He Knoweth the Souls of the East. *Unknown.* *Fr.* Book of the Dead. AWP
I expect to pass thru this world but once. But Once. *Unknown.* BLP
I Explain. Stephen Crane. War Is Kind, VI. AA; AmP; TCAP
I faced the Gods upon a peak of snow. Birds of Prey. Leconte de Lisle. TrFP
I fain would be a sculptor of the soul. Sculptor of the Soul. Toyohiko Kagawa. MaRV
I fall and stumble as I grope my way. Clinging to Thee. *Unknown.* SoLD
I falter where I firmly trod. The Larger Hope. Tennyson. *Fr.* In Memoriam A. H. H., LV. MaRV
I fancy that I'm an unrequited lover. The Unrequited Lover. T'ai Wang-shu. ChLP
I favor most in flowers the shyest ones. Noctiflora. Maurice Lesemann. NP
I fear, I fear the rarity. Death by Rarity. Marguerite Young. LiTA
I fear, I shall begin to grow in love. The Parasite. Ben Jonson. *Fr.* Volpone. CoEV
I Fear No Power a Woman Wields. Ernest McGaffey. AA; BLP; HBV; LBAP
I fear not henceforth death. Madrigal. William Drummond of Hawthornden. ElSeCe; LO
I fear that Puck is dead—it is so long. The Death of Puck. Eugene Lee-Hamilton. HBMV; OBVV
I fear the poor. Noblemen. Miles M. Dawson. BAP
I Fear Thy Kisses, Gentle Maiden. Shelley. EmBrPo; GTBS; GTBS-D; GTBS-W; GTSE; HBV; LiTL; LPS-1; ViBoPo
(To ——.) BPN; EM-2; EnRP; EPN; ERP; GTSL; InPo
I fear to love thee, Sweet, because. To Olivia. Francis Thompson. BMEP; MBP; MoBrPo
I feast my eyes upon you. Song of Songs. Tzu Yeh. ChLP; PoHN
I feast on the grape hill. The Grape Hill. Endre Ady. OnPM
I Feed a Flame Within [Which So Torments Me]. Dryden. *See* Song: "I feed a flame within . . ."
I feel a breath from other planets blowing. Rapture. Stefan George. AWP; JAWP; WBP
I feel a newer life in every gale. May. J. G. Percival. BAV; BoTP; LPS-2
I feel a poem in my heart to-night. Embryo. Mary Ashley Townsend. AA; HBV
I feel an air from other planets flowing. Transport. Stefan George. LiTW
I Feel I Am. John Clare. SeCePo
I feel it when the game is done. Footnote to Tennyson. Gerald Bullett. FiBHP
I Feel Like My Time Ain't Long ("I feel like"), *with music.* *Unknown.* BoAN-2
I Feel Like My Time Ain't Long ("Oh, de hearse keep a-rollin'"), *with music.* *Unknown.* OuSiCo
I feel my genial spirits droop. With Them That Rest. Milton. *Fr.* Samson Agonistes. LiA
I feel myself in need. George Moses Horton, Myself. George Moses Horton. NoCaPo
I feel myself like the flame. The Candle Flame. Janet Lewis. CrMA
I feel remorse for all that Time has done. Love's Remorse. Edwin Muir. LiTL
I feel so exceedingly lazy. A Hot-Weather Song. Don Marquis. HBMV; StVeCh; WhC; YaD
I feel that deep within me burns. Dmitri Venevitinov, *tr. fr. Russian by* C. M. Bowra. BoRS
I feel that in the days gone by. In Days Gone By. Ida M. Mills. BoTP
I feel the breath of the summer night. A Summer Night. Elizabeth Stoddard. AA
I feel the spring far off, far off. Spring in War-Time. Sara Teasdale. OHIP
I feel this barque of mine. Seas. Juan Ramón Jiménez. TeCS
I feel towards God just as a woman might. Spiritual Passion. George Barlow. OBVV
I feel towards you as toward a meagre few. Saint Teresa of Avila. Sister Mary St. Virginia. PraNu
I feel very sorry for/ Toys not played with. Not Any More. Dorothy Aldis. BoChLi
I feele my selfe endaungered beyond reason. Sonnet. Thomas Lodge. PoP
I fell into a sleep at midnight, while the frost. The Frost Elves. Archibald Lampman. UnW
I felt a cleavage in my mind. Emily Dickinson. MOAP; OxBA; TwP

I felt a funeral in my brain. Emily Dickinson. AnFE; APA; CoAnAm; CoV; ExPo; InPo; LiTA; MAPA; MOAP; OxBA; PoEL-5; PoRA; TwAmPo; TwP
I Felt a Spirit of Love Begin to Stir. Dante, *tr. fr. Italian by* Dante Gabriel Rossetti. *Fr.* La Vita Nuova. AWP; JAWP; PreP; WBP
I felt most deeply in what world I was. Wordsworth. *Fr.* The Prelude, X. NBE
I felt no tremor and I caught no sound. The White Dust. W. W. Gibson. MoBrPo; NeMA
I felt the lurch and halt of her heart. Lightning. D. H. Lawrence. LiTL; MBP; MoAB; MoBrPo
I felt the wind soft from the land of souls. Traveling South toward Italy. Elizabeth Barrett Browning. *Fr.* Aurora Leigh, VII. BCEP
I felt the world a-spinning on its nave. The Last Journey. John Davidson. *Fr.* The Testament of John Davidson. BSV; GoTS
I fight a battle every day. The Fighter. S. E. Kiser. BLPA
I Fights Mit Sigel! Grant P. Robinson. BLPA
I fill this cup to one made up. A Health. Edward Coote Pinkney. AA; AnAmPo; APW; BAP; HBV; IAP; InP; LA; LBAP; LPS-1; MOAP; PR; SPP; TCAP; TreFS
I find it normal, passing these great frontiers. Manchouli. William Empson. CoBMV
I Find My God. V. Sackville-West. *Fr.* Solitude. QS
I find no peace, and all my war is done. Description of the Contrarious Passions in a Lover [*or* Love's Inconsistency]. Petrarch, *tr. by* Sir Thomas Wyatt. Sonnets to Laura: To Laura in Life, CIV. AWP; BLV; ElSeCe; EnLi-1 (1949 ed.); JAWP; LiTB; LiTL; OAEP; OuHeWo; PeBoSo; PoFS; PreP; ReEn; ReIE; SiPS; TrGrPo; TuPP; WBP
I find no peace and bear no arms for war. Sonnet. Petrarch, *tr. by* T. G. Bergin. Sonnets to Laura: To Laura in Life, CIV. LyPI
I find no peace, yet from all wars abstain me. Petrarch, *tr. by* Joseph Auslander. Sonnets to Laura: To Laura in Life, CIV. PrPoCR
I first adventure, with foolhardy might. Prologue. Joseph Hall. *Fr.* Virgidemiarum. ReEn; ReIE; SiCE; ViBoPo
I first informed them that we were to fly. Ulysses and the Sirens. Homer. *Fr.* The Odyssey. ReEn
I first tasted under Apollo's lips. Evadne. Hilda Doolittle ("H. D."). AV; LoPS; MAPA; MOAP
I fish for minnows in the lake. Epigram. Su T'ung-po. OnPC
I fix mine eye on thine and there. Witchcraft by a Picture. John Donne. PoFS
I fled Him, down the nights and down the days. The Hound of Heaven. Francis Thompson. ACP; AnFE; ATP; BEL; BLV; BMEP; BoLiVe; CaAE; CAW; CBPC; CoBE; CP; EmBrPo; EnL; EnLi-2; EnLit; EPN; EPP; EV-5; FaFP; GTBS-W; GoBC; GoTL; GrCo-2; GTSL; HBV; JKCP; LBBV; LEAP; LiA; LiTB; LiTM; LoBV; MaRV; MBP; MCCG; MM; MoAB; MoBrPo; OAEP; OBMV; OtMeF; OxBoCh; PIAE; PIR; PoE; PoEL-5; PoLi; POTT; PoVP; PreP; SeCePo; SeCeV; TCEP; TCPD; TOP; TreF; TrGrPo; TwCrTr; TyEnPo; UnPo (1st ed.); ViBoPo; ViP; ViPP; VLEP; WGRP; WHA
I fling my soul to the air like a falcon flying. *See* I flung my soul . . .
I fling myself against the ground. The Good Ground. Virginia Moore. YT
I Flung Me Round Him. Roden Noel. *Fr.* The Water-Nymph and the Boy. HBV; OBEV (1st ed.); OBVV (Song of the Water-Nymph.) BMEP
I flung [*or* fling] my soul to the air like a falcon flying. The Falconer of God. William Rose Benét. BAP; CAW; CP; CV; GBV (1952 ed.); HBMV; LEAP; MaRV; NP; NV; PC; PG; PoeMoYo; POT; PoTo; QS; SBMV; TCAP; TCPD; WGRP
I fly the crowded roads where thousands hurry. Sonnet. Pierre de Ronsard. LiA
I fold my two hands o'er my face. Lover's Memory. F. Tennyson Jesse. DiM
I Follow, Lo, the Footing. Ben Jonson. LiTL
I followed a barbed-wire fence. Holding-Paddock. William Hart-Smith. AnNZ
I followed my Duke ere I was a lover. Sir Richard's Song. Kipling. OtMeF
I followed once a fleet and mighty serpent. A Subterranean City. Thomas Lovell Beddoes. HoPM
I followed, splendid season. Trouble at Sea. Thomas Prys. PrWP
I followed where they led. His Throne Is with the Outcast. James Russell Lowell. ChIP
I, for long days a stranger. Petition. Clinton Scollard. BAP; MaRV
I for thy sake was pierced with heavy sorrow. Good Friday. Girolamo Savonarola. ChIP; OQP; QP-1
I fought under Lee and Stonewall. Enlisted. "Eliza Calvert Hall." MDAH
I found a ball of grass among the hay. Mouse's Nest. John Clare. ChTr; ExPo; LiTB; LoBV; SeCeV
I found a bird's nest in a tree. Misfortune. Ralph Bergengren. FAOV
I found a calf in the goldenrod. Calf in the Goldenrod. Judy Van der Veer. MuM
I found a dimpled spider, fat and white. Design. Robert Frost. CoBMV; CrMA; Po; SeCeV
I found a flower in a desolate plot. The Black Wall-Flower. Frances Anne Kemble. VA
I found a flower in the wood. Wood Flower. Richard Le Gallienne. HBMV
I Found a Horseshoe, *with music. Unknown.* AS
I found a little brown purse. Found in the Woods. Irene F. Pawsey. BoTP
I found a little fairy flute. Fairy Music. Enid Blyton. BoTP
I found a little old elfin man. The Dandelion. Katharine Pyle. DD
I found a little record of her days. Mother's Diary. Elsie Duncan Sanders. DDA
I found a pigeon's skull on the machair. Perfect. "Hugh MacDiarmid." NeBP
I found a torrent falling in a glen. The Torrent. E. A. Robinson. MaPo; NePA
I found a yellow flower in the grass. A Summer Sanctuary. John Hall Ingham. AA
I found at daybreak yester morn. Medieval Norman Songs, V. *Unknown, tr. by* John Addington Symonds. AWP; JAWP; WBP
I Found God. Mary Afton Thacker. MaRV
I Found Her Out There. Thomas Hardy. CH; LO; MoVE; PoEL-5
I found him in a shell hole. Frenchie. Frank C. McCarthy. AlBD
I found Him in the shining of the stars. Arthur's Disillusionment. Tennyson. *Fr.* Idylls of the King. TreFS
I found him openly wearing her token. A Conquest. Walter Herries Pollock. OBVV; VA
I found in dreams a place of wind and flowers. A Ballad of Life. Swinburne. HBV; PoVP; VLEP
I found in Innisfail the fair. Aldfrid's Itinerary through Ireland. *Unknown.* OnYI
I found myself one day all, all alone. Three Ballate, I. Angelo Poliziano. AWP
I found myself, young girls, while it was May. Dance Song. Angelo Poliziano. LyPI
I found no beauty on the mountain heights. Beauty. Joel Elias Spingarn. HBMV
I found ten kinds of wild flowers growing. Late October. Sara Teasdale. YeAr
I found that ivory image there. Crazy Jane Grown Old Looks at the Dancers. W. B. Yeats. AtBAP
I found the phrase to every thought. Emily Dickinson. AnFE; APA; CoAnAm; OBAV (Utterance.) AA; TOP
"I found the place last winter." Eric's voice. The Dreaming Trout. Charles Bruce. *Fr.* The Flowing Summer. CaP
I found the task that I had dreaded so. The Dreaded Task. Margaret E. Bruner. PoToHe
I found Thee in my heart, O Lord. Edward Dowden. *Fr.* New Hymns for Solitude. TrPWD
I found them lying on the shore. The Dolls. Frederic Prokosch. LiTM (1946 ed.)
I found you fluttering. Caught by Chance. T. W. Ramsey. HaMV
I found you in a newspaper. Idea of a Swimmer. Jean-Richard Bloch. TrJP
I, François Villon, ta'en at last. Would I Be Shrived? Villon. BLPA
I gaed to spend a week in Fife. The Annuity. George Outram. BOHV; BSV; EBSV; HBV
I Gained a Greater Strength. Cullen Jones. *Fr.* Sonnets in Wartime. MuM
I gat your letter winsome Willie. To William Simpson of Ochiltree [*or* Epistle to William Simpson, Ochiltree]. Burns. BSV; EBSV; MCCG
"I gather my poems out of the heart of the clover." The Poet's Harvesting. Charles J. O'Malley. CAW
I gather thyme upon the sunny hills. Immalee. Christina Rossetti. ThWaDe
I gather where I hope to gain. *Unknown.* SeCSL
I gathered in my rod and line. Toyo, *tr. fr. Japanese by* Lois J. Erickson. SoLD
I gathered marble Venus in my arms. A Parable for Poetasters. Oliver St. John Gogarty. WhC
I gathered with a careless hand. Fallen Cities. Gerald Gould. PoeT; PtOT
I gave a beggar from my scanty store. The True Gift. *Unknown.* ChIP; MaRV
I Gave Her Cakes; I Gave Her Ale. *Unknown.* AtBAP; TreFS

I Gave Her Cakes (*continued*)
(Cakes and Ale.) FaFP; SiTL
("I gave her cakes; [and] I gave her ale.") EG; LO

I gave into a brown and tired hand. Christmas Roses. May Riley Smith. PEOR

I gave my heart to a woman. W. E. Henley. Echoes, XXXVI. BPN

I Gave My Life for Thee. Frances Ridley Havergal. OlF; VA

I Gave My Love. Lexie Dean Robertson. PR

I gave my love a cherry without a stone. Captain Wedderburn's Courtship (B *vers.*). *Unknown.* ViBoFo

I gave the commons their sufficient meed. The Lawgiver's Boast. Solon, *tr. by* Gilbert Highet. OxBG

I gave the people freedom clear. Rule of Fair Play. Solon, *tr. by* Henry Nelson Coleridge. GrR; PoFr

I gave to Hope a watch of mine: but he. Hope. George Herbert. PoEL-2

I gave you. Gifts. Huang Pien. PoHN

I gave you immortality and what did you give me? Dain do Eimhir, XIX. Sorley Maclean. NeBP

I gaze across the Nile; flamelike and red. The Sphinx. Lord Alfred Douglas. PtOT

I gaze upon the beauty of the stars. The Beauty of the Stars. Moses ibn Ezra. TrJP

I gaze with grief upon our generation. A Thought. Mikhail Yurevich Lermontov. AWP; WoL

I gazed, and lo! Afar and near. Battle of Somerset. Cornelius C. Cullen. PAH

I gazed forth from my wintry tent. In Camp. William Haines Lytle. BlG

I gazed upon her picture. The Picture. Heine. OnPM

I Gazed upon the Cloudless Moon. Emily Brontë. ChTr

I gazed upon the glorious sky. June. Bryant. AA; CoBA; HBV; IAP; LPS-2; MOAP; SN; TCAP

I gazed with faith upon the sea. On the Ferry. Douglas V. Kane. MuM

I Gazed Within. Emily Jane Brontë. ViBoPo

I Get Up at Dawn. Lu Yu, *tr. fr. Chinese by* Kenneth Rexroth. OnPC

I get up. I am sick. Morning. Chu Shu Chen. OnPC

I gits my chillun up 'fo' day. Dew. John Charles McNeill. NoCaPo

I give more praise to Troy's redoubt. On Troy. Oliver St. John Gogarty. WhC

I Give My Heart to Thee. Standish James O'Grady. TIP

I Give My Heart to Thee. *Unknown, tr. fr. Latin by* Ray Palmer. BePJ

I Give My Soldier Boy a Blade. William Maginn. BlG; HBV; PAH
(Soldier-Boy, The.) VA

I Give Thanks. Grace Fallow Norton. NP

I give thee all, I can no more. A Sum. "Lewis Carroll." BoN

I give thee thanks, Adonai! My Soul in the Bundle of Life. *Unknown. Fr.* The Dead Sea Scrolls. TrJP

I give thee treasures hour by hour. Then. Rose Terry Cooke. HBV

I give these flowers and fruits, these leafy sprays. Green. Paul Verlaine. LiTW

I give you a house of snow. The Dove of New Snow. Vachel Lindsay. MAP; MoAmPo

I give you a land of sun and flow'rs, and summer the whole year long. Oklahoma. Harriet Parker Camden. PoRL

I give you horses for your games in May. Sonnets of the Months: May [*or* Of the Months: May]. Folgore da San Germiniano. AWP; LyMA; LyPI

I give you meadow-lands in April, fair. Sonnets of the Months: April [*or* Of the Months: April]. Folgore da San Geminiano. AWP; LyMA; LyPI

I give you my hand. Microcosmos, VIII. Nigel Heseltine. NeBP

I give you now Professor Twist. The Purist. Ogden Nash. FiBHP; MoAmPo (1950 ed.); MoShBr; NeMA; PreP

I Give You the End of a Golden String. Blake. *See* To the Christians.

I give you these verses. Jet Eyes. Baudelaire. LiA

I give you this Bible and more to take. Inscription on the Flyleaf of a Bible. Dannie Abse. TrJP

I glance from humble toil and see. Kitchen Window. J. E. H. MacDonald. CaP; OCL; TwCaPo

I gnarled me where the spinster tree. Waterwall Blues. Howard Moss. MoPo; NePA

I go about dumbfoundedly, and show a dullard's glance. The Glorious Game. Richard Burton. HBMV

I go a-fishing. Angler. Isabel Fiske Conant. PC

I Go a-Walking. Barbara Young. DDA

I Go by Road. Catulle Mendès, *tr. fr. French by* Alice Meynell. AWP; JAWP; TrJP; WBP

I go down from the hill in gladness. A Farewell. "Æ." AnIV

I go down to Dupont Street. Chinatown Chant. Tom MacInnes. CaP; OCL

I Go Fishin'. Richard S. Powell. IHA

I go in vesture spun by hands. The Secret. Jessie B. Rittenhouse. PC

I go North to cold, to home, to Kinnaird. Kinnaird Head. George Bruce. NeBP; PoN

I go not where I will but must. The Journey. John T. McFarland. OQP; QP-1

I go out of the darkness. Lady Izumi Shikibu, *tr. fr. Japanese by* Kenneth Rexroth. OnPJ

I go separately. Santa Fe Trail. Barbara Guest. NeAP

I go through the fields of blue water. Essex. Arthur Shearly Cripps. PoeT

I go to concert, party, ball. My Rival. Kipling. OnPP

I go to knit two clans together. The Wedding of the Clans. Aubrey Thomas De Vere. AnIL; GTIV; IrPN; TIP

I Go to Prove My Soul. Robert Browning. *See* In His Good Time.

I Go to School. Sister Mary Madeleva. SaFP

I Go to This Window. E. E. Cummings. NAMP

I go with earth, experiencing light. Time in the Sun. Louise Townsend Nicholl. NePoAm-2

I go with silent feet and slow. The Monk. "Seumas O'Sullivan." GTIV

I, God, that all the world have wrought. Noah's Flood. *Unknown.* BEL

I, Gonzalo de Berceo, in the gentle summertide. The Praise of Spring. Gonzalo de Berceo. *Fr.* The Miracles of Our Lady. AnSpL-1; TeCS

I got a cross. Shout All over God's Heaven. *Unknown.* IHA

I Got a Gal at the Head of the Holler. *Unknown. See* Sourwood Mountain.

I Got a Home in [*or* in-a] Dat Rock. *Unknown.* APW; BoAN-1, *with music;* OlF

I got a kite on New Year's Day. Kite-flying. Mary McNeil Fenollosa. RAR

I Got a Letter from Jesus, *with music. Unknown.* AS

I got a robe, you got a robe. All God's Chillun Got Wings [*or* Goin' to Walk All ovah God's Heb'n]. *Unknown.* BoAN-1; HiLiAm; OlF; SiTL; TreFS

I got me flowers to straw Thy way. Easter. George Herbert. AtBAP; BoTP; CH; EG; FaBoCh; FaBoEn; LEAP; LoGBV; OBEV; OBS; OHIP; PCH; SeEP; TrGrPo

I got so I could hear his name. Emily Dickinson. CoBA; LoPS; MOAP; ReMP

I Got to Go to School. Nixon Waterman. PTA-2

I Got to Roll, *with music. Unknown.* OuSiCo

I got up one mornin' jes' 'bout four o'clock. Stagolee (B *vers.*). *Unknown.* BaBo; ViBoFo

I gotta lov' for Angela. Between Two Loves. T. A. Daly. BOHV; MAP; MoAmPo (1942 ed.); PoeMoYo; PoMa; StVeCh (1940 ed.); VOD

I grant indeed that fields and flocks have charms. Truth in Poetry. George Crabbe. *Fr.* The Village. SeCePo

I grant thou wert not married to my Muse. Sonnets, LXXXII. Shakespeare. PeBoSo

I Grant Your Eyes Are Much More Bright. *At. to* John Bulteel. SeCL

I grasped a thread of silver; it cut me to the bone. A Rhyme Out of Motley. Amy Lowell. TBM

I grazed the green as I fell. Summer. P. K. Page. PeCV

I greet my love with wine and gladsome lay. Sabbath, My Love. Judah Halevi. TrJP

I greet thee, my Redeemer sure. Salutation to Jesus Christ. John Calvin. MaRV; WGRP

I greet you, Bellerophon, as you come. The Airmail Arrives. Ethel Romig Fuller. PoTo

I greet you now, my schoolmates dear. School Greeting. G. Scott. MeMeAg

I greet you, son, with joy and winter rue. Muse in Late November. Jonathan Henderson Brooks. PoNe

I grew assured, before I asked. Sweet Meeting of Desires. Coventry Patmore. LPS-1

I grew up at Jung-yang. Stopping the Night at Jung-yang. Po Chü-i. TrCh

I grieve about my fellow-men. Wednesday. "Elspeth." WhC

I grieve; and dare not show my discontent! Self and the Otherself. Elizabeth, Queen of England. DiM; LO

I Grieve for Beauty Wasted. Grace Noll Crowell. LS

I Grieve Not That Ripe Knowledge. James Russell Lowell. IAP

I grieve to think of you alone. Prescience. Donald Jeffrey Hayes. PoNe

I grieve when I think on the dear happy days of my youth. Draherin O Machree. *Unknown.* AnIV

I Grieved for Buonaparté. Wordsworth. BPN; EmBrPo; EnLP; EnRP; GEPC; PeBoSo; Po; REAL

I grieved to learn 'twas just a myth. Still Undaunted. George B. Ryan. CIV

I groan as I put out. An Island Fisherman. Katharine Tynan. TIP

I guess I'm bad as I can be. Incorrigible. Burges Johnson. PoMa

I guess my health is gittin' poor. Headaches Jes' 'fore School. Maurice C. Johnson. FAOV

I. H. B. William Winter. AA; OBAV
I. H. S. Sean Jennett. MeRV
I Had a Black Man. *Unknown.* OxBoLi
I had a cat and the cat pleased me. Barnyard Song. *Unknown.* OxNR; TrAS
I had a chair at every hearth. The Lamentation of the Old Pensioner. W. B. Yeats. TIP
I had a dog/ Whose name was Buff. *Unknown.* OxNR
I Had a Dove. Keats. CBPC; CH; OTPC
(Dove, The.) HBV
(Song: "I had a dove, and the sweet dove died.") CG; FaPON; PRWS; ThWaDe; TVSH
I had a dream, and in that dream. William Snowden Battles. *Fr.* The Doctor's Dream. PoP
"I had a dream last night." E. A. Robinson. *Fr.* Captain Craig. PC
I had a dream last night. I dreamed. Andre. Gwendolyn Brooks. TiPo (1959 ed.)
I had a dream of death: that I returned. The Vision. Virginia Moran Evans. UnW
I had a dream of some great house of stone. Conspiracy. George Sterling. UnW
I had a dream, one glorious, summer night. Beauty. William Winter. LPS-3
I had a dream, which was not all a dream. Darkness. Byron. BCEP; BPN; EmBrPo; EnRP; EPN; LiTB; OAEP; PoEL-4
I Had a Duck-billed Platypus. Patrick Barrington. CenHV; FiBHP
(Diplomatic Platypus, The.) SHBV-4
I Had a Fair Young Son. Sara Bard Field. MuM
I had a feeling in my neck. Mumps. Elizabeth Madox Roberts. FaPON; GaP; LiL; MPB; TSW
I had a friend, but he. False Friend. Al-Hajjam. MooP
I had a friend: or thought I had a friend. The Mantis Friend. Vincent McHugh. NePoAm-2
I had a garden where for sunless days. The Music of a Friend. Louis V. Ledoux. OQP; QP-2
I had a heart as good as gold. The Golden Heart. Witter Bynner. HBMV
I Had a Hippopotamus. Patrick Barrington. CenHV
I had a horse. Full Sky. Jules Supervielle. MiCF
I had a hoss, his name was Bill. The Crazy Dixie. *Unknown.* SoAF
I had a kinsman; he. Bereavement. Euripides. *Fr.* Alcestis. OxBG
I had a little bird. The Orphan's Song. Sydney Dobell. CH; GTBS-D; LEAP; OTPC; PPL
I had a little cow/ Hey diddle, ho diddle! *Unknown.* OxNR
I had a little dog and his name was Blue Bell. *Unknown.* OxNR; SAS
I had a little dog, and my dog was very small. The Little Dog. Frances Cornford. RIS
I Had a Little Doggy. *Unknown.* BoChLi; MPB; OTPC
("I had a little Doggy that used to sit and beg.") PPL; SAS
I had a little hen, the prettiest ever seen. Mother Goose. BoTP
I had a little hobby horse. Mother Goose. BoChLi; BoTP; GFA; OxNR; SiTL; WP
I had a little horse, his name was Dappled [*or* Dobbin] Grey. *Unknown.* BoN; OxNR
I had a little husband. Mother Goose. BoTP; ExPo; FaFP; HBV; HBVY; OTPC; OxNR; PPL
I had a little moppet. *Unknown.* OxNR
I had a little nag. *Unknown.* OxNR
I had a little nut-tree; nothing would it bear. Mother Goose. BoChLi; BoTP; CBPC; CH; ExPo; GBV (1952 ed.); LiTG; MoShBr; OTPC; OxBoLi; OxNR; PoRh; PPL; RIS; SiTL; StVeCh; TiPo (1952 ed.) WP
I had a little pony. Mother Goose. BoChLi; BoTP; GFA; OTPC; OxNR; PCH; PPL; RIS; SiTL; StVeCh; TiPo (1959 ed.); WP
I had a little pussy. Catkin. *Unknown.* GFA; MPB
I had a little snowball once. *Unknown.* GFA
I had a little sorrow. The Penitent. Edna St. Vincent Millay. ALV; BOHV; DDA; YaD
I had a little wife. *Unknown.* OxNR
I had a mother who read to me. The Reading Mother. Strickland Gillilan. BLPA; DDA
I had a nickel and I walked around the block. *Unknown.* SiTL
I had a penny. Market Square. A. A. Milne. TiPo (1959 ed.)
I had a rich old great-aunt. Legacy. Nancy Byrd Turner. BrR; MoSiPe
I had a sailor uncle once. A Sailor Uncle. *Unknown.* OnHT
I had a silver buckle. The Buckle. Walter de la Mare. BrR; PoRh
I had a sudden vision in the night. The Ladder. Leonora Speyer. BAP; HBMV; PG; TBM
"I had a true love but she left me." The Quaker's Wooing. *Unknown.* AS
I had a true love, if ever a girl had one. The Tri-colored Ribbon. Peadar Kearney. OnYI
I had a true-love, none so dear. Fortune's Wheel. Lord De Tabley. OBVV; PoVP; VA
I had a trusty comrade. The Good Comrade. Ludwig Uhland. LiA
I had a vision at last. Euripides Alexopoulos. Edgar Lee Masters. *Fr.* The New Spoon River. ChMo; CMP
I had a vision of a drooping band. Processional. Stanton A. Coblentz. UnW
I had a vision; was it in my sleep? Help, Sure Help [*or* At Torcello]. Arthur Hugh Clough. *Fr.* Dipsychus, Pt. II, sc. vii. BMV; PoVP; VLEP
I had a vision when the night was late. The Vision of Sin. Tennyson. BPN; EmBrPo; LiA; PoVP; ViPo; ViPP; VLEP
I had a wife, but she is gone. The Drunkard. Fenton Johnson. AnAmPo; LA
I had a willow whistle. The Piper. Rachel Field. PoRh
I had almost grown grey before my time. Resurgent. Richard Linn Edsall. JKCP (1955 ed.)
I had always thought. I Have Never Been Here Before. Jacob Glatstein. OnCuPl
I had ambition, by which sin. Ambition. W. H. Davies. MBP; MoBrPo; TrGrPo
I had an image of the bright, bare day. Pearl Diver. William Rose Benét. AnAmPo; BLV; LA
I had approached, like other youths, the shield. The Poet and the French Revolution. Wordsworth. *Fr.* The Prelude, XI. EPN
I had as lief be embraced by the porter at the hotel. Two Figures in Dense Violet Light [*or* Night]. Wallace Stevens. CoV; MAP; MoAB; MoAmPo; OnPM
I had been hungry all the years. Emily Dickinson. LiTA; LiTM (rev. ed.); MAP; MoAmPo
(Hunger.) CoBA; NeMA
I had been ill; and when I saw. Recovery from Mental Illness. H. C. Bosman. BoSA
I had been rowing for a long time. The White Water Lily. Stéphane Mallarmé. AnFP
I Had but Fifty Cents. *Unknown.* BeLS; BLPA; TreF
I had but one illusion—a pleasant fancy. Our Lives Are Rivers. Luis G. Urbina. AnMP
I had come to the house, in a cave of trees. Medusa. Louise Bogan. AWP; HoPM; InPo; MAP; MoAB; MoAmPo; MOAP; MoPo; MoVE; PoeMoYo; TCPD
I had expected. To Stephen Spender. Timothy Corsellis. WaP
I had for my winter evening walk. Good Hours. Robert Frost. RG
I had forgotten how to pray. When I Had Need of Him. S. E. Kiser. BLRP
I had found the secret of a garret-room. The Poets. Elizabeth Barrett Browning. *Fr.* Aurora Leigh, I. VA
I had gone broke, and got set to come back. Epigram. J. V. Cunningham. NePoAm
I had gone fruitless and defenceless, Lady. A Nun to Mary, Virgin. Sister Mary St. Virginia. ISi
I had heard of these things before—of chariots rumbling. Dido of Tunisia. Phyllis McGinley. NeTW
I had loved him for a year. Was There a Summer? Irene Rathbone. DiM
I had just gone to bed. Three Lyrics. Petronius Arbiter. LaP; LiTW
I had ma clothes cleaned. Dressed Up. Langston Hughes. GoSl
I had my birth where stars were born. My Birth. Minot Judson Savage. AA; WGRP
I had never before held death, pale and polished, in my hands. The Captain of the Oberon. Francis Webb. *Fr.* A Drum for Ben Boyd. NeLNL
I had no God but these. Christ and the Pagan. John Banister Tabb. CAW; JKCP; MeRV
I had no heart to join the dance. The Lonely Dancer. Richard Le Gallienne. BMEP
I had no thought of violets of late. Sonnet. Alice Dunbar Nelson. BANP; CDC; PoNe
I had no time to hate, because. Emily Dickinson. IAP; TCAP
(Little Toil of Love, The.) LiTL
(No Time to Hate.) BAP
I had not heard that there could be such blue. In Hawaiian Seas. Clifford Gessler. PoTo
I had not known that I was dead. On Easter Morn. Edith M. Thomas. EOAH
I had not known what life might be. The Lesson. Sister Mary Eleanore. JKCP (1955 ed.)
I had not minded walls. Emily Dickinson. AWP; InPo; MOAP
I had not noticed scarlet haw. Remembrance. John Richard Moreland. PR
I had not seen my son's dear face. San Lorenzo Giustiniani's Mother [*or* San Lorenzo's Mother]. Alice Meynell. HBV; POTT; TriL

I had not thought to have unlockt my lips. Temperance and Virginity. Milton. *Fr.* Comus. OBS
I had over-prepared the event. Villanelle; the Psychological Hour. Ezra Pound. MOAP; NP
I had returned from dreaming. Dream. Witter Bynner. NP
I Had Scarcely Fallen Asleep. John Gould Fletcher. MOAP
I had seen, as dawn was breaking. La Nuit Blanche. Kipling. MBP; MoBrPo
I had sworn to be a bachelor, she had sworn to be a maid. Platonic. William Terrett. LPS-I
I Had the Courage. Guillaume Apollinaire, *tr. fr. French by* Daisy Aldan. AnFP
I had to laugh. Horizons. Gwendolen Haste. BAP
I had two friends a while ago. De Gustibus. John Erskine. TBM
I had two pigeons bright and gay. *Unknown.* OxNR
I had walked a long way. Ballad of Thread for a Needle. Marjorie Allen Seiffert. TBM
I had walked life's way [*or* path] with an easy tread. I Met the Master Face to Face. *Unknown.* BePJ; BLRP
I had watched the ascension and decline of the moon. W. J. Turner. *Fr.* The Seven Days of the Sun. OBMV
I had written him a letter which I had, for want of better. Clancy of The Overflow. Andrew Barton Paterson. BoAu
I had written to Aunt Maud. Waste [*or* Aunt Maud]. Harry Graham. LiTG; MoShBr; SiTL
I had yesterday happiness gladly rejected. Semyon Yakovlevich Nadson, *tr. fr. Russian by* Sir Cecil Kisch. WaL
I Hae Laid a Herring in Saut. James Tytler. BOHV
I hae seen great anes and sat in great ha's. My Ain Fireside. Elizabeth Hamilton. FaBoBe; HBV; LPS-I
I haf von funny leedle poy. Leedle Yawcob Strauss. Charles Follen Adams. BOHV; PTA-I
I hafe set my hert so hye. I Have Set My Heart So High. *Unknown.* CoBE
I hail from high in the alkali. When West Comes East. Corey Ford. InMe
I hailed me a woman from the street. My Madonna. Robert W. Service. BLPA
I hailed the bus and I went for a ride. Bus Ride. Selma Robinson. *Fr.* Ferry Ride. FaPON
I halted at a pleasant inn. The Wayside Inn. *Unknown.* ADAH; TVSH
"I hardly ever ope my lips," one cries. Epigram [*or* Silence and Speech]. Richard Garnett. ALV; HBV; OtMeF
I hardly know you, and already I say to myself. Etude. Carlos Pellicer. AnCL
I hardly suppose I know anybody who wouldn't rather be a success than a failure. Kindly Unhitch That Star, Buddy. Ogden Nash. LiTA; LiTM
I Hate. Joachim du Bellay, *tr. fr. French by* Alan Conder. Regrets, LXVIII. TrFP
(Sonnet: "I hate the money-lending avarice," *tr. by* Ralph N. Currey.) FoS
I hate/ To wait. What Literature Needs. John Holmes. InMe
I hate a prologue to a story. The Duke of Benevento. Sir John Henry Moore. CEP; OBEC
I hate and love/ And if you ask me why. Catullus, *tr. fr. Latin by* Horace Gregory. RoL
I hate and love—the why I cannot tell. Love's Unreason. Catullus, *tr. fr. Latin.* OuHeWo
I hate my beauty in the glass. Thomas Hardy. *Fr.* The Beauty. LO
"I hate my verses, every line, every word." Love the Wild Swan. Robinson Jeffers. AnFE; CoAnAm; MAP; MoAB; MoAmPo; PoFr; TwAmPo
I hate that drum's discordant sound. The Drum [*or* Retort on the Foregoing]. John Scott of Amwell. OBEC; OBEV (new ed.); ViBoPo
I hate the country's dirt and manners, yet. Epistle to a Friend. William Habington. EV-2
I hate the cunning mantis, lean, mimetic. Notes for a Bestiary. Terence Heywood. LiTM
I hate the Cyclic poem, nor approve. Uncommon. Callimachus. OnPM
I hate the dreadful hollow behind the little wood. Maud. Tennyson. EmBrPo; OAEP; PIR; PoVP; ViPo; ViPP; VLEP
I hate the Florentine's rapacious greed. I Hate. Joachim du Bellay. Regrets, LXVIII. TrFP
I hate the man who builds his fame. The Poet and the Rose. John Gay. TCEP
I hate the money-lending avarice. Sonnet. Joachim du Bellay. *Fr.* Regrets. FoS
I hate thee, Death! Mors, Morituri Te Salutamus. Francis Burdett Money-Coutts. OBVV
I Hate Their Empty Shows. Horace. *See* Persian Fopperies.
I hate those pants that mother makes. The Small Boy's Loquitur. *Unknown.* CH
I hate to sing your hackneyed birds. A Panegyric on Geese. Francis S. Mahony. OnYI
I hate to spend the night. Thanks, Just the Same. *Unknown.* DDA
I hate to talk about it, 'cause. Little Danny Donkey. Helen Cowles LeCron. GFA
I hate your hackneyed epic, have no taste. Fastidious [*or* Odi Profanum Vulgus]. Callimachus. GrR; OxBG
I hated a fellow-man long ago. Hate. Herbert E. Palmer. POTE
I hated thee, fallen tyrant! I did groan. Feelings of a Republican on the Fall of Bonaparte. Shelley. AnEnPo
"I hates to think of dyin'," says the skipper to the mate. The Worried Skipper. Wallace Irwin. BLPA
I Haue a Yong Suster. *Unknown. See* I Have a Young Sister.
I Haunt the Hills That Overlook the Sea. John Davidson. *Fr.* The Testament of a Man Forbid. BSV
I have a bird of paradise. Hope. Mikhail Lermontov. BoR
I Have a Blue Piano. Else Lasker-Schüler, *tr. fr. German by* Ralph Manheim. TrJP
I have a bookcase, which is what. Shake, Mulleary, and Go-ethe. H. C. Bunner. ALV; AnAmPo; BOHV; FiBHP; InMe; LA; PFE
I have a boy of five years old. Anecdote for Fathers. Wordsworth. EmBrPo; EnRP; FAOV
I have a brother. Envy. Edgar Daniel Kramer. PoMa
I have a child of four years old. God Has Put It Away. Jörgen Moe. AnNoLy
I have a child; so fair. A Girl. Sappho. GrL; OxBG
I have a copper penny and another copper penny. Logic. *Unknown.* BOHV; PCH
I have a cup of common clay. The Common Things. Barbara Young. OQP; QP-I
I have a daughter,/ Clais fair. Clais. Sappho, *tr. by* H. De Vere Stacpoole. GrR
I have a dog,/ His name is Jack. My Doggie. C. Nurton. BoTP
I have a dream for you, Mother. For You, Mother. Hilda Conkling. HH
I have a fancy: how shall I bring it. The Secret. James Russell Lowell. IAP
I have a feeling for those ships. The Stone Fleet. Herman Melville. BAV; EtS
I Have a Friend. Anne Spencer. CDC
I have a friend who would give a price for those long fingers all of one length. Snakes, Mongooses, Snake-Charmers and the Like. Marianne Moore. ExPo
I have a funny Airedale dog. My Airedale Dog. W. L. Mason. GFA; UTS
I have a garden of my own. Child's Song. Thomas Moore. AlDL; ERP; GoBC; GTIV; OxBI; SUS; ViBoPo
I Have a Gentil Cok. *Unknown.* KN; NBE; SeCePo; ViBoPo
(Gentle Cock, The.) OxBoLi
I have a golden ball. A Rune of Riches. Florence Converse. BoTP; NLK; SUS
I have a grief. Agitato Ma Non Troppo. John Crowe Ransom. OxBA
I have a Gumbie Cat in mind, her name is Jennyanydots. The Old Gumbie Cat. T. S. Eliot. GoTP
I have a heart that cries to God. And with No Language but a Cry. Amos Niven Wilder. MaRV; QS
I have a horse—a ryghte goode horse. Ye Carpette Knyghte. "Lewis Carroll." AlDL
I have a kindly neighbor, one who stands. The Kindly Neighbor. Edgar A Guest. MaRV; PoToHe
I have a king who does not speak. Emily Dickinson. MAPA; TwAmPo
I Have a Life with Christ to Live. John Campbell Shairp. MaRV
I have a little boat. My Little Boat. Sarah Jane S. Harrington. RAR
I have a little daughter. At Singing Time. Anne P. L. Field. MOAH
I have a little hobby of saving odds and ends. A Nun's Hobby. Sister Mary of the Angels. PraNu
I have a little house. My Little House. J. M. Westrup. BoTP
I have a little inward light, which still. The Inward Light. Henry Septimus Sutton. WGRP
I have a little kinsman. The Discoverer. Edmund Clarence Stedman. AA; EOAH; HBV
I have a little pussy. Catkin. *Unknown.* GFA; MPB; OTPC (1946 ed.); TiPo
I have a little shadow that goes in and out with me. My Shadow. Robert Louis Stevenson. FaBoBe; FaPON; GFA; GoBP; HBV; HBVY; LiTG; MPB; NeHB; OnHT; OTPC; PCH; PECK; PoVP; RIS; StVeCh; TiPo; TreF; VLEP
I have a little sister, she is only two years old. My Little Sister. *Unknown.* OTPC (1923 ed.)
I have a little sister, they call her Peep, Peep. Mother Goose. BoChLi; BoTP; CBPC; OTPC (1946 ed.); OxNR; RIS; StVeCh; TiPo

I have a little valentine. My Valentine. Mary Catherine Parsons. TiPo (1952 ed.)
I have a little wat'ring pot. Thirsty Flowers. Arthur A. Knipe. GFA
"I have a Love I love too well." The Sacrilege. Thomas Hardy. VLEP
I have a mackintosh shiny brown. Chestnut Buds. Evelyn M. Williams. BoTP
I have a mistress, for perfections rare. A Devout Lover [*or* Love and Reverence]. Thomas Randolph. BCEP; EG; HBV; HoPM; LiTL; OBEV
I have a mother gone to glory. The Other Shore. *Unknown.* ABF
I have a name, a little name. The Pet Name. Elizabeth Barrett Browning. HBV; LPS-1
I Have a Need. Bilhana, *formerly at. to* Chauras, *tr. fr. Sanskrit by* E. Powys Mathers. *Fr.* Black Marigolds. OnPM
I have a need of dreaming. Autumn Song. Philip Clark Horton. CAG
I have a need of silence and of stars. Home. William Alexander Percy. *Fr.* In New York. LS; TBM
I have a new umbrella. My New Umbrella. M. M. Hutchinson. BoTP
I have a new vegetable garden, about two acres. Autobiography. Lu Yu. WhP
I Have a Noble Cock. *Unknown.* MeEV
I have a pair of boots so rare. The Sandman. *Unknown.* RIS
I have a passion for the name of Mary. Mary. Byron. *Fr.* Don Juan, V. GEPC
I have a picture in my room in which. Intaglio. Henri Coulette. NePoEA
I have a pin. The Keepsake. Hsü Ching Fan. PoHN
I have a proved, unerring Guide. The Unerring Guide. Anna Shipton. BLRP
I Have a Rendezvous with Death. Alan Seeger. AOAH; BAP; BAV; BBV; BLPA; BTP; CaAE; CDC; CP; DD; FaFP; HBV; InP; LEAP; LiTM; LPS-1; MaRV; MCCG; MM; NeHB; NeMA; NP; NV; OBAV; OHFP; PaA; PFY; PoeMoYo; PoMa; POT; PoTo; PTA-2; PYM; SBMV; SoV; TCAP; TOP; TreF; ViBoPo; VOD (1931 ed.); WaP; YT
(Rendezvous, The.) OtMeF; WGRP
I Have a Rendezvous with Life. Countee Cullen. LPS-1; MaRV; OQP; PoTo; QP-1
I have a river in my mind. Six o'Clock. Owen Dodson. PoNe
I Have a Roof. Ada Jackson. TrPWD
I have a room whereinto no one enters. Memory. Christina Rossetti. CoEV
"I have a ship in the North Countrie." The Sweet Trinity; or, The Golden Vanity (B *vers.*). *Unknown.* BaBo
I have a smiling face, she said. The Mask. Elizabeth Barrett Browning. OBVV; VLEP
I Have a Son. Emory Pottle. PEDC
I have a son, a little son, a boy just five years old. The Three Sons. John Moultrie. LPS-1
I have a son who goes to France. I Have a Son. Emory Pottle. PEDC
I have a story fit to tell. The Strong Swimmer. William Rose Benét. PoNe
I have a strain of a departed bard. Forerunners. Alexander Smith. *Fr.* A Life-Drama. VA
I have a suit of new clothes in this happy new year. When I Think of the Hungry People. O-Shi-O. MaRV
I have a surprise for you, Mother. For You, Mother. Hilda Conkling. HH
I have a thousand pictures of the sea. Muna Lee. Sonnets, IV. HBMV
I have a tree, a graft of love. Arbor Amoris. Villon. AWP
I have a tree in my arm. Maze. Richard Eberhart. AnAmPo
I have a white dog. My Dog, Spot. Rodney Bennett. BoTP
I have a wife of my own. Nobody. Burns. LiTL
I Have a Word I Fain Would Say. Sayat Nova, *tr. fr. Armenian by* Zabelle C. Boyajian. ArmLP
I Have a Yong Suster. *Unknown. See* I Have a Young Sister.
I have a young love. The Sailor. Sylvia Townsend Warner. NV; OBMV
I Have a Young Sister (*orig. and mod. vers.*). *Unknown.* CH
(I Have [*or* Haue] a Yong Suster.) ExPo; NBE; PoEL-1; SeCeV
(Love without Longing.) OxBoLi
I have achieved. That which the lonely man. The Seeker. Lascelles Abercrombie. *Fr.* The Fools' Adventure. WGRP
I have achieved the life of contemplation. House Dog. George Boas. AlBD
I have always acted for the best. C. Day Lewis. *Fr.* The Magnetic Mountain. QS
I Have Always Found It So. Birdie Bell. BLRP
I have always had one lode-star, now. My Lode-Star. Robert Browning. *Fr.* Pauline. MaRV
I have always hated the rain. Rain. Jean Starr Untermeyer. AV
I have always known. Ariwara no Narihira, *tr. fr. Japanese by* Kenneth Rexroth. OnPJ
"I have always lived, and I always must." The Violet Star. Eugene Fitch Ware. DDA
I have an arrow that will find its mark. Emerson. WhC
I have an Easter house today. Easter. Mary Hoge Wardlaw. PraP
I have an Orchard. Christopher Marlowe *and* Thomas Nashe. *Fr.* The Tragedy of Dido. ChTr
I have an uncle I don't like. Manners. Mariana Griswold Van Rensselaer. FaPON; HBMV; HBVY; MPB
I have an understanding with the hills. After Sunset. Grace Hazard Conkling. AnAmPo; BAP; EPN; HBMV; LA; MaRV; NLK; NV; SBMV; VOD; YT
I have awakened from the unknowing to the knowing. For William Edward Burghardt Dubois on His Eightieth Birthday. Bette Darcie Latimer. PoNe
I have baptized thee Withy, because of thy slender limbs. To ——? Richard Dehmel. AWP
I have been,/ Three separate times, in war. James Harold Manning. *Fr.* What Is Truth? CaP
I have been a censor for fifteen months. Censorship. Arthur Waley. WaP
I have been a snob to-day. Threnody. Alfred Kreymborg. MAPA
I have been abus'd of late/ by some of the poets crew. The Scolding Wives Vindication; or, An Answer to the Cuckold's Complaint. *Unknown.* CoMu
I have been back to my home again. Some Old School-Books. *Unknown.* PEOR
I have been blind, so blind! Discovery. José Moreno Villa. CoSP
I have been cherish'd and forgiven. Lines ——. Hartley Coleridge. PoEL-4
I have been drunk of life's commingled wines. David. Edmund Vance Cooke. TBM
I have been figuring that in a way. The Time Is Today. John Farrar. GoYe
I have been frequently astonished, letting go. Requiem: To Paula Modersohn-Becker. Rainer Maria Rilke. AnGP
I have been given my charge to keep. The Fairies' Siege. Kipling. OtMeF; VLEP
I have been here before. Sudden Light. Dante Gabriel Rossetti. BMEP; BrBE; EmBrPo; FaBoEn; GTBS-D; InP; LO; LoBV; LoPS; NBE; OAEP; Po; POTT; PoVP; TrGrPo; TwHP; UnW; VA; VLEP
I have been ill so long that I do not count the days. Being Visited by a Friend during Illness. Po Chü-i. TrCh
I Have Been in Love and in Debt. Alexander Brome. *See* Mad Lover, The.
I have been mounted on life's topmost wave. Sonnets. George Henry Boker. MOAP
I have been one acquainted with the night. Acquainted with the Night. Robert Frost. AmP; ChMo; ChTr; CoBMV; CoV; InP; LiTM; MaPo; NePA; NP; PoFS; PoLFOT; TwP; VOD (1935 ed.)
I have been profligate of happiness. To Olive. Lord Alfred Douglas. OBEV (new ed.); OBVV
I have been searching for some metaphor. Traveler. Sister Mary Thérèse. JKCP (1955 ed.)
I have been searching for the end of the world. End of the World. Raymond Kresensky. PSO
I have been silent a lifetime. After Dunkirk. Alun Lewis. SoV
I have been so great a lover. The Great Lover. Rupert Brooke. BEL; BLV; BoLiVe; CaAE; EnLit; EPP; FaFP; HoPM; LiTB; LiTM; MBP; MCCG; MoBrPo; NeMA; PIAE; PoeMoYo; PoMa; POT; PoTo; POTT; TCEP; TCPD; TreF; TrGrPo; TwCV; VOD; WaP
I have been so misused by chaste men with one wife. Ship near Shoals. Anna Wickham. HBMV
I have been sure of three things all my life. Clement Wood. Eagle Sonnets, III. HBMV
I have been temperate always. Anticipation. Amy Lowell. LEAP
I have been thinking to-day. Rounded Up in Glory. *Unknown.* CSF
I Have Been through the Gates. Charlotte Mew. AV; BLV; CBOV; GTML; MBP; MoAB; MoBrPo; TrGrPo; TwCV
I have been to market, my lady, my lady. *Unknown.* SAS
I have been treading on leaves all day until I am autumn-tired. A Leaf-Treader. Robert Frost. MAP; MoAmPo
I have been wandering in the lonely valleys. Mountain Laurel. Alfred Noyes. EPP; POTT; TCPD
I have been young, and now am not too old. Report on Experience. Edmund Blunden. FaBoEn; FaBoTw; LO; MoPW; OBMV; POTE

"I have beene all day looking after." The Witches' Song. Ben Jonson. CH
I have begun to die. The Sentry. Alun Lewis. MoWP
I have beheld thee in the morning hour. Sappho to Hesperus. Walter Savage Landor. *Fr.* Pericles and Aspasia. BPN
I have berries purple-blue. Invitation. Ella Young. BoChLi (1950 ed.)
I have blown, sir,/ Hard for your worship. Ben Jonson. *Fr.* The Alchemist. LO
I have borne the anguish of love, which ask me not to describe. Odes, XI. Hafiz. AWP; JAWP; OuHeWo; WBP
I have borne too long this burden. Wyn Griffith. *Fr.* Branwen. MoWP
I have bound in bundles the branches. The Bundles of Firewood. *Unknown.* ChLP
I have broken the panes of the night. The Night Was Going. Raúl Otero Reiche. AnCL
I have broken the rainbow. Pamphlet. Luis Muñoz Marín. AnCL; PoFr; WoL
I have brought berries on a grape-leaf. Keepsake from Quinault. Dorothy Alyea. GoYe
I have brought my pillow and am lying at the northern window. A "Tzu-yeh" Song. *Unknown.* ChLP; TrCh
I have brought the wine. This Is My Love for You. Grace Fallow Norton. HBV
I have builded my house; deep, deep have I digged in the earth. Achievement. Berta Hart Nance. MaRV
I Have Built Myself, with Honour and Dignity. "St.-J. Perse," *tr. fr. French by* T. S. Eliot. *Fr.* Anabasis. AtBAP
I have but one story. Summer Is Gone. *Unknown.* AnIL; LyMA; SiB
I Have Cared for You, Moon. Grace Hazard Conkling. HBMV
I Have Cast the World. Yone Noguchi. NP
I have chased fugacious woodchucks over many leagues of land. Woodchucking. *Unknown.* DDA
I have climbed ladders through the blue! Ladders through the Blue. Hermann Hagedorn. PC
I have closed fast my window. The Weeping. Federico García Lorca. CoSP; OnPM
I have closed the door on doubt. Closing the Doors. Irene Pettit McKeehan. MaRV; OQP; QP-1
I have come again, gentlemen and ladies. Spring Song. Theodore Spencer. AnFE; CoAnAm; TwAmPo
I have come again with greeting. Afanasi Afanasievich Fet, *tr. fr. Russian by* C. M. Bowra. BoRS
I have come and brought you greeting. Afanasi Afanasievich Fet, *tr. fr. Russian by* Sir Cecil Kisch. WaL
I have come back from the mountains. The Silent Places. Harold M. Hildreth. OQP; QP-2
I have come down to the garden. At the Place of the Roman Baths. "Richard Scrace." CaP; CPG; OCL
I have come far for this cleansing. Escape. James Rorty. PC
"I have come for the myrrh," the angel said. The King's Gifts. C. Frances Loomis. CAG
I have come from pride all the way. Dawns. Alfred Kreymborg. MAP
I have come into the desert. Charles Erskine Scott Wood. *Fr.* The Poet in the Desert. NP
I have come to bury love. Buried Love. Sara Teasdale. ChMo; CMP
I have come to the borders of sleep. Lights Out. Edward Thomas. CoEV; GTBS-D; MoP; POTE
I have come to the quiet place. The Quiet Place. George A. McCauliff. JKCP (1955 ed.)
I have come to where the world drops off. Visit to a Hospital. Jean Valentine Chace GoYe
I have consider'd it, and finde. The Second Thanksgiving; or, The Reprisal. George Herbert. OAEP
I have courage and hardihood. Besieged. Zalman Schneour. TrJP
I have crossed the river and gathered hibiscus. *Unknown, tr. fr. Chinese.* The Nineteen Han Poems, VI. WhP
I Have Cursed Winter. John Russell McCarthy. MuM
I have dark-blooming heather and white-gleaming sands. Denmark Speaks. Søren Hallar. BoDS
I have desired to go. Heaven-Haven. Gerard Manley Hopkins. ACP; BLV; BoLiVe; CAW; CBOV; ChMo; CoBE; EmBrPo; EnL; EnLi-2; FaBoEn; GoBC; LoBV; MBP; MoAB; MoBrPo; MoP; NeMA; OAEP; OBEV (new ed.); POTT; PoVP; TrGrPo; ViBoPo; ViP; VLEP; WaKn
I have discovered finally to-day. The Silent Pool. Harold Monro. ChMo; CMP
I have done all I could. The Tree and the Lady. Thomas Hardy. MBP; MoAB; MoBrPo
I have done my bit of carving. The Old Figurehead Carver. H. A. Cody. EtS
I have done one braver thing. The Undertaking. John Donne. AnFE; BLV; BoLiVe; EPS; GPE; MePo; ReEn; SeEP; TuPP
I have done the deed. Didst thou not hear a noise? Macbeth Does Murder Sleep [*or* Multitudinous Seas Incarnadine]. Shakespeare. *Fr.* Macbeth, II, ii. FiP; LiA
I have done the State some service, and they know 't. Othello Reviews His Career. Shakespeare. *Fr.* Othello, V, ii. BCEP
I have done with being judged. Robert Browning. *Fr.* The Ring and the Book. OAEP
I Have Drank My Last Glass. *Unknown.* PTA-2
I have dreamed so much of you. Poem to the Mysterious Woman. Robert Desnos. MiCF
I have driven North after midnight, machined. Poem for My Thirty-second Birthday. John Ciardi. MiAP
I have drunk ale from the Country of the Young. He Thinks of His Past Greatness When a Part of the Constellations of Heaven. W. B. Yeats. OAEP (2d ed.); PoEL-5
I have drunk the Sea's good wine. A Pagan Hymn. John Runcie. NLK
I have eaten. This Is Just to Say. William Carlos Williams. AmP
I have eaten apples and have kissed your lips. Fleeting Restlessness. Juana de Ibarbourou. LiTW
I have eaten your bread and salt. Prelude to "Departmental Ditties." Kipling. BPN
I have fallen in love with American names. American Names. Stephen Vincent Benét. AmP; BoLiVe (1945 ed.); DDA; InP; LaNeLa; LoGBV; NP; OxBA; PG; WaKn; YaD
I Have Felt a Presence. Wordsworth. *Fr.* Lines Composed a Few Miles above Tintern Abbey. MaRV
I have felt the thrill of passion in the poet's mystic book. The Ultimate Joy. *Unknown.* BOHV
"I have finished another year," said God. New Year's Eve. Thomas Hardy. MBP; MoBrPo; POTT; PreP
I have five hundred crowns. The Constant Service of the Antique World. Shakespeare. *Fr.* As You Like It, II, iii. EV-1
I have floated far too long on the surface of the wave. The Eel. Evan Morgan. CAW
I have forebodings of Thee. Time is going. Aleksandr Blok, *tr. fr. Russian by* C. M. Bowra. BoR
I Have Foreknown Thee. Aleksandr Blok, *tr. fr. Russian by* Babette Deutsch. TrRV
I have forgot them all. The White Veil. Grace Fallow Norton. PraNu
I have fought no mighty fight. Finis. John McClure. LS
I have found God on a high hill alone, alone. Discovery. Raymond Kresensky. OQP; QP-2
I have found out a gig-gig-gift. An Invitation to the Zoölogical Gardens. *Unknown.* BOHV
I Have Found Romance. Victor Starbuck. NoCaPo
I Have Found Such Joy. Grace Noll Crowell. PoToHe (new ed.)
I have four loves, four loves are mine. My Estate. John Drinkwater. HBMV
I have gathered luss/ At the wane of the moon. The Herb-Leech. Joseph Campbell. AnIL; OnYI
I Have Golden Shoes. Lesbia Harford. MoAuPo
I have gone back in boyish wonderment. Return. Sterling A. Brown. CDC
I have gone far from my beloved ones. Jerusalem the Dismembered. Uri Zvi Greenberg. *Fr.* Jerusalem. TrJP
I have gone out and seen the lands of Faery. Dreams within Dreams. "Fiona Macleod." PoVP
"I have gone the whole round of creation: I saw and I spoke." Robert Browning. *Fr.* Saul. EPP
I have got a new-born sister. Choosing a Name. Mary Lamb. HBV; LPS-1; OTPC (1923 ed.)
I have got her. Fujiwara no Kamatari, *tr. fr. Japanese by* Arthur Waley. LiTW
I Have Got My Leave. Rabindranath Tagore. Gitanjali, XCIII. OBMV
I have got patronage, but am too lazy to use it. Lazy Man's Song. Po Chü-i. TrCh
I have great faith in this boy. Students. Haniel Long. AnAmPo; LA
I have great need that the Saint grant help. Cynewulf. *Fr.* Juliana. AnOE
I have grown past hate and bitterness. Nationality. Mary Gilmore. BoAV; NeLNL
I have grown tired of routine work. Afternoon in a Church. Raymond Kresensky. ChIP
I have grown tired of sorrow and human tears. In the Wood of Finvara. Arthur Symons. BLV; MBP; MoBrPo; NeMA; PoVP
I have grown tired of you. More Letters Found near a Suicide. Frank Horne. BANP
I have grown weary of the mesa's splendor. The Patio. Rose Henderson. VOD
I have grown weary of the open sea. The Wanderer. William Alexander Percy. LS; SPP
I have had asthma for a/ Long time. Visitors. Tu Fu. OnPC

I have had courage to accuse. The Crowning Gift. Gladys Cromwell. BAP; HBMV; MAP; NP
I have had enough. I gasp for breath. Sheltered Garden. Hilda Doolittle ("H. D."). PG
I have had enough of women, and enough of love. Wanderer's Song. Arthur Symons. BMEP; MBP; MoBrPo; POTT; ViBoPo
I have had playmates, I have had companions. The Old Familiar Faces. Charles Lamb. AWP; BCEP; BLPA; BoFr; EnLit; EPN; EPP; ERP; EV-4; FaBoBe; FaFP; GTBS; GTBS-D; GTBS-W; GTSE; GTSL; HBV; JAWP; LEAP; LiTG; LPS-1; NeHB; OBEV; OBRV; PCD; PG; PIAE; PoeMoYo; PYM; TCEP; TOP; TreF; ViBoPo; WBP
I have had to learn the simplest things. Maximus, to Himself. Charles Olson. NeAP
I have halted my horse by the tree of the doves. Song. "St.-J. Perse." *Fr.* Anabasis. LiTW
I Have Heard ("I have heard the stirring chorus"). *Unknown.* FiBHP
I have heard/ He does not bestow horses for poems. A Miserly Patron. *Unknown.* AnIL
I have heard a lady this night. Bewitched. Walter de la Mare. PoMS
I have heard a mother bird. Welcome to Spring. Irene Thompson. BoTP
I have heard echoes and seen visions of you. Jerked Heartstrings in Town. Emily B. C. Jones. HBMV
I have heard music and the long wave falling. Inclusion. George Sterling. MuM
I have heard song through the leaves. Marginalia for Pentecost. Leo L. Ward. JKCP (1955 ed.)
I have heard talk of bold Robin Hood. Robin Hood's Golden Prize. *Unknown.* BaBo; ESPB; OBB
I have heard that a certain princess. The Jonquils. Allen Upward. *Fr.* Scented Leaves from a Chinese Jar. NP
I have heard that hysterical women say. Lapis Lazuli. W. B. Yeats. ChMP; CoBMV; FaBoTw; GTBS-W; LiTB; LiTM; MoPo; MoVE; OAEP (2d ed.)
I have heard the curlew crying. Wild Geese. Katharine Tynan. GoTP
I have heard the foxes. Burial. Edward Weismiller. MuM
I have heard the pigeons of the Seven Woods. In the Seven Woods. W. B. Yeats. ChMo; CMP; LoBV
I have heard the stirring chorus. I Have Heard. *Unknown.* FiBHP
I have heard the wild geese. Old Age. Cale Young Rice. NLK (1947 ed.); SBMV
I have heard them in the night. The New-born. Helen Hoyt. BAP; NP
I have heard what the talkers were talking, the talk of the beginning and the end. Song of Myself, III. Walt Whitman. CoV; PoLFOT
I have heard whispers that I cannot speak. An Unanswered Question. Leonard Bacon. MuM
I have hoped, I have planned, I have striven. Unsubdued. Samuel Ellsworth Kiser. MaRV; PoToHe
"I have it here," he said and stroked the rust. The Horror on Dagoth Wold. Frank Belknap Long. DaM
I have it in my heart to serve God so. Sonnet: Of His Lady in Heaven. Jacopo da Lentini. AWP; JAWP; LyPI; WBP
"I have just come from the salt, salt sea." The House Carpenter. *Unknown.* AS
I have just seen a beautiful thing. The Black Finger. Angelina W. Grimké. PoNe
I have just seen three ducks rise up from the rushes. Etching at Dusk. Frederic Prokosch. BLA
I have just seen you go down the mountain. Departure. Wang Wei. WhP
I have killed the moth flying around. Moth-Terror. Benjamin De Casseres. BAP; SBMV; TrJP
I have kissed the summer dawn. Dawn. Arthur Rimbaud. AnFP
I have known a woman. Woman. Isabel Fiske Conant. TBM
I have known cities with the strong-armed Rhine. Aged Cities. Frederick William Faber. BMEP
I have known honey from the Syrian hills. Bee-Master. V. Sackville-West. PtOT
I have known life's hunger. Hunger. Hazel Hall. NP
I have known love and hate [*or* woe] and work [*or* toil] and fight. To a Photographer. Berton Braley. LEAP; PoeMoYo; POT; PoTo
I have known many men, and many men. Dedicatory. Mary Gilmore. BoAV
I Have Known Poets. Mary Austin. DDA
I have known the inexorable sadness of pencils. Dolor. Theodore Roethke. AmP; CoBMV; FiMAP; MoVE
I have known the silence of the stars and of the sea. Silence. Edgar Lee Masters. LaNeLa; MAP; MoAmPo; NP; PoMa; PoToHe (new ed.); SBMV
I have known the strange nurses of kindness. But I Do Not Need Kindness. Gregory Corso. NeAP
I have known two worlds. T. S. Eliot. *Fr.* The Rock. OxBoCh
I have laid sorrow to sleep. Love and Sleep. Arthur Symons. VLEP
I have laied these sheetes you bad me on the bed. Shakespeare. *Fr.* Othello, IV, iii. AtBAP
I have lain in the sun. Fortunatus Nimium [*or* Nimium Fortunatus]. Robert Bridges. ChMo; CMP; MBP; MoAB; MoBrPo; PoP
I have learned/ To look on nature. Nature. Wordsworth. *Fr.* Lines Composed a Few Miles above Tintern Abbey. CBE; GrCo-1; SN
I have led a good life, full of peace and quiet. The Good Boy. *Unknown.* AS
I have led her home, my love, my only friend. Tennyson. *Fr.* Maud. BEL; BMEP; BPN; ChER; EV-5; FiP; GEPC; GTBS-D; PoEL-5
I have left a basket of dates. The Little Sister of the Prophet. Marjorie Pickthall. HBV
I have lifted my eyes to the strength of the hills. His Name. Charles Poole Cleaves. OQP; QP-1
I Have Lived and I Have Loved. *Unknown, at. to* Charles Mackay. HBV; ReTS
I have lived and worked in Pennsylvania. Steel. Henri DeWitt Saylor. PoMa
I have lived in important places, times. Epic. Patrick Kavanagh. OxBI
I Have Lived Long Enough. Shakespeare. *Fr.* Macbeth, V, iii *and* V, ii. TrGrPo
I have lived long enough, having seen one thing, that love hath an end. Hymn to Proserpine. Swinburne. BEL; BPN; EmBrPo; EnL; EnLi-2; EPN; OAEP; OBVV; PoEL-5; POTT; PoVP; SeCeV; TCEP; ViP; ViPo; ViPP; VLEP
I have lived long enough: my way of life. I Have Lived Long Enough. Shakespeare. *Fr.* Macbeth, V, iii *and* V, ii. TrGrPo
I have lived so many years. The Old Shepherd. Zacharias Papondoniou. MoGP
I have lived through these times and for a thousand years. Epitaph. Robert Desnos. MiCF
I Have Lived with Shades. Thomas Hardy. BrBE
I Have Looked Inward, *sels.* Don Marquis.
"I rose . . I rose . . . ," VIII. PFY
"There was a locked door," IV. PFY
I have lost, and lately, these. Upon the Loss of His Mistresses. Robert Herrick. BEL; EM-1; EnLi-1 (1949 ed.); EPS; OAEP; ReEn; SeCV-1; SeEP
I have lost her, I know. Mother. Daniel Lawrence Kelleher. NeIP
I have lost my mistress, horse and wife. Epigram. *Unknown.* ALV
"I have lost my portmanteau." The Bishop and His Portmanteau. *Unknown.* ALV
I Have Lost My Shoes. Constantino Suasnavar, *tr. fr. Spanish by* Muna Lee. *Fr.* Numbers. AnCL; FaPON
I have lost my turtle-doo. Villanelle. Jean Passerat. LiA
I have loved—but then who has not? Frolicked—who has not tasted. Years of Discretion. Philodemus of Gadara. GrPE
I have loved colours [*or* colors], and not flowers. Amends to Nature. Arthur Symons. BMEP; CBOV; GTML; GTSL; HBMV; PoVP; YT
I Have Loved Flowers That Fade. Robert Bridges. BMEP; EG; GTBS; GTBS-D; LO; MBP; MoAB; MoBrPo; POTT; PoVP; VLEP
(Elegy: "I have lov'd flowers that fade.") VA
I Have Loved Hours at Sea. Sara Teasdale. ChMo; CMP
I have loved large cities, capitals of the world. The Master City. Rose J. Orente. GoYe
I have loved to-night; from love's last bordering steep. The Happy Night. J. C. Squire. BMEP; HBMV
I have loved two things deeply: the earth and silence. A Pioneer of Monaro. Francis Webb. MoAuPo
I have loved wind and light. To Night. Arthur Symons. POTT
"I have loved your winsome face." Dance Song. *Unknown.* ArmLP
I have lyric aspiration. The Curse of Faint Praise. Irwin Edman. InMe
I have made a sirventes against the city of Toulouse. Sirventes. Paul Blackburn. NeAP
I have marked, as on the heather now I strayed. As on the Heather. Reinmar von Hagenau. AWP
I have met them at close of day. Easter 1916. W. B. Yeats. ChMP; CoBMV; CoEV; EnLP; FaBoMo; GTIV; LiTM; MoAB; OxBI; PoFS; SeCeV; ShBV-4
I have milked well the breast. Aleppo. Ibn Kharuf. MooP
I Have My Cruse of Oil. William Wetmore Story. *Fr.* Tired. PSO
I have neither plums nor cherries. Nicholas Breton. EG
I Have Never Been Here Before. Jacob Glatstein, *tr. fr. Yiddish by* Sarah Zweig Betsky. OnCuPl

I have never been rich before. To My Friend. Anne Campbell. PoToHe
I have never seen him, this invisible member of the panel, this thirteenth juror. The People vs. the People. Kenneth Fearing. MoAmPo (1950 ed.)
I have never seen volcanoes. Emily Dickinson. PoEL-5
I have new shoes in the Fall-time. New Shoes. Alice Wilkins. GFA; SUS; TiPo
I have no brother—they who meet me now. Thy Brother's Blood. Jones Very. OnAP; PoEL-4
I have no care for systematic theology. Eschatology. Morris Bishop. WhC
I have no chill despondence that I am. Farewell to the Muses. John Hamilton Reynolds. OBRV
I have no dog, but it must be. My Dog. John Kendrick Bangs. BLPA; FaBoBe; MPB; OTPC (1946 ed.); StVeCh; UTS
I have no ears or eyes. The Tugged Hand. W. H. Davies. MoPW
I have no faith in Heaven. Religion. Heine. LiTW
I have no folded flock to show. The Battle-Flag of Sigurd. Dora Greenwell. OBVV
I have no happiness in dreaming of Brycelinde. Under the Moon. W. B. Yeats. EG
I have no heart for any other joy. An End. Sara Teasdale. NV
I have no love for the winecup. If thou wouldst have me taste it. A Kiss within the Cup. Agathias Scholasticus. GrPE
I have no more gold. Advent. John Gould Fletcher. MAP; MaRV; MoAmPo
"I have no name." Infant Joy. Blake. *Fr.* Songs of Innocence. BCEP; EiPP; EM-1; EnLi-2; EnLit; FaPON; GoTP; GTSL; HBV; HBVY; KN; LEAP; LoBV; NeHB; OTPC; PRWS; SiSoSe; ThWaDe; TiPo (1952 ed.); ViBoPo
I have no natural craving for the name. Creon. Sophocles. *Fr.* Oedipus Rex. PoFr
"I have no penny," quoth Piers, "pullets to buy." William Langland. *Fr.* The Vision of Piers Plowman. MyFE
I have no solid horse to share with Joan. Joan of Arc, 1926. Virginia Moore. TBM; YT
I have no strength nor substance, yet I shake. Here I Am. Nancy Birckhead. RIS
I Have No Surety. Bilhana, *formerly at. to* Chauras, *tr. fr. Sanskrit by* E. Powys Mathers. *Fr.* Black Marigolds. OnPM
I have no temple and no creed. After the Order of Melchisedec. Robert Norwood. MaRV
I have no thing that is mine sure. Serenader. George Dillon. NP
I have no wings, but yet I fly. Mary Austin. *Fr.* Rhyming Riddles. TiPo
I have no wit, no words, no tears. A Better Resurrection. Christina Rossetti. HBV; OxBoCh; POTT; PoVP; StJW; TrPWD; ViPo; VLEP
I have no word to match with its white wonder. Of Wounds. Sister Mary Madeleva. ISi
I have no words—alas!—to tell. Poe. *Fr.* Tamerlane. LO
I have no words to tell what way we walked. Christina Rossetti. *Fr.* From House to Home. MBP
I Have Not Forgotten. Baudelaire, *tr. fr. French by* Vernon Watkins. AnFP
I have not gathered gold. To Death. Padraic Pearse. AnIV
I have not heard lutes beckon me, nor the brazen bugles call. Recompense. Robert Ervin Howard. DaM
I have not known a quieter thing than ships. Ships in Harbor [*or* Harbour]. David Morton. EtS; OBAV; VOD
I have not loved the world, nor the world me. Defiance. Byron. *Fr.* Childe Harold's Pilgrimage. OBRV; RO
I have not read a rotten page. A Ballade of a Book-Reviewer. G. K. Chesterton. PtOT
"I have not sought Thee, I have not found Thee." Love Is Strong as [*or* Stronger than] Death. Christina Rossetti. LO; MaRV; MeRV; TriL
I have not spent the April of my time. Sonnet [*or* Youth]. Bartholomew Griffin. Fidessa, More Chaste than Kind, XXXV. ElL; ElSeCe; OBSC; ReEn; SiCE; TuPP
I have not told my garden yet. Emily Dickinson. OBAV (Secret, The.) AA; TOP
I have not where to lay my head. Mountain Song. Harriet Monroe. HBV; NP; NV
I have often dreamed. Dreams of Flying. George Darley. UnW
I have often played with man, saith the Lord. Charles Péguy. *Fr.* The Mystery of the Innocent Saints. CAW
I have oh such a yearning. I Am a Grown Man. Franz Werfel. TwGV
I Have Overcome the World. Laura Simmons. ChIP (World Conqueror.) MaRV
I have picked this heatherstalk. The Goodbye. Guillaume Apollinaire. OnPM
I have planted a garden. Home. Liu Ping. PoHN
I have praised many loved ones in my song. Mother. Theresa Helburn. FaPON; HBV; LBMV; MOAH; OHIP; TSW
I have prayed for you, prayed that your path may be. For a Novice. Sister Mary Edwardine. PraNu
I have put my days and dreams out of mind. The Triumph of Time. Swinburne. ViBoPo
I have put out my candlelight. Night. Hermann Hesse. TwGV
I have read, in some old marvellous tale. The Beleaguered City. Longfellow. CG; IAP; TriL; UnW
I have received jewels of conspicuous beauty. Egan O'Rahilly. *Fr.* On a Pair of Shoes Presented to Him. OnYI
I have recovered it. Eternity. Arthur Rimbaud. AnFP
I have remembered beauty in the night. To E. Sara Teasdale. ChMo; CMP
I have renounced already that hope. I renounce the sudden Whole. Spring Song. Rayner Heppenstall. NeBP
I have ridden the wind. Cale Young Rice. *Fr.* The Mystic. NLK
I have said that the soul is not more than the body. Letters from God [*or* A Hub for the Universe]. Walt Whitman. Song of Myself, XLVIII. BAV; CoBA; CBOV; CoV; FaFP; TrGrPo
I have seen/ A curious child. Faith [*or* Tidings of Invisible Things]. Wordsworth. *Fr.* The Excursion, IV. GrCo-1; MaRV; OBRV
I have seen a lovely thing. Blight. Arna Bontemps. BANP
I have seen also your angel. Companions of the Morass. Léonie Adams. MOAP
I have seen an old faith falter. And the Greatness of These. J. R. Perkins. OQP; QP-2
I have seen an old street weeping. La Rue de la Montagne Sainte-Geneviève. Dorothy Dudley. HBMV
I have seen beauty where light stabs the hills. Sonnets of a Portrait Painter, XVI. Arthur Davison Ficke. AnAmPo; LA
I Have Seen Black Hands. Richard Wright. PoNe
I have seen cliffs that met the ocean foe. St. Bee's Head. Thomas Edward Brown. VLEP
I have seen dawn and sunset on moors and windy hills. Beauty. John Masefield. BEL; LoPS; PoeT
I have seen death too often to believe in death. A Journey Ends. Don Blanding. MaRV
I have seen full many a sight. Dinah Kneading Dough. Paul Laurence Dunbar. PR
I Have Seen Higher, Holier Things than These. Arthur Hugh Clough. *See* Τὸ Καλόν.
I have seen in the Virginia forest. Apparition. John Peale Bishop. MoVE
I have seen lace-makers in Madeira. Grisaille. Terence Heywood. BoSA
I have seen many things. Miser. Harold Vinal. MCCG
I have seen Mary at the cross. The Holy Women. William Alexander Percy. LS
I have seen men binding their brothers in chains. The Hate and the Love of the World. Max Ehrmann. PoToHe (new ed.)
I have seen morning break within his eyes. Dereliction. Edward Shillito. ChIP
I have seen much to hate here—much to forgive. The White Cliffs. Alice Duer Miller. OtMeF
I have seen, O desolate one, the voice has its tower. Bell Tower. Léonie Adams. AnAmPo; LA; MAP; MoAB; MoAmPo
I have seen, O, the miller's daughter. Miller's Daughter. John Crowe Ransom. MOAP
I have seen old ships sail like swans asleep. The Old Ships. James Elroy Flecker. AnFE; CaAE; CBE; CH; EnLit; EtS; GTBS-D; GTML; GTSL; MBP; MoBrPo; MoVE; OBMV; OtMeF; PC; PoeMoYo; PoRA; POTE; POTT; ShBV-3; TCPD; TwCV; WHA
I have seen Our Lady in Ireland, being carried in procession in May. Heart for All Her Children. Albert J. Hebert, Jr. ISi
I have seen rare sunshine held in the first birch leaves. Annunciation. Ken Etheridge. MoWP
I have seen such Junes in gardens without people. The Needed Word. Jorge Guillén. CoSP
I have seen tall chimneys without smoke. Soliloquy. Frederick E. Laight. BoCaPo (1943 ed.); CaP
I have seen that which is mysterious. The Grand Canyon of the Colorado. John Gould Fletcher. ChMo; CMP; TwCV
I have seen the proudest stars. To One Unknown. Helen Dudley. AV; NP
I Have Seen the Robins Fall. Louis Dudek. CaP
I Have Seen the Spring. Sara Teasdale. ChMo; CMP
I have seen the swelling sun. My Jewels. Mary Dixon Thayer. TBM
I have seen wildernesses made. Wilderness. Leslie Nelson Jennings. MuM
I have seen you, O king of the dead. In the Desert. Alice Corbin. NP

I have seen you suffer in the midst of winters. Harlem. Jean Brierre. PoNe
I Have Set My Heart So High. *Unknown.* CoBE
I have ships that went to sea. Ships at Sea. Robert Barry Coffin. EtS; LPS-1
I have shut my little sister in from life and light. The Factories. Margaret Widdemer. BAP; CV; HBV; LEAP; MaRV; NeMA; PC; PFE; PoeMoYo; PoMa; POT; PoTo; PYM; TCAP
I have slain none except my Mother. An Only Son. Kipling. LiA
I have slipped the world between my palm. Mood. Winifred Kohn. CAG
I have smelled all the perceptible smells. Looking Back. Heine. AnGP
I have so loved you I can never find. Resurgence. Margaret Tod Ritter. TBM
I have sojourned in the Muse's land. Necessity. Euripides. *Fr.* Alcestis. GrR
I have some dainty pussies here. Pussy Willows. Mary E. Plummer. GFA; MPB; RAR
I have sought beauty through the dust of strife. The Final Lesson. Arthur Stringer. MaRV
I have sought long with steadfastness. Songs and Lyrics, XXXIX. Sir Thomas Wyatt. SiPS
I Have Sought Thee Daily. Solomon ibn Gabirol, *tr. fr. Hebrew by* Israel Zangwill. LiTW
I have sown beside all waters in my day. A Black Man Talks of Reaping. Arna Bontemps. BANP; CDC; PoNe
I have sown upon the fields. The Idle Flowers. Robert Bridges. ChTr
I have spoken with the dead. Communion. Hildegarde Flanner. NP
I have spot-resistant trousers. Summer Song. W. W. Watt. FiBHP
I have spread wet linen. Today. Ethel Romig Fuller. PoToHe (new ed.)
I have stayed [*or* stay'd] too long from your grave, it seems. At Her Grave. Arthur O'Shaughnessy. PoVP; VA
I have stood gazing down at newly turned sod. The Atheist's Wail. Dorothy Ducas. QS
I have studied many times. George Gray. Edgar Lee Masters. *Fr.* Spoon River Anthology. TOP
"I have subdued at last the will to live." The Sanyassi. Philip Gilbert Hamerton. VA
I have sung, to deceive the evil-sounding clock of time. Plain Song. Jean Cocteau. MiCF
I have taken that vow. The Red-haired Man's Wife. James Stephens. HBMV; MBP; MoBrPo; OBVV
I have taken the woman of beauty. The Bear's Song. *Tr. by* Constance Lindsay Skinner. AWP; JAWP; WBP
I have tasted Sorrow. Bitter Bread and Weak Wine. Jean Starr Untermeyer. TBM
I have the greatest fun at night. The Quilt. Mary Effie Lee Newsome. CDC
I have the most exacting little house. My Little House. Hazel Harper Harris. DDA
I have this deal of death about my hands. Blood. Ray Bremser. NeAP
I have this to say, if I can say it. Before Sentence Is Passed. R. P. Blackmur. LiTA
I have thought long this wild wet night that brought no rest. A Sleepless Night. Egan O'Rahilly. AnIL; KiLC
I have thought of beaches, fields. Bundles. Carl Sandburg. MAP; MoAmPo
I have thought very much about heat. The Heat. Gertrude Stein. AtBAP
I have threatened Theology a thousand times over. Theology [*or* Grace for Theology]. William Langland. *Fr.* The Vision of Piers Plowman. GoBC; PoLi
I have three candles in my room. Candle-lighting Song. Arthur Ketchum. HBMV
I Have Three Pearls. Tove Meyer, *tr. fr. Danish by* Charles W. Stork. BoDS
I have thrown wide my window. Midnight. Michael Roberts. OBMV; POTE
I have to live with myself, and so. Myself. Edgar A. Guest. BLP; BLPA; MaRV; NeHB; OQP; QP-1
I have to thank God I'm a woman. The Affinity. Anna Wickham. BMEP; HBMV; MBP; MoBrPo
I have tossed hours upon the tides of fever. Bout with Burning. Vassar Miller. NePoEA
I have traveled this wide world all over. Rosin the Bow [*or* Rosen the Bow]. *Unknown.* ABS; CSF
I have travelled my land, my heart big with pride. Song of an Australian. Flexmore Hudson. BoAu
I have travelled sometime up and down our coast. Gazeteer of Newfoundland. Michael Harrington. CaP
I have travelled to Euboea and her plains with vineyards growing. The Wanderer. Theognis. GrPE
I Have Trod. Robert Louis Stevenson. VLEP
I have turned back. Night Reverie. Ling Ju Jung. PoHN
I Have Twelve Oxen. *Unknown.* ChTr; TwHP
(My Twelve Oxen.) TMEV
(Song: "I have twelve oxen that be fair and brown.") ThWaDe
(Twelve Oxen.) CH
I have two friends—two glorious friends. The Two Friends. Charles Godfrey Leland. AA; BLP; LBAP; LEAP
I have two servants. Blue Persian. Isabella Fiske Conant. CIV
I have two sons and a son-in-law. The Frenchman's Ball. *Unknown.* OuSiCo
I have two sons, Wife. Two Sons. Robert Buchanan. TVSH; VA
I have waited, I have longed. The Stay-at-Home. Josephine Preston Peabody. CV
I have waked, I have come, my beloved! I might not abide. Sunrise. Sidney Lanier. AA; ADAH; SPP; TCAP
I have walked a great while over the snow. The Witch. Mary Elizabeth Coleridge. GTBS-D; PoVP
I have walked always in a veil. Imprisoned. Eunice Tietjens. HBMV
I have walked and prayed for this young child an hour. W. B. Yeats. *Fr.* A Prayer for My Daughter. ViBoPo; WoL
I have wandered like a sheep that's lost. Thomas Heywood. *Fr.* The Cherubim. WGRP
I Have Wandered to a Spring. Edna Wahlert McCourt. AV
I have wasted nothing. O Lord, I have saved. The Miser. Laura Bell Everett. OQP; QP-2
I have watch'd thee with rapture, and dwelt on thy charms. Lines: Addressed to —— on the 29th of September, When We Parted for the Last Time. *Unknown.* BOHV
I have watched a thousand days. Salonikan Grave. Kipling. *Fr.* Epitaphs of the War, 1914–18. LiA; OAEP (2d ed.)
I have wept a million tears. The Man to the Angel. "Æ." OBVV; VA
I have wished a bird would fly away. A Minor Bird. Robert Frost. AlDL; BLA; ChMo; CMP
I have with fishing-rod and line. The Wounded Hawk. Herbert Palmer. FaBoTw; HaMV
I have within my hand some lilies of the valley. Lilies of the Valley. Jo Gardner. BePJ
I have worshipped in churches and chapels. My Altar. John H. Styles, Jr. MaRV
I have woven shrouds of air. The Earth-Spirit. William Ellery Channing. AnNE; APW; PFY
I Have Wrapped My Dreams in a Silken Cloth. Countee Cullen. *See* For a Poet.
I have written high school teachers down SAVANTS. Chant Royal from a Copydesk. Rufus Terral. InMe
I haven't a palace. Any Bird. Ilo Orleans. RIS
I haven't got a cent. Penny Whistle Blues. E. H. L. Island. InMe
I hear a brown bird sing. Nostalgia. Theognis. GrR
I hear a cricket at my window sill. Touch. Joseph Auslander. MAP; MoAmPo (1942 ed.)
"I hear a cry from the Sansard cave." The Feud. Frederick George Scott. CPG; PCN
I hear a distant clarion blare. Adieu. Edmond John Armstrong. TIP
I hear a mouse. The Mouse. Elizabeth J. Coatsworth. PCD; RIS; SUS; UTS
I hear a rainbird singing. The Rainbird. Bliss Carman. BLA
I hear a savage tale of you. Blue Jay. Leonora Speyer. BLA; WhBS
I hear a sudden [*or* the sullen] cry of pain! The Snare. James Stephens. BMEP; BoTP; CBE; CH; ChMo; CMP; HBMV; LEAP; MM; MoSiPe; OxBI; PCN; PoRL; ReaPo; ShBV-1; TCPD; TiPo; UTS; YT
I hear a whisper in the heated air. Ceylon. A. Hugh Fisher. HBV
I hear a young girl singing. Beside the Blackwater. Norreys Jephson O'Conor. HBMV
I hear again the tread of war go thundering through the land. Albert Sidney Johnston. Kate Brownlee Sherwood. BlG; GA; MC; PAH
I hear along our street. Christmas Carols. Gui Barozai, *par. by* Longfellow. BoTP
I Hear America Singing. Walt Whitman. APW; AWP; BBV (1951 ed.); BoChLi (1950 ed.); CoBA; CV; DDA; FaBoBe; FaFP; FaPON; GoTP; IAP; LiTA; LoGBV; MAP; MoAmPo; MOAP; MPB; NeHB; NeMA; PaA; PCD; PCH; PoeMoYo; PoFr; PoFS; PoMa; PreP; PYM; REAL; StVeCh; TCAP; TiPo (1952 ed.); TreFS; TrGrPo; VOD (1935 ed.); YaD
I Hear an Army [Charging upon the Land]. James Joyce. Chamber Music, XXXVI. AnIV; AWP; ExPo; GTIV; JAWP; JKCP (1926 ed.); LiTL; LiTM; MBP; MoBrPo; NAMP; OxBI; PoRA; POTE; ShBV-4; TwCV; ViBoPo; WBP
I hear and behold God in every object, yet understand God not in the least. Walt Whitman. *Fr.* Song of Myself. WGRP
I Hear and See Not Strips of Cloth Alone. Walt Whitman. WaaP

I hear enormous noises in the night. March Winds. Cecil Francis Lloyd. CaP; OCL

I hear, far up the mountain trail. Twanging Gold. Winifred Welles. MuM

I hear footsteps over my head all night. The Walker. Arturo Giovannitti. AnAmPo; LA; PoFr

I hear His low voice say to me. His Grace. Ishii. SoLD

I hear in my heart, I hear in its ominous pulses. The Wild Ride. Louise Imogen Guiney. AA; BAP; CAW; CBOV; CP; HBV; JKCP; MAP; MoAmPo (1942 ed.); NV; OBAV; PC; PFY; POT; PoTo; TCAP

I Hear It Said. Barbara Young. BLPA; NeHB

I Hear It Was Charged against Me. Walt Whitman. BoFr; IAP; LiTA; MAP; MCCG; MoAmPo; MOAP

I hear leaves drinking rain. The Rain. W. H. Davies. BoTP; ChMo; CMP; EnLit; NV; PCH; POTE; RIS; TiPo

I hear men cry on every hand. Chess. Ibn Sharaf. MooP

I Hear My Sacred Heart Beat. Jules Laforgue, *tr. fr. French by* William Jay Smith. AnFP

I hear no voice, I feel no touch. Evening Song [*or* Evening Hymn]. *Unknown.* BOL; OTPC (1946 ed.); RAR

I hear of late, but hold it very strange. To a Dear Friend Lately Given Over to Covetousness. Thomas Lodge. *Fr.* A Fig for Momus. SiCE

I hear some say, "This man is not in love!" Laughing at Fortune. Michael Drayton. Idea, XXIV. BEL; BLV; LO; OAEP; TrGrPo

I hear the angels marching. October of the Angels. James J. Daly. WHL

I hear the beat of the hoofs of wild horses. Hallucinations? Beverley Randolph Tucker. PoP

I hear the bells at eventide. End of the Day. Duncan Campbell Scott. VA

I hear the clock in the half gloom. Refuge. John Thompson. BoAu

I Hear the Cries of Evening. Stephen Spender. CaAE; ReaPo

I hear the engine pounding. The Ways of Trains. Elizabeth J. Coatsworth. BoChLi (1950 ed.); TiPo

I hear the former beauty, she. Lament of the Old Woman Remembering Her Youth. Villon. FoS

I hear the halting footsteps of a lass. Harlem Shadows. Claude McKay. BANP; PoNe

I hear the little black cricket. The Cricket and the Star. Mary Effie Lee Newsome. GoSl

I hear the low wind wash the softening snow. The Flight of the Geese. Sir Charles G. D. Roberts. *Fr.* Songs of the Common Day. BLA; PeCV; SN; VA

I hear the music of the murmuring breeze. By an Open Window in Church. Corinne Roosevelt Robinson. BLP; POT; PoTo

I hear the noise about thy keel. In Memoriam A. H. H., X. Tennyson. BPN; EmBrPo; EnLi-2; EPN; GEPC; GTSL; OAEP; OBEV (1st ed.); ReaPo; ViPo; VLEP

I hear the robins singing in the rain. On a Gloomy Easter. Alice Freeman Palmer. OHIP; MaRV

I hear the sea-song of the blood in my heart. The Undersong. "Fiona Macleod." NLK

I hear the Shadowy Horses, their long manes a-shake. He Bids His Beloved Be at Peace. W. B. Yeats. Po

I hear the stern decree: I bow to what is fated. Afanasi Fet, *tr. fr. Russian by* Oliver Elton. BoRS

I hear the sullen cry of pain! *See* I hear a sudden cry of pain!

I Hear the Wave. *Unknown, tr. fr. Middle Irish by* Eugene O'Curry. OnYI

I hear the wind a-blowing. Mad Song. Hester Sigerson. AnIV

I hear the wings, the winds, the river pass. Out of Doors. Walter Conrad Arensberg. AnAmPo; BAP; LA; PoeMoYo

I Hear the Woodlands Calling. Madison Cawein. TSW; TSWC

I hear them grinding, grinding through the night. Machines. Daniel Whitehead Hicky. MuM; PoeMoYo; PoMa; VOD (1935 ed.)

I hear them say, "By all this stir." The Right above the Wrong, 1857. William Cox Bennett. PoFr

I hear throughout the silent night. Night. Sophus Michaëlis. BoDS

I hear thy spirit calling unto me. Burdens of Unrest [*or* Mary's Lament for Shelley Lost at Sea]. Thomas Holley Chivers. APW; SPP

I hear within my heart of hearts. The Cello. Ernst Josephson. AnSL

I hear you have gone to live among the village mounds. Visiting the Hermit Cheng. Po Chü-i. WhP

I hear you, little bird. Joy of the Morning. Edwin Markham. AA; BLA; FaPON; HBV; LBAP; MPB; PoRL

I hear you, little spirit, in the bushes. To Puck. Beatrice Llewellyn Thomas. HBMV

I hear your familiar footsteps all about me. Second Life of My Mother. Jorge Carrera Andrade. AnCL

. . . I heard/ After the hour of sunset yester-even. The Glow-Worm. Wordsworth. *Fr.* The Prelude. RO

I heard a/ Couple of fleas. Archy, the Cockroach, Speaks. Don Marquis. *Fr.* Certain Maxims of Archy. FaPON

I heard a bird at break of day. Overtones. William Alexander Percy. BAP; BLA; DD; HBMV; HBVY; LS; MaRV; NLK; SBMV; SPP

I heard a bird at dawn. The Rivals. James Stephens. AlDL; BoTP; FaPON; GTBS-D; InvP; MoVE; OBEV (new ed.); OBMV; OTPC (1946 ed.); PoRh; RAR; SP; UTS

I Heard a Bird Sing. Oliver Herford. MoSiPe; SiSoSe; TiPo (1952 ed.); YeAr

I heard a brooklet gushing. Whither? Wilhelm Müller. AWP

I heard a cow low, a bonnie cow low. The Queen of Elfland's Nourrice. *Unknown.* ESPB; FaBoCh; OBB

I heard a cry in the night, a thousand miles. Message. Sara Teasdale. SBMV

I heard a cry in the night from a far-flung host. Memorial Day. William E. Brooks. GrCo-2; HH; MaRV; OQP; PEDC; PGD; PoRL; PSO; QP-2

I heard a fairy tapping at my window. Half-asleep. Thelma Harrington Bell. RAR

I heard a fly buzz when I died. Emily Dickinson. AmPP (4th ed.); CoBA; ExPo; GTBS-W; InPo; MAP; MoAB; MoAmPo; MOAP; MoPW; MoVE; NePA; OxBA; PoE; PoFS; PoRA; ReaPo; ReMP; RiBV; SeCeV; TwP (Dying.) AnFE; APA; CoAnAm; LiTA; LiTM; MAPA; TwAmPo

I heard a halloo in the wood. Adventure. Mary Fullerton. BoAV

I heard a herald's note announce the coming of a king. Rex Mundi. David Gascoyne. ChMP

I heard a horseman. The Horseman. Walter de la Mare. AlDL; SUS; TiPo (1959 ed.)

I Heard a Linnet Courting. Robert Bridges. GTBS-W; LiTB; LiTM; OBMV; TwCV (Linnet, The.) LiTL; OBEV (new ed.)

I heard a man explaining. Barabbas Speaks. Edwin McNeill Poteat. MaRV

I Heard a Mess of Merry Shepherds. *Unknown.* AnEC

I heard a mouse. The Mouse. Elizabeth J. Coatsworth. BoTP; FaPON; MoShBr; MoSiPe; OTPC (1946 ed.); PCD; RIS; SUS; TiPo; UTS

I Heard a Noise. *Unknown.* ElSeCe; InvP; TuPP (Shadow, A.) ElL

I heard a red-winged black-bird singing. A June Day. Sara Teasdale. YeAr

I Heard a Sailor. W. W. Gibson. CMP

I heard a small sad sound. The To-be-forgotten. Thomas Hardy. PoVP

I Heard a Soldier. Herbert Trench. AnFE; CH; HBV; LBBV; LEAP; MBP; PoeMoYo

I heard a sound of voices. Godfrey Thring. OlF

I heard a thousand blended notes. Lines Written in Early Spring [*or* Written in Early Spring *or* What Man Has Made of Man]. Wordsworth. ADAH; BEL; BPN; CBOV; CoBE; EM-2; EmBrPo; EnLi-2; EnLit; EnRP; EPN; ERP; GEPC; GTBS; GTBS-D; GTBS-W; GTSE; GTSL; HBV; MaRV; MCCG; OAEP; OBRV; PG; PoE; PoMa; REAL; SN; TCEP; TOP; TyEnPo

I heard a tiny hammering as of wee bells a-clamoring. The Wood of Tara. Harry Noyes Pratt. MuM

I heard a voice at evening softly say. Day by Day. Julia Harris May. BLRP; MaRV

I heard a Voice by night, that called to me. Uriel. "Owen Meredith." UnW

I heard a voice say "Look into your heart." Christopher Hassall. *Fr.* Soliloquy to Imogen. LO

I heard a voice that cried, "Balder the Beautiful." Tegnér's Drapa. Esaias Tegnér, *tr. by* Longfellow. TCAP

I heard a voice that cried, "Make way for those who died!" The March. J. C. Squire. HBMV; LBBV; OHIP; TCEP

I heard a woman's voice that wailed. In Ruin Reconciled. Aubrey Thomas De Vere. IrPN

I heard a wood thrush in the dusk. Wood Song. Sara Teasdale. Interlude: Songs Out of Sorrow, VI. BAP; BLA; PoeMoYo; PYM

I heard an angel singing. An Angel Singing [*or* The Two Songs]. Blake. CBOV; MeMeAg; RIS

I heard an angel speak last night. A Curse for a Nation [*or* Prologue]. Elizabeth Barrett Browning. EPP; PoVP

I heard an old farm-wife. The Son. Ridgely Torrence. BAP; HBMV; InP; InvP; MAP; MoAmPo (1942 ed.); MotAn; NP; PFY; PoeMoYo; SBMV; TCPD; WaKn

"I heard at night your long sighs." Dreaming of a Dead Lady. *Unknown.* TrCh

I heard beneath the quiet stars last night. Sonnet. Florence Wilson Roper. *Fr.* Return of Proserpine. UnW

I Heard de Preachin' of de Word o' God, *with music. Unknown.* BoAN-2

I heard from Rémon, Rémon. Rémon. *Unknown.* TrAS

I heard God calling. Spring's Answer. Edwin Osgood Grover. NLK
I heard great Hector sounding war's alarms. Hector in Hades. Robert Bridges. Growth of Love, LIII. CBOV
I Heard Her Whisper. Ruth Guthrie Harding. UnW
I heard him faintly, far away. The Corn Crake. James H. Cousins. OnYI
I heard how, to the beat of some quick tune. The Dancer. Sadi. *Fr.* The Bustan. AWP; JAWP; OuHeWo; WBP
I Heard Immanuel Singing. Vachel Lindsay. ChMo; CMP; QS; TBM; TriL
I heard in the night the pigeons. No Child. Padraic Colum. AnFE; GTIV; OBMV; POTE
I heard it all, each, every note. Ralph Hodgson. *Fr.* The Song of Honour. TwCV
I Heard It in the Valley. Annette Wynne. MoSiPe
I heard it whispered in the cryptic streets. The Cryptic Streets. Abu-l-Ala al-Maarri. LiTW
I heard last night a little child go singing. Juliet of Nations. Elizabeth Barrett Browning. *Fr.* Casa Guidi Windows. VA
I heard men cry, "The sun shall die." Phoenix. E. Merrill Root. MuM
I heard men saying, Leave hope and praying. The Voice of Toil. William Morris. AnFE; BMEP; BPN; CoBE; EmBrPo; EPN; HBV; POTT; PoVP; TCEP
I heard my ancient sea-blood say. A Life. George Edward Woodberry. EtS
I heard my love was going to Yang-chou. A "Tzu-yeh" Song. *Unknown.* ChLP; OnPM; TrCh
I heard no sound where I stood. The Sleeping House. Tennyson. *Fr.* Maud. FaBoEn
I heard, O Polypaides, I heard the bird's shrill crying. The Refugee. Theognis. GrPE
I heard one who said: "Verily." Cassandra. E. A. Robinson. AmPP; ExPo; LiTA; LiTM (rev. ed.); MaPo; NePA; NP; OxBA; PoFr; SeCeV
I heard or seemed to hear the chiding Sea. Seashore [*or* Sea-Shore]. Emerson. AmPP (4th ed.); AnAmPo; EtS; IAP; LA; LiTA; MOAP; OBAV; OxBA
I heard strange pipes when I was young. An Outland Piper. Donald Davidson. LS
I heard that Faustus oftentimes rehearses. Of Faustus, a Stealer of Verses. Sir John Harington. SiCE; TuPP
I heard that you ask'd for something to prove this puzzle the New World. To Foreign Lands. Walt Whitman. AmPP (3d ed.); IAP
I heard the bells across the trees. Victory Bells. Grace Hazard Conkling. AOAH; HBV; MC; PaA; PAH
I heard the bells of Bethlehem ring. Birds of Bethlehem. Richard Watson Gilder. AA
I Heard the Bells on Christmas Day. Longfellow. *See* Christmas Bells.
I heard the carping [*or* herde a carpyng] of a clerk. Robyn and Gandeleyn [*or* Robin and Gandelyn]. *Unknown.* BaBo; EnSB; ESPB; OBB
I heard the centuries tick slowly. Soul's Adventure. Stanley J. Kunitz. NP
I heard the crane cry unto men his greeting. The Crane's Message. Theognis. GrL; OxBG
I heard the dogs howl in the moonlight night. A Dream. William Allingham. BMEP; CBOV; EV-5; GTIV; OxBI; UnW; VA
I heard the farm cocks crowing loud, and faint, and thin. Daybreak in a Garden. Siegfried Sassoon. BoTP
I heard the harp of Alfred. The Harp of Alfred. Robert Ervin Howard. DaM
I heard the hymn of being sound. Ralph Hodgson. *Fr.* The Song of Honour. LO
I Heard the Old Men. Edward Davison. PtOT
I heard the old, old men say. The Old Men Admiring Themselves in the Water. W. B. Yeats. BMEP; FaBoCh; LoGBV; VLEP
I heard the Poor Old Woman say. Lament for the Poets: 1916. Francis Ledwidge. AnIV; AWP; JAWP; JKCP (1926 ed.); LBBV; OnYI; OxBI; WBP
I Heard the Ruffian-Shepherd Rudely Blow. Ovid, *tr. fr. Latin by* Dryden. *Fr.* Metamorphoses, XIII: The Fable of Acis, Polyphemus and Galatea. AtBAP
I heard the sighing of the reeds. By the Pool at the Third Rosses. Arthur Symons. POTT; VLEP
I heard the snowflakes whisper in the still dark night. Snowflakes. Ruth M. Arthur. BoTP
I heard the song of the breath. The Song of the Breath [*or* A Song of Breath]. Stephen Vincent Benét. *Fr.* John Brown's Body. AmP; MoVE
I heard the spring light whisper. Bliss Carman. *Fr.* Earth Voices, II. OCL
I heard the trailing garments of the Night. Hymn to the Night. Longfellow. AA; AmP; AmPP; AnAmPo; AnEnPo; AnFE; AnNE; APA; APW; BAP; BAV; CoAnAm; ExPo; HBV; HBVY; IAP; LA; LaNeLa; LEAP; LoBV; LPS-2; MOAP; NePA; OBAV; OTPC; OuHeWo: OxBA; PoFS; StVeCh (1940 ed.); TCAP; TOP; TreFS; TrGrPo; ViBoPo; WHA
I heard the train's shrill whistle call. The Rendition. Whittier. IAP
I heard the verdict, stern and grim. Injustice. Sheldon Shepard. ChIP
I Heard the Voice of Jesus Say. Horatius Bonar. BePJ; BPP; MaRV; OIF
(Voice from Galilee, The.) HBV; VA
I heard the waterfall rejoice. In the Wood. Sara Teasdale. PC
I heard the wild beasts in the wood complain. Mundus Morosus [*or* The World Morose]. Frederick William Faber. ACP; CAW; OBVV
I heard the wild geese flying. Wild Geese. Elinor Chipp. BLA; FaPON; HBMV; MPB; TiPo
I heard the wild storm as I lay at rest. Parting in Autumn. Holger Drachmann. BoDS
I heard the wind all day. Watching by a Sick-Bed. John Masefield. NP
I heard the wind[s] among the trees. Ecstasy. Harold Trowbridge Pulsifer. BAP; PC
I heard thee, joyous votary. To a Robin. T. A. Daly. JKCP
I heard them in their sadness say. Dust. "Æ." BMEP; HBMV; LBBV; OQP; QP-1; WGRP
I heard them say "He died last night." Songs of La Mouche. Sir Henry Head. PoP
I heard them say, "Her hands are hard as stone." Her Beauty. Max Plowman. HBMV
I heard—'twas on a morning, but when it was and where. Singing Water. Rudolph Chambers Lehmann. HBMV
I heard two workers say, "This chaos/ Will soon be ended." Idiom of the Hero. Wallace Stevens. OxBA
I heard you singing, singing alone. A Child's Song Overheard. Grace Hazard Conkling. PC
I Heard You, Solemn-Sweet Pipes of the Organ. Walt Whitman. LoPo; LoPS; MOAP; NePA; OxBA
I heard your voice, you told. Separation. Laurence Housman. BMEP
I heare the whistling plough-man all day long. On the Plough-Man. Francis Quarles. OBS
I hedge rebellious grasses in. The Stranger. Daniel Henderson. HBMV; TBM
"I heeard da ole folks talkin' in our house da other night." Why Adam Sinned. Alex Rogers. BANP
I heed not that my earthly lot. To ——. Poe. IAP
I held a jewel in my fingers. Emily Dickinson. WHA
I Held a Lamb. Kim Worthington. TiPo (1959 ed.)
I Held Her Hand. Walter Savage Landor. *Fr.* Ianthe. EmBrPo
(Epigrams.) ALV
(Lyrics to Ianthe.) BPN
(Test, The.) HBV; VA
I held it truth, with him who sings. In Memoriam A. H. H., I. Tennyson. BEL; BoFr; BoLiVe; CoBE; EM-2; EmBrPo; EnL; EnLi-2; EnLit; EPN; EPP; GEPC; HBV; LEAP; LiTB; LiTG; OAEP; OQP; QP-1; TCEP; ViPo; VLEP
I helped a little lame dog. My Little Dog. Pearl Forbes MacEwen. BoTP
I herde a carpyng of a clerk. *See* I heard the carping of a clerk.
"I hereby bequeath to the Bide-a-Wee Home all people." Lines in Dispraise of Dispraise. Ogden Nash. NAMP
I Hereby Swear That to Uphold Your House. Elinor Wylie. *Fr.* One Person. LoPS; NePA; ReaPo
(House Sonnet.) LiTL
(Sonnet from "One Person.") LiTA; MAP; MoAB; MoAmPo
(Sonnets from "One Person.") NP; OxBA
I hesitate to write about the spring. The Faithful Lover. Robert Pack. NePoEA
I hid my heart. The Robber. Ivy O. Eastwick. SiSoSe
I hid my heart in a nest of roses. A Ballad[e] of Dreamland. Swinburne. BPN; EmBrPo; EPN; HBV; MBP; PoVP; TCEP; VLEP
I Hid My Love. John Clare. *See* Secret Love.
I hide my grief throughout the weary days. To Richard. Vera Bax. DiM
I hide myself within a flower. With a Flower. Emily Dickinson. LiTL
I hoe and I plow. Farmer. Liberty Hyde Bailey. YeAr
I Hoed and Trenched and Weeded. A. E. Housman. A Shropshire Lad, LXIII. BPN; EmBrPo; InP; LiTM (rev. ed.); MoAB; MoBrPo; PoVP; TrGrPo; UnPo (3d ed.); ViPo
I hoes an' I plows. Rain or Shine. *Unknown.* APW
I hold a letter in my hand. A Poem for the Meeting of the American Medical Association. Oliver Wendell Holmes. PoEL-5
I hold as faith. *Unknown.* SeCSL
I hold him, verily, of mean emprise. Canzone: He Perceives His Rashness in Love. Guido Guinicelli. AWP; JAWP; WBP

I hold it truth, with him who sings. *See* I held it truth . . .
"I hold no cause worth my son's life," one said. Mothers of Men. Amelia Josephine Burr. OQP; QP-2
I hold no dream of fortune vast. Success. Edgar A. Guest. TreF
I hold that Christian grace abounds. My Creed. Alice Cary. WGRP
I hold that when a person dies. A Creed. John Masefield. HBMV; WGRP
I hold the splendid daylight in my hands. Litany. George Campbell. PoNe
I hold to my heart when the geese are flying. Wild Geese. Grace Noll Crowell. BLA
I hold you at last in my hand. The Butterfly. Alice Freeman Palmer. HBV; MaRV; POT; PoTo
I honor the land that gave me birth. Brothers. George E. Day. MaRV
I Honour You in Dread. Ramón López Velarde, *tr. fr. Spanish by* Samuel Beckett. AnMP
I hope. Wish. *Unknown.* DDA
I hope for nothing better than your smile. Alley Cat. Frank Stevens. CIV
I hope he doesn't see me walking past his bed. Letter. Alexander Bergman. TrJP
I hope I'm fond of much that's good. Rotten Row. Frederick Locker-Lampson. ALV
I hope that soon, dear mother. To Mother. Louisa M. Alcott. MOAH
I hope there is a little boy somewhere. Father to Daughter. Mary Ballard Duryee. FAOV
I hope there is a resurrection day. Resurrection. Harry Kemp. HBV
I hope when I am dead that I shall lie. Oblivion. Jessie Redmond Fauset. BANP; PoNe
I hope when you're yourself and twice my age. Metaphor for My Son. John Holmes. MiAP
I hoped that he would love me. The Kiss. Sara Teasdale. ChMo; CMP; HBV
I hoped that with the brave and strong. He Doeth All Things Well. Anne Brontë. MaRV
I hug my pillow and do not speak a word. Poems in Depression, at Wei Village. Po Chü-i. TrCh
I hug my sleep, and in blocklike rock rejoice. Night. Michelangelo. LyPI
I hung my verses in the wind. The Test. Emerson. AA; BAP; IAP
I hurried by the legless beggar. The Quality of Mercy. Mary M. Walsh. CAG
I idle stand that I may find employ. The Idler. Jones Very. AA; HBV; LEAP
I idly cut a parsley stalk. On a Midsummer [*or* Midsummer's] Eve. Thomas Hardy. FaBoTw; GTML; GTSL; VLEP
"I, if I perish, perish"—Esther spake. Monna Innominata, VIII. Christina Rossetti. EmBrPo; ViPo
I imagine him still with heavy brow. Beethoven's Death Mask. Stephen Spender. UnS
I in a vision/ Saw my lost sweetheart. Meeting of Phantoms. Anders Österling. AnSL
I, in My Intricate Image. Dylan Thomas. LiTB
I, in My Pitiful Flesh. Glenway Wescott. NP
I in the Grayness Rose. Stephen Phillips. BMEP; EnLit; LBBV; LEAP
I in Thee, and Thou in Me. Christopher Pearse Cranch. HBV; IAP
I in these flowery meads would be. The Angler's Wish. Izaak Walton. *Fr.* The Compleat Angler. HBV; LPS-2; SeCL
I intend to slip away. Happy Valley, The. Páll Olafsson. IcP
I intended a handspring. Triolet. Margaret Hoover. PCD
I intended an Ode. "Urceus Exit" [*or* Triolet]. Austin Dobson. *Fr.* Rose-Leaves. ATP (1935 ed.); BMEP; BPN; GTSL; HBV; LEAP; MBP; MoBrPo (1942 ed.); OBEV; PIAE; PreP; TCEP; TOP
I invoke the land of Ireland. Invocation to Ireland [*or* Aimirgin's Invocation]. *At. to* Amergin. AnIV; OnYI
I jabbed a jack-knife in my thumb. My Sore Thumb. Burges Johnson. HBVY
I jes' don' know ef de kohn'll grow. De Good Lawd Know My Name. Frank Lebby Stanton. WBLP
I Johon Schep, som tyme Seynte Marie prest of/ York. Sermon to the Rebels at Blackheath. John Ball. PoFr
I joined the army when I was fifteen. Soldier's Song. *Unknown.* WhP
I, Jones, Soldier, *sel.* Joseph Schull.
"Sound smashes through the dark. It is a wall." TwCaPo
"I, Joseph, wonder how this may be." Marvel Not, Joseph, on Mary Mild. *Unknown.* AnEC
I journeyed from my native spot. His Country. Thomas Hardy. BoFr
I journeyed, on a winter's day. Jane Smith. Kipling. PA
I Journeyed South to Meet the Spring. Robert Underwood Johnson. PR
I joy, dear mother, when I view. The British Church. George Herbert. PoE
I joy not in no earthly bliss. The Quiet Mind. *Unknown.* OBSC; SiCE
I joy to see now in your drawèn work. Amoretti, LXXI. Spenser. PeBoSo; SiCE
I just beheld a monstrous crow. Ebony and Ivory. Ibn Hamdin. MooP
I just said I didn't know. Parachutes, My Love, Could Carry Us Higher. Barbara Guest. NeAP
I keep in memory one lovely hour. White Anemone. Lucille Evans. MuM
I keep my eyes wide open. Seeking, Finding. Pedro Salinas. CoSP
I keep the rustic gate closed. Idleness. Lu Yu. OnPC
I Keep Three Wishes Ready. Annette Wynne. MoSiPe; TiPo (1952 ed.)
I keep walking around myself, mouth open with amazement. Immoral. James Oppenheim. HBV
I Keep Wondering. Hilda Conkling. PFE; PFY
I Kenning through Astronomy. Edward Taylor. *See* Meditation Eight.
I kept my answers small and kept them near. Answers. Elizabeth Jennings. NePoEA
I kept my jay for seven years. Jamais je nourrirai de geai. *Unknown.* BoCaPo (1948 ed.)
I kept neat my virginity. Song. Glyn Jones. NeBP
I kept two singing birds. The Maid's Tragedy. Sylvia Townsend Warner. AV
I killed a robin. The little thing. Remorse. Sydney Dayre. DD
I killed her? Ah, why do they cheer? Out. Ernest Radford. PIAE
I killed them, but they would not die. The Immortals. Isaac Rosenberg. FaBoTw; TrJP
I Kilt er Cat. Virginia Frazer Boyle. CIV
I kiss my hand to you. To the Lighted Lady Window. Marguerite Wilkinson. CAW; ISi; WHL
I kiss you good-bye, my darling. The Virgin Mother. D. H. Lawrence. ViBoPo
I kissed a kiss in youth. Scintilla. William Stanley Braithwaite. BANP; CDC
I kissed her hand and it smelt of soap. Clean Clothes. Rafael Arévalo Martínez. AnCL
I Kissed You. *Unknown.* BLPA
I kneel beside you quietly, my son. Cradle Song of a Celtic Queen. James Edward Tobin. JKCP (1955 ed.)
I kneel not now to pray that Thou. A Prayer. Harry Kemp. BAP; HBV; MaRV; WGRP
I kneel on Holy Thursday with the faithful worshipping. The Mother of the Rose. James M. Hayes. JKCP
I kneel to pray. My Prayer. Mark Guy Pearse. OQP; PraP; QP-2
I knelt to pray when day was done. Revelation. Whitney Montgomery. PraP
I knew a black beetle, who lived down a drain. Nursery Rhymes for the Tender-hearted, IV. Christopher Morley. HBMV; TCAP; YaD
I knew a boor—a clownish card. The Folly of Brown. W. S. Gilbert. InMe
I knew a boy who took long walks. Stalky Jack. William Brighty Rands. BoTP; RIS
I Knew a Cappadocian. A. E. Housman. FiBHP
I knew a little Serval cat. Never Get Out! John Galsworthy. OtMeF
I knew a most superior camper. The Bunyip and the Whistling Kettle. John Manifold. LiTB; LiTM; NeLNL; PoMS; SiTL; WaP
I knew a much-loved mariner. "He Bringeth Them unto Their Desired Haven." Lewis Frank Tooker. HBV
I Knew a Woman [Lovely in Her Bones]. Theodore Roethke. NePA; NePoAm-2; UnPo (3d ed.) (Poem.) TrGrPo (rev. ed.)
I knew an old lady. Antique Shop. Carl Carmer. FaPON; MoSiPe
I knew an old wife lean and poor. The Goose. Tennyson. BOHV; EV-5; GBV (1952 ed.); PIR
I Knew by the Smoke That So Gracefully Curled. Thomas Moore. LPS-1
I knew by their eyes when they came. Missing. Irene Rutherford McLeod. BMEP
I Knew Her. Feodor Ivanovich Tyutchev, *tr. fr. Russian by* Babette Deutsch. TrRV
("I knew her erst in days afar," *tr. by* Sir Cecil Kisch.) BoRS; WaL
I knew her first as food and warmth and rest. My Mother. Amelia Josephine Burr. DD; HBMV
I knew his face the moment that he passed. The One. Everard Jack Appleton. MaRV
I knew his house by the poplar trees. Norah. Zoë Akins. AV; HBV
I knew, I felt (perception unexpressed). The Development of Man. Robert Browning. *Fr.* Paracelsus. EPN

I knew once,/ In your embrace. Poem about Waking. David Ferry. NePoAm-2
I knew quite well that some day. Narihira, *tr. fr. Japanese by* I. W. Furukami. LiTW
I knew she lay above me. The White Jessamine. John Banister Tabb. HBV
I knew that an essence, close. The Moment. Germán Pardo García. AnCL
I knew that Disaster. Disaster. James Clarence Mangan. IrPN
I knew that you were coming, June. June. Douglas Malloch. POT; PoTo; YeAr
I knew the black earth of the North. Red Earth. Grace Noll Crowell. HiLiAm
I knew the man. I see him as he stands. Lincoln. George Henry Boker. *Fr.* Our Heroic Times. DD; GA; LBAH; MC; OHIP
I knew thee not, nor durst attendance strive. Upon Mr. Fletchers Playes, Published, 1647. Henry Vaughan. PtP
I knew Thee not, Thou wounded Son of God. Knowledge through Suffering. George Wallace Briggs. MaRV
I knew you long before great motors buzzed. Big Thompson Canon. Jean Milne Gower. PoOW
I knock again and try [again] the key. A Pagan Reinvokes the Twenty-third Psalm. Robert L. Wolf. HBMV; NV; TBM; TrPWD
I knock at the door of a romance. Federico. Nicolás Guillén. PoNe
I Know. Elsa Barker. AV; HBMV; VOD
I know. "Andrei Bely." *Fr.* Christ Is Risen. TrRV
I know/ that it's a heavy task. Wine. Nikolai Ushakov. RuPo
I know/ Where the wind flowers blow! Song from "April." Irene Rutherford McLeod. CP; SUS; VOD
I Know a Bank. Shakespeare. *See* Violet Bank, A.
I know a barber. Edward Anthony. *Fr.* Oddity Land. TiPo (1959 ed.)
I know a barn in Breckenridge on the Blue. Old Men on the Blue. Thomas Hornsby Ferril. PoOW
I know a boy who went to meet the morning. Morning. Dorothy Hamilton Gallagher. SiSoSe
I know a city on a hill, a mountain's castled crown. Assisi. Alfred Noyes. GoBC; SaFP
I know a country of bright anonymous beaches. [In] Memory of Lake Superior. George Dillon. MAP; MoAmPo (1942 ed.); PoTo
I know a dog called Isaac. Three Dogs. E. C. Brereton. BoTP
I know a faithful dog who sits beside. The Faithful Friend. Margaret E. Bruner. AlBD
I know a Flower of beauty rare. The Lay of the Captive Count. Goethe. AWP
I know a flower so sweet and fair. I Am the Rose of Sharon. Catherine Winkworth. BePJ
I know a funny little man. Mr. Nobody. *Unknown.* BoTP; DDA; FaPON; GaP; GoBP; HBVY; MPB (1956 ed.); OnHT; OTPC; PoMS; RAR; StVeCh
I know a garden with three strange gates. The Last Gate. Stella Mead. BoTP
I know a girl who for present purposes let us call by the name of Emily. I Want to Sit Next to Emily. Ogden Nash. BOHV
I know a girl with teeth of pearl. "Wouldn't You Like to Know." John Godfrey Saxe. HBV
I know a green grass path that leaves the field. The Green River. Lord Alfred Douglas. HBMV; MBP; MoBrPo (1942 ed.); OBEV (new ed.); OBVV; PIAE; PoVP
I know a Jew fish crier down on Maxwell Street. Fish Crier. Carl Sandburg. MOAP; OxBA; WoL
I know a little butterfly with tiny golden wings. The Butterfly. Margaret Rose. BoTP
I know a little clock shop. The Clock Shop. Jeannette C. Shirk. GFA
I know a little creature. An Autumn Riddle. *Unknown.* OTPC (1946 ed.)
I know a little cupboard. The Cupboard. Walter de la Mare. BrR; FaPON; GoBP; PCH; PoRh; RAR; TiPo
I Know a Little Garden-Close. William Morris. *Fr.* The Life and Death of Jason, IV. AtBAP; CH; EG; EmBrPo; GTSE; PoE; POTT; ViBoPo; ViPo; ViPP; VLEP
(Garden by the Sea, A.) BMEP; GTML; PoEL-5; PoVP
(Nymph's Song To Hylas, The.) BPN; CBOV; HBV; LEAP; LoPS, 5 *ll.*; OBEV; TOP
(Sweet Song Sung Not Yet to Any Man, A.) AEV
I know a little garden path. A Hint to the Wise. Pringle Barret. HBVY; PCH
I know a little island. Aloha. William Griffith. HBMV
I know a little man who is happy all day long. Happy as a King. "Gabriel Setoun." TVSH
I know a little zigzag boy. The Zigzag Boy and Girl. *Unknown.* GFA
I Know a Lovely Lady Who Is Dead. Struthers Burt. HBMV; MuM
I know a maiden fair to see. Beware. *Tr. by* Longfellow. PR
I know a Mount, the gracious Sun perceives. Rudel to the Lady of Tripoli. Robert Browning. BPN; EmBrPo; LoBV; NBE; OtMeF; PoVP
I know a mountain, lone it lies. The Granite Mountain. Lew Sarett. HBMV
I Know a Name. *Unknown.* BLRP; MaRV; OQP; QP-1
I know a nunnery which no man heeds. The White Alder. *Unknown.* CAG
I know a place. Deep in the Woods. Mildred D. Shacklett. GFA
I know a place, in the ivy on a tree. The Bird's Nest. John Drinkwater. StVeCh
I know a place that holds the Sky. The Upside-down World. Hamish Hendry. BoTP
I know a place where summer strives. Emily Dickinson. NePA
I know a place where the sun is like gold. Four-Leaf Clover. Ella Higginson. AA; ADAH; FaPON; HBV; OTPC (1946 ed.); POT; PoTo; PTA-1
I Know a Quiet Vale. Thomas S. Jones, Jr. VOD
I know a renegade hotel. Traveler's Rest. Ogden Nash. InMe
I know a road that leads from town. The Road to the Pool. Grace Hazard Conkling. HBMV; VOD
I know a room where tulips tall. Song. V. Sackville-West. *Fr.* Mirage. AlDL
I Know a Secret. Christopher Morley. MPB
I know a secret, such a one. The Serf's Secret. William Vaughn Moody. HBV
"I know a solemn secret to keep between ourselves." The Elfin People Fill the Tubes. Winifred M. Letts. BoTP
I know a soul that is steeped in sin. I Know a Name! *Unknown.* BLRP; MaRV; OQP; QP-2
I know a spot where love delights to dream. Sacred Grove. Edward Cracroft Lefroy. *Fr.* Echoes from Theocritus. AWP
I know a story, fairer, dimmer, sadder. My Babes in the Wood. Sarah Morgan Bryan Piatt. AA
I know a tavern in the town. Table for One. John Holmes. WhC
I know a thing that's most uncommon. On a Certain Lady at Court. Pope. ALV; BCEP; BLV; CEP; HBV; OAEP; OBEC; OBEV
I know a town tormented by the sea. Galway. Mary Devenport O'Neill. NeIP; OxBI
I know a vale where I would go one day. A Mountain Gateway. Bliss Carman. CPG
I know a wasted place high in the Alps. Two Poems on the Catholic Bavarians, II. Edgar Bowers. PtPa
I know a way. The Song in the Dell. Charles Edward Carryl. AA
I know a wind-swept hill where all day long. Silentium Altum. Blanche Mary Kelly. CAW
I know, although when looks meet. Crazy Jane and Jack the Journeyman. W. B. Yeats. AtBAP
I know an ice handler who wears a flannel shirt. Ice Handler. Carl Sandburg. OxBA
I know, as my life grows older. Whatever Is—Is Best. Ella Wheeler Wilcox. BLPA; TreFS
I know, blue modest violets. Violets. *Unknown.* BoTP
I Know de Lord's Laid His Hands on Me, *with music. Unknown.* BoAN-2
I know derisive men and women. Aboriginal Sin. John Hay. NePoAm-2
I know four winds with names like some strange tune. Weather Words. David McCord. ImOP
I know her, the thing of laces, and silk. A Musical Box. William Wetmore Story. PR
I know him, February's thrush. The Thrush in February. George Meredith. EmBrPo
I know him now, not now to know demanding. Nunc Scio, Quid Sit Amor. L. A. MacKay. BoCaPo
I know how it would be . . . a rainy moon. After Storm. David Morton. HBMV
I know how poems come. Poems. Hilda Conkling. NP
I know how to hold. How to Go and Forget. Edwin Markham. HBMV
I Know I Am but Summer to Your Heart. Edna St. Vincent Millay. AmPP; ChMo; CMP; TwCV
(Sonnet: "I know I am but summer to your heart.") HBMV
I Know I Am Deathless. Walt Whitman. *Fr.* Song of Myself, XX. MaRV
I know, I know. Song. Arthur Cleveland Coxe. SDH
I know, I know where violets blow. God's Will. Robert Munger. AA
I know I look the kind of dolt. To a Junior Waiter. A. P. Herbert. FiBHP
I know I never did devise. Daughters. William Rose Benét. FAOV

I know I shall remember. The Cathedral of St. Louis. Carl Carmer. MoSiPe
I know it must be winter (though I sleep). Winter Sleep. Edith M. Thomas. AA; EOAH; LBMV
I know it will not ease the smart. Edith and Harold. Arthur Gray Butler. OBVV
I know just what my father was to me. What My Father Was to Me. D. G. Bechers. FAOV
I know, Justine, you speak me fair. Justine, You Love Me Not! John Godfrey Saxe. HBV; PR
I know, Lord, Thou hast sent Him. Mary at Nazareth. Cale Young Rice. StJW
I know lots of men who are in love. I Never Even Suggested It. Ogden Nash. FiBHP; LiTA; LiTL; LiTM; SiTL
I know mine own, our Shepherd says. The Good Shepherd. J. Harold Gwynne. BePJ
I Know Moonlight, *with music*. *Unknown*. AS (Group of Negro Songs, A.) NAMP
I know my body's of so frail a kind. Man [*or* I Know Myself a Man]. Sir John Davies. *Fr.* Nosce Teipsum. ChTr; EIL; EM-1; WHA
I Know My Love. *Unknown*. AnIV
I Know My Princess. Bilhana, *formerly at. to* Chauras, *tr. fr. Sanskrit by* E. Powys Mathers. *Fr.* Black Marigolds. OnPM
I know my soul hath power to know all things. Man [*or* The Vanity of Human Learning]. Sir John Davies. *Fr.* Nosce Teipsum. BCEP; MaRV; OBEV
I Know Myself a Man. Sir John Davies. *See* Man.
I know no sleep you do not stand beside. The Unborn. Judith Wright. MoAuPo
I know no song to sing you. Stars and Silence. *Unknown*. OnPM
I know not but in every leaf. Fraternity. John Banister Tabb. HBV
I know not by what methods rare. This I Know [*or* Prayer]. Eliza M. Hickok. BLRP; PraP
I know not how, but I am brought. Opium Dream. George Crabbe. *Fr.* The World of Dreams. RO
I know not how, but sometimes I remember. The Other People. Lilith Lorraine. MuM
I Know Not How It Falls on Me. Emily Brontë. VLEP
I know not how it may be with others. Old Furniture. Thomas Hardy. MoVE
I know not how that Bethlehem's Babe. Our Christ. Harry Webb Farrington. BePJ; MaRV; OQP; QP-1; QS
I know not how to call you light. To La Sanscœur. William Caldwell Roscoe. VA
I know not how to meet the tempest's rage! The Ship of State. Alcaeus. GrR
I know not if from uncreated spheres. Michelangelo, *tr. fr. Italian by* George Santayana. AWP
I know not if I love her overmuch. Sonnets after the Italian. Richard Watson Gilder. HBV
I know not if the voice of man can reach to the sky. Faith. *Tr. fr. Pawnee Indian*. GrCo-1
I know not of what we pondered. Companions. Charles Stuart Calverley. BOHV; HBV; NA; PoVP; TOP; TSW; VA
I know not Seville. Seville. L. D'O. Walters. HBMV
I know not that the men of old. The Men of Old. Richard Monckton Milnes. EV-5; GTBS; GTSL; LPS-3; OBEV (new ed.); OBVV
I know not, Theodora, if this robe. Estrella Learns That Her Lover Has Killed Her Brother. Lope de Vega Carpio. *Fr.* La Estrella de Sevilla. LiA
I know not these my hands. Amaze. Adelaide Crapsey. LA
I know not—'tis a sorry state. Nec Odi Nec Amo. Theognis. GrR
I know not too well how I found my way home in the night. Robert Browning. *Fr.* Saul. LoBV
I know not what in other men may sleep. Ideal Passion, XXIX. George Edward Woodberry. MOAP
I know not what is in the well, mother! The Well. Manuel de la Parra. AnMP
I know not what my secret is. Andrew Lang. CBE
I know not what spell is o'er me. Lorelei. Heine. TrJP
I know not what the future hath. Whittier. *Fr.* The Eternal Goodness. BAP; BLRP; OQP; QP-1; TreF
I know not what to do. Fragment Thirty-six [*or* Hesperides]. Hilda Doolittle ("H. D."). ChMo; CMP; NP; OxBA; TwCV
I know not what will befall me: God hangs a mist o'er my eyes. Not Knowing. Mary Gardiner Brainard. AA
I know not when your bill I'll see. Some Day. F. P. Doveton. PA
I Know Not Whether I Am Proud. Walter Savage Landor. BPN; EmBrPo; EnRP (Lyrics and Epigrams, XV.) ERP
I know not whether laws be right. In Prison. Oscar Wilde. *Fr.* The Ballad of Reading Gaol. ACP (1926 ed.); MaRV; OQP; QP-2
I know not who thou art to whom I pray. Ideal Passion, XXXIX. George Edward Woodberry. MOAP
I Know Not Why. Morris Rosenfeld. AA; LBMV
I Know Not Why. Paul Verlaine, *tr. fr. French by* Muriel Kittel. AnFP
I Know Not Why, but All This Weary Day. Henry Timrod. AmP; TCAP (Sonnet: I Know Not Why.) SPP
I know not why, but even to me. A Trifle. Henry Timrod. HBV
I know not why I yearn for thee again. Dreams of the Sea. W. H. Davies. EtS; NLK; TCEP
I know not why my soul is rack'd. Changed. Charles Stuart Calverley. ALV; FiBHP
I know not why or whence he came. The Deserter. Joseph S. Cotter, Jr. CDC
I know not why nor whence it came. Reality. Herman Eugene Kittredge. UnW
I know now how it feels to be a ghost. Ghost. Alexa Lane. MuM; UnW
I Know on a Night Overcast. Hayyim Nahman Bialik, *tr. fr. Hebrew by* Jacob Sloan. LiTW
I know seven mice. Edward Anthony. *Fr.* Oddity Land. TiPo (1959 ed.)
I know some lonely houses off the road. Emily Dickinson. MW; OxBA; PoE; PoMS; PoRA; WaKn (Lonely House, The.) AnEnPo; MoAB; MoAmPo (1950 ed.); PFY; YT
I Know Something Good about You. *Unknown*. BLPA; PoToHe
I Know That All beneath the Moon Decays. William Drummond of Hawthornden. BSV (Sonnet: "I know . . .") EPS; LEAP
I Know That Any Weed Can Tell. Louis Ginsberg. TBM (Song.) TrJP
I know that behind these walls is the city, over these rooftops is the sun. Foghorn in Horror. Muriel Rukeyser. FiMAP
I know that death is God's interpreter. Death the Revealer. Albert E. S. Smythe. CPG
I know that Europe's wonderful, yet something seems to lack. Henry van Dyke. *Fr.* America for Me. MaRV
I know that face! Daphne. Bliss Carman. BoCaPo
I Know That He Exists. Emily Dickinson. AmPP; AnFE; APA; CoAnAm; CoV
I Know That I Am a Great Sinner. Purohit. OBMV
I know that I have one Pal. Old Pal. Marty Hale. AlBD
I Know That I Have Savoured. Bilhana, *formerly at. to* Chauras, *tr. fr. Sanskrit by* E. Powys Mathers. *Fr.* Black Marigolds. OnPM
I Know That I Must Die Soon. Else Lasker-Schüler, *tr. fr. German by* Ralph Manheim. TrJP
I know that I shall meet my fate. An Irish Airman Foresees His Death. W. B. Yeats. AnEnPo; CoBMV; EnL; EnLi-2 (1949 ed.); FaBoCh; FaBoMo; LiTG; LiTM (rev. ed.); LoGBV; MoAB; MoBrPo; OBMV; OnPM; OtMeF; PoF; PoFr; TrGrPo; TwP; WaaP; WaP; WoL
I know that if thou please thou canst provide. George Wither. *Fr.* Brittan's Remembrancer. SeCV-1
I know that Jenny loves the whispering corn. Jenny. Jesse Stuart. *Fr.* Man with a Bull-Tongue Plow. BoFr
I know that my dog has a soul. To "Silk." Marty Hale. AlBD
I know that my Redeemer lives. Charles Wesley. OlF; PoFr; TreFS
I know that my Redeemer lives & I. *Unknown*. SeCSL
I Know that My Redeemer Liveth. Virginia Frazer Boyle. BePJ
I know that my Redeemer liveth—but out of the depths of time. The Redeemer. "Fiona Macleod." WGRP
I know that perfect self-esteem. Self-Esteem. Edward Coote Pinkney. SPP
I know that the knell shall sound once more. The Knell Shall Sound Once More. *Unknown*. BlG
I know that the Master walked on earth. The Way of the Master. Albert E. S. Smythe. CPG
I know that there are dragons. Serious Omission. John Farrar. GoBP; RIS; UTS
I know that these poor rags of womanhood. Afterwards. "Violet Fane." HBV; OBVV; VA
I know that this my crying, like the crying. Night. Hayyim Nahman Bialik. AWP; LiTW
I know that this was Life—the track. In Memoriam A. H. H., XXV. Tennyson. EmBrPo; EnLi-2; EPN; GEPC; LPS-1; TOP; ViPo; VLEP
I know that to die is to be dead to the world. To His Sons. Lu Yu. WhP
I know that to the winds my reason is cast! The Conquest of Love. Racine. *Fr.* Phèdre. LiTW
I know that virtue to be in you, Brutus. A Swimmer. Shakespeare. *Fr.* Julius Caesar, I, ii. BHV
I know that when she dies and goes to Heaven. Busybody. Loretta Lee. DDA

I know that you have tried, dear friend. For a Friend Who Thinks Himself Urbane. Robert Penn Warren. BoFr
I know the hedge in Briar Lane. I Must Away. May Sarson. BoTP
I know the injured pride of sleep. Night and Morning. Austin Clarke. AnIL; MoAB; NeIP
I know the month, I know the week. First Born. Frances O'Connell Corridan. JKCP (1926 ed.)
I know the night is near at hand [*or* drawing near]. Vespers [*or* Evening *or* From Dark to Light]. S. Weir Mitchell. BPP; LBAP; MaRV; OQP; QP-1; WGRP
I know the road to Jericho. The Jericho Road. Edwin McNeill Poteat. ChIP; MaRV; QS
I know the ships that pass by day. The Lights. J. J. Bell. BoTP
I know the sky will fall one day. Child's Song. Gerald Gould. BoTP
I know the song that the bluebird is singing. The Bluebird. Emily Huntington Miller. GFA; MPB; OTPC (1946 ed.); PRWS; PTA-1; RAR
I know the sorrows of the last abyss. Compensation. William Ellery Leonard. SBMV
I know the sun shines, and the lilacs are blowing. Enlisted Today. *Unknown.* BlG
I know the thing that's most uncommon. On a Certain Lady at Court. Pope. ALV; BCEP; BLV; BoLiVe; CaAE; CEP; CoBE; EnLit; HBV; OAEP; OBEC; OBEV; TrGrPo
I know the ways [*or* wayes] of learning; both the head. The Pearl. George Herbert. EPS; FaBoEn; MePo; OxBoCh; PoEL-2; ReEn; SeCV-1
I know thee well, brown friar. The Wolf of Gubbio Speaks to Saint Francis. Sister Mary Monica. SaFP
I know there shall dawn a day. Reverie. Robert Browning. OHIP
I know *Thou art.* Thou Art. Kawabuchi. SoLD
I know to God, full of myght. Confiteor. *Unknown.* CoBE
I know two things about the horse. The Horse. Naomi Royde-Smith. CenHV; FiBHP; LiTM; SiTL
I know very well, goddess, she is not beautiful. Calypso's Island. Archibald MacLeish. MoAB
I know very well what I'd rather be. Rathers. Mary Austin. FaPON
I know well I am mortal, a feeble thing and fleeting. The Scientist. Ptolemy. GrPE
I know well this body of mine. Vain Wish. Otomo Yakamochi. OnPM
I know what beer is. Beer and Skittles. Diana Barrett. StaSt
I know what fainting means, the heady sweetness. Address to Death. Afanasi Afanasievich Fet. TrRV
I know what mother's face is like. The Blind Child. *Unknown.* MaRV
I know what the caged bird feels, alas! Sympathy. Paul Laurence Dunbar. CDC; PoNe
I know what will happen, sweet. You and I. Timothy Daniel Sullivan. JKCP (1926 ed.); TIP
"I know what you're going to say," she said. Candor. H. C. Bunner. HBV; PR
I know what you're saying, yellow girl. Yellow Girl. Nicolas Guillén. TwSpPo
I know when milk does flies contain. All Things Except Myself I Know. Villon. BOHV
I know, where Hampshire fronts the Wight. "Hold." Patrick R. Chalmers. HBV
I Know Where I'm Going. *Unknown.* AnIV; IrPN; LO; LoPS; MoShBr; OnYI; PG (1955 ed.); ViBoPo (Irish Song.) AtBAP
I know where is a thief, and long hath been. Ad Eandem. Thomas Bastard. SiCE
I know where stands a linden. Song of the Falcon. *Unknown.* BoDaBa
I know where the wind flowers blow. Song from "April." Irene Rutherford McLeod. CP; SUS; VOD
I know where there's a treasure. The Secret. Marchette Chute. GoBP
I know who won the peace of God. King Ailill's Death. *Tr. by* Whitley Stokes. TIP
I know why lilies ring their bells. Secret. Esther Hull Doolittle. YeAr
I know, within my mouth, for bashful fear. Love's Despair. Richard Lynche. *Fr.* Diella. ElL
I know you after sixty years. Two of You. Mark Van Doren. UnPo (1st ed.)
I know you are too dear to stay. Prevision. Aline Kilmer. SBMV
I know you by the blade. Dionysios Solomos. *Fr.* Hymn to Liberty. MoGP
I know. You cannot keep your passion hid. Dostoievsky to a Young Communist. Daniel J. Honan. JKCP (1955 ed.)
I know you, rider, gonna miss me when I'm gone. Woman Blue. *Unknown.* ABF
I know you: solitary griefs. The Precept of Silence. Lionel Johnson. ACP (1926 ed.); BMEP; CAW; HBV; LBBV; LEAP; MBP; MoBrPo; PoeT; PoToHe (1941 ed.); PoVP; ViBoPo; ViPP; VLEP
I know your barren belief—that a rose will grow. For a Materialist. Adelaide Love. MaRV; OQP; QP-2
I Know Your Heart, O Sea! Cale Young Rice. VOD
I knowed a man, which he lived in Jones. Thar's More in the Man than Thar Is in the Land. Sidney Lanier. CoBA
I labored long, I strove with might and main. Of Impatience Which Brings All Our Gains to Nothing. Jacopone da Todi. CAW
I lack in service, lack in love. To Holy Jesus. Princess Philipa. CAW
I lack the braver mind. Confession of Faith. Elinor Wylie. AnAmPo; AnFE; APA; CoAnAm; LA; MAP; MoAmPo; TwAmPo
I laid me down upon a bank. Poems from MSS. Blake. EnLoPo; ViBoPo
I laid me down upon the shore. Pre-Existence. Frances Cornford. DiM; HBMV; PoeT; POTE; TwCV; WaKn
I laid my ear to the brooklet's brim. The Nixie. Johan Sebastian Cammermeyer Welhaven. AnNoLy
I laid my haffet on Elfer Hill. Elfer Hill. *Unknown.* AWP
I laid my wife beneath this stone. *Unknown.* WhC
I Lais whose laughter was scornful in Hellas. Dedication of a Mirror. Plato, *tr. by* Dudley Fitts. LiTW
I Lais, whose proud laughter mocked Hellas; whose alluring. "Quand Vous Serez Bien Vieille." Plato, *tr. by* F. L. Lucas. GrPE
I laks to go to coht en see. Punishment. John Charles McNeill. NoCaPo
I laks yo' kin' of lovin'. Long Gone. Sterling A. Brown. BANP; CDC
I landed on Iona's holy isle. Iona. Frederick Tennyson. GoBC
I lang hae thought, my youthfu' friend. Epistle to a Young Friend. Burns. BLP; MCCG; OHFP
I lately lived in quiet case. Love Is Like a Dizziness. James Hogg. BOHV; HBV; InMe
I lately lost a preposition. The Naughty Preposition. Morris Bishop. FiBHP
I Lately Vowed, but 'Twas in Haste. John Oldmixon. HBV
I laugh and sing, but cannot tell. To Lucasta. Richard Lovelace. OBS
I laugh at each dull bore, taste's parasite. Heine. Fresco-Sonnets to Christian Sethe, 1. AWP; JAWP; WBP
I laugh with you because I dare not cry. The Day Will Come. Marion Strobel. TBM
I laughed at the lovers I passed. Terenure. Blanaid Salkeld. NeIP
I laved my hands. Lost for a Rose's Sake. *Unknown.* AWP; JAWP; WBP
I lay among the ferns. Edward Carpenter. *Fr.* Among the Ferns. OQP; QP-2
I lay and speculated on the impact of a bullet. Terror. Thomas O'Brien. NeIP
I lay beside you . . . on your lips the while. The Haunted House. George Sylvester Viereck. AnAmPo; LA
I lay face-downward on the grass. The Barrier. Louis Lavater. MoAuPo
I lay i' the bosom of the sun. Palabras Grandiosas. Bayard Taylor. *Fr.* The Echo Club. BOHV
I lay in my tent at mid-day. The Crossing at Fredericksburg. George Henry Boker. PAH
I lay in silence, dead. A woman came. Another Way. Ambrose Bierce. AA; BAP; LEAP; LHV
I lay me down and slumber. A. E. Housman. More Poems, XIII. EmBrPo
I lay me down to rest me. Prayers. *Unknown.* BOL
I lay me down to sleep. In the Hospital. Mary Woolsey Howland. HBV; LPS-1; MaRV
I lay my harp on the curved table. The Harp. Po Chü-i. WhP
I Lay My Lute beside Thy Door. Clarence Urmy. HBMV
I Lay My Sins on Jesus. Horatius Bonar. BePJ
I lay on Delos of the Cyclades. The Ship. Lloyd Mifflin. AA; LEAP
I lay sick. Fevered Sleep. Shan Ho Yü. PoHN
I lay upon the summer grass. The Oracle. Arthur Davison Ficke. HBV; OBAV
I leaned on the horn of the yellow moon. Egotist. John Bruce MacCallum. PoP
I leaned out of [*or* my] window, I smelt the white clover. Songs of Seven: Seven Times Three. Jean Ingelow. AV; GBV (1922 ed.); HBV; LPS-1; PTA-1
I leant out over a ledging cliff and looked down into the sea. Atavism. Cale Young Rice. BAP; UnW
I leant [*or* leaned] upon a coppice gate. The Darkling Thrush. Thomas Hardy. AnFE; ATP (1953 ed.); BLA; BLV; BoLiVe; ChMo; CMP; CoBE; CoBMV; EmBrPo; EnL; EnLi-2 (1949 ed.); EPN; ExPo; FaFP; GTBS-W;

I leant [*or* leaned] upon a coppice gate (*continued*)
GTML; GTSL; HBMV; InP; KN; LiTB; LiTG; LiTM; MBP; MoAB; MoBrPo; MoPo; NeMA; OAEP; OBEV (new ed.); OBVV; PG (1955 ed.); PoFS; POTE; POTT; PoVP; ReaPo; ReMP; SeCeV; ShBV-4; TCEP; TCPD; TrGrPo; TwCV; TwHP; ViP; ViPo; ViPP; VLEP; WaP
I learn as the years roll onward. Life's Lesson. *Unknown.* BLRP
I learn'd his greatness first at Lavington. Cardinal Manning. Aubrey Thomas De Vere. JKCP; VA
I learned today the world is round. The Road to China. Olive Beaupré Miller. MPB
I leave behind me the elm-shadowed square. Outward Bound. Thomas Bailey Aldrich. AA; EtS
I leave mortality, and things below. The Ecstasy. Abraham Cowley. Po
I leave the world to-morrow. Farewell. Enid Derham. BoAu
I leave thee, beauteous Italy! no more. Farewell to Italy. Walter Savage Landor. BPN; VA
I leave thy praises unexpress'd. In Memoriam A. H. H., LXXV. Tennyson. EmBrPo; EPN; GEPC; ViPo; VLEP
I leave with unreverted eye the towers. Florence. Walter Savage Landor. SeCePo
I led him on into the frosted wood. Fable. George O'Neil. NP
I left a lei, Lady. Lady of Peace. Fray Angelico Chavez. ISi
I left great Rome. Aricia offered me. Horace. Satires, I, 5. LaP
I left my home in Virginia. The Roving Rebel. D. F. Lemarr. BlG
I left the crowded streets behind. The Greater Birth. Hermann Hagedorn. UnW
I left the dusty travelled road the proper people tread. The Road to Tartary. Bernard Freeman Trotter. CPG
I left the streets of Galway town. The Tramp's Song. Mary Devenport O'Neill. AnIV
I left thee last, a child at heart. Rosalind's Scroll. Elizabeth Barrett Browning. *Fr.* The Poet's Vow. HBV; OBEV (1st ed.)
I Left Ye, Jeanie. Hew Ainslie. EBSV
I left you once in madness and disgrace. To His Mother. Heine. OnPM
I lent my love a book one day. An Experience and a Moral. Frederick Swarthout Cozzens. LPS-1
I let you flick your sleek fork-lightning spear. To a King Snake. LeGarde S. Doughty. MuM
I licked it and it felt so nice. The Ice Man. Dorothy Aldis. GoBP
I Lie Down with God. *Tr. fr. Modern Irish by* Eleanor Hull. *Fr.* Four Prayers. AnIV; GTIV
(Four Prayers.) OnYI
I lie enveloped in a dream of pain. The Inner Voice. Antero de Quental. UnW
I lie here on the hill of spring. In Spring. Eduard Mörike. AnGP
I lie in the hay. Swallow Tails. Tom Robinson. FaPON
I lie in the tall grass by the berry trail. Love Song. *Unknown, tr. fr. Kootenai Indian.* BAP
I lie long abed. Otomo no Yakamochi, *tr. fr. Japanese by* Kenneth Rexroth. OnPJ
I lie upon my bed and hear and see. The Largest Life. Archibald Lampman. CaP; CPG; OCL
I lift mine eyes against the sky. I Know Not Why. Morris Rosenfeld. AA; LBMV
I lift mine eyes and all the windows blaze. Divina Commedia, V [*or* On Translating the "Divina Commedia"]. Longfellow. AmP; AmPP; AnAmPo; AnFE; AnNE; APA; APW; CoAnAm; CoBA; CoV; ES; GoBC; IAP; LA; LPS-2; MOAP; NePA; OBAV; OuHeWo; OxBA; PIAE; PtP; ReaPo; SeCeV; TCAP; TOP; TriL
I lift my cap to beauty. A Song of the Road. Fred G. Bowles. MaRV; NLK; OQP; QP-2
I lift my eyes, but I cannot see. A Seeker in the Night. Florence Earle Coates. TrPWD
I Lift My Gaze. John Hall Wheelock. MaRV
I lift my head and watch. Thoughts in Exile. Su T'ung-po. OnPC
I lift my head from lowly bed. Moschatel. Daniel James O'Sullivan. NeIP
I lift my heavy heart up solemnly. Sonnets from the Portuguese, V. Elizabeth Barrett Browning. BPN; EmBrPo; TOP; VA; ViPo
I lift the latch. Swifts in the Chimney. Rose Mills Powers. BLA
I lift the Lord on high. Père Lalement. Marjorie Pickthall. BoCaPo; CaP; MM; OCL; PeCV; TwCaPo; TwCV
I lift these hands with iron fetters banded. South Carolina to the States of the North. Paul Hamilton Hayne. PAH
I lift this sumach-bough with crimson flare. Torch-Light in Autumn. John James Piatt. AA; LEAP
I like a church; I like a cowl. The Problem. Emerson. AA; AmP; AmPo; AmPP; AnAmPo; AnNE; AWP; BAP; CoBA; CoV; EV-4; HBV; IAP; JAWP; LA; LBAP; LiTA; LPS-3; MaRV; MOAP; NePA; OBAV; OuHeWo; OxBA; PECK; TCAP; TOP; WBP; WGRP
I like a dog at my feet when I read. The Dog. Edgar A. Guest. AlBD
I like a half day on one day. Page IX. Gertrude Stein. WaKn
I like a look of agony. Emily Dickinson. ReMP
(Real.) OnPM
I like a mouse Wild Animals. Elizabeth Fleming. StVeCh
I like a road that leads away to prospects white and fair. The Best Road of All. Charles Hanson Towne. HBMV; NLK; OQP; POT; PoTo; QP-2
I like a storm at May's beginning. Spring Thunder. Feodor Tyutchev. BoR
I Like Americans. Edna St. Vincent Millay. DDA; YaD
I like best those crotchety ones. The Odd Ones. Ruth Suckow. MCCG
I like blowing bubbles, and swinging on a swing. Things I Like. Marjorie H. Greenfield. BoTP
I Like Christmas. James S. Tippett. ChBR
I like coffee, I like tea. *Unknown.* FaFP; SiTL
I like days. December. Aileen Fisher. SiSoSe
I like her gentle hand that sometimes strays. Richard Watson Gilder. *Fr.* Sonnets after the Italian. HBV
I Like House Cleaning. Dorothy Brown Thompson. BrR; FaPON
I Like Little Pussy. Jane Taylor. CIV; FaBoBe; GFA; HBV; HBVY; PPL; PTA-1
(I Love Little Pussy.) FaPON; OTPC; OxNR, *abr.*; PCH; RAR, *abr.*; TiPo, *st.* 1.
("I love little pussy, her coat is so warm," *st.* 1.) RIS
(Kitty; How to Treat Her, *st.* 1.) CBPC; PoC
(Little Pussy.) GoTP
(Pussy, *abr.*) SAS
I like men./ They stride about. Men. Dorothy E. Reid. DDA; NeMA; StaSt
I Like My Body. E. E. Cummings. LiTG
I like my friend Meng. A Few Words to Meng Hao-jan. Li Po. WhP
I like nature strained through a town. City Nature. Esther Pinch. PoMa
I like not lady-slippers. Tiger-Lilies. Thomas Bailey Aldrich. BAV; GN; GoTP; OBAV
I like not tears in tune, nor do I prize. On the Memory of Mr. Edward King [Drowned in the Irish Seas]. John Cleveland. EPS (1942 ed.); OBS; SeEP
I like old houses that are weather-stained. To an Old Farmhouse. Edna Jacques. DDA
I like old houses, with steps that sag. Old Houses. Jennie Romano. PoToHe (new ed.)
I like old streets with quiet names. Quiet Streets. Victor Starbuck. NoCaPo
I like our house because it is so big and old. Our House. Nellie Burget Miller. GFA
I like rumpled little boys. Little Boys. Margaretta Scott. DDA
I like sitting alone when the moon is shining. Song of the Pines. Po Chü-i. WhP
I like that ancient Saxon phrase, which calls. God's-Acre. Longfellow. HBV; LPS-1; PoRL
I like that old, kind [*or* sweet] legend. The Little Mud-Sparrows; Jewish Legend. Elizabeth Stuart Phelps Ward. ChrBoLe; CLS; PEOR; SDH
I like the boss' daughter. Constantino Suasnavar. *Fr.* Numbers. AnCL
I like the Chinese laundryman. Mar Quong, Chinese Laundryman. Christopher Morley. MPB; MW
I like the clouds. Summer Sky. Ruth McKee Gordon. TiPo (1959 ed.)
I like the fall. The Mist and All. Dixie Willson. BrR; FaPON; MPB; YeAr
I like the hunting of the hare. The Old Squire. Wilfrid Scawen Blunt. HBV; OBEV (new ed.); OBVV; VA
I like the man who faces what he must. The Inevitable. Sarah Knowles Bolton. AA; MaRV; OQP; PCD; QP-1; WGRP
I like the old house tolerably well. Bliss Carman. *Fr.* Behind the Arras. BAP
I like the people who keep shops. Shops. Winifred M. Letts. MoSiPe; MW
I like the story of the circus waif. The Road. Herbert Morris. NePoAm-2
I like the tangled brakes and briers. Days Like These. Ella Elizabeth Egbert. NLK; PoMa
I like the town on rainy nights. Rainy Nights. Irene Thompson. BoTP
I like the way that the world is made. Contentment. Burges Johnson. AlBD
I like the whistle of trains at night. Trains at Night. Frances Frost. BrR; TiPo
I like the wide and common road. The Knapsack Trail. Edwin Osgood Grover. OQP; QP-2

I like the woods. Autumn Woods. James S. Tippett. BoChLi; SUS; TiPo
I like to chase the fireflies. Fireflies. Grace Wilson Coplen. GFA; UTS
I like to find. Pleasures. Denise Levertov. NeAP
I like to look at pamphlets. Illustrated Booklet on Request. Betty Frye Leach. DDA
I like to look at the blossomy track of the moon upon the sea. Main Street. Joyce Kilmer. JKCP
I like to look out of my window and see. Rain. Helen Wing. GFA
I like to move. There's such a feeling. Moving. Eunice Tietjens. GaP; TiPo
I like to play close by my father's den. Are You There? Strickland Gillilan. PoToHe (new ed.)
I Like to Quote. Mitchell D. Follansbee. WhC
I like to ride in a tramcar. Travelling. Dorothy Gradon. BoTP
I like to see a thing I know. New Sights. *Unknown.* BoTP
I like to see it lap the miles. Emily Dickinson. AmPo; AmPP; MAP; MoAB; MoAmPo; MOAP; MoShBr; MoVE; OxBA; PoE; PoeMoYo; ReaPo; TwP
(Amherst Train, The.) LoGBV
(Locomotive, The.) CoBA; FaPON; MPB
(Railroad Train, The.) PCD
(Railway Train, The.) MCCG
(Train, The.) LiTA; LiTG; LiTM (rev. ed.); MW
I like to see the airplane and hear the buzzing sound. The Airplane. Annette Wynne. GFA
I like to see the eager-faced old woman. An Old Woman with Flowers. Agnes Lee. NP
I like to see the patience of a leafless tree. A Leafless Tree. Ann Louise Thompson. OQP; QP-2
I Like to Sing Also. John Updike. FiBHP
I like to sit and watch my cat. Sport for Gods. Jewell Bothwell Tull. CIV
I like to sit by the fire. A Man Speaks. Ethel Romig Fuller. DDA
I like to sit here by the hearth. Movies in the Fire. Mildred D. Shacklett. GFA
I like to think/ That, long ago. Snowdrops. Mary Vivian. BoTP
I like to walk. Crows. David McCord. TiPo (1959 ed.)
I like to wear my party frock. Best. Rose Fyleman. BrR
I Like Wood Roads. *Unknown.* DDA
I like you, Mrs. Fry! I like your name! A Friendly Address. Thomas Hood. PoEL-4
I like your muse because she's gay and witty. W. H. Auden. *Fr.* Letter to Lord Byron. PtP
I Liked but Never Loved Before. *Unknown.* SeCL
I liked to go to the branch today. At the Water. Elizabeth Madox Roberts. LS
I liked to walk in the river meadows. The Midnight Court. Brian Merriman. KiLC
I linger on the flathouse roof, the moonlight is divine. The Flathouse Roof. Nathalia Crane. TCAP; YT
I List ("I list as sounds from the town float by"). Guillaume Apollinaire, *tr. fr. French by* Alan Conder. TrFP
I 'listed at home for a lancer. Lancer. A. E. Housman. EnLit; MBP; MoBrPo
I listen and my hand thy letter presses. An Old Woman's Answer to a Letter from Her Girlhood. Susan L. Emory. CAW
I listen to the agony of God. The Agony of God. Georgia Harkness. MaRV
I listen'd to the music broad and deep. Love and Music. Philip Bourke Marston. VA
I listened, there was not a sound to hear. Full Moon; Santa Barbara. Sara Teasdale. BrR; TSW; TSWC
I listened to a man and he. Psychometrist. James Stephens. POTE
I listened to the Phantom by Ontario's shore. The Poet. Walt Whitman. *Fr.* By Blue Ontario's Shore. IAP; MoAmPo (1950 ed.)
I listened to them talking, talking. A Man. Louis Untermeyer. FAOV
I little know or care. Forever and a Day. Thomas Bailey Aldrich. HBV; LHV
I live among the grasses. The Field-Mouse. Enid Blyton. BoTP
I Live, and Yet Methinks I Do Not Breathe. *Unknown.* ElSeCe
I live at the upper end of the river. A River-long Love. Li Chih-yi. ChLP
I live for the good of my nation. Rosin the Bow [*or* Old Rosin, the Beau]. *Unknown.* CoSo; CSF
I live for those who love me. What I Live For. George Linnaeus Banks. BLPA; FaBoBe; MaRV; NeHB; PTA-1; PoToHe (new ed.); TreFS
I live in light and love. Heaven. Takamoto. SoLD
I live in poverty; day by day. The Yellow River. Lu Yu. WhP
I live in the town. The Town Child. Irene Thompson. BoTP
I live in this house, walls being plastered. Keep Me Still, for I Do Not Want to Dream. Larry Eigner. NeAP
I live my life in circles that grow wide. Rainer Maria Rilke. *Fr.* The Book of Hours. UnW
I live, sweet love, whereas the gentle wind. Licia, XXVI. Giles Fletcher. SiCE; TuPP
I live: this much I know; and I defy. Immortality. Willis Fletcher Johnson. OQP; QP-2
I live where James B. Duke persists. Tar Heel. Helen Bevington. NoCaPo (rev. ed.)
I live, yet no true life I know. I Die because I Do Not Die. St. Theresa of Avila. AnSpL-1
I lived a life without love, and saw the being. The Mirage. Oscar Williams. CrMA; LiTL; LiTM; NePA
I lived among great houses. The Statesman's Holiday. W. B. Yeats. AtBAP
I lived here nearly 5 years before I could. Chicago Poem. Lew Welch. NeAP
I Lived in a Town, *with music.* *Unknown.* TrAS
I lived my days apart. A Mystic as Soldier. Siegfried Sassoon. CP; LBBV; NP; WGRP
I lived to tell the truth, and truth was wrong. Laocoon. Donald Hall. NePoAm-2
"I lived with Mr. Punch, they said my name was Judy." Variations. Randall Jarrell. MiAP
I lived with Pride; the house was hung. The House of Pride. William J. Dawson. MaRV; PoToHe
I lived with visions for my company. Sonnets from the Portuguese, XXVI. Elizabeth Barrett Browning. BEL; BPN; CoBE; EmBrPo; EnLi-2; EnLit; OAEP; TOP; VA; ViPo
"I loathe a man that's evil. My face in my veil I'll cover." Loyalty. Theognis. GrPE
I loathe, abhor, destest, despise. Dried Apple Pies. *Unknown.* BLPA
I loathe an uninitiate ear! Simplicity. Horace. Odes, III, 1. RoL
I loathe bards' commonplaces. No beaten track delights me. The Aesthete. Callimachus. GrPE
I Loathe That I Did Love. Thomas, Lord Vaux. *See* Aged Lover Renounceth Love, The.
I loathe the very thought of her. Morning Star. James J. Galvin. ISi
I loathed you, Spoon River. I tried to rise above you. Archibald Higbie. Edgar Lee Masters. *Fr.* Spoon River Anthology. InP; NP
I Lo'ed Ne'er a Laddie but Ane. Hector MacNeill. EBSV
I loitered weeping with my bride for gladness. Lyrics. James Agee. MAP; MoAmPo
I long have had a quarrel set with Time. The Two Highwaymen. Wilfrid Scawen Blunt. MBP; MoBrPo (1942 ed.); OBEV (1st ed.)
I long not now, a little while at least. Protest. Countee Cullen. CDC; PFE
I long to go over there to the further bank of the river. The Further Bank. Rabindranath Tagore. AlDL
I long to know/ How my dear mistress fares. An Invocation [*or* Invocation to Spirit]. George Chapman. *Fr.* Bussy d'Ambois, V, iii. EV-1; LiA; ViBoPo
I long to talk[e] with some old lover's ghost. Love's Deity [*or* Deitie]. John Donne. ATP; AWP; BEL; ElL; ElSeCe; EM-1; EnLi-2; EnLit; EnLP; EPP; EPS; EV-2; InPo; KN; LiTB; LiTG; LiTL; MaPo; MePo; OAEP; OuHeWo; PIAE; PoE; PreP; ReEn; SeCePo; SeCV-1; SeEP; TOP; TuPP; TwP; WBP; WHA
I longed for joy and peace and deep content. A Bleeding Heart Aflame. James M. Hayes. PraNu
I Look. Sigbjörn Obstfelder, *tr. fr. Norwegian by* Charles W. Stork. AnNoLy
I look at my shadow over and over in the lake. Looking in the Lake. Po Chü-i. WhP
I look at the crisp golden-thread hair. Canzone: His Portrait of His Lady. Fazio degli Uberti. AWP
I look at the Greek-derived design that nourished my infancy. Hellenistics. Robinson Jeffers. OnAP
I look at the swaling sunset. In Trouble and Shame. D. H. Lawrence. OBMV
I look at the white heavens. I Look. Sigbjörd Obstfelder. AnNoLy
I look at your eyes and your mouth's red flower. You Were Much Too Near. Arnulf Øverland. AnNoLy
I look before, and do not see the ancients. The Ancients. Ch'en Tzu-ang. WhP
I Look Down. Po Chü-i, *tr. fr. Chinese by* Arthur Waley. OnPM
I look down. Halfway Up the Mountain. Liu Tzu Hui. PoHN
I look down on the Twelve City Streets. I Look Down. Po Chü-i. OnPM
I Look Forward. Claire Goll, *tr. fr. French by* Claire Goll. OnPM
I Look into My Glass. Thomas Hardy. EG; FaBoTw; LO; MoPW; POTE
I look into the Stars. Jane Draper. HBMV

I Look Not Back. Annie Johnson Flint. BePJ
I look on kingship in high pines. Exile. Jennette Yeatman. GoYe
I look on the specious electrical light. A Rhyme about an Electrical Advertising Sign. Vachel Lindsay. InP
I look out into the yonder. Last Call. Langston Hughes. NePoAm-2
I look to Thee in ev'ry need. The Christian Life. Samuel Longfellow. PraP; WGRP
I look up and see/ his curtains and bed. On the Death of His Father. Wei Wen-ti. TrCh
I Look Up Hotels. Constantino Suasnavar, *tr. fr. Spanish by* Muna Lee. *Fr.* Numbers. AnCL; OnPM
I look upon my native city's wall. Death Warnings. Francisco de Quevedo y Villegas. CAW
I look upon the world—and she resembles a garden. The End of Man Is Death. Moses ibn Ezra. TrJP
I look upon thy happy face. To a Child. George Edgar Montgomery. AA
I look with awe upon the human race. Two Somewhat Different Epigrams, II. Langston Hughes. NePoAm-2
I look'd to find a man who walk'd with God. Enoch. Jones Very. APW
I lookd upon my true loves eye. *Unknown.* SeCSL
I looked across and beyond the churned-up lake. A Dream. Hugh Connell. NeIP
I looked and saw your eyes. Three Shadows. Dante Gabriel Rossetti. BPN; EmBrPo; HBV; PoVP; ViBoPo; VLEP
I looked and the shore was still faraway. The Cretan. Dionysios Solomos. MoGP
I Looked at England. Mabel E. Allan. NeTW
I looked far back into other years, and lo, in bright array. Mary, Queen of Scots. Henry Glassford Bell. BeLS; BLPA; FaBoBe
I looked for Christ on Madison Street. Christ on Madison Street. Raymond Kresensky. ChIP
I looked for Heaven, high on a hill. Heaven in My Hand. Raymond Kresensky. OQP; QP-2
I looked for him everywhere. A Child Asleep. Elizabeth Madox Roberts. AnAmPo; LA
I looked for that which is not, nor can be. Three Stages [*or* A Pause of Thought]. Christina Rossetti. EmBrPo; FaBoEn
I looked from my window this morning and found. Winter Feathers. Mildred D. Shacklett. GFA
I looked in my heart while the wild swans went over. Wild Swans. Edna St. Vincent Millay. BAP; MAP; MoAmPo; MM
I looked into a lake and saw a forest. Playmates. Lillian Everts. GoYe
I looked into my body. X-Ray. Leonora Speyer. ImOP
I looked into my heart to write. Summer Song. George Barker. ChMP; FaBoTw; GTBS-D
I looked like Abraham Lincoln. Elliott Hawkins. Edgar Lee Masters. *Fr.* Spoon River Anthology. OxBA
I looked on that prophetic land. Presences Perfected. Siegfried Sassoon. MBP; MoBrPo
I looked one night and there Semiramis. A Look into the Gulf. Edwin Markham. AA; LBAP; LEAP
I Looked Out into the Morning. James Thomson. Sunday up the River, I. EmBrPo; OAEP; PoVP; ViBoPo; VLEP
I looked over Jordan and what did I see. Swing Low, Sweet Chariot. *Unknown.* BlG; FaPON; GoSl; InP
I looked to find Spring's early flowers. The Lament of the Flowers. Jones Very. OxBA
I looked upon the dreary waste. The Message of the Bells. Thomas Curtis Clark. PGD
I looked upon the earth: it was a floor. Our Lady in the Middle Ages. Frederick William Faber. ACP; CAW; ISi
I lose the sunlight, lovely above all else. The Lost World of Adonis. Praxilla. OxBG
I lost my heart the other day. *Unknown.* SeCSL
I lost my mare in Lincoln Lane. *Unknown.* OxNR
I Lost the Love of Heaven. John Clare. GTBS-D; LoBV; RO; TriL
(Vision, A.) ChTr
I lothe that I did love. *See* I loathe that I did love.
I Lov'd Thee Once. Sir Robert Ayton. *See* I Loved Thee Once.
I love a book, if there but run. The Book Lover. Clinton Scollard. MOB
I love a busy, hustling town! A Busy Street. *Unknown.* DDA
I Love a Flower. Heine, *tr. fr. German by* Herman Salinger. AnGP
I Love a Flower. Robert Nichols. ChMP
I love a lass as fair as e'er was seen. Of a Mistress. Sir Aston Cokayne. SeCL
I love a noble lady, the reason why is clear. I Serve. Meinloh von Sevelingen. OnPM; WoL
I love a prayer-book. A Girl's Mood. Lizette Woodworth Reese. HBMV
I Love All Beauteous Things. Robert Bridges. BoTP; ChMo; CMP; ExPo; HBMV; HBVY; LEAP; PoeT; POTT; PoVP; ShBV-4; TwCV; VLEP
(All Beauteous Things.) BLV
(To L. B. C. L. M.) OAEP; ViBoPo
I love all hardy exercise. Sunday up the River, V. James Thomson. EmBrPo
I love all shining things. Shining Things. Elizabeth Gould. BoTP
I love all things that God has made. Prairie Winds. Helena Coleman. CPG; OCL
I love all waves and lovely water in motion. Five Degrees South. Francis Brett Young. EtS
I love and fear him. Lady Kasa, *tr. fr. Japanese by* Kenneth Rexroth. OnPJ
I love, and have some cause to love, the earth. Delight in God Only. Francis Quarles. *Fr.* Emblems. BCEP; EPS (1942 ed.); LPS-2
I love and he loves me again. A Nymph's Passion [*or* A Nymph's Secret]. Ben Jonson. ElSeCe; EnLit; OBEV (new ed.)
I love and worship thee in that thy ways. Madonna Natura. "Fiona Macleod." WGRP
I love as though I were not born to die. Samis Idyll. Dachine Rainer. NePoAm
I love at early morn, from new-mown swath. John Clare. *Fr.* Summer Images. ChTr; EG; ERP
I love at eventide to walk alone. Summer Moods. John Clare. LPS-2
I love but dare not show it for why. *Unknown.* SeCSL
I Love but thee. Heine, *tr. fr. German by* Louis Untermeyer. AWP
(Wenn ich in deine Augen seh', *tr. by* Sir Theodore Martin.) OuHeWo
I love contemplating—apart. Napoleon and the British Sailor [*or* Soldier and Sailor]. Thomas Campbell. BeLS; CG; LH; LPS-2; ShGoBo
I love daffodils. Spring Song. Hilda Conkling. GBV (1922 ed.); HH; MPB; PoTo; TSW; TSWC
I love her always; in that is my pain. He Desires Her Husband's Death. Dafydd ap Gwilym. LyMA
"I love, I love, and whom love ye?" *Unknown.* LO
I love it, I love it; and who shall dare. The Old Arm-Chair [*or* A Contrast in Styles]. Eliza Cook. ATP; LPS-1; MotAn; OTPC (1923 ed.); ShGoBo; WBLP
I love Kentucky. Daniel Boone. Cotton Noe. BoHiPo
I Love Little Pussy. Jane Taylor. *See* I Like Little Pussy.
I love little pussy, her coat is so warm. The Wild Home-Pussy. Emma Rounds. RIS
I Love Little Willie, *with music. Unknown.* ABF
I Love Long Black Eyes. Bilhana, *formerly at. to* Chauras, *tr. fr. Sanskrit by* E. Powys Mathers. *Fr.* Black Marigolds. OnPM
I love Love! Of Roses. Mary Carolyn Davies. PR
I love, lovėd, and so doth she. Sir Thomas Wyatt. SiPS
I love my country, but that love is odd. My Country. Mikhail Lermontov, *tr. by* Babette Deutsch. TrRV
I love my country with a singular love. My Country. Mikhail Lermontov, *tr. by* Frances Cornford and E. P. Salaman. LiTW
I love, my God, but with no love of mine. By Thy Life I Live [*or* Adoration]. Mme Guyon. MaRV; WGRP
I love my hour of wind and light. Swallow Flight. Sara Teasdale. NP
I Love My Jean. Burns. *See* Of A' the Airts.
I love my Lady; she is very fair. My Beautiful Lady. Thomas Woolner. OBVV; VA
I love my lady with a deep purple love. Imagiste Love Lines. *Unknown.* BOHV
I Love My Life, but Not Too Well. Harriet Monroe. *See* Love Song.
I love my little gowns. "Vanity, Saith the Preacher." Josephine Preston Peabody. InP
I love my little son, and yet when he was ill. The Two Parents. "Hugh MacDiarmid." FaBoTw
I Love My Love. Helen Adam. NeAP
I Love My Love. Charles Mackay. NeHB
I Love My Love in the Morning. Gerald Griffin. ACP; GoBC; IrPN; OnYI
I love my prairies, they are mine. My Prairies. Hamlin Garland. FaPON; PTA-2
I love my queer cellar with its dusty smell. The Cellar. Hilda Conkling. PCH
I love not Colorado. Westward Ho. *Unknown.* CoSo; CSF
I love not thy perfections. When I hear. Depreciating Her Beauty. Wilfrid Scawen Blunt. The Love Sonnets of Proteus. OBMV
I love not wine, but shouldst thou wish. Agathias Scholasticus, *tr. fr. Greek by* Lilla Cabot Perry. GrPo
I love not wine; yet if thou'ldst make. Leave a Kiss within the Cup. Agathias Scholasticus, *tr. by* J. M. Edmonds. GrL; OxBG; WoL
I love Octopussy, his arms are so long. The Octopussycat. Kenyon Cox. *Fr.* Mixed Beasts. FaPON; RIS; TiPo

I love old gardens best, gardens where cloistering walls. Old Gardens. Frances Beatrice Taylor. CPG
I love old gardens best—tired old gardens. A Charleston Garden. Henry Bellamann. LS
I love old maps made long ago. Old Maps. Eunice Tietjens. BrR
I love old mothers—mothers with white hair. Dear Old Mothers [*or* Old Mothers]. Charles S. Ross. MOAH; OQP; PGD; PoToHe (new ed.); PSO; QP-1
I Love Old Things. Wilson MacDonald. OCL
I love our old pear tree. The Pear Tree. E. Elizabeth Longwell. BrR
I love sea words. Sea Words. Mary Sinton Leitch. EtS
I love sixpence, jolly [*or* pretty] little sixpence. Mother Goose. OTPC; OxNR
I love snow and all the forms. Shelley. *Fr.* Song: "Rarely, rarely, comest thou." TiPo (1959 ed.)
I Love the Beginning of All Rain. Geoffrey Scott. POTE
I Love the Blue Violet. John Clare. AtBAP
I love the call of horns from woods at night. The Horn. Alfred de Vigny. TrFP
I love the chalice and the pyx. God Speaks in All Religions. Thomas Lake Harris. BAP; MaRV
I love the cradle songs the mothers sing. Desire in Spring. Francis Ledwidge. CP; NV; VOD
I love the evenings, passionless and fair, I love the evens. A Sunset. Victor Hugo. AWP; JAWP; WBP
I love the festive board. Gay Feast. Pushkin. OnPM; TrRV
I love the fitful gust that shakes. Autumn. John Clare. BoTP; EG; EnSW; GTBS-D; MW; PCH; WP
I Love the Friendly Faces of Old Sorrows. Karle Wilson Baker. PC
I love the glamour of English towns. Homesick in England. Robert Haven Schauffler. PC
I love the hours when wild geese fly. Hour of Autumn. Myrtle Alice McCarcy. DDA
I love the jocund dance. Song. Blake. EG; EiPP
I love the lad no longer; I have spurned my bitter sadness. The Broken Chain. Theognis. GrPE
I love the little rain. After the Rain. Tristan Corbière. AnFP
I love the little winding lanes. Lanes in Summer. Malcolm Hemphrey. BoTP
I love the locust tree. The Library. William Carlos Williams. *Fr.* Paterson, Bk. III. AtBAP
I love the man who dares to face defeat. Courage. Ozora Stearns Davis. OQP; QP-1
I love the mellow minds. Old Women. Frances Alexander. HiLiAm
I love the modest violet. The Sunflower. Gilles Durant. TrFP
I love the name of Christ the Lord, the Man of Galilee. The Christ of Common Folks. George T. Liddell. BPP; OQP; QP-1
I love the old melodious lays. Proem. Whittier. AA; AmPP; AnNE; CoBA; CoV; HBV; IAP; LEAP; MOAP; NePA; OBAV; OxBA; TCAP
I love the ragged veterans of June. The Ragged Regiment. Alice Williams Brotherton. NLK
I love the silver-shaken. The Wind's Life. Harry Kemp. NLK
I love the sound of the horn in the deep, dim woodland. The Sound of the Horn. Alfred de Vigny. AWP; JAWP; WBP
I love the stillness of the wood. "Lewis Carroll." *Fr.* Solitude. AlDL
I love the stony pasture. The Deserted Pasture. Bliss Carman. HBV; NLK
I love thee and I love thee not. The Reason Why. Thomas Lovell Beddoes. OBRV
I love thee, Avon! though thy banks have known. The Avon. Henry Jacobs. AnNZ
I love thee, Baby! for thine own sweet sake. To Ianthe. Shelley. ATP
I love thee, Betty. *Unknown.* OxNR
I love thee, Chromis; hither, god-like youth! To Chromis. André Chénier. TrFP
I love thee, dear, and knowing mine own heart. In Deep Places. Amelia Josephine Burr. AV
I love thee, dear, for what thou art. To a Plain Sweetheart. T. A. Daly. JKCP
I love thee for thy fickleness. *Unknown.* SeCSL
I Love Thee, Gracious Lord. C. C. Cox. BePJ
I Love Thee, Lord. Connie Calenberg. BePJ
I love thee, love thee, Giulio! Parting Lovers. Elizabeth Barrett Browning. LPS-1
I love thee, Mary, and thou lovest me. The Chemist to His Love. *Unknown.* BOHV; InMe
I love thee, nature, with a boundless love. Love of Nature. John Clare. RO
I love thee not, Sabidius. To Sabidius. Martial, *tr. by* Timothe Kendall. TuPP
I love Thee, O most gracious Lord. I Love Thee, Gracious Lord. C. C. Cox. BePJ
I love thee, pious ox, through whom my heart. The Ox. Giosuè Carducci. WoL
I love thee then. Stephen Phillips. *Fr.* Marpessa. LoPS
I love thee when thy swelling buds appear. The Tree. Jones Very. ADAH; AnAmPo; AnNE; APW; DD; GN; GoTP; HBV; LA; OHIP; PEDC; PoRL
I love them—and I hearken. The Carillon. Rosalia Castro de Murguía. CAW
I love thine inland seas. America. Henry van Dyke. HiLiAm
I love this land of forest grand! Young Canada; or, Jack's as Good as His Master. Alexander McLachlan. BoCaPo
I love this little house because. Motto for a Dog House. Arthur Guiterman. AlBD
I love those spirits. Débris. Lola Ridge. BAP; NP
I Love Thy Kingdom, Lord. Timothy Dwight. IAP; MaRV (Love to the Church.) AA; HBV; HiLiAm; TCAP
I love to go to see Aunt Flo. Farm Life. Ruth Edna Stanton. GFA
I love to hear the autumn crows go by. Autumn Evening. John Clare. ThWaDe
I love to hear the little bird. The Bird. Samuel Hoffenstein. FiBHP
I love to hear the train go by. 'Spress! Jimmy Garthwaite. GFA
I love to hear thine earnest voice. To an Insect. Oliver Wendell Holmes. APW; DDA; HBV; HBVY; IAP; LPS-2; OTPC; SN; StaSt; TCAP; TreF
I love to lie awake and hear. Raindrops. Isla Paschal Richardson. GFA
I love to lie under the lemon. Fantasy. Hugh McCrae. MM; MoAuPo
I Love to Love. Marion Ward. ATP; PreP
I love to meet/ A sudden turn like this. James Hurdis. *Fr.* The Village Curate. EnSW
I love to rise in a summer morn. The School Boy. Blake. *Fr.* Songs of Experience. CH; EM-1; EV-3; FaBoCh; GTBS-D
I love to see the old heath's withered brake. Emmonsail's Heath in Winter. John Clare. FaBoEn; PoEL-4
I love to see, when leaves depart. Autumn. Roy Campbell. JKCP (1955 ed.); MBP; MoBrPo; OBMV; POTE; TrGrPo (1942 ed.)
I love to see you in your oval frames. Pastel. Théophile Gautier. TrFP
I Love to Steal Awhile Away. Phoebe H. Brown. BPP; PraP (Private Devotion.) AA
I love to step inside a church. Within the Gates. David W. Foley. MaRV
I love to tell the story. Katherine Hankey. OlF
I love to think of them at dawn. His Peace. William Alexander Percy. QS
I love to think of things I hate. The Complete Misanthropist. Morris Bishop. FiBHP; SiTL
I love to think this fragrant air. Winds of Eros. "Æ." HBMV
I love to wander through the woodlands hoary. October [*or* A Still Day in Autumn]. S. W. Whitman. BoTP; LPS-2
I Love You. Ella Wheeler Wilcox. BLPA; FaBoBe
I love you,/ Not only for what you are. Love. *Unknown, at. to* Roy Croft. BLPA; FaBoBe; MaRV; NeHB; PoToHe (new ed.)
I love you and hate you, but if I can tell. Love and Hate. Catullus. OnPM
I love you, as the sum of all those forms. Venetian Sonnets, VIII. August, Graf von Platen. AnGP
I Love You, Dear. William Allingham. PCH
I love you first because your face is fair. V-Letter. Karl Shapiro. CoBMV; FiMAP; MiAP; TrJP; WaP
I love you for your brownness. To a Dark Girl. Gwendolyn B. Bennett. BANP; CDC
I love you, great new Titan! Soldier: Twentieth Century. Isaac Rosenberg. ChMP
I Love You, Ha! You Brown-Skin Devil. Björnstjerne Björnson, *tr. fr. Norwegian by* Charles W. Stork. AnNoLy
"I love you, mother," said little John. Which Loved Best? "Joy Allison." HH; OHIP; PEDC; WBLP
"I love you, my lord!" Triolet. Paul T. Gilbert. BOHV
I love you opposite the seas. Tiki. André Breton. MiCF
I love you, ox, who pour into my heart. The Ox. Giosuè Carducci. OnPM
I love you, pretty maid, for you are young. Glauce. Aubrey Thomas De Vere. IrPN
"I love you, sweet: how can you ever learn." Youth's Antiphony. Dante Gabriel Rossetti. The House of Life, XIII. BPN; PoVP; TOP; ViPo
I Love You Truly. Carrie Jacobs Bond. TreFS
I love you well, my steel-white dagger. Dagger. Mikhail Yurevich Lermontov. AWP; JAWP; WBP
I love your hands. Your Hands. Angelina Weld Grimké. CDC

I love your lips when they're wet with wine. I Love You. Ella Wheeler Wilcox. BLPA; FaBoBe
I Loved a Lass. George Wither. CH; EnLi-1; EV-2; HBV; LO; OBEV; PG
(Love Sonnet, A.) ElL; ElSeCe; LiTL; OBS; SeEP; ViBoPo
I loved a love—a royal love. Ireland. Edmund Leamy, Sr. JKCP
I loved a woman. The stars fell from heaven. Ezra Pound. *Fr.* Near Périgord. NP
I loved her for that she was beautiful. My Lady. Philip James Bailey. *Fr.* Festus. LO; OBVV
I loved her one/ Not learned, save in gracious household ways. Happy He with Such a Mother. Tennyson. *Fr.* The Princess. PGD; PSO
I loved him in my dawning years. A Life's Love. *Unknown.* LPS-3
I loved him not; and yet now he is gone. The Maid's Lament. Walter Savage Landor. *Fr.* The Citation and Examination of William Shakespeare. BPN; EV-4; GTBS; HBV; LPS-1; OBEV; OBRV; OBVV; ReTS; VA
I loved him three storms ere he loved me again. Love's Flight. Else Lasker-Schüler. TrJP
I loved, I kissed, I was happy, I was conquered, her love is mine. The Secret. *Unknown.* GrPE
I Loved, I Love You. Byron. LiTL
I loved, I played, I drank my wine. Philodemus, *tr. fr. Greek by* the Earl of Cromer. GrPo
I loved my lord, my black-haired lord, my young love. The Magnet. Ruth Stone. NePA
I Loved Thee. Robert, Earl Nugent. *See* Epigram: "I loved thee, beautiful and kind."
I Loved Thee, Atthis, in the Long Ago. Bliss Carman. CaP; OCL
I loved thee long and dearly. Florence Vane. Philip Pendleton Cooke. AA; HBV; SPP
I Loved [*or* Lov'd] Thee Once. Sir Robert Ayton. LiTL; OBS; ViBoPo
(I'll Love No More.) EV-2
(On a Woman's Inconstancy.) ElL
(To an Inconstant.) HBV
(To an Inconstant Mistress.) BSV; EBSV
(To an Inconstant One.) OBEV
(Woman's Inconstancy.) LPS-1
I loved you. Toward the Piraeus. Hilda Doolittle ("H. D."). TBM
I loved you, Atthis, once, long, long ago. To Atthis. Sappho. GrL; OxBG
I loved you dearly, Stone Fish Lake. Stone Fish Lake. Yüan Chieh. TrCh
I loved you first: but afterwards your love. Monna Innominata, IV. Christina Rossetti. EmBrPo; ViPo
I Loved You Once. Pushkin, *tr. fr. Russian.* BoR, *tr. by* C. M. Bowra; TrRV, *tr. by* Babette Deutsch
I. M. H. Maurice Baring. ACP (1952 ed.)
I. M. Margaritae Sorori. W. E. Henley. *See* Margaritae Sorori.
I. M.—R. T. Hamilton Bruce. W. E. Henley. *See* Invictus.
I made a far journey. Descent. Jalal ed-Din Rumi. PeP
I made a footing in the wall. Byron. *Fr.* The Prisoner of Chillon. OBRV
I Made a House of Houselessness. Rose O'Neill. BAP
(Established.) AV
I made a loaf of bread. The White Bird. Roy McFadden. NeIP
I made a pilgrimage to find the God. Revelation. Edwin Markham. MaRV; OQP; QP-1; WGRP
I made a posy [*or* posie], while the day ran by. Life. George Herbert. EG; ElSeCe; HBV; LiTB; LPS-3; MeLP; MePo; OBS; PoFS; RiBV; SeCeV; SeCL; SeCV-1; SeEP
I made a song for my dear love's delight. A Song's Worth. Susan Marr Spalding. AA
I made a song one morning. Merchandise. Amy Lowell. LaNeLa; MAPA
I made a sort of promise I might go. A Boy's Trust. Leo C. Turner. FAOV
I made a vow once, one only. Make No Vows. Grace Fallow Norton. NP
I made another garden, yea. Song. Arthur O'Shaughnessy. PoVP
I made god upon god. Pygmalion. Hilda Doolittle ("H. D."). LA; WGRP
I made my song a coat. A Coat. W. B. Yeats. GTBS-W; LiTG; LiTM (rev. ed.); PoEL-5; TwP
I made myself a little boat. The Voyage with the Nautilus. Mary Howitt. TVSH
I made myself as a tree. March Hares. Andrew Young. HaMV; MoVE; POTE
I made myself the friend of all. Strategy. Ibn Sa'id of Alcala la Real. MooP
I made new speech for you—a secret tongue. Language. Winifred Welles. NP
I made of my sorrow. Fandango for Sorrow. Catherine Graham Miller. CAG
I made the cross myself whose weight. A Little Parable. Anne Reeve Aldrich. AA; BAP; HBV; LBAP; LEAP; MaRV
I made the newssheets rustle, opening. So What. Vladimir Mayakovsky. TrRV
I made the test in God's own Laboratory. William Ellery Leonard. *Fr.* Two Lives, Pt. III. LA; MOAP
I made them lay their hands in mine and swear. Their Conscience as Their King. Tennyson. *Fr.* Guinevere. MaRV
I made up my mind to change my way. The Trail to Mexico. *Unknown.* AS, *with music;* CoSo; CSF; IHA
I made you many and many a song. The Net. Sara Teasdale. LoP; MOAP
I make a pact with you, Walt Whitman. A Pact. Ezra Pound. CoV; LiTA; MoPW; NePA; OxBA; Po
I make complaint incessantly. Night. Al-Liss. MooP
I make his crescent fill or lack. Emily Dickinson. CoBA
I make my shroud, but no one knows. Song. Adelaide Crapsey. AnAmPo; HBV; LA; MAP; MoAmPo (1942 ed.); NP; SBMV; TOP
I make no question of your right to go. Sonnets, III. Muna Lee. HBMV
I make not my division of the hours. Patrick Moloney. Sonnets—Ad Innuptam, I. BoAu
I make this in a warring absence when. Poem for Caitlin. Dylan Thomas. MoWP
I many times thought peace had come. Emily Dickinson. AmP; AmPP; TwP
(Peace.) LBAP
I march'd three miles through scorching sand. On a Curate's Complaint of Hard Duty. Swift. GTIV
I marked a cross upon a lonely spot. Traditions. Ramón Campoamor. OnPM
I marked all kindred powers the heart finds fair. Love Enthroned. Dante Gabriel Rossetti. The House of Life, I. BMEP; BPN; CoBE; EmBrPo; PIAE; PoVP; ViPo; VLEP
I marked the slow withdrawal of the year. In Memorabilia Mortis. Francis Sherman. CaP; OCL
I married a man of the Croydon class. Nervous Prostration. Anna Wickham. DiM
I marry'd a wife of late. Keep a Good Tongue in Your Head. Martin Parker. CoMu
I marvel at the gilliflowers. The Hypocrites. Ibn al-Batti. MooP
I Marvel at the Ways of God. E. B. White. WhC
I marvell'd why a simple child. Only Seven. Henry S. Leigh. BOHV; HBV; LPS-3; PA
I mastered pastoral theology, the Greek of the Apostles. The Minister. Fenton Johnson. AnAmPo; LA
I maun tae the sea, gang doon I maun tae the sea. Tuscan Folk Songs, 8. *Unknown, tr. into Scottish by* Edwin Morgan. LyPI
I, Maximus of Gloucester, to You. Charles Olson. NeAP
I may as well. The Retired Pork-Butcher and the Spook. G. E. Farrow. BOHV
I may be dead to-morrow, uncaressed. For the Book of Love. Jules Laforgue. AWP; LiTW
I may be smelly and I may be old. The River God. Stevie Smith. FaBoTw
I may live on until. Fujiwara no Kiyosuke, *tr. fr. Japanese by* Kenneth Rexroth. OnPJ
I may not claim. Host and Guest. Henry W. Clark. OQP; PSO; QP-1
I may not hold to sacred strain. To a Nun. Mary Terry Gill. PraNu
I may not keep the heights I gain. For an Hour. Winfred Ernest Garrison. OQP; QP-1
I may not put my finger forth. Faith. John Richard Moreland. LS; OHIP
I may not venture to your door. I Send Our Lady. Sister Mary Thérèse. ISi
I may sing of a may. The Five Joys. *Unknown.* AnEC
I may speak with the tongues of men and of angels. The Greatness of Love. First Corinthians, Bible, *N.T.*, *tr. by* James Moffatt. MaRV
I meane not to defend the scapes of any. Ovid. Amores, II, 4. LaP
I Meant to Do My Work Today. Richard Le Gallienne. GoTP; MPB; NLK; PoMa; SP; StaSt; TiPo; VOD
(Called Away.) SUS
I meant to find her when I came. Emily Dickinson. BoFr
I meant to have but modest needs. Emily Dickinson. IAP
I measure every grief I meet. Emily Dickinson. MAP; MoAB; MoAmPo; TwP
I measure years by days and days by hours. Subjectivity. Helen Pinkerton. PtPa
I measured myself by the wall in the garden. Day Dreams, or Ten Years Old. Margaret Johnson. BLPA
I meditate upon a swallow's flight. Coole Park, 1929. W. B. Yeats. OBMV; OxBI

I meditate upon the heresy of the degenerate age—Christianity's magical Deus. The Precious Music of Heresy. Hakushu Kitahara. PoLJ

I meet thy pensive, moonlight face. A Lost Love. Henry Francis Lyte. GTSL

I meet you in an evil time. An Eclogue for Christmas. Louis MacNeice. FaBoMo; MoPo; MoVE; OBMV; TwHP

I meet you in the mystery of the night. Robert Norwood. His Lady of the Sonnets, II. CPG

I met a child upon the moor. On the Moor. Cale Young Rice. HBV

I met a friar in a hood. Hilda Doolittle ("H. D."). *Fr.* Claribel's Way to God. MeRV

I met a Jack-o'-Lantern, Hallowe'en. Smiling. Dixie Willson. GFA

I met a lady from the South who said. New Hampshire. Robert Frost. AmPP (4th ed.); CoV

I met a little cottage girl. We Are Seven. Wordsworth. BLPA; BPN; EM-2; EPN; EPP; ERP; GEPC; GN; HBV; LPS-1; PTA-1; TCEP; WBLP

I met a little Elf-man, once. The Little Elf-Man [*or* The Little Elf]. John Kendrick Bangs. AA; BoChLi; BoTP; FaBoBe; GaP; GFA; GoBP; GoTP; HBV; HBVY; MPB; OnHT; OTPC (1946 ed.); PCH; PRWS; RAR; SP; TiPo; WaKn

I met a little mountain boy. In the Mountains. Cotton Noe. LS

I met a man as I went walking. Puppy and I. A. A. Milne. BoTP; FaPON; TiPo

I met a man in older lands. On the Safe Side. Lord Dunsany. OxBI

I met a man in South Street, tall. Cutty Sark. Hart Crane. *Fr.* The Bridge. AmPP; FaBoMo; LiTA; NP

I met a man late yesternight. Song of the Old Man. John Gould Fletcher. MOAP

I met a man mowing. Hay Harvest. Patrick R. Chalmers. BoTP

I met a man the other day. The Counselor. Dorothy Parker. InMe

I met a ragged man. The Song. Theodore Roethke. CrMA; FiMAP

I met a sailor in the woods. The Englishman. Walter de la Mare. PtOT

I met a seer. The Book of Wisdom. Stephen Crane. *Fr.* The Black Riders. CoBA; HoPM; MAP; MoAmPo

I met a toad. Warty Bliggens, the Toad. Don Marquis. *Fr.* Archy and Mehitabel. FiBHP

I met a traveler [*or* traveller] from an antique land. Ozymandias [of Egypt]. Shelley. ATP; AWP; BCEP; BEL; BeLS; BLP; BLV; BoLiVe; BPN; CaAE; CBE; CBOV; CH; CoBE; EM-2; EmBrPo; EnL; EnLi-2; EnLit; EnRP; EPN; EPP; ERP; ES; EV-4; ExPo; FaBoBe; FaBoCh; FaBoEn; FaFP; FiP; GEPC; GoTP; GTBS; GTBS-D; GTBS-W; GTSE; GTSL; HBV; HBVY; HoPM; InP; InPo; JAWP; LoBV; LoGBV; LPS-2; MaPo; MaRV; MCCG; MyFE; NeHB; OAEP; OTPC (1946 ed.); OuHeWo; PC; PeBoSo; PECK; PFE; PG (1955 ed.); PIAE; PIR; Po; PoE; PoeMoYo; PoFS; PoRA; PreP; PYM; REAL; RiBV; RO; SeCeV; ShBV-3; TCEP; TOP; TreF; TrGrPo; TyEnPo; UnPo (1st ed.); WaKn; WBP; WHA

I met a traveller from an antique land. Ozymandias Revisited. Morris Bishop. ALV

I met a woman old and grey. The One Who Stayed. Ada Foster Murray. LEAP

I met an elf-man in the woods. How to Treat Elves. Morris Bishop. FiBHP

I Met at Eve. Walter de la Mare. HBMV; PtOT

I met ayont the cairney. Empty Vessel. "Hugh MacDiarmid." FaBoTw

I met brightness of brightness upon the path of loneliness. The Enchanted Mistress. Egan O'Rahilly. GTIV

I Met by Chance. Heine, *tr. fr. German by* John Todhunter. AWP

I met four chaps yon birks amang. Jenny's Bawbee. Sir Alexander Boswell. EBSV

I met God in the morning. The Secret [*or* His Presence Came Like Sunrise]. Ralph Spaulding Cushman. BLRP; MaRV; PraP

I met her as a blossom on a stem. The Dream. Theodore Roethke. AmP; MoVE

I Met Her in the Garden Where the Praties Grow, *with music. Unknown.* AS

I met her on the poetry page. On a Certain Nun. Sister Mary Ignatius. PraNu

I met her on the Umbrian Hills. The Lady Poverty. Evelyn Underhill. CAW; CP; GTML; HBV; SaFP

I met him again, he was trudging along. I Fights Mit Sigel! Grant P. Robinson. BLPA

I met Louisa in the shade. Louisa. Wordsworth. EmBrPo; EnRP

I met my dead self on the street. Encounter. William Griffith. BAP

I met ol' Satan on the way. Hell and Heaven. *Unknown.* OxBoLi

I met Poetry, an old prostitute walking. Moral Story II. David Wright. ChMP

I met Poor Sorrow on the way. Alms. Josephine Preston Peabody. POT; PoTo

I met the Bishop on the road. Crazy Jane Talks with the Bishop. W. B. Yeats. AtBAP; CoBMV; CoEV; EnLP; ExPo; LiTG; LiTM (rev. ed.); OAEP (2d ed.); TwP

I met the boss; he wanted me to go. On the Trail to Idaho. *Unknown.* CoSo; PoRL

I met the boy from Donegal, sez I, "Come here a minute." Sheskinbeg. Elizabeth Shane. HBMV

I met the Love-Talker one eve in the glen. The Love-Talker. "Ethna Carbery." AnIV; BMEP; CH; OnYI; OxBI

I Met the Master Face to Face. *Unknown.* BePJ (I Met the Master.) BLRP

I met the one I loved. Unexpected Fortune. Abul Qasim of Silves. MooP

I met the wife who'd left me bed. Sour Wine. Arthur Stringer. BoCaPo (1943 ed.)

I met the yawning of my appetite. The North of Wales. Herbert Morris. NePoAm-2

I met them on the trail today. Thanks. Marty Hale. AlBD

I met three children on the road. Three Children near Clonmel. Eileen Shanahan. OnYI; OxBI

I met upon the woodland ways. Heredity. Frederick Peterson. PoP

I met with a country lass. The Thankful Country Lass; or, The Jolly Batchelor Kindly Entertained. *Unknown.* CoMu

I met with a jovial girl. The Roaring Lad and the Ranting Lass; or, A Merry Couple Madly Met. *Unknown.* CoMu

I met with Death in his country. Lord Dunsany. Songs from an Evil Wood, III. LBBV; MBP; MoBrPo (1942 ed.)

I met you often when you were visiting princes. On Meeting Li Kuei-Nien down the River. Tu Fu. LiTW

I mid the hills was born. Harold the Valiant. Mary Elizabeth Hewitt Stebbins. AA

I might be better busied; I grant so. Ad Zoilum. John Heath. TuPP

I might have been like the migratory eagles. The Stygian Oath. Angelos Sikelianos. MoGP

I might have climbed up Calvary. A Follower. Daisy Conway Price. ChIP

I might have touched you where you lay. Quarrel. Jean McDougall. GoBC; JKCP (1955 ed.)

I might not, if I could. Lines by a Medium. *Unknown.* NA

I might—unhappy word—oh me, I might. Astrophel and Stella, XXXIII. Sir Philip Sidney. OBSC; ReEn; SiPS; TuPP

I mind, love how it ever was this way. Bed-Time. Ralph M. Jones. HBMV

I mind me in the days departed. The Deserted Garden. Elizabeth Barrett Browning. EmBrPo; EV-4; HBV; OBEV (1st ed.); VLEP

I Mind That I Went Round with Men and Women. Bilhana, *formerly at. to* Chauras, *tr. fr. Sanskrit by* E. Powys Mathers. *Fr.* Black Marigolds. OnPM

I Mind the Coming. Bilhana, *formerly at. to* Chauras, *tr. fr. Sanskrit by* E. Powys Mathers. *Fr.* Black Marigolds. OnPM

I Mind the Time of the Falling of Blossoms. Bilhana, *formerly at. to* Chauras, *tr. fr. Sanskrit by* E. Powys Mathers. *Fr.* Black Marigolds. OnPM

I mingle with your bones. The One Lost. Isaac Rosenberg. MBP; MoBrPo

I miss the polished brass, the powerful black horses. On the Road to Woodlawn. Theodore Roethke. FiMAP

I Miss Thee, My Mother. Eliza Cook. MOAH

I miss you in the morning, dear. Miss You. *Unknown.* PoToHe (new ed.)

I missed him when the sun began to bend. Lost and Found. George Macdonald. BoFr; MaRV; OQP; QP-1; StJW; WGRP

I missed one night, but the next I went. The Second Night. Thomas Hardy. VLEP

I mock thee not, though I by thee am mockèd. To Flaxman [*or* Epigram]. Blake. OxBoLi; SiTL

I mount the turret steps to welcome spring. The Twelve Moons. Li Ho. WhP

I mourn Adonis, lovely Adonis slain. Lament for Adonis. Bion, *tr. by* Henry Harmon Chamberlin. GrR

I mourn for Adonis—Adonis is dead. Bion's Lament for Adonis. Bion, *tr. by* Elizabeth Barrett Browning. ATP; GrPo

I mourn for Polyanthus, who died new-wed, O stranger. Lost at Sea. Phaedimus. GrPE

I mourn not those who lose their vital breath. Better to Be Brave. Lucillius. OnPM

I mourn "Patroclus," whilst I praise. My Last Terrier. John Halsham. HBV

I mourn you not, best friend. Much good and fair. "Nothing Is Here to Wail." Philetas. GrPE

I mourned with thousands. On Burns. Wordsworth. BoHiPo

I move amid your throng, I watch you hold. Sonnets to Miranda, VI. Sir William Watson. HBV
I Mun Be Married a Sunday. Nicholas Udall. *Fr.* Ralph Roister Doister. ElL
I Must and I Will Get Married, *with music. Unknown.* TrAS
I Must Away. May Sarson. BoTP
I must be dreaming through the days. Experience. Lesbia Harford. BoAu
I must be flattered. The imperious. Modern Love, XXVIII. George Meredith. ViPo
I must be ill: my mind is dumb and bored. Sonnet. Nikolai Gumilev. BoRS
I must be mad, or very tired. Meeting-House Hill. Amy Lowell. AmPP (3d ed.); LoGBV; MAP; MoAmPo; NeMA; NP; OxBA; PFY; TCAP
I Must Be Silent. Anne Blackwell Payne. NoCaPo
I must complayne she doth enioye my love. *At. to* Thomas Campion. SeCSL
I must confess that often I'm. *Time* Like an Ever-rolling Stream. P. G. Wodehouse. FiBHP
I must get out to the woods again, to the whispering tree and the birds awing. The Call. Edgar A. Guest. NLK
I must go all my days. Maternity. Babette Deutsch. TBM
I must go back to a vest again, to a winter vest with sleeves. April. Godfrey Fox Bradby. ShBV-1
I must go down to the seas again, to the lonely sea and the sky. Sea Fever. John Masefield. BEL; BLV; BMEP; BoChLi; BoLiVe; CaAE; CBOV; ChMo; CMP; CV; EnLi-2 (1949 ed.); EnLit; EtS; FaBoBe; FaPON; GBV; GTBS; GTSL; HBV; HBVY; HiLiEn; LBBV; LEAP; MBP; MCCG; MoAB; MoBrPo; MPB; NeHB; NeMA; NLK; OBVV; OHFP; OtMeF; OTPC (1946 ed.); PCD; PFE; PoeMoYo; PoMa; POT; PoTo; POTT; PreP; PYM; RG; ShBV-1; SP; StVeCh; TCEP; TiPo; TOP; TreF; TrGrPo; TwCV; VOD; WHA; YT
I must go down to the seas again, where the billows romp and reel. Sea-Chill. Arthur Guiterman. NLK (1947 ed.)
I must have passed the crest a while ago. The Long Hill. Sara Teasdale. ChMo; CMP; HBMV; LiTA; LiTM; MAP; MoAmPo; MOAP
I must have wanton poets, pleasant wits. Christopher Marlowe. *Fr.* Edward the Second, I, i. ViBoPo
I must laugh and dance and sing. Youth. Aline Thomas. MPB
I must leave you. Ariwara no Yukihira, *tr. fr. Japanese by* Kenneth Rexroth. OnPJ
I Must Light a Candle. Gertrude Hanson. ChIP
I must needs say, were thou mine own brother. Aliud. Thomas Freeman. TuPP
I must not gaze at them although. The Barrier. Claude McKay. BANP
I must not grieve my Love, whose eyes would read. To Delia, XLVIII. Samuel Daniel. ElL; HBV; OBEV
I Must Not Tease My Mother. Lydia Huntley Sigourney. OTPC (1923 ed.)
I must not think of thee; and, tired yet strong. Renouncement. Alice Meynell. AnFE; AV; BLV; BMEP; CAW; CBOV; EnLit; EPP; ES; EtPaEn; GTML; GTSL; HBV; LBBV; LEAP; LiTL; LO; LoPo; LoPS; MBP; MM; MoBrPo; OBEV; OBMV; OBVV; PIAE; POTT; PoVP; TCEP; TOP; VA; ViBoPo
I must not throw upon the floor. The Crust of Bread. *Unknown.* HBV; HBVY; OTPC (1923 ed.)
I Must Not Yield. Nora May French. AV
I Must Out and Play Again. Kathleen Millay. NLK (1947 ed.)
I must possess you utterly. Possession. Richard Aldington. MBP; MoBrPo
I must return. My fields and my orchards. The Return. Tao Yuan-ming. WhP
I Must to Prayer. Frank Buchanan. QS
I must watch over this day. Prayer for Each Awakening. Luis Cané. AnCL
I, my dear, was born to-day. On My Birthday, July 21. Matthew Prior. OBEV
I Myself Am Heaven and Hell. *Br. sel. fr.* The Rubáiyát of Omar Khayyám, *tr. by* Edward Fitzgerald. GrCo-1
I myself saw furious with blood. Aeneas at Washington. Allen Tate. LiTA; MoPo; MoVE; NePA; OxBA
"I myself will now go home and see." Homer. *Fr.* The Iliad, VI. ReIE
I-N spells "in." I-n and O-u-t. *Unknown.* MuP
I nebber see de like since I been [*or* bin] born. Johnny Come Down to Hilo [*or* Oh, Wake Dat Girl!]. *Unknown.* ABF; MuP; SoAmSa
I need no assurances, I am a man who is preoccupied of his own soul. Assurances. Walt Whitman. IAP
I need no world more spacious than the region here. Greenock. John Davidson. *Fr.* A Ballad in Blank Verse of the Making of a Poet. BSV
I need not die to go. Where, O, Where? Elinor Wylie. LoPS
I Need Not Go. Thomas Hardy. ChMo; CMP; EG; LoPS; OBEV (new ed.); OBVV
I need not leave the jostling world. The Shut Door. *Unknown.* PraP
I need not praise the sweetness of his song. To Henry Wadsworth Longfellow [*or* To H. W. L.]. James Russell Lowell. LPS-3; PtP
I need not seek or pray, my newly born. New Mother. Anita Laurie Cushing. MotAn
I need not shout my faith. Thrice eloquent. Silence. Charles Hanson Towne. BPP; MaRV; OQP; QP-1; WGRP
I need not your needles, they're needless to me. The Baker's Reply to the Needle Peddler. *Unknown.* OxNR; SiTL
I need so much the quiet of your love. At Nightfall. Charles Hanson Towne. BLPA; FaBoBe; NeHB; PoToHe (new ed.)
I Need Thee. George Macdonald. MaRV
I Need Thee. Frederick Whitfield. BePJ
I need Thee every hour. Annie S. Hawks. OlF
I Need Thee, Precious Jesus. *Unknown.* BePJ
I need Thee, precious Jesus! I Need Thee. Frederick Whitfield. BePJ
I ne'er could any luster see. Air. Sheridan. *Fr.* The Duenna. HBV
I ne'er deserved the glorious name of poet. Of His Muse. Sir John Harington. SiCE
I ne'er had ventured e'en to hope for this. Robert Browning. *Fr.* Pauline. PtP
I ne'er on the border. Serranilla VI. Marqués de Santillana. AnSpL-1
I ne'er was struck before that hour. First Love. John Clare. ChTr; EnLoPo
I never believed much in a golden city. A Holy City. Maxwell Anderson. *Fr.* The Star Wagon. QS
I never bought a young gazelle. *See* I never reared a young gazelle.
I never build a song by night or day. My Comrade. Edwin Markham. AA
I never call that gentle name. My Mother! George W. Bethune. MotAn
"I never can do it," the little kite said. How the Little Kite Learned to Fly. *Unknown.* GFA; HBV; HBVY; OnHT; OTPC; TVC; TVSH
I never cared for life: life cared for me. Epitaph. Thomas Hardy. TriL
I never crossed your threshold with a grief. The Closed Door. Theodosia Garrison. BLPA; PoToHe
I never cut my neighbor's throat. Guilty. Marguerite Wilkinson. MaRV; OQP; QP-1
I never did on cleft Parnassus dream. Prologue to the First Satire. Persius. *Fr.* Satires. AWP
I never drank of Aganippe well. Astrophel and Stella, LXXIV. Sir Philip Sidney. OBSC; ReEn; ReIE; SiCE; SiPS; TuPP
I never even hear. Whistles. Rachel Field. GFA; StVeCh (1955 ed.); TiPo
I Never Even Suggested It. Ogden Nash. FiBHP; LiTA; LiTL; LiTM; SiTL
I never forget a face. You're So Kind. Groucho Marx. SiTL
I never gave a lock of hair away. Elizabeth Barrett Browning. Sonnets from the Portuguese, XVIII. BPN; HBV; LEAP; LPS-1; VA
I never got a telegram before. Telegram. William Wise. TiPo (1959 ed.)
I never had a happier time. One Saturday. "Marian Douglas." AA
I never had a piece of toast. James Payn. CenHV
I never had walked quite so far. Alone. Joseph Paget-Fredericks. StVeCh
I never have got the bearings quite. The Flag. James Jeffrey Roche. PaA; PAH
I never have had a look at the sea. Recompense. Grace Noll Crowell. PCD
I never have seen the snow so white. Christmas Birthday. Grace Ellen Glaubitz. SiSoSe
I never hear it ring without. The Door-Bell. Charlotte Becker. PoToHe (new ed.)
I never hear that one is dead. Emily Dickinson. MoVE
I never hear the word "escape." Escape. Emily Dickinson. NeMA
"I never hurt maid in all my time." The Death of Robin Hood. *Unknown.* ViBoPo
I Never Knew a Night So Black. John Kendrick Bangs. MaRV; PoToHe
. . . I never knew before/ The meaning of this love. Thomas Lovell Beddoes. *Fr.* Death's Jest Book. LO
I never knew before freedom could be. Sonnets from Camp, I. Jesse Stuart. MuM
I never knew how words were vain. Rain. Kenneth Slade Alling. HBMV; NLK
I never knew the earth had so much gold. Feuerzauber. Louis Untermeyer. NP; SBMV; TrJP
I never knew thee, child; but this I knew. S. M. S. (Sister Mary Stanislaus, O.P.). Patrick Augustine Sheehan. PraNu

I never laie me downe to rest. *Unknown.* SeCSL
I never look upon the sea. Aunt Zillah Speaks. Herbert Palmer. FaBoTw
I never look'd that he should live so long. John of Launoy. Sir Henry Taylor. *Fr.* Philip van Artevelde. VA
I never lost as much but twice. Emily Dickinson. MAP; MoAB; MoAmPo
I never loved ambitiously to climb. Ambition. Thomas Nashe. EV-2
I never loved your plains! Hills. Arthur Guiterman. BAP; HBVY; MaRV; NLK; PoeMoYo; PoMa; POT; PoTo; VOD; YT
I never may believe. The Poet Greatly Pictured. Shakespeare. *Fr.* A Midsummer Night's Dream, V, i. BCEP
I never met the Spring alone before. Alone in Spring. Caroline Giltinan. LS; TBM
I never muse upon my lady's grace. George Edward Woodberry. Ideal Passion, XXV. HBMV
I never prayed for Dryads, to haunt the woods again. An Invocation. William Johnson Cory. HBV; OBVV
I never quite know/ How the Pooka looks. Shape-Changer. Ella Young. BoChLi (1950 ed.)
I never *quite* saw fairy-folk. Very Nearly. Queenie Scott-Hopper. FaPON; GoBP; MeMeAg; MPB; OTPC (1946 ed.); RAR; TVC; TVSH
I never read the story but I wonder. The Servant of the Prophet. Abbie Huston Evans. QS
I never realized God's birth before. Robert Browning. *Fr.* The Ring and the Book. ChIP
I never really like this cat though she is. V Is for Victory, as You Can Plainly See. Marsden Hartley. LiTM
I never reared [*or* bought] a young gazelle. 'Twas Ever Thus. Henry S. Leigh. BOHV; HBV; PA
I never saw a lovelier sky. An Evening Walk. Andrew Young. AlDL
I never saw a man who looked. Oscar Wilde. *Fr.* The Ballad of Reading Gaol. PoFr
I never saw a moor. Emily Dickinson. AmPo; AmPP; AnNE; CoBA; FaFP; FaPON; GTBS-W; LiTA; LiTM (rev. ed.); MAP; MaRV; MoAB; MoAmPo; MPB; NePA; OBAV; PoLFOT; SP; TCAP; TiPo (1952 ed.); TrGrPo; TwP; VOD (1935 ed.)
(Certainty.) GoTP
(Chartless.) AA; ATP; BAP; BBV; DDA; GN; HBV; LBAP; LEAP; NeMA; OQP; OTPC; PFE; PYM; QP-1; TOP; TreF; WGRP
I never saw a puppy that. Hot Weather. Dorothy Aldis. GFA
"I never saw a Purple Cow." Diversions of the Re-echo Club. Carolyn Wells. BOHV
I never saw a Purple Cow. The Purple Cow. Gelett Burgess. BOHV; CenHV; FaFP; FaPON; FiBHP; HBV; HBVY; InP; LBN; LEAP; LiL; LiTM; MeMeAg; NA; NeHB; NePA; PIAE; PoeMoYo; SiTL; StaSt; TiPo; TreFS; TSW; TSWC; YaD
I never saw my father old. A Celebration. May Sarton. NePoAm-2
I never saw that you did painting need. Sonnets, LXXXIII. Shakespeare. PeBoSo
I never saw the cliffs of snow. The Canadian. Jesse Edgar Middleton. CPG; OCL
I never saw the hills so far. A Journey. Josephine Preston Peabody. RAR
I never saw the morning till to-day. Chariots. Witter Bynner. HBMV
I never saw you. madam, lay [*or* sawe my ladye laye] apart. The Cornet [*or* Complaint That His Ladie . . . Kept Her Face Alway Hidden from Him]. Earl of Surrey. ES; OBSC; PoEL-1; SiPS
I never see the newsboys run. Fleet Street. Shane Leslie. LBBV; OnYI; PoeT
I Never See the Red Rose [Crown the Year]. John Masefield. *Fr.* Sonnets ("Long long ago"). ChMo; CMP; EnLi-2 (1949 ed.); EPP; InP; PeBoSo
(Sonnet: "I never see the red rose crown the year.") GoYe
I never see upon a hill. Symbols. John Richard Moreland. ChIP; PGD
I never set my two eyes on a head was so fine as your head. A Translation from Walther von der Vogelweide. J. M. Synge. MoBrPo
I Never Shall Love the Snow Again. Robert Bridges. CH; ChMo; CMP; OAEP; PoeT; POTT; VLEP
I never speak a word. Mary Austin. *Fr.* Rhyming Riddles. TiPo
I never stooped so low, as they. Negative Love. John Donne. ReEn
I never swung a staff and deep, oh deep. Sonnet. Roy Daniells. PeCV
I never thought that youth would go. Youth. Jessie B. Rittenhouse. HBMV
I never used to think myself so fine. Sonnet. Michelangelo. LyPI
I never was attached to that great sect. The Longest Journey. Shelley. *Fr.* Epipsychidion. NBE; OtMeF
I never watch the sun set a-down the Western skies. Visions. Edmund Leamy. BBV; GBV (1922 ed.); JKCP
I never went to Mamble. Mamble. John Drinkwater. AlDL; LBBV; PoeT
I never will complain of my dear husband, Mrs. Henn. He Didn't Oughter. A. P. Herbert. ALV; FiBHP
I never yet could understand. Proud Lover. Richard Henry Stoddard. PR
I never yet went down to the sea. Down to the Sea. Isabel Taylor. SOS
I not care for Gyges' sway. *Unknown, tr. fr. Greek by* Thomas Stanley. GrPo
I notic'd how the spent and speechless year. Time Lags Abed. D'Arcy Cresswell. AnNZ
I, now at Carthage. He, shot dead at Rome. *Vale* from Carthage (Spring, 1944). Peter Viereck. MiAP; MoAmPo (1950 ed.)
I now have a master of great literature. Windy Weather. Jorge Carrera Andrade. TwSpPo
I now have lunched alone, I have had. Trilce, XXVIII. César Vallejo. TwSpPo
I now mean to be serious—it is time. Lady Adeline Amundeville. Byron. *Fr.* Don Juan. PoEL-4
I now remembered slowly how I came. The Journey. Yvor Winters. MoVE
I now think[e] Love is rather deaf[e] than blind. My Picture Left in Scotland. Ben Jonson. LiTL; MePo; PoEL-2; SeCV-1
I objurgate the centipede. The Centipede. Ogden Nash. FaPON
I observe: "Our sentimental friend, the moon!" Conversation Galante. T. S. Eliot. HBMV; MAP; MoAmPo (1942 ed.)
I offer Thee. A Rune of Praise. *Unknown.* WHL
I Offer You This Verse. Baudelaire, *tr. fr. French by* Vernon Watkins. AnFP
I offered the donkey. Ilo Orleans. RIS
I oft have heard men say there be. William Browne. LO
I oft stand in the snow at dawn. Don Marquis. *Fr.* To a Lost Sweetheart. FiBHP
I often dream strange penetrating dreams. My Familiar Dream. Paul Verlaine. TrFP
I often have been told. The *Constitution* and the *Guerrière.* *Unknown.* PAH
I often have pondered and puzzled and wondered. Plautus. *Fr.* Mostellaria. LaP
I often picture you among the flowers, Mother. Sister M. Eulalia. WHL
I often say my prayers. Prayer. John Burton. MaRV
I often say to my sad heart. Prose Poem: The Irremediable. Emile Hennequin. OnPM
I often see flowers from a passing car. A [*or* The] Passing Glimpse. Robert Frost. InP; NeMA
I often sit and wish that I. A Wish [*or* A Kite]. Frank Dempster Sherman. BoChLi (1950 ed.); PCH; TiPo; TVC; TVSH
I Often Watch Thee Musing Dreamily. Pierre de Ronsard, *tr. fr. French by* Alan Conder. TrFP
I often wish that I had been alive. God's Youth. Louis Untermeyer. PFY
I often wonder how it is. My Playmate. Mary I. Osborn. BoTP
I on Hesiod idly browsing. Reading Hesiod. Marcus Argentarius. OxBG; WoL
I on my horse, and love on me, doth try. Astrophel and Stella, XLIX. Sir Philip Sidney. ReEn; SiPS
I once had a gal and I loved her well. When I Was a Brave Cowboy. *Unknown.* CoSo
I once had a sweet little doll, dears. The Lost Doll. Charles Kingsley. *Fr.* The Water Babies. FaPON; MPB; MoShBr; OTPC; PRWS; TiPo; TVC; TVSH
I once had money and a friend. Money and a Friend. *Unknown.* BLPA; NeHB
I once knew a soldier just from the war. The Soldier. *Unknown.* ABS
I once may see, when years shall [*or* may] wreck my wrong. To Delia, XXXIV [*or* Beauty's Glass]. Samuel Daniel, *after* Philippe Desportes. OnPM; ReIE
I once possessed this happiness: to bind. The Master of Time. Jan van Nijlen. LiTW
I once praised loneliness and said. Aureole. Helene Magaret. BPP
I once was a guest at a nobleman's wedding. The Nobleman's Wedding. William Allingham. IrPN
I Once Was a Maid. Burns. KN; OxBoLi; SiTL
I Only Am Escaped Alone to Tell Thee. Howard Nemerov. NePA
I only ask a mod'rate [*or* moderate] fate. The Wish. Thomas Godfrey. IAP; NoCaPo
I only kissed her hand. A Possibility. Carolyn Wells. ALV; PR

I only knew one poet in my life. How It Strikes a Contemporary. Robert Browning. EmBrPo; GEPC; PoVP; ViPo; ViPP
I only knew she came and went. My Love. *Unknown.* LPS-3
I open my scuttle at night and see the far-sprinkled systems. Walt Whitman. *Fr.* Song of Myself. PFY
I opened a book. Bunch, a Cat. Claude Colleer Abbott. PoC
I opened the blinds; the day was bright. Frightening Death. Charles Anson Ingraham. PoP
I opened the window wide and leaned. John Masefield. *Fr.* The Everlasting Mercy. WGRP
I owe, says Metius, much to Colon's care. Epigram. Leonard Welsted. ALV
I own I like not Johnson's turgid style. Lines on Dr. Johnson. "Peter Pindar." CoEV
I own John Graydon's place. John Graydon. Wilson MacDonald. CaP
I owned a little boat a while ago. The Master of My Boat [*or* The Boat]. Joseph Addison Richards, *wr. at. to* George Macdonald. MaRV; OQP; QP-2
I pace the sounding sea-beach and behold. Milton. Longfellow. AA; AmP; AmPP; APW; AWP; BLV; IAP; InPo; MOAP; NePA; PeBoSo; PtP; TOP; TrGrPo
I Paint What I See. E. B. White. LiTM; NAMP; OnAP; PoFr
I painted her a gushing thing. Disillusioned. "Lewis Carroll." CenHV
I painted on the roof of a skyscraper. People Who Must. Carl Sandburg. SAS
I paints and paints. Shirley Brooks. CenHV
I pant for the music which is divine. Music [*or* Fragment: Music]. Shelley. CBE; EmBrPo; ERP
I Pass a Lighted Window. Clement Wood. HBMV; PFE; SBMV
I pass a thousand leagues inland. Ambition. J. Hinckley. CAG
I pass all my hours in a shady old grove. Song. *At. to* Charles II, King of England. SeCL
I pass my days among the quiet places. Hallowed Places. Alice Freeman Palmer. HBV
I Pass the Great Hall. Li Ho, *tr. fr. Chinese by* Ho Chih-yuan. WhP
I Pass the Night at General Headquarters. Tu Fu, *tr. fr. Chinese by* Kenneth Rexroth. OnPC
I pass the vale. I breast the steep. Onward and Upward. John Charles Earle. MaRV
I passed a tomb among green shades. Her Rival for Aziza. *Unknown. Fr.* The Thousand and One Nights. AWP
I passed a wood of beech trees yesterday. Beech Trees. Sister Mary Madeleva. BBV (1951 ed.)
I passed along the water's edge below the humid trees. The Indian upon God. W. B. Yeats. ChMo; CMP; GTIV; MBP; MoBrPo; POTT; WGRP
I passed by a garden, a little Dutch garden. A Little Dutch Garden. Harriet Whitney Durbin. OTPC (1946 ed.)
I passed by the beach. Three Poems from the Japanese, I. Yamabe no Akahito, *tr. fr. Japanese by* Kenneth Rexroth. HoPM; OnPJ
I passed Olympus in the night. Tourist. Mark Van Doren. NePoAm-2
I passed the night most blissfully. Night of Bliss. Ibn al-Zaqqaq. MooP
I passed this very moment by thy doors. The Bankrupt. Thomas Otway. *Fr.* Venice Preserved. EV-3
I passed through the gates of the city. Life and Nature. Archibald Lampman. PeCV
I past [*or* passed] beside the reverend walls. In Memoriam A. H. H., LXXXVII. Tennyson. BoFr; BPN; CoBE; EM-2; EmBrPo; EnSW; EPN; GEPC; OAEP; ViPo; VLEP
I pause beside the stream, and hear. Barbarians. James Stephens. ChMo; CMP
I pause not now to speak of Raleigh's dream. John Smith's Approach to Jamestown. James Barron Hope. MC; PAH
I paused last eve beside the blacksmith's door. *See* Last eve I passed beside a blacksmith's door.
I peeped through the window. *Unknown.* OxNR
I peer into myself. Island. Wilberto L. Cantón. AnCL
I pick it up, I turn it over, I scoff. "Will He Give Him a Stone?" Abbie Huston Evans. QS
I picked a primrose, pale as death. Phyllis M. Lubbock. LO
I picked fresh mint. My Garden. Norah Hussey. BoTP
I picked up my mother. Ishikawa Takuboku, *tr. fr. Japanese by* Kenneth Rexroth. LiTW
I picked up the clod. The Clod. Edwin Curran. BAP; HBMV
I picture her there in the quaint old room. Dreaming in the Trenches. William Gordon McCabe. AA; SPP
I pile the chill sea-shingle with my hands above thee sleeping. The End of a Venture. Zonas. GrPE
I pinned a butterfly against the wall. Birthday Again. Fuyue Anzai. PoLJ
I pitch my tent on this camp ground, few days, few days. Few Days. *Unknown.* ABF
I pitched my day's leazings in Crimmercrock Lane. The Dark-eyed Gentleman. Thomas Hardy. MBP; MoAB; MoBrPo
I pity the slender Mother-maid. The Lonely Crib. Leonard Feeney. WHL
I place thee back upon the shelf. On Rereading Télémaque. James Jeffrey Roche. PR
I placed a jar in Tennessee. Anecdote of the Jar. Wallace Stevens. CoBMV; CoV; ExPo; GTBS-W; LiTA; MoAB; MoAmPo; MOAP; MoVE; NePA; OxBA
I plant on thy behalf this green young pine. Sacred to Helen. Pierre de Ronsard. TrFP
I planted a hand. Christina Rossetti. *Fr.* Sing-Song. MBP
I planted a willow. The Willow by the River. Po Chü-i. PoHN
I planted beans at the foot of the Southern Mountain. Planting Beans. T'ao Ch'ien. OnPM
I Planted Little Trees To-day. James B. Carrington. PEDC
I Planted My Bright Paradise. Aleksandr Blok, *tr. fr. Russian by* Frances Cornford *and* Esther Polianowsky Salaman. TrRV
("I planted my bright Paradise," *tr. by* C. M. Bowra.) BoRS
"I play for Seasons, not Eternities!" Modern Love, XIII. George Meredith. EmBrPo; EPN; FaBoEn; ViP; ViPo
I play my garden is a church. An Easter Surprise. Leona Covey. GFA
I play with stones and sit beside the stream. At I-ye Temple. Po Chü-i. WhP
I played a game of baseball, I belong to Casey's Nine. Slide, Kelly, Slide. J. W. Kelly. FaFP; TreFS
I played I was two polar bears. The Bear Hunt. Margaret Widdemer. FaPON; GoBP; MPB; UTS
I played with you 'mid cowslips blowing. Love and Age. Thomas Love Peacock. *Fr.* Gryll Grange. EV-4; HBV; OBEV; ViBoPo
I plead that the ancient wisdoms. The Wells of Our Fathers. Inez Barclay Kirby. MuM
I pluck the white hibiscus. Mr. A. E. Housman on the Olympic Games, *parody.* E. V. Knox. WhC
I plucked a honeysuckle where. The Honeysuckle. Dante Gabriel Rossetti. BPN; EmBrPo; PoVP
I plucked a throstle from the throat of God. The Thrush. Timothy Corsellis. LiTM; WaaP; WaP
I plucked pink blossoms from mine apple-tree. An Apple Gathering. Christina Rossetti. PoVP; TCEP
I Plucked the Berry. William Motherwell. *See* Sing On, Blithe Bird.
I plunge my hand among the leaves. Pot-Pourri. Austin Dobson. POTT
I ply with all the cunning of my art. The Craftsman. Marcus B. Christian. PoNe
I Ponder on Life. Max Ehrmann. PoToHe (new ed.)
I pop my whip, I bring the blood. Ox-driving Song. *Unknown.* OuSiCo
I Praise. Rainer Maria Rilke. *See* O Tell Us, Poet.
I praise a snakeskin or a stone. Snakeskin and Stone. Keith Douglas. NePoEA
I praise the Frenchman, his remark was shrewd. William Cowper. *Fr.* Retirement. BLPA; NeHB
I Praise the Tender Flower. Robert Bridges. EG; RiBV
I praise Thee not, with impious pride. Sir Lewis Morris. *Fr.* A Heathen Hymn. TrPWD
I praised the speech, but cannot now abide it. Of the Warres in Ireland. Sir John Harington. LPS-2
I pray attend unto this jest. The Fair Maid of the West. *Unknown.* CoMu
I pray for poverty for you. Mellin de Saint-Gelais. *Fr.* On a Detractor. FoS
I pray for you, and yet I do not frame. A Prayer. Mary Dixon Thayer. MaRV
I pray! My little body and whole span. Supplication of the Black Aberdeen. Kipling. BLPA
I pray not for the joy that knows. A Prayer. Marion Franklin Ham. TrPWD
"I pray," said Rolfe, "a word." Ungar and Rolfe. Herman Melville. *Fr.* Clarel. OxBA
I pray that when I die. Lines after Visiting a Cemetery. Richard K. Corbin. CAG
I pray that you may never have. I Bid You Keep Some Few Small Dreams. Helen Frazee-Bower. MoSiPe
I Pray Thee. *Unknown, tr. fr. Chinese by* E. D. Edwards. ChLP
I pray thee, Dante, shouldst thou meet with Love. Sonnet: To Dante Alighieri (He Mistrusts the Love of Lapo Gianni). Guido Cavalcanti. AWP
I Pray Thee Leave, Love Me No More. Michael Drayton. *See* To His Coy Love.
I pray thee, Master Chung. I Pray Thee. *Unknown.* ChLP
I pray Thee O Lord. A Prayer. Juljan Tuwim. TrJP

I Pray to Venus. Elizabeth of York. DiM
I Pray You. Thomas Moore. OBRV
I pray you all give [*or* gyve] your audience [*or* audyence]. Everyman. *Unknown.* BEL; EnLi-1; MeEV; PoEL-1; TCEP
I Pray You, Be Merry and Sing with Me. *Unknown.* AnEC
I pray you, in your letters. Shakespeare. *Fr.* Othello, V, ii. InP
I pray you, leave this man in peace. Flame and Clarity. Georges Duhamel. BoFr
I pray you, let us roam no more. I Pray You. Thomas Moore. OBRV
I pray you not, Leuconöe, to pore. Horace. Odes, I, 11. LaP
"I pray you, reverend Sir, this letter write." If Only I Could Write! Ramón de Campoamor. *Fr.* Doloras. AnSpL-2
I pray you, Sadness, leave me soon. Sadness and Joy. W. H. Davies. PC
I pray you what's asleep? As the Day Breaks. Ernest McGaffey. AA
I prayed for strength, and then I lost awhile. The Answered Prayer. Annie Johnson Flint. PraP
I prayed then to the beam, blithe in mood. The Poet Prays to the Cross. *Unknown.* *Fr.* The Dream of the Rood. PoLi
I prayed to see the face of God. The Back of God. J. R. Perkins. MaRV; OQP; QP-2
I Prayed Today. Grace Noll Crowell. PraP
I preach my sermons through a joke. The Bore; a Dramatic Version of Horace. Horace. *Fr.* Satires. RoL
I preached as never sure to preach again. A Preacher's Urgency. Richard Baxter. MaRV
I press my ear to my pillow as a child his ear to a shell. Night Pulse. Ruth Guthrie Harding. MuM
I press [*or* presse] not to the choir [*or* quire], nor dare I greet. To My Worthy Friend Mr. [*or* Master] George Sands [on His Translation of the Psalmes]. Thomas Carew. EV-2; MeLP; MePo; OBS; SeCV-1; SeEP
I prethee, Clodius, tell me what's the reason. To Clodius. Everard Guilpin. *Fr.* Skialetheia. ReIE
I prithee let my heart alone. Song. Thomas Stanley. ElSeCe; ViBoPo
I Prithee Send Me Back My Heart. Sir John Suckling. EnLit; EV-2; LPS-1; SeCL
(Song: "I prithee send me back my heart.") ElSeCe; EPS; HBV; LiTL; SeEP; ViBoPo
(To My Love.) ALV
I prithee Sweet to me be kind. *Unknown.* SeCSL
I proclaim Thee great and wonderful. Psalm. Murilo Mendes. AnCL
I, proclaiming that there is. The Dancer at Cruachan and Cro-Patrick. W. B. Yeats. UnS
I Promise You, *in mod. Eng.* *Unknown.* TMEV
I promised Sylvia to be true. Song. Earl of Rochester. SeCePo
I purchased my love for money. A Love-Song. Gustaf Fröding. AnSL
I purposed once to take my pen and write. Prefatory Sonnet. Henry Kendall. BoAV
I put him on the train in Albury. Returned Soldier. E. G. Moll. MoAuPo
I put my hand upon my heart. Head and Heart. C. D. B. Ellis. LiTM; SiTL
I put my hat upon my head. Hats and the Man. Samuel Johnson. FiBHP
I put the idols by. I left the place. Idols of Imagination. Richard Eberhart. FiMAP
I put those things there.—See them burn. The Song of the Demented Priest. John Berryman. MoPo
I put thy hand aside, and turn away. A Farewell. "Madeline Bridges." AA
I quarreled with my brother. The Quarrel. Eleanor Farjeon. FaPON
"I quite realized," said Columbus. Clerihews. E. C. Bentley. FiBHP; OnPP
I, Rain[e]y Betha, 22. Plaint. Charles Henri Ford. AtBAP; MoVE
I raise my cup and invite. Moon, Flowers, Man. Su T'ung-po. OnPC
I raise . . . my glass to all good dogs. A Toast. June Provine. AlBD
I raise the curtains and go out. Alone. Chu Shu Chen. OnPC
I raised a dog and his name was Blue. Old Blue. *Unknown.* OuSiCo
I raised a noble falcon. The Falcon. "The Knight of Kürenberg." LyMA
I raised my eyes aloft, and I beheld. One World. Dante. *Fr.* Divina Commedia. MaRV
I ran along the daisy fields. The Daisy Field. Margaret Widdemer. RAR
I ran along the yellow sand. Pete at the Seashore. Don Marquis. AlBD
I ran for a catch. Coulson Kernahan. CenHV
I ran onto Mehitabel again. The Old Trouper. Don Marquis. *Fr.* Archy and Mehitabel. MoP
I ran out in the morning, when the air was clean and new. Autumn Morning at Cambridge. Frances Cornford. HBMV; MoVE; OBVV; TCPD
I ran over a pig. Two Triolets. *At. to* Maurice Baring. AlDL
I ranted to the knave and fool. Remorse for Intemperate Speech. W. B. Yeats. TwP
I rather like the music. To a Katydid. James J. Montague. LPS-1
I reach among the plain and lovely words. Definition. Grace Noll Crowell. MotAn
I reach out arms of love to you. Franciscan. Katherine Brégy. SaFP
I reach out with my barbaric hands above the ebony night. God. Gonzalo Escudero. AnCL
I reached the highest place in Spoon River. Henry C. Calhoun. Edgar Lee Masters. *Fr.* Spoon River Anthology. AmP; LiTA; LiTM (rev. ed.); NP
I read a legend of a monk who painted. The Monk's Vision. *Unknown.* PEOR
I read, before my eyelids dropped [*or* dropt] their shade. A Dream of Fair Women. Tennyson. BEL; BPN; EmBrPo; EPP; EV-5; GEPC; OBRV; PtP; ViPo; VLEP
I read how Troilus served in Troy. A Comparison of His Love with the Faithful and Painful Love of Troilus to Cressid. *Unknown.* ReIE
I read last night of the Grand Review. A Second Review of the Grand Army. Bret Harte. BlG; HBV; MC; MDAH; PAH
I read last night with many pauses. Troy. Robin Flower. MM; SeCePo
I read my sentence steadily. Emily Dickinson. NePA; TCAP
I read once more this care-worn, patient face. On a Picture of Lincoln. John Vance Cheney. PGD
I read somewhere that a swan, snow-white. The Watch of a Swan. Sarah Morgan Bryan Piatt. AA
I read the marble-lettered name. A Grave in Hollywood Cemetery, Richmond. Margaret Junkin Preston. AA
I read the pain and pathos of your eyes. Unfulfilled. Corinne Roosevelt Robinson. AV
I read the verses from my copy. In Parenthesis. Frank Dempster Sherman. PR
I read with varying degrees. Edna St. Vincent Millay. *Fr.* Journal. ImOP
I reade in ancient times of yore. The Map of Mock-Begger Hall. *Unknown.* CoMu
I really meant to do my work to-day. A Plea. Hazel Miners. CAG
I really take it very kind. Domestic Asides; or, Truth in Parentheses. Thomas Hood. EnRP; ERP
I reason, earth is short. What of That? Emily Dickinson. OnPM
I recall the time. Memories. Shen Yo. ChLP
I recalled my heart's desire. In Battle. Abul Hasan of Badajoz. MooP
I reckon I git your drift, gents. Banty Tim. John Hay. DDA; LPS-3; MAP; MoAmPo (1942 ed.)
I reckon the first day I saw those eyes. To Calista. Charles Cotton. LO; NBE
I reckon, when I count at all. Emily Dickinson. MAP; MoAmPo
I recognized him by his skips and hops. Pan and the Cherries. Paul Fort. AWP; PoMS
I recollect a nurse call'd [*or* called] Ann. A Terrible Infant. Frederick Locker-Lampson. ALV; BOHV; FiBHP; HBV; InMe; LauV; TreFS; WhC
I recollect in early life. My First Love. Harry Graham. FiBHP
I recollect my master tenderly. The Flute. André Chénier. TrFP
I recommend for plain dis-ease. Convalescence, VII. David McCord. WhC
I regret that before people can be reformed they have to be sinners. Piano Tuner, Untune Me That Tune. Ogden Nash. UnS
I regretted the arrival of my death. What Profit? Immanuel di Roma. TrJP
I Remember. Robert G. Burlingham. CAG
I Remember. Denis Glover. AnNZ
I Remember. Thomas Hood. *See* I Remember, I Remember.
I remember. A Memory. Lola Ridge. AV
I remember,/ There lived a Spanish Princess of our name Thomas Heywood. *Fr.* A Challenge for Beauty. LO
I remember a day, and if it were then. Recollections of Oisin *Unknown.* SiB
I remember a house where all were good. In the Valley of the Elwy. Gerard Manley Hopkins. EG; InPo; LiTG; ViBoPo

I remember, as if it were yesterday. One and One. C. Day Lewis. OAEP (2d ed.); UnS
I remember distinctly the tired tumult of my urges. Journey to a Parallel. Bruce McM. Wright. PoNe
I remember ever so long. Tragic Memory. *Unknown. Fr.* Manyo Shu. OnPM
I remember forgotten faces. I Remember. Robert G. Burlingham. CAG
I remember how I lay. Two Taverns. Edwin Markham. TSW
I remember how we stood. The Last Corn Shock. Glenn Ward Dresbach. FaPON
I Remember, I Remember, *parody.* Phoebe Cary. PA
I Remember, I Remember. Thomas Hood. BEL; BLPA; BTP; EnLi-2 (1949 ed.); EnLit; EnRP; ERP; EV-4; FaBoBe; FaFP; FaPON; GoTP; HBV; LiTB; LiTG; LPS-1; MaRV; MyFE; NeHB; OBRV; PECK; PG (1945 ed.); PIR; PoEL-4; PRWS; TreF; TVSH (I Remember.) CH; MPB (1956 ed.); OTPC; PCD (Past and Present.) GTBS; GTBS-D; GTBS-W; GTSE; GTSL; PoeMoYo; PYM; ShBV-1; ShGoBo; WP
I remember, I remember,/ The house where I was wed. I Remember, I Remember. Phoebe Cary. PA
I remember, I remember, ere my childhood flitted by. As to the Weather. *Unknown.* BOHV
I remember it well; 't was a morn dull and gray. Macdonald's Raid. Paul Hamilton Hayne. PAH
I remember once a glorious thing. The Chilterns. John Davidson. VLEP
I remember once, on a journey to the west. I Remember the River at Wu Sung. Mei Yao Ch'en. OnPC
I remember paddocks opening green. I Remember. Denis Glover. AnNZ
I Remember the Blue River. Mei Yao Ch'en, *tr. fr. Chinese by* Kenneth Rexroth. OnPC
I remember the cleared streets, the strange suspense. On the Passing of the Last Fire Horse from Manhattan Island. Kenneth Slade Alling. TBM
I remember the lowering wintry morn. The Risks of the Game. Adam Lindsay Gordon. OtMeF
I remember the neckcurls, limp and damp as tendrils. Elegy for Jane. Theodore Roethke. AmP; FiMAP; GTBS-W; MoAB; NePA
I Remember the River at Wu Sung. Mei Yao Ch'en, *tr. fr. Chinese by* Kenneth Rexroth. OnPC
I remember Wednesday was the day. Two Lean Cats. Myron O'Higgins. PoNe
I remember well the way. His New Suit. Samuel Ellsworth Kiser. MDAH
I remember when the changeful earth. In Childhood and Youth. Wordsworth. GrCo-2
I Remembered. Sara Teasdale. LoPo; LoPS; TCPD
I, Remembering. Roger Mais. PoNe
I rent the Veil where the Dead dwell. Blake. *Fr.* The Gates of Paradise. PoD
I resent great instruments. Independence. Mary Fullerton. BoAV
I reside at [the] Table Mountain, and my name is Truthful James. The Society upon the Stanislaus. Bret Harte. AA; BAP; BeLS; BOHV; HBV; InMe; LEAP; LPS-3; MaC; SiTL
I Resolve. Charlotte Perkins Gilman. *See* Resolve.
I resolved,/ How much the destiny of Man had still. Residence in France. Wordsworth. *Fr.* The Prelude, X. ERP
I Rest with Thee, O Jesus. *Unknown, tr. fr. Modern Irish by* Eleanor Hull. *Fr.* Four Prayers. JKCP (1926 ed.) (Four Prayers.) OnYI
I rested on the breezy height. Above St. Irénée. Duncan Campbell Scott. VA
I, restless in the military train. City by Night. Vittorio Sereni. OnPM
I return the bitterness. Transformation. Lewis Alexander. CDC; PoNe
I Return unto Zion. Zechariah, VIII: 3-5, Bible, *O.T.* TrJP
I, Richard Kent, beneath these stones. Epitaph. Sylvia Townsend Warner. MBP; MoBrPo; NeMA
I Ride an Old Paint, *with music. Unknown.* AS; TrAS
I ride on the mountain tops, I ride. The Joy of the Hills. Edwin Markham. LBMV; PoMa; POT; PoTo
I Ride the Great Black Horses of My Heart. Robert Nathan. MAP
I ride through a dark, dark land by night. Ichabod! Thy [*or* The] Glory Has Departed. Ludwig Uhland. AWP; IrPN
I rise, & greive. *Unknown.* SeCSL
I rise and leave the town in morning haze. Town of France. Henri de Régnier. TrFP
I rise as from a bath of sparkling water. Shelley. *Fr.* Prometheus Unbound. NBE
I rise before the dawn has come. Comfort. Miyauchi. SoLD
I rise from the earth, I fall from on high. Everywhere. Nancy Birckhead. RIS
I rise in the dawn, and I kneel and blow. The Song of the Old Mother. W. B. Yeats. AnIV; BEL; CV; GTSL; MBP; MCCG; MOAH; MoBrPo; MotAn; NeMA; VA
I 'rived in the camp, and all I could see. Burns's Log Camp. *Unknown.* ShS
I roamed with wine along the lakes and rivers. Happy Regret. Tu Mu. WhP
I rock in the heart of the rose. Joy. Matilda Hutchinson Turner. RAR
I rode a line on the open range. The Old Cowboy. *Unknown.* CoSo
I rode across a valley range. The Old Cowman. Badger Clark. SCC
I rode in Montana and old Idaho. Up the Trail. *Unknown.* CoSo
I rode in the dark of the spirit. Beyond Good and Evil. George Edward Woodberry. TCPD
I rode my horse to the hostel gate. Both Less and More. Richard Watson Dixon. LoBV
I rode through Indiana, and the ragged hedges cried. This Is New England. Margery Mansfield. DDA
I rode through the Bush in the burning noon. Bannerman of the Dandenong. Alice Werner. TVSH
I rose . . . I rose . . . Don Marquis. *Fr.* I Have Looked Inward. PFY
I rose not from my knees and called on her for comfort. The Maiden Meed. William Langland(?). *Fr.* The Vision of Piers the Plowman, Passus 2. CoBE
I rose up when the battle was dead. Comrades. Laurence Housman. BoFr; HBV
I Roused, Started Up, in the Night. August, Graf von Platen, *tr. fr. German by* Dwight Durling. AnGP
I row in my boat in the twilight, half-purple, half-grey, overhead. John Francis O'Donnell. *Fr.* In the Twilight. IrPN
I rue the day, a rueful day I trow. Thursday; or, The Spell. John Gay. *Fr.* The Shepherd's Week. CEP
I rush to your dwelling. Pursuit. Juljan Tuwim. TrJP
I said: All is [*or* now] complete! Twelve by the Clock. Jorge Guillén. CoSP; WoL
I said, "I have shut my heart." Over the Roofs. Sara Teasdale. BAP; NP; OBAV
I said I splendidly loved you; it's not true. Sonnet. Rupert Brooke. POTT
I said I stood upon thy grave. Arisen at Last. Whittier. IAP
I said, "I will find God"; and forth I went. Seeking God. Edward Dowden. GrCo-1; MaRV; WGRP
I said: I will go down. The Eagle Hunter. Rose O'Neill. TBM
I said: "I will take heed to my ways." Lord, Make Me to Know Mine End. Psalm XXXIX, Bible, *O.T.* TrJP
I said, "I will walk in the fields." *See* I said, "Let me walk in the fields."
I said I would have my fling. The Price He Paid. Ella Wheeler Wilcox. WBLP
I said, in drunken pride of youth and you. Challenge. Sterling A. Brown. CDC
I said in my heart, "I am sick of four walls and a ceiling." Richard Hovey. *Fr.* Spring. ADAH; BBV (1951 ed.); NLK; PoMa
I said it in the meadow-path. Shared. Lucy Larcom. NLK
I said, "It is good to live in the country." The Somerset Farmer. Marguerite Wilkinson. CP
I said: "Let me walk [*or* I will walk] in the fields." Obedience [*or* What Christ Said]. George Macdonald. BePJ; BLRP; ChIP; HBV; MaRV; OQP; OTPC; QP-1; WGRP
I said: "My heart, now let us sing a song." A Wedding-Song. John White Chadwick. AA
I said my pleasure shall not move. Our Thrones Decay. "Æ." TIP
I said: "Nay, pluck not,—let the first fruit be." Hoarded Joy. Dante Gabriel Rossetti. The House of Life, LXXXII. BPN; PoVP; ViPo
I said: "O let me sing the praise." He Inadvertently Cures His Love-Pains. Thomas Hardy. ChMo; CMP
I said of laughter: it is vain. A Testimony. Christina Rossetti. EmBrPo
I Said Sometimes with Tears. Samuel Crossman. OxBoCh
I said, "Sweet Master, hear me pray." The Blessed Task. Harriet McEwen Kimball. BePJ
"I," said the duck. "I call it fun." Who Likes the Rain? Clara Doty Bates. BoTP; GFA; GoBP; OTPC (1946 ed.); PCH; PPL; RAR; TiPo
I said—Then, dearest, since 'tis so. The Last Ride Together. Robert Browning. BEL; BMEP; BoLiVe; BPN; CBOV; EM-2; EmBrPo; EnLi-2; FiP; GEPC; GTML; GTSL; HBV; LEAP; LiTB; LoBV (1949 ed.); OAEP; OBEV; OBVV; OuHeWo; PoEL-5; PoVP; RiBV; TyEnPo; UnPo (1st ed.); ViPP; VLEP; WHA
I said: "There is an end of my desire." Vain Resolves. Ernest Dowson. VLEP

I said, "This horse, sir, will you shoe?" Logical English. *Unknown.* BOHV

I Said, This Misery Must End. Christopher J. Brennan. BoAu; BoAV; NeLNL

I said to Death: "Supposing it were true." Dancing Partners. Philip Child. CaP

I said to Heart, "How goes it?" Heart replied. For [*or* The] False Heart. Hilaire Belloc. FaBoCh; HBMV; LoGBV; MBP; MoBrPo

I said to heaven that glowed above. Odes, XII. Hafiz, *tr. by* Emerson. AWP; OuHeWo

I said to Lettice, our sister Lettice. Lettice. Dinah Maria Mulock Craik. HBV

I Said to Love. Thomas Hardy. BrBE; EmBrPo; ViPo; VLEP

I said to my companion, this is walking. Victoria Market. Francis Brabazon. BoAV

I said to my Heart, between sleeping and waking. Chloe. Earl of Peterborough. CEP; OBEC

I said to Sorrow's awful storm. The Soul's Defiance. Lavinia Stoddard. AA

I said to the cuckoo: "Till I die." "Anna Akhmatova," *tr. fr. Russian by* V. de S. Pinto. BoR

I said, when evil men are strong. Two Victories. Wordsworth. *Fr.* Song at the Feast of Brougham Castle. LH

I said, when the word came, "She will break." Of Little Faith. Harold T. Pulsifer. EtS

I said: "Within the garden trimly bordered." Inspiration. E. V. Knox. CenHV

I Sail in the Fall. Davíd Stefánsson, *tr. fr. Icelandic by* Watson Kirkconnell. IcP

I sail over the ocean blue. I Catcha da Plenty of Feesh. Unknown. AS; TrAS

I sail'd from the Downs in the *Nancy.* The Tar for All Weathers. Charles Didbin. CG; OTPC (1923 ed.)

I sailed in my dreams to the Land of Night. Fantasy. Gwendolyn B. Bennett. CDC

I sang a song at dusking time. The Song for Colin. Sara Teasdale. ChMo; CMP; MOAP

I sang a song of joy to one grown sad. An Echo. Grace Hyde Trine. BAP

I sang as one. The Conflict. C. Day Lewis. AnEnPo; EnLit; FaBoMo; LiTB; LiTM; MBP; MoAB; MoBrPo

I sang the songs of red revenge. Homer. Albert Ehrenstein. TrJP

I sat alone with my conscience. Conscience [and Future Judgment]. Charles William Stubbs. BLPA; MaRV; PTA-2

I Sat among the Green Leaves. Marjorie Pickthall. AV; BMEP; HBMV; NV

I sat, and held the book upon my knees. The Poet Considers Perfection. Elizabeth Virginia Raplee. MaRV

I sat and read Anacreon. Philander's Song. Sir Charles G. D. Roberts. BoCaPo (1948 ed.)

I sat at Berne, and watched the chain. Below the Heights. William Herries Pollock. VA

I sat at my loom in silence. The Weaver. *Unknown.* BLRP

I sat beside a stream. Beside a Stream. Hamda. MooP

I sat beside the red stock route. Harry Pearce. David Campbell. NeLNL

I sat beside the streamlet. Remember or Forget. Hamilton Aidé. HBV; VA

I sat by my window one night. Musings. Longfellow. PEOR

I sat by the granite pillar, and sunlight fell. Commemoration. Sir Henry Newbolt. FaBoTw; OBVV

I sat down on a bumblebee. Suffering. Nathalia Crane. TSWC

I sat drinking and did not notice the dusk. Self-Abandonment. Li Po. TrCh

I sat here this morning, detached, summoning up, I think. The Deviator. Bertram Warr. BoCaPo (1948 ed.)

I sat in a friendly company. The Lover. John Crowe Ransom. LS

I sat in the school of sorrow. The School of Sorrow. Harold Hamilton. BLRP

I sat me down upon a green bank-side. Bronx. Joseph Rodman Drake. AnAmPo; LA

I sat me weary on a pillar's base. The Sphinx. James Thomson. The City of Dreadful Night, XX. EPN; OAEP; POTT; ViP

I sat on cushioned otter skin. The Madness of King Goll. W. B. Yeats. ChMo; CMP

I sat one night beside a blue-eyed girl. Categorical Courtship. *Unknown.* BOHV; CIV

I sat unsphering Plato ere I slept. The Fall of a Soul. John Addington Symonds. PoVP; VA

I sat upon a windy mountain height. Sunset on the Cunimbla Valley, Blue Mountains. Douglas Brooke W. Sladen. VA

I sat upon my little porch. Thoughtfulness. Yamaguchi. SoLD

I sat with Doris, the shepherd maiden. Doris; a Pastoral. Arthur Joseph Munby. HBV; VA

I sat with her, and spoke right goldenly. The Lady of Life. Thomas Michael Kettle. ACP; JKCP (1926 ed.)

I sat with Love upon a woodside well. Willowwood, I. Dante Gabriel Rossetti. The House of Life, XLIX. BPN; EmBrPo; HBV; OAEP; PoEL-5; POTT; PoVP; ReaPo; TCEP; TyEnPo; ViP; ViPo; VLEP; WHA

I sat with May upon a midnight hill. The Seasons of the Gods. Albert E. S. Smythe. CPG

I sat with one I love last night. Last Night. George Darley. GTIV; HBV; OnYI

I sat within the temple of her heart. Sonnet. Charles Sangster. CPG

I saunter by the shore and lose myself. A Hymn to the Sea. Richard Henry Stoddard. EtS

I saunter home in the evening. The Bricklayer. Vasili Kazin. BoR

I sauntered down through Europe. The Jackpot. Eugene Fitch Ware. DDA

I saw a bee, I saw a flower. The Bee-Orchis. Andrew Young. ChTr

I saw a boy in a black-jack wood. The Maul. Mary E. Nealy. GA; MC

I saw a boy with eager eye. The Two Boys. Mary A. Lamb. OBRV

I saw a brown squirrel to-day in the wood. Mr. Squirrel. V. M. Julian. BoTP

I saw a bug/ with twenty feet. A Bug. Aileen Fisher. GoBP

I saw a bus marked XANADU. Thoughts. Roy Davis. WhC

I saw a certain sailorman who sat beside the sea. All at Sea. Frederick Moxon. BOHV

I Saw a Chapel All of Gold. Blake. EM-1; EnRP; LiTB; LiTG

I saw a cherry weep, and why? The Weeping Cherry. Robert Herrick. AtBAP

I saw a dead man's finer part. His Immortality. Thomas Hardy. ChMo; CMP

I saw a dog. Ilo Orleans. RIS

I saw a faire maiden sit and sing. *See* Lullay, Mine Liking.

I saw a faun! The Faun. Sara King Wiley. OBAV

I Saw a Fish Pond All on Fire. *Unknown.* BoN; ChTr; OxNR

I saw a fly within a bead. The Amber Bead. Robert Herrick. ChTr

I saw a frieze on whitest marble drawn. Ecstasy. W. J. Turner. AlDL; CH; POTE; PtOT; TwCV

I Saw a Ghost. Joan Boilleau. TiPo

I saw a Gnome. The Gnome. Harry Behn. FaPON; TiPo (1959 ed.)

I saw a great barge. The Barge. Rose Fyleman. BrR

I saw a grown girl coming down. Glenn Ward Dresbach. Songs of the Plains, I. NP

I saw a history in a poet's song. Symbols. John Drinkwater. BMEP; NV; TCEP

I saw a holly sprig brought from a hurst. A Vision of the World's Instability. Richard Verstegan. ElL

"I saw a light," Columbus said. Light in the Darkness. Aileen Fisher. YeAr

I saw a little boy who made. The Boy and His Playthings. Anna Maria Lenngren. AnSL

I saw a little dog today. Lost Dog. Margaret E. Sangster. AlBD

I saw a little snail [*or* a snail]. Little Snail. Hilda Conkling. FaPON; GFA; MPB; PoRh; RAR; TiPo; TVC; TVSH; UTS

I saw a little squirrel. A Little Squirrel. *Unknown.* TiPo

I Saw a Maid. Ellery Husted. LoPS

I Saw a Maiden. *Unknown.* ISi

I Saw a Man. Stephen Crane. The Black Riders, XXIV. BAP; HoPM; MAP; MoAmPo; NeMA; PoeMoYo
(I Saw a Man Pursuing the Horizon.) CoBA; LiTA; LoGBV; NePA

I saw a man at the dawn of day. The Drunkard's Doom. *Unknown.* ABF

I saw a man, by some accounted wise. Erastus Wolcott Ellsworth. *Fr.* What Is the Use? AA

I saw a man come down to the furious sea. The Antagonist. David Ferry. NePoAm-2

I saw a man on a horse. Mirage. Richard Church. AlDL

I Saw a Man Pursuing the Horizon. Stephen Crane. *See* I Saw a Man.

I saw a man whose face was white as snow. The Uninfected. E. L. Mayo. MiAP

I saw a maniac's frozen form. As They Fell. Edward A. Blount, Jr. PoP

I saw a marble shaft gleam white. The Washington Monument. Alma Adams Wiley. PEDC

I Saw a Monk of Charlemain [*or* Charlemaine]. Blake. *Fr.* Jerusalem. EnRP; MeRV; NBE; OBRV
(Monk, The.) LoBV

I saw a mountain. I Keep Wondering. Hilda Conkling. PFE; PFY

I Saw a New World. William Brighty Rands. VA

I Saw a Peacock [with a Fiery Tail]. *Unknown.* BoN; CH; ChTr; FaBoCh; ImOP; LiL; LiTG; LoGBV; OxBoLi;

I Saw a Peacock (*continued*) OxNR; PoMS; SiTL
(Ambiguous Lines, *longer vers.*) BOHV
(Not So Impossible.) GoTP
I saw a people rise before the sun. Yom Kippur. Israel Zangwill. TrJP
I Saw a Phoenix in the Wood Alone. Petrarch, *tr. by* Spenser. *Fr.* The Visions of Petrarch. ChTr; EnLi-1
I saw a picture once by Angelo. An Unpraised Picture. Richard Burton. AA
I saw a poor old woman on the bench. By the Salpêtrière. Thomas Ashe. VA
I saw a proud, mysterious cat. The Mysterious Cat. Vachel Lindsay. ChTr; FaPON; MPB; PoRh; RAR; SP; StVeCh; TiPo; UTS
I saw a querulous old man, the tobacconist of Eighth Street. The Tobacconist of Eighth Street. Richard Eberhart. MiAP
I saw a reindeer, strayed from star-pastures. The Lost Dream. Fannie Stearns Davis. PoTo
I saw a rose in snow. Early Snow. Ken Etheridge. MoWP
I saw a shadow on the ground. The Sky. Elizabeth Madox Roberts. GFA; MAP; MoAmPo; VOD
I saw a ship a-sailing. Mother Goose. BoChLi; BoN; BoTP; CBPC; FaBoBe; GFA; HBV; HBVY; MoShBr; MPB; OTPC; OxNR; PCH; PoRh; PPL, *sl. diff. vers.;* RIS; SAS; StVeCh; TiPo
I saw a ship a-sailing. Romance. "Gabriel Setoun." BoTP; OTPC; PRWS
I saw a ship a-sailing, a-sailing, a-sailing. An Old Song Resung. John Masefield. AlDL; ExPo; LiTB; PtOT
I saw a ship of martial build. The Berg. Herman Melville. AmP; AtBAP; LiTA; PoEL-5; PoFS
I saw a sickly cellar plant. The Incentive. Sarah N. Cleghorn. HBMV
I saw a slowly-stepping train. God's Funeral. Thomas Hardy. QS; WGRP
I saw a snail. *See* I saw a little snail.
I Saw a Stable. Mary Elizabeth Coleridge. MBP; OxBoCh
(I Saw a Stable Low and Very Bare.) TCPD
I saw a star slide down the sky. The Falling Star. Sara Teasdale. BrR; MoShBr; MoSiPe; PoRh; StVeCh; SUS; TiPo
I saw a staring virgin stand. Two Songs from a Play, I. W. B. Yeats. *Fr.* The Resurrection. CoBMV; EnLP; ExPo; FaBoTw; LiTB; MoPo; PoFS; RiBV; SeCeV; UnPo
I saw a stately lady. The Stately Lady. Flora Sandstrom. BoTP
I saw a stranger yestereen [*or* yestreen]. The Rune of Hospitality [*or* Gaelic Rune of Hospitality]. *Unknown.* BoFr; CAW; WHL
I Saw a Sweet and Silly Sight. *Unknown, at. to* John Brackley. AnEC
(Carol: "I saw a sweet and seemly sight.") BOL
(O Jesu Parvule.) ISi
I saw a terrible river. The Sin; a Definition. Francis Maguire JKCP (1955 ed.)
I saw a thing, and stopped to wonder. The Pine Bough. Richard Aldridge. NePoAm
I saw a thousand fearful wrecks. Shakespeare. King Richard III, *fr.* I, iv. SG
I saw a Tiger's golden flank. The Lion and the Lamb. Elinor Wylie. CoBA
I saw a tiny pebble fall. What Price. Lulu Minerva Schultz. GoYe
I saw a tomb by the wayside, as I went towards Corinth City. "Here Lies a Most Beautiful Lady." Agathias Scholasticus. GrPE
I saw a Vision yesternight. To the State of Love, or the Senses Festival. John Cleveland. MePo
I saw a vulture in the sky. Life and Death. W. J. Turner. FaBoTw
I saw a war, yet none the trumpet blew. The War. Jones Very. IAP; TCAP
I saw a white bird once. Yosano Akiko, *tr. fr. Japanese by* Kenneth Rexroth. LiTW
I saw a woman in a green field. The Postures of Love, I. Alex Comfort. NeBP
I saw a wonder as I came along. The Shepherds. Sophie Jewett. ChrBoLe
I saw a youth and maiden on a lonely city street. Take Back Your Gold. Louis W. Pritzkow. TreF
I saw again the spirits on a day. Bethesda. Arthur Hugh Clough. BPN; EmBrPo; PoVP; VLEP
I saw along each noisy city street. Christmas Trees. Violet Alleyn Storey. SDH; StJW
I saw an aged beggar in my walk. The Old Cumberland Beggar. Wordsworth. EnRP; ERP; GEPC; LaA; PoE
I saw an ass who bore a load. The Loaded Ass. Bhartrihari. OnPM
"I saw an elephant walking down the road." April Fool. Elizabeth J. Coatsworth. YeAr
I saw, and trembled for the day. A Warning. Coventry Patmore. EnLoPo
I saw, at noon, Alexa on the road. Two Fires. Meleager. OnPM
I saw at times a star, that through the night afar. Hebrew Melody. Mikhail Yurevich Lermontov. WaL
I saw Castara pray, and from the skie. To Castara Praying. William Habington. *Fr.* Castara. MeRV
I saw cold thunder in the grass. Herons. Robin Blaser. NeAP
I saw dawn creep across the sky. A Summer Morning. Rachel Field. BoChLi; StVeCh (1955 ed.); SUS; TiPo
I Saw Death Slain. William Capell. ChIP
I saw death this afternoon lurking near the tennis courts. Near the Base Line. Samuel L. Albert. NePoAm-2
I saw Ecclesiasticus. Ecclesiasticus. Donald Davidson. LS
I Saw Eternity. Louise Bogan. LiTA; MOAP
I saw Eternity the other night. The World [*or* Eternity *or* A Vision]. Henry Vaughan. AtBAP; ATP; AWP; BBV; BCEP; BEL; BLV; BoLiVe; CBOV; CoBE; ElSeCe; EM-1; EnL; EnLi-1; EnLit; EPP; EPS; EV-2; ExPo; FaBoEn; GoTL; GTBS-W; GTSL; HBV; ImOP; InPo; LiTB; LiTG; LoBV; MaPo; MaRV; MePo; NBE; OAEP; OBEV (new ed.); OBS; OuHeWo; OxBoCh; PC; Po; PoE; PoEL-2; PoeMoYo; PoFr; PoFS; PreP; ReaPo; ReEn; SeCeV; SeCV-1; SeEP; TCEP; TOP; TreFS; TrGrPo; TwCrTr; TwHP; TyEnPo; ViBoPo; WGRP; WoL
I saw fair Chloris walk alone. On Chloris Walking in the Snow [*or* Chloris in the Snow]. William Strode. EG; ElSeCe; EV-2; GTBS-W; HBV; OBEV; OBS; SeCL; SeEP
I saw five birds all in a cage. *Unknown. Fr.* Riddles. CoBE
I Saw from the Beach. Thomas Moore. GTIV; OxBI
I saw, from yonder silent cave. The Two Streams. Thomas Moore. *Fr.* Evenings in Greece. GoBC
I Saw God. William L. Stidger. PGD
I saw God! Do you doubt it? What Tomas [an Buile] Said in a Pub. James Stephens. AnFE; BMEP; ChMo; CMP; GTSL; LBBV; LiTM; MBP; MoAB; MoBrPo; NeMA; NP; TCPD; TrGrPo; TwCV; WGRP
I Saw God Wash the World. William L. Stidger. BLPA; MaRV; MPB (1956 ed.); OQP; QP-1
I saw green banks of daffodil. E. Wyndham Tennant. TiPo (1959 ed.)
I saw her crop a rose. John Clare. EG; LO, 8 *ll.*
I saw her first abreast the Boston light. The *William P. Frye.* Jeanne Robert Foster. MC; PAH
I saw her in childhood. Agnes. Henry Francis Lyte. ATP (1935 ed.); GTSL
I saw her last night at a party. The Mourner à la Mode. John Godfrey Saxe. LHV
I Saw Her Once. Richard Henry Dana. BAV
I saw her once, one little while, and then no more. And Then No More. Friedrich Rückert, *tr. by* James Clarence Mangan. AnIV; BLPA; GTIV; IrPN
I saw her plucking cowslips. The Witch. Percy H. Ilott. BoTP
I saw her scan her sacred scroll. Alma Mater's Roll. Edward Everett Hale. AA
I saw him coming up the street. Welcome Home. Louella C. Poole. AlBD
I saw him dead, a leaden slumber lies. Cromwell Dead. Andrew Marvell. *Fr.* A Poem upon the Death of Oliver Cromwell. ChTr; OBS; ViBoPo
"I saw him kiss your cheek!" "'Tis true." Sly Thoughts. Coventry Patmore. The Angel in the House, II, viii, 3. LPS-1
I saw him leave his pagan century. The Centurion. Helen Purcell Roads. ChIP
I saw him lying there—my father—with eyes. The Addict. Larry Rubin. GoYe
I saw him naked on a hill. The Shepherd Boy. Edward J. O'Brien. HBMV
I saw him once before. The Last Leaf. Oliver Wendell Holmes. AA; AmPP; AnAmPo; AnFE; AnNE; APA; APW; BAV; BLV; CoAnAm; CoBA; FaBoBe; FaPON; HBV; HiLiAm; IAP; InP; LA; LBAP; LEAP; OnPP; OuHeWo; PFE; PFY; PG (1945 ed.); PIAE; PIR; PR; PTA-2; SeCeV; SiTL; TCAP; TOP; TreF; TSW; TSWC; WaKn; WBLP
I saw him peeping from my lawn. Dandelion. Kate L. Brown. TVC; TVSH
I saw him sitting in his door. The Philosopher. Sara Teasdale. PoToHe
I saw him where the rose was red. The Stranger. John Richard Moreland. ChIP; OQP; QP-1
I saw Him with flesh all bespred—He came from the East. Conquering and to Conquer [*or* The Coming of Christ]. *Unknown.* ACP; TMEV
I saw history in a poet's song. Symbols. John Drinkwater. BMEP; NV; TCEP

I Saw, 1 Saw the Lovely Child. Frederic William Henry Myers. VA
(Evanescence.) OBVV

I Saw in a Vision. Jean Ingelow. *Fr.* The Dreams That Came True. UnW

I saw in dream a dapper mannikin. Im Traum sah ich ein Männchen klein und putzig. Heine. AWP

I saw in dreams a mighty multitude. No Death. Philip Bourke Marston. BMEP; VA

I Saw in Louisiana a Live-Oak Growing. Walt Whitman. ADAH; AWP; BoFr; CoBA; GBV (1952 ed.); HiLiAm; InPo; JAWP; LiTA; MCCG; MOAP; NePA; OxBA; TCAP; WBP

I saw in Siena pictures. Sodoma's Christ Scourged. George Edward Woodberry. StJW

I saw in Ulm a castle high. The Blacksmith. *Unknown.* SAS

I saw it all in Fancy's glass. The Torch of Liberty. Thomas Moore. DD; IDAH; PEDC

I saw it all, Polly, how when you had call'd for sop. Poor Poll. Robert Bridges. MoPo; OxBoLi

I saw it in a shell-torn town. The Cross. Donald Earl Edwards. ChIP

I saw it in Bellagio. Green Shawl. Helen Bayley Davis. PoTo

I saw it once where myriad works adorn. On a Sculptured Head of the Christ. Mahlon Leonard Fisher. HBV

I saw it—pink and white—revealed. A Thought in Two Moods. Thomas Hardy. EPN

I saw Love stand. Forgiven? Jeannette Bliss Gillespy. *Fr.* Cameos. AA

I saw my face. A Coffeepot Face. Aileen Fisher. MPB

I Saw My Father. E. L. Mayo. MiAP

I saw my lady by a cool, fresh stream. Sonnet. Lorenzo de' Medici. LyPI

I Saw My Lady Weep. *Unknown.* CoEV; EIL; EG; ElSeCe; EnLoPo; GTBS-W; HBV; LiTB; LO; OBSC; TrGrPo; ViBoPo
(In Lacrimas.) GTSL
(My Lady's Tears.) EV-1; OBEV

I saw my luve in black velvet. Exile. Sidney Goodsir Smith. PoN

I saw my scattered hopes upon the floor. The Phallic Symbol. Nicholas Moore. NeBP

I saw Nelson at the Battle of the Nile. Limerick. *Unknown.* LiBL

I saw new worlds beneath the water lie [*or* ly]. On Leaping over the Moon. Thomas Traherne. AtBAP; LiTB; LoBV; SeCV-2

I saw no doctor, but, feeling queer inside. *Unknown, tr. fr. Greek by* Humbert Wolfe. PIAE; WhC

I saw not they were strange, the ways I roam. After Music. Josephine Preston Peabody. AA

I saw old Autumn in the misty morn. Autumn [*or* Ode: Autumn]. Thomas Hood. ERP; EV-4; HBV; LiTB; OBEV; OBRV; PCD; PoEL-4; VA; ViBoPo

I saw old Duchesses with their young loves. Vanity. Anna Wickham. FaBoTw

I Saw Old General at Bay. Walt Whitman. IAP

I saw old Time, destroyer of mankind. Time and Death. William Henry Whitworth. EtS

I saw on earth another light. The Light from Within. Jones Very. WGRP

I saw on the slant hill a putrid lamb. For a Lamb. Richard Eberhart. FiMAP; MiAP

I saw one hung upon a cross. Gallows and Cross. J. E. H. MacDonald. CaP

I saw, one sultry night above a swamp. Fireflies. Edgar Fawcett. AnAmPo; BAP; HBV; LBAP

I saw red clay gullies. Homing Song. Rebecca Cushman. NoCaPo

I saw Saleianus in mourning array. A Golden Sorrow. Martial. LiTW

I saw someone by the white syringa. Ballad: White Rose. Sacheverell Sitwell. POTE (1959 ed.)

I Saw That Shattered Thing. Leonard Bacon. TBM

I saw the archangels in my apple-tree last night. The Apple-Tree. Nancy Campbell. AnIV; NP

I Saw the Beauty Go. Mary Gilmore. NeLNL

I saw the beauty of the world. The Beauty of the World. William Brighty Rands. UnW

I saw the best minds of my generation. Squeal. Louis Simpson. FiBHP

I saw the best minds of my generation destroyed by madness, starving hysterical naked. Howl. Allen Ginsberg. AmP; NeAP

I saw the blackthorn blaze. Vivian's Speech. John Davidson. BSV

I saw the bodies of earth's men. The Navigators. W. J. Turner. OBMV

I saw the civil sun drying earth's tears. The Thaw. Henry David Thoreau. CoV

I Saw the Clouds. Hervey White. HBV

I saw the Connaught Rangers when they were passing by. The Connaught Rangers. Winifred M. Letts. HBMV; TCEP

I saw the Conquerors riding by. The Conquerors. Harry Kemp. AnAmPo; BAP; ChIP; HBV; LA; LEAP; MaRV

I saw the constellated matin choir. Prelude. Edmund Clarence Stedman. AA

I saw the day's white rapture. Song. Charles Hanson Towne. HBV; OBAV

I saw the Devil's Darning Needle. Devil's Darning Needle. C. Lindsay McCoy. GFA

I saw the eyes, where Amor took his place. Sonnet. Guido Cavalcanti. LyPI

I saw the farmer plough the field. Harvest. M. M. Hutchinson. BoTP

I Saw the Figure of a Lovely Maid. Wordsworth. GEPC; LO
(Sonnet: "I saw the figure of a lovely maid.") UnW

I saw the first pear. Orchard [*or* Keeper of the Orchards]. Hilda Doolittle ("H. D."). AnFE; APA; AtBAP; BAP; CoAnAm; CoBA; ExPo; LEAP; LiTA; MAP; MoAmPo; OxBA; PoTo; SBMV

I saw the fog grow thick. The Fog. W. H. Davies. TiPo (1959 ed.); WaKn

I saw the ghostesses. Ghostesses. *Unknown.* ChTr

I saw the grave of Shakespeare in a dream. Shakespeare's Mourners. John Banister Tabb. AmP

I saw the green Spring. The Grey Spring. Alfred Noyes. BMEP

I saw the Lord Christ tonight. Inasmuch. William E. Brooks. PGD

I saw the Lord in a field where a humble laborer. The Laborer. Galatea Kazantzakis. MoGP

I saw the lovely arch. The Rainbow. Walter de la Mare. PtOT; TiPo

I saw the marsh-grass blowing. Marsh-Grass. Jessie B. Rittenhouse. TBM

I saw the Master of the Sun. He stood. The Sun God. Aubrey Thomas De Vere. ACP; BMEP; ES; OBVV; PoVP; TIP

I saw the meadow sweetly set. A Meadow and My Lady. Reinmar von Hagenau. LyMA

I saw the midlands. Kisses in the Train. D. H. Lawrence. MBP; MoAB; MoBrPo

I saw the moon,/ One windy night. Flying. J. M. Westrup. BoTP

I saw the moonlight before my couch. On a Quiet Night [*or* My Far-off Home]. Li Po. OnPM; WoL

I saw the mountain oak with towering form. Seek Those Things Which Are Above. William Newell. EOAH

I saw the object of my pining thought. Sonnet. Thomas Watson. *Fr.* The Tears of Fancy. EIL; TuPP

I saw the old man pause, then turn his head. The Old Conservative. L. Frank Tooker. EtS

I saw the Piper hanging on a tree. Pan Crucified. Leonora Speyer. BAP

I saw the pride of all the meadows. Narcissus. William Cowper. OTPC

I saw the Prince of Darkness, with his staff. At the Cenotaph [*or* Make Them Forget]. Siegfried Sassoon. ChMo; CMP; MaRV

I saw the racer coming to the jump. The Racer. John Masefield. PreP

I saw the ramparts of my native land. Sonnet: Death Warnings. Francisco Gómez de Quevedo y Villegas. AnSpL-1; AWP; JAWP; TeCS; WBP; WoL

I saw the shapes that stood upon the clouds. London Nightfall. John Gould Fletcher. MAP; MoAmPo; NeMA

I saw the shepherd fold the sheep. The Folded Flock. Wilfrid Meynell. CAW; GoBC; JKCP; TrPWD

I saw the sky descending, black and white. Where the Rainbow Ends. Robert Lowell. AmP; AnNE; CoBMV; FiMAP; MoAB; MoAmPo (1950 ed.); NePoEA; OnHM; TrGrPo (rev. ed.)

I saw the smiling bard of pleasure. Odes of Anacreon. *Tr. by* Thomas Moore. OuHeWo

I saw the Son of God go by. The Question. Rachel Annand Taylor. ChIP; HBV; MaRV

I saw the spiders marching through the air. Mr. Edwards and the Spider. Robert Lowell. AmP; MoAB; MoPo; MoVE; NePoEA; ReMP; SeCeV

I saw the spires of Oxford. The Spires of Oxford. Winifred M. Letts. BEL; BLP; BMEP; CV; EnLit; FaFP; HBV; HiLiEn; InP; LBBV; LEAP; MaRV; MCCG; NeHB; OHFP; OnYI; PoMa; PoRA; POT; PoTo; PYM; TCEP; TOP; TreF; VOD (1931 ed.); WGRP

I saw the spot where our first parents dwelt. The Garden. Jones Very. AmP; OxBA

I saw the sunlit vale. and the pastoral fairy-tale. The Sunlit Vale. Edmund Blunden. ChMP; GTBS-D; MoVE

I saw the swans fly westward to the hills. The Swans. John Irvine. UnW

I saw the throng, so deeply separate. A General Communion. Alice Meynell. JKCP
I saw the twinkle of white feet. Hebe. James Russell Lowell. AA; AnFE; AnNE; APA; CoAnAm; HBV; IAP; MOAP; TCAP
I Saw the Vision of Armies. Walt Whitman. WaaP
I saw the wild rose on its parent thorn. A Simile. Mrs. J. Hunter. DiM
I saw the wind to-day. Padraic Colum. SUS
I Saw the Winter Weaving. Jalal ed-Din Rumi, *tr. fr. Persian by* Professor Hastie. LiTW
I Saw Thee. Ray Palmer. HBV; LPS-2
I saw Thee in a dream, Beloved! Dream of Love. Bhai Vir Singh. OnPM
I saw thee on thy bridal day. To ——. Poe. IAP
I saw thee once, and nought discerned. The Discovery. Cardinal Newman. OBRV
I saw thee once—once only—years ago. To Helen. Poe. AmPo; CoV; IAP; UnW
I saw thee when, as twilight fell. I Saw Thee. Ray Palmer. HBV; LPS-2
I saw them chase the gypsies [*or* gipsies]. The Gypsies [*or* Gipsies]. "Richard Scrace." CaP; OCL
I saw them coming in the eyeless day. And the Dead. Sean Jennett. NeBP
I saw them from our car today. The Women Toilers. Grace Bowen Evans. OQP; QP-2
I saw them kissing in the shade and knew the sum of all my lore. The Young Lovers. Ridgely Torrence. *Fr.* The House of a Hundred Lights. AA
I saw them passing endlessly. Crucified. Patrick Dacus Moreland. StJW
I saw them shining in the sun. The Little Stones of Arlington. Barbara Young. OQP; QP-2
I saw them walk that lane again. On Seeing Swift in Laracor. Brinsley MacNamara. AnIV; OxBI
I saw these dreamers of dreams go by. The Gold-Seekers. Hamlin Garland. AA; FaBoBe; MC; OBAV; YaD
I saw this day sweet flowers grow thick. The Happy Child. W. H. Davies. AtBAP; POTE
I saw this eve the wandering sun. Prodigals. Charles L. O'Donnell. HBMV
I saw three black pigs riding. Girl's Song. W. W. Gibson. ChMo; CMP
I Saw Three Ships (*diff. versions*). *Unknown.* ACP; AnEC; BLPA; CAW; GoTP; HH; OBB; OTPC; OxBoCh; PRWS; SDH; WHL; WP
(As I Sat on a Sunny Bank.) ChTr; OxBoLi; OxNR
(As I Sat under a Sycamore Tree.) AnEC; ChBr; LiTB; ViBoPo
I saw three ships a-sailing. An Old Song Re-sung. Katharine Tynan. QS
I saw three ships come sailing by. Mother Goose. MeMeAg; OxNR; RIS
I Saw Three Witches. Walter de la Mare. HOAH
I saw thy beauty in its high estate. To a Magnolia Flower in the Garden of the Armenian Convent at Venice. Silas Weir Mitchell. AA; OBAV
I saw Time in his workshop carving faces. Time. Frederick George Scott. VA
I saw—'twas in a dream, the other night. Montefiore. Ambrose Bierce. AA; AnAmPo; BAP; LA; PFY
I Saw Two Clouds at Morning. John Gardiner Calkins Brainard. HBV; LPS-1; PoToHe
(Epithalamium.) AA
I Saw Two Lions. Clayton Hoff. TwCaPo
I saw where in the shroud did lurk. On an Infant Dying as Soon as Born. Charles Lamb. BCEP; EV-4; GTBS; GTBS-D; GTBS-W; GTSE; GTSL; MotAn; OBEV; OBRV
I saw with open eyes. Stupidity Street. Ralph Hodgson. AtBAP; BLA; BMEP; CaAE; CBOV; CH; ChMo; CMP; EnLit; HBV; LiTM (rev. ed.); MBP; MoAB; MoBrPo; NeMA; NP; PoeMoYo; PoFr; PtOT; PYM; SiSoSe; SP; TCEP; TOP; TreFS; TwCV; UTS; WP
I saw you dance that summer before the war. Grand Ballet. Frances Cornford. MoP
I saw you die. Murdered Little Bird. *Unknown.* FiBHP
I saw you down on the beach today. Two Stanzas about Eve. Herman Wildenvey. AnNoLy
I saw you go beyond the river to guard over the frontier. Gazing after Her Husband. Lu Yu. WhP
I saw you hunched and shivering on the stones. The Monkey. Nancy Campbell. NP; POT
"I saw you take his kiss!" "'Tis true." The Kiss [*or* Sly Thoughts]. Coventry Patmore. The Angel in the House, II, viii, 3. ALV; EnLoPo; FiBHP; LiTL; OBVV; PC
I saw you toss the kites on high. The Wind. Robert Louis Stevenson. BoTP; GBV (1922 ed.); GFA; GN; HBVY; MPB; OnHT; OTPC; PCH; PoVP; RAR; StVeCh; SUS; TiPo; YT
I say it, though none believe me. I say that clear for ever. The Artist's Last Word. Parrhasius. GrPE
I say it to comfort me over and over. The Cynic. Theodosia Garrison. AV; HBMV; PR
I say it under the rose. Thalia. Thomas Bailey Aldrich. AA; HBV; InMe; LHV; OBAV
I say no more for Clavering. Clavering. E. A. Robinson. CrMA; HBMV; OxBA
I say now, Fernando, that on a day. Hibiscus on the Sleeping Shores. Wallace Stevens. NP
I say, old man, your horse will die. Poor Old Man. *Unknown.* SoAmSa
I say that I am wise. Yet dead leaves know. Wisdom. Daniel Whitehead Hicky. OQP; QP-2
I say that I think for myself, but what is this Self of mine. Heir and Serf. Don Marquis. HBMV
I say, the acknowledgment of God in Christ. Robert Browning. *Fr.* A Death in the Desert. ChIP
I say the whole earth and all the stars in the sky. For Religion's Sake [*or* The Necessity of Religion]. Walt Whitman. *Fr.* Starting from Paumanok. GrCo-1; MaRV
I say to thee, do thou repeat. The Kingdom of God. Richard Chenevix Trench. WBLP
I say unto you: Cherish your doubts. Honest Doubt. Robert Weston. MaRV
I scarce believe [*or* beleeve] my love to be so pure. Love's Growth. John Donne. GTBS-W; MePo; NBE; ReEn; SeCV-1; TuPP
I Scarcely Grieve, O Nature! Henry Timrod. PoMa
I scarcely think. The Zoo. Humbert Wolfe. GBV (1952 ed.); MoShBr; WaKn
I search among the plain and lovely words. Definition. Grace Noll Crowell. PoToHe (new ed.)
I see—/ In the recess of the ruined garden. Song of Departing May. Rofu Miki. PoLJ
I see a blind man every day. The Blind Man. Margaret E. Sangster. PoToHe
I see a dog—no stone to shy at him. Dilemma. Bhartrihari. LiTW
I see a farmer walking by himself. The Farmer, 1917. Fredegond Shove. TwCV
I see a monster. The Mammon Monster. Charles Erskine Scott Wood. BAP
I see a nest in a green elm-tree. The Child and the World. Kate Douglas Wiggin. PPL
I see a schooner in the bay. Memory. Duncan Campbell Scott. BoCaPo (1948 ed.)
I See a Star That Plummets. Heine, *tr. fr. German by* Kurt J. Fickert. AnGP
I see a tiny fluttering form. The Southern Snow-Bird. William Hamilton Hayne. AA
I see a white river bird, and I see the women. By the River. Harold Lenoir Davis. NP
I see above each joy soon hover. Ended! Nikolaus Lenau. AnGP
I see all human wits. Shakespeare. Emerson. AnNE
I see amid the fields of Ayr. Robert Burns. Longfellow. PtP
I see an eagle winging to the sun. On the Death of a Kinsman. James Matthew Legaré. SPP
I see around me here. Wordsworth. *Fr.* The Excursion, I. OBRV
I see before me now a traveling army halting. Bivouac on a Mountain Side. Walt Whitman. AA; AmP; AmPo; APW; ChTr; CoBA; CoV; IAP; MDAH; MOAP; OxBA; Po; TCAP
I see before me the Gladiator lie. The Dying Gladiator. Byron. *Fr.* Childe Harold's Pilgrimage, IV. CBE
I see black dragons mount the sky. Shapes and Signs. James Clarence Mangan. ERP; OnYI; TIP
"I see by the pa-apers, Hennessy," said Mr. Dooley. The Poets at a House-Party. Carolyn Wells. PA
I see by the sun the day's getting on. The Sæter Girl's Sunday. Jörgen Moe. AnNoLy
I see enslavement to a mistress closing on me. Tibullus. Elegies, II, 4. LaP
I See Her. Bilhana, *formerly at. to* Chauras, *tr. fr. Sanskrit by* E. Powys Mathers. *Fr.* Black Marigolds. OnPM
I see her in the festal warmth to-night. Ursula. Robert Underwood Johnson. HBV
I see her on a lonely forest track. The Maroon Girl. Walter Adolphe Roberts. PoNe
I see him come from far. The Ballad of the Bore. Austin Dobson. VLEP
I see him old, trapped in a burly house. A Pauper. Allen Tate. LiTM
I see Him: on thy lap He lies. Dei Genitrix. Aubrey Thomas De Vere. IrPN
I see him sit, wild-eyed, alone. The Last Aboriginal. "Fiona Macleod." PoVP; VA
I See His Blood upon the Rose. Joseph Mary Plunkett. CAW; ChIP; GoBC; HBMV; JKCP; MaRV; MBP; NeHB; NV; OnYI; OQP; OxBI; QP-1; StJW; WGRP
I see Hunger watching at every house door. Cha Liang-cheng. *Fr.* Hungry China. LiTW

I see, I hear, I feel, I know, I rue. Fidessa, More Chaste than Kind, XLVII. Bartholomew Griffin. ReIE
I see in his last preached and printed booke. On John Donne's Book of Poems. John Marriott. CH
I see in you the estuary that enlarges and spreads. To Old Age. Whitman. InP
I see in your eyes. To a Certain Woman. Albert Rice. CDC
I See My Plaint. *At. to* John Harington. ElL
I see my way as birds their trackless way. Guidance. Robert Browning. *Fr.* Paracelsus. BPP
I see my white-faced sisters of the foul tenements. Sweat-Shop Slaves. Charles Erskine Scott Wood. BAP
I see no bird arise. My Sun-killed Tree. Marguerite Harris. GoYe
I see no equivalents. The Poet at Night-Fall. Glenway Wescott. LiTM (1946 ed.); NP
I see Phantoms of Hatred and of the Heart's Fullness and of the Coming Emptiness. W. B. Yeats. Meditations in Time of Civil War, VII. LiTB
I see skies more bright and blue. Sight. Cora Ball Moton. GoSl
I see that chance hath chosen me. Sir Thomas Wyatt. SiPS
I see that wreath which doth the wearer arm. To the Memory of My Friend, Ben Jonson. Henry King. BoFr
I See the Boys of Summer. Dylan Thomas. LiTB
I see the cloud-born squadrons of the gale. A Storm in the Distance. Paul Hamilton Hayne. AA; HiLiAm; OBAV
I see the curse on gestures proud and cold. The Curse. Shelley. *Fr.* Prometheus Unbound, I. PoFr
I see the dawn e'en now begin to peer. *Unknown. Fr.* Popular Songs of Tuscany. AWP
I see the dun, low western house. The Good Fates. Mark Van Doren. MuM
I See the Heavy Startled Hair. Bilhana, *formerly at. to* Chauras, *tr. fr. Sanskrit by* E. Powys Mathers. *Fr.* Black Marigolds. OnPM
I see the horses and the sad streets. The Eye. Allen Tate. LiTA
I see the house. My heart thyself contain! Astrophel and Stella, LXXXV. Sir Philip Sidney. SiPS
I see the moon. The Moon. *Unknown.* GoTP; OxNR; PCH; TiPo
I see the moonlight shining on my couch. Meditation on a Quiet Night. Li Po. WhP
I see the star-lights quiver. The Flight from the Convent. Theodore Tilton. AA
I see the wealthy miller yet. The Miller's Daughter. Tennyson. VLEP
I see the wild flowers, in their summer morn. John Clare. *Fr.* Summer Images. CoEV
I see thee ever in my dreams. The Karamanian Exile. James Clarence Mangan. IrPN; OBVV; TIP
I See Thee in a Thousand Pictures. "Novalis," *tr. fr. German* by Herman Salinger. *Fr.* Sacred Songs. AnGP
I see Thee in the distant blue. God. John Banister Tabb. MaRV
I see thee pine like her in golden story. Coleridge. Theodore Watts-Dunton. HBV; OBVV; PtP; VA
I see thee still! thou art not dead. A Remembrance. Willis Gaylord Clarke. AA
I see them a mother and daughter. On the Bridge of Athlone; a Prophecy. Donagh MacDonagh. OxBI
I see them all, far-linked in aeons past. Ancestral Ghosts. John W. Garvin. CPG
I see them—crowd on crowd they walk the earth. The Dead. Jones Very. AA; AnNE; APW; IAP; LEAP; OxBA; TCAP
I see them nightly in my sleep. Eyes of God. Hermann Hagedorn. HBMV; TBM
I see them on my trellises and walls. Wistaria Blossoms. Charles Dalmon. *Fr.* Three Pictures. TSW; TSWC
I see them totter in, the very old. In the Public Library. Althea Todd Alderson. BLP
I see they're packing up once more. Tabitha Soliloquizes. Minnie Leona Upton. CIV
I see thou holdest cheap two things. On the Sultan Mahmúd. Firdausi. LiTW
I see ye like a flooer. Lovely as a Flower. Heine, *tr. fr. German into Scottish by* Edwin Morgan. AnGP
I see you, a child. The Album. C. Day Lewis. ChMP; EnLoPo; FaBoEn; OxBI
I see you dart, swift pirate of the air. Hawk. Clinton Scollard. BLA
I see you in the silver. Arctic Tern in a Museum. Mary Effie Lee Newsome. PoNe
I see you, Juliet, still, with your straw hat. Farewell to Juliet. Wilfrid Scawen Blunt. The Love Sonnets of Proteus, XLVII. EnLoPo
I see you not, though well. Pedro Salinas, *tr. fr. Spanish by* Eleanor L. Turnbull. CoSP
I see you, Odysseus, with your hand in hiding. Polyxena. Euripides. *Fr.* Hecuba. OxBG
I see your face as on that calmer day. To My Mother. Robert Haven Schauffler. MOAH
I seek a being to invade. Impulses. Henri Michaux. OnHM
I seek a teacher and a rule. I Go to School. Sister Mary Madeleva. SaFP
I seek about this warld unstable. Of the Changes of Life. William Dunbar. EBSV
I seek but one thing—to make sure of You. Six Sonnets. Mary, Queen of Scots. DiM
I seek, in prayerful words, dear friend. God Bless You. *Unknown.* PoToHe
I seek salvation. Aleksandr Blok, *tr. fr. Russian by* V. de S. Pinto. BoRS
I Seek Thee in the Heart Alone. Herbert Trench. WGRP
I seem but a drudge, yet I pass any king. The Praise of Husbandry [*or* As True as Thy Faith, This Riddle Thus Saith]. Thomas Tusser. SiCE; TuPP
I seem to hear a long, undying "alas." Venetian Sonnets, V. August, Graf von Platen. AnGP
I Seem to See My Prison Walls. Bilhana, *formerly at. to* Chauras, *tr. fr. Sanskrit by* E. Powys Mathers. *Fr.* Black Marigolds. OnPM
I seen a dunce of a poet once, a-writin' a little book. Gelett Burgess. *Fr.* The Protest of the Illiterate. FiBHP
I seen her last night. A Lament. L. A. G. Strong. YT
I seize the sphery harp. I strike the strings. Enitharmon's Song. Blake. *Fr.* Vala. ChTr
I selfish and forsaken do still long for you. Deus Absconditus. Anne Ridler. FaBoMo
I sell clouds of many colours. Street Cry. Rafael Alberti. AnSpL-2; CoSP
I sell the best brandy and sherry. O'Tuomy's Drinking Song. John O'Tuomy. OnYI
I send a garland to my love. The Lover's Posy. Rufinus. AWP; JAWP; WBP
I send, I send here my supremest kiss. His Tears to Thamesis. Robert Herrick. OAEP
I send my heart up to thee, all my heart. In a Gondola. Robert Browning. BEL; BLV; BPN; EmBrPo; EPN; EtPaEn; GEPC; PoVP; REAL; TCEP; VA; ViBoPo; ViPo; VLEP
I Send Our Lady. Sister Mary Thérèse. ISi
I send thee a shell from the ocean beech. With a Nantucket Shell. Charles Henry Webb. AA
I send thee here a posy that my hand. Roses. Pierre de Ronsard. TrFP
I send thee here of ribbon a whole yard. *Unknown.* LO
I send thee myrrh, not that thou mayest be. Not of Itself but Thee. *Unknown.* AWP
I send thee, Rhodocleia, this garland's flowery splendour. "This Same Flower That Smiles To-Day." Rufinus. GrPE
I send to you a nosegay that but now. Pierre de Ronsard, *tr. fr. French by* Curtis Hidden Page. PrPoCR
I send you a box/ Of glowing pearls. Otomo no Yakamochi, *tr. fr. Japanese by* Kenneth Rexroth. OnPJ
I send you here a sort of allegory. To —— [with the Following Poem]. Tennyson. *Fr.* The Palace of Art. ViPo; ViPP
I send you here a wreath of blossoms blown. Roses. Pierre de Ronsard. AWP; JAWP; WBP
I sent a letter to my love. George Barker. *Fr.* The True Confession of George Barker. FaBoTw
I sent a ring—a little band. To Helene. George Darley. OBEV (1st ed.)
I Sent for Ratcliffe. Matthew Prior. *See* Remedy Worse than the Disease, The.
I sent my Collie to the wash. Nonsense Quatrains. Gelett Burgess. CenHV
I sent my love a parcel. By Parcels Post. George R. Sims. BOHV
I sent my love two roses—one. White Flag. John Hay. HBV; PR
I sent my Soul through the Invisible. The Soul Is All [*or* Heaven and Hell]. Omar Khayyám, *tr. by* Edward Fitzgerald. *Fr.* The Rubáiyát. MaRV; OnPM
I sent out invitations. Inviting Guests. Ch'eng-kung Sui. BoFr; TrCh
I sent thee to the frontiers, quickly tell. The Spanish Ships Reach Mexico. Dryden. *Fr.* The Indian Emperor, I, ii. BeR
I, Seraphion, hermit of Mount Athos. Seraphion. James K. Baxter. AnNZ
I Serve. Meinloh von Sevelingen, *tr. fr. German by* Jethro Bithell. OnPM; WoL
I Serve. *Unknown.* TMEV
I Serve a Mistress. Anthony Munday, *ad. fr. the Italian of* Luigi Pasqualigo. *Fr.* Fedele and Fortunio. ElL; LO (Fedele's Song.) ElSeCe; OBSC
I serve my master: you, and countless others. Who Is Free? Philemon. OxBG
I serve where I no truth can find. I Serve. *Unknown.* TMEV

I serve. With unaggressive mien. Ich Dien. Susie M. Best. OQP; QP-1
I Served in a Great Cause. Horace L. Traubel. AA; LEAP
"I served the great cause," *sel.* BAP
I served my time in [*or* on] the Black Ball Line. The Black Ball Line [*or* Blow, Boys, Blow]. *Unknown.* ABF; ShS (*vers.* IV); SoAmSa
I set a charm upon your hurrying breath. A Marriage Charm. Nora Hopper. HBV
I set a jumpy mouse trap. A Change of Heart. Valine Hobbs. SiSoSe
I set apart a day for wandering. A Day for Wandering. Clinton Scollard. CP; NV
I set my heart to sing of leaves. Anticipation. Lord De Tabley. GTBS-D
I set on this barren board. Choice. Muna Lee. NV; TBM
I shake my hair in the wind of morning. Triumph of Love. John Hall Wheelock. MAP; MoAmPo; NP
I shake-shake. Do Not Open until Christmas. James S. Tippett. ChBR
I shall always come to find you here. Orpheus. J. F. Hendry. NeBP
"I shall arise." For centuries. Resurgam. *Unknown.* WGRP
I shall be beautiful when you come back. Transformation. Jessie B. Rittenhouse. HBMV
"I shall be careful to say nothing at all." How She Resolved to Act. Merrill Moore. MAP; MoAmPo; MOAP; NeMA; PIAE
I Shall Be Loved as Quiet Things. Karle Wilson Baker. HBMV; MCCG; TBM
I Shall Be Satisfied. M. Behemb. BePJ
I shall be shapen. A Pair of Lovers. Jeanne Robert Foster. HBMV
I Shall Break a Heavy Bough. Gertrude Callaghan. TBM
I shall come back in ways I think you'll know. Unregenerate. Jacqueline Embry. HBMV
I shall come back to die. In This Dark House. Edward Davidson. OBMV
I shall come this way again. Auf Wiedersehen. Donald Jeffrey Hayes. CDC
I shall cry God to give me a broken foot. Flash Crimson. Carl Sandburg. MAP; MoAmPo
I shall die on Cotswold hills. Cotswold Hills. Mary Colborne-Veel. MM
I shall foot it. The Road and the End. Carl Sandburg. NP
I shall gather myself into myself again. The Crystal Gazer. Sara Teasdale. MAP; MoAmPo; NeMA
I shall go among red faces and virile voices. Cattle Show. "Hugh MacDiarmid." GoTS; MoBrPo; OBMV
I shall go as my father went. The Tenancy. Mary Gilmore. BoAV
I shall go away. And the birds will stay. The Last Journey. Juan Ramón Jiménez. TeCS
I Shall Go Back. Edna St. Vincent Millay. AnNE; MoAmPo; MOAP; NePA
(I Shall Go Back Again.) MAP
("I shall go back again to the bleak shore.") GTBS-W
I shall go by lightly. Who Goes By Lightly. Gertrude Callaghan. JKCP (1955 ed.)
I shall go down from the stark, gray-stone towers. Refuge. Hervey Allen. HBMV
I shall go forth one day to joust with death. The Last Tourney. Frederic F. Van de Water. BLP; HBMV
I shall go on the gypsies' road. The Gypsies' Road. Dora Sigerson Shorter. OBVV
I shall go out as all men go. I Accept. Harold Trowbridge Pulsifer. HBMV; OQP; QP-2
I shall go out when the light comes in. Death at Daybreak. Anne Reeve Aldrich. AA; OQP; QP-2
I shall hate you. Hatred. Gwendolyn Bennett. BANP; CDC
I shall have a gold room. Chanson d'Or. Ann Hamilton. HBMV
I shall have pearls blacker than caviar. Capriccio. Babette Deutsch. HBMV; TSW
I shall have three grey poplar trees above me when I sleep. The Three Poplars. Philip Francis Little. GTIV; OxBI
I Shall Laugh Purely. Robinson Jeffers. CrMA; LiTA; LiTM (rev. ed.); WaP
I shall lie hidden in a hut. Prophecy. Elinor Wylie. AnAmPo; LA; MOAP
I Shall Live On. Ralph S. Cushman. PSO
I Shall Live to Be Old. Sara Teasdale. MOAP
I shall make a song like your hair. Secret. Gwendolyn B. Bennett. CDC
I shall make a song of the Queen of Crete. The Queen of Crete. John Grimes. HBMV
I shall make offering in a new basket of marsh-grass. Intervals. Beatrice Ravenel. HBMV; TBM
I shall never forget my mother's voice singing. Now That Can Never Be Done. Sister Maris Stella. GoBC
I shall not ask Jean Jacques Rousseau. Pairing-Time Anticipated. William Cowper. BOHV
I Shall Not Be Afraid. Aline Kilmer. BAP; HBMV; JKCP; NP; PoeMoYo; VOD
I shall not call for help until they coffin me. Last Lines. Egan O'Rahilly. KiLC
I Shall Not Care. Sara Teasdale. AnEnPo; BAP; BTP; ChMo; CMP; HBV; LBMV; MAP; MoAmPo; NeMA; PFY; TCPD; TrGrPo; TwCV
I Shall Not Cry Return. Ellen M. H. Gates. HBV
I Shall Not Die. *Unknown, tr. fr. Irish by* Frank O'Connor. KiLC
I shall not die entirely from this earth. One Generation to Another. Carla Lanyon Lanyon. ReTS
I Shall Not Die for Thee. *Unknown, tr. fr. Modern Irish by* Douglas Hyde. AnIL; GTIV; MBP; OxBI
I shall not get my poem done. Karle Wilson Baker. *Fr.* Poet Songs. HBMV
I shall not go to the autumn woods again. Disillusion. Sister Mary Edwardine. JKCP (1955 ed.)
I shall not lie to you any more. The Modern Woman to Her Lover. Margaret Widdemer. BAP; HBMV; PR; TCAP
I Shall Not Make a Garment of My Grief. Roselle Mercier Montgomery. BLP; LS
I shall not miss the roses, fading. Grapes. Pushkin. OnPM; TrRV
I Shall Not Pass Again This Way ("The bread that bringeth strength"). Ellen H. Underwood. BLRP; MaRV; OQP; QP-1; TreF; WBLP
I Shall Not Pass This Way Again ("Through this toilsome world, alas!"). *Unknown.* BLPA; NeHB; TreFS
I Shall Not Pass This Way Again. Eva Rose York. FaFP; MaRV; OHFP; WBLP
I shall not say/ That I am busy. Work. Toyohiko Kagawa. SoLD
I shall not see the faces of my friends. The Dying Reservist. Maurice Baring. HBV
I shall not see thee. Dare I say. In Memoriam A. H. H., XCIII. Tennyson. EmBrPo; EPN; GEPC; ViPo; VLEP
I shall not see you for a hundred days. Parting. Robert Gittings. ES
I shall not tarry over scrolls. Bethlehem. Harry Webb Farrington. OQP; QP-2
I shall not tell, although of love I'm dying. Happy Martyrdom. Pierre de Ronsard. TrFP
I Shall Not Weep. Belle MacDiarmid. HBMV
I shall not wonder more, then. Change. Raymond Knister. BoCaPo; CaP; PeCV
I shall note first/ the ones I loved. The Chronicler. Alexander Bergman. TrJP
I Shall Remember. H. D. Carberry. PoNe
I shall remember then. Youth. Thomas S. Jones, Jr. BAP; OQP; QP-2
I shall saddle my [*or* a] horse. Old Man's Song. Aleksey Vasilyevich Koltsov. BoR; TrRV
I shall say, Lord, "Is it music, is it morning." Resurgam. Marjorie Pickthall. BoCaPo
I shall see a star tonight. Star Thought. Frances Shaw. NP
I shall slough my self as a snake its skin. "I." Louis Golding. TrJP
I shall steal upon her. Chanson Naïve. John McClure. HBMV
I shall strike you without anger. Heautontimoroumenos. Baudelaire. AnFP
I shall take flight from Death on sudden wings. The Victory. John Hall Wheelock. NP
I shall tell you. Strangers. Mark Turbyfill. NP
I shall unsheathe my soul. Manuel Altolaguirre, *tr. fr. Spanish by* Eleanor L. Turnbull. CoSP
I shall walk down the road. Death. Maxwell Bodenheim. AnAmPo; BAP; LA; LiTM; MAP; MAPA; MoAmPo (1942 ed.); NP; PFY; TrJP
I shall walk in the sun alone. To a Siamese Cat. Michael Joseph. PoC
I shall wear laughter on my lips. Hope. Anna Blake Mezquida. MaRV
I Shall Weep. Peretz Hirshbein, *tr. fr. Yiddish by* Joseph Leftwich. TrJP
I shall you tell a great marvel. What, Heard Ye Not. *Unknown.* AnEC
"I Shame to Wear a Heart So White." Euripides, *tr. fr. Greek by* Hugh Owen Meredith. *Fr.* Hecuba. GrR
I shape the vessel of my life. Misdirection. Eleanor Slater. MoSiPe
I sheath my sword. In mercy go. Victory. Aline Kilmer. MaRV
I shed no outward tears, but my heart wept. Meeting. Joseph Rodman Drake. UnW
I shepherd of boulevards. Clouds. Gerardo Diego. CoSP
I shipped, dy'e see, in a Revenue sloop. The Darned Mounseer. W. S. Gilbert. *Fr.* Ruddigore. TSW; TSWC
I shipped on board of th' *Ebenezer.* The *Ebenezer.* *Unknown.* ShS
I shiver, Spirit fierce and bold. At the Grave of Burns. Wordsworth. *Fr.* Memorials of a Tour in Scotland, 1803. BEL; BPN; EM-2; EmBrPo; EnLi-2; EnRP; ERP; GEPC; PtP

I shoot the Hippopotamus. The Hippopotamus. Hilaire Belloc. CenHV; FiBHP; ShBV-2; UTS; WhC
I shot a partridge in the air. The Birds and the Pheasant. *Unknown.* PA
I shot an arrow into the air. A Shot at Random. D. B. Wyndham Lewis. FaFP; FiBHP; SiTL
I shot an arrow into the air. The Arrow and the Song. Longfellow. AA; AnAmPo; AnNE; BAP; BBV (1951 ed.); BTP; DD; FaFP; HBV; HBVY; IAP; LA; LEAP; MaRV; NeHB; OBAV; OnHT; OQP; OTPC; PECK; PG (1933 ed.); PoToHe (new ed.); PTA-1; PYM; QP-2; TCAP; TreF; TSWC; TVSH
I shot him where the Rio flows. Marta of Milrone. Herman Scheffauer. SCC
I shot my friend to save my country's life. The Body Politic. Donald Hall. NePoEA
I should be wretched as a cold lone house. Stanyan Bigg. *Fr.* Night and the Soul. BMEP
I should grieve to desperation. Anacreon to the Sophist. "B. H." InMe
I should have cut my life. Eviction. Elizabeth Brewster. CaP
I should have seen the sign: "Fresh paint." Fresh Paint. Boris Pasternak. TrJP; TrRV
I should have thought. At Baia. Hilda Doolittle ("H. D."). AnFE; APA; CoAnAm; LiTA; MOAP; NP; TwAmPo
I should like a great lake of ale. The Feast of Saint Brigid of Kildare. *At. to* St. Bridget. CAW; OnYI
I should like to be a dancer. Caprice. Anne Morrow Lindbergh. DDA
"I should like to buy you a birthday present," said Billy to Betsy Jane. Betsy Jane's Sixth Birthday. Alfred Noyes. SiSoSe
I should like to creep. A Mona Lisa. Angelina Weld Grimké. CDC
I Should Like to Have a Great Pool of Ale. *At. to* St. Bridget. *See* Feast of Saint Brigid of Kildare, The.
I should like to imagine. Clair de Lune. Ford Madox Ford. BMEP
I should like to rise and go. Travel. Robert Louis Stevenson. FaBoCh; FaPON; GoBP; GoTP; LoGBV; MoShBr; MPB; OnHT; PoVP; StVeCh; TiPo; WaKn
I should like to see that country's tiled bedrooms. Keeping Their World Large. Marianne Moore. WaP
I should not dare to be so sad. Emily Dickinson. InPo; MOAP
I should not have waited. Lady Akazome Emon, *tr. fr. Japanese by* Kenneth Rexroth. OnPJ
I should not say. Thomas Lovell Beddoes. *Fr.* The Second Brother, II, i. AtBAP
I should not wonder. *Unknown.* *Fr.* Abusive Snatches. SiB
I should rather say one prayer to the Mother of God. Preference. Daniel Sargent. ISi
I should worry, I should care. *Unknown.* ExPo
I shut the careful door of my room and leave. Election Day. Patricia K. Page. BoCaPo (1948 ed.)
I sicken of men's company. The Green Inn. Theodosia Garrison. HBMV; NLK
I Sigh All the Night. Edward Ravenscroft. *Fr.* The Citizen Turned Gentleman. SeCL
I sigh for the heavenly country. The Heavenly City. Stevie Smith. FaBoTw
I Sigh for the Land of the Cypress and Pine. Samuel Henry Dickson. SPP; TCAP
I sighed [*or* sigh'd] and owned [*or* own'd] my love. *Unknown.* EG; GTBS-W
I, sighing o'er the happy past. George Henry Boker. *Fr.* The Book of the Dead. MOAP
I sing a legend of the sea. The Captain and the Mermaids. W. S. Gilbert. YT
I Sing a Maiden. *Unknown.* *See* I Sing of a Maiden.
I sing a song of sixpence, and of rye. An Ode. Anthony C. Deane. PA
I Sing an Old Song. Oscar Williams. LiTM; NePA
I sing. But do I really sing? My Voice. "Demyan Bedny." RuPo
I sing divine Astrea's praise. A Dialogue between Two Shepherds. Thenot and Piers, in Praise of Astrea. Countess of Pembroke. ReIE
I sing no longer of the skies. The Song of the King's Minstrel. Richard Middleton. HBV
I Sing No New Songs. Frank Marshall Davis. PoNe
I sing no out-of-date matter. "Contemporaneity." Timotheus. GrPE
I sing not of Angelica the fair. Richard Barnfield. *Fr.* Lady Pecunia; or, The Praise of Money. ReIE
I sing not of the draper's praise, nor yet of William Wood. An Excellent New Song upon His Grace Our Good Lord Archbishop of Dublin. Swift. CoMu
I sing not old Jason, who travell'd thro' Greece. Down-Hall; a Ballad. Matthew Prior. CEP
I sing of a frigate, a frigate of fame. The Flash Frigate. *Unknown.* AmSS; SG
I Sing of a Maiden. *Unknown.* AtBAP; BoW; CaAE; CH; EG; EV-2; ExPo; FaBoCh; GoTP; InPo; ISi; KN; LiTB; LoGBV; MeEV; PoEL-1; SDH; SeCeV; TreFS; TrGrPo; TyEnPo; ViBoPo
(As Dew in April.) AnEC
(Carol: "I sing of a Maiden.") CBOV; CoEV; MotAn; OBEV; OxBoCh; PoLi; ShBV-2; ThWaDe
(Carol to Our Lady.) CAW; GoBC
(I Sing a Maiden.) OnPM
(I Syng[e] of a Mayden.) BrBE; OAEP
(Maiden Makeles, The.) ChTr
(Mother and Maiden.) BLV
(On the Virgin.) LiA
(Two Carols to Our Lady, 1.) ACP
Ancient Christmas Carol, An, *sel.* OHIP; PCH; RG
(Carol: "He came all so still.") BoTP; DD; HBV; HBVY
I sing of autumn and the falling fruit. Ship of Death. D. H. Lawrence. KN; MoAB; NAMP; ViBoPo
I sing of brooks, of blossom[e]s, birds, and bowers. The Argument of His Book [*or* His Theme]. Robert Herrick. *Fr.* Hesperides. AtBAP; AWP; BEL; BLV; BoLiVe; BrBE; CoBE; ElSeCe; EM-1; EnL; EnLi-1; EnLit; EPS; HBV; HBVY; InP; InPo; InvP; LEAP; MyFE; OAEP; OBS; PoE; PoEL-3; PoRA; ReEn; SeCePo; SeCeV; SeCV-1; SeEP; TrGrPo; TyEnPo; ViBoPo; WHA
I sing of Dionysus, an old story. To Dionysus. *Unknown.* *Fr.* Homeric Hymns. OxBG
I sing of George Augustus Chadd. The Ballad of Private Chadd. A. A. Milne. CenHV
I sing of ghosts and people under ground. The End. Mark Van Doren. ViBoPo
I sing of men and angels, and the days. Ebenezer Elliott. *Fr.* Spirits and Men. OBRV
I sing of Olaf [Glad and Big]. E. E. Cummings. AmP; LiTA; LiTM; NePA; SiTL; WaP
I sing of Pope. A Dialogue. Austin Dobson. BPN; PoVP
I sing of sorrow. Borrower. Mary Carolyn Davies. *Fr.* A Girl's Songs. SBMV
I sing of the cliffs that descend to. Sorrento. Carl Snoilsky. AnSL
I sing of the decline of Henry Clay. Conquistador. A. D. Hope. MoAuPo
I sing of the Good Samaritan. The Song of the Good Samaritan. Vernon Watkins. LiTM (rev. ed.)
I sing of the life of the wild sea-gulls. Sea Gulls. R. W. Page. CAG
I sing the birth was born tonight. A Hymn[e] on [*or* for *or* of] the Nativity of My Saviour [*or* Savior]. Ben Jonson. AnEC; COAH; EV-2; SDH; SeCV-1; StJW
I Sing the Body Electric. Walt Whitman. AmPo
I sing the civil wars, tumultuous broils. Samuel Daniel. *Fr.* The Civil Wars. ReIE
I sing the fates of Gebir. Walter Savage Landor. Gebir, I. BPN
I sing the first green leaf upon the bough. Song in March. Clinton Scollard. NLK
I sing the glorious power with azure eyes. Hymn to Athena. *Unknown.* *Fr.* Homeric Hymns. AWP
I sing the hymn of the conquered, who fell in the battle of life. Io Victis! William Wetmore Story. AA; APW; GrCo-2; HBV; MaRV; OQP; QP-2; WGRP
I sing the man who Judah's scepter bore. Abraham Cowley. *Fr.* Davideis, I. SeEP
I sing the Name which none can say. Hymn to [the Name above Every Name] the Name of Jesus. Richard Crashaw. LEAP; NBE; SeCV-1
I sing the praise of honored wars. The Soldier's Song. *Unknown.* ElSeCe; ReEn; TuPP
I sing the sofa, I, who lately sang. The Sofa. William Cowper. *Fr.* The Task. CEP; OAEP
I sing the song of a new dawn waking. Song of the New World. Angela Morgan. BAP; CP; CV; HBMV; HBVY; OQP; QP-2
I sing the song of the workman. The Song of Labor. Ninette M. Lowater. PEDC
I sing the uplift and the up-welling. The Redeeming Mercy. Israel Zangwill. *Fr.* Jehovah. GrCo-2; WGRP
I sing to him that rests below. In Memoriam A. H. H., XXI. Tennyson. BPN; EmBrPo; EnL; EnLi-2; EPN; GEPC; RiBV; ViPo; VLEP
I sing what was lost and dread what was won. What Was Lost. W. B. Yeats. POTE
I sing with myself. Duet. Leonora Speyer. BAP; HBMV; PC
I, singularly moved. Winter. Coventry Patmore. The Unknown Eros, I, iii. LEAP; LO; NBE; POTT; VLEP
I Sit Alone. Walter de la Mare. POTE
I sit alone and listen. Kijo, *tr. fr. Japanese by* Lois J. Erickson. SoLD
I sit alone and silent. Gethsemane. *Unknown.* SoLD
I sit among my flasks and jars. The Story of the Alchemist. Eugene Williams. PCD
I sit and dream. Lost Happiness. Chang Miao Ching. PoHN

I Sit and Look Out. Walt Whitman. MaRV; OxBA
I Sit and Sew. Alice Dunbar Moore Nelson. CDC
I Sit as I Have Always Sat. Holger Drachmann, *tr. fr. Danish by* Charles W. Stork. BoDS
I sit at eve within the curtain's fold. L'Angelo. Thomas Caulfield Irwin. IrPN
I sit at home. Hitomaro, *tr. fr. Japanese by* Kenneth Rexroth. OnPJ
I sit at home and sew. Needle Travel. Margaret French Patton. HBMV
I sit at the door between two worlds. Heaven and Earth. Annabel Ledlie Berry. DDA
I sit beside my darling's grave. To God and Ireland True. Ellen O'Leary. TIP; VA
I sit beside the brazier's glow. Before Action. W. W. Gibson. BEL; ChMo; CMP; TOP; TwCV; VOD (1931 ed.)
I sit by the trail in the misty moonlight. Six Yoke. Edwin Ford Piper. NV
I sit forsaken in the evening chill. In Absence. Benedikt Gröndal. IcP
I sit here at the window. Poetry and Thoughts on Same. Franklin P. Adams. HBMV
I sit in an office at 244 Madison Avenue. Spring Comes to Murray Hill. Ogden Nash. FiBHP
I sit in my garden among the roses. Prisoners. Nancy Barr Mavity. HBMV
I sit in one of the dives. September 1, 1939. W. H. Auden. CoBMV; ExPo; FaBoEn; InPo; LiTA; LiTM; MaPo; MoAB; MoBrPo (1950 ed.); MoVE; NePA; OAEP (2d ed.); OxBA; PoFS; ReMP; SeCeV; TwHP; WaP
I sit in sad soliloquy. Melancholia. Louis J. Karnosh. PoP
I sit in the dusk. I am all alone. Tableau at Twilight. Ogden Nash. FiBHP
I sit in the early twilight. A Lifetime. Bryant. IAP
I sit on the back platform of the train. The Train Butcher. Thomas Hornsby Ferril. GoYe
I sit on the surge called ten stories tall. The Seesaw. Oscar Williams. LiTA; LiTG
I sit through the long night. Night Rain. Ch'eng Wang. PoHN
I Sit with My Dolls. *Unknown, tr. fr. Yiddish by* Joseph Leftwich. TrJP
I sleep and rest, my heart makes moan. Seven Times Five—Widowhood. Jean Ingelow. *Fr.* Songs of Seven. GBV (1922 ed.); HBV
I Sleep, but My Heart Waketh. The Song of Solomon, V: 2–VI: 3, Bible, *O.T.* TrJP
I sleep with thee and wake with thee. To Mary. John Clare. EnLoPo
I slept and dreamed that life was Beauty. Duty. Ellen S. Hooper. BLPA; HBV; LPS-2; NeHB; OQP; QP-1; TreFS
I slept. I dreamed. I seemed to climb a hard, ascending track. Africa. *Unknown.* MaRV; StJW
I slept in a sleepy field. Airship. Hy Sobiloff. NePA
I slept in an old homestead by the sea. Chimney Swallows. Horatio Nelson Powers. HBV; OTPC (1923 ed.)
I slept in spring not conscious of the dawn. Spring Dawn. Li Po. WhP
I slumbered, and the white waves washed me thus. Loneliness. Nikolai Gumilev. BoR
I smile to see how you devise. A Proper Sonnet Intituled: I Smile to See How You Devise. *Unknown.* ReIE
I so love water laughter. Streams. Clinton Scollard. NLK; PoMa
I so loved once, when Death came by I hid. The Rival. James Whitcomb Riley. LBMV
I sometimes hold it half a sin. In Memoriam A. H. H., V. Tennyson. BPN; EM-2; EmBrPo; EnLi-2; EPN; GEPC; LPS-1; OAEP; OuHeWo; ViPo; VLEP
I Sometimes Think. *Unknown. See* To Be or Not to Be.
I sometimes think I'd like to be. The Best of All. Margaret G. Rhodes. BoTP
I sometimes think I'd rather crow. To Be or Not to Be. *Unknown.* AlDL; BOHV; FaFP; GoTP; LiTM; MoShBr; SiTL
I sometimes think that I will. Don Marquis. Grotesques, III. FiBHP
I sometimes think that mountains are not worth. Praise of Engineers. James J. Donohue. JKCP (1955 ed.)
I sometimes think that never blows so red. So Red the Rose. Omar Khayyám, *tr. by* Edward Fitzgerald. *Fr.* The Rubáiyát. InP; LO; OnPM
I sometimes think Thou art my secret love. Weariness. William Alexander Percy. *Fr.* In New York. SPP
I sometimes walk uncharted ways. The Wayfarer. Verna Loveday Harden. PSO
I sometimes wonder if it's really true. Hill-born. W. W. Gibson. NP
I sometimes wonder where he lives. Echo. *Unknown.* GFA
I sought a soul in the sea. Jalal ed-Din Rumi, *tr. fr. Persian by* A. J. Arberry. PeP
I sought a theme and sought for it in vain. The Circus Animals' Desertion. W. B. Yeats. ChMo; FaBoTw; LiTB; OAEP (2d ed.)
I sought for Peace, but could not find. Peace [*or* On Peace]. *At. to* Samuel Speed. OxBoCh; SeCL; SeEP
I sought Him in a great cathedral, dim. Search. Anne Marriott. MaRV
I sought Him in the still, far place where flowers blow. God's Way. Dorothy Clarke Wilson. MaRV
I sought Him where my logic led. The Search. Sara Henderson Hay. MaRV
I sought his love in sun and stars. The Search. Thomas Curtis Clark. MaRV; WGRP
I sought immortality. The Crib. Christopher Morley. FAOV
I Sought My Soul. *Unknown.* MaRV
I sought not from thee a return. Abraham Cowley. *Fr.* The Vain-Love. LO
I sought of bishop and priest and judges. On Christians, Mercy Will Fall. *Unknown. Fr.* The Black Book of Carmarthen. PrWP
I Sought on Earth. George Santayana. Sonnets, I. AnEnPo (Sorrow.) WGRP
I Sought the Living God. John Calvin Slemp. ChIP
I Sought the Lord. *Unknown.* MaRV
I sought Thee round about, O Thou my God. The Search for God. Thomas Heywood. *Fr.* Hierarchie of the Blessed Angels. MaRV; OxBoCh; WGRP
I sought to hear the voice of God. The Voice of God. Louis I. Newman. OQP; PoToHe; QP-2; TreF
I sought to hold her, but within her eyes. The Angel at the Ford. William James Dawson. VA
I sought you through the world. Pilgrim. Ibn al-Batti. MooP
I sowed the seeds of love. The Seeds of Love. *Unknown, at. to* Mrs. Fleetwood Habergham. FaBoCh; LoGBV; OxBoLi, *sl. diff.*
I span and Eve span. Eve Song. Mary Gilmore. MoAuPo
I speak/ Not for myself, but for the age unborn. The Torch Bearers. Alfred Noyes. *Fr.* Watchers of the Sky. GrCo-1
I speak for all—for them that fly. Praise. Christopher Smart. RO
I speak for each no-tonguéd tree. Sidney Lanier. *Fr.* The Symphony. ViBoPo
I speak of that famed damsel, by whose spear. Ariosto. *Fr.* Orlando Furioso, II. PrPoCR
I speak of that great house. Beyond the Hunting Woods. Donald Justice. NePoEA
I speak of wants, of frauds, of policies. De Subiecto Operis Sui. Thomas Bastard. SiCE
I speak this poem now with grave and level voice. Immortal Autumn. Archibald MacLeish. BoLiVe (1945 ed.); ChMo; CMP; CoBMV; LiTA; MAP; MoAB; MoAmPo; NeMA; NP; ReaPo; ReMP; TrGrPo; TwCV
I speak with a proud tongue of the people who were. Slainthe [*or* Dedication]. Patrick MacGill. AnIV; LBBV; OnYI
I Spend My Days Vainly. Frank Kendon. MBP; MoBrPo (1942 ed.); POTE
I spend my sad life in sighs and in cries. To Celia. Daniel Kenrick. SeCL
I spent a night in the Green Hill. Night in the Green Hill. Clara Platt Meadowcroft. BAP
I spent a night turning in bed. The Whip. Robert Creeley. NeAP
I spied beside the garden bed. In the Garden. Ernest Crosby. HBV; HBVY
I spoiled the day. A Wasted Day. Frances Cornford. HBMV; MBP; MoBrPo; NeMA; TSW; TSWC
I spoke the sea, that reaches green. Gray shore. James Rorty. EtS; MOAP
I spoke to the pale and heavy-lidded woman, and said. The Pale Woman. Arthur Symons. FaBoTw
I Spoke to the Violet. John Shaw Neilson. BoAV
I spoke to thee. Orientale. E. E. Cummings. NP; PG; TBM
I spot the hills. Theme in Yellow. Carl Sandburg. MPB; PCD; StVeCh (1955 ed.); TiPo; YeAr
I sprang to the rollocks and Jorrocks and me. How I Brought the Good News from Aix to Ghent (or Vice Versa). Robert Julian Yeatman *and* Walter Carruthers Sellar. FiBHP; WhC
I sprang to the stirrup, and Joris, and he. How They Brought the Good News from Ghent to Aix. Robert Browning. BBV (1923 ed.); BEL; BeLS; BMEP; BoChLi; BPN; CG; EM-2; EmBrPo; EnLi-2 (1949 ed.); EPP; EV-5; FaBoBe; FaFP; GEPC; GN; GoTP; HBV; HBVY; HoPM; LPS-2; MCCG; MW; OnHT; OnSP; PCD; PECK; PFE; PoVP; PYM; ShBV-1; StVeCh; TCEP; TiPo (1952 ed.); TOP; TreF; TSWC; TVSH; VA; ViPo; ViPP; VLEP
I Spy. N. E. Hussey. BoTP
I staid the night for shelter at a farm. *See* I stayed the night . . .
I stand above a white-rimmed sea. The Sea of Peace. Ruth McEnery Stuart. MaRV

I stand alone through each long day. The Blind Peddler [*or* Pedlar]. Sir Osbert Sitwell. BMEP; MBP; MoBrPo (1942 ed.)

I stand amid the roar. A Dream within a Dream. Poe. ChTr; RO

I stand and watch. Waiting. Ts'ui Ying Ying. ChLP; PoHN

I stand before your cage to make my sketch. Artist and Ape. Gordden Link. GoYe

I stand beneath the tree, whose branches shade. St. John's, Cambridge. Longfellow. OBEV

I stand beside a comrade tree. At Lanier's Grave. John Banister Tabb. AmP

I stand between them and the outer winds. Mater in Extremis. Jean Starr Untermeyer. TBM

I Stand Corrected. Margaret Fishback. WhC

I stand here every afternoon. The Balloon Man. E. Herbert. BoTP

I stand high in the belfry tower. On the Tower. Annette von Droste-Hülshoff. AnGP

I stand in my door and look over the low field[s] of Drynam. The Widow of Drynam. Patrick MacDonogh. NeIP; OnYI; OxBI

I stand in the dark light in the dark street. Birthplace Revisited. Gregory Corso. NeAP

I stand in the forest shadows. At Night. Joseph von Eichendorff. AnGP

I stand most humbly. Wisdom. Langston Hughes. TiPo

I stand on the cliff and watch the veiled sun paling. The Voice of Nature. Robert Bridges. ChMo; CMP; PoVP

I stand on the mark, beside the shore. The Runaway Slave at Pilgrim's Point. Elizabeth Barrett Browning. PoNe

I stand on the rim of the world. The Soul of Man Seeketh. John W. Garvin. CPG

I stand serene beside the struggling marts. Your Sanctuary. Walter Lyman French. MaRV

I stand upon the summit of my life. Thalatta! Thalatta! Joseph Brownlee Brown. AA; BAP; BTP; HBV; LBAP

I stand upon the threshold of two years. Backward—Forward. *Unknown.* BLRP

I stand with roses beside the highway. Introductory Song. Carl Snoilsky. *Fr.* Travel Scenes. AnSL

I stand within the stony, arid town. The City Tree. Isabella Valancy Crawford. CaP; OCL

I started early, took my dog. Emily Dickinson. AnAmPo; LA; PoEL-5; ThWaDe
(By the Sea.) LiTA; LiTM (rev. ed.)

I started on a journey just about a week ago. I Want to Go to Morrow. *Unknown.* PTA-1

I started on the trail on June twenty-third. The Lone Star Trail. *Unknown.* AS; CSF

I started out with Maw and Paw. The Bank of the Arkansaw. *Unknown.* OuSiCo

I staun at the winnock, my een are on thon sea. Tuscan Folk Songs, 6. *Unknown, tr. into Scottish by* Edwin Morgan. LyPI

I staun at the winnock, the sea-faem blins my een. Tuscan Folk Songs, 1. *Unknown, tr. into Scottish by* Edwin Morgan. LyPI

I staun at the winnock, the sea liggs ootby. Tuscan Folk Songs, 10. *Unknown, tr. into Scottish by* Edwin Morgan. LyPI

I stayed [*or* staid] the night for shelter at a farm. The Witch of Coös. Robert Frost. *Fr.* Two Witches. AmP; AnNE; AtBAP; CoBMV; DaM; ExPo; LiTM (rev. ed.); MoAB; NePA; ReMP; ViBoPo (1958 ed.)

I steadfastly will. To Safeguard the Heart from Sadness. Sarah N. Cleghorn. PC

I steal across the sodden floor. The Dream House. Marjorie Allen Seiffert. HBMV

I stepped from plank to plank. Emily Dickinson. Po

I still bear in mind the picture of the globe. The Philosophic Apology. Samuel Greenberg. MoPo; NePA

I still keep open Memory's chamber; still. Memory. Earl of Rosslyn. VA

I stirred not, but stood long and pondered. Afanasi Afanasievich Fet, *tr. fr. Russian by* Sir Cecil Kisch. WaL

I Stole Brass. *Unknown.* ChTr

I stole forth dimly in the dripping pause. Moon Compasses. Robert Frost. CoV; MoVE

I stole through the dungeons, while everyone slept. Alternative Endings to an Unwritten Ballad. Paul Dehn. FiBHP

I stood and leant upon the mast. The Voyage. Heine. AWP

I stood and saw my mistress dance. Upon His Mistress [*or* M.] Dancing. James Shirley. SeCL; SeEP

I stood at eve, as the sun went down, by a grave where a woman lies. 'Ostler Joe. George R. Sims. BeLS; BLPA; HBV; TreF

I stood at sunset on a gentle hill. Sympathy. James B. Kenyon. UnW

"I stood at the back of the shop, my dear." At the Draper's. Thomas Hardy. *Fr.* Satires of Circumstance. EnLi-2 (1949 ed.); MBP; MoAB; MoBrPo; NeMA

I stood at the foot of Rocky Carradon. Rapture on the Cornish Hills. Robert Stephen Hawker. EnSW

I stood before the bars of Fate. The Bars of Fate. Ellen M. H. Gates. BLP

I stood beside a hill. February Twilight. Sara Teasdale. FaPON; MoSiPe; YeAr

I stood beside a pool, from whence ascended. Sonnet. Richard Chenevix Trench. IrPN

I stood beside the grave of him who blazed. Churchill's Grave. Byron. EmBrPo

I stood between two mirrors when you died. Elegy. William Jay Smith. NePoEA

I stood by the Holy City. At Jerusalem. Edna Dean Proctor. BPP

I stood by the window while she made the bed. North and South. Florida Watts Smyth. StaSt

I stood in a meadow. Green Valley. Dorothy Vena Johnson. PoNe

I stood in the gloom of a spacious [spurious, *wr.*] room. Awake, My Lute! C. S. Lewis. BoN; CenHV

I stood in the ride, and the glamour. My Woodcock. Patrick Reginald Chalmers. CenHV

I stood in Venice on the Bridge of Sighs. Venice [*or* Refuge in Venice]. Byron. *Fr.* Childe Harold's Pilgrimage, IV. BEL; BPN; EnRP; EPN; ERP; EV-4; HBV; MCCG; OAEP; OBRV; TCEP; ViBoPo

I stood on a mighty mountain. Ich Stand auf Hohen Berge. Charles *and* Janet Ashbee. SG

I stood on a roof top and they wove their cage. On the Pilots Who Destroyed Germany in the Spring of 1945. Stephen Spender. NeBP; Po

I stood on Brocken's sovran height, and saw. Lines Written in the Album at Elbingerode. Samuel Taylor Coleridge. BPN; EmBrPo

I Stood on the Bridge. *Unknown.* LiTG
("I stood on the bridge at midnight.") FaFP; SiTL

I stood on the bridge at midnight. The Bridge. Longfellow. BPP; CoBA; HBV; IAP; REAL; SN; TCAP; TreF

I stood on the shore of the beautiful sea. The Sorrow of the Sea. *Unknown.* PEOR

I stood on the sidewalk in Tucson. Arizona Nights: Rodeo Parade. Berta Hart Nance. HiLiAm

I stood one day by the breezy bay. A Nautical Extravagance [*or* Extravaganza]. Wallace Irwin. MW; StPo; StVeCh

I stood, one Sunday morning. London Churches. Richard Monckton Milnes. LPS-1

I stood still and was a tree amid the wood. The Tree. Ezra Pound. APA; ChMo; CMP; CoAnAm; InPo; MOAP; TwAmPo

I Stood Tiptoe [upon a Little Hill]. Keats. EmBrPo; EnRP; ERP; EV-4; FaPON; GEPC
Sels.
"How silent comes the water round that bend." MyFE
(From the Bridge, *br. sel.*) PCH
(Minnows.) FaPON; GN; GoTP; RIS
"I stood tiptoe upon a little hill," *first* 14 *ll.* OTPC
(Sigh of Silence, The.) GN
(Upon a Hill, 22 *ll.*) RIS; StaSt
Marigolds. ADAH
Sweet Peas. ADAH; GN; MPB (1956 ed.); PCH

I stood upon a beach one starry night. Ecstasy. Victor Hugo. TrFP

I stood upon a church spire. The Poets at a House-Party. Carolyn Wells. PA

I Stood upon a High Place. Stephen Crane. The Black Riders, IX. AmP; LiTA; NePA

I stood upon a lawn whose greensward spread. Sir Charles Abraham Elton. *Fr.* Boyhood. EnSW

I stood upon a shore, a pleasant shore. The Shell's Song. Keats. EtS

I stood upon the Plain. The Plains of Abraham. Charles Sangster. CPG

I stood upon the threshold. Prayer. George Sylvester Viereck. BAP; LPS-1

I stood where Love in brimming armfuls bore. Love's Baubles. Dante Gabriel Rossetti. The House of Life, XXIII. PoVP; ViPo

I stood with the Dead. Siegfried Sassoon. ChMP

I stood within the city disinterred. Shelley. *Fr.* Ode to Naples. EPN

I stood within the cypress gloom. Implora Pace. Charles Lotin Hildreth. AA; TBV

I stood within the heart of God. Pandora's Song. William Vaughn Moody. *Fr.* The Fire-Bringer. AnFE; APA; BAP; CBOV; CoAnAm; GBV; IAP; LBAP; MAP; MoAmPo (1942 ed.); MOAP; OQP; QP-1; QS; WGRP

I stoop to gather a seabird's feather. The Feather. Vernon Watkins. FaBoTw; MoVE

I stooped to the silent earth and lifted a handful of her dust. A Handful of Dust. James Oppenheim. BAP; LEAP; TrJP

I stopped for him. The Rabbit. John Lewisohn. PCD

I stopped to watch a man strike at the trunk. The Axe in the Wood. Clifford Dyment. POTE

I strayed along the strand with mussels strewn. Along the Strand. Alfred Mombert. TrJP
I stretch My Thoughts. Jeanette E. Perkins. PraP
I strive to live my life in whitest truth. George Henry Boker. *Fr* Sonnets; a Sequence of Profane Love. MOAP
I strolled beside the shining sea. The Cumberbunce. Paul West. BOHV; NA
I strove, O Lord, to grasp a star for Thee. Failure. Mary Sinton Leitch. ChIP
I Strove with None. Walter Savage Landor. *See* On His Seventy-fifth Birthday.
I struck for what I deemed the right. After the Battle. George Sylvester Viereck. GoYe
I struck the board, and cried [*or* cry'd], "No more!" The Collar. George Herbert. AtBAP; ATP; AWP; BEL; BrBE; CaAE; CoBE; CoEV; ElSeCe; EM-1; EnL; EnLi-1; EnLit; EPP; EPS; EV-2; ExPo; FaBoEn; GTBS-W; HBV; InPo; JAWP; KN; LiTB; LiTG; LoBV; MaPo; MaRV; MeLP; MePo; NBE; OAEP; OBS; OuHeWo; OxBoCh; PC; PoE; PoEL-2; PoFS; PoRA; PreP; ReEn; RiBV; SeCePo; SeCeV; SeCL; SeCV-1; SeEP; TCEP; TOP; TrGrPo; TwCrTr; TwHP; TyEnPo; UnPo (1st ed.); ViBoPo; WBP; WHA
I struck the trail in seventy-nine. The Gal I Left behind Me. *Unknown.* ABF; CoSo; CSF
I studied my tables over and over. A Mortifying Mistake [*or* A Little Mistake]. Anna Maria Pratt. AA; DDA; HBV; HBVY; OnHT; RIS
I stumble, groping in the labyrinth of laughter. For a Young Musician. Marion Eells. CAG
I Stumbled upon Happiness. DuBose Heyward. LS
I suddenly saw I was wrang when I felt. Deep-Sea Fishing. "Hugh MacDiarmid." SeCePo
I suffered so much from printer's errors. The Author's Epitaph. *Unknown.* FiBHP
I summon to the winding ancient stair. A Dialogue of Self and Soul. W. B. Yeats. ExPo; FaBoMo; LiTB; LiTM; MoP; OAEP (2d ed.); Po; ReMP
I sundry see, for beauty's gloss. That He Findeth Others as Fair, but Not So Faithful as His Friend. George Turberville. ElL; ElSeCe; SiCE; TuPP
I suppose it just depends on where you're raised. The Mallee Fire. Charles Henry Souter. BoAu
I swear, Aurora, by thy starry eyes. Earl of Stirling. Aurora, Sonnet X. EV-2
I swear by swayings of that form so fair. The Mock Caliph. *Unknown. Fr.* The Book of a Thousand Nights and a Night. EnLi-1
I swear I have not deliberately returned to the street. July Avenue. Jorge Luis Borges. TwSpPo
I sweare to thee I will begone. *Unknown.* SeCSL
I sweat and tremble when I see. Glad Flow'ring Time. Mimnermus. GrR
I sweep the cloisters. Hide and Seek. Sister Mary Philip. PraNu
I sweep the street and lift me hat. The Old Man at the Crossing. L. A. G. Strong. OBMV
I swept my house of life and garnished it. Perfection. Ruth Scofield Fargo. OQP; QP-2
I Syng of a Mayden. *Unknown. See* I Sing of a Maiden.
I tak the Queenis Grace, thy mother. The Childhood of James V. Sir David Lindsay. *Fr.* The Complaynt of Schir David Lindesay. AtBAP
I take a comfort from my very badness. Oneness with Him. George Macdonald. MaRV
I Take 'Em and Like 'Em. Margaret Fishback. WhC
I take four devils with me when I ride. Poem. Gervase Stewart. WaP
I take him down upon the beach. Son and Surf. Julia Hurd Strong. GoYe
I take my chaperon to the play. The Chaperon. H. C. Bunner. AA; HBV
I take my leave with sorrow of Him I love so well. Multiplication. Joyce Kilmer. WHL
I take no books, nor I read no papers. The Gull Decoy. Larry Gorman. ShS
I take no shame that still I sing the rose. The Eternal Way. Richard Le Gallienne. InP
I Take Thee, Life. Margot Ruddock. DiM; OBMV; POTE
I take this time to think what Nature meant. Earl of Rochester. *Fr.* Letter from Artemisa, in the Town, to Cloe, in the Country. NBE
I take what never can be taken. The Poet. Haniel Long. HBMV
I take your poems in my hand and read them beside the candle. On Board Ship; Reading Yüan Chen's Poems. Po Chü-i. TrCh
I takes and I paints. Poem by a Perfectly Furious Academician. *Unknown.* FiBHP
I talked one midnight with the jolly ghost. All in a Garden Green. W. E. Henley. OBMV
I talked to old Lem. Old Lem. Sterling A. Brown. PoNe
I taste a liquor never brewed. Emily Dickinson. AmP; AmPo; AmPP (4th ed.); AnAmPo; CoV; LA; LiTA; LiTM (rev. ed.); MAP; MaPo; MCCG; MoAmPo; MOAP; MoPW; NePA; OnAP; OxBA; PoEL-5; ReMP; SeCeV; TreFS; TwP
(Inebriate of Air.) ATP; CoBA; NeMA; PFE
(Intoxication.) BAP
I taste of tunnel benefits. To Engineers. Roberta Teale Swartz. PoeMoYo
I teach-a da bird an' I blow-a da ring. The Educated Love Bird. Peter Newell. FiBHP
I teach how we cheat the young. A 4 Part Geometry Lesson. Robin Blaser. NeAP
I Teach School. *Unknown.* BLP
I tear the jade pins. Forsaken. Kao Shuang. PoHN
I Tell of Another Young Death. Cesar Tiempo, *tr. fr. Spanish by* Donald Devenish Walsh. TrJP
I tell thee Dick where I have been. A Ballad [*or* Ballade] upon [*or* of] a Wedding. Sir John Suckling. AtBAP; BOHV; CoMu; EV-2; HBV; InvP; LEAP; LiA; LoBV; NBE; OBS; ReEn; SeCeV; SeCL; SeCV-1; SeEP; ViBoPo
I Tell Thee, Priest. George Gascoigne. BHV
I tell thee, stationer—why, never fear! To the Stationer. Thomas Freeman. SiCE; TuPP
I tell thee that the self-willed pride of Zeus. The Overthrow of Zeus. Aeschylus. *Fr.* Prometheus Bound. OxBG
I tell thee truly, herald. After the Battle. Shakespeare. King Henry V, *fr.* IV, vii *and* viii. BHV
I tell them where the wind comes from. People with Proud Chins. Carl Sandburg. PFY
I tell yeh whut! The chankin'. Horses Chawin' Hay. Hamlin Garland. StVeCh
I tell you a poet must be free. Freedom. Leonard Mann. NeLNL
I tell you a tale to-night. The Admiral's Ghost. Alfred Noyes. BBV; PoMS; TiPo (1952 ed.)
I tell you again that I discovered silence. The Sounds of Dawn. Efraín Huerta. AnCL; LiTW
I tell you, hopeless grief is passionless. Grief. Elizabeth Barrett Browning. AnFE; BLV; BPN; ES; GTBS-D; GTML; GTSL; HBV; LoBV; OBEV; OBVV; PoVP; TrGrPo; ViPo
I tell you that I see her still. I Only Am Escaped Alone to Tell Thee. Howard Nemerov. NePA
I tend my flowers for thee. Emily Dickinson. TriL
I 'tend that in the garden. The Nugly Little Man. Marion St. John Webb. TVC; TVSH
I thank all who have loved me in their hearts. Sonnets from the Portuguese, XLI. Elizabeth Barrett Browning. BPN; CoBE; VA; ViPo
I Thank God I'm Free at Las', *with music. Unknown.* BoAN-2
I Thank My God. Geoffrey Anketell Studdert-Kennedy. PSO
I thank the goodness and the grace. A Child's Hymn of Praise. Jane Taylor. OTPC (1923 ed.)
I thank the Lord for little things! Little Things. Helen Rowland. DDA
I thank the Lord for quiet things. Quiet Things. "I. W." OQP; QP-2
I thank thee and I praise thee, O thou radiant grace. Thanksgiving. "Yehoash." TrJP
I thank Thee, Father, for my rest. *Unknown.* PraP
I thank thee, Father, once again. Thanksgiving for Thanksgiving. Amos R. Wells. PEDC
I thank thee, Father, that the night is near. Night. Jones Very. APW
I thank Thee for so many things. Thanksgiving Day. Marie Barton. PraP
I thank Thee, God, for New Year's Day. New Year. Marie Barton. PraP
I Thank Thee, Lord. Oliver Huckel. *See* Unanswered Prayer.
I thank Thee, Lord, for quiet rest. A Child's Morning Prayer. Mary Lundie Duncan. OTPC
I Thank Thee, Lord, for Strength of Arm. Robert Davis. MaRV
I thank Thee, Lord, for this good life. For Having Thee. Francis X. Connolly. JKCP (1955 ed.)
I thank Thee that I learn. Thanksgiving. Emily Read Jones. TOAH
I thank You for these gifts, dear God. Gratitude. Margaret E. Sangster. MaRV; PraP
I Thank You God. E. E. Cummings. *See* I Thank You God for Most This Amazing.
I thank you God,/ For a hundred things. Ilo Orleans. RIS
I thank you, God,/ That swallows know their way. Thanksgiving. Louise Driscoll. YeAr
I Thank You God for Most This Amazing. E. E. Cummings. MoAB
(I Thank You God.) MeRV
I thank you, God in Heaven, for friends. In Gratitude for Friends. Margaret E. Sangster. PraP
I thank you indeed that, sure of me, you assume such license. To Cerinthus. Sulpicia. LaP

I that am clothed with the sun. Our Lady of the Apocalypse. Sister Mary Bertrand. JKCP (1955 ed.)
I that had found the way so smooth. The Return. Jessie Fauset. CDC
I that had yearned for youth, my own, again. My Son. Douglas Malloch. FAOV; MaRV
I that in heill wes [*or* health was] and gladnes[s]. Lament for the Makaris [*or* Makars]. William Dunbar. ACP; AEV; AtBAP; BSV; ChTr; CoEV; GoTS; OAEP; OBEV; PoD; PoEL-1; SiCE; ViBoPo
I that lived ever about you. English Girl. *Tr. by* E. Powys Mathers. OBMV
I that my slender oaten pipe in verse was wont to sound. Virgil. *Fr.* The Aeneid, I. ReIE
I that tremble at your feet. The Missive. Sir Edmund Gosse. HBV
I that whilom lived secure. A Testament. *Unknown.* OBSC
I' the how-dumb-deid o the cauld hairst nicht. The Eemis-Stane. "Hugh MacDiarmid." NeBP
I, the image of godhead, who thought myself. Faust Struggles with His Soul. Goethe. *Fr.* Faust. LiTW
I, the Old Woman of Beare. The Old Woman of Beare [Regrets Lost Youth]. *Unknown.* KiLC; OBMV
I, the poet William Yeats. To Be Carved on a Stone. W. B. Yeats. MM
I the Preacher was king over Israel in Jerusalem. Vanity. Ecclesiastes, Bible, *O.T.* OuHeWo
I, Theris, who lie buried on this shore. Archias, *tr. fr. Greek by* the Earl of Cromer. GrPo
I, Thespis, in dramatic mould. Dioscorides, *tr. fr. Greek by* W. C. Lawton. GrPo
I think/ I never loved her more than now. Noonday. Fan Tseng Hsiang. ChLP; PoHN
I think a stormless night-time shall ensue. The World's Death-Night. James Chapman Woods. VA
I think a time will come when you will understand. For My Father. Paul Potts. FaBoTw
I think about God. God. Gamaliel Bradford. WGRP
I think and think; yet still I fail. The Veil. Walter de la Mare. ChMo; CMP; MM
I think before they saw me the giraffes. The Giraffes. Roy Fuller. ChMP; NeBP
I think between my cradle-bars. Ballade of Faith. Tom MacInnes. CaP; OCL
I think, by God! It is no lie. Confession. Hervey Allen. TBM
I Think Continually of Those Who Were Truly Great. Stephen Spender. AnFE; AtBAP; CaAE; EnL; EnLit; ExPo; FaBoEn; LiTB; LiTG; LiTM; NAMP; OAEP (2d ed.); PG (1945 ed.); PoLFOT; PoRA; ReMP; TwCV; TwHP; WaP
(I Think Continually.) CoEV; MoP; POTE; ShBV-4
(I Think Continually of Those.) BoLiVe; ChMo; ChTr; GTBS-W; MaRV; MoAB; MoBrPo; NeMA; PoeMoYo; PoFr; PoFS; TrGrPo; ViBoPo (1958 ed.)
I think, could I have kept you here with me. Released. Anne Blackwell Payne. NoCaPo
I think ere any early poet awed. The Masterpiece. Walter Conrad Arensberg. AnAmPo; BAP; LA
I think flowers can see. Thoughts of a Little Girl. María Enriqueta. FaPON
I think God loves new temples built to Him. New Temples. Lexie Dean Robertson. OQP; QP-2
I think God loves simplicity. Thanksgiving. Margaret E. Sangster. PEDC
I think God loves the little towns. The Little Towns. Irene Mary Davidson. HiLiAm
I think God sang when He had made. The Star. Beatrice Redpath. CaP; CPG; OCL
I think God seeks this house, serenely white. A Country Church. Violet Alleyn Storey. OQP; QP-2
I think God took the fragrance of a flower. Mothers. *Unknown.* PGD
I think he had not heard of the far towns. St. John Baptist. Arthur O'Shaughnessy. HBV
I think he would have hated this white shrine. At the Lincoln Memorial. William E. Brooks. OQP; QP-2
I think I could turn and live with animals. Animals [*or* The Beasts]. Walt Whitman. Song of Myself, XXXII. AnEnPo; EV-5; FaFP; GTBS-W; HBV; LiTG; LoBV (1949 ed.); MCCG; NePA; OBVV; PC; PG (1955 ed.); PoMa; SiTL; TrGrPo; WGRP
I think I hear them stirring there, today. Armistice Day. Roselle Mercier Montgomery. MC; PoRL
I Think I Know No Finer Things than Dogs. Hally Carrington Brent. AlBD; BBV (1951 ed.); BLPA; NeHB
I think I never shall forget. Macroom on Market Day. Virginia Lyne Tunstall. LS
I think I remember this moorland. We Have Been Here Before. Morris Bishop. FiBHP; InMe; WhC
I Think I See Her. Jessie Fauset. *See* Oriflamme.
I Think I See Him There. Waring Cuney. CDC
I think if I lay dying in some land. The Harbour [*or* The Harbor]. Winifred M. Letts. PoMa; VOD
I think if I should cross the room. The Room's Width. Elizabeth Stuart Phelps Ward. AA
I think if I should wait some night in an enchanted forest. Fantasy. Ruth Mather Skidmore. PoMS
I think if I were a tree. If I. T. C. O'Donnell. GFA
I think I'll do a fearful deed. The Madman. L. A. G. Strong. PC
I think it better that in times like these. On Being Asked for a War Poem. W. B. Yeats. MoVE; TwP
I think it is his blindness makes him so. An Afternoon in Artillery Walk. Leonard Bacon. AnAmPo; ATP; LA; PreP
I think it is over, over. In Harbor. Paul Hamilton Hayne. AA; BAP; HBV; IAP; LBAP; PoeMoYo; SPP; TCAP
I think it very nice to take. Perhaps. Pringle Barret. PCH
I think it was in such a greenery. Saint Francis. Amanda Benjamin Hall. SaFP
I think it was Spring—but not certain I am. Epicurean Reminiscences of a Sentimentalist. Thomas Hood. ERP
I think mice/ Are rather nice. Mice. Rose Fyleman. BoTP; FaPON; GoBP; MoSiPe; MPB; StVeCh; SUS; TiPo
I Think Myself to Be Alive. Dorothy Wellesley. POTE
I think now of latitudes solitary, Asian, and velvet. In a Valley of This Restless Mind. Ewart Milne. NeIP
I think October must have loved in vain. Artist. "Joseph Upper." MuM
I think Odysseus, as he dies, forgets. Odysseus Dying. Sheila Wingfield. OxBI
I think of a flower that no eye has ever seen. Beauty. Laurence Binyon. MBP; MoBrPo
I think, of all the things at school. Johnny's Hist'ry Lesson. Nixon Waterman. PTA-1
I think of Gaspard that certainly was not. Star. Guillaume Apollinaire. AnFP
I Think of Him as One Who Fights. Anna Hempstead Branch. HBMV
I think of robins. Passport beyond Tyranny. David Ross. PG (1945 ed.)
I think of the days. Fujiwara no Atsutada, *tr. fr. Japanese by* Kenneth Rexroth. OnPJ
I think of the tribes: the women prized for fatness. The Tribes. Roy Fuller. BoSA
I think of thee!—my thoughts do twine and bud. Sonnets from the Portuguese, XXIX. Elizabeth Barrett Browning. BPN; EPN; VA
I think of you, Myrtho, divine enchantress. Myrtho. Gérard de Nerval. AnFP
I think of you when sun with sudden splendor. The Lover Is Near. Goethe. LiTW
I Think of Your Generation. Charles Brasch. AnNZ
I Think on Thee. Thomas Kibble Hervey. VA
I think she sleeps: it must be sleep, when low. Modern Love, XV. George Meredith. ViPo
I think some saint of Eirinn wandering far. Fuchsia Hedges in Connacht. Padraic Colum. GoBC
I Think That God Is Proud. Grace Noll Crowell. PoToHe
I think that God, when I was born. Ghosts. Henri Charles Read. LO
I think that I shall never make. In a Garden. Donald C. Babcock. NePoAm
I think that I shall never see/ A billboard. Song of the Open Road. Ogden Nash. LiTM; NAMP; NLK (1947 ed.); SiTL; TreFS; WhC
I think that I shall never see/ A poem. Trees. Joyce Kilmer. BAP; BAV; BBV (1923 ed.); BLPA; BTP; CP; CV; DD; FaBoBe; FaFP; FaPON; HBV; HBVY; HH; InP; JKCP; LEAP; MAP; MaRV; MCCG; MPB; NeHB; NeMA; NP; NV; OBAV; OHFP; OIF; OTPC (1946 ed.); PEDC; PoMa; POT; PoTo; PYM; SBMV; TCAP; TreF; UnPo; VOD; WBLP; WGRP; YT
I think that if some faery spirit strewed. The Salesman. Robert Mezey. NePoEA
I think that life has spared those mortals much. Vigil. Faith Baldwin. MaRV; MuM
I think that look of Christ might seem to say. The Meaning of the Look. Elizabeth Barrett Browning. ChIP; MaRV
I think that man hath made no beauteous thing. To Melody. George Leonard Allen. CDC
I think that Mary Magdalene. Mary Magdalene [*or* One Version]. Leonora Speyer. HBMV; NP; NV; TBM
I think that no one ever knew. Shoes. Louis Untermeyer. StaSt
I think that surely there's a god. Little Woodland God. Judy Van der Veer. MuM
I Think That There Is Laughter. Robert Avrett. MuM
I think that we retain of our dead friends. Remembrance. John Henry Boner. AA
I think the city's iron tide. The Romantic. "Sagittarius" (Olga Katzin). DiM
I think the fairies to my christening came. Fairy Godmothers. Eugene Lee-Hamilton. OBVV
I think the ghost of Leerie. Daffodils over Night. David Morton. PCH; VOD

I think the hemlock likes to stand. The Hemlock. Emily Dickinson. OnPM
I think the lovely shooting stars. Shooting Stars. Grace Noll Crowell. BoChLi
I think the wind is curious. Lonely Wind. Eleanor Hammond. GFA
I think they must be sorry. The Sleepy Maple Trees. Eleanor Hammond. GFA
I think they were about as high. The Shade-Catchers. Charlotte Mew. AlDL
I think thou waitest, Love, beyond the gate. The Lonely Road. Kenneth Rand. HBV
"I think" thought Sam Butler. English Liberal. Geoffrey Taylor. LiTM; SiTL
I think true love is never blind. True Love. Phoebe Cary. PoToHe
I think we are too ready with complaint. Cheerfulness Taught by Reason. Elizabeth Barrett Browning. EOAH; PoVP
I think we can all remember when a Greaser hadn't no show. The Texas Cowboy and the Mexican Greaser. *Unknown.* SCC
I Think When I Read That Sweet Story of Old. Jemima Luke. MaRV; OlF; OTPC (1946 ed.); PCH
(Child's Desire, The.) BOL
I think when you have ridden toward the sun. Echo. Amory Hare. MuM
I think you know, Annas, the price is low. Thirty Pieces of Silver for Jesus. Helene Mullins. StJW
"I Thirst . . ." Katherine Brégy. CAW
I thirst, but not as once I did. My Soul Thirsteth for God. William Cowper. MeRV
I thirst for God, to Him my soul aspires. The Living God. Abraham ibn Ezra. TrJP
I thought, belovèd, to have brought to you. The Gift. "Æ." ChMo; CMP; HBMV; LEAP; LoPo; LoPS; TCPD
I Thought by Tears. Sara Coleridge. DiM
I thought he was dumb. Tortoise Shout. D. H. Lawrence. LiTM
I thought how once Theocritus had sung. *See* I thought once how Theocritus had sung.
I thought I could saw, and I thought I could plane. Carpenter. E. V. Lucas. StVeCh
I Thought I Had Outlived My Pain. Elisabeth Scollard. TBM
I thought I heard the captain [*or* Old Man] say. L'Envoi—Leave Her Johnny [*or* Leave Her, Johnny]. *Unknown.* SG; SoAmSa
I thought I saw a fallen flower. Moritake, *tr. fr. Japanese by* Lois J. Erickson. SoLD
I thought I saw an angel flying low. Nocturne at Bethesda. Arna Bontemps. BANP; CDC; PoNe
I thought I saw the fallen leaves. Hokku. Arakida Moritake. InP
I thought I saw white clouds, but no! Lilies. Shiko. SUS; TiPo
I thought I was so tough. Tamer and Hawk. Thom Gunn. NePoEA
I thought it strange he asked for me. Riding through Jerusalem. Marion Susan Campbell. ChIP
I thought it was the little bed. Half-waking. William Allingham. MOAH; VA
I Thought Joy Went by Me. Willard Wattles. HBMV
I thought love lived in the hot sunshine. Blake. *Fr.* William Bond. LO
I thought my heart had lost the power [*or* quite forgot]. Pushkin, *tr. fr. Russian.* BoR, *tr. by* V. de S. Pinto; WaL, *tr. by* Sir Cecil Kisch
I thought my net was full of shining fish. Oto, *tr. fr. Japanese by* Lois J. Erickson. SoLD
I thought no more was needed. A Song. W. B. Yeats. AtBAP
I thought of Chatterton, the marvellous boy. The Progress of Poets. Wordsworth. *Fr.* Resolution and Independence. PtP; RO
I thought of death beside the lonely sea. Life and Death. Duncan Campbell Scott. VA
I thought of Ennerdale as of a thing. Ennerdale. Frederick William Faber. EnSW
I thought of killing myself because I am only a bricklayer. Bricklayer Love. Carl Sandburg. AmP
I thought of thee, my partner and my guide. After-Thought. Wordsworth. The River Duddon, XXXIV. BPN; CoEV; EM-2; EnL; EnLi-2; EnRP; EPN; EPP; ES; FaBoEn; MeRV; OAEP; OBEV; OBRV; PIAE; SeCePo; TCEP
I thought of your beauty, and this arrow. The Arrow. W. B. Yeats. EG
I thought on war with horrors rife. Nikolai Nekrasov, *tr. fr. Russian by* Sir Cecil Kisch. BoRS; WaL
I thought once how Theocritus had sung. Sonnets from the Portuguese, I. Elizabeth Barrett Browning. AnFE; BCEP; BEL; BoHiPo; BPN; CaAE; CoBE; EmBrPo; EnLi-2; EnLit; EPN; EPP; EtPaEn; EV-4; GTBS; GTBS-D; GTSL; HBV; HiLiEn; LEAP; OAEP; OBEV; OuHeWo; PeBoSo; PFE; PoE; PoVP; TCEP; TOP; VA; ViBoPo; ViP; ViPo
I thought one spring [that] just for fun. The Horse Wrangler. D. J. O'Malley. CoSo (B *vers.*); CSF
I thought our love at full, but I did err. Sonnet. James Russell Lowell. LPS-1
I thought that I could follow Him. There Was No Room on the Cross. *Unknown.* GoBC
I thought that it would bring me luck. The Gift. Abu Aiyub. MooP
I thought that Love had been a boy. *Unknown.* EnLoPo
I thought that nature was enough. Emily Dickinson. MaRV
I thought the feud was ended last Christmas Day. Black Christmas. DuBose Heyward. LS
I thought the night without a sound was falling. How Infinite Are Thy Ways. William Force Stead. *Fr.* Uriel. OBMV; TrPWD
I thought the winner had been found. Brooklynese Champion. Margaret Fishback. WhC
I thought they'd be strangers aroun' me. The Curate's Kindness. Thomas Hardy. CoBMV; PoVP
I thought this day to bring to thee. A Birthday Song. Richard Watson Gilder. PoRL
I Thought to Deal the Death-Stroke. Christina Rossetti. Three Stages, III. EmBrPo
I thought to die that night in the solitude. The Edge. Lola Ridge. AnAmPo; LA; NP; OnYI
I thought to meet no more, so dreary seem'd. Burial of the Dead. John Keble. OBEV (1st ed.)
I thought to pass away before, and yet alive I am. Conclusion to the May Queen and New Year's Eve. Tennyson. *Fr.* The May Queen. OTPC (1923 ed.)
I thought to shoulder Time but those sad birds. The Birds. Herbert Gorman. BLA; TBM
"I thought you loved me." In the Orchard. Muriel Stuart. AV; NP
I threw a penny in the air. *Unknown.* CenHV
I thrilled to hear the heavenly singing of the nightingale. Yaha, *tr. fr. Japanese by* Lois J. Erickson. SoLD
I, through all chances that are given to mortals. To Ausonius. Paulinus of Nola. LaP; LiA
I throw my apple towards you. Love's Apple. Plato. GrPE; GrR
I throw on my clothes, and wait for the Moon. Poems Translated from the Chinese. *Unknown, tr. by* John Francis Davis. RO
I thumped on you the best I could. W. D. Snodgrass. Heart's Needle, VIII. NePoEA
I, thy servant, full of sighs, cry unto thee. Penitential Psalm. *Unknown.* WGRP
I tink I hear my brother say. Stars Begin to Fall. *Unknown.* AA
I to my home shall be going. The Parting of Hector and Andromache. Homer, *tr. by* William B. Smith *and* Walter Miller. *Fr.* The Iliad, VI. TreFS
I to My Perils. A. E. Housman. More Poems, VI. EnLi-2 (1949 ed.); ViBoPo
I told my little boy a story. Night, Stars, Glow-Worms. H. Leivick. LiTW
I told my love, I told my love. Blake. *Fr.* Love's Secret. CaAE
I told myself in singing words. As It Was. Lila Cabot Perry. Meeting after Long Absence, II. AA; OBAV
I told the sun that I was glad. The Sun. John Drinkwater. FaPON; TiPo
I, Too. Langston Hughes. CDC
(Epilogue: "I, too, sing America.") PreP
(I, Too, Sing America.) PoNe
I too, dislike it: there are things that are important beyond all this fiddle. Poetry. Marianne Moore. AmP; AnFE; APA; ATP (1953 ed.); CoAnAm; CoBMV; ExPo; InPo; LiTA; LiTM; MoAB; MoAmPo (1950 ed.); NAMP; NePA; NP; OxBA; PreP; ReMP; SeCeV; TwAmPo; ViBoPo (1958 ed.)
I, too, have been a wanderer; but, alas! Wordsworth. *Fr.* The Prelude, VI. PtP
I too, have been Yogi. Yogi. Benjamin De Casseres. BAP
I too, have gone down. Kinship. Wade Oliver. PoP
I, too, have heard strange whispers, seen. Those That Come Back. Don Marquis. LEAP
I, Too, Have Known. Marguerite George. OQP; QP-2
I Too Have Travelled. Maurice Baring. JKCP (1955 ed.)
I, too, O Christ, denied you. Easter Joy. Daisy Conway Price. ChIP
I too remember distant golden days. Reincarnation. E. Wyndham Tennant. UnW
I too remember, in the after years. Frederick Tennyson. *Fr.* Niobe. MOAP; VA
I, too, saw God through mud. Apologia pro Poemate Meo. Wilfred Owen. ChMP; CoBE; CoBMV; LBBV; LiTM (rev. ed.); MBP; MoAB; MoBrPo; NeMA; NP; PoFr; TwCV
I, Too, Sing America. Langston Hughes. *See* I, Too.

I too, yes I, trust Zeus. Need I say more? Athena's Faith. Aeschylus. *Fr.* Eumenides. LiA
I took a day to search for God. Vestigia. Bliss Carman. CaP; GrCo-2; MaRV; OCL; OQP; QP-1; QS; WGRP
I Took a Hansom on To-Day. W. E. Henley. HBV
I took a piece of plastic clay. A Piece of Clay [*or* Sculpture *or* The Sculptor]. *Unknown.* MaRV; OQP; PoToHe (new ed.); QP-1
I took a reed and blew a tune. The Find. Francis Ledwidge. SP
I took away three pictures. Sandhill People. Carl Sandburg. ChMo; CMP
I took her dainty eyes, as well. Villanelle of His Lady's Treasures. Ernest Dowson. HBV
I took her to the river. The Faithless Wife. Federico García Lorca. LiTW
I took Love to task. Love's Argument. Father Andrew. MaRV
I took money and bought flowering trees. Planting Flowers on the Embankment. Po Chü-i. TrCh
I took my dolly for a walk. *Unknown.* GFA
I took my girl to a fancy ball. I Had but Fifty Cents. *Unknown.* BeLS; BLPA; TreF
I took my heart in my hand. Twice. Christina Rossetti. GTML; GTSL; OBEV; OBVV; TyEnPo; ViBoPo
I took my power in my hand. Emily Dickinson. NeMA; NePA
I took one draught of life. Emily Dickinson. CoBA; TwP
I took the crazy short-cut to the bay. Swimmers. Louis Untermeyer. PFY; PoeMoYo; TCPD
I took this time to think what Nature meant. Earl of Rochester. *Fr.* Letter from Artemisa in Town, to Cloe, in the Country. NBE
I toss my black hair. The Song of Freedom and the Sea. Yiannis Sphakianakis. MoGP
I tossed my friend a wreath of roses, wet. Gifts. Mary Elizabeth Coleridge. PoVP
I tossed my golden anchor to the sea. Sonnet. Idris Davies. MoWP
I touch and recollect/ Less than the shape and shade. Tiresias' Lament. Ellen de Young Kay. NePoEA
I touched a shining mote of sand. Lyric. Philip Child. CaP
I touched—amid the blond. Core. Jaime Torres Bodet. AnCL
I towered far, and lo! I stood within. God-forgotten. Thomas Hardy. BEL; PoVP; TOP; ViP; VLEP
I Tramp a Perpetual Journey. Walt Whitman. *Fr.* Song of Myself, XLVI. OQP; QP-2
(Perpetual Journey, The.) GrCo-2
I tramped the pavement, blaming [*or* cursing] God. Comrade Jesus. Ralph Cheyney. ChIP; PGD
I travel over you a swift railway track. Gimli. Miriam Waddington. BoCaPo (1948 ed.)
I travel'd thro' a land of men. The Mental Traveller. Blake. EnRP; PoEL-4
I Traveled among Unknown Men. Wordsworth. *Fr.* Lucy. AWP; BoLiVe; BPN; EM-2; EnL; EnRP; EPN; ERP; GEPC; GTBS; GTBS-D; GTBS-W; GTSL; InPo; JAWP; OAEP; OBRV; OuHeWo; PoFS; REAL; TCEP; TOP; TrGrPo; TwP; WBP
(Lucy.) BLV; EmBrPo; EnLi-2; EnLit; FiP; HBV; LoPo; OBEV
I Traveled with Them. Mu'tamid, King of Seville, *tr. fr. Arabic by* J. B. Trend. AWP
I travelled [*or* travell'd] on, seeing the hill, where lay. The Pilgrimage. George Herbert. ChTr; EPS (1942 ed.)
I traversed a dominion. Mute Opinion. Thomas Hardy. ChMo; CMP; ViPo
I tread on many autumns here. Walking in Beech Leaves. Andrew Young. MoVE
I treasure in secret some long, fine hair. The Wind-Harp. James Russell Lowell. CAP
I Tremble to Think. Oliver St. John Gogarty. PoP
I Tremble When with Looks Benign. Sara Coleridge. DiM
I tried but I could not remember my dream. The Hills of Pomeroy. Ewart Milne. NeIP
I tried to live by bread alone. Satisfied. Edgar Cooper Mason. BLRP
I tried to love your mountains. Mountains. John Richard Moreland. LS
I tripped along a narrow way. Forthfaring. Winifred Howells. AA
I triumphed, fleeing gorgeous suicide. Royalty. Stéphane Mallarmé. TrFP
I trod that day the sacred shadows. The Oak Grove. Nikolaus Lenau. AnGP
I trod the January snows. Communion. Wallace Gould. AnAmPo; LA
I trod the mellow earth between the rows. Distribution. Elsie B. Purcell. PoMa
I Trod upon the Age's Heels. Nikolay Lvov, *tr. fr. Russian by* Babette Deutsch. TrRV
"I trow that gude ending." Bruce Consults His Men. John Barbour. *Fr.* The Bruce. GoTS
I truly wonder what they mean by sin. Ideal Passion, X. George Edward Woodberry. MOAP
I trust I have not wasted breath. In Memoriam A. H. H., CXX. Tennyson. CoBE; EmBrPo; EPN; GEPC; ImOP; SeCePo; TOP; ViPo; VLEP
I try to capture rhythm. Futility. Mary S. Hawling. DDA; PoMa; VOD (1935 ed.)
I try to forget, but it is in vain. To the Distant One. Po Chü-i. WhP
I try to knead and spin, but my life is low the while. In Leinster [*or* Irish Peasant Song]. Louise Imogen Guiney. AA; GoBC; HBV; JKCP; LBMV; OBAV; OBVV; PFY
I try to remember the things. Youth. Keidrych Rhys. MoWP
I tuned in to a symphony. E Tenebris. Helen Spalding. NeTW
I turn my steps where the lonely road. In Dark Hour. Seumas MacManus. JKCP; WGRP
I turn the corner of prayer and burn. Dylan Thomas. *Fr.* Vision and Prayer. MeRV
I Turn the Key. Winifred Corrigan. JKCP (1955 ed.)
I turn the page and read. At the British Museum. Richard Aldington. BLV; MBP; MoBrPo
I turned and gave my strength to woman. Two Generations. L. A. G. Strong. GTIV; OBMV
I turned to the parlor in panic. Frustrate. Louis Untermeyer. HBMV; InMe; YaD
I twined a wreath of heather white. Corona Inutilis. James Lister Cuthbertson. BoAu
I understand the large hearts of heroes. Heroes. Walt Whitman. *Fr.* Song of Myself. AA; PoFr
I understand the roseate mystery. Ideal Passion, XVII. George Edward Woodberry. MOAP
I understand what you are running for. For Eager Lovers. Genevieve Taggard. AnAmPo; LA; NP
I understood thy hint, and thank thee for it. Schiller. *Fr.* Don Carlos. BoFr
I urged my mind against my will. The Heart Looks On. Leonora Speyer. NP
I used to be stout-hearted. Light-shy. Ibsen. AnNoLy
I used to delve in classic lore. Astrology. Sennett Stephens. PR
I used to go to bed at night. Bed during Exams. Clara Warren Vail. PA
I used to have a comrade. The Good Comrade. Ludwig Uhland. BoFr
I used to have a ol' gray hoss [*or* old grey horse]. Goin' Down to Town. *Unknown.* AS; SoAF
I used to live on Cottonwood and owned a little farm. A Mormon [Immigrant] Song. *At. to* George Hicks. CoSo; CSF
I used to live on mountain top. Old Joe Clarke. *Unknown.* TrAS
I Used to Love My Garden. C. P. Sawyer. LiTG
I used to see her in the door. Paul. James Wright. NePoEA
I used to walk on solid gr'und. To a Sea Eagle. "Hugh MacDiarmid." MoBrPo
I ust to read in the novel books 'bout fellers that got the prod. Cowboy's Worrying Love. James Barton Adams. SCC
I uster own the Double D. Cyclone Blues. *Unknown.* CoSo
I, Valour, wretched maid, sit here forlorn. Asclepiades, *tr. fr. Greek by* Lord Neaves. GrPo
I vanquished the angel of sleep, he of mournful allegory. Nocturnal Collection. "Pablo Neruda." AnCL
I veil thy face, Child.—Would that so. Friendship's Servitude. Euripides. *Fr.* Hippolytus. GrR
I Vex Me Not with Brooding on the Years. Thomas Bailey Aldrich. OBAV; UnW
I vex my heart with fancies dim. In Memoriam A. H. H., XLII. Tennyson. EmBrPo; EPN; GEPC; ViPo; VLEP
I, Virgin of the Snows, have liv'd. The Jungfrau's Cry. Stopford Brooke. VA
I Visit Carmel. Sister Mary Madeleva. PraNu
I Visited Again. Pushkin, *tr. fr. Russian by* Babette Deutsch. TrRV
I vow I won't be gagged, I won't be tied! Prologue: Written for the Re-opening of the Theatre Royal, Richmond, Yorkshire, 1942. "Sagittarius" (Olga Katzin). DiM
I Vow to Thee, My Country. Sir Cecil Spring-Rice. BoTP; MM; ShBV-3; TVSH
(Homeland, The.) MaRV
I vow'd unvarying faith; and she. Constancy. Coventry Patmore. *Fr.* The Angel in the House. OBVV
I Vowed. Fray Angelico Chavez. SaFP
I voyage north, I journey south. The Vagrant of Time. Sir Charles G. D. Roberts. OCL
I wad ha'e gi'en him my lips tae kiss. Mary's Song. Marion Angus. LO
I wad I were where Helen lies. *See* I wish I were where Helen lies.
I wadna gi'e my ain wife. My Ain Wife. Alexander Laing. HBV; VA

I wage not any feud with Death. Tennyson. In Memoriam A. H. H., LXXXII. EmBrPo; EnLi-2; EPN; GEPC; LiTB; LiTG; ReaPo; TOP; ViPo; VLEP

I waigh not Fortunes frowne or smile. A Contented Mind [*or* Contentment]. Joshua Sylvester. EV-1; HBV; LPS-3

I wait and he does not come. *Unknown, tr. fr. Japanese by* Kenneth Rexroth. LiTW

I wait and watch: before my eyes. The Waiting. Whittier. APW; BLV; IAP

I wait for wonder, or the weather's turn. Absent Creation. D. S. Savage. NeBP

I wait in the night. The Tryst. Shen Yüeh. PoHN

I Wait My Lord. *Unknown. See* Gourd Has Bitter Leaves, The.

I waited and worked. Koheleth. Louis Untermeyer. TrJP

I waited for my/ Lover until I could hear. *At. to* Hitomaro, *tr. fr. Japanese by* Kenneth Rexroth. OnPJ

I waited for the train at Coventry. Godiva. Tennyson. BPN; HBV; PoVP; VLEP

I waited in the little sunny room. Eve's Daughter. Edward Rowland Sill. PR

I waited years today . . . one year for every hour. Entry November 12. Walter Benton. LoPS

I Wake and Feel the Fell of Dark. Gerard Manley Hopkins. ChMo; CoBE; CoBMV; EnLi-2; GTBS-W; LiTB; LiTG; OAEP; MaPo; MoPW; PoEL-5; POTT; PoVP; ReaPo; ReMP; SeCeV; TwHP; ViP; ViPP; VLEP
(Sonnet.) CoEV; PoLi
(Terrible Sonnets, The, III.) MoPo

I wake and hear it raining. Morning Worship. Mark Van Doren. NePoAm-2

I wake at the touch of morning: and the City is shaken with a Song! Peace at Morning. Dana Burnet. AOAH

I wake! I feel the day is near. Chanticleer. Celia Thaxter. PRWS; TVC; TVSH

I wake, I rise: from end to end. Tennyson. In Memoriam A. H. H., C. BrBE

I wake in the morning early. Singing-Time. Rose Fyleman. SiSoSe; TiPo

I wake in the night with such uncertain gladness. The Girl Takes Her Place among the Mothers. Marya Zaturenska. HBMV

I wake to sleep, and take my waking slow. The Waking. Theodore Roethke. CoBMV; CrMA; FiMAP; Po

I waked; the sun was in the sky. On Waking from a Dreamless Sleep. Annie Fields. AA

I waken in the early dawn. Morning Prayer. Utako Hayashi. SoLD

I wakened on my hot, hard bed. The Watch. Frances Cornford. HBMV; LiTM; MBP; MoBrPo

I wald noght spare forto speke wist I to spede. How King Edward and His Menge Met with the Spaniardes in the Sea. Laurence Minot. NBE

I walk a road—an ancient, trodden way. Another While. Morris Rosenfeld. TrJP

I walk across the meadow, dreaming of Parnassus. To the Commonplace. Gloria Goddard. BAP

I walk and cinder bats riddle my cloak. The Circle of C. Lynette Roberts. MoWP

I walk and I wonder. Spring. Isaac Rosenberg. TrJP

I walk beside the prisoners to the road. A Camp in the Prussian Forest. Randall Jarrell. MiAP; MoAmPo (1950 ed.); NeMA

I walk by Mother Arax. The Tears of Araxes. Raphael Patkanian. ArmLP

I walk down a long. A Poem for Museum Goers. John Wieners. NeAP

I walk down the garden-paths. Patterns. Amy Lowell. AmPP; AnFE; AnNE; APA; ATP; AWP; BAP; BAV; BLV; BoLiVe; ChMo; CMP; CoAnAm; CoBA; FaFP; HBV; IAP; JAWP; LiTA; MAP; MoAmPo; MOAP; NeMA; NePA; NP; NV; OBAV; OxBA; PFE; PoFr; POT; PoTo; PreP; ReaPo; SBMV; TCAP; TCPD; TOP; TreFS; TrGrPo; UnPo (1st ed.); WBP

I walk down the Valley of Silence. Song of the Mystic. Abram J. Ryan. JKCP; SPP

I walk, I only. Nocturn. Francis Thompson. POTE; TCPD

I walk, I trust, with open eyes. Love's Reality. Coventry Patmore. *Fr.* The Angel in the House. PoVP

I walk in London. Belle Isis; Ballad of a Rose. Sacheverell Sitwell. Rosario d'Arabeschi; Poems and Rose Portraits, I. POTE (1959 ed.)

I walk in nature still alone. Great Friend. Henry David Thoreau. CoV; PoEL-4

I walk like a legend through cathedrals and markets. Swansea Market. Peter Hellings. MoWP

I walk of grey noons by the old canal. Sonnet. Thomas Caulfield Irwin. EnSW; IrPN

I walk on grass as soft as wool. An Old Woman Laments in Springtime. Edith Sitwell. LO; ViBoPo

I Walk Out into the Country at Night. Lu Yu, *tr. fr. Chinese by* Kenneth Rexroth. OnPC

I walk out into the night and it is strange. Winter Moonlight. Gillespie Evans. CAG

I walk the dusty ways of life. The Troubadour of God. Charles Wharton Stork. WGRP

I walk the old frequented ways. Behind the Closed Eye. Francis Ledwidge. MCCG; VOD

I walk through the long schoolroom questioning. Among School Children. W. B. Yeats. AnIL; ATP (1953 ed.); ChMo; ChMP; CMP; CoBMV; CoEV; EnLP; FaBoEn; LiTB; LiTG; LiTM (rev. ed.); MaPo; MBP; MoAB; MoBrPo; MoVE; OAEP (2d ed.); PoVP; ReMP; RiBV; SeCeV; TrGrPo; TwHP; UnPo

I walk to the river's bank before the night. Water. Hermann Claudius. TwGV

I walk upon the rocky shore. My Mother. Josephine Rice Creelman. DD; MOAH; OHIP

I walk with bare, hushed feet the ground. Whittier. *Fr.* The Eternal Goodness. BAP

I walk'd [*or* walked] along a stream for pureness rare. Fragment. Gervase Markham, *at. to* Christopher Marlowe. CaAE; LoBV; OBSC

I walk'd in the lonesome evening. Song [*or* Song: "Across the Sea"]. William Allingham. EnLoPo; IrPN

I walked a mile with Pleasure. Along the Road [*or* Pleasure and Sorrow]. Robert Browning Hamilton. BLPA; BPP; MaRV; NeHB; TreFS

I walked abroad in a snowy day. Soft Snow. Blake. AtBAP; BoW

I walked alone to my Calvary. Calvary. *Unknown.* OQP; QP-2

I walked along a stream for pureness rare. *See* I walk'd along . . .

I walked along the cedar grove. A Psalm for Moderns. Thomas P. McDonnell. JKCP (1955 ed.)

I walked amid the lilies, at the morn. The Lilies. John Francis O'Donnell. IrPN

I walked and came upon a picket fence. Wordsworthian Reminiscence. *Unknown.* BOHV; TOP

I walked beside the deep, one night of stars. Nocturne. Victor Hugo. CAW

I walked beside the evening sea. Ebb and Flow. George William Curtis. AA; HBV; LBAP; LEAP; OBAV

I walked down the lane. In September. Eleanor Hammond. GFA

I walked entranced/ Through a land of Morn. King Cahal Mór of the Wine-red Hand [*or* A Vision of Connaught in the Thirteenth Century]. James Clarence Mangan. AnIL; AnIV; GoBC; IrPN; TIP

I walked in loamy Wessex lanes, afar. The Pity of It. Thomas Hardy. ChMo; CMP; InP; LiTM (rev. ed.); WaP

I walked, in meditation that was pain. Sonnet. Arthur Davison Ficke. MuM

I walked in Palestine one summer day. The Good Shepherd. Clyde Edwin Tuck. BePJ

I walked in Tara's Wood one summer night. Moon Mockery. Robert Ervin Howard. DaM

I walked my fastest down the twilight street. Apparition. John Erskine. HBMV

I walked on the banks of the tincan banana dock and sat down. Sunflower Sutra. Allen Ginsberg. NeAP

I walked out in my Coat of Pride. The Fur Coat. James Stephens. BMEP

I Walked Out to the Graveyard to See the Dead. Richard Eberhart. MiAP; MoPo

I walked that day out to the death-marked hill. Simon of Cyrene. Georgia Harkness. ChIP

I walked the hills. Earth Angel. Barbara Young. BAP

I walked the mountains. Microcosmos, XLIII. Nigel Heseltine. NeBP

I Walked [*or* Walkt] the Other Day [to Spend My Hour]. Henry Vaughan. EnL; FaBoEn; MePo; OBS; OxBoCh; ReEn; SeCL; SeEP
(Flower, The.) EV-2
(Hidden Flower, The.) EPS

I Walked the Road of the Dawn. Dionysios Solomos, *tr. fr. Modern Greek by* Rae Dalven. *Fr.* The Free Besieged. MoGP

I walked the sthreets o' Paris, an' I walked the sthreets o' Rome. Sthreets of Home. Denis A. McCarthy. PoTo

I walked this Easter morning in the wood. Assurance. Grace Noll Crowell. PoRL

I walked through Ballinderry in the spring-time. Lament for [the Death of] Thomas Davis. Sir Samuel Ferguson. AnIV; GTIV; IrPN; OnYI; OxBI; PoFr; TIP

I walked through the woodland meadows. The Broken Pinion. Hezekiah Butterworth. MaRV; PTA-2

I walked where in their talking graves. At the British War Cemetery, Bayeux. Charles Causley. POTE (1959 ed.)

I walked with Maisie long years back. The Ballad of Camden Town. James Elroy Flecker. EnLit; HBV

I Walked with My Reason. Sorley Maclean. *See* Dain do Eimhir, XXII.

I walked with you tonight. You did not know. Strange Meeting. Harper Poulson. UnW

I Walkt the Other Day. Henry Vaughan. *See* I Walked the Other Day.

I wander afield, thriving in sturdy thought. Unpathed Haunts. Lucretius, *tr. by* William Ellery Leonard. *Fr.* De Rerum Natura. LiA

I wander aimless, to and fro. Aimless. Louis Palagyi. TrJP

I wander all night in my vision. The Sleepers. Walt Whitman. AmP

I wander at random, silent, alone. Wandering at Night. K'ung P'ing Chung. PoHN

I wander far and unrestrained. Spring. John Alden Carpenter. RIS

I wander homeward at evening. The Bricklayer. Vasili Kazin. TrRV

I wander thro' [*or* through] each charter'd street. London. Blake. *Fr.* Songs of Experience. AtBAP; AWP; CEP; ChER; CoEV; EiPP; EM-1; EnL; EnLi-2 (1949 ed.); EnRP; ExPo; FaBoEn; InPo; LiTB; LO; MaPo; NBE; OnPM; PoE; PoEL-4; PoFS; RiBV; SeCePo; SeCeV; TwHP; TyEnPo; UnPo; ViBoPo; WoL

I wander thro' each dirty street, *sel., sl. diff.* ChTr

I wander through a crowd of women. At Piccadilly Circus. Vivian de Sola Pinto. OBMV

I wander through the silent night. Nocturne. Joseph von Eichendorff. AnGP

I wander'd [*or* wandered] by the brookside. The Brookside. Richard Monckton Milnes. HBV; LPS-1; TreFS; VA

I wandered by the brookside. Love and Science. *Unknown.* PA

I wandered down the dying afternoon. Birch-Wood. Leo Cox. BoCaPo (1943 ed.)

I Wandered Lonely as a Cloud. Wordsworth. AEV; AtBAP; BEL; BoTP; BPN; CaAE; CoBE; EG; EM-2; EmBrPo; EnLi-2; EnLit; EnRP; EPN; EPP; ERP; ExPo; GEPC; HBV; HBVY; InP; LEAP; LoBV; MaPo; OAEP; OBRV; OTPC; OuHeWo; PECK; PFE; PoE; PoFS; PoRA; PreP; RG; SUS; TCEP; ThWaDe; TOP; TwHP; TyEnPo; UnPo; ViBoPo; WHA

(Daffodils.) ADAH; AnEnPo; AnFE; BCEP; BLPA; BLV; BoChLi; BoLiVe; BTP; CBOV; CBPC; DD; EV-3; FaBoBe; FaFP; FaPON; FiP; GBV; GN; GoTP; GTBS; GTBS-D; GTBS-W; GTSE; GTSL; HiLiEn; HoPM; LiTB; LiTG; LPS-2; MaRV; MCCG; MPB; MW; NeHB; OBEV; OHFP; OnHT; PC; PCD; PCN; PG (1945 ed.); PIAE; PIR; PoeMoYo; PoMa; PTA-1; PYM; SeCeV; ShBV-1; SN; StVeCh; TreF; TrGrPo; TVSH; WBLP; WP

I wandered lonely [*or* lone] where the pine-trees made. The Trailing Arbutus. Whittier. AnAmPo; BLP; CoBA; IAP; LA; PEOR; PTA-2; REAL; TCAP

I wandered on through field and fold. The Ploughman. Gilbert Thomas. HBMV

I Wandered Out. George Wither. *Fr.* Fair Virtue, the Mistress of Philarete. SeCL

(Divided Heart, The.) TrGrPo

("I wandered out a while agone.") ElSeCe

I wandered through Scoglietto's far retreat. Sonnet on Holy Week. Oscar Wilde. JKCP (1926 ed.)

I wandered [*or* wander'd] today to the hill, Maggie. When You and I Were Young, Maggie. George W. Johnson. OlF; TreF

I wandering went/ Among the haunts and dwellings of mankind. Shelley. *Fr.* Prometheus Unbound. FiP

I Want a Girl (Just Like the Girl That Married Dear Old Dad). Will Dillon. TreFS

"I want a green parrot." The Green Parrot. Humbert Wolfe. TwCV

I want a hero: an uncommon want. Byron. *Fr.* Don Juan, I. EnL; EnLit; EnRP; ERP; OAEP; Po; PreP

I want a little house upon a little hill. Needs. Charles Hanson Towne. DDA

I want a little witch cat. Witch Cat. Rowena Bennett. SiSoSe

I want a poem, I want/ a Polish song. Death over the Air. Jacinto Fombona Pachano. AnCL

I want a Puppy Dog. For Christmas. Dorothy Aldis. ChBR; GoBP; UTS

I want an egg for Easter. An Egg for Easter. Irene F. Pawsey. BoTP

I want free life and I want fresh air. Lasca. Frank Desprez. BeLS; BLPA; FaBoBe; HBV; NeHB; PTA-1; SCC; TreF

I Want God's Heab'n to Be Mine, *with music. Unknown.* BoAN-2

I want my boy to have a dog. Example. Marty Hale. AlBD

I want my buddies and all my friends. Dupree (A *vers.*). *Unknown.* ViBoFo

I Want My Time. *Unknown.* SCC

I want no horns to rouse me up to-night. Nuit Blanche. Amy Lowell. TBM

I want nothing but your fire-side now. Hearthstone. Harold Monro. HBMV

I want, the more chastely to compose my verse. Landscape. Baudelaire. AnFP

I want the New Year's opening days. A Prayer for the New Year. *Unknown.* BLRP

I want three days to read the Iliad through! Pierre de Ronsard, *tr. fr. French by* Curtis Hidden Page. PrPoCR

I want to be a carpenter. Trades. Amy Lowell. OTPC (1946 ed.)

I Want to Be a Cowboy. *Unknown.* ABS

I want to be alone with you. The Testament. Mikhail Lermontov. BoR

I Want to Be Married and Cannot Tell How. *Unknown.* OnYI

"I want to be new," said the duckling. The New Duckling. Alfred Noyes. *Fr.* Touchstone on a Bus. BoTP; FaPON; MPB

I want to be ready. Walk in Jerusalem Jus' like John. *Unknown.* BoAN-2

I want to be where all is very still. Lyric. Gertrude MacGregor Moffat. CPG

I want to be your pinkie. Le Désert de l'Amour. Stevie Smith. DiM

I Want to Die Easy When I Die, *with music. Unknown.* BoAN-2

I Want to Die While You Love Me. Georgia Douglas Johnson. BANP; CDC

I want to die with the dying day. When the Day Comes. Manuel Gutiérrez Nájera. AnMP

I want to give you something my child. The Gift. Rabindranath Tagore. MOAH

I want to go aboard my ship, and sail and sail away. The Dream Ship. W. K. Holmes. BoTP

I Want to Go to Morrow. *Unknown.* PTA-1

I want to go to Peachtree. Peachtree. Archibald Rutledge. LA

I Want to Go Wandering. Vachel Lindsay. TSW; TSWC

I Want to Know. John Drinkwater. BoChLi; FaPON

I want to know, am I the only stooge. All Awry. Justin Richardson. SiTL

I want to know why when I'm late. I Want to Know. John Drinkwater. BoChLi; FaPON

I want to learn to whistle. Whistles [*or* Whistle]. Dorothy Aldis. BoChLi (1950 ed.); GFA; TiPo (1952 ed.)

I want to lie alone beside the sedges. An Old Man's Weariness. Arthur L. Phelps. CPG

I want to see the slim palm-trees. Heritage. Gwendolyn Bennett. BANP

I want to see the wagons in the wood. Christmas. Margaret Avison. TwCaPo

I want to sing lyrics, lyrics. How Can I Sing? *Unknown.* MaRV

I Want to Sit Next to Emily. Ogden Nash. BOHV

I want to stride the hills! My feet cry out. Hill Hunger. Joseph Auslander. NLK; VOD

I want to tell you of a trip I did take. George Britton. *Unknown.* CoSo

I want to travel the common road. The Common Road. Silas H. Perkins. BLPA; FaBoBe; NeHB

I want ye. Cowboy Boasting Chants. *Unknown.* ABF

I Want You. Arthur L. Gillom. BLPA; FaBoBe; NeHB

I wanted a rifle for Christmas. Presents. Marchette Chute. BrR; ChBR; SiSoSe; StVeCh

I wanted the gold, and I sought it. The Spell of the Yukon. Robert W. Service. BLPA; FaBoBe; FaFP; NeHB; TreF

I wanted this morning to bring you a gift of roses. The Roses of Sa'adi. Marceline Desbordes-Valmore. LiTW

I wanted to be more human. Forms of the Human. Richard Eberhart. FiMAP

I wanted to bring you this Jap iris. For C. Philip Whalen. NeAP

I Wanted to Die in the Desert. *Unknown.* CoSo

I wanted you, nameless woman of the South. Southern Cross. Hart Crane. *Fr.* The Bridge: Three Songs. LiTA

I wanted you to come today. How Like a Woman. Caroline Duer *and* Alice Duer Miller. PR

I wanted you when skies were red. Unanswered. Martha Dickinson Bianchi. AA

I wants a piece of calico. Mattie's Wants and Wishes. Grace Gordon. DDA

I war against the folly that is War. The New Mars. Florence Earle Coates. PGD

I warmed both hands before the fire of life. Envoi. D. B. Wyndham Lewis. FiBHP

I warn, like the one drop of rain. The Voice of the Void. George Parsons Lathrop. AA

"I warn ye all, ye gay ladies." Child Waters. *Unknown.* ESPB; OAEP; OBB

I was a bachelor, I lived by myself. The Weaver. *Unknown.* AS
I was a boy when I heard three red words. Threes. Carl Sandburg. OxBA
I Was a Brook. Sara Coleridge. *Fr.* Phantasmion. OBRV
I Was a Bustle-Maker Once, Girls. Patrick Barrington. WhC
I Was a Child. Rainer Maria Rilke, *tr. fr. German by* Herman Salinger. TwGV
I was a child and overwhelmed: Mozart. The Corner-Knot. Robert Graves. BLV
I was a dreamer: I dreamed. The Dream-Teller. Padraic Gregory. HBMV; OnYI
I was a goddess ere the marble found me. A Statue in a Garden. Agnes Lee. HBMV; NP
I was a high-born gentleman. Gypsy Davy. *Unknown.* AS
I was a jay-bird, screeching back the noise. Imitatrix Ales. Archias. OxBG
I was a joke at dinners; aye, any would-be wit. Revenge to Come. Propertius. *Fr.* Elegies. AWP; JAWP; LiTW; WBP
I Was a King in Babylon. W. E. Henley. *See* To W. A.
I Was a Labourer. Sean Jennet. Cycle; Seven War Poems, II. OnYI
I was a lady of high renown. Jamie Douglas. *Unknown.* BaBo (*A vers.*); ESPB; OBB; ViBoFo (*A vers.*); WHA
I was a peasant girl from Germany. Elsa Wertman. Edgar Lee Masters. *Fr.* Spoon River Anthology. OxBA
I was a peasant of the Polish plain. Five Souls. W. N. Ewer. AOAH; MaRV; OQP; QP-2
I was a Roman soldier in my prime. A Guard of the Sepulcher. Edwin Markham. StJW; WGRP
I was a scholar: seven useful springs. The Scholar and the Dog. John Marston. AlBD
I was a stricken deer, that left the herd. The Stricken Deer [*or* Dreams, Empty Dreams *or* Self-Portrait]. William Cowper. *Fr.* The Task. BHV; BrBE; CoBE; EnRP; FiP; LEAP; LoBV; LPS-3; MaRV; OAEP; OxBoCh; RO
I Was a Wandering Sheep. Horatius Bonar. *See* Lost but Found.
I was a wild and wayward boy. Song: The Harp. Sir Walter Scott. *Fr.* Rokeby. EV-4
I was a woman always liked spangles. Sleep, Madame, Sleep. Annemarie Ewing. NePoAm
I was a young girl hidden deep in her chamber. A Second Song of Chang-kan. Li Po. WhP
I was a young maid truly. The Sandgate Girl's Lamentation. *Unknown.* CoMu
I was about to sail away in a junk. To Wang Lun. Li Po. BoFr
I was afraid/ and I came back from madness. Madhouse Poem. Carlos Oquendo de Amat. AnCL
I was always a lover of ladies' hands! Your Hands [*or* Ad Manus Puellae]. Ernest Dowson. LoPo; LoPS
I was always the Elephant's Friend. A Ballade of the Grotesque. G. K. Chesterton. PIAE
I was an armed warrior, but now. The Horn. *Unknown.* EPP
I was an elephant. Elephant! Tom Scherman. PCD
I was an English shell. An English Shell. A. C. Benson. VA
I was angry with my friend. A Poison Tree. Blake. *Fr.* Songs of Experience. AnFE; AWP; BoLiVe; CaAE; EG; EM-1; EnL; EnLi-2; EnLit; EnRP; EPP; FaFP; GTBS-W; HoPM; InPo; JAWP; LEAP; LiTB; LiTG; MaPo; OAEP; OtMeF; PoEL-4; PoFS; PoMS; PreP; TOP; TreFS; TrGrPo; TyEnPo; WBP
I was ashamed! I dared not lift my eyes! Shame. James Stephens. ChMo; CMP
I was asked to tell my station and name. Abroad. Sophus Claussen. BoDS
I was asking for something specific and perfect for my city. Mannahatta. Walt Whitman. MoAmPo; OuHeWo; REAL
I was astonished by no grace. A Woman Passes the Door. George O'Neil. NP
"I was bat seven year alld." *See* "I was but seven year auld."
I was bored with old Seville. Seville. Al-Tutili. MooP
I Was Born Almost Ten Thousand Years Ago, *with music. Unknown.* AS
I was born at night on the crossways. Nikolai Tikhonov, *tr. fr. Russian by* C. M. Bowra. BoRS
I was born downtown on a wintry day. Karl Shapiro. Recapitulations, I. FiMAP
I was born for deep-sea faring. A Son of the Sea. Bliss Carman. EtS; NLK
I was born forty years ago. La Femme de Quarante Ans. Stuart Cloete. NeTW
I was born in a bad slum. Plot Improbable, Character Unsympathetic. Elder Olson. NePA
I was born in a stall. Shall I, Mother, Shall I, Shall I Do So? *Unknown.* AnEC
I was born in Belfast between the mountain and the gantries. Carrickfergus. Louis MacNeice. AnIL; OnYI
I was born in Boston, a city [*or* place] you [*or* we] all know well. The Boston Burglar. *Unknown.* ABS; CoSo; CSF
I was born in Illinois. My Fathers Came from Kentucky. Vachel Lindsay. *Fr.* Alexander Campbell. HBMV
"I was born in Indiany," says a stranger, lank and slim. Like His Mother Used to Make. James Whitcomb Riley. IHA
I was born in the century of the death of the rose. Biography for the Use of the Birds. Jorge Carrera Andrade. AnCL
I was born in the suburbs of Bologna. Queroqué the Frog; an Autobiography. Shimpei Kusano. PoLJ
I was born in the town of Boston. The Boston Burglar. *Unknown.* ViBoFo
I was born on the prairie. Prairie. Carl Sandburg. ChMo; CMP; HeT; IAP; LaNeLa; MM; NP
I was born on the prairie. Prairie Birth. Grace Stone Coates. DDA; PaA
I was born, they say, in tears. Tears and Song. *Unknown.* OnPM
I was born under a kind star. Katharine Tynan. EG
I Was Born upon Thy Bank, River. Henry David Thoreau. PoEL-4
I was borned and raised in east Virginia. East Virginia. *Unknown.* OuSiCo
I was broke and out of a job in the city of London. Paddy Get Back. *Unknown.* AmSS; ShS; SoAmSa
I was brought up in a rampart. The Stolen Fifer. Padraic Fiacc. NeIP
I was brought up under the Stone Castle. Song. Tsang Chih. TrCh
"I was but [*or* bat] seven year auld [*or* alld]." The Laily Worm and the Machrel of the Sea. *Unknown.* ChTr; ESPB; InvP; LoBV; OBB; PoEL-1
I was carried to a font. Dithyramb in Retrospect. Peter Hopegood. BoAV
I was climbing up a mountain path. An Obstacle. Charlotte Perkins Gilman. DDA; OBAV
I was driving the cows and the frogs were soothsaying. Twilight. Eileen Duggan. JKCP (1955 ed.)
I was even wearier where I waited. Migrants. Ethel Anderson. BoAV
I was first of all the kings who drew. King Arthur's Order of Chivalry. Tennyson. GrCo-1
I was five when we moved to England, and the strange voices. Anton Vogt. *Fr.* For England, in Grateful Appreciation. AnNZ
I was foolish about windows. Foolish about Windows. Carl Sandburg. MOAP
I was foretold, your rebel[l] sex. A Deposition from Love. Thomas Carew. CoEV; ElSeCe; EV-2; MeLP; NBE; OAEP; OBS
I was going to the city to sell the herbs I had plucked. The Politician. Po Chü-i. TrCh
I was happy. Shadow. William Griffith. BAP
I was in a garden, she said. Death in Carmel. Jessica Powers. PraNu
"I was in a hooker once," said Karlssen. Cape Horn Gospel—I. John Masefield. StPo
I was in a summery dale. The Owl and the Nightingale. *Unknown, at. to* Nicholas de Guildford. MeEV
I was in Margate last July, I walked upon the pier. Misadventures at Margate. "Thomas Ingoldsby." BOHV; HBV; LPS-3
I was in the boy scouts once. Butchers. Redmond Phillips. NeLNL
I was in the harbor. Resolution. "Wiolar." InMe
I was in the sand near to the seawall. The Husband's Message. *Unknown.* EnLit
I was just about to take a drink. To Hear Him Tell It. *Unknown.* SCC
I was laying around town, just spending my time. The Strawberry Roan. *Unknown.* ABF
I was lost/ In doubt and fear. Lost, but Won. Henry von Schlichten. BePJ
I was lying still in a field one day. Zhenya Gay. TiPo (1959 ed.)
I Was Made Erect and Lone. Henry David Thoreau. FaBoEn; PoEL-4
I was made Father-of-the-Multitude. Abraham. Edmund Vance Cooke. QS
I Was Made of This and This. Gertrude Robison Ross. HBMV
I was [*or* wus] mighty good lookin' when I was [*or* wus] young. Spacially [*or* Specially] Jim. Bessie Morgan. BOHV; HBV; PTA-2
I was milking in the meadow when I heard the Banshee keening. The Warnings. Alice Furlong. AnIV
I was mistuk, once, for the Poape of Roame . . . The Silver Crook. Alfred Noyes. ChMo; CMP
I was near the King that day. I saw him snatch. Devotion to Duty. Siegfried Sassoon. MoPW
I was nine when my father died. Kit Carson. Arthur Guiterman. GA

I was not asked if I should like to come. The Bewildered Guest. William Dean Howells. BAP
I was not aware of the moment. Rabindranath Tagore. Gitanjali, XCV. NP
I was not blind,/ you must not think that I was blind. Priam. Dudley Fitts. OnHM
I was not born to Helicon, nor dare. A Gratulatory to Mr. Ben. Johnson for His Adopting of Him to Be His Son. Thomas Randolph. OBS
I was not, I was made: I was. To Be and Not to Be. *Unknown.* OnPM
I was not meant to kneel at the cool high altar. A Nonconformist. Emyr Humphreys. MoWP
I was not meant to stand in a sea-edge garden. Figurehead. Dorothy Paul. EtS
I was not sorrowful, I could not weep. Spleen. Ernest Dowson. MBP; MoBrPo
I was not train'd in academic bowers. Written at Cambridge. Charles Lamb. EnRP; OBRV
I was of delicate mind. I stepped aside for my needs. The Refined Man. Kipling. *Fr.* Epitaphs of the War. FaBoTw
I was on a tower in the midst of the stars. Lightning of the Abyss. Jules Laforgue. AnFP
I was on the drive in Eighty. Silver Jack. *Unknown.* CoSo; CSF
I was on the ocean once. Sanctuary. Elinor MacArthur. BLA
I was once an armed warrior. Now the worthy youth. A Horn. *Unknown.* OuHeWo
I was out walking an' a-ramblin' one day. The Wild Rippling Water. *Unknown.* CoSo
I was playing golf that day. *Unknown.* FiBHP
I was Polyxene in life. A Young Mother. Dioscorides. OxBG
I was reared/ In the great city, pent 'mid cloisters dim. Samuel Taylor Coleridge. *Fr.* Frost at Midnight. AlDL
I was sat in the church of their Lord. Microcosmos, XXXV. Nigel Heseltine. NeBP
I was selling my white horse. Song of Past Feelings. Po Chü-i. TrCh
I was sent adrift on the waves of the world. The Sad Song of Finian. "Ethna Carbery." DiM
I was seventy-seven, come August. The Little Old Lady in Lavender Silk. Dorothy Parker. InMe; YaD
I was sitting in my study. Papa's Letter. *Unknown.* PTA-2
I was smitten by the beauty. Football Is a Woman's Game. Al Graham. LauV
I was so chill and overworn, and sad. Song. Anna Wickham. BLV; CBOV; LoPS; MBP; MoBrPo; NeMA
I was spawned from the glacier. The Iceberg. Sir Charles G. D. Roberts. CaP
I was strolling one day down the Lawther Arcade. The Tin Gee Gee. Fred Cape. PTA-2
I was stung by a man-of-war. The Lesson. Larry Rubin. GoYe
I was takin' off my bonnet. Darwinism in the Kitchen. *Unknown.* FiBHP
I was taught prayer as a child, to bend the knee. Prayer at Dawn. Diarmuid O'Shea. KiLC
I was that dancer. On the screen. Re-run. Winfield Townley Scott. FiMAP
I was the chief of the race—he had stricken my father dead. The Voyage of Maeldune. Tennyson. PoEL-5
I was the first fruits of the battle of Missionary Ridge. Knowlt Hoheimer. Edgar Lee Masters. *Fr.* Spoon River Anthology. OxBA
I Was the Man. Cyril Tourneur. *Fr.* The Revengers Tragedy, IV, iv. LiA
I Was the Midmost. Thomas Hardy. MaPo
I was the milliner. Mrs. Williams. Edgar Lee Masters. *Fr.* Spoon River Anthology. NAMP
I was the moon. Dead. Rhoda Coghill. OnYI
I was the Moorish maid, Moraima. Moraima. *Unknown.* AnSpL-1
I was the only child of Frances Harris of Virginia. Hamilton Greene. Edgar Lee Masters. *Fr.* Spoon River Anthology. OxBA
I was the Other Shepherd. The Other Shepherd. Margaret Widdemer. SDH
I was the patriarch of the shining land. John Sutter. Yvor Winters. MoVE
I was the third man running in a race. The Service. Burges Johnson. HBMV; PreP; StaSt; VOD
I was thy Neighbour once, thou rugged Pile! Elegiac Stanzas, Suggested by a Picture of Peele Castle, in a Storm [*or* Nature and the Poet]. Wordsworth. BEL; BPN; ChER; EM-2; EmBrPo; EnRP; EPN; ERP; GEPC; GTBS; GTBS D; GTBS-W; GTSE; GTSL; HBV; MyFE; OAEP; OBRV; PoFS; TOP
I was too ambitious in my deed. Content. Elizabeth Barrett Browning. MaRV
I was upon the high and blessed mound. Sonnet: Of [*or* At] the Grave of Selvaggia. Cino da Pistoia. AWP; JAWP; OnPM; WBP
I was walking on the sea-shore. The Seagulls. Sir John Morris-Jones. PrWP
"I was with Grant—" the stranger said. The Aged Stranger. Bret Harte. AA; CaAE; LHV; MaC; MAP; MoAmPo (1942 ed.); NeMA; TreFS
I was wrought of walnut blocks and rolled rod steel. The Springfield Calibre Fifty. Joseph Mills Hanson. PoOW
I was yesterday in Ben Dorain and in her precincts I was not at a loss. Last Leave of the Hills. Duncan Ban MacIntyre. GoTS
I was young and happy and my heart was light and gay. Snagtooth Sal. Lowell O. Reese. ABF; SCC
I Wash My Face in a Golden Vase. *Unknown.* ChBR
I washed my face in water. Riddle. *Unknown.* ChTr
I wasn't well, and at my call. Martial, *tr. fr. Latin by* "G. I. C." Epigrams, V, 9. LaP
I Waste Away. Isaiah, XXIV: 16–20, Bible, *O.T.* TrJP
I watch afar the moving mystery. The Flying Mist. Edwin Markham. SN
I watch beside you in your silent room. Morton Luce. *Fr.* Thysia. HBV
I watch her fingers where they prance. Enigma. Hugh McCrae. BoAV; MoAuPo
I watch her in the corner there. Arachne. Rose Terry Cooke. AA; AnAmPo; LA
I watch him with his Christmas sled. His Christmas Sled. James Whitcomb Riley. FAOV
I watch the battle in the orange-grove. The Rout of San Romano. Jon Manchip White. NePoEA
I watch the curious hastened trait of twilight. Sadness, Glass, Theory. Roy Fuller. WaP
I watch the doctors walking with the nurses to and fro. The Memory. Lord Dunsany. OxBI
I watch the dung-cart stumble by. In December. Andrew Young. SeCePo
I watch the farmers in their fields. Farmers. William Alexander Percy. MaRV; WGRP
I watch the great spokes of this wheel. Beside a Balance Wheel. MacKnight Black. NP
I watch the leaves that flutter in the wind. Leaves at My Window. John James Piatt. AA
I Watch the Ships. Arthur W. H. Eaton. CPG
I watch the shore of gladness. Night Thoughts. John Sebastian Cammermeyer Welhaven. AnNoLy
I watch them on the drill field, the awkward and the grave. The Drill. Harry Brown. NeTW; TwAmPo; WaaP
I watch them through the bee's wing of the great bridge. River Traffic. Frederick Mortimer Clapp. VOD (1935 ed.)
I watch thy little bells of blue. To a Bluebell. Helena Coleman. CPG
I watch your gentle current as it flows. Sonnet: To the River Seine. Luigi Alamanni. LyPI
I Watched a Blackbird. Thomas Hardy. WhBS
I watched a sail until it dropped from sight. 'Tis Life Beyond [*or* Horizon]. *Unknown.* BPP; MaRV
I watched her as she stooped to pluck. On the Brink. Charles Stuart Calverley. VA
I watched her at her spinning. No and Yes. Theodore Tilton. PR
I watched him at the banquet wait. Lazarus. A. S. Cripps. BoSA
I watched the agony of a mountain farm. The Farm Died. Malcolm Cowley. *Fr.* Blue Juniata. MAP; MoAmPo (1942 ed.)
I watched the blind attack. Snow in April. Leonora Speyer. PG (1955 ed.)
I watched the Captains. The Captains of the Years. Arthur R. Macdougall, Jr. ChIP; MaRV; OQP; QP-2
I watched the day come up the road. To a Mocking Bird. Edwin Osgood Grover. BLA
I watched the hills drink the last color of light. Thought's End. Léonie Adams. MAP; MoAB; MoAmPo; PIAE
I watched the Lady Caroline. Lovelocks. Walter de la Mare. MoVE
I watched the pretty, white sea gull. The Sea Gull. Leroy F. Jackson. GFA; UTS
I watched the sea for hours blind with sun. Sonnet. Winfield Townley Scott. MiAP
I watched thee sleeping, child, as long ago. To My Daughter Adèle. Victor Hugo. TrFP
I watched them playing there upon the sand. The Castle. Sidney Alexander. PoNe
I watched your red lips move. Through Your Window. Tzu Yeh. ChLP; PoHN
I wear a cloak of laughter. Cloak of Laughter. Abigail Cresson. PoToHe
I Wear a Crimson Cloak To-Night. Lois Seyster Montross. HBMV
"I wear a cross of bronze," he said. The Cross. Leon Gellert. BoAu
I wear a snow-white rose today. Love's Tribute. Lorena W. Sturgeon. PGD; PSO

I wear your kiss like a feather. Two Kisses. Stephen Spender. ChMo; LoPo; LoPS
I weary of these noisy nights. Away. Max Ehrmann. PoToHe
I Weep. Angelina Weld Grimké. CDC
I weep. To Gottfried Benn. Else Lasker-Schüler. OnPM
I weep a sight which was not seen. Doom-devoted. Louis Golding. HBMV
I weep, but with no bitterness I weep. Souvenir. Alfred de Musset. AWP; WoL
I weep for Adonais—he is dead! Adonais. Shelley. AEV; AtBAP; ATP; BCEP; BEL; BoLiVe; BPN; ChER; EM-2; EmBrPo; EnL; EnLi-2; EnLit; EnRP; EPN; EPP; ERP; EV-4; FiP; GEPC; GoTL; HBV; HoPM; LiA; LoBV; MaPo; MCCG; NBE; OAEP; OBRV; PIAE; PoE; PoEL-4; PtP; REAL; ReaPo; TOP; TrGrPo; TriL; TwCrTr; UnPo (1st ed.); ViBoPo; WHA; WoL
I weep—not as the young do. I Weep. Angelina Weld Grimké. CDC
I weep those dead lips, white and dry. Linen Bands. Vance Thompson. AA
I weigh not fortune's frown or smile. A Contented Mind [*or* Contentment]. Joshua Sylvester. EV-1; HBV; LPS-3; PoToHe (1941 ed.); ReTS
I went a roaming, maidens, one bright day. Angelo Poliziano. Three Ballate, 3. AWP
I went across the pasture lot. The Cornfield. Elizabeth Madox Roberts. SUS
I went a-riding, a-riding. Texas. Amy Lowell. InP; PoMa; PoTo
I went a-roaming through the woods alone. The Nightingale. John Addington Symonds. VA
I went back an old-time lane. In the Fall o' Year. Thomas S. Jones, Jr. HBV
I went back to a place I knew. Remembrance. Aline Kilmer. CAW
I went but once to San Antonio. Some Towns of Texas. Karle Wilson Baker. HiLiAm
I went by star and planet shine. The Well-beloved. Thomas Hardy. ViP
I Went Down into the Desert to Meet Elijah. Vachel Lindsay. WGRP
I went down the garden, and what should I see. My Garden. Roger Lancelyn Green. BoN
I Went Down to the Depot, *with music*. *Unknown*. AS
I went down to the river. Life Is Fine. Langston Hughes. WaKn
I went down to the river, poor boy. Bow Down Your Head and Cry. *Unknown*. CoSo
I went down to the shouting sea. Sand-between-the-Toes. A. A. Milne. TiPo (1959 ed.)
I went down town one day in a lope. Ida Red. *Unknown*. ABF
I went into a public-'ouse to get a pint o' beer. Tommy. Kipling. BPN; EnLi-2 (1949 ed.); EnLit; MBP; MoBrPo; NeMA; PoVP; PTA-2; TreFS; ViPP
I went into a sort of house. The Wheelgoround. Robert Clairmont. PoMS
I went into my grandmother's garden. *Unknown*. OxNR
I went into my stable, to see what I might see. Old Wichet. *Unknown*. StPo
I went into the amphitheatre for the first time. Remembrance. Francisco Castillo Nájera. PoP
I went into the deserts of dim sleep. Fragment. Shelley. RO
I went into the flea circus. Small Talk. Don Marquis. *Fr.* Archy Does His Part. StPo
I went into the larder. Phosphorescence. Rosamond Langbridge. ReTS
I went out at the eastern gate. The Eastern Gate. *Unknown*. TrCh
I Went Out into the Garden. Moses ibn Ezra, *tr. fr. Hebrew by* Solomon Solis-Cohen. LiTW; TrJP
I went out on an April morning. Morning. Sara Teasdale. NP
I went out to the farthest meadow. Love Is a Terrible Thing. Grace Fallow Norton. AV; BAP; HBV; NV; PFY; PoeMoYo; SBMV
I went out to the hazel wood. The Song of Wandering Ængus. W. B. Yeats. AEV; BLV; BMEP; BoLiVe; CBOV; CH; ChMo; CMP; CP; EnLi-2 (1949 ed.); EnLit; FaBoCh; GoTP; GTIV; InP; KN; LoGBV; MaPo; MBP; MoAB; MoBrPo; NV; OnSP; PG; PoEL-5; PoMS; PoRA; POTT; RG; SP; TCPD; ThWaDe; TiPo; TwCV; TyEnPo; VLEP; WaKn
I went out to the woods today. Paradox. Jessie B. Rittenhouse. PR; TBM
I went this morning down to where the Johnny-Jump-Ups grow. The Faithless Flowers. Margaret Widdemer. MPB; SP
I went through the market-place crying, There is no death. A. R. D. Fairburn. *Fr.* Disquisition on Death. AnNZ
I went to bring. The Skippery Boo. Earl L. Newton. GoTP
I went to call on the Lord in His house on the high hill. The Bomb That Fell on America. Hermann Hagedorn. QS
I went to church. Worship. Helen Welshimer. BPP
I went to court last night. Puck Goes to Court. Fenton Johnson. CDC; GoSl
I went to dances at Chandlerville. *See* I went to the dances at Chandlerville.
I went to dig a grave for Love. Love's Change. Anne Reeve Aldrich. AA; AV; LBAP
I went to Frankfort, and got drunk. Epigram on an Academic Visit to the Continent. Richard Porson. OnPM; OxBoLi; WhC
I went to heaven. Emily Dickinson. NePA
I went to her who loveth me no more. Enchainment. Arthur O'Shaughnessy. HBV
I went to ma daddy. Hard Daddy. Langston Hughes. BANP
I went to market and bought me a cat. An Old Rhyme. *Unknown*. BoTP
I went to Noke. *Unknown*. OxNR
I went to San Francisco. Trip; San Francisco. Langston Hughes. GoSl
I went to school with the tutor, Law. The Teachers. C. V. Pilcher. OQP; QP-2
I went to seek for Christ. The Search. James Russell Lowell. MaRV; StJW
I went to sleep, and now I am refreshed. Cardinal Newman. *Fr.* The Dream of Gerontius. UnW
I went to sleep smiling. Prescience. Margaret Widdemer. HBMV
I went to someone's dinner and a play. Moan in the Form of a Ballade. Maurice Baring. WhC
I went to Strasbourg, where I got drunk. On a German Tour. Richard Porson. FiBHP
I went to sup with Cinna t'other night. Of Good Sauce. Sir John Harington. SiCE
I went to tea at Elizabeth's house. A Strange Interlude. Margaret Fishback. BOHV
I went to the animal fair. Animal Fair. *Unknown*. AS; BLPA; FaBoBe; GoTP; MoShBr; SiTL; YaD
I went to the captain with my hat in my hand. Take This Hammer. *Unknown*. OuSiCo
I went to the dances at Chandlerville. Lucinda Matlock. Edgar Lee Masters. *Fr.* Spoon River Anthology. BAP; BAV; ChMo; CMP; CP; InP; LaNeLa; LiTA; LiTL; LiTM; MAP; MCCG; MoAmPo; MotAn; MoVE; NeMA; NP; NV; OnPP; OxBA; ReMP
I went to the fields with the leisure I got. The Frightened Ploughman. John Clare. PoEL-4
I went to the Garden of Love. The Garden of Love. Blake. *Fr.* Songs of Experience. AWP; EM-1; EnLi-2 (1949 ed.); EnLoPo; EnRP; ExPo; InPo; JAWP; LEAP; LiTB; LiTG; LiTL; LO; LoBV; OAEP; PoE; PoFS; SeCeV; TOP; TyEnPo; ViBoPo; WBP
I went to the road that lies under the wall. *See* I went to the toad . . .
I went to the theatre. No Coaching. Christopher Morley. QS
I went to the toad [road, *wr.*] that lies under the wall. *Unknown*. OxNR; SiTL
I went to the wood and got it. Mother Goose. PPL, *longer vers.*; RIS
I went to the Wood of Flowers. The Wood of Flowers. James Stephens. BoTP
I went to turn the grass once after one. The Tuft of Flowers. Robert Frost. AmP; AmPP; AnNE; AtBAP; AWP; CoBMV; CV; GoYe; HBV; HBVY; IAP; InP; JAWP; LaNeLa; LiTA; MAP; MoAB; MoAmPo; MoPW; NeMA; OxBA; PC; ReaPo; SeCeV; TSW; TSWC; TwP; WBP
I went to worship in a house of God. Prayer in a Country Church. Ruth B. Van Dusen. TrPWD
I went up and down the streets. Doc Hill. Edgar Lee Masters. *Fr.* Spoon River Anthology. BAP; NP
I went up one pair of stairs. Just like Me. Mother Goose. BoTP; PPL
I went up to a high hill. The High Hill. Clinton Scollard. MaRV
I went up to London Town. Devilish Mary. *Unknown*. OuSiCo
I went up to the light of truth as if into a chariot. To Truth. *Unknown*. *Fr.* Solomon. WGRP
I went visiting Miss Melinda. Strawberry Jam. May Justus. FaPON
I wept a tear. Tears for Sale. Leonora Speyer. HBMV
I Wept as I Lay Dreaming. Heine, *tr. fr. German by* John Todhunter. AWP
I wept, still hoping tears might be the key. Barrier. Dorothy Quick. MuM; UnW
I wept Theonoe's loss; but one fair child. Loss after Loss. Bianor. OnPM
I were unkind unless that I did shed. Lines on His Com-

panions Who Died in the Northern Seas. Thomas James. SeCL
I wet my feet in the river. Ballad of the Doorstone. Louise Ayres Garnett. TBM
I . . . What a fine statue! Victory. Arthur B. Rhinow. MaRV
I which was once a happy wight. A Proper New Song Made by a Student in Cambridge. Thomas Richardson. TuPP
I whispered, "I am too young." Brown Penny. W. B. Yeats. ExPo; FaBoCh; LoGBV
I whispered my great sorrow. The Sedges. "Seumas O'Sullivan." AnIV; LBBV
I, who all my life had hurried. Epitaph for Any New Yorker. Christopher Morley. PC; PIAE
I who am dead a thousand years. To a Poet a Thousand Years Hence. James Elroy Flecker. BMEP; CaAE; ChTr; HBV; InP; LEAP; MBP; MoBrPo; MoPW; PoRA; POT; PoTo; POTT; ReTS; ShBV-4; TCPD; TrGrPo (1942 ed.); TwCV
I, who am known as London, have faced stern times before. London under Bombardment. Greta Briggs. OtMeF
I who am nothing and this tissue. Hoc Est Corpus. Alex Comfort. LiTB; LiTM; POTE
I who am street-known am also street knowing. Investigator. Miriam Waddington. BoCaPo (1948 ed.); CaP
I who employ a poet's tongue. Timid Lover. Countee Cullen. BANP
I who erst while the worlds sweet aire did draw. *Unknown.* SeCSL
I, Who Fade with the Lilacs. William Griffith. BAP; HBMV
I Who Had Been Afraid. Sister Maris Stella. GoBC
I, who had slept the dreamless sleep of Death. Dying-Day of Death. Ronald Campbell Macfie. EBSV
I who have favour'd many, come to be. To the Most Learned, Wise, and Arch-Antiquary, M. John Selden. Robert Herrick. SeCV-1
I who have heard solemnities of sound. The Great Voice. Clinton Scollard. BLP; MaRV
I, who have lost the stars, the sod. On a Subway Express. Chester Firkins. BAP; LBMV; PC; PFY; QS; VOD (1935 ed.); YaD
I who have no lover. Hero's Invocation to Death. Margaret Tod Ritter. TBM
I—who have the healing creed. Christ in Introspect. Charlotte Brontë. MaRV
I who have walked splay-footed in hobnailed boots. Imaginary Correspondence, *parody.* Frank Sidgwick. WhC
I, who knew Circe, have come back. Ulysses in Autumn. Joseph Auslander. MAP; MoAmPo (1942 ed.); PoeMoYo
I who love beauty in the open valleys. He, Too, Loved Beauty. Edwin McNeill Poteat. ChIP
I who love you bring. Song. Theodore Spencer. AnFE; CoAnAm; TwAmPo
I who once was free. Seguidilla. José de Valdivielso. CAW
I who sang only from the exquisite. Gentle Fatherland. Ramón López Velarde. TwSpPo
I, who was always counted, they say. Over the Hill from the Poor-House. Will M. Carleton. PTA-2
I who was once a golden woman like those who walk. Invocation. Edith Sitwell. AtBAP
I, who was the flower of my day among the beauties. The Beautiful Woman. Tu Fu. WoL
I will a round unvarnished tale deliver. Othello's Wooing. Shakespeare. *Fr.* Othello. BCEP
I Will Accept. Christina Rossetti. OxBoCh
(Bruised Reed Shall He Not Break, A.) EV-5
I will accomplish that and this. In After Days. George Frederick Cameron. BoCaPo; CaP; CPG
I will and bequeath. Testament. F. Tennyson Jesse. DiM
I will arise and go hence to the west. A Connaught Lament. Nora Hopper. AV; LBBV
I Will Arise and Go Now. Ogden Nash. WaKn
I will arise and go now, and go to Innisfree. The Lake Isle of Innisfree. W. B. Yeats. ATP; BEL; BLV; BMEP; BoLiVe; CaAE; CBE; ChMo; CMP; CoBMV; EnL; EnLi-2 (1949 ed.); EnLit; EPP; FaFP; FaPON; GBV; GTBS; GTBS-W; GTSL; HBV; HiLiEn; InP; LBBV; LEAP; LiTG; LiTM (rev. ed.); MaPo; MBP; MCCG; MoAB; MoBrPo; NeMA; OAEP (2d ed.); OBEV; OBVV; OnYI; OTPC (1946 ed.); PC; PoeT; PoRA; POT; PoTo; POTT; PoVP; PreP; PYM; ShBV-2; SP; TCEP; TCPD; TIP; TOP; TreF; TrGrPo; TSW; TSWC; TVSH; VLEP; WHA; YT
I will arise and go now, and go to Inverness. The Cockney of the North. Harry Graham. CenHV
I will arise and go; the wind is fain of me. The Sojourner. Sara Hamilton Birchall. NLK
I will arise and to my Father go. Seeking and Finding God. John C. Earle. MaRV
I will be a lion. Wild Beasts. Evaleen Stein. MPB (1956 ed.); RAR; UTS
I will be happy if but for once. Dubiety. Robert Browning. PoVP; ViPo
I will be quiet and talk with you. Along the Beach. Robert Browning. *Fr.* James Lee's Wife. VLEP
I will be the gladdest thing. Afternoon on a Hill. Edna St. Vincent Millay. BAP; BoTP; FaPON; LEAP; MPB; NLK; OxBA; POT; PoTo; SBMV; StVeCh (1955 ed.); TiPo (1952 ed.); TSW; TSWC; VOD
I will be what God made me, nor protest. Robert Bridges. The Growth of Love, LXII. PoVP
I Will Believe. William H. Roberts. BLRP
I will carry my coat and not put on my belt. A "Tzu-yeh" Song. *Unknown.* ChLP; TrCh
I will cast out wisdom and reject learning. Taoist Song. Chi K'ang. TrCh
I will come to you. Otomo no Yakamochi, *tr. fr. Japanese by* Kenneth Rexroth. OnPJ
I will confront Death smiling, and no tremor. Death, Life, Fear. Lilla Cabot Perry. BOL
I will consider my Cat Jeoffry. The Cat. Christopher Smart. *Fr.* Jubilate Agno. BoW
I will convince thee. Recrimination. Euripides. *Fr.* Iphigenia in Aulis. GrR
I will defy you down until my death. The Quiet Woman. Genevieve Taggard. AnEnPo; NP
I will drink, I will gamble, I will play wild again. O-Bar Cowboy. *At. to* Bill Wagon. CoSo
"I will ease my breast." Endymion's Vision. Keats. *Fr.* Endymion. ERP
I Will Enjoy Thee Now. Thomas Carew. LiTL
(Rapture, A.) ViBoPo
I will exchange a city for a sunset. Barter. Marie Blake. PoToHe (new ed.)
I will explain the eagle's nature. The Eagle's Nature. *Unknown, tr. fr. Middle English. Fr.* The Bestiary. MeEV
I will fare up White Creek Water. Indigo Bird. Stephen Crombie. BLA
I will fling wide the windows of my soul. Sonnet. Robert Hillyer. HBMV
I will give to you diamonds and rubies. To a Lady. John McClure. PR
I Will Give You. Blake. *See* To the Christians.
I will give you a golden ring. The Keys of Heaven. *Unknown.* FTB
I will give you the end of a golden string. *See* I give you the end of a golden string.
I will go back—I will go back. Château de Monthiers. Katherine Mann. EBSV
I will go back to the great sweet mother. The Sea [*or* The Return]. Swinburne. *Fr.* Triumph of Time. BLV; BMEP; BoLiVe; EtS; GTSL; HBV; LEAP; LPS-2; MBP; NLK; OAEP; PIAE; POTT; TrGrPo; TSW
I will go down to the sea again. Sea Song. Norah Holland. CaP; OCL
I will go out to grass with that old king. Richard Hovey. *Fr.* The Faun. NLK
I will go up the mountain after the moon. Moon Folly. Fannie Stearns Davis. *Fr.* Songs of Conn the Fool. CP; NV; RG; SP
I will go walking on Eighth Street. Eighth Street West. Rachel Field. ChBR; SiSoSe
I Will Go with My Father a-Ploughing. Joseph Campbell. AnIL; FaPON; GaP; GoBC; JKCP; OnYI; SiSoSe; TiPo (1959 ed.)
I will go with the first air of morning. Fishing. Dorothy Wellesley. OBMV
I will have a little house. The Little House. Katharine Tynan. LBBV
I will have all my beds blown up; not stuffed. Ben Jonson. *Fr.* The Alchemist, II, ii. NBE
I will have few cooking-pots. Domestic Economy. Anna Wickham. BLV; NeMA
I will have one built/ Like Pompey's theatre. John Day. *Fr.* The Parliament of Bees. ViBoPo
I Will Help You. Wolstan Dixey. PEOR
I will hew great windows for my soul. Windows For My Soul. Angela Morgan. OQP; QP-2
I will hold beauty as a shield against despair. Beauty as a Shield. Elsie Robinson. BLPA; PoToHe (new ed.)
I Will Keep Christmas. P. A. Ropes. BoTP
I will keep the fire of hope ever burning on the altar of my soul. Realization. Sri Ananda Acharya. WGRP
I will leave the dust of the city street and the noise of the busy town. The Vagrant. Pauline Slender. HBMV; NLK; PoTo
I Will Leave This House. Joseph Auslander. DDA
I Will Lift Up Mine Eyes unto the Hills. Psalms, CXXI, Bible, *O.T* AWP; BBV (1951 ed.); BLP; EnLi-1; FaPON; HiLiEn; JAWP; OnPM; OuHeWo; PC; TreF
(Pilgrim's Song, *Moulton, Modern Reader's Bible.*) WGRP
(Song of Safety, A.) PCH
(Song of Trust, A.) PCD; TrGrPo
I will live in Ringsend. Ringsend. Oliver St. John Gogarty. AnIL; LiTM; OBMV

I will love thee, O Lord, my strength. David Praiseth God for His Manifold and Marveilous Blessings. Psalm XVIII, Bible, *O.T.* LiA
I will make a new song of the word. Paul Engle. *Fr.* Break the Heart's Anger: Prologue. PoFr
I will make a small statue. Boy in the Dusk. Humbert Wolfe. MM
I will make a song for these States. A Song for the States. Walt Whitman. PoRL
I Will Make You Brooches. Robert Louis Stevenson. *See* Romance.
I will move quietly within this place. San Francesco d'Assisi. Catherine Parmenter. SaFP
I will never be able to stop my tears. On the Death of His Baby Son. Su T'ung-po. OnPC
I will never buy the pig in the poke. Buying a Pig. John Heywood. SiCE
"I will never eate nor drinke," Robin Hood said. Robin Hood's Death. *Unknown.* BaBo; ESPB
I will not break the tryst, my dear. A Tryst. Louise Chandler Moulton. HBV
I will not change my horse with any that treads. The Horse. Shakespeare. *Fr.* King Henry V. GoTP
I will not change my path with you. Dreams. Philip M. Raskin. OQP; QP-2
I will not cling forever to you, Tristram. Isolte of Brittany. Peter B. Yates, Jr. CAG
I will not comb my morning hair. Morning Hair. *Unknown.* OnPM
I will not doubt for evermore. Henry David Thoreau. *Fr.* Inspiration. MaRV
I will not doubt, though all my ships at sea. Faith. Ella Wheeler Wilcox. BLRP; MaRV; OQP; PoToHe; QP-2
I will not fear myself, will not fear truth. William Ellery Leonard. *Fr.* Two Lives, Pt. III. MOAP
I will not gather the vervain sweet. Sorrow. *Unknown.* OnPM
I Will Not Give Thee All My Heart. Grace Hazard Conkling. AV
"I will not go," he said, "for well." Infirm. Edward Sandford Martin. ALV; PR
I Will Not Grieve. Heine, *tr. fr. German by* Kurt J. Fickert. AnGP
I will not have the mad Clytie. Flowers. Thomas Hood. HBV; LPS-2; OTPC (1923 ed.); VA
I will not have you think me less. A Jewish Poet Counsels a King. Santob de Carrion. TrJP
I Will Not Hurry. Ralph Spaulding Cushman. MaRV
I will not kiss you country fashion. A Calvinist in Love. Jack R. Clemo. ChMP
I Will Not Let Thee Go. Robert Bridges. AnFE; BeLS; ChMo; CMP; CoBMV; EnLoPo; FaBoBe; LiTL; PoeT; POTT; PoVP; TCPD; TyEnPo; VA
I will not let you say a woman's part. A Woman's Answer. Adelaide Anne Procter. LPS-1
I will not look for him. A Woman's Pride. Helen Hay Whitney. AA
I will not make a bargain; I but ask. W. B. Yeats. *Fr.* Deirdre. ReTS
I will not perturbate/ Thy Paradisal state. To the Dead Cardinal of Westminster. Francis Thompson. POTT; PoVP
I will not rail, or grieve when torpid eld. Age [*or* Sonnet—Age]. Richard Garnett. OBVV; VA
I will not say to you, "This is the Way; walk in it." To My Son. *Unknown.* PoMa
I will not shut me from my kind. In Memoriam A. H. H., CVIII. Tennyson. BPN; EM-2; EmBrPo; EnLi-2; EPN; GEPC; ViPo; VLEP
I will not sing in Parker's praise. A New Song on Parker the Delegate. *Unknown.* SG
I will not sob myself to sleep, nor waken. Release. Margaret Tod Ritter. AV
I will not try the reach again. Hilaire Belloc. *Fr.* Dedicatory Ode. PoeT
I will not weep, for 'twere as great a sin. Conjectured to Be upon the Death of Sir Walter Raleigh. Henry King. EG
I will now address myself to the problem of writing. A Week of Doodle. Reed Whittemore. NePoEA
I will paint her as I see her. A Portrait. Elizabeth Barrett Browning. GN; HBV; LPS-1; OTPC
I will pluck from my tree a cherry-blossom wand. The Cherry Blossom Wand. Anna Wickham. MBP; MoBrPo; TSW; TwCV
I Will Praise the Lord at All Times. William Cowper. (Olney Hymns.) CEP
I will praise thee, O Lord, with my whole heart. I Will Sing Praise. Psalm IX, Bible, *O.T.* FaPON
I will put enmities/ Between thee and the woman. Genesis, Bible, *O.T.* (*Douay vers.*). ISi
I will report a twofold truth. Now grows. Empedocles, *tr. fr. Greek by* William Ellery Leonard. GrPo
I will repudiate the lie. If a Man Die, Shall He Live Again? John Richard Moreland. ChIP; MaRV; PGD
I will rise, I will go from the places that are dark with passion and pain. Seaward. George E. Woodberry. Wild Eden, XLI. AA
I will row my boat on Muckross Lake. The Wings of Love. James H. Cousins. AnIV
I will seek the heart of the hills far from the toils of the town. Where White Creek Goes. Clinton Scollard. PoTo
I will sing a song. The Song of the Lark. George Macdonald. BMEP
I will sing a song of battle. The Song of Chess. *At. to* Abraham ibn Ezra. TrJP
I will sing, I will go, and never ask me why. The Tramp Sings. Ridgely Torrence. *Fr.* Eye-Witness. PFY
I will sing, if ye will hearken. The Laird of Logie. *Unknown.* BaBo; CH; ESPB
I will sing in my cage. Bravura. *Unknown, tr. by* Mary Austin. APW
I will sing no more songs: the pride of my country I sang. O'Bruidar [*or* O Bruadair]. James Stephens, *after* O'Bruaidar. GTIV; OxBI
I will sing of myself a song that is true. The Seafarer. *Unknown.* EnLi-1 (1949 ed.)
I Will Sing Praise. Psalms, IX, Bible, *O.T.* FaPON
I will sing unto the Lord, for he hath triumphed gloriously. Triumphal Chant [*or* War Song of the Red Sea *or* The Song of Moses]. Exodus, Bible, *O.T.* BHV; LiTW; TrGrPo
I will sing unto the Lord, for He is highly exalted. Then Sang Moses. Exodus, Bible, *O.T.* TrJP
I will sing unto thee. Song to the Sun. Esaias Tegnér. AnSL
I will sing you a song full of quiet fire. Song: To a Lady with Many Names. John Wickham. JKCP (1955 ed.)
I will sing you a song of that beautiful land. Home of the Soul. Ellen M. Huntington Gates. BLRP
I will speak of your deeds. An Oration, Entitled "Old, Old, Old, Old Andrew Jackson." Vachel Lindsay. ATP (1935 ed.); GA; YaD
I will start anew this morning with a higher fairer creed. A New Start. *Unknown.* OQP; QP-1
I will take my pipes and go now, for the bees upon the sill. The Piper. Donn Byrne. BPP; PoTo
I will teach you my townspeople. Tract. William Carlos Williams. AmP; AmPP; CoBMV; LiTA; LiTM; MoAB; MoAmPo; MOAP; NePA; OnAP; TrGrPo; WoL
I will tell you a tale tonight. The Admiral's Ghost. Alfred Noyes. BBV
I Will Tell You of a Fellow. *Unknown.* *See* Common Bill.
I Will Trust. Jean Ingelow. MaRV
I will weave the violet white. Heliodora's Wreath [*or* A Spring Garland]. Meleager. GrR; OxBG
I will with engines never exercised [*or* exercisde]. Christopher Marlowe. *Fr.* Tamburlaine the Great, Pt. II. BCEP; BrBE
I, Willie Wastle. *Unknown.* OxNR
I winged my bird. Bert Kessler. Edgar Lee Masters. *Fr.* Spoon River Anthology. AnFE; APA; CoAnAm
I Wish. Nancy Byrd Turner. SiSoSe
I wish a cricket in a wicker boat. A Japanese Birthday Wish. Thomas Burnett Swann. GoYe
I wish all the/ mandragora. Blue Funk. Joel Oppenheimer. NeAP
I wish 'at I'd of been here when. When Pa Was a Boy. S. E. Kiser. FAOV
I wish, because the sweetness of your passing. Wild Wishes. Ethel M. Hewitt. HBV
I wish for rain—and I wish for snow. Nearing Cold-Dale. Hannes Hafstein. IcP
I wish he were the Polar Star in Heaven. Anchises. Blanaid Salkeld. OxBI
I wish, how I wish that I had a little house. The Shiny Little House. Nancy M. Hayes. BoTP; SUS
I wish I could lend a coat. Akahito. *Fr.* Manyo Shu. AWP
I wish I could remember. To a Child. David McCord. AnAmPo
I wish I could remember that [*or* the] first day. The First Day. Christina Rossetti. Monna Innominata, II. EmBrPo; EnLi-2; EPP; FaBoBe; HBV; LiTL; LO; TCEP; ViPo
I wish I had a penguin playmate. My Penguin Playmate. Donald E. Cooke. MPB (1956 ed.)
I wish I had a pony or a trot. I Wish I Had Great Knowledge or Great Art. Delmore Schwartz. FiMAP
I wish I had a yellow cat. Three Wishes. *Unknown.* DDA
I wish I had an aeroplane. A Penny Wish. Irene Thompson. BoTP
I wish I had been his apprentice. The Nazareth Shop [*or* In the Carpenter Shop]. *Unknown.* ChIP; GoTP; OQP; QP-2; StJW
I Wish I Had Great Knowledge or Great Art. Delmore Schwartz. FiMAP
I wish I knew geography—for that would tell me why. Lines

on a Mysterious Occurrence. Alfred Denis Godley. CenHV

I wish I lived in a caravan. The Pedlar's [or Peddler's] Caravan. William Brighty Rands. BoChLi; BoTP; GaP; GFA; HBV; HBVy; MPB; OTPC; PCH; PRWS; RIS; StVeCh (1940 ed.); TVC; TVSH

I wish I loved the human race. The Wishes of an Elderly Man. Sir Walter Raleigh. CenHV; FaBoCh; FiBHP; LoGBV; SiTL; ShBV-4; WhC

I wish I owned a Dior dress. Reflections at Dawn. Phyllis McGinley. FiBHP

I wish I was a' apple, a-hangin' on a tree. *Unknown. See* I wish I was an apple . . .

I wish I was a happy bird. Love Scorned by Pride. John Clare. RO

I Wish I Was a Little Bird. *Unknown.* AS

I wish I was a little egg. A Wish. *Unknown.* DDA

I Wish I Was a Mole in the Ground. *Unknown.* ABF

I wish I was an [or a'] apple, a hangin' on [or in] the tree. Cindy. *Unknown.* SoAF; TrAS; TreFS

I Wish I Was by That Dim Lake. Thomas Moore. ERP; GoBC; LiA; PoEL-4

I wish I was in de [or the] land ob [or of] cotton. Dixie. Daniel Decatur Emmett. ABF; APW; BlG; BoHiPo; FaFP; FaPON; HBV; LEAP; OlF; PaA; PoFr; SPP; TrAS; TreF; TrGrPo; YaD

I wish I was in the land of cotton. The New Dixie. Maria Louisa Eve. BlG

I Wish I Was Single Again. *Unknown. See* When I Was Single.

I Wish I Were. *Unknown.* FaFP; OxBoLi; SiTL

I wish I were a little bird. A Wish. Christina Rossetti. BPN

I wish I were an Emperor. Wishes. F. Rogers. BoTP

I wish I were an ivory lyre. Wishes. Callistratus. OnPM

I wish I were close. Three Poems from the Japanese, III. Yamabe no Akahito, *tr. fr. Japanese by* Kenneth Rexroth. HoPM; LiTW; OnPJ

I wish I were in the Dutchman's Hall. Lowlands, *vers.* III. *Unknown.* AmSS

I wish I were now. The Isle of the Heather. Murdo Mac-Leod. EBSV

I wish I were the little key. A Child's Wish. Abram J. Ryan. AA; CAW; JKCP

I wish I were the little man. To an Andalusian Fan. J. Rodriguez la Orden. OnPM

I wish I were where Helen lies. Helen of Kir[k]connell [or Fair Helen]. *Unknown.* AnFE; AWP; BBV (1923 ed.); BCEP; BrBE; BSV; CBE; CBOV; CH; EBSV; EtPaEn; EV-2; FaFP; GBV (1922 ed.); GoTS; GTBS; GTBS-D; GTBS-W; GTSE; GTSL; HBV; InP; InPo; LEAP; LH; LiTB; LiTG; LiTL; LO; LoBV; OBB; OBEV; OTPC; SeCeV; UnPo (1st ed.); ViBoPo; WP

I wish my enemies would go to hell. Greetings of the Season. Hilaire Belloc. SiTL

I wish my eyes were big and blue. Wishes. Edna Kingsley Wallace. MoSiPe

I wish my hair cut. Jones at the Barber Shop. *Unknown.* LPS-3

I wish my heart. Ballad of the Rag-Bag Heart. Marjorie Allen Seiffert. AV

I wish my mother could see me now. M. I. (Mounted Infantry of the Line). Kipling. BPN

I Wish My Tongue Were a Quiver. L. A. Mackay. *Fr.* The Ill-tempered Lover. BoCaPo; CaP; SiTL

I wish not Thasos rich in mines. Mimnermus Incert. Walter Savage Landor. PoEL-4

I wish, O son of the Living God. The Wish of Manchin of Liath [or The Hermit's Song]. *Unknown.* AnIL; OnYI

"I wish she had not died," she said. Motherless. Mary Mapes Dodge. FAOV

I wish she would not ask me if I love the kitten more than her. Concerning Love. Josephine Preston Peabody. CIV; WhC

I wish that Easter eggs would do. If Easter Eggs Would Hatch. Douglas Malloch. MPB

I wish that I could have my wish to-night. Shakespeare. Henry Ames Blood. AA

I wish that I could see to-night. The Silver Tree. Francis Keppel. BLA

I wish that I could understand. The Wonderer. Robert W. Service. BBV

I wish that I were rubber-skinned. Wish at Meal-Time. John Farrar. BoChLi

I Wish That My Room Had a Floor. Gelett Burgess. FiBHP; GoTP; InvP; LiL
(Floorless Room, The.) HBVy
(Limerick.) ALV; CenHV; HBV; LiBL; NA; TSW; TSWC; WhC

I wish that my soul could perish with my body. To His Wife. Ovid. *Fr.* Tristia. LaP

I wish that there were some wonderful place. The Land of Beginning Again. Louise Fletcher Tarkington. BLPA; OQP; PTA; QP-2

I wish that when you died last May. May and Death. Robert Browning. GEPC; GTML

I wish there were some wonderful place. Louise Fletcher Tarkington. *See* I wish that there were . . .

I wish they would hurry up their trip to Mars. A Projection. Reed Whittemore. NePoEA; WaKn

I wish to cast off my body. Oedipus. Robert Garnier. *Fr.* Antigone. LiA

I wish to make my sermon brief,—to shorten my oration. Praise of Little Women. Juan Ruiz, Archpriest of Hita. *Fr.* The Book of Good Love. AnSpL-1; AWP

I wish to tune my quivering lyre. The Bard of Love. *Unknown, tr. by* Byron. OuHeWo

I wish we could take a statistic with more grace, beloved. Enlightenment. Josephine Miles. FiMAP

I wish we might go gypsying one day the while we're young. The Gypsying. Theodosia Garrison. NLK; VOD

"I wish, when summer's drawing near about the end of May." I Wish. Nancy Byrd Turner. SiSoSe

I wish you were a pleasant wren. Child's Talk in April. Christina Rossetti. GN; OTPC (1923 ed.)

I wish you were real! Phantasus: VI–14. Arno Holz. LiTW

I wish you'd speak to Mary, Nurse. The Game of Cricket. Hilaire Belloc. FiBHP

I wish you'd write me a letter about the frost. Frost. Yevgeny Aronovich Dolmatovsky. TrRV

I wish your breast were made of glass. The Lover's Lament (B vers.) *Unknown.* AS

I wished so long that I could pass. Rediscovery. Geoffrey Johnson. UnW

I wished to shirk my task one day. Discovery. Benjamin Keech. PoToHe

I wisht I wus a hummin' bird. Wishing. John Charles McNeill. NoCaPo

I with the morning's love have oft made sport. Sunrise on the Sea. Shakespeare. *Fr.* A Midsummer Night's Dream, III, ii. ChTr

I with the sea-shell sounding heart. Heredity and Ego. Mary Josephine Benson. CPG

I with uncovered head. James Russell Lowell. *Fr.* Ode Recited at the Harvard Commemoration, July 21, 1865. OHIP

I, with Whose Colo[u]rs Myra Dressed [or Drest] Her Head. Fulke Greville. Caelica, XXII. AtBAP; EG; ElSeCe; InvP; PoE
(Myra.) CoEV; EIL; EV-1; GTBS-W; LoBV; OBEV; OBSC
(To Myra.) LiTB; LiTG; LiTL; ViBoPo

I within me holding. The Soldier. Alun Lewis. MoWP

I woke at three; for I was bid. Going to Church. Coventry Patmore. *Fr.* The Angel in the House. LoBV

I woke by first light in a wood. Sestina. Donald Justice. NePoEA

I woke from death and dreaming. A Shepherd's Coat. Lilian Bowes-Lyon. ChMP; GTBS-D

I woke up this mornin' 'bout four o'clock. Casey Jones (G vers.). ViBoFo

I woke up with morning yawning in my mouth. Dawn. Louis Dudek. PeCV

I won a noble fame. Sir Marmaduke's Musings. Theodore Tilton. AA

I won the prize essay at school. John Horace Burleson. Edgar Lee Masters. *Fr.* Spoon River Anthology. CrMA

I Wonder. Jeannie Kirby. BoTP

I wonder about the trees. The Sound of [the] Trees. Robert Frost. AnFE; APA; AtBAP; BrBE; ChMo; CMP; CoAnAm; MAPA; NV; OxBA; PG; PoeMoYo; TwAmPo; TwCV; VOD

I wonder by my troth what thou and I. The Good-Morrow. John Donne. AnFE; AtBAP; AWP; BLV; BoLiVe; CoEV; EG; EIL; EnLi; EnLoPo; EnLP; EPS; EV-2; ExPo; FaBoBe; FaBoEn; GTBS-W; HBV; HoPM; InPo; InvP; LEAP; LiTB; LiTG; LiTL; LoBV; LoPo; LoPS; MaPo; MeLP; MePo; NBE; OBS; Po; PoE; PoEL-2; PoFS; PoRA; ReaPo; ReEn; SeCeV; SeCV-1; SeEP; TrGrPo; TuPP; TwHP; TwP; ViBoPo

I wonder, dear, if you had been. A Conjecture. Charles Francis Richardson. AA

I wonder do they sit in endless rest. The Dead. Victor Starbuck. BLP; LS; NoCaPo

I wonder do you feel today. Two in the Campagna. Robert Browning. BLV; BMEP; BoLiVe; BPN; CoEV; EM-2; EmBrPo; EnLi-2 (1949 ed.); EPN; EtPaEn; ExPo; FaBoEn; GEPC; GTBS-D; GTML; HBV; OAEP; PoEL-5; PoVP; SeCePo; SeCeV; TOP; TrGrPo; TyEnPo; ViPo; ViPP; VLEP; WHA

I wonder, Duddon, if you still remember. To the River Duddon. Norman Nicholson. FaBoMo

I wonder how it happens. I Change. Witter Bynner. HBMV

I wonder how it would be here with you. Altitude. Lola Ridge. NP

I wonder how the organist can do so many things. The Organist. *Unknown.* BLPA

"I wonder if Brougham thinks as much as he talks." A Voice, and Nothing Else. *Unknown.* LPS-3

I wonder if Christ had a little black dog. The Little Black Dog. Elizabeth Gardner Reynolds. AlBD

I wonder if, sunning in Eden's vales. Ballade of the Ancient Wheeze. Nate Salsbury *and* Newman Levy. InMe

I wonder if that cypress tree. Question. Howard McKinley Corning. ChIP

I wonder if the cabbage knows. Affinity. "Ricketty Kate." MoAuPo

I wonder if the engine. Engine. James S. Tippett. BoChLi; SUS

I wonder if the hawk knew. The Different Day. Grace Hazard Conkling. TCPD

I Wonder If the Lion Knows. Annette Wynne. UTS

I wonder if the name is right. The Address. *Unknown.* PCH

I wonder if the old cow died or not. The Question. W. W. Gibson. BEL

I wonder if the sap is stirring yet. The First Spring Day. Christina Rossetti. BPN

I wonder if the tides of Spring. Beyond. Thomas S. Jones, Jr. TBM

I wonder if they like it—being trees? Tree Feelings. Charlotte Perkins Gilman. GFA; MW; NLK; PGD

I wonder if, when Galatea woke. A Question. Edna Livingston. GoYe

I wonder in what fields today. On Her Child's Death. Kaga no Chiyo. LiTW

I Wonder in What Isle of Bliss. Justin Huntly M'Carthy, *par. fr. the French of* Villon. *Fr.* If I Were King. PFE
  (Ballad of Dead Ladies, A.) HBV
  ("Sigh, my lute, sigh.") ReTS, *longer sel.*

I Wonder Not That Youth Remains. Walter Savage Landor. BPN
  (Epigram: "I wonder not that youth remains.") EV-4

I wonder poet, can you take it. The Muse to an Unknown Poet. Paul Potts. FaBoTw

I wonder sometimes if the soldiers lying. Song for the Heroes. Alex Comfort. MoBrPo (1950 ed.); NeBP

I wonder that the grot was bare of birds. Didymus. Eileen Duggan. JKCP (1955 ed.)

I wonder that the metal stands the test. The Anvil of God's Mercy. Anna Hamilton Wood. OQP; QP-2

I wonder—were there flowers there. Were Flowers There? George William Allison. ChIP

I Wonder What Became of Rand, McNally. Newman Levy. InMe; WhC

I wonder what day of the week. Untimely Thought. Thomas Bailey Aldrich. AnNE

I wonder what he charged for chairs at Nazareth. The Carpenter. G. A. Studdert-Kennedy. ChIP; OQP; QP-1; StJW

I Wonder What It Feels Like to Be Drowned. Robert Graves. MBP; MoBrPo; TSW; TSWC

I wonder what my kite can see. The Kite. Pearl Forbes MacEwen. BoTP

I wonder what spendthrift chose to spill. March. Celia Thaxter. GoTP

I wonder what the Clover thinks. A Song of Clover. Helen Hunt Jackson. GN; OTPC

I wonder what your thoughts are, little Cloud. The Cloud. Oliver Herford. BOHV

I wonder where I may gather some sweet pretty flowers. Garden Song. *Unknown.* PCH

I wonder where it could of went to. Legend. John V. A. Weaver. PFY; TCPD; YaD

I wonder where the rabbits go. Tracks. John Farrar. GFA

I wonder whether the girls are mad. William Bond. Blake. MyFE

I wonder who is haunting the little snug café. At the Lavender Lantern. Charles Divine. HBMV

I wonder why the grass is green. I Wonder. Jeannie Kirby. BoTP

I wonder why the inlaid psaltery has fifty strings. The Inlaid Psaltery. Li Shang-yin. WhP

I wonder will he be gentle. The Young Bride's Dream. Rhoda Coghill. OxBI

I wondered at the mighty horse. The Overworked Horse. Gerald Gould. MoBrPo (1942 ed.)

I Won't Be My Father's Jack. *Unknown.* OxNR; UnS

I won't print and you won't see. World War III. *Unknown.* SiTL

I woo unseen, this groaning winter's night. The Wooing of Saint Francis. Hyacinth Blocker. SaFP

I work at night, surrounded by city. Burial in the East. "Pablo Neruda." AnCL

I work or play, as I think best. Emancipation. *Unknown.* BLPA

I worship the greatest first. Hippolytus Temporizes. Hilda Doolittle ("H. D."). MOAP

I worship thee, sweet will of God! The Will of God. Frederick William Faber. MaRV; VA

I worshipped, when my veins were fresh. Revelation. William Baylebridge. *Fr.* Life's Testament. BoAV; MM

I Wot Full Well that Beauty Cannot Last. George Turberville. *See* To His Friend, Promising . . .

I wot not how the world's degenerate. Satire. Joseph Hall. *Fr.* Virgidemiarum. ReIE

I Would. Pierre de Ronsard, *tr. fr. French by* Alan Conder. TrFP

I would all womankind were dead. The Lay of the Lover's Friend. William E. Aytoun. BOHV

I would ask of you, my darling. Will You Love Me When I'm Old? *Unknown.* BLPA; FaBoBe; NeHB

I would be a bird, and straight on wings I arise. Robert Bridges. The Growth of Love, XXII. GTML

I would be as ignorant as the dawn. *See* I would be ignorant . . .

I would be bread. Lover's Wish. F. Tennyson Jesse. DiM

I would be dismal with all the fine pearls of the crown of a king. To a Blue Flower. John Shaw Neilson. BoAV

I Would Be Great. Hattie B. McCracken. OQP; QP-2

I would be ignorant [or as ignorant] as the dawn. The Dawn. W. B. Yeats. MaPo; MoVE; NP

I would be left alone with this great love. The Cloister. Richard Le Gallienne. LBBV

I would be married, but I'd have no wife. On Marriage. Richard Crashaw. ReEn

I would be one with Thee. Communion. Loren W. Burch. ChIP

I would be only. Love Song. Iwan Goll. OnPM

I would be thine when morning breaks. Lines to My . . . George Moses Horton. NoCaPo

I Would Be True. Howard Arnold Walter. *See* My Creed.

I would beat out your face in brass. Face. Carl Sandburg. ReMP

I would build myself a house. Songs of the Plains, IV. Glenn Ward Dresbach. NP

I Would Comprehend Thee. Rainer Maria Rilke, *tr. fr. German by* Jessie Lemont. OnPM

I would, dear Jesus, I could break. A Prayer. John D. Long. OQP; QP-1

I Would Define My Love. Jessica Powers. JKCP (1955 ed.)

I would flee from the city's rule and law. A Country Summer Pastoral. Sam Walter Foss. BOHV

I Would Forgo. Hilda Doolittle ("H. D."). LO; MoP
  (I Would Forego.) LoPS

I would give all my old razor-blades. Louvre. Rhys Davies. MoWP

I Would Go Back. Mary M. Curchod. ChIP; PSO

I would go to the white beach. Manuel Altolaguirre, *tr. fr. Spanish by* Eleanor L. Turnbull. CoSP

I would have a man live in manly fashion. Volo Virum Vivere Viriliter. *Unknown.* *Fr.* Carmina Burana. LaF

I would have gone; God bade me stay. Weary in Well-doing. Christina Rossetti. RiBV; SeCePo; TrPWD; ViPo; VLEP

I would have my own vision. The Analysis of Love. Sir Herbert Read. FaBoMo; LiTG

I would I had been island-born. A Ballade of Islands. Lucy Catlin Robinson. AA

I would I had something to do—or to think! All in the Downs. Tom Hood. ALV; CenHV

I would I had thrust my hands of flesh. Edmund Pollard. Edgar Lee Masters. *Fr.* Spoon River Anthology. AnFE; APA; CoAnAm

I would I had thy courage, dear, to face. To Manon, on Her Lightheartedness. Wilfrid Scawen Blunt. The Love Sonnets of Proteus, XI. VA

I would I knew of some wise wight. This World Fares But as a Fantasy. *Unknown.* TMEV

I would I might forget that I am I. Sonnets, IV. George Santayana. AWP; JAWP; LBMV; MOAP; TOP; WBP

I would I were a bird so free. Popular Songs of Tuscany. *Unknown, tr. by* John Addington Symonds. AWP

I would I were a damask rose. Would I Were a Rose. *Unknown.* OxBG

I would I were a god, with all the scope. Clark Ashton Smith. *Fr.* Nero. BAP

I Would I Were Actaeon. *Unknown, at. to* ——— Bewe. EIL
  (Actaeon.) OBSC

I Would I Were an Excellent Divine. Nicholas Breton. LPS-2

I would I were beneath a tree. The Three Woulds. *Unknown.* DDA

I would I were on yonder hill. Shule Aroon. *Unknown.* GTIV; TIP

I would I were the little flower. Valentine. Charles G. Blanden. DD

I would, if I could. *Unknown.* OxNR

I would immortalize these nymphs: so bright. L'Après-Midi d'un faune [or The Afternoon of a Faun]. Stéphane Mallarmé. AWP; LiA; LiTW; MiFP

I would in rich and golden-colored rain. Phyllis, XXXIV. Thomas Lodge. ReEn

I would in that sweet bosom be. James Joyce. Chamber Music, VI. ReMP
I Would Know. Vicente Aleixandre, *tr. fr Spanish by* Eleanor L. Turnbull. CoSP
I would lie low—the ground on which men tread. The Earth. Jones Very. AmP; OxBA
I would like to dive. The Diver. W. W. E. Ross. BoCaPo; PeCV
I would like to have the men of Heaven. The Heavenly Banquet. *At. to* St. Bridget. OnYI; SiB
I would like to speak. A Kindergarten Orator. Julia H. May. MeMeAg
I Would Like You for a Comrade. Edward Abbott Parry. PCH; TVC; TVSH
I would live all my life in nonchalance and insouciance. Introspective Reflection. Ogden Nash. WhC
I would live for a day and a night. The Song-Maker. Anna Wickham. MBP; MoBrPo
I Would Live in Your Love. Sara Teasdale. NV
I would live this life so well. A Creed. Edgar A. Guest. HH; PEDC
I Would Love to Be a Shepherd. Kostas Krystallis, *tr. fr. Modern Greek by* Rae Dalven. MoGP
I would make a list against the evil days. A Ballade-Catalogue of Lovely Things. Richard Le Gallienne. CBOV; CP; HBMV; PIAE; POT; PoTo
I would make songs for you. Songs. Babette Deutsch. HBMV
I would make you. Petition for a Miracle. David Morton. *Fr.* Boke of Two Ladies. ISi
I would not alter thy cold eyes. Flos Lunae. Ernest Dowson. OBMV; ViPP
I would not always reason. The Conjunction of Jupiter and Venus. Bryant. IAP; OQP; QP-2
I would not, as the light-hearts do. The Dying Year. Clyde Walton Hill. PEDC
I would not ask Thee that my days. A Prayer for Faith. Alfred Norris. BLRP
I would not be a serving-man. Merrythought's Song. Beaumont *and* Fletcher. *Fr.* The Knight of the Burning Pestle. OBS
I would not be the moon, the sickly thing. In Dispraise of the Moon. Mary Elizabeth Coleridge. CH
I would not call him in, my heart decried. The Architect. Molly Anderson Haley. ChIP
I would not change one little jot. His Will. Kanda. SoLD
I would not, could I, make thy life as mine. A Vain Wish. Philip Bourke Marston. VA
I would not enter on my list of friends. Heedless Cruelty [*or* Humanity]. William Cowper. *Fr.* The Task. BCEP; LPS-3
I would not from the wise require. The Merry Heart. Henry Hart Milman. TVSH
I would not give my Irish wife. The Irish Wife. Thomas D'Arcy McGee. HBV; VA
I would not go to old Joe's house. Old Joe Clark. *Unknown.* ABF
I would not have a god come in. Mastery. Sara Teasdale. *Fr.* Interlude: Songs Out of Sorrow. ChMo; CMP; HBV; QS; WGRP
I would not have my general be. A General. Archilochus. GrR
I would not have the world to know. Mikhail Yurevich Lermontov, *tr. fr. Russian by* Sir Cecil Kisch. WaL
I Would Not Have This Perfect Love of Ours. James Russell Lowell. APW
(Sonnet: "I would not have this perfect love of ours.") CoBA
I Would Not Live Alway. William Augustus Muhlenberg. AA; HBV
I would not paint a picture. Emily Dickinson. CoV
I would not spare for to speak, wist I to speed. Winchelsea Fight, or the Humbling of the Spaniards. Laurence Minot. SG
I would not that immortal soul reclaim. He Lives at Last. Lucile Lippitt. MaRV
I would prisoner in this tower. The Tower of Iznajar. Rafael Alberti. CoSP
I Would Remember Constant Things. John Urban Nicholson. TBM
I would run swiftly past the blossomy copse. Tropical Pool. Muna Lee. NV
I would say a few words. Perhaps a Prayer. James Schevill. FiMAP
"I would," says Fox, "a tax devise." Epigram. Sheridan. HBV
I would sit in the windows ledge. Education. Josephine Miles. FiMAP
I would spend a morning. April Morning. George Elliston. NLK
I would that all men my hard case might know. Behold the Deeds! H. C. Bunner. ALV; BOHV; HBV; InMe; LEAP; LHV; PA
I Would That All My Verses. Juan Ramón Jiménez, *tr. fr. Spanish by* J. B. Trend. AnSpL-2
I would that even now. Princess Shoku, *tr. fr. Japanese by* Curtis Hidden Page. *Fr.* Hyaku-Nin-Isshu. AWP; JAWP; WBP
I would that folk forgot me quite. Tess's Lament. Thomas Hardy. FaBoTw
I would that free from sickness, untouched by cares and tears. "The Sated Guest." Mimnermus. GrPE
I would that I might fold my tent. On the Advantages of Travel. *Unknown.* CAG
I would that I were a mighty man. Dreams and Life. Erik Axel Karlfeldt. AnSL
I would that, richly gilding me, I might. I Would. Pierre de Ronsard. TrFP
I Would That Wars Should Cease. Tennyson. *Fr.* The Charge of the Heavy Brigade at Balaclava: Epilogue. AOAH
I would that we were, my belovèd, white birds on the foam of the sea! The White Birds. W. B. Yeats. EnL; VA
I would the gift I offer here. Dedication. Whittier. *Fr.* Songs of Labor. AmPP (4th ed.); AnNE; CoBA; CoV; IAP; OxBA
I Would the World Were Mine. Caroline E. S. Norton. DiM
I Would Thou Wert Not Fair. Nicholas Breton. *See* His Wisdom.
I would to God I were quenched and fed. The Anguish. Edna St. Vincent Millay. BAP; ChMo; CMP; NeMA
I would to God, that mine old age might have. His Wish to God. Robert Herrick. OxBoCh
I would to heaven that I were so much clay. Fragment. Byron. ERP; FiP; OAEP
I would unto my fair restore. Of Joan's Youth. Louise Imogen Guiney. AA; HBV; LBMV; LEAP
I Wouldna Gie a Copper Plack. Mary A. Barr. BCEP
I wrastled wid Satan, I wrastled wid sin. *Unknown.* NAMP
I wreathe him in my arms; I wail his wrong. The Solitary Mourner. Euripides. *Fr.* Rhesus. GrR
I write about a silly ass. Hero and Leander. Joseph S. Newman. FiBHP
I write. He sits beside my chair. A New Poet. William Canton. BMEP; HBV; VA
I write. My mother was a Florentine. Motherless. Elizabeth Barrett Browning. *Fr.* Aurora Leigh, I. MOAH; VA
I write my name as one. An Autograph. Whittier. AA
I write no poem men's hearts to thrill. I Teach School. *Unknown.* BLP
I write to soothe that inward grief alone. Sonnet. Vittoria Colonna. LyPI
I write to you . . . And yet, so great is the silence. Letter from the Front. Angelos Sikelianos. MoGP
I Write Verses. Walter Savage Landor. *See* Yes, I Write Verses.
I write you; is my act not serving. Tatyana's Letter to Onegin. Pushkin. *Fr.* Eugene Onegin. TrRV
I wrote, and in my heart was burning. The Letter. Mu'tamid, King of Seville. MooP
I wrote some lines once on a time. The Height of the Ridiculous. Oliver Wendell Holmes. AA; ALV; AnNE; APW; BAP; BBV (1951 ed.); BOHV; DDA; FaFP; FiBHP; HBV; HiLiAm; IAP; LauV; LEAP; LHV; LPS-3; MCCG; MOAP; MoShBr; MPB; NeHB; OTPC (1946 ed.); PFE; PIR; PoeMoYo; PTA-2; SiTL; StVeCh; WhC; YaD
I wrought and battled and wept, near and afar. The Last Port. Frank Wilmot. BoAu
I wrought them like a targe of hammered gold. On His "Sonnets of the Wingless Hours." Eugene Lee-Hamilton. VA
I wus mighty good-lookin' when I wus young. *See* I was mighty good lookin' when I was young.
I Wuz Borned on the Rivuh, *with music. Unknown.* StDa
I yearn more hungrily to see your face. Upon the Same. Joachim du Bellay. Les Amours, XXVII. TrFP
I yearn to bite on a colloid. Amazing Facts about Food. *Unknown.* BOHV
I years had been from home. Emily Dickinson. AmP; AmPP (4th ed.); OxBA; PoRA
I yield, I yield! Divine Althea, see. The Surrender. Thomas Flatman. EV-3
I Yield Thee Praise. Philip Jerome Cleveland. TrPWD
Iago Prytherch his name, though, be it allowed. A Peasant. R. S. Thomas. MoWP
Iambicum Trimetrum. Spenser. EIL; OBEV (new ed.); PoEL-1; ReIE
(Iambica.) OxBoLi; SiTL
Ianthe, *sels.* Walter Savage Landor.
Do You Remember Me? EnRP; GTBS-D; ViBoPo
(Ianthe's Question.) OBEV
(Lyrics to Ianthe.) BPN
(Years After.) EV-4
"From you, Ianthe, little troubles pass." BLV; BoLiVe;

Ianthe (*continued*) CaAE; EV-4; OBEV; PIAE; TrGrPo; TyEnPo
(Ianthe's Troubles.) OnPM; VA; ViBoPo
(Lyrics and Epigrams, III.) CBOV
(Your Pleasures Spring like Daisies.) EmBrPo; EPN
I Held Her Hand. EmBrPo
(Epigrams.) ALV
(Lyrics to Ianthe.) BPN
(Test, The.) HBV; VA
"Ianthe, you resolve [*or* are call'd] to cross the sea." OBVV
(Absence.) EnRP; OBRV
(Lyrics to Ianthe.) BPN
"Mild is the parting year, and sweet." BPN; CaAE; EmBrPo; ERP; OBRV; PG; TrGrPo
(Autumn.) BLV; BoLiVe; OBEV (1st ed.)
(Lament: "Mild is the parting year, and sweet.") BCEP
(Lyrics and Epigrams, I.) CBOV
"Past ruin'd [*or* ruined] Ilion Helen lives." AnFE; AWP; BoLiVe; CaAE; EmBrPo; EnLoPo; EnRP; EPN; ExPo; FaBoEn; GTBS-D; InPo; JAWP; LiTL; LO; LoBV; OAEP; OBRV; OQP; Po; PoE; PoEL-4; QP-2; ReaPo; RiBV; TrGrPo; TyEnPo; UnPo (1st ed.); ViBoPo; WBP
(Ianthe.) LiTB
(Lyrics and Epigrams, II.) CBOV
(Lyrics to Ianthe.) BPN
(Verse: "Past ruined Ilion . . .") BCEP; BLV; HBV; OBEV
Pleasure! Why Thus Desert [the Heart]. BPN; EmBrPo
"Proud word you never spoke, but you will speak." BPN; CaAE; EmBrPo; EnLoPo; EPN; ERP; EV-4; GTBS; GTSL; OBEV; TOP; ViBoPo
(Lyrics and Epigrams, V.) CBOV
(Prophecy, A.) VA
"Well I remember how you smiled." BCEP; BPN; EmBrPo; FaBoEn; GTBS; LoBV; TrGrPo; ViBoPo
(Epigram.) EV-4
(Her Name.) OBVV
Ibant Obscuri; Vision of Aeneas. Virgil, *tr. fr. Latin by* Robert Bridges. *Fr.* The Aeneid, VI. LaP
Ibbety bibbety gibbety goat. *Unknown.* ExPo
Ibbity, bibbity, sibbity, sab. *Unknown.* RIS
Iberia. Leo Kirschenbaum. UnS
Iberian God. Antonio Machado, *tr. fr. Spanish by* Ruth Matilda Anderson. TeCS
"O master of fortunes and of poverties," *sel.* PoFr
Iberian! palter no more! By thine hands. To Spain—a Last Word. Edith M. Thomas. MC
Ibis. *Unknown.* BLA
Ibn Sawa, Lord of Bahrien, in the field. Al-Maumin. Sir Edwin Arnold. BoFr
Ibnul Husain wrote verses eloquent. On Hearing al-Mutanabbi Praised. Ibn Wahbun. MooP
Icarus. Alfred Raymond Bellinger. LPS-1
Icarus. Philippe Desportes, *tr. fr. French by* Alan Conder. TrFP
(Sonnet, A: "Icarus is fallen here, the marvelous boy," *tr. unknown.*) PoF
Icarus. Valentin Iremonger. NeIP; OnYI; OxBI
Icarus. Harry Lyman Koopman. AA
Icarus, *abr.* Earl Marlatt. GA
Icarus. Kendrick Smithyman. AnNZ
Icarus. *Unknown. See* Love Winged My Hopes.
Icarus in November. Alec B. Stevenson. SPP
Icarus is fallen here, the marvelous boy. A Sonnet. Philippe Desportes. PoF
Icarus made himself wings. Icarus. Earl Marlatt. GA
Icarus on wings of steel. The Winged Horseman. Joseph Auslander. PoTo
Ice. Dorothy Aldis. GFA; SUS; TiPo
Ice, The. W. W. Gibson. EPN
Ice. Sir Charles G. D. Roberts. BoCaPo; ExPo
Ice. Stephen Spender. AtBAP; FaBoMo; SeCePo
Ice and Fire. Spenser. *See* Amoretti, XXX.
Ice built, ice bound, and ice bounded. Alaska. Joaquin Miller. PAH
Ice cannot shiver in the cold. Howard Lamson. Edgar Lee Masters. *Fr.* The New Spoon River. LEAP; NAMP; ViBoPo
Ice-Cart, The. W. W. Gibson. POT; PoTo; PtOT; ShBV-2; TCPD; TwCV; WP
Ice-Cream Man, The. Rachel Field. BoChLi; FaPON; GaP; SiSoSe
Ice-Floes, The. E. J. Pratt. CaP; OCL
Ice-Flumes Owregie Their Lades. Douglas Young. SeCePo
Ice Handler. Carl Sandburg. OxBA
Ice in a Stream. Liu Tsung-yuan, *tr. fr. Chinese by* Robert Payne. OnPM; WhP
Ice-King opened his frozen gates to hold high court one day, The. The Triumph of Spring. Mary Bayard Clarke. NoCaPo
Ice Man, The. Dorothy Aldis. GoBP
Ice on the Round Pond. Paul Dehn. AlDL
Ice rushes down the Indian river, The. Sudden Spring. Margaret Coulby. TwCaPo
Iceberg, The. E. J. Pratt. *Fr.* The *Titanic.* TwCaPo
Iceberg, The. Sir Charles G. D. Roberts. CaP
Icebergs. William Prescott Foster. EtS
Icebound Swans, The. *Unknown, tr. fr. Old Irish by* Seán O'Faoláin. SiB
Iced Branches. Kenneth Slade Alling. MuM
Iceland. Andreas Munch, *tr. fr. Norwegian by* Charles W. Stork. AnNoLy
Iceland First Seen. William Morris. BPN; EmBrPo; PoVP; ViP; VLEP
Iceland's Song. Grimur Thomsen, *tr. fr. Icelandic by* Jakobina Johnson. IcP; LiTW
Ich aem eldre then Ich wes, a wintre and a lore. *Unknown. Fr.* Poema Morale. EPP
Ich Am of Irlonde. *Unknown. See* Irish Dancer, The.
Ich Dien. Susie M. Best. OQP; QP-1
Ich stand auf hohen Berge. Charles Ashbee *and* Janet Ashbee, *ad. fr. German.* SG
Ich sterbe . . . Life ebbs with an easy flow. The End of a War. Sir Herbert Read. OBMV; WaP
Ich was in one sumere dale. The Owl and the Nightingale. *At. to* Nicholas de Guildford. EPP
Ich weiss nicht, was soll es bedeuten. Heine. *See* Loreley, The.
Ichabod. Whittier. AA; AmP; AmPP; AnAmPo; AnFE; AnNE; APA; APW; BAP; CoAnAm; CoBA; CoV; DD; GA; HBV; IAP; LA; LBAP; LiTA; LPS-3; MOAP; OxBA; PAH; PG; PIAE; Po; PoEL-4; REAL; TCAP; TOP
Ichabod! Thy [*or* The] Glory Has Departed. Ludwig Uhland, *tr. fr. German by* James Clarence Mangan. AWP; IrPN
Icham of Irlaundë. The Irish Dancer. *Unknown.* EnL
Ichneumon, The. Oppian, *tr. fr. Greek by* Gilbert Highet. *Fr.* Cynegetica. OxBG
Ichot a burde in boure bryht. Blow [*or* Blou] Northern[e] Wind [*or* Wynd]. *Unknown.* AtBAP; OBEV
Ichthyosaurus, The. *Unknown.* MeMeAg; OTPC (1946 ed.)
"Ici Repose." Bernard Freeman Trotter. MaRV
Icker-backer. *Unknown.* RIS
Ickle ockle, blue bockle. *Unknown.* OxNR
Icosasphere, The. Marianne Moore. ImOP
Icy cold the night was, in heaven the brilliant/ Stars. Sapphic Stanzas. Aleksandr Radishchev. BoRS; LiTW
Icy-eyed Caucasus. From Gombor. Nikolai Tikhonov. RuPo
Icy sun rises silently, The. Quail Sky. Li Ch'ing-chao. OnPC
I'd a dream to-night. Mater Dolorosa [*or* The Mother's Dream]. William Barnes. BCEP; CH; EV-4; HBV; MaRV; MotAn; OBEV; PoVP; RO
I'd asked the grocer. The Grocer and the Gold-Fish. Wilfrid Thorley. BrR
I'd Be a Butterfly. Thomas Haynes Bayly. HBV
I'd been away from her three years—about that. The Faithful Lovers. *Unknown, at. to* Sir Francis Cowley Burnand. LPS-1
I'd been on duty from two till four. Stand-to; Good Friday Morning. Siegfried Sassoon. FaBoTw
I'd Choose to Be a Daisy. *Unknown.* BoTP
I'd climbed beyond the clouds, the eagles, too. Sierra Nevada. Théophile Gautier. TrFP
I'd draw all this into a fine element,—a color. The Rug. Michael McClure. NeAP
I'd fill up the house with guests this minute. A Revel. Donagh MacDonagh. NeIP
I'd Know You! Rose Mazan. SaFP
I'd Laugh Today. *Unknown, wr. at. to* Christina Rossetti. MeMeAg
I'd Leave. Andrew Lang. FaPON
I'd liefer be nothing. For the Records. Joseph Easton McDougall. MM
I'd like a different dog. Dogs and Weather. Winifred Welles. FaPON; StVeCh; TiPo
I'd like a little. *Unknown.* FaFP; SiTL
I'd like a stocking made for a giant. A Christmas Wish. Eugene Field. ChBR
I'd like now, yet had haply been afraid. The Soldier Relieved. Robert Browning. CBPC
I'd like to/ pull. The Intelligent Sheep-Man and the New Cars. William Carlos Williams. NePoAm-2
I'd like to be a bee. Epigram. Tasso. LyPI
I'd like to be a dentist with a plate upon the door. The Dentist. Rose Fyleman. GaP; TiPo
I'd Like to Be a Lighthouse. Rachel Field. GFA; OTPC (1946 ed.)
I'd like to be a scarecrow. Summer Wish. John Farrar. GFA
I'd like to be a water-lily sleeping on the river. Water Lily. John Farrar. GFA
I'd like to be a worm. Zhenya Gay. TiPo (1959 ed.)
I'd like to be alone with you. Testament. Mikhail Yurevich Lermontov. TrRV

I'd like to be the sort of friend that you have been to me. A Friend's Greeting. Edgar A. Guest. BLPA
I'd like to be walking the cranberry road. Cranberry Road. Rachel Field. MoSiPe
I'd like to hear a sermon done. S. P. C. A. Sermon. Stuart Hemsley. FiBHP
I'd like to hunt the Injuns 'at roam the boundless plain. I Got to Go to School. Nixon Waterman. PTA-2
I'd like to peddle toy balloons. The Balloon Seller. Elizabeth Fleming. BoTP
I'd like to run like a rabbit in hops. Rabbit. Tom Robinson. FaPON
I'd like to think when life is done. When Life Is Done. Edgar A. Guest. MaRV
I'd like to write the sort of things. A Wish. John P. Mulgrew. DDA
I'd Love to Be a Fairy's Child. Robert Graves. BoTP; FaPON; HBVY; TSW; TSWC
I'd love to give a party. A Wish. Elizabeth Gould. BoTP
I'd mind me of my love, for that's my mood. Delay Not! Pierre de Ronsard. TrFP
I'd never dare to walk across. The Invisible Bridge [or Queer Quatrains]. Gelett Burgess. BOHV; NA; RIS
I'd niver seen the face av her. The Meeting. Arthur Stringer. CPG
I'd oft heard of this Sledburn Fair. Sledburn Fair. *Unknown.* CH
I'd often seen before. The Sheaf. Andrew Young. ChTr
I'd open room for millions on the earth. Goethe. *Fr.* Faust. PoFr
I'd rather be the ship that sails. The Ship That Sails. *Unknown.* PoToHe (new ed.)
I'd Rather Have Fingers than Toes. Gelett Burgess. BOHV; HBV; LBN; MeMeAg; PoeMoYo; TSW; TSWC
(Hair.) SiTL
(On Digital Extremities.) FaPON; HBVY
I'd rather have habits than clothes. Limerick. Gelett Burgess. NA
I'd rather have Jesus than all earth can give. My Choice. Grace B. Renfrow. BePJ
I'd rather have the thought of you. Choice. Angela Morgan. SBMV
I'd rather hear a rattler rattle. The Bloody Injians [or A Fragment]. *Unknown.* CoSo; CSF
I'd rather listen to a flute. Samuel Hoffenstein. FiBHP
I'd rather live in Bohemia than in any other land. In Bohemia. John Boyle O'Reilly. LHV
I'd rather see a sermon than hear one any day. Sermons We See. Edgar A. Guest. MaRV
I'd "read" three hours. Both notes and text were fast a mist becoming. A Dialogue from Plato. Austin Dobson. BOHV; HBV
I'd really hate to go to bed. Bats. Mary Effie Lee Newsome. GoSl
I'd rock my own sweet childie to rest. The Cradle of Gold. Alfred Perceval Graves. BOL
I'd watched the sorrow of the evening sky. Pine Trees and the Sky: Evening. Rupert Brooke. MCCG
I'd weave a wreath for those who fought. Through Fire in Mobile Bay. *Unknown, at. to* David Glascoe Farragut. BlG; PAH
I'd wed you without herds, without money, or rich array. Cashel of Munster. *At. to* William English, *tr. by* Sir Samuel Ferguson. AnIV; GTIV; IrPN; OBEV; OBVV; OnYI; OxBI
Ida Red. *Unknown.* ABF; StDa, *with music*
Idaho Cowboy Dance, An. James Barton Adams. **See** At a Cowboy Dance.
Idas Te Diliget Unam. Seaforth Mackenzie. MM
Idbury bells are ringing. Country Thought. Sylvia Townsend Warner. MBP; MoBrPo; NeMA
Idea, *sels.* Michael Drayton.
"As in some countries, far remote from hence," L. ReIE
"As Love and I, late harbour'd in one inn," LIX.
(Love's Proverbs.) EV-1
(Play with Proverbs, A.) ES
"As other men, so I myself do muse," IX. EnLi-1 (1949 ed.) (XII); ReEn; SiCe; TuPP
"Bright star of beauty, on whose eyelids sit," IV. ElSeCe; EPP; HBV; SiCE
"Calling to mind[e] since first my love begun," LI. OBSC; PoEL-2; RiBV; SiCE
"Cleere Ankor [or Clear Anker], on whose silver-sanded shore," LIII (*also given as XIII in* Idea's Mirrour). BrBE; TuPP
"Cupid, I hate thee, which I'd have thee know," XLVIII. LO
"Dear [or Deare or Deere], why should you comma[u]nd me to my rest," XXXVII. EG; ElL; EPP; FaBoEn; HBV; LiTL; LO; LoPo; OAEP; PoEL-2; ReEn; TuPP; ViBoPo
(Night and Day.) LiTB; LiTG
(Sonnets to "Idea," II.) OBSC
"Evil spirit, your beauty haunts me still, An," XX. CoBE; ElL; ElSeCe; EPP; LoBV; OAEP; OBSC; ReEn; ReIE; SiCE; TuPP
"How many paltry, foolish, painted things," VI. ElL; EnLoPo; HBV (XLII); InP; LoBV; NBE; OBSC; ReEn; ReIE; RiBV; SiCE; TuPP
(Her Fame.) ES
(Immortality in Song.) BCEP
"I hear some say, 'This man is not in love!'" XXIV. BEL; LO; OAEP; TrGrPo
(Laughing at Fortune.) BLV
"In pride of wit, when high desire of fame," XLVII. SiCE; TuPP
"Into these loves who but for passion looks," *introd. sonnet.* BEL; HBV; TuPP; ViBoPo
(To the Reader of These Sonnets.) ReEn; ReIE; SiCE
"Like an adventurous sea-farer am I," I. EnLi-1 (1949 ed.); EtS; ReEn; SiCE; TuPP
"Love, banished heaven, in earth was held in scorn," XXIII. (Guest, The.) ES
"Many there be excelling in this kind," LXXIII (*last sonnet in Esdaile ed.; also in* England's Heroical Epistles). NBE; SiCE; TuPP
"Methinks I see some crooked mimic jeer," XXXI. TuPP
(Sonnet—To the Critic.) LoBV
(To the Critic.) SiCE
"My heart the anvil where my thoughts do beat," XL (*also given as XLIV in* Idea's Mirrour). HBV; ReIE
"Nothing but No and I, and I and No," V. PoEL-2
"Our floods' queen, Thames, for ships and swans is crowned," XXXII. TuPP
(To the River Anker.) SiCE
"Since there's no help[e], come let us kiss[e] and part," LXI. AEV; AtBAP; ATP; AWP; BEL; BrBE; CaAE; CoEV; EG; ElL; ElSeCe; EM-1; EnL; EnLi-1; EnLit; EnLoPo; EPP; ExPo; FaBoEn; HBV; InP; JAWP; LO; LoBV; LoPo; OAEP; OBSC; PeBoSo; PoE; PoEL-2; ReEn; ReIE; RiBV; SeCePo; ShBV-4; SiCE; TCEP; TOP; TrGrPo; TuPP; TwHP; TyEnPo; ViBoPo; WBP; WHA
(Come Let Us Kisse and Part[e].) LPS-1; TreFS
(Farewell, A.) ES
(Love's Farewell.) EV-1; GTBS; GTBS-D; GTBS-W; GTSE; GTSL
(Love's Parting.) CBOV
(Parting, The.) AnEnPo; BCEP; BLV; EtPaEn; HoPM; LEAP; LiTB; LiTG; LiTL; LoPS; OBEV; OtMeF; PIAE; SeCeV
(Sonnet from "Idea.") OuHeWo
"Some men there be which like my method well," XLII. SiCE; TuPP
"Some misbelieving and profane in love," XXXV. TuPP
(To Miracle.) SiCE
"Stay, speedy Time, behold, before thou pass," XVII. OBSC
(To Time.) SiCE
"There's nothing grieves me but that age should haste," VIII. ReEn; ReIE; SiCE
"To nothing fitter can I thee compare," X. BEL; ElL; HBV; OBSC; SiCE; TrGrPo; TuPP; ViBoPo
"Truce, gentle love, a parley now I crave!" LXIII. ReIE; TuPP
"When conquering love did first my heart assail," XXIX. (To the Senses.) OAEP
"When first I ended, then I first began," LXII (*also given as L in* Idea's Mirrour). TrGrPo
(Paradox, The.) BLV; PIAE
"Whilst thus my pen strives to eternize thee," XLIV. BEL; OBSC; ReEn; SiCE; TuPP; ViBoPo
"Why should your fair eyes with such sovereign grace," XLIII. OBSC
(Against Knowledge in Loving.) ES
"Witless gallant, a young wench that wooed, A," XXI. PeBoSo; SiCE; TuPP
"You're [or You] not alone when you are still alone," XI. LoPS (XII); PoEL-2; TrGrPo
(Give Me My Self.) BLV; LO
(You're Not Alone.) LiTL
Idea, The. Agnes Mary Frances Robinson. UnW
Idea is exciting, surely, The. Errors of Observation. Gordon Wharton. PoN
Idea of a Swimmer. Jean-Richard Bloch, *tr. fr. French by* "S. P." TrJP
Idea of Joy. Josephine Miles. FiMAP
Idea of justice may be precious, An. Ode. Frank O'Hara. NeAP
Idea of Order at [or in] Key West, The. Wallace Stevens. AmP; AmPP; CoBMV; MAP; MoAB; MoAmPo; MoPo; OxBA; Po
Idea of Wealth, An. Christopher Marlowe. *Fr.* The Jew of Malta, I, i. BCEP
Idea; or, The Shepherd's Garland. Michael Drayton. *See* Shepherd's Garland, The.
Idea ran around the world, An. The Return. Muriel Rukeyser. FiMAP

Ideal. Sister Miriam Clare. PraNu
Ideal. Padraic Pearse, *tr. fr. Modern Irish by* Thomas MacDonagh. AnIV; AWP; CAW; JAWP; JKCP; LBBV; LiTW; NP; OnYI; TIP; WBP
Ideal, The. Francis Saltus Saltus. AA
Ideal, The. Shelley. *See* Demogorgon's Last Words.
Ideal. Wordsworth. *See* London, 1802.
Ideal Beauty. Fernando de Herrera, *tr. fr. Spanish by* Longfellow. CAW; TeCS
Ideal City, The. Washington Gladden. OQP; QP-2
Ideal General, The. Archilochus, *tr. fr. Greek by* A. Watson Bain. OxBG
(General, A, *tr. by* A. C. Benson.) GrR
Ideal Husband to His Wife, The. Sam Walter Foss. BOHV; InMe
Ideal Memory. William James Dawson. VA
Ideal Passion (*Complete,* I–XLII). George Edward Woodberry. MOAP
Sels.
"Between my eyes and her so thin the screen," XXXVII. HBMV
"'Evil thing is honor,' once of old, An," XXVIII. HBMV
"Farewell, my Muse! for, lo, there is no end," XLII. HBMV
"I never muse upon my lady's grace," XXV. HBMV
"Immortal Love, too high for my possessing," XL. HBMV
"In what a glorious substance did they dream," XXVI. HBMV
"My lady ne'er hath given herself to me," I. NV
"Oh, how with brightness hath Love filled my way," XXX. HBMV
"Why, Love, beneath the fields of asphodel," XXXIII. HBMV
Idealism and Realism. Gustaf Fröding, *tr. fr. Swedish by* Charles W. Stork. AnSL
Idealist, The. James Coale Sappington, Jr. CAG
Idealists. Alfred Kreymborg. BAP; CP; NV; PoMa; SBMV; TSW
Ideality. Hartley Coleridge. VA
Ideals. Robert Greene. PoToHe (new ed.)
Ideals of Satire, The. Pope. *Fr.* First Epistle of the Second Book of Horace. FiP
Idea's Mirrour, *sels.* Michael Drayton.
"Beauty sometime, in all her glory crowned," IX. NBE
"Black pitchy night, companion of my woe," XLV. LoBV (LXX); OBSC; ReIE; SiCE; TuPP
"Cleere Ankor [*or* Clear Anker], on whose silver-sanded shore," XIII (*also given as LIII in* Idea). BrBE; TuPP
"Glorious sun went blushing to his bed, The," XXV. OBSC
"If chaste and pure devotion of my youth," XXXVIII. OBSC; SiCE; ViBoPo
"Letters and lines, we see, are soon defaced," XXI. ReIE
"My fair, look from those turrets of thine eyes," XXXIV. OBSC; SiCE
"My heart, imprisoned in a hopeless isle," XXII. OBSC; SiCE
"My heart the anvil where my thoughts do beat," XLIV (*also given as XL in* Idea). HBV; ReIE
"Read here (sweet Maid) the story of my woe," I. OBSC; ReIE
"Stay, stay, sweet Time! Behold, or ere thou pass," VII. ReIE
"Sweet secrecy, what tongue can tell thy worth?" XLVI. SiCE; ViBoPo
To the Dear Child of the Muses and His Ever Kind Maecenas, Master Anthony Cooke, Esquire. ReIE; SiCE; TuPP
"When first I ended, then I first began," L (*also given as LXII in* Idea). TrGrPo
(Paradox, The.) BLV; PIAE
Identity. Thomas Bailey Aldrich. AA; AnNE; BAP; BPP; MAP; PFY; PoeMoYo; UnW
Identity. Sister Mary Helen. GoBC
Identity. Elizabeth Jennings. NePoEA
Identity. Hyam Plutzik. FiMAP
Ideogram. Alfred G. Bailey. BoCaPo
Idiom of the Hero. Wallace Stevens. OxBA
Idiot, The. Hart Crane. PoFS
Idiot, The. Frederick Peterson. PoP
Idiot. Allen Tate. AnAmPo; FaBoMo; LA; LiTA; NAMP
Idiot Boy, The. Wordsworth. ERP
Idiot greens the meadow with his eyes, The. Idiot. Allen Tate. AnAmPo; FaBoMo; LA; LiTA; NAMP
Idiots will prate and prate of suicide. Leonard Bacon. Sonnets, III. TBM
Idle Charon. Eugene Lee-Hamilton. BMEP; ES; LEAP; OBVV
Idle chatter, rising like a fountain, The. Lèse-Majesté. Herbert S. Gorman. BAP; HBMV
Idle dayseye, the laborious wheel, The. O. Richard Wilbur. LiTA; MoPo
Idle Flowers, The. Robert Bridges. ChTr
Idle Fyno. *Unknown. See* A Ha Ha Ha! This World Doth Passe.
Idle Housewife. Samuel Rowlands. SiCE
Idle Lake, The. Spenser. The Faerie Queene, II, 6. PC
Idle Life I Lead, The. Robert Bridges. EG; LiTM
Idle poet, here and there, An. The Revelation. Coventry Patmore. *Fr.* The Angel in the House. EG; EnLoPo; EPP; POTT; ViBoPo
Idle Singer, The. William Morris. *See* Apology, An: "Of Heaven or Hell . . ."
Idle Thoughts. V. Sackville-West. AlDL
Idle to Grieve. Duncan Campbell Scott. PC
Idle Verse. Henry Vaughan. AtBAP; ElSeCe; NBE; OAEP
Idle youth/ By all availed. Song of the Highest Tower. Arthur Rimbaud. AnFP
Idleness. Lu Yu, *tr. fr. Chinese by* Kenneth Rexroth. OnPC
Idleness. Silas Weir Mitchell. AA; OBAV
Idleness. T. Sturge Moore. PoeT
(To Idleness.) TCPD
Idleness. Andrew Young. POTE
Idler, The. Elizabeth Jennings. NePoEA
Idler, The. Jones Very. AA; HBV; LEAP
Idler holds that rose as always rose, An. The Idler. Elizabeth Jennings. NePoEA
Idlers, The. Edmund Blunden. BoTP; CH
Idly I cut me a reed by the shore where the sea heaves and thunders. Art. Apollon Nikolayevich Maikov. TrRV
Idly sings the shepherd. Juan Ramón Jiménez. *Fr.* Autumnal Aria. AnSpL-2
Idmon, a dyer in purple. The Birth of Arachne, the Spider. James Schevill. FiMAP
Idol, The. Louise Driscoll. BAP; HBMV
Idol in the Porch, The. José Juan Tablada, *tr. fr. Spanish by* Samuel Beckett. AnMP
Idol-Maker Prays, The. Arthur Guiterman. SBMV
Idolatry. Arna Bontemps. PoNe
Idols. Richard Burton. TrPWD
Idol's Eye, The, *sel.* Harry B. Smith.
Tattooed Man, The. InMe; LauV
Idols of Imagination. Richard Eberhart. FiMAP
Idols of the mind, The. Pygmalion. W. Wesley Trimpi. PtPa
Idyl: "And my young sweetheart sat at board with me." Alfred Mombert, *tr. fr. German by* Ludwig Lewisohn. AWP; JAWP; WBP
Idyl, An: "Come down, O maid, from yonder mountain height." Tennyson. *See* Come Down, O Maid.
Idyl in Idleness, An. Robert Pack. NePoEA
Idyll: "Among the flowers, among the lilies." Jean Vauquelin de la Fresnaye, *tr. fr. French by* Alan Conder. TrFP
Idyll: "In Switzerland one idle day." Hugh Macnaghten. HBMV
Idyll: "There see the clover, pea, and bean." Matthew Green. *Fr.* The Spleen. BeR
Idyll of Phatte and Leene, An. *Unknown.* BOHV; PA
Idyll of the Rose. Decimus Magnus Ausonius, *tr. fr. Latin by* John Addington Symonds. AWP
Idylls, sels. Theocritus, *tr. fr. Greek.*
Amycus, *fr.* XXII, *tr. by* C. S. Calverley. OxBG
"And Thou Beside Me Singing in the Wilderness," *fr.* VIII, *tr. by* F. L. Lucas. GrPE
Cyclops, The, XI, *tr. by* Elizabeth Barrett Browning. AWP; EnLi-1; JAWP; WBP
(Cyclops in Love, The, *pr. tr. by* Andrew Lang.) GrL
Daphnis, I, *tr. by* F. L. Lucas. GrPE
(Daphnis Song, The, *pr. tr. by* Andrew Lang.) GrL
(Death of Daphnis, The, *tr. by* C. S. Calverley.) AWP; JAWP; WBP
(Song of the Death of Daphnis, The, *tr. by* J. H. Hallard.) EnLi-1
Cup, The, *sel.* GrR, *tr. by* R. C. Trevelyan; OxBG, *tr. by* Sir William Marris
Passing of Daphnis, The, *sel., tr. by* Sir William Marris. OxBG
Dogs at the Homestead, The, *fr.* XXV, *tr. by* C. S. Calverley. OxBG
Domestic Scene, *fr.* XXIV, *tr. by* Henry Harmon Chamberlin. GrR
Fisherman, The, XXI, *tr. by* C. S. Calverley. AWP
Dream of a Golden Catch, *sel., tr. by* R. C. Trevelyan. GrR
Fisherman's Hut, *sel., tr. by* Henry Harmon Chamberlain. GrR; OxBG
Harvest-Home, VII, *tr by* C. S. Calverley. AWP; GrR, *sel.;* GrL, *pr. tr. by* Andrew Lang
("Once on a time did Eucritus and I," *tr. by* C. S. Calverley.) GrPo
Bound for the Harvest-Home, *sel., tr. by* Walter Headlam. OxBG
Festival, The, *sel., tr. by* F. L. Lucas. GrPE
Late Summer in the Country, *sel., pr. tr. by* Walter Pater. OxBG
"Season of Mellow Fruitfulness," *sel., tr. by* R. C. Trevelyan. GrR
Summer Joys, *sel., tr. by* J. M. Edmonds. LiA
Herdsman, The, IV, *tr. by* C. S. Calverley. AWP

Hylas, XIII. GrPE, *tr. by* F. L. Lucas; GrR, *sel., tr. by* C. S. Calverley; OxBG, *shorter sel., tr. by* C. S. Calverley
In Praise of Bombyca, *fr.* X. *tr. by* T. F. Higham. OxBG
(Transfiguring Love, *tr. by* C. S. Calverley.) GrR
Incantation, The, II, *tr. by* C. S. Calverley. AWP; JAWP; WBP
(Love-Magic, *tr. by* R. C. Trevelyan.) GrR
(Pharmaceutria, The, *pr. tr. by* Andrew Lang.) GrL
(Second Idyll, The, *tr. by* Jack Lindsay.) LiTW
(Simaetha, *tr. by* Jack Lindsay.) OxBG
(Sorceress, The.) GrPE, *tr. by* F. L. Lucas; LiA, *tr. by* C. S. Calverley
("Where are the bay-leaves, Thestylis, and the charms?" *tr. by* C. S. Calverley.) GrPo
Lines Written to Accompany the Gift of a Distaff to Theugenis. XXVIII, *tr. by* T. F. Higham. OxBG
(Gift-Card Enclosed, *tr. by* R. C. Trevelyan.) GrR
Lovers' Meeting, *fr.* XII, *tr. by* F. L. Lucas. GrPE
Lovesick Cyclops, A, VI, *tr. by* R. C. Trevelyan. GrR
Coy Polyphemus, *sel.* OxBG
Neatherd's Lament, The, XX, *pr. tr. by* Andrew Lang. GrL
"O Galatea faire, why dost thou shun thy lover true?" *fr.* XI. GrPo
(Giant's Wooing, The, *tr. by* C. S. Calverley.) GrR
(Polyphemus to Galatea.) OxBG
Reapers' Song, *fr.* X. GrR, *tr. by* Henry Harmon Chamberlin; OxBG, *tr. by* T. F. Higham
Rustic Serenade, *fr.* III, *tr. by* R. C. Trevelyan. GrR
(Serenade.) OxBG
Syracusan Women, The, XV, *pr. tr. by* Andrew Lang. GrL
("Praxinoa in?" *tr. by* Leigh Hunt.) GrPo
Adonis Song, The, *sel., tr. by* R. C. Trevelyan. GrR
Syracusan Women [at the Adonis Festival], The, *fr.* XV. GrR, *tr. by* R. C. Trevelyan; WoL, *tr. by* J. M. Chapman
(Gorgo and Praxinoa, *tr. by* Jack Lindsay.) OxBG
Transience, *fr.* XXIII, *tr. by* F. L. Lucas. GrPE
Two Boxers, The, *fr.* XXII, *tr. by* Henry Harmon Chamberlin. GrR
Wooing of Daphnis, The, XXVII, *pr. tr. by* Andrew Lang. GrL
Idylls and Epigrams, *sel.* Johan Ludvig Runeberg, *tr. fr. Swedish by* Charles W. Stork.
"From a lover's trysting came the maiden." AnSL
Idylls of the King, *sels.* Tennyson.
Balin and Balan.
Fire of Heaven, The. EPN
Coming of Arthur, The. VLEP
King, The. BHV
Merlin's Riddle. BPN
Song: "Blow, trumpet, for the world is white with May." (Trumpet Song.) BPN
(War Song.) BHV
Dedication: "These to his memory—since he held them dear." PoVP; ViPP
(To the Queen.) BHV
Albert the Good. BMEP
Gareth and Lynette. HeT
Follow the Christ, 4 *ll.* MaRV
("Man am I grown, a man's work must I do," 4 *ll.*) ChIP
Geraint and Enid.
O Purblind Race, 7 *ll.* OQP; QP-2
Guinevere. BPN; EnLit; EPN; GEPC; VLEP
"But I was first of all the kings who drew." GTSL
(King Arthur's Order of Chivalry.) GrCo-1
Foolish Virgins. LPS-3
Queen Becomes an Abbess, A. PraNu
Remorse ("Shall I kill myself?"). MaRV
Their Conscience as Their King. MaRV
Too Late. MaRV; OQP; QP-2
We Needs Must Love the Highest, 7 *ll.* MaRV
Holy Grail, The. PoVP; ViPo; ViPP; VLEP
Lancelot and the Grail. GoBC
Quest of the Grail, The. BHV
Lancelot and Elaine. HeT; PoVP; ViPo; ViPP; VLEP
"Elaine the fair, Elaine the loveable." ReTS
Elaine's Song. BPN
Last Tournament, The. ViPo
Marriage of Geraint, The.
Turn, Fortune, Turn Thy Wheel. TVSH; VLEP
(Enid's Song.) BPN; LPS-3
(Fortune.) BHV
Merlin and Vivien.
In Love, if Love Be Love. AEV; EV-5; GTBS; GTSL; LoPS; PoEL-5; TrGrPo; VLEP
(All in All.) GTBS-W; LiTB
(If Love Be Ours.) OQP; QP-2
(Little Rift within the Lute, The.) LoPo
(Vivien's Song.) BPN; FaBoEn
Passing of Arthur, The. CoBE; EM-2; EPN; HeT; PCN; REAL
(Morte d'Arthur, *incorporated in the Idylls, with changes, as* The Passing of Arthur.) AnEnPo; ATP; BBV; BEL; BMEP; BoLiVe; BPN; CBOV; EmBrPo, *with add. ll.* 324-354; EnLi-2; EPP; EV-5; FaBoBe; FiP; GEPC; GTSL; HBV; LPS-2; OAEP; OnSP; PIR; PoE; PoEL-5; TCEP; TOP; TwCrTr; UnPo (1st ed.); ViPo; VLEP; WHA
"And answer made King Arthur, breathing hard." ReTS
"And slowly answered Arthur from the barge." GTSL
Arthur's Disillusionment. TreFS
Prayer ("[Pray for my soul] More things are wrought by prayer"), 9 *ll.* BLRP; OQP; PraP; QP-1; TreF; WGRP
Prayer ("The old order changeth, yielding place to new"). MaRV
(Prayer for the Dead.) GoBC
"Then rose the King and moved his host." NBE
"Then saw they how there hove a dusky barge." VA
Pelleas and Ettarre.
"Rose, A, but one, none other rose had I." PoEL-5
(Worm within a Rose.) VLEP
To the Queen. PoVP
Iena's Song. Charles Mair. *Fr.* Tecumseh. VA
Iersch brybour baird, vyle beggar with thy brattis. William Dunbar. *Fr.* The Flyting of Dumbar and Kennedie. AtBAP
Iesu. George Herbert. *See* Jesu.
Iesu, Dulcis Memoria. St. Bernard of Clairvaux. *See* Jesu Dulcis.
Iesu, swete sone dere! Our Lady's Song [*or* The Virgin's Song]. *Unknown.* AtBAP; OBEV (new ed.). *See also* Jesu, my sweet Son dear.
If. Carolyn Sherwin Bailey. PCH
If. Mortimer Collins. BOHV; FiBHP; HBV; PA
If. H. C. Dodge. BOHV
If. Oswald Durand, *tr. fr. French by* Edna Worthley Underwood. PoNe
If. Rebecca Foresman. *See* How To Forget.
If. William Dean Howells. AA; LBAP; OBAV
If. Kipling. BBV (1951 ed.); BLPA; BMEP; BPN; BTP; CBE; ChMo; EnLit; FaBoBe; FaFP; FAOV; GoTP; GrCo-1; HBV; HBVY; HiLiEn; LiTM; MaRV; NeHB; OHFP; OtMeF; OTPC (1946 ed.); PoeMoYo; PoMa; POT; PoTo; PTA-1; PYM; ShGoBo; TreF; TSW; TSWC; VLEP; WBLP
If. James Jeffrey Roche. HBV; PR
If. P. A. Ropes. BoTP
If. Alice Todd. BoTP
If. *Unknown.* *See* If All the World Were Paper.
If/ ice shall melt. If Ice. W. W. E. Ross. BoCaPo
If a body meet a body. *See* Gin a body meet a body.
If a daughter you have, she's the plague of your life. Song. Sheridan. *Fr.* The Duenna. CEP; NeHB
If a fairy should come from Babyland. Pop. Elinor Maxwell. FAOV
If a feller's been a-straddle. When You're Throwed. *Unknown.* SCC
If a lad's but a lad in the heart of a town. The Ditty the City Sang. Alfred Kreymborg. NeMA
If a leaf rustled, she would start. The White Moth. Sir Arthur Quiller-Couch. VA
If a Maid Be Fair. Laura Goodman Salverson. CaP
If a man could live a thousand years. If. H. C. Dodge. BOHV
If a Man Die. Florence Hamilton. MaRV
(Conjecture.) BAP
If a Man Die, Shall He Live Again? John Richard Moreland. ChIP; MaRV; PGD
If a Man Who Turnips Cries. Samuel Johnson. *See* If the Man Who Turnips Cries.
If a man would be a soldier, he'd expect, of course, to fight. A Little Rhyme and a Little Reason. Henry Anstadt. BLRP
If a Pig Wore a Wig. Christina Rossetti. *Fr.* Sing-Song. BoChLi
If a star can grow. Mystery. Scudder Middleton. NV
If a stranger sojourn with thee in your land, ye shall not vex him. Strangers. Leviticus, Bible, *O.T.* BoFr
If a task is once begun. Always Finish. *Unknown.* BLPA; FaBoBe; NeHB; WBLP
If a thousand pinks and lilies are embraced. Celestial Dream. Pierre de Ronsard. TrFP
If a wished-for thing and a thing past hoping for. Catullus, *tr. fr. Latin by* Arthur Symons. LaP
If a woman be loved, hated and envied. Translations from Modern Japanese Poetry. Akiko Yanagiwara. PFE
If a Woodchuck Would Chuck. *Unknown.* FaPON
("How much wood would a woodchuck chuck.") StVeCh; TiPo
If a wren can cling. Faith. F. B. Meyer. OQP; QP-2
If after kirk ye bide a wee. An Angel Unawares. *Unknown.* BLRP; MaRV
If Ah evah git to glory, an' Ah hope to mek it thoo. Black Mammies. John Wesley Holloway. BANP; MotAn
If Alcibiades kill my countrymen. Shakespeare. *Fr.* Timon of Athens, V, i. MyFE

If All Be True That I Do Think. Henry Aldrich. *See* Reasons for Drinking.
If all my days were summer, could I know. Revelation. Warren F. Cook. BLRP
If all our life were one broad glare. The Joy of Incompleteness. Albert Crowell. PoToHe (new ed.)
If all the carts were painted gay. Holiness. John Drinkwater. BMEP; CP
If all the earthe were paper white. *Unknown.* SeCL
If all the flowers of all the fields on earth. On Lamb's Specimens of Dramatic Poets. Swinburne. EPP
If all the grief and woe and bitterness. Planh for the Young English King. Bertrans de Born. LiTW
If all the harm that women have done. A Thought. James Kenneth Stephen. BOHV; FiBHP; VA
If all the land were apple-pie. *See* If all the world were apple-pie.
If all the little Christmas trees. If. Carolyn Sherwin Bailey. PCH
If All the Pens That Ever Poets Held. Christopher Marlowe. *See* Poet's Pen, The.
If all the seas were one sea. Mother Goose. BoTP; LiL; OTPC (1946 ed.); OxNR; Po; PPL; SiTL; StVeCh
If all the ships I have at sea. My Love Ship. Ella Wheeler Wilcox. PTA-1
If All the Skies [Were Sunshine]. Henry van Dyke. NLK; WBLP; WGRP
If all the sorrows of this weary earth. Friends. Thomas Curtis Clark. PoToHe
If All the Tears Thou Madest Mine. Margaret Louisa Woods. GTML
If all the trees in all the woods were men. Cacoëthes Scribendi. Oliver Wendell Holmes. AA; APW; BOHV
If all the verse what I have wrote. Archys Autobiography. Don Marquis. *Fr.* Archys Life of Mehitabel. CrMA
If All the Voices of Men. Horace L. Traubel. AA; BAP
If all the women in the town were bundled up together. The Agricultural Irish Girl. *Unknown.* OnYI
If All the World. Dollie Radford. VA
If all the world and love were young. The Nymph's Reply to the [Passionate] Shepherd [*or* Answer to Marlowe *or* Reply . . .]. Sir Walter Ralegh. ATP; BLV; CBOV; CenL; CoBE; EiL; ElSeCe; EM-1; EnL; EnLi-1; EPP; EV-1; ExPo; GTBS-W; HBV; HoPM; LEAP; LiTB; LiTG; LiTL; LoBV; LPS-1; OAEP; OBEV; OBSC; OuHeWo; PG (1945 ed.); Po; PoE; PoFS; ReaPo; ReEn; ReIE; RiBV; SeCePo; SeCeV; SiCE; SiPS; SiTL; TCEP; TOP; TreFS; TrGrPo; TuPP; UnPo (1st ed.); ViBoPo; WHA
If all the world were apple pie. Mother Goose. BOHV; CG; FaFP; HBV; HBVY; LiL; NA; OnHT; OTPC; PCH; PPL; RIS
If all the world were candy. The Ambitious Mouse. John Farrar. PCH; TSW
If All the World Were Paper. *Unknown.* CenL; LiTG; LoBV; OxNR; SeCL; SiTL
(If.) AIDL; BoN
(Interrogativa Cantilena.) SeEP
If all the world were right. If All the World. Dollie Radford. VA
If all that love and man hath sworne. *Unknown.* SeCSL
If all were rain and never sun. Sun and Rain. Christina Rossetti. PPL
If Along the Highroad. *Unknown, tr. fr. Chinese by* Arthur Waley. *Fr.* Shi King. LiTW
If Amorous Faith. Petrarch, *tr. fr. Italian by* C. B. Cayley. Sonnets to Laura: To Laura in Life, CLXXXVIII. OnPM
(Signs of Love.) AWP; JAWP; WBP
If an unkind word appears. On File. John Kendrick Bangs. PoToHe (new ed.); WBLP
If any ask the reason I went wrong. A Plague the Meddling Female! Euripides. *Fr.* Andromache. GrR
If any ask why roses please the sight? Description of Mercy. John Fletcher. *Fr.* Christ's Victory and Triumph. EV-2
If any ask why there's no great She-Poet. Dedication of the Cook. Anna Wickham. MBP; MoBrPo
If any flower that here is grown. Inscription in a [*or* His] Garden. George Gascoigne. OBSC; TrGrPo; TuPP
If Any God. Mark Van Doren. QS
If any God should say. Rebirth [1914–18]. Kipling. GTML; GTSL; LoBV
If any good may come to me. George Henry Boker. *Fr.* The Book of the Dead. MOAP
If any have a stone to shy. The Pebble. Elinor Wylie. BoFr; MAP; MoAmPo
If any little word of mine [*or* ours]. A Good Creed [*or* A New Year Prayer]. *Unknown.* PoToHe; PraP
If Any Man Would Come after Me. Edwin McNeill Poteat. ChIP
If any man would know the very cause. Sonnet: He Is Out of Heart with His Time. Guerzo di Montecanti. AWP
If any mourn us in the workshop, say. Batteries Out of Ammunition. Kipling. *Fr.* Epitaphs of the War. PoVP
If any question why we died. Common Form. Kipling. *Fr.* Epitaphs of the War. FaBoTw; LiA; PoVP
If any vague desire should rise. In Memoriam A. H. H., LXXX. Tennyson. EmBrPo; EnLi-2; EPN; GEPC; ViPo; VLEP
If any vision should reveal. In Memoriam A. H. H., XCII. Tennyson. EmBrPo; EPN; GEPC; ViPo; VLEP
If any wench Venus's girdle wear. Song. John Gay. *Fr.* The Beggar's Opera. PoEL-3
If any would portray thee. Before the Ikon of the Mother of God. Constantine of Rhodes. ISi
If anybody's friend be dead. Emily Dickinson. IAP
If anyone long for a musical song. The Wanton Trick. *Unknown.* CoMu
If apples were pears. To My Valentine. *Unknown.* PCH
If as a flower [*or* flowre] doth spread and die. Employment. George Herbert. AtBAP; ElSeCe; SeCV-1
If, as they say, some dust thrown in my eyes. Dust in the Eyes. Robert Frost. CoV
If, as they tell in stories old. The Eye of the Beholder. James Lionel Michael. BoAu
If asked the day that this man dies. At a Loss. James L. Weil. GoYe
If at this time I am derided. The Sympathy. *Unknown.* SeCL
If at your coming princes disappear. Comets—On the Italian Duke Who Ran Away for Fear of the Comet of 1742. Samuel Johnson. BeR
If aught can teach us aught, Affliction's looks. Affliction. Sir John Davies. *Fr.* Nosce Teipsum. CoEV; OBSC
If aught I may have said or done. An Evening Prayer. Laura E. Kendall. BLRP
If aught, my Cleobulus, befall (for what shall save me). Love's Last Sacrament. Meleager. GrPE
If aught [*or* ought] of oaten stop, or pastoral song. Ode to Evening [*or* To Evening]. William Collins. AEV; AnEnPo; AnFE; AtBAP; ATP; AWP; BCEP; BEL; BLV; BrBE; CaAE; CBOV; CEP; CoBE; CoEV; EG; EiPP; EM-1; EnL; EnLi-2; EnRP; EnSW; EPP; EV-3; ExPo; FaBoBe; FaBoEn; GTBS; GTBS-D; GTBS-W; GTSE; GTSL; HBV; InP; InPo; JAWP; KN; LEAP; LiTB; LiTG; LoBV; OAEP; OBEC; OBEV; OuHeWo; PIAE; Po; PoE; PoEL-3; PoFS; PreP; ReaPo; RiBV; SeCePo; SeCeV; ShBV-4; TCEP; TOP; TrGrPo; TwHP; TyEnPo; UnPo (1st ed.); ViBoPo; WBP; WHA
If aught of simple song have power to touch. The Birthday Crown. William Alexander. OBVV
If aught that stumbles in my speech. Abstemia. Gelett Burgess. NA
If baby only wanted to, he could fly up to heaven this moment. Baby's Way. Rabindranath Tagore. MOAH
If bees stay at home. Weather Wisdom [*or* Signs and Seasons]. *Unknown.* GoTP; OxNR; RIS; TreF
If, before being earth, the thought of sound. Anticipation. Joseph Tusiani. GoYe
If Bet bedecks herself with gems, bestirs herself when bid. Why Not? *Unknown.* WhC
If Bethlehem were here today. Christmas Morning. Elizabeth Madox Roberts. ChBR; ChrBoLe; GoTP; LS; MAP; MaRV; MoAmPo; MPB; PCH; PoRh; StJW; StVeCh; SUS; TSW; WHL
"If black was white." William Brighty Rands. *Fr.* Topsy-turvy World. BoN
If Brother Francis pardoned Brother Flea. A Broad Minded Bishop Rebukes the Verminous Saint Francis. G. K. Chesterton. SaFP
If but some vengeful god would call to me. Hap. Thomas Hardy. AWP; ChMo; CMP; CoBMV; EmBrPo; EnLi-2 (1949 ed.); InPo; JAWP; MoBrPo; OAEP (2d ed.); PeBoSo; PoE; PoLFOT; ViPo; ViPP; WBP
"If but the Gods, of their mercy." The Water of Dirce. Edith M. Thomas. TBM
If buttercups buzz'd after the bee. *Unknown.* LoGBV
If . . . by chance . . . we should meet. I'd Know You! Rose Mazan. SaFP
If by dull rhymes our English must be chain'd. On the Sonnet [*or* The Sonnet Claims More Freedom]. Keats. ERP; ES
If by hoards of gold a man. Not by Gold Alone. *Unknown. Fr.* Anacreontea. GrR
If by the dairy's hatch I chance to hie. Blouzelinda's Death. John Gay. *Fr.* The Shepherd's Week. BeR
If Candlemas Day be dry and fair. Candlemas. *Unknown.* PoRL
If care do cause men cry, why do not I complain? Earl of Surrey. SiPS
If caring profits, then for care take thought. God's Concern. Palladas. OxBG
If chance assign'd. Sir Thomas Wyatt. SiPS
If Charon drove a hearse along the beach. Variations on a Theme. Alfred G. Bailey. BoCaPo
If chaste and pure devotion of my youth. Idea's Mirrour, XXXVIII. Michael Drayton. OBSC; SiCE; ViBoPo

If childhood were not in the world. The Salt of the Earth. Swinburne. BPN; EmBrPo; EPP; PoVP
If Christ, as thou affirmest, be of men. The Illimitable God. Robert Browning. *Fr.* A Death in the Desert. MaRV
If Christ could ever be born again. The Christmas Tree. Edward Shillito. ChIP; OQP; QP-1; SDH
If Christmas brought me nothing more. A Poem for Christmas. C. A. Snodgrass. PoToHe (new ed.)
If close hauled on the starboard tack. Rules of the Road. *Unknown.* SoAmSa
If come into this world again I must. Dew on a Dusty Heart. Jean Starr Untermeyer. MAP; MoAmPo
If "compression is the first grace of style." To a Snail. Marianne Moore. FaBoMo; OnPM
If Crost with All Mishaps Be My Poor Life. William Drummond of Hawthornden. BSV
If Cupid Were a Child. Thomas Watson. *Fr.* Hecatompathia; or, Passionate Century of Love. TuPP
If Cynthia Be a Queen. Sir Walter Ralegh. SiPS
If Dante mourns, there wheresoe'er he be. To One Who Had Censured [*or* A Tribute to Dante]. Boccaccio. *Fr.* Sonnets. AWP; GoBC
If Days were nights, I could their weight endure. The Nettle. Bayard Taylor. PA
If dead, we cease to be; if total gloom. Human Life; on the Denial of Immortality. Samuel Taylor Coleridge. ChER
If dear[e] Anthea, my hard fate it be. To Anthea. Robert Herrick. OBS; SeEP
If death and time are stronger. Strong Love. A. E. Housman. OtMeF
If death had come here with me, to New Haven. Nocturne in Which Death Speaks. Xavier Villaurrutia. AnCL
If Death Is Kind. Sara Teasdale. ChMo; CMP
If death should come with his cold, hasty kiss. Life and Death. Carroll Carstairs. DDA
If dogma errs, and if there is no Hell. To a Lost Spirit. Lord Dunsany. UnW
If Doughty Deeds [My Lady Please]. Robert Graham. BSV; GoTS; GTBS; GTBS-D; GTBS-W; GTSE; GTSL; LPS-1; OBEV; TVSH
(Cavalier's Song.) HBV
(O Tell Me How to Woo Thee.) EBSV; OBEC
(To His Lady.) LH
If down his throat a man should choose. An Unsuspected [*or* Unexpected] Fact. Edward Cannon. BOHV; BoN; NA
If dreaming of thee be a waste of time. Sonnet. George Henry Boker. Sonnets; a Sequence of Profane Love, XXXV. MOAP
If dumb too long the drooping Muse hath stayed. To the Earl of Warwick on the Death of Mr. Addison. Thomas Tickell. CEP; EiPP; EV-3; HBV; LPS-3; OBEC; PtP
If duty to your country means. A Soldier's Wife to Her Husband. Liu Chi. ChLP; OnPM; PoHN
If Easter Be Not True. Henry H. Barstow. BLRP; MaRV; OQP; PGD; PSO; QP-1
If Easter Eggs Would Hatch. Douglas Malloch. MPB
If echoes from the fitful past. Abstrosophy. Gelett Burgess. CenHV; NA
If e'er for human bliss or woe. To My Mother. Felicia Dorothea Hemans. MOAH
If e'er my rhyming be at fault. Erring in Company. Franklin P. Adams. BOHV; TCAP; TOP
If England were what England seems. England. Kipling. OtMeF
If ever a garden was Gethsemane. For Jim, Easter Eve. Anne Spencer. PoNe
If ever a sailor was fond of good sport. Jack's Fidelity. Charles Dibdin. EtS
If ever aching heart can speed across the years. Catullus, *tr. fr. Latin by* H. W. Household. LaP
If ever against this easy blue and silver. Interruption. Robert Graves. GTBS-W; LiTB; LiTM
If ever age. Bitten. Mark Van Doren. AnAmPo; LA
If ever, as I struck thy strings. To His Lyre. Franklin P. Adams. LHV
If ever I dig out. Via Lucis. Charles G. Blanden. OQP; QP-1
If ever I git off this warpath. That Pretty Little Gal. *Unknown.* ABF
If ever I go to Stony Town, I'll go as to a fair. Stony Town. John Shaw Neilson. BoAV; NeLNL
If ever I had dreamed of my dead name. To My Friend. Wilfred Owen. NAMP
If Ever I Marry [I'll Marry a Maid]. *Unknown.* ElL; ElSeCe
(Maids and Widows.) PreP
If ever I render back your heart. Song for a Slight Voice. Louise Bogan. NP
If ever I saw blessing in the air. April Rise. Laurie Lee. GTBS-D; OnHM
If ever I should [*or* If I should ever] condescend to prose. Poetical Commandments [*or* Poet's Credo]. Byron. *Fr.* Don Juan. BPN; FiP; GEPC; OBRV; OxBoLi; SeCePo
If ever I suspect thee of a lie. To L——. D'Arcy Cresswell. AnNZ
If ever I travel this road again. The Gal I Left behind Me. *Unknown.* ABF
"If ever I walk to church to wed." The Satin Shoes. Thomas Hardy. CoBMV
If ever I'd known Italy. If. Oswald Durand. PoNe
If ever it were time for the nation's dead to ride. Australia Day, 1942; in Memoriam W. J. Miles. Ian Mudie. BoAu
If ever man had love too dearly bought. A Lover, Disdained, Complaineth. Thomas, Lord Vaux. TuPP
If ever man might him avaunt. Sir Thomas Wyatt. SiPS
If ever round our domicile you chance to be a-wandering. "Everybody Works but Father" as W. S. Gilbert Would Have Written It. Arthur G. Burgoyne. FiBHP
If ever Sorrow spoke from soul that loves. Sonnet. Henry Constable. *Fr.* Diana. ElL; SiCE
If ever there is something nice. Five Years Old. Lysbeth Boyd Borie. SiSoSe
If ever there lived a Yankee lad. Darius Green and His Flying-Machine. John Townsend Trowbridge. BeLS; BoChLi; BOHV; FaBoBe; HBV; HBVY; IHA; InMe; MoShBr; MW; PTA-1; PYM; StVeCh (1940 ed.); YaD
If ever there was man who justly stank. Two Poems against His Rival, 1. Catullus. LiTW
If Ever Time Shall Come. Alison Brown. PEDC
If ever two were one, then surely we. To My Dear and Loving Husband. Anne Bradstreet. AmP; AmPP; BAV; IAP; NePA; OxBA; PoEL-3
If ever you come to Phthia, with her vineyards greenly growing. "He Fell among Thieves." *Unknown.* GrPE
If ever you go riding on the road through Lincoln Town. Where Billy the Kid Still Rides. S. Omar Barker. HiLiAm
If ever you go to Dolgelly. Thomas Hughes. CenHV
If Ever You Go to Dublin Town. Patrick Kavanagh. AnIL
If ever you should come to Modena. Ginevra. Samuel Rogers. *Fr.* Italy. EV-3; LPS-3
If ever you should follow. Belden Hollow. Leslie Nelson Jennings. GoYe
If ever you should go by chance. How to Tell [*or* Know] the Wild Animals. Carolyn Wells. FaFP; FaPON; FiBHP; GoTP; HBVY; MaC; MPB; TiPo; TSW; UTS
If every man's internal care. Without and Within. Pierre A. B. D. Metastasio. LPS-3
If everyone had a flying machine. Chairoplane Chant. Nancy Byrd Turner. RIS
If Everything. Paul Engle. SiTL
If everywhere in the street. Songs, II. Denis Glover. AnNZ
If, fairest, through thy heart. To His Mistress. Gilles Durant. LiA
If faith most true, a heart that cannot feign. Petrarch. *Fr.* Sonnets to Laura: To Laura in Life. PrPoCR
If faithful soul[e]s be alike glorified. Holy Sonnets, VIII. John Donne. OBS; SeEP
If Fancy would favour. Sir Thomas Wyatt. SiPS
If Fathers Knew [but How To Leave]. *Unknown.* EG; ElL; ElSeCe
If few are won to read my lays. A Song to One. T. A. Daly. PIAE; YT
If flowers could speak. Nature in War-Time. Herbert Palmer. HaMV
If for a moment only, and then ineptly. People as Flowers. Francis Maguire. JKCP (1955 ed.)
If for a woman I would die. A Song. Countess of Winchilsea. ViBoPo
If for all the promises you regard so lightly. Horace. Odes, II, 8. LaP
"If" for Girls, An. Elizabeth Lincoln Otis. FAOV; PTA-2
If Fortune's dark eclipse cloud glory's light. Illusion. Sir William Alexander. *Fr.* Darius. EBSV
If Frequently to Mass. Christine de Pisan, *tr. fr. French by* J. G. Legge. LyMA
If Friday's dream is on Saturday told. Signs and Charms. *Unknown.* StaSt
If from my painting one hue. An Evening Song. Wilson MacDonald. OCL
If from the public way you turn your steps. Michael [a Pastoral Poem]. Wordsworth. AEV; BEL; BPN; EM-2; EmBrPo; EnL; EnLi-2; EnLit; EnLP; EnRP; EPN; ERP; EV-3; GEPC; GoTL; OAEP; PoE; ShBV-3; TOP; TyEnPo; UnPo (1st ed.); WHA
If girls were as charming after the fact as before it. Andante, ma Non Assai. Rufinus Domesticus. LiTW
If God compel thee to this destiny. A Thought for a Lonely Death-Bed. Elizabeth Barrett Browning. MaRV
If God hath made this world so fair. The Earth Is Full of God's Goodness James Montgomery. MaRV
If God is thrilled by a battle cry. Wonder. John Galsworthy. QS
If Goghtan's bards no longer crown. Lament over the Heroes

If Goghtan's bards no longer crown (*continued*)
Fallen in the Battle of Avarair. Karekin Srvanstian. ArmLP
If granny but knew how. Hush Rhymes—Italian. *Unknown.* BOL
If graver heads shall count it overlight. To the Author. George Peele. *Fr.* Hecatompathia (*by* Thomas Watson). ReIE
If Gray Had Had to Write His Elegy in the Cemetery of Spoon River Instead of in That of Stoke Poges. J. C. Squire. WhC
If great Apollo offered as a dower. Fidessa, More Chaste than Kind, LIV. Bartholomew Griffin. ReIE; TuPP
If grief come early. First or Last. Thomas Hardy. ChMo; CMP; VLEP
If grief for grief can touch thee. The Appeal. Emily Brontë. EmBrPo; EnLoPo; LoBV
If grief should come to me. Comfort. Margaret French Patton. PC
If gutter-puddles after rain. Dirt and Deity. Louis Ginsberg. OQP; QP-2
If handycraftmen have great praise for working well. George Turbervile in Praise of the Translator of This Book [Sir Geoffrey Fenton]. George Turberville. ReIE
If He be truly Christ. Second Seeing. Louis Golding. WGRP
If he could doubt on his triumphal cross. Calvary. William Dean Howells. ChIP; OQP; QP-1
If He could speak, that victim torn and bleeding. The Suffering God. G. A. Studdert-Kennedy. MaRV
If he play, being young and unskilful, for shekels of silver and gold. Maxim. Kipling. OtMeF
If He Should Come. Lilith Lorraine. ChIP; MaRV; MuM
If He Should Come. Edwin Markham. ChIP; OQP; QP-1
If He Should Come Again. Maeterlinck, *tr. fr. French by* Lord Alfred Douglas. MiFP
If he should come tomorrow, the Meek and Lowly One. If He Should Come. Lilith Lorraine. ChIP; MaRV; MuM
If he that erst the form so lively drew. Earl of Surrey. SiPS
If he were living—dare I ask? Bereaved. Emily Dickinson. CoBA
If he will be heaven after death. Prelude to Objects. Wallace Stevens. CoV
If Hearts Are Dust. James Terry White. OQP; QP-1
If heaven and earth were both not fully bent. His Complaint against Love and Fortune. Nicholas Breton. ReIE
If Heaven had no love for [*or* did not love] wine. Drinking Alone in Moonlight. Li Po. AWP; WhP
If Heaven the grateful liberty would give. The Choice. John Pomfret. CEP; EiPP; OBEC; PoE; PoFS; PreP; TOP
If Heaven were to do again. The Peaceful Shepherd. Robert Frost. *Fr.* A Sky Pair. MAP; MoAB; MoAmPo; OS
If heav'n be pleased when sinners cease to sin. Epigrams: Elegy on Coleman. *Unknown.* ALV
If He'd Be a Buckaroo, *with music. Unknown.* OuSiCo
If here and now be but a timely span. Here and Now. Catharine Cater. PoNe
If High Heaven had no love for wine. Drinking Alone by Moonlight, 3. Li Po. TrCh
If homely virtues draw from me a tune. Envoy. James Weldon Johnson. TrPWD
If hope grew on a bush. Christina Rossetti. *Fr.* Sing-Song. MBP
If hours be years the twain are blest. At a Hasty Wedding. Thomas Hardy. ViP
If humility and purity be not in the heart. T. S. Eliot. *Fr.* The Rock. TiPo
If hungry, Lord, I need bread. In Harbor. Lizette Woodworth Reese. TrPWD
If I. T. C. O'Donnell. GFA
If I/ or anybody. 306. E. E. Cummings. AnEnPo
If I Am but the Water. Christopher La Farge. LoPS
If I am ever forced to leave this land. My Greenup Friends. Jesse Stuart. *Fr.* Man with a Bull-Tongue Plow. BoFr
If I am not a fool in prophecy. Dreams Come True. Sophocles. *Fr.* Electra. OxBG
If I am slow forgetting. In April. Margaret Lee Ashley. OBAV
If I am to live or be in the studios. John Standish, Artist. Kenneth Fearing. AnAmPo; LA
"If I ascend to heaven, thou art there." Without and Within. Norman Ault. MaRV; StJW
If I ask why/ You need not reply. The Question Is Proof. Elizabeth Bartlett. NePoAm-2
If I, athirst by a stream, should kneel. A Drifting Petal. Mary McNeil Fenollosa. AA
If I be a diviner and full of the divining spirit. The Seven Seals. Nietzsche. *Fr.* Also sprach Zarathustra. LiA
"If I Be Lifted Up." E. P. Dickie. *See* "And I, if I Be Lifted Up, Shall Draw All Men."
If I But Knew. Amy E. Leigh. AA
If I but knew. The Pine against the Blue. Victor Starbuck. LS; NoCaPo
If I but knew what the tree-tops say. If I But Knew. Amy E. Leigh. AA
If I can bear your love like a lamp before me. The Lamp. Sara Teasdale. ChMo; CMP; InP; NV
If I can do some good today. My Daily Prayer. Grenville Kleiser. BLRP; MaRV; PraP
If I can lead a man who has been blind. The Reward. Grace G. Bostwick. MaRV
If I can stop one heart from breaking. Emily Dickinson. CV; MaRV; PoToHe
(Helping the Handicapped.) TreF
(Not in Vain.) OHFP
If I Come Back. Victor Starbuck. LS
If I come in, you must leave the door ajar. Cat's World. Bernice Kenyon. CIV
If I could be a gipsy-boy. The Caravan. Madeleine Nightingale. BoTP; GaP; MPB
If I could catch that moth. Under Glass. Alfred Kreymborg. AnAmPo; LA; MAPA
If I could choose my paradise. No and Yes. Thomas Ashe. HBV
If I could climb the garden wall. There—and Back. Rodney Bennett. BoTP
If I Could Come Again to That Dear Place. John Masefield. *Fr.* Sonnets ("Long, long ago"). CMP; EPP; HBV
(Revelation.) ChMo
(Sonnet, *wr. at. to* Herbert P. Horne.) LEAP
(Sonnet XXIX.) TwCV
If I could do so, lovely girl of mine. *Unknown, tr. fr. Italian by* L. R. Lind. LyPI
If I could drive steel like John Henry. Drivin' Steel. *Unknown.* AS
If I could ever sing the songs. Silent Songs. Richard Henry Stoddard. TCAP
If I could feel my hand, dear Lord, in Thine. Faith. Sarah K. Bolton. PraP
If I could gather up the threads of time. The Perfect Round. Hilda Mary Hooke. CPG
If I could get within this changing I. Sonnets ("Long long ago"). John Masefield. EPP; WGRP
If I Could Grasp a Wave from the Great Sea. John Richard Moreland. EtS
If I could have/ Two things in one. Moriturus. Edna St. Vincent Millay. AnAmPo; GTBS-W; LA; LiTA; NAMP
If I could hold within my hand. Jesus the Carpenter. Charles M. Sheldon. ChIP; MaRV; OQP; QP-1
If I could I surely would. Pharaoh's Army Got Drownded. *Unknown.* AS
If I could know that here about. Evelyn. Rossiter Johnson. AA
If I could live without the thought of death. On the Shortness of Time. Wilfrid Scawen Blunt. The Love Sonnets of Proteus, XCVI. MBP; MoBrPo (1942 ed.)
If I could live year-round upon this hill. In Conclusion. Abbie Huston Evans. NP
If I Could Love. John Gardner Calkins Brainard. PR
If I could not be the girl I am. Her Choice. Mattie Lee Hausgen. GFA
If I Could Only Live at the Pitch That Is Near Madness. Richard Eberhart. FiMAP; MiAP; MoAB
If I could only serve him. Service. Anna Hempstead Branch. AV
If I could paint you, friend, as you stand there. A Football-Player. Edward Cracroft Lefroy. VA
If I could put my woods in song. My Garden. Emerson. IAP
If I could see a little fish. On the Bridge. Kate Greenaway. MCCG; MPB; RAR; SAS
If I could see, as once, my face. Innocence. Alfred Gordon. CPG
If I Could Shut the Gate [against My Thoughts]. *Unknown.* ElL; ElSeCe; HBV; LoBV; OxBoCh; SiCE
If I could smell smells with my ears. Curious Something. Winifred Welles. TiPo
If I could stand, gel, goldenly. Come Michaelmas. A. Newberry Choyce. HBMV
If I could take your mountains in my heart. Frank Wilmot. *Fr.* The Gully. BoAV; NeLNL
If I could trust mine own self with your fate. Trust. Christina Rossetti. Monna Innominata, XIII. EmBrPo; HiLiEn; VA; ViPo
If I deny my kinship to a man. A Gentle Park. Moss Herbert. GoYe
If I Desire. Thomas Burbidge. VA
If I did come of set intent. To Archinus. Callimachus. AWP
If I did not love you more than my very eyes. Catullus, *tr. fr. Latin by* Frances Fletcher. LaP
If I Die a Railroad Man, *with music. Unknown.* AS
If I die of love, why, let me die. My Love Who Loves Me Not. Hitomaro. PFE

If I don't drive around the park. Some Beautiful Letters [*or* Observation]. Dorothy Parker. FiBHP; InMe

If I drink water while this doth last. Chorus. Thomas Love Peacock. *Fr.* Crotchet Castle. ViBoPo

If I entreat this lady that all grace. Sonnet: To a Friend Who Does Not Pity His Love. Guido Cavalcanti. AWP

If I err not, the sylvan sprites rejoice. Olympia. Boccaccio. WoL

If I esteemed you less, Envy would kill. Sonnet to Byron. Shelley. PtP

If I ever attain, in this splendid domain. Reverse English. *Unknown.* CAG

If I Ever Have Time for Things That Matter. Vilda Sauvage Owens. BOHV

If I Felt Less. Morris Wintchevsky, *tr. fr. Yiddish by* Joseph Leftwich. TrJP

If I Forget Thee. Emanuel Litvinoff. TrJP

If I forswear the art divine. The Exile's Devotion. Thomas d'Arcy McGee. VA

If I Freely May Discover. Ben Jonson. *Fr.* The Poetaster, II, ii. EG; ElSeCe; ReEn; TuPP (Song.) ElL

If I from universal mud. Ballad of the Mystic and the Mud. Tom MacInnes. CPG

If I go to see the play. Old Stuff. Bert Leston Taylor. BOHV; HBMV; LHV

If I Got My Ticket, Can I Ride? *with music. Unknown.* OuSiCo

If I grieve often, thinking of the dead. To a Believer. Marjorie Pickthall. PeCV

If I Had a Boy. *Unknown.* PEDC

If I Had a Broomstick. Patrick R. Chalmers. TVC; TVSH

If I had a donkey that wouldn't go. *Unknown.* OxNR

If I had a farm, an' no need to be beggin' my bread. The Beggar. H. L. Doak. HBMV

If I had a hundred dollars to spend. The Animal Store. Rachel Field. AlBD; GoBP; OTPC (1946 ed.); TiPo; UTS

If I had a-listened what my mother said. Prison Moan. *Unknown.* OuSiCo

If I had a son! A little child. Barren. "Rachel." TrJP

If I had [*or* I'd] as much money as I could spend. Mother Goose. FaFP; HBV; OTPC; OxNR

If I had been a Heathen. The Song of the Strange Ascetic. G. K. Chesterton. HBMV

If I had been in Palestine. Judge Me, O Lord! Sarah N. Cleghorn. ChIP; MaRV; StJW

If I had but one year to live. One Year to Live. Mary Davis Reed. PoToHe (new ed.)

If I Had but Two Little Wings. Samuel Taylor Coleridge. BoTP; CH; OHIP; OTPC (1923 ed.); PECK (Something Childish, but Very Natural.) EV-4; OBRV

If I had chosen thee, thou shouldst have been. To Manon, as to His Choice of Her. Wilfrid Scawen Blunt. *Fr.* The Love Sonnets of Proteus. HBV; ViBoPo

If I had feet to dance before the holy arc. Corpus Christi: Invocation. Margery Mansfield. NV

If I had just one penny. Choice. John Farrar. BrR; SiSoSe

If I Had Known. Mary Carolyn Davies. BLPA

If I had known how narrow a prison is love. Liadain to Curither. Moireen Fox. NP

If I had known what trouble you were bearing. If I Had Known. Mary Carolyn Davies. BLPA

If I had known what would come later. Boris Pasternak, *tr. fr. Russian by* C. M. Bowra. BoRS

If I had left at my going. A Form of Flight. Emilio Prados. CoSP

If I had never known your face at all. Sonnets to Miranda, VIII. Sir William Watson. FaBoBe; HBV

If I had only loved your flesh. Song. V. Sackville-West. HBMV

If I had peace to sit and sing. The Singer. Anna Wickham. BMEP; HBMV; MBP; MoBrPo; NeMA; NP; TSW; TSWC

If I Had Ridden Horses. Theodore Maynard. HBMV

If I had sat at supper with the Lord. With Me in Paradise. Alexander Harvey. ChIP

If I had seen Thee, Master. The Prayer of a Teacher. Elizabeth McE. Shields. PraP

If I had stood, waiting for you to come. Two Sonnets; to a Spiritual Entity, II. Helen Pinkerton. PtPa

If I had thought thou couldst have died. To Mary [*or* Song: To Mary *or* Lines Written to Music]. Charles Wolfe. EV-4; GTSL; HBV; LO; OBEV; OBRV; TIP; ViBoPo

If I had wit for to indite. A Secret. *Unknown.* OBSC

If I had won my Wendy. Luck. Evan V. Shute. CaP

If I Had Youth. Edgar A. Guest. POT; PoTo

If I have any taste, it is hardly. Hunger. Arthur Rimbaud. AWP

If I have faltered more or less. The Celestial Surgeon. Robert Louis Stevenson. BBV; BMEP; BPP; EBSV; EPN; GBV (1922 ed.); GoTP; HBV; HBVY; LBBV; MaRV; MBP; MoBrPo; MW; OQP; PC; PIAE; PoeT; PoToHe (new ed.); POTT; PoVP; QP-1; TreFS; TrGrPo; TrPWD; ViBoPo; WGRP

If I Have Lifted Up Mine Eyes to Admire. Amos N. Wilder. TrPWD

If I Have Made, My Lady. E. E. Cummings. ChMo; MOAP; NAMP; PoRA

If I have run my course and seek the pearls. The Marathon Runner. Fenton Johnson. CDC

If I have since done evil in my life. The Sinner-Saint. Wilfrid Scawen Blunt. ACP; CAW

If I have wounded any soul to-day. Evening Prayer [*or* My Evening Prayer]. *At. to* C. Maud Battersby, *also to* Charles H. Gabriel. BLPA; FaBoBe; NeHB; OQP; PraP; QP-1

If I hope, I pine; if I fear, I faint and die. Hope and Fear. Thomas Campion. PoP

If I in woemen would take my delight. *Unknown.* SeCSL

If I knew You and You Knew Me. Nixon Waterman. *See* "To Know All Is to Forgive All."

If I knew you, and you knew me. At Church Next Sunday. *Unknown.* BLRP

If I knocked in this dead night. Threshold. Edmund Blunden. HBMV

If I lay waste and wither up with doubt. Faith [*or* What Shall It Profit?]. William Dean Howells. AA; LBAP; MaRV; OQP; QP-1; WGRP

If I leave all for thee, wilt thou exchange. Sonnets from the Portuguese, XXXV. Elizabeth Barrett Browning. BEL; BPN; EmBrPo; EnLi-2; EnLit; TOP; VA; ViBoPo; ViPo

If I, like Solomon. O to Be a Dragon. Marianne Moore. GoYe

If I live till my fighting days are done. Against the Wall. Aline Kilmer. FAOV; NV

If I live to grow old, for I find I go down. The Old Man's Wish [*or* The Wish]. Walter Pope. CoMu; OBS; PoP; SeCL; SeEP

If I Loved You. Oscar Hammerstein, II. Po

"If I may trust your love," she cried. Tantalus; Texas [*or* The Llano Estacado]. *Unknown, at. to* Joaquin Miller. CoSo; HBV

If I might alter kind. The Lover, Whose Mistresse Feared a Mouse, Declareth that He Would Become a Cat if He Might Have His Desire. George Turberville. PoC

If I Might Choose. John Anster. OnYI (Sonnet: "If I might choose where my tired limbs shall lie.") IrPN

If I might guess, then guess I would. Dorcas. George Macdonald. OBVV

If I might only love my God and die! If Only. Christina Rossetti. OxBoCh

If I mistake not, thou art Harry Monmouth. A Combat. Shakespeare. King Henry IV, Pt. I, *fr.* V, iv. BHV

If I Must. Lloyd Roberts. CPG

If I must die. Youth. George Cabot Lodge. AA

If I must go, let it be easy, slow. Improvisation on an Old Theme. Dorothy Livesay. CaP

If I, Mycenae, moulder in dust and desolation. Mycenae Fallen. Pompeius. GrPE

If I only had not chanced. Two Others, on Either Side. Edith Mirick. ChIP

If I Only Was the Fellow. Will S. Adkin. BLPA (Just Try to Be the Fellow That Your Mother Thinks You Are.) WBLP

If I really, really trust Him. A Question. *Unknown.* BLRP

If I remain and fight. The Prayer of Calcas. *Unknown.* *Fr.* Troelus a Chresyd. PrWP

If I say to you: "I have given up everything." The One for All Time. Paul Eluard. MiCF

If I See in My Soul. Bilhana, *formerly at. to* Chauras, *tr. fr. Sanskrit by* E. Powys Mathers. *Fr.* Black Marigolds. OnPM

If I seeke t'enjoy the fruit of my paine. *Unknown.* SeCSL

If I shall ever win the home in Heaven. Daniel Gray. Josiah Gilbert Holland. AA; HBV; LEAP

If I should choose, yea, for my life. In Nigellum. John Weever. TuPP

If I should die. Emily Dickinson. MoAB

If I should die and leave you here a while. Turn Again to Life. Mary Lee Hall. MaRV

If I should die out there on the battle-front. Poem to Lou. Guillaume Apollinaire. LiTW

If I should die, think only this of me. The Soldier. Rupert Brooke. *Fr.* 1914. AEV; AnFE; AOAH; BBV; BEL; BLV; BMEP; BoLiVe; BTP; CaAE; CBOV; CP; EnLit; EPN; EPP; ES; EV-5; ExPo; FaBoEn; FaFP; GTBS; GTBS-W; GTML; GTSL; HiLiEn; InP; LBBV; LEAP; LiTB; LiTM; MaC; MaRV; MBP; MCCG; MoBrPo; MoVE; NeHB; NeMA; OBEV (new ed.); OTPC (1946 ed.); PIAE; PoeT; PoMa; PoRA; POT; POTE; PoTo; POTT; PreP; PYM; ShBV-3; TCEP; TCPD; TOP; TreF; TrGrPo; TVSH; TwCV; ViBoPo; VOD; WaP; WHA; WP; YT

If I Should Die Tonight. *parody.* Ben King. BOHV; FiBHP; HBV; InMe; LEAP; PA; TreFS; YaD
If I Should Die Tonight. Arabella Eugenia Smith, *wr. at. to* Robert C. V. Meyers. BAP; BLPA; HBV; LPS-1; PoeMoYo; PYM; TreF
If I should dwell now on the pain. Sunshine. Fujita. SoLD
If I Should Ever by Chance. Edward Thomas. BLV; CP; EPP; FaBoCh; GTSL; HBMV; LBBV; LoGBV; MBP; MoAB; MoBrPo; MoShBr; NeMA; OBMV; TwCV
If I should ever condescend to prose. *See* If ever I should condescend to prose.
If I should hasten or cry out. Entry to the Desert. James Rorty. MOAP; TBM
If I should labor through daylight and dark. Philosophy. Dorothy Parker. InMe
If I should lift my look for yours to-night. Realization. Mahlon Leonard Fisher. AnAmPo; LA
If I should live in a forest. Old Poets. Joyce Kilmer. LEAP
If I should lose my sight and never see again. Prisoners. Helen M. Lehman. DDA
If I should meet with the boy that I was. Excavation. Clifford Bax. PtOT
If I should paint thy portrait, mother dear. My Mother. Bertha Nolan. PGD
If I should pamphleteer twenty years against royalists. To the Ghost of John Milton. Carl Sandburg. ReMP
If I should pass the tomb of Jonah. Losers. Carl Sandburg. ChMo; CMP; HBMV; MAP; MoAB; MoAmPo; MoVE; NP; TrGrPo
If I should pray this lady pitiless. Sonnet. Guido Cavalcanti. LyPI
If I shouldn't be alive. Emily Dickinson. CoBA; MAPA; PG; TwAmPo
(Crumb for Robin.) OnPM
If I speak with the tongues of men and of angels. *See* Though I speak . . .
If I take an acorn. If. Alice Todd. BoTP
If I think music. Music. Hilda Conkling. HH; MPB
If I turn to the lady on my left, and say. Conversation. William F. Walsh. JKCP (1955 ed.)
If I was drawn here from a distant place. To —— in Church. Alan Seeger. HBV
If I were a bear. Furry Bear. A. A. Milne. StVeCh (1955 ed.); TiPo (1959 ed.)
If I were a boy again—ah, me! Looking Back. Mary Mapes Dodge. FAOV
If I were a Cassowary. Some Cannibal. *At. to* Samuel Wilberforce. BoN; CenHV
If I Were a Cat. *Unknown.* CIV
If I were a chipmunk. No Escape. Harriet L. Delafield. GoYe
If I were a cloud in heaven. Lise. Rose Terry Cooke. AA
If I were a mermaid clad in scales. Foam of Fancy. Mary Josephine Benson. CPG
If I were a mouse. The Furry Home. J. M. Westrup. BoTP
If I Were a One-legged Pirate. Mildred Plew Meigs. GoBP
If I Were a Pig. Elizabeth Fleming. BoTP
If I Were a Pilgrim Child. Rowena Bennett. YeAr
If I Were a Poet. Albert Ulrik Bååth, *tr. fr. Swedish by* Charles W. Stork. AnSL
If I Were a Queen. Christina Rossetti. *Fr.* Sing-Song. CoBE; GaP; PoVP; SiSoSe
If I were a tailor, I'd make it my boast. The Tradesman. *Unknown.* PCH
If I Were a Voice. Charles Mackay. TreF
If I Were an Apple. *Unknown.* BoTP
If I were asked to give a thought which in one word would speak. You Mean My Mother. *Unknown.* PEDC
If I Were Dead. Coventry Patmore. The Unknown Eros, I, xiv. ACP; CAW; GoBC; HBV; JKCP; OBEV (1st ed.); POTT; VLEP
If I were dead, and in my place. A Song to Amoret. Henry Vaughan. AEV; HBV; LiTL; NBE; ViBoPo
If I were dead in the Desert—as you would like me to be. To a Depraved Lying Woman. Sorley Maclean. NeBP
"If I were dead, you'd sometimes say, 'Poor Child!'" If I Were Dead. Coventry Patmore. *Fr.* The Unknown Eros. ACP; CAW; GoBC; HBV; JKCP; OBEV (1st ed.); POTT; VLEP
If I were fierce and bald and short of breath. Base Details. Siegfried Sassoon. MBP; MoBrPo; NeMA; TwCV
If I were fire I'd burn the world away. Sonnet: Of All He Would Do. Cecco Angiolieri da Siena. AWP; JAWP; LyMA; LyPI; OnPM; WBP
If I were hanged on the highest hill. Mother o' Mine [*or* Dedication]. Kipling. *Fr.* The Light That Failed. FaFP; MaRV; MOAH; MotAn; NeHB; OQP; PSO; PTA-2; QP-1; WBLP
If I were in a fairy tale. The Duck. Edith King. BoTP; GFA; HBVY; StVeCh
If I were just a fairy small. A Fairy Voyage. *Unknown.* OTPC (1946 ed.); PCH
If I Were King, *sels.* Justin Huntly M'Carthy.
I Wonder in What Isle of Bliss, *fr. ch.* 9, *par. fr. the French of* Villon. PFE
(Ballad of Dead Ladies, A.) HBV
("Sigh, my lute, sigh," *longer sel.*) ReTS
If I Were King ("All French folk, whereso'er ye be"), *fr. ch.* 2, *par. fr. the French of* Villon. HBV
If I Were King ("If I were king—ah, love, if I were king"), *introd. poem, par. fr. the French of* Villon. FaFP; LEAP; PFE; TreF
If I were King of France, that noble fine land. The Heather. Neil Munro. EBSV; OBVV
If I were king of this broad land. Much Virtue in If. T. Sturge Moore. TCPD
If I were less the man, I might have kept. Two Sonnets for a Lost Love, II. Samuel A. De Witt. GoYe
If I were Lord of Tartary. Tartary [*or* Lord of Tartary]. Walter de la Mare. BMEP; CP; EPP; GaP; GoTP; HBMV; MW; PC; PoRh; PtOT; PYM; ShBV-1; SP
If I were mild, and I were sweet. Dilemma. Dorothy Parker. InMe
If I were oh, so very small. If. P. A. Ropes. BoTP
If I were only dafter. Witter Bynner. *Fr.* Spectra: Opus 6. LiTM
If I were queen of all the land. The Chain of Princes Street. Elizabeth Fleming. PCH
If I were rich what would I do? Why Tomas Cam Was Grumpy. James Stephens. ChMo; CMP; WhC
If I Were Santa's Little Boy. Mary Carolyn Davies. DD; HH
If I were stone dead and buried under. Felo de Se. Richard Hughes. OBMV
If I Were the Lord God. Claudia Cranston. VOD
If I were thine, I'd fail not of endeavour. The Third Proposition. "Madeline Bridges." BOHV
If I Were to Tell of Our Labours, Our Hard Lodging. Aeschylus, *tr. fr. Greek by* Louis MacNeice. *Fr.* Agamemnon. WaaP
If I were told that I must die tomorrow. When. "Susan Coolidge." HBV; LPS-2
If I were told that I must go tonight. Songs. Grace Noll Crowell. LS
If I were very sure. The Coup de Grace. Edward Rowland Sill. AA
If I were you, when ladies at the play, Sir. Tu Quoque. Austin Dobson. BOHV
If I when my wife is sleeping. Danse Russe. William Carlos Williams. MOAP
If I, who only sing, in other ways. The New Physician. Stephen Chalmers. HBMV
If I woke in Bombay it would be possible. Bombay. Josephine Miles. FiMAP
If Ice. W. W. E. Ross. BoCaPo
If I'd a little money. Plans. Luisa Hewitt. PCH
If I'd as much money as I could spend. *See* If I had as much money . . .
If I'd as much money as I could tell. *Unknown.* OxNR
If "ifs" and "ands." Proverbs [*or* Some Proverbs in Verse]. *Unknown.* FaBoBe; HBV
If I'm at church these days. Rondel. Christine de Pisan. FoS
If in a picture, Piso, you should see. The Art of Poetry. Horace, *tr. by* the Earl of Roscommon. EnLi-1
If in a wildwood where no sunbeam falls. To a Nun of the Good Shepherd. Michael Earls. PraNu
If in all the world there be more woe. *See* If in the World There Be More Woe.
If in an odd angle of the hutment. Eighth Air Force. Randall Jarrell. MiAP; MoVE; ReMP
If in his study he hath so much care. Antiquary. John Donne. TuPP
If in some far-off, future day. Epitaph for a Cat. Margaret E. Bruner. CIV
If in that secret place. Barter. Margaret Widdemer. HBMV; WGRP
If in that Syrian garden, ages slain. Easter Hymn. A. E. Housman. ChMP; MaRV; MoAB; ReaPo; SeCeV; TriL
If in the fight my arm was strong. The Warrior to His Dead Bride. Adelaide Anne Procter. DiM; OBVV
If in the material world. The Soul Eternal. Sir John Bowring. MaRV
If, in the month of dark December. Written after Swimming from Sestos to Abydos. Byron. ALV; BOHV; InMe; LauV; OBRV; PoE; PoeMoYo
If in the Sacred Garden Jesus said. Silence. Alfred de Vigny. TrFP
If, in the silent mind of One all-pure. In Utrumque Paratus. Matthew Arnold. EmBrPo; GEPC; NBE; OAEP; PoEL-5; PoVP; ViPP; VLEP
If in the summer of thy bright regard. To M. William Gay. BoAu
If in the World There Be More Woe. Sir Thomas Wyatt. EG; ElL; SiPS
(Disdain.) TrGrPo

(Treizaine.) OBSC
If in the years that come such thing should be. Ideal Memory. William James Dawson. VA
If in this book dullness do chance to lurk. Ad Collegium Wintoniensem. John Heath. TuPP
If, in thy second state sublime. In Memoriam A. H. H., LXI. Tennyson. EmBrPo; EPN; GEPC; ViPo; VLEP
If it/ Were lighter touch. The Guarded Wound. Adelaide Crapsey. AnAmPo; LA; NP; NV
If it be all for nought, for nothingness. Resurrection. *Unknown.* ChIP; MaRV
If It Be Destined. Petrarch, *tr. fr. Italian by* Edward Fitzgerald. Sonnets to Laura: To Laura in Life, XI. AWP; JAWP; OnPM; WBP
If it be pleasant to look on, stalled in the packed serai. Certain Maxims of Hafiz. Kipling. HBV
If it be sin so dearly for to love thee. Coelia, VII. William Percy. ReIE
If It Be True That Any Beauteous Thing. Michelangelo, *tr. fr. Italian by* J. E. Taylor. LPS-1
(Madrigal.) BoFr
If it chance your eye offend you. A. E. Housman. A Shropshire Lad, XLV. PoVP
If It Do Come to Pass. Shakespeare. *Fr.* As You Like It, II, v. ViBoPo
If it form the one landscape that we the inconstant ones. In Praise of Limestone. W. H. Auden. CoBMV; MaPo; MoAB; MoVE; NePA
If it had not been for Cotton-eyed Joe. Cotton-eyed Joe. *Unknown.* ABF
If it had not been the Lord who was on our side. Psalm CXXIV, Bible, *O.T.* OnPM
If It Is Not My Portion. Rabindranath Tagore. Gitanjali, LXXIX. OBMV
If it is the use. White for Mourning. Al-Fata al-Kafif. MooP
If it is true that we no longer seek. The Fear of Trembling. John Hollander. NePoEA
If it must be; if it must be, O God! Sonnet. David Gray. EBSV
If it only had been acid. Elegy on the Death of Virginia Woolf. Ronald Hambleton. BoCaPo (1948 ed.)
If It Rained Tonight. César Vallejo, *tr. fr. Spanish by* Donald Devenish Walsh. AnCL
If it so hap this offspring of my care. To Delia, III. Samuel Daniel. ReEn
If it wasn't for me and the likes of me. Madeline at Jefferson Market Night Court. Margaret McGovern. WhC
If it were but a wall between us. Small Song. Daniel Whitehead Hicky. MaRV
If it were done when 'tis done, then 'twere well. Duncan's Murder [*or* Macbeth's Murder Meditation *or* Vaulting Ambition]. Shakespeare. *Fr.* Macbeth, I, vii. BCEP; EV-1; FiP; NBE; PIR; WHA
If it were not for the voice. Nakatsukasa. *Fr.* Shui Shu. AWP
If it were only a dream. The Father. George Francis Savage-Armstrong. VA
If it were right that goddesses for men should weep. His Own Epitaph. Naevius. LaP
If it were so—a sudden turn in the track. Deep Woods. Leslie Nelson Jennings. MuM
If it would walk at all. Shadow to Shadow. Hervey Allen. HBMV
If it's true that Nature can. Epitaph on Rabelais. Pierre de Ronsard. FoS
If-itty-teshi-mow Jays. Limerick. *Unknown.* BOHV
If I've a babe in town, Babe. Belle. *Unknown.* OuSiCo
"If, Jerusalem, I Ever Should Forget Thee." Heine, *tr. fr. German by* Margaret Armour. TrJP
If Jesus Came Back Today, *sel.* Vincent Godfrey Burns.
"If Jesus came back today." ChIP; OQP; QP-2
If Jesus came to earth again. Christ's Sympathy. Sir Edward Bulwer-Lytton. BePJ
If Jesus Christ is a man. The Song of a Heathen. Richard Watson Gilder AA; BAP; BePJ; ChIP; LEAP; MaRV; OQP; QP-1; StJW; WGRP
If Jesus should tramp the streets tonight. If He Should Come. Edwin Markham. ChIP; OQP; QP-1
If Jove himself be subject unto love. Passion XXXVII. Thomas Watson. *Fr.* Hecatompathia. ElSeCe
If, knowing all that now is known. Presage. Thomas Thornely. QS
If ladies' manners with their gauds agree. Against the Fantastical Attire That Many Ladies Wear Nowadays. John Davies of Hereford. SiCE
If learned in other things you be. Abraham Cowley. *Fr.* Resolved to Love. LO
If life be as a flame that death doth kill. A Rhyme of Life. Charles Warren Stoddard. HBV; LBAP; MaRV
If life be gone, fresh life to you. Jalal ed-Din Rumi, *tr. fr. Persian by* A. J. Arberry. PeP
If life on earth be less than is a day. Sonnet. Joachim du Bellay. *Fr.* Olive. CAW
If life seems drab and difficult. The Bridge You'll Never Cross. Grenville Kleiser. MaRV
If life were never bitter. If. Mortimer Collins. BOHV; FiBHP; HBV; PA
If life's pleasures cheer thee. Our Rock. Francis Scott Key. BePJ
If light of life outlive the set of sun. Swinburne. After Sunset, III. BEL; EPN; EPP; OQP; QP-1
If lilies now had come to candid birth. To Queen Radigunde with Herbs and Violets. Venantius Fortunatus. LyMA
If Lincoln Should Return. Margaret E. Bruner. PoToHe
If livelihood by knowledge were endowed. Mesnevi. Sadi. *Fr.* The Gulistan. AWP; JAWP; LiTW; WBP
If, Lord, Thy Love for Me Is Strong. St. Theresa of Avila, *tr. fr. Spanish by* Arthur Symons. AnSpL-1; AWP; CAW; JAWP; LiTW; WBP
If, Lord, your splendid gift the Word I truly hold. Request for a Song. Julian Tuwim. LiTW
If love be life, I long to die. Dispraise of Love, and Lovers' Follies. "A. W." BLV; ElL; HBV; LO; OBSC; TrGrPo
If love be like the flower that in the night. Anthony Munday, *ad. fr. the Italian of* Luigi Pasqualigo. *Fr.* Fedele and Fortunio. TuPP
If Love Be Ours. Tennyson. *See* In Love, if Love Be Love.
If love came up the valley. A Change of Face. Harrison Smith Morris. PR
If Love, for Love of Long Time Had. John Heywood. ElL
If love should count you worthy, and should deign. Decision. *Unknown.* PoToHe (new ed.)
If love thou hast for me, not hate. Youth and Age. Sappho. GrR
If love were but a little thing. Song. Florence Earle Coates. HBMV; LBMV; NV
If Love Were Jester at the Court of Death. Frederic Lawrence Knowles. HBV
If love were what the rose is. A Match. Swinburne. ALV; BEL; BMEP; BPN; EmBrPo; EnLi-2; EnLit; GTBS-D; GTBS-W; GTML; GTSL; HBV; LEAP; LiTL; LoPo; LPS-1; OBVV; PFE; PG (1945 ed.); PIR; PoVP; TOP; VA; VLEP
If Luther's day expand to Darwin's year. Epilogue. Herman Melville. *Fr.* Clarel. AnAmPo; APW; ImOP; LA
If made of gold were brown leaves when. Good Old Finn. *Unknown.* LyMA
If man can find rich consolation, remembering his good deeds. Catullus, *tr. fr. Latin by* Horace Gregory. RoL
. . . If man could see / The perils and diseases that he elbows. Thomas Lovell Beddoes. *Fr.* Death's Jest-Book. PoP
If Man, That Angel of Bright Consciousness. Conrad Aiken. NePA
If, Marchioness, you can descry. Stanzas. Corneille. LiTW
If Mary goes far out to sea. Stately Verse. *Unknown.* FaPON; TiPo (1959 ed.)
If medals were ordained for drinks. To a Boon Companion [*or* The Boon Companion]. Oliver St. John Gogarty. OBMV; OtMeF
If Mercie be so large, where's Justice place? Justice and Mercy. Fulke Greville. *Fr.* Mustapha. EV-1
If men be judged wise by their beards and their girth. Epigram. Joseph Solomon del Medigo. TrJP
If men may credit give to true-reported fames. In Praise of a Gentlewoman Who, though She Were Not Very Fair, Yet Was She as Hard-favored as Might Be. George Gascoigne. ReIE
If Michael, leader of God's host. The Rose of Peace. W. B. Yeats. OBVV
If mine eyes can speak to do hearty errand. Sapphics. Sir Philip Sidney. *Fr.* Arcadia. SiPS
If Mother Nature patches. Sewing. William H. Hayne. *Fr.* Pine Needles. ADAH; GFA; MeMeAg; OTPC (1946 ed.); PCH
If Music and Sweet Poetry. Richard Barnfield. *See* To His Friend Master R. L., in Praise of Music and Poetry.
If Music Be the Food of Love. Shakespeare. *Fr.* Twelfth Night, I, i. BCEP; EV-1; PoFS; UnS
(Food of Love, The.) TrGrPo
(Music.) TreFS
If Music Might but Assuage! Euripides, *tr. fr. Greek by* R. C. Trevelyan. *Fr.* Medea. GrR
If my bark sink. Emily Dickinson. MaRV
If my best wines mislike thy taste. Quits. Thomas Bailey Aldrich. AA
If my body come from brutes, tho' somewhat finer than their own. Tennyson. *Fr.* By an Evolutionist. MaRV
If my books easy of digestion be. Ad Lectorem. Thomas Bastard. SiCE
If my boy sleep quietly. *Unknown.* BOL
If my dark grandam had but known. Little Gray Songs from St. Joseph's, VI. Grace Fallow Norton. LBMV
If my dear love were but the child of state. Sonnets, CXXIV. Shakespeare. PeBoSo
If my face could only promise that its color would remain. Face to Face. Frances Cochrane. HBV

If my feeble prayer can reach Thee. Mystic's Prayer. *Unknown.* MaRV

If my garden oak spares one bare ledge. Creed. Anne Spencer. CDC

If My Girl with Lotus Eyes. Bilhana, *formerly at. to* Chauras, *tr. fr. Sanskrit by* E. Powys Mathers. *Fr.* Black Marigolds. OnPM

If my harsh, humble style and rimes ill-dressed. Sonnet I: Dedication of These Rimes to His First Love. Francis Davison. ReIE

If my ill-tuned rhymes content the wise. To the Ungentilized Censurer. Henry Parrot. SiCE

If my peculiar pulchritude in Paris seemed to please. An Intermezzo for the Fourth Act. William Allen White. InMe

If, my religion safe, I durst embrace. To Sir Henrie Savile [upon His Translation of Tacitus]. Ben Jonson. OBS; SeCV-1

If my tears desert me, why. Love's Evidence. Ibn Baqi. MooP

If my vain soul needs blows and bitter losses. Ella Wheeler Wilcox. *Fr.* The Christian's New-Year Prayer. TrPWD

If Nancy Hanks/ Came back as a ghost. Nancy Hanks. Rosemary Benét *and* Stephen Vincent Benét. BAP; FaPON; GBV (1952 ed.); LaNeLa; NeMA; SiSoSe; StVeCh (1955 ed.); TiPo

If Nature, for a favorite child. Matthew. Wordsworth. BPN; EmBrPo; ERP; GEPC

If never sin were, Mercy were none. Mercy. *Unknown.* TMEV

If no love is, O god, what fele I so? Song of Troilus [*or* Troilus Soliloquizes *or* Canticus Troili]. Chaucer. *Fr.* Troilus and Criseyde. AtBAP; AWP; EG; LO; LoPS

If no man had invented human word. The Bird at Dawn. Harold Monro. WhBS

If No One Ever Marries Me. Laurence Alma-Tadema. GoTP; OTPC; RIS

If not a human being lived on earth. The Laughter of the Spheres. Herman Eugene Kittredge. MuM

If not now soft airs may blow. Absence. John Arthur Blaikie. VA

If now, as is too true. Absent Friends. Ibn Hazm. MooP

If now thou seest me a wreck, worn out and minished out of sight. Old Age. Al-Aswad, Son of Ya'fur. *Fr.* The Mufaddaliyat. AWP

If now unto my lips be raised. The Cup. Frederick T. Roberts. ChIP

If now you cannot hear me, it is because. The Barricades. Denise Levertov. NeBP

If, of a wretched state and all forlorn. Sonnet. Leonard Digges. LO; SeCL; SeEP

If of our life the span be not a day. Sonnet. Joachim du Bellay. *Fr.* Olive. WoL

If of thy mortal goods thou art bereft. Hyacinths to Feed Thy Soul. Sadi. *Fr.* The Gulistan. BLPA; FaBoBe; MaRV; NeHB

If of us two might only one be glad. The Greatest Gift. Blanche Edith Baughan. BoAu

If on a spring night I went by. Courage [*or* The Prayer]. John Galsworthy. OtMeF; QS

If, on Account of the Political Situation. W. H. Auden. *Fr.* For the Time Being. LiTA; WaP

If on my theme I rightly think. Why I Drink. Henry Aldrich. ALV; LauV; WhC

If on some balmy summer night. Edith Nesbit. LEAP

If on the Book itself we cast our view. The Scriptures. Dryden. *Fr.* Religio Laici. OBS

If on this night of still, white cold. Faith. Hortense Flexner. PoMa; VOD

If once I could gather in song. Song. W. W. Gibson. OBVV; TOP

If once might have been, once only. Youth and Art. Robert Browning. BOHV; BPN; EV-5; GEPC; HBV; VA; VLEP

If Once the Great Archangel of our Dreams. Struthers Burt. NoCaPo

If once we feared that Fear itself might come. Personal Valour. V. Sackville-West. NeTW

If Once You Have Slept on an Island. Rachel Field. BrR

If one could have that little head of hers. A Face. Robert Browning. BPN; GEPC; PoVP; VA; VLEP

If one could only be certain beyond all question. The Anti-Symbolist. Sidney Keyes. MoPo

If One Might Live. Ethelwyn Wetherald. CPG

If one of the comedy-makers of old had attempted to order the Knights. The Poet and His Rivals. Aristophanes, *tr. by* Gilbert Murray. *Fr.* The Knights. OxBG

If one of the old-fashioned comedy-bards. To the Fickle Gallery. Aristophanes, *tr. by* Benjamin Bickley Rogers. *Fr.* The Knights. GrR

If one pure love, if one supreme devotion. Sonnet XXXI. Michelangelo. BoFr

If one should bring me this report. In Memoriam A. H. H., XIV [*or* Of One Dead]. Tennyson. BPN; EM-2; EmBrPo; EnLi-2; EPN; GEPC; LiTB; LiTG; ViPo; VLEP

If one should tell them what's clearly seen. Crumbs or the Loaf. Robinson Jeffers. ChMo; CMP

If one were soundproof, like a well-built house. Machines—or Men. Elizabeth Newport Hepburn. PoMa

If Only . . . Rose Fyleman. StVeCh; UTS

If Only. Christina Rossetti. OxBoCh

If only a single rose is left. If Only Thou Art True. George Barlow. VA

If only I could send you one small slice. Letter from the Vieux Carre. Ethel Green Russell. GoYe

If Only I Could Write! Ramón de Campoamor, *tr. fr. Spanish by* Ida Farnell. *Fr.* Doloras. AnSpL-2

If only I'd some money. If Only . . . Rose Fyleman. StVeCh; UTS

If only in dreams may man be fully blest. The First Kiss. Theodore Watts-Dunton. *Fr.* The Coming of Love. HBV; VA

If only Mr. Roosevelt. E. C. Bentley. *Fr.* Biography for Beginners. CenHV

If only my song, that soon must exalt me to the band of Immortals. To the Ashes of Claude Colet. Etienne Jodelle. LiA

If only the brown leaf were gold. Generosity. *Unknown.* KiLC

If Only the Dreams Abide. Clinton Scollard. BLP; HBV; LBAP

If only the world. Minamoto no Sanetomo, *tr. fr. Japanese by* Kenneth Rexroth. OnPJ

If Only Thou Art True. George Barlow. VA

If only we might live as we choose! To His Cousin. Martial. PoFr

If Only, When I Made My Debut. Boris Pasternak, *tr. fr. Russian by* Babette Deutsch. TrRV

If only, when one heard. *Unknown. Fr.* Kokin Shu. AWP; LiTW; PFE

If Orpheus' Voice. Sir Philip Sidney. Astrophel and Stella: Third Song. SiPS
(If Orpheus Voyce Had Force.) PoEL-1
(Astrophel to Stella, His Third Song.) ReIE

If other men could clearly see your moon-white face. Silent Sufferer. John Gilland Brunini. JKCP (1926 ed.)

If ought of oaten stop or pastoral song. *See* If aught of oaten stop, or pastoral song.

If oxen, or lions, or horses had hands like men, they too. Anthropomorphism. Xenophanes. GrPE

If panegyric shakes him, then. Royal Bounty. Ibn Sa'id of Alcala la Real. MooP

If parting be decreed for the two of us. Parting. Judah Halevi. AWP; TrJP

If Paw Could Have His Way. Samuel Ellsworth Kiser. FAOV

If Peace and Silence could arise. To a Cat. Samuel Hoffenstein. CIV

If pleasures where not wastinge. *Unknown.* SeCSL

If Poisonous [*or* Poysonous] Mineral[l]s, and If That Tree. John Donne. Holy Sonnets, IX. AnEnPo; AtBAP; ATP (1953 ed.); EnLP; ExPo; GTBS-W; LiTB; MaPo; MePo; OBS; PeBoSo; PoEL-2; ReEn; RiBV; TuPP; TwP; UnPo
(Forget.) EPP; WHA

If Pope Had Written "Break, Break, Break." J. C. Squire. CenHV

If prating from morning to night. Prattling Swallows. Nicostratus. OnPM

If publique weal or country's claim might languish and bewail. An Epitaph upon the Death of the Right Reverent Father in God J. Jewel. Nicholas Bourman. ReIE

If quiet after music is more still. Sonnet for a Marriage. Ann Louise Hayes. PtPa

If radio's slim fingers can pluck a melody. Proof [*or* God Hears Prayer]. Ethel Romig Fuller. DDA; MaRV; MoSiPe; OQP; PraP; QP 2; QS

If recollecting were forgetting. With Flowers. Emily Dickinson. AA

If rest is sweet at shut of day. A Roundel of Rest. Arthur Symons. HBV

If right be wracked and overrun. They of the Mean Estate Are Happiest. *Unknown.* SiCE

If rightly tuneful bards decide. Amoret. Mark Akenside. OBEV

If Rome so great, and in her wisest age. To Edward Allen [*or* Alleyne]. Ben Jonson. OAEP; OBS; ReIE

If sad complaint would show a lover's pain. Giles Fletcher. *Fr.* Licia. TuPP

If sadly thinking, with spirits sinking. The Deserter [*or* The Deserter's Meditation *or* Let Us Be Merry before We Go]. John Philpot Curran. AnIV; BLV; EV-3; IrPN; LH; RO; SeCePo; TIP; ViBoPo

If Scars Are Worth the Keeping. Glenn Ward Dresbach. TBM

If seeing all the fiends rebel. The Terms. Thorsteinn Erlingsson. IcP

If seen by many minds at once your image. By the Lake. Lawrence Durrell. *Fr.* Eight Aspects of Melissa. NeBP
If self-regard has golden wit. Five Epigrams, 3. Donald Hall. NePoAm-2
If She Be Made of White and Red. Herbert P. Horne. HBV; VA
If She Be Not as Kind as Fair. Sir George Etherege. *Fr.* The Comical Revenge; or, Love in a Tub. SeCL
(Song: "If she be not as kind as fair.") CEP
If she but has her purring-throated. Ninetta's Tom-Cat. Christian Richardt. BoDS
If She But Knew. Arthur O'Shaughnessy. HBV; VA
If She Frown My Heart Would Break. Vicente Espinel, *tr. fr. Spanish by* Sir John Bowring. AnSpL-1
If she had been beautiful, even. Of a Woman, Dead Young. Dorothy Parker. DDA
If she had—Well! She longed, and knew not wherefore. Oliver Wendell Holmes. *Fr.* Iris. LO
If she should die (as well suspect we may). Upon Thought Castara May Die. William Habington. *Fr.* Castara. ACP
If shoemakers' children are left with feet bare. Left Out. Mary Carolyn Davies. HH
If Sleep and Death be truly one. In Memoriam A. H. H., XLIII. Tennyson. EM-2; EmBrPo; EnLi-2; EPN; GEPC; LPS-1; ViPo; VLEP
If so be a toad be laid. A Charm, or an Allay for Love. Robert Herrick. FaBoCh; LoGBV
If So Tomorrow Saves. Christina Rossetti. *See* Heaven Overarches Earth and Sea.
If solitude hath ever led thy steps. Sunset. Shelley. *Fr.* Queen Mab. LPS-2
If Some Grim Tragedy. Ninna May Smith. HBMV
If someone said, Escape. Longface Mahoney Discusses Heaven. Horace Gregory. ChMo; ExPo
If Someone, Something, somehow (as man dreams). A Musical Critic Anticipates Eternity. Siegfried Sassoon. UnS
If sometimes I must hear good men debate. Witness of God. James Russell Lowell. *Fr.* The Cathedral. OQP; QP-2
If sometimes strangeness seems on me to fall. The New House. Joseph Easton McDougall. CaP
If Spirits Walk. Sophie Jewett. AA; HBV
If stars dropped out of heaven. Christina Rossetti. *Fr.* Sing-Song. RIS
If Still They Live. Edith M. Thomas. *Fr.* The Inverted Torch. AA; BLP; OBAV; OQP; QP-1
If Stones Can Dream. Daniel Berrigan. JKCP (1955 ed.)
If stores of dry and learned lore we gain. The Memory of the Heart. Daniel Webster. LPS-1
If strange things happen where she is. On Portents. Robert Graves. FaBoMo
If Suddenly a Clod of Earth. Harold Monro. *Fr.* Strange Meetings. EPP; MBP; MoBrPo
(Strange Meetings.) LBBV
If suddenly blackness crawled. Cat's Eye. Paul Engle. PoMa
If suddenly, wonderfully, glittering among the leaves. The Daily Manna. Sara Henderson Hay. GoYe
If suppliant palms, upraised at the sacrifice. Horace. Odes, III, 23. LaP
If That High World. Byron. EmBrPo
If that I for thy sweet sake. *Unknown.* SeCSL
If that my King should say. Roses for My King. Sister Mary Madeleva. SaFP
If that thou hast the gift of strength, then know. The Burden of Strength. George Meredith. EPN
If that thou love me and thy heart be true. All or Nothing. Theognis. GrR
If that we thus are guilty doth appear. Thesis and Antithesis. Arthur Hugh Clough. ViPP
If that which warns the young beware of vice. Barnabe Rich, Gentleman Soldier, in Praise of the Author. Barnabe Rich. ReIE
If the autumn ended. The Enduring. John Gould Fletcher. TBM; TSW; TSWC
If the bull is quiet and the bird is sleeping. Power-driven. José Moreno Villa. CoSP
If the butterfly courted the bee. Topsy-turvy World. William Brighty Rands. BoN; MPB; OTPC (1946 ed.); TSW; TSWC; VA
If the day looks kinder gloomy. Just Try This. *Unknown.* WBLP
If the deep wood is haunted, it is I. Nocturne. Robert Hillyer. UnW
If the distrait verdure cleave not to the branch. Croesus in Autumn. Robert Penn Warren. AnAmPo; LA
If the dull substance of my flesh were thought. Sonnets, XLIV. Shakespeare. PeBoSo
If the evening's red and the morning gray. A Weather Rule [*or* Weather Signs]. *Unknown.* MPB (1956 ed.); OTPC; RIS
If the fat butcher thinks he slays. Mutton. *Unknown.* PA
If the French have a notion. The Island. *Unknown.* *Fr.* Ballads on Napoleon. CoBE
If the good God were suddenly. Paradox. Huw Menai. MaRV
If the green cedar is bitter, you can eat it. Empty Purse. Tu Fu. OnPM
If the Heart Be Homeless. Annemarie Ewing. NePoAm-2
If the Heart of a Man. John Gay. *Fr.* The Beggar's Opera, II, i. ATP (1935 ed.)
("If the heart of a man is depress with cares.") CEP; EnLoPo
(Song: "If the heart . . .") CaAE
If the high counsels of the Lord of Thunder. Si Vis Celsi Iura Tonantis. Boethius, *tr. by* Helen Waddell. TriL
If the lady hath any loveliness, let it die. Blackberry Winter. John Crowe Ransom. OnHM; OxBA; PoRA
If the lone bird lament or the green leaves. Petrarch. *Fr.* Sonnets to Laura: To Laura in Death. PrPoCR
If the lost word is lost, if the spent word is spent. T. S. Eliot. *Fr.* Ash Wednesday. BrBE; OxBoCh
If the Man Who Turnips Cries. Samuel Johnson. BOHV; WhC
(Burlesque [of Lope de Vega].) FaFP; LiTG; SiTL
(Epigram: "If a man who turnips cries.") HBV
(If a Man Who Turnips Cries.) LBN; OxNR
(Turnip Seller. The.) BoN
If the Moonbeam. Unnur Benediktsdóttir, *tr. fr. Icelandic by* Skuli Johnson. IcP
If the neighbor-lands three should cry: "Forget." Invocation and Promise. Verner von Heidenstam. AnSL
If the night's so full of darkness. *Unknown.* *Fr.* Four Songs. LyMA
If the oak is out before the ash. A Few Old Proverbs. *Unknown.* ADAH; OxNR
If the quick spirits in your eye. Persuasions to Joy [*or* Persuasions to Enjoy *or* Song: Perswasions to Enjoy]. Thomas Carew. BrBE; ElSeCe; EnLi-1; EPS; HBV; MePo; OBEV; RiBV; SeCL; SeCV-1
If the red slayer think[s] he slays. Brahma. Emerson. AA; AmP; AmPo; AmPP; AnAmPo; AnFE; AnNE; APA; APW; AWP; BAP; BAV; BLV; BoLiVe; CBOV; CoAnAm; CoBA; CoV; DDA; EV-4; GTBS; GTBS-D; GTBS-W; HBV; IAP; InPo; JAWP; LA; LEAP; LiTA; LiTG; LPS-3; MOAP; NePA; OBAV; OBEV; OBVV; OxBA; PFY; Po; PoLFOT; PoRA; REAL; SeCeV; ShBV-4; TCAP; TreF; TrGrPo; UnPo; ViBoPo; WBP; WGRP; WHA; WoL
If the rose in meek duty. Dedication. Francis Thompson. CoBE
If the sea were one great ink-pot/ And of paper all the sky. The Lies of Men. *Unknown.* OnPM
If the sea were one great ink-pot/ And the sky of paper made. The Evil in Women. *Unknown.* OnPM
If the Seas Dry. Clement Wood. BAP
If the "shut-ins" all united. Secret Service. Gertrude Robinson Dugan. PraP
If the silent grave can receive any pleasure. Elegy on Quintilia. Catullus. LiA
If the sudden tidings came. The World's Justice. Emma Lazarus. HBV
If the sun low down in the West, my friend. A Lady to a Lover. Roden Noel. OBVV
If the things of earth must pass. If Only the Dreams Abide. Clinton Scollard. BLP; HBV; LBAP
If the truth were but known when she came at last. Lady Godiva. Edward Shanks. HBMV
If the unfortunate fate engulfing me. Farewell to My Mother. "Plácido." BANP; PoNe
If the voice were perceived with the eyes. Pedro Salinas, *tr. fr. Spanish by* Eleanor L. Turnbull. CoSP
If the way be rough with thorns and stones. My Prayer. Lucy Carruth. PraP
If the weather's wet and weary. "We Have with Us To-night." Bert Leston Taylor. PFE
If the wild bowler thinks he bowls. Brahma. Andrew Lang. CenHV
If the winds of heaven. The Abbot Henjo, *tr. fr. Japanese by* Kenneth Rexroth. OnPJ
If the woman in the purple petticoat. Give No White Flower. Brenda Chamberlain. NeIP
If their bee nothing new, but that which is. *See* If there be nothing new, but that which is.
If There Are Any Heavens. E. E. Cummings. MoAB; MoAmPo (1950 ed.)
If There Be Any Gods. "Seumas O'Sullivan." BMEP
If There Be Any One. Christina Rossetti. Monna Innominata, XII. MBP
(Abnegation.) VA
("If there be any one can take my place.") EmBrPo; ViPo
If there be graveyards in the heart. God Bless You, Dear. To-Day! John Bennett. AA; HBV
If There Be Music. Hellen Gay Miller. MuM
If there be [*or* their bee] nothing new, but that which is. Sonnets, LIX. Shakespeare. FaBoEn; PeBoSo; ReEn

If there be some weaker one. Whittier. *Fr.* Andrew Rykman's Prayer. MaRV
If there be time enough before the slaughter. Poem. Wyn Griffith. MoWP
If there be truth in ancient saws. A Name for My Love. W. K. Welsh. PR
If there exists a hell—the case is clear. To Sir Toby. Philip Freneau. CoBA
If There Had Anywhere Appeared. Richard Chenevix Trench. *See* God Our Refuge.
If there is a natural body, there is also a spiritual body. Natural and Spiritual. First Corinthians, Bible, *N.T.* GrCo-1
If there is a vile, pernicious. School. James Kenneth Stephen. BOHV
If there is any life when death is over. On the Dunes. Sara Teasdale. NP; TCAP
If there is any pleasure to repeat. Prayer against Love. Catullus. LiTW
If there is any way, dear Lord. A Message. Anna Nelson Reed. OQP; QP-1
If there is no God for thee. To a Dog. Anna Hempstead Branch. MAP; MoAmPo (1942 ed.)
If There Is Thought among the Daffodils. Florence Wilson Roper. MuM
If there is to be freedom of mind and face. To the Priest of the Middles. Lynette Roberts. MoWP
If there was a broken whispering by night. Parting at Dawn. John Crowe Ransom. AnAmPo; LA
If there were any of the sons of men. Retrospection. Hubert Church. AnNZ
If there were dreams to sell. Dream-Pedlary [*or* Dreams to Sell]. Thomas Lovell Beddoes. AlDL; AnFE; AtBAP; BCEP; BLV; BoTP; CaAE; CBPC; CH; EG; EnRP; EPN; EPP; ERP; EV-4; FaBoBe GTBS-W; LEAP; LiA; LiTB; LoBV; NeHB; OBEV; OBRV; OBVV; OQP; OtMeF; OTPC (1946 ed.); PCD; PFE; PG (1945 ed.); PoEL-4; PoP; QP-2; TCEP; TOP; TreFS; TrGrPo; VA; ViBoPo; WP; YT
If there were no past, but specious present only. Speculative Evening. Marguerite Young. LiTA
If there were not a wonder in the world. Leaves. Rowena Baker. CAG
If there were, oh! an Hellespont of cream. The Author Loving These Homely Meats [*or* Homely Meats *or* Buttered Pippin-Pies]. John Davies of Hereford. ChTr; ElL; ElSeCe; FaBoCh; LoGBV
If there were sound, the slapping. Tall Tale God. Mark Van Doren. CrMA
If there's a fox, he said, I'll whistle the beggar. Mahony's Mountain. Douglas Stewart. SeCePo
If there's no sun, I still can have the moon. Philosophy. John Kendrick Bangs. PoToHe (new ed.)
If these brief lays, of Sorrow born. In Memoriam A. H. H., XLVIII. Tennyson. BPN; EM-2; EmBrPo; EnLi-2; EPN; GEPC; ViPo; VLEP
If these clerics or commoners take Christ for their topic. Preaching and Not Doing. William Langland. *Fr.* The Vision of Piers Plowman. PoLi
If These Endure. Lilith Lorraine. PGD
If these, quoth Potus, prove not things admired. Nemo Nascitur Artifex. Henry Parrot. SiCE
If they hint, O Musician, the piece that you played. The Ballad of Imitation. Austin Dobson. HBV; VLEP
If They Honoured Me, Giving Me Their Gifts. "Michael Field." OBMV; TCPD
If They Meant All They Said. Alice Duer Miller. BOHV
If They Spoke. Mark Van Doren. ImOP
If thine were wings, and in thy hand were bow. The Better Eros. Asclepiades. OnPM
If this ain't the Holy Ghost, I don't know. Holy Ghost. *Unknown.* OuSiCo
If This Be All. Anne Brontë. TrPWD
If this be all, for which I've listened long. A Word with a Skylark. Sarah Piatt. BLA; JKCP (1926 ed.); NLK; SN
If This Be Love. Henry Constable. *See* Diana: "To live in hell . . ."
If This Be Love. Richard Eberhart. LiTL
If this be love, to draw a weary breath. To Delia, IX. Samuel Daniel. OBSC; ReEn; SiCE; TrGrPo
If this bright lily. A Song at Easter. Charles Hanson Towne. BLRP; ChIP; MaRV
If this fair rose offend thy sight. The White Rose. *Unknown.* LPS-1
If This Great World of Joy and Pain. Wordsworth. BPN; EM-2; EmBrPo; EPN
If This Is All. Alban Asbury. OQP; QP-2
If this is life—a bed in which to lie. A Relief [*or* WPA] Worker Reflects on Suicide. Stewart Atkins. NoCaPo
If this is peace, this dead and leaden thing. Dead Fires. Jessie Redmond Fauset. BANP; PoNe
If this life-saving rock should fail. On Middleton Edge. Andrew Young. POTE
If this little world tonight. Earth [*or* Proem]. Oliver Herford. *Fr.* The Bashful Earthquake. AA; BTP
If This Old Place. Mary Kolars. JKCP
If this our life be but a single day. Home. Joachim du Bellay, *tr. by* Alan Conder. Olive, CXIII. TrFP
If this our little life is but a day. Sonnet to Heavenly Beauty. Joachim du Bellay, *tr. by* Andrew Lang. AWP; JAWP; WBP
If this pale rose offend your sight. Presenting [*or* On Presenting] to a Lady a White Rose and a Red on the Tenth of June. William Somervile. AEV; CEP; OBEC
If this should not be Love, O God, what shakes me? Petrarch. *Fr.* Sonnets to Laura: To Laura in Life. PrPoCR
If this that has befallen were of some such sort. Plight of a Forsaken Lover. Menander. *Fr.* Perikeiromene. GrR
If this town should tumble down. Ditty. Audrey Beecham. PoD
If this uncertain age in which we dwell. The Lesson for Today. Robert Frost. LiTA; LiTM (rev. ed.); NePA; SiTL; WaP
If This Were Faith. Robert Louis Stevenson. BLP; BMEP; EPP; MaRV; PC; PoeT; POTT; TrPWD; WGRP
(If This Were Enough.) OQP; QP-2
"If to feel, in the ink of the slough," *sel.* PoFr
If this world's friends might see but once. The Seed Growing Secretly. Henry Vaughan. OxBoCh; SeCV-1
If thou a reason dost desire to know. To Cynthia, on her Embraces. Sir Francis Kynaston. EG; LO
If thou art merely conscious clay—ah, well. Surrender. "S. M. M." JKCP
If thou art sleeping, maiden. Song. Gil Vicente, *tr. by* Longfellow. AWP; JAWP; LiTW; WBP
If thou canst make the frost be gone. Valentine. Edith M. Thomas. PR
If thou canst wake with me, forget to eate. John Ford. *Fr.* The Lover's Melancholy. PoEL-2
If thou couldst empty all thyself of self. Indwelling. Thomas Edward Brown. VLEP
If Thou Desire to Live in Rest ("If thou delight in quietness"). William Hunnis. ShGoBo
If thou disdain the sacred muse. Epilogue. Sir Edmund Gosse. TCEP
If thou dislik'st the piece thou light'st on first. To the Sour Reader. Robert Herrick. OAEP
If thou doest not love sacke. *Unknown.* SeCSL
If thou dost bid thy friend farewell. Parting. Coventry Patmore. PoToHe
If thou dost love. *Unknown.* SeCSL
If thou dost love me as thou sayst. *Unknown.* SeCSL
If thou dost the number know. *Unknown, tr. fr. Greek by* Thomas Stanley. GrPo
If thou hast loving thoughts of me. Tucked-up Skirts. *Unknown.* ChLP
If thou hast squander'd years to grave a gem. A Charge. Herbert Trench. HBV; LEAP; OBEV (new ed.); OBVV; TVSH
If thou hast wisdom, hear me, Celia. Ben Jonson. *Fr.* Volpone. ViBoPo
If thou in surety safe wilt sit. Look or You Leap [*or* The Lookers-on]. Jasper Heywood. ACP (1952 ed.); ElL; SiCE; TuPP
If Thou Indeed Derive Thy Light from Heaven. Wordsworth. BPN; EmBrPo; EnRP; OBRV
If Thou Longest So Much to Learn. Thomas Campion. LoPS
If thou must love me, let it be for naught. Sonnets from the Portuguese, XIV. Elizabeth Barrett Browning. AnFE; ATP (1935 ed.); AV; BCEP; BEL; BLV; BoFr; BPN; CaAE; CBOV; CoBE; DiM; EmBrPo; EnLi-2; EnLit; EPN; EPP; ES; EV-4; FaFP; GTBS; GTBS-W; GTSE; GTSL; HBV; LEAP; LiTB; LiTG; LiTL; LoPS; LPS-1; MaRV; OBEV; OBVV; PG; PIAE; PoToHe (new ed.); TCEP; TOP; TreFS; TrGrPo; TyEnPo; ViBoPo; ViPo; WHA
If Thou, O God, the Christ didst leave. Prayer of a Modern Thomas. Edward Shillito. ChIP; MaRV; PGD
If thou of fortune be bereft. Not by Bread Alone. James Terry White. OQP; QP-1
If thou seekest the dread throne of God on earth. On Our Lady of Blachernae. *Unknown.* ISi
If thou shouldst bid thy friend farewell. Counsel. Mollie E. Moore. HBV
If thou shouldst ever come by choice or chance. Ginevra. Samuel Rogers. *Fr.* Italy. BeLS; EV-3; LPS-3
If thou survive my well-contented day. Sonnets, XXXII. Shakespeare. BEL; BLV; BoLiVe; ElL; EM-1; EnL; EnLit; EPP; ES; EtPaEn; EV-1; GTBS; GTBS-D; GTBS-W; GTSE; GTSL; HBV; LiTL; OBSC; PeBoSo; SiCE; TOP
If thou wast still, O stream. Richard Watson Dixon. CBE
If Thou Wert by My Side, My Love. Reginald Heber. HBV; LPS-1
If thou wert lying cold and still and white. Reconciliation. Caroline Atherton Briggs Mason. AA
If thou wilt come and dwell with me at home. Daphnis to

Ganymede. Richard Barnfield. *Fr.* The Affectionate Shepherd. ElL; ThWaDe
If Thou Wilt Ease Thine Heart. Thomas Lovell Beddoes. *See* Dirge: "If thou wilt ease thine heart."
If thou wilt mighty be, flee from the rage. He Ruleth Not though He Reign over Realms That Is Subject to His Own Lust. Sir Thomas Wyatt. BrBE; ReIE; SiCE; SiPS
If thou wouldst have me speak, Lord, give me speech. The Preacher's Prayer. George Macdonald. MaRV
If Thou Wouldst Know. Hayyim Nahman Bialik, *tr. fr. Hebrew by* Harry H. Fein. TrJP
If thou wouldst learne, not knowing how, to pray. A Forme of Prayer. Francis Quarles. MePo
If thou wouldst speak unto my grief, beware. The Secret. Henri de Régnier. TrFP
If thou would'st stand on Etna's burning brow. Our Traveller. Henry Cholmondeley-Pennell. BOHV; InMe
If thou would'st view fair Melrose aright. Melrose Abbey. Sir Walter Scott. *Fr.* The Lay of the Last Minstrel. EV-4; OBRV; SeCePo
If thought can reach to Heaven. The Rabbi's Song. Kipling. GTML
If thoughts had wings. A Little Valentine. Elizabeth Winton. PCH
If through my perjured lips Thy voice may speak. A Prayer for a Preacher. Edward Shillito. TrPWD
If through the garden's flowery tribes I stray. Bloom the Jasmines. William Shenstone. LiA
If thus my heart should summon you again. Three Sonnets, II. Cathleen Keegan. MuM
If thus we needs must go. The Heart. Michael Drayton. SeEP
If thy brother shall trespass against thee. Forgiveness. St. Matthew, Bible, *N.T.* BoFr
If thy mistress be too coy. *Unknown.* SeCSL
If thy sad heart, pining for human love. To Edgar Allan Poe. Sarah Helen Whitman. *Fr.* Sonnets from the Series Relating to Edgar Allan Poe. AA; BAP; LBAP; LEAP
If thy soul check thee that I come so near. Sonnets, CXXXVI. Shakespeare. PeBoSo
If thy soul, Herrick, dwelt with me. Hesperides. Thomas Bailey Aldrich. BAV
If tired of trees I seek again mankind. The Vantage Point. Robert Frost. CoBMV; MaPo; OxBA; PoLFOT
If to be absent were to be. To Lucasta, [on] Going beyond the Seas. Richard Lovelace. AtBAP; CaAE; ElSeCe; EPS; EV-2; FaBoEn; GTBS; GTBS-D; GTBS-W; GTSE; GTSL; HBV; LiTB; LiTG; LiTL; LO; LoBV; MeLP; OAEP; OBEV; OBS; ReEn; SeCL; SeCV-1; SeEP; TriL; ViBoPo
If to Die. Myrtle Romilu. BLRP
If to feel, in the ink of the slough. Robert Louis Stevenson. *Fr.* If This Were Faith. PoFr
If to grow old in Heaven is to grow young. True Woman—III: Her Heaven. Dante Gabriel Rossetti. The House of Life, LVIII. BMEP; BPN; EmBrPo; EPN; GTML; PoVP; ViPo
If, to one who remembers his past beneficences. Catullus, *tr. fr. Latin by* Frances Fletcher. LaP
If to your twilight land of dream. In Memoriam—Leo, a Yellow Cat. Margaret Sherwood. BLPA; CIV; NeHB
If transmigration e'er compel. In Praise of Gilbert White. William John Courthope. *Fr.* The Paradise of Birds. VA
If trees were tall and grasses short. By the Babe Unborn. G. K. Chesterton. AlDL
If true love is there. True Love. *Unknown.* SoLD
If truth in hearts that perish. A. E. Housman. A Shropshire Lad, XXXIII. PoVP
If Valour's best be gallantly to die. The Athenian Monument. Simonides. *tr. by* William C. Lawton. GrL; OxBG
If valour's noblest part is to die well. On Those Who Fell at Plataea. Simonides, *tr. by* Walter Leaf. GrR; PoFr
If virtue be thy guide. To the Christian Reader. Robert Southwell. SiCE
If wandering in a wizard's car. To Helen. Winthrop Mackworth Praed. HBV
If wandering through some silent forest aisle. A. C. S. Alexander M. Stephen. CPG
If War Be Kind. Stephen Crane. *See* War Is Kind, I.
If War Is Right. Alice Corbin. OQP; QP-2
If we are marked to die, we are enow. King Henry before the Field of Saint Crispian. Shakespeare. King Henry V, *fr.* IV, iii. BBV (1951 ed.)
If We Believed in God. Jessie Wiseman Gibbs. BLRP
If we but knew what forces helped to mold. Plea for Tolerance. Margaret E. Bruner. PoToHe (new ed.)
If we could get the hang of it entirely. Entirely. Louis MacNeice. ChMo; LiTB; MoPW
If we could go again. Ode: The Eumenides. A. J. M. Smith. BoCaPo (1948 ed.)
If we could hear the voice of Lincoln saying. The Deaf. L. Lamprey. *Fr.* Days of the Leaders, 1925. BBV (1951 ed.)
If We Could Only Be! Lee Shippey. PEDC
If we could push ajar the gates of life. God's Plans. May Riley Smith. BLRP; MaRV
If we could salvage Babylon. The Unchanged. Isabel Ecclestone Mackay. OCL
If We Didn't Have to Eat. Nixon Waterman. BOHV
"Life would be an easy matter," *sel.* FiBHP
If we dreamed that we loved Her aforetime. To San Francisco. S. J. Alexander. PAH
If we gave unto the living as we lavish on the dead. Give to the Living. Ida Goldsmith Morris. WBLP
If we give love and sympathy. The Human Touch, 2. Helen King. PoToHe
If we go walking on the streets. Angleworm. Herbert Cahoon. SiTL
If We Had Met. Wilfrid Scawen Blunt. VLEP
If we have never sought, we seek Thee now. *See* If we never sought . .
If we have not learned that God's in man. For Us. Charlotte Perkins Gilman. OQP; PSO; QP-1
If We Knew. May Riley Smith. BLPA
If We Knew ("If we knew the cares and crosses"). *Unknown.* MaRV
If we knew the woe and heartache. If We Knew. May Riley Smith. BLPA
If We Must Die. Claude McKay. BANP; MAP; PoNe
If we never [*or* have never] sought, we seek Thee now. Jesus of the Scars. Edward Shillito. ChIP; MaRV; OQP; QP-1
If we offend it is with our good will. Shakespeare. *Fr.* A Midsummer Night's Dream, V, i. BoN
If we shadows have offended. Shakespeare. *Fr.* A Midsummer Night's Dream, V, ii. OBSC
If we shall live, we live. Meeting. Christina Rossetti. LO
If we should be shipwrecked together. Chums. James William Foley. PTA-2
If we should find unfinished, incomplete. Fulfillment. Charlotte Newton. OQP; QP-1
If we speak less of love, let none suppose. To Be Etched in Silver. Carolyn Wilson Link. MuM
If we square a lump of pemmican. Scientific Proof. J. W. Foley. BOHV
If We Understood. *Unknown.* PTA-2
If we with earnest effort could succeed. This Were to Pray. Richard Chenevix Trench. MaRV
If what I am could only step. The Element. Struthers Burt. NoCaPo (1941 ed.)
If what I find I do not love. Resignation. Santob de Carrion. TrJP
If what we fought for seems not worth the fighting. Lines for the Hour. Hamilton Fish Armstrong. BAP; HBMV; MaRV; MC
If wheels bar up the road, where streets are crossed. Of Crossing the Streets. John Gay. *Fr.* Trivia. EnLi-1 (1949 ed.)
If When I Die. *At. to* William Fowler. ElL
If, when I kneel to pray. Prayer. Charles Francis Richardson. AA
If, when the century is done. Twenty-fourth Day—Evening. Richard Church. *Fr.* Twentieth Century Psalter. SoV
If when the sun at noon[e] display[e]s. A Beautifull Mistress [*or* Song]. Thomas Carew. EG; OBS; SeEP
If when the wind blows. Daniel Webster's Horses. Elizabeth J. Coatsworth. AnNE; MAP; MoAmPo; PoMS
If, when your mother bore you, you were born. The Common Lot. Menander. OxBG
If, while turtle round is flowing. The Warning. Thomas Brown. PoP
If wind could talk, and the birds. Ted Birkett. August Derleth. DaM
If wine and music [*or* musick] have the power. A Song. Matthew Prior. ATP (1935 ed.); CEP; LoBV
If wisdom's height is only disenchantment. A Word to the Wise. Caroline Duer. AA
If wishes were horses, beggars would ride. Mother Goose. BoChLi; FaBoBe; HBV; OTPC; OxNR; PPL; SiTL
If with complaint the pain might be express'd. Sir Thomas Wyatt. SiPS
If with exultant tread. Francis Thompson. *Fr.* Ode to the Setting Sun. OHIP
If with light head erect I sing. Inspiration. Henry David Thoreau. AA; AmPP; AnAmPo; AnFE; AnNE; APA; BAP; CoAnAm; FaBoBe; HBV; LA; LBAP; LEAP; OBAV; TCAP; WGRP
If with my sleeve I hide the faint color of the dawning sun. Four Folk-Songs in Hokku Form, 4. *Unknown.* LiTW
If with pleasure you are viewing any work a man is doing. Do It Now. Berton Braley. BLPA; FaFP; WBLP
If with water you fill up your glasses. The Poet's Inspiration. Cratinus. OxBG
If Women Could Be Fair. Edward de Vere, Earl of Oxford. CoBE; ElL; ElSeCe; OAEP; ReEn; TuPP

If Women Could Be Fair (*continued*)
(Fair Fools.) EV-1
(If Women Would Be Fair.) LiTL
(Renunciation, A.) GTBS; GTBS-D; GTBS-W; GTSE; HBV; LPS-3
If ye fear to be affrighted. A Charm. Robert Herrick. ChTr
If ye fear to be benighted. Another Charm. Robert Herrick. OTPC (1923 ed.)
If ye will with Mab find grace. The Fairies. Robert Herrick. EPS; FaPON; MPB; OBS; OTPC (1946 ed.); SeEP
If ye would drink delight. Song. Clément Marot. TrFP
If yet I have not all thy love. Lover's [*or* Love's] Infiniteness[e]. John Donne. CaAE; EIL; ElSeCe; EnLi-1 (1949 ed.); EPS; FaBoEn; GTBS-W; LiTB; LiTG; LiTL; MaPo; MeLP; OBS; PoE; PoEL-2; SeCV-1; SeEP; TuPP
If yet there be a few that take delight. Prologue. Dryden. *Fr.* The Loyal General (*by* Nahum Tate). CEP; SeCV-2
If yielding fear, or cankered villainy. Audaces Fortuna Iuvat. George Gascoigne. CaAE
If yo' brother done you wrong. You Fight On. *Unknown.* AS
If yonder children asleep beneath the dawn of opened lilies should die. Before the Coming of the Planes That Burn the Cities. Otto D'Sola. AnCL
If You. Robert Creeley. NeAP
If you a wrinkle on the sea have seene. *Unknown.* SeCSL
If you and your folks like me and my folks. *Unknown.* SiTL
If you are a gentleman. *Unknown.* OxNR; SiTL
If you are a little girl. It's a Fib. "Elspeth." ALV
If you are bound to till a soil where farms. A Letter from the Country. Howard Baker. TwAmPo
If You Are Fire. Isaac Rosenberg. ChMP
If you are on the Gloomy Line. Get a Transfer. *Unknown.* BLPA; WBLP
If you are tempted to reveal. Three Gates. Beth Day, *after the Arabian.* BLP; BLPA; MaRV; NeHB; OQP; PoToHe; QP-1; TreFS
If you ask for the cause of our national flaws. Eureka! Alfred Denis Godley. CenHV
If you ask me whence the story. Goosey Goosey Gander—by Various Authors (Longfellow's Version). William Percy French. CenHV
If you ask why my heart so swells with rage. Anteros. Gérard de Nerval. AnFP
If You Be a Nun. Leigh Hunt. *See* Nun, The.
If you be that May Margaret. May Margaret. Théophile Marzials. HBV; VA
If you become [*or* be] a nun, dear. The Nun. Leigh Hunt. ALV; BOHV; HBV; InMe; OBRV; OBVV; PG (1945 ed)
If You But Knew. *Unknown.* BLPA; FaBoBe; NeHB
If You Came. Ruth Pitter. DiM; LoPS
If you came back, perhaps you would not find. The Wastes of Time. Lord Alfred Douglas. ES
If you came to my secret glade. If You Came. Ruth Pitter. DiM; LoPS
If you can catch a leaf, so they say. October Boy. Virginia Graham. AlDL
If you can dress to make yourself attractive. An "If" for Girls. Elizabeth Lincoln Otis. FAOV; PTA-2
If you can finde a hart sweet love to kill. *Unknown.* SeCSL
If you can fry flour fritters. Flour Fritters. *Tr. by* Isaac Taylor Headland. PCH
If you can keep your head when all about you. If. Kipling. BBV (1951 ed.); BLPA; BMEP; BPN; BTP; CBE; ChMo; EnLit; FaBoBe; FaFP; FAOV; GoTP; GrCo-1; HBV; HBVY; HiLiEn; LiTM; MaRV; NeHB; OHFP; OtMeF; OTPC (1946 ed.); PoeMoYo; PoMa; POT; PoTo; PTA-1; PYM; ShGoBo; TreF; TSW; TSWC; VLEP; WBLP
If you can take your dreams into the classroom. The Teacher's "If." R. J. Gale. PTA-2
If you can tell the number. Catalogue. *Unknown. Fr.* Anacreontea. GrPE
If you cannot on the ocean. Your Mission. Ellen M. Huntington Gates. BLPA; BLRP; NeHB; PTA-1
If you can't be a pine on the top of the hill. Be the Best of Whatever You Are. Douglas Malloch. BLPA; YaD
If You Can't Eat [You Got To]. E. E. Cummings. ChMo; PoLFOT
If you come my way that is. Poem from Llanybri. Lynette Roberts. MoWP; NeBP
If you could bring her glories back! Babylon. Ralph Hodgson. HBMV; TCEP
If you could creep out on a summer's night. A Midnight Performance. Helen Wing. GFA
If you could crowd them into forty lines! Limitations. Siegfried Sassoon. MBP; MoBrPo
If you could lie upon this berth, this berth whereon I lie. Through a Porthole. Leon Gellert. BoAu
If you could look into my heart. For a Valentine. Mary Elizabeth Newell. PCH
If you could see, fair brother, how dead beat. Prolonged Sonnet: When the Troops Were Returning from Milan [*or* Troops Returning from Milan]. Niccolò degli Albizzi. AWP; LyPI; OnPM; WaaP
"If you dare," she said. Love among the Clover. Odell Shepard. PR
If you deemed his face was fair. Violet. Ibn A'isha. MooP
If you do love as well as I. The Thought. Lord Herbert of Cherbury. ElSeCe; InvP; LoBV (2d ed.); SeCL; SeEP
"If you do love me weel, Willie." Fair Janet (B *vers.*). *Unknown.* ESPB
If you don't know the kind of person I am. A Ritual to Read to Each Other. William Stafford. NePA
If you don't like my apples. Nursery Rhymes. *Unknown.* OxBoLi
If you don't quit monkeying with my Lulu. Lulu. *Unknown.* ABF; CoSo
If you ever, ever, ever meet a grizzly bear. Grizzly Bear. Mary Austin. FaPON; TiPo
If you ever [*or* evah] go to Houston. The Midnight Special. *Unknown.* AS; SoAF
If you feel for it pressing back the glossy leaves. Orange Tree by Night. Sacheverell Sitwell. *Fr.* The Red-gold Rain. AtBAP
If you find a paddling pool. The Paddling Pool. E. M. Adams. BoTP
If you for orders, and a gown design. John Oldham. *Fr.* A Satyr Address'd to a Friend That Is About to Leave the University, and Come Abroad in the World. OBS
If you give me your attention, I will tell you what I am. The Disagreeable Man. W. S. Gilbert. *Fr.* Princess Ida. ALV; FiBHP; MPB; PoVP
If you go a-picnicking and throw your scraps about. Picnics. *Unknown.* BoTP
If you go down the garden path. The Garden Path. Charlotte Druitt Cole. GFA
If you go over desert and mountain. The Fountain of Tears. Arthur O'Shaughnessy. OBEV (1st ed.); OBVV; PoVP; VLEP
If You Had a Friend. Robert Lewis. PoToHe (new ed.)
If you had already resolved to blight my joyless love. Tibullus. Elegies, I, 9. LaP
If you had asked of me. The Idol. Louise Driscoll. BAP; HBMV
If you had died. This Will Pass. Semyon Osipovich Kirsanov. TrRV
If you had eyes to view. The Blind Man. Nazhun. MooP
If you had lived in that more stately time. Sonnets to Miranda, II. Sir William Watson. HBV
If you have a carrier-dove. Art, II. James Thomson. EPP
If You Have a Dog. Douglas Malloch. AlBD
If you have a friend worth loving. Say It Now [*or* Seeds of Kindness *or* A Sermon in Rhyme]. *Unknown.* BLPA; FaFP; PoToHe; PTA-2; WBLP
If you have a gray-haired mother. Before It Is Too Late. George Bancroft Griffith. MOAH
If you have a tender message. Before It Is Too Late. Frank Herbert Sweet. PoToHe (new ed.)
If you have a thing to do. Do It Right. Samuel O. Buckner. WBLP
If you have a word of cheer. Tell Him So. James Arthur Edgerton. MaRV
If you have climbed a laden apple tree. Afternoon in a Tree. Sister Maris Stella. GoBC
If you have ever, like me. Please Excuse Typing. J. B. Boothroyd. FiBHP; SiTL
If you have forgotten water-lilies floating. Water-Lilies. Sara Teasdale. MAP; MoAmPo; NeMA
If you have heard a kind word spoken. Tell Him So. *Unknown.* BLPA; WBLP
If you have lost the radio beam. Any Man's Advice to His Son. Kenneth Fearing. ChMo; PoLFOT
If You Have Made Gentler the Churlish World. Max Ehrmann. OQP; QP-2
(If You Made Gentler the Churlish World.) PoToHe (new ed.)
If You Have Nothing. Jessica Powers. JKCP (1955 ed.)
If you have revisited the town, thin Shade. To a Shade. W. B. Yeats. LiTB; PoE; PoEL-5
If You Have Seen. Thomas Moore. BOHV
(Nonsense.) InMe; NA
If you have spoken something beautiful. If You Have Made Gentler the Churlish World. Max Ehrmann. OQP; PoToHe (new ed.); QP-2
If you haven't any ideas. Deny Yourself. Christopher Morley. LHV; YaD
If you hear a kind word spoken. Tell Him So. *Unknown.* BLPA; WBLP
If you hear a prayer that moves you. Prayer. *Unknown.* PraP
If you hold the Great Form. Tao Teh Ching, XII. *Unknown, tr. fr. Chinese.* WhP

If You Keep Faith with Me. John Edward Spear. JKCP (1955 ed.)

If you love God, take your mirror between your hands and look. Song. Mahmud Djellaladin Pasha. LiTW

If You Love Me. Samuel Hoffenstein. ALV

("If you love me, as I love you.") FiBHP

If You Made Gentler the Churlish World. Max Ehrmann. *See* If You Have Made Gentler the Churlish World.

If you must draw mere beauty. Design for a Stream-lined Sunrise. Sister Mary Madeleva. GoBC; JKCP (1955 ed.)

If you never came with a pigeon rainbow purple. Sumach and Birds. Carl Sandburg. YT

If you never do anything for anyone else. The Immoral Proposition. Robert Creeley. NeAP

If you only spend. Song for a 'Fraid Cat. Patience Eden. DDA

If you refuse me once, and think again. Song. Sir John Suckling. BrBE

If you searched the county o' Carlow, ay, and back again. Old Pedhar Carthy from Clonmore. Patrick Joseph McCall. TIP

If you see a bittern. The Bittern. Roberta Teale Swartz. WhBS

If You See a Fairy Ring. *Unknown.* BoTP

If you see a package. Secrets. E. Kathryn Fowler. ChBR

If you see a tall fellow ahead of the crowd. Forget It. *Unknown.* WBLP

If you see the crow, my love. The Crow. Ibn Sa'id of Alcala la Real. MooP

If you should bid me make a choice. The Windmill. E. V. Lucas. BoTP

If you should go, and beauty still be hidden. For a Poet Growing Old. Lawrence Lee. TBM

If you should go before me, dear, walk slowly. Walk Slowly. Adelaide Love. BLPA

If you should look for this place after a handful of lifetimes. Tor House. Robinson Jeffers. AnAmPo; LA; LoBV

If You Should Tire of Loving Me. Margaret Widdemer. HBMV; OBAV; PR; SBMV

If you sit down at set of sun. Count That Day Lost [*or* A Day Well Spent *or* At Set of Sun]. "George Eliot." MaRV; NeHB; OQP; PoToHe (new ed.); PTA-1; QP-2

If you sneeze on [*or* Sneeze on a] Monday, you sneeze for danger. Mother Goose. HBV; HBVY; PPL; RIS; StaSt; TreF

If You Stick a Stock of Liquor. Newman Levy. ALV

If you strike a thorn or rose. Keep a-Goin'. Frank L. Stanton. FaFP; OHFP; PreP; WBLP

If you, that have grown old, were the first dead. The New Faces. W. B. Yeats. MoVE

If you think well of me. To Hsü Ling. Yü Hsin. BoFr; PoHN

If you think you are beaten, you are. Thinking. Walter D. Wintle. WBLP

If you wake at midnight, and hear a horse's feet. A Smuggler's Song. Kipling. *Fr.* Puck of Pook's Hill. ShBV-1

If you want a receipt for that popular mystery. The Heavy Dragoon. W. S. Gilbert. *Fr.* Patience. PC

If you want to drive wrinkles from belly and brow. Eating Song. Sir Walter Raleigh. WhC

If you Want to Go a-Courting, *with music.* *Unknown.* TrAS

If you want to go to heaven. The Blood-strained Banders. *Unknown.* OuSiCo

If you want to have the kind of a church. It Isn't the Church—It's You. *Unknown.* BLPA; WBLP

If You Want to Know Where the Privates Are. *Unknown.* ABF

(Where They Were, *sl. diff.*) AS

If you want to live in the kind of a town. It Isn't the Town, It's You. R. W. Glover. BLPA

If you wants to hear ol' Rattler moan. Ol' Rattler. *Unknown.* ABF

If you were a white rose, Columbine. A Fantasy. Crosbie Garstin. PFE

If you were an Eskimo baby. An Eskimo Baby. Lucy Diamond. BoTP

If you were busy being kind. How to Forget [*or* If]. Rebecca Foresman. PoToHe (new ed.); WBLP

If you were coming in the fall. Emily Dickinson. AmPo; AmPP (4th ed.); AnAmPo; LA; LaNeLa; MOAP; OxBA; PoRA

If you were going to get a pet. If You. Robert Creeley. NeAP

If you were gone afar. To Rosemary. Stephen Vincent Benét. LaNeLa; LoPS

If You Were Here. Philip Bourke Marston. HBV; VA

If you were queen of bloaters. A Catch. Tom Hood. CenHV

If you were riding in a coach. Oath[s] of Friendship. *Unknown.* BoFr; TrCh

If you were to ask me why I dwell among green mountains. Conversation in the Mountains. Li Po. WhP

If you were true or not, what matter? Inevitability. Valery Yakovlevich Bryusov. TrRV

If you will come on such a day. The Gardener. Sidney Keyes. ChMP; MoAB

If you will listen a while I will sing you a song. *See* If you'll listen awhile . . .

If you will love know such to be. *Unknown.* SeCSL

If you with your true self would be acquainted. Here Are Sands, Ignoble Things. Menander. OxBG

If you would do a kindness to the dead. Justice Protects the Dead. Aeschylus. *Fr.* Phryges. OxBG

If you would do good, then do it today. Generosity. Steingrímur Thorsteinsson. *Fr.* Epigrams. IcP

If you would have a good hound. The Perfect Greyhound. *Unknown.* PCH

If you would have dark themes and high-flown words. Insights. Catherine Davis. NePoEA

If you would know the love which I you bear. Sir John Davies. *Fr.* Sonnets to Philomel. SiPS

If you would know why men dread nonchalance. The King of Spain. Maxwell Bodenheim. TCPD

If you would like to see the height of hospitality. The Donovans. Francis A. Fahy. TIP

If you would see him. The Eagle. James Daly. AnAmPo; LA

If you would sing of heroes, sing of her. Lot's Wife. Elizabeth Morrow. BAP

If you your lips would keep from slips. Our Lips and Ears [*or* Caution]. *Unknown.* BLPA; NeHB; PFE; StaSt; TreF; WBLP

If you'd have me go on loving you. Ezra Pound. *Fr.* Impressions of François-Marie Arouet (de Voltaire). MoAB

If you'd rather not to kiss then say so then. Rebuff. Samuel L. Albert. NePoAm-2

If you'll come gather round me, I'll sing you a song. Lone Driftin' Riders. *Unknown.* CoSo

If you'll [*or* you will] listen awhile I will sing you a song. Jim Fisk. *Unknown.* AS; ViBoFo

If you'll listen awhile I'll sing you a song. The Road to Cook's Peak. *Unknown.* CoSo; CSF

If your miraculous DDT. Natural Selection. David Brock. TwCaPo

If your nose is close to the grindstone rough. A Timely Warning. *Unknown.* PoMa

If you're anxious for to shine in the high aesthetic line as a man of culture rare. Bunthorne's Song [*or* The Aesthete]. W. S. Gilbert. *Fr.* Patience. ALV; EnLi-2; FiBHP; LiTB; PoVP; SiTL; ViP

If You're Ever Going to Love Me. *Unknown.* BLPA; NeHB

If you're in London, Will'um, then I take it you're en route. To William Allen White. Edna Ferber. InMe

If you're longing for fun or enjoyment. Duffy's Hotel. *Unknown.* ShS

If you're told to do a thing. Obedience. Phoebe Cary. PCH

If you're Volunteer Artist or Athlete, or if you defend the Home. "Form Fours." Frank Sidgwick. WhC

If you're waking call me early, call me early, mother dear. New Year's Eve. Tennyson. *Fr.* The May Queen. OTPC (1923 ed.)

If you're waking, please don't call me, please don't call me, Currie dear. A Laureate's Log. *Unknown.* PA

If youth be thine. Juventa Perennis. Thomas Edward Brown. MBP

If you've got a job to do. Do It Now! *Unknown.* BLPA; FaFP; WBLP

If You've Never. Elsie M. Fowler. GFA

If you've tried and have not won. Don't Give Up. Phoebe Cary. PCH; PTA-1

I'faith, sweetheart, methinks now you are in an excellent good temporality. Shakespeare. King Henry IV, Pt. II, *fr.* II, iv. MyFE

Ignorance. John Masefield. BEL

Ignorance, error, cupidity, and sin. To the Reader. Baudelaire. AnFP

Ignorance of Death. William Empson. CoBMV; LiTM (rev. ed.); ReMP

Ignorance of Man, The. James Merrick. OxBoCh

Ignorant present has scribbled over the past, The. Louis Dudek. *Fr.* Europe. PeCV

Ignore dull days; forget the showers. Lesson from a Sun-Dial. *Unknown.* RIS; TiPo

Igstrawnary tail I vill tell you this week, An. A Wofle New Ballad of Jane Roney and Mary Brown. Thackeray. BOHV

Ike Walton's Prayer. James Whitcomb Riley. AA

"Il Est Cocu—le Chef de Gare!" H. S. Mackintosh. WhC

Il était un' bergère. *Unknown, tr. fr. French.* CIV

Il Flor degli Eroici Furori. John Addington Symonds. VA

I'l gaze no more on her bewitching face. Murdering Beauty. Thomas Carew. OAEP

Il Insonio Insonnado, *sel.* Nathaniel Whiting. Office of Poetry, The. OBS

Il Pastor Fido, *sels.* Sir Richard Fanshawe, *after the Italian of* Giovanni Battista Guarini.

Il Pastor Fido (*continued*)
Fall, The. *After the Spanish of* Luis de Góngora. MePo; OBS
Golden Age, The. LyPI
Hope. OBS
"How I forsook." AWP
Now War Is All the World About. LoBV
(Ode, An, upon Occasion of His Majesties Proclamation in the Year 1630, Commanding the Gentry to Reside upon Their Estates in the Countrey.) MePo; OBS
Of Time. SeCL
(Of Beauty.) InMe
Rose, A. *After the Spanish of* Luis de Góngora. ES; HBV; OBEV; OBS; PoEL-2; SeCePo; SeCL; SeEP; TeCS
(Rose of Life, The.) AWP
Il Penseroso. Milton. AEV; AWP; BCEP; BLV; BoLiVe; BrBE; CBE; CBOV; CEP; EM-1; EnL; EnLi-1; EnLit; EPP; EV-2; FiP; GEPC; GTBS; GTBS-D; GTBS-W; GTSE; GTSL; HBV; HiLiEn; HoPM; InPo; LEAP; LiA; LiTB; LiTG; LPS-3; MaPo; MyFE; OBEV; OBS; OuHeWo; PIAE; PIR; Po; PoE; ReaPo; SeCeV; ShBV-3; TCEP; TOP; TrGrPo; TVSH; TwCrTr; UnPo (1st ed.); ViBoPo; WHA
Sels.
"But let my due feet never fail." PC
Come Pensive Nun. PraNu
"Oft on a plat of rising ground." PC
"Sweet bird that shunn'st the noise of folly." CH; SN
"There is close cover by some brook." PC
Il pleut doucement sur la ville. Paul Verlaine, *tr. fr. French by* Ernest Dowson. AWP; JAWP; PG (1945 ed.); WBP
(Tears, *tr. by* Alan Conder.) TrFP
(Tears and Rain, *tr. by* Ernest Dowson.) OnPM
(Tears Fall within Mine Heart, *tr. by* Ernest Dowson.) EnLi-2
(Tears Flow in My Heart, *tr. by* Muriel Kittel.) AnFP
Ile sooth his plots: and strow my hate with smiles. George Chapman. *Fr.* Bussy d'Ambois, IV, ii. PoEL-2
I'le tell you a tale of my love and I. The Shepheard and the Milkmaid. *Unknown.* CoMu
Ile wear those golden spurres upon my heeles. George Chapman. *Fr.* The Conspiracy of Charles, Duke of Byron, III, i. PoFr
Ilex Tree, The. Agnes Lee. NP
Iliad, The, *sels.* Homer, *tr. fr. Greek.*
Achaeans Renew the Battle, The, *fr.* IV, *tr. by* F. L. Lucas. GrPE
Achilles and Agamemnon; the Fatal Feud, *fr.* I, *tr. by* the Earl of Derby. GrR
("Have you the face to utter such a threat, most grasping Atrides?" *longer sel., tr. by* George Ernle.) GrPo
("O tyrant, armed with insolence and pride," *tr. by* William Hyde Appleton.) PoFr
Achilles and Lycaon, *fr.* XXI. GrR, *tr. by* the Earl of Derby; OxBG, *shorter sel., tr. by* C. M. Bowra
(Achilles Refuses to Spare Lycaon's Life, *shorter sel., pr. tr. by* A. T. Murray.) LiA
(Achilles to Lycaon, *shorter sel., tr. by* Richmond Lattimore.) LiTW; WaaP
Achilles and Patroclus, *fr.* XVI, *tr. by* Sir William Marris. OxBG
("Meanwhile Patroclus stood beside his friend," *tr. by* Bryant.) GrPo
(Patroclus to Achilles, *tr. by* the Earl of Derby.) GrR
Achilles' Arms, *fr.* XIX, *tr. by* F. L. Lucas. GrPE
Achilles Goes Forth to Battle, *fr.* XIX, *tr. by* George Chapman. EV-1
Achilles over the Trench, *fr.* XVIII, *tr. by* F. L. Lucas. GrPE
(Achilles on the Rampart, *tr. by* Tennyson.) OxBG
(Achilles' Shout, *tr. by* Tennyson.) LiA
("So saying, light-foot Iris past away," *tr. by* Tennyson.) GrPo
Achilles' Prayer, *fr.* XVI, *tr. by* the Earl of Derby. OxBG
("Achilles then within his tent withdrew," *tr. by* the Earl of Derby.) GrPo
(Prayer of Achilles, The, *pr. tr. by* Andrew Lang, Walter Leaf, *and* Ernest Myers.) GrR
Achilles Rejects the Embassy, *fr.* IX, *tr. by* F. L. Lucas. GrPE
Achilles' Remorse, *fr.* XVIII, *tr. by* F. L. Lucas. GrPE
(Achilles and Thetis, *tr. by* Sir William Marris.) OxBG
(So Ends the Wrath of Achilles, *tr. by* William Cowper.) GrR
(Thetis and Achilles, *tr. by* Sir William Marris.) LiTW
Achilles Shows Himself in the Battle by the Ships, *fr.* XVIII, *tr. by* George Chapman. OBS
Achilles Unreconciled, *fr.* IX, *tr. by* the Earl of Derby. GrR
(Achilles' Reply to the Embassy, *abr., tr. by* Maurice Hewlett.) OxBG
("Most valiant and noble Odysseus, seeing Atrides," *tr. by* George Ernle.) GrPo
Advance of the Trojans, The, *fr.* III, *tr. by* William Cowper. OxBG
("But when the bands were mustered round their leaders on each side," *tr. by* F. L. Lucas.) GrPE
(Trojans and Greeks, *tr. by* the Earl of Derby.) GrR
After the Chariot-Race, *fr.* XXIII, *tr. by* Pope. OxBG
(Sequel to the Chariot Race, *pr. tr. by* Lang, Leaf, *and* Myers.) GrR
Agamemnon; Peace Offerings to Achilles, *fr.* IX, *tr. by* Maurice Hewlett. GrR
Ajax Covers the Flight of the Greeks, *fr.* XI, *tr. by* William Cowper. GrR
(Ajax in the Fight, *tr. by* William Cowper.) OxBG
("But now Zeus throned in the highest made Ajax' heart turn cold," *shorter sel., tr. by* F. L. Lucas.) GrPE
("But the eternal father throned on high," *tr. by* William Cowper.) GrPo
Ajax on the Decks, *fr.* XV, *pr. tr. by* Lang, Leaf, *and* Myers. OxBG
Ajax Prays for Light, *fr.* XVII, *tr. by* the Earl of Derby. LiA
"And there illustrious Vulcan also wrought," *fr.* XVIII, *tr. by* Bryant. GrPo
Andromache, *fr.* XXII, *pr. tr. by* Samuel Butler. OxBG
(Andromache the Desolate, *pr. tr. by* Lang, Leaf, *and* Myers.) GrR
("So she spoke in tears but the wife of Hektor had not yet/ heard," *tr. by* Richmond Lattimore.) GrPo
Apollo Destroys the Wall, *fr.* XV, *tr. by* the Earl of Derby. OxBG
Appeal of Phoenix, The, *fr.* IX, *tr. by* George Ernle. OxBG
(Old Knight Phoenix, The, *pr. tr. by* Lang, Leaf, *and* Myers.) GrR
"As when, high up the mountains, through the endless woodland ways," *fr.* II, *tr. by* F. L. Lucas. GrPE
"At the report agony like dark mist clouded his eyesight," *fr.* XVIII, *tr. by* George Ernle. GrPo
Atrides Goes into Battle, *fr.* XI, *tr. by* George Chapman. KN
Barren Battlefield, The, *fr.* XIX, *tr. by* F. L. Lucas. GrPE
Battle of the Curetes and Aetolians, *fr.* IX, *tr. by* Pope. LiA
Beginning of the Wrath, The, *fr.* I, *tr. by* Sir William Marris. OxBG
Briseis, the Slave Girl; Tears for Patroclus, *fr.* XIX, *tr. by* William Cowper. GrR
("Briseis, fair as golden Venus, saw," *tr. by* the Earl of Derby.) GrPo
"But among the immortals uncontrollable laughter," *fr.* I, *tr. by* Richmond Lattimore. GrPo
"But as o'er some parched mountain sweeps a portentous blaze," *fr.* XX *and* XXI, *tr. by* F. L. Lucas. GrPE
"But as some star of bale amid night's misty skies," *fr.* XI, *tr. by* F. L. Lucas. GrPE
"But when now they came unto the ford of the fair-flowing river," *fr.* XXI, *pr. tr. by* Lang, Leaf, *and* Myers. GrPo
Camp at Night, The, *br. sel. fr.* VIII, *tr. by* George Chapman. LPS-2
(Trojans outside the Walls, The, *sl. longer sel.*) OBS
Chariot Race, The, *fr.* XIII, *tr. by* George Chapman. EV-1
Clouds upon Windless Peaks, *fr.* V, *tr. by* F. L. Lucas. GrPE
Dead Is Patroclus, *fr.* XVIII, *tr. by* Pope. LiA
Death of Gorgythian, The, *fr.* VIII, *tr. by* Pope. GrR
(Death of Gorguthion, The, *br. sel., tr. by* F. L. Lucas.) GrPE
Death of Patroclus, The, *fr.* XVI, *tr. by* Sir William Marris. OxBG
(Death of Patroklos, The, *pr. tr. by* Lang, Leaf, *and* Myers.) GrR
("Now while the sun was going about mid-heaven," *pr. tr. by* Lang, Leaf, *and* Myers.) GrPo
Elders of Troy Behold Helen, The, *fr.* III, *tr. by* the Earl of Derby. LiA
Fallen Olive-Tree, The, *fr.* XVII, *tr. by* F. L. Lucas. GrPE
"For Hectors glorie still he stood; and ever went about," *fr.* XV, *tr. by* George Chapman. LiA
Ghost of Patroclus, The, *fr.* XXIII, *tr. by* William Cowper. OxBG
(Shade of Patroclus, The, *shorter sel., tr. by* the Earl of Derby.) LiA
Glaukos and Diomedes, *fr.* VI, *pr. tr. by* Lang, Leaf, *and* Myers. GrR
(Story of Bellerophon, The, *shorter sel., pr. tr. by* Hallam Tennyson *and* Alfred Tennyson.) OxBG
"He heard, and madly at the motion pleased," *fr.* IV, *tr. by* Pope. GrPo
Helen, *fr.* III. GrR, *tr. by* Maurice Hewlett; OxBG, *tr. by* William Cowper
Helen on the Walls of Troy Looking for Her Brothers, *fr.* III, *tr. by* Edward Craven Hawtrey. LiA
(Helen Seeks for Her Brothers among the Army of the Greeks before Troy.) CBOV
Helen; the Penitent, *fr.* VI, *tr. by* the Earl of Derby. GrR

Helen Unreproached by Hector, *fr.* XXIV, *tr. by* William Cowper. LiA
Homeric Moonlight, A, *fr.* VIII, *tr. by* Pope. BeR
Horse Xanthus Warns Achilles, The, *fr.* XIX, *tr. by* F. L. Lucas. GrPE
Immortal Steeds of Achilles, The, *fr.* XVII, *tr. by* the Earl of Derby. GrR
(Horses of Achilles, The.) GrPE, *shorter sel., tr. by* F. L. Lucas; OxBG, *tr. by* the Earl of Derby
("Meantime, at distance from the scene of blood," *tr. by* Pope.) GrPo
Lamentations, The, *fr.* XXIV, *tr. by* Sir William Marris. LiTW; OxBG
(Lamentations of the Women, The, *tr. by* the Earl of Derby.) GrR
(Wail for Hector, The, *tr. by* F. L. Lucas.) GrPE
Last Fight, The, *fr.* XXII, *pr. tr. by* Lang, Leaf, *and* Myers. OxBG
(Death of Hector, The, *tr. by* George Chapman. OBS
(Slaying of Hector, The, *pr. tr. by* Lang, Leaf, *and* Myers.) GrR
("Thus as he spoke, his sharp-edged sword he drew," *tr. by* the Earl of Derby.) GrPo
Last Stand at the Ships, The, *fr.* XV, *tr. by* F. L. Lucas. GrPE
"Meantime the goddess-born in secret pin'd," *fr.* I, *tr. by* Dryden. GrPo
"Meanwhile Achilles, plung'd," *fr.* I, *tr. by* the Earl of Derby. GrPo
Meeting of Priam and Achilles, The, *fr.* XXIV, *tr. by* F. L. Lucas. GrPE
Menelaos; Blasphemy under Duress, *fr.* XIII, *tr. by* William Cowper. GrR
Menelaus and Odysseus, *fr.* III, *tr. by* William Cowper. OxBG
Nestor's Doubt, *fr.* XIV, *tr. by* F. L. Lucas. GrPE
Nestor's Speech to Achilles and Agamemnon, *fr.* I, *tr. by* George Chapman. ReEn
"No longer I avoid thee as of late," *fr.* XXII, *tr. by* Bryant. GrPo
"Now when the goddess, white-armed Hera," *fr.* V, *tr. by* F. L. Clark. GrPo
"O father Zeus, if ever among the Gods I gave," *fr.* I, *tr. by* F. L. Lucas. GrPE
"O Heav'n! the veriest child might plainly see," *fr.* XVII, *tr. by* the Earl of Derby. GrPo
"O that I were as sure to live, immortal, and sustain," *fr.* VIII, *tr. by* George Chapman. AtBAP
Old Traveller, The, *fr.* XV, *tr. by* F. L. Lucas. GrPE
Paris Is Worsted by Menelaus and Returns to Helen, *fr.* III, *tr. by* F. L. Lucas. GrPE
Paris Rescued by Aphrodite, *fr.* III, *tr. by* Maurice Hewlett. GrR
Parting of Hector and Andromache, The, *fr.* VI. SeEP, *tr. by* George Chapman; TreFS, *tr. by* William B. Smith *and* Walter Miller
"Chief, The, replied: 'That post shall be my care,'" *tr. by* Pope. EPP
"Chief, The, reply'd: This time forbids to rest," *tr. by* Pope. ATP, *abr.*; CEP
Hector and Andromache. GrPE, *tr. by* F. L. Lucas; GrR, *tr. by* William Cowper; OBEC, *tr. by* Pope
"Hector left in haste," *tr. by* Bryant. GrPo
Hektor and Andromache, *tr. by* Maurice Hewlett. LiTW; OxBG, *shorter sel.*
Hektor [*or* Hector] to Andromache. ReEn, *tr. by* George Chapman; WaaP, *tr. by* Richmond Lattimore
"I myself will now go home and see," *tr. by* George Chapman. ReIE
Last Parting of Hector and Andromache, The, *tr. by* Dryden. SeEP
"She with his sight made breathless haste to meet him," *tr. by* George Chapman. ViBoPo
Patroclus' Body Saved, *fr.* XVII, *tr. by* E. R. Dodds. OxBG; WaaP
Patroclus Goes to Battle, *fr.* XVI, *tr. by* F. L. Lucas. GrPE
Patroclus Intercedes for the Achaeans, *fr.* XVI, *tr. by* F. L. Lucas. GrPE
"Patroclus lights, impatient for the fight," *fr.* XVI, *tr. by* Pope. GrPo
Plight of Wounded Aphrodite, The, *fr.* V, *tr. by* George Chapman. GrR
Priam and Achilles, *fr.* XXIV. OBEC, *tr. by* Pope; OBS, *shorter sel., tr. by* George Chapman; OxBG, *tr. by* Robert Bridges
(Priam at the Feet of Achilles, *tr. by* the Earl of Derby.) GrR
(Priam's Prayer to Achilles, *tr. by* Robert Bridges.) LiA
Priam and Helen on the Wall, *fr.* III, *tr. by* F. L. Lucas. GrPE
("And then came Iris as a messenger," *shorter sel., tr. by* H. N. Couch.) GrPo
Pursuit round the Walls, The, *fr.* XXII, *tr. by* William Cowper. OxBG
("Thus pondering he stood; meantime approach'd.") GrPo
Pyre of Patroclus, The, *fr.* XXIII, *tr. by* Pope. OBEC
(Preparation of the Pyre for Patroclus, *shorter sel.*) UnPo (1st ed.)
Rally, The, *fr.* V, *tr. by* Sir William Marris. OxBG
Reconciliation of Achilles and Agamemnon, The, *fr.* XIX, *tr. by* the Earl of Derby. GrR
Sarpedon and Glaucus, *fr.* XII. GrR, *tr. by* William Cowper; OxBG, *tr. by* Maurice Hewlett
("Nor had great Hector and his friends the rampire overrun," *tr. by* George Chapman.) AtBAP
Sarpedon's Speech, *fr.* XII, *tr. by* George Chapman. OBS
(Sarpedon to Glaukos, *shorter sel., tr. by* Richmond Lattimore.) WaaP
("Whence is it, Glaucus, that in Lycian land," *shorter sel., tr. by* the Earl of Derby.) GrPo
Scales of War, The, *fr.* VIII, *tr. by* F. L. Lucas. GrPE
(Scales of Zeus, The, *shorter sel.*) GrR, *tr. by* George Chapman; OxBG, *tr. by* William Cowper
Scamander the River God, *fr.* XXI, *tr. by* the Earl of Derby. GrR
(Achilles and the Scamander, *shorter sel., tr. by* Sir William Marris.) OxBG
("Now bursting on his head with thundering sound," *shorter sel., tr. by* Pope.) GrPo
Sere and Yellow Leaf, The, *fr.* VI, *tr. by* F. L. Lucas. GrPE
Shield of Achilles, The, *fr.* XVIII. GrPE, *tr. by* F. L. Lucas; GrR, *tr. by* Pope; OxBG, *abr., tr. by* Pope
(Achilles' Shield, *tr. by* George Chapman.) ReEn
("This said, he left her there, and forth did to his bellows go," *tr. by* George Chapman.) TuPP
(Vulcan Forges the Shield of Achilles, *tr. by* George Chapman.) KN
Slaying of Hector, The, *fr.* XXII, *tr. by* F. L. Lucas. GrPE
("Thus they throughout the city, scared like fawns," *longer sel., pr. tr. by* Lang, Leaf, *and* Myers.) GrL
Slaying of Patroclus, The, *fr.* XVI, *tr. by* F. L. Lucas. GrPE
Sleep of Bronze, A, *fr.* XI, *pr. tr. by* A. T. Murray. LiA
Snow of Stones, The, *fr.* XII, *tr. by* Michael Balkwill. OxBG
"So spoke Priam's noble son, with many and many a word," *fr.* XXI, *tr. by* F. L. Lucas. GrPE
"So was the dread fray of Trojans and Achaians," *fr.* VI, *pr. tr. by* Lang, Leaf, *and* Myers. GrL
Stag and Jackals, *fr.* XI, *tr. by* F. L. Lucas. GrPE
"Standing on high Olympus' topmost peak," *fr.* XIV, *tr. by* the Earl of Derby. GrPo
Steeds of Heaven, The, *fr.* V, *tr. by* F. L. Lucas. GrPE
Storming of the Achaean Wall, The, *fr.* XII *and* XIII, *tr. by* F. L. Lucas. GrPE
Struggle for Patroclus, The, *fr.* XVII *and* XVIII, *tr. by* F. L. Lucas. GrPE
"Sun went down, and the work of the Achaians was accomplished, The," *fr.* VII, *pr. tr. by* Lang, Leaf, *and* Myers. GrPo
"Then in the field the Trojans supped; but the Argives kept," *fr.* XVIII, *tr. by* F. L. Lucas. GrPE
"Then the assembly was broken up," *fr.* XXIV, *pr. tr. by* Lang, Leaf, *and* Myers. GrL
"Then thou, Achilles, reverence the Gods," *fr.* XXIV, *tr. by* the Earl of Derby. GrPo
"Then up sprang storm-foot Iris to bear the word He gave," *fr.* XXIV, *tr. by* F. L. Lucas. GrPE
Thersites, *fr.* II, *tr. by* Maurice Hewlett. OxBG
("Rest now took their seats and kept to their own several places, The," *longer sel., pr. tr. by* Samuel Butler.) GrPo
(Thersites Out of Bounds, *tr. by* George Chapman.) GrR
Thetis and Hephaestus, *fr.* XVIII, *tr. by* Sir William Marris. OxBG
(Visit of Thetis to Hephaistos, *longer sel., tr. by* George Chapman.) GrR
Thetis to Achilles, *fr.* I, *pr. tr. by* Samuel Butler. LiA
Thunder of Zeus, The, *fr.* XX, *tr. by* Sir William Marris. LiA
"Thus kept the Trojans watch," *fr.* IX, *pr. tr. by* Lang, Leaf, *and* Myers. GrL
"Thus, weeping bitterly, the aged pair," *fr.* XXII, *tr. by* Bryant. GrPo
Trojan Camp-Fires, The, *fr.* VIII. GrR, *tr. by* the Earl of Derby; OxBG, *tr. by* Tennyson
Trojans Encamp before the Achaean Wall, The, *fr.* VIII *and* IX, *tr. by* F. L. Lucas. GrPE
("So Hector spake; the Trojans roared applause," *shorter sel., fr.* VIII, *tr. by* Tennyson.) GrPo
Two Hosts, The, *fr.* IV, *tr. by* W. E. Gladstone. OxBG
(Strife, War's Sister Urges On the Host, *longer sel., tr. by* Pope.) GrR
"Urge not, divine Achilles, me to sit," *fr.* XXIV, *tr. by* William Cowper. GrPo
Vow of Vengeance, The, *fr.* XVIII, *tr. by* William Cowper. GrR

Iliad, The (*continued*)
Wall of the Greeks, The, *fr.* XII, *tr. by* William Cowper. GrR
(Wall, The.) OxBG
Wasps, *fr.* XII, *tr. by* F. L. Lucas. GrPE
"When every least commander's will best soldiers had obeyed," *fr.* III, *tr. by* George Chapman. ReEn
Women Who Wait, *fr.* VI, *tr. by* Maurice Hewlett. GrR
Wraith of Patroclus, The, *fr.* XXIII, *tr. by* F. L. Lucas. GrPE
Wrath of Achilles, The, *fr.* I, *tr. by* F. L. Lucas. GrPE
("Achilles' baneful wrath resound, O goddess that impos'd," *shorter sel., tr. by* George Chapman.) ReIE
("O Goddess! sing the wrath of Peleus' son," *tr. by* Bryant.) EnLi-1
(Quarrel, The, *tr. by* Sir William Marris.) WoL
("Sing, goddess, the anger of Peleus' son Achilleus," *br. sel., tr. by* Richmond Lattimore.) GrPo
("Sing, goddess, the wrath of Achilles Peleus' song," *longer sel., pr. tr. by* Lang, Leaf, *and* Myers.) GrL
(Sing, O Muse, *br. sel., tr. by* the Earl of Derby.) LiA
Wrath of Achilles, The, *abr., fr.* XIX, *tr. by* Bryant. BBV (1923 ed.)
Wrestling Match, The, *fr.* XXIII, *tr. by* George Chapman. GrR
Zeus on Olympus, *fr.* I, *pr. tr. by* A. T. Murray. LiA
"Zeus spake; and storm-foot Iris leapt forth to bear His Word," *fr.* XXIV, *tr. by* F. L. Lucas. GrPE
Iliad. Humbert Wolfe. BLV; MBP; MoBrPo; PFE; PIAE; TCPD; TwCV
Ilicet. Swinburne. EmBrPo; PoD, *abr.*; PoVP; VLEP
Ilion, Ilion. Tennyson. LoBV
Ilion Overthrown. Euripides, *tr. fr. Greek by* Hugh Owen Meredith. *Fr.* Hecuba. GrR
(Troy, *tr. by* J. T. Sheppard.) OxBG
Ill. Bernard Spencer. NeBP
I'll Aye Ca' In by Yon Town. Burns. BSV
I'll be an otter, and I'll let you swim. River-Mates. Padraic Colum. AnIV; AWP; JAWP; LEAP; WBP
I'll Be as True. Thomas Lovell Beddoes. *Fr.* Early Fragments. AtBAP
"I'll be the goodest little girl." Wash Dolly Up like That. "Eleanor Kirk." PEOR
I'll be the strongest amid you. The Strongest. "Yehoash." TrJP
I'll Be Your Epitaph. Leonora Speyer. HBMV
I'll build a house of arrogance. Haven. Donald Jeffrey Hayes. PoNe
I'll Build My House. Amanda Benjamin Hall. HBMV
Ill busied man! why shouldst thou take such care. My Midnight Meditation. *At. to* Henry King *and to* John King. MePo; OBS; SeCL
I'll buy you a tartan bonnet. *Unknown.* OxNR
I'll call thy frown a headsman, passing grim. To My Lady. George Henry Boker. *Fr.* Sonnets. AA; MOAP
I'll carry you off. Fragment of an Agon. T. S. Eliot. LiTB
I'll do what the raids suggest. A Boy. John Ashbery. NeAP
I'll eat when I'm hungry, I'll drink when I'm dry. Rye Whisky. *Unknown.* ABF; CoSo; GoTP; OxBoLi; SiTL
Ill fares the land, to hastening ills a prey. The Common Man [*or* Where Wealth Accumulates]. Goldsmith. *Fr.* The Deserted Village. BHV; GrCo-1; MaRV
I'll find me a spruce. Christmas Tree. Aileen Fisher. ChBR
I'll follow you down to the spring. The Spring. Luis Fabio Xammar. AnCL
I'll frame, my Heliodora! a garland for thy hair. A Garland for Heliodora [*or* Wreath for Heliodora]. Meleager. AWP; EnLi-1; JAWP; OnPM; OuHeWo; WBP
I'll gallop away to market town. A Ballad of Riding. Marjorie Allen Seiffert. NP
I'll Give My Love a Light and Friendly Kiss. *Unknown. See* Je caresserai la belle par amitié.
"I'll give thee a paper of pins." Paper of Pins. *Unknown.* ABF; ABS
I'll give thee, good fellow, a twelvemonth or twain. The Barefooted Friar. Sir Walter Scott. *Fr.* Ivanhoe. EmBrPo; EV-4
I'll give you now, both great and small. The Gift. *Unknown.* SAS
I'll go no more on fancy flights. She No Longer Loves Him. Charles Dalmon. TCPD
I'll go, said I, to the woods and hills. The Apostate. A. E. Coppard. OBMV
I'll Go to Bethlehem. *Unknown, tr. fr. Czecho-Slovakian carol by* Edward Bliss Reed. ChrBoLe
I'll go to my Love where he lies in the deep. On a Gentleman in a Late Engagement against the Turks, Was Slain and Thrown Overboard, and She Since Mad. *Unknown.* SeCL
I'll go up on the mountain top. Mountain Top [*or* Liza Jane]. *Unknown.* AS; SoAF
I'll hold my candle high, and then. High Resolve. *Unknown.* PoToHe
I'll hope no more. To His Dear God. Robert Herrick. WP
Ill Humour. Jorge Carrera Andrade, *tr. fr. Spanish by* Donald Devenish Walsh. AnCL
I'll keep a little tavern. Tavern. Edna St. Vincent Millay. GaP; OTPC (1946 ed.)
I'll kick your walls to bits, I'll die scratching a tunnel. Gulliver. Kenneth Slessor. BoAV
I'll Live in This Poor Rime. Shakespeare. *See* Sonnets, CVII.
I'll lop them, it will be easier so to tend them. The Tall Fruit Trees. Ruth Pitter. DiM
I'll Love No More. Sir Robert Ayton. *See* I Loved Thee Once.
Ill Merchandise. *At. to* Automedon of Aetolia *and to* Theocritus, *tr. fr. Greek by* F. L. Lucas. GrPE
I'll never be a nun, I trow. Nightingale Weather. Andrew Lang. BSV; POTT
I'll Never Get Drunk Any More. *Unknown.* OnYI
I'll Never Love Thee More. James Graham, Marquess of Montrose. *See* My Dear and Only Love.
I'll Niver Go Home Again. Arthur Stringer. CPG
I'll not believe the dullard dark. Rubric. Josephine Preston Peabody. AA
. . . I'll not bow/ To the gentle Jesus of the women. Him I Follow. "Clemence Dane." *Fr.* Will Shakespeare. QS
I'll Not Confer with Sorrow. Thomas Bailey Aldrich. OBAV
I'll Not Marry at All. *Unknown.* ABS
I'll not weep that thou art going to leave me. Stanzas. Emily Brontë. LoBV
Ill Omens. Thomas Moore. PoEL-4
I'll put you, myself, my baby, to slumber. Lullaby. *Unknown.* BOL
I'll Remember You, Love, in My Prayers. *Unknown.* BLPA; FaBoBe; NeHB
When the Curtains of Night Are Pinned Back, *br. sel., with music.* AS
I'll Sail upon the Dog-Star. Thomas D'Urfey. *Fr.* A Fool's Preferment. FaBoCh; LoGBV; OxBoLi
Ill sat to be with the calm, The. Essentials. Samuel Greenberg. LiTA
I'll seek the spewing little copper-kettle creek. Not Alone. Thad Stem, Jr. NoCaPo (rev. ed.)
"I'll send you now sailing across the sea." Lullaby. Witter Bynner. BOL
I'll show you one who might have been an abbot. A Quaint Character. Alexander Smith. *Fr.* A Life Drama. BMEP
I'll sing of heroes and of kings. Love. Abraham Cowley. AWP; PG (1945 ed.)
I'll Sing Thee Songs of Araby. William Gorman Wills. OIF
I'll sing you a good old song. The Fine Old English Gentleman. *Unknown.* CH; HBV; LPS-3; OnPP
I'll sing you a new ballad, and I'll warrant it first-rate. The Fine Old English Gentleman; New Version. Charles Dickens. CoMu
I'll sing you a song/ Nine verses long. *Unknown.* OxNR
I'll sing you a song/ The days are long. *Unknown.* OxNR
I'll sing you a song, and a merry, merry song. The Ballad of Jenny the Mare. Edward Fitzgerald. EV-5
I'll sing you a song, it won't take long. The Man That Wouldn't Hoe Corn. *Unknown.* ABS; IHA
I'll sing you a song, not very long. His Heart Was True to Poll [*or* True to Poll]. F. C. Burnand. BOHV; HBV
I'll sing you a song of a schooner of fame. The Loss of the *Druid. Unknown.* ShS
I'll sing you a song of peace and love. Whack Fol the Diddle. Peadar Kearney. FiBHP; OnYI
I'll sing you a song of the world and its ways. Six Feet of Earth. *Unknown.* BLPA
I'll sing you a song that has often been sung. Brigham Young. *Unknown.* CoSo; CSF
I'll sing you a song, though it may be a sad one. Sioux Indians. *Unknown.* CoSo; CSF
I'll sing you a true song of Billy the Kid. Billy the Kid. *Unknown.* ABF; CoSo (B *vers.*); FaBoBe; SoAF
I'll sing you twelve O. Green Grow the Rushes O. *Unknown.* OxBoLi; SiTL
I'll sit down again, Steve, with your shy ghost. For Steve. Earle Birney. BoCaPo (1948 ed.); WaP
I'll strike thee calmly, not in hate. Heauton Timoroumenos. Baudelaire. TrFP
I'll Take You Home Again, Kathleen. Thomas P. Westendorf. OIF; TreF
I'll teach my sons. My Sons. Ron Loewinsohn. NeAP
I'll teach thee, lovely Phillis, what love is. Phyllis, XXVI. Thomas Lodge. TuPP
I'll Tell Her. George Granville. SeCL
(Song: "I'll tell her the next time, said I.") SeEP
I'll tell my own daddy. *Unknown.* OxNR
"I'll tell St. Peter that I know." Cowboy Songs. *Unknown.* OuSiCo
I'll Tell Thee Everything I Can. "Lewis Carroll." *See* White Knight's Song, The.
I'll tell thee everything I can. Alice in Cambridge. R. C. Evarts. CAG

I'll tell thee now deare Love what thou shalt doe. A Valediction; of the Booke. John Donne. NBE
I'll tell you a doleful tragedy. Guy Fawkes. *Unknown.* ABS
I'll tell you a story/ About Jack a Nory. Mother Goose. BoN; HBV; MeMeAg; MPB (1956 ed.); OnHT; OTPC; OxNR; PPL; RIS; SAS; SiTL
I'll tell you a story, a story anon. King John and the Bishop. *Unknown.* ESPB
I'll tell you a story that will thrill you. Pattonio, the Pride of the Plain. *Unknown.* CoSo
"I'll tell you how the leaves came down." How the Leaves Came Down. "Susan Coolidge." DD; HBV; HBVY; MPB; OTPC; PECK; PRWS; TVC; TVSH
I'll tell you how the sun rose. Emily Dickinson. AmPo; BrR; IAP; LaNeLa; MOAP; MoShBr; MW; NeHB; OBAV; PoEL-5; SiSoSe; StaSt
(Day, A.) AnNE; GoTP; PRWS; TCAP
(Poem.) ThWaDe
(Sun, The.) StVeCh
(Sunrise and Sunset.) TreFS; YT
(Sunset and Sunrise.) SUS
I'll tell you of a false hearted knight. The False-hearted Knight. *Unknown.* BaBo
I'll tell you of a fellow. Hardly Think I Will. *Unknown.* ABF
I'll tell you of a sailor now, a tale that can't be beat. The Story of Samuel Jackson. Charles Godfrey Leland. StPo
I'll tell you what I heard that day. Upon the Hill before Centreville. George Henry Boker. PAH
I'll tell you whence the rose did first grow red. William Strode. EG
Ill-tempered Lover, The, *sel.* L. A. MacKay.
I Wish My Tongue Were a Quiver. BoCaPo; CaP; SiTL
I'll Try. Ann Hawkshaw. *See* Robin Redbreasts, The.
I'll twine white violets and the myrtle green. Meleager, *tr. fr. Greek by* Goldwin Smith. GrPo
"I'll wager, I'll wager, I'll wager with you." The Broomfield Hill (B *vers.*). *Unknown.* ESPB
I'll wake you and shake you. To the Laggards. Joseph Bovshover. TrJP
I'll Wear a Shamrock. Mary Carolyn Davies. BrR; SiSoSe; TiPo (1952 ed.); YeAr
Ill Will. Arthur Rimbaud, *tr. fr. French by* William M. Davis. AnFP
I'll wish no more thou shouldst love me. The Contented Lover. *Unknown.* SeCL
I'll wreathe my sword in myrtle bough. Patriotic Song. Callistratus. PoFr
I'll write a poem, then sink to dreams. Poem. Guillaume de Poitiers. LyMA
Illegitimate Things. William Carlos Williams. MoAB; MoAmPo
Illimitable. Gamaliel Bradford. TBM
Illimitable God, The. Robert Browning. *Fr.* A Death in the Desert. MaRV
Illinois. C. H. Chamberlain. PoRL
Illness ("Dear friends, there is no cause for so much sympathy"). Po Chü-i, *tr. fr. Chinese by* Arthur Waley. TrCh
Illness ("Sad, sad—lean with long illness"). Po Chü-i, *tr. fr. Chinese by* Arthur Waley. MoPW; TrCh
Illness and Idleness. Po Chü-i, *tr. fr. Chinese by* Arthur Waley. TrCh
Illuminated Canticle, The. Florence Wilkinson Evans. PFY
Illuminating lamps, ye orbs crystallite. *Unknown. Fr.* Zepheria. ReIE
Illumination for Victories in Mexico. "Grace Greenwood." PAH
Illusion. Earl of Stirling. *Fr.* Darius. EBSV
Illusion. Ján Rak, *tr. fr. Slovak by* Michael Flach. LiTW
Illusion. Nevah Trebor. PC
Illusion. Ella Wheeler Wilcox. WGRP
Illusion forms before us like a grove. The Triumph of Death. Barbara Howes. NePoAm-2
Illusion of Love, The. Sarojini Naidu. MM
Illusion of War. Richard Le Gallienne. *See* This Is War.
Illustrated Booklet on Request. Betty Frye Leach. DDA
Illustrated World, The. "César Moro," *tr. fr. Spanish by* Muna Lee. AnCL
Illustration, The/ is nothing to you without the application. To a Steam Roller. Marianne Moore. MAP; MoAB; MoAmPo; OxBA
Illustrious Holland! hard would be his lot. Byron. *Fr.* English Bards and Scotch Reviewers. OBRV
Illustrious monarch of Iberia's soil. Columbus to Ferdinand. Philip Freneau. PAII
Illyrian woodlands, echoing falls. To E. L., on His Travels in Greece. Tennyson. SeCePo
Illyria's hair fell down. The Oracular Portcullis. James Reaney. PeCV
I'm a bird that's free. Aretina's Song. Sir Henry Taylor. VA
I'm a blizzard from the Brazos on a tear, hear me hoot. The Bad Man from the Brazos. *Unknown.* CoSo
I'm a broken-hearted gardener, and don't know what to do. The Broken-hearted Gardener. *Unknown.* ChTr
I'm a Decent Boy from Ireland, *with music. Unknown.* ShS
I'm a fashionable beau, just turn'd out the newest go. The Dandy O. *Unknown.* CoMu
I'm a gay puncher, fresh from the Pecos Flat. The Pecos Puncher. *Unknown.* CoSo
I'm a gay tra, la, la. Serenade [*or* Swiss Air]. Bret Harte. LBN; NA
I'm a goin' [*or* a gwine] to tell you 'bout de comin' of de Saviour. In Dat Great Gittin' Up Mornin'. *Unknown.* AA; BoAN-2
I'm a Good Old Rebel. Innes Randolph. *See* Rebel, The.
I'm a grandchild of the gods. The Complaint of New Amsterdam. Jacob Steendam. PAH
I'm a gwine to tell you bout de comin' ob de Saviour. *See* I'm a goin' to tell you . . .
I'm a happy little thing. *See* I'm a pretty little thing.
I'm a happy miner, I love to sing and dance. The Happy Miner. *Unknown.* CoSo; CSF; IHA
I'm a heartbroken raftsman. Jack Haggerty. Dan McGinnis. ViBoFo
I'm a howler from the prairies of the West. The Desperado [*or* The Boozer]. *Unknown.* CoSo; CSF; TreFS
I'm a lean dog, a keen dog, a wild dog and lone. Lone Dog. Irene R. McLeod. AlBD; AlDL; BMEP; FaPON; MCCG; MPB; NeMA; PoMa; SP; StVeCh (1940 ed.); TiPo; TVSH; UTS
I'm a little butterfly. *Unknown.* OxNR
I'm a little Hindoo. *Unknown.* FaFP; SiTL
I'm a lonely bullwhacker. The Bullwhacker. *Unknown.* ABF; CoSo; CSF
I'm a new contradiction; I'm new and I'm old. *See* I'm a strange contradiction . . .
I'm a peddler, I'm a peddler. The Connecticut Peddler. *Unknown.* ABF
I'm a peevish old man with a penny-whistle. Beggar's Serenade. John Heath-Stubbs. NeBP
I'm a plain girl whose hands are stained with earth. A Song. Ivan Alekseyevich Bunin. TrRV
I'm a poor lonesome cowboy. Poor Lonesome Cowboy. *Unknown.* ABF; AS; CSF
I'm a pretty [*or* happy] little thing. The Field Daisy [*or* The Daisy]. Jane Taylor. BoTP; PCH; PPL
I'm a pup dog and I know it. The Pup Dog's Opinion of the Quick Tempered Man. Rowland C. Bowman. AlBD
I'm a racing success. The Greyhound Speaks. Edward Anthony. AlBD
I'm a rambler and a gambler. Rambling Gambler. *Unknown.* CoSo
I'm a rambling wretch of poverty, from Tip'ry town I came. The Son of a Gambolier. *Unknown.* AS
I'm a Round-Town Gent. *Unknown.* GoSl
I'm a rowdy cowboy just off the stormy plains. The Lone Star Trail. *Unknown.* AS; CSF
I'm a rowdy soul. Rowdy Soul. *Unknown.* StDa
I'm a six foot t'ree from Brooklyn. Situation Normal. Hank Chernick. WhC
I'm a spent arrow shouldered from the sun. The Unknown Warrior Sings and Curses in the Street. Herbert Palmer. FaBoTw
I'm [*or* I am] a strange [*or* new] contradiction; I'm new and I'm old. A Book [*or* A Riddle: A Book]. Hannah More. GN; HH; OTPC; PoRL
I'm a Stranger Here, *with music. Unknown.* OuSiCo
I'm a stranger in your city, my name is Paddy Flynn. Portland County Jail. *Unknown.* AS
I'm a very highly educated man. The Highly Educated Man. *Unknown.* ABF
I'm a young married man that is tired in life. Cod Liver Ile. *Unknown.* OuSiCo
"I'm after axin', Biddy dear." Diffidence. Wade Whipple. PTA-1
I'm a-goin' down this road feelin' bad. I'm Goin' down This Road Feelin' Bad. *Unknown.* TrAS
I'm Alabama Bound, *with music. Unknown.* StDa
(Alabama Bound, *diff. vers., with music.*) ABF, *longer vers.*; SoAF
I'm always told to hurry up. Going to Bed. Marchette Chute. BoChLi (1950 ed.)
I'm an alley-cat. A Roving Alley-Cat. Mary Cockburn Bomke. CIV
I'm a-Rollin', *with music. Unknown.* BoAN-1
I'm as friendly as can be. Chickadee. Marion Mitchell Walker. GFA
I'm as restless as a willow in a windstorm. It Might as Well Be Spring. Oscar Hammerstein II. Po
I'm a-tellin' you the truth and not lying nor joking. Cheyenne. *Unknown.* CoSo
I'm Black and Blue. Heine, *tr. fr. German by* John Todhunter. AWP; JAWP; WBP

I'm bound away to leave you, good-bye, my love, good-bye. Goodbye, My Love, Goodbye. *Unknown.* SoAmSa
I'm bound to Alabama, Oh, roll the cotton down. Roll the Cotton Down. *Unknown.* SoAmSa
I'm bound to follow the long-horn cows. The Lone Star Trail. *Unknown.* CoSo
"I'm busy!/ No, I cannot stay." Too Busy? Ralph S. Cushman. PraP
I'm called by the name of a man. *Unknown.* OxNR
I'm Called Little Buttercup. W. S. Gilbert. *Fr.* H. M. S. Pinafore. OIF
(Little Buttercup.) TreFS
I'm Captain Jinks of the Horse Marines. Captain Jinks. *Unknown, at. to* T. Maclagan. BLPA; FaFP; OnPP; TreF
I'm ceded, I've stopped being theirs. Emily Dickinson. ViBoPo
I'm comin' back and haunt you, don't you fret. Ghost. John V. A. Weaver. BAP; HBMV
I'm dead, and yet must thole the sleepless surge. A Tomb by the Sea. Archias. OxBG
I'm determined to live an old maid. I'll Not Marry at All. *Unknown.* ABS
I'm done with hope and chance. Freedom. Palladas. OxBG
I'm doubtful that he knew how well he taught. Dew-Plants. Ernest G. Moll. NeLNL
I'm down, good Fate, you've won the race. Thrown. Ralph Hodgson. HBMV
I'm dreaming now of Hallie [*or* Hally]. Listen to the Mocking Bird. Septimus Winner. OIF; TrAS
I'm far frae my hame, an' I'm weary aftenwhiles. My Ain Countree. Mary Augusta Demarest. HBV; WGRP
I'm folding up my little dreams. My Little Dreams. Georgia Douglas Johnson. BANP; CDC; GoSl; PoNe
I'm fonder of carats than carrots. I Take 'Em and Like 'Em. Margaret Fishback. WhC
I'm frae St. Mungows, waes my heart. The Glasgow Chap's Story; or, Confessions over a Bottle. Alexander McLachlan. BoCaPo (1948 ed.)
I'm full of everything I do not want. Sonnet: Of the 20th June 1291. Cecco Angiolieri da Siena. AWP
I'm giving a party to-morrow at three. My Party. Queenie Scott-Hopper. BoTP
I'm Glad. Elizabeth McE. Shields. PraP
I'm Glad. *Unknown.* GFA; GoBP; HBVY; MeMeAg; OTPC (1946 ed.); WhC
(I'm Glad the Sky Is Painted Blue.) LiL
I'm glad I am living this morning. God's World. Mildred Keeling. BLRP
I'm glad our house is a little house. Song for a Little House. Christopher Morley. BoTP; FaPON; MPB; StVeCh; TreF; TSW; TSWC
I'm glad that I/ Live near a park. The Park. James S. Tippett. BrR; SUS; TiPo
I'm glad that I am born to die. Burges. *Unknown.* ABF
I'm glad that I am not to-day. Something to Be Thankful For. Clara J. Denton. HH; TOAH
I'm Glad the Sky Is Painted Blue. *Unknown. See* I'm Glad.
I'm glad the stars are over me. Stars. *Unknown.* GFA
I'm glad to lie on a sack of leaves. What the Shuiler Said as She Lay by the Fire in the Farmer's House. Padraic Colum. TwCV
I'm goin' away for to stay a little while. He's Gone Away. *Unknown.* APW; AS; TrAS
I'm Goin' down the Rivuh, *with music.* *Unknown.* StDa
I'm Goin' down the Rivuh, Baby, *with music.* *Unknown.* StDa
I'm Goin' down the Rivuh befo' Long, *with music.* *Unknown.* StDa
I'm Goin' down This Road Feelin' Bad, *with music.* *Unknown.* TrAS
I'm goin' out West, down on the Rio Grande. Alice B. *Unknown.* AS
I'm Goin' to Ship on the *Mike Davis, with music.* *Unknown.* StDa
I'm Goin' up the Rivuh, *with music.* *Unknown.* StDa
I'm goin' up the rivuh to carry them sacks. Carryin' Sacks. *Unknown.* StDa
I'm goin' where them chilly winds won't [*or* don'] blow, darlin' baby. Chilly Winds. *Unknown.* OuSiCo; TrAS
"I'm going down," she said, tying her yellow scarf. Going down the Mountain [*or* Descending]. Valentin Iremonger. EnLoPo; NeIP
I'm going out! I'm tired of tables, chairs. House-weary. Ian Drag. OQP; QP-2
I'm going out to clean the pasture spring. The Pasture. Robert Frost. AmPP; AnNE; ChMo; CMP; CoV; DDA; FaPON; LaNeLa; MAP; MoAB; MoAmPo; MOAP; MoShBr; NeMA; OxBA; Po; PoRh; RAR; SP; StVeCh; SUS; TiPo; TSW; TSWC; TwCP; TwP; UTS; ViBoPo
I'm going out to dine at Gray's. Ballade of Hell and of Mrs. Roebeck. Hilaire Belloc. MoVE
I'm going softly all my years in wisdom if in pain. Babylon. Viola Taylor. HBV
I'm going to be a pirate with a bright brass pivot-gun. The Tarry Buccaneer. John Masefield. MCCG; TCPD
I'm going to leave old Texas now. The Texas Song. *Unknown.* CoSo
"I'm going to school tomorrow, just." Patrick Goes to School. Alicia Aspinwall. MPB
I'm going to write a letter to our oldest boy who went. Father's Letter. Eugene Field. IHA
I'm going to write a novel, hey. An Ode. John Updike. FiBHP
I'm going to write a story. The Nicest Story. Abbie Farwell Brown. HH
I'm go'n' to lay down my sword and shield. Ain' Go'n' to Study War No Mo'. *Unknown.* AS
I'm gonna preach to my diamond, hammer ring. Drive It On. *Unknown.* OuSiCo
I'm gonna take those shoes I bought you. Good-by, Pretty Mama. *Unknown.* ABF
"I'm growing old, I've sixty years." Carcassonne. Gustave Nadaud. BLPA; FaBoBe; HBV; MW; NeHB
I'm growing very big and tall. Growing Up. Edna Kingsley Wallace. MoSiPe
I'm gwine to Alabamy, oh. Gwine to Alabamy. *Unknown.* TrAS
I'm Gwine Up to Heab'n Anyhow, *with music.* *Unknown.* BoAN-2
I'm Happiest When Most Away. Emily Brontë. SeCePo
I'm happy, Kerouac, your madman Allen's. Malest Cornifici Tuo Catullo. Allen Ginsberg. NeAP
I'm here at Clifton, grinding at the mill. Clifton. Thomas Edward Brown. POTT
I'm hiding, I'm hiding. Hiding. Dorothy Aldis. BoChLi; FaPON; MPB; SUS; TiPo
I'm holdin' down the Boar's Nest, an a-cookin' for myself. Batchin'. S. Omar Barker. IHA
I'm hungry, oh so hungry! The Birds on the School Windowsill. Evelyn Dainty. BoTP
I'm in a toder mood today. OIC. *Unknown.* SiTL; WhC
I'm in disgrace/ And degradation. Notice Given. Berton Braley. AlBD
I'm in love with you, Baby Louise! Baby Louise. Margaret Eytinge. LPS-1
I'm jilted, forsaken, outwitted. The Jilted Nymph. Thomas Campbell. EnLoPo
I'm just a poor wayfaring stranger. *See* I am a poor wayfaring stranger.
I'm just the grocery store cat. The Grocery Store Cat. Margaret E. Bruner. CIV
I'm king of the road! I gather. His Majesty. Theron Brown. AA
I'm learning how to dive and swim. Learning to Swim. Anna Medary. GFA
I'm like a skiff on the ocean tost. John Gay. EnLoPo
I'm longing for the forest. Home. Verner von Heidenstam. AnSL
I'm looking at your lofty head/ Away up in the air. Pikes Peak. *Unknown.* PoOW
I'm lovely as a dream in stone, O mortal! Beauty. Baudelaire. LO
I'm makin' a road. Florida Road Workers. Langston Hughes. GoSl; MAP; MoAmPo
I'm making another trip. Taciturn Sea Captain. Kotaro Takamura. PoLJ
I'm night guard all alone tonight. I Want My Time. *Unknown.* SCC
I'm nobody! Who are you? Emily Dickinson. AmPo; AnNE; BBV (1951 ed.); GoTP; NeMA; PC; TCAP; TiPo (1952 ed.); TreFS; WHA; YaD
(Nobody, A.) MaC
I'm not a chicken; I have seen. The September Gale. Oliver Wendell Holmes. PTA-2
I'm Not a Single Man. Thomas Hood. HBV
(Lines in a Young Lady's Album.) ALV
I'm not afraid of rats and mice. The Escape. Emily Rose Burt. GFA
I'm not here. Halcyon. Hilda Doolittle ("H. D."). MAP; MoAmPo
I'm now a gude farmer, I've acres o' land. Rural Content. Andrew Scott. EBSV
I'm O'er [*or* Owre] Young to Marry Yet. Burns. EBSV; LoPS; ViBoPo
("I am my mammie's ae bairn.") LO
I'm offering for sale today. A Bargain Sale. S. E. Kiser. PoToHe (new ed.)
I'm only a dog—/ Not much, you say? Only a Dog. Grenville Kleiser. AlBD
I'm only four score year, my sons, and a few. Daniel Boone's Last Look Westward. Cale Young Rice. LS; SPP
I'm out to find the new, the modern school. The Fledgling Bard and the Poetry Society. George Reginald Margetson. BANP
I'm Owre Young to Marry Yet. Burns. *See* I'm O'er Young to Marry Yet.

I'm ready now for my last trip. The Last Voyage. Henrik Wergeland. AnNoLy

I'm ready now to cat-chase those porcelain people. Imprecation for an Aesthetic Society with Newts, Warts, Waxes and Pins. Rosalie Moore. OnHM

I'm ridin' tonight round the dam bed-ground. Up the Trail. *Unknown.* CoSo

I'm Sad and I'm Lonely, *with music. Unknown.* AS; TrAS

I'm sad for, loving thee, I know full well. Why. Mikhail Lermontov. BoR

I'm sending you a valentine. Valentine for My Mother. Harry Lee. MPB

I'm sharp as a needle today. The Tailor. Piotr Vasilyevich Oreshin. TrRV

I'm sick o' New York City an' the roarin' o' the thrains. Ould Kilkinny. James B. Dollard. CPG

I'm sick of all this silly rot. A Dog's Life. Milly Walton. AlBD

I'm sick of fog and yellow gloom. Homesick. Dorothy Frances McCrae. BoAu

I'm sick of this new-fangled schism. Idealism and Realism. Gustaf Fröding. AnSL

I'm sittin' on the stile, Mary. Lament of the Irish Emigrant. Helen Selina Sheridan. GTIV; HBV; LPS-1; OBEV (1st ed.); OBVV; TIP; VA

I'm sitting alone by the fire. Her Letter. Bret Harte. CoBA; HBV; InP; LPS-1; PR; YT

I'm sitting here a-thinking. We've Done Our Hitch in Hell. *Unknown.* ABF

I'm so sorry for old Adam. Old Adam. *Unknown.* AS

I'm Sorry, Love, I Bring So Small a Bone. Burges Johnson. DDA

I'm sorry you are wiser. For the Birthday of a Middle-aged Child. Aline Kilmer. FAOV

I'm such a quiet little ghost. The Superstitious Ghost. Arthur Guiterman. DaM

I'm such a very little girl. Only Five. *Unknown.* MeMeAg

I'm sure I make no claim to be. Lines on Death, and Ballade. Villon. FoS

I'm sure I see it all now as it was. Aretemias. E. A. Robinson. MOAP

I'm sure that I like Christmas best. I Like Christmas. James S. Tippett. ChBR

I'm sure that no one ever knows. Underneath the Clothes. Madeleine Nightingale. RIS

I'm sure that Spring is on the way. Signs. Beatrice M. Murphy. GoSl

I'm taught p-l-o-u-g-h. O-U-G-H. Charles B. Loomis. BOHV

"I'm tell j'you what, thees sheeps beezness." The Sheep Beezness. S. Omar Barker. IHA

I'm Thankful that My Life Doth Not Deceive. Henry David Thoreau. PoEL-4

I'm thankful that the sun and moon. Lines by an Old Fogy. *Unknown.* HSP

I'm that distinguished twice-born hero. The Death of Digenes Akritas. John Heath-Stubbs. NePoEA

I'm the Dog. Grenville Kleiser. AlBD

I'm the gardener today. Lawn-Mower. Dorothy W. Baruch. SUS

I'm the king of the castle. *Unknown.* OxNR

I'm the Man That Kin Raise So Long, *with music. Unknown.* StDa

I'm the oats here, I have bells for dress. The Oats. Jeppe Aakjaer. BoDS

I'm the pert little pimpernel. Pimpernel. Charlotte Druitt Cole. BoTP

I'm the sub-average male *Time* reader. The Sub-average *Time* Reader. Ernest Wittenberg. FiBHP

"I'm thinking and thinking," said old Sam Shore. Sam's Three Wishes; or, Life's Little Whirligig. Walter de la Mare. ChMo; CMP; PCN

I'm thinking that to-night, if not before. The Young Gray Head. Caroline Anne Bowles. LPS-3

I'm tired of Love: I'm still more tired of Rhyme. Fatigue. Hilaire Belloc. MoVE; SiTL

I'm tired of symbols, of laws divine. To My Generation. Benyamin Galai. TrJP

I'm tired of trying to think. Existentialism. Lloyd Frankenberg. FiBHP

"I'm tired—oh, tired of books," said Jack. The Bookworm. Walter de la Mare. TiPo (1959 ed.)

I'm told that certain insect wives. Insect Wives. Rudolph Altrocchi. WhC

Im Traum sah ich ein Männchen klein und putzig. Heine, *tr. fr. German by* Sir Theodore Martin. AWP

I'm travellin' down the Castlereagh, an' I'm a station-hand. A Bushman's Song. Andrew Barton Paterson. BoAu

I'm Troubled in Mind, *with music. Unknown.* BoAN-1

I'm up and down and round about. As the World Turns. Swift. OTPC (1946 ed.); RIS

I'm very happy where I am. The Exiled Mother [or A Peasant Woman's Song]. Dion Boucicault. GTIV; TIP

I'm very, very glad indeed. The Centipede. Samuel Hopkins Adams. InMe

I'm voluble; I'm voiceless; I am Echo: I reply. Echo. Archias. OxBG

I'm wearin' [or wearing] awa', John [or Jean]. The Land o' [or of] the Leal. Lady Nairne. BCEP; EBSV; EV-3; GTBS; GTBS-D; GTBS-W; GTSE; GTSL; HBV; LPS-1; MaRV; MCCG; NA; OBEV; TCEP; WBLP; WGRP

I'm wife; I've finished that. Emily Dickinson. ViBoPo

I'm wild and wool[l]y and full of fleas. The Drunken Desperado [or Cowboy Boasting Chants]. Baird Boyd. ABF; ChTr; SCC

I'm Wishing the Whole World Christmas. Annette Wynne. MoSiPe

I'm Worried Now but I Won't Be Worried Long, *with music. Unknown.* OuSiCo

I'm Wukin' My Way Back Home, *with music. Unknown.* StDa

Image, The. Roy Fuller. ChMP; PoN

Image, The. Richard Hughes. OBMV

Image, The. Sylvia Townsend Warner. BLV; BoLiVe (1939 ed.); InP; PIAE

Image dance of change, An. Conclusion. Siegfried Sassoon. MBP; MoBrPo

Image Imagination. Elizabeth Sewell. JKCP (1955 ed.)

Image in a Lilac Tree. Terence Tiller. NeBP

Image in a Mirror. Mae Winkler Goodman. GoYe

Image in the bulb-ringed mirror. Mask. Elizabeth Cox. GoYe

Image in the Forum, The. Robert Buchanan. ChIP

Image in the Sand, The, *sel.* E. F. Benson. Prayer: "Dawn of the everlasting day, The." PC

Image-Maker, The. Oliver St. John Gogarty. OBEV (new ed.); OBMV; PoRA

Image of beauty, when I gaze on thee. Janus. "Æ." TIP

Image of Death, The, *sel.* Robert Southwell. "Gown which I do use to wear, The." ViBoPo

Image of Death. The. Thomas, Lord Vaux. *See* Aged Lover Renounceth Love, The.

Image of Delight, The. William Ellery Leonard. AnFE; APA; CoAnAm; HBMV; MAP; MoAmPo (1942 ed.)

Image of God, The. Francisco Aldana, *tr. fr. Spanish by* Longfellow. CAW; WGRP

Image of Lethe, An. The Coming of War; Actaeon. Ezra Pound. NP; TwCV

Image of Silenus. Douglas Le Pan. BoCaPo (1948 ed.)

Imageries of dreams reveal a gracious age. The Age of a Dream. Lionel Johnson. OBMV; TIP; ViPP

Images. Richard Aldington. BMEP; MBP; MoBrPo; NeMA; NP; PFE; PIAE; TOP

Images. Richard Schaukal, *tr. fr. German by* Ludwig Lewisohn. AWP

Images break upon a sad day, The. Gladstone. Julian Symons. WaP

Images of J—— assail him. The Bus Trip. Joel Oppenheimer. NeAP

Imaginary Correspondence, *parody.* Frank Sidgwick. WhC

Imaginary Dialogue. Antiphilus of Byzantium, *tr. fr. Greek by* Dudley Fitts. TriL

Imaginary Elegies, I–IV. Jack Spicer. NeAP

Imaginary Iceberg. The. Elizabeth Bishop. LiTM; MoAB; MoAmPo (1950 ed.); MoVE; ReMP

Imagination. John Davidson. *Fr.* New Year's Eve. MBP; MoBrPo

Imagination. Shakespeare. *See* Lunatic, the Lover, and the Poet, The.

Imagination. Christopher Smart. *Fr.* Reason and Imagination. BeR

Imagination. Wordsworth. *Fr.* The Prelude, VI. FiP (Cambridge and the Alps, *shorter sel.*) ERP ("Imagination—here the power so called," *shorter sel.*) NBE

Imagination and Taste, How Impaired and Restored. Wordsworth. *See* Prelude, The.

Imagination flies out on the airman's wings. "They Also Serve . . ." Oliffe Richmond. NeTW

Imagination—here the Power so called. Imagination [or Cambridge and the Alps]. Wordsworth. *Fr.* The Prelude. ERP; FiP; NBE

Imaginative Crisis, The. *Unknown.* BOHV

Imagine a road as straight as a wish. The Road. Hyam Plutzik. FiMAP

Imagine him still with heavy brow. Beethoven's Death Mask. Stephen Spender. CaAE

Imagine, mother, that you are to stay home and I to travel into strange lands. The Merchant. Rabindranath Tagore. MOAH

Imagine nothing: you will find. Ode on Nothing Edward Harry William Meyerstein. MM

Imagine the South. George Woodcock. NeBP

Imagined Happiness. Erik Axel Karlfeldt, *tr. fr. Swedish by* Charles W. Stork. AnSL; LiTW

Imagining How It Would Be to Be Dead. Richard Eberhart. FiMAP; LiTA

Imagiste Love Lines. *Unknown.* BOHV

Imitated from the Persian. Robert Southey. *See* Lord, Who Art Merciful.
Imitation. H. C. Bunner. PA
Imitation. Anthony C. Deane. BOHV; PA
Imitation of a Psalm [CXLV]. François de Malherbe, *pr. tr. fr. French.* LiA
Imitation of Christ. Wilma C. Ludlow. ChIP
Imitation of Christ, *sels.* Thomas à Kempis, *tr. fr. Latin.*
Immunity. ChIP; OQP; QP-1
Man Proposes. TreF
Of Love of Silence and of Solitude. TreF
Thoughts of Death, The. OuHeWo
Imitation of Faust, The. Alfred Hayes. LiTM (1946 ed.)
Imitation of Robert Browning. James Kenneth Stephen. InMe; PA
Imitation of Spenser. Keats. ATP; BPN; EmBrPo; EnRP; ERP
Morning, *st.* 1. GN
Imitation of the First Epistle of the Second Book of Horace. Pope. *See* First Epistle of the Second Book of Horace.
Imitation of the Seventeenth Epistle of the First Book of Horace, An, *sel.* William Diaper.
Mr. Diaper Wants Advancement. BeR
Imitation of the Sixth Satire of the Second Book of Horace, An, *sel.* Pope.
Two Mice, The. BeR
Imitation of Walt Whitman. "Judy." BOHV; PA
Imitation of Walt Whitman. James Kenneth Stephen. PA
(Of W. W.—Americanus.) FiBHP; WhC
(Sincere Flattery.) HBV; InMe
Imitation of Wordsworth, An. Catherine Fanshawe. *See* Fragment in Imitation of Wordsworth.
Imitatrix Ales. Archias, *tr. fr. Greek by* Sir William Marris. OxBG
Immaculate Conception, The. John Banister Tabb. ISi
Immaculate Palm. Joseph Joel Keith. ISi
Immalee. Christina Rossetti. ThWaDe
Immanence. F. Barrie Flint. OQP; QP-1
Immanence. Edmond G. A. Holmes. MaRV
Immanence. Richard Hovey. OQP; QP-1; WGRP
Immanence. Thomas Durley Landels. MaRV
Immanence. Evelyn Underhill. GrCo-2; MaRV; QS; StJW
Immanence. *Unknown.* BPP
Immanent, The. Gerard Manley Hopkins. *See* As Kingfishers Catch Fire, Dragonflies Draw Flame.
Immanent God, The. Emerson. *Fr.* Woodnotes, II. MaRV
Immeasurable haze. To the Holy Spirit. Yvor Winters. MoVE
Immediates. Charles Bruce. BoCaPo
Immediates? Let us take for text. Immediates. Charles Bruce. BoCaPo
Immediates? Well we have birth and sickness and death. Alternative. Charles Bruce. BoCaPo
Immensitie cloysterd in thy deare wombe. Nativitie. John Donne. OBS
Immensity. John Hall Wheelock. BAP
Immigrant, The. Frank Kendon. MBP; MoBrPo (1942 ed.); POTE
Immigrants. Nancy Byrd Turner. PoeMoYo
Immobile Wind, The. Yvor Winters. NP
Immolated. Herman Melville. APW; ViBoPo
Immolation. Robert Farren. OnYI
Immoral. James Oppenheim. HBV
Immoral Arctic, The. Morris Bishop. FiBHP; WhC
Immoral Proposition, The. Robert Creeley. NeAP
Immorality, An. Ezra Pound. ChMo; CMP; HBV; LiTL; LiTM; MAP; MoAB; MoAmPo; NeMA; NePA; OBAV; SiTL
Immortal, The. Blake. *Fr.* The Book of Los, *ch.* 2. LiTB; LoBV
Immortal. Richard Church. MoBrPo (1942 ed.)
Immortal. Florence Earle Coates. MaRV
Immortal, The. Marjorie Pickthall. CaP; OCL
Immortal, The. Cale Young Rice. NLK; VOD
Immortal. Sara Teasdale. WGRP
Immortal. Mark Van Doren. MAP; MoAmPo; PoeMoYo; TBM
Immortal Aphrodite. Sappho. *See* Ode to Aphrodite.
Immortal Autumn. Archibald MacLeish. BoLiVe (1945 ed.); ChMo; CMP; CoBMV; LiTA; MAP; MoAB; MoAmPo; NeMA; NP; ReaPo; ReMP; TrGrPo; TwCV
Immortal Babe, who this dear day. For Christmas Day. Joseph Hall. AnEC
Immortal bard! for whom each muse has wove. An Epistle to Mr. Pope. George Lyttelton. Po
Immortal Choirs, The. *Unknown, tr. fr. Greek by* Arthur S. Way. *Fr.* Homeric Hymns. GrR
(Choirs of Heaven, The, *tr. by* T. F. Higham.) OxBG
Immortal Flowers. Wallace Rice. AA
Immortal Flowers of Poesy. Christopher Marlowe. *See* Poet's Pen, The.
Immortal Imogen, crowned queen above. The Two Swans. Thomas Hood. CH
Immortal is an ample word. Emily Dickinson. TwP
Immortal Israel. Judah Halevi, *tr. fr. Hebrew by* Solomon Solis-Cohen. TrJP
Immortal Living. Harold Trowbridge Pulsifer. MaRV
Immortal Love, Author of This Great Frame. George Herbert. TwHP
(Love.) EPS (1936 ed.); MeRV; SeCV-1
Immortal Love, forever full. Our Master. Whittier. BLRP; IAP; MaRV; StJW; WBLP; WGRP
Immortal Love, too high for my possessing. Ideal Passion, XL. George Edward Woodberry. HBMV; MOAP
Immortal Mind, The. Byron. *See* When Coldness Wraps This Suffering Clay.
Immortal Morn. Hezekiah Butterworth. PEDC; PoRL
Immortal Muse, The. Richard Watson Dixon. CBE
Immortal Nature. Erasmus Darwin. *Fr.* The Economy of Vegetation. OBEC
Immortal Newton Never Spoke. Earl of Chesterfield. InP
(On a Full-Length Portrait of Beau Marsh, *wr.* [Nash], *st.* 1 *by* the Earl of Chesterfield, *st.* 2 *by* Jane Brereton.) BOHV
Immortal on thy many-splendoured throne. To Aphrodite. Sappho. GrL; OxBG
Immortal Panoply, The. Wallace B. Nichols. *Fr.* Prometheus in Piccadilly. ReTS
Immortal Part, The. A. E. Housman. A Shropshire Lad, XLIII. BrBE; MBP; MoBrPo; Po; POTT; PoVP; UnPo (3d ed.); VLEP
Immortal Perfume. Leconte de Lisle, *tr. fr. French by* Alan Conder. TrFP
Immortal Residue, The. Adelaide Crapsey. MaRV; MoAmPo (1942 ed.)
Immortal spirit hath no bars, The. Dawn. Frederick George Scott. CaP; CPG; MaRV; OCL; UnW
Immortal Springtime and Its Tokens. Bernardo de Balbuena, *tr. fr. Spanish by* Samuel Beckett. *Fr.* Grandeza Mexicana. AnMP
Immortal Steeds of Achilles, The. Homer, *tr. fr. Greek by* the Earl of Derby. *Fr.* The Iliad, XVII. GrR
(Horses of Achilles, The.) GrPE, *tr. by* F. L. Lucas; OxBG, *tr. by* the Earl of Derby
("Meantime, at distance from the scene of blood," *tr. by* Pope.) GrPo
Immortal stood frozen amidst, The. The Immortal. Blake. *Fr.* The Book of Los. LiTB; LoBV
Immortal Words. Aline Badger Carter. ChIP
Immortalia Ne Speres. Alcaeus, *tr. fr. Greek by* C. M. Bowra. GrL; OxBG
Immortalis. David Morton. HBV
Immortality. "Æ." AnIV; AWP; GTIV; JAWP; OBMV; VA; WBP; WGRP
Immortality. Addison. *See* Cato.
Immortality. Matthew Arnold. BPN; EmBrPo; EPN; FiP; MaRV; PC; PoVP; VLEP
Immortality. Richard Henry Dana. AA; WGRP
Immortality. Emily Dickinson. *See* It is an honourable thought.
Immortality. Joachim du Bellay, *tr. fr. French by* Alan Conder. Antiquities of Rome, XXXII. TrFP
Immortality. W. W. Gibson. ChMo; CMP
Immortality. Samuel Greenberg. LiTA
Immortality. Arthur Sherburne Hardy. AA
Immortality. Frank Horne. BANP
Immortality. Joseph Jefferson. BLPA; DDA; NeHB
Immortality. Job, XIV: 1–2, 7–12, XIX: 25–27, Bible, *O.T.* (*Moulton, Modern Reader's Bible*). WGRP
Immortality. Willis Fletcher Johnson. OQP; QP-2
Immortality. Milton. *Fr.* Lycidas. MaRV
Immortality. "Nicolai Maksimovich Minski," *tr. fr. Russian by* Babette Deutsch. TrJP; TrRV
Immortality. Susan L. Mitchell. GTIV; OnYI
Immortality. Frederic William Henry Myers. VA
Immortality. Ptolemy, *tr. fr. Greek by* Robert Bridges. GrCo-1
(Starry Heavens Without.) OxBG
Immortality. Lizette Woodworth Reese. AA; BAP; HBMV; HBVY; LEAP; POT; PoTo
Immortality. Sir Philip Sidney. *See* Who Hath His Fancy Pleased.
Immortality. *Unknown, tr. fr. Greek by* William Hay. OnPM
Immortality Conferred in Vain. Theognis, *tr. fr. Greek by* J. M. Edmonds. GrL; LiTW; OxBG
Immortality in Song. Michael Drayton. *See* Idea: "How many paltry foolish painted things."
Immortality of Love. Robert Southey. *Fr.* The Curse of Kehama. EV-4
("They sin who tell us.") OBRV
Immortality of the Soul, The ("All moving things to other things do move"). Sir John Davies. *Fr.* Nosce Teipsum. EV-2
Immortality of the Soul, The ("For why should we the busy soul believe"). Sir John Davies. *Fr.* Nosce Teipsum. ViBoPo

Immortality of Verse, The. Pope, *after the Latin of* Horace. AWP; JAWP; WBP
Immortality she gave, The. There Is No Trumpet like the Tomb. Emily Dickinson. BLV; BoLiVe
Immortall Love, authour of this great frame. *See* Immortal Love, Author of This Great Frame.
Immortals, The. Isaac Rosenberg. FaBoTw; TrJP
Immortals in Exile. Arthur Davison Ficke. PFY
Immovable, unchanging. Two Songs. Heine. WoL
Immunity. Thomas à Kempis, *tr. fr. Latin. Fr.* Imitation of Christ. ChIP; OQP; QP-1
Immunity. Ibn Maimun, *tr. fr. Arabic by* A. J. Arberry. MooP
Immutabilis. Alice Learned Bunner. *Fr.* Vingtaine. AA
Immutabilis. Mahlon Leonard Fisher. MuM
Imogen. Sir Henry Newbolt. HBMV
Imogen. Richard Henry Stoddard. IAP
Imogen—in Wales. Thomas Caulfield Irwin. IrPN
Impar Impares Odit. Henry Parrot. SiCE; TuPP
Impassive god with baneful threatening hand. The Clock. Baudelaire. LO; TrFP
Impatience. Ts'ao Ho, *tr. fr. Chinese by* Henry H. Hart. OnPM
Impatient Poet, The. D'Arcy Cresswell. AnNZ
Impatient with Desire. George Granville. SeCL
Impenitentia Ultima. Ernest Dowson. HBV; POTT; VLEP
Imperator Augustus. Sir Rennell Rodd. VA
Imperator Victus. Hart Crane. OxBA
Imperatrix. Gustav Davidson. TBM
Imperceptible/ It withers in the world. Ono no Komachi, *tr. fr. Japanese by* Kenneth Rexroth. OnPJ
Imperceptively the world became haunted by her white dress. The White Dress. Marya Zaturenska. MoAmPo; TwAmPo
Impercipient, The. Thomas Hardy. ChMo; CMP; MaPo; MaRV; OAEP; PoLFOT; POTT; TrGrPo; ViBoPo; ViPo; WGRP
Imperial bloom, whose every curve we see. A White Camellia. Edgar Fawcett. SN
Imperial boy had fallen in his pride, The. My Fatherland. William Cranston Lawton. AA
Imperial Consort of the Fairy King, The. Sonnet: The Wild Duck's Nest. Wordsworth. ChER; EnSW
Imperial Man. James Russell Lowell. *Fr.* Under the Old Elm, VIII. PGD
Imperiled stands the day. Up the bright street. For the Undefeated. Eleanor Wells. NeTW
Impertinence at first is borne. The Hound and the Huntsman. John Gay. TCEP
Impertinent, we tease the weary Heaven. The Man and the Flea. La Fontaine. OnPM
Impetuous Lover, The. A. R. D. Fairburn. AnNZ
Impetuous Samuel. Harry Graham. NA
Impiety, *sel.* Helene Margaret.
"Lord, I have not time to pray." TrPWD
Impious Feast, The, *sels.* Robert Eyres Landor. OBRV
Babylon, *fr.* Bk. I.
Festival, The, *fr.* Bk. III.
Historic Time, *fr.* Bk. VIII.
Jew's Home, The, *fr.* Bk. I.
Nineveh, *fr.* Bk. V.
Sleep, *fr.* Bk. VII.
Implacable angel, The. Epitaph. Leone da Modena. TrJP
Implacable as are thy arctic floes. Russia. Elliott Napier. BoAu
Implicit Faith. Aubrey Thomas De Vere. *Fr.* May Carols. GoBC; MaRV
Implora Pace. Charles Lotin Hildreth. AA
Imponderable the dinosaur. Cape Hatteras. Hart Crane. *Fr.* The Bridge. CoV; LiTA; OnAP
Important Evidence. "Lewis Carroll." *See* Evidence Read at the Trial of the Knave of Hearts.
Important People. Louis Untermeyer, *and others.* StaSt
Importune Me No More. Elizabeth I, Queen of England. *See* When I Was Fair and Young.
Impossible, The. Jules Laforgue, *tr. fr. French.* AnFP, *tr. by* William Jay Smith; TrFP, *tr. by* Alan Conder
Impossible Fact, The. Christian Morgenstern, *tr. fr. German by* Herman Salinger. TwGV
Impossible—the eagle's flight! The Proof. Lucy Larcom. EOAH
Impossible the years have fled away so fast! The Mice at the Door. Vincent McHugh. NePoAm-2
Impossible, you say, that man survives. The Unbelievable. Edwin Markham. MaRV; PSO
Impossibility, The. Coventry Patmore. *Fr.* The Angel in the House. PoVP
Impossibly, Motivated by Midnight. E. E. Cummings. NAMP
Imposture, The, *sels.* James Shirley.
O Fly My Soul, *fr.* II, ii. AtBAP; EG; OBS; OxBoCh
(Hymn, A: "O fly, my soul!"). GoBC; OBEV (1st ed.)
(Song of Nuns, A.) ACP; CAW; PraNu
Piping Peace. ACP; LoBV
(Io.) OBS; SeCL
(Peace.) EV-2
(Song: "You Virgins that did late despair.") PoEL-2
(You Virgins.) ViBoPo
Imprecation for an Aesthetic Society with Newts, Warts, Waxes and Pins. Rosalie More. OnHM
Impress of the Crucifix. Mother Mary Alphonsa. PraNu
Impression. E. E. Cummings. *See* Sunset.
Impression. Sir Edmund Gosse. BMEP; HBV; LEAP
Impression at Reno. C. R. Holmes. PtPa
Impression de Nuit; London. Lord Alfred Douglas. ES; OBEV (new ed.); OBVV; PoVP
Impression du Matin. Oscar Wilde. MBP; MoBrPo; PoVP; ViP
Impression—IV. E. E. Cummings. MAP; MoAmPo; PIAE; TwCV
(Hours Rise Up [Putting Off Stars], The.) ChMo; OxBA
Impression: Le Réveillon. Oscar Wilde. PoVP
Impression of a Fountain. Hakushu Kitahara, *tr. fr. Japanese by* Katue Kitasono. LiTW
Impression of Autumn. Rachel Annand Taylor. EBSV
Impression of Exile. Luis Cernuda, *tr. fr. Spanish by* Eleanor L. Turnbull. CoSP
Impressions. Harold Monro. BMEP
Impressions. Oscar Wilde.
La Fruite de la Lune, II. Po; PoVP
Les Silhouettes, I. Po; PoVP; VLEP
Impressions of François-Marie Arouet (de Voltaire), *sel.* Ezra Pound.
"If you'd have me go on loving you." MoAB
Impressions of My Father, *sel.* Marcia Masters.
Country Ways, I. GoYe
Imprimis he was "broke." Thereafter left. Giffen's Debt. Kipling. ViP
Imprisoned. Eunice Tietjens. HBMV
Imprisoned. John Hall Wheelock. PR
Imprisoned in the marble block. Sleeping Beauty. Elinor Wylie. MuM
Imprisoned Revolutionist, The, *abr.* Mihran Damadian, *tr. fr. Armenian by* Alice Stone Blackwell. PoFr
Imprisoned Soul, The. Walt Whitman. *See* Last Invocation, The.
Impromptu. Ch'iu T'ung, *tr. fr. Chinese by* Henry H. Hart. PoHN
Impromptu. Thomas Gray. HoPM; MyFE; SeCePo
(Impromptu, Suggested by a View, in 1766, of the Seat and Ruins of a Nobleman, at Kingsgate, Kent.) CoEV
(On Lord Holland's Seat near Margate, Kent.) SeCeV
Impromptu on Charles II. Earl of Rochester. ChTr
Impromptu, Suggested by a View, in 1766, of the Seat and Ruins of a Nobleman, at Kingsgate, Kent. Thomas Gray. *See* Impromptu.
Impromptus. Byron. BPN
Improvisation. Louis Dudek. BoCaPo (1948 ed.)
Improvisation. Alfred Kreymborg. MAP
Improvisation. Boris Pasternak, *tr. fr. Russian by* Babette Deutsch. Po; TrRV
Improvisation on an Old Theme. Dorothy Livesay. CaP
Improvisation III. Harold Silverman. TwCaPo
Improvising. Louise Townsend Nicholl. NePoAm-2
Impulse, The. Robert Frost. *Fr.* The Hill Wife. AWP; ChMo; CMP; IAP; LiTM; LO; MOAP; NePA; NP; SBMV
Impulse. José Moreno Villa, *tr. fr. Spanish by* Eleanor L. Turnbull. CoSP
Impulses. Henri Michaux, *tr. fr. French by* Eunice Clark. OnHM
Impulsive Dialogue. Maxwell Bodenheim. NP
In. Vicente Huidobro, *tr. fr. Spanish by* H. R. Hays. TwSpPo
In a Balcony. Robert Browning. EnLi-2 (1949 ed.); PoVP; ViPP
In a Bamboo Grove. Wang Wei, *tr. fr. Chinese.* WhP
In a bank of flowers, against a wall of roses, they stand. The Graduating Class. Eunice Tietjens. FAOV
In a bark, methought, lone steering. Thomas Campbell. *Fr.* A Dream. UnW
In a basement tavern,/ amid smoke and swearing. Doomed. Kostas Varnalis. MoGP
In a Bath Teashop. John Betjeman. EnLoPo
In a Bird Sanctuary. Richard Wilbur. FiMAP
In a Boat. Hilaire Belloc. AlDL; ISi
In a bowl to sea went wise men three. The Wise Men of Gotham. Thomas Love Peacock. BoN
In a branch of willow hid. To a Caty-did. Philip Freneau. AA; AmP; AmPP; APW; CoBA; IAP; LHV; SN; TCAP
In a British Cemetery Overseas, May, 1940. Richard Elwes. NeTW
In a Bye-Canal. Herman Melville. PoFS
In a Cathedral City. Thomas Hardy. EnLoPo
In a cavern, in a canyon. Paul Dehn. *Fr.* Rhymes for a Modern Nursery. FiBHP
In a cavern in a canyon. Oh, My Darling Clementine. U

In a cavern in a canyon (*continued*)
known, at. to Percy Montross. FaBoBe; FaFP; OlF; TreF
In a certain region grew a great banyan tree. The Panchatantra: How the Crow-Hen Killed the Black Snake. *Unknown, tr. by* Arthur W. Ryder. OuHeWo
In a certain town lived a merchant named Naduk. The Panchatantra: The Mice That Ate Iron. *Unknown, tr. by* Arthur W. Ryder. OuHeWo
In a chariot of light from the regions of day. Liberty Tree. Thomas Paine. MC; PAH; PoFr
In a Child's Album. Wordsworth. GN; PCH
In a China Shop. George Sidney Hellman. AA
In a Church of Padua. Herman Melville. MeRV
In a church where I could kneel. Deo Gracias. *Unknown.* TMEV
In a church which is furnish'd with mullion and gable. All Saints. Edmund Yates. BOHV; HBV; SiTL
In a City Square. Eleanor Glenn Wallis. NePoAm-2
In a Class of Moral Theology. Francis Sweeney. JKCP (1955 ed.)
In a clear space he lay. The Shade of Patroclus. Homer, *tr. by* the Earl of Derby. *Fr.* The Iliad, XXIII. LiA
In a cleft that's christened Alt. The Man and the Echo. W. B. Yeats. TwHP
In a Closed Universe. James Hayford. NePoAm-2
In a cloud of time, this dust of locusts, in which we move. O Contemporaries. Louis Dudek. TwCaPo
In a [*or* the] coign of the cliff between lowland and highland. A Forsaken Garden. Swinburne. BoLiVe; BPN; EmBrPo; EPN; FaBoEn; GTBS; GTBS-D; GTML; GTSL; HBV; InP; LiTB; LiTG; LoBV; MBP; OBVV; PIAE; PoE; PoFS; PoVP; ShBV-4; TCEP; TOP; VA; ViP; ViPo; VLEP; WHA
In a cool curving world he lies. The Fish. Rupert Brooke. GTML; MM
In a Convex Mirror. Rosemary Dobson. MoAuPo
In a Copy of Browning. Bliss Carman. HBMV
In a Copy of Omar Kháyyám. James Russell Lowell. AA; TCAP
In a corner. Dissembler. Charles Shaw. GoYe
In a cottage embosom'd within a deep shade. Blue Ey'd Mary. *Unknown.* CoMu
In a Cottage in Fife. *Unknown.* BoN; LiL; OxNR; RIS
In a crack near a cupboard, with dainties provided. The Young Mouse. Jefferys Taylor. OnHT; OTPC (1923 ed.)
In a dark and dismal alley where the sunshine never came. Tommy's Prayer. John F. Nicholls. PTA-2
In a dark corner of the room the harp. Rimas, VII. Gustavo Adolfo Bécquer. TeCS
In a dark garden, by a dreadful tree. Quorum Porum. Ruth Pitter. PoC
In a dark hour, tasting the Earth. Tasting the Earth. James Oppenheim. BAP; MAP; MoAmPo (1942 ed.); PFY; TBM; TCPD
In a dark little crack, half a yard from the ground. The Spider and His Wife. Jane Taylor. OTPC (1923 ed.)
In a Day, *sel.* Augusta Davies Webster.
Deaths of Myron and Klydone, The. VA
In a dazzle of lights and goodbyes. North Star West. Earle Birney. TwCaPo
In a dear little home of tarpaulin and boards. No Thoroughfare. Ruth Holmes. BoTP
In a Desert Town. Lionel Stevenson. StVeCh
In a Devonshire lane as I trotted along. The Devonshire Lane. John Marriott. BOHV
In a dim corner of my room for longer than my fancy thinks. The Sphinx. Oscar Wilde. PoVP; ViPP; VLEP
In a dingy kitchen. Lamentations. Alter Brody. TrJP
In a dirty old house lived a Dirty Old Man. The Dirty Old Man. William Allingham. LPS-1; PCD
In a doomed and empty house in Houndsditch. The Vindictive Staircase; or, The Reward of Industry. W. W. Gibson. AnFE; POTT
In a dream I saw a beautiful island. Island of Night. Galway Kinnell. NePoAm
In a dream not long sped. Sisters. "Robin Hyde." AnNZ
In a Drear-nighted December. Keats. *See* Stanzas: "In a drear-nighted December."
In a drowsy warmth I lie. Kindred. Theodore Morrison. MuM
In a factory building there are wheels and gearings. Our Father's Hand. Annie Johnson Flint. BLRP
In a fair place. The Vision. "Fiona Macleod." *Fr.* Sospiri di Roma. BMEP; VLEP
In a false dream I saw the Foe prevail. Nightmare. Sir William Watson. LEAP
In a far corner. *See* In the far corner.
In a far country, in the days before Jesus was born in Judea. The Three Holy Kings. *Unknown.* CLS
In a far country that I cannot name. The Proud King. William Morris. *Fr.* The Earthly Paradise. EV-5
In a far eastern country. The Sending of the Magi. Bliss Carman. ChrBoLe
In a far land upon a day. The Riding of the Kings. Eleanor Farjeon. ChBR; YeAr
In a far-away northern country in the placid pastoral region. The Ox-Tamer. Walt Whitman. MOAP
In a field by Cahirconlish. The Man Who Trod on Sleeping Grass. Dora Sigerson Shorter. GTIV
In a Forest. Andrew Marvell. *Fr.* Upon Appleton House. EV-2
In a funny little garden not much bigger than a mat. The Proud Vegetables. Mary McNeil Fenollosa. GFA
In a Garden. Donald C. Babcock. NePoAm
In a Garden. Theda Kenyon. NLK
In a Garden. Stephen Spender. TwHP
In a Garden. Swinburne. BOL; PRWS; VLEP
In a Garden by Moonlight. Thomas Lovell Beddoes. *Fr.* Torrismond. VA
In a garden of shining sea-weed. The Sea Princess. Katharine Pyle. PCH
In a garden shady this holy lady. Song for St. Cecilia's Day. W. H. Auden. FaBoTw
In a garden where the whitethorn spreads her leaves. Alba Innominata. *Unknown.* AWP; LiTW
In a Garret. Elizabeth Akers Allen. AA; LEAP
In a Gay Jar. "Feodor Sologub." *See* Amphora, The.
In a Girls' School. David Morton. PoRL
In a glade of an elfin forest. The Elfin Artist. Alfred Noyes. CV
In a Glass. Swift. RIS
In a Glorious Garden Grene. *Unknown.* EG
In a Gondola. Robert Browning. BEL; BLV; BPN; EmBrPo; EPN; EtPaEn; GEPC; PoVP; REAL; TCEP; VA; ViBoPo, *abr.;* ViPo; VLEP
Moth's Kiss, First, The, *sel.* AtBAP; GTSL; LPS-1; OBEV; OBVV; PIR
(Song: "Moth's kiss, first, The.") BoLiVe; HBV; TrGrPo
(Song from "In a Gondola.") LEAP
In a great land, a new land, a land full of labour and riches and confusion. Longfellow. Henry van Dyke. CV
In a green place lanced through. The Blue Heron. Theodore Goodridge Roberts. BoCaPo; CaP; PeCV; TwCaPo
In a grey cave, where comes no glimpse of sky. Waiting. Katharine Tynan. TIP
In a Grove Most Rich of Shade. Sir Philip Sidney. Astrophel and Stella: Eighth Song. OBSC; SiPS
(Eighth Sonnet, The.) OAEP
In a gust of wind the white dew. Bunya no Asayasu, *tr. fr. Japanese by* Kenneth Rexroth. OnPJ
In a happy reign there should be no hermits. To Chi Wu Ch'ien Bound Home after Failing in an Examination. Wang Wei. BoFr
In a harbour grene aslepe whereas I lay. *See* In a herber green . . .
In a hard, burned land of ash, stripped of leaves. Beatrice. Baudelaire. AnFP
In a Hard Intellectual Light. Richard Eberhart. FiMAP; LiTM (rev. ed.); MoVE
In a herber [*or* harbour] green, asleep where as I lay. In Youth Is Pleasure [*or* Of Youth He Singeth *or* Youth]. Robert Wever. *Fr.* Lusty Juventus. ChTr; EG; ElL; OBEV; OBSC; SiCE; TuPP
In a hidden valley a pale blue flower grows. The Valley of Pale Blue Flowers. "Fiona Macleod." PoVP
In a high valley of the hills. From an Upland Valley. Richard Church. MBP; MoBrPo (1942 ed.)
In a hole of the heel of an old brown stocking. Stocking Fairy. Winifred Welles. FaPON; TiPo
In a hollow oak-tree. Wood Wife. Leah Bodine Drake. DaM
In a hollow of the forest. The Bomber. Brian Vrepont. BoAV
In a Hundred Years. Elizabeth Doten. BLPA
In a Lady's Album. Marcus Clarke. BoAu
In a Land. *Unknown, at. to* Lao-tzu, *tr. fr. Chinese by* Witter Bynner. *Fr.* Tao Teh King. OnPM
In a land for antiquities greatly renowned. The Toad's Journal. Jane Taylor. LPS-3
In a Lecture-Room. Arthur Hugh Clough. BPN; EmBrPo; EPN; PoVP; TCEP; VA; ViPo; VLEP
In a Library. Richard Burton. MOB
In a Library. Emily Dickinson. *See* Precious, mouldering pleasure 'tis, A.
In a little piece of wood. Mr. and Mrs. Spikky Sparrow. Edward Lear. SAS
In a little precious stone what splendor meets the eyes! Juan Ruiz, Archpriest of Hita. *Fr.* Praise of Little Women. TeCS
In a little white house. The Return of the Fairy. Humbert Wolfe. PoMS
In a London Square. Arthur Hugh Clough. BPN; EmBrPo; EnLi-2; EPN; PoVP; VLEP
(Put Forth Thy Leaf, Thou Lofty Plane.) ViPP

In a London Street. Edward Ward. *Fr.* Hudibras Redivivus. BeR
In a London Terminus. John Lehmann. AtBAP
In a loose robe of tinsel forth [*or* tynsell foorth] she came. Corinna Bathes [*or* Natures Naked Jem]. George Chapman. *Fr.* Ovid's Banquet of Sense. FaBoEn; OBSC
In a Lovely Garden Walking. Ludwig Uhland, *tr. fr. German by* George MacDonald. AWP; JAWP; WBP
In a Low Rocking-Chair. Helen Coale Crew. BOL; HBMV
In a lumber camp. The Peon's Mother. Jewel Wurtzbaugh. HiLiAm
In a luminous valley once I awoke. Amber Lands. Tom MacInnes. BoCaPo; CPG
In a Meadow. John Swinnerton Phillimore. OBEV (new ed.); OBVV
In a meadow/ Beside the chapel three boys were playing football. Father Mat. Patrick Kavanagh. AnIL; MoAB
In a meadow by the roadway. Ukrainian Song. Ivan Surikov. BoR
In a melancholy [*or* melancholie] fancie [*or* fancy], out of my self [*or* myself]. Hallow [*or* Hollo] My Fancie [*or* Fancy]. William Cleland, *and others.* CH; LPS-3; NBE; SeCL
In a milkweed cradle. Baby Seeds. *Unknown.* MeMeAg; OTPC (1946 ed.); PCH
In a minute the doctor will find out what is wrong. A Utopian Journey. Randall Jarrell. FiMAP
In a Moonlight Wilderness. Samuel Taylor Coleridge. *See* Fruit Plucker, The.
In a Museum. Babette Deutsch. HBMV
In a Museum. Thomas Hardy. UnS
In a Museum. Anne Elizabeth Wilson. CIV
In a narrow road where there was not room to pass. Meeting in the Road. *Unknown.* TrCh
In a nation of one hundred fine, mob-hearted, lynching, relenting, repenting millions. Bryan, Bryan, Bryan, Bryan. Vachel Lindsay. CrMA; LiTA; OxBA; OxBoLi
In a net of mist the moon depends on the wood. Spring Song. George Brandon Saul. GoYe
In a nook/ That opened south. In May. J. M. Synge. MBP; MoBrPo
In a palace of pearl and sea-weed. The Sea Princess. Katherine Pyle. TVC; TVSH
In a park, delightful and fair. Villancico for His Three Daughters. Marqués de Santillana. LyMA
In a pellucid calm of summer sunset. Mandarin on the Air. Christopher Morley. PoMa
In a pioneer's cabin out West, so they say. Betty and the Bear. *Unknown.* PTA-2
In a pitchy midnight air. Cupid—Ungrateful Guest. *Unknown.* *Fr.* Anacreontea. GrR
In a plain pleasant cottage, conveniently neat. The Miller. John Cunningham. CEP; OBEC
In a Poem. Robert Frost. CoV
In a pool of shadow floating on the sand. Asleep. Witter Bynner. *Fr.* Chapala Poems. NP
In a Province. F. T. Prince. BoSA; MoVE
In a puddle by the roadside. Reflections. Cyrus E. Albertson. MaRV
In a quiet water'd land, a land of roses. The Dead at Clonmacnois[e]. Angus O'Gillan. AnIL; AnIV; GTIV; HBV; IrPN; OBEV; OBMV; OBVV; OnYI; OxBI; PoD; TIP
In a race-course box behind the stand. Right Royal. John Masefield. OtMeF
In a realm that shall be nameless. The Tale of the Golden Cockerel. Pushkin. TrRV
In a Restaurant. W. W. Gibson. PoeMoYo; VOD
In a room that we love. Swallows. Cale Young Rice. VOD
In a Rosary. Swinburne. VLEP
In a Rose Garden. John Bennett. BLPA; FaBoBe; HBV; NeHB
In a rusty, worn-out cabin sat a broken-hearted leaser. The Miner's Song. Charles E. Winter. CSF; IFA
In a scented wood. The Night. Helen Leuty. BoTP
In a September Night. F. Wyville Home. VA
In a shady nook one moonlit night. The Leprahaun. Robert Dwyer Joyce. OnYI; PoMS
In a Shop Window. Margaret E. Sangster. AlBD
In a sick shade of spruce, moss-webbed, rock-fed. As It Looked Then. E. A. Robinson. MaPo; NePA
In a sky of methylene blue. Fantasia. Carlos Drummond de Andrade. AnCL
In a slumber visional. The Vision of Mac Conglinne. *Unknown.* CAW
In a small chamber, friendless and unseen. William Lloyd Garrison. James Russell Lowell. LPS-3
In a snug little court as I stood t'other day. The Pleasing Constraint. Aristaenetus. ALV
In a solitude of the sea. The Convergence of the Twain. Thomas Hardy. CaAE; CoBMV; EnL; FaBoTw; InPo; LiTB; MaPo; MoAB; MoBrPo; MoPo; MoVE; OAEP (2d ed.); SeCeV; ShBV-3; ViP; ViPP
In a somer sesun [*or* summer season], when softe [*or* soft] was the sonne [*or* sun *or* when the sun was softest]. Prologue [*or* The Induction *or* The Field Full of Folk]. William Langland. *Fr.* The Vision of Piers Plowman. BCEP; BEL; CoBE; EnLi-1; EnLit; EPP; MeEV; PoEL-1; PoLi; TCEP
In a Southern Garden. Dorothea Mackellar. BoAu
In a Spring Grove. William Allingham. IrPN
In a stable bare. Yuletide. Alice Furlong. JKCP
In a Staffordshire Churchyard. *Unknown.* WhC (Four Country Epitaphs.) GoTP
In a stately hall at Brentford, when the English June was green. The Last Meeting of Pocahontas and the Great Captain. Margaret Junkin Preston. GA; MC; PAH
In a Station of the Metro. Ezra Pound. AmP; CoV; ExPo; InP; MAP; MoAB; MoAmPo; NeMA; OxBA; UnPo
In a still room at hush of dawn. The Eavesdropper. Bliss Carman. BAP
In a Storm. Harry Kemp. PFY
In a stormwind, single, undying. Liberty for All. Viktor Khlebnikov. BoRS
In a Strange House. Stanley J. Kunitz. NP
In a summer season, when soft was the sun. *See* In a somer sesun, when softe was the sonne.
In a Sunny Nook. Hans Vilhelm Kaalund, *tr. fr. Danish by* Charles W. Stork. BoDS
In a sweet springtime. Easter Prayer. Nancy Byrd Turner. PraP
In a tabernacle of a toure [*or* tower]. *Unknown.* *Fr.* Quia Amore Langueo. ACP; CoBE
In a tangled, scented hollow. Sleep. Lewis Frank Tooker. AA
In a temple at Kioto in far-away Japan. The Three Wise Monkeys. Florence Boyce Davis. WBLP
In a throng, a festal company. Wordsworth. *Fr.* The Prelude. OBRV
In a Time of Crisis. Lawrence Durrell. LiTM
In a Time of Pestilence. Thomas Nashe. *See* Adieu, Farewell, Earth's Bliss!
In a Town Garden. Donald Mattam. FiBHP
In a Troubled Dream. Stanton A. Coblentz. UnW
In a Troubled World. Stanton A. Coblentz. ChIP
In a valley, centuries ago. The Petrified Fern. Mary Lydia Bolles Branch. AA; CV; LPS-3; PTA-2
In a Valley of This Restless Mind. Ewart Milne. NeIP
In a valley [*or* valey *or* the vale *or* the vaile] of this restless [*or* of restles] mind [*or* minde *or* mynd]. Quia Amore Langueo. *Unknown.* AtBAP; CoEV; EnLit; LiA; LiTG; LiTL; LO; OBEV; OxBoCh; PoEL-1; PoLi; WoL
In a Vermont bedroom closet. A Record Stride. Robert Frost. NePA
In a Volume of Austin Dobson. Mary Elizabeth Coleridge. PoVP
In a week of perpetual rain. The Tray. Thomas Cole. NePoAm
In a while they rose and went out aimlessly riding. Merlin Enthralled. Richard Wilbur. NePoEA
In a white gully among fungus red. Native-born. Eve Langley. BoAV; NeLNL
In a wild moraine of forgotten books. The Old School List. James Kenneth Stephen. CenHV
In a Woman's Face. Richard Church. LO; LoPS
In a Wood. Thomas Hardy. *Fr.* The Woodlanders. InP; OAEP; POTT; ViP
In a Wood Clearing. Wilson MacDonald. CaP; OCL
In a wood they call the Rouge Bouquet. Rouge Bouquet. Joyce Kilmer. CV; DD; DDA; HBV; MC; NV; OBAV; PaA; PAH; PFY; SBMV; TreFS
In a world of battlefields there came. When the Dead Men Die. Rose O'Neill. HBMV
In a world of orange serenity. The Lacemaker (Vermeer). Anne Marx. GoYe
In a wreath of myrtle I'll wear my glaive. Callistratus, *tr. fr. Greek by* John Conington. GrPo
In a Year. Robert Browning. AtBAP; BMEP; EPN; LPS-1; PIR; VLEP
In Absence. Avenzoar, *tr. fr. Arabic by* A. J. Arberry. MooP
In Absence. Benedikt Gröndal, *tr. fr. Icelandic by* Watson Kirkconnell. IcP
In Absence. James Russell Lowell. BAV
In Absence. Robert Cameron Rogers. PR
In Absence. Tu Fu, *tr. fr. Chinese by* Herbert A. Giles. OuHeWo
In Acceptance Lieth Peace. Amy Carmichael. MaRV
In Action. *Unknown.* MDAH
In Adam's Fall. The New England Primer. *Unknown.* HiLiAm
In Africa. Roy Fuller. BoSA
In Africa (a quarter of the world). Timbuctoo. Thackeray PA
In Afric's fabled mountains I have panned the golden sand. The Alien. Charles Murray. MM
In After Days. George Frederick Cameron. BoCaPo; CaP; CPG
In After Days. Austin Dobson. BLV; BMEP; BPN;

In After Days (*continued*)
CBOV; EnLit; HBV; InP; LEAP; MaRV; MBP; MoBrPo (1942 ed.); NeMA; OBEV; OBVV; OQP; POT; PoTo; POTT; PoVP; QP-2; TCEP; TOP; TreFS; TSW; TSWC; VA; VLEP
(In After Days When Grasses High.) VOD
In After Time. Walter Savage Landor. VA
(Epigram: "No, my own love of other years.") EV-4
(No, My Own Love of Other Years.) BPN
In after times when strength or courage fail. Buffel's Kop. Roy Campbell. ChMP
In after years, when you look back upon. The Window. Francis Scarfe. NeBP
In all complaints that show a threat'ning form. Physician's Advice. Augustus Peck Clarke. PoP
In all good Greek of Plato. *See* In all the good Greek of Plato.
In all happiness and peace of mind. What Followed. Josephine Miles. FiMAP
In all his life and teaching. Certainties. Kenneth W. Porter. ChIP
In all my Emma's beauties blest. Emma. Goldsmith. OnYI
In all my life, oh God,/ This hour stands first. Love. Victor Hugo. *Fr.* Ruy Blas. LiA
In all my loving, dreaming, suffering. To My Friends in São Paulo. Olavo Bilac. BoFr
In all senses, forever, the silence palpitates. Apotheosis. Jules Laforgue. AnFP
In All the Argosy of Your Bright Hair. Dunstan Thompson. WaP
In all the Eastern hemisphere. The Fall of J. W. Beane. Oliver Herford. StPo
In all the four seas. The Taoist Monk. Tu Hsün Hao. OnPM
In all the good Greek of Plato. Survey of Literature. John Crowe Ransom. FaBoCh; LiTA; LoGBV; LS; SiTL
In All the Humors. Martial. *See* Temperament.
In all the land, range up, range down. Langley Lane. Robert Buchanan. HBV
In all the lands there are, from Cadiz to. The Vanity of Human Wishes. Juvenal. Satires, X. LaP
In all the towns and cities fair. Thomas Winterbottom Hance. W. S. Gilbert. InMe
In all the world. Fujiwara no Toshinari, *tr. fr. Japanese by* Kenneth Rexroth. OnPJ
In all they brood. Numbers. Agnes Lee. NP
In All Things, Victory. Nagata, *tr. fr. Japanese by* Lois J. Erickson. PraP; SoLD
In all thy humors, whether grave or mellow. Temperament [*or* To a Capricious Friend *or* In All the Humors]. Martial. AWP; BOHV; JAWP; OnPM; WBP
In alternate measure chanting, daily sing we Mary's praise. Irish Hymn to Mary. *Unknown.* CAW
In amaze. Ode to Quinbus Flestrin. Pope. OAEP
In among the silver birches winding ways of tarmac wander. Indoor Games near Newbury. John Betjeman. MoPW; MoVE
In Ampezzo ("In days of summer let me go"). Trumbull Stickney. TwAmPo
In Ampezzo ("Only once more and not again"). Trumbull Stickney. AnFE; APA; CoAnAm; CrMA; TwAmPo
In Amsterdam there dwells [*or* dwelt *or* lived] a maid. The Maid of Amsterdam [*or* A-Roving]. *Unknown.* AmSS; OxBoLi; SG; ShS; SoAmSa
In an age of fops and toys. Voluntaries, III [*or* Duty *or* So Nigh Is Grandeur]. Emerson. AnNE; HBVY; LiTA; MaRV; PoeMoYo; TreFS; YT
In an Age of Science. Thomas Curtis Clark. MaRV
In an Alameda Field. Anna Catherine Markham. BAP
In an arboure of green may. *Unknown.* SeCSL
In an Artist's Studio. Christina Rossetti. EnLi-2; OAEP; POTT; VLEP
In an attic bare and cheerless, Jim the newsboy dying lay. The Dying Newsboy. Emily Thornton. PTA-2
In an Auction Room. Christopher Morley. OBAV
In an Autumn Wood. William Alexander Percy. HBMV
In an autumnal evening, cool and still. The Cathedral-Walk. George Crabbe. *Fr.* Tales of the Hall. EnSW
In an Empty House. Ivan Alekseyevich Bunin, *tr. fr. Russian by* Babette Deutsch. TrRV
In an envelope marked:/ Personal. Personal. Langston Hughes. PoNe
In an idle hour I thought of former days. Thinking of the Past. Po Chü-i. TrCh
In an ocean, 'way out yonder. The Dinkey-Bird. Eugene Field. AA; BOHV; HBVY; HiLiAm; LBN; NA; PFY; TreFS; TSW; TSWC; UTS
In an old and ashen island. Sappho's Tomb. Arthur Stringer. CaP; OCL
In an Old Barn. Sir Charles G. D. Roberts. BoCaPo
In an old book at even as I read. "Ex Libris." Arthur Upson. HBV; LBMV; LEAP
In an old chamber softly lit. During a Chorale by César Franck. Witter Bynner. *Fr.* To Celia. AnAmPo; HBMV; LA; NP
In an old city by the storied shores. Opportunity. Edwin Markham. OQP; QP-2
In an Old Library. Yuan Mei, *tr. fr. Chinese by* L. Cranmer-Byng. LiTW
In an Old Nursery. Patrick R. Chalmers. HBMV; VOD
In an old print. The Lake Boats. Edgar Lee Masters. NP
In an Oriental Harbour. Cale Young Rice. VOD
In ancient days there lived [*or* dwelt] a Turk. Kafoozalum [*or* Kafoozelum]. *Unknown.* BeLS; BLPA; SoAF
In ancient time old men observed that. Of Clergymen and Their Livings. Sir John Harington. TuPP
In ancient [*or* antient] times, as story tells. Baucis and Philemon. Swift. CEP; CG; EiPP; GN; GoTL; KN; OBEC; OTPC (1946 ed.); StPo
In ancient times I heard of the south acres. Remembering the Ancient Farmstead. Tao Yuan-ming. WhP
In ancient times the hungry gods. The Ways of the Gods. Stanton A. Coblentz. OQP; QP-2
I-n and O-u-t. *Unknown.* MuP
In Angel-Court the sunless air. For a Charity Annual. Austin Dobson. TCEP
In another country, black poplars shake themselves over a pond. The North Country. D. H. Lawrence. OAEP (2d ed.)
In Answer to a Lady Who Advised Retirement. Lady Mary Wortley Montagu. DiM; OBEC
In Answer to a Question. Wilfrid Scawen Blunt. The Love Sonnets of Proteus, XXVIII. ViBoPo
In any hour the singers with mouths of gold. Two Musics. Norman McCaig. NeBP
In any medium except that of verse. One-Way Song, XXIV. Wyndham Lewis. SiTL
In Apia Bay. Sir Charles G. D. Roberts. PAH
In April. Elizabeth Akers Allen. OTPC (1946 ed.); PRWS
(Spring at the Capital.) MDAH
In April. Emily Gail Arnold. PEDC
In April. Margaret Lee Ashley. OBAV
In April. John Richard Moreland. LS
In April. Ethelwyn Wetherald. CaP; OCL
In April/ Come he will. The Cuckoo. *Unknown.* BoTP
In April cuckoos come. Signs and Charms. *Unknown.* StaSt
In April Once, *sel.* William Alexander Percy.
Spring of God, The. OQP; QP-2
In April sun the dead march played. Appomattox. MacKinlay Kantor. AnAmPo
In April the moon is a thin feather of bloom. A Spring Garland. James Rorty. MOAP
In Arabia's book of fable. Princess Sabbath. Heine. TrJP
In Arcadia. Lawrence Durrell. FaBoMo
In Arcadie. Helen Merrill Egerton. CPG
In Arcady. Cosmo Monkhouse. OBVV
In Ariostum Orlandi Furiosi Autorem. John Heath. SiCE
In Arizona, *sels.* William Haskell Simpson.
Bareback. NP
Burdens. NP
Hoppi Ghosts. NP
Pity Not. HBMV; NP
Trees. NP
In Armorik, that called is Britayne. The Franklin's Tale. Chaucer. *Fr.* The Canterbury Tales. OAEP
In arrogance and vanity. Only One King. John Richard Moreland. ChIP; PGD
In as Much . . . "Æ." ChMo; CMP
In Asinum Christi Vectorem. Richard Crashaw, *tr. fr. Latin by* D. C. Allen. Epigrammata Sacra, I, 2. LaP
In Auchtermuchty there dwelt ane man. The Wife of Auchtermuchty. *Unknown.* EBSV; GoTS
In August. William Dean Howells. GN; PoRL
In August the cool wind blows to drive the heat away. August. Lu Yu. WhP
In Autumn. Frances Kiely. CAG
In Autumn. George Sterling. MOAP; UnW
In autumn down the beechwood path. Beech Leaves. James Reeves. AlDL
In autumn pastures where a bird had flown. Autumn Bird. Howard McKinley Corning. MAP; MoAmPo (1942 ed.)
In Autumn tomboy winds begin to throw. Old Nurse Winter. Jean Starr Untermeyer. TSW
In autumpn whan the sun in Virgine. The Bowge of Court. John Skelton. ReIE
In awe before life's penny show. Poet. Nat Henry. PFE
In Baalbec there were lovers. The Passing Flower. Harry Kemp. HBMV
In Babylon, where first her queen, for state. Pyramus and Thisbe. Ovid. OuHeWo
In Ballades things always contrive to get lost. A Ballade of Ballade-Mongers. Augustus M. Moore. BOHV; PA
In Baltimore there lived a boy. The Boy Who Laughed at Santa Claus. Ogden Nash. CenHV; MaC; StPo
In Barracks. Siegfried Sassoon. FaBoTw
In Battle. Abul Hasan of Badajoz, *tr. fr. Arabic by* A. J. Arberry. MooP

In Battle. Wallace Stevens. NP
In battle-line of sombre gray. The Spirit of the *Maine.* Tudor Jenks. AA; MC; PAH
In Beatae Virginis Verecundiam. Richard Crashaw, *tr. fr. Latin by* D. C. Allen. Epigrammata Sacra, II, 11. LaP
In Beatricem Praepropere Defunctam ("In Beatrice did all perfections grow"). John Heath. TuPP
In Bed. Jacqueline Green. CAG
In bed, asleep, I dream. Leaving the Monastery Early in the Morning. Lu Yu. OnPC
In Bertram's Garden. Donald Justice. NePoEA
In Bethlehem, that [*or* in that] fair city. To Bliss God Bring Us All and Some. *Unknown.* AnEC
In Bethlehem, That Noble Place. *Unknown.* AnEC
In Bethlehem, Today. Madeleine Sweeney Miller. PSO
In Beverley town a maid did dwell. The Beverley Maid and the Tinker. *Unknown.* CoMu
In Bibberley Town, *with music. Unknown.* SaSa
In black skies a storm is streaming. Winter Evening. Pushkin. BoR
In blessèd silence vegetates the place. The Parish Church. Julio Herrera y Reissig. CAW
In bloody fields she sits as gay. Honour. Bernard Mandeville. *Fr.* On Honour. BeR
In blossoms white my cherry tree stands framed. Cherry Tree. Hermann Claudius. TwGV
In blows the loitering air of spring. Spring Air. Gene Derwood. FaFP; GTBS-W; LiTL
In Bodenstown Churchyard there is a green grave. Tone's Grave. Thomas Osborne Davis. OnYI
In Bodleian and Harleian/ Lurk ambushes of grace. Our Lady of the Libraries. Sister Mary Ignatius. ISi
In bodnie (bonnie), bright and fair Scotland, where bluebells they did grow. The Paisley Officer, *vers.* II. *Unknown.* ShS
In body alone was Zosime. "The Vasty Halls of Death." Damascius. GrPE
In Bohemia. John Boyle O'Reilly. LHV
In bower fair Ingelil. The Dragon. *Unknown.* BoDaBa
In bower sat Hillelil. The Griefs of Hillelille. *Unknown.* BoDaBa
In Bowre and Field he sought, where any tuft. Eve. Milton. *Fr.* Paradise Lost, IX. OBS
In boxes lined with faded satin. Pawnshop Window. R. H. Grenville. GoYe
In Breughel's great picture, The Kermess. The Dance. William Carlos Williams. AmP; ExPo; LoGBV; OxBA
In Brittany ("In Brittany the churches"). E. V. Lucas. WHL
In Brittany ("In Brittany I lost my way"). Charles Weekes. OnYI
In Brittany there lived a lad. The Heart. *Unknown.* MaC
In broad daylight I dream I. A Dream at Night. Mei Yao Ch'en. OnPC
In Broad Daylight I Dream of My Dead Wife. Mei Yao Ch'en, *tr. fr. Chinese by* Kenneth Rexroth. OnPC
In Broad Street building (on a winter night). The Gouty Merchant and the Stranger. Horace Smith. BeLS; BOHV; LPS-3
In Broken Images. Robert Graves. CoEV; MoP
In Brunton Town. *Unknown.* BaBo
(Bruton Town, *diff. vers.*) EnSB
"In Buckinghamshire hedgerows." The Icosasphere. Marianne Moore. ImOP
In Cabin'd Ships at Sea. Walt Whitman. IAP
In Cacum. Thomas Bastard. SiCE
In Caium. Thomas Bastard. SiCE
In calm and cool and silence, once again. First-Day Thoughts. Whittier. AmPP; CoV; IAP; PreP
In calm and heavenly dream she seems to float. Epiphany. Leconte de Lisle. TrFP
In came her sister. Lady Maisry (B *vers.*). *Unknown.* ESPB
In Camp. William Haines Lytle. BIG
In candent ire the solar splendor flames. Aestivation [*or* Intramural Aestivation]. Oliver Wendell Holmes. *Fr.* The Autocrat of the Breakfast-Table. AmPP; AnNE; BOHV; ChTr; InMe; NA; REAL; WhC
In careless days now dim. Native Land. Gina Ballantyne. BoAu
In Carmel Bay the people say. Abalone. *Unknown.* AS
In Carnival we were, and supp'd that night. Versailles. Stopford Augustus Brooke. VA
In Caroline, whar I was born. Walk, Jaw-Bone. S. S. Steele. TrAS
In Cavan of little lakes. A Song of Freedom. Alice Milligan. AnIV; OnYI; PoFr
In caves emptied of their workers, turning. The Angels at Hamburg. Randall Jarrell. AmP
In Cawsand Bay lying, with the Blue Peter flying. Cawsand Bay [*or* Fine New Ballad of Cawsand Bay]. *Unknown.* OBB; PC
In cerements of painted linen wound. The Vase of Myrrh. Thomas S. Jones, Jr. MuM
In Chains. Albrecht Haushofer, *tr. fr. German by* Herman Salinger. *Fr.* Sonnets from Moabite Prison. TwGV
In Cherbourg Roads the pirate lay. The Eagle and Vulture. Thomas Buchanan Read. PAH
In Cherry Lane. William Livingston. JKCP
In Childhood and Youth. Wordsworth. *Fr.* The Prelude, I *and* II. GrCo-2
In childhood, when with eager eyes. The Trance of Time. Cardinal Newman. OxBoCh
In childhood's pride I said to Thee. The Soul's Prayer. Sarojini Naidu. MaRV
In Childhood's unsuspicious hours. Epicurean. William James Linton. VA
In Christ I feel the heart of God. Our Christ. Lucy Larcom. MaRV; OQP; QP-1; StJW
In Christ there is no East or [*or* nor] West. All One in Christ [*or* No East or West *or* Brothers of the Faith]. John Oxenham. BLRP; ChIP; MaRV; OQP; QP-1
In Christian world Mary the garland wears! The Names. Charles Lamb. OTPC (1923 ed.)
In Christophorum. Thomas Freeman. SiCE
In Church. Thomas Hardy. Satires of Circumstance, II. MBP; MoAB; MoBrPo
In church your grandsire cut his throat. On the Upright Judge [Who Condemned the "Drapier's" Printer]. Swift. ALV; SiTL
"In churches," said the Pardoner, "when I preach." Prologue to the Pardoner's Tale. Chaucer. *Fr.* The Canterbury Tales. EnL
In Chus. *Unknown.* TuPP
In cinemas we sought. Sing, Brothers, Sing! W. R. Rodgers. MoAB; MoBrPo (1950 ed.)
In Ciprium. Sir John Davies, *after the Latin of* Martial. ReIE; SiCE; TuPP
In City Streets. Ada Smith. HBV; NLK; OTPC (1923 ed.); PoeT; PYM
In cleft of valley and slope of hill. Flanders Roses. Nikolai Tikhonov. RuPo
In Clementina's Artless Mien. Walter Savage Landor. *See* Of Clementina.
In Cleversulzbach under the wold. The Old Church Cock. Eduard Mörike. AnGP
In cloisters dim and haunted. An Eastern Legend. Margaret L. Woods. UnW
In Clonmel Parish Churchyard. Sarah Morgan Bryan Piatt. AA
In clouds she shines, and so obscurely shineth. Thomas Watson. *Fr.* The Tears of Fancy. TuPP
In cock-wattle sunset or grey. Nostalgia. Louis MacNeice. GTBS-D; OnYI
In college days I studied Greek and Latin Composition. Ain't Education Grand? Jean Gillespie. DDA
In colleges and halls, in ancient days. Discipline in Education. William Cowper. *Fr.* The Task. CoBE
In Collins Street standeth a statue tall. Gone. Adam Lindsay Gordon. BoAu
In coming down to Manchester to gain my liberty. The Soldier's Farewell to Manchester. *Unknown.* CoMu
In coming to the feast I found. The Horn. Léonie Adams. AnAmPo; InPo; LA; MAP; MoAB; MoAmPo
In Commendation of George Gascoigne's Steel Glass. Sir Walter Ralegh. SiPS
In Commendation of Music. William Strode. OBEV (new ed.)
(Commendation of Music, The.) SeCL
In Common. Gene Derwood. NePA
In Conclusion. Abbie Huston Evans. NP
In concord then they set up hasty ways. Freighter. Bruce Ruddick. CaP
In Conjunction. Charles Madge. FaBoMo; NeBP
In Controversial Foul Impureness. Arthur Hugh Clough. ViPP
(Noli Aemulari.) PoVP
In Conway town there did dwell. O Johnny Dear, Why Did You Go? *Unknown.* ABS
In coolness of a valley. The Broken Ring. Joseph von Eichendorff. AnGP
In Córdoba within the drowsing Plaza. Quién Sabe? Ruth Comfort Mitchell. PoMa; VOD
In Country Sleep. Dylan Thomas. LiTB; LiTM (rev. ed.)
In country towns at sunrise, languid bells. Morning Bells. Georges Rodenbach. TrFP
In Course of Time. W. W. Gibson. ChMo; CMP
In court to serve, decked with fresh array. The Courtier's Life. Sir Thomas Wyatt. ReIE
In Coventry. James J. Daly. CAW
In Crystal Towers. Geffrey Whitney. ElSeCe
(Content.) ElL
("In crystal towers, and turrets richly set.") SiCE
(Song: "In crystal towers [towns, *wr.*] and turrets richly set.") ACP
In Cumberland city, as you shall all hear. Villkins and His Dinah (A *vers.*). *Unknown.* BaBo
In Cypres Sat Fair Venus by a Fount. Robert Greene. ReIE

In Cyprus springs—whereas dame Venus dwelt. Complaint of the Lover Disdained. Earl of Surrey. BEL; SiPS
In Dacum. Sir John Davies. TuPP
In dangerous times we two came south. To a Friend Bound North after the Rebellion. Ssu-k'ung Shu. BoFr
In Dark Hour. Seumas MacManus. JKCP; WGRP
In dark Thermopylae they lie. On Those Who Fell at Thermopylae. Simonides, *tr. by* Robert Bland. GrR; PoFr
In darkest hours I hear a voice. Jesus Is Near. Robert Cassie Waterston. BePJ
In darkness the loud sea makes moan. The Charm. Rupert Brooke. LoPo
In Dat Great Gittin' Up Mornin'. *Unknown.* AA; BoAN-2, *with music*
In Days Gone By. Ida M. Mills. BoTP
In days gone by, when a baby I. Three Lullabies. Fred Emerson Brooks. BOL
In Days like These. Thomas H. Stacy. MDAH
In days long gone God spake unto our sires. The Call. Thomas Curtis Clark. PGD
In days of ease, when now the weary sword. Court of Charles II. Pope. *Fr.* To Augustus. OBEC
In days [*or* the days] of old, when Englishmen were—men. Italian Opera. James Miller. OBEC; UnS
In days of old when knights caught cold. Thoughts on Progress. David Daiches. SiTL
In days of old, when knights were bold. A Warrior Bold. Edwin Thomas. OlF
In days of old when Spenser sang. Ballade of the Goth. Sir Walter Raleigh. WhC
In days of peace my fellow-men. From a Full Heart. A. A. Milne. BOHV; InMe
In days of summer let me go. In Ampezzo, II. Trumbull Stickney. TwAmPo
In days of yore, from Britain's shore. The Maple Leaf Forever. Alexander Muir. BoHiPo
In days when Albion's seamen knew. Sea-Birds. Fray Angelico Chavez. ISi
In days when George the Third was King. Miss Nancy's Gown. Zitella Cocke. AA
In de ebening by de moonlight when dis darkie's work was over. In the Evening by the Moonlight. James A. Bland. TreFS
In de Lord, in de Lord. My Soul's Been Anchored in de Lord. *Unknown.* BoAN-2; OlF
In de Mornin', *with music. Unknown.* SoAmSa
In de Vinter Time, *with music. Unknown.* AS
In Deadly Fear. Blake. *Fr.* Jerusalem. SeCePo
In Death. Mary Emily Bradley. AA
In Debtor's Yard the stones are hard. Oscar Wilde. *Fr.* The Ballad of Reading Gaol. ViBoPo
In December. Andrew Young. SeCePo
In December, when the days draw to be short. Little John Nobody. *Unknown.* OxBoLi
In Decium. Sir John Davies. TuPP
In deep blue sky the sun is bright. Alfred Domett. *Fr.* Ranolf and Amohia. AnNZ
In Deep Places. Amelia Josephine Burr. AV
In Defense of Felons. Robert Mezey. NePoEA
In Defence of Humanism. David Gascoyne. LiTM (rev. ed.)
In Defence of Satire. Pope. *See* Satire: "Ask you what provocation I have had?"
In Defense of Children. Arthur Guiterman. FAOV
In Defense of Their Inconstancy. Ben Jonson. ReEn
In Defense of Youth. Robbins Wolcott Barstow. QP-2
In Derision of a Country Life. Edward Ravenscroft. *Fr.* The Italian Husband. SeCL
In Description. Ann Louise Hayes. PtPa
In Desert Places. Sister Mary Madeleva. GoTP
In desolation, here a lost world lies. Epitaph, Found Somewhere in Space. Hugh Wilgus Ramsaur. MaRV; MuM
In despair at not being able to rival the creations of God. Hymn to Her Unknown. Walter James Turner. LiTL; LiTM; OBMV
In Die Nativitatis ("Nowell, nowell, nowell, nowell,/ Tidings good I think to tell"). *Unknown.* AnEC (Christmas Carol, A: "Borys hede that we bryng here, The.") EnLit
In Die Nativitatis ("Nowell, nowell, nowell, nowell."/ "Who is there that singeth so nowell"). *Unknown.* AnEC
In digging up your bones, Tom Paine. Tom Paine. Byron. BoHiPo
In dim green depths rot ingot-laden ships. Sunken Gold. Eugene Lee-Hamilton. EtS; VA
In Dispraise of the Moon. Mary Elizabeth Coleridge. CH
In distant countries have I seen. The Last of the Flock. Wordsworth. CG
In distant days of wild romance. Now and Then. Jane Taylor. OTPC (1923 ed.)
In distant lands the statesmen scheme and plot. Sonnet for My Dog. Thomas Curtis Clark. AlBD
In distant Yith past crested, ragged peaks. Dreams of Yith. Duane W. Rimel. DaM
In Distrust of Merits. Marianne Moore. AmPP; CoBMV; LiTA; LiTM; MoAB; MoAmPo (1950 ed.); NePA; OxBA; PoRL; SeCeV; TrGrPo (rev. ed.); UnPo (3d ed.); ViBoPo (1958 ed.); WaaP; WaP
In dog-days plowmen quit their toil. The Swimmer. John Crowe Ransom. PFY
In Domrèmy a maid. The Maid of Arc. Gordon Bottomley. GoTL (1949 ed.)
In Doubt of Doubt. Robert Browning. *Fr.* Bishop Blougram's Apology. MaRV
In dream, again within the clean cold hell. The Gorse. W. W. Gibson. AtBAP; TCPD
In dream I saw two Jews that met by chance. Moses and Jesus. Israel Zangwill. TrJP
In dreams a dark château. The Dark Château. Walter de la Mare. POTT
In dreams I see the Dromedary still. The Dromedary. Archibald Y. Campbell. HBMV; PFE; PoMa; PtOT; StaSt
In Dresden, in the square one day. The Violinist. Archibald Lampman. CaP; OCL
In dressing a calve's head, although. A Calf's Head Meeting. Samuel Butler. *Fr.* Hudibras. BeR
In Dublin's fair city, where the girls are so pretty. Cockles and Mussels [*or* Molly Malone]. *Unknown.* LO; MaC; OnYI
In due course of course you will be issued with. Unarmed Combat. Henry Reed. Lessons of the War, III. LiTB
In due season the amphibious crocodile. Amphibious Crocodile. John Crowe Ransom. AnAmPo; LA
In Dulci Iubilo [*or* Jubilo]. John Wedderburn, *after the German.* AnEC; ChTr
In Dulci Jubilo. *Unknown, tr. fr. Middle High German by* Paul Crowley. CAW
In each green leaf a memory let lie. With Roses. Beatrix Demarest Lloyd. AA
In each mans heart that doth begin. Loves World. Sir John Suckling. SeCV-1
In Earliest Spring. William Dean Howells. AA; FaBoBe; PFY
In Early Morning. Tao Yuan-ming, *tr. fr. Chinese by* Yang Chi-sing. WhP
In Early Spring. Victor Hugo, *tr. fr. French by* Alan Conder. TrFP
In Early Spring. Alice Meynell. AnFE; HBV
In early spring when Samuel plows. On Our Farm. Esther Antin. RIS
In Early Summer Lodging in a Temple to Enjoy the Moonlight. Po Chü-i, *tr. fr. Chinese by* Arthur Waley. LiTW; TrCh
In early summer the woods and herbs are thriving. Reading "The Book of Strange Places and Seas." Tao Yuan-ming. WhP
In early winter before the first snow. An Elegy. E. J. Scovell. ChMP
In early youth, as you may guess. The Young Gazelle. Walter Parke. BOHV
In early youth I made a vow. Brown Eyes. Mrs. S. L. Dempsey. AlBD
In earth is a little thing. The Rule of Money. *Unknown.* PoFr
In Earthen Vessels. Whittier. *Fr.* The Friend's Burial. BLRP
In easy dialogue is Fletcher's praise. To My Dear Friend, Mr. Congreve, on His Comedy Called "The Double-Dealer." Dryden. CEP; FiP; GEPC; NBE; OBS; PoE; PoEL-3; PtP
In Ed. Allen. John Weever. ReIE
In eddying course when leaves began to fly. On Echo and Silence. Sir Samuel Egerton Brydges. ES
In Egypt they worshipped me. I Am the Cat. Leila Usher. BLPA
In eighteen hundred and forty-five. Greenland Whale Fishery. *Unknown.* OuSiCo
In eighteen hundred and forty one [*or* forty-wan]. Paddy [*or* Pat] Works on the Railway [*or* the Erie]. *Unknown.* ABF; TrAS
In eighteen hundred and forty-six. A-Working on the Railway. Arthur H. Clark. IHA
In eighteen hundred and sixty-one. The *Alabama, vers.* II. *Unknown.* ShS
In eighteen ninety 'twas a sleigh. Enter Saint Nicholas! *Unknown.* CAG
In either hand the hastening angel caught. The Departure from Paradise. Milton. *Fr.* Paradise Lost, XII. LPS-1
In either mood, to bless or curse. Doom. Arthur O'Shaughnessy. MBP; MoBrPo (1942 ed.); OBVV
In elder times an ancient custom 'twas. Swearing. Henry Fitzsimon. ACP (1952 ed.)
In eloquence no man could equal him. Pericles. Eupolis. OxBG
In England from the train you see. From the Train. Marjorie Wilson. BoTP

In England, on the downs. The Refugee. Lord Dunsany. NeTW
In England there was a lordling born. Hynd [*or* Hynde] Horn. *Unknown.* GN; OBB
In enterprise of martial kind. The Duke of Plaza-Toro. W. S. Gilbert. *Fr.* The Gondoliers. ALV; FaPON; FiBHP; OnPP; PCD
In Epitaphium Pingui Minerva Compositum. Thomas Freeman. TuPP
In Eternum I Was Once Determed. Sir Thomas Wyatt. MaPo; NBE; SiPS
In every clime, from Ganges' distant stream. The Vanity of Human Wishes. Juvenal. *Fr.* Satires, X. RoL
In every leaf that crowns the plain. Faith. John Richard Moreland. LS; OHIP
In every line a supple beauty. A Likeness. Willa Cather. HBMV
In every meanest face I see. Sons of Promise. Thomas Curtis Clark. PoToHe
In every race, in every creed. Universal Language. Josephine Robinson. BoHiPo
In every seed to breathe the flower. Faith. John Banister Tabb. WGRP
In every solemn tree the wind. Love Song from New England. Winifred Welles. AV; HBMV; MAP
In every trembling bud and bloom. An Easter Canticle. Charles Hanson Towne. ChIP; MaRV, *abr.*; OHIP; QS; TrPWD
In every village marked with little spire. The Village Schoolmistress. William Shenstone. *Fr.* The Schoolmistress. LPS-2
In every war, strange legends circulate. Philippine Madonna. Louise Crenshaw Ray. ISi
In every way of life true pleasure flows. Metrodorus, *tr. fr. Greek by* John Beaumont. GrPo
In Evil Long I Took Delight. John Newton. MaRV; OxBoCh
(Looking at the Cross.) BePJ
In ev'ry thought, in ev'ry wish I own. Joseph Howe. *Fr.* Acadia. CaP
In Excelsis. Thomas S. Jones, Jr. SBMV
In Excelsis. Amy Lowell. MAP; MoAmPo
In Excelsis Gloria, *abr.* *Unknown.* COAH
(Christo Paremus Canticam, Excelsis Gloria.) AnEC
(When Christ Was Born of Mary Free.) MeEV
In Exile. B. E. Baughan. AnNZ
In Exile. Mary Elizabeth Blake. LBAP
In Exile. Heine, *tr. fr. German by* Kate Flores. AnGP
In Exile. Andrew Marvell. *See* Bermudas.
In Exile, VIII. Charles Ould. MM
In Exile; Reply. Sir Ronald Ross. *See* Lines Written after the Discovery . . . of the Germ of Yellow Fever.
In Explanation. Walter Learned. AA; HBV; LBAP
(Explanation, An.) ALV; PR
In Extremis. Fray Angelico Chavez. JKCP (1955 ed.)
In Extremis. Margaret Fishback. FiBHP
In Extremis. Vera Larminie. QS
In Extremis. George Sterling. HBV
In Extremity. Phoebe Cary. PraP
In Fable all things hold discourse. Ay and No. John Gay. CBOV
In facile natures fancies quickly grow. Perseverance. Leonardo da Vinci. LPS-3
In fair Calabria's woods a snake is bred. The Snake. Virgil, *tr. by* Dryden. *Fr.* Georgics. LiA
In fair Lo Yang. Joy. Fan Yün. PoHN
In fair Provence, the land of lute and rose. Sestina. Sir Edmund Gosse. InP
In fair Worcester City and in Worcestershire. The Gosport Tragedy (A *vers.*). *Unknown.* BaBo
In Fairyland. Joyce Kilmer. TSW
In faith, good Histor, long is your delay. Geron and Histor. Sir Philip Sidney. *Fr.* Arcadia. SiPS
In faith, I do not love thee with mine eyes. Sonnets, CXLI. Shakespeare. EtPaEn; MaPo; PeBoSo; PoEL-2; TrGrPo
In faith I wot not what to say. Sir Thomas Wyatt. SiPS
In faith methinks it is no right. Resignation. Sir Thomas Wyatt. OBSC
In Falmouth Harbour—I. Lionel Johnson. POTT
In far-famed Bagdad, in a druggist's shop. The Parrot of Bagdad. Jalal ed-Din Rumi. PeP
In far forests' leafy twilight, now is stealing gray dawn's shy light. Music of the Dawn. Virginia Bioren Harrison. HBV
In far Tibet/ There live a lama. I Will Arise and Go Now. Ogden Nash. WaKn
In fashion as a snow-white rose, lay then. Paradiso: The Saints in Glory. Dante. *Fr.* Divina Commedia. WGRP
In fathoms five the anchor gone. Hatteras. Philip Freneau. CoV
In Favor of One's Time. Frank O'Hara. NeAP
In fear of death do not neglect small bounty. Poem. John Prichard. MoWP
In fear of the rich mouth. The Frightened Man. Louise Bogan. MOAP
In Februar come foul days, flee them gin ye may. The Anatomy o Winter. Hesiod, *tr. by* Robert Garioch. *Fr.* Works and Days. PoN
In February. P. A. Ropes. BoTP
In February. Henry Simpson. HBV
In February. John Addington Symonds. DD; PRWS; YeAr
In February I give you gallant sport. Of the Months, February. Folgore da San Geminiano. AWP
In February there are days. When. Dorothy Aldis. SiSoSe
In February, when the sap's below. Pruning Vines. Howard McKinley Corning. MAP; MoAmPo (1942 ed.)
In fellowship of living things. A Creed. Ellen Glasgow. OQP; QP-1
In fellowship Religion has its founts. George Meredith. *Fr.* The Test of Manhood. WGRP
In Festubert. Edmund Blunden. OBMV
In fiction tales we keep performing. The Collies. Edward Anthony. GoTP
"In Fields Where Roses Fade." Pompeius, *tr. fr. Greek by* F. L. Lucas. GrPE
In fifty years, when peace outshines. Song-Books of the War Siegfried Sassoon. InP; PtOT
In '59 Pike's Peakers were a sight. The Pike's Peakers Lawrence N. Greenleaf. PoOW
In Fisherrow. W. E. Henley. VOD
In five-score summers! All new eyes. 1967. Thomas Hardy PG (1945 ed.)
In Flaccum. Sir John Davies. TuPP
In Flanders Fields. John McCrae. AOAH; BBV; BEL; BLPA; BMEP; BoCaPo; BTP; CaP; CP; CPG; DD; DDA; EnLit; FaFP; GrCo-1; GTSL; HBV; HH; InP; LEAP; MaRV; MBP; MCCG; MM; MPB; NeHB; NeMA; OCL; OHFP; OQP; OtMeF; OTPC (1946 ed.); PaA; PCD; PeCV; PEDC; PFE; PGD; PoFr; PoMa; PoP; PoRL; POT; PoTo; PTA-1; PYM; QP-2; SiSoSe; SoV; SP; StVeCh (1940 ed.); TreF; TVSH; TwCaPo; ViBoPo; YT
In Flanders Fields. *Unknown.* WBLP
In Flanders Fields; an Answer. C. B. Galbreath. *See* Another Reply to "In Flanders Fields."
In Flanders fields peace reigns to-night. A Flanders Grave. Nathaniel Nathanson. POT
In Flanders Fields the cannon boom. Another Reply to "In Flanders Fields" [*or* In Flanders Fields; an Answer]. C. B. Galbreath. BLPA; HH; PTA-1
In Flanders Fields the poppies grow. Far Away from Flanders Field. L. S. Uphoff. PSO
"In Flanders fields, where poppies blow." Old Soldier Dead. Annette Kohn. HH
In Flanders Now. Edna Jaques. CaP; MaRV
In Flanders once there dwelt a company. The Pardoner's Tale. Chaucer. *Fr.* The Canterbury Tales. RiBV
In Flanders there was once a desperate set. Death and the Ruffians. Chaucer. *Fr.* The Canterbury Tales: The Pardoner's Tale. BCEP
In Flaundres whylom [*or* whilom] was a companye [*or* compaignye]. The Pardoner's Tale. Chaucer. *Fr.* The Canterbury Tales. BEL; CoBE; EM-1; EnLit; EV-1; FiP; LiA; OAEP; PoEL-1; WHA
In flow'ry Japan, the home of the fan. The Feast of the Doll. Nora Archibald Smith. PPL
In fond delusion once I left thy side. A Sonnet to My Mother. Heine. TrJP
In foreign land, with faith unshaken. The Bird. Pushkin. WaL
In foreign lands you will reside. The Hallowe'en Party: Nonsense Rimes for the Men. *Unknown.* HOAH
In Foreign Parts. Laura E. Richards. HBV; HBVY; LiL
In Forest Depths. Richard Henry Horne. *Fr.* Orion. VA
In form and feature, face and limb. The Twins. Henry Sambrooke Leigh. BOHV; CenHV; FaPON; GaP; GoTP; HBV; HBVY; MaC; OTPC (1946 ed.); PoeMoYo; PoMa; PYM; StaSt; StVeCh (1940 ed.); TiPo; TSW; TSWC; WaKn
In former days my father and mother. Cuckoo. *Unknown.* *Fr.* Riddles. AnOE
In former times, when Israel's ancient creed. Absolute and Abitofhell. Ronald Arbuthnott Knox. CenHV
In Fountain Court. Arthur Symons. PoeT; POTT; VLEP
In fourteen hundred and ninety-two. Christopher Columbus. Franklin Pierce Adams. InMe
In fourteen hundred and ninety-two. Christofo Columbo. *Unknown.* AmSS
In fourteen hundred and ninety-two. Moosehead Lake. *Unknown.* OuSiCo
In fourteen hundred ninety-two, Columbus sailed the ocean blue. The History of the U.S. Winifred Sackville Stoner. BLPA; TreF; YaD
In France. Frances Cornford. HBMV
In Freedom's War, of "Thirty Years" and more. Enfant Perdu [*or* Lost Child—Enfant Perdu]. Heine, *tr. by* Richard Monckton Milnes. AWP; OuHeWo; PoFr; WoL

In 'Frisco Bay there lay three ships. A Long Time Ago (C *vers.*). *Unknown.* SoAmSa
In front of our mouths, wherever we swim. Goldfish on the Writing Desk. Max Brod. LiTW; TrJP
In front of these came Addison. William Cowper. *Fr.* Table Talk. PtP
In front the awful Alpine track. Stanzas in Memory of the Author of "Obermann." Matthew Arnold. BPN; EM-2; EPN; GEPC; PoVP; ViPo; ViPP; VLEP
In front the horse's rump bright as a lantern. Sleighride. Patrick Anderson. CaP
In full-blown dignity, see Wolsey stand. Ambition. Samuel Johnson. *Fr.* The Vanity of Human Wishes. BHV
In Galilee. Mary Frances Butts. AA
In Galilee. Jessie Mackay. AnNZ
In Gayer Hours, when high my Fancy run. The Bastard's Lot. Richard Savage. *Fr.* The Bastard. OBEC
In Genesis, the world was made. Old Testament Contents. *Unknown.* BLPA
In Genoa a friar walked. The Friar of Genoa. Scharmel Iris. JKCP
In Genoa the superb O'Connell dies. The Dead Tribune. Denis Florence MacCarthy. ACP
In Gerontem. Sir John Davies. ReIE
In Gethsemane. Giles Fletcher. MaRV; StJW
In Gettysburg at break of day. The Charge of Pickett's Brigade. *Unknown.* PTA-2
In gladness past all words her white arms flung. Musaeus. *Fr.* Hero and Leander. GrPo
In Glencullen. J. M. Synge. OBMV; OxBI; ThWaDe
In Go-Cart So Tiny. Kate Greenaway. *See* Around the World.
In God's Eternal Studios. Paul Shivell. *Fr.* The Studios Photographic. HBV
In God's name, cheerly on, courageous friends. Shakespeare. King Richard III, *fr.* V, ii. PoFr
In God's own name, as I have said. Villon. *Fr.* The Testament. TrFP
In going to my naked bed, as one that would have slept. Amantium Irae. Richard Edwards. BOL; EIL; EV-1; HBV; KN; LEAP; LoBV; OBEV; OBSC; PoE; ReEn; ReIE; SiCE; TuPP
In good condition. For Sale, a Horse. Charles Edward Taylor. AA
In good King Charles's golden days. The Vicar of Bray. *Unknown.* ALV; CEP; EV-4; HBV; InvP; LPS-3; OBEC; OxBoLi; ViBoPo
In good old Benjamin Franklin's time. The Truth about B. F. Albert Stillman. InMe
In good old Colony times. Old Colony Times. *Unknown.* ABS
In good old days such sort of love held sway. Old-Time Love. Clément Marot. LiA
In Goya's greatest scenes we seem to see. A Coney Island of the Mind, 1. Lawrence Ferlinghetti. NeAP
In graceful windings, trailing their white exhaust. Sky Writers. William Rose Benét. PoF
In Gratitude for Friends. Margaret E. Sangster. PraP
In Grato Jubilo. David McCord. UnS
In graves where drips the winter rain. The Song of the Graves. *Unknown.* OBMV
In Great Bitterness. Cino da Pistoia. *See* Sonnet: To Love, in Great Bitterness.
In Greece the shadows slept as still. Hawaiian Hilltop. Genevieve Taggard. PoMa
In green Caledonia they ne'er were two lovers. Burns and His Highland Mary. *Unknown.* ShS
In Green Old Gardens. "Violet Fane." HBV; VA
In greenwoods once these relics must have known. Driftwood. Richard Wilbur. FiMAP
In grey April when the bud rounded. The Flute of May. Harry Woodbourne. GoYe
In grey-haired Celia's withered arms. A Paraphrase from the French. Matthew Prior. OxBoLi
In grief and anguish of my heart my voice I did extend. The Song of Jonah in the Whale's Belly. Michael Drayton. *Fr.* The Harmony of the Church. ReIE
In Guernica the dead children. Pastorale. Norman Rosten. SePoSe
In Guernsey. Swinburne. ATP (1935 ed.); BPN; PoVP; VLEP
In guilty night & hid in false disguise. *Unknown.* SeCSL
In Gusts of Music. Sister Davida. JKCP (1955 ed.)
In gutter and on sidewalk swells. Second Avenue. Orrick Johns. BAP
In Hades. Anna Callender Brackett. AA
In half-forgotten days of old. The Writing on the Image. William Morris. *Fr.* The Earthly Paradise. EmBrPo
In halls of sleep you wandered by. Among Shadows. Arthur Davison Ficke. NP
In Hampton Roads, the airs of March were bland. The Attack. Thomas Buchanan Read. PAH
In Hans' old mill his three black cats. Five Eyes. Walter de la Mare. PoC; UTS
In happier climes, for luckier men. The Player's Christmas. William Lackaye. CAG
In happy climes the seat of innocence. America. George Berkeley. *Fr.* Verses on the Prospect of Planting Arts and Learning in America. BeR
In Harbor. Paul Hamilton Hayne. AA; BAP; HBV; IAP; LBAP; PoeMoYo; SPP; TCAP
In Harbor. Lizette Woodworth Reese. TrPWD
In Hardin County, 1809. Lulu E. Thompson. BoHiPo; PoMa; StPo
In Harmony with Nature. Matthew Arnold. EPN; GEPC; MaRV; OAEP; PoVP; ViPP; VLEP
(To an Independent Preacher.) EmBrPo; PeBoSo; TOP
In haste the sons of Achaea, where the huts of their leaguer lay. The Scales of War. Homer. *Fr.* The Iliad, VIII. GrPE
In Havenpool Harbour the ebb was strong. The Mongrel. Thomas Hardy. AlBD
In having all things, and not Thee, what have I? Delight in God Only. Francis Quarles. *Fr.* Emblems. MaRV
In Hawaiian Seas. Clifford Gessler. PoTo
In Haywodum. Sir John Davies. ReIE; SiCE; TuPP
In health and ease am I. Francis Davison. EG
In hearts too young for enmity there lies the way. Disarm the Hearts. Ethel Blair Jordan. PGD
In Heaven,/ Some little blades of grass. The Blades of Grass. Stephen Crane. The Black Riders, XVIII. AmP; BAP; MAP; MaRV; MoAmPo; NeMA; PoeMoYo; PYM; TCAP
In Heaven a spirit doth dwell. Israfel. Poe. AA; AmP; AmPo; AmPP; AnAmPo; AnFE; APA; APW; AWP; BAP; BAV; BLV; BoLiVe; CoAnAm; CoBA; HBV; IAP; InPo; LA; LBAP; LEAP; LiTA; MOAP; NePA; OxBA; PoEL-4; PreP; PFY; REAL; RG; SPP; TCAP; TreFS; TSW; WHA
In heaven a Spirit doth dwell. Israfiddlestrings, *parody.* *Unknown.* BOHV
In heaven-high musings and many. The Strength of Fate. Euripides, *tr. by* A. E. Housman. *Fr.* Alcestis. AWP; JAWP; WBP
In Heaven, I Suppose, Lie Down Together. C. Day Lewis. ChMo; MoPo
In heaven soaring up I dropt an ear. The Joy of Church Fellowship [Rightly Attended]. Edward Taylor. *Fr.* God's Determinations. AmP; AmPP; CoV; OxBA
In heaven there is a star I call my own. Sonnets. Irene Rutherford McLeod. HBMV
In Heavenly Love Abiding. Anna L. Waring. MaRV; OIF
In heav'n the blessed angels have their being. Ode VIII: That All Other Creatures Have Their Abiding in Heaven, Hell, Earth, Air, Water, or Fire; but He in All of Them. Francis Davison. ReIE
In Heavy Mind. James Agee. MAP; MoAmPo
In heavy sleep the Caliph lay. The Caliph and Satan. James Freeman Clarke. LPS-3
In Hellbrunn. Georg Trakl, *tr. fr. German.* AnGP, *tr. by* Kate Flores; LiTW, *tr. by* Werner Heider
In her coffin, satin-shirred. A Poor Relation. Audrey McGaffin. NePoAm-2
In her ear he whispers gaily. The Lord of Burleigh. Tennyson. BPN; CG; OTPC (1923 ed.); PECK
In Her Entirety. Baudelaire, *tr. fr. French by* Alan Conder. TrFP
In her lone cottage on the downs. Miss Thompson Goes Shopping. Martin Armstrong. ShBV-2
In Her Paths. Francis Thompson. VLEP
In here, I feel the soul of someone dead. The Dead Youth. Kostes Palamas. *Fr.* Life Immovable. MoGP
In here—this room holds all my treasures, friend. Wanderlust. Alba Zizzamia. CAG
In higher natures, poetic or mystical. Robert Bridges. *Fr.* The Testament of Beauty. LO; PtP
In highest Heaven, at Mary's knee. The Cherub-Folk. Enid Dinnis. CAW
In highest way of heaven the sun did ride. Astrophel and Stella, XXII. Sir Philip Sidney. OBSC; SiPS
In Him. James Vila Blake. WGRP
In Him. Annie Johnson Flint. BLRP
In Him Confiding. William Cowper. MaRV
("Sometimes a light surprises.") OIF
In Him We Live. Henry More. MaRV
In Him We Live. Jones Very. AmP; OxBA
In Him Ye Are Made Full. William H. Hudnut, Sr. ChIP
In His Blanket on the Ground. Caroline H. Gervais. BlG
In his chamber, weak and dying. A Strike among the Poets. *Unknown.* BOHV; FiBHP; SiTL
In his cool hall, with haggard eyes. The Pagan World [*or* West and East]. Matthew Arnold. *Fr.* Obermann Once More. CBPC; GTML
In His Extreme Sickness. Thomas, Lord Vaux. ReIE
In His Good Time. Robert Browning. *Fr.* Paracelsus. OQP; QP-1
(Guidance.) BPP
(I Go to Prove My Soul.) MaRV

In his heroic mould were cast. David Glasgow Farragut. Wallace Rice. GA
In his last bin [*or* binn] Sir Peter lies. Song. Thomas Love Peacock. *Fr.* Headlong Hall. EnRP; OBRV; ViBoPo
In his lone cave the lion sleeps. The Lion at Noon. Victor Hugo. LiTW
In his malodorous brain what slugs and mire. God. Isaac Rosenberg. MoPo
In his narrow cassock straight and red. Acolyte. Mary Brent Whiteside. LS
In his old gusty garden of the North. Robert Louis Stevenson. Lizette Woodworth Reese. HBV
In his own image the Creator made. On Man [*or* Man]. Walter Savage Landor. OBRV; TriL; VA
In His Sight. Anna R. Baker. OQP; QP-2
In His Steps. Katharine Lee Bates. PGD
In his tall senatorial. The Drum; the Narrative of the Demon of Tedworth. Edith Sitwell. *Fr.* Façade. BoW; FaBoTw
In His Will. Howard Mumford Jones. LS
In Hoc Signo. Godfrey Fox Bradby. *See* Kingdoms.
In Holland children set their shoes. Shoe or Stocking. Edith M. Thomas. SDH
In holly hedges starving birds. Christmas Eve. John Davidson. CBPC; MPB; OHIP; SDH
In holy night we made the vow. Writ in Water [*or* The Vow]. Meleager. LPS-1; OuHeWo
In honnour of this heghe fest, of custume yere by yere. A Lover's New Year's Gift. John Lydgate. PoEL-1
In Honor of His Mistress. Cecco Angiolieri da Siena. *See* Sonnet: Of Love, in Honor of His Mistress Becchina.
In Honor of Taffy Topaz Christopher Morley. CIV; PoMa; TiPo
In Honour of St. David's Day. *Unknown.* PrWP
In Honour of the City of London. William Dunbar. CoEV; EV-1; OBEV
(London.) EBSV
(To the City of London.) ChTr
In Hospital, *sels.* W. E. Henley.
Apparition, XXV. BEL; EnLi-2 (1949 ed.); POTT; PoVP; TCEP; TrGrPo
Ave, Caesar! XIV. POTT
Before, IV. BEL; BMEP; BPN; EnLi-2; MBP; MoBrPo; OuHeWo; PoVP; TCEP; ViP
Casualty, XIII. PoVP
Clinical, XI. TCEP
Discharged, XXVIII. BPN; POTT; PoVP; VLEP
Enter Patient, I. BPN; PoVP
House-Surgeon, XVI. PoVP
Music, XXIII. BPN
Nocturn, XXVII. BPN
Operation, V. EPP; LEAP; PoVP; ViP
(From "In Hospital.") LEAP
Pastoral, XXII. Po
Romance, XXI. EnLit; MC; PAH; POTT
Scrubber, XIX. PoVP
Staff-Nurse: New Style, X. PoVP
Staff-Nurse: Old Style, VIII. BPN; InP; PIAE; PoVP
Vigil, VII. LoBV; POTT
Visitor, XX. PIAE
Waiting, II. BPN; PoVP; VLEP
In hospital. My Friends. Mikhail Lukonin. RuPo
In Hospital; Poona. Alun Lewis. MoPW; NeBP; SeCePo
In hot career or ranging far and wide. The Huntress. José Joaquín Pesado. AnMP
In houses where no snakes are found. *Unknown. Fr.* The Panchatantra. LiTW
In Hsü-chou, in the District of Ku-feng. Chu-ch'en Village. Po Chü-i. TrCh
In Humbleness. Daniel G. Hoffman. NePA
In humbleness, in tenderness, upon the tomb enthralling. The Seeming Dead. Paul Valéry. TrFP
"In Huts Where Poor Men Lie." Bianor, *tr. fr. Greek by* F. L. Lucas. GrPE
"In Huts Where Poor Men Lie." Phocylides, *tr. fr. Greek by* F. L. Lucas. GrPE
In idle dalliance now it welcomes weeds. An Abandoned Tow-Path. Elias Lieberman. PFE; PoeMoYo
In Illness. *Unknown.* PraP
In Imagine Pertransit Homo. Thomas Campion. *See* Follow Thy Fair Sun.
In Imitation of Anacreon. Matthew Prior. CEP
(On Critics.) SeCeV
In Imitation of Pope. Isaac Hawkins Browne. *Fr.* A Pipe of Tobacco. OBEC
In Imitation of Spenser. William Shenstone. *See* School-Mistress, The.
In Imitation of Young. Isaac Hawkins Browne. *Fr.* A Pipe of Tobacco. OBEC
In Immemoriam. "Cuthbert Bede." NA; PA
(In Memoriam.) BOHV
In inexperienc'd infancy. Shadows in the Water. Thomas Traherne. AtBAP
In innocence that this could be. Three Persons. Louise Townsend Nicholl. CAW
In Ionia whence sprang old poets' fame. Phoebe on Latmus. Michael Drayton. *Fr.* Endimion and Phoebe. OBSC; ReIE
In it despair has married wildest mirth. Death's Jest Book. Thomas Lovell Beddoes. *Fr.* Letters in Verse . . . 1826. RO
In Italy, in Belgium, in France. Our Dead, Overseas. Edwin Markham. OQP; QP-2
In its double skirt enwrapped. The Walnut. Ibn al-Qutiya. MooP
In Jaën where I'm abiding. The Jolly Supper. Baltasar del Alcázar. AnSpL-1
In January. Gordon Bottomley. MM; TCPD
In jealousy of cause and pride of plan. Autonomous. Mark Van Doren. LiTA; PG (1955 ed.)
In Jericho. *Unknown.* SiTL
In Jersey City where I did dwell. The Butcher's Boy. *Unknown.* ABS
In Jerusalem. *Unknown.* StJW
In journeyings my weak soul makes. Cowardice. Emyr Humphreys. NeTW
In July month, ae bonny morn. My Winsome Dear. Robert Fergusson. *Fr.* Leith Races. SeCePo
In June. Nora Perry. SN; YeAr
In June, amid the golden fields. The Groundhog. Richard Eberhart. AmP; AnFE; CoAnAm; ExPo; FaBoMo; FaFP; GTBS-W; LiTA; LiTG; LiTM; MiAP; MoAB; MoPo; MoVE; NePA; OnAP; PG (1955 ed.); ReMP; SeCeV; TwAmPo; UnPo (3d ed.); WaP
In June and Gentle Oven. Anne Wilkinson. PeCV
In June I give you a close-wooded fell. Of the Months: June. Folgore da San Geminiano. AWP
In June I saw the withering of my mother. Bedside. Francis Reginald Scott. BoCaPo (1948 ed.)
In June the early signs. For a Christening. Anne Ridler. DiM; MoPo
In just proportion, as the gods ordain. Fortune's Wheel. Euripides. *Fr.* Children of Heracles. GrR
In Just-Spring When the World. E. E. Cummings. *See* Chanson Innocent.
In Kalamazoo, in Kalamazoo. Why I No Longer Travel. Laura E. Richards. MPB
In Kensington Gardens. Arthur Symons. EnLoPo
In Kerry. J. M. Synge. AWP; JAWP; MBP; MoBrPo; WBP
In Kirkland glen the snows are deep. Harding Hill. Clinton Scollard. MuM
In kirtle of myrtle the goose girl goes. The Goose Girl. Dorothy Roberts. CaP; OCL
In kohl mines and estaminets of gold. The Vole. Marvin Solomon. NePoAm-2
In Köln [*or* Köhln], a town of monks and bones. Cologne. Samuel Taylor Coleridge. ALV; BoHiPo; BOHV; HBV; InMe; LPS-3; WhC
In Lacrimas. *Unknown. See* I Saw My Lady Weep.
In Lady Street. John Drinkwater. WP
In lands I never saw, they say. Emily Dickinson. NePA
In Larch Wood/ Is a little grey pool. Larch Wood Secrets. Ivy O. Eastwick. BoTP
In Leinster. Louise Imogen Guiney. AA; JKCP; OBVV
(Irish Peasant Song.) LBMV; OBAV
(Song: "I try to knead and spin.") GoBC; HBV
(Song in Leinster.) PFY
In less than two and twenty years. Asclepiades, *tr. fr. Greek by* William Wallace *and* Mary Wallace. GrPo
In letters large upon the frame. What's in a Name? Richard Kendall Munkittrick. BOHV; InMe
In life, Manes the slave; but, since he died. Death the Leveller. Anyte, *tr. by* F. L. Lucas. GrPE; GrR
In Life Our Absent Friend Is Far Away. Christina Rossetti. BoFr
In life still death is here. Media Vita. *At. to* Notker Balbulus. CAW
In life there are blows so heavy. The Black Messengers. César Vallejo. TwSpPo
In life this man was Manes, and a slave. Death the Leveller. Anyte, *tr. by* Sir William Marris. OxBG
In life three ghostly friars were we. Glee—The Ghosts. Thomas Love Peacock. *Fr.* Melincourt. ViBoPo
In life we had not seen her once. Mother. Helen Frazee-Bower. MuM
In Limine. Struthers Burt. NoCaPo (1941 ed.)
In little Annie's garden. Annie's Garden. Eliza Lee Follen. PPL
In little faces pinched with cold and hunger. As Ye Do It unto These. *Unknown.* ChIP
In little white dresses and little white pants. The Popcorn Party. "E. R. B." GFA
In Liverpool there liv'd a man. The Big Five-Gallon Jar. *Unknown.* ShS
In Locksley town, in merry Nottinghamshire. Robin Hood's Birth, Breeding, Valor, and Marriage. *Unknown.* ESPB
In Loco. Peter Jackson. BoSA

In London city was Bicham born. Young Beichan. *Unknown.* ESPB; ViBoFo

In London City where I once did dwell, there's where I got my learning. Barbara Allen. *Unknown.* AS; BeLS

In London I never know what I'd be at. The Contrast. C. Morris. BOHV

In London once I lost my way. A Plain Direction. Thomas Hood. OTPC (1946 ed.); TVSH

In London, September, 1802. Wordsworth. *See* Written in London, September, 1802.

In London there I was bent. London Lackpenny [*or* Lickpenny]. *Unknown.* ChTr; CoMu

In London-town Dame Trottypeg. D'Arcy Wentworth Thompson. *Fr.* Nursery Nonsense. BoN

In London town where I did dwell. The Butcher Boy. *Unknown.* ViBoFo

In London was young Beichan born. Young Beichan [and Susie Pye]. *Unknown.* HBV; LoEn; OBB

In lonely forests pensively I pace. Wild Beast. Pierre de Ronsard. TrFP

In lonely silence. From an Old House. Harold Monro. TCEP

In lonely watches night by night. Requiescant. Frederick George Scott. DD; OHIP

In loopy links the canker crawls. Indifference. *Unknown.* NA

In Louisiana. Albert Bigelow Paine. AA

In Love for Long. Edwin Muir. GTBS-W; LiTM (rev. ed.)

In love his kingdom great two fools there be. Laura, VIII. Robert Tofte. ElSeCe; ReIE; TuPP

In Love, if Love Be Love. Tennyson. *Fr.* Idylls of the King: Merlin and Vivien. AEV; EV-5; GTBS; GTSL; LoPS; PoEL-5; TrGrPo; VLEP
(All in All.) GTBS-W; LiTB
(If Love Be Ours.) OQP; QP-2
(Little Rift within the Lute, The.) LoPo
(Vivien's Song.) BPN; FaBoEn

In love they wore themselves in a green embrace. Adolescence. P. K. Page. BoCaPo (1948 ed.); CaP; TwCaPo

In love to be sure what disasters we meet. The Lover's Arithmetic. *Unknown.* OxBoLi

In love with all earth's loveliness. The Parable of the Mustard Weed. Dora Hagemeyer. StaSt

In love with you I all things elce doe hate. *Unknown.* SeCSL

In loving thee thou know'st I am forsworn. Sonnets, CLII. Shakespeare. PeBoSo; ReIE

In loving you, sweet land, we love a thing. Sweet Land. Francis Maguire. JKCP (1955 ed.)

In lowly dale, fast by a river's side. Vale [*or* Land] of Indolence [*or* Enchanted Ground]. James Thomson. *Fr.* The Castle of Indolence. BSV; CBOV; EBSV; EnRP; EPP; OBEC; SeCePo; ViBoPo

In Lucem Transitus, October, 1892. Henry van Dyke. *See* Tennyson.

In Lydia's golden city, gleaming Sardis. The Bride of Sardis. Sappho. GrR

In Lyonesse, beneath the waves. Lyonesse. Godfrey Fox Bradby. ReTS

In Maidstone Gaol, I am lamenting. Farewell to the World of Richard Bishop. *Unknown.* CoMu

In manner brusk, pompous in air and style. The Consultation. William Green Brownson. *Fr.* The Country Doctor. PoP

In Mantua-territory half is slough. Sordello's Birth-Place. Robert Browning. *Fr.* Sordello. MyFE

In Manus Tuas, Domine. *Unknown.* CoBE
(Three Devout Fragments, 3.) TMEV

In many a distant, unknown land. The Sorrows of Armenia. *Unknown.* ArmLP

In many forms we try. The Bohemian Hymn. Emerson. APW; IAP; MOAP; OQP; PFY; QP-1; WGRP

In marble halls as white as milk. Mother Goose. CBPC; ChTr; HBV; HBVY; OTPC; OxNR; PPL; RIS; SiTL; StVeCh

In Marcellum. Thomas Freeman. SiCE

In March. Archibald Lampman. CPG

In March. Wordsworth. *See* Written in March.

In March come the March winds. The March Winds. George Washington Wright Houghton. YeAr

In March I give you plenteous fisheries. Sonnets of the Months: March. Folgore da San Geminiano. AWP; LyMA

In March sow thy barley, thy lond not too cold. March. Thomas Tusser. ReIE

In martial sports I had my cunning tried. Astrophel and Stella, LIII. Sir Philip Sidney. ReEn; ReIE; SiPS

In mathematicks he was greater. Samuel Butler. *Fr.* Hudibras, I, 1. ImOP

In Mather's Magnalia Christi. The Phantom Ship. Longfellow. DaM; EtS

In matters of commerce the fault of the Dutch. Epigrams: The Dutch. George Canning. OxBoLi

In May. W. H. Davies. OBVV; TCEP

In May. J. M. Synge. MBP; MoBrPo

In May. *Unknown.* BoTP

In May. Robert Kelley Weeks. SN

In May I go a-walking to hear the linnet sing. In May. *Unknown.* BoTP

In May my heart was breaking. Autumn Valentine. Dorothy Parker. NeMA

In May, when sea-winds pierced our solitudes. The Rhodora. Emerson. AA; ADAH; AmPo; AmPP; AnAmPo; AnEnPo; AnFE; AnNE; APA; APW; AWP; BAP; BAV; BLV; BoLiVe; BTP; CoAnAm; CoBA; DD; FaFP; GA; GN; GoTP; GTSE; HBV; HBVY; HiLiAm; IAP; InPo; JAWP; LA; LEAP; LiTA; LiTG; LPS-2; MCCG; MOAP; MPB; NeHB; NLK; OBAV; OHFP; OTPC; OxBA; PEOR; PFE; PIAE; PIR; PoLFOT; PTA-2; PYM; REAL; SeCeV; TCAP; TOP; TreFS; TrGrPo; TVSH; WBP; WHA; YT

In May, when sea-winds pierced our solitudes. Variation on a Line by Emerson. W. S. Merwin. NePA

In Mayan Splendor. Frank Belknap Long. DaM

In me is a little painted square. Old Age. Maxwell Bodenheim. MAP; MoAmPo (1942 ed.)

In Me, Past, Present, Future Meet. Siegfried Sassoon. ChMo; CMP; OBEV (new ed.)

In Me Two Worlds. C. Day Lewis. AnFE

In mean time flew our ships, and straight we fetched. Homer. *Fr.* The Odyssey, XII. TuPP

In Measure Time We'll Row, *with music. Unknown.* ShS

In Media Vita. Willa Cather. OBAV

In melancholic fancy. Hallo My Fancy. William Cleland, *and others.* CH; LPS-3; OxBoLi

In Memorabilia Mortis. Francis Sherman. CaP; OCL

In Memoriam. "Cuthbert Bede." *See* In Immemoriam.

In Memoriam. Thomas Edward Brown. VLEP

In Memoriam. Frank A. Collymore. PoNe

In Memoriam. Dorothy Frances Gurney. SaFP

In Memoriam. Ada Jackson. PGD

In Memoriam. Mary Lamb. *See* Parental Recollections.

In Memoriam. F. L. Lucas. CaAE

In Memoriam. Alexander William Mair. MM

In Memoriam. Richard Monckton Milnes. HBV

In Memoriam. Sir William Stirling-Maxwell. EBSV

In Memoriam, A. C. M. L., *sel.* Cecil Arthur Spring-Rice.
"God of all power and might." TrPWD

In Memoriam, A. H., *sel.* Maurice Baring.
"God, who had made you valiant, strong, and swift." CAW

In Memoriam A. H. H. Tennyson. BMEP, *much abr.;* BPN, *abr.;* EM-2, *abr.;* EmBrPo; EnLi-2, *abr.;* EPN; GEPC; OAEP, *abr.;* PIR, *much abr.;* PoVP; TriL; ViPo; ViPP; VLEP

Sels.

"Again at Christmas did we weave," LXXVIII. EnL; EnLit

"And all is well, tho' faith and form," CXXVII. BEL; CoBE; HBV; TCEP

"And rise, O moon, from yonder down," *fr.* Epilogue. BrBE; EPP; LEAP; RiBV
"And, star and system rolling past," *shorter sel.* ImOP

"As sometimes in a dead man's face," LXXIV. LiTB; LiTG; ReaPo

"Be near me when my light is low," L. AnFE; AtBAP; BEL; CoBE; EnL; LiTB; LiTG; PoE; PoEL-5; PoFS; ReaPo; TOP

"By night we linger'd on the lawn," XCV. AnFE; EnL; EnSW; LoBV; PoEL-5; ReaPo

"Calm is the morn without a sound," XI. BoLiVe; CaAE; ChTr; CoBE; CoEV; EnSW; ExPo; FaBoEn; FiP; GTBS-D; GTML; LiTB; LPS-1; OBEV (1st ed.); PoE; PoEL-5; PoFS; ReaPo; SeCeV; ShBV-4; TrGrPo; TVSH
(Autumn.) SN

"Contemplate all this work of Time," CXVIII. BEL; CoBE; EnL; MaPo; PIAE; PoFS; SeCeV; TCEP; TOP

"Danube to the Severn gave, The," XIX. EnL; LoBV; TOP

"Dark house, by which once more I stand," VII. BEL, *abr.;* BoFr; CoBE; EnL; EnLit; FaBoEn; LiTB; MaPo, PoD; PoE; PoEL-5; ReaPo; SeCeV; TwHP; UnPo

"Dear friend, far off, my lost desire," CXXIX. BoFr; MaPo; TOP
(Truths That Never Can Be Proved, The.) MaRV
"Strange friend, past, present and to be," *br. sel.* LO

"Dip down upon the northern shore," LXXXIII. MaPo
(April Days.) ADAH; SN
(Spring.) HBV; LPS-2

"Do we indeed desire the dead," LI. AtBAP; BEL; BoFr; PIAE; TOP

"Doors, where my heart was used to beat," CXIX. PoEL-5

"Dost thou look back on what hath been," LXIV. BHV

"Fair ship, that from the Italian shore," IX. BoLiVe; GTSL; LEAP; LPS-1; OBEV (1st ed.); ReaPo

"Her eyes are homes of silent prayer," XXXII. EPP; TOP

"How fares it with the happy dead," XLIV. OBEV (1st ed.)
"How many a father have I seen," LIII. BEL; TOP
"How pure at heart and sound in head," XCIV. CoBE; LPS-1
"I cannot love thee as I ought," LII. BEL; EnLit; RiBV
"I cannot see the features right," LXX. EnL; LiTB; PoEL-5; UnW
"I climb the hill: from end to end," C. PoEL-5; TOP
("I wake, I rise: from end to end.") BrBE
"I dream'd there would be spring no more," LXIX. UnW
"I envy not in any moods," XXVII. BEL; CoBE; EnL; EnLit; EPP; FaBoEn; GTSL; HBV; LEAP; LiTB; LiTG; LiTL; OuHeWo; PIAE; TCEP; TOP; TyEnPo
(Lost Love.) TreFS
(Tis Better to Have Loved and Lost.) MaRV
"I falter where I firmly trod," *fr.* LV.
(Larger Hope, The.) MaRV
"I hear the noise about thy keel," X. GTSL; OBEV (1st ed.); ReaPo
"I held it truth, with him who sings," I. BEL; BoFr; BoLiVe; CoBE; EnL; EnLit; EPP; HBV; LEAP; LiTB; LiTG; OQP; QP-1; TCEP
"I know that this was Life—the track," XXV. TOP
(Dead Friend, The.) LPS-1
"I past beside the reverend walls," LXXXVII. BoFr; CoBE; EnSW
"I sing to him that rests below," XXI. EnL; RiBV
"I sometimes hold it half a sin," V. LPS-1; OuHeWo
"I trust I have not wasted breath," CXX. CoBE; ImOP; SeCePo; TOP
"I wage not any feud with death," LXXXII. LiTB; LiTG; ReaPo; TOP
"If one should bring me this report," XIV.
(Of One Dead.) LiTB; LiTG
"If sleep and death be truly one," XLIII. LPS-1
"In those sad words I took farewell," LVIII. TCEP
"Is it, then, regret for buried time," CXVI. BEL; MaPo; TCEP
"Lo, as a dove when up she springs," XII. LoBV
"Love is and was my lord and king," CXXVI. BEL; BoFr; CoBE; HBV; OBEV; ReaPo; SeCeV; TCEP
(My Lord and King.) ChTr
"My own dim life should teach me this," XXXIV. CoBE; EnL; MaPo; SeCePo
(Life Shall Live for Evermore.) MaRV; OQP; QP-2
"Now fades the last long streak of snow," CXV. AlDL; BEL; BrBE; CaAE; CoBE; EOAH; FaBoEn; GTBS-D; MaPo; OBEV (1st ed.); PoE; SeCeV; ShBV-4; TCEP
(Spring.) ADAH; DD; HBV; LPS-2; SN; YT
"Now, sometimes in my sorrow shut," XXIII. OBEV (1st ed.); TOP
"O days and hours, your work is this," CXVII. BEL; HBV; MaPo; TCEP
(Dead Friend, The.) LPS-1
"O living will that shalt endure," CXXXI. BEL; BoLiVe; CBE; CoBE; EnL; EnLit; FaBoBe; HBV; PIAE; TOP
(Prayer, The: "O Living will that shalt endure.") WGRP
(Truths That Never Can Be Proved, The.) MaRV
"O Sorrow, cruel fellowship," III. EnL; MaPo; TOP
"O sorrow wilt thou live with me," LIX. GTSL
"O thou that after toil and storm," XXXIII. TOP
"O wast thou with me, dearest, then," CXXII. TOP
"Oh yet we trust that somehow good," LIV. AnFE; AtBAP; BEL; BoLiVe; BPP; EnL; EnLit; EPP; ExPo (LIV–LVI); GTBS-W; GTSL; HBV; LEAP; LiTB; LiTG; LoBV; LPS-2; MaPo; OQP; OuHeWo; PIAE; PoE; PoFS; QP-1; ReaPo; RiBV; SeCeV; TCEP; TOP; TrGrPo; TyEnPo; UnPo
(Larger Hope, The.) GrCo-1, *fr.* LIV *and* LV; MaRV, *fr.* LIV *and* LV; TreFS; WGRP
"Old warder of these buried bones," XXXIX. PoEL-5
"Old yew, which graspest at the stones," II. CoEV; EmBrPo; EnLi-2; EPN; FaBoEn; GEPC; GTBS-D; MaPo; OAEP; PoEL-5; ReaPo; SeCeV; TyEnPo; ViPo; VLEP
(Yew in the Graveyard, The.) UnPo (3d ed.)
"On that last night before we went," CIII. PoEL-5; UnW
"One writes, that 'Other friends remain,'" VI. BEL; PoEL-5
"Path by which we twain did go, The," XXII. TOP; TVSH
(Dead Friend, The.) LPS-1
"Peace; come away: the song of woe," LVII. BoFr
"Ring out, wild bells, to the wild sky," CVI. BEL; BoFr; BoLiVe; CBPC; CoBE; DD; EnL; EnLit; EPP; EV-5; FaFP; FaPON; FiP; GTBS; GTBS-W; GTSL; HBV; HH; HiLiEn; InP; LEAP; LiTB; LiTG; MaPo; MaRV; MCCG; MPB; NeHB; OlF; OQP; OTPC; PEDC; PG (1945 ed.); PGD; PoE; PoRL; PTA-2; PYM; QP-1; SeCeV; ShBV-2; TCEP; TiPo (1959 ed.); TOP; TreF; TrGrPo; TVSH; TyEnPo; UnPo; WP
(Christmas.) BHV
(New Year, The.) GrCo-1
(New Year's Eve.) CBE; LPS-3
(Ring Out the Old, Ring in the New.) WBLP
Thousand Years of Peace, The, 3 *sts.* AOAH
"Risest thou thus, dim dawn, again," LXXII. GTBS-D; PoEL-5
"Risest thou thus, dim dawn, again," XCIX. BrBE
"'So careful of the type?' but no," LVI. AnFE; CoBE; EnL; HBV; InP; LoBV; MaPo; OBEV (1st ed.); OuHeWo; PIAE; ReaPo; SeCeV; TCEP; TOP
"So many worlds, so much to do," LXXIII. HBV; LPS-1
"Strong Son of God, immortal love," Proem [*or* Prologue]. BBV; BEL; BoLiVe; ChIP; CoBE; EnL; EnLit; EPP; GTBS-W; HBV; LEAP; LiTB; LPS-2; MaRV; NeHB; OQP; OuHeWo; OxBoCh; PIAE; PoFS; QP-1; REAL; RiBV; SeCeV; StJW; TOP; TreF; TrGrPo; TrPWD; TyEnPo; UnPo (1st ed.); WGRP; WHA
"Sweet after showers, ambrosial air," LXXXVI. BEL; TOP
"That each, who seems a separate whole," XLVII. LPS-1; PIAE
"That which we dare invoke to bless," CXXIV. EnL; GTSL; WGRP
(Intuition.) MaRV
"There rolls the deep where grew the tree," CXXIII. CaAE; CoBE; GTML; MaPo; SeCePo; SeCeV
"Tho' truths in manhood darkly join," XXXVI. ChIP
(Word, The.) GoBC
(Word Incarnate, The.) MaRV
"Thou comest, much wept for; such a breeze," XVII. EnLi-2; OBEV (1st ed.)
"Thy voice is on the rolling air," CXXX. BoFr; EnL; EPP; HBV; HiLiEn; MaPo; PIAE; PoFS; ReaPo; TOP; TyEnPo; UnPo; UnW
(Truths That Never Can Be Proved, The.) MaRV
"Till now the doubtful dusk reveal'd," *fr.* XCV. AlDL
"Time draws near the birth of Christ, The," XXVIII. ChIP, 3 *sts.*; EnLit; PGD, 3 *sts.*; SDH; TOP; TVSH
(Bells of Yule.) PEOR
(Birth of Christ, The, *fr.* XXVIII *and* XXX.) COAH
(Christmas Bells, 3 *sts.*) MaRV
(Rise, Happy Morn, 4 *sts., incl.* 1 *st. fr.* XXX.) BePJ
(Time Draws Near, The.) OQP; QP-1
"Time draws near the birth of Christ, The," CIV. EnLit; PoE; TCEP
"To Sleep I give my powers away," IV. MaPo
"Tonight the winds begin to rise," XV. AnFE; CaAE; CoEV; EnSW; FaBoEn; GTBS-D; LiTB; OBEV (1st ed.); PoEL-5; PoFS; ReaPo; ShBV-4
"Unwatch'd the garden bough shall sway," CI. BrBE; CaAE; EnSW; GTBS-D; OBEV (1st ed.); PoEL-5; SeCeV
"We leave the well-beloved place," CII. PoEL-5
"What hope is here for modern rhyme," LXXVII. CoBE; LPS-1
"What words are these have fall'n from me," XVI. CoBE
"Whatever I have said or sung," CXXV. TCEP
"When Lazarus left his charnel cave," XXXI. EPP
"When on my bed the moonlight falls," LXVII. EnL; LoBV; NeHB; PoE; ReaPo; SeCePo; SeCeV; TOP; UnW
"When rosy plumelets tuft the larch," XCI. FaBoEn; ViBoPo
"Wild bird, whose warble, liquid sweet," LXXXVIII. BEL
"Wish, that of the living whole, The," LV. AnFE; AtBAP; BEL; EnL; EnLit; HBV; LoBV; MaPo; OBEV (1st ed.); OQP; OuHeWo; PIAE; PoFS; QP-1; ReaPo; SeCeV; TCEP; TOP; UnPo
"With trembling fingers did we weave," XXX. CoBE; EnL; EnLit; RiBV
"Yet if some voice that man could trust," XXXV. MaPo; ViBoPo
"You say, but with no touch of scorn," XCVI. BEL; EnL; EnLit; EPP; LEAP; OQP; PIAE; QP-1; TOP
(Doubt.) WGRP
Stronger Faith, A ("Perplext in faith, but pure in deeds"), 3 *sts.* MaRV
In Memoriam A. M. W. Gordon Bottomley. LEAP
In Memoriam; Easter 1915. Edward Thomas. SoV
In Memoriam Egon von Rilke. Rainer Maria Rilke, *tr. fr. German by* J. B. Leishman. BoFr
In Memoriam F. A. S. Robert Louis Stevenson. GTBS
In Memoriam; Francis Ledwidge. Norreys Jephson O'Conor. HBMV
In Memoriam; Ho Chi-chang. Li Po, *tr. fr. Chinese by* Shigeyoshi Obata. BoFr
In Memoriam; Ingvald Bjorndal and His Comrade. Malcolm Lowry. BoCaPo (1948 ed.)
In Memoriam; John Davidson. Ronald Campbell Macfie. GoTS
In Memoriam; Lady Blessington. Walter Savage Landor. TriL

In Memoriam—Leo, a Yellow Cat. Margaret Sherwood. BLPA; CIV; NeHB
In Memoriam Margaritae Sororis. W. E. Henley. *See* Margaritae Sorori.
In Memoriam; Nelson, Pitt, Fox. Sir Walter Scott. *See* To William Stewart Rose, Esq.
In Memoriam R. T. Hamilton Bruce. W. E. Henley. *See* Invictus.
In Memoriam; Roy Campbell. R. N. Currey. BoSA
In Memoriam Technicam. Tom Hood. BOHV
In Memoriam—W. G. Ward. Tennyson.
 (Valedictory, I.) GoBC
In Memory, *sel.* Lionel Johnson.
 "Ah! fair face gone from sight." FaBoEn; PoEL-5
In Memory of a Child. Vachel Lindsay. InP
In Memory of Ann Jones. Dylan Thomas. *See* After the Funeral.
In Memory of Arthur Winslow. Robert Lowell. *See* Death from Cancer.
In Memory of "Barry Cornwall." Swinburne. HBV
In Memory of Con and Eva Gore-Booth. W. B. Yeats. *See* In Memory of Eva Gore-Booth and Con Markiewicz.
In Memory of Edward Wilson, *parody.* James Clerk Maxwell. *See* Rigid Body Sings.
In Memory of Ernst Toller. W. H. Auden. AtBAP
In Memory of Eva Gore-Booth and Con Markiewicz. W. B. Yeats. MoAB; OBMV; TriL
 (In Memory of Con and Eva Gore-Booth.) OxBI
In Memory of G. K. Chesterton. Walter de la Mare. GoBC
In Memory of Garcia Lorca. Eldon Grier. PeCV
In Memory of General Grant. Henry Abbey. AA
In Memory of James T. Fields. Whittier. OBVV
In Memory of Jane Frazer. Geoffrey Hill. NePoEA
In Memory of John Lothrop Motley. Bryant. AA
In Memory of Kathleen. Kenneth Patchen. MoAmPo
In Memory of Lake Superior. George Dillon. *See* Memory of Lake Superior.
In Memory of Lewis Carroll. *Unknown.* PoRL
In Memory of Major Robert Gregory. W. B. Yeats. AnIL; OAEP (2d ed.); PoFS; TriL
In Memory of Marie A. Bertolt Brecht, *tr. fr. German by* H. R. Hays. LiTW
In Memory of Mother Seraphine Ireland. Sister Maris Stella. PraNu
In Memory of My Dear Grandchild Ann. Anne Bradstreet. BAV
In Memory of My Feelings. Frank O'Hara. NeAP
In Memory of Radio. LeRoi Jones. NeAP
In Memory of Rex Whistler. Dorothy Wellesley. DiM
In Memory of Robin Hyde, 1906–39. Charles Brasch. AnNZ
In Memory of Saon of Acantus. Callimachus. *See* Saon of Acanthus.
In Memory of Sigmund Freud. W. H. Auden. AtBAP; CoBMV; FaBoMo; LiTB; OxBA
In Memory of the Circus Ship *Euzkera,* Wrecked in the Caribbean Sea, 1 September 1948. Walker Gibson. NePoAm
 (Circus Ship *Euzkera,* The.) FiBHP
In Memory of Vachel Lindsay. Sara Teasdale. PIAE
In Memory of W. B. Yeats. W. H. Auden. ATP (1953 ed.); BoLiVe (1945 ed.); ChMo; CoBMV; EnL; FaFP; GTBS-W; HoPM; InPo; LiTB; LiTM; MaPo; MoAB; MoBrPo; MoVE; NePA; OAEP (2d ed.); OnHM; Po; PoFS; PreP; PtP; ReMP; TrGrPo; TwHP; UnPo (3d ed.); ViBoPo (1958 ed.)
 "Earth, receive an honoured guest," *sel.* ChMP; ChTr; FaBoTw; NeMA; PG (1955 ed.)
In Memory of Walter Savage Landor. Swinburne. BPN; EmBrPo; HBV; PoEL-5; PoFS; PoTT; PoVP; PtP; VA; ViP; VLEP
In Men Whom Men Condemn [as Ill]. Joaquin Miller. *Fr.* Byron. BAP; HBV; MaRV; NeMA; OQP; QP-2
 (Byron.) BLP; LBAP; MAP; MoAmPo; PC
 (Charity.) PoeMoYo
 (Lines.) BBV (1951 ed.)
In Mercer Street the light slants down. The Lark's Song. "Seumas O'Sullivan." BLA
In Merioneth, over the sad moor. Dead. Lionel Johnson. FaBoEn; GTBS-D; PoEL-5
In merry Scotland, in merry Scotland. Henry Martyn. *Unknown.* BaBo; ESPB
In Mexico. Evaleen Stein. AA
In mid whirl of the dance of Time ye start. Exit. Sir William Watson. VA
In Middle Row, some years ago. The Ghost. Thomas Hood. DaM
In midnight sleep of many a face of anguish. Old War-Dreams. Walt Whitman. DDA
In Midst of Woods. *Unknown.* TuPP
 (Blackbird, The.) EIL
In minds pure glasse when I my selfe behold. Sonnet. William Drummond of Hawthornden. OBS
In Misery's darkest cavern known. Samuel Johnson. *Fr.* On the Death of Mr. Robert Levet. ViBoPo
In Misty Blue. Laurence Binyon. HBMV; PoeT
In misty dreams and shadowed memories. In Mayan Splendor. Frank Belknap Long. DaM
In mole-blue indolence the sun. The Jungle. Alun Lewis. MoPo
In Montana [a Land of Contrasts]. Washington Jay McCormick. SiTL; WhC
In Mornigan's park there is a deer. Riddle. *Unknown.* ChTr
In morning light my damson show'd. The Plum Tree by the House. Oliver St. John Gogarty. OBEV (new ed.); PoRA
In Mortem Venerabilis Andreae Prout Carmen. Francis Sylvester Mahony. IrPN
In moss-prankt dells which the sunbeams flatter. Lovers, and a Reflection. Charles Stuart Calverley. BOHV; LPS-3; NA; PA; WhC
In most men's eyes one virtue, alone, is worth endeavour. Plutocracy. Theognis. GrPE
In mount or vale, throughout the changeful year. Beauty Everywhere. Albert Durrant Watson. CPG
In moving-slow he has no peer. The Sloth. Theodore Roethke. FiBHP; NePA; NePoAm; SiTL; WaKn
In my beginning is my end. East Coker. T. S. Eliot. *Fr.* Four Quartets. ChMP; FaBoMo; MoVE; NePA; PoLFOT
In my boat that goes. Saigyo Hoshi, *tr. fr. Japanese by* Arthur Waley. AWP
In my childhood trees were green. Autobiography. Louis MacNeice. FaBoTw
In My Craft or Sullen Art. Dylan Thomas. ChMP; GTBS-W; InvP; LiTM (rev. ed.); NeBP; OAEP (2d ed.); OnHM; Po; PoLFOT; PrWP; SeCeV
In my deep heart these chimes would still have rung. To W. P., IV. George Santayana. OBAV
In my defence. God me defend. Three Devout Fragments, 1. *Unknown.* TMEV
In my dream I seem to be/ sailing on the deserted sea. Maria's Dream. Dionysios Solomos. *Fr.* Lambros. MoGP
In My End Is My Beginning. Rosemary Dobson. BoAV; NeLNL
In my father's garden, oh, beauteous, oh, fair. The Wondrous Apple Tree. *Unknown.* SaSa
In My Father's House. Robert Freeman. OQP; QP-1
In My Father's House, *with music.* *Unknown.* AS
In my former days of bliss. On the Muse of Poetry. George Wither. *Fr.* The Shepherd's Hunting. EV-2
In My Garden. Alma L. Gray. SaFP
In My Garden. *Unknown.* BoTP
In my garden grows a tree. The Apple Rhyme. Madeleine Nightingale. BoTP
In my garden stands an arbor. The Pool in My Garden. Ku Shih. PoHN
In my home by the great pagoda. Waiting. Dorothy Choate Herriman. CPG
In My Infancy. David Ross. PG (1955 ed.)
In My Late Age. Tu Fu, *tr. fr. Chinese.* WhP
In my little garden. In My Garden. *Unknown.* BoTP
In my life. Haiku. Issa. LiTW; OnPJ
In my little log cabin. Rye Whisky. *Unknown.* ABF
In my narrow room, I throw. Mist. Li Ch'ing-chao. OnPC
In My Old Verses. Charles Guérin, *tr. fr. French by* Joseph T. Shipley. CAW
In My Own Album. Charles Lamb. OBRV
 (Lines Written in My Album.) EV-4
In my own shire, if I was sad. A. E. Housman. A Shropshire Lad, XLI. EmBrPo; PoVP; TyEnPo
In my poor mind it is most sweet to muse. Childhood. Charles Lamb. LPS-1
In my quiet room I talked with my Friend today. I Prayed Today. Grace Noll Crowell. PraP
In my room, the world is beyond my understanding. On the Surface of Things. Wallace Stevens. NP
In my sleep I was fain of their fellowship, fain. Sunrise. Sidney Lanier. *Fr.* Hymns of the Marshes. AA; ADAH; HiLiAm; PoEL-5; SPP; TCAP
In my song my love is prisoned. Imprisoned. John Hall Wheelock. PR
In my stone eyes I see. What Riddle Asked the Sphinx. Archibald MacLeish. HoPM
In my sunny girlhood's vernal life. A Portrait. Joseph Ashby-Sterry. HBV; VA
In My Thirtieth Year. Archibald MacLeish. *See* L'An Trentiesme de Mon Eage.
In My Time. Edmund Blunden. MoPW
In my young days I drank a/ Lot of wine. A Friend Advises Me to Stop Drinking. Mei Yao Ch'en. HoPM; OnPC
In my youth's summer I did sing of One. The Wandering Outlaw. Byron. *Fr.* Childe Harold's Pilgrimage, III. FiP
In Natales et Pascha Concurrentes. George Herbert, *tr. fr. Latin by* D. C. Allen. LaP
In nature apt to like, when I did see. Astrophel and Stella, XVI. Sir Philip Sidney. SiPS

In "nature" there's no choice. Beyond the End. Denise Levertov. NeAP
In Nazareth. Leslie Savage Clark. ChIP
In Nazareth he knew each narrow street. Sight. Ida Norton Munson. ChIP
In Nazareth, the narrow road. The Carpenter of Nazareth. George Blair. StJW
In New Ross. Valentin Iremonger. NeIP
In New York. William Vaughn Moody. *Fr.* Song-Flower and Poppy. LEAP
In New York. William Alexander Percy.
Home, V. LS; SPP
(In New York.) TBM
In the Night, IV. SPP
On Sunday Morning, I. QS; SPP
Song You Love, The, II. SPP
Weariness, III. SPP
In Nigellum. John Weever. TuPP
In 1929. Stephen Spender. *See* Whim of Time, A.
In no one sin couldst thou abide. Last Supper; Jesus to Judas. S. Foster Damon. TBM
In No Strange Land. Francis Thompson. AnFE; AtBAP; BLV; BMEP; BoLiVe; ChIP; CoEV; GTBS; GTML; HBMV; LBBV; LiTB; LiTG; MBP; MoAB; OBEV (new ed.); OQP; QP-2; ShBV-4; TCEP; TrGrPo; TwCrTr; WGRP
(Kingdom of God, The.) CoBE; CP; EmBrPo; EPN; GoBC; MaRV; OxBoCh; Po; PoeT; PoLi; POTE; POTT; PoVP; ReaPo; RiBV; SeCeV; TriL; VLEP; WoL
In no way that I chose to go. The Snow. Clifford Dyment. MoVE; POTE
In Norgum. *Unknown.* TuPP
In Normandy. E. V. Lucas. GaP
In Norway lands there lived a maid. The Great Silkie of Sule Skerry. *Unknown.* BaBo (A *vers.*); ViBoFo (B *vers., with music*)
In Nottamun Town not a soul would look up. Nottamun Town. *Unknown.* OxBoLi; SiTL
In Nottingham there lives a jolly tanner. Robin Hood and the Tanner. *Unknown.* BaBo; ESPB; MaC
In November. Anne Reeve Aldrich. AA
In November. Archibald Lampman. BoCaPo
In November. Susan Kelly Phillips. TOAH
In November. Duncan Campbell Scott. VA
In numbers, and but these few. An Ode on the Birth of our Saviour. Robert Herrick. AnEC; COAH; GN; OTPC (1923 ed.)
In obedience to the imperial command. A Soldier. *Unknown.* OnPM
In Obitum Alienius. Henry Parrot. SiCE
In Obitum Ed. Spenser Poetae Prestaniss. John Weever. ReIE
In Obitum M. S., X Maii, 1614. William Browne. *See* Epitaph: "May, be thou never graced with birds that sing."
In Ocean's wide domains. The Witnesses. Longfellow. AtBAP
In October. Bliss Carman. YeAr
In October. Michael Hamburger. NePoEA
In October at midnight in the olive groves. Thoughts from Abroad. Patrick Maybin. NeIP
In October the pregnant woman walked by the river. In October. Michael Hamburger. NePoEA
In October, when they know. Winter Coats. Dorothy Aldis. RIS
In old days those who went to fight. Hearing that His Friend Was Coming Back from the War. Wang Chien. BoFr; LiTW; TrCh
In old Kentuck in de arternoon. Clare de Kitchen. *Unknown.* BLPA
In old Nevers, so famous for its. Vert-Vert, the Parrot. Louis Gresset. CAW
In old Pekin a monarch reigned. The Street of Doctors. Thomas Walsh. PoMa
In old time they were called the church's pillars. Of the Pillars of the Church. Sir John Harington. SiCE
In one corner the nimble incest. Max Ernst. Paul Eluard. MiFP
In one of the Assyrian wars. Wading at Wellfleet. Elizabeth Bishop. AmP
In One of Those Excursions. Wordsworth. *Fr.* The Prelude, XIV. MaPo
In one short word/ Take all the truth of this. Embittered Youth. Sophocles. *Fr.* Philoctetes. GrR
In only thee, my timid, fleet gazelle. The Timid Gazelle. Kasmuneh. TrJP
In Order To. Kenneth Patchen. Po
In order to escape from Time I arrive at a time. Suicide? Elias Nandino. PoP
In order to escape you. Love. Jaime Torres Bodet. AnCL
In Orknay. William Fowler. GoTS
In Ortygia the Dawn land the old gods dwell. Ortygia. Jessie Mackay. BoAu
In other men we faults can spy. The Turkey and the Ant. John Gay. OTPC (1923 ed.)
In other thing who that recordeth. The Story of Ulysses. John Gower. *Fr.* Confessio Amantis. SG
In other time long gone. The Spinner's Song. Clemens Brentano. AnGP
In other years—lost youth's enchanted years. Bayard Taylor. Thomas Bailey Aldrich. GA
In Our Boat. Dinah Maria Mulock Craik. HBV
In our country, in our country. The Merry Hay-Makers; or, Pleasant Pastime between the Young-men and Maids, in the Pleasant Meadows. *Unknown.* CoMu
In our crazed brains words are visions. Prose Poem: Words. Emile Hennequin. OnPM
"In our darkness the sun is a lamp." Angelos Sikelianos. *Fr.* Daedalus in Crete. MoGP
In our Durham County I am sorry for to say. The Durham Lock-out. *Unknown.* CoMu
In our fields, fallow and burdened, in grass and furrow. Christopher Fry. *Fr.* The Boy with a Cart. LiTB
In our hearts is the Great One of Avon. Jocosa Lyra. Austin Dobson. BOHV; InP
In our hills the girls are plenty. Circassian Song. Mikhail Lermontov. BoR
In Our Lane. *Unknown, tr. fr. Chinese by* Arthur Waley. *Fr.* Shi King. LiTW
In our Museum galleries. The Burden of Nineveh. Dante Gabriel Rossetti. BPN; EmBrPo; OAEP; PoVP; TwCrTr; ViP; VLEP
In our old shipwrecked days there was an hour. Modern Love, XVI [*or* Love Dies]. George Meredith. BEL; BMEP; CBOV; EnLi-2; GTBS; GTBS-D; GTML; HBV; LO; PIAE; PoFS; SeCePo; ViPo; WHA
In Our Time. Huw Menai. MaRV
In Our Time. Michael Roberts. WaP
In our town people live in rows. The Fired Pot. Anna Wickham. FaBoTw; TrGrPo (1942 ed.)
In Owenni Epigrammata. Thomas Freeman. SiCE
In Pace. Arthur Reed Ropes. VA
In Pace in Idipsum Dormiam et Requiescam. Patrick O'Connor. CAW
In Paco town and in Paco tower. The Ballad of Paco Town. Clinton Scollard. PAH
In pain she bore the son who her embrace. Elegy. Moses ibn Ezra. TrJP
In pairs,/ as if to illustrate their sisterhood. For the Sisters of the Hôtel Dieu. A. M. Klein. BoCaPo (1948 ed.)
In Palestine. George W. Carlin. ChIP
In Panelled Rooms. Ruth Herschberger. LiTA
("Love-grip, first excited by the eye, The.") GTBS-W
In Paradise. Arlo Bates. AA
In Parenthesis. Frank Dempster Sherman. PR
In Paris. Thomas MacDonagh. OnYI
In Paris, at the Louvre, there have I seen. Modern Love, XXXIII. George Meredith. ViP; ViPo
In Paris dwelt the lady fair. Lady Alda's Dream. *Unknown.* TeCS
In Paris the tottering tower of St. James. Vigilance. André Breton. MiCF
In paschall feast, the end of ancient rite. Of the Blessèd Sacrament of the Altar. Robert Southwell. GoBC
In Passing. Roy Helton. HBMV
In passing with my mind. The Right of Way. William Carlos Williams. MoVE
In "pastures green"? Not always; sometimes He. He Leadeth Me [*or* On the Twenty-third Psalm]. *Unknown.* BLRP; MaRV; OQP; QP-1
In Paths Untrodden. Walt Whitman. APW; NePA; OxBA
In Patris Mei Memoriam. John Myers O'Hara. SBMV
In peace, Love tunes the shepherd's reed. Sir Walter Scott. *Fr.* The Lay of the Last Minstrel, III. ViBoPo
In pearls and rubies rich the hawthorns show. Glittering Frost. Ambrose Philips. *Fr.* A Winter Piece. BeR
In petticoat of green. Phyllis [*or* Of Phyllis]. William Drummond of Hawthornden. EIL; ElSeCe; GN; HBV; LiTL; OTPC
In Phaeacia. James Elroy Flecker. HBMV; ReTS
In Phaedram. Thomas Freeman. TuPP
In Philistia. Bliss Carman. ALV
In Philonem. Thomas Bastard. SiCE
In pious times, ere [*or* e'r] priestcraft did begin. Absalom and Achitophel, Pt. I. Dryden. BrBE; CEP; EiPP; EM-1; EnLi-1; EPS; GEPC; LiA; OAEP; REAL; SeCV-2; SeEP; TOP; TyEnPo
In pity for man's darkening thought. Two Songs from a Play, II. W. B. Yeats. *Fr.* The Resurrection. EnLP; ExPo; LiTB; MoPo; PoFS; RiBV; SeCeV; UnPo
In place of fire God a woman gave. Palladas, *tr. fr. Greek by* F. A. Wright. GrPo
In place where wants Apollo with his lute. An Epitaph upon the Death of Sir William Drury. Barnabe Rich. ReIE
In placid hours well-pleased we dream. Art. Herman Melville. APW; PoFS; ViBoPo

In Plague Time. Thomas Nashe. *See* Adieu, Farewell, Earth's Bliss!
In planting trees you must select a spot. Friendship. Meng Chia. BoFr
In Plimmerton, in Plimmerton. Threnody. Denis Glover. AnNZ
In Polar noons when the moonshine glimmers. The Weaver of Snow. "Fiona Macleod." PoVP
In Ponce I remembered. Recuerdo. Grace Hazard Conkling. TBM
In Porcum. John Heath. SiCE; TuPP
In Portugal, 1912. Alice Meynell. OxBoCh
In Postures That Call. Oscar Williams. WaP
In Praesepio. Charles L. O'Donnell. MM
In Praise of a Beggar's Life. "A. W." EIL, *2 sts.;* ElSeCe; TrGrPo
(Play, Beggars, Play!) WHA
(Song in Praise of a Beggar's Life, A.) OBSC; SiCE
In Praise of a Gentlewoman Who, though She Were Not Very Fair, Yet Was She as Hard-favored as Might Be. George Gascoigne. ReIE
In Praise of a Girl. Huw Morus, *tr. fr. Welsh by* Gwyn Williams. PrWP
In Praise of a Harp. *Unknown, tr. fr. Old Irish by* Osborn Bergin. SiB
In Praise of Aed [the Chieftain]. *Unknown, tr. fr. Old Irish by* Robin Flower. AnIL; LyMA
In Praise of Ale ("I cannot eat but little meat"). *At. to* William Stevenson. *See* Back and Side Go Bare, Go Bare.
In Praise of Ale ("Whenas the chill sirocco blows"). *Unknown, at. to* Thomas Bonham. ALV; CenL; ElSeCe; EV-2; FaBoCh; OBS; SeCL; SeEP; ViBoPo
(Give Me Ale.) HBV
(Pipe and Can, 2.) OBEV
In Praise of Angling. Sir Henry Wotton. LPS-2
In Praise of Bombyca. Theocritus, *tr. fr. Greek by* T. F. Higham. *Fr.* Idylls, X. OxBG
(Transfiguring Love, *tr. by* Charles Stuart Calverley.) GrR
In Praise of Cocoa, Cupid's Nightcap. Stanley J. Sharpless. FiBHP
In Praise of Common Things. Lizette Woodworth Reese. LS
In Praise of Commonplace. Sir Owen Seaman. InMe
In Praise of Country Life. Horace, *tr. fr. Latin by* John Marshall *and* Christopher Smart. Epodes, II.
(Country Life, *tr. by* Dryden.) AWP
(Revery of a Business Man, *tr. by* Dryden.) WoL
In Praise of Diversity. Phyllis McGinley. SiTL
In Praise of Fidelia. Mildmay Fane, Earl of Westmorland. ElSeCL; SeCL
In Praise of Gilbert White. William John Courthope. *Fr.* The Paradise of Birds. VA
In Praise of His Daphnis. Sir John Wotton. EIL
In Praise of His Lady. Matthew Grove. *Fr.* Pelops and Hippodamia. EIL
In Praise of His Love. Sir John Wotton. EIL
(Damaetas' Jig.) ElSeCe
In Praise of His Loving and Best-beloved Fawnia. Robert Greene. *See* Fawnia.
In Praise of Hope. Abraham Cowley. EV-2
In Praise of Hunting. *Unknown, tr. fr. Greek by* T. F. Higham. OxBG
In Praise of Isabel Pennell. John Skelton. *See* To Mistress Isabel Pennell.
In Praise of Johnny Appleseed. Vachel Lindsay. PoRL; StVeCh; TSW; TSWC
In Praise of Leaves, *sel.* Lilian Shuman Dreyfus.
Dedication: "Stumbling, we see the future as a cup." MOAH
In Praise of Limestone. W. H. Auden. CoBMV; MaPo; MoAB; MoVE; NePA
In praise of little children I will say. Laus Infantium. William Canton. HBV; VA
In Praise of Llamas. Arthur Guiterman. FiBHP
In Praise of Love. Juan Ruiz, Archpriest of Hita, *tr. fr. Spanish by* Ida Farnell. TeCS
In Praise of Music and Poetry. Richard Barnfield. *See* To His Friend Master R. L., in Praise of Music and Poetry.
In Praise of Rosamund. Robert Greene. *See* Hexametra Alexis in Laudem Rosamundi.
In Praise of the King. Ibn Ammar, *tr. fr. Arabic by* A. J. Arberry. MooP
In Praise of the Royal Scots Fusiliers. John Buchan. POT
In Praise of the Sun. "A. W." OBSC
("Golden sun that brings the day, The.") SiCE
In Praise of Wisdom. Solomon ibn Gabirol, *tr. fr. Hebrew by* Solomon Solis-Cohen. TrJP
In Praise of Wyatt's Psalms. Earl of Surrey. SiPS
In Praise of Young Girls. Raymond Asquith. OtMeF
In pride of May. *Unknown.* OBSC
In pride of wit, when high desire of fame. Idea, XLVII. Michael Drayton. SiCE; TuPP
In Prison. Sir Roger L'Estrange. *See* Loyalty Confin'd.
In Prison. William Morris. AtBAP; BPN; PoVP; ViP
(Knight in Prison, The.) SoV
In Prison. Frederick Peterson. PR
In Prison. Oscar Wilde. *Fr.* The Ballad of Reading Gaol. OOP; QP-2
("I know not whether laws be right.") ACP; MaRV
In Prison. Tamiko Yamamuro, *tr. fr. Japanese by* Lois J. Erickson. SoLD
In Prize. Cicely Fox Smith. WhC
In Provence. Jean Aicard, *tr. fr. French by* Thomas Walsh. CAW
In Puritan New England a year had passed away. The First Thanksgiving Day. Alice Williams Brotherton. DD; OHIP; TOAH
In purple fire spoke the heavenly wrath. Stefan George. *Fr.* The Star of the Covenant. TwGV
In pyntarris. *Unknown.* WhC
In Quebec. Kipling. *See* Limerick: "There was a small boy of Quebec."
In quest of the garden of roses. Red Rose. Hafiz. PeP
In quietness and confidence. A Hymn of Trust. Nettie M. Sargent. BLRP
In Railway Halls [on Pavements]. Stephen Spender. ChMo; FaBoMo
("In railway halls, on pavements near the traffic.") EnLit
In rain and twilight mist the city street. This Is My Hour. Zoë Akins. HBV; LEAP
In rain or shine; in heat or snow. Pushcart Row. Rachel Field. BrR
In Rama. George Alfred Townsend. AA
In re Solomon Warshawer. A. M. Klein. BoCaPo
In Reading Gaol by Reading Town. Oscar Wilde. *Fr.* The Ballad of Reading Gaol. FaFP; LiTB
In regard to Eternity (said the Old Mandarin). Eternity and the Tooth. Christopher Morley. QS
In Regent's Park. Anne Ridler. DiM; POTE
In Remembrance. Julia Benson Parker. PraP
In revel and carousing. Theodosia Burr; the Wrecker's Story. John Williamson Palmer. GA; PAH
In Richard's days, when lost his pastur'd plain. The Country Justice. John Langhorne. LaA
In right I have no power to live. The Soul's Bitter Cry. *Unknown.* WGRP
In Ringlets Curl'd Thy Tresses Flow. Mary Balfour. IrPN
In Robin Hood Cove. Marsden Hartley. AnFE; CoAnAm
In Rock Springs, snow beside the tracks. Five Times Zero. Donald F. Drummond. PtPa
In Romney Marsh. John Davidson. BSV; EV-5; GoTS; GTBS; GTBS-D; LBBV; OBVV; PC; PoeT; POTE; ShBV-3; ViBoPo
In Rose Time. Willa Cather. OBAV
In Rudionem. John Weever. SiCE; TuPP
In Rufum. Sir John Davies. ReIE
In Ruin Reconciled. Aubrey Thomas De Vere. IrPN
In ruling well what guerdon? Life runs low. The Two Old Kings. Lord De Tabley. ES; OBEV (new ed.); OBVV; VA
In S Street trod the fantom [*or* phantom] guard. The Warrior Passes. Hubert Kelley. DD; GA; LPS-1
In sailing it were good to have a chart. The Voyage. W. W. Gibson. ChMo; CMP
In Saint-Avoye, and not elsewhere. Villon. *Fr.* The Testament. TrFP
In Salamis, filled with the foaming. Troy [*or* Song of Troy]. Euripides. *Fr.* Trojan Women. GrR; OxBG; WoL
In Salem seasick spindrift drifts or skips. Salem. Robert Lowell. AnNE; NePoEA
In Salutation to My Father's Spirit. Sarojini Naidu. FAOV
In Samarcand. Laura E. Richards. PoRh
In Sana, O, in Sana, God, the Lord. Prince Adeb. George Henry Boker. LPS-2
In Saturday Market, there's eggs a-plenty. Charlotte Mew. *Fr.* Saturday Market. FaPON
In Saturn's Reign. Juvenal, *tr. fr. Latin by* Dryden. *Fr.* Satires. BeR
In Scarlet Town where I was born [*or* bound]. Barbara Allen [*or* Bonny Barbara Allan *or* Barbara Allen's Cruelty]. *Unknown.* BCEP; BSV; CBOV; ESPB (B *vers.*); FaFP; HBV; LEAP; LO; OBB; OBEV; OnSP; OTPC (1923 ed.); TreF; TrGrPo; ViBoFo (C *vers.*); ViBoPo
In scented gardens of the south. The Nightingale. Elizabeth Belloc. JKCP (1955 ed.)
In schomer, when the leves spring [*or* spryng]. Robin Hood and the Potter. *Unknown.* BaBo; ESPB
In School Days. Whittier. AA; AnNE; BLPA; BTP; CoBA; FaBoBe; IAP; MPB (1956 ed.); MW; NeHB; OTPC (1946 ed.); PCD; PTA-1; PYM; StVeCh (1940 ed.); TCAP; TreF
"Still sits the schoolhouse by the road," *sel.* FaPON
In Schraffi's. W. H. Auden. MaPo
In Scotland there was a babie born. Hind Horn. *Unknown.* ATP; BaBo (A *vers.*); EPP; ESPB; TOP; ViBoFo

"In Scotland was I bred and born." Bonny Barbara Allen [*or* Ellen]. *Unknown.* BaBo (B *vers.*); Po
In Scotland, where the porridge grows. Of the Stalking of the Stag. Sir Owen Seaman. CenHV
In Scotland's realm, forlorn and bare. The Chaffinch's Nest at Sea. William Cowper. OTPC (1923 ed.)
In sea-cold Lyonesse. Sunk Lyonesse. Walter de la Mare. CoBMV; FaBoCh
In seaboard town there was a merchant. In Brunton Town. *Unknown.* BaBo
In Search of the Picturesque. William Combe. *Fr.* Dr. Syntax in Search of the Picturesque. OBRV
In search of wisdom, far from wit I fly. Wit and Wisdom. Ambrose Philips. EV-3
In season what time every growing thing. The Spider and the Fly. John Heywood. ReIE
In secret mountain fastnesses we stored. Sara Bard Field. *Fr.* Barabbas. PoFr
In secret place where once I stood. The Flesh and the Spirit. Anne Bradstreet. AmP; AmPP; AnAmPo; AnFE; APA; APW; CoAnAm; IAP; LA; LiTA; MOAP; NePA; OxBA
In seed time learn, in harvest teach, in winter enjoy. Proverbs of Hell. Blake. *Fr.* The Marriage of Heaven and Hell. AtBAP; EM-1; EnLi-2; RO
In Senecam. John Heath. SiCE
In sensuous coil. Kings. *Unknown. Fr.* The Panchatantra. AWP; LiTW; PoFr
In September. Eleanor Hammond. GFA
In September. Francis Ledwidge. POTE; TCPD
In serene irony the infinite azure. The Azure. Stéphane Mallarmé. AnFP
In Service. Winifred M. Letts. CV; HBMV; POT; PoTo; VOD; YT
In seventeen hundred and fifty-nine. Hawke. Sir Henry Newbolt. BBV
In seventeen hundred and ninety-four. The Greenland Fishery. *Unknown.* OBB
In seventeen hundred and seventy-five. The Bombardment of Bristol. *Unknown.* PAH
In seventeen hundred thirty-two. George Washington. *Unknown, at. to* M. Alice Bryant. HH
In Severum. Sir John Davies. ReIE
In Seville, when the feast was long. Remember Me. Winthrop Mackworth Praed. ERP
In shade of death's sad tree/ Stood dolefull shee. Sancta Maria Dolorum, or the Mother of Sorrows. Richard Crashaw. LiA
In Shadow. Hart Crane. TwAmPo
In Shadow. Caroline Hazard. GoBC
In shadowy calm the boat. Hope. Phillips Stewart. CaP; OCL
In shantung suits we whites are cool. The Devil-Dancers. William Plomer. BoSA
In shards the sylvan vases lie. The Ravaged Villa. Herman Melville. GTBS-D; PoEL-5
In shelter of the vaulted yews. The Owls. Timeus Gaylord. DaM
In Sherwood lived stout Robin Hood. *Unknown.* OBSC
In shining groups, each stem a pearly ray. Ghost-Flowers. Mary Potter Thacher Higginson. AA
In shrouds distinct, on palls apart. Meek Candidates for Grave Space. Leo Kennedy. BoCaPo
In Siberia's wastes. Siberia. James Clarence Mangan. CBOV; ERP; GTIV; IrPN; TIP
In Sickness. Swift. CEP; OBEC
In Sight of the Town of Cockermouth, Where the Author Was Born, and His Father's Remains Are Laid. Wordsworth. ES
In Silence. Lorenzo Mavilis, *tr. fr. Modern Greek by* Rae Dalven. MoGP
In silence, and at night, the conscience feels. The Cardinal's Soliloquy. Sir Edward Bulwer-Lytton. *Fr.* Richelieu; or, The Conspiracy. VA
In silence and in darkness memory wakes. Memory. Edward Shanks. MM
In silence, solitude and stern surmise. Trumbull Stickney. George Cabot Lodge. LBMV
In silence stark and bitter. The Day of the Slaves. Leonard Bacon. PoFr
In silent gaze the tuneful choir among. Stanzas to Mr. Bentley. Thomas Gray. EiPP; EV-3
In silent horror o'er the desert-waste [*or* boundless waste]. Hassan; or, The Camel Driver. William Collins. Persian Eclogues, II. CEP; EV-3
In silent night when rest I took. Upon the Burning of Our House. Anne Bradstreet. AmP; AmPP (4th ed.); OxBA
In silken, milken Samarcand. In Samarcand. Laura E. Richards. PoRh
In simple muslin delicately dressed. New Orleans Balcony. Dorothy Haight. CAW
In simple wise the revelation came. Pentecost. Laura Simmons. ChIP
In simpler verse than triolets. An Old-fashioned Poet. Ada Foster Murray. HBV
In Sleep. Richard Burton. AA
In sleeplessness of London rooms. Dawn in London. Nikolai Tikhonov. RuPo
In sleepy dreams of family-men. The Epoch. Nikolai Tikhonov. RuPo
In Sligo the country was soft; there were turkeys. County Sligo. Louis MacNeice. OnYI
In slow and smoky fires thou burn'st and art consumèd. St. Sebastian. Valery Yakovlevich Bryusov. TrRV
In slow recuperative hours. Convalescence, V. David McCord. WhC
In slumbers of midnight the sailor boy lay. The Mariner's Dream. William Dimond. BeLS; HBV; LPS-2
In small green cup an acorn grew. The Acorn. *Unknown.* BoTP
In smokey inns whose loft is reached by ladders. The Old Masters. Emile Verhaeren. AnEnPo
In Smyrna, Melpo,/ Hero in Salonika. Sinner. Galatea Kazantzakis. MoGP
In snake-coloured tights. Memory of a Witch. Iku Takenaka. PoLJ
In snorts of wind, the tawny meadow. Runaway. Kim Kurt. NePoAm-2
In Snow. William Allingham. IrPN
In so much as the lily and the rose. Sonnet. Garcilaso de la Vega. TeCS
In Soapsuds Street. Manuel Bandeira, *tr. fr. Portuguese by* Dudley Poore. AnCL
In sober mornings do[e] not thou rehearse. When He Would Have His Verses Read. Robert Herrick. EnL; NBE; OAEP; OBS; SeCV-1; SeEP
In Soft Moss, Muted Steps. David Einhorn, *tr. fr. Yiddish by* Sarah Zweig Betsky. OnCuPl
In solemn conclave vow and swear. Constitution for a League of Nations. Arthur Guiterman. InMe
In solemn pause the forest waits. The Untended Field. Robert Hillyer. AnNE
In solitary august, like a story. Passage of an August. Eithne Wilkins. NeBP
In Solitude. Virna Sheard. CPG
In some small hamlet on the lonely plain. Thomas Tickell. *Fr.* To a Lady before Marriage. EnSW
In some unused lagoon, some nameless bay. The Dismantled Ship. Walt Whitman. AmPP (4th ed.); OxBA
In somer, when the shawes be sheyne. Robin Hood and the Monk [*or* In Summer *or* May in the Green-Wood *or* Whitsuntide]. *Unknown.* BaBo; CBOV; CH; ESPB; OBB; OBEV; TCEP; ViBoFo; ViBoPo. *See also* In summer when the shaws be sheen.
In Sorrow. Thomas Hastings. AA; HBV
In sorrowes drown'd I wast my weary dayes. *Unknown.* SeCSL
In sorrow's cell I laid me down to sleep. Rosader's Sonnet. Thomas Lodge. *Fr.* Rosalynde; or, Euphues' Golden Legacy. EPP; ReIE
In Spain. Emily Lawless. AnIV
(Spain.) TIP
In Spain. Sir Thomas Wyatt. OBSC; SeCePo
In Spain; Drinking Song. Emily Lawless. AnIV
In Spain, where the courtly Castilian hidalgo twangs lightly each night his romantic guitar. Carmen. Newman Levy. ALV; FiBHP
In Sparta once Aristodemus. Money Makes the Man. Alcaeus. GrR
In speculation. Chorus. A. E. Housman. *Fr.* Fragment of a Greek Tragedy. BMEP
In Spirit Senses Are. "Angelus Silesius," *tr. fr. German by* Paul Carus. OnPM
In spite of a day a day lost in the heat a day. A Day Lost. Gertrude Stein. AtBAP
In spite of all the learned have said. The Indian Burying Ground. Philip Freneau. AA; AmP; AmPP; AnAmPo; AnFE; APA; APW; BAV; CoAnAm; CoBA; HBV; HiLiAm; IAP; LA; LBAP; LiTA; LiTG; MOAP; NePA; OBAV; OxBA; Po; PoEL-4; RiBV; TCAP; TriL; UnW
In spite of cold and chills. Daffodils. Kikurio. SUS; TiPo
In spite of my efforts. Taira no Kanemori, *tr. fr. Japanese by* I. W. Furukami. LiTW
In spite of rice, in spite of wheat. Epigram on the Poor of Boston . . . 1774. *Unknown.* PAH
In Spite of Sorrow. Adoniram Judson. MaRV
In Spite of War. Angela Morgan. CV; SBMV
In sport a vessel's crew will often take. The Albatross. Baudelaire. TrFP
In Spring. Michael Lewis. *See* April Winds.
In Spring. Li Po, *tr. fr. Chinese by* Witter Bynner. LiTW
In Spring. Eduard Mörike, *tr. fr. German by* Vernon Watkins. AnGP
In Spring. Georg Sannikov, *tr. fr. Russian by* C. M. Bowra. BoRS

In spring and summer winds may blow. Walter Savage Landor. GTML; PG
In spring before the dawn we see. Summer Day. Boris Pasternak. BoRS
In spring Cydonian apple-trees. Reflections of Spring. Ibycus. GrR
In spring I look gay. A Tree. *Unknown.* BoTP; OxNR; RIS
In spring of youth [*or* youth's spring] it was my lot. The Lake: To——. Poe. AmP; APW; IAP; OBRV; OnPM; TriL
In Spring the day is early. April Winds [*or* In Spring]. Michael Lewis. StaSt; TSW; TSWC
In spring time birds are born and sing. In the Woods. Gérard de Nerval. TrFP
In spring, when branches of woodbine. Trailing Arbutus. Henry Abbey. SN
In spring, when the green gits back in the trees. When the Green Gits Back in the Trees. James Whitcomb Riley. ADAH; YT
In Springfield Mountain. *Unknown. See* Springfield Mountain.
In Springfield, where his ashes lie. The Lincoln Circuit. E. O. Laughlin. LPS-1
In Springtime. Samuel Taylor Coleridge. *Fr.* Work without Hope. BoTP
In Spring-Time. W. H. Davies. MM; NLK (1947 ed.); TwCV
In springtime the eider cleaves its way. The Eider Duck. Ibsen. AnNoLy
In springtime when the leaves are young. Seasons. Christina Rossetti. YeAr
In State. Forceythe Willson. BIG; LPS-2
"O keeper of the sacred key," *sel.* AA
In stature the Manlet was dwarfish. The Manlet. "Lewis Carroll." PA
In stifling mows the men became oppressed. An August Afternoon. J. P. Irvine. SN
In storm he lived and with the storm he died. The Death of Shelley. Donald Parson. MuM
In Stratis Viarum. Arthur Hugh Clough. PoVP; VLEP
In streets, among the rocks of time and weather. The Mountains. Louis Dudek. CaP
In such a marvellous night so fair. The Night of Marvels. Sister Violante do Ceo. CAW
In Such a Night. Shakespeare. *Fr.* The Merchant of Venice, V, i. ChTr; FiP; LiA; WHA
(Divine Harmony, The.) GoBC
In such a night, when every louder wind. A Nocturnal Reverie. Countess of Winchilsea. BCEP; CEP; EiPP; EnSW; EPP; EV-3; FaBoEn; GoTL; LoBV; OBEC; PoEL-3; SeCePo
In such a spot, with radiant flowers for halo. She of the Garden. Emile Verhaeren. CAW
In Such an Age. Angela Morgan. *See* Today.
In Summer. Charles Hanson Towne. HBMV
In Summer. *Unknown. Fr.* Robin Hood and the Monk. CH
("In somer, when the shawes be sheyne.") ViBoPo
(In the Fair Forest, *2 sts., mod.*) BoTP
(May in the Green-Wood.) OBEV
(Morning of May, A, *mod.*) PoLi
(Whitsuntide.) CBOV
In summer all is bright and gay. The Death of Lailí. Nizami. *Fr.* Lailí and Majnún. PeP
In summer elms are made for me. Dilemma of the Elm. Genevieve Taggard. MAP; MoAmPo
In summer, ere the Ascension. Mane Nobiscum Domine. *Unknown.* TMEV
In summer-heat or in wintertime glistening. Artist. Aleksandr Blok. BoR
In summer I am very glad. Playgrounds. Laurence Alma-Tadema. BoTP; HBV; HBVY; OTPC; PCH; PPL
In summer I'm disposed to shirk. The Lazy Writer. Bert Leston Taylor. ALV; PFE; PoMa
In summer, in the open air. Summer Sabbath. Jessie E. Sampter. TrJP
In summer, in the sunlight. Story Books. E. V. Lucas. MOB
In summer, on the headlands. The Neckan. Matthew Arnold. GBV (1952 ed.); TVSH
In Summer, Spring, and also Fall. A Desk Motto. Don Marquis. DDA
In summer the garden where we played. The Crack. J. C. Hall. HaMV
In summer time, I took my road. Sheep in the Shade. William Barnes. EnSW
In summertime on Bredon. Bredon Hill [*or* Summer Time on Bredon]. A. E. Housman. A Shropshire Lad, XXI. BEL; BPN; ChMo; CMP; EmBrPo; EnLi-2; GBV (1952 ed.); LiTL; MBP; MoAB; MoBrPo; NeMA; PoTo; POTT; PoVP; RiBV; TCEP; TCPD; TreF; TwCV; TyEnPo; ViP; ViPo; WHA
In summer time, when leaves grew green and birds were singing. King Edward the Fourth and a Tanner of Tamworth. *Unknown.* BaBo; ESPB
In summer time, when leaves grow green/ Down a down a down. Robin Hood and the Tinker. *Unknown.* BaBo; ESPB
In summer time, when leaves grow green and flowers are fresh and gay. Robin Hood and the Curtal Friar. *Unknown.* BaBo; ESPB
In summer time, when leaves grow green, when they doe grow both green and long. The Noble Fisherman; or, Robin Hood's Preferment. *Unknown.* ESPB; OBB
In summer, when the days were long. Summer Days. Wathen Marks Wilks Call. LPS-1; VA
In summer, when the grass is thick, if mother has the time. The Fairy Book. Norman Gale. HBV; HBVY; OHIP; OTPC (1946 ed.); RAR; TVC; TVSH
In summer when the rose-bushes. Song. Edith Sitwell. NP
In summer when the shaws be [*or* are] sheen. Robin Hood and the Monk [*or* A Morning of May], *mod. Unknown.* MeEV; PoLi. *See also* In somer, when . . .
In summer when the woods are green. In the Fair Forest. *Unknown.* BoTP
In summers heate and mid-time of the day. Ovid. Amores, I, 5. LaP
In summer's mellow midnight. The Night Wind. Emily Brontë. ChER; ChTr; OAEP
In sunburnt parks where Sundays lie. Cobb Would Have Caught It. Robert Fitzgerald. InvP
In sunny girlhood's vernal life. A Portrait. Joseph Ashby-Sterry. HBV; VA
In Superbum. Thomas Freeman. SiCE
In surety and obscurity twice mailed. Not Always. E. A. Robinson. CoV
In swaddling clothes he came across the sea. The Round Trip. McLandburgh Wilson. BLP
In Switzerland one idle day. Idyll. Hugh Macnaghten. HBMV
In Syon lodge me (Lord) for pitty. Hildebert of Lavardin. *Fr.* Prayer to the Holy Trinity. LiA
In Taberna Quando Sumus. *Unknown, tr. fr. Latin by* George F. Whicher. *Fr.* Carmina Burana. LaP
In talking/ You are very like. To a Lady Holding the Floor. Mildred Weston. FiBHP
In tangled wreaths, in clustered gleaming stars. Yellow Jessamine. Constance Fenimore Woolson. AA; HBV
In tattered old slippers that toast at the bars. The Cane-bottomed Chair. Thackeray. FAOV; HBV; OTPC; PoVP
In Teacup Times. Austin Dobson. *See* Rondeau to Ethel, A.
In tears I tossed my coin from Trevi's edge. Italian Rhapsody. Robert Underwood Johnson. HBV
In tedious exile now too long detain'd. Daedalus and Icarus. Ovid. *Fr.* Metamorphoses, VIII. RoL
In Tempestiva. Henry Longan Stuart. CAW
In temporary pain. The New God. Witter Bynner. *Fr.* The New World. WGRP
In Tempore Senectutis. Ernest Dowson. POTT; VLEP
In Temptation. Charles Wesley. *See* Jesus, Lover of My Soul.
In tender May when the sweet laugh of Christ. The Puritan. Karl Shapiro. MoAmPo (1950 ed.)
In Tenebris. Thomas Hardy. FaBoEn; LiTB; PoLFOT; SeCePo; ViP; ViPo
Sels.
"When the clouds' swoln bosoms," II. BrBE; ChMo; CMP; LiTM (rev. ed.)
"Wintertime nighs," I. OAEP (2d ed.); TreFS; UnPo
In Tenebris. Sister Mary of the Visitation. JKCP (1955 ed.)
In Tennessee, the dogwood tree. Tennessee. Francis Brooks. AA
In Tesla's Laboratory. Robert Underwood Johnson. AA
In th' olde dayes of the Kyng [*or* King] Arthour. The Wife of Bath's Tale [*or* The Tale of the Wyf of Bathe]. Chaucer. *Fr.* The Canterbury Tales. EnLit; LiA; REAL; ViBoPo
In Thankfull Remembrance for My Dear Husband's Safe Arrivall Sept. 3, 1662. Anne Bradstreet. TrPWD
In that age, the great anagram of God. The Incarnation of Sirius. James McAuley. MoAuPo
In that bad year and city of your birth. For an Emigrant. Randall Jarrell. OxBA
In that day I had hoped for a pair of boots to guard my feet on the terrible trek. My Head on My Shoulders. Jeremy Ingalls. GoYe
In that desolate land and lone. The Revenge of Rain-in-the-Face. Longfellow. BBV; GA; PaA; PAH
In That Dim Monument Where Tybalt Lies. Arthur Davison Ficke. HBMV
In that fell strife, when force with force engages. William Tell. Schiller. PoFr
In that forest whitish tree-trunks loom. The Forest. Nikolai Gumilev. BoRS

In that furious, final wake for Flannagan. The Dancers with a Hop. James Schevill. FiMAP
In that hour came the disciples unto Jesus, saying. Jesus and the Children. St. Matthew, Bible, *N.T.* GrCo-1
In that I have so greatly failed thee, Lord. So Little and So Much. John Oxenham. BLRP
In that land all Is, and nothing's Ought. Neither Here nor There. W. R. Rodgers. FaBoMo; GTBS-W; LiTB; LiTM; MoAB; MoBrPo (1950 ed.); NeBP; ViBoPo (1958 ed.)
In that land of dopy dreams, happy peaceful Philippines. Damn the Filipinos. *Unknown.* ABF
In that miraculous sunset, wonder-spent. Down Channel. A. G. Prys-Jones. UnW
In that moment you sailed for all of death. Elegy for Your Absence. Eugenio Florit. TwSpPo
In that most wretched hovel. In the Wretched Hovel. *Unknown.* OnPM
In that new world toward which our feet are set. Compensation. Celia Thaxter. HBV
In that November off Tehuantepec. Sea Surface Full of Clouds. Wallace Stevens. AnAmPo; AnFE; CoAnAm; CoBA; CoBMV; LA; MAP; MoAB; MoAmPo; TwAmPo
In that, O queen of queens, thy birth was free. To Our Blessed Lady [*or* To Our Lady]. Henry Constable. ACP; CAW; CoBE; GoBC; ISi; OBSC
In that proud port which her so goodly graceth. Amoretti, XIII. Spenser. EV-1; PeBoSo; ReIE
In that rapacious littoral now slaked by sea. Shore Birds. Vi Gale. GoYe
In that same gardin all the goodly flowres. The Garden of Adonis. Spenser. *Fr.* The Faerie Queene, III. NBE
In that soft mid-land where the breezes bear. Rodney's Ride. Elbridge Streeter Brooks. GA; MC; OTPC; PAH
In that sore hour around thy bed there stood. Deliverance. William James Dawson. OBVV
In that strange city. Hunger. Mary Carolyn Davies. AnAmPo
In thaws like cloth-of-gold blithe noonday goes. Lent. Lubov Nikitishna Stolitza. TrRV
In the Acadian land, on the shores of the Basin of Minas. Longfellow. *Fr.* Evangeline. CoBA; IAP
In the Afterglow. Flora S. Rivola. MotAn
In the age that was golden, the halcyon times. Pessimism. Newton Mackintosh. BOHV
In the air of the room. Rendezvous. Antonia Pozzi. OnPM
In the air there are no coral. A Song. Duncan Campbell Scott. PeCV; TwCV
In the Album of a Composer. Henrik Ibsen, *tr. fr. Norwegian by* Charles W. Stork. AnNoLy
In the Allegheny Mountains. The Barn-Swallow. William Sargent. RIS
In the amber morning by the inlet's high shore. Hands. Earle Birney. BoCaPo (1943 ed.); TwCV
In the Ambulance. W. W. Gibson. BMEP; PYM
In the American Grain, *sel.* William Carlos Williams.
Sir Walter Raleigh. OnHM
In the ancestral chest lies a watery sword, three feet long. A Sword in the Spring Office. Li Ho. WhP
In the ancestral presence of the dead. Necessity. Letitia E. Landon. BCEP
In the ancient town of Bruges. Carillon. Longfellow. *Fr.* The Belfry of Bruges. CoBA; IAP; LPS-2
In the Annals of Tacitus. Philip Murray. NePoAm
In the April Rain. Mary Anderson. BoTP
In the Arena. Antero de Quental, *tr. fr. Portuguese by* S. Griswold Morley. UnW
In the Art Museum. Gertrude Hall. OBAV
In the austere November sky. A Song for Saint Cecilia. Marya Zaturenska. TriL
In the Autumn mountains. Hitomaro, *tr. fr. Japanese by* Kenneth Rexroth. OnPJ
In the Autumn sky the clouds are thinned. After Rain. Tu Fu. OnPM
In the Azure Night. Bartolomé Galindez. CAW
In the Backs. Frances Cornford. DiM
In the bad old days it was not so bad. The Managers. W. H. Auden. EnLit
In the Baggage Coach Ahead. Gussie L. Davis. TreFS
(Baggage Coach Ahead.) ABS
In the bare midst of Anglesey they show. East and West. Matthew Arnold. BPN
In the Barn. Josephine Pinckney. NP
In the barn the tenant Cock. Day; a Pastoral. John Cunningham. OBEC
In the Barnyard. Dorothy Aldis. UTS
In the Barn-Yard's Southerly Corner. Sir Charles G. D. Roberts. BoCaPo; TwCaPo
In the Bay. Swinburne. BMEP; VLEP
In the Bay. Arthur Symons. PoVP
In the Bay of Sumi. Fujiwara no Toshiyuki, *tr. fr. Japanese by* Kenneth Rexroth. OnPJ
In the Bazaars of Hyderabad. Sarojini Naidu. FaPON; GaP; MoSiPe
In the Beginning. Harriet Monroe. AA
In the Beginning. Jenny Lind Porter. GoYe
In the Beginning. Dylan Thomas. MaPo
In the beginning, at every step, he turned. The Sickness of Adam. Karl Shapiro. *Fr.* Adam and Eve. AmP; CoBMV; FiMAP; MoAB; ReMP
In the beginning, earth gave forth, around. The Origins of Life. Lucretius. *Fr.* De Rerum Natura. LiTW
In the beginning God created the heaven and the earth. The Creation [*or* Creator]. Genesis, Bible, *O.T.* GrCo-1; ImOP; TreF; WoL
In the beginning God created the world. T. S. Eliot. *Fr.* The Rock. OxBoCh
In the beginning God made woman's mind apart from man's. On Women. Semonides, *tr. by* J. M. Edmonds. GrL
In the beginning God made various kinds of women. Semonides, *tr. fr. Greek by* Richmond Lattimore. GrPo
"In the beginning," said the old man. Genesis. Ray Mathew. NeLNL
In the beginning the Great Spirit gave the prairie rare gifts. The Western Trail. Robert V. Carr. PoOW
In the beginning there arose the Golden Child. To the Unknown God. *Unknown. Fr.* The Rig-Veda. GrCo-1; OuHeWo
In the beginning, there was nought. Creation. Alfred Noyes. GoBC; OBVV; TCPD
In the beginning there were transports. Genesis. Jules Alan Wein. TrJP
In the beginning this was Self alone, in the shape of a person. The Universal Self. *Unknown. Fr.* The Upanishads. WoL
In the Beginning Was the Bird. Henry Treece. LiTB; LiTM; MoWP; WaP
In the beginning was the three-pointed star. In the Beginning. Dylan Thomas. MaPo
In the Beginning Was the Word. St. John, I: 1-17, Bible, *N.T.* TreF
(Word, The, I: 1-5.) MaRV; TrGrPo
In the Beginning Was the Word. Anna Hempstead Branch. NV; TBM
In the beginning was the Word. The Eternal Word. Longfellow. ChIP
In the beginning, when green came on the pasture. In the Beginning. Jenny Lind Porter. GoYe
In the belovèd hour that ushers day. To Doctor Hake. Robert Louis Stevenson. VLEP
In the big-flaked sugar-snow. Maple Feast. Frances Frost. SiSoSe
In the Birdless Country. Toson Shimazaki, *tr. fr. Japanese by* Takamichi Ninomiya *and* D. J. Enright. PoLJ
In the bitter waves of woe. Ultima Veritas. Washington Gladden. OQP; QP-1
In the Black Ball Line I served my time. Banks of the Sacramento. *Unknown.* SG
In the black furrow of a field. The Hare. Walter de la Mare. TiPo
In the Bleak Mid-Winter. Christina Rossetti. *See* Christmas Carol, A.
In the blossom-land Japan. An Old Song. "Yehoash." AWP; JAWP; LiTW; WBP
In the Blue Ridge. Olive Tilford Dargan. NoCaPo
In the Blue Sky. Bocho Yamamura, *tr. fr. Japanese by* Takamichi Ninomiya *and* D. J. Enright. PoLJ
In the bluebell forest. Bluebells. Olive Enoch. BoTP
In the bowl of buildings alias the back yard. Milk at the Bottom of the Sea. Oscar Williams. GTBS-W; LiTA; MoPo
In the Breeze. Boris Pasternak, *tr. fr. Russian by* C. M. Bowra. TrJP
("In the breeze, on a bough that is asking.") BoR
In the bright bay of your morning, O God. Prayer. Claire Goll. TrJP
In the bright season when He, most high Jove. The Golden Sestina. Giovanni Pico della Mirandola. LiTW
In the Busy Streets, Domains of Trade. Henry David Thoreau. CoV
In the cage my life began. Bagheera's Song. Kipling. *Fr.* The Second Jungle Book. PoFr
In the capital spring comes late. Buying Flowers. Po Chü-i. WhP
In the Carpenter Shop. Robert McIntyre. *See* Nazareth Shop, The.
In the Carpenter's Shop. Sara Teasdale. HBMV; StJW
In the castle of my soul. The Little Gate to God. Walter Rauschenbusch. MaRV; QS
In the Catacombs. Harlan Hoge Ballard. BOHV; YaD
In the Cathedral Close. Edward Dowden. GTIV; OBVV; OxBI
In the cavern of cold. London Revisited—1946. Dorothy Livesay. BoCaPo (1948 ed.)
In the Caves of Auvergne. W. J. Turner. HBMV; POTE; TCPD
In the Cemetery of the Sun. Wilfred Watson. PeCV
In the Chaotic Age. C. Day Lewis. ChMo

In the Children's Hospital. Tennyson. HBV; PoVP
In the chill of Autumn. Love's Temperature. Walter of Chatillon. LaP
In the church, fallen like dancers. Enfidaville. Keith Douglas. HaMV
In the Churchyard at Cambridge. Longfellow. PoEL-5
In the City. T. P. Cameron Wilson. *Fr.* The City Tramp. MW
In the City. Israel Zangwill. WGRP
In the Clear Cold. Sergei Aleksandrovich Yesenin, *tr. fr. Russian by* Babette Deutsch. TrRV
In the Cloister. William J. Fischer. PraNu
In the cloud-gray mornings. Hoar-Frost. Amy Lowell. *Fr.* Chinoiseries. AnAmPo; LA; NP
In the Coach, *sel.* Thomas Edward Brown. Pazons, The, V. POTT
In the coign of the cliff between lowland and highland. *See* In a coign . . .
In the coiled shell sounds Ocean's distant roar. The Tutelage. Robert Mowry Bell. AA
In the cold I will rise, I will bathe. The Lonely Death. Adelaide Crapsey. AnFE; APA; BAP; CoAnAm; LEAP; MAP; MoAmPo (1942 ed.); NP; SBMV
In the cold October night-time. *See* In the wild October night-time.
In the convent of Drontheim. The Nun of Nidaros. Longfellow. *Fr.* Tales of a Wayside Inn. PraNu
In the cool autumn month—the Eighth or the Ninth. An Invitation to Li Po. Ts'ui Tsung-chi. BoFr
In the cool, impersonal room. The Egoist Dead. Elizabeth Brewster. CaP
In the Cool of the Evening. Alfred Noyes. HBV
In the cool of twilight, now the sun has gone. My Two Daughters. Victor Hugo. LO; TrFP
In the cool, sweet hush of a wooded nook. Missing. *Unknown.* BIG
In the copper marsh. Heron. Philip Booth. NePoEA
In the corner of the bedroom is a great big curtain. Brownie. A. A. Milne. CBPC
In the Country. W. H. Davies. BMEP; ChMo; CMP
In the County Tyrone, in the town of Dungannon. The Ould Orange Flute. *Unknown.* OxBoLi
In the Courts of Evil/ Borgias dine. Saint Francis Borgia; or, A Refutation for Heredity. Phyllis McGinley. NePoAm-2
In the courtyard grows a rare tree. *Unknown, tr. fr. Chinese.* The Nineteen Han Poems, IX. ChLP; WhP
In the courtyard there grows a strange tree. *Unknown, tr. fr. Chinese by* Arthur Waley. Seventeen Old Poems, 8. TrCh
In the Cove. Mary Fanny Youngs. HH
In the cowslip pips I lie. Clock-a [*or* o']-Clay. John Clare. BLV; FaPON; LiTB; LoBV; PoEL-4; PoFS; SeCeV; ThWaDe; TrGrPo; WHA
In the cradle of my heart my sweet one will I lay. A Hush Song. Paul Gregan. BOL
In the cream gilded cabin of his steam yacht. Mr. Nixon. Ezra Pound. *Fr.* Hugh Selwyn Mauberley. CoBMV; CoV; LiTA; LiTM (rev. ed.); MoPo
In the crimson of the morning, in the whiteness of the noon. The Coming of His Feet. Lyman W. Allen. BLPA; MaRV; NeHB
In the crocus-bed I saw her. Cat and Crocuses. Eva Martin. PoC
In the Cross of Christ I Glory. Sir John Bowring. HBV; MaRV; OIF; WGRP (Towering o'er the Wrecks of Time.) BePJ
In the crowd's multitudinous mind. Crucifixion. Eva Gore-Booth. MaRV; WGRP
In the Dark. George Arnold. HBV
In the Dark. Frances Louisa Bushnell. AA
In the Dark. Mary Potter Thacher Higginson. AA
In the Dark. Sophie Jewett. LBAP; TrPWD
In the dark and peace of my final bed. Little Pagan Rain Song. Frances Shaw. HBMV; NP
In the dark beneath the earth. Dead Waters. Manuel Gutiérrez Nájera. AnMP
In the dark caverns of the night. Poem. Henry Treece. NeBP
In the dark crevasses the smoke-white fish. Leviathan. Margaret R. Gould. TwCaPo
In the dark days, the early evenings of December. The Bell-Ringers. James Rorty. MOAP
In the dark dungeons of the mind. The Praying-Mantis. Annie Charlotte Dalton. BoCaPo (1943 ed.); TwCaPo
In the Dark, in the Dew. Mary Newmarch Prescott. HBV
In the dark of the wood, silence. No leaf stirred. The Dark Wood. John Hall Wheelock. PG (1955 ed.)
In the dark pathways of his Gothic mind. Sketch. "Seumas O'Sullivan." AnIV
In the dark pine-wood. James Joyce. Chamber Music, XX. ReaPo
In the dark room of her disinclination. Chorus for Refusal. Margaret Marks. MAP
In the dark womb where I began. C. L. M. [*or* To His Mother]. John Masefield. BLV; BMEP; BoLiVe; ChMo; CMP, HBV; LiTM; MBP; MoBrPo; MotAn; OBVV; POTE; POTT
In the darkened alcove. Cradle Song. Victor Hugo. BOL
In the darkening church. Rufus Prays. L. A. G. Strong. MBP; MoBrPo; PC
In the darkness before dawn. Paean of Dawn in May. Herbert Trench. GTIV
In the darkness deep. The Song of the Turnkey. Harry Bache Smith. AA
In the darkness he sings of the dawning. The Poet. Mary Sinton Leitch. BoHiPo; HBMV; LS; PoMa
In the darkness, who would answer for the color of a rose. The Blind Girl. Nathalia Crane. MAP; MCCG; MoAmPo (1942 ed.); PFE
In the Dawn. Odell Shepard. WGRP
"We are standing in the great dawn of a day they did not know," *sel.* MaRV
In the dawn, although I know. Fujiwara no Michinobu, *tr. fr. Japanese by* Kenneth Rexroth. OnPJ
In the dawn I gathered cedar-boughs. Song of Whip-plaiting. Constance Lindsay Skinner. *Fr.* Songs of the Coast-Dwellers. BoCaPo; NP
In the dawn's first light. Sister Sun. Ibn Malik of Granada. MooP
In the day the sun is darkened. Lines. Stopford Augustus Brooke. IrPN
In the Days of Crinoline. Thomas Hardy. WhC
In the days of my season of salad. A Song of Renunciation. Sir Owen Seaman. CenHV; PA
In the Days of Old. Thomas Love Peacock. *Fr.* Crotchet Castle. HBV
In the Days of Old Rameses, *with music. Unknown.* AS
In the days of old, when Englishmen were—men. *See* In days of old . . .
In the days of President Washington. In Praise of Johnny Appleseed. Vachel Lindsay. PoRL; TSW; TSWC
In the Days of Thy Youth. Bhartrihari, *tr. fr. Sanskrit by* Arthur W. Ryder. OnPM
In the days that have passed, in the days that have flown. Lemme Go Back! *Unknown.* CAG
In the days that tried our fathers. National Anthem by Gen. George P. M—— "Orpheus C. Kerr." *Fr.* The Rejected "National Hymns." LPS-3
In the days when Arthur bold. Sir Launfal. Thomas Chester. ATP
In the days when my hair first fell over my forehead. A Ballad of Ch'ang Kan. Li Po. ChLP
In the Days When the Cattle Ran. Hamlin Garland. MPB
In the Day's Work. Jessie Litchfield. MoAuPo
In the dead middle of night. The Exile. Gerald Bullett. POTE
In the dead of night. Dead of Night. Manuel Bandeira. AnCL
In the dead of night I heard a sound of storm. The Messiah. David Frishman. LiTW
"In the Dead Unhappy Midnight." Gerald Massey. UnW
In the Dean's porch a nest of clay. In the Cathedral Close. Edward Dowden. GTIV; OBVV; OxBI
In the December weather, grey and grim. John Francis O'Donnell. *Fr.* Happy Christmases. IrPN
In the deep heart of man a poet dwells. The Enchanter. Emerson. HiLiAm; IAP
In the deep shadows of the porch. Bind-Weed. "Susan Coolidge." GN; OTPC
In the deep violet air. Chanson sans Paroles. Ernest Dowson. PoVP
In the depth of your hopes and desires. Kahlil Gibran. *Fr.* The Prophet. UnW
In the Depths. Arthur Hugh Clough. BPN; EmBrPo; PoVP; VLEP
In the Depths of Night. Manuel Gutiérrez Nájera, *tr. fr. Spanish by* Thomas Walsh. CAW
In the Desert. Alice Corbin. NP
In the Desert. Herman Melville. MeRV
In the desert/ I saw a creature. The Heart [*or* Eating]. Stephen Crane. The Black Riders, III. BAP; CrMA; HoPM; MAP; MoAmPo; NeMA
In the deserted garden on weed-grown terraces the willows are fresh again. The Deserted Garden. Li Po. OnPM
In the deserted moon-blanch'd street. A Summer Night. Matthew Arnold. BMEP; BPN; EM-2; EmBrPo; EnLi-2; EPN; EV-5; ExPo; GEPC; GTBS; GTSE; GTSL; MCCG; OAEP; PoVP; SeCePo; SeCeV; TyEnPo; ViPo; ViPP; VLEP
In the deserted streets, nobody. The Cathedral at Evening. Luis Cernuda. CoSP
In the dim and distant ages, in the half-forgotten days. A Soldier of Weight. John Kendall. WhC
In the distance. A Bell at Evening. K'ung Hsiang Shu. PoHN
In the Dock. Walter de la Mare. ChMP

In the dome of my Sires as the clear moonbeam falls. Newstead Abbey. Byron. ChER
In the Dordogne. John Peale Bishop. AnAmPo
In the downhill of life, when I find I'm declining. To-Morrow. John Collins. GTBS; GTBS-D; GTBS-W; GTSE; GTSL; HBV
In the dream, in the charmed dream we are flying. The Eye of Humility. Kay Smith. BoCaPo (1948 ed.)
In the drifting rain the cows in the yard are as black. Milking before Dawn. Ruth Dallas. AnNZ
In the drinking-well. Aunt Eliza. Harry Graham. ALV; ChTr; FaFP; MaC; NA; SiTL; WhC
In the Dumps. *Unknown.* NA; SiTL
("We're all in the dumps.") BoN
In the dungeon-crypts idly did I stray. The Prisoner. Emily Brontë. AnFE; EmBrPo; EnLi-2 (1949 ed.); EV-5; OAEP; ViP
In the Dusk. Francis Ledwidge. VOD
In the dusk of the forest shade. The Men. Maurice Bell. BlG
In the Dusky Path of a Dream. Rabindranath Tagore. The Gardener, LXII. OBMV
In the dusty glare of a humid morning. Slums. James Oppenheim. BAP
In the early days in our own wild way we hurried the time along. The Ruin of Bobtail Bend. James Barton Adams. PoOW
In the early morning-shine. Life's Hebe. James Thomson. VA
In the Early, Pearly Morning. "Laurence Hope." LoPo
Carpe Diem, 4 *ll.* OtMeF
In the early spring, the fattening young weeds. The Spirit. Harold Lenoir Davis. NP
In the earth, the earth, thou shalt be laid. Warning and Reply. Emily Brontë. GTIV; OBVV; OxBI; PoVP; TriL; VA; VLEP
In the East, in the East is my heart. My Heart Is in the East. Judah Halevi. TrJP
In the east of the city. The Morning Bell of Fang T'a. Hsi P'ei Lan. OnPM; PoHN; WoL
In the eastern quarter dawn breaks, the stars flicker pale. Cock-Crow Song. *Unknown.* LiTW; TrCh
In the eighth moon of autumn, the wind howling viciously. The Roof Whirled Away by Winds. Tu Fu. WhP
In the Elegy Season. Richard Wilbur. FiMAP; MoAB; NePoEA
In the Elk Season. Erik Axel Karlfeldt, *tr. fr. Swedish by* Charles W. Stork. AnSL
In the embers shining bright. Cradle Song. Richard Watson Gilder. BOL
In the empty mountains. Hitomaro, *tr. fr. Japanese by* Kenneth Rexroth. OnPJ
In the end. For the Magi. J. Patrick Walsh. JKCP (1955 ed.)
In the end it comes to this: you weigh the alternatives. The Steelyards. Charles Bruce. BoCaPo (1948 ed.)
In the End of Days. Isaiah, II: 2–4, Bible, *O.T.* TrJP
In the end of the sabbath, as it began to dawn. Easter Morning. St. Matthew, Bible, *N.T.* TreF
In the endless nights, from my bed, where sleepless in anguish I lie. Mater Tenebrarum. James Thomson. EmBrPo
In the enormous tragic silence of the night. Brother Dog. Luis Anibal Sanchez. CAW; SaFP
In the eternal/ Light of the spring day. Ki no Tomonori, *tr. fr. Japanese by* Kenneth Rexroth. OnPJ
In the Environs of the Funeral Home. Robert Mezey. NePoEA
In the Evening. Thomas Hardy. ImOP
In the evening/ Quiet of the country town. Tanka. Noin Hoshi. Po
In the evening/ The rice leaves in the garden. Minamoto no Tsunenobu, *tr. fr. Japanese by* Kenneth Rexroth. OnPJ
In the evening/ The sun goes down. At Sunset. Ivy O. Eastwick. BoTP
In the evening after the rain. Home. Ivan Swift. BAP
In the Evening by the Moonlight. James A. Bland. TreFS
In the evening dusk when the storm raged high. Snowfrid. Viktor Rydberg. AnSL
In the evening from my window. *Unknown.* SUS
In the Evening I Walk by the River. Ou-yang Hsiu, *tr. fr. Chinese by* Kenneth Rexroth. OnPC
In the evening things stand no longer blind. Houses Have Open Eyes. Paul Zech. OnPM
In the evening, when the world knew he was dead. In the Evening. Thomas Hardy. ImOP
In the eye is the wound. The Wounded Prince. Douglas Le Pan. BoCaPo (1948 ed.)
In the Face of Grief. Sister Juana Inés de la Cruz, *tr. fr. Spanish by* Thomas Walsh. CAW
In the fair days when God. To Victor Hugo. Swinburne. OBVV; PtP
In the Fair Forest. *Unknown. See* In Summer.
In the fair gardens of celestial peace. Lines to the Memory of "Annie," Who Died at Milan, June 6, 1860. Harriet Beecher Stowe. LPS-1
In the Fall o' Year. Thomas S. Jones, Jr. HBV
In the family drinking well. Sister Nell. *Unknown.* FaPON
In the far and mighty West. Wyoming. Charles E. Winter. PoRL
In the far corner. The Blackbird. Humbert Wolfe. BLA; BoTP; FAOV; FaPON; HBMV; HBVY; MPB; NLK; PCH; StVeCh; SUS; TiPo; TSW; UTS
In the far north stands a pine tree, lone. The Pine Tree. Heine. PCH
In the far spaces of eternity. Harmony. Thomas Grant Springer. PoToHe
In the Far Years. Wilson MacDonald. CaP; OCL
In the Fashion. A. A. Milne. CBPC
In the Field. Harold Lenoir Davis. NP
In the Fields. Charlotte Mew. AlDL; MBP; MoAB; MoBrPo; MoP; POTE; TwCV
(Spring.) StaSt
In the Fields. *Unknown. See* Out in the Fields with God.
In the fields where, long ago. A Christmas Hymn. *Unknown.* COAH
In the Firelight. Eugene Field. AA
(My Mother's Faith.) MotAn
In the First House. Joseph Joel Keith. GoYe
In the first rank of these did Zimri stand. Zimri [*or* The Duke of Buckingham]. Dryden. *Fr.* Absalom and Achitophel. CoEV; PoFS; SeCePo; ShBV-4; ViBoPo
In the first year of the last disgrace. News of the World II. George Barker. FaBoTw; LiTB
In the flash of the singing dawn. The Yellow Swan. Sir Gilbert Parker. CPG
In the fog we drift hither. Rain on the River. Lu Yu. OnPC
In the foil-and-pastel tea room. Non-Euclidean Elegy. John Frederick Nims. MoVE
In the fold. The Little Young Lambs. Patrick Chalmers. TiPo (1952 ed.)
In the Forest. Longfellow. *See* Prologue to "Evangeline."
In the Forest. Alexander McLachlan. *Fr.* The Emigrant. BoCaPo
In the Forest. Alexander Petofi, *tr. fr. Hungarian by* Henry Phillips, Jr. LiTW
In the Forest. Jules Supervielle, *tr. fr. French.* MiFP, *tr. by* James Kirkup; TrFP, *tr. by* Alan Conder
In the "foursome" some would fain. Ballade of the Golfer in Love. Clinton Scollard. BOHV
In the Fourth Year. Lord Gorell. NeTW
In the full ripeness of thy beauty's prime. Pluto and Venus. *Unknown.* OnPM
In the Furies' Grasp. Euripides, *tr. fr. Greek by* R. Potter. *Fr.* Orestes. GrR
(Orestes and Electra, *tr. by* J. A. Symonds.) OxBG
In the galaxy of nations. The Southern Republic. Olivia Thomas. BlG
In the Garb of Old Gaul. Sir Henry Erskine. EBSV
In the Garden. Ernest Crosby. HBV; HBVY
In the Garden. Emily Dickinson. *See* Bird came down the walk, A.
In the Garden. Richard Eberhart. NePoAm-2
In the Garden. F. S. Flint. NP
In the Garden. John S. B. Monsell. OQP; QP-1
In the Garden. Ilo Orleans. RIS
In the Garden. *Unknown.* MaRV
In the Garden at Swainston. Tennyson. OBEV (new ed.); OBVV; PoVP; TCEP; ViPo; VLEP
(Valedictory, II.) GoBC
In the Garden Blossoms the Rose. Gil Vicente, *tr. fr. Spanish by* Eleanor L. Turnbull. TeCS
In the garden of death, where the singers whose names are deathless. In Memory of "Barry Cornwall." Swinburne. HBV
In the Garden of Eden, planted by God. Trees. Bliss Carman. DD; NLK; OHIP; PoRL
In the Garden of Regrets. The Garden of Regrets. Andrew Lang. BoN
In the garden of spring. Blossoms. Otomo Yakamochi. OnPM
In the Garden of the Lord. Helen Keller. BPP; MaRV; OQP; QP-2; WGRP
In the garden there strayed/ A beautiful maid. *Unknown.* LO
In the Garden; Villa Cleobolus. Lawrence Durrell. ChMP
In the garret under the sloping eaves. The Wedding Gift. Minna Irving. BLPA
In the gathering gloom they lie. Terror. "Yehoash." TrJP
In the Gentlemanly Interest. Donald Evans. NP
In the glittering collection of paste diamonds one in particular ranks very high. Oh, Stop Being Thankful All over the Place. Ogden Nash. NePA; SiTL
In the Gloaming. James C. Bayles. NA
In the Gloaming ("In the gloaming, Oh my darling"). Meta Orred. FaFP; OlF; TreF

In the Gloaming ("In the gloaming to be roaming"), *parody.* Charles Stuart Calverley. ALV; InMe; PA

In the gloom of whiteness. Snow. Edward Thomas. FaBoTw; MoVE

In the gloomy ocean bed. The *Kearsarge.* James Jeffrey Roche. AA; OBAV; PAH

In the Glorious Assumption of Our Blessed Lady. Richard Crashaw. *See* On the Glorious Assumption . . .

In the Glorious Epiphanie of Our Lord God. Richard Crashaw. PoEL-2

In the glow of their youth they have come, and they pass. A Mascot. Arthur Guiterman. AlBD

In the Gold Room. Oscar Wilde. CaAE

In the golden air, the risky autumn. Piazzas. Barbara Guest. NeAP

In the Golden Birch. Jane Elizabeth Gostwycke Roberts. VA

In the golden glade the chestnuts are fallen all. North Wind in October. Robert Bridges. BrBE; TCEP

In the Golden Morning of the World. Thomas Westwood. VA

In the golden twilight the rain. The Terrace in the Snow. Su T'ung-po. OnPC

In the Good Old Summer Time. Ren Shields. TreF

In the Grass. Hamlin Garland. LBAP; POT; PoTo

In the Grass. Annette von Droste-Hülshoff, *tr. fr. German by* James Edward Tobin. AnGP

In the grass. Little Folks in the Grass. Annette Wynne. BoChLi; SP; UTS

In the Grave No Flower. Edna St. Vincent Millay. CrMA

In the gray [*or* grey] beginning of years, in the twilight of things that began. Hymn of Man. Swinburne. EmBrPo; PoVP; VLEP

In the gray dawn they left Jerusalem. The Ascension. Edwin Markham. StJW

In the gray dawning across the white lake. Wild March. Constance Fenimore Woolson. YeAr

In the gray of the twilight and glow of the fire. Waiting for Father. Mary Mapes Dodge. FAOV

In the Great Green Commonwealth of Thought. John Masefield. LiTM

In the Great House, and in the House of Fire. He Holdeth Fast to the Memory of His Identity. *Unknown. Fr.* Book of the Dead. AWP; JAWP; WBP

In the Great Metropolis. Arthur Hugh Clough. EmBrPo; PoVP; ViP; ViPP; VLEP

In the great world—which, being interpreted. Byron. *Fr.* Don Juan, XI. OxBoLi

In the green boughs on the tree-top. Birdie in the Cradle. *Unknown.* BOL

In the green garden the nightingale. Ivan Surikov, *tr. fr. Russian by* V. de S. Pinto. BoR

In the green hedge tall and thick. June in Wiltshire. Geoffrey Grigson. WaP

In the green light of water, like the day. The Swans. Edith Sitwell. FaBoMo; GTBS-D; MoVE

In the green quiet wood, where I was used. Mortality. Gerald Gould. MBP; MoBrPo (1942 ed.)

In the green sky I saw the new moon reaping. Harvest. Hafiz. PeP

In the green spaces of the listening trees. Pan Pipes. *Unknown.* VOD (1935 ed.)

In the greenest growth of the Maytime. An Interlude. Swinburne. EmBrPo; ViBoPo

In the greenest of our valleys. The Haunted Palace. Poe. *Fr.* The Fall of the House of Usher. AA; AmP; AmPP; AnFE; APA; APW; BAP; BeLS; BoLiVe; CBOV; CH; ChTr; CoAnAm; DDA; EV-5; HBV; IAP; LiTA; LiTG; MCCG; MOAP; NePA; OBAV; OBVV; OnAP; OTPC; OxBA; PFE; PFY; Po; PoE; PoEL-4; PoeMoYo; SPP; TCAP; TOP; TreFS; TrGrPo; ViBoPo

In the greenhouse lives a wren. *Unknown.* OxNR

In the Greenwood. Shakespeare. *See* Under the Greenwood Tree.

In the grey beginning of years. Swinburne. *See* In the gray . . .

In the grey solitudes. Night Laughter. Leonard Bacon. BAP

In the grey wastes of dread. Horses on the Camargue. Roy Campbell. AtBAP; POTE; SeCePo; ShBV-3

In the grey wilderness—a dog! Lost. John Galsworthy. AlBD

In the grip of Spring sorrow. Spring Sorrow. Wei Chuang. ChLP

In the groined alcoves of an ancient tower. The Second Volume. Robert Mowry Bell. AA

In the growing haste of the world must this thing be. Sails. George Sterling. EtS

In the gutter. Beggar. F. S. Flint. MBP; MoBrPo (1942 ed.)

In the hall-gate sate Capys. The Prophecy of Capys. Macaulay. BHV

In the hall the coffin waits, and the idle armourer stands. Laus Deo. Sydney Dobell. OBEV (1st ed.)

In the happier years gone by me. February 14, 22 B.C. Franklin P. Adams. InMe

In the harbour, in the island, in the Spanish Seas. Trade Winds. John Masefield. FaBoCh; OBMV; ShBV-4

In the Haunts of Bass and Bream. Maurice Thompson. SN

In the Heart. Anna Bunston de Bary. MaRV

In the Heart of a Seed. Kate L. Brown. *See* Little Plant, The.

In the Heart of Contemplation. C. Day Lewis. FaBoMo; MoPo

In the Heart of Jesus. Murdoch O'Daly, *tr. fr. Irish by* George Sigerson. CAW

In the heart of night. The Two Houses. Thomas Hardy. NP

In the heart of the busy city. The Old Stone Basin. "Susan Coolidge." PEOR

In the heart of the hills of life, I know. My Springs. Sidney Lanier. UnPo

In the heart of the white summer mist lay a green little piece of the world. Karma. William Canton. VA

In the Heat of the Day. Kyukin Susukida, *tr. fr. Japanese by* Takamichi Ninomiya *and* D. J. Enright. PoLJ

In the Hedgeback. "Hugh MacDiarmid." NeBP

In the Henry James Country. William Abrahams. WaP

In the high forest dew drips this clear summer night. The Cuckoo Sings. Wei Ying-wu. WhP

In the high, high grass of Guinée. Country Graveyard. Charles F. Pressoir. PoNe

In the high places lo! there is no light. Lighten Our Darkness. Lord Alfred Douglas. HBMV

In the high trees—many doleful winds. The Liberator. Wu Ti. TrCh

In the high turret chamber sat the sage. Death as the Fool. Frank T. Marzials. VA

In the high watch-tower of the soul. The Watch-Tower of the Soul. Anna Hempstead Branch. MOAP

In the Highlands. Robert Louis Stevenson. BSV; GoTS; GrCo-2; GTBS-D; HBV; LEAP; OBEV; OBVV; PoeT; POTT
("In the highlands, in the country places.") FaBoCh

In the Hills. Wang Wei, *tr. fr. Chinese by* Li Fu-ning. WhP

In the hole of a heel of an old brown stocking. Stocking Fairy. Winifred Welles. BoChLi

In the hollow tree, in the old grey tower. The Owl [*or* The Horned Owl]. "Barry Cornwall." BCEP; BLA; CG; LPS-2; OTPC; SN; TVSH

In the hollows of the mountains. The Oven-Bird. Frank Bolles. SN

In the Holy Nativity of Our Lord God. Richard Crashaw. BEL; CoBE; ElSeCe; EnL; EPP, *sl. abr.*; EPS; PoEL-2; TCEP, *sl. abr.*; SeCeV; SeCV-1; SeEP; TCEP; *sl. abr.*; UnPo (1st ed.)
(Holy Nativity of Our Lord God, *sl. abr.*) WGRP
(Hymn of the Nativity.) AtBAP; MeLP; OBS
(Hymne of the Nativity, Sung as by the Shepheards, An.) MePo
(Nativity, The.) OxBoCh; PoLi
(Shepherds' Hymn, The, *sl. abr.*) EV-2
Sels.
"Gloomy night embraced the place."
(Hymn of the Nativity, A.) ViBoPo
Shepherds' Hymn: "We saw thee in thy balmy nest." ACP; CAW; TrGrPo, 3 *sts.*
(Hymn Sung as by the Shepherds, A.) GoBC
(Shepherds Hymn Their Saviour, 2 *sts.*) EG
(Verses from the Shepherds' Hymn.) OBEV
"Welcome to our wondering sight," 6 *ll.* ChIP
(Chorus, 6 *sts.*) MeRV

In the Honour of Christës Birth. *Unknown.* AnEC

In the Hospital. Patrick Anderson. BoCaPo

In the Hospital. Arthur Guiterman. MaRV; SBMV; VOD; WGRP

In the Hospital. Mary Woolsey Howland. HBV; MaRV
(Rest.) LPS-1

In the hot malodorous pen. Goat-Pen. Luis L. Franco. AnCL

In the Hour of Death. Richard Doddridge Blackmore. *See* Dominus Illuminatio Mea.

In the Hour of My Distress. Robert Herrick. *See* His Litany to the Holy Spirit.

In the Hour of Trial. James Montgomery. PraP

In the Hours of Darkness. James Flexner. FaPON; MPB

In the Humpbacked Sky. Nikolai Tikhonov, *tr. fr. Russian by* Jack Lindsay. RuPo

In the House of Idiedaily. Bliss Carman. BoCaPo; OBVV; PFY

In the hush and the lonely silence. Autumn Leaves. Angelina Wray. PTA-2

In the hush of a shivery Christmas-tide dawn. A Christmas Insurrection. Anne P. L. Field. COAH

In the hush of early even. The Fugitive. John Freeman. MBP

In the jolly, jolly spring. What the Toys Are Thinking. ffrida Wolfe. GoBP; TiPo
In the kitchen the servant Hagar sits. Hagar's Last Night at Abraham's. Itzik Manger. OnCuPl
In the knoll that is the greenest. The Wee Folk. Donald A. MacKenzie. EBSV
In the Land of Magic. Henri Michaux, *tr. fr. French by* Richard Ellmann. LiTW
In the land of Ra the flaming, by the shores of Nile's slow waters. The Tryst. Valery Yakovlevich Bryusov. TrRV
In the land of Tao-chou. The People of Tao-chou. Po Chü-i. ChTr; TrCh
In the land of turkeys in turkey weather. Dance of the Macabre Mice. Wallace Stevens. NePA; OxBA; SeCeV
In the Land Where We Were Dreaming. Daniel Bedinger Lucas. *See* Land Where We Were Dreaming, The.
In the Lane. L. A. G. Strong. HaMV
In the late evening, when the house is still. The Anodyne. Sarah N. Cleghorn. OQP; PC; QP-2
In the leaf-strewn cavern, Daphnis, thy wearied limbs lie sleeping. The Hunter Hunted. Theocritus. GrPE
In the leafage, verdant casket stained with gold. Head of a Faun. Arthur Rimbaud. TrFP
In the leafy tree-tops. Echo. Otomo Yakamochi. OnPM
In the least flowering weed she lies. Dear Perfection. Ruth Pitter. AlDL
In the leaves the raindrops gently. Aleksey Konstantinovich Tolstoy, *tr. fr. Russian by* C. M. Bowra. BoR
In the Lecture Room. James K. Baxter. Cressida, I. AnNZ
In the Library. Clinton Scollard. *Fr.* Lyrics from a Library. MOB
In the light of the moon, by the side of the water. My Daughter Louise. Homer Greene. HBV
In the Lighthouse at Point Lookout, North Carolina. Henry Jerome Stockard. NoCaPo
In the Lilac-Rain. Edith M. Thomas. HBV
In the loam we sleep. Loam. Carl Sandburg. ChMo; CMP; NV; SBMV; TwCV
In the lone night she comes. My Silent Guest. Benjamin Sledd. NoCaPo
In the lonesome latter years. The Promissory Note. Bayard Taylor. BOHV; HBV; PA
In the long, sleepless watches of the night. The Cross of Snow. Longfellow. AmP; AmPP; AnAmPo; APW; CoBA; IAP; LA; LEAP; MaRV; OxBA; TriL
In the Longer Novitiate. Catharine McPartlin. PraNu
In the loud waking world I come and go. Nihil Humani Alienum. Titus Munson Coan. AA
In the Lovely Half-Daylight. André Breton, *tr. fr. French by* Wallace Fowlie. MiCF
In the low house, whose thick lights. Lady Day. Padraic Fallon. NeIP
In the low-raftered garret, stooping. Dorothy in the Garret. John Townsend Trowbridge. LPS-1
In the lower lands of day. Swinburne. EG
In the Lybian desert I. Modo and Alciphron. Sylvia Townsend Warner. MBP; MoBrPo
In the magnificence of autumn eves. Autumn Evening. Feodor Tyutchev. BoRS
In the maple-sugar bush. March. Elizabeth J. Coatsworth. YeAr
In the market-place of Bruges stands the belfry old and brown. Longfellow. *Fr.* The Belfry of Bruges. EV-5; HBV
In the Matter of Two Men. James David Corrothers. BANP
In the mazes of loitering people, the watchful and furtive. Chance Meetings. Conrad Aiken. BAP
In the Meadow. Charles Campbell Washburn. CAG
In the Meadows at Mantua. Arthur Symons. PoeT
In the merry month of May. Phyllida [*or* Phillida] and Corydon [*or* A Pastoral *or* The Ploughman's Song]. Nicholas Breton. *Fr.* The Honourable Entertainment Given to the Queen's Majesty in Progress at Elvetham, 1591. ALV; BCEP; BLV; CenL; EG; EIL; ElSeCe; EM-1; EPP; EV-1; FaBoEn; HBV; LiTL; LPS-1; OAEP; OBEV; OBSC; ReEn; ReIE; SeCePo; SiCE; TrGrPo; TuPP
In the middle of a wilderness a band of wagons halted. Wilderness. Katsumi Tanaka. PoLJ
In the middle of August when the southwest wind. The Lesser Children. Ridgely Torrence. BLA; LBMV
In the middle of countries, far from hills and sea. Out of the Window. Aldous Huxley. AlDL
In the middle of the night. Silver Wedding. Ralph Hodgson. HBMV; TrGrPo
In the middle of the night the Balshem rests. Saint Balshemtov. Itzik Manger. OnCuPl
In the middle of this life's journey. An American Takes a Walk. Reed Whittemore. MoVE
In the midmost of ocean. The Sea. Lloyd Frankenberg. AnFE; CoAnAm; TwAmPo
In the Midst of Life. Dora Sigerson Shorter. GTIV
In the midst of my garden. The Palm-Tree. Abd-ar-Rahman I. AWP; JAWP; WBP
In the midst of words your wordless image. The Heart. Harvey Shapiro. HoPM
In the midway of this our mortal life. Dante. *Fr.* Divina Commedia: Inferno. OuHeWo
In the mildest, greenest grove. Lost and Found. Charles Sangster. BoCaPo
In the Mile End Road. Amy Levy. VA
In the Mirror. Elizabeth Fleming. BoTP
In the Mist. "Susan Coolidge." LPS-3
In the misty hollow, shyly greening branches. The Whisper of Earth. Edward J. O'Brien. NLK
In the Mohave. Patrick Orr. BANP; LiTM; NV
In the Monastery. Norreys Jephson O'Conor. CAW; SBMV
In the moneth of May when the new tender green. The Prologue. *Unknown.* ReIE
In the month of April. *Unknown.* RIS
In the month of February. February. *Unknown.* BoTP; PCH
In the Month of Green Fire. Sophie Himmell. GoYe
In the month of June the grass grows high. Reading the Book of Hills and Seas. T'ao Ch'ien. Twelve Poems, 11. TrCh
In the Mood of Blake. William Soutar. HaMV
In the Moonlight. Thomas Hardy. BMEP; LEAP; NP
In the Moonlight. Jens Peter Jacobsen, *tr. fr. Danish by* Charles W. Stork. BoDS
In the Moonlight. Norreys Jephson O'Conor. HBMV; SUS
In the Moonlight. David McKee Wright. AnNZ; BoAu
In the moonlight, in this night. Clair de lune. Luis Palés Matos. AnCL
In the Morgue. Israel Zangwill. TrJP
In the morn we met the proud array. The March of the Three Kings. *Unknown.* ChrBoLe
In the Morning. Paul Laurence Dunbar. GoSl; MW
In the Morning. Cecilia Loftus. GFA
In the morning as the fine rain falls. The Fine Rain. Shinkichi Takahashi. PoLJ
In the morning in the blue snow. Annual Gaiety. Wallace Stevens. MAP; MoAB; MoAmPo
In the morning, in the dark. The Night Hunt. Thomas MacDonagh. OxBI
In the Morning, in the Morning. A. E. Housman. TwP
In the morning light trills the gay swallow. Hezekiah Butterworth. *See* In the rosy light . . .
In the morning the city. City [San Francisco]. Langston Hughes. FaPON; GoSl
In the morning the hawk and the sun flew up together. Night and the Child. Judith Wright. SeCePo
In the morning, very early. Barefoot Days. Rachel Field. FaPON; YeAr
In the morning we enter the barracks at the east gate. At the Frontier. Tu Fu. WhP
In the morning when I swing. My Swinging Shadow. Grace Wilson Coplen. GFA
In the morning when ye rise. A Charm. Robert Herrick. OTPC (1923 ed.)
In the morning wood a deer reclines. The Deer. Tatsuji Miyoshi. PoLJ
In the Mosque. Ibn Malik of Murcia, *tr. fr. Arabic by* A. J Arberry. MooP
In the motionless haze of interior heat. Louise Townsend Nicholl. *Fr.* Recital. UnS
In the mountain village. Minamoto no Morotada, *tr. fr. Japanese by* Kenneth Rexroth. OnPJ
In the Mountains. Cotton Noe. LS
In the Mountains on a Summer Day. Li Po, *tr. fr. Chinese.* AWP, *tr. by* Arthur Waley; TrCh, *tr. by* Arthur Waley; WhP
In the mud of the Cambrian main. A Ballade of Evolution. Grant Allen. ATP (1935 ed.)
In the muscadine-glowing noon. Fête Galante. Edith Sitwell. CaAE
In the Mushroom Meadows. Thomas Walsh. SBMV
In the mustardseed sun. Poem on His Birthday. Dylan Thomas. PoLFOT
In the Naked Bed, in Plato's Cave. Delmore Schwartz. ExPo; FiMAP; GTBS-W; LiTA; LiTG; LiTM; MiAP; MoAB; MoAmPo; MoVE; NePA; ReMP; TwAmPo
In the name of God—Who shall open. The Lord. José Maria Gabriel y Galán. CAW
In the name of Him who died. Follow Me! Sheldon Shepard. ChIP
In the Name of Jesus Christ. Claudia Cranston. HBMV
In the Name of Our Sons. Dorothy Gould. PGD
In the Name of the Empress of India, make way. The Overland Mail. Kipling. CV; PECK
In the narrow street. Return. H. D. Carberry. PoNe
In the negro gardens negro birds. To Eliza, Duchess of Dorset. Joseph Bennett. LiTA; NePA
In the neighborhood slums. Sad Sunsets. Zacharias Papondoniou. MoGP
In the Neolithic Age, *br. sel.* Kipling. Wide, Wide World, The. OtMeF

In the new city of marble and bright stone. The Unknown Soldier. Conrad Aiken. *Fr.* The Soldier. WaaP; WaP
In the niggard, sickly desert. The Upas Tree. Pushkin. TrRV
In the Night. Elizabeth Jennings. NePoEA
In the Night. William Alexander Percy. *Fr.* In New York. SPP
In the Night. James Stephens. OBMV
In the Night. *Unknown.* NA
In the night/ Gray, heavy clouds. The Peaks. Stephen Crane. War Is Kind, XVIII. AA; AmP; HBV; TCAP; WGRP
In the night a golden cloudlet straying. The Crag. Mikhail Lermontov. BoR
In the night, in the night, as I turned upon my bed. The Passion of Man: 1918–1938. J. C. Squire. QS
In the night, in the night, O my Country, the stream calls out from afar. Parvuli Ejus. Aubrey Thomas De Vere. IrPN
In the Night of the Full Moon. Carl Busse, *tr. fr. German by* Jethro Bithell. AWP
In the night the agile mole. The Unfortunate Mole. Mary Kennedy. GoYe
In the night the man could hear the wind walking. Harvest. Gene Shuford. GoYe
In the Night Watches. Sir Charles G. D. Roberts. PeCV
In the night when all are sleeping. The Hoopskirt. John Gould Fletcher. LaNeLa
In the Nine Provinces there is not room enough. A Vision. Ts'ao Chih. TrCh
In the noisy street. Conrad Aiken. Discordants, V. MOAP
In the nook of a wood—where a pool freshed with dew. The Stranger. Walter de la Mare. OAEP (2d ed.)
In the north city. The House of Chung. Han Shan. PoHN
In the northern hemisphere. Kangaroo. D. H. Lawrence. BrBE; MoVE; ShBV-4
In the North-west there is a floating cloud. The Campaign against Wu, 2. Wei Wen-ti. TrCh
In the north-west there is a high house. *Unknown, tr. fr. Chinese by* Arthur Waley. Seventeen Old Poems, 5. TrCh
In the numb time when foam froze. All That Is, and Can Delight. Robert Farren. OxBI
In the Nuns' Garden. Denis A. McCarthy. PraNu
In the ocean of the sky. Hitomaro, *tr. fr. Japanese by* Arthur Waley. LiTW
In the ocean of the sky. The Moon Ship. *Unknown.* GFA
In the ocean, 'way out yonder. The Dinkey-Bird. Eugene Field. AA; BOHV; HBVY; LBN; NA; PFY; TSW; TSWC; UTS
In the old age black was not counted fair. Sonnets, CXXVII. Shakespeare. PeBoSo; ReIE; TwP
In the old back streets o' Pimlico. The Rambling Sailor. Charlotte Mew. HBMV; PoRA
In the Old Church. Jean Blewett. CPG
In the old church tower. Thanksgiving Day. Thomas Bailey Aldrich. TOAH
In the Old Churchyard at Fredericksburg. Frederick Wadsworth Loring. AA
In the Old City. Jacob Fichman, *tr. fr. Hebrew by* Sholom J. Kahn. TrJP
In the old colony days, in Plymouth the land of the Pilgrims. The Courtship of Miles Standish. Longfellow. BeLS; TreFS
In the old days (a custom laid aside). Abraham Davenport. Whittier. AmPP; AnNE; CBOV; CoBA; CoV; DDA; IAP; MOAP; OBAV
In the old days, Lesbia, you said Catullus alone. Catullus, *tr. fr. Latin by* Frances Fletcher. LaP
In the old days the white gates swung. Pastoral. Clifford Dyment. MoVE
In the old days when King Arthur ruled the nation. The Wife of Bath's Tale. Chaucer. *Fr.* The Canterbury Tales. EnL
In the old garden. Reverie. Fan Ch'eng Ta. PoHN
In the old Hebrew myth the lion's frame. The Hive at Gettysburg. Whittier. APW
In the old, lonely park all white with frost. Sentimental Colloquy. Paul Verlaine, *tr. by* Alan Conder. LO
In the old park, frozen and deserted. Sentimental Dialogue. Paul Verlaine, *tr. by* Muriel Kittel. AnFP
In the old park, solitary and vast. Colloque sentimentale. Paul Verlaine, *tr. by* Arthur Symons. MiFP
In the "Old South." Whittier. AA; APW
In the Open Air. John Gould Fletcher. ChMo; CMP
In the open sea. Peasant and Geisha Songs. *Unknown.* LiTW
In the Orchard. Ibsen, *tr. fr. Norwegian by* Sir Edmund Gosse. AWP; JAWP; WBP
In the Orchard. Muriel Stuart. AV; NP
In the Organ-Loft with a Poetess. John Henry Boner. NoCaPo (rev. ed.)
In the other gardens. Autumn Fires. Robert Louis Stevenson. BrR; GFA; SUS; TiPo; YeAr
In the outer world that was before this earth. Genesis. Swinburne. ViP
In the pain, in the loneliness of love. Love Knocks at the Door. John Hall Wheelock. LBMV
In the palace of a certain king stood an incomparable bed. Leap and Creep. *Unknown. Fr.* The Panchatantra. OuHeWo
In the pale mauve twilight, streaked with orange. Even-song. Conrad Aiken. HBMV; PG
In the pallid soughing of the dawn. Bucolic Funeral. Justo Sierra. AnMP
In the Paralelo a one-legged/ Man. Entered in the Minutes. Louis MacNeice. LiTB
In the Park. Rose Fyleman. StVeCh (1955 ed.)
In the Park. Helen Hoyt. AV; HBMV
In the Pass. Clinton Scollard. TBM
In the Past. Trumbull Stickney. MAP; MoAmPo (1942 ed.); MOAP; OxBA
In the Pasture. Dora Hagemeyer. MuM
In the path of the silver Star. Epiphany. Katherine Burton. PSO
In the pathways of heaven. To the Memory of John Burroughs. Catherine Parmenter. PEDC; PoRL
In the Pauper's Turnip-Field. Herman Melville. APW; PoEL-5
In the penetrating damp. A Restless Night in Camp. Tu Fu. OnPC
In the Person of Woman Kind. Ben Jonson. SeCV-1
In the Piazza at Night. Arthur Hugh Clough. *Fr.* At Venice. ViPo
In the picture the people stroll and stroll all day. Public Holiday; Paris. Joyce Horner. GoYe
In the Pioneer Camp. "Anna Akhmatova," *tr. fr. Russian by* Jack Lindsay. RuPo
In the Place de la Bastille. Richard Burton. BAP
In the placid summer midnight. Street Scene. W. E. Henley. BoTP
In the pleasant green garden. A [*or* The] Tea Party. Kate Greenaway. MPB; OTPC; PPL; TiPo (1952 ed.)
In the pleasant orchard closes. The Lost Bower. Elizabeth Barrett Browning. CBPC
In the Poppy Field. James Stephens. CP; NV; TCPD; WP
In the prison cell I sit. Tramp, Tramp, Tramp. George Frederick Root. FOAH; MDAH; OlF; TreFS
In the Prison Pen. Herman Melville. PoEL-5
In the Proscenium. Gene Derwood. GTBS-W; LiTA; LiTM (rev. ed.)
(War's Clown in the Proscenium.) NePA
In the public-house to die. Drinking Song. "The Archpoet of Cologne," *tr. by* John Addington Symonds. LiA
In the Public Library. Alethea Todd Alderson. BLP
In the Public Ward. Florence Randal Livesay. CPG
In the pure soul, although it sing or pray. Eternal Christmas. Elizabeth Stuart Phelps Ward. ChIP; MaRV; PGD
In the purple light, heavy with redwood, the slopes drop seaward. Apology for Bad Dreams. Robinson Jeffers. AmP; AmPP; AnFE; CoAnAm; CoBMV; LiTA; MAP; MoAB; MoAmPo; MOAP; OnAP; OxBA; SeCeV; TwAmPo
In the Queen's Room. Norman Cameron. Three Love Poems, II. FaBoTw
In the quiet of the morning I heard a knock at my door. T'ao Ch'ien. Twelve Poems, 2. TrCh
In the raftered barn we lie. Out of Trenches; the Barn, Twilight. Robert Nichols. NV
In the rain's push and the wind's hand. From My Thought. Daniel Smythe. GoYe
In the Rangitaki Valley. Katherine Mansfield. DiM
In the ranks of the Austrian you found him. The Forced Recruit. Elizabeth Barrett Browning. PoVP
In the rarest of English valleys. A Bunch of Cowslips. *Unknown.* PEOR
In the Ravine. W. W. E. Ross. PeCV
In the red April dawn. Birds in April. W. E. Henley. YT
In the red country. The Red Country. William Rose Benét. AOAH
In the region of clouds, where the whirlwinds arise. The Castle in the Air. Thomas Paine. LPS-3
In the Restaurant. Thomas Hardy. Satires of Circumstance, XI. MBP; MoAB; MoBrPo
In the Rhine, in the beautiful river. A Madonna. Heine. OnPM
In the Ringwood. Thomas Kinsella. OxBI
In the Room. James Thomson. OBVV
In the room at Warm Springs. At Warm Springs. William Rose Benét. PoRL
In the room below the young man sat. The Young Man Waited. Edmund Vance Cooke. PTA-1
In the room, in a corner all darkened. Rima VII. Gustavo Adolfo Bécquer. *Fr.* Rimas. AnSpL-2
In the room the women come and go. T. S. Eliot. *Fr.* The Love Song of J. Alfred Prufrock. BAP
In the roses, snuggled deep. A Surprise. Elizabeth Winton. PCH

In the rosy [*or* morning] light trills the gay swallow. The Snowbird. Hezekiah Butterworth. PCH; PRWS

In the round park the old men sitting on benches. Fifth Elegy. Alex Comfort. FaBoMo

In the Round Tower at Jhansi. Christina Rossetti. EmBrPo

In the Royal City spring is almost over. The Flower Market. Po Chü-i. TrCh; WoL

In the royal path. The Triumph of Joseph. Charles Jeremiah Wells. *Fr.* Joseph and His Brethren. VA

In the rude age, when knowledge was not rife. Another Tribute to Wyatt. Earl of Surrey. SiPS

In the ruined chapel. Vespers. Georgios Drossinis. MoGP

In the rush of the merry morning. Merry Christmas. *Unknown.* COAH

In the rustle of the twilight dream. Magic Refrains. Apostolos Melachrinos. *Fr.* Variations. MoGP

In the rutted soil of the household patio. The Puddle. Jacinto Fombona Pachano. TwSpPo

In the sad Southwest, in the mystical Sunland. Homes of the Cliff Dwellers. Stanley Wood. PoOW

In the sad spirit. To the Unknown Light. Edward Shanks. NV; TrPWD

In the salt terror of the stormy sea. The City of the Soul. Lord Alfred Douglas. HBMV; LBBV

In the sand I grew, by the rocky sea-wall. The Husband's Message. *Unknown.* AnOE

In the sanded desert stands a tree. The Tree in the Desert. Friedrich Hebbel. LiTW

In the Santa Clara Valley, far away and far away. On the Great Plateau. Edith Franklin Wyatt. HBMV; NP; NV

In the scented bud of the morning—O. The Daisies. James Stephens. AnIV; AWP; JAWP; PreP; TIP; WBP

In the School of Coquettes. Circe [*or* To Rose]. Austin Dobson. *Fr.* Rose-Leaves. BPN; PFE; VLEP

In the sea, Biscayne, there prinks. Homunculus et la Belle Etoile. Wallace Stevens. MAP; MoAB; MoAmPo

In the sea-marsh where I carve the harsh shallows. Poem for a Neighbour. Keidrych Rhys. MoWP

In the sea of ivy clothed Iwami. Hitomaro, *tr. fr. Japanese by* Kenneth Rexroth. OnPJ

In the seaport of Saint Malo 'twas a smiling morn in May. Jacques Cartier. Thomas D'Arcy McGee. CaP; OCL

In the Season. Robert Louis Stevenson. *See* It Is the Season Now to Go.

In the season of Spring is the season of growing. In the Spring. Ibycus. OxBG

In the Secret Rose Garden. Sa'd ud-din Mahmud Shabistari, *tr. fr. Persian by* Florence Lederer. LiTW

In the secret Valley of Silence. The Valley of Silence. "Fiona Macleod." PoVP

In the Selkirks. Duncan Campbell Scott. CaP; OCL

In the Servants' Quarters. Thomas Hardy. MBP; MoAB; MoBrPo; QS

In the Seven Woods. W. B. Yeats. ChMo; CMP; LoBV

In the shabby train no seat is vacant. The Refugees. Randall Jarrell. MoAB; MoAmPo (1950 ed.)

In the shade of a tree, we two sat, him and me. Jim Haggerty's Story. *Unknown.* ABF

In the shade of the gardens, in the blue night. Midnight at Mestre. Alfonso Gatto. OnPM

In the shadow of a broken house. A Glimpse of Time. Laurence Binyon. AnFE

In the shadow of the tall bamboos. The Temple Bells of Yün Sui. Yang Wan Li. PoHN

In the Shadows. Leah Bodine Drake. DaM

In the Shadows. David Gray. *See* I Die, Being Young.

In the Shadows. E. Pauline Johnson. CPG

In the shadowy passageway. The Girl with the Blue Lamp. José María Eguren. AnCL

In the Shadowy Whatnot Corner. Robert Silliman Hillyer. NePoAm

In the shaking of a sieve the refuse remaineth. The Test of Men. Ecclesiasticus, Bible, Apocrypha. TrJP

In the shape of this night, in the still fall of snow, Father. At the New Year. Kenneth Patchen. AnFE; CoAnAm; TwAmPo

In the Shenandoah Valley, one rider grey and one rider blue. Shenandoah. Carl Sandburg. PaA

In the shut drawer, even now, they rave and grieve. Packet of Letters. Louise Bogan. LiTL

In the Silence. Josephine Preston Peabody. QS

In the Silence of Night. Francis Jammes, *tr. fr. French by* Alan Conder. TrFP

In the silence that falls on my spirit. My Father's Voice in Prayer. May Hastings Nottage. BLRP

In the silent midnight watches, list—thy bosom door! He Standeth at the Door. Arthur Cleveland Coxe. HBV

In the Silent Night. Isaac Leibush Peretz, *tr. fr. Yiddish by* Joseph Leftwich. TrJP

In the Skies. E. J. Pratt. *Fr.* Dunkirk. BoCaPo

In the sky the bright stars glittered. The Quilting Party. Frances Kyle. OIF

In the sleepy forest where the bluebells. The Awakening of Dermuid. Austin Clarke. *Fr.* The Vengeance of Finn. AnIV

In the slow lapse of unrecorded afternoon. No Answer. Laurence Whistler. MoVE

In the Small Canals. John Addington Symonds. *Fr.* In Venice. PoVP

In the Small Stove. Aleksey Surkov, *tr. fr. Russian by* Jack Lindsay. RuPo

In the smoke-blue cabaret. Ecclesiastes. Morris Bishop. HBMV

In the smoky outhouses of the court of love. In the Queen's Room. Norman Cameron. Three Love Poems, II. FaBoTw

In the Snow. W. H. Davies. POTE

In the snowing and the blowing. Nearly Ready. Mary Mapes Dodge. PRWS

In the soldier's helmet doves. Petronius, *tr. fr. Latin by* Jack Lindsay. LaP

In the solitude amid the pine trees. To a Woodbine Tendril. August, Graf von Platen. AnGP

In the sorrow and the terror of the nations. The Mother. Nettie Palmer. BoAu

In the South There Are Fine Fish. *Unknown, tr. fr. Chinese.* WhP

In the southern land many birds sing. The South. Wang Chien. AWP; TrCh

In the southern village the boy who minds the ox. The Herd Boy. Lu Yu. ChTr; TrCh

In the Spring, *sl. abr.* William Barnes. RO

In the Spring. Ibycus, *tr. fr. Greek by* Walter Headlam. OxBG

In the Spring. Meleager, *tr. fr. Greek by* Andrew Lang. AWP; JAWP; WBP

(Spring.) ADAH; VOD

In the spring garden. Otomo no Yakamochi, *tr. fr. Japanese by* Kenneth Rexroth. LiTW; OnPJ

In the spring, on the trees. Fluttering Leaves. Rodney Bennett. BoTP

In the spring twilight, in the colour'd twilight. An Even-Song. Sydney Dobell. OBVV

In the spring when the green gits back in the trees. When the Green Gits Back in the Trees. James Whitcomb Riley. ADAH; YT

In the spring, when winds blew and farmers were plowing fields. American Spring Song. Sherwood Anderson. NP

In the springtime I am always. Old Age. Ou-yang Hsiu. OnPC

In the squdgy river. The Hippopotamus. Georgia R. Durston. GFA; TiPo; UTS

In the Stable. Elizabeth Goudge. ChBR

In the stagnant pride of an outworn race. Santiago. Thomas A. Janvier. MC; PAH

In the States. Robert Louis Stevenson. PoVP; VA; VLEP

In the still air the music lies unheard. The Master's Touch. Horatius Bonar. BePJ; HBV; LPS-2; MaRV; TrPWD; VA

In the still cold before the sun. A Saint's Hours. Sarah N. Cleghorn. POT; SBMV

In the still light/ I see Thee. The Mystic. Gertrude Bone. QS

In the Still, Star-lit Night. Elizabeth Stoddard. AA

In the Stillness of Dawn. Euripides, *tr. fr. Greek by* R. Potter. *Fr.* Iphigenia in Aulis. GrR

(Watch before Dawn, *tr. by* F. Melian Stawell.) OxBG

In the stirred waters the white stones are shining. The Stirred Waters. *Unknown. Fr.* Shi King. ChLP

In the stony night move the stars' white mouths. The Postures of Love, III. Alex Comfort. NeBP

In the Storm. Stanton A. Coblentz. ChIP

In the Storm. Peter Andreas Jensen, *tr. fr. Norwegian by* Charles W. Stork. AnNoLy

In the stove the fire has fallen. Winter. Tosaburo Ono. PoLJ

In the Strand. Havelock Ellis. PoP

In the strange city of life. Nostalgia. Walter de la Mare. CoBMV

In the Strange Isle. Michael Roberts. FaBoMo; POTE

In the Streets of Catania. Roger Casement. AnIV

In the Study. Burges Johnson. FAOV

In the subtraction of my yeares. *Unknown.* SeCSL

In the Subway. Louis Untermeyer. PoeMoYo

In the Sultan's Garden. Clinton Scollard. InP

In the summer, by the river. Peasant and Geisha Songs. *Unknown.* LiTW

In the summer even. Ballad. Harriet Prescott Spofford. HBV; LBAP

In the Summer of Sixty. *Unknown.* ABS; CoSo; IHA; PoOW

In the summer palace the fireflies have lost their way. Ninth Moon. Li Ho. LiTW

In the summit of my head. Ad Majorem Hominis Gloriam. John Gould Fletcher. MAP; MoAmPo

In the sunny orchard closes. In the Orchard. Ibsen. AWP; JAWP; WBP

In the sweet shire of Cardigan. Simon Lee [the Old Huntsman]. Wordsworth. BEL; BPN; EM-2; EmBrPo;

In the sweet shire of Cardigan (*continued*)
EnRP; EPN; ERP; GEPC; GTBS; GTBS-D; GTBS-W; GTSE; GTSL; REAL
In the sweet solitude, the Mountain's life. The Mountain. William Ellery Channing. PFY
In the tender spreading tropical mornings. Lizard. K. E. Ingram. PoNe
In the Tenth Circle. *Unknown.* CAG
In the theatre. The Fates. Stephen Spender. TwHP
In the third-class seat sat the journeying boy. Midnight on the "Great Western." Thomas Hardy. CH; CoBMV
In the third day of May. The Boy and the Mantle. *Unknown.* BaBo; ESPB; OBB
In the third month, a sudden flow of blood. The Vow. Anthony Hecht. NePoEA
In the third month after the children of Israel were gone forth. The Ten Commandments. Exodus, Bible, *O.T.* GrCo-1
In the third month the town of Hsien-yang. Drinking Alone by Moonlight, 2. Li Po. TrCh
In the Third Year of War. Henry Treece. WaP
In the tides of the warm south wind it lay. Verazzano. Hezekiah Butterworth. PAH
In the time of old sin without sadness. Variations on an Air: After Swinburne. G. K. Chesterton. InP
In the Time of Strife. Frank L. Stanton. FOAH
In the time of the flower of the linden and the bay? When? José Moreno Villa. CoSP
In the Time of the Persecution. L. Aaronson. NeTW; QS
In the Time of Trouble. Leslie Savage Clark. TrPWD
In the time of wild roses. Bab-Lock-Hythe. Laurence Binyon. MoVE; PoeT
In the time when herbs and flowers. Caelica and Philocell. Fulke Greville. Caelica, LXXVI. OBSC
In the town of Athy one Jeremy Lanigan. Lanigan's Ball. *Unknown.* OxBoLi
In the Township. Denis Glover. AnNZ
In the Trades. Cicely Fox Smith. EtS
In the Train. Clifford Bax. InP; TCPD
In the Train. Bodil Bech, *tr. fr. Danish by* Charles W. Stork. BoDS
In the Train. James Thomson. *See* As We Rush, as We Rush in the Train.
In the Tree-Top. Lucy Larcom. BOL
In the Trench. Leon Gellert. BoAV; MoAuPo
In the tub on Monday morning. Monday Morning. Helen Wing. GFA; MeMeAg
In the turret's great glass dome, the apparition, death. Siegfried. Randall Jarrell. MiAP; ReMP
In the Twilight. George Cotterell. VA
In the Twilight. James Russell Lowell. AA; HBV; IAP
In the Twilight, *sel.* John Francis O'Donnell.
"I row in my boat in the twilight, half-purple, half-grey, overhead." IrPN
In the twilight of yellow clouds. The Crows at Nightfall. Li Po. ChLP
In the Unending Tedium. Paul Verlaine, *tr. fr. French by* Muriel Kittel. AnFP
In the uproar and stench. The Great Armistice [*or* Worlds at War]. Robert Haven Schauffler. ADAH; GDAH
In the vaile [*or* vale] of restles mynd. *See* In a valley of this restless mind.
In the Vale of Glamorgan. Huw Menai. MoWP
In the Valley of Cauteretz. Tennyson. BPN; EmBrPo; EPN; OBVV; PoVP; TCEP; TOP; UnW; ViPo; VLEP
In the Valley of Shanganagh, where the songs of skylarks teem. The Valley of Shanganagh. John Martley. TIP
In the Valley of the Elwy. Gerard Manley Hopkins. InPo; LiTG; ViBoPo
("I remember a house where all were good.") EG
In the valley of the Pegnitz, where across broad meadow-lands. Nuremberg. Longfellow. AmPP; CoBA; HBV; IAP; LPS-2
In the valley the birches are bored. Russian Spring. Ivan Alekseyevich Bunin. TrRV
In the vast glow of sun at evening. Song before Night. Richard Dehmel. OnPM
In the vast vague gray. Sunday up the River, III. James Thomson. EmBrPo
In the Vastness, a God. *Unknown.* OQP; QP-2
In the very early morning when the light was low. The Interpreter. Orrick Johns. AnAmPo; HBMV; LA; MAP; NP; PFY; SBMV
In the Vices. Donald Evans. HBMV; NP
In the village churchyard she lies. In the Churchyard at Cambridge. Longfellow. PoEL-5
In the village squares. The Unemployed. LeVan Roberts. PGD
In the Virginia lowlands I was born. Lowlands, *vers.* II. *Unknown.* ShS
In the warm hush of the autumnal night. An Autumn Cricket. Clinton Scollard. MuM
In the Water. Swinburne. *Fr.* A Midsummer Holiday. BPN; PoVP; VLEP
In the wax works of Nature they strike. Note. Anthony Euwer. *Fr.* The Limeratomy. HBMV
In the Way of Peace. Lauchlan MacLean Watt. ChIP; OQP; QP-1
In the Web. E. L. Mayo. MiAP
In the Week When Christmas Comes. Eleanor Farjeon. ChBR; SiSoSe; TiPo (1952 ed.)
In the wet dusk silver-sweet. The Memory of Earth. "Æ." BMEP; LEAP; OBVV; PoVP; TIP
In the Wet Shadows. Ramón López Velarde, *tr. fr. Spanish by* Samuel Beckett. AnMP
In the white-flowered hawthorn brake. Song from "Ogier the Dane" [*or* Antiphony]. William Morris. *Fr.* The Earthly Paradise. BPN; EG; OAEP; POTT; PoVP; VA; ViBoPo; VLEP
In the White Giant's Thigh. Dylan Thomas. AtBAP; LiTB; PoLFOT; ReMP
In the white moonlight, where the willow waves. The Graveyard Rabbit. Frank L. Stanton. AA; LHV
In the white of noon-day's brightness the city seems blotted out. In the Old City. Jacob Fichman. TrJP
In the wide and rocky pasture where the cedar trees are gray. Connecticut Road Song. Anna Hempstead Branch. OBAV
In the Wide Awe and Wisdom of the Night. Sir Charles G. D. Roberts. CaP; OCL
In the wild autumn weather, when the rain was on the sea. Love and Death. Rosa Mulholland. HBV; VA
In the wild [*or* cold] October night-time, when the wind raved round the land. The Night of Trafalgar [*or* The Boatman's Song *or* Trafalgar]. Thomas Hardy. *Fr.* The Dynasts. AIDL; CH; ChTr; FaBoCh; MBP; MoBrPo; OBMV; PoVP; ReTS; ShBV-1; WaaP
In the wild soft summer darkness. Summer Night, Riverside. Sara Teasdale. TCPD
In the Wilderness. Robert Graves. CH; GTBS-D; MBP; MoAB; MoBrPo; OxBI; SeCePo; ShBV-3
In the Wilderness. Edith Lovejoy Pierce. TrPWD
In the winding folds of old capitals. The Little Old Women. Baudelaire. AnFP
In the window of a grange. Love and Honour. Fulke Greville. Caelica, LXXIV. OBSC
In the Wind's Eye. R. P. Blackmur. Scarabs for the Living. II. CrMA
In the winged cradle of sleep I lay. Cradle Song. Celia Thaxter. BOL
In the winter, in the winter. The Organ Grinders' Garden. Mildred Plew Meigs. GaP
In the winter the rabbits match their pelts to the earth. White Season. Frances M. Frost. FaPON; TiPo
In the winter time we go. White Fields. James Stephens. FaPON; MoShBr; SiSoSe; SUS
In the winter when the wet lanes hissed and sucked. Microcosmos, XXXIII. Nigel Heseltine. NeBP
In the Winter Woods. Frederick George Scott. CPG
In the Wood. Herbert Edwin Clarke. VA
In the Wood. Eileen Mathias. BoTP
In the Wood. Boris Pasternak, *tr. fr. Russian by* C. M. Bowra. BoRS
In the Wood. Sara Teasdale. PC
In the Wood Lay a Dead Doe. *Unknown, tr. fr. Chinese.* WhP
(Maytime, *tr. by* L. Cranmer-Byng.) AWP
In the Wood of Finvara. Arthur Symons. BLV; MBP; MoBrPo; NeMA; PoVP
In the Woods. Dorothy Baker. BoTP
In the Woods. Emerson. *Fr.* Good-bye. OQP; QP-2
In the Woods. Gérard de Nerval, *tr. fr. French by* Alan Conder. TrFP
In the Woods. Frederick George Scott. CaP; OCL
In the Woods. Paul Verlaine, *tr. fr. French by* Muriel Kittel. AnFP
In the woodyard were green and dry. The Rick of Green Wood. Edward Dorn. NeAP
In the worst inn's worst room, with mat half-hung. The Duke [*or* Second Duke *or* Death] of Buckingham. Pope. *Fr.* Moral Essays, Epistle III. CoEV; ExPo; FiP; OBEC
In the wrath of the lips that assail us. Stigmata. Charles Warren Stoddard. JKCP; TrPWD
In the wrecks [*or* wracks] of Walsingham. A Lament for Our Lady's Shrine at Walsingham [*or* The Wreck of Walsingham]. *Unknown.* ACP; ISi; PoEL-2; SiCE; TriL
In the Wretched Hovel. *Unknown, tr. fr. Japanese by* Ishii *and* Obata. OnPM
In the year 1910—and I give the date without uncertainty. Versos de Montalgo. *Unknown.* AS
In the Year of Many Conversions and the Private Soul. John Ciardi. MiAP
In the year of ninety-four in the city of Mazatlán. Tragedia de Heraclio Bernal. *Unknown.* ABF
In the year since Jesus died for men. The Siege of Corinth. Byron. GoTL

In the year that King Uzziah died. Here Am I—Send Me. Isaiah, Bible, *O.T.* GrCo-2
In the years about twenty. An Irish Love-Song. Robert Underwood Johnson. HBV
In the Year's Morning. David Ross. PG (1955 ed.)
In the years of her age the most beautiful. He Wishes He Might Die and Follow Laura. Petrarch. *Fr.* Sonnets to Laura: To Laura in Death. OBMV; TwCV
In the young merry time of spring. Cornfields. Mary Howitt. OTPC (1923 ed.)
In the youth of summer. The Hills of Cualann. Joseph Campbell. AnIV
In their heaven the sainted hosts. George Meredith. *Fr.* The Song of Theodolinda. MeRV
In their ragged regimentals. Carmen Bellicosum [*or* The Old Continentals]. Guy Humphreys McMaster. AA; ALV; DD; DDA; GN; HBV; LPS-2; MC; OBAV; PaA; PAH; PAP
In these cold evenings, when the rain. Fear of the Earth. Alex Comfort. MoBrPo (1950 ed.); NeBP
In These Dark Woods. Faith Baldwin. MuM
In these days of indigestion. Some Little Bug. Roy Atwell. BOHV
In these deep solitudes and awful cells. Eloïsa to Abelard. Pope. CEP; EiPP; EnL; EnLi-1; GEPC; LoBV; OAEP; PoEL-3; ReaPo
In these drear wastes of sea-born land, these wilds where none may dwell but He. Sir Richard Francis Burton. *Fr.* The Kasidah. HBV
In these far cleaner days no armies clash. Security. Denis Glover. AnNZ
In these fresh meadows, yet his quiet spirit. Charles Doughty. *Fr.* Wayfaring, to the Valley of the Dove. TCPD
In these gay thoughts, the Loves and Graces shine. Epistle to Mrs. Blount, with the Works of Voiture. Pope. CBOV
In these latter days. Twentieth Century Love-Song. Richard Church. HaMV
In these long winter nights when moon doth steer. Four Sonnets to Helen, 3. Pierre de Ronsard. *Fr.* Sonnets pour Hélène. LiTW; PrPoCR
In These Our Winter Days. C. Day Lewis. ChMo; POTE
In these pure white yards where the south wind blows. The Mad Pomegranate Tree. "Odysseus Elytis." MoGP
In these restrained and careful times. Impression. Sir Edmund Gosse. BMEP; HBV; LEAP
In Thessaly. Clark Ashton Smith. DaM
In thickest fight triumphantly he fell. General Albert Sidney Johnston. Mary Jervey. GA
In Thine hour of holy sadness. St. Bernard of Clairvaux. *Fr.* Of Our Lord's Passion. ChIP
In Thine Image; a Negro Speaks. Fania Kruger. QS
In Thine Own Heart. "Angelus Silesius," *tr. fr. German.* ChIP; MaRV
In this age of Bigger Business, there's a crying need for men. The Optimist. "G. O. R." CAG
In this air. One of the Regiment. Douglas Le Pan. CaP
In this base world, one must love many things. To Mr. Victor Hugo. Alfred de Musset. BoFr
In this beloved marble view. On the Bust of Helen by Canova. Byron. EmBrPo
In this book every line has been clean. Limerick. H. I. Brock. LiBL
In this book I see your face and in your face. Frontispiece. May Swenson. NePoEA
In this broad earth of ours. In This Earth Perfection. Walt Whitman. *Fr.* Birds of Passage. OQP; QP-2
In this brown seed, so dry and hard. Resurrection. Agnes W. Storer. ChIP; OQP; QP-1
In this buff-gray cliff. Sandstone. Anne Marriott. CaP; TwCV
In this choice work, with wisdom penned, we find. On a Book Called Unitarian Theology. Philip Freneau. CoV
In this city I loved you, where light. Chicago. Galway Kinnell. NePoAm
In this clear shining climate. Wind of September in the Poplars. Luis Cernuda. CoSP
In this congealit season sharp and chill. An Evening and Morning in Winter. Gawin Douglas. *Fr.* Prologues to the Aeneid. BSV
In This Dark House. Edward Davidson. OBMV
In this deep hush and quiet of my soul. Sonnet. George Henry Boker. MOAP
In this dread hour for thee and all mankind. The Prophetic Hour. Michael Thwaites. PoFr
In This Earth, Perfection. Walt Whitman. *Fr.* Birds of Passage. OQP; QP-2
In this enemy city where your winged danger. Epitaph for an American Bomber. James Bertram. AnNZ
In this fair niche above the unslumbering sea. A Singer Asleep. Thomas Hardy. OAEP; POTE; POTT; PtP
In this fair stranger's eyes of gray. Absence. Matthew Arnold. Switzerland, VI. OAEP; PoVP; ViPP
In this friend's face I know. Time-Bomb. Earle Birney. TwCaPo
In this green chest is laid away. On a Fair Woman. Francis Burdett Money-Coutts. OBVV
In this green valley where the Ouse. Cowper at Olney. Sylvia Lynd. POTE
In this high pasturage, the Blunden time. The Archaeological Picnic. John Betjeman. EnLoPo
In This Hotel. Emanuel Carnevali. AnAmPo; LA; NP
In this hour of pure sunlight. Brazil. Ronald de Carvalho. AnCL; WoL
In this hour of worship. Prayer. *Unknown.* PraP
In this house, she said, in this high second storey. Under. J. C. Squire. FaBoTw
In this hush of night. Lullaby. Henry D. Muir. BOL
In this imperfect, gloomy scene. The Amateur Bard on Woman. *Unknown.* PC
In this laborious world of Thine, tumultuous with toil and struggle. India. Rabindranath Tagore. LPS-1
In this life/ Of error, ignorance, and strife. Shelley. *Fr.* The Sensitive Plant. LO
In this little urne [*or* urn] is laid. Upon Prue [*or* Prew] His Maid. Robert Herrick. EM-1; EPS; OAEP; SeCV-1; SeEP; TyEnPo
In this lone, open glade I lie. Lines Written in Kensington Gardens. Matthew Arnold. BPN; EM-2; EmBrPo; EnLi-2; EPN; PoVP; TCEP; ViPo; ViPP; VLEP
In this marble, buried lies. Epitaph [*or* On a Beautiful Virgin]. Thomas Jordan. SeCL; TriL
In this May-month, by grace. Asian Birds. Robert Bridges. VA
In this meadow starred with spring. Morning Glory. Siegfried Sassoon. ChMo; CMP; TwCV
In this merry morn of May. *Unknown, tr. fr. French by* John Addington Symonds. Medieval Norman Songs, VII. AWP
In this mountain village, I have grown accustomed. The Voices of Pine Trees. Rengetsu. OnPM
In this, O Nature, yield I pray to me. Indian Fevers. Sir Ronald Ross. PoP
In this orchestra full of vain deceit. The Changing World. Jami. OnPM
In this our English coast much blessed blood is shed. A Song of Four Priests Who Suffered Death at Lancaster. *Unknown.* ACP
In this pleasant beechen shade. A Poet's Grave. Thomas Bailey Aldrich. GA
In this quiet town, it is odd to discover. In New Ross. Valentin Iremonger. NeIP
In this red wine, where Memory's eyes seem glowing. Toast to Omar Khayyám. Theodore Watts-Dunton. VA
In This River. Valentin Iremonger. NeIP
In this sad place. The Haunted Garden. Henry Treece. NeBP
In this savage place the sun stands still. Margaret Allonby. *Fr.* Lustration of the Winter Tree. BoSA
In this secluded shrine. To a Wood-Violet. John Banister Tabb. HBV
In this short span. The Cragsman. Geoffrey Winthrop Young. PtOT
In this shrill moon the scouts of winter ran. Isabella Valancy Crawford. *Fr.* Malcolm's Katie. PeCV
In this small character is sent. Upon a Braid of Hair in a Heart. Henry King. EnLoPo
In this squalid, dirty dooryard. The Pear Tree. Edna St. Vincent Millay. MAP; MoAmPo
In This Stern Hour. Josephine Johnson. MaRV
In this still place, remote from men. Glen-Almain, the Narrow Glen. Wordsworth. GTSL
In this sudden tempest at the night's heart. Gale. John Holloway. PoN
In this sweet book, the treasury of wit. To His Lady. Sir John Davies. SiPS
In this sweet curving place. The Outdoor Theatre. Anne Goodwin Winslow. LS
In this sweet solitude, the mountain sits. William Ellery Channing. *Fr.* The Mountain. PFY
In this theayter they has plays. An Old Woman, outside the Abbey Theater. L. A. G. Strong. FiBHP; MBP; MoBrPo
In this time Christ hath us sent. Man, Be Glad in Hall and Bower. *Unknown.* AnEC
In this timē God hath sent. Make We Merry in Hall and Bower. *Unknown.* AnEC
In this time of Christmas. In the Honour of Christēs Birth. *Unknown.* AnEC
In This Trembling Shadow. *Unknown.* TuPP
In this vale of wretchedness. Pray for Us that We Savēd Be. *Unknown.* AnEC
In this wide inland sea, that hight by name. The Idle Lake. Spenser. *Fr.* The Faerie Queene, II, 6. PC
In this world I shall not find. Wind-Litany. Margaret Widdemer. NLK
In this world (the Isle of Dreams). The White Island; or, Place of the Blest. Robert Herrick. ChTr; EPS; EV-2; HBV; MeRV; OBS; OxBoCh; SeCL; SeEP

In this worlds raging sea. Regret [*or* Regrat]. William Drummond of Hawthornden. AtBAP; PoEL-2
In this year, as before I said. Christmas Time. Villon, *tr. by* John Payne. *Fr.* Le Petit Testament. LiA
In tholde dayes of the Kyng Arthour. *See* In th' olde dayes . . .
In those days, Francis smiled a revolution. Genealogy. Sister Mary Francis. SaFP
In those fields haunted by fear. Three Barrows Down. Jocelyn Brooke. ChMP
In those great days adventure called. Adventure. T. W. Earp. PoMa
In those old days which poets say were golden. Beer. Charles Stuart Calverley. CenHV
In those sad words I took farewell. In Memoriam A. H. H., LVIII. Tennyson. BPN; EmBrPo; EPN; GEPC; TCEP; ViPo; VLEP
In those sweet days. Dreams of My Youth. Edward Kenealy. RO
In Thought. Stéphane Mallarmé, *tr. fr. French by* Alan Conder. TrFP
In thought I traveled to the high abode. Sonnets on the Death of Laura. Petrarch, *tr. by* Brooks Vaughan. *Fr.* Sonnets to Laura: To Laura in Death, XXXIV. UnW
In thought that brought no rest nor peace of heart. The Sages. Adam Mickiewicz. CAW
In thoughts from the visions of the night, when deepe sleepe falleth on men. Visions of the Night. Job, Bible, *O.T.* LiA
In thousands toward the south the swallows fly. Sonnet. Arthur Davison Ficke. MuM
In Three Days. Robert Browning. BPN; EmBrPo; EPN; EtPaEn; GEPC; PoVP
In through every lattice-bar/ Where the trellis gapes ajar. Annunciation Night. Abby Maria Hemenway. *Fr.* Mary of Nazareth. ISi
In thy coach of state. A Crowned Poet. Anne Reeve Aldrich. AA
In thy fair domain. Landscape. William Mason. *Fr.* The English Garden. OBEC
In Thy garden, in Thy garden, though the rain. The Garden of the Holy Souls. Eleanor Hamilton King. *Fr.* Hours of the Passion. ACP; JKCP (1926 ed.)
In thy hammock gently sleeping. Baby Dear. Samuel Lover. BOL; OTPC (1946 ed.)
In Thy Presence. Richard Chenevix Trench. *See* Prayer: "Lord, what a change within us one short hour."
In thy white bosom Love is laid. Song. John Arthur Blaikie. VA
In Tilbury Town did Old King Cole. Old King Cole. E. A. Robinson. HBV; MOAP; SBMV
In Time. Kathleen Raine. NeBP
In Time like Glass. W. J. Turner. MoBrPo; NAMP; OBMV; POTE
In Time of Grief. Lizette Woodworth Reese. AA; ATP (1953 ed.); LBAP; PFY; TCPD
In Time of Mistrust, XIII. Robert Hillyer. QS
In Time of Mourning. Swinburne. BPN; VLEP
In Time of Need. Katharine Tynan. TrPWD
In Time of Peace. Michael Roberts. MoP
In Time of Pestilence. Thomas Nashe. *See* Adieu, Farewell, Earth's Bliss!
In Time of Pestilence. Sophocles, *tr. fr. Greek by* J. T. Sheppard. *Fr.* Oedipus Rex. OxBG
In Time of Silver Rain. Langston Hughes. GoSl; TiPo
In time of sorrow one should be. Thought for the Winter Season. Mary Elizabeth Osborn. NePoAm
In Time of Suspense. Laurence Whistler. NeTW; POTE
"Draw-to the curtains then, and let it rain," *sel.* LoPS
In Time of "The Breaking of Nations." Thomas Hardy. AnEnPo; BMEP; CaAE; CBOV; ChMo; CMP; CoBMV; EnLi-2 (1949 ed.); EnLit; EPP; EV-2; ExPo; GTBS-W; GTML; GTSL; InP; LiTB; LiTM; LoBV; MBP; MM; MoAB; MoBrPo; NeMA; NP; OAEP (2d ed.); OBEV (new ed.); POTE; PoVP; SeCeV; ShBV-3; TreF; TwCV; ViP; VLEP
In Time of War, *sels.* W. H. Auden.
"As a young child the wisest could adore him." ChMo
"But in the evening the oppression lifted." EnLit
"Far from the heart of culture he was used." ChMo
"He stayed: and was imprisoned in possession." ChMo; EnLit
"He was their servant—some say he was blind." ChMo
"He watched the stars and noted birds in flight." ChMo
"Here war is simple like a monument." EnLit
"His generous bearing was a new invention." ChMo
"Life of man is never quite completed, The." EnLit
"So from the years the gifts were showered." ChMo
"They wondered why the fruit had been forbidden." ChMo
"Wandering lost upon the mountains of our choice." ChMo; EnLit
In time of yore when shepherds dwelt. Olden Love-making. Nicholas Breton. ElSeCe; OBSC
In time the peasant's bull endures the ploughshare. Time Is No Remedy. Ovid. *Fr.* Tristia. LaP
In time the snowman always dies. Thaw. Walker Gibson. NePoAm
In Time the Strong and Stately Turrets Fall. Giles Fletcher. Licia, XXVIII. PeBoSo; ReEn; ReIE; SiCE; TuPP (Time.) OBSC
In Time We See That Silver Drops. Robert Greene. *Fr.* Arbasto. ReIE; SiCE
(Doralicia's Song.) LoBV; OBSC
In times o'ergrown with rust and ignorance. Priestcraft and Private Judgement. Dryden. *Fr.* Religio Laici. OBS
In times of calm or hurricane, in days of sun or shower. The Dog Parade. Arthur Guiterman. AlBD
In times of quietness. Silence. Toyohiko Kagawa. SoLD
In Tir-na'n-Og. "Ethna Carbery." JKCP
In Titum. Sir John Davies. ReIE; TuPP
In to [*or* In-to] thir dirk and drublie dayis. Meditation [*or* Meditatioun] in Wyntir. William Dunbar. BSV; EBSV; SeCePo
In torrid heats of late July. Of the Book-Hunter. Andrew Lang. VA
In touching gently like a golden finger. Visible and Invisible. Helen Pinkerton. PtPa
In Town. Austin Dobson. InP
In Town. *Unknown.* ABF
In Tribute. Vernal House. CaP
In Trinity Churchyard. Thomas S. Jones, Jr. VOD
In tropical climes there are certain times of day. Mad Dogs and Englishmen. Noel Coward. CenHV; FiBHP; WhC
In Trouble and Shame. D. H. Lawrence. OBMV
In Trust. Mary Mapes Dodge. PPL; SiSoSe
In truth how glorious was the High Priest. The High Priest. *Unknown.* TrJP
In truth, O Love, with what a boyish kind. Astrophel and Stella, XI. Sir Philip Sidney. ElL; ElSeCe; InvP; ReEn; SiCE; SiPS
In Tuaim Inbhir. Robin Flower, *fr. the Irish.* GTIV; TriL
(Ivy Crest, The.) AnIL
In Tumulum Abrahami Simple. John Weever. SiCE; TuPP
In Tumulum Avari. John Weever. SiCE
In Tune with the Infinite. Shakespeare. *See* How Sweet the Moonlight Sleeps upon This Bank.
In Tuscany. Eric Mackay. VA
In Tuscany, the vintage season reigns. The Vintage. Belle Cooper. GoBC
In twelve chambers the ladies, decked for the day. A Palace Poem. Hsüeh Feng. LiTW
In twice five years the "greatest living poet." Contemporary Poets. Byron. *Fr.* Don Juan, XI. OBRV
In Two Months Now. George Dillon. MAP; MoAmPo (1942 ed.); PoMa
In unexperienced infancy. Shadows in the Water. Thomas Traherne. EnLi-1; EPS (1942 ed.); LiTB; MePo; OBS; PoEL-2; SeCL; UnPo (1st ed.)
In Utrumque Paratus. Matthew Arnold. EmBrPo; GEPC; NBE; OAEP; PoEL-5; PoVP; ViPP; VLEP
In vacant intraterminal hush. Vacation Exercise. M. K. Joseph. AnNZ
In Vain. Rose Terry Cooke. AA; LEAP
In Vain. Emily Dickinson. *See* I cannot live with you.
In vain. Irony of God. Eva Warner. ChIP
In Vain Earth Decks Herself. Moses ibn Ezra, *tr. fr. Hebrew by* Solomon Solis-Cohen. *Fr.* The World's Illusion. TrJP
In vain I look around. To the Memory of a Lady. George Lyttelton. OBEC
In vain I seek and sue to her for grace. Amoretti, XX. Spenser. PeBoSo
In Vain I Seek to Flee. Pushkin, *tr. fr. Russian by* Babette Deutsch. TrRV
In vain, in vain—the all-composing Hour. Conclusion [*or* Chaos *or* The Triumph of Ignorance]. Pope. *Fr.* The Dunciad. CoBE; EnLi-1; FiP; LoBV; ReTS; RiBV; ViBoPo
In Vain, Mine Eyes. Sir Philip Sidney. *Fr.* Arcadia. SiPS
In vain, poor Nymph, to please our youthful sight. An Elegy: To an Old Beauty. Thomas Parnell. CEP
In vain the cords and axes were prepared. William Falconer. *Fr.* The Shipwreck. LPS-2; OBEC
In vain they roll and scatter, the vagrant, straying stones. Ad Judaeos Mactatores Stephani. Richard Crashaw. Epigrammata Sacra, I, 38. LaP
In vain this fair bouquet do I compose. Love's Own Home. Pierre de Ronsard. TrFP
In vain thy altars do they heap. May Carol. Aubrey Thomas De Vere. CAW
In vain to me the smiling [*or* smileing] mornings shine. Sonnet on the Death of [Mr.] Richard West. Thomas Gray. CEP; EiPP; EM-1; EnLit; EnRP; ES; OAEP; OBEC; PeBoSo; PoE; PoEL-3; SeCePo; TrGrPo; ViBoPo
In Vain Today. Austin Dobson. MBP; MoBrPo (1942 ed.); YT
(To Brander Matthews.) ALV

In vain we call old notions fudge. Stealing [*or* International Copyright]. James Russell Lowell. AA; IAP; MaRV; TreF
In vain you tell your parting lover. Song. Matthew Prior. HBV
In Valleys Green and Still. A. E. Housman. Last Poems, VII. FaBoTw; SoV
In Valleys of Springs of Rivers. A. E. Housman. *See* Clunton and Clunbury.
In vaulted place where shadows flit. In a Church of Padua. Herman Melville. MeRV
In Venice, *sels.* John Addington Symonds.
In the Small Canals. PoVP
Invitation to the Gondola, The. PoVP
In Vinculis, *sels.* Wilfrid Scawen Blunt.
Deeds That Might Have Been, The. TrGrPo
Liberty, Equality, Fraternity. PoFr
In Virgine [*or* Virgyne] the sweltry [*or* sultry] sun 'gan [*or* did] sheene. An Excelente Balade of Charitie. Thomas Chatterton. BCEP; CEP; EiPP; EnRP; EV-3; GoTL; LiTB; LiTG; OBEC; SeCePo; TCEP
In visions of the dark night. A Dream. Poe. IAP
In Wakefield there lives a jolly pinder. The Jolly Pinder of Wakefield [*or* Robin Hood and the Pinder of Wakefield]. *Unknown.* BaBo; ESPB; EV-2
In Walpi. Elizabeth J. Coatsworth. *Fr.* The Painted Desert. PoeMoYo
In War Time. W. H. Auden. TwHP
In Waste Places. James Stephens. *See* Waste Places, The.
In waters still as a burnished mirror's face. Fishing in the Wei River. Po Chü-i. TrCh
In Weary Night. Blake. *Fr.* The Gates of Paradise. LiA
In Western Mountains, *sel.* Glenn Ward Dresbach.
Life or Death. HBMV
In Westminster Abbey. *At. to* Francis Beaumont *and to* William Basse. *See* On the Tombs in Westminster Abbey.
In Westminster Abbey. John Betjeman. LiTM
In Westminster not long ago. The Ratcatcher's Daughter. *Unknown.* ChTr; OxBoLi
In wet and cloudy mists I slowly rise. Night's Song. *At. to* Sir William Davenant. *Fr.* Luminalia. SeCL
In what a glorious substance did they dream. Ideal Passion, XXVI. George Edward Woodberry. HBMV
In what a strange bewilderment do we. Morn. Helen Hunt Jackson. AA
In what bright realm, what sphere of radiant thought. Petrarch, *tr. by* Joseph Auslander. Sonnets to Laura: To Laura in Life, CXXVI. PrPoCR
In what dark silent grove. Cogitabo pro Peccato Meo. William Habington. CoBE
In what dead summer came her petals here? A Rose Found in a Greek Dictionary. Edmund Wilson. CAG
In what divine ideal, what lofty sphere. Sonnet. Petrarch, *tr. by* T. G. Bergin. Sonnets to Laura: To Laura in Life, CXXVI. LyPI
In what far, Judean field. The Glory of the Grass. Claire Wallace Flynn. StJW
In what finite tendon dost thou rise? Spirituality. Samuel Greenberg. LiTA
In What Manner the Soul Is United to the Body. Sir John Davies. *See* Soul and the Body, The.
In what torn[e] ship soever I embark[e]. A Hymn [*or* Hymne] to Christ, at the Authors Last Going into Germany. John Donne. AnEnPo; EPS (1942 ed.); EV-2; FaBoEn; LiTB; LiTG; MeLP; MePo; MeRV; OAEP; OBS; OxBoCh; Po; SeCV-1; SeEP; TuPP; ViBoPo; WoL
In white splendors and red terrors my thoughts. Michael the Archangel. Michael Williams. JKCP (1955 ed.)
In whitest hour of pain the iron air. Prayer in Time of War. Henry Treece. WaP
In Whom Is No Variableness. Edith Hickman Divall. *See* Changeless.
In Whom We Live and Have Our Being. James Rhoades. MaRV
In whomsoe'er since Poesy began. On Burns. Dante Gabriel Rossetti. BPN
In Wicklow. Rhoda Coghill. NeIP
In wild October when the low hills lie. Two States of Prayer. Thomas Merton. JKCP (1955 ed.)
In William Rufus's hall the galleries reached. Fifth Day. R. D. Fitzgerald. MoAuPo
In Wiltshire. Edmund Blunden. POTE
In Windsor Castle. Earl of Surrey. *See* Prisoned in Windsor, He Recounteth His Pleasure There Passed.
In Windsor Castle lives the king. Home Thoughts. Denis Glover. AnNZ
In Winnipeg at Christmas. Winnipeg at Christmas. Rose Fyleman. ChBR
In Winter. C. H. Bretherton. InMe
In Winter. Emily Dickinson. *See* In winter, in my room.
In winter I get up at night. Bed in Summer. Robert Louis Stevenson. CPN; GFA; OnHT; OTPC; PCH; PoVP; RIS; StVeCh
In winter, in my room. Emily Dickinson. LiTA; OxBA; PoE; SeCeV
(In Winter.) MAPA; TwAmPo
In winter, when the dismal rain. A Fragment from a Ballad. Alexander Smith. BMEP
In winter, when the fields are white. Humpty Dumpty's Recitation [*or* Song]. "Lewis Carroll." *Fr.* Through the Looking-Glass. BOHV; ChTr; FiBHP; GoTP; OxBoLi; SAS; SiTL
In winter when the rain rain'd cauld. Tak Your Auld Cloak about Ye. *Unknown.* EBSV
In winter, when the wind I hear. The Four Winds. Frank Dempster Sherman. TVC; TVSH
In winter's just return, when Boreas gan his reign. Earl of Surrey. SiPS
In wintertime I have such fun. Quoits. Mary Effie Lee Newsome. CDC; GoSl
In winter-time we go. White Fields. James Stephens. BoTP
In Wintry Midnight, o'er a Stormy Main. Petrarch, *tr. fr. Italian by* William Barnes. ChTr
In wiser days, my darling rosebud, blown. To My Daughter Betty, the Gift of God. Thomas Michael Kettle. CAW; HBMV; JKCP (1955 ed.); OnYI
In wishing nothing we enjoy still most. Human Happiness. Dryden. *Fr.* The Indian Emperor, IV, i. FiP
In Wolfen Teeth. Chaim Grade, *tr. fr. Yiddish by* Sarah Zweig Betsky. OnCuPl
In wonder and time-mists. Chorus. Lord De Tabley. *Fr.* Philoctetes. PoVP
In Wonted Walks, Since Wonted Fancies Change. Sir Philip Sidney. MaPo; ReIE
(In Wonted Walkes.) PoEL-1
In Woods near the Frontline. Mikhail Isakovsky, *tr. fr. Russian by* Jack Lindsay. RuPo
In woods so long time bare. Cuckoo! Hilaire Belloc. MoVE
In woods still winter bare. Shadbush. Christina Rainsford. GoYe
In Xanadu did Kubla Khan. Kubla Khan. Samuel Taylor Coleridge. AnFE; AtBAP; ATP; AWP; BBV; BCEP; BEL; BLV; BoLiVe; BPN; BrBE; CaAE; CBE; CBOV; CBPC; CH; ChER; ChTr; CoBE; CoEV; DaM; EG; EM-2; EmBrPo; EnL; EnLi-2; EnLit; EnRP; EPN; EPP; ERP; EV-4; ExPo; FaBoBe; FaBoCh; FaBoEn; FaFP; FiP; GBV (1952 ed.); GN; GTBS-W; GTSL; HBV; HiLiEn; HoPM; InP; InPo; InvP; JAWP; KN; LEAP; LH; LiA; LiTB; LiTG; LoBV; LoGBV; LPS-3; MaC; MCCG; MyFE; NeHB; OAEP; OBEV; OBRV; OtMeF; OTPC; OuHeWo; PC; PG (1945 ed.); PIAE; PIR; Po; PoE; PoEL-4; PoeMoYo; PoFS; PoRA; PreP; REAL; ReaPo; RG; RiBV; SeCeV; ShBV-3; TCEP; ThWaDe; TOP; TreFS; TrGrPo; TVSH; TwHP; TyEnPo; UnPo (3d ed.); ViBoPo; WBP; WHA
In yon hollow Damon lies. In Arcady. Cosmo Monkhouse. OBVV
In yon post-town there lived a margent. The Apprentice Boy. *Unknown.* ABS
In yonder dim and pathless wood. The Lost Church. Ludwig Uhland. UnW
In yonder grave a Druid lies. Ode on the Death of Mr. Thomson. William Collins. EiPP; EV-3; OBEC; PtP; SeCePo
In yonder valley there dwelt, alone. The Mountain Sprite. Thomas Moore. OTPC
In Your Absence. Elizabeth Baxter. PoToHe (new ed.)
In your arms was still delight. Retrospect. Rupert Brooke. NP
In your face I sometimes see. To My Little Son. Julia Johnson Davis. FAOV; HBMV
In your garb and outward clothing. Neatness in Apparel. Charles *and* Mary Lamb. OTPC
In your hesitant moments, remember Cornford and Fox. They Live. Randall Swingler. WaP
In your hollow, hoary olive tree. Olive Tree. Lorenzo Mavilis. MoGP
In your mother's apple orchard. Yvonne of Brittany. Ernest Dowson. PoVP
In your next letter I wish you'd say. Letter to New York. Elizabeth Bishop. LiTL
In your quick face and in your pulsing throat. To One Singing. Russell Mayo Spear. CAG
In Youth. Evaleen Stein. AA
In youth from rock to rock I went. To the Daisy. Wordsworth. BPN; EmBrPo; EnRP; ERP; GEPC
In youth, gay scenes attract our eyes. The Vanity of Existence. Philip Freneau. CoV
In youth I frowned. Old Woman's Song. Thomas Cole. NePoAm-2
In youth I served my time. Retirement. *Unknown.* KiLC
In Youth, in Age. Robert Cooper. TuPP

In Youth Is Pleasure. R. Wever. *Fr.* Lusty Juventus. ChTr; OBEV
("In a herber green asleep whereas I lay.") EG
(Of Youth He Singeth.) EIL
(Youth.) OBSC
In youth my wings were strong and tireless. Alexander Throckmorton. Edgar Lee Masters. *Fr.* Spoon River Anthology. BAP; SBMV
In youth, when blood was warm and fancy high. At Last. Paul Hamilton Hayne. EOAH
In youth's spring it was my lot. *See* In spring of youth it was my lot.
In Ystrad Fflur a soft breeze blows. Ystrad Fflur. T. Gwynn Jones. PrWP
In zummer, leäte at evenèn tide. The Rwose in the Dark. William Barnes. AtBAP
Inalienable/ for the humbly dying. And Then There. František Halas. LiTW
Inarticulate. Mabel Ruggles Cobb. DDA
Inasmuch! William E. Brooks. PGD
Inasmuch. S. V. R. Ford. PTA-2
Inaudible move day and night. Silence. John Lancaster Spalding. AA
Inauguration Day. Richard Watson Gilder. PoRL
Inbetweentimes. Sir Herbert Read. *See* Day's Affirmation.
Inbrothered ("There is a destiny"). Edwin Markham. *Fr.* A Creed. BLPA; GrCo-1
Incantation, The. *At. to* Amergin. *See* Invocation to Ireland.
Incantation, An. Byron. *Fr.* Manfred, I, i. OBRV
("When the moon is on the wave.") UnW
Incantation, The. Theocritus, *tr. fr. Greek by* C. S. Calverley. Idylls, II. AWP; JAWP; WBP
(Love-Magic, *tr. by* R. C. Trevelyan.) GrR
(Pharmaceutria, *pr. tr. by* Andrew Lang.) GrL
(Second Idyll, The, *tr. by* Jack Lindsay.) LiTW
(Simaetha, *tr. by* Jack Lindsay.) OxBG
(Sorceress, The.) GrPE, *tr. by* F. L. Lucas; LiA, *tr. by* C. S. Calverley
("Where are the bay-leaves, Thestylis, and the charms?" *tr. by* C. S. Calverley.) GrPo
Incantation, An. Marguerite Wilkinson. AV; NP
Incantation for Healing. Constance Lindsay Skinner. NV
Incantation for Rain. *Unknown, tr. fr. Navajo Indian by* Washington Matthews. ExPo
Incantation in "Oedipus." Dryden. *Fr.* Oedipus, III, i. TriL
Incantations. Annie Charlotte Dalton. CPG
Incapable now of the classical despair. Respects. Alan Brownjohn. PoN
Incarnate for our marriage you appeared. The Marriage. Yvor Winters. MoVE
Incarnate Love. Christina Rossetti. ChIP; MaRV
Incarnate Love. Wilbur Fisk Tillett. BLRP
Incarnatio Est Maximum Donum Dei. William Alabaster. MePo
Incarnation, The. Giles Fletcher. StJW
Incarnation. "Maurine Halliburton." MuM; UnW
Incarnation, The. William Langland. *Fr.* The Vision of Piers Plowman. PoEL-1
Incarnation. Edith Lovejoy Pierce. MaRV; MuM
Incarnation of Sirius, The. James McAuley. MoAuPo
Incendiary Sex, The. Don Marquis. LPS-1
Incense. Leslie Savage Clark. ChIP
Incense. Zabelle Essayan, *tr. fr. Armenian by* Zabelle C. Boyajian. ArmLP
Incense. Louise Townsend Nicholl. NePoAm-2
Incense, and flesh of swine, and this year's grain. To Phidyle. Horace. *Fr.* Odes. AWP
Incense and Moonlight. Kan Ju Yü, *tr. fr. Chinese by* Henry H. Hart. ChLP
Incense at the altar slowly burns, The. Incense. Zabelle Essayan. ArmLP
Incense Burner, The. Abus Salt, *tr. fr. Arabic by* A. J. Arberry. MooP
Incentive, The. Sarah N. Cleghorn. HBMV
Incest represented by a frockcoated gentleman. Vision of Moth-eaten Pianos Falling to Pieces. "César Moro." AnCL
Inchcape Rock, The. Robert Southey. BeLS; CaAE; CG; ChTr; EV-4; FaBoBe; GN; GoTP; HBV; HBVY; LPS-2; MW; OBRV; OnSP; OTPC; PECK; TreFS; TVSH
Incident. Countee Cullen. BoChLi (1950 ed.); CDC; MoSiPe; OQP; PoNe; QP-2
(Incident; Baltimore.) GoSl
Incident, An. Douglas Le Pan. PeCV
Incident, An. Frederick Tennyson. GoBC
Incident at Matauri. Kendrick Smithyman. AnNZ
Incident Characteristic of a Favorite Dog. Wordsworth. CG
Incident Here and There, An. Hilda Doolittle ("H. D."). CrMA
Incident of French History, An. James I. Whitman. PCD
Incident of the French Camp. Robert Browning. BBV; BEL; BeLS; BMEP; BPN; EmBrPo; EnLi-2 (1949 ed.); EPN; EV-5; GEPC; GN; GoTP; HBV; HBVY; HiLiEn; LPS-2; MaC; MCCG; MW; NeHB; OnSP; OTPC; PECK; PFE; PIR; PoeMoYo; PoVP; PTA-1; PYM; SoV; TCEP; TreF; TrGrPo; TSW; TSWC; TVSH; VA
Incident on a Journey. Thom Gunn. NePoEA
Incidents in Playfair House. Nicholas Moore. NeBP
Incidents in the Life of My Uncle Arly. Edward Lear. AIDL; MoShBr; NA; OxBoLi; SiTL; TrGrPo; WhC
Incipit Vita Nova. William Morton Payne. AA
Incline, O Maiden,/ Thou sorrow-laden. Prayer. Goethe. *Fr.* Faust. LiA
Incline Thine ear, O God. Therefore, We Thank Thee, God. Reuben Grossman. TrJP
Inclosed within a hedge. Emily Dickinson. PoeMoYo
Inclusion. George Sterling. MuM
Inclusions. Elizabeth Barrett Browning. BPN; EmBrPo; HBV; OBVV; TOP
Inclusiveness. Dante Gabriel Rossetti. The House of Life, LXIII. EmBrPo; EnLi-2; PoVP; VA; ViPo
Incognita. Austin Dobson. CenHV; PoVP
Incognita of Raphael. William Allen Butler. AA
Incognitos of masquerading moons. Festoons of Fishes. Alfred Kreymborg. HBMV; TCPD
Incommunicable Glory, The. Dante, *tr. fr. Italian by* Wendell Phillips Stafford. *Fr.* Divina Commedia: Paradiso, I. GrCo-2
Incomparable Kiss, An. *Unknown.* SeCL; SeEP
(Give Me a Kiss from Those Sweet Lips of Thine.) InvP
Incompatibility. Aubrey Thomas De Vere. IrPN
Incomprehensible, The. Isaac Watts. CEP; WGRP
Incomprehensible—/ O Master—fate and mystery. Sanctus. David Gascoyne. *Fr.* Miserere. NeBP
Incongruously gray he sits. Balloon Man. Hazel I. Dannecker. PoMa
Inconsistency of Women's Love. Catullus, *tr. fr. Latin by* George Lamb. OnPM
Inconstancy. Abraham Cowley. EPS (1942 ed.)
(Love.) PoFS
Inconstancy. John Donne. *See* Sonnet: "Oh, to vex me . . ."
Inconstancy. Joseph Rodman Drake. PR
Inconstancy Reproved. *At. to* Sir Robert Ayton. *See* To His Forsaken Mistress.
Inconstant Mistress, The. *At. to* Sir Robert Ayton. *See* To His Forsaken Mistress.
Inconvenience, An. John Banister Tabb. UTS
Incorporation, The. Stefan George, *tr. fr. German by* David Luke. AnGP
Incorrigible. Burges Johnson. PoMa
Incorrigible one, still groping with your eyes. Thought and the Poet. "Peter Yates." ChMP
Increase Our Faith. Frances Ridley Havergal. PraP
Increasing moonlight drifts across my bed, The. Fredericksburg. Thomas Bailey Aldrich. BAP; MDAH; PaA; PAH; PAP; PFY
Incredibly near the vital edge of tears. From J. Haydn to Constanze Mozart (1791). Edgar Bowers. PtPa
Incredulous, he stared at the amused. Vocation. W. H. Auden. ChMo
Incremation, The. Matthew Arnold. *See* Burning of Balder's Ship, The.
Incurable. Dorothy Parker. PR
Incurables, The. Arthur Upson. AnAmPo; LA
Indeed a sweet and knowing lady. Anemones for Miss Austen. Bernard Bergonzi. HaMV; PoN
Indeed I live in the dark ages! To Posterity. Bertolt Brecht. OnHM
Indeed I must confess. Platonic[k] Love. Abraham Cowley. *Fr.* The Mistress. SeCV-1; SeEP
Indeed, it will soon be over, I shall be done. Intimations of Mortality. Phyllis McGinley. NeMA
Indeed, my Caelia, 'tis in vain. Song. Sir John Henry Moore. LO; OBEC
Indeed, Sir Peter, I could wish, I own. On Clergymen Preaching Politics. John Byrom. SeCePo
Indeed this is sweet life! my hand. No Master. W. H. Davies. PoFr; POTT
Indeed, this world is flat: as for the other, nonsense. The Cigarette. Jules Laforgue. LiTW
Indeed this very love which is my boast. Sonnets from the Portuguese, XII. Elizabeth Barrett Browning. BPN; HBV; LPS-1
Indeede I am studying Alcumye. John Webster. *Fr.* The White Devil, I, ii. AtBAP
Independence. Mary Fullerton. BoAV
Independence. Roy McFadden. OxBI
Independence. Guy Mason. CaP
Independence. Tobias George Smollett. *Fr.* Ode to Independence. OBEC
("Thy spirit, Independence, let me share!") PoFr
Independence. Henry David Thoreau. AmPP (3d ed.); AnNE; CoBA; PoFr; TreFS

Independence Bell, July 4, 1776 (*sl. diff. versions*). *Unknown.* BLPA; DD; *abr.*; FaBoBe
(Independence Bell.) BoHiPo; MC, *abr.*; PEDC, *abr.*
(Independence Bell, Philadelphia, *sl. abr.*) IDAH
(Liberty and Independence, *sl. abr.*) TreFS
Independence Day. Royall Tyler. PAH
Independence Day To-Day. Margaret E. Sangster. PEDC
Independence Square, Christmas 1783. Arthur Guiterman. PEDC
India. Florence Earle Coates. AA
India. Rabindranath Tagore. LPS-1
India. W. J. Turner. MoBrPo
India became his jasmined youth, Goa. Roy Macnab. *Fr.* The Man of Grass. BoSA
India the Magic. H. A. Jules-Bois, *tr. fr. French by* Thomas Walsh. CAW
Indian, The. Arthur S. Bourinot. BoCaPo
Indian, The. *Unknown. See* American Indian, The.
Indian at the Burial-Place of His Fathers, An. Bryant. CoBA
Indian Burying Ground, The. Philip Freneau. AA; AmP; AmPP; AnAmPo; AnFE; APA; APW; BAV; CoAnAm; CoBA; HBV; HiLiAm; IAP; LA; LBAP; LiTA; LiTG; MOAP; NePA; OBAV; OxBA; Po; PoEL-4; RiBV; TCAP; TriL; UnW
Indian Children. Annette Wynne. BoChLi; GaP; GFA; MPB; OTPC (1946 ed.); PCH; StVeCh; SUS; TiPo
Indian children squat upon the ground. Chairs. Annette Wynne. GFA
Indian Cradle Song. *Unknown.* BoChLi; BOL
Indian Dance. Frederick Niven. CaP; OCL
Indian Elephant, The. C. J. Kaberry. FiBHP
Indian Emperor, The, *sels.* Dryden.
Ah, Fading Joy, *fr.* IV, iii. ChTr; FiP; LoBV; OAEP; ViBoPo
("Ah, fading joy, how quickly art thou past!") ElSeCe; MaPo
(Song: "Ah, fading joy.") BeR; EPS (1942 ed.); FaBoEn; TCEP
Human Happiness, *fr.* IV, i. FiP
Spanish Ships Reach Mexico, The. *fr.* I, ii. BeR
Indian Epigram: "Communion with the good is friendship's root." *Unknown, tr. fr. Sanskrit by* Paul Elmer More. BoFr
Indian Epigrams. *Unknown, tr. fr. Sanskrit by* Arthur W. Ryder. BoFr
Indian Fevers. Sir Ronald Ross. PoP
Indian-footed move the mists. Ghosts of Indians. Witter Bynner. OBAV; PoeMoYo; PoTo; VOD
Indian Ghost Dance and War, The. W. H. Prather. PoOW
Indian Girl. Emilio Vásquez, *tr. fr. Spanish by* Blanca López Castillón. AnCL
Indian Hunter, The. Eliza Cook. BLPA
Indian Hymn of Thanks to Mother Corn, An. *Unknown.* PCH
Indian Love-Song. "Owen Meredith." VA
Indian Lullaby, An. Claude Bryan. BOL
Indian Lullaby. Sarah Comstock. BOL
Indian Lullaby. Charles Myall. BOL; MPB; RAR
Indian Lullaby, An. *Unknown.* BOL; RAR
Indian Maid, The. Keats. *Fr.* Endymion, IV. ERP
Indian Massacre, The. Joseph Howe. *Fr.* Acadia. BoCaPo
Indian Names. Lydia Huntley Sigourney. BAP; BAV; FaPON; HBV; LEAP; MC; MPB; OTPC; PAH; PoRL; PTA-2
Indian Night Tableau. Hyman Edelstein. CaP
Indian Pipe and Moccasin Flower. Arthur Guiterman. BrR; SUS
Indian Pipes. Winifred Welles. AnAmPo; LA
Indian Point. Marsden Hartley. TwAmPo
Indian Queen, The, *sels.* Sir Robert Howard *and* John Dryden.
Death like a Rose. BeR
Song of Aerial Spirits. AtBAP
Zempoalla's Dream. BeR
Indian Rebellion. Jorge Carrera Andrade, *tr. fr. Spanish by* H. R. Hays. TwSpPo
Indian Runner, The. W. L. Stoddard. CAG
Indian Serenade, The. Shelley. AnFE; ATP; AWP; BCEP; BEL; BLV; BoLiVe; BPN; CaAE; EM-2; EmBrPo; EnLi-2; EnLit; EnRP; EPP; ERP; EtPaEn; EV-4; ExPo; GEPC; GTSL; HoPM; InPo; JAWP; KN; LiTB; LiTG; LiTL; LoBV; LoPo; LoPS; MCCG; OAEP; OBEV; OBRV; OuHeWo; PFE; PG; PIAE; REAL; TCEP; TOP; TreF; TrGrPo; TyEnPo; UnPo (1st ed.); ViBoPo; WBP
(I Arise from Dreams of Thee.) PIR
(Lines to an Indian Air.) FaBoBe; FiP; GTBS; GTBS-D; GTBS-W; GTSE; HBV; LEAP; LPS-1; NeHB
Indian Sky. Alfred Kreymborg. NP
Indian Song, An. W. B. Yeats. VA
Indian Songs. Louis Mertins. StVeCh (1955 ed.)
Rain Chant.
Prayer to the Sun God.
Indian Student, The; or, Force of Nature. Philip Freneau. AmPP (4th ed.); APW; OxBA
Indian Summer, The. John Howard Bryant. TOAH
Indian Summer. Eudora S. Bumstead. TOAH
Indian Summer. Wilfred Campbell. BoCaPo (1948 ed.); CaP; OCL
Indian Summer. Helena Coleman. CPG
Indian Summer ("These are the days"). Emily Dickinson. AnNE; BoLiVe (1945 ed.); CoBA; CoV; DDA; GoTP; HBV; MAP; MoAmPo; NeMA; NLK; PFE
Indian Summer. A. S. Draper. YeAr
Indian Summer. Erle Reiter Hannum. CAG
Indian Summer. J. P. Irvine. SN
Indian Summer. William Ellery Leonard. Two Lives, Pt. III. AnAmPo; HBMV; LA; MOAP; MuM; NP; NV; PG (1945 ed.); SBMV
Indian Summer. Susanna Strickland Moodie. CaP; OCL
Indian Summer. Lydia Huntley Sigourney. BAV
Indian Summer. John Banister Tabb. AA; DD
Indian Summer. *Unknown.* LPS-2
Indian Summer. Henry van Dyke. VOD
Indian Summer. Whittier. *Fr.* Eve of Election. PCH; PEOR
Indian Summer—Buffalo Summer. Winfield Townley Scott. FiMAP
Indian Summer Day on the Prairie, An. Vachel Lindsay. StVeCh; WaKn; YT
Indian summer is with us now. Indian Summer. A. S. Draper. YeAr
Indian summer sky is sapphirine, The. A Country House in the South. John Henry Boner. NoCaPo
Indian upon God, The. W. B. Yeats. ChMo; CMP; GTIV; MBP; MoBrPo; POTT; WGRP
Indian war was over, The. The Captive's Hymn. Edna Dean Proctor. PAH
Indian weed [now] witherèd quite, The. A Religious Use of Taking Tobacco [*or* Pipe and Can]. *At. to* Robert Wisdome. CenL; ElL; HBV; OBEV; OBS; SeEP
Indian Wind Song, An. Peter McArthur. CPG
Indian Woman, The. Walt Whitman. *Fr.* The Sleepers. PCD; PCH
Indiana. Hart Crane. *Fr.* The Bridge: Powhatan's Daughter. AnFE; CoAnAm; LiTA; TwAmPo
Indiana: no blustering summit or coarse gorge. Midwest. John Frederick Nims. MoVE
Indians. Charles Sprague. *Fr.* Centennial Ode. GN
Indians chant and dance about, The. Not a Cloud in the Sky. Richard Armour. WhC
Indians Come down from Mixco, The. Miguel Angel Asturias, *tr. fr. Spanish by* Donald Devenish Walsh. AnCL; FaPON
Indian's Grave, The. George J. Mountain. BoCaPo (1943 ed.); CaP
Indians stole fair Annie, The. Fair Annie (C *vers.*). *Unknown.* ViBoFo
Indian's Welcome to the Pilgrim Fathers, The. Lydia Huntley Sigourney. AA; DD
Indictment. Margaret Todd Ritter. AnAmPo; LA
Indifference. Louise Driscoll. MW; PoMa
Indifference, The. Sir Charles Sedley. CEP; SeCV-2
Indifference. G. A. Studdert-Kennedy. BPP; ChIP; MaRV; OQP; PGD; QP-1; QS
(Crucifixion, The.) StJW
Indifference ("The cat is in the parlour"). *Unknown.* BOHV
Indifference ("In loopy links the canker crawls"). *Unknown.* NA
Indifference to Fortune. James Thomson. *Fr.* The Castle of Indolence, II. OBEC
Indifferent, The. Francis Beaumont. ElL; ElSeCe; EnLit; HBV
Indifferent, The. John Donne. ATP (1935 ed.); BEL; ElSeCe; EM-1; EnL; EnLit; EnLP; EPP; EPS; OAEP; OuHeWo; ReEn; ReIE; SeCV-1; TOP; TuPP; TwP
("I can love both fair and brown.") EG
Indifferent, flippant, earnest, but all bored. The Conscript. W. W. Gibson. ChMo; CMP; MaRV; PoeMoYo; POTT
Indignant at the fumbling wits, the obscure spite. Paudeen. W. B. Yeats. MaPo; PoEL-5
Indignant Male, An. A. B. Ross. BrR; MPB
Indignantly he spoke, and dashed to earth. The Web. Homer. *Fr.* The Odyssey, II. OxBG
Indignation. Victor Hugo, *tr. fr. French.* WoL
Indignation Dinner, An. James David Corrothers. BANP; PoNe
Indignation's fiery flood. The Confession of Golias. "The Archpoet of Cologne." LyMA
Indigo Bird. Stephen Crombie. BLA
Indigo Bird, The. Ethelwyn Wetherald. CPG
Indirection. Richard Realf. AA; AnAmPo; AnFE; APA; BAP; CoAnAm; HBV; LA; LEAP; MaRV; OBAV; OQP; QP-1
Indispensability. Arthur Guiterman. WaKn
Individualist Speaks, The. Louis MacNeice. MoVE; OBMV
Individuality. Sidney Lanier. SPP

Indolence, *sel.* Robert Bridges.
Thou Didst Delight My Eyes. GTBS-D; LoPS; MBP; MoAB; MoBrPo; VA; VLEP
Indolence. Vernon Watkins. FaBoTw
Indolent and kitten-eyed. Cheetah. Charles Eglington. BoSA
Indolent Heart. Franz Werfel, *tr. fr. German by* Elizabeth Selden. BoFr
Indolent vicar of Bray, An. Limerick. Langford Reed. TSWC
Indoor Games near Newbury. John Betjeman. MoPW; MoVE
Indra, the Supreme God. *Unknown, tr. fr. Sanskrit by* Romesh Dutt. *Fr.* The Rig-Veda. AWP
Induced Current. Herbert Mayo. PoMa
Induction, The: "In a summer season . . ." William Langland. *See* Prologue: "In a somer sesun . . ."
Induction: "O sovereign power of love." Keats. *See* Invocation to the Power of Love.
Induction to Endymion. Keats. *See* Thing of Beauty Is a Joy Forever, A.
Induction to "The Mirror for Magistrates." Thomas Sackville, Earl of Dorset. *See* Mirror for Magistrates, The.
Indulge no more may we. The End of the Episode. Thomas Hardy. LO; LoPS
Indulgent giants burned to crisp. Lavish Kindness. Elinor Wylie. AtBAP; CrMA
Indweller of a peaceful vale. To Southey, 1833. Walter Savage Landor. PtP
Indwelling. Thomas Edward Brown. VLEP
Indwelling God, The. Frederick Lucian Hosmer. MaRV; OQP; QP-2; WGRP
Inebriate of Air. Emily Dickinson. *See* I taste a liquor never brewed.
Inebriety, *sel.* George Crabbe.
Vicar, The. AnFE
Inefficacious Egg, The. Roy Bishop. HBMV
Inert he lies on the saltgold sand. The Sunbather. Vernon Watkins. MoPo; MoVE; MoWP
Inertia. Audrey McGaffin. NePoAm
Inescapable romance, inescapable choice. Wallace Stevens. *Fr.* An Ordinary Evening in New Haven. ReMP
Inevitability. Valery Yakovlevich Bryusov, *tr. fr. Russian by* Babette Deutsch. TrRV
Inevitable, The. Sarah Knowles Bolton. AA; MaRV; OQP; PCD; QP-1; WGRP
Inexhaustible. Israel Zangwill. TrJP
Inexorable. William Drummond of Hawthornden. *See* Madrigal: "My thoughts hold mortal strife."
Inexorable, The. Huw Menai. MoWP
Inexorable Death. Aeschylus, *tr. fr. Greek by* C. M. Bowra. *Fr.* Niobe. OxBG
Inexorably bound/ As my hope launching high. Little Air, II. Stéphane Mallarmé. AnFP
Inexperience. June Breining. PoMa
Infallibility. Thomas Stephens Collier. AA
Infancy. Hugh Downman. PoP
Infant Heracles, The. Pindar, *tr. fr. Greek by* C. J. Billson. *Fr.* Nemean Odes, I. OxBG
Infant Innocence. A. E. Housman. ChTr; EnLi-2 (1949 ed.), *sl. diff.*; FaBoCh; FaFP; LiTB; LiTM; LoGBV; OxBoLi; SiTL; WhC, *sl. diff.*
("Grizzly Bear is huge and wild, The.") CenHV
Infant Joy. Blake. *Fr.* Songs of Innocence. BCEP; EiPP; EM-1; EnLi-2; EnLit; FaPON; GoTP; GTSL; HBV; HBVY; KN; LEAP; LoBV; NeHB; OTPC; PRWS; SiSoSe; ThWaDe; TiPo (1952 ed.); ViBoPo
Infant Moses, The. Max Jacob, *tr. fr. French by* Cecily Mackworth. MiFP
Infant Noah. Vernon Watkins. NeBP
Infant Roses in Their Bloom. John Oldham. *Fr.* To the Memory of Mr. Charles Morwent. BeR
Infant Sorrow. Blake. *Fr.* Songs of Experience. BLV; BoLiVe; EiPP; EnL; FaBoEn; PoEL-4; PoFS
Infant Spring. Fredegond Shove. HBMV
Infant—wailing in nameless fear, An. Life. Ella Wheeler Wilcox. PoToHe
Infantryman, An. Edmund Blunden. ViBoPo
Infants die with a cry. The Hades of Science. Edward Willard Watson. PoP
Infant's Eye, An. Thomas Traherne. CoBE
Infants' gravemounds are steps of angels, where. Graves of Infants. John Clare. OBVV
Infants' Petition, The. Michael Wigglesworth. *Fr.* The Day of Doom. AnNE
(Damnation of the Infants.) APW
Infelix Felix. Thomas D'Arcy McGee. TIP
Inferno. Dante, *tr. fr. Italian. Fr.* Divina Commedia. EnLi-1 (*fr.* V *and* XIII), *tr. by* Frances Winwar; OuHeWo, *abr., tr. by* Henry F. Cary
Sels.
Dante Enters the Gate of Hell, *fr.* III, *tr. by* J. A. Carlyle. LiA
Francesca da Rimini, *fr.* V, *tr. by* Dante Gabriel Rossetti. EmBrPo; EPN; EPP
Paolo and Francesca, *fr.* V, *tr. by* Byron. LiA
Pier delle Vigne, *fr.* XIII, *tr. by* John Ciardi. HoPM
Ugolino, *fr.* XXXIII, *tr. by* Laurence Binyon. LiA
"While I was all absorbed," *fr.* XXVIII, *tr. by* Longfellow. CAW
Infida's Song. Robert Greene. *Fr.* Never Too Late. AtBAP; OBSC
("Sweet Adon', dar'st not glance thine eye?") LO
Infidelity. Louis Untermeyer. NP; TrJP
Infinite, The. Giacomo Leopardi, *tr. fr. Italian.* LiA, *tr. by* Romilda Rendel; LiTW, *tr. by* Kenneth Rexroth; OnPM, *tr. by* Glauco Cambon; WoL, *tr. by* R. C. Trevelyan
(Infinito, L', *tr. by* Lorna de' Lucchi.) AWP; JAWP; WBP; Po, *tr. by* John Heath-Stubbs
(Infinity, *tr. by* Brooks Vaughan.) UnW
Infinite, The. John Boyle O'Reilly. OnYI; UnW
Infinite consanguinity it bears. Voyages, III. Hart Crane. MoPo; MoVE; Po
Infinite gentleness, infinite irony. Effigy of a Nun. Sara Teasdale. MAP; MoAmPo; NP
Infinite! let me not think on you. Simple Things. Paul Jean Toulet. CAW
Infinite orderliness of the natural world, The. The Spiral. John Holmes. MiAP
Infinite Power, eternal Lord. The Comparison and Complaint. Isaac Watts. TrPWD
Infinite Time. Hugo von Hofmannsthal, *tr. fr. German by* Michael Hamburger. AnGP
Infinite Truth and Might! whose love. Thy Name We Bless and Magnify. John Power. BLRP
"Infinite," The. Word horrible! at feud. Legem Tuam Dilexi. Coventry Patmore. OxBoCh; PoEL-5; PoLi
Infinitely apart lie the Herd Boy star. *Unknown, tr. fr. Chinese.* The Nineteen Han Poems, X. WhP
Infinitesimal James. Limerick. *Unknown.* BOHV
Infinito, L'. Giacomo Leopardi. *See* Infinite, The.
Infinity. Giacomo Leopardi. *See* Infinite, The.
Infinity. Philip Henry Savage. AA; LBAP
Infinity. Walt Whitman. *Fr.* Song of Myself, XLIV–XLV. AA
Infinity and Motor. José Moreno Villa, *tr. fr. Spanish by* Eleanor L. Turnbull. CoSP
Infinity of Wishes. *Unknown, tr. fr. Spanish by* Sir John Bowring. OnPM
Infinity, when all things it beheld. The Preface. Edward Taylor. *Fr.* God's Determinations. AmPP; CoV; OxBA
Infir Taris. *Unknown.* BoN; ChTr; OxNR
Infirm. Edward Sandford Martin. ALV; PR
Inflamed Disciple, The. Arthur Kramer. InMe
Inflatable Globe, The. Theodore Spencer. LiTA; LiTM; NePA; WaP
Inflictis. Archibald Stodart-Walker. *Fr.* The Moxford Book of English Verse. CenHV
Influence. Joseph Morris, *wr. at. to* Joseph Norris. MaRV
Influence. Robert Haven Schauffler. CAG
Influence. John Banister Tabb. PoMa
Influence. *Unknown.* MaRV
Influence of Natural Objects. Wordsworth. *Fr.* The Prelude, I. AWP; BPN; InPo; JAWP; LoBV; MCCG; OBRV; RO; WBP
(Boyhood.) WHA
(Nature's Ministry.) GrCo-2
("Wisdom and spirit of the universe.") AtBAP; CoEV
Influence of Time on Grief. William Lisle Bowles. *See* Time and Grief.
Infold us with thy peace, dear moon-lit night. Nocturne. Virna Sheard. OCL
Informing Spirit, The. Emerson. *Fr.* History. AWP; IAP; InPo; MOAP; WGRP
(History.) BBV
(No Great, No Small.) MaRV
Infusorial earthmounds of the Upper Amazon, The. Lost Explorer. Edmund Pennant. GoYe
Ingenious Little Old Man, The. John Bennett. FaPON; GaP
Ingle-Side, The. Hew Ainslie. HBV; OTPC (1923 ed.)
Inglorious friend! most confident I am. Sonnet to a Clam. John Godfrey Saxe. AnNE; APW; BOHV
Ingoldsby Legends, The, *sels.* "Thomas Ingoldsby."
City Bells. *Fr.* The Lay of St. Aloys. LPS-2
Forlorn One, The. BOHV
Hand of Glory, The. DaM
Hon. Mr. Sucklethumbkin's Story. OBRV
Jackdaw of Rheims, The. BOHV; EV-4; HBV; LPS-3; OTPC (1923 ed.); PoeMoYo; ShBV-1; TSW; VA
Knight and the Lady, The. BOHV
Lay of St. Cuthbert, The. OtMeF
Misadventures at Margate. BOHV; HBV; LPS-3
Mr. Barney Maguire's Account of the Coronation. VA
Not a Sou Had He Got. *Fr.* The Cynotaph. HBV; PA
Verses Prefixed to the "Lay of St. Gengulphus." EV-4
Ingrateful Beauty Threatened. Thomas Carew. CBOV; CoEV; ElSeCe; EnLi-1; EPS; HBV; InvP; LO; MeLP; OBEV; OBS; SeCV-1; SeEP; TOP

(Celia Threatened.) EV-2
("Know, Celia, since thou art so proud.") EG
(Ungrateful Beauty Threatened.) BCEP
Ingratitude. Shakespeare. *See* Blow, Blow, Thou Winter Wind.
Inhabitants of old Jerusalem, The. The Popish Plot. Dryden. *Fr.* Absalom and Achitophel. ACP; TCEP
Inhaling the air, a boy on a tricycle. Improvisation. Louis Dudek. BoCaPo (1948 ed.)
Inheritance. "Æ." ChMo; CMP; EPN; PoVP; TIP
Inheritance. Anna Hempstead Branch. TBM
Inheritance. Mary Potter Thacher Higginson. AA; LBAP
Inheritance. Alfonsina Storni, *tr. fr. Spanish by* Jessie Read Wendell. OnPM
Inheritance. *Unknown, tr. fr. Irish by* Frank O'Connor. KiLC
Inheritors, The. Dorothy Livesay. CaP
Inhibited Persian, An. Richard Hart. CIV
Inhuman Henry. A. E. Housman. FiBHP
Inhuman man! curse on thy barb'rous art. On Seeing a Wounded Hare Limp by Me. Burns. BPP; OTPC; SN
Inhuman Wolf and the Lamb sans Gene, The. Guy Wetmore Carryl. ALV
Inis Fal. *Unknown, tr. fr. Irish by* James Stephens. GTIV; OBMV
Inisgallun. Darrell Figgis. OnYI
Initial Love, The, *sel.* Emerson.
Cupid. APW
Initiates. Aristophanes, *tr. fr. Greek by* Benjamin Bickley Rogers. *Fr.* The Frogs. GrR
Initiation. Laurence Binyon. GTML
Initiation. Rainer Maria Rilke, *tr. fr. German by* C. F. MacIntyre. TrJP
(Eingang [Prelude], *tr. by* M. D. Herter Norton.) Po
Injian Ocean sets an' smiles, The. For to Admire. Kipling. MBP; MoBrPo
"Injun, The." John E. Logan. BoCaPo (1943 ed.)
Injunction. Blake. *Fr.* Gnomic Verses. BLV; BoLiVe
(Gnomic Verses.) OBRV; TrGrPo
Injurious time now with a robbers hast. A Single Famished Kiss. Shakespeare. *Fr.* Troilus and Cressida, IV, iv. LiA
Injustice. Sheldon Shepard. ChIP
Inkstand, The. Ibn Lubbal, *tr. fr. Arabic by* A. J. Arberry. MooP
Inky Mouth, The. Al-Barraq, *tr. fr. Arabic by* A. J. Arberry. MooP
Inlaid Psaltery, The. Li Shang-yin, *tr. fr. Chinese.* WhP
Inland City. John Crowe Ransom. ChMo
Inland my life is set. Seaward. Jeannette Bliss Gillespy. CAG
Inland, within a hollow vale, I stood. Near Dover, September, 1802 [*or* Sonnet: September, 1802]. Wordsworth. BPN; ChER; EM-2; EmBrPo; EnLi-2; EnRP; EPP; ERP; ES; GEPC; MaPo; OAEP; REAL; TOP
Inmate of smoaking cots, whose rustic shed. Ode on Lyric Poetry. Sir James Marriott. Po
Inn, The. "John Presland." VOD
Inn by the Road, The. C. E. Warner. OQP; QP-1
Inn of Care, The. Samuel Waddington. OBVV; VA
Inn of Earth, The. Sara Teasdale. ChMo; CMP; LiTA
Inn of the Silver Moon, The, *sel.* Herman Knickerbocker Viele.
Good Inn, The. HBV
Inn That Missed Its Chance, The. Amos Russel Wells. ChrBoLe
Innate Helium. Robert Frost. ImOP
Inner Brother. Stephen Stepanchev. WaP
Inner Light. Milton. *Fr.* Paradise Lost, III. MaRV
Inner Light, The. Frederic William Henry Myers. *Fr.* Saint Paul. BMEP; HBV; LEAP; MaRV; WGRP
Inner Significance of the Statues Seated outside the Boston Public Library, The. Walter Conrad Arensberg. AnAmPo; LA
Inner Silence, The. Harriet Monroe. HBMV; NP
Inner Temple Masque, The, *sels.* William Browne.
Sirens' Song. BCEP; EtS; EV-2; LPS-3, *sl. abr.;* OBEV
(Siren Song.) EG
(Song of the Sirens.) ChTr; CoEV; ElL
(Song of the Syrens, *sl. abr.*) OBS
("Steer hither, steer your wingèd pines.") ElSeCe; ViBoPo
"Son of Erebus and Night." ElSeCe; ViBoPo
Inner Vision. *Unknown, tr. fr. Sanskrit by* Joseph Nadin Rawson. *Fr.* The Upanishads. OnPM
Inner Vision, The. Wordsworth. GTBS; GTBS-D; GTBS-W; GTSE; GTSL; HBV; LPS-3
(Most Sweet It Is with Unuplifted Eyes.) BPN; EM-1; EmBrPo; EnLit; EnRP; EPN; EPP; ERP; LO; PeBoSo; TOP
(Walk in Meditation.) ES
Inner Voice, The. Antero de Quental, *tr. fr. Portuguese by* S. Griswold Morley. UnW
Innocence. "Æ." ChMo
Innocence. George S. Chappell. DDA; YaD
Innocence, The. Robert Creeley. NeAP
Innocence. Alfred Gordon. CPG
Innocence. Anne Spencer. CDC
Innocence. Thomas Traherne. EPS
Innocent, The. Gene Derwood. NePA; WaP
Innocent Country-Maid's Delight, The; or, A Description of the Lives of the Lasses of London. *Unknown.* CoMu
Innocent eyes not ours. All Things Wait upon Thee. Christina Rossetti. GN
Innocent Fears. Gerasimos Markoras, *tr. fr. Modern Greek by* Rae Dalven. MoGP
Innocent Landscape. Elinor Wylie. OxBA
Innocent paper! whom too cruel hand. Amoretti, XLVIII. Spenser. PeBoSo
Innocent spirits, bright, immaculate ghosts! From Generation to Generation. William Dean Howells. AA; PFY
Innocent, sweet Day is dead, The. Night and Day. Sidney Lanier. AA; AnAmPo; LA; MAP; MoAmPo (1942 ed.); MOAP
Innocents, The. *Unknown.* OBB
Innocents, The. Elinor Wylie. StJW
Innominata. Benjamin Sledd. NoCaPo
Innominatus. Sir Walter Scott. *See* Breathes There the Man.
Innumerable Beauties. Lord Herbert of Cherbury. *See* Sonnet: "Innumerable Beauties, thou white haire."
Innumerable Friend. May Sarton. WaKn
Inquiry, The. Thomas Hardy. At Casterbridge Fair, V. BEL; EmBrPo; EnLi-2 (1949 ed.); EnLit; PoVP
Inquiry, The. Charles Mackay. *See* Tell Me, Wingèd Winds.
Inquisition upon Fame and Honor, An. Fulke Greville. SiCE
Inquisitive Barn. Frances Frost. BrR
Inquisitive Cock Sparrow, An. D'Arcy Wentworth Thompson. *Fr.* Nursery Nonsense. BoN
Inquisitors, The. Robinson Jeffers. MoAmPo (1950 ed.); PoLFOT
Insane in the Garden, The. Rainer Maria Rilke, *tr. fr. German by* Ruth Speirs. AnGP
Insatiableness. Thomas Traherne. OxBoCh
"This busy, vast, inquiring soul," *sel.* ElSeCe
(Enquiring Soul, The, 1 *st.*) MaRV
"Insatiate brute, whose teeth abuse." The Small Silver-coloured Bookworm. Thomas Parnell. OnYI
Inscribed on a Jade Tablet of Yu. *Unknown, tr. fr. Chinese. Fr.* The Fountain of Old Poems. WhP
Inscribed on the Collar of a Dog. Pope. *See* Epigram: "I am his Highness' dog at Kew."
Inscription. William Cowper. MeRV
Inscription, An: "Grass of levity." *Unknown.* ElL
Inscription: "He wrote upon his heart." Donald Jeffrey Hayes. CDC
Inscription: "It is not hard to tell a rose." Ann Hamilton. HBMV
Inscription: "Oh, in the quiet haven, safe for aye." William Alexander. TIP
Inscription: On a Tablet against a Root-House. William Shenstone. EiPP
Inscription: On the Back of a Gothic Seat. William Shenstone. EiPP
Inscription: "Sea-fowls build in wrinkles on my face, The." Sir William Watson. BLP
Inscription, The: "Sealed with the seal of Life, thy soul and mine." Elsa Barker. *Fr.* The Spirit and the Bride. HBMV
Inscription: "Ye powers unseen, to whom the bards of Greece." Mark Akenside. OBEC
Inscription at Mount Vernon. *Unknown.* PoRL
Inscription at the City of Brass. *Unknown. See* Inscriptions at the City of Brass.
Inscription by the Sea, An. *Unknown, tr. fr. Greek by* E. A. Robinson. *Fr.* The Greek Anthology. AWP; ChTr; InP; JAWP; TOP; WBP
(Variations of Greek Themes, XI.) MOAP
Inscription for a Fountain. "Barry Cornwall." *See* For a Fountain.
Inscription for a Fountain. Stephen Gwynn. GTIV
Inscription for a Fountain on a Heath. Samuel Taylor Coleridge. EV-4; MCCG; OAEP
Inscription for a Grotto. Mark Akenside. CEP; OBEC; PoEL-3; RO
(For a Grotto.) SeCePo
Inscription for a Hospital. E. O. Laughlin. PoP
Inscription for a Mirror in a Deserted Dwelling. William Rose Benét. LoPS; MAP; MoAmPo; TriL
Inscription for a Portrait of Dante. Boccaccio, *tr. fr. Italian by* Dante Gabriel Rossetti. *Fr.* Sonnets. AWP; JAWP; WBP
(Inscription for Portrait of Dante.) OnPM
(Tribute to Dante, A.) GoBC
Inscription for a Smyrna Privy. Agathias Scholasticus, *tr. fr. Greek by* Dudley Fitts. LyMA
Inscription for a Statue of Love. Voltaire, *tr. fr. French by* Henry Carrington. LiTW

Inscription for a Tablet on the Banks of a Stream. Robert Southey. OBEC
Inscription for an Old Bed. William Morris. OBEV (new ed.); OBVV; WP
(For the Bed at Kelmscott.) EmBrPo; PoEL-5; PoVP; ViP
(Lines for a Bed at Kelmscott Manor.) CH
Inscription for an Old Well. John Fallon. PoP
Inscription for My Little Son's Silver Plate. Eugene Field. FAOV; PPL
Inscription for Portrait of Dante. Boccaccio. *See* Inscription for a Portrait of Dante.
Inscription for the Entrance to a Wood. Bryant. ADAH; AmP; AmPP; AnNE; APW; BAV; CoBA; CoV; IAP; MCCG; MOAP; OxBA
Inscription in a Garden. George Gascoigne. OBSC; TrGrPo
(Inscription in His Garden.) TuPP
Inscription in a Hermitage. Thomas Warton, the Younger. *See* Retirement.
Inscription in a Library. W. G. Wendell. WhC
Inscription on a Grot. Samuel Rogers. *Fr.* The Pleasures of Memory. OBEC
Inscription on a Shrine near Ischl. Elizabeth, Empress of Austria-Hungary, *tr. fr. German by* Thomas Walsh. CAW
Inscription on an Ancient Bell. *Unknown, tr. fr. Latin by* Fr. Bridgett. ISi
Inscription on Melrose Abbey. *Unknown.* LPS-1
Inscription on Stone over Shakespeare's Grave. *Unknown.* TreFS
Inscription on the Flyleaf of a Bible. Dannie Abse. TrJP
Inscription on the Pyramid of Pepi I. *Unknown, tr. fr. Egyptian by* Lindley W. Hubbell. LiTW
Inscription on the Pyramid of Unas. *Unknown, tr. fr. Egyptian by* Lindley W. Hubbell. LiTW
Inscription on the Statue of Liberty. Emma Lazarus. *Fr.* The New Colossus. PaA; PoRL
("Give me your tired, your poor.") PoFr
Inscription on the Tomb of the Lady Mary Wentworth, The. Thomas Carew. *See* Maria Wentworth.
Inscription Set upon the Great Gate of Theleme, The, *abr.* Rabelais, *tr. fr. French by* Sir Thomas Urquhart. *Fr.* Gargantua. PoFr
Inscription to Spartans Dead at Thermopylae. Simonides. *See* Thermopylae.
Inscriptions at the City of Brass. *Unknown, tr. fr. Arabic by* E. Powys Mathers. *Fr.* The Thousand and One Nights. AWP; PG (1945 ed.); PoFr, 2 *sts.;* WaaP, 3 *sts.*
Inscription at the City of Brass ("Drunkenness of youth has passed like a fever"), *sel.* LiTW
Inscriptions on Dials, *sel.* Isaac Watts.
Thus Steal the Silent Hours Away. AEV
Inscrutable Mystery, The. Job, XXXVIII–XL, Bible, *O.T.* GrCo-2
Insect or blossom? Fragile, fairy thing. The Mariposa Lily. Ina Donna Coolbrith. AA
Insect Wives. Rudolph Altrocchi. WhC
Insectarian, An. John Banister Tabb. UTS
Insects. Isidor Schneider. AnAmPo; LA; TrJP
Insects from the Nile. Pope. *Fr.* An Essay on Criticism, Pt. I. BeR
Insensibility. Wilfred Owen. BrBE; ChMP; CoEV; ExPo; FaBoTw; GTBS-W; LiTB; LiTM; MoAB; OAEP (2d ed.); SeCeV; WaP
Insert Myself within Your Story. Stéphane Mallarmé, *tr. fr. French by* Frederick Morgan. AnFP
Insets, *sel.* Laurence Housman.
"Dear heart, when with." BMEP
Inside a jar with painted flowers. The Jar. "Feodor Sologub." BoR
Inside its zig-zag lines the little camp is asleep. The Magazine Fort, Phoenix Park, Dublin. William Wilkins. IrPN; SeCePo; TIP
Inside my father's close. My Father's Close. *Unknown.* AWP; PoVP
Inside of King's College Chapel, Cambridge. Wordsworth. Ecclesiastical Sonnets, XLIII. BPN; EM-2; EmBrPo; EnLi-2; EnLP; EnRP; EPN; ES; GEPC; GoBC; MaRV; OAEP; OBRV; OxBoCh
(King's College Chapel, Cambridge.) CBE
(Within King's College Chapel, Cambridge.) GTBS; GTBS-D; GTBS-W; GTSE; GTSL
Inside the city's throbbing heart. St. Michan's Churchyard. Rose Kavanagh. TIP
Inside the house I sit alone. Meditation in Winter. Leonard Mann. BoAV
Inside the sombre walls the neat quadrangles still are green. Knole. Roy Fuller. PoN
Inside the ten acres, the pickers of mulberry-leaves are moving leisurely. The Ten Acres. *Unknown.* ChLP
Inside this northern summer's fold. Siena. Swinburne. ViPo
Insights. Catherine Davis. NePoEA
Insignificance of the World. Thomas Lovell Beddoes. *Fr.* Fragments Intended for the Dramas. ERP
Insignificant Existence. Isaac Watts. LPS-3
(Horace Paraphrased.) LoBV; UnPo (3d ed.)
Insinuation. Paul Valéry, *tr. fr. French by* Barbara Howes. AnFP
Insistently through sleep—a tide of voices. The Harbor Dawn. Hart Crane. *Fr.* The Bridge: Powhatan's Daughter. AmP; CoV; LiTA; MoPo; NePA; OxBA
Insolence. Homer C. House. MuM
Insomnia. Tristan Corbière, *tr. fr. French by* Kenneth Koch *and* Georges Guy. AnFP
Insomnia. Ethna MacCarthy. NeIP
Insomnia. Dante Gabriel Rossetti. BPN; PoVP; VLEP
Insomnia. Jules Supervielle, *tr. fr. French by* Wallace Fowlie. MiCF
Insomnia. John Banister Tabb. TrPWD
Insomnia. Edith M. Thomas. AA
Insomniac Poem. Ron Loewinsohn. NeAP
Inspect Us. Edith Daniell. BOHV
Inspection. Wilfred Owen. WaP
Inspection, The. Frederick B. Watt. CaP
Inspiration. "John Crichton." CPG
Inspiration. W. W. Gibson. WGRP
Inspiration. Per Hallström, *tr. fr. Swedish by* Charles W. Stork. AnSL
Inspiration. Hilda Mary Hooke. CPG
Inspiration. Samuel Johnson. AA; HBV; TrPWD; WGRP
(Life of Ages, *abr.*) GrCo-1
Inspiration. E. V. Knox. CenHV
Inspiration, The. James Montgomery. *See* Columbus.
Inspiration. Shakespeare. *See* Lunatic, the Lover, and the Poet, The.
Inspiration. John Banister Tabb. WGRP
Inspiration. Henry David Thoreau. AA; AmPP; AnAmPo; AnFE; AnNE; APA; BAP, *abr.;* CBOV; CoAnAm; FaBoBe; HBV; IAP; LA; LBAP; LEAP; MOAP; OBAV; OxBA; TCAP; TriL; WGRP, *abr.*
"I will not doubt for evermore," *br. sel.* MaRV
Inspiration ("As the hand moves over the harp and the strings speak"). *Unknown. Fr.* Solomon. WGRP
Inspiration, An. Ella Wheeler Wilcox. WGRP
Inspirations. William James Dawson. MaRV; WGRP
Instans Tyrannus. Robert Browning. PoFr; VLEP
Instant splendour, the swung bells that speak, The. Prothalamion. Terence Tiller. NeBP
Instead of incense (Blessed Lord) if wee. Nathaniel Wanley. *Fr.* Royal Presents. TrPWD
Instead of Neat Inclosures. Robert Herrick. *Fr.* An Ode on the Birth of Our Saviour. ChTr
Instead of the endless quest for perfection. Take a Chance. Al Ringgold. WeGO
Instead of the Puritans landing on Plymouth Rock. Thoughts for St. Stephen. Christopher Morley. WhC
Instruction. Hazel Hall. NP
Instruction Manual, The. John Ashbery. NeAP
Instruction sore long time I bore. Charles Kingsley. CenHV
Instructions of King Cormac. Cormac, King of Cashel, *tr. fr. Irish.* PoToHe (new ed.)
Instruments, The. Dryden. *Fr.* A Song for St. Cecilia's Day. BLV
(Fife and Drum, 8 *ll.*) GN
Insubordination. Margaret Evelyn Singleton. ChIP
Insufficiency. Elizabeth Barrett Browning. AV; BPN; EmBrPo
Insult, The. Robert Layzer. NePoEA
Insult, The. *Unknown.* SCC
Intaglio. Henri Coulette. NePoEA
Intaglios. Francis Brooks. AA
On the Plains.
Tennessee.
Intangibly the intricate vein. Dark Flower. Louis Untermeyer. PIAE
Integer Vitae. Thomas Campion. *See* Man of Life Upright, The.
Integer Vitae. Horace, *tr. fr. Latin by* Sir Theodore Martin. Odes, I, 22. EnLi-1
(Purity.) RoL
(To Aristius Fuscus.) OuHeWo
Integrity. William L. Stidger. ChIP; OQP; QP-2
Intellect. Emerson. OnPM
Intellect of man is forced to choose, The. The Choice. W. B. Yeats. TwP
Intelligent Sheep-Man and the New Cars, The. William Carlos Williams. NePoAm-2
Intemperance. Isaiah, V: 11–12, Bible, *O.T.* (Moulton, *Modern Reader's Bible*). MaRV
Intempestiva. Henry Longan Stuart. JKCP (1926 ed.)
Intended for Sir Isaac Newton. Pope. *See* Epitaph Intended for Sir Isaac Newton.
Intended to Allay the Violence of Party Spirit. John Byrom. *See* Jacobite Toast, A.
Intense and terrible beauty, how has our race with the frail naked nerves. Gale in April. Robinson Jeffers. AmPP; ChMo; CMP; MAP; MoAB; MoAmPo; NeMA
Intensity abstracted in air, ready to break, V. Frances Crawford. PtPa

Inter, mitzy, titzy, tool. *Unknown.* OxNR
Inter Sodales. W. E. Henley. HBV
Interceding. Opal Leonore Gibbs. BePJ; PraP
Intercepted Salute. Thomas Edward Brown. POTT
Intercession. L. M. Hollingsworth. PraP
Intercession in Late October. Robert Graves. MoAB
Intercession, on Sulpicia's Birthday, to Her Guardian Spirit. Tibullus, *tr. fr. Latin by* Hubert Creekmore. LaP
Interests of a black man in a cellar, The. Black Tambourine. Hart Crane. CoBMV; NAMP; OxBA; PoNe
Interim. Clarissa Scott Delany. CDC; PoNe
Interior. Ronald de Carvalho, *tr. fr. Portuguese by* Dudley Poore. AnCL
Interior. Padraic Colum. MBP; MoBrPo; TSW; TSWC
Interior. Marjorie Allen Seiffert. NP
Interior. Paul Valéry, *tr. fr. French.* AnFP, *tr. by* Barbara Howes; TrFP, *tr. by* Alan Conder
Interior Decorator Gets in My House, An. Wilfred J. Funk. LauV
Interior of the Rose. Rainer Maria Rilke, *tr. fr. German by* Kate Flores. AnGP
Interior; the Suburbs. Horace Gregory. AnAmPo; LA; NP
Interlude, An. John Peale Bishop. LiTA
Interlude. Maxwell Bodenheim. MAPA
Interlude. Euripides, *tr. fr. Greek by* Gilbert Murray. *Fr.* Medea. GrR
Interlude. Idris Davies. MoWP
Interlude. Eileen Duggan. AnNZ
Interlude. Holger Lundbergh. PoMa
Interlude. Scudder Middleton. BAP; NV; SBMV
Interlude. Keidrych Rhys. MoWP
Interlude. Theodore Roethke. MiAP
Interlude, The. Karl Shapiro. MoVE
Interlude. Edith Sitwell. MoAB; MoBrPo; NeMA
Interlude, An. Swinburne. EmBrPo; ViBoPo
Interlude. Ella Wheeler Wilcox. BLP; HBV; LBAP (Growing Old.) BLPA
Interlude, for a Solitary Flute, *sel.* Samuel Hoffenstein. "Little I knew, when morning-white." QS
Interlude: Songs Out of Sorrow, *sels.* Sara Teasdale.
Lessons, III. PC
Mastery, II. ChMo; CMP; HBV; QS; WGRP
Spirit's House, I. OQP; QP-1; QS
Wisdom, IV. BAP; InP; LoPo; MAP; MoAmPo; MuM
Wood Song, VI. BAP; BLA; PoeMoYo; PYM
Intermezzo. Robert Hillyer. NePoAm
Intermezzo for the Fourth Act, An. William Allen White. InMe
Interminable contingency. Contingency. W. Wesley Trimpi. PtPa
Interminable, not to be divined. The Sea. Richard Hovey. *Fr.* Seaward. NLK
Interminable ocean lay beneath, The. Sunrise at Sea. Edwin Atherstone. EtS
Interminable palaces front on the green parterres. Fontainebleau. Sara Teasdale. TriL
Intermission, Please! Irwin Edman. SiTL; WhC
Internal Cerberus, whose griping fangs. Conscience. Sir Edward Sherburne. ACP
Internal Harmony. George Meredith. EPN
International Brigade Arrives at Madrid, The. "Pablo Neruda," *tr. fr. Spanish by* Angel Flores. WaaP
International Brigade Dead. Thomas O'Brien. NeIP
International Copyright. James Russell Lowell. AA; IAP
International Episode, An. Caroline Duer. AA; PAH
International Hymn. George Huntington. MaRV
International Ode. Oliver Wendell Holmes. PEOR; TCAP
Interne, The. Maxwell Bodenheim. NP
Interpretation. Sheldon Shepard. ChIP
Interpreter, The. Orrick Johns. AnAmPo; HBMV; LA; MAP; NP; PFY; SBMV
Interpreters, The. Swinburne. BPN; PoEL-5
Interracial. Georgia Douglas Johnson. PoNe
Interred [*or* Interr'd] beneath this marble stone. An Epitaph. Matthew Prior. CEP; EiPP; OBEC; PoE; PoEL-3
Interred in ages past thou keepest. Ravenna. Aleksandr Blok. BoRS
Interrogation, The. Edwin Muir. LiTB; SeCePo
Interrogativa Cantilena. *Unknown. See* If All the World Were Paper.
Interruption. Robert Graves. LiTB; LiTM ("If ever against this easy blue and silver.") GTBS-W
Interruption. Edith Benedict Hawes. DDA
Interval. Joseph Auslander. MAP; MoAmPo (1942 ed.)
Interval. Dorothy E. Hanbury Rowe. MM
Interval with Fire. Dorothy Livesay. CaP
Intervals. Beatrice Ravenel. HBMV; TBM
Interview. Lila Terry. DDA
Intery, mintery, cutery, corn. Mother Goose. OTPC; OxNR; PCH; PPL; StVeCh; TiPo
Intice not me with thy alluringe eye. *Unknown.* SeCSL
Intil ane garth, under ane reid rosere. The Praise of Age. Robert Henryson. BSV
Intimate music never ceases, An. The Sound of the Heart. Ramón López Velarde. TwSpPo
Intimations of Immortality from Recollections of Early Childhood. Wordsworth. *See* Ode: Intimations of Immortality . . .
Intimations of Mortality. Phyllis McGinley. NeMA
Into a famous toy shop. A Schemer. Edgar L. Warren. PEOR
Into a gentle wildness and confusion. Sea Side. Robert Graves. MoPo
Into a high-walled nunnery had fled. The Parting of Launcelot and Guinevere. Stephen Phillips. BMEP; ReTS
Into a little close of mine I went. Two Lyrics, 1. Lorenzo de' Medici. AWP
Into a Mountain Apart. Alice E. Sherwood. PraP
Into a sweet May morning. John of Hazelgreen. *Unknown.* BaBo (A *vers.*); ESPB; ViBoFo
Into a ward of the whitewashed halls. Somebody's Darling. Marie La Coste [*or* La Conte]. BIG; BLPA; DD; HBV; LPS-2; PTA-2; TreF; WBLP
Into azure cloudland searching. To My Distant Beloved. Alois Jeitteles. TrJP
Into Battle. Julian Grenfell. HBV; KN; LBBV; LoBV; MM; OBEV (new ed.); OBMV; OtMeF; POTE; ShBV-3; ShGoBo; TwCV; WaaP
Into Chin Shih. Youth Rides Forth. Li Po. PoHN
Into ethereal meads. Life's Testament, XII. William Baylebridge. BoAV
Into exile with only a few shirts. The Exile. Robert Graves. MoP
Into his hands, utterly into his power. Six Sonnets. Mary, Queen of Scots. DiM
Into Life. Stephen Spender. TwHP
Into love and out again. Theory. Dorothy Parker. BOHV
Into my eyes he loving looked. The Mirror. Judah Halevi. TrJP
Into My Heart an Air That Kills. A. E. Housman. A Shropshire Lad, XL. BPN; CBE; ChMo; ChTr; CMP; EmBrPo; EnL; GTBS-W; LiTB; MoAB; MoBrPo; OAEP (2d ed.); Po; POTT; PoVP; TwP; ViBoPo; ViPo (Yon Far Country.) LiTM; SeCePo
Into my heart's treasury. The Coin. Sara Teasdale. CP; HBMV; SP; TiPo (1952 ed.)
Into My Own. Robert Frost. TwP
Into my room to-night came June. June Night. Hazel Hall. HBMV
Into Norway's/ Open coastline. Greetings to Norway. Jóhann Sigurjónsson. IcP
Into Slumbers. John Fletcher. *See* Care-charming Sleep.
Into the basin put the plums. The Christmas Pudding. *Unknown.* TiPo (1952 ed.)
Into the bosom of the one great sea. God Is One [*or* The Unity of God]. Panatattu. MaRV; WGRP
In-to the calendis of Januarie. Prologue. Sir David Lindsay. *Fr.* The Dreme. EBSV
Into the caverns of the sea. Joy Enough. Barrett Eastman. AA
Into the crucible of life. Onwardness. Doris Hedges. CaP
Into the dark death cloud they passed, to set. The Spartan Monument. Simonides. GrL; OxBG
Into the Darkness. Basho, *tr. fr. Japanese by* H. G. Henderson. OnPM
Into the darkness and hush of night. Night. Longfellow. IAP
Into the Devil tavern. The Three Troopers. George Walter Thornbury. BeLS; BMEP; HBV; VA
Into the dusk and snow. A Traveller. *Unknown.* WGRP
Into the dust of the making of man. The Builders. Henry van Dyke. OQP; QP-2
Into the endless dark. City Lights. Rachel Field. FaPON; GFA
Into the Endless Night. Lilith Lorraine. UnW
Into the fountain. The Fountain. James Russell Lowell. GoTP
Into the furnace let me go alone. Baptism. Claude McKay. AnEnPo; PoNe
Into the gold of the setting sun. The Indian Runner. W. L. Stoddard. CAG
Into the golden vessel of great song. Edna St. Vincent Millay. *Fr.* Unnamed Sonnets. NP
Into the inmost temple thus I came. The Temple of Venus. Spenser. *Fr.* The Faerie Queene. WHA
Into the justice of eternity. Dante. *Fr.* Divina Commedia: Paradiso. PoFr
Into the lonely park all frozen fast. Colloque sentimental. Paul Verlaine. EnLi-2
Into the loud surf. O Altitudo! Sarah N. Cleghorn. PC
Into the mists of the pagan island. The Sons of Patrick. James B. Dollard. JKCP
Into the night, into the blanket of night. Slabs of the Sunburnt West. Carl Sandburg. CoV
Into the Noiseless Country. Thomas William Parsons. AA; LEAP

Into the Ocean, long ago. Lost Wine. Paul Valéry. TrFP
Into the sad cold heart. They Bury Him. Marya Zaturenska. *Fr.* Elegies over John Reed. BAP
Into the Salient. Edmund Blunden. ViBoPo
Into the scented woods we'll go. Green Rain. Mary Webb. CH; FaPON
Into the Silent Land! Song of the Silent Land. Johann Gaudenz Salis-Seewis. AWP; HBV; JAWP; LEAP; OQP; WBP
Into the Silent Places. The Old Year and the New. Annie Johnson Flint. BLRP
Into the silver night. Revelation. Sir Edmund Gosse. BMEP; OBEV; OBVV; TCPD
Into the skies, one summer's day. The Thought. William Brighty Rands. BMEP; OBEV; OBVV; UnW
Into the street the Piper stept. Robert Browning. *Fr.* The Pied Piper of Hamelin. BoTP
Into the Sunset. S. Hall Young. QP-1
(Let Me Die Working.) MaRV
Into the sunshine, full of the light. The Fountain. James Russell Lowell. BAV; BoTP; CG; MW; OTPC; PCH; PRWS; PTA-1; RG; TVSH
Into the thick of the fight he went, pallid and sick and wan. Wheeler at Santiago. James Lindsay Gordon. PAH
Into the tomb they took Him, sad of heart. Tell the Disciples. *Unknown.* PSO
Into the town of Conemaugh. The Man Who Rode to Conemaugh. John Eliot Bowen. GA; PAH
Into the Twilight. W. B. Yeats. *Fr.* Celtic Twilight. BEL; ChMo; EPN; EV-4; HBV; PC; PoeT; POTT; PoVP
Into the valley of Death am I come. Elysium. Agnes Mary Frances Robinson. UnW
Into the west of the waters on the living ocean's foam. Homeward Bound. George Edward Woodberry. *Fr.* Wild Eden. AA
Into the wilderness. Tempted. Katharine Lee Bates. ChIP; StJW
Into the wood at close of rainy day. Sonnet. Thomas Caulfield Irwin. IrPN
Into the woods my Master went. A Ballad of Trees and the Master [*or* The Cross]. Sidney Lanier. AA; ADAH; AmP; AnAmPo; BAV; BePJ; BTP; CAW; ChIP; CoBA; CoV; DDA; GoBC; GTBS-W; HBV; IAP; LA; LaNeLa; LBAP; LiTA; MAP; MaRV; MoAmPo (1942 ed.); NLK; OBAV; OQP; OxBA; PC; PFE; PFY; PoEL-5; PoeMoYo; PoRL; QP-1; SPP; StJW; TCAP; TOP; WGRP; WHL
Into the World and Out. Sarah Morgan Bryan Piatt. HBV
Into the yard the farmer goes. Evening at the Farm [*or* Farmyard Song]. John Townsend Trowbridge. BBV; BTP; GN; MPB; PECK; RIS
Into these loves who but for passion looks. To the Reader of These Sonnets. Michael Drayton. Idea, *introd. sonnet.* BEL; HBV; ReEn; ReIE; SiCE; TuPP; ViBoPo
Into this place whereas the elfin knight. The Dance of the Graces. Spenser. *Fr.* The Faerie Queene, VI, 10. BCEP
Into This World Now Is Come/ Christe Redemptor Omnium. *Unknown.* AnEC
Into this world, this day did come. I Pray You, Be Merry and Sing with Me. *Unknown.* AnEC
Into Thy Hands. Loren W. Burch. ChIP
Intolerably sad, profound. Before the Anaesthetic; or, A Real Fright. John Betjeman. SeCePo
Intolerance. Molly Anderson Haley. DDA; MaRV
Intolerance. John Richard Moreland. ChIP
Intolerance. Winthrop Mackworth Praed. MaRV
Intoxicated Poet, The. Allen Upward. *Fr.* Scented Leaves from a Chinese Jar. NP
Intoxication. Emily Dickinson. *See* I taste a liquor never brewed.
Intra Sepulchrum. Thomas Hardy. MaPo
Intramural Aestivation, or Summer in Town, by a Teacher of Latin. Oliver Wendell Holmes. *See* Aestivation.
Intreat Me Not to Leave Thee. Ruth, I: 16–17, Bible, *O.T.* InP; TreF
(Address of Ruth to Naomi.) GBV (1952 ed.)
("And Ruth said, Intreat me not to leave thee.") LO
(Ruth to Naomi.) MaRV; TrGrPo
Intrepid Ricardo, The. E. C. Bentley. *Fr.* Biography for Beginners. CenHV
Intro, The. C. J. Dennis. WhC
Introduction: "Camille St. Saëns was racked with pains." Ogden Nash. *Fr.* The Carnival of Animals. UnS
Introduction: "Forget six counties overhung with smoke." William Morris. *See* Prologue: "Forget six counties . . ."
Introduction: "Hear the voice of the bard!" Blake. *See* Hear the Voice of the Bard.
Introduction, The: "Most noble Excellence." Al-Dhahabi, *tr. fr. Arabic by* A. J. Arberry. MooP
Introduction: "Piping down the valleys wild." Blake. *See* Piping down the Valleys Wild.
Introduction: "Tired Nature's sweet restorer, balmy sleep!" Edward Young. *See* Complaint, The.
Introduction: "'Twas late in my long journey, when I had clomb to where." Robert Bridges. *Fr.* The Testament of Beauty. MoVE
Introduction and Anecdotes. "Peter Pindar." *Fr.* Bozzy and Piozzi. PoEL-3
Introduction—Childhood and School-Time. Wordsworth. *See* Prelude, The.
Introduction; Combinations of Atoms; Creation and Destruction of Worlds. Lucretius, *pr. tr. fr. Latin by* W. H. D. Rouse. *Fr.* De Rerum Natura. RoL
Introduction of a refrain, The. 'Twixt Cup and Lip. Mark Hollis. FiBHP
Introduction to Dogs, An. Ogden Nash. AlBD; GoTP; MoShBr
Introduction to "Songs of Experience." Blake. *See* Hear the Voice of the Bard.
Introduction to "Songs of Innocence." Blake. *See* Piping down the Valleys Wild.
Introduction to "Spastara's Death." Bengt Lidner, *tr. fr. Swedish by* Charles W. Stork. AnSL
Introduction to "The Last Fruit off an Old Tree." Walter Savage Landor. *See* On His Seventy-fifth Birthday.
Introduction to the Man of Law's Prologue. Chaucer. *Fr.* The Canterbury Tales. FiP
Introductory. Dante Gabriel Rossetti. *See* Sonnet, The ("A sonnet is a moment's monument").
Introductory Song: "I stand with roses beside the highway." Carl Snoilsky. *tr. fr. Swedish by* Charles W. Stork. *Fr.* Travel Scenes. AnSL
Introspective Reflection. Ogden Nash. WhC
Introversion. Evelyn Underhill. MaRV; WGRP
Intrudinge hopes what make you heere. *Unknown.* SeCSL
Intuition. Tennyson. *See* In Memoriam A. H. H.: "That which we dare invoke to bless."
Intuitive guilt and the sun's harsh light. On the Seventh Anniversary of the Death of My Father. Robert Pack. NePoEA
Invader, The. Norman Cameron. POTE
Invalid, The. Virginia J. Foley. PFE
Invalid. Audrey McGaffin. NePoAm-2
Invariably when wine redeems the sight. The Wine Menagerie. Hart Crane. OxBA
Invasion. Hubert Witheford. AnNZ
Invasion of Greece, The. Jeremy Ingalls. PoFr
Invasion Song. *Unknown.* PoOW
Invasion Weather. Douglas Newton. NeBP
Invective. Pearce Young. PtPa
Invective against the Wicked of the World, An, *sel.* Nicholas Breton.
"Let but a fellow in a fox-furred gown." ViBoPo
Invented a Person. Lenore G. Marshall. GoYe
Inventin'est Man, The. "J. B. H." IHA
Invention. Sir William Watson. HBV
Inventor's Wife, The. Mrs. E. T. Corbett. PTA-2
Inventor's Wife, An. Jeannie Pendleton Ewing. PTA-2
Inventory. Dorothy Parker. AnAmPo; LA
Inventress and virgin,/ Martyred Cecilia. Verses to St. Cecilia. David Wright. POTE (1959 ed.)
Inverberg. J. F. Hendry. NeBP
Inverey cam doun Deeside, whistlin and playin. The Baron of Brackley. *Unknown.* BaBo; EBSV; ESPB; OBB
Inverse Ratio. *Unknown.* WhC
Inversnaid. Gerard Manley Hopkins. ACP; AlDL; ChMo; EmBrPo; FaBoMo; GTBS-W; GTML; LiTB; LiTG; LiTM (rev. ed.); LoBV; MoAB; MoBrPo; PoRA; POTT; PoVP; ShBV-3; UnPo (3d ed.)
Wildness, *last 4 ll.* OtMeF
Inverted Eyelids. Ibn Haiyun, *tr. fr. Arabic by* A. J. Arberry. MooP
Inverted Torch, The. Edith M. Thomas. LBMV
Sels.
If Still They Live. AA; BLP; OBAV; OQP; QP-1
Tell Me. AA
(Cure-All.) TBM
(Lyric.) OBAV
When in the First Great Hour. AA
Will it Be So? AA
Investigator. Miriam Waddington. BoCaPo (1948 ed.); CaP
Investment, The. Robert Frost. ChMo; OxBA
Investor's Soliloquy. Kenneth Ward. FaFP; SiTL
Invictus. W. E. Henley. Echoes, IV. AnEnPo; AnFE; BBV; BEL; BLPA; BLV; BMEP; BPN; BTP; CBOV; CP; DD; EnLi-2; EnLit; EPP; FaBoBe; FaFP; GoTP; GTBS-W; GTSE; GTSL; HBV; HBVY; HiLiEn; HoPM; LBBV; LEAP; LiTB; LiTG; LiTM (rev. ed.); MaRV; MBP; MCCG; MoBrPo; NeHB; NeMA; OBEV; OBMV; OBVV; OHFP; OQP; OtMeF; OTPC (1946 ed.); OuHeWo; PC; PCD; PFE; PIAE; PIR; PoeMoYo; PoMa; POT; PoTo; PoVP; PTA-1; PYM; QP-1; ShBV-3; TCEP; TOP; TreF; TrGrPo; TSW; TSWC; VLEP; VOD; WGRP; YT
(Echoes.) LoBV
(I. M.—R. T. Hamilton Bruce.) POTT; ViBoPo
(In Memoriam, R. T. Hamilton Bruce.) GrCo-1

(Out of the Night.) EPN; EV-5
(Out of the Night That Covers Me.) GTBS
(R. T. Hamilton Bruce.) CaAE
Invincible. Sir Gilbert Parker. *Fr.* A Lover's Diary. VA
Invincible. Winnie Lynch Rockett. OQP; QP-2
Inviolable. Margaret Willy. DiM
Invisible, The. Richard Watson Gilder. WGRP
Invisible atoms of the air, The. Three Rimas, 1. Gustavo Adolfo Bécquer. *Fr.* Rimas. LiTW
Invisible Bride, The. Edwin Markham. HBV; LBMV; OBAV
Invisible Bridge, The. Gelett Burgess. BOHV; NA
(Queer Quatrains.) RIS
Invisible gulls with human voices cry in the sea-cloud. Fog. Robinson Jeffers. TBM
Invisible Playmate, The. Margaret Widdemer. FaPON; MPB; RAR
Invisible Trumpets Blowing. E. J. Pratt. *Fr.* Brébeuf and His Brethren. CaP
Invitation. Al-Mutawakkil, *tr. fr. Arabic by* A. J. Arberry. MooP
Invitation, An. Basho, *tr. fr. Japanese by* H. G. Henderson. OnPM
Invitation. Harry Behn. FaPON
Invitation. Solomon ibn Gabirol, *tr. fr. Hebrew by* Israel Zangwill. TrJP
Invitation, The. Thomas Godfrey. AnFE; APA; CoAnAm; IAP; TCAP
Invitation, The. George Herbert. TriL
Invitation, The. Robert Herrick. OAEP
Invitation. Ibn Sa'id of Seville, *tr. fr. Arabic by* A. J. Arberry. MooP
Invitation, The. Donagh MacDonagh. OnYI
Invitation, The. Goronwy Owen, *tr. fr. Welsh by* George Borrow. LiTW, *abr.*; PrWP
Invitation, The. Shelley. *See* To Jane: The Invitation.
Invitation. Ridgely Torrence. NP; PCH
Invitation, The. *Unknown.* OxBoCh
Invitation, The. Nathaniel Wanley. SeEP
Invitation. Ella Young. BoChLi (1950 ed.)
Invitation to Daphnis, An, *sel.* Countess of Winchilsea. Nature's Colours. BeR
Invitation to Death. Emilio Prados, *tr. fr. Spanish by* Eleanor L. Turnbull. CoSP
Invitation to Eternity. John Clare. PoEL-4; TriL; UnW
Invitation to Hsiao Chü-shih. Po Chü-i, *tr. fr. Chinese by* Arthur Waley. TrCh
Invitation to Jane, The. Shelley. *See* To Jane: The Invitation.
Invitation to Juno. William Empson. AtBAP; FaBoMo
Invitation to Li Po, An. Ts'ui Tsung-chi, *tr. fr. Chinese by* Shigeyoshi Obata. BoFr
Invitation to Lubberland, An. *Unknown. See* Ho, for Lubberland.
Invitation to Miss Marianne Moore. Elizabeth Bishop. MoVE
Invitation to Selborne, The, *sel.* Gilbert White.
"Oft on some evening, sunny, soft, and still." EnSW
Invitation to Sleep. Christina Rossetti. *See* Come, Blessèd Sleep.
Invitation to the Country, An. Bryant. ADAH; SN
Invitation to the Dance. Sidonius Apollinaris, *tr. fr. Latin by* Howard Mumford Jones. AWP
Invitation to the Gondola, The. John Addington Symonds. *Fr.* In Venice. PoVP
Invitation to the Voyage. Baudelaire, *tr. fr. French by* Richard Wilbur. AnFP
(Invitation to Travel, *tr. by* Alan Conder.) TrFP
Invitation to the Zoölogical Gardens, An. *Unknown.* BOHV
Invitation to Travel. Baudelaire. *See* Invitation to the Voyage.
Invitation to Youth. *Unknown, tr. fr. Latin by* John Addington Symonds. OnPM
Invite me to dinner, I'm sure to accept. Epicharmus, *tr. fr. Greek by* Charles H. Kahn. GrPo
Invites His Nymph to His Cottage. Philip Ayres. EnLoPo
Inviting a Friend to Supper. Ben Jonson, *after the Latin of* Martial. AWP; ElSeCe; JAWP; LiTB; LoBV; MaPo; OAEP; OBS; OxBoLi; Po; PoE; PoEL-2; ReEn; RiBV; SeCV-1; SeEP; TuPP; WBP
(Epigram: "Tonight, grave Sir, both my poor house and I," *sl. abr.*) MyFE
Inviting Guests. Ch'eng-kung Sui, *tr. fr. Chinese by* Arthur Waley. TrCh
("I sent out invitations.") BoFr
Invocatio ad Mariam. Chaucer, *mod. vers. by* Frank Ernest Hill. *Fr.* The Canterbury Tales: The Second Nun's Tale. ISi
("Thou maid and mother, daughter of thy son," *mod. vers.*) GoBC
(Two Invocations of the Virgin, 1.) ACP
Invocation: "American muse, whose strong and diverse heart." Stephen Vincent Benét. *Fr.* John Brown's Body. CrMA; MPB; NP, *shorter sel.*; PaA
America ("You are the buffalo-ghost . . ."), *sel.* PoeMoYo
Invocation: "As pools beneath stone arches take." John Drinkwater. HBMV; NP
Invocation: "Awake, awake, my Lyre!" Abraham Cowley. *See* Supplication, A.
Invocation: "Bob Southey! You're a poet—Poet laureate." Byron. *See* Dedication: "Bob Southey! . . ."
Invocation: "Come down from heaven to meet me when my breath." Siegfried Sassoon. MBP; MoBrPo
Invocation: "Earth, ocean, air, beloved brotherhood." Shelley. *See* Invocation to Nature.
Invocation: "Empty my heart, Lord of daily vices," *sel.* Theodore Spencer. TrPWD
Invocation: "Eternal God omnipotent! The One." Caelius Sedulius, *tr. fr. Latin by* George Sigerson. *Fr.* Carmen Paschale. OnYI
Invocation: "Give me a spirit that on this life's rough sea." George Chapman. *See* Master Spirit, The.
Invocation: "Goddess of Cyprus come." Sappho, *tr. fr. Greek by* H. De Vere Stacpoole. GrR
Invocation, An: "Hear, sweet spirit." Samuel Taylor Coleridge. *Fr.* Remorse (Osorio), III, i. EmBrPo; KN; OAEP
(Hear, Sweet Spirit.) ViBoPo
(Song: "Hear, sweet spirit.") MCCG; RO
(Song from "Osorio.") BPN; TOP
(Voice Sings, A.) CAW; CH; MeRV
Invocation: "Help me to make this working day." Francesca Falk Miller. PEDC
Invocation, An: "I long to know." George Chapman. *Fr.* Bussy d'Ambois, V, iii. EV-1
("I long to know/ How my dear mistress fares.") ViBoPo
(Invocation to Spirit.) LiA
Invocation, An: "I never prayed for Dryads, to haunt the woods again." William Johnson Cory. HBV; OBVV
Invocation: "I who was once a golden woman like those who walk." Edith Sitwell. AtBAP
Invocation: "Let me be buried in the rain." Helene Johnson. BANP; PoNe
Invocation: "Maiden, and mistress of the months and stars." Swinburne. *Fr.* Atalanta in Calydon. PoEL-5; PoVP
Invocation: "Maidens young and virgins tender." Horace, *tr. fr. Latin by* Louis Untermeyer. Odes I, 21. AWP; JAWP; WBP
Invocation: "Mother of God, mother of man reborn." Arthur J. Little. *Fr.* Christ Unconquered. ISi
Invocation: "O Glass-Blower of time." Clara Shanafelt. SBMV
Invocation: "O mother-maid! O maiden-mother free!" Chaucer, *mod. vers. by* Frank Ernest Hill. *Fr.* The Canterbury Tales: The Prioress's Tale. ISi
(O Mooder Mayde.) BoW
(Prayer to the Blessed Virgin, *shorter sel., mod. vers.*) CAW
(Two Invocations of the Virgin, 2, *mod. vers.*) ACP
Invocation: "O Thou, Creator from original chaos." G. Rostrevor Hamilton. BoFr; NeTW; QS
Invocation: "O Thou whose equal purpose runs." Wendell Phillips Stafford. MaRV; TrPWD
Invocation: "Of Man's first disobedience, and the fruit." Milton. *See* Invocation to the Heavenly Muse.
Invocation: "Phoebus, arise!" William Drummond of Hawthornden. *See* Phoebus, Arise!
Invocation: "Rarely, rarely, comest thou." Shelley. *See* Song: "Rarely, rarely, comest thou."
Invocation: "There is no balm on earth." Gilbert Thomas. TrPWD
Invocation: "Thou,—whose enduring hand once laid in sooth." Edmund Clarence Stedman. AA
Invocation, An: "To God, the everlasting, who abides." John Addington Symonds. WGRP
"O God, unknown, invisible, secure," *sel.* MaRV; TrPWD
Invocation: To the Spirit of Delight. Shelley. *See* Song: "Rarely, rarely comest thou."
Invocation: "Truth, be more precious to me than the eyes." Max Eastman. BAP; CP; NV; OQP; QP-1; WGRP
(Truth.) MaRV
Invocation, An: "We are what suns and winds." Walter Savage Landor. *See* Regeneration.
Invocation and Prelude. Stefan George, *tr. fr. German by* Ludwig Lewisohn. AWP
Invocation and Promise. Verner von Heidenstam, *tr. fr. Swedish by* Charles W. Stork. AnSL
Invocation and Proposition. Carlos de Sigüenza y Góngora, *tr. fr. Spanish by* Samuel Beckett. *Fr.* Eastern Evangelic Planet. AnMP
Invocation by the Priest of Pan. John Fletcher. *See* Evening Song.
Invocation of Agamemnon's Ghost. Aeschylus. *See* "Dies Irae."
Invocation of Comus, The. Milton. *See* Star That Bids the Shepherd Fold, The.
Invocation of Death. Kathleen Raine. MoAB

Invocation of Peace, *sel.* "Fiona Macleod."
"Deep peace, pure white of the moon to you." BoTP
Invocation of Silence. Richard Flecknoe. SeCL
(Silence Invoked.) GoBC
Invocation, An, Read at the Celebration of Independence Day in San Francisco, in 1888. Ambrose Bierce. BAP
Invocation; the Bondage of Religion. Lucretius, *pr. tr. fr. Latin by* W. H. D. Rouse. *Fr.* De Rerum Natura. RoL
Invocation to Chaucer. William Morris. *Fr.* The Life and Death of Jason, XVII. BPN
(To Chaucer.) EmBrPo
Invocation to Death. Emanuel Carnevali. NP
Invocation to Fancy. Joseph Warton. *Fr.* Ode to Fancy. OBEC
Invocation to Ireland. *At. to* Amergin, *tr. fr. Old Irish by* R. A. S. Macalister *and* Eoin MacNeill. OnYI
(Aimirgin's Invocation, *tr. by* R. A. S. Macalister *and* Eoin MacNeill.) AnIV
(Incantation, The, *tr. by* George Sigerson.) OnYI
Invocation to Light. Milton. *See* Hail, Holy Light.
Invocation to Love. William Drummond of Hawthornden. *See* Phoebus, Arise!
Invocation to Misery. Shelley. EmBrPo
Invocation to Nature. Shelley. *Fr.* Alastor; or, The Spirit of Solitude. EPN
(Invocation: "Earth, ocean, air, beloved brotherhood.") WHA
Invocation to Rain in Summer. William C. Bennett. GN; LPS-2
(Summer Invocation.) HBV; OTPC
Invocation to Sleep. Beaumont *and* Fletcher. *Fr.* The Woman-Hater. *See* Come, Sleep.
Invocation to Sleep. John Fletcher. *Fr.* The Tragedy of Valentinian. *See* Care-charming Sleep.
Invocation to Sleep, An. Josiah Gilbert Holland. BOL
Invocation to Spirit. George Chapman. *See* Invocation, An: "I long to know."
Invocation to the African Muse. Roy Campbell. *Fr.* The Flaming Terrapin. BoSA
Invocation to the Faerie Queene. Spenser. *See* Legend of the Knight of the Red Cross.
Invocation to the Genius of Greece. Mark Akenside. *Fr.* The Pleasures of Imagination. OBEC
Invocation to the Heavenly Muse. Milton. *Fr.* Paradise Lost, I. TreFS
(Fallen Angels, The, *longer sel.*) WoL
(Invocation: "Of Man's first disobedience, and the fruit.") FaBoEn; PoEL-3; PoFS
(Of Man's First Disobedience.) FiP
("Of Man's first disobedience, and the fruit.") ATP; BEL; BoLiVe; CBE; *sel.*; CoBE; EM-1; EnL; EnLi-1; EnLit; EPP; EV-2; GEPC; OAEP; OuHeWo; REAL; SeEP; TCEP; TOP; TyEnPo
(Opening Argument, The.) BCEP
Invocation to the Muse. Richard Hughes. MBP; MoBrPo
Invocation to the Power of Love. John Keats. *Fr.* Endymion, II. BPN
(Induction.) ERP
("O sovereign power of love! O grief! O balm!") EnRP; ViBoPo
Invocation to the Social Muse. Archibald MacLeish. CoV; LiTM; NAMP; OnAP
Invocation to the Wind. Joseph Kalar. AnEnPo
Invocation to Urania. Milton. *Fr.* Paradise Lost, VII. FiP; OBS
("Descend from heav'n Urania, by that name.") BrBE; NBE; TCEP
Invocation to Youth. Laurence Binyon. OBEV; OBVV
Involuntary/ I may live on. Emperor Sanjo, *tr. fr. Japanese by* Kenneth Rexroth. OnPJ
Inward and outward to northward and southward the beach-lines linger and curl. The Marshes of Glynn. Sidney Lanier. AA; ADAH; ATP; HBV; IAP; LEAP; MAP; MCCG; MoAmPo (1942 ed.); PC; PG (1933 ed.); SPP; TCAP; TOP; WGRP; WHA
Inward Light, The. Henry Septimus Sutton. WGRP
Inward Morning, The. Henry David Thoreau. AmP; AmPP (3d ed.); MOAP
Inward Peace. Matthew Arnold. *Fr.* Lines Written in Kensington Gardens. MaRV
Inwardly fired with vehement wrath. The Confession of Bishop Golias. "The Archpoet of Cologne." LaP
Io. Aeschylus, *tr. fr. Greek by* Walter Headlam. *Fr.* Suppliants. OxBG
Io. James Shirley. *See* Piping Peace.
Io! Paean! Io! sing. Triumph of the Whale. Charles Lamb. EtS; ImOP; OBRV
Io Victis. William Wetmore Story. AA; APW; GrCo-2; HBV; MaRV; OQP; QP-2; WGRP
"Speak, History! Who are life's victors?" *sel.* ChIP
Iolanthe, *sels.* W. S. Gilbert.
Contemplative Sentry, The. ALV; EnLi-2; FiBHP; PoVP
House of Peers, The. InMe; MBP
(House of Lords, The.) TrGrPo
(Song: "When Britain really ruled the waves.") InP
Lord Chancellor's Song ("When you're lying awake"). CoBE; PCD, *much abr.*
(Nightmare.) CoEV; LiTM; OxBoLi; ShBV-3; SiTL; YT
Said I to Myself, Said I. PoVP
Susceptible Chancellor, The. ALV; PoVP
Iölas' Epitaph. William Drummond of Hawthornden. AtBAP; PoEL-2; TriL
Ion, *sels.* Euripides, *tr. fr. Greek.*
Apollo the Betrayer, *tr. by* C. M. Bowra. OxBG
Dawn. GrR, *tr. by* A. W. Verrall; OxBG, *shorter sel., tr. by* C. M. Bowra
Divine Betrayal, The, *tr. by* A. W. Verrall. GrR
Ion and Creusa; Recognition, *tr. by* A. W. Verrall. GrR
"You that make music from the seven voices of the lyre," *tr. by* Moses Hadas *and* J. H. McLean. GrPo
Ion, *sel.* Sir Thomas Noon Talfourd.
Sympathy, *fr.* I, ii. LPS-3
(Friend, A.) PoToHe
Ion and Creusa; Recognition. Euripides, *tr. fr. Greek by* A. W. Verrall. *Fr.* Ion. GrR
Iona. Arthur Cleveland Coxe. AA
Iona. Frederick Tennyson. GoBC
Ione. Aubrey Thomas De Vere. GTSE; IrPN
Ione, Dead the Long Year. Ezra Pound. TwCV
Ione, fifteen years have o'er you passed. Ione. Aubrey Thomas De Vere. GTSE; IrPN
Ionian Holiday. *Unknown, tr. fr. Greek by* T. F. Higham. *Fr.* Homeric Hymns. OxBG
Ionian Song. C. P. Cavafy, *tr. fr. Modern Greek by* Rae Dalven. MoGP
"Ionis, I swear it, there never shall be." Callignotus and Ionis. Callimachus. GrL
Ipecacuanha. George Canning. ChTr
Iphigeneia and Agamemnon ("Iphigeneia, when she heard her doom"). Walter Savage Landor. *Fr.* The Hellenics. BEL; BeLS; BPN; EmBrPo; EnLi-2; EPN; ERP; EV-4; LPS-3; TwCrTr
(Iphigeneia.) EnRP
(Sacrifice.) LH
Iphigeneia in Aulis. Euripides. *See* Iphigenia in Aulis.
Iphigenia. Tennyson. *Fr.* A Dream of Fair Women. BHV
(Helen and Iphigenia.) TwCrTr
Iphigenia [*or* Iphigeneia] in Aulis, *sels.* Euripides, *tr. fr. Greek.*
Aftermath, The, *tr. by* Richmond Lattimore. WaaP
Chorus: "And Pergamos," *tr. by* Hilda Doolittle ("H. D."). AWP; LiTW
For Hellas! *tr. by* Arthur S. Way. GrR
"Had I, my father, Orpheus' gift of speech," *tr. by* G. M. A. Grube. GrPo
"Had I, my father, the persuasive voice." EnLi-2
"Hear then what to my mind/ Deliberate thought presents." EnLi-2
In the Stillness of Dawn, *tr. by* R. Potter. GrR
(Watch before Dawn, *tr. by* F. Melian Stawell.) OxBG
Prayer of Iphigenia, The, *tr. by* Arthur S. Way. GrR
Recrimination, *tr. by* R. Potter. GrR
Iphigenia in Tauris, *sels.* Euripides, *tr. fr. Greek.*
Agamemnon's Children, *tr. by* Gilbert Murray. OxBG
Bird of the Sea, *tr. by* Gilbert Murray. OxBG
("Halcyon, that from the wave-swept reef," *tr. by* J. C. Wordsworth.) GrPo
(O Halcyon Bird, *tr. by* Gilbert Murray.) GrR
By Friendship's Ties, *tr. by* Gilbert Murray. GrR
Iphigenia's Dream, *tr. by* Witter Bynner. GrR
Pylades, *tr. by* Gilbert Murray. OxBG
Stratagem, *tr. by* Witter Bynner. GrR
Tidings of Home, *tr. by* Gilbert Murray. GrR
Woman without Tears, A, *tr. by* Witter Bynner. GrR
Iphione. Thomas Caulfield Irwin. EnLoPo; IrPN
Ipsa Quae. Nicholas Breton. *See* Pastoral of Phillis and Corydon, A.
Ipsey Wipsey spider. *Unknown.* OxNR
Ipsissimus. Eugene Lee-Hamilton. BMEP
Ipswich Bar. Esther Willard Bates *and* Brainard L. Bates. HBMV
I'r hen iaith a'i chaneuon. Walter Dowding. MoWP
Iram Indeed Is Gone. Omar Khayyám, *tr. fr. Persian by* Edward Fitzgerald. *Fr.* The Rubáiyát. OnPM
Ireland. Stephen Lucius Gwynn. HBV
Ireland. Lionel Johnson. HBV
Ireland. Walter Savage Landor.
(Ireland Never Was Contented.) OxBoLi
Ireland. Edmund Leamy, Sr. JKCP
Ireland. Denis Florence MacCarthy. LPS-2; PoFr, *abr.*
Ireland. John James Piatt. AA; LBAP
Ireland. Dora Sigerson Shorter. BMEP; GTIV; LBBV; LEAP; OBEV; OBVV; OxBI
Ireland. Francis Stuart. NeIP
Ireland, Mother of Priests. Shane Leslie. JKCP
Ireland Never Was Contented. Walter Savage Landor. *See* Ireland.

Ireland, O Ireland, center of my longings. Ireland. Stephen Lucius Gwynn. HBV
Ireland Weeping. William Livingston, *tr. fr. Gaelic.* GoTS
Irene, *sel.* Samuel Johnson.
Tomorrow, *fr.* III, iii. LPS-3
Irene, do you yet remember. The Chess-Board. "Owen Meredith." HBV; LPS-1; OBVV; VA
Iridescent trifle of a king, The. The Silent Cockatoo. H. P. Stoddard. MuM
Iridescent vibrations of midsummer light, The. Irradiations, II [IV]. John Gould Fletcher. AnFE; APA; MAPA; TwAmPo
Iris. "Michael Field." VA
Iris, The. Gasetsu, *tr. fr. Japanese.* TiPo
Iris, *sel.* Oliver Wendell Holmes.
"If she had—Well! She longed, and knew not wherefore." LO
Iris. Hilda Mary Hooke. CPG
Iris. *Unknown, tr. fr. Japanese by* William N. Porter. MPB
Iris by the riverside. Iris. Hilda Mary Hooke. CPG
Iris-flower with topaz leaves, An. At Delos. Duncan Campbell Scott. BoCaPo; PeCV
Iris Flowers. Mary McNeil Fenollosa. RAR
Iris was yellow, the moon was pale, The. Iris. "Michael Field." VA
Irish, The. Francis Carlin. JKCP (1926 ed.)
Irish. Edward J. O'Brien. MoSiPe; SiSoSe
Irish Airman Foresees His Death, An. W. B. Yeats. AnEnPo; CoBMV; EnL; EnLi-2 (1949 ed.); FaBoCh; FaBoMo; LiTG; LiTM (rev. ed.); LoGBV; MoAB; MoBrPo; OBMV; OnPM; OtMeF; PoF; PoFr; TrGrPo; TwP; WaaP; WaP; WoL
Irish Astronomy. Charles G. Halpine. HBV
Irish Council Bill, 1907, The [*parody on the* Shan Van Vocht], *sel.* Susan Mitchell.
"Is it this you call Home Rule?" OnYI
Irish Dancer, The. *Unknown.* AnIL; EnL; FaBoCh; LoGBV; OBEV (new ed.); SeCePo; TMEV, *mod. vers.*
(I Am of Ireland.) OnYI
(Ich Am of Irlonde.) AtBAP; PoEL-1
Irish Emigrant, The. Helen Selina Sheridan. *See* Lament of the Irish Emigrant.
Irish Face, An. "Æ." ChMo; CMP
Irish faults are not so very new, The. Written on the Sense of Isolation in Contemporary Ireland. Robert Greacen. NeIP
Irish Girl's Lament, The, *with music. Unknown.* ShS
Irish Franciscan, The. Rosa Mulholland. CAW; SaFP
Irish Grandmother. Katherine Edelman. SiSoSe
Irish Harper and His Dog, The. Thomas Campbell. *See* Harper, The.
Irish History. William Allingham. IrPN
Irish Hurrah, The. Thomas Osborne Davis. OnYI
Irish Hymn to Mary. *Unknown.* CAW
Irish Lady, The, *with music. Unknown.* OuSiCo
Irish Lamentation, An. Goethe, *tr. fr. German by* James Clarence Mangan. AWP
Irish Love-Song, An. Robert Underwood Johnson. HBV
Irish Love Song. Margaret Widdemer. *See* Mary, Helper of Heartbreak.
Irish Lullaby: "I'd rock my own sweet childie to rest." Alfred Perceval Graves. BOL; TIP
Irish Lullaby: "I've found my bonny babe a nest." Alfred Perceval Graves. BOL; HBV
Irish Molly O. Francis A. Fahy. TIP
Irish Molly O. *Unknown.* HBV; TIP
Irish Mother in the Penal Days, The. John Banim. AnIV; TIP
Irish Mother's Lament, The. Cecil Frances Alexander. TIP
Irish Peasant Girl, The. Charles Joseph Kickham. AnIV; JKCP (1926 ed.); TIP
Irish Peasant Song. Louise Imogen Guiney. *See* In Leinster.
Irish Peasant to His Mistress, The. Thomas Moore. ACP; EV-4; OBEV (1st ed.); PoFr; TIP
Irish Rapparees, The. Sir Charles Gavan Duffy. AnIV; PoFr; TIP; VA
Irish Reaper's Harvest Hymn, The. John Keegan. TIP
Irish Riddle, An. *Unknown. See* Lane, A.
Irish Schoolmaster, The. James A. Sidey. BOHV; FiBHP
Irish Song: I Know Where I'm Going. *Unknown. See* I Know Where I'm Going.
Irish Spinning-Wheel, The. Alfred Perceval Graves. TIP
Irish Te Deum, The. *Unknown.* WHL
Irish Wife, The. Thomas D'Arcy McGee. HBV; VA
Irish Wild-Flower, An. Sarah Morgan Bryan Piatt. AA
Irish Wolf, The. James McCarroll. TIP
Irish Wolf-Hound, The. Denis Florence MacCarthy. *Fr.* The Foray of Con O'Donnell. SN; VA
Irishman, The. James Orr. DD
Irishman and the Lady, The. William Maginn. BOHV; HBV; VA
Irishman's Christening, An. *Unknown.* OnYI
Irmeline Rose. Jens Peter Jacobsen, *tr. fr. Danish by* Charles W. Stork. BoDS
Iron cities swim upon the sea. Autobiography. John Gould Fletcher. MOAP
Iron cross is black as death and hard as human hate, The. The Three Crosses. Edmund Vance Cooke. PEDC
Iron dragon nuzzles paving crust, The. House Demolished. Charles Malam. PoMa
Iron Fare. Marjorie Allen Seiffert. NP
Iron Gate, The, *sel.* Oliver Wendell Holmes.
"As on the gauzy wings." AA
Iron-Gray Horses, The. *Unknown, tr. fr. Chinese.* WhP
Iron Horse, The. Israel Newman. PoMa
Iron, left in the rain. Rust. Mary Caroline Davies. BAP; HBMV
Iron long time hid in our mother earth. Volucre Ferrum. John Heath. SiCE
Iron Messiah, The. Vladimir Timofeevich Kirillov, *tr. fr. Russian by* George Z. Patrick. PoFr
Iron Music, The. Ford Madox Ford. HBMV; VOD (1931 ed.)
Iron Pot proposed, An. The Earthen Pot and the Iron Pot. La Fontaine. BoChLi
Iron-red rose-leaf, tinctured with. Rose. Lewis Thompson. AtBAP
Iron-Wind Dances. Lew Sarett. Thunderdrums, V. MAP
Iron Wine. Lola Ridge. NP
Ironic: LL.D. William Stanley Braithwaite. BANP
Ironical. Violet Alleyn Storey. DDA
Irony. Mabel Wing Castle. BLP
Irony, An. Plato, *tr. fr. Greek by* Sir Alexander Croke. OuHeWo
Irony. Louis Untermeyer. NP; TrJP
Irony of God. Eva Warner. ChIP
Irradiations, *sels.* John Gould Fletcher.
"Ant, An, crawling up a grass blade," XVI. LaNeLa
"As I wandered over the city through the night," XXV. LEAP
"Balancing of gaudy broad pavilions, The," IV [VI]. AnFE; APA; CoAnAm; MAPA; TwAmPo
"Blue, brown, blue: sky, sand, sea," XVIII. ChMo; CMP
"Brown bed of earth, still fresh and warm with love," VIII [XIV]. MAPA; TwAmPo
"Flickering of incessant rain," V [VII]. AnFE; APA; CoAnAm; MAP; MAPA; MoAmPo; NePA; PFE; TwAmPo
"Fountain blows its breathless spray, The," VI [VIII]. AnFE; APA; CoAnAm; MAPA; TwAmPo
"Iridescent vibrations of midsummer light, The," II [IV]. AnFE; APA; CoAnAm; MAPA; TwAmPo
"It is evening, and the earth," XXIX. LaNeLa
"Morning is clean and blue, The," XXII. AnAmPo; LA; MAP; MoAmPo; NePA; NP
"Not noisily, but solemnly and pale," XXI. AnAmPo; LA; NePA; NP
"O seeded grass, you army of little men," IX [XV]. AnAmPo; LA; MAP; MAPA; MoAmPo; NeMA; NP; PFE; TwAmPo
"Over the roof-tops race the shadows of clouds," III [V]. AnFE; AnAmPo; APA; CoAnAm; LA; LaNeLa; MAP; MAPA; MoAmPo; NeMA; NePA; NP; PFE; PFY; TwAmPo
"Spattering of the rain upon pale terraces, The," I. AnFE; APA; CoAnAm; MAPA; TwAmPo
"Today you shall have but little song from me," X [XXXII]. MAPA; TwAmPo
"Trees, The, like great jade elephants," VII [X]. MAP; MAPA; MoAmPo; NeMA; NePA; PFE; TwAmPo
Irreparable Rose. Meleager. *See* Heliodora.
Irresistible bacilli are at work, The. With the Most Susceptible Element, the Mind, Already Turned under the Toxic Action. Walter Benton. WaP
Irresponsive silence of the land, The. Aloof. Christina Rossetti. *Fr.* The Thread of Life. BLV; BoLiVe; ES; FaBoEn; MBP; OBEV; OBVV; TrGrPo; TyEnPo; VA; YT
Irreverent Brahmin, The. Arthur Guiterman. LHV
Irrevocable. Mary Wright Plummer. WGRP
Irrigate the high wasteland and the slopes for plowing. Old Age. Lu Yu. WhP
Irrigation. Ann Nolan Clark. StVeCh (1955 ed.)
Irving. James Russell Lowell. *Fr.* A Fable for Critics. AnNE
("What! Irving? thrice welcome, warm heart and fine brain.") CoBA
Is a caterpillar ticklish? Only My Opinion. Monica Shannon. FaPON; MPB; StVeCh (1955 ed.); TiPo
I's a little Alabama coon. Little Alabama Coon. Hattie Starr. AA; BOL
"Is a tide a thing of a day?" The Dragon's Warning. Lyon Sharman. CPG
Is a welling fountain hid. Inverted Eyelids. Ibn Haiyun. MooP
Is an enchanted thing. The Mind Is an Enchanting Thing. Marianne Moore. CoBMV; CrMA; InvP; MoAB; MoAmPo (1950 ed.); MoPo; OnAP; OxBA; Po; ReMP

"Is anybody there?" said the Travel[l]er. *See* "Is there anybody there?"
I's boun' to see my gal to-night. On the Road. Paul Laurence Dunbar. AA
Is Earth My Enemy or No? Frances Kiely. CAG
Is 5, *sels.* E. E. Cummings.
"It really must/ be Nice," I. AnAmPo; LA; YaD
My Sweet Old Etcetera, III. AnAmPo; LA; NAMP; NePA; OxBA; WaaP; WaP
(Two XI.) MM
"Poets yeggs and thirsties," II. AnAmPo; LA
Is God invisible? This very room. Sonnet XI. Adele Greeff. GoYe
Is heaven a physician? Emily Dickinson. TwP
Is It a Dream? G. A. Studdert-Kennedy. MaRV; PoToHe
Is it a dream? Ah yet, it seems. Slumber-Songs of the Madonna, II. Alfred Noyes. BOL
Is it a dream, and nothing more—this faith. Is It a Dream? G. A. Studdert-Kennedy. MaRV; PoToHe
"Is it a dream?" I asked. To which my fellow. The Fulfillment. Delmore Schwartz. FiMAP
Is it a mocking jest that Christmas bells. Christmas, 1917. Brent Dow Allinson. AOAH
"Is it a sail?" she asked. From the Harbor Hill. Gustav Kobbé. HBV
Is It a Sin to Love Thee? *Unknown.* BLPA
Is it a wish—that tiny tin whistle. Peewee. Alfred Kreymborg. TCPD
Is it as plainly in our living shown. On Seeing Weather-beaten Trees. Adelaide Crapsey. BLV; CBOV; InP; MAP; MCCG; MoAmPo (1942 ed.); NeMA; PIAE
Is it bad to have come here. Gallant Château. Wallace Stevens. MAP; MoAB; MoAmPo
Is It Because I Am Black? Joseph Seamon Cotter, Jr. BANP
Is It Because of Some Dear Grace. Louis Golding. TrJP
Is it birthday weather for you, dear soul? Birthday Poem for Thomas Hardy. C. Day Lewis. CoBMV
Is it enough to think to-day. Memorial Day. Annette Wynne. MaRV; OHIP
Is It Far to Go? C. Day Lewis. AtBAP; GTBS-D
Is it for fear to wet a widow's eye. Sonnets, IX. Shakespeare. PeBoSo
Is it good-by. The Troop-Ship Sails. Robert W. Chambers. MDAH
Is it her nature or is it her will. Amoretti, XLI. Spenser. OAEP; PeBoSo
Is it illusion? or does there a spirit from perfecter ages. Arthur Hugh Clough. *Fr.* Amours de Voyage, II. EPN
Is it indeed so? If I lay here dead. Sonnets from the Portuguese, XXIII. Elizabeth Barrett Browning. BPN; VA
Is it life or is it death? By the Sea. Bayard Taylor. PA
Is it naught? Is it naught. Cuba. Edmund Clarence Stedman. PAH
Is it news you ask for, strangers, as you stand and gaze around. The Jamestown Flood. *Unknown.* ABS
Is it no comfort that a million share. Thus Answered. E. H. W. Meyerstein. *Fr.* Two War Sonnets. NeTW
Is it not a delicious fancy. Thinking of a Master. Richard Church. HaMV
Is It Not Better at an Early Hour. Walter Savage Landor. BPN; CBOV; EmBrPo
(On Timely Death.) TOP
(On Living Too Long.) VA
Is it not by his high superfluousness we know/ Our God? The Excesses of God. Robinson Jeffers. CoV; MaRV; QS
Is it not fine to walk in spring. Winter's Beauty. W. H. Davies. ChMo; CMP
Is it not strange that men can die. Reflection. W. J. Turner. OBMV
Is it not sure a deadly pain. *Unknown.* EG; EnLoPo
Is it not sweet beloved youth. To a Boy, with a Watch. Thomas Moore. FAOV
Is It Nothing to You? L. James Kindig. BePJ
"Is It Nothing to You?" May Probyn. GoBC; JKCP; OBEV (new ed.); OBVV; VA
Is it nothing to you, all ye that pass by. Is It Nothing to You? L. James Kindig. BePJ
Is it only to-day. A Song. Tzu Yeh. PoHN
Is It Possible? Sir Thomas Wyatt. LoBV; MaPo
("Is it possible that so high debate.") SiPS
(Varium et Mutabile.) OBSC
(Ys Yt Possyble.) PoEL-1
Is it raining, little flower? Rain. *At. to* Lucy Larcom, *also to* Mary Frances Butts. NLK
"Is it really very far." Little Miss Pitt. William Wise. TiPo (1959 ed.)
Is It Really Worth the While? *Unknown.* BLPA
Is it serious, or funny? B. Larry Eigner. NeAP
Is it so far from thee. The Chamber over the Gate. Longfellow. OBAV
Is it so small a thing. Matthew Arnold. *Fr.* Empedocles on Etna. OBEV; OBVV
Is it the beauty of the rose. The Reversible Metaphor. "Troubadour." InMe
Is it the palm, the cocoa-palm. The Palm-Tree. Whittier. LPS-2
Is it the tinkling of mandolins which disturbs you? Little Ivory Figures Pulled with String. Amy Lowell. AnFE; APA; CoAnAm; MAPA; NAMP; TwAmPo; ViBoPo
Is it the wind, the many-tongued, the weird. The Draft Riot. Charles De Kay. PAH
Is it, then, regret for buried time. In Memoriam A. H. H., CXVI. Tennyson. BEL; EmBrPo; EnLi-2; EPN; GEPC; MaPo; OAEP; TCEP; ViPo; VLEP
Is it this sky's vast vault or ocean's sound. The Monochord. Dante Gabriel Rossetti. The House of Life, LXXIX. CaAE; PoVP; TCEP; ViPo
Is it this you call Home Rule? Susan Mitchell. *Fr.* The Irish Council Bill, 1907 [*parody on the* Shan Van Vocht]. OnYI
Is it thus, O Shane the haughty! Shane the valiant! that we meet. Shane's Head. John Savage. TIP
Is it thy will that I should wax and wane. Apologia. Oscar Wilde. PoVP
Is it thy will thy image should keep open. Sonnets, LXI. Shakespeare. LO; LoPo; PeBoSo; PoEL-2
Is it True? Sarah Williams. BLPA
Is it true, Cynthia, that throughout Rome you are notorious. Propertius. Elegies, II, 5. LaP
Is it true, then, my girl, that you mean it. Yes? H. C. Bunner. HBV
Is It True, Ye Gods, Who Treat Us. Arthur Hugh Clough. *See* "Wen Gott Betrügt, Ist Wohl Betrogen."
Is it Ulysses that approaches from the east. The World as Meditation. Wallace Stevens. MoAB
Is It Well with the Child? Christina Rossetti. OBEV (1st ed.)
Is It Worth While? Joaquin Miller. PTA-1
Is it your command/ That we must pass through this life. Lady Ise, *tr. fr. Japanese by* Kenneth Rexroth. OnPJ
Is it your hope, hope's hearth, heart's home, here at the lane's end? Moving In. C. Day Lewis. ReaPo
"Is John Smith within?" Mother Goose. GaP; OTPC; OxNR; RIS; SAS
Is Life itself but many ways of thought? Substitution. Anne Spencer. CDC
Is Life Worth Living? Alfred Austin. LH; OTPC (1946 ed.)
"Is life worth living? Yes, so long," *sel.* MaRV; TreFS
Is Love a Boy. *Unknown.* ReIE
Is Love Not Everlasting? Ronald McCuaig. BoAV
Is love, then only liking. Always. Harrison Smith Morris. OBAV
Is Love, Then, So Simple? Irene Rutherford McLeod. BMEP; HBMV; LBBV; WHA
Is man's destructive lust insatiable? Kyrie. David Gascoyne. *Fr.* Miserere. NeBP
Is Mary in the dairy? Where's Mary? Ivy O. Eastwick. TiPo
Is My Lover on the Sea? "Barry Cornwall." EtS
Is My Team Plowing? A. E. Housman. A Shropshire Lad, XXVII. AnEnPo; AtBAP; BLV; BoLiVe; BPN; ChMo; CMP; CoBMV; EnL; LBBV; LiTM (rev. ed.); MaPo; MBP; MoAB; MoBrPo; OAEP (2d ed.); OBEV (new ed.); OnPP; OuHeWo; PG; PoVP; PreP; ReaPo; SeCeV; TrGrPo; TwP; ViP; ViPo; VLEP; VOD (1935 ed.); WHA
(From "A Shropshire Lad.") LEAP
(Voice from a Grave, A.) BMEP
Is my wrath splendid? Yet I become. Not Revenge . . . but These. Emanuel Litvinoff. NeTW
Is nature then a niggard of her bliss? The Smart Lady. Edward Young. *Fr.* The Love of Fame. BeR
Is not man's greatest heart's desire. Omnia Vanitas. Dugald Buchanan. GoTS
Is not one's life itself an act of daring. The Venture of Faith. Francis Greenwood Peabody. MaRV
Is not the work done? Nay, for still the scars. A Prayer for the Healing of the Wounds of Christ. Laurence Housman. MaRV
Is not thilke same a goteheard prowde. July. Spenser. *Fr.* The Shepheardes Calender. ReIE
Is not this April of our brief desire. April of Our Desire. Lola Ridge. MAP; MoAmPo (1942 ed.)
Is not this hearth, where goats now feed? The Hearth of Urien. Llywarch the Aged. ChTr
Is our time worse than all the times that went before it. "Anna Akhmatova," *tr. fr. Russian by* C. M. Bowra. BoRS
Is Praxinoa at home? The Syracusan Women. Theocritus, *tr. by* J. M. Chapman. *Fr.* Idylls. WoL
Is Praxinoe at home? The Syracusan Women. Theocritus, *tr. by* Andrew Lang. *Fr.* Idylls. GrL
Is seacoast fog, is starfish caught. New England Is New England Is New England. Brenda Heloise Green. GoYe
Is she/ Thoughtless of life. Nun Snow. Alfred Kreymborg. AnFE; APA; CoAnAm; MAPA; TwAmPo

Is she dead?/ She is what you would have her. John Webster. *Fr.* The Duchess of Malfi. AnFE
Is she not come? The messenger was sure. Tristram and Iseult. Matthew Arnold. PoVP; ViPo; ViPP; VLEP
Is she to bee buried in Christian buriall, that wilfully seekes her owne salvation? Shakespeare. *Fr.* Hamlet, V, i. AtBAP
"Is Sin, then, fair?" The Sting of Death. Frederick George Scott. BoCaPo; PeCV
Is some such word. Propriety. Marianne Moore. UnS
Is that dance slowing in the mind of man. The Dance. Theodore Roethke. Four for Sir John Davies, I. CoBMV; CrMA; FiMAP; NePoAm; ReMP; UnS
"Is that you, Peggy? my goodness me!" Peggy's Wedding. Thomas Edward Brown. EnLit; VLEP
Is the gateway to India at Bombay. Conversation Piece. Smith Dawless. PreP
Is the Moon Tired? Christina Rossetti. *Fr.* Sing-Song. BoTP; StVeCh
Is the noise of grief in the palace over the river. A Mother in Egypt. Marjorie Pickthall. CaP; CPG; HBV; MOAH; OCL; PCN
Is the way o'ercast with shadows? Jesus Understands. *Unknown.* BLRP
Is there a cause why we should wake the dead? The Yew-Tree. Vernon Watkins. LiTB
Is there a great green commonwealth of Thought. Sonnet. John Masefield. *Fr.* Sonnets ("Long long ago"). LiTM; MBP; MoBrPo
Is there a madness underneath the sun. The Starred Mother. Robert Whitaker. PGD
Is there a pious pleasure that proceeds. Grant Me Peace. Catullus. LiA
Is there a song for the New Year. New Year's Eve. Wyn Griffith. MoWP
Is there a Spanish love. Two Loves, Hyacinth! José Moreno Villa. CoSP
Is there a tuft of grass. New Song to an Old Air. Victor Hugo. LiA
Is there a whim-inspirèd fool. A Bard's Epitaph. Burns. EiPP; EPP; InP; LPS-3; PIR
"Is there any news of the war?" she said. Reading the List. *Unknown.* BlG; MDAH
"Is there anybody there?" said the Traveller. The Listeners. Walter de la Mare. AnFE; AWP; BBV (1952 ed.); BLV; BMEP; BoLiVe; CBOV; ChMo; CMP; CoBMV; CoEV; DaM; EnLit; EPP; FaFP; FaPON; GTBS-D; GTBS-W; GTML; GTSL; HBV; HBVY; HoPM; InP; InvP; JAWP; LBBV; LEAP; LiTB; LiTM; MaC; MaRV; MBP; MoAB; MoBrPo; MoPo; MoVE; NAMP; NeMA; NP; NV; OAEP (2d ed.); OBEV (new ed.); OBMV; OBVV; OtMeF; PCD; PFE; PIAE; Po; PoeMoYo; PoRA; POTE; PreP; PtOT; PYM; SeCeV; ShBV-3; ThWaDe; TOP; TreF; TrGrPo; TVSH; TwCV; UnW; ViBoPo; VOD; WBP; WHA
"Is there anything." Wise Sarah and the Elf. Elizabeth J. Coatsworth. PoMS
Is there anything as I can do ashore for you. A Valediction (Liverpool Docks). John Masefield. FaBoTw; OBMV
Is there anything I can do. The Key to Everything. May Swenson. NePoEA
Is there anything in spring so fair. Apple Blossoms. Helen Adams Parker. BoTP
Is there but emptiness from sky to sky. Today. Lizette Woodworth Reese. SPP
Is There for Honest Poverty. Burns. *See* Man's a Man for A' That, A.
Is there moonlight where you are? Moonlight. Nils Collett Vogt. AnNoLy
Is there never a man in all Scotland. Johnnie Armstrong (B *vers.*). *Unknown.* ESPB
Is there no greater good than health and ease. Deliver Us From. Amelia Josephine Burr. OQP; QP-2
Is there no hope? the sick man said. The Sick Man and the Angel. John Gay. CEP
Is there no landmark; no north-growing moss. Who Has Gone through the Wood. Floris Clark McLaren. BoCaPo
Is there no place/ Left for repentance. Satan's Pride. Milton. *Fr.* Paradise Lost, IV. MaRV
Is there no secret place on the face of the earth? The Moneyless Man. Henry Thompson Stanton. BLPA
Is there no splendid Himalayan height. The Better Part. Bhartrihari. OnPM
Is there no voice in the world to come crying. New Dreams for Old. Cale Young Rice. HBV; SBMV
Is there one desires to hear. Killarney [*or* Epilogue to "Fand"]. William Larminie. *Fr.* Fand. AnIV; TIP
Is there so small a range. Keats. *Fr.* Sleep and Poetry. BEL
Is there still any shadow there. Memo. Kenneth Fearing. ChMo
Is there virtue in the sweet medium? Poem. John Prichard. MoWP
Is there, when the winds are singing. The Mother's Hope. Laman Blanchard. LPS-1; MOAH
Is this a dagger, which I see before me. A Dagger of the Mind [*or* Night]. Shakespeare. *Fr.* Macbeth, II, i. LiA; LPS-3; PIR; TreFS
Is this a fast, to keep. To Keep a True Lent [*or* A True Lent]. Robert Herrick. BEL; DD; EM-1; EnLi-1; EPP; GrCo-1; HBV; LPS-2; MaRV; OHIP; PoRL; TOP
Is this a holy thing to see. Holy Thursday. Blake. *Fr.* Songs of Experience. CEP; CoBE; EiPP; EM-1; EnL; EnLi-2 (1949 ed.); EnRP; OAEP; PoE; ReaPo
Is this a time to be cloudy and sad. The Gladness of Nature. Bryant. ADAH; DD; HBV; HBVY; OTPC; SN
Is This Presumption? Louise H. Toness. ChIP
Is this Sir Philip Sidney, this loud clown. The Knight in Disguise. Vachel Lindsay. HBV
Is this the country of immortal love. The Land. W. J. Turner. QS
Is this the end of all adventuring. Trail's End. Beulah May. MuM
Is this the face that thrills with awe. The Face of Jesus Christ. Christina Rossetti. *Fr.* The Descent from the Cross. BePJ; ChIP
Is this the front—this level sweep of life. At the Front. John Erskine. HBMV
Is this the Lake, the cradle of the storms. Written on the Banks of Wastwater during a Calm. "Christopher North." OBRV
Is This the Lark! Joseph Auslander. BLA; PFE; PoeMoYo; PoTo
Is this the man by whose decree abide. Imperator Augustus. Sir Rennell Rodd. VA
Is this the night the world must burn like Troy? Like Ilium. Thomas Merton. JKCP (1955 ed.)
Is this the price of beauty! Fairest, thou. Charleston. Richard Watson Gilder. PAH
Is this the region, this the soil, the clime. The Fall of the Angels [*or* Satan's Kingdom]. Milton. *Fr.* Paradise Lost, I. CBE; FiP; MyFE; NBE; TreFS
Is this the Seine? An Ode to Spring in the Metropolis. Sir Owen Seaman. FiBHP; WhC
Is this the street? Never a sign of life. Stormy Night. W. R. Rodgers. OxBI
Is This the Time to Halt? Charles Sumner Hoyt. MaRV (Is This the Time to Sound Retreat?) BLRP
Is this the time to speak? Shall we tell the strong. Easter Evening, 1942. Leonard Bacon. NeTW
Is this the tribute you have brought to Me. Voice in a Cathedral. Thomas Curtis Clark. ChIP
"Is this the way to the Town?" I said. Figures in a Nightmare. Leah Bodine Drake. UnW
Is thy face like thy mother's, my fair [*or* my own sweet] child! Byron. *Fr.* Childe Harold's Pilgrimage, III. BEL; BoLiVe; BPN; ChER; CoBE; EM-2; EmBrPo; EnL; EnLi-2; EnLit; EnRP; EPN; ERP; GEPC; OAEP; REAL; TOP
"Is thy husband hang'd?" "He was, but he is nat." Of a Husband Hang'd. John Heywood. ReIE
Is thy name Mary, maiden fair? L'Inconnue. Oliver Wendell Holmes. BAV
"Is Thy Servant a Dog?" John Banister Tabb. JKCP
Is Time on my hands? Yes, it is. Thoughts Thought While Waiting for a Pronouncement from a Doctor, a Big Executive, the Department of Internal Revenue, or Any Other Momentous Pronouncer. Ogden Nash. SiTL
Is to love, this—to nurse a name. Poem. Rhoda Coghill. NeIP
Is true Freedom but to break. Stanzas on Freedom. James Russell Lowell. GN
"Is water nigh?" The Gift of Water. Hamlin Garland. AA; AnAmPo; LA
Is Yo' Lamps Gone Out? *with music.* *Unknown.* StDa
Is your place a small place? Your Place. John Oxenham. BLRP; MaRV; OQP; QP-2
Isaac a ransom while he lay. Didn't Old Pharaoh Get Los'? *Unknown.* BoAN-1; OIF
Isaac and Archibald. E. A. Robinson. AmPP; CBOV; OxBA
"So I proposed, without an overture," *sel.* BoFr
Isabeau s'y promène. *Unknown, tr. fr. French-Canadian folk song by* George T. Lanigan. BoCaPo (1948 ed.)
Isabel. Sydney Dobell. OBVV
Isabel Jones & Curabel Lee. David McCord. GoTP
Isabel met an enormous bear. Adventures of Isabel. Ogden Nash. AlDL; CenHV; MoAmPo; MoShBr; NeMA; TiPo (1959 ed.)
Isabel of the lily-white hand. Isabeau s'y promène. *Unknown.* BoCaPo (1948 ed.)
Isabella, *sel.* Sir Charles Hanbury Williams.
Old General, The. OBEC
Isabella; or, The Pot of Basil. Keats. BPN; EmBrPo; EnRP; ERP; EV-4; GEPC; ViBoPo, *much abr.*
Sels.

Isabella (*continued*)
Beginning of Love, The. UnPo (1st ed.)
"It was a vision. In the drowsy gloom." UnW
Kernel of the Grave, The. LiA
Proud Florentines, The. PoFr
Isabellita, do not pine. The Guardian Angels—Spanish. *Unknown.* BOL
Isador and Ida Strauss. E. J. Pratt. *Fr.* The *Titanic.* TwCaPo
Isadore. Thomas Holley Chivers. APW; SPP
Isaiah, *sels.* Bible, O.T.
All Flesh Is Grass, XL: 6–8. TrJP
"And it shall come to pass in the day that the Lord shall give thee rest," XIV: 3–19. PoFr
"But they that wait upon the Lord shall renew their strength," XL: 31. TiPo (1952 ed.)
Comfort Ye, Comfort Ye My People, XL. EM-1; LiA; TrJP (1–5); WoL, XL *and* LV
(Comfort Ye My People, XL: 1–11.) TreFS
Death of the King of Babylon ("The whole earth is at rest, and is quiet"), XIV: 7–12. PoD
Downfall of the Tyrant ("How hath the oppressor ceased"), XIV: 4–19. TrGrPo
"For Zion's sake will I not hold my peace," LXII: 1, 6, 10. PoFr
(For Zion's Sake, 1–5.) TrJP
Hear the Word of the Lord, I: 10–23. TrJP
Here Am I—Send Me, VI: 1–8. GrCo-2
Ho, Everyone That Thirsteth, LV: 1–3, 6–7. MaRV
(Divine Compassion, The, LV: 1–3, 6–13). GrCo-2
How Beautiful Upon the Mountains, LII: 7–10. TrJP
I Waste Away, XXIV: 16–20. TrJP
In the End of Days, II: 2–4. TrJP
(Swords and Plowshares.) GrCo-1
Intemperance, V: 11–12 (*Moulton, Modern Reader's Bible*). MaRV
Israel, My Servant, XLI: 8–16. TrJP
Let Me Sing of My Well-Beloved, V. TrJP
Man of Sorrows, The ("Who hath believed our report?"), LIII. EM-1
Messiah, The ("Behold, a virgin shall conceive"), VII: 14–25. AWP
My Thoughts Are Not Your Thoughts, LV: 8–13. TrJP
Peaceable Kingdom, The, XI: 6. FaPON; LiTW (6–9)
Power to the Faint ("Hast thou not known"), XL: 28–31. GrCo-1
Prince of Peace, The ("The people that walked in darkness"), IX: 2, 6–7. ChrBoLe
Proclamation ("Thus saith the Lord, the Redeemer of Israel"), *arr. fr.* XLIX. StaSt
Rod of Jesse, The, XI: 1–10. AWP; OuHeWo, XI:1–9, LIII: 10–12
(And There Shall Come Forth, XI: 1–9.) TrJP
Servant of God, The, LII: 13–LIII: 11. GrCo-1
(Behold, My Servant, LII: 13–LIII: 9.) OuHeWo
Song of the Harlot, XXIII: 16. TrJP
"Therefore the Lord Himself shall give you a sign," VII: 14–15, *Douay vers.* ISi
Vision of the Day of Judgment, LXIII (*Moulton, Modern Reader's Bible*). WGRP
Watchman, What of the Night? XXI: 11–15. AWP
Whom Shall One Teach, XXVIII: 9–13. TrJP
"Woe to thee that spoilest," XXXIII: 1–4. PoFr
Zion Redeemed ("Arise, shine, for thy light is come"), LX. LiA
Isaiah Beethoven. Edgar Lee Masters. *Fr.* Spoon River Anthology. NV
Isaias. Bible, *O.T.* (*Douay vers.*). *See* Isaiah.
Isbrand's Song. Thomas Lovell Beddoes. *Fr.* Death's Jest Book, III, iii. PoE
(Squats on a Toad-Stool under a Tree.) InvP
I'se de niggah, I'se de niggah. The Song of Dark Waters. Roy Helton. IHA; PC
I'se got religion an' I doan care. Mandy's Religion. Alice Corbin. *Fr.* Echoes of Childhood. PoNe
Iseult of Brittany. Matthew Arnold. Tristram and Iseult, III. GEPC; PoVP
Iseult of Ireland. Matthew Arnold. Tristram and Iseult, II. PoVP
("Raise the light, my Page, that I may see her.") ReTS
Ishmael. Herbert Edward Palmer. OBEV (new ed.); POTE
Isis Wanderer. Kathleen Raine. FaBoMo
Island, The. Audrey Alexandra Brown. BoCaPo
Island, The, *sel.* Byron.
Highlands Swelling Blue, The. OBRV
Island. Wilberto L. Cantón, *tr. fr. Spanish by* Dudley Fitts. AnCL
Island, The. Richard Henry Dana. *Fr.* The Buccaneer. AnNE; LPS-2
Island, The. Seán Jennett. JKCP (1955 ed.); NeIP; SeCePo
Island, The. V. Sackville-West. *Fr.* The Land. MM
Island, The. Giuseppe Ungaretti, *tr. fr. Italian by* Creighton Gilbert. LiTW
Island, The ("Daddy Neptune one day to Freedom did say"). *Unknown.* BHV
Island, The ("If the French have a notion"). *Unknown. Fr.* Ballads on Napoleon. CoBE
Island, The. George Woodcock. NeBP
Island, The, *sel.* Francis Brett Young.
Atlantic Charter; 1942. BBV (1951 ed.)
(Atlantic Charter, A.D. 1620–1942.) TiPo (1952 ed.)
Island Battlefield. C. R. Holmes. PtPa
Island Boatman's Love-Croon, The. Robert Farren. CoBE
Island Cemetery, The. W. H. Auden. NePoAm-2
Island Dogs ("The island crawls with dogs"). Charles G. Bell. NePoAm-2
Island etched on a silver sky, An. Basho, *tr. fr. Japanese by* Lois J. Erickson. SoLD
Island Fisherman, An. Katharine Tynan. TIP
Island in the Moon, An, *sels.* Blake.
Doctor Johnson. RO
Good English Hospitality. CoMu
(Mayors, The.) CH
Island lies nine leagues away, The. The Island. Richard Henry Dana. *Fr.* The Buccaneer. AnNE; LPS-2
Island of bitter memories, thickly sown. Irish History. William Allingham. IrPN
Island of Night. Galway Kinnell. NePoAm
Island of Saints, still constant, still allied. Erin. Kenelm H. Digby. CAW
Island of Shadow/ Silk of the Kine. Nostalgie d'Automne. Leslie Daiken. NeIP
Island of Shadows, The. Richard Garnett. VA
Island of Sleep, The. W. B. Yeats. *Fr.* The Wanderings of Oisin. TIP
Island [*or* Islands] of the Blest, The. Pindar, *tr. fr. Greek. Fr.* Olympian Odes, II. GrR, *tr. by* C. J. Billson; OBEC, *tr. by* Gilbert West; OxBG, *tr. by* C. J. Billson
Island Quarry. Hart Crane. CrMA
Island Tea. William Aspenwall Bradley. PR
Island that had flowered to the sun, The. The Coming of Dusk upon a Village in Haiti. Henry Rago. HoPM
Islanders, The. Kipling. BPN
Islands, The. Hilda Doolittle ("H.D."). AV; MAP; MoAmPo; PG; TBM
Islands. Rachel Field. GFA
Islands; a Song. John Malcolm Brinnin. AnFE; CoAnAm
Islands and peninsulas, continents and capes. Geography. Eleanor Farjeon. BrR; FaPON
Islands and the mountains in the day, The. Shelley. *Fr.* The Revolt of Islam. ChER
Islands are subtle places, still. Islands; a Song. John Malcolm Brinnin. AnFE; CoAnAm
Islands called me far away, The. The Cloud. Josephine Preston Peabody. LBMV; OBAV
Islands of the Blest, The. Pindar. *See* Island of the Blest, The.
Islands of the Ever Living, The. *Tr. fr. Irish by* Padraic Colum. AnIV
Islands of the Sea, The. George Edward Woodberry. MC; PAH
Islands, The: Puget Sound. James Rorty. MOAP
Islands which whisper to the ambitious, The. At Epidaurus. Lawrence Durrell. LiTB; MoPo
Isle of a summer sea. Cuba. Harvey Rice. PAH
Isle of Apple-Trees, The. Fritz S. Burnell. BoAu
Isle of Lone, The. Walter de la Mare. PtOT
Isle of [the] Long Ago, The. Benjamin Franklin Taylor. FaFP; HBV; PTA-2; TreFS; WBLP
(Long Ago, The.) BLPA; NeHB
Isle of Lost Dreams. "Fiona Macleod." VA
Isle of Portland, The. A. E. Housman. MoBrPo; PoVP
Isle of the Dead, The. Otto Freund. MuM
Isle of the Heather, The. Murdo Macleod, *tr. fr. Gaelic by* Henry Whyte. EBSV
Isle of the Long Ago, The. Benjamin Franklin Taylor. *See* Isle of Long Ago, The.
Isle of trees full foliaged in a meadow, An. Sonnet. Thomas Caulfield Irwin. IrPN
Isled in the midnight air. The Moth. Walter de la Mare. FaBoEn; MoVE; ShBV-3; TwCV
Isles, The. Sir Charles G. D. Roberts. VA
Isles of Greece, The. Byron. *Fr.* Don Juan, III. AEV; AnFE; AWP; BCEP, *abr.*; BEL, *longer sel.*; BHV; BPN; BTP; ChTr; CoBE; EM-2, *longer sel.*; EmBrPo; EnLit; ERP; EV-4; FaBoEn; FiP; GEPC; HBV; InPo; LEAP; LiTB; OBEV; OBRV; OTPC, *sts.* 1–3; PFE, *abr.*; PoFr; RiBV; SeCeV; TCEP, *longer sel.*; TOP; TreFS; TVSH; TwCrTr; ViBoPo; WHA; WP
(Glory That Was Greece, The.) CBPC; LH
(Isles of Greece: Ways of Poets, *longer sel.*) EPN
(Song of the Greek Bard.) LPS-2
(Song of the Greek Poet.) CBOV; PIR
Islesman's Home, The. Thomas Pattison. EBSV
Isn't it strange [*or* funny]/ That princes and kings. A Bag of Tools [*or* Builders]. R. L. Sharpe. BLPA; DDA; MaRV; NeHB; PoToHe (new ed.); YaD

Isn't it strange some people make. Some People. Rachel Field. FaPON
Isn't the violet a dear little flower? and the daisy, too. The Lay Preacher Ponders. Idris Davies. FaBoTw
"Isn't this Joseph's son?"—ay, it is He. Jesus the Carpenter. Catherine C. Liddell. DD; HBV; PECK; VA
Isolate and full, the moon. Full Moon. Tu Fu. OnPC
Isolation. Matthew Arnold. *See* To Marguerite.
Isolation. Arthur Hugh Clough. *Fr.* Dipsychus, Pt. II, sc. ii. OBVV
("Where are the great, whom thou would'st wish to praise thee?") BPN; EPN
Isolation. Albert Teodor Gellerstedt, *tr. fr. Swedish by* Charles W. Stork. AnSL
Isolation. Josephine Preston Peabody. AA; AnAmPo; LA
Isolation of Genius, The. Byron. *See* He Who Ascends to Mountain-Tops.
Isolation; to Marguerite. Matthew Arnold. Switzerland, IV. BPN; GEPC; PoVP; ViPP; VLEP
Isolationist. P. K. Page. BoCaPo
Isoida was an Irish queen who always spoke in German. Tristan and Isolda. Newman Levy. InMe
Isolte of Brittany. Peter B. Yates, Jr. CAG
Israel. William Ellery Leonard. QS
Israel. Israel Zangwill. TrJP
Israel Freyer's Bid for Gold. Edmund Clarence Stedman. PAH
Israel, My Servant. Isaiah, XLI: 8-16, Bible, *O.T.* TrJP
Israelite Graveyard. César Tiempo, *tr. fr. Spanish by* Rolfe Humphries, Donald Devenish Walsh, *and* Dudley Fitts. AnCL
Israel's Duration. Judah Halevi, *tr. fr. Hebrew by* Nina Davis Salaman. TrJP
Israfel. Poe. AA; AmP; AmPo; AmPP; AnAmPo; AnFE; APA; APW; AWP; BAP; BAV; BLV; BoLiVe; CoAnAm; CoBA; HBV; IAP; InPo; LA; LBAP; LEAP; LiTA; MOAP; NePA; OxBA; PFY; PoEL-4; PreP; REAL; RG; SPP; TCAP; TreFS; TSW; WHA
Israfel. Karl Shapiro. PtP
Israfiddlestrings. *Unknown.* BOHV
Issa's more full of sport and wanton play. Martial, *tr. fr. Latin by* W. F. Gosling. Epigrams, I, 109. LaP
Issue of great Jove, draw near, you muses nine, The! The Garden. Nicholas Grimald. ReIE
"Issues from the hand of God, the simple soul." Animula. T. S. Eliot. AmPP; ChMo; LiTB; MAP; MoAmPo (1942 ed.); MoPW; MoVE; PoLFOT; TwAmPo; TwP
Is't only you who think, free-thinking Man. All Things Are Sentient. Gérard de Nerval. TrFP
Isthmian Odes. Pindar. *See* Odes.
It. James Whitcomb Riley. *Fr.* A Session with Uncle Sidney. MeMeAg
It aids the dancer's heel, the writer's head. The Love of Praise. Edward Young. *Fr.* The Love of Fame. BeR
It ain't gonna rain, it ain't gonna snow. Ain't Gonna Rain. *Unknown.* AS
It ain't the failures he may meet. The Quitter. *Unknown.* BLPA; WBLP
It ain't the funniest thing a man can do. The First Settler's Story. Will Carleton. IHA; PTA-1
It ain't the guns nor armament. Co-operation. J. Mason Knox. BLPA; YaD
It all began so easy. Christina. Louis MacNeice. OxBI
It almost makes me cry to tell. The Dreadful Story about Harriet and the Matches. Heinrich Hoffmann. BoN
It autumne was, and on our hemisphere. Song. William Drummond of Hawthornden. OBS
It avails not [neither] time nor place—distance avails not. Walt Whitman. *Fr.* Crossing Brooklyn Ferry. NeMA; PIAE
It baffles the foreigner like an idiom. Drug Store. Karl Shapiro. AmPP (4th ed.); FiMAP; MoVE; OxBA
It befell at Martynmas [*or* Marynmas]. Captain Car; or, Edom o Gordon. *Unknown.* BaBo; EnLit; EPP; ESPB (A *vers.*); OAEP; TOP; ViBoFo (A *vers.*)
It being in this life forbidden to move. The Death-Wish. Louis MacNeice. AnFE
It being time, I look again for holly. Holly. Helen Bevington. NoCaPo (rev. ed.)
It bends far over Yell'ham Plain. The Comet at Yell'ham. Thomas Hardy. ExPo; ViP
It blows, it blows, the east wind blows. Friendship Veers with Fortune. *Unknown.* BoFr
It came so quietly—the first gray light. Resurrection. Ida Norton Munson. ChIP
It came to pass. Brother Ass and St. Francis. John Banister Tabb. AnAmPo; LA; SaFP
It came to pass after this, that Absalom the son of David had a fair sister. Second Samuel, Bible, *O.T.* LO
It came to pass also, that seven brethren. A Mother and Her Seven Sons. Second Maccabees, Bible, Apocrypha. BHV
It Came upon the Midnight Clear. Edmund Hamilton Sears. FaPON; MaRV; OlF; OTPC (1946 ed.); PCH, *st.* 1; SDH; YaCaBo, *with music*
(Angels' Song, The.) AA; BePJ; PEDC
(Christmas Carols.) HBV; HBVY
(Glorious Song of Old, The.) COAH
(Peace on Earth.) FaFP
It Can Be Done. *Unknown.* PoToHe (new ed.)
It Cannot Be. David Banks Sickels. *See* Reincarnation.
It cannot be that men who are the seed. Our First Century. George Edward Woodberry. PAH
It chanced as on a winter's night. The Debate of the Body and the Soul. *Unknown.* BCEP
It chanced his lips did meet her forehead cool. Modern Love, VI. George Meredith. ViBoPo; ViPo
It chanced of late, a shepherd's swain. A Fiction. "A. W." TuPP
It chanced one day they met. Each in surprise. Seven Sad Sonnets, VII. Mary Aldis. HBMV
It chanced that I, the other day. The Bore. Horace. *Fr.* Satires. EnLi-1; OuHeWo
It chanced to be our washing day. Oliver Wendell Holmes. *Fr.* The September Gale. FiBHP
It chanced to me upon a time to sail. My Native Land. John Boyle O'Reilly. LPS-2
It chanced upon a winter's day. William Cowper. *Fr.* Pairing Time Anticipated. CG
It chanced when the dance was pealing. Aleksey Konstantinovich Tolstoy, *tr. fr. Russian by* C. M. Bowra. BoR
It comes from childhood land. The Vesper Sparrow. Edith M. Thomas. SN
It comes, it comes, the day of meeting. Complaint. Evgeni Baratynsky. BoRS
It comes! the dire catastrophe draws near. William Falconer. *Fr.* The Shipwreck. EV-3
It comes to me more and more. The Love of the Father. *Unknown.* BLRP
It comes to me yet like a sunlight blur. A Drive. Otto Gelsted. BoDS
It comes to this. Revelation. David Meltzer. NeAP
It comes to this, in plain words. Victory. Eileen Duggan. AnNZ
It costs me never a stab nor squirm. Thought for a Sunshiny Morning. Dorothy Parker. PoMa
It Couldn't Be Done. Edgar A. Guest. BLPA; FaBoBe; FaFP; NeHB; TreFS; WBLP; YaD
It crawled away from 'neath my feet. That Hill. Blanche Taylor Dickinson. CDC
It did not last; the Devil shouting Ho! J. C. Squire. ExPo
It does no good to speak of the big, blue bush. Study of Images, I. Wallace Stevens. ReMP
It does not fly, does not sing. José Moreno Villa, *tr. fr. Spanish by* Eleanor L. Turnbull. CoSP
It does not hurt. She looked along the knife. "Non Dolet." Swinburne. BPN; PoVP; ViPP
It does not make sense in terms of historical fact. Sans Souci. Lisel Mueller. NePoAm-2
It does not matter/ That I am forgotten. Lady Ukon, *tr. fr. Japanese by* Kenneth Rexroth. OnPJ
It doesn't always do to let a mug know everything. Charlie Piecan. F. Murray *and* F. Leigh. OxBoLi
It don't seem hardly right, John. Jonathan to John. James Russell Lowell. *Fr.* The Biglow Papers. CoBA; IAP; PaA; PAH; PAP
It don't take sech a lot o' laws. Code of the Cow Country. S. Omar Barker. PoOW
It dreams in the deepest sleep, it remembers the storm last month. Ocean. Robinson Jeffers. MOAP
It drooped and it faded, my rose of beauty rare. The Rose. Gudmundur Gudmundsson. IcP
It dropped into the well one evening. Lament for Lost Love. Genaro Estrada. AnCL
It dropped so low in my regard. Emily Dickinson. AmPP; OxBA
(Disillusioned.) CoBA
(Life, CXVIII.) BAV
It ended, and the morrow brought the task. Modern Love, II. George Meredith. BEL; EmBrPo; EnLi-2; HBV; OAEP; POTT; ViPo; VLEP
It faded on the crowing of the cock. Shakespeare. *Fr.* Hamlet, I, i. MyFE
It Feels Good as It Is without the Giant. Wallace Stevens. Notes toward a Supreme Fiction, VII. MoPo; NePA
It fell about a Marti[n]mas time. Barbara Allen (B *vers., with music*). *Unknown.* ViBoFo
It fell about the Lambmass tide. Bonny Lizie Baillie. *Unknown.* BaBo; ESPB
It fell about [*or* upon *or* and about] the Lammas tide [*or* time]. The Battle of Otterbourne [*or* Otterburn]. *Unknown.* BaBo (B *vers.*); BSV; EBSV; EM-1; EPP; ESPB; EV-2; FaBoCh; GoTS; HBV; OBB
It fell about the Lammas time. Lord Livingston. *Unknown.* ESPB
It fell about the Martinmas [time]. Edom o' Gordon [*or* Captain Car]. *Unknown.* BSV; EBSV; ESPB (F *and* H

It fell about the Martinmas [time] (*continued*) *vers.*); EV-2; HBV; OBB; OBEV (1st ed.); ViBoFo (B *vers.*)
It fell about the Martinmas [tyde]. Jamie Telfer in the Fair Dodhead. *Unknown.* BSV; EBSV; ESPB; EV-2
It fell about the Martinmas time. Get Up and Bar the Door. *Unknown.* ATP; BaBo; BEL; BLV; BoChLi; BoLiVe; BSV; EBSV; EnL; EnLi-1; EnLit; ESPB; GoTP; GoTS; MaC; OBB; StPo; TiPo (1952 ed.); TrGrPo; TyEnPo; ViBoPo
It fell in the ancient periods. Uriel. Emerson. AnFE; AnNE; APA; APW; CoAnAm; IAP; LiTA; MOAP; NePA; OBEV (1st ed.); OxBA; PFY
It fell on a day, and a bonny summer [*or* simmer] day. The Bonnie House of Airlie. *Unknown.* BaBo (A *vers.*); EBSV; ESPB; OBB; OBEV
It Fell upon a Holy Eve. Spenser. *See* Perigot and Willie's Roundelay.
It fell upon a time when Eucritus and I were walking. The Harvest-Home. Theocritus. *Fr.* Idylls. GrL
It fell upon a Wednesday [*or* Wodensday]. Brown Robin's [*or* Robyn's] Confession. *Unknown.* ACP; CH; ESPB; OBB; SG; WHL
It fell upon the Lammas time. Young Ronald. *Unknown.* ESPB
It fell upon us like a crushing woe. Colonel Ellsworth. Richard Henry Stoddard. PAH
It fills the sky like wind made visible. P-51. John Ciardi. PreP
It fleeth away, my heart, quickly. Stand Fast, O My Heart. *Unknown.* LiTW
It flows through old [*or* all] hushed Egypt [*or* Aegypt] and its sands. The Nile [*or* The River Nile]. Leigh Hunt. BTP; EnRP; ES; EV-4; OBRV; PeBoSo; ViBoPo
It follows up the hill and down. Market Day. Abigail Cresson. HBMV
It Fortifies My Soul to Know. Arthur Hugh Clough. *See* "With Whom Is No Variableness . . ."
It grows late autumn, and the rooks are flown. The Unreaped Field. Nikolai Nekrasov. BoR
It had an autumn smell. Autumn. Allen Tate. Seasons of the Soul, II. MoVE
It had never seemed to me until I met. Silhouette and Oil. Rebecca Cushman. NoCaPo
It had to be. She from his weariness. Seven Sad Sonnets, I. Mary Aldis. HBMV
It hain't no use fer me to say. Love Lyrics of a Cowboy. R. V. Carr. SCC
It happened in Milan one summer night. Crushed Fender. Rosa Zagnoni Marinoni. MaRV; PoToHe (1941 ed.)
It happened in New Mexico. They Have Blown the Trumpet. Florence Converse. QS
It happened on a certain day. The Ship *Rambolee.* *Unknown.* ShS
It happened, on a solemn eventide. The Walk to Emmaus. William Cowper. StJW
It happened on a summer's day. The Castle Builder. La Fontaine. OTPC
It happened on a Sunday. Camp. Patrick Anderson. BoCaPo (1948 ed.)
It happened on an April day. Resurgam. John Richard Moreland. ChIP
It happened once, some men of Italy. The Lady of the Land. William Morris. *Fr.* The Earthly Paradise. EmBrPo; EPP; PoVP; TOP; VLEP
It happened once upon a time. James Hatley. *Unknown.* BaBo; ESPB
It Happened So Very Long Ago. W. C. Starkweather. CAG
It Happens, Often. Edwin Meade Robinson. BAP; HBMV
It hardly seems that he is dead. A Dead Friend. Norman Gale. VA
It has always been King Herod that I feared. Twelfth Night. Elinor Wylie. MM
It has broken us. *Unknown.* *Fr.* Sea Snatches. SiB
It has happened before. Four Preludes on Playthings of the Wind, III. Carl Sandburg. AnAmPo; AnFE; BLV; CoBA; InP; LA; MAP; MoAB; MoAmPo; NePA; NP; SeCeV
It has happened suddenly. Je Suis une Table. Donald Hall. NePoEA
It Is a Beauteous Evening, Calm and Free. Wordsworth. ATP; AWP; BoLiVe; BPN; ChTr, 8 *ll.*; CoBE; EM-2; EmBrPo; EnL; EnLi-2; EnLit; EnLP; EnRP; EPN; ERP; EV-3; FiP; GEPC; HBV; HBVY; HiLiEn; InPo; JAWP; LiTB; MaPo; MCCG; NeHB; OAEP; OuHeWo; PFE; PIAE; PoE; PoEL-4; PoFS; ReaPo; RiBV; SeCePo; SeCeV; TCEP; TOP; TreFS; TwHP; TwP; TyEnPo, ViBoPo; WBP; WHA
(At Sunset.) ES
(By the Sea.) EtS; GTBS; GTBS-D; GTBS-W; GTSE; GTSL; WP
(Composed upon the Beach near Calais.) PeBoSo
(Evening on Calais Beach.) CaAE
(Evening on the Beach.) BLV
(On the Beach at Calais.) TrGrPo
(On the Sea-Shore near Calais.) BEL; CBE; EPP
(Sonnet.) ChER; LoBV
(Sunset and Sea.) LEAP
It is a beauteous morning, calm and free. Country Club Sunday. Phyllis McGinley. CrMA
It is a crude thing as it shapes up here. New Construction; Bath Iron Works. G. Stanley Koehler. NePoAm-2
It is a curious thing that you. The Kangaroo. Elizabeth J. Coatsworth. StVeCh (1955 ed.); TiPo (1952 ed.)
It is a door. What Is This Coming Year? William Olney. PSO
It is a fair death, fighting in the front of battle. "Dulce et Decorum." Tyrtaeus. GrPE
It is a funny thing, but true. Folks and Me. Lucile Crites. WBLP
It is a good plan, and began with childhood. Monologue of a Deaf Man. David Wright. POTE (1959 ed.)
It Is a Gracious House and Ever Was. Euripides, *tr. fr. Greek by* Dudley Fitts *and* Robert Fitzgerald. *Fr.* Alcestis. LiTW
It is a hollow garden, under the cloud. Winter Swan. Louise Bogan. AnAmPo; LA
It is a huge spider that can not crawl farther. The Spider. César Vallejo. AnCL
It is a lie—their priests, their pope. The Confessional. Robert Browning. PoVP; OtMeF; ViBoPo
It is a long while since I have seen you, Li Po. Thinking of Li Po. Tu Fu. WhP
It is a memory now—that vesper hour. In the Organ-Loft with a Poetess. John Henry Boner. NoCaPo (rev. ed.)
It is a miracle to me. Miracles. E. Merrill Root. TBM
"It is a month, and isna mair." The White Fisher. *Unknown.* ESPB
It is a peaceful end of all desire. Death—What Is It? James Newton Matthews. PoP
It is a pilgrim coming from the East. The Pilgrim from the East. Gustave Kahn. TrJP
It is a piteous thing to be. Heresy Indeed. Sara Henderson Hay. QS
It is a place where poets crowned may feel the heart's decaying. Cowper's Grave. Elizabeth Barrett Browning. EmBrPo; EV-4; HBV; OBVV; PoVP; PtP; ViPo; VLEP
It Is a Pleasant Day. *Unknown.* BoTP
It is a secret sorrow, IV. Frances Crawford. PtPa
It is a strange, miraculous thing. Enigma in Altman's. Phyllis McGinley. PoMa; WhC
It is a sultry day; the sun has drunk. Summer Wind. Bryant. AA; APW; BAV; PoEL-4; TCAP
It is a summer gloaming, balmy-sweet. A Summer Twilight. Charles Tennyson Turner. OBRV
It is a Thracian trick to brawl in wine. Horace. Odes, I, 27. LaP
It is a thread—a tiny, shining thread. Vision. Ida Norton Munson. ChIP
It is a venerable place. Coventry Patmore. *Fr.* The River. EnSW
It is a wee, sad-colored thing. Phoebe. *Unknown.* BLA
It is a whisper among the hazel bushes. The Twilight People. "Seumas O'Sullivan." OnYI
It is a willow when summer is over. Willow Poem. William Carlos Williams. NP
It is a winter's tale. A Winter's Tale. Dylan Thomas. AtBAP; FaBoMo; LiTB; PoLFOT; SeCeV
It is a wolf's hunched back that bristles. Fields. "Andrei Bely." TrRV
It is a wond'rous thing how fleet. A Maiden Lamenting for Her Fawn. Andrew Marvell. BCEP
It is all one in Venus' wanton school. Song. John Lyly. SeCePo
It is almost as hard for friends to meet. To My Retired Friend Wei. Tu Fu. LiTW
It is an ancient Mariner. The Ancient Mariner, *parody.* *Unknown.* PA
It is an ancient Mariner. The Rime of the Ancient Mariner. Samuel Taylor Coleridge. AEV; AnFE; AtBAP; ATP; BCEP; BEL; BeLS; BLV; BoLiVe; BPN; BrBE; CaAE; CBE; CG; CH; ChER; CoBE; CoEV; EM-2; EmBrPo; EnL; EnLi-2; EnLit; EnRP; EPN; EPP; ERP; EV-4; ExPo; FaBoBe; FaBoCh; FaFP; FiP; GBV (1922 ed.); HBV; HiLiEn; HoPM; LEAP; LiTB; LiTG; LoGBV; LPS-3; MaPo; MCCG; OAEP; OBEV; OBRV; OnSP; OtMeF; OTPC; OuHeWo; PCN; PIAE; PIR; Po; PoE; PoEL-4; PoFS; PYM; ReaPo; RiBV; SeCeV; SG; ShBV-2; TCEP; TOP; TreF; TrGrPo; TyEnPo; UnPo (1st ed.); ViBoPo; WHA
It is an August evening in a free roof-garden. Ernest Crosby. *Fr.* Town Pictures. PC
It is an enormous spider that no longer moves. The Spider. César Vallejo. TwSpPo
It is [*or* 'Tis] an honourable thought. Emily Dickinson. EG
(Immortality.) MAPA; TwAmPo

It is an old belief. Beyond. John Gibson Lockhart. MaRV
It is as though some babe, that loveth hues. The Missal. Ruth Pitter. CAW
It is as though we never flirted. Flirtation. Ibn Zaydun. MooP
It is as true as strange, else trial feigns. Sonnet. John Davies of Hereford. EIL
It Is at Moments after I Have Dreamed. E. E. Cummings. OxBA
It is at morning, twilight they expire. After Midnight. Charles Vildrac. AWP; JAWP; WBP
It is autumn now. Mosquito Net. Fuyuji Tanaka. PoLJ
It is because they troubled me. The Pupil Returns to His Master [*or* The Pupil to His Master]. Fannie Stearns Davis. PFY; TBM
It is because you were my friend. Mortal Combat. Mary Elizabeth Coleridge. DiM; MBP; OBVV
It Is Becoming Now to Declare My Allegiance. C. Day Lewis. LiTM (rev. ed.)
It Is Better . . . Ecclesiastes, Bible, *O.T.* *See* Better Path, The.
It is bitter and sweet, during the Winter nights. The Cracked Bell. Baudelaire. AnFP
It is bleak December noon. December. Thomas Caulfield Irwin. IrPN
It is blue-butterfly day here in spring. Blue-Butterfly Day. Robert Frost. BAP; NeMA
It is borne in upon me that pain. The Human Being Is a Lonely Creature. Richard Eberhart. FiMAP; NePoAm
It is buried and done with. Farewell. John Addington Symonds. OBVV; PG (1945 ed.); VA
It is Cascorach the Bloody, who killed. *Unknown.* *Fr.* Sea Snatches. SiB
It is Christmas Day in the workhouse, and the cold, bare walls are bright. Christmas Day in the Workhouse. George R. Sims. BeLS; BLPA; PTA-2; TreF
It is Christmas in the mansion. Christmas in the Heart. *Unknown.* ChBR; MaRV; OHIP; SiSoSe
"It is cold outside, you will need a coat." The Arabian Shawl. Katherine Mansfield. *Fr.* Two Nocturnes. HBMV
It is cold without flesh, without bones. Dead in Wars and in Revolutions. Mary Devenport O'Neill. NeIP
. . . It is colder now/ there are many stars/ we are drifting. Epistle to Be Left in the Earth. Archibald MacLeish. BoLiVe (1945 ed.); ChMo; CMP; ImOP; MAP; MoAmPo; MoAB; PoLFOT; TrGrPo
It Is Coming. M. Florence Mosher. PEOR
It is common knowledge to every schoolboy. Portrait of the Artist as a Prematurely Old Man. Ogden Nash. CrMA; FaFP; LiTA; LiTM; NePA; SiTL
It is creation's morning. Now. Harriet Monroe. HBV
It is cruel for a woman with her man gone. Black Christmas. DuBose Heyward. LS
It is daffodil time, so the robins all cry. Daffodil Time. Clinton Scollard. PR
It is dangerous for a woman to defy the gods. Letter to My Sister. Anne Spencer. PoNe
It is dark and lonesome here. The Lover. Richard Henry Stoddard. AA
It is dark as a cave. The Clock-Winder. Thomas Hardy. PoVP
It is dawn. The horizon. Names. Jorge Guillén. AnSpL-2; CoSP; LiTW
It is done!/ Clang of bell and roar of gun. Laus Deo! Whittier. AmP; AmPP; AnNE; CoBA; CoV; DD; IAP; LPS-2; MC; PaA; PAH; PoFr; TriL
It is dusk on the Lost Lagoon. The Lost Lagoon. Pauline Johnson. CPG
It is early morning within this room; without. Laurence Binyon. *Fr.* Winter Sunrise. ChMP
It is easy enough to be pleasant. Worth While. Ella Wheeler Wilcox. BLPA; PoToHe; TreF
It is easy to mold the yielding clay. Clay Hills. Jean Starr Untermeyer. CP; HBMV; MAP; MoAmPo (1942 ed.); NeMA; NP; NV; PCD
It is enough that in this burdened time. Love Is Enough. Sir Gilbert Parker. CPG
It is equal to living in a tragic land. Dry Loaf. Wallace Stevens. AtBAP; CrMA; OxBA; PoRA
It is evening. The Yellow Crane Tower. Li Po. PoHN
It is evening, Senlin says, and in the evening. Evening Song of Senlin. Conrad Aiken. *Fr.* Senlin; a Biography. HBMV; MOAP
It is fallen! it is fallen! At Dawn. Charles Williams. FaBoTw
It is far into the night. At the Close of Day. Iku Takenaka. PoLJ
It is fifteen years since peace was declared with the Tartars. The Moon over the Pass. Lu Yu. WhP
It is fine to say we're thankful. Thanksgiving. William Ludlum. PraP
It Is Finished. Horatius Bonar. BePJ
It Is Finished. Jonathan Evans. BePJ
It Is Finished. Christina Rossetti. VA
It Is Finished. Sir Henry Wotton. BePJ
It is finished! Man of Sorrows. Via Crucis, Via Lucis. T. H. Hedge. BePJ
"It is finished." The last nail. Tenebrae. David Gascoyne. *Fr.* Miserere. FaBoMo; NeBP
"It is finished!" Thou didst cry like the roar. Miguel de Unamuno. *Fr.* The Christ of Velazquez, Pt. II. TeCS
It is fitting that you be here. On Seeing Two Brown Boys in a Catholic Church. Frank Horne. BANP; CDC; PoNe
It is folly for any man in the world. The Praises of God. *Unknown.* AnIL
It is for us/ to praise the Lord of all. The Kingdom of God. Rab. TrJP
It is from a heart sickness. Song of the Little Hypertrophic Child. Jules Laforgue. AnFP
It is good-by. The Troop-Ship Sails. Robert W. Chambers. MDAH
It is good for strength not to be merciful. To a Young Artist. Robinson Jeffers. CoBA
It is good to be out on the road, and going one knows not where. Tewkesbury Road. John Masefield. BoTP; CV; EPN; EPP; GBV; MCCG; PoeT; POT; PoTo; StaSt; TCEP; TSW; TSWC; VOD
It is good to strive against wind and rain. A Mood. Amélie Rives. AA
It is good under sea where trees grow. Under Sea. Konstantin Balmont. BoRS
It Is Great for Our Country to Die. James Gates Percival. *See* Elegiac.
It is green, it is made of willow. The Day-Bed. Richard Eberhart. FiMAP
It is hard for those who have never known persecution. Chorus VI. T. S. Eliot. *Fr.* The Rock. LiTM; QS
It is hard going to the door. The Door. Robert Creeley. NeAP
It is held, that valour is the chiefest virtue. Valour. Shakespeare. *Fr.* Coriolanus, II, ii. BHV
It is humiliating. Wormwood. Sappho. WoL
It is I, America, calling! A Call to Arms. Mary Raymond Shipman Andrews. MC; PAH
It Is I, Be Not Afraid. A. B. Simpson. BePJ
It is I, Odysseus—Elpenor. 1933. Archibald MacLeish. TwCV
It is I that am under sorrow at this time. Another Song. William Ross. GoTS
It is impossible to find anything good. Flood. Mary Grant Charles. GoYe
It is in captivity. The Bull. William Carlos Williams. MoVE
It is in loving—not in being loved. Christian Paradox. *Unknown.* MaRV
It is in many ways made plain to us. Retractions, V. James Branch Cabell. HBMV
It is in the rock, but not in the stone. Riddle. *Unknown.* ChTr
It Is in Winter that We Dream of Spring. Robert Burns Wilson. AA
It is, indeed, a pleasant thing to know. A Snowfall on Plum Trees after They Had Bloomed. Charles Dalmon. *Fr.* Three Pictures. TSW; TSWC
It is Jesukin. The Vision of Ita. *Unknown.* SiB
It Is July. Susan Hartley Swett. *See* July.
It is late afternoon at the beach; I lie on the swaying dock. "And All the While the Sky Is Falling . . ." Lora Dunetz. NePoAm
It is late, already, it is night. Soldier and Girl Sleeping. Sheila Shannon. SoV
It is late in the year. Night in the House by the River. Tu Fu. OnPC
It is late last night the dog was speaking of you. Donall Oge [*or* The Grief of a Girl's Heart]. *Unknown, tr. by* Lady Gregory. ChTr; DiM; GTIV
It is leviathan, mountain and world. History. Robert Fitzgerald. MoVE
It is lighted, we know, like a palace. Don't Go In. Mrs. M. A. Kidder. PreP
It is likely enough that lions and scorpions. Ante Mortem. Robinson Jeffers. CoV; MAP; MoAmPo; MoVE
"It is long since we met," she said. One End of Love. James Branch Cabell. SPP
It is May, it is May! Song for a May Morning. Herbert Trevelyan. AlDL
It is mellowed and soft as an apple's cheek. An Old Face. Francesca Falk Miller. PEDC
It is memory speaking, preternaturally clear. Elizabeth at the Piano. Horace Gregory. UnS
It is midnight, my wedded. The Ghosts' Moonshine. Thomas Lovell Beddoes. DaM; LO; NBE
It is midnight; the great dwelling. Miserere. Gaspar Nuñez de Arce. CAW
It is midnight, yet sleep will not come to me. Strolling under the Moon. Lu Yu. WhP

It is moonlight. Alone in the silence. Evening Song of Senlin. Conrad Aiken. *Fr.* Senlin; a Biography. SBMV

It is more than a year. Lung Men Temple. Po Chü-i. PoHN

It is morning, Senlin says, and in the morning. Morning Song of Senlin. Conrad Aiken. *Fr.* Senlin; a Biography. AmP; CBOV; ChMo; CMP; HBMV; InP; LiTA; LiTM; MAP; MoAB; MoAmPo; MOAP; NeMA; NP; NV; OxBA; PIAE; PoMa; PoTo; ReMP; SBMV; TrGrPo; WoL

It is most true, that eyes are form'd [*or* formed] to serve. Astrophel and Stella, V. Sir Philip Sidney. MaPo; OBSC; ReEn; SiCE; SiPS; TuPP; TwHP

It is my body leaves my love, not I. Struggling Fancies. Bhartrihari. OnPM

It is my heart that must remain. Canzone: Of Distance. Ruggieri d'Amici. LyPI

It is my joy in life to find. A Prayer. Frank Dempster Sherman. POT; PoTo; TreFS

It is my lady's holiday. Four and Twenty Drummers. *Unknown.* MuP

It is my own door that is shut. Dialogue. John Erskine. HBMV

It is my sorrow that this day's troubles. Slievenamon. *Unknown.* KiLC

It is myself. To a Dog Injured in the Street. William Carlos Williams. MoAB; NePoAm; SeCeV

It is night-time; all the waters round me. Swimming by Night. Alice Blaine Damrosch. LEAP

It Is No Dream of Mine. Henry David Thoreau. CoV

It is no idle fabulous tale, nor is it fayned newes. Newes from Virginia. Richard Rich. BAV; PAH

It is no vulgar nature I have wived. Modern Love, XXXV. George Meredith. ViPo

It is not a whirlwind rolling along the valley. The Murder of the Tsarevich Dimitri by Boris Godunov. *Unknown.* LiTW

It Is Not a Word. Sara Teasdale. NP

It is not bad. Let them play. The Bloody Sire. Robinson Jeffers. ChMo; LiTM; NePA

It Is Not Beauty I Demand. George Darley. *See* Loveliness of Love, The.

It is not blessed sleep. It looms as hateful. Sonnets of the Midnight Hours. Donald Wandrei. DaM

It is not, Celia, in our power. To a Lady Asking [Him] How Long He Would Love Her. Sir George Etherege. BrBE; CEP; EG; ElSeCe; HBV; LiTL; LO; LoBV; LoPS; OBEV; OnPM; SeCL; SeEP; ViBoPo

It Is Not Death. Thomas Hood. *See* Death.

It is not death. The Young Soldier. Wilfred Owen. BLV

It is not death I fear, nor that the gold. A Fear. Ruth Messenger. BLP

It is not death so much we dread. Poem for Combatants. Alan White. MaRV

It is not death that is bitter—that for all men stands fated. Death in Boyhood. *Unknown.* GrPE

It is not death, that sometime in a sigh. Death [*or* Sonnet]. Thomas Hood. EG; ES; LoBV; OBEV; OBRV; PeBoSo; ViBoPo

It Is Not Death to Die. George Washington Bethune. AA

It Is Not Death to Die. H. Malan. BePJ

It is not down this road I walk. Denial. Lancaster Pollard. NLK

It is not easy to be good. On Being Good. John Kendrick Bangs. PR

It is not easy to be less than lovers. For M——. Bruce Williamson. NeIP

It is not fair to visit all. Eve. Oliver Herford. HBMV; YaD

It Is Not Far. Sara Teasdale. *See* Night.

"It is not fear of death." Execution of Major André. Nathaniel P. Willis. BoHiPo

It Is Not Finished, Lord. G. A. Studdert-Kennedy. ChIP

It is not for nothing that the sun looks like a young-again old-timer. For Harry and June. Ray Mathew. NeLNL

It is not grief or pain. After Soufrière. "Michael Field." MBP

It Is Not Growing like a Tree. Ben Jonson. *Fr.* A Pindaric Ode. AnFE; BBV (1951 ed.); BEL; CBE; ChTr; CoBE; EnLi-1 (1949 ed.); EPP; EPS; LEAP; LiTB; LiTG; OBEV; OQP; QP-2; RiBV; TOP
(Good Life, Long Life.) LPS-3
(Greatness in Littleness.) BCEP
(Honour in Bud.) LH
(Noble Nature, The.) BTP; CG; EV-2; GN; GoBC; GTBS; GTBS-D; GTBS-W; GTSE; GTSL; HBV; HBVY; MaRV; MCCG; MW; OTPC; PECK; PG; TVSH
(Oak and Lily.) BoLiVe; TrGrPo
(Perfect Life.) WP
(Perfection in Small Things.) GrCo-1
(Proportion.) FaBoEn
(Short Measures.) BLV

It is not hard to tell of a rose. Inscription. Ann Hamilton. HBMV

It is not—I swear it by every fiery omen. Readings, Forecasts, Personal Guidance. Kenneth Fearing. MoAmPo; PoLFOT

It Is Not Likely Now. Frances Bellerby. ChMP

It is not, Lord, the sound of many words. Henry Lok. *Fr.* Sonnets of Christian Passions. SiCE; TuPP

It is not raining rain to me. *See* It isn't raining rain to me.

It is not right for you to know, so do not ask, Leuconoë. Ad Leuconoen. Franklin P. Adams, *after* Horace. AWP; JAWP; WBP

It is not right to judge a man. First Impressions. Alfred Grant Walton. PoToHe (new ed.)

It is not so much where you live. How—When—Where. John Oxenham. MaRV

It Is Not So with Me. Blake. *Fr.* Vala; or, The Four Zoas. SeCePo

It is not spring—not yet. Berkshires in April. Clement Wood. SBMV; VOD

It is not streets where proud-roofed mansions stand. A Country's Greatness. Alcaeus. GrPE

It is not sweet content, be sure. In the Depths. Arthur Hugh Clough. BPN; EmBrPo; PoVP; VLEP

It is not that I love you less. The Self[e]-banished. Edmund Waller. EPS; FaBoEn; MePo; OBS; SeEP

It is not the fear of death. Andre's Request to Washington. Nathaniel Parker Willis. MC; PAH

It is not the foreignness *per se* of heroes. Why the British Girls Give In So Easily. Nicholas Moore. WaP

It is not the mountains that tower. Mountain and River. Louis Ginsberg. PFE

It is not the young whom we find feeding the pigeons. The Pigeon-Feeders in Battery Park. Julia Cooley Altrocchi. GoYe

It Is Not to Be Thought Of. Wordsworth. BPN; EM-2; EmBrPo; EnLP; EnRP; EPN; ERP; FiP; MaRV; PeBoSo; PoFr; ShGoBo; TOP
(Destiny.) LH
(England, 1802, IV.) EV-3; HBV; OBEV
(London, 1802, III.) ES
(Sonnet: "It is not to be thought of that the flood.") LoBV; OBRV

It Is Not Too Late. Lucia Trent. PGD

It is not true that every day. Gold Hair. William Morris. BPN

It is not true, this tale. Palinode on Helen. Stesichorus. OxBG

It is not vertue, wisdom, valour, wit. Woman. Milton. *Fr.* Samson Agonistes. OBS

It is not what we say or sing. All Here. Oliver Wendell Holmes. IAP

It is not, y' are deceav'd, it is not blisse. To Pentadius. Jacopo Sannazaro. LaP

It is not you that move, but the running sand. The Eye. Eithne Wilkins. NeBP

It Is Not Yours, O Mother, to Complain. Robert Louis Stevenson. MOAH
(Mother and Son.) LH

Almighty Will, The, *br. sel.* GrCo-1

It is now the tenth hour of this October night. October. John Bayliss. NeBP

It is of a fearless highwayman a story I will tell. Quantrell (B *vers.*). *Unknown.* CoSo

It is of a flash packet, flash packet of fame. The *Dom Pedro.* *Unknown.* SoAmSa

It is on the sea and under the waves of the sea. Cycle. Seán Jennett. WaP

It is one thing to sing the beloved; another, alas! The Third Duino Elegy. Rainer Maria Rilke. *Fr.* The Duino Elegies. AnGP

It is only in the open air. In the Open Air. John Gould Fletcher. ChMo; CMP

It is only that this warmth and movement are like. The Woman in Sunshine. Wallace Stevens. CoV; MoVE

It is ordained, or so Politian said. Epitaph for the Poet V., I. Arthur Davison Ficke. BAP; HBMV

It is over, the ceaseless search is over. Over. Robert Finch. BoCaPo

It is pleasant to lie in the gloaming. The Sweet, Low Speech of the Rain. Ella Higginson. NLK

It is portentous, and a thing of state. Abraham Lincoln Walks at Midnight. Vachel Lindsay. AmPP; AnFE; ATP (1935 ed.); BoHiPo; CaAE; CoAnAm; CoBA; CP; FaFP; FaPON; GrCo-2; HBV; InP; LaNeLa; LiTA; MAP; MaRV; MC; MCCG; MoAmPo; MOAP; MoVE; MPB; NAMP; NP; OBAV; OHFP; OHIP; OnPP; OQP; OxBA; PaA; PAH; PEDC; PFE; PG (1945 ed.); PoRL; QP-2; SBMV; TCAP; TreF; TriL; VOD

It is posted in the clubrooms. SOS. Kenneth Fearing. AmP

It Is Raining. Lucy Sprague Mitchell. BrR; TiPo

It Is Raining Again. Apostolos Melachrinos, *tr. fr. Modern Greek by* Rae Dalven. MoGP

It is raining on the river. Nanking. Wei Chuang. PoHN

It is raining . . . Wait, do not sleep. Rainy Night. Juana de Ibarbourou. AnCL

It is related that the Caliph Harun al-Rashid. The Mock Caliph. *Unknown, tr. by* Sir Richard Francis Burton. EnLi-1
It is rest full of light, neither fever nor languor, on the bed or on the road. Evenings. Arthur Rimbaud. AnFP
It is said that many a king in troubled Europe. Rulers; Philadelphia. Fenton Johnson. GoSl; PoNe
It is said the Bedouins cry, on the Syrian hills, a clear. On Syrian Hills. Richard Burton. ChIP
It is she alone that matters. Bouquet of Belle Scavior. Wallace Stevens. MoAB; MoAmPo
It is simple, it is easy. "Anna Akhmatova," *tr. fr. Russian by* C. M. Bowra. BoRS
It is so good to be alive. A Song of Living. William Stanley Braithwaite. BPP
"It is so late, it grows so cold." Conversation in the Forest. Joseph von Eichendorff. AnGP
It is so long gone by, and yet. A Reminiscence. Amy Levy. AV
It Is So Long Since My Heart. E. E. Cummings. ChMo
It is so much easier to forget than to have been Mr. Whittier. Mr. Whittier. Winfield Townley Scott. CrMA; OnHM
It is so peaceful on the ceiling! Sleeping on the Ceiling. Elizabeth Bishop. MiAP
It is some school, brick, green, a sleepy hill. An Officer's Prison Camp Seen from a Troop-Train. Randall Jarrell. WaP
It is some time since the last rainfall was heard. The Body of Summer. "Odysseus Elytis." LiTW
It is spring. The West River. Yü Hsüan Chi. PoHN
It is spring. To One Afar. Chang Jung. PoHN
It Is Spring and All Is Well. Charles Erskine Scott Wood. PFY
It is spring in the mountains. Written on the Wall at Chang's Hermitage. Tu Fu. HoPM; OnPC
It is spring on the lake. Sailing on the Lake to the Ching River. Lu Yu. OnPC
It is springtime, to the south and north of my cottage the floods are out. The Arrival of a Guest. Tu Fu. WoL
It is strange how we travel the wide world over. Reality. John Drinkwater. BMEP
It is strange to think of the Annas, the Vronskys, the Pierres. Fate and the Younger Generation. D. H. Lawrence. OxBoLi; SiTL; WhC
It is strange we trust each other. Why Doubt God's Word? A. B. Simpson. BLRP
It is such a long way to the east, and my sleeves. On Meeting a Messenger to the Capital. Ts'en Ts'an. WhP
It is suddenly known that we have captured Chi-peh. On Hearing that Our Arms Have Captured Honan and Hupeh. Tu Fu. WhP
It is summer, says a fairy. Roses. *Unknown.* PEOR
It is sweet and bitter, on the winter nights. The Cracked Bell. Baudelaire. OnPM
It is talked the warld all over. Sheath and Knife. *Unknown.* ESPB; ViBoFo
It Is That Bane of Self in Love. Richard Eberhart. LiTL
It is that pale, delaying hour. Evening Songs, II. John Vance Cheney. AA
It is the association after all. A Way of Looking. Elizabeth Jennings. NePoEA
It is the bell of death I hear. The Bell. W. H. Davies. ChMo; CMP
It is the bittern's solemn cry. Solitude. Frederick Peterson. AA
It is the calm and solemn night! Alfred Domett. *Fr.* A Christmas Hymn. PGD
It is the cause, it is the cause, my soule. Othello and Desdemona. Shakespeare. *Fr.* Othello, V, ii. AtBAP; FiP
It Is the Celestial Ennui of Apartments. Wallace Stevens. *Fr.* Notes toward a Supreme Fiction. MoPo; NePA
It is the counterpoise that minds. Noble Love. Richard Flecknoe. ACP
It is the day of all the year. *Unknown.* OxNR
It is the day when he was born. In Memoriam A. H. H., CVII. Tennyson. EmBrPo; EnLi-2; EPN; GEPC; OAEP; ViPo; VLEP
It is the duty of the student. Duty of the Student. Edward Anthony. GoTP
It is the East we dream of: there. The Rider. Leah Bodine Drake. NePoAm-2
It is the evening hour. Mary [*or* To Mary: It Is the Evening Hour]. John Clare. ChTr; EnLoPo; FaBoEn; RO
It is the evening hour; the rapid sky. Canzone. Petrarch. LyMA; LyPI
It is the fall, the eternal fall of water. The Fall. Kathleen Raine. MoPo
It is the first mild day of March. To My Sister [*or* A Change in the Year]. Wordsworth. BoTP; BPN; EmBrPo; EnRP; ERP; GEPC; OBRV; PoE; SN
It is the harvest moon! On gilded vanes. The Harvest Moon. Longfellow. GN
It is the hour when Arno turns. A Song of Arno. Grace Ellery Channing. AA
It Is the Hush of Night. Byron. *Fr.* Childe Harold's Pilgrimage, III. LiTB
(Night.) LoBV
It is the littleness I would keep. To a Photograph. Parker Tyler. NePA
It is the memory of the peacock and the muses. Letter to R. Willard Maas. WaP
It is the midnight hour; the beauteous sea. Calm as the Cloudless Heaven. "Christopher North." EtS
It is the miller's daughter. Song. Tennyson. *Fr.* The Miller's Daughter. BLV; BPN; EG; GTBS; GTBS-W; GTSL; HBV; LiTG; LiTL; LPS-1; OBEV; OBVV; PIR; RiBV; TrGrPo
It is the month of falling stars. The Month of Falling Stars. Ella Higginson. YeAr
It is the pain, it is the pain, endures. Villanelle. William Empson. ChMP; EnLoPo
It is the reaching out into the dark. The Moment. David Rowbotham. BoAV
It Is the Reed. Sister Maris Stella. GoBC
It is the road, the chart. Faith. John Richard Moreland. ChIP
It is the same infrequent star. The Star of Calvary. Nathaniel Hawthorne. AA
It is the sea: dead calm—and the spring tide. Paris at Night. Tristan Corbière. AnFP
It Is the Season Now to Go. Robert Louis Stevenson. BSV; POTT; VLEP
(In the Season.) VA
It is the season of the sweet wild rose. Modern Love, XLV. George Meredith. EmBrPo; PoEL-5; ViPo
It is the sigh of languid bliss. Wind in the Wood. Paul Verlaine. LO; TrFP
It is the slow encroachment, word by word. Scarabs for the Living, VIII. R. P. Blackmur. TwAmPo
It is the spot I came to seek. An Indian at the Burial-Place of His Fathers. Bryant. CoBA
It is the tenderness you feel you know. The Catharsis. Alfred Alvarez. PoN
It is the third watch. Moonlight on the West Tower. Pao Ssu Hsien. PoHN
It is the very error of the moon. Shakespeare. *Fr.* Othello, V, ii. MyFE
It is the white Plum Tree. 'Tis the White Plum Tree. John Shaw Neilson. BoAV
It is the word pejorative that hurts. Sailing after Lunch. Wallace Stevens. MoPo
It is their way to find the surface. Poem by the Charles River. Robin Blaser. NeAP
It is 3.42 A.M. on a troop train. The Kid in Upper 4. Nelson C. Metcalf. TreFS
It is time for me to go, mother; I am going. The End. Rabindranath Tagore. MOAH
It is time, it is time. Viktor Khlebnikov, *tr. fr. Russian by* C. M. Bowra. BoRS
It Is Time That I Wrote My Will. W. B. Yeats. The Tower, III. MoVE; TCPD
It is time to be old. Terminus. Emerson. AA; AmPo; AmPP; AnNE; APW; AWP; CoBA; CoV; EOAH; HBV; IAP; InPo; LBAP; MOAP; OnAP; OuHeWo; OxBA; PoEL-4
It Is Time to Build. Elias Lieberman. MaRV
It is time to explain myself—Let us stand up. Walt Whitman. *Fr.* Song of Myself, XLIV. MaRV
It is to pick dead leaves. Yard Man. Andrew Hewitt. NoCaPo (rev. ed.)
It is told by seafarers. Told by Seafarers. Galway Kinnell. NePoAm-2
It is told, in Buddhi-theosophic schools. Transcendentalism. *Unknown.* BOHV; NA
It is too calm to be a dream. Easter Dawn. Frances Ridley Havergal. EOAH
"It is too late!" Ah, nothing is too late. Too Late? Longfellow. WBLP
It is too late—of her has all been said. Malibran. Alfred de Musset. LiA
It Is toward Evening. *Unknown.* BePJ
It is true that, older than man and ages to outlast him. Gray Weather. Robinson Jeffers. ChMo
It is true the haggard has nested. H. L. R. Edwards. From Knees Up, Muvver Brown, IV. MoWP
It is 12:20 in New York a Friday. The Day Lady Died. Frank O'Hara. NeAP
It is very aggravating. The Truth about Horace. Eugene Field. BOHV; InMe; InP; LHV
It is very nice to think. A Thought. Robert Louis Stevenson. MeMeAg; OTPC; PCH; PPL
It is well to give when asked, but it is better to give unasked. On Giving Kahlil Gibran. BoFr
It is well with this noble prince. The happy destiny hath come to pass. Song of the Harper. *Unknown.* LiTW
It is what he does not know. On a Squirrel Crossing the Road in Autumn, in New England. Richard Eberhart. NePA

It is when they come with questions. Poem for the Atomic Age. Emanuel Litvinov. NeBP

It is when we are near the end of a book that we enjoy it. Books. Ch'en Shih-tao. WhP

It Is Winter, I Know. Merrill Moore. MAP; MoAmPo

It is written in the skyline of the city. Pact. Kenneth Fearing. ChMo

It is young Sir Marstig. Marstig and His Lady. *Unknown.* BoDaBa

It Isn't Far to Bethlehem. Arthur R. Macdougall, Jr. PGD

It isn't hard/ To drive a car. Ilo Orleans. RIS

It isn't raining rain to me. April Rain [*or* Rain Song]. Robert Loveman. BAP; BoTP; DD; HBV; HBVY; LEAP; MaRV; MBP; NLK; OQP; POT; PoTo; QP-1; RIS; SUS; TrJP; WBLP

It Isn't the Church—It's You. *Unknown.* BLPA; WBLP

It Isn't the Cough. *Unknown.* FaFP; LiTM; SiTL

It isn't the thing you do. The Sin of Omission. Margaret E. Sangster. BLPA; HBV; MaRV; PoToHe; PTA-2; TreFS

It isn't the Town, It's You. R. W. Glover. BLPA

It joins a dark pine to another tree. Cobweb. Winifred Welles. AnAmPo; LA

It keeps eternal whisperings around. On the Sea [*or* Sonnet on the Sea]. Keats. ATP (1935 ed.); BLV; BoLiVe; BPN; CBE; CoBE; EM-2; EmBrPo; EnL; EnRP; EPN; EPP; ERP; EtS; EV-4; ExPo; GEPC; GTBS-W; HBV; KN; LiTB; MaPo; MCCG; PeBoSo; PIAE; PreP; SeCePo; SeCeV; SG; TCEP; TrGrPo; TwHP; ViBoPo

It Kindles All My Soul. Casimir the Great, *tr. fr. Latin.* LPS-2

It later befell in the years that followed. The Fire-Dragon and the Treasure. *Unknown. Fr.* Beowulf. AnOE

It lies around us like a cloud. The Other World. Harriet Beecher Stowe. AA; HBV; LPS-2; WGRP

It Lies Not in Our Power to Love or Hate. Christopher Marlowe. *Fr.* Hero and Leander, First Sestiad. BoLiVe; TrGrPo; WHA

(First Sight.) BLV; CoEV

(Love at First Sight.) EV-1; FaBoEn

(Who Ever Loved, That Loved Not at First Sight?) BCEP; FaFP; LiTB; LiTG; LiTL

It lies not on the sunlit hill. The White Peace. "Fiona Macleod." EPN; FaBoBe; HBV; OQP; PoVP; QP-2

It lies there now an ingot black and cold. The Smelting Furnace. Hugo Tigerschiöld. AnSL

It little profits that an idle king. Ulysses. Tennyson. AEV; ATP; AWP; BEL; BHV; BLV; BMEP; BoLiVe; BPN; CaAE; CBOV; CoBE; CoEV; EM-2; EmBrPo; EnL; EnLi-2; EnLit; EPN; EPP; EV-5; ExPo; FiP; GDAH; GEPC; GTSE; HBV; HoPM; InP; InPo; LEAP; LiTB; LoBV; MaPo; MCCG; MyFE; NBE; OAEP; OnPP; OuHeWo; PIAE; PIR; Po; PoE; PoeMoYo; PoFS; PoVP; PoRA; PreP; REAL; ReaPo; ReTS; SeCePo; SeCeV; ShBV-4; TCEP; TOP; TreF; TrGrPo; TriL; TwCrTr; TwHP; UnPo; VA; ViBoPo; ViPo; ViPP; VLEP; WHA; YT

It looked extremely rocky for the Mudville [*or* Boston] nine that day. Casey at the Bat. Ernest Lawrence Thayer. BBV (1951 ed.); BeLS; BLPA; BOHV; FaBoBe; FaFP; HBV; IHA; InMe; LHV; MaC; NeHB; OnSP; PoRA; PreP; PTA-1; PYM; StPo; TreF; YaD

It looks a piece of golden, broken glass. Onion Skin in Barn. Kenneth Slade Alling. NePoAm

It looks as if in dreams the soul was free. Dreams. Thomas Edward Brown. GTML; VLEP

It looks like any building. The Library. Barbara A. Huff. FaPON

It matters little where I was born. A Swedish Poem. *Unknown.* PEOR

It matters not that Time has shed. To My Father. William Hamilton Hayne. SPP

It matters not, when I am dead. Heart's Haven. Kendall Banning. MaRV; MuM

It May Be. Max Jacob, *tr. fr. French by* Wallace Fowlie. MiCF

It May Be. S. E. Kiser. BLP

It may be/ I'll join with thee in a most just revenge. John Webster. *Fr.* The Duchess of Malfi. PoFr

It may be good, like it who list. Sir Thomas Wyatt. SiPS

It may be on a quiet mountain-top. Autumn. James Stephens. ChMo; CMP

It may be so,—perhaps thou hast. To the Portrait of "A Gentleman." Oliver Wendell Holmes. BOHV; InMe

It May Be So with Us. John Masefield. *Fr.* Sonnets ("Long long ago"). ATP; TOP

(Life Is a Miracle.) GrCo-2

It may be that a strange dream. It May Be. Max Jacob. MiCF

It may be that the sun was bright. Mary Shakespeare. Ada Jackson. PoMa

It may be that the words I spoke. The Heartening. Winifred Webb. PTA-2

It may be that you cannot stay. It May Be. S. E. Kiser. BLP

It may be these things never did occur. Kinnereth. "Rachel." LiTW; TrJP

It may be 'tis observ'd, I want relations. George Wither. *Fr.* The Tired Petitioner. SeCV-1

It may be when the sunlight strikes the sill. In Your Absence. Elizabeth Baxter. PoToHe (new ed.)

It may be you don't care for dogs. Just Plain Dog. Lyla Myers. AlBD

It may have been a sunset such as this. Plain Chant of the Hill Country. Sister Mary David. JKCP (1955 ed.)

It may have been the pride in me for aught. The Corridor. E. A. Robinson. BoFr

It may indeed be phantasy when I. To Nature. Samuel Taylor Coleridge. ES; MaRV

It May Not Always Be So; and I Say. E. E. Cummings. *Fr.* Sonnets—Unrealities. AnAmPo; LA; MOAP

It Might as Well Be Spring. Oscar Hammerstein II. Po

It Might Be Ávila. Pedro Salinas, *tr. fr. Spanish by* Anne Sawyer Durand. AnSpL-2

It might have been in the heart of a deep forest. The False Summer. Marya Zaturenska. CrMA

It Might Have Been Worse. G. J. Russell. PoToHe (new ed.)

It moves me not, my God, to love of Thee. To Christ Crucified. *Unknown.* TeCS

It Must Be Abstract. Wallace Stevens. OnAP

It must be by his death; and, for my part. Murder of Julius Caesar. Shakespeare. *Fr.* Julius Caesar, II, i. EV-1

It must be fun like dad to play. Child's Play of Men. Michael Earls. FAOV

It must be so—Plato, thou reason'st well. Cato's Soliloquy [on Immortality]. Addison. *Fr.* Cato. BCEP; BPP; LPS-3; MaRV; OQP; QP-1; ReTS; TreFS; WBLP

It must have been for one of us, my own. Not Thou but I. Philip Bourke Marston. BLPA; LEAP

It Never Comes Again. Richard Henry Stoddard. *See* Flight of Youth, The.

It nods and curtsies and recovers. A. E. Housman. A Shropshire Lad, XVI. PoVP

It Often Comes into My Head. Walter Savage Landor. EmBrPo

It often rains in our town. And you know. The Discovery. Mary Carolyn Davies. MOB

It ofttimes has been told. The *Constitution* and the *Guerrière.* *Unknown.* AmSS; SoAmSa; ViBoFo

It once might have been, once only. Youth and Art. Robert Browning. BOHV; BoLiVe; BPN; EmBrPo; EV-5; GEPC; HBV; MaPo; PoVP; VA; ViBoPo; ViPo; VLEP

It ought to come in April. Wearing of the Green. Aileen Fisher. YeAr

It owned not a color that vanity dons. My Grandmother's Turkey-Tail Fan. Samuel Minturn Peck. PR

It pains me less, to stand. The Miser. Ibn Sa'id of Alcala la Real. MooP

It Pays. Arnold Bennett. *See* Limerick: "There was a young man of Montrose."

It piles up, thick and formidable, on the marble terrace. The Shadow of Flowers. Su T'ung-po. OnPC

It pleased the Lord of Angels (praise His name!). A Legend of Service. Henry van Dyke. GBV (1922 ed.)

It pricked like needles slashed into his face. Philip Dagg. W. W. Gibson. *Fr.* Casualties. VOD

It pulses through the twilight. Robin Song. Elisabeth Scollard. BLA

It quickned next a toyfull Ape, and so. John Donne. *Fr.* The Progresse of the Soule. PoEL-2

It rained a mist, it rained a mist. The Jewish Lady. *Unknown.* ABS; BaBo

It Rained in the Night. Jorge Carrera Andrade, *tr. fr. Spanish by* Muna Lee. AnCL

It rained, it poured, it rained so hard. Sir Hugh (B *vers.*). *Unknown.* ViBoFo

It rained quite a lot, that spring. You woke in the morning. Metropolitan Nightmare. Stephen Vincent Benét. DaM; ImOP

It rained toward day. The morning came sad and white. Robert Penn Warren. *Fr.* To a Little Girl, One Year Old, in a Ruined Fortress. MoVE

It Rains. Edward Thomas. BrBE; MoVE

It rains and then it rains and still it rains. Rain Inters Maggiore. Alfred Kreymborg. AnAmPo; LA

It rains on Berwyn hills, the night draws on. The Poet's Welcome. Edward Richard. *Fr.* Pastoral Poem. PrWP

It really must. E. E. Cummings. *Fr.* Is 5. AnAmPo; LA; YaD

It rely is ridikkelus. Bobby's First Poem. Norman Gale. MoShBr

It ripen'd by the river banks. Circumstance. Frederick Locker-Lampson. BOHV

It Rolls On. Morris Bishop. ImOP

It rose upon the sordid street. Music in the Street. *Unknown.* TIP
It sat between my husband and my children. Seele im Raum. Randall Jarrell. CoBMV; FiMAP
It say in de Bible. Ku Kluck Klan. Lawrence Gellert. TrAS
It Scarcely Seems Worth While. Vladislav Khodasevich, *tr. fr. Russian by* Babette Deutsch. LiTW; TrRV ("What is the use of time and rhyme?" *tr. by* Vladimir Nabokov.) BoRS
It seconds the crickets of the province. The Rocking Chair. A. M. Klein. CaP; PeCV
It seemed corrival of the world's great prime. A Fallen Yew. Francis Thompson. EmBrPo; MBP; MoAB; MoBrPo; VLEP
It seemed so mad a thing to do. The Rich Young Man. Laura Simmons. BAP; ChIP
It seemed that he would rather hear. Epitaph. Edward Weismiller. PoMa
It seemed that out of the battle I escaped. Strange Meeting. Wilfred Owen. AnFE; AtBAP; BMEP; CaAE; ChMP; CoBE; CoBMV; CoEV; EnLi-2 (1949 ed.); ExPo; FaBoEn; FaBoMo; GTBS-W; KN; LBBV; LiTB; LiTM; LoBV; MBP; MM; MoAB; MoBrPo; MoP; MoPo; MoVE; NAMP; NP; NV; OAEP (2d ed.); PoE; POTE; SeCeV; ShBV-4; TrGrPo; TwCV; WaaP; WaP
It seemed to be but chance, yet who shall say. May 30, 1893. John Kendrick Bangs. AA
It seemed to me in the night. The Hour Is Late. Winfield Townley Scott. FiMAP
It seemed too late for roses. An Autumn Rose-Tree. Michael Earls. JKCP
It seemeth such a little way to me. The Beyond. Ella Wheeler Wilcox. MaRV
It seems a day. Nutting. Wordsworth. BPN; EM-2; EmBrPo; EnRP; EnSW; ERP; GEPC
It seems a flower, but not a flower. A Flower? Po Chü-i. WhP
It seems as if . . . or did the actual chance. With Christopher Smart. Robert Browning. *Fr.* Parleyings with Certain People of Importance. PtP
It seems I have no tears left. They should have fallen. Tears. Edward Thomas. LiTB; MoPW; PoE
It seems like a dream. An Autumn Morning. *Unknown.* BoTP
It seems like a dream—that sweet wooing of old. Bachelor Hall. Eugene Field. BLPA
It seems no work of man's creative hand. Pedra [*or* Petra]. John William Burgon. BLPA; NeHB
It seems so simple now, that life of thine. Washington. Geraldine Meyrich. OHIP
It seems so strange that I once loved you so. Twenty Years After. Evan V. Shute. CaP
It seems so strange that man, full-blooded man. Quail. Bernard O'Dowd. BoAu
It seems that I hear that beauty who. Lament of the Lovely Helmet-Dealer. Villon. LyMA
It seems that rifles fire blanks, or they're all cock-eyed. Phony War. Raymond Souster. BoCaPo (1948 ed.)
It seems that Rome through the long roars of war. The Appian Way. Geoffrey Johnson. JKCP (1955 ed.)
It seems to me I'd like to go. Far from the Madding Crowd [*or* Vacation]. Nixon Waterman. BLPA; FaBoBe; MPB (1956 ed.); NeHB; NLK; WBLP
It seems to me that I can almost taste. Azaleas. Muda. SoLD
It settles softly on your things. The Dust. Gertrude Hall. AA; OBAV
It shall be said I died for Coelia! Coelia, XIX [*or* Sonnet]. William Percy. ElL; ReEn; ReIE; TuPP
It Shall Not Be Again! Thomas Curtis Clark. *See* Apparitions.
It Shall Suffice. Thomas Campion. *See* Follow Your Saint.
It shifts and shifts from form to form. The Name. Don Marquis. HBV; LEAP; OBAV
It Should Be Easy. Mark Van Doren. CrMA
It sifts from leaden sieves. The Snow. Emily Dickinson. GoTP; RG
It singeth low in every heart. The Abiding Love [*or* Auld Lang Syne]. John White Chadwick. BLPA; FaBoBe; MaRV; NeHB; WGRP
It sings to me in sunshine. Segovia and Madrid. Rose Terry Cooke. AA; OBAV
It slaps and laps at the city's wharves. The River of Commerce. "O. L." CAG
It sleeps among the thousand hills. The Unnamed Lake. Frederick George Scott. BoCaPo; CaP; CPG; OCL
It snowed in spring on earth so dry and warm. Our Singing Strength. Robert Frost. AnAmPo; AtBAP; CoBA; InP; LA
It so happens I am tired of being a man. Walking Around. "Pablo Neruda." AnCL; LiTW
It softens now. April snow. The Turning. Philip Booth. NePoAm-2
It sometimes happens that two friends will meet. Why Should We Mourn? *Unknown.* BPP
It sounded as if the streets were running. Emily Dickinson. NePA
It stands upon a plain in far Cathay. The Tower of Genghis Khan. Hervey Allen. TCPD
It started into raining. Me an' My Doney-Gal. *Unknown.* CoSo
It stood at bay in its own dark sea. Sardinia from a Liner. Leonora Speyer. PoeMoYo
It stood embosom'd in a happy valley. Norman Abbey. Byron. *Fr.* Don Juan. OBRV
It stood in the cellar low and dim. The Apple-Barrel. Edwin L. Sabin. DD
It stood on a bleak country corner. The Old Brown Schoolhouse. *Unknown.* TreF
It stops the town we come through. Troop Train. Karl Shapiro. OxBA; WaaP; WaP
It stuns. The Crane. J. Redwood Anderson. MM; TCPD
It suiteth well that when at table. Table Manners for the Hostess. Jean de Meun. *Fr.* The Romance of the Rose. EnLi-1
It sushes. Cynthia in the Snow. Gwendolyn Brooks. TiPo (1959 ed.)
It sweeps gray-winged across the obliterated hills. The Squall. Leonora Speyer. POT; VOD
It swings upon the leafless tree. The Snow-filled Nest. Rose Terry Cooke. SN
It takes a heap o' children to make a home that's true. Edgar A. Guest Syndicates [*or* Considers] "The Old Woman Who Lived in a Shoe" [*or* Just Home]. Louis Untermeyer. FiBHP; MoAmPo; PreP; StaSt; WhC
It takes a heap o' livin' in a house t' make it home. Home. Edgar A. Guest. BLPA; FaBoBe; OHFP; PTA-2; TreF; YaD
It takes a little courage. The Only Way to Win. *Unknown.* WBLP
It takes a lot of letters to make up the alphabet. P's and Q's. Rupert Sargent Holland. OTPC
It takes much art. La Carte. Justin Richardson. FiBHP; SiTL
It talks and talks, but the words. The Typewriter. Mariana Griswold Van Rensselaer. GFA
It tis hir voice, deare mistress, sweetest hart. *Unknown.* SeCSL
It took me ten days. In the Beginning Was the Word. Anna Hempstead Branch. NV; TBM
It took the sea a thousand years. Erosion. E. J. Pratt. CaP; CoBE; OnPM; TwCaPo
It trembled off the keys—a parting kiss. Her Music. Martha Dickinson Bianchi. AA
It troubled me as once I was. Once a Child. Emily Dickinson. ImOP
It Was a Beauty That I Saw. Ben Jonson. *Fr.* The New Inn, IV, iv. OBS; ReEn; SeCL; SeEP (Lovel's Song.) TrGrPo (Vision of Beauty, A.) LPS-1
It was a black Bunny, with white in its head. Black Bunny. William Brighty Rands. CBPC
It was a blind beggar, had long lost his sight. The Blind Beggar's Daughter of Bednall-Green. *Unknown.* EV-2; LoEn; OBB; OTPC
It was a bowl of roses. A Bowl of Roses. W. E. Henley. BPN; EnLi-2; EPP; MBP; MoBrPo; OuHeWo
It was a bright and cheerful afternoon. Summer and Winter. Shelley. EV-4; UnPo (3d ed.)
It was a bright and lovely summer's morn. The Two Pictures. *Unknown.* PTA-2
It was a bright day and all the trees were still. Silence. W. J. Turner. MoBrPo
It was a chilly winter's night. A Winter Night. William Barnes. ChTr
It was a close, warm, breezeless summer night. Conclusion [*or* Majestic Intellect]. Wordsworth. *Fr.* The Prelude. PoEL-4; RO
It was a comely young lady fair. Dark-eyed Canaller. *Unknown.* OuSiCo
It was a cough that carried him off. *Unknown.* WhC
It was a dark and stormy night. The Sailor Boy. *Unknown.* ShS
It was a day like any other. No One Knew. "Demyan Bedny." TrRV
It was a day of sun and rain. At Fontainebleau. Arthur Symons. VA
It was a day of turning when you came. The Turning. Philip Murray. NePoAm
It was a den where no insulting light. The Den of the Titans. Keats. *Fr.* Hyperion. WHA
It was a dismal and a fearful night. On the Death of Mr. William Hervey. Abraham Cowley. BoFr; CoEV; EPS; EV-2; GTSL; OBEV; OBS; SeCV-1; SeEP; ViBoPo
It was a dismal day when chilling rain. The Greater Gift. Margaret E. Bruner. PoToHe (new ed.)

It was a dismal land. The Haunt of Grendel. *Unknown. Fr.* Beowulf. BCEP
It was a draper eminent. The Seraph and the Snob. May Kendall. CenHV
It was a dream (ah! what is not a dream?). On the Death of Southey. Walter Savage Landor. BPN
It was a dreary day in Padua. Countess Laura. George Henry Boker. BeLS; LPS-3
It was a famous story, proclaim it far and wide. The Famous Light Brigade. *Unknown.* ShS
"It Was a Famous Victory." Franklin P. Adams. LauV
It was a fancy'd noise, for all is hush'd. Among the Dead. Congreve. *Fr.* The Mourning Bride. BeR; LiA
It was a fatal trick to play upon him. Holy Matrimony. Harold Monro. ChMo; CMP
It was a fiery circus horse. The Day of the Circus Horse. T. A. Daly. RIS; TSWC; UTS
It Was A' for Our Rightfu' King. Burns. *See* Farewell, The: "It was a' for our rightfu' king."
It was a friar of orders free. Song. Thomas Love Peacock. *Fr.* Maid Marian. ViBoPo
It was a friar of orders grey. The Friar of Orders Grey. *Unknown.* ACP; BCEP; CAW; CEP; EV-3; GoBC; HBV; LPS-1; OBEC; WHL
It was a frosty-cold midwinter night. A Boy in the Piney Woods. John Henry Boner. NoCaPo
It was a gallant sailor man. The Two Anchors. Richard Henry Stoddard. BeLS
It was a German town that we awoke in. Long Roads. Mikhail Matusovsky. LiTW; TrRV
It Was a Goodly Co. E. E. Cummings. CrMA; LiTA; LiTM; MoVE; SiTL; WaP
It was a grey day. Tom Thomson. Arthur S. Bourinot. CaP
It was a heavenly time of life. The Quest. Ellen Mackay Hutchinson Cortissoz. HBV
It was a hundred years ago. The White-footed Deer. Bryant. AnNE; PTA-1
It was a hungry pussy cat. A Thanksgiving Fable. Oliver Herford. HH; OnHT; PRWS; TOAH; UTS
It was a hunter's tale that rolled like wind. Donald Davidson. *Fr.* The Tall Men. SPP
It was a kind and northern face. Praise for an Urn (In Memoriam: Ernest Nelson). Hart Crane. AmP; AnFE; ATP (1953 ed.); AWP; ChMo; CoAnAm; CoBMV; InPo; LiTG; LiTM (rev. ed.); MAP; MoAB; MoAmPo; MOAP; MoVE; OxBA; PoE; ReMP; UnPo (3d ed.)
It was a knight in Scotland borne. The Fair Flower of Northumberland. *Unknown.* BaBo; ESPB; LoEn; OBB
It was a lady of the north she lov'd a gentleman. Room for a Jovial Tinker: Old Brass to Mend. *Unknown.* CoMu
It was a little yellow dog. The Yellow Dog. Edgar A. Guest. AlBD
It was a long, long trip on the Erie. Erie Canal. *Unknown.* ABF
It was a long time ago. As I Grew Older. Langston Hughes. BANP
It Was a Lording's Daughter. *Unknown, at. to* Shakespeare. *Fr.* The Passionate Pilgrim. ElL
(Contentions.) HBV
It Was a Lover and His Lass. Shakespeare. *Fr.* As You Like It, V, iii. BEL; CBE; CH; EG; ElL; ElSeCe; EM-1; EnL; EnLi-1; EnLit; EV-1; ExPo; GTBS; GTBS-D; GTBS-W; GTSE; GTSL; HBV; InPo; LiTB; LiTG; LiTL; LO; LoBV; OBEV; PIR; PoRA; ReaPo; ShBV-1; SiCE; SiTL; TOP; ViBoPo
(Country Song.) TrGrPo
(Love in Spring-Time.) MCCG
(Lovers Love the Spring.) BLV
(Pages' Song, The.) OBSC; SeCePo
(Song: "It was a lover and his lass.") FiP
(Song of the Two Pages.) BoLiVe
(Songs from "As You Like It.") LEAP
(Songs from the Plays.) AWP; JAWP; WBP
It was a merry time. The Courtship, Merry Marriage, and Picnic Dinner of Cock Robin and Jenny Wren. *Unknown.* HBV; OTPC; PPL
It was a mighty monarch's child. Mir träumte von einem Königskind. Heine. AWP
It was a millinger most gay. The Fair Millinger. Fred W. Loring. BOHV
It was a miniature country once. Japan. Anthony Hecht. CrMA; LiTM (rev. ed.)
It was a mischievous wind that pushed him; a murderous gust that jarred young Jan from the scaffold. Monument. A. M. Sullivan. GoYe
It was a Moorish maiden was sitting by a well. The Broken Pitcher. William E. Aytoun. BOHV; InMe; PoVP
It was a mother and a maid. The Milk White Doe. *Unknown.* AWP
It was a night of early spring. Wisdom. Sara Teasdale. BAP; LoPo; MAP; MoAmPo; MuM
It was a noble Roman. Find a Way. John Godfrey Saxe. PEDC
It was a noble Roman. On Fort Sumter. *Unknown.* MC; PAH
It was a perfect day. Sowing. Edward Thomas. AlDL; BMEP; CBOV; HBMV; NP; POTE
It was a puritanicall ladd. Off a Puritane. *Unknown.* CoMu
It was a quiet way. Emily Dickinson. CoBA; LoPo; LoPS; MeRV
It was a railway passenger. Striking. Charles Stuart Calverley. CenHV; PA
It was a rich merchant man. The Merchant and the Fidler's Wife. *Unknown.* CoMu
It was a robber's daughter, and her name was Alice Brown. Gentle Alice Brown. W. S. Gilbert. BOHV; FiBHP; InMe; MBP; NA; OnSP; PIAE
It was a rule of Leonardo da Vinci's. Clerihews. E. C. Bentley. OnPP
It was a saying used a great while since. To Master Bastard, Taxing Him of Flattery. Sir John Harington. SiCE
It was a sea uncharted that you sailed. Dead Aviator. Zoë Akins. LPS-1
It was a sergeant, old and gray. Picciola. "Orpheus C. Kerr." AA; PTA-2
It was a shabby house, lacking grace or dignity. The Cost. Mary Elizabeth Colman. NeTW
It was a starry night in June, the air was soft and still. The Battle of Bunker's Hill. Frederick S. Cozzens. PTA-2
It was a still autumnal day. We Walked among the Whispering Pines. John Henry Boner. AA
It was a stormy night in early spring. Easter Advent. John Henry Boner. NoCaPo
It was a summer [*or* summer's] evening. The Battle of Blenheim [*or* After Blenheim]. Robert Southey. BBV; BCEP; BeLS; BLV; BoChLi; BOHV; BTP; CG; EnLit; EnRP; EPN; ERP; EV-4; GN; GoTP; GTBS; GTBS-D; GTBS-W; GTSE; GTSL; HBV; HBVY; InMe; LPS-2; MCCG; MW; NeHB; OBRV; OnSP; OTPC; PC; PCN; PECK; PIAE; PIR; PoeMoYo; PYM; SoV; StVeCh (1940 ed.); TCEP; TOP; TreF; TrGrPo; TVSH; WBLP
It was a summer evening. "It Was a Famous Victory." Franklin P. Adams. LauV
It was a summer's night, a close warm night. Conclusion. Wordsworth. *Fr.* The Prelude. FaBoEn
It was a tall young oysterman lived by the river-side. The Ballad of the Oysterman. Oliver Wendell Holmes. AmPP; AnAmPo; AnNE; BOHV; EtS; FaFP; HBV; HBVY; LA; MCCG; MOAP; MoShBr; OnSP; PCD; PoeMoYo; PYM; TreFS; YT
It was a time of sadness, and my heart. The Changed Cross. Mrs. Charles Hobart. LPS-2
It was a time of trouble—executions. Chesspieces. Joseph Campbell. OxBI
It was a valorous music poured upon us. Parade. Harry Brown. TwAmPo
It was a violent time. Wheels, racks, and fires. A Mirror for Poets. Thom Gunn. NePoEA
It was a vision. In the drowsy gloom. Keats. *Fr.* Isabella. UnW
It was a waning crescent. July Dawn. Louise Bogan. NePoAm-2
It was a weakness of Voltaire's. Clerihews. E. C. Bentley. OnPP
It was a wild black nicht. In the Hedgeback. "Hugh MacDiarmid." NeBP
It was a Yule Day that Arthur lay in London. The Round Table. Layamon. *Fr.* The Brut. EnLi-1
It was about the deep of night. A Ballad of Christmas. Walter de la Mare. SDH; StJW
It was about the Martinmas time. Barbara Allan. *Unknown.* EnSB
It was after hearing the parish priest. Virgins. Francis Carlin. HBMV
It was all over now. The populace. Fishers in the Night. Beulah May. ChIP
It was always the time for a laugh, when the name. The "Lily's" Thanksgiving. Mrs. Dawson M. Phelps. TOAH
It was amusing on that antique grass. Recorders in Italy. Adrienne Cecile Rich. UnS
It Was an April Morning. Wordsworth. Poems on the Naming of Places, I. BPN; EmBrPo; ERP
(April Morning, An, *abr.*) RO
It was an artless Bandar, and he danced upon a pine. Divided Destinies. Kipling. BOHV
It was an early day of spring. Aleksey Konstantinovich Tolstoy, *tr. fr. Russian by* C. M. Bowra. BoR
It was an earthly place, but strangely made. To the Memory of Yale College. Phelps Putnam. AnAmPo; LA
It Was an English Ladye Bright. Sir Walter Scott. *Fr.* The Lay of the Last Minstrel, VI. ATP; BSV
(Song of Albert Graeme.) EmBrPo; EnRP; ERP
It was an hairy oubit, sae proud he crept alang. The Oubit. Charles Kingsley. BOHV; PoVP
It was an hill placed in an open plain. The Dance of the

Graces [*or* The Dance]. Spenser. *Fr.* The Faerie Queene, VI, 10. OBSC; RiBV; TrGrPo

It was an old house; and there seemed to live. Arthur Davison Ficke. *Fr.* Rue des Vents. UnW

It was an old, old, old, old lady. One, Two, Three. H. C. Bunner. FaPON; HBV; InP; MPB; OTPC; PCH; PRWS; PTA-2; RAR; TSW; TSWC; TVC; TVSH

It was April, blossoming spring. The Mother. Wilfred Campbell. CPG; OCL

It was, as if the devil of evil had got. García Lorca. Louis Dudek. BoCaPo (1948 ed.)

It was as if thunder took form upon. Woman Looking at a Vase of Flowers. Wallace Stevens. CrMA

It was at dinner as they sat. The Laird of Wariston (B *vers.*). *Unknown.* ESPB

It was at sundown that I saw it. Little Birch Tree. Sergey Ostrovoy. TrRV

It was beside the fire that I had lit. Yea. John Crowe Ransom. Two Sonnets, I. LO; LoPS

It was bold Sir Nilus. Nilus and Hillelille. *Unknown.* BoDaBa

It was brave young Parson Webster. The Fighting Parson. Henry Ames Blood. IDAH

It was broken. Then he commanded each of the warriors. The Battle of Maldon. *Unknown.* LiA

It was but now their sounding clamours sung. On the Crucifixion. Giles Fletcher. *Fr.* Christ's Victory and Triumph. OxBoCh

It was but some few nights ago. An Evening Walk in Spring. Arthur Hugh Clough. VLEP

It was but the lightest word of the King. The King. Mary Elizabeth Coleridge. OBVV

It was but yesterday, my love, thy little heart beat high. Lament of Anastasius. William Bourn Oliver Peabody. AA

It was by these men's valor that wide-lawned Tegea. Epigram for the Dead at Tegea. *Unknown.* WaaP

It was by yonder thorn I saw the fairy host. The Fairy Lover. Moireen Fox. AnIV

It was Captain Pierce of the *Lion* who strode the streets of London. The First Thanksgiving [Day]. Clinton Scollard. DD; MC; PAH

It was cause for laughter of a special brand. The Fish. Ralph Gustafson. BoCaPo (1948 ed.)

It was Chrismus Eve. I mind hit fu' a mighty gloomy day. Chrismus on the Plantation. Paul Laurence Dunbar. IHA

It was Christmas Eve in the year fourteen. Under the Snow. Robert Collyer. AA

It was dark and frosty, pain congealed into ice. Deportation. "M. J." TrJP

It was down in a lone green valley. The Jealous Lover. *Unknown.* ShS

It was down in old Joe's barroom. Gambler's Blues [*or* Those Gambler's Blues]. *Unknown.* AS; TrAS

It was down to Red River I came. The Skew-Ball Black. *Unknown.* CoSo; CSF

It was Earl Haldan's Daughter. Ballad of Earl Haldan's Daughter. Charles Kingsley. EV-5; GN; OTPC

It was early, early in the spring. The Croppy Boy. *Unknown.* AnIV; GTIV; OxBoLi; PoFr

It was early in the month of May. Barbery Allen. *Unknown.* ABS

It was early in the season in the spring of '63. Lumberjacks and Teamsters. *Unknown.* OuSiCo

It was early last September nigh to Framlin'am-on-Sea. Roundabouts and Swings. Patrick R. Chalmers. PCN; PoeT; ShGoBo

It was early Monday morning Willie Leonard arose. Willie Leonard or the Lake of Cold Finn. *Unknown.* BaBo

It was early one mornin' as I passed St. James Hospital. Cowboy's Lament (Iron Head's Version). *Unknown.* CoSo

It was early Sunday morning, in the year of sixty-four. *Kearsarge* and *Alabama.* *Unknown.* PAH

It was eight bells in the forenoon and hammocks running sleek. How They Do It. J. C. Squire. HBMV; InMe

It was eight bells ringing. The Fighting *Téméraire.* Sir Henry Newbolt. BBV (1923 ed.); HBV

It was Einar Tamberskelver. Einar Tamberskelver. Longfellow. *Fr.* Tales of a Wayside Inn: The Saga of King Olaf. AmPP (4th ed.); YT

It was far in the sameness of the wood. The Demiurge's Laugh. Robert Frost. OxBA

It was fifty years ago. The Fiftieth Birthday of Agassiz. Longfellow. ImOP; LPS-1; OBAV

It was for beauty like a fleet at sea. The Faun Tells of the Rout of the Amazons. T. Sturge Moore. AnFE

It was for you that the mountains shook at Sinai. Epitaph. *Unknown.* TrJP

It was frosty winter's season. Philomela's Second Ode. Robert Greene. *Fr.* Philomela, the Lady Fitzwater's Nightingale. OBSC; SiCE

It was good to lie in the Cove. Tide Trapped. Floris Clark McLaren. TwCaPo

It was her first sweet child, her heart's delight. Her First-born. Charles Tennyson Turner. MOAH; VA

It was in a pleasant deepô, sequestered from the rain. The Ballad of Charity. Charles Godfrey Leland. BOHV; InMe

It was in and about the Martinmas time. Barbara Allen [*or* Bonny Barbara Allan *or* Sir John Graeme and Barbara Allan]. *Unknown.* AWP; BaBo (A *vers.*); BoLiVe; CH; CoBE; EBSV; EM-1; EnLi-1 (1949 ed.); EnLit; ESPB; InPo; JAWP; LiTB; LiTL; LoEn; OuHeWo; OxBoLi; ReaPo; RiBV; TOP; TyEnPo; ViBoFo (A *vers.*); WBP

It was in October the woe began. The Fire of Frendraught (C *vers.*). *Unknown.* ESPB

It was in the days when Claverhouse. Jamie Douglas. *Unknown.* PTA-2

It was in the lovely month of May. The Troubled Soldier. *Unknown.* AS

It was in the merry, merry month of May. Sweet William. *Unknown.* OuSiCo

It was in the merry month of May. The Trail to Mexico. *Unknown.* AS; CSF; IHA

It was in the month of May. Bonny Barbara Allen (C *vers.*). *Unknown.* BaBo

It was in the prime. "George Eliot." *Fr.* The Spanish Gipsy. DiM

It was in the schooner *Ambition.* The Spring Trip of the Schooner *Ambition.* *Unknown.* ShS

It was in the town of Liverpool, all in the month of May. *Unknown.* LO

It was in the town of Waterford. The Wexford Girl. *Unknown.* ShS (*vers.* II); ViBoFo

It was in the town of Wexford. The Wexford Girl, *vers.* I. *Unknown.* ShS

It was in the Wars of the Roses white and red. The Bonnie House of Airlie (B *vers.*). *Unknown.* BaBo

It was in the year eighteen hundred and forty-nine. Sacramento, *vers.* I. *Unknown.* ShS

It was in the year of forty-four [*or* ninety-four]. The Whale. *Unknown.* AmSS; SG

It was intill a pleasant time. Earl [of] Mar's Daughter. *Unknown.* BaBo; CH; ESPB; GN; HBV; OBB; OnSP

It was kept out in the kitchen, and 'twas long and deep and wide. The Wood-Box. Joseph C. Lincoln. DDA; PTA-2

It was last Monday morning as I have heard them say. Lancashire Lads. *Unknown.* CoMu

It was last spring. Impression of Exile. Luis Cernuda. CoSP

It was late in mild October, and the long autumnal rain. The Huskers. Whittier. HOAH; IAP; MOAP; PTA-1; REAL

It was late in the night when the Squire came home. The Gipsy Laddie. *Unknown.* FaBoCh; LoGBV; OxBoLi; SiTL

It was laughing time, and the tall Giraffe. Laughing Time. William Jay Smith. FaPON

It was less than two thousand we numbered. With Corse at Allatoona. Samuel H. M. Byers. GA; PAH

It was Lilith the wife of Adam. Eden Bower. Dante Gabriel Rossetti. EmBrPo; PoVP

It was lonely in the zero dark, Admetus. Alcestis. Isabel Williams Verry. GoYe

It was long ago, but I seem to see. The Legend of the Christmas Rose. Florence Boyce Davis. PEDC

It was long ago, I yet remember. The Cross Speaks. *Unknown.* *Fr.* The Dream of the Rood. PoLi

It was long past the noon when I pushed back my chair. Through the Solitudes. George Francis Savage-Armstrong. TIP

It was Love that built the mountains. The Work of Love. Margaret E. Sangster. BLRP

It was many and many a year ago. Andrew M'Crie. Robert Fuller Murray. CenHV

It was many and many a year ago. Annabel Lee. Poe. AA; AmP; AmPo; AmPP; AnFE; APA; APW; AWP; BAP; BAV; BBV; BeLS; BLPA; BLV; BoLiVe; BTP; CaAE; CH; CoAnAm; CoBA; DDA; EtS; EV-5; FaFP; FaPON; GoTP; GTBS-W; GTSE; HBV; HBVY; HoPM; IAP; InPo; JAWP; LEAP; LiTA; LiTG; LiTL; LoEn; LoGBV; LoPo; LPS-1; MaC; MCCG; MOAP; MPB; MW; NeHB; NePA; OBAV; OBEV (1st ed.); OBVV; OtMeF; OTPC; OuHeWo; OxBA; PCD; PG; PIR; PoFS; PTA-2; PYM; SeCeV; SPP; StaSt; StPo; StVeCh; TCAP; TOP; TreF; TrGrPo; TVSH; ViBoPo; WBP; WBLP; YT

It was many and many a year ago/ In a district called E. C. The Cannibal Flea. Tom Hood. PA

It was many and many a year ago/ On an island near the sea. A Poe-'em of Passion. C. F. Lummis. BOHV

It was many and many a year ago/ In a dwelling down in town. Samuel Brown. Phoebe Cary. PA

It was May, the month of May. The Prisoner. *Unknown.* TeCS

It was maybe eight o'clock. Phyllis and the Philosopher. Josephine Pinckney. NP
It was much later in his life he rose. Muriel Rukeyser. *Fr.* Gibbs. ImOP
It Was My Blood. Hans Egon Holthusen, *tr. fr. German by* Herman Salinger. *Fr.* Lament for My Brother. TwGV
It was my choice, it was no chance. Sir Thomas Wyatt. SiPS
It Was My June. Daryl Duke. TwCaPo
It was my thirtieth year to heaven. Poem in October. Dylan Thomas. CoBMV; EnL; GTBS-W; LiTB; LiTM (rev. ed.); MaPo; MoVE; NeBP; OAEP (2d ed.); PoLFOT; PoRA; SeCePo
It was near evening, the room was cold. The Oath. Allen Tate. LiTM; OxBA
It was near the first cock-crowing. The Song of the Shepherds. Edwin Markham. SDH
It was neere a thicky shade. The Description of a Shepherd and His Wife. Robert Greene. *Fr.* Never Too Late. EV-1
It was night in the village of Nazareth. Annunciation Night. Katherine E. Conway. CAW; ChIP
It was night time! God, the Father Good. What the Devil Said. James Stephens. ChMo; CMP
It was night with the shine of the moon amid the smaller stars shining. Horace. Epodes, XV. LaP
It was no dull though lonely strand. Abertawy. Walter Savage Landor. EmBrPo
It was no enemy which did this wrong. The Sop. *Unknown.* StJW
It was not by vile loitering in ease. The Praise of Industry. James Thomson. *Fr.* The Castle of Indolence. OBEC
It was not death, for I stood up. Emily Dickinson. AtBAP; MAPA; MaPo; MoPo; NePA; PoE; TwAmPo
It was not death to me. The Kiss of God. G. A. Studdert-Kennedy. BLRP
It was not dying: everybody died. Losses. Randall Jarrell. AmP; CoBMV; FiMAP; MoVE; OxBA; UnPo (3d ed.); WaP
It Was Not Fate. William H. A. Moore. BANP
It was not God that told us. Le Secret Humain. Archibald MacLeish. ChMo; CMP
It Was Not in the Winter. Thomas Hood. *See* Time of Roses.
It was not like your great and gracious ways! Departure. Coventry Patmore. The Unknown Eros, I, viii. ACP; BMEP; CoBE; GTBS-D; GTML; GTSL; HBV; JKCP; LEAP; LO; OBEV; OBVV; PG (1945 ed.); PoLi; POTT; PoVP; SeCePo; VLEP
It was not long e're he perceiv'd the skies. Michael Drayton. *Fr.* The Moone-Calfe. PoEL-2
It was not meant for human eyes. The Combat. Edwin Muir. ChMP; GTBS-D; LiTB
It Was Not Strange. Esther Lloyd Hagg. PGD
It Was Not You. André Spire, *tr. fr. French by* Jethro Bithell. TrJP
"It was not you I came to please." The Dissemblers. Thomas Hardy. VLEP
It was not you I was waiting for. It Was Not You. André Spire. TrJP
It was not Zeus, I think, made this decree. The Undying Law. Sophocles. *Fr.* Antigone. OxBG
It was nothing but a rose I gave her. A Sigh. Harriet Prescott Spofford. AA; HBV; PR
It was of a sea captain that followed the sea. The Sea Captain. *Unknown.* ViBoFo
It was on a cold and stormy night. The Drunkard's Hell. *Unknown.* CSF
It was on a cold winter's night. When Poor Mary Came Wandering Home. *Unknown.* AS
It was on a May, on a midsummer's day. Sir Hugh; or, The Jew's Daughter (N *vers.*). *Unknown.* ESPB
It was on a merry time. Mother Goose. *See* 'Twas on a merry time.
It was on a Sunday morning, the church was far away. The Duff. David McKee Wright. AnNZ
It was on a Wednesday night, the moon was shining bright. Jesse James. *Unknown.* AmPP (3d ed.); APW; AS; BeLS; FaBoBe; PIAE; UnPo; YaD
It was on a Yule Day that Arthur in London lay. The Round Table. Layamon. *Fr.* The Brut. MeEV
It was on an evning sae saft and sae clear. The Broom of Cowdenknows (B *vers.*). *Unknown.* ESPB
It was on one Monday morning just about one o'clock. The *Titanic* (A *vers.*) *Unknown.* ViBoFo
It was on one munday morning in may. The Lover's Return. *Unknown.* ABS
It was on Saturday eve, in the gorgeous bright October. Autumn in the Highlands. Arthur Hugh Clough. GTSE
It was on the fourteenth day of January. Bold Daniels. *Unknown.* SoAmSa
It was on the Mount Cithaeron, in the pale and misty morn. William Wilkins. *Fr.* Actaeon. TIP
It was on the seventeenth, by break of day. The Battle of Bunker Hill. *Unknown.* PAH
It was on the western frontier. The Clown's Baby. "Margaret Vandegrift." SCC
It was one fine day in the month of May. The *River Lea.* Sam Peck. SoAmSa
It was one November—the second day. The Second of November. *Unknown.* SG
It was one summer's morning on the fourteenth day of May. The Mower. *Unknown.* CoMu
It was only a few short years ago. The Cowboy. *Unknown.* CoSo
It was only a tiny seed. Only a Little Thing. Mrs. M. P. Handy. PEOR; PoToHe
It was only my own voice that I had heard. This One Heartshaken. Sister Maris Stella. GoBC
It was only the clinging touch. The Child. George Edward Woodberry. Wild Eden, XXX. AA
It was our hard general's false treachery. Braddock's Defeat. *Unknown.* ABF
It was our King and our fair young Queen. Germand Gladensvend. *Unknown.* BoDaBa
It was our love's Gethsemane, and you wept. The Dark Memory. John Hall Wheelock. LiTL
It was our war-ship *Clampherdown.* The Ballad of the *Clampherdown.* Kipling. PECK; PIR
"It was our wedding-day." Possession. Bayard Taylor. LPS-1
It was peeping through the brambles that little wild white rose. The Wild White Rose. Ellen H. Willis. PTA-1
It was Private Blair, of the regulars, before dread El Caney. Private Blair of the Regulars. Clinton Scollard. PAH
It was roses, roses, all the way. The Patriot. Robert Browning. BHV; BPN; CBPC; EPN; EV-5; GTBS-D; MW; PCN; PoRA; PoVP; TCEP; TrGrPo; ViPP; VLEP
It was running down to the great Atlantic. The Stream. Lula Lowe Weeden. CDC
It was Saint Olaf the King so bold. Saint Olaf and the Trolls. *Unknown.* BoDaBa
It was six men of Indostan [*or* Hindostan]. The Blind Men and the Elephant. John Godfrey Saxe. AnNE; APW; BBV (1951 ed.); BLPA; BoTP; FaBoBe; GoTP; HBV; HBVY; MaC; MaRV; MW; NeHB; OTPC; PCD; PoeMoYo; PoToHe (new ed.); PreP; StPo; StVeCh (1940 ed.); TreF; TSW; TVSH; WBLP
It was so cold the skyline seemed to splinter. Contrast. Eileen Duggan. AnNZ
It was so dark along my little street. Light. Helen Welshimer. PraP
It was so mild a thing to see. The Friendship. Mark Van Doren. MOAP
It was something to see that their white was different. Holiday in Reality. Wallace Stevens. NePA; OxBA
It was sometime in the P.M. of the fall of '92. Doing Railroads for *The Rocky Mountain News.* Cy Warman. PoOW
It was surprising, after all the years. On Meeting a Lady. Charles L. O'Donnell. MM
It was taken a long time ago. The Verdict. Norman Cameron. SeCePo
It was that fierce contested field when [*or* where] Chickamauga lay. Thomas at Chickamauga. Kate Brownlee Sherwood. BIG; GA; PAH
It was the autumn of the year. Left Behind. Elizabeth Akers Allen. HBV; LPS-1
It was the barren Easter. The Barren Easter. Clinton Scollard. EOAH
It was the busy hour of 4. Spring Arithmetic. *Unknown.* FiBHP
It was the calm and silent night! A Christmas Hymn. Alfred Domett. BMEP; COAH; DD; GN; GTBS; HBV; OBVV; OTPC; TVSH; VA; WGRP
It Was the Cat. W. S. Gilbert. *Fr.* H.M.S. Pinafore. CIV
It was the charming month of May. Chloe. Burns. GN; HBV; OTPC
It was the cooling hour. Haidee. Byron. *Fr.* Don Juan, II. OBRV; ViBoPo
It was the day of the preparation. The First Easter. St. Luke, Bible, *N.T.* EOAH
It was the day the sun had overcast. Sonnet: Good Friday 1327. Petrarch. *Fr.* Sonnets to Laura: To Laura in Life. LyPI
It was the doughty Sverker. The Battle of Lena. *Unknown.* BoDaBa
It was the Earl from Orkney. Hildina. *Unknown.* PaOS
It was the earth that Dante trod. About an Allegory. Walter Conrad Arensberg. AnAmPo; LA
It was the fairy of the place. The Three Counsellors. "Æ." TIP
It was the flame. Genius. Gertrude MacGregor Moffat. CPG
It was the flowery season of the year. A Shipwrecked Youth Reaches Land. Luis de Góngora. *Fr.* The Solitudes. TeCS

It was the fruit on high. Soul's Kiss. Samuel Greenberg. LiTA
It was the good ship *Billycock,* with thirteen men aboard. The Ballad of [*or* to] the *Billycock.* Anthony C. Deane. ALV; BMEP; NeMA; TSW
It was the hour of night, when thus the Son. The Son of God in the Wilderness; His Dream. Milton. *Fr.* Paradise Regained, II. EV-2
It was the hour when all grows dark. Hymn to Passion. Kostes Palamas. MoGP
It was the King of Denmark. Niels Strangeson's Stone Tower. *Unknown.* BoDaBa
It was the little Isabel. Bell's Dream. Frederic Edward Weatherly. OTPC
It Was the Love of Life. Siegfried Sassoon. ChMo; CMP
It Was the Lovely Moon. John Freeman. POTE; TwCV
It was the middle of the spring. The Dance Ring. Eleanor Farjeon. DiM
It was the month in which the righteous maide. Prosopopoia; or, Mother Hubberd's Tale. Spenser. ReIE
It was the month of April. Flerida and Don Duardos. Gil Vicente. TeCS
It was the month of May. Far down the Beautiful River. Longfellow. *Fr.* Evangeline. BAV; IAP
It was the morning of that blessed day. Petrarch. *Fr.* Sonnets to Laura: To Laura in Life. PrPoCR
It was the morning of the first of May. Popular Songs of Tuscany. *Unknown.* AWP; JAWP; WBP
It was the pleasant harvest time. The Witch's Daughter. Whittier. *Fr.* Mabel Martin. PTA-2
It was the Queen of Bejerland. The Bridal of Queen Dagmar. *Unknown.* BoDaBa
It was the rainbow gave thee birth. The Kingfisher. W. H. Davies. BLA; CBE; GTBS-D; MoVE; OBEV (new ed.); POTE; POTT; PtOT; ShBV-2; TCPD; TSW; TSWC; TwCV
It was the schooner *Hesperus.* The Wreck of the *Hesperus.* Longfellow. AnNE; ATP (1935 ed.); BeLS; BoChLi (1939 ed.); CBOV; CG; CoBA; EtS; FaBoBe; FaFP; FaPON; GN; HBV; HBVY; IAP; MOAP; MW; NeHB; OnSP; OTPC; PAH; PECK; TCAP; TreF; TVSH; WBLP
It was the season, when through all the land. The Birds of Killingworth. Longfellow. *Fr.* Tales of a Wayside Inn. APW; IAP; OxBA; PCN
It was the sixth dawn. Still the *Fiat Lux.* Eve. Manuel M. Flores. AnMP
It was the soul of Karnaghan Buidhe. The Soul of Karnaghan Buidhe. James B. Dollard. JKCP
It was the stage driver's story, as he stood with his back to the wheelers. The Stage Driver's Story. *Unknown.* IHA
It was the Stately Southerner, that carried the Stripes and Stars. The Stately Southerner. *Unknown.* SoAmSa
It was the Sun that drew her up from the earth. Our Lady's Assumption. Sister Agnes. JKCP (1955 ed.)
It was the swain young Engel. Young Engel. *Unknown.* BoDaBa
It Was the Time of Roses. Thomas Hood. *See* Time of Roses.
It was the time of year. A Prehistoric Camp. Andrew Young. MoPW
It was the time when lilies blow. Lady Clare. Tennyson. AIDL; BeLS; FaPON; HBV; LoEn; MW; OTPC; PECK; StPo; StVeCh; TVSH
It was the time, when rest, soft sliding downe. Sonnet. Joachim du Bellay. *Fr.* Visions. AWP; OnPM
It was the twilight hour. An Old Man's Dreams. Eliza M. Sherman. PTA-2
It was the very noon of night: the stars above the fold. The Story of the Shepherd. *Unknown.* OHIP; SDH
It was the wild midnight. The Death of Leonidas. George Croly. BeLS; LPS-2
It was the wildest vanity. Interlude. Eileen Duggan. AnNZ
It was the winter wild[e]. Hymn. Milton. *Fr.* On the Morning of Christ's Nativity. BCEP; CBE; CBOV; COAH; EV-2; FiP; KN; MotAn; OBEV; OtMeF; StJW; WHA
It was the worthy Lord of Learne [*or* Lorn]. The Lord of Lorn and the False Steward. *Unknown.* ESPB; OBB
It was then night; the sounde and quiet slepe. Virgil. *Fr.* The Aeneid, IV. PoEL-1
It was then she struck—from behind. The Wanderer; Broadway. William Carlos Williams. TwAmPo
It was there on the hillside, no tall traveller's story. Pegasus. C. Day Lewis. AtBAP
It was this way. "Rumoresque Senum Severiorum." Marcus Argentarius. LiTW
It was three slim does and a ten tined buck in the bracken lay. The Revenge of Hamish. Sidney Lanier. AnEnPo; CoBA; HoPM; OnAP; PFE; PoEL-5; SPP; TCAP; TOP
It was too late for man. Early for God. Emily Dickinson. OnPM
It was too lonely for her there. The Impulse. Robert Frost. *Fr.* The Hill Wife. AWP; ChMo; CMP; IAP; LiTM; LO; MOAP; NePA; NP; SBMV
It was touching when I started. Aunt Nerissa's Muffin. Wallace Irwin. FiBHP
It was twenty years ago I saw the fox. The Fox. Phoebe Hesketh. HaMV
It was upon a Lammas night. The Rigs o' Barley. Burns. BSV; LiTB; LoBV; RO; ViBoPo
It was upon an April morn. The Heart of the Bruce. William Edmonstoune Aytoun. LPS-2
It was very early in the spring. The Croppy Boy. *Unknown.* AnIL
It was water I was trying to think of all the time. Appoggiatura. Donald Jeffrey Hayes. PoNe
It was when weather was Arabian I went. Allegory of the Adolescent and the Adult. George Barker. LiTB
It was worth the while of a boy to live. In the Days When the Cattle Ran. Hamlin Garland. MPB
It Was Wrong to Do This, Said the Angel. Stephen Crane. The Black Riders, LIV. AmP; LiTA; NePA
It was yesterday she roller-skated down. Eighteen. Sister Mary Honora. NePoAm-2
It was young David, lord of sheep and cattle. Five Smooth Stones. Stella Benson. MBP; MoBrPo (1942 ed.)
It was young Sir Karel. Sir Karel's Lykewake. *Unknown.* BoDaBa
It wasn't Ernest; it wasn't Scott. Song for the Squeeze-Box. Theodore Roethke. NePoAm
It waved not through an Eastern sky. The Palm Tree. Felicia Dorothea Hemans. ERP
It went many years. The Lockless Door. Robert Frost. PoLFOT
It were a double grief, if the true-hearted. Longfellow. *Fr.* Auf Wiedersehen. OQP; QP-2
It were as if the heavens. Moon-Night. Joseph von Eichendorff. AnGP
It were easiest to say, "The moon and lake." Sonnet. Muna Lee. NP
It were my soul's desire. The Soul's Desire. *Tr. by* Eleanor Hull. OxBI
It will always be like this. Departure Platform. Kenneth Allott. NeBP
It Will Be a Hard Winter. Olive Tilford Dargan. TBM
It will be all the same in a hundred years. In a Hundred Years. Elizabeth Doten. BLPA
It will be easy to love you when I am dead. Sonnet. Muna Lee. BAP; HBMV
It will be look'd [*or* looked] for, book[e], when some but see. To My Book[e]. Ben Jonson. MaPo; OAEP; Po; ReIE; SeCV-1; TuPP
It will not meet us where the shadows fall. "And the Life Everlasting." Percy Clough Ainsworth. MaRV
It worries me to beat the band. Ain't It Awful, Mabel? John Edward Hazzard. BOHV
It would be easier for me to come. Preface to Confessional. "C. H. W." CAG
It would have starved a gnat. Emily Dickinson. MoVE
It would never be morning, always evening. Memory of Brother Michael. Patrick Kavanagh. MoAB; OnYI; OxBI
It would take an angel's eye. Humming Bird. Robert P. Tristram Coffin. BLA
It wouldn't be so bad if he. In Extremis. Margaret Fishback. FiBHP
It wound through strange scarred hills, down cañons lone. The Old Santa Fé Trail. Richard Burton. PAH
It wus at our Augus' meetin'. The August Meeting. John Charles McNeill. NoCaPo (rev. ed.)
It wuz one day, I believe in May, when old Si Hubbard to me did say. Si Hubbard. *Unknown.* AS; IHA
Italia, Io Ti Saluto! Christina Rossetti. LO; OBVV; POTT; VLEP
Italia, mother of the souls of men. On the Monument Erected to Mazzini at Genoa [*or* Lines on the Monument of Giuseppe Mazzini]. Swinburne. BMEP; BPN; TCEP; VA; VLEP
Italia! Oh Italia! thou who hast. Italy. Vincenzo da Filicaja, *tr. by* Byron. AWP; OnPM; WoL
Italia, O Italia, upon whom. Sonnet. Vincenzo da Filicaja, *tr. by* Lorna de' Lucchi. PoFr
Italian boy that liked to play, An. Columbus. Annette Wynne. HH; MPB; TiPo
Italian Chest, An. Marjorie Allen Seiffert. HBMV (Lorenzo's Bas-Relief for a Florentine Chest.) NP
Italian Garden, An. Agnes Mary Frances Robinson. *See* Ah Me, Do You Remember Still.
Italian Husband, The, *sel.* Edward Ravenscroft. In Derision of a Country Life. SeCL
Italian in England, The. Robert Browning. BPN; EmBrPo; GEPC; OAEP; PCN; PoVP; ViPo; VLEP
Italian lakes, transparent blue. The Return. George Arthur Greene. TIP
Italian Lullaby. *Unknown, tr. fr. Italian.* FaPON
Italian Music in Dakota. Walt Whitman. AmP; TCAP

Italian Opera. James Miller. OBEC
"In days of old, when Englishmen were—men," *sel.* UnS
Italian Poppies. Joel Elias Spingarn. HBMV
Italian Rhapsody. Robert Underwood Johnson. HBV
Italian Song, An. Samuel Rogers. *See* Dear Is My Little Native Vale.
Italy. Byron. *Fr.* Beppo. OBRV; SeCePo
Italy. Vincenzo da Filicaja, *tr. fr. Italian by* Byron. AWP; WoL
(Italia! Oh Italia! *tr. by* Byron.) OnPM
(Sonnet: "Italia, O Italia," *tr. by* Lorna de' Lucchi.) PoFr
Italy, *sels.* Samuel Rogers.
Bologna, and Byron. OBRV
Descent, The. LPS-2
Ginevra. EV-3; LPS-3
Italy ("O Italy, how beautiful thou art!"). LPS-2
Jorasse. LPS-2
Naples. LPS-2
Rome. LPS-2
"There is, within three leagues and less of Padua." PtP
Venice, *abr.* LPS-2
Italy and Britain. Addison. *Fr.* A Letter from Italy. OBEC
Itch to Etch, The. Harold A. Larrabee. WhC
Ité. Ezra Pound. MAP; MoAB; MoAmPo; TwAmPo
Ite Domum Saturae, Venit Hesperus. Arthur Hugh Clough. BEL; BPN; EmBrPo; EnLit; EPN; PoVP; TCEP; VA; VLEP
(Home, Rose, and Home, Provence and La Palie.) EV-5
(Les Vaches.) OAEP; ViP
Item. E. E. Cummings. MoAB; MoAmPo
"Item: for fret and wrath and panic-fear." William Ellery Leonard. *Fr.* Two Lives, Pt. III. MOAP
"Item: not only a bastard Hamlet,—nay." William Ellery Leonard. *Fr.* Two Lives, Pt. III. MOAP
"Item: you would not meet the issue." William Ellery Leonard. *Fr.* Two Lives, Pt. III. MOAP
Iter Supremum. Arthur Sherburne Hardy. AA; LBAP
Ithaca. C. P. Cavafy, *tr. fr. Modern Greek.* LiTW, *tr. by* Edward Fenton; MoGP, *tr. by* Rae Dalven
Ithaca. Oscar Levertin, *tr. fr. Swedish by* Charles W. Stork. AnSL
'Ithin the woodlands flow'ry gleaded. Linden Lea. William Barnes. GTSE
Itiskit, Itaskit, *with music. Unknown.* TrAS
(Kitty, Kitty Casket, *diff. vers., with music.*) OuSiCo
(Tisket, a Tasket, A.) RIS
It's a certain voice, it's the sound. The Homeland. Emile Cammaerts. PoFr
It's a comfort to me in life's battle. The Little Child's Faith. Louis E. Thayer. PoToHe
It's a Far, Far Cry. Patrick MacGill. HBMV; VOD
It's a Fib. "Elspeth." ALV
It's a Gay Old World. *Unknown.* FaFP
It's a good day I saw again those I will not forget. To Pablo Picasso. Paul Eluard. MiCF
It's a great separation my friends they have caused me. Adieu to Bon County. *Unknown.* ABF
It's a lang time yet till the kye gae hame. The Herd Laddie. Alexander Smart. EBSV
It's a lonely road through bogland to the lake at Carrowmore. Carrowmore [*or* The Gates of Dreamland]. "Æ." BEL; ChMo; CMP; HBMV; HBV
It's a Long Way. William Stanley Braithwaite. GoSl
It's a mournful tune the rain is making. Spinster Song. Virginia Lyne Tunstall. HBMV
It's a Queer Time. Robert Graves. BMEP; MBP; MoBrPo; MCCG; MoAB; NeMA
It's a *rum*—/ Ba band. "And Now . . ." J. B. Boothroyd. FiBHP
It's a strange courage. El Hombre. William Carlos Williams. LiTA
It's a strange courage. Nuances of a Theme by Williams. Wallace Stevens. LiTA
It's a sunny pleasant anchorage, is Kingdom Come. Port of Many Ships. John Masefield. OBMV
It's a very odd thing. Miss T. Walter de la Mare. CenHV; FaBoBe; GFA; GoBP; MoShBr; MPB (1956 ed.); PoRh; RAR; SUS; TiPo; TSW; TSWC
"It's a very warm day," observed Billy. Limerick. Tudor Jenks. BOHV
It's a warm wind, the west wind, full of birds' cries. The West Wind. John Masefield. BEL; ChMo; CMP; CV; EnLi-2 (1949 ed.); EnLit; FaFP; GTBS-W; GTSL; InP; LiTB; LiTM; MBP; MoAB; MoBrPo; PG; POT; PoTo; TOP; TreF; TSW; TSWC; VOD
It's a wicked night and the sea is wild. The Legend of Ghost Lagoon. Joseph Schull. HeT
It's a wild night for a soul to go. The Journey. L. Le Mesurier. VOD
Its Ain Drap o' Dew. James Ballantine. HBV
It's all a trick, quite easy when you know it. Villanelle. W. W. Skeat. FiBHP; SiTL
It's all very well to write reviews. Lasca. Frank Desprez. BLPA; HBV; PTA-1; SCC
It's autumn in the country I remember. Mnemosyne. Trumbull Stickney. AnFE; CoAnAm; CrMA; LiTA; MOAP; OxBA; TwAmPo; ViBoPo (1958 ed.)
It's awf'lly bad luck on Diana. Hunter Trials. John Betjeman. FiBHP
It's better if at the Duke's court I am fed. Satires: In the Service of the Duke. Ariosto. LyPI
Its blossoms dried, its glories brief. Midsummer. Hermann Hesse. LiTW
Its cloven hoofprint on the sand. How to Catch Unicorns. William Rose Benét. CV; HBMV; TSW
It's co-existence. A Message for the Nations of the World. Bertrand Russell. SiTL
It's cold and raw the north winds blow. The Maid That Sold Her Barley. *Unknown.* OnYI
"It's cold," said the cricket. Halloween Concert. Aileen Fisher. SiSoSe
It's cold, says Crean at the tiller. Douglas Stewart. *Fr.* Worsley Enchanted. NeLNL
It's coming, boys. In Trust. Mary Mapes Dodge. PPL; SiSoSe
Its cry is mournful. Tanka: The Cry of the Crane. Tsurayuki. InP
It's cuddle-me-time by the nursery clock. A Rock-a-bye Song. Helen Wing. GFA
It's dark, child, snatcher of sparks! Rondel. Tristan Corbière. AnFP
It's doing your job the best you can. Success [*or* That's Success]. Berton Braley. PoToHe; WBLP
It's Dowie in the Hint o' Hairst. Hew Ainslie. *Fr.* Mary. EBSV
It's dreadfully monotonous. Thoughts in School. Dorothy M. Young. DDA
It's easy to die 'mid the world's applause. The Greater Glory. Myra Brooks Welch. MaRV
It's easy to fight when everything's right. Carry On! Robert W. Service. HBV; MaRV
It's easy to talk of the patience of Job. Humph! Job had nothin' to try him! The Inventor's Wife. Mrs. E. T. Corbett. PTA-2
Its edges foamed with amethyst and rose. The Great Breath. "Æ." CBOV; CMP; EPN; EPP; GTIV; LBBV; MBP; MoBrPo; OBEV; OBMV; OxBI; PFE; VA; WGRP; WHA
Its eyes are gray. A Sketch from the Life. Arthur Guiterman. BOHV
It's far I must be going. Via Longa. Patrick McDonough. HBMV
It's farewell to the drawing-room's civilized cry. Song for the New Year. W. H. Auden. EnLi-2 (1949 ed.)
It's fifty miles to Sittingen's Rocks. Prince Robert (B *vers.*). *Unknown.* ESPB
It's Fine Today. Douglas Malloch. BLPA
("Ain't It Fine Today!") WBLP
It's foolish to bring money. Spring Market. Louise Driscoll. HBMV; HBVY; NLK
It's foolish to mourn for a dog, I guess. Lines for "Tops." "Jazbo of Old Dubuque." AlBD
Its former green is blue and thin. The Garden Seat. Thomas Hardy. TriL
It's forty in the shade to-day, the sprouting eaves declare. Pan in Vermont. Kipling. ViP; WhC
It's four o'clock, and I shan't sleep till morning. Snowflake. Stepan Shchipachev. BoRS
Its friendship and its carelessness. The Path to the Woods. Madison Cawein. LBMV
It's Fun to Be a Pup. James J. Montague. AlBD
It's fun to clean house. I Like House Cleaning. Dorothy Brown Thompson. BrR; FaPON
It's fun to go out and buy new shoes to wear. Mary Ann Hoberman. TiPo (1959 ed.)
Its gates are griffin-guarded gates. The Sorceress of the Moon. William Rose Benét. DaM
Its gaze filled my abyss, its gaze melted. Pain. Enrique González Martinez. AnMP
It's gettin' bits o' posies. Sweethearts. Mary Gilmore. BoAu
It's going to come out all right—do you know? Caboose Thoughts. Carl Sandburg. AnAmPo; ChMo; CMP; IAP; LA; OnAP
It's good to be back. In the Garden. Ilo Orleans. RIS
It's good to take the dusty road. Daddy. Robert Freeman. FAOV
It's Good Up Here. "Anna Akhmatova," *tr. fr. Russian by* Jack Lindsay. RuPo
It's great to be alive and be. It's Simply Great. Sidney Warren Mase. PoToHe
It's hair and dress, framing old portrait faces. Eternal Contour. Florida Watts Smyth. GoYe
It's hard for a dead man to play at passion. Dance of Death. Aleksandr Blok. BoRS

It's Hard on We Po' Farmers, *with music.* *Unknown.* OuSiCo
"It's hard to be without a wage," I said. Unemployed. Ralph Cheyney. ChIP
It's hard to breathe in a tenement hall. Song of a Factory Girl. Marya Zaturenska. HBMV; NP
It's hard to know if you're alive or dead. It's a Queer Time. Robert Graves. BMEP; MBP; MCCG; MoAB; MoBrPo; NeMA
It's hard to think. To a Human Skeleton. Richard Armour. WhC
It's home for me and a snug roof-tree. Road Song. James Stuart Montgomery. NLK
It's in Bolton Hall, and the clock strikes one. The Lay of St. Cuthbert. "Thomas Ingoldsby." OtMeF
It's in Connacht in Munster that yourself might travel wide. The Kerry Cow. Winifred M. Letts. MW; TSW; TSWC
It's Jim Farrow and John Farrow and little Simon, too. Jim Farrow. *Unknown.* CoSo; CSF
It's jolly to play at make-believe. The Bowman. Hugh Chesterman. MW
It's just because I like you that I'm sellin'. Horse-Chestnut Tree. Witter Bynner. DDA
It's just the little homely things. Little Things. *Unknown.* PoToHe (new ed.)
It's kind of you to let me have my hat. Hattage. A. P. Herbert. FiBHP
It's Lamkin was a mason good. Lamkin. *Unknown.* BaBo (A *vers.*); ESPB; OBB; ViBoFo
Its legs unlooping. The Skiff. Al-Munsafi. MooP
It's Little for Glory I Care. Charles James Lever. *Fr.* Charles O'Malley, the Irish Dragoon. OnYI (Mickey Free's Song.) ALV
It's little I care what path I take. Departure. Edna St. Vincent Millay. MAP; MoAmPo
It's Little Joe, the wrangler. Little Joe, the Wrangler. *At. to* N. Howard Thorp. CoSo; CSF
It's lonely in lodgings above the street. A Lonely Man. Agnes Lee. NP
Its masts of might, its sails so free. The Wreck. John Ruskin. VA
It's Me, O Lord. *Unknown.* BoAN-1, *with music;* OIF
"It's mending worse," he said. Old Man at a Cricket Match. Norman Nicholson. HaMV
It's Midsummer Day. Haytime. Irene F. Pawsey. BoTP
It's more than just an easy word for casual good-bye. Aloha Oe. Don Blanding. PoToHe (new ed.)
It's my fear that my wake won't be quiet. A Connachtman. Padraic Colum. LBBV
Its Name Is Known. Daniel Lawrence Kelleher. NeIP
"It's narrow, narrow, make [*or* mak] your bed." Fair Annie. *Unknown.* AnFE; BaBo (A *vers.*); BSV; EBSV; ESPB; OBB; ViBoFo (A *vers.*)
It's no aye rainin' on the misty Achils. Hughie Seeks to Console a Brother Shepherd, Over-grieving for the Loss of His Son. James Logie Robertson. BSV
It's no go the merry-go-round [*or* merrygoround], it's no go the rickshaw. Bagpipe Music. Louis MacNeice. ExPo; LiTB; LiTM; OAEP (2d ed.); OnYI; PoE; ReaPo; SeCePo; SeCeV; SiTL; ViBoPo (1958 ed.)
It's no joke at all, I'm not that sort of poet. The Confession. Wen Yi-tuo. ChTr; LiTW
It's No Use Raising a Shout. W. H. Auden. HoPM; LiTM; OBMV; ReMP; TwCV
It's noon when "Thirty-five" is due. The Engineers' Making Love. Robert J. Burdette. PTA-1
It's not a bit windy. Toadstools. Elizabeth Fleming. BoTP
It's not a case of poisoned cup. Martial, *tr. fr. Latin by* "T. W. M." Epigrams, VI, 19. LaP
It's not adultery, the lawyers say. Stop, Science—Stop! A. P. Herbert. FiBHP
It's not so much what you say. The Tone of Voice. *Unknown.* PoToHe (new ed.)
It's not so much your presence that I miss. Regret. Winifred Kohn. CAG
It's not the age,/ Disease, or accident. Apologia. David Gascoyne. ChMP
It's not the thickened midriff that I mind. So This Is Middle Age! Francis Whiting Hatch. WhC
It's not the tunes that it can play. The Old Music Box. Rachel Field. BoChLi
It's not very far to the edge of town. Adventure. Harry Behn. TiPo (1959 ed.)
It's of a blind beggar, and he lost his sight. The Blind Beggar of Bednall (Bethnal) Green. *Unknown.* BaBo
It's of a brisk young butcher, as I have heard 'em say. Leicester Chambermaid. *Unknown.* CoMu
It's of a fair young creature that dwelt by the sea side. Mary on the Silvery Tide. *Unknown.* ShS
It's of a famous American ship, for New York we are bound. The *Shenandoah.* *Unknown.* SoAmSa
It's of a famous [*or* fearless] highway-man a story I will [*or* now I'll] tell. Brennan on the Moor. *Unknown.* OnYI; ViBoFo
It's of a rich squire in Bristol doth dwell. Squire and Milkmaid; or, Blackberry Fold. *Unknown.* CoMu
It's of a young lord o the Hielands. Lizie Lindsay (B *vers.*). *Unknown.* ESPB
It's of those Texas cowboys a story I'll tell. The Lone Buffalo Hunter [*or* The Texas Cowboys]. *Unknown.* CoSo; CSF
It's once I courted as pretty a lass. *Unknown.* OxNR
"It's only a little grave," they said. The Little Grave. *Unknown.* PEOR
It's only a tale of a life-boat, of the dying and the dead. The Women of Mumbles Head. Clement Scott. PTA-2
It's only we, Grimalkin, both fond and fancy free. The Ride to Cherokee. Amelia Walstein Carpenter. AA
It's Over a (See Just). E. E. Cummings. MoPW; OxBA
It's pleasant lazily to pass. Twelve Blades of Grass. Mikhail Isakovsky. RuPo
Its presence is not impeded by visible form. The Human Mind. Ai Shih-te. TrJP
It's primrose petals for a gown. The Fairy Frock. Katharine Morse. UTS
It's queer about my Uncle Frank. Uncle Frank. Monica Shannon. GaP
"It's queer," she said, "I see the light." The Maid-Servant at the Inn. Dorothy Parker. QS; StJW
Its quick soft silver bell beating, beating. Auto Wreck. Karl Shapiro. LiTM; MiAP; MoVE; NePA; ReMP
It's quiet in Hell just now, it's very tame. Lament of an Idle Demon. R. P. Lister. FiBHP
It's quite the vogue to own a dog. Ownership. Isla Paschal Richardson. AIBD
It's rainin'. Weet's the gairden sod. The Blast—1875. Robert Louis Stevenson. POTT
It's Raining, It's Pouring. *Unknown.* OxNR; TrAS, *with music*
It's raining, it's raining. *Unknown.* OxNR
It's rare to see the morning breeze. The Ingle-Side. Hew Ainslie. HBV; OTPC (1923 ed.)
It's real fall on the one-night stands. The Call of the Road. Florence Nash. DDA
It's really almost past belief. Harriet and the Matches. Heinrich Hoffmann. RIS
It's right to have a little maid. Song against Servants. Gertrude Jane Codd. JKCP (1926 ed.)
Its roof among the stars projected. Phantasus. Arno Holz. AWP; JAWP; WBP
It's seldom wise to generalize. Homage to Texas. Robert Graves. LiTB
It's Simply Great. Sidney Warren Mase. PoToHe
It's singin' in an' out. Marri'd. Mary Gilmore. BoAu
It's so cold and shiny till the birds can't hardly sing. Lines from the Blues. *Unknown.* OuSiCo
It's something to be born at sea, as I. Poe's Mother. Beatrice Ravenel. LS
It's sport for gentlemen, but rage and pain. Dicing. Agathias Scholasticus. OxBG
It's spring, I leave a street where poplars are astonished. Spring. Boris Pasternak. BoRS
It's spring. The gentle breezes rustle. In Spring. Georg Sannikov. BoRS
It's springtime in Donegal. Springtime in Donegal. Mabel Rose Stevenson. StVeCh
It's step her to your weev'ly wheat. Weevily Wheat. *Unknown.* AS
"It's strange," my mother said, "to think." My Mother's House. Eunice Tietjens. HBMV; NP; TBM
It's such a little thing to weep. Emily Dickinson. AmP; AmPP; TwP
It's ten years ago today you turned me out o' doors. The Winged Horse. Hilaire Belloc. AIDL
It's the anarchy of poverty. The Poor. William Carlos Williams. MoAB; MoAmPo; NeMA
It's the long road to Guinea. Guinea. Jacques Roumain. AnCL; PoNe
It's the mixture of peasantry. Peasant. Alfred Kreymborg. MAP
It's the spring. Pastoral. W. E. Henley. *Fr.* In Hospital. Po
It's the Syme the Whole World Over. *Unknown.* AS, *with music;* TrAS, *with music;* TreFS (It's the Syme the Wide World Over.) BeLS
It's there you'll see confectioners with sugar sticks and dainties. Galway Races. *Unknown.* GTIV; OxBoLi
It's Three No Trumps. Guy Innes. FiBHP
It's time that I began/ the tale of Lenin. The Death of Lenin. Vladimir Mayakovsky. *Fr.* Vladimir Ilyich-Lenin. RuPo
It's time to make love. Douse the glim. Limberick. Conrad Aiken. FiBHP; SiTL
It's time to say farewell. My horse I stay. Parting. Wang Wei. OnPM

It's Tuesday morning, Cook, my dear. Backstair Ballad. David McCord. BOHV
It's Two o'Clock. Vladimir Mayakovsky, *tr. fr. Russian by* Babette Deutsch. TrRV
Its unobtrusive force leaves you so free. The Catholic Faith. Kenelm H. Digby. CAW
It's very hard to be polite. Under-the-Table Manners. *Unknown.* DDA
It's very nice to think of how. A Kitten's Thought. Oliver Herford. RIS
It's Very Unwise to Kill the Goose. Philip H. Rhinelander. WhC
It's we two, it's we two, it's we two for aye. Like a Laverock in the Lift. Jean Ingelow. HBV; LPS-1
Its wingéd lion stands up straight to hide. Venice. Howard Moss. MoAB
It's wiser being good than bad. Robert Browning. *Fr.* Apparent Failure. BMEP; MaRV; PC
It's wonderful dogs they're breeding now. Tim, an Irish Terrier. Winifred M. Letts. TVSH
Itt rely is ridikkelus. Bobby's First Poem. Norman Gale. FiBHP
'Ittle Touzle Head. Ray Garfield Dandridge. BANP
Itylus. Swinburne. BLA; ChTr; EmBrPo; EnLi-2; EPP; EV-5; GTBS; GTSL; HBV; MBP; OBEV (1st ed.); PIR; POTT; PoVP; ReaPo; ViPo; ViPP; VLEP; WHA
Iulus. Eleanor Glenn Wallis. NePoAm-2
Ivan. G. D. Martineau. NeTW
Ivanhoe, *sels.* Sir Walter Scott.
  Anna-Marie, Love, Up Is the Sun, *fr. ch.* 40. EmBrPo; ViBoPo
  Barefooted Friar, The, *fr. ch.* 17. EmBrPo; EV-4
  Rebecca's Hymn, *fr. ch.* 40. BPN; EmBrPo; EnRP; LPS-2
  ("When Israel . . .") ViBoPo
I've a friend, over the sea. Time's Revenges. Robert Browning. BPN; GEPC; PoVP; PR; VLEP
I've a humble little motto. Keep a-Pluggin' Away. Paul Laurence Dunbar. MCCG
I've a pal called Billy Peg-Leg, with one leg a wood leg. Peg-Leg's Fiddle [*or* Billy Peg-Leg's Fiddle]. Bill Adams. BBV; EtS; MW
I've a secret in my heart, sweet Marie. Sweet Marie. Cy Warman. TreFS
I've aften wished for Burns's pen. John Kearsley Mitchell. *Fr.* To N. Chapman, M.D. PoP
I've an excellent scheme, if you will but believe it. Communism? Aristophanes. *Fr.* The Ecclesiazusae. GrR
I've an ingle, shady ingle, near a dusky bosky dingle. Midsummer Jingle. Newman Levy. WhC
I've beat my way wherever any winds have blown. Once You Git the Habit [*or* The Habit]. *At. to* Berton Braley. CoSo; CSF
I've been a moonshiner for sev'nteen long years. Kentucky Moonshiner. *Unknown.* AS; TrAS
I've been along the quarry road. Shells in Rock. Elizabeth Madox Roberts. AnAmPo; LA
I've been in love for long. In Love for Long. Edwin Muir. GTBS-W; LiTM (rev. ed.)
I've been sortin' the mail at Jonesville fer going on fifteen year. Sortin' the Mail. W. Scott Stranahan. DDA
I've been thinkin' of it over, an' it 'pears to me to-day. Reunited. Frank L. Stanton. MDAH
I've been thinking, sadly thinking. The Cogitative Bass Crank. Joseph B. Cawthorn. DDA
I've been thinking today. Rounded Up in Glory. *Unknown.* CoSo
I've been to California, and I haven't got a dime. Alas! *Unknown.* IHA
I've been to Palestine. John Brown. Vachel Lindsay. *Fr.* The Booker Washington Trilogy. AnAmPo; LA; MAP; MoAmPo; NP; TBM; TriL
I've been to Red Hoss Mountain, where Field once dwelt and wrote. Old Red Hoss Mountain. Cy Warman. PoOW
I've been travlin' all de day. Ride On, Moses. *Unknown.* BoAN-1
I've been trying to fashion a wifely ideal. A Plea for Trigany. Sir Owen Seaman. BOHV
I've been upon the prairie. Bronc Peeler's Song. *Unknown.* CoSo; CSF
I've been wandering, listening for a song. The Singer's Quest. Odell Shepard. NLK
I've Been Workin' on the Railroad. *Unknown.* FaFP; TreF
I've borne full many a sorrow, I've suffered many a loss. The Heaviest Cross of All. Katherine Eleanor Conway. AA; JKCP
I've brought you nuts and hops. October. Christina Rossetti. *Fr.* The Months; a Pageant. BoTP
I've built a castle in the sand. Castles in the Sand. Dorothy Baker. BoTP
I've built my monument, but not with hands I made it. Monument. Pushkin. BoR
I've busted bronchos off and on. The Bronc That Wouldn't Bust. *Unknown.* SCC
I've closed my door and I am all alone. Pax Beata. Mary Rachel Norris. VOD
I've come by the May-tree all times o' the year. The May Tree. William Barnes. LiTB; LoBV
I've come from the street, Spring, where the poplar stands. Spring. Boris Pasternak. TrRV
I've come to give you fruit from my orchard. The Crossed Apple. Louise Bogan. NP
I've done a very frightful thing. The Liar. Rue Carpenter. RIS
I've dug up all my garden. Sowing Seeds. Ursula Cornwall. BoTP
I've eaten bitter bread. Whalin' up the Lachlan. Louis Esson. NeLNL
I've entered every gateway. The Little Samaritan. Eleanor Halbrook Zimmerman. AlBD
I've explained to St. Peter I'd rather stay here. Message from a Little Ghost. Muriel Whitehead Jarvis. DDA
I've forgotten what day, but late in December. The Basilisk. Philip Child. CaP
I've found a Friend, O such a Friend! James G. Small. OIF
I've found my bonny babe a nest. An Irish Lullaby. Alfred Perceval Graves. BOL; HBV
I've found the place where Darkness goes. The Railway Tunnel. Queenie Scott-Hopper. TVC; TVSH
I've given thee wings shall waft thee forth with ease. Immortality Conferred in Vain. Theognis. GrL; LiTW; OxBG
I've gone about for years I find. Dedication. Edward Salisbury Field. *Fr.* The Quest. MOAH
I've got a barrow; it's a very small. My Barrow. Elizabeth Fleming. GFA
I've got a bow and arrow. Robin Hood. Rachel MacAndrew. BoTP
I've Got a Dog. Ethel M. Kelley. AlBD; PCD
I've got a letter, parson, from my son away out West. Billy, He's in Trouble [*or* Bill's in the Legislature]. James Barton Adams. DDA; PTA-2; YaD
I've got a lovely home. Best of All. J. M. Westrup. BoTP
I've got a mule, her name is Sal. The Erie Canal [*or* Low Bridge, Everybody Down]. William S. Allen. ABF; AS; IHA; TrAS
I've Got a New Book from My Grandfather Hyde. Leroy F. Jackson. BrR; FaPON; SiSoSe
I've got a pony. The Pony. Rachel MacAndrew. BoTP
I've Got a Rocket. *Unknown.* SiSoSe; TiPo (1959 ed.)
I've got a sister nine feet tall. 'Way Down in Cuba. *Unknown.* AmSS
I've Got the Giggles Today. A. P. Herbert. FiBHP
I've grown a goitre by dwelling in this den. To Giovanni da Pistoia on the Painting of the Sistine Chapel, 1509. Michelangelo. LyPI
I've had my share of pastime, and I've done my share of toil. The Sick Stockrider. Adam Lindsay Gordon. OtMeF
I've heard in old times that a sage used to say. Let Us Be Happy as Long as We Can. Joseph Stansbury. IAP
I've heard it said that Sir Barnabas Beer. Endurance Test. Dacre Balsdon. FiBHP
I've heard many times. *Unknown. Fr.* Four Short Poems. LyMA
I've heard the sea upon the troubled rocks. The Man Whom the Sea Kept Awake. Robert Bly. NePoEA
I've Heard Them Lilting at Loom and Belting. C. Day Lewis. OBMV; TwCV
I've heard them lilting at our ewe [*or* yowe]-milking. The Flowers of the Forest [*or* A Lament for Flodden]. Jane Elliot. BSV; CH; EBSV; EiPP; EPP; EV-3; FaBoCh; GoTS; GTBS; GTBS-D; GTBS-W; GTSE; GTSL; HBV; LiTG; OBEC; OBEV; ShBV-3; ViBoPo
I've just got here, through Paris, from the sunny southern shore. The Man Who Broke the Bank at Monte Carlo. Fred Gilbert. TreF
I've kept a haughty heart thro' grief and mirth. To My Mother. Heine. AWP; JAWP; WBP
I've kissed thee, sweetheart, in a dream at least. Sleep. Théophile de Viau. AWP
"I've known a cherry tree to blossom full." Unto the End. Jessie B. Rittenhouse. MuM
I've known a Heaven like a tent. Emily Dickinson. BLV; BoLiVe
I've known ere now an interfering branch. The Axe-Helve. Robert Frost. AmPo; CoV; OxBA
I've known rivers. The Negro Speaks of Rivers. Langston Hughes. BANP; CaAE; CDC; GoSl; PoeMoYo; PoNe
I've known the spring in England. The Fields o' Ballyclare. Denis A. McCarthy. CV
I've landed today in a peaceful nook. Literary Gruk. Piet Hein. LiTW
I've learned a precious secret. The Secret of the Cross. M. J. Clarkson. BePJ
I've learned to say it carelessly. The Name. Williamina Parrish. AV
I've Learned to Sing. Georgia Douglas Johnson. GoSl

I've left my own old home of homes. John Clare. *Fr.* The Flitting. EV-4; OBRV
I've listened now a full half hour. The Corn-Crake. David Gray. EBSV
I've lived my life in careless ease. Epitaph on Himself. Mathurin Regnier. LiTW
I've lived to bury my desires. Pushkin, *tr. fr. Russian by* Maurice Baring. BoR
(Elegy: "Outlived are all my aspirations," *tr. by* Sir Cecil Kisch.) WaL
I've loops o' string in the place of buttons. The Traveller. Cicely Fox Smith. POT; PoTo
I've Lost My ——. Harry Cholmondeley Pennell. CenHV
I've love songs of my springtime pride. Dedication. Holger Drachmann. BoDS
I've never been to London. Fifty Acres. James Larkin Pearson. DDA; NoCaPo
I've never ceased to curse the day I signed. The Old Huntsman. Siegfried Sassoon. ChMo; CMP
I've never known a dog to wag. The Dog. *Unknown.* AlBD; WBLP
I've never travelled for more'n a day. On the Quay. John Joy Bell. HBV
I've not sung of my country. To My Country. "Rachel." LiTW
I've not the gold of Gyges. To Himself. Anacreon. LiTW
I've not the heart to pick the violets. Naojo, *tr. fr. Japanese by* Lois J. Erickson. SoLD
I've noticed how the woolly lamb. All Wool. Abbie Farwell Brown. TiPo (1952 ed.)
I've oft been asked by prosing souls. A Reason Fair to Fill My Glass. Charles Morris. HBV
I've oft been told by learned friars. An Argument. Thomas Moore. EnLoPo
I've often heard my mother say. The Unknown Color. Countee Cullen. FaPON; GoSl
I've often thought that headstrong youths. The Periwinkle Girl. W. S. Gilbert. MBP
I've paid for your sickest fancies; I've humoured your crackedest whim. The *Mary Gloster.* Kipling. BeLS; BPN; OtMeF
I've Plucked the Berry. William Motherwell. *See* Sing On, Blithe Bird!
I've put some/ Ashes in my sweet papa's bed. A Group of Negro Songs. W. C. Handy. NAMP
I've rambled and gambled all my money away. Rabble Soldier. *Unknown.* AS
I've Rambled This Country Both Earlye and Late, *with music.* *Unknown.* OuSiCo
I've reached the land of corn and wine. Edgar Page. OlF
I've said goodbye to the three black kittens. First Departure. Frances Frost. SiSoSe
I've sailed among the Yankees, the Spaniards and Chinees. The Sailor's Way. *Unknown.* ShS
I've Searched the Year. Konstantin Simonov, *tr. fr. Russian by* Jack Lindsay. RuPo
I've seen a dying eye. Emily Dickinson. CoV; InPo; MAPA; MOAP; NePA; PoEL-5; TwAmPo
(Dying Eye, A.) OnPM
I've seen caravans/ Going to the fair! Caravans. Irene Thompson. BoTP
I've seen her, I've seen her. Vision. Rose Fyleman. PCH
I've seen her pass with eyes upon the road. Muy Vieja Mexicana [*or* Una Anciana Mexicana]. Alice Corbin. NP; OBAV; SBMV
I've seen one flying saucer. Only when. Go Fly a Saucer. David McCord. FaPON; ImOP
I've seen the moonbeam's shining light. Life. *Unknown.* PoToHe
I've seen the smiling/ Of fortune beguiling. The Flowers of the Forest. Alison Cockburn. BSV; EBSV; OBEC
I've seen the Thousand Islands. Tadoussac. Charles Bancroft. BLPA
I've seen them in the morning light. Red Poppies in the Corn. W. Campbell Galbraith. POT
I've seen this dell in July's shine. The Outcast Mother. Emily Brontë. EmBrPo
I've studied all the lore of separation. Tristia. Osip Mandelstam. BoR
I've swum the Colorado where she runs close down to hell. The Insult. *Unknown.* SCC
I've taken my fun where I've found it. The Ladies. Kipling. ALV; BPN; EnLit; MBP; MoBrPo; ViP; ViPP
I've taught me other tongues—and in strange eyes. To England. Byron. *Fr.* Childe Harold's Pilgrimage, IV. WHA
I've taught thee love's sweet lesson o'er. Song [*or* Romanzo to Sylvia]. George Darley. *Fr.* Sylvia; or, The May Queen. OBRV; VA
I've Thirty Months. J. M. Synge. OBMV
I've told you many a tale, my child, of the old heroic days. Madeleine Verchères. William Henry Drummond. CaP; CPG; OCL
I've traveled all around this world and Tonawanda, too. The Erie Canal Ballad. *Unknown.* ABF
I've Travelled Far in Many Lands. Hinton White. MaRV
I've tried, dear God. I'm Glad. Elizabeth McE. Shields. PraP
I've tried the new moon tilted in the air. The Freedom of the Moon. Robert Frost. PFE
I've walked through all the lodgings. John Fletcher. *Fr.* The Night-Walker; or, The Little Thief. MyFE
I've wandered east, I've wandered west. Jeanie Morrison. William Motherwell. EBSV; EV-4; HBV; LO; LPS-1
I've wandered to the village, Tom, I've sat beneath the tree. Forty Years Ago [*or* Twenty Years Ago]. *Unknown.* BLPA; HBV
I've watched the clouds by day and night. Watching Clouds. John Farrar. StVeCh
I've watched, with microscopic eye. On the Rising Generation. Howard Dietz. ALV
I've watched you now a full half-hour. To a Butterfly. Wordsworth. CG; GoTP; HBV; OTPC; PTA-1; SeCeV; SN
I've wet no lip in the Nag's spring. Choliambs. Persius. LaP
I've Worked for a Silver Shilling. Charles W. Kennedy. HBMV
Ivenimus eum in campis silvae. The Five Unmistakable Marks. David Jones. MoWP
Iver and Esbern both were merry. Esbern Snare. *Unknown.* BoDaBa
Ives, *sel.* Muriel Rukeyser.
"This is Charles Ives." UnS
Ivory, coral, gold, The. Madrigal. William Drummond of Hawthornden. EIL; ElSeCe; EV-2
Ivory Gate, The, *sel.* Thomas Lovell Beddoes.
Mighty Thoughts of an Old World, The. CoEV; EG; NBE
(Song of Thanatos, The.) CaAE
(Stanzas: "Mighty thought of an old world, The.") ERP; TrGrPo
(Stanzas from "The Ivory Gate.") EnRP
Ivory Gate, The. Mortimer Collins. VA
Ivry. Macaulay. BHV; GN; HBV; HBVY; OBRV; OTPC; PECK; RG; TVSH; VA
(Battle of Ivry, The.) WBLP
Ivy. Frank Dempster Sherman. MAP
Ivy Chief of Trees It Is. *Unknown.* AnEC
Ivy Crest, The. Robin Flower, *fr. the Irish.* *See* In Tuaim Inbhir.
Ivy Green, The. Charles Dickens. *Fr.* The Pickwick Papers, *ch.* 6. BPP; HBV; HBVY; LPS-2; OTPC (1946 ed.); PECK; PIR; RIS; TVSH; VA
Ivy in the dungeon grew, The. Climbing to the Light. Charles Mackay. RIS
Ivy o'er the mouldering wall, The. The Sun-Dial. Thomas Love Peacock. *Fr.* Melincourt. OBRV
Izaac Walton, Cotton, and William Oldways. Walter Savage Landor. PoEL-4
Izaak Walton to River and Brook. Eugene Lee-Hamilton. VA

J

J. A. G. Julia Ward Howe. GA; PAH
J. B. H. C. Bunner. AA
J. D. R. Oliver Wendell Holmes. IAP
J. Milton Miles. Edgar Lee Masters. *Fr.* Spoon River Anthology. CrMA
J. S. Mill. E. C. Bentley. *Fr.* Biography for Beginners. BOHV; OxBoLi; WhC
("John Stuart Mill.") FiBHP
Ja, Ja, Ja! *with music.* *Unknown.* ShS
Ja-Nez—burro with the long ears. Burro with the Long Ears. *Tr. by* Hilda Faunce Wetherill. FaPON
Jabberwocky. "Lewis Carroll." *Fr.* Through the Looking Glass, *ch.* 1. AlDL; ALV; BLV; BoChLi; BoN; EnLi-2 (1949 ed.); FaBoBe; FaFP; FaPON; FiBHP; GoTP; HBV; HoPM; InP; LBN; LEAP; LiTB; LiTG; MBP; NA; NAMP; OnSP; OTPC; PIAE; PoRA; PoVP; PreP; PYM; RAR; RIS; SeCeV; ShBV-2; SiTL; TiPo; TreF; TrGrPo; ViP; WhC
(Stanza of Anglo-Saxon Poetry.) BoN
Jabberwocky. R. C. Evarts. CAG
Jabberwocky (as the Author of "The Faerie Queene" Might Have Written It). Julius Cooper. InMe
Jabberwocky of Authors, The. Harry Persons Taber. BOHV
Jabesh Gilead. Victor Starbuck. *Fr.* Saul, King of Israel. MuM
Jack. Louis Golding. TrJP
Jack ("He ain't much of a dog to look at"). *Unknown.* AlBD

Jack and Gye. *Unknown.* OxNR
Jack and His Father. John Heywood. TuPP
Jack and Jill. Anthony C. Deane. *See* Here Is the Tale.
Jack and Jill. Charles Battell Loomis. PA
  As Austin Dobson Might Have Written It.
  As Swinburne Might Have Written It.
  As Walt Whitman Might Have Written It.
Jack and Jill. Harriet S. Morgridge. *Fr.* Mother Goose Sonnets. AA
Jack and Jill. Elisabeth Cavazza Pullen. PA
Jack and Jill—as Kipling Might Have Written It. Anthony C. Deane. *See* Here Is the Tale.
Jack and Jill went up the hill/ To fetch some heavy water. Paul Dehn. *Fr.* Rhymes for a Modern Nursery. FiBHP
Jack and Jill [*or* Gill] went up the hill. Mother Goose. FaBoBe; FaFP; HBV; HBVY; OnHT; OTPC; OxBoLi; OxNR; PCH; PPL; SAS; SiTL; StVeCh; TiPo
Jack and Jille. Gillian. *Unknown.* BOHV; PA
Jack and Joan. Thomas Campion. EnL; FaBoCh; HBV; TuPP; WP
  (Fortunati Ninium.) GTSL
  ("Jack and Joan they think no ill.") CenL; EG; EV-2; OAEP; OBSC; ReEn; SiCE
  (Song: "Jack and Joan they think no ill.") TVSH
Jack and Roger. Benjamin Franklin. ChTr
  (Quatrain: "Jack eating rotten cheese, did say.") WhC
Jack Barrett went to Quetta. The Story of Uriah. Kipling. LEAP; PIR
Jack, be nimble. Mother Goose. BoChLi; OxNR; PCH; RIS; SiTL; StVeCh; TiPo
Jack Bridges, Scotch-Irish farmer of an inch of dirt on the Greenbrier River. John Henry; an American Episode. Alfred V. Frankenstein. CAG
Jack Creamer. James Jeffrey Roche. GA; MC; PAH
Jack Dempsey's Grave. —— MacMahon. SCC
Jack Donahoo [*or* Donahoe]. *Unknown.* ABS; CoSo; CSF
Jack, eating rotten cheese, did say. Jack and Roger [*or* Quatrain]. Benjamin Franklin. ChTr; WhC
Jack Frenchman's Lamentation. *Unknown.* CoMu
Jack Frost. Helen Bayley Davis. GFA; MPB
Jack Frost. Hannah Flagg Gould. *See* Frost, The.
Jack Frost. Cecily E. Pike. BoTP
Jack Frost. "Gabriel Setoun." BoTP; DD; GFA; HBV; HBVY; MPB; OnHT; OTPC; RAR
Jack Frost ("When Jack Frost comes—Oh the fun"). *Unknown.* GFA
Jack Frost in the Garden. John P. Smeeton. BoTP
Jack Frost must be a caterer. Winter Treats. Mildred D. Shacklett. GFA
Jack Frost was in the garden. Jack Frost in the Garden. John P. Smeeton. BoTP
Jack Haggerty. *Unknown, at. to* Dan McGinnis. ShS, *with music;* TrNE, *with music;* ViBoFo
  (Flat River Girl, *with music.*) AS
Jack Hall, he is so small. Mother Goose. RIS
Jack Horner ("Jack Horner was a pretty lad"). *Unknown.* OTPC; PPL
Jack Horner. Adeline D. T. Whitney. *Fr.* Mother Goose for Grown Folks. LPS-3
Jack Horner was a pretty lad. Jack Horner. *Unknown.* OTPC; PPL
Jack-in-the-Box. Elder Olson. NePA
Jack-in-the-Pulpit. Rowena Bennett. MPB (1956 ed.)
Jack-in-the-Pulpit. Ivy O. Eastwick. YeAr
Jack-in-the-Pulpit. Rupert Sargent Holland. OTPC; StVeCh (1940 ed.)
Jack-in-the-pulpit is preaching a sermon. Jack-in-the-Pulpit. Rowena Bennett. MPB (1956 ed.)
Jack in the pulpit, out and in. *Unknown.* OxNR
Jack Kelso, *sel.* Edgar Lee Masters.
  Portrait of a Poet. ATP
Jack o' Diamonds, *with music.* *Unknown.* OuSiCo
Jack o' Diamonds; or, The Rabble Soldier. *Unknown.* *See* Rebel Soldier, The.
Jack o' the Inkpot. Algernon Blackwood. BoTP
Jack of all trades, he was master of none, A. Master of None. Margites. OxBG
Jack of Newbury, *sels.* Thomas Deloney.
  "Maiden fair I dare not wed, A." ReIE
  "My masters, I thank you, it's time to pack home." ReIE
  Weavers' Song, The. EV-2; SiCE
Jack Overdue. John Pudney. AlDL
Jack (quoth his father) how shall I ease take? Jack and His Father. John Heywood. TuPP
Jack Riley. *Unknown.* ABS
Jack Robinson. Thomas Hudson. SG
Jack Rose. Maxwell Bodenheim. HBMV
Jack Shows His Qualities and Great Good Will to Jone. Thomas Howell. ReIE; TuPP
Jack Sprat/ Had a cat. *Unknown.* OxNR
Jack Sprat [*or* Spratt] could eat no fat. Mother Goose. BoChLi; FaBoBe; FaFP; HBV; HBVY; OTPC; OxNR; PCH; PPL; RIS; SiTL
Jack Sprat's pig. Mother Goose. BrR
Jack Tar. Emile Jacot. BoTP
Jack Tar, *with music.* *Unknown.* ShS
Jack the Guinea Pig. *Unknown.* AmSS
Jack the Jolly Tar. *Unknown.* BaBo
Jack the Piper. *Unknown.* ChTr
  ("As I was going up the hill.") OxNR
Jack the Ripper. Allan M. Laing. FiBHP
Jack Williams. *Unknown.* ABS
Jack Wrack. *Unknown.* *See* Off to Sea Once More.
Jackals prowl, the serpents hiss, The. Elegy. Arthur Guiterman. BOHV; InMe
Jackaro, *with music.* *Unknown.* IHA
  (Lily Munro, *with music.*) OuSiCo
Jackdaw, The. Vincent Bourne, *tr. fr. Latin by* William Cowper. CBOV; HBV; HBVY; OTPC (1923 ed.); TCEP
Jackdaw of Rheims, The. "Thomas Ingoldsby." *Fr.* The Ingoldsby Legends. BOHV; EV-4; HBV; LPS-3; OTPC (1923 ed.); PoeMoYo; ShBV-1; TSW; VA
Jacket of Gray, The. Caroline A. Ball. BIG
Jackie Faa. *Unknown.* *See* Wraggle Taggle Gipsies, The.
Jackman's Song, The. Ben Jonson. *See* Gipsy Song ("The faery beam upon you").
Jackpot, The. Eugene Fitch Ware. DDA
Jack's Fidelity. Charles Dibdin. EtS
Jack's wondrous sick, who thinks he shall go mad. Nil Perdunt Mendici. Henry Parrot. SiCE
Jackson, *with music.* *Unknown.* AS
Jackson at his counter packing tea. The Tea Trader. Daniel Henderson. PFE
Jackson at New Orleans. Wallace Rice. DD; GA; PAH
Jackson is on sea, Jackson is on shore. Jackson. *Unknown.* AS
Jacky, Come Give Me Thy Fiddle. *Unknown.* OxNR; UnS
Jacob. Phoebe Cary. BOHV; InMe; PA
Jacob. Arthur Hugh Clough. BHV; ViPP
Jacob Godbey. Edgar Lee Masters. *Fr.* Spoon River Anthology. ChMo; CMP; LiTA
Jacob, hear! Jacob's Destiny. Richard Beer-Hofmann. *Fr.* Jacob's Dream. TrJP
Jacob! I do not like to see thy nose. The Pig. Robert Southey. BOHV
Jacob rose that night and passed over the ford of Jabbok. Wrestling with God. Genesis, Bible, *O.T.* GrCo-1
Jacob Tonson, His Publisher. Dryden. BeR; ChTr
Jacobean. Clifton Fadiman. FiBHP
Jacobite in Exile, A. Swinburne. *See* Jacobite's Exile.
Jacobite on Tower Hill, The. George Walter Thornbury. VA
Jacobite Toast, A. John Byrom. EV-3; OtMeF
  (Epigram: "God bless the King—I mean the faith's defender.") HBV
  (Extempore Verses Intended to Allay the Violence of Party Spirit.) OBEC
  (Intended to Allay the Violence of Party Spirit.) PIAE
  (Toast, A.) ViBoPo
  (Which Is Which?) BOHV
Jacobite's Epitaph, A. Macaulay. CBOV; GTBS; InP; LH; OBEV; OBVV; WP
  (Epitaph on a Jacobite.) CBE; EV-4; VA; ViBoPo
Jacobite's Exile, 1746, A. Swinburne. OBVV; OtMeF
  (Jacobite in Exile, A.) LH
Jacobite's Farewell, A. Swinburne. POTT; PoVP; TOP
Jacob's Dream, *sel.* Richard Beer-Hofmann, *tr. fr. German by* Ida Bension Wynn.
  Jacob's Destiny. TrJP
Jacob's Ladder. *Unknown.* MaRV
Jacopone da Todi. Matthew Arnold. *See* Austerity of Poetry.
Jacquerie, The, *sels.* Sidney Lanier.
  Betrayal. AA
  Hound, The. AA; AlBD; PFY; PoMS
  (Song for "The Jacquerie.") MAP; MoAmPo (1942 ed.); MOAP; SPP
Jacques Cartier. Thomas D'Arcy McGee. CaP; OCL
Jade faces of the girls on Yueh Stream, The. The Girls of Yueh. Li Po. WhP
Jade Flower Palace. Tu Fu, *tr. fr. Chinese by* Robert Payne. LiTW; WhP; OnPC, *tr. by* Kenneth Rexroth
Jaffar. Leigh Hunt. BCEP; BeLS; CG; HBV; LPS-1; OTPC; TVSH
Jaffier Parting with Belvidera. Thomas Otway. *Fr.* Venice Preserved. LPS-1
Jagg'd mountain peaks and skies ice-green. Breughel's Winter. Walter de la Mare. SeCePo
Jaguar, The. Ted Hughes. POTE (1959 ed.)
Jahr der Seele, Das, *sels.* Stefan George, *tr. fr. German.*
  After Harvest, *tr. by* Herman Salinger. TwGV
  "No way too long, no path too steep," *tr. by* Daisy Broicher. AWP
Jahwar's sons! Your tyranny. Cruel Masters. Ibn Zaydun. MooP
Jail would have killed me. Nathan Suffrin. Edgar Lee Masters. *Fr.* The New Spoon River. ChMo; CMP

Jake Diefer, the barrel-chested Pennsylvanian. The Enlistments. Stephen Vincent Benét. *Fr.* John Brown's Body. ATP
Jake was a dirty Dago lad, an' he gave the skipper chin. Cape Horn Gospel. John Masefield. ShBV-3
Jam on Gerry's Rock, The. *Unknown.* AS, *with music;* BaBo; ShS, *vers.* I, *with music;* ViBoFo, *with music*
(Gerry's Rocks, *with music.*) ABF
(Jam on Jerry's Rock, The, *vers.* II, *with music.*) ShS
(Young Monroe at Gerry's Rock, *with music.*) AmSS
Jam-Pot, The. Kipling. HBV; PA
Jamaica Market. Agnes Maxwell-Hall. PoNe
Jamais je nourrirai de geai. *Unknown, tr. fr. French-Canadian folk song by* William McLennan. BoCaPo (1948 ed.)
James Bird. *Unknown.* ABS
James Fitz-James and Ellen. Sir Walter Scott. *Fr.* The Lady of the Lake, VI. LPS-2
James Garber. Edgar Lee Masters. *Fr.* Spoon River Anthology. ChMo; CMP
James Grant. *Unknown.* ESPB
James Harris. *Unknown. See* Daemon Lover, The.
James Hatley. *Unknown.* BaBo; ESPB
James Lee's Wife. Robert Browning. ViPP
Sels.
Ah, Love, but a Day, I. EPN
Along the Beach, IV. VLEP
Among the Rocks, VII. BLV; BoLiVe; BPN; VLEP
(Ancient Doctrine, The.) OBVV
("O good gigantic smile.") EPN; YT
On Deck, IX. EtPaEn
James McCosh. Robert Bridges. AA
James Russell Lowell ("This is your month"). Oliver Wendell Holmes. PEOR
James Russell Lowell ("Thou shouldst have sung the swan-song for the choir"). Oliver Wendell Holmes. DD; GA
James Russell Lowell. Whittier. DD; GA
James Russell Lowell's Birthday Festival. Oliver Wendell Holmes. PEOR
James went to the door of the kitchen and said. Rudeness. Elizabeth Turner. OTPC (1923 ed.)
James Wetherell. E. A. Robinson. MoAmPo
James Whaland. *Unknown.* AS, *with music;* IHA
Jamestown Flood, The. *Unknown.* ABS
Jamestown had its starving time. Hard Rows to Hoe. Daniel Henderson. PaA
Jamestown Homeward Bound, The, *with music. Unknown.* SoAmSa
Jamie Douglas ("I was a lady of high renown"). *Unknown.* ESPB, *shorter vers.;* OBB; WHA
Jamie Douglas ("It was in the days when Claverhouse"). *Unknown.* PTA-2
Jamie Douglas ("O waly, waly up the bank"). *Unknown. See* Waly, Waly.
Jamie Telfer [in the Fair Dodhead]. *Unknown.* BSV; EBSV; ESPB, *sl. diff.;* EV-2
Jan. G. D. Martineau. NeTW
Ján Ibn Ján. Rena Carey Sheffield. BAP
Jan., Jan., is a jeweler-man. January Snow. Aileen Fisher. YeAr
Jan! Jan! Oh, God of Mercy! The Piper. Josephine Preston Peabody. CV
Jan Kubelik. Carl Sandburg. NP
Jane Addams. Marguerite Wilkinson. CAG
Jane and Eliza. Ann Taylor. HBV; HBVY; OnPP
Jane awoke Ralph so gently on one morning. Morning. John Crowe Ransom. LS
Jane Conquest. *Unknown.* PTA-1
Jane, do you see these little dots. Silkworms. Mary Elliott. OTPC (1923 ed.)
Jane, Jane,/ Tall as a crane. Aubade. Edith Sitwell. ExPo; InP; MBP; MoAB; MoBrPo; NeMA; NP; PoRA; TrGrPo
Jane Jones. Ben King. IAP; IHA; PTA-1
Jane looks down at her organdy skirt. In Bertram's Garden. Donald Justice. NePoEA
Jane Retreat. Edwin Honig. LiTL
Jane, she could not. Man's Way. L. A. G. Strong. HBMV
Jane Smith. Kipling. HBV; PA
Jane Was a Neighbor. *Unknown. See* Death of Queen Jane, The.
Jane Williams had a lover true. Shocking Rape and Murder of Two Lovers. *Unknown.* CoMu
Janet Waking. John Crowe Ransom. AmP; AnAmPo; ExPo; LA; MAP; MoAB; MoAmPo; ReaPo; ThWaDe
Janette's Hair. Charles Graham Halpine. HBV
Janitor's Boy, The. Nathalia Crane. GoTP; NeMA; StaSt; TSWC
January. Elizabeth J. Coatsworth. BoChLi (1950 ed.)
January. Rosaline E. Jones. PEOR
January. Sylvia S. Lambdin. YeAr
January. Lucy Larcom. OOP; QP-1
January. Michael Lewis. GoTP
January. James Russell Lowell. *See* Winter Morning, A.
January. Daniel James O'Sullivan. NeIP
January. Frank Dempster Sherman. YeAr
January. Spenser. *See* January Eclogue.
January. William Carlos Williams. MAP; MoAB; MoAmPo; NP
January, angry at the whole damned town. Spleen LXXV. Baudelaire. ReMP
January, bleak and drear. January. Frank Dempster Sherman. YeAr
January brings the snow. The Garden Year [*or* The Months]. Sara Coleridge. CBPC; DD; FaBoBe; GoTP; HBV; HBVY; MeMeAg; MPB; OTPC; PCH; PPL; RAR; RIS; StaSt; StVeCh; TiPo; TSW
January cold [and] desolate. The Months. Christina Rossetti. *Fr.* Sing-Song. FaPON; RIS
January Eclogue. Spenser. *Fr.* The Shepheardes Calender. FiP
(January.) ReIE
January falls the snow. Calendar Rhyme. Flora Willis Watson. BoTP
January 1, 1828. Nathaniel Parker Willis. BAV
January Is Here. Edgar Fawcett. YeAr
January Jasmine. Zoe Kincaid Brockman. NoCaPo
January Morning, A. Archibald Lampman. CPG; MW
January Night. Rafael Alberto Arrieta, *tr. fr. Spanish by* Muna Lee. AnCL; OnPM
January 1940. Roy Fuller. HoPM; LiTM; OnHM; SeCePo; WaP
January, 1919. Boris Pasternak, *tr. fr. Russian by* C. M. Bowra. BoRS
January sky is deep and calm, The. Reason for Not Writing Orthodox Nature Poetry. John Wain. HaMV
January Snow. Aileen Fisher. YeAr
January snowy, February flowy, March blowy. The Months. Sheridan. PCH
January sparkles. January. Sylvia S. Lambdin. YeAr
January Tenth. Emilio Prados, *tr. fr. Spanish by* Eleanor L. Turnbull. CoSP
Janus. "Æ." TIP
Janus. Madeline Mason. GoYe
Japan. Anthony Hecht. CrMA; LiTM (rev. ed.)
Japan Can Teach, *cond.* Toyohiko Kagawa, *tr. fr. Japanese by* Lois J. Erickson. SoLD
Japan for Sightseeing. Iku Takenaka, *tr. fr. Japanese by* Takamichi Ninomiya *and* D. J. Enright. PoLJ
Japanese, The. Ogden Nash. InMe; WhC
Japanese Birthday Wish, A. Thomas Burnett Swann. GoYe
Japanese Cherries. Katherine Brégy. JKCP (1926 ed.)
Japanese have funny things, The. A Rhyme Sheet of Other Lands. Hugh Chesterman. BoTP
Japanese Hokku. Lewis Alexander. CDC
Japanese Love-Song, A. Alfred Noyes. LEAP; OBVV
Japanese Lovers, The. *Unknown.* BeLS; BLPA
Japanese Lullaby. Eugene Field. *See* Little Blue Pigeon.
Japanese poetry. *See* Haikai; Haiku; Hokku; Tanka; Hyaku-Nin-Isshu; Kokin Shu; Manyo Shu; Shui Shu; *also individual titles and first lines.*
Japanese Print, A. Ruth Mason Rice. BAP
Japanese Vase Wrought in Metals, A. Marjorie Allen Seiffert. NP
Japanesque. Oliver Herford. FiBHP
Jar, The. "Feodor Sologub." *See* Amphora, The.
Jar, The. Richard Henry Stoddard. AA; DDA; LEAP; OBAV
(Day and Night My Thoughts Incline.) HBV
Jar of cider and my pipe, A. The Sluggard. W. H. Davies. OBMV
Jar of Nations, The. A. E. Housman. *See* Oh Is It the Jar of Nations.
Jardin de la Chapelle Expiatoire. Robert Finch. PeCV
Jardin des Fleurs. Charles David Webb. NePoAm-2
Jardin du Palais Royal. David Gascoyne. MoPo
Jarring the air with rumour cool. Small Fountains. Lascelles Abercrombie. *Fr.* Emblems of Love. CH
Jason and Medea. John Gower. *Fr.* Confessio Amantis, V. ACP
"Flees he tok and goth to bote, The," *sel.* AtBAP
Jason, what scheme is framed, what's laid in store. Medea Betrayed. Apollonius Rhodius. *Fr.* Argonautica, IV. OxBG
Jason, which sih his fader old. John Gower. *Fr.* Confessio Amantis, V. EPP
Jason's Father Sees His Returning Son. Pindar, *pr. tr. fr. Greek by* Sir John Sandys. *Fr.* Pythian Odes, IV. LiA
Jason's Sowing and Reaping. Apollonius Rhodius, *tr. fr. Greek by* George Allen. *Fr.* Argonautica, III. OxBG
Javanese Dancers. Arthur Symons. POTT; PoVP; VA
Jay-bird, jay-bird, settin' on a rail. *Unknown.* GoTP
Jay Gould's Daughter, *with music. Unknown.* AS
Jay Hawkins. Edgar Lee Masters. *Fr.* The New Spoon River. ChMo; CMP
Jay in the Feathers of the Peacock, The. La Fontaine, *tr. fr. French by* Elizur Wright. OnPM

Jazz Band in a Parisian Cabaret. Langston Hughes. BANP; MAP; MoAmPo
Jazz band struck up Dixie, The . . . I could see. Victory in the Cabarets. Louis Untermeyer. HBMV
Jazz Fantasia. Carl Sandburg. AnFE; CoAnAm; MAP; MoAB; MoAmPo; NeMA; PoNe; TwAmPo
Jazz of This Hotel, The. Vachel Lindsay. ATP
Jazzonia. Langston Hughes. BANP
Je caresserai la belle par amitié, *with music. Unknown, tr. fr. French.* OuSiCo
Je Ne Sçay [*or* Sais] Quoi, The. William Whitehead. LO; OBEC
Je ne veux de personne auprès de ma tristesse. Henri de Régnier, *tr. fr. French by* "Seumas O'Sullivan." AWP; JAWP; WBP
Je Suis une Table. Donald Hall. NePoEA
Jealous Adam. Itzig Manger, *tr. fr. Yiddish by* Jacob Sonntag. TrJP
Jealous breeze, a-shiver, The. Amulet. Ibn Sa'id of Alcala la Real. MooP
Jealous Doggerel. Burges Johnson. AIBD
Jealous Enemy, The. Petrarch, *tr. fr. Italian by* Thomas LeMesurier. Sonnets to Laura: To Laura in Death, XLVII. LiTW
Jealous girls these sometimes were. How Marigolds Came Yellow. Robert Herrick. ChTr
Jealous, I Own It. Walter Savage Landor. EmBrPo
Jealous Lover, The (*diff. versions*). *Unknown.* ABS; ShS, *with music,* ViBoFo
(Fair Florella or the Jealous Lover, A *and* B *vers.*) BaBo
(Weeping Willow, The.) ABS
Jealous Lovers, The, *sel.* Thomas Randolph.
Charm, A. SeCL
Jealous Man, A. *Unknown, tr. fr. Irish by* Frank O'Connor. KiLC
Jealousy. Mary Elizabeth Coleridge. EnLoPo; PoVP
(Myrtle Bush Grew Shady, The.) CH
Jealousy. Earl of Rochester. *See* Song: "My dear mistress has a heart."
Jealousy. Shakespeare. *Fr.* Othello, III, iii. LiA
(Not Poppy, nor Mandragora.) WHA
Jealousy. *Unknown, tr. fr. Irish by* Frank O'Connor. KiLC
Jealousy. Countess of Winchilsea. SeCL
Jealousy's an awful thing and foreign to my nature. I Can't Think What He Sees in Her. A. P. Herbert. FiBHP
Jean. Burns. *See* Of A' the Airts.
Jean. Paul Potts. NeBP
Jean Desprez. Robert W. Service. CV
Jean François. *Unknown. See* Boney.
Jean Richepin's Song. Herbert Trench. LiTG; LiTM (rev. ed.); OBMV; OxBI; POTE
Jeane. William Barnes. LO
Jeane's Wedden Day in Mornen. William Barnes. PoVP
Jeanie, come tie my. *See* Jennie, come tie my.
Jeanie Morrison. William Motherwell. EBSV; EV-4; HBV; LO; LPS-1
Jeanie with the Light Brown Hair. Stephen Collins Foster. FaFP; OlF; TrAS, *with music;* TreF
Jeannette. Otto Julius Bierbaum, *tr. fr. German by* Jethro Bithell. AWP
Jeannette and Jeannot. Charles Jefferys. BLPA
Jeannie Marsh. George Pope Morris. AA
Jeat Ring Sent, A. John Donne. PoEL-2
Jeff Davis. *Unknown.* BoHiPo
Jefferson and Liberty, *with music. Unknown.* TrAS
Jefferson D. H. S. Cornwell. PAH
Jefferson Davis. Walker Meriwether Bell. BoHiPo, *st.* 1; GA; PAH
Jefferson Davis. Harry Thurston Peck. GA
"And now he slinks through dark oblivion's gate," *br. sel.* BoHiPo
Jefferson Highway, The. Sister Mariella. JKCP (1955 ed.)
Jehovah. Israel Zangwill. WGRP
Redeeming Mercy, The, *sel.* GrCo-2
Jehovah Buried, Satan Dead. E. E. Cummings. NePA
Jehovah's Immovable Throne. Psalms, XCIII, Bible, *O.T.* (Moulton, *Modern Reader's Bible*). WGRP
Jehu. Louis MacNeice. LiTG; LiTM (rev. ed.); MoAB; WaP
Jellicle Cats are black and white. The Song of the Jellicles. T. S. Eliot. FaBoCh; LiL; LoGBV
Jellon Grame. *Unknown.* BaBo; ESPB (A *and* B vers.); OBB
Jelly Fish, The. Robert P. Tristram Coffin. CAW
Jellyfish, The. Ogden Nash. FaPON
Jem writes his verses with more speed. A Rhymester. Samuel Taylor Coleridge. BOHV
Jemima. *Unknown. See* There Was a Little Girl.
Jenghiz upon the mountains white and high. The Endless Error. Donald F. Drummond. PtPa
Jenner. Pasteur, Koch and Yersin. Dragons. Edward Lovelle Stewart. PoP
Jennie [*or* Jeanie *or* Jenny], come tie my. Mother Goose. BoTP; BrR; OxNR; TiPo (1952 ed.)
Jennie Jenkins, *with music. Unknown.* OuSiCo
Jennifer Gentle and Rosemary. *Unknown. See* Riddles Wisely Expounded.
Jenny. Dante Gabriel Rossetti. EmBrPo; LiA; PoEL-5; POTT; ViP; ViPo; ViPP; VLEP
Jenny. Jesse Stuart. *Fr.* Man with a Bull-Tongue Plow. BoFr
Jenny and Johnny. Dorothy King. BoTP
Jenny and Me were engaged, you see. Pink Dominoes. Kipling. CenHV
Jenny come tie my. *See* Jennie, come tie my.
Jenny Dang the Weaver. Sir Alexander Boswell. EBSV
Jenny from Ballinsloe. *Unknown.* TIP
Jenny gay and Johnny grim. Jenny and Johnny. Dorothy King. BoTP
Jenny Kiss'd [*or* Kissed] Me. Leigh Hunt. ALV; BCEP; BLPA; BLV; BTP; EnLi-2; EV-4; FaBoBe; FaFP; GTBS-W; HBV; InMe; LEAP; LiTG; LiTL; LoPo; LoPS; LPS-1; NeHB; OBEV; OBVV; OTPC (1946 ed.); PC; PCD; PG (1945 ed.); PIR; PoMa; PoRA; SiTL; TreF; TyEnPo
(Rondeau, A: "Jenny kiss'd me when we met.") ATP (1935 ed.); CBOV; EnLit; EnRP; EPP; ERP; GTBS; GTSL; HoPM; InP; MCCG; OnPM; PoE; TCEP; TOP; ViBoPo
Jenny kiss'd me in a dream. "Such Stuff as Dreams." Franklin P. Adams. FiBHP; PC
Jenny kiss'd me when we met. Paul Dehn. *Fr.* A Leaden Treasury of English Verse. FiBHP
Jenny White and Johnny Black. Eleanor Farjeon. FaPON
Jenny wi' the Airn Teeth. Alexander Anderson. BOL; HBV
Jenny Wren. W. H. Davies. CMP; MBP; MoBrPo; PIAE; StaSt
Jenny Wren fell sick. Mother Goose. CBPC; CG; OTPC; OxNR; RIS
Jenny Wren's got a house. The Secret. Elizabeth Fleming. BoTP
Jenny's Bawbee. Sir Alexander Boswell. EBSV
Jephthah's Daughter. Judges, XI: 30–40, Bible, *O.T.* OuHeWo
Jephthah's Daughter, *sel.* Charles Heavysege.
"Oh, think how hard it is to die when young!" CaP
Jephthah's Daughter. Tennyson. BHV
Jephthah's Daughter. "Yehoash," *tr. fr. Yiddish by* Alter Brody. TrJP
Jephtha's Daughter. Byron. EmBrPo
Jerboa, The. Marianne Moore. AtBAP; MoPo
Jeremiad. Oscar Williams. LiTA
Jeremiah, *sels.* Bible, *O.T.*
As Fowlers Lie in Wait, V: 26–31. TrJP
But Fear Thou Not, O Jacob, XLVI: 27–28. TrJP
Call for True Repentance, A, VII: 1–20. WoL
Cry of the Daughter of My People, The, VIII: 18–23. TrJP
Cursed Be the Day, XX: 14–18. TrJP
New Covenant, A, XXXI: 31–34. GrCo-2
O Lord, Thou Hast Enticed Me, XX: 7–10. TrJP
Oh That I Were in the Wilderness, IX: 1–10. TrJP
Peace! and There Is No Peace, VIII: 1–22. WoL
Potter and the Clay, The, XVIII: 1–11. WoL
"Therefore thus saith the Lord; Ye have not hearkened unto me," XXXIV: 17. PoFr
Jeremiah. Witter Bynner. CrMA
Jeremiah, *sels.* Stefan Zweig, *tr. fr. German by* Eden Paul *and* Cedar Paul.
Chosen of God. TrJP
Flowering without End. TrJP
Jeremiah, blow the fire. *Unknown.* OxNR
Jeremy Hobbler. *Unknown.* BoTP
Jericho. Willard Wattles. HBMV; SBMV
Jericho is on the inside. The Walls of Jericho. Blanche Taylor Dickinson. CDC
Jericho, Jericho, round and round the walls I go. Jericho. Willard Wattles. HBMV; SBMV
Jericho Road, The. Edwin McNeill Poteat. ChIP; MaRV; QS
Jericho's Blind Beggar. Longfellow. *See* Blind Bartimeus.
Jerked Heartstrings in Town. Emily B. C. Jones. HBMV
Jeronimo's House. Elizabeth Bishop. MiAP
Jerry and Me. Hiram Rich. HBV
Jerry, Go an' Ile That Car. *Unknown.* AS, *with music;* CSF; IHA
Jerry Hall/ He is so small. *Unknown.* BoN; OxNR; SiTL
Jerusalem. Bernard of Cluny. *See* Jerusalem, the Golden.
Jerusalem, *sels.* Blake.
"Ah! weak and wide astray," *fr. ch.* 2. OBRV
"England! awake! awake! awake," *fr. prologue to ch.* 4. CBE; EnRP; OBRV
"Fields from Islington to Marybone, The," *fr. prologue to ch.* 2. ChTr; OBRV
(From Islington to Marybone.) TriL

"He who would do good to another," *fr. ch.* 2. NBE
"I give you the end of a golden string," *fr. prologue to ch.* 4. OBRV; ShBV-4
(I Will Give You.) OTPC (1946 ed.)
(To the Christians.) EnRP; WGRP
"I saw a monk of Charlemain[e]," *fr. prologue to ch.* 3. EnRP; MeRV; NBE; OBRV
(Monk, The.) LoBV
In Deadly Fear. SeCePo
"Jesus replied: 'Fear not Albion,'" *fr. ch.* 4.
(Brotherhood.) CoEV
"Jesus said: 'Wouldst thou love one who never died,'" *fr. ch.* 4. NBE
(Written 1811.) MaRV; StJW
"Rhine was red with human blood, The," *fr. prologue to ch.* 2. ViBoPo
"So spoke London, immortal guardian," *fr. ch.* 2. NBE
"What are those golden builders doing," *fr. ch.* 1. OBRV
"What shall I do? what could I do," *fr. ch.* 2. NBE
Jerusalem. Blake. *Fr.* Milton. *See* And Did Those Feet in Ancient Time.
Jerusalem. William Drummond of Hawthornden. EV-2
Jerusalem, *sel.* Uri Zvi Greenberg, *tr. fr. Hebrew by* Charles A. Cowen.
Jerusalem the Dismembered. TrJP
Jerusalem. *Unknown. See* New Jerusalem, The.
Jerusalem Delivered [*or* Godfrey of Bulloigne], *sels.* Tasso, *tr. fr. Italian.*
Armida, the Sorceress, *fr.* IV, *tr. by* Edward Fairfax. EnLi-1
"But better hopes inspirit and make blithe," *fr.* VI, *tr. by* J. H. Wiffen. PrPoCR
Crusaders Reach Jerusalem, The, *fr.* III, *tr. by* Edward Fairfax. EnLi-1
(Crusaders Behold Jerusalem, The, *tr. by* J. H. Wiffen.) CAW
Erminia Wanders in the Fields and Dreams of Love, *fr.* VII, *tr. by* Edward Fairfax. LiA
"Know, he assists the cause of God, who toils," *fr.* IV, *tr. by* J. H. Wiffen. PoFr
"Lark was warbling sweet her evening song, The," *fr.* XIX, *tr. by* J. H. Wiffen. PrPoCR
"Moors, the Ethiops, and the Arabs then, The," *fr.* XX, *tr. by* J. H. Wiffen. PrPoCR
"Now from the fresh soft lap and twilight bower," XIV, *tr. by* J. H. Wiffen. PrPoCR
"Odorous air, morn's messenger, now spread, The," *fr.* III, *tr. by* J. H. Wiffen. PrPoCR
Pluto's Council, *tr. by* Edward Fairfax. OBSC
Prayer Brings Rain, A, *tr. by* Edward Fairfax. OBSC
"Round is the spacious pile; and in its heart," *fr.* XVI, *tr. by* J. H. Wiffen. PrPoCR
"Sacred armies and the godly knight, The," *fr.* I, *tr. by* Edward Fairfax. CAW
"Scarce had Aurora ris'n with grateful ray," XV, *tr. by* J. H. Wiffen. PrPoCR
"Through the brown shade of forests ivied o'er," *fr.* VII, *tr. by* J. H. Wiffen. PrPoCR
"'Twas night; nor yet had either wearied host," XII, *tr. by* J. H. Wiffen. PrPoCR
"When they had passed all those troubled ways," *fr.* XVI, *tr. by* Edward Fairfax. TuPP
"Whilst thus in fervent toil the artisan," IV, *tr. by* J. H. Wiffen. PrPoCR
Jerusalem Delivered. Louis Untermeyer. MAP
Jerusalem, My Happy Home. *Unknown. See* New Jerusalem, The.
Jerusalem, Rejoice for Joy, *in mod. Eng. At. to* William Dunbar. TMEV
Jerusalem, that place divine. Jerusalem. William Drummond of Hawthornden. EV-2
Jerusalem the Dismembered. Uri Zvi Greenberg, *tr. fr. Hebrew by* Charles A. Cowen. *Fr.* Jerusalem. TrJP
Jerusalem, the Golden. Bernard of Cluny, *tr. fr. Latin by* John Mason Neale. *Fr.* De Contemptu Mundi. CAW; MaRV; OlF, 4 *sts.*; WGRP
(Celestial Country, The.) GoBC, *abr.*; GrCo-1, *much abr.*; LPS-2
(Jerusalem, *abr.*) HBV; OBVV
Jerusalem, thy joys divine. The Under Song. *Unknown.* ACP
Jes' beyan a clump o' pines. The Corn Song. John Wesley Holloway. BANP
Jes' the sort o' weather and jes' the sort of sky. God Made This Day for Me. Edgar A. Guest. NLK
Jesous Ahatonhia. Jesse Edgar Middleton, *after* Jean de Brébeuf. CaP; ChrBoLe; OCL
Jess, a wild cowboy, loves whisky and beer. Jess's Dilemma. *Unknown.* CoSo
Jessamine. Ibn al-Abbar, *tr. fr. Arabic by* A. J. Arberry. MooP
Jessamine shows like a star, The. Queen Rose. Christina Rossetti. BPN
Jesse James. William Rose Benét. BBV (1951 ed.); InP; MAP; MoAmPo; NAMP; NeMA; OnAP; PoeMoYo; PreP; StPo; TrGrPo
Jesse James (*diff. versions*). *Unknown.* ABF (A *vers., with music;* B *vers.*); ABS (A *and* B *vers., much abr.*); AmPP (3d ed.); APW; AS; ATP; BaBo (A, B, *and* C *vers.*); BeLS; CoSo (A *vers., with music;* B, C, *and* D *vers.*); CSF, *with music;* FaBoBe; IHA; InP; MaC; TrAS, *with music;* TreFS; UnPo; ViBoFo (A *and* B *vers.*); YaD
(Death of Jesse James.) BoHiPo
Jesse James was a lad who [*or* that] killed many a man. Jesse James. *Unknown.* BaBo (C *vers.*); MaC; ViBoFo (A *vers.*)
Jesse James was a two-gun man. Jesse James. William Rose Benét. BBV (1951 ed.); StPo; TrGrPo
Jesse James was one of his names, another it was Howard. Jesse James (B *vers.*). *Unknown.* BaBo; ViBoFo
Jessica's my sister. Richard Has Something to Say. Rose Fyleman. GaP
Jessie. Thomas Edward Brown. EtPaEn; HBV; OBEV (1st ed.)
Jessie. Eugene Field. InMe
Jessie. Bret Harte. GN
Jessie, the Flower o' Dunblane. Robert Tannahill. EBSV; EV-4; HBV
(Flower o' Dumblane, The.) LPS-1
Jess's Dilemma. *Unknown.* CoSo
Jest a-wearyin' for you. Wearyin' for You. Frank L. Stanton. BAP; HBV
Jest 'fore Christmas. Eugene Field. ChBR; DD; FaFP; FaPON; HBV; HBVY; HH; MPB; MW; OHFP; OTPC; SDH; TreF; YT
Jest rain and snow! and rain again! The First Bluebird. James Whitcomb Riley. CV
Jester and His Daughter, The. Tom Taylor. *Fr.* The Fool's Revenge. VA
Jester Bee. Frank Dempster Sherman. UTS
Jester Condemned to Death, The. Horace Smith. BOHV; PoeMoYo
Jester shook his hood and bells, and leap'd upon a chair, The. The Jester's Sermon. George Walter Thornbury. BeLS; BMEP; LPS-2; TreFS
Jester walked in the garden, The. The Cap and Bells. W. B. Yeats. BMEP; ChTr; GTSL; LEAP; MBP; OBVV
Jester's Plea, The. Frederick Locker-Lampson. CenHV
Jester's Sermon, The. George Walter Thornbury. BeLS; BMEP; LPS-2; TreFS
Jesu. George Herbert. MeLP
(Iesu.) EV-2; OBS
Jesu,/ If thou wilt make. A Page's Road Song. William Alexander Percy. LS; TrPWD; YeAr
Jesu, as Thou Art Our Saviour. *Unknown.* AnEC
Jesu! by that shuddering dread which fell on Thee. Angel of the Agony. Cardinal Newman. *Fr.* The Dream of Gerontius. OxBoCh
Jesu Christ, sooth God, sooth man. Prison Songs, II. *Unknown.* TMEV
Jesu Dulcis. St. Bernard of Clairvaux, *tr. fr. Latin.* CAW
(Iesu, Dulcis Memoria, *tr. by* Gerard Manley Hopkins.) LaP
Jesu, Dulcis Memoria. *Unknown, tr. fr. Latin.* WHL
Jesu, Fili Dei. *At. to* John Trouluffe *and* Richard Smert. AnEC
Jesu, Fili Virginis. *At. to* Richard Smert. AnEC
Jesu, Fili Virginis. *Unknown.* AnEC
Jesu [*or* Iesu] is in my heart, his sacred name. Jesu [*or* Iesu]. George Herbert. EV-2; MeLP; OBS
Jesu, Jesu, Jesu, Jesu,/ Save us all through Thy virtue. Jesu, as Thou Art Our Saviour. *Unknown.* AnEC
Jesu, joy of man's desiring. Johann Sebastian Bach. *Fr.* Herz und Mund. OlF
Jesu, Lover of My Soul. Charles Wesley. *See* Jesus, Lover of my Soul.
Jesu, Maria—I am near to death. Cardinal Newman. *Fr.* The Dream of Gerontius. ACP; CoBE; EnLi-2; PoVP
Jesu, my sweet Son dear. Cradle Song of the Virgin [*or* Christmas Night]. *Unknown.* ISi; TMEV. *See also* Jesu [*or* Iesu], swete sone dere!
Jesu, no more! it is full tide. On the Bleeding Wounds of Our Crucified Lord [*or* Upon the Bleeding Crucifix]. Richard Crashaw. SeCV-1; TrGrPo
Jesu, swetë sonë derë. *Unknown.* EnL. *See also* Iesu, swete sone dere! *and* Jesu, my sweet Son dear.
Jesu! The very thought of Thee. Jesu, Dulcis Memoria. *Unknown.* WHL
Jesu, to Thee I cry and greed. *Unknown. Fr.* Jesus the Comforter. MaRV
Jesukin. *At. to* St. Ita, *tr. fr. Old Irish by* George Sigerson. CAW; OnYI
(Saint Ita's Fosterling, *tr. by* Robin Flower.) OnYI
(Vision of Ita, The, *tr. by* Whitley Stokes.) AnIL; SiB

Jesus. Robert Bridges. *Fr.* The Testament of Beauty, I. MaRV
("So it was when Jesus came in his gentleness.") MeRV
Jesus. Joseph Eliyia, *tr. fr. Modern Greek by* Rae Dalven. MoGP
Jesus ("Jesus, there is no dearer name than thine"). Theodore Parker. AA
Jesus ("O thou great friend to all the sons of men"). Theodore Parker. *See* Way, the Truth, and the Life, The.
Jesus. Ramón Pimentel Coronel, *tr. fr. Spanish by* Joseph I. C. Clarke. CAW
Jesus. *Unknown.* ChIP; OQP; QP-1; QS
Jesus/ Wracked on your cross. Unity. Lloyd Frank Merrell. ChIP
Jesus—all Thy labor vast. Father, into Thy Hands. Thomas B. Pollock. BePJ
Jesus, and didst Thou condescend. Thou Alone Canst Save. Amelia Wakeford. BePJ
Jesus—and didst Thou leave the sky. Compassion So Divine. Anne Steele. BePJ
Jesus and I. Dan Crawford. BLRP
Jesus and Lazarus. St. John, XI: 1-44, Bible, *N.T.* BoFr
Jesus! and shall it ever be. Ashamed of Jesus. Joseph Grigg. BePJ; OlF
Jesus and the Children. St. Matthew, XVIII: 1-6, XIX: 13-14, Bible, *N.T.* GrCo-1
Jesus and the Sinner. Sadi, *tr. fr. Persian by* W. C. Mackinnon. PeP
Jesus Answers the Pharisees. St. John, VIII: 12-32, Bible, *N.T.* TreFS
Jesus at Play with His School-Mates. Longfellow. *Fr.* Christus; a Mystery, Pt. II, iii. APW
Jesus, at whose supreme command. The Cup of Blessing. Charles Wesley. BePJ
Jesus Calls Us o'er the Tumult. Cecil Frances Alexander. MaRV; OlF
Jesus came, the heavens adoring. Jesus Comes on Clouds Triumphant. Godfrey Thring. BePJ
Jesus, Child and Lord. Frederick William Faber. BePJ
Jesus Christ—and We. Annie Johnson Flint. OQP; QP-1
(Christ—and We.) MaRV
Jesus Christ is risen to-day. *Unknown, tr. fr. Latin by* Nahum Tate *and* Nicholas Brady, *st.* 4 *by* Charles Wesley. OlF
Jesus Christ the Appletree. *Unknown.* BeR
Jesus Christ to-day is risen. Easter. Martin Luther, *after* John Huss. EOAH
Jesus Christ, who stands between. The Covenant of His Grace. Charles Wesley. BePJ
Jesus Comes on Clouds Triumphant. Godfrey Thring. BePJ
Jesus, Deliverer. Anatolius. *See* Fierce Was the Wild Billow.
Jesus First and Jesus Last. Thomas MacKellar. BePJ
Jesus, Friend of sinners, hear. Bid Me Sin No More. Charles Wesley. BePJ
Jesus, gentlest Saviour. Frederick William Faber. OlF
Jesus Goin' to Make Up Mah Dyin' Bed, *with music. Unknown.* SoAF
Jesus, great Shepherd of the sheep. Great Shepherd of the Sheep. Charles Wesley. BePJ
Jesus hath died that I might live. Dying that I Might Live. Charles Wesley. BePJ
Jesus Himself. Henry Burton. BLRP
Jesus His Mother meets. Fourth Station. Padraic Colum. ISi
Jesus, How Much Thy Name Unfolds. Mary Peters. BePJ
Jesus, I kneel down to say. Just for Jesus. Lysbeth Boyd Borie. GaP
Jesus, I Love Thy Charming Name. Philip Doddridge. BePJ
Jesus, I my cross have taken. Lo, We Have Left All. Henry Francis Lyte. VA
Jesus I saw, crossing Times Square. The Flower in the Sea. Malcolm Cowley. NP
Jesus, immortal King, arise. Christ, the Conqueror. Aaron C. H. Seymour, *wr. at. to* Henry Foster Burder. BePJ
Jesus in the Temple. John Donne. *See* Temple.
Jesus, in whom the Godhead's rays. Wash Me Whiter than Snow. Charles Wesley. BePJ
Jesus Is Near. Robert Cassie Waterston. BePJ
Jesus is our common Lord. Walking with Him in White. Charles Wesley. BePJ
Jesus is tenderly calling thee home. Fanny Crosby. OlF
Jesus, Judas, and Peter. St. Luke, XXII: 31-62, Bible, *N.T.* BoFr
Jesus, keep me near the cross. Fanny Crosby. OlF
Jesus, let Thy pitying eye. Break My Heart of Stone. Charles Wesley. BePJ
Jesus Lives, and So Shall I. Christian Fürchtegott Gellert, *tr. fr. German.* BePJ
(Jesus Lives, *abr.*) PGD
(Ye Shall Live Also, *diff. vers., tr. by* Frances E. Cox, *wr. at. to* Arthur Coxe.) BePJ
Jesus, Lord mickle of might. Sir Cawline. *Unknown.* OBB
Jesus, Lord, that madest me. Richard de Castre's Prayer to Jesus. *Unknown.* TMEV
Jesus [*or* Jesu], Lover of My Soul. Charles Wesley. BePJ; HBV; MaRV; NeHB; OlF, *abr.*; OxBoCh; TreF; TriL; WGRP
(Divine Lover, The, *sl. abr.*) BLRP
(In Temptation.) CEP; EiPP; PoE; PoEL-3; TOP
Jesus loves me, this I know. Anna Warner. OlF
Jesus' mother never had no man. Conception. Waring Cuney. BANP; PoNe
Jesus, my chief pleasure. Peace and Joy in Jesus Christ. Johann Franck. BePJ
Jesus, My God and My All. Frederick William Faber. BePJ
Jesus, my Lord, attend. For Perfect Peace. Charles Wesley. BePJ
Jesus, my Lord, my chief delight! The Glorious Gift of God. Benjamin Beddome. BePJ
Jesus, my Lord, my God, my all. Henry Collins. OlF
Jesus, my one Love, behold me draw near. Scattering Flowers. St. Thérèse of Lisieux. WHL
Jesus, my Saviour, Brother, Friend. Fly Back to Christ. Charles Wesley. BePJ
Jesus, My Saviour, Look on Me! John Macduff. BePJ
Jesus! my Shepherd, Husband, Friend. John Newton. *Fr.* The Name of Jesus. TrPWD
Jesus, my strength and righteousness. Thy Conquering Name. Charles Wesley. BePJ
Jesus Nevuh Come in the Mornin', *with music. Unknown.* StDa
Jesus, of a maid Thou wouldst be born. Jesu, Fili Virginis. *At. to* Richard Smert. AnEC
Jesus, of a maid Thou wouldst be born. Jesu, Fili Virginis. *Unknown.* AnEC
Jesus of Nazareth. Ernest Cadman Colwell. ChIP; MaRV; QS
Jesus of Nazareth, King of the Jews. Villanelle. A. M. Sullivan. OQP; QP-2
Jesus of Nazareth Passes By. George T. Liddell. ChIP
Jesus of Nazareth Passeth By. Lydia Huntley Sigourney. BePJ; StJW
Jesus of the Scars. Edward Shillito. ChIP; MaRV; OQP; QP-1
Jesus Only. Elias Nason. BePJ
Jesus Only. A. B. Simpson. BePJ
Jesus our brother, kind [*or* strong] and good. The Friendly Beasts. *Unknown.* ChrBoLe; ChBR; FaPON; SiSoSe
Jesus Praying. Hartley Coleridge. MaRV; StJW
Jesus Prays Alone. William Bingham Tappan. BePJ
Jesus, Refuge of the Weary. Savonarola, *tr. fr. Latin.* MaRV
Jesus replied: "Fear not Albion." Brotherhood. Blake. *Fr.* Jerusalem. CoEV
Jesus said, "Wouldst thou love one who never died." Written 1811. Blake. *Fr.* Jerusalem. MaRV; NBE; StJW
Jesus, Saviour, Pilot Me. Edward Hopper. BLRP; BPP; OlF
Jesus Shall Reign Where'er the Sun. Isaac Watts. BePJ; EV-3, *abr.*; MaRV; OlF; WGRP, *sl. abr.*
(King Triumphant, *abr.*) BLRP
Jesus' sisters—two or three. Names. Edwin McNeill Poteat. NoCaPo (rev. ed.)
Jesus, stand beside them. A Wedding Hymn. Thomas Tiplady. MaRV
Jesus, Sun and Shield art Thou. The First and the Last. Horatius Bonar. BePJ
Jesus, sweet is love of Thee. Jesu Dulcis. St. Bernard of Clairvaux. CAW
Jesus, teach me how to be. The Housewife. Catherine Cate Coblentz. BLRP; ChIP; StJW; TrPWD
Jesus, Tender Shepherd [Hear Me]. Mary Duncan. *See* Child's Evening Prayer, A.
Jesus, the Blessed Agitator. The Blessed Agitator. Lucia Trent. ChIP
Jesus the Carpenter. Catherine C. Liddell. DD; HBV; PECK; VA
Jesus the Carpenter. Charles M. Sheldon. ChIP; MaRV; OQP; QP-1
Jesus the Comforter, *sel. Unknown.*
"Jesu, to Thee I cry and greed." MaRV
Jesus, the friend of lonely, beaten folk. Mary's Son. Lucia Trent. ChIP; PGD
Jesus, the gift divine I know. The Well of Living Water. Charles Wesley. BePJ
Jesus, the Lamb of God, hath bled. Graven on the Palms of His Hands. Charles Wesley. BePJ
Jesus, the Lord of glory, died. Our Ever-present Guide. *Unknown.* BePJ
Jesus the Name Most High. Charles Wesley. BePJ
Jesus, the poet of Galilee. The Miracle Songs of Jesus. Wilson MacDonald. CPG
Jesus, the Soul of Our Joys. Charles Wesley. BePJ
Jesus the Very Thought of Thee. *At. to* St. Bernard of Clairvaux, *tr. fr. Latin by* Edward Caswall. MaRV
(Sweetest Name, The.) BePJ

Jesus, there is no dearer name than thine. Jesus. Theodore Parker. AA
Jesus, These Eyes Have Never Seen. Ray Palmer. MaRV (Blessed Face, The.) BePJ
Jesus, Thou Art the King. Charles Wesley. BePJ
Jesus! Thou art the sinner's Friend. Friend of Sinners. Richard Burnham. BePJ
Jesus, Thou Divine Companion. Henry van Dyke. MaRV
Jesus, Thou everlasting King. Accept Our Tribute. Isaac Watts. BePJ
Jesus, Thou Joy of Loving Hearts. *At. to* St. Bernard of Clairvaux, *tr. fr. Latin by* Ray Palmer. MaRV; WGRP (Thou Light of Life.) BePJ
Jesus, thou soul of all our joys. Jesus, the Soul of Our Joys. Charles Wesley. BePJ
Jesus, Thou source divine. The Only Name Given under Heaven. Anne Steele. BePJ
Jesus, Thy blood and righteousness. I Believe Thy Precious Blood. John Wesley. BePJ
Jesus! Thy church, with longing eyes. The Triumphs of Thy Conquering Power. William H. Bathurst. BePJ
Jesus! thy Crucifix. Emily Dickinson. MoVE
Jesus, Thy far-extended fame. Christ, the Good Physician. Charles Wesley. BePJ
Jesus! Thy love shall we forget. Shall We Forget. William Mitchell. BePJ
Jesus to cast one thought upon. Iesu, Dulcis Memoria. St. Bernard of Clairvaux. LaP
Jesus Understands. *Unknown.* BLRP
Jesus, united by Thy grace. The Loadstone of His Love. Charles Wesley. BePJ
Jesus was a carpenter. He gladly plied. The Carpenter. Amy Bruner Almy. ChIP
Jesus Was a Humble Man. Raymond Kresensky. ChIP
Jesus Was Sitting in Moses' Chair. Blake. *Fr.* The Everlasting Gospel. EV-3; OxBoCh (New Law, The.) StJW
Jesus, we lift our souls to Thee. Bless, Dear Saviour, This Child. Thomas Beck. BePJ
Jesus, we look to Thee. Claiming the Promise. Charles Wesley. BePJ
Jesus went unto the mount of Olives. Neither Do I Condemn Thee. St. John, Bible, *N.T.* GrCo-1
Jesus, when from Thy Mother's clasp I see Thee go. The Unpetalled Rose. St. Thérèse of Lisieux. CAW
Jesus! When my soul is parting. Jesus First and Jesus Last. Thomas MacKellar. BePJ
Jesus, where'er Thy people meet. Hymn: On Opening a Place for Social Prayer. William Cowper. BrBE
Jesus, while our hearts are bleeding. Thy Will Be Done. *Unknown.* BePJ
Jesus, who knows full well. All Our Griefs to Tell. John Newton. BePJ
Jesus, whose lot with us was cast. Jesus. *Unknown.* ChIP; OQP; QP-1; QS
Jesus, whose love rekindles dying fires. In the Way of Peace. Lauchlan MacLean Watt. ChIP; OQP; QP-1
Jesus, whoso with Thee. Lauda. Girolamo Benevieni. CAW
Jesus, Won't You Come B'm-By? *with music. Unknown.* AS
Jet Eyes. Baudelaire, *pr. tr. fr. French.* LiA
Jet form swaying in the morning mist, A. Intolerance. John Richard Moreland. ChIP
Jet Plane. A. M. Sullivan. JKCP (1955 ed.)
Jetsam, *sel.* William Vaughn Moody.
"Once at a simple turning." MAP; MoAmPo (1942 ed.)
Jeune Parque, La, *sel.* Paul Valéry, *pr. tr. fr. French.*
"I buried my head in my thick arms." LiA
Jew, The. Moyshe Kulbak, *tr. fr. Yiddish by* Sarah Zweig Betsky. *Fr.* The Secret Saint. OnCuPl
Jew, The. Isaac Rosenberg. MBP; MoBrPo; PoFr
Jew Lady, The. *Unknown. See* Sir Hugh.
Jew of Malta, The, *sels.* Christopher Marlowe.
"Fye, what a trouble 'tis to count this trash," *fr.* I, i. NBE (Barabas in His Counting-House.) CoEV
Idea of Wealth, An, *fr.* I, i. BCEP
Mine Argosy from Alexandria, *fr.* I, i. ChTr ("Give me the merchants of the Indian mines.") LO
Precious Stones, *br. sel. fr.* I, i. EV-1
Song of Ithamore, The, *fr.* IV, iv. WHA
Jew to Jesus, The. Florence Kiper Frank. BPP; ChIP; GrCo-1; HBMV; MaRV; NP; NV; StJW; WGRP
Jew Walks in Westminster Abbey, A. Aubrey Hodes. TrJP
Jew Wrecked in the German Cell, The. W. H. Auden. PeBoSo; WaP (Diaspora, The.) LiTA; QS
Jewel, The. Wan Tse, *tr. fr. Chinese by* Alan Lee Simms. ChLP
Jewel-blue electric flowers, The. Three o'Clock; Morning. Ridgely Torrence. NP; TBM
Jewel of the Secret Treasury, The. Hafiz. Odes, VI. AWP; JAWP; LiTW; WBP
Jewelled mine of the pomegranate, whose hexagons of honey, The. The Pomegranate. Louis Dudek. PeCV
Jewels. Asayasu, *tr. fr. Japanese by* Basil Hall Chamberlain. OnPM
Jewels, The. Austin Clarke. MoAB
Jewess, The, *sel.* Henrik Wergeland, *tr. fr. Norwegian by* Charles W. Stork.
"Tangled briars intertwisting." AnNoLy
Jewish Arabic Liturgies. *Unknown, tr. fr. Arabic by* Hartwig Hirschfeld. TrJP
Jewish Cemetery at Newport, The. Longfellow. AmP; AmPP; AnNE; APW; CoV; OnAP; OxBA; PoE; RiBV
Jewish Conscript, The. Florence Kiper Frank. BPP; OQP; QP-2; QS; TrJP
Jewish Hymn in Babylon. Henry Hart Milman. LPS-2
Jewish king now walks at large and sound, The. Zaph Describes the Haunts of Malzah. Charles Heavysege. *Fr.* Saul. BoCaPo
Jewish Lady, The. *Unknown. See* Sir Hugh.
Jewish Lullaby. Louis Untermeyer. RIS
Jewish Main Street. Irving Layton. CaP
Jewish May, The. Morris Rosenfeld, *tr. fr. Yiddish by* Rose Pastor Stokes *and* Helena Frank. TrJP
Jewish Poet Counsels a King, A. Santob de Carrion, *tr. fr. Spanish.* TrJP
Jewishness. Jacob Glatstein, *tr. fr. Yiddish by* Sarah Zweig Betsky. OnCuPl
Jews, The. Henry Vaughan. OBS
Jews, a headstrong, moody, murm'ring race, The. The English in 1680. Dryden. *Fr.* Absalom and Achitophel. NBE
Jews at Haifa. Randall Jarrell. MoAmPo (1950 ed.)
Jew's Daughter, The. *Unknown. See* Sir Hugh.
Jew's Home, The. Robert Eyres Landor. *Fr.* The Impious Feast, I. OBRV
Jews sit in the House of Study, learn Torah, voices raised. Elijah in the House of Study. Mani Leib. OnCuPl
Jezebel. Scudder Middleton. HBMV; TBM
Jhesu cryst, myn leman swete. *Unknown. Fr.* A Prayer of the Five Wounds. AtBAP
Jig. C. Day Lewis. OxBI
Jig, A. Robert Greene. *See* Doron's Jig.
Jigsaw III. Louis MacNeice. HaMV
Jill Came from the Fair. Eleanor Farjeon. GoBP; TiPo
Jillian of Berry. Beaumont *and* Fletcher. *Fr.* The Knight of the Burning Pestle. ElL (Merrythought's Song: "For Jillian of Berry.") OBS
Jilted Nymph, The. Thomas Campbell. EnLoPo
Jim. Hilaire Belloc. AlDL; CenHV; ChTr; HBMV; LiL; MaC; OnSP; ShBV-2; TSW; TSWC
Jim. Perceval Gibbon. BoSA
Jim. Bret Harte. AA; BOHV; IAP; LEAP; LPS-3; MAP; MoAmPo (1942 ed.); NeMA; TCAP; WhC
Jim and Bill. Franklin P. Adams. LHV
Jim and I as children played together. Oh Lucky Jim! *Unknown.* ChTr
Jim at the Corner. Eleanor Farjeon. GaP; SUS
Jim Bludso [of the *Prairie Belle*]. John Hay. AA; AmPP (3d ed.); AnAmPo; BAP; BAV; BBV; BeLS; BOHV; CoBA; DDA; FaBoBe; FaFP; HBV; HiLiAm; IHA; LA; LEAP; MaC; MCCG; MoAmPo (1942 ed.); NeMA; OBAV; PaA; PCD; PFY; PoeMoYo; PoMa; TreFS; YaD
Jim Bowker, he said, if he'd had a fair show. Then Ag'in. Sam Walter Foss. BAP; BOHV; HBV
Jim Brady's Big Brother. James William Foley. PTA-2
Jim-Dog. Margaret E. Sangster. AlBD
Jim Farrow. *Unknown.* CoSo; CSF
Jim Finley's Pig. *Unknown.* FTB
Jim Fisk. *Unknown.* AS, *with music;* ViBoFo
Jim Haggerty's Story. *Unknown.* ABF
Jim-Jam King of the Jou-Jous, The. Alaric Bertrand Stuart. BOHV
Jim Jay. Walter de la Mare. CenHV; CV; GaP; GoTP; HBMV; NV; RG; RIS; SiSoSe
Jim Keene was a reporter on the Trib. The Unknown Reporter. Lee Shippey. DDA
Jim Porter's Shanty Song. *Unknown.* IHA
Jim says a sailor man/ He means to be. When We Are Men. E. Stella Mead. BoTP
Jim was a sailor. Jim at the Corner. Eleanor Farjeon. GaP; SUS
Jimmie Randall was a-hunting, a-hunting in the dark. Molly Bawn. *Unknown.* ViBoFo
Jimmy Randolph. *Unknown. See* Lord Randal.
Jimmy the Mowdy. *Unknown.* OxNR
Jimmy's Enlisted; or, The Recruited Collier. *Unknown.* CoMu
Jimson lives in a new. A Call to the Wild. Lord Dunsany. OnYI
Jingle. John O'Keeffe. *See* Amo, Amas.
Jingle Bells. James S. Pierpont, *wr. at. to* John Pierpont. FaFP; OlF; TreF; YaD
Jingle, bells! jingle, bells! *Unknown.* OxNR
Jingle, Jingle, clear the way. Sleigh Song. G. W. Pettee. LPS-2
Jinny Git Around, *with music. Unknown.* OuSiCo

Jinny the Just. Matthew Prior. CEP; OBEC; OBEV (new ed.); PoEL-3
Jippy and Jimmy. Laura E. Richards. MPB; TiPo
Jist after the war, in the year '98. Shemus O'Brien. Joseph Sheridan Le Fanu. TIP
Jo Jo, My Child. *Unknown, tr. fr. Hebrew by* Immanuel Olsvanger. TrJP
Joan, be swift at the parapet. To Joan of Arc on D-Day. Sister Mary Thérèse. MuM
Joan of Arc at Domremy. Charles Buxton Going. VOD
Joan of Arc, 1926. Virginia Moore. TBM; YT
Joan of Arc to the Tribunal. Anthony Frisch. CaP
Job, *sels.* Bible, *O.T.*
"And Job spake, and said: 'Let the day perish wherein I was born,'" III: 3-25; XXXVIII; XXXIX. BrBE
"Behold, God is great, and we know him not," XXXVI: 26-30, 32. ImOP
Immortality ("For I know that my vindicator liveth"), XIX: 25-27, *Moulton, Modern Reader's Bible.* WGRP
Job's Comforters, XI: 7-10, *Moulton, Modern Reader's Bible.* WGRP
(Eternal Quest, The, XI: 7-8, *Moulton, Modern Reader's Bible.*) MaRV
Job's Curse, III: 3-26. AWP; JAWP; WBP
(Job Complains.) TrGrPo
(Job Longeth for Death, III: 13-19.) PoD
(Let the Day Perish, III: 1-26.) TrJP
Job's Entreaty, XIV. AWP; JAWP; WBP
(Immortality: "Man that is born of woman," XIV, 1-2, 7-12, *Moulton, Modern Reader's Bible.*) WGRP
(Job Cries Out, XIV.) TrGrPo
(Job's Questions, XIV.) OuHeWo
Lord Gave, The, I: 20-21. TreF
Man That Is Born of a Woman, XIV: 1-2. ChTr
Not Flesh of Brass, VI: 1-13. TrJP
Oh That I Knew Where I Might Find Him, XXIII, 3, 8-10. MaRV
Price of Wisdom, The, XXVIII. TrGrPo
(Wisdom, XXVIII: 12-28.) BHV
Visions of the Night, IV: 13-17. LiA
Voice Out of the Whirlwind Answers Job, The, XXXVIII-XLII. EM-1
God Replies, XXXVIII: 2-41. TrGrPo
"Hast thou given the horse his might?" XXXIX: 19-XL: 2. ChTr; InP
Horse, The, XXXIX: 19-25. FaPON; GoTP; StaSt, *abr.*; TrGrPo
(War-Horse, The.) BHV; ShBV-2
Inscrutable Mystery, The, *sels. fr.* XXXVIII-XL. GrCo-2
Leviathan, XLI: 1-21. TrGrPo
Leviathan, the Crocodile, XLI: 13-24, 26-34. MuP
Out of the Whirlwind, XL: 7-24; XLI. AWP; JAWP; WBP
Then the Lord Answered, XXXVIII: 2-24; XXXIX. AWP; JAWP; ShBV-4 (XXXVIII: 1-11, 31-35); WBP
Treasures, The, XXXVIII: 22-32. BoW
Voice from the Whirlwind, The; God's Majesty, XXXVIII. PG (1955 ed.)
Voice of God Out of the Whirlwind, The, XXXVIII-XL. CBOV
Voice Out of the Whirlwind, The. MaRV (XXXVIII: 2-XL: 2, *Moulton, Modern Reader's Bible*); OuHeWo (XXXVIII: 2-XLII: 6)
"Where wast thou when I laid the foundations of the earth?" XXXVIII: 4-38, *abr.* ImOP
Job. Samuel Taylor Coleridge. BOHV
(Epigram: "Sly Beelzebub took all occasions.") LPS-3
Job. E. W. Mandel. PeCV
Job ("O Job, Job"), *with music. Unknown.* OuSiCo
Job Reviles. A. M. Klein. *Fr.* Design for Mediaeval Tapestry. QS
Jobson's Amen. Kipling. AnFE; POTT; VLEP
Jocasta. Euripides, *tr. fr. Greek by* M. Wodhull. *Fr.* Phoenician Maidens. GrR
Jocasta's Death. Sophocles, *tr. fr. Greek by* J. T. Sheppard. *Fr.* Oedipus Rex. LiA; OxBG
(Death of Jocasta, The, *tr. by* Gilbert Murray.) GrR
Jock Johnstone, the Tinkler. James Hogg. BCEP *abr.*; LPS-2
Jock o' Dreams. Rose Fyleman. BoTP
Jock o' the Side. *Unknown.* ESPB (A *and* B *vers.*); OBB; ViBoFo
Jock of [*or* o'] Hazeldean. Sir Walter Scott. BEL; BeLS; BPN; CoBE; EBSV; EmBrPo; EnLi-2 (1949 ed.); EnLit; EnRP; EPN; ERP; EV-4; GN; GTBS; GTBS-D; GTBS-W; GTSE; GTSL; HBV; HiLiEn; MCCG; OAEP; OBRV; OTPC; TCEP; TOP
Jock the Leg and the Merry Merchant. *Unknown.* ESPB
Jockey was a dowdy lad. Scotch Song. Thomas D'Urfey. *Fr.* The Campaigners; or, The Pleasant Adventures at Brussels. CEP
Jocky Fou, Jenny Fain. *Unknown.* EBSV
Jocky said to Jenny, Jenny wilt thou do't. A Dainty Sang [*or* For the Love of Jean]. Allan Ramsay. *Fr.* The Gentle Shepherd. EBSV; OBEC
Jocosa Lyra. Austin Dobson. BOHV; InP
Joculator Domini. Sister Mary John Frederick. GoBC
Joe. David McCord. TiPo (1959 ed.)
Joe Baratta's Giuseppina. Leetla Giuseppina. T. A. Daly. TSWC
Joe Beauchamp ees conceited man. De Baby Show. Wilson MacDonald. WhC
Joe Bowers. *Unknown.* ABF, *with music*; ABS; APW; ATP; BaBo; BoHiPo; CoSo, *with music;* CSF; TrAS, *with music;* TreFS; ViBoFo
Joe Dobson, *with music.* "B.A.T." FTB
Joe Fowler Blues, The, *with music. Unknown.* StDa
Joe Greene. Merrill Moore. WoL
Joe hates a sycophant. It shows. Epigram [*or* On Joe]. P. Dodd. ALV; SiTL
Joe Tinker. Amanda Benjamin Hall. HBMV
Joe Turner [Blues], *with music. Unknown.* AS; TrAS
Joe, you prefatory mortal. Apostrophe to a Pram Rider. E. B. White. InMe
Jog On, Jog On [the Foot-Path Way]. Shakespeare. *Fr.* The Winter's Tale, IV, ii. CBE; ChTr; EG; FaBoCh; GN; HBV; HBVY; LoGBV; OBSC; SiCE; TiPo (1952 ed.); TVC; TVSH; ViBoPo
(Autolycus.) EV-1
(Autolycus' Song.) WhC
(Footpath Way, The.) RIS
(Merry Heart, The.) BoTP; ElL; PCH; ShGoBo; SiTL; TrGrPo
(Songs of Autolycus, The.) OTPC (1923 ed.)
Johannes Agricola in Meditation. Robert Browning. EmBrPo; OBVV; PoVP; TwP; ViPo; ViPP
Johannes Milton, Senex. Robert Bridges. EPP; LiTB; NAMP; PoEL-5
Johannesburg. William Plomer. BoSA
John. Bible, *N.T. See* First Epistle of John *and* St. John.
John Alcohol, my foe, John. My Foe. *Unknown.* BOHV; PA
John and Peter and Robert and Paul. The Chemistry of Character. Elizabeth Dorney. BLPA
John Anderson. Burns. *See* John Anderson, My Jo.
"John Anderson, My Jo." Charles G. Blanden. HBV
John Anderson, My Jo ("John Anderson, my jo, John,/ When we were first acquent"). Burns. AEV; AWP; BEL; BLV; BoLiVe; CaAE; CBOV; CEP; CoBE; EBSV; EiPP; EM-1; EnLi-2; EnLit; EnRP; EV-3; InPo; JAWP; LiTL; LPS-1; MaRV; MCCG; NeHB; OAEP; OBEC; OBEV; OtMeF; OuHeWo; PFE; PG; PIR; Po; PoE; PoMa; ReaPo; RiBV; ShBV-1; TCEP; TOP; TrGrPo; TVSH; ViBoPo; WBP; WHA; WP
(Hymn of Marriage.) PoToHe
(John Anderson.) CBE; GTBS; GTBS-D; GTBS-W; GTSE; GTSL; HBV; InP; LEAP; LiTB; LiTG; LoPo; OTPC; PECK; WBLP
John Anderson, My Jo ("John Anderson, my jo, John/ I wonder what ye mean"). *At. to* Robert Burns. CoMu
John B. Sails, The, *with music. Unknown.* AS
John Ball shot them all. *Unknown.* PPL
John Barleycorn. Burns. BOHV; CG, *sl. abr.*; CoEV; EV-3; FaBoCh; HBV; LoGBV; LPS-3; PECK; SeCeV; ShBV-1
John Baynham's Epitaph. Thomas Dermody. OnYI
John Bird, a laborer, lies here. Epitaph. Sylvia Townsend Warner. BLV; MBP; MoBrPo; NeMA; PIAE
John Bright. Francis Barton Gummere. AA
John Brown. Stephen Vincent Benét. *Fr.* John Brown's Body. WoL
John Brown. Harry Lyman Koopman. AA
John Brown. Vachel Lindsay. Booker Washington Trilogy, II. AnAmPo; LA; MAP; MoAmPo; NP; TBM; TriL
John Brown. Edna Dean Proctor. PAH
John Brown. Allen Tate. SPP
John Brown. Eugene F. Ware. GA
John Brown; a Paradox. Louise Imogen Guiney. DD; GA
John Brown and Jeanne at Fontainebleau. Students. Florence Wilkinson Evans. HBV; SBMV
John Brown died on the scaffold for the slave. John Brown. Edna Dean Proctor. PAH
John Brown of Osawatomie. Edmund Clarence Stedman. *See* How Old Brown Took Harper's Ferry.
John Brown of Osawatomie [*or* Ossawatomie] spake on his dying day. Brown of Osawatomie [*or* Ossawatomie]. Whittier. BHV; DD; GA; HBV; LEAP; LPS-2; MC; OTPC; PAH; PIR
John Brown of Ossawatomie. John Brown. Allen Tate. SPP
John Brown's Body, *sels.* Stephen Vincent Benét.
Battle of Gettysburg, The. BeLS
Pickett's Charge. PoeMoYo
Enlistments, The. ATP
Invocation: "American muse, whose strong and diverse heart." CrMA; MPB; NP, *shorter sel.*; PaA

America ("You are the buffalo-ghost . . ."). PoeMoYo
John Brown. WoL
John Brown's Body Lies a-Moldering. TwCV
John Brown's Prayer. AtBAP; NP; PoNe
"Lincoln, six feet one in his stocking feet." PreP
(Lincoln Calls for Volunteers.) ATP
Love Came By from the Riversmoke. MAP; MoAmPo
Out of John Brown's Strong Sinews. WHA
Significance of John Brown, The. PaA
("Out of his body grows revolving steel," *shorter sel.*) VOD (1935 ed.)
Slaver, The, Prelude. AmPP; TwCV
Soliloquy of Lincoln before Manassas. PaA
Song of Breath, A. MoVE
(Song of the Breath, The.) AmP
Song of the Riders. MAP; MoAmPo
Thirteen Sisters, The. TreF
"This is the hidden place that hiders know." ViBoPo

John Brown's Body (*diff. versions*). *Unknown, at. to* Charles Sprague Hall *and to* Thomas Brigham Bishop. ABF, *with music;* BoHiPo; FaFP; GA; InP; MC; OIF; PoFr; ShS, *with music;* SiTL; TrAS, *with music*
(Glory Hallelujah! or, John Brown's Body.) PaA; PAH
John Brown's Body Lies a-Mouldering. Stephen Vincent Benét. *Fr.* John Brown's Body. TwCV
John Brown's Prayer. Stephen Vincent Benét. *Fr.* John Brown's Body. AtBAP; NP; PoNe
John Bull, Esquire, my jo John. A New Song to an Old Tune. *Unknown.* PAH
John Bull for pastime took a prance. Nongtongpaw. Charles Dibdin. BOHV; CG; HBV
John Bun. *Unknown. See* On John Bun.
John Burns of Gettysburg. Bret Harte. DDA; GA; HBV; LHV, *abr.;* MC; OHIP; PaA; PAH; PAP
John Butler Yeats. Jeanne Robert Foster. GoYe
John Calvin was a man of God. House of Calvin. Leonora Speyer. QS
John Calvin whose peculiar fad. Ballade of the Heresiarchs. Hilaire Belloc. MoVE
John Charles Frémont. Charles F. Lummis. PAH
John Charles Frémont. Whittier. LPS-3
John Cherokee, *with music. Unknown.* SoAmSa
John Cook had a little grey mare. *Unknown.* OxNR
John could not sleep, though swaddled from the cold. Light Sleeping. Thom Gunn. PoN
John Damascene, *sel.* Aleksey Konstantinovich Tolstoy, *tr. fr. Russian by* Maurice Baring.
Troparion. BoR
John Dameray, *with music. Unknown.* ShS
John Darrow. Donald Davidson. HBMV
John Dobbins was so captivated. The Eggs and the Horses. *Unknown.* LPS-3
John Done Saw That Number, *with music. Unknown.* OuSiCo
John Donne's Defiance. J. R. Hervey. AnNZ
John Dory. *Unknown.* BHV, *sl. abr.;* ESPB; SG
John Endicott, *sels.* Longfellow.
Proclamation, The. PAH
Prologue, The: "Tonight we strive to read." PAH
John Evereldown. E. A. Robinson. AmPP (4th ed.); MOAP; NePA; OBAV; OxBA
John Fane Dingle by Rumney Brook. Glaucopis. Richard Hughes. OBMV
John Filson. William Henry Venable. PAH
John François. *Unknown. See* Boney.
John Frost. William Miller. PCH
John Garner's Trail Herd. *Unknown.* CoSo; CSF
John Gilbert, with music. Unknown. StDa
John Gilpin [*or* John Gilpin's Ride]. William Cowper. *See* Diverting History of John Gilpin, The.
John Gorham. E. A. Robinson. ChMo; CMP; MAP; MAPA; MoAB; MoAmPo; NP
John Graydon. Wilson MacDonald. CaP
John Greenleaf Whittier. Phoebe Cary. DD; GA
John Greenleaf Whittier. John Cameron Grant. DD; GA
John Grumlie. Allan Cunningham. BOHV; HBV
John had. Happiness. A. A. Milne. TiPo
John Hancock Otis. Edgar Lee Masters. *Fr.* Spoon River Anthology. PoFr; TOP
John Hardy. *Unknown.* BaBo (A *and* B *vers.*); TrAS, *with music;* ViBoFo (A *and* B *vers.*)
(John Harty, *diff. vers., with music.*) ABF
John Henry. Lucy Cherry Crisp. NoCaPo (rev. ed.)
John Henry (*diff. versions*). *Unknown.* ABF, *2 vers., with music;* AmPP (3d ed.); APW; AS, *with music;* BaBo (A *and* B *vers.*); BeLS; FaBoBe; FaFP; GoSl; MaC; OuSiCo, *with music;* OxBoLi; SiTL; SPP; TiPo (1959 ed.); TrAS, *with music;* TrGrPo; ViBoFo (A, B, C, D, E, *and* F *vers.*)
("John Henry tol' his cap'n," *much abr.*) NAMP
John Henry; an American Episode. Alfred V. Frankenstein. CAG
John Henry, dat's one wurrisome boy. John Henry. Lucy Cherry Crisp. NoCaPo (rev. ed.)
John Henry in Harlem. M. B. Toleson. GoSl
John Henry tol' his cap'n. John Henry. *Unknown.* AmPP (3d ed.); AS; BeLS; NAMP
John Henry was a lil [*or* little] baby. John Henry. *Unknown.* ABF; FaFP; MaC; OxBoLi; SiTL; TrGrPo
John Henry was a railroad man. John Henry (B *vers.*). *Unknown.* BaBo
John Henry was a steel drivin' man. John Henry. *Unknown.* ABF
John Henry was a very small boy. John Henry (A *vers.*). *Unknown.* ViBoFo
John Henry, who was a baby. John Henry (C *vers.*). *Unknown.* ViBoFo
John Henry's mother had a little baby. John Henry. *Unknown.* OuSiCo
John Horace Burleson. Edgar Lee Masters. *Fr.* Spoon River Anthology. CrMA
John Hoskins to His Little Child Benjamin, from the Tower. John Hoskins. TuPP
John-John. Thomas MacDonagh. AnIV; AWP; HBMV; JAWP; LBBV; OnYI; OxBI; TIP; WBP
John Jones. Swinburne. *Fr.* The Heptalogia. NA; OAEP
John Keats. Byron. *Fr.* Don Juan, XI. BCEP
John Keats. T. A. Daly. PoeMoYo
John Keats. Dante Gabriel Rossetti. Five English Poets, 4. BPN; EmBrPo; EPN; PtP
John Keats, who was killed off by one critique. John Keats. Byron. *Fr.* Don Juan, XI. BCEP
John Kinsella's Lament for Mrs. Mary Moore. W. B. Yeats. AtBAP; EnLP; LiTM; MoAB; OAEP (2d ed.); SiTL
John Knox's Indictment of the Queen. Swinburne. *Fr.* Bothwell. VA
John Landless beside the Road. Iwan Goll, *tr. fr. French by* Claire Goll. OnPM
John Landless Leads the Caravan. Iwan Goll, *tr. fr. French by* William Carlos Williams. TrJP
John Littlehouse the redhead was a large ruddy man. The Blacksmith's Serenade. Vachel Lindsay. StPo
John Littlewit, friends, was a credulous man. Littlewit and Loftus. Pamelia Vining Yule. BoCaPo (1943 ed.)
John Marr, *sel.* Herman Melville.
"Since as in night's deck-watch ye show." ViBoPo
John Masefield Relates the Story of Tom, Tom, the Piper's Son, *parody.* Louis Untermeyer. MoAmPo
John Maynard. Horatio Alger, Jr. BeLS; BLPA; FaBoBe; PTA-2
John o' Badenyon. John Skinner. EBSV
John o' Dreams. Theodosia Garrison. HBMV
John o' Lorn. Neil Munro. EBSV
John O'Dwyer of the Glen. *Tr. fr. Irish by* Thomas Furlong. AnIV
John of Gaunt's Dying Speech. Shakespeare. *See* This England ("This royal throne of kings.")
John of Hazelgreen. *Unknown.* BaBo (A, B, *and* C *vers.*); ESPB (A *and* E *vers.*); ViBoFo
John of Launoy. Sir Henry Taylor. *Fr.* Philip van Artevelde. VA
John of Tours. *Unknown, tr. fr. French by* Dante Gabriel Rossetti. AWP; JAWP; PCN; PoVP; WBP
John Pattison Gibson. W. W. Gibson. MM
John Paul Jones. Richard Watson Gilder. PoRL
John Peel. John Woodcock Graves. CH; OxBoLi
John Pegram. William Gordon McCabe. BIG
John Pelham. James Ryder Randall. AA; BIG; GA; PAH
John Popham. Robert P. Tristram Coffin. OnPP
John Quincy Adams. Stephen Vincent Benét. NAMP
John Richard William Alexander Dwyer. Horace Smith *and* James Smith. *Fr.* The Theatre. OBRV
John Riley, *with music. Unknown.* OuSiCo
John Saw the Holy Number, *with music. Unknown.* BoAN-1
John Sevier. Donald Davidson. *Fr.* The Tall Men. SPP
John Smith, fellow fine. *Unknown.* OxNR
John Smith's Approach to Jamestown. James Barron Hope. MC; PAH
John Standish, Artist. Kenneth Fearing. AnAmPo; LA
John Stuart Mill. J. S. Mill. E. C. Bentley. *Fr.* Biography for Beginners. BOHV; FiBHP; OxBoLi; WhC
John Sutter. Yvor Winters. MoVE
John the Baptist. William Drummond of Hawthornden. *See* For the Baptist.
John the Baptist. Louis Simpson. NePoEA
John the Pilgrim. Theodore Watts-Dunton. MaRV
John Thompson's Daughter. Phoebe Cary. BOHV; PA; PTA-2
John Thomson and the Turk (A *and* B *vers.*). *Unknown.* ESPB
John Tompkins lived in a house of logs. The Second Concession of Deer. William Wye Smith. BoCaPo (1943 ed.)
John Underhill. Whittier. PAH; TCAP
John Was a-Writin', *with music. Unknown.* OuSiCo
John Wasson. Edgar Lee Masters. *Fr.* Spoon River Anthology. LaNeLa
John Webster. Swinburne. *Fr.* Sonnets on English Dramatic Poets (1590–1650). InvP; PtP; VLEP

John Wesley Gaines. *Unknown.* FiBHP
John Wesley's Rule. John Wesley. HBVY; PCH
(Rule, 4.) FaFP
(What to Do.) MeMeAg
John Winter. Laurence Binyon. PtOT; SG; TCPD
John woke on Jan. first and felt queer. Limerick. *Unknown.* BOHV
John Woodvil; a Tragedy, *sel.* Charles Lamb.
Helen, *by* Mary Lamb. OBRV
John Wylie sold his father's farm and went. Exchange. W. H. Gerry. CAG
John you are my husbandes'man you knowe. *Unknown.* SeCSL
John-a-Dreams and Harum-Scarum. Ballad of Low-lie-down. Madison Cawein. HBV
Johneen. Patrick J. Carroll. WHL
Johneen. "Moira O'Neill." TIP
Johnie Armstrong. *Unknown.* BaBo; BoLiVe; EBSV; EnLi-1 (1949 ed.); ESPB (A, B, *and* C *vers.*); GDAH; HoPM; OBB; PC; ReaPo; TOP; TrGrPo; UnPo; ViBoFo (A *and* B *vers.*)
(Johnny Armstrong.) MaC; StaSt, *abr.*
"King he wrytes a luving letter, The," *sel.* PoFr
Johnie Cock. *Unknown.* BaBo (A, B, C, *and* D *vers.*); ESPB (A, B, C, D, *and* K *vers.*); TCEP, *diff. vers.*; ViBoFo (A *and* B *vers.*)
Johnie Faa. *Unknown.* *See* Wraggle Taggle Gipsies, The.
Johnie rose up in a May morning. Johnie Cock. *Unknown.* BaBo (C *vers.*); ViBoFo (B *vers.*)
Johnie Scot. *Unknown.* BaBo (A *and* B *vers.*); ESPB
Johnnie Bought a Ham, *with music.* *Unknown.* OuSiCo
Johnnie, Cock Up Your Beaver. Burns. AtBAP
(Cock Up Your Beaver.) CBE
Johnnie Cope. Adam Skirving. CBOV; EBSV
(Hey Johnnie Cope.) EV-3
Johnnie Courteau. William Henry Drummond. BoCaPo; CaP; CPG; OCL; PeCV
Johnnie Crack and Flossie Snail. Dylan Thomas. *Fr.* Under Milk Wood. FaPON
(Song: "Johnnie Crack and Flossie Snail.") FiBHP
Johnnie Norrie. *Unknown.* OxNR
Johnnie of Cockerslee. *Unknown.* OBB
Johnnie's First Moose. William Henry Drummond. CP
Johnny and Betsy. *Unknown.* ABS
Johnny Appleseed. Rosemary Benét *and* Stephen Vincent Benét. BoChLi (1950 ed.); MPB; OTPC (1946 ed.); TrAS, *with music*
Johnny Appleseed. Arthur S. Bourinot. CaP
Johnny Appleseed, *sel.* Vachel Lindsay.
"Johnny Appleseed, Johnny Appleseed." FaPON
Johnny Appleseed. Edgar Lee Masters. CP
Johnny Appleseed. William Henry Venable. PaA; PAH
Johnny Appleseed Still Further West. Vachel Lindsay. HiLiAm
Johnny Armstrong. *Unknown.* *See* Johnie Armstrong.
Johnny Armstrong killed a calf. *Unknown.* OxNR
Johnny Boker, *with music.* *Unknown.* AmSS; ShS; SoAmSa
Johnny Cock, in a May morning. Johnie Cock. *Unknown.* BaBo (B *vers.*); ESPB (C *vers.*)
Johnny Come Down to Hilo, *with music.* *Unknown.* ABF; SoAmSa, *st.* 1
(Johnny Walk Along to Hilo, *with music.*) ShS
(Oh, Wake Dat Girl!) MuP
Johnny Dow. *Unknown.* WhC
("Wha lies here?") FiBHP; SiTL
Johnny Faa, the Gypsy Laddie. *Unknown.* *See* Wraggle Taggle Gipsies, The.
Johnny Faa, the Lord of Little Egypt. *Unknown.* *See* Wraggle Taggle Gipsies, The.
Johnny Fife and Johnny's Wife. Mildrew Plew Meigs. GaP; TiPo
Johnny had a little dove. Johnny's Farm. H. M. Adams. BoTP
Johnny he's risen up in the morn. Johnny of Cockley's Well. *Unknown.* EnSB
Johnny, I Hardly Knew Ye. *Unknown.* AnIV; GTIV; OnYI; OxBoLi; TIP; WaaP
Johnny, I Hardly Knew Ye: In Dublinese, *parody.* *Unknown.* OnYI
Johnny, I Hardly Knew Ye: In Miltonese, *parody.* Oliver St. John Gogarty. OnYI
Johnny, I Hardly Knew Ye: In Swinburnese, *parody.* Robert Yelverton Tyrrell. OnYI
Johnny Jones has lost a leg. The Wail of the Well. *Unknown.* DDA
Johnny McCardner, *with music.* *Unknown.* OuSiCo
Johnny of Cockley's Well. *Unknown.* EnSB
Johnny of the Avenue. Rondel. Villon. TrFP
Johnny O'May; Johnny O'May. To a Friend Recently Married. Struthers Burt. NoCaPo
Johnny Randall. *Unknown.* *See* Lord Randal.
Johnny Raw and Polly Clark. *Unknown.* CoMu
Johnny Sands. *Unknown, at. to* John Sinclair. ABS (A *and* B *vers.*); CoMu; ViBoFo
Johnny shall have a new bonnet. Mother Goose. HBV; HBVY; OTPC; OxNR; WP
Johnny Stiles, or the Wild Mustard River, *with music.* *Unknown.* OuSiCo
Johnny, though clear mine eyes, to speculate. Johnny, I Hardly Knew Ye: In Miltonese, *parody.* Oliver St. John Gogarty. OnYI
Johnny Walk Along to Hilo. *Unknown.* *See* Johnny Come Down to Hilo.
Johnny, Won't You Ramble? *with music.* *Unknown.* OuSiCo
Johnnycake, The. *Unknown.* MPB
Johnny's By-low Song. Laura E. Richards. BoChLi; BOL
Johnny's Farm. H. M. Adams. BoTP
Johnny's Hist'ry Lesson. Nixon Waterman. PTA-1
Johnny's the Lad I Love. *Unknown.* AnIV; GTIV; OxBoLi
Johny he has risen up i' the morn. Johnie Cock. *Unknown.* BaBo (A *vers.*); ESPB; ViBoFo (A *vers.*)
Joi, the Glug. C. J. Dennis. NeLNL
Join all the world's delights. Poem for Gwyn and Käthe. Davies Aberpennar. MoWP
Join hands and circle to the left. Rhymed Dance Calls. *Unknown.* CoSo
Join mates in mirth to me. Upon His Meeting with His Two Worthy Friends and Fellow-Poets. Sir Philip Sidney. *Fr.* Two Pastorals. SiCE; TuPP
Join once again, my Celia, join. Song. Charles Cotton. ViBoPo
Join the Caroling. Rowena Bastin Bennet. SDH
Join together thirty spokes—you have a wheel. Tao Teh Ching, XXIII. *Unknown, tr. fr. Chinese.* WhP
Join with the noble-hearted. Distich. Shuraikh. TrJP
Joined the Blues. John Jerome Rooney. AA
Joke Versified, A. Thomas Moore. *See* On Taking a Wife.
Jokesmith's Vacation, The. Don Marquis. ALV; FiBHP
Joliet. Carl Sandburg. CoV
Jolly Batchelor Kindly Entertained, The. *Unknown.* *See* Thankful Country Lass, The.
Jolly Beggar, The. *At. to* James V, King of Scotland. CoMu
Jolly Beggars, The. Burns. BEL; CEP; EiPP; EM-1; EnRP; OAEP; PoEL-4
See the Smoking Bowl before Us, *sel.* ALV, *abr.*; ATP (1935 ed.); BSV; GoTS
(Jolly Mortals, Fill Your Glasses.) EnLi-2 (1949 ed.)
Drinking Song: "Fig for those by law protected, A." PoFr; TrGrPo
Jolly Cowboy, The, *with music.* *Unknown.* CoSo
Jolly Days. Ivy O. Eastwick. MPB (1956 ed.)
Jolly Driver, The. *Unknown.* CoMu
Jolly fat friar loved liquor good store, A. Gluggity Glug. George Colman. *Fr.* The Myrtle and the Vine. HBV; LPS-3
Jolly Good Ale and Old. *At. to* William Stevenson. *See* Back and Side Go Bare, Go Bare.
Jolly icicles ringing in their throats, The. The Snowshoers. A. M. Klein. BoCaPo (1948 ed.)
Jolly Jack. Thackeray. HBV
Jolly Jankyn. *Unknown.* OxBoLi
Jolly Lumbermen, The. *Unknown.* *See* Buffalo Skinners, The.
Jolly men at Feckenham, The. The Feckenham Men. John Drinkwater. CP; GBV; GTSL; TVSH
Jolly Miller, The. Isaac Bickerstaffe. *See* There Was a Jolly Miller.
Jolly Mortals, Fill Your Glasses. Burns. *See* See the Smoking Bowl before Us.
Jolly Old Pedagogue, The. George Arnold. HBV; LPS-2; OnPP; TreFS
Jolly old sow once lived in a sty, A. The Three Little Pigs. Sir Alfred Scott-Gatty. BoTP
Jolly Phoebus his car to the coach-house had driven. Homecoming. *Unknown.* AnIV
Jolly Pinder of Wakefield, The. *Unknown.* BaBo; ESPB
(Robin Hood and the Pinder of Wakefield.) EV-2
Jolly Shepherd, The. Shakespeare. Fr. King Lear, III, vi. PCH
Jolly Shepherd, shepherd on a hill. In Praise of His Love [*or* Damaetas' Jig]. Sir John Wotton. EIL; ElSeCe
Jolly Shepherd Wat, The. *Unknown.* *See* Can I Not Sing.
Jolly Supper, The. Baltasar del Alcázar, *tr. fr. Spanish by* Thomas Walsh. AnSpL-1
Jolly Swain, A. Aphra Behn. *Fr.* The City Heiress; or, Sir Timothy Treat-All. DiM
Jolly Trades-Men, The. *Unknown.* CoMu
Jolly Wagoner, The, *with music.* *Unknown.* TrAS
Jolly Wassail-Bowl, A. *Unknown.* AnEC
Jolly Wat. *Unknown.* *See* Can I Not Sing.
Jolly Woodchuck, The. Marion Edey. FaPON; TiPo
Jolly Young Sailor and the Beautiful Queen, The, *with music.* *Unknown.* ShS
Jolly Young Waterman, The. Charles Dibdin. EV-3
Joly Wat. *Unknown.* *See* Can I Not Sing.
Jonah, *sels.* Bible, *O.T.*
Jonah's Prayer, II: 3-11. TrJP
Story of Jonah, The, I: 3-17. SG

Jonah. Aldous Huxley. ChTr
Jonah. *Unknown. Fr.* Patience. ACP
Jonah and the Whale. Viola Meynell. EtS; MBP; MoBrPo (1942 ed.)
Jonah and the Whale. *Unknown.* BLPA
Jonah rose up to flee unto Tarshish from the presence of the Lord. Jonah, Bible, *O.T.* SG
Jonah was an immigrant, so runs the Bible tale. Darky Sunday School. *Unknown.* ABF; OxBoLi; SiTL
Jonah's Prayer. Jonah, II: 3–11, Bible, *O.T.* TrJP
Jonas Kindred's Household. George Crabbe. *Fr.* Tales. FaBoEn
Jonathan. "Rachel," *tr. fr. Hebrew by* L. V. Snowman. TrJP
Jonathan. Rose Fyleman. TiPo
Jonathan Bing. Beatrice Curtis Brown. FaPON; GaP; LiL; PCD; RIS; TiPo
Jonathan Bing Dances for Spring. Beatrice Curtis Brown. GoBP; SiSoSe
Jonathan Bing Does Arithmetic. Beatrice Curtis Brown. GaP; RIS
Jonathan Bing's Tea. Beatrice Curtis Brown. WaKn
Jonathan Blake. After the Party. William Wise. FaPON
Jonathan Gee. Jonathan. Rose Fyleman. TiPo
Jonathan Houghton. Edgar Lee Masters. *Fr.* Spoon River Anthology. OxBA
Jonathan Smith, *with music.* Karl N. Llewellyn. SoAF
Jonathan to John. James Russell Lowell. *Fr.* The Biglow Papers, 2d Series, No. II. CoBA; IAP; PaA; PAH; PAP
Jones at the Barber Shop. *Unknown.* LPS-3
Jones's Pasture. Abbie Huston Evans. NP
Jonquils, The. Allen Upward. *Fr.* Scented Leaves from a Chinese Jar. NP
Jonquils and violets smelling sweet. Before Spring. P. A. Ropes. BoTP
Jonson, to tell the world what I to thee. To My Friend Mr. Jonson. Sir Thomas Roe. BoFr
Jorasse. Samuel Rogers. *Fr.* Italy. LPS-2
Jordan ("When first my lines [*or* verse]"). George Herbert. ATP; EPS; MePo; OBS; PoFS; SeEP
Jordan ("Who says that fictions"). George Herbert. CoEV; ElSeCe; FaBoEn; LiTB; MeLP; MePo; OBS; Po; PoEL-2; PoFS; PrWP; ReEn; SeEP; TriL; TwCrTr
Jordan Dove, The, *sel.* Sergei Aleksandrovich Yesenin, *tr. fr. Russian by* Babette Deutsch.
"Moon is the tongue, The." TrRV
Jorridge and Porridge. Louise Ayres Garnett. GaP; OTPC (1946 ed.)
Joseph and His Brethren. Genesis, XXXVII: 3–36, XXXIX: 1–XLVI: 30, Bible, *O.T.* OuHeWo
Joseph and His Brethren, *sels.* Charles Jeremiah Wells. VA
Patriarchal Home, The.
Phraxanor to Joseph.
Rachel.
Triumph of Joseph, The.
Joseph and the Shopkeeper. *Unknown, tr. fr. French by* Alfred R. Bellinger. ChrBoLe
Joseph Being an Aged Man. *Unknown.* AnEC
Joseph, honored from sea to sea. The Man of the House. Katharine Tynan. CAW; ChrBoLe; JKCP; WHL
Joseph Mary Plunkett. Wilfrid Meynell. ISi
Joseph Mica. *Unknown. See* Wreck of the Six-Wheel Driver, The.
Joseph Mickel was a good engineer. The Wreck of the Six-Wheel Driver. *Unknown.* ABF
Joseph, mild and noble, bent above the straw. Mary's Baby. Shaemas O'Sheel. CAW; HBV; HBVY; JKCP
Joseph Was an Old Man. *Unknown. See* Cherry-Tree Carol, The.
Joseph was an old man. A Carol. Lizette Woodworth Reese. StJW
Joseph Rodman Drake. Fitz-Greene Halleck. *See* On the Death of Joseph Rodman Drake.
Joseph Sturge. Whittier. BHV
Joseph's Suspicion. Rainer Maria Rilke, *tr. fr. German by* Paul Engle. ReMP
Joses, the Brother of Jesus. Harry Kemp. HBMV; MaRV; OQP; QP-2
Joshua Fit de Battle ob Jerico [*or* of Jericho]. *Unknown.* APW; ATP; BoAN-1; MaC; OlF; PreP; TrAS, *with music;* TrGrPo
(Group of Negro Songs, A.) NAMP
Joshua Peabody. John Holmes. BPP
Josie. *Unknown. See* Frankie and Johnny.
Joslin Murdoch, an actor no more could act. A Visit to the Sea. Edgar Lee Masters. BoFr
Journal, *sel.* Edna St. Vincent Millay.
"I read with varying degrees." ImOP
Journal of an Airman, *sel.* W. H. Auden.
Airman's Alphabet, The. PoF
Journals, *sel.* Emerson.
"America, my country, can the mind." AmPP
Journey, The. Thomas Curtis Clark. MaRV
Journey, The. Aidan Clarke. BoTP
Journey, The. Walter de la Mare. InP
Journey, The. Mary Berri Hansbrough. AA
Journey. Sam Harrison. NeIP
Journey, The. L. Le Mesurier. VOD
Journey, IV. Erik Lindegren, *tr. fr. Swedish by* Martin S. Allwood. LiTW
Journey, The. John T. McFarland. OQP; QP-1
Journey, The. Scudder Middleton. HBMV
Journey. Edna St. Vincent Millay. NLK; TCAP; VOD
Journey, *sel.* Harold Monro.
"Oh the wild engine! Every time I sit." AlDL
Journey, The. Edwin Muir. MoVE
Journey. Salvador Novo, *tr. fr. Spanish by* H. R. Hays. AnCL
Journey, A. Josephine Preston Peabody. RAR
Journey, The. Yvor Winters. MoVE
Journey among Ruins. Li Ho, *tr. fr. Chinese by* Ho Chih-yuan. WhP
Journey Ends, A. Don Blanding. MaRV
Journey from New Zealand. "Robin Hyde." AnNZ
Journey into France, The. *Unknown.* CoMu
Journey of the Magi. T. S. Eliot. AmP; ChMo; CMP; CoBA; FaBoCh; FaBoMo; FaFP; GTBS-D; GTBS-W; InPo; LiTA; LiTM; LoGBV; MAP; MaPo; MoAB; MoAmPo; NePA; OAEP (2d ed.); OBMV; PoE; PoLFOT; PtOT, *sl. abr.;* ReaPo; RiBV; ShBV-3; StJW; TrGrPo; TriL; TwCV; TwHP; TwP; UnPo (3d ed.)
Journey Onwards, The. Thomas Moore. EV-4; GTBS; GTBS-D; GTBS-W; GTSE; GTSL; HBV; SeCePo (As Slow Our Ship.) LPS-1; TIP
Journey through the Night. John Holloway. NePoEA
Journey to a Parallel. Bruce McM. Wright. PoNe
Journey to Brundusium, *abr.* Horace, *tr. fr. Latin by* William Cowper. WoL
Journey to Exeter, A, *abr.* John Gay. WoL
Journey to Iceland. W. H. Auden. BrBE
Journey to Jerusalem, *sel.* Maxwell Anderson.
"For ten days now they have done no work. The walls." QS
Journey to the North. Tu Fu, *tr. fr. Chinese by* Pu Hsiang-hsing. WhP
Journey toward Evening. Phyllis McGinley. GoYe
Journeying Alone. Princess Oku, *tr. fr. Japanese by* Ishii *and* Obata. OnPM
Journeyman, The. Ralph Hodgson. AtBAP
Journeyman, The. *Unknown, tr. fr. Irish by* Frank O'Connor. KiLC
Journey's End. Evelyn H. Healey. MaRV
Journey's End, The. Henry Lee Smith. PoP
Journey's End. Humbert Wolfe. TrJP; TwCV; YT
Jove descends in sleet and snow. The Storm. Alcaeus. AWP; JAWP; OnPM; WBP
Jove for Europa's love took shape of bull. Parthenophil and Parthenophe, LXIII. Barnabe Barnes. ReEn
Jove thundered out of heaven, and straight was known. Coelo Tonantem. Horace. *Fr.* Odes. SoV
Jovial Beggar, The. *Unknown.* BoTP; CG
Jovial Crew, A; or, The Merry Beggars, *sels.* Richard Brome.
"Round, a round, a round, boys, a round, A," *fr.* IV, i. TuPP
Song of the Beggars, *fr.* I, i. CenL; SeCL
Jovial Marriner, The; or, The Sea-Man's Renown. John Playford. CoMu
Jovial Priest's Confession, The. Leigh Hunt. BOHV
Jovial Tinker, The; or, The Willing Couple. *Unknown.* CoMu
Jovial Shepheard's Song, The. Michael Drayton. *See* Sirena.
Jovial Welshmen, The. *Unknown. See* Three Jovial Welshmen, The.
Joy. Hilda Conkling. PC
Joy. W. H. Davies. POTT
Joy. Clarissa Scott Delany. CDC; PoNe
Joy. Fan Yün, *tr. fr. Chinese by* Henry H. Hart. PoHN
Joy. Paul Fort, *tr. fr. French by* Alan Conder. TrFP
Joy. Sister Mary Irma. JKCP (1955 ed.)
Joy. Robinson Jeffers. ChMo; CMP; NeMA; NP
Joy. Rose Hawthorne Lathrop. *Fr.* Give Me Not Tears. AA
Joy. Carl Sandburg. BAP; LEAP; NP; PC
Joy. Matilda Hutchinson Turner. RAR
Joy. Oscar Wilde. *Fr.* Humanitad. PCH
Joy and Dream. Goethe, *tr. fr. German by* L. R. Lind. LiTW
Joy and Pleasure. W. H. Davies. OBMV
Joy and Sorrow. Aubrey Thomas De Vere. OQP; QP-2
Joy and Sorrow. Sadi, *tr. fr. Persian by* A. J. Arberry. PeP
Joy, and the triumph and the doom of gladness. The Dear Mystery. John Hall Wheelock. TBM
Joy and woe are woven fine. Life. Blake. *Fr.* Auguries of Innocence. CBE
Joy as Old as Breathing, A. Etta May Van Tassel. JKCP (1955 ed.)

Joy Awaiting, The. James Henry Darlington. BAP
Joy, beauty, awe, supremest worship blending. At Benediction. Eleanor Rogers Cox. JKCP
Joy cannot be found in the star. José Moreno Villa, *tr. fr. Spanish by* Eleanor L. Turnbull. CoSP
Joy comes and goes; hope ebbs and flows. A Question [*or* To Fausta]. Matthew Arnold. EmBrPo; PoVP; VLEP
Joy Enough. Barrett Eastman. AA
Joy for the sturdy trees. Tree-planting. Samuel Francis Smith. OHIP
Joy in Insecurity. Emily Dickinson. *See* Go not too near a house of rose.
Joy in rebel Plymouth town, in the spring of sixty-four. "Albemarle" Cushing. James Jeffrey Roche. PAH
Joy in the Flowers. Blake. *See* Nightingale and Flowers.
Joy is a trick in the air. Birth-Dues. Robinson Jeffers. MAP; MoAB; MoAmPo
Joy is everywhere on earth. Chant of the Ninth Order of Seraphim. Inigo de Mendoza. CAW
Joy is in the meadow gay. Joy. Paul Fort. TrFP
Joy Is in the Morning Veiled, A. Lola Ridge. TCPD
Joy is not a thing you can see. Joy. Hilda Conkling. PC
Joy is the best of healers, when the pains. Music's Anodyne. Pindar. *Fr.* Nemean Odes, IV. GrR
Joy is the blossom, sorrow is the fruit. Epigram. Walter Savage Landor. HBV
Joy! joy! the day is come at last, the day of hope and pride. The Muster of the North. Sir Charles Gavan Duffy. TIP
Joy lights the candles in my heart. Candles. Babette Deutsch. VOD
Joy May Kill. Michelangelo, *tr. fr. Italian by* John Addington Symonds. AWP; JAWP; WBP
(Fearful Joy.) OnPM
Joy Meets Boy. Robert P. Tristram Coffin. OTPC (1946 ed.)
Joy-Month. David Atwood Wasson. HBV; SN
Joy o' Living. Amanda Benjamin Hall. HBMV
Joy of a Dog, The. Edgar A. Guest. AlBD
Joy of Battle, The. John Fletcher. *Fr.* The Mad Lover, IV, iv. EV-2; LH
("Arm, arm, arm, arm!") CenL; ElL
Joy of Church Fellowship [Rightly Attended], The. Edward Taylor. *Fr.* God's Determinations. AmP; AmPP; CoV; OxBA
Joy, of flame celestial fashioned. Ode to Joy. Schiller. LiA; LiTW
Joy of Giving, The. Whittier. ChBR
Joy of Incompleteness, The. Albert Crowell. PoToHe (new ed.)
Joy of Knowledge. Isidor Schneider. TrJP
Joy of Life, The. W. H. Davies. ChMo; CMP; TriL
Joy of Life. Moses ibn Ezra, *tr. fr. Hebrew by* Solomon Solis-Cohen. *Fr.* The Book of Tarshish. TrJP
Joy of Life. Mary Russell Mitford. OTPC
Joy of Living, The. Robert Browning. *See* Wild Joys of Living, The.
Joy of My Life! Henry Vaughan. *See* Joy of My Life! While Left Me Here.
Joy of my life! full oft for loving you. Amoretti, LXXXII. Spenser. BEL; PeBoSo; ReIE
Joy of My Life! While Left Me Here. Henry Vaughan. SeCV-1
(Joy of My Life!) OBS
Joy of the Hills, The. Edwin Markham. LBMV; PoMa; POT; PoTo
Joy of the Morning. Edwin Markham. AA; BLA; FaPON; HBV; LBAP; MPB; PoRL
Joy of your opulent atoms! wouldst thou dare. Democritus. Robert Bridges. MeRV
Joy, rose-lipped dryad, loves to dwell. Thomas Warton, the Elder. *Fr.* Retirement, an Ode. ViBoPo
Joy shakes me like the wind that lifts a sail. Joy. Clarissa Scott Delany. CDC; PoNe
Joy, Shipmate, Joy! Walt Whitman. AmP; BBV (1923 ed.); BHV; BPP; DD; EOAH; HBVY; IAP; MCCG; MoAmPo (1950 ed.); OHIP; PCH; TCAP; TOP
Joy so short alas, the pain so near, The. Sir Thomas Wyatt. SiPS
Joy, Sorrow and Happiness. Axel Juel, *tr. fr. Danish by* Charles W. Stork. BoDS
Joy stands on the hilltops. The Call. Edgar A. Guest. NLK
Joy, the triumph, the delight, the madness, The! Shelley. *Fr.* Prometheus Unbound. AtBAP
Joy, thou goddess, fair, immortal. Hymn to Joy. Schiller, *tr. by* Edgar A. Bowring. GrCo-2
Joy to none be wanting. King Horn. *Unknown.* EPP
Joy to Philip, he this day. Going into Breeches. Charles *and* Mary Lamb. EV-4; OTPC (1923 ed.); PRWS
Joy to the present, hope of future ages. To James VI, King of Scotland. Sir John Harington. SiCE
Joy to the World! The Lord Is Come. Isaac Watts. OlF; YaCaBo, *with music*
Joy to You. Francis Carlin. PFY
Joyce Kilmer. Amelia Josephine Burr. DD; HBMV
Joyce's Repentance, The. *Unknown, tr. fr. Irish by* Douglas Hyde. GTIV; MeRV
Joyful, joyful, we adore Thee. Hymn of Joy. Henry van Dyke. MaRV
Joyful lady, sing! To a Lady Playing and Singing in the Morning. Thomas Hardy. TOP
Joyful Mother of Children, A. *Unknown, tr. fr. Greek by* A. J. Butler. OxBG
Joyful [*or* Joyfull] New Ballad, A. Thomas Deloney. CoMu
"O noble England," *sel.* ViBoPo
Joyful Wisdom, The. Coventry Patmore. The Angel in the House, I, x, 1. HBV
Joyous birds shrouded in cheerful shade, The. The Music at the Bower of Bliss. Spenser. *Fr.* The Faerie Queene, II. MyFE
Joyous festival hath dawned, the holy Easter Day, The. Easter Day. Juan Ruiz, Archpriest of Hita. TeCS
Joyous-Gard. Thomas S. Jones, Jr. LBMV
Joyous morning ran and kissed the grass, The. The Wakers. John Freeman. HBMV; MBP; TSW
Joyous springtime wooed me with a breath, The. Early Spring. Helge Rode. BoDS
Joys. James Russell Lowell. BoTP
Joy's Crown of Joy. Asclepiades, *tr. fr. Greek by* F. L. Lucas. GrPE
Joys of Art, The. Rachel Annand Taylor. OBVV
Joys of Heaven, The. Thomas à Kempis, *tr. fr. Latin by* Erastus C. Benedict. CAW
Joys of living wreathe my face, The. The Circling Year. Ramona Graham. PTA-2
Joys of Marriage, The. Charles Cotton. BOHV; InMe
Joys of Paradise. St. Augustine, *tr. fr. Latin by* Prioress Augustine. CAW
Joys of the Road, The. Bliss Carman. DDA; HBV; HBVY, *sl. abr.;* NLK; OBVV; PCN; PIR; SN; TCAP; TSW; TSWC
Joys of the Virgin Mary, The. Juan Ruiz, Archpriest of Hita, *tr. fr. Spanish by* Elisha K. Kane. *Fr.* The Book of Good Love. AnSpL-1
Joy's Peak. Robert Farren. ISi
Joys Seven. *Unknown.* *See* Twelve Good Joys, The.
J's the Jumping Jay-Walker. Phyllis McGinley. *Fr.* All Around the Town. FaPON; TiPo (1952 ed.)
Juan and Haidee; Ways of Love. Byron. *Fr.* Don Juan, II. EPN; MaPo, *shorter sel.*
(Haidee, *shorter sel.*) OBRV
("It was the cooling hour," *shorter sel.*) ViBoPo
Juan Belmonte, Torero. Donald Finkel. NePoEA
Juan de Juni the priest said. Aodh Ruadh O'Domhnaill [*or* Red Hugh]. Thomas McGreevy. AnIV; OBMV; OnYI; OxBI
Juan in England. Byron. *Fr.* Don Juan, XI. FiP
Juan knew several languages—as well. London Literature and Society. Byron. *Fr.* Don Juan, XI. BPN
Juan Murray. *Unknown.* CoSo, *with music;* CSF
Juan Quintana. Alice Corbin. BAP; HBMV; NP
Juana. Alfred de Musset, *tr. fr. French by* Andrew Lang. AWP; JAWP; WBP
Juanita. Joaquin Miller. AA
Jubalee, *with music.* *Unknown.* BoAN-2
Jubilant the music through the fields a-ringing. World Music. Frances Louisa Bushnell. AA
Jubilate. George Arnold. EtS
Jubilate Agno, *sels.* Christopher Smart.
Flowers Are Great Blessings. MeRV
(Flowers, *shorter sel.*) RO
"For I am not without authority in my jeopardy, which I derive inevitably from the glory of the name of the Lord." EiPP
"For the feast of Trumpets should be kept up that being the most direct and acceptable of all instruments." UnS
For the Letter ל Which Signifies God. AtBAP
Let Elizur Rejoice with the Partridge. PoEL-3
Let Lotan Rejoice with Sauterelle. AtBAP
Let Peter Rejoice with the Moon Fish. AtBAP
My Cat Jeoffry. ChTr; FaBoCh; GoTP; LiTB; SeCePo; SiTL
(Cat, The.) BoW, *abr.;* PoC; RO
(For I Will Consider My Cat Jeoffry.) AtBAP; EiPP; PoEL-3; SeCeV
(Rejoice in the Lamb, *br. sel.*) PoD
Rejoice in God. AtBAP
("Rejoice in God, O ye Tongues; give the glory to the Lord, and the Lamb.") EiPP
Search for Pearls, The. RO
Jubilo. Allen Tate. WaP
Judaeus Errans. Louis Golding. TrJP
Judaism. Cardinal Newman. ACP
Judas. Gamaliel Bradford. OQP; QP-1
Judas. Howard McKinley Corning. ChIP
Judas. Edward Davison. NV
Judas. *Unknown.* BaBo; ESPB; OBB, 5 *sts.;* ViBoFo

Judas. Harold Vinal. BAP
Judas Iscariot. Robert Buchanan. LEAP; OBVV; OxBoCh
Judas Iscariot. Margaret Nickerson Martin. ChIP; PGD
Judas Iscariot. R. A. K. Mason. AnNZ
Judas Iscariot. Stephen Spender. MoAB; MoBrPo (1950 ed.)
Judas Iscariot dour and dark. Descent for the Lost. Philip Child. CaP
Judas Maccabeus. First Maccabees, Bible, Apocrypha. TrJP
Judas smoothed his heavy beard. Judas. Harold Vinal. BAP
Judas was I! Ah, the mockery! Judas Iscariot. Margaret Nickerson Martin. ChIP; PGD
Judean Hills Are Holy. William L. Stidger. ChIP; MaRV; OQP; QP-1
Judg'd [*or* Judged] by my goddess' doom to endless pain. Coelia, I. William Percy. ReIE; TuPP
Judge, judge, tell the judge. Nursery Rhymes, II. *Unknown.* OxBoLi
Judge me, O God, and plead my cause against an ungodly nation. Psalm XLIII, Bible, *O.T.* OnPM
Judge Me, O Lord! Sarah N. Cleghorn. ChIP; MaRV; StJW
Judge mildly the tasked world; and disincline. The World's Advance. George Meredith. EPN
Judge Not. Adelaide Anne Procter. LPS-3
Judge Not According to the Appearance. Christina Rossetti. TrPWD
Judge not, that ye may not be judged. Fairness. St. Matthew, Bible, *N.T.* BoFr
Judge Not the Preacher for He Is Thy Judge. George Herbert. EV-2
Judge not; the workings of his brain. Judge Not. Adelaide Anne Procter. LPS-3
Judge of modes in silks and satins, A. Harriet Simper Has Her Day. John Trumbull. *Fr.* The Progress of Dulness. AmPP (4th ed.)
Judge Roy Bean of Vinegarroon. The Law West of the Pecos. S. Omar Barker. IHA
Judge, who lives impeccably upstairs, The. Upstairs Downstairs. Hervey Allen. HBMV; PoNe
Judged by my goddess' doom to endless pain. *See* Judg'd by my goddess' doom . . .
Judged by the Company One Keeps. *Unknown.* BLPA; NeHB; YaD
Judgement in Heaven, A. Francis Thompson. *See* Judgment in Heaven, A.
Judgement of God, The. William Morris. *See* Judgment of God, The.
Judges, *sels.* Bible, *O.T.*
  "Awake, awake, Deborah," V: 12–28. PoFr
  Jephthah's Daughter, XI: 30–40. OuHeWo
  Song of Deborah, The, V: 2–31. LiTW
   (Song of Deborah and Barak, The, 2–21.) AWP
   (Then Sang Deborah and Barak, 1–31.) TrJP
   (War Song of Kishon, 1–23.) BHV
Judge's Song, The. W. S. Gilbert. *Fr.* Trial by Jury. PoVP
Judging by Appearances. Emilie Poulsson. MPB
Judging Distances. Henry Reed. Lessons of the War, II. ChMP; FaBoMo; LiTB; MoAB
Judgment, The. Katharine Lee Bates. OQP; QP-2
Judgment. William Rose Benét. AnAmPo; BAP; LA
Judgment. Grace Ellery Channing. AA
Judgment, The. Dora Read Goodale. AA; AnAmPo; LA; LEAP
Judgment. Eleanor Graham. DDA
Judgment. Kenneth W. Porter. ChIP
Judgment and cash and health and faith in God go wrong. But Choose. John Holmes. MiAP
Judgment and Mercy. Dorothy L. Sayers. *Fr.* The Devil to Pay, sc. iv. MaRV
Judgment Day. William Dean Howells. AA; PFY
Judgment [*or* Judgement] in Heaven, A, *sels.* Francis Thompson.
  "Athwart the sod which is treading for God." CoBE
  Epilogue: "Heaven, which man's generations draws." MBP; MoAB; MoBrPo
  Epilogue: "Virtue may unlock hell." EmBrPo; PoLi
Judgment of God, The. William Morris. POTT; SoV; ViPP; VLEP
   (Judgment of God, The.) OBVV
Judgment of Paris, The, *sels.* Ralph Schomberg.
  Ay or Nay? TrJP
  Courtier's a Riddle, A. TrJP
  Like Birds of a Feather. TrJP
Judgment of Paris, The, 4 *ll.* *Unknown.* *Fr.* Goddesses Three *in* Winchester College Songs. OtMeF
Judgment! two syllables can make. A Dooms-Day Thought. Thomas Flatman. CEP
Judith, *sel.* Lascelles Abercrombie. *Fr.* Emblems of Love, III.
  Balkis. BMEP; HBV; LEAP
   (Song: "Balkis was in her marble town.") MBP; MoBrPo
Judith, *sels.* Bible, Apocrypha.
  Tyrant's Death, The. BHV (XIII: 6–19); PoFr (XIII: 6–15)
  ". . . With Timbrels," XVI: 2–21. TrJP
Judith. William Young. AA
Judith of Bethulia. John Crowe Ransom. CrMA; FaBoMo; LiTA; LiTM (rev. ed.); LS; MM; MoPo; NePA; SPP
Judith of Minnewaulken, *sel.* Maxwell Anderson.
  Judith Remembers. WHA
"Jug and a book and a dame, A." The Rubáiyát. Edwin Meade Robinson. *Fr.* Limericised Classics. HBMV
Jug, jug! Fair fall the nightingal. The Nightingale. Richard Brathwaite. *Fr.* Nature's Embassy. EIL
Jug of water in the hand, and on, A. Dawn. "Rachel." TrJP
Juggernauting trams and the prolonged, The. The Towers at Evening. Frank Wilmot. *Fr.* Melbourne and Memory. NeLNL
Juggler, The. Bliss Carman. LBAP
  "Look how he throws," *sel.* BAP; CV
Juggler. Richard Wilbur. AmP; FiMAP; LiTM (rev. ed.); MoAB; NePA; NePoEA
Jugglers, The. John Gay. EV-3
Juggling Jerry. George Meredith. BEL; BeLS; BoLiVe; EmBrPo; EnLit; EPN; EPP; HBV; HiLiEn; OAEP; OnPP; PoeT; POTT; SeCePo; TCEP; VA; ViPo; VLEP
   (Last Words of Juggling Jerry, The.) TOP
Jugurtha. Longfellow. AA; CoBA; CoV; IAP
Juley, *with music.* *Unknown.* SoAmSa
Julia. Robert Herrick. *See* Rock of Rubies, The.
Julia, a Novel, *sel.* Helen Maria Williams.
  To Hope. OBEC
Julia and I did lately sit. Cherry-Pit. Robert Herrick. OAEP
Julia, if I chance to die. His Request to Julia. Robert Herrick. EM-1; EPS (1942 ed.); OBS; SeEP
Julia Miller. Edgar Lee Masters. *Fr.* Spoon River Anthology. MoVE
Julia, my dear, how long, I wonder. Lovers and Friends. Henry Luttrell. *Fr.* Advice to Julia. OBRV
Julian, *sel.* Earl of Rochester.
  More Dullness. BeR
Julian Grenfell. Maurice Baring. HBMV; POTE
Julian the Apostate. Ernest Denny. QS
Juliana, *sel.* Cynewulf, *tr. fr. Anglo-Saxon by* Charles W. Kennedy.
  "I have great need that the Saint grant help." AnOE
Juliana. *Unknown, tr. fr. Latin by* George F. Whicher. *Fr.* Carmina Burana. LaP
Julia's Letter. Byron. *Fr.* Don Juan, I. EV-4
   ("They tell me 'tis decided; you depart.") ViBoPo
Julie Ann Johnson, *with music.* *Unknown.* ABF
Julie-Jane. Thomas Hardy. MoVE
Julie Plante, The. William Henry Drummond. *See* Wreck of the *Julie Plante*, The.
Juliet. Hilaire Belloc. EnLoPo
Juliet, farewell. I would not be forgiven. Farewell [to Juliet]. Wilfrid Scawen Blunt. The Love Sonnets of Proteus, XXXIX. AnEnPo; TrGrPo
Juliet has lost her little downy owl. Elegy on the Death of Juliet's Owl. Maurice Baring. MM
Juliet of Nations. Elizabeth Barrett Browning. *Fr.* Casa Guidi Windows. VA
Juliet's Yearning. Shakespeare. *Fr.* Romeo and Juliet, III, ii. TreFS
Julius Brink. Edgar Lee Masters. *Fr.* The New Spoon River. ChMo; CMP
Julius Caesar, *sels.* Shakespeare.
  Antony's Oration, *fr.* III, ii. TrGrPo
   (Antony's Oration over Caesar's Body.) LiTB
  Brutus and Cassius, *fr.* IV, iii. CBE
  Brutus and Portia, *fr.* II, i. GrCo-2
  "Brutus has riv'd my heart," *fr.* IV, iii. BoFr
  Cassius Poisons Brutus' Mind, *fr.* I, ii. TreFS
  Cowards ("Cowards die many times before their deaths"), *fr.* II, ii. BLP; MaRV, 2 *ll.*
   (Death of Cowards, The.) TreFS
   (That Men Should Fear.) TrGrPo
  Farewell, A: "Now, most noble Brutus," *fr.* V, i. BHV
  "Friends, Romans, countrymen," *abr. fr.* III, ii. PIR
   (Antony's Oration, *abr.*) TrGrPo
   (Antony's Oration over Caesar's Body.) TreF
   (Antony's Oration over the Body of Caesar.) EV-1
   (I Come to Bury Caesar.) WHA
   (Mark Antony's Oration, *shorter sel.*) BCEP; PYM
  Julius Caesar's Preference, *fr.* I, ii. TreFS
  Murder of Julius Caesar, *fr.* II, i. EV-1
  "O mighty Caesar! dost thou lie so low?" *fr.* III, i. BHV. *fr.* i *and* ii
   (Antony's Oration over the Body of Caesar, *abr.*) LPS-3
   (Mark Antony's Lament.) TreFS
  "O, pardon me, thou bleeding piece of earth," *fr.* III, i. PIR
  "Our course will seem too bloody, Caius Cassius," *fr.* II, i. PIR

Julius Caesar (*continued*)
Perfect Tribute, The ("His life was gentle"), *fr.* V, v. MaRV
"Remember March, the ides of March remember," *fr.* IV, iii. PIR
Swimmer, A, *fr.* I, ii. BHV
There Is a Tide [in the Affairs of Men], *fr.* IV, iii. BCEP; BTP; MaRV
(Time to Strike, The.) TreFS
"This was the noblest Roman of them all," *fr.* V, v. PIR
(Brutus.) BCEP; GoTP
(Fragment from Mark Antony's Speech.) PECK
(Man, A.) BHV
(Noblest Roman, The.) FaFP; TreFS
(Portrait of Brutus.) TrGrPo
(Shakespeare Gallery, A: Brutus.) MaC
"Why, man, he doth bestride the narrow world," *fr.* I, ii. PIR
(Portrait of Caesar.) TrGrPo
(Shakespeare Gallery, A: Caesar.) MaC
"You are dull, Caska," *fr.* I, iii. NBE
July, *sel.* John Clare. *Fr.* The Shepherd's Calendar.
"Loud is the summer's busy song." GoTP; OBRV
July. Spenser. *Fr.* The Sheapheardes Calender. ReIE
July. Susan Hartley Swett. GN; OTPC (1946 ed.); PoRL; StVeCh (1940 ed.)
(It Is July.) YeAr
July. Thomas Tusser. ReIE
July. *At. to* Whittier. YeAr
July Avenue. Jorge Luis Borges, *tr. fr. Spanish by* H. R. Hays. TwSpPo
July Dawn. Louise Bogan. NePoAm-2
July Dawn, A, *sel.* John Francis O'Donnell.
"We left the city, street and square." IrPN
July, 1850. Feodor Ivanovich Tyutchev, *tr. fr. Russian by* Sir Cecil Kisch. WaL
July 14, at Night. Feodor Ivanovich Tyutchev, *tr. fr. Russian by* Babette Deutsch. OnPM; TrRV
July ghost, aghast at the strange winter, A. Midsummer Frost. Isaac Rosenberg. MoBrPo (1950 ed.); MoPo
July in the Jardin des Plantes. Claire McAllister. NePA
July is honored with the labor of fields. Labor of Fields. Elizabeth J. Coatsworth. TiPo (1959 ed.)
July is just in the nick of time! The Mowers. Myron B. Benton. YeAr
July Meadow. Louise Driscoll. YeAr
July sun burns down on the sandy beaches. To the Atoyac. Ignacio Manuel Altamirano. AnMP
July the first, of a morning clear, one thousand six hundred and ninety. The Boyne Water. *Unknown.* AnIV; OnYI; TIP
July the redbird (*hanh!*), redbird, Augus' the fly (*hanh!*). Don't Talk about It. *Unknown.* OuSiCo
July; the Succession of the Four Sweet Months. Robert Herrick. *See* Succession of the Four Sweet Months, The.
July the twenty-second day. The Descent on Middlesex. Peter St. John. PAH
July's dry emperies have fired a snake. Crotalus Rex. Brewster Chiselin. MoVE
Jumbled in the Common Box. W. H. Auden. PoRA
Jumblies, The. Edward Lear. BOHV; BoN; ChTr; CoEV; EnLi-2 (1949 ed.); FaBoBe; FaFP; GFA; HBV; HBVY; KN; LBN; LiL; LiTB; NA; OtMeF; OTPC; OxBoLi; PC; PoE; PoRA; PoVP; RIS; SAS; SeCeV; SiTL; TiPo; VA; ViP
Jumbo Jee. Laura E. Richards. GaP; SUS
Jump Jim Crow. *Unknown.* APW
Jump—jump—jump. The Little Jumping Girls. Kate Greenaway. FaPON; MPB; TiPo
Jump or Jiggle. Evelyn Beyer. TiPo
Jumpin' Judy, *with music.* *Unknown.* ABF
June. Bryant. AA; CoBA; HBV; IAP; LPS-2; MOAP; SN; TCAP
June. Mary Carolyn Davies. SiSoSe; TiPo (1959 ed.)
June. Nora Hopper. YeAr
June. Francis Ledwidge. CBOV; CP; GTIV; HBMV; NV; OnYI; PIAE; PoeMoYo; TCEP; VOD
June. James Russell Lowell. *Fr.* The Vision of Sir Launfal: Prelude to Part First. BBV; BTP; DD; EV-5; GoTP; HBV; HBVY; LPS-2; OHFP; PECK; PIR; PoRL; PTA-1; StaSt
("And what is so rare as a day in June?") OBAV
(Day in June, A.) FaPON; GrCo-1; HiLiAm; PoeMoYo; PYM; StVeCh (1955 ed.)
("Earth gets its price for what Earth gives us.") TreF
("For a cap and bells.") AA; LEAP
(June Weather.) GN
(What Is So Rare as a Day in June.) FaBoBe; FaFP; NePA
June. Wilson MacDonald. CaP
June. Douglas Malloch. POT; PoTo; YeAr
June. Harrison S. Morris. BAP; HBV
June. William Morris. *Fr.* The Earthly Paradise. BPN; POTT; PoVP; ViPo, *abr.*; VLEP
("O June, O June, that we desired so," *abr.*) ViBoPo
June. Irene F. Pawsey. BoTP
June. Theodore Harding Rand. CaP; OCL
June. Spenser. *Fr.* The Sheapheardes Calender. EnLit
June. Jane G. Stewart. BoTP
June. *Unknown.* PEOR
June Bracken and Heather. Tennyson. EnLoPo; GEPC; PoVP; VLEP
June-bug's got the golden wing, The. Bedbug. *Unknown.* GoSl
June Day, A. Sara Teasdale. YeAr
June in Wiltshire. Geoffrey Grigson. WaP
"June! June! June!" A Spring Lilt. *Unknown.* PCH
June Morning. Hugh McCrae. BoAV
June Night. Hazel Hall. HBMV
June Nights. Victor Hugo, *tr. fr. French by* Alan Conder. TrFP
June Rapture. Angela Morgan. HBMV
June Song of a Man Who Looks Two Ways. Leslie Daiken. NeIP
June sunlight slants across the path. Commencement. Margaret E. Sangster. PEDC
June Thunder. Louis MacNeice. ChMo; ChMP; GTBS-D; MoPo
June, too soon. Rules of the Road. *Unknown.* SoAmSa
June Twilight. John Masefield. GoYe
June was not over. Another Way of Love. Robert Browning. BPN; EmBrPo; GEPC; PoVP; VLEP
June Weather. James Russell Lowell. *See* June.
June's bridesman, poet o' the year. The Bobolink. James Russell Lowell. *Fr.* The Biglow Papers, 2d Series, No. VI. BLA
Junes, The, were free and full, driving through tiny/ Roads. June Thunder. Louis MacNeice. ChMo; ChMP; GTBS-D; MoPo
Jung Idea, The. "P. H." SiTL
Jungfrau's Cry, The. Stopford Brooke. VA
Jungle, The. Louis Dudek. PeCV
Jungle, The. Alun Lewis. MoPo
Jungle, The, *sel.* Archibald Fleming MacLiesh.
Report. NAMP
Jungle:/ Glaze green and red feathers, jungle. Ezra Pound. *Fr.* Canto XX. MoPo
Jungle Book, The, *sels.* Kipling.
Road-Song of the Bandar-Log. NV; OAEP (2d ed.); VLEP
Shiv and the Grasshopper. VLEP
White Seal, The, 8 *ll.* CaAE
(Seal Lullaby.) NV; PRWS
(White Seal's Lullaby, The.) RAR
Jungle is the frame for the machine, The. The Bulldozer. Donald A. Stauffer. WaP
Jungle Mammy Song, *with music.* *Unknown.* AS
Jungle necklaces are hung. Here She Is. Mary Britton Miller. TiPo (1959 ed.)
Jungle Pest, The. Roland Young. BOHV
Jungle Taste. Edward S. Silvera. CDC
Jungle Trees, The. Marjorie Wilson. BoTP
Junior Arbiter of Fate, The. Chu Yuan, *tr. fr. Chinese by* Shen Yu-ting. *Fr.* The Nine Songs. WhP
Junior's Foxy Friends, The. Raymond W. Walker. CAG
Juniper. Eileen Duggan. CAW; ChBR; MoSiPe
Juniper. Laurie Lee. ChMP; NeBP
Juniper Jim. "F. Anstey." YT
Juniper, Juniper,/ Green in the snow. *Unknown.* BoTP
Juniper Tree, The. Wilfred Watson. PeCV
Junk man passed the house today, The. Ol' Clothes. *Unknown.* PoToHe (new ed.)
Jupiter Feretrius? His origin? I'll make a start: write. Propertius. Elegies, IV, 10. LaP
Jupiter, have compassion, finally, on that sick girl, my sweetheart. Propertius. Elegies, II, 28 A *and* B. LaP
Jupiter Sends a Fury to Baffle Turnus in Battle. Virgil, *pr. tr. fr. Latin by* H. R. Fairclough. *Fr.* The Aeneid, XII. LiA
Just a Fishing Smack at Empson. George Barker. SiTL
Just a path that is sure. A Wish. Walter C. Smith. TVSH
Just a picture of somebody's child. Somebody's Child. Louise Chandler Moulton. HBV
Just a Smack at Auden. William Empson. FaBoTw; LiTM (rev. ed.); SiTL; UnPo (3d ed.)
Just a Smack at Smacking. *Unknown.* SiTL
Just a song at twilight, when the lights are low (refrain). Love's Old Sweet Song. G. Clifton Bingham. TreF
Just a Wearyin' for You. Frank L. Stanton. *See* Wearyin' for You.
Just after the Board had brought the schools up to date. Modern Ode to the Modern School. John Erskine. YaD
Just & Unjust. Lord Bowen. *See* Rain It Raineth, The.
Just are the ways of God. The Transcendence of God. Milton. *Fr.* Samson Agonistes. OBS
Just a-Ridin'. Badger Clark. SCC
Just as a flower, about to unfold. Mary Singing. Alfred de Musset. TrFP

Just as a mother, with sweet, pious face. Providence. Vincenzo da Filicaja. CAW
Just as Abel offered sacrifices to God. Cain. Théodore Agrippa d'Aubigné. *Fr.* Les Tragiques. LiA
Just as eternity transforms him at last unto Himself. The Tomb of Edgar Poe. Stéphane Mallarmé. AnFP
Just as, from a well-blazing fire, sparks. The Universal Fire. *Unknown. Fr.* The Upanishads. OnPM
Just as He Feared. Edward Lear. *See* Limerick: "There was an old man with a beard."
Just as I Am. Charlotte Elliott. HBV; VA
("Just as I am, without one plea.") OlF
Just as I am, Thine own to be. Consecration. "Marianne Farningham." MaRV
Just as I thought I was growing old. The Prime of Life. Walter Learned. HBV
Just as I'd found the huckle-berries. Interruption. Edith Benedict Hawes. DDA
Just as in the ages gone before. When We Are No More. Lucretius. *Fr.* De Rerum Natura. LiA
Just as my finger on these keys. Peter Quince at the Clavier. Wallace Stevens. AmPP (4th ed.); AnFE; AnNE; APA; ATP (1953 ed.); BLV; CoAnAm; CoBMV; CoV; ExPo; HBMV; InPo; LiTM; MAP; MAPA; MM; MoAB; MoAmPo; MOAP; NAMP; NP; OxBA; PreP; ReaPo; ReMP; RiBV; TCPD; TrGrPo; TwAmPo; UnPo (3d ed.); ViBoPo; WoL
Just as of yore the friendly rain. Mater Dolorosa. Elliott Napier. BoAu
Just as she was, the painter has caught Theodote. Her Picture. Julianus. GrPE
Just as soon as summer's done. The Weather Factory. Nancy Byrd Turner. SUS
Just as the body is one and yet has many parts. Many Parts, One Body. First Corinthians, Bible, *N.T.* GrCo-1
Just as the even-bell rang, we set out. Recollections after an Evening Walk. John Clare. ERP
Just as the hour was darkest. The Ballad of New Orleans. George Henry Boker. PAH
Just as the moon was fading amid her misty rings. Kriss Kringle. Thomas Bailey Aldrich. BoChLi (1939 ed.); HBVY; MPB; PEDC; PEOR; SDH; TSW
Just as the school came out. The Snow. W. W. Gibson. BEL
Just as the spring came laughing through the strife. John Pelham. James Ryder Randall. AA; BlG; GA; PAH
Just as those swans are, poets must be rare. Ariosto. *Fr.* Orlando Furioso, XXXV. LyPI
Just as those who gaze get higher than those who climb. The Glacier. Louis MacNeice. AnFE
Just at the self-same beat of time's wide wings. Keats. *Fr.* Hyperion. OBRV
Just Be Glad. James Whitcomb Riley. WBLP
Just before the Battle, Mother. George Frederick Root. BlG; OlF; TreFS
Just Beguiler. Thomas Campion. AtBAP
Just behind the Battle, Mother, *parody. Unknown.* FiBHP
Just bent on viewing cherries. Issa. Satirical Poems on Daimyos, II. PoFr
Just beyond the rainbow's rim a river ripples down. The Sleepytown Express. James J. Montague. HBMV
Just Dropped In. William Cole. FiBHP
Just ere the darkness is withdrawn. Sleep and His Brother Death. William Hamilton Hayne. AA
Just Exchange. Sir Philip Sidney. *Fr.* Arcadia. *See* My True Love Hath My Heart.
Just Folks. Edgar A. Guest. FaFP; TreFS
Just for a day I fled the town. The Return to Nature. William T. Allison. CPG
Just for a handful of silver he left us. The Lost Leader. Robert Browning. BEL; BMEP; BPN; CaAE; EM-2; EmBrPo; EnL; EnLi-2; EnLit; EPN; EV-5; GEPC; GTBS; GTBS-D; GTBS-W; GTSL; HBV; MCCG; OtMeF; PIAE; PIR; PoFr; PoFS; PoVP; PtP; REAL; TCEP; TreFS; TrGrPo; TwP; VA; ViBoPo; ViPo; ViPP; VLEP
Just for a space that I met her. Incognita. Austin Dobson. CenHV; PoVP
Just for Jesus. Lysbeth Boyd Borie. GaP
Just for the Ride. *Unknown.* FaFP; SiTL
Just for Today (*sl. diff. versions*). Sybil F. Partridge, *wr. at. to* Samuel Wilberforce *and to* Frederick William Faber. HBV; MaRV; OQP, *abr.*; PraP; QP-1, *abr.*; TreF; VA, *abr.*
(To-Day.) WHL
Just 'fore Christmas. Eugene Field. *See* Jest 'fore Christmas.
Just Forget. Myrtle May Dryden. WBLP
Just Friends. Robert Creeley. NeAP
Just from Dawson, *with music. Unknown.* ABF
Just God! and these are they. Clerical Oppressors. Whittier. PAH
Just Home. Louis Untermeyer. *See* Edgar A. Guest Syndicates "The Old Woman Who Lived in a Shoe."
Just imagine yourself seated on a shadowy terrace. That Reminds Me. Ogden Nash. FiBHP
Just in the dubious point, where with the pool. Angling. James Thomson. *Fr.* The Seasons: Spring. LPS-2
Just in the gray of the dawn, as the mists uprose from the meadows. The Expedition to Wessagusset. Longfellow. *Fr.* The Courtship of Miles Standish. PAH
Just Jumbo. Eileen Mathias. BoTP
Just Keep Fishin'. Harry M. Dean. DDA
Just Keep On. Clifton Abbott. WBLP
Just like a Man. *Unknown, at. to* Lizzie M. Hadley. BoTP
Just like Me. P. W. Sinks. BLRP
Just like This. D. A. Olney. BoTP
Just look, Manetto, at that wry-mouth'd minx. Sonnet: Of an Ill-favored Lady. Guido Cavalcanti. AWP; JAWP; WBP
Just lost when I was saved! Emily Dickinson. CoBA; OBAV; PoLFOT
(Called Back.) AA; AnFE; APA; BAP; BLP; CoAnAm; LEAP; MoAmPo (1950 ed.)
Just mark that schooner westward far at sea. The Schooner. Thomas Edward Brown. MBP
Just now/ Out of the strange. The Warning. Adelaide Crapsey. AnAmPo; BAP; BAV; BLV; CBOV; InP; LA; MAP; MCCG; MoAmPo (1942 ed.); NeMA; NP; NV; PFE; PIAE; SBMV
Just now I visited the monkeys. The Petty Officers' Mess. Roy Fuller. ChMP
Just now the lilac is in bloom. The Old Vicarage, Grantchester. Rupert Brooke. GoTL (1949 ed.); MBP; MoBrPo; MoVE; PoeT; PoRA; POTT; ShBV-3; TCPD; TOP
Just One Book. *Unknown.* BLRP
Just One More Spring. Nicephorus Vrettakos, *tr. fr. Modern Greek by* Rae Dalven. MoGP
Just One Signal. *Unknown.* PAH
Just one song more, then the long sleep and silence. One Song More. Clinton Scollard. MuM
Just one thing, O Master, I ask today. My Only Plea. Walter J. Kuhn. PraP
Just Passing. *Unknown.* BLRP
Just Plain Dog. Lyla Myers. AlBD
Just Sixteen. Hsü Chien, *tr. fr. Chinese by* Henry H. Hart. ChLP; OnPM
Just-so Stories, *sels.* Kipling.
Camel's Hump, The. BoChLi
First Friend, The. MPB
(Playing Robinson Crusoe.) PECK
True Royalty. PECK
Just stand aside and watch yourself go by. Watch Yourself Go By [*or* A Cure for Fault-finding]. Strickland W. Gillilan. BLPA; PoToHe; WBLP
Just take a trifling handful, O philosopher! Sky-making. Mortimer Collins. BOHV
Just tell her this, Dorkas. Got it? Good. The Message. Meleager. LiTW
Just Tell Them That You Saw Me. Paul Dresser. TreFS
"Just the place for a Snark!" the Bellman cried. The Hunting of the Snark. "Lewis Carroll." BoN; FiBHP; NA; PoEL-5; SiTL; WhC
Just the Same To-day. *Unknown.* BLRP; WBLP
Just Then the Door. Merrill Moore. AnEnPo; DaM
Just to Be Needed. Mary Eversley. PoToHe
Just Try This. *Unknown.* WBLP
Just Try to Be the Fellow That Your Mother Thinks You Are. Will S. Adkin. *See* If I Only Was the Fellow.
Just twenty years to-day! Twenty. Albert Durrant Watson. CPG
Just Wait for Me. Konstantin Mikhailovich Simonov, *tr. fr. Russian by* Babette Deutsch. TrRV
Just watch them, comrade . . . with an owner's eye. Nepman. "Demyan Bedny." TrRV
Just when each bud was big with bloom. Birth. Grace Raymond. AA
Just where the tide of battle turns. John Burns of Gettysburg. Bret Harte. DDA; GA; HBV; LHV; MC; OHIP; PAH; PAP
Just where the Treasury's marble front. Pan in Wall Street. Edmund Clarence Stedman. AA; AnAmPo; BAP; HBV; IAP; LA; LEAP; PFY
Justice. Shakespeare. *See* Thrice Armed.
Justice and Mercy. Fulke Greville. *Fr.* Mustapha. EV-1
Justice Denied in Massachusetts. Edna St. Vincent Millay. CoBA; MAP; MoAmPo
Justice Protects the Dead. Aeschylus, *tr. fr. Greek by* C. M. Bowra. *Fr.* Phryges. OxBG
Justice to Scotland. *Unknown.* BOHV; InMe
Justice walking o'er the frozen Thames, A. Epigram. *Unknown.* ALV
Justified Mother of Men, The. Walt Whitman. *See* Whitman's Mother.
Justify all those renowned generations. The Renowned Generations. W. B. Yeats. OxBoLi
Justine, You Love Me Not! John Godfrey Saxe. HBV; PR

Justus Quidem Tu Es, Domine. Gerard Manley Hopkins. *See* Thou Art Indeed Just, Lord.
Jutlander, The. Steen Steensen Blicher, *tr. fr. Danish by* Charles W. Stork. BoDS
Juvenilities. Juan Meléndez Valdés. *See* Of Love's Awakening.
Juventa Perennis. Thomas Edward Brown. MBP
Juxta. Grover Jacoby. GoYe
Juxtaposition. Arthur Hugh Clough. *Fr.* Amours de Voyage, Canto III, vi. VA

K

K. K. Can't Calculate. Frances Miriam Whitcher. BOHV
Kaaba of the generous hand. Petition. Abur Rabi. MooP
Kabul town's by Kabul river. Ford o' Kabul River. Kipling. FaBoTw; POTT
Kacelyvo's slope still felt. The Last Redoubt. Alfred Austin. HBV
Kaddish, *sel.* Allen Ginsberg.
"Strange now to think of you, gone without corsets and eyes." NeAP
Kaddish. Levi-Yitzhok of Berditchev, *tr. fr. Yiddish by* Joseph Leftwich. TrJP
Kadia the Young Mother Speaks. Jessie Sampter. TrJP
Kafoozalum. *Unknown.* BeLS; BLPA
(Kafoozelum, *with music.*) SoAF
Kai Khosrau sat in a garden bright. Rustam and Akwan Dev. Firdausi. *Fr.* Shah Namah. PeP
Kais Declares His Love. Nizami, *tr. fr. Persian by* James Atkinson. *Fr* Lailí and Majnún. PeP
Kais in the Desert. Nizami, *tr. fr. Persian by* James Atkinson. *Fr.* Lailí and Majnún. PeP
Kaiser & Co. Alexander Macgregor Rose, *sometimes at. to* Rodney Blake. BLPA; BoHiPo; HBV
(Hoch! Der Kaiser.) BOHV
Kaiser Dead. Matthew Arnold. AlBD; TCEP
Kaiser of dis Vaterlandt, Der. Teddy unt Me unt Gott. *Unknown.* BLPA
Kaleidoscope. Frances Angevine Gray. MuM
Kalevala, *sel.* *Unknown, tr. fr. Finnish.*
Prayer for Rain. WGRP
Kallundborg Church. Whittier. BeLS; GBV
Kallyope Yell, The. Vachel Lindsay. BLV; BoLiVe
Kamal is out with twenty men to raise the Border side. A Ballad of East and West. Kipling. BEL; BPN; CP; FaBoBe; HBV; LBBV; LH; POT; PTA-2; PYM; TCEP; TSW; TSWC; VA
Kanaris. Alexandros Pallis, *tr. fr. Modern Greek by* Rae Dalven. MoGP
Kanawâki—"By the Rapid." The Caughnawaga Beadwork Seller. William Douw Lighthall. CaP; OCL
Kane. Fitz-James O'Brien. LPS-3; PAH
Kangaroo, The. Elizabeth J. Coatsworth. StVeCh (1955 ed.); TiPo (1952 ed.)
Kangaroo. D. H. Lawrence. BrBE; MoVE; ShBV-4
Kangaroo, The. Ogden Nash. WhC
Kangarooster, The. Kenyon Cox. *Fr.* Mixed Beasts. RIS; TiPo
Kansas. Vachel Lindsay. TOP
Kansas Boys (*diff. versions*). *Unknown.* AS (B *vers.*); IHA, *abr.*; SoAF, *with music*
(Hello, Girls, A *vers., with music.*) AS
("Hello, girls, listen to my voice.") CoSo
(Mississippi Girls.) CSF
(Texian Boys, *with music.*) CoSo
Kansas Cowboy, A, *with music.* *Unknown.* CoSo
Kansas Emigrants, The. Whittier. CoBA; MC; PaA; PAH
Kansas Line, The ("Come all you jolly cowmen, don't you want to go"). *Unknown.* CSF
Kansas Line, The ("A cowboy's life is a dreary, dreary life"). *Unknown.* *See* Dreary, Dreary Life, The.
Karamanian Exile, The. James Clarence Mangan, *after the Turkish.* IrPN; OBVV; TIP
Karl. Charles Spear. AnNZ
Karl, from your beachhead on that hollow island. V-Letter to Karl Shapiro in Australia. Selden Rodman. WaP
Karma. William Canton. VA
Karma. Empedocles, *tr. fr. Greek by* F. L. Lucas. GrPE
Karma. E. A. Robinson. AmPP; AnNE; ChMo; CMP; CoBMV; MoAB; MoAmPo (1950 ed.)
Karolin's Song. Ben Jonson. *See* Though I Am Young.
Karroo, The, *sel.* Francis Carey Slater.
"Gone are those resolute trekkers—pilgrims who passed through the desert." MM
Karshish and Lazarus. Robert Browning. *See* Epistle, An, Containing the Strange Medical Experience of Karshish, the Arab Physician.
Karshish, the Arab Physician ("Karshish, the picker-up of learning's crumbs"). Robert Browning. *See* Epistle, An, Containing the Strange Medical Experience of Karshish, the Arab Physician.
Kashmiri Song ("Pale hands I love"). "Laurence Hope." BLPA; FaBoBe; FaFP; LBBV; NeHB; OlF; TreF
Kashmiri Song by Juma ("You never loved me"). "Laurence Hope." DiM
Kasidah, The, *sel.* Sir Richard Francis Burton.
"In these drear wastes." HBV
Kate. Helen Underwood Hoyt. RIS
Kate Adams, The, *with music.* *Unknown.* StDa
Kate Kearney. Lady Morgan. BLPA; FaBoBe; NeHB
Kate Ketchem. Phoebe Cary. PTA-1
Kate o' Belashanny. William Allingham. IrPN
Kate of Aberdeen. John Cunningham. HBV
Kate rose up early as fresh as a lark. Wind's Work. T. Sturge Moore. AlDL; HBMV; HBVY; TVSH
Kate Shelly. Eugene J. Hall. PTA-1
Kate Temple's Song. Mortimer Collins. HBV; VA
Kate was a pretty child. Kate. Helen Underwood Hoyt. RIS
Kathaleen Ny-Houlahan. *Unknown, tr. fr. Gaelic by* James Clarence Mangan. CoBE; ERP; TIP
(Kathleen-Ni-Houlahan.) AnIV
Katharine Jaffray. *Unknown.* BaBo; ESPB (A, B, *and* C *vers.*); InP; TCEP; ViBoFo (A *vers.*; B *vers., with music*)
(Katharine Johnstone.) OBB
Katherine Milton: Died MDCLVIII. Milton. *See* On His Deceased Wife.
Katherine Veitch. W. W. Gibson. CV
Kathleen Mavourneen. Louisa Macartney Crawford, *sometimes at. to* Julia Crawford. FaBoBe; HBV; OlF; TreF; VA
Kathleen-Ni-Houlahan. *Unknown.* *See* Kathaleen Ny-Houlahan.
Kathleen O'More. George Nugent Reynolds. TIP
Katie an' the *Jim Lee* Had a Little Race, *with music.* *Unknown.* StDa
(*Katie* an' the *Jim Lee* Had a Race, 1 *st., diff. vers.*) *Unknown.* StDa
Katie Lee and Willie Grey. *Unknown, at. to* Josie R. Hunt *and to* J. H. Pixley. BeLS; BLPA; PTA-1
Katie's Secret. *Unknown.* ABS
(Hawthorne Tree, The, B *vers.*) ABS
Katy Dorey, *with music.* *Unknown.* OuSiCo
Katy-did. C. Lindsay McCoy. GFA
Katy's Answer. Allan Ramsay. CEP; EiPP
Katzenjammer Kids, The. James Reaney. PeCV; TwCaPo
Kavanagh, The. Richard Hovey. HBV; LBAP; LHV
Kayak, The. *Unknown.* FaPON; GFA; OTPC (1946 ed.); PCH
Kayak Song, A. Lucy Diamond. BoTP
Kazoo. Tristan Corbière, *tr. fr. French by* Kate Flores. AnFP
Kearny at Seven Pines. Edmund Clarence Stedman. AA; DD; DDA; GA; HBV; HBVY; MC; MDAH; OTPC; PaA; PAH; PAP
Kearsarge. S. Weir Mitchell. PAH
Kearsarge, The. James Jeffrey Roche. AA; OBAV; PAH
Kearsarge and *Alabama.* *Unknown.* PAH
Keats. Longfellow. AmP; IAP; MOAP
Keats. William Wilberforce Lord. *Fr.* Ode to England. AA
Keats. Lizette Woodworth Reese. AA; BAP
Keats. John Banister Tabb. AmP
Keats' Last Sonnet. Keats. *See* Bright Star! Would I Were Steadfast as Thou Art.
Keel Row, The. *Unknown.* EV-4
(Weel May the Keel Row.) WP
Keen. Edna St. Vincent Millay. HBMV
Keen blaws the wind o'er the braes o' Gleniffer. The Braes o' Gleniffer. Robert Tannahill. EBSV; EV-4; OBRV
Keen, Fitful Gusts Are Whisp'ring Here and There. Keats. BEL; BPN; EM-2; EmBrPo; EnLit; EnRP; ERP; EV-4; GTBS-W; MaPo; OAEP; PeBoSo
(Sonnet.) CaAE; GEPC; PoEL-4; REAL
(Wayfarer, The.) CBE
Keen gleams the wind, and all the ground. Peace. Charles De Kay. SN
Keen is the wind, bare the hill, it is difficult to find shelter. Winter. *Unknown.* *Fr.* The Black Book of Carmarthen. PrWP
Keen Stars Were Twinkling, The. Shelley. LoPo
(To Jane.) EPN; ThWaDe
Keen, sweet fragrance lies along the air, A. The Canadian Pine. William T. Allison. CPG
Keen Thyself, Poor Wight. Geoffrey Keating, *tr. fr. Late Middle Irish by* Padraic Pearse. OnYI
Keen was the air, the sky was very light. Garden Fairies. Philip Bourke Marston. VA
Keen winds of cloud and vaporous drift. Nocturne. Richard Garnett. OBVV
Keenan's Charge. George Parsons Lathrop. AA; BBV (1923

ed.); HBV; MC; MDAH; OBAV; PAH; PAP, *abr.*; PFY
Keener tempests come, The: and, fuming dun. Winter [*or* A Snow Scene]. James Thomson. *Fr.* The Seasons. EnRP; EPP; EV-3; LPS-2; TOP; ViBoPo
Keening of Mary, The. *Unknown, tr. fr. Irish by* Padraic Pearse. ISi
Keep a brave spirit, and never despair. Press Onward. *Unknown.* FaFP
Keep a Good Tongue in Your Head. Martin Parker. CoMu
Keep a red heart of memories. Haze. Carl Sandburg. OnHM
Keep a Stiff Upper Lip. Phoebe Cary. FaFP
Keep a-Goin'. Frank L. Stanton. FaFP; OHFP; PreP; WBLP
Keep a-Inchin' Along, *with music. Unknown.* BoAN-1
Keep a-Pluggin' Away. Paul Laurence Dunbar. MCCG
Keep a-runnin'! Keep a-runnin'! Fiah gwinter obertake you. Lonesome Grabeya'ad. Josephine Pinckney. TCPD
Keep away from roads' webs, they always lead. Direction to a Rebel. W. R. Rodgers. LiTM (rev. ed.)
Keep back the one word more. Reserve. Lizette Woodworth Reese. AA
Keep dis in min', an' all'll go right. Don't Tell All You Know. *Unknown.* PCH
Keep heart, O comrade, God may be delayed. Walt Whitman. BBV (1951 ed.)
Keep in the Heart the Journal Nature Keeps. Conrad Aiken. *Fr.* Preludes for Memnon. ChMo; CMP; NePA; OxBA
Keep Innocency. Walter de la Mare. SoV
Keep Love in Your Life. Thomas Curtis Clark. WBLP
Keep Me f'om Sinkin' Down, *with music. Unknown.* BoAN-1
Keep me from bitterness. It is so easy. Prayer in Affliction. Violet Alleyn Storey. MaRV; TrPWD
Keep me from fretting, Lord, today. Prayer. May Carleton Lord. PGD
Keep me, I pray, in wisdom's way. The Bibliomaniac's Prayer. Eugene Field. AA
Keep Me, Jesus. Keep Me. Waverly Turner Carmichael. BANP
Keep me quiet, Master. A Prayer for Peace. William Adams Brown. MaRV
Keep Me Still, for I Do Not Want to Dream. Larry Eigner. NeAP
Keep my riband, take and keep it. Elizabeth Barrett Browning. *Fr.* Catarina to Camoens. GTSE
Keep Not Thou Silence. Psalms, LXXXIII, Bible, *O.T.* TrJP
Keep off your thoughts from things that are past and done. Resignation. Po Chü-i. TrCh
Keep On Praying. Roger H. Lyon. BLRP
Keep on your mask and hide your eye. *Unknown.* LO
Keep open house; dabble in bricks and mortar. The Way to Poverty. *Unknown.* OxBG
Keep out of the forest. Forest God. Dorothy Quick. DaM
Keep Silence, all created things. God's Dominion and Decrees. Isaac Watts. OBEC
Keep Smiling. *Unknown.* WBLP
Keep the dream alive and growing always. Song (2). Edwin Rolfe. TrJP
Keep the Glad Flag Flying. *Unknown.* FaFP
"Keep the peace, Borso!" Where are we? Canto XXI. Ezra Pound. ChMo; CMP
"Keep this for me." Faith. *Unknown.* PoToHe (new ed.)
Keep this little light, O Father. A Birthday Prayer. John Finley. TrPWD
Keep thou/ Thy tearless watch. Anguish. Adelaide Crapsey. PFE
Keep Thou My Heart. Buel P. Colton. BLP
Keep Thou My Way, O Lord. Fanny Crosby. TrPWD
Keep Ye Holy Sabbath Rest. *Unknown, tr. fr. Hebrew by* Herbert Loewe. TrJP
Keep you these calm and lovely things. To the Liffey with the Swans. Oliver St. John Gogarty. AnIL; OxBI
Keep your copper coin, save your cup of wheat. Never Ask Me Why. Silvia Margolis. GoYe
Keep Your Grit. Louis E. Thayer.
Hang to Your Grit! *sel.* WBLP
Keep Your Hands on That Plow, *with music. Unknown.* OuSiCo
Keeper, The. Arthur Stringer. MaRV
Keeper of the Orchards. Hilda Doolittle ("H. D."). *See* Orchard.
Keepers of the Pass, The. Sir Charles G. D. Roberts. VA
Keeping Endless Holiday. Petronius Arbiter, *tr. fr. Latin by* Ben Jonson. LiA
(Foeda Est in Coitu.) LiTW
Keeping On. Arthur Hugh Clough. *See* Say Not the Struggle Nought Availeth.
Keeping Store. Mary Frances Butts. GFA; OTPC (1946 ed.); PCH; PPL
Keeping the Sabbath. Emily Dickinson. *See* Some keep the Sabbath going to church.
Keeping Their World Large. Marianne Moore. WaP
Keepsake, The. Hsü Ching Fan, *tr. fr. Chinese by* Henry H. Hart. PoHN
Keepsake from Quinault. Dorothy Alyea. GoYe
Keepsake Mill. Robert Louis Stevenson. TSW; TSWC
Keith of Ravelston. Sydney Thompson Dobell. *See* Ballad of Keith of Ravelston, The.
Kelpius's Hymn. Arthur Peterson. AA
Kelvin Grove. Thomas Lyle. EBSV
Kemp Owyne. *Unknown.* BaBo; BEL; BoLiVe; CoBE; EM-1; EnLi-1 (1949 ed.); EnSB; ESPB (A *and* B *vers.*); OBB, *var.*; SeCeV; TOP; ViBoFo
Ken. Charlotte Mew. TCPD
Ke-ni-ga Song. *Tr. fr. American Indian song by* Natalie Barnes. MPB
Kensington Gardens, *sels.* Thomas Tickell.
Fairies. OBEC
Tulips, The. BeR
Kensington Gardens, *sels.* Humbert Wolfe. *Poems indexed separately by titles and first lines.*
Kentish hamlets gray and old. The Memory of Kent. Edmund Blunden. HBMV
Kentish Petition, The, 1701, *sel.* Defoe.
"'Tis fatal to tyrannic power, when they." PoFr
Kentish Sir Byng stood for his King. Marching Along. Robert Browning. Cavalier Tunes, I. ATP (1935 ed.); BEL; BLV; BMEP; BPN; EM-2; EmBrPo; EnLi-2; EnLit; EPN; EPP; EV-5; GEPC; HBV; LEAP; MCCG; MW; OAEP; PIR; PoVP; PreP; PYM; ShBV-1; TCEP; TOP; VA; ViPo; VLEP; YT
Kenton and Deborah, Michael and Rose. Ambition. Aline Kilmer. HBMV; LHV; SBMV; WHL
Kentucky Babe. Richard Henry Buck. AA; BOL; HBV
Kentucky Belle. Constance Fenimore Woolson. BeLS; BlG; BLPA; FaBoBe; GoTP; MaC; PAH; PTA-1; StaSt; StPo
Kentucky Birthday; February 12, 1815. Frances Frost. SiSoSe; YeAr
Kentucky Moonshiner, *with music. Unknown.* AS; TrAS
Kentucky Mountain Farm. Robert Penn Warren. SPP
Sels.
Cardinal, The, IV. MoVE
History among the Rocks, III. MAP; MoAmPo; MoVE
Kentucky Mountaineer. Jesse Stuart. *Fr.* Man with a Bull-Tongue Plow. PoeMoYo
"Farewell to Springtime," *st.* 661.
"I came the Womack Road," *st.* 295.
"Last night the rain," *st.* 283.
"Spring in Kentucky hills," *st.* 149.
Kentucky Philosophy. Harrison Robertson. BOHV; HBV; IHA; PTA-1
Kentucky water, clear springs: a boy fleeing. The Swimmers. Allen Tate. MoVE
Kepe well x, and flee fro vii. Ten Commandments, Seven Deadly Sins, and Five Wits. *Unknown.* ChTr
Kepler. Albert Durrant Watson. CPG; OCL
Kept for Jesus. Edith E. Cherry. BePJ
Kept Waiting in the Boat at Chiu-k'ou Ten Days by an Adverse Wind. Po Chü-i, *tr. fr. Chinese by* Arthur Waley. TrCh
Kera Phrosini, *sel.* Aristotelis Valaoritis, *tr. fr. Modern Greek by* Rae Dalven.
"Wind carries me on its wings, The." MoGP
Kéramos, *much abr.* Longfellow. PoEL-5; ReTS
(Potter's Song, The.) YT
Kernel, The. Frank Kendon. MBP; MoBrPo (1942 ed.)
Kernel of the Grave, The. Keats. *Fr.* Isabella. LiA
Kerry Cow, The. Winifred M. Letts. MW; TSW; TSWC
Kerry Dance, The. James Lyman Molloy. OlF; OnYI
Kerry Lads, The. Theodosia Garrison. HBMV
Kestrels, The. Sidney Keyes. FaBoMo; POTE
Kettle descants in a cozy drone, The. At Tea. Thomas Hardy. *Fr.* Satires of Circumstance. EPP; PoVP; TyEnPo
Kettle sang the boy to a half-sleep, The. Halibut Cove Harvest. Kenneth Leslie. CaP
Kevin Barry, *with music. Unknown.* AS
Kevin Barry. Terence Ward. OnYI
Key, The. John Oxenham. BePJ
Key-Board, The. Sir William Watson. HBV
Key into the Language of America, A; or, An Help to the Language of the Natives, *sels.* Roger Williams.
Boast Not, Proud English. AmPP (4th ed.)
Courteous Pagan Shall Condemn, The. AmPP (4th ed.)
(Brother Indian, The.) GrCo-1
Key of the Kingdom, The. *Unknown. See* This Is the Key.
Key of yesterday, The. The Lost Key. Priscilla Leonard. MaRV; OQP; QP-2
Key to Everything, The. May Swenson. NePoEA
Key West. Hart Crane. ChMo
Key will stammer, and the door reply, The. Week-End, II. Harold Monro. CP; MoBrPo (1950 ed.); YT
Keyhole in the Door, The. *Unknown.* CoMu
Keys of Heaven, The, *with music. Unknown.* FTB
(Paper of Pins, *sl. diff.*) ABF; ABS

Keys of Morning, The. Walter de la Mare. AtBAP; MoVE
Keys of the Jail, The. *Unknown. See* Clefs de la prison, Les.
Khalif's fury raged, The. John Masefield. *Fr.* Enslaved. ReTS
Khamsin. Clinton Scollard. AA; LBAP; PFY
Khristna and His Flute. "Laurence Hope." HBV
Khrushchev is coming on the right day! Poem. Frank O'Hara. NeAP
Khustina—the Kerchief. Fedkovich, *tr. fr. Ukrainian by* Florence Randal Livesay. CPG
Kick at the rock, Sam Johnson, break your bones. Epistemology. Richard Wilbur. NePoEA
Kicking his mother until she let go of his soul. Mundus et Infans. W. H. Auden. LiTB; LiTM; MoAB; MoBrPo (1950 ed.)
Kicking my heels in the street. At the Stage-Door. Arthur Symons. LEAP; POTT
Kid, The, *sels.* Conrad Aiken.
 Awakening, The, VII. MoVE
 Proem to "The Kid" ("Where now he roves, by wood or swamp whatever"). MoAB
Kid, The. William Shenstone. OTPC (1923 ed.)
Kid and His Dog, A. Leroy J. Fleury. AlBD
Kid Has Gone to the Colors, The. William Herschell. PTA-1
Kid in Upper 4, The. Nelson C. Metcalf. TreFS
Kid March had the stuff but his style was hard. The Up-Set. Corey Ford. WhC
Kid Stuff. Frank Horne. PoNe
Kiddush. Leah Rachel Yoffie. FAOV
Kiddy cars of little tikes. Transportation Problem. Richard Armour. WhC
Kidnapping of Sims, The. John Pierpont. PAH
Kids. Witter Bynner. MPB
Kid's Last Fight, The. *Unknown.* TreF
Kilbarchan now may say alas! The Epitaph of Habbie Simpson [*or* The Life and Death of the Piper of Kilbarchan]. Robert Sempill. EBSV; OBS
Kilcash. *Unknown, tr. fr. Irish by* Frank O'Connor. KiLC; OBMV; OxBI; ThWaDe
Kildee. John Banister Tabb. SPP
Kilimandjaro. Bayard Taylor. AmP
Kilissa, the Nurse. Aeschylus, *tr. fr. Greek by* Lewis Campbell. *Fr.* Choephoroe. GrR
Kilkenny Boy, The. Eileen Shanahan. NeIP
Kilkenny Cats, The. *Unknown.* BOHV; CIV; FaFP; LiL; LiTG; TreF
 (Limerick: "There once were two cats of Kilkenny," *sl. diff.*) CenHV
Kill yourselves with knives and poisoned gas. Strangers Are We All upon the Earth. Franz Werfel. TrJP
Killarney. Edmund Falconer. OlF; TreFS
Killarney. Charles Kingsley. WhC
Killarney. William Larminie. *Fr.* Fand. AnIV
 (Epilogue to "Fand.") TIP
Killed at the Ford. Longfellow. BBV; IAP; OHIP; TCAP
Killed in Action. Terence Tiller. NeBP
Killed in the trenches! How cold and bare. "A Rebel Soldier Killed in the Trenches before Petersburg, Va., April 15, 1865." *Unknown.* BIG
Killer, The. *Unknown.* ABF; CoSo
Killers ("I am put high over all others in the city today"). Carl Sandburg. MoVE
Killers ("I am singing to you"). Carl Sandburg. NP
Killing. Samuel Greenberg. LiTA
Killing, The. Edwin Muir. ChMP
Killing No Murder. Sylvia Townsend Warner. MBP; MoBrPo
Killyburn Brae. *Unknown.* OnYI
Kilmallock. Sir Aubrey De Vere. IrPN
Kilmeny. James Hogg. *Fr.* The Queen's Wake. CBPC; DaM; EBSV; EV-3; GBV (1922 ed.); HBV; LPS-3; OBEV; OBRV; OnSP, *abr.*; OtMeF, *abr.*
 (Bonny Kilmeny Gaed up the Glen.) GoTS; BSV
Kilmeny. Alfred Noyes. EnLit; POT
Kilroy. Peter Viereck. MoAmPo (1950 ed.); NeMA
 (Kilroy Was Here.) OnAP; PoRA
Kin. Carl Sandburg. BAP; NP
Kinchinjunga. Cale Young Rice. AnAmPo; HBV; LA; LBMV
Kincora. *Unknown, tr. fr. Middle Irish by* James Clarence Mangan. AnIV; GTIV; OnYI; OxBI
 (Lamentation of Mac Liag for Kincora.) AnIL
Kind. Josephine Miles. FiMAP
Kind Are Her Answers. Thomas Campion. AnFE; EG; HBV; LiTL; OBSC; SeCeV; TrGrPo
 (Kinde Are Her Answeres.) AtBAP; FaBoEn; PoEL-2
 (Lost Freedom.) BLV
Kind bird, thy praises I design. The Bird. Countess of Winchilsea. EiPP
Kind Christian souls who pass me by. The Monkey's Carol. Winifred M. Letts. CV
Kind country-men listen I pray. All Things Be Dear but Poor Mens Labour; or, The Sad Complaint of Poor People. "L. W." CoMu
Kind Deeds. Julia A. Fletcher Carney. *See* Little Things.
Kind Friend, A. Jami, *tr. fr. Persian.* BoFr
Kind friends, if you will listen, a story I will tell. Browneyed Lee. *Unknown.* CoSo
Kind friends, we welcome you today. Opening Address. *Unknown.* MeMeAg
Kind friends, you must pity my horrible tale. The Dreary Black Hills. *Unknown.* ABF; CoSo; CSF
Kind gentlemen, will you be patient awhile? Robin Hood's Birth, Breeding, Valor, and Marriage. *Unknown.* ESPB
Kind Hearts. *Unknown.* HBV
Kind Heaven, assist the trembling muse. Wyoming Massacre. Uriah Terry. PAH
Kind Inn, A. George Dillon. GoYe
Kind Keeper, The. Dryden. *See* Limberham; or, The Kind Keeper.
Kind Look, The. Willard Maas. LiTM (1946 ed.)
Kind Lovers, Love On. John Crowne. *See* Song: "Kind lovers, love on."
Kind Marcus me to supper lately bade. Against Feasting. Sir John Harington. SiCE
Kind Miss, *with music. Unknown.* AS
Kind Mousie, The. Natalie Joan. BoTP
Kind of Act of, The. Robert Creeley. NeAP
Kind of an Ode to Duty. Ogden Nash. TrGrPo; UnPo (3d ed.); WhC
Kind of grass that a spit-bug chooses, The. The Spit-Bug. William H. Matchett. WaKn
Kind of heart, of beauty bright. The Rendezvous. Catullus. OnPM
Kind pity [*or* Kinde pitty] chokes my spleen[e]; brave scorn forbids. Satire [*or* Satyre] III: On Religion. John Donne. *Fr.* Satires. EnLP; EPS (1942 ed.); MaPo; MeLP; MePo; OBS; PoEL-2; ReEn; ReIE; SeCV-1; SeEP; TuPP
Kind Shepherd, see, Thy little lamb. The Good Shepherd. H. P. Hawkins. BOL
Kind Sir: These Woods ("Kind Sir: This is an old game"). Anne Sexton. GoYe
Kind Sleep. Isabel Fiske Conant. PC
Kind solace in a dying hour! Tamerlane. Poe. AmP; IAP
Kind to the world, but to itself unkind. Sonnet: The Silkworm. Michelangelo. LyPI
Kind voice, A, calls, "Come, little ones." Crocuses. Anna M. Platt. BoTP
Kind was my friend who, in the Eastern land. The Crescent and the Cross. Thomas Bailey Aldrich. EOAH
Kinde Are Her Answeres. Thomas Campion. *See* Kind Are Her Answers.
Kinde pitty chokes my spleene; brave scorn forbids. *See* Kind pity chokes my spleen . . .
Kindergarten Orator, A. Julia H. May. MeMeAg
Kindest and the happiest pair, The. Forbearance. William Cowper. MaRV
Kindle, O Lord, along the way. Nearing the Ford. Dwight Edwards Marvin. PraP
Kindle the Christmas brand, and then. The Ceremonies for Candlemas Day. Robert Herrick. COAH; EnLit; EPS; OAEP
Kindler of glory's embers. In Praise of Aed. *Unknown.* AnIL; LyMA
Kindliest thing God ever made, The. Shade. Theodosia Garrison. MaRV; OHIP; PoeMoYo
Kindling impulse seized the host, A. Chattanooga. Herman Melville. APW
Kindly Advice. *Unknown.* BOHV
 (Panther, The.) NA
Kindly cock is the fairies' friend, The. The Cock. Rose Fyleman. UTS
Kindly Neighbor, The. Edgar Guest. PoToHe
 "I have a kindly neighbor, one who stands," *sel.* MaRV
Kindly Screen, The. Belle Chapman Morrill. MaRV
Kindly Unhitch That Star, Buddy. Ogden Nash. LiTA; LiTM
Kindly Vision. Otto Julius Bierbaum. AWP; JAWP; WBP
Kindly watcher by my bed, lift no voice in prayer. Music. George Du Maurier. OBEV (new ed.); OBVV
Kindly word and a tender tone, A. A Gentle Word. *Unknown.* PoToHe (new ed.)
Kindness. T. Sturge Moore. GTML; OBMV
Kindness to Animals. J. Ashby-Sterry. BOHV; InMe; NA
Kindness to Animals. Laura E. Richards. TiPo
Kindness to Animals. *Unknown.* BoTP; GoTP; HBV; HBVY; OTPC; PPL
Kindred. Theodore Morrison. MuM
Kindred. George Sterling. MuM; OBAV
Kindred Harmonies. Paul Verlaine, *tr. fr. French by* Alan Conder. TrFP
Kinds of Trees to Plant. Spenser. *Fr.* The Faerie Queene, I, i. OHIP
Kine of My Father, The. Dora Sigerson Shorter. OnYI; OxBI
King, The. Mary Frances Butts. OQP; QP-2
King, The. Mary Elizabeth Coleridge. OBVV
King, The. Kipling. BPN; InP; PoVP

King, The. Tennyson. *Fr.* Idylls of the King: The Coming of Arthur. BHV
"King, a flock is feeding." Montoro's Song against Count Alvaro de Luna, High Constable of Castile. Eduardo Marquina, *tr. by* Dorothea Mackellar. MoAuPo
King Ailill's Death. *Tr. fr. Early Middle Irish by* Whitley Stokes. TIP
King Alexander led the van. Allegro. "McM." InMe
King Alfred Answers the Danes. G. K. Chesterton. *Fr.* Ballad of the White Horse. OxBoCh
King Alfred sensed among his country's words. Anglo-Saxon. E. L. Mayo. MiAP
King Alfred's Metres of Boethius, *sel.* Boethius, *tr. fr. Latin by* King Alfred.
"Why will ye ever/ With unjust hatred," XXVII. BoFr
King and his brother both were fain, The. King Oluf and His Brother. *Unknown.* BoDaBa
King and his knights went to church [*or* to the church went], The. The Confessions of the Seven Deadly Sins. William Langland. *Fr.* The Vision of Piers Plowman. BEL; EnLi-1 (1949 ed.)
King and Queen of Cantelon. Babylon. *Unknown.* ChTr
King and Queen of the Pelicans we. The Pelican Chorus. Edward Lear. LiL
King and queen were riding, The. *See* King and the queen were riding, The.
King and the Child, The. Eugene J. Hall. PTA-2
King and the Clown, The. *Unknown, ad. fr. Persian by* Michael Lewis. MaC
King and the Oak, The. Robert Ervin Howard. DaM
King and the Pope, The. Charles Henry Webb. PR
King and the queen were riding, The. Child's Song [*or* The Naughty Blackbird]. Kate Greenaway. HBVY; OTPC (1946 ed.); PCH
King Arthur, *sels.* Dryden.
Harvest Song, *fr.* V, i. BeR
(Song: "Your hay it is mowed and your corn is reap'd.") CEP; SeCV-2
How Happy the Lover, *fr.* IV, i. ElSeCe; LoBV; OnPM; ViBoPo
(Song: "How happy the lover.") SeEP
(Song to a Minuet.) EPS (1942 ed.); SeCL
Song of Venus, *fr.* V, i. LoBV; OxBoLi; PoEL-3; SeCeV
(Song Sung by Venus in Honor of Britannia.) EPS (1942 ed.)
Syren's Song, *fr.* IV, i. BeR
King Arthur, *sel.* Richard Hovey.
Hunting Song. HBV; NLK
King Arthur. Layamon. *Fr.* The Brut. LEAP
King Arthur and His Round Table, *sel.* John Hookham Frere.
Bees and Monks, *fr.* Canto III. OBRV
King Arthur and King Cornwall. *Unknown.* ESPB, *sl. abr.;* OBB
King Arthur, growing very tired indeed. Salad—after Tennyson. Mortimer Collins. CenHV
King Arthur's Death. *Unknown.* ACP
King Arthur's Dream. *Unknown.* ACP
King Arthur's Order of Chivalry. Tennyson. *Fr.* Idylls of the King: Guinevere. GrCo-1
("But I was first of all the kings who drew.") GTSL
King Arthur's Round Table. John Owen, *tr. fr. Latin by* Thomas Harvey. *Fr.* Four Epigrams. PrWP
King Arthur's Waes-hael. Robert Stephen Hawker. ISi; JKCP; OBEV; OBVV; OxBoCh; SDH
King asked, The. The King's Breakfast. A. A. Milne. CenHV
King Borborigmi. Conrad Aiken. ChMo; CMP; MAPA; MOAP
King Bruce and the Spider. Eliza Cook. OTPC (1923 ed.); StVeCh (1940 ed.)
(Try Again.) BoTP
King but an his nobles a', The. Brown Robin. *Unknown.* ESPB
King Cahal Mór of the Wine-red Hand. *Tr. by* James Clarence Mangan. *See* Vision of Connaught in the Thirteenth Century, A.
King Canute, *abr.* Thackeray. OTPC
King Charles, and who'll do him right now? Give a Rouse. Robert Browning. Cavalier Tunes, II. BEL; BLV; BoLiVe; BPN; EM-2; EmBrPo; EnLi-2; EnLit; EPN; EPP; EV-5; GEPC; HBV; MCCG; OAEP; PC; PoVP; PreP; PYM; ShBV-1; TCEP; TOP; VA; ViPo; VLEP
King Charles he is King James's son. The White Cockade. *Unknown.* OnYI
King Charles II. Earl of Rochester. *See* Epitaph on Charles II.
King Charles the First walked and talked. *Unknown.* OxNR
King Charles upon the Scaffold. Andrew Marvell. *Fr.* An Horatian Ode upon Cromwell's Return from Ireland. ChTr
King Christian. Johannes Evald, *tr. fr. Danish by* Longfellow. AWP; JAWP; WBP
King Cophetua and the Beggar Maid. Don Marquis. HBMV; InMe
King Cotton, *sel.* Sir Leo Money.
"Mills of Lancashire grind very small, The." MaRV; OQP; QP-2
King Croesus carried to Apollo's sibyl. Oracle at Delphi. Robert Bagg. NePoAm-2
King-Cups and a Stream. Richard Savage. *Fr.* The Wanderer, V. BeR
King David. Stephen Vincent Benét. HBMV; TCPD
King David. Walter de la Mare. UnPo (1st ed.)
King David. Heine, *tr. fr. German by* Louis Untermeyer. PoFr
King David and King Solomon. James Ball Naylor. CenHV; GoTP
King David, knowing well. An Example of the Praise of God for His Omnipotency, out of the CXIII Psalm. John Hall. ReIE
King David's limbs were weary. He had fled. David's Lament for Absalom. Nathaniel P. Willis. PTA-2
King did a Mermaid catch and keep, The. The Mermaid's Spaeing. *Unknown.* BoDaBa
King Don Sancho. *Unknown, tr. fr. Spanish.* AnSpL-1, *tr. by* Nicholson B. Adams; TeCS, *tr. by* William J. Entwistle
King Drinks Wine, A. Li Ho, *tr. fr. Chinese by* Ho Chih-yuan. WhP
King Dying on the Battle-Field, The. Alexander Smith. BMEP
King Easter has courted her for her lands [*or* gowd]. Fause Foodrage. *Unknown.* ESPB; OBB
King Edward the Fourth and a Tanner of Tamworth. *Unknown.* BaBo; ESPB
King Edward the Third, *sels.* Blake.
"Let liberty, the charter'd right of Englishmen." PoFr
War Song to Englishmen, A. CH; MeRV; RO; WaaP
(War.) BHV
(War Song, A.) OHIP
King Edwards, *with music.* *Unknown.* SoAmSa
King Edwin's Feast. John White Chadwick. OTPC
King Enjoys His Own Again, The. Martin Parker. OBS
King Erik. Carl Snoilsky, *tr. fr. Swedish by* Charles W. Stork. AnSL
King Erik and the Scornful Maid. *Unknown, tr. fr. Danish by* E. M. Smith-Dampier. BoDaBa
King Estmere. *Unknown.* ESPB; OBB
King Eternal, The. James Montgomery. MaRV
King Evander/ Began the story. Aeneas at the Site of Rome. Virgil. *Fr.* The Aeneid, VIII. LaP
King Fisher courted Lady Bird. The King-Fisher Song. "Lewis Carroll." *Fr.* Sylvie and Bruno Concluded. BoN; RIS
King Francis was a hearty king, and loved a royal sport. The Glove and the Lions. Leigh Hunt. BeLS; BHV; EnLit; EV-4; FaPON; GN; HBV; HBVY; HoPM; LPS-2; MaC; OnSP; OTPC; PCD; PCN; PECK; PoMa; PreP; TreF; WBLP
King Goodheart. W. S. Gilbert. *See* There Lived a King.
King Hancock sat in regal state. A Song about Charleston. *Unknown.* PAH
King Hart, *sel.* Gawin Douglas.
Hart's Castle. AtBAP; PoEL-1
King has called for priest and cup, The. The Last Rhyme of True Thomas. Kipling. OtMeF
King has passed along the great highway, The. The King Passes. Anne Hunter Temple. ChIP
King has written a braid letter, The. Lord Derwentwater. *Unknown.* ESPB
King he hath been a prisoner, The. Willie o Winsbury. *Unknown.* BaBo; ESPB
King he reigns on a throne of gold, The. The Leveller. "Barry Cornwall." EV-4
King he wrytes a luving letter, The. *Unknown.* *Fr.* Johnie Armstrang. PoFr
King Henry. *Unknown.* BaBo; ESPB; OBB
King Henry IV, Pt. I, *sels.* Shakespeare.
Bravery, *fr.* V, ii. BHV
Combat, A, *fr.* V, iv. BHV
King's Army, The, *fr.* IV, i. LiA
(Armed.) BHV
My Liege, I Did Deny No Prisoners, *fr.* I, iii. WaaP
("But I remember, when the fight was done.") PIR
(Hotspur.) BHV; ShGoBo
(Hotspur's Description of a Fop.) LPS-2
(Staff Officer, The.) OtMeF
King Henry IV, Pt. II, *sels.* Shakespeare.
Henry IV's Soliloquy on Sleep, *fr.* III, i. TVSH
(Cares of Majesty, The.) LiTB; TreF
(Sleep.) BCEP; EV-1; LPS-3
(Soliloquy on Sleep.) FiP
(Uneasy Lies the Head.) BLP
Mortality, *fr.* III, ii. LiA
"Nay, you shall see mine orchard," V, iii. MyFE
"O my worshipful lord, an't please your grace," *fr.* II, i. LO
Tavern, The, II, iv. LiA

King Henry IV, Pt. II (*continued*)
("I'faith, sweetheart, methinks now you are in an excellent good temporality," *abr.*) MyFE
King Henry V, *sels.* Shakespeare.
After the Battle, *fr.* IV, vii *and* viii. BHV
Death of Falstaff, The, *fr.* II, iii. LiA
("Boy, bristle thy courage up; for Falstaff he is dead.") LO
("Prithee, honey-sweet husband, let me bring thee to Staines.") MyFE
Goodness in Things Evil, *fr.* IV, i. EV-1
Horse, The, *fr.* III, vii. GoTP
King Henry before the Field of Saint Crispian, *fr.* IV, iii. BBV (1951 ed.)
(Agincourt [Battle of St. Crispian's Day].) BHV
(England at War [St. Crispin's Day].) EV-1
"Marry, if you would put me to verses or to dance," *fr.* V, ii. LO
Once More unto the Breach, Dear Friends, Once More, III, i. WaaP
(Blast of War, The.) TrGrPo
(England at War; Harfleur, England, and St. George.) EV-1
(Henry V at Harfleur.) TreF
(Henry V before Harfleur.) ShBV-2; TVSH
(Henry Fifth's Address to His Soldiers.) WHA
(Henry V to His Soldiers.) PoFS
(King Henry before Harfleur.) PC
(King to His Soldiers before Harfleur, The.) LPS-2
Prologues to Henry V (*to all Acts*) BHV
(Agincourt, *abr.*) LH
(England at War.) EV-1
Before Agincourt, *fr.* Prologue to IV. ChTr
Eve of Agincourt, The, *fr.* Prologue to IV. ShBV-3
Muse of Fire, A, *2 ll., fr.* Prologue to I. ChTr
Now Entertain Conjecture of a Time, Prologue to IV. NBE; WaaP
So Work the Honey-Bees, *fr.* I, ii. BCEP
(Commonwealth of the Bees, The.) GN
Traitors, *fr.* II, ii. BHV
King Henry VI, Pt. I, *sels.* Shakespeare.
Father and Son, *fr.* IV, v *and* vii. BHV
King Is Dead, A, *fr.* I, i. ChTr
King Henry VI, Pt. II, *sels.* Shakespeare.
Gratitude, *3 ll., fr.* II, i. MaRV
Thrice Armed ("What stronger breastplate than a heart untainted!"), *4 ll., fr.* III, ii. BLP, *3 ll.;* MaRV
(Justice.) BTP
King Henry the Sixth, Pt. III, *sels.* Shakespeare.
Content ("My crown is in my heart"), *4 ll., fr.* III, i. MaRV
("My crown is in my heart, not on my head," *3 ll.*) PoToHe (new ed.)
King Henry VI Yearns for the Simple Life, *fr.* II, v. TreFS
(Kingship and the Shepherd's Life.) EV-1
(Shepherd's Life, A, *abr.*) LPS-1
King Henry VIII, *sels.* Shakespeare *and probably* John Fletcher.
Ambition ("Cromwell, I charge thee, fling away ambition"), *fr.* III, ii. TrGrPo
(Higher Loyalty, The.) MaRV
Cranmer's Prophecy of Queen Elizabeth, *fr.* V, v. WGRP
(England at Peace. A Vision.) EV-1
For a Patriot, *3 ll., fr.* III, ii. PGD
Orpheus with His Lute, *fr.* III, i, *song by* Fletcher, *also at. to* Shakespeare. AtBAP; CBE; ChTr; CoEV; EIL; EV-1; GN; KN; OAEP; OBEV; OTPC; SiCE; TrGrPo; TuPP; TVSH; ViBoPo
(Music.) BLV; FaBoCh
(Orpheus.) PoRL; UnS
(Song: "Orpheus with his lute made trees.") OBS; PoEL-2
(Sweet Music.) PIAE
Vision, The, IV, ii. LiA
Wolsey's Farewell to Cromwell ("Cromwell, I did not think to shed a tear"), *fr.* III, ii. EV-1
("Cromwell, I did not think to shed a tear.") InP; PIR
(Wolsey.) OTPC (1923 ed.)
(Wolsey's Advice to Cromwell.) LPS-1
(Wolsey's Regrets.) TreFS
Wolsey's Farewell to His Greatness, *fr.* III, ii. OHFP; PTA-2
(Cardinal Wolsey's Farewell.) LiTB; MaRV; TreF
("Farewell, a long farewell, to all my greatness!") PIR
(Farewell to All My Greatness.) BCEP; LiTG
(Farewell to Greatness.) TrGrPo
(Wolsey, on His Downfall.) TVSH
(Wolsey's Fall.) LPS-1
King Henry before Harfleur. Shakespeare. *See* Once More unto the Breach . . .
King Henry before the Field of Saint Crispian. Shakespeare.
King Henry V, *fr.* IV, iii. BBV (1951 ed.)
(Agincourt [Battle of St. Crispian's Day].) BHV
(England at War [St. Crispin's Day].) EV-1
King Henry Fifth's Conquest of France. *Unknown.* BaBo (A *and* B *vers.*); ESPB
King Henry VII and the Shipwrights. Kipling. PCN
King Henry VI Yearns for the Simple Life. Shakespeare.
King Henry VI, Pt. III, *fr.* II, v. TreFS
(Kingship and the Shepherd's Life.) EV-1
(Shepherd's Life, A, *abr.*) LPS-1
King Henry to Rosamond. Michael Drayton. *Fr.* England's Heroical Epistles. OBSC
King Henry was sent for. The Death of Queen Jane (D *vers.*). *Unknown.* BaBo
King Honor's Eldest Son. Elinor Wylie. CoBA
King Horn, *abr. Unknown.* EPP
King in Egypt, A. David Morton. MuM
King in His Beauty, The. St. Bernard of Clairvaux, *tr. fr. Latin.* BePJ
King in His Beauty, The. James G. Deck. BePJ
King in the Cradle, The. *Unknown.* BOL
(Old Carol, with Lullaby, An.) AnEC
King Is Cold, The. Robert Browning. LPS-3
King Is Dead, A. Shakespeare. King Henry VI, Pt. I, *fr.* I, i. ChTr
"King is gone, The," the old man said. The Deserted Kingdom. Lord Dunsany. AnIV
King is out a-hunting, The. The King's Wood. C. S. Holder. BoTP
King is sick, The. His cheek was red. *See* King was sick, The. His cheek was red.
King James and Brown. *Unknown.* ESPB
King James II. Dryden. *Fr.* The Hind and the Panther. ACP
King Jamie hath made a vow. Flodden Field. *Unknown.* ESPB
King John [*or* Kynge Johan], *sel.* John Bale.
Wassail, Wassail. ChTr
(Wassail.) AnEC
("Wassail, wassail, out of the milk-pail.") TuPP
King John, *sels.* Shakespeare.
Citizens Defend Angiers, The, *fr.* II, i. BHV
"Death, death:—O amiable lovely death," *fr.* III, iv. PoD
"Grief fills the room up of my absent child," *fr.* III, iv. MotAn
Hubert and Arthur, IV, i. ShGoBo
"O, let us pay the time but needful woe," *fr.* V, vii. PoFr
This England, *fr.* V, vii. BoTP; EV-1
(England, 2.) OTPC
(Words of Faulconbridge, The.) BHV
To Gild Refinèd Gold, IV, ii. BCEP; LiTB; LiTG
King John and Matilda, *sel.* Robert Davenport.
Requiem: "Matilda, now go take thy bed." SeCL
("Matilda, now go take thy bed.") TuPP
King John and the Abbot of Canterbury. *Unknown.* BLV; BoTP; CG; ESPB; GN; GoTP; HBV; LPS-3; OBB; OnSP; OTPC; RG; StaSt; TrGrPo
(Abbot of Canterbury, The.) EV-2
(King John and the Abbot.) BoChLi; BOHV; EnSB
(King John and the Bishop.) BaBo; ESPB, *longer vers.*
King John's Castle. Thomas Kinsella. OxBI
King Kyr Manuel Komninos, The. Manuel Komninos. C. P. Cavafy. MoGP
King Lear, *sels.* Shakespeare.
Blow, Winds, *fr.* III, ii. TrGrPo; WHA
("Blow windes, and crack your cheeks; rage, blow.") AtBAP
(Father's fury, A, *longer sel.*) BCEP
Cod-Piece That Will House, The, *fr.* III, ii. ViBoPo
Death of Lear, *fr.* V, iii. FiP
("And my poor fool is hang'd!") PoD
(My Poore Foole.) LiA
Dover Cliffs, *fr.* IV, vi. LPS-2; SN
"Good morrow to you both," *fr.* II, iv. AtBAP
(O Foole, I Shall Go Mad.) LiA
He That Has and a Little Tiny Wit, *fr.* III, ii. ViBoPo
"Heare Nature, heare deere Goddesse," *fr.* I, iv. NBE
"Heere is better then the open ayre, take it thankfully," *fr.* III, vi. AtBAP
"Here is the place my Lord, good my Lord enter," *fr.* III, iv. AtBAP
"Howle, howle, howle, howle: O you are men of stones," *fr.* V, iii. AtBAP
Jolly Shepherd, The, *fr.* III, vi. PCH
Lear and Cordelia ("How does my Royall Lord? . . ."), *fr.* IV, vii. LiA
Lear and Cordelia ("Some officers take . . ."), *fr.* V, iii. FiP
Lear's Prayer, *fr.* II, iv. BCEP
"Let it be so, thy truth then be thy dowre," *fr.* I, i. NBE
"No, no, no, no: Come let's away," *fr.* V, iii. NBE
"No, they cannot touch me for coyning. I am the King himselfe," *fr.* IV, vi. AtBAP
"O reason not the need: our basest beggars," *fr.* II, iv. NBE
Take Physic, Pomp, *fr.* III, iv. TrGrPo

(Discovery of Pity.) UnPo (1st ed.)
When Priests Are More in Word, *fr.* III, ii. ViBoPo
"With hey, ho, the wind and the rain," *2 ll., fr.* III, ii. TiPo (1952 ed.)
King Lear and His Three Daughters, *sl. abr. Unknown.* CG
King Lear Blinded Oedipus in a Dream. Malcolm Lowry. BoCaPo (1948 ed.)
King Lear once ruled in this land. King Lear and His Three Daughters. *Unknown.* CG
King Lily-o'-th'-Valley so stately. Home-coming. Gustaf Fröding. AnSL
King lived long ago, A. Robert Browning. *Fr.* Pippa Passes. EV-5
King looked on him kindly, as on a vassal true, The. Bavieca. *Unknown.* AnSpL-1
King Louis on his bridge is he. Le Père Sévère. *Unknown.* AWP; JAWP; WBP
King must rule kingdom. Cities are seen from afar. Maxims (Cotton MS.). *Unknown.* AnOE
King o' Spain's Daughter, The. Jeanne Robert Foster. BAP; HBMV
King Oedipus. Sophocles. *See* Oedipus Rex.
King of Brentford, The. Thackeray, *after* Béranger. HBV; OtMeF
King of Canoodle-Dum, The. W. S. Gilbert. CenHV
King of China's Daughter, The. Edith Sitwell. BoTP; MBP; MoBrPo; PoRh
(Two Nut Trees, 2.) CH
(Variations on an Old Nursery Rhyme.) HBMV; TSW; TSWC
King of Connacht, The. *Unknown, tr. fr. Irish by* Frank O'Connor. KiLC
King of Denmark's Ride, The. Caroline Norton. BBV; BeLS; GN; HBV; LPS-1; VA
King of Dreams, The. Clinton Scollard. HBV
King of Elves, The. Janice Wiewel. CAG
King of France and four thousand men, The. *Unknown.* PPL
King of France, the king of France, The,/ with forty [*or* fifty] thousand men. Mother Goose. OxNR; RIS
King of Guzzlemuchgate, The. Pierre Jean de Béranger, *tr. fr. French by* Alan Conder. TrFP
King of Heaven, make me whole. Prayer. Yevgeny Abramovich Boratynsky. TrRV
King of Ireland's Son, The. Nora Hopper. AnIL; GTIV
King of Kings, The. James Shirley. *See* Death the Leveller.
King of Kings, The. Lon Woodrum. BePJ
King of Love, The. Henry W. Baker. BePJ; MaRV
King of Spain, The Maxwell Bodenheim. TCPD
King of stars. The Open Door. *Unknown.* KiLC
King of the Belgians. Marion Couthouy Smith. PAH
King of the Cradle, The. Joseph Ashby-Sterry. HBV
King of the Crocodiles, The. Robert Southey. CG
King of the day is exerting his power, The. Spring. Meta E. B. Thorne. *Fr.* Songs of the Seasons. PEOR
King of the Doctors, The, *sel.* Joseph Rodman Drake.
"How stately yon palace uplifts its proud head." PoP
King of the Rainy Country, The. Baudelaire, *tr. fr. French by* Edna St. Vincent Millay. WoL
King of the sea, and Ruler of the shore. Dedication of a Ship. Macedonius. OnPM
King of this people, good lord Eteocles. News of War. Aeschylus. *Fr.* Seven against Thebes. OxBG
King of Thule, The. Goethe, *tr. fr. German by* James Clarence Mangan. *Fr.* Faust. AWP; JAWP; WBP; LPS-3, *tr. by* Bayard Taylor
King of Triolets, The. Jacques Ranchin, *tr. fr. French by* J. G. Legge. LiA
King of Ulster, The. *Unknown, tr. fr. Irish by* Frank O'Connor. KiLC
King of Yueh, K'u-chien, conquered the men of Wu, The. An Elegy for Yueh. Li Po. WhP
King of Yvetot, The. Pierre Jean de Béranger, *tr. fr. French by* William Toynbee. AWP; JAWP; WBP; WoL
——*Tr. by* Thackeray. OnPP; RIS
King, oh boon for my aspiring mind, A! Another, of Another Mind. "F. M." TuPP
King Olaf's Death-Drink. Longfellow. Tales of a Wayside Inn: The Musician's Tale, Pt. I, xxi. AmPP (4th ed.)
King Olaf's Return. Longfellow. Tales of a Wayside Inn: The Musician's Tale, Pt. I, ii. AmPP (4th ed.)
King Olaf's War-Horns. Longfellow. Tales of a Wayside Inn: The Musician's Tale, Pt. I, xix. AmPP (4th ed.); PFY
King Oluf and His Brother. *Unknown, tr. fr. Danish by* E. M. Smith-Dampier. BoDaBa
King on the Tower, The. Ludwig Uhland, *tr. fr. German by* Thackeray. OBVV
King Orfeo. *Unknown.* ESPB; OBB; OxBoLi
King Passes, The. Anne Hunter Temple. ChIP
King Philip had vaunted his claims. A Ballad to Queen Elizabeth [*or* A Ballad of the Armada]. Austin Dobson. ALV; GTBS; LH; MuP; OBVV; ShBV-2; TVSH
King Philip's Last Stand. Clinton Scollard. PAH
King Philip's Men. Audrey Alexandra Brown. BoCaPo
King Pippin. *Unknown.* LiL
("Little King Pippin he built a fine hall.") BoN; OxNR
King Richard II, *sels.* Shakespeare.
"And wilt thou pluck my fair son from mine age," *fr.* V, ii. MotAn
Banishment ("All places that the eye of heaven visits"), *fr.* I, iii. EV-1
Bolingbroke ("Oh, to what purpose"), *fr.* I, iii. CBE
Dying Men ("The tongues of dying men"), *fr.* II, i. MaRV
"For heaven's [*or* God's] sake, let us sit upon the ground," *fr.* III, ii. HoPM; PoFr
(Death of Kings, The.) TrGrPo
(Kingship.) EV-1
(". . . Of comfort no man speak.") PIR
(Of the Death of Kings.) ChTr
(Richard II's Dejection.) TreFS
(Sad Stories of the Death of Kings.) BCEP
Gentle Richard, *fr.* V, ii. LiA
Richard II Banishes Bolingbroke, *fr.* I, iii. PoFS
This England, *fr.* II, i. LiA; MuP; TreF; TrGrPo
(England.) OTPC
(Gaunt's Dying Speech.) CBE
(John of Gaunt's Dying Speech, *longer sel.*) FiP
(This Royal Throne of Kings.) BHV; EV-1, *longer sel.*; ShBV-2
King Richard III, *sels.* Shakespeare.
Address of Richard III to His Army, The, *fr.* V, iii. UnPo (1st ed.)
"Ah, my young princes! ah, my tender babes," *fr.* IV, iv. MotAn
Dream of Clarence, The, *fr.* I, iv. UnW
(Dream of Wrecks, A.) ChTr
("I saw a thousand fearful wrecks," *shorter sel.*) SG
(Methought I Saw a Thousand Fearful Wrecks, *shorter sel.*) EtS
"In God's name, cheerly on, courageous friends," *fr.* V, ii. PoFr
"Why, then, 'tis time to arm and give direction," *fr.* V, iii. PoFr
Winter of Our Discontent, *fr.* I, i. LiA
(Evil Designs.) TreF
(Hate the Idle Pleasures.) TrGrPo
King Richard hearing of the pranks. The King's Disguise and the Friendship with Robin Hood. *Unknown.* ESPB
King Robert of Sicily. Longfellow. Tales of a Wayside Inn: The Sicilian's Tale, Pt. I. AnNE; BeLS; MW; OHIP; OnSP; PCD; PCN; PFE; PTA-1; TCAP; YT
(Sicilian's Tale, The.) CoV
King sat silent in the hall, his queen, The. The Queen of Eleusis. Robert Morse. MuM
King sent for his wise men all, The. W. James Reeves. ChTr
King sent his lady on the first Yule day, The. The Yule Days. *Unknown.* ChTr
King Siegfried sat in his lofty hall. The Three Songs. Bayard Taylor. StPo
King sits in Dunfermline [*or* Dumferling] town [*or* toune], The. Sir Patrick Spens [*or* Spence]. *Unknown.* AnFE; AtBAP; ATP; AWP; BaBo (A *and* B *vers.*); BBV (1923 ed.); BCEP; BEL; BLV; BoChLi; BoLiVe; BSV; CaAE; CBOV; CH; CoBE; CoEV; EBSV; EM-1; EnL; EnLi-1; EnLit; EnRP; EnSB; EPP; ESPB; EtS; EV-2; ExPo; FaBoCh; GN; GoTS; HBV; HoPM; InP; InPo; InvP; JAWP; LH; LiTB; LoBV; LoGBV; MCCG; OAEP; OBB; OBEV; OnSP; OtMeF; OTPC (1946 ed.); OuHeWo; PCN; PFE; PIAE; PoEL-1; PoMa; PoRA; PYM; REAL; ReaPo; RG; RiBV; SeCeV; SG; ShBV-1; TCEP; TiPo (1952 ed.); TOP; TreF; TrGrPo; UnPo; ViBoPo (A *and* B *vers.*); ViBoPo; WBP; WHA
King-slaying in Finderup, The. *Unknown, tr. fr. Danish by* E. M. Smith-Dampier. BoDaBa
King Solomon. "Owen Meredith." BMEP
King Solomon and King David. *Unknown.* DDA; RIS, *diff. vers.*
King Solomon, before his palace gate. Azrael. Longfellow. AnAmPo; LA
King Solomon stood in the house of the Lord. The Dead Solomon. John Aylmer Dorgan. AA
King Solomon was the wisest man. A Song of Solomon. Josephine Preston Peabody. NP; OBAV
King Stephen. Robert Graves. WaKn
King stood crowned, The; around in the gate. The Crowning of Arthur. Charles Williams. FaBoMo
King stood still, The. David's Lament over Absalom. Nathaniel P. Willis. PTA-2
King Sverrir. Grímur Thomsen, *tr. fr. Icelandic by* Eiríkur Magnússon. IcP
King, that hast reign'd [*or* reigned] six hundred years, and grown. To Dante. Tennyson. EPP; TCEP
King to His Soldiers before Harfleur, The. Shakespeare. *See* Once More unto the Breach . . .

King to Oxford sent a troop of horse, The. Oxford & Cambridge [*or* Epigram]. Sir William Browne. ALV; WhC
King Triumphant. Isaac Watts. *See* Jesus Shall Reign Where'er the Sun.
King Valdemar sailed by isle and eyre. Valdemar and Tove (A *vers.*). *Unknown.* BoDaBa
King walked in his garden green, The. The Three Singing Birds. James Reeves. PoMS
King was embarked along with a Persian slave, A. Purgatory May Be Paradise. Sadi. OuHeWo
King was on his throne, The. The Vision of Belshazzar. Byron. GN; HBV; OTPC; ShGoBo; TOP
King was [*or* is] sick, The. His cheek was red. The Enchanted Shirt. John Hay. BBV; BLPA; BOHV; GN; GoTP; MaC; OnSP; PIAE; TiPo (1952 ed.); TSW; TSWC
King was sitting on his throne, A. King Henry Fifth's Conquest of France (B *vers.*). *Unknown.* BaBo
King Who Died Young, The. Ibn al-Khabbaza, *tr. fr. Arabic by* A. J. Arberry. MooP
King William Was King George's Son, *with music. Unknown.* OuSiCo
King Winter sat in his Hall one day. Outside. Hugh Chesterman. BoTP
King with all his kingly train, The. Louis XV. John Sterling. BeLS; VA
King Witlaf's Drinking-Horn. Longfellow. CoBA; TCAP
Kingcups. Eleanor Farjeon. GBV (1952 ed.)
Kingcups. Sacheverell Sitwell. BLV; MBP; MoBrPo
Kingdom, The. Thomas Curtis Clark. ChIP; MaRV
Kingdom. Sir Edward Dyer. *See* My Mind to Me a Kingdom Is.
Kingdom, The, *sels.* Louis MacNeice.
"Little dapper man but with shiny elbows, A." ChMP
"Under the surface of flux and of fear there is an underground movement." LiTM
Kingdom of Death, The. Homer, *tr. fr. Greek by* F. L. Lucas. *Fr.* The Odyssey, XI. GrPE
Kingdom of God, The. Rab, *tr. fr. Hebrew.* TrJP
Kingdom of God, The. Francis Thompson. *See* In No Strange Land.
Kingdom of God, The. Richard Chenevix Trench. WBLP
Kingdom of God Is within You, The. Toyohiko Kagawa, *tr. fr. Japanese by* Lois J. Erickson. SoLD
Kingdom of Heaven. Léonie Adams. MAP; MoAB; MoAmPo
Kingdom of Heaven, The. G. K. Chesterton. OQP; QP-1
Kingdom of Number is all boundaries, The. W. H. Auden. *Fr.* Numbers and Faces. ImOP
Kingdom Within, The. Percy Clough Ainsworth. MaRV
Kingdoms. Godfrey Fox Bradby. ChIP
(In Hoc Signo.) MaRV
Kingdoms. Oliver St. John Gogarty. AlDL
Kingdoms. Charles Oluf Olsen. OQP; QP-2
Kingdoms of the Earth go by, The. Kingdoms [*or* In Hoc Signo]. Godfrey Fox Bradby. ChIP; MaRV
Kingdoms of this world shall pass away, The. The Realm of Love. George Tucker Bispham, Jr. CAG
Kinge Arthur lives in merry Carleile, and seemely is to see. The Marriage of Sir Gawain. *Unknown.* BaBo; ESPB; OBB
Kingfisher, The. W. H. Davies. BLA; CBE; GTBS-D; MoVE; OBEV (new ed.); POTE; POTT; PtOT; ShBV-2; TCPD; TSW; TSWC; TwCV
Kingfisher, The. Blanche Mary Kelly. GoBC
Kingfisher, The. Andrew Marvell. *Fr.* Upon Appleton House. AtBAP; ChTr; FaBoEn
King-Fisher Song, The. "Lewis Carroll." *Fr.* Sylvie and Bruno Concluded. BoN; RIS
Kingfishers, The. Charles Olson. NeAP
Kingis Quair [*or* Quhair], The, *abr.* James I, King of Scotland. MeEV
Sels.
"Bewailling [*or* Bewailing] in my chamber thus allone." BSV; LEAP, *abr.*
(Coming of Love, The.) GoTS
(He Sees His Beloved, *longer sel.*) PoEL-1
"Blissit mot be the heye goddis all." AtBAP
Dawn of Love, The, 5 *sts.* EBSV
(Walking under the Tour, 3 *sts.*) SeCePo
"To reckon of everything the circumstance." BSV; NBE
"Worshipe, ye that lovers been, this May," 7 *ll.* TrGrPo
(Spring Song of the Birds.) OBEV
Kings, The. Louise Imogen Guiney. BAP; GoBC; HBV; LBMV; MAP; MoAmPo (1942 ed.); OBAV; PC; PoeMoYo
Kings. Victor Hugo, *tr. fr. French by* Alan Conder. TrFP
Kings. Joyce Kilmer. WHL
Kings. John Richard Moreland. ChIP; MaRV
Kings. *Unknown, tr. fr. Sanskrit by* Arthur W. Ryder. *Fr.* The Panchatantra. AWP; PoFr
("In sensuous coil.") LiTW
Kings and Tyrants. Robert Herrick. PoFr
Kings are but guardians who the poor should keep. Guardians. Sadi. PeP
Kings Are Passing Deathward, The. David Morton. OQP; QP-2; SBMV
King's Army, The. Shakespeare. King Henry IV, Pt. I, *fr.* IV, i. LiA
(Armed.) BHV
King's Ballad, The. Joyce Kilmer. HBV
King's Breakfast, The. A. A. Milne. CenHV
King's College Chapel, Cambridge. Wordsworth. *See* Inside of King's College Chapel, Cambridge.
Kings come riding home from the Crusade, The. Crusade. Hilaire Belloc. GoBC
King's Dancer, The. Hilda Mary Hooke. CPG
King's Daughter, *sel.* V. Sackville-West.
Greater Cats, The. DiM; GTBS-D; MoP; OBMV; PoC; POTE; ShBV-4
("Greater cats with golden eyes, The.") LO
King's Disguise, and Friendship with Robin Hood, The. *Unknown.* ESPB
King's Dochter Lady Jean, The. *Unknown.* ESPB
King's Entertainment, The, *sel.* Thomas Dekker.
Troynovant. LoBV
King's Epitaph, The. Earl of Rochester. *See* Epitaph on Charles II.
Kings from the East, The. Heine, *tr. fr. German.* ChTr; GoTS, *tr. into Scottish by* Alexander Gray
King's Gifts, The. C. Frances Loomis. CAG
Kings Go By, The. John Masefield. *See* Choice, The.
King's Hand, The. Mu'tamid, King of Seville, *tr. fr. Arabic by* A. J. Arberry. MooP
King's Highway, The. John Steven McGroarty. DDA; HBV; MW; NLK; POT; PoTo
King's Highway, The. John Masefield. BLRP
King's Hunt Is Up, The. William Gray. *See* Hunt Is Up, The.
King's Missive, The. Whittier. PAH; TCAP
King's most faithful Subjects we, The. England's Triumph; or, The Subjects' Joy. *Unknown.* CoMu
Kings must be dauntless; subjects will contemn. Upon Kings. Robert Herrick. PoFr
Kings of Europe, The; a Jest. Robert Dodsley. CEP
Kings of France. Mary W. Lincoln. BLPA
Kings of the earth are men of might, The. Kings. Joyce Kilmer. WHL
Kings of the East, The. Katharine Lee Bates. ChIP, *abr.;* MaRV; OQP; QP-1; SDH; WGRP
Kings of Troy, The. Euripides. *See* Chorus: Kings of Troy, The.
King's Own Regulars, The. *Unknown.* PAH
King's poet was his captain of horse in the wars, The. Mount Badon. Charles Williams. FaBoTw
King's Quhair, The. James I, King of Scotland. *See* Kingis Quair, The.
King's Ring, The. Theodore Tilton. *See* Even This Shall Pass Away.
King's road is a troublous summons calling day and day, The. A Leaf from a Fly-Book. Seaforth Mackenzie. MM
King's Son, The. Thomas Boyd. AnIV; GTIV; OBMV; OxBI
Kings they came from out the south, The. Christmas Carol. Sara Teasdale. ChrBoLe; SDH; StJW
Kings to the Stable, The. A Song for the Season. Katharine Tynan. SDH
King's Tragedy, The. Dante Gabriel Rossetti. BPN; EmBrPo; EPN; PoVP; TOP; ViPo; VLEP
King's Visit, The. William Morris. *Fr.* The Earthly Paradise. VA
Kings' wares; and dreams; and April dusks. The Portrait of a Florentine Lady. Lizette Woodworth Reese. HBMV
Kings who without control the sceptre sway'd. George Wither. *Fr.* The Conquered King. PoFr
King's Wood, The. C. S. Holder. BoTP
King's young dochter was sitting in her window, The. The King's Dochter Lady Jean. *Unknown.* ESPB
Kingship. Joachim du Bellay, *tr. fr. French by* Alan Conder. Antiquities of Rome, XVI. TrFP
Kingship ("Let's talk of graves"). Shakespeare. *See* Death of Kings, The.
Kingship and the Shepherd's Life ("O God! methinks it were a happy life"). Shakespeare. *See* King Henry VI Yearns for the Simple Life.
Kingship is passing down the yellow road. Bonfire of Kings. Donald Evans. AnAmPo; LA
Kingston Church. Thomas D'Urfey. SeCL
Kinkaiders, The. *Unknown.* AS. *with music;* CoSo
(Kinkaider's Song, The.) ABS
Kinmont Willie. *Unknown.* BaBo; BEL; BSV; CBOV; EBSV; ESPB; EV-2; LH; OBB
Kinnaird Head. George Bruce. NeBP; PoN
Kinnereth. "Rachel," *tr. fr. Hebrew by* A. M. Klein. LiTW; TrJP

Kinsey! Thy pages studiously rehearse. Volume II (Kinsey). David Daiches. SiTL
Kinship. Angela Morgan. BPP
Kinship. Wade Oliver. PoP
Kinship. Sir Charles G. D. Roberts. CaP; OCL
Kinship. Edward H. S. Terry. MaRV; OQP; QP-2
Kinship with the Stars. George Meredith. *Fr.* Modern Love, IV. GTBS-W; LiA
Kinsman. Jean Ingelow. MaRV
Kinsmen of Francis, The. A Rhyme for Francis: October 4th. Eleanor Farjeon. SaFP
Kinsmen, you shall behold. John Drinkwater. *Fr.* Abraham Lincoln. TwCV
Kiph. Walter de la Mare. AlDL; TiPo (1959 ed.)
Kirkland Lake. James Wreford Watson. BoCaPo
Kirk's Alarm, The. Burns. OxBoLi
Kirov Is with Us. Nikolai Tikhonov, *tr. fr. Russian by* Jack Lindsay. RuPo
Kiss, The. Mary Carolyn Davies. *Fr.* A Girl's Songs. SBMV
Kiss, A. Austin Dobson. *Fr.* Rose-Leaves. ALV; BPN; CBOV; EnLit; HBV; InP; MBP; MoBrPo (1942 ed.)
Kiss, A. William Drummond of Hawthornden. ElL
Kiss, The. Robert Herrick. LPS-1
Kiss, The ("For love's sake, kiss me once again"). Ben Jonson. *See* Begging Another, on Colour of Mending the Former.
Kiss, The ("Oh, that joy so soon should waste"). Ben Jonson. *See* Song: "O, that joy so soon should waste."
Kiss, The. Walter Savage Landor. *See* Maid I Love, The.
Kiss, The. Tom Masson. BOHV; LauV
Kiss, The. Thomas Moore. EnLoPo
Kiss, The ("My ghostly father"). Charles d'Orléans. *See* Confession.
Kiss, The. Coventry Patmore. *Fr.* The Angel in the House, II, viii, 3. ALV; EnLoPo; FiBHP; LiTL; OBVV; PC
(Sly Thoughts.) LPS-1
Kiss, The. Dante Gabriel Rossetti. The House of Life, VI. PoVP
("What smouldering senses in death's sick delay.") ViPo
Kiss, The. Siegfried Sassoon. LBBV; NP; NV
(To These I Turn, in These I Trust.) LEAP
Kiss, The. Sara Teasdale. ChMo; CMP; HBV
Kiss, A ("He's my doll"). *Unknown, tr. fr. Irish by* Frank O'Connor. KiLC
Kiss, The ("O keep your kisses, young provoking girl!"). *Unknown, tr. fr. Late Middle Irish by* the Earl of Longford. OnYI; OxBI
Kiss, The ("Since for kissing thee, Minguillo"). *Unknown.* *See* Minguillo's Kiss.
Kiss, The. Franz Werfel, *tr. fr. German by* Elizabeth Selden. BoFr
Kiss, a word of thanks, away, A. Fatherhood. Henry Charles Beeching. PoeT
Kiss, Dear Maid, The. Byron. LPS-1
Kiss-Fest, The. Irwin Edman. InMe
Kiss, A? for a child's kiss? Francis Thompson. *Fr.* Sister Songs. BMEP
Kiss her, kiss her, kiss her a thousand times. Ersatz. Raymond Souster. BoCaPo (1948 ed.); PeCV
Kiss I begged, A; but, smiling, she. Weeping and Kissing. Sir Edward Sherburne. ElSeCe; SeCL; SeEP
Kiss in the Rain, A. Samuel Minturn Peck. BOHV
Kiss in the Ring. *Unknown.* OxBoLi
Kiss is maypole where my seven, The. The First Cycle of Love Poems, III. George Barker. MoPo
Kiss me but once, and in that space supreme. Love's Kiss. Helen Hay Whitney. AA
Kiss me softly and speak to me low. To My Love. John Godfrey Saxe. HBV
Kiss [*or* Kisse] me, sweet; the wary lover. To Celia [*or* Song to Celia]. Ben Jonson. AWP; ElL; ElSeCe; JAWP; LiTL; LO; LoBV; LoPS; SeCV-1; WBP
Kiss me then, my merry May. Medieval Norman Songs, III. *Unknown, tr. by* John Addington Symonds. AWP
Kiss me, though you make believe. Make Believe. Alice Cary. HBV; LPS-1; PR; PreP
Kiss my grey hair, oh, my love. Healing. Abraham Reisen. LiTW; TrJP
Kiss of God, The. Geoffrey Anketell Studdert-Kennedy. BLRP
Kiss thou nor deny'st, nor givest one, A. To Polla. John Owen. *Fr.* Four Epigrams. PrWP
Kiss within the Cup, A. Agathias Scholasticus. *See* Leave a Kiss within the Cup.
Kiss'd Yestreen. *Unknown.* OtMeF
Kisse me, sweet; the warie lover. *See* Kiss me, sweet; the wary lover.
Kissed me from the saddle, and I still can feel it burning. The Smoke-blue Plains. Badger Clark. YaD
Kissed we not and said good-bye? Since We Said Good-Bye. Arthur Upson. PR
Kisses. *At. to* Thomas Campion. ElL; OBSC
(Kisses Make Men Loath to Go.) LiTL
(My Love Bound Me.) ElSeCe; TuPP
(Song: "My Love bound me with a kiss.") HBV
Kisses. Cristóbal de Castillejo, *tr. fr. Spanish by* Jeanne Pasmantier. AnSpL-1
Kisses. William Strode. LPS-1; NeHB
Kisses. Arthur Symons. VLEP
Kisses. Esaias Tegnér, *tr. fr. Swedish by* Charles W. Stork. AnSL
Kisses Desired. William Drummond of Hawthornden. EnLoPo
Kisses in the Train. D. H. Lawrence. MBP; MoAB; MoBrPo
Kisses Make Men Loath to Go. *At. to* Thomas Campion. *See* Kisses.
Kisses on the breast, like water from a pitcher! Sparrow Hills. Boris Pasternak, *tr. by* C. M. Bowra. BoRS
Kisses upon your breast, like water from a jug. Vorobyev Hills. Boris Pasternak, *tr. by* J. M. Cohen. OnHM
Kissin'. *Unknown.* FiBHP; LiTG; LiTL; SiTL; TreF
(Kissing's No Sin.) HBV; LPS-1
Kissing. Lord Herbert of Cherbury. EnLoPo; LiTL; ViBoPo
Kissing and Bussing. Robert Herrick. OAEP
Kissing Her Hair. Swinburne. *See* Rondel: "Kissing her hair I sat against her feet."
Kissing's No Sin. *Unknown.* *See* Kissin'.
Kit Carson. Arthur Guiterman. GA
Kit Carson's Last Smoke. "Stanley Vestal." PoOW
Kit Carson's Ride. Joaquin Miller. AmPP (3d ed.); HiLiAm; IAP; TreFS
Kit Logan and Lady Helen. Robert Graves. HBMV
Kit, the recording angel wrote. Kitty's "No." Arlo Bates. Conceits, II. AA
Kitchen Clock, The. John Vance Cheney. BOHV
Kitchen door was opened, The. Coming of Winter. Boris Pasternak. RuPo
Kitchen fire that wakes so soon, The. Fires. Elizabeth Fleming. BoTP
Kitchen Window. J. E. H. MacDonald. CaP; OCL; TwCaPo
Kitchenette Building. Gwendolyn Brooks. PoNe
Kitchie-Boy, The. *Unknown.* BaBo; ESPB
Kite, The. Harry Behn. FaPON; TiPo (1959 ed.)
Kite, The. Fang Che Chai, *tr. fr. Chinese by* Henry H. Hart. OnPM; PoHN
Kite, The. Pearl Forbes MacEwen. BoTP
Kite, The. José Moreno Villa, *tr. fr. Spanish by* Eleanor L. Turnbull. CoSP; OnPM
Kite, A. Frank Dempster Sherman. *See* Wish, A.
Kite, A. *Unknown.* TiPo
Kite, a sky, and a good firm breeze, A. Kite Days. Mark Sawyer. BrR; SiSoSe; TiPo
Kite and a string, A. She Would. Dixie Willson. GFA
Kite Days. Mark Sawyer. BrR; SiSoSe; TiPo
Kite-flying. Mary McNeil Fenollosa. RAR
Kite of rags, A. Contrast. Issa. PoFr
Kite Tales. Rose Waldo. GFA
Kite, while devouring a skylark, A. The Stupid Kite. Allen Upward. *Fr.* Scented Leaves from a Chinese Jar. NP
Kit's conscience shall ne'er bring him in trouble. In Christophorum. Thomas Freeman. SiCE
Kit's Cradle. Juliana Horatia Ewing. CIV; SAS, *abr.*
Kitsos. *Unknown, tr. fr. Modern Greek by* Rae Dalven. MoGP
Kitten, The. Joanna Baillie. CIV; DiM; PoC
Kitten, A. Eleanor Farjeon. TiPo
Kitten, The. Ogden Nash. FaPON; MoShBr; WhC
Kitten and Falling Leaves, The. Wordsworth. CIV, *much abr.*; PoC
Sels.
"See the kitten on the wall." CG; PRWS, *shorter sel.*
(Kitten at Play, The.) BoTP; FaPON; MPB (1956 ed.); OTPC
(Kitten Playing with the Falling Leaves, The.) GoTP
"That way look, my infant, lo!" HBVY
Kitten and Firefly. Marie Grimes. CIV
Kitten at Play, The. Wordsworth. *See* Kitten and Falling Leaves, The.
Kitten once to its mother said, A. The Robber Kitten. *At. to* George M. Baker. CIV; FTB
Kitten Playing with the Falling Leaves, The. Wordsworth. *See* Kitten and Falling Leaves, The.
Kitten Speaks, The. William Brighty Rands. *See* Cat of Cats, The.
Kitten went a-walking, A. A Serious Question. Carolyn Wells. CIV
Kittens, The. F. Hey. SAS
Kittens. Catherine Parmenter. CIV
Kittens. Michael Scot. PoC
Kitten's Eclogue, The. Ruth Pitter. PoC
Kitten's Night Thoughts. Oliver Herford. BoChLi; MPB
"Kittens, now I'll find names for you." The Kittens. F. Hey. SAS
Kitten's Thought, A. Oliver Herford. RIS

Kittiwakes and cormorants go to sleep, The. Nightfall in Inishtrahull. Daniel James O'Sullivan. NeIP
Kitty. Elizabeth Prentiss. *See* Long Time Ago.
Kitty Bhan. Edward Walsh. ACP
Kitty Caught a Hornet. Leroy F. Jackson. UTS
Kitty Hawk is a Caesar among monuments. The Structure of the Plane. Muriel Rukeyser. PoF
Kitty; How to Treat Her. Jane Taylor. *See* I Like Little Pussy.
Kitty in the Basket. Eliza Lee Follen. SAS
Kitty, Kitty,/ Wash your paws. *Unknown.* RIS
Kitty, Kitty Casket. *Unknown.* *See* Itiskit, Itaskit.
"Kitty, Kitty, you mischievous elf." Both Sides. Mary Abigail Dodge. CIV
Kitty Neil. John Francis Waller. HBV; TIP; VA
(Dance Light.) LPS-1
Kitty of Coleraine. *Unknown, at. to* Charles Dawson Shanly *and to* Edward Lysaght. BOHV; HBV; LPS-1; MCCG; OnYI; StPo; TIP
Kitty Wants to Write. Gelett Burgess. BOHV
Kitty Wells. *Unknown.* ABS
Kitty: What She Thinks of Herself. William Brighty Rands. *See* Cat of Cats, The.
Kitty's Feet. Norah M. Holland. CPG
Kitty's Laugh. Arlo Bates. Conceits, I. AA
Kitty's "No." Arlo Bates. Conceits, II. AA
Kiumers. Firdausi, *tr. fr. Persian by* Joseph Champion. *Fr.* Shah Namah. PeP
Klare von Reuter. Jorge Carrera Andrade, *tr. fr. Spanish by* Muna Lee. AnCL
Klaxon. James Reaney. TwCaPo
Kleisoura. Angelos Sikelianos, *tr. fr. Modern Greek by* Rae Dalven. MoGP
Kleptomaniac. Leonora Speyer. AnAmPo; HBMV; LA
Klondike, The. E. A. Robinson. PaA; PAH
Klondike Miner. The. *Unknown.* IHA
Knapsack Trail, The. Edwin Osgood Grover. OQP; QP-2
Knapweed. A. C. Benson. HBV; VA
Knavish Merman, The. *Unknown, tr. fr. Danish by* E. M. Smith-Dampier. BoDaBa
Knee, The. Christian Morgenstern, *tr. fr. German by* Lola Gruenthal. AnGP
Knee-deep in June. James Whitcomb Riley. OHFP
Knee walks through the world, alone, A. The Knee. Christian Morgenstern. AnGP
Kneel always when you light a fire! The Sacrament of Fire. John Oxenham. BMEP; POT; PoTo; VOD (1935 ed.)
Kneel down, fair Love, and fill thyself with tears. A Ballad of Death. Swinburne. PoVP; VLEP
Kneel then with me, fall worm-like on the ground. Night. George Chapman. *Fr.* The Shadow of Night. OBSC
Kneel to the beautiful women who bear us this strange brave fruit. Chanty. John Masefield. *Fr.* The Tragedy of Pompey the Great. BMEP
Kneel to the Lord. Christopher Smart. *Fr.* On the Goodness of the Supreme Being. BeR
Kneeling Camel, The. Anna Temple Whitney. BLPA
(Rest and Work.) MaRV
(Submission and Rest.) BLRP
Kneeling he spoke the names he loved the most. A Martyr's Mass. Alfred Barrett. GoBC; JKCP (1955 ed.)
Knell. George Chapman. MaRV
Knell nor deep minute-gun gave the world warning. Cid of the West. Edna Dean Proctor. DD; GA
Knell Shall Sound Once More, The. *Unknown.* BlG
Knell that dooms the voiceless and obscure, The. Survival. Florence Earle Coates. AA
Knew'st thou the edicts which forbade these things? The Higher Command. Sophocles. *Fr.* Antigone. MaRV
Knicht had two sons o sma fame, A. Sir Lionel (B *vers.*). *Unknown.* ESPB
Knife, The. Milton Kaplan. TrJP
Knife, The. "J. R." MoAuPo
Knife-Grinder, The. George Canning *and* John Hookham Frere. *See* Friend of Humanity and the Knife-Grinder, The.
Knife within his hand he stood, A. Chicago Idyll. E. Merrill Root. AnAmPo; LA; PreP
Knight, A. Chaucer, *mod. vers. by* Louis Untermeyer. *Fr.* The Canterbury Tales: Prologue. GoTP
Knight, The. Sister Maryanna. WHL
Knight, The. Rainer Maria Rilke, *tr. fr. German by* Charles Issawi. AnGP
Knight and a lady, A/ Went riding one day. *Unknown.* BoTP
Knight and a lady once met in a grove, A. Sympathy. Reginald Heber. BeLS; BOHV
Knight and Shepherd's Daughter[s], The (A *and* B *vers.*). *Unknown.* BaBo; ESPB
(Knight and the Shepherd's Daughter. The.) ViBoFo
Knight and the Lady, The. "Thomas Ingoldsby." *Fr.* The Ingoldsby Legends. BOHV
Knight and the Shepherd's Daughter, The. *Unknown.* *See* Knight and Shepherd's Daughter, The.
Knight, Death, and the Devil, The. Randall Jarrell. CrMA
Knight Errant, The. Arthur Stringer. BoCaPo (1943 ed.)
Knight-errant of the never-ending quest. Shelley. Henry van Dyke. VOD
Knight Fallen on Evil Days, The. Elinor Wylie. MAP; MoAmPo
Knight had ridden down from Wensley Moor, The. Hart-Leap Well. Wordsworth. BeLS; CG; LPS-2; MyFE
Knight in Disguise, The. Vachel Lindsay. HBV
Knight in Prison, The. William Morris. *See* In Prison.
Knight in the Bower, The. *Unknown.* *See* Heron, The.
Knight in the Feather-Fell, The. *Unknown, tr. fr. Danish by* E. M. Smith-Dampier. BoDaBa
Knight is away in the merry greenwood, The. The Ballad of Baby Bunting. Henry S. Leigh. BOL
Knight knock'd at the castle gate, The. Desire. William Cornish. EG; OBSC; SeCeV
Knight of Bethlehem, A. Henry Neville Maugham. *Fr.* The Husband of Poverty. CBPC; ChIP; MaRV; OQP; QP-2
(Song: "There was a Knight of Bethlehem.") BoTP
Knight of Curtesy, The, *sel. Unknown, tr. fr. Middle English by* Pearl London.
Eaten Heart, The. TrGrPo
Knight of Ghosts and Shadows, A. Dunstan Thompson. NePA
Knight of La Mancha, A. Frank Belknap Long. DaM
Knight of Liddesdale. *Unknown.* ESPB
Knight of the Burning Pestle, The, *sels.* Beaumont *and* Fletcher.
"Better music ne'er was known," *fr.* V, iii. SiCE; TuPP
Come, You Whose Loves Are Dead, *fr.* IV, iv. AtBAP; EIL; SiCE; TuPP
(Dirge: "Come, you whose loves are dead.") EV-2
Jillian of Berry, *fr.* IV, v. EIL
(Merrythought's Song: "For Jillian of Berry.") OBS
Merrythought's Song: "I would not be a servingman," *fr.* IV, v. OBS
Mirth, *fr.* II, viii. EIL
("Tis mirth that fills the veins with blood.") SiCE
(Laugh and Sing.) TrGrPo
Month of May, The, *fr.* IV, v. ChTr
"Nose, nose, jolly red nose," *fr.* I, iii. FaBoCh; LoGBV
"Tell me, dearest, what is love?" *fr.* III, i. *Diff. vers.*, 3 *sts., given in* The Captain. ElSeCe
Knight of the Grail, The. *Unknown.* *See* Falcon, The.
Knight of the Holy Ghost, he goes his way. In Memory of G. K. Chesterton. Walter de la Mare. GoBC
Knight stands in the stable-door, The. Young Johnstone. *Unknown.* BaBo; ESPB
Knight ther [*or* there] was, and that a worthy man, A. A Knight [*or* Seven Pilgrims *or* Some Characters]. Chaucer. *Fr.* The Canterbury Tales: Prologue. BLV; GoTP; LEAP; MaC; TrGrPo
"Knight there is, A," a lady said. Reward of Service. *Unknown.* LyMA
Knight, with Umbrella. Elder Olson. FiBHP
Knightes Tale, The. Chaucer. *See* Knight's Tale, The.
Knighting of the Sirloin of Beef by Charles the Second, The. *Unknown.* COAH
Knightliest of the knightly race, The. The Virginians of the Valley. Francis Orrery Ticknor. AA; AnAmPo; BlG; DD; HBV; LA; PaA; PAH; SPP; TCAP
Knightly Code, The. Eustache Deschamps, *tr. fr. French by* Daniel J. McKenna. CAW
Knights, The, *sels.* Aristophanes, *tr. fr. Greek.*
Demos and His Flatterer, *tr. by* T. Mitchell. OxBG
(Political Cartoon, *tr. by* Benjamin Bickley Rogers.) GrR
Demos Rejuvenated, *tr. by* Gilbert Murray. OxBG
(Demus; a Return to His Better Self, *tr. by* Benjamin Bickley Rogers.) GrR
Demus Shriven, *tr. by* Benjamin Bickley Rogers. GrR
Old-Time Virtues, *tr. by* Benjamin Bickley Rogers. GrR
Poet and His Rivals, The, *tr. by* Gilbert Murray. OxBG
(To the Fickle Gallery, *tr. by* Benjamin Bickley Rogers.) GrR
Sausage-Seller's Triumph, The, *tr. by* Benjamin Bickley Rogers. GrR
Knights, The. Ibn Sa'id of Alcala la Real, *tr. fr. Arabic by* A. J. Arberry. MooP
Knights Errant. Sister Mary Madeleva. CAW
Knight's Ghost, The. *Unknown.* ESPB
Knight's Leap, The. Charles Kingsley. BHV; PCD; StPo; TVSH
Knight's Prayer, The. Sarum Primer. *See* God Be in My Head.
Knights ride off to war, The. The Tale of Battle. Ibn Sa'id of Alcala la Real. MooP
Knight's Song, The. *Unknown.* *See* Wandering Knight's Song, The.
Knight's [*or* Knightes] Tale, The. Chaucer. *Fr.* The Canterbury Tales. BEL; GEPC; GoTL; TOP
Sels.
Arcite's Farewell, *mod. vers. by* John Hall Wheelock. LiTL
"Allas the Wo! Allas, the peynes stronge." LO

Emily's Prayer To Diana. MyFE
Morning in May. LPS-2
(Dawn, *shorter sel.*) CBOV
"Whan that Arcite to Thebes comen was." LiA
Knights to Chrysola, The. Rachel Annand Taylor. OBVV
Knight's Toast, The. *At. to* Sir Walter Scott. MotAn; PCD; PTA-2
Knight's Tomb, The. Samuel Taylor Coleridge. AEV; BCEP; BHV; EM-2; EmBrPo; EnRP; EPN; ERP; EV-4; FaBoCh; GN; InP; LEAP; LoGBV; LPS-2; ShBV-1; TCEP; TVSH
Knightsbridge of Libya. Sorley Maclean. NeBP
Knitting is the maid o' the kitchen, Milly. The Kitchen Clock. John Vance Cheney. BOHV
Knock, and the door shall open: ah, we knocked. The Seekers. Arthur Stringer. CPG
Knock at the door [*or* dooric]. *Unknown.* OxNR; SAS
"Knock-me-down sermon, and worthy of Birch, A." An Old Buffer. Frederick Locker-Lampson. CenHV
Knocking at the Door. John Freeman. HBMV
Knole. Roy Fuller. PoN
Knot, The. Henry Vaughan. ISi
Knot of Blue and Gray, A. *Unknown.* PEDC
Knot of knaves are early met together, A. Henry Parrot. SiCE
Knot which first my heart did strain, The. Sir Thomas Wyatt. SiPS
Knotting Song, The. Sir Charles Sedley. *See* Hears Not My Phyllis.
Know all to whom these few sad lines shall come. Sir Aston Cokayne. ReEn
Know, Celia, since thou art so proud. Ingrateful [*or* Ungrateful] Beauty Threatened [*or* Celia Threatened]. Thomas Carew. BCEP; CBOV; CoEV; EG; ElSeCe; EnLi-1; EPS; EV-2; HBV; InvP; LO; MeLP; OBEV; OBS; SeCV-1; SeEP; TOP
"Know, he assists the cause of God, who toils." Tasso. *Fr.* Jerusalem Delivered, IV. PoFr
Know I not who thou mayst be. At the Hacienda. Bret Harte. AA; OBAV
Know in Vain. Dante Gabriel Rossetti. The House of Life, LXV. PoVP
Know lady that my life depends. *Unknown.* SeCSL
Know, Nature's children all divide her care. Pope. *Fr.* An Essay on Man, Epistle III. BeR
Know, that I would accounted be. To Ireland in the Coming Times. W. B. Yeats. OxBI
Know that the age of Pyrrha is long passed. Patrick Moloney. Sonnets—Ad Innuptam, IV. BoAu
Know the male. Tao Teh Ching, XXVIII. *Unknown, tr. fr. Chinese.* WhP
Know then, I was born in a strange country. To My People. Edwin Seaver. TrJP
Know then this truth, enough for man to know. Pope. *Fr.* An Essay on Man, Epistle IV. EV-3
Know Then Thyself. Pope. An Essay on Man, Epistle II. LiTB, *fr.* II *and* IV; LiTG, *fr.* II *and* IV; MaRV, 18 *ll.*; OBEC, 18 *ll.*; SeCePo, 18 *ll.*
("Know then thyself, presume not God to scan.") AnFE, *fr.* II *and* IV; EnLi-1 (1949 ed.); EnLit; EV-3; ExPo; GoTL; MaPo; NBE, *abr.*; PG (1955 ed.); PoEL-3; TCEP; TOP, *abr.*; TrGrPo, 18 *ll.*; TwP; ViBoPo, 18 *ll.*
(Know Thyself, 18 *ll.*) TwCrTr
(Lines from "An Essay on Man," 18 *ll.*) GoBC
(Man, 18 *ll.*) BLV; BoLiVe; CBE, *longer sel., abr.*
(Paragon of Animals, The, 18 *ll.*) ACP
(Proper Study of Man, The, 18 *ll.*) TreFS
(Proper Study of Mankind, The, 30 *ll.*) FiP
(Riddle of the World, 18 *ll.*) FaFP; GTBS-W
Know this./ Spent bullets die. Manifesto of the Soldier Who Went Back to War. Angel Miguel Queremel. PoFr; WaaP
Know thou, O Virgin, noble-blest. Prudentius. *Fr.* Cathemerinon. ISi
Know Thyself. Pope. *See* Know Then Thyself.
Know, 'twas well said, that spirits are too high. Sir Francis Kynaston. EG
Know ye, fair folk who dwell on earth. Epitaph. Iraj. PeP
Know Ye Not That Lovely River. Gerald Griffin. OnYI
Know ye the land where the cypress and myrtle. The Bride of Abydos [*or* The Land of the Sun *or* The Orient]. Byron. BEL; BPN; EmBrPo; EPP; EV-4; LPS-2; MCCG; OAEP
Know ye the willow-tree. The Willow-Tree. Thackeray. BOHV; CenHV; HBV; PA
Know you, fair[e], on what you look. On Mr. G. Herbert's Book [*or* On George Herbert's "The Temple"]. Richard Crashaw. EV 4; OxBoCh; PtP; SeCV 1
Know you her secret none can utter? Alma Mater. Sir Arthur T. Quiller-Couch. OBVV; PoeT
Know you, like me, the piquancy of sorrow. A Sight-Seer's Dream. Baudelaire. TrFP
Know you that land where forest shadows fold. Mignon. Goethe. *Fr.* Wilhelm Meister. LiTW
Know Yourself, *sels.* John Arbuthnot.
Godlike Brute, The. BeR
"What am I? how produc'd?" PoP
Knowed him more 'n twenty year'. Greetings for Two. James W. Foley. IHA
Knowest Thou Isaac Jogues? Francis W. Grey. CAW
Knowest thou the land where bloom the lemon [*or* citron] trees. Mignon [*or* Mignon's Song]. Goethe. *Fr.* Wilhelm Meister. AWP; JAWP; LPS-3; WBP
Knowing that it would burn she courted fire. The Little Flower. Leonard Feeney. PraNu
Knowing the heart of man is set to be. Samuel Daniel. *Fr.* To the Lady Margaret Countesse of Cumberland. FaBoEn
Knowing this man, who calls himself comrade. Definition. Edwin Rolfe. BoFr; NAMP
Knowing What Time It Is at Night. Louise Townsend Nicholl. PG (1955 ed.)
Knowledge. Archilochus, *tr. fr. Greek.* OxBG
Knowledge. Louise Bogan. HBMV
Knowledge. Thomas Curtis Clark. OQP; QP-2
Knowledge. Frederic W. H. Myers. *Fr.* Saint Paul. OQP; QP-1
Knowledge. Frederick George Scott. VA
Knowledge. "Jan Struther." OS
Knowledge. Whittier. *See* Bible, The.
Knowledge after Death. Henry Charles Beeching. OBVV; VA
Knowledge and Reason. Sir John Davies. *See* Much Knowledge, Little Reason.
Knowledge and wisdom, far from being one. Wisdom. William Cowper. *Fr.* The Task, VI. MaRV
Knowledge of Age. Margaret Avison. PeCV
Knowledge; Solomon Discourses. Matthew Prior. *Fr.* Solomon on the Vanity of the World. BeR
Knowledge Studies Others. *Unknown, at. to* Lao-tzu, *tr. fr. Chinese by* Witter Bynner. *Fr.* Tao Teh King. OnPM
Knowledge through Suffering. George Wallace Briggs. MaRV
Knowledge without Wisdom. T. S. Eliot. *See* Eagle Soars in the Summit of Heaven, The.
Knowledgeable Child, The. L. A. G. Strong. OBMV
Knowlt Hoheimer. Edgar Lee Masters. *Fr.* Spoon River Anthology. OxBA
Known in Vain. Dante Gabriel Rossetti. The House of Life, LXV. BPN; EmBrPo; EnLi-2; EPP; TCEP; ViPo
Known Soldier, The. Mark Antony De Wolfe Howe. AOAH
Known Soldier, The. Kenneth Patchen. WaaP
Known World, The. Brewster Ghiselin. MoVE
Knows he that never took a pinch. To My Nose. Alfred A. Forrester. BLPA; BOHV; LPS-3
Knows he who tills this lonely field. Dirge. Emerson. BoFr; OBAV
Know'st thou, Lorenzo, what a friend contains? The Fruits of Friendship. Edward Young. *Fr.* Night Thoughts. BoFr; GrCo-1
Know'st thou not at the fall of the leaf. Autumn Song. Dante Gabriel Rossetti. BPN; ViBoPo; VLEP
Know'st thou the land where the fair citron blows. Mignon. Goethe. LiA
Know'st thou the land where the herd houseless stray'd. The Isleman's Home. Thomas Pattison. EBSV
Know'st thou what task the man's may be. Man and Wife. Parvin. PeP
Kochia. Thomas Hornsby Ferril. NePoAm-2
Koheleth. Louis Untermeyer. TrJP
Κοινα τὰ τῶν Φίλων (Koina ta ton Philon). John Addington Symonds. OBVV
Kokin Shu [*or* Sho], *sels.* *Tr. fr. Japanese by* Arthur Waley.
"Although it is not plainly visible to the eye." Fujiwara no Toshiyuki. AWP; JAWP; PFE, *tr. wr. at. to* Curtis Hidden Page; WBP
"Beloved person must I think, The." Ki no Akimine. AWP
"Did I ever think." Ono no Takamura. AWP
"Hoping all the time." *Unknown.* AWP
"If only, when one heard." *Unknown.* AWP; LiTW; PFE, *tr. wr. at. to* Curtis Hidden Page
"My love/ Is like the grasses." Ono no Yoshiki. AWP; LiTW; PFE; *tr. wr. at. to* Curtis Hidden Page
(Unknown, *tr. by* Basil Hall Chamberlain.) OnPM
"O cuckoo." *Unknown.* AWP
"Since I heard/ Faintly the voice." Mitsune. AWP
"Thing which fades, A." Ono no Komachi. AWP; JAWP
"When the dawn comes." *Unknown.* AWP
Ko-Ko's Song ("As some day it may happen that a victim must be found"). W. S. Gilbert. *Fr.* The Mikado. LiTB; SiTL
(They'll None of 'em Be Missed.) EnLi-2 (1949 ed.); PoVP
Ko-Ko's Song ("On a tree by a river a little tom-tit"). W. S. Gilbert. *See* Suicide's Grave, The.
Ko-Ko's Song ("There is beauty in the bellow of the blast"), *much abr.* W. S. Gilbert. *Fr.* The Mikado. PCD
Kol Nidra. Joseph Leiser. *Fr.* The Day of Atonement. AA; TrJP

Kolendy for Christmas. *Unknown, tr. fr. Polish by* Irena Dalgiewicz. CAW
Kookaburra, *sel.* T. Inglis Moore.
"Over the multiple terrors of Mars." NeLNL
"Kookoorookoo! kookoorookoo!" Christina Rossetti. *Fr.* Sing-Song. EmBrPo; RIS
Koran, The, *sel.* Mohammed, *tr. fr. Arabic by* J. M. Rodwell.
Teaching of Mohammed, The. WoL
Kore. Frederic Manning. HBV; LoBV, *wr. at. to* Ezra Pound
Korea. Vincent Buckley. BoAV
Korean Woman Seated by a Wall, A. William Meredith. NePoEA
Korf has invented a new kind of joke. Korf's Joke. Christian Morgenstern. AnGP
Korf meets a giant trained to hold. The Pious Giant. Christian Morgenstern. AnGP
Korf's Joke. Christian Morgenstern, *tr. fr. German by* R. F. C. Hull. AnGP
Korosta Katzina Song. *Tr. fr. Hopi Indian by* Natalie Curtis. AWP; JAWP
Korsør. Adam Oehlenschläger, *tr. fr. Danish by* Charles W. Stork. *Fr.* Langelands Rejsen. BoDS
Koskiusko. Samuel Taylor Coleridge. EnRP
Kossuth. James Russell Lowell. BHV
Kotatsu, from which to watch, A. Issa. Satirical Poems on Daimyos, I. PoFr
Kotytto's ritual feast they keep. The Worship of Cotys. Aeschylus. *Fr.* Edoni. OxBG
Kowhai. A. R. D. Fairburn. MM
Kraken, The. Tennyson. GTBS-D; NBE; OBRV; Po; PoEL-5; PoVP; ViPP; VLEP
Krazy; Reflection No. 5. "Baron Ireland." PoMa
Kree. A. C. Gordon. AA
Krinken. Eugene Field. BTP; PECK
Kris Kringle. Clinton Scollard. ChBR; GaP
Krishna. "Æ." *See* Oversoul.
Krishna, Krishna,/ Now as I look on. Considerations of Murder [*or* Debate between Arjuna and Sri Krishna]. *Unknown. Fr.* Bhagavad-Gita. LiTW; WaaP
Kriss Kringle. Thomas Bailey Aldrich. BoChLi (1939 ed.); HBVY; MPB; PEDC; SDH; TSW
(Quite like a Stocking.) PEOR
Ku Kluck Klan, *with music.* Lawrence Gellert. TrAS
Ku Klux. Madison Cawein. AA; PAH
Ku Li. "Robin Hyde." AnNZ
Ku! Listen! in Alahiyi you repose, O Terrible Woman. Sacred Formula to Attract Affection. *Unknown.* LiTA
Kubla Khan; or, A Vision in a Dream. Samuel Taylor Coleridge. AnFE; AtBAP; ATP; AWP; BBV; BCEP; BEL; BLV; BoLiVe; BPN; BrBE; CaAE; CBE; CBOV; CBPC; CH; ChER; ChTr; CoBE; CoEV; DaM; EM-2; EmBrPo; EnL; EnLi-2; EnLit; EnRP; EPN; EPP; ERP; EV-4; ExPo; FaBoBe; FaBoCh; FaBoEn; FaFP; FiP; GBV (1952 ed.); GN; GTBS-W; GTSL; HBV; HiLiEn; HoPM; InP; InPo; InvP; JAWP; KN; LEAP; LiA; LiTB; LiTG; LoBV; LoGBV; LPS-3; MaC; MCCG; MyFE; NeHB; OAEP; OBEV; OBRV; OtMeF; OTPC; OuHeWo; PC; PG (1945 ed.); PIAE; PIR; Po; PoE; PoEL-4; PoeMoYo; PoFS; PoRA; PreP; REAL; ReaPo; RG; RiBV; SeCeV; ShBV-3; TCEP; ThWaDe; TOP; TreFS; TrGrPo; TVSH; TwHP; TyEnPo; UnPo (3d ed.); ViBoPo; WBP; WHA
("In Xanadu did Kubla Khan.") EG
(Romance.) LH
Kukkuu, kukkuu, sounds the distant voice. Two Folk Songs, 2. *Unknown.* LiTW
Kung's Wisdom ("Kung walked"). Ezra Pound. *See* Canto XIII.
Kunming Pool is the great glory of Han, The. Song of Autumn. Tu Fu. WhP
Kwang-kwang cry the mallards. The Mallards. *Unknown.* WhP
Kyng Jamy/ Jamy your joye is all go. A Ballade of the Scottyshe Kynge. John Skelton. CoMu
Kynge Johan. John Bale. *See* King John.
Kyrie. David Gascoyne. *Fr.* Miserere. NeBP
Kyrie Eleison! The Funeral of Philip Sparrow. John Skelton. *Fr.* Phyllyp Sparowe. ACP
"Kyrie, so kyrie." Jolly Jankyn. *Unknown.* OxBoLi
Kyrielle. John Payne. HBV

L

L. E. L. Christina Rossetti. EmBrPo
L of G's Purport. Walt Whitman. *See* "Leaves of Grass's" Purport.
La Bella Bona Roba. Richard Lovelace. AtBAP; PoEL-3
La Bella Donna. Dante Gabriel Rossetti. TCEP
La Belle Confidente. Thomas Stanley. FaBoEn; MeLP; MePo; OBS
La Belle Dame sans Merci. A. R. D. Fairburn. AnNZ
La Belle Dame sans Merci. Keats. AEV; AnFE; AtBAP; ATP; AWP; BBV; BCEP; BEL; BeLS; BLV; BoLiVe; BPN; CaAE; CBE; CBOV; CG; CH; ChTr; CoBE; CoEV; DaM; EM-2; EmBrPo; EnL; EnLi-2; EnLit; EnRP; EPP; ERP; EtPaEn; ExPo; FaBoBe; FaBoCh; FaFP; FiP; GBV; GEPC; GoTP; GTBS; GTBS-D; GTBS-W; GTSE; GTSL; HBV; HOAH; HoPM; InP; InPo; InvP; JAWP; KN; LEAP; LiA; LiTB; LiTG; LO; LoBV; LoEn; LoGBV; MaC; MCCG; MyFE; OAEP; OBEV; OBMV; OBRV; OnSP; OtMeF; OTPC (1923 ed.); PFE; PG; PIAE; PoE; PoEL-4; PoFS; PoRA; PreP; REAL; ReaPo; RG; RiBV; SeCeV; ShBV-3; ShGoBo; StPo; TCEP; TOP; TrGrPo; TVSH; TwHP; TwP; UnPo; WaKn; WHA; WoL; WP
(Ballad: La Belle Dame sans Merci.) EV-4; ViBoPo
La Belle Sauvage. John Hunter-Duvar. *Fr.* De Roberval; a Drama. BoCaPo (1948 ed.)
La Bête Humaine. James Kirkup. NeBP
La Carte. Justin Richardson. FiBHP; SiTL
La Ci Darem la Mano. John Frederick Nims. MiAP
La Condition Botanique. Anthony Hecht. NePoEA
La Corona. John Donne. OBS
La Donna E Mobile. "A. K." FiBHP; InMe
La Donna E Perpetuum Mobile. Irwin Edman. FiBHP
La Femme de Quarante Ans. Stuart Cloete. NeTW
La Figlia Che Piange. T. S. Eliot. APA; BLV; BoLiVe; CaAE; ChMo; CMP; CoAnAm; FaBoTw; LiTA; LoPo; LoPS; MAP; MoAmPo (1942 ed.); NP; NV; PG (1945 ed.); POTE; PreP; ReMP; TCPD; TwP; ViBoPo
La Fraisne. Ezra Pound. NP; PG (1933 ed.)
La Fuite de la Lune. Oscar Wilde. *Fr.* Impressions. Po; PoVP
La Galisse now I wish to touch. The Happy Man. Gilles Ménage. BOHV
La Gialletta Gallante; or, The Sun-burn'd Exotique Beauty. Lord Herbert of Cherbury. AtBAP
La Grande Jatte; Sunday Afternoon. Thomas Cole. NePoAm
La Grisette. Oliver Wendell Holmes. AA; HBV; IAP
La Guerre. E. E. Cummings. MAP; MoAB; MoAmPo
O Sweet Spontaneous, II. AnNE; BoLiVe (1945 ed.); PoLFOT
(O Sweet Spontaneous Earth.) OxBA; TrGrPo
La' laha, il Allah! The Three Khalandeers. James Clarence Mangan. OBVV
La Madonna di Lorenzetti. John Williams Andrews. HBMV
La Marche des Machines. A. S. J. Tessimond. MoP
La Mélinite; Moulin-Rouge. Arthur Symons. POTT
La Nuit Blanche. Kipling. MBP; MoBrPo
La Perouse. William Hart-Smith. BoAu
La Plata chants silver, The/ Where its glittering waters roll. Rivers of the West. "Sunset Joe." PoOW
La Preciosa. Thomas Walsh. ISi
La Prière de Nostre Dame. Chaucer. *See* A. B. C., An.
La Rose des Vents. Richard Wilbur. MiAP
La Rue de la Montagne Sainte-Geneviève. Dorothy Dudley. HBMV
La Saisiaz, *sel.* Robert Browning.
Prologue. BPN; EmBrPo; PoVP
La Terre. Frank Oliver Call. *Fr.* A Sonnet Series of French Canada. CPG
La Tricoteuse. George Walter Thornbury. BeLS; BMEP
La Vie C'est la Vie. Jessie Redmond Fauset. BANP; CDC; PoNe
Labor. James Russell Lowell. *Fr.* A Glance behind the Curtain. MaRV
(Work.) PEDC
Labor. Frances Sargent Osgood. PEDC; PoRL
Labour. V. Sackville-West. *Fr.* The Land. TwCV
Labor ("We have fed you all"). *Unknown.* PGD; OQP; QP-1
Labor and Love. Sir Edmund Gosse. HBV
Labor is wealth—in the sea the pearl groweth. Labor. Frances Sargent Osgood. PEDC; PoRL
Labour Lost. Archias, *tr. fr. Greek by* F. L. Lucas. GrPE
Labor of Fields. Elizabeth J. Coatsworth. TiPo (1959 ed.)
Labor raises honest sweat. The Dignity of Labor. Robert Bersohn. WhC
Labor Song. Denis Florence MacCarthy. *Fr.* The Bell-Founder. DD; LPS-2
Laborare Est Orare. Francis Albert Rollo Russell. MaRV
Laboratory, The; Ancien Régime. Robert Browning. ATP; BLV; BoLiVe; CBOV; GTML; OBEV (new ed.); OBVV; PoFS; PoVP; REAL; ReTS; ShBV-3; ViPo; ViPP; VLEP; YT
Laboratory Midnight, The. Reuel Denney. ImOP; NePA
Laborer, The. John Clare. LPS-2
Laborer, The. Richard Dehmel, *tr. fr. German by* Jethro Bithell. AWP; JAWP; WBP; WoL
Laborer, The. William Davis Gallagher. APW
Laborer, The. José Maria de Heredia, *tr. fr. French by* Wilfrid Thorley. AWP; JAWP; WBP

Laborer, The. Galatea Kazantzakis, *tr. fr. Modern Greek by* Rae Dalven. MoGP
Labourer, The. Aleksey Khomyakov, *tr. fr. Russian by* Sir Bernard Pares. BoR
Laborer, The. Evan Thomas. PSO
Labourer in the Vineyard, The. Stephen Spender. NeBP
Laborer, The, to the lady: Yes, there are. Madonna; 1936. John Louis Bonn. ISi
Laborers, The. Kostes Palamas, *tr. fr. Modern Greek by* Rae Dalven. MoGP
"Laborers Together with God." Lucy Alice Perkins. BLRP
Labouring man, that tills the fertile soil, The. Pains and Gains. Edward de Vere, Earl of Oxford. ElL
Labors of Hercules, The. Marianne Moore. AnAmPo; LA; OxBA
Labours of the Sun, The. Mimnermus, *tr. fr. Greek by* F. L. Lucas. GrPE
Labrador Night. Leo Cox. BoCaPo (1943 ed.)
Labuntur Anni. Anacreon, *tr. fr. Greek by* J. M. Edmonds. GrR
Labuntur Anni. Byron. *See* At Thirty Years.
Laburnum. Humbert Wolfe. MBP; MoBrPo
. . . Laburnum, rich/ In streaming gold. Flowering Shrubs. William Cowper. *Fr.* The Task, VI. RO
Labyrinth, The W. H. Auden. GTBS-W; LiTA; LiTM (rev. ed.); NePA; SiTL
Labyrinth of Fortune, *sel.* Juan de Mena, *tr. fr. Spanish by* Jeremiah Holmes Wiffen.
Macías in the Circle of Venus. AnSpL-1
Labyrinths, The/ that time creates. Afterwards. Federico García Lorca. CoSP
Lace Pedlar, The. Catherine A. Morin. BoTP
Lacedaemon. *Unknown, tr. fr. Greek by* Hugh Macnaghten. OxBG
(Humbling of Sparta, The, *tr. by* F. L. Lucas.) GrPE
Lacedaemon, hast thou seen it? The Home of Helen. T. Sturge Moore. LBBV
Lacedaemon, land unconquered, that no foeman's foot molested. The Humbling of Sparta. *Unknown.* GrPE
Lacemaker, The (Vermeer). Anne Marx. GoYe
Lacewing has lighted upon the wall, A. A Dirge. Mokichi Saito. PoP
Lachin y Gair. Byron. BPN
Lachrimae. *Unknown.* AtBAP
("Flow my teares fau from your springs.") SeCSL
Lachrymae. David Gascoyne. *Fr.* Miserere. AtBAP; BoW; NeBP; POTE
Lachrymae Christi. Hart Crane. ReMP
Lachrymae Musarum. Sir William Watson. *See* Lacrimae Musarum.
Lachrymatory, The. Charles Tennyson Turner. VA
Lack of Steadfastness. Chaucer. *See* Lak of Stedfastnesse.
Lackey Bill. *Unknown.* CoSo; CSF
Lacking my love, I go from place to place. Amoretti, LXXVIII. Spenser. ElL; PeBoSo; ViBoPo
Lacking samite and sable. Christmas Carol. May Probyn. ACP; CAW; GoBC; HBMV; ISi; OBVV
Lacking Sense, The. Thomas Hardy. PoEL-5
Lacquer Liquor Locker, The. David McCord. FiBHP; InMe
Lacrimae Musarum. Sir William Watson. HBV; PtOT; VA
(Lachrymae Musarum.) PoVP
Lacrimae Rerum. Palladas, *tr. fr. Greek by* Walter Leaf. OxBG
Lacrimae Rerum. "Lambros Porphyras," *tr. fr. Modern Greek by* Rae Dalven. MoGP
Lad, and a lass, aforetime it was my lot to be, A. Pre-Existence. Empedocles. GrPE
Lad came to the door at night, The. The True Lover. A. E. Housman. A Shropshire Lad, LIII. ATP; BLV; BoLiVe; DaM; LiTL; PoVP; TwP
Lad, for overfancy clothing. Simplicity. Franklin P. Adams. PoeMoYo
Lad of the Curly Locks. *Unknown, tr. fr. Irish by* Frank O'Connor. KiLC
Lad Philisides, The. A Country Song. Sir Philip Sidney. *Fr.* Arcadia. OBSC; SiPS
Lad That Is Gone, A. Robert Louis Stevenson. *See* Sing Me a Song.
Lad that was a fowler, deep in a leafy grove, A. Love Hunted. Bion. GrPE
Lad, who was new to the city's ways, A. The Snake in Paradise. Tove Ditlevsen. BoDS
Lad, will you draw the lightning down. To Lovers. Amelia Josephine Burr. PR; TBM
Lad, you took the soul of me. Lindbergh. Angela Morgan. DD; GA
Ladder, The. Leonora Speyer. BAP; HBMV; PG; TBM
Ladder of St. Augustine, The. Longfellow. IAP; PTA-2; REAL; TCAP
Heights, The, *br sel.* TreF
Ladder to Thrift, The. Thomas Tusser. ReIE; SiCE
Ladders through the Blue. Hermann Hagedorn. PC
Laddie. Katharine Lee Bates. POT; PoTo
Laddie. Dana Burnet. AlBD
Laddie, little laddie, come with me over the hills. A Cry from the Canadian Hills. Lilian Leveridge. BLPA
Laden with spoil of the South, fulfilled with the. The Death of Admiral Blake. Sir Henry Newbolt. GTML
Laden with yellowing pears. The Half of Life. Friedrich Hölderlin. LiTW
Ladie Greensleeves. *Unknown. See* My Lady Greensleeves.
Ladie stude in her bour-door, The. Young Hunting (C *vers.*). *Unknown.* ESPB
Ladies, The. Kipling. ALV; BPN; EnLit; MBP; MoBrPo; ViP; ViPP
Ladies' Aid, The. *Unknown.* DDA
Ladies and gentlemen:/ This broadcast comes to you from the city. Voice of the Studio Announcer. Archibald MacLeish. *Fr.* The Fall of the City. HoPM; MoAmPo
Ladies and gentlemen/ Whose mother is no more. Complaint on the Oblivion of the Dead. Jules Laforgue, *tr. by* William Jay Smith. AnFP; LiTW
Ladies and gentlemen/ You whose mother is dead. Lament of Forgetfulness of the Dead. Jules Laforgue, *tr. by* Cecily Mackworth. MiFP
Ladies, as ye may perceive, fair and happy girls are we. Carnival Song: Song of the Girls and the Tattlers (Cicadas). Lorenzo de' Medici. LyPI
Ladies at a ball. Glimpse in Autumn. Jean Starr Untermeyer. StVeCh (1940 ed.); TSW; TSWC
Ladies' Eyes Serve Cupid Both for Darts and Fire. "A. W." OBSC
Ladies, Farewell! James Howard. *Fr.* The English Monsieur. SeCL
Ladies' Gard. William Morris. *Fr.* Golden Wings. BMEP (Ancient Castle, An.) SeCePo
("Midways of a walled garden.") ChTr; LiA
Ladies in Clovelly streets. Why Travel. Patience Eden. DDA
Ladies in the Dinin' Room, *with music.* *Unknown.* OuSiCo
Ladies men admire, The, I've heard. Some Beautiful Letters: Interview. Dorothy Parker. InMe
Ladies of Bourges, The. Johannes Secundus, *tr. fr. Latin by* F. A. Wright. LaP
Ladies of London, both wealthy and fair. Advice to the Ladies of London in the Choice of Their Husbands. *Unknown.* CoMu
Ladies of St. James's, The. Austin Dobson. BPN; HBV; LEAP; PCN; PoRA; POTT; PoVP; TVSH; VA; VLEP
Ladies rose, The. I held the door. The Dean's Consent. Coventry Patmore. *Fr.* The Angel in the House. VA
Ladies sat in Lindholm hold, The. Sir Verner's Escape. *Unknown.* BoDaBa
Ladies That Have Intelligence in Love. Dante, *tr. fr. Italian by* Dante Gabriel Rossetti. La Vita Nuova, X. LiTW; WoL
(Canzone: "Ladies that have intelligence in love.") LiA; LyMA; LyPI
(Vita Nuova, La, X.) AWP; OuHeWo
Ladies, though to your conquering eyes. Song. George Etherege. *Fr.* The Comical Revenge. HBV; LO; OBEV (1st ed.); OBS
Ladies, to this advice give heed. A Maxim Revised. *Unknown.* BLPA; NeHB; WBLP
Ladies, well I deem, delight. My Lady Nature and Her Daughters. Cardinal Newman. GoBC
Ladies, where were your bright eyes glancing. Imogen. Sir Henry Newbolt. HBMV
Lads and lasses gathering. The Willow-Boughs. Aleksandr Blok. BoTP
Lads in Their Hundreds, The. A. E. Housman: A Shropshire Lad, XXIII. ATP (1953 ed.); CoBMV; MBP; MoBrPo; Po; PoVP; PreP; UnPo (1st ed.); VLEP
Lad's Love. Esther Lilian Duff. HBMV
Lads of Wamphray, The. *Unknown.* BaBo; ESPB
Lads were hanging baskets, The. The May Basket. Dora Read Goodale. PCH
Lady, The. Elizabeth J. Coatsworth. InP; MaC
Lady, A Amy Lowell. BAP; MAP; MAPA; MoAmPo; NeMA; NP; PoeMoYo; SBMV
Lady,/ Baby. *Unknown.* OxNR
Lady Adeline Amundeville. Byron. Don Juan, XIII. PoEL-4
Lady Again Complains, The. Earl of Surrey. SiPS
Lady Alda's Dream. *Unknown, tr. fr. Spanish by* James Young Gibson. TeCS
Lady Alice. *Unknown.* CG; ESPB (A, B *and* C *vers.*); OBB
Lady Alice, Lady Louise. The Blue Closet. William Morris. BPN; EmBrPo; PoVP; TCEP; VA; ViPo; ViPP; VLEP
Lady Alice was sitting in her bower window. Lady Alice. *Unknown.* CG; ESPB; OBB
Lady, although we have not met. Woman. Fitz-Greene Halleck. PR
Lady and an Ape, A. W. S. Gilbert. GBV
Lady and Crocodile. Charles Burgess. NePoAm-2
Lady and gentlemen fays, come buy! Nephon's Song [*or* The Elfin Pedlar]. George Darley. *Fr.* Sylvia. BoTP; VA

Lady and Queen and Mystery manifold. Ballade to Our Lady of Czestochowa. Hilaire Belloc. ACP (1952 ed.); ISi; QS
Lady and the Dwarf-King, The. *Unknown. See* Hind Etin.
Lady and the Magpie, The. *Unknown, tr. fr. Chinese by* Arthur Waley. AtBAP
Lady and the Swine, The. *Unknown. See* Lady Who Loved a Swine, The.
Lady Anne Bothwell's Lament. *Unknown. See* Balow.
Lady Anne Dewhurst on a crimson couch. Daughters of Philistia. Walter C. Smith. *Fr.* Olrig Grange. VA
Lady Apple Blossom. Apple Blossom. Kate Louise Brown. GFA; OTPC (1946 ed.)
Lady April. Richard Le Gallienne. YeAr
Lady, as I know thy power. Song to the Virgin Mary. Pero López de Ayala. CAW
Lady asks me, A. Canzone. Guido Cavalcanti. LiTW
Lady Barbara. Alexander Smith. LPS-1
Lady Bates. Randall Jarrell. MiAP; NoCaPo (rev. ed.)
"Lady, beside the great green wall of sea." Hymn to Venus. Edith Sitwell. FaBoMo
Lady, better bards than I. As to Eyes. Franklin P. Adams. PR
Lady-Bird. *See* Ladybird.
Lady-Bug. *See* Ladybug.
Lady by Renoir au bord de la Seine. Portrait. Miriam Waddington. BoCaPo (1948 ed.)
Lady Byron's Reply to Lord Byron's "Fare Thee Well." *Unknown.* BLPA
Lady Clara V. de V., The. An Answer. Henry S. Leigh. YT
Lady Clara Vere de Vere. Tennyson. BPN; HBV; LPS-1; PoVP; YT
Nobility, *br. sel.* OTPC (1946 ed.)
Lady Clara Vere de Vere! The Wedding. Tom Hood. BOHV; InMe
Lady Clare. Tennyson. BeLS; FaPON; CoTP; HBV; LoEn; MW; OTPC; PECK; StPo; StVeCh; TVSH
"It was the time when lilies blow," *sel.* AlDL
Lady Comes to an Inn, A. Elizabeth J. Coatsworth. MAP; MoAmPo; NeMA; StPo
Lady Complains of Her Lover's Absence, A. Earl of Surrey. *See* Complaint of the Absence of Her Lover Being upon the Sea.
Lady Day. Padraic Fallon. NeIP
Lady Day in Harvest. Sheila Kaye-Smith. ISi
Lady Day in Ireland. Patrick J. Carroll. JKCP
Lady Diamond. *Unknown.* BaBo; ESPB
Lady, do not hold your parasol. By the Beautiful Sea. Thomas Cole. NePoAm-2
Lady Dying in Childbed, A. Robert Herrick. EG
Lady dying of diabetes, A. The Mechanical Optimist. Wallace Stevens. NAMP
Lady Elgin, The. *Unknown.* ABS
Lady Elspat. *Unknown.* ESPB; OBB
Lady Erskine sits in her chamber. Child Owlet. *Unknown.* ESPB
Lady fair, if on the page. Stanzas. Corneille. LiA
Lady fair, of lineage high, A. A Lady and an Ape. W. S. Gilbert. GBV
Lady, farewell, whom I in silence serve! A Poem Put into My Lady Laiton's Pocket. Sir Walter Ralegh. SiPS
Lady Fortune is both friend and foe, The. The Fortune. *Unknown.* ACP
Lady Franklin's Lament, *2 vers., with music. Unknown.* ShS
Lady from Harlem, The. Malcolm Cowley. NP
Lady Geraldine's Courtship, *sel.* Elizabeth Barrett Browning. Poets, The. BCEP
Lady, giver of bread. Litany to Our Lady. Caryll Houselander. ISi
Lady Godiva. Edward Shanks. HBMV
Lady Greensleeves. *Unknown. See* My Lady Greensleeves.
Lady Hamilton. Muriel Stuart. DiM
Lady Heron's Song. Sir Walter Scott. *See* Lochinvar.
Lady hold your horses, sit down in your seat. Driver Saying. Josephine Miles. FiMAP
Lady I Know, A. Countee Cullen. *See* For a Lady I Know.
Lady, I loved you all last year. A Song of Impossibilities. Winthrop Mackworth Praed. BOHV; InMe; NA
Lady, I thank thee. Look on Me with Thy Sweet Eyes. *Unknown.* MeEV
Lady, I thank thee for thy loveliness. The Moonstar. Dante Gabriel Rossetti. The House of Life, XXIX. PoVP; ViPo
Lady! if for the cold and cloudy clime. The Prophecy of Dante. Byron. EmBrPo
Lady, if grace to me so long be lent. He Hopes That Time Will Render Her More Merciful. Petrarch. Sonnets to Laura: To Laura in Life, XI. EnLi-1; OuHeWo
Lady, If You So Spight Me. *Unknown.* ReIE
Lady in a Limousine. Lucia Trent. PR
Lady in the latest gown, A. Appreciation à la Mode. Armel O'Connor. SaFP
Lady Inger is fair as a rose, The. Sir David and His Stepsons. *Unknown.* BoDaBa
Lady is smarter than a gentleman, maybe, A. Trial and Error. Phyllis McGinley. SiTL
Lady Isabel. *Unknown.* BaBo; ESPB
Lady Isabel and the Elf-Knight (*diff. versions*). *Unknown.* BaBo (A, B, *and* C *vers.*); ESPB (A, B, *and* H *vers.*); OAEP; OBB; ViBoFo (A *and* B *vers.*)
(False-hearted Knight, The.) BaBo
Lady, it is to be presumed. Milady's Face. Ben Jonson. BoHiPo
Lady Jane (Sapphics). Sir Arthur Quiller-Couch. FiBHP; InMe; PA; WhC
Lady Jane was tall and slim, The. The Knight and the Lady. "Thomas Ingoldsby." *Fr.* The Ingoldsby Legends. BOHV
Lady! Lady!/ Upon Heaven-height. In a Boat. Hilaire Belloc. AlDL; ISi
Lady, lady, should you meet. Some Beautiful Letters: Social Note. Dorothy Parker. BOHV; InMe
Lady Lost. John Crowe Ransom. AnFE; CoAnAm; MAP; MoAB; MoAmPo; NeMA; TrGrPo; TwAmPo
Lady Lost in the Wood, The. Milton. *Fr.* Comus. LPS-3
Lady loved a swaggering rover, A. Pirate Treasure. Abbie Farwell Brown. EtS: TBM
Lady Macbeth. Yu Min-chuan, *tr. fr. Chinese.* WhP
Lady Maisdry was a lady fair. Lord Ingram and Chiel Wyet (C *vers.*). *Unknown.* ESPB
Lady Maisry. *Unknown.* BaBo (A *and* B *vers.*); ESPB (A *and* B *vers.*); OBB; ViBoFo
Lady Maisry lives intill a bower. Thomas o Yonderdale. *Unknown.* ESPB
Lady Margaret sat in her bower-door. Prince Heathen (B *vers.*). *Unknown.* ESPB
Lady Margaret sat in her bowry all alone. Sweet William's Ghost (B *vers.*). *Unknown.* ViBoFo
Lady Margaret sits in her bower door. Hind Etin. *Unknown.* BaBo (A *vers.*); ESPB
Lady Margery May sits in her bower. Prince Heathen. *Unknown.* ESPB
Lady Marjorie, Lady Marjorie. Sweet William's Ghost [*or* William and Marjorie]. *Unknown.* DaM; EBSV
Lady Mary. Henry Alford. VA
Lady Mary, blissful Dame. The Mother of God. *Unknown. Fr.* Horologium. ISi
Lady Mary Villiers [*or* Villers] lies, The. Epitaph on the Lady Mary Villiers. Thomas Carew. EV-2; LEAP; OAEP; OBEV; SeCL; SeCV-1; SeEP; ViBoPo
Lady may allow me be so bold, A. Hope for Miracles. Wolfram von Eschenbach. LiTW; LyMA
Lady Mine. Herbert Edwin Clarke. BOHV
Lady Moon, The. Kate Louise Brown. BoTP
Lady Moon. Kate Kellogg. PPL
Lady Moon. Richard Monckton Milnes. BoTP; MoShBr; OTPC; PCH; PRWS; RAR; SAS, *st.* 1
Lady Moon. Christina Rossetti. *See* O Lady Moon.
Lady moon is sailing, The. The Lady Moon. Kate Louise Brown. BoTP
Lady moon, lady moon, sailing so high! Lady Moon. Kate Kellogg. PPL
Lady Moon, Lady Moon, where are you roving? Lady Moon. Richard Monckton Milnes. BoTP; MoShBr; OTPC; PCH; PRWS; RAR; SAS
Lady, my lady, come from out the garden. To a Certain Lady, in Her Garden. Sterling A. Brown. CDC
Lady of Arngosk, The. *Unknown.* ESPB
Lady of Carlisle, The, *with music. Unknown.* OuSiCo
Lady of Castlenoire. Thomas Bailey Aldrich. BeLS; LoEn
Lady of Heaven. Guittone d'Arezzo, *tr. fr. Italian by* Dante Gabriel Rossetti. CAW
Lady of Heaven and earth, and therewithal. His Mother's Service to Our Lady. Villon, *tr. by* D. G. Rossetti. AWP; CAW; ISi; LiTW; LyMA; MeRV
Lady of Heaven, Regent of the earth. Ballad. Villon, *tr. by* John Payne. LiA
Lady of Heaven, the mother glorified. Lady of Heaven. Guittone d'Arezzo. CAW
Lady of High Degree, A. *Unknown, tr. fr. French by* Andrew Lang. AWP
Lady of Hsiang, The. Chu Yuan, *tr. fr. Chinese by* Shen Yuting. *Fr.* The Nine Songs. WhP
Lady of Letters. Raymond F. Roseliep. ISi
Lady of Lidice. Fray Angelico Chavez. ISi; JKCP (1955 ed.)
Lady of Life, The. Thomas Michael Kettle. ACP; JKCP (1926 ed.)
Lady of Light, I would admit a dream to you. The Buried Lake. Allen Tate. CrMA
Lady of Night, twy-hornéd, lover of nightlong dances. Moonlit Love. Philodemus of Gadara. GrPE
Lady of O. James J. Galvin. ISi
Lady of Peace. Fray Angelico Chavez. ISi
Lady of Shalott, The. Tennyson. AnFE; ATP (2 *vers.*); BEL; BeLS; BMEP; BoLiVe; BPN; CBE; CBOV; CBPC; EM-2; EmBrPo; EnL; EnLi-2; EnLit; EPN; EPP;

EV-5; FaFP; FiP; GBV; GEPC; GN; GTML; GTSL; HBV; InP; LEAP; LiTG; MaC; MCCG; MW; OAEP; OBEV; OBRV, *diff. vers.;* OBVV; OnSP; OTPC; PIAE; PoE; PoVP; ReaPo (2 *vers.*); RG; SeCeV; ShBV-1; TCEP; TOP; TreF; TyEnPo; ViPo; ViPP; VLEP; WHA

Lady of sorrow! What though laughing blue. Grey. Archibald T. Strong. BoAu

Lady of the dark head-dress. Boabdil. José Zorrilla. AnSpL-2

Lady of the depths. Madame. Jules Supervielle. MiCF

Lady of the hills with crimes untold, The. Natura Maligna. Theodore Watts-Dunton. MeRV

Lady of the Lake, The. *sels.* Sir Walter Scott.

Alice Brand, *fr.* IV. EmBrPo; HBV; HBVY; OTPC (1946 ed.); TVSH
(Ballad, Alice Brand.) EV-4

Battle of Beal' an Duine, *fr.* VI. TCEP, *abr.*
(Beal' an Dhuine.) LPS-2

Boat Song, *fr.* II. BEL; BHV; EBSV; EnLi-2 (1949 ed.); EV-4; OAEP; PoEL-4
(Hail to the Chief Who in Triumph Advances.) BCEP, *sl. abr.;* BPN; EmBrPo; EnRP
(Song of Clan-Alpine.) LPS-2

Chase, The, *fr.* I. EnRP; LH, *sl. abr.*
(Stag Hunt, The.) LPS-2

Coronach, *fr.* III. AnFE; BEL; BHV; BPN; BSV; CaAE; CH; EBSV; EmBrPo; EnLi-2 (1949 ed.); EnLit; EnRP; ERP; EV-4; GTBS; GTBS-D; GTBS-W; GTSL; HBV; InP; LPS-1; MW; OAEP; OBRV; OHIP; PCD; PCN; PoRA; ShBV-1; TCEP; TOP; TreFS; TrGrPo; ViBoPo; WHA
("He is gone upon the mountain.") EPN

Dawn on Lake Katrine, *fr.* III. EV-4

Fiery Cross, The, *fr.* III. ERP

Fitz-James and Roderick-Dhu, *fr.* V. EPP; LPS-2
(Roderick Dhu, *shorter sel.*) OBRV
(Roderick Dhu and Fitz-James; a Noble Action, *shorter sel.*) EV-4

Flowers and Trees, The, *fr.* I *and* III. EV-4

Harp of the North. Prologue. BHV; EmBrPo; EnLi-2 (1949 ed.); ERP; ViBoPo
("Harp of the North that moldering long hast hung.") OAEP

Harp of the North, Farewell. Epilogue. BPN; CoBE; EV-4
("Harp of the North, farewell! The hills grow dark.") OAEP; ViBoPo

Hymn to the Virgin, *fr.* IV. EnRP; GoBC
(Ave Maria.) ISi

James Fitz-James and Ellen, *fr.* VI. LPS-2

"Rose is fairest when 'tis budding new, The," *fr.* IV. ViBoPo

Soldier, Rest! [Thy Warfare O'er], *fr.* I. AOAH; ATP (1935 ed.); AWP; BCEP; BEL; BPN; BTP; CBPC; CoBE; DD; EmBrPo; EnLi-2; EnLit; EPN; EPP; ERP; GN; HBV; HBVY; HH; JAWP; LPS-2; MoShBr; OTPC (1946 ed.); PIAE; PoRA; PYM; TCEP; TOP; TreFS; TrGrPo; WaKn; WBP
(Ellen's Song, *abr.*) CBE
(Song: "Soldier rest! thy warfare o'er.") BHV; OAEP; OBRV

Soldier's Song ("Our vicar still preaches that Peter and Poule"), *fr.* VI. ViBoPo

Song: "Heath this night must be my bed, The," *fr.* III. EV-4; LPS-1
(Heath This Night Must Be My Bed, The.) ERP

Song: "Not faster yonder rowers might," *fr.* II. EV-4

Song: "Toils are pitched, The," *fr.* IV. EmBrPo
(Toils Are Pitched, The.) EnRP; ERP

"Time rolls his ceaseless course," *fr.* III. ViBoPo

"Twice have I sought Clan-Alpine's glen," *fr.* V. OBRV

Western Waves of Ebbing Day, The, *fr.* I. OTPC; PoEL-4

Lady of the Lake, The. *Unknown.* ShS

Lady of the Lambs, The. Alice Meynell. *See* Shepherdess, The.

Lady of the Land, The. William Morris. *Fr.* The Earthly Paradise. EmBrPo; EPP; PoVP; TOP; VLEP, *abr.*

Lady of the legless world I have. Notes after Blacking Out. Gregory Corso. NeAP

Lady of the manor was dressing for the ball, The. The Highland Tinker. *Unknown.* CoMu

Lady Pecunia; or, The Praise of Money, *sel.* Richard Barnfield.
"I sing not of Angelica the fair." ReIE

Lady Poverty, The. Alice Meynell. EPP; GTSL; HBV; OBMV; PoeT; POTT; PoVP; SaFP; TCPD

Lady Poverty, The. Evelyn Underhill, *sometimes at. to* Jacob Fischer. CAW; CP; GTML; HBV; SaFP

Lady Prayeth the Return of Her Lover Abiding on the Seas, The. *Unknown.* EIL
(Seafarer, The.) OBSC
(To Her Sea-faring Lover.) OBEV

Lady put off her fur, it was so warm in the outer office, The. Appointment in Doctor's Office. Josephine Miles. FiMAP

Lady Queen Anne she sits in the sun. *Unknown.* OxNR

Lady, receive, receive in gracious wise. He Wrote unto a Scottish Dame . . . as Followeth. George Gascoigne. ReIE

Lady red upon the hill, A. The Waking Year. Emily Dickinson. AA; EOAH; HBV; LHV; OHIP
(Life, IX.) OBAV

Lady, The, Says: "It is Cockcrow." *Unknown, tr. fr. Chinese.* WhP

Lady, scholar, poet, saint, you ask. The Tower of Lowliness. Sister Miriam. PraNu

Lady Sleep. Rowena Bastin Bennett. GaP

Lady Sloe. Juan Ruiz, Archpriest of Hita, *tr. fr. Spanish by* Elisha K. Kane. TeCS

Lady stands in her bower door, The. The Twa Magicians. *Unknown.* BaBo; ESPB

Lady Stood, A. Dietmar von Aist, *tr. fr. German by* Jethro Bithell. AWP; LiTW

Lady, take care; for in the diamond eyes. Light and Dark. Barbara Howes. MoVE

Lady, take my broken heart. Christ and His Mother at the Cross. Jacopone da Todi. CAW

Lady That Hast My Heart. Hafiz, *tr. fr. Persian by* Gertrude L. Bell. *Fr.* Odes. LiTW
("Lady that hast my heart within thy hand.") AWP

Lady, that in the prime of earliest youth. To a Virtuous Young Lady. Milton. EM-1; ES; TOP

Lady that was so fair and bright, A. Enixa Est Puerpera. *Unknown.* AnEC

Lady, the glass you lift has sleep's bright fever in it. Homage to Circe. Horace Gregory. MoAmPo (1950 ed.)

"Lady, the loveliest ever the sun looked down upon, A." A Mother's Picture. Alice Cary. MotAn

Lady—the lyre thou bid'st me take. To ——. Jeremiah Joseph Callanan. IrPN

Lady, the meshes of your coiling hair. He Praises Her Hair. *Unknown.* AnIL

Lady! the songs of spring were in the grove. Sonnet: To the Lady Beaumont. Wordsworth. ChER

Lady, the sunlit hour is beautiful. Children. Euripides. OxBG; WoL

Lady, there is a hope that all men have. William Ellery Channing. *Fr.* A Poet's Hope. AA; AnAmPo; IAP; LA; LEAP

Lady there was of Antigua, A. Limerick. Cosmo Monkhouse. HBV; TSW; TSWC

Lady! thine upward flight. The Assumption of the Virgin. Luis de León. AnSpL-1

Lady, three white leopards sat under a juniper tree. Salutation. T. S. Eliot. *Fr.* Ash Wednesday. AnAmPo; LA; LO; LoBV; TCPD

Lady, thy soldier I would be. Ave Maria. John Jerome Rooney. JKCP

Lady to a Lover, A. Roden Noel. OBVV

Lady Turned Serving-Man, The. *Unknown.* CG; OBB
(Famous Flower of Serving-Men, The.) ESPB

Lady up on yonder hill. Legend. Sister Mary Jeremy. JKCP (1955 ed.)

Lady, up to your high and shining crown. Madrigal 178. Michelangelo. LyPI

Lady Venetia Digby, The. Ben Jonson. GoBC

Lady, very fair are you. Ad Chloen, M. A. Mortimer Collins. BOHV; HBV

Lady walked by the ocean strand, The. Strand-Thistle. Gustav Falke. AWP

Lady, Was It Fair of Thee. Thomas Lovell Beddoes. HoPM

Lady Weasel one fine morn. The Cat, the Weasel, and the Little Rabbit. La Fontaine. TrFP

Lady, Weeping at the Crossroads. W. H. Auden. MoVE

Lady, When I Behold. *Unknown.* ElSeCe
(Her Lips.) LiTL
("Lady, when I behold the roses sprouting.") EG

Lady, when we sat together. The Seamy Side of Motley. Sir Owen Seaman. InMe

Lady, when your lovely head. Dawn Shall over Lethe Break [*or* On a Sleeping Friend]. Hilaire Belloc. MM; POTE

Lady who intervenes, The. Virgin. Padraic Fallon. OnYI

Lady who liked to crochet, A. *Unknown.* SiTL

Lady Who Loved a Swine, The, *with music. Unknown.* OuSiCo
(Hunc, Said He.) ChTr
(Lady and the Swine, The, *sl. diff.*) RIS
(Silver Sty, The.) Po
("There was a lady loved a swine.") OxNR

Lady Who Offers Her Looking-Glass to Venus, The. Matthew Prior, *after* Plato. CaAE; OBEV; PIAE; ViBoPo
(Farewell, A: "Venus take my votive glass.") AWP
(Lais' Mirror.) WoL

Lady, who with tender word. The Housewife's Prayer. Blanche Mary Kelly. DDA; GoBC; JKCP; WHL

Lady, whose ancestor/ Fought for Prince Charlie. The Stirrup Cup. Douglas Ainslie. ESBV; GoTS

Lady, whose shrine stands on the promontory. T. S. Eliot. *Fr.* Four Quartets: The Dry Salvages. ISi

Lady Will You Come with Me into. E. E. Cummings. ThWaDe
Lady with Arrows. Margaret Marks. MAP
Lady with Technique, The. Hughes Mearns. *Fr.* Later Antigonishes. FiBHP; InMe; SiTL; WhC
Lady with the broom beheld dismayed, The. The Puddle. Morris Abel Beer. LEAP
Lady with the Sewing-Machine, The. Edith Sitwell. NV
Lady with the Unicorn, The. Vernon Watkins. LiTB
Lady, you are with beauties so enriched. Song. Francis Davison. ElL
Lady, you think too much of speeds. Statistics. Stephen Spender. MBP; MoBrPo
Lady-Bird. Caroline Anne Bowles. GFA; GoTP; OTPC; RAR
(To the Ladybird.) PCH; TVC; TVSH
Ladybird, ladybird [*or* Lady-bug, lady-bug] fly away home! Mother Goose. BoChLi (1950 ed.); BoN; FaPON; OxNR; PPL; RIS; SAS; SiTL
Lady Bug. C. Lindsay McCoy. GFA
Ladye Chapel at Eden Hall. Eleanor Cecilia Donnelly. JKCP
Ladye Marye! today/ Let me say my own say. The Spotless Maid. Vincent McNabb. ISi
Ladyes, you that seeme soe nice. *Unknown.* SeCSL
Lady's Answer, The. Samuel Butler. *Fr.* Hudibras. BeR
Lady's-Maid Song, The. John Hollander. NePoEA
Lady's Receipt for a Beau's Dress, The. *Unknown.* CoMu
Lady's Sepulcher, A. Li Ho, *tr. fr. Chinese by* Ho Chih-yuan. WhP
Lady's Song, The. Dryden. EV-3; LoBV; SeCeV
Lady's Song. Milton. *See* Sweet Echo.
Lady's Third Song, The. W. B. Yeats. *Fr.* The Three Bushes. FaBoTw
Lady's Trial, The, *sel.* John Ford.
Pleasures, Beauty, Youth Attend Ye. LiTL; ViBoPo
Lady's "Yes," The. Elizabeth Barrett Browning. BPN; HBV; LiTL; LPS-1
Laegaire, son of the king of Connacht, was out one day. Army of the Sidhe. Lady Gregory. SP
Laertes. Homer, *tr. fr. Greek.* *Fr.* The Odyssey, XXIV. GrR, *tr. by* William Morris; OxBG, *longer sel.*, *tr. by* Sir William Marris
Laetus did in his mistress' quarrel die. Thomas Bastard. TuPP
La Fayette. Samuel Taylor Coleridge. BPN; EmBrPo; EnRP
La Fayette. Dolly Madison. PaA; PAH
Lagoon, The. Ashton Greene. NePoAm
Laid in My Quiet Bed. Earl of Surrey. *See* How No Age Is Content.
Laid Off. Francis Webb. BoAV
Laid on Thine Altar. *Unknown.* TrPWD
(Sacrifice of the Will, The.) PraP
Laid out for dead, let thy last kindness be. To Robin Redbreast. Robert Herrick. EPS; OBS; SeEP; TrGrPo
Laili and Majnún, *sels.* Nizami, *tr. fr. Persian by* James Atkinson. PeP
Death of Kais, The.
Death of Laili, The.
Envoi: "O ye, who thoughtlessly repose."
Kais Declares His Love.
Kais in the Desert.
Laili Disconsolate.
Laily Worm and the Machrel of the Sea, The. *Unknown.* ChTr; ESPB; InvP; LoBV; OBB; PoEL-1
Laird, a lord, A. *Unknown.* OxNR
Laird o' Cockpen, The. Lady Nairne, *2 added sts. by* Susan Ferrier. BeLS; BOHV; BSV; EBSV; EV-3; HBV; LPS-1; OBRV
Laird o' Drum, The. *Unknown.* ESPB
Laird o' Lamington, The. James Hogg. EBSV
Laird o Logie, The. *Unknown.* CH; ESPB (*A and B vers.*)
(Laird of Logie, The.) BaBo
Laird of Bristoll's daughter was in the woods walking, The. Captain Wedderburn's Courtship. *Unknown.* BaBo (*A vers.*); ESPB
Laird of Leys is on to Edinburgh, The. The Baron o Leys. *Unknown.* ESPB
Laird of Logie, The. *Unknown.* *See* Laird o Logie, The.
Laird of Schelynlaw, The. John Veitch. VA
Laird of Wariston, The (*A and B vers.*). *Unknown.* BaBo; ESPB
Lairdless Place, The. Kate Rennie Archer. GoYe
Lais. Hilda Doolittle ("H. D."). MAP; MoAmPo
Lais' Mirror. Plato, *tr. fr. Greek.* OnPM, *tr. by* Matthew Prior; OxBG, *tr. by* F. E. Garrett; WoL, *tr. by* Matthew Prior
(Dedication to Aphrodite, *tr. by* J. M. Edmonds.) GrR
("Lais of the haughty smile," *tr. by* F. E. Garrett.) GrPo
(Lais to Aphrodite, *tr. by* E. A. Robinson.) MOAP
Lak of Stedfastnesse. Chaucer. AWP; CoEV
(Lack of Steadfastness.) PoLi
Lake, The. Louis O. Coxe. MoVE
Lake, The. Alphonse de Lamartine, *tr. fr. French.* LiA, *tr. by* John Payne; WoL, *tr. by* Katherine Hillard
Lake, The. Herman Melville. APW
Lake, The. Eleanour Norton. NLK
Lake, The. Poe. *See* Lake, The: To ——.
Lake, The. James Stephens. AnEnPo; MoBrPo
Lake, The. John Banister Tabb. AmP
Lake allows an average father, walking slowly, A. Lakes. W. H. Auden. NePA; NePoAm
Lake and a Fairy Boat, A. Thomas Hood. *See* Song: "Lake and a fairy boat, A."
Lake at Newstead, The. Byron. *Fr.* Don Juan, XIII. GEPC
Lake Boats, The. Edgar Lee Masters. NP
Lake comes throbbing in with voice of pain, The. A Lake Memory. Wilfred Campbell. BoCaPo; VA
Lake Coriskin. Sir Walter Scott. *Fr.* The Lord of the Isles, III. EV-4
Lake Harvest. Raymond Knister. PeCV
Lake is calm, The; and, calm, the skies. The Heart and Nature. "Owen Meredith." GTML
Lake Isle, The. Ezra Pound. CrMA; SiTL
Lake Isle of Innisfree, The. W. B. Yeats. ATP; BEL; BLV; BMEP; BoLiVe; CaAE; CBE; ChMo; CMP; CoBMV; EnL; EnLi-2 (1949 ed.); EnLit; EPP; FaFP; FaPON; GBV; GTBS; GTBS-W; GTSL; HBV; HiLiEn; InP; LBBV; LEAP; LiTG; LiTM (rev. ed.); MaPo; MBP; MCCG; MoAB; MoBrPo; NeMA; OAEP (2d ed.); OBEV; OBVV; OnYI; OTPC (1946 ed.); PC; PoeT; PoRA; POT; PoTo; POTT; PoVP; PreP; PYM; ShBV-2; SP; TCEP; TCPD; TIP; TOP; TreF; TrGrPo; TSW; TSWC; TVSH; VLEP; WHA; YT
Lake lay blue below the hill, The. L'Oiseau Bleu. Mary Elizabeth Coleridge. BoTP; CH; PoVP; WhBS
Lake Leman ("Clear, placid Leman!"). Byron. *Fr.* Childe Harold's Pilgrimage, III. MaPo
(Calm and Storm on Lake Leman, *abr.*) LPS-2
(Night and Storm in the Alps, *abr.*) MCCG
(Night on Lake Leman.) TCEP
Lake Leman ("Lake Leman woos me"). Byron. *Fr.* Childe Harold's Pilgrimage, III. PoEL-4
(Man and Nature.) EPP
Lake Leman lies by Chillon's walls. Byron. *Fr.* The Prisoner of Chillon. OBRV
Lake Memory, A. Wilfred Campbell. BoCaPo; VA
Lake, Mountain, Tree. Denis Glover. AnNZ
Lake of Gaube, The. Swinburne. PoVP; VLEP
Lake of the Dismal Swamp, The. Thomas Moore. BLPA; DaM
Lake of Van, The. Raffi, *tr. fr. Armenian by* George M. Green. ArmLP
Lake Poets, The. Byron. *Fr.* Don Juan, III. UnPo (1st ed.)
Lake Song. Jean Starr Untermeyer. AnAmPo; AV; HBMV; LA; MAP; MoAmPo (1942 ed.); NP; TrJP
Lake Superior. Samuel Griswold Goodrich. AA
Lake, The: To ——. Poe. AmP; APW; IAP; OBRV; OnPM; TriL
Lakes. W. H. Auden. NePA; NePoAm
Lakes of astonishment break open. The Mountain Climber. Antonia Pozzi. OnPM
Lakes of the Atchafalaya, The. Longfellow. *Fr.* Evangeline. PoEL-5
Lakka-trees ripen two by two. A Song of a Pure-hearted Girl. Meng Chiao. ChLP
Lalage. "S. W. D. M." CAG
Lalla Rookh, *sels.* Thomas Moore.
Alas! How Light a Cause May Move, *fr.* The Story of the Sultana Nourmahal, or, Light of the Harem. LPS-1
By Bendemeer's Stream, *fr.* The Veiled Prophet of Korassan. BLP; OTPC (1946 ed.); RG
(Bendemeer.) OBRV
(Girl's Song, A.) CBPC
Farewell to Thee, Araby's Daughter, *fr.* The Fire-Worshippers. LPS-1
Fly to the Desert, Fly with Me, *fr.* The Story of the Sultana Nourmahal, or, Light of the Harem. GTIV; LPS-1
Linda to Hafed, *fr.* The Fire-Worshippers. LPS-1
(Fire Worshippers, The.) EV-4
(Flight of Fondest Hopes, The, *shorter sel.*) BCEP
Syria, *fr.* Paradise and the Peri. LPS-2
Vale of Cashmere, The, *fr.* The Story of the Sultana Nourmahal, or, Light of the Harem. LPS-2
(Light of the Haram, The.) EnRP
Lalla Rookh/ Is a naughty book. On Thomas Moore's Poems. *Unknown.* FiBHP; SiTL
La-la-llamas rate as mammals. In Praise of Llamas. Arthur Guiterman. FiBHP
L'Allegro. Milton. AnFE; AWP; BCEP; BEL; BLV; BoLiVe; BrBE; CBE; CBOV; CoBE; EM-1; EnL; EnLi-1; EnLit; EPP; EV-2; FaFP; FiP; GEPC; GN; GTBS; GTBS-D; GTBS-W; GTSE; GTSL; HBV; HiLiEn; HoPM; InPo; LEAP; LiA; LiTB; LiTG; LoBV; LPS-3; MaPo; MCCG; MyFE; OBEV; OBS; OTPC, *abr* (1923 ed.); OuHeWo; PIAE; PIR; PoE;

ReaPo; SeCePo; SeCeV; ShBV-3; TCEP; TOP; TreFS; TrGrPo; TVSH; TwCrTr; ViBoPo; WHA; WoL
Sels.
"Haste thee, Nymph, and bring with thee." OTPC (1946 ed.); PC; YT
Part of L'Allegro ("To hear the lark"). SN
Sometimes, with Secure Delight. MPB
L'Allegsho—Invitation au Bal. *Unknown.* CAG
Lama, The. Ogden Nash. FaPON; FiBHP; LiL; SiTL
("One-l lama, The.") FaBoCh; LoGBV
Lamarck Elaborated. Richard Wilbur. NePoEA
Lamb, The. Blake. *Fr.* Songs of Innocence. AnFE; BCEP; BEL; BLV; BoChLi; BoLiVe; BoTP; BTP; CAW; CBPC; CEP; CH; CoBE; EiPP; EM-1; EnL; EnLi-2; EnLit; EnRP; EV-3; ExPo; FaBoBe; FaBoCh; FaPON; GoTP; HBV; LiTB; LiTG; LoBV; LoGBV; MaPo; MaRV; MeMeAg; MPB; NeHB; OAEP; OBEC; OTPC; OuHeWo; OxBoCh; PG (1945 ed.); PoFS; PoRh; PRWS; PTA-2; RAR; RIS; SeCeV; StaSt; StVeCh (1940 ed.); SUS; TOP; TreF; TrGrPo; TVC; TVSH; TwCrTr; TwHP; UTS; WaKn; WGRP; WHA
(Little Lamb.) StVeCh (1955 ed.)
Lamb, The. Kate Greenaway. OTPC (1923 ed.); PPL; SAS
Lamb, The. *Unknown.* OTPC (1923 ed.)
Lamb. Humbert Wolfe. MBP; MoBrPo; TwCV
Lamb-Child, The. John Banister Tabb. ChBR; SDH
Lamb of God wears a scarlet robe, The. Futile Sacrifice. Murray Skinner. ChIP
Lamb, whan the hert is laich. Whan the Hert Is Laich. Sidney Goodsir Smith. NeBP
Lambros, *sels.* Dionysios Solomos, *tr. fr. Modern Greek by* Rae Dalven. MoGP
Easter Day.
Maria's Dream.
Maria's Prayer.
Lambro's Return, *sl. abr.* Byron. *Fr.* Don Juan, III. OBRV
Lambs. Katharine Tynan. GTIV
Lambs at Play. Robert Bloomfield. LPS-2
Lambs at Play. Christina Rossetti. *See* On the Grassy Banks.
Lambs in the Meadow. Laurence Alma-Tadema. PRWS
Lambs on the Green Hills Stood Gazing on Me, The. *Unknown.* AnIV
Lamb's wool and leopard's cuffs. Ode I/X/7. *Unknown.* BoFr
Lame Beggar, A. John Donne. TuPP
Lame, impotent conclusion to youth's dreams. Farewell to Juliet. Wilfrid Scawen Blunt. The Love Sonnets of Proteus, LII. ViBoPo
Lame Man and the Blind Man. Waring Cuney. PoNe
Lame One, The. Sherwood Anderson. AnAmPo; LA
Lame Shepherd, The. Katharine Lee Bates. SDH
Lame Soldier, The, *with music. Unknown.* OuSiCo
Lament: "All is far/ And long gone by." Rainer Maria Rilke, *tr. fr. German by* Randall Jarrell. AnGP
(Lament: "Oh, everything is far," *tr. by* C. F. MacIntyre.) TrJP
Lament: "As I walked under the African moon." George Malcolm. NeTW
Lament: "Ban of Time there is no disobeying, The." Gelett Burgess. InMe
Lament: "Chaste maids which haunt fair Aganippe's well." William Drummond of Hawthornden. *Fr.* Tears on the Death of Meliades. LoBV
Lament: "Cry has left in the wind, The." Federico García Lorca, *tr. fr. Spanish by* Eleanor L. Turnbull. CoSP
Lament: "Fall now, my cold thoughts, frozen fall." Laurence Binyon. MoVE
Lament: "Farewell Mercy, farewell thy piteous grace." John Lydgate. *Fr.* Court of Sapience. PoEL-1
Lament, A: "Five long years." Ch'en Yü Hui, *tr. fr. Chinese by* Henry H. Hart. PoHN
Lament: "I am lying in thy tomb, love." Roden Noel. MOAH; VA
Lament, A: "I seen her last night." A. G. Strong. YT
Lament: "Listen, children:/ Your father is dead." Edna St. Vincent Millay. LEAP; PoeMoYo
Lament: "Lo, now he shineth yonder." Hugh Holland. PoD
Lament: "Mild is the parting year, and sweet." Walter Savage Landor. *See* Mild Is the Parting Year.
Lament: "My man is a bone ringèd with weed." Brenda Chamberlain. *See* First Woman's Lament.
Lament, A: "My thoughts hold mortal strife." William Drummond of Hawthornden. *See* Madrigal: "My thoughts hold mortal strife."
Lament: "Nashe's old queens who bartered young and fair." Richard Wilbur. FiMAP
Lament: "Oh, everything is far." Rainer Maria Rilke. *See* Lament: "All is far."
Lament: "O! wither'd is the garland of the war." Shakespeare. *Fr.* Antony and Cleopatra, IV, xiii. KN
Lament, A: "O world! O life! O time!" Shelley. AtBAP; BCEP; BLV; BoLiVe; BPN; CBE; CBOV; ChER; ChTr; EG; EmBrPo; EnLi-2 (1949 ed.); EnLit; EnRP; EPN; ERP; EV-4; GEPC; GTBS; GTBS-D; GTBS-W; GTSE; KN; LoBV; LPS-1; OAEP; OBRV; PIR; PoRA; TCEP; TOP; TrGrPo; WHA
("O world! O life! O time!") BrBE
(Threnos.) GTSL
Lament: "Sigh, wind in the pine." Douglas Stewart. MoAuPo
Lament: "Sleep and death, the darkling eagles." George Trakl, *tr. fr. German by* Kate Flores. AnGP
Lament: "Snows cloaked/ Mountain cliffs." Gudmundur Gudmundsson, *tr. fr. Icelandic by* Watson Kirkconnell. IcP; LiTW
Lament: "We who are left, how shall we look again." W. W. Gibson. BMEP; CaAE; ChMo; CMP; PtOT; TwCV
Lament: "Weariness of the bones." "Pablo de Rokha," *tr. fr. Spanish by* H. R. Hays. OnPM; TwSpPo
Lament: "What moved me, was the way your hand." Dorothy Livesay. CaP
Lament: "When the folk of my household." *Tr. fr. Irish by* Edward Walsh. OBVV
Lament: "Within my bosom stirs once more tonight." Princess Zeb-un-Nissa, *tr. fr. Persian by* Paul Whalley. LiTW
Lament: "Youth's bright palace." Denis Florence MacCarthy. JKCP (1926 ed.); OBVV
Lament at the Day's End. Jules Laforgue, *tr. fr. French by* Cecily Mackworth. MiFP
Lament, A; 1547. Alexander Scott. *See* Lament of the Master of Erskine.
Lament for a Dead Burro. Joaquin Antonio Peñalosa, *tr. fr. Spanish by* Arthur Train, Jr. SaFP
Lament for a Dead Cow. Francis Cary Slater. BoSA
Lament for a Dead Wine-Maker. Li Po, *tr. fr. Chinese by* Henry H. Hart. PoHN
Lament for a Man Who Loved God. James Schevill. FiMAP
Lament for a Poor Poet. Myles Connolly. CAW
Lament for a Quince Tree Uprooted by the Storm. Tu Fu, *tr. fr. Chinese by* Hsieh Wen Tung. WhP
Lament for a Sailor. Paul Dehn. WaP
Lament for Adonis. Bion, *tr. fr. Greek by* John Addington Symonds. AWP; JAWP; LiA; WBP; WoL; GrL, *pr. tr. by* Andrew Lang; GrR, *abr., tr. by* Henry Harmon Chamberlin; OxBG, *tr. by* George Allen
(Bion's Lament for Adonis, *tr. by* Elizabeth Barrett Browning.) ATP
("I mourn for Adonis—Adonis is dead," *tr. by* Elizabeth Barrett Browning.) GrPo
"For Adonis I am crying, for Adonis' beauty dead," *sel., tr. by* George Allen. LiTW
Lament for Alcuin. Fredugis, *tr. fr. Latin by* Helen Waddell. TriL
Lament for Art O'Leary, The. Eileen O'Leary, *tr. fr. Modern Irish by* Frank O'Connor. AnIL; KiLC
Lament for Banba. Egan O'Rahilly, *tr. fr. Irish by* James Clarence Mangan. AnIV; AWP; JAWP; WBP
Lament for Bion, A. *At. to* Moschus, *tr. fr. Greek by* George Chapman. AWP; JAWP; WBP; EnLi-2, *tr. by* J. H. Hallard; GrL, *pr. tr. by* Andrew Lang; GrPE, *tr. by* F. L. Lucas; LiA, *pr. tr. by* Andrew Lang
("Mingle your sighs with mine, ye dales, thou Dorian water," *tr. by* L. P. Chamberlayne.) GrPo
Nox Est Perpetua una Dormienda, *sel., tr. by* E. J. Myers. OxBG
Lament for Cael. *Unknown, tr. fr. Old Irish by* Seán O'Faoláin. SiB
Lament for Capt. Paton. John Gibson Lockhart. OBRV
(Captain Paton's Lament.) EBSV
Lament for Chaucer. Thomas Hoccleve. *Fr.* De Regimine Principum. OBEV; PtP
Lament for Corc and Niall of the Nine Hostages. *At. to* Torna, *tr. fr. Old Irish by* Sir Samuel Ferguson. OnYI
Lament for Corinth. Antipater of Sidon. *See* Ruins of Corinth, The.
Lament for Culloden. Burns. BoHiPo; GTBS; GTBS-D; GTBS-W; GTSE; GTSL; HBV; OBEV
(Lovely Lass o' Inverness, The.) EBSV; EM-1; EV-3; GoTS
Lament for Daphnaida. Spenser. FiP
Lament for Flodden. Jane Elliot. *See* Flowers of the Forest, The.
Lament for Ignacio Sanchez Mejias. Federico García Lorca. *See* Lament for the Death of a Bullfighter.
Lament for Imogen. Shakespeare. *See* Fear No More the Heat o' the Sun.
Lament for Ireland, A. Shemus Cartan, *tr. fr. Irish by* Lady Gregory. GTIV
Lament for King Ivor. Whitley Stokes, *fr. Old Irish.* TIP
Lament for Lost Love. Genaro Estrada, *tr. fr. Spanish by* Donald Devenish Walsh. AnCL
Lament for My Brother, *sel.* Hans Egon Holthusen, *tr. fr. German by* Herman Salinger.
It Was My Blood. TwGV
Lament for My Son Ts'ui, A. Po Chü-i, *tr. fr. Chinese by* Henry H. Hart. PoHN
Lament for O'Sullivan Beare, The. *Tr. fr. Irish by* Jeremiah Joseph Callanan. AnIV

Lament for O'Sullivan Beare, The (*continued*)
(Dirge of O'Sullivan Bear.) IrPN; TIP
(Lament of O'Sullivan Bear.) GTIV
Lament for Our Lady's Shrine at Walsingham, A. *Unknown, at. to* Philip Howard, Earl of Arundel. ISi; PoEL-2; TriL
("In the wracks of Walsingham.") SiCE
(Wreck of Walsingham, The.) ACP
Lament for Pasiphae. Robert Graves. FaBoTw
Lament for Prince Henry. Thomas Campion. *See* Lamentation, A.
Lament for Richard Rolston. Sir Osbert Sitwell. ChMP
Lament for Seán. Daniel James O'Sullivan. NeIP
Lament for Sean MacDermott. "Seumas O'Sullivan." AnIV
Lament for Tabby. *Unknown.* CIV
Lament for the Death of a Bullfighter. Federico García Lorca, *tr. fr. Spanish.* CoSP, *abr., tr. by* Eleanor L. Turnbull; ReMP, *tr. by* Warren Carrier
(Lament for Ignacio Sanchez Mejias, *tr. by* Stephen Spender *and* J. L. Gili.) LiTW
Lament for the Death of Eoghan Ruadh O'Neill. Thomas Osborne Davis. AnIV; GTIV; OxBI; TIP
(Lament for the Death of Owen Roe O'Neill.) IrPN; OnYI
Lament for the Death of Thomas Davis. Sir Samuel Ferguson. *See* Lament for Thomas Davis.
Lament for the Great Yachts. Patric Dickinson. HaMV
Lament for the Makaris [*or* Makars]. William Dunbar. ACP; AEV; AtBAP; BSV; ChTr; CoEV; GoTS; PoD, *abr.*; SiCE; ViBoPo, *abr.*
(Lament for the Makaris Quhen He Wes Seik, The.) OAEP
(Lament for the Makers.) OBEV; PoEL-1
Lament for the Poets: 1916. Francis Ledwidge. AnIV; AWP; JAWP; JKCP (1926 ed.); LBBV; OnYI; OxBI; WBP
Lament for the Princes of Tyrone and Tyrconnel, A. *Tr. fr. Irish by* James Clarence Mangan. AnIV
(Lament for the Princes of Tir-Owen and Tirconnell.) TIP
Lament for the Priory of Walsingham, A, *sel. Unknown.*
"Bitter was it, Oh to view." ChTr
Lament for the Sailing of the Crusade. Rinaldo d'Aquino, *tr. fr. Italian by* Thomas G. Bergin. LyPI
Lament for the Son of Leod. Mari Nighean Alisdair Ruaidh. *See* Cumha Mhic Leoid.
Lament for the Two Brothers Slain by Each Other's Hand. Aeschylus, *tr. fr. Greek by* A. E. Housman. *Fr.* The Seven against Thebes. AWP; JAWP; WBP
Lament for the Woodlands. *Unknown, tr. fr. Irish by* Frank O'Connor. KiLC
Lament for Thomas Davis. Sir Samuel Ferguson. AnIV; GTIV; PoFr, 6 *sts.*; TIP
(Lament for the Death of Thomas Davis.) IrPN; OnYI; OxBI
Lament for Thomas MacDonagh. Francis Ledwidge. *See* Thomas MacDonagh.
Lament for Urien, The. *Unknown, tr. fr. Middle Welsh by* Ernest Rhys. *Fr.* The Red Book of Hergest. OBMV
Lament for Yellow-haired Donough, The. *Unknown, tr. fr. Irish by* Frank O'Connor. KiLC
Lament him, Mauchline husbands a'. On a Wag in Mauchline [*or* Epitaph for James Smith]. Burns. ALV; FiBHP
Lament in Exile, A. Psalms, CXXXVII, Bible, *O.T. See* Song of Exile, A.
Lament in Old Age. Rudagi, *tr. fr. Persian by* A. V. Williams Jackson. PeP
Lament in rhyme, lament in prose. Poor Mailie's Elegy. Burns. EBSV
Lament in Time of Pestilence. Thomas Nashe. *See* Adieu, Farewell, Earth's Bliss!
"Lament not thy path of woe, O loved man." Christ to the Sufferer. *Unknown. Fr.* Andreas. PoLi
Lament of a Despised Lover. Juan Ruiz, Archpriest of Hita, *tr. fr. Spanish by* Ida Farnell. TeCS
Lament of a Man for His Son. *Unknown, tr. fr. Paiute Indian by* Mary Austin. AWP; FAOV; JAWP; WBP
Lament of a Mocking-Bird. Frances Anne Kemble. AA; HBV
Lament of Ahania, *sel.* Blake.
"Where is my golden palace?" LoPS
Lament of an Idle Demon. R. P. Lister. FiBHP
Lament of Anastasius. William Bourn Oliver Peabody. AA
Lament of Barbara, Marchioness of Douglas. *Unknown. See* Waly, Waly.
Lament of Edward Blastock, The. Edith Sitwell. OBMV
Lament of Eve, The. *Unknown.* ACP (1952 ed.)
Lament of Flora Macdonald, The. James Hogg. BoHiPo; EBSV
Lament of Forgetfulness of the Dead. Jules Laforgue. *See* Complaint on the Oblivion of the Dead.
Lament of Granite. David Ross. PG (1945 ed.)
Lament of Guiderius and Arviragus. Shakespeare. *See* Fear No More the Heat o' the Sun.
Lament of Hsi-chün. Hsi-chün, *tr. fr. Chinese by* Arthur Waley. TrCh
Lament of Ian the Proud, The. "Fiona Macleod." VLEP
Lament of "La Belle Heaulmière," The. Villon. *See* Lament of the Lovely Helmet-Dealer.
Lament of Maev Leith-Dherg, The. *Unknown, tr. fr. Middle Irish by* Thomas W. H. Rolleston. OnYI; TIP
Lament of Mary Queen of Scots. Burns. BoHiPo
Lament of O'Sullivan Bear. *Tr. by* Jeremiah Joseph Callanan. *See* Lament for O'Sullivan Beare, The.
Lament of Quarry, The. Léonie Adams. NP
Lament of Saint Anne, The. *Unknown. Fr.* The Protevangelium of James. CAW
Lament of Tasso, The. Byron. EmBrPo
Lament of the Border Widow, The. *Unknown.* CBOV; EBSV; HBV; LPS-2; OBB; OTPC (1923 ed.), *sl. diff.*
(Bonnie Bower.) CH
(Border Widow's Lament.) BSV
("My love he built me a bonny bower.") LO
Lament of the Damned in Hell, The. Edward Young. OxBoCh
Lament of the Flowers, The. Jones Very. OxBA
Lament of the Frontier Guard. Li Po, *tr. fr. Chinese by* Ezra Pound. CoAnAm; CoBMV; TwAmPo; WaaP
Lament of the Irish Emigrant. Helen Selina Sheridan. GTIV; HBV; LPS-1; OBEV (1st ed.); OBVV; TIP; VA
Lament of the Irish Maiden, The. Denny Lane. TIP
Lament of the Lovely Helmet-Dealer. Villon, *tr. fr. French by* Hubert Creekmore. LyMA
(Lament of "La Belle Heaulmière," The, *tr. by* Lewis Wharton.) LiTW
(Lament of the Old Woman Remembering Her Youth, *abr., tr. by* Ralph N. Currey.) FoS
Lament of the Mangaire Sugach. Andrew Magrath, *tr. fr. Modern Irish by* Edward Walsh. OnYI; TIP
Lament of the Master of Erskine. Alexander Scott. BSV
("Depart, depart, depart!" *abr.*) LO
(Lament, A; 1547, *abr.*) CH
Lament of the Mole-Catcher, The. Sir Osbert Sitwell. LBBV
Lament of the Old Woman Remembering Her Youth. Villon. *See* Lament of the Lovely Helmet-Dealer.
Lament of the Organist of Notre-Dame de Nice. Jules Laforgue, *tr. fr. French by* Vernon Watkins. AnFP
Lament of the Pianos Which Are Overheard in Well-to-do Quarters. Jules Laforgue, *tr. fr. French by* Joseph Bennett. AnFP
Lament of the Players. Roland Burke Hennessy. LPS-1
Lament of the Scotch-Irish Exile. James Jeffrey Roche. BOHV
Lament of the Troops on the Death of Peter the Great. *Unknown, tr. fr. Russian by* N. Kershaw Chadwick. BoFr
Lament of the Voiceless, The. Laura Bell Everett. OQP; PGD; QP-2
Lament of This Good Moon. Jules Laforgue, *tr. fr. French by* Joseph Bennett. AnFP
Lament over Saul. Second Samuel, Bible, *O.T. See* David's Lament.
Lament over Sir Philip Sidney. *Unknown. See* Funerall Song, A.
Lament over the Heroes Fallen in the Battle of Avarair. Karekin Srvanstian, *tr. fr. Armenian by* Zabelle C. Boyajian. ArmLP
Lament the Night before His Execution, A. Chidiock Tichborne. *See* Elegy: "My prime of youth is but a frost of cares."
Lament to Nana of Erech. *Unknown, tr. fr. Babylonian tablets by* Stephen Langdon. LiTW
Lament who will, in fruitless tears. The Lapse of Time. Bryant. BAV
Lamentable Ballad of the Bloody Brook, The. Edward Everett Hale. HBV; PAH
Lamentable Tragedy of Locrine, The. *At. to* George Peele, *also at. to* Charles Tilney. *See* Locrine.
Lamentation, A. Thomas Campion. CH; OHIP
(Lament for Prince Henry.) TriL
Lamentation. Ezekiel, XIX: 2–9, Bible, *O.T.* TrJP
Lamentation. Lynette Roberts. MoWP
Lamentation for Celin, The. *Unknown, tr. fr. Spanish by* John Gibson Lockhart. AWP; JAWP; OuHeWo; WBP
"At the gate of old Granada, when all its bolts are barred," *sts.* 1–5. PoFr
Lamentation for the Death of Sir Maurice Fitzgerald, Knight of Kerry, A. Pierce Ferriter, *tr. fr. Late Middle Irish by* James Clarence Mangan. IrPN
Lamentation for the Fall of Jerusalem. Lamentations, Bible, *O.T. See* Misery of Jerusalem, The.
Lamentation for the Three Sons of Turann, Which Turann, Their Father, Made over Their Grave, The. John Todhunter. TIP
Lamentation of Beckles, The. Thomas Deloney. SiCE
Lamentation of Chloris, The. *Unknown.* CoMu
Lamentation of Danaë, The. Simonides. *See* Danaë.
Lamentation of Don Rodrigo [*or* Roderick], The. *Unknown,*

tr. fr. Spanish by John Gibson Lockhart. AnSpL-1; TeCS
Lamentation of Hugh Reynolds, The. *Unknown.* TIP
Lamentation of Mac Liag for Kincora. *Unknown. See* Kincora.
Lamentation of Nippur. *Unknown, tr. fr. Babylonian tablets by* Stephen Langdon. LiTW
Lamentation of the Old Pensioner, The. W. B. Yeats. MaPo; TIP
Lamentation of the Virgin, A, *abr.* *Unknown.* TMEV
Lamentations, *sels.* Bible, *O.T.*
Affliction, III: 1–15. TrJP
Desolation in Zion, I: 12–17. TrJP
How Is the Gold Become Dim, IV: 1–5. ChTr
Lamentation for the Fall of Jerusalem, I. LiTW
(Misery of Jerusalem, The.) AWP
Lamentations. Alter Brody. TrJP
Lamentations, The. Homer, *tr. fr. Greek by* Sir William Marris. *Fr.* The Iliad, XXIV. LiTW; OxBG
(Lamentations of the Women, The, *tr. by* the Earl of Derby.) GrR
(Wail for Hector, The, *tr. by* F. L. Lucas.) GrPE
Lamentations of the Fallen Angels. Cædmon (?), *tr. fr. Anglo-Saxon by* Charles W. Kennedy. *Fr.* Christ and Satan. AnOE
Laments. *Unknown, tr. fr. Arabic by* E. Powys Mathers. *Fr.* The Thousand and One Nights. AWP; JAWP; WBP
Lamia. Keats. BEL; EM-2; EmBrPo; EnLi-2; EnRP; EPN; ERP; GEPC; OAEP; PIR; TwCrTr
Sels.
Banquet, The, *fr.* Pt. II. SeCePo
"Love in a hut, with water and a crust," *fr.* Pt. II. EV-4
Wide-spreaded Night, *br. sel. fr.* Pt. I. LiA
Lamillia's Song. Robert Greene. *See* Fie, Fie on Blind Fancy!
L'Amitié et L'Amour. John Swanwick Drennan. IrPN
Lamkin. *Unknown.* BaBo (A, C, *and* D *vers.*); ESPB (A, B, *and* K *vers.*); OBB; ViBoFo
(False Linfinn, B *vers.*) BaBo
L'Amour sans Ailes. Charles Fenno Hoffman. PR
Lamp, The. Sarah Pratt Greene. AA
Lamp, The. Sara Teasdale. ChMo; CMP; InP; NV
Lamp, The. Henry Vaughan. SeCL
Lamp, The. Charles Whitehead. OBEV (new ed.); OBVV
(As Yonder Lamp.) VA
Lamp and the Moon, The. Shan Ho Yü, *tr. fr. Chinese by* Henry H. Hart. PoHN
Lamp burns long in the cottage, The. There's Money in Mother and Father. Morris Bishop. FiBHP
Lamp burns sure, within, The. Emily Dickinson. LiTA
Lamp Flower, The. Margaret Cecilia Furse. BoTP
Lamp in the West, The. Ella Higginson. AA; HBV
Lamp must be replenished, but even then, The. Manfred. Byron. BEL; BPN; EmBrPo; EnLi-2 (1939 ed.); EnRP; EPN; ERP; GEPC
Lamp of Life, The. Amy Lowell. MaRV
Lamp of Poor Souls, The. Marjorie Pickthall. CPG; HBV; TwCV
Lamp of the body is the eye, The. The Pure Light. St. Matthew, Bible, *N. T.* GrCo-1
Lamp of valor flickered low, The. Lindbergh; Ballad. Alexander Laing. PoeMoYo
Lamp Posts. Helen Hoyt. YT
Lamplighter, The. "Seumas O'Sullivan." OxBI
Lamplighter, The. Robert Louis Stevenson. FaFP; GaP; MPB; OTPC; PCH; PoVP; TreF; TVC; TVSH
Lampoon; in the School of Socrates. Aristophanes. *See* Socrates' Experiments.
Lamps Are Burning, The. Charles Reznikoff. TrJP
Lamps have been put out, and now the night is hushed and clear, The. The Milky Way. Zakarias Topelius. AnSL
Lamp's Shrine, The. Dante Gabriel Rossetti. The House of Life, XXXV. PoVP; ViPo
Lampus extinct at last in ashes lies. In Obitum Alienius. Henry Parrot. SiCE
L'An Trentiesme de Mon Eage [*or* Age]. Archibald MacLeish. AnFE; APA; CoAnAm; LiTM; MoVE; NePA; NP; TBM; TriL; TwAmPo
(In My Thirtieth Year.) MAP; MoAmPo
Lancashire Doxology, A. Dinah Maria Mulock Craik. LPS-2
Lancashire Lads. *Unknown.* CoMu
Lancashire Puritane, The. *Unknown.* CoMu
Lancaster bore him—such a little town. A Hundred Collars. Robert Frost. YaD
Lancelot. Arna Bontemps. CDC
Lancelot and Elaine. Tennyson. *Fr.* Idylls of the King. HeT; PoVP; ViPo; ViPP; VLEP
Sels.
"Elaine the fair, Elaine the loveable." ReTS
Elaine's Song. BPN; FaBoEn
Lancelot and Guinevere. Gerald Gould. HBV
Lancelot and the Grail. Tennyson. *Fr.* Idylls of the King: The Holy Grail. GoBC
Lancer. A. E. Housman. Last Poems, VI. EnLit; MBP; MoBrPo
L'Ancien Régime. James Thomson. PoVP
Land, The, *sel.* Struthers Burt.
"Be not afraid, O Dead." AOAH; DD; HBMV
Land, The. Kipling. MBP; MoBrPo; ViPP
Land, The, *sels.* V. Sackville-West.
"Country habit has me by the heart, The." AlDL
"Far from shrewd companies." AlDL
Labour. TwCV
Peddler and the Reddleman, The. TCPD
Ploughing. TCPD
"Shepherds and stars are quiet with the hills." ShBV-4
Spring. MoP
Spring Was Late That Year, The. AtBAP
Vintage. TwCV
Weed Month. MBP; MoBrPo (1942 ed.)
Winter Song. MBP; MoBrPo (1942 ed.)
Land, The. W. J. Turner. OS
Land across the Sea, A. William Morris. *Fr.* The Earthly Paradise. VA
Land and Sea. Moschus, *tr. fr. Greek by* J. H. Hallard. GrR
Land and Sea. *Unknown, tr. fr. Greek by* Sir William Marris. OxBG
Land beloved of horsemen, fair, The. Choral Poem. Sophocles. *Fr.* Oedipus at Colonus. LiTW
Land Dirge, A. John Webster. *See* Call for the Robin Redbreast and the Wren.
Land grew bright in a single flower, The. Christmas Carol. Sister Francisca Josefa del Castillo. CAW
"Land Is Ours, The." Sir Samuel Ferguson. *Fr.* Congal. IrPN
Land it is the landlord's, The. The Song of the Wage-Slave. Ernest Charles Jones. PoFr
Land lies in water; it is shadowed green. The Map. Elizabeth Bishop. LoGBV; ReMP
Land o' Nae Surprise, The. John Stevenson. BOL
Land o' the Leal, The. Lady Nairne. BCEP; EBSV; GTBS; GTBS-D; GTBS-W; GTSE; GTSL; HBV; LPS-1; MaRV; MCCG; NA; OBEV; TCEP; WBLP; WGRP
(Land of the Leal, The.) EV-3
Land of Beginning Again, The. Louise Fletcher Tarkington. BLPA; OQP; PTA-2; QP-2
Land of Biscay, The. A. E. Housman. More Poems, XLVI. ReaPo
Land of brown heath and shaggy wood. Scotland. Sir Walter Scott. *Fr.* The Lay of the Last Minstrel. BSV; LPS-2
Land of Cokaigne, The. *Unknown, tr. fr. Middle English.* CAW, *br. sel.;* TMEV
(Cokaygne.) AnIL
(Land of Cockayne, The.) MeEV
(Land of Cokaygne, The, *at. to* Friar Michael of Kildare, *mod. vers. by* Russell K. Alspach.) OnYI
Land of Counterpane, The. Robert Louis Stevenson. BoChLi; FaBoBe; FaFP; FaPON; GoBP; HBV; HBVY; MPB; NeHB; OTPC; PCH; PoVP; RIS; StVeCh; TreF; VA
Land of Destiny. Catherine Parmenter. PEDC
Land of Dreams, The. Blake. BeLS; BOL; CBPC; CH; OBRV
Land of Dreams, The. Henry Martyn Hoyt. HBMV
Land of Dreams, The. H. F. Sargent. BOL
Land of Dreams and Sleep, A—a poppied land! Nubia. Bayard Taylor. HBV
Land of gold!—thy sisters greet thee. California. Lydia Huntley Sigourney. MC; PAH
Land of Heart's Desire, The. Emily Huntington Miller. HBV
Land of Heart's Desire, The. W. B. Yeats. PoVP
"Wind blows out of the gates of the day, The," *sel.* ViBoPo
(Faerie's Song, *abr.*) GBV
(Fairy Song.) MBP; MoBrPo; OnYI
(From "The Land of Heart's Desire.") GTSL
(Lyric from "The Land of Heart's Desire.") CP; NV
(Song: "Wind blows out of the gates of day, The.") BEL; InP; TSW
(Song of the Faeries [*or* Fairies], The.) ChMo; CMP
(Voice, The.) PtOT
Land of Indolence. James Thomson. *See* Vale of Indolence.
Land of leaning ice, A. North Labrador. Hart Crane. ChMo; FaBoMo
Land of Masters. Mikhail Yurevich Lermontov, *tr. fr. Russian by* Babette Deutsch. OnPM; TrRV
Land of mine, where I was bred. Aleksey Konstantinovich Tolstoy, *tr. fr. Russian by* C. M. Bowra. BoR
Land of Muravia, The, *sel.* Aleksandr Tvardovsky, *tr. fr. Russian by* Jack Lindsay.
"Morgunok listened. His grand-dad said." RuPo
Land of my heart,/ What future is before thee? William Dudley Foulke. *Fr.* Ad Patriam. PGD
Land of Nations, *sel.* Gertrude Stein.
"Here is a poem." AtBAP
Land of Nod, The. Robert Louis Stevenson. GoTP; MPB (1956 ed.); PoVP; VA; VLEP

Land of Nod, The. Elizabeth Hays Wilkinson. BOL
Land of Our Birth. Kipling. *Fr.* Puck of Pook's Hill. BoTP; MaRV
(Children's Song, The.) MW; PoVP; TVSH
Land of Our Fathers. Clinton Scollard. *See* Ad Patriam.
Land of Story-Books, The. Robert Louis Stevenson. CBPC; FaBoBe; FaPON; GoTP; HBV; HBVY; MOB; MPB; NeHB; OTPC; PoVP; PRWS; TiPo; TreFS; TSW; TSWC
"There, in the night, where none can spy," *sel.* YT
Land of the Empire Builders. Oregon State Song. J. A. Buchanan. PoRL
Land of the Evening Mirage, The. *Unknown, tr. fr. Sioux Indian by* A. M. Beede. WGRP
Land of the Free. Arthur Nicholas Hosking. BLPA; PaA
Land of the Free, *sel.* Archibald MacLeish.
"We wonder whether the dream of American liberty." MoAB; MoAmPo; NeMA
Land of the Free. Sister Mary Honora. NePoAm-2
Land of the Leal, The. Lady Nairne. *See* Land o' the Leal, The.
Land of the masters, land of slaves, farewell. Land of Masters. Mikhail Lermontov. OnPM
Land of the mountains high. Utah, We Love Thee. Evan Stephens. PoRL
Land of the South, whose stricken heart and brow. North to the South. Richard Watson Gilder. MDAH
Land of the Sun, The. Byron. *See* Bride of Abydos, The.
Land of the West! though passing brief the record of thine age. Washington. Eliza Cook. WOAH
Land of the Wilful Gospel. Sidney Lanier. *Fr.* The Psalm of the West. PAH
Land of unconquered Pelayo! land of the Cid Campeador! The Surrender of Spain. John Hay. AA
Land, that, from the rule of kings, The. The Bartholdi Statue. Whittier. PaA; PAH
Land that is lonelier than ruin, A. By the North Sea, I. Swinburne. EmBrPo; PoEL-5; PoVP
Land That Man Has Newly Trod, A. Joaquin Miller. AmPP (3d ed.)
Land That We Love. Richard Watson Gilder. PaA
Land War, The. "Seumas O'Sullivan." GTIV; OxBI
Land was ours before we were the land's, The. The Gift Outright. Robert Frost. AmP; AmPP (4th ed.); CoBMV; CrMA; FaBoEn; InPo; LiTM; LoGBV; MaPo; MoAB; MoAmPo (1950 ed.); NeTW; OxBA; WaKn; WaP
Land was overmuch like scenery, The. Beowulf. Richard Wilbur. CrMA
Land was white, The. Riddle. *Unknown.* ChTr; OxNR
Land we from our fathers had in trust, The. Feelings of the Tyrolese. Wordsworth. ERP
Land We Must Have, A. Per Sivle, *tr. fr. Norwegian by* Charles W. Stork. AnNoLy
Land Where Hate Should Die, The. Denis A. McCarthy. PGD; PSO; PTA-2
Land Where I Was Born, The. Shaw Neilson. BoAu
"Land where I was born sits by the seas, The." Paolo and Francesca. Dante, *tr. by* Byron. *Fr.* Divina Commedia: Inferno. LiA
Land where the banners wave last in the sun. Freedom, Our Queen. Oliver Wendell Holmes. PEDC
Land Where the Columbines Grow. Arthur J. Fynn. PoOW
Land Where the Taffy Birds Grow, The. Margaret McBride Hoss. GFA
Land Where We Were Dreaming, The. Daniel Bedinger Lucas. SPP
(In the Land Where We Were Dreaming.) PAH, *abr.*
Land Which No One Knows, The. Ebenezer Elliott. *See* Plaint.
Land Within, The. Mary Webb. MM
Land without Ruins, A. Abram Joseph Ryan. SPP
Land-Fall. George M. Brady. NeIP
Landfall in Unknown Seas. Allen Curnow. AnNZ
Landing, The. "Lewis Carroll." *Fr.* The Hunting of the Snark. WhC
Landing, The. Padraic Colum. TIP
Landing of the Pilgrim Fathers [in New England], The. Felicia Dorothea Hemans. BCEP; BeLS; BLPA; BoHiPo; DD; ERP; FaBoBe; FaFP; FaPON; GN; GoTP; HBV; HBVY; HH; LPS-2; MaRV; MC; MW; NeHB; OHIP; OnSP; OTPC; PaA; PAH; PCH; PGD, *abr.;* PIR; PoFr; PoRL; TreF; WBLP
(Landing of the Pilgrims, The.) PECK; PTA-1
(Pilgrim Fathers.) BoTP; LH
Landlady. P. K. Page. CaP; TwCaPo
Landlady's Daughter, The. Ludwig Uhland. *See* Hostess' Daughter, The.
Landlocked. Charles Buxton Going. VOD
Land-locked I lie, in idleness. Rondeau. Theodora Bates. CAG
Landlubber's Chantey, The. James Stuart Montgomery. HBMV
Landmarch by camel and shipsail we take. Cargoes of the Radanites. Harry Alan Potamkin. TrJP
Landmark, The. Dante Gabriel Rossetti. The House of Life, LXVII. BPN; EmBrPo; EPN; EPP; PoVP; TCEP; ViPo
Landmark. John Short. PoN
Landor. John Albee. AA; LEAP
Landor. Alexander Hay Japp. PtP; VA
Landore. George Woodcock. MoWP
Landowner, some years ago, A. The Young Forest. "Demyan Bedny." TrRV
Landrail, The. Sir Aubrey De Vere. IrPN
Land's End (Point Lobos, California). Stanton A. Coblentz. EtS
Landscape. Baudelaire, *tr. fr. French.* AnFP, *tr. by* Vernon Watkins; TrFP, *tr. by* Alan Conder
Landscape. Maxwell Bodenheim. MOAP
Landscape. William Cowper. *Fr.* The Task. CoBE
Landscape, A. John Cunningham. CEP; EnSW; RO, *abr.*
Landscape. R. N. Currey. BoSA
Landscape, A, *sel.* James Hurdis.
"Behold that vale, whose sides are cloth'd with wood." EnSW
Landscape. William Mason. *Fr.* The English Garden. OBEC
Landscape. Alfred W. Purdy. CaP
Landscape. Henri de Régnier, *tr. fr. French by* Alan Conder. TrFP
Landscape, The. William Shenstone. *See* Song: Landskip, The.
Landscape as a Nude. Archibald MacLeish. Frescoes for Mr. Rockefeller's City, I. AmPP (4th ed.); ReaPo
(Frescoes for Mr. Rockefeller's City.) UnPo
Landscape as Metal and Flowers. Winfield Townley Scott. HoPM; MiAP
Landscape: Beast/ Yonder, by the eastward sea. Figure for an Apocalypse. Thomas Merton. CrMA
Landscape Fading, The. Goronwy Rees. MoWP
Landscape lies in snow: brown leafless woods, The. Landscape of the Heart. Charles Abraham Elton. *Fr.* The Brothers. RO
Landscape Lies within My Head, The. Gervase Stewart. WaaP
Landscape near an Aerodrome, The. Stephen Spender. AnEnPo; AnFE; CoBMV; EnLit; LiTM; MBP; MoAB; MoBrPo; MoVE; OAEP (2d ed.); PoLFOT; ReMP; ShBV-4; WoL
Landscape of Evil. Tristan Corbière. *See* Evil Landscape.
Landscape of Love, The. Thomas Cole. NePoAm
Landscape of Love. P. K. Page. BoCaPo (1943 ed.)
Landscape of the Heart. Charles Abraham Elton. *Fr.* The Brothers. RO
Landscape of the Heart, The. Geoffrey Grigson. LiTB; LiTM; WaP
Landscape Painting, *sel.* William Gilpin.
"Far up yon river, opening to the sea." EnSW
Landscape where I lie, The. Song for a Lyre. Louise Bogan. LiTA
Landscape with Children. Sister Maris Stella. JKCP (1955 ed.)
Landscape with Figures. Keith Douglas. NePoEA
Landscape with Figures. A. R. D. Fairburn. AnNZ
Landscape with the Giant Orion, *sel.* Sacheverell Sitwell.
Orion Seeks the Goddess Diana. MoVE
Landscapes (I–V). T. S. Eliot. KN; LoGBV
Sels.
Cape Ann, V. ThWaDe
New Hampshire, I. FaBoCh; LoBV; ThWaDe
Rannoch by Glencoe, IV. FaBoEn
Usk, III. CoBE; FaBoCh
Landscapes. Louis Untermeyer. HBV; LEAP
Landscape's private and all that it contains, The. Artillery Shoot. James Forsyth. WaP
Landsman, The. Moschus. *See* Ocean, The.
Lane, A. *Unknown.* PCH
("From house to house he goes.") BoTP; OTPC (1946 ed.)
(Irish Riddle, An, *sl. diff.*) RIS
Lane, The. Andrew Young. HaMV
Lane County Bachelor, The, *with music. Unknown.* AS; SoAF, *shorter vers.*
(Starving to Death on a Government Claim.) ABS; IHA, *diff. vers.*
Lane of elms in June, A—the air. Forby Sutherland. George Gordon M'Crae. VA
Lanes in Summer. Malcolm Hemphrey. BoTP
Lang Johnny More. *Unknown.* ESPB
Langelands Rejsen, *sel.* Adam Oehlenschläger, *tr. fr. Danish by* Charles W. Stork.
Korsør. BoDS
L'Angelo. Thomas Caulfield Irwin. IrPN
Langland's Life. William Langland, *tr. fr. Middle English.* *Fr.* The Vision of Piers Plowman. MeEV
Langley Lane. Robert Buchanan. HBV
Langston Hughes. Jacques Roumain, *tr. fr. French by* Edna Worthley Underwood. PoNe

Langsyne, When Life Was Bonnie. Alexander Anderson. HBV
Language. Winifred Welles. NP
Language has not the power to speak what love indites. Fragment. John Clare. PoEL-4
Languages. Carl Sandburg. CoV
Languid, and sad, and slow, from day to day. Sonnet. William Lisle Bowles. CEP
Languid lady next appears in state, The. Characters of Women. Edward Young. *Fr.* Love of Fame, the Universal Passion, Satire V. OBEC
Languid river, like, The. Wave Wing. Ibn Sa'id of Alcala la Real. MooP
Languish and dispaire my hart. *Unknown.* SeCSL
Languor. Stéphane Mallarmé, *tr. fr. French by* Ithell Colquhoun. MiFP
Lanigan's Ball. *Unknown.* OxBoLi
Lanky hank of a she in the inn over there, The. A Glass of Beer [*or* Righteous Anger]. James Stephens, *after* O'Bruaidar. AnFE; AnIV; ExPo; FiBHP; LiTM; LiTW; MBP; MoAB; MoBrPo; OBMV; SeCePo; ShBV-4; SiTL; WhC
Lantern, The. Richard Church. MBP; MoBrPo (1942 ed.)
Lantern Festival, The. Ou-yang Hsiu, *tr. fr. Chinese.* ChLP
Lantern light from deeper in the barn, A. The Fear. Robert Frost. ATP; BeLS; MAPA; NAMP; TwAmPo
Lantern Out of Doors, The. Gerard Manley Hopkins. ChMo; EmBrPo; LiTB; OxBoCh
Lanty Leary. Samuel Lover. BOHV
Lanty Leary. *Unknown.* ChTr
Laocoon. Don Gordon. WaaP
Laocoon. Donald Hall. NePoAm-2
Laodamia, *sels.* Audrey Alexandra Brown.
"At dawn they launched the ships; and all went well." TwCV
Laodamia. Wordsworth. BEL; BPN; EM-2; EmBrPo; EnRP; EPN; ERP; EV-3; GEPC; OAEP; TwCrTr
Lao-lao Ting, a Tavern. Li Po, *tr. fr. Chinese by* Shigeyoshi Obata. BoFr
Laon and Cythna. Shelley. *See* Revolt of Islam, The.
Lao-tse. Thomas S. Jones, Jr. AnAmPo; LA
Lao-tzu. Po Chü-i, *tr. fr. Chinese by* Arthur Waley. LiTW; OnPM; WoL
(Philosophers, The.) TrCh; WhC
Lapful of Nuts, The. *Unknown, tr. fr. Irish by* Sir Samuel Ferguson. GTIV; IrPN; WP
Lapis Lazuli. W. B. Yeats. ChMP; CoBMV; FaBoTw; GTBS-W; LiTB; LiTM; MoPo; MoVE; OAEP (2d ed.)
Lapping of lake water, The. Lake Song. Jean Starr Untermeyer. AnAmPo; AV; HBMV; LA; MAP; MoAmPo (1942 ed.); NP; TrJP
Lapse of Time, The. Bryant. BAV
Lapse of Time, The. Edward Young. *See* Time.
Lapsus Calami. James Kenneth Stephen. *See* To R. K.
Lapsus Linguae. Keith Preston. WhC
Lapwing, The. Blake. *See* O Lapwing!
Lapwing. Rex Warner. ShBV-3
Lara, *sel.* Byron.
"There was in him a vital scorn of all." OBRV
Laramie Trail. Joseph Mills Hanson. PoOW
Larbowlins stout, you must turn out. Rules of the Road. *Unknown.* SoAmSa
Larch Hill. Leslie Daiken. OnYI
Larch Tree. Laurie Lee. NeBP
Larch-tree gives them needles, The. Trees and Fairies. Rose Fyleman. RAR
Larch Trees. Frederick William Faber. EnSW
Larch Wood Secrets. Ivy O. Eastwick. BoTP
Larches about this retrospective town. Naseby; Late Autumn. Basil Dowling. AnNZ
Large Bad Picture. Elizabeth Bishop. MiAP
Large, calm harbour lies below, The. In Falmouth Harbour, I. Lionel Johnson. POTT
Large glooms were gathered in the mighty fane. James Thomson. The City of Dreadful Night, XIV. OAEP; POTT; ViP
Larger Hope, The. Tennyson. *See* In Memoriam A. H. H.: "Oh yet we trust . . ."
Larger Prayer, The. Ednah Dow Cheney. BLRP; MaRV; OQP; PraP; QP-1; WGRP
Largess, The. Richard Eberhart. LiTA; LiTM (rev. ed.); TwAmPo
Largest Life, The. Archibald Lampman. CaP; CPG; OCL
There Is a Beauty, *sel.* MaRV
Largo. Sidney Goodsir Smith. NeBP
Largo. Dunstan Thompson. LiTA; LiTM; MoPo; WaP
Lariat snaps; the cowboy rolls, The. The Closing of the Rodeo. William Jay Smith. NePoEA
Larissa. Thomas Love Peacock. *Fr.* Rhododaphne. OBRV
Lark, The. W. W. Gibson. ChMo; CMP
Lark, The. James Hogg. *See* Skylark, The.
Lark. Josephine Miles. FiMAP
Lark, The. Lizette Woodworth Reese. BLA; GFA; HBMV; NLK; OTPC (1946 ed.); TCAP; VOD
Lark, The. Pierre de Ronsard, *tr. fr. French by* Alan Conder. TrFP
Lark, The. *Unknown.* OBS; SeCL
Lark above our heads doth know, The. A Violinist. Francis William Bourdillon. OBVV; VA
Lark and the Nightingale, The. Hartley Coleridge. OTPC (1923 ed.)
(Song: "'Tis sweet to hear the merry lark.") HBV
Lark and the Rook, The. *Unknown.* OTPC; PRWS
Lark as small as a flint arrow, A. The Round Barrow. Andrew Young. SeCePo
Lark Ascending, The. George Meredith. CoBE; EmBrPo; EnLi-2; EPN; LoBV; OAEP; PoeT; POTT; PoVP; VA
"For singing till his heaven fills," *sel.* BLA
Lark Descending. Edmund Blunden. MoP
Lark hit us in the face with his rising sound. Lark. Josephine Miles. FiMAP
Lark in the mesh of the tangled vine, A. Kyrielle. John Payne. HBV
Lark in the Morning, The. *Unknown.* ChTr
Lark is singing in the blinding sky, The. Sea-Marge [*or* Autumn]. Alexander Smith. *Fr.* A Life-Drama. GTSE; VA
Lark is up to meet the sun, The. Morning. Jane Taylor. HBV
Lark knows no such rapture, The. To a Seamew. Swinburne. BLA; MBP
Lark Now Leaves His Wat'ry [*or* Watery] Nest, The. Sir William Davenant. AnEnPo; CenL; CH; ChTr; EG; EV-2; InvP; LO; PoRA; ReEn; SeCL; ViBoPo; WHA
(Aubade.) ATP (1935 ed.); OBEV
(Awake! Awake!) BLV; PIAE
(Morning.) ACP; HBV
(Morning Song.) LEAP; TrGrPo
(Song: "Lark now leaves his wat'ry [*or* watery] nest, The.") AWP; ElSeCe; FaBoEn; GoBC; JAWP; LiTL; MeLP; MePo; OBS; SeCV-1; SeEP; TOP; WBP
Lark sings for joy in her own loved land, The. Lines to the Stormy Petrel. *Unknown.* LPS-2
Lark, skylark, spilling your rubbed and round. The Ecstatic. C. Day Lewis. AlDL
Lark was warbling sweet her evening song, The. Tasso. *Fr.* Jerusalem Delivered, XIX. PrPoCR
Lark Went Singing, A. Ruth Guthrie Harding. UnW
Larks. Katharine Tynan. GTIV; OnYI; TIP
Larks and the angels make a stir. Brother Clement. *Fr.* The Death of an Italian Beggar. SaFP
Lark's Grave, The. Thomas Westwood. TVC; TVSH
Lark's Nest, A. Christopher Smart. *Fr.* Hymns for the Amusement of Children. FaBoCh; LoGBV
Lark's Song, The. "Seumas O'Sullivan." BLA
Larkspur and Hollyhock. Names. Dorothy Aldis. BoChLi; SUS
Larrie O'Dee. William W. Fink. BOHV; HBV; OTPC (1946 ed.)
Larry and Gogo love mushrooms. Making Mushrooms. Esther Antin. RIS
Larry M'Hale. Charles James Lever. *Fr.* Charles O'Malley, the Irish Dragoon. OnYI; TIP
Larry O'Toole. Thackeray. ALV
Lars Porsena of Clusium. Horatius at the Bridge. Macaulay. *Fr.* Lays of Ancient Rome. BBV; BCEP; BeLS; BHV; CBPC; EV-4; FaBoCh; FaFP; HBV; HBVY; LH; LoGBV; LPS-2; MCCG; OHFP; OnSP; PECK; PIR; ShBV-1; TreF
L'Art, 1910. Ezra Pound. OxBA
Las Sierpes Street. Oliverio Girondo, *tr. fr. Spanish by* Milton Ben Davis. AnCL
Lasca. Frank Desprez. BeLS; BLPA, *sl. abr.*; FaBoBe; HBV; NeHB; PTA-1; SCC; TreF
Lass o' Arranteenie, The. Robert Tannahill. EBSV
Lass o' Gowrie, The. Lady Nairne. HBV
Lass of Ballochmyle, The. Burns. EBSV
Lass of Islington, The. *Unknown.* CoMu
Lass of Lochroyan, The. *Unknown.* EBSV; HBV; OBB; OBEV (1st ed.); SG
(Fair Annie of Lochroyan, *with music.*) AS
(Lass of Roch Royal, The.) *Unknown.* BaBo; EBSV (A *and* D *vers.*); VIBoFo (A *vers., with music;* B *and* C *vers.*)
(True Lover's Farewell, The, *diff. vers.*) AS
(Who Will Shoe Your Pretty Little Foot?) AS
Lass of Lynn's New Joy, for Finding a Father for Her Child, The. *Unknown.* CoMu
Lass of Mohea, The. *See* Little Mohee, The.
Lass of Patie's Mill, The. Allan Ramsay. BSV; EBSV; EV-3
Lass of Richmond Hill, The. James Upton. HBV; LPS-1
Lass of Roch Royal. *Unknown. See* Lass of Lochroyan, The.
Lass That Died of Love, The. Richard Middleton. HBV
Lass That Made the Bed to Me, The. Burns. InvP; RO

Lass there lives upon the green, A. Pastorella. *At. to* Sir Henry Sheers. SeCL
Lass, when they talk of love, laugh in their face. Love. Francis Jammes. AWP
Lass with the Delicate Air, The. Michael Arne. OlF
Lass with the Golden Locks, The. Christopher Smart. RO
Lassie all alone was making her moan, A. As I Stood by Yon Roofless Tower. Burns. EBSV
Lassie, What Mair Wad You Hae? Heine, *tr. fr. German into Scottish by* Alexander Gray. GoTS
Lassie wi' the Lint-white Locks. Burns. EV-3; RO
Lassie, with the lips sae rosy. Mädchen mit dem rothen Mündchen. Heine. AWP; JAWP; WBP
Last Abbot of Gloucester, The. Wilfred Rowland Childe. CAW
Last Aboriginal, The. "Fiona Macleod." PoVP; VA
Last All Saints' holy-day, even now gone by. Sonnet [*or* To Beatrice on All Saints' Day]. Dante, *tr. by* D. G. Rossetti. AWP; GoBC; JAWP; OnPM; WBP
Last Ally, The. William Rose Benét. *See* His Ally.
Last and greatest herald of heaven's King, The. For the Baptist [*or* Saint John Baptist]. William Drummond of Hawthornden. BSV; CBOV; EBSV; EPS (1942 ed.); ES; EV-2; GoTS; GTBS-D; GTBS-W; GTSE; GTSL; HBV; LoBV; OBEV; OBS; OnPP; OxBoCh; PeBoSo; PIAE; SeEP; TrGrPo
Last Antelope, The. Edwin Ford Piper. PCN; PoMa; TCPD
Last Antiphon: To Mary. James J. Donohue. ISi
Last Appeal, A. Frederic William Henry Myers. MaRV; VA
Last Appendix to "Yankee Doodle," The. *Unknown.* PAH
Last April, when the winds had lost their chill. Dover Cliff. F. Wyville Home. VA
Last Ascent, The. John Lehmann. ChMP
Last autumn. Mourning for Li San. Po Chü-i. PoHN
Last Battle, The. *Unknown, tr. fr. Old French by* C. K. Scott Moncrieff. *Fr.* The Song of Roland. LiTW
Last Boats, The. Endre Ady, *tr. fr. Hungarian by* Antal Nyerges. LiTW
Last Bob White, The. Whitney Montgomery. BLA
Last Booke of the Ocean to Scinthia, The. Sir Walter Ralegh. *See* Ocean to Cynthia, The.
Last Bowstrings, The. Edward Lucas White. AA
Last bright star of dawn, The. Easter Day. Dionysios Solomos. *Fr.* Lambros. MoGP
Last Buccaneer, The. Charles Kingsley. BeLS; EtS; GoTP; HBV; MCCG; PoVP; SG; ShBV-1; VA
(Old Buccaneer, The.) CBPC; FaBoBe
(Pleasant Isle of Aves, The.) EV-5; LH
Last Buccaneer, The. Macaulay. EtS; EV-4; HBV; LH; SG
Last Call. Langston Hughes. NePoAm-2
Last came Anarchy; he rode. Shelley. *Fr.* The Masque of Anarchy. PoFr
Last came, and last did go. Milton. *Fr.* Lycidas. PoFr
Last Camp-Fire, The. Sharlot Mabridth Hall. HBV
Last Cargo. Silence Buck Bellows. EtS
Last chair finally was carried out, The. The House. Paula Nelson. GoYe
Last Chantey, The. Kipling. AnFE; BLV; BMEP; BoLiVe; ChMo; EPN; EtS; FaBoCh; GTBS; LoGBV; MBP; MoBrPo; MuP; OBVV; OtMeF; POTT; PoVP; SG; VA; VLEP
Last Chapter, The. Walter de la Mare. ChMo; MoBrPo
Last Charge at Appomattox, The. Henry Jerome Stockard. BlG
Last Chorus: "All is best, though we oft doubt." Milton. *See* All Is Best.
Last Chrysanthemum, The. Thomas Hardy. ChMo; CMP; LiTB; PG (1955 ed.); PoVP; TwCV; ViP
Last Cigar, The. *Unknown.* PA
Last cloud of a storm that is scattered and over. The Cloud. Pushkin. BoR
Last clouds in a throng above us sailing, The. Afanasi Fet, *tr. fr. Russian by* V. de S. Pinto. BoRS
Last Coachload, The. Walter de la Mare. SeCePo
Last Communion, The. Leo Ward. CAW; GoBC
Last Confession, A. Dante Gabriel Rossetti. ViPP
Last Confession, A. W. B. Yeats. LiTL; LO; TwP
Last Confessional. John Drinkwater. LBBV
Last Conqueror, The. James Shirley. *See* Victorious Men of Earth.
Last Corn Shock, The. Glenn Ward Dresbach. FaPON
Last Cowboy, The. Glenn Ward Dresbach. HiLiAm
Last Cradle Song, The. James Hogg. BOL
Last Cup of Canary, The. Helen Gray Cone. AA; PFY
Last Dance, The. May Riley Smith. BAP
Last Day, The. Dryden. *See* Poet's Resurrection.
Last Day, The. Daniel Sargent. CAW
Last Day of the Year, The. Annette von Droste-Hülshoff, *tr. fr. German by* James Edward Tobin. AnGP
Last Day of the Year, The. Alexander Smart. PCH
Last Day of the Year, The. Su T'ung-po, *tr. fr. Chinese by* Kenneth Rexroth. OnPC
Last Days, The. George Sterling. AnAmPo; CP; HBMV; LA; NP; NV; OBAV; TCAP
Last Days. Elizabeth Stoddard. AA; AnAmPo; LA
Last Days of Alice. Allen Tate. AmP; AtBAP; MOAP; OxBA; UnPo
Last Days of Pompeii, The, *sel.* Sir Edward Bulwer-Lytton.
Nydia's Song. OBVV
Last Defile, The. Amy Carmichael. MaRV
Last Dying Words of Bonnie Heck, The. William Hamilton. EBSV
Last Easter Jim put on his blue. Easter Zunday. William Barnes. PoVP
Last eve I passed [*or* I paused last eve] beside a [*or* the] blacksmith's door. The Anvil [of] God's Word [*or* Hammers and Anvil *or* God's Word]. John Clifford. BLPA; BLRP; BPP; MaRV; NeHB; OQP; PoToHe (new ed.); QP-1; WBLP
Last Evening. Rainer Maria Rilke, *tr. fr. German.* OnPM, *tr. by* Jessie Lemont; WaaP, *tr. by* C. F. MacIntyre
Last evening when I went to bed. Our Birthday. Marion Edey. SiSoSe
Last Fairy, The. Rosamund Marriott Watson. OBVV
Last Fairy-Tale, The. "Lambros Porphyras," *tr. fr. Modern Greek by* Rae Dalven. MoGP
Last farewell is on my tongue, The. The Vain Farewell. Paulus Silentiarius. OxBG
Last few prayers are done, The. Miserere. Herman Schefauer. BAP
Last Fierce Charge, The. *Unknown.* ViBoFo
Last Fight, The. Homer, *pr. tr. fr. Greek by* Andrew Lang, Walter Leaf, *and* Ernest Myers. *Fr.* The Iliad, XXII. OxBG
(Death of Hector, The, *tr. by* George Chapman.) OBS
(Slaying of Hector, The.) GrPE, *longer sel., tr. by* F. L. Lucas; GrR, *pr. tr. by* Lang, Leaf, *and* Myers
("Thus as he spoke, his sharp-edged sword he drew," *longer sel., tr. by* the Earl of Derby.) GrPo
("Thus they throughout the city, scared like fawns," *longer sel., pr. tr. by* Lang, Leaf, *and* Myers.) GrL
Last Fight, The. Lewis Frank Tooker. AA; FaBoBe; MDAH
Last Fire. Dante Gabriel Rossetti. The House of Life, XXX. PoVP; ViPo
Last, for December, houses on the plain. Sonnets of the Months: December. Folgore da San Gemignano. AWP; LyPI
Last Frontier, The. John Gould Fletcher. InPo; MOAP
Last Fruit off an Old Tree, The, *sels.* Walter Savage Landor.
On His Seventy-fifth Birthday. AEV; AnEnPo; AnFE; BEL; BLV; BoLiVe; BPN; CoEV; EmBrPo; EPN; EPP; InP; InPo; LiTB; MaRV; OAEP; PFE; PIAE; PIR; PoE; PreP; SeCeV; TOP; TreF; TrGrPo; TyEnPo; WHA; WP
(Dying Speech of an Old Philosopher.) ViBoPo
(End, The.) EV-4; SeCePo
(Envoi.) FaBoEn
(Finis.) BCEP; BTP; GTBS-W; OBEV; OBVV; OnPP; PC
("I strove with none, for none was worth my strife.") CaAE; ChTr; EG; EnRP; GTBS; GTML; GTSL; HBV; LEAP; MCCG
(Introduction: "I strove with none, for none was worth my strife.") EnLi-2
(Lyrics and Epigrams.) CBOV; ERP
(On Himself.) VA
"There falls with every wedding chime." SeCePo; VA
Last Furrow, The. Edwin Markham. AA
Last Gate, The. Stella Mead. BoTP
Last Gloucesterman, The. Gordon Grant. EtS
Last glow from the orchid candle now fails, The. A Dream of Chiangnan. Huang-fu Sung. OnPM
Last Good-by, The. Louise Chandler Moulton. AA; LBAP
Last Guest, The. Frances Shaw. HBMV; NP
Last heiress she of many a rood. Miss Penelope Leith. Walter C. Smith. EBSV
Last Hero, The. G. K. Chesterton. OtMeF
Last Hill. Edith Mirick. ChIP
Last Hound, The. Howard McKinley Corning. MuM
Last Hour, The. Ethel Clifford. HBV; NLK
Last Hour, The. Robert Ervin Howard. DaM
Last Hour, The. Henry Augustus Rawes. CAW
Last Hour of Faustus, The. Christopher Marlowe. *See* End of Dr. Faustus, The.
Last Hour of Leave. Arthur Gordon. LoPo
Last Hunt, The. William Roscoe Thayer. AA; FaBoBe; HBV
Last Hymn, The. "Marianne Farningham." BLPA; PTA-1
Last Instructions to a Painter, *sels.* Andrew Marvell.
Charles II. OBS
Dutch in the Medway, The. OBS
Last Invocation, The. Walt Whitman. AmP; AnFE; APA; APW; BLV; BoLiVe; CoAnAm; GTBS-D; HBV; IAP; LBAP; MAP; MaRV; MoAmPo; MOAP; NeMA; OnAP;

OQP; OxBA; PoEL-5; QP-1; RiBV; TCAP; TOP; TrGrPo; TrPWD
(Imprisoned Soul, The.) OBEV; WGRP
Last Journey, The. John Davidson. *Fr.* The Testament of John Davidson. BSV; GoTS
Last Journey. Enrique González Martínez, *tr. fr. Spanish by* Samuel Beckett. AnMP
Last Journey, A. Thomas Hardy. FAOV
Last Journey, The. Juan Ramón Jiménez, *tr. fr. Spanish by* Eleanor L. Turnbull. TeCS
Last Journey, The. Leonidas of Tarentum, *tr. fr. Greek by* Charles Merivale. AWP; JAWP; WBP
Last Journey, The. Sophocles, *tr. fr. Greek by* T. F. Higham. *Fr.* Antigone. OxBG
Last Journey of the Wooers, The. Homer, *tr. fr. Greek by* William Cowper. *Fr.* The Odyssey, XXIV. OxBG
(Limbo; the Shades of the Suitors.) GrR
Last Judgment, The. Revelation, XX: 11–XXI: 7, Bible, *N.T.* TreF
Last Judgment. Stanton A. Coblentz. MaRV
Last Judgment, The. Cynewulf, *tr. fr. Anglo-Saxon by* Charles W. Kennedy. *Fr.* Christ. AnOE
(Human Race Comes to Be Judged, The, *diff. tr.*) PoLi
Last Judgment. John Gould Fletcher. AWP; MOAP
Last Landlord, The. Elizabeth Akers Allen. AA
Last Lauch. Douglas Young. SeCePo
Last Leaf, The. Thomas Hardy. CMP
Last Leaf, The. Oliver Wendell Holmes. AA; AmPP; AnAmPo; AnFE; AnNE; APA; APW; BAV; BLV; CoAnAm; CoBA; FaBoBe; FaPON; HBV; HiLiAm; IAP; InP; LA; LBAP; LEAP; LHV; LPS-1; MCCG; MOAP; OBAV; OBVV; OnPP; OuHeWo; PFE; PFY; PG (1945 ed.); PIAE; PIR; PR; PTA-2; SeCeV; SiTL; TCAP; TOP; TreF; TSW; TSWC; WaKn; WBLP
Last Leap, The. Adam Lindsay Gordon. BoAu
Last Leave. Gilean Douglas. MuM
Last Leave of the Hills. Duncan Ban MacIntyre, *tr. fr. Gaelic.* GoTS
Last light has gone out of the world, except, The. Liberty. Edward Thomas. MoAB
Last Lines. Emily Brontë. BLV; BMEP; ChER; CoEV; EmBrPo; EnLi-2 (1939 ed.); EV-5; FaBoBe; GoBC; HBV; LEAP; MaRV; NeHB; OBEV; OBVV; PC; TrGrPo; WGRP; WHA
(Her Last Lines.) VA
(Lines.) CaAE
(No Coward Soul [Is Mine].) CBE; DiM; EnLi-2 (1949 ed.); EnLit; EPN; FaBoEn; FaFP; GTBS-W; GTIV; GTML; GTSL; LiTB; OAEP; OxBI; PoEL-5; PoVP; TreFS; TrPWD; ViP; VLEP
Last Lines. "Thomas Ingoldsby." *See* As I Laye a-Thynkynge.
Last Lines, *sel.* "Owen Meredith."
"Lord! if in love, though fainting oft, I have tended thy gracious vine." TrPWD
Last Lines. Egan O'Rahilly, *tr. fr. Irish by* Frank O'Connor. KiLC
Last Lines. Sir Walter Ralegh. *See* Conclusion, The.
Last Lines. Sergei Yesenin, *tr. fr. Russian by* C. M. Bowra. BoRS
Last Lines of the Dunciad. Pope. *Fr.* The Dunciad, LV. GEPC
Last Longhorn, The. *At. to* R. W. Hall. CoSo; CSF
Last Love. Feodor Ivanovich Tyutchev, *tr. fr. Russian.* LiTW, *tr. by* Vladimir Nabokov; TrRV, *tr. by* Babette Deutsch; WaL, *tr. by* Sir Cecil Kisch
Last Man, The, *sels.* Thomas Lovell Beddoes.
Crocodile, A. AnFE; NBE
Fragment: "Or I will burst/ Damnation's iron egg, my tomb." RO
Last Man, The. Thomas Campbell. BSV; EnRP; EV-4; OBRV; UnW
Last Man, The. Thomas Hood. ERP; NBE; OBRV; RO
Last March, an angel of the night. A Son in December. Frank Kendon. POTE
Last Mathematician. Hyman Edelstein. CaP
Last May a Braw Wooer. Burns. EnLi-2; PCN
Last Meeting of Pocahontas and the Great Captain, The. Margaret Junkin Preston. GA; MC; PAH
Last Memory, The. Arthur Symons. HBV
Last Minstrel, The. Sir Walter Scott. *Fr.* The Lay of the Last Minstrel. TreFS
(Minstrel, The.) EV-4
("Way was long, the wind was cold, The.") OTPC, *abr.*
Last month of the winter was for the most part clear and mild, The. Poems Translated from the Chinese. *Unknown, tr. by* John Francis Davis. RO
Last Mowing, The. Robert Frost. InP
Last Music, The. Lionel Johnson. GTIV; PoVP
Last Night. George Darley. GTIV; HBV; OnYI
Last Night, The. Orrick Johns. PR; TBM
Last Night. Christian Winther, *tr. fr. Danish by* Theophilus Marzials. OlF; VA
Last night. Sky. Betty Shippe. DDA
Last night a song woke in my silent room. In the Silence of Night. Francis Jammes. TrFP
Last night a sword-light in the sky. Stone Trees. John Freeman. LBBV; MBP; TCPD
Last night a wind from Lammermoor came roaring up the glen. The Raiders. Will H. Ogilvie. EBSV; ShBV-2
Last night, against the wall of the moon. Roses. J. Corson Miller. CAW
Last night, ah, yesternight, betwixt her lips and mine. Non Sum Qualis Eram Bonae sub Regno Cynarae [*or* Cynara]. Ernest Dowson. AnEnPo; AnFE; AWP; BeLS; BLPA; BLV; BMEP; CaAE; EnLi-2; EnLit; EnLoPo; EPP; FaBoBe; FaFP; GTBS-D; GTBS-W; GTML; HBV; InPo; LBBV; LEAP; LiTB; LiTG; LiTL; LiTM (rev. ed.); LO; LoPo; MBP; MoBrPo; NeHB; NeMA; OBEV (new ed.); OBMV; OBVV; OtMeF; PG; PoFS; PoRA; POTT; PoVP; PreP; TreF; TrGrPo; UnPo; ViBoPo; ViPP; VLEP
Last night Alicia wore a Tuscan bonnet. Alicia's Bonnet. Elisabeth Cavazza Pullen. AA
Last night along the river banks. The Boats Are Afloat. Chu Hsi. OnPC
Last night, among his fellow roughs. The Private of the Buffs. Sir Francis Hastings Doyle. BMEP; EV-5; GTBS; HBV; InP; LH; LPS-2; OBEV (new ed.); OBVV; PoVP; VA
Last night as I lay on the prairie. The Cowboy's Dream. Charles J. Finger. CoSo; CSF; IHA; MaC; YT
Last night, as I slept. Spring Dreams. Ts'en Ts'an. PoHN
Last night as I was marching on the road. Fata Morgana. Kathleen Raine. MoP
Last night, as through the crowd on Market Street. Glimpses. Roy Helton. HBMV
Last night at black midnight I woke with a cry. The Ghosts of the Buffaloes. Vachel Lindsay. AnAmPo; AnEnPo; CoBA; LA; MAP; MoAmPo; NePA; PreP; RG; TCPD
Last night, by the side of the mountain lake. The Lost Shoe. Norah M. Holland. CPG
Last night for the first time since you were dead. To L. H. B. Katherine Mansfield. AnNZ; HBMV
Last night God barr'd the portals of the East. Holiday. Henry Dawson Lowry. OBVV
Last night he lay within my arm. The Mother. Isabel Ecclestone Mackay. CPG
Last night I crept across the snow. Prayer. John Farrar. ChrBoLe; OTPC (1946 ed.); PoRL; SDH
Last night I did not fight for sleep. In Hospital; Poona. Alun Lewis. MoPW; NeBP; SeCePo
Last night I got to thinking, when I couldn't go to sleep. Thanksgiving Night. Wilbur Nesbit. DD; HH; PEDC
Last night I heard a *rat-tat-too.* Rain Riders. Clinton Scollard. GaP; TiPo
Last night I heard him in the woods. The Woodpecker. Joyce Sambrook. BoTP
Last night I heard the eager rain. No One Knows the Countryside. Struthers Burt. TBM
Last night I kissed you with a brutal might. Sonnets of a Portrait Painter, XXXVII. Arthur Davison Ficke. AnAmPo; LA
Last night I lay a-sleeping. The Holy City. Frederick Edward Weatherly. BLRP; WBLP
Last night I lay in an open field. Starlight. J. C. Squire. PtOT
Last night I looked into a dream; 'twas drawn. A Dream. Thomas Lovell Beddoes. HoPM
Last night I saw a Silver Road. The Silver Road. Hamish Hendry. BoTP
Last night I saw the monster near; the big. The White Monster. W. H. Davies. LiTB
Last night I saw the Pleiades again. The Pleiades. Arthur Adams. BoAu
Last night I saw you in my sleep. Bad Dreams. Robert Browning. OAEP; PoVP
Last night I saw you in the sky. Starfish. Winifred Welles. FaPON; SiSoSe
Last night I supped on lobster. The Dream. *Unknown.* OxBoLi
Last night I tossed and could not sleep. God Prays. Angela Morgan. GrCo-2; MaRV; WGRP
Last night I was sleeping, dear mother. The Hawthorne Tree. *Unknown.* ABS
Last Night I Woke. Sir Edmund Gosse. LoPo
(Fear of Death, The.) LBBV
Last night in a land of triangles. Zalinka. Tom MacInnes. BoCaPo; PeCV
Last night in my sleep, I saw. The Dream. Georgios Vizinos. MoGP
Last night in sleep I seemed a king. Voltaire, *tr. fr. French.* BoHiPo
Last night, in snowy gown and glove. At the Comedy. Arthur Stringer. HBV
Last night in the open shippen. Christmas Day. Andrew Young. AlDL

Last night it was the whip-poor-will. A Southern Whip-Poor-Will. Clinton Scollard. BLA
Last night lingers in the west, The. Influence. Robert Haven Schauffler. CAG
Last night, my darling, as you slept. Some Time. Eugene Field. MOAH
Last night my fayre resolv'd to goe. *Unknown.* SeCSL
Last night my friend—he says he is my friend. I Hear It Said. Barbara Young. BLPA; NeHB
Last night my kisses drowned in the softness of black hair. Black Hair. Muhammadji. LiTW
Last night my little boy confessed to me. Two Prayers. Andrew Gillies. BLRP; MaRV; PoToHe
Last Night of Winter, The. Winifred Welles. NP
Last night rain fell over the scarred plateau. Dawn on the Somme. Robert Nichols. POTE
Last night returning from my twilight walk. A Ballad of Past Meridian. George Meredith. EV-5; POTT; PoVP
Last night that she lived, The. Emily Dickinson. AmP; AmPP; AnFE; APA; CoAnAm; CoBA; CoV; ExPo; GTBS-D; LiTA; NePA; OxBA; PoEL-5; TwP
Last night the carol-singers came. The Carol Singers. Margaret G. Rhodes. BoTP
Last night the gypsies came. Gypsies. Rachel Field. BoTP; GoBP; PoRh
Last night the nightingale woke me. Last Night. Christian Winther. OlF; VA
Last night the southwest wind shook through the trees. Burning Leaves. Charles Edward Eaton. NoCaPo (rev. ed.)
Last night the thunder began to roll. Broadcasting. Mildred D. Shacklett. GFA
Last night the wind was up to tricks. Picking Up Sticks. Eleanor Farjeon. PCH
Last night they came across the river and. The Enemies. Elizabeth Jennings. MoPW
Last night 'twas witching Hallowe'en. The Charms. Emma A. Opper. DD
Last night was the second time you have appeared in my dream. To a Person. Haruo Sato. PoLJ
Last night we marked the twinkling stars. The End of the Drought. Peter McArthur. CPG
Last night when all the stars were still. Three White Birds of Angus. Eleanor Rogers Cox. HBMV
Last Night, When Fevered Minutes. Ronald Hambleton. BoCaPo
Last night when I had fallen asleep, wearied with our sea-toils. Dream of a Golden Catch. Theocritus. *Fr.* Idylls, XXI. GrR
Last night, when my tired eyes were shut with sleep. A Gazelle. Richard Henry Stoddard. AA
Last night, while we were fast asleep. New Year's Day. Rachel Field. TiPo
Last night, within my dreaming. Pine Music. Kate Louise Brown. BoTP
Last night, within the stifling train. Martial in Town. Andrew Lang. POTT; PtP
Last night you stirred in your sleep as the night went through. Before Dawn. Elinor Chipp. HBMV
Last night your heart was mine. Wisdom. Virginia Lawrence. PR
Last Ode, The. Kipling. MeRV
"Last of England, The! O'er the sea, my dear." For the Picture, "The Last of England." Ford Madox Brown. VA
Last of His Tribe, The. Henry Clarence Kendall. VA
Last of last words spoken is, Good-bye, The. Good-bye. Walter de la Mare. FaBoEn
Last of October, The. Fall. Aileen L. Fisher. TiPo (1952 ed.); YeAr
Last of our steers on the board has been spread, The. The Foray. Sir Walter Scott. EmBrPo; EPN
Last of the *Eurydice*, The. Sir Joseph Noel Paton. VA
Last of the Flock, The. Wordsworth. CG
Last of your tribe and long departed hence. Commandant's Isle. William Douw Lighthall. CPG
Last Oracle, The. Swinburne. BMEP; VLEP
Last pale gleam of spring, The. Farewell to Spring. Hsü Ying Yü. PoHN
Last Parting of Hector and Andromache, The. Homer. *See* Parting of Hector and Andromache, The.
Last Party, The. *Unknown.* CAG
Last peaks of the world, beyond all seas. The Edge of the World. Sophocles. OxBG
Last Pilot, The. Duncan Tovey. POT
Last Piper, The. Edward J. O'Brien. BAP; SBMV
Last Plea. Jean Starr Untermeyer. TrPWD
Last Poem. Po Chü-i, *tr. fr. Chinese by* Arthur Waley. TrCh
Last Port, The. Frank Wilmot. BoAu
Last Portage, The, *sel.* Wilson MacDonald.
"As the stars go out so let me go." MaRV
Last pose flickered, failed, The. Rain after a Vaudeville Show. Stephen Vincent Benét. MAP; MoAmPo
Last Prayer, The. Wilfred Campbell. CPG
Last Prayer, A. Helen Hunt Jackson. AA; MaRV; OBAV; PCD; TrPWD
(Prayer, A: "Father, I scarcely dare to pray.") OQP; PraP; QP-2
Last Prayer. Christina Rossetti. *See* Before the Beginning.
Last Quarter Moon of the Dying Year, The. Jonathan Henderson Brooks. CDC
Last Rally. Clifford J. Laube. JKCP (1955 ed.)
Last Redoubt, The. Alfred Austin. HBV
Last Refuge. Michelangelo, *tr. fr. Italian by* George Santayana. LiTW
(Three Poems, 2.) AWP
Last Request, The. Philetas, *tr. fr. Greek by* T. F. Higham. OxBG
Last Reservation, The. Walter Learned. AA; PaA; PAH
Last Resort, The. *Unknown, tr. fr. Danish by* E. M. Smith-Dampier. BoDaBa
Last Review, The. Emily J. Bugbee. BLPA
Last Rhyme of True Thomas, The. Kipling. OtMeF
Last Ride Together, The. Robert Browning. BEL; BMEP; BoLiVe; BPN; CBOV; EM-2; EmBrPo; EnLi-2; FiP; GEPC; GTML; GTSL; HBV; LEAP; LiTB; LoBV (1949 ed.); OAEP; OBEV; OBVV; OuHeWo; PoEL-5; PoVP; RiBV; TyEnPo; UnPo (1st ed.); ViPP; VLEP; WHA
Last Ride Together, The (from Her Point of View). James Kenneth Stephen. BOHV; CenHV; PA
Last Romantic, The. Alexander Laing. AnAmPo; LA
Last Rose, The. John Davidson. OBEV (1st ed.)
Last Rose of Summer, The. Thomas Moore. *See* 'Tis the Last Rose of Summer.
Last Round, The. Anna Wickham. MBP; MoBrPo
Last Saturday night I called at the house. Johnny McCardner. *Unknown.* OuSiCo
Last sea-thing dredged by sailor Time from Space. Australia. Bernard O'Dowd. BoAu; NeLNL
Last Sleep, The. Charles Hanson Towne. TBM
Last Snow. Andrew Young. AlDL; MoBrPo (1942 ed.); POTE; StaSt
Last snow is going, The. Spring. Harry Behn. TiPo
Last Song, The. Eileen Duggan. CAW
Last Song. James Guthrie. TiPo
Last Song of Callicles. Matthew Arnold. *See* Callicles' Song.
Last Song to a Girl of the Waterfront. Otto D'Sola, *tr. fr. Spanish by* Angel Flores. AnCL
Last Sonnet. Keats. *See* Bright Star, Would I Were Steadfast as Thou Art.
Last Spinning Wheel, The. Hubbard Fulton Page. NoCaPo
Last Spring. Thomas S. Jones, Jr. Four Sonnets, II. SBMV
Last Stand at the Ships, The. Homer, *tr. fr. Greek by* F. L. Lucas. *Fr.* The Iliad, XV. GrPE
Last Stanzas of "The Bush." Bernard O'Dowd. *Fr.* The Bush. BoAu
("Where is Australia, singer, do you know?") PoFr
Last step taken found your heft, The. To a Thinker. Robert Frost. PoLFOT; TwHP
Last sunbeam, The/ Lightly falls from the finished Sabbath. Dirge for Two Veterans [*or* Two Veterans]. Walt Whitman. BLV; BoLiVe; GN; IAP; LH; MDAH; MoAmPo (1950 ed.); NeMA; PIAE; PoEL-5
Last Supper, The. St. John, XIII: 1–XVI: 17, Bible, *N.T.* OuHeWo
Last Supper, The. Joaquin Miller. StJW
Last Supper, The. Oscar Williams. FaFP; GTBS-W; LiTA; LiTM; NePA; TwAmPo
Last Supper. Elinor Wylie. ChMo
Last Supper; Jesus to Judas. S. Foster Damon. TBM
Last tall son of Lot and Bellicent, The. Gareth and Lynette. Tennyson. *Fr.* Idylls of the King. HeT
Last Tavern, The. Frances Beatrice Taylor. CPG
Last, the long-haired casuarina, The. Casuarina. Roland Robinson. BoAV
Last thin acre of stalks that stood, The. Immortal. Mark Van Doren. MAP; MoAmPo; PoeMoYo; TBM
Last Thoughts of a Fighting Man. Frances Angermayer. *See* Conversion.
Last time I slept with the queen, The. Dylan Thomas. SiTL
Last to leave—the first to go, The. The First Division Marches. Grantland Rice. DDA; PaA; YaD
Last Tournament, The. Tennyson. *Fr.* Idylls of the King. ViPo
Last Tourney, The. Frederic F. Van de Water. BLP; HBMV
Last Trams, *sel.* Kenneth Slessor.
"Then, from the skeletons of trams." MoAuPo
Last Trial, The. Petrarch. *See* Set Me Where Phoebus' Heat.
Last Trial, The. *Unknown.* OBSC
Last Verses. Thomas Chatterton. BCEP; PoFS; TrGrPo
Last Verses. Michael Drayton. *See* Soe Well I Love Thee.
Last Verses. William Motherwell. HBV
Last Verses. Edmund Waller. *See* Old Age.
Last Voyage, The, *sels.* Alfred Noyes. The Torch Bearers, **III.**

Messages, *fr.* XIII. GoBC
Strong City, The, *fr.* Dedication. GoBC
Under the Pyrenees, *fr.* Dedication. GoBC
You That Sing in the Blackthorn, *fr.* II. GoBC
(Bird Song.) BLA
(Tell Me You That Sing.) POTT
(Unconscious, The.) MM
Last Voyage, The. Katharine Tynan. HBMV
Last Voyage, The. Henrik Wergeland, *tr. fr. Norwegian by* Charles W. Stork. AnNoLy
Last Voyage of Sir Francis Drake, and Sir John Hawkins, The, *abr.* Charles Fitzgeffrey. *Fr.* Sir Francis Drake. SG
Last Voyage of the Fairies, The. William H. Davenport Adams. HBVY; PRWS
Last Walk in Autumn, The. Whittier. IAP
Last Week of February (1890). Robert Bridges. POTT
Last week—the Lord be praised for all His mercies. Letter from a Missionary. Whittier. IAP
Last Whiskey Cup, The. Paul Engle. ATP; YaD
Last wild element is mastered now, The. The Discipline of Consequences. Eileen Duggan. JKCP (1955 ed.)
Last winter a snowman; and after snow an iceman. Farmer. Padraic Fallon. OxBI
Last winter we were/ short of firewood. A Letter to Hitler. James Laughlin. LiTA; WaP
Last winter when the snow was deep. One Night. Marchette Chute. ChBR
Last Wish, The. "Owen Meredith." LoPS; OBEV (1st ed.); OBVV
Last Word, The. Matthew Arnold. BEL; BLV; BMEP; BoLiVe; BPN; BPP; EM-2; EnLi-2; EPP; FaBoEn; FiP; GTBS-D; HBV; MaRV; MCCG; NBE; OBVV; PG; PIAE; PoEL-5; PoFS; PoRA; PoVP; PreP; SoV; TCEP; TOP; TrGrPo; ViPo; VLEP
"They out-talked thee, hissed thee, tore thee." GrCo-1
Last Word, The. Damagetus, *tr. fr. Greek by* F. L. Lucas. GrPE
Last Word, A. Ernest Dowson. MBP; MoBrPo; PoVP; VLEP
Last Word, The. Frederic Lawrence Knowles. HBV
Last Word of a Bluebird, The. Robert Frost. FaPON; StVeCh (1955 ed.); TiPo; WhBS
Last Words. Annette von Droste-Hülshoff, *tr. fr. German by* Margarete Münsterberg. CAW
Last Words, The. Maurice Maeterlinck, *tr. fr. French by* Frederick York Powell. AWP; JAWP; WBP
Last Words before Winter. Louis Untermeyer. GoTP; MAP; MoAmPo; NeMA
Last Words; Napoleon and Wellington, *sel.* Arthur Hugh Clough.
Serve in Thy Post, 4 *ll.* PGD
Last Words of Byron. George Chapman. *Fr.* The Tragedy of Charles, Duke of Byron, V, i. CoEV
Last Words of Don Henriquez, The. Zalman Schneour, *tr. fr. Yiddish by* Joseph Leftwich. TrJP
Last Words of Juggling Jerry, The. George Meredith. *See* Juggling Jerry.
Last Words to a Dumb Friend. Thomas Hardy. OAEP (2d ed.); PoC; PoFS
Last Words to Miriam. D. H. Lawrence. CoBMV
Last year at the Lantern Festival. The Lantern Festival. Ou-yang Hsiu. ChLP
Last year I trod these fields with Di. Mrs. Smith. Frederick Locker-Lampson. BOHV; HBV
Last year, my Love, it was my hap. The Noble Art of Murdering. Thackeray. BMEP
Last year the war was in the northeast. War. Li Po. ChTr
Last year we fought by the head-stream of the So-kan. The Nefarious War. Li Po. WoL
Last year we fought by the springs of San-kan River. Fighting on the South Frontier. Li Po. WhP
Last year when I accompanied you. To a Traveler. Su T'ung-po. HoPM; OnPC
Last year, when I lay sick. Drunk Again. Po Chü-i. PoHN
Last year you went with your troops to Tibet. Thinking of a Friend Lost in the Tibetan War. Chang Chi. BoFr
Lastlie stode warre in glittering armes yclad. A Vision of War. Thomas Sackville. *Fr.* Induction to "A Mirror for Magistrates." FaBoEn
Lastly came Winter clothèd all in frize. Winter. Spenser. *Fr.* The Faerie Queene, VII, 7. GN; OTPC
Lat never a man a wooing wend. King Henry. *Unknown.* BaBo; ESPB; OBB
Lat Noman Booste of Konnyng nor Vertu. John Lydgate. *See* Like a Midsummer Rose.
Lat Take a Cat. Chaucer. *Fr.* The Canterbury Tales: The Manciple's Tale. ChTr
Late. Helen Salz. GoYe
Late Air. Elizabeth Bishop. FiMAP
Late April and you are three; today. W. D. Snodgrass. Heart's Needle, II. NePoEA
Late at een, drinkin' the wine. The Dowie Houms [*or* Dens] o' Yarrow [*or* The Braes o' Yarrow]. *Unknown.* BaBo; BSV; CBOV; EBSV; ESPB; GoTS; OBB; OBEV; OBS; PCN
Late at morning's prime I roved. A Hidden Rose-Tree. Marguerite A. Power. TIP
Late Autumn. William Allingham. IrPN
Late Autumn. Sakutaro Hagiwara, *tr. fr. Japanese by* Takamichi Ninomiya *and* D. J. Enright. PoLJ
Late Autumn. A. M. Sullivan. GoBC
Late Autumn. Andrew Young. HaMV; MoVE
Late Comer. Fanny de Groot Hastings. GoYe
Late Corner. Langston Hughes. NePoAm-2
Late in an evening forth as I went. Archie o' Cawfield. *Unknown.* BaBo (A *vers.*); ESPB
Late in March, when the days are growing longer. Honey Harvest. Martin Armstrong. MM; TwCV
Late, in the louring sky, red, fiery, streaks. James Thomson. *Fr.* The Seasons: Winter. FaBoEn
Late in the month a rough east wind had sway. The Charming of the East Wind. Charles Tennyson Turner. EnSW
Late Lark Twitters, A. W. E. Henley. *See* Margaritae Sorori.
Late las' night I was a-makin' my rounds. Bad Man Ballad. *Unknown.* ABF
Late, Last Rook, The. Ralph Hodgson. MBP; MoBrPo
Late, late: and grey day darkens into eve. Evening. Ch'en Tzu-ang. OnPM
Late, late. But lift now the diffident fiddle and fill. Spring-Dance. W. R. Rodgers. PoN
Late, late, so late! and dark the night and chill. Too Late. Tennyson. *Fr.* Idylls of the King: Guinevere. MaRV; OQP; QP-2
Late Leaves. Walter Savage Landor. HBV; OBEV (1st ed.)
("Leaves are falling, The: so am I.") CaAE; EG; GTSE
Late lies the wintry sun abed. Winter-Time. Robert Louis Stevenson. GFA; GoTP; MBP; MoBrPo; StVeCh
Late Light. Edmund Blunden. EnLoPo
Late lingers Clephantis. And now begins to flicker. Broken Tryst. Paulus Silentiarius. GrPE
Late Love. Dorothy Wellesley. DiM
Late Massacre in Piedmont, The. Milton. *See* On the Late Massacre in Piedmont.
Late, my grandson! half the morning have I paced these sandy tracts. Locksley Hall Sixty Years After. Tennyson. EnLi-2 (1949 ed.); PoVP; ViPo; VLEP
Late November. Archibald Lampman. TwCV
Late October. Sara King Carleton. GoYe
Late October. Sara Teasdale. YeAr
Late of the jungle, wild and dim. Billiards. Walker Gibson. NePoAm
Late One Night. *Unknown.* *See* Bad Man Ballad.
Late, retarding, and unsettled season, The. Autumn; an Ode. Charles Gullans. NePoEA
Late Rising. Jacques Prévert, *tr. fr. French by* Selden Rodman. OnHM
Late Snow. J. C. Squire. PtOT
Late snow beats, A. Faces. Lola Ridge. MAP; MoAmPo (1942 ed.)
Late Spring, The. Louise Chandler Moulton. LPS-1
(Spring Is Late, The.) HBV
Late Summer, The. John Malcolm Brinnin. TwAmPo
Late summer changes to autumn. A Woman Standing by a Gate with an Umbrella. John Gould Fletcher. ChMo; CMP
Late Summer in the Country. Theocritus, *pr. tr. by* Walter Pater. *Fr.* Idylls, VII. OxBG
("Season of Mellow Fruitfulness," *tr. by* R. C. Trevelyan.) GrR
Late sun in the winter sky, The. Vision. Giosuè Carducci. OnPM
Late tired with woe, even ready for to pine. Astrophel and Stella, LXII. Sir Philip Sidney. EnLit; HBV; ReEn; SiPS
Late travelling along in London way. A Coxcomb. Joseph Hall. *Fr.* Virgidemiarum. EV-2
Late 'twas in June, the fleece when fully grown. Eclogue. Michael Drayton. *Fr.* The Shepherd's Garland. OBSC
Late When the Autumn Evening Fell. Sir Walter Scott. *Fr.* Waverley. EBSV
Late Winter. Hazel Hall. HBMV
Late Winter. J. P. McAuley. NeLNL
Late Winter. Philip Henry Savage. PCH
Late Wisdom. George Crabbe. *Fr.* Reflections. EV-3; HBV, *abr.*; OBEV, *abr.*; TrGrPo
("We've trod the maze of error round.") OBRV
Lately, alas! I knew a gentle boy. Sympathy. Henry David Thoreau. MOAP
Lately having escaped three-kinded death. A Birth. Muriel Rukeyser. FiMAP
Lately Our Songsters [*or* Poets] Loiter'd [*or* Loitered] in Green Lanes. Walter Savage Landor. BPN; EmBrPo; EPN; LiTB; PoEL-4; RiBV; RO

Lately Written by Thomas, Earl of Strafford. *Unknown.* EV-2
Later Antigonishes. Hughes Mearns.
Alibi. InMe
Crime Note. InMe
Frustrated Male. InMe; SiTL
Lady with Technique, The. FiBHP; InMe; SiTL; WhC
Me. InMe
Reveille. InMe; SiTL
Later Life, *sels.* Christina Rossetti.
"Did Adam love his Eve from first to last?" 3 *ll.*, *fr.* XV. LO
"Star Sirius and the Pole Star dwell afar," IX. VA
"To love and to remember; that is good," 4 *ll.*, *fr.* VII. LO
Tread Softly! All the Earth Is Holy Ground, X. PeBoSo
"We lack, yet cannot fix upon the lack," VI. VA
Later, to Cerinthus. Sulpicia, *tr. fr. Latin by* Hubert Creekmore. LaP
Latest Decalogue, The. Arthur Hugh Clough. BEL; BOHV; BPN; ChTr; CoEV; EmBrPo; EnLi-2 (1949 ed.); EnLit; EPN; ExPo; HoPM; InMe; LiTG; LoBV; OAEP; OBVV; OtMeF; PIAE; PoE; PoFS; PoVP; PreP; RiBV; SiTL; TOP; ViBoPo, 4 *add. ll.*; ViP, 4 *add. ll.*; ViPo; ViPP, 4 *add. ll.*; VLEP; WGRP
Latest, earliest, of the year. Primroses. Alfred Austin. BMEP; OBVV
Latet Anguis. *Unknown, at. to* William Cornish. OBEV (new ed.)
Lather and shave. Barber's Cry. *Unknown.* TrAS
Latin. *Unknown.* ChTr
Latin Hymn [to the Virgin]. Winthrop Mackworth Praed. CoBE; ERP
Latin is a dead tongue. Latin. *Unknown.* ChTr
Latin Lullaby. *Unknown. See* Lullaby: "Slumber, Jesu, o'er thy dreaming."
Latin Tongue, The. James J. Daly. CAW; GoBC
Latter Day, The. Thomas Hastings. AA
Latter Day, The. Thomas, Lord Vaux. PoLi
(Bethinking Himself of His End, Writeth Thus.) SiCE
Latter-Day Warnings. Oliver Wendell Holmes. *Fr.* The Autocrat of the Breakfast Table, *ch.* 1. IAP; OnAP; PCD
Latter Rain, The. Jones Very. AmP; GN; LPS-2; OxBA
Lattice at Sunrise, The. Charles Tennyson Turner. OBVV; VA
Laud of Saint Catherine, The. Swinburne. *Fr.* Siena. CAW
Laud to my Lord who gave thee all of loveliness. The Mock Caliph. *Unknown. Fr.* The Thousand and One Nights. EnLi-1
Lauda. Girolamo Benevieni, *tr. fr. Italian by* John Addington Symonds. CAW
Lauda Anima Mea. Psalms, CXLVI, Bible, *O.T.*, *tr. by* John Hopkins. ReIE
Lauda Sion, *much abr.* St. Thomas Aquinas, *tr. fr. Latin.* WHL
Laudate Dominum. Psalms, CL, Bible, *O.T.* ChTr
Laudate for Christmas. Prudentius, *tr. fr. Latin by* H. T. Henry. CAW
Laude, honor, praisingis, thankis infinite. The Difficulties of Translation. Gawin Douglas. *Fr.* Prologues to the Aeneid. GoTS
Lauded lilies of the field, The. Mrs. Seymour Fentolin. Oliver Herford. HBMV
Lauds. Leonard Mahoney. SaFP
Laugh and Be Merry. John Masefield. EnLit; FaFP; MBP; MoBrPo; NeMA; PC; PoeT
Laugh and Sing (" 'Tis mirth that fills the veins with blood"). Beaumont *and* Fletcher. *See* Mirth.
Laugh, and the World Laughs with You. Ella Wheeler Wilcox. *See* Solitude.
Laugh at all my dreams, my dearest. Credo. Saul Tchernichowsky. LiTW
Laugh in Church, A. *Unknown.* PTA-2
Laugh is just like sunshine, A. Sunshine and Music. Ripley Dunlap Saunders. PoToHe (new ed.)
Laugh It Off. Henry Rutherford Elliot. WBLP
Laugh not fond foole cause I a face. *Unknown.* SeCSL
Laugh now but by tomorrow you may weep. After Laughter. Grace Buchanan Sherwood. GoYe
Laugh on, laugh on at all the dreams. I Believe. Saul Tchernichowsky. TrJP
Laughed at the old deliberate ways. Repression. Timothy Corsellis. WaP
Laughters, The. Louis Untermeyer. GDAH
Laughin' wif yo' dinnah in de cohneh ob yo' mouf. A Dixie Lullaby. Strickland W. Gillilan. LHV
Laughing and teasing. A Glimpse of Beauty. Chien Liang Tse. OnPM
Laughing Ann. A. P. Herbert. OnPP
Laughing at Fortune. Michael Drayton. *See* Idea: "I hear some say, 'This man is not in love.'"
Laughing Chorus. *Unknown. See* Flower Chorus.
Laughing Corn. Carl Sandburg. MOAP; TCAP
Laughing Hyena, by Hokusai, The. D. J. Enright. PoN
Laughing It Out. William Stanley Braithwaite. Sandy Star and Willie Gee, II. BANP
Laughing knot of village maids, A. The Shaded Pool. Norman Gale. HBV; OBVV
Laughing, panting little Pan, A. The Birthday. Witter Bynner. FAOV
Laughing reds that children love, toy wagon wheels and tops, The. Childhood Reds. Don Blanding. DDA
Laughing Song. Blake. *Fr.* Songs of Innocence. BoTP; BrR; CBOV; EiPP; EnLi-2; EnRP; GoTP; KN; OTPC; PCH; PoRh; SUS; TiPo; ThWaDe; WaKn; WP
(When the Green Woods Laugh.) CH
Laughing sun has followed on the rain, The. The Magpie. Tristan Klingsor. TrFP
Laughing Time. William Jay Smith. FaPON
Laughing Willow, The. Oliver Herford. BOHV; HBV
Laughter. Isabella Valancy Crawford. CaP; OCL
Laughter. Olive Enoch. BoTP
Laughter. Johan Ludvig Runeberg, *tr. fr. Swedish by* Charles W. Stork. AnSL
Laughter and Death. Wilfrid Scawen Blunt. The Love Sonnets of Proteus, XCI. BMEP; MBP; MoBrPo (1942 ed.); PoMa; VA
Laughter and Tears. Tertius van Dyke. MaRV
Laughter in Heaven. Sister Mary Angeline. PraNu
Laughter not time destroyed my voice. The Friends of His Youth. W. B. Yeats. *Fr.* A Man Young and Old. AtBAP
Laughter of the lesser lynx, The. The Lesser Lynx. E. V. Rieu. CenHV; FiBHP
Laughter of the Spheres, The. Herman Eugene Kittredge. MuM
Laughter to the Last. Julianus, *tr. fr. Greek by* F. L. Lucas. GrPE
Laughter wears a lilied gown. Laughter. Isabella Valancy Crawford. CaP; OCL
Laughter, with us, is no great undertaking. Mrs. Reece Laughs. Martin Armstrong. POTE
Laughter without a home. Laughter. Johan Ludvig Runeberg. AnSL
Launch Out into the Deep. Ida Norton Munson. ChIP
Launched upon ether float the worlds secure. Authority. William Reed Huntington. AA
Laung time sense Ah tole 'bout de Haug-eye man. The Haug-Eye Man. Opie Read. BoHiPo
Laura. Thomas Campion. *See* Rose-cheeked Laura.
Laura, *sels.* Robert Tofte.
"As burnish'd gold, such are my sovereign's hears." ReIE
"Down from the neck unto that dainty breast." ReIE
"In love his kingdom great two fools there be." ElSeCe; ReIE; TuPP
"Rich damask roses in fair cheeks do bide." EIL
"Strange is this thing! My horse I cannot make." ReIE; TuPP
"Two winds, one calm, another fierce to see." ReIE
"Unto thy favor, which when nature formed." TuPP
"What time with brow the loveliest gins to scowl." ReIE
"When I did part from thee the other night." ReIE
"When she was born she came with smiling eye." ElSeCe; ReIE; TuPP
Laura Sleeping. Charles Cotton. ElSeCe; FaBoEn; LoBV; OBS; SeCL; ViBoPo
Laura Sleeping. Louise Chandler Moulton. AA
Laura Waits for Him in Heaven. Petrarch, *pr. tr. fr. Italian by* J. M. Synge. *Fr.* Sonnets to Laura: To Laura in Death. OBMV; TwCV
Laurana's Song. Richard Hovey. AA
Laura's Song. Oliver Madox Brown. OBVV; VA
Laureate, The. William Aytoun. PA
Laureate, The. Robert Graves. FaBoTw
(Wretch, The.) MoP
Laureate of Dulness, The. Dryden. *See* Shadwell.
Laureate's Log, A. *Unknown.* PA
Laureate's Tourney. William Aytoun. PA
Laurel-crowned Horatius. Lauriger Horatius [*or* Time's Flying]. *Unknown.* HBV; OnPM
Laurel-leaf which you this day do wear, The. Amoretti, XXVIII. Spenser. PeBoSo; ReIE
Laurella, *sel.* John Todhunter.
Morning in the Bay of Naples. TIP
Laurels and Immortelles. *Unknown.* BLPA
Laurence Bloomfield in Ireland, *sel.* William Allingham.
Ballytullagh. IrPN
Laurentians, The. Arthur S. Bourinot. OCL
Lauriger Horatius. *Unknown, tr. fr. Latin by* John Addington Symonds. HBV
(Time's Flying.) OnPM
Laus Deo. Robert Bridges. TriL
Laus Deo. Sydney Dobell. OBEV (1st ed.)
Laus Deo! Whittier. AmP; AmPP; AnNE; CoBA; CoV; DD; IAP; LPS-2; MC; PaA; PAH; PoFr; TriL
Laus Infantium. William Canton. HBV; VA
Laus Mortis. Frederic Lawrence Knowles. HBV

Laus Veneris. Louise Chandler Moulton. AA; HBV; OBAV; VLEP

Laus Veneris. Swinburne. EmBrPo; PoVP; ViPP
"Ah, love, there is no better life than this," *sel.* PIAE

Laus Virginitatis. Arthur Symons. EnLoPo

Lausanne. Thomas Hardy. EmBrPo; FaBoTw; TriL; ViPo

Laval; Noble Educator. John Daniel Logan. CPG

Lavender. Alfred Noyes. VOD

Lavender Beds, The. William Brighty Rands. CBPC

Lavender Bush, The. Elizabeth Fleming. BoTP

Lavender Cowboy, The, *with music.* *Unknown.* CoSo

Lavender for old loves. The Answer. Sara Hamilton Birchall. NLK

Lavender, lavender. Lavender. Alfred Noyes. VOD

Lavender's Blue. *Unknown.* CH; HH; LiTL
("Lavender's blue, diddle, diddle," *sl. diff.*) OxNR

Lavender's for Ladies. Patrick R. Chalmers. HBMV

Lavengro, *sel.* George Borrow.
"Life is sweet, brother." BBV (1951 ed.)

Lavinia. James Thomson. *Fr.* The Seasons: Autumn. OBEC

Lavish Kindness. Elinor Wylie. AtBAP; CrMA

Law, The. Abraham ibn Ezra, *tr. fr. Hebrew by* Alice Lucas. TrJP

Law against Lovers, The, *sel.* Sir William Davenant.
Wake All the Dead! What Ho! What Ho! FaBoCh; LoGBV; PoD; SeCePo; SeCL
(Song: "Wake all the dead!") LoBV

Law and Liberty. E. J. Cutler. PTA-2

Law firm commanding, A. Help Wanted. Franklin Waldheim. BLPA

Law is the true embodiment, The. The Susceptible Chancellor. W. S. Gilbert. *Fr.* Iolanthe. ALV; PoVP

Law like Love. W. H. Auden. CoBMV; FaBoTw; PoFS; PoLFOT
(Law, Say the Gardeners, Is the Sun.) MoAB; MoBrPo; TrGrPo

Law makes long spokes of the short stakes of men. Legal Fiction. William Empson. CoEV; ExPo; FaBoMo; LiTB; LiTM; MoP; MoVE; ReMP

Law of Averages, The. "Troubadour." FiBHP; InMe

Law of Jehovah is perfect, restoring the soul, The. *See* Law of the Lord is perfect, The.

Law of Love, The. John Oxenham. *Fr.* Chaos—and the Way Out. OQP; QP-2

Law of the Jungle, The. Kipling. *Fr.* The Second Jungle Book. BoChLi; LiTB; PoEL-5; PoVP; ShBV-1; VA

Law of the Lord [*or* Jehovah] is perfect, restoring the soul, The. The Law Within [*or* God's Precepts Perfect]. *Fr.* Psalm XIX, Bible, *O.T.* (*Moulton, Modern Reader's Bible*). BLRP; MaRV

Law of the Yukon, The. Robert W. Service. CaP; CPG; HBV; OCL; TreFS

Law, Say the Gardeners, Is the Sun. W. H. Auden. *See* Law like Love.

Law West of the Pecos, The. S. Omar Barker. IHA

Law Within, The. Psalms, XIX: 7–14, Bible, *O.T.* (*Moulton, Modern Reader's Bible*). MaRV

Lawd he thought he'd make a man, De. *See* Lord he thought he'd make a man, De.

Lawd, if I got my ticket, can I ride? If I Got My Ticket, Can I Ride? *Unknown.* OuSiCo

Lawd knows I'se glad fer ter see dis rain. After a Rain. Lucy Cherry Crisp. NoCaPo (rev. ed.)

Lawd, Lawd,/ Seems lak I heerd the *Joe Fowler* blow. The *Joe Fowler* Blues. *Unknown.* StDa

Lawful Wine. Hafiz, *tr. fr. Persian by* Walter Leaf. PeP

Lawgiver's Boast, The. Solon. *See* Rule of Fair Play.

Lawlands o' Holland, The. *Unknown.* *See* Lowlands of Holland, The.

Lawn as White as Driven Snow. Shakespeare. *Fr.* The Winter's Tale, IV, iii. ElSeCe; EM-1; EV-1; OAEP; OBSC; SiCE; ViBoPo; WP
(Autolycus' Song.) KN; LoBV
(Come Buy! [Come Buy!]) ElL; GaP
(Pedlar's Song.) CH
(Songs of Autolycus, The.) OTPC (1923 ed.)

Lawn-Mower. Dorothy W. Baruch. SUS

Lawn Roller, The. Robert Layzer. NePoEA

Lawns were dry in Euston park, The. The Fakenham Ghost. Robert Bloomfield. EV-3

Lawrence of Virtuous Father Virtuous Son. Milton. *See* To Mr. Lawrence.

Lawrence; the Last Crusade, *sel.* Selden Rodman.
"Out of the east the plane spun; over rolling." NAMP

Laws-a-massey, what have you done? Negro Reel. *Unknown.* AS

Laws are the secret avengers, The. The Avengers. Edwin Markham. MAP; MoAmPo; NeMA

Laws of God, the Laws of Man, The. A. E. Housman. Last Poems, XII. EmBrPo; EnLi-2 (1949 ed.); MoAB; MoBrPo; OxBoLi; PoLFOT; QS

Lawyer and Child. James Whitcomb Riley. FAOV

Lawyer asked Jesus a question, A. The Greatest Commandments. St. Matthew, Bible, *N.T.* GrCo-2

Lawyer in Search of Six Poets. *Unknown.* SiTL

Lawyer Patelin. *Unknown, pr. tr. fr. French.* LiA

Lawyers, Bob, know too much, The. The Lawyers Know Too Much. Carl Sandburg. HBMV; MOAP; YaD

Lawyer's Farewell to His Muse, The. Sir William Blackstone. EV-3

Lawyer's head to draw a crafty deed, A. Description of Cozeners. George Whetstone. TuPP

Lawyer's Invocation to Spring. Henry Howard Brownell. BOHV; LPS-3; PR

Lawyers Know Too Much, The. Carl Sandburg. HBMV; MOAP; YaD

Lay a Garland on My Hearse. Beaumont *and* Fletcher. *See* Aspatia's Song.

Lay aside phrases; speak as in the night. This Is Not Death. Humbert Wolfe. MBP; MoBrPo

Lay by your pleading, Love lies a-bleeding. *Unknown.* LO

Lay Called The Short Lay of Sigurd, The. *Unknown.* *See* Short Lay of Sigurd, The.

Lay Dis Body Down, *with music.* *Unknown.* ABF

Lay down, boys, and take a little nap. Cumberland Gap. *Unknown.* ABF

Lay down one hand before you like a tool. Scarabs for the Living, III. R. P. Blackmur. CoAnAm; TwAmPo

Lay down the axe; fling by the spade. Our Country's Call. Bryant. AnNE; MC; PaA; PAH

Lay down these words. Riprap. Gary Snyder. NeAP

Lay down your stake at play, lay down your passion. A Rule to Play. Sir John Harington. SiCE

Lay him beneath his snows. The Dead Czar Nicholas. Dinah Maria Mulock Craik. LPS-3

Lay him down where the fern is thick and fair. Night Burial in the Forest. Duncan Campbell Scott. BoCaPo; CPG

Lay his dear ashes where ye will. President Lincoln's Grave. Caroline Atherton Briggs Mason. DD; GA; OHIP

Lay It Bare. *Unknown, tr. fr. Japanese by* Ishii *and* Obata. OnPM

Lay me down beneaf de willers in de grass. A Death Song. Paul Laurence Dunbar. AA; BANP; CDC; PoNe

"Lay me in a cushioned chair." The Ballad of the Foxhunter. W. B. Yeats. EnLit

Lay me low, my work is done. Valedictory. Adam Lindsay Gordon. VA

Lay me on an anvil, O God! Prayers of Steel. Carl Sandburg. AnAmPo; BAP; ChMo; CMP; CV; FaPON; IAP; LA; MAP; MoAmPo; MPB; NeMA; NP; PFY; PoMa; PoTo; TrPWD; YaD

Lay me to rest in some fair spot. Traveller's Hope. Charles Granville. HBV; OBVV

Lay me to rest on yon towering height. Simpson's Rest. George S. Simpson. PoOW

Lay me to sleep in sheltering flame. The Mystic's Prayer. "Fiona Macleod." HBV; MaRV; TrPWD; WGRP

Lay Not a Memory Low. Elizabeth Selden. BoFr

Lay not up for yourselves treasures upon earth. Treasures [in Heaven]. St. Matthew, Bible, *N.T.* GoTP; TrGrPo

Lay of Ancient Rome. Thomas R. Ybarra. BOHV; CAG; HBV; InMe; LauV; LHV; WhC

Lay of Finn, The. *Unknown, tr. fr. Anglo-Saxon by* Charles W. Kennedy. *Fr.* Beowulf. AnOE

Lay of Hakon, The. Eyvindr Finsson. *See* Death Song of Haakon the Good.

Lay of Macaroni, The. Bayard Taylor. PA

Lay of Norse-Irish Sea-Kings. Arthur MacGurcaich, *tr. fr. Irish by* George Sigerson. TIP

Lay of Prince Marvan, The. *Tr. fr. Irish by* Eleanor Hull. AnIV

Lay of Rosabelle, The. Sir Walter Scott. *See* Rosabelle.

Lay of St. Aloys, The, *sel.* "Thomas Ingoldsby." *Fr.* The Ingoldsby Legends.
City Bells. LPS-2

Lay of St. Cuthbert, The. "Thomas Ingoldsby." *Fr.* The Ingoldsby Legends. OtMeF

Lay of Sigurd, The. *Unknown.* *See* Short Lay of Sigurd, The.

Lay of the Battle of Tombland, The. Dunstan Thompson. LiTA; NePA

Lay of the Captive Count, The. Goethe, *tr. fr. German by* James Clarence Mangan. AWP

Lay of the Cid, The. *Unknown.* *See* Cid, The.

Lay of the Deserted Influenzaed. Henry Cholmondeley-Pennell. BOHV; InMe

Lay of the Famine, A. *Unknown, at. to* Rosa Mulholland. OnYI; TIP

Lay of the Forlorn. George Darley. OnYI; TriL

Lay of the Laborer. Thomas Hood. DD; ERP; HH; VA

Lay of the Last Frontier. Harold Hersey. PoOW

Lay of the Last Minstrel, *sels.* Sir Walter Scott.
Breathes There the Man [with Soul So Dead], *fr.* VI. BBV; BHV; BLPA; CBE; EnRP; ERP; FaFP; InP; LPS-2; MaRV; NeHB; OAEP; OBRV; PGD; PIR; PTA-1; PYM; TreF
(From "The Lay of the Last Minstrel.") LEAP
(Innominatus.) OBEV; TOP

Lay of the Last Minstrel (*continued*)
(Love of Country.) BTP; OHFP; OQP; PSO; QP-1; WBLP
(Love of Fatherland.) GS; TVSH
(My Native Land.) GN; MPB (1956 ed.); OnHT; OTPC (1923 ed.); StaSt
(My Own, My Native Land.) EBSV; StVeCh (1940 ed.)
(Native Land.) PIAE; TrGrPo
(Patriotism.) BCEP; EV-4; PCD; PG (1945 ed.)
"Call it not vain; they do not err," *fr.* V. OBRV
"Feast was over in Branksome tower, The," *fr.* I. OBRV
"He paused: the listening dames again," Interlude *after* IV OBRV
"Humble boon was soon obtain'd, The," *fr. introd. and* I. OBRV
Hymn for the Dead, *fr.* VI, *par. fr. the Latin* Dies Irae *of* Thomas of Celano. BSV; EmBrPo
(Dies Irae.) GoBC; MaRV
("Nought of the bridal will I tell," *longer sel.*) OBRV
"If thou would'st view fair Melrose aright," *fr.* II. EV-4; OBRV
(Melrose Abbey.) SeCePo
It Was an English Ladye Bright, *fr.* VI. ATP; BSV
(Song of Albert Graeme.) EmBrPo; EnRP; ERP
Love. *fr.* III. BSV; EV-4; LPS-2, *fr.* III *and* V
"In peace, Love tunes the shepherd's reed." ViBoPo
Minstrel's Lowly Bower, The. Conclusion. EV-4
Nature's Sympathy with the Poet, *fr.* V. EV-4
Rosabelle, *fr.* VI. BeLS; BSV; CG; EBSV; GTBS; GTBS-D; GTBS-W; GTSE; GTSL; HBV; OTPC (1923 ed.)
(Dirge of Lovely Rosabelle, The.) EV-4
(Harold's Song [to Rosabelle].) EmBrPo; EnLi-2; EnRP; ERP
(Lay of Rosabelle, The.) EPP
Scotland, *fr.* VI. BSV; LPS-2
Sweet Teviot, *fr.* IV. ERP; OBRV
("Sweet Teviot! on thy silver tide.") BSV
True Love's the Gift, *fr.* V. OBRV
(True Love.) EV-4
"Way was long, the wind was cold, The." *Introd.* OTPC
(Last Minstrel, The.) TreFS
(Minstrel, The.) EV-4
Lay of the Levite, The. William E. Aytoun. HBV
Lay of the Love-lorn, The. William E. Aytoun *and* Sir Theodore Martin. BOHV; PA
(Cry of the Lovelorn, The.) CenHV
Lay of the Lover's Friend, The. William E. Aytoun. BOHV
Lay of the Trilobite, The. May Kendall. CenHV
Lay of the Vigilantes, The. *Unknown.* PoOW
Lay of Thrym, The. *Unknown, tr. fr. Icelandic by* Henry Adams Bellows. *Fr.* The Elder Edda. LiTW; OuHeWo
(Thor Gets Back His Hammer, *tr. by* Bertha S. Phillpotts.) PaOS
(Thrymskvitha, *tr. by* Henry Adams Bellows.) LiA
Lay of Wayland, The. *Unknown, tr. fr. Icelandic by* Henry Adams Bellows. *Fr.* The Elder Edda. PaOS
Lay on the fire their ancient hold. Burning the Bee-Tree. Ruth Pitter. POTE
Lay out the minutes, row on ordered row. Time Out. Frances Westgate Butterfield. GoYe
Lay Preacher Ponders, The. Idris Davies. FaBoTw
Lay Thou, O God, Thy quickening hand. Prayer for the President. Amos R. Wells. PraP
Lay thy head upon this pillow. Lullaby. Fred Emerson Brooks. BOL
Lay up nearer, brother, nearer. The Dying Californian. *Unknown.* ABS; TrAS
Lay willows under Walsingham. The Holy Land of Walsingham. Benjamin Francis Musser. ISi
Lay Your Head. Iwan Goll, *tr. fr. French by* Iwan Goll. OnPM
Lay Your Sleeping Head [My Love]. W. H. Auden. BoLiVe (1945 ed.); ChMP; CoBMV; FaBoEn; GTBS-D; LiTB; LO; LoPS; MaPo; MoAB; MoBrPo; MoPo; MoVE; PoE; POTE; ReMP; SeCePo; UnPo (3d ed.)
(Song XI.) EnLoPo
Laye of ye Woodpeckore, Ye. Henry A. Beers. NA
Layer above layer—the moving clouds! Rain. Tu Fu. OnPM
Lays of Ancient Rome, *sels.* Macaulay.
Battle of Lake Regillus, The, *sels.*
Battle, The. BHV
Death of Herminius, The. OtMeF
Fight in the Centre, The. OtMeF
"Men said he saw strange visions." UnW
War-Horse, The. BHV
Horatius [at the Bridge]. BBV, *abr.*; BCEP, *abr.*; BeLS; BHV; CBPC; EV-4; FaBoCh, *abr.*; FaFP; HBV; HBVY; LH; LoGBV; LPS-2; MCCG; OHFP, *abr.*; OnSP; PECK; PIR, *abr.*; ShBV-1; TreF
"Then out spake brave Horatius," *sel.* LEAP, 6 *sts*; PoFr, 5 *sts.*
"And in the nights of winter," *sel.* AlDL
Fight at the Bridge, The, *sel.* MaC; OtMeF
Virginia, *sel.*
Roman Father's Sacrifice, The. LPS-3
Lays of Tom-Cat Hiddigeigei. Joseph Viktor von Scheffel, *tr. fr. German by* William Fitzgerald. PoC
Lazarus. Wilfred Campbell. BoCaPo
Lazarus. A. S. Cripps. BoSA
Lazarus. José Asunción Silva, *tr. fr. Spanish by* "Anthony Boucher." DaM
Lazarus. *Unknown. See* Dives and Lazarus.
Lazarus. Ursula Wood. DiM
Lazarus Walks in the Alps. Ernest Walsh. MeRV
Lazily I stir a white feather fan. In the Mountains on a Summer Day. Li Po. WhP
Lazily through the clear. The Goldfish. Audrey Alexandra Brown. CaP
Lazy-bones, lazy-bones, wake up and peep. Nonsense Verses. Charles Lamb. BOHV; NA
Lazy deuks that sit i' the coal-neuks. *Unknown.* OxNR
Lazy laughing languid Jenny. Jenny. Dante Gabriel Rossetti. EmBrPo; LiA; PoEL-5; POTT; ViP; ViPo; ViPP; VLEP
Lazy Man's Song. Po Chü-i, *tr. fr. Chinese by* Arthur Waley. TrCh
Lazy petals of magnolia-bloom float down the sluggish river. Elegy on a Nordic White Protestant. John Gould Fletcher. PoNe
Lazy Roof, The. Gelett Burgess. BOHV; NA
(Queer Quatrains.) RIS
Lazy sheep, pray tell me why. The Sheep [*or* The Boy and the Sheep]. Ann Taylor. BoChLi; BoTP; MBP; OTPC; PRWS; RAR; UTS
Lazy Writer, The. Bert Leston Taylor. ALV; PFE; PoMa
Le Cœur de l'Immaculée. Benjamin Francis Musser. WHL
Le Dernier Jour d'un Condamné. George Augustus Baker, Jr. PR
Le Désert de l'Amour. Stevie Smith. DiM
Le Diner. Arthur Hugh Clough. Spectator ab Extra, II. OxBoLi
Le Hore di Recreatione; or, The Pleasant Historie of Albino and Bellama, *sel.* Nathaniel Whiting.
Tinker and the Monks, The. SeCL
Le Jardin ("The lily's withered chalice falls"). Oscar Wilde. CaAE; GTIV; SeCePo; ViPP
(Garden, The.) PoRA
Le Jardin des Tuileries ("This winter air is keen"). Oscar Wilde. JKCP (1926 ed.)
Le Jeune Homme Caressant Sa Chimère. John Addington Symonds. OBVV; PoVP
Le Marais du Cygne. Whittier. PAH
Le Mauvais Larron. Rosamund Marriott Watson. VA
Le Médecin Malgré Lui. William Carlos Williams. PoP
Le Monocle de Mon Oncle. Wallace Stevens. AnAmPo; AnFE; APA; CoAnAm; CoBMV; LA; LiTM; MAPA; MoAB; NP; TwAmPo
Le Repos en Egypte; the Sphinx. Agnes Repplier. CAW; ISi; JKCP
(Sphinx, The.) StJW
Le Roi Est Mort. Agnes Mary Frances Robinson. OBVV
Le Secret Humain. Archibald MacLeish. ChMo; CMP
Le Vieux Temps. William Henry Drummond. BoCaPo
Lea Rig [The]. Burns. BSV; EBSV
(My Ain Kind Dearie, O.) GoTS
Lead gently, Lord, and slow. A Hymn. Paul Laurence Dunbar. MaRV; TrPWD
Lead, Kindly Light. Cardinal Newman. *See* Pillar of the Cloud, The.
Lead me, O God, and thou my Destiny. God Leads the Way. Cleanthes. OxBG
Lead on, lead on, America. Louise Ayres Garnett. *Fr.* Song of Liberty. PGD
Lead On, O King Eternal. Ernest W. Shurtleff. MaRV
Lead the soul whom letters have well nourished. Lament of the Pianos Which Are Overheard in Well-to-do Quarters. Jules Laforgue. AnFP
Lead us, heavenly Father, lead us. Prayer to the Trinity [*or* Hymn]. James Edmeston. HBV; NeHB; OIF; VA
Lead us, O Father, in the paths of peace. William H. Burleigh. OIF
Lead ye me on, O God and Destiny. The Stoic's Resignation. Cleanthes. GrPE
Leadbelly's Chisholm Trail. *Unknown. See* When I Was a Cowboy.
Leade the black bull to slaughter, with the bore. Upon Master W. Montague. Thomas Carew. SeEP
Leaden Echo and the Golden Echo, The. Gerard Manley Hopkins. ChMo; CoBMV; EnLi-2 (1949 ed.); FaFP; GTBS-D; GTBS-W; LiA; LiTB; LiTM; LoBV; MoVE; OAEP (2d ed.); OBMV; PreP; ReaPo; TwCV; ViPo; VLEP
Golden Echo, The. MBP; MoAB; MoBrPo
Leaden Echo, The. CaAE; MBP; MoAB; MoBrPo
Leaden Echo and the Golden Echo, The. T. Sturge Moore, *par. of* Gerard Manley Hopkins. ReaPo

Leaden Treasury of English Verse, A, *sels.* Paul Dehn. FiBHP
"Jenny kiss'd me when we met."
"Nuclear wind, when wilt thou blow."
Leaden-eyed, The. Vachel Lindsay. ATP; BLV; BoLiVe; ChMo; CMP; GrCo-1; GTBS-W; LiTA; LiTM; MaRV; NAMP; NePA; NP; NV; PoeMoYo
Leader, A. "Æ." HBMV
Leader, The. Hilaire Belloc. ACP (1952 ed.)
Leader, The. Second Samuel, XXIII: 3-4, Bible, *O.T.* PCD; PCH
Leader, The. Robert Underwood Johnson. GA
Leader-Haughs and Yarrow. *Unknown.* EBSV
"Leader" they have called you—they who followed in your lead. The Old Name. Katherine D. M. Simons. LS
Leaders. *Unknown.* WBLP
Leaders and Friends of Mankind. Matthew Arnold. *Fr.* Rugby Chapel. GrCo-1
Leaders, New Style; the General (1917). Siegfried Sassoon. *See* General, The.
Leaders of the Crowd, The. W. B. Yeats. EnLit; MBP; MoAB; MoBrPo; TwP
Leaders, Old Style. Sir Walter Scott. *Fr.* Marmion, III. OtMeF
Leading. Mary Carolyn Davies. MaRV
Leading. Nagata, *tr. fr. Japanese by* Lois J. Erickson. SoLD
Leadsman's Song, The. *At. to* J. Pearce *and to* Charles Dibdin. *See* Heaving the Lead.
Leaf. John Hewitt. NeIP
Leaf, A. Ludwig Uhland, *tr. fr. German by* John S. Dwight. AWP; JAWP; WBP
Leaf, The. John Williams. NePoAm-2
Leaf after Leaf Drops Off. Walter Savage Landor. OQP; QP-2; ViBoPo
Leaf after leaf forsakes me. Transition. Hermann Hesse. TwGV
Leaf and Soul. John Banister Tabb. PoMa
Leaf falls softly at my feet, A. A Leaf. Ludwig Uhland. AWP; JAWP; WBP
Leaf for Hand in Hand, A. Walt Whitman. BoFr
Leaf from a Fly-Book, A. Seaforth Mackenzie. MM
Leaf is no more now than corruption's scent. Twilight of the Wood. Léonie Adams. NLK (1947 ed.)
Leaf moved up on me, like a tattered old sailor dropped from the long winds, A. Punchinello. Hugh de Burgh. CAW
Leaf-Movement. Arthur Davison Ficke. MAP; NP
Leaf of Grass, A. Walt Whitman. *See* Miracles ("I believe a leaf of grass").
Leaf on the Water, The. Ouan-tsi, *tr. into English by* James Whitall *fr. the Chinese-to-French translation of* Judith Gautier. ChLP
Leaf-picking, The. Frédéric Mistral, *tr. fr. Provençal by* Harriet Waters Preston. AWP; JAWP; WBP
Leaf-Treader, A. Robert Frost. MAP; MoAmPo
Leaf turns, A. The Walker. Yvor Winters. NP
Leaf will wrinkle to decay, The. The Crest Jewel. James Stephens. AnIL; MBP; MoAB; MoBrPo
Leafless are the trees; their purple branches. The Golden Mile-Stone. Longfellow. PoEL-5
Leafless, stemless, floating flower. The Butterfly. John Banister Tabb. UTS
Leafless Tree, A. Ann Louise Thompson. OQP; QP-2
Leafless trees, the untidy stack, The. A Lonely Place. Edward Shanks. TCPD
Leaflight to lamplight, blind with so much sight. The Brahms. Herbert Morris. NePoAm-2
League of broomgrass, rose and mauve and umber, A. Dusk in the Low Country. DuBose Heyward. BAP; TCAP
League of Love in Action, The. Edwin Markham. PEDC
League of Nations, A. Joel Barlow. *See* Union of the World, A.
League of Nations, The. Mary Siegrist. MC; PAH
League of Nations. Nancy Byrd Turner. AOAH
Leagues north, as fly the gull and auk. The *Palatine.* Whittier. EtS
Leak in the Dike, The. Phoebe Cary. FaFP; FaPON; OnSP; OTPC; PTA-1; StVeCh (1940 ed.); TreF
Lean and tall and stringy are the Navajo. The Painted Desert: The Navajo. Elizabeth J. Coatsworth. PoeMoYo
Lean back, and get some minutes' peace. Faustine. Swinburne. BeLS; EmBrPo; PoVP; ViPo; ViPP; VLEP
Lean close and set thine ear against the bark. Heart of Oak. Charles Henry Luders. AA
Lean coyote, prowler of the night, The. Sunrise. Charles Erskine Scott Wood. *Fr.* The Poet in the Desert. GoTP; MAP; PFY
Lean in the greenhood of my fearful years. Fool Song. Cornel Lengyel. GoYe
Lean, lanky son of desert sage. To a Jack Rabbit. S. Omar Barker. IHA
Lean out of the window. Goldenhair [*or* Song]. James Joyce. *Fr.* Chamber Music. BoTP; ChTr; HBMV; LEAP; MoSiPe; POTE; TwCV
Lean out the window: down the street. A Man with a Little Pleated Piano. Winifred Welles. FaPON; GaP
Lean Street. G. S. Fraser. NeBP
Lean tyke, supple, A. Allendale Dog. Lilian Bowes-Lyon. DiM
Lean your small head against the Spring. Walking to Dedham. David Wright. NeBP
Leander. the fool. Columbine. Paul Verlaine. TrFP
Leander's Death. Musaeus, *tr. fr. Greek by* Michael Balkwill. *Fr.* Hero and Leander. OxBG
Leaners or Lifters. Ella Wheeler Wilcox. *See* Lifting and Leaning.
Leaning/ On my shoulder. Impatience. Ts'ao Ho. OnPM
Leaning against the wind across the paddock ways. Winter Westerlies. James Devaney. BoAV; MoAuPo
Leaning his chin in his small hard hands. Kentucky Birthday [February 12, 1815]. Frances Frost. SiSoSe; YeAr
Leans now the fair willow, dreaming. The Willow. Walter de la Mare. CBE
Leap and Creep. *Unknown, tr. fr. Sanskrit by* Arthur W. Ryder. *Fr.* The Panchatantra. OuHeWo
Leap from the crags, brave boy! The Dhoon. Thomas Edward Brown. POTT
Leap of Roushan Beg, The. Longfellow. MW; PTA-1; StVeCh
Leap out, chill water, over reeds and brakes. The River God. Sacheverell Sitwell. MBP; MoBrPo
Leap, Santa, down our chimney. Letter to Santa Claus. John Wain. PoN
Leap to the highest height of spring. An Early Bluebird. Maurice Thompson. AA
Leaping Falls. Galway Kinnell. NePoAm-2
Leaping Laughers, The. George Barker. OBMV
Lear. Thomas Hood. VA
Lear and Cordelia ("How does my royall lord"). Shakespeare. *Fr.* King Lear, IV, vii. LiA
Lear and Cordelia ("Some officers take them away"). Shakespeare. *Fr.* King Lear, V, iii. FiP
Lear and Cordelia! 'twas an ancient tale. To England. George Henry Boker. AA; AnAmPo; HBV; LA; OTPC
Learn how to hope, to wait the proper tide. Counsels. Antonio Machado. AnSpL-2
Learn to speak this little word. "No!" Eliza Cook. PoToHe (new ed.)
Learn to Wait. *Unknown.* PoToHe
Learn Truly. Stepan Petrovich Shchipachev, *tr. fr. Russian by* Jack Lindsay. RuPo
Learn, you who wonder at my many forms. Propertius. Elegies, IV, 2. LaP
Learned and a happy ignorance, A. Eden. Thomas Traherne. BLV; PoEL-2; ReaPo; SeCV-2; TrGrPo
Learned Ass, The. Francis Jammes, *tr. fr. French by* Alan Conder. TrFP
Learned Ladies. Byron. *Fr.* Don Juan, IV. GEPC
Learned Man, A. Stephen Crane. The Black Riders, XX. LiTA; MoAmPo (1950 ed.); NePA
Learned man, whom once a week, A. A Satire on the Royal Society. Samuel Butler. BeR
Learned Men, The. Archibald MacLeish. MoAB; MoAmPo (1950 ed.)
Learned Mistress, A. *Unknown, tr. fr. Irish by* Frank O'Connor. KiLC; OBMV
Learned Negro, The. *Unknown.* BOHV
Learned society of late, A. The Elephant in the Moon. Samuel Butler. BeR
Learnedest crew that I ever knew was the crew of the *Let-Her-Rip*, The. The Yarn of the *Let-Her-Rip.* Thomas R. Ybarra. PFE
Learning. William Barnes. MOB
Learning. George Chapman. *Fr.* Euthymiae Raptus; or, The Tears of Peace. SeCePo
("But this is learning; to have skill to throwe.") BrBE
Learning. Mary Fullerton. NeLNL
Learning and dignity. Flaming Banners. Bhartrihari. OnPM
Learning, that cobweb of the brain. Samuel Butler. *Fr.* Hudibras, Pt. I. NBE
Learning to Draw. Ann *or* Jane Taylor. SAS
Learning to Play. Abbie Farwell Brown. HH; PPL
Learning to Skate. Emilie Blackmore Stapp. GFA
Learning to Swim. Anna Medary. GFA
Lear's Prayer. Shakespeare. *Fr.* King Lear, II, iv. BCEP
Least little sound sets the coyotes walking, The. Outside. William Stafford. NePoAm-2
Least of Carols, The. Sophie Jewett. ChrBoLe; OHIP; SDH
Leather Bottel, The. John Wade. SeCL
Leather handles gripped. Subway Engineer. C. R. Holmes. PtPa
L'Eau Dormante. Thomas Bailey Aldrich. HBV; PR
Leaute to lufe is gretumly. Loyalty. John Barbour. *Fr.* The Bruce. EBSV
Leave a Kiss within the Cup. Agathias Scholasticus, *tr. fr. Greek by* J. M. Edmonds. GrL; OxBG; WoL
("I love not wine, but shouldst thou wish," *tr. by* Lilla Cabot Perry.) GrPo

Leave a Kiss within the Cup (*continued*)
(Kiss within the Cup, A, *tr. by* F. L. Lucas.) GrPE
"Leave all and follow—follow!" The Forbidden Lure. Fannie Stearns Davis. HBV
Leave Caelia, leave the woods to chase. On His Mistris That Lov'd Hunting. *Unknown.* OBS
Leave Helen to her lover. Draw away. The White Isle of Leuce. Sir Herbert Read. BrBE; FaBoTw
Leave her alone. The Seals. L. A. G. Strong. LO; POTE
Leave Her, Johnny. *Unknown.* SG; SoAmSa, *with music*
(Leave Her, Bullies, Leave Her, *diff. vers., with music.*) AS
(Time for Us to Leave Her, *diff. vers., with music.*) ShS
(Time to Leave Her, *diff. vers., with music.*) AmSS
Leave her now, go out and learn. To Himself. Richard Aldridge. NePoAm
Leave her that; and thou shalt leave her. Richard Crashaw. *Fr.* The Flaming Heart. PraNu
Leave him: he's quiet enough: and what matter. Here Lies a Prisoner. Charlotte Mew. MoBrPo
Leave Him Now Quiet [by the Way]. Trumbull Stickney. CrMA; LiTA; MOAP; TwAmPo
Leave him, sweet Eros, give him peace at last. In Memory of Rex Whistler. Dorothy Wellesley. DiM
Leave husbandry sleeping a while, ye must do. A Digression to Hospitality. Thomas Tusser. SiCE
Leave It All Quietly to God. Psalms, LXII: 1–8, Bible, *O.T.*, *tr. by* James Moffatt. MaRV
Leave It with Him. *Unknown.* BLRP
Leave, Lady! in your glass of crystal clean. Amoretti, XLV. Spenser. PeBoSo
Leave, leave, converted publican! lay down. Christus Matthaeum et Discipulos Alloquitur. Sir Edward Sherburne. ACP
Leave leave to weepe Ornone, & now, move. *Unknown.* SeCSL
Leave me a little while alone. At His Grave. Alfred Austin. VA
Leave me a while, for you have been too long. Lover to Lover. David Morton. HBMV
Leave me, all sweet refrains my lip hath made. Sonnet. Luis de Camões. AWP; CAW; JAWP; WBP
Leave Me in Peace to Meditate. Charles d'Orléans, *tr. fr. French by* Alan Conder. TrFP
Leave Me, O Love [Which Reachest but to Dust]. Sir Philip Sidney. *Sometimes considered Sonnet CX of* Astrophel and Stella; *also in* Certain Sonnets. BCEP; EG; EIL; ElSeCe; EnLit; ExPo; LEAP; LiTB; LiTG; MaPo; OAEP; OxBoCh; PoE; PoRA; ReaPo; ReEn; ReIE; RiBV; SeCePo; SeCeV; SiCE; TOP; TriL; TrPWD; TuPP; TyEnPo; ViBoPo; WHA
(Farewell, A.) CBOV; UnPo (1st ed.)
(Farewell World.) FaBoEn
(Love.) PeBoSo
(Sonnet: "Leave me, O love.") BrBE; CoEV
(Splendidis Longum Valedico Nugis.) ES; EV-1; LO; OBEV; OBSC; SiPS
Leave me, O world, O to myself! Withdrawal. Eduard Mörike. AnGP
Leave Me to My Own. Lew Sarett. LEAP
Leave now the beach, and even that perfect friendship. End of Season. Robert Penn Warren. TwAmPo
Leave, Philomel, to make thy moan! To Philomel. John Tatham. SeCL
Leave prolonging thy distress! A Little Breath I'll Borrow. Thomas Campion. PoP
Leave-taking, A. Sir Frederick Napier Broome. AnNZ
Leave-taking, A. Arno Holz, *tr. fr. German by* Jethro Bithell. AWP; JAWP; WBP
Leave Taking. Milton, *Fr.* Paradise Lost, XII. FaBoEn
Leave-taking, A. Swinburne. CH; FaBoEn; HBV; MBP; OAEP; OBVV; PIR; PoEL-5; PoVP; TCEP; ViBoPo; VLEP
("Let us go hence, my songs; she will not hear.") EG
Leavetaking ("Pass, thou wild light"). Sir William Watson. AEV; HBV; PoVP; TCPD
Leave-taking of Artemis, The. Euripides, *tr. fr. Greek by* Gilbert Murray. *Fr.* Hippolytus. GrR
Leave tarnished sorrow, disappointment, doubt. Thought for a New Year. Gail Brook Burket. PGD
Leave the chicory where it stands. Bavarian Roadside. Leonora Speyer. NP
Leave the early bells at chime. Road-Hymn for the Start. William Vaughn Moody. MAP; MoAmPo (1942 ed.)
Leave the flurry/ To the masses. *Unknown.* WhC
Leave the gods to order all things. Archilochus, *tr. fr. Greek by* J. H. Merivale. GrPo
Leave the lady, Willy, let the racket rip. Willy and the Lady. Gelett Burgess. HBMV
Leave the Miracle to Him. Thomas H. Allan. BLRP
Leave the rest, and take the wine. Wine and Citron. Abu Abd Allah. MooP
Leave the Thread with God. *Unknown.* BLRP
Leave the uproar! At a leap. Nature and Life. George Meredith. Po; ViP; VLEP
Leave the Word Alone. Edward Marshall. NeAP
Leave thine own home, O youth, seek distant shores! Encouragement to Exile. Petronius. AWP; JAWP; WBP
Leave this barren spot to me! The Beech Tree's Petition. Thomas Campbell. ADAH; GTSL; HBV; SN
Leave Train. Alan Ross. ChMP
Leave Us Religion. Blanaid Salkeld. NeIP
Leave we awhile without the turmoil of the town. Our Lady of France. Lionel Johnson. ISi
Leave wealth where wealth is found. Contentment. Al-Tutili. MooP
Leave your home behind, lad. The Recruit. A. E. Housman. A Shropshire Lad, III. PoVP
Leaves. Rowena Baker. CAG
Leaves, The. William Barnes. ChTr
Leaves. W. H. Davies. MBP; MoBrPo
Leaves. Sara Teasdale. HBV; NP; NV
Leaves. Katharine Tynan. BoTP
Leaves, The. *Unknown.* BoTP
Leaves. J. M. Westrup. BoTP
Leaves/ Murmuring by myriads. From My Diary, July 1914. Wilfred Owen. CoBMV; FaBoMo; LiTM (rev. ed.); MBP; MoAB; MoBrPo
Leaves are always beautiful, I think. Leaves. J. M. Westrup. BoTP
Leaves are dropping from the trees, The. Autumn Leaves. Margaret P. Sutphen. PCH
Leaves are fading and falling, The. November. Alice Cary. PTA-1
Leaves are falling, The. The Wild Geese. *Unknown.* PoHN
Leaves are falling, falling, The. Autumn Leaves. W. Hodgson Burnet. PoMa
Leaves are falling, falling, as from far away, The. Autumn. Rainer Maria Rilke. AnGP
Leaves are falling, The; so am I. Late Leaves. Walter Savage Landor. CaAE; EG; GTSE; HBV; OBEV (1st ed.)
Leaves are fresh after the rain, The. April Showers. James Stephens. TiPo (1959 ed.)
Leaves are uncurling, The. Spring. Marchette Chute. TiPo (1959 ed.)
Leaves at My Window. John James Piatt. AA
Leaves before the Wind. May Sarton. NePoAm
Leaves Drink, The. Alice Wilkins. GFA
Leaves fall. The City of Falling Leaves. Amy Lowell. *Fr.* 1777. MAPA; SUS; TCPD; TiPo; TwAmPo
Leaves fall, fall as from far, The. Autumn. Rainer Maria Rilke. OnPM; TrJP
Leaves had a wonderful frolic, The. The Leaves. *Unknown.* BoTP
Leaves have their time to fall. The Hour of Death. Felicia Dorothea Hemans. HBV; LoBV
Leaves make a slow. Spring Rain. Harry Behn. TiPo
Leaves of autumn burning through the grey, The. Chorale for Autumn. Marya Zaturenska. NP
"Leaves of Grass's" Purport. Walt Whitman. CaAE
(L of G's Purport.) IAP
Leaves of the summer, lovely summer's pride. The Leaves. William Barnes. ChTr
Leaves of the Tree of Love are fears and sighs and tears, The. The Tree of Love. Ramon Lull. CAW
Leaves, summer's coinage spent, golden are all together whirled. Lapwing. Rex Warner. ShBV-3
Leaves that cling to the tired ground. Memories. Claire Morris. CAG
Leaves, the little birds, and I, The. The Little Shepherd's Song. William Alexander Percy. GFA; POT; PoTo; YeAr
Leaves throng thick above, The. The Last Leaf. Thomas Hardy. CMP
Leaves were reddening to their fall, The. The Gray Doves' Answer. Frederic Edward Weatherly. TVC; TVSH
Leaves will fall again sometime and fill, The. Sunday Morning Apples. Hart Crane. NAMP
Leavetaking. *See* Leave-taking.
Leaving Barra. Louis MacNeice. ChMo; POTE; ReaPo
Leaving behind us the puddling swamp-woods. Released. Olive Tilford Dargan. NoCaPo
Leaving Ching-k'ou. Su T'ung-po, *tr. fr. Chinese by* Yu Min-chuan. WhP
Leaving of Liverpool, The, *with music.* *Unknown.* ShS
Leaving Sunnyside behind, the high weaving clarinet. Girl Asleep. Raymond Souster. TwCaPo
Leaving the bar slack-watered, I have left. Two Voyages. Maurice James Craig. NeIP
Leaving the Homestead. *Unknown.* PTA-2
Leaving the Monastery Early in the Morning. Lu Yu, *tr. fr. Chinese by* Kenneth Rexroth. OnPC
Leaving the viaduct on the left, and coming over the hill. St. Ursanne. Michael Roberts. LiTM
Leaving Troy. Thomas Caulfield Irwin. IrPN

Leaving White Emperor City at Dawn. Li Po, *tr. fr. Chinese.* WhP
Lecompton's Black Brigade. Charles Graham Halpine. PAH
Lectori Quomodo Legat. Thomas Freeman. SiCE
Lecture upon the Shadow, A. John Donne. AnEnPo; AtBAP; AWP; ElSeCe; EPS (1942 ed.); EV-2; InPo; OBS; Po; ReEn; SeEP; TuPP
Lecturer's impartial prose, The. In the Lecture Room. James K. Baxter. Cressida, I. AnNZ
Led on through many years to my last hours. Madrigal 139. Michelangelo. LyPI
Leda. Hilda Doolittle ("H. D."). HBMV; InPo; MOAP; TCPD
Leda. W. Wesley Trimpi. PtPa
Leda and the Swan. Oliver St. John Gogarty. AnIL; OnYI
Leda and the Swan. W. B. Yeats. AnIL; AtBAP; ChMP; CoBMV; CoEV; EnL; EnLi-2 (1949 ed.); EnLP; ExPo; FaBoEn; InPo; LiTM; MaPo; MBP; MoAB; MoBrPo; MoVE; OAEP (2d ed.); PeBoSo; PoE; PoFS; PoLFOT; SeCeV; TrGrPo; TwHP; TwP
Leda release/ The sensuous swan. Leda. W. Wesley Trimpi. PtPa
Leda, the Lost. Eda Lou Walton. AnAmPo
Ledger, The. Crates, *tr. fr. Greek by* J. M. Edmonds. GrR
"Lee." Mary Sinton Leitch. *See* Statue Inscribed "Lee," Richmond.
Lee, *sel.* Edgar Lee Masters.
"No grief for the great ones." ChMo; CMP
Lee. Archibald Rutledge. LS
Lee at the Wilderness. Mary Evelyn Moore Davis. BlG
Lee in the Mountains. Donald Davidson. MoVE; SPP; UnPo
Lee to the Rear. John Reuben Thompson. BlG; GA; MC; MDAH; PaA; PAH; SPP
Leech-Gatherer, The. Wordsworth. *See* Resolution and Independence.
Leech's brother walked slowly in the forest, The. "Comte de Lautréamont." *Fr.* The Song of Maldoror. MiFP
Leedle Yawcob Strauss. Charles Follen Adams. BOHV; PTA-1
Lee's Parole. Marion Manville. BlG; GA, *abr.*; PAH
Leesome Brand. *Unknown.* BaBo (A *vers.*); ESPB (A *and* B *vers.*); OBB
(Medelwold and Sidselille, B *vers.*) BaBo
Leetla Boy, Da. T. A. Daly. CP; CV; HBV; NV; PoTo; YT
Leetla Giorgio Washeenton. T. A. Daly. FaPON; MPB; OTPC (1946 ed.); TSW; TSWC
Leetla Giuseppina. T. A. Daly. TSWC
Leetle Bateese. William Henry Drummond. *See* Little Bateese.
Leezie Lindsay. *Unknown. See* Lizie Lindsay.
Lefroy in the Forest, *abr.* Charles Mair. *Fr.* Tecumseh, II, i. VA
("This region is as lavish of its flowers.") CPG
Left and right and swing around! Dance. James Stephens. ChMo; CMP
Left Behind. Elizabeth Akers Allen. HBV; LPS-1
Left by his friend to breakfast alone on the white/ Italian shore. Edward Lear. W. H. Auden. InvP; PtP
Left leg flung out, head cocked to the right. Poet. Karl Shapiro. AnFE; CoAnAm; MoAB; MoAmPo (1950 ed.); TwAmPo
Left like an unknown's breath on mirrors. Visitations. Lawrence Durrell. *Fr.* Eight Aspects of Melissa. NeBP
Left March. Vladimir Mayakovsky, *tr. fr. Russian by* C. M. Bowra. BoRS
Left on the Battle-Field, *abr.* Sarah Tittle Bolton. LPS-2
Left Out. Mary Carolyn Davies. HH
Leg, The. Karl Shapiro. MoAB; MoAmPo (1950 ed.); NeMA; TrGrPo (rev. ed.); UnPo (3d ed.)
Leg in a Plaster Cast, A. Muriel Rukeyser. MoAmPo
Leg in the Subway, The. Oscar Williams. AnFE; CoAnAm; LiTM; NePA; TwAmPo
Leg over leg. *Unknown.* OxNR
Legacie, The. John Donne. *See* Legacy, The.
Legacies. Ethelwyn Wetherald. CPG; MaRV; OQP; QP-2
Legacy, The. Proverbs, IV: 1-13, Bible, *O.T.* TrJP
Legacy [*or* Legacie], The. John Donne. AtBAP; EPS; TrGrPo
Legacy. Frederick Ebright. NeTW
Legacy, A. Karl Gustaf af Leopold, *tr. fr. Swedish by* Charles W. Stork. AnSL
Legacy. Gladys McKee. JKCP
Legacy, A. Martial. *See* Hinted Wish, A.
Legacy, *with music.* Thomas Moore. AS
Legacy. Nancy Byrd Turner. BrR; MoSiPe
Legacy. Ruth Winant Wheeler. ChIP
Legacy, A. Whittier. BoFr
Legal Fiction. William Empson. CoEV; ExPo; FaBoMo; LiTB; LiTM; MoP; MoVE; ReMP
Legem Tuam Dilexi. Coventry Patmore. The Unknown Eros, II, vi. OxBoCh; PoEL-5; PoLi
Legend. Hart Crane. InPo; MOAP; MoVE; OxBA; TwAmPo
Legend. Ralph Gustafson. CaP
Legend. Sister Mary Jeremy. JKCP (1955 ed.)
Legend, A. May Kendall. VA
Legend. Theodore Morrison. MuM
Legend, A. Adelaide Anne Procter. GoBC; JKCP
Legend. Vincent Starrett. DaM
Legend. Ridgely Torrence. EtS
Legend, A: "Christ, when a child, a garden made." *Unknown, at. to* Peter Ilich Tchaikovsky, *tr. fr. Russian by* Nathan Haskell Dole. ChIP; MaRV; OHIP; SDH
Legend. John Waller. NeBP
Legend. John V. A. Weaver. PFY; TCPD; YaD
Legend. John Hall Wheelock. LiTL
Legend. Judith Wright. BoAV
Legend about Color, A. Edwin McNeill Poteat. NoCaPo (rev. ed.)
Legend Beautiful, The. Longfellow. Tales of a Wayside Inn: The Theologian's Tale, Pt. II. CBPC; PTA-2
Legend of Babe Jesus and the Weeders, The. *Unknown.* ChrBoLe
Legend of Bishop Hatto, The. Robert Southey. *See* God's Judgment on a Wicked Bishop.
Legend of Boastful Bill, The. Badger Clark. SCC
Legend of Bregenz, A. Adelaide Anne Procter. PTA-1
Legend of Camelot, A. George Du Maurier. CenHV
Legend of Cherries, A. Charles Dalmon. HBMV; TSW
Legend of Felix is ended, the toiling of Felix is done, The. Envoy. Henry van Dyke. *Fr.* The Toiling of Felix. BLPA
Legend of Gethsemane, A. Teresa Hooley. StJW
Legend of Ghost Lagoon, The, *sel.* Joseph Schull.
"It's a wicked night, and the sea is wild," I *and* II. HeT
(Pirates' Fight, The, I *and* II, *much abr.*) CaP
Legend of Good Women, The, *sels.* Chaucer.
Prologue.
"And as for me, though that my wit be lite." ViBoPo
("And as for me, thogh that I can but lyte.") CH
Balade: "Hyd, Absolon, thy gilte tresses clere." AtBAP; AWP; BrBE; ChTr; FiP; InPo; JAWP; LiTG; LoBV; OBEV; SeCeV; WBP
(Ballade.) LyMA
(Hyd, Absolon, Thy Gilte Tresses Clere.) ExPo
(Of His Lady, *sl. diff.*) EG
"Of all the floures in the mede." LO
(Daisy, The, *longer sel.*) LPS-2
"She is the clernesse and the verray light." LO
This Fresshe Flour. SeCePo
"Thousand tymes have I herd men telle, A." NBE
Whan That the Month of May. AtBAP
Story of Thisbe of Babylon, Martyr, The. TCEP
Legend of Grand Lake, The. Joseph L. Westcott. PoOW
Legend of Heinz von Stein, The. Charles Godfrey Leland. BOHV; HBV
Legend of His Lyre. Aaron Schmuller. GoYe
Legend of Lake Okeefinokee, A. Laura E. Richards. PoRh; RIS; StPo
(Legend of Okeefinokee, A.) BoChLi
Legend of Montrose, The, *sel.* Sir Walter Scott.
Annot Lyle's Song: "Birds of Omen." EmBrPo; EnRP
Legend of Noël. Frances Frost. PoTo
Legend of Okeefinokee, A. Laura E. Richards. *See* Legend of Lake Okeefinokee, A.
Legend of Provence, A, *sel.* Adelaide Anne Procter.
"Of all the nuns no heart was half so light." PraNu
Legend of Qu'Apelle Valley, The. Emily Pauline Johnson. UnW
Legend of Rabbi Ben Levi, The. Longfellow. Tales of a Wayside Inn: The Spanish Jew's Tale, Pt. I. AnNE; BAV; DaM; EV-5; GBV (1952 ed.)
Legend of Robert, Duke of Normandy, The, *sel.* Michael Drayton.
Fame and Fortune. OBSC
Legend of Service, A. Henry van Dyke. GBV (1922 ed.)
Legend of Sir Guyon, or of Temperance, The, *abr.* Spenser. The Faerie Queene, II, 12. WHA
Legend of the Admen, The. Everett W. Lord. BLPA
Legend of the Christmas Rose, The. Florence Boyce Davis. PEDC
Legend of the Cornstalk, The. Longfellow. *Fr.* The Song of Hiawatha. GrCo-1
Legend of the Dead Lambs, The. "Owen Meredith." VA
Legend of the Dogwood Tree, The. Geraldine Farrar. StJW
Legend of the Dove, A. George Sterling. LEAP; NP
Legend of the Easter Eggs, The. Fitz-James O'Brien. BeLS
Legend of the First Cam-u-el, The. Arthur Guiterman. ALV; BAP; BOHV; CenHV; PFE; PoeMoYo; PYM
Legend of the Glaive, The. Joseph Sheridan Le Fanu. DaM
Sels.
Fionula. TIP
Song of the Spirits, The. OnYI
Legend of the Knight [*or* Knyght] of the Red Cross, or of Holiness. Spenser. The Faerie Queene, I, 1-12. BEL;

Legend of the Knight of the Red Cross (*continued*)
EM-1 (1-3); EnLi-1 (*1 and 2*); GEPC; OAEP; TOP (*1 and 4*)
(Invocation to the Faerie Queene, *prologue*.) FiP
("Lo! I, the man whose Muse whylome did maske.") EnLit, *prologue, 1 and 2*; REAL, *prologue and 1*; TCEP, *prologue, 1, 3, 4, 5, and 12, abr.*
(Story of the Red Cross Knight, or of Holiness, The, *sels. fr. 1, 4, 9, 11, and 12*.) EV-1
Legend of the Northland, A. Phoebe Cary. GoTP; HBV; HBVY; OTPC; PTA-2; RIS
Legend of the Organ-Builder, The. Julia C. R. Dorr. BeLS; BLPA; FaBoBe; PTA-1
Legend of the Saintfoin, The. Pamela Tennant. GBV (1922 ed.)
Legend of the Tortoise, The. Pamela Tennant. GBV (1922 ed.)
Legend of Viable Women, A. Richard Eberhart. MiAP; MoVE
Legend of Walbach Tower, The. George Houghton. PAH
Legend of Waukulla, The. Hezekiah Butterworth. PAH
Legends for Trees, *sels.* Arthur Ketchum.
Countersign. HBMV
Spirit of the Birch, The. MPB; MW; OHIP
Legends of Christmas. Aileen Fisher. ChBR
Legends of Evil, The. Kipling. MoShBr
"This is the sorrowful story," I.
"'Twas when the rain fell steady," II.
Legerdemain. Kenneth Mackenzie. BoAV
Legion cries of battle die, The. The Bookworm. J. M. Moore. CAG
Legion of Honor, The. H. L. Flash. BIG
Legion of Iron, The. Lola Ridge. NAMP
Legomoton. *Unknown.* BoN
Legree's big house was white and green. Simon Legree—a Negro Sermon [*or* A Negro Sermon: Simon Legree]. Vachel Lindsay. The Booker Washington Trilogy, I. AnAmPo; ATP (1935 ed.); CoBA; HBMV; InMe; LA; LiTA; LoGBV; MAP; MoAmPo; MoVE; NAMP; NePA; PCN; PFY; ShBV-2
Legs, The. Robert Graves. FaBoMo; HaMV; LiTB; LiTM; MoP
Lehayyim, my brethren, Lehayyim, I say. Simhat Torah. Judah Leib Gordon. TrJP
Leicester Chambermaid. *Unknown.* CoMu
Leif was a man's name. Hervey Allen. *Fr.* Saga of Leif the Lucky. EtS
Leila. George Hill. APW
Leipsydrion. *Unknown, tr. fr. Greek by* C. M. Bowra. OxBG
Leir and His Daughters. Layamon, *tr. fr. Middle English. Fr.* The Brut. MeEV
Leisure. W. H. Davies. AnFE; AWP; BLV; BMEP; BoTP; CaAE; CH; ChMo; CMP; EnLit; FaBoBe; FaFP; FaPON; GTSE; HBV; HiLiEn; JAWP; LBBV; LiTB; LiTM; MBP; MoShBr; NBE; OBEV (new ed.); OBMV; OBVV; OtMeF; PC; PoeMoYo; PoeT; PoTo; POTT; PYM; SeCePo; ShBV-1; TCPD; TiPo; TOP; TrGrPo; TSW; TSWC; TVSH; WaKn; WBP; WHA; WoL; WP
Leisure the serfs will not forget. Reading Tolstoy. John Peter. BoSA
Leisurely Indulgence, A. Sakutaro Hagiwara, *tr. fr. Japanese by* Takamichi Ninomiya *and* D. J. Enright. PoLJ
Leisurely with some rustic fellow beside the wild river. Strolling in a Village. Liu Teh-jen. WhP
Leith police dismisseth us, The. *Unknown.* OxNR
Leith Races, *sel.* Robert Fergusson.
My Winsome Dear. SeCePo
Leitrim Woman, A. Lyle Donaghy. OnYI; OxBI
Lementable New Ballad upon the Earle of Essex Death, A. *Unknown.* CoMu
Lemme be wid Casey Jones. Odyssey of Big Boy. Sterling A. Brown. BANP; CDC
Lemme Go Back! *Unknown.* CAG
Lemmings, The. John Masefield. ChMo; CMP
Lemmings, The. Donald A. Stauffer. LiTG; SiTL; WaP
Lemon Sherbet. Marvin Solomon. NePoAm
Lemonade Stand. Dorothy Brown Thompson. SiSoSe
Lend a Hand. Edward Everett Hale. *See* Look Up.
Lend me, a little while, the key. The Pedler [*or* Pedlar]. Charlotte Mew. HBMV; TCPD
Lend me thy fillet, Love! The Lover's Song. Edward Rowland Sill. AA; HBV; PR
Lend me your song, ye nightingales! The Woodland Choir. James Thomson. *Fr.* The Seasons: Spring. CoBE
Length o' days ageän do shrink, The. The Fall. William Barnes. PoEL-4
Length of days is in her right hand. Wisdom. Proverbs, Bible, *O.T.* BPP
Length of Life. Hesiod, *tr. fr. Greek by* Sir William Marris. *Fr.* Precepts of Chiron. OxBG
Length of Moon. Arna Bontemps. CDC; PoNe
Lengthy Symphony. Persis Greely Anderson. WhC
Lenin, *sel.* Dorothy Wellesley.
"So I came down the steps." OBMV
Leningrad: 1943. Vera Inber, *tr. fr. Russian by* Dorothea Prall Radin *and* Alexander Kaun. *Fr.* The Pulkovo Meridian. WaaP
Lennavan-mo. Lullaby. "Fiona Macleod." BOL
Lenore. Poe. AA; AmP; AmPo; AmPP; AnFE; APA; BAP; CoAnAm; CoBA; IAP; LiTA; MOAP; SPP; TreFS; WHA
Lenox Avenue. Sidney Alexander. PoNe
Lens. Anne Wilkinson. PeCV
Lens and line/ Across the map deploy. Toponymy. Ralph Gustafson. BoCaPo (1943 ed.)
Lens of morning, polished sheer by sleep, The. Celestial Body. Louise Townsend Nicholl. NePoAm
Lent. Miriam LeFevre Crouse. ChIP
Lent. Jane McKay Lanning. MaRV
Lent. W. R. Rodgers. AnIL; NeBP; OxBI
Lent. Lubov Nikitishna Stolitza, *tr. fr. Russian by* Babette Deutsch. TrRV
Lent Lily, The. A. E. Housman. A Shropshire Lad, XXIX. AlDL; MPB; OHIP; PoRL; PoVP; ViP
Lent lily, pasque flower, herb trinity. Sea Sorrow. Rose Mills Powers. TBM
Lente, Lente. Ovid. *See* Slowly, Slowly.
Lenten Is [*or* Ys] Come. *Unknown.* BrBE; TyEnPo; ViBoPo
(Alysoun.) GoBC
(Spring.) AtBAP
(Spring Has Come.) PoLi
(Spring Song.) EnLi-1, *mod. vers.*; LyMA; PoEL-1
(Spring-Tide.) EV-1; OBEV
(Springtime.) CBOV; EPP, *Middle English and mod. vers.*
Lenten Lines to Lydia. Sennett Stephens. PR
Lenten stuff is come to the town. Two Old Lenten Rhymes, I. *Unknown.* ACP; WHL
Lenten Ys Come. *Unknown.* *See* Lenten Is Come.
"Lenten Ys Come with Love to Toune." Meleager, *tr. fr. Greek by* F. L. Lucas. GrPE
Lenton has brought us, as I understand. Two Old Lenten Rhymes, II. *Unknown.* ACP
L'Envoi: "Here are we for the last time face to face." William Morris. *Fr.* The Earthly Paradise. BPN; EmBrPo; EnLi-2; PoVP; ViP; ViPo
L'Envoi: "I end as I began." Robert Buchanan. TVSH
L'Envoi: "My towers at last! these rovings end." Herman Melville. *See* L'Envoi: Return of the Sire de Nesle, The.
L'Envoi: "Now in a thought, now in a shadowed word." E. A. Robinson. *Fr.* The Children of the Night. GrCo-2; MeRV; TwP
L'Envoi: "Oh, bubbles of the vanished wine." *Unknown.* DDA
L'Envoi: "O love triumphant over guilt and sin." Frederic Lawrence Knowles. OQP; QP-1; TrPWD
L'Envoi: Return of the Sire de Nesle, The. Herman Melville. AnFE; CoAnAm; ViBoPo
(L'Envoi: "My towers at last! these rovings end.") APA
L'Envoi: "Seek not for me within a tomb." John G. Neihardt. *See* Envoi: "O seek me not within a tomb."
L'Envoi: "There's a whisper down the field where the year has shot her yield." Kipling. *See* Long Trail, The.
L'Envoi: "What is the moral? Who rides may read." Kipling. *Fr.* The Story of the Gadsbys. MoBrPo; NeMA; TrGrPo
(Winners, The.) BLPA
L'Envoi: "When earth's last picture is painted, and the tubes are twisted and dried." Kipling. BTP; DD; FaFP; HBV; MaRV; OHFP; PECK; PTA-1; WGRP
(Envoy.) PoVP
(When Earth's Last Picture Is Painted.) BMEP; BPN; ChMo; EnLit; LiTB; POT; PoTo; TCPD; TreFS; VLEP
L'Envoi: "Where are the loves that we loved before." Willa Cather. HBV
L'Envoi: "Who findeth comfort in the stars and flowers." Thomas Lovell Beddoes. *Fr.* Death's Jest Book. LO
L'Envoi–Leave Her Johnny. *Unknown.* *See* Leave Her Johnny.
L'Envoy to W. L. H. Ainsworth, Esq. Francis S. Mahony. OnYI
Leo to His Mistress. Henry Dwight Sedgwick. BLPA; CIV
Leodogran, the King of Cameliard. The Coming of Arthur. Tennyson. *Fr.* Idylls of the King. VLEP
Leolin and Edith. Tennyson. *Fr.* Aylmer's Field. GN
Leonard: "Sun upon the lake is low, The." Sir Walter Scott. *See* Sun upon the Lake Is Low, The.
Leonardo da Vinci. Thomas S. Jones, Jr. MuM
Leonardo's "Monna Lisa." Edward Dowden. *See* Mona Lisa.
Leonidas. George Croly. HBV
Leonora. E. A. Robinson. MaPo; NePA
Lepanto. G. K. Chesterton. AlDL; AnFE; BEL; BMEP; CAW; CoBE; CP; GDAH; GoBC; GoTL (1949 ed.); HBMV; HBVY; InP; JKCP (1955 ed.); LBBV; MBP; MoBrPo; NeMA; NV; OBMV; OnSP; OtMeF; PC;

PFE; PoRA; POT; POTE; PoTo; PYM; ShBV-3; TreFS; TwCV; WHA
Lepanto marks the spot of victory. Our Lady of the Rosary. Francis A. Gaffney. JKCP
Leper, The. Swinburne. LO; VLEP
Leper, The. Nathaniel P. Willis. LPS-2, *abr.;* StJW; WGRP
Leper Cleansed, The. John Collop. BCEP; TrGrPo
Leper Island. Patricia Avis. PoN
Leper of London, The. Herman Scheffauer. BAP
Leprahaun, The. Robert Dwyer Joyce. OnYI; PoMS
Leprecaun, or Fairy Shoemaker, The. William Allingham. *See* Fairy Shoemaker, The.
Lerians are bad: not some bad, and some not. Problem in Logic. Phocylides, *tr. by* Lord Neaves. OnPM
Lerians are evil, The; all!—and not just a few. The Exception That Proves the Rule. Phocylides, *tr. by* F. L. Lucas. GrPE
Les Amours. Charles Cotton. ElSeCe; HBV
Les Belles Roses sans Mercie. Arthur Shearly Cripps. OBVV
Les Chantiers. S. Frances Harrison. *Fr.* Down the River. CPG
Les Chasse-Neige. Ralph A. Lewin. FiBHP
"Le's go down to Jurdon, le's go down to Jurdon." 'Ligion So Sweet. *Unknown.* ABF
Les Millwin. Ezra Pound. CoV; MOAP
Les Morts Vont Vite. H. C. Bunner. AA
Les Noyades, *sel.* Swinburne.
"Could I change you, help you to love me, sweet." LoPS
Les Planches-en-Montagne. Michael Roberts. OBMV
Les Roses Mortes. Rosamund Marriott Watson. PFE
Les Savants Ne Sont Pas Curieux. Merrill Moore. PoP
Les Silhouettes. Oscar Wilde. *Fr.* Impressions. Po; PoVP; VLEP
Les Sylphides. Louis MacNeice. CoBMV
Les Vaches. Arthur Hugh Clough. *See* Ite Domum Saturae, Venit Hesperus.
Lesbia. Richard Aldington. NP
Lesbia. Catullus, *tr. fr. Latin by* Richard Crashaw. LiA
(Counting Kisses.) LiTW
Lesbia. Congreve. BCEP
(Silly Fair.) LPS-2
Lesbia forever on me rails. Lesbia Railing. Catullus, *tr. by* Swift. AWP; JAWP; LiTW; WBP
Lesbia, my love, let's be gay and enjoy ourselves. The Kiss-Fest. Irwin Edman. InMe
Lesbia Railing. Catullus, *tr. fr. Latin by* Swift. AWP; JAWP; LiTW; WBP
("Lesbia swears at me continually; she's never quiet," *tr. by* L. R. Lind.) LaP
(Upon Lesbia's Abuse, *tr. by* George Lamb.) OnPM
Lesbia Sewing. Harold Vinal. HBMV
Lesbia still rails at me when by. Upon Lesbia's Abuse. Catullus, *tr. by* George Lamb. OnPM
Lesbia swears at me continually; she's never quiet. Catullus, *tr. by* L. R. Lind. LaP
Lesbia, whom some thought a lovely creature. Lesbia's Rule of Praise. Sir John Harington. SiCE
Lesbia's Disgrace. Catullus, *tr. fr. Latin by* George Lamb. OnPM
Lesbia's Rule of Praise. Sir John Harington. SiCE
Lesbia's Vow. Catullus, *tr. fr. Latin by* Francis Hodgson. OnPM
Lesbos. Baudelaire, *tr. fr. French by* Barbara Gibbs. AnFP
Lèse-Majesté. Herbert S. Gorman. BAP; HBMV
Less and less often now, the horny young men. Horace. Odes, I, 25. LaP
Less Lonely. Alfred Kreymborg. AnAmPo; LA
Less said the better. Missing. John Pudney. HaMV
Less than the Dust. "Laurence Hope." AV
Less the dog begged to die in the sky. Love Poem. George Barker. *Fr.* Fourth Cycle of Love Poems. NeBP
Lesser Children, The. Ridgely Torrence. BLA; LBMV
Lesser griefs that may be said, The. In Memoriam A. H. H., XX. Tennyson. EmBrPo; EnLi-2; EPN; GEPC; ViPo; VLEP
Lesser Lynx, The. E. V. Rieu. CenHV; FiBHP
Lesser Testament, The. Villon. *See* Petit Testament, Le.
Lesson, The. W. H. Auden. FaBoMo
Lesson. Harry Behn. TiPo (1959 ed.)
Lesson, The. Sister Mary Eleanore. JKCP (1955 ed.)
Lesson, A. Christina Rossetti. RIS
Lesson, The. Larry Rubin. GoYe
Lesson, The. Anne Goodwin Winslow. LS
Lesson, A. Wordsworth. CoEV; GTBS; GTBS-D; GTBS-W; GTSE; GTSL
(Small Celandine, The.) EM-2; HBV; OBRV
Lesson for Today, The. Robert Frost. LiTA; LiTM (rev. ed.); NePA; SiTL; WaP
Lesson from a Sun-Dial. *Unknown, ad. fr. German by* Louis Untermeyer. TiPo
Lesson from Van Gogh, A. Howard Moss. MoAB
Lesson in Geography, A. Frances Wynne. TIP
Lesson of Mercy, A. George Murray. VA
Lesson of the Flowers, The. Hafiz, *tr. fr. Persian by* E. H. Palmer. PeP
Lesson of the Water Mill, The. Sarah Doudney. *Fr.* The Man o' Airlie. HBV; PoToHe, *abr.;* TreFS
(Water Mill, The.) BLPA; BPP, *abr.;* PTA-2. *sl. diff. vers.;* WGRP
Lesson of Water. *Unknown, at. to* Lao-tzu, *tr. fr. Chinese by* Witter Bynner. *Fr.* Tao Teh King. OnPM
Lesson to Lovers, A. Moschus. *See* Love's Lesson.
Lessons. Sara Teasdale. Interlude: Songs Out of Sorrow, III. PC
Lessons. Helen Weber. PGD
Lessons for a Boy. Samuel Taylor Coleridge. *See* Metrical Feet.
Lessons from the Gorse. Elizabeth Barrett Browning. HBV
Lessons in Limericks. David McCord. InMe
Lessons of Nature, The. William Drummond of Hawthornden. *See* Book of the World, The.
Lessons of the War (I–III). Henry Reed. LiTB
Sels.
Judging Distances, II. ChMP; FaBoMo; MoAB
Naming of Parts, I. HoPM; LiTM; MoAB; MoVE; SeCePo; ShBV-3; SiTL; ViBoPo (1958 ed.); WaP
("Today we have naming of parts.") TrGrPo (rev. ed.)
Lessons of the Year. *Unknown.* BLRP
Lest it may more quarrels breed. Twelve Articles. Swift. BOHV; InMe
Lest men suspect your tale to be untrue. The Devil's Advice to Story-Tellers. Robert Graves. LiTM (rev. ed.)
Lest men suspect your tale untrue. The Painter Who Pleased Nobody and Everybody. John Gay. BeLS; CEP
Lest the young soldiers be strange in heaven. The Old Soldier. Katharine Tynan. AOAH
Lest Thou Forget. William L. Stidger. PoToHe
Lest, tortured by the world's strong sin. Desideravi. Theodore Maynard. HBMV
Lest We Forget. Deuteronomy, VI–VIII, *sels.*, Bible, *O.T.* GrCo-1
Lest We Forget! Kipling. *See* Recessional.
Lest We Forget. Curtis Wheeler. AOAH
Lest we forget! The months swing into years. Armistice Night. Curtis Wheeler. HH
Lest you should think that verse shall die. The Immortality of Verse. Pope. AWP; JAWP; WBP
Lestynt, lordynges, both elde and ynge. Of a Rose, a Lovely Rose. *Unknown.* BoW; OBEV; OxBoCh
Let/ Thy mother rather feel thy pride than fear. Shakespeare. *Fr.* Coriolanus, III, ii. MotAn
Let a child live by this river. The Hudson. Harriet Plimpton. VOD (1935 ed.)
Let a joy keep you. *See* Let joy keep you.
Let all men see the ruins of the shrine. Robert Hillyer. Sonnets, XIV. HBMV
Let All the Earth Keep Silence. Lucy A. K. Adee. OQP; QP-2
Let all the fish that swim the sea. Herring Is King. Alfred Perceval Graves. TIP
Let all the world in every [*or* ev'ry] corner sing. Antiphon. George Herbert. CBE; EPS (1942 ed.); EV-2; PreP
Let All Things Pass Away, *sel.* W. B. Yeats.
"Rivery field spread out below, A." ChTr
Let America Be America Again. Langston Hughes. PoFr; PoNe
Let Bacchus's sons be not dismayed. Garryowen. *Unknown.* OnYI
Let baths and wine-butts be November's due. Of the Months: November. Folgore da San Geminiano. AWP
Let Be. *Unknown.* WBLP
Let be at last; give over words and sighing. Venite Descendamus. Ernest Dowson. POTT
Let be the herds and what the harvest brings. The Fourth of July. Charles Leonard Moore. IDAH
Let Bourbons fight for status quo. Status Quo. Binga Dismond. PoNe
Let but a fellow in a fox-furred gown. An Invective against the Wicked of the World. Nicholas Breton. ViBoPo
Let but a thrush begin. Lyric. John Hewitt. NeIP
Let but the son of earth. The Ages of Man. *At. to* Abraham ibn Ezra. TrJP
Let certain holdings of stocks and bonds. Codicil. Mabel MacDonald Carver. GoYe
Let Christmas not become a thing. Christmas Prayer. Madeline Morse. PGD; PSO
Let courage stiffen. Iron Fare. Marjorie Allen Seiffert. NP
Let dainty wits cry on the sisters nine. Astrophel and Stella, III. Sir Philip Sidney. OBSC; ReEn; ReIE; SiCE; SiPS; TuPP
Let de peoples know (unnh). Blues for Bessie. Myron O'Higgins. PoNe
Let deeds be our quest. Vow of the European. Ulrich Becher. TwGV
Let Deirdre be her name: harm will come through her. The Foretelling of Cathbad the Druid at Deirdre's Birth. *Unknown.* LiTW

Let Dogs Delight to Bark and Bite. Isaac Watts. HBVY; OTPC; PECK; TreFS
(Against Quarrelling and Fighting.) OBEC; SeCePo
(Quarrelling.) BLPA
Let Dreamers Wake. Lilith Lorraine. PGD
"Let Earth give thanks," the deacon said. Give Thanks fer What? W. F. Croffut. TOAH
Let Elizur Rejoice with the Partridge. Christopher Smart. *Fr.* Jubilate Agno. PoEL-3
Let 'em censure: what care I? In Imitation of Anacreon [*or* On Critics]. Matthew Prior. CEP; SeCeV
Let England, and Ireland, and Scotland rejoice. The Royal Victory. *Unknown.* SG
Let Erin Remember the Days of Old. Thomas Moore. EnRP; ERP; PoE
Let fame. Vladimir Mayakovsky. *Fr.* At the Top of My Voice. TrRV
Let fate or insufficiency provide. To J. M. George Meredith. EPN
Let folly praise that fancy loves, I praise and love that Child. A Child My Choice. Robert Southwell. CAW; GoBC; HBV; OxBoCh; PoLi; SiCE
Let four captains/ Bear Hamlet, like a soldier, to the stage. Shakespeare. *Fr.* Hamlet, V, ii. MyFE
Let from its dream the soul awaken. The Coplas on the Death of His Father, the Grandmaster of Santiago. Jorge Manrique. CAW
Let Glory's sons manipulate. The Politician. Ambrose Bierce. BAP
Let go the Limb? Leaf and Soul. John Banister Tabb. PoMa
Let Go the Peak Halyards, *frag.* *Unknown.* AmSS
Let Go the Reef Tackle, *with music.* *Unknown.* ShS
Let gouty monarchs share their shams. Yankee Doodle. *Unknown.* APB
Let half-starv'd slaves in warmer skies. Postscript to a Letter on the Excise Laws. Burns. PIR
Let hammer on anvil ring. The Armorer's Song. Henry Bache Smith. AA; MW; OHIP
Let hands be about him white, O his mother's first. The Mother and Child. Vernon Watkins. NeBP
Let heathen sing thy heathen praise. The Greek Fathers. Cardinal Newman. JKCP
Let her lie naked here, my hand resting. News of the World III. George Barker. AtBAP; FaBoTw; LiTB; LiTM (rev. ed.)
Let her who walks in Paphos. Lais. Hilda Doolittle ("H. D."). MAP; MoAmPo
Let here the brow be bared. At the Tomb of Washington. Clinton Scollard. DD; GA; MC; OHIP; PEDC
Let him alone and when he is one year older. A Young Boy. Jessica Nelson North. NP
Let him be safe in sleep. Spell of Sleep. Kathleen Raine. HaMV
Let him be sold, though still he sleep. Meleager, *tr. fr. Greek by* Walter Headlam. GrPo
Let him kiss me with the kisses of his mouth. The Song of Songs. Song of Solomon, Bible, *O.T.* AWP; TrGrPo
Let Him Return. Leona Ames Hill. PoToHe (new ed.)
Let him who wishes seek pomp and honor, follow. Sonnet. Lorenzo de' Medici. LyPI
Let immortality of earth and men's lips hold you. To Jean. Duncan B. M. Emrich. CAG
Let It Be Forgotten. Sara Teasdale. BAP; BAV; BLV; BPP; CBOV; CP; HBMV; LoPS; MAP; MoAmPo; NP; PG (1945 ed.); TCPD; TrGrPo
(Song.) PFY; SBMV
Let it be Sabbath, Sabbath! Eternal Sabbath. Isaac Leibush Peretz. TrJP
Let it be so, thy truth then be thy dowre. Shakespeare. *Fr.* King Lear, I, i. NBE
Let it be understood that I am Don Juan Gomez! Conquistador [*or* Announcement]. Elizabeth J. Coatsworth. GoTP; MAP
Let it flame or fade and the war roll down like a wind. England. Tennyson. *Fr.* Maud. BHV
Let it idly droop, or sway. The Flag. Lucy Larcom. DD; FOAH; HH
Let it no longer be a forlorn hope. On the Baptized Ethiopian [*or* Aethiopian]. Richard Crashaw. SeCV-1; SeEP
Let it not be, love, underneath a roof. Golden Bough. Helen Hoyt. HBMV
"Let it not come unto you, all ye that pass by!" Desolation in Zion. Lamentations, Bible, *O.T.* TrJP
Let it not your wonder move. His Excuse for Loving. Ben Jonson. *Fr.* A Celebration of Charis. PoEL-2; SeCV-1; SeEP; TuPP
Let joy [*or* a joy] keep you. Joy. Carl Sandburg. BAP; LEAP; NP; PC
Let Liberty run onward with the years. A Holy Nation. Richard Realf. *Fr.* Of Liberty and Charity. PoFr
Let liberty, the charter'd right of Englishmen. Blake. *Fr.* King Edward the Third. PoFr
Let Loneliness be mute. Accuse. To Losers. George Dillon. NP
Let Lotan Rejoice with Sauterelle. Christopher Smart. *Fr.* Jubilate Agno. AtBAP
Let lovers that like honey-flies. To Cynthia on His Love after Death. Sir Francis Kynaston. SeEP
Let man be free! The mighty word. Whittier. *Fr.* The Emancipation Group. PGD
Let man's soul [*or* soule] be a sphere [*or* spheare], and then, in this. Good Friday, 1613. Riding Westward. John Donne. AtBAP; ATP (1953 ed.); ExPo; MeLP; MePo; OBS; OxBoCh; Po; PoEL-2; ReaPo; ReEn; SeCV-1; SeEP; TriL; TuPP
Let me alone, I prithee, in this cell. Satyra Quinta. Everard Guilpin. *Fr.* Skialetheia. SiCE; TuPP
Let me at last be laid. At Last. Sir Lewis Morris. VA
Let Me Be a Giver. Mary Carolyn Davies. PoToHe
Let me be a little kinder. My Daily Creed. *Unknown.* BLP; MaRV
Let me be buried in the rain. Invocation. Helene Johnson. BANP; PoNe
Let me be like that lonely house, O Lord. A Prayer. André Lafon. TrFP
Let me be marble, marble once again. Galatea Again. Genevieve Taggard. WHA
Let me be my own fool. A Counterpoint. Robert Creeley. NeAP
Let me be the one. By Myself. Robert Frost. RIS
Let me be what I am, as Virgil cold. An Elegie. Ben Jonson. PoEL-2
Let Me Be with Thee. Charlotte Elliott. VA
Let me be your servant. Old Age of Temperance. Shakespeare. *Fr.* As You Like It, II, iii. LPS-2
Let me but do my work from day to day. Work. Henry van Dyke. *Fr.* The Three Best Things. BTP; MaRV; OQP; PoeMoYo; PoMa; PoRL; POT; PoTo; PYM; QP-1; SP; TCAP; YT
Let me but live my life from year to year. Life. Henry van Dyke. *Fr.* The Three Best Things. BLP; MaRV; OQP; QP-1
Let me close my eyes tight. Invocation to Death. Emanuel Carnevali. NP
Let me come in where you sit weeping—aye. Bereaved. James Whitcomb Riley. AA; BAP; LBAP; LEAP; MaRV; OBAV
Let me confess that we two must be twain. Sonnets, XXXVI. Shakespeare. OAEP; PeBoSo
Let Me Die Working. S. Hall Young. *See* Into the Sunset.
Let me do my work each day. A Prayer. Max Ehrmann. BLPA; FaBoBe; MaRV; NeHB; PoToHe
Let Me Enjoy ("Let me enjoy the earth no less"). Thomas Hardy. AnFE; AWP; ChMo; CMP; HBV; InPo; JAWP; PoVP; ViBoPo; VLEP; WBP
Let me enjoy myself in drunkenness. Drinking. Hsin Ch'i-chi. LiTW; WhP
Let me enlighten. 'Tis no metaphor. William Ellery Leonard. *Fr.* Two Lives, III. MOAP
Let Me Flower as I Will. Lew Sarett. TrPWD
Let Me Go Back. Mary E. Albright. BLRP
Let Me Go Down to Dust. Lew Sarett. TBM; TrPWD
Let me go forth, and share. Ode in May. Sir William Watson. BMEP; CBOV; GTML; MBP; MoBrPo (1942 ed.); OBEV; OBVV; PC; PoeT; PoVP; WGRP
Let Me Go Warm. Luis de Góngora, *tr. fr. Spanish by* Longfellow. AnSpL-1; AWP; JAWP; WBP; WoL
Let Me Go Where'er I Will. Emerson. *See* Music.
Let Me Grow Lovely. Karle Wilson Baker. BLPA; FaBoBe; HBMV; NeHB; TrPWD
(Growing Old.) DDA; OQP; QP-2
Let Me Guide a Little Child. *Unknown.* PraP
Let me have a scarlet maple. The Grave-Tree. Bliss Carman. CaP; CPG; OCL
Let me have men about me that are fat. Julius Caesar's Preference. Shakespeare. *Fr.* Julius Caesar, I, ii. TreFS
Let Me Kiss Him for His Mother. *Unknown.* BlG
Let Me Laugh. *Unknown.* SeCL
Let me lay it to you gently, Mr. Gone! Poem of Holy Madness, IV. Ray Bremser. NeAP
Let me learn now where Beauty is. Questing. Anne Spencer. CDC
Let me lie down beside you, prince. By a British Barrow. Andrew Young. NeTW
Let Me Lift Jesus, Lord. Jo Gardner. BePJ
Let Me Live. Shakespeare. *See* On Death.
Let Me Live for a Time Way Back from the Road. C. G. Farnum. PoP
Let me live harmlessly; and near the brink. The Angler's Song. John Dennys. *Fr.* The Secrets of Angling. ElL; MyFE
Let me live, O Mighty Master. A Sportsman's Prayer. *Unknown.* MaRV
Let Me Live Out My Years. John G. Neihardt. BAP; BLP; GrCo-2; HBMV; MAP; MaRV; PC; PoMa; TBM; TreFS; YaD
Let Me Love Bright Things. A. Newberry Choyce. HBMV
Let Me No More a Mendicant. Arthur Colton. LBMV

Let Me Not Die. Edith Lovejoy Pierce. TrPWD

Let me not know how sins and sorrows glide. Prayer. James Elroy Flecker. TrPWD

Let me not pray to be sheltered from dangers. Prayer for Courage. Rabindranath Tagore. MaRV

Let me not to the marriage of true minds. Sonnets, CXVI [or The Marriage of True Minds or True Love or Love's Not Time's Fool]. Shakespeare. AnEnPo; AnFE; ATP; AWP; BBV; BCEP; BEL; BLV; BoFr; BoLiVe; CaAE; CoBE; CoEV; EG; EIL; ElSeCe; EM-1; EnL; EnLi-1; EnLit; EnLoPo; EPP; ES; EtPaEn; EV-1; ExPo; FaBoEn; FaFP; GBV; GoBC; GrCo-2; GTBS; GTBS-D; GTBS-W; GTSE; GTSL; HBV; InPo; InvP; JAWP; KN; LEAP; LiA; LiTB; LiTG; LiTL; LO; LoBV; LoPo; LPS-1; MaPo; MaRV; MCCG; OAEP; OBEV; OBSC; OuHeWo; PeBoSo; PFE; PG; PIAE; PIR; Po; PoE; PoEL-2; PoeMoYo; PoRA; PreP; REAL; ReaPo; ReEn; ReIE; RiBV; SeCePo; SeCeV; ShBV-4; SiCE; TOP; TreF; TrGrPo; TwP; TyEnPo; UnPo; ViBoPo; WBP; WHA

Let me now set down a picture of New England that will show it to you and explain it. Praise of New England. Thomas Caldecot Chubb. GoYe

Let Me Play the Fool. Shakespeare. Fr. The Merchant of Venice, I, i. TrGrPo (Why Should a Man.) BLP

Let me poure [or powre] forth. A Valediction: Of Weeping. John Donne. AtBAP; ATP; EG; EnLP; MeLP; MePo; OBS; ReIE; TuPP

Let me remember music. Prayer. Sydney King Russell. MuM

Let me remember you or dream you. The Wall. Octavio Paz. AnCL

"Let me see if Philip can." The Story of Fidgety Philip. Heinrich Hoffmann. BoN

Let Me Sing of My Well-Beloved. Isaiah, V, Bible, O.T. TrJP

Let me sit down a minute, stranger. Down in Lehigh Valley. Unknown. TreF

Let me sit here by this adobe wall. Summer Comes. Edith Agnew. SiSoSe

Let Me Sleep. Christina Rossetti. PC

Let me sleep among the shadows of the mountains when I die. Whence Cometh My Help. Odell Shepard. OBAV

Let Me Speak of Pure Things. Ho Chih-fang, tr. fr. Chinese by Chiang Shao-yi. LiTW

Let me speak, sir. Cranmer's Prophecy of Queen Elizabeth [or England at Peace]. Shakespeare and probably John Fletcher. King Henry VIII, fr. V, v. EV-1; WGRP

Let me stand still upon the height of life. Forward. "Susan Coolidge." PEOR

Let me stop here. Let me, too, see nature awhile. Morning Sea. C. P. Cavafy. MoGP

Let me take this other glove off. In Westminster Abbey. John Betjeman. LiTM

Let me tell to you the story. "Los Pastores." Edith Agnew. ChBR; GaP

Let me thy properties explain. On an Ill-managed House. Swift. AnIV

Let me today do something that will take. A Morning Prayer. Ella Wheeler Wilcox. MaRV; OQP; PoToHe; QP-2

Let Me Walk Alone Where Breaks the Sea. Luis de Góngora. See Loveliest Girl, The.

Let Me Walk with the Men in the Road. Walter J. Gresham. See Crowded Ways of Life.

Let me work and be glad. A Prayer. Theodosia Garrison. TrPWD

Let men intently strip your grace. Three Love Poems, I. Stepan Petrovich Shchipachev. RuPo

Let Mine Eyes See Thee. St. Theresa of Avila, tr. fr. Spanish by Arthur Symons. AWP; CAW; JAWP; WBP

Let mine not be the saddest fate of all. Uselessness. Ella Wheeler Wilcox. TrPWD

Let Minions Marshal Every Hair. Unknown. ALV

Let mother earth now deck[e] herself[e] in flowers. Epithalamium. Sir Philip Sidney. Fr. Arcadia. EV-1; SiPS

Let my soul, a shining tree. Tree and Sky. Siegfried Sassoon. TSW

Let my spear lie down for the spider to weave its thread. Old Age. Euripides. OxBG

Let my sweet song be pleasing unto Thee. A Love Song. Judah Halevi. TrJP

Let my voice ring out and over the earth. Song. James Thomson. Sunday up the River, XVII. EmBrPo; HBV; MaRV; OBVV; POTT; PoVP; VLEP

Let Myron muse at Nature's passing might. The Lover Extolleth the Singular Beauty of His Lady. George Turberville. ReIE

Let Nature Be Your Teacher. Wordsworth. Fr. The Tables Turned. MaRV

Let never a man a wooing wend. King Henry. Unknown. ESPB; OBB

Let no blasphemer till the sacred earth. Benediction. Mark Turbyfill. NP; TBM

Let No Charitable Hope. Elinor Wylie. AnAmPo; ChMo; HBMV; InP; LA; LEAP; LiTA; LiTM; MAP; MoAB; MoAmPo; MOAP; NePA; NV; OxBA; PoE; TBM; TrGrPo

Let no heart in sorrow weep for other days. Ho! for Carolina! William Bernard Harrell. NoCaPo

Let no man ask thee of anything. Soothsay. Dante Gabriel Rossetti. BPN; EmBrPo

Let no man come into this hall. Make We Merry, Both More and Less. Unknown. AnEC; SDH

"Let no man write my epitaph; let my grave." Written Immediately after Reading [or On] the Speech of Robert Emmet [or Emmet's Epitaph]. Robert Southey. ERP; LPS-3; PoFr

Let no one awaken/ This child so fast asleep. Deep Sleep. "Gabriela Mistral." AnCL

Let no one say he is adored. Warning. Unknown. APW

Let no pirate's sword storm these veins of yours. For Her on the First Day Out. Robert Bagg. NePoAm-2

Let Noble thy protector be. The Protector. Ibn Sharaf. MooP

Let noman booste of konnyinge nor vertu. See Lat noman booste of konnyng nor vertu.

Let none but guests or clubbers hither come. Ben Jonson's [or Johnsons] Sociable Rules for the Apollo. Ben Jonson. SeCV-1; TuPP

Let none who have not wisdom govern you. Canzone: He Rebukes the Evil of That Time. Siciliano Inghilfredi. PoFr

Let not any withering Fate. Oracles, I. Lionel Johnson. VLEP

Let not Chloris think, because. Unknown. OBSC

Let not dark nor shadows fright thee. A Song of Dalliance. William Cartwright. ALV; NBE

Let not Death boast his conquering power. On Eleanor Freeman, Who Died 1650, Aged 21. Unknown. OBEV (new ed.)

Let not his humble vesture make thee blind. The Poor Scholar. Abraham ibn Chasdai. TrJP

Let Not My Death Be Long. Leonora Speyer. BAP

Let not my jealous foes. Mutability. Ibn Hazm. MooP

Let not my love be call'd [or called] idolatry. Sonnets, CV. Shakespeare. BoFr; PeBoSo

Let not old age disgrace my high desire. Old Age. Sir Philip Sidney. Fr. Arcadia. SiPS

Let not one spark of filthy lustful fire. Amoretti, LXXXIII. Spenser. PeBoSo

Let not our hearts be busy inns. Christmas Prayer. Ralph Spaulding Cushman. MaRV

Let not our town be large, remembering. On the Building of Springfield. Vachel Lindsay. AmPP (3d ed.); InP; LBMV; MOAP; NAMP; OHFP; PaA; TOP; WHA

Let not, sweet saint, let not these lines offend you. Sonnet I: He Demands Pardon for Looking, Loving, and Writing. Walter Davison. ReIE

Let not the ballad-singer's shrilling strain. Of Ballad-Singers. John Gay. Fr. Trivia; or, The Art of Walking the Streets of London, III. EnLi-1 (1949 ed.)

Let Not the Sluggish Sleep. Unknown. CenL; OxBoCh (Song, A: "Let not the sluggish sleep.") ACP; GoBC

Let not the sun go down upon your wrath. Forgiveness. Ephesians, Bible, O.T. BoFr

Let not us that youngmen be. Youth. Unknown. OBSC

Let Not Woman E'er Complain. Burns. LPS-1

Let not young souls be smothered out before. The Leaden-eyed. Vachel Lindsay. ATP; BLV; BoLiVe; ChMo; CMP; GrCo-1; GTBS-W; LiTA; LiTM; MaRV; NAMP; NePA; NP; NV; PoeMoYo

Let not your heart be altogether lonely. Good-by—to My Mother. Margaret Larkin. BLP

Let not your heart be faint. The Peace of Christ. John Antes La Trobe. BePJ

Let not your heart be troubled. The Peace of Christ [or My Peace I Give unto You or The Way, the Truth, and the Life]. St. John, Bible, N.T. EM-1; TreFS; WoL

Let Not Your Heart Be Troubled. Alice Mortenson. BePJ

Let Nothing Disturb Thee. St. Theresa of Avila. See Santa Teresa's Book-Mark.

Let now the dead be hidden in the earth. The Voice of Enlightenment. Euripides. Fr. Suppliants. GrR

Let now your soul in this substantial world. An End of Travel. Robert Louis Stevenson. VLEP

Let observation, with extensive view. The Vanity of Human Wishes. Samuel Johnson. ATP; BEL; CEP; CoBE; EiPP; EPP; EV-3; LaA; LoBV; Po; PoE; PoEL-3; PoFS; TOP; TriL; UnPo (1st ed.)

Let one another this embrace. Unknown. LO

Let other servants boast a snowy glove. Upon Scarlet and Blush-coloured Ribbands, Given by Two Ladies. James Shirley. GoBC

Let others better mold the running mass. The Sixth Book of the Aeneis. Virgil, tr. by Dryden. Fr. The Aeneid. SeCV-2

Let others chaunt a country praise. London Town. Lionel Johnson. PoVP

Let others cheer the winning man. A Smile. *Unknown.* BLPA; WBLP
Let others from the town retire. Nonpareil. Matthew Prior. EnLoPo
Let others give you wealth and love. The Gift. Louis V. Ledoux. SBMV
Let others keep to the beaten track. Ballade of the Road Unknown. Richard Le Gallienne. CV
Let others of the world's decaying tell. Sonnet. Earl of Stirling. Aurora, XCVIII. ElL
Let others pile their yellow ingots high. Pastoral Elegy [*or* An Elegy]. Albius Tibullus. AWP; LiTW
Let Others Share. Edward Anthony. GoTP
Let others sing of knights and paladins. To Delia, LII [*or* Beauty, Time, and Love *or* Trophies]. Samuel Daniel. BCEP; BEL; CoBE; ElL; ElSeCe; EnLi-1 (1949 ed.); EPP; ES; FaBoEn; HBV; OAEP; OBEV; OBSC; ReEn; ReIE; SiCE; TuPP; ViBoPo
Let others sing of Mars, and of his train. To Love; a Sonnet. Philip Ayres. CEP
Let others write about you, or leave you all unknown. Propertius. Elegies, II, 11. LaP
Let others write of battles fought. True Heroism. *Unknown.* PEOR
Let Our Love Be. Samuel Hoffenstein. PR
Let our smooth modern laughter still deride. Meditation. Dorothy Hobson. MuM
Let our song begin with the choir of Muses that own. The Muses' Gift. Hesiod. *Fr.* Theogony. OxBG
Let Peter Rejoice with the Moon Fish. Christopher Smart. *Fr.* Jubilate Agno. AtBAP
Let Pilate and let Judas holy be. The Perjured. Albert E. Johnson. QS
Let pious Damon take his seat. Sermon in a Churchyard. Macaulay. OBRV
Let Poets chant of clouds and things. A Pure Mathematician. Arthur Guiterman. PoMa
Let praise devote thy work, and skill employ. Laus Deo. Robert Bridges. TriL
Let readers say (description or abuse). The Lemmings. Donald A. Stauffer. LiTG; SiTL; WaP
Let Rome in Tiber melt, and the wide arch. Shakespeare. *Fr.* Antony and Cleopatra, I, i. EtPaEn
Let sailors watch the waning Pleiades. Cleonicos. Edward Cracroft Lefroy. Echoes from Theocritus, XXVII. AWP; JAWP; WBP
Let schoolmasters puzzle their brain. The Three Jolly Pigeons [*or* Song]. Goldsmith. *Fr.* She Stoops to Conquer. EnLi-1 (1949 ed.); OAEP; PoRA; ViBoPo
Let scoffers doubt it if they will. Concerning Brownie. Nancy Byrd Turner. AlBD; PC
Let Sol his annual journeys run. Hint from Voiture. William Shenstone. EnLoPo
Let Some Great Joys Pretend to Find. Thomas Shadwell. *Fr.* The Woman-Captain. OAEP
Let Something Good Be Said. James Whitcomb Riley. MaRV
Let Sporus tremble—"What? that thing of silk." Sporus [*or* Lord Hervey]. Pope. *Fr.* Epistle to Dr. Arbuthnot. AWP; ChTr; CoEV; InPo; JAWP; LPS-3; MaPo; NBE; ViBoPo; WBP
Let such pure hate still underprop. Love. Henry David Thoreau. AnNE
Let Swedish bosoms deep and strong. Swedish National Hymn. Karl Vilhelm August Strandberg. AnSL; PoFr
Let Taylor preach, upon a morning breezy. Morning Meditations. Thomas Hood. LPS-3
Let tears be for all men, all children. Pray Pity for Bill Smith. Paul L. Grano. BoAu
Let th' ayre complayne, and eke the parent great. Chorus. Seneca. *Fr.* Hercules Furens. LaP
Let that which is to come be as it may. John Masefield. *Fr.* Sonnets ("Long, long ago"). HBV
Let the bells ring, and let the boys sing. Song. John Fletcher. *Fr.* The Spanish Curate, III, ii. OBS; TuPP
Let the bird of loudest lay. The Phoenix and the Turtle. Shakespeare. CaAE; FaBoEn; GTBS-W; KN; LiTB; LiTG; LiTL; LoBV; MaPo; MePo; MyFE; OBEV; OBSC; PoEL-2; SeCePo; SeCeV; SiCE
Let the Boat Go. "Kostes Hatzopoulos," *tr. fr. Modern Greek by* Rae Dalven. MoGP
Let the boy try along this bayonet-blade. Arms and the Boy. Wilfred Owen. AnEnPo; FaFP; GTBS-W; LiTB; LiTM; MBP; MoAB; MoBrPo; NAMP; NP; OAEP (2d ed.); WaP
Let the brass dome of heaven, wide and great. An Oath. Theognis. OxBG
Let the bright blood flow; starve and liquidate. Song above Death. James Edward Tobin. JKCP (1955 ed.)
Let the Catholic Church be now arrayed. Bishop Butler of Kilcash. *Unknown.* OnYI
Let the day glare, O memory, your tread. Ode to Fear. Allen Tate. BLV; MM
Let the Day Perish. Job, Bible, *O.T. See* Job's Curse.
Let the door be open wide. Christmas Eve. Liam P. Clancy. ISi
Let the dull merchant curse his angry fate. Elegy: The Unrewarded Lover. William Walsh. CEP; EV-3
Let the earth eat up her dead. A Note on the Continuity of Life. John Ransom Palmer. PoP
Let the eye remember the loved face. The Soul Remembers. Richard Burdick Eldridge. GoYe
Let the farmer praise his grounds. The Cruiskeen Lawn. *Unknown.* HBV; OnYI; TIP
Let the flame be fed on the altar of the ideal. Théophile Gautier. *Fr.* Le Triomphe de Pétrarque. LiA
Let the Florid Music Praise. W. H. Auden. MoPo
Let the foul scene proceed. The Marionettes. Walter de la Mare. AtBAP
Let the green Succatash with thee contend. Joel Barlow. *Fr.* The Hasty Pudding. LoGBV
Let the knowing speak. Adjuration. Charles Enoch Wheeler. PoNe
Let the Light Enter. Frances E. W. Harper. PoNe
Let the lover his mistress's beauty rehearse. My Bonny Black Bess. *Unknown.* ABS; ViBoFo
Let the mad poets say whate'er they please. A Real Woman. Keats. LiTL
Let the mighty and great. The Happy Farmer. *Unknown.* GoTP
Let the mountains stand forth! Requiem. Hamilton Warren. GoYe
Let the Nations Be Glad. Psalms, LXVII, Bible, *O.T.* FaPON (1-5)
("God be merciful unto us, and bless us.") OnPM
Let the night keep/ What the night takes. Night. William Rose Benét. MAP; MoAmPo; NeMA
Let the night weep on your hand. Admonition before Grief. Hazel Hall. NP
Let the Nile cloak his head in the clouds, and defy. On the Discoveries of Captain Lewis. Joel Barlow. GA; MC; PAH
Let the place of the solitaires. The Place of the Solitaires. Wallace Stevens. NP
Let the Pulse Speak. Louis Untermeyer. BoFr
Let the Punishment Fit the Crime. W. S. Gilbert. *See* Humane Mikado, The.
Let the rain kiss you. April Rain Song. Langston Hughes. FaPON; PoRh; SUS; TiPo
Let the rain plunge radiant. The Way Through. Denise Levertov. NeAP
Let the Rich Man Fill His Belly. *Unknown, tr. fr. Spanish by* Havelock Ellis. OnPM
(Folk Songs. 1.) LiTW
(Spanish Folk Songs.) AWP; JAWP; WBP
Let the snake wait under. A Sort of a Song. William Carlos Williams. HoPM; SeCeV
Let the tale's sailor from a Christian voyage. Sonnets, X. Dylan Thomas. LiTM
Let the thick curtain fall. My Triumph. Whittier. BHV; IAP; TCAP
Let the Toast Pass. Sheridan. *Fr.* The School for Scandal, III, iii. HBV; LPS-1; OnYI; OxBI; PreP
(Famous Toast, A.) TreF
(Here's to the Maiden.) ALV; EV-3; LiTL; SiTL
(Song: "Here's to the maiden [*or* maid] of bashful fifteen.") CEP; NeHB; OBEC; OxBoLi; PoRA; ViBoPo
Let the toper regale in his tankard of ale. The Pipe of Tobacco. *At. to* John Usher. HBV
Let the Traveller Pause. Junzaburo Nishiwaki, *tr. fr. Japanese by* Takamichi Ninomiya *and* D. J. Enright. PoLJ
Let the vain courtier waste his days. Country Life. Lope de Vega. AnSpL-1
Let the waves of slumber billow. To a Lady Troubled by Insomnia. Franklin P. Adams. InMe
Let the wise man place his seat. The Confession of Golias. "The Archpoet of Cologne." LiTW
Let the youth hardened by a sharp soldier's life. Horace. Odes, III, 2. LaP; WaaP
Let them bestow on every airth a limb. Verses Composed on the Eve of His Execution [*or* On Himself]. James Graham, Marquess of Montrose. ChTr; EBSV; OBS; SeCePo
Let them bury your big eyes. Elegy. Edna St. Vincent Millay. *Fr.* Memorial to D. C. AnNE; BAP; HBMV; InP; MAP; MoAB; MoAmPo; NeMA; NePA; PoRA
Let them come, come never so proudly. God Save Elizabeth! Frances Turner Palgrave. HBV
Let them devour and be devour'd! Christopher Brennan. *Fr.* The Burden of Tyre. NeLNL
Let them go by—the heats, the doubts, the strife. Oasis. Edward Dowden. OxBI; TIP
Let them say to my Lover. Amor Mysticus. Sister Marcela de Carpio de San Félix. AnSpL-1; AWP; CAW; JAWP; LiTW; WBP
Let there be laid, when I am dead. Posthumous Coquetry. Théophile Gautier. AWP

Let there be life, said God. The Power and the Glory. Siegfried Sassoon. GrCo-2; OBMV; OS

Let there be Light! The Apple Tree. Oliver St. John Gogarty. AIDL; OS

"Let there be light!" God spake of old. The Library. Whittier. MOB

Let there be many windows to your soul. Progress. Ella Wheeler Wilcox. BLPA

Let There Be No More Battles! Edwin Markham. PSO

Let there be violet dusk and a cool air. In Pace in Idipsum Dormiam et Requiescam. Patrick O'Connor. CAW

Let there be within these phantom walls. Dream House. Catherine Parmenter Newell. PoToHe

Let those complain that feel Love's cruelty. To the Blest Evanthe. John Fletcher. *Fr.* A Wife for a Month. SeCL; SeEP

Let those love now, who never loved before. The Vigil of Venus. *Unknown.* WoL

Let those who are in favor with their stars. Sonnets, XXV. Shakespeare. EM-1; EnL; EnLi-1; OBSC; PeBoSo; ReIE; SiCE; WoL

Let those who will on science meditate. The Pain of Stone. Sophie Himmell. MuM

Let thunder burst. Anacreontic. Francisco Martínez de la Rosa. AnSpL-2

Let thy gold be cast in the furnace. Cleansing Fires. Adelaide Anne Procter. WGRP

Let thy tears, Le Vayer, let them flow. To Monsieur de la Mothe le Vayer. Molière. AWP; JAWP; WBP

Let time and chance combine, combine. Adieu. Thomas Carlyle. HBV; OBRV; VA

"Let trees be made, for Earth is bare." The Coming of the Trees. Arthur Guiterman. PEDC

Let Trouble-Makers trouble make. A Line o' Cheer. John Kendrick Bangs. LPS-1

Let true love amongst us be. The Duty of Christian Folk. *Unknown.* TMEV

Let tyrants shake their iron rods. Chester. William Billings. TrAS

Let us abandon then our gardens and go home. Justice Denied in Massachusetts. Edna St. Vincent Millay. CoBA; MAP; MoAmPo

Let Us All Be Unhappy on Sunday. Charles Neaves. EBSV

Let us, as by this verdant bank we float. The Water-Party. Robert Bridges. CaAE

Let us ask ourselves some questions; for that man is truly wise. The Higher Catechism. Sam Walter Foss. WGRP

Let us ask you a few questions, without rancor. For Any Member of the Security Police. Josephine Jacobsen. NePoAm

Let us be guests in one another's house. Any Wife or Husband. Carol Haynes. BLPA; NeHB; PoToHe

Let Us Be Happy as Long as We Can. Joseph Stansbury. IAP

Let us be just with life. Although it bear. The Balance. George Sterling. PC

Let Us Be Kind. W. Lomax Childress. PTA-2

Let Us Be Men. D. H. Lawrence. MoPW

Let Us Be Merry [before We Go]. John Philpot Curran. *See* Deserter, The.

Let Us Be Off! C. Day Lewis. WoL

Let us be still. There is nothing that we can do. Silence. Humbert Wolfe. ReTS

Let us begin to carry up this corpse. A Grammarian's Funeral. Robert Browning. AnFE; BEL; BMEP; BoLiVe; BPN; CoBE; EM-2; EmBrPo; EnLit; EPN; EPP; EV-5; GEPC; GTBS; HBV; LEAP; LoBV; MaRV; OAEP; PoE; PoVP; TOP; TyEnPo; ViPo; ViPP; VLEP; WGRP

Let us begin with Zeus, the power we mortals never leave. Aratus. *Fr.* Phaenomena. GrPo

Let us break bread togedder. When I Fall on My Knees. *Unknown.* BoAN-2

Let Us Break Down the Barriers. Ormond Thomas. MoWP

Let us bury him here. Between the Battles. Francis Sherman. BoCaPo (1943 ed.)

Let us cheer the weary traveler. Weary Traveler. *Unknown.* BoAN-1

Let Us Come before His Presence. William Ludlum. PraP

Let Us Consider Where the Great Men Are. Delmore Schwartz. *Fr.* Shenandoah. MoAB; MoAmPo

Let us dance and let us sing. The Fairy Ring. *Unknown.* BoTP

Let us deal kindly with a heart of old by sorrow torn. Saadabad. James Elroy Flecker. SeCePo

Let Us Declare! *sel.* Angela Morgan.
"Come, workers! Poets, artists, dreamers, more and more." PGD

Let us deliberately sit into design. Shapes. Mark Turbyfill. NP

Let Us Drink. Alcaeus, *tr. fr. Greek by* John Hermann Merivale. AWP

Let us drink and be merry, dance, joke, and rejoice. The Careless Gallant [*or* Coronemus Nos Rosis antequam Marcescant]. Thomas Jordan. CoMu; HBV; OBEV; OxBoLi; SeCL; SeEP; SiTL

Let us drink old wine, at the sight of which I rejoice. Five Arabic Verses in Praise of Wine, I. *Unknown.* TrJP

Let us dry our tears now, laddie. Daddy Knows. James William Foley. FAOV

Let us evoke no phantom throng. Armistice Day. Lucia Trent. AOAH; PGD

Let Us Forget. Agnes Mary Frances Robinson. AV; WHA

Let us forget these principalities. Innumerable Friend. May Sarton. WaKn

Let us gather us the sunshine. Scatter Seeds of Kindness. May Riley Smith. BLPA; WBLP

Let Us Give Thanks. "Marianne Farningham." PEDC

Let us give thanks before we turn. Louis Untermeyer. *Fr.* Food and Drink. PreP

Let Us Go Down. Christopher Brennan. BoAV

Let us go hence, my songs; she will not hear. A Leave-taking. Swinburne. CH; EG; FaBoEn; HBV; MBP; OAEP; OBVV; PIR; PoEL-5; PoVP; TCEP; ViBoPo; VLEP

Let us go hence: the night is now at hand. A Last Word. Ernest Dowson. MBP; MoBrPo; PoVP; VLEP

Let us go, lassie, go. The Braes o' Balquhither. Robert Tannahill. EBSV

"Let us go off on a candid cadenza." Lincoln. Delmore Schwartz. FiMAP

Let us go on with experiments. We Creators. Olive Tilford Dargan. LS; NoCaPo

Let us go then, you and I. The Love Song of J. Alfred Prufrock. T. S. Eliot. AmPo; AmPP; AnFE; APA; ATP (1953 ed.); AWP; ChMo; CMP; CoAnAm; CoBA; CoBMV; CoEV; EnL; EnLit; ExPo; HBMV; HoPM; InPo; LEAP; LiTB; LiTM (1946 ed.); MAP; MAPA; MaPo; MoAB; MoAmPo; MoPW; MoVE; NeMA; NePA; NP; OAEP (2d ed.); OnAP; Po; PoFS; PoLFOT; PoRA; PreP; ReaPo; ReMP; RiBV; SeCeV; TrGrPo; TwAmPo; TwP; UnPo; ViBoPo

"Let us go to the wood," said this pig. Song to Five Toes. *Unknown.* OTPC (1946 ed.); PCH

Let us go up and look him in the face. Lord De Tabley. *Fr.* Orestes. BMEP; LEAP

Let us haste to Kelvin Grove, bonnie lassie, O. Kelvin Grove. Thomas Lyle. EBSV

Let us hasten—let us fly. Aristophanes. *Fr.* The Frogs. MaRV

Let Us Have Peace. Nancy Byrd Turner. MaRV; OQP; PoToHe; QP-2

Let us have winter loving that the heart. Winter Love. Elizabeth Jennings. NePoEA

Let Us Keep Christmas. Grace Noll Crowell. MaRV (Eternal Values.) PoToHe (new ed.)

Let us keep him warm. Dirge. Thomas Bailey Aldrich. OBAV

Let us keep splendid loyalties. Loyalties. Walter A. Cutter. OQP; QP-2

Let us leave talking of angelic hosts. Sonnets from "One Person." Elinor Wylie. OxBA

Let us, Lesbia darling, still. Love Is All. Catullus, *tr. by* Sir Theodore Martin. EnLi-1; OuHeWo

Let us live, O my Lesbia, and go on loving! Catullus, *tr. by* Asa M. Hughes. LaP

Let us live, then, and be glad. Gaudeamus Igitur. *Unknown.* *Fr.* Carmina Burana. HBV; LaP; WoL

Let us make haste, make haste! Impulse. José Moreno Villa. CoSP

Let us make love, let us make war. Paying a Debt. Chevalier de Boufflers. OnPM

Let us mind the tenth of October. The Battle of Point Pleasant. *Unknown.* ABS

Let us, my Lesbia! live and love. To Lesbia. Catullus, *tr. by* Charles Abraham Elton. OnPM

Let us not fear for the creative word. Liberté, Egalité, Fraternité. Florence Converse. NeTW; PoFr

Let Us Not Pretend. Ray Mathew. BoAV

Let Us Not Say the Skin Is Dark. Joseph Joel Keith. MuM

"Let us not speak, for the love we bear one another." In a Bath Teashop. John Betjeman. EnLoPo

Let us not think of our departed dead. Our Dead [*or* An Epitaph]. Edwin Markham. MaRV; OQP; QP-2

Let us now enjoy a famous feast. *Unknown, tr. fr. Chinese.* The Nineteen Han Poems, IV. WhP

Let Us Now Praise Famous Men, *sel.* James Agee.
Prologue: "Against time and the damages of the brain." OnAP

Let Us Now Praise Famous Men. Ecclesiasticus, XLIV: 1-14, Bible, Apocrypha. BHV; ChTr
(Our Fathers, XLIV: 1-15.) TrJP
(Praise of Famous Men, XLIV: 10-14.) MaRV

"Let Us Now Praise Famous Men." C. Day Lewis. ChMo

Let us pass on, for it is the law which no one can evade. Victor Hugo. *Fr.* Toute la Lyre. LiA

Let us play, and dance, and sing. The Vision of Delight. Ben Jonson. PoEL-2; SeCV-1
Let us pour a libation. To Apollo and the Muses. Terpander. OxBG
Let us praise our mighty fathers. Old-Time Virtues. Aristophanes. *Fr.* The Knights. GrR
Let us put by some hour of every day. Sanctuary. Clinton Scollard. MaRV; OQP; QP-1
Let us put feathers. Feathers. Olive Hopegood. MoAuPo
Let us rejoice and sing. The Conception of Christ. *Unknown.* AnEC
Let us remember how we came. For Remembrance. Edward Shanks. LBBV
Let us remember the yellow. In the Month of Green Fire. Sophie Himmell. GoYe
Let us return from Ilium, and no more. Independence. Guy Mason. CaP
Let us return, meantime, to the round of song. Propertius. Elegies, III, 2. LaP
Let us ride together. Riding Song. *Unknown.* SCC
Let us rise in early morning. Risen with Healing in His Wings. St. John of Damascus. BePJ; CAW
Let Us Rise Up and Live. Francis Sherman. CaP; OCL
Let Us See Jesus. Anna B. Warner. *See* We Would See Jesus.
Let us sit by a hissing steam radiator a winter's day. Horses and Men in Rain. Carl Sandburg. MOAP
Let Us Smile. Wilbur D. Nesbit. WBLP
Let Us Take the Road. John Gay. *Fr.* The Beggar's Opera, II, i. ATP (1935 ed.); CEP
Let us take to our hearts a lesson. The Tapestry Weavers. Anson G. Chester. BLPA; BLRP; PTA-1; WBLP
Let us thank Almighty God. Creatrix. Anna Wickham. BMEP; LBBV; MBP; MoBrPo; TrGrPo (1942 ed.)
Let us thank God for unfulfilled desire. For Transient Things. James A. S. McPeek. OQP; QP-2
Let us to-day. Song for Memorial Day. Clinton Scollard. OHIP
Let us trust no longer, my soul, in the promises of the world. Imitation of a Psalm. François de Malherbe. LiA
Let us turn, now, from the rigid clocks. Subject for Prophecy. Gemma D'Auria. JKCP (1955 ed.)
Let us, under rays that peep. Muted. Paul Verlaine. TrFP
Let us use time [*or* it] whilst we may. Of Time [*or* Of Beauty]. Sir Richard Fanshawe. *Fr.* Il Pastor Fido. InMe; SeCL
Let us walk in the white snow. Velvet Shoes. Elinor Wylie. AV; CH; ChMo; FaPON; MAP; MoAB; MoAmPo; MPB; NeMA; NP; NV; OTPC (1946 ed.); PCH; PFY; PG; PIAE; PoeMoYo; PoTo; ReaPo; SiSoSe; SP; StVeCh; TCPD; TiPo (1952 ed.); TreFS; TrGrPo; TSW; TSWC; WHA
Let us walk softly, friends. New Year's Thoughts. Lillian Gray. OQP; QP-2
Let Us with a Gladsome Mind. Milton. MaRV; OlF; WGRP
(Praise the Lord.) FaBoCh; LoGBV
Let vain excitement's shrine be covered with new grasses. My Anguish. Innokenti Annenski. BoR
Let verse be as a key. The Art of Poetry. Vicente Huidobro. AnCL
Let War's Tempests Cease. Longfellow. OHIP
Let wits contest. The Posy. George Herbert. EPS (1942 ed.)
Let Y stand for you who says. You. Kenneth Rexroth. *Fr.* A Bestiary. HoPM
Let your hands meet. The Death of Meleager. Swinburne. *Fr.* Atalanta in Calydon. BMEP; BPN; OBVV; PoVP; VLEP
Let your song be delicate. Song Be Delicate. John Shaw Neilson. BoAV
Let Zeus Record, *sel.* Hilda Doolittle ("H. D.").
"Stars wheel in purple, yours is not so rare." MAP; MoAmPo
Lethal Thought, The. Mary Boyd Wagner. GoYe
Lethe. Baudelaire, *tr. fr. French by* Barbara Gibbs. AnFP
Lethe. Hilda Doolittle ("H. D."). BLV; CBOV; ChMo; CMP; MAP; MoAmPo; NeMA; PG (1945 ed.); PoRA; ReaPo; TCPD; TrGrPo; ViBoPo
Lethe. Georgia Douglas Johnson. CDC
Lethe. Lorenzo Mavilis, *tr. fr. Modern Greek by* Rae Dalven. MoGP
Lethe. Edna St. Vincent Millay. PG
Letrilla. *Unknown, tr. fr. Spanish by* Ada Marshall Johnson. TeCS
Letrilla; the Lord of Dollars. Francisco de Quevedo y Villegas. *See* Lord of Dollars, The.
Let's away with study. Obmittamus Studia. *Unknown. Fr.* Carmina Burana. LaP
Let's Be Merry. Christina Rossetti. *Fr.* Sing-Song. FaPON
("Mother shake the cherry-tree.") PoVP; TiPo
Let's build bridges here and there. Interracial. Georgia Douglas Johnson. PoNe
Let's contend no more, Love. A Woman's Last Word. Elizabeth Barrett Browning. BEL; BLPA; BMEP; BoLiVe; BPN; EmBrPo; EPN; EV-5; FaBoBe; FaFP; GEPC; GTBS; GTBS-D; HBV; InPo; LiTL; LO; LoPS; OAEP; PIR; PoVP; TreFS; TrGrPo; ViBoPo; ViPo; VLEP
Let's dance now, all of us, all of us, oh my maidens. Bailada. Airas Núñez. LyMA
Let's Drink and Love. *Unknown, tr. fr. Greek by* J. M. Edmonds. GrL
Let's enjoy, while the season invites us. Giovinette, che fate all' amore. Lorenzo da Ponte. *Fr.* Don Giovanni. TrJP
Let's Forget. Charles L. H. Wagner. PoToHe
Let's Go Fishin'. Robert S. Holmes. DDA
"Let's go huntin'," says Risky Rob. Billy Barlow. *Unknown.* OuSiCo
Let's Go to Bed. *Unknown.* ChTr
Let's go to the wood, says this pig. *Unknown.* OxNR
Let's Go to the Woods ("'Let's go to the woods,' says Richard to Robin"). *Unknown.* ABS
"Let's go! we have still time." The Coca Tree. Jacinto Fombona Pachano. TwSpPo
Let's Have a Picnic Out-of-Doors. Mary Carolyn Davies. PCH
Let's not be slow in knowing. On Calvary's Lonely Hill. Herbert Clark Johnson. PoNe
Let's not use eyes anymore. Dialogue—2 Dollmakers. Gregory Corso. NeAP
Let's play we are a tune. Invitation. Ridgely Torrence. PCH
Let's say, the opposition knows the ring. Anthony Delius. *Fr.* The Great Divide. BoSA
Let's shake wild music from gray belfry chimes. Resurrection. Lady Margaret Sackville. HBMV
Let's sing a song together once. Song. Louis Simpson. NePoAm
Let's skip a few short years of hollow peace. George the Third. Byron *Fr.* The Vision of Judgment. FiP
Let's speak of good omens only: The Spirit of Birth draws near. He Need Speak No Longer in Behalf of Sulpicia and Cerinthus. Tibullus. LaP
Let's straighten this out, my little man. To a Small Boy Standing on My Shoes While I Am Wearing Them. Ogden Nash. ALV; FiBHP
Let's talk about some unpretentious things. A Change of Subject. Daniel Sargent. JKCP (1955 ed.)
Let's talk of graves, of worms and epitaphs. The Death of Kings [*or* Kingship *or* Richard II's Dejection]. Shakespeare. King Richard II, *fr.* III, ii. EV-1; TreFS; TrGrPo
Let's think of eggs. The Poultries. Ogden Nash. AlDL; CenHV
Letter. Olga Berggolts, *tr. fr. Russian by* Jack Lindsay. *Fr.* Parting. RuPo
Letter. Alexander Bergman. TrJP
Letter, A. John Malcolm Brinnin. LoPS; TwAmPo
Letter, A. Chang Chi, *tr. fr. Chinese by* Henry H. Hart. ChLP; PoHN
Letter, A. Emerson. OxBA
Letter I ("You were amused to find you too could fear"). William Empson. ChMP; LiTB
Letter IV ("Hatched in a rasping darkness of dry sand"). William Empson. LiTB
Letter II ("Burned in this element"). W. S. Graham. NePoEA
Letter V ("Lie where you fell and longed"). W. S. Graham. PoN
Letter VI ("A day the wind was hardly"). W. S. Graham. ChMP
Letter, The. John Holmes. NePoAm
Letter, The. Amy Lowell. AV
Letter, The. Beatrice M. Murphy. PoNe
Letter, The [*or* A]. Mu'tamid, King of Seville, *tr. fr. Arabic.* LiTW, *tr. by* Dulcie L. Smith; MooP, *tr. by* A. J. Arberry
Letter, The. Po Chü-i, *tr. fr. Chinese by* Arthur Waley. BoFr; LoBV; TrCh
Letter, A. Matthew Prior. *See* Letter to the Hon. Lady Miss Margaret Cavendish-Holles-Harley, A.
Letter, A. Sir Arthur Quiller-Couch. CenHV
Letter, A. Anne Ridler. LiTL; LiTM
Letter, A, *sel.* Earl of Rochester.
"Love—the most generous passion of the mind." LO
Letter I ("The midnight streets as I walk back"). Randall Swingler. WaP
Letter VIII ("On the first day of snow, my train"). Randall Swingler. WaP
Letter, The. Elizabeth Turner. Mrs. Turner's Object-Lessons, IX. OTPC (1923 ed.)
Letter, The. John Hall Wheelock. AnEnPo; LiTL
Letter across Doubt and Distance. M. Carl Holman. PoNe
Letter Containing a Panegyric on Bath, *abr.* Christopher Anstey. The New Bath Guide, VI. OBEC
Letter for You, A. Catharine M. Fanshawe. *See* Riddle, A: "'Twas whispered in Heaven, 'twas muttered in hell."

Letter from a Coward to a Hero. Robert Penn Warren. MAP
Letter from a Girl to Her Own Old Age, A. Alice Meynell. CaAE; GoTL; GTBS-W; LiTB; MBP; MoBrPo; ViBoPo
Letter from a Missionary. Whittier. IAP
Letter from a Postulant. Sister Mary Irma. PraNu
Letter from a State Hospital. Frank Mundorf. GoYe
Letter from Artemisa in the Town, to Cloe, in the Country, A. Earl of Rochester. SeCV-2
Sels.
"I took this time to think what Nature meant," II. NBE
"Y'expect to hear, at least, what Love has past," I. NBE
Letter from Home, A. Yüan K'ai, *tr. fr. Chinese by* Henry H. Hart. PoHN
Letter from Italy, A. Addison. CEP
Sels.
Italy and Britain. OBEC
"O Liberty, thou goddess heavenly bright." PoFr
Letter from Mexico. Tristan Corbière, *tr. fr. French by* Kate Flores. AnFP
Letter from Mr. Ezekiel Biglow of Jaalam to the Hon. Joseph T. Buckingham, A ("Thrash away, you'll hev to rattle"). James Russell Lowell. The Biglow Papers, 1st Series, No. I. AmPP; OxBA; TCAP
(Biglow Papers, The.) IAP
(Ez for War, *abr.*) APW
(Mr. Hosea Biglow Speaks.) PAH
("Thrash away, you'll hev to rattle.") CoBA
(To a Recruiting Sergeant.) AnNE
War, *sel.*, 1 *st.* MaRV
Letter from Mr. Hosea Biglow to the Hon. J. T. Buckingham, A ("This kind o' sogerin'"). James Russell Lowell. The Biglow Papers, 1st Series, No. II. OxBA
"Letter from my love today, A!" A Ballad of Hell. John Davidson. AnEnPo; AnFE; BLV; CBOV; HoPM; MBP; MoBrPo; PoVP; WHA
Letter from Newport, A. Frederic William Henry Myers. VA
Letter from Paparua. Colin Newbury. AnNZ
Letter from Rome, A. Arthur Hugh Clough. Amours de Voyage, Canto I, v. LoBV
Letter from the Country, A. Howard Baker. TwAmPo
Letter from the Front. Angelos Sikelianos, *tr. fr. Modern Greek by* Rae Dalven. MoGP
Letter from the Metropolis, A. Mildred D. Ingalls. CAG
Letter from the South. Robert E. Hayden. PoNe
Letter from the Vieux Carre. Ethel Green Russell. GoYe
Letter from Town; the Almond Tree. D. H. Lawrence. MoPW
Letter Home, A. Li Shang-yin. *See* Sent to Home.
Letter Is a Gypsy Elf, A. Annette Wynne. SUS
Letter of a Mother. Robert Penn Warren. MAP; MoAmPo
Letter of Advice. A. Winthrop Mackworth Praed. HBV; OBRV; OxBoLi; TOP; WhC
Letter Received, A. Emily Dickinson. *See* Way I read a letter's this, The.
Letter that was three weeks late, A. These Things Have I Loved. Codman Hislop. CAG
Letter to a Friend. John Thompson. BoAV
Letter to a Friend. Robert Penn Warren. MAP; MoAmPo
Letter to a Teacher of English. Robert Hillyer. AnFE; CoAnAm; TwAmPo
Letter to a Young Friend. Burns. *See* Epistle to a Young Friend.
Letter to a Young Poet. George Barker. ChMP
Letter to Alex Comfort. Dannie Abse. FaBoTw
Letter to Ben Jonson. Francis Beaumont. *See* Master Francis Beaumont's Letter to Ben Jonson.
Letter to Claudia. Wrenne Jarman. DiM
Letter to Daphnis [*or* Dafnis], A. Countess of Winchilsea. DiM; EnLoPo
Letter to Elsa, A. Grace Hazard Conkling. HBMV; HBVY
Letter to Heine. Louis Ginsberg. MuM
Letter to Her Husband, A ("Phoebus, make haste"). Anne Bradstreet. AmP; AmPP; AnFE; APA; CoAnAm; LiTA; MOAP
Letter to Her Husband, Absent upon Publick Employment, A. Anne Bradstreet. OxBA
Letter to His Friend Isaac, A. Judah Halevi, *tr. fr. Hebrew by* Emma Lazarus. TrJP
Letter to Hitler, A. James Laughlin. LiTA; WaP
Letter to Karl Shapiro. E. L. Mayo. MiAP
Letter to Lady Margaret Cavendish-Holles-Harley When a Child, A. Matthew Prior. *See* Letter to the Hon. Lady Miss Margaret Cavendish-Holles-Harley, A.
Letter to Lord Byron, *sels.* W. H. Auden.
"Autumn is here," Pt. V. MoP
"Great War had begun, The: but masters' scrutiny," *fr.* Pt. IV. PoLFOT
"I like your muse because she's gay and witty." PtP
"My passport says I'm five feet and eleven," Pt. IV. ChMo
Letter to Manlius Torquatus. Catullus, *tr. fr. Latin by* Jack Lindsay. LiTW
Letter to Maria Gisborne. Shelley. GEPC
"You are now/ In London, that great sea," *sel.* ChER; OBRV
Letter to My Sister. Anne Spencer. PoNe
Letter to My Wife. Roy Fuller. NeBP; POTE
Letter to My Wife. Keidrych Rhys. WaP
Letter to New York. Elizabeth Bishop. LiTL
Letter to R. Willard Maas. WaP
Letter to Robert Frost, A. Robert Hillyer. MoAmPo; PtP
Letter to Rome, A. Steven Peele. ReIE
Letter to Santa Claus. John Wain. PoN
Letter to Sir H. Wotton at His Going Ambassador to Venice. John Donne. OBS
Letter to Sir Robert Walpole, A. Henry Fielding. CEP
Letter to the City Clerk. Frederick A. Wright. FaFP
Letter to the Countess of Denbigh against Irresolution and Delay in Matters of Religion, A. Richard Crashaw. *See* To the Noblest and Best of Ladies, the Countess of Denbigh.
Letter to the Dead in Spring. Mary Cecile Ions. MuM
Letter to the Front. Muriel Rukeyser. WaP
Sels.
Even during War. TrJP
To Be a Jew in the Twentieth Century. TrJP
Letter to the Hon. Lady Miss Margaret Cavendish-Holles-Harley, A. Matthew Prior. CEP; LoBV; OBEC
(Letter, A.) SeCePo; WP
(Letter to Lady Margaret Cavendish-Holles-Harley, When a Child, A.) OBEV; PRWS
(To a Child of Noble Birth.) OTPC (1923 ed.)
Letter to the Night. Lloyd Frankenberg. AnAmPo
Letter to the World. Emily Dickinson. *See* This is my letter to the world.
Letter to Viscount Cobham. Congreve. LoBV
Letter to William Carlos Williams, A. Kenneth Rexroth. OnHM
Letter today, official, buff, A. Letter from Paparua. Colin Newbury. AnNZ
Lettergae, The. Charles Murray. EBSV
Letters. Emerson. LPS-3; TCAP
Letters, The. Lawrence Lee. MuM
Letters. Bernard Spencer. NeBP; WaP
Letters, The. Tennyson. HBV
Letters and lines, we see, are soon defaced. Idea's Mirrour, XXI. Michael Drayton. ReIE
Letters are comforting to get. Convalescence, VI. David McCord. WhC
Letters at School, The. *Unknown.* OTPC (1923 ed.)
Letters Found near a Suicide. Frank Horne. CDC; PoNe
Letters from God. Walt Whitman. Song of Myself, XLVIII. CBOV
("I have said that the soul is not more than the body.") BAV; CoBA; CoV; TrGrPo
(Hub for the Universe, A.) FaFP
Letters from Teignmouth, *sel.* Winthrop Mackworth Praed. Our Ball. EnRP; TCEP
Letters I cannot read, I have no skill. Six Letters. Euripides. OxBG
Letters, I, your lone friend, write in sorrow, The. From William Tyndale to John Frith. Edgar Bowers. NePoEA
Letters, like blood along a weakening body. Letters. Bernard Spencer. NeBP; WaP
Letters to Dead Imagists. Carl Sandburg. AmPP (3d ed.)
Letters to Malaya, *sel.* Martyn Skinner.
"Then came Dunkirk to mitigate the news," *fr.* IV. AlDL
Lettice. Dinah Maria Mulock Craik. HBV
Lettice. "Michael Field." VA
Letty's Globe. Charles Tennyson Turner. BTP; EPN; ES; HBV; OBEV; OBVV; PECK; VA
Leukothea. Keith Douglas. NeBP
Levantine, A. William Plomer. OBMV
Levee Camp "Holler," *with music. Unknown.* ABF
Levee Moan (A *and* B *vers., with music*). *Unknown.* AS
Level and the Square, The. Robert Morris. BLPA
Level of Abstraction, A. Robert Conquest. PoLFOT
Level with duty, days ride a city-express across the calendar page. Coin in the Fist. Florence Kerr Brownell. GoYe
Level with the summit of that eastern mount. Eos. Richard Henry Horne. *Fr.* Orion. VA
Leveller, The. "Barry Cornwall." EV-4
Levelling Dust, The. James Shirley. *See* Death the Leveller.
Leves Amores. Arthur Symons. AnEnPo
Levi, thou art a load, I'll lay thee down. Dryden. *Fr.* Absalom and Achitophel, Pt. II. AtBAP; SeEP
Leviathan. Job, XLI: 1-21, Bible, *O.T.* TrGrPo
Leviathan. Margaret R. Gould. TwCaPo
Leviathan. W. S. Merwin. NePoEA
Leviathan. Peter Quennell. POTE; TCPD
"Music met Leviathan returning, A," *sel.* MBP; MoBrPo
Leviathan. Louis Untermeyer. GoTP
Leviathan. Edward Young. *Fr.* A Paraphrase on Part of the Book of Job. BeR
Leviathan drives the eyed prow of his face. Leviathan. Peter Quennell. POTE; TCPD

Leviathan, the Crocodile. Job, XLI: 13-24, 26-34, Bible, *O.T.* MuP
Leviticus, *sel.* Bible, *O.T.*
Strangers, XIX: 33-34. BoFr
Levy Silver. Edgar Lee Masters. *Fr.* The New Spoon River. ChMo; CMP
Lewd Love Is Loss. Robert Southwell. ACP; EV-1
Lewesdon Hill, *sel.* William Crowe.
"From this proud eminence on all sides round." EnSW
Lewie Gordon. Alexander Geddes. EBSV
Lewis, the Lost Lover. Sir Thomas More. *See* Fortune.
Lewti; or, The Circassian Love-Chant. Samuel Taylor Coleridge. BPN; EmBrPo; EV-4
(Lewti.) EnRP; ERP
Lexington. Oliver Wendell Holmes. DD; MC; PAH
Lexington. Sidney Lanier. *Fr.* The Psalm of the West. PaA; PAH
Lexington. Whittier. MC; PAH
Lexington Murder, The. *Unknown.* BaBo; OuSiCo, *with music*
(Lexington Miller, The.) BaBo
Li Ling. *Unknown, tr. fr. Chinese by* Arthur Waley. TrCh
Li Po. Ruth Gilbert. AnNZ
Li Po was about to sail in his boat. A Poem for Wang Lung. Li Po. ChLP
Liadain. *Unknown, tr. fr. Old Irish by* Frank O'Connor. KiLC
(Liadain and Cuirithir, *sl. diff. vers.*) SiB
Liadain to Curither. Moireen Fox. NP
Liadin and Curither. *Unknown, tr. fr. Old Irish by* Kuno Meyer. OnYI
Liady-Day an' Ridden House. William Barnes. OBRV
Liar, The. Rue Carpenter. RIS
Liar, The. *Unknown, tr. fr. Irish by* Frank O'Connor. KiLC
Liar and bragger. Peregrine. Elinor Wylie. HBMV; LEAP; TCPD
'Lias! 'Lias! Bless de Lawd! In the Morning. Paul Laurence Dunbar. GoSl; MW
Libation Bearers. Aeschylus. *See* Choephoroe.
Libel of Divorce, A. George Gascoigne. ReEn
Libera Nos a Malo. Eric Bruno. JKCP (1955 ed.)
Libera Nos, Domine—Deliver us, O Lord, not only from British dependence, but also. Emancipation from British Dependence [*or* A Political Litany]. Philip Freneau. IAP; IDAH; PAH
Liberals raised this in their finest hour. Norris Dam. Selden Rodman. PoNe
Liberator, The. Wu Ti, *tr. fr. Chinese by* Arthur Waley. TrCh
Liberté, Egalité, Fraternité. Florence Converse. NeTW; PoFr
Libertine, The. Aphra Behn. OBEV (1st ed.)
Liberty. Blake. *See* Eternity.
Liberty. Abraham Cowley. *Fr.* Ode upon Liberty. GrCo-1
Liberty. John Hay. AA; PoFr
Liberty. John Ceiriog Hughes. PoFr
Liberty. Michael Chazarian Nalbandian, *tr. fr. Armenian.* ArmLP, *tr. by* Zabelle C. Boyajian; PoFr, *tr. by* Alice Stone Blackwell
Liberty. Leopold Staff, *tr. fr. Polish by* Watson Kirkconnell. PoFr
Liberty. Edward Thomas. MoAB
Liberty, *sel.* James Thomson.
British Commerce, *fr.* IV. OBEC
Liberty, *sel.* Wordsworth.
"Beetle loves his unpretending track, The." FiBHP
Liberty. Sir Thomas Wyatt. *See* Lover Rejoiceth, The.
Liberty and Independence. *Unknown.* *See* Independence Bell, July 4, 1776.
Liberty and Requiem of an Imprisoned Royalist, The. Sir Roger L'Estrange. *See* Loyalty Confin'd.
Liberty Enlightening the World. Edmund Clarence Stedman. PAH
Liberty, Equality, Fraternity. Wilfrid Scawen Blunt. *Fr.* In Vinculis. PoFr
Liberty for All. William Lloyd Garrison. AA; GrCo-1; IDAH
Liberty for All. Viktor Khlebnikov, *tr. fr. Russian by* C. M. Bowra. BoRS
Liberty of the Press. Sir Aubrey De Vere. PoFr; TIP
Liberty Pole, The. John Trumbull. *Fr.* M'Fingal. AmPP (3d ed.); APW, *abr.*; TCAP, *abr.*
Liberty Pole, The. *Unknown.* *See* Derry-Down.
Liberty Song, The. John Dickinson. AmPP; TrAS, *with music*
(Song of American Freedom, A.) PoFr
Liberty Tree. Thomas Paine. MC; PAH; PoFr
Liberty's Latest Daughter. Bayard Taylor. *See* America.
Library, The, *sels.* George Crabbe.
Books. EV-3, *abr.*; OBEC
Crusty Critics. OBEC
Library, The. Barbara A. Huff. FaPON
Library, The. Mary Mills. NePoAm
Library, The. Frank Dempster Sherman. AA; OBAV
Library, The. Whittier. MOB
Library, The. William Carlos Williams. *Fr.* Paterson, III. AtBAP
Lice Seekers, The. Arthur Rimbaud. *See* Chercheuses de poux, Les.
Licences? Yes. Poetic licence. Ode to Himself. Sir Walter Raleigh. WhC
Licht begouth to quenschyng out and fall, The. An Evening and Morning in June. Gawin Douglas. *Fr.* Prologues to the Aeneid. BSV
Lichtenberg. Kipling. EnLit
Licia, *sels.* Giles Fletcher.
Elegy, An: "Down in a bed, and on a bed of down." ReIE
"First did I fear, when first my love began," XX. SiCE; TuPP
"I live, sweet love, whereas the gentle wind," XXVI. SiCE; TuPP
"If sad complaint would show a lover's pain," Elegie III. TuPP
"In time the strong and stately turrets fall," XXVIII. PeBoSo; ReEn; ReIE; SiCE; TuPP
(Time.) OBSC
"Like Memnon's rock, touched [*or* touch'd] with the rising sun," XLVII. ElL; ReEn; ReIE; SiCE; TuPP
"Love was laid down, all weary, fast asleep," IX. ReIE
"My love was mask'd and armed with a fan," XXIII. ReIE
"O sug'red talk, wherewith my thoughts do live," LII. ReIE
"Sad, all alone, not long I musing sat," I. ReIE; SiCE; TuPP
"Seven are the lights that wander in the skies," XXV. ReEn; ReIE; SiCE; TuPP
"Whenas her lute is tuned to her voice," XXXI. TuPP
Licus, thou art deceived in saying that. To Licus. Everard Guilpin. *Fr.* Skialetheia. SiCE
Liddell and Scott; on the Completion of Their Lexicon. Thomas Hardy. OxBoLi
Liddesdale Crosiers hae ridden a race, The. The Death of Parcy Reed. *Unknown.* BaBo (A *vers.*); ESPB; OBB
Lidice. Mary Sinton Leitch. NeTW
Lidice. "Lucio." NeTW
Lidice. Charles Schiff. NeTW
Lie, The. Howard Moss. AtBAP; MoAB; NePoAm
Lie, The. Sir Walter Ralegh. AtBAP; BCEP; BHV; BLV; ChTr; CoEV; ElSeCe; EnLi-1 (1949 ed.); ExPo; HBV; InvP; LiTB; OAEP; OBSC; PoEL-2; PoFr; PoFS; ReEn; RiBV; SeCeV; SiCE; SiPS; SiTL; TrGrPo; TuPP; ViBoPo; WoL, *abr.*
(Lye, The.) PECK
(Soul's Errand, The.) LPS-3; WGRP
Lie a-bed,/ Sleepy head. Baby, Sleep. Christina Rossetti. *Fr.* Sing-Song. BOL; OTPC (1946 ed.)
Lie heavy on him, earth! for he. For Sir John Vanbrugh, Architect. Abel Evans. PIAE; WhC
Lie low; my little one. Roman Lullaby. *Unknown.* RIS
Lie not; but let thy heart be true to God. George Herbert. *Fr.* The Church Porch. EPS (1942 ed.)
Lie of the Land, The. Margaret Fishback. SiTL
Lie on the Sand. Alistair Campbell. AnNZ
"Lie still, my newly married wife." The Griesly Wife. John Manifold. ATP (1953 ed.); MoBrPo (1950 ed.)
Lie still, old Dane, below thy heap. A Danish Barrow. Francis Turner Palgrave. VA
Lie where you fell and longed. Letter V. W. S. Graham. PoN
Liebesweh. Dora Wilcox. BoAu
Lied V. José Maria Eguren, *tr. fr. Spanish by* Donald Devenish Walsh. AnCL
Liefer would I turn and love. Deranged. Padraic Fiacc. NeIP
Liege lady! believe me. Lover Loquitur. Louise Imogen Guiney. PR
Lien, The. Adelaide Love. MoSiPe
Lies have short wings. He lies that so sings. John Davies of Hereford. SiCE
Lies of Men, The. *Unknown, tr. fr. Spanish by* Havelock Ellis. OnPM
Lieutenant who went out to shoot, A. Limerick. Morgan Taylor. LiBL
Life. Franklin P. Adams. InMe
Life. Francis Bacon. EV-1; GTBS; GTBS-D; GTBS-W; GTSE
(Life of Man, The.) ElL; OBSC; WHA
(On the Life of Man.) ElSeCe
(World, The.) HBV; LPS-1; PIR
Life. Anna Letitia Barbauld. AlDL, *abr.*; BCEP; BLPA; DiM; EV-3; FaFP; HBV; LEAP; LPS-1; MaRV, *abr.*; NeHB, *abr.*; OBEV; OBRV; TreFS, *abr.*
(Life! I Know Not What Thou Art.) BTP; GTBS; GTBS-D; GTBS-W; GTSE; GTSL; PECK; PTA-2
Life ("Joy and woe are woven fine"). Blake. *Fr.* Auguries of Innocence. CBE
Life. Horatius Bonar. OQP; QP-2

Life. Paul C. Boomer. PoP
Life. Charlotte Brontë. OQP; QP-2
Life. Alice Brown. AA
Life. Robert Browning. *Fr.* Christmas Eve and Easter-Day. OQP; QP-2
Life. Francis Burrows. PtOT
Life. "N. C." SeCL
Life. Samuel Taylor Coleridge. BPN; EmBrPo; EnRP
Life. "Barry Cornwall." VA
Life. George Crabbe. OBEC
Life. W. H. Davies. ChMo
Life. Margaret Deland. *See* By One Great Heart.
Life. *Comp. by* Mrs. H. A. Deming. *Fr. various poems.* BOHV
Life. Emily Dickinson. *See* Our share of night to bear.
Life. Paul Laurence Dunbar. CDC
Life, A. John Gould Fletcher. ChMo; CMP
Life. Wayne Gard. OQP; QP-1
Life. Amory Hare. HBMV
Life. George Herbert. ElSeCe; HBV; LiTB; LPS-3; MeLP; MePo; OBS; PoFS; RiBV; SeCeV; SeCL; SeCV-1; SeEP
("I made a posie, while the day ran by.") EG
Life. Frederick Lawrence Knowles. ChIP; MaRV
Life. Lizzie M. Little. VA
Life. Longfellow. *Fr.* The Psalm of Life. GN
Life. Sarojini Naidu. BPP
Life. Edward H. Pfeiffer. UnW
Life. Nan Terrell Reed. BLPA
Life. Sir Walter Scott. *Fr.* The Abbot. BPN
Life. Shakespeare. *See* All the World's a Stage.
Life. Edward Rowland Sill. BLP; BLRP; LBAP; MaRV; OQP; QP-1
Life. Charles Swain. VA
Life. *Unknown, at. to* Lao-tzu, *tr. fr. Chinese by* Witter Bynner. *Fr.* Tao Teh King. OnPM
Life ("I've seen the moonbeam's shining light"). *Unknown.* PoToHe
Life. Henry van Dyke. *Fr.* The Three Best Things. BLP; MaRV; OQP; QP-1
Life. William Merrell Vories. MaRV; OQP; QP-2
Life. John Hall Wheelock. LBMV
Life, *abr.* Ella Wheeler Wilcox. PoToHe
Life. Richard Henry Wilde. *See* My Life Is like the Summer Rose.
Life. T. P. Cameron Wilson. VOD
Life, A. George Edward Woodberry. EtS
Life, a Bubble. William Drummond of Hawthornden. *See* Madrigal: "This life, which seems so fair."
Life a Cheat. Dryden. *See* When I Consider Life.
Life, a Question. Corinne Roosevelt Robinson. HBV
Life a right shadow is. The Permanency of Life. William Drummond of Hawthornden. BSV
Life a Voyage. Palladas, *tr. fr. Greek by* R. A. Furness. OxBG
("Life is a perilous voyage. The seas o'erwhelm," *tr. by* L. P. Chamberlayne.) GrPo
("Sailor Home from the Sea, The," *tr. by* F. L. Lucas.) GrPE
Life Above, the Life on High, The. St. Theresa of Avila, *tr. fr. Spanish by* Edward Caswall. WGRP
Life after Death. Pindar, *tr. fr. Greek by* Walter Headlam. OxBG
(After-Life.) GrR
Life Again. Keats. *See* Sleep.
Life and Art. Archilochus, *tr. fr. Greek by* F. L. Lucas. GrPE
Life and Death. Edward Benlowes. *Fr.* Theophila. FaBoEn
Life and Death. Carroll Carstairs. DDA
Life and Death. Herbert E. Clarke. PSO
Life and Death. Ernest H. Crosby. *See* How Did He Live.
Life and Death. Sir William Davenant. *Fr.* The Christians Reply to the Philosopher. OBS
Life and Death. Lilla Cabot Perry. AA
Life and Death. Christina Rossetti. POTT; VLEP
Life and Death. Duncan Campbell Scott. VA
Life and Death. Shakespeare. *See* Fear of Death.
Life and Death. W. J. Turner. FaBoTw
Life and Death of Dr. Faustus, The. Christopher Marlowe. *Fr.* Dr. Faustus. LEAP
Life and Death of Jason, The, *sels.* William Morris.
Alas! for Saturn's days of Gold, *fr.* X. EmBrPo
I Know a Little Garden Close, *fr.* IV. AtBAP; CH; EG; EmBrPo; GTSE; PoE; POTT; ViBoPo; ViPo; ViPP; VLEP
(Garden by the Sea, A.) BMEP; GTML; PoEL-5; PoVP
(Nymph's Song to Hylas, The.) BPN; CBOV; HBV; LEAP; LoPS, 5 *ll.*; OBEV; TOP
(Sweet Song Sung Not Yet to Any Man, A.) AEV
Invocation to Chaucer, *fr.* XVII. BPN
(To Chaucer.) EmBrPo
O Bitter Sea, *fr* IV. EmBrPo; PoVP
(Song of the Argonauts, *abr.*) EtS
(To the Sea.) BPN
O Death, That Maketh Life So Sweet, *fr.* XII. EmBrPo; PoVP; ViPo; VLEP
(Orpheus' Song of Triumph.) BPN
"O happy seafarers are ye," *fr.* XIV. ViBoPo
(Songs of Orpheus and the Sirens.) BPN
"'Sing on,' he said, 'but let me dream of bliss,'" *fr.* IV. EV-5
Song of Orpheus ("O surely now the fisherman"), *fr.* IX. LEAP
"'Upon the day thou weariest of me,'" *fr.* IX. LoPS
Life and Death of the Piper of Kilbarchan, The. Robert Sempill. *See* Epitaph of Habbie Simpson, The.
Life and Death of William Longbeard, The, *sels.* Thomas Lodge.
Fancy, A. ElL
"My mistress when she goes." EG; SiCE; TuPP
(Her Rambling.) OBSC; LoBV
(My Mistress.) TrGrPo
Rose, The. OBSC
Life and Fame. Abraham Cowley. AnEnPo; LiTG
Life and Genuine Character of Dean Swift, The. Swift. EiPP
Life and Love. Elizabeth Barrett Browning. BPN; PoVP
Life and Love. Whittier. *Fr.* Snow-bound. BLRP
(Yet Love Will Dream.) MaRV
Life and Nature. Archibald Lampman. PeCV
Life and the Universe show spontaneity. The Positivists. Mortimer Collins. BOHV
Life and the Weaver. A. W. Dewar. BLRP; WBLP
Life and Thought. Matthew Arnold. *Fr.* Empedocles on Etna, II. FiP
Life and Thought have gone away. The Deserted House. Tennyson. VA
Life? and worth living? Life, a Question. Corinne Roosevelt Robinson. HBV
Life at last I know is terrible. What Is Terrible. Roy Fuller. WaP
Life at Rome. Juvenal, *tr. fr. Latin by* Miriam Allen deFord. Satires, III. LaP
Life, being careful, such a husbandry shows. Small Things. Lizette Woodworth Reese. MuM
Life, believe, is not a dream. Life. Charlotte Brontë. OQP; QP-2
Life Boat. *Filed as* Lifeboat.
Life brings our all: long Time leaves nought abiding. Time the Changer. Plato. OxBG
Life burns us up like fire. Life. John Hall Wheelock LBMV
Life can hold such lovely things! Thank You, God. Nina Stiles. PoToHe (new ed.)
Life contracts and death is expected. Death of a [*or* the] Soldier. Wallace Stevens. AmPP; SoV
Life Death Does End. Gerard Manley Hopkins. *See* No Worst, There Is None.
Life did not bring me silken gowns. Red Geraniums. Martha Haskell Clark. BLPA; NeHB; VOD
Life-Drama, A, *sels.* Alexander Smith.
Forerunners. VA
Quaint Character, A. BMEP
Minor Poet, A. VA
Sea-Marge. VA
(Autumn.) GTSE
Life-Drunk. Arthur Stringer. PC
Life ever flies with course that nought may stay. Petrarch, *tr. by* Lady Dacre. Sonnets to Laura: To Laura in Death, IV. PrPoCR
Life from the Lifeless. Robinson Jeffers. ChMo
Life Half Lived. Friedrich Hölderlin. *See* Half of Life, The.
Life has conquered, the wind has blown away. Hope. *Unknown.* KiLC
Life has loveliness to sell. Barter. Sara Teasdale. ChMo; CMP; FaPON; MCCG; MPB; OBAV; OQP; OTPC (1946 ed.); QP-2; SP; TreFS; VOD
Life Hidden. Christina Rossetti. VLEP
Life holds no sweeter thing than this—to teach. No Sweeter Thing. Adelaide Love. PGD
Life hurries on, a frantic refugee. Sonnet. Petrarch, *tr. by* Morris Bishop. Sonnets to Laura: To Laura in Death, IV. LyPI
Life! I Know Not What Thou Art. Anna Letitia Barbauld. *See* Life.
Life Immovable, *sel.* Kostes Palamas, *tr. fr. Modern Greek by* Rae Dalven.
Dead Youth, The. MoGP
Life impaled him high on a cliff. Biography of an Agnostic. Louis Ginsberg. TrJP
Life in a day: he took his girl to the ballet. Les Sylphides. Louis MacNeice. CoBMV
Life in a Half-Breed Shack. *Unknown.* CoSo; CSF
Life in a Love. Robert Browning. BMEP; BPN; EM-2; EmBrPo; EV-5; GEPC; GTBS; HBV; OAEP; OBVV; PIR; PoFS; PoVP; TOP; TrGrPo; VLEP
(Escape Me?—Never.) LiTL; LoPo

Life in her creaking shoes. To K. de M. W. E. Henley. Echoes, XXXIV. POTT; PoVP
Life in Laconics. Mary Mapes Dodge. BOHV
Life-in-Love. Dante Gabriel Rossetti. The House of Life, XXXVI. PoVP; ViPo; VLEP
Life, in one semester. Song. Charles G. Blanden. OQP; QP-2
Life in the Autumn Woods. Philip Pendleton Cooke. LPS-2; SPP
Life in the Chem. Lab. Henry W. Eliot, Jr. CAG
"Life in the world is but a big dream." Waking from Drunkenness on a Spring Day. Li Po. TrCh
Life Is a Dream, *sel.* Pedro Calderón de la Barca, *tr. fr. Spanish.*
"We live, while we see the sun," *tr. by* Arthur Symons. AWP; JAWP; LiTW; PoFr; WBP
("Truth—and let us then restrain," *tr. by* Richard C. Trench.) TeCS
Life is a gift that most of us hold dear. Fin de Siècle. *Unknown.* BOHV
Life is a jest, and all things show it. My Own Epitaph [*or* His Own Epitaph *or* Epitaph]. John Gay. ALV; HBV; InP; OnPM; PIAE; PreP; SeCePo; SeCeV; TOP; ViBoPo
Life is a leaf of paper white. James Russell Lowell. *Fr.* For an Autograph. MaRV
Life is a long discovery, isn't it? Discovery. Hilaire Belloc. ViBoPo
Life Is a Lovely Thing. Minnie Case Hopkins. DDA
Life Is a Miracle. John Masefield. *See* It May Be So with Us.
Life is a most extraordinary thing. Tomato Juice. A. P. Herbert. WhC
Life is a perilous voyage. Tempest-tossed. Life a Voyage. Palladas, *tr. by* R. A. Furness. OxBG
Life is a perilous voyage. The seas o'erwhelm. Palladas, *tr. fr. Greek by* L. P. Chamberlayne. GrPo
Life is a pilgrimage, they say. Cockle-Shell and Sandal-Shoon. Herbert T. J. Coleman. CaP
Life is a poet's fable. *Unknown.* OBSC; SiCE
Life is a shepherd lad who strides and sings. Life. Amory Hare. HBMV
Life is a sorry mélange of gold and silver and stubble. Nonsense. Robert Haven Schauffler. HBMV
Life is a trifle. The New Crusade. Katharine Lee Bates. CV; MC
Life is a voyage of peril. Before its tempests driven. "The Sailor Home from the Sea." Palladas. GrPE
Life is a woven fabric. Life and the Weaver. A. W. Dewar. BLRP; WBLP
Life is but a flying slave. Palladas, *tr. fr. Greek by* F. A. Wright. GrPo
Life is but a game of ball. Variation on a Theme. G. T. Hellman. CAG
Life Is but Loss. Robert Southwell. SiCE
Life Is Fine. Langston Hughes. WaKn
Life Is Leaving One Strange Port. Raymond Boesch. JKCP (1955 ed.)
Life is like a wayside bloom. Life. Wayne Gard. OQP; QP-1
Life is long that loathsomely doth last, The. Elegy Wrote in the Tower, 1554 [*or* Comparison of Life and Death]. John Harington. ElL; ReIE
Life Is Love. William Johnson Fox. VA
Life Is More True. E. E. Cummings. WaP
Life is myself, I keep the life of all. An Enigma of Sleep. James I, King of England. PeBoSo
Life is not dear or gay. The Lass That Died of Love. Richard Middleton. HBV
Life is not sweet. One day it will be sweet. Life and Death. Christina Rossetti. POTT; VLEP
Life is real, life is earnest. A Parody on "A Psalm of Life." *Unknown.* BLPA
Life is seldom if ever dull. Gull. William Jay Smith. TiPo (1959 ed.)
Life Is Short. Horace, *tr. fr. Latin by* J. H. Deazeley. Odes, II, 3. RoL
Life Is Struggle. Arthur Hugh Clough. BEL; BPN; EmBrPo; EnLi-2; PoVP; VLEP
Life is sweet, brother. George Borrow. *Fr.* Lavengro. BBV (1951 ed.)
Life is the fool of hope, till one last morning. Deceitful Hope. Julius Polyaenus. OxBG
Life is too brief. Life. William Merrell Vories. MaRV; OQP; QP-2
Life is too grim with anxious, eating care. The Higher Kinship. Wilfred Campbell. OCL
Life is vile. Green Sunday. Katue Kitasono. LiTW
Life isn't dreary. A Word about Woodpiles. Nancy Byrd Turner. BrR
Life knows no dead so beautiful. Joaquin Miller. *Fr.* Myrrh. BAP
Life Laughs Onward. Thomas Hardy. TwCV
Life-Lesson, A. James Whitcomb Riley. AA; BAP; HBV; LEAP; OBAV; TreFS
Life like a Matador Goes Forth. John Ransom Palmer. PoP
Life like the billow rolls, and youthful bloom. The Heart in Brahma. Bhartrihari. OnPM
Life-long, Poor Browning. Anne Spencer. CDC; PoNe
Life may be given in many ways. The Martyr Chief. James Russell Lowell. *Fr.* Ode Recited at the Harvard Commemoration. LBAH; LPS-3
Life May Change, but It May Fly Not. Shelley. *Fr.* Hellas. BPN; EmBrPo; EPN
(Choruses from Hellas.) EnRP
Life met me on the threshold—young, divine. The Forgotten Countersign. Corinne Roosevelt Robinson. OQP; QP-2
Life-Mosaic. Frances Ridley Havergal. TrPWD
Life Must Burn. John Hay. NePoAm
Life Not Death. Tennyson. *Fr.* The Two Voices. MaRV
Life of a Beau, The. James Miller. OBEC
Life of a Fairy, The. *Unknown. See* Fairy Queen, The.
Life of Ages. Samuel Johnson. *See* Inspiration.
Life of Guthlac, The, *sel. Unknown.*
Death in Bed. PoLi
Life of itself will be cruel and hard enough. Sonnets, V. Muna Lee. HBMV
Life of Life. Johannes Edfelt, *tr. fr. Swedish by* Martin S. Allwood. LiTW
Life of Life. Coventry Patmore. The Angel in the House, I, viii, 1. EPP
Life of Life. Shelley. *Fr.* Prometheus Unbound, II, v. CH; FiP; ReTS
(Chorus: "Life of Life! thy lips enkindle.") LoBV
(Hymn to the Spirit of Nature.) GTBS; GTBS-D; GTBS-W; GTSE
("Life of Life! thy lips enkindle.") AnFE; AtBAP; LO; OBRV; PoEL-4; TCEP; ViBoPo
(Voice in the Air [Singing].) BCEP; LiA
Life of Man, The. Francis Bacon. *See* Life.
Life of Man, The. Barnabe Barnes. *Fr.* A Divine Century of Spiritual Sonnets. OBSC
(Blast of Wind, A, a Momentary Breath.) PeBoSo; SiCE; TuPP
Life of Man, The. Keidrych Rhys, *fr. the Welsh.* TriL
Life of Man, The. Swinburne. *See* Before the Beginning of Years.
Life of Man, The. Lucius H. Thayer. OQP; QP-2
Life of man [*or* men], The/ Is an arrow's flight. The Flight of the Arrow [*or* The Arrow]. Richard Henry Stoddard. AA; MaRV
Life of man is full of grief and sorrow, The. The Misery of Man. Alexander Craig. SeCL
Life of man is never quite completed, The. W. H. Auden. *Fr.* In Time of War. EnLit
Life of Men, The. Aristophanes, *tr. fr. Greek by* John Hookham Frere. *Fr.* The Birds. RO
Life of my learning, fire of all my Art. A Dedication. Mary Elizabeth Coleridge. TrPWD
Life of my life, I shall ever try. Because of Thee. Rabindranath Tagore. Gitanjali, IV. GrCo-1
Life of my life, take not so soon thy flight. To His Dying Brother, Master William Herrick. Robert Herrick. EV-2; OAEP; PoD; SeCV-1
Life of Nature, The. Samuel Taylor Coleridge. *Fr.* Dejection; an Ode. RO
Life of Our Life. Henry Burke Robins. MaRV
Life of Primitive Man, The. Lucretius, *tr. fr. Latin by* W. Taylor McLeod. *Fr.* De Rerum Natura, V. LaP
Life of St. Cellach of Killala, The, *sels. Unknown, tr. fr. Late Middle Irish by* Standish Hayes O'Grady.
Dear Was He. OnYI
Hail, Fair Morning. OnYI
He Who Forsakes the Clerkly Life. OnYI
Life of San Millán, The, *sels.* Gonzalo de Berceo, *tr. fr. Spanish.*
Battle of Simancas, The, *tr. by* Longfellow. TeCS
"He walked those mountains wild, and lived within that nook," *tr. by* John Hookham Frere. AnSpL-1; CAW
Life of the Blessed, The. Luis de León, *tr. fr. Spanish by* Bryant. AnSpL-1; AWP
(Heavenly Home, The, *tr. by* Ida Farnell.) TeCS
Life on its way returns into a mist. Life. *Unknown, at. to* Lao-tzu. *Fr.* Tao Teh King. OnPM
Life on the Ocean Wave, A. Epes Sargent. AA; EtS; FaBoBe; GN; HBV; LEAP; LPS-2; MW; NeHB; OlF; PECK; PIR; TreFS
Life or Death. Glenn Ward Dresbach. *Fr.* In Western Mountains. HBMV
Life Owes Me Nothing. *Unknown.* OQP; PoToHe; QP-2
Life (priest and poet say) is but a dream. The Dragon-Fly [*or* Lines to a Dragon Fly]. Walter Savage Landor. OBEV (new ed.); OBRV; OBVV
Life Removed, The. Luis de León, *tr. fr. Spanish by* Aubrey F. G. Bell. TeCS; WoL
Life ripens swiftly in these lonely hills. The Mountain Girl. DuBose Heyward. BLP; LS; MuM; NV
Life said: "My house is thine with all its store." The Outer Gate. Nora May French. LBMV

Life Sculpture. George Washington Doane. BAP; BLPA; MaRV; OHFP; WBLP
(Sculptors of Life.) OQP; QP-1
Life Shall Live for Evermore. Tennyson. *See* In Memoriam A. H. H.: "My own dim life . . ."
Life should be very pleasant for. Reflections on an Ideal Existence. Sara Henderson Hay. CIV
Life surges from It in an endless sea. The Absolute. Hugh Wilgus Ramsaur. MuM
Life That Counts, The. "A. W. S." FaFP; WBLP
Life that walketh without rule, The. The Golden Mean. Aeschylus. *Fr.* Eumenides. GrR
Life the Beloved. Dante Gabriel Rossetti. The House of Life, XCVI. BPN; PoVP; ViPo
Life through Death. Richard Chenevix Trench. EOAH
Life through Verse. Alpheus of Mitylene, *tr. fr. Greek by* Lord Neaves. OnPM
Life to Come, The. Edward Shillito. OQP; QP-2
Life to the bigot is a whip. Epitaph for a Bigot. Dorothy Vena Johnson. PoNe
Life Upright, The. Thomas Campion. *See* Man of Life Upright, The.
Life was to us an amphora of wine. The Wine-Cup. Richard Aldington. LBBV
Life went whistling a catch, between the plum and the cherry. Flood Tide. Stephen Vincent Benét. PFY
Life—What Is It? James Newton Matthews. PoP
Life, where your lone candle burns. Holy Light. John Hall Wheelock. LiTM (1946 ed.); PG (1955 ed.)
Life with yon Lambs, like day, is just begun. Composed on a May Morning, 1838. Wordsworth. ES
Life within Our Forms, The. Jami, *tr. fr. Persian by* F. Hadland Davis. OnPM
Life without Passion, The. Shakespeare. *See* Sonnets, XCIV.
Life would be an easy matter. If We Didn't Have to Eat. Nixon Waterman. BOHV; FiBHP
Life-Boat, The. Erik Lindorm, *tr. fr. Swedish by* Charles W. Stork. AnSL
Lifeboat that's kept at Torquay, The. Limerick. *Unknown.* LiBL
Lifeless solitude—an angry waste, A. On the Telescopic Moon. John Swanwick Drennan. IrPN
"Life's a cat with nine sharp tails." Feline Anyway. Eden Phillpotts. BMEP
Life's a Dream. Pedro Calderón de la Barca. *See* Life Is a Dream.
Life's a Game. *Unknown.* BLPA
Life's a jail where men have common lot. The Gamblers. Vachel Lindsay. ChMo; CMP
Life's a Jest. Glycon, *tr. fr. Greek by* F. L. Lucas. GrPE
Life's all getting and giving. The Wishing-Caps. Kipling. OtMeF
Life's Angel watched a happy child at play. The Angel of Life. Richard Rowe. BoAu
Life's Best. Simonides, *tr. fr. Greek by* F. L. Lucas. GrPE
Life's Brevity. Francisco de Quevedo, *tr. fr. Spanish by* Eleanor L. Turnbull. TeCS
Life's Brevity. Simonides, *tr. fr. Greek by* J. H. Merivale *and* Lord Neaves. OnPM
Life's burnished grail I take from him. The Potion. Winnie Lynch Rockett. ChIP
Life's but a puppet-play. Play out your own. The World's Stage. Palladas. GrPE
Life's Circumnavigators. W. R. Rodgers. AnIV; FaBoMo; OxBI
Life's Cloudy Quest. John Richard Moreland. MuM
Life's Common Duties. Minot Judson Savage. WBLP
Life's Common Things. Alice E. Allen. WBLP
Life's Evening. William Dudley Foulke. OQP; QP-2; WGRP
Life's Finest Things. Bangs Burgess. OQP; QP-2
Life's Forest Trees. Ella Wheeler Wilcox. ADAH
Life's Hebe. James Thomson. VA
Life's Illusion. Alexander Louis Fraser. OQP; QP-1
Life's Last Scene. Samuel Johnson. *See* Burden of Age, The.
Life's Lesson. *Unknown.* BLRP
Life's Love, A. *Unknown.* LPS-3
Life's Made Up of Little Things. Mary R. Hartman. PoToHe (new ed.)
Life's Medley. Philetas, *tr. fr. Greek by* Hugh Macnaghten. OxBG
Life's Mirror. "Madeline Bridges." BLPA; FaBoBe; MaRV; NeHB; PoToHe; PTA-1; TreF; WBLP
Life's not our own,—'tis but a loan. Life. Charles Swain. VA
Life's Parallels, A. Christina Rossetti. PoEL-5; TriL
Life's Poor Play. Pope. *Fr.* An Essay on Man, Epistle II. OBEC; SeCePo
Life's Purpose. "George Eliot." *Fr.* A Minor Prophet. MaRV
Life's Purpose. James Russell Lowell. *Fr.* The Cathedral. MaRV
Life's Scars. Ella Wheeler Wilcox. BLPA
Life's sweetest joys are hidden. The Tree-Top Road. May Riley Smith. HBV; NLK
Life's Testament, *sels.* William Baylebridge.
"All that I am to Earth belongs," XI. BoAV
"Brain, the blood, the busy thews, The," II. BoAV
"I worshipped, when my veins were fresh," VI. BoAV
(Revelation.) MM
"Into ethereal meads," XII. BoAV
Life's Uncertainty. Ecclesiastes, Bible, *O.T.* *See* Cast Thy Bread upon the Waters.
Life's Ways Are Devious. Friedrich Hölderlin, *tr. fr. German by* Kate Flores. AnGP
Lifesaver. Elizabeth Riddell. NeLNL
Lifetime, A. Bryant. IAP
Lifetime. Winifred Welles. VOD
Lift as he will a wordless face. Defeated Farmer. Mark Van Doren. AnAmPo; LA
Lift Every Voice and Sing. James Weldon Johnson. GoSl; PoNe
Lift her up tenderly. Song of the Ballet. J. B. Morton. FiBHP
Lift it high, our glorious banner. The American Flag. Lena E. Faulds. HH
Lift me higher. Fools! Can nurses. In Extremis. Vera Larminie. QS
Lift me, O God, above myself. Per Ardua ad Astra. John Oxenham. TrPWD
Lift Not the Painted Veil. Shelley. *See* Sonnet: "Lift not the painted veil."
Lift, O dark and glorious Wonder. A Hymn to God in Time of Stress. Max Eastman. QS; TrPWD
Lift the receiver. Hear the young word, "Hi!" Long Distance, 1944. James Boyd. NoCaPo (rev. ed.)
Lift up the banner of our love. The Raising of the Flag. Condé Benoist Pallen. JKCP
Lift Up the Curtain. Hermann Hagedorn. *Fr.* The Heart of Youth. QS
Lift . . . up the drooping head. Welcome to the Prince of Ossory. William Heffernan the Blind. IrPN
Lift up the shuttered eyelids that were drawn. A King in Egypt. David Morton. MuM
Lift Up Your Heads. Psalms, Bible, *O.T.* *See* Twenty-fourth Psalm, The.
Lift up your heads, great gates, and sing. The Ascension. Joseph Beaumont. OxBoCh
Lift Up Your Heads, O Ye Gates. Psalms, Bible, *O.T.* *See* Twenty-fourth Psalm, The.
Lift Up Your Heads, Rejoice! Thomas T. Lynch. WGRP
Lift up your heartës and be glad! What Cheer? Good Cheer! Good Cheer! Good Cheer! *Unknown.* AnEC
Lift Up Your Hearts! Henry Montague Butler. MaRV
Lift up your hearts in Gumber, laugh the Weald. Sonnet. Hilaire Belloc. AlDL
Lift your arms to the stars. Love and Liberation. John Hall Wheelock. MAP; MoAmPo
Lift your foot high in the dance. Euripides. *Fr.* Trojan Women. GrPo
Lifting and Leaning. Ella Wheeler Wilcox. BLPA; WBLP
(Leaners or Lifters.) MaRV
(Two Kinds of People.) PoToHe; PTA-2
Lifting the thunder of their acclamation. Shelley. *Fr.* The Revolt of Islam. ChER
Li Fu, a Chinese poet, long ago. A Chinese Poet. Frank Oliver Call. CPG
Li Fu-jen. Wu Ti, *tr. fr. Chinese by* Arthur Waley. AtBAP; BoW; TrCh
("Sound of her silk skirt has stopped, The.") LO
Ligeia ("Ligeia! Ligeia!"), *poem.* Poe. *Fr.* Al Aaraaf. APW
Ligeia, *pr. tale, sel.* Poe.
Conqueror Worm, The. AA; AmP; AnAmPo; AnFE; APA; AWP; BAV; CoAnAm; CoBA; HBV; IAP; InPo; LA; LiTA; MOAP; PIAE; SPP; TCAP
("Lo! 'tis a gala night.") AmPP
Ligeia! Ligeia!/ My beautiful one! Ligeia. Poe. *Fr.* Al Aaraaf. APW
Light. Vicente Aleixandre, *tr. fr. Spanish by* Eleanor L. Turnbull. CoSP
Light. Francis William Bourdillon. *See* Night Has a Thousand Eyes, The.
Light. Carol Coates. CaP
Light, The. John Holloway. NePoEA
Light. George Macdonald. VA
Light. Milton. *See* Hail, Holy Light.
Light. Helen Welshimer. PraP
Light. Grace Wilkinson. OQP; QP-2
Light after darkness, gain after loss. Afterwards. Frances Ridley Havergal. BLRP
Light and Dark. Barbara Howes. MoVE
Light and Darkness. Henri de Régnier, *tr. fr. French by* Alan Conder. TrFP
Light and Life. Victor Hugo, *tr. fr. French by* George Burnham Ives. *Fr.* Les Burgraves, Pt. I, sc. iii. LiA

Light and Love. Francis William Bourdillon. *See* Night Has a Thousand Eyes, The.
Light and Rejoicing to Israel. *Unknown, tr. fr. Hebrew by* Israel Abrahams. TrJP
Light and rosy be thy slumbers. Cradle Song. *Unknown.* BOL
Light and Shadow. Sophocles, *tr. fr. Greek by* Sir George Young. *Fr.* Electra. GrR
Light as a flake of foam upon the wind. Sea Life. James Montgomery. *Fr.* The Pelican Island. LPS-2
Light as a leaping faun! Nijinsky. Doris Ferne. CaP
Light at Equinox. Léonie Adams. CrMA
Light at Evening Time. R. H. Robinson. PraP
Light at last begun. Creation. Joel Barlow. *Fr.* The Columbiad. APW
Light beats upon me, The. Mid-Day. Hilda Doolittle ("H. D."). ViBoPo (1941 ed.)
Light between the Trees. Henry van Dyke. GBV (1922 ed.)
Light Breaks Where No Sun Shines. Dylan Thomas. EnL; FaBoMo; LiTB; LiTL; LiTM; MoAB; MoBrPo; OAEP (2d ed.); SeCePo; ViBoPo
Light breeze rustles the reeds, A. Night Thoughts while Travelling. Tu Fu. OnPC
Light broke in upon my brain, A. Byron. *Fr.* The Prisoner of Chillon. OBRV
Light comes in your face, a sudden glow, A. A Question of Sacrifice. Sister M. Eulalia. WHL
Light diffusing my likeness. Legend of His Lyre. Aaron Schmuller. GoYe
Light do I see within my Lady's eyes. Ballata 5. Guido Cavalcanti. LyPI
Light exists in spring, A. Emily Dickinson. ExPo; LiTA; PoFS; RiBV
Light falls gently from the dormer panes, The. On a Spring Board. Edward Cracroft Lefroy. OBVV; ShGoBo
Light flower leaves its little core, The. The Changed Woman. Louise Bogan. HBMV
Light flows our war of mocking words, and yet. The Buried Life. Matthew Arnold. BEL; BMEP; BoLiVe; BPN; EmBrPo; EnL; EnLi-2; EnLit; EPN; ERP; GEPC; LEAP; OAEP; OuHeWo; PoFS; PoVP; SeCeV; VA; ViPo; ViPP; VLEP
Light foot hears you and the brightness begins, The. A Poem Beginning with a Line by Pindar. Robert Duncan. NeAP
Light-footed Iphiclus. Hesiod, *tr. fr. Greek by* Sir William Marris. *Fr.* Eoiae. OxBG
Light from Within, The. Jones Very. WGRP
Light had gone out from his vanquished eyes, A. The Old Eagle. E. J. Pratt. BoCaPo (1943 ed.)
Light has come again and found. Ark of the Covenant. Louise Townsend Nicholl. ImOP
Light has transformed them. Their utility gone. Apples. Lisel Mueller. NePoAm-2
Light Heart. T. Sturge Moore. POTE
Light-hearted Fairy, The. *Unknown.* BoChLi; BoTP; FaPON; GaP; MeMeAg; MPB (1956 ed.); OTPC; PCH; SUS; TiPo (1952 ed.); TVSH
(Fairy, The.) PPL
Light-hearted I walked into the valley wood. Conversion. T. E. Hulme. FaBoMo; LoBV; MBP; MoBrPo (1942 ed.); ViBoPo
Light in the Darkness. Aileen Fisher. YeAr
Light in the Darkness. Cardinal Newman. *See* Pillar of the Cloud, The.
Light in the window seemed perpetual, The. The Room above the Square. Stephen Spender. ChMo; ChMP
Light is like a spider, The. Tattoo. Wallace Stevens. AnFE; APA; CoAnAm; LiTA; NP
Light is music, and the first note breaks, The. Genesis. A. M. Sullivan. JKCP (1955 ed.)
Light is out in Italy, A. Mazzini. Laura C. Redden Searing. LPS-3
Light Is Sweet, The. Ecclesiastes, XI: 7, Bible, *O.T.* FaPON
"Light, light, light, my little Scotch-ee." Little Scotch-ee. *Unknown.* AS
Light, Light of My Eyes. Propertius, *tr. fr. Latin by* Ezra Pound. LiTW
Light looked down and beheld Darkness. "And the Word Was Made Flesh." Laurence Housman. MaRV
Light Love. Asclepiades, *tr. fr. Greek by* F. L. Lucas. GrPE
Light Love. Charles Hanson Towne. PR
Light Love. *Unknown, tr. fr. Japanese by* Basil Hall Chamberlain. OnPM
Light Lover. Aline Kilmer. HBMV; LEAP
Light may be had for nothing. Little Candle. Carl Sandburg. GoYe
"Light! more light! the shadows deepen." Let the Light Enter. Frances E. W. Harper. PoNe
Light, my light, the world-filling light, the eye-kissing light, heart-sweetening light! A Song-Offering. Rabindranath Tagore. LiTW
Light of Asia, The, *sels.* Sir Edwin Arnold.
End Which Comes, The, *fr.* III. LoBV
Nirvana, *fr.* VIII. VA
Power That Moves to Good, The. GrCo-2
Light of autumn evenings falls serene, The. Autumn Evening. Feodor Ivanovich Tyutchev. OnPM; TrRV
Light of Bethlehem, The. John Banister Tabb. CAW; ChIP; MaRV; PoRL
Light of dim mornings, shield from heat and cold. To Duty. Thomas Wentworth Higginson. AA; AnAmPo; LA; LEAP
Light of evening, Lissadell, The. In Memory of Eva Gore-Booth and Con Markiewicz. W. B. Yeats. MoAB; OBMV; OxBI; TriL
Light of Faith, The. Edgar Dupree. BLRP
Light of Faith, The. George Santayana. *See* O World.
Light of God is Falling, The. Louis Fitzgerald Benson. MaRV; OQP; QP-1
Light of Life, The. *Unknown, tr. fr. Arabic by* Sir Edwin Arnold. OnPM
Light of Other Days, The. Alfred Bunn. TreFS
Light of Other Days, The. Thomas Moore. *See* Oft in the Stilly Night.
Light of our father's eyes, and in our own. To Louis Kossuth. Swinburne. BPN
Light of spring, The. Song. Alice Duer Miller. AA
Light of Stars, The. William H. Furness. *See* Evening Hymn.
Light of Stars, The. Longfellow. OTPC
Little Moon, The, *sel.* BoTP
Light of the Haram, The. Thomas Moore. *See* Vale of Cashmere, The.
Light of the Soul. *Tr. fr. Latin by* Edward Caswall. BePJ
Light of the Sun over Arctic Regions. David Gascoyne. CaAE
Light of the World, The. St. John, XII: 44–50, Bible, *N.T.* WoL
Light of the World. Sylvester Judd. BePJ
Light of the World. John S. B. Monsell. TrPWD
Light of the World, How Long the Quest. Edwin McNeill Poteat. MaRV
Light of this world, whom the world tries to darken. In Time of Mistrust, XIII. Robert Hillyer. QS
Light on Cape May, The, *with music.* *Unknown.* ShS
Light on the dark horizon, A. Go Tell Them that Jesus Is Living. *Unknown.* BePJ
Light on the Erie Canal, A. The Erie Canal Ballad. *Unknown.* ABF
Light passes, The. Evening. Hilda Doolittle ("H. D."). ChMo; CMP; FaBoMo; LoBV; OTPC (1946 ed.); Po; TwCV; YT
Light rued false Ferdinand to leave a lovely maid forlorn. The Spectre Boat. Thomas Campbell. UnW
Light Shining Out of Darkness. Jane Borthwick. BLRP
Light Shining Out of Darkness. William Cowper. AEV; AtBAP; BLRP; EiPP; EnRP; FaBoCh; FaFP; HBV; LiTB; LoGBV; MaRV; OBEC; PoE; PoEL-3; SeCePo; SeCeV; TCEP; TreF; TrGrPo
(God Moves in a Mysterious Way.) CoBE; FiP
(Hymn: "God moves in a mysterious way.") CoEV; OIF
(Providence.) BPP, *abr.*; WGRP
Light Shoes. Patrick Kelly. JKCP (1926 ed.)
Light-shy. Ibsen, *tr. fr. Norwegian by* Charles W. Stork. AnNoLy
Light Sleeping. Thom Gunn. PoN
Light, stillness and peace lie on the broad sands. The Estuary. Ruth Pitter. MoVE
Light That Failed, The, *sel.* Kipling.
Mother o' Mine. FaFP; MaRV; MotAn; NeHB; OQP; PSO; PTA-2; QP-1; WBLP
(Dedication: "If I were hanged on the highest hill.") MOAH
Light that fills thy house at morn, The. The Gifts of God. Jones Very. AA
Light That Is Felt, The. Whittier. PEOR
Light that labored to an early fall, The. The Lake. Louis O. Coxe. MoVE
Light That Lies, The. Thomas Moore. *Fr.* The Time I've Lost in Wooing. BTP
Light, that out of the west looked back once more. Night Thoughts in Age. John Hall Wheelock. MoVE
Light the Lamp Early. Raymond Holden. MAP; MoAmPo (1942 ed.)
Light the Lamps Up, Lamplighter. Eleanor Farjeon. CH; GaP; RIS; SiSoSe; TiPo (1959 ed.)
Light to dusk is turning. The Woman of the North. Jens Christian Hostrup. BoDS
Light up My World for Me. God to Man. *Fr.* The Talmud. TrJP
Light up thy homes, Columbia. Illumination for Victories in Mexico. Grace Greenwood. PAH
Light upon the Mountains, A. Henry Burton. MaRV
Light was gone, and there wasn't a sound, The. Lost. Maurice Lesemann. NP

Light will never open sightless eyes, The. Morning. Jones Very. AnNE; APW
Light will shine again, The; it cannot die. There Will Be Peace. Margaret Miller Pettengill. PGD
Light-winged Smoke, Icarian Bird. Henry David Thoreau. *See* Smoke.
Light-winged wilding meadowlark, The. Out of Darkness. Sister Maris Stella. JKCP (1955 ed.)
Light [*or* Cleanse] with the burning log of oak. Yule-Tide Fires. *Unknown.* PCD; PCH; PoRL; SDH
Light Within. Milton. *See* He That Has Light Within.
Light Woman, A. Robert Browning. AEV; BPN; HBV; PoVP; VLEP
Light words they were, and lightly, falsely said. A Protest. Arthur Hugh Clough. VA
Light Yoke and Easy Burden, The. Charles Wesley. BePJ
Lighted Night. Jorge Guillén, *tr. fr. Spanish by* Eleanor L. Turnbull. CoSP
Lighten Our Darkness. Lord Alfred Douglas. HBMV
Lighteneth she night's darkness, ay, as an evening lamp. The Night Long. Imr El Kais. LiTW
Lighter scarf of richer fold, A. Baby Zulma's Christmas Carol. Augustus Julian Requier. LPS-1
Lighter than dandelion down. Silkweed. Philip Henry Savage. AA; OBAV
Lighter than thistledown. First Snow. Ivy O. Eastwick. TiPo
Lightest foam, straightest spray. Waters of the Sea. Cecil Goldbeck. EtS
Lighthouse, The. Sir Walter Scott. OTPC (1946 ed.); PCH
Light-House, The. *Unknown.* PEOR
Lighthouse, The. Marjorie Wilson. BoTP
Lighthouse Keeper's Offspring, The. James Broughton. CrMA
Lighting rooms perfect a chequerboard, The. Dusk on English Bay. Earle Birney. BoCaPo
Lightless Suburb. "Pablo Neruda," *tr. fr. Spanish by* H. R. Hays. TwSpPo
Lightless, unholy, eldritch thing. The Bat. Ruth Pitter. AlDL
Lightly an ignorant boor is made content. Half-Way Knowledge. Bhartrihari. OnPM
Lightly, gently, on the city. The Awakening of Spring. Ku Shih. PoHN
Lightly he laugh'd, as one that read my thought. Tennyson. *Fr.* The Gardener's Daughter. EnSW
Lightly he touched her soft and rosy hand. Musaeus. *Fr.* Hero and Leander. GrPo
Lightly, lightly,/ Summer breezes playing. Bokujin, *tr. fr. Japanese by* Lois J. Erickson. SoLD
Lightly like Music Running. Jean Garrigue. MoVE
Lightly, O lightly, we bear her along. Palanquin Bearers. Sarojini Naidu. MoSiPe
Lightly She Whipped o'er the Dales. John Mundy. ReIE
Lightly stepped a yellow star. Emily Dickinson. MAP; MoAmPo; MoShBr; OxBA
Lightly the breath of the spring wind blows. By Wood and Wold. Adam Lindsay Gordon. BoAu
Lightness. Richard Wilbur. FiMAP
Lightning. *At. to* Diotimus *and to* Leonidas of Tarentum, *tr. fr. Greek by* F. L. Lucas. GrPE
Lightning. D. H. Lawrence. LiTL; MBP; MoAB; MoBrPo
Lightning bug got, A. The Flattered Lightning Bug. Don Marquis. StPo
Lightning flashed, The. He saw that welcome sign. Theseus. Bacchylides, *tr. by* Arthur S. Way. GrR
Lightning flashed, and lifted, The. The Thunder-Shower. John Hall Wheelock. NP
Lightning for Atmosphere. Marya Zaturenska. TwAmPo
Lightning is a yellow fork, The. Emily Dickinson. OnAP
Lightning of a summer, The. Lady Bates. Randall Jarrell. MiAP; NoCaPo (rev. ed.)
Lightning of the Abyss. Jules Laforgue, *tr. fr. French by* Vernon Watkins. AnFP
Lightning spoke one stormy night, The. Fate. Christian Morgenstern. AnGP
Lightning, The, spun your garment for the night. The Lights of New York. Sara Teasdale. PoMa
Light'ood Fire. The. John Henry Boner. AA
Lights, The. John Joy Bell. BoTP
Lights. Mary Lanier Magruder. VOD
Lights along the shore at night, The. The Hub. Oscar Williams. MaRV
Lights are on the harbor, The. Deep Down. James Stuart Montgomery. NLK
Lights are out and gone are all the guests, The. The Hanging of the Crane. Longfellow. IAP
Lights begin to twinkle from the rocks, The. Tennyson. *Fr.* Ulysses. MuP
Lights from the parlor and kitchen shone out, The. Escape at Bedtime. Robert Louis Stevenson. AlDL; BrR; GoTP; HBVY; OTPC; PCH; PoRh; PoVP; TiPo; TreFS; TrGrPo; TSW; TSWC; VLEP
Light's Glittering Morn. John Mason Neale. OxBoCh
"Lights go out." Lola Ridge. *Fr.* The Ghetto. LEAP; MAP; MoAmPo (1942 ed.); TCPD
Lights in the Quarters Burnin' Mighty Dim, *with music. Unknown.* OuSiCo
Lights of heaven (which are the world's fair eyes), The. Of the Soul of Man and the Immortality Thereof. Sir John Davies. *Fr.* Nosce Teipsum. ReIE
Lights of Home, The. Alfred Noyes. EOAH
Lights of New York, The. Sara Teasdale. PoMa
Lights of Saturday night beat golden, golden over the pillared street, The. Saturday Night. James Oppenheim. HBV; TSW
Lights Out. Edward Thomas. CoEV; GTBS-D; MoP; POTE
Lights out! And a prow turned towards the South. The Race of the *Oregon.* John James Meehan. PAH
Lights out. Shades up. Girl in a Nightgown. Wallace Stevens. OxBA
Lightship, The. Josephine Winslow Johnson. MoSiPe
'Ligion. John Charles McNeill. NoCaPo
'Ligion So Sweet, *with music. Unknown.* ABF
Like a bird that trails a broken wing. Prodigal. Ellen Gilbert. GoBC; MaRV
Like a black enamoured king whispered low the thunder. Dunedin in the Gloaming. Jessie Mackay. BoAu
Like a blind spinner in the sun. Spinning. Helen Hunt Jackson. BLP; CV; HBV; LBAP; OQP; QP-1; TCAP
Like a bread without the spreadin'. Smile. *Unknown.* BLPA; WBLP
Like a bulwark against fate. At Rest in the Blast. Marianne Moore. MoAB; MoAmPo (1950 ed.)
Like a butterfly, my nostalgia. Nostalgia. Tatsuji Miyoshi. PoLJ
Like a chained brute beast howling in the heat. The Showmen. Leconte de Lisle. TrFP
Like a clamorous flock of startled birds. The Nightingale. Paul Verlaine. AnFP
Like a Cloud, like a Mist. Helen Hoyt. AV
Like a coy maiden, ease, when courted most. Nature and God. William Cowper. *Fr.* The Task. CoBE
Like a crescent of autumn shines the moon of Omei. Song for the Moon on Mount Omei. Li Po. ChLP; WhP
Like a damask rose you see. *See* Like as the damask rose you see.
Like a dog with a bottle, fast ty'd to his tail. The Batchelors Song. Thomas Flatman. CEP
Like a donkey's back. Thasos. Archilochus. OxBG
Like a dream it all comes over me as I hear the Christmas bells. A Christmas Long Ago. *Unknown.* PTA-2
Like a drop of water is my heart. Youth and Maidenhood. Sarah Williams. OBVV
Like a drowsy, rain-browned saint. Hill-Side Tree. Maxwell Bodenheim. MAP; MAPA; MoAmPo (1942 ed.)
Like a fairy spirit I leave the gate of the city. Autumn. Lu Yu. WhP
Lake a faun my head uplifted. Curfew. Sir Herbert Read. *Fr.* Eclogues. BrBE
Like a flight of arrows the wind. Stormy Night in Autumn. Chu Shu Chen. OnPC
Like a forsaken theatre art thou. By Cobequid Bay. Alexander Louis Fraser. CaP
Like a gaunt, scraggly pine. Lincoln. John Gould Fletcher. ChMo; CMP; HBMV; LaNeLa; MoAmPo; MAP; MOAP; NeMA; PaA; PCN; PFE; PoRL; SBMV; SP; VOD
Like a glacier man advances. All Too Slowly. Lucia Trent. ChIP
Like a gondola of green scented fruits. Images. Richard Aldington. BMEP; MBP; MoBrPo; NeMA; NP; PFE; PIAE; TOP
Like a great burst of singing came the day. Morning in the Bay of Naples. John Todhunter. *Fr.* Laurella. TIP
Like a great rock, far out at sea. Lady Sanuki. *Fr.* Hyaku-Nin-Isshu. AWP; JAWP; WBP
Like a great wheel. Incense and Moonlight. Kan Ju Yü. ChLP
Like a hidden spring. My Love-Song. Else Lasker-Schüler. TrJP
Like a hound with nose to the trail. Michaelmas. Norman Nicholson. FaBoTw; MoBrPo (1950 ed.)
Like a huge Python, winding round and round. Our Casuarina Tree. Toru Dutt. VA
Like a jewel golden-rimmed. An Autumn Day. Margaret Sangster. PEOR
Like a king from a sunrise-land. Days and Nights. T. Sturge Moore. HBMV
Like a Laverock in the Lift. Jean Ingelow. HBV; LPS-1
Like a lizard in the sun, though not scuttling. The Laureate [*or* The Wretch]. Robert Graves. FaBoTw; MoP
Like a lone Arab, old and blind. Love's Apparition and Evanishment. Samuel Taylor Coleridge. EnRP; EV-4
Like a loose island on the wide expanse. To a Deaf and Dumb Little Girl. Hartley Coleridge. PoEL-4

Like a loud-booming bell shaking its tower. The Latin Tongue. James J. Daly. CAW; GoBC

Like a Midsummer Rose. John Lydgate. *Fr.* The Fall of Princes. CoEV
(Lat Noman Booste of Konnyng nor Vertu.) AtBAP; NBE

Like a mist of the sea at morn it comes. The Wraith of Roanoke. Benjamin Sledd. NoCaPo

Like a Mourningless Child. Kenneth Patchen. MoAmPo

Like a musician that with flying finger. The Master-Chord. William Caldwell Roscoe. VA

Like a regiment filing across the sky. Brooklyn Bridge. Frederick Mortimer Clapp. VOD (1935 ed.)

Like a ship, that through the ocean wide. *See* Like as a ship . . .

Like a Shower of Rain. Ennius, *tr. fr. Latin by* John Wight. *Fr.* Annales. LaP; WaaP

Like a skein of loose silk blown against a wall. The Garden. Ezra Pound. AWP; CoV; InPo; JAWP; LiTA; MoAB; MoAmPo (1950 ed.); NP; WBP

Like a sleeping swine upon the skyline. Muckish Mountain (The Pig's Back). Shane Leslie. AnIV

Like a small gray/ coffee pot. The Gray [*or* Grey] Squirrel. Humbert Wolfe. BLV; MBP; MoBrPo; NeMA; PIAE

Like a stone toppled from an endless hill. The Fall of Satan. Roy Campbell. *Fr.* The Flaming Terrapin. BoSA

Like a strong bow bent forcefully. The Dive. Ted Robins. PreP

Like a tower of brass is Punch. Conrad Aiken. *Fr.* Punch, the Immortal Liar. NP

Like a wave crest. Emperor Uda, *tr. fr. Japanese by* Kenneth Rexroth. LiTW; OnPJ

Like a Whisper. Ethan Ayer. GoYe

Like a white cat. Moonlight. Maud E. Uschold. StVeCh (1955 ed.)

Like a White Stone. "Anna Akhmatova," *tr. fr. Russian by* Babette Deutsch. OnPM; TrRV

Like a white wall whereon forever breaks. Octaves, XVIII. E. A. Robinson. CoV

Like a young child who to his mother's door. Doors. Hermann Hagedorn. AnAmPo; BAP; CBOV; LA; OBAV; PFY; SBMV

Like air on skin, coolness of yachts at mooring. Yachts on the Nile. Bernard Spencer. ChMP

Like an adventurous seafarer am I. Idea, I. Michael Drayton. EnLi-1 (1949 ed.); EtS; ReEn; SiCE; TuPP

Like an apple burnt-up by winter. Girl's Song. Aleksey Surkov. RuPo

Like an April Day. Johan Sebastian Cammermeyer Welhaven, *tr. fr. Norwegian by* Charles W. Stork. AnNoLy; LiTW

Like an arrow shot. Wine. Micah Joseph Lebensohn. LiTW; TrJP

Like an empty stage. The Snow-Gardens. Zoe Akins. AV

Like an hart, the live-long day. The Relief on Easter Eve. Thomas Pestel. MeRV; OxBoCh; SeCL

Like an ill husband, though I knew the same. Thomas Dekker. *Fr.* The Honest Whore. LO

Like an invader, not a guest. Winter's Troops. Charles Cotton. *Fr.* Winter. ChTr

Like an Ocean Is This World. Hovhannes Erzingatzi, *tr. fr. Armenian by* Zabelle C. Boyajian. ArmLP

Like an old battle, youth is wild. Keep Innocency. Walter de la Mare. SoV

Like angels with great tawny eyes. The Ghost. Baudelaire. TrFP

Like any merchant in a store. The Ticket Agent. Edmund Leamy. HBMV; MW; PoMa; StVeCh

Like any of us—you or me. Old Man Pot. Lyon Sharman. CaP; OCL

Like apple-blossom, white and red. To Daphne. Sir Walter Besant. HBV; VA

Like April morning clouds, that pass. To William Erskine, Esq. Sir Walter Scott. Marmion, *introd. to* III. EBSV; OBRV

Like architects of a sumptuous palace. Olympian Ode, VI. Pindar. *Fr.* Odes. LiTW

Like [*or* Lyke] as a huntsman after weary chase [*or* chace]. Amoretti, LXVII. Spenser. BLV; BoLiVe; BrBE; ES; OAEP; PeBoSo; PoEL-1; ReEn; RiBV; SeCePo; SiCE; TrGrPo; TwHP

Like [*or* Lyke] as a ship, that through the ocean wide [*or* wyde]. Amoretti, XXXIV. Spenser. AnFE; BEL; BrBE; CoBE; EnLi-1; EnLit; EPP; ES; EtS; HBV; KN; OBSC; PeBoSo; PIAE; PoFS; REAL; ReaPo; ReEn; ReIE; SiCE; TwHP

Like as herb and tree in May. True Love. Ernest Rhys. POTE

Like as the armèd Knighte. The Fight of Faith. Anne Askewe. LPS-2

Like as the bay, that bears on branches sweet. In Praise of His Lady. Matthew Grove. *Fr.* Pelops and Hippodamia. EIL

Like as the bird in the cage enclosed. Songs and Lyrics, XXIII. Sir Thomas Wyatt. SiPS

Like as the culver, on the barèd bough. Amoretti, LXXXVIII. Spenser. EG; ES; PeBoSo

Like as the damask rose you see. Man's Mortality [*or* Of Man's Mortalitie]. *At. to* Simon Wastell. *Fr.* Microbiblion. AlDL; EV-1; FaBoCh; HBV; LoBV; LoGBV; LPS-1; OBS; SeCL; SeEP; WBLP. *See also* Like to the damask rose you see.

Like as the divers-fretchled butterfly. The Muse Reviving. Sir John Davies. SiPS

Like as the doleful dove delights alone to be. No Pains Comparable to His Attempt. William Hunnis. ReIE

Like as the Dove. Sir Philip Sidney. SiPS

Like as the dumb solsequium, with care ourcome. The Solsequium. Alexander Montgomerie. GoTS

Like as the fountaine of all light created. Incarnatio Est Maximum Donum Dei. William Alabaster. MePo

Like as the hart, athirst in desert dreary. Where Is Thy God? J. Lewis Milligan, *par. fr.* Psalm XLII, Bible, *O.T.* MaRV

Like as the lark that, soaring higher and higher. Thomas William Parsons. AA

Like as the lark within the marlian's foot. The Lover Showeth His Woeful State and Prayeth Pity. *Unknown.* TuPP

Like as the lute delights or else dislikes. To Delia, LIV. Samuel Daniel. OAEP

Like as the rage of rain. The Uncertain State of a Lover. *Unknown.* EIL

Like as the swan towards her death. Songs and Lyrics, LI. Sir Thomas Wyatt. SiPS

Like as the sweet red apple that ripens on high in the branches. The Highest Fruit. Sappho. OnPM

Like as the tide that comes from th' ocean main. Spenser. *Fr.* The Faerie Queene. HoPM

Like as the waves make towards the pebbled shore. Sonnets, LX. Shakespeare. AnFE; ATP (1953 ed.); BEL; BLV; BoFr; BoLiVe; ChTr; CoBE; CoEV; EIL; ElSeCe; EM-1; EnL; EnLi-1; EnLit; ES; EtPaEn; EV-1; ExPo; FaBoEn; FaFP; GTBS; GTBS-D; GTBS-W; GTSE; GTSL; HBV; LEAP; LiTB; LiTL; LoBV; NBE; OBSC; PeBoSo; Po; PoRA; ReaPo; ReEn; ReIE; SeCeV; ShBV-4; SiCE; TwHP; UnPo; ViBoPo

Like as, to make our appetites more keen. Sonnets, CXVIII. Shakespeare. PeBoSo; UnPo (1st ed.)

Like autumn winds that rustle in the leaves. The Old Bard Speaks. Joseph R. N. Maxwell. JKCP (1955 ed.)

Like Barley Bending. Sara Teasdale. CP; HBMV

Like bees that suck the morning dew. An Thou Were My Ain Thing. Allan Ramsay. EBSV; EV-3

Like Birds of a Feather. Ralph Schomberg. *Fr.* The Judgment of Paris. TrJP

Like buckskin and broadcloth and strange American shillings. Tanglewood. Francis Sweeney. JKCP (1955 ed.)

Like cattle-raiding heroes in the Tain. Address of Welcome. Maurice James Craig. *Fr.* Three Cat Poems. PoC

Like children in a starry night. The Relapse. John Sheffield. NBE

Like crown'd athlete that in a race has run. Landor. Alexander Hay Japp. PtP; VA

Like Crusoe with the bootless gold we stand. Experience. Edith Wharton. AA

Like Desert Woods. Thomas Lodge. SiCE; TuPP

Like five moving fingers. Translations from Modern Japanese Poetry. Akiko Yosano. PFE

Like Flakes of Snow. B. Y. Williams. MuM

Like Flowers We Spring. *Unknown.* EIL

Like gods who are fêted. They Came to the Wedding. Babette Deutsch. NePoAm

Like gossamer/ On the swift breath of morn, the vessel flew. Ever as We Sailed. Shelley. *Fr.* The Revolt of Islam. SeCePo

Like gript stick. The Sermons. Richard Hughes. OBMV

Like Groping Fingers. Abraham Sutzkever, *tr. fr. Yiddish by* Joseph Leftwich. TrJP

Like Hermit Poor. *At. to* Sir Walter Ralegh. *See* Like to a Hermit.

Like Him, whilst friends and lovers slept. Gethsemane. M. Betham-Edwards. BePJ

Like Him Whose Spirit. Arthur Davison Ficke. NP

Like His Mother Used to Make. James Whitcomb Riley. IHA

Like Ilium. Thomas Merton. JKCP (1955 ed.)

Like intuition, starlight pierced the twelve. Starlight like Intuition Pierced the Twelve. Delmore Schwartz. MiAP

Like labor-laden moonclouds faint to flee. The House of Life, XLI: Through Death to Love. Dante Gabriel Rossetti. BPN; PoVP; ViPo; VLEP

Like labouring bees on a long summer day. Bees. Dryden. *Fr.* Annus Mirabilis. BeR

Like lamp of intricate stained glass which hangs. From Ancient Fangs. Peter Viereck. LiTA; MiAP

Like liquid gold the wheat field lies. Color in the Wheat. Hamlin Garland. HiLiAm; PTA-2

Like many a one, when you had gold. The Old Story.

E. A. Robinson, *after* Marcus Argentarius. AWP; JAWP; LiTW; MOAP; WBP
Like marble, nude, against the purple sky. The Diver. John Frederic Herbin. CaP
Like Memnon's rock, touched [*or* touch'd] with the rising sun. Licia, XLVII. Giles Fletcher. ElL; ReEn; ReIE; SiCE; TuPP
"Like men riding." Nelly Trim. Sylvia Townsend Warner. MBP; MoAB; MoBrPo
Like Michinoku/ Cloth, printed with tangled ferns. Minamoto no Toru, *tr. fr. Japanese by* Kenneth Rexroth. OnPJ
Like mirrored paintings done by Fragonard. The Flamingos. Rainer Maria Rilke. OnPM
Like Mother, Like Son. Margaret Johnston Grafflin. BLPA; NeHB
(To My Son.) PoToHe (new ed.)
Like Music. John Hall Wheelock. NP
Like old astrologers I'll sleep on high. Landscape. Baudelaire. TrFP
Like One I Know. Nancy Campbell. JKCP
Like one pale, flitting, lonely gleam. Sense, if You Can Find It. Hartley Coleridge. UnW
Like one who in her third widdowhood doth professe. To Mr. Rowland Woodward. John Donne. MePo
Like one who solves some curious alphabet/ On desert stele . . . and then solves a word. William Ellery Leonard. *Fr.* Two Lives, Pt. III. AnAmPo; LA; MOAP
Like one who solves some curious alphabet/ Upon a desert stele . . . But perhaps. William Ellery Leonard. *Fr.* Two Lives, Pt. III. AnAmPo; LA; MOAP
Like pensive herds at rest upon the sands. The Accursed. Baudelaire. LiTW
Like Plimsoll lines on British hulls. Convalescence, II. David McCord. WhC
Like savage wood-nymphs with their hair on end. John Davidson. *Fr.* The Testament of a Prime Minister. BSV
Like silver dew are the tears of love. Epitaph. Alfred Edgar Coppard. OBMV
Like silver lamps in a distant shrine. Silver Lamps. W. C. Dix. BePJ
Like small curled feathers, white and soft. While Shepherds Watched Their Flocks by Night [*or* The First Best Christmas Night]. Margaret Deland. COAH; DD; GN; HBVY; SDH; StJW
Like smoke I vanish though I burn like flame. Human Life. William H. Mallock. ACP (1926 ed.); JKCP (1926 ed.); OQP; QP-2
Like snails I see the people go. From a Street Corner. Eleanor Hammond. HBMV
Like snakes of golden autumn fire. Nevada. Lawrence Gurney. GoYe
Like snooker balls thrown on the table's faded green. A Poet's Progress. Michael Hamburger. NePoEA
Like Snow. Robert Graves. AtBAP
Like Snow. Omar Khayyám. *See* Worldly Hope, The.
Like snowflakes, or like petals of sweet flowers. Easter. Miyoshi. SoLD
Like some great pearl from out the Orient. Night-Wind. Beatrix Demarest Lloyd. AA
Like some huge bird that sinks to rest. Sunset. Herbert Bashford. AA
Like some lone miser, dear, behold me stand. Morton Luce. *Fr.* Thysia. HBV
Like some lost monster of the Saurian Age. Gargantua. Hugh Wilgus Ramsaur. MuM
Like some old voyager out of the past. Captain's Walk; Salem. Oliver Jenkins. PoMa
Like some poor bark on the rough ocean tost. Drifting. George Crabbe. CaAE
Like some school master, kind in being stern. Unanswered Prayers. Ella Wheeler Wilcox. WGRP
Like some small hungry bird that sees and hears. Sonnet. Vittoria Colonna. LyPI
Like some weak lords, neighbour'd by mighty kings. Astrophel and Stella, XXIX. Sir Philip Sidney. SiPS
Like souls that balance joy and pain. Sir Launcelot and Queen Guinevere. Tennyson. PIR; VA
Like South-Sea Stock, expressions rise and fall. Time's Changes. James Bramston. *Fr.* The Art of Politicks. OBEC
Like spectral hounds across the sky. Minot's Ledge. Fitz-James O'Brien. OnYI
Like the blooming rose/ Which on its native stem unsully'd grows. The Rose. Ariosto. *Fr.* Orlando Furioso. LiA
Like the bole of a fallen mountain tree. The Corpse. Salvador Díaz Mirón. AnMP
Like the crash of the thunder. Zionist Marching Song. Naphtali Herz Imber. TrJP
Like the ears of wheat in a wheat-field. Epilog. Heine. *Fr.* The North Sea. AWP; JAWP; WBP
Like the Eyes of Wolves. Nachum Yud, *tr. fr. Yiddish by* Joseph Leftwich. TrJP
Like the fire it came to birth. The Water-Cooler. Sharaf al-Din. MooP
Like the first seed before man's birth. The Baptism. L. Aaronson. FaBoTw
Like the first swallow in the spring returning. Beatrice. Oscar Levertin. AnSL
Like the ghost of a dear friend dead. Time Long Past. Shelley. BPN; EmBrPo; EPN; ERP; HBV
Like the glorious red of the sunrise. Your Death. Takamoto. SoLD
Like the Idalian Queen. William Drummond of Hawthornden. *See* Madrigal: "Like the Idalian queen."
Like the idle fingers of wind caressing the forehead of God. The Falling of the Snow. Raymond Souster. CaP
Like the last stone at the bridge's end. The Return of the Men. Luc Durtain. BoFr
"Like the leaves in their generations, such is the race of men." The Sere and Yellow Leaf. Homer. *Fr.* The Iliad, VI. GrPE
Like the Light Sound. Luis Cernuda, *tr. fr. Spanish by* Eleanor L. Turnbull. CoSP
Like the moon her kindness is. Human Dignity. W. B. Yeats. A Man Young and Old, II. TwP
Like the pippin blushing high. Beyond the Vulgar Reach. Sappho, *tr. by* J. M. Edmonds. GrR
Like the soul of a stream. To a Cloud. Manuel Altolaguirre. LiTW
Like the stalks of wheat in the fields. Epilogue. Heine. *Fr.* The North Sea. TrJP
Like the steps of footsore armies. Waiting for Death. Mordecai Gebirtig. TrJP
Like the swarthy son of some tropic shore. The Voyageur. S. Frances Harrison. *Fr.* Down the River. CPG
Like the sweet apple which reddens upon the topmost bough. One Girl [*or* Beauty *or* A Young Bride]. Sappho, *tr. by* Dante Gabriel Rossetti. AWP; BMEP; EnLi-1; GrL; GrPo; JAWP; LEAP; LiTW; OuHeWo; OxBG; ViBoPo; WBP
Like the Touch of Rain. Edward Thomas. EnLoPo
Like the tribes of Israel. Sherman's in Savannah. Oliver Wendell Holmes. GA; MC; PAH
Like the violet, which alone. Castara. William Habington. *Fr.* Castara, I. LiTL
Like the white wave following. The White Wave Following. Alice Milligan. GTIV
Like thee I once have stemmed the sea of life. Epitaph, Intended for Himself. James Beattie. EBSV; HBV; OBEV
Like this, unto a wounded crane. "Anna Akhmatova," *tr. fr. Russian by* C. M. Bowra. BoRS
Like those boats which are returning. Saigyo Hoshi, *tr. fr. Japanese by* Arthur Waley. AWP
Like to a baker's oven is the grave. Epitaphs. Francis Jeffrey. OxBoLi
Like to a Coin. Arlo Bates. AA
Like to a god he seems to me,/ Above the gods. Catullus' Translation of the Ode to Anactoria (*by* Sappho). Catullus, *tr. by* Sir William Marris. LiA
Like to a god he seems to me,/ O more than god. Sappho. Catullus, *tr. by* William Ellery Leonard. AWP; JAWP; WBP
Like to a Hermit. *At. to* Sir Walter Ralegh. PoFS; TuPP
(Hermit, The.) OBSC; PeBoSo
(Like Hermit Poor.) SiPS
("Like to a hermit poor in place obscure.") EG; ReEn
(Like to an Hermit Poor.) ReIE
(Poem, A: "Like to an Hermit poore in place obscure.") SiCE
(Sonnet: "Like to an hermit poor . . .") ElL
Like to a stranger in a foreign strand. Ithaca. Oscar Levertin. AnSL
Like to Ahasuerus, that shrewd prince. The Pope. Robert Browning. The Ring and the Book, X. ViPo; ViPP
Like to an Hermit Poor. *At. to* Sir Walter Ralegh. *See* Like to a Hermit.
Like to clear in highest sphere. *See* Like to the clear . . .
Like to Diana in her summer weed[e]. Doron's Description of Samela [*or* Samela]. Robert Greene. *Fr.* Menaphon. AtBAP; ElL; ElSeCe; EV-1; HBV; LoBV; OBEV; OBSC; PoEL-2; ReIE; SiCE; TuPP; ViBoPo
Like to the Arctic Needle. Francis Quarles. Emblems, V, 4. OxBoCh
(I Am My Beloved's, and His Desire Is towards Me.) OBS
("Like to the Arctic needle, that does guide.") SeEP
(Unsettled Soul, The.) CoEV
"Eternal God! O Thou that only art," *sel.* MaRV
Like to the clear in highest sphere. Rosaline. Thomas Lodge. *Fr.* Rosalynde; or, Euphues' Golden Legacy. BLV; ElL; ElSeCe; EV-1; GoBC; GTBS; GTBS-D; GTBS-W; GTSE; GTSL; LiTB; LiTG; LO; LPS-1; OBEV; OBSC; TrGrPo
Like to the damask rose you see. Hos Ego Versiculos. Francis Quarles. *Fr.* Argalus and Parthenia. CaAE; CenL; OBS; SeEP. *See also* Like as the damask rose you see.

Like to the Falling of a Star. Henry King. *See* Sic Vita.
Like to the fatal, ominous raven which tolls. To Deloney. Everard Guilpin. *Fr.* Skialetheia. ReIE
Like to the leaf that falls. Epicedium. Horace L. Traubel. AA
Like to the leaves of the forest that bloom in the flowery season. Elegiac. Mimnermus. LiTW
Like to the Marigold. Edward Taylor. *Fr.* Sacramental Meditations. AnNE
Like to the seely fly. Francis Davison. EG
Like to the Thundering Tone. Richard Corbet. BOHV; NA
Like to [*or* unto] these unmeasurable mountains. The Lover's Life Compared to the Alps. Jacopo Sannazaro, *tr. by* Sir Thomas Wyatt. ReEn; ReIE; SiCE; TuPP
Like torn-up newsprint the nonchalant snow. 1894 in London. Charles Spear. AnNZ
Like trains of cars on tracks of plush. The Bee. Emily Dickinson. AnNE; GN; MoAB; MoAmPo (1950 ed.); NeMA; OTPC
Like Truthless Dreams. Sir Walter Ralegh. *See* Farewell to the Court.
Like two bats in the birdless country. In the Birdless Country. Toson Shimazaki. PoLJ
Like two cathedral towers these stately pines. My Cathedral. Longfellow. BAV
Like two pale stars at distance seen. St. Simon and St. Jude's Day. Cecil Frances Alexander. IrPN
Like two proud armies marching in the field. Your Beauty and My Reason. *Unknown.* OBSC; TrGrPo
Like unto Like, Quoth the Devil to the Collier. *Unknown. See* Westminster Wedding, A.
Like unto Them That Dream. Psalms, CXXVI, Bible, *O.T.* TrJP
Like unto these unmeasurable mountains. *See* Like to these unmeasurable mountains.
Like violets pale i' the spring o' the year. Song. James Thomson. Sunday up the River, IX. OBVV
Like vultures flocking from their charnel house. The Conquerors. José Maria de Heredia. TrFP
Like Washington ("We cannot all be Washingtons"). *Unknown.* DD; GA; HH; MeMeAg
Like Water down a Slope. Zalman Schneour, *tr. fr. Hebrew by* Harry H. Fein. TrJP
Like wretched sores/ like bloody scourges. The Damned. Manuel Moreno Jimeno. AnCL
Like your window that does not exist. The Illustrated World. "César Moro." AnCL
Likeness, A. Robert Browning. NBE; PoVP
Likeness, A. Willa Cather. HBMV
Likeness has made them animal and shy. The Twins. Karl Shapiro. AnFE; CoAnAm; MiAP; MoAmPo (1950 ed.); Po; TrJP; TwAmPo
Likeness of heaven!/ Agent of Power! The Ocean. John Augustus Shea. EtS
Li'l' Gal. Paul Laurence Dunbar. GoSl
Li'l Jesus-Baby, De. Louise Ayres Garnett. BOL
L'il Pickaninny Coon. "P. H." CAG
Li'l Road to Res', De. Leigh Richmond Miner. BOL
Li'l Yaller Cradle. Louise Ayres Garnett. BOL
Lilac, The. Williams Barnes. EV-4
Lilac. F. S. Flint. HBMV
Lilac, The. Humbert Wolfe. FaPON; HBVY; MBP; MoBrPo; NeMA; OTPC (1946 ed.); YT
Lilac alone. Night Lilac. Mark Van Doren. MOAP
Lilac bushes were small with winter, The. Exercise in Aesthetics. Winfield Townley Scott. FiMAP
Lilac Dusk. Lizette Woodworth Reese. VOD
Lilac heat was heavy on the meadow, A. In the Wood. Boris Pasternak. BoRS
Lilac ribbon is unbound, A. Country of No Lack. Jean Starr Untermeyer. MAP; MoAmPo
Lilacs. Hilda Conkling. NP; TBM
Lilacs. Amy Lowell. AmPP; AnAmPo; AnNE; AtBAP; CBOV; IAP; LA; LaNeLa, *abr.;* MAP; MoAmPo; MoVE; OxBA; PIAE; PoeMoYo; PoTo; TCPD
Lilacs blossom just as sweet. Threnody. Dorothy Parker. InMe
Lilacs for Remembrance. Irene Shirley Moran. PoMa
L'Ile du Levant; the Nudist Colony. Barbara Howes. NePoAm-2
L'ile Sainte Croix. Arthur W. H. Eaton. CPG
Lilian. Tennyson. HBV; PoVP; VLEP
Lilian Adelaide Neilson. Clement Scott. VA
Lilies. Padraic Colum. NePoAm
Lilies. Ibn Darraj, *tr. fr. Arabic by* A. J. Arberry. MooP
Lilies. Don Marquis. BOHV
Lilies, The. John Francis O'Donnell. IrPN
Lilies. Shiko, *arr. by* Olive Beaupré Miller. SUS; TiPo
Lilies and Roses. Ibn al-Qutiya, *tr. fr. Arabic by* A. J. Arberry. MooP
Lilies are white,/ Rosemary's green. Hearts and Lace Paper [*or* Flower Tokens]. *Unknown.* BoTP; OxNR; PCH; RIS
Lilies lie in my lady's bower, The. Oh! Weary Mother. Barry Pain. The Poets at Tea, VIII. NA
Lilies, lilies, white lilies and yellow. Lilies. Don Marquis. BOHV
Lilies of the Field, The. Daniel Henderson. MaRV; StJW
Lilies of the Field, The. Compton Mackenzie. OBVV
Lilies of the Valley. Jo Gardner. BePJ
Lilies of the Valley. Marion Mitchell Walker. GFA
Lilies of White. Unnur Benediktsdóttir, *tr. fr. Icelandic by* Watson Kirkconnell. IcP
Lilies say on Easter day, The. The Song of the Lilies. Lucy Wheelock. OHIP
Lilies That Fester. Shakespeare. *See* Sonnets, XCIV.
Lilith. Calvin Holmes. CAG
Lilith. Dante Gabriel Rossetti. *See* Body's Beauty.
Lilium Regis. Francis Thompson. HBMV; JKCP
(Lillium Regis.) WGRP
Lill' Angels. Beatrice Ravenel. LS
Lilli Burlero. Thomas, Lord Wharton. OxBoLi
(Lilliburlero, *with music.*) ViBoFo
(New Song, A; or, Lilliburlero.) CoMu
Lilliput Levee. William Brighty Rands. CenHV; TSW; TSWC
Lillium Regis. Francis Thompson. *See* Lilium Regis.
Lilly in a Christal, The. Robert Herrick. AtBAP; PoEL-3
(Lily in a Crystal, The.) SeCePo
Lily Adair. Thomas Holley Chivers. SPP
Lily and the Rose, The. *Unknown. See* Maidens Came, The.
Lily Bed, The. Isabella Valancy Crawford. PeCV
Lily Bright and Shine-a. *Unknown. See* Here Comes a Lusty Wooer.
Lily castles gleam. Lilies. Ibn Darraj. MooP
Lily floated white and red, The. The Water-Lily. Robert Nichols. TCPD
Lily, Germander, and Sops-in-Wine. *Unknown. See* And Can the Physician Make Sick Men Well.
Lily has a smooth stalk, The. Christina Rossetti. *Fr.* Sing-Song. MBP; OuHeWo
Lily has an air, The. There's Nothing like the Rose. Christina Rossetti. PRWS
Lily in a Crystal, The. *See* Lilly in a Christal, The.
Lily in my garden grew, A. The Maiden and the Lily. John Fraser. HBV
Lily McQueen. Sara Jackson. DiM
Lily Munro. *Unknown. See* Jackaro.
Lily of Shavarshan, The. Leo Alishan, *tr. fr. Armenian by* Alice Stone Blackwell. ArmLP
Lily of the Resurrection. Lucy Larcom. EOAH
Lily of the Valley, The. Thomas Lovell Beddoes. EG
Lily of Yorrow, The. Henry van Dyke. AA
Lily on liquid roses floating. Champagne Rosée [*or* Rosé]. John Kenyon. OBEV; OBRV; OBVV; VA
Lily Princess, The. *Unknown, tr. fr. Japanese by* William N. Porter. MPB
Lilya, *sel.* Eysteinn Asgrímsson, *tr. fr. Icelandic by* Eiríkur Magnússon.
Author's Entreaty for His Lay. ISi
"Lily's" Thanksgiving, The. Mrs. Dawson M. Phelps. TOAH
Lily's withered chalice falls, The. Le Jardin [*or* The Garden]. Oscar Wilde. CaAE; GTIV; PoRA; SeCePo; ViPP
Limb and Mind. John Waller. NeBP
Limbed in a God's likeness that lacks no courage. Man, the Metal-Worker. D. G. Bridson. MuP
"Limber-limbed, lazy god, stretched on the rock." Pan Learns Music. Henry van Dyke. PCH
Limberham; or, The Kind Keeper. *sel.* Dryden.
Song from the Italian, A, *fr.* III. i. CEP; SeCV-2
Limberick. Conrad Aiken. FiBHP; SiTL
Limbo, *sel.* Samuel Taylor Coleridge.
"'Tis a strange place." ERP; NBE
Limbo. Georg Trakl, *tr. fr. German by* Christopher Middleton. AnGP
Limbo; the Shades of the Suitors. Homer. *See* Last Journey of the Wooers, The.
Limbs remember blood and fire, The. Time Regained. Sir Herbert Read. FaBoMo
Limbs that erstwhile charmed your sight, The. Dear, They Have Poached the Eyes You Loved So Well. Rupert Brooke. WhC
Lime-trees by the open door, The. "Anna Akhmatova," *tr. fr. Russian by* R. M. Hewitt. BoR
Limeratomy, The. Anthony Euwer. HBMV
Sels.
Face, The. TreF; TSWC
(Limerick: "As a [*or* For] beauty I'm not a great star.") BOHV; GoTP; HBV; HBVY; InvP; LiBL
(My Face.) FaFP; LiTM; NePA; SiTL; WhC
Hands, The. TSWC
Smile, The. TSWC
(Limerick: "No matter how grouchy you're feeling.") LiBL; WhC
Limericised Classics. Edwin Meade Robinson. HBMV

Limerick: "All young men should take note of the case." M. B. Thornton. LiBL
Limerick: "Amateur, driving too fast, An." Aristophanes, *ad. fr. Greek by* F. A. Wright. *Fr.* The Wasps. LiBL
Limerick: "Amorous M. A., An." *Unknown.* LiBL
Limerick: "And let the canakin clink, [clink]." Shakespeare. *Fr.* Othello, II, iii. LiBL
Limerick: "And those two young ladies of Birmingham." *Unknown. See* Limerick: "There were three young women of Birmingham."
Limerick: "Angry young husband called Bicket, An." John Galsworthy. CenHV
Limerick: "Ankle's chief end is exposiery, The." Anthony Euwer. The Limeratomy: The Ankle. HBMV
Limerick: "As a [*or* For] beauty I'm not a great star." Anthony Euwer. *Fr.* The Limeratomy. BOHV; GoTP; HBV; HBVY; InvP; LiBL
(Face, The.) HBMV; TreF; TSWC
(My Face.) FaFP; LiTM; NePA; SiTL; WhC
Limerick: "At the village emporium in Woodstock." Frederick Winsor. WhC
Limerick: "Beautiful lady named Psyche, A." *Unknown.* LiBL; LiTG; SiTL; WhC
Limerick: "Book and a jug and a dame, A." Edwin Meade Robinson. *See* Limerick: "Jug and a book and a dame, A."
Limerick: "Bottle of perfume that Willie sent, The." *Unknown.* GoTP; TSWC; WhC
Limerick: "Bright little maid of St. Thomas, A." *Unknown.* HBV
Limerick: "But he [*or* He *or* Pa] followed the pair to Pawtucket." *Unknown.* LiBL; LiTG
(More Limericks.) HBV (8th ed.)
(That Nantucket Limerick and What Followed.) TreF
Limerick: "Canner, exceedingly [*or* remarkably] canny, A." Carolyn Wells. HBV; HBVY; LiBL; PoeMoYo; TSW; TSWC
(Canner, Exceedingly Canny, A.) FaPON
(Two Limericks.) YaD
Limerick: "Cannibal bold of Penzance, A." *Unknown.* LiBL
Limerick: "Canny old codger at Yalta, A." *Unknown.* LiBL
Limerick: "Cautious collapsible cow, The." *Unknown.* LiBL
Limerick: "Certain young fellow, named Bobbie, A." *Unknown.* LiBL
Limerick: "Certain young gourmet of Crediton, A." Charles Cuthbert Inge. CenHV; LiBL; WhC
Limerick: "Cleopatra, who thought they maligned her." Newton Mackintosh. LiBL; NA
Limerick: "Clergyman [*or* Evangelical vicar] in want, A." Ronald Arbuthnott Knox. CenHV; LiBL; OxBoLi; WhC
Limerick: "Clergyman out in Dumont, A." Morris Bishop. LiBL; WhC
Limerick: "Consider the lowering lynx." Langford Reed. CenHV
Limerick: "Dear Sir: Your astonishment's odd." *Unknown.* LiBL
Limerick: "Decrepit old gasman, named Peter, A." *Unknown.* LiBL; SiTL
(Decrepit Old Gasman, A.) FaFP
Limerick: "Eccentric old person of Slough, An." George Robey. CenHV
Limerick: "Epicure [*or* Diner while . . . , A], dining at Crewe, An." *Unknown.* CenHV; LiBL; LiTG; RIS; StaSt; WhC
(Epicure, An [Dining at Crewe].) GoTP; LiL; LiTM (rev. ed.); SiTL
Limerick: "Evangelical vicar in want." Ronald Arbuthnott Knox. *See* Limerick: "Clergyman in want, A."
Limerick: "Flea and a fly [*or* Fly and a flea] in a flue, A." *Unknown.* GoTP; LiBL; LiL; LiTG; PoeMoYo; TiPo (1959 ed.); TSWC; WhC
Limerick: "For beauty I am not a star." Anthony Euwer. *See* Limerick: "As a beauty I'm not a great star."
Limerick: "Funny old lady named Borgia, A." *Unknown.* WhC
Limerick: "Funny old person of Slough, A." *Unknown.* RIS
Limerick: "God's plan made a hopeful beginning." *Unknown.* LiBL
Limerick: "H was an indigent hen." Bruce Porter. NA
Limerick: "Half baked potato, named Sue, A." George Libaire. LiBL
Limerick: "Hands they were made to assist, The." Anthony Euwer. The Limeratomy: The Hands. HBMV; TSWC
Limerick: "He died in attempting to swallow." Roy Campbell. LiBL
(Death of Polybius Jubb, The.) LiTG; SiTL; WhC
Limerick: "He followed the pair to Pawtucket." *Unknown. See* Limerick: "But he followed . . ."
Limerick: "Hungry old man from the Rhine, A." *Unknown. See* Limerick: "There was an old man of the Rhine."
Limerick: "I am gai. I am poet. I dvell." George Du Maurier. *See* Vers Nonsensiques.
Limerick: "I saw Nelson at the Battle of the Nile." *Unknown.* LiBL
Limerick: "'I think' thought Sam Butler." Geoffrey Taylor. LiTM
Limerick: "I wish that my room had a floor!" Gelett Burgess. *See* I Wish That My Room Had a Floor.
Limerick: "I'd rather have fingers than toes." Gelett Burgess. *See* I'd Rather Have Fingers than Toes.
Limerick: "I'd rather have habits than clothes." Gelett Burgess. NA
Limerick: "If-itty-teshi-mow Jays." *Unknown.* BOHV
Limerick: "In the wax works of Nature they strike." Anthony Euwer. The Limeratomy: Note. HBMV
Limerick: "In this book every line has been clean." H. I. Brock. LiBL
Limerick: "Indolent vicar of Bray, An." Langford Reed. TSWC
Limerick: "Infinitesimal James." *Unknown.* BOHV
Limerick: "'It's a very warm day,' observed Billy." Tudor Jenks. BOHV
Limerick: "John woke on Jan. first and felt queer." *Unknown.* BOHV
Limerick: "Jug and a book [*or* Book and a jug] and a dame, A." Edwin Meade Robinson. LiBL
(Limericised Classics: The Rubaiyat.) HBMV
Limerick: "Lady there was of Antigua, A." Cosmo Monkhouse. HBV; TSW; TSWC
Limerick: "Lieutenant who went out to shoot, A." Morgan Taylor. LiBL
Limerick: "Lifeboat that's kept at Torquay, The." *Unknown.* LiBL
Limerick: "Limerick packs laughs anatomical, A." *Unknown.* LiBL
(Limerick on Limericks, A.) SiTL
Limerick: "'Lucasta,' said Terence O'Connor." Edwin Meade Robinson.
(Limericised Classics: To Lucasta, on Going to the Wars.) HBMV
Limerick: "Man to whom illness was chronic, A." *Unknown.* LiBL
(Beer.) SiTL
Limerick: "Man went a-hunting at Reigate [*or* Rygate], A." *Unknown.* BoTP; RIS
Limerick: "Miss Minnie McFinney of Butte." *At. to* Carolyn Wells. LiBL; WhC
Limerick: "Mussolini's pet Marshal, Graziani." T. R. Ybarra. LiBL
Limerick: "My name's Mister Benjamin Bunny." Frederic Edward Weatherly. CenHV
Limerick: "Nice old lady named Tweedle, A." *Unknown.* LiBL
Limerick: "No matter how grouchy you're feeling." Anthony Euwer. *Fr.* The Limeratomy. LiBL; WhC
(Smile, The.) HBMV; TSWC
Limerick: "Now the ears, so I always had thunk." Anthony Euwer. The Limeratomy: The Ears. HBMV
Limerick: "Now the sneeze is a joy-vent, I s'pose." Anthony Euwer. The Limeratomy: The Sneeze. HBMV
Limerick: "O God, inasmuch as without Thee." *Unknown.* LiBL
Limerick: "Pa followed the pair to Pawtucket." *Unknown. See* Limerick: "But he followed the pair . . ."
Limerick: "Poor benighted Hindoo, The." Cosmo Monkhouse. HBV; PCD; TSW; TSWC
Limerick: "Pretty young actress, a stammerer, A." Eille Norwood. CenHV
Limerick: "Remarkable truly, is art!" Gelett Burgess. HBV
Limerick: "Reverend Henry Ward Beecher, The." *At. to* Oliver Wendell Holmes. CenHV; HBVY; TSWC
(Eggstravagance, An.) PCD
(Henry Ward Beecher.) ChTr
(Limerick: "Said a great Congregational preacher.") LiBL; WhC
("Said a great Congregational preacher.") GoTP; SiTL
Limerick: "Rheumatic old man in White Plains, A." *Unknown.* LiBL
Limerick: "Said a bad little youngster named Beauchamp." *At. to* Carolyn Wells. PIAE; TSW; TSWC
Limerick: "Said a girl from beyond Pompton Lakes." Morris Bishop. LiBL
Limerick: "Said a great Congregational preacher." *At. to* Oliver Wendell Holmes. *See* Limerick: "Reverend Henry Ward Beecher, The."
Limerick: "Said a lady whose surname was Beaulieu." Franklin P. Adams. PIAE
Limerick: "Said Nero to one of his train." *Unknown.* LiBL
Limerick: "Said old Peeping Tom of Fort Lee." Morris Bishop. LiBL; WhC
Limerick: "Said the Reverend Jabez McCotton." James Montgomery Flagg. LiBL

Limerick: "She frowned and called him Mr." *Unknown.* GoTP; TSWC
(She Called Him Mr.) FaPON
Limerick: "Should a plan we suggest just that minute." "R. K. B." LiBL
Limerick: "Silly young fellow named Hyde, A." *Unknown.* LiBL; WhC
Limerick: "Sleeper from the Amazon, A." *Unknown.* WhC
(Sleeper from the Amazon, A.) LiL
Limerick: "Styles that at present are regnant, The." *Unknown.* LiBL
Limerick: "Then the pair followed Pa to Manhasset." *Unknown.* LiBL
(That Nantucket Limerick and What Followed.) TreF
Limerick: "There is a creator named God." James Abbott McNeill Whistler. BOHV; LiBL
Limerick: "There is a wonderful family called Stein." *Unknown.* BOHV
(Limerick: "Wonderful family is Stein, A.") LiBL
Limerick: "There is a young artist called [*or* named] Whistler." Dante Gabriel Rossetti. BOHV; LiBL
Limerick: "There is a young lady whose nose/ Continually prospers and grows." Edward Lear. OTPC (1946 ed.). *See also* Limerick: "There was a young lady whose nose/ Was so long . . ."
Limerick: "There is an old he-wolf named Gambart." Dante Gabriel Rossetti. CenHV
Limerick: "There once was a bonnie Scotch laddie." *Unknown.* LiBL; WhC
Limerick: "There once was a boy of Bagdad." *Unknown.* RIS; StaSt
Limerick: "There once was a girl of New York." Cosmo Monkhouse. LiBL; NA
Limerick: "There once was a girl of Pitlochry." *Unknown.* CenHV
Limerick: "There once was a happy hyena." Carolyn Wells. PCH
Limerick: "There once was a man from Nantucket." *Unknown. See* Limerick: "There was an old man of Nantucket."
Limerick: "There once was a man of Bengal." *Unknown. See* Limerick: "There was a young man of Bengal."
Limerick: "There once was a man of Calcutta." *Unknown.* LiBL; TSWC; WhC
(There Once Was a Man of Calcutta.) LiL
Limerick: "There once was a man [*or* was a young man] who said: 'Damn!'" Maurice Evan Hare. CenHV; LiBL; OxBoLi
Limerick: "There once was a man [*or* was a young man] who said, 'God.'" Ronald Arbuthnott Knox. LiBL; OxBoLi
Limerick: "There once was a man who said, 'How.'" *Unknown.* LiBL; NA
Limerick: "There once was a painter named Scott." Dante Gabriel Rossetti. CenHV
Limerick: "There once was a person of Benin." Cosmo Monkhouse. LiBL; NA
Limerick: "There once was a pious young priest." *Unknown.* TSWC
Limerick: "There once was a popular crooner." M. B. Thornton. LiBL
Limerick: "There once was a sculptor called [*or* named] Phidias." Oliver Herford. BOHV; LiBL
Limerick: "There once was an arch armadillo." Carolyn Wells. PCH
Limerick: "There once was an Ichthyosaurus." *Unknown.* MeMeAg; OTPC (1946 ed.)
Limerick: "There once was an old man of Lyme." *Unknown, at. to* Edward Lear, *also to* Cosmo Monkhouse. NA; PreP
(Limerick: "There was an old party [*or* a young fellow] of Lyme.") LiBL; LiTG; OxBoLi; PIAE
(Limerick: "There was an old person of Lyme.") CenHV
Limerick: "There once were some learned M.D.'s." Oliver Herford. BOHV; LiBL
Limerick: "There once were two cats of Kilkenny." *Unknown. See* Kilkenny Cats, The.
Limerick: "There was a dear lady of Eden." *Unknown.* LiBL; NA
Limerick: "There was a fair maid from Decatur." *Unknown.* LiBL
Limerick: "There was a faith-healer of Deal." *Unknown.* CenHV; LiBL; LiTM; PIAE; PreP; TSWC; WhC
(Faith-Healer.) FaFP; SiTL
("There was a faith-healer of Deal.") GoTP
Limerick: "There was a fat canon of Durham." *Unknown.* WhC
Limerick: "There was a fat man of Bombay." *Unknown.* BoChLi; RIS
Limerick: "There was a gay damsel of Lynn." *Unknown.* LiBL; NA
Limerick: "There was a good canon of Durham." William Ralph Inge. CenHV
Limerick: "There was a kind curate of Kew." *Unknown.* CenHV
Limerick: "There was a poor chap called Rossetti." Dante Gabriel Rossetti. CenHV
Limerick: "There was a princess of Bengal." Walter Parke. NA
Limerick: "There was a queer fellow named Woodin." "Cuthbert Bede." BoN; CenHV
Limerick: "There was a small boy of [*or* young man from] Quebec." Kipling. HBV; HBVY; LiBL; NA
(In Quebec.) TSWC
Limerick: "There was a trim maiden named Wood." William A. Lockwood. LiBL
Limerick: "There was a young bard of Japan." *Unknown.* CenHV
Limerick: "There was a young belle of Old Natchez." Ogden Nash. LiBL
Limerick: "There was a young critic of King's." Arthur Clement Hilton. CenHV
Limerick: "There was a young curate of Hants." E. V. Knox. CenHV
Limerick: "There was a young curate of Salisbury." *Unknown, at. to* George Libaire. LiBL
("There was once a young curate of Salisbury," *sl. diff.*) BoN
Limerick: "There was a young farmer of Leeds." *Unknown.* RIS; StaSt
Limerick: "There was a young fellow called Green." *Unknown.* CenHV
Limerick: "There was a young fellow from Fife." T. R. Ybarra. LiBL
Limerick: "There was a young fellow named Clyde." *Unknown.* BOHV
Limerick: "There was a young fellow named Dice." *Unknown.* LiBL
Limerick: "There was a young fellow named Hall." *Unknown.* LiTG; WhC
(Happy Time, A.) LiTM; SiTL
Limerick: "There was a young fellow named Hatch." *Unknown.* LiBL
Limerick: "There was a young fellow named Sydney." Don Marquis. LiBL
(Young Fellow Named Sydney, A.) SiTL
Limerick: "There was a young fellow [*or* person] named Tate [*or* Tait]." *At. to* Carolyn Wells. GoTP; HBV; HBVY; LiBL; PIAE; PoeMoYo; PreP; TSW; TSWC; WhC
Limerick: "There was a young fellow of Ceuta." *Unknown.* CenHV
Limerick: "There was a young fellow of Lyme." *Unknown. See* Limerick: "There once was an old man of Lyme."
Limerick: "There was a young fellow of Perth." *Unknown.* RIS; StaSt; WhC
Limerick: "There was a young genius of Queens'." Arthur Clement Hilton. CenHV
Limerick: "There was a young girl of Lahore." Cosmo Monkhouse. HBV
Limerick: "There was a young girl of Majorca." Edward Lear. LiBL
Limerick: "There was a young gourmand of John's." Arthur Clement Hilton. CenHV
Limerick: "There was a young lady at Bingham." *Unknown.* LiBL
Limerick: "There was a young lady called Starky." *Unknown. See* Mendelian Theory.
Limerick: "There was a young lady from Joppa." *Unknown.* BOHV; LiBL
Limerick: "There was a young lady [*or* woman] named [*or* called] Bright." *Unknown, at. to* Arthur Buller. CenHV; LiBL; OxBoLi; WhC
(Relativity.) FaFP; ImOP; LiTM; SiTL
(Young Lady Named Bright, A.) FaPON
Limerick: "There was a young lady named Wemyss." *Unknown.* TSWC
Limerick: "There was a young lady of Bute." Edward Lear. OTPC (1946 ed.); StVeCh
Limerick: "There was a young lady of Byde." *Unknown.* LiBL
Limerick: "There was a young lady of Corsica." Edward Lear. BoN; CenHV; ChTr
Limerick: "There was a young lady of Ealing." *Unknown.* CenHV
Limerick: "There was a young lady of Flint." *Unknown.* CenHV
Limerick: "There was a young lady of Hull." Edward Lear. MoShBr
Limerick: "There was a young lady of Kent." *Unknown.* CenHV; LiBL; SiTL
Limerick: "There was a young lady of Limerick." Andrew Lang. CenHV
Limerick: "There was a young lady of Lynn,/ Who was deep in original sin." *Unknown.* BOHV; LiBL; TSWC
Limerick: "There was a young lady of Lynn/ Who was so exceedingly thin." *Unknown.* CenHV; InP; OnPP
(Young Lady of Lynn, The.) ChTr

Limerick: "There was a young lady of Milton." *Unknown.* NA
Limerick: "There was a young lady of Niger." *Unknown, at. to* Cosmo Monkhouse. BOHV; HBV; HBVY; InP; LiBL; NA; PCD; PoeMoYo; TiPo (1959 ed.); TSW; TSWC
(Not Just for the Ride.) FaFP; LiTM; SiTL
(There Was a Young Lady of Niger.) InvP; LiL
(Young Lady of Niger, The.) FaPON
Limerick: "There was a young lady of Norway." Edward Lear. OTPC (1946 ed.); StVeCh; TiPo; TSW; TSWC
(Young Lady of Norway, A.) FaPON
Limerick: "There was a young lady of Oakham." *Unknown.* BOHV
Limerick: "There was a young lady of Portugal!" Edward Lear. LiTG; OxBoLi
Limerick: "There was a young lady of Riga." *Unknown.* BoN; CenHV
Limerick: "There was a young lady of Russia." Edward Lear. MoShBr
Limerick: "There was a young lady of Ryde/ Who ate a green apple and died." *Unknown.* CenHV
("There was once a young lady of Ryde.") BoN
Limerick: "There was a young lady of Ryde/ Whose shoe-strings were seldom untied." Edward Lear. OxBoLi; WhC
Limerick: "There was a young lady of Spain." *Unknown.* LiTG
(Young Lady of Spain, A.) LiTM
Limerick: "There was a young lady of station." "Lewis Carroll." BOHV; CenHV; GoTP
Limerick: "There was a young lady of Truro." *Unknown.* BOHV
Limerick: "There was a young lady of Twickenham." Oliver Herford. BOHV; LiBL; WhC
Limerick: "There was a young lady of Venice." *Unknown.* BOHV; LiBL
Limerick: "There was a young [*or* an old] lady of Wales." *Unknown.* NA; RIS
Limerick: "There was a young lady of Warwick." *Unknown.* ATP; PIAE
Limerick: "There was a young lady of Wilts." *Unknown.* HBV
Limerick: "There was a young lady of Woosester." *Unknown.* GoTP; LiBL; WhC
Limerick: "There was a young lady whose bonnet." Edward Lear. GFA; PCH; StVeCh
Limerick: "There was a young lady whose chin." Edward Lear. BoChLi; BoN; RIS; StaSt; TiPo
Limerick: "There was a young lady whose eyes." Edward Lear. RIS; StaSt; TSW; TSWC
Limerick: "There was a young lady whose nose/ Was so long . . ." Edward Lear. BoChLi; BoN; FaPON; SAS. *See also* Limerick: "There is a young lady whose nose/ Continually prospers . . ."
Limerick: "There was a young maid of Manila." *Unknown.* OnPP
Limerick: "There was a young maid who said, 'Why.'" *Unknown.* LiBL; NA; RIS; StaSt
Limerick: "There was a young maiden, a Sioux." *Unknown.* LiBL
Limerick: "There was a young man at St. Kitts." *Unknown.* *See* Limerick: "There was a young man of St. Kitts."
Limerick: "There was a young man down in Ga." *Unknown.* OnPP
Limerick: "There was a young man from Cornell." *Unknown.* BOHV
Limerick: "There was a young man from Japan." *Unknown.* LiBL; LiTM; SiTL
Limerick: "There was a young man from Quebec." Kipling. *See* Limerick: "There was a small boy of Quebec."
Limerick: "There was a young man named Achilles." Edwin Meade Robinson.
(Limericised Classics: How Homer Should Have Written the Iliad.) HBMV
Limerick: "There was a young man of Bengal." *Unknown.* GoTP; OxBoLi; TSWC
(Limerick: "There once was a man of Bengal," *sl. diff.*) CenHV
Limerick: "There was a young man of Cohoes." Robert J. Burdette. BOHV; NA
Limerick: "There was a young man of Devizes." *Unknown, at. to* Archibald Marshall. CenHV; WhC
Limerick: "There was a young man of Fort Blain[e]ly." *Unknown.* BOHV; LiBL
Limerick: "There was a young man of Hong Kong." *Unknown.* LiBL
Limerick: "There was a young man of Laconia." *Unknown.* BOHV
Limerick: "There was a young man of Madrid." *Unknown.* LiBL; WhC
Limerick: "There was a young man of Montrose." Arnold Bennett. CenHV; OxBoLi
(It Pays.) FaFP; LiTM; SiTL
Limerick: "There was a young man of Ostend." *Unknown.* BOHV; LiBL
Limerick: "There was a young [*or* an old] man of St. Bees." W. S. Gilbert. BOHV; InvP; LBN; LiBL; LiTG; TSWC
(Limerick in Blank Verse, A.) LBN
(Old Man of St. Bees.) SiTL
Limerick: "There was a young man of [*or* at] St. Kitts." *Unknown.* BOHV; LiBL; NA
Limerick: "There was a young man of Sid. Sussex." Arthur C. Hilton. WhC
Limerick: "There was a young man of the Cape." *At. to* Robert Louis Stevenson. *See* Limerick: "There was an old man of the Cape."
Limerick: "There was a young man so benighted." *Unknown.* HBV; OnPP
Limerick: "There was a young man who said, 'Damn!'" Maurice Evan Hare. *See* Limerick: "There once was a man who said, 'Damn!'"
Limerick: "There was a young man who said, 'God.'" Ronald Arbuthnott Knox. *See* Limerick: "There once was a man who said, 'God.'"
Limerick: "There was a young man who said, 'Run.'" *Unknown.* LiBL
Limerick: "There was a young man who was bitten." *At. to* Walter Parke. LiBL; NA; TSWC
Limerick: "There was a young person named Tate." *At. to* Carolyn Wells. *See* Limerick: "There was a young fellow named Tate."
Limerick: "There was a young person of Ayr." Edward Lear. BoN
Limerick: "There was a young person of Crete." Edward Lear. OTPC (1946 ed.)
Limerick: "There was a young person of Janina." Edward Lear. BoN
Limerick: "There was a young person of Smyrna." Edward Lear. OxBoLi
Limerick: "There was a young poet of Thusis." *Unknown.* OxBoLi
Limerick: "There was a young poet of Trinity." *Unknown.* HBMV; TSWC
Limerick: "There was a young servant at Drogheda." *Unknown.* TSWC
Limerick: "There was a young woman called Starkie." *Unknown.* *See* Mendelian Theory.
Limerick: "There was a young woman named Bright." *Unknown.* *See* Limerick: "There was a young lady named Bright."
Limerick: "There was an Archdeacon who said." *Unknown.* OxBoLi
Limerick: "There was an auld birkie ca'ed Milton." Andrew Lang. CenHV
Limerick: "There was an old fellow of Lynn." *Unknown.* LiBL
Limerick: "There was an old Fellow of Trinity,/ A doctor well versed in Divinity." *Unknown.* CenHV; LiBL
Limerick: "There was an old fellow of Trinity/ Who solved the square root of Infinity." *Unknown.* LiBL; WhC
Limerick: "There was an old lady of Chertsey." Edward Lear. BoN
Limerick: "There was an old lady of Wales." *Unknown.* RIS
Limerick: "There was an old lady who said,/ When she found a thief under her bed." *Unknown.* RIS; StaSt
Limerick: "There was an old lady whose folly." Edward Lear. RIS; StaSt
Limerick: "There was an old man from [*or* of] Peru/ Who dreamt he was eating his shoe." *Unknown.* CenHV; LiTG; TSWC
(Old Man from Peru, An.) FaFP; LiTM (rev. ed.); SiTL
Limerick: "There was an old man from the Rhine." *Unknown.* *See* Limerick: "There was an old man of the Rhine."
Limerick: "There was an old man in a barge." Edward Lear. PoVP
(Nonsense Pictures in Rhyme.) MPB
Limerick: "There was an old man in a boat." Edward Lear. BoChLi (1950 ed.); HBV; OTPC; StVeCh
Limerick: "There was an old man in a pew." Edward Lear. MoShBr
Limerick: "There was an old man in a pie." *Unknown.* BOHV
Limerick: "There was an old man in a tree." Edward Lear. BoChLi; BOHV; GoTP; HBV; InvP; LBN; LiBL; NA; OTPC; PoVP; SAS; TiPo (1952 ed.)
Limerick: "There was an old man in a trunk." Ogden Nash. CenHV
Limerick: "There was an old man of Ancona." Edward Lear. BoN
Limerick: "There was an old man of Aosta." Edward Lear. BoN
Limerick: "There was an old man of Bengal." "F. Anstey." CenHV

Limerick: "There was an old man of Berlin." Edward Lear. PoVP
Limerick: "There was an old man of Blackheath." *Unknown.* CenHV; LiL; TSWC
Limerick: "There was an old man of Boulogne." *Unknown.* CenHV; OxBoLi
(Old Man of Boulogne, An.) LiTM; SiTL
Limerick: "There was an old man of Cape Horn." Edward Lear. TSW; TSWC
Limerick: "There was an old man of Cashmere." Edward Lear. BoN
Limerick: "There was an old man of Coblenz." Edward Lear. BoN
Limerick: "There was an old man of Kamschatka." Edward Lear. NA
Limerick: "There was an old man of Khartoum." *Unknown.* LiBL; OxBoLi
Limerick: "There was an old man of Leghorn." Edward Lear. BoN; NA
Limerick: "There was an old man of Madras." Edward Lear. BoN
Limerick: "There was an old man of Melrose." Edward Lear. LBN
Limerick: "There was [*or* once was] an old man of [*or* a man from] Nantucket." Dayton Voorhees. HBV; LiBL; LiTG; TreF
Limerick: "There was an old man of Nepaul." Edward Lear. BoN
Limerick: "There was an old man of Peru/ Who dreamt he was eating his shoe." *Unknown. See* Limerick: "There was an old man from Peru."
Limerick: "There was an old man of Peru/ Who never knew what he should do." Edward Lear. BoN
Limerick: "There was an old man of Peru/ Who watched his wife making a stew." Edward Lear. BoN
Limerick: "There was an old man of Port Grigor." Edward Lear. BoN
Limerick: "There was an old man of St. Bees." W. S. Gilbert. *See* Limerick: "There was a young man of St. Bees."
Limerick: "There was an old man of Spithead." Edward Lear. BoN
Limerick: "There was an old man of Tarentum." *Unknown.* HBV; LiBL; LiL; PoeMoYo; TSWC; WhC
Limerick: "There was an old [*or* a young] man of the Cape." *At. to* Robert Louis Stevenson. ATP; BOHV; LiBL; TSWC
(Wear and Tear.) PIAE
Limerick: "There was an old man of the coast." Edward Lear. BoN; CenHV; LiBL; MoShBr; PoVP; RIS; StaSt
Limerick: "There was an old man of the Dargle." Edward Lear. BoN; ChTr
Limerick: "There was an old man of The Hague." Edward Lear. BoN
Limerick: "There was an old man of the Isles." Edward Lear. OTPC (1946 ed.); StVeCh
Limerick: "There was an old man of [*or* from] the Rhine." *Unknown.* BOHV; GoTP
(Limerick: "Hungry old man from the Rhine, A.") StaSt
Limerick: "There was an old man of the South." Edward Lear. BoN
Limerick: "There was an old man of the West." Edward Lear. BoN; RIS; StaSt
Limerick: "There was an old man of Thermopylae." Edward Lear. BoN; CenHV; LBN; LiBL; NA
Limerick: "There was an old man of Tobago." *Unknown.* BOHV; LiBL; RIS
Limerick: "There was an old man of Vesuvius." Edward Lear. LiBL
Limerick: "There was an old man of West Dumpet." Edward Lear. BoN
Limerick: "There was an old man on the Border." Edward Lear. CenHV; PoVP
Limerick: "There was an old man on whose nose." Edward Lear. BoChLi; BoN
Limerick: "There was an old man who said, 'Do.'" *Unknown.* FaPON; ImOP; LiBL; MeMeAg; NA; RIS; StaSt
Limerick: "There was an old man who said 'Gee!'" *Unknown.* BOHV
Limerick: "There was an old man who said, 'How.'" Edward Lear. BoChLi; BoN; GFA; PIAE; SAS; StVeCh; TSW; TSWC
Limerick: "There was an old man who said, 'Hush!'" Edward Lear. BoN; GoTP; HBV; LiTG; NA; OTPC; OxBoLi; PIAE; StVeCh
Limerick: "There was an old man who said, 'Well!'" Edward Lear. OTPC (1946 ed.); RIS; StaSt
Limerick: "There was an old man who supposed." Edward Lear. BoN; LBN; LiBL; NA; RIS; StaSt; WhC
Limerick: "There was an old man, who when little." Edward Lear. BoN; GoTP
Limerick: "There was an old man with a beard,/ Who said, 'It is just as I feared!'" Edward Lear. BoChLi; BoN; ChTr; HBV; LBN; LiBL; NA; OTPC; PoVP; StVeCh; TiPo; TSW; TSWC
(Just as He Feared.) RAR
(Old Man with a Beard.) FaPON
Limerick: "There was an Old Man with a beard,/ Who sat on a horse when he reared." Edward Lear. LiBL
Limerick: "There was an old man with a nose." Edward Lear. BoN
Limerick: "There was an old man with a poker." Edward Lear. HBV; OTPC
Limerick: "There was an old monk of Siberia." *Unknown.* LiBL
Limerick: "There was an old party of Lyme." *Unknown. See* Limerick: "There once was an old man of Lyme."
Limerick: "There was an old person of Anerly." Edward Lear. LiBL
Limerick: "There was an old person of Blythe." Edward Lear. BoN
Limerick: "There was an old person of Bray." Edward Lear. BoN
Limerick: "There was an old person of Burton." Edward Lear. RIS; StaSt
Limerick: "There was an old person of Cassel." Edward Lear. BoN
Limerick: "There was an old person of Dean." Edward Lear. BoChLi; MoShBr; PCH
Limerick: "There was an old person of Ewell." Edward Lear. BoN
Limerick: "There was an old person of Grange." Edward Lear. BoN
Limerick: "There was an old person of Gretna." Edward Lear. BoN; ChTr
Limerick: "There was an old person of Ickley." Edward Lear. BoN
Limerick: "There was an old person of Leeds." *Unknown.* WhC
Limerick: "There was an old person of Lyme." *Unknown. See* Limerick: "There once was an old man of Lyme."
Limerick: "There was an old person of Pinner." Edward Lear. BoN
Limerick: "There was an old person of Rheims." Edward Lear. BoN
Limerick: "There was an old person of Rye." Edward Lear. BoN
Limerick: "There was an old person of Slough." Edward Lear. BoN
Limerick: "There was an old person of Spain." Edward Lear. BoN
Limerick: "There was an old person of Sparta." Edward Lear. BoChLi (1939 ed.)
Limerick: "There was an old person of Tring/ Who embellished his nose with a ring." Edward Lear. BoN
Limerick: "There was an old person of Tring/ Who, when somebody asked her to sing." *Unknown.* LiBL; WhC
Limerick: "There was an old person of Ware." Edward Lear. BoChLi; BoN; CenHV; GoTP; LiBL; NA; PCH
(Moppsikon Floppsikon Bear, The.) SAS
Limerick: "There was an old person of Wick." Edward Lear. NA
Limerick: "There was an old person of Wilts." Edward Lear. BoN
Limerick: "There was an old person of Woking." Edward Lear. NA
Limerick: "There was an old person whose habits." Edward Lear. BoChLi (1950 ed.); BoN; FaPON; LBN
Limerick: "There was an old soldier of Bister." *Unknown.* BOHV
Limerick: "There was an old stupid who wrote." Walter Parke. LiBL; NA
Limerick: "There was an old tailor of Bicester." *Unknown.* CenHV
Limerick: "There was an old woman of Leeds." *Unknown.* RIS
Limerick: "There was once a man with a beard." Edward Lear. *See* Limerick: "There was an old man with a beard."
Limerick: "There was once a pious young priest." *Unknown. See* Limerick: "There once was a pious young priest."
Limerick: "There was once a small boy in Quebec." Kipling. *See* Limerick: "There was a small boy of Quebec."
Limerick: "There was once a young lady of Riga." *Unknown. See* Limerick: "There was a young lady of Niger."
Limerick: "There were three young women of Birmingham." *Unknown.* HBV
(Limerick: "And those two young ladies of Birmingham.") LiBL
Limerick: "There's a combative artist named Whistler." Dante Gabriel Rossetti. CenHV
Limerick: "There's a Portuguese person named Howell." Dante Gabriel Rossetti. CenHV
Limerick: "There's a vaporish maiden in Harrison." Morris Bishop. LiBL; WhC

Limerick: "There's an Irishman, Arthur O'Shaughnessy." Dante Gabriel Rossetti. CenHV
(On the Poet O'Shaughnessy.) ChTr
Limerick: "These places abound in the old." George Libaire. LiBL
Limerick: "They say that I was in my youth." *Unknown.* CenHV
Limerick: "This bird is the keel-billed toucan." Howard Ketcham. LiBL
Limerick: "To smash the simple atom." Ethel Jacobson. LiTM
Limerick: "Tutor who tooted the [*or* a] flute, A." Carolyn Wells. BOHV; HBV; HBVY; LBN; LiBL; TSW; TSWC; WhC
(Tutor, The.) MoShBr
(Tutor Who Tooted the [*or* a] Flute, A.) GoTP; LiL; TiPo (1959 ed.)
(Two Limericks.) YaD
Limerick: "Unpopular youth of Cologne, An." *Unknown.* TSWC
Limerick: "Well, it's partly the shape of the thing." *Unknown.* WhC
Limerick: "When a jolly young fisher named Fisher." *Unknown.* LiBL
Limerick: "When that Seint George hadde sleyne ye dragone." *Unknown. See* When That St. George Had Slain His Dragon.
Limerick: "When you go to a store in Ascutney." Richard H. Field. WhC
Limerick: "When you think of the hosts without No." *Unknown.* SiTL; TSWC
Limerick: "With a conscience we're able to see." Anthony Euwer. The Limeratomy: The Conscience. HBMV
Limerick: "Wonderful bird is the pelican, A." Dixon Lanier Merritt. CenHV; LiBL; LiTG
Limerick: "Wonderful family is Stein, A." *Unknown. See* Limerick: "There is a wonderful family called Stein."
Limerick: "Yes, theirs was a love that was tidal." Paul Kieffer. LiBL
Limerick: "You remember that pastoral frolic." "R. K. B." LiBL
Limerick: "Young lady of fair Mytilene, A." *Unknown.* CenHV
Limerick: "Young man on a journey had met her, A." *Unknown.* LiBL
Limerick: "Your verses, dear friend, I surmise." *Unknown.* LiBL
Limerick gets laughs anatomical, A. *See* Limerick packs laughs anatomical, A.
Limerick in Blank Verse, A. W. S. Gilbert. *See* Limerick: "There was a young man of St. Bees."
Limerick Lasses, The. Alfred Perceval Graves. TIP
Limerick packs [*or* gets] laughs anatomical, A. Limerick [on Limericks]. *Unknown.* LiBL; SiTL
Limerick Town, *sel.* John Francis O'Donnell.
"Here I've got you, Philip Desmond, standing in the market-place." IrPN
Limitary nature of a wall, The. Divisibility. Hyam Plutzik. FiMAP
Limitations. Siegfried Sassoon. MBP; MoBrPo
Limitations of Knowledge, The. Empedocles, *tr. fr. Greek by* T. F. Higham. OxBG
Limited. Carl Sandburg. AmP; LoGBV; MAP; MoAB; MoAmPo; NeMA; OxBA
Limits. Emerson. PoEL-4
Limits. Sister Rita Agnes. JKCP (1955 ed.)
Limousine up to my brass facade, The. After Mardi Gras. Sister Mary Honora. NePoAm-2
Limp in lambing weather. Sheep. Keidrych Rhys. MoWP
Limpid shimmering sea is like a turquoise, The. The Silent Day. Luis G. Urbina. AnMP
Limpopo and Tugela churned. The Scorpion. William Plomer. AtBAP; BoSA; OBMV; POTE
Lincoln. George Henry Boker. *Fr.* Our Heroic Times. DD; GA; LBAH; MC; OHIP
Lincoln. John Vance Cheney. DD; GA; LBAH; OHIP; PEDC
Lincoln. Thomas Curtis Clark. BAP; HH
Lincoln. Rembrandt William B. Ditmars. HBMV
Lincoln. Paul Laurence Dunbar. LBAH; OQP; QP-1
Lincoln. John Gould Fletcher. ChMo; CMP; HBMV; LaNeLa; MAP; MoAmPo; MOAP; NeMA; PaA; PCN; PFE; SBMV; SP; VOD
Sels.
"Like a gaunt, scraggly pine." PoRL
"There was a darkness in this man." PoFr
Lincoln. Florence Kiper Frank. PGD
Lincoln. Jane L. Hardy. OHIP
Lincoln. Clyde Walton Hill. PEDC; PGD
Lincoln. Julia Ward Howe. GA; PoRL
Lincoln. Vachel Lindsay. *Fr.* The Litany of the Heroes. MW; OHIP
Lincoln ("Nature, they say, doth dote"). James Russell Lowell. *See* Martyr Chief, The.
Lincoln ("Such was he, our Martyr-Chief"). James Russell Lowell. *See* Abraham Lincoln.
Lincoln. Walter Malone. PSO
("Blend of mirth and sadness, A.") InP
(Masterpiece, The.) PGD
Lincoln. S. Weir Mitchell. PAH; PSO
Lincoln. Harriet Monroe. *Fr.* Commemoration Ode. AA
Lincoln. James Larkin Pearson. BAP; NoCaPo
Lincoln. Edna Dean Proctor. LBAH
Lincoln. James Whitcomb Riley. DD; OHIP
Lincoln. Corinne Roosevelt Robinson. MaRV; OHIP
Lincoln. Delmore Schwartz. FiMAP
Lincoln. Laura Simmons. LPS-1; PSO
Lincoln. Wendell Phillips Stafford. HH
Lincoln. Maurice Thompson. PEDC
Lincoln. John Townsend Trowbridge. LBAH; PGD
Lincoln. Nancy Byrd Turner. FaPON; MOB; MPB; TiPo
Lincoln. Henry Tyrrell. PEDC
(Lincoln's Way, *much abr.*) HH
(Masterful Man, The, *first 5 ll.*) PGD
Lincoln ("Lincoln! When men would name a man"). *Unknown.* LBAH; OHIP
Lincoln?/ He was a mystery in smoke and flags. Carl Sandburg. The People, Yes, Sec. 57. PoLFOT
"Lincoln?—/ Well, I was in the old Second Maine." A Farmer Remembers Lincoln. Witter Bynner. BAP; HH; MAP; MoAmPo (1942 ed.)
Lincoln; an Ode, *sel.* Hermann Hagedorn.
Master, Make Us One! PSO
Lincoln and Liberty, *with music.* F. A. Simpson. AS; TrAS
Lincoln arose! the masterful great man. Lincoln [*or* The Masterful Man *or* Lincoln's Way]. Henry Tyrrell. HH; PEDC; PGD
Lincoln at Gettysburg. Thomas Curtis Clark. PSO
Lincoln at Gettysburg. Bayard Taylor. *Fr.* The Gettysburg Ode. BlG; PAH
("After the eyes that looked.") LBAH; OHIP
Lincoln Calls for Volunteers. Stephen Vincent Benét. *Fr.* John Brown's Body. ATP
("Lincoln, six feet one in his stocking feet.") PreP
Lincoln Child, The. James Oppenheim. GA, *abr.;* HBMV; MAP; MoAmPo (1942 ed.)
Lincoln Circuit, The. E. O. Laughlin. LPS-1
Lincoln, Come Back. Thomas Curtis Clark. PGD
Lincoln is not dead. He lives. Lincoln Triumphant. Edwin Markham. HH; PEDC; PoRL
Lincoln Leads. Minna Irving. HH; OHIP
Lincoln Memorial, The. Alma Adams Wiley. PEDC
Lincoln Portrait, *abr.* Aaron Copland. MaRV
Lincoln, six foot one in his stocking feet. Lincoln Calls for Volunteers. Stephen Vincent Benét. *Fr.* John Brown's Body. ATP; PreP
Lincoln Statue, The. W. F. Collins. OHIP; PGD
Lincoln, the Man of the People. Edwin Markham. BAP; BoChLi; CP; CV; DDA; GA; GrCo-2, *abr.;* HBV; HH; HiLiAm; LBAH; LBMV; LEAP; MAP; MC; MCCG; MoAmPo; NeMA; NV; OHFP; OHIP; OnPP; PaA; PAH; PFY; PIAE; PoeMoYo; PoMa; POT; PoTo; PTA-2; PYM; TCAP; TreFS; TrGrPo; VOD; YT
(Lincoln, the Great Commoner.) GN
"Color of the ground was in him, The," *sel.* MaRV; OQP; PGD; PSO; QP-1
Lincoln, the man who freed the slave. A Tribute. *Unknown.* PGD
Lincoln, the woodsman, in the clearing stood. Abraham Lincoln. Florence Evelyn Pratt. LBAH
Lincoln! "Thou shouldst be living at this hour!" "Thou Shouldst Be Living at This Hour." Kenyon West. PGD
Lincoln Triumphant. Edwin Markham. HH; PEDC; PoRL
Lincoln was a long man. Abraham Lincoln. Rosemary Benét *and* Stephen Vincent Benét. NAMP; TiPo; YeAr
Lincoln! When men would name a man. Lincoln. *Unknown.* LBAH; OHIP
Lincoln's Birthday. John Kendrick Bangs. MeMeAg; PGD
(Lincoln's Birthday—1918.) DD; HH
Lincoln's Birthday. Nathan Haskell Dole. GA
Lincoln's Birthday. Richard Henry Stoddard. *See* Abraham Lincoln.
Lincoln's Birthday. Ida Vose Woodbury. LBAH; PEOR
Lincoln's Birthday—1918. John Kendrick Bangs. *See* Lincoln's Birthday.
Lincoln's Grave, *sels.* Maurice Thompson.
At Lincoln's Grave. GA
He Is Not Dead. PSO
(Lincoln's Grave.) LBAH
(Prophecy, A.) AA
Lincoln's Way. Henry Tyrrell. *See* Lincoln.
Lincolnshire Poacher, The. *Unknown.* CH; OxBoLi
Lincolnshire Remembered. Frances Cornford. HaMV
L'Inconnue. Oliver Wendell Holmes. BAV
Linda to Hafed. Thomas Moore. *Fr.* Lalla Rookh. LPS-1
(Fire Worshippers, The.) EV-4
Lindbergh. Aline Michaelis. DD; GA
Lindbergh. Angela Morgan. DD; GA

Lindbergh. Wendell Phillips Stafford. GA
Lindbergh; a Ballad. Alexander Laing. PoeMoYo
Linden blossomed, the nightingale sang, The. Farewell. Heine. AWP
Linden Lea. William Barnes. GTSE
Linden of the millennium. Tribal Lay. "Pablo de Rokha." TwSpPo
Linden Tree, The. Dietmar von Aist, *tr. fr. German by* Edgar Taylor. LyMA
Line in long array where they wind betwixt green islands, A. Cavalry Crossing a Ford. Walt Whitman. AA; AmP; AmPo; AmPP; APW; ChTr; CoBA; IAP; MDAH; MOAP; OxBA; Po; TCAP; UnPo (3d ed.)
Line o' Cheer, A. John Kendrick Bangs. LPS-1
Line of an American Poet, The. Reed Whittemore. MoVE
Line of Beauty, The. Edward Dowden. OnYI
Line of light, A! it is the inland sea. Mare Mediterraneum. John Nichol. VA
Line-Storm Song, A. Robert Frost. LoPo; LoPS
Line-up, A. *Unknown.* PCH
("One to make ready.") OxNR
Line Up, Brave Boys. Hamlin Garland. SN
Lineage. Robert Farren. CoBE
Lined coat, warm cap and easy felt slippers. Ease. Po Chü-i. TrCh
Lineman, The. William Hurd Hillyer. PoeMoYo
Lineman. Gerald Raftery. PoMa
Lineman Calling. Josephine Miles. FiMAP
Linen Bands. Vance Thompson. AA
Lines, The. Randall Jarrell. CrMA
Lines: Addressed to —— on the 29th of September, When We Parted for the Last Time. *Unknown.* BOHV
Lines: "And this was she! the peerless and the bright." Miss Holford. DiM
Lines: "Ay, if a madman could have leave." Keats. PoP
Lines: "By this the sun was all one glitter." John Masefield. *Fr.* The Everlasting Mercy. GBV
Lines: "Child, A, said, *'What is the grass?'*" Walt Whitman. *See* Grass.
Lines: "Clear had the day been from the dawn." Michael Drayton. *See* Fine Day, A.
Lines: "Cold earth slept below, The." Shelley. AnEnPo; ChER; EmBrPo; EnRP; LoBV
Lines: "Come hither, child—who gifted thee." Emily Brontë. UnW
Lines: "Cool is the autumn wind." Li Po, *tr. fr. Chinese by* Shigeyoshi Obata. ChLP
Lines: "Homeless man goes, even on life's sunniest slope." William Hurrell Mallock. ACP (1926 ed.); JKCP (1926 ed.)
Lines: "Hurry me Nymphs! O, hurry me." George Darley. *See* Sea, The.
Lines ——: "I have been cherish'd and forgiven." Hartley Coleridge. PoEL-4
Lines: "In men whom men condemn as ill." Joaquin Miller. *See* In Men Whom Men Condemn.
Lines: "In the day the sun is darkened." Stopford Augustus Brooke. IrPN
Lines: "Love within the lover's breast." George Meredith. HBV
Lines: "Mine ears have heard your distant moan." J. C. Squire. WhC
Lines: "Nay, traveller! rest." Wordsworth. *See* Lines Left upon a Seat in a Yew-Tree.
Lines: "No coward soul is mine." Emily Brontë. *See* Last Lines: "No coward soul is mine."
Lines: "Old lover of the sun, who thus made moan." Leconte de Lisle, *tr. fr. French.* UnW
Lines: "Shall earth no more inspire thee." Emily Brontë. *See* Shall Earth No More Inspire Thee?
Lines: "Sights o'er yonder snowy range, The." Aubrey Thomas De Vere. BMEP
Lines: "Slumber did my spirit seal, A." Wordsworth. *See* Slumber Did My Spirit Seal, A.
Lines: "Soul, secure in her existence, smiles, The." Addison. *Fr.* Cato: Cato's Soliloquy. UnW
Lines: "Sun that brief December day, The." Whittier. *See* Winter Day.
Lines: "Surely a Voice hath called her to the deep." George Arthur Greene. TIP
Lines: "This living hand, now warm and capable." Keats. ChER
Lines: "Though all the Fates should prove unkind." Henry David Thoreau. MOAP
Lines: "To you, dear mother heart." John Charles McNeill. NoCaPo
Lines: "Unwarmed by any sunset light." Whittier. *Fr.* Snowbound. GBV
Lines: "When I am lost in the deep body of the mist on a hill." Yone Noguchi. NP
Lines: "When the lamp is shattered." Shelley. BCEP; BPN; CaAE; CBOV; EM-2; EmBrPo; EnL; EnLi-2; EnLit; EnRP; EPN; ERP; GEPC; LoBV; MaPo; OAEP; OBEV; PoE; PoEL-4; RiBV; TOP; TyEnPo; ViBoPo
(Flight of Love, The.) GTBS; GTBS-D; GTBS-W; GTSE; GTSL; HBV
(When the Lamp Is Shattered.) AnFE; BEL; BoLiVe; BrBE; CBE; CH; CoBE; EG; FiP; LiTG; LoPo; LPS-1; MCCG; OBRV; PG; PoFS; ReaPo; ShBV-4; TCEP; TrGrPo; UnPo (1st ed.); WHA
Nest of Love, The, *sel.* RO
Lines: "When youthful faith hath fled." John Gibson Lockhart. OBEV (new ed.); OBVV
(When Youthful Faith Hath Fled.) BSV
Lines: "You drop a tear for those that die." Aubrey Thomas De Vere. *See* You Drop a Tear.
Lines Addressed to a Seagull. Gerald Griffin. OnYI; TIP
Lines after Visiting a Cemetery. Richard K. Corbin. CAG
Lines and Squares. A. A. Milne. BoN
Lines are straight and swift between the stars, The. Stars at Tallapoosa. Wallace Stevens. MOAP
Lines around Petersburg, The. Samuel Davis. BlG
Lines beneath the Portrait of Milton. Dryden. *See* Lines Printed under the Engraved Portrait of Milton.
Lines by a Fond Lover. *Unknown.* NA
Lines by a Medium. *Unknown.* NA
Lines by a Person of Quality. J. B. B. Nichols. VA
Lines by a Person of Quality. *At. to* Pope *and to* Swift. InMe; NA
(Love Song, A.) PA
(Song by a Person of Quality.) ReaPo
Lines by Claudia, *abr.* Emily Brontë. UnW
Lines Composed a Few Miles above Tintern Abbey, on Revisiting the Banks of the Wye during a Tour, July 13, 1798. Wordsworth. BCEP; BEL; BoLiVe; BPN; BrBE; CBOV; ChER; CoBE; EM-2; EmBrPo; EnL; EnLi-2; EnLit; EnLP; EnRP; EPN; EPP; ERP; EV-3; ExPo; FiP; GEPC; GoTL; HBV; InP; LoBV; MaPo; MCCG; NBE; OAEP; OBRV; OuHeWo; PIAE; PoEL-4; PoFS; PreP; REAL; SeCePo; SeCeV; TCEP; TOP; TreFS; TrGrPo; TriL; TwHP; TyEnPo; UnPo (1st ed.); WHA
(Tintern Abbey.) LiTB; LPS-2; PoE; ReaPo; TwP
Sels.
"And now, with gleams of half-extinguished thought." (Tintern Abbey.) ViBoPo
"For I have learned/ To look on nature." OQP; PC; QP-2
("I have learned/ To look on nature.") CBE; SN
(Lines Written above Tintern Abbey.) BBV
(Nature.) GrCo-1
I Have Felt a Presence. MaRV
"And I have felt/ A presence," *br. sel.* UnW
"Sounding cataract, The/ Haunted me." FaBoEn; WGRP
"That best portion of a good man's life," *br. sel.* PoToHe
"That blessed mood," *abr.* LEAP
This Prayer I Make. PoToHe
Lines Composed at Grasmere. Wordsworth. OBRV
Lines Composed in a Wood on a Windy Day. Anne Brontë. DiM
Lines for a Bed at Kelmscott Manor. William Morris. *See* Inscription for an Old Bed.
Lines for a Drawing of Our Lady of the Night. Francis Thompson. ISi; MeRV; POTT; VLEP
Lines for a Feast of Our Lady. Sister Maris Stella. ISi
Lines for a Friend's House. Edgar A. Guest. PraP
Lines for a Girl's Study. Nancy Byrd Turner. MOB
Lines for a Sundial. Thomas Herbert Warren. OBVV
Lines for a Wedding Gift. Wesley Trimpi. NePoEA
Lines for an Interment. Archibald MacLeish. ChMo; CMP; InP; MaRV; ReaPo
Lines for an Old Man. T. S. Eliot. FaBoTw; MoPW; OnAP
Lines for Cuscuscaraway and Mirza Murad Ali Beg. T. S. Eliot. FiBHP
Lines for Insomnia. Anne Mary Lawler. DDA
Lines for the Hour. Hamilton Fish Armstrong. BAP; HBMV; MaRV; MC
Lines for the Margin of an Old Gospel. Sheila Wingfield. ChMP; PoN
Lines for the Tombstone of a Singing-Master. *Unknown.* LauV
Lines for Those Invited in T. Stefan George, *tr. fr. German by* Reginald H. Phelps. AnGP
Lines for "Tops." "Jazbo of Old Dubuque." AlBD
Lines Found in His Bible. Sir Walter Ralegh. *See* Conclusion, The.
Lines from a Ghazel. Mir Alishir, *tr. fr. Persian.* BoFr
Lines from an Elegy on the Death of His Wife. Kakinomoto no Asomi Hitomaro, *tr. fr. Japanese by* Clara A. Walsh. LiTW
Lines from Catullus ("The sun may set and rise"). Sir Walter Ralegh, *after the Latin of* Catullus. SiPS
Lines from Love Letters. *Unknown.* OBEV (new ed.)
Lines from the Blues. *Unknown.* OuSiCo
Lines grow slack in our hands at full high-water, The. Rock Carving. Douglas Stewart. NeLNL; SeCePo

Lines in a Young Lady's Album. Thomas Hood. *See* I'm Not a Single Man.
Lines in Dispraise of Dispraise. Ogden Nash. NAMP
Lines in Memory of Edmund Morris, *sel.* Duncan Campbell Scott.
"Here Morris, on the plains that we have loved." CPG
Lines Inscribed upon a Cup Formed from a Skull. Byron. RO
Lines Left upon a Seat in a Yew-Tree. Wordsworth. BPN; EM-2; EmBrPo; EPN; ERP; GEPC
(Lines: "Nay, traveller! rest.") MCCG
Lines of the Lords of Tartary, The. The Pipe of Peace. F. L. Lucas. HaMV
Lines on a Bill of Mortality, 1790. William Cowper. OxBoCh
Lines on a Mysterious Occurrence. Alfred Denis Godley. CenHV
Lines on a Re-reading of Parts of the Old Testament, *sel.* Wilfred Campell.
"Sublimity! Sublimity! I lay thee down." InP
Lines on a Young Lady's Photograph Album. Philip Larkin. EnLoPo; PoN
Lines on an Album. Mary Bayard Clarke. NoCaPo
Lines on an Autumnal Evening. Samuel Taylor Coleridge. BPN
Lines on Carmen Sylva. Emma Lazarus. TrJP
Lines on Death, and Ballade. Villon, *tr. fr. French by* Ralph N. Currey. FoS
Lines on Dr. Johnson. "Peter Pindar." CoEV
Lines on First Looking into Chapman's Homer. Keats. *Fr.* On First Looking into Chapman's Homer. PFE
Lines on Hearing That Lady Byron Was Ill. Byron. EmBrPo
Lines on Hearing the Organ. Charles Stuart Calverley. CenHV; FiBHP; InMe
Lines on His Companions Who Died in the Northern Seas. Thomas James. SeCL
Lines on Isabella Markham. John Harington. *See* Sonnet Made on Isabella Markham, A.
Lines on Mountain Villages. "Sunset Joe." PoOW
Lines on Receiving His Mother's Picture. William Cowper. *See* On the Receipt of My Mother's Picture Out of Norfolk.
Lines on Seeing a Lock of Milton's Hair. Keats. TriL
Lines on the Antiquity of Microbes. Strickland Gillilan. *See* On the Antiquity of Microbes.
Lines on the Back of a Confederate Note. Samuel Alroy Jonas. BLPA; PaA
(Confederate Note, The.) BlG
Lines on the Celebrated Picture by Leonardo da Vinci, Called the Virgin of the Rocks. Charles Lamb. ISi
Lines on the Death of Bismarck. John Jay Chapman. PoEL-5
Lines on the Death of Mr. Levett. Samuel Johnson. *See* On the Death of Mr. Robert Levet, a Practiser in Physic.
Lines on the Execution of King Charles I. James Graham, Marquess of Montrose. *See* Epitaph on King Charles I.
Lines on the Loss of the *Titanic.* Thomas Hardy. *See* Convergence of the Twain, The.
Lines on the Mermaid Tavern. Keats. AWP; BCEP; BEL; BPN; CoBE; EM-2; EmBrPo; EnLi-2; EnLit; EnRP; EPN; EPP; ERP; EV-4; GEPC; HBV; InMe; InPo; LoBV; OAEP; OBRV; OTPC (1923 ed.); PoRA; PreP; SeCeV; TCEP; TOP; TreFS; TwP; ViBoPo
(Mermaid Tavern, The.) ATP; FaBoBe; GTBS; GTBS-D; GTBS-W; GTSE; GTSL; InvP; PoFS; ReTS
Lines on the Monument of Giuseppe Mazzini. Swinburne. TCEP; VLEP
(On the Monument Erected to Mazzini at Genoa.) BMEP; BPN; VA
Lines on the Tombs in Westminster. *At. to* Francis Beaumont *and to* William Basse. *See* On the Tombs in Westminster Abbey.
Lines on the Wall of His Prison Cell. Luis de León. *See* Written on the Walls of the Dungeon.
Lines Printed under the Engraved Portrait of Milton. Dryden. BEL; CEP; EiPP; EPP; EV-3; InP; LiA; SeCeV; SeCV-2; TCEP; TOP
(Epigram on Milton.) BoLiVe; EnLi-1 (1939 ed.); EnLit; GEPC; PtP; TrGrPo
(Lines beneath the Portrait of Milton.) SeEP
(Milton.) BLV
(Portrait of Milton.) ACP
(Under the Portrait of [John] Milton.) BCEP; HBV; LEAP; LPS-3; PIR; WHA
Lines Suggested by the Fourteenth of February ("Darkness succeeds to twilight"). Charles Stuart Calverley. ALV
Lines Suggested by the Fourteenth of February ("Ere the morn the East has crimsoned"). Charles Stuart Calverley. InMe
Lines to a Blind Girl. Thomas Buchanan Read. AA
Lines to a Book Borrower. "F. C." MOB
Lines to a Critic. Shelley. EPN
Lines to a Dictator. Mary Sinton Leitch. NeTW
Lines to a Don. Hilaire Belloc. MBP; MoBrPo; OtMeF
Lines to a Dragon Fly. Walter Savage Landor. *See* Dragon-Fly, The.
Lines to a Future Historian. Kathleen Nott. PoN
Lines to a Lady Weeping. Byron. ERP
Lines to a Lady, Who Asked of Him How Long He Would Love Her. Sir George Etherege. *See* To a Lady Asking Him How Long He Would Love Her.
Lines to a Man Who Thinks that Apple Betty with Hard Sauce Is Food for a Human Being. George S. Kaufman. InMe
Lines to a Nasturtium. Anne Spencer. CDC; PoNe
Lines to a Young Lady. Edward Lear. *See* How Pleasant to Know Mr. Lear.
Lines to an Indian Air. Shelley. *See* Indian Serenade, The.
Lines to Dr. Ditmars. Kenneth Allan Robinson. ImOP; PoMa
Lines to Ellen. Emerson. IAP
Lines to Fanny, *sels.* Keats.
"O, for some sunny spell." LoPS
"Where shall I learn to get my peace again?" ChER
Lines to Homo Somejerktensis. Earnest A. Hooton. WhC
Lines to Miss Florence Huntingdon. *Unknown.* BOHV; NA
Lines to Mr. Hodgson. Byron. PoE
Lines to My . . . George Moses Horton. NoCaPo
Lines to My Father. Countee Cullen. FAOV
Lines to My Father. Leslie Daiken. NeIP; OxBI
Lines to Our Elders. Countee Cullen. CDC
Lines to Ratclif. Earl of Surrey. *See* Exhortation to Learn by Others' Trouble.
Lines to Sigrún. Bjarni Thorarensen, *tr. fr. Icelandic by* Watson Kirkconnell. IcP
Lines to the Blessed Sacrament. James Joseph Callanan. OnYI
Lines to the Memory of "Annie," Who Died at Milan, June 6, 1860. Harriet Beecher Stowe. LPS-1
Lines to the Stormy Petrel. *Unknown.* LPS-2
Lines to the Unborn. Patrick D. Waddington. TwCaPo
"Lines twelve to twenty are in great dispute." Classical Criticism. George Lynde Richardson. AA
Lines (2) on the Questionable Importance of the Individual. Eli Siegel. *See* Shortest Poem in the World, The.
Lines Written above Tintern Abbey. Wordsworth. *See* Lines Composed a Few Miles above Tintern Abbey . . .
Lines Written after a Battle. *Unknown.* BOHV; InMe
Lines Written after a Very Severe Tempest Which Cleared Up Extremely Pleasant. Mercy Warren. BAV
Lines Written after the Discovery by the Author of the Germ of Yellow Fever. Sir Ronald Ross. ImOP; MaRV; PoeMoYo
Lines Written among the Euganean Hills. Shelley. BCEP, *abr.;* BPN; EmBrPo; EnRP; EPP, *much abr.;* ERP; GEPC; PoEL-4
("Many a green isle needs must be," *abr.*) GTBS
(View from the Euganean Hills, North Italy, *abr.*) LPS-2
(Written among the Euganean Hills, North Italy.) GTSE, *abr.;* GTSL, *much abr.*
(Written in the Euganean Hills, North Italy.) GTBS-D; GTBS-W
" 'Mid the mountains Euganean," *sel.* ViBoPo
Lines Written at Cambridge, to W. R., Esquire. Phineas Fletcher. ElL
Lines Written at Geneva; July, 1824. Thomas Lovell Beddoes. ERP
Lines Written at the Grave of Alexandre [*or* Alexander] Dumas. Gwendolyn B. Bennett. CDC; PoNe
Lines Written at the Temple of the Holy Sepulchre. George Sandys. BePJ
Lines Written by One in the Tower. Chidiock Tichborne. *See* Elegy: "My prime of youth is but a frost of cares."
Lines Written by Request. Sir Owen Seaman. PA
Lines Written during a Period of Insanity. William Cowper. FiP; InPo; NBE
(Lines Written under the Influence of Delirium.) AtBAP; PoEL-3
Lines Written in a Country Parson's Orchard. Leslie Daiken. OnYI
Lines Written in a Mausoleum. Lillian Grant. GoYe
Lines Written in a Moment of Vibrant Ill-Health. Morris Bishop. WhC
Lines Written in a Nunnery Chapel. James Clarence Mangan. PraNu
Lines Written in a Small Inn While Staying in the Capital in the Late Spring. Yang W'an-li, *tr. fr. Chinese by* Yang Chi-sing. WhP
Lines Written in an Album. Willis Gaylord. LPS-3
Lines Written in an Album at Malta. Byron. InP
Lines Written in Early Spring. Wordsworth. ADAH; BEL; BPN; CBOV; CoBE; EM-2; EmBrPo; EnLi-2; EnLit; EnRP; EPN; ERP; GEPC; HBV; MCCG; OAEP; OBRV; PG; PoE; PoMa; REAL; SN; TCEP; TyEnPo
(What Man Has Made of Man.) MaRV
(Written in Early Spring.) GTBS; GTBS-D; GTBS-W; GTSE; GTSL; TOP
Lines Written in Her Breviary. St. Theresa of Avila, *tr. by* Longfellow. *See* Santa Teresa's Book-Mark.

Lines Written in Kensington Gardens. Matthew Arnold. BPN; EM-2; EmBrPo; EnLi-2; EPN; PoVP; TCEP; ViPo; ViPP; VLEP
Calm Soul of All Things, *sel.* WGRP
("Calm soul of all things! make it mine.") TrPWD
(From "Lines Written in Kensington Gardens.") LEAP
(Inward Peace.) MaRV
Lines Written in My Album. Charles Lamb. *See* In My Own Album.
Lines Written in Ridicule of Certain Poems Published in 1777. Samuel Johnson. EiPP
Lines Written in the Album at Elbingerode. Samuel Taylor Coleridge. BPN; EmBrPo
Lines Written in the Highlands after a Visit to Burns's Country, *br. sel.* Keats.
World outside the World, The. RO
Lines Written in the Realization that I Must Die. Robert Ervin Howard. DaM
Lines Written near Richmond, upon the Thames, at Evening. Wordsworth. OBEC
Lines Written on Hearing the News of the Death of Napoleon. Shelley. ChER
Lines Written on Her Death-Bed. Mary Monk. DiM
Lines Written on November 15, 1933, by a Man Born November 14, 1881, to Another Born November 15, 1881. Clayton Hamilton. InMe
Lines Written the Night before His Execution. Sir Walter Ralegh. *See* Conclusion, The.
Lines Written to Accompany the Gift of a Distaff to Theugenis. Theocritus, *tr. fr. Greek by* T. F. Higham. Idylls, XXVIII. OxBG
(Gift-Card Enclosed, *tr. by* R. C. Trevelyan.) GrR
Lines Written to Music. Charles Wolfe. *See* To Mary.
Lines Written under the Influence of Delirium. William Cowper. *See* Lines Written during a Period of Insanity.
L'Inferno. Benjamin Sledd. NoCaPo
Linford Newman. Edgar Lee Masters. *Fr.* The New Spoon River. GrCo-2
Linger not in my library. Mine Host. *Unknown.* AlDL
Linger not long. Home is not home without thee. The Wife to Her Husband. *Unknown.* HBV; LPS-1
Lingering clouds, rolling, rolling, The. Flood. T'ao Ch'ien. Twelve Poems, 12. AlDL; TrCh
Lingering, lingering. Love. Wu Yung. ChLP
Lingering sunset across the plain, The. The Gila Monster Route. L. F. Post *and* Glenn Norton. ABF; APW; OnAP; SCC
Ling-ling Go the Hounds. *Unknown, tr. fr. Chinese.* WhP
Lingua, *sel. At. to* Thomas Tomkis.
Gordian Knot, The. ElL
Link o' Day, *with music. Unknown.* TrAS
Linked to a clod, harassed, and sad. Circumstance. Thomas Bailey Aldrich. AA
Links of Chance, The. Edward Rowland Sill. PFY
Linnet, The. Robert Bridges. *See* I Heard a Linnet Courting.
Linnet, The. Walter de la Mare. BLA; BMEP; BrBE; GTML; HBMV; LiTB; LoBV; NP
Linnet, The. Ralph Hodgson. ChMo; CMP
Linnet in a Gilded Cage, A. Christina Rossetti. UTS
Linnet in the rocky dells, The. Song [*or* My Lady's Grave]. Emily Brontë. EmBrPo; EnLit; EV-5; HBV; OAEP; OBEV (1st ed.); OBVV; OTPC; PoVP; TOP; VA
Linnet on the Bough, The. John Gay. *Fr.* Dione; a Pastoral Tragedy. BeR
Linnet who had lost her way, A. Tenebris Interlucentem. James Elroy Flecker. BMEP; MBP; MoBrPo; POTT
Linos. *Unknown, tr. fr. Greek by* T. F. Higham. OxBG
Linota Rufescens. Lyle Donaghy. OnYI
Lion, The. Hilaire Belloc. MBP; MoBrPo; RAR; TSW; TSWC; UTS
Lion, A. Joseph G. Francis. MPB
Lion, The. Mary Howitt. FaPON; OTPC
Lion, The. Vachel Lindsay. HBMV (2d ed.); InP; UTS
Lion. Mary Britton Miller. UTS
Lion, The. Ogden Nash. CenHV
Lion. Kenneth Rexroth. *Fr.* A Bestiary. HoPM
Lion, The. W. J. Turner. MBP; MoBrPo; TrGrPo (1942 ed.)
Lion and Lioness. Edwin Markham. LBAP
Lion and the Cub, The. John Gay. CG; GN; HBV; OTPC (1923 ed.)
Lion and the Lamb, The. Elinor Wylie. CoBA
Lion and the Mouse, The. Jefferys Taylor. HBV; HBVY; OnHT; OTPC
Lion and the Terrapin, The. William Hill Brown. NoCaPo (rev. ed.)
Lion and the unicorn, The. Mother Goose. BoN; BoTP; HBV; OTPC; OxBoLi, *diff. vers.;* OxNR; PPL; SiTL
Lion at Noon, The. Victor Hugo, *tr. fr. French by* Eva Martin. LiTW
Lion Cub, of sordid mind, A. The Lion and the Cub. John Gay. CG; GN; HBV; OTPC (1923 ed.)
Lion emerged from his lair, A. A Lion. Joseph G. Francis. MPB
Lion Fountain. Al-Tutili, *tr. fr. Arabic by* A. J. Arberry. MooP
Lion Grown Old, The. La Fontaine, *tr. fr. French by* Elizur Wright. OnPM
Lion has a tail and a very fine tail, A. In the Fashion. A. A. Milne. CBPC
Lion, he prowleth far and near, The. The Hunters. Ruth Temple Lindsay. JKCP
Lion-House, The. John Hall Wheelock. BAP; HBMV; TBM
Lion-hunger, tiger-leap! The Way of Cape Race. E. J. Pratt. CoBE; EtS
Lion is a beast to fight, The. *See* Lion is the beast to fight, The.
Lion is a kingly beast, The. The Lion. Vachel Lindsay. HBMV (2d ed.); InP; UTS
Lion is called the king, The. Lion. Kenneth Rexroth. *Fr.* A Bestiary. HoPM
Lion is the [*or* a] beast to fight, The. Sage Counsel. Sir Arthur Quiller-Couch. CenHV; HBV; HBVY; LBN; LiL; NA
Lion is the desert's king, The; through his domain so wide. The Lion's Ride. Ferdinand Freiligrath. LPS-2
Lion, mourning, in his age, the wane, A. The Lion Grown Old. La Fontaine. OnPM
Lion, A? No: if I. Lion Fountain. Al-Tutili. MooP
Lion of St. Mark's upon the glass, The. Her Dead Brother. Robert Lowell. NePoEA
Lion oft hungers, and yet, The. Lions and Swine. Steingrimur Thorsteinsson. *Fr.* Epigrams. IcP
Lion over the Tomb of Leonidas, The. *Unknown, tr. fr. Greek by* Walter Leaf. AWP; JAWP; WBP
Lion Path, The. Charlotte Perkins Gilman. BLP
Lion Roars at the Enraging Desert, The. Wallace Stevens. Notes toward a Supreme Fiction, V. MoPo; NePA
Lion standeth on a hill, The; if he hear a man hunting. The Lion's Nature. *Unknown. Fr.* The Bestiary. MeEV
Lion tamers wrestle with the lions in a cage, The. Apex. Nate Salsbury. InMe; WhC
Lion, the Ape, and the Two Asses, The. La Fontaine, *tr. fr. French by* Alan Conder. TrFP
Lion, the lion, he dwells in the waste, The. The Lion. Hilaire Belloc. MBP; MoBrPo; RAR; TSW; TSWC; UTS
Lion, thou are girt with might! The Lion. Mary Howitt. OTPC
Lion walks on padded paws, The. How Creatures Move. *Unknown.* GFA
Lion with the heat oppressed, A. The Lion and the Mouse. Jefferys Taylor. HBV; HBVY; OnHT; OTPC
Lion, you were once the King. Lion. Mary Britton Miller. UTS
Lionel Grierson. Edgar Lee Masters. *Fr.* The New Spoon River. ChMo; CMP
Lionel Johnson. Joyce Kilmer. PtP
Lioness whelped, and the sturdy cub, The. The Eagle's Song. Richard Mansfield. DD; HBV; HBVY; MC; MDAH; PaA; PAH
Lions and Dragons. Oppian, *tr. fr. Greek by* William Diaper. *Fr.* Halieuticks. BeR
Lions and Swine. Steingrimur Thorsteinsson, *tr. fr. Icelandic by* Vilhjalmur Stefansson. *Fr.* Epigrams. IcP
Lion's Cub, The. Maurice Thompson. AA
Lion's Nature, The. *Unknown, tr. fr. Middle English. Fr.* The Bestiary. MeEV
Lions of the hill are gone, The. Deirdre's Lament for the Sons of Usnach. *Unknown.* GTIV; IrPN; OnYI; SeCePo
Lions on the mountains I've drove them to their lairs, The. Dodge City, the End of the Trail. *Unknown.* CoSo
Lion's Ride, The. Ferdinand Freiligrath, *tr. fr. German.* LPS-2
Lions Running over the Green. Annette Wynne. UTS
Lion's Skeleton, The. Charles Tennyson Turner. VA
Lip and the Heart, The. John Quincy Adams. AA; LHV; PR
"Lip of This Poor Earthen Urn, The." Zonas, *tr. fr. Greek by* F. L. Lucas. GrPE
Li Po was about to sail in his boat. A Poem for Wang Lung. Li Po. WhP
Lips and Eyes. Thomas Middleton. *See* Song: "Love for such a cherry lip."
Lips, lips, open. A Sleeping Child [*or* To a Sleeping Child]. Arthur Hugh Clough. BOL; PRWS
Lips of the Christ-child are like to twin leaves, The. The Christ-Child. St. Gregory of Narek. ArmLP; CAW
Lips of the Wise, The. Proverbs, XV: 1-5, 7-8, 15-17, Bible, *O.T.* TrGrPo
(Merry Heart, A, XV: 1, 13, 15-17.) StVeCh
("Soft answer turneth away wrath, A," XV: 1.) TiPo (1952 ed.)
Lips sealed in iron stillness, no more henceforth for ever. The Dead Ballet-Dancer. Paulus Silentiarius. GrPE
Lips That Touch Liquor Must Never Touch Mine, The. George W. Young. PTA-1
Lips that touch wine jelly. Wine Jelly. *Unknown.* WhC

Liquids. Merrill Moore. PoMa
Liquor & Longevity. *Unknown.* LiTG; SiTL; WhC
Lisabetta [*or* Lizabetta], Marianina, Fiametta, Teresina. The Flower Factory. Florence Wilkinson Evans. CP; GrCo-1; HiLiAm; NV; PC; PFE
Lisa's Golden Hair. Francisco de Quevedo y Villegas, *tr. fr. Spanish by* Roy Campbell. TeCS
(On Lisa's Golden Hair.) AtBAP
Lise. Rose Terry Cooke. AA
Lis'en to de Lam's, *with music. Unknown.* BoAN-1
Lissen to my story. John Henry (B *vers.*). *Unknown.* ViBoFo
Lissom goddess came with the south wind, A. Rain. Junzaburo Nishiwaki. PoLJ
List all you California boys. California Trail. *Unknown.* CSF
List no more the ominous din. George Darley. *Fr.* Nepenthe. OBRV
List to an old-time lay of the Spear-Danes. Beowulf. *Unknown.* EM-1; EnLi-1
List to me, as when ye heard our father. *See* Listen to me . . .
List to that bird! His song—what poet pens it? The Mocking-Bird. Ednah Proctor Clarke. AA
List to the song of the chickadee. Song of the Chickadee. *Unknown.* OTPC (1946 ed.); PCH
List while the poet trolls. The Rival Curates. W. S. Gilbert. CenHV; MBP
Listed by beauty's conquering charms. Proud Chloe's Heart. Horace. OnPM
Listen. E. E. Cummings. WaaP
Listen. Vladimir Mayakovsky, *tr. fr. Russian by* C. M. Bowra. BoRS
Listen. Albert Durrant Watson. CPG
Listen! Humbert Wolfe. AlDL
Lis/ -ten/ you know what I mean. Listen. E. E. Cummings. WaaP
Listen!/ Just because the stars light up their fires. Listen. Vladimir Mayakovsky. BoRS
Listen:/ There roams, far away, by the waters of Clead. Nikolai Gumilev. *Fr.* The Giraffe. FaPON
Listen . . ./ With faint dry sound. November Night. Adelaide Crapsey. AnAmPo; BAP; BLV; FaPON; LA; MAP; MoAmPo (1942 ed.); MPB; NeMA; NP; NV; PFE; PFY; PIAE; VOD (1935 ed.)
Listen a moment, I pray you; what was that sound that I heard. A Sign of Spring. Eben Eugene Rexford. PCH; PEDC
Listen a while, the moon is a lovely woman. Night Stuff. Carl Sandburg. ChMo; CMP; NP; TSW
Listen all ye, 'tis the Feast o' St. Stephen. Feast o' St. Stephen. Ruth Sawyer. OHIP
Listen and I'll tell you about Willie the Weeper. Willie the Weeper. *Unknown.* ABF; APW; BLPA
Listen and learn what manner of god I am. The Living God. Oracle of Serapis. OxBG
Listen, and the battle I shall begin. The Sea-Fight at Sluys. Laurence Minot. SG
Listen, and when thy hand this paper presses. A Letter from a Girl to Her Own Old Age. Alice Meynell. CaAE; GoTL; GTBS-W; LiTB; MBP; MoBrPo; ViBoPo
Listen, children:/ Your father is dead. Lament. Edna St. Vincent Millay. LEAP; PoeMoYo
Listen, children, listen, won't you come into the night? Who Calls? Frances Clarke. HH; PoRh; SiSoSe; StaSt; TSW; TSWC
Listen, David! Josephine Jacobsen. JKCP (1955 ed.)
Listen! Do you hear the winging. Angel Voices. Mary B. Stevenson. ChIP
Listen, gallants, to my words. The Commonwealth of Birds. James Shirley. GoBC
Listen! I will be honest with you. Walt Whitman. *Fr.* Song of the Open Road. PoFr
Listen! I will make a small statue. Boy in the Dusk. Humbert Wolfe. MM
Listen! In the April rain. In the April Rain. Mary Anderson. BoTP
Listen! It is the summer's self that ambles. The Good Humor Man. Phyllis McGinley. MoShBr
Listen jealous man. A Jealous Man. *Unknown.* KiLC
Listen, listen! The small song bird. Song to Imogen (in Basic English). Richard L. Greene. WhC
Listen, lively lordings all. The Rising in the North. *Unknown.* ACP; BaBo; ESPB
Listen, Lord. James Weldon Johnson. BANP
Listen lordings both great and small. The Murder of Saint Thomas of Kent. *Unknown.* ACP
Listen, lordings, unto me, a tale I will you tell. Christmas Carol. *Unknown.* COAH
Listen, men!/ The scratching friar. Ballyhoo for a Mendicant. Carlton Talbott. AnAmPo; LA
Listen! My August bird. Song-Bird. Brian Vrepont. NeLNL
Listen, my children, and you shall hear. Paul Revere's Ride. Longfellow. *Fr* Tales of a Wayside Inn. AmPP (4th ed.); AnNE; APW; BAP; BAV; BBV; BeLS; BLPA; BoHiPo; CoBA; DD; EV-5; FaBoBe; FaFP; FaPON; GA; GoTP; HBV; HBVY; IAP; IDAH; LoGBV; LPS-2; MC; NeHB; OBAV; OHFP; OnHT; OnSP; PaA; PAH; PAP; PEDC; PIR; PoFr; PoRL; PTA-1; PYM; REAL; RIS; StPo; StVeCh; TCAP; TiPo (1952 ed.); TreF; TrGrPo; WBLP; YaD
Listen, my son, to the silence. The Silence. Federico García Lorca. CoSP
Listen now and ye may lere. The Burgesses of Calais. Laurence Minot. ACP
Listen! Now I have come to step over your soul. Sacred Formula to Destroy Life. *Unknown.* LiTA
Listen, Pigeon, Bend an Ear. H. W. Haenigsen. WhC
Listen. Put on Morning. W. S. Graham. FaBoTw
Listen sweet Dove unto my song. Whitsunday. George Herbert. AtBAP
Listen, the hay-bells tinkle as the cart. The Holy Innocents. Robert Lowell. ATP (1953 ed.); InPo; InvP; MoAB; MoAmPo (1950 ed.); NePoEA
Listen! the somber foliage of the Pine. The Pine's Mystery. Paul Hamilton Hayne. SPP; TCAP
Listen. The tale of one of my follies. The Alchemy of Words. Arthur Rimbaud. AnFP
Listen! the wind is rising. Listen! Humbert Wolfe. AlDL
Listen [*or* List] to me, as when ye heard our father. Canadian Boat Song. *Unknown, at. to* John Galt. BLPA; BSV; CaP; EBSV; FaBoCh; GoTS; LoGBV; NBE; OBEV (new ed.); OBRV; OCL
Listen to me, listen to me, my dear! Modern Sonnet. Grace Hazard Conkling. BAP
Listen to my story—'tis a story true. John Henry. *Unknown.* TrAS
Listen to the exhortation of the Dawn! The Salutation of the Dawn. *Unknown.* MaRV
Listen to the kitchen clock. The Old Kitchen Clock. Ann Hawkshaw. BoTP; OTPC (1923 ed.)
Listen to the lyre! The Lyre [*or* The Enchanted Lyre]. George Darley. LO; OBVV
Listen to the Mocking-Bird. Septimus Winner. OlF; TrAS, *with music*
Listen to the Muse's lyre. Odes of Anacreon, *tr. by* Thomas Moore. OuHeWo
Listen to the roar of your liberation! Angelos Sikelianos. *Fr.* On Death. LiTW
Listen to the song. Wandering Jack. Emile Jacot. BoTP
Listen to the story of Willie the Weeper. Willie the Weeper. *Unknown.* ABF; APW; BeLS; BLPA; YaD
Listen to the tale. Slim Greer. Sterling A. Brown. BANP
Listen to the tawny thief. Bacchus. Frank Dempster Sherman. BAP; LBMV; MAP
Listen to the water mill. The Lesson of the Water Mill [*or* The Water Mill]. Sarah Doudney. *Fr.* The Man o' Airlie. BLPA; BPP; HBV; PoToHe; PTA-2; TreFS; WGRP
Listen to what startled the neighbors, one night. Propertius. Elegies, IV, 8. LaP
Listeners, The. Walter de la Mare. AnFE; AWP; BBV (1951 ed.); BLV; BMEP; BoLiVe; CBOV; ChMo; CMP; CoBMV; CoEV; DaM; EnLit; EPP; FaFP; FaPON; GTBS-D; GTBS-W; GTML; GTSL; HBV; HBVY; HoPM; InP; InvP; JAWP; LBBV; LEAP; LiTB; LiTM; MaC; MaRV; MBP; MoAB; MoBrPo; MoPo; MoVE; NAMP; NeMA; NP; NV; OAEP (2d ed.); OBEV (new ed.); OBMV; OBVV; OtMeF; PCD; PFE; PIAE; Po; PoeMoYo; PoRA; POTE; PreP; PtOT; PYM; SeCeV; ShBV-3; ThWaDe; TOP; TreF; TrGrPo; TVSH; TwCV; UnW; ViBoPo; VOD; WBP; WHA
Listeneth, lordings, both great and small. A, A, A, A,/ Nunc Gaudet Ecclesia. *Unknown.* AnEC
Listening Dryads hushed the woods, The. The Pewee. John Townsend Trowbridge. HBV; OTPC; SN
Listening, listening; it is never still. The Märchen. Randall Jarrell. FiMAP
Listening to a Broadcast. John Manifold. WaP
Listening to the Monk of Szechuan Playing on His Lute. Li Po, *tr. fr. Chinese by* Chiang Shao-yi. WhP
Listening to the River. Su T'ung-po, *tr. fr. Chinese by* Yu Min-chuan. WhP
Listening to the storm, the wind and the rain. Sonnets, IV. Feng Chih. *Fr.* Twenty-seven Sonnets. WhP
Listeth, lordes, in good entent. Sir Thopas. Chaucer. *Fr.* The Canterbury Tales. BEL; EM-1
Listless he eyes the palisades. In the Prison Pen. Herman Melville. PoEL-5
Lists, The. Sir Philip Sidney. *See* Astrophel and Stella: Sonnets, XLI.
Lisy's Parting with Her Cat. James Thomson. CIV; PoC
Liszt. E. C. Bentley. *Fr.* Biography for Beginners. UnS
Litanie, The. John Donne. *See* Litany, The.
Litanies of Satan, The. Baudelaire, *tr. fr. French by* Frances Winwar. EnLi-2

Litany [*or* Litanie], The. John Donne. AtBAP; PoEL-2
Sels.
"From being anxious, or secure." EnLit; NBE; OxBoCh, *4 sts.*
Litanie from "Holy Sonnets," A ("From tempting Satan to tempt us"). MeRV
Litany, A: "Drop, drop, slow tears." Phineas Fletcher. *See* Hymn, An: "Drop, drop, slow tears."
Litany: "From all that terror teaches." G. K. Chesterton. *Fr.* A Hymn. OtMeF
Litany: "I hold the splendid daylight in my hands." George Campbell. PoNe
Litany: "Oh, by Thy cross and passion." Marie LeNart. ChIP
Litany, A: "Ring out your bells." Sir Philip Sidney. *See* Ring Out Your Bells.
Litany: "Saviour, when in dust to thee." Sir Robert Grant. LPS-2
Litany: "When my feet have wander'd." John S. B. Monsell. VA
Litany: "When the sun rises on another day." Charles Angoff. TrPWD
Litany at [*or* of] Atlanta, A. William Edward Burghardt Du-Bois. BANP; CDC; PoNe
Litany for Argos. Aeschylus, *tr. fr. Greek by* Lewis Campbell. *Fr.* Suppliants. GrR
Litany for Dictatorships. Stephen Vincent Benét. AmPP; AnEnPo; NAMP; OxBA; PoFr
Litany for Halloween. *Unknown.* PoRL; SiSoSe
Litany for Latter-Day Mystics, A. Cale Young Rice. WGRP
Litany for Old Age, A. Una W. Harsen. TrPWD
Litany for Peace. Leslie Savage Clark. PGD
Litany for Peace, A. Pearce Young. PtPa
Litany in Time of Plague. Thomas Nashe. *See* Adieu, Farewell, Earth's Bliss.
Litany of Atlanta, A. W. E. B. DuBois. *See* Litany at Atlanta, A.
Litany of Night. Hugh Robert Orr. GrCo-2
Litany of the Black People. Countee Cullen. *See* Litany of the Dark People.
Litany of the Comfortable, The. Viola Chittenden White. QS
Litany of the Dark People. Countee Cullen. MaRV; NV; QS; TrPWD
(Litany of the Black People.) SDH; StJW
Litany of the Heroes, *sel.* Vachel Lindsay.
Lincoln. MW; OHIP
Litany of the Rooms of the Dead. Franz Werfel, *tr. fr. German by* Edith Abercrombie Snow. TrJP
Litany to Our Lady. Caryll Houselander. ISi
Litany to Pan. Eden Phillpotts. MBP
Litany to Satan. Baudelaire, *tr. fr. French by* James Elroy Flecker. AWP
Litany to the Holy Spirit. Robert Herrick. *See* His Litany to the Holy Spirit.
Literary Dinner. Vladimir Nabokov. FiBHP
Literary Gruk. Piet Hein, *tr. fr. Danish by* Piet Hein, Stephen Schwartz, *and* Martin S. Allwood. LiTW
Literary Importation. Philip Freneau. IAP
Literary Lady, The. Sheridan. *Fr.* The Fatal Falsehood (*by* Hannah More): Epilogue. BOHV
Literary Landscape with Dove and Poet. Phyllis McGinley. NePoAm-2
Literary Love. Harry Kemp. HBMV
Literary Poet to his Patron, A. Pope. *Fr.* An Essay on Man, IV. CBE
(Henry St. John, Viscount Bolingbroke.) OBEC
(Poet's Friend, The.) LPS-3
Literary Squabble, A. James Robinson Planché. CenHV
Literary Vampire, The. *Unknown.* CAG
Lithe and listen, gentlemen,/ That be of free-born blood. A Gest of Robyn Hode [*or* A Little Geste of Robin Hood and His Meiny]. *Unknown.* ESPB; OBB
Lithe and listen, gentlemen:/ Other knight of sword or pen. Holiday. John Davidson. OBVV
Lithe and listen, gentlemen to sing a song. The Heir of Linne. *Unknown.* EV-2
Lithe and long as the serpent train. The Grape-Vine Swing. Samuel Minturn Simms. AnAmPo; POT
Lithe beautiful fear, A. Python. Grace Hazard Conkling. NP; PoeMoYo; TCPD
Lit'le David Play on Yo' Harp. *Unknown.* BoAN-1, *with music;* OIF
Little. Dorothy Aldis. FaPON; SUS; TiPo
Little, A. George Du Maurier. *See* Little Work, A.
Little Adam. Arnulf Øverland, *tr. fr. Norwegian by* Charles W. Stork. AnNoLy
Little Aglae. Walter Savage Landor. *Fr.* Pericles and Aspasia, CXIII. BPN; VA
Little Ah Sid, *with music. Unknown.* AS
Little Air, I ("Somehow a solitude"). Stéphane Mallarmé, *tr. fr. French by* Kate Flores. AnFP
Little Air, II ("Inexorably bound"). Stéphane Mallarmé, *tr. fr. French by* Kate Flores. AnFP
Little Alabama Coon. Hattie Starr. AA; BOL
Little am I among lesser gods; but call in season. The God of the Lowly. Perses. GrPE
Little and Brown have lost their cat. The Lost Cat. Lilian Whiting. CIV
Little and Great. Charles Mackay. *See* Small Beginnings.
Little and Lonely under the Evening Star. George Brandon Saul. TBM
Little and plain seem now those red brick walls. The Nation's Shrine. Alma Adams Wiley. PEDC
Little *and,* the tiny *if,* The. Alliances. Nathalia Crane. MAP
Little Angels, The. Jacopone da Todi, *tr. fr. Italian by* Anne Macdonnell. CAW
Little angels of heaven, The. "There Shall Be More Joy . . ." Ford Madox Ford. MBP; MoBrPo (1942 ed.)
Little Annie Rooney. Michael Nolan. TreF
Little Ants, The. Ann *or* Jane Taylor. SAS
Little ants in leafy wood. Little Brothers of the Ground. Edwin Markham. SN
Little babe, while burns the west. Song for a Babe. Jean Ingelow. BOL
Little baby, lay your head. Good Night! Jane Taylor. BOL; CBPC; HBV; HBVY; OTPC; PPL; RAR; SAS
Little bat, little bat. To the Bat. Edith King. BoTP
Little Bateese. William Henry Drummond. BMEP; CPG; POT; PoTo; PTA-2
(Leetle Bateese.) CaP; MW; OCL
Little Beach-Bird, The. Richard Henry Dana. AA; AnAmPo; AnFE; AnNE; APA; APW; BLA; CoAnAm; EtS; HBV; LA; LBAP; LEAP; LPS-2; OTPC (1923 ed.); SN; TCAP
Little Bell. Thomas Westwood. GN; HBV; LPS-1; OTPC (1946 ed.), *sl. abr.;* TVC
Little Bess, with laughing eyes. What's the Lesson for Today? *Unknown.* PEOR
Little betrothed has washed her linen, The. Whiteness. "Isobel Hume." HBMV
Little Betty Blue. Agnes Grozier Herbertson. BoTP
Little Betty Blue/ Lost her holiday shoe. Mother Goose. OxNR; SAS; StVeCh
Little Betty Pringle she had a pig. *Unknown.* OxNR
Little Big Horn. Ernest McGaffey. GA; PAH
Little Billee. Thackeray. BOHV; CBOV; CenHV; EtS; EV-5; FaBoCh; GaP; HBV; HBVY; LBN; LoGBV; LPS-3; MPB; NA; OnSP; OTPC; PECK; PoVP; TreFS; TSW; TSWC; TVSH
Little billow, glassy-breasted. Barcarole. Johan Ludvig Heiberg. BoDS
Little Billy. Sir Arthur Conan Doyle. FAOV
Little Billy Breek. *Unknown.* OxNR
Little Birch Tree. Sergey Ostrovoy, *tr. fr. Russian by* Babette Deutsch. TrRV
Little Birches. Mary Effie Lee Newsome. PoNe
Little birches, white and slim, The. The Birches. Walter Prichard Eaton. StVeCh
Little Bird, The. Walter de la Mare. BrR
Little bird flew through the dell, A. Autumn Song. Johann Ludwig Tieck. AWP
Little Bird, Go through My Window, *with music. Unknown.* OuSiCo
Little Bird I Am, A. Mme Guyon, *tr. fr. French.* WGRP
(Prisoner's Song, A.) MaRV
Little bird, little bird, go through my window. *Unknown.* OuSiCo
Little bird of paradise. *Unknown.* OxNR
Little Birdie. Tennyson. *See* What Does Little Birdie Say?
Little Birds. "Lewis Carroll." *Fr.* Sylvie and Bruno Concluded. BoN; WhC
Little Birds Are Playing, *sel.* KN; OxBoLi
Little Birds. Jacob Sternberg, *tr. fr. Yiddish by* Joseph Leftwich. TrJP
Little Birds are dining. Little Birds. "Lewis Carroll." *Fr.* Sylvie and Bruno Concluded. BoN; WhC
Little Birds Are Playing. "Lewis Carroll." *Fr.* Little Birds. KN; OxBoLi
Little birds in a row. Little Birds. Jacob Sternberg. TrJP
Little birds now seek their nests, The. Evening Hymn. Mathilda Barbara Betham-Edwards. TVSH
Little birds praise you, The. Cradle Carol. Eleanor Slater. MaRV
Little birds sing with their beaks. Singing. Dorothy Aldis. GFA
Little birds sit on the telegraph wires. Sparrows. Adeline D. T. Whitney. PEOR
Little birds sleep sweetly in their soft round nests. Evening Song. Cecil Frances Alexander. DD; OHIP; OTPC (1923 ed.); RAR; TVC
Little Bird's Song, A. Margaret Rose. BoTP
Little bit of blowing, A. After Winter. Carolyn Sherwin Bailey. PCH
Little bit of blowing, A. Thoughts for a Cold Day. *Unknown.* BoTP
Little black ant found a large grain of wheat, A. The Little Ants. Ann *or* Jane Taylor. SAS

Little Black Boy, The. Blake. *Fr.* Songs of Innocence. AnFE; AtBAP; AWP; BCEP; BEL; CEP; CH; CoEV; EiPP; EM-1; EnL; EnLi-2; EnLit; EnRP; EV-3; HBV; InPo; LoGBV; MotAn; MyFE; OAEP; OBEC; OBEV; OxBoCh; PoEL-4; PoFr; PoNe; RiBV; SeCeV; TOP; TreFS; TrGrPo
Little Black boy/ Chased down the street. Nigger. Frank Horne. BANP; CDC
Little Black Bug. Margaret Wise Brown. FaPON
Little black bull kem down de medder, De. Hoosen Johnny. *Unknown.* AS
Little Black Dog, The. Elizabeth Gardner Reynolds. AlBD
Little black dog ran round the house, The. *Unknown.* OxNR
Little Black-eyed Rebel, The. Will Carleton. FaPON; GoTP; PAH; PAP; PTA-1
Little Black Hen, The. Armel O'Connor. SaFP
Little Black Man, A. Aleksandr Aleksandrovich Blok, *tr. fr. Russian by* Babette Deutsch. TrRV
Little Black Man with a Rose in His Hat. Audrey Wurdemann. YaD
Little Black Rose, The. Aubrey Thomas De Vere. ACP; GTIV; OnYI; TIP
(Song: "Little Black Rose shall be red at last, The!") IrPN
Little Black Sheep, The. *At. to* Paul Laurence Dunbar, *also to* Sarah Pratt McLean Greene. *See* Sheepfol', De.
Little black thing among the snow, A. The Chimney Sweeper. Blake. *Fr.* Songs of Experience. AtBAP; BoW; CBOV; EiPP; EnL; EnLi-2 (1949 ed.); EnLit; EV-3
Little Black Train, A, *with music. Unknown.* OuSiCo
Little blind girl wandering, A. The Brook. William Wilberforce Lord. AA
Little Blue Apron. *Unknown.* BoTP
Little Blue Ben, who lives in the glen. *Unknown.* OxNR
Little Blue Betty lived in a den. *Unknown.* OxNR
Little Blue Pigeon. Eugene Field. BOL; GBV (1922 ed.); TVSH
(Japanese Lullaby.) MOAH
Little Blue-Ribbons. Austin Dobson. OnPP
Little Blue Shoes. Blue Shoes. Kate Greenaway. MPB; RAR; TiPo
Little Boatie. Henry van Dyke. BOL
Little Boats of Britain, The. Sara E. Carsley. CaP
Little body I would hold. Unborn. Irene Rutherford McLeod. HBMV
Little Bonny, *with music. Unknown.* OuSiCo
Little boots and big boots. Rubber Boots. Rowena Bastin Bennett. GFA
Little Bo-Peep/ Had lost her sheep. The Fairy Sleep and Little Bo-Peep. *Unknown.* BoTP
Little Bo-Peep has lost her sheep. Mother Goose. FaBoBe; HBV; HBVY; OlF; OnHT; OTPC; OxNR; PCH; PPL; RIS; SAS; StVeCh; TiPo
Little bo-peepals. Boston Nursery Rhymes. Joseph Cook. BOHV; PA
Little Bob Robin. *Unknown.* OxNR
Little Bow to Books on How To, A. Irwin Edman. WhC
Little boy and a little girl, A. Mother Goose. PPL. *See also* There was a little boy and a little girl.
Little Boy Blue. Guy Wetmore Carryl. *See* Harmonious Heedlessness of Little Boy Blue, The.
Little Boy Blue. Thomas Holley Chivers. MOAP
Little Boy Blue. Eugene Field. AA; BAP; BeLS; BTP; CP; FaFP; FaPON; HBV; HBVY; IAP; LBAP; LEAP; LiTG; MAP; MoAmPo (1942 ed.); MotAn; NeHB; NeMA; OBAV; OHFP; OnHT; PC; PCD; PFE; PIR; PoeMoYo; PTA-1; PYM: TreF; VOD
Little Boy Blue. John Crowe Ransom. LiTM; TwAmPo
Little Boy Blue, come blow [up] your horn. Mother Goose. BoChLi; BoTP; FaBoBe; FaFP; HBV; HBVY; OTPC; OxNR; PCH; PPL; RIS; SAS; StVeCh; TiPo
Little Boy Found, The. Blake. *Fr.* Songs of Innocence. EnRP; TiPo (1952 ed.)
Little boy had bought a top, A. The Boy and His Top. John Hookham Frere. OTPC (1923 ed.)
Little Boy in the Morning, A. Francis Ledwidge. MCCG; OnYI; POT; TIP
Little boy is fishing, The. The Fisherman. David McCord. TiPo (1959 ed.)
Little boy leaned down his head, A. The Visitant. Walter de la Mare. UnW
Little Boy Lost, The ("Father, father, where are you going?"). Blake. *Fr.* Songs of Innocence. EnRP; FAOV; TiPo (1952 ed.)
Little Boy Lost, A ("Nought loves another as itself"). Blake. *Fr.* Songs of Experience. CEP; EM-1; EnLi-2; EnLit; EnRP; OAEP; ViBoPo
Little boy lost in the lonely fen, The. The Little Boy Found. Blake. *Fr.* Songs of Innocence. EnRP; TiPo (1952 ed.)
Little Boy Lost, The. Stevie Smith. FaBoTw
Little Boy of heavenly birth, A. Out of Bounds. John Banister Tabb. JKCP; MaRV
Little boy once played so loud, A. Extremes. James Whitcomb Riley. FaPON; GoBP; HBVY; MPB; PCH; PPL
Little Boy Prays for His Dog, A. *Unknown.* DDA
Little boy pressed his face against the windowpane, The. The Paper Windmill. Amy Lowell. CP
Little boy sat dreaming, A. Stars. *Unknown.* GFA
Little Boy Speaks, A. E. V. Emans. DDA
Little Boy to the Locomotive, The. Benjamin R. C. Low HBMV
Little boy was set to keep, A. The Boy and the Wolf. John Hookham Frere. HBV; HBVY; OnHT; OTPC (1923 ed.)
Little Boys. Margaretta Scott. DDA
Little boys and little maidens. Little Catkins. Aleksandr Aleksandrovich Blok. TrRV
Little Boy's Good-Night, The. Eliza Lee Follen. OTPC (1923 ed.)
Little Boys of Texas. Robert P. Tristram Coffin. WaKn
Little Boy's Pocket, A. *Unknown.* PPL
Little Boy's Vain Regret, A. Edith M. Thomas. AA
Little Breath I'll Borrow. A. Thomas Campion. PoP
Little Breeches. John Hay. AA; AmPP (3d ed.); BeLS; BOHV; CoBA; DDA; FaBoBe; GoTP; HBV; LPS-3; OBAV; StaSt, *abr.*; TreFS; TSW; TSWC
Little broken bones of men, The. I Would Remember Constant Things. John Urban Nicholson. TBM
Little brook! Little brook! The Brook Song. James Whitcomb Riley. CG
Little Brother of the Rich, A. Edward Sandford Martin. AA; HBV
Little Brothers of the Ground. Edwin Markham. SN
Little Brother's Secret. Katherine Mansfield. FaPON; MoSiPe; TiPo
Little Brown Baby. Paul Laurence Dunbar. BANP; BTP; PoNe
Little brown baby-bird, lapped in your nest. Lullaby of the Iroquois. E. Pauline Johnson. BOL
Little Brown Bear. Alice Wilkins. GFA
Little Brown Bobby. Laura Elizabeth Richards. SAS
Little Brown Boy. Helene Johnson. *See* Poem: "Little brown boy."
Little brown brother, oh! little brown brother. Baby Seed Song. Edith Nesbit. BoChLi; DD; FaPON; HBV; HBVY; MPB; OTPC; PCH; PRWS; RAR; SP; TVC; TVSH
Little Brown Bulls, The. *Unknown.* BaBo; OuSiCo, *with music*
Little Brown Church in the Vale, The. William S. Pitts. OlF
Little brown gopher explored one day, A. The Little Gopher Man. Nancy Bockius Scott. PCH
Little Brown Hands. Mary Hannah Krout. PTA-1
Little Brown Jug, The. *Unknown.* ABF, *with music;* FaFP; TrAS, *with music;* TreF; YaD
Little brown maid wailing sore, The. *Unknown, tr. fr. Spanish by* Eleanor L. Turnbull. TeCS
Little Brown Seed. Rodney Bennett. BoTP
Little Brown Seed in the Furrow, The. Ida W. Benham. PEOR
Little brown seed, round and sound. Little Brown Seed. Rodney Bennett. BoTP
Little brown squirrel hops in the corn, The. The Rejected "National Hymns," VII. "Orpheus C. Kerr." BOHV; InMe; LPS-3; PA
Little brown surf-bather of the mountains! The Water Ouzel. Harriet Monroe. BLA; CP; NP; OTPC (1946 ed.); SBMV
Little Brown Wren, The. Clinton Scollard. WhBS
Little Busy Bee. Isaac Watts. *See* How Doth the Little Busy Bee.
Little but Great. Charles Mackay. *See* Small Beginnings.
Little Buttercup. W. S. Gilbert. *See* I'm Called Little Buttercup.
Little by little we subtract. Observation. Samuel Hoffenstein. PoMa
Little Cabin, A. Charles Bertram Johnson. BANP
Little Calathine. *Unknown, tr. fr. Greek by* Lord Neaves. OnPM
Little Callimachus harsh Death bore hence. On a Child. Lucian. GrPE
Little Candle. Carl Sandburg. GoYe
Little cares that fretted me, The. Out in the Fields with God [*or* In the Fields *or* Cares]. *Unknown, at. to* Louise Imogen Guiney *and to* Elizabeth Barrett Browning. BLP; BLPA; BLRP; DD; GoTP; HBV; HBVY; MaRV; MPB; MW; NeHB; NLK; OQP; OTPC (1946 ed.); PTA-1; QP-2; TreFS; WBLP; WGRP
Little Cart, The. Ch'en Tzu-lung, *tr. fr. Chinese by* Arthur Waley. AtBAP; LoBV; TrCh
Little Carved Bowl. The. Margaret Widdemer. BrR; YT
Little Cat Angel, The. Leontine Standfield. BLPA; CIV
Little cat played on a silver flute, A. The Boston Cats. Arthur Macy. CIV
Little Catkins. Aleksandr Blok, *tr. fr. Russian by* Babette Deutsch. TrRV
(Willow-Boughs, The, *tr. unknown.*) BoTP
Little Chap Who Follows Me, The. *Unknown.* PoToHe (new ed.)

Little chapel of pink tile, A. Saint Francis' Wood. Alexander J. Cody. SaFP
Little Charlie Chipmunk. Helen Cowles LeCron. FaPON; GFA; TiPo
Little Child, The. Albert Bigelow Paine. AA; ChIP; MaRV
Little Child, A. Bethlehem of Judea. *Unknown.* ChBR
Little Child, a joy-of-heart, with eyes, A. At Nazareth. Katharine Lee Bates. StJW
Little Child, a Limber Elf, A. Samuel Taylor Coleridge. *Fr.* Christabel. LoBV; ViBoPo
Little child, good child, go to sleep. Evening Song. Fannie Stearns Davis. BOL; GFA; SP; VOD
Little Child, I Call Thee. *Unknown, tr. fr. Irish by* Douglas Hyde. TIP
Little Child of Mary. H. T. Burleigh. StJW
Little Child There Is Yborn, A. *Unknown.* AnEC
Little Children, The. Irwin Granich. MaRV
Little Children. Mary Howitt. PRWS
Little children, never give. Kindness to Animals. *Unknown.* BoTP; GoTP; HBV; HBVY; OTPC; PPL
Little Child's Faith, The. Louis Edwin Thayer. PoToHe
Little Child's Hymn, A. Francis Turner Palgrave. BOL; VA
Little Child's Prayer, A. John Banister Tabb. *See* Child's Prayer, A.
Little Christ Child. Elsie M. Fowler. PoRL
Little Christ was good, and lay. Like One I Know. Nancy Campbell. JKCP
Little Christel. William Brighty Rands. PRWS
Little Christmas Donkey, The. Geraldine Farrar. StJW
Little Christmas Tree, The. "Susan Coolidge." DD; PEDC; PEOR; SDH
Little Christmas tree that stands, The. What the Christmas Tree Thinks. Mary Carolyn Davies. PCH
Little City. Robert Horan. CrMA; LiTM (rev. ed.); NePA
Little Clan, The. Frederick Robert Higgins. OBMV
Little clock is friends with me, The. The Gymnastic Clock. Mary Carolyn Davies. TVC; TVSH
Little Clotilda. *Unknown.* BoTP
Little Cloud, The. John Howard Bryant. LPS-2
Little Clown Puppet. Carolyn Haywood. BrR
Little cock sparrow sat on a [green] tree, A. Mother Goose. BoTP; MeMeAg; OTPC; OxNR; SiTL
Little Colt. *Unknown.* DDA
Little colt-broncho, loaned to the farm, A. The Broncho That Would Not Be Broken. Vachel Lindsay. ATP (1935 ed.); BAP; BBV (1951 ed.); ChMo; CMP; CP; CV; LaNeLa; LiTM (rev. ed.); NePA; NV; PFY; TBM; YT
Little colt, you can't help wobbling. Little Colt. *Unknown.* DDA
Little Commodore, The. J. C. Squire. HBMV
Little Cossack, The. Laura E. Richards. PoRh
Little cottage stood alone, the pride, The. The Old Cottagers. John Clare. OBRV
Little Count of Lemonade, The. Look Out for the Snake! Luis Palés Matos. AnCL
Little cousin is dead, by foul subtraction, The. Dead Boy. John Crowe Ransom. LiTA; LS; MoPW; OxBA
Little cowboy, what have you heard. The Fairy Shoemaker [*or* The Leprecaun *or* The Lupracaun]. William Allingham. EV-5; OnYI; PCH; RG
Little cramped words scrawling all over the paper. The Letter. Amy Lowell. AV
Little creatures of the under earth, The. They Are Forewarned. Winifred Gray Stewart. MuM
Little cross, A/ To tell my loss. Robin's Cross. George Darley. OnYI
Little cross of weather-silvered wood, A. "Ici Repose." Bernard Freeman Trotter. MaRV
Little Dame Crump. *Unknown.* BoTP; FTB, *with music;* PCH
Little Dancers, The. Laurence Binyon. BoTP; CH; MBP; MoBrPo; MoVE; OBVV; PoeT
Little Dandelion. Helen Barron Bostwick. DD; HBV; HBVY; OTPC (1923 ed.); PRWS
Little Dandelion, The. Lula Lowe Weeden. CDC
Little Danny Donkey. Helen Cowles LeCron. GFA
Little dapper man but with shiny elbows, A. Louis MacNeice. *Fr.* The Kingdom. ChMP
Little Dark Rose, The. *Unknown.* *See* Dark Rosaleen.
Little daughter of the grove. The Unripe Orange. Al-Asamm. MooP
Little David. *Unknown.* APW; TrAS, *with music*
(Little David, Play on Yo' Harp.) GoSl
Little Day Moon. Nellie Burget Miller. GFA
Little Dead Child, The. Josephine Daskam Bacon. DaM
Little Death, The. Carolyn Wilson Link. MuM
Little Derwent's Breakfast, *sel.* *Unknown.*
Little Gentleman, The. HBV; HBVY
"Little dew." Epic. Virginia Moore. TSWC
Little Dicky Dilver. *Unknown.* OxNR
"Little did I, the young one, slumber at night." The Child's Dream. *Unknown.* OnPM
Little Dirge. Jean Starr Untermeyer. HBMV
Little Disaster, The. *Unknown.* SAS
Little Distance Off, A. John Lehmann. MoP
Little Dog, The. Frances Cornford. RIS
Little Dog-Angel, The. Norah M. Holland. CPG
Little Dog Barked, The. *Unknown.* AlBD
Little Dog's Day, The. Rupert Brooke. ShBV-1
Little Dove. Mary's Lullaby. Ivy O. Eastwick. ChBR
Little Doves, The. *Unknown.* PPL; SAS
Little Dreamers, The. Frank L. Stanton. BOL
Little dreams of maidenhood, The. The Wife. Theodosia Garrison. HBV
Little drop of dew. A Dewdrop. Frank Dempster Sherman. PPL
Little drops of water. Little Things. Julia A. Fletcher Carney, *wr. at. to* E. C. Brewer *and to* Frances S. Osgood. BoTP; FaBoBe; FaFP; FaPON; GFA; GoTP; HBV; HBVY; NeHB; OnHT; OTPC; PECK; TreF
Little Drummer, The. Richard Henry Stoddard. AA; PAH
Little Dutch Garden, A. Harriet Whitney Durbin. OTPC (1946 ed.)
Little Dutch Gretchen sat in the kitchen. *Unknown.* SAS
Little Dutch Soldier, The. *Unknown.* *See* Snapoo.
Little Dutchman, The. Mary Mapes Dodge. GaP
Little Eau Pleine, The. *Unknown.* IHA
Little elbow leans upon your knee, A. Tired Mothers. May Riley Smith. HBV; MOAH
Little Elegy. Elinor Wylie. BoFr
Little elephant was crying, The. Cradle Song of the Elephants. Adriano del Valle. FaPON
Little Elf, The. John Kendrick Bangs. AA; FaBoBe; GaP; GFA; GoBP; GoTP; HBV; HBVY; MPB; OnHT; PRWS; SP; WaKn
(Little Elf-Man, The.) BoChLi; BoTP; PCH
(Little Elfman, The.) OTPC (1946 ed.); RAR; TiPo
Little Ellie sits alone. Romance of the Swan's Nest. Elizabeth Barrett Browning. BPN; CG; GN; LPS-1; OTPC
Little enough of that wide country. The Spell of France. Edmund Blunden. POTE
Little Epithalamium. Chester Kallman. CrMA
Little Exercise. Elizabeth Bishop. CrMA; MoAB; MoAmPo (1950 ed.); UnPo (3d ed.)
Little face there was, A. In Rama. George Alfred Townsend. AA
Little Fair Soul, The. Menella Bute Smedley. VA
Little fairy comes at night, A. Queen Mab [*or* The Dream Fairy]. Thomas Hood. BoTP; DD; EV-4; HBV; HBVY; HOAH; OTPC, *abr.;* PCH; PPL; RAR, *abr.;* StVeCh; TVC; TVSH
Little Fairy Flitabout had such a craze for fleetness. The Careless Fairy. Nancy Byrd Turner. BoChLi
Little fairy snowflakes. Santa Claus. *Unknown.* MeMeAg; OTPC (1946 ed.)
Little Family, The. *Unknown.* BaBo
Little Fan. James Reeves. PoMS
Little Farm, The; or, The Weary Ploughman. *Unknown.* CoMu
Little Fauns to Proserpine, The. Marjorie Pickthall. OCL
Little Feet. Elizabeth Akers Allen. HBV; LPS-1
Little feet too young and soft to walk. The Stranger's Grave. Emily Lawless. OnYI
Little fields are very green, The. Dutch Slumber Song. Viola Chittenden White. VOD
Little Finger Game, A. E. J. Falconer. BoTP
Little Fir Tree, The. Margaret Rose. BoTP
Little Fir-Trees, The. Evaleen Stein. PTA-2
Little Firs, The. *Unknown.* DDA
Little Fish That Would Not Do as It Was Bid, The. Ann *or* Jane Taylor. OHIP
Little fishes in a brook. *Unknown.* OxNR
Little Flag on Our House, The. William Curtis Demorest. PaA
Little Flags, The. John Clair Minot. DD; HH; PEDC
Little flock of clouds go down to rest, A. Evening Clouds. Francis Ledwidge. MPB; VOD
Little Flower, The. Leonard Feeney. PraNu
Little flower grew in a lonely vale, A. To Mrs. Ann Flaxman. Blake. OBRV
Little flowers came through the ground, The. At Easter Time. Laura E. Richards. BoChLi; DD; EOAH; HH; MPB; OHIP; OTPC (1946 ed.)
Little flutt'rer! swifter flying. To a Hedge-Sparrow. *Unknown.* OTPC (1923 ed.)
Little fly,/ Thy summer's play. The Fly. Blake. *Fr.* Songs of Experience. BLV; BoLiVe; EiPP; EM-1; EnL; GoTP; MaPo; OTPC (1923 ed.); TrGrPo
Little Folk. Carrie Ward Lyon. HOAH
Little Folks in the Grass. Annette Wynne. BoChLi; SP; UTS
Little Fox, The. Marion Edey. TiPo
Little fox, the wolf and bear made peace, The. The Fox, The Wolf, and the Bear. *Unknown.* ArmLP
Little foxes in their holes, The. The Fugitive. William Rose Benét. MOAP
Little French Dog, The. Tom Robinson. AlBD
Little French doll was a dear little doll, The. The Doll's Wooing. Eugene Field. RIS

Little French Lawyer, The, *sel.* John Fletcher.
Song in the Wood. EIL; ThWaDe
"Little Friend's" Grave. Frederick George Scott. BoCaPo
Little Frog, A. Alice Wilkins. GFA
Little Gal at Our House. *with music.* *Unknown.* ABF
Little Garaine. Sir Gilbert Parker. FaPON; OTPC (1946 ed.); PRWS
Little Garden, A. Amy Lowell. GBV
Little garden little Jowett made, A. *Unknown, sometimes at. to* Richard Porson. WhC
Little Garment, A. Diodorus, *tr. fr. Greek by* Lord Neaves. OnPM
Little Gate to God, The. Walter Rauschenbusch. MaRV, *abr.*; QS
Little gate was reached at last, The. Auf Wiedersehen. James Russell Lowell. AA; BAV; CoBA; HBV; IAP; LPS-1; PR; TCAP
Little General Monk. *Unknown.* OxNR
Little Gentleman, The. *Unknown.* *Fr.* Little Derwent's Breakfast. HBV; HBVY
Little Geste of Robin Hood and His Meiny, A. *Unknown.* *See* Gest of Robyn Hode, A.
Little Ghost, The. Katharine Tynan. HBV
Little Ghost, The. Zonas of Sardis, *tr. fr. Greek by* F. L. Lucas. GrPE
Little Ghost Who Died for Love, The. Edith Sitwell. CaAE; MoP
Little Ghosts, The. Thomas S. Jones, Jr. HBV
Little Gidding. T. S. Eliot. *Fr.* Four Quartets. AmPo; ExPo; FaBoEn; OAEP (2d ed.)
Sels.
"Ash on an old man's sleeve," II. FaBoTw; GTBS-W; PoFS
"We shall not cease from exploration," *fr.* V. ImOP
Little Giffen. Francis Orrery Ticknor. AA; BlG; BoHiPo; CoBA; DD; GA; HBV; IAP; MaC; MC; OBAV; PaA; PAH; PCD; PoP; SPP; TCAP; TreFS
Little Gift of Laughter, The. Kathleen Millay. BAP
Little Girl, A. Charles Angoff. GoYe
Little Girl, The. Nicholas Moore. NeBP
Little girl, A/ Had wandered in the night. John W. Lynch. *Fr.* A Woman Wrapped in Silence. ISi
Little Girl, Be Careful What You Say. Carl Sandburg. GoYe
Little Girl in Bloom, A. Anne Blackwell Payne. GFA
"Little girl, little girl." Mother Goose. BoTP; OxNR
Little girl that I used to know, The. Lost Child. Charles Fletcher Lummis. FAOV
Little Girl That Lost a Finger, The. "Gabriela Mistral," *tr. fr. Spanish by* Muna Lee. AnCL; FaPON
Little Girl That Mother Used to Be. Nancy Byrd Turner. HH
Little Girl to Her Dolly, The. Ann Taylor. SAS
Little girl went for a walk, A. A Summer Walk. Elizabeth Winton. PCH
Little girls' frocks are frilly, The. Ballroom Dancing Class. Phyllis McGinley. MoShBr
Little girl's new present was a bear, The. The Bear. Vladimir Lugovskoi. RuPo
Little Girl's Songs, A. Hilda Conkling. NP
Little girls that are dancing around me, break off from your play. Song of the Figurehead. Kai Friis-Møller. BoDS
Little Gods, The. Abigail Cresson. PoMa
Little gold head, my house's candle. Lullaby of a Woman of the Mountain. *Unknown.* BOL; NP
Little Golden Ring, The, *with music.* *Unknown.* ShS
Little golden son, the rain is coming, coming. A Servian Lullaby. Nora Hopper. BOL
Little Goldenhair. F. Burge Smith. LPS-1
Little Goose, A. Eliza Sproat Turner. BOHV
Little Gopher Man, The. Nancy Bockius Scott. PCH
Little Gottlieb. Phoebe Cary. OTPC (1946 ed.); TVC; TVSH
Little granite church upholds, The. Sheepstor. L. A. G. Strong. HBMV
Little Grave, The. *Unknown.* PEOR
Little gray cat was walking prettily, The. The Little White Cat. *Unknown.* OnYI
Little gray dog, don't run, don't fear. Apology to a Small Dog. Teddy Webb. AIBD
Little gray [*or* grey] hill-glade, A, close-turfed, withdrawn. Marsyas. Sir Charles G. D. Roberts. PeCV; VA
Little Gray Lamb, The. Archibald Beresford Sullivan. ChrBoLe; CLS; SDH
Little Gray Songs from St. Joseph's, *sels.* Grace Fallow Norton.
"If my dark grandam had but known," VI. LBMV
"My little soul I never saw," XLVII. HBV; LBMV
"With cassock black, baret and book," XXX. HBV; LBMV
Little gray wonder, in pride of fur. To an Enchantress. Alice Brown. CIV
Little green bird sat on a fence rail, A. Mother Goose. BoChLi
Little green frog lived under a log, A. Strange Talk. L. E. Yates. BoTP
Little green frog once lived in a pool, A. The Frog. Rose Fyleman. BoTP
Little green lizard on Solomon's wall, The. The Biographer. Louise Lamprey. DDA
Little Green Orchard, The. Walter de la Mare. DaM; MPB; MW; POTT; TiPo (1952 ed.)
Little Green Tents. Walt Mason. OQP; PSO; QP-1
Little Green Tree Blues. Langston Hughes. PoNe
Little Gregory. Theodore Botrel, *tr. fr. French by* Richard C. Savage. CAW
Little Gretchen, little Gretchen wanders up and down the street. The Little Match-Girl. Hans Christian Andersen. LPS-1
Little grey hill-glade, A, close-turfed, withdrawn. *See* Little gray hill-glade . . .
Little Guinever. Annie Fields. AA
Little Gunver. Johannes Ewald, *tr. fr. Danish by* Charles W. Stork. BoDS
Little Gustava. Celia Thaxter. BoChLi; FaPON; HBV; HBVY; PRWS; RAR
"Little Haly! Little Haly!" cheeps the robin in the tree. On the Death of Little Mahala Ashcraft. James Whitcomb Riley. AA; OBAV
Little hand is knocking at my heart, A. The Return. Arthur Symons. BMEP; HBMV; LoPS; VLEP
Little Hands. Laurence Binyon. HBV; MaRV
Little hare new-littered, from my mother's breast they tore me, A. The Baby Hare. Meleager. GrPE; GrR
Little harp, at thy cry. Brechva's Harp Song. Ernest Rhys. VA
Little head against my shoulder. The Sigh. Thomas Hardy. VLEP
Little Hector Philips. Katherine Philips. DiM
Little hedgerow birds, The. An Old Man [*or* Animal Tranquillity and Decay]. Wordsworth. ERP; FaBoCh; LoGBV
Little herdboy, sitting there. The Pilgrim and the Herdboy. Robert Buchanan. OBVV
Little Herd-Boy's Song, The. Robert Buchanan. *Fr.* The Pilgrim and the Herdboy. BoTP
Little Hermogenes is so small. Old Greek Nonsense Rhymes. Lucilius. BoN
Little Hobby-Horse, A. Eliza Grove. OTPC
Little honey, A! Ay, a little sweet. Wilfrid Scawen Blunt. *Fr.* Esther. LEAP
Little honey baby, shet yo' eyes up tight. A Southern Lullaby. Virna Sheard. CPG
Little Horned Toad. *Tr. fr. Navajo Indian by* Hilda Faunce Wetherill. FaPON
Little House, The. Struthers Burt. NoCaPo
Little House, A. Abigail Cresson. DDA
Little House, The. John Richard Moreland. LS
Little House, The. Sir Gilbert Parker. CPG
Little House, The. Katharine Tynan. LBBV
Little hungry baby—do not cry! A Belgian Lullaby. Martha S. Gielow. BOL
Little Hymn, A. Jane Taylor. *See* God Is So Good.
Little I ask; my wants are few. Contentment. Oliver Wendell Holmes. *Fr.* The Autocrat of the Breakfast Table, *ch.* 11. AmPP (4th ed.); AnNE; BOHV; HBV; HiLiAm; IAP; InMe; OnPP; OxBA; PIR; PR; REAL; TCAP; TOP; TreF
Little I knew, when morning-white. Samuel Hoffenstein. *Fr.* Interlude, for a Solitary Flute. QS
Little I ween, did Mary guess. His Mother's Joy. John White Chadwick. AA
Little Indian, Sioux or Crow. Foreign Children. Robert Louis Stevenson. BoChLi; BoTP; GaP; GFA; MPB; OTPC (1946 ed.); RIS; SUS; TVSH
Little Ink More or Less, A. Stephen Crane. War Is Kind, II. AmPP (3d ed.); AnAmPo; LA
Little inmate, full of mirth. The Cricket. Vincent Bourne, *tr. by* William Cowper. HBV; HBVY; LPS-2; OTPC; SN
Little inn in Bethlehem first heard the echo of his voice, A. Echoes of Jesus. Lucile Coleman. ChIP
Little is he victor here, A. Tactic. Margaret Marks. MAP
Little island, you may fancy. Isolation. Albert Teodor Gellerstedt. AnSL
Little Ivory Figures Pulled with String. Amy Lowell. AnFE; APA; CoAnAm; MAPA; NAMP; TwAmPo; ViBoPo
Little Jack Dandy-prat. *Unknown.* OxNR
Little Jack Frost. *Unknown.* GFA; PPL
Little Jack Horner, *parody.* Anthony C. Deane. PA
Little Jack Horner/ Sat in the corner. Mother Goose. BoChLi; FaBoBc; FaFP; HBV; HBVY; OnHT; OTPC; OxNR; PCH; RIS; SAS; SiTL
Little Jack Horner sat in the corner eying the pies all day. A Medley. Michael Lewis. TSW; TSWC
Little Jack of Christ, The. St. Stephen's Word. Rayner Heppenstall. ChMP
Little Jack Pumpkin Face. *Unknown.* PCH
Little Jack Sprat/ Once had a pig. *Unknown.* OxNR

Little Jenny Wren/ Fell sick upon a time. Mother Goose. BoChLi (1950 ed.); BoTP
Little Jesus. Francis Thompson. *See* Child's Prayer, A.
Little Jesus came to town, The. A Christmas Folk-Song. Lizette Woodworth Reese. ChBR; ChrBoLe; DD; FaPON; GFA; HBMV; HBVY; MPB; NV; OHIP; OTPC (1946 ed.); PoRh; PoRL; RAR; SDH; SP; StJW; SUS; TiPo (1952 ed.); TSW; UTS; VOD
Little Jesus, little Jesus. A Child at a Crèche. Alice Isabel Hazeltine. ChrBoLe
Little Jesus, sweetly sleep, do not stir. Rocking. *Unknown.* ChrBoLe
Little Jesus wast Thou shy. A Child's Prayer [*or* Little Jesus *or* Ex Ore Infantium]. Francis Thompson. BoTP; ChrBoLe; DD; EmBrPo; GTSE; HBV; HBVY; MaRV; OBVV; OHIP; PoRh; PoRL; POTT; PoVP; SDH; StJW; SUS; TreFS; TSW; TSWC; VOD
Little Jew lived in a little straw hut, A. Biography. Abraham M. Klein. TrJP
Little Joe-Johnny. Gustaf Fröding, *tr. fr. Swedish by* Charles W. Stork. AnSL
Little Joe, the Wrangler, *with music. At. to* N. Howard Thorp. CoSo; CSF
Little John a Begging. *Unknown.* BaBo; ESPB (A *and* B *vers.*)
Little John Bottlejohn. Laura E. Richards. LiL; PoMS; RIS
Little John Jiggy Jag. *Unknown.* OxNR
Little John Nobody. *Unknown.* OxBoLi
Little Johnny-jump-up said. Wise Johnny. Edwina Fallis. SiSoSe; SUS; TiPo
Little Johnny Mine, The. Daisy L. Detrick. PoOW
Little Johnny Morgan. *Unknown.* OxNR
Little Joke. Elinor Wylie. LHV
Little Jumping Girls, The. Kate Greenaway. FaPON; MPB ("Jump—jump—jump.") TiPo
Little King, The. Irene Gass. ChrBoLe
Little King Boggen, he built a fine hall. Mother Goose. StVeCh
Little King Pippin he built a fine hall. King Pippin. *Unknown.* BoN; LiL; OxNR
Little Kings and Queens of the May. Juliana Horatia Ewing. *See* For Good Luck.
Little Kirsteen was so fair a maid. Sir John the Outlaw. *Unknown.* BoDaBa
Little Kiss When No One Sees, A. Samuel Minturn Peck. PreP
Little Kittens, The. Eliza Lee Follen. GFA; TiPo; UTS
Sels.
"Where are you going,/ My little cat?" BoTP
"Where are you going,/ My little kittens?" BoTP
"Little kittens, be quiet—be quiet, I say!" A Cat to Her Kittens. Eliza Grove. OTPC (1923 ed.)
Little Kitty. Elizabeth Prentiss. *See* Long Time Ago.
Little Knight in Green, The. Katharine Lee Bates. AA
Little lad, little lad. *Unknown.* OxNR
Little ladies, white and green. Snowdrops. Laurence Alma-Tadema. BoTP; PRWS
Little lady lairdie, The. *Unknown.* OxNR
Little Lady of Ch'ing-hsi, The. *Unknown, tr. fr. Chinese by* Arthur Waley. ChLP; TrCh
Little lady of my heart! Ad Domnulam Suam. Ernest Dowson. HBV; PG
Little Lady Wren. Tom Robinson. FaPON; TiPo
Little Lake, The. Bedros Tourian, *tr. fr. Armenian by* Alice Stone Blackwell. ArmLP
Little Lamb. Blake. *See* Lamb, The.
Little lamb had Mary, A; sweet. An Old Song by New Singers. A. C. Wilkie. BOHV; PA
Little Lamb Went Straying, A. Albert Midland. OTPC (1923 ed.)
Little lamb, who made thee? The Lamb. Blake. *Fr.* Songs of Innocence. AnFE; BCEP; BEL; BLV; BoChLi; BoLiVe; BoTP; BTP; CAW; CBPC; CEP; CH; CoBE; EiPP; EM-1; EnL; EnLi-2; EnLit; EnRP; EV-3; ExPo; FaBoBe; FaBoCh; FaPON; GoTP; HBV; LiTB; LiTG; LoBV; LoGBV; MaPo; MaRV; MeMeAg; MPB; NeHB; OAEP; OBEC; OTPC; OuHeWo; OxBoCh; PG (1945 ed.); PoFS; PoRh; PRWS; PTA-2; RAR; RIS; SeCeV; StaSt; StVeCh; SUS; TOP; TreF; TrGrPo; TVC; TVSH; TwCrTr; TwHP; UTS; WaKn; WGRP; WHA
Little lambkin, The, says "Ba, Ba!" Buttercup Farm. *Unknown.* SAS
Little lambs, little lambs. Baby Beds. *Unknown.* BoTP
Little lamps of the dusk. Fireflies. Carolyn Hall. FaPON; GFA; HBMV; HBVY; MPB; PCH; TSW; TSWC; UTS
Little Land, The. Robert Louis Stevenson. GoBP; OnHT; PoVP; PRWS; StVeCh (1955 ed.); TVC; TVSH
Little lane—the brook runs close beside, A. On a Lane in Spring. John Clare. EnSW
Little lass of Plymouth—gentle, shy, and sweet. Boy and Girl of Plymouth. Helen L. Smith. PTA-2
Little Learning Is a Dangerous Thing, A. Pope. *Fr.* An Essay on Criticism, Pt. II. BCEP; HoPM; PG (1955 ed.); TreF; TrGrPo
(Alps on Alps.) FaFP; GTBS-W
(Little Learning, A.) ChTr; CoEV; LiTB; LiTG; OBEC; SeCePo
Little Lettice is dead, they say. Lettice. "Michael Field." VA
Little Libbie. Julia A. Moore. ATP
Little light is going by, A. Firefly. Elizabeth Madox Roberts. GFA; GoBP; LS; OTPC (1946 ed.); PoRh; SUS; TiPo; UTS
Little Litany to St. Francis, A. Philip Murray. NePoAm
Little, little puppy on a great big street. First Airing. John E. Donovan. AlBD
Little lonely child am I, A. The Moon-Child. "Fiona Macleod." CH; EtS; VLEP
Little Lord Jesus, The. *Unknown.* ChrBoLe
Little Lost Child, The. Edward B. Marks. TreFS
Little Lost Pup. Arthur Guiterman. AlBD; BBV (1951 ed.); PCD; TreFS
Little Lough, The. John Hewitt. NeIP
Little Love-God, The. Meleager, *tr. fr. Greek by* Walter Headlam. AWP
Little love-god lying once asleep, The. Sonnets, CLIV. Shakespeare. EM-1; PeBoSo; ReIE
Little Love, A, of heaven a little share. Sufficiency. Gleeson White. VA
Little love serves my turne. *Unknown.* SeCSL
Little Love Song, A. Helen Cecilia Willis. CAG
Little Lover. Leonora Speyer. BAP; HBMV
Little lowly hermitage it was, A. Archimago's Hermitage. Spenser. *Fr.* The Faerie Queene, I, 1. BCEP
Little Lucy Lavender. Lucy Lavender. Ivy O. Eastwick. BoTP; SiSoSe
Little Lucy Lester. M. Steel. BoTP
Little Maia. Zakarias Topelius, *tr. fr. Swedish by* Charles W. Stork. AnSL
Little Maid and the Cowslips, The. John Clare. BoTP
Little maid of Astrakan, A. The Divan. Richard Henry Stoddard. AA
Little Maid of Far Japan. Annette Wynne. MPB
Little maid, pretty maid,/ Whither goest thou? Mother Goose. OxNR; PPL
Little maid upon my fan. Little Maid of Far Japan. Annette Wynne. MPB
Little maiden climbed an old man's knee, A. After the Ball. Charles Kassell Harris. TreF
Little maiden, dost thou pine. Valentine to a Little Girl. Cardinal Newman. GoBC
Little maiden met me in the lane, A. The Intercepted Salute. Thomas Edward Brown. POTT
Little Mamma. Charles Henry Webb. BOHV; FAOV
Little Man, The. Hughes Mearns. *See* Antigonish.
Little man/ Little man. Ilo Orleans. RIS
Little man in coal pit. *Unknown.* OxNR
Little man, little man. First Trousers. Susie Dawson Brown. FAOV
Little man, now greyed with years of books, The. Greek, Four Credits. James L. MacKavanaugh. CAG
Little Man Who Wasn't There, The. Hughes Mearns. *See* Antigonish.
Little Marine, The. *Unknown.* *See* Snapoo.
Little marsh-plant, yellow green, A. The Sundew. Swinburne. CoEV; ViP
Little Mary Bell had a fairy in a nut. Long John Brown and Little Mary Bell. Blake. SiTL
Little Mary Cassidy. Francis A. Fahy. HBV
Little masters, hat in hand. Clover. John Banister Tabb. AA; AnAmPo; AnFE; APA; CoAnAm; LA; NLK; OBAV
Little Match-Girl, The, *abr.* Hans Christian Andersen, *tr. fr. Danish.* LPS-1
Little Matthy Groves [*or* Mathie Grove]. *Unknown.* *See* Little Musgrave and Lady Barnard.
Little Men, The. William Allingham. *Fr.* The Fairies. OtMeF
Little Men, The. Flora Fearne. BoTP
Little men all in a row. Little Rain Men. Ruth Anne Hussey. PCH
Little men of meadow land, The. Adventure. Nancy Byrd Turner. StVeCh (1955 ed.)
Little Messenger of Love, The. *Unknown.* PEOR
Little Milliner, The. Robert Buchanan. BeLS; LPS-1
Little Millwins attend the Russian Ballet, The. Les Millwin. Ezra Pound. CoV; MOAP
Little Miss Muffet, *parody.* *Unknown.* PA
Little Miss Muffet/ Crouched on a tuffet. Paul Dehn. *Fr.* Rhymes for a Modern Nursery. FiBHP
Little Miss Muffet/ Sat on a tuffet. Mother Goose. BoChLi; FaBoBe; FaFP; HBV; HBVY; OnHT; OTPC; OxNR; PCH; PPL; RIS; SAS; SiTL; StVeCh; TiPo
Little Miss Muffet discovered a tuffet. The Embarrassing Episode of Little Miss Muffet. Guy Wetmore Carryl. FaPON; MPB; StPo; TSW; TSWC

Little Miss Muffet is eating her whey. The Eternal Young. Edgar A. Guest. OnHT
Little Miss Pitt. William Wise. TiPo (1959 ed.)
Little Mistake, A. Anna Maria Pratt. *See* Mortifying Mistake, A.
Little Mr. Browny Bee. Browny Bee. Irene F. Pawsey. BoTP
Little Mister Polliwog. Ways of Traveling. Alice Wilkins. GFA
Little Mistress Comfort got up early one fine day. Mistress Comfort. Elizabeth Gould. BoTP
Little moat that fronts our fortress-wall, The. The Moat. Oliffe Richmond. NeTW
Little Moccasins. Robert W. Service. CPG
Little Mohee, The. *Unknown.* ABF, *with music;* AmSS, *with music;* APW, *diff. vers.;* BaBo
(Lass of Mohea, The, *with music.*) SoAmSa
(Pretty Mohea, The.) ABS
Little Moon, The. Longfellow. *Fr.* The Light of Stars. BoTP
Little moon was restless in eternity, A. Night Note. James Oppenheim. MAP; MoAmPo (1942 ed.)
Little more kindness and a little less creed, A. The World Needs. *Unknown.* PoToHe (new ed.)
Little more tired at close of day, A. As We Grow Older [*or* Growing Old]. Rollin J. Wells. BLPA; PoToHe; WBLP
Little more toward the light, A. Growing Gray. Austin Dobson. HBV; LPS-3
Little More West. Roy Helton. ElSeCe
Little Mother. "M. P. D." PEDC
Little Mother Maybe. *Unknown.* SAS
Little moths are creeping, The. Interior. Padraic Colum. MBP; MoBrPo; TSW; TSWC
Little mountain spring I found, A. The Spring. Rose Fyleman. BrR; FaPON
Little mouse in gray velvet. Mouse. Hilda Conkling. GoBP; StVeCh; TiPo
Little mouse nibbled a Limburger cheese, A. A Mouse, a Cat, and an Irish Bull. John Banister Tabb. CIV
Little Mud-Sparrows, The; Jewish Legend. Elizabeth Stuart Phelps Ward. ChrBoLe; CLS; PEOR; SDH
Little Musgrave and Lady Barnard. *Unknown.* BaBo (A *vers.*); ESPB (A *and* B *vers.*); InvP; OBB; ViBoFo
(Little Mathie Grove, B *vers.*) BaBo
(Little Matthy Groves, *diff. vers.*) ABS
(Lord Banner, C *vers.*) BaBo
Little mushroom table spread, A. Robert Herrick. *Fr.* Oberon's Feast. OTPC (1923 ed.); ViBoPo
Little Music, A. Victor Hugo, *tr. fr. French by* Alan Conder. TrFP
Little my lacking fortunes show. Expenses. Adelaide Crapsey. NP; TOP
Little Nan. *Unknown.* MDAH; PEOR
Little Nancy [*or* Nanny *or* Nan] Etticoat. Mother Goose. BoChLi; ChTr; HBV; HBVY; OTPC; OxNR; PCH; PPL; RIS; SiTL; StVeCh; TiPo
Little Nellie Cassidy has got a place in town. In Service. Winifred M. Letts. CV; HBMV; POT; PoTo; VOD; YT
Little new neighbor, have you come to be. Welcome. Rose Waldo. MPB
Little New Year, my friend-to-be. Gifts for the New Year. Ruby E. Weyburn. PSO
Little newt, The. The Newt. David McCord. TiPo (1959 ed.)
Little Nipper an' 'Is Ma, The. George Fauvel Gouraud. AA
Little Nun, A. Edith Loomis. PraNu
Little Old Lady, The. Rodney Bennett. BoTP
Little old lady, The. Tea. Dorothy E. Reid. PFE
Little Old Lady in Lavender Silk, The. Dorothy Parker. InMe; YaD
Little old man came riding by, A. *Unknown.* GoTP
Little old man lived in the west, A. Dandoo. *Unknown.* ABS
Little old man lived up in a cloud, A. The Cloud House. Adrian Mott. GaP
Little old man of Derby, A. *Unknown.* OxNR
Little old man of the sea, A. The Ingenious Little Old Man. John Bennett. FaPON; GaP
Little Old Sod Shanty, The. *Unknown.* AS, *with music;* CoSo, *with music;* CSF; IHA
(Little Old Sod Shanty on My Claim, The, 4 *sts.*) ABS
Little old tailor that came from Mayo, The. The Tailor That Came from Mayo. Denis A. McCarthy. OnYI
Little old woman, A. Behind the Waterfall. Winifred Welles. PoMS; StVeCh; TiPo
Little old woman, A. Bramble Jam. Irene F. Pawsey. BoTP
Little Old Women, The. Baudelaire, *tr. fr. French by* Barbara Gibbs. AnFP
Little one, come to my knee! A Story for a Child [*or* A Night with a Wolf]. Bayard Taylor. GN; HBV; HBVY; OTPC (1923 ed.); PCD; PTA-2; TVC; TVSH
Little one sleeps in its cradle, The. Song of Myself, VIII. Walt Whitman. MaPo; TrGrPo
Little One Smiles, The. Oscar Stjerne, *tr. fr. Swedish by* Charles W. Stork. AnSL
Little one, thy mother's weeping. The Lullaby of Danäe. Edmund Clarence Stedman. BOL; MOAH
Little One Weary. Christina Rossetti. BOL
Little Ones, The. W. H. Davies. MaRV
Little onward lend thy guiding hand, A. Samson Agonistes. Milton. AtBAP; BrBE; EnLi-1; NBE; PoEL-3; TwCrTr; ViBoPo
Little or nothing said soon mended is. John Davies of Hereford. SiCE
Little Orphant Annie. James Whitcomb Riley. AA; BAP; BoChLi; BOHV; FaFP; FaPON; GoBP; HBV; HBVY; HOAH; MoShBr; MPB; OBAV; OTPC; PECK; PFY; PYM; StVeCh; TiPo; TreF; TSW; TSWC
Little owlet in the glen. A Word to the Wise. Louise M. Laughton. MeMeAg
Little Pagan Rain Song. Frances Shaw. HBMV; NP
Little Page's Song, A. William Alexander Percy. HBV
Little Papoose. Hilda Conkling. FaPON; GaP
Little Parable, A. Anne Reeve Aldrich. AA; BAP; HBV; LBAP; LEAP; MaRV
Little park that I pass through. Ellis Park. Helen Hoyt. HBMV; NLK; NP; PoMa; POT; PoTo; SBMV; SP; VOD; YT
"Little, passionately, not at all, A." Villanelle of Marguerites. Ernest Dowson. EnLi-2; MBP; MoBrPo; PIAE; POTT
Little Peach, The. Eugene Field. BOHV; LauV; LBN; TSW; TSWC
Little Peach, The. *Unknown.* NA
Little peach in the orchard grew, A. The Little Peach. Eugene Field. BOHV; LauV; LBN; TSW; TSWC
Little Penelope Socrates. Christmas Chimes. *Unknown.* BOHV
Little People, The. Joseph Joel Keith. MuM
Little People. Isaac Leibush Peretz, *tr. fr. Yiddish by* Joseph Leftwich. TrJP
Little Person, A. Brian Hooker. HBMV
Little Pig Asleep, A. Leroy F. Jackson. BrR
Little pig lived in a sty, A. The Greedy Little Pig. Irene F. Pawsey. BoTP
Little Piggies, The. Thomas Hood. *See* Precocious Piggy.
Little pitiful, worn, laughing faces, The. The Beggars. Margaret Widdemer. NP
Little Pixie Piper went, A. Pipes and Drums. Lilian Holmes. GFA
Little Plant, The. Kate Louise Brown. DD; EOAH; HH; OTPC (1946 ed.); PTA-1
(In the Heart of a Seed.) MeMeAg
Little Poll Parrot. *Unknown.* OxNR
Little Polly Flinders/ sat among the cinders. Mother Goose. HBV; HBVY; OTPC; OxNR; RIS; SAS
Little Ponds. Arthur Guiterman. HBMV
Little Pony. Robert M. B. Nichols. PoTo; TCPD
Little Prayer, A. Paul Goodman. LiTA
Little Prayer, A. Samuel Ellsworth Kiser. BLP; MaRV; PraP
Little Pretty Bonny Lass, A. *Unknown.* EIL
Little pretty Nancy girl. *Unknown.* OxNR
Little pretty nightingale, [*or* Lytyll prety nyghtyngale], The. The Nightingale. *Unknown.* BLV; EG; EPP; LO; LyMA; OAEP; TrGrPo
Little pretty petty hints. An Interior Decorator Gets in My House. Wilfred J. Funk. LauV
Little priest of Felton, The. *Unknown.* OxNR; PPL
Little prince of long ago, A. Sons of the King. Joan Agnew. BoTP
Little Prince Tatters has lost his cap! Prince Tatters. Laura E. Richards. GaP; HBV; HBVY; MPB; TVSH
Little Puppy. *Tr. fr. Navajo Indian by* Hilda Faunce Wetherill. FaPON; TiPo (1959 ed.)
Little Pussy. Jane Taylor. *See* I Like Little Pussy.
Little Pussy Whitey-toes. *Unknown.* SAS
Little quids, the monstrous quids, The. The Quids. Laura Riding. MoP
Little ragged girl, our ball-boy, A. A Game at Salzburg. Randall Jarrell. MiAP
Little Rain. Elizabeth Madox Roberts. PoRh; SUS; TiPo (1952 ed.)
Little Rain, The. Tu Fu, *tr. fr. Chinese by* L. Cranmer-Byng. FaPON
Little Rain Men. Ruth Anne Hussey. PCH
Little Raindrops. *At. to* Ann Hawkshaw. BoTP; HBV; HBVY; OTPC (1923 ed.)
Little Rebel, The. Joseph Ashby-Sterry. VA
Little Red Hen, The. Eudora Bumstead. FTB
Little Red Lark, The. Alfred Perceval Graves. HBV
Little Red Lark, The. Katharine Tynan. POT; PoTo
Little red lark, The/ Arises with dawn. Morning. Ivy O. Eastwick. BoTP
Little Red Ribbon, The. James Whitcomb Riley. HBV
Little Red Riding Hood. Guy Wetmore Carryl. FiBHP

Little Red Sled, The. Jocelyn Bush. PCH; TiPo
Little Responsory for a Republican Hero. César Vallejo, *tr. fr. Spanish by* H. R. Hays. TwSpPo
Little Rhyme and a Little Reason, A. Henry Anstadt. BLRP
Little Rift within the Lute, The. Tennyson. *See* In Love, If Love Be Love.
Little Road, The. Nancy Byrd Turner. RIS; TiPo
Little road goes up the hill, A. A Conversation. Sara Hamilton Birchall. NLK
Little road grows narrow up the hill, The. No Season for Our Season. Willard Maas. AnAmPo
Little road says, Go, The. The House and the Road. Josephine Preston Peabody. CP; CV; LBMV; NV
Little road was straying, A. The Little Road. Nancy Byrd Turner. RIS
Little roads I travel, The. Nugatory. E. B. White. BOHV
Little Roads to Happiness. Wilhelmina Stitch. PoToHe (new ed.)
Little Robin red breast I hear you sing your song. Robin Red Breast. Lula Lowe Weeden. CDC
Little Robin Redbreast came to visit me. *Unknown.* OxNR
Little Robin Redbreast sat upon a tree [*or* rail]. Mother Goose. BoChLi; BoTP (*2 vers.*); GFA; GoBP; HBV; HBVY; MPB; OxNR; PPL; RIS; SAS; SiTL; StVeCh
Little room, depressing, old, A. The Tailor. "S. Ansky." TrJP
Little Rose, be not sad for all that hath. The Little Dark Rose. *Unknown.* OnYI
Little Rose Is Dust, My Dear, The. Grace Hazard Conkling. HBV; NP; OBAV
Little Rose Tree, The. Rachel Field. FaPON; SUS; TiPo
Little saint best fits a little shrine, A. A Ternary [*or* Ternarie] of Littles. Robert Herrick. ALV; BOHV; BoTP; EPS; EV-2; FaBoCh; HBV; HBVY; LoGBV; MaPo; MyFE; OTPC (1923 ed.); PG (1955 ed.); PoEL-3; PoRA; WhC
Little Salamander, The. Walter de la Mare. BMEP; LBBV; NP
Little Saling. Olaf Baker. HBMV
Little Sally Sand, *with music. Unknown.* TrAS
Little Sally Waters. Mother Goose. TiPo
Little Samaritan, The. Eleanor Halbrook Zimmerman. AlBD
Little Sandman's Song. *Unknown, tr. fr. German by* Louis Untermeyer. RIS
Little Sarah she stood by her grandmother's bed. The Johnny-cake. *Unknown.* MPB
Little Saxon words, they say, The. Heritage. Dorothy Paul. VOD
Little scarlet emblem, A. The Red Cross. Edna Jacques. PoRL
Little Scotch-ee, *with music. Unknown.* AS
Little screech owl sits polite, The. The Warning. Robert P. Tristram Coffin. DaM
Little Senorita. Charles Divine. MPB
Little Sequence, A, *sels.* Francis Burdett Money-Coutts.
"Forgive!" OBVV
"No wonder you so oft have wept." OBVV
Little Serenade. Kenton Kilmer. WHL
Little Servant, The. Sophia Mavroidi Papadaky, *tr. fr. Modern Greek by* Rae Dalven. MoGP
Little Shade, The. Edwina Stanton Babcock. BAP
Little sharp vexations, The. Our Burden Bearer [*or* The Unfailing One]. Phillips Brooks. BLRP; MaRV; PraP
Little shepherd maiden, A. Il Etait un' Bergère. *Unknown.* CIV
Little Shepherdess to Her Lambs, The. Rose Fyleman. GoBP
Little Shepherd's Song, The. William Alexander Percy. GFA; POT; PoTo; YeAr
Little ship was tossed about, The. On Top of Troubled Waters. Dorothy J. Langford. BePJ
Little Ships in the Air. Edward A. Rand. TVSH
Little ships of whitest pearl. A Mother's Song. Francis Ledwidge. EtS
Little ships two abreast. On the Beach. Manuel Altolaguirre. CoSP
Little shoes of fairies are, The. Fairy Shoes. Annette Wynne. MPB (1956 ed.)
Little shop at Nazareth, The. Carpenter's Son. Annie Johnson Flint. BePJ
Little shrivelled and humpbacked creature, The! Tim, the Fairy. Florence Randal Livesay. CaP; CPG; OCL
Little shrivelled up old woman rejoiced, The. The Despair of the Old Woman. Baudelaire. OnPM
Little siren of the stage. To Signora Cuzzoni. Ambrose Philips. CEP; LoBV; OBEC
Little Sister Left in Charge, The. Cecil Frances Alexander. OTPC (1923 ed.)
Little Sister of the Prophet, The. Marjorie Pickthall. HBV
Little Sister Rose-Marie. Rose-Marie of the Angels. Adelaide Crapsey. HBV
Little sisters, the birds. Saint Francis to the Birds. Katharine Tynan. SaFP
Little sleeping and much grieving,—the traveller. On the Way to Hang-chow; Anchored on the River at Night. Po Chü-i. TrCh
Little Snail. Hilda Conkling. FaPON; GFA; MPB; PoRh; RAR; TiPo; TVC; TVSH; UTS
Little snail. Snail. Langston Hughes. FaPON; GoSl; TiPo
Little snail, little snail,/ With your hard stony bed. The Snail. *Unknown.* PCH
Little snake now grieves, The. A Spring Serpent. Yvor Winters. ExPo
Little snatch of an ancient song. Of an Old Song. William E. H. Lecky. WGRP
Little snow people are hurrying down, The. Putting the World to Bed. Esther W. Buxton. TVC; TVSH
Little Soldier, The. J. L. Molloy. BlG
Little soldiers thread the hills, The. Small Soldiers with Drum in Large Landscape. Robert Penn Warren. Mexico Is a Foreign Country, IV. FiMAP
Little Son. Georgia Douglas Johnson. CDC; FAOV
Little son looks in the father's face, The. Father. Arthur Vine Hall. FAOV
Little son whom I lift with the wings of my dream. To a Mother. Sophia Mavroidi Papadaky. MoGP
Little Song, A. Robert Grosseteste, *tr. fr. Latin by* William de Shoreham, *mod. vers. by* F. M. Capes. ISi
Little Song, A. Duncan Campbell Scott. VA
Little Song in the Air. Genaro Estrada, *tr. fr. Spanish by* Donald Devenish Walsh. AnCL
Little Song of Life, A. Lizette Woodworth Reese. BrR; FaPON; HBMV; MPB; MW; PC; PoMa; SP; TiPo (1959 ed.)
Little Song of Spring, A. Mary Austin. YeAr
Little Song of Work, A. Sarah Elizabeth Sprouse. BLRP
Little Songs. Marjorie Pickthall. CaP; OCL
Little songs are prettiest. To the Littlest of All. Arthur Guiterman. FAOV
Little songs of summer are all gone today, The. End-of-Summer Poem. Rowena Bastin Bennett. FaPON; SiSoSe
Little Sooth Sermon, A, *in mod. Eng. Unknown.* TMEV
Little Sorrow. "Marian Douglas." SAS; TVC; TVSH
Little soul, like a cloud, like a feather. To His Soul. Emperor Hadrian, *tr. by* Elinor Wylie. LaP
Little soul, little tease, little stray. Animula Blandula Vagula. Emperor Hadrian, *tr. by* Charles Glenn Wallis. LiTW
Little soul scarce fledged for earth, A. A Baby's Death. Swinburne. TCEP; VLEP
Little sound, A. Many a Mickle. Walter de la Mare. GTSE
Little sparrows, The. Pastoral. William Carlos Williams. MOAP
Little Spring. *Unknown.* GFA
Little Spring Flows Clear Again, The. Glenn Ward Dresbach. NP
Little Squirrel, A. *Unknown.* TiPo
Little Star. Jane Taylor. *See* Twinkle, Twinkle, Little Star.
Little Star, The ("Scintillate, scintillate"). *Unknown.* BOHV; InMe
Little stars have five sharp wings. Stars. Carolyn Hancock. RIS
Little Stones of Arlington, The. Barbara Young. OQP; QP-2
Little strokes/ Fell great oaks. Well-packed Wisdom. Benjamin Franklin. *Fr.* Poor Richard's Almanac. StaSt
Little sun, a little rain, A. The Earth and Man. Stopford Augustus Brooke. HBV; OnYI; OTPC; TIP
Little Swirl of Vers Libre, A. Thomas R. Ybarra. BOHV
Little Sycamore, The. *Unknown, tr. fr. the* Turin Papyrus *by* James Baikie. RAR
Little Talk. Aileen Fisher. FaPON
Little Talk wid Jesus Makes It Right, A, *with music. Unknown.* BoAN-2
Little taper set tonight. The Christ [*or* Christmas] Candle. Kate Louise Brown. OTPC (1946 ed.); PoRL; VOD
Little Te Deum of the Commonplace, A, *sels.* John Oxenham.
"For all the wonders of this wondrous world." PGD; PSO
"With hearts responsive." TrPWD
Little Tee-wee. *Unknown.* OxNR
Little Testament, The. Villon. *See* Petit Testament, Le.
Little thatched house I was born in, The. Sergei Yesenin, *tr. fr. Russian by* R. M. Hewitt. BoRS
Little Theocritus. Caroline Wilder Paradise. AA
Little thing, ah, little mouse. To Christina at Nightfall. Ford Madox Ford. GTML
Little Things. Julia A. Fletcher Carney, *wr. at. to* E. C. Brewer *and to* Frances S. Osgood. FaBoBe; FaFP; GoTP; HBV; HBVY; NeHB, *2 sts.;* OnHT; OTPC; TreF, *2 sts.*
(Kind Deeds.) BoTP
("Little drops of water.") FaPON, *2 sts.;* GFA, *st. 1;* PECK
Little Things, The. Gerald Gould. GTML
Little Things, The. Elizabeth Isler. PoToHe (new ed.)
Little Things. Orrick Johns. AnAmPo; LA; MAP; NLK; NP; NV; PG (1945 ed.); PoToHe (new ed.); SBMV
Little Things. Eileen Mathias. BoTP
Little Things. Helen Rowland. DDA

Little Things. James Stephens. AnEnPo; ChMo; CMP; FaPON; HBMV; MBP; MoBrPo; MPB; NeMA; PoeMoYo; SiSoSe; TiPo (1959 ed.); UTS
Little Things. Marion Strobel. HBMV; NP
Little Things ("It's just the little homely things"). *Unknown.* PoToHe (new ed.)
Little Things of Life, The ("The little things of life are all so sweet"). *Unknown.* BTP
Little Things That Happen, The. Marjorie Wilson. BoTP
Little things, that run, and quail. Little Things. James Stephens. AnEnPo; ChMo; CMP; FaPON; HBMV; MBP; MoBrPo; MPB; NeMA; PoeMoYo; SiSoSe; TiPo (1959 ed.); UTS
Little things, the little restless things, The. The Little Things. Gerald Gould. GTML
Little thinkest thou, poor flower. *See* Little think'st thou, poor flower.
Little thinks, in the field, yon red-cloaked clown. Each and All. Emerson. AA; AmP; AmPo; AmPP; AnNE; AWP; CoBA; CoV; HBV; HiLiAm; IAP; LPS-2; MCCG; MOAP; NePA; OBAV; OHFP; OQP; OxBA; QP-2; REAL; WGRP
Little think'st [*or* thinkest] thou, poor [*or* poore] flower. The Blossom[e]. John Donne. AWP; ElSeCe; EV-2; InPo; LiTB; MeLP; OBS; SeEP; UnPo (1st ed.)
Little tigers are at rest, The. Tom Hood. CenHV
Little Tillie Turtle. Road Fellows. Barbara Young. BrR
Little time for laughter, A. After. Philip Bourke Marston. HBV
Little Toil of Love, The. Emily Dickinson. *See* I had no time to hate, because.
Little Tom Tittlemouse,/ Lived in a bell-house. *Unknown.* OxNR
Little Tommy Tacket. *Unknown.* OxNR
Little Tommy Tiddler. Paul Edmonds. BoTP
Little Tommy Tittlemouse/ Lived in a little house. *Unknown.* OxNR
Little Tommy Tucker/ Sings for his supper. Mother Goose. HBVY; OTPC; OxNR; PCH; PPL; RIS; SAS
Little tongue of red-brown flame. On the Hearth-Rug. Mary Elizabeth Coleridge. CBE
Little too abstract, a little too wise, A. Return. Robinson Jeffers. GoYe
Little Tower, The. William Morris. POTT
Little Town. Federico García Lorca, *tr. fr. Spanish by* Eleanor L. Turnbull. CoSP; OnPM
Little Town, The. Clinton Scollard. SDH
(Bethlehem.) MaRV
Little Towns, The. Irene Mary Davidson. HiLiAm
Little toy dog is covered with dust, The. Little Boy Blue. Eugene Field. AA; BAP; BeLS; BTP; CP; FaFP; FaPON; HBV; HBVY; IAP; LBAP; LEAP; LiTG; MAP; McAmPo (1942 ed.); MotAn; NeHB; NeMA; OBAV; OHFP; OnHT; PC; PCD; PFE; PIR; PoeMoYo; PTA-1; PYM; TreF; VOD
Little Toy Land of the Dutch, The. *Unknown.* GFA; MPB; OTPC (1946 ed.)
Little Tramp Dog. Rena Manning. AIBD
Little Trotty Wagtail. John Clare. BoTP; FaPON; PCH; RIS; UnPo (3d ed.); WP
Little Tumescence, A. Jonathan Williams. NeAP
Little Turtle, The. Vachel Lindsay. BoChLi; FaPON; GFA; GoBP; MeMeAg; PCH; RAR; StVeCh; SUS; TiPo; UTS
Little unpretentious country church, The. The Country Churches. Maysie Tulie Klein. DDA
Little Vagabond, The. Blake. BOHV; CEP; EM-1; SeCeV
Little Valentine, A. Elizabeth Winton. PCH
Little virgin is like unto a rose, A. Ariosto. *Fr.* Orlando Furioso, I. LyPI
Little waves, happy waves. Seaside Nursery Song. "M. La T." BOL
Little Waves of Breffny, The. Eva Gore-Booth. AnIV; CP; HBV; HBVY; LBBV; OnYI; POT; PoTo; TVSH; YT
(Waves of Breffny, The.) BMEP; MBP; NLK; StaSt; TSW; TSWC
Little Way, A. Frank L. Stanton. AA; LBAP; OBAV
Little way below her chin, A. On Some Buttercups. Frank Dempster Sherman. AA
Little way, more soft and sweet, A. First Footsteps. Swinburne. EmBrPo; GrCo-1; NeHB
Little way to walk with you, my own, A. A Little Way. Frank L. Stanton. AA; LBAP; OBAV
Little, Wee Froggies, The. J. K. Nutting. *Fr.* How the Froggies Go to Sleep. SAS
Little While, A. Horatius Bonar. *See* Beyond the Smiling and the Weeping.
Little While, A. Emily Brontë. *See* Little While, a Little While, A.
Little While, A. Don Marquis. HBV
Little While, A. Dante Gabriel Rossetti. VA; ViBoPo; VLEP
Little While, a Little While, A. Emily Brontë. GTML; OAEP; OxBI; ViBoPo
(Little While, A.) EnLi-2 (1949 ed.); TreFS
(Stanzas: Little While, a Little While, A.) GTIV
(Weary Task, The.) EmBrPo
"There is a spot, 'mid barren hills," *sel.* EnSW
Little While I Fain Would Linger Yet, A ("A little while. my life is almost set!"). Paul Hamilton Hayne. AA; BLP; HBV; IAP; LBAP; LEAP; OBAV; PoeMoYo; SPP; TCAP
Little while my love and I, A. A May Song. "Violet Fane." DiM; OBVV; VA
Little while the tears and laughter, A. A Little While. Don Marquis. HBV
Little While to Love and Rave, A. Samuel Hoffenstein. ALV
Little Whistler, The. Frances Frost. StVeCh (1955 ed.); TiPo
Little White Cat, The. *Unknown, tr. fr. Modern Irish by* Mrs. Costello of Tuam. OnYI
Little white clouds are racing over the sky, The. Magdalen Walks. Oscar Wilde. MBP; MoBrPo; YT
Little white face that looks into mine. Metempsychosis. Luella C. Poole. CIV
Little white feathers. Snowflakes. Mary Mapes Dodge. MPB
Little White Fox. David Rowbotham. BoAV
Little white horses are out on the sea. White Horses. Winifred Howard. BrR; SUS; UTS
Little White Lily. George Macdonald. CG; HBV; HBVY; MPB; OTPC; PECK; PRWS; SAS
Little white mermaidens live in the sea, The. The Mermaidens. Laura E. Richards. BrR; StVeCh (1955 ed.)
Little white prayers, The. Cologne Cathedral. Frances Shaw. NP
Little white snowdrop just waking up. Waiting to Grow. Frank French. PEDC
Little Wild Baby. "Margaret Vandegrift." AA; HBV
Little wild bird sometimes at my ear, A. Ballata: Of True and False Singing. *Unknown.* AWP; OnPM; UnS
Little wild birds have come flying, The. Love-Song. *Unknown.* AWP
Little Willie ("Little Willie from his mirror"). *Unknown.* MoShBr
("Little Willie from his mirror.") GoTP; WhC
Little Willie ("Little Willie hung his sister"). *Unknown.* NA; TreFS
Little Willie ("Willie saw some dynamite"). *Unknown.* FaPON
Little Willie, in the best of sashes. Tender-Heartedness. Harry Graham. ALV; NA
Little Willie's Hearing. *Unknown.* FAOV; PTA-2
Little Willie's My Darlin', *with music. Unknown.* OuSiCo
Little Wind. Kate Greenaway. GFA; GoBP; SUS
("Little wind, blow on the hill-top.") TiPo
Little window-garden plot, A. Memorial Day. Margaret Sidney. PEOR
Little winter cottontails. The Outdoor Christmas Tree. Aileen Fisher. SiSoSe
Little Woodland God. Judy Van der Veer. MuM
Little Words, The. Edith Daley. BAP
Little Words. Benjamin Keech. PoToHe
Little words that wear silk dresses. The Words. Opal Whiteley. TSW; TSWC
Little Work, A. George Du Maurier. *Fr.* Trilby, Pt. VIII. FaBoBe; HBV; NeHB; OQP; QP-2
(Little, A.) MaRV
(Little Work, a Little Play, A.) PoToHe (new ed.); TreFS
Little world of olden days is gone, The. In an Age of Science. Thomas Curtis Clark. MaRV
Little yellow buttercup, A. A Buttercup. *Unknown.* BoTP
Little yellow flame of fur. To a Kitten. Martha Haskell Clark. CIV
Little you think, my lovely friend. Walter Savage Landor. ERP
Little Young Lambs, The. Patrick Chalmers. TiPo (1952 ed.)
Little young lambs, oh! why do you stay. The Wolf and the Lambs. Ivy O. Eastwick. BoTP
Littles. Robert Herrick. *See* Ternarie of Littles, A.
Littlest door, the inner door, The. The Door. Mary Carolyn Davies. HBMV; PC
Littlewit and Loftus. Pamelia Vining Yule. BoCaPo (1943 ed.)
Liturgy of My Legs. "Pablo Neruda," *tr. fr. Spanish by* Dudley Fitts. AnCL
Live a-Humble, *with music. Unknown.* SoAF
Live-a humble, humble, Lord. Humble Yo'self de Bell Done Ring. *Unknown.* BoAN-2
Live all thy sweet life through. A Summer Wish. Christina Rossetti. BPN
Live and Help Live. Edwin Markham. MaRV; OQP; QP-1
Live and Love. Elizabeth Barrett Browning. *Fr.* A Drama of Exile. OQP; QP-2
Live as you like, long as you like, secure. For Haroun Al Raschid. Abu'l-Atahija. LiTW
Live Blindly. Trumbull Stickney. AnAmPo; AnFE; APA; CoAnAm; LA; LBMV; LiTA; NePA; TwAmPo
(Live Blindly and upon the Hour.) MAP; MoAmPo (1942 ed.); MOAP; PeBoSo; TrGrPo
Live Christ. John Oxenham. BLRP; ChIP; OQP; QP-1
Live Each Day. Goethe, *tr. fr. German.* OQP; QP-1

Live ever here, Lorenzo?—shocking thought! Edward Young. *Fr.* Night Thoughts. EnRP
Live here, great heart; and love and dy [*or* die] and kill. Upon the Book and Picture of the Seraphicall Saint Teresa. Richard Crashaw. *Fr.* The Flaming Heart. AtBAP; OBS; RiBV
Live in a Love. Robert Browning. TrGrPo
Live in the Present. Sarah Knowles Bolton. OQP; QP-1 (Live Today.) MaRV
Live in these conquering leaves; live all the same. Richard Crashaw. *Fr.* The Flaming Heart. EV-2; LiA
Live Joyfully. Ecclesiastes, IX: 7-11, Bible, *O.T.* TreFS
"Live like the wind," he said, "unfettered." The Wind Bloweth Where It Listeth. Countee Cullen. NP
Live, live with me, and thou shalt see. To Phyllis [to Love and Live with Him]. Robert Herrick. AnEnPo; EPS (1942 ed.); LiTL; OAEP; ReaPo
Live long, Elisa, that the wolf of Spain. Ad Reginam Elizabetham. Thomas Bastard. SiCE
Live man victorious, The. The Victor. Theodosia Garrison. UnW
Live on? But forty years, I'm twenty now. For Fifty Years. Arthur C. Coe. CAG
Live, prince of poets! Thy affections guide. Ad Gulielmum Warner. John Weever. ReIE
Live so that you. Certain Maxims of Archy. Don Marquis. InMe
Live, Spenser, ever in thy *Faerie Queene* [*or Fairy Queene*]. A Remembrance of Some English Poets. Richard Barnfield. ReIE; SiCE; TuPP
Live thy life/ Young and old. The Oak. Tennyson. BPN; EmBrPo; EPN; FaPON; MPB; PoVP; YT
Live Today. Sarah Knowles Bolton. *See* Live in the Present.
Live, trifling incidents, and grace my songs. Robert Bloomfield. *Fr.* The Farmer's Boy. OBRV
Live unlamenting though obscure remaining. To J. S. Collis. Ruth Pitter. OxBoCh
Live While You Live. Philip Doddridge. OxBoCh (Dum Vivimus, Vivamus.) OBEC
Live with me; be my wife. The Passionate Clerk to His Love. Ronald McCuaig. MoAuPo
Live with Me Still. Thomas Dekker *and* John Ford. *Fr.* The Sun's Darling. EV-2; SeCL
Live You by Love Confined. C. Day Lewis. ChMo; LO; MoP
Lived on one's back. Vigil. W. E. Henley. *Fr.* In Hospital. LoBV; POTT
Lively sparks that issue from those eyes, The. The Lover Describeth His Being Striken with Sight of His Love. Sir Thomas Wyatt. ReIE
Lively young turtle lived down by the banks, A. The Turtle and Flamingo [*or* The Song of the Turtle and Flamingo]. James T. Fields. BOHV; GN; HBV
Lives. Henry Reed. LiTB
Lives. Arthur Rimbaud, *tr. fr. French by* Angel Flores. AnFP
Lives in winter. Mother Goose. HBV; TiPo
Lives of Great Men. *Unknown.* FaFP
Lives of Great Men All Remind Us. Longfellow. *Fr.* A Psalm of Life. DD
Lives of great men all remind us/ As their pages o'er we turn. Lives of Great Men. *Unknown.* FaFP
Lives of Gulls and Children, The. Howard Nemerov. FiMAP; NePoEA
Lives of many men are, The. To Wei Pa, a Retired Scholar. Tu Fu. OnPC
Lives there a man with soul so dead. Whatever Is, Is Right. Laman Blanchard. BOHV
Livid sky on London, A. The Old Song. G. K. Chesterton. FaBoTw
Living. Harold Monro. ChMo; CMP; FaBoMo; LiTB; LiTM; SeCePo
Living. D. S. Savage. NeBP
Living. *Unknown.* BLPA; FaBoBe; NeHB; TreFS
Living Book, The. Charlotte Fiske Bates. AA
Living Bread. Eva Weaver Sefton. BePJ
Living Chalice, The. Susan Mitchell. HBMV
Living Christ, The. Toyohiko Kagawa, *tr. fr. Japanese by* Lois J. Erickson. SoLD
"Living Dog" and "The Dead Lion," The. Thomas Moore. OBRV
Living Flame of Love, The. St. John of the Cross, *tr. fr. Spanish by* E. Allison Peers. LiTW; TeCS (O Flame of Living Love, *tr. by* Arthur Symons.) AnSpL-1; AWP; CAW
Living, giant, all, in, little, pieces, A. Poem. José Garcia Villa. MeRV
Living God, The. Daniel ben Judah, *tr. fr. Hebrew by* Israel Zangwill. TrJP (Magnified Be the Living God, *tr. by* Simeon Singer.) GrCo-2
Living God, The. Charlotte Perkins Gilman. WGRP
Living God, The. Abraham ibn Ezra, *tr. fr. Hebrew by* Alice Lucas. TrJP
Living God, The. Oracle of Serapis, *tr. fr. Greek by* T. F. Higham. OxBG
Living God O magnify and bless, The. The Living God. Daniel ben Judah. TrJP
Living in a wide landscape are the flowers. Desert Flowers. Keith Douglas. FaBoTw
Living in Missouri wuz a bold, bad man. Jesse James (B *vers.*). *Unknown.* ABF
Living in retirement beyond the World. The Valley Wind. Lu Yün. OnPM; TrCh
Living in Sin. Adrienne Cecile Rich. NePoEA
Living in the Country. Tao Yuan-ming, *tr. fr. Chinese by* Yang Chi-sing. WhP
Living Juliet, The. Shakespeare. *See* He Jests at Scars . . .
Living Lustres, The. Horace Smith. EV-4
Living Memory, A. William Augustus Croffut. AA
Living Sacrifice, A. Romans, XII, Bible, *N.T. Tr. by* Edgar J. Goodspeed. GrCo-1
Living sacrifice, the pyre, The. A Fire Shall Burn before Him. Benjamin Francis Musser. PraNu
Living Temple, The. Oliver Wendell Holmes. *Fr.* The Autocrat of the Breakfast Table, *ch.* 7. AmPP (3d ed.)
Living Tithe, The Mabel Munns Charles. ChIP
Living unto Thee. John Ellerton. MaRV (God of the Living.) WGRP
Living Water. Ruth M. Williams. BePJ
Living water should be cooked. Boiling Tea. Su T'ung-po. WhP
Living Waters. Caroline S. Spencer. LPS-3
Liz-Town Humorist, A. James Whitcomb Riley. IHA
Liza, go steep your long white hands. Spring Pastoral. Elinor Wylie. AnEnPo
Liza in the Summer Time, *with music.* *Unknown.* AS
Liza Jane, *with music.* *Unknown.* ABF, *with add. sts.*; AS (Mountain Top, *diff. vers., with music.*) AS; SoAF
Liza Lee, *with music.* *Unknown.* SoAmSa
Lizabetta [*or* Lisabetta], Marianina, Fiametta, Teresina. The Flower Factory. Florence Wilkinson Evans. GrCo-1; HiLiAm
Lizard, The. Abbie Farwell Brown. UTS
Lizard. K. E. Ingram. PoNe
Lizard. Agnes Maxwell-Hall. PoNe
Lizard Head, star-thirsty stone. To Lizard Head. Clifford J. Laube. CAW
Lizard, lover of heat, of high. The Old Man to the Lizard. Archibald MacLeish. CoV
Lizie Lindsay (A *and* B *vers.*). *Unknown.* ESPB (Leezie Lindsay.) FaBoCh; LoGBV (Lizzy Lindsay.) EBSV
Lizie Wan. *Unknown.* BaBo (A *and* B *vers.*); ESPB; ViBoFo
Lizzie Borden. *Unknown.* BOHV; TreFS (Crimes of Lizzie Borden, The.) FaFP; LiTM; SiTL ("Lizzie Borden took an axe.") CenHV
Lizzie's Sister. *Unknown.* SiTL
Lizzy Liberty, *abr.* John Skinner. PoFr
Lizzy Lindsay. *Unknown.* *See* Lizie Lindsay.
Llama, The. Hilaire Belloc. BOHV; FaBoCh; FiBHP; LoGBV
Llano Estacado, The. *Unknown.* *See* Tantalus; Texas.
Llewellyn and the Tree. E. A. Robinson. BeLS; HBMV; TwP
Llewelyn's Chariot. Vernon Watkins. MoWP
Llyn-y-Dreiddiad-Vrawd; the Pool of the Diving Friar. Thomas Love Peacock. *Fr.* Crotchet Castle, *ch.* 16. KN
Llyric of the Llama, A. Burges Johnson. LauV
Lo! above the mournful chanting. Kol Nidra. Joseph Leiser. *Fr.* The Day of Atonement. AA; TrJP
Lo! all in Silence, all in Order stand. Books. George Crabbe. *Fr.* The Library. EV-3; OBEC
Lo! all thy glory gone! Nekros. John Banister Tabb. AmP
Lo, amidst London I lift thee. Mother and Son. William Morris. GTML
Lo! an old song, yellow with centuries! Love, Weeping, Laid This Song. Lizette Woodworth Reese. LS
Lo, as a careful housewife runs to catch. Sonnets, CXLIII. Shakespeare. OAEP; PeBoSo; ReEn
Lo, as a dove when up she springs. In Memoriam A. H. H., XII. Tennyson. EmBrPo; EnLi-2; EPN; GEPC; LoBV; ViPo; VLEP
Lo, as some bard on isles of the Aegean. The Inner Light. Frederic William Henry Myers. *Fr.* Saint Paul. MaRV; VA
Lo! as some venturer, from his stars receiving. Advent. Frederic William Henry Myers. *Fr.* Saint Paul. ChIP; MaRV; PGD
Lo! as the Potter Mouldeth. *Unknown, tr. fr. Hebrew by* Elsie Davis. TrJP
Lo, as the sun from his ocean bed rising. There She Blows! *Unknown.* EtS; SoAmSa
Lo, as the thrushes' throats. Lyric. Al-Barraq. MooP
Lo at last the poor little beetle also attains to the word. The Beetle. Vicente Aleixandre. CoSP
Lo, Collin, here the place whose pleasaunt syte. June. Spenser. *Fr.* The Shepheardes Calender. EnLit
"Lo, Death has come for thee." Colloquy. Al-Munsafi. MooP

Lo! Death has reared himself a throne. The City in the Sea. Poe. AA; AmP; AmPo; AmPP; AnAmPo; AnEnPo; AnFE; APA; APW; BAP; BLV; BoLiVe; CaAE; CBOV; CoAnAm; CoBA; CoV; FaBoEn; GTBS-D; HBV; IAP; LEAP; LiTA; MOAP; NePA; OBAV; OBRV; OnAP; OxBA; PoE; PoEL-4; PoFS; ReaPo; RiBV; RO; SPP; TCAP; TrGrPo; ViBoPo; WHA

Lo, fainter now lie spread the shades of night. Morning Hymn. Gregory the Great. CAW; WGRP

Lo, from our loitering ship a new land at last to be seen. Iceland First Seen. William Morris. BPN; EmBrPo; PoVP; ViP; VLEP

Lo! from the Livid East. James Thomson. *Fr.* The Seasons: Winter. AtBAP
("Lo! from the livid East, or piercing North.") FaBoEn

Lo! from the woodland skirting the old town. Autumn. Thomas Caulfield Irwin. IrPN

Lo, God, our God, has come! Bless the Blessed Morn. Horatius Bonar. BePJ

Lo, had begun again for her the time. William Ellery Leonard. *Fr.* Two Lives. AnEnPo

Lo, Helen came from her chamber fragrant, high-vaulted of old. Homer. *Fr.* The Odyssey, IV. GrPo

Lo here a little volume, but great [*or* large] book! On a Prayer Book Sent to Mrs. M. R. [*or* Prayer]. Richard Crashaw. BCEP; BrBE; HBV; MeRV; SeEP

Lo, here I am all prepared. Invitation to Death. Emilio Prados. CoSP

Lo, here is fellowschippe. To Vida D. Scudder. Florence Converse. BoFr

Lo, here is God, and there is God! The New Sinai. Arthur Hugh Clough. BPN; PoVP; ViPo; VLEP

Lo! Here the Gentle Lark. Shakespeare. *Fr.* Venus and Adonis. ChTr

Lo, here the impost of a faith entire. To Delia, LVII. Samuel Daniel. TuPP

Lo, here the state of every mortal wight. Respice Finem. Thomas Proctor. OBSC; ReIE; SiCE; TuPP

Lo! here we come a-reaping. George Peele. *Fr.* The Old Wives' Tale. BLV; OBSC

Lo, how have Apollo's bay-boughs shaken stormily! To Apollo. Callimachus. GrL

Lo, how I seek and sue to have. Sir Thomas Wyatt. SiPS

Lo! how the lark soars upward and is gone. The Death of Leander. Thomas Hood. *Fr.* Hero and Leander. EnRP

Lo how the messenger-eagle on high. On Wings of Song. Bacchylides. GrR

Lo, how the terraced towers, and monstrous round. No Single Thing Abides. Lucretius. *Fr.* De Rerum Natura. AWP; JAWP; PG (1945 ed.); WBP

Lo, I, a maiden knight. Petition of Youth before Battle. John Bunker. CAW

Lo, I am black, but I am comely too. The Dark Brother. Lewis Alexander. CDC

Lo! I am Death! With aim as sure as steady. *Unknown.* *Fr.* The Dance of Death. AnSpL-1

"Lo! I am Saul." Charles Heavysege. *Fr.* Saul. BoCaPo

Lo, I Am Stricken Dumb. *Unknown, tr. fr. Hebrew by* Theodor H. Gaster. *Fr.* The Dead Sea Scrolls. TrJP

Lo, I am weary of all. A Cry. Herbert Edwin Clarke. VA

Lo, I Am with You Always. John Charles Earle. ChIP; MaRV; OQP; QP-1

Lo, I Am with You Always. Martha Snell Nicholson. BePJ

Lo, I beheld Maurus. On Maurus the Rhetor. Palladas of Alexandria. LiTW

Lo, I have given thee plumes wherewith to skim. To Cyrnus. Theognis. GrPo; GrR

Lo! I have learned of the loveliest of lands. *Unknown.* *Fr.* The Phoenix. AnOE

Lo, I have opened unto you the wide gates of my being. Psalm to My Beloved [*or* Fulfillment]. Eunice Tietjens. LoPS; PoToHe (new ed.)

Lo! I must tell a tale of chivalry. Specimen of an Induction to a Poem. Keats. EmBrPo; ERP

Lo, I shall tell you the truest of visions. The Dream of the Rood. *Unknown, at. to* Cynewulf. EnLi-1; OuHeWo

Lo! I sing cheerily. Opening Poem. Boethius. *Fr.* Consolation of Philosophy. LaP

Lo! I, the man whose Muse whylome did maske. The Legend of the Knight of the Red Crosse, or of Holinesse. Spenser. *Fr.* The Faerie Queene, I. BEL; EM-1; EnLi-1; EnLit; FiP; GEPC; OAEP; REAL; TCEP; TOP

Lo! I will tell tne dearest of dreams. A Dream of the Rood. *Unknown, at. to* Cynewulf. AnOE

Lo, if some pen should write upon your rafter. The Inner Light. Frederic William Henry Myers. BMEP; HBV; LEAP; WGRP

Lo, in a thousand citadels. Stacking the Needles. Theda Kenyon. AOAH

Lo! in the mute, mid wilderness. The Unicorn. George Darley. *Fr.* Nepenthe. ChTr; FaBoEn; NBE; OBRV; PoEL-4

Lo, in the orient when the gracious light. Sonnets, VII. Shakespeare. PeBoSo; ReIE; SiCE

Lo! in the painted oriel of the West. The Evening Star. Longfellow. AnNE

Lo, in the sanctuaried East. Orient Ode. Francis Thompson. CoBE

Lo! in the vigils of the night, ere sped. In Whom We Live and Have Our Being. James Rhoades. MaRV

Lo, in the west. Slumber Song. John Banister Tabb. BOL

Lo! in this unlovely shell. The Chrysalis. John James Piatt. InP

"Lo, it is I, be not afraid!" James Russell Lowell. *Fr.* The Vision of Sir Launfal. OQP; QP-1; TreF

Lo, Joseph dreams his dream again. The League of Nations. Mary Siegrist. MC; PAH

Lo, ladies, here (if you can use it well). Epilogus. George Whetstone. TuPP

Lo! Leman Sweet. *Unknown.* CoBE

Lo, Lord, Thou ridest! The Hurricane. Hart Crane. AmP; ChMo; CoBMV; MoAB; MoAmPo; OxBA

Lo, Love again with glancing eyes. Love. Ibycus. OxBG

Lo, Love's obeyed by all. 'Tis right. The Impossibility. Coventry Patmore. *Fr.* The Angel in the House. PoVP

Lo! Mid the splendor of eternal spaces. Resurrection. Angela Morgan. OQP; QP-1

Lo, my prophetic dreams are very truth at last. On the Emperor's Departure, December 7, 1812. Gavril Derzhavin. TrRV

Lo, now he shineth yonder. Lament. Hugh Holland. PoD

Lo now I bid ye, my merry men all. Lovel and John. *Unknown.* BoDaBa

Lo, now to a song thy heart incline. The Eagle of Song. Bacchylides. OxBG

Lo, praise of the prowess of people-kings. Beowulf. *Unknown.* BEL

Lo Que Digo, *with music. Unknown, tr. fr. Spanish.* AS

Lo, quhat it is to love. *See* Lo, what it is to love.

Lo, she cometh to us from afar. Assumpta Est Maria. Liam Brophy. ISi

Lo, soul, seest thou not God's purpose from the first? Brotherhood. Walt Whitman. *Fr.* Passage to India. MW

Lo! sun and moon, these minister for aye. Israel's Duration. Judah Halevi. TrJP

Lo, that doves. A Song for Souls under Fire. Mark Turbyfill. NP

Lo the bat with leathern wing. Doctor Johnson. Blake. *Fr.* An Island in the Moon. RO

Lo, the copse unbosoms. Treachery. Ibn Khafaja. MooP

Lo, the Day-Spring, brightest Angel. Prayer to Christ Our Lord. Cynewulf. PoLi

Lo! the foolish fell. Killing. Samuel Greenberg. LiTA

Lo, the Lilies of the Field. Reginald Heber. *See* Providence.

Lo, the moon's self! Phases of the Moon. Robert Browning. *Fr.* One Word More. ChTr

Lo, the Poor Indian. Pope. *Fr.* An Essay on Man, Epistle I. TreFS

Lo! the Southland Queen, emerging. Pro Memoria. Ina M. Porter. BlG

Lo! the unbounded sea! The Ship Starting. Walt Whitman. MOAP

Lo, the Winter Is Past. Song of Solomon, Bible, *O.T.* *See* For, Lo, the Winter Is Past.

Lo! there he lies, our Patriarch Poet, dead! Bryant Dead. Paul Hamilton Hayne. DD; GA

Lo, there the hermit of the waste. The Heron. Mary Howitt. TVSH

Lo, these are they that move 'twixt land and sky. Fields of Soria, IV. Antonio Machado. AnSpL-2; TeCS

Lo, thou, my Love, art fair. Christ to His Spouse [*or* The Beloved to the Spouse]. William Baldwin. ElL; OBSC; OxBoCh

Lo, thou the glory of the great earth. A Maiden Ring-adorned. Cynewulf. *Fr.* Christ. PoLi

Lo! through a shadowy valley. The Funeral of Time. Henry Beck Hirst. AA; APW

Lo, thus, as prostrate, "In the dust I write." The City of Dreadful Night. James Thomson. DaM; EmBrPo; EnLit; GoTS; OAEP; POTT; PoVP; ViBoPo; ViP; VLEP

Lo! 'tis a gala night. The Conqueror Worm. Poe. *Fr.* Ligeia. AA; AmP; AmPP; AnAmPo; AnFE; APA; AWP; BAV; CoAnAm; CoBA; HBV; IAP; InPo; LA; LiTA; MOAP; PIAE; SPP; TCAP

Lo—to the battle-ground of life. On the Birth of a Child. Louis Untermeyer. CP; NeMA

Lo, Victress on the Peaks. Walt Whitman. CoV

Lo, we have heard of the fame in old time. Beowulf. *Unknown, tr. by* Benjamin Thoye. TCEP

Lo, we have heard of the glory in days of old of the Spear-Danes. Beowulf. *Unknown, tr. by* Albert C. Baugh. EnLit

Lo! we have learned of the glory of the kings who ruled the Spear-Danes. Beowulf. *Unknown, tr. by* C. B. Tinker. EnL; OuHeWo; TOP

"Lo, We Have Left All." Henry Francis Lyte. VA
Lo, what a golden day it is! Thorgerda. John Payne. VA
Lo! what [*or* quhat] it is to love. A Rondel of Love. Alexander Scott. BSV; EBSV; OBEV
Lo, what wonders the day hath brought. Snow. Elizabeth Akers Allen. HBV; SN
Lo, when back mine eye. Thomas Campion. SiCE
Lo, when the Lord made North and South. The Rose of the World. Coventry Patmore. *Fr.* The Angel in the House. HBV; LPS-2
Lo, when we wade the tangled wood. Drawing near the Light. William Morris. BPN
Lo, where enviousness and lies. Lines on the Wall of His Prison Cell. Luis de León, *tr. by* Thomas Walsh. CAW
Lo, where envy and where lies. Written on the Walls of His Dungeon. Luis de León, *tr. by* Thomas Walsh. OnPM; TrJP
Lo, where he loometh, a hulk elephantine. Government Official. Paul Dehn. WaP
Lo [*or* Loe]! where she comes along with portly pace. The Bride. Spenser. *Fr.* Epithalamion. LPS-1
Lo! where the four mimosas blend their shade. For an Epitaph at Fiesole [*or* His Epitaph]. Walter Savage Landor. BPN; OBRV; OBVV; TOP; VA
Lo! where the rosy-bosom'd Hours. Ode on the Spring [*or* Spring]. Thomas Gray. BrBE; CEP; EV-3; GTBS; GTBS-D; GTBS-W; GTSE; GTSL; HBV; LPS-2
Lo, Who Could Stand. *Unknown, tr. fr. Hebrew by* Israel Zangwill. TrJP
Lo! yon phantom army marching across Heaven. Indian Night Tableau. Hyman Edelstein. CaP
Load. John Hewitt. OnYI
Load of brushes and baskets and cradles and chairs, A. No Buyers; a Street Scene. Thomas Hardy. LiTB
Load of hay! *Unknown.* RIS
Load of Sugar Cane, The. Wallace Stevens. NP
Loaded Ass, The. Bhartrihari, *tr. fr. Sanskrit by* Paul Elmer More. OnPM
Loaded with gallant soldiers. Ready. Phoebe Cary. PAH; PAP
Loadstone of His Love, The. Charles Wesley. BePJ
Loam. Carl Sandburg. ChMo; CMP; NV; SBMV; TwCV
Loan of a Stall, The. James L. Duff. ISi
Loathing both seas of Life and Death. Upland of Nirvana. *Unknown.* OnPM
Loathsome mask has fallen, the man remains, The. The End of Tyranny. Shelley. *Fr.* Prometheus Unbound. ShBV-3
Lob. Edward Thomas. MoVE
Lob Lie-by-the Fire. Walter de la Mare. CV
Lobster, The. "Lewis Carroll." *See* Voice of the Lobster, The.
Lobster, The. *Unknown.* GoTP
Lobster and the Maid, The. Frederic Edward Weatherly. OTPC
Lobster Quadrille, The. "Lewis Carroll." *Fr.* Alice's Adventures in Wonderland, *ch.* 10. BoChLi; BoTP; FaPON; MoShBr; OTPC (1946 ed.); PA; PCD; PCH; PRWS; RAR; RIS; SAS; StVeCh; UTS
(Mock Turtle's Song, The.) ChTr; MPB (1956 ed.); PoVP
(Quadrille, A.) EnLi-2
(Whiting and the Snail, The.) HBV; HBVY
("'Will you walk a little faster?' said a whiting to a snail.") TiPo (1952 ed.)
Local I'll bright my tale on, how. The Children of Greenock. W. S. Graham. FaBoTw
Local Train of Thought, A. Siegfried Sassoon. AtBAP
Localities. Carl Sandburg. Po
Locate your love, you lose your love. To No One in Particular. Witter Bynner. PR
Loch Achray was a clipper tall, The. The Yarn of the *Loch Achray.* John Masefield. CV; InP; SeCeV; StPo
Loch Lomond. *Unknown, at. to* Lady John Scott. *See* Bonnie Banks o' Loch Lomond, The.
Lochaber No More. Allan Ramsay. EBSV; HBV; LPS-1
Lochiel's Warning. Thomas Campbell. EnRP; ERP; EV-4; LPS-2
Lochinvar. Sir Walter Scott. *Fr.* Marmion, V. ATP; BBV; BCEP; BEL; BeLS; BHV; BoChLi; BoTP; BSV; CBOV; CBPC; CoBE; EBSV; EmBrPo; EnLi-2 (1949 ed.); EnLit; EnRP; EPN; ERP; EV-4; FaBoBe; FaFP; FaPON; GN; GoTP; GoTS; HBV; HiLiEn; InP; LH; LoEn; LoPo; LPS-1; MaC; MCCG; MW; NeHB; OAEP; OBRV; OnHT; OnSP; OtMeF; OTPC; PCD; PECK; PFE; PIAE; PIR; PoE; PoRA; PYM; ShBV-1; StPo; StVeCh; TCEP; TOP; TreF; TVSH; WHA
(Lady Heron's Song.) CaAE
(Young Lochinvar.) CG; HBVY; RG
Lochmaben Harper, The. *Unknown.* BaBo; ESPB; OBB, *sl. diff. vers.*
Lochnagar cam frae the west. Katharine Jaffray (B *vers.*). *Unknown.* ViBoFo
Lock and form had first to burst. Form Is Delight. Ernst Stadler. OnPM
Lock the dairy door. *Unknown.* OxNR
Lock the Door, Lariston. James Hogg. BSV; EBSV; GoTS; MuP; TVSH
Lock up, fair lids, the treasure of my heart. Sleep [*or* Sonnet]. Sir Philip Sidney. *Fr.* Arcadia. EG; ElL; OBSC; SiCE; SiPS
Lock up thy heart within thy breast alway. Volto Sciolto e Pensieri Stretti. James Clarence Mangan. IrPN
Lock your bedroom doors with terror. Admonition. John Peale Bishop. TwAmPo
Locked arm in arm they cross the way. Tableau. Countee Cullen. BANP; TCPD
Locked in the stillness of this mighty wheel. New Dynamo. Gerald Raftery. PoMa
Lockless Door, The. Robert Frost. PoLFOT
Locks and Bolts, *with music. Unknown.* TrAS
(I Dreamed Last Night of My True Love, *with music.*) AS
Locks between her chamber and his will, The. Midnight. Shakespeare. *Fr.* The Rape of Lucrece. OBSC; SiCE
Locksley Hall. Tennyson. ATP (1935 ed.); BEL; BMEP; BPN; EM-2; EmBrPo; EnL; EnLi-2; EnLit; EPN; EPP; FaBoBe; FaFP; GEPC; HBV; LiTG; LPS-1; OAEP; PIAE; PIR; PoVP; REAL; TCEP; TOP; ViPo; ViPP; VLEP; WHA
Sels.
Federation of the World, The, *abr.* MaRV
"For I dipped into the future, far as human eye could see." PGD; PYM
(Federation of the World.) PoRL
(Poet's Prophecy, A.) PTA-1
(Prophecy.) CBE; GTBS-W; TreF; WBLP
(Universal Peace, The.) AOAH
(Vision, A.) BoHiPo
(Vision of the World, The.) GrCo-1
"Slowly comes a hungry people, as a lion creeping nigher." PoFr
Locksley Hall Sixty Years After. Tennyson. EnLi-2 (1949 ed.); PoVP; ViPo; VLEP
Sels.
Saint Francis. SaFP
That Which Made Us. OQP; QP-2
Locomotive, The. Emily Dickinson. *See* I like to see it lap the miles.
Locomotive. Shigeharu Nakano, *tr. fr. Japanese by* Takamichi Ninomiya *and* D. J. Enright. PoLJ
Locomotive to the Little Boy, The. Benjamin R. C. Low. HBMV
Locrine, *sel. At. to* George Peele, *also at. to* Charles Tilney.
"We cobblers lead a merry life," *fr.* II, iii. ElSeCe
(Cobbler's Song, The.) OBSC
(Strumbo, Dorothy, Trumpart, Cobbling Shoes.) TuPP
Locust, The. *Tr. fr. Zuni Indian by* Frank Cushing. *See* Coyote and the Locust, The.
Locust, because the meadow is warm in the present, The. The Acolyte. James Rorty. MOAP
Locust drones along the drowsy noon, The. Bush Goblins. H. M. Green. BoAu
Locust Hunt, The. Philip Murray. NePoAm-2
Locust, locust, playing a flute. The Coyote and the Locust [*or* The Locust]. *Tr. by* Frank Cushing. AWP; FaPON; JAWP; SUS; WBP
Locust Swarm, The. Hsu Chao, *tr. fr. Chinese by* Kenneth Rexroth. OnPC
Locusts have no king, yet they go forth, The. No King. Arthur Guiterman. MuM
Locusts laid their eggs in the corpse. The Locust Swarm. Hsu Chao. OnPC
Locusts, or Apollyonists, The, *sels.* Phineas Fletcher.
Canto I. EPS
("Of Men, nay Beasts: worse, Monsters: worst of all.") SeCV-1; SeEP
Sin, Despair, and Lucifer, *fr.* I. OBS
Lodge Room over Simpkins' Store, The. Lawrence N. Greenleaf. PoOW
Lodged. Robert Frost. BAP
Lodging for the Night, A. James Rorty. MOAP
Lodging with the Old Man of the Stream. Po Chü-i, *tr. fr. Chinese by* Arthur Waley. AWP; JAWP; TrCh; WBP
Loe here the precious dust is laid. Epitaph on Maria Wentworth. Thomas Carew. PoEL-3
Loërd, thou clepedest me. Prayer for Forbearance. *Unknown.* LoBV
Loftier Race, A. John Addington Symonds. MaRV
(Church Triumphant, The.) WBLP
(Coming Day, The.) GrCo-1
(Human Outlook, The.) WGRP
(These Things Shall Be.) PoFr
Lofty against our Western dawn uprises Achilles. Song, Youth, and Sorrow. William Cranston Lawton. AA
Lofty Column and the Laurel fall, The. Petrarch. *Fr.* Sonnets to Laura: To Laura in Death. PrPoCR
Lofty House, The. John Gould Fletcher. MAP; MoAmPo
Lofty Mind, A. Thomas Lovell Beddoes. *Fr.* Fragments Intended for the Dramas. ERP

Lofty ship from Salcombe came, A. The Salcombe Seaman's Flaunt to the Proud Pirate [*or* High Barbary]. *Unknown.* CBPC; ChTr; EtS; SG
Lofty stands the sun. The Young Reaper. Aleksey Koltsov. BoRS
Lofty vision of thornless sleep. Heads and Tails. "Claudia Lars." AnCL
Logan at Peach Tree Creek. Hamlin Garland. GA; MC; PAH
Logan Braes ("O Logan, sweetly didst thou glide"). Burns. RO
Logan Braes ("By Logan's streams that rin sae deep"). John Mayne, *wr. at. to* Burns. EBSV; MotAn
(Logan's Braes.) BSV
Logic. *Unknown.* BOHV; PCH
Logic is my eye. Seeing. John Lyle Donaghy. NeIP
Logic of Hudibras. Samuel Butler. *See* **Presbyterian Knight.**
Logical English. *Unknown.* BOHV
Logical Story, A—The Deacon's Masterpiece; or, The Wonderful "One-Hoss Shay." Oliver Wendell Holmes. *See* Deacon's Masterpiece, The; or, The Wonderful "One-Hoss Shay."
Logical Vegetarian, The. G. K. Chesterton. CenHV; LiTG; SiTL
Logie o' Buchan. George Halket. EV-3
(Logic of Buchan.) EBSV
Lohengrin. William Morton Payne. AA
Lois Malone. August Derleth. DaM
L'Oiseau Bleu. Mary Elizabeth Coleridge. BoTP; CH; PoVP; WhBS
"Loitering with a vacant eye." A. E. Housman. A Shropshire Lad, LI. EmBrPo; PoVP
Lola. Federico García Lorca, *tr. fr. Spanish by* Eleanor L. Turnbull. CoSP
Lollai, Lollai, Litil Child! *Unknown.* BOL; BrBE; KN
Lollingdon Downs, *sels.* John Masefield. LiTB (I–XV)
Choice, The, VIII. MBP; MoAB; MoBrPo
(Kings Go By, The.) PoeMoYo
"I could not sleep for thinking of the sky," V. ChMP; GTBS-W; LiTM (rev. ed.)
(Sonnet.) LiTG; NV
"Night is on the downland, on the lonely moorland," XVIII. CP; GoYe
(Night on the Downland.) GTBS-W; LiTM; MBP; MoBrPo; MoPo
Lollocks. Robert Graves. ChTr; MoPW
Lolly Too-Dum, *with music. Unknown.* OuSiCo
Lolotte, who attires my hair. Noblesse Oblige. Jessie Fauset. CDC
L'Onda dal Mar' Divisa. Vladimir Soloviev, *tr. fr. Russian by* Babette Deutsch. TrRV
London ("I wander thro' each Charter'd street"). Blake. *Fr.* Songs of Experience. AtBAP; AWP; CEP; ChER; ChTr; CoEV; EiPP; EM-1; EnL; EnLi-2 (1949 ed.); EnRP; ExPo; FaBoEn; InPo; LiTB; LO; MaPo; NBE; OnPM; PoE; PoEL-4; PoFS; RiBV; SeCePo; SeCeV; TwHP; TyEnPo; UnPo; ViBoPo; WoL
London ("There souls of men are bought and sold"). Blake. *Fr.* The Human Image. ChTr
London. John Davidson. BSV; PoeT; VA
London. Dryden. *See* New London, The.
London. William Dunbar. *See* In Honour of the City of London.
London. F. S. Flint. LBBV; MBP; MoBrPo (1942 ed.); NP; PFE; TwCV
London [a Poem in Imitation of the Third Satire of Juvenal]. Samuel Johnson. GoTL; PoEL-3
Sels.
London Delights. BeR
Poverty in London. BeR; ChTr; CoEV; OBEC
("By numbers here from shame or censure free.") EnLi-1 (1949 ed.); EPP; ViBoPo
London. Irene Rutherford McLeod. VOD
London. Peter Anthony Motteux. *See* Slaves to London.
London. Ernest Rhys. POTE
London. T. P. Cameron Wilson. HBMV; VOD
London Bells. *Unknown. See* Bells of London, The.
London Bridge, *sel.* Francis Turner Palgrave.
Margaret Roper's Vision of Her Father, Sir Thomas More. FAOV
London Bridge. *Unknown.* CH; ChTr; OTPC; OxBoLi; PCH; 4 *ll.*
("London Bridge is broken down.") OxNR
London Bridge. Frederic Edward Weatherly. VA
London Bridge is broken down. After London. John Dynham Cornish Pellow. GTBS
London Bridge is broken [*or* falling] down. London Bridge. *Unknown.* CH; ChTr; OTPC; OxBoLi; OxNR; PCH
London Bridge is falling down, Rome's burnt, and Babylon. Spring MCMXL. David Gascoyne. MoVE
London Churches. Richard Monckton Milnes. LPS-1
London City, *with music. Unknown.* AS
(Go Bring Me Back My Blue-eyed Boy, *diff. vers.*) AS
London Delights. Samuel Johnson. *Fr.* London. BeR
London Despair. Frances Cornford. OBMV
London, 1802 ("It is not to be thought of that the flood"). Wordsworth. *See* It Is Not to Be Thought Of.
London, 1802 ("Milton! thou should'st be living . . ."). Wordsworth. AnFE; ATP; AWP; BEL; BPN; CBE; CoBE; EM-2; EmBrPo; EnL; EnLi-2; EnLit; EnLP; EnRP; EPN; EPP; ERP; ES; ExPo; FiP; GEPC; GTSL; InP; InPo; InvP; JAWP; LiTB; MaPo; MCCG; OAEP; OBRV; OuHeWo; PeBoSo; PFE; PoE; PoEL-4; PoFr; PoFS; PoRA; PreP; REAL; ReaPo; RiBV; SeCeV; ShBV-3; TCEP; TOP; TreF; TwHP; TwP; TyEnPo; WBP
(England, 1802.) BCEP; HBV; LEAP; OBEV; PoeMoYo; PtP
(Ideal.) LH
(Milton.) PoMa
(Milton, Thou Shouldst Be Living at This Hour.) GTBS; GTBS-D; GTBS-W; GTSE; HiLiEn; WHA
(Sonnet: "Milton! Thou shouldst be living at this hour.") EV-3; LoBV
(To Milton.) BLV; BoLiVe; LPS-3; TrGrPo
London, 1802 ("O Friend! I know not which way I must look"). Wordsworth. *See* Written in London, September, 1802.
London Elegies, II. Fred Marnau, *tr. fr. German by* E. O. Sigler. BoFr
London, England. Epilogue to a Human Drama. Stephen Spender. EnLit
London Feast. Ernest Rhys. VA
London, Hast Thou Accused Me. Earl of Surrey. *See* Satire on London, A.
London Idyll, A. "John Presland." VOD
London Interior. Harold Monro. ChMo; CMP
London Is a Fine Town. *Unknown.* CoMu
London Lickpenny. *Unknown, wr. at. to* John Lydgate, *tr. fr. Middle English.* CoMu; GoTL; MeEV; TMEV
(London Lackpenny.) ChTr; EV-1, *abr.*
London Literature and Society. Byron. *Fr.* Don Juan, XI. BPN
London, my beautiful. London. F. S. Flint. LBBV; MBP; MoBrPo (1942 ed.); NP; PFE; TwCV
London Night. Kathleen Raine. NeBP
London Nightfall. John Gould Fletcher. MAP; MoAmPo; NeMA
London, 1940. A. A. Milne. MaRV
London, 1941. Mervyn Peake. NeTW
London Plane-Tree, A. Amy Levy. DiM; VA
(Plane-Tree, The.) MW; OBVV
London Poets. Amy Levy. DiM; OBVV
London Prentice, The. *Unknown.* CoMu
London Rain. Nancy Byrd Turner. MoSiPe
London Revisited—1946. Dorothy Livesay. BoCaPo (1948 ed.)
London River. Frederic Edward Weatherly. TVSH
London Sad London. *Unknown.* OBS
London shall perish—arch and spire and wall. Lines to a Dictator. Mary Sinton Leitch. NeTW
London Snow. Robert Bridges. AlDL; AnFE; CBOV; CBPC; CH; ChMo; ChTr; CMP; CoBMV; EPP; EV-5; GTBS-W; GTML; GTSE; LiTB; LiTG; LiTM (rev. ed.); LoBV; MBP; MM; MoAB; MoBrPo; PIAE; Po; PoE; PoEL-5; PoeMoYo; PoeT; PoMa; PoVP; ReMP; SeCePo; SeCeV; ShBV-3; TCEP; TrGrPo; VLEP; VOD (1935 ed.)
London Spring. Antoni Slonimski, *tr. fr. Polish by* Frances Notley. TrJP
London Squares. Sir Osbert Sitwell. LBBV
London, the "Flower of Cities All." London. Ernest Rhys. POTE
London Thoroughfare Two A.M., A. Amy Lowell. PoeMoYo; VOD
London, thou art of townes *A per se.* In Honour of the City of London [*or* To the City of London]. William Dunbar. ChTr; CoEV; EBSV; EV-1; OBEV
London to Paris, by Air. Lord Gorell. PoeMoYo
London, to thee I do present the merry Month of May. The Month of May. Beaumont *and* Fletcher. *Fr.* The Knight of the Burning Pestle. ChTr
London Town. Byron. *Fr.* Don Juan. GEPC
London Town. Lionel Johnson. PoVP
London Town. John Masefield. ChMo; CMP; OtMeF
London Trees. Beryl Netherclift. BoTP
London under Bombardment. Greta Briggs. OtMeF
London Voluntaries. W. E. Henley. Po (I–II); PoVP
Allegro Maëstoso, V. ViP
London Voluntary, II. PIAE
Night Cat, The, *br. sel. fr.* II. BMEP
Scherzando, III. POTT
("Down through the ancient Strand.") BPN
(From "London Voluntaries," III–IV, *abr.*) LEAP
(London Voluntary, A, III.) AlDL
(Wind-Fiend, The, *fr.* III–IV, *abr.*) BMEP
Londoner in the Country, The. Richard Church. HaMV
Londoners Gent to the King do present, The. On the Lord Mayor and Court of Aldermen, Presenting the Late King

Londoners Gent to the King do present, The (*continued*) and Duke of York Each with a Copy of Their Freedoms, Anno Dom. 1674. Andrew Marvell. CoMu
London's full of statues. Temple Bar. Rose Fyleman. UTS
London's Tempe; *or,* The Field of Happiness, *sel.* Thomas Dekker.
"Brave iron! brave hammer! from your sound." TuPP
(Song of the Cyclops, The.) NBE; ShBV-1
Lone and forgotten/ Through a long sleeping. The Lonely. "Æ." AWP; JAWP; OnYI; WBP
Lone Bather. A. M. Klein. TwCaPo
Lone Buffalo Hunter, The. *Unknown.* CoSo; CSF
(Texas Cowboys, The, *same.*) CoSo
Lone Dog. Irene R. McLeod. AlBD; AlDL; BMEP; FaPON; MCCG; MPB; NeMA; PoMa; SP; StVeCh (1940 ed.); TiPo; TVSH; UTS
Lone Driftin' Riders. *Unknown.* CoSo
Lone eagle of the wild Atlantic plain. Lindbergh. Wendell Phillips Stafford. GA
Lone Flower, hemmed in with snows and white as they. To a Snowdrop. Wordsworth. BPN; EmBrPo
Lone Founts. Herman Melville. AnFE; CoAnAm; LiTA; OnPM; ViBoPo
Lone Gentleman. "Pablo Neruda," *tr. fr. Spanish by* Dudley Fitts. AnCL
Lone heart, learning. Vigils. Siegfried Sassoon. ChMo; CMP
Lone Huntsman. Christie Jeffries. GoYe
Lone, I wander where the pathway glistens. Mikhail Lermontov, *tr. fr. Russian after* J. S. Phillimore. BoR
Lone in the North a Pine Tree. Heine, *tr. fr. German by* Kate Flores. AnGP
("Yonder's a lanely fir-tree," *tr. into Scottish by* Edwin Morgan.) AnGP
Lone in the wood she sang, the pretty Rose-Marie. Rose-Marie. Zakarias Topelius. AnSL
Lone kingfisher skims the river's crest, A. The Kingfisher. Blanche Mary Kelly. GoBC
Lone lake, half lost amidst encircling hills. Arts Lough. George Arthur Greene. TIP
Lone-Land. John Banister Tabb. OQP; QP-2
Lone, lone and lone I stand. The Myall in Prison. Mary Gilmore. BoAV
Lone Man, The. *Unknown, tr. fr. Old English. Fr.* Widsith. PoLi
Lone midnight-soothing melancholy bird. The Nightingale. Edward Moxon. OBRV
Lone o'er the moors I stray'd. The Hand. Ebenezer Jones. OBVV
Lone Prairie, The. *Unknown. See* Dying Cowboy, The ("Oh, bury me not . . .").
Lone seas are ominous. Lone Huntsman. Christie Jeffries. GoYe
Lone Sentry, The. James R. Randall. BlG
Lone Star State secretes the clay, The. Grave of Albert Sidney Johnston. J. B. Synnott. BlG
Lone Star Trail, The. *Unknown.* AS; CoSo, *diff. vers., with music;* CSF, *diff. vers.*
Lone Swan. Rose Mills Powers. BLA
Lone the dove of thought goes lagging. The Dove of Thought. Verner von Heidenstam. AnSL
Lone walks and the lonelier midnights come to half. William Ellery Leonard. *Fr.* Two Lives, Pt. III. MOAP
Lone watch of the moon over mountains old, The. Mortality. James Devaney. BoAV
Lone white gull with sickle wings. To a Solitary Sea-Gull. Cale Young Rice. BLA
Loneliness. Edwin Essex. JKCP (1926 ed.); TrPWD
Loneliness. Robert Frost. *Fr.* The Hill Wife. AmPo; BAP; ChMo; CMP; FaBoEn; IAP; MOAP; NP; SBMV; TwP
Loneliness. Nikolai Gumilev, *tr. fr. Russian by* C. M. Bowra. BoR
Loneliness. Hanshin, *tr. fr. Japanese by* Harold Gould Henderson. WoL
Loneliness. Hsiao Wu Ti, *tr. fr. Chinese by* Henry H. Hart. PoHN
Loneliness. Ignace M. Ingianni. MuM
Loneliness. Rainer Maria Rilke. *See* Solitude.
Loneliness. Tu Fu, *tr. fr. Chinese by* Kenneth Rexroth. OnPC
Loneliness. Franz Werfel, *tr. fr. German by* Edith Abercrombie Snow. TrJP
Loneliness has two faces: one that looks. Strange Meeting. Leslie Nelson Jennings. MuM
Loneliness is like the rain. Loneliness. Rainer Maria Rilke. AnGP
Loneliness of her old age flashed clear, The. Aged Ninety Years. Wilbert Snow. AnAmPo; LA
Lonely, The. "Æ." AWP; JAWP; OnYi; WBP
Lonely. Lizette Woodworth Reese. MOAP
Lonely. André Spire, *tr. fr. French by* Jethro Bithell. AWP; JAWP; TrJP; WBP
Lonely, A/ Sick old man. Taxes. Tu Hsün Hao. OnPM
Lonely and cold and fierce I keep my way. Gulf Stream. "Susan Coolidge." AA; EtS
Lonely and sad. The Waning Moon. P'an Shih. PoHN
Lonely and wild it rose. The Mysterious Music of Ocean. *Unknown.* EtS
Lonely Are the Fields of Sleep. Mary Newton Baldwin. GoYe
Lonely Beauty. Samuel Daniel. *Fr.* The Complaint of Rosamond. OBSC
Lonely-Bird, The. Harrison Smith Morris. AA; SN
Lonely Bugle Grieves, The. Grenville Mellen. *Fr.* Ode on the Celebration of the Battle of Bunker Hill, June 17, 1825. AA; BAP; IDAH; LEAP
Lonely Burial. Stephen Vincent Benét. BAP; SBMV
Lonely Child, The. Ernest Briggs. NeLNL
Lonely Child, The. James Oppenheim. LEAP; NP
Lonely Christ, The. Edward Shillito. ChIP
Lonely Crib, The. Leonard Feeney. WHL
Lonely Dancer, The. Richard Le Gallienne. BMEP
Lonely Death, The. Adelaide Crapsey. AnFE; APA; BAP; CoAnAm; LEAP; MAP; MoAmPo (1942 ed.); NP; SBMV
Lonely Dog, The. Margaret E. Bruner. AlBD; PoToHe
Lonely House, The. Emily Dickinson. *See* I know some lonely houses off the road.
Lonely I lay in the heather-soft hollow. The Heather. Steen Steensen Blicher. BoDS; LiTW
Lonely Isle, The. Claudian, *tr. fr. Latin by* Howard Mumford Jones. AWP; JAWP; WBP
Lonely lake, a lonely shore, A. The Loon. Lew Sarett. BAP; BLA; HBMV; TBM
Lonely Land, The. A. J. M. Smith. CaP; TwCV
Lonely, lonely lay the hill. As Rivers of Water in a Dry Place. Anna Bunston De Bary. HBMV
Lonely Man, A. Agnes Lee. NP
Lonely Month, The. Ruthven Todd. NeBP
Lonely Mother, The. Fenton Johnson. GoSl; NP; PoNe
Lonely Night. Sappho. *See* Night.
Lonely Night in Early Autumn. Po Chü-i, *tr. fr. Chinese by* Ching Ti. ChLP; WhP
Lonely o'er the dying ember. Shadows. Sebastian Evans. PrWP
Lonely Old Age. Yüan Chen, *tr. fr. Chinese by* Henry H. Hart. PoHN
Lonely orchid grows in the courtyard, The. The Orchid. Tao Yuan-ming. WhP
Lonely Pine Is Standing, A. Heine. *See* Fichtenbaum steht einsam, Ein.
Lonely Place, A. Edward Shanks. TCPD
Lonely pond in age-old stillness sleeps, A. Basho, *tr. fr. Japanese by* Curtis Hidden Page. AWP; JAWP; WBP
Lonely Road, The. Kenneth Rand. HBV
Lonely, save for a few faint stars, the sky. The Little Dancers. Laurence Binyon. BoTP; CH; MBP; MoBrPo; MoVE; OBVV; PoeT
Lonely season in lonely lands, when fled, The. November. Robert Bridges. PoEL-5
Lonely Shell, The. Martha Eugenie Perry. CaP
Lonely Spring. Saisei Muro, *tr. fr. Japanese by* Takamichi Ninomiya *and* D. J. Enright. PoLJ
Lonely student in a silent room, A. International Brigade Dead. Thomas O'Brien. NeIP
Lonely task it is to plow, A. Plowing; a Memory. Hamlin Garland. StVeCh
Lonely Trek. Joseph Joel Keith. MuM
Lonely Tryst. Kathleen Sutton. MuM
Lonely wanderer, wounded with iron, A. Shield. *Unknown. Fr.* Riddles. AnOE
Lonely way, A, and as I went my eyes. Two Infinities. Edward Dowden. VA
Lonely Wife, The. Li Po, *tr. fr. Chinese by* Florence Ayscough *and* Amy Lowell. ChLP
Lonely Wind. Eleanor Hammond. GFA
Lonely Woman, The. M. Forrest. BoAu
Lonely workman, A, standing there. In the Moonlight. Thomas Hardy. BMEP; LEAP; NP
Lonesome. Paul Laurence Dunbar. MPB; PoRL
Lonesome, dear Lord, how can I ever be. Living Bread. Eva Weaver Sefton. BePJ
Lonesome Grabeya'ad. Josephine Pinckney. TCPD
Lonesome Grove, The, *with music. Unknown.* TrAS
Lonesome Road. *Unknown. See* Long Lonesome Road.
Lonesome Valley. *Unknown.* OIF
Lonesome Water. Roy Helton. DaM; DDA; MAP; MoAmPo; PoMS; WaKn
Lonesome? Well, I guess so! A Nevada Cowpuncher to His Beloved. *Unknown.* SCC
Long after both of us are scattered dust. Sonnets, XXXIV. Robert Hillyer. OBAV
Long after the days and seasons, the beings and countries. Barbarian. Arthur Rimbaud. LiTW
Long after the last wall is swept away. Kimball Flaccus. *Fr.* Sonnet Sequence. CAG
Long Ago. Siegfried Sassoon. AlDL
Long Ago, The. Benjamin Franklin Taylor. *See* Isle of Long Ago, The.

Long ago I blazed a trail. The Pioneer. Arthur Guiterman. MPB

Long ago I learned how to sleep. Wind Song. Carl Sandburg. GBV (1952 ed.); MAP; MoAB; MoAmPo; MoShBr; NeMA; TwAmPo; YT

Long ago I used to pray. Seedtime and Harvest. Sir Henry Head. PoP

Long ago, November. Fireworks. Phyllis Reid. DiM

Long ago, on a bright spring day. Old and Young. Francis William Bourdillon. VA

Long ago powerful snake when men also. The Deluge. *Unknown. Fr.* Wallam Olum. LiTA

Long ago the thunder went talking. Before Winter. Frederick R. McCreary. MAP

Long ago to a white-haired gentleman. The Hat Given to the Poet by Li Chien. Po Chü-i. AtBAP; BoW; TrCh

Long and a Sad Tale, A. "Lewis Carroll." *Fr.* Alice's Adventures in Wonderland. ViP

Long and final passage over the breathtaking height. To Rafael Cansinos Assens. Jorge Luis Borges. AnCL

Long and grey and gaunt he lies. At the Dog Show. Christopher Morley. AlBD; MoShBr; MPB

Long and Lovely. Arthur Davison Ficke. TCPD

Long annoys and short contentings. Of Love. *Unknown.* SeCL

Long are the hours the sun is above. Robert Bridges. EG; LO; POTT

Long are the years since he fell asleep. Washington. B. Y. Williams. PGD; OQP; QP-1

Long as I can call to mind. A Childish Game. Reinmar von Hagenau. AWP; JAWP; WBP

Long as I was able, in the town of my birth. Harvest Moon. Josephine Miles. FiMAP

Long as thine Art shall love true love. Dear Land of All My Love. Sidney Lanier. *Fr.* The Centennial Meditations of Columbia. DD; GA; GN; HBVY; MPB; PGD; StVeCh

Long Autumn rain. Autumn Song. Edward Dowden. OnYI

Long awaited day, The. Walter Savage Landor. *Fr.* Gebir, VII. OBRV

Long Ballad of Marsk Stig, The. *Unknown, tr. fr. Danish by* E. M. Smith-Dampier. BoDaBa

Long before he reached our age. Lines Written on November 15, 1933, by a Man Born November 14, 1881, to Another Born November 15, 1881. Clayton Hamilton. InMe

Long betwixt Love and Fear. Dryden. *Fr.* The Assignation. LiTL; SeCL; ViBoPo
(Song: "Long betwixt love and fear Phillis tormented.") SeEP

Long-billed Gannets. Frances D. Emery. GoYe

Long 'bout June, when everything's. I Go Fishin'. Richard S. Powell. IHA

Long by the willow-trees. The Willow-Tree. Thackeray. BOHV; HBV; InMe; PA

Long canoe, The. Lullaby. Robert Hillyer. FaPON

Long Centuries of Centuries. Konstantin Dmitreyevich Balmont, *tr. fr. Russian by* Babette Deutsch. TrRV

Long centuries past by lonely barrows grew. The Holy Thorn. Thomas S. Jones, Jr. PSO

Long-closed door, oh open it again, The. Love Song. Judah Alharizi. LiTW; TrJP

Long coast curves and the cliffs rise up, The. On the Beach. Cale Young Rice. VOD

Long cool corridor alive with fame, A. Winged Victory. Harold Trowbridge Pulsifer. BAP

Long Did I Toil. John Quarles *and* Henry F. Lyte. MaRV

Long did the heroes with King Phineus bide. Apollonius Rhodius. *Fr.* Argonautica, II. GrPo

Long Distance, 1944. James Boyd. NoCaPo (rev. ed.)

Long do I sorrow that the spring should end. Farewell to Chao Ta-lin. Su T'ung-po. BoFr

Long ere the morn. The Hunter's Song. William Basse. SeCL

Long-expected one and twenty. One-and-twenty [*or* A Short Song of Congratulation *or* To a Young Heir]. Samuel Johnson. BCEP; BeR; InvP; LEAP; LoBV; OBEC; OBEV; PoEL-3; TyEnPo; UnPo (3d ed.)

Long fed on boundless hopes, O race of man. The Better Part. Matthew Arnold. BPN; ChIP; EM-2; EPN; GrCo-1; MaRV; PoVP; StJW; TOP; ViPP; VLEP

Long Feud. Louis Untermeyer. AnAmPo; AnFE; APA; CoAnAm; LA; MAP; MoAmPo; NeMA

Long from the lists of love I stood aloof. Omnia Vincit. Alfred Cochrane. HBV

Long Gone. Sterling A. Brown. BANP; CDC

Long Gone, *with music. Unknown.* ABF

Long, gray moss that softly swings, The. In Louisiana. Albert Bigelow Paine. AA

Long green swell, A. Chill of the Eve. James Stephens. ChMo; CMP; OnYI

Long grey street with balconies, A. Calle de Toledo, Madrid. John Dos Passos. *Fr.* Winter in Castile. VOD (1935 ed.)

Long had Amyntor free from love remained. Amyntor. Thomas Godfrey. IAP

Long had the giant-form on Gallia's plains. The French Revolution. Erasmus Darwin. PoFr

Long-haired kittens of Damascus, why are you playing in the streets of St. Paul? Damascus. Edna Holroyd Yellan. CIV

Long-haired preachers come out ev'ry night. The Preacher and the Slave. *Unknown.* AS; TrAS

Long-haired Yak has long black hair, The. Yak. William Jay Smith. GoTP; TiPo (1959 ed.)

Long Harbour, The. Mary Ursula Bethell. AnNZ

Long Has the Furious Priest. William Byrd. SPP

Long has the summer sunlight shone. Incognita of Raphael. William Allen Butler. AA

Long hast thou, friend! been absent from thy soil. Mr. Pope's Welcome from Greece. John Gay. OBEC; OxBoLi; PoEL-3; PtP

Long hath she slept, forgetful of delight. Vita Nuova. Sir William Watson. OBVV

Long have I beat with timid hands upon life's leaden door. The Suppliant. Georgia Douglas Johnson. CDC; PoNe

Long have I dreamed of love's adventure. The Spell. Medora Addison. HBMV

Long have I framed weak phantasies of Thee. ΑΓΝΩΣΤΩι ΘΕΩι (To an Unknown God). Thomas Hardy. MoPo; WGRP

Long have I loved the terrible clouds that loom. Prayer for Dreadful Morning. E. Merrill Root. TrPWD

Long have I searched the Earth for liberty. Liberty, Equality, Fraternity. Wilfrid Scawen Blunt. *Fr.* In Vinculis. PoFr

Long have I wooed thee through the slow winged hours. Sleep. John Bruce MacCallum. PoP

Long heron feather, The. The Gray [*or* Grey] Plume. Francis Carlin. HBMV; TBM

Long Hill, The. Sara Teasdale. ChMo; CMP; HBMV; LiTA; LiTM; MAP; MoAmPo; MOAP

Long hours we toiled up through the solemn wood. Mount Rainier. Herbert Bashford. AA

Long I followed [*or* follow'd] happy guides. Forerunners. Emerson. AA; AnNE; IAP; MoAP; OBAV; OBEV (new ed); OBVV; OxBA; TCAP

Long I Have Loved to Stroll. T'ao Ch'ien, *tr. fr. Chinese by* William Acker. ChTr

Long in thy shackles, Liberty. To Lucasta, from Prison. Richard Lovelace. PoFr

Long Irish melancholy of lament! "To Weep Irish." Lionel Johnson. VLEP

Long is the day without Usnagh's [*or* Usnech's] Children. Deirdre's Lament [*or* Deirdre's Lament over Naoisi]. *Unknown.* LiTW; OnYI; SiB

Long is the road 'twixt town and town that runs. Afoot. Cicely Fox Smith. NLK

Long John. Padraic Fallon. NeIP

Long John Brown and Little Mary Bell. Blake. SiTL

Long languishing in double malady. Amoretti, L. Spenser. PeBoSo

Long Last Mile, The. Lauchlan MacLean Watt. MaRV

Long lay the ocean-paths from man concealed. Columbus [*or* The Inspiration]. James Montgomery. *Fr.* The West Indies. PAH; PEDC

Long-legged Fly. W. B. Yeats. FaBoEn; FaBoTw; LiTM; PoE

Long legs, crooked thighs. Mother Goose. HBV; HBVY; OTPC; OxNR; PPL; RIS

Long lines of cliff breaking have left a chasm. Enoch Arden. Tennyson. BeLS; VLEP

Long Lonesome Road, *with music. Unknown.* OuSiCo
(Lonesome Road, *diff. vers., with music.*) AS
(Look Down That Lonesome Road, *diff. vers., with music.*) OuSiCo

Long, Long Ago. Thomas Haynes Bayly. OlF; TreF

Long, Long Ago. *Unknown.* BrR; ChBR; DD; FaPON; GFA; MPB; OHIP; OTPC (1946 ed.); PEDC; RAR; TiPo (1952 ed.)
(Christmas Song, A: "Winds through the olive trees.") BoTP

Long, long ago. The Carpenter. Gumpei Yamamuro. SoLD

Long long ago, as it appears. The Rat Who Withdrew from the World. La Fontaine. TrFP

Long, long ago, beyond the misty space. The Celts. Thomas D'Arcy McGee. GTIV; OnYI; OxBI

Long, long ago, when all the glittering earth. John Masefield. *Fr.* Sonnets ("Long long ago"). EPP; HBV

Long, long ago, when it was spring. Life Is a Lovely Thing. Minnie Case Hopkins. DDA

Long, long and dreary is the night. Simonides, *tr. fr. Greek by* John Herman Merivale. GrPo

Long, Long Be My Heart with Such Memories Filled. Thomas Moore. FaBoBe

Long, long before the Babe could speak. At Bethlehem [*or* The Child at Bethlehem]. John Banister Tabb. *Fr.* The Child. AA; PRWS

Long, long legs, The. From the Country to the City. Elizabeth Bishop. CrMA

Long, long, long the trail. Light between the Trees. Henry van Dyke. GBV (1922 ed.)

Long, long river, The. Haiku. Boncho. LiTW; OnPJ

Long, long time, and a long time ago, A. A Long Time Ago. *Unknown.* AmSS; SG

Long, long wished-for hour has come, The. A Cushla Gal Mo Chree. Michael Doheny. TIP

Long love that in my thought doth harbor [*or* harbour], The. The Lover for Shamefastness Hideth His Desire within His Faithful Heart. Petrarch, *tr. by* Sir Thomas Wyatt. Sonnets to Laura: To Laura in Life, CIX. CoBE; ReEn; ReIE; SiCE; TuPP
Long Love that is sovereign to my mind, The. Petrarch, *tr. by* Joseph Auslander. Sonnets to Laura: To Laura in Life, CIX. PrPoCR
Long march of the unnumerable hours, The. Ajax! to All Farewell! Sophocles. *Fr.* Ajax. GrR
Long may the shamrock. The Shamrock. *Unknown.* HH
Long months He lay within the womb. Signum Cui Contradicetur. Sister Mary Angelita. GoBC; JKCP (1926 ed.)
Long Nature travailed, till at last she bore. Nature's Travail. *Unknown.* AWP
Long Night, The. Harry Bache Smith. AA
Long Night Moon, The; December. Frances Frost. YeAr
Long night succeeds thy little day. Margaret Love Peacock. Thomas Love Peacock. OBRV; VA
Long, O Protesilaus, long shall thy fame be chanted. The Elms of Protesilaus. Antiphilus of Byzantium. GrPE
Long past midnight I sit here. Forsaken. Zalman Schneour. TrJP
Long poles support the branches of the orchards in New Hampshire. Apples in New Hampshire. Marie Gilchrist. PoMa
Long pored St. Austin o'er the sacred page. A Passage in the Life of St. Augustine. *Unknown.* LPS-2
Long Race, The. E. A. Robinson. CrMA
Long rain, The, falls on the empty forest. After Long Rain. Wang Wei. WhP
Long resounding marble corridors, The, the shining parlors with shining women in them. The Hotel. Harriet Monroe. AnAmPo; LA; NP
Long, rich breadth of Holland lace, A. Old Flemish Lace. Amelia Walstien Carpenter. AA
Long Road, The, *sel.* John Gray. Gazelles and Unicorn. ChTr
Long Road, The. A. E. Housman. *See* White in the Moon the Long Road Lies.
Long road and a village, A. Holy Family. Muriel Rukeyser. MoAmPo
Long Road Blossoms, The. Samuel Marshak, *tr. fr. Russian by* Jack Lindsay. RuPo
Long Road West, The. H. H. Knibbs. IHA
Long Roads. Mikhail Matusovsky, *tr. fr. Russian by* Babette Deutsch. LiTW; TrRV
Long-rolling, The,/ Steady-pouring. The Main-Deep. James Stephens. MBP; MoBrPo; OBMV; ShBV-1; UnPo
Long scythe biting through the grain, The. The Hare. Stanley Snaith. HaMV
Long Shadow of Lincoln, The. Carl Sandburg. MoAmPo (1950 ed.)
Long since, a dream of heaven I had. Divine Compassion. Whittier. TriL
Long since her warrior sons abroad did wend. The Sons of Aeacus. Pindar. *Fr.* Isthmian Odes. OxBG
Long since I'd ceased to care. The Parrot. W. W. Gibson. OBMV
Long since, in sore distress, I heard one pray. A Warrior's Prayer. Paul Laurence Dunbar. MaRV; OQP; QP-1
Long since the first fruits have been laid. Forever on Thanksgiving Day. Wilbur D. Nesbit. PEDC
Long since your bones have mouldered; long, Doricha, the binding. Sappho. Poseidippus. GrPE
Long sobbings, The. Autumn Song. Paul Verlaine. LiTW
Long Song after Short Songs, A. Li Ho, *tr. fr. Chinese by* Ho Chih-yuan. WhP
Long Summer Day, *with music. Unknown.* OuSiCo
Long-tailed pig, A. *Unknown.* OxNR
Long-tailed ponies go nosing the pine-lands. Parochial Theme. Wallace Stevens. LiTA
Long temple banners flutter, The. Morning Prayer. Ch'eng Tsung Lo. PoHN
Long the proud Spaniard[s] advanced [*or* had vaunted] to conquer us. The Winning of Cales. Thomas Deloney. CoMu; SG
Long the tyrant of our coast. On the Capture of the *Guerrière.* Philip Freneau. GA; PAH
Long, their fixed eyes to Heaven bent. Lord Herbert of Cherbury. *Fr.* An Ode upon a Question Moved, Whether Love Should Continue for Ever? LO
Long they pine in weary woe, the nobles of our land. Kathleen-Ni-Houlahan [*or* Kathaleen Ny-Houlahan]. *Tr. by* James Clarence Mangan. AnIV; CoBE; ERP; TIP
Long Time a Child. Hartley Coleridge. EnRP; HBV; OBRV; PoEL-4
Long Time Ago. Elizabeth Prentiss. ABF, *sl. diff.*; GFA; TVC; TVSH
(Kitty.) BoTP; CBPC; MoShBr; MPB
(Little Kitty.) CIV; SAS
Long Time Ago, A. *Unknown.* AmSS, *with music*; SG; ShS, *6 vers., with music*; SoAmSa, *diff. vers., with music*
Long Time Ago, A/ I went on a journey. T'ao Ch'ien, *tr. fr. Chinese by* Arthur Waley. FaBoCh; LoGBV; TrCh
Long time ago, when I was a child, A. The Snow Globe. Howard Nemerov. FiMAP
Long time he lay upon the sunny hill. Childhood. Edwin Muir. SeCePo
Long time in some forgotten churchyard earth of Warwickshire. Who Were before Me. John Drinkwater. OBMV
Long time of the sea had old England been Queen. The Brave Tars of Old England. *Unknown.* SG
Long time those gay and spotted hides. Your Chase Had a Beast in View. John Peale Bishop. LiTA
Long, Too Long America. Walt Whitman. AmPo; CoV
Long Trail, The. Kipling. HBV; OtMeF; POTT; ViBoPo; VLEP
(Envoy: "There's a whisper down the field where the year has shot her yield.") PoVP
(L'Envoi: "There's a whisper . . .") LEAP; OBEV; OBVV
Long tyme hathe Christ (long tyme I must confesse). On the Reed of Our Lord's Passion. William Alabaster. PoEL-2
Long up and down I paced the House of Pain. The Incurables. Arthur Upson. AnAmPo; LA
Long View. Genevieve Taggard. MoAmPo
Long Voyage, The. Malcolm Cowley. AnFE; CoAnAm; GBV (1952 ed.); NePA; TwAmPo; WaKn
Long War, The. Li Po, *tr. fr. Chinese by* Cheng Yu Sun. WaaP
Long was I, Lady Luck, your serving-man. Davy, the Dicer. Sir Thomas More. *Fr.* Two Short Ballettes . . . Made for His Pastime While He Was Prisoner in the Tower of London. TuPP
Long was the great Figg by the prize fighting Swains. Extempore Verses upon a Trial of Skill between the Two Great Masters of the Noble Science of Defence, Messrs. Figg and Sutton. John Byrom. OBEC
Long Was the Road. Nikolai Tikhonov, *tr. fr. Russian by* Jack Lindsay. RuPo
Long was the road to Bethlehem, where Joseph. Bethlehem. Bliss Carman. SDH
Long was the splendid/ Trunk of the Northland. The Unity of the North. Parmo Carl Ploug. BoDS
Long was the way to Bethlehem to those who sought. The Way to Bethlehem. Clinton Scollard. OQP; PSO; QP-1
Long While, The. Omar Khayyám, *tr. fr. Persian by* Edward Fitzgerald. *Fr.* The Rubáiyát. OnPM
Long while I sought to what I might compare. Amoretti, IX. Spenser. PeBoSo; PoE; TwHP
Long white barn, A. Riddle. *Unknown.* ChTr
Long white clouds are Morning's wash, The. Morning Clouds. Nellie Burget Miller. GFA
Long White Seam, The. Jean Ingelow. GN; HBV; OTPC; VA
Long white shaft of the moon, The. Moonspath. Don Carlos Pamplin. CAG
Long-winged terns dart wild and dive, The. As the Tide Comes In. Cale Young Rice. NLK; VOD
Long year is at an end, The. To His Brother. Wei Ying-wu. PoHN
Long years ago, beneath another sky. The Revelation. Havelock Ellis. PoP
Long years ago I blazed a trail. The Pioneer. Arthur Guiterman. MPB; TiPo
Long years ago I wandered here. On Recrossing the Rocky Mountains after Many Years. John Charles Frémont. PoOW
Long years have men been seeking for Wisdom's light. Hymn to Truth. James Byers Colton, II. CAG
Long years I lived under vast porticoes. The Former Life. Baudelaire. AnFP
Long years!—It tries the thrilling frame to bear. The Lament of Tasso. Byron. EmBrPo
Long years, methinks, of sorrow and of care. The Cascade. Tadamine. OnPM
Long years of pleasant friendship may be broken. True to the Best. Benjamin Keech. PoToHe
Long years their cabin stood. Eviction. William James Linton. VA
Long years you've kept the door ajar. Dedication. Robert Bridges. *Fr.* Overheard in Arcady. MOAH
Longer life, the more offence, The. Upon Consideration of the State of This Life He Wisheth Death. *Unknown.* SiCE; TuPP
Longer on this earth we live, The. Unwasted Days. James Russell Lowell. *Fr.* Under the Old Elm. MCCG
Longer to muse. Sir Thomas Wyatt. SiPS
Longest day in the year had come, The. Midsummer Night. Marion Edey. YeAr
Longest Journey, The. Shelley. *Fr.* Epipsychidion. OtMeF
("I never was attached to that great sect.") NBE
Longest tyranny that ever sway'd, The. To My Honor'd Friend, Dr. Charleton. Dryden. CEP; EiPP; EnL; SeCV-2; SeEP
Longface Mahoney Discusses Heaven. Horace Gregory. ChMo; ExPo
Longfellow. Thomas Bailey Aldrich. GA
Longfellow. Craven Langstroth Betts. DD; GA

Longfellow ("The winds have talked with him confidingly"). James Whitcomb Riley. AA; DD; PoRL
Longfellow. Henry van Dyke. CV
Longfellow Alphabet, A. *Comp. by* Caroline B. Le Row, *fr. various poems by* Longfellow. PEOR
Longford Legend, A. *Unknown.* OnYI; StPo
Longing. Matthew Arnold. HBV; LO, *st.* 1; OAEP; VLEP
Longing. Ch'ang Pi Lan, *tr. fr. Chinese by* Henry H. Hart. PoHN
Longing. Euripides. *See* O for the Wings of a Dove.
Longing. Judah Halevi, *tr. fr. Hebrew by* Nina Davis Salaman. TrJP
Longing, *abr.* George Herbert. SeCV-1
"Bowels of pitie heare!" *sel.* BrBE
Longing, *sel.* James Russell Lowell.
Thing We Long For, The. OQP; QP-2
Longing. Viktor Rydberg, *tr. fr. Swedish by* Charles W. Stork. AnSL
Longing. Sara Teasdale. ChMo; CMP
Longing. Christian Winther, *tr. fr. Danish by* Charles W. Stork. BoDS
Longing. Clement Wood. TBM
Longing a wife must bear, The. Esparsa. Gil Vicente. LyMA
Longing at twilight the lovesick Adam saw. The Begetting of Cain. Hyam Plutzik. FiMAP
Longing for Heaven. Anne Bradstreet. *See* As Weary Pilgrim.
Longing for Home. Jean Ingelow. *See* Seven Times Seven.
Longing for Jerusalem. Judah Halevi, *tr. fr. Hebrew by* Emma Lazarus. TrJP
Longings. José Moreno Villa, *tr. fr. Spanish by* Eleanor L. Turnbull. CoSP; OnPM
Lon's away/ Cill Garad is sad today. St. Columcille. *Fr.* On a Dead Scholar. AnIL
Look, The. Elizabeth Barrett Browning. MaRV
(Lord Turned, and Looked upon Peter, The.) ChIP
Look, The. Sara Teasdale. ALV; HBV; LiTL; LiTM; MOAP; PR
Look ahead, look astern, look the weather and the lee. The Coasts of High Barbary. *Unknown.* OnSP
Look and remember. Look upon this sky. Travelogue for Exiles. Karl Shapiro. AnFE; CoAnAm; MoAmPo (1950 ed.); NeMA; PG (1945 ed.); TrJP; TwAmPo
Look and See. Tom Robinson. BoChLi (1950 ed.)
Look at her, calm and benign. A Bronze Statuette of Kwan-yin. Charles Wharton Stork. GoYe
Look at her—there she sits upon her throne. The Turbine. Harriet Monroe. NP
Look at him there in his stovepipe hat. American Primitive. William Jay Smith. NePoAm; NePoEA
Look at Marcus and take warning. Old Greek Nonsense Rhymes. Lucilius. BoN
Look at me. I am Ishmael. The Old Convict. H. A. Vaughan. PoNe
Look at me with thy large brown eyes. Philip, My King. Dinah Maria Mulock Craik. HBV; LPS-1; VA
Look at my knees. I Wonder What It Feels Like to Be Drowned. Robert Graves. MBP; MoBrPo; TSW; TSWC
Look at Six Eggs. Carl Sandburg. *Fr.* Prairie. FaPON
Look at that sky—so blue, so clear! A Sigh in Winter. August, Graf von Platen. AnGP
Look at the aeroplane. The Aeroplane. Jeannie Kirby. BoTP
Look at the little darlings in the corn! Fireflies in the Corn. D. H. Lawrence. NP; NV
Look at the peace of inanimate things. Reading Giraldus Cambrensis. T. H. White. NeTW
Look at the stars! look, look up at the skies! The Starlight Night. Gerard Manley Hopkins. ACP; AlDL; CaAE; CAW; EmBrPo; EV-5; GoBC; GTBS; GTBS-W; JKCP; LiTM; MBP; MeRV; MoAB; MoBrPo; MoPW; MoVE; OBVV; OxBoCh; PoVP; SeCePo; ShBV-4; ThWaDe; ViBoPo; ViP; WoL
Look at this ancient house; it has survived. A House in Wartime. Richard Church. NeTW; POTE
Look at this skin—at fourscore years. Robert Barnabas Brough. *Fr.* The Marquis of Carabas. FiBHP
Look at this village boy, his head is stuffed. Farm Child. R. S. Thomas. ChMP
Look away now from the high lonesome hills. Admonition for Spring. L. A. Mackay. BoCaPo; CaP; PeCV; TwCV
Look back. Two powers have raised Rome's lofty head. Sulpicia II. *Fr.* The Satire. LaP
Look back with longing eyes and know that I will follow. The Flight. Sara Teasdale. BAP; CMP; HBMV; LEAP; MAP; NP; TBM; WHA
Look, Barker, when you wrote me I lay cringing. Mailed to G. B. Gene Derwood. NePA
Look [*or* Looke], Delia, how we esteem the half-blown rose. To Delia, XXXVI. Samuel Daniel. ElL; ElSeCe; EnLit; HBV; ReEn; SeCePo; SiCE; TuPP; WHA
Look Down Fair Moon. Walt Whitman. CoV; IAP; OnPM; TCAP
Look down from the lip of the hill. The Quiet Street. Nan McDonald. NeLNL
Look down, look down. Lonesome Road [*or* Look Down That Lonesome Road]. *Unknown.* AS; OuSiCo
Look down on me, a little one. A Child's Morning Prayer. Jeannie Kirby. BoTP
Look Down That Lonesome Road. *Unknown.* *See* Long Lonesome Road.
Look down. The dead have life. Gravestones. Vernon Watkins. ChMP
Look down the long valley and there stands a mountain. Too Anxious for Rivers. Robert Frost. MoPW
Look ere thou leap; nay, thou canst in no wise brook. Looking and Leaping. John Heywood. ReIE
Look, everyone, look! Easter Joy. Nancy Byrd Turner. YeAr
Look: Florentines and Umbrians have made whole. For a Nativity. Lisel Mueller. NePoAm-2
Look for Me on England. H. B. Mallalieu. WaP
Look for rebellion, look to be depos'd. Christopher Marlowe. *Fr.* Edward the Second. PoFr
Look forth and say, "Lo, on the left, from where tumultuous Moyle." "The Land Is Ours." Sir Samuel Ferguson. *Fr.* Congal. IrPN
Look from the [*or* thy] sphere of endless day. Other Sheep I Have, Which Are Not of This Fold [*or* A Home Mission Prayer]. Bryant. PraP; TrPWD
Look, God, I have never spoken to You. Conversion [*or* Last Thoughts of a Fighting Man]. Frances Argermayer. PGD; TreFS
Look, great Ceres, at this band. To Ceres. Joachim du Bellay. TrFP
Look he comes! how tall he is! Conrad Aiken. *Fr.* Punch; the Immortal Liar. NP
"Look here," I said, "Hawk." The Shepherd and the Hawk. William Hart-Smith. AnNZ
Look: Here our bodies lie in a long, long line. But We Shall Bloom. Haim Guri. TrJP
Look Home. Robert Southwell. EV-1; TuPP
Look, how he shakes for cold! Crucifixus pro Nobis [*or* Hymn]. Patrick Carey. OxBoCh; SeCL
Look how he throws them up and up. Bliss Carman. *Fr.* The Juggler. BAP; CV
Look how her close defences laddered like. Apollo and Daphne. W. R. Rodgers. LiTB
Look how it sparkles, see it great. A Diamond. Robert Loveman. AA
Look, how the daffodils arise. John Hall. *Fr.* The Lure. LO
Look How the Flower. William Drummond of Hawthornden. *See* No Trust in Time.
Look how the girl up there. Herodas, *tr. fr. Greek by* Hugo Sharpley. GrPo
Look how the industrious bee in fragrant May. The Bee. Charles Fitzgeffrey. *Fr.* Sir Francis Drake. ElL
Look how the lark soars upward and is gone. False Poets and True. Thomas Hood. HBV
Look [*or* Looke] how the pale queen [*or* queene] of the silent night. A Sonnet of the Moon [*or* The Moon]. Charles Best. CH; ElL; ElSeCe; ES; EtS; HBV; OBSC; TuPP
Look, I Have Thrown All Right. L. A. MacKay. PeCV
Look, I see him! Phaedra Declares Her Love for Her Stepson. Racine. *Fr.* Phèdre. LiA
Look! I stand among workbenches, hammers, furnaces, forges, and/ among a hundred comrades. We Grow Out of Iron. Aleksey Kapitonovich Gastev. TrRV; WoL
Look in mine eyes, Beloved! Is it true. Consummation. Elsa Barker. *Fr.* The Spirit and the Bride. HBMV
Look in my face; my name is Might-have-been. A Superscription. Dante Gabriel Rossetti. The House of Life, XCVII. BEL; BMEP; BPN; EmBrPo; EnL; EnLi-2; EnLit; EPP; FaBoEn; HBV; LEAP; LO; LPS-3; NBE; PG (1955 ed.); PoEL-5; PoVP; SeCePo; TOP; VA; ViPo; ViPP; VLEP; WHA
Look, in the attic, the unentered room. Before the Carnival. Thom Gunn. NePoEA
Look, in the Labyrinth of Memory. Delmore Schwartz. TrJP
Look in Their Eyes, The. Robert Haven Schauffler. AOAH
Look in this mirror, tell me what you see. Glass Dialectic. Howard Nemerov. WaP
Look in thy glass, and tell the face thou viewest. Sonnets, III. Shakespeare. EG; GTBS-W; LiTB; OBSC; PeBoSo; SiCE; TwP
Look Inland Now. Percy MacKaye. JKCP (1955 ed.)
Look into the Gulf, A. Edwin Markham. AA; LBAP; LEAP
Look into Thy Heart. Sir Philip Sidney. *See* Astrophel and Stella, I.
Look into Water, A. A. E. Housman. *See* Oh Fair Enough Are Sky and Plain.
Look! it is as though the sun. Fern House at Kew. Paul Dehn. ChMP
Look! Look at me! Tree Birthdays. Mary Carolyn Davies. OHIP
Look, look! Day dies and the evening has come! Amitié Amoureuse. Luc Grimard. PoNe
Look, look, my lord! Dialogue from "The Dream Queen." Bhasa. *Fr.* The Dream Queen. LiTW

Look! look! the spring is come. First Spring Morning. Robert Bridges. BoTP; YeAr
Look, Mother! the Mariner's rowing. The Mariner's Bride. James Clarence Mangan. IrPN
Look, my countrymen. The Last Journey. Sophocles. *Fr.* Antigone. OxBG
Look, my lady, what I've brought here. With a Water Lily. Ibsen. AnNoLy
Look my love! The Fifth Watch of the Night. Chien T'ang. ChLP; PoHN
Look, my love, on the wall, and here, at this Eastern picture. Morning. Henry Reed. MoVE; NeBP
Look not in my eyes, for fear. A. E. Housman. A Shropshire Lad, XV. PoEL-5; PoVP
Look not on me with scorn because. Simon the Cyrenian Speaks. Glen Baker. ChIP
Look Not Thou. Sir Walter Scott. *See* Lucy Ashton's Song.
Look Not to Me for Wisdom. Charles Divine. HBMV
Look not upon me, seek no more to stay me. M. Kirwan. LO
Look not upon me with such eyes, my son. Miguel de Unamuno. *Fr.* Domestic Scenes. LiTW; WoL
Look Not What Others Do. Christian Morgenstern, *tr. fr. German by* Eileen Hutchins *and* Ursula Grahl. AnGP
Look now, at this February street in April. A Street in April. Louis Dudek. BoCaPo (1948 ed.)
Look now, directed by yon candle's blaze. Fiction. Charles Sprague. *Fr.* Curiosity. AA
Look, O Stranger, at the danger. The T.B.'s Progress. Norman Bethune. PoP
Look of sympathy, the gentle word, The. These Are Not Lost. *At. to* Richard Metcalf *and to* Sarah Doudney. PoToHe
Look off, dear Love, across the sallow sands. Evening Song. Sidney Lanier. AmPP (3d ed.); BAP; CoBA; IAP; LBAP; LEAP; LoPo; LoPS; MOAP; NeHB; OBAV; PG; PoeMoYo; PR; TCAP; TOP
Look on Me with Thy Sweet Eyes. *Unknown, tr. fr. Middle English by* Mabel Van Duzee. MeEV
Look! On the great bronze bell. Buson, *tr. fr. Japanese by* Lois J. Erickson. SoLD
Look—on the topmost branches of the world. Sunday Evening in the Common. John Hall Wheelock. HBV; MAP; MoAmPo; NP; PFY
Look on these waters, with how soft a kiss. An Aestuary. George Croly. IrPN
Look on this cast, and know the hand. The Hand of Lincoln. Edmund Clarence Stedman. AA; OHIP
Look on this maid of honour, now. Philip Massinger. *Fr.* The Maid of Honour. ACP (1952 ed.); GoBC
Look once more e're we leave this specular Mount. Athens. Milton. *Fr.* Paradise Regained, IV. OBS; SeEP; ViBoPo
Look or You Leap. Jasper Heywood. ElL; SiCE; TuPP (Lookers-on, The.) ACP (1952 ed.)
Look our ransomed shores around. Additional Verses to Hail Columbia. Oliver Wendell Holmes. PAH
Look out, boys, better wash your hands. The Marrowbone Itch. *Unknown.* OuSiCo
Look Out for the Snake! Luis Palés Matos, *tr. fr. Spanish by* Donald Devenish Walsh. AnCL
Look out how you use proud words. Primer Lesson. Carl Sandburg. FaPON; MAP; MoAmPo; MoShBr; StVeCh; TSW; TSWC
Look out! look out! Jack Frost. Cecily E. Pike. BoTP
Look out! Look out, boys! Clear the tracks! The Broomstick Train; or, Return of the Witches. Oliver Wendell Holmes. FaPON; HOAH; MCCG; PoMS
Look out upon the stars, my love. A Serenade. Edward Coote Pinkney. AA; AnFE; APA; APW; BAP; BAV; BLV; CoAnAm; HBV; MOAP; OBAV; PIAE; PR; SPP
Look over Yonder, *with music.* Lawrence Gellert. TrAS
Look round our world, behold the chain of love. Nature's Chain. Pope. *Fr.* An Essay on Man. BCEP; LPS-2
Look round the habitable world, how few. The Tenth Satire of Juvenal. *Tr. by* Dryden. WoL
Look round: You see a little supper room. De Coenatione Micae. Martial. FaBoCh; LaP; LoGBV
Look, sisters, look! Chorus of the Furies. Aeschylus. *Fr.* Eumenides. WoL
Look, Stranger! *sel.* W. H. Auden.
  Dedication: "Since the external disorder, and extravagant lies." CaAE
Look, Stranger, on [*or* at] This Island Now. W. H. Auden. CaAE; CoBMV; InvP; MaPo; OAEP (2d ed.); ReaPo (Look, Stranger.) AlDL; MoAB; MoBrPo; MoP; Po; PoFS; ShBV-4; TrGrPo
Look, sunset's all undone! Emblems of Evening. Robert Horan. CrMA
Look, the raft, a signal flying. Far Off-Shore. Herman Melville. AmPP (4th ed.)
Look, the Soldiers! Felix V. Ramos, *tr. fr. Spanish by* Muriel Rukeyser. PoFr
Look! the valleys are thick with grain. Bob White. Dora Read Goodale. BLA; WhBS
Look! . . . There—beyond the window-pane. All-Saints' Eve. Leah Bodine Drake. DaM
Look [*or* See] thou character. Give thy thoughts no tongue. Polonius' Advice to Laertes. Shakespeare. *Fr.* Hamlet, I, iii. BBV; FAOV
Look through this glass. The Telescope. J. C. Hall. HaMV
Look thy last on all things lovely. Farewell. Walter de la Mare. CBE
Look to the blowing Rose about us—"Lo." Careless Delight. Omar Khayyám, *tr. by* Edward Fitzgerald. *Fr.* The Rubáiyát. OnPM
Look to the lattice above. At the Window. Praxilla. OxBG
Look to This Day. *Unknown. See* Salutation of the Dawn, The.
Look Up. Edward Everett Hale. FaBoBe; FaFP; NeHB; OQP; QP-2
  (Lend a Hand.) TreFS
Look Up. Martha Snell Nicholson. BePJ
Look up at Mount Soracte's dazzling snow. Horace. Odes, I, 9. LaP
Look up, languishing soul! Lo, where the fair. The Hymn of the Holy Cross. Richard Crashaw. StJW
"Look up," she said; and all the heavens blazed. Starlight. John White Chadwick. AA
Look up this river in the book of rivers. Border River. Alfred Goldsworthy Bailey. CaP
Look Up to Pentland's Tow'ring Tap. Allan Ramsay. BSV
Look up, you loose-haired women in the field. Running Vines in a Field. H. L. Davis. AnAmPo; LA; NP
Look upward at the hill that must be climbed. Progression. Inez Clark Thorson. MaRV
Look, we don't give a hoot if Zippo-Fasteners have gone to war. Memorial to the Great Big Beautiful Self-sacrificing Advertisers. Frederick Ebright. WaP
Look what immortal floods the sunset pours. The Sea—in Calm. "Barry Cornwall." EtS
Look, wild and wide. The Sea. *Unknown.* KiLC
Look, William, how the morning mists. The Morning Mist. Robert Southey. OTPC
Look, yes, look for them. Dead Angels. Rafael Alberti. CoSP
Look yonder, belovèd, where day reclining. Sunset Clouds. Henrik Wergeland. AnNoLy
Look-a How Dey Done My Lord, *with music. Unknown.* BoAN-2
Looke Delia how we 'steeme the half-blowne rose. *See* Look, Delia, how we esteem the half-blown rose.
Looke heere upon this picture, and on this. Shakespeare. *Fr.* Hamlet, III, iv. NBE
Looke here my boies, see what a world of ground. Tamburlaine's Dying Speech to His Sons. Christopher Marlowe. *Fr.* Tamburlaine the Great. PoD
Looke how a bird lyes tangled in a net. Shakespeare. *Fr.* Venus and Adonis. BrBE
Looke How the Pale Queene. Charles Best. *See* Sonnet of the Moon, A.
Looker-on, The. Frank Kendon. POTE
Lookers-on, The. Jasper Heywood. *See* Look or You Leap.
Lookin' Back. "Moira O'Neill." TIP
Lookin' for the Bully of the Town. *Unknown.* BaBo
Looking and Leaping. John Heywood. ReIE
Looking at the Cross. John Newton. *See* In Evil Long I Took Delight.
Looking at the Moon and Thinking of One Far Away. Chang Chiu-ling, *tr. fr. Chinese by* Witter Bynner. ChLP
Looking Back. Mary Mapes Dodge. FAOV
Looking Back. Heine, *tr. fr. German by* Christopher Middleton. AnGP
Looking back across the years, O Christ, we see Thee go. Palm Sunday Hymn. "George Klingle." ChIP; PSO
Looking by chance in at the open window. The Foreboding. Robert Graves. ChMP; GTBS-D
Looking cautiously down they saw two men fishing. Drama. William Hart-Smith. BoAV; NeLNL
Looking Down on Mesopotamia. Mary Ursula Bethell. AnNZ
Looking Forward. Christina Rossetti. EmBrPo
Looking Forward. Robert Louis Stevenson. InP; OTPC (1946 ed.); PoVP; VLEP
  ("When I am grown to man's estate.") CenHV
Looking from the hut door one dawn in June. Frank Wilmot. *Fr.* The Gully. BoAV; NeLNL
Looking from the Pavilion over the Lake. Su T'ung-po, *tr. fr. Chinese by* Kenneth Rexroth. OnPC
Looking Glass, The. Kipling. FaBoTw; GTSL; OBMV; OnPP
Looking Glass, The. James Shirley. LiTL; LO
Looking-Glass Pussy, The. Margaret Widdemer. RAR; UTS
Looking in the Lake. Po Chü-i, *tr. fr. Chinese by* Ching Ti. WhP
Looking into History. Richard Wilbur. PoLFOT
Looking into the windows that doom has broken. Sonnet. George Woodcock. NeBP
Looking on the peaceful face. A Dirge. Hisaki. OnPM
Looking one day toward the coast of France. Ballade. Charles d'Orléans. LiTW

Looking over the water shows nothing but trees. Windowed Habitations. Charles G. Bell. NePoAm-2
Looking to the sea, it is a line. The Innocence. Robert Creeley. NeAP
Looking toward Mount Wu. Li Po, *tr. fr. Chinese.* WhP
Looking Up. Hiromi, *tr. fr. Japanese by* Lois J. Erickson. SoLD
Looking Within. John Lehmann. MBP
Lookout, The. William Collins. EtS
Look-out seaman loudly bawled, The. The Fight. John Mitford. *Fr.* The Adventures of Johnny Newcome in the Navy. SG
Lookout watch must climb and climb, The. Crow's Nest. Richard F. Armknecht. GoYe
Looks like to me. Little Green Tree Blues. Langston Hughes. PoNe
Looks of a Lover Enamoured, The. George Gascoigne. EIL; SeCePo
Loom, The. Edgar Lee Masters. TBM
Loom of Dreams, The. Arthur Symons. PoVP
Loom of Time, The ("Man's life is laid"). *Unknown.* BLPA; MaRV; NeHB
Loom of Years, The, *sel.* Alfred Noyes.
"O, woven in one wide Loom." MaRV
Loon, The. Theodore Harding Rand. CaP; OCL
Loon, The. Lew Sarett. BAP; BLA; HBMV; TBM
Loon, The. Alfred Billings Street. AA; BLA
Loons, The. Archibald Lampman. VA
Loose earth falls in the grave like a peaceful regular breathing, The. A Dog's Death. J. C. Squire. TCEP
Loose eyes of an old man, The. Negroes. Maxwell Bodenheim. PoNe
Loose Saraband, A. Richard Lovelace. PoEL-3
Loping along on the day's patrol. The Sheepherder. Lew Sarett. FaPON; GaP
Loping and sloped with heat, face thatched and red. Drinker. Patrick Anderson. PeCV
Loppèd tree in time may grow again, The. Times [*or* Tymes] Go [*or* Time Goes] by Turns. Robert Southwell. ACP; AEV; CoBE; EIL; ElSeCe; FaBoEn; GoBC; GTBS-W; HBV; LiTB; LiTG; OBEV (1st ed.); OBSC; OxBoCh; PG; PoEL-2; SiCE; WP
Lopsided with God. On the Road to Vicenza. Ralph Gustafson. CaP
Lord, The. José María Gabriel y Galán, *tr. fr. Spanish by* Thomas Walsh. CAW
Lord, a big fat woman with the meat shakin' on her bones. Big Fat Woman. *Unknown.* OuSiCo
Lord above gave man an arm of iron, The. With a Little Bit of Luck. Alan Jay Lerner. FaFP
Lord above, in tender love, The. Thanksgiving Hymn. *Unknown.* PAH
Lord Alfred Tennyson/ Lived upon venison. Important People. Louis Untermeyer, *and others.* StaSt
Lord and Judge, The. Mikhail Lomonosov, *tr. fr. Russian by* Sir John Bowring. BoRS
Lord Apollo, who has never died, The. Many Are Called. E. A. Robinson. BAP; InP; MoVE; OnAP; OxBA; TBM
Lord Arnaldos. James Elroy Flecker. StPo
Lord, art Thou at the table-head above. The Reflection [*or* Reflexion]. Edward Taylor. AmPP; AtBAP; NePA; OxBA
Lord, as thou wilt, bestow. Prayer. Eduard Mörike. TrPWD
Lord Banner. *Unknown. See* Little Musgrave and Lady Barnard.
Lord Bateman. *Unknown. See* Young Beichan.
Lord Bayham. *Unknown. See* Young Beichan.
Lord Beichan and Susie Pye. *Unknown. See* Young Beichan.
Lord, bless my playmates. A Prayer for My Playmates. *Unknown.* PraP
Lord bless thee and keep thee, The. Benediction [*or* Blessing of the Priests]. Numbers, Bible, *O.T.* TrGrPo; TrJP
Lord Buddha, on thy Lotus-throne. To a Buddha Seated on a Lotus. Sarojini Naidu. MM
Lord Buffington. Lucy W. Rhu. DDA
Lord, but it's cold and wretchedly I'm wrapped. The Second Shepherds' Play. *Unknown.* MeEV
"Lord Byron was a very famous poet." Epitaphic Sonnets. *Unknown.* CAG
"Lord Byron" was an Englishman. Julia A. Moore. *Fr.* Sketch of Lord Byron's Life. FiBHP
Lord Caesar, when you sternly wrote. After Construing. A. C. Benson. VA
Lord, call thy pallid angel. Corn-Law Hymn. Ebenezer Elliott. BCEP; LPS-2
Lord! canst Thou see and suffer? Is Thy hand. Francis Quarles. *Fr.* Emblems. EPS
Lord Chancellor's Song ("When you're lying awake"). W. S. Gilbert. *Fr.* Iolanthe. CoBE; PCD, *much abr.*
(Nightmare.) CoEV; LiTM; OxBoLi; ShBV-3; SiTL; YT
Lord Chancellours Villanies Discovered, The; or His Rise and Fall in the Four Last Years. *Unknown.* CoMu
Lord Christ, beneath Thy starry dome. Hymn for a Household. Daniel Henderson. ChIP; HBMV; MaRV; OQP; PraP; QP-1; StJW
Lord Christ Came to Notre Dame, The. Richard Le Gallienne. SDH
Lord Christ, if I might serve Thee in my heart. Joan of Arc at Domremy. Charles Buxton Going. VOD
Lord Christ, when first thou cam'st to men. O Love That Triumphs over Loss. Walter Russell Bowie. MaRV
Lord Clive. E. C. Bentley. *Fr.* Biography for Beginners. BOHV; MoShBr; OxBoLi; WhC
(Clive.) ShBV-3
("What I like about Clive.") CenHV
Lord, Come Away! Jeremy Taylor. *See* Christ's Coming in Triumph.
Lord comes not, and stays his steps, The. The Lord of Hsiang. Chu Yuan. *Fr.* The Nine Songs. WhP
Lord, confound this surly sister. The Curse. J. M. Synge. ChTr; SiTL
Lord Cornwallis and a Carolina Spring. Helen Bevington. NoCaPo (rev. ed.)
Lord Delamere. *Unknown.* ESPB
Lord Derwentwater. *Unknown.* BaBo; ESPB (A *and* D *vers.*)
Lord descended from above, The. The Majesty of God. Thomas Sternhold. WGRP
Lord, dismiss us with thy blessing. John Fawcett. OlF
Lord Donald. *Unknown. See* Lord Randal.
Lord, Dost Thou Look on Me. Christina Rossetti. EPN
Lord Erlinton had ae daughter. Erlinton. *Unknown.* ESPB
Lord Erskine, at women presuming to rail. A Wife. Sheridan. BOHV
Lord Finchley. Hilaire Belloc. FiBHP; OxBoLi
Lord, for the erring thought. The Undiscovered Country [*or* A Thanksgiving *or* A Prayer]. William Dean Howells. HBV; MaRV; OQP; PEOR; PraP; QP-2; TrPWD; WGRP
Lord, for tomorrow and its needs. Just for Today [*or* To-Day]. Sybil F. Partridge, *wr. at. to* Samuel Wilberforce *and to* Frederick W. Faber. HBV; MaRV; OQP; PraP; QP-1; TreF; VA; WHL
Lord, forgive. Prayer. Pauline Schroy. OQP; QP-2
Lord frowned down from every wall, The. Childhood. Donagh MacDonagh. NeIP
Lord Gabriel, wilt thou not rejoice. Cradle Song. Josephine Preston Peabody. BOL; HBV; NP; SBMV
Lord Galloway. Burns. OxBoLi
Lord Gave, The. Job, I: 20–21, Bible, *O.T.* TreF
Lord, Give Me Faith. Dwight Edwards Marvin. PraP
Lord, give me faith!—to live from day to day. Faith. John Oxenham. MaRV
Lord, give me vision that shall see. Beyond the Profit of Today. *Unknown.* PoToHe (new ed.)
Lord, give them freedom who are weak. A Hymn. Nikolai Alekseyevich Nekrasov. LiTW
Lord, give Thy people hearing ears. A Pastor's Prayer for His Congregation. Grace E. Troy. PraP
Lord, give us more of faith. A Prayer. Nancy Byrd Turner. PraP
Lord God, how full our cup of happiness! The Cup of Happiness. Gilbert Thomas. MaRV; TrPWD
Lord God in Paradise. Grace for Gardens. Louise Driscoll. NLK; TrPWD
Lord God of Hosts, be with us here! Prayer in the Trenches, I. Brent Dow Allinson. AOAH
Lord God of hosts, we render thanks. Our Refuge and Strength. Grenville Kleiser. PraP
Lord, God of love, the wedded hearts'. The Sanctum. T. A. Daly. TrPWD
Lord, God of peace, my spirit's high ideal. Prologue from "Peace on Earth." Gudmundur Gudmundsson. IcP
Lord God of the oak and the elm. Prayer. George Villiers. TrPWD
Lord God of trajectory and blast. Man unto His Fellow Man. Norman Corwin. *Fr.* On a Note of Triumph. QS; TrJP
Lord God Planted a Garden, The. Dorothy Frances Gurney. DD; FaBoBe; HBMV; NeHB; WGRP
(God's Garden.) MaRV
Lord God said to His angel, The: "Let the old things pass away." Revelation. John Jerome Rooney. JKCP
Lord God smiled, The. The Preachers. Norman Nicholson. NeBP
Lord God! this was a stone. The Stone. Thomas Vaughan. OBS; PrWP
Lord God walked in the morning cool, The. First Mother. Vivian Yeiser Laramore. MotAn
Lord God, who let Your baby Son. Father-Prayer. Margaret Widdemer. PraP
Lord Gorbals. Harry Graham. ShBV-2
Lord, Grant Us Calm. Christina Rossetti. EPN; OxBoCh
Lord, grant us eyes to see, and ears to hear. Prayer. Christina Rossetti. ChIP
Lord Guy. George F. Warren. BOHV
Lord had a job for me, The. Get Somebody Else [*or* Too

Lord had a job for me, The (*continued*)
Busy]. *At. to* Paul Laurence Dunbar. BLRP; MaRV; WBLP
Lord Harry has written a novel. A Novel of High Life. Thomas Haynes Bayly. EV-4
Lord, hast Thou set me here. The Priest's Lament. Robert Hugh Benson. ACP
Lord hath builded for Himself, The. The Unknown God. Henry Francis Lyte. MaRV
"Lord hath need of thee, The; do thou be good." One Day at Rouen. Sister Mary Bernetta. JKCP (1955 ed.)
Lord, Have Mercy on Us. Thomas Nashe. *See* Adieu, Farewell, Earth's Bliss!
Lord Hay's Mask, *sel.* Thomas Campion.
Roses. OBSC
(Now Hath Flora Robbed Her Bowers.) EV-2
Lord [*or* Lawd] he thought he'd make a man, De. Dese Bones Gwine to Rise Again. *Unknown.* ABF; APW; AS; OxBoLi; SoAF
Lord, help me live from day to day. Others. Charles D. Meigs. MaRV; OQP; QP-1; WBLP
Lord, her watch thy Church is keeping. Henry Downton. OlF
Lord Hervey. Pope. *See* Sporus.
Lord Heygate. Hilaire Belloc. OxBoLi
Lord High-Bo. Hilaire Belloc. FiBHP
Lord, how can man preach Thy eternal word? The Windows [*or* The Church Windows]. George Herbert. CoBE; ElSeCe; EPS; MaPo; MeLP; OAEP; OBS; SeCV-1
Lord, how is Gamester chang'd! His hair close cut. On Reformed Gamester. Ben Jonson. ReIE
Lord! how this weather is cold, and I am ill happed. The Second Shepherds' Play. *Unknown.* EM-1; EnLit
Lord, I am glad for the great gift of living. Prayer to the Giver. Charles Hanson Towne. OQP; PSO; QP-1
Lord, I Am Here. Christina Rossetti. *Fr.* Christ Our All in All. MeRV
("Lord, I am here.—But, child, I look for thee.") ViP
Lord, I am humbled by the great. Scatheless. Marguerite Wilkinson. BAP; HBMV; TBM
Lord, I am like to Misletoe. To God. Robert Herrick. TrPWD; WGRP
Lord, I am poor; but it becomes. I Have a Roof. Ada Jackson. TrPWD
Lord, I am thankful for this day. Thanksgiving. Whitney Montgomery. PraP
Lord, I am weeping. As Thou wilt, O Lord. The Absent Soldier Son. Sydney Dobell. MOAH
Lord, I confess my sin is great. Repentance. George Herbert. OAEP
Lord, I do not ask for houses of steel. Prayer of the Unemployed. Raymond Kresensky. OQP; QP-2
Lord, I doubt no more Thy mercy. The Other Room. *Unknown.* PraP
Lord, I give thanks! Thanksgiving. Susie M. Best. QS; TrPWD
Lord, I have fasted, I have prayed. Weakness of Nature. Richard Hurrell Froude. OBRV
Lord, I have knelt and tried to pray to-night. Communion. Edward Dowden. MaRV; TrPWD
Lord, I have not time to pray. Helene Magaret. *Fr.* Impiety. TrPWD
Lord, I have passed another day. An Evening Hymn. Ann *or* Jane Taylor. BOL
Lord, I have sinn'd, and the black number swells. The Penitent. Jeremy Taylor. OBS; OxBoCh
Lord, I remember, and am sore amazed. Hymn of Weeping. Amittai ben Shefatiah. TrJP
Lord, I say nothing; I profess. Christ the Man. W. H. Davies. ChMo; CMP; MaRV; WGRP
Lord, I Want to Be a Christian in-a My Heart. *Unknown.* BoAN-2, *with music;* OlF
Lord, I would follow, but. Follow Me! John Oxenham. ChIP; MaRV
Lord, I would thank You for these things. Gifts without Season. Joseph Auslander. MaRV
Lord, if I dare not sing of seraphs' flaming wings. Earthbound. Theodore Maynard. QS
Lord! if in love, though fainting oft, I have tended thy gracious Vine. "Owen Meredith." *Fr.* Last Lines. TrPWD
Lord, if this night my journey end. Hymn in Contemplation of Sudden Death. Dorothy L. Sayers. QS
Lord, If Thou Art Not Present. John Gray. CAW; TrPWD
Lord, I'm done for: now Margot. Rondeau. William Jay Smith. FiBHP
Lord, I'm just a little boy. Child's Christmas Song. T. A. Daly. OBAV
Lord, in all the stir. A Prayer at Christmas Time. Nancy Byrd Turner. PraP
Lord, in an age of steel and stone. A Prayer for Today. Charles Nelson Pace. MaRV; OQP; QP-2
Lord in His wisdom made the fly, The. The Fly. Ogden Nash. FaPON
Lord, in mercy pardon me. A Prayer. Frances Ridley Havergal. PraP
Lord, in my silence how do I despise. Frailty. George Herbert. ElSeCe; OxBoCh
Lord, in the strength of grace. Dedication. Charles Wesley. MaRV
Lord! in the temple of thy love. Song of Adoration to God. Thomas Holley Chivers. SPP
Lord, in this day of battle. Prayer during Battle. Hermann Hagedorn. TrPWD
Lord, in this dust Thy sovereign voice. A Thanksgiving. Cardinal Newman. TrPWD
Lord, in this hour of tumult [*or* day of battle]. Prayer during Battle. Hermann Hagedorn. POT; SBMV; VOD
Lord, in thy name thy servants plead. Seed Time Hymn. John Keble. VA
Lord! in whose sight a thousand years but seem. Sacred Ode. Juan Meléndez Valdés. AnSpL-2
Lord indeed is risen, The. He Is Risen. John Oxenham. ChIP
Lord Ingram and Chiel Wyet. *Unknown.* BaBo; ESPB (A, B, *and* C *vers.*); OBB
Lord Is a Man of War, The. Exodus, XV: 3-10, Bible, *O.T.* WaaP
Lord Is King, The. *Unknown, tr. fr. Hebrew by* Solomon Solis-Cohen. TrJP
Lord is my friend, so I shall not be lonely, The. A One Hundred Fifty-first Psalm. Henry B. Robins. MaRV
Lord is my light and my salvation, The. My Light and My Salvation [*or* The Deliverance of Jehovah]. Psalm XXVII, Bible, *O.T.* MaRV; WGRP
Lord Is My Shepherd, The. Psalms, XXIII, Bible, *O.T.* EnLi-1; FaPON; HiLiEn; MaRV; OuHeWo; StVeCh; TrJP; TreF
(Protection of Jehovah, The, *Moulton, Modern Reader's Bible.*) WGRP
(Psalm of David.) SUS
(Psalm of the Shepherd, The.) GrCo-1
(Psalm XXIII.) AWP; EM-1; ExPo; JAWP; OHIP; OnPM; PC; PG (1955 ed.); ReIE; TiPo (1952 ed.); WBLP; WoL
(Shepherd's Psalm.) PCD; PCH
(Twenty-third Psalm, The.) FaBoBe; NeHB; OTPC (1946 ed.); PoeMoYo; PreP; PYM; StaSt; TrGrPo
Lord Is My Shepherd, The. John Knox, *par. fr.* Psalms, XXIII, Bible, *O.T.* BePJ
Lord, It Belongs Not to My Care. Richard Baxter. MaRV; OxBoCh
(Entering by His Door, *abr.*) BePJ
Lord it is my chief complaint. William Cowper. *Fr.* Lovest Thou Me? TrPWD
Lord! It Is Not Life to Live. Augustus Montague Toplady. *Fr.* Happiness Found. MaRV; OxBoCh; TrPWD
Lord, it is time. Most great the summer was. Autumn's Day. Rainer Maria Rilke, *tr. by* Kate Flores. AnGP
Lord, it is time. The summer was too long. Autumn Day. Rainer Maria Rilke, *tr. by* C. F. MacIntyre. TrJP
Lord, It's All, Almost Done, *with music.* *Unknown.* OuSiCo
Lord Jesus Christ, my life, my light. I Shall Be Satisfied. M. Behemb. BePJ
Lord Jesus, make Thyself to me. My Prayer. *Unknown.* BePJ; BLRP; PraP
Lord Jesus, Thou hast known. A Mother's Birthday. Henry van Dyke. MaRV; OHIP
Lord Jesus! when I think of Thee. The King in His Beauty. James G. Deck. BePJ
Lord Jesus, When We Stand Afar. William Walsham How. ChIP
Lord Jesus, who would think that I am thine? Hold Thou Me Fast. Christina Rossetti. BePJ
Lord Jesus! with what sweetness and delights. Ascension-Day. Henry Vaughan. OxBoCh
Lord Jesus, You were always good. In Illness. *Unknown.* PraP
Lord, kill my restless spirit. And There Shall Be No Night. Amelia Kathleen Blessington. DuMV
Lord, lay the taste of prayer upon my tongue. The Taste of Prayer. Ralph W. Seager. TrPWD
Lord, lay your fingers on. Closing Prayer. Johnstone G. Patrick. TrPWD
Lord, let me be the torch that springs to light. The Torch. Theodosia Garrison. BLPA
Lord, let me live like a regular man. A Prayer. Berton Braley. BLPA
Lord, let me make this rule. School Days. Maltbie D. Babcock. MaRV
Lord, let me not die until I've done for Thee. My Work. *Unknown.* MaRV
Lord, let me not in service lag. A Creed. Edgar A. Guest. HH; PEDC
Lord let me work! At singing I have failed. My Song. Eunice K. Biddle. PSO
Lord, let my heart be always young at Christmas. A Christmas Prayer. Ruby Dell Baugher. PraP

Lord, let not my religion be. A Prayer. Clarence M. Burkholder. OQP; QP-2
Lord, let the angels praise thy name. Miserie. George Herbert. PoEL-2
Lord let the house of a brute to the soul of a man, The. By an Evolutionist. Tennyson. BEL; EmBrPo; EnLi-2; EPN; PoVP; TCEP
Lord, let war's tempests cease. Let War's Tempests Cease. Longfellow. OHIP
Lord, life is good! Thanksgiving. Charles Hanson Towne. PoMa
Lord Livingston. *Unknown.* ESPB
Lord, Lord to Thee. A Sailor's Prayer. George Hornell Morris. TrPWD
Lord Lovel. *Unknown.* ABS (A *and* B *vers.*); AS, *with music;* BaBo (A *and* B *vers.*); BLPA; BoChLi; ESPB (A, B, *and* D *vers.*); FaPON; LoEn; OBB; OnSP; OTPC; PoMS; TreFS; ViBoFo (A *and* B *vers.*)
Lord Lovell he stood at his own front door. The Tale of Lord Lovell, *parody. Unknown.* PA
Lord Lundy. Hilaire Belloc. OxBoLi; ShBV-3
Lord, Make a Regular Man Out of Me. Edgar A. Guest. BLPA; NeHB
Lord, Make Me an Instrument of Your Peace. St. Francis of Assisi, *tr. fr. Italian.* TreFS
("Prayer: Lord, make me an instrument of Thy Peace.") PoToHe (new ed.)
(Prayer for Peace.) SaFP
(St. Francis' Prayer.) MaRV
Lord, make me coy and tender to offend. Unkindness. George Herbert. HBV
Lord, Make Me to Know Mine End. Psalms, XXXIX, Bible, *O.T.* TrJP
Lord, make me sensitive to the sight. Prayer. Barbara Marr. TrPWD
Lord, make my childish soul stand straight. A Prayer. "William Laird." HBMV
Lord, make my loving a guard for them. Mother-Prayer. Margaret Widdemer. HBMV; PraP
Lord, make my soul. The Mirror. Blanche Mary Kelly. GoBC; TrPWD
Lord, Many Times I Am Aweary Quite. Richard Chenevix Trench. BePJ; OBRV
Lord Maxwell's Last Goodnight. *Unknown.* BaBo; ESPB (A *and* B *vers.*); OBB
(Lord Maxwell's Good-Night.) EBSV
Lord, may I be a sparrow in a tree. Sparrow. Stephen Vincent Benét. DDA
Lord, may there be no moment in her life. Prayer of Any Husband. Mazie V. Caruthers. MaRV; PoToHe
Lord, mind your trees to-day! The Bushfeller. Eileen Duggan. AnNZ; JKCP (1955 ed.)
Lord, must I bear the whole of it, or none? Crucifixion. Frederick George Scott. ChIP; MaRV; OQP; QP-1
Lord, my first-fruits present themselves to thee. The Dedication. George Herbert. OAEP
Lord my pasture shall prepare, The. Pastoral Hymn [*or* Trust in God]. Addison. EV-3; OBEC; OlF
Lord never grant me what I ask for. The Unforeseen. Conrado Nalé Roxlo. AnCL; LiTW
Lord North's Recantation. *Unknown.* PAH
Lord, not for light in darkness do we pray. A Prayer. John Drinkwater. HBV; MaRV; OBVV; QS; TrPWD; WGRP
Lord, now lettest thou thy servant depart in peace. Nunc Dimittis. St. Luke, Bible, *N.T.* WGRP; WHL
Lord, now that Spring is in the world. An Easter Prayer [*or* Easter]. Charles Hanson Towne. ChIP; OQP; PSO; QP-1
Lord. Oh, hear me prayin' Lord. Oh, Hear Me Prayin'. *Unknown.* BoAN-2
Lord of All, The. Edwin Markham. BCEP; CAW
Lord of All Being. Oliver Wendell Holmes. *See* Sun-Day Hymn, A.
Lord of all growing things. Growing. *Unknown.* MaRV
Lord of All I Survey. Keith Sinclair. AnNZ
Lord of all light and darkness. At a Burial. Sir William Watson. MaRV
Lord of all pots and pans and things, since I've no time to be. Prayer Hymn. "M. K. H." ChIP; OQP; QP-2
Lord of all the lore that man had found, The. Saint Thomas Aquinas. Thomas S. Jones, Jr. CAW
Lord of Athene's holy hill. The Coming of Theseus towards Athens. Bacchylides. GrPE
Lord of Burleigh, The. Tennyson. BPN; CG; OTPC (1923 ed.); PECK
Lord of Butrago, The. *Unknown, tr. fr. Spanish by* John Gibson Lockhart. LPS-2
Lord of days and nights that hear thy word of wintry warning. A Word with the Wind. Swinburne. BPN
Lord of Dollars, The. Francisco de Quevedo y Villegas, *tr. fr. Spanish by* Thomas Walsh. AnSpL-1; TeCS
(Letrilla; the Lord of Dollars.) WoL
Lord of Eden. Marie de L. Welch. AnAmPo
Lord of Europa's Tyrian line. Song of the Initiated. Euripides. OxBG
Lord of Heaven to Earth Came Down, The. Kathryn Blackburn Peck. BePJ
Lord of Himself. Sir Henry Wotton. *See* Character of a Happy Life, The.
Lord of Hsiang, The. Chu Yuan, *tr. fr. Chinese by* Shen Yu-ting. *Fr.* The Nine Songs. WhP
Lord of life, look smiling down. A Marriage Prayer. Gerald Massey. PraP
Lord of Lorn and the False Steward, The. *Unknown.* ESPB
(Lord of Lorn, The, *shorter vers.*) OBB
Lord of My Heart's Elation. Bliss Carman. BoCaPo; HBV; LBMV; NV; TrPWD
(Veni Creator.) MaRV
Lord of my love, to whom in vassalage. Sonnets, XXVI. Shakespeare. PeBoSo; PoFS; ReEn
Lord of my years, can life be bare. Common Blessings. Thomas Curtis Clark. TrPWD
Lord of Nature. Pindar, *tr. fr. Greek by* Lionel W. Lyde. GrR
Lord of our fathers, hear our prayer. Decoration Day Prayer. Arthur Roszelle Bemis, Jr. OQP; QP-1
Lord of Rosslyn's daughter gaed through the wud her lane, The. Captain Wedderburn's Courtship. *Unknown.* ViBoFo (A *vers.*); ESPB (B *vers.*)
Lord of Sea and Earth and Air. Prayer for a Pilot. Cecil Roberts. BBV; FaPON; OTPC (1946 ed.); TrPWD
Lord of Tartary. Walter de la Mare. *See* Tartary.
Lord of the Brave and Strong. *Unknown, tr. fr. Russian by* John Brownlie. GrCo-1
Lord of the Celtic dells. To Joseph Ablett. Walter Savage Landor. BPN; EmBrPo
Lord of the East, The. Chu Yuan, *tr. fr. Chinese by* Shen Yu-ting. *Fr.* The Nine Songs. LiTW; WhP
Lord of the Far Horizons. Bliss Carman. MaRV; TrPWD
Lord of the grass and hill. Overlord [*or* Veni Creator]. Bliss Carman. CaP; OCL; WGRP
Lord of the Isle, The. Stefan George, *tr. fr. German by* Ludwig Lewisohn. AWP; JAWP; WPB
(Lord of the Island, The, *tr. by* Charles E. Passage.) AnGP
Lord of the Isles, The, *sels.* Sir Walter Scott.
Bannockburn, *fr.* VI. BSV
Fading Autumn, *fr.* I. EV-4
Lake Coriskin, *fr.* III. EV-4
Savage Grandeur. *fr.* IV. EV-4
Tempest, A, *fr.* III. EV-4
Lord of the land. Prayer of a Patriot. Henry J. von Schlichten. BePJ
Lord of the lands, beneath Thy bending skies. A Hymn for Canada. Albert Durrant Watson. CaP; CPG; OCL
Lord of the Mountain. Navajo Prayer [*or* Prayer to the Mountain Spirit]. *Unknown.* PoRL; StVeCh; WGRP
Lord of the odored alleys green! who on the silence flings. The Mocking Bird. Irving Bacheller. BLA
Lord of the pots and pipkins, since I have not time to be. The Divine Office of the Kitchen. Cecily Hallack. BLRP
Lord of the Pythian treasure. Sophocles. *Fr.* Oedipus Rex. GrPo
Lord of the Sabbath, hear us pray. Hear Us, in This Thy House. Philip Doddridge. BePJ
Lord of the seas' great wilderness. Watchmen of the Night. Cecil Roberts. VOD (1931 ed.)
Lord of the strong, when earth you trod. Lord of Us All. Donald Hankey. MaRV
Lord of the tender twilight sky. Vespers. Claribel Weeks Avery. PraP
Lord of the Winds. Mary Elizabeth Coleridge. OxBoCh; TrPWD
Lord of the winds! I feel thee nigh. The Hurricane. Bryant. LPS-2; PEOR
Lord of the World, The. G. A. Studdert-Kennedy. PGD; PSO
Lord of the World. *Unknown, tr. fr. Hebrew by* D. A. de Sola. TrJP
Lord of Us All. Donald Hankey. MaRV
Lord of wind and water. A Sea-Prayer. William Stanley Braithwaite. OBAV; PraP
Lord over all! whose power the sceptre swayed. Lord of the World. *Unknown.* TrJP
Lord over life and all the ways of breath. Ernest Dowson. *Fr.* De Amore. TrPWD
Lord Phoebus, when our Lady, the gracious Leto, bore Thee. Nativity. Theognis. GrPE
Lord possessed me in the beginning of his ways, The. Proverbs, Bible, *O.T.* (*Douay vers.*). ISi
Lord preserve thy going out, The. A Friend's Prayer. *Unknown.* PraP
Lord, purge our eyes to see. Judge Not According to the Appearance. Christina Rossetti. TrPWD

Lord Rameses of Egypt sighed. Birthright. John Drinkwater. AlDL; CH; HBV; LBBV; MM; POTE; WHA
Lord Randal. *Unknown.* AtBAP; ATP; AWP; BaBo (A, B, C, *and* D *vers.*); BEL; BLV; BoLiVe; BSV; CaAE; CBOV; CG; CoBE; EM-1; EnL; EnRP; EnSB; EPP; ESPB (A, B, *and* J *vers.*); GBV (1952 ed.); HBV; HoPM; InP; InPo; JAWP; LiTB; LiTG; LoBV; OBB; OnSP; OuHeWo; PCN; PFE; PIAE; PreP; RiBV; SeCeV; ShBV-1; TOP; TreF; TrGrPo; TwHP; UnPo; ViBoFo (A, B, *and* C *vers.*); WBP; WP
(Jimmy Randolph.) ABS
(Johnny Randall.) ABS; PIAE
(Lord Donald.) BrBE
(Lord Randall.) LiTL; MaC; ReaPo
Lord, The, reigneth, he is apparelled with majesty. Jehovah's Immovable Throne. Psalms, XCIII, Bible, *O.T.* WGRP
Lord Ronald. *Unknown.* LoEn
Lord Ronald courted Lady Clare. Lady Clare. Tennyson. GoTP
Lord Ronald was a mighty man. Lord Ronald. *Unknown.* LoEn
Lord said, The,/ "Say 'We.'" Pronouns. Karle Wilson Baker. GrCo-2; LS; QS
Lord Saltoun and Auchanachie. *Unknown.* BaBo; ESPB
Lord, Save Us, We Perish. Christina Rossetti. TrPWD
Lord Shaftesbury. Dryden. *See* Achitophel.
Lord, since the night has come, I say my prayer to Thee. The Prayer of the Humble. Zacharias Papondoniou. MoGP
Lord, since the strongest human hands I know. In the Dark. Sophie Jewett. LBAP; TrPWD
Lord, spare to them this very little child. Prayer That an Infant May Not Die. Francis Jammes. CAW
Lord, Speak to Me, that I May Speak. Frances Ridley Havergal. MaRV; OlF
(For Every Day.) BLRP
(Worker's Prayer, A.) PraP
Lord, Take Away Pain. *Unknown.* BPP; OQP; QP-1
(Pain.) MaRV
Lord, teach a little child to pray. A Child's Prayer. *Unknown.* BOL
Lord that purposed for his more avail, A. Of Inclosing a Common. Sir John Harington. SiCE
Lord, the newness of this day. Prayer. Henry van Dyke. PraP
Lord, the people of the land. Hymn. *Unknown.* IDAH
Lord, the Roman hyacinths are blooming in bowls. A Song for Simeon. T. S. Eliot. BLV; BoLiVe; CoBE; LiTB; MAP; MaRV; MM; MoAmPo (1942 ed.); OxBoCh; POTE; TwCV
Lord, the snowful sky. Sailor's Carol. Charles Causley. AtBAP
Lord, Thine humble servants hear. Hymn for Atonement Day. Judah Halevi. TrJP
Lord, this humble house we'd keep. Edgar A. Guest. *Fr.* Prayer for the Home. MaRV
Lord Thomas and Fair Annet (*diff. versions*). *Unknown.* BaBo (A *and* B *vers.*); EnLit; ESPB (A, D, *and* I *vers.*); OBB; ViBoFo
(Brown Girl, The, C *vers.*) BaBo
(Brown Girl, or Fair Eleanor, The, *with music.*) AS
(Brown Girl, or Fair Ellender, The.) SPP
(Lord Thomas.) ABS
(Lord Thomas and Fair Ellinor.) CG
(Nut-brown Bride, The.) EBSV
(Sir Peter's Leman, D *vers., tr. fr. Danish by* E. M. Smith-Dampier.) BaBo; BoDaBa
Lord Thomas and Lady Margaret. *Unknown.* BaBo; ESPB
Lord Thomas he was a bold forrester. Lord Thomas and Fair Annet (B *vers.*). *Unknown.* BaBo
Lord Thomas is to the hunting gone. Lord Thomas and Lady Margaret. *Unknown.* BaBo
Lord Thomas Stuart. *Unknown.* BaBo; ESPB
Lord Thomas's Wedding. *Unknown. See* Lord Thomas and Fair Annet.
Lord, thou art mine, and I am thine. Clasping of Hands. George Herbert. PoEL-2
Lord, thou dost know with what implacable hand. The Calling. Luis Felipe Contardo. CAW
Lord, thou hast been our dwelling place in all generations. God, Our Dwelling Place [*or* The Span of Man *or* Thou Art God]. Psalm XC, Bible, *O.T.* AWP; BPP; EM-1; MaRV
Lord, thou hast given me a cell. A Thanksgiving to God for His House [*or* A Thankful Heart]. Robert Herrick. AEV; BCEP; BEL; CenL; ChTr; ElSeCe; EM-1; EnLi-1; EnLit; EPS; EV-2; FaBoBe; HBV; InPo; LEAP; MaRV; NeHB; OBS; OHIP; OQP; OTPC; PEOR; PGD; Po; PoE; PoRA; PoToHe; QP-1; ReEn; SeCeV; SeCV-1; SeEP; TiPo (1952 ed.); TOP; TrPWD; UnPo (1st ed.); ViBoPo; WGRP; WoL; WP
Lord, Thou hast made this world below the shadow of a dream. M'Andrew's Hymn. Kipling. OtMeF; PoEL-5; ViPP
Lord, Thou knowest how I live. Bedtime Prayer. Henry van Dyke. PraP
Lord, thou who didst teach, forgive me for teaching. The Teacher's Prayer. "Gabriela Mistral." MaRV
Lord, Thy peaceful gift restore. Night-Watch Prayer. Henry van Dyke. PraP
Lord, Thy power knows no declining. Rallying Hymn for the Church. Alexander Louis Fraser. PraP
Lord Turned, and Looked upon Peter, The. Elizabeth Barrett Browning. *See* Look, The.
Lord Ullin's Daughter. Thomas Campbell. BBV (1923 ed.); BCEP; BeLS; BoTP; CG; EBSV; EnRP; ERP; EV-4; FaPON; GN; GTBS; GTBS-D; GTBS-W; GTSE; GTSL; HBV; HBVY; LoEn; LPS-1; MW; OBRV; OnSP; OTPC; PECK; PYM; TreF; TVSH; WBLP; WP
Lord, very fair my lot and beautiful my story. Very Fair My Lot. Jacob David Kamzon. TrJP
Lord Vyet. A. C. Benson. OBVV
Lord Walter's Wife. Elizabeth Barrett Browning. BeLS; LPS-1
Lord Waterford. *Unknown.* ChTr
Lord we have not forgotten them, the pioneers. Lord of All I Survey. Keith Sinclair. AnNZ
Lord, we look to once for all, The. The Heretic's Tragedy. Robert Browning. NBE
Lord, we whose sturdy sires. A Supplication. Clinton Scollard. QS
Lord! what a busy [*or* busie], restless thing. The Pursuit. Henry Vaughan. OAEP; TrPWD
Lord, what a change within us one short hour. Prayer [*or* In Thy Presence *or* An Hour with Thee]. Richard Chenevix Trench. BePJ; BLRP; GrCo-1; MaRV; OQP; PoToHe; PraP; QP-1; TrPWD; WBLP; WGRP
Lord what a stately piece was Man. The Fall. Nathaniel Wanley. SeEP
Lord, what am I, that with unceasing care. Tomorrow. Lope de Vega. AnSpL-1; AWP; CAW; MeRV; TeCS; TrPWD
Lord what is man, that he should find. Psalm VIII, Bible, *O.T. Paraphrased by* Christopher Smart. TrPWD
Lord, what is man? why should he cost thee. Charitas Nimia; or, The Dear Bargain. Richard Crashaw. EPS; MaRV; MePo; OxBoCh; PoFS; PoLi; ReEn; SeEP
Lord, what these weders ar cold. The Second Shepherds' Play. *Unknown.* PoEL-1
Lord, what unvalued pleasures crown'd. The Invitation. Nathaniel Wanley. OxBoCh; SeEP
Lord, when I find at last thy paradise. She Asks for New Earth. Katharine Tynan. HBMV
Lord, when I look at lovely things which pass. In the Fields [*or* Spring]. Charlotte Mew. AlDL; MBP; MoAB; MoBrPo; MoP; POTE; StaSt; TwCV
Lord, when my bedtime comes tonight, I pray. Prayer of a Tired Woman. Mazie V. Caruthers. PraP
Lord, when my strength is weakness hitherto unknown. Strength in Weakness. Philip E. Howard. PraP
Lord, when on my bed I lie. A Prayer. John Oxenham. PraP
Lord, when the fields are gripped by cold. The Ravens. Arthur Rimbaud. TrFP
Lord, when the sense of Thy sweet grace. A Song of Divine Love [*or* An Ecstasy *or* Divine Love]. Richard Crashaw. ElSeCe; EPS (1942 ed.); EV-2; GoBC; MaRV; MeRV; PoE; SeCeV; TriL; TrPWD; TwHP; ViBoPo
Lord When the Wise Men Came from Far[r]. Sidney Godolphin. MeLP; OBS
(Hymn: "Lord when the wise men came from farr.") BrBE; MePo
(Wise Men and Shepherds.) OxBoCh
Lord, when they kill me, let the job be thorough. Merthyr. Glyn Jones. PrWP
Lord! When Those Glorious Lights I See. George Wither. LPS-2
Lord, when Thou seest that my work is done. After Work. John Oxenham. MaRV
Lord! when Thou wentest from this place. The Lament of Eve. *Unknown.* ACP (1952 ed.)
Lord, When We Leave the World. Francis Quarles. BCEP
Lord, Where Shall I Find Thee? Judah Halevi, *tr. fr. Hebrew by* Nina Davis Salaman. TrJP
Lord, where Thou art our holy dead must be. Easter Eucharist. *Unknown.* MaRV
Lord, While for All Mankind We Pray. John R. Wreford. MaRV; TrPWD
Lord, who am I to teach the way. The Teacher. Leslie Pinckney Hill. BANP; GrCo-1; MaRV; PoNe; PraP; TrPWD
Lord who are infinitely absent. Nada. Pierre Emmanuel. MiCF
Lord, Who Art Merciful. *Tr. fr. Persian by* Robert Southey. MaRV; TrPWD
(Imitated from the Persian.) EnRP; ERP
Lord, who createdst man in wealth and store. Easter Wings.

George Herbert. ATP; ElSeCe; EOAH; EPS; ExPo; LiTB; MeLP; MePo; OAEP; OBS; PoEL-2; PoFS; PreP; SeEP; TwCrTr
Lord! who desirest that the sin should die. Penitence. Pedro Soto de Rojas. OnPM
Lord Who Dwells in the Clouds, The. Chu Yuan, *tr. fr. Chinese by* Shen Yu-ting. *Fr.* The Nine Songs. WhP
Lord, who lovest little children. "M. R." PraP
Lord, who ordainest for mankind. The Mother's Hymn. Bryant. DD; MaRV; MOAH; MotAn; OHIP
Lord, who shall abide in thy tabernacle? Psalm XV, Bible, *O.T.* OuHeWo
Lord Will Happiness Divine, The. William Cowper. *See* Contrite Heart, The.
Lord William; or, Lord Lundy. *Unknown.* BaBo; ESPB
Lord Willoughby. *Unknown.* CoMu; TuPP
(Brave Lord Willoughby.) EV-2; LH
Lord, with glowing heart I'd praise thee. Hymn. Francis Scott Key. TrPWD
Lord, with what care hast Thou begirt us round! Sin. George Herbert. BCEP; EPS; ES; EV-2; PeBoSo; ViBoPo
Lord! within Thy Peace I Rest Me. Clemens Brentano, *tr. fr. German by* Mabel Cotterell. AnGP
Lordinges, I wol you singen of a grotē. Sing a Song of Sixpence, *parody.* Frank Sidgwick. WhC
"Lordings," he said, "in churches when I preach." The Prologue to the Pardoner's Tale. Chaucer, *mod. by* Frank Ernest Hill. *Fr.* The Canterbury Tales. RiBV
Lordings [*or* Lordingees], listen, and hold you still. Durham Field. *Unknown.* ESPB; OBB
Lordings, Listen to Our Lay. *Unknown, tr. fr. Anglo-Norman carol by* F. Douce. OHIP; SDH
(Anglo-Norman Carol.) AnEC
"Lordings," quod he, "in chirches whan I preche." Prologue to the Pardoner's Tale. Chaucer. *Fr.* The Canterbury Tales. BEL; CoBE; EM-1; EnLi-1; OAEP
Lordly and Isolate Satyrs, The. Charles Olson. NeAP
Lords and ladies all bydene. A New Carol of Our Lady. *Unknown.* AnEC
Lords, knights, and 'squires, the numerous [*or* num'rous] band. To a Child of Quality, Five Years Old. Matthew Prior. AEV; CBOV; CoBE; EiPP; EPP; EV-3; ExPo; GN; GTBS-W; HBV; InP; LiA; LiTB; OBEC; OBEV; PoEL-3; SeCeV; TCEP
Lords' Mask, The, *sel.* Thomas Campion.
Song: To the Masquers Representing Stars. LoBV
(Stars Dance, The.) OBSC
Lords of life, the lords of life, The. Experience. Emerson. AnAmPo; AnNE; IAP; LA; LiTA; MOAP; PoEL-4; TCAP
Lords of the land, the ways my thought hath trod. Fatal Discovery. Sophocles. *Fr.* Oedipus Rex. GrR
Lords of the Main, The. Joseph Stansbury. IAP; PAH
Lords of the Wilderness. John Leyden. OBRV
Lord's Prayer, The. St. Matthew, VI: 9-13, Bible, *N.T.* MaRV; TrGrPo
(Poem of the Our Father, The.) CAW
Lore. Edna Ethel Davis. ChIP
Lore Lay. Clemens Brentano, *tr. fr. German by* Mabel Cotterell. AnGP
Loreine, a Horse. Arthur Davison Ficke. TCPD
Lorelei [*or* Loreley], The. Heine, *tr. fr. German.* AnGP, *tr. into Scottish by* Edwin Morgan; GoTP, *tr. by* Louis Untermeyer; OuHeWo, *tr. by* Sir Theodore Martin; PoMS, *tr. by* William Ellery Leonard; TrJP, *tr. by* Emma Lazarus
(Ich weiss nicht. was soll es bedeuten.) AWP, *tr. by* Alexander MacMillan; PreP, *trs. by* MacMillan *and by* Louis Untermeyer
Lorena. H. D. L. Webster, *wr. at. to* J. P. Webster. BlG; BLPA
Lorenzo's Bas-Relief for a Florentine Chest. Marjorie Allen Seiffert. *See* Italian Chest, An.
Lorraine. Charles Kingsley. VA
(Lorraine Lorèe.) BBV
(Lorraine, Lorraine, Lorrèe.) PoVP
Los is by mortals nam'd Time, Enitharmon is nam'd Space. Blake. *Fr.* Milton, I. OBRV
"Los Pastores." Edith Agnew. ChBR; GaP
Losers. Carl Sandburg. ChMo; CMP; HBMV; MAP; MoAB; MoAmPo; MoVE; NP; TrGrPo
Losers, The. William Young. *See* Pawns, The.
Losing a Slave-Girl. Po Chu-i, *tr. fr. Chinese by* Arthur Waley. AWP; TrCh
Loss. Julia Johnson Davis. HBMV
Loss. Paul Eluard, *tr. fr. French by* Patricia Terry. OnPM
Loss. Randall Jarrell. FiMAP
Loss after Loss. Bianor, *tr. fr. Greek by* Goldwin Smith. OnPM
Loss and Gain. Longfellow. PEOR; PTA-2
Loss at Sea. Callimachus, *tr. fr. Greek by* John Addington Symonds. OnPM
Loss falls from the air as the tables turn. Complaint. Joseph Bennett. LiTA
Loss in Delay[s]. Robert Southwell. OBSC; SiCE
Loss may grieve you, love may leave you. If You Have a Dog. Douglas Malloch. AlBD
Loss of Love, The. Countee Cullen. PoNe
Loss of My Sons, The. Egill Skallagrimsson, *tr. fr. Icelandic by* W. C. Green. PaOS
Loss of the *Birkenhead,* The. Sir Francis Hastings Doyle. HBV
Loss of the *Cedar Grove,* The, *with music. Unknown.* ShS
Loss of the *Druid,* The, *with music. Unknown.* ShS
Loss of the Mortal Maiden. Keats. *Fr.* Endymion, IV. ERP
Loss of the *Ramillies,* The. *Unknown. See* Ship *Rambolee,* The.
Loss of the *Royal George,* The. William Cowper. *See* On the Loss of the *Royal George.*
Losses. Frances Brown. *See* Greatest Loss, The.
Losses. Randall Jarrell. AmP; CoBMV; FiMAP; MoVE; OxBA; UnPo (3rd ed.); WaP
Lost. John Galsworthy. AlBD
Lost. Maurice Lesemann. NP
Lost. Carl Sandburg. BrR; ChMo; CMP; MOAP; NP; ReaPo; TCAP; VOD; WHA
Lost. Celia Thaxter. PPL
Lost a boy! A runaway! Runaway Cupid. Meleager. GrPo; GrR
Lost Acres. Robert Graves. FaBoMo; LiTG; MoPW
Lost—an April. Mary Brent Whiteside. TBM
Lost and alien lie the leas. Fantaisie d'Antan. Clark Ashton Smith. DaM
Lost and Found. George Macdonald. BoFr; MaRV; OQP; QP-1; StJW; WGRP
Lost and Found. Charles Sangster. BoCaPo
Lost and Given Over. E. J. Brady. BoAu
Lost Angel, The. Al-Kasad, *tr. fr. Arabic by* A. J. Arberry. MooP
Lost Ape, The. "J. W. G. W." PA
Lost at Sea. Phaedimus, *tr. fr. Greek by* F. L. Lucas. GrPE
Lost at Sea ("Ah, misty Geraneia"). Simonides, *tr. fr. Greek by* F. L. Lucas. GrPE
Lost at Sea ("From Sparta to Apollo we"). Simonides, *tr. fr. Greek by* G. Arundell Esdaile. GrL; OxBG
Lost at Sea ("Go, topless Geraneia, and gaze, foul precipice"). Simonides, *tr. fr. Greek by* T. F. Higham. GrL; OxBG
Lost at Sea ("A strange land holds thy bones"). Simonides, *tr. fr. Greek by* Walter Leaf. GrL; OxBG; WoL
Lost at Sea ("Thou hast but foreign earth"). Simonides, *tr. fr. Greek by* F. L. Lucas. GrPE
Lost Ball, The. Lucy Sprague Mitchell. TiPo (1959 ed.)
Lost Bower, The. Elizabeth Barrett Browning. CBPC
Lost but Found. Horatius Bonar. HBV; VA
(I Was a Wandering Sheep.) BePJ
Lost, but Won. Henry von Schlichten. BePJ
Lost Cat, The. Lilian Whiting. CIV
Lost Child, A. H. C. Bunner. PR
Lost Child. Heine. *See* Enfant Perdu.
Lost Child. Charles Fletcher Lummis. FAOV
Lost Children, The. Richard Eberhart. NePoAm-2
Lost Chord, The. Adelaide Anne Procter. BPP; CAW; FaFP; HBV; LPS-3; MaRV; OlF; PTA-1; TreF; WBLP; WGRP
Lost Christ, The. Thomas Curtis Clark. ChIP; OQP; QP-2
Lost Christ, The. Franklin D. Elmer, Jr. ChIP
Lost Church, The. Ludwig Uhland, *par. by* Sarah Helen Whitman. UnW
Lost City. Marion Strobel. NP
Lost Colony, The, *sels.* Paul Green. NoCaPo
Old Tom's Song.
Prologue to "The Lost Colony."
Lost Colors, The. Elizabeth Stuart Phelps Ward. AA; HBV; HBVY
Lost Corner. John Gould Fletcher. ChMo; CMP
Lost day. A Certain Saturday. Edith Lovejoy Pierce. ChIP
Lost Days, The. "Susan Coolidge." PSO
Lost Days. Dante Gabriel Rossetti. The House of Life, LXXXVI. BPN; EmBrPo; EnL; EnLi-2; EnLit; EPN; EPP; ES; GoBC; GTML; MaRV; NBE; OAEP; PIAE; POTT; PoVP; TOP; ViPo; ViPP; WHA
Lost Desire. Meleager, *tr. fr. Greek by* William M. Hardinge. AWP
Lost Dog. Frances Rodman. AlBD; PoRL
Lost Dog. Margaret E. Sangster. AlBD
Lost Doll, The. Charles Kingsley. *Fr.* The Water Babies. FaPON; MoShBr; MPB; OTPC; PRWS; TVC; TVSH
("I once had a sweet little doll, dears.") TiPo
Lost Dream, The. Fannie Stearns Davis. PoTo
Lost Eden. Kendall Banning. MuM
Lost Explorer. Edmund Pennant. GoYe
Lost for a Rose's Sake. *Unknown, tr. fr. French by* Andrew Lang. AWP; JAWP; WBP

Lost Fox. Frances Frost. PoTo
Lost Freedom. Thomas Campion. *See* Kind Are Her Answers.
Lost Friend, The. Sappho, *tr. fr. Greek by* F. L. Lucas. GrPE
Lost Garden. "Katherine Hale." CaP; OCL
Lost Genius, The. John James Piatt. AA; OBAV
Lost God, A, *sel.* Francis W. Bourdillon.
"Ah happy, who have seen." WGRP
Lost Happiness. Chang Miao Ching, *tr. fr. Chinese by* Henry H. Hart. PoHN
Lost Harbor. Leslie Nelson Jennings. TBM
Lost Heart. Sappho, *tr. fr. Greek by* F. L. Lucas. GrPE
Lost Heifer, The. Austin Clarke. OxBI
Lost Heir, The. Thomas Hood. LPS-1
Lost Illusion, A. George Du Maurier. CenHV
Lost Illusions. Georgia Douglas Johnson. BANP
Lost in a Blizzard. Arthur W. Monroe. PoOW
Lost in a troubled dream, I roamed alone. In a Troubled Dream. Stanton A. Coblentz. UnW
Lost in France. Ernest Rhys. POTE; SoV
Lost in Hades. Andrew Lang. UnW
Lost in Heaven. Robert Frost. MAP; MoAmPo
Lost in the vastness of the void Pacific. Homecoming. Karl Shapiro. MiAP
Lost Is My Quiet. *Unknown.* ElSeCe
(Song: "Lost is my quiet for ever.") SeCL
Lost Jewel, A. Robert Graves. EnLoPo
Lost Jimmie Whalen. *Unknown.* ABF, *with music;* BaBo
Lost Key, The. Priscilla Leonard. MaRV; OQP; QP-2
Lost Lady, The, *sel.* Sir William Berkeley.
Where Did You Borrow That Last Sigh? SeCL; TuPP
Lost Lagoon, The. Pauline Johnson. CPG
Lost Lamb, The. Thomas Westwood. OTPC (1923 ed.); PCH
Lost Leader, The. Robert Browning. BEL; BMEP; BPN; CaAE; EM-2; EmBrPo; EnL; EnLi-2; EnLit; EPN; EV-5; GEPC; GTBS; GTBS-D; GTBS-W; GTSL; HBV; MCCG; OtMeF; PIAE; PIR; PoFr; PoFS; PoVP; PtP; REAL; TCEP; TreFS; TrGrPo; TwP; VA; ViBoPo; ViPo; ViPP; VLEP
Lost Legion, The. Aneirin, *tr. fr. Welsh by* D. S. Evans. LyMA
Lost Light. Elizabeth Akers Allen. HBV
Lost Little Sister, The. William Barnes. PoEL-4
Lost! lost! Forever lost! I have betrayed. Aceldama. Longfellow. StJW
Lost! lost! lost! Advertisement of a Lost Day. Lydia H. Sigourney. WBLP
Lost, Lost! Yet Come. Robert Browning. *Fr.* Paracelsus, Pt. II. EmBrPo
Lost Love. Robert Graves. AWP; CH; ChMP; FaBoCh; JAWP; LoGBV; MBP; MoAB; MoBrPo; POTE; WBP
Lost Love, The. Fenton Johnson. NP
Lost Love. Andrew Lang. BMEP; BSV; HBV; LEAP
Lost Love, A. Henry Francis Lyte. GTSL
Lost Love. Tennyson. *See* In Memoriam, A. H. H.: "I envy not in any moods."
Lost Love, The. Wordsworth. *See* She Dwelt among the Untrodden Ways.
Lost Maidenhead. Sappho, *tr. fr. Greek by* F. L. Lucas. GrPE
Lost manor where I walk continually. The Pier-Glass. Robert Graves. CoBMV; MoAB
Lost Mr. Blake, The. W. S. Gilbert. EnLi-2 (1949 ed.); InMe; ViP
Lost Mistress, The. Robert Browning. AEV; EmBrPo; EV-5; FaBoEn; FiP; GTSE; HBV; LiA; OBEV; OBVV; PoVP; VLEP
Lost music returns, The: a few bring it. Of the New Prosody. Brewster Ghiselin. MoVE
Lost my partner, skip to my Lou. Skip to My Lou. *Unknown.* ABF
Lost now are the homes of the heroes. Scarce here and there a city. Mycenae Fallen. Alpheus. GrPE
Lost Occasion, The. Whittier. CoBA; GA, *abr.;* IAP; PTA-2; TCAP
Lost on Both Sides. Dante Gabriel Rossetti. The House of Life, XCI. BPN; GTML (XCVII); GTSL; PoVP; SeCePo; ViPo; ViPP
Lost Ones, The. Francis E. Ledwidge. TCEP
Lost Orchard, The. Edgar Lee Masters. ChMo; CMP; LaNeLa; MoPo
Lost Playmate, The. Abbie Farwell Brown. HBVY
Lost Playmate, The. Walter de la Mare. *See* Autumn.
Lost Pleiad, The. Arthur Reed Ropes. BOHV
Lost Pleiad, The. William Gilmore Simms. AA; APW; OBAV; SPP
Lost Range, The. Harry Herbert Knibbs. DDA
Lost Sheep, The. St. Luke, XV: 4-7, Bible, *N.T.* TreF
Lost Shepherd, The. James Thomson. *Fr.* The Seasons: Winter. CoBE
(Winter.) SeCePo
Lost Shipmate, The. Theodore Goodridge Roberts. BoCaPo; CaP; CPG; OCL
Lost Ships. Thomas Hornsby Ferril. EtS
Lost Shoe, The. Walter de la Mare. BoChLi (1939 ed.); BrR; TSW; TSWC
Lost Shoe, The. Norah M. Holland. CPG
Lost Son, The. Theodore Roethke. CoBMV; FiMAP; MiAP; MoPo; NePA; ReMP
Flight, The, *sel.* TrGrPo (rev. ed.)
Lost Spectacles, The. *Unknown.* BOHV
Lost Steamship, The. Fitz-James O'Brien. DaM
(Second Mate, The.) AA
Lost—Three Little Robins. *Unknown.* DD; PEDC
Lost, tortured by the world's strong sin. Desideravi. Theodore Maynard. HBMV
Lost Tribe, The. Robert Finch. CaP
Lost Tribune, The. George Sigerson. TIP
Lost Voice, The. "A. H. S." PA
Lost War-Sloop, The. Edna Dean Proctor. PAH
Lost Wine, The. Paul Valéry, *tr. fr. French.* AnFP, *tr. by* Barbara Howes; TrFP, *tr. by* Alan Conder
Lost Word, The. Charles Henry Webb. PA
Lost Word of Jesus, A. Henry van Dyke. WGRP
Lost World. Louis Ginsberg. MuM
Lost World of Adonis, The. Praxilla, *tr. fr. Greek by* T. F. Higham. OxBG
Lost Years. Eugene Lee-Hamilton. OBVV
Lost Youth. Roger Casement. CAW; JKCP (1926 ed.)
Lost Youth. Longfellow. SG
Lot would be no loss, the slender stand, The. Wild Cherry. Louise Townsend Nicholl. NePoAm
Loth to depart, but yet at last, each one. The Parting Verse, the Feast There Ended. Robert Herrick. SeCV-1
Lotos-Eaters, The. Tennyson. AtBAP; BEL; BMEP; BoLiVe; BPN; BrBE; EM-2; EmBrPo; EnL; EnLi-2; EnLit; EPN; EV-5; ExPo; FiP; GEPC; GoTL; LEAP; LiTB; MaPo; MCCG; OAEP; OBRV, *abr.;* PoE; PoEL-5; PoFS; PoVP; ReaPo; RiBV; SeCeV; ShBV-4; TOP; TVSH; TwCrTr; TwHP; VA; ViPo; ViPP; VLEP
Sels.
Choric Song: "There is sweet music here that softer falls." GTML; GTSL; LiTG; OuHeWo; PC, *st.* 1; ReTS, 4 *sts.;* WHA
(Choric Song of the Lotos-Eaters.) GTBS-W; ViBoPo
(Song of the Lotos-Eaters.) BMEP; CBE; CBOV; CoEV; OBEV
"'Courage!' he said, and pointed toward the land." ChTr; CoBE; HBV; OTPC, *abr.;* PECK; SG; TCEP
Lotosblume ängstigt, Die. Heine, *tr. fr. German by* James Thomson. AWP
(Lotus-Flower, The.) OnPM
Lots of truisms don't have to be repeated. The Anatomy of Happiness. Ogden Nash. LiTA; LiTM; SiTL
Lot's Wife. "Anna Akhmatova," *tr. fr. Russian by* Babette Deutsch. TrRV
Lot's Wife. Elizabeth Morrow. BAP
Lotus. *Unknown, tr. fr. Japanese by* Lois J. Erickson. SoLD
Lotus, The. Johan Sebastian Cammermeyer Welhaven, *tr. fr. Norwegian by* Charles W. Stork. AnNoLy
Lotus Eaters, The. Tennyson. *See* Lotos-Eaters, The.
Lotus-Flower, The. Heine. *See* Lotosblume ängstigt, Die.
Lotus-Land and the Cyclops' Cave. Homer. *tr. fr. Greek by* F. L. Lucas. *Fr.* The Odyssey, IX. GrPE
Lotus Leaves. Mitsukuni, *tr. fr. Japanese by* Asataro Miyamori. OnPM
Lotus of the Nile, The. Arthur W. H. Eaton. CPG
Loud and clear. City Bells. "Thomas Ingoldsby." *Fr.* The Ingoldsby Legends: The Lay of St. Aloys. LPS-2
Loud Boreas opened wide his mouth. A Gale of Wind. John Mitford. *Fr.* The Adventures of Johnny Newcome in the Navy. SG
Loud brayed an ass. Quoth Kate, "My Dear." Epigram. *Unknown.* ALV
Loud chatter in a thousand minor lines. Short Story in Sonnet Form. Maxwell Bodenheim. MOAP
Loud deep calls me home even now to feed it, The. Shelley. *Fr.* Prometheus Unbound, III, ii. ChER
Loud drums are rolling, the mad trumpets blow, The! Battle Cry. William Henry Venable. PAH
Loud is the summer's busy song. July. John Clare. *Fr.* The Shepherd's Calendar. GoTP; OBRV
Loud is the vale! the voice is up. Lines Composed at Grasmere. Wordsworth. OBRV
Loud mechanical voices of the sirens, The. Letter to My Wife. Roy Fuller. NeBP; POTE
Loud mockers in the roaring street. The Second Crucifixion. Richard Le Gallienne. HBV; MaRV; OBEV (1st ed.); OBVV; WGRP
Loud pianist summons from the dark, The. Melodie Grotesque. Persis Greely Anderson. WhC
Loud roared the dreadful thunder. The Bay of Biscay. Andrew Cherry. LPS-2

Loud roared the tempest. The Requital. Adelaide Anne Procter. VA
Loud roared the winds, dark grew the night. The Old Oak Tree. *Unknown.* ShS
Loud through the still November air. The Church of the Revolution. Hezekiah Butterworth. PAH
Loud, tumultuous and troubled world, The. Holy Night. Nathaniel A. Benson. CaP
Loud were they, loud, as they rode o'er the hill. Charm for a Sudden Stitch. *Unknown.* AnOE
Loudens the sea-wind, downward plunge the bows. To D'Annunzio; Lines from the Sea. Robert Nichols. OBMV
Loudon Hill, or, Drumclog. *Unknown.* ESPB
Loudoun's Bonnie Woods and Braes. Robert Tannahill. HBV
Lough, The. William Allingham. IrPN
Lough Bray. Standish James O'Grady. IrPN; TIP
Loughareema, Loughareema. The Fairy Lough. "Moira O'Neill." DiM; OBVV; TVSH; YT
Louis XV. John Sterling. BeLS; VA
Louisa. Wordsworth. EmBrPo; EnRP
Louisa May Alcott. Louise Chandler Moulton. AA
Louisburg. *Unknown.* PAH
Louise, have you forgotten yet. Old Loves. Henry Murger. AWP
Louise Hedeen. Edgar Lee Masters. *Fr.* The New Spoon River. LEAP
Louisiana Girls, *with music. Unknown.* ABF
Louisiana! Louisiana! That dear old state of ours. Song of Louisiana. Vashti R. Stopher. PoRL
Loulou and Her Cat. Frederick Locker-Lampson. ALV
Lounge Bar. James K. Baxter. Cressida, XII. AnNZ
Louse-Catchers, The. Arthur Rimbaud. *See* Chercheuses de poux, Les.
Louse Crept Out of My Lady's Shift, A. Gordon Bottomley. ChTr
Lousy Peter. Sir Osbert Sitwell. HaMV
Louvre. Rhys Davies. MoWP
Lovable Child, The. Emilie Poulsson. HBV; MPB
Love. Sarah Flower Adams. VA
Love. Anacreon, *tr. fr. Greek by* T. F. Higham. GrL; OxBG
Love. Joseph Beaumont. OBS
Love. The Song of Solomon, VIII: 6–7, Bible, *O.T.* CBOV; LiA; MaRV
(As a Seal upon Thy Heart.) TrJP
("Set me as a seal upon thine heart.") LiTW; LoPo
Love. Maxwell Bodenheim. NP
Love ("How do I love thee?"). Elizabeth Barrett Browning. *See* Sonnets from the Portuguese.
Love ("If thou must love me"). Elizabeth Barrett Browning. *See* Sonnets from the Portuguese.
Love. Robert Browning. *Fr.* Earth's Immortalities. BPN; EnLoPo; PIR; PoVP; VLEP
Love. Samuel Butler. *Fr.* Hudibras. BeR; SeCL
Love. Byron. *See* Bitter Meditation.
Love. Charles Stuart Calverley. ALV; FiBHP
Love. John Clare. *See* Song: "Love lives beyond the tomb."
Love. Samuel Taylor Coleridge. BEL; BeLS; BPN; ChER; EM-2; EmBrPo; EnRP; EPN; ERP; EV-4; GTBS; GTBS-D; GTBS-W; GTSE; GTSL; HBV; LEAP; LiTL; LoBV; LPS-1; OAEP; OBEV; TOP
(Genevieve.) BCEP
"All impulses of soul and sense," *sel.* LO
Love. Rodrigo Cota de Maguaque. *See* Such Is Love.
Love ("Five years ago"). Abraham Cowley. *See* Inconstancy.
Love ("I'll sing of heroes and of kings"). Abraham Cowley, *after the Greek of* Anacreon. AWP; PG (1945 ed.)
Love. *At. to* Roy Croft. BLPA; FaBoBe; NeHB
(Why Do I Love You?) PoToHe (new ed.)
"I love you,/ Not only for what you are," *sel.* MaRV
Love. Samuel Daniel. *See* Love Is A Sickness.
Love. Dante, *tr. fr. Italian by* Philip Henry Wicksteed. *Fr.* Divina Commedia: Paradiso, XXXIII. LiA
Love. Sir William Davenant. *Fr.* The Unfortunate Lovers. SeCL
Love. John Swanwick Drennan. IrPN
Love. William Drummond of Hawthornden. *See* Love Which Is Here a Care.
Love. Dryden. *Fr.* The Conquest of Granada, Pt. II, Act III, sc. iii. FiP
Love. Euripides, *tr. fr. Greek by* Arthur S. Way. *Fr.* Hippolytus. WoL
Love. Walker Gibson. NePoAm-2
Love ("Immortal Love, author of this great frame"). George Herbert. *See* Immortal Love, Author . . .
Love ("Love bade me welcome"). George Herbert. AWP; BLV; BoLiVe; BrBE; CaAE; CBOV; CenL; CH; ChTr; CoEV; EG; ElSeCe; EM-1; EnL; EnLit; EPP; EPS (1936 ed.); ExPo; FaBoEn; HBV; InPo; LiTB; LO; MaPo; MaRV; MeLP; MePo; OBEV; OBS; OxBoCh; Po; PoE; PoEL-2; ReEn; RiBV; SeCePo; SeCeV; SeCL; SeCV-1; SeEP; ShBV-4; StJW; TOP; TrGrPo; TwCrTr; TyEnPo; ViBoPo; WHA
(Love Bade Me Welcome.) LiTL
Love. Robert Herrick. PIAE
("Love is a circle . . .") LO
Love, *abr.* Thomas Kibble Hervey. LPS-1
Love. Victor Hugo, *tr. fr. French by* Mrs. Newton Crosland. *Fr.* Ruy Blas, III, iv. LiA
Love. Ibycus, *tr. fr. Greek by* C. M. Bowra. OxBG
Love. Immanuel di Roma, *tr. fr. Italian by* Joseph Chotzner. TrJP
Love. Francis Jammes, *tr. fr. French by* Jethro Bithell. AWP
Love. Juan Ramón Jiménez, *tr. fr. Spanish by* Eleanor L. Turnbull. TeCS
Love. Gordon LeClaire. CaP
Love, *sel.* James Russell Lowell.
True Love. OQP; QP-2
Love. James Clarence Mangan. IrPN
Love. Itzik Manger, *tr. fr. Yiddish by* Sarah Zweig Betsky. OnCuPl
Love. Anthony Munday. *Fr.* Zelanto, the Fountain of Fame. OBSC
Love. John Oxenham. BLRP
Love. Kostes Palamas, *tr. fr. Modern Greek by* Rae Dalven. *Fr.* The Twelve Songs of the Gypsy. MoGP
Love. George Peele. *See* What Thing Is Love?
Love. Richard Rolle of Hampole. *Fr.* Love Is Life. BCEP
("For now, love thou, I rede, Christ, as I thee tell.") ACP; CAW
Love. Samuele Romanelli, *tr. fr. Hebrew by* A. B. Rhine. TrJP
Love. Sappho, *tr. fr. Greek.* AWP, *tr. by* William Ellery Leonard; GrL, *tr. by* C. M. Bowra; OxBG, *tr. by* C. M. Bowra
(Captive, The, *tr. by* H. De Vere Stacpoole.) GrR
Love. Sir Walter Scott. *Fr.* The Lay of the Last Minstrel, III. BSV; EV-4; LPS-2 (*fr.* III *and* V)
Love ("Tell me where is fancy bred"). Shakespeare. *See* Tell Me Where Is Fancy Bred.
Love. Shelley. *See* One Word Is Too Often Profaned.
Love. Sir Philip Sidney. *See* Leave Me O Love . . .
Love. Alexander Smith. OBEV (1st ed.)
Love. Spenser. The Faerie Queene, *introd. to* IV. OBSC
Love. Tasso. *See* Love, the Master of True Eloquence.
Love. Henry David Thoreau. AnNE; OBVV; OQP; QP-2
Love. Johann Ludwig Tieck, *tr. fr. German by* Herman Salinger. LiTW
Love. Henry Timrod. *See* Quatorzain.
Love. Jaime Torres Bodet, *tr. fr. Spanish by* Muna Lee. AnCL
Love. Thomas Traherne. SeCV-2
Love. Katrina Trask. AA
Love. Herbert Trench. *Fr.* Come, Let Us Make Love Deathless. MaRV
Love. *Unknown, tr. fr. Arabic by* E. Powys Mathers. *Fr.* The Thousand and One Nights. AWP; LiTW
Love. Louis Untermeyer. HBMV
Love. Henry van Dyke. *Fr.* The Three Best Things. TCAP
Love. Charles Russell Wakeley. OQP; QP-1
Love. Sir William Watson. *See* Epigram: "Love, like a bird . . ."
Love. Herman Wildenvey, *tr. fr. Norwegian by* Charles W. Stork. AnNoLy
Love ("By love subsists"). Wordsworth. *Fr.* The Prelude, XIV. RO
Love. Wu Yung, *tr. fr. Chinese.* ChLP
Love a bee, that lurked among. Stung. *Unknown.* OuHeWo
Love, a Thousand Sweets Distilling. James Shirley. *Fr.* The Witty Fair One. SeCL
(Song.) SeEP
Love a woman! you're an ass. A Song. Earl of Rochester. BeR
Love above Beauty. Henry Reynolds. TuPP
Love after Death. Arthur O'Shaughnessy. GTIV
Love against Love. David A. Wasson. LPS-3
Love all the senses doth beguile. Of Love. James Sandford. EIL
Love among the Clover. Odell Shepard. PR
Love among the Ruins. Robert Browning. BEL; BoLiVe; BPN; CoBE; EM-2; EmBrPo; EnL; EnLi-2 (1949 ed.); EnLit; EPN; EtPaEn; GEPC; GTML; GTSE; HBV; MaPo; MCCG; OAEP; OBEV (new ed.); OBVV; PoEL-5; PoVP; ReTS; TOP; UnPo (1st ed.); ViPo; ViPP; VLEP
Love and a Bottle, *sel.* George Farquhar.
Song: "How blest are lovers in disguise!" SeCL
Love and a Day. Madison Cawein. PR
Love and Age. Thomas Love Peacock. *Fr.* Gryll Grange. EV-4; HBV; OBEV; ViBoPo
Love and Death. Catullus, *tr. fr. Latin by* H. W. Garrod. AWP; JAWP; WBP
Love and Death. Margaret Deland. AA; HBV
Love and Death. Ben Jonson. *See* Though I Am Young.
Love and Death. Rosa Mulholland. HBV; VA
Love and Death. Tennyson. PIR

Love and Death. *Unknown, tr. fr. Spanish by* James Young Gibson. AnSpL-1
Love and Discipline. Henry Vaughan. EPS; TrPWD
Love and Folly. La Fontaine, *tr. fr. French by* Bryant. AWP
Love and forgetting might have carried them. Two Look at Two. Robert Frost. AnAmPo; CoBA; CoBMV; CrMA; LA; LiTL; MAP; MoAB; MoAmPo
Love and Fortune. Fulke Greville. Caelica, XXIX. OBSC
Love and Friendship. Emily Brontë. GTBS-D
Love and Friendship. Keats. *Fr.* Endymion, I. OBRV
Love and Glory. Thomas Dibdin. CG
Love and harmony combine. Song. Blake. EnRP; LiTL
Love and Hate. Catullus, *tr. fr. Latin by* Thomas Moore. OnPM
Love and Hate. Longfellow. *Fr.* Christus; a Mystery, Pt. I, 1st Interlude. MaRV
Love and Hate. *Unknown, tr. fr. Irish by* Frank O'Connor. KiLC
Love and Honour. Fulke Greville. Caelica, LXXIV. OBSC
Love and Hope. Dante Gabriel Rossetti. The House of Life, XLIII. PoVP; ViPo
Love and Hope. *Unknown. See* Love Winged My Hopes.
Love & I of late did parte. *Unknown.* SeCSL
Love and Italy. Robert Underwood Johnson. LBAP
Love and Jealousy. Robert Greene. *See* When Gods Had Fram'd the Sweet of Women's Face.
Love and Jealousy. Sir Philip Sidney. *Fr.* Arcadia. SiPS
Love and Know Not Why. *Unknown. See* Love Not Me.
Love and Law. Vachel Lindsay. OQP; QP-1
Love and Liberation. John Hall Wheelock. MAP; MoAmPo
Love and Life. Abraham Cowley. *Fr.* The Mistress. SeEP
Love and Life. Winfred Ernest Garrison. OQP; QP-2
Love and Life. Julie Mathilde Lippmann. AA; HBV
Love and Life. Earl of Rochester. BLV; CaAE; CEP; ElSeCe; EnLoPo; EPP; EPS; EV-3; FaBoEn; HBV; LiTL; LoBV; MePo; OBEV; OBS; PoEL-3; SeCL; SeCV-2; SeEP; TrGrPo; ViBoPo
("All my past life is mine no more.") EG
(Song: "All my past life . . .") PreP
Love and Life. Henry Timrod. *Fr.* Quatorzain. OQP; QP-2
Love and Love's Mates. Swinburne. *See* We Have Seen Thee, O Love.
Love and Lust. Isaac Rosenberg. ChMP; TrJP
Love and Music. Philip Bourke Marston. VA
Love and Philosophy. George Chapman. *See* Sonnet: "Muses that sing love's sensual empery."
Love and Poverty. Elisabeth Cavazza Pullen. AA
Love and Reason. Arthur Hugh Clough. VLEP
Love and Reason. George Hill. APW
Love and Reason. Matthew Prior. *Fr.* Solomon, II. OBEC
Love and Reason. Sir Philip Sidney. *Fr.* Arcadia. SiPS
Love and Reverence. Thomas Randolph. *See* Devout Lover, A.
Love and Sacrifice. Bernard O'Dowd. BoAu; BoAV
Love and Science. *Unknown.* PA
Love and Sleep. Arthur Symons. VLEP
Love and Sorrow. Swinburne. *Fr.* The Sisters. POTT
Love and the Bee. *Unknown, tr. fr. Greek by* F. L. Lucas. *Fr.* Anacreontea. GrPE
Love and the Child. William Brighty Rands. PRWS
Love and the Child. Francis Thompson. VLEP
Love and the gentle heart are one same thing. La Vita Nuova, XI. Dante. AWP; OuHeWo
Love and the Lady Lagia, Guido and I. Sonnet: On the Detection of a False Friend. Guido Cavalcanti. AWP
Love and the Poet. Shakespeare. *Fr.* Love's Labour's Lost, IV, iii. CoEV
Love and the Poets. Byron. *Fr.* Don Juan, III. GEPC
Love and the Skull. Baudelaire, *tr. fr. French by* Alan Conder. TrFP
Love and Timarion matched their wings and eyes. *Unknown. tr. fr. Greek by* Humbert Wolfe. PIAE
Love and Time. Beatrix Demarest Lloyd. AA
Love and Time. Denis Florence MacCarthy. LPS-1
Love and Time. Sir Walter Ralegh. *See* Nature, That Washed Her Hands.
Love and War. Arthur Patchett Martin. VA
Love and Wine. Hafiz, *tr. fr. Persian by* John Richardson. PeP
Love and Wine. Julianus, *tr. fr. Greek by* Lord Neaves. OnPM
Love and Youth. William James Linton. VA
Love, any devil else but you. Love's Exchange. John Donne. LiTL
Love Armed. Aphra Behn. *See* Song: "Love in fantastic triumph sate."
Love, as a Warrior Lord. Ovid, *tr. fr. Latin by* the Earl of Rochester. LiTW
Love assumes the color of unlove. Separation. Tu Mu. WhP
Love at a Rout. Winthrop Mackworth Praed. ERP
Love at Ebb. Swinburne. *See* Mary Beaton's Song ("Between the Sunset . . .").
Love at First Sight. Christopher Marlowe. *See* It Lies Not in Our Power to Love or Hate.
Love at First Sight. Christopher Morley. FAOV
Love at Large. Coventry Patmore. *Fr.* The Angel in the House. HoPM; PoVP
Love at Sea. Swinburne, *after the French of* Théophile Gautier. AWP; BPN; HBV; TOP; VA; VLEP
Love at the closing of our days. Last Love. Feodor Tyutchev. LiTW
Love at the Door. Meleager, *tr. fr. Greek by* John Addington Symonds. AWP
Love at the lips was touch. To Earthward. Robert Frost. AnFE; APA; BLV; BoLiVe; CoAnAm; CoBMV; GTBS-D; HBMV; InPo; LiTA; LO; MAP; MoAB; MoAmPo; MOAP; MoPo; MoVE; NePA; OnAP; OxBA; PoeMoYo; PreP; ReMP; TBM; TCPD; TwAmPo; TwP; WoL
Love at Two Score. Thackeray. *See* Age of Wisdom, The.
Love Bade Me Welcome. George Herbert. *See* Love ("Love bade me welcome").
Love, banished heaven, in earth was held in scorn. The Guest. Michael Drayton. Idea, XXIII. ES
Love bathed my soul in the electric flame. Ideal Passion, XIII. George Edward Woodberry. MOAP
Love between Brothers and Sisters. Isaac Watts. CaAE; PECK
Love, born in Greece, of late fled from his native place. Astrophel and Stella, VIII. Sir Philip Sidney. SiPS
Love born of knowledge, love that gains. George Meredith. *Fr.* The Thrush in February. FaBoEn
Love, brave vertues younger brother. Love's Horoscope. Richard Crashaw. HBV; MeLP; OBS
Love brought by night a vision to my bed. Lost Desire. Meleager. AWP
Love brought me to a silent grove. Upon Love. Robert Herrick. BLV; BoLiVe; TrGrPo
Love built a stately house; where Fortune came. The World. George Herbert. BEL; OBS; SeCL; SeCV-1; SeEP; StJW; TOP
Love built this shrine; these hallowed walls uprose. On Entering a Chapel. John Davidson. MaRV; OQP; QP-2
Love, by sure proof I may call thee unkind. Astrophel and Stella, LXV. Sir Philip Sidney. SiPS
Love, by that loosened hair. Song. Bliss Carman. BAP; HBV; VA
Love called me like a beacon on a hill. The Swamp. Beatrice Ravenel. TBM
Love Calls Us to the Things of This World. Richard Wilbur. FiMAP; NePA; NePoEA; PoLFOT; PoRA; TrGrPo (rev. ed.)
Love Came Back at Fall o' Dew. Lizette Woodworth Reese. AV; BAP; HBV; LBMV; LO; LoPS; NV
Love Came By from the Riversmoke. Stephen Vincent Benét. *Fr.* John Brown's Body. MAP; MoAmPo
Love came down at Christmas. Incarnate Love. Christina Rossetti. ChIP; MaRV
Love came into a world of hate. Yet Love Was Born. Charles Hannibal Voss. BePJ
Love can do all but raise the dead. Emily Dickinson. LiTA; NePA
Love Cannot Live. *Unknown.* ElL
Love-Cave, The. Seami Motokiyo, *tr. fr. Japanese by* Ernest Fenollosa. LiTW
Love-Chain, The. Moschus. *See* Love's Lesson.
Love chill'd with cold & missing in the skyes. *Unknown.* SeCSL
Love Comes. Ernest Crosby. OQP; QP-2
Love comes back to his vacant dwelling. The Wanderer [*or* Rondel: The Wanderer]. Austin Dobson. HBV; InP; MBP; MoBrPo (1942 ed.); TOP
Love comes laughing up the valleys. The Call. Reginald Wright Kauffman. HBV
Love Concealed. Shakespeare. *See* She Never Told Her Love.
Love, Conquering and Unconquerable. Sophocles, *tr. fr. Greek by* John Swinnerton Phillimore. *Fr.* Antigone. GrR
(Power of Love, The.) LiA
(Unconquerable Love.) OxBG
Love controls the gods above. Amor Habet Superos. *Unknown. Fr.* Carmina Burana. LaP
Love dances with yellow-haired April. Temptation. Dionysios Solomos. *Fr.* The Free Besieged. MoGP
Love-dazed, on rosy paths I sought thee far. A Man's Last Word to a Woman. Verner von Heidenstam. AnSL
Love Dead. Heine. *See* Sag', wo ist dein schönes Liebchen.
Love Dialogue. *Unknown.* CoBE
Love Dies. George Meredith. *See* Modern Love: "In our old shipwrecked days there was an hour."
Love Dissembled. Shakespeare. *Fr.* As You Like It, III, v. LPS-1

Love distills desire upon the eyes. Euripides. *Fr.* Hippolytus. GrPo
Love Divine. Charles Wesley, *wr. at. to* Augustus Toplady. MaRV
(Divine Love.) WGRP
("Love divine, all love excelling.") LPS-2; OlF
Love, do not count your labour lost. Sullen Moods. Robert Graves. LBBV
Love doth again. Sir Thomas Wyatt. SiPS
Love, Drink and Debt. Alexander Brome. *See* Mad Lover, The.
Love drooped when beauty fled the bower. On the Death of a Recluse. George Darley. GTIV; OBVV; OxBI; TriL
Love Elegies, *sels.* James Hammond.
Elegy: On Delia's Being in the Country, VII. CEP
Elegy: To Delia, XII. CEP
Love-Ending. Rose O'Neill. LEAP
"Go, go, complete the overthrow," *sel.* BAP
Love Endures. John Nichol. EBSV
Love Enslaved. Benedetto Guidi, *tr. fr. Italian by* Thomas Moore. OnPM
Love entered in my heart one day. The Wayfarer. Sara Teasdale. ChMo; CMP
Love Enthroned. Dante Gabriel Rossetti. The House of Life, I. BMEP; BPN; CoBE; EmBrPo; PIAE; PoVP; ViPo; VLEP
Love Epigram. *Unknown, tr. fr Old Irish by* Seán O'Faoláin. SiB
Love ere he bleeds, an eagle in high skies. Modern Love, XXVI. George Meredith. HBV; ViPo; VLEP
Love ever gives. Love's Prerogative. John Oxenham. BLRP
Love-Faith. Harry Kemp. HBMV
Love, felt from far, long sought, scarce found. In the Small Canals. John Addington Symonds. *Fr.* In Venice. PoVP
Love fled that bitter house one day. The Mask. Jessie M. Heiner. MuM
Love flows like a river. In Silence. Lorenzo Mavilis. MoGP
Love for a Hand. Karl Shapiro. FiMAP
Love for Love, *sels.* William Congreve.
Nymph and a Swain, A. SeCL
(Song; Set by Mr. John Eccles.) SeEP
Song: "Soldier and a sailor, A," *fr.* III, iv. EV-3; OAEP
(Buxom Joan.) BOHV; InMe
(Soldier and a Sailor, A.) CoMu
Love for Patsy, A. John Thompson, Jr. GTBS-W; LiTA; LiTL; LiTM; NePA; WaP
Love for Sale. Meleager. *See* Child for Sale, A.
Love for such a cherry lip. Song [*or* Lips and Eyes]. Thomas Middleton. *Fr.* Blurt, Master Constable. EG; ElL; ElSeCe; HBV; ViBoPo
Love forged for me a golden chain. Wildness. Blanche Shoemaker Wagstaff. BAP; HBMV
Love, forget me when I'm gone! Love's Last Suit. Thomas Davidson. BSV
Love Forsworn. Shakespeare. *See* Take, O Take Those Lips Away.
Love Found Me. Richard Chenevix Trench. MaRV
Love Freed from Ignorance and Folly, *sel.* Ben Jonson.
Song: "How near to good is what is fair." LPS-2
Love gaily squats upon the skull. Love and the Skull. Baudelaire. TrFP
Love, give me leave to serve thee, and be wise. An Elegie. Thomas Randolph. MePo
Love, Give Me the Feel of To-Morrow. Ralph Cheyney. AOAH
Love gives every gift, whereby we long to live. Echoes of Love's House. William Morris. GTML; GTSL
Love gives its best. Love. John Oxenham. BLRP
Love Goes a-Hawking. Thomas Lovell Beddoes. *Fr.* The Bride's Tragedy. VA
(Song: "A ho! A ho!") ChER
Love-grip, first excited by the eye, The. In Panelled Rooms. Ruth Herschberger. GTBS-W; LiTA
Love growne proude would governe me. *Unknown.* SeCSL
Love Grows by What It Feeds On. Bhartrihari, *tr. fr. Sanskrit by* Arthur W. Ryder. OnPM
Love Guards [*or* Guides] the Roses of Thy Lips. Thomas Lodge. Phyllis, Sonnet XIII. EG; ElL; ElSeCe; OBEV; ReEn; SiCE; TuPP
(Fidelity.) OBSC
(To Phyllis.) ViBoPo
Love has been sung a thousand ways. Songs Ascending. Witter Bynner. *Fr.* To Celia. HBV; LoPS; NP
Love has gone and left me, and the days are all alike. Ashes of Life. Edna St. Vincent Millay. AV; FaBoBe; HBV; LiTL; NP
Love has its secrets, joy has its revealings. The Love Secret. *Unknown.* AWP
Love has never read the *Ave Maria.* Love. Immanuel di Roma. TrJP
Love has unbound my limbs and set me shaking. Love. Sappho. GrL; OxBG
Love, Hate, Compassion. First Epistle of John, II: 9–IV: 20, Bible, *N.T.* BoFr
Love Hath a Language. Helen Selina Sheridan. *Fr.* To My Son. HBV
Love hath great store of sweetness, and 'tis well. R. W. Dixon. *Fr.* Love's Consolation. LO
Love hath his poppy-wreath. Love in Dreams. John Addington Symonds. HBV
Love hath me brought in evil thought. A Rhyme-beginning Fragment. *Unknown.* AnIL
Love Hath No Physic for a Grief Too Deep. Robert Nathan. TBM
Love hath so long possessed me for his own. La Vita Nuova, XVIII. Dante. AWP; OuHeWo
Love he to-morrow, who loved never. The Vigil of Venus. *Unknown.* AWP; OuHeWo
Love heeds no more the sighing of the wind. The Garden of Shadow. Ernest Dowson. BrBE; FaBoEn; HBV
Love held a harp between his hands, and, lo! Love's Music. Philip Bourke Marston. VA
Love, how ignobly hast thou met thy doom! He Has Fallen from the Height of His Love. Wilfrid Scawen Blunt. The Love Sonnets of Proteus, XIV. ViBoPo
Love, how thou'rt tired out with rhyme! *See* O Love, how thou art tired out with rhyme!
Love Hunted. Bion, *tr. fr. Greek by* F. L. Lucas. GrPE
Love, I am sick for thee, sick with an absolute grief. The Grief of Love. *Unknown.* AWP
Love I have placed on you, The. Misplaced? *Unknown, tr. by* Havelock Ellis. OnPM
Love, I Marvel What You Are. Trumbull Stickney. HBV
Love I obey shoot home thy dart. *Unknown.* SeCSL
Love, I proclaim, the vagrant child. Love, the Vagrant [*or* The Child Eros]. Meleager. OnPM; WoL
Love, I should be content. Duality. Katherine Thayer Hobson. GoYe
Love Idyll, A. The Song of Solomon, II: 1–14, 16–17, III: 1–5, Bible, *O.T.* CBOV
(I Am the Rose of Sharon, II.) ChTr
(Song of Songs, II: 1–17.) GBV, *abr.*; PG
Love, if a god thou art. Madrigal I: To Cupid [*or* To Cupid]. Francis Davison. EG; ElSeCe; OBSC; SiCE; TuPP
Love in a Cottage. Nathaniel Parker Willis. BAV; HBV; LHV; PR
Love in a Cotton Mill. Stewart Atkins. NoCaPo
Love in a hut, with water and a crust. Keats. *Fr.* Lamia. EV-4
Love in a Life. Robert Browning. BMEP; BPN; EM-2; EmBrPo; EPN; GEPC; HBV; InvP; LiTL; OAEP; OBVV; PoVP; TOP; VLEP
Love in a Tub. Sir George Etherege. *See* Comical Revenge, The.
Love in a Village, *sels.* Isaac Bickerstaffe.
Song: "How happy were my days." OBEC
There Was a Jolly Miller. GoTP; HBV; OnPP; OTPC (1946 ed.); ViBoPo; WP, *shorter sel.*
(Jolly Miller.) RIS
(Song: "There was a jolly miller once.") OBEC, *shorter sel.*; OnYI
("There was a jolly miller once," *st.* 1.) OxNR
Love in a Wood, *sel.* William Wycherley.
Spouse I Do Hate, A. OAEP
Love in Action. Coventry Patmore. *Fr.* The Angel in the House, II, x. EG
Love in Age. Ethel Anderson. MoAuPo
Love in Age. Charles G. Bell. NePoAm-2
Love in Disguise. *Unknown.* CSF
Love in Dreams. John Addington Symonds. HBV
Love in Exile, *sels.* Mathilde Blind.
"I charge you, O winds of the West." TrJP; VA
"Why will you haunt me unawares." VA
Love in Fantastick Triumph. Aphra Behn. *See* Song: "Love in fantastic triumph sate."
Love in Her Eyes Sits Playing. John Gay. *Fr.* Acis and Galatea. EnLi-1 (1949 ed.); EV-3; OBEC; OnPM; ViBoPo
(Song: "Love in her eyes sits playing.") FaBoEn; LoPo
Love in Her Hair. *Unknown, tr. fr. Greek by* Andrew Lang. OxBG
(Changeful Beauty.) EnLoPo
Love in her sunny eyes does basking play. The Change. Abraham Cowley. *Fr.* The Mistress. BEL; CoBE; FaBoEn; LO; MeLP; MePo; OBS; ReEn; SeCV-1
Love in Hunger. Philip Oakes. PoN
Love-in-Idleness. Thomas Lovell Beddoes. LiTL; ViBoPo
Love-in-Idleness. Shakespeare. *Fr.* A Midsummer Night's Dream, II, i. TrGrPo
Love in Jeopardy. Humbert Wolfe. NeMA
Love in May. Jean Passerat, *tr. fr. French by* Andrew Lang. AWP
Love in Men and Devils. Cecco Angiolieri da Siena. *See* Sonnet: Of Love in Men and Devils.

Love in Moonlight. Bhartrihari, *tr. fr. Sanskrit by* Paul Elmer More. LiTW
Love in My Bosom like a Bee. Thomas Lodge. *See* Rosalynde: Rosalind's Madrigal.
Love in my heart: oh, heart of me, heart of me! Song. "Fiona Macleod." AA
Love in Spring. Meleager. *See* Persuasion's Rose.
Love in Spring-Time. Shakespeare. *See* It Was a Lover and His Lass.
Love in the Calendar. Robert Underwood Johnson. PR
Love in the Dark, *sel.* Sir Francis Fane.
Cupid, I Scorn to Beg the Art. SeCL; SeEP
Love in the Museum. Adrienne Cecile Rich. NePoEA
Love in the Springtime. Theognis, *tr. fr. Greek by* J. M. Edmonds. GrR
Love in the Valley. George Meredith. AEV; AnEnPo; AWP; BEL; BMEP, *abr.*; EmBrPo; EnL; EnLi-2; EPN; GTSL; HBV; InPo; LEAP, *abr.*; LiTB, *abr.*; LiTG, *abr.*; LiTL, 4 *sts.*; LoPS, 5 *sts.*; OBEV (1st ed., *complete*; new ed., *abr.*); OBVV; OnPP, *abr.*; PIAE; POTT; PoVP; TOP; TriL; TyEnPo; ViBoPo; ViP; ViPo; VLEP; WHA, *abr.*
Sels.
"Hither she comes; she comes to me; she lingers," 3 *sts.* EtPaEn
"Shy as the squirrel and wayward as the swallow," 5 *sts.* PoeT
"Under yonder beech-tree single on the green-sward." GTBS-D, 7 *sts.*; GTBS-W, 2 *sts.*; ShBV-4, 3 *sts.*; TrGrPo, 6 *sts.*
White Owl, The, 2 *ll.* ChTr
Love in the Winds. Richard Hovey. AA; HBV; LEAP; LoPo; MAP; MoAmPo (1942 ed.); PoeMoYo; PoMa
Love in Thy Youth. *Unknown.* ElSeCe; HBV; ViBoPo
("Love in thy youth, fair maid; be wise.") EG; GTSL; LO
(Madrigal.) SeCL
Love in Time's Despite. Edwin Muir. LiTL
Love Indivisible. Pierre de Ronsard, *tr. fr. French by* Alan Conder. TrFP
Love is a circle, that doth restless move. Love. Robert Herrick. LO; PIAE
Love Is a God. Bilhana, *formerly at. to* Chauras, *tr. fr. Sanskrit by* E. Powys Mathers. *Fr.* Black Marigolds. OnPM
Love Is a Hunter Boy. Thomas Moore. OnYI
Love Is a Keeper of Swans. Humbert Wolfe. MBP; MoBrPo
Love Is a Law. *Unknown. Fr.* The Thracian Wonder. ElL
("Love is a law, a discord of such force.") TuPP
Love is a light burden that gladdeneth young and old. Richard Rolle of Hampole. *Fr.* Love Is Life. GoBC
Love is a light burthen; love gladdens young and old. Love. Richard Rolle of Hampole. *Fr.* Love Is Life. BCEP
Love is a little golden fish. The Golden Fish. George Arnold. HBV; LPS-1; PR
Love is a pain with purest joy combined. Melting Ice. Sophocles. OxBG
Love is a proud and gentle thing, a better thing to own. The Door. Orrick Johns. LoPS; NP; TBM
Love Is a Sickness[e]. Samuel Daniel. *Fr.* Hymen's Triumph. BEL; EV-1; LiTG; LiTL; LoBV; LPS-1; OAEP; OBEV; PG; PoEL-2; TreFS; TuPP; ViBoPo
(Love.) ElL; OBSC
(Love Is a Sickness[e] Full of Woes.) AtBAP; LO; SiCE
(Song: "Love is a sickness.") HBV
Love is a sluggard, and for these things lives. Love Is Idle. Euripides. OxBG
Love is a sour delight, a sug'red grief. Thomas Watson. *Fr.* Hecatompathia. ReIE
Love Is a Terrible Thing. Grace Fallow Norton. AV; BAP; HBV; NV; PFY; PoeMoYo; SBMV
Love is a torment. Lay It Bare. *Unknown.* OnPM
Love Is All. Catullus, *tr. fr. Latin by* Theodore Martin. EnLi-1; OuHeWo
("Let us live, O my Lesbia, and go on loving!" *tr. by* Asa M. Hughes.) LaP
(To Lesbia, *tr. by* Charles Abraham Elton.) OnPM
"Love is all/ Unsatisfied." Crazy Jane on the Day of Judgment. W. B. Yeats. AtBAP
Love is and was my lord and king. In Memoriam A. H. H., CXXVI. Tennyson. BEL; BoFr; BPN; ChTr; CoBE; EM-2; EmBrPo; EnLi-2; EPN; GEPC; HBV; OAEP; OBEV; ReaPo; SeCeV; TCEP; ViPo; VLEP
Love Is Best. Asclepiades, *tr. fr. Greek by* Hugh Macnaghten. GrL
Love is cruel, Love is sweet. Song. Thomas Macdonagh. ACP
Love Is Dead. Sir Philip Sidney. *See* Ring Out Your Bells.
Love Is Enough, *sels.* William Morris.
"Dawn talks to-day." AtBAP
(Day of Love, The.) BPN
"Love is enough: cherish life that abideth." VLEP
"Love is enough: draw near and behold me." VLEP
"Love is enough: have no thought for to-morrow." EmBrPo; VLEP
"Love is enough: ho ye who seek saving." OBVV; VLEP
(Final Chorus.) BPN
"Love is enough: it grew up without heeding." VLEP
"Love is enough: though the World be a-waning." AnEnPo; BLV; BMEP; EPN; LEAP; LiTL; MBP; NeHB; OBEV; OBVV; PoEL-5; TOP; ViBoPo
(Song for Music.) TCEP
"Love is enough: through the trouble and tangle." VLEP
"Love is enough: while ye deemed him a-sleeping." VLEP
Love Is Enough. Sir Gilbert Parker. CPG
"Love is enough," I read somewhere. To an Unknown Poet. Countee Cullen. BAP
Love is ever bought at best. The Misogynist. L. F. Gerlach. PtPa
Love is for some a heavy cross. Boris Pasternak, *tr. fr. Russian by* C. M. Bowra. BoRS
Love is heavens fayre aspect. *See* Love is the heaven's fair aspect.
Love Is Idle. Euripides, *tr. fr. Greek by* C. M. Bowra. OxBG
Love Is Kind. Benjamin Keech. PoToHe
Love Is Life, *sels.* Richard Rolle of Hampole.
"For now, love thou, I rede, Christ, as I thee tell." ACP; CAW, 4 *sts.*
Love ("Love is a light burthen"), 2 *sts.* BCEP
"Love is a light burden that gladdeneth young and old." 3 *sts., mod. vers. by* Alfred Noyes. GoBC
Love Is like a Dizziness. James Hogg. BOHV; HBV; InMe
Love is like a lamb, and love is like a lion. Song: Love Is like a Lamb. Thomas Middleton. *Fr.* Blurt, Master Constable. AtBAP
Love is like the wild rose-briar. Love and Friendship. Emily Brontë. GTBS-D
Love Is Love. Sir Edward Dyer. *See* Lowest Trees Have Tops, The.
Love Is More Thicker than Forget. E. E. Cummings. AnFE; CoAnAm; Po; PoLFOT
Love Is My Betrayer. August, Graf von Platen, *tr. fr. German by* Edwin Morgan. AnGP
Love is my sin and thy dear virtue hate. Sonnets, CXLII. Shakespeare. PeBoSo
Love Is Not All; It Is Not Meat nor Drink. Edna St. Vincent Millay. The Fatal Interview, XXX. ChMo; LoPo; MOAP; OxBA; TwCV
Love Is Not Love Which Alters. Shakespeare. *See* Sonnets, CXVI.
Love Is Not Solace. Sister Maris Stella. GoBC
Love Is Not Winged. Eubulus, *tr. fr. Greek by* T. F. Higham. OxBG
Love Is of God. Horatius Bonar. MaRV
Love is sharper than stones or sticks. Ballade of Unfortunate Mammals. Dorothy Parker. ALV; BOHV; InMe
Love Is Strong. Richard Burton. AA; HBV
Love Is Strong as Death. Christina Rossetti. MaRV; MeRV; TriL
(Love Is Stronger than Death.) LO
Love is that later thing than death. Emily Dickinson. LiTA; NePA
Love is that madness which all lovers have. Love. Dryden. *Fr.* The Conquest of Granada, Pt. II. FiP
Love is that orbit of the restless soul. Sonnets. George Henry Boker. MOAP
Love is the blossom where there blows. Wooing Song. Giles Fletcher, the Younger. *Fr.* Christ's Victory and Triumph: Christ's Victory on Earth. ElL; ElSeCe; EV-2; HBV; LO; OBEV; ViBoPo
Love is the bread that feeds the multitudes. George Edward Woodberry. *Fr.* The Roamer. MaRV
Love is the cause of war and death in battle. Affidavit in Platitudes. E. B. White. InMe
Love Is the Every Only God. E. E. Cummings. ChMo
Love Is the God of Peace. Propertius, *tr. fr. Latin by* John Nott. Elegies, III, 5. RoL
Love is the heaven's fair [*or* fayre] aspèct. Batte's Song. Michael Drayton. *Fr.* The Shepherd's Garland. LO; NBE
Love is the key of life and death. A Song for the Least of All Saints. Christina Rossetti. BePJ
Love is the mainspring of existence. The Exile. John Clare. RO
Love is the sunne it selfe from whence. *Unknown.* SeCSL
Love is too young to know what conscience is. Sonnets, CLI. Shakespeare. PeBoSo; PoEL-2; ReEn
"Love is too young to know what conscience is." Eighth Type of Ambiguity. John Wain. PoN
Love is witty, but not wise. A Displeasure against Love. Nicholas Breton. CaAE; SiCE
Love kept me one and twenty years a slave. Petrarch. Sonnets to Laura: To Laura in Death, LXXXV. PrPoCR
Love Knocks at the Door. John Hall Wheelock. LBMV
Love-Knot, The. Nora Perry. AA; BOHV; HBV; LPS-1

Love laid his sleepless head. Song. Swinburne. BLV; BoLiVe; PIAE; TrGrPo
Love Lesson, A. Clément Marot. *See* Yes and No.
Love, let us live as we have lived, nor lose. To His Wife. Decimus Magnus Ausonius. LaP; LiTW
Love-Letter. The. Dante Gabriel Rossetti. The House of Life, XI. BPN; EmBrPo; PoVP; REAL; ViPo; VLEP
Love Letter, A. Thomas of Hales. *See* Luve Ron, A.
Love-Letter, A. *Unknown, tr. fr. Anglo-Saxon by* Francis A. Blackburn. EPP
Love Letter from an Impossible Land. William Meredith. WaP
Love-Letters Made in Flowers. Leigh Hunt. LPS-1
Love Lies Sleeping. Plato, *tr. fr. Greek by* F. L. Lucas. GrPE
Love, lift me up upon thy golden wings. An Hymn[e] of Heavenly Love. Spenser. EV-1; ReIE; StJW
Love, light for me/ Thy ruddiest blazing torch. Deliciae Sapientiae de Amore: Hail Virgin in Virginity a Spouse. Coventry Patmore. *Fr.* To the Unknown Eros. OxBoCh; PoVP; PraNu
Love Lightens Labor. *Unknown.* LPS-1
Love, like a bird, hath perch'd upon a spray. Epigram [*or* Love]. Sir William Watson. ALV; MBP; MoBrPo (1942 ed.); TrGrPo
Love, Like a Drop of Dew. W. H. Davies. ChMo; CMP
Love, like a mountain-wind upon an oak. Love. Sappho. AWP
Love like heat and cold. Jealousy. *Unknown.* KiLC
Love, like Ulysses. Counsel. Roselle Mercier Montgomery. HBMV
Love-Lily. Dante Gabriel Rossetti. AtBAP; BPN; EmBrPo; POTT; PoVP; VLEP
Love Lives beyond the Tomb. John Clare. *See* Song: "Love lives beyond the tomb."
Love Looks Tenderly. Ibycus, *tr. fr. Greek by* J. M. Edmonds. GrR
Love Looks to the Future. Gerald Gould. POTE
Love-Lord God, in hands of Thine. In Manus Tuas. *Unknown.* TMEV
Love, love, a lily's my care. Words for the Wind. Theodore Roethke. FiMAP
Love, love alone, cause King Edwards to leave the t'rone. King Edwards. *Unknown.* SoAmSa
Love, love me only. Song. Robert Crawford. BoAu
Love, love today, my dear. Song. Charlotte Mew. MBP; MoBrPo
Love, love, what wilt thou with this heart of mine. Rondel: To His Mistress. Jean Froissart. AWP
Love Lyric. Max Michelson. NP
Love Lyrics. Song of Solomon, II: 8-14, Bible, *O.T.* OuHeWo
Love Lyrics of a Cowboy. R. V. Carr. SCC
Love Lyrics of Proteus, The, *sel.* Wilfrid Scawen Blunt.
Song: "Oh fly not, Pleasure," *fr.* A Rhapsody. JKCP; OBEV (1st ed.); OBVV; ViBoPo
Love-Madness. Paulus Silentiarius, *tr. fr. Greek by* F. L. Lucas. GrPE
Love-Magic. Theocritus. *See* Incantation, The.
Love Me Again. *Unknown.* ElL
Love me and leave me; what love bids retrieve me? can June's fist grasp May? John Jones. Swinburne. *Fr.* The Heptalogia. NA; OAEP
Love Me and Never Leave Me. Ronald McCuaig. BoAV; MoAuPo
Love Me at Last. Alice Corbin. AV; BAP; HBMV; NP
Love me because I am lost. Song. Louise Bogan. AV; MOAP; NP; PG (1955 ed.)
Love me brought. Love on the Cross. J. Grimstone. TMEV
"Love me, for I love you"—and answer me. Monna Innominata, VII. Christina Rossetti. EmBrPo; ViPo
Love Me—I Love You. Christina Rossetti. *Fr.* Sing-Song. BoTP; EmBrPo
(Mother's Song, A.) BOL; OTPC (1946 ed.)
Love Me Little, Love Me Long. *Unknown.* BLPA, *abr.;* ElL; EM-1; FaBoBe; FaFP; LiTL; LPS-1; NeHB; PG (1955 ed.); TreF
Love me, love my dog: by love to agree. Of Loving a Dog. John Heywood. SiCE; TuPP
Love Me Not for Comely Grace. *Unknown.* *See* Love Not Me.
Love Me or Not. Thomas Campion. ElL; ElSeCe; EV-2; HBV; ViBoPo
"Love me, sweet girl! your love is all I ask!" Light Love. *Unknown.* OnPM
Love me, sweet, with all thou art. A Man's Requirements. Elizabeth Barrett Browning. BPN; EmBrPo
Love Means Adventure. Toyohiko Kagawa, *tr. fr. Japanese by* Lois J. Erickson. SoLD
Love, meet me in the green glen. Meet Me in the Green Glen. John Clare. GTBS-D
Love, men's honour, many ripening deeds. The Impatient Poet. D'Arcy Cresswell. AnNZ
Love-Messenger. Meleager. *See* Mosquito Turned Messenger, The.
Love met me at noonday. Stephen Crane. Intrigue, IX. MOAP
Love, mine! seek not to grope. Ad Leuconoen. Francis Sylvester Mahony. IrPN
Love mistress is of many minds. Love's Servile Lot. Robert Southwell. ReIE; SiCE; TuPP
Love mocks us all. Then cast aside. Albi, Ne Doreas *wr.* [Doleas]. Horace. Odes, I, 33. AWP
Love-Moon, The. Dante Gabriel Rossetti. The House of Life, XXXVII. PoVP; ViPo
Love much. Earth has enough of bitter in it. Ella Wheeler Wilcox. PoToHe (new ed.)
Love must be a fearsome thing. Wood-Song. Josephine Preston Peabody. AA; ADAH
Love must think in music sweetly. Love. Johann Ludwig Tieck. LiTW
"Love my heart for an hour, but my bone for a day." Street Song. Edith Sitwell. CoBMV; MoPo; MoVE; OnHM; POTE
Love needs no pondered words. Song for Lovers. T. I. Moore. MoAuPo
Love Not. Caroline Elizabeth Sarah Norton. HBV; IrPN; LPS-1; OBVV; VA
Love not a loveliness too much. Ownership. Lizette Woodworth Reese. MAP; MoAmPo
Love, Not Duty. Arthur Hugh Clough. VLEP
Love not, love not, ye hapless sons of clay! Love Not. Caroline Elizabeth Sarah Norton. HBV; IrPN; LPS-1; OBVV; VA
Love Not Me [for Comely Grace]. *Unknown.* ALV; BLV; CBOV; CH; ElL; ElSeCe; EV-1; FaFP; GTBS; GTBS-D; GTBS-W; GTSE; GTSL; HBV; LiTB; LiTG; LiTL; LO; LPS-1; OBEV; PG; PreP; SiTL; ViBoPo
(Love and Know Not Why.) OnPM
(Love Me Not for Comely Grace.) BCEP; EG; PIAE; RiBV; SiCE; TOP
(Love's Unreason.) TrGrPo
(Madrigal.) EV-2
Love not too much. The Affliction of Richard. Robert Bridges. TriL
Love Note II: Flags. Gwendolyn Brooks. PoNe
Love, oh love, oh careless love. Careless Love. *Unknown.* AS, *with music;* StDa; TrAS
Love of a Boy, The. Richard Hovey. PR
Love of a King, The. Tu Fu, *tr. fr. Chinese by* Edna Worthley Underwood *and* Chi Hwang Chu. ChLP
Love of Books, The. James R. Clemens. PIAE
"Love of Christ Which Passeth Knowledge, The." Christina Rossetti. StJW
(I Bore with Thee, Long, Weary Days.) BePJ
Love of Country. Sir Walter Scott. *See* Breathes There the Man.
Love of Deceit, The. Baudelaire, *tr. fr. French by* Dwight Durling. AnFP
Love of England. William Cowper. *See* England.
Love of Fame, the Universal Passion, *sels.* Edward Young.
Characters of Women, *fr.* Satire V. OBEC
Love of Praise, The, *fr.* Satire I. BeR
Smart Lady, The, *fr.* Satire V. BeR
Love of Fatherland. Sir Walter Scott. *See* Breathes There the Man.
Love of field and coppice, The. My Country. Dorothea Mackellar. BoAu
Love of God, The. Bernard Rascas, *tr. fr. Provençal by* Bryant. CAW; LPS-2; WGRP
Love of God, The. Eliza Scudder. LPS-2
Love of God Supreme, The. John Wesley. *See* Hymn: "Thou hidden love of God, whose height."
Love of Hell, The. Abraham Burstein. TrJP
Love of King David and Fair Bethsabe, The. George Peele. *See* David and Bethsabe.
Love of life that captained him could brook, The. Lost Harbor. Leslie Nelson Jennings. TBM
Love of man and woman is as fire, The. My Comrade. James Jeffrey Roche. AA
Love of my life came not, The. The Deep-Sea Pearl. Edith M. Thomas. AV
Love of Nature. John Clare. RO
Love of Nature. James Thomson. *Fr.* The Seasons: Autumn. OBEC
Love of One's Neighbor. Max Jacob, *tr. fr. French by* Wallace Fowlie. MiCF
Love of Praise, The. Edward Young. *Fr.* The Love of Fame, Satire I. BeR
Love of Swans, The. Leonard Mann. MoAuPo
Love of the Father, The. *Unknown.* BLRP
Love of Women, The. Byron. *Fr.* Don Juan, II. BCEP; CoBE
Love Omnipresent. *At. to* Joshua Sylvester. *See* Were I as Base as Is the Lowly Plain.
Love on a day, wise poets tell. How Violets Came Blue. Robert Herrick. EnL; EPS (1942 ed.)

Love on the Cross. J. Grimstone. TMEV
Love on the Farm. D. H. Lawrence. MBP; MoAB; MoBrPo; TrGrPo
Love on the Mountain. Thomas Boyd. AnIV; GTIV; HBV; OxBI
Love once kiss'd me. A Sad Song. William Allingham. GTIV
Love once more looks tenderly. Love Looks Tenderly. Ibycus. GrR
Love Once Was like an April Dawn. Robert Underwood Johnson. HBV
Love One Another. Bedros Tourian, *tr. fr. Armenian by* Zabelle C. Boyajian. ArmLP
Love or Death. Paulus Silentiarius, *tr. fr. Greek by* A. J. Butler. OxBG
Love over All. *Unknown, tr. fr. Latin.* OQP; QP-2 (Found on an English Sun Dial.) PC
Love Pagan. Arthur Shearly Cripps. MM
Love Passing By. Gustavo Adolfo Bécquer, *tr. fr. Spanish by* Alice Jane McVan. OnPM
Love, Peace, and Repose! the tenderest trio. My Early Home. John Clark. HBV; OTPC (1923 ed.)
Love Planted a Rose. Katharine Lee Bates. InP; PFE; PoTo; VOD
Love Poem: "Flowers upon your lips and hands." Maurice James Craig. NeIP
Love Poem: "Less the dog begged to die in the sky." George Barker. *Fr.* Fourth Cycle of Love Poems. NeBP
Love Poem, A: "My chosen she is." Hywel ab Owain Gwynedd, *tr. fr. Welsh by* H. Idris Bell. LyMA (Ode to a Chosen Girl, *tr. by* Gwyn Williams.) PrWP
Love Poem: "My clumsiest dear, whose hands shipwreck vases." John Frederick Nims. HoPM; MiAP
Love Poem: "My joy, my jockey, my Gabriel." George Barker. *See* My Joy, My Jockey, My Gabriel.
Love Poem: "O Golden Fleece she is where she lies tonight." George Barker. *See* O Golden Fleece.
Love Poem: "O tender under her right breast." George Barker. *See* O Tender under Her Right Breast.
Love Poem: "Then like the ship at rest in the bay." George Barker. First Cycle of Love Poems, IV. FaBoMo ("Then like the ship at rest in the bay.") MoPo
Love Poem: "Where you (in this saying) lag in the waving woods." W. S. Graham. FaBoMo
Love Poem: "You say that in your eyes alone is all the world." Jiri Wolker, *tr. fr. Czech by* E. Osers *and* J. K. Montgomery. LiTW
Love Poem: "Yours is the face that the earth turns to me." Kathleen Raine. LiTB; LoPS; MoAB; MoPo; NeBP
Love Poem—1940. Miriam Hershenson. GoYe
Love, Pride, and Forgetfulness. Tennyson. BoFr
"Love purifies his acts," my lady said. Ideal Passion, XXIII. George Edward Woodberry. MOAP
Love, Reason, Hate, did once bespeak. Barley-break. Sir John Suckling. SeCV-1
Love Redeemed, *sels.* William Baylebridge. BoAV
"Utile canons, the set codes of priests, The," XXXIII.
"Who questions if the punctual sun unbars," LXXXII.
Love Restored, *sel.* Ben Jonson.
"This motion was of love begot." UnS
Love Rides the Lion. Karl Gjellerup, *tr. fr. Danish by* Charles W. Stork. BoDS
Love sat at ease upon Time's bony knee. Sonnets: A Sequence of Profane Love. George Henry Boker. MOAP
Love sat down like a tired tinker. Stop Thief. Herman Knickerbocker Vielé. PR
Love scorch'd my finger, but did spare. Upon Love. Robert Herrick. SeCV-1
Love Scorned by Pride. John Clare. RO
Love Scorns Degrees. Paul H. Hayne. *Fr.* The Mountain of the Lovers. LPS-1
Love Secret, The. *Unknown, tr. fr. Arabic by* Wilfrid Scawen Blunt. AWP
"Love seeketh not itself to please." The Clod and the Pebble. Blake. *Fr.* Songs of Experience. AWP; BEL; BoLiVe; CoEV; EiPP; EM-1; EnL; EnLi-2; EnLit; EnLoPo; EnRP; EPP; FaBoEn; JAWP; LO; LoBV; NBE; OAEP; OBEC; OnPM; OtMeF; TOP; TrGrPo; ViBoPo; WBP
Love Serviceable. Coventry Patmore. The Angel in the House, I, vi, 3. EnLoPo; MaRV
Love Sets Order in the Elements. Thomas Nabbes. *Fr.* Microcosmus. UnS
Love, should I fear death most for you or me? Cloud and Wind. Dante Gabriel Rossetti. The House of Life, XLIV. PoVP; ViPo
Love should I set my heart upon a crown. Oh, Ask Me Not. John Charles McNeill. NoCaPo
Love-Sight. Dante Gabriel Rossetti. *See* Lovesight.
Love signed the contract blithe and leal. Epigram. John Swanwick Drennan. IrPN
Love Sleeping. Plato, *tr. fr. Greek by* Thomas Stanley. AWP; OnPM; WoL
Love Slumbers On. Shelley. *See* Music, When Soft Voices Die.
Love Somebody, Yes I Do, *with music. Unknown.* AS
Love Song. Judah Alharizi, *tr. fr. Hebrew by* Emma Lazarus. LiTW; TrJP
Love Song. Rudolf G. Binding, *tr. fr. German by* Herman Salinger. TwGV
Love Song. Björnstjerne Björnson, *tr. fr. Norwegian by* Charles W. Stork. AnNoLy
Love Song. Mary Carolyn Davies. AV
Love Song. "Adam Drinan." NeBP; OnHM
Love Song ("Now the lusty spring is seen"). John Fletcher. *See* Love's Emblems.
Love Song ("Take, oh take those lips away"). John Fletcher. *Fr.* The Bloody Brother, V, ii. FaBoEn
Love-Song, A. Gustaf Fröding, *tr. fr. Swedish by* Charles W. Stork. AnSL
Love-Song, A. Norman Gale. LEAP
Love Song, A. Theodosia Garrison. OBAV; SBMV
Love Song. Iwan Goll, *tr. fr. French by* Claire Goll. OnPM
Love Song, The. Ivor Gurney. EnLoPo
Love Song, A. Judah Halevi, *tr. fr. Hebrew by* Nina Davis Salaman. TrJP
Love-Song, The. Bernice Lesbia Kenyon. AV
Love-Song. Else Lasker-Schüler, *tr. fr. German by* Jethro Bithell. TrJP
Love Song. Luis de León, *tr. fr. Spanish by* Thomas Walsh. TrJP
Love Song. Harriet Monroe. AV; LBAP; NP; NV; OBAV (I Love My Life, but Not Too Well.) HBV
Love Song. Sophia Mavroidi Papadaky, *tr. fr. Modern Greek by* Rae Dalven. MoGP
Love Song. Dorothy Parker. InMe; NeMA
Love Song, A. *At. to* Pope *and to* Swift. *See* Lines by a Person of Quality.
Love Song. Rainer Maria Rilke, *tr. fr. German by* Kate Flores. AnGP
Love Song. Margot Ruddock. OBMV
Love Song. George Brandon Saul. TBM
Love Song. Arthur Symons. PoVP ("O woman of my love, I am walking with you on the sand.") GTML
Love-Song, A. Thomas of Hales. *See* Luve Ron, A.
Love Song, A. Steingrímur Thorsteinsson, *tr. fr. Icelandic by* Jakobina Johnson. IcP
Love Song. Henry Treece. MaRV
Love-Song, A. W. J. Turner. OBMV
Love Song ("Beautiful is she"). *Unknown, tr. fr. Haida Indian by* Constance Lindsay Skinner. AWP; JAWP; WBP
Love Song ("Early I rose"). *Unknown, tr. fr. Papago Indian by* Mary Austin. AWP; JAWP; LiTA (Papago Love-Songs.) APW
Love Song, A ("He is a heart"). *Unknown, tr. fr. Old Irish by* Myles Dillon. AnIL
Love Song ("Herself hath given back my life to me"). *Unknown, tr. fr. Latin by* Helen Waddell. LiTW
Love Song ("I lie in the tall grass by the berry trail"). *Unknown, tr. fr. Kootenay Indian by* Constance Lindsay Skinner. (Two Lyrics from the Kootenay.) BAP
Love-Song ("The little wild birds"). *Unknown, tr. fr. Russian by* W. R. S. Ralston. AWP
Love Song, A ("One alone, a sister without her peer"). *Unknown, tr. fr. Egyptian by* Alan H. Gardiner. LiTW
Love-Song, A ("Sabina has a thousand charms"). *Unknown.* ElSeCe; SeCL; SeEP
Love Song, A ("Up, for mercy, and be going"). *Unknown, tr. fr. Greek by* T. F. Higham. OxBG
Love-Song ("Whomsoe'er look I upon"). *Unknown, tr. fr. Winnebago Indian by* Natalie Curtis. APW
Love Song. William Carlos Williams. LoPS; MoAB; MoAmPo (1950 ed.); NP; TCPD
Love-Song by a Lunatic, A. *Unknown.* NA
Love Song from New England. Winifred Welles. AV; HBMV; MAP
Love Song of Har Dyal, The. Kipling. EtPaEn; GBV; OtMeF
Love Song of J. Alfred Prufrock, The. T. S. Eliot. AmPo; AmPP; AnFE; APA; ATP (1953 ed.); AWP; ChMo; CMP; CoAnAm; CoBA; CoBMV; CoEV; EnL; EnLit; ExPo; HBMV; HoPM; InPo; LEAP; LiTB; LiTM (1946 ed.); MAP; MAPA; MaPo; MoAB; MoAmPo; MoPW; MoVE; NePA; NP; OAEP (2d ed.); OnAP; Po; PoFS; PoLFOT; PoRA; PreP; ReaPo; ReMP; RiBV; SeCeV; TrGrPo; TwAmPo; TwP; UnPo; ViBoPo
Sels.
"In the room the women come and go," *br. sel.* BAP
"Let us go then, you and I," *22 ll.* NeMA
Love Song of Polyphemus, The. Luis de Góngora, *tr. fr. Spanish by* Frances Fletcher. *Fr.* Polyphemus and Galatea. LiTW
Love Song Out of Nothing. Vassar Miller. NePoEA
Love Song to Eohippus. Peter Viereck. MoAmPo (1950 ed.)
Love Songs. Mina Loy. AnAmPo; LA
Love Sonnet, A. George Wither. *See* I Loved a Lass.

Love Sonnets of Proteus, The, *sels.* Wilfrid Scawen Blunt.
Depreciating Her Beauty, VI. OBMV
Farewell to Juliet, *sels.*
Farewell ("Farewell, then, it is finished"), LIII. MBP; MoBrPo (1942 ed.)
Farewell to Juliet ("I see you, Juliet, still, with your straw hat"), XLVII. EnLoPo
Farewell to Juliet ("Juliet, farewell. I would not be forgiven"), XXXIX. AnEnPo
(Farewell.) TrGrPo
Farewell to Juliet ("Lame, impotent conclusion"), LII. ViBoPo
He Has Fallen from the Height of His Love, XIV. ViBoPo
In Answer to a Question, XXVIII. ViBoPo
Laughter and Death, XCI. BMEP; MBP; MoBrPo (1942 ed.); PoMa; VA
On a Lost Opportunity, LVII. EtPaEn
On the Nature of Love, XXII. ViBoPo
On the Shortness of Time, XCVI. MBP; MoBrPo (1942 ed.)
St. Valentine's Day, LV. EnLoPo; ES; EtPaEn; OBEV (1st ed.); OBVV; PoeT; ViBoPo
To Manon, as to His Choice of Her, VIII. HBV
(As to His Choice of Her.) ViBoPo
To Manon, Comparing Her to a Falcon, II. OBVV; VA
(Falcon, The.) ACP
To Manon, on Her Lightheartedness, XI. VA
To Manon, on His Fortune in Loving Her, III. CaAE; GTSL; LEAP; OBEV (1st ed.)
To One on Her Waste of Time, LVIII. ViBoPo
To One Who Would Make a Confession, LXII. HBV; LEAP; ViBoPo
Two Highwaymen, The, LXXI. MBP; MoBrPo (1942 ed.); OBEV (1st ed.)
Love steered my course, while yet the sun rode high. Of Fiammetta Singing [or Fiammetta]. Boccaccio. *Fr.* Sonnets. AWP; GoBC
Love still a boy, and oft a wanton is. Astrophel and Stella, LXXIII. Sir Philip Sidney. EG; HBV; MyFE; OAEP; ReEn; SiPS
Love Still Has Something of the Sea. Sir Charles Sedley. *See* Song: "Love still has . . ."
Love Story, A. Robert Graves. AtBAP; FaBoTw; LiTB; MoVE
Love Story, A. Oliver Herford. PoMS
Love, strong as Death, is dead. An End. Christina Rossetti. EmBrPo
Love suffereth all things. Sacrifice. Frederic Manning. NP
Love Suffereth Long. Sara Henderson Hay. ChIP; OQP; QP-2
Love-Sweetness. Dante Gabriel Rossetti. The House of Life, XXI. BEL; BPN; EmBrPo; EnLit; EPN; EPP; EtPaEn; EV-5; OAEP; POTT; PoVP; TOP; ViPo; VLEP
Love Symphony, A. Arthur O'Shaughnessy. HBV; VLEP
Love-Talker, The. "Ethna Carbery." AnIV; BMEP; CH; OnYI; OxBI
Love than Death More Strong. *Unknown, tr. fr. Spanish by* Elizabeth du Gué Trapier. TeCS
Love that doth reign and live within my thought. *See* Love that liveth and reigneth in my thought.
Love, that drained her, drained him she'd loved, though each. The Turtle Dove. Geoffrey Hill. NePoEA
Love, that dwarfs our life. Yamabo no Akahito, *tr. fr. Japanese by* I. W. Furukami. LiTW
Love that I had for you, my dear, The. El Amor Que Te Teniá. *Unknown.* ABF
Love [or Luve] that I have [or hae] chosen, The. The Lowlands [or Lawlands] o' Holland. *Unknown.* AmSS; BSV; CBOV; CH; EBSV; OBB; SG
Love That Is Dead and Buried. Christina Rossetti. DiM
Love That Is First and Last. Swinburne. *See* Tristram and Iseult.
Love that is hoarded, moulds at last. Song. Louis Ginsberg. MaRV; PoToHe (new ed.)
Love that is not quite love, The. Light Love. Charles Hanson Towne. PR
Love that liveth and reigneth [or doth reign and live] in my thought. Complaint of a Lover Rebuked. Petrarch, *tr. by* the Earl of Surrey. Sonnets to Laura: To Laura in Life, CIX. AWP; BEL; CoBE; ElSeCe; EnLi-1 (1949 ed.); EnLit; EPP; LiTW; LyMA; OAEP; OnPM; ReEn; ReIE; SiCE; SiPS; TrGrPo; TuPP; TyEnPo
Love, that long since hast to thy mighty power. An Hymn in Honor of Love. Spenser. ReIE
Love that looks still on your eyes. Song. William Browne. EG
"Love That Never Told Can Be." John Erskine. CAG
Love that rose on stronger wings, The. In Memoriam A. H. H., CXXVIII. Tennyson. EmBrPo; EPN; GEPC; ViPo; VLEP
Love that the heart is feeling, The. Mouth and Eyes. *Unknown.* OnPM
Love the Archer. Rufinus, *tr. fr. Greek by* F. A. Wright. OxBG
Love the Beautiful. Felix Mendelssohn. *See* Every Day.
Love, the Delight of All Well-thinking Minds. Fulke Greville. Caelica, I. OBSC; PoE; SiCE
Love, the Fisher. Bhartrihari, *tr. fr. Sanskrit by* Arthur W. Ryder. OnPM
Love the Foe. Sadi, *tr. fr. Persian by* A. J. Arberry. PeP
Love, the great master of true eloquence. Love, the Master of True Eloquence. Tasso. AWP; OnPM
Love the Indispensable and Crowning Grace. First Corinthians, Bible, *N.T.* *See* Charity.
Love, the inevitable, here appears. Love's Tyranny. Marcus Argentarius. OnPM
Love, the Light-Giver. Michelangelo, *tr. fr. Italian by* John Addington Symonds. AWP; LiTW
Love, the Master of True Eloquence. Tasso, *tr. fr. Italian by* John Herman Merivale. OnPM
(Love.) AWP
Love—the most generous passion of the mind. Earl of Rochester. *Fr.* A Letter. LO
Love the Rascal. Meleager. *See* Runaway Cupid.
Love the Shepherd. Myrinus, *tr. fr. Greek by* F. L. Lucas. GrPE
Love the unholy, that frost which quickens summer. Didactic Sonnet. Melvin Walker La Follette. NePoEA
Love, the Vagrant. Meleager. *See* Runaway Cupid.
Love the Wild Swan. Robinson Jeffers. AnFE; CoAnAm; MAP; MoAB; MoAmPo; PoFr; TwAmPo
Love, thou art absolute sole lord. A Hymn to the Name and Honour of the Admirable Saint Teresa. Richard Crashaw. ACP; CaAE; CoEV; EPS; EV-2; FaBoEn; KN; LiA; LoBV; MeLP; MePo; OAEP; OBEV; OBS; OxBoCh; PoEL-2; PoFS; PraNu; ReEn; SeCL; SeCV-1; SeEP; TriL; WGRP
Love, thou art best of human joys. A Song [or On Love]. Countess of Winchilsea. DiM; SeCL; SeEP
Love Thou Thy Land, with Love Far-brought. Tennyson. BPN; EmBrPo; EPN; PoVP; ViPo; VLEP
Love, through your spirit and mine what summer eve. Last Fire. Dante Gabriel Rossetti. The House of Life, XXX. PoVP; ViPo
Love throwes more dangerous darts than death I spy. *Unknown.* SeCSL
Love thy bright monarchy I now defy. *Unknown.* SeCSL
Love thy country, wish it well. Ode [or Shorten Sail]. George Bubb Dodington. CEP; OBEC; OBEV (1st ed.)
Love thy God and love Him only. Reality. Sir Aubrey De Vere. WGRP
Love thy mother, little one! To a Child Embracing His Mother. Thomas Hood. MOAH
Love Thyself Last. Ella Wheeler Wilcox. MaRV
Love, Time and Death. Frederick Locker-Lampson. HBV
Love, Time and Measure. *At.* to John Lilliat. *See* Song: "When love on time and measure makes his ground."
Love to faults is always blind. Blake. *Fr.* Poems from MSS. ViBoPo
Love to his singer held a glistening leaf. Love's Last Gift. Dante Gabriel Rossetti. The House of Life, LIX. BPN; PoVP; ViPo
Love to love calleth. Robert Bridges. *Fr.* Ode to Music. TwCV
Love to My Lord. Louisa Van Plattenhaus. BePJ
Love to the Church. Timothy Dwight. *See* I Love Thy Kingdom, Lord.
Love to the foolish giveth wit by great and potent art. In Praise of Love. Juan Ruiz, Archpriest of Hita. TeCS
Love Token, The. *Unknown.* *See* Bailiff's Daughter of Islington, The.
Love too in season riseth in the sky. Love in the Springtime. Theognis. GrR
Love took my life and thrilled [or thrill'd] it. Song [or The Surface and the Depths]. Lewis Morris. HBV; OBVV; VA
Love Triumphant, *sel.* Dryden.
Prologue: "So now, this poet, who forsakes the stage." OxBoLi
(Prologue to "Love Triumphant.") SiTL
Love Triumphant. Frederic Lawrence Knowles. BAP; HBV; LBMV; PR
Love 20¢ the First Quarter Mile. Kenneth Fearing. LoPS
Love Unchangeable. Rufus Dawes. AA
Love, under thy dominion unbending hearts bow low. Love. Euripides. WoL
Love Unfeigned, The. Chaucer. *See* Exhortation to Youth.
Love unreturn'd, how ere the flame. Constancye. Sidney Godolphin. MePo
Love Unseen. Byron. *See* Bitter Meditation.
Love Unsought. Emma Catharine Embury. AA
Love Vagabonding. William Drummond of Hawthornden. ElSeCe
Love vs. Marriage. Jean de Meun, *tr. fr. French by* Bernard D. N. Grebanier. *Fr.* The Romance of the Rose. EnLi-1
Love Virtue. Milton. *Fr.* Comus. GrCo-1

Love wakes and weeps. Cleveland's Song. Sir Walter Scott. *Fr.* The Pirate, *ch.* 23. EmBrPo
Love wakes men, once a life-time each. Coventry Patmore. *Fr.* The Angel in the House: The Revelation. LO
Love, wandering through the golden maze. Love Enslaved. Benedetto Guidi. OnPM
Love was a minstrel, singing. Counterpoint. Mary H. Blodgett. CAG
Love was before the light began. Love. *Unknown. Fr.* The Thousand and One Nights. AWP; LiTW
Love was laid down, all weary, fast asleep. Licia, IX. Giles Fletcher. ReIE
Love Was Once Light as Air. C. Day Lewis. *Fr.* Two Songs (Written to Irish Airs). OAEP (2d ed.)
Love Was True to Me. John Boyle O'Reilly. GTIV
(Song: "Love was true to me.") ACP
Love We as Brothers. William Langland, *mod. by* Henry W. Wells. *Fr.* The Vision of Piers Plowman. PoLi
Love, we have heard together. Moonlight North and South. Robert Fuller Murray. BSV; EBSV
Love we the warmth and light of tropic lands. The Tropics. Douglas Brooke Wheelton Sladen. VA
Love, Weeping, Laid This Song. Lizette Woodworth Reese. LS
Love well and pray for all thy dead. Pray for the Dead. Arthur Dentworth Hamilton Eaton. PoRL
Love, What Art Thou? Lady Mary Wroth. *Fr.* The Countess of Montgomery's Urania. SeCL
Love, when all the years are silent, vanished quite and laid to rest. Hereafter. Harriet Prescott Spofford. HBV
Love Which Is Here a Care. William Drummond of Hawthornden. OxBoCh
(Love.) EPS (1942 ed.)
Love which me so cruelly tormenteth, The. Amoretti, XLII. Spenser. PeBoCo
Love Who Will, for I'll Love None. William Browne. HBV (8th ed.); SeCL
Love Whom Ye List and Spare Not. *Unknown.* ReIE
Love, Whose Month Was Ever May. Ulrich von Lichtenstein, *tr. fr. German by* Jethro Bithell. AWP; JAWP; WBP
Love will die that very hour. Love vs. Marriage. Jean de Meun. *Fr.* The Romance of the Rose. EnLi-1
Love Will Find Out the Way. *Unknown.* BLV; CBOV; FaBoCh; GN, *abr.;* HBV; LiTG; LiTL; LoGBV; OBEV; OTPC, *abr.* (1923 ed.); PCD; SeCL; TreFS
(Great Adventurer, The.) FaFP; GTBS; GTBS-D; GTBS-W; GTSE; GTSL
("Over the mountains.") LO
(Truth's Integrity.) SeEP; TuPP
Love will not have me cry. Canzonetta: He Will Neither Boast nor Lament. Jacopo da Lentino. AWP
Love will outwatch the stars, and light the skies. Love's Vigil. Edwin Markham. OQP; QP-2
Love will stay,/ And it will stay forever. Phaedra Jealous. Racine. *Fr.* Phèdre. LiA
Love Winged My Hopes. *Unknown.* ElL; TrGrPo
(Icarus.) OBEV
(Love and Hope.) BLV
("Love winged my hopes and taught me how to fly.") OBSC
"And none but Love their woeful hap did rue," *sel.* LO
Love with a liquid ecstasy. Self-Esteem. Anna Wickham. PIAE
Love within the lover's breast. Lines. George Meredith. HBV
Love without Hope. Robert Graves. ChTr; OxBI
Love without Longing. *Unknown. See* I Have a Young Sister.
Love, won or lost, is countless gain. Coventry Patmore. *Fr.* The Angel in the House, I, v, 2. LO
Love writes surrender as its due. Beauty, Too, Seeks Surrender. Jessica Powers. JKCP (1955 ed.)
Love, you have broken my wings—I cried. Answer. Leonora Speyer. PG (1945 ed.)
Love, You have struck me straight, my Lord! Resolution. Charles L. O'Donnell. GoBC; TrPWD
"Love you?" said I, then I sighed, and then I gazed upon her sweetly. Ferdinando and Elvira; or, The Gentle Pieman. W. S. Gilbert. BOHV; LBN; NA; PC
Love you seek for, presupposes. Question and Answer. Elizabeth Barrett Browning. BPN
Love Your Enemies. St. Matthew, V: 38-48, Bible, *N.T.* GrCo-1
"Love your neighbor as yourself!" Thoughts on the Commandments. George Augustus Baker, Jr. AA; HBV; PR
Loved for themselves, too. Oft as I behold. Paul Veronese: Three Sonnets, II. Sir Samuel Ferguson. IrPN
Loved I Am, and Yet Complaine of Love. Sir Philip Sidney. *Fr.* Arcadia. PoEL-1
(Complaint of Love.) SiPS
Loved of My Soul. Israel Najara, *tr. fr. Hebrew by* Nina Davis Salaman. TrJP
Lovel and John. *Unknown, tr. fr. Danish by* E. M. Smith-Dampier. BoDaBa
Lovelier than all the rest. With Her Beauty. Tu Fu. OuHeWo
Loveliest dawn of gold and rose. The Least of Carols. Sophie Jewett. ChrBoLe; OHIP; SDH
Loveliest Girl, The. Luis de Góngora, *tr. fr. Spanish by* John Pierrepont Rice. AnSpL-1
(Let Me Walk Alone Where Breaks the Sea.) TeCS
Loveliest of Trees [the Cherry Now]. A. E. Housman. A Shropshire Lad, II. AlDL; AnFE; ATP; AWP; BEL; BLV; BMEP; BoLiVe; BPN; CaAE; CBOV; ChMo; ChTr; CMP; CoBE; CoBMV; CP; EmBrPo; EnL; EnLi-2 (1949 ed.); EnLit; FaBoBe; FaFP; GTBS-W; GTSL; InP; InPo; JAWP; LiTB; LiTM; MBP; MoAB; MoBrPo; MPB (1956 ed.); NeMA; OAEP; OHIP; OQP; OTPC (1946 ed.); OuHeWo; PCH, *st.* 1; PoE; PoeMoYo; PoLFOT; POT; PoTo; POTT; PoVP; QP-1; ShBV-3; StVeCh; TCEP; TCPD; TOP; TrGrPo; TSW; TSWC; TwCV; TwHP; TwP; ViBoPo; ViP; ViPo; VLEP; VOD (1935 ed.); WBP
Loveliest of trees, the cherry now. In a Town Garden. Donald Mattam. FiBHP
Loveliest things of earth are not, The. The Forest-Bird. W. J. Turner. POTE
Lovelilts. Marion Hill. BOHV
Loveliness. Hilda Conkling. TiPo
Loveliness. *Unknown, tr. fr. Japanese by* Lois J. Erickson. SoLD
Loveliness of Love, The. George Darley. EV-4; GTBS; GTBS-D; GTBS-W; GTSE; LPS-1; TIP
(It Is Not Beauty I Demand.) EG; HBV; LiTL; OBRV; PoE
(Song: "It is not Beauty I demand.") OBVV
Loveliness that dies when I forget. Loveliness. Hilda Conkling. TiPo
Lovelocks. Walter de la Mare. MoVE
Lovel's Song. Ben Jonson. *See* It Was a Beauty That I Saw.
Lovely am I as dream in stone, O mortal! Beauty. Baudelaire. TrFP
Lovely as a Flower. Heine, *tr. fr. German by* Kate Flores. AnGP
("I see ye like a flooer," *tr. into Scottish by* Edwin Morgan.) AnGP
Lovely as is the rose to men, when first it flowers in spring. *Unknown. Fr.* Carmina Epigraphica. LaP
Lovely are curves of the white owl sweeping. The White Owl. George Meredith. *Fr.* Love in the Valley. ChTr
Lovely Bed, A. Mattie Lee Hausgen. GFA
Lovely boy, thou art not dead. Three Epitaphs upon the Death of a Rare Child of Six Years Old, II. Francis Davison. OBSC; ReIE
Lovely Chance. Sara Teasdale. CP
Lovely cherries on the tree. Adjectives. Moishe Nadir. TrJP
Lovely Chloris, though thine eyes. Love above Beauty. Henry Reynolds. TuPP
Lovely Colonus! Sophocles. *See* Grove of Colonus, The.
Lovely courier of the sky. Anacreon's Dove. Samuel Johnson. AWP; JAWP; WBP
Lovely dainty Spanish needle. The Spanish Needle. Claude McKay. GoSl
Lovely Dames. W. H. Davies. PtOT
Lovely days of spring have clothed the plains, The. The Round-up. Sarah Elizabeth Howard. PoOW
Lovely Delightful Song of Thy Sister, The. *Unknown, tr. fr. Egyptian by* T. Eric Peet. LiTW
Lovely form there sate beside my bed, A. Phantom or Fact. Samuel Taylor Coleridge. BPN; EmBrPo; EnRP
Lovely fountain leaps, The. The Fountain. Ibn al-Ra'i'a. MooP
Lovely grapes and apples. A Tabernacle Thought. Israel Zangwill. TrJP
Lovely Green Lady, A. The Green Lady. Charlotte Druitt Cole. BoTP
Lovely hill-torrents are. Song. W. J. Turner. MBP; MoBrPo
Lovely homeland once was mine, A. In Exile. Heine. AnGP
Lovely in Decay. Samuel Taylor Coleridge. *Fr.* Remorse. RO
Lovely Infanta, The. *Unknown, tr. fr. Spanish by* Alice Jane McVan. AnSpL-1
Lovely kind, and kindly loving. An Odd Conceit [*or* Song]. Nicholas Breton. ElL; LO; OBSC; SiCE; TuPP
Lovely lady, Christabel, The. Samuel Taylor Coleridge. *Fr.* Christabel. LO
Lovely Lady dressed in blue. To Our Lady. Mary Dixon Thayer. TreFS
Lovely lady, rein thy will. Death's Warning to Beauty. *Unknown.* AnIL
Lovely lady sat and sange, A. Mary and Her Child. *Unknown.* OxBoCh
Lovely Lass o' Inverness, The. Burns. *See* Lament for Culloden.

Lovely Lass to a Friar Came, A. *At. to* the Earl of Rochester. CoMu
"Lovely, lasting peace of mind!" A Hymn to Contentment. Thomas Parnell. CEP; EiPP; OBEC
Lovely light of stars, The. New Year. Fujita. SoLD
Lovely little daughter. The Artichoke. Ibn al-Talla. MooP
Lovely Lo-fu in the land of Chin, The. The Song of the Four Seasons. Li Po. WhP
Lovely looseness of your body laves, The. The Heads and Tails of Love. James Wreford Watson. BoCaPo (1948 ed.)
Lovely, lost, italic curve, The. The Missal. Rosemary Dobson. BoAV; MoAuPo
Lovely, lovely is my son! *Unknown.* BOL
Lovely Maid. Ibn Khafaja, *tr. fr. Arabic by* A. J. Arberry. MooP
Lovely maid, with rapture swelling. Lines by a Fond Lover. *Unknown.* NA
Lovely Mary Donnelly. William Allingham. AnIV; GTSE; HBV; IrPN; LPS-1; VA
Lovely morn, A, so still, so very still. May, 1840. Hartley Coleridge. OBVV
Lovely of hair and breast and face. The Question. Norman Gale. FiBHP
Lovely River. Ibn Khafaja, *tr. fr. Arabic by* A. J. Arberry. MooP
Lovely Rivers and Lakes of Maine, The. George B. Wallis. BLPA
Lovely Rose Is Sprung, A. *Unknown, tr. fr. German by* Margarete Münsterberg. AWP
Lovely Semiramis. The Fan. Edith Sitwell. HBMV
Lovely Shall Be Choosers, The. Robert Frost. AmP; CoBMV; CoV; MAP; MoAB; MoAmPo; OxBA
Lovely spring breeze has come, The. Spring Day on West Lake. Ou-yang Hsiu. OnPC
Lovely spring, gone on thy ways. Autumn Complaint. Nikolaus Lenau. AnGP
Lovely the Earth Is. Bernhard Severin Ingemann, *tr. fr. Danish by* Charles W. Stork. BoDS
Lovely the rose; and yet—its beauty Time deflowers. Transcience. Theocritus. *Fr.* Idylls, XXIII. GrPE
Lovely Things. H. M. Sarson. BoTP
Lovely Things. *Unknown, tr. fr. Japanese by* Lois J. Erickson. SoLD
Lovely Village Fair, The; or, I Dont Mean to Tell You Her Name. *Unknown.* CoMu
Lovely was that night in May. The Postilion. Nikolaus Lenau. AnGP
Lovely was the death. A Desultory Poem, Written on the Christmas Eve of 1794. Samuel Taylor Coleridge. *Fr.* Religious Musings. EmBrPo; EnRP; ERP
Lovely Woman, A. W. H. Davies. FaBoTw
Lovely woman rolls up, A/ The delicate bamboo blind. The Night of Sorrow. Li Po. WoL
Lovely world, how ardently. A Dead Maiden's Complaint. Gerasimos Markoras. MoGP
Lovely years went lightly by, The. A Child's Song to Her Mother. Winifred Welles. HBMV
Lovely young lady I mourn in my rhymes, A. An Epitaph. George John Cayley. BOHV; FiBHP; HBV
Lovely young Lavinia once had Friends, The. Lavinia. James Thomson. *Fr.* The Seasons: Autumn. OBEC
Lovely Youth, The. Aneirin, *tr. fr. Welsh by* H. Idris Bell. LiTW
Lovely Youth. Pushkin, *tr. fr. Russian by* Babette Deutsch. TrRV
Lover, The. Coventry Patmore. The Angel in the House, I, iii, 1. EPP; EV-5; PoVP
Lover, The. John Crowe Ransom. LS
Lover, The. Richard Henry Stoddard. AA
Lover, The; a Ballad. Lady Mary Wortley Montagu. CEP; LO; OBEC
Lover Abused Renounceth Love, The, *sel.* George Turberville.
"Was never day came on my head." ElL
Lover and Birds, The. William Allingham. GTIV; OBVV
Lover and Echo. Carrol O'Daly, *tr. fr. Middle Irish or fr. Late Middle Irish by* George Sigerson. OnYI
Lover and His Lass, A. Ronald Hambleton. BoCaPo
Lover and Philosopher. Sir William Davenant. *See* To a Mistress Dying.
Lover and the Belovèd, The. Ramon Lull, *tr. fr. Spanish by* Garret Strange. CAW
Lover and the stern philosopher, The. The Cats. Baudelaire. MiFP
Lover Approving His Lady Unkind Is Forced Unwilling to Utter His Mind, A. *Unknown.* ReIE
Lover Beseecheth His Mistress Not to Forget His Steadfast Faith and True Intent, The. Sir Thomas Wyatt. *See* Forget Not Yet.
Lover breeze to the roses pleaded, A. "Treasure Island." Patrick R. Chalmers. ReTS
Lover Comforteth Himself with the Worthiness of His Love, The. Earl of Surrey. EV-1; PoE; SiCE; TuPP
("When raging love with extreme pain.") EnLoPo; SiPS
Lover Compareth His Heart to the Overcharged Gun, The. Sir Thomas Wyatt. ReIE
Lover Compareth His State to a Ship in Perilous Storm Tossed on the Sea, The. Petrarch, *tr. fr. Italian by* Sir Thomas Wyatt. Sonnets to Laura: To Laura in Life, CLVI. BEL; CoBE; ElL; ElSeCe; EnLi-1; EnLit; PoE; PoEL-1; PoFS; ReIE; TuPP
(Galley, The.) OBSC
(Lover Like to a Ship Tossed on the Sea.) EtS
(My Galley.) LiTB
(My Galley Charged with Forgetfulness.) EnL; MaPo; NBE; ReEn; SiCE; SiPS; TwHP
Lover Complaineth of His Lady's Unconstancy, The. *Unknown.* ReIE
Lover Complaineth [*or* Complayneth] the Unkindness of His Love, The. Sir Thomas Wyatt. AtBAP; BrBE; CaAE; CenL; ElL; ElSeCe; EM-1; EnLit; EPP; FaBoEn; OAEP; PoE; PoEL-1; ReIE; TCEP; TrGrPo; TriL; TyEnPo; ViBoPo
(My Lute, Awake!) AEV; CoBE; EG; EnL; LEAP; MaPo; ReIE; *diff. vers.;* SiPS
(To His Lute.) CoEV; OBEV; OBSC; PG
Lover Consults with Reason, The. Thomas Carew. TrGrPo
Lover Deceived by His Lady's Unconstancy Writeth unto Her as Followeth, The. Thomas Churchyard. ReIE; TuPP
(Farewell to a Fondling, A.) ElL
Lover Deceived Writes to His Lady, The, *sel.* Thomas Howell.
Who Would Have Thought. ElL
Lover Declareth His Affection, Together with the Cause Thereof, The. George Gascoigne. TuPP
Lover Describeth His Being Striken with Sight of His Love, The. Sir Thomas Wyatt. ReIE
Lover, Disdained, Complaineth, A. Thomas, Lord Vaux. TuPP
Lover divine and perfect Comrade. Gods. Walt Whitman. AnAmPo; LA
Lover Envies an Old Man, The. Shaemas O'Sheel. SBMV
Lover Exhorteth His Lady to Be Constant, The. *Unknown.* OBSC; TuPP
Lover Exhorteth His Lady to Take Time While Time Is, The. George Turberville. ReIE
Lover Extolleth the Singular Beauty of His Lady, The. George Turberville. ReIE
Lover for Death, A. Ralph Cheyney. TBM
Lover for Shamefastness Hideth His Desire within His Faithful Heart, The. Petrarch, *tr. fr. Italian by* Sir Thomas Wyatt. Sonnets to Laura: To Laura in Life, CIX. CoBE; ReIE; TuPP
("Long love that in my thought doth harbor, The.") ReEn; SiCE
Lover Having Dreamed of Enjoying of His Love, Complaineth That the Dream Is Not either Longer or Truer, The. Sir Thomas Wyatt. BEL; CoBE; EnLi-1; ReIE; TCEP; WHA
(Unstable Dream, According to the Place.) OAEP
Lover I Am, A. *Unknown.* SeCL
Lover in Distress Exclaimeth against Fortune, The. *Unknown.* ReIE
Lover in Liberty Smileth at Them in Thraldom. *Unknown.* ElL; ElSeCe
Lover in the Praise of His Beloved and Comparison of Her Beauty, The. *Unknown.* ReIE; TuPP
Lover in Winter Plaineth for the Spring, The. *Unknown.* *See* Western Wind, When Wilt Thou Blow?
Lover Is Near, The. Goethe, *tr. fr. German by* Werner Heider. LiTW
Lover is of colour deed and pale, The. The X Properte. Sir Thomas More. *Fr.* The XII Properties or Condicyons of a Lover. CoBE
Lover Like to a Ship Tossed on the Sea, The. Sir Thomas Wyatt. *See* Lover Compareth His State to a Ship in Perilous Storm Tossed on the Sea, The.
Lover Loquitur. Louise Imogen Guiney. PR
Lover Mourns for the Loss of Love, The. W. B. Yeats. Po
Lover of Child Marjory, The. A Sea Child. Bliss Carman. HBV; VA
Lover of children! Fellow heir with those. In Memory of Lewis Carroll. *Unknown.* PoRL
Lover of her body said, The. The Two Lovers. Richard Hovey. HBV
Lover of His Country, The. Andreas Calvos, *tr. fr. Modern Greek by* Rae Dalven. MoGP
Lover Rejected Complaineth, A. Edward de Vere, Earl of Oxford. ReIE
Lover Rejoiceth [That He Hath Broken the Snares of Love], The. Sir Thomas Wyatt. BLV; LoPS; TrGrPo
(Liberty.) OBSC
(Love's Snare.) LiTL
(Tangled I Was.) TuPP
("Tangled I was in love's snare.") ReEn; SiPS

Lover Rejoiceth the Enjoying of His Love, The. Sir Thomas Wyatt. FaBoEn; ReIE
(Promise, A.) OBSC
("Once, as methought, Fortune me kiss'd.") SiPS
Lover Renounceth Love, The. Sir Thomas Wyatt. *See* Renouncing of Love, A.
Lover Sendeth Sighs to Move His Suit, The. Sir Thomas Wyatt. LiTL
Lover Showeth His Woeful State and Prayeth Pity, The. *Unknown.* TuPP
Lover Showeth [*or* Sheweth] How He Is Forsaken of Such as He Sometime Enjoyed, The. Sir Thomas Wyatt. AtBAP; BLV; BrBE; CaAE; ElL; ElSeCe; FaBoEn; HoPM; OAEP; PoE; PoEL-1; PoFS; PoRA; ReIE; TrGrPo; TuPP; ViBoPo
(How Like You This?) SeCePo
(Lover Shows How He Has Been Forsaken, The.) TriL
(Remembrance.) CoEV; OBSC
(They Flee from Me.) AnEnPo; ATP (1953 ed.); EG; EnL; ExPo; GTBS-W; InPo; LiTB; LoBV; RiBV; SeCeV; SiPS; UnPo (3d ed.)
("They flee from me that sometime did me seek.") EnLoPo; MaPo; ReEn; SiCE
(Vixi Puellis Nuper Idoneus.) LiTG; LiTL; LO; OBEV
Lover Sings of a Garden, The. Helen Hoyt. NP
Lover Tells of the Rose in His Heart, The. W. B. Yeats. ChMo; CMP; CoBE; EnLi-2 (1949 ed.); GTML; POTT; ViBoPo
(Aedh Tells of the Rose in His Heart.) MBP; MoBrPo
Lover, the lover will always remember, The. Act of Love. Nicholas Moore. NeBP
Lover Thinks of His Lady in the North, The. Shaemas O'Sheel. HBV
Lover to His Bed, with Describing of His Unquiet State, The. Sir Thomas Wyatt, *after the Italian of* Petrarch. ReIE; TuPP
("Restful place, reviver of my smart.") SiPS
Lover to His Lady, The. *At. to* Plato, *tr. fr. Greek by* George Turberville. OBSC; TuPP
(Lover to His Lady That Gazed Much Up to the Skies, The.) SiCE
(My Girl, Thou Gazest Much.) RiBV
Lover to Lover. David Morton. HBMV
Lover to the Thames of London, to Favour His Lady Passing Thereon, The. George Turberville. ChTr; ElL; ElSeCe; OBSC; ReIE
Lover under burthen of his [mistress'] love, The. A Gulling Sonnet. Sir John Davies. Gulling Sonnets, I. ElL; TuPP
Lover, The, Whose Mistresse Feared a Mouse, Declareth that He Would Become a Cat if He Might Have His Desire. George Turberville. PoC
Loverd Godd, in hondes tine. In Manus Tuas, Domine. *Unknown.* CoBE
Lovers, The. Byron. LiTL
Lovers, The. Phoebe Cary. HBV; LPS-3
(Love's Moods and Tenses.) BOHV
Lovers, The. Alex Comfort. NeBP
Lovers, The. Edward Davison. LO; LoPS
(Willow and Water.) PG (1955 ed.)
Lovers. Mary Fullerton. BoAV
Lovers. Miriam Waddington. TwCaPo
Lovers, The. Marya Zaturenska. MoAmPo
Lovers, and a Reflection. Charles Stuart Calverley. BOHV; LPS-3; NA; PA; WhC
Lovers and Friends. Henry Luttrell. *Fr.* Advice to Julia. OBRV
Lovers and madmen have such seething brains. The Lunatic, the Lover, and the Poet [*or* Imagination *or* Inspiration]. Shakespeare. *Fr.* A Midsummer Night's Dream, V, i. CoEV; FiP; GTBS-W; LiTB
Lovers and the City, The, *sel.* M. K. Joseph.
Old Montague. AnNZ
Lover's Anger, A. Matthew Prior. LO; LoPS; SeCL
Lover's Appeal, The. Sir Thomas Wyatt. *See* Earnest Suit to His Unkind Mistress Not to Forsake Him, An.
Lover's Arithmetic, The. *Unknown.* OxBoLi
Lovers, avoid the shafts that fly. Song. Charles d'Orléans. FoS
Lover's Choice, The. Thomas Bedingfield. HBV
Lover's Complaint, A. *Unknown, at. to* Sir Walter Ralegh. *See* As You Came from the Holy Land.
Lovers conceits are like a flattring glasse. *Unknown.* OBS
Lover's Curse, A. Meleager, *tr. fr. Greek by* Dudley Fitts. LiTW
Lover's Death, The. Propertius, *tr. fr. Latin by* John Nott. Elegies, II, 13a. RoL
Lover's Death, The. *Unknown, tr. fr. Danish by* E. M. Smith-Dampier. BoDaBa
Lovers' Dialogue. Sir Philip Sidney. *See* Astrophel and Stella: Eleventh Song.
Lover's Diary, A, *sels.* Sir Gilbert Parker.
Art. VA
Invincible. VA
Love's Outset. VA
Reunited. OBVV; OQP; QP-2
(Envoy: "When you and I have played the little hour.") VA
Woman's Hand, A. VA
Lover's Envy, A. Henry van Dyke. HBV
Lover's Farewell, The. James Clarence Mangan. IrPN
Lovers Flee, The. Jami, *tr. fr. Persian by* Edward Fitzgerald. *Fr.* Salámán and Absál. PeP
Lovers, forget your love. Wind and Window-Flower. Robert Frost. YT
Lovers How They Come and Part. Robert Herrick. AtBAP; LO; OxBoLi; PoEL-3
Lovers in the act dispense. The Thieves. Robert Graves. GTBS-W; LiTM (rev. ed.); OxBI
Lovers in Winter. Robert Graves. Po
Lovers' Infiniteness[e]. John Donne. CaAE; ElL; ElSeCe; EnLi-1 (1949 ed.); EPS; FaBoEn; GTBS-W; LiTB; MaPo; MeLP; OBS; PoE; PoEL-2; SeCV-1; SeEP; TuPP
(Love's Infiniteness.) LiTG; LiTL
Lover's Journey, The. George Crabbe. *Fr.* Tales. EnSW; EPP, *abr.*
Lover's Lament, A. Shakespeare. *See* Come Away, Come Away, Death.
Lover's Lament, The ("My dearest dear, the time draws near"). *Unknown.* AS
Lover's Lament, A ("My little breath"). *Unknown, tr. fr. Tewa Indian by* H. J. Spinden. AWP; JAWP; WBP
Lover's Lane. Paul Laurence Dunbar. BANP
Lover's Lane, Saint Jo. Eugene Field. PR
Lover's Legacy, A. *Unknown.* SeCL
("Faine would I Cloris ere I dye.") SeCSL
Lover's Life Compared to the Alps, The. Jacopo Sannazaro, *tr. fr Italian by* Sir Thomas Wyatt. ReIE; TuPP
("Like to these unmeasurable mountains.") ReEn; SiCE
Lovers Love the Spring. Shakespeare. *See* It Was a Lover and His Lass.
Lover's Lullaby, A. George Gascoigne. *See* Lullaby of a Lover, The.
Lovers may find similitudes. The Cascade. Edgell Rickword. ChMP; FaBoTw
Lovers' Meeting. Theocritus, *tr. fr. Greek by* F. L. Lucas. *Fr.* Idylls, XII. GrPE
Lover's Melancholy, The, *sels.* John Ford.
"Cunning arts man, The/ Faltered not in a line." MyFE
Fly Hence, Shadows, *fr.* V, i. CenL; OnPM; SeCL; ViBoPo
(Dawn.) OBEV
(Matin Song.) EV-2
(Song: "Fly hence, shadows, that do keep.") LoBV
"If thou canst wake with me, forget to eate," *fr.* IV, ii. PoEL-2
"Minutes are numbered by the fall of sands," *fr.* IV, iii. PoD; PoEL-2
Musical Duel, *fr.* I, i. LPS-2
"Parthenophil is lost, and I would see him." PoD
Lover's Memory. F. Tennyson Jesse. DiM
Lover's New Year's Gift, A. John Lydgate. PoEL-1
Lovers of Marchaid, The. Marjorie Pickthall. HBV
Lovers Parted. Lesbia Harford. BoAu
Lover's Play of Words. Martial, *tr. fr. Latin by* Thomas Moore. OnPM
Lover's Posy, The. Rufinus, *tr. fr. Greek by* W. H. D. Rouse. AWP; JAWP; WBP
Lover's Prison, The. Ariosto, *tr. fr. Italian by* Leigh Hunt OnPM
Lover's Progress, The, *sel.* John Fletcher.
Dead Host's Welcome, The, *fr.* III, i. EV-2; SeCL; TrGrPo
('Tis Late and Cold.) ViBoPo
Lover's Protestation, A. Thomas Lodge. *See* Fancy, A ("First shall the heavens . . .").
Lover's Quarrel, A. Robert Browning. EtPaEn
Lovers, Rejoice [*or* Rejoyce]! Beaumont *and* Fletcher. *Fr.* Cupid's Revenge. ElL; FaBoEn
Lover's Reply to Good Advice. Richard Hughes. MBP; MoBrPo
Lover's Resolution, The. George Wither. *See* Shall I, Wasting in Despair.
Lover's Return, The. *Unknown.* ABS
Lover's Song, The. Alfred Austin. OBVV
Lover's Song, The. Edward Rowland Sill. AA; HBV; PR
Lovers' souls 'gin dance with glee. Dance. Sadi. PeP
Lover's Tale, The, *sel.* Tennyson.
"And yet tonight." VLEP
Lovers tread the water, lovers go. Lovers. Miriam Waddington. TwCaPo
Lovers' Walk, The. Dante Gabriel Rossetti. The House of Life, XII. BPN; OAEP; PoVP; TOP; ViPo
Lovers whose lifted hands are candles in winter. For a Child Expected. Anne Ridler. LiTM; MoVE; NeBP; SeCePo
Lovers' Wine. Baudelaire, *tr. fr. French by* Alan Conder. TrFP
Lover's Wish. F. Tennyson Jesse. DiM

Loves. Jean Antoine de Baïf, *pr. tr. fr. French.* LiA
Love's a hussy when you know her. You'll Know Love. F. T. Macartney. MoAuPo
Love's a Jest, *sel.* Peter Anthony Motteux.
Slaves to London. OAEP
(London.) SeCL
(Song, A: "Slaves to London, I'll deceive you.") SeEP
Love's Absence in the Spring. Abraham Cowley. *See* Spring, The.
Love's Adventure, *in mod. Eng. Unknown.* TMEV
Loves Alchemy [*or* Alchymie]. John Donne. EnLP; LiTL; MePo; OAEP; ReEn; TuPP; ViBoPo
Love's an Enchanter. Pierre de Ronsard, *tr. fr. French by* Alan Conder. TrFP
Loves and Losses of Pierrot, *sels.* William Griffith.
Pierrette in Memory. BAP; HBV; SBMV
Pierrot Makes a Song. PR
Loves and sorrows of those who lose an orchard. The Lost Orchard. Edgar Lee Masters. ChMo; CMP; MoPo
Love's Anniversary to the Sun. William Habington. ES
Love's Apparition and Evanishment. Samuel Taylor Coleridge. EnRP; EV-4
Love's Apple. Plato, *tr. fr. Greek by* F. L. Lucas. GrPE; GrR
Love's Argument. Father Andrew. MaRV
Love's Autumn. John Payne. VA
Love's Assize. Guido Cavalcanti, *tr. fr. Italian by* Hubert Creekmore. LiTW
(Sonnet: Love's Assize.) LyPI
Love's Baubles. Dante Gabriel Rossetti. The House of Life, XXIII. PoVP; ViPo
Love's Blindness. William James Linton. VA
Love's Blindness. Theognis, *tr. fr. Greek by* F. L. Lucas. GrPE
Love's but the Frailty of the Mind. Congreve. *Fr.* The Way of the World. EnLi-1; SeCL
(Song.) SeEP
Love's Calendar. William Bell Scott. HBV
Love's Capriciousness. Callimachus, *tr. fr. Greek by* Robert Allason Furness. OxBG
(Hunting Code, *tr. by* R. A. Furness.) GrR
(Love's Chase, *tr. by* G. M. Young.) GrL
Love's Caution. W. H. Davies. ChMP
Love's Change. Anne Reeve Aldrich. AA; AV; LBAP
Love's Chase. Callimachus. *See* Love's Capriciousness.
Love's Code. Mutarrif, *tr. fr. Arabic by* A. J. Arberry. MooP
Love's Coming. Shaw Neilson. BoAu; MoAuPo
Love's Concession. Shakespeare. *See* Sonnets, CXXX.
Love's Consolation, *sel.* R. W. Dixon.
"Love hath great store of sweetness, and 'tis well." LO
Love's Cosmopolitan. Annie Matheson. OBVV
Love's Cure, *sel.* Beaumont *and* Fletcher.
Turn, Turn Thy Beauteous Face Away. AtBAP
(Song.) PoEL-2
Love's Daring. *Unknown.* EV-2
Love's Deity [*or* Deitie]. John Donne. ATP; AWP; BEL; EIL; ElSeCe; EM-1; EnLi-1; EnLit; EnLP; EPP; EPS; EV-2; InPo; KN; LiTB; LiTG; LiTL; MaPo; MePo; OAEP; OuHeWo; PIAE; PoE; PreP; ReEn; SeCePo; SeCV-1; SeEP; TOP; TuPP; TwP; WBP; WHA
Love's Delights. Nahum Tate. *Fr.* The History of King Richard II. SeCL
Love's Despair. Dryden. *See* Farewell, Ungrateful Traitor.
Love's Despair. Richard Lynche. *Fr.* Diella. EIL
Love's Despair. Diarmad O'Curnain, *tr. fr. Modern Irish by* George Sigerson. GTIV; OnYI; OxBI; TIP
Love's Despair. Shakespeare. *See* Come Away, Come Away, Death!
Love's Detective. Gamaliel Bradford. PR
Love's Diet. John Donne. OAEP; PoFS
Love's Emblems. John Fletcher. *Fr.* The Tragedy of Valentinian, II, iv. EIL; HBV; LEAP; OBEV
(Love Song.) FaBoEn
("Now the lusty spring is seen.") EG; ElSeCe; ViBoPo
(Song.) SeEP
Love's Ending. *Unknown. See* Sought by the World.
Love's Entreaty. Michelangelo, *tr. fr. Italian by* John Addington Symonds. AWP
(Sonnet LV: "Thou knowest, love, I know that thou dost know.") BoFr
Love's equinoctial gales are past. Winter. Maurice James Craig. OnYI
Love's Eternity. Shakespeare. *See* Sonnets, CXVI.
Love's Evidence. Ibn Baqi, *tr. fr. Arabic by* A. J. Arberry. MooP
Love's Exchange. John Donne. LiTL
Love's Extremes. Antonio Villegas, *tr. fr. Spanish by* Sir John Bowring. OnPM
Love's Fancy. Tamuke, *tr. fr. Japanese by* Ishii *and* Obata. OnPM
Love's Farewell. Michael Drayton. *See* Idea: "Since there's no help . . ."
Love's Fatality. Dante Gabriel Rossetti. The House of Life, LIV. PoVP; ViPo
Love's Fidelity. Petrarch. *See* Vow to Love Faithfully, Howsoever He Be Rewarded, A.
Love's Flight. Else Lasker-Schüler, *tr. fr. German by* Jethro Bithell. TrJP
Love's Forget-Me-Not. Isabella Valancy Crawford. CPG
Love's Fragility. Alan Porter. POTE
Love's Franciscan. Henry Constable. ACP; GoBC; SaFP
Love's fruit in all the world is only this. Two as One. Bhartrihari. OnPM
Love's Glory. Fulke Greville. Caelica, XVI. OBSC
("Fie [*or* Fye] foolish Earth, think you the heaven wants glory.") LO; PoEL-1
Love's god is a boy. Cupid. *Unknown.* EIL
Love's Grave. George Meredith. *See* Modern Love: "Mark where the pressing wind."
Love's Grave. Thomas Watson. *See* My Love Is Past.
Love's Growing Pains. James Gallagher. JKCP (1955 ed.)
Love's Growth. John Donne. GTBS-W; MePo; NBE; ReEn; SeCV-1; TuPP
Loves Horoscope. Richard Crashaw. HBV; MeLP; OBS
Love's Immaturity. E. J. Scovell. LiTB
Love's Immortality. Elsa Barker. *Fr.* The Spirit and the Bride. HBMV
Love's Immortality. *Unknown. See* Crowned with Flowers.
Love's Inconsistency. Petrarch, *tr. by* Sir Thomas Wyatt. *See* Description of the Contrarious Passions in a Lover.
Love's Infiniteness. John Donne. *See* Lovers' Infiniteness.
Love's Insight. *Unknown.* GTSL
Love's Justification. Michelangelo, *tr. fr. Italian by* Wordsworth. AWP; JAWP; WBP
(Deathless Flower, A.) WoL
(Sonnet: "Yes! hope may with my strong desire keep pace.") LyPI
("Yes! hope may with my strong desire keep pace.") RO
Love's Kiss. Helen Hay Whitney. AA
Love's Labour Lost. Robert Tofte. *Fr.* Alba. EIL
Love's Labour's Lost, *sels.* Shakespeare.
Did Not the Heavenly Rhetoric of Thine Eye, *fr.* IV, iii. LiTB; LiTG
(Heavenly Rhetoric, The.) GTBS-W
(Sonnet: "Did not the heavenly rhetoric . . .") ViBoPo
Love and the Poet, *fr.* IV, iii. CoEV
"O we have made a vow," *fr.* IV, iii. NBE
On a Day—Alack the Day! *fr.* IV, iii. EIL; ElSeCe; EV-1; ViBoPo
(Blossom.) OBEV
(Dumain's Rhymes.) OBSC
(Love's Perjuries.) GTBS; GTBS-D; GTBS-W; GTSE; GTSL; HBV
(Passionate Shepherd's Song, The.) ReIE
So Sweet a Kiss, *fr.* IV, iii. EIL; InvP
When Daisies Pied and Violets Blue, *fr.* V, ii. AnFE; EG; EM-1; MyFE; OBEV; OBSC; PoEL-2; PoRA; SeCeV; SiCE; TyEnPo
(Song[s]: Spring and Winter.) ExPo; LoBV
(Song: "When daisies pied and violets blue.") FiP; HBV; TwHP
(Songs from "Love's Labour's Lost," 1.) LEAP
(Spring.) BoTP; EIL; ElSeCe; EV-1; InPo; MaPo; PoFS; PreP; ReaPo; SeCePo; SiTL; TrGrPo; UnPo; ViBoPo
(Spring and Winter.) KN; OBEV; ThWaDe
(Ver and Hiems.) ALV
When Icicles Hang by the Wall, *fr.* V, ii. AEV; AnFE; ATP; BBV (1923 ed.); BEL; CoBE; EG; EM-1; EnLi-1; EnLit; EPP; FaPON; GN; LiTB; LPS-2; MyFE; OBSC; OTPC; OuHeWo; PIR; PoEL-2; PoRA; SeCeV; SiCE; TOP; TyEnPo
(Hiems.) FaBoCh; LoGBV
(Song: "When icicles hang by the wall.") FiP; HBV; WP
(Songs: Spring and Winter.) ExPo
(Songs from "Love's Labour's Lost," 2.) LEAP
(Songs from the Plays.) AWP; JAWP; WBP
(Spring and Winter, 2.) OBEV
(Tu-Whit To-Who.) CH
(Winter.) BCEP; BLV; CBE; CBOV; CenL; CG; ChTr; EIL; ElSeCe; EnL; EV-1; GBV (1952 ed.); GTBS; GTBS-D; GTBS-W; GTSE; GTSL; InPo; LiTG; MaPo; MCCG; MPB; PCD; PCH; PIAE; PoE; PoFS; PreP; ReaPo; RG; SeCePo; ShBV-1; TreFS; TrGrPo; UnPo; ViBoPo; WaKn; WHA
(Winter Song.) BoLiVe
(Winter's Song.) FaBoEn
Love's Labyrinth, *sel.* Thomas Forde.
Fond Love, No More. SeCL
Love's Land. Isabella Valancy Crawford. CaP; OCL
Love's Language. Hafiz, *tr. fr. Persian by* Richard Le Gallienne. PeP
Love's Language. Donagh MacDonagh. NeIP
Love's Last Gift. Dante Gabriel Rossetti. The House of Life, LIX. BPN; PoVP; ViPo

Love's Last Resource. Sadi, *tr. fr. Persian by* L. Cranmer-Byng. *Fr.* The Gulistan. AWP; LiTW
Love's Last Sacrament. Meleager, *tr. fr. Greek by* F. L. Lucas. GrPE
Love's Last Suit. Thomas Davidson. BSV
Love's Lesson. Moschus, *tr. fr. Greek by* Ernest Myers. AWP
(Lesson to Lovers, A, *tr. by* Shelley.) OxBG
(Love-Chain, The, *tr. by* J. H. Hallard.) GrR
Love's Likeness. George Darley. OBVV
Love's Limit. *Unknown.* TrGrPo
("Ye bubbling springs that gentle music makes.") EG
Love's Lord. Edward Dowden. HBV
Love's Lovers. Dante Gabriel Rossetti. The House of Life, VIII. BPN; EmBrPo; PoVP; ViPo
Love's Madness. Catullus. *See* True or False.
Love's Magic. Clara Carson LeLand. PSO
Love's Martyr, *sels.* Sir Robert Chester. ElL
Ditty: "O holy Love, religious saint!"
Her Hair.
Love's Matrimony. Duke of Newcastle. *See* Love's Vision ("There is no happy life").
Love's Memory. Shakespeare. *Fr.* All's Well That Ends Well, I, i. LPS-1
Love's Miracle. Lucy Maud Montgomery. MaRV
Love's Moods and Tenses. Phoebe Cary. *See* Lovers, The.
Love's Mortality. Richard Middleton. LBBV; WHA
Love's multitudinous boneyard. Chorus. Jack Kerouac. *Fr.* Mexico City Blues. NeAP
Love's Music. Philip Bourke Marston. VA
Love's Nestlings. *Unknown, tr. fr. Greek by* F. L. Lucas. *Fr.* Anacreontea. GrPE
Love's Nightingale. Richard Crashaw. LoBV
Love's Nobility. Emerson. *Fr.* Celestial Love. TreF
Love's Nocturn. Dante Gabriel Rossetti. BPN; EmBrPo
Love's Not Time's Fool. Shakespeare. *See* Sonnets, CXVI.
Loves of the Lions, The. Charles Madge. MoP
Loves of the Plants, The. Erasmus Darwin. *See* Botanic Garden, The.
Love's Old Sweet Song. G. Clifton Bingham. FaBoBe; OlF; TreF
Love's Omnipresence. *At. to* Joshua Sylvester. *See* Were I as Base as Is the Lowly Plain.
Love's on the highroad. Song. Dana Burnet. HBV; PFE; PoMa; POT; PoTo; PR; VOD
Love's Outset. Sir Gilbert Parker. *Fr.* A Lover's Diary. VA
Love's Own Home. Pierre de Ronsard, *tr. fr. French by* Alan Conder. TrFP
Love's pallor and the semblance of deep ruth. Dante. *Fr.* La Vita Nuova. AWP; JAWP; WBP
Love's Parting. Michael Drayton. *See* Idea: "Since there's no help."
Love's perfect blossom only blows. Courtesy. Coventry Patmore. *Fr.* The Angel in the House. OBVV
Love's Perjuries. Shakespeare. *See* On a Day—Alack the Day!
Love's Philosophy. Shelley. AEV; AtBAP; BLPA; BPN; CoBE; EM-2; EmBrPo; EnLi-2 (1949 ed.); EnLit; EnRP; EPN; ERP; EV-4; FaBoBe; GTBS; GTBS-D; GTBS-W; GTSE; GTSL; HBV; HoPM; LiA; LiTG; LiTL; LoPo; LPS-1; NeHB; OAEP; OBRV; PG; PoFS; PoToHe (new ed.); TOP; TrGrPo; TyEnPo; ViBoPo; WP
Love's Pilgrims. Thomas Campion. OBSC
(Pilgrimage towards Loves Holy Land, A.) FaBoEn
(What Faire Pompe Have I Spide of Glittering Ladies.) AtBAP; PoEL-2
Love's Poor. Richard Le Gallienne. VA
Love's Prayer. James Whitcomb Riley. *See* Prayer Perfect, The.
Love's Prerogative. John Oxenham. BLRP
Love's priestess, mad with pain and joy of song. Sappho. Swinburne. *Fr.* On the Cliffs. GTML; VA
Love's Prime. Thomas May. *Fr.* The Old Couple, III, i. SeCL
("Dear, do not your fair beauty wrong.") EG; ElSeCe; TuPP; ViBoPo
Love's Priority. Jorge Luis Borges, *tr. fr. Spanish by* Robert Stuart Fitzgerald. AnCL
Love's Prisoner. Mariana Griswold Van Rensselaer. HBV
Love's Progress. John Donne. Elegies, XVIII. LiTB; LiTG; ViBoPo
Love's Progress. Theodore Roethke. FiMAP
Love's Protestation. Thomas Lodge. *See* Fancy, A ("First shall the heavens . . .").
Love's Proverbs. Michael Drayton. Idea, LIX. EV-1
(Play with Proverbs, A.) ES
Love's Reality. Coventry Patmore. *Fr.* The Angel in the House. PoVP
Love's Rebel. Earl of Surrey. OBSC
(Complaint of a Lover That Defied Love and Was by Love After the More Tormented.) ReIE; SiCe
("When summer took in hand the winter to assail.") SiPS
Love's Remorse. Edwin Muir. LiTL
Love's Résumé. Heine, *tr. fr. German by* "J. F. C." TrJP
Love's Resurrection Day. Louise Chandler Moulton. AA; HBV; LEAP
Love's Riddle, *sel.* Abraham Cowley.
Song: "Merry waves dance up and down, and play, The." AlDL
(Sport.) EPS (1942 ed.); SeCL
Love's Ritual. Charles Hanson Towne. LBMV
Love's Rosary. Alfred Noyes. HBV
Love's Rosary. George Edward Woodberry. AA
Love's Schooling. John Lyly. *See* O Cupid! Monarch over Kings.
Love's Secret. Blake. BCEP; BLV; BoLiVe; CBOV; EnLi-2 (1939 ed.); EPP; FaFP; GTSL; NeHB; OBEV; OtMeF; PG; PIAE; PoeMoYo; PoFS; TrGrPo
(Never Seek to Tell Thy Love.) AnFE; ChER; EG; EM-1; EnL; EnLoPo; EnRP; GTBS-D; LiTL; LO; LoPo; LoPS; OAEP; OBEC; OnPM; PoE; PoEL-4; TrEV
(Poems from MSS.) ViBoPo
(Song: "Never seek to tell thy love.") ExPo; LoBV
"I told my love, I told my love," *sel., sl. diff.* CaAE
Love's Secret Name. John Arthur Blaikie. VA
Love's Servile Lot. Robert Southwell. ACP; ReIE; SiCE; TuPP
Love's Shadow. George Sterling. MuM
Loves She like Me? Samuel Woodworth. AA
Love's Silence. Sir Philip Sidney. *See* Astrophel and Stella: Sonnets, LIV.
Love's Slavery. John Sheffield. Duke of Buckingham and Normanby. CEP
Love's Snare. Sir Thomas Wyatt. *See* Lover Rejoiceth That He Hath Broken the Snares of Love, The.
Love's Spite. Aubrey Thomas De Vere. HBV; VA
Love's Springtide. Frank Dempster Sherman. LBMV
Love's Storm. Ibn Sa'id of Alcala la Real, *tr. fr. Arabic by* A. J. Arberry. MooP
Love's Stratagem. *Unknown, tr. fr. Greek by* F. L. Lucas. *Fr.* Anacreontea. GrPE
Love's Strength. Harriet Eleanor Hamilton King. MaRV; OQP (4 *ll.*); QP-2 (4 *ll.*)
Love's stricken "why." Emily Dickinson. BLV; BoLiVe
Love's Temperature. Walter of Chatillon, *tr. fr. Latin by* L. R. Lind. LaP
Love's Terror. *Unknown, tr. fr. Japanese by* Arthur Waley. WoL
Love's Testament. Dante Gabriel Rossetti. The House of Life, III. BPN; PoVP
("O thou who at Love's hour.") ViPo
Loves that doubted, the loves that dissembled, The. Lines by a Person of Quality. J. B. B. Nichols. VA
Love's tongue within my heart speaks plain to thee. The Mock Caliph. *Unknown.* EnLi-1
Love's Tribute. Lorena W. Sturgeon. PGD; PSO
Love's Trinity. Alfred Austin. OBVV
Love's Tryst. Bion, *tr. fr. Greek by* F. L. Lucas. GrPE
Love's Tyranny. Marcus Argentarius, *tr. fr. Greek by* Lord Neaves. OnPM
Love's Unreason. Catullus, *tr. fr. Latin.* OuHeWo
("I hate and love/ And if you ask me why," *tr. by* Horace Gregory.) BOL
Love's Unreason. *Unknown. See* Love Not Me for Comely Grace.
Love's Unveiling. Tessa Sweazy Webb. MuM
Love's Usury. John Donne. SeEP
Love's Victories. James Shirley. *Fr.* Cupid and Death. GoBC
Loves Victory. Aurelian Townsend. *See* To the Countesse of Salisbury.
Love's Vigil. Edwin Markham. OQP; QP-2
Love's Vision. Edward Carpenter. WGRP
Love's Vision ("Dear, let us two each other spy"). Duke of Newcastle. LO, *abr.;* SeCL
Love's Vision ("There is no happy life"). Duke of Newcastle. LO; LoPS
(Love's Matrimony.) SeCePo; SeCL
Love's Wisdom. Margaret Deland. AA
Love's Witchery. Thomas Lodge. *See* My Bonny Lass, Thine Eye.
Love's without Reason. Alexander Brome. OBS; SeEP
Loves World. Sir John Suckling. SeCV-1
Love's worshipers alone can know. Love and Folly. La Fontaine. AWP
Love's Young Dream. Thomas Moore. HBV; LPS-1; OlF; PIR; WBLP
Lovesick Cowboy, The. Charles A. Bobston. CoSo
Lovesick Cyclops, A. Theocritus, *tr. fr. Greek by* R. C. Trevelyan. Idylls, VI. GrR
Coy Polyphemus, *sel.* OxBG
Love-sicke Poet, The. Joseph Hall. *Fr.* Virgidemiarum. FaBoEn
(Satire: "Great is the folly of a feeble brain.") ReIE

Lovesight [*or* Love-Sight]. Dante Gabriel Rossetti. The House of Life, IV. BEL; BLV; BMEP; BoLiVe; BPN; CaAE; CoBE; EmBrPo; EnLi-2; EnLit; EPN; EPP; ES; EV-5; FaBoEn; GTBS-D; GTSL; HBV; LEAP; OAEP; OBVV; PIAE; POTT; PoVP; ReaPo; TCEP; TOP; TrGrPo; TyEnPo; VA; ViBoPo; ViPo; ViPP; VLEP; WHA

Lovest Thou Me? William Cowper. HBV; NBE; OBEC; TriL
(Hark, My Soul! It Is the Lord.) BePJ; OlF
"Lord it is my chief complaint," *sel.* TrPWD

Lovewell's Fight ("Of worthy Captain Lovewell I purpose now to sing"). *Unknown.* BaBo; HBV; PAH

Lovewell's Fight ("What time the noble Lovewell came"). *Unknown.* PAH

Loving and Beloved. Sir John Suckling. FaBoEn; OBS; SeEP

Loving and Liking. Dorothy Wordsworth. OTPC

Loving Ballad of Lord Bateman, The. *Unknown. See* Young Beichan.

Loving friend is Jesus, A. A Heavenly Friend. Paul Tucker. BePJ

Loving friend, the gift of one. To Flush, My Dog. Elizabeth Barrett Browning. AlBD; BoFr

Loving Henry. *Unknown. See* Young Hunting.

Loving in truth, and fain in verse my love to show. Astrophel and Stella, I. Sir Philip Sidney. AEV; AnFE; AWP; BCEP; BEL; CoBE; EG; ElSeCe; EnL; EnLi-1; EnLit; EPP; EV-1; FaBoEn; GTBS-W; HBV; InPo; JAWP; LEAP; LiTB; LiTG; LiTL; LoPo; MaPo; NBE; OAEP; OBSC; PeBoSo; Po; PoFS; ReaPo; ReEn; ReIE; SeCePo; SeCeV; SiCE; SiPS; TCEP; TOP; TrGrPo; TuPP; TwHP; ViBoPo; WBP

Loving looks the large-eyed cow. A Christmas Prayer. George Macdonald. BOL; SUS

Loving Mad Tom. *Unknown. See* Tom o' Bedlam's Song.

Loving she is, and tractable, though wild. Characteristics of a Child Three Years Old. Wordsworth. OBRV

Low-anchored Cloud. Henry David Thoreau. *See* Mist.

Low and mournful be the strain. Voluntaries. Emerson. IAP; TCAP

Low-backed Car, The. Samuel Lover. HBV; LPS-1

Low Barometer. Robert Bridges. CoBMV; LiTB; LoBV (2d ed.); MeRV; RiBV; UnPo (3d ed.)

Low beating of the tom-toms, The. African Dance. Langston Hughes. FaPON; MoSiPe; TiPo (1952 ed.)

Low blowing winds from out a midnight sky. An Old Song. Thomas S. Jones, Jr. POT; PoTo

Low Bridge, Everybody Down. William S. Allen. *See* Erie Canal, The ("I've got a mule").

Low burns the summer afternoon. Nightfall; a Picture. Alfred B. Street. LPS-2

Low Doun in the Broom. *Unknown.* BSV; GoTS

Low Down Chariot, *with music. Unknown.* OuSiCo

Low-down, Lonesome Low, The. *Unknown. See* Golden Vanity, The.

Low full sweep of instrumental string, A. Sonnet. *Unknown.* CAG

Low hangs the moon above the hard white road. To William Morris. W. C. Greene. CAG

Low hut rests in Lookout's shade, A. The Coat of Faded Gray. G. W. Harris. BlG

Low! I, the man whose Muse whylome did maske. *See* Lo I the man . . .

Low in the eastern sky. To the Maiden in the East. Henry David Thoreau. MOAP; OxBA

Low in the troubled west. Cradle Song. *Unknown.* BOL

Low in thy grave with thee. David's Lament for Jonathan. Peter Abelard. LiTW

Low lie your heads this day. The Lamentation for the Three Sons of Turann. John Todhunter. TIP

Low lies the land upon the sea. The Lookout. William Collins. EtS

Low, like another's, lies the laureled head. Lacrimae [*or* Lachrymae] Musarum. Sir William Watson. HBV; PoVP; PtOT; VA

Low, Lute, Low! Tennyson. *See* Hapless Doom of Woman.

Low moon shone on the desert land and the sage was silver white, A. Charley Lee. Henry Herbert Knibbs. WaKn

Low on his fours the Lion. Unstooping. Walter de la Mare. UTS

Low on the utmost boundary of the sight. Moonlight in Summer. Robert Bloomfield. LPS-2

Low spake the knight to the peasant maid. The Rose and the Gauntlet. "Christopher North." BeLS; LPS-3

Low stream by a winding track, A. Festival in Tuscany. William Force Stead. POTE

Low sun whitens on the flying squalls, The. Rounding the Cape. Roy Campbell. BoSA

Low Sunday and Monday, *sel.* Gerard Manley Hopkins. To Oxford. NBE

Low Tide. Lynette Roberts. NeBP

Low Tide on Grand-Pré. Bliss Carman. BoCaPo; CaP; CPG; OCL; PeCV; TwCV

Low Trade, A. Herodas, *tr. fr. Greek by* Gilbert Highet. OxBG

Low-voiced girls that go, The. The Invisible Bride. Edwin Markham. HBV; LBMV; OBAV

Low was our pretty cot: our tallest rose. Reflections on Having Left a Place of Retirement. Samuel Taylor Coleridge. BPN; EmBrPo; EnRP; OBEC

Low whispers the wind from Malaya. A Song. Jayadeva. *Fr.* The Gita Govinda. LiTW

Lowell. James Russell Lowell. *Fr.* A Fable for Critics. AmPP (4th ed.); OxBA
(On Himself.) AA
("There is Lowell, who's striving Parnassus to climb.") CoBA

Lowell Alphabet, A. *Comp. by* Caroline B. Le Row, *fr. various poems by* James Russell Lowell. PEOR

Lower Animals. Alan Anderson. PCD

Lower Forms of Life. Mary Winter. GoYe

Lower him gently, gently, now, into the quiet deep. Sea Burial. Robina Monkman. EtS

Lower World, The (the Sibyl Speaks). Virgil, *tr. fr. Latin by* Rolfe Humphries. *Fr.* The Aeneid, VI. LaP

Lowering night, with muggy sultry air, A. The Stampede. Earl Alonzo Brininstool. PoOW

Lowery Cot. L. A. G. Strong. MBP; MoBrPo

Lowest Place, The. Christina Rossetti. EnLi-2; EPP; MaRV; TrPWD; ViPo

Lowest Trees Have Tops [*or* Topps], The. Sir Edward Dyer. AtBAP; EG; ElL; ElSeCe; FaBoEn; InPo; PoEL-1; PoRA; SiCE
(Love Is Love.) TrGrPo
(Modest Love, A.) LiTG; LiTL; OBSC

Lowland Sea, The. *Unknown. See* Golden Vanity, The.

Lowland Witch Ballad, A. William Bell Scott. DaM

Lowlands, *diff. versions. Unknown.* AmSS (*3 vers., with music*); ChTr; OxBoLi; SG; ShS (*3 vers., with music*); SoAmSa (*A and B vers., with music*); TrAS, *with music*
("I dreamt a dream the other night.") LO
(Lowlands, Away.) MuP

Lowlands Low. Kenneth Leslie. BoCaPo

Lowlands Low, The. *Unknown. See* Golden Vanity, The.

Lowlands, lowlands, away [*or* hurrah], my John. Lowlands. *Unknown.* AmSS; SoAmSa; TrAS. *See also* I dreamt a dream the other night.

Lowlands o' [*or* of] Holland, The. *Unknown.* BSV; CBOV, *diff. vers.*; EBSV; OBB; SG
(Lawlands o' Holland, The.) AmSS; CH

Lowly Bethlehem, *with music.* Count Zinzendorf, *tr. fr. German.* TrAS

Lowly hillock raised its head, A. Mountain and Hillock. Steingrímur Thorsteinsson. *Fr.* Epigrams. IcP

Lowly the soul that waits. Laddie. Katharine Lee Bates. POT; PoTo

Lowly woman, A. Morning Prayer. Utako Hayashi. SoLD

Low'ring heaven had mask'd her in a cloud, The. Michael Drayton. *Fr.* Mortimeriados. ReIE

Loyal Effusion. Horace Smith *and* James Smith. OBRV

Loyal General, The, *sel.* Nahum Tate.
Prologue: "If yet there be a few that take delight," *by* Dryden. CEP; SeCV-2

"Loyal hearts of London City, come, I pray, and sing my ditty." The Dutchess of Monmouth's Lamentation for the Loss of Her Duke. *Unknown.* CoMu

Loyal Scot, The, *sel.* Andrew Marvell.
"But who considers well will find indeed." ViBoPo

Loyal to country and comrades and then. February Twelfth. Mary F. Hepburn. PCH

Loyalties. Walter A. Cutter. OQP; QP-2

Loyalty. John Barbour. *Fr.* The Bruce. EBSV

Loyalty. Berton Braley. BLPA

Loyalty. Allan Cunningham. *See* Hame, Hame, Hame.

Loyalty. Theognis, *tr. fr. Greek by* F. L. Lucas. GrPE

Loyalty Confin'd. Sir Roger L'Estrange. OBS
(In Prison.) LPS-3
(Liberty and Requiem of an Imprisoned Royalist, The.) EV-2
(Mr. Le Strange His Verses in the Prison at Linn.) SeCL

Loyalty Hymn. Edith Lovejoy Pierce. ChIP; MaRV

Lo-yang. Emperor Ch'ien Wen-ti, *tr. fr. Chinese by* Arthur Waley. AtBAP; AWP; JAWP; TrCh; WBP

Lo-yu Tombs, The. Li Shang-yin, *tr. fr. Chinese.* WhP

Lubber Breeze. T. Sturge Moore. CH

Lubly Fan, *with music.* Cool White. TrAS

Lucasta frown and let me die. To Lucasta: Her Reserved Looks. Richard Lovelace. SeCV-1

Lucasta Laughing. Richard Lovelace. PoEL-3

"Lucasta," said Terence O'Connor. "To Lucasta, on Going to the Wars." Edwin Meade Robinson. *Fr.* Limericised Classics. HBMV

Lucia. Francesco Franchini, *pr. tr. fr. Latin by* Richard Aldington. LaP

Lucid instant comes upon, The. Teufelsdröckh Minor. Morton Dauwen Zabel. NP
Lucid Interval. George O'Neil. TBM
Lucifer, The. Guy Glover. CaP
Lucifer. D. H. Lawrence. OAEP (2d ed.)
Lucifer. Milton. *Fr.* Paradise Lost, I. UnPo (1st ed.)
Lucifer and Elissa. Philip James Bailey. *Fr.* Festus. VA
Lucifer at Leisure. Sister Mary Maura. JKCP (1955 ed.)
Lucifer in Starlight. George Meredith. AnEnPo; AnFE; ATP; BEL; BLV; BMEP; BoLiVe; CBOV; CH; CoBE; EmBrPo; EnL; EnLi-2; EnLit; EPN; EPP; ES; ExPo; GTML; HBV; HoPM; InP; InPo; LEAP; LiTB; LiTG; LoBV; OAEP; OBEV; OBVV; PG (1955 ed.); PIAE; PoEL-5; PoeT; PoFS; POTT; PoVP; ReaPo; RiBV; SeCeV; ShBV-4; TCEP; TOP; TrGrPo; TwCV; UnPo; VA; ViBoPo; ViP; ViPo; ViPP; VLEP
Lucifer Sings in Secret. Elinor Wylie. MM
Lucifer's Song. Philip James Bailey. *Fr.* Festus. BMEP
Lucile, *sels.* "Owen Meredith."
  Dinner Hour, The. VA
  Mission, The, of Sister Seraphine, a Sister of Charity. PraNu
  Sister of Charity Comforts a Wounded Soldier, A. PraNu
  What We May Live Without. TreF
  ("We may live without poetry, music and art.") PoToHe (new ed.)
Lucilia, wedded to Lucretius, found. Lucretius. Tennyson. EmBrPo; EV-5; PtP; ViPo; ViPP; VLEP
Lucilius was the man, who, bravely bold. The Art of Poetry. Nicolas Boileau. EnLi-1
Lucinda. *Unknown.* SeCL
Lucinda Matlock. Edgar Lee Masters. *Fr.* Spoon River Anthology. BAP; BAV; ChMo; CMP; CP; InP; LaNeLa; LiTA; LiTL; LiTM; MAP; MCCG; MoAmPo; MotAn; MoVE; NeMA; NP; NV; OnPP; OxBA; ReMP
Lucinda Prattle. Palmer Brown. LiL
Lucinda wink or vaile those eyes. *Unknown.* SeCSL
Lucius Junius Brutus over the Body of Lucretia. John Howard Payne. *Fr.* Brutus; or, The Fall of Tarquin. LPS-3
Luck. W. W. Gibson. EtS; MoShBr; OBMV
Luck. Evan V. Shute. CaP
Luck in the Square Stone, The, *sel.* H. C. Bosman.
  "At the safari's end a porter." BoSA
Luck is a star. The Fireborn Are at Home in Fire. Carl Sandburg. MoAmPo (1950 ed.)
Luck of Edenhall, The. Ludwig Uhland, *tr. fr. German by* Longfellow. AWP; StPo
Luckless man/ Avoids the miserable bodkin's point. Man's Anxious, but Ineffectual Guard against Death. Thomas Lovell Beddoes. ChER
Luckless Prince Aladdin, The. Prince Aladdin of the Lamp. Gustaf Fröding. AnSL
Lucky are the dead who forget/ life's bitterness. Lethe. Lorenzo Mavilis. MoGP
Lucky Chance, The, *sel.* Aphra Behn.
  Of Love, *at. to* Aphra Behn, *also to* —— Ousley. SeCL
  (Song: "O Love! that stronger art than wine.") BrBE; LO
Lucky Coin, The. Austin Clarke. NeIP
Lucky like Cook to travel and return. "Heureux Qui Comme Ulysse." John Manifold. WaaP; WaP
"Lucky magpie, holy bird, what hateful lies you tell!" The Lady and the Magpie. *Unknown.* AtBAP
Lucky Snail, The. Winifred Welles. StVeCh (1940 ed.)
Lucky Strike. Merrill Moore. MOAP
Lucrative offices are seldom lost. Absence of Occupation. William Cowper. *Fr.* Retirement. OBEC
Lucrece and Nara. Laura Riding. FaBoMo
Lucretius. Lionel Johnson. PtP
Lucretius. Tennyson. EmBrPo; EV-5; PtP; ViPo; ViPP; VLEP
Lucretius could not credit centaurs. Invitation to Juno. William Empson. AtBAP; FaBoMo
Lucretius felt the change of the world in his time. Prescription of Painful Ends. Robinson Jeffers. CoV; LiTA; MoAB; MoAmPo; OxBA
Lucretius! King of men, that are. Lucretius. Lionel Johnson. PtP
Lucy. Walter de la Mare. ChMo; CMP
Lucy, *complete, in 5 parts.* Wordsworth. BPN; EM-2; EmBrPo; EnLi-2; EnLit; EnRP; EPN; ERP; FiP; GEPC; HBV; OAEP; OBEV; OBRV; PoFS; TCEP; TrGrPo
  Sels.
  "I traveled [*or* travell'd] among unknown men." AWP; BLV; BoLiVe; BPN; EM-2; EmBrPo; EnL; EnLi-2; EnLit; EnRP; EPN; ERP; FiP; GEPC; GTBS; GTBS-D; GTBS-W; GTSL; HBV; InPo; JAWP; LoPo; OAEP; OBEV; OBRV; OuHeWo; PoFS; REAL; TCEP; TOP; TrGrPo; TwP; WBP
  "She dwelt among the untrodden ways." AnFE; ATP; AWP; BCEP; BEL; BLPA; BoLiVe; BPN; BTP; CBE; CBOV; CoBE; EG; EM-2; EmBrPo; EnLi-2; EnLit; EnRP; EPN; EPP; ERP; EtPaEn; EV-3; FaBoEn; FiP; GEPC; GTSL; HBV; HBVY; InP; JAWP; LEAP; LiTB; LiTG; LiTL; LoBV; LoPo; LPS-1; MaC; MaPo; MCCG; NeHB; OAEP; OBEV; OBRV; OTPC; OuHeWo; PECK; PG; PoE; PoFS; ReaPo; TCEP; TOP; TreF; TrGrPo; TVSH; TwHP; TyEnPo; ViBoPo; WBP; WHA; WP
  (Lost Love.) GTBS; GTBS-D; GTBS-W; GTSE
  Violet, The, *sel.* PCH
  "Slumber did my spirit seal, A." AnEnPo; AnFE; AWP; BEL; BLV; BoLiVe; BPN; CBOV; CoEV; EG; EM-2; EmBrPo; EnLi-2; EnLit; EnRP; EPN; EPP; ERP; EtPaEn; ExPo; FaBoCh; FaBoEn; FiP; GEPC; GTBS; GTBS-D; GTBS-W; GTSE; GTSL; HBV; InPo; JAWP; LEAP; LiTB; LiTG; LiTL; MaPo; OAEP; OBEV; OBRV; OnPM; OuHeWo; PoE; PoEL-4; PoFS; ReaPo; RiBV; TCEP; TOP; TreFS; TrGrPo; TwHP; TyEnPo; ViBoPo; WBP
  (Lines.) LoBV
  "Strange fits of passion have I known." BPN; CoBE; EG; EM-2; EmBrPo; EnL; EnLi-2; EnLit; EnRP; EPN; ERP; EV-3; FiP; GEPC; HBV; LEAP; LiTB; LiTG; LiTL; LO; OAEP; OBEV; OBRV; Po; PoE; PoFS; REAL; TCEP; TrGrPo; TwP; ViBoPo
  "Three years she grew in sun and shower." AtBAP; AWP; BEL; BPN; CBOV; EM-2; EmBrPo; EnLi-2; EnLit; EnRP; EPN; EPP; ERP; EtPaEn; EV-3; FiP; GBV; GEPC; GN; HBV; HBVY; LEAP; LiTL; LoBV; LPS-1; OAEP; OBEV; OBRV; OnPP; OTPC (1923 ed.); OuHeWo; PoE; PoEL-4; PoFS; REAL; ReaPo; SN; TCEP; TOP; TreFS; TrGrPo; TWP; TyEnPo
  (Education of Nature, The.) GTBS; GTBS-D; GTBS-W; GTSE; GTSL
  Nature's Gifts to Lucy, *sel.* LiA
Lucy and Colin. Thomas Tickell. *See* Colin and Lucy.
Lucy Ashton's Song. Sir Walter Scott. *Fr.* The Bride of Lammermoor, *ch.* 3. BSV; CBE; EBSV; EnRP; EV-4; GoTS; LEAP; OBEV; OtMeF
  (Look Not Thou.) OBRV
Lucy Gray; or, Solitude. Wordsworth. BEL; BeLS; BPN; CBOV; CG; CH; EM-2; EmBrPo; EnRP; EPN; EPP; ERP; EV-3; FiP; GEPC; GTSL; HBV; HiLiEn; OAEP; OBRV; OnSP; OTPC; PoFS; PRWS; PYM; REAL; SeCeV; TCEP; TOP; TreFS; TVSH; TwP; UnPo (1st ed.)
Lucy is a golden girl. A Golden Girl. "Barry Cornwall." LPS-1
Lucy Lake. Newton Mackintosh. BOHV; HBV; PA
Lucy Lavender. Ivy O. Eastwick. BoTP; SiSoSe
Lucy Locket lost her pocket. Mother Goose. BoChLi; OxBoLi; OxNR; PCH; PPL; SiTL; TiPo (1959 ed.)
Lucy, you brightness[e] of our sphere [*or* spheare], who are. To Lucy, Countess[e] of Bedford, with Mr. Donnes Satires [*or* Satyres]. Ben Jonson. OBS; ReIE; SeCV-1; SeEP; TuPP
Lucy's Birthday. Thackeray. OTPC (1923 ed.)
Lucy's Canary. Adelaide O'Keeffe. OTPC (1923 ed.)
Lucy's Flittin'. William Laidlaw. EBSV
Ludmilla; an Ode on the Occasion of Her Departure from These Shores. Ernest W. Thiele. WhC
Luf es lif that lastes ay, thar it in Criste es feste. A Song of the Love of Jesus. Richard Rolle of Hampole. PoEL-1
Lufoten. Quentin Stevenson, *ad. fr.* O. V. De Lubicz-Milosz. POTE (1959 ed.)
Lugano, August 1937. H. L. R. Edwards. MoWP
Lugete O Veneres Cupidinesque. Godfrey Elton. ReTS
Lugnaquillia, *sel.* George Francis Savage-Armstrong.
  Wicklow Scene, A. TIP
Lugubrious Whing-Whang, The. James Whitcomb Riley. BOHV; NA; YaD
Luini in porcelain! Medallion. Ezra Pound. *Fr.* Hugh Selwyn Mauberley. CoBMV; CoV; LiTA; LiTM (rev. ed.); MoPo
Luis de Camões. Roy Campbell. BoSA; FaBoTw
Luke. Bible, *N.T.* *See* St. Luke.
Luke Havergal. E. A. Robinson. AA; AmP; AmPP; AWP; CoBA; CoBMV; CoV; CrMA; DaM; InPo; JAWP; LEAP; LiTA; LiTM (rev. ed.); MAP; MoAB; MoAmPo; MOAP; MoPo; MoVE; NePA; PFY; Po; PoEL-5; PoRA; TriL; TwP; UnPo (3d ed.)
Luke tells us how the boy Jesus. The Temple. Clifford Dyment. ChMP
Lull in the racket and brattle, A. The Lark. W. W. Gibson. ChMo; CMP
Lull, lullaby, all is still and the sea lakes are. An Unmarried Mother Sings. F. R. Higgins. POTE
Lull-lully, my baby, oh, would that thy mother. The Widow's Lullaby. *Unknown.* BOL
Lulla by [*or* Lullaby] baby, lulla by baby. Lullaby. John Phillip. *Fr.* Comedy of Patient and Meek Grissell. EIL; EM-1; ReEn; TuPP
Lulla, la lulla, lulla lullaby./ My sweet little baby. Lulla, My Sweet Little Baby. *Unknown.* ReEn; TuPP
Lulla-lullaby,/ Hush, my babe. *Unknown.* BOL

Lulla, My Sweet Little Baby. *Unknown.* TuPP
("Lulla, la lulla, lulla lullaby.") ReEn
Lullaby, The: "As through the palms ye wander." Lope de Vega Carpio, *tr. fr. Spanish by* Thomas Walsh. CAW
Lullaby: "At sunset our white butterflies." Joseph Russell Taylor. BOL
Lullaby, A: "Baby, baby, hush-a-bye." Laurence Alma-Tadema. BOL
Lullaby: "Baby child of Mary, The." *Unknown, tr. fr. Spanish.* BOL
Lullaby: "Baby wants a lullaby." William Brighty Rands. BOL; PPL
Lullaby: "Baloo, loo, lammy, now baloo, my dear." Lady Nairne. HBV
Lullaby, A: "Because some men in khaki coats." G. R. Glasgow. BOL
Lullaby: "Bedtime's come fu' little boys." Paul Laurence Dunbar. BoChLi; GoSl; LBAP; MPB; StVeCh (1940 ed.); TSW; TSWC; VOD
Lullaby: "Beloved, may your sleep be sound." W. B. Yeats. EnLP; FaBoTw; OBMV; POTE
Lullaby: "Birds in their nests are softly calling." Grace Mitchell. BOL
Lullaby, A: "Cease, warring thoughts, and let his brain." James Shirley. *Fr.* The Triumph of Beauty. BOL; TuPP
Lullaby, A: "Close to the heart that is throbbing in love to you." Willis Walton Franz. BOL
Lullaby: "Come sleep, and with the sweet deceiving." Beaumont *and* Fletcher. *See* Come, Sleep.
Lullaby: "Day is ending; night is falling." John White Chadwick. BOL
Lullaby: "Day is stealing down the west." Florence Earle Coates. BOL
Lullaby: "Dear mother, in dreams I see her." Claxson Bellamy *and* Harry Paulton. *Fr.* Erminie. BOL
Lullaby, A: "Dollie, the night has come." Louis C. Elson. BOL
Lullaby: "Dream, dream, thou flesh of me!" "Patience Worth." BOL
Lullaby: "Evening shades are falling." *Unknown.* BOL
Lullaby, A: "For wars his life and half a world away." Randall Jarrell. FiMAP
Lullaby: "Girl with eyes like dying flowers." Max Harris. BoAV; MoAuPo
Lullaby: "Golden dreamboat's ready, all her silken sails are spread, The." Edgar A. Guest. OnHT
Lullaby: "Golden slumbers kiss your eyes." Thomas Dekker, *and others. See* Golden Slumbers Kiss Your Eyes.
Lullaby: "Hush dove the summer." Miriam Waddington. CaP
Lullaby, A: "Hush, hush, rest my sweet." Mary Newmarch Prescott. BOL
Lullaby: "Hush, lullay,/ Your treasures all." Léonie Adams. BLV; BoLiVe (1939 ed.); MAP; MoAB; MoAmPo; NeMA
Lullaby: "Hush! the waves are rolling in." *Unknown. See* Gaelic Lullaby.
Lullaby: "Hush thee, hush." "R. D. H." CAG
Lullaby, A: "Hush thee, my baby boy, hush thee to sleep." *Unknown, tr. fr. Gaelic by* Alexander Stewart. BOL; EBSV
Lullaby: "Hush thee, sweet baby." Thomas Davidson. BOL
Lullaby: "Husheen, the herons are crying." "Seumas O'Sullivan." BOL; GBV; OnYI; TVSH
Lullaby: "I'll put you, myself, my baby, to slumber." *Unknown, tr. fr. Irish by* George Sigerson. BOL
Lullaby: "I'll send you now sailing across the sea." Witter Bynner. BOL
Lullaby: "In this hush of night." Henry D. Muir. BOL
Lullaby: "Lay thy head upon this pillow." Fred Emerson Brooks. BOL
Lullaby: "Lennavan-mo." "Fiona Macleod." BOL
Lullaby: "Long canoe, The." Robert Hillyer. FaPON
Lullaby: "Lullaby baby, lullaby baby." John Phillip. *Fr.* Comedy of Patient and Meek Grissell. ElL; EM-1
("Lulla by baby, lulla by baby.") ReEn; TuPP
Lullaby: "Lullaby, lullaby,/ Shadows creep across the sky." Phyllis Garlick. BoTP
Lullaby: "Lullaby, oh lullaby." Christina Rossetti. *Fr.* Sing-Song. BoChLi; BOL; OTPC (1946 ed.); RIS
Lullaby, A: *"Mo cheann ban beag,* lie still and rest." Mary Anne O'Reilly. BOL
Lullaby: "My heart makes mock at the long day's harms." Nannie Fitzhugh Maclean. BOL
Lullaby: "My little one, sleep softly." Harriet Monroe. BOL; NP
Lullaby: "Now bylow, baby, and slumber sweet and soundly." *Unknown.* BOL
Lullaby, A: "Now while rest the happy herds." Helen Gray Cone. BOL
Lullaby: "Oh, honey, li'l honey, come and lay yo' wooly head." Edmund S. Leamy. BOL; GBV (1922 ed.)
Lullaby: "O! hush thee, my darling, sleep soundly my son." *Unknown, tr. fr. Yiddish by* Alice Lucas. TrJP
Lullaby, A: "O hushaby, baby! Why weepest thou?" Owen Roe O'Sullivan, *tr. fr. Irish by* James Clarence Mangan. BOL
Lullaby: "O Mary, mother, if the day we trod." Arthur Sherburne Hardy. BOL
Lullaby, A: "O saftly sleep, my bonnie bairn!" Alexander A. Ritchie. BOL; EBSV
Lullaby: "O sleep, sweet infant, for we all must sleep." Hartley Coleridge. BOL
Lullaby: "O'er the haycocks comes the moon." Alice Archer Sewall James. BOL
Lullaby: "Plump little baby clouds." *Unknown.* BOL
Lullaby: "Puva—puva—puva." *Tr. fr. Hopi Indian by* Natalie Curtis. SUS
Lullaby: "Rest, my babe, rest!" *Unknown.* BOL
Lullaby: "Rockaby, lullaby, bees in the clover!" Josiah Gilbert Holland. *Fr.* The Mistress of the Manse. AA; HBV
Lullaby: "Rooks' nests do rock on the tree top, The." William Barnes. BOL
Lullaby, A: "See how the poppies nod." Agnes H. Begbie. BOL
Lullaby, A: "Sich a li'l feller." Frank L. Stanton. BOL
Lullaby: "Sleep, baby, sleep, I can see two little sheep." *Unknown.* BOL
Lullaby, A: "Sleep, baby, sleep, the wind." Robert Ellice Mack. BOL
Lullaby: "Sleep, baby, sleep, waiting near." Virginia Bioren Harrison. BOL
Lullaby, A: "Sleep, child, lie quiet, let be." James Agee. OnHM
Lullaby: "Sleep, little baby, sleep and rest." Elinor Chipp. HBMV
Lullaby: "Sleep, little one, and be good." *Unknown, tr. fr. German.* BOL
Lullaby: "Sleep, mouseling, sleep." Elizabeth J. Coatsworth. SiSoSe
Lullaby: "Sleep, my babe, lie still and slumber." *Unknown, tr. fr. Welsh.* BOL
Lullaby: "Sleep, my baby, all the night!" Wendell Phillips Stafford. BOL
Lullaby: "Sleep, my baby, sleep, my boy." *At. to* Eliza Lee Follen, *also to* Jane Taylor. BOL
(Sweetly Sleep.) MOAH
Lullaby, A: "Sleep, my darling, sleep!" Celia Thaxter. BOL
Lullaby, A: "Sleep, my dear one, sleep." George Edgar Montgomery. BOL
Lullaby: "Sleep, my little baby, sleep." Samuel Hoffenstein. TrJP
Lullaby: "Sleep, my little one, sleep." Sarah Jane S. Harrington. RAR
Lullaby: "Sleep, O my babe, not thine a manger." James B. Kenyon. BOL
Lullaby: "Sleep, sleep, lovely white soul." Walter de la Mare. BOL; GBV
Lullaby: "Sleep, sleep, my darling." *Unknown, tr. fr. French.* BOL
Lullaby: "Sleep soft and long, no morn is worth the waking." Alice Herbert. BLP
Lullaby, A: "Sleep soft, baby mine!" Monica Peveril Turnbull. BOL
Lullaby: "Sleepy little, creepy little goblins in the gloaming." James W. Foley. BOL; PTA-2
Lullaby: "Slumber, Jesu, lightly dreaming." *Unknown, tr. fr. Latin by* Raymond F. Roseliep. ISi
(Latin Lullaby, *tr. by* Garrett Strange.) CAW
Lullaby: "Slumber, slumber, little one, now." Frank Dempster Sherman. BOL
Lullaby: "Softly now the burn is rushing." Seumas MacManus. AnIV; BOL
Lullaby: "Softly sink in slumbers golden." Gerald Massey. BOL
Lullaby: "Song for the baby, sweet little Bopeep, A." Shirley Dare. BOL
Lullaby, A: "Suppose I put my baby to sleep." Kate Wisner McClusky. BOL
Lullaby: "Sweet and low, sweet and low." Tennyson. *See* Sweet and Low.
Lullaby, A: "Sweet baby, sleep! what ails my dear." George Wither. *See* Rocking Hymn, A.
Lullaby: "They are fluttering and fluttering, like birds upon the tree." Virginia Frazer Boyle. BOL
Lullaby: "Though the world has slipped and gone." Edith Sitwell. AtBAP; ChMP; LiTM; POTE; WaP
Lullaby: "Upon my lap my sovereign sits." Richard Verstegan. CH; ElL; GTSL; HBV; LoBV; MotAn; OBEV
(Our Blessed Lady's Lullaby.) BOL; ElSeCe; LO
(Our Lady's Lullaby.) ACP; CAW; GoBC; ISi
(Upon My Lap My Sovereign Sits.) ViBoPo
Lullaby: "Weep you no more, sad fountains." *Unknown. See* Weep You No More, Sad Fountains.

Lullaby, A: "We've wandered all about the upland fallows." Ford Madox Ford. BOL
Lullaby: "When little birdie bye-bye goes." *Unknown. See* When Little Birdie Bye-bye Goes.
Lullaby: "Wide as this night, old as this night." Kenneth Fearing. ChMo
Lullaby, A: "Wind is tapping the window-pane, The." William Noble Roundy. BOL
Lullaby: "Wind whistled loud at the window-pane, The." William Brighty Rands. BOL; BoTP
Lullaby./ Adult and child. Songs for a Colored Singer, III. Elizabeth Bishop. PoNe
Lullaby and good-night. The Guardian Angels—German. *Unknown.* BOL
Lullaby baby, lullaby baby. *See* Lulla by baby, lulla by baby.
Lullaby Carol. *Unknown. See* Lullay, Mine Liking.
Lullaby, child of the Madonna. The Baby's Charms. *Unknown.* BOL
Lullaby for a Baby Fairy. Joyce Kilmer. BOL
Lullaby for a Baby Toad. Stella Gibbons. AlDL
Lullaby for a Man-Child. Jean Starr Untermeyer. BOL; YT
Lullaby for a Sick Child. *Unknown, tr. fr. Italian.* BOL
Lullaby for Christmas, A. John Addington Symonds. BOL
Lullaby for Titania. Shakespeare. *See* You Spotted Snakes.
Lullaby in Bethlehem. Henry Howarth Bashford. BOL; HBV; HBVY
Lullaby in Undertones. "Feodor Sologub," *tr. fr. Russian by* R. M. Hewitt. BoR
Lullaby, little Jesus, my little pearl. Kolendy for Christmas. *Unknown.* CAW
Lullaby, lullaby baby. Thomas Goffe. *Fr.* The Tragedy of Orestes. TuPP
Lullaby, my little one. *Unknown.* BOL
Lullaby, my little one. Cradle Song. Carl Michael Bellman. FaPON
Lullaby, my pretty baby. Cradle Song. *Unknown.* BOL
Lullaby-O, By-O, Babe. Harry Noyes Pratt. BOL
Lullaby, O Lullaby. William Cox Bennett. BOL; HBV; OTPC
Lullaby, oh lullaby! Lullaby. Christina Rossetti. *Fr.* Sing-Song. BoChLi; BOL; OTPC (1946 ed.); RIS
"Lullaby, oh lullaby." A Serenade. Thomas Hood. BOL
Lullaby of a Female Convict to Her Child, the Night Previous to Execution, The. Henry Kirke White. BOL
Lullaby of a Lover, The. George Gascoigne. ElL; ElSeCe; EV-1; OAEP; ReIE; SiCE
(Gascoigne's Lullaby [*or* Lullabie].) PoE; PoEL-1; PoFS; ReEn; TrGrPo; TuPP
(Lover's Lullaby, A.) HBV; OBEV
(Sing Lullaby, as Women Do.) InvP
Lullaby of a [*or* the] Woman of the Mountain. Padraic Pearse, *tr. fr. Modern Irish by* Thomas MacDonagh. BOL; NP; OnYI
Lullaby of an Infant Chief. Sir Walter Scott. BHV; BOL; CBE; EmBrPo; EnRP; ERP; EV-4; FaPON; GoTP; HBV; MPB; OTPC; PCH, *st.* 1; PoRh; PRWS; RIS; TVC; TVSH
(Cradle Song.) CBPC
Lullaby of Danaë, The. Edmund Clarence Stedman, *par. fr. the Greek of* Simonides. BOL; MOAH
Lullaby of Nokomis, *abr.* Longfellow. *Fr.* The Song of Hiawatha, III. PCH
Lullaby of the Catfish and the Crab. William Rose Benét. WhC
Lullaby of the Iroquois. E. Pauline Johnson. BOL
Lullaby of the Pict Mother. Louise Lamprey. BOL
Lullaby of the Virgin. Lope de Vega. *See* Madonna, to Her Sleeping Child, The.
Lullaby of the Virgin. *Unknown, tr. fr. Latin by* Alma Strettell. BOL
Lullaby of the Woman of the Mountain. Padraic Pearse. *See* Lullaby of a Woman of the Mountain.
Lullaby Song. William P. M'Kenzie. BOL
Lullaby, sweet baby mine!/ Mother spins the thread so fine. A Danish Cradle Song. *Unknown.* BOL; BoTP
Lullaby, sweet lullaby. The Baby's Charms—Sardinian. *Unknown.* BOL
Lullaby Town. John Irving Diller. BLPA; NeHB
Lullay, Jesu, Lullay, Lullay! *Unknown.* AnEC
Lullay, Lullay. John Skelton. AtBAP; PoEL-1
(Here Foiowith Divers Balettis and Dities Solacious, Devised by Master Skelton, Laureate.) PoFS
(With Lullay, Lullay, like a Child.) InvP
Lullay, Lullay ("Lullay, lullay, litel child,/ Thu that were so sterne"). *Unknown.* OxBoCh
Lullay, Lullay ("Lullay, lullay, thou lytill Child"). *Unknown. See* Lullay, My Child, and Weep No More.
Lullay! lullay! lytel Child, myn owyn dere fode. *Unknown.* BOL
Lullay, lullay, thou little tiny child. *See* Lully, lulla . . .
Lullay, Mine Liking, My Dear Son, Mine Sweeting. *Unknown.* AnEC
("I saw a faire maiden.") EG
(Lullaby Carol.) BOL
("Lullay, mine lyking, my dere sone, myn swetying.") NBE
(Of the Virgin and Child.) LiA
Lullay, My Child, and Weep No More. *Unknown.* AnEC
(Lullay, Lullay, *shorter vers.*) BOL
Lullay, thou little tiny child. *See* Lully, lulla, thou little tiny child.
Lulled, at silence, the spent attack. Baggot Street Deserta. Thomas Kinsella. PoN
Lulled by La Belle Dame sans Merci he lies. The Enchanted Knight. Edwin Muir. MoVE
Lully, lulla [*or* Lullay, lullay], thou little tiny child. The Coventry Carol [*or* A Carol at the Manger]. *Unknown.* AnEC; BOL; YaCaBo
Lully, Lulley. *Unknown. See* Falcon, The.
Lulu, *with music. Unknown.* ABF; CoSo
(My Lulu, *diff.*) AS
Lumber Camp Song, The. *Unknown.* ShS
Lumbering tractor rolls its panting round, The. A Melbourne Ode; the Agricultural Show, Flemington, Victoria. Frank Wilmot. BoAu
Lumberman's Alphabet, The, *with music. Unknown.* ShS
Lumbermen, The. Whittier. BHV; WoL
Lumberyak, The. William F. Kirk. IHA
Lumberyard, The. Ruth Herschberger. LiTA; LiTL; LiTM (rev. ed.)
Lumen de Lumine. Shelley. *Fr.* Adonais. GoBC
("One remains, the many change and pass, The.") InP
Luminalia, *sel. At. to* Sir William Davenant.
Night's Song. SeCL
Luminary of the Birds expires, The. To the Admirable Transubstantiation of the Roses. Luis de Sandoval y Zapata. AnMP
Luminol is what you take. Hymn for Grief. Margaret Widdemer. QS
Luminous Hands of God, The. Eleanor Kenly Bacon. OQP; QP-1
Luna. Victor Hugo, *tr. fr. French by* Alan Conder. TrFP
Lunar Stanzas. Henry Coggswell Knight. BOHV; NA
Lunar Valley of Lost Things, The. Ariosto, *tr. fr. Italian by* Sir John Harington. *Fr.* Orlando Furioso, XXXIV. LiTW
Lunaria, *sel.* Maximilian Aleksandrovich Voloshin, *tr. fr. Russian by* Babette Deutsch.
Sonnet XV: "Pure pearl of silence brooding on the sky." TrRV
Lunatic, A. Mokichi Saito, *tr. fr. Japanese by* Shio Sakanishi. PoP
Lunatic, the Lover, and the Poet, The. Shakespeare. *Fr.* A Midsummer Night's Dream, V, i. FiP; InP; PIR
(Imagination.) EV-1; GTBS-W; LiTB; LiTG
(Inspiration, *sl. longer sel.*) CoEV
(Poet Greatly Pictured, The, *sl. longer sel.*) BCEP
("'Tis strange, my Theseus," *sl. longer sel.*) NBE
(Tricks of Imagination, The.) TreFS
Lunch. F. S. Flint. PFE
Lunchroom bus boy who looked like Orson Welles, The. The Passion of M'Phail, IV. Horace Gregory. TwAmPo
Lung Men Temple. Po Chü-i, *tr. fr. Chinese by* Henry H. Hart. PoHN
Lupracaun, or Fairy Shoemaker, The. William Allingham. *See* Fairy Shoemaker, The.
Lupus in Fabula. Malcolm Lowry. BoCaPo (1948 ed.); PeCV
Lupus, you question carefully. How to Raise a Son. Martial. LaP; LiTW
Lure, The, *sel.* John Hall.
"Look, how the daffodils arise." LO
Lure, The. John Boyle O'Reilly. HBV; LauV
"Lured," little one? Nay, you've but heard. Nested. Habberton Lulham. HBV
Luscious and Sorrowful. Christina Rossetti. PoEL-5; SeCePo
Lush green the grass that grows between. The Willow Bottom. Madison Cawein. VOD
Lusiads, The (Os Lusíadas), *sels.* Luis de Camões, *tr. fr. Portuguese.*
Cape of Tempests, The, *tr. by* Sir Richard Fanshawe. LiTW
Episode of Adamastor off the Cape of Good Hope, *tr. by* Sir Richard Fanshawe. LiA
Passage to India, *abr., tr. by* J. J. Aubertin. WoL
Lust. Shakespeare. *See* Sonnets, CXXIX.
Lust for the breezes. Poem for Keith Scott. Davies Aberpennar. MoWP
Lust in Song. Robert Graves. *See* Bards, The.
Lust is the oldest lion of them all. An Italian Chest [*or* Lorenzo's Bas-Relief for a Florentine Chest]. Marjorie Allen Seiffert. HBMV; NP
Lust of Gold, The. James Montgomery. *Fr.* The West Indies. PAH
Lust of mind is pride, The. Affliction. W. Wesley Trimpi. PtPa

Lustily, lustily, let us sail forth. Song of the Pirates. *Unknown. Fr.* Common Conditions. MuP; ReEn; SiCE; TuPP
Lustral sweat in its fine slow beads, The. Grave Piece. Richard Eberhart. ReMP
Lustration of the Winter Tree, *sel.* Margaret Allonby.
"In this savage place the sun stands still." BoSA
Lustrous face, A. Beardless Youth. Ibn Iyad. MooP
Lusty Fryer of Flanders, The. *Unknown.* CoMu
Lusty Juventus. Charles Madge. FaBoMo
Lusty Juventus, *sel.* R. Wever.
In Youth Is Pleasure. ChTr; OBEV
("In a herber green asleep whereas I lay.") EG; SiCE; TuPP
(Of Youth He Singeth.) EIL
(Youth.) OBSC
Lusty May. *Unknown. See* O Lusty May.
Lute, The. Ibn Qadi Mila, *tr. fr. Arabic by* A. J. Arberry. MooP
Lute, The. Rainer Maria Rilke, *tr. fr. German by* Jessie Lemont. OnPM
Lute and Furrow. Olive Tilford Dargan. LS; SPP; TBM
Lute in the Attic, The. Kenneth Patchen. OnHM
Lute, no longer hang upon your peg unstirred. Fecundi Calices [*or* Song and Wine]. Bacchylides. LiTW; OxBG
Lute Obeys, The. Sir Thomas Wyatt. *See* Blame Not My Lute.
Luther, they say, was unwise. A Letter from Rome. Arthur Hugh Clough. *Fr.* Amours de Voyage. LoBV
Luve Ron, A, *abr.* Thomas of Hales, *tr. fr. Middle English.* EPP, *orig. and mod. vers.*
(Love-Song, A, *abr., tr. by* Henry S. Pancoast.) MeEV
Where Is Paris and Heleyne? *sel.* ChTr
"Luve that I hae chosen, The." *See* Love that I have chosen, The.
Luveli Ter of Loveli Eyghe. *At. to* Johan de Grimestone. AtBAP
Lux Advenit Veneranda. Adam of St. Victor, *tr. fr. Latin by* H. T. Henry. CAW
Lux Aeterna. Irwin Edman. TBM
Lux Est Umbra Dei. John Addington Symonds. VA
Lux in Tenebris. Katharine Tynan. GTIV; OxBI; TIP; TrPWD
Lux in Tenebris. *Unknown.* GoBC
Lux, my fair falcon, and thy [*or* your] fellows all. Of Such as Had Forsaken Him [*or* Epigram]. Sir Thomas Wyatt. SiCE; SiPS; TuPP
Luxuriant, fragrant, fresh the new-blown rose. Sonnet. José de Espronceda. TeCS
Luxurious man, to bring his vice in use. The Mower against Gardens. Andrew Marvell. LiTB; OAEP; PoEL-2; ReEn; SeCV-1; SeEP
Lycaenis calls thee; Ilithya, come. To the Goddess of Childbirth. Callimachus. GrR
Lychee, The. Wang I, *tr. fr. Chinese by* Arthur Waley. FaBoCh
Lycidas. Milton. AEV; AnEnPo; AnFE; AtBAP; ATP; AWP; BEL; BLV; BoLiVe; CaAE; CBE; CBOV; ChTr; CoEV; EM-1; EnL; EnLi-1; EnLit; EPP; EPS; EV-2; ExPo; FaBoEn; FiP; GEPC; GTBS; GTBS-D; GTBS-W; GTSE; GTSL; HBV; InPo; JAWP; LEAP; LH; LiA; LiTB; LiTG; LoBV; MaPo; MCCG; MyFE; OAEP; OBEV; OBS; OuHeWo; PIAE; PIR; Po; PoE; PoEL-3; PoFS; PreP; REAL; ReaPo; RiBV; SeCeV; SeEP; TCEP; TOP; TrGrPo; TriL; TwCrTr; TwHP; TyEnPo; UnPo; ViBoPo; WBP; WGRP; WHA; WoL
Sels.
"Alas! What boots it with incessant." PC
"But O the heavy change, now thou art gon." PoD
Flowers. ADAH
Immortality. MaRV
"Last came, and last did go." PoFr
"Yet once more, o ye laurels." BCEP
Lycidas and Moeris. Virgil. Eclogues, IX. AWP
Lycidus, *sel.* Aphra Behn.
Song: "Not to sigh and to be tender." CaAE
Lycon begin—begin the mournful tale. Eclogue. William Diaper. *Fr.* Nereides; or, Sea-Eclogues. SeCePo
Lycon, the rising down that first appeared. Good Expectations. *Unknown.* OnPM
Lycosa the Spider. Annie Charlotte Dalton. BoCaPo (1943 ed.)
Lydia. Madison Cawein. PR
Lydia. Leconte de Lisle, *tr. fr. French by* Alan Conder. TrFP
Lydia. Lizette Woodworth Reese. AA; OBAV
Lydia Is Gone This Many a Year. Lizette Woodworth Reese. CH; GBV (1952 ed.); HBV
Lydia, now that days are ashen. Lenten Lines to Lydia. Sennett Stephens. PR
Lydia Pinkham, *with music. Unknown.* AS
Lydia, why do you ruin by lavishing. Questioning Lydia. Horace, *tr. by* Louis Untermeyer. *Fr.* Odes. InP
Lydian I, a Lydian slave, A; and yet, O master. The Old Slave. Dioscorides, *tr. by* F. L. Lucas. GrPE
Lydian, yes, a Lydian I, A. A Faithful Servant [*or* A Slave's Epitaph]. Dioscorides, *tr. by* R. A. Furness. GrR; OxBG
Lydian? Yes; to Timanthes foster father, and slave. Dioscorides, *tr. by* William Stebbing. GrPo
Lye, The. Sir Walter Ralegh. *See* Lie, The.
Lyell's Hypothesis Again. Kenneth Rexroth. MoVE; OnHM
Lyf so short, the craft so long to lerne, The. The Parlement of Foules: Proem. Chaucer. FiP; MyFE; NBE; ViBoPo
Lying. Thomas Moore. BOHV; FiBHP
Lying a-dying. Young Death. Christina Rossetti. EmBrPo
Lying alone in this dark bamboo grove. In a Bamboo Grove. Wang Wei. WhP
Lying at night poised between sleep and waking. East Coast—Canada. Elizabeth Brewster. CaP
Lying by the fireside. Fire Pictures. Emma Rounds. MPB
Lying in bed this morning, just a year. A Letter. Anne Ridler. LiTL; LiTM
Lying in the Grass. Sir Edmund Gosse. LBBV; OBVV; PoeT; TCEP; TOP; VA
Lying in the sunshine among the buttercups. Tribute to Grass. John J. Ingalls. WBLP
Lyke as a huntsman after weary chace. *See* Like as a huntsman . . .
Lyke as a ship, that through the ocean wyde. *See* Like as a ship . . .
Lyke-Wake Carol, A. Arthur Shearly Cripps. PoeT
Lyke-Wake Dirge, A. *Unknown.* AnFE; AtBAP; BCEP; CBOV; CH; ChTr; DaM; EBSV; FaBoCh; GoBC; HBV; HoPM; LoBV; MeRV; OBB; OBEV; OtMeF; OxBoCh; PoD; PoEL-1; PoLi; ReaPo; SeCeV; ShBV-2
(Cleveland Lyke-Wake Dirge.) BrBE; EnSB
(Final Dirge.) ACP
Lyke-Wake Song, A. Swinburne. PoVP; ViP
Lynchburg Town, *with music. Unknown.* OuSiCo
Lynched Negro. Maxwell Bodenheim. PoNe
Lynching, The. Claude McKay. BANP
Lynching Bee, The. William Ellery Leonard. PoNe
Lynmouth Widow, A. Amelia Josephine Burr. AV; BAP; NV; SBMV
Lynx. R. A. D. Ford. CaP
Lyonesse. Godfrey Fox Bradby. ReTS
Lyre, The. George Darley. *See* Listen to the Lyre *and* Solitary Lyre, The.
Lyre and the Crown, The. Marcus Argentarius, *tr. fr. Greek by* Walter Leaf. OxBG
Lyric: "Give me a light that I may see her." John Masefield. CaAE
Lyric, A: "How can I sing light-souled." Lorenzo de' Medici, *tr. fr. Italian by* John Addington Symonds. JAWP; WBP
Lyric: "I touched a shining mote of sand." Philip Child. CaP
Lyric: "I want to be where all is very still." Gertrude MacGregor Moffat. CPG
Lyric: "Let but a thrush begin." John Hewitt. NeIP
Lyric: "Lo, as the thrushes' throats." Al-Barraq, *tr. fr. Arabic by* A. J. Arberry. MooP
Lyric: "Songs of adolescence, The." John Thompson. BoAu
Lyric: "Tell me, is there sovereign cure." Edith M. Thomas. *See* Tell Me.
Lyric, A: "There's nae lark loves the lift, my dear." Swinburne. *See* There's Nae Lark.
Lyric, A: "You smiled, you spoke." Walter Savage Landor. *See* You Smiled, You Spoke.
Lyric: "You would have understood me, had you waited." Ernest Dowson. *See* You Would Have Understood Me.
Lyric Barber. Liboria E. Romano. GoYe
Lyric Deed, The. John G. Neihardt. DD; GA; TBM
Lyric from "Maud." Tennyson. *See* Come into the Garden, Maud.
Lyric Love. Robert Browning. *See* O Lyric Love.
Lyric sound of laughter, The. April Music. Clinton Scollard. NLK
Lyric Stanzas of Empedocles. Matthew Arnold. *See* Empedocles on Etna: Empedocles' Song.
Lyric to the Isles. Charles Sangster. CPG
Lyrical Epigram, A: "My little old dog." Edith Wharton. PC
Lyrical Poem, The. Richard Garnett. VA
Lyrick for Legacies. Robert Herrick. OBS
Lyrics, *sels.* James Agee.
"I loitered weeping with my bride for gladness." MAP; MoAmPo
"No doubt left. Enough deceiving." MAP; MoAmPo
"Not met and marred with the year's whole turn of grief." MAP; MoAmPo
Lyrics. Ezra Pound. *See* E. P. Ode pour l'Election de Son Sepulchre.
Lyrics from a Library, *sel.* Clinton Scollard.
In the Library. MOB
Lyrics from "The Princess." Tennyson. *See* Princess, The.

Lyrics of Earth, *sel.* Archibald Lampman.
Dedication: "Mother to whose valiant will." MOAH
Lyrics to Inez and Jane. What She Said About It. Charles Henry Webb. PR
Lysistrata, *sels.* Aristophanes, *tr. fr. Greek by* Benjamin Bickley Rogers.
How the Women Will Stop War. OxBG; WaaP
Hymn of Peace. OxBG
(Rejoicings for Peace.) GrR
Woman's Antidote for War, A. GrR
Lyth and listen, gentlemen. Robin Hood and the Beggar, II. *Unknown.* BaBo; ESPB
Lythe and listin, gentilmen. A Gest of Robyn Hode. *Unknown. See* Lithe and listen, gentlemen.
Lyttel Boy, The. Eugene Field. AA; LEAP
Lyttelton Harbour, *sels.* D'Arcy Cresswell. AnNZ
"Home did I say, ye homeless? Not to ye," VIII.
"Thou bent and only motion of our lives," XXXIII.
"Ye barren hearts and bitter, steep'd in brine," XXXVIII.
Lytyll prety nyghtyngale, The. *See* Little pretty nightingale.
Lyubka. Boris Pasternak, *tr. fr. Russian by* Babette Deutsch. TrRV

M

M. Edward Lear. WhC
M and A and R and I. *Unknown.* AnEC
M. Crashaw's Answer for Hope. Richard Crashaw. *See* For Hope.
M. Edwards' May. Richard Edwards. TuPP
(Master Edwards' May.) SiCE
(May.) OBSC
M. Francis Beaumont's Letter to Ben Jonson. Francis Beaumont. *See* Master Francis Beaumont's Letter to Ben Jonson.
M. I. (Mounted Infantry of the Line). Kipling. BPN
M. P.; or, The Blue Stockings, *sel.* Thomas Moore.
Orator Puff. LPS-3
M., Singing. Louise Bogan. CrMA; LiTA; NePA
M was once a little mouse M. Edward Lear. WhC
Ma an' Pa'd been raisin' chickens. Pa's Chickens. Homer Roberts. IHA
Ma Jesus/ Was a troubled man. Troubled Jesus. Waring Cuney. BANP; GoSl
Ma Lord. Langston Hughes. GoSl
Ma says no, it's too much care. The Joy of a Dog. Edgar A. Guest. AlBD
Ma Wei. Li Shang-yin, *tr. fr. Chinese.* WhP
Mab the Mistress-Fairy. Ben Jonson. *See* Queen Mab.
Mabel, in New Hampshire. James T. Fields. HBV; PR
Mabel, little Mabel. The Face against the Pane. Thomas Bailey Aldrich. TreFS
Mabel Martin; a Harvest Idyl. Whittier. BAV
Sels.
Husking, The, *abr., fr.* II. APW
I Call the Old Time Back. Proem. ViBoPo
Witch's Daughter, The, *abr., fr.* II–VI. PTA-2
Mac and Daisy, Carl and Marie. Hornets. C. Lindsay McCoy. GFA
Macadam, gun-gray as the tunny's belt. Van Winkle. Hart Crane. *Fr.* The Bridge. AmP; AmPP; CrMA; LiTA; MAP; MoAB; MoAmPo; ReMP
Macaffie's Confession. *Unknown.* BeLS; CoSo, *with music;* CSF
M'Andrew's Hymn. Kipling. OtMeF; PoEL-5
(McAndrew's Hymn.) ViPP
Macaria and Iolaus. Euripides, *tr. fr. Greek. Fr.* Children of Heracles. GrR, *tr. by* Arthur S. Way; OxBG, *tr. by* George Allen
Macaulay. Walter Savage Landor. LPS-3; VA
Macaulay at Tea. Barry Pain. *See* Poets at Tea, The.
Macavity; the Mystery Cat. T. S. Eliot. AlDL; CenHV; EnL; HaMV; KN; LiTM; NeMA; PoC; PoLFOT; PoRA; ShBV-3; TiPo; TwP; WaKn
Macaw preens upon a branch outspread, A. Decoration. Louise Bogan. MAP; MoAB; MoAmPo
Macbeth. Walter de la Mare. TCEP
Macbeth, *sels.* Shakespeare.
". . . Better be with the dead," *fr.* III, ii. PIR
"Blood hath been shed ere now, i' the olden time," *fr.* III, iv. MyFE
"Canst thou not minister to a mind diseased?" *fr.* V, iii.
(Mind Diseased, A.) BCEP
(Remorse.) MaRV
"Give me my sword./ Who's there?" *fr.* II, i. MyFE
"Here's a knocking indeede," *fr.* II, iii. AtBAP
"I have lived long enough; my way of life," *fr.* V, iii. TrGrPo
"If it were done when 'tis done, then 'twere well," *fr.* I, vii. NBE; PIR
(Duncan's Murder.) EV-1
(Macbeth's Murder Meditation.) BCEP
(Murder Pact, The.) WHA
(Vaulting Ambition.) FiP
"Is this a dagger which I see before me," *fr.* II, i. PIR
(Dagger of the Mind, A.) LPS-3
(Macbeth's Words before Murdering.) TreFS
(Night.) LiA
Murder, The, II, ii. CBOV; LPS-3
(Deed, The, *shorter sel.*) EV-1
(Macbeth Does Murder Sleep, *shorter sel.*) FiP
(Multitudinous Seas Incarnadine, *shorter sel.*) LiA
(Murderers, The.) WHA
("That which hath made them drunk, hath made me bold.") AtBAP; MyFE
"My liege,/ They are not yet come back," *fr.* I, iv. PIR
"Now o'er the one half world," *fr.* II, i. NBE
O! Full of Scorpions, *fr.* III, ii. FiP
Sleep—Innocent Sleep, *fr.* II, ii. EV-1
(Conscience.) MaRV
(Sleep.) TreFS
"They met me in the day of successe," *fr.* I, v. AtBAP
"This guest of summer, the temple-haunting martlet," *fr.* I, vi.
(Fragments from the Old Masters: The Temple-haunting Martlet.) PoF
"Tomorrow, and tomorrow, and tomorrow," *fr.* V, v. BLP; BrBE; FaFP; LiTB; OQP; PFE; PG; PIR; QP-1; TrGrPo; WHA
(Empty Life, The.) MaRV
(Macbeth Learns of His Wife's Death.) TreF
(Macbeth on His Wife's Death.) CoEV
(Out, Out, Brief Candle!) ChTr
(She Should Have Died Hereafter.) FiP; InP; NBE
(Tomorrow.) BCEP
(Tomorrow and Tomorrow.) NeHB; UnPo
(Way to Dusty Death, The.) EV-1
"We have scotch'd the snake, not kill'd it," *fr.* III, ii. AtBAP; NBE
Witches' Song, The, *fr.* IV, i. OnHT
(Charm, The.) ElL
("Thrice the brinded cat hath mewed.") ElSeCe; InvP; MyFE
(Witches' Charm.) SiTL
(Witches' Meeting, The, *fr.* I, i *and* IV, i.) CG
(Witches' Spell, The.) PoMS
McCullam Camp. Larry Gorman. *See* Winter of '73, The.
MacDiarmod's Daughter. Francis Carlin. HBMV
Macdonald's Raid. Paul Hamilton Hayne. PAH
McDonogh Day in New Orleans. Marcus B. Christian. PoNe
Macer has joined the army, and what's to become of peaceable Cupid? Tibullus. Elegies, II, 6. LaP
M'Fingal, *sels.* John Trumbull.
Liberty-Pole, The, III. AmPP (3d ed.); APW, *abr.;* TCAP, *abr.*
"This said, our 'Squire, yet undismayed," *fr.* III. IAP
Town Meeting, The, *abr.* AnNE
Town-Meeting, A.M., The, *fr.* I. IAP; TCAP
Town-Meeting, P.M., The, *fr.* II. TCAP
MacFlecknoe; or, A Satire upon the True-Blue Protestant Poet, T. S. Dryden. ATP (1953 ed.); BEL; CEP; EiPP; EnLi-1; EnLit; GEPC; MaPo; OAEP; OxBoLi; Po; PoE; PoFS; PtP; ReaPo; SeCV-2; SeEP; SiTL; TCEP, *abr.;* TwHP
Sels.
"All human things are subject to decay." AtBAP; CoBE; ExPo; TrGrPo; ViBoPo
(Laureate of Dulness, The.) CoEV
(Poet Shadwell. The.) FiP
(Primacy of Dullness, The.) OBS
(Shadwell.) AnFE; EV-3; NBE
Poet Shadwell's Coronation, The. BeR
MacGregor's Gathering. Sir Walter Scott. AnFE; BrBE; EBSV; EmBrPo; PoFr
Machberoth, *sel.* Immanuel di Roma, *tr. fr. Hebrew by* Joseph Chotzner.
Virtue. TrJP
Macheath and Polly. John Gay. *See* Song: "Were I laid on Greenland's coast."
Machine, The. W. W. Gibson. PCN; PoTo; PtOT
Machine Hand, A. Thomas Ashe. OBVV
Machine stitched rivets ravel on a tree. The Pilot in the Jungle. John Ciardi. MiAP
Machines. Daniel Whitehead Hicky. MuM; PoeMoYo; PoMa; VOD (1935 ed)
Machines in haughty and presumptuous pride. Ode to Machines. Louis Ginsberg. PoMa
Machines of death from east to west. Revelation. William Soutar. HaMV
Machines—or Men. Elizabeth Newport Hepburn. PoMa
Macías in the Circle of Venus. Juan de Mena, *tr. fr. Spanish*

by Jeremiah Holmes Wiffen. *Fr.* Labyrinth of Fortune. AnSpL-1
McIlrath of Malate. John Jerome Rooney. PAH
MacKenna's Dream. *Unknown.* OnYI
Mackerel skies and mares' tails. Rules of the Road. *Unknown.* SoAmSa
Mackerel sky,/ Mackerel sky. *Unknown.* OxNR
McKinley. *Unknown.* GA; MC; PAH
McKinley Brook, *with music.* George Calhoun. ShS
Mackrimmon's Lament. Sir Walter Scott. EBSV; EmBrPo
M'Lean's Welcome. James Hogg. EBSV
Macleod's wizard flag from the gray castle sallies. Mackrimmon's Lament. Sir Walter Scott. EBSV; EmBrPo
MacLugach! says Finn. *Unknown. Fr.* The Colloquy of the Ancients. OnYI
Macombrey Queen, The, *with music. Unknown.* StDa
MacPhairson Clonglocketty Angus McClan [*or* M'Clan]. Ellen McJones [*or* M'Jones] Aberdeen. W. S. Gilbert. HBV; InMe; PCD; TSW; TSWC
Macpherson's [*or* M'Pherson's] Farewell. Burns. BSV; EBSV; MCCG; OtMeF
(Defiance.) LH
Macrocosm. Philip Child. CaP
Macroom on Market Day. Virginia Lyne Tunstall. LS
Mac Tulchain, by his own wish. *Unknown. Fr.* Penitentes. SiB
Mad as the Mist and Snow. W. B. Yeats. AtBAP; ChTr
Mad Berkeley believed, with his gay cavaliers. The Burning of Jamestown. Thomas Dunn English. PAH
Mad Blake. William Rose Benét. BAP; HBMV; SBMV
Mad Boy's Song. Leo Kennedy. BoCaPo; TwCaPo
Madboy's Song. Muriel Rukeyser. MoAmPo; TrJP
Mad Dogs and Englishmen. Noel Coward. CenHV; FiBHP; WhC
Mad Farmer's Song. *Unknown.* BrR; RIS
("My father left me three acres of land.") OxNR
(Sing Ivy.) BoTP
(Three Acres of Land.) NA
Mad Gardener's Song, The. "Lewis Carroll." *See* Gardener's Song, The.
Mad girl with the staring eyes and long white fingers, The. Cassandra. Robinson Jeffers. LiTA; LiTM; NePA; WaP
Mad Girl's Song. L. E. F. Barry. ReTS
Mad Jasper. Max Harris. MoAuPo
Mad Lover, The. Alexander Brome. ElSeCe; SeCL; SeEP
(I Have Been in Love and in Debt.) ALV
(Love, Drink, and Debt.) OtMeF
Mad Lover, The, *sels.* John Fletcher.
Joy of Battle, The, *fr.* V, iv. EV-2; LH
("Arm, arm, arm, arm!") CenL; ElL
Prayer to Venus, *fr.* V, iii. SeCL
"To the fair fields where loves eternal dwell," *fr.* IV, i. MyFE
Mad Lover, The. Speer Strahan. CAW
Mad Maid's Song, The. Robert Herrick. AWP; BLV; BoLiVe; CaAE; CH; EG; EnLoPo; EPS (1942 ed.); EV-2; InPo; LoBV; OBEV; PoFS; SeCL; SeCV-1; SeEP; TrGrPo; ViBoPo; WP
Mad Margaret's Song. W. S. Gilbert. *Fr.* Ruddigore. RIS
Mad Maudlin to Find Out Tom of Bedlam. *Unknown.* SiTL
Mad Merry Pranks of Robin Good-Fellow, The. *Unknown. See* Robin Goodfellow ("From Oberon, in fairy land").
Mad Patsy said, he said to me. In the Poppy Field. James Stephens. CP; NV; TCPD; WP
Mad Poem Addressed to My Nephews and Nieces, A. Po Chü-i, *tr. fr. Chinese by* Arthur Waley. TrCh
Mad Poll. J. Corson Miller. JKCP (1955 ed.)
Mad Pomegranate Tree, The. "Odysseus Elytis," *tr. fr. Modern Greek by* Rae Dalven. MoGP
Mad River. Longfellow. PTA-2
"Mad Scene, The." Aeschylus, *tr. fr. Greek by* G. M. Cookson. *Fr.* Choephoroe. GrR
Mad Song. Blake. BCEP; BEL; CEP; EiPP; EM-1; EnLi-2; EnLit; EnRP; NBE; PoE; PoEL-4; PoRA; TrGrPo
Mad Song. Hester Sigerson. AnIV
Mad Song; or, Tom o' Bedlam's Song. *Unknown. See* Tom o' Bedlam's Song.
Mad Sweeney. *Unknown. See* Sweeney the Mad.
Mad Woman of Punnet's Town, The. L. A. G. Strong. MBP; MoBrPo
Mad World, My Masters, A, *sel.* Thomas Middleton.
O for a Bowl of Fat Canary. *Also in* Alexander and Campaspe (*by* John Lyly). OnPM; ViBoPo
Madaket Beach. Isabel Harriss Barr. GoYe
Madam Hickory. Wilbur Larremore. AA
"Madam, I have come a-courting." Quaker's Courtship. *Unknown.* ABS
Madam Life. W. E. Henley. MBP; MoBrPo; TrGrPo
(Madam Life's a Piece in Bloom.) VLEP
Madam Rumour. Wyn Griffith. MoWP
Madam, Were you but only great, there are some men. To the Excellent Pattern of Beauty and Virtue, Lady Elizabeth, Countess of Ormond. James Shirley. GoBC
Madam, when we two walked, the rest unheeding. Pierre de Ronsard. *Fr.* Sonnets pour Hélène. PrPoCR
Madam [*or* Madame], withouten many words. To His [*or* a] Lady to Answer Directly with Yea or Nay. Sir Thomas Wyatt. EG; ElL; EnLoPo; LO; OBSC; PoFS; ReEn; ReIE; SeCePo; SiPS; TuPP
Madam would speak with me? So, now it comes. Modern Love, XXXIV. George Meredith. ViPo
Madam, you are right; the fight was a great pity. To the Woman in Bond Street Station. Edward Weismiller. LiTA; NePA; WaP
Madame. Jules Supervielle, *tr. fr. French by* Wallace Fowlie. MiCF
Madame d'Albert's [*or* d'Albret's] Laugh. Clément Marot, *tr. fr. French by* Leigh Hunt. ALV; AWP; JAWP; WBP
(On Her Laugh.) OnPM
Madame de Courament excels at Bridge. An Old Lady. "Katherine Hale." CPG
Madame Dill. *Unknown.* FiBHP
Madame, had all antiquitie been lost. To Mary Lady Wroth. Ben Jonson. OBS
Madame, his grace will not be absent long. Cyril Tourneur. *Fr.* The Revenger's Tragedy. AtBAP; NBE; PoEL-2
Madame Louise sleeps well o' nights. Aux Carmélites. Katharine Tynan. OnYI
Madame Mouse Trots. Edith Sitwell. *Fr.* Façade. FaBoCh
Madame—O Lady of the jeweled brain. For Madame Chiang Kai-shek. Amanda Benjamin Hall. NeTW
Madame Sans Souci. *Unknown.* BOHV
Madame, whose nose is not of the smallest, greetings! Catullus, *tr. fr. Latin by* Frances Fletcher. LaP
Madame, withouten many words. *See* Madam, withouten many words.
Madame, ye ben of al beauté shryne. To Rosemounde; a Balade [*or* Ballad]. Chaucer. InP; LoPS
Mädchen mit dem rothen Mündchen. Heine, *tr. fr. German by* Sir Theodore Martin. AWP; JAWP; WBP
Made in the Hot Weather. W. E. Henley. *See* Ballade Made in the Hot Weather.
Made Lake, The. Louise Townsend Nicholl. NePoAm-2
Madeleine in Church, *sel.* Charlotte Mew.
"How old was Mary out of whom you cast." LO; MBP; MoAB; MoBrPo
Madeleine Verchères. William Henry Drummond. CaP; CPG; OCL
Madeline at Jefferson Market Night Court. Margaret McGovern. WhC
Madelon. *Unknown.* BoHiPo
Mademoiselle from Armentières. *Unknown.* BoHiPo; SiTL; SoAmSa, *with music*
(Hinky Dinky, *with music.*) TrAS
(Hinky Dinky, Parlee-Voo.) ABF; AS
Mademoiselle Richarde. Edith Sitwell. MoVE
Madhouse Poem. Carlos Oquendo de Amat, *tr. fr. Spanish by* H. R. Hays. AnCL
Madly Singing in the Mountains. Po Chü-i, *tr. fr. Chinese by* Arthur Waley. AlDL; MoPW; OuHeWo; TrCh
Madman, The. L. A. G. Strong. PC
Madman's Song, The. John Webster. *See* Oh, Let Us Howl Some Heavy Note.
Madman's Song. Elinor Wylie. BAP; MAP; MoAB; MoAmPo; MoSiPe; PoRA
Madness. Harry Lee. MaRV
Madness of Heracles, The. Euripides, *tr. fr. Greek by* Hugh Owen Meredith. *Fr.* Heracles. GrR
Madness of King Goll, The. W. B. Yeats. ChMo; CMP
Madness of Winds, The. Lloyd Roberts. CPG
Madonna, A. Heine, *tr. fr. German by* James Thomson. OnPM
Madonna. Pushkin, *tr. fr. Russian by* Babette Deutsch. TrRV
Madonna and Child, The. *Unknown. See* This Endernight I Saw a Sight.
Madonna di Campagna. Alfred Kreymborg. HBMV
Madonna loves. Madonna Remembers. Sister Mary Edwardine. WHL
Madonna, Madonna,/ Sat by the grey road-side. Cradle-Song. Adelaide Crapsey. BOL; HBMV; ISi
Madonna Mia. Swinburne. HBV; MBP; VLEP
Madonna Natura. "Fiona Macleod." WGRP
Madonna; 1936. John Louis Bonn. ISi
Madonna of the Carpenter Shop, The. Ruth Guthrie Harding. SDH
Madonna of the Dons. Arthur MacGillivray. ISi; JKCP (1955 ed.)
Madonna of the Empty Arms. Maurice Francis Egan. ISi
Madonna of the Evening Flowers. Amy Lowell. BAV; ChMo; CMP; MAP; MM; MoAmPo; NeMA; OBAV; PoeMoYo; SBMV; TOP
Madonna of the Exiles. James Edward Tobin. ISi
Madonna Remembers. Sister Mary Edwardine. WHL

Madonna, to Her Sleeping Child, The. Lope de Vega, *tr. fr. Spanish by* George Ticknor. ChrBoLe
(Christmas Cradlesong, A.) TeCS
(Lullaby of the Virgin.) AnSpL-1
(Whispering Palms.) BOL
Madonna's Lamp, The. Wilhelm, Prince of Sweden, *tr. fr. Swedish by* Thomas Walsh. CAW
Madonna's Lullaby. St. Alphonsus Liguori, *tr. fr. Italian by* James J. Galvin. ISi
Madrigal V: Allusion to the Confusion of Babel. Francis Davison. ReIE
Madrigal: "Ay me, alas, heigh ho, heigh ho!" *Unknown. See* Ay Me, Alas.
Madrigal: "Beautie [*or* Beauty], and the life, The." William Drummond of Hawthornden. AtBAP; EBSV; ElL; PoEL-2; TriL
(Her Passing.) OBEV
Madrigal: "Beside the rivers of the midnight town." John Frederick Nims. MiAP
Madrigal: "Clear eyes, sweet and serene." Gutierre de Cetina. *See* Madrigal: "Eyes that are clear, serene."
Madrigal: "Come let's begin to revel 't out." *Unknown.* BoTP
Madrigal, A: "Crabbed age and youth." Shakespeare. *See* Crabbed Age and Youth.
Madrigal: "Dear night, the ease of care." William Drummond of Hawthornden. EV-2
Madrigal: "Dear, when I did from you remove." Lord Herbert of Cherbury. ElL; ElSeCe
Madrigal 52: "Diana, naked in the shadowy pool." Petrarch, *tr. fr Italian by* Morris Bishop. LyPI
Madrigal, A: "Easter-glow and Easter-gleam!" Clinton Scollard. EOAH
Madrigal: "Eyes that are clear, serene." Gutierre de Cetina, *tr. fr. Spanish by* L. R. Lind. LiTW
(Madrigal: "Clear eyes, sweet and serene," *tr. by* Nicholson B. Adams.) AnSpL-1
Madrigal: "Fain would I change that note." *Unknown. See* Fain Would I Change That Note.
Madrigal: "Faustina hath the fairer face." *Unknown.* ElSeCe; EV-1
("Faustina hath the fairer face.") OBSC
Madrigal: "Ha ha! ha ha! This world doth pass." *Unknown. See* Fara Diddle Dyno.
Madrigal: "He comes again!" Sir Edmund Gosse. PtP
Madrigal: "How should I love my best?" Lord Herbert of Cherbury. PoEL-2; ViBoPo
Madrigal: "I always loved to call my lady Rose." *Unknown.* ElL
Madrigal: "I fear not henceforth death." William Drummond of Hawthornden. ElSeCe; LO
Madrigal: "If it be true that any beauteous thing." Michelangelo. *See* If It Be True That Any Beauteous Thing.
Madrigal: "Ivory, coral, gold, The." William Drummond of Hawthornden. ElL; ElSeCe; EV-2
Madrigal 178: "Lady, up to your high and shining crown." Michelangelo, *tr. fr. Italian by* Creighton Gilbert. LyPI
Madrigal 139: "Led on through many years to my last hours." Michelangelo, *tr. fr. Italian by* Creighton Gilbert. LyPI
Madrigal: "Like the Idalian queen." William Drummond of Hawthornden. EBSV; ElL; ElSeCe; EV-2; FaBoEn; InvP; LiTL; OBEV; OBS; PoEL-2; SeEP; ViBoPo
(Like the Idalian Queen.) BSV; GoTS; SeCePo
Madrigal: "Love in thy youth, fair maid; be wise." *Unknown. See* Love in Thy Youth.
Madrigal: "Love not me for comely grace." *Unknown. See* Love Not Me for Comely Grace.
Madrigal: Love Vagabonding. William Drummond of Hawthornden. LoBV
Madrigal: "My Love in her attire doth show her wit." *Unknown. See* My Love in Her Attire.
Madrigal: "My mistress frowns when she should play." *Unknown, at. to* John Hilton. *See* Fa La La.
Madrigal: "My mistress is as fair as fine." Thomas Ravenscroft. CH; SiTL
("My mistress is as fair as fine.") OxBoLi
Madrigal: "My thoughts hold mortal strife." William Drummond of Hawthornden. AtBAP; EBSV; ElL; ElSeCe; EV-2; GTBS; GTBS-D; GTBS-W; GTSE; LoBV; OBS; OnPM
(Inexorable.) OBEV
(Lament, A.) GTSL
(My Thoughts Hold Mortal Strife.) BSV
Madrigal: "O I do love, then kiss me." Robert Jones. OxBoLi; SiTL
Madrigal: "Once in an arbor was my mistress sleeping." Barnabe Barnes. *Fr.* Parthenophil and Parthenophe. TuPP
Madrigal 109: "Ravished by all that to the eyes is fair." Michelangelo, *tr. fr. Italian by* George Santayana. LyPI
(Poems.) JAWP; WBP
(Three Poems.) AWP
Madrigal: Restless Lover, The. Francisco de Quevedo y Villegas, *tr. fr. Spanish by* Philip Ayres. TeCS
Madrigal: "Since Bonny-boots was dead, that so divinely." *Unknown. See* Since Bonny-Boots Was Dead.
Madrigal: "Sing with me, you little amorous birds." Matteo Maria Boiardo, *tr. fr. Italian by* L. R. Lind. LyPI
Madrigal: "Sister, awake, close not your eyes." *Unknown. See* Sister, Awake!
Madrigal: "Some there are as fair to see to." Francis Davison. *See* Her Commendation.
Madrigal: "Sound of thy sweet name, my dearest treasure, The." Francis Davison. *See* Sound of Thy Sweet Name, The.
Madrigal, A: "Swans, The, whose pens as white as ivory," *sel.* Robert Greene. ViBoPo
Madrigal: "Sweet rose, whence is this hue." William Drummond of Hawthornden. ElSeCe
Madrigal: "Take, O take those lips away." Shakespeare. *See* Take, O Take Those Lips Away.
Madrigal: "Tell me where is Fancy bred." Shakespeare. *See* Tell Me Where Is Fancy Bred.
Madrigal: "This life, which seems so fair." William Drummond of Hawthornden. EBSV; EG; ElL; ElSeCe; EPP; EPS; EV-2, *sl. diff.*; LiTG; OBS; SeCePo
(Life, a Bubble.) TOP
(This Life.) CH; TrGrPo
(This Life a Bubble.) OnPM
(This Life, Which Seems So Fair.) BSV; GTBS; GTBS-D; GTBS-W; GTSE; GTSL
Madrigal: "This saith my Cloris bright." *Unknown, par. fr.* Giovanni Battista Guarini. LO
Madrigal 95: "Though time may prod against me and insist." Michelangelo, *tr. fr. Italian by* Creighton Gilbert. LyPI
Madrigal: "Thule, the period of Cosmography." *Unknown. See* Wonders.
Madrigal I: To Cupid. Francis Davison. *See* To Cupid.
Madrigal: To His Lady Selvaggia Vergiolesi. Cino da Pistoia, *tr. fr. Italian by* Dante Gabriel Rossetti. AWP; JAWP; WBP
Madrigal: "Unhappy [*or* Unhappie] light." William Drummond of Hawthornden. AtBAP; EPS; OBS
Madrigal: "What dewdrops or what tears." Tasso, *tr. fr. Italian by* Cecil Clifford Palmer. LyPI
Madrigal: "When in her face mine eyes I fix." Earl of Stirling. Aurora, Madrigal I. ElL
Madrigal 86: "While life is running out in me through time." Michelangelo, *tr. fr. Italian by* Creighton Gilbert. LyPI
Madrigal: "Why dost thou haste away." Sir Philip Sidney. *Fr.* Arcadia. EG; OBSC; SiPS
Madrigal: "Your love is dead, lady, your love is dead." R. S. Thomas. EnLoPo
Madrigal to a Streetcar Token. Rafael Alberti, *tr. fr. Spanish by* Lloyd Mallan. LiTW
Madroño. Bret Harte. AA; OBAV
Mae Christie. Hubbard Fulton Page. NoCaPo
Maerchen. Walter de la Mare. CoBMV
Maesia's Song. Robert Greene. *See* Sweet Are the Thoughts That Savor of Content.
Maeve. Mervyn Peake. LO
Magalu. Helene Johnson. CDC; PoNe
Magazine Fort, Phoenix Park, Dublin, The. William Wilkins. IrPN; SeCePo; TIP
Magdalen. Henry Kingsley. HBV; MaRV; OBVV
(At Glastonbury.) PoRA
Magdalen. James Ryder Randall. JKCP
Magdalen, The. Sir Edward Sherburne. *See* And She Washed His Feet with Her Teares . . .
Magdalen at Michael's gate. Magdalen [*or* At Glastonbury]. Henry Kingsley. HBV; MaRV; OBVV; PoRA
Magdalen Walks. Oscar Wilde. MBP; MoBrPo; YT
Mage of music, deaf to outward sound, The. Beethoven. Roden Noel. BMEP
Magellan. Allen Curnow. AnNZ
Maggie and Milly and Molly and May. E. E. Cummings. NePoAm-2
Maggie Lauder. Francis Sempill. EBSV (*A and B vers.*); OBS
Maggie's Visit to Oxford, *sel.* "Lewis Carroll."
"To Worcester gardens next." CIV
Maggots of Flattery. Samuel Butler. BeR
Magi. Leslie Savage Clark. ChIP
Magi, The. Milton. *Fr.* On the Morning of Christ's Nativity. ChTr
Magi, The. W. B. Yeats. CoBMV; MaPo; NP; TwHP
Magi came out of the Orient Land, The. Three Kings' Song. *Unknown.* BOL
Magi Visit Herod, The. Caelius Sedulius, *tr. fr. Latin by* H. T. Henry. *Fr.* Carmen Paschale. CAW
Magian Wine. Abu Jaafar, *tr. fr. Arabic by* A. J. Arberry. MooP
Magic. John Farrar. LEAP; VOD (1931 ed.)
Magic. Hamlin Garland. NP; PoeMoYo
Magic, *sel.* Lionel Johnson.
"They wrong with ignorance." POTT
Magic. José Moreno Villa, *tr. fr. Spanish by* Eleanor L. Turnbull. CoSP

Magic. Po Chü-i, *tr. fr. Chinese by* Arthur Waley. TrCh
Magic. Shakespeare, *after the Latin of* Ovid. *Fr.* The Tempest, V, i. AWP; JAWP; WBP
(Shakespeare's Fairies; Some of Them.) CBPC
Magic Car Moved On, The. Shelley. *Fr.* Queen Mab, I. GN
Magic Landscape, A. Afanasi Afanasievich Fet, *tr. fr. Russian by* Babette Deutsch. TrRV
Magic Lariat. Glenn Ward Dresbach. BrR
Magic Mirror, The. Henry Mills Alden. HBV
Magic Month, The. Gelett Burgess. SDH
Magic of Melody, The. Pindar. *See* O Golden Lyre!
Magic Piper, The. E. L. Marsh. BoTP; SiSoSe
Magic Refrains. Apostolos Melachrinos, *tr. fr. Modern Greek by* Rae Dalven. *Fr.* Variations. MoGP
Magic Vine, The. *Unknown.* GFA
Magic Waves. Gertrude Van Winkle. GFA
Magic Whistle, The. Margaret Rose. BoTP
Magic Window, The. Eleanor Hammond. MPB
Magical Nature. Robert Browning. BPN; PoVP; VLEP
Magico prodigioso, El, *sel.* Pedro Calderón de la Barca, *tr. fr. Spanish by* Shelley.
Demon Speaks, The. CAW
Magna Charta. *Unknown.* OHFP; WBLP
Magna Est Veritas. Coventry Patmore. *Fr.* The Unknown Eros. AnFE; BMEP; CaAE; CAW; CoBE; GoBC; GTML; MaRV; OBEV (new ed.); OBVV; OQP; PC; PG (1945 ed.); POTT; PoVP; QP-2; ViP; VLEP
(Truth.) BLV; TrGrPo
(Truth Is Great, The.) OnPM
Magnanimous, The. Ellen de Young Kay. NePoEA
Magnet, The. Thomas Stanley. MePo
Magnet, The. Ruth Stone. NePA
Magnet hung in a hardware shop, A. The Fable of the Magnet and the Churn. W. S. Gilbert. *Fr.* Patience. FaPON; MPB
Magnetic Lady to Her Patient, The. Shelley. EmBrPo
Magnetic Mountain, The, *sels.* C. Day Lewis.
"God is a proposition," XXI. QS
"I have always acted for the best," XI. QS
Nearing Again the Legendary Isle, VI. CoBMV; FaBoTw; GTBS-W; LiTB; MBP; MoAB; MoBrPo; MoPW; NeMA; PeBoSo; ReMP
"Tempt me no more; for I," XXIV. CaAE; EnLit; NAMP
(Tempt Me No More.) AnFE; MBP; MoAB; MoBrPo; OAEP (2d ed.); OBMV; PoFr; POTE
"Though winter's barricade delays," XXVIII. ChMo; EnLit
Magnets. Laurence Binyon. HBMV
Magnificat, The. St. Luke, I: 46-55, Bible, *N.T.* ISi (*Douay vers.*); MaRV; WGRP; WHL
(Hymn of the Blessed Virgin.) CAW
Magnificence, *sel.* John Skelton.
"So merrily singeth the nightingale!" *fr.* IV, xxix. PoFr
Magnificent strong sun! in these last days. September Sun; 1947. David Gascoyne. AtBAP; FaBoMo; POTE (1959 ed.)
Magnificent the beast! Look in the eyes. A New Idol. Laurence Binyon. PoFr
Magnificently, here, you stand, alone. To Craske's Statue at Gloucester. Russell Mayo Spear. CAG
Magnified Be the Living God. Daniel ben Judah. *See* Living God, The.
Magnolia Cemetery. Henry Timrod. *See* At Magnolia Cemetery.
Magnolia Tree. Sacheverell Sitwell. NV
Magnolia Tree, The. Hubert Witheford. AnNZ
Magpie, The. Tristan Klingsor, *tr. fr. French by* Alan Conder. TrFP
Magpie has a nest. The Nest of the Magpie. *Unknown.* WhP
Magpie, magpie, flutter and flee. *Unknown.* OxNR
Magpies, The. Denis Glover. AnNZ
Magpies and Swans. Sir Philip Sidney. *See* Astrophel and Stella: Sonnets, LIV.
Magpies in Picardy. T. P. Cameron Wilson. BLA; HBV; OtMeF
Magpie's Nest. Charles *and* Mary Lamb. OTPC (1923 ed.); PRWS
Magpie's Song, The. Frank S. Williamson. BoAu
Magruder's Lullaby. *Unknown.* BOL
Mag's Song. *Unknown.* *See* Orphan Girl, The.
Magus would needs, forsooth, this other day. Henry Parrot. SiCE; TuPP
Mah Mammy Stoled a Cow, *with music.* *Unknown.* SoAF
Mah mule is white, mah chahcoal is black. Charcoal Man. *Unknown.* TrAS
Mahabharata, *sel.* *Unknown, tr. fr. Sanskrit by* Sir Edwin Arnold.
Great Journey, The. BoFr
Mahmoud. Leigh Hunt. CG; LPS-2
Mahmud and Ayaz; a Paraphrase on Sa'di. Sir Edwin Arnold. *Fr.* With Sa'di in the Garden. VA
Mahogany Tree, The. Thackeray. COAH; HBV; LPS-1; VA
Mahoney. Seán Jennett. NeIP
Mahony's Mountain. Douglas Stewart. SeCePo
Maia was one, all gold, fire, and sapphire. A Legend of Viable Women. Richard Eberhart. MiAP; MoVE
Maid, The. Katherine Brégy. CAW; GoBC
Maid, The. Theodore Goodridge Roberts. CBPC; CPG; HBV; MoShBr
Maid and the Palmer, The. *Unknown.* ACP; BaBo; ESPB (*A and B vers.*); OBS
Maid, The (and thereby hangs a tale). Sir John Suckling. *Fr.* A Ballad upon a Wedding. LO; LoPS
Maid Antibia, The. Anyte, *tr. fr. Greek by* William Hay. OnPM
Maid Freed from the Gallows, The. *Unknown.* AnFE; AS (*American vers., with music*); BaBo (*A and C vers.*); ESPB (*A and I vers.*); InPo; TOP; ViBoFo (*A, B, C, and D vers.*)
(Gallows Tree, The, *D vers.*) BaBo
(Golden Ball, The, *B vers.*) BaBo
(Hangman's Song, The, *abr., sl. diff.*) ABS
(Hangman's Tree, The.) ExPo
(Hangsaman, *with music.*) TrAS
(Maid Saved from the Gallows, The.) AWP
Maid I Left Behind, The, *with music.* *Unknown.* ShS
Maid I Love, The. Walter Savage Landor. EPN
(Kiss, The.) OBVV
(Lyrics and Epigrams, X.) ERP
Maid in the Mill, The, *sel.* John Fletcher *and* William Rowley.
Come Follow Me, You Country Lasses. SeCL
Maid in the Rice-Fields, The. Viola Meynell. MBP; MoBrPo (1942 ed.)
Maid is out in the clear April light, The. Ellen Hanging Clothes. Lizette Woodworth Reese. PoeMoYo; VOD
Maid Marian, *sels.* Thomas Love Peacock.
For the Slender Beech and the Sapling Oak. EnRP; ERP
(Song: "For the tender beech and the sapling oak.") ADAH; OHIP; PRWS
(Greenwood Tree, The.) GTSE
(Oak and the Beech, The.) OTPC
Over, Over. EV-4
Robin Hood and the Grey Friars. EV-4
Song: "It was a friar of orders free." ViBoPo
Though I Be Now a Gray, Gray Friar. ERP
Maid Marjory sits at the castle gate. Medieval Norman Songs, XVII. *Unknown, tr. fr. French by* John Addington Symonds. AWP; JAWP; WBP
Maid Mary came to Bethlehem town. The First Christmas. Norah M. Holland. ChrBoLe
Maid Me Loved, A. Patrick Hannay. ALV; SeCL
Maid my true heart loves would not my true love be, The. Round Robin. Bhartrihari. LiTW
Maid of Amsterdam. *Unknown.* AmSS, *with music;* SG
Maid of Arc, The. Gordon Bottomley. GoTL (1949 ed.)
Maid of Athens, Ere We Part. Byron. BEL; BPN; EM-2; EmBrPo; EnLi-2 (1949 ed.); EnLit; EnRP; ERP; FaFP; HBV; LPS-1; MCCG; NeHB; OAEP; OuHeWo; TCEP; TreF
Maid of Christ doth plead with [*or* entreateth] me, A. A Luve Ron [*or* A Love-Song]. Thomas of Hales. EPP; MeEV
Maid of Cloghroe, The. *Unknown.* TIP
Maid of fifteen, in childlike beauty dight. Pierre de Ronsard. *Fr.* Amours de Cassandre. PrPoCR
Maid of Honour, The, *sel.* Philip Massinger.
"Look on this maid of honour, now," *fr.* V, ii. ACP (1952 ed.); GoBC
Maid of Kent, A. *Unknown.* OxBoLi
(There Was a Maid.) ElL
("There was a mayde cam out of Kent.") LO
Maid of Neidpath, The. Thomas Campbell. GoTS; GTBS; GTBS-D; GTBS-W; GTSE
("Earl March look'd on his dying child.") GTSL
(Song.) EBSV; HBV
Maid of Neidpath, The. Sir Walter Scott. BeLS; BPN; EBSV; EmBrPo; EnRP; ERP; GTBS; GTBS-D; GTBS-W; GTSE; GTSL
Maid of Orleans, The (*play*), *sel.* Schiller, *tr. fr. German by* John Eliot Drinkwater-Bethune.
"Farewell, ye mountains, and ye much-loved paths," *fr.* Prologue, sc. iv. PoFr
Maid of Orleans, The (*poem*). Schiller, *tr. fr. German by* James Clarence Mangan. AWP; JAWP; WBP
Maid of the Meerschaum, The. Kipling. PA
Maid of the Sweet Brown Knowe, The. *Unknown.* AnIV; OnYI
Maid of Tottenham, The. *Unknown.* CoMu
Maid of Wu. Li Po, *tr. fr. Chinese by* Shigeyoshi Obata. ChLP
Maid, Out of Thine Unquarried Mountain-Land. *Unknown, tr. fr. Greek by* G. R. Woodward. ISi
Maid peerless hath born God's Son, A. She May Be Called a Sovereign Lady. *Unknown.* AnEC

Maid Saved from the Gallows, The. *Unknown. See* Maid Freed from the Gallows, The.
Maid-Servant at the Inn, The. Dorothy Parker. QS; StJW
Maid she [*or* shee] went to the well to wash[e], The. The Maid and the Palmer. *Unknown.* ACP; BaBo; ESPB; OBS
Maid That Sold Her Barley, The. *Unknown.* OnYI
Maid Unwed, The. Sappho, *tr. fr. Greek by* F. L. Lucas. GrPE
Maid who binds her warrior's sash, The. The Brave at Home. Thomas Buchanan Read. *Fr.* The Wagoner of the Alleghanies. BLP; HBV; LBAP; LPS-2; MDAH; PAP
Maid who mindful of her playful time, A. The Sibyl. Thomas Gordon Hake. VA
Maid who, on the first of May, The. Old Superstitions. *Unknown.* HBVY; TreF
Maiden, The. Peter Hille, *tr. fr. German by* Jethro Bithell. AWP
Maiden, A. Kageki, *tr. fr. Japanese by* Asataro Miyamori. OnPM
Maiden, and mistress of the months and stars. Atalanta in Calydon. Swinburne. PoEL-5; PoVP; ViPo
"Maiden and Mother, daughter of thine own son." Vision of the Divine Mystery [*or* St. Bernard's Prayer to the Virgin Mary]. Dante. *Fr.* Divina Commedia: Paradiso, XXXIII. LiTW; MeRV
Maiden and the Lily, The. John Fraser. HBV
Maiden and the lither lad, The. The Last Resort. *Unknown.* BoDaBa
Maiden at the Thing, The. *Unknown, tr. fr. Danish by* E. M. Smith-Dampier. BoDaBa
Maiden caught me in the wild, The. The Crystal Cabinet. Blake. CH; FaBoCh; LoGBV; OBRV; PoEL-4
Maiden City, The. Charlotte Elizabeth Tonna. HBV
Maiden Eyes. Gerald Griffin. HBV
"Maiden fair I dare not wed, A." Thomas Deloney. *Fr.* Jack of Newbury. ReIE
Maiden from the Bosphorus, A. How the Helpmate of Blue-Beard Made Free with a Door. Guy Wetmore Carryl. InMe
Maiden Gown, The. William Cavendish, Duke of Newcastle. SeCL
Maiden Hind, The. *Unknown, tr. fr. Danish by* E. M. Smith-Dampier. BoDaBa; LiTW; LyMA
Maiden in Bird's Plumage, The. *Unknown, tr. fr. Danish by* E. M. Smith-Dampier. BoDaBa
Maiden in the Moor [*or* Mor]. *Unknown.* AtBAP; LoBV; PoEL-1
Maiden Lies in Her Chamber, A. Heine, *tr. fr. German by* Louis Untermeyer. AWP; JAWP; WBP
Maiden Makeles, The. *Unknown. See* I Sing of a Maiden.
Maiden Meditation. Mikhail Isakovsky, *tr. fr. Russian by* Jack Lindsay. RuPo
Maiden Meed, The. William Langland. *Fr.* The Vision of Piers Plowman, Passus 2. CoBE
Maiden most beautiful, mother most bountiful, lady of lands. The Song of the Standard. Swinburne. PoVP; VLEP
Maiden of late, A. The Maid's Longing. Thomas d'Urfey. *Fr.* Pills to Purge Melancholy. SiTL
Maiden of Passamaquoddy, The. James De Mille. WhC
Maiden of the laughing eyes. Song of Life. Florence Earle Coates. BAP; POT; PoTo
Maiden once, of certain age, A. Any One Will Do. *Unknown.* BOHV
Maiden Queen, The. Dryden. *See* Secret Love; or, The Maiden Queen.
Maiden Ring-adorned, A. Cynewulf, *tr. fr. Anglo-Saxon by* Mother Margaret Williams. *Fr.* Christ. ISi; PoLi, *shorter sel.*
Maiden sat in an apple tree, A. The Apple Tree. Brian Vrepont. BoAu
Maiden that bore the heaven's King. Prison Songs, V. *Unknown.* TMEV
Maiden, thy cheeks with tears are wet. April. Robert Loveman. AA
Maiden who gazes dreamily from her window, The. The Willow Leaf. Tchan Tiou-lin. ChLP
Maiden with a Milking-Pail, A. Jean Ingelow. LPS-1
Maiden! with the meek, brown eyes. Maidenhood. Longfellow. HBV; IAP; LPS-1; MOAP; TCAP
Maiden wooes the handsome knight, The. Sir Magnus and the Elf-Maid. *Unknown.* BaBo
Maidenhead Well Lost, A, *sel.* Thomas Heywood.
Hence with Passion, Sighs and Tears. SeCL
Maidenhood. Longfellow. HBV; IAP; LPS-1; MOAP; TCAP
Maidenhood! Maidenhood! where hast thou gone from me. Farewell to Maidenhood. Sappho, *tr. by* H. De Vere Stacpoole. GrR
Maidenhood, O Maidenhood. Wedding Songs. Sappho, *tr. by* C. M. Bowra. GrL; OxBG
Maidens, The. *Unknown, tr. fr. Russian by* W. R. S. Ralston. OnPM
Maidens at Rest. Chaeremon, *tr. fr. Greek by* George Allen. GrL; OxBG
Maidens Came, The. *Unknown.* AtBAP; EG; KN; LO; PoEL-1, *longer vers.*; ViBoPo
(Bailey Beareth the Bell Away, The.) ExPo; LiTB; SeCePo, *longer vers.*; SeCeV
(Bridal Morning.) OBEV (new ed.)
(Lily and the Rose, The.) OxBoLi
(Song: "Maidens [*or* Maydens] came, The.") BrBE; ThWaDe
(Young Girl's Song.) TrGrPo
Maiden's Choice, The. Samuel Bishop. PIAE
(Epigram: "Fool and knave with different views, A.") ALV
(Touch-Stone, The.) HBV
Maiden's Complaint, The. Brian Merriman, *tr. fr. Modern Irish by* Arland Ussher. *Fr.* The Midnight Court. LiTW
Maiden's Complaint in Spring-Time, A. *Unknown, tr. fr. Latin by* Helen Waddell. LiA
Maidens, gather not the yew. Prologue to a Saga. Dorothy Parker. InMe
Maidens have come forth, The. The Maidens. *Unknown.* OnPM
Maiden's Ideal of a Husband, A. Henry Carey. *Fr.* The Contrivances. HBV; LPS-1
Maidens, in Thebes Athene loved once a nymph past measure. The Bathing of Pallas. Callimachus. GrPE
Maidens, kilt your skirts and go. Celia's Home-coming. Agnes Mary Frances Robinson. OBEV (new ed.); OBVV; VA
Maiden's Morning-Dream, The. *Unknown, tr. fr. Danish by* E. M. Smith-Dampier. BoDaBa
Maidens, O you pretty things. Girls' Song. Pushkin. *Fr.* Eugene Onegin. BoR
Maidens rise & come away. *Unknown.* SeCSL
Maidens shall weep at merry morn. The Summer Malison. Gerard Manley Hopkins. PoEL-5
Maidens' Song. *Unknown, tr. fr. Greek by* T. F. Higham. OxBG
Maiden's song in the choir was telling, A. Aleksandr Blok. BoR
Maidens who this bursting [*or* burning] May. A Young Man's Song. William Bell. FaBoTw; NePoEA
Maidens, why spare ye? To Cupid. Michael Drayton. ElL
Maidens young and virgins tender. Invocation. Horace. *Fr.* Odes. AWP; JAWP; WBP
Maids and Widows. *Unknown. See* If Ever I Marry.
Maids Are Simple. Thomas Campion. TuPP
Maid's Complaint, The. Agathias Scholasticus, *tr. fr. Greek by* F. L. Lucas. GrPE
Maid's Complaint for Want of a Dil Doul, The. *Unknown.* CoMu
Maids Conjuring Book, The. *Unknown.* CoMu
Maids from the south through Myrkwood flew. The Lay of Wayland. *Unknown.* *Fr.* The Elder Edda. PaOS
Maid's Lament, The. Walter Savage Landor. *Fr.* The Citation and Examination of William Shakespeare. BPN; EV-4; GTBS; HBV; LPS-1; OBEV; OBRV; OBVV; ReTS; VA
Maid's Last Prayer, The, *sel.* Thomas Southerne.
Though You Make No Return. SeCL
(Song, A, Set by H. Purcell, and Sung by Mrs. Hodgson.) SeEP
Maid's Longing, The. Thomas d'Urfey. *Fr.* Pills to Purge Melancholy. SiTL
Maid's Metamorphosis, The. *Unknown. See* Mayde's Metamorphosis, The.
Maids must be wives and mothers to fulfil. Woman's Heart. Frances Anne Kemble. MotAn
Maids of Elfin-Mere, The. William Allingham. GTIV; IrPN; OnYI
"Maids of Honour, The." *Unknown.* CoMu
Maids of Simcoe, The, *with music.* *Unknown.* ShS
Maid's Remonstrance, The. Thomas Campbell. LPS-1
Maid's Revenge, The, *sel.* James Shirley.
"Take heed; do not profane." BoFr
Maid's Thought, The. Robinson Jeffers. BAV
Maids to bed and cover coal. The [*or* A] Bellman's Song. *Unknown.* CenL; ElL; ElSeCe; SeCePo
Maid's Tragedy, The, *sels.* Beaumont *and* Fletcher.
"All joys upon him! for he is my friend." *fr.* I, i. BoFr
Aspatia's Song, *fr.* II, i. AWP; BCEP; BLV; CBOV; EV-2; HBV; InPo; JAWP; LEAP; OBEV; OBS; PIAE; TOP; TrGrPo; WBP
(Dirge: "Lay a garland on my hearse.") EPP
(I Died True.) CH
(Lay a Garland on My Hearse.) AtBAP; CenL; ElL; ElSeCe; InP; OAEP; SiCE; TuPP; ViBoPo; WHA
Bridal Song: "Cynthia, to thy power," *fr.* I. ii. OBEV
("Cynthia, to thy power and thee.") TuPP
Bridal Song: "Hold back thy hours, dark Night," *fr.* I, ii. ElL; LoPS; TrGrPo
("Hold back thy hours, dark Night, till we have done.") EG; ElSeCe; RiBV; ViBoPo

"I could never have the power," *fr.* II, i. TuPP
Maid's Tragedy, The. Sylvia Townsend Warner. AV
Mail has come from home, The. To My Friend, Grown Famous. Eunice Tietjens. HBMV
Mailed to G. B. Gene Derwood. NePA
Mailligh Mo Stor. George Ogle. IrPN
Maimed, beggared, grey; seeking an alms; with nod. Bellerophon. George Meredith. EPP
Maimed [*or* Maim'd] Debauchee, The. Earl of Rochester. PoEL-3; UnPo (3d ed.)
Main artery of fighting. War. Guillaume Apollinaire. WaaP
Main-Deep, The. James Stephens. MBP; MoBrPo; OBMV; ShBV-1; UnPo
Main Range. James Picot. BoAu
Main-Sheet Song, The. Thomas Fleming Day. EtS
Main Street. Joyce Kilmer. JKCP
Main Truck, The; or, A Leap for Life. George Pope Morris. PTA-1
Maine comes marching on as one. States Crowning Washington, The. Kate Bowles Sherwood. WOAH
Maine Trail, A. Gertrude Huntington McGiffert. HBV; NLK
Maine Woods in Winter. Grace Hazard Conkling. CP
Mainsail Haul, *2 vers., with music. Unknown.* ShS
Mainspring, The. Martha Eugenie Perry. CaP
Maire My Girl. John Keegan Casey. AnIV; IrPN; JKCP (1926 ed.); OnYI; TIP
Mairgread ni Chealleadh. Edward Walsh. IrPN
Mais où est le preux Charlemagne? *Unknown, tr. fr. Greek by* T. F. Higham. OxBG
Maisrie. Jessie Mackay. AnNZ
Maister and the Man, The. John Heywood. ReIE
Maize, The. William W. Fosdick. LPS-2
"Majestic Bird! so proud and fierce." Eagle on a Tombstone. Antipater of Sidon. OnPM
Majestic Intellect. Wordsworth. *See* Conclusion: "It was a close, warm, breezeless summer night."
Majestic Sweetness. Samuel Stennett. BePJ
Majestuous and sapphirine, it rears. The Chest of Perote. Joaquin Arcadio Pagaza. AnMP
Majesty and Mercy of God, The. Sir Robert Grant. OHIP; WGRP
("O worship the King, all glorious above.") OlF
Majesty of God, The. Thomas Sternhold. WGRP
Major-General, The. W. S. Gilbert. *See* Modern Major-General, The.
Major-General Scott. On to Richmond. John R. Thompson. PAH
Major-General's Song. W. S. Gilbert. *See* Modern Major-General, The.
Majuba Hill. Roy Macnab. BoSA
Make a joyful noise unto the Lord, all ye lands. Thanksgiving [*or* Psalm of Praise *or* Be Thankful unto Him]. Psalm C, Bible, *O.T.* BoChLi (1950 ed.); FaPON; MPB; OHIP; OnPM; PG (1955 ed.); SiSoSe; StVeCh; SUS; TiPo (1952 ed.); UnS
Make Believe. Alice Cary. HBV; LPS-1; PR; PreP
Make Friends. *At. to* Ali Ben Abu Taleb, *tr. by* Emerson. *See* Friends and Enemies.
Make haste, O God, to deliver me. Psalm LXX, Bible, *O.T.* OnPM
Make Haste, Sweet Love. Spenser. *See* Amoretti, LXX.
"Make it sweet and delicate to eat." The Eaten Heart. *Unknown. Fr.* The Knight of Curtesy. TrGrPo
Make it where the winds may sweep. The Old Man's Grave. L. M. Montgomery. CPG
Make me a bowl, a mighty bowl. The Cup. John Oldham. AWP
Make me a captive, Lord. Christ's Bondservant [*or* Christian Freedom]. George Matheson. MaRV; TrPWD
Make Me a Garment, *with music. Unknown.* OuSiCo
Make me a handle as straight as the mast of a ship. To the Blacksmith with a Spade. *Unknown.* KiLC
Make me content, O Lord, with daily bread. Prayer for Contentment. Edwin McNeill Poteat. NoCaPo (rev. ed.); TrPWD
Make me, dear Lord, polite and kind. A [Little] Child's Prayer. John Banister Tabb. DDA; FaPON; GaP; OBAV; TreF; YaD
Make me feverish, sleepless, and breathless. Prayer. "Anna Akhmatova." OnPM; TrRV
Make Me Kind. Duncan McNeil. PraP
Make Me Merry Both More and Less. *Unknown.* RiBV
Make me no vows of constancy, dear friend. Until Death. Elizabeth Akers Allen. HBV
Make me, O Lord, Thy spinning-wheel complete. Housewifery [*or* Huswifery]. Edward Taylor. AmP; AmPP; AnNE; GTBS-W; LiTA; NePA; OnAP; OxBA
Make me over, mother April. Spring Song. Bliss Carman. BAP; CPG; HBV; HBVY; LEAP; NLK; OCL; VA; YT
Make me thy lyre, even as the forest is. Shelley. *Fr.* Ode to the West Wind. MaRV
Make me Thy warden. Wild Larkspur. Annie Charlotte Dalton. CPG
Make me too brave to lie or be unkind. A Prayer for Every Day. Mary Carolyn Davies. BLPA; FaBoBe; NeHB; PoToHe
Make merry, heart within me. Others shall come to birth. Dust to Dust. Theognis. GrPE
Make my mortal dreams come true. Whittier. *Fr.* Andrew Rykman's Prayer. TrPWD
Make new friends, but keep the old. Friends Old and New [*or* New Friends and Old Friends]. Joseph Parry. BLPA; NeHB; OQP; PoToHe; QP-2
Make No Vows. Grace Fallow Norton. NP
Make of my heart an upper room, I pray. A River of Grace. Molly Anderson Haley. ChIP
Make room, all ye kingdoms, in history renown'd. American Independence. Francis Hopkinson. PAH
Make room for the World-man! The World-Man. Henry Victor Morgan. OQP; QP-1
Make room on our banner bright. Song of Texas. William Henry Cuyler Hosmer. PAH
Make the great God thy fort, and dwell. Psalm XCI. *Paraphrased by* Thomas Carew. MeRV
Make Them Forget. Siegfried Sassoon. *See* At the Cenotaph.
Make this thing plain to us, O Lord! Clean Hands. Austin Dobson. AOAH; TrPWD
Make three-fourths of a cross, and a circle complete. Riddles. *Unknown.* HBV; HBVY; OxNR
Make Thy Way Mine. "George Klingle." PraP
Make thyself known, Sibyl, or let despair. Mona Lisa [*or* Leonardo's "Monna Lisa"]. Edward Dowden. OnYI; VA
Make us Thy mountaineers. The Last Defile. Amy Carmichael. MaRV
Make Way! Florence Crocker Comfort. PGD
Make Way for Liberty. James Montgomery. *See* Arnold von Winkelried.
Make way, make way. The Stream's Song. Lascelles Abercrombie. OBMV; POTE
Make way, my lords! for Death now once again. Charles II of Spain to Approaching Death. Eugene Lee-Hamilton. VA
Make We Joy in This Feast. *Unknown.* AnEC
Make We Merry, Both More and Less. *Unknown.* AnEC; EPP, *Middle English vers.;* SDH
Make We Merry in Hall and Bower. *Unknown.* AnEC
Make We Merry in This Feast. *Unknown.* AnEC
Make We Merry This New Year. *Unknown.* AnEC
Make We Mirth for Christës Birth. *Unknown.* AnEC
(Twelve Days of Christmas, The.) TMEV
Make your cotton and make your corn. Farmers of the South. *Unknown.* OuSiCo
Maker Alone Knows, The. *Unknown.* PoLi
Maker-of-Sevens in the scheme of things. The Wife-Woman. Anna Spencer. BANP
Maker of Songs. Hazel Hall. HBMV
Maker of Toy Boats, The. Frank Oliver Call. CPG
Makers of fables and of verses tell. Legend. Theodore Morrison. MuM
Making a Garden. William Mason. *Fr.* The English Garden, I. BeR
Making a Man. Carolyn R. Freeman. FAOV
Making a Man. Nixon Waterman. BLPA
Making Land. Thomas Fleming Day. EtS
Making Life Worth While. "George Eliot." MaRV; OQP; QP-2
Making mountain war, here river wandered. Waitaki Dam. Denis Glover. AnNZ
Making Mushrooms. Esther Antin. RIS
Making of Birds, The. Katharine Tynan. BMEP, *abr.;* DD; GTIV; HBMV; JKCP; OxBI
Making of Man, The. John White Chadwick. AA; LBAP
Making of Man, The. Priscilla Leonard. *See* This Is the Making of Man.
Making of Man, The. Swinburne. *See* Before the Beginning of Years.
Making of Man, The. Tennyson. EPN
Making of Master Messerin, The. Rustico di Filippo. *See* Sonnet: Of the Making of Master Messerin.
Making of the Soul of Man, The. Upton Sinclair. OQP; QP-2
Making of Viola, The. Francis Thompson. POTT; PoVP
Making Port. J. T. McKay. EtS
Making Tens. M. M. Hutchinson. BoTP
Making toast at the fireside. Misfortunes Never Come Singly [*or* Nurse]. Harry Graham. FaFP; MaC; NA; SiTL
Malady of Love Is Nerves, The. Petronius Arbiter, *tr. fr. Latin by* Howard Mumford Jones. AWP
Malbecco and Hellenore. Spenser. *Fr.* The Faerie Queene, III, 9 *and* 10. MaPo
Malbrouck. Francis Sylvester Mahony, *after the French.* BOHV
Malbrouck. *Unknown, tr. fr. French-Canadian folk song by* William McLennan. BoCaPo

Malchus. Ida Norton Munson. ChIP
Malchus' Ear. Richard Crashaw. StJW
Malcolm Bryler. *Unknown.* SiTL
Malcolm's Katie, *sels.* Isabella Valancy Crawford.
"In this shrill moon the scouts of winter ran." PeCV
"Mighty morn strode laughing up the land, The." CPG
"South Wind laid his moccasins aside, The." BoCaPo
Malcontent, The, *sel.* John Marston.
"I cannot sleepe, my eyes ill neighbouring lids." PoEL-2
Malcontents, The. Dryden. *See* Zimri.
Maldive Shark, The. Herman Melville. AmP; AmPP (4th ed.); APW; LoGBV; NePA; OxBA; PoEL-5; PoFS
♂ and ♀. W. Craddle. WhC
Male and Female Created He Them. Aldous Huxley. ALV
Male Inconsistency. Aristophanes, *tr. fr. Greek by* Benjamin Bickley Rogers. *Fr.* The Thesmophoriazusae. GrR
(Chorus of Women.) BOHV
("They're always abusing the women.") GrPo
Malediction upon Myself. Elinor Wylie. AnAmPo; LA
Malefic Return, The. Ramón López Velarde, *tr. fr. Spanish by* Samuel Beckett. AnMP
Malemute Dog, A. Pat O'Cotter. BLPA
Malest Cornifici Tuo Catullo. Allen Ginsberg. NeAP
Malevolent or droll they brood. Gargoyles at Oxford. Margaret Willy. DiM
Malibran. Alfred de Musset, *tr. fr. French by* Marie Agathe Clarke. LiA
Malice. Robert Southey. *Fr.* The Curse of Kehama. BCEP
("I charm thy life.") LoBV; OBRV
Malice and love, in their ways opposite. Caelica, XCV. Fulke Greville. SiCE
Mall Feball deserves reward. *Unknown. Fr.* Eulogistic Snatches. SiB
Mallard. Rex Warner. PoF
Mallards, The. *Unknown, tr. fr. Chinese.* WhP
Mallee Fire, The. Charles Henry Souter. BoAu
Maltese Dog, A. Tymnes, *tr. fr. Greek by* Edmund Blunden. FaBoCh; LoGBV; OxBG; TiPo (1959 ed.)
Maltworm's Madrigal, The. Austin Dobson. HBV
Malum Opus. James Appleton Morgan. NA
Malvern Hill. Herman Melville. AmPP; MC; PAH
Malzah and the Angel Zelehtha. Charles Heavysege. *Fr.* Saul. VA
Malzah Speaks. Charles Heavysege. *Fr.* Saul. BoCaPo
Malzah's Song. Charles Heavysege. *Fr.* Saul. BoCaPo
Mama Have You Heard the News? *Unknown. See* Casey Jones.
Mama, they're gonna give me the keys to this jail. Les Clefs de la Prison. *Unknown.* OuSiCo
Mama's Advice. Kurt M. Stein. InMe
Mamble. John Drinkwater. AlDL; LBBV; PoeT
Mambo dans le Hounfort, La. Charles F. Pressoir, *tr. fr. French by* Edna Worthley Underwood. PoNe
Mamma and Nurse went out one day. The Dreadful Story of Pauline and the Matches. Heinrich Hoffmann. CIV
Mamma and Papa/ Wo-ho Lawdy. Godamighty Drag. *Unknown.* OuSiCo
Mamma, as I went out to-day. Little Maia. Zakarias Topelius. AnSL
Mamma gave us a single peach. The Peach. Charles *and* Mary Lamb. OTPC (1923 ed.)
Mamma, I have been in the lane to see. The Fishes. Mrs. Motherly. SAS
Mamma, let's go and see the lambs. A Visit to the Lambs. *Unknown.* OTPC (1923 ed.); SAS
Mamma, Mamma, *with music. Unknown.* OuSiCo
Mamma, Mamma, make me a garment. Make Me a Garment. *Unknown.* OuSiCo
Mamma's Gone to the Mail Boat, *with music. Unknown.* OuSiCo
Mammon. Milton. *Fr.* Paradise Lost, I. MaRV
Mammon emovèd was with inward wrath. Spenser. *Fr.* The Faerie Queene, II. ViBoPo
Mammon Marriage. George Macdonald. OBVV
Mammon Monster, The. Charles Erskine Scott Wood. BAP
Mammon, the least erected spirit that fell. Mammon. Milton. *Fr.* Paradise Lost, I. MaRV
Mammon's House. Spenser. *Fr.* The Faerie Queene, II, 7. MyFE
Mammy Hums. Carl Sandburg. PoNe
Mammy rocks the baby. Lill' Angels. Beatrice Ravenel. LS
Mammy's Li'l Boy. Harry Stillman Edwards. BOL
Mammy's li'l pickaninny coon. Li'l Pickaninny Coon. "P. H." CAG
Mammy's Lullaby. Strickland W. Gillilan. BOL
Mamua, when our laughter ends. Tiare Tahiti. Rupert Brooke. POTT; SeCeV
Man. Elizabeth Barrett Browning. *Fr.* Aurora Leigh, I. BCEP
Man. Harold Lewis Cook. NP
Man, The. Stephen Crane. *See* Man Said to the Universe, A.
Man. Sir John Davies. *Fr.* Nosce Teipsum. BCEP, *2 sts.*; EIL; EM-1; OBEV, *2 sts.*
(I Know Myself a Man.) ChTr
(Vanity of Human Learning, The, *2 sts.*) MaRV
(Which Is a Proud, and Yet a Wretched Thing.) WHA
Man. Samuel Greenberg. CrMA
Man, A. Arthur Guiterman. LPS-1
Man. George Herbert. BLV; BoLiVe; GrCo-2, *abr.*; InPo; MaPo; MePo; OAEP; PoEL-2; SeCV-1; TrGrPo; TrPWD, *abr.*
Man. Friedrich Hölderlin, *tr. fr. German by* R. F. C. Hull. AnGP
Man. Walter Savage Landor. *See* On Man.
Man. Pope. *See* Human Folly *and* Know Then Thyself *and* Worth Makes the Man.
Man, A. Clinton Scollard. OHIP; PEDC
Man ("Man, proud man"). Shakespeare. *See* But Man, Proud Man.
Man, A ("This was the noblest Roman of them all"). Shakespeare. *See* Portrait of Brutus.
Man ("What a piece of work is a man!"). Shakespeare. *Fr.* Hamlet, II, ii. TreF
("What a piece of work is man!") InP
Man. Marvin Stevens. MaRV
Man. Swinburne. *See* Before the Beginning of Years.
Man, A ("Often, when I would sit, a dreamy, straight-haired child"). Jean Starr Untermeyer. FAOV
Man, A ("I listened to them talking"). Louis Untermeyer. FAOV
Man. Henry Vaughan. AnEnPo; CoEV; EPS; EV-2; FaBoEn; HBV; MeLP; MePo; OBEV (new ed.); OBS; PoEL-2; PoFS; SeCV-1; TwCrTr
Man, The. Helen Hay Whitney. AV
Man. Humbert Wolfe. *Fr.* Requiem. MBP; MoBrPo
Man. Edward Young. *Fr.* Night Thoughts. BCEP; LPS-3; MaRV
"Man, a man, a kingdom for a man, A!" Satire VII. John Marston. *Fr.* The Scourge of Villainy. ReIE
Man, A! a man! There is a man loose in Canada. The Stone. Peter McArthur. PCN
Man a Microcosm. John Collop. PoP
Man adrift on a slim spar, A. Stephen Crane. Four Poems, IV. CrMA
Man, afraid to be alive. The Cage. Martin Armstrong. BLV; PoFr; POTE
Man against the Sky, The. E. A. Robinson. AmPP; APA; ChMo; CMP; CoAnAm; CoBMV; CoV; IAP; LiTA; MAP; MOAP; MoVE; NAMP; OxBA; TwAmPo
Man am I grown, a man's work must I do. Follow the Christ. Tennyson. *Fr.* Idylls of the King: Gareth and Lynette. ChIP; MaRV
Man and Beast. Francis Meynell. MBP; MoBrPo (1942 ed.)
Man and Bird and God. *Unknown, tr. fr. Old Irish by* Owen Masters. LyMA
Man and boy—said the old sailor. Sea Story. Vincent Starrett. DaM
Man and His Books. Eiluned Lewis. DiM
Man and His Makers. Muriel Stuart. NP
Man and his man chanced late to be, A. The Maister and the Man. John Heywood. ReIE
Man and Nature ("Lake Leman woos me"). Byron. *See* Lake Leman ("Lake Leman woos me").
Man and Nature ("Oh, that the desert"). Byron. *See* Ocean, The.
Man and Nature. Robert Kelley Weeks. AA
Man and the Ascidian. Andrew Lang. HBV
Man and the Echo, The. W. B. Yeats. TwHP
Man and the Flea, The. La Fontaine, *tr. fr. French by* Elizur Wright. OnPM
Man and the Machine, The. E. J. Pratt. WoL
Man and the pitiless waters. Death-Grapple. Laura Bell Everett. OQP; QP-2
Man and the Sea. Tu Hsün Hao, *tr. fr. Chinese by* Henry H. Hart. OnPM
Man and the Universe. Matthew Prior. *Fr.* Solomon on the Vanity of the World. BeR
Man and the Weasel, The. Phaedrus, *tr. fr. Latin by* Christopher Smart. AWP; OnPM
Man and Wife. Parvin, *tr. fr. Persian by* A. J. Arberry. PeP
Man and Woman Made One Unity. Milton. *See* Adam and Eve in the Garden.
Man and woman walking, A. The Feather. Lilian Bowes-Lyon. ChMP
Man as God. John Davidson. *Fr.* A Ballad in Blank Verse of the Making of a Poet. BMEP
Man at Peace. Antipater of Sidon, *tr. fr. Greek by* John Addington Symonds. OnPM
Man at the Window. August Derleth. DaM
Man at Work. John Holmes. WhC
Man, Be Glad in Hall and Bower. *Unknown.* AnEC
Man, Be Joyful and Mirth Thou Make. *Unknown. See* Et Incarnatus.
Man, Be Merry as Bird on Berry. *Unknown.* AnEC
Man, be merry, I thee rede. Et Incarnatus [*or* Man, Be Joyful and Mirth Thou Make]. *Unknown.* ACP; AnEC; TMEV

Man Beholdeth God, A. "Angelus Silesius," *tr. fr. German by* Paul Carus. OnPM
Man bent over his guitar, The. The Man with the Blue Guitar. Wallace Stevens. LiTA; UnS
Man Besmitten so, A. Alfred Kreymborg. TBM
Man born of desire. Dirge. Robert Bridges. *Fr.* Ode to Music. TwCV
Man, born to toil, in his labour rejoiceth. A Hymn to Nature. Robert Bridges. YeAr
Man-brained and man-handed ground-ape, The. Original Sin. Robinson Jeffers. MoAB; MoAmPo (1950 ed.); MoVE
Man, by fortune raised, that holds, The. Isthmian Ode III: To Melissus of Thebes, Victor in the Horse-Race. Pindar. *Fr.* Odes. PreP
Man by the Name of Bolus, A. James Whitcomb Riley. AA; OBAV
Man by the wall snores, The. *Unknown. Fr.* Mad Sweeney. AnIL
Man Called Dante, I Have Heard, A. Georgiana Goddard King. HBV
Man came slowly, from the setting sun, A. Cuchulain's Fight with the Sea [*or* The Death of Cuchulain]. W. B. Yeats. AnIL; ChMo; ChTr; CMP; GoTL; PoVP
Man cannot look round the roadway's curve. Boundaries. Catherine Cate Coblentz. BPP; OQP; QP-1
Man Carries Woman. Tore Örjasæter, *tr. fr. Norwegian by* Charles W. Stork. AnNoLy
Man Carrying Bale. Harold Monro. MBP; MoBrPo; MoP; PoeMoYo; TCEP; TCPD
Man-Child. Michael Breathnach. JKCP (1926 ed.)
Man Christ, The. Therese Lindsey. BePJ; BPP; ChIP; MaRV
Man Closes the Shutters, The. Lionello Fiumi, *tr. fr. Italian by* Creighton Gilbert. LiTW
Man comes a pilgrim of the universe. The Pilgrim. Edwin Markham. MaRV
Man Coming toward You, The. Oscar Williams. AnAmPo; AnFE; CoAnAm; LiTA; LiTM; TwAmPo
"Man coming toward you is falling forward on all fronts, The," I *and* II. NePA
Man; Creation's Masterpiece. Sophocles. *See* Choral Ode: "Wonders are many . . ."
Man, do not despair. On the Eve of New Wars. Louis Untermeyer. MAP
Man, dreame no more of curious mysteries. Fulke Greville. Caelica, LXXXVIII [LXXXIX]. MePo; OBS
Man Flammonde, from God knows where, The. Flammonde. E. A. Robinson. AmPP; AnAmPo; BLV; BoLiVe; ChMo; CMP; CoBA; IAP; InP; LA; LiTA; LiTM (rev. ed.); MAPA; NV; OBAV; PoLFOT; SBMV; SeCeV; TOP; TwP; UnPo (1st ed.)
Man! Foolish man! On Exodus III, 14, I Am That I Am. Matthew Prior. CEP
Man fools about with self-analysis. The Collective Portrait. Robert Finch. BoCaPo (1948 ed.)
Man for Galway, The. Charles James Lever. OnYI
Man found a treasure, A; and, what's very strange. An Irony. Plato. OuHeWo
Man Frail and God Eternal. Isaac Watts. *See* O God, Our Help in Ages Past.
Man, free thinker! do you believe you alone can reason. Golden Verses. Gérard de Nerval. AnFP
Man from his blindness attaining the succor of sight. Death Song in "Taliesin." Richard Hovey. *Fr.* Taliesin. PC
Man from Sangamon, at Gettysburg, The. Eleanor G. R. Young. OQP; QP-2
Man from Snowy River, The. A. B. Paterson. NeLNL
Man Goin' Round [*or* Roun'], *with music. Unknown.* ABF; AS
Man grows up. Proem. Robert Nathan. DDA
Man had something in the look of him, The. Karshish and Lazarus. Robert Browning. *Fr.* An Epistle Containing the Strange Medical Experience of Karshish, the Arab Physician. GoBC
Man has a soul of vast defines. Putney Hymn. *Unknown.* TrAS
Man has his unseen friend, his unseen twin. John Masefield. *Fr.* Sonnets ("Long long ago"). PoeMoYo
Man has, to pay his ransom here. The Ransom. Baudelaire. LO
Man He Killed, The. Thomas Hardy. ChMo; CMP; CoBE; CoBMV; EnL; FaFP; GTBS-W; InP; LEAP; LiTB; LiTM; MBP; MoAB; MoBrPo; NP; OQP; PoeMoYo; SoV; TCEP; TreF; UnPo; VLEP; WaaP; WHA
Man His Own Star. John Fletcher. *See* Man Is His Own Star.
Man Hunt, The. Madison Cawein. AnAmPo; LA; MAP; PoeMoYo; SPP
Man-Hunt, The. Carl Sandburg. *Fr.* The Four Brothers. OQP; QP-2
Man I Am and Man Would Be. Robert Browning. *Fr.* Ferishtah's Fancies. VLEP
Man I had a love for, The. An Old Woman's Lamentations. Villon, *pr. tr. by* J. M. Synge. MoBrPo; OBMV; TwCV
Man I Was of Old, The. Pushkin, *tr. fr. Russian by* Babette Deutsch. TrRV
Man I would not name, I would not prize, A. Tyrtaeus, *tr. fr. Greek.* GrPo
Man in a Room. William Carlos Williams. NP
Man in Nature. William Roscoe Thayer. AA
Man in righteousness arrayed, The. To Sally. John Quincy Adams, *after* Horace. AA; ALV; AWP; JAWP; LHV; PR, WBP
Man in That Airplane, The. Oscar Williams. WaP
Man in the Bowler Hat, The. A. S. J. Tessimond. HaMV; POTE
Man in the Dress Suit, The. Robert L. Wolf. HBMV
Man in the Moon, The. "Hugh MacDiarmid." NeBP
Man in the Moon, The. James Whitcomb Riley. BOHV; HBV; HBVY; InMe; NA; OTPC; YT
Man in the Moon, The ("The Man in the Moon as he sails the sky"). *Unknown.* GaP; GFA; OTPC (1946 ed.)
Man in the moon, The/ Came tumbling down [*or* down too soon]. Plum-Pudding or Plum Porridge. Mother Goose. BoChLi; BoN; OTPC; OxBoLi; OxNR; PPL; SAS; SiTL
Man in the Moon Drinks Claret, The ("Bacchus, the father of drunken Nowls"). *Unknown.* CoMu
Man in the moon drinks claret, The. *Unknown.* BoN; OxNR
Man in the moon looked out of the moon, The. The Children's Bedtime. Mother Goose. PCH
Man in the moon was caught in a trap, The. *Unknown.* OxNR
Man in the mune, The/ is making shune. *Unknown.* OxNR
Man in the Street Is Fed, The. Carl Sandburg. *Fr.* The People, Yes. AmPP (4th ed.); OxBA
Man in the wilderness asked of [*or* said to] me, The [*or* A]. Mother Goose. BOHV; BoTP; FaBoCh; LiTG; LoGBV; NA; OTPC; OxNR; PPL; SiTL
Man, in those early days. Corruption. Henry Vaughan. CAW; EPS; OBS
Man, introverted man, having crossed. Science. Robinson Jeffers. AmPP; CoBA; OxBA
Man Is a Fool. *Unknown.* FaFP; SiTL
Man is a fool and a bag of wind! Hakluyt Unpurchased. Franklin McDuffee. EtS
Man is a little world and bears the face. De Microcosmo. Thomas Bastard. SiCE
Man is a lumpe, where all beasts kneaded bee. To Sir Edward Herbert at Julyers. John Donne. SeCV-1
Man Is a Prisoner. Edwin Wiley Fuller. *Fr.* The Angel in the Cloud. NoCaPo
Man is a sacred city, built of marvellous earth. The Chief Centurions. John Masefield. *Fr.* The Tragedy of Pompey the Great. POTE; TCPD; WGRP
Man is a shadow's dream! Cadgwith. Lionel Johnson. CoBE; PoVP
Man Is a Snow. Earle Birney. PeCV
Man is a torch borne in the wind; a dream. The Pilot. George Chapman. *Fr.* Bussy d'Ambois. EtS
Man Is a Weaver. Moses ibn Ezra, *tr. fr. Hebrew by* Emma Lazarus. TrJP
Man is blest that hath not gone, The. Beatus Vir. Psalm I, Bible, *O.T., tr. by* Thomas Sternhold. ReIE; SiCE
Man is blind because of sin. Pis-Aller. Matthew Arnold. BMEP; BPN; EmBrPo; EPN; PoVP; VLEP
Man is born, a man dies, A. Tir-Nan-Og. J. F. Hendry. NeBP
"Man Is Born to Sorrow." Philitas, *tr. fr. Greek by* F. L. Lucas. GrPE
Man Is but a Castaway. Clarence Day. ImOP
Man is coming out of the mountains. Touch and Go. Stevie Smith. DiM
Man Is Dear to Man: the Poorest Poor. Wordsworth. PoToHe
Man is for woman made. A Rondelay. Peter Anthony Motteux. BOHV
Man Is His Own Star. John Fletcher. *Fr.* Upon an Honest Man's Fortune. OQP; QP-2
(Man His Own Star.) EV-2
Man Is in Pain. Philip Lamantia. NeAP
Man is in the fields, let us look with his eyes, A. Enigma. R. S. Thomas. ChMP
Man is most anxious not to stir. That Corner. Blanaid Salkeld. OnYI; OxBI
Man is my darling, my love and my pain. God Speaks to the Man in Despair. Stevie Smith. DiM
Man is no mushroom growth of yesterday. Social Heredity. John Kells Ingram. TIP
Man is permitted much. The Elements [*or* Chorus of the Elements]. Cardinal Newman. GoBC; OBRV; OBVV; PoVP; VA
Man is the world, and death th' ocean. John Donne. *Fr.* Elegie on the Lady Marckham. PoD
Man knows not love—such love as women feel. Woman's Love. *Unknown.* WBLP

Man, like others, formed by God, A. The Saxons of Flint. Lewys Glyn Cothi. PrWP
Man, like the sordid earth, from which he sprung. Sir Charles Sedley. *Fr.* The Happy Pair. BeR
Man looking into the sea. A Grave [*or* A Graveyard]. Marianne Moore. AnAmPo; CrMA; ExPo; FaBoEn; LA; LiTA; MoPo; MoVE; NP; PoFS; SeCeV; UnPo (3d ed.)
Man loved, heart and soul, his favorite cat, A. The Cat Changed into a Woman. La Fontaine. CIV
Man-made laws and doctrines pass. The Day Breaks. Thomas Curtis Clark. ChIP
Man-making. Edwin Markham. MaRV; OQP; PGD; QP-1
Man, Man, Man. *Unknown.* ALV; FaFP; LiTL; SiTL
Man, matron, maiden. Robert Baden-Powell. CenHV
Man may be marytred in bondage. The Mainspring. Martha Eugenie Perry. CaP
Man may escape from rope and gun. John Gay. *Fr.* The Beggar's Opera, II, ii. CEP
Man May Live Thrice Nestor's Life, A. Thomas Norton. *See* Against Women either Good or Bad.
Man more kindly, in his careless way, A. A Portrait. Caroline Duer. AA; OBAV
Man morose and dull and sad, A. Metaphysics. Franklin P. Adams. LHV
Man-Moth, The. Elizabeth Bishop. LiTA; MiAP; MoAB; MoAmPo (1950 ed.)
Man, Move Thy Mind, and Joy This Feast. *Unknown.* AnEC
"Man Must Live, A." Charlotte Perkins Gilman. MaRV; OQP; PIAE; QP-2
Man must serve his time to every trade, A. Byron. *Fr.* English Bards and Scotch Reviewers. EPP
Man Named Hods, A. *Unknown.* CoSo; CSF
Man Named Legion, The. Sara Henderson Hay. PoFr
Man never knows precisely what is right. Essay on Man. *Unknown.* PoToHe (new ed.)
Man New Made. Shakespeare. *Fr.* Measure for Measure, II, ii. GoBC
Man, Not His Arms. Selden Rodman. WaP
Man o' Airlie, The, *sel.* Sarah Doudney.
Lesson of the Water Mill, The. HBV; PoToHe, *abr.;* TreFS
(Water Mill, The.) BLPA; BPP, *abr.;* PTA-2, *sl. diff.;* WGRP
Man-o'-War, The. Byron. *Fr.* Childe Harold's Pilgrimage, II. SG
Man Octipartite. *Tr. fr. Middle Irish by* Whitley Stokes. TIP
Man of Athens on a summer's day, A. Babrius, *tr. fr. Greek by* James Davies. GrPo
Man of Calvary, The. "Sin Killer" Griffin. OuSiCo
Man of Crete. J. R. Hervey. AnNZ
Man of Culture, A. A. S. J. Tessimond. HaMV
Man of Experience, A. Laoiseach Mac an Bhaird, *tr. fr. Irish by* Frank O'Connor. KiLC
Man of Galilee. Mary Louise Deissler. BePJ
Man of Galilee, The. Hildegarde Hoyt Swift. ChIP
Man of Grass, The, *sel.* Roy Macnab.
"India became his jasmined youth, Goa." BoSA
Man of Kerioth, The, *sels.* Robert Norwood.
"Blind minstrel, come." CPG
"But, this I found." CaP
Man of kind and noble mind, A. How the Babes in the Wood Showed They Couldn't Be Beaten. Guy Wetmore Carryl. RIS
Man of Life Upright, The. Thomas Campion, *after* Horace. CenL; CoBE; EIL; EV-2; MaRV; OAEP; OBSC; PoRA; PYM; ReEn; SiCE; TOP; TuPP; TyEnPo; ViBoPo; WP
(Integer Vitae.) BCEP; GTSL; HBV; OBEV; PG (1945 ed.)
(Life Upright, The.) HBVY
(Upright Life, The.) BHV
Man of Many Devices, The. Homer, *pr. tr. fr. Greek by* A. T. Murray. *Fr.* The Odyssey, I. LiA
Man of Men, A. Leonard Charles Van Noppen. PGD
Man of Mode, The; or, Sir Fopling Flutter, *sels.* Sir George Etherege.
As Amoret with Phyllis Sat, *by* Sir Carr Scrope. SeCL
Song: "Pleasures of love, and the joys of good wine, The," *fr.* IV, i. CEP
Man of Peace, The. Bliss Carman. DD; HH, *diff.;* OHIP
Man of Prayer, The. Christopher Smart. *See* Strong Is the Horse upon His Speed.
Man of Ross, The. Pope. *Fr.* Moral Essays, Epistle III. CoBE
Man of Science Speaks, The. Harriet Monroe. MaRV; PoeMoYo
Man of Sense, A. Richard Eberhart. MiAP
Man of song and man of science. The Priest [*or* My Father's House]. James Oppenheim. *Fr.* Night. MaRV; QS
Man of Sorrows, The. Isaiah, LIII, Bible, *O.T.* EM-1
Man of Sorrows, The. *Unknown.* ChIP; MaRV; OQP; PGD; QP-2
Man of the House. Katharine Tynan. CAW; ChrBoLe; JKCP; WHL
Man of the Marne, The. Bliss Carman. AOAH
Man of the North Countrie, The. Thomas D'Arcy McGee. OnYI
Man of the Open West, The. Arthur W. Monroe. PoOW
Man of the rugged frame and calm, worn face. The Lincoln Memorial. Alma Adams Wiley. PEDC
Man of Thessaly, The. *Unknown.* LiTG; SiTL
("There was a man of Thessaly.") BoN; OxNR
Man of Tyre, The. D. H. Lawrence. MeRV
Man of Words, A. *Unknown.* BOHV; FaFP; SiTL; TreFS
(Man of Words and Not of Deeds, A.) FaBoCh; LoGBV; OxBoLi
(Proverbs.) HBV
(Some Proverbs in Verse.) FaBoBe
Man on the Flying Trapeze, The. George Leybourne. ABF, *with music;* BeLS; BLPA, *with music;* FaBoBe; FaFP; LiTG; LoGBV; NeHB; OxBoLi; SiTL; YaD
(Flying Trapeze, The, *sl. diff. vers.*) TreF
Man on the Hill, The. Maurice Hewlett. *Fr.* The Song of the Plow. POTE
Man, one harmonious soul of many a soul. Shelley. *Fr.* Prometheus Unbound. CBE
Man paused at the window to look in, A. Man at the Window. August Derleth. DaM
Man Plowing. Edith Mirick. MuM
Man possessed a cat on which he doted, A. Cat into Lady. La Fontaine. PoC
Man prayed his way up from the beast. Reply. Janet Norris Bangs. OQP; QP-1
Man prepared against all ills to come, A. The Christian Militant. Robert Herrick. HoPM
Man Proposes. Thomas à Kempis. *Fr.* Imitation of Christ, I, 19. TreF
Man proposes, God in His time disposes. On a Dead Child. Richard Middleton. OBVV
Man, proud man. Man. Shakespeare. *Fr.* Measure for Measure, II, ii. BCEP
Man Returns to the Gates of Eden. Dorothy Hobson. MuM
Man rives the granite from its ledge. Dream across the Dark. Clifford J. Laube. JKCP (1955 ed.)
Man Said to the Universe, A. Stephen Crane. *Fr.* War Is Kind. AmPP; CoBA; ImOP; InP; YaD
(Four Poems, III.) CrMA
(Man, The.) BOHV
(War Is Kind, IV.) AnAmPo; LA
Man said unto his angel, A. The Kings. Louise Imogen Guiney. BAP; GoBC; HBV; LBMV; MAP; MoAmPo (1942 ed.); OBAV; PC; PoeMoYo
Man sat in the gallery, The. Words without Music. *Unknown.* WhC
Man sat on a rock and sought, A. Prehistoric Smith. David Law Proudfit. BOHV
Man Saw a Ball of Gold in the Sky, A. Stephen Crane. The Black Riders, XXXV. AmP; LiTA; NePA
Man Seven Years Standing, The. Vladimir Mayakovsky, *tr. fr. Russian by* Jack Lindsay. *Fr.* About This. RuPo
Man shall come into this land, A. Bard's Chant. James Shirley. *Fr.* Saint Patrick for Ireland. ACP
Man should kindle once a year, A. A Fire at Night. Robert P. Tristram Coffin. TwCV
Man should live in a garret aloof, A. The Flight of the Goddess. Thomas Bailey Aldrich. HBV; LBAP
Man so various that he seemed to be, A. Zimri. Dryden. *Fr.* Absalom and Achitophel. BCEP
Man Speaks, A. Ethel Romig Fuller. DDA
Man, tak heed to me. Epitaph. *Unknown.* BSV
Man, take your gun: and put to shame. Take Your Gun. Jacob Bronowski. POTE
Man that had six mortal wounds, a man, A. Cuchulain Comforted. W. B. Yeats. LiTG; LiTM (rev. ed.)
Man that I know likes the bare tree best, A. Full Moon. Clifford Bax. POTE
Man that is born of a woman. Job, Bible, *O.T.* AWP; ChTr; JAWP; OuHeWo; TrGrPo; WBP; WGRP
Man that joins in life's career, The. The Parting Glass. Philip Freneau. AA; AmP; IAP; LEAP; LHV; TCAP
Man that never will declare his thought, The. On the Deception of Appearances. Sadi. *Fr.* The Gulistan. AWP; LiTW
Man that was old came a-courtin' one day, A. Old Shoes and Leggin's. *Unknown.* OuSiCo
Man that would of truth tell, A. The Quest of Saint Truth. *Unknown.* TMEV
Man That Wouldn't Hoe Corn, The. *Unknown.* ABS; IHA
Man, the egregious egoist. Cold-blooded Creatures. Elinor Wylie. ChMo; ImOP
Man the Enemy of Man. Sir Walter Scott. *Fr.* Rokeby. WBLP
Man, the Feeblest of Earth's Creatures. Homer, *tr. fr. Greek by* William Cowper. *Fr.* The Odyssey. GrR
Man, the Metal-Worker. D. G. Bridson. MuP

Man there came, whence none could tell, A. The Touchstone. William Allingham. LPS-3
Man there is of fire and straw, A. William Wilson. Malcolm Cowley. AnAmPo; LA; MoVE
Man thinks he plays a lot of parts. It's Fun to Be a Pup. James J. Montague. AlBD
Man to Man. John McClure. HBMV
Man to the Angel, The. "Æ." OBVV; VA
Man to the plough. Farmers. *Unknown.* OtMeF
Man to whom illness was chronic, A. Limerick [*or* Beer]. *Unknown.* LiBL; SiTL
Man, twisted so with loves and hates. Man. Harold Lewis Cook. NP
Man unto His Fellow Man. Norman Corwin. *Fr.* On a Note of Triumph. TrJP
("Lord God of trajectory and blast.") QS
Man upon mould, whatsoever thou be. "Put Money in Thy Purse." *Unknown.* TMEV
Man Walks in the Wind, A. Maurice Lesemann. AnAmPo; LA; LiTL
"Man wants but little here below." The Wants of Man. John Quincy Adams. LPS-3; PR
Man was all shot through that came to-day, The. Connolly. Liam MacGowan. OnYI
Man was called Methuselah, The. I remember. The Devil and the Angel (6). Rosemary Dobson. BoAV
Man Was Drawing Near to Me, A. Thomas Hardy. InPo
Man Was Made to Mourn; a Dirge. Burns. CEP; LPS-1
Man's Inhumanity to Man, *sel.* BLPA; FaFP; MaRV; NeHB
Man was sitting underneath a tree, A. Seumas Beg. James Stephens. FaPON; GaP; PCN; TSW; TSWC
Man was the first guilt, A. All That 'Lieve in Christian Lay. *Unknown.* AnEC
Man was to be hanged, A . . . an ancient story. The Wings of Azrael. Edwin Björkman. NoCaPo (1941 ed.)
Man went a-hunting at Reigate [*or* Rygate], A. *Unknown.* BoTP; RIS
Man went down to Panama, A. Goethals, the Prophet-Engineer. Percy MacKaye. BAP; PoeMoYo; PoRL; StVeCh
Man went forth one day at eve, A. Tragedy. "Æ." MoBrPo
Man Who Broke the Bank at Monte Carlo, The. Fred Gilbert. TreF
Man who cloaked his bitterness within, The. Thomas Hood. E. A. Robinson. HBMV; PtP
Man who doubts if he should marry, A. Anaxandrides, *tr. fr. Greek by* F. A. Paley. GrPo
Man Who Dreamed of Faeryland, The. W. B. Yeats. GTIV; OAEP (2d ed.)
Man Who Dreamed of Fairies, The. Po Chü-i, *tr. fr. Chinese by* Arthur Waley. TrCh
Man who drew his strength from all, A. The Lincoln Statue. W. F. Collins. OHIP; PGD
Man who feels not, more or less, somewhat, The. Sonnet: Of Love in Men and Devils [*or* Love in Men and Devils]. Cecco Angiolieri da Siena. AWP; OnPM
Man who follow English ways. Civil Irish and Wild Irish. Laoiseach Mac an Bhaird. AnIL
Man Who Frets at Worldly Strife, The. Fitz-Greene Halleck *and* Joseph Rodman Drake. *Fr.* The Croaker Papers. AA
Man who goes for Christian resignation, The. Epigram. J. V. Cunningham. NePoAm
Man Who Had Fallen among Thieves, A. E. E. Cummings. CoBMV; LiTM; MoVE; OxBA
Man Who Hid His Own Front Door, The. Elizabeth MacKinstry. FaPON; GaP; TiPo
Man who in his life trusts in this world, A. Epitaph. *Unknown.* TrJP
Man who invented the women's waists that button down behind, The. Nemesis. James William Foley. BOHV
Man Who Married Magdalene, The. Louis Simpson. NePoEA
Man who met a phalanx with their spears, The. The Good Hour. Louise Driscoll. HBMV
Man who misses all the fun, The. It Can Be Done. *Unknown.* PoToHe (new ed.)
Man Who Rode to Conemaugh, The. John Eliot Bowen. GA; PAH
Man who saw the light hanging on the tall end, The. The Borrower of Salt. Oscar Williams. *Fr.* Variations on a Theme. LiTA; NePA
Man who seeks one thing in life, and but one, The. One Thing. "Owen Meredith." OQP; QP-2; WBLP
Man who shuns wine, woman, and song, The. Fool. *Unknown.* PIAE
Man Who Thought He Was a Horse, The. Thomas Hornsby Ferril. NePoAm-2
Man Who Trod on Sleeping Grass, The. Dora Sigerson Shorter. GTIV
Man Who Wanted to Be a Seagull, The. J. R. Hervey. AnNZ
Man who with undaunted toils, The. The Elephant and the Bookseller. John Gay. LoBV
Man Whom Men Deplore, A. Alfred Kreymborg. HBMV
(Call Him High Shelley Now.) TBM
Man Whom the Sea Kept Awake, The. Robert Bly. NePoEA
Man whose name was Johnny Sands, A. Johnny Sands. John Sinclair. ABS; CoMu; ViBoFo
Man Whose Thoughts, The. Sir Edward Dyer. TuPP
Man will need, A/ before his death. Winter Breath. Edward Weismiller. PoMa
Man with a Bull-Tongue Plow, *sels.* Jesse Stuart.
Jenny, *st.* 12. BoFr
Kentucky Mountaineer. PoeMoYo
"Farewell to Springtime in Kentucky hills," *st.* 661.
"I came the Womack Road from Sandy Bridge," *st.* 295.
"Last night the rain thumped on the clapboard roof," *st.* 283.
"Spring in Kentucky hills will soon awaken," *st.* 149.
My Greenup Friends, *st.* 388. BoFr
"There is shrill music in high winds at night," *st.* 293. PoMa
Man with a Hammer, The. Anna Wickham. AV
Man with a Little Pleated Piano, A. Winifred Welles. FaPON; GaP
Man with an Eagle on His Shoulder, The, *sel.* Ilya Selvinsky, *tr. fr. Russian by* Jack Lindsay.
Song of Babek. RuPo
Man with Crow's-Feet round His Eyes, A. E. Leslie Spaulding. DDA
Man with his burning soul. Truth. John Masefield. WGRP
Man with his lion under the shed of wars, The. The Song of the Borderguard. Robert Duncan. NeAP
Man with the acid face, The. The Face. A. J. M. Smith. BoCaPo (1943 ed.)
Man with the Blue Guitar, The. Wallace Stevens. LiTA
"Man bent over his guitar, The," *sel.* UnS
Man with the Broken Fingers, The. Carl Sandburg. PoFr
Man with the Hoe, The. Edwin Markham. AA; AnAmPo; AnFE; APA; BAP; BAV; BLPA; BLV; BTP; CoAnAm; CP; CV; DD; FaFP; GTBS-W; HBV; HiLiAm; LA; LBMV; LEAP; LiTA; LiTM; MAP; MaRV; MCCG; MoAmPo; NAMP; NeHB; NeMA; NV; OBAV; OHFP; OQP; PC; PECK; PEDC; PFE; PFY; PoeMoYo; PoFr; PoMa; POT; PoTo; PreP; PTA-1; PYM; QP-1; TCAP; TCPD; TreF; TrGrPo; VOD; WBLP; WGRP; WoL
Man with the Hoe, The; a Reply. John Vance Cheney. AA; DD, *abr.*
(Man with the Hoe, The.) BAP; HBV
Man with Three Friends, The. Dora Greenwell. OBVV
Man Within, The. Annemarie Ewing. NePoAm-2
Man without a Road, The, X. Erik Lindegren, *tr. fr. Swedish by* Richard B. Vowles. LiTW
Man without Faith, The. Richard Church. POTE
Man without Sense of Direction. John Crowe Ransom. LiTM (rev. ed.); OxBA
Man—Woman. Lydia Huntley Sigourney. LPS-3
"Man, you too, aren't you, one of these rough followers of the criminal?" In the Servants' Quarters. Thomas Hardy. MBP; MoAB; MoBrPo; QS
Man Young and Old, A, *sels.* W. B. Yeats.
First Love. TwP
Friends of His Youth, The. AtBAP
Human Dignity. TwP
Mermaid, The. TwP
Mana Aboda. T. E. Hulme. FaBoMo
Management Area of Cherokee, The. The Trout Map. Allen Tate. FaBoMo
Managers, The. W. H. Auden. EnLit
Manager's desk revolves in business circles, The. The Daily Round. Ronald McCuaig. BoAV
Manahatta . . ./ A lovely name, he thought, and a lovely island. Early Dutch. Jennie M. Palen. GoYe
Mananaan to Bran. *Unknown, tr. fr. Old Irish by* Seán O'Faoláin. SiB
Mañanitas de Jalisco. *Unknown. See* Early Mornings.
Manassas. Catherine Anne Warfield. BlG; MC; MDAH; PAH
Manchouli. William Empson. CoBMV
Manchy, The. Leconte de Lisle, *tr. fr. French by* Thomas Walsh. LiA
Manciple's Tale, The, *sel.* Chaucer. *Fr.* The Canterbury Tales.
Lat Take a Cat. ChTr
Mandalay. Kipling. ATP; BEL; BLV; BoLiVe; BPN; ChMo; EnLi-2; EnLit; EPP; HBV; LEAP; LiTB; LiTM (rev. ed.); MBP; MoBrPo; PIAE; PoVP; PTA-1; ShBV-2; SiTL; StaSt; TCPD; TOP; TreF; TrGrPo; VLEP; YT
(On the Road to Mandalay.) OlF
Mandan Priest, The. Edward William Thomson. CPG
Mandarin on the Air. Christopher Morley. PoMa
Mandevil's river of dry jewels grows. Part of Mandevil's Travels. William Empson. AtBAP
Mandoline. Paul Verlaine, *tr. fr. French by* Arthur Symons. AWP; JAWP; OBMV; WBP
(Mandolines, *tr. by* Alan Conder.) TrFP
Mandrake, The. Leland Davies. BAP
Mandrake Hert, The. Sidney Goodsir Smith. AtBAP

Mandrake's Song. Thomas Lovell Beddoes. *Fr.* Death's Jest Book, I, i. NBE
Mandy's Lay. Louis Untermeyer. StaSt
Mandy's Religion. Alice Corbin. *Fr.* Echoes of Childhood. PoNe
Mane Nobiscum Domine, *in mod. Eng. Unknown.* TMEV
Manere of the Crying of ane Playe, The. William Dunbar. AtBAP
Manfred. George Meredith. EPN
Manfred; a Dramatic Poem. Byron. BEL; BPN; EmBrPo; EnLi-2 (1939 ed.); EnRP; EPN; ERP; GEPC
Sels.
Coliseum, The, *fr.* III, iv. MCCG
(Coliseum by Moonlight, *abr.*) LPS-2
(Manfred, *abr.*) BCEP
"Hear me, hear me," *fr.* II, iv. ReTS
"When the moon is on the wave," *fr.* I, i. UnW
(Incantation, An.) OBRV
Mangoes, The. Duraciné Vaval, *tr. fr. French by* Donald Devenish Walsh. AnCL; PoNe
Mangroves Dance, The. Rose Strong Hubbell. NLK (1947 ed.)
Mangy and gaunt I walk the tiles tonight. An Alley Cat. Nancy Byrd Turner. CIV; PoeMoYo
Manhattan. Morris Abel Beer. BAP; BoHiPo; PoTo
Manhattan. John Gould Fletcher. VOD (1935 ed.)
Manhattan. Margaret Elward Lawless. PoMa
Manhattan, *sels.* Charles Hanson Towne.
City, The, *fr.* XIV. CV; SBMV
Spring in Town, *fr.* V. TBM
Manhattan! All your symmetry of steel. Manhattan. Margaret Elward Lawless. PoMa
Manhattan Arming. Walt Whitman. *See* First O Songs for a Prelude.
Manhattan Menagerie. Joseph Cherwinski. GoYe
Manhood. Oliver Wendell Holmes. *Fr.* The Poet at the Breakfast Table. AWP
Manhood ("Manhood I am: therefore I me delight"). Sir Thomas More. TuPP
Maniac, The. Matthew Gregory Lewis. LPS-1
Maniac, The. Thomas Russell. OBEC
Manichaean's Prayer, The. Longfellow. *Fr.* Tales of a Wayside Inn. APW
Manifesto, A. Timotheus, *tr. fr. Greek by* Gilbert Highet. OxBG
Manifesto of the Soldier Who Went Back to War. Angel Miguel Queremel, *tr. fr. Spanish by* Donald Devenish Walsh. PoFr; WaaP
Manikin and Minikin. Alfred Kreymborg. MAPA; TwAmPo
Manila. Eugene Fitch Ware. BOHV; FiBHP; InMe; YaD
Manila Bay. Arthur Hale. PAH
Manitou. Wilfred Campbell. OCL
Mankind has cast me out. John Davidson. *Fr.* The Testament of a Man Forbid. BrBE
Mankind Is Sick. Thomas Traherne. *Fr.* Christian Ethics. OxBoCh
Manlet, The. "Lewis Carroll." PA
Manly Heart, The. George Wither. *See* Shall I, Wasting in Despair.
Manly Man, The. *Unknown.* BLPA; WBLP
Mannahatta ("I was asking for something specific"). Walt Whitman. AA; HBV; IAP; MAP; MoAmPo; OuHeWo; REAL
Manner, The. Sir Osbert Sitwell. MoP
Manner of her death was thus, The. *Unknown.* WhC
Mannerly Margery Milk and Ale. John Skelton. ReEn
Manners. Mariana Griswold Van Rensselaer. FaPON; HBMV; HBVY; MPB
Manners in the dining-room. *Unknown.* OxNR
Mano; a Poetical History, *sels.* Richard Watson Dixon. VA
Of a Vision of Hell, Which a Monk Had.
Of Temperance in Fortune.
Skylark, The.
Manor Farm, The. Edward Thomas. EV-5; ExPo; HaMV; NP; SeCeV
Manor Lord, The. George Houghton. AA
"Man's a dreamer, The!" Good! That places him. God's Dream. William Norris Burr. OQP; QP-1
Man's a Man for A' That, A. Burns. BBV (1923 ed.); BEL; BoLiVe; CBE; CoBE; EnLi-2; EPP; GTBS-W; HiLiEn; InPo; LoBV; MaRV; OuHeWo; PFE; PIAE; PoMa; TCEP; TOP; TrGrPo; ViBoPo; WoL
(For A' That.) BCEP; PECK; PYM
(For A' That and A' That.) AnFE; BTP; CBOV; CEP; EiPP; EnLit; EV-3; FaBoBe; FaFP; GrCo-1, *3 sts.;* HBV; HBVY; LiTB; LiTG; LPS-1; MCCG; NeHB; OAEP; OHFP; OQP; OTPC; PIR; PoeMoYo; QP-1; RiBV; WBLP
(Is There for Honest Poverty?) EBSV; EM-1; EnL; EnRP; OBEC; PoFr; TreF
Man's a poor deluded bubble. Song. Robert Dodsley. CEP
Man's Amazement. *Unknown.* CoMu
Man's Anxious, but Ineffectual Guard against Death. Thomas Lovell Beddoes. ChER
Man's body doth obey o'er-mastering death. The Soul. Pindar. GrR
Man's Bread, A. Josephine Preston Peabody. YeAr
Man's Civil War. Robert Southwell. SiCE
Man's Daughter, A. John Drinkwater. LEAP
Man's Days. Eden Phillpotts. HBV; OBEV (new ed.); OBVV
(Gaffer's Song, The.) MBP
Man's Destiny. Robert Browning. *Fr.* Paracelsus, V. MaRV
(Awakening of Man, The.) WGRP
("Progress is/ The law of life.") OQP; QP-2
Man's earthliness which saints deplore. Compliment to Mariners. George H. Dillon. TBM
Man's flitting life finds surest stay. John Thorn. SiCE
Man's Hidden Side. Nathan Haskell Dole. BAP
Man's home is everywhere. On ocean's flood. Man—Woman. Lydia Huntley Sigourney. LPS-3
Man's hopes are spirits with fast-fleeting wings. Epitaph on a Flute-Player. Diotimus of Athens. LiA
Man's hour is such a puny thing and slight. Insolence. Homer C. House. MuM
Man's Ingratitude. Shakespeare. *See* Blow, Blow, Thou Winter Wind.
Man's ingress into the world is naked and bare. A Brief Sermon. *Unknown.* TreFS
Man's Inhumanity to Man. Burns. *Fr.* Man Was Made to Mourn; a Dirge. BLPA; FaFP; MaRV; NeHB
Man's Inhumanity to Man. Martial, *tr. fr. Latin by* Paul Nixon. RoL
Man's inhumanity to man is hard. Inverse Ratio. *Unknown.* WhC
Man's Last Word to a Woman, A. Verner von Heidenstam, *tr. fr. Swedish by* Charles W. Stork. AnSL
Man's Life. William Hammond. OBS
Man's Life, after Posidonius or Crates. *At. to* Posidippus, *tr. fr. Greek by* Nicholas Grimald. ReIE; SiCE; TuPP
("What course of life should wretched mortals take?" *tr. by* John Beaumont.) GrPo
Man's life is but vain, for 'tis subject to pain. The Angler's Song. *Unknown.* AlDL; SeCL
Man's life is death. Yet Christ endured to live. Wednesday in Holy Week. Christina Rossetti. ChIP; PGD
Man's life is laid in the loom of time. The Loom of Time. *Unknown.* BLPA; MaRV; NeHB
Man's life is like a sparrow, mighty King! Persuasion. Wordsworth. Ecclesiastical Sonnets, XVI. MaRV; OQP; QP-2
Man's life is well compared to a feast. A Comparison of the Life of Man. Richard Barnfield. AEV; OBSC; SiCE
Man's life, like any weaver's shuttle, flies. The Life of Man. Keidrych Rhys. TriL
Man's Life Likened to a Stage Play. Thomas Howell. SiCE
Man's life was once a span; now one of those. Man's Life. William Hammond. OBS
Man's life's a tragedy. His mother's womb. De Morte. *Unknown, at. to* Sir Henry Wotton. CenL; OBS
Man's Littleness in Presence of the Stars. Henry Kirke White. WBLP
Man's Love. Byron. *Fr.* Don Juan, I. BCEP
("Man's love is of man's life a thing apart.") TreF
Man's Love, A. Tove Ditlevsen, *tr. fr. Danish by* Martin S. Allwood. LiTW
Man's Medley. George Herbert. ViBoPo
Man's mind is larger than his brow of tears. To the Victor. William Ellery Leonard. MAP; MoAmPo (1942 ed.); PoFr
Man's Mortality. *At. to* Simon Wastell. *Fr.* Microbiblion. FaBoCh; HBV; LoGBV; LPS-1; SeCL; WBLP. *See also* Hos Ego Versiculos, *sl. diff. vers. by* Francis Quarles, *fr.* Argalus and Parthenia.
(Of Man's Mortalitie.) EV-1
(Verses of Man's Mortality [*or* Mortalitie].) OBS; SeEP
"Like as the damask rose you see," *sel.* AlDL
Man's Natural Element. Abu-l-Ala al-Maarri, *tr. fr. Arabic by* R. A. Nicholson. LiTW
Man's Need. David Ross. PG (1945 ed.)
Man's noisy pleasures are at rest. Evening. Joseph von Eichendorff. AnGP
Man's Pillow. Irving Browne. AA; LEAP
Man's Place in Nature. *Unknown.* BOHV; PA
Man's Prayer, The. T. A. Daly. TrPWD
(Father's Prayer, A.) PraP
Man's Prime Desire. Jami, *tr. fr. Persian by* F. Hadland Davis. OnPM
Man's Requirements, A. Elizabeth Barrett Browning. BPN; EmBrPo
Man's Road. Enrique Peña Barrenechea, *tr. fr. Spanish by* Muna Lee. AnCL
Man's Roots, *sel.* R. N. Currey.
"Man's roots are not in earth; while trees and flowers." BoSA
Man's Service. Fulke Greville. *Fr.* Of Humane Learning. PoFr

("Chiefe use then in man of that he knowes, The.") OBS; SiCE
Man's spirit with spread wings. Limits. Sister Rita Agnes. JKCP (1955 ed.)
Man's Testament. Adam Lindsay Gordon. *See* Question Not.
Man's Way. L. A. G. Strong. HBMV
Manshape, that shone. Of a Death in Winter, I. Gerard Manley Hopkins. *Fr.* That Nature Is a Heraclitean Fire and of the Comfort of the Resurrection. BoW
Mansion of a robin, The. Definitions for a Tree. Anne Blackwell Payne. NoCaPo
Mansong, *sel.* Marcus Adeney.
Choral: "We the proper ancients speak not out of turn." BoCaPo (1943 ed.)
Mantis. Terence Heywood. BoSA
Mantis Friend, The. Vincent McHugh. NePoAm-2
Mantle of Mary, The. Patrick O'Connor. ISi
Manual System. Carl Sandburg. TiPo (1952 ed.)
Manuel Komninos. C. P. Cavafy, *tr. fr. Modern Greek by* Rae Dalven. MoGP
Manufactured Gods. Carl Sandburg. WGRP
MS of Benedictbeuern. *Tr. fr. Latin by* Helen Waddell. DiM
MS of St. Martial of Limoges. *Tr. fr. Latin by* Helen Waddell. TriL
Manuscripts of God, The. Longfellow. *Fr.* The Fiftieth Birthday of Agassiz. MaRV
Many, The. Swinburne. *Fr.* Sonnets on English Dramatic Poets (1590–1650). PoVP
Many a fairer face than yours. To a Lady. Franklin P. Adams. FiBHP
Many a flower hath perfume for its dower. Exultate Deo. Christina Rossetti. MeRV
Many a flower have I seen blossom. Gibberish. Mary Elizabeth Coleridge. MoVE; PoeT
Many a gray-haired sire has died. The Southern Homes in Ruin. R. B. Vance. BIG
Many a green-fezz pilgrim falters. The Pilgrims. Anthony Delius. BoSA
Many a green isle needs must be. Lines Written among the Euganean Hills. Shelley. BCEP; BPN; EmBrPo; EnRP; EPP; ERP; GEPC; GTBS; GTBS-D; GTBS-W; GTSE; GTSL; LPS-2; PoEL-4
Many a hearth upon our dark globe sighs after many a vanished face. Vastness. Tennyson. BMEP; BPN; EM-2; EmBrPo; GEPC; PoVP; TCEP; VA; VLEP
Many a lip is gaping for drink. Eliza Cook. *Fr.* Song of the Seaweed. FiBHP
Many a long, long year ago. The Alarmed Skipper [*or* The Nantucket Skipper]. James T. Fields. AmSS; BOHV; DDA; EtS; GoTP; HBV; LHV; LPS-3; YaD
Many a man can sleep as he desires. Rooming-House Melancholy. Eric Kästner. LiTW
Many a Mickle. Walter de la Mare. GTSE
Many a night far-faring. The Night Traveller. Ibn Atiya. MooP
Many a solemn conference. When the Minister Came to Tea. Juliet Tompkins. DDA
Many a starry night had they known. The Dogs of Bethlehem. Katharine Lee Bates. AlBD; ChrBoLe; CV
Many a summer is dead and buried, A. Spirits Everywhere. Ludwig Uhland. AWP
Many a Tear. Paulus Silentiarius, *tr. fr. Greek by* William Hay. LiA
Many a tree is found in the wood. A Salute to Trees. Henry van Dyke. NLK; StVeCh
Many a trick the wise fox knows. Too Versatile. Archilochus. GrPE
Many a year is in its grave. The Passage. Ludwig Uhland. LPS-1
Many and sharp the numerous ills. Man's Inhumanity to Man. Burns. *Fr.* Man Was Made to Mourn. BLPA; FaFP; MaRV; NeHB
Many Are Called. E. A. Robinson. BAP; InP; MoVE; OnAP; OxBA; TBM
Many are praised, and some are fair. In Spain; Drinking Song. Emily Lawless. AnIV
Many are the doors of the spirit that lead. Doors of the Temple. Aldous Huxley. HBMV; OS
Many are the notes. The Solitary. Wordsworth. *Fr.* The Excursion, II. ERP
Many are the sayings of the wise. The Ways of God to Man. Milton. *Fr.* Samson Agonistes. OBS; SeCeV
Many are the wand-bearers. Evoe! Edith M. Thomas. BAP; HBV; LBAP; LEAP
Many-coloured clouds make me think of her upper garments, of her lower garments, The. Songs to the Peonies. Li Po. ChLP
Many days have come and gone. For a Copy of Herrick. Austin Dobson. PtP; VLEP
Many desire, but few or none deserve. The Advice. Sir Walter Ralegh. SiPS
Many do not break their bread with me, The. A Toast. Marguerite Wilkinson. SDH
Many have painted her. But there was one. Rainer Maria Rilke. *Fr.* The Book of Hours. CAW
Many have planted. Landscape. R. N. Currey. BoSA
Many have sung the rose. The Perfect Sign. Marion Couthoy Smith. BAP
Many have sung the summer's songs. Winter Song. V. Sackville-West. *Fr.* The Land. MBP; MoBrPo (1942 ed.)
Many in aftertimes will say of you. Monna Innominata, XI. Christina Rossetti. AV; EmBrPo; PoVP; TCEP; ViBoPo; ViPo
Many Indeed Must Perish in the Keel. Hugo von Hofmannsthal, *tr. fr. German by* Jethro Bithell. AWP; JAWP; TrJP; WBP
(Many Truly, *tr. by* Vernon Watkins.) AnGP
Many ingenious lovely things are gone. Nineteen Hundred and Nineteen. W. B. Yeats. LiTB; MoAB; MoPo; OnHM
Many Inventions, *sel.* Kipling.
Song of the Galley-Slaves. ChTr; PoEL-5; PoFr
Many Joys. Pierre de Ronsard, *tr. fr. French by* Alan Conder. TrFP
Many know you now by virtue of that music. Musician. Clifford Bax. TCPD
Many love music but for music's sake. On Music. Walter Savage Landor. BPN; HBV; TriL; VA
Many loved truth, and lavished life's best oil. James Russell Lowell. *Fr.* Ode Recited at the Harvard Commemoration, July 21, 1865. PFY; PoFr
Many, many welcomes. Snowdrop. Tennyson. OTPC (1946 ed.); PCH; PoRL
Many men of many minds. *Unknown.* WhC
Many now had left him, melting fast, The. The Lonely Christ. Edward Shillito. ChIP
Many Parts, One Body. First Corinthians, XI: 12–27, Bible, *N.T. Tr. by* Edgar J. Goodspeed. GrCo-1
Many people seem to think. Nonsense Quatrains. Gelett Burgess. CenHV
Many shapes of wings. Environs. Larry Eigner. NeAP
Many Sisters to Many Brothers. Rose Macaulay. PoeT
Many sit at Jesus' table. Few Wholly Faithful. *Unknown.* BePJ
Many sow, but only the chosen reap, The. Lines to My Father. Countee Cullen. FAOV
Many stars will shine tomorrow. Star-Song. Hans Carossa. TwGV
Many thanes sat at Seaford. Proverbs of King Alfred. *At. to* King Alfred. TCEP
Many the Bacchi that brandish the rod. Few There Be. *Unknown.* OxBG
Many the forms of life. Sophocles. *Fr.* Antigone. GrPo
Many there be excelling in this kind. Michael Drayton. *Fr.* England's Heroical Epistles (*also in* Idea). NBE; SiCE; TuPP
Many Things. Oliver Wendell Holmes. PoToHe (new ed.)
Many Things Thou Hast Given Me, Dear Heart. Alice Wellington Rollins. AA
Many T'ousand Go, *with music. Unknown.* ABF
Many Truly. Hugo von Hofmannsthal. *See* Many Indeed Must Perish in the Keel.
Many water cannot quench love. An Old Saying. Swinburne. MeRV
Many weary weeks divide me. The Ship's Cook, a Captive Sings. Hugo von Hofmannsthal. TrJP
Many weary weeks I passed. Garden at Sunset. Marj Kuhl. MooP
Many winds, flowing edge to edge. The Winds. William Carlos Williams. AnAmPo; LA
Many Wings. Isabel Fiske Conant. HBMV
Many, without discrimination, mention your name. Sonnets, VII. Feng Chih. *Fr.* Twenty-seven Sonnets. WhP
Many Workmen. Stephen Crane. The Black Riders, XXXI. LiTA; NePA
Many years ago, stood our Alma Mater. Alma Mater. Robert Dye. PreP
Manyo Shu, *sels. Tr. fr. Japanese by* Arthur Waley.
"Because he is young." Okura. AWP; JAWP; LiTW; WBP
"By way of pretext." Yakamochi. AWP; JAWP; LiTW; WBP
(Pretext.) WoL
Come to Me. *Unknown, tr. by* Ishii *and* Obata. OnPM
"Dress that my brother has put on is thin, The." "The Lady of Sakanoye." AWP; JAWP; WBP
Elegy, An: "Though I see the white azaleas on the shore." *Unknown, tr. by* Ishii *and* Obata. OnPM
Endless, The. *Unknown.* OnPM
"For my sister's sake." Hitomaro. AWP; LiTW
Foreboding. *Unknown, tr. by* Ishii *and* Obata. OnPM
"How will you manage." Princess Daihaku. AWP; JAWP; WBP
(Crossing the Mountain Alone.) WoL
"I wish I could lend a coat." Akahito. AWP
"May the men who are born." Hitomaro. AWP

Manyo Shu (*continued*)
("May those who are born after me," *tr. by* Kenneth Rexroth.) LiTW; OnPJ
"Men of valor, The." Akahito. AWP; PFE, *tr. wr. at. to* Curtis Hidden Page
(Tanka.) InP
"My heart thinking." "The Lady of Sakanoye." AWP; JAWP; LiTW; PFE, *tr. wr. at. to* Curtis Hidden Page; WBP
"O boy cutting grass." Hitomaro. AWP
"O pine-tree standing." Hakutsu. AWP; JAWP; PFE, *tr. wr. at. to* Curtis Hidden Page; WBP
"On the moor of Kasuga." Hitomaro. AWP
"On the shore of Nawa." Hioki no Ko-okima. AWP
"Plum-blossom, The." Akahito. AWP
Referring to Flowers. *Unknown, tr. by* Ishii *and* Obata. OnPM
River of Heaven, The. *Unknown, tr. by* Lafcadio Hearn. AWP; LiTW
"Shall we make love." *Unknown.* AWP; LiTW
(Bright Night, A.) WoL
Tragic Memory. *Unknown, tr. by* Ishii *and* Obata. OnPM
"Unknown love." "The Lady of Sakanoye." AWP; JAWP; WBP
"What am I to do with my sister?" Prince Yuhara. AWP; JAWP; WBP
"When evening comes." Yakamochi. AWP; JAWP; LiTW; WBP
Maori Girl's Song, A. Alfred Domett. OBVV
Map, The. Elizabeth Bishop. LoGBV; ReMP
Map of Mock-Begger Hall, The. *Unknown.* CoMu
Map of My Country. John Holmes. MiAP
Map of Places, The. Laura Riding. FaBoMo; LiTA
Map of Verona, A. Henry Reed. ChMP; PoN
Map Reference T994724. John Pudney. WaP
Maple, The. James Russell Lowell. ADAH
Maple and Sumach. C. Day Lewis. CoBMV; FaBoMo
Maple buds are red, are red, The. A Song of Waking. Katharine Lee Bates. DD; OHIP; PEOR
Maple Feast. Frances Frost. SiSoSe
Maple, from the leafy wildwood. Song of the Maple. R. M. Streeter. PEOR
Maple Hangs Its Green Bee Flowers, The. John Clare. AtBAP
Maple is a dainty maid, The. Autumn Fancies. *Unknown.* FaPON; MPB; StVeCh
Maple Leaf Forever, The. Alexander Muir. BoHiPo
Maple Leaves. Thomas Bailey Aldrich. AnNE; GN; TOP
(October.) GoTP
Maple Leaves. Shiko, *tr. fr. Japanese by* H. G. Henderson. OnPM
Maple owned that she was tired, The/ of always wearing green. Autumn Fashions. Edith M. Thomas. DD; YeAr
Maple puts her corals on in May, The. The Maple. James Russell Lowell. ADAH
Maple's bloom is red, The. Of Red in Spring. David McCord. MAP; MoAmPo (1942 ed.)
Maples flare among the spruces, The. Harvest Home. Arthur Guiterman. YeAr
Mappemounde. Earle Birney. BoCaPo (1948 ed.); PeCV
Maps. Dorothy Brown Thompson. BrR; TiPo
Mar Quong, Chinese Laundryman. Christopher Morley. MPB; MW
Marathon. Clinton Scollard. VOD
Marathon Runner, The. Fenton Johnson. CDC
Marbhan, O hermit. The Hermit and the King. *Unknown.* SiB
Marble, bosomed in the mountain hoar, The. The Unattained. Henry Jerome Stockard. NoCaPo
Marble is veined as leaves and fruit. Braque. M. K. Joseph. AnNZ
Marble ruin nigh forgotten, A. Tempio di Venere. T. Sturge Moore. GTML
Marble Statuette Harpist. Sara Van Alstyne Allen. CoYe
Marble-Top. E. B. White. FiBHP; WhC
Marble, weep, for thou dost cover. On Margaret Ratcliffe. Ben Jonson. ReIE; TriL
Marble woman, naked among her violets, The. Waltz in Yungay Square. "Winétt de Rokha." AnCL
Marcela. George Henry Miles. PraNu
Marcellus. Virgil, *tr. fr. Latin by* Dryden. *Fr.* The Aeneid, VI. OBS
Marcellus, if you mark how he doth go. In Marcellum. Thomas Freeman. SiCE
March. Bryant. DD; GN; OTPC
March. Madison Cawein. MW
March. Elizabeth J. Coatsworth. YeAr
March. Isabella Valancy Crawford. OCL
March. Emily Dickinson. *See* Dear March, come in!
March. Camilla Doyle. MBP
March. Arthur Guiterman. YeAr
March. Eleanor Hammond. GFA
March. Raymond Peckham Holden. CAG
March. Nora Hopper. HBV
March. A. E. Housman. A Shropshire Lad, X. FaBoCh; LoGBV; PoVP; ViP
March. Lucy Larcom. OTPC (1946 ed.); PCH; TVSH
March. Robert Loveman. AA
March. William Morris. *Fr.* The Earthly Paradise. HBV; LPS-2; OtMeF, *abr.;* POTT; VLEP
March. Folgore da San Geminiano, *tr. fr. Italian by* D. G. Rossetti. *Fr.* Sonnets of the Months. LyMA
March, The. J. C. Squire. HBMV; LBBV; OHIP; TCEP
March. Celia Thaxter. GoTP
March. Thomas Tusser. ReIE
March. Charles Henry Webb. AA
March. Wordsworth. *See* Written in March.
March brings the lamb. *Unknown.* RIS
March Dreams. Rose Henderson. MoSiPe
March Evening. L. A. G. Strong. MBP; MoBrPo
March for Youth, A. K. G. Ossian-Nilsson, *tr. fr. Swedish by* Charles W. Stork. AnSL; PoFr
March Hares. Andrew Young. HaMV; MoVE; POTE
March in the Ranks Hard-prest, and the Road Unknown, A. Walt Whitman. AmPo; AmPP (4th ed.); IAP; MOAP; OxBA; TCAP
March into Virginia, The. Herman Melville. AmP; LiTA; LiTG; OnAP; TrGrPo; UnPo (3d ed.); ViBoPo; WaaP
March is a worker, busy and merry. March. Eleanor Hammond. GFA
March, March [Ettrick and Teviotdale]. Sir Walter Scott. *See* Border Ballad.
March, march, head erect. *Unknown.* OxNR
March! March! March! from sunrise till it's dark. The Marching Song of Stark's Men. Edward Everett Hale. GA; MC; PAH
March! March! March! They are coming. March. Lucy Larcom. OTPC (1946 ed.); PCH; TVSH
March, 1941. Paul Goodman. LiTA
March, A, November Sixth, 1832. Erik Gustaf Geijer, *tr. fr. Swedish by* Charles W. Stork. AnSL
March of Humanity, The. J. Corson Miller. HBMV
March of the Men of Harlech. *Unknown.* *See* Men of Harlech.
March of the Spirit. Angelos Sikelianos, *tr. fr. Modern Greek by* Rae Dalven. MoGP
March of the Three Kings, The. *Unknown, tr. fr. Old French.* ChrBoLe; OHIP
March of the Volunteers. Shih Ee. *See* Ch'i Lai'.
March of the Workers, The. William Morris. *Fr.* Chants for Socialists. BMEP; ViP
March-Patrol of the Naked Heroes. Herbert S. Gorman. TCPD
March Thoughts from England. Margaret L. Woods. LBBV; OBVV
March to Moscow, The. Robert Southey. BOHV; SiTL
March to Tuna Town, lads! Dalecarlian March. Erik Axel Karlfeldt. AnSL
March Twilight. Louise Bogan. NePoAm-2
March Wind, The. E. H. Henderson. BoTP
March Wind, The. *Unknown.* GFA
March Wind. Maud E. Uschold. YeAr
March Wind. Helen Wing. GFA
March-wind sang in a frosty wood, A. The Friendly Blight. Aubrey Thomas De Vere. IrPN
March Winds. Cecil Francis Lloyd. CaP; OCL
March Winds, The. George Washington Wright Houghton. YeAr
March winds and April showers. Weather Wisdom [*or* Weather Signs]. *Unknown.* FaBoBe; GoTP; HBV; HBVY; OTPC; OxNR; PPL; RIS; StaSt; TreF
March with his wind hath struck a cedar tall. On Queen Anne's Death. *Unknown.* ElL
Marché aux Oiseaux. Richard Wilbur. FiMAP
Märchen, The. Randall Jarrell. FiMAP
Marching Along. William B. Bradbury. BlG
Marching Along. Robert Browning. Cavalier Tunes, I. ATP (1935 ed.); BEL; BLV; BPN; EM-2; EmBrPo; EnLi-2; EnLit; EPN; EPP; EV-5; GEPC; HBV; MCCG; MW; OAEP; PIR; PoVP; PreP; PYM; ShBV-1; TCEP; TOP; VA; ViPo; VLEP
(From "Cavalier Tunes.") LEAP
Marching armies of the past, The. Confederate Memorial Day. *Unknown.* BlG
Marching down to Armageddon. Armegeddon. Sir Edwin Arnold. PTA-2
Marching Song. Dana Burnet. AOAH; MC; PAH
Marching Song. Ebenezer Elliott. BCEP
Marching Song, A. Kao Ang, *tr. fr. Chinese by* Henry H. Hart. PoHN
Marching Song. Robert Louis Stevenson. BoTP; FaPON; OTPC; TiPo; VLEP
Marching Song. Ernst Toller, *tr. fr. German.* MaRV
Marching Song. Tyrtaeus, *tr. fr. Greek by* C. M. Bowra. GrL; OxBG; GrR, *tr. by* H. Rushton Fairclough
Marching Song of Stark's Men, The. Edward Everett Hale. GA; MC; PAH

Marching through Georgia. Henry Clay Work. BlG; GA; MDAH; OTPC; PaA; PAH
Marcia and I went over the curve. Millions of Strawberries. Genevieve Taggard. FaPON; GoTP; MoShBr; MPB; TiPo
Marco Bozzaris. Fitz-Greene Halleck. AA; BAP; BeLS; GN; HBV; HoPM; IAP; LEAP; LPS-2; OBAV; OnHT; PECK; PFY; PIR; TCAP; TreF; WBLP
Marco Polo. Clarence Day. BOHV; LauV
Marcus Antoninus Cui Cognomen Erat Aurelius. Burns Singer. PoN
Marcus Argentarius. Kenneth Rexroth. CrMA
Marcus Curtius. Oliver St. John Gogarty. OBMV
Marcus, thou maker of idols, inspector of portents. Epigram on Marcus the Gnostic. St. Pothinus. CAW
Marcus Tullius Cicero's Death. Theodore Beza, *tr. fr. Latin by* Nicholas Grimald. ReIE
"Now have I lived, O Rome, enough for me," *sel.* TuPP
Marcus, when running in the armored race. *Unknown, tr. fr. Greek by* Humbert Wolfe. PIAE
Mardi, *sel.* Herman Melville.
We Fish. GoTP
Mardi Gras. Joseph Auslander. MuM
Mare, A. Mnasalcas, *tr. fr. Greek by* T. F. Higham. OxBG
Mare Liberum. Henry van Dyke. PaA; PAH
Mare Mediterraneum. John Nichol. VA
Mare Nostrum. Joel Oppenheimer. NeAP
Mares of the Camargue, The. Frédéric Mistral, *tr. fr. French by* George Meredith. *Fr.* The Mirèio. AWP
Margaret. Charles Cotton. TrGrPo
(Concerning Four Rural Sisters.) PeBoSo
("Margaret of humbler stature by the head.") EG
(Resolution in Four Sonnets.) PoEL-3
(Two Rural Sisters.) EnLoPo
Margaret. Walter Savage Landor. *See* Mother, I Cannot Mind My Wheel.
Margaret and Dora. Thomas Campbell. HBV
Margaret, are you grieving? Spring and Fall. Gerard Manley Hopkins. AnFE; ChTr; CoEV; EmBrPo; EnL; ExPo; GTBS-W; KN; LiTB; LiTM; MoAB; MoPo; MoVE; OAEP; PoE; PoEL-5; PoFS; PoRA; POTT; ReaPo; ReMP; SeCeV; ThWaDe; TwHP; ViP; ViPP
Margaret Fuller. Amos Bronson Alcott. AA
Margaret Fuller. James Russell Lowell. *Fr.* A Fable for Critics. APW
Margaret Grady—I fear she will burn. The Witch. Katharine Tynan. OnYI
Margaret Love Peacock. Thomas Love Peacock. OBRV; VA
Margaret my sweetest, Margaret I must go. The Souldiers Farewel to His Love. *Unknown.* CoMu
Margaret [*or* Marg'ret] of humbler stature by the head. Concerning Four Rural Sisters: Margaret. Charles Cotton. EG; EnLoPo; PeBoSo; PoEL-3; TrGrPo
Margaret; or, The Ruined Cottage. Wordsworth. *Fr.* The Excursion, I. EnRP; ERP
Margaret Roper's Vision of Her Father, Sir Thomas More. Francis Turner Palgrave. *Fr.* London Bridge. FAOV
Margaret to Dolcino. Charles Kingsley. HBV
Margaret's beauteous—Grecian arts. Margaret and Dora. Thomas Campbell. HBV
Margaret's Song. Lascelles Abercrombie. *Fr.* The New God; a Miracle. GTBS; LBBV; PoeT
Margarita first possest. The Chronicle; a Ballad. Abraham Cowley. BOHV; BrBE; CEP; EV-2; GoTL; LPS-1; SeCV-1; ViBoPo
Margaritae Sorori [*or* Sororis]. W. E. Henley. Echoes, XXXV. BLV; BMEP; CaAE; CP; EPP; GBV; GTSL; InP; LBBV; MBP; MCCG; MoBrPo; NeHB; NeMA; OBEV; OBVV; OuHeWo; PFE; PIAE; PoFS; TrGrPo; UnPo (1st ed.); WGRP; WHA
(I. M. Margaritae Sorori [*or* Sororis].) BEL; BPN; EnLi-2 (1949 ed.); OQP; POTT; PoVP; QP-1; TCEP; TOP; ViP; VOD
(In Memoriam Margaritae Sororis.) GrCo-1
(Late Lark, A.) BLA; PoRA
(Late Lark Twitters [from the Quiet Skies], A.) HBV; HiLiEn; LEAP; VLEP
(So Be My Passing.) BLP; HBVY; MaRV
Margarite of America, A, *sel.* Thomas Lodge.
Sonnet: "O shady vales, O fair enriched meads." ElL; OBSC
(All Things Revive Save the Lover.) ES
(O Shady Vales! O Fair Enrichèd Meads.) PeBoSo
(Song: "O shadie vales, O faire inriched meades.") BrBE
Margery Daw. Daniel Henry Holmes. BAP
Margery Daw. Ruth Manning-Sanders. QS
Margery Mutton-pie. *Unknown.* OxNR
Margie's Thanksgiving. Eudora S. Bumstead. TOAH
Marginal. José Maria Eguren, *tr. fr. Spanish by* Donald Devenish Walsh. AnCL
Marginal Dark, The. John Malcolm Brinnin. TwAmPo
Marginalia for Pentecost. Leo L. Ward. JKCP (1955 ed.)
Margot. George O'Neil. VOD
Margrave. Robinson Jeffers. ChMo; CMP
Marg'ret of humbler stature by the head. *See* Margaret of humbler stature . . .
Marguerite. Ibn Billita, *tr. fr. Arabic by* A. J. Arberry. MooP
Mari Magno, *sel.* Arthur Hugh Clough.
Currente Calamo. LoBV
Maria Aegyptiaca. John Heath-Stubbs. FaBoMo
Maria Bright. Walther von der Vogelweide, *tr. fr. Medieval German by* Ian G. Colvin. ISi
Maria Immaculata. Condé Benoist Pallen. JKCP
Maria intended a letter to write. How to Write a Letter. Elizabeth Turner. MoShBr; OTPC (1923 ed.)
Maria Minor. Margaret Avison. BoCaPo
Maria Wentworth. Thomas Carew. ATP; MeLP; MePo; SeCV-1; SeEP; TriL
(Inscription on the Tomb[e] of the Lady Mary Wentworth, The.) CoEV; OBS
Mariale, *sel.* Bernard of Cluny, *tr. fr. Latin.*
"Every day/ To Mary pay." CAW
Mariam, *sels.* Lady Elizabeth Carew.
Chorus: "'Tis not enough for one that is a wife." LiTL
Revenge of Injuries. LPS-3
Marian. Thomas Ashe. VA
Marian. George Meredith. EV-5; GTML; HBV
Marian Drury. Bliss Carman. HBV; VA
Mariana. Tennyson. AWP; BLV; BMEP; BPN; CH; ChER; EmBrPo; EV-5; GEPC; GTML; GTSL; HBV; InPo; JAWP; LiTL; MaPo; MyFE; OAEP; OBEV; OBRV; OBVV; OnPP; Po; PoE; PoEL-5; PoFS; PoVP; ShBV-4; TOP; TrGrPo; TwHP; UnPo (3d ed.); ViBoPo; ViPo; ViPP; VLEP; WBP
"Her tears fell with the dews at even," *sel.* LO
Mariana in the South. Tennyson. GEPC; PoVP; VLEP
Marianson. *Unknown, tr. fr. French-Canadian folk song by* William McLennan. BoCaPo
Maria's Dream. Dionysios Solomos, *tr. fr. Modern Greek by* Rae Dalven. *Fr.* Lambros. MoGP
Maria's Prayer. Dionysios Solomos, *tr. fr. Modern Greek by* Rae Dalven. *Fr.* Lambros. MoGP
Marie. Lola Ridge. MAP; MoAmPo (1942 ed.)
Marie, arise, my indolent sweet saint! Pierre de Ronsard. *Fr.* Amours de Marie. PrPoCR
Marie de Meranie, *sel.* John Westland Marston.
Parting of King Philip and Marie, The. VA
Marie Hamilton. *Unknown. See* Mary Hamilton.
Marie Magdalens Complaint at Christs Death. Robert Southwell. MePo
Marie Stuart, *sel.* Björnstjerne Björnson.
Taylor's Song, *tr. fr. Norwegian by* Charles W. Stork. AnNoLy
"Marie, will you marry me?" Bobby Shaftoe. *Unknown.* PTA-1
Marien Lee. Mary Howitt. OTPC (1923 ed.)
Marie's face is a weathered sign. Marie. Lola Ridge. MAP; MoAmPo (1942 ed.)
Marigo. Zacharias Papondoniou, *tr. fr. Modern Greek by* Rae Dalven. MoGP
Marigold, The. Blake. *Fr.* Visions of the Daughters of Albion. AtBAP
Marigold, The ("The God above, for man's delight"). William Forrest. *See* New Ballade of the Marigolds, A.
Marigold, The ("To Mary our Queen"). William Forrest. ACP; CAW
Marigold. Richard Garnett. CIV
Marigold. Bayard Taylor. BAV
Marigold, The. Allen Upward. *Fr.* Scented Leaves from a Chinese Jar. NP
Marigold, The. George Wither. OBS; SeCL; SeEP
Marigold and Myrrh. Alcaeus, *tr. fr. Greek by* Walter Petersen. GrR
Marigold So Likes the Lovely Sun[ne], The. Thomas Watson. AtBAP; LO
Marigolds. Bliss Carman. NLK
Marigolds. Louise Driscoll. BoTP; LEAP
Marigolds. Keats. *Fr.* I Stood Tiptoe upon a Little Hill. ADAH
Marigolds are nodding, The. Marigolds. Bliss Carman. NLK
Mariline, *abr.* Charles Sangster. BoCaPo
Marina. T. S. Eliot. AmP; BrBE; ChMo; ChMP; CoEV; EnLit; FaBoMo; GTBS-D; InPo; LiTA; MM; MoP; NP; PoE; PoFS; ReaPo; TwAmPo
Marina of the Rocks. "Odysseus Elytis," *tr. fr. Modern Greek by* Rae Dalven. MoGP
Marina's gone, and now sit I. Memory [*or* So Shuts the Marigold Her Leaves *or* Celadyne's Song]. William Browne. *Fr.* Britannia's Pastorals. ChTr; HBV; OBS
Marine. Arthur Rimbaud, *tr. fr. French by* Francis Golffing. AnFP
Marine Cemetery, The. Paul Valéry. *See* Cemetery by the Sea, The.
Mariner, The. Allan Cunningham. EtS
Mariner, ask not whose these ashes be. The Blessing of the Dead. *Unknown.* GrPE

Mariner, in the green spire. Land-Fall. George M. Brady. NeIP
Mariner sat on the shrouds one night, A. The Drowned Mariner. Elizabeth Oakes Smith. AA
Mariner, what of the deep? Deep Sea Soundings. Sarah Williams. EtS; WGRP
Mariners. David Morton. EtS; PoMa; VOD
Mariners, The. Margaret L. Woods. OBVV
Mariner's Adieu, The. George Hill. APW
Mariner's Bride, The. James Clarence Mangan, *after the Spanish.* IrPN
Mariner's Dream, The. William Dimond. BeLS; HBV; LPS-2
Mariners sleep by the sea, The. The Mariners. Margaret L. Woods. OBVV
Mariners' Song. Thomas Lovell Beddoes. *See* To Sea, To Sea.
Mariner's Song, The. Sir John Davies. OBSC
Mariners the while provide, The. The Taking of Cartagena. Thomas Greepe. *Fr.* The True and Perfecte Newes of the Worthy Enterprises of Sir Francis Drake, 1586. SG
Mariner's Wife, The. William Julius Mickle, *also at. to* Jean Adam. *See* Sailor's Wife, The.
Mariner's Wife, The. *Unknown.* EBSV
Marines Hymn, The. *Unknown, at. to* L. Z. Phillips. OlF; PoRL; TreF; YaD
Marionette. Fray Angelico Chavez. SaFP
Marionettes, The. Walter de la Mare. AtBAP
Marionettes. "Michael Field." TCPD
Marionettes, The. Puppets. Ming Huang. PoHN
Mariposa Lily, The. Ina Donna Coolbrith. AA
Maris Stella. Mother Francis Raphael. JKCP
Maritae Suae. William Philpot. OBEV; OBVV
Marital Tragedy. Keith Preston. WhC
Marizibill. Guillaume Apollinaire, *tr. fr. French by* Frederick Morgan. AnFP
Marjorie's Almanac. Thomas Bailey Aldrich. FaPON; GFA; MPB; PRWS; RAR
Mark. Bible, *N.T.* *See* St. Mark.
Mark, The. Louise Bogan. MOAP; MoPo; MoVE; NP
Mark. Ernest McGaffey. AA
Mark Antony. John Cleveland. ALV; ElSeCe; EPS; InvP; ReaPo; SeCL; SeEP; ViBoPo
("Whenas the nightingale chanted [*or* chaunted] her vespers.") EG; LiTL
Mark Antony's Lament. Shakespeare. *Fr.* Julius Caesar, III, i. TreFS
(Antony's Oration over the Body of Caesar, *abr.*) LPS-3
("O mighty Caesar! dost thou lie so low?" *fr.* i *and* ii.) BHV
Mark Antony's Oration. Shakespeare. *See* Antony's Oration.
Mark but the semblance of Fucata's face. Sic Ars Diluditur Arte. Henry Parrot. SiCE
Mark [*or* Marke] but this flea, and mark[e] in this. The Flea. John Donne. ATP; EnLP; HoPM; LiTB; LiTG; LiTL; MePo; Po; ReaPo; ReEn; ReIE; SeCV-1; SiTL; TrGrPo; TuPP; TwP
Mark Hopkins sat on one end of a log. Education. Arthur Guiterman. MaRV
Mark How the Bashful Morn [in Vain]. Thomas Carew. *See* Boldness in Love.
Mark how the lark and linnet sing. On the Death of Mr. Purcell. Dryden. UnS
Mark Lee was born a month before M. L. Black Boy. Carl Carmer. AnAmPo; LA
Mark me how still I am! The sound of feet. The Statue of Lorenzo de' Medici. J. E. Nesmith. AA
Mark of Man, Mark of Beast. August Derleth. DaM
Mark then my words, for I will speak, O King. Lycophron. *Fr.* Alexandra. GrPo
Mark this: for I know not where it will end. "The Mad Scene." Aeschylus. *Fr.* Choephoroe. GrR
Mark this song, for it is true. The Innocents. *Unknown.* OBB
Mark Twain; a Pipe Dream. Oliver Herford. BOHV
Mark well my heavy doleful tale. A Carol for Twelfth Day. *Unknown.* COAH; OHIP; SDH
Mark well what time thou hearest the crane's harsh-pealing cry. The Crane's Flight. Hesiod, *tr. by* Arthur S. Way. *Fr.* Works and Days. GrR
Mark when she smiles with amiable cheer. Amoretti, XL. Spenser. CBOV; ES; OBSC; PeBoSo
Mark, when you hear aloft in the clouds of the sky. When the Crane Flies South. Hesiod, *tr. by* Jack Lindsay. *Fr.* Works and Days. OxBG
Mark where the pressing wind shoots javelin-like. Modern Love, XLIII. George Meredith. AnFE; BEL; CaAE; CoEV; EnLi-2; EnLoPo; FaBoEn; GTBS-D; GTML; HBV; InPo; OAEP; OBEV; PoEL-5; RiBV; SeCeV; ViP; ViPo
Mark you the floor[e]? that square and speckled [*or* spekled] stone. The Church Floor [*or* The Church-Floore]. George Herbert. ATP; ExPo; MeLP; OBS; PoE; SeCePo; SeCeV
Marke but this flea, and marke in this. *See* Mark but this flea, and mark in this.
Marke how the bashful morne, in vaine. *See* Mark How the Bashful Morn.
Marke well this stone, it hydes a precious treasure. *Unknown.* SeCSL
Market Day. Abigail Cresson. HBMV
Market Day. Mary Webb. CH
Market-Girl, The. Thomas Hardy. At Casterbridge Fair, IV. BEL; EmBrPo; EnLi-2 (1949 ed.); EnLit; PoVP
Market of Trinidad/ in the warm moist morning! Trinidad Market. Ronald de Carvalho. AnCL
Market Place, The. Lucilius, *tr. fr. Latin by* Geoffrey Johnson. LaP
Market Place, The. J. Corson Miller. MuM
Market Square. A. A. Milne. TiPo (1959 ed.)
Market Town, The. Francis Carlin. HBMV
Market Women's Cries. Swift. *See* Verses for Fruitwomen.
Marketing. E. J. Falconer. BoTP
Markham. Robert Underwood Johnson. BAP
Marlborough, *sel.* Charles Hamilton Sorley.
"So, there, when sunset made the downs look new." WGRP
Marlow Madrigal, A. Joseph Ashby-Sterry. VA
Marmion, *sels.* Sir Walter Scott.
Abbess, The, *fr.* II. GoBC; PraNu
Challenge, *fr.* V. OtMeF
Christmas in the Olden Time, *fr. Introd. to* VI. COAH, *sl. abr.;* EPP; GoBC; LPS-2; OTPC; PCH, 3 *ll.;* PEOR, *abr.*
(Christmas: "And well our Christian sires of old," *abr.*) ERP
(Christmas: "The damsel donned her kirtle sheen," *abr.*) PCH
(Christmas in England, *abr.*) GN
(Christmas in Olden Time.) PoRL
("Heap on more wood!—the wind is chill," 3 *ll.*) TiPo
(Old Christmastide.) ChBR, 3 *ll.;* DD; MPB; SDH
Flodden, *fr.* VI. BHV; BSV; NBE, *shorter sel.;* PoFr, *abr.*
(Battle, The.) ERP, *longer sel., abr.;* PoEL-4
(Flodden Field.) LiA, *shorter sel.;* LPS-2, *abr.*
(Flodden; the Attack.) LH
(Flodden; the March.) LH
(Flodden; the Last Stand.) EV-4, *abr.;* LH
Leaders, Old Style, *fr.* III. OtMeF
Lochinvar, *fr.* V. ATP; BBV; BCEP; BEL; BeLS; BHV; BoChLi; BoTP; BSV; CBOV; CBPC; CoBE; EBSV; EmBrPo; EnLi-2 (1949 ed.); EnLit; EnRP; EPN; ERP; EV-4; FaBoBe; FaFP; FaPON; GN; GoTP; GoTS; HBV; HiLiEn; InP; LH; LoEn; LoPo; LPS-1; MaC; MCCG; MW; NeHB; OAEP; OBRV; OnHT; OnSP; OtMeF; OTPC; PCD; PECK; PFE; PIAE; PIR; PoE; PoRA; PYM; ShBV-1; StPo; StVeCh; TCEP; TOP; TreF; TVSH; WHA
(Lady Heron's Song.) CaAE
(Young Lochinvar.) CG; HBVY; RG
Marmion and Douglas, *fr.* VI. LPS-2; OHFP, *abr.;* OtMeF; WHA, *abr.*
(Battle, The.) EnRP
(Parting of Marmion and Douglas, The.) PTA-2, *abr.*
Norham Castle, *fr.* I. LPS-2
O, Woman! In Our Hours of Ease, *fr.* VI. BCEP
(O, Woman!) TreFS
Shepherd, The, *fr. Introd. to* IV. ERP
(Shepherd in Winter, The.) OTPC (1923 ed.)
To William Erskine, Esq., *Introd. to* III. EBSV
("Like April morning clouds.") OBRV
("Thus while I ape the measure wild.") OBRV
To William Stewart Rose, Esq., *Introd. to* I. EBSV
(In Memoriam; Nelson, Pitt, Fox.) EV-4; LH
(Nelson, Pitt, [and] Fox.) BSV; OBEV
(November in Ettrick Forest.) BSV
("November's sky is chill and drear.") OBRV
(Pitt and Fox.) BCEP
"When dark December glooms the day," *fr. Introd. to* V. OBRV
Where Shall the Lover Rest, *fr.* III. CBE; CBOV; CH, *abr.;* EBSV; EmBrPo; EnRP; GTBS; GTBS-D; GTBS-W; GTSE, 4 *sts.;* GTSL
(Song: "Where shall . . .") EV-4; OBRV; PoEL-4; ViBoPo
Maroon Girl, The. Walter Adolphe Roberts. PoNe
Marpessa, *sels.* Stephen Phillips.
"As he was speaking, she with lips apart." BrBE
"I love thee then." LoPS
"O brief and breathing creature." BMEP; LEAP
Marquette on the Shores of the Mississippi. John Jerome Rooney. CAW; JKCP
Marquis de Sade, The. André Breton, *tr. fr. French by* Wallace Fowlie. MiCF
Marquis of Carabas, The. Robert Barnabas Brough. HBV
"Look at this skin—at fourscore years," *sel.* FiBHP
Marriage. Blake. OxBoLi
(When a Man Has Married a Wife.) SiTL
Marriage. Austin Clarke. OxBI

Marriage. Gregory Corso. NeAP
Marriage, A. Robert Creeley. NeAP
Marriage. Babette Deutsch. AV
Marriage. W. W. Gibson. HBV; MaRV
"I dreamt not that love's way," *sel.* LO
Marriage. Donald Hall. NePoEA
Marriage. Hesiod, *tr. fr. Greek by* Jack Lindsay. *Fr.* Works and Days. OxBG
Marriage. Samuel Rogers. *Fr.* Human Life. LPS-1
Marriage. Ina Seidel, *tr. fr. German by* Herman Salinger. TwGV
Marriage ("That wife is best"). *Unknown, tr. fr. Greek.* OxBG
Marriage. Mark Van Doren. BAP
Marriage. Anna Wickham. BMEP
Marriage, The. Yvor Winters. MoVE
Marriage a-la-Mode, *sel.* Dryden.
Why Should a Foolish Marriage Vow, *fr.* I, i. InPo; LiTL; ViBoPo
(Song: "Why should a foolish marriage vow.") AWP; CEP; EiPP; SeCV-2
(Songs from the Plays.) OAEP
Marriage and the Care o't. Robert Lochore. HBV
Marriage Charm, A. Nora Hopper. HBV
Marriage-Hater Match'd, The, *sel.* Thomas D'Urfey.
Hunting Song, *fr.* II, i. SeCL
(Solon's Song.) CEP; SeEP
Marriage of a Virgin, The. Dylan Thomas. LiTM; PoE
(On the Marriage of a Virgin.) EnLoPo
Marriage of Claudia. Martial, *tr. fr. Latin by* John Arthur Pott. LiA
Marriage of Geraint, The. Tennyson. *See* Idylls of the King.
Marriage of Guenevere, The, *sel.* Richard Hovey.
Song: "Flower-born Blodueda, The." OBAV
Marriage of Heaven and Earth, The. Aeschylus, *tr. fr. Greek by* C. M. Bowra. *Fr.* Danaides. OxBG
Marriage of Heaven and Hell, The. Blake. CEP; EiPP; EnRP
Sels.
Proverbs of Hell. AtBAP; EM-1; EnLi-2; RO
"Rintrah roars and shakes his fires in the burden'd air." LoBV
Marriage of Pocahontas, The. Mrs. M. M. Webster. GA; MC; PAH
Marriage of Sir Gawain, The. *Unknown.* BaBo; ESPB; OBB
Marriage of Sir John Smith, The. Phoebe Cary. PA
Marriage of the Frog and the Mouse, The. *Unknown.* EV-1
Marriage of Thetis, The. Pindar, *tr. fr. Greek by* C. J. Billson. *Fr.* Isthmian Odes, VIII. OxBG
Marriage of True Minds, The. Shakespeare. *See* Sonnets, CXVI.
Marriage of Two. C. Day Lewis. ChMP
Marriage of Wit and Science, The, *sel.* *Unknown.*
"Come, come, lie down, and thou shalt see." TuPP
Marriage Prayer, A. Gerald Massey. PraP
Marriage Ring, A. George Crabbe. EV-3; LO; OBEV
(His Wife's Wedding Ring.) OBRV
("Ring, so worn as you behold, The.") EnLoPo
Marriage Secret. *Unknown, tr. fr. Spanish by* Havelock Ellis. OnPM
Marriage Song. Lascelles Abercrombie. *Fr.* Emblems of Love. BMEP, *abr.*; BrBE
(From "Marriage Song," *abr.*) LEAP
Marriage Song. Judah Halevi, *tr. fr. Hebrew by* Alice Lucas. TrJP
Marriage Song. William Thomas Walsh. JKCP (1955 ed.)
Marriage—Two Views. Menander, *tr. fr. Greek by* C. M. Bowra. OxBG
Marri'd. Mary Gilmore. BoAu
Married and the Single, The. Cardinal Newman.
(Fragment from Saint Gregory Nazianzen, A, *abr.*) PraNu
"Married!" he says,/ And looks at me quite sharply. On the Road. W. W. Gibson. HiLiEn
Married Lover, The. Coventry Patmore. The Angel in the House, II, xii, 1. EPN; EV-5; GoBC; GTBS; HBV; LiTL; LoPS; OBEV; PIAE; POTT; PoVP; TrGrPo; VA
("Why, having won her, do I woo?") EG
Married Man Gonna Keep Your Secret, *with music.* *Unknown.* OuSiCo
Married man I was asking, A. Marriage Secret. *Unknown.* OnPM
Married Me a Wife, *with music.* *Unknown.* OuSiCo
Marrowbone Itch, The, *with music.* *Unknown.* OuSiCo
Marry, I lent my gossip my mare, to fetch home coals. A Carman's Account of a Law-Suit. Sir David Lindsay. BOHV
Marry, if you would put me to verses or to dance. Shakespeare. King Henry V, *fr.* V, ii. LO
Marry Monday, marry for wealth. Old Superstitions. *Unknown.* HBV; HBVY; TreF
Mars and Venus. Robert Greene. *Fr.* Tullie's Love. OBSC
(Song: "Mars in a fury 'gainst love's brightest queen.") CaAE
(Sonnet or Dittie: "Mars in a fury . . .") LoBV
Mars is braw in crammasy. The Bonnie Broukit Bairn. "Hugh MacDiarmid." FaBoCh; GoTS
Mars, most-strong, gold-helm'd, making chariots crack. To Mars [*or* Hymn to Mars]. *Unknown.* *Fr.* Homeric Hymns. KN; LoBV
Marseillaise, The [*or* La]. Claude Joseph Rouget de Lisle, *tr. fr. French by* Charles H. Kerr. BoHiPo; HBV; LPS-2; PoFr; TreFS; WBLP
Marsh, The. W. D. Snodgrass. NePoEA
Marsh Blackbird, A. Harriet Sennett. BLA
Marsh-Grass. Jessie B. Rittenhouse. TBM
Marsh grass silvered by the frost. One Remembering the Marshes. Loren C. Eiseley. CAG
Marsh Marigolds. Godfrey Fox Bradby. ReTS; TVSH
Marsh Song—at Sunset. Sidney Lanier. CoBA; MOAP; SPP; TOP
Marshal Lyautey. R. N. Currey. BoSA
Marshes of Glynn, The. Sidney Lanier. AA; ADAH; AmPP; AnFE; ATP; CoAnAm; CoBA; HBV; IAP; LEAP; LiTA; LiTG; MCCG; NeMA; NePA; OxBA; PC; PoMa; SPP; TCAP; TOP; WGRP; WHA
Sels.
"As the marsh-hen secretly builds on the watery sod." BAP; MaRV; OQP; QP-1
"Beautiful glooms, soft dusks in the noonday fire." PFY
"Inward and outward to northward and southward." MAP; MoAmPo (1942 ed.)
"Oh, what is abroad in the marsh and the terminal sea?" EtS
"To the edge of the wood I am drawn, I am drawn." BBV (1951 ed.)
"Ye marshes, how candid and simple and nothing-withholding and free." PG
(Marshes, The.) NLK
Marsiliun at Saragossa, Charles at the siege. Charles at the Siege. George Hetherington. AnIV
Marsk Stig Made an Outlaw. *Unknown, tr. fr. Danish by* E. M. Smith-Dampier. BoDaBa
Marsk Stig's Daughters. *Unknown, tr. fr. Danish by* E. M. Smith-Dampier. BoDaBa
Marstig and His Lady. *Unknown, tr. fr. Danish by* E. M. Smith-Dampier. BoDaBa
Marstig woke all at the mirk midnight. The Long Ballad of Marsk Stig. *Unknown.* BoDaBa
Marston ("Marston, dropping it in the grate, broke his pipe"). Stephen Spender. FaBoTw
Marston Moor. Winthrop Mackworth Praed. BHV; ShGoBo
Marston, thy muse enharbors Horace' vein. Ad Jo. [*or* Io.] Marston et Ben. Jonson [*or* Ionson]. John Weever. ReIE; SiCE; TuPP
Marsyas. Sir Charles G. D. Roberts. PeCV; VA
Marta of Milrone. Herman Scheffauer. SCC
Martha. Walter de la Mare. GBV; MBP; MoBrPo; OTPC (1946 ed.); PoeT; TreFS; TwCV
Martha has daughters. Children of Martha. Gilean Douglas. TwCaPo
Martha is not so tall, nor yet so fair. Charles Cotton. *Fr.* Resolution in Four Sonnets . . . Concerning Four Rural Sisters. PeBoSo; PoEL-3
Martha with joy received her blessed Lord. Mary and Martha. Francis Quarles. StJW
Marthy Had a Baby, *with music.* *Unknown.* OuSiCo
Marthy Virginia's Hand. George Parsons Lathrop. BlG; MC; PAH
Martial Cadenza. Wallace Stevens. NePA; NeTW; OxBA
Martial Elegy for Some Lead Soldiers, A. Robert Louis Stevenson. SoV
Martial Friendship. Shakespeare. *Fr.* Coriolanus, IV, v. LPS-1
Martial in London. Mortimer Collins. ALV; BOHV; InMe
Martial, in sooth none should presume to write. De Poeta Martiali. Thomas Bastard. SiCE
Martial in Town. Andrew Lang. POTT; PtP
Martial Rage. Horace, *tr. fr. Latin by* William Boscawen. OnPM
Martial [*or* My friend(s)], the things that do [*or* things for to] attain. The Means to Attain a Happy Life [*or* Martial's Quiet Life *or* The Things That Cause a Quiet Life]. Martial, *tr. by* the Earl of Surrey. AEV; BCEP; CBOV; EIL; ElSeCe; EM-1; EnLi-1 (1949 ed.); EnLit; EPP; EV-1; HBV; LPS-1; OBEV; OBSC; OnPM; ReEn; SiCE; SiPS; TrGrPo; TuPP; ViBoPo
Martial, thou gav'st farre nobler epigrammes. To the Ghost of Martial. Ben Jonson. OAEP
Martial's Quiet Life. Martial. *See* Means to Attain Happy Life, The.
Martian Maid, The. Brian Lazarus. SiTL
Martin. Joyce Kilmer. BAP; CP; DDA; LBMV; MAP; NeMA; NV; OBAV; OnPP; PFY; PoeMoYo; PYM; VOD
Martin Buber in the Pub. Max Harris. BoAV

Martin Elginbrodde. *Unknown. See* Epitaph: "Here lie I, Martin Elginbrodde."
Martin Luther at Potsdam. Barry Pain. ALV; BOHV; NA
Martin Luther to His Son, Hans. Martin Luther. FAOV
Martin said to his man. Martin to His Man [*or* Who's the Fool Now?]. *Unknown.* NA; SiTL
Martin sat young upon his bed. St. Martin and the Beggar. Thom Gunn. ShBV-3
Martin to His Man. *Unknown.* NA
(Who's the Fool Now?) SiTL
Martin's Puzzle. George Meredith. EmBrPo
Martyr, The. Natalie Flohr. ChIP; PGD
Martyr, The. Herman Melville. PoEL-5; TrGrPo
"Good Friday was the day," *sel.* PoFr
Martyr Chief, The ("Nature, they say, doth dote"), *abr.* James Russell Lowell. *Fr.* Ode Recited at the Harvard Commemoration, July 21, 1865, VI. OQP; PSO; QP-1
(Abraham Lincoln.) PEOR
(Commemoration Ode, The.) PGD
(Lincoln.) DD
Martyr Chief, The ("Such was he, our Martyr-Chief"). James Russell Lowell. *See* Abraham Lincoln.
Martyr worthiest of the bleeding name, The. The True Martyr. Thomas Wade. EPN; OBVV
Martyrdom. "Rufus Learsi." TrJP
Martyrdom. Leonard Van Noppen. BAP
Martyrdom of Father Campion, The. Henry Walpole. ACP; GoBC
Martyrdom of Mary, Queen of Scots, The. Robert Southwell. *Fr.* At Fotheringay. ACP
Martyrdom of Saint Sebastian, The. Eugenio Florit, *tr. fr. Spanish by* Donald Devenish Walsh. AnCL
Martyrdom of Two Pagans. Philip Whalen. NeAP
Martyred Saint, he lies upon his bier, A. Lincoln. Corinne Roosevelt Robinson. MaRV; OHIP
Martyred Soldier, The, *sel.* Henry Shirley.
"What are earthly honors." TuPP
Martyr's Death, A. Menahem ben Jacob, *tr. fr. Hebrew.* TrJP
Martyr's Hymn, The. Martin Luther, *tr. fr. German by* William Johnson Fox. LPS-2
Martyr's Hymn, The, *ad.* Francis H. Rose. MaRV
Martyr's Mass, A. Alfred Barrett. GoBC; JKCP (1955 ed.)
Martyr's Memorial. Louise Imogen Guiney. AA
Martyrs of Nazareth. Sister Margaret Maria. PraNu
Martyrs of the *Maine,* The. Rupert Hughes. PAH
Martyrs' Song. Christina Rossetti. EmBrPo
Marvel No More. Sir Thomas Wyatt. OBSC; PoE; ReIE; SiPS
Marvel Not, Joseph, on Mary Mild. *Unknown.* AnEC
Marvel of Marvels. Christina Rossetti. MBP; OBEV (1st ed.); OxBoCh
Marvel Ye Not. Dante, *tr. fr. Italian by* Thomas Okey. *Fr.* Divina Commedia: Purgatorio, III. LiA
Marvell, still your fragrant rhyme. The Poet of Gardens. Daniel Henderson. HBMV
Marvelous thing I have mused in my mind, A. Mirabile Misterium!/ The Son of God Is Man Become. *Unknown.* AnEC
Mary, *sel.* Hew Ainslie.
It's Dowie in the Hint o' Hairst. EBSV
Mary. "W. B." ChIP; PSO
"Mary." Byron. Don Juan, V, 4. GEPC
Mary. Fray Angelico Chavez. ISi
Mary. John Clare. EnLoPo; FaBoEn; RO
(To Mary: It Is the Evening Hour.) ChTr
Mary. Thomas Curtis Clark. ChIP
Mary. Eleanor Downing. JKCP
Mary. Robert Farren. ISi
Mary. Sara Henderson Hay. BAP
Mary. Nellie Knight. ChIP
Mary. Margaret E. Sangster. DD; EOAH
Mary. Tavallali, *tr. fr. Persian by* A. J. Arberry. PeP
Mary. Rose Trumbull. MaRV
Mary Ambree. *Unknown.* OBB, *sl. abr.;* OTPC (1923 ed.), *abr.*
(Valorous Acts Performed at Gaunt by the Brave Bonny Lass, Mary Ambree, The.) TuPP
Mary Ames. *Unknown.* NA
Mary an' Martha Jes' Gone 'Long, *with music. Unknown.* BoAN-2
Mary and Darnley. Humbert Wolfe. ReTS
Mary and Elizabeth. St. Luke I: 39–45, Bible, *N.T.* (*Douay vers.*). ISi
Mary and Gabriel. St. Luke I: 26–38, Bible, *N.T.* (*Douay vers.*). ISi
Mary and Gabriel. Rupert Brooke. ISi
Mary and Her Child. *Unknown.* OxBoCh
Mary and Her Lamb. Sarah Josepha Hale. *See* Mary Had a Little Lamb.
Mary and Martha. Francis Quarles. StJW
Mary and Simeon. St. Luke II: 34–35, Bible, *N.T.* (*Douay vers.*). ISi
Mary and the Bramble. Lascelles Abercrombie. OBMV
Mary and the Lamb. Frank Dempster Sherman. InMe; PA
Mary and Willie. *Unknown.* ABS
Mary Ann. *Unknown.* LiTG
Mary-Ann was alone with her baby in arms. Mary-Ann's Child. William Barnes. CG
Mary Anne Lowder. *Unknown.* WhC
Mary-Ann's Child. William Barnes. CG
Mary Arden. Eric Mackay. VA
Mary at Nazareth. Cale Young Rice. StJW
Mary at the Cross. Clyde McGee. BPP; MaRV; PGD
Mary Beaton's Song ("Between the sunset and the sea"). Swinburne. *Fr.* Chastelard. HBV; PIR
(Between the Sunset and the Sea.) PoVP
(Love at Ebb.) BPN
Mary, beautiful and bright. Maris Stella. Mother Francis Raphael. JKCP
Mary Booth. Thomas William Parsons. AA; OBAV
Mary, daughter of Saint Anne. Slumber-Song of the Blessed Mother. *Unknown.* ChrBoLe
Mary, flower of flowers all. Now Sing We with Joy and Bliss. *Unknown.* AnEC
Mary, for the love of thee. Carol: The Five Joys of the Virgin. *Unknown.* ACP; ISi
Mary full of grace, well may thou be. Three Devout Fragments: Ave. *Unknown.* TMEV
Mary Gloster, The. Kipling. BeLS; BPN; OtMeF
Mary gould of golden hew, The. *Unknown.* SeCSL
Mary Had a Baby, Yes, Lord, *with music. Unknown.* BoAN-2
Mary had a little bird. The Canary. Elizabeth Turner. OTPC (1923 ed.)
Mary Had a Little Lamb. Sarah Josepha Hale. OlF; OxNR; SiTL, 4 *ll.*
(Mary and Her Lamb.) OnSP; SAS; TreFS
(Mary's Lamb.) FaBoBe; FaFP; FaPON; GFA; GoTP; HBV; HBVY; OnHT; OTPC; RIS; TiPo (1959 ed.); WP
Mary had a little lamb/ She set it on the shelf. *Unknown.* SiTL
Mary had a little lamb. An Old Song by New Singers. A. C. Wilkie. BOHV; PA
Mary had a little llama. Happy Ending. Harry Silleck Grannatt. StaSt
Mary had a pretty bird. Mother Goose. PPL
Mary Had a William Goat, *with music. Unknown.* AS
Mary [*or* Marie] Hamilton. *Unknown.* BaBo; BSV; CBOV, *abr.;* EBSV; ESPB (A and B *vers.*); OAEP; OuHeWo; PoFS; ReaPo; ViBoFo, *with music*
(Queen's Marie, The.) OBB; OBEV
("Word's gane to the kitchen.") LO
Mary Hamilton's Last Goodnight. *Unknown.* ViBoFo
Mary has a thingamajig clamped on her ears. Manual System. Carl Sandburg. TiPo (1952 ed.)
Mary, Helper of Heartbreak. Margaret Widdemer. BAP; HBMV
(Irish Love Song.) SBMV
Mary Hynes. Padraic Fallon, *after the Irish of* Anthony Raftery. AnIV; OxBI
Mary Hynes. Lady Gregory, *after the Irish of* Anthony Raftery. DiM; GTIV
Mary Hynes. Frank O'Connor, *after the Irish of* Anthony Raftery. KiLC
Mary! I want a lyre with other strings. To Mary Unwin [*or* Sonnet to Mrs. Unwin *or* To Mrs. Unwin]. William Cowper. BEL; BoFr; CBOV; CoBE; ES; EV-3; GTBS; GTBS-D; GTBS-W; GTSE; GTSL; HBV; LEAP; OAEP; OBEC; OBEV; PeBoSo; RiBV; TCEP; TrGrPo
Mary Immaculate. Eleanor C. Donnelly. CAW; JKCP
Mary, in a dream of love. Dialogue between Mary and Gabriel. W. H. Auden. *Fr.* For the Time Being—A Christmas Oratorio. ISi
Mary, in the house of John. The Mother of Judas. Amelia Josephine Burr. WHL
Mary is a gentle name. Gentle Name. Selma Robinson. MoShBr; MoSiPe
Mary is a lady bright. A, A, A, A [*or* Nunc Gaudet Maria]. *Unknown.* AnEC; ISi
Mary is black, and taller than the last. Charles Cotton. *Fr.* Resolution in Four Sonnets . . . Concerning Four Rural Sisters. PeBoSo; PoEL-3
Mary Jane. *Unknown.* NA
Mary Knew. Ida Norton Munson. ChIP
Mary laid her Child among. Carol. Norman Nicholson. NeBP; StJW
Mary Le More. George Nugent Reynolds. OnYI
Mary, long by Boss's kisses bored. Don't Look Now but Mary Is Everybody. Peter Viereck. LiTA; LiTM (rev. ed.); ReMP
Mary McGuire's our Cook, you know. This and That. Florence Boyce Davis. FaPON; GaP; TiPo (1952 ed.)
Mary Magdalene. Richard Burton. BPP; ChIP
Mary Magdalene. Dante Gabriel Rossetti. *See* Mary Magdalene at the Door of Simon the Pharisee.
Mary Magdalene. Leonora Speyer. HBMV; NP
(One Version.) NV; TBM

Mary Magdalene and the Other Mary. Christina Rossetti. StJW
Mary Magdalene at the Door of Simon the Pharisee. Dante Gabriel Rossetti. BPN; EmBrPo; GoBC; POTT; PoVP; VA
Mary Magdalene, that easy woman. Lent. W. R. Rodgers. AnIL; NeBP; OxBI
Mary, maiden, mild and free. A Little Song. Robert Grosseteste. ISi
Mary, Mary [*or* Mistress Mary], quite contrary. Mother Goose. BoChLi; BoN; BrR; FaBoBe; FaFP; HBV; HBVY; OnHT; OTPC; OxNR; PCH; PPL; RIS; SAS; SiTL; StVeCh; TiPo
Mary Middling. Rose Fyleman. SUS
Mary Modyr, Cum and See. *Unknown.* OxBoCh
Mary Morison. Burns. AnFE; BEL; BLV; BoLiVe; CEP; CoBE; EBSV; EM-1; EnLi-2; EnLit; EnRP; EV-3; GTBS; GTBS-D; GTBS-W; GTSE; HBV; InPo; LPS-1; MCCG; OAEP; OBEC; OBEV; OuHeWo; REAL; TrGrPo; TyEnPo; WHA
(Devotion.) LH
("O Mary, at thy window be.") EG
(Song: Mary Morison.) AWP; JAWP; TOP; WBP
Mary, most serenely fair. To the Sistine Madonna. Cornelia Otis Skinner. ISi
Mary Mother, Heart Sublime. Mother's Petition, in Wartime. Helen M. Burgess. ChIP
Mary mother, meek and mild. Nowell, ell, ell, ell . . . *Unknown.* AnEC
Mary, Mother of our Maker. The Annunciation. St. Nerses. ISi
Mary Mother, well with thee! A Very Popular Prayer. *Unknown.* TMEV
Mary o' the Wild Moor. *Unknown.* *See* Mary of the Wild Moor.
Mary O'Brian. J. Redwood Anderson. LBBV; OnPP
Mary of Bethlehem. Mary King. ISi
Mary of Nazareth, *sel.* Abby Maria Hemenway.
Annunciation Night. ISi
Mary of [*or* o'] the Wild Moor (*diff. versions*). *Unknown.* ABS; BaBo
(When Poor Mary Came Wandering Home, *frag., with music.*) AS
Mary on Her Way to the Temple. Ruth Schaumann, *tr. fr. German by* Edwin Buers. ISi
Mary on the Silvery Tide. *Unknown.* ShS
Mary Passes. *Unknown, tr. fr. German.* ISi
Mary Pondered All These Things. Edwin McNeill Poteat. ChIP
Mary, Queen of Scots. Henry Glassford Bell. BeLS; BLPA; FaBoBe
Mary Queen of Scots. Burns. BHV
(Lament of Mary Queen of Scots.) BoHiPo
Mary Queen of Scots. Charles Tennyson Turner. HBV
Mary Queen of Scots Landing at the Mouth of the Derwent, Workington. Wordsworth. ES
Mary Ross, The. Blanche Edith Baughan. BoAu
Mary Salome, Widow. Anne Ryan. JKCP (1926 ed.)
Mary sat in the corner dreaming. In the Carpenter's Shop. Sara Teasdale. HBMV; StJW
Mary sat musing on the lamp-flame at the table. The Death of the Hired Man. Robert Frost. AmPP; AnNE; ATP; BAV; CBOV; ChMo; CMP; CoBA; CoV; DDA; HoPM; MaC; MAP; MoAB; MoAmPo; MOAP; NeMA; OxBA; PCN; PFE; PIAE; PreP; SeCeV; TCAP; TCPD; TOP; TrGrPo; TwHP; UnPo (1st ed.)
Mary Sets the Table. David Morton. POT; PoTo
Mary Shakespeare. Ada Jackson. PoMa
Mary Shepherdess. Marjorie Pickthall. ISi; VOD; WHL
Mary Singing. Alfred de Musset, *tr. fr. French by* Alan Conder. TrFP
Mary Sings. Norah M. Holland. ChrBoLe
Mary Star of the sea! Lionel Johnson. *Fr.* Cadgwith. ISi
Mary Stuart, *sel.* Schiller, *tr. fr. German.*
"Well! Have I acted right at last, my lady?" ReTS
Mary Stuart, *sel.* Swinburne.
Song: "And ye maun braid your yellow hair." BPN
Mary Stuart said to Darnley, "Nay, do not scold me!" Mary and Darnley. Humbert Wolfe. ReTS
Mary, the Christ long slain, passed silently. Motherhood. Agnes Lee. BAP; BLPA; HBMV; MOAH; NP; NV
Mary the Cook-Maid's Letter to Dr. Sheridan. Swift. LoBV; OnYI; OxBoLi
Mary, the Maid of the Inn. Robert Southey. CG
Mary, the maiden, walked out in the country. After the Annunciation. Eileen Duggan. ISi
Mary the mother and Jesu the child. Christmas Night. Alice Isabel Hazeltine. ChrBoLe
Mary the Mother of Jesus. The Spinner. Charles L. O'Donnell. GoBC; ISi
Mary the Mother sang to her Son. A Carol. Lizette Woodworth Reese. HBMV
Mary, the mother, sits on the hill. Carol [*or* Song]. Langdon Elwyn Mitchell. BOL; ChrBoLe; OHIP; SDH
Mary to Her Babe. "L. L. O'K." BOL
"Mary, uplifted to our sight." On the Feast of the Assumption. Eleanor Downing. JKCP
Mary, Virgin and Mother. Elizabeth Seton. JKCP
Mary walked in the daisies. Gabriel. Willard Wattles. HBMV
Mary Was a Red Bird, *with music. Unknown.* OuSiCo
Mary Was Watching. *Unknown, tr. fr. Czech by* Mary Cochrane Vojacek. ISi
Mary, we hail thee, Mother and Queen compassionate. Salve Regina. *At. to* Hermanus Contractus. ISi
Mary Weeps for Her Child. *Unknown.* OxBoLi
Mary went through the thorn-wood wild. Mary Passes. *Unknown, tr. fr. German.* ISi
Mary,—what melodies mingle. Mary and the Lamb. Frank Dempster Sherman. InMe; PA
Mary, when that little child. Mary. Rose Trumbull. MaRV
Mary Will Smile. William Cliffton. BAV
Mary Winslow. Robert Lowell. AnNE; MiAP; MoVE
Mary wore her red dress. Mary Was a Red Bird. *Unknown.* OuSiCo
Mary Wore Three Links of Chain, *with music. Unknown.* AS
(All Mah Sins Been Taken Away, *with music.*) SoAF
Maryland. James Ryder Randall. *See* My Maryland.
Maryland Battalion, The. John Williamson Palmer. AA; HBV; IDAH; MC; PaA; PAH
Maryland! My Maryland! James Ryder Randall. *See* My Maryland.
Maryland Resolves. *Unknown.* PAH
Maryland Virginia Caroline. Emblems. Allen Tate. AmPP (3d ed.); AWP; InPo; MOAP
Maryland Yellow-Throat, The. Henry van Dyke. BAP; DDA; HBV; OBAV
Mary's Assumption. Alfred J. Barrett. ISi
Mary's Baby. Shaemas O'Sheel. CAW; HBV; HBVY; JKCP
Mary's Dream. John Lowe. EBSV
Mary's Easter. Marie Mason. DD; EOAH
Mary's Ghost. Thomas Hood. FiBHP
Mary's Girlhood. Dante Gabriel Rossetti. BPN; CAW; EmBrPo; GBV; GoBC; ISi; MeRV; PoVP; SDH; VLEP; WGRP
Mary's gone a-milking. Milking Pails. *Unknown.* CH
Mary's Lamb. Sarah Josepha Hale. *See* Mary Had a Little Lamb.
Mary's Lament for Shelley, Lost at Sea. Thomas Holley Chivers. *See* Burdens of Unrest.
Mary's Lullaby. Elizabeth J. Coatsworth. ChrBoLe
Mary's Lullaby. Ivy O. Eastwick. ChBR
Mary's Manger-Song. William Channing Gannett. BOL
Mary's Son. Lucia Trent. ChIP; PGD
Mary's Song. Marion Angus. LO
Mary's Vision. *Unknown, tr. fr. Irish by* Eleanor Hull. ISi
Ma's Tools. *Unknown.* DDA; PEDC
Masar. Walter Savage Landor. *Fr.* Gebir, V. LoBV
("Once a fair city, courted then by kings.") OBRV
Mascot, A. Arthur Guiterman. AlBD
Mashona Husbandman, A. Arthur Shearly Cripps. MM
Mask, The. Elizabeth Barrett Browning. OBVV; VLEP
Mask. Elizabeth Cox. GoYe
Mask, The. Clarissa Scott Delany. CDC; PoNe
Mask. Ken Etheridge. MoWP
Mask, The. Jessie M. Heiner. MuM
Mask, A. Milton. *See* Star That Bids the Shepherd Fold, The.
Mask. Stephen Spender. MoAB; MoBrPo; NeMA
Mask, The. *Unknown.* BoFr
Mask [*or* Masque] of Anarchy, The. Shelley. CoEV, *abr.;* EM-2, *much abr.;* EmBrPo; EnRP
Sels.
"Last came Anarchy," *much abr.* PoFr
"Stand ye calm and resolute," *sts.* 79–91. LoBV
Mask of Cupid, The. Spenser. *See* Masque of Cupid, The.
Mask of Mutability, The. Spenser. *See* Pageant of the Seasons and the Months, The.
Mask Presented at Ludlow-Castle, A. Milton. *See* Comus.
Masked Ball, The. Wilson MacDonald. MaRV
Masked Shrew, The. Isabella Gardner. ImOP
Masks. Thomas Bailey Aldrich. AA
Mason, The. Robert Farren. JKCP (1955 ed.); OnYI; OxBI
Masque of Anarchy, The. Shelley. *See* Mask of Anarchy, The.
Masque of Augurs, The, *sel.* Ben Jonson.
Apollo's Song. LoBV
Masque of Balliol, The, *sels.* Henry Charles Beeching, *and others.* CenHV
"First come I. My name is Jowett." Henry Charles Beeching.
"I am a most superior person." Henry Charles Beeching.
"I am Andrew Cecil Bradley." Cecil Arthur Spring-Rice.
"I am featly-tripping Lee." Henry Charles Beeching.

Masque of Balliol, The (*continued*)
"I am Huxley, blond and merry." John B. B. Nichols.
"I am the Dean of Christ Church, Sir." Cecil Arthur Spring-Rice.
"Old tips come out as good as new." John William Mackail.
"Roughly, so to say, you know." John William Mackail.
"Upright and shrewd, more woo'd of fame." Henry Charles Beeching.
Masque of Beauty, The, *sel.* Ben Jonson.
Song: "When love at first did move." GoBC
Masque of Christmas, The. Ben Jonson. OxBoLi
Masque of Cupid, The. Spenser. *Fr.* The Faerie Queene, III, 11 *and* 12. EV-1; PoEL-1 (*fr.* 12)
(Mask of Cupid, The, *fr.* 12.) OBSC
(Procession of Cupid, The, *fr.* 12.) NBE
Masque of Life and Death, A. Witter Bynner. AnAmPo; LA
Masque of Loved Ladies, A. Anne Goodwin Winslow. LS
Masque of Oberon, The. Ben Jonson. *See* Oberon, the Fairy Prince.
Masque of Pandora, The, *sel.* Longfellow.
All-seeing Gods, The. OQP; QP-2
Masque of Queen Bersabe, The, *sel.* Swinburne.
"I am the queen Herodias." AtBAP
Masque of Queens, The, *sel.* Ben Jonson.
Witches' Charms, The, I–III. ElL; PoMS, *sl. shorter;* ThWaDe; TwHP
Witches' Charm, III: "Owl is abroad, The." FaBoCh; LoBV; LoGBV; ReEn
(Charm.) KN
Masque of Reason, A, *sel.* Robert Frost.
God's Speech to Job. OnHM
Masque of Souls, A. "Richard Scrace." CPG
Masque of the Gypsies, The. Ben Jonson. *See* Gypsies Metamorphosed, The.
Masque of the Inner-Temple and Gray's Inne, The, *sels.* Francis Beaumont.
"More pleasing were these sweet delights," III. OBS
"On blessed youths, for Love doth pause," II. OBS
"Peace and silence be the guide," V. OBS
(Three Songs, 3.) GoBC
"Shake off your heavy trance," I. ElSeCe; EV-2; OBS; OnPM; TrGrPo; ViBoPo
(Dance, A.) BLV
(Fit Only for Apollo.) ChTr
(Song for a Dance.) ElL; FaBoCh; LoGBV
(Three Songs, 1.) GoBC
(Superlative Dance and Song.) UnS
"Ye [*or* We] should stay longer if we durst," IV. OBS; TrGrPo; ViBoPo
(Three Songs, 2.) GoBC
Masque of the Metamorphosed Gipsies, A. Ben Jonson. *See* Gypsies Metamorphosed, The.
Masque of the Middle Temple and Lincoln's Inn, The, *sels.* George Chapman.
Descend, Fair Sun! ElL; TuPP
Now, Sleep, Bind Fast. TuPP
(Bridal Song.) ElL; LO
Masque of the Twelve Months, The, *sel. Unknown, at. to* George Chapman.
Shine Out, Fair Sun, With All Your Heat. ChTr
(Song.) ElL
Masque Presented at Ludlow Castle, A. Milton. *See* Comus.
Masquerade. Faith Baldwin. MuM
Masquerader, The. Aline Kilmer. HBMV
Mass of Love. *Unknown, tr. fr. Spanish by* Anna Pursche. LiTW; TeCS
Mass was sung, and prayers were said, The. *See* Then mass was sung . . .
Massa bin an' sol' yeh. O! Link o' Day. *Unknown.* TrAS
Massa had a old gray rooster. Bile Dem Cabbage Down. *Unknown.* SoAF
Massa ob de Sheepfol', De. Sarah Pratt McLean Greene. *See* Sheepfol', De.
Massachusetts Song of Liberty. Mercy Warren. PAH
Massachusetts to Virginia. Whittier. AmPP; AnNE; CoBA; IAP; WoL
Massacre of the Innocents, The. André Salmon, *tr. fr. French by* W. J. Strachan. MiFP
Massacre of the Macpherson, The. William Edmondstoune Aytoun. CenHV; ChTr; OtMeF; VA
Massa's in de Cold, Cold Ground. Stephen Collins Foster. AA; APW; IHA; LEAP; OBAV; OlF; TreF
Massasauga, The. Hamlin Garland. AA
Massenet/ Never wrote a Mass in A. Antony Butts. FiBHP
Masses, The. Benjamin De Casseres. DDA
Masses. Carl Sandburg.
(Poor, The.) NP
Masses. César Vallejo, *tr. fr. Spanish by* H. R. Hays. TwSpPo
Masses, The! The masses! The Masses. Benjamin De Casseres. DDA
Massive gates of Circumstance, The. Trifles. *Unknown.* HBV
Master, The. Thomas Curtis Clark. *See* Abraham Lincoln, the Master.
Master, The. "C. G. L." ImOP
Master, The. W. S. Merwin. NePoEA
Master, The. S. D. Robbins. BePJ
Master, The. E. A. Robinson. AmP; BAP; GTBS-W; HBV; HH; InP; LBMV; LEAP; LiTA; LiTG; LiTM (rev. ed.); MAP; MoAB; MoAmPo; NeMA; NP; OHIP; OTPC (1946 ed.); PaA; PFY; PIAE; PoLFOT; PoRL; TCPD; TriL
Master and Man. Sir Henry Newbolt. WhC
Master Artisan, make me over. "Tell Ye the Faint of Heart." Francis J. Rock. JKCP (1955 ed.)
Master Blacksmith, The. Arnold Andrews. OQP; QP-1
Master Brunetto, this my little maid. Sonnet: To Brunetto Latini. Dante. AWP
Master calls for thee, The. The Divine Call. Sister Mary Genevieve. PraNu
Master-Chord, The. William Caldwell Roscoe. VA
Master City, The. Rose J. Orente. GoYe
Master divine. Thanks for New Opportunities. *Unknown.* PSO
Master Edwards' May. Richard Edwards. *See* M. Edwards' May.
Master-Foe, The. William Baylebridge. *Fr.* Sextains. BoAV
Master Francesco, I have come to thee. Petrarch. Giosuè Carducci. AWP
Master Francis Beaumont's Letter to Ben Jonson. Francis Beaumont. BEL; ElSeCe; EPP, *abr.;* PtP
(Letter to Ben Jonson, A.) LoBV
(M. Francis Beaumont's Letter to Ben Jonson.) SeEP
(Mr. Francis Beaumont's Letter . . . *abr.*) OBS; ViBoPo
Sels.
"Methinks the little wit I had is lost." LEAP
"What things have we seen." EnLit
Master Had a Bran' New Coat, *with music. Unknown.* StDa
"Master has come over Jordan, The." Christ and the Little Ones. Julia Gill. BLPA
Master He was hungry, The. The Blessing. Mary Colborne-Veel. BoAu
Master, I hail you from my heart. A Message to Meng Hao-jan. Li Po. BoFr
Master I have, and I am his man. Master and Man. Mother Goose. NA; OxNR; TiPo
Master, I see thee with the locks of grey. Ronsard. Andrew Lang. PtP
Master, in memory of that Verse of Thine. Lines Written by Request. Sir Owen Seaman. PA
Master-Knot, The. Omar Khayyám, *tr. fr. Persian by* Edward Fitzgerald. *Fr.* The Rubáiyát. OnPM
Master, Make Us One. Hermann Hagedorn. *Fr.* Lincoln; an Ode. PSO
Master Mariner, The. George Sterling. HBV; MAP; MoAmPo (1942 ed.); PoTo; TCAP
Master, may thy mercy hold me. Springtime—a Humble Cry from the Depths. Clemens Brentano. AnGP
Master mind, that taste and genius grace, A. Lord Leigh. *Fr.* On Uvedale Price's Essay. EnSW
Master Musician. Margaret Evelyn Singleton. ChIP
Master of discords John. The Harper. *Unknown.* AnIL; KiLC
Master of human destinies am I. Opportunity. John James Ingalls. AA; BAP; BTP; FaFP; HBV; HBVY; LBAP; MaRV; OHFP; OQP; PTA-1; QP-1; TreF; WBLP; YaD
Master of Laborers, The. George Edward Day. PGD; PSO
Master of life, the day is done. The Last Prayer. Wilfred Campbell. CPG
Master of metaphor, at three. David. Walker Gibson. CrMA; NePoAm
Master of My Boat, The. Joseph Addison Richards, *wr. at. to* George Macdonald. OQP; QP-2
(Boat, The.) MaRV
Master of None. Margites, *tr. fr. Greek by* T. F. Higham. OxBG
Master of the murmuring courts. Love's Nocturn. Dante Gabriel Rossetti. BPN; EmBrPo
Master of Time, The. Jan van Nijlen, *tr. fr. Dutch by* A. J. Barnouw. LiTW
Master-Player, The. Paul Laurence Dunbar. MaRV
Master Singers, The. Rhys Carpenter. WGRP
Master Sky-Lark, *sels.* John Bennett.
Sky-Lark's Song, The. AA
Song of the Hunt, The. AA
Master-songs are ended, and the man, The. Walt Whitman. E. A. Robinson. AmP; CoV; NePA; OxBA
Master Spirit, The. George Chapman. *Fr.* The Conspiracy of Charles, Duke of Byron, III, i. EtS
(Brave Spirit, A.) EV-1
("Give me a spirit that on this life's rough sea.") MyFE; ViBoPo
(Invocation: "Give me a spirit that on this life's rough sea.") KN

Master stood in His garden, The. For the Master's Use [*or* The Watered Lilies]. *Unknown.* BLPA; BLRP
Master stood upon the mount, and taught, The. Progress. Matthew Arnold. ChIP; EmBrPo; EPN; MaRV; StJW
Master Surgeon. Lucia Trent. ChIP
Master, the Swabber, The. Shakespeare. *Fr.* The Tempest, II, ii. InPo; ViBoPo
(None of Us Cared for Kate.) OnPM
(Stephano's Song.) SG; WhC
Master, this very hour. This Very Hour. Lizette Woodworth Reese. AnAmPo; HBMV; LA
Master, to do great work for Thee my hand. Life-Mosaic. Frances Ridley Havergal. TrPWD
Master-Welder, The. Sarah Wingate Taylor. JKCP (1955 ed.)
Master, where abidest Thou? Rabbi, Where Dwellest Thou? Come and See. *Unknown.* BePJ
Master, whose fire kindled our glad surprise. The Master. "C. G. L." ImOP
Masterful Man, The. Henry Tyrrell. *See* Lincoln.
Masterpiece, The. Walter Conrad Arensberg. AnAmPo; BAP; LA
Masterpiece, The. Walter Malone. *See* Lincoln.
Masterpiece, The. Kathleen Millay. BAP
Masters. Kingsley Amis. NePoEA; PoLFOT
Masters, The. "Laurence Hope." HBV
Masters, The. Margaret Widdemer. HBMV
Masters, in This Hall. William Morris. AnEC; ChTr; COAH
Master's Invitation, The. Anson Davies Fitz Randolph. AA
Master's Man, The. William G. Tarrant. MaRV; OQP; PSO; QP-1
Masters of the Heart Touched the Unknown, The. Delmore Schwartz. FiMAP
Master's Touch, The. Horatius Bonar. BePJ; HBV; LPS-2; MaRV; TrPWD; VA
Mastery. Charles F. Lummis. BAP
Mastery. Sara Teasdale. Interlude: Songs Out of Sorrow, II. ChMo; CMP; HBV; QS; WGRP
Mastiff, The. John Gay. AlBD
Mastiff is a stately brute, The. Dogs and Dogs. *Unknown.* AlBD
Masts rise white to the stars, The. Veneta Marina. Arthur Symons. VLEP
Match, The. Andrew Marvell. NBE
Match, A. Swinburne. ALV; BEL; BMEP; BPN; EmBrPo; EnLi-2; EnLit; GTBS-D; GTBS-W, *abr.*; GTML; GTSL; HBV; LEAP; LiTL; LoPo; LPS-1; OBVV; PFE; PG (1945 ed.); PIR; PoVP; TOP; VA; VLEP
Match's Way, The. Vladimir Kazin, *tr. fr. Russian by* Jack Lindsay. RuPo
Mated to the Millennium,—Time's last heir. Columbia. Frederic Lawrence Knowles. IDAH
"Mater á Dios, preserve us." With Cortez in Mexico. Wilfred Campbell. PAH
Mater Amabilis. Aubrey Thomas De Vere. ISi
Mater Amabilis. Emma Lazarus. BOL; MOAH; OHIP
Mater Christi. Aubrey Thomas De Vere. *Fr.* May Carols. PoVP
Mater Dei. Katharine Tynan. GTIV; ISi
Mater Desiderata. Winthrop Mackworth Praed. OBVV
Mater Dolorosa. William Barnes. BCEP; CH; HBV; MaRV; MotAn; OBEV
(Mother's Dream, The.) EV-4; PoVP; RO
Mater Dolorosa. John Fitzpatrick. JKCP
Mater Dolorosa. J. Grimstone. TMEV
Mater Dolorosa. Louis V. Ledoux. BAP; SBMV
Mater Dolorosa. Elliott Napier. BoAu
Mater Dolorosa. Swinburne. BMEP; VLEP
Mater Dolorosa. John Banister Tabb. AnAmPo; LA; StJW
Mater Dulcissima. *Unknown.* *See* Quid Petis, O Fili?
Mater Hierusalem Civitas Sancta Dei. *Unknown.* MeRV
Mater in Extremis. Jean Starr Untermeyer. TBM
Mater Incognita. Sister Mary Benvenuta. ISi
Mater Misericordiae. Sister St. Miriam of the Temple. JKCP (1955 ed.)
Mater Salutaris. *Unknown.* AnEC
Mater Severa. Stephen Lucius Gwynn. TIP
Mater Tenebrarum. James Thomson. EmBrPo
Mater Triumphalis. Swinburne. EmBrPo; POTT; VLEP
"I am thine harp between thine hands, O mother," *sel.* BMEP; BPN
Maternal Earth stirs redly from beneath. The Flaming Terrapin, I. Roy Campbell. MBP; MoBrPo
Maternal Grief. Wordsworth. MOAH
Maternal Lady with the Virgin Grace. Mary Lamb. ISi
(Aspiration.) CAW
Maternity. Babette Deutsch. TBM
Maternity. Anne P. L. Field. MOAH
Maternity. Jean Ingelow. *See* Seven Times Four.
Maternity. Alice Meynell. NP; NV; POTE
(Mother.) MaRV
(One Wept Whose Only Child Was Dead.) AnFE
Mathematical. Jessica Nelson North. NP
Mathematics. Lionel Wiggam. PoMa
Mathematics or the Gift of Tongues. Anna Hempstead Branch. ImOP
Mathmid, The. Hayyim Nahman Bialik, *tr. fr. Hebrew by* Maurice Samuel. AWP; PoFr, *abr.*
Matilda. Hilaire Belloc. CenHV; FaBoCh; LoGBV; StPo; YT
Matilda, come hither, I pray. The Crocus. Mary Elliott. OTPC (1923 ed.)
Matilda Jane, you never look. Doll's Song. "Lewis Carroll." OTPC (1946 ed.)
Matilda, Matriarch. Mazie V. Caruthers. CIV
Matilda Maud Mackenzie frankly hadn't any chin. How a Girl Was Too Reckless of Grammar by Far. Guy Wetmore Carryl. BOHV; FiBHP
Matilda, now go take thy bed. Requiem. Robert Davenport. *Fr.* King John and Matilda. SeCL; TuPP
Matilda postures on the window-sill. Fish-Day. Mazie V. Caruthers. CIV
Matilda told such dreadful lies. Matilda. Hilaire Belloc. CenHV; FaBoCh; LoGBV; StPo; YT
Matilda's busy mothering these days. Mothering. Mazie V. Caruthers. CIV
Matilda's grown grandmotherly these days. Matilda, Matriarch. Mazie V. Caruthers. CIV
Matilda's Manners. Mazie V. Caruthers. CIV
Matin Song. Nathaniel Field. *See* Rise, Lady Mistresse, Rise!
Matin Song. John Ford. *See* Fly Hence Shadows.
Matin Song. Thomas Heywood. *See* Pack, Clouds, Away.
Matin-Song. *Unknown, tr. fr. German by* Jethro Bithell. WoL
Matins. John Finley. PraP
Matins. George Herbert. CBE
(Mattens.) TrPWD
Matins. John Banister Tabb. SPP
Matins. Henry van Dyke. MaRV
Matres Dolorosae. Robert Bridges. MOAH
Matriarch of your chain and consort of the clouds. That Far Lone Mountain. Sister Mary Stephanie. JKCP (1955 ed.)
Matrix, *sel.* Dorothy Wellesley.
"Spiritual, the carnal, are one, The." OBMV
Matron Cat's Song, The. Ruth Pitter. PoC
Matronalia, March 1, The. Tibullus, *tr. fr. Latin by* Hubert Creekmore. LaP
Matt Casey formed a social club that beat the town for style. The Band Played On. John F. Palmer. TreF
Mattens. George Herbert. *See* Matins.
Matter. Louis Untermeyer. YT
Matter is indestructible. Smoke Stack. A. M. Sullivan. WaKn
Matter of Life and Death, A. Richard Aldridge. NePoAm
Matter whose movement moves us all. Entropy. Theodore Spencer. ImOP
Matthew. Bible, *N.T.* *See* St. Matthew.
Matthew. Clive Sansom. HaMV
Matthew. Sister Margaret Teresa. JKCP (1955 ed.)
Matthew. Wordsworth. BPN; EmBrPo; ERP; GEPC
Matthew and Mark and Luke and holy John. Epi-strauss-ium. Arthur Hugh Clough. ViP; ViPP
Matthew and Mark, and Luke and John. The New Testament. Thomas Russell. TreFS
Matthew, Mark, Luke and John. *Unknown.* FaBoCh; GoTP; LoGBV; OTPC; OxNR; RIS; SiTL
(Bed Charm.) HBVY; PCH
(Before Sleeping.) CAW; CH; MeRV; TreF
(Prayer.) OxBoLi
(Prayer before Sleeping.) WHL
(Safe in Bed.) CBPC
(White Paternoster, The.) PC
Matthew, Mark, Luke, and John,/ Hold my horse till I leap on. *Unknown.* OxNR
Mattie's Wants and Wishes. Grace Gordon. DDA
Maturity. J. Elgar Owen. WaP
Mauberley. Ezra Pound. *Fr.* Hugh Selwyn Mauberley. CoBMV; CoV; LiTA; LiTM (rev. ed.); MoPo
Mauberley, 1920, II. NP
Maud. Henry S. Leigh. BOHV
Maud. Tennyson. EmBrPo; OAEP; PIR, *abr.*; PoVP; ViPo; ViPP; VLEP
Sels.
"Birds in the high Hall-garden," Pt. I, xii. BPN; CBOV; EV-5; GEPC; OTPC (1923 ed.)
"Cold and clear-cut face," Pt. I, iii. GEPC
Come Into the Garden, Maud, Pt. I, xxii. BEL; BPN; EM-2; EnLit; EPN; EPP; EV-5; ExPo; FiP; GEPC; GTBS; GTSE; GTSL; HBV; LEAP; LiTG; LiTL; LPS-1; MCCG; OBVV; PIAE; TreF; TyEnPo; UnPo (1st ed.); VA
(Lyric from "Maud.") EnLi-2
(Maud.) BMEP; GTBS-W; OBEV
(Song [from "Maud"].) AWP; InPo; JAWP; TCEP; TOP; WBP

Maud (*continued*)
Dead, Long Dead, Pt. V, i. AtBAP
England, Pt. III, v. BHV
"Go not, happy day," Pt. I, xvii. BPN; LiTL; OBVV; TOP
(Song: "Go not, happy day.") ATP
I Have Led Her Home, Pt. I, xviii. BEL; BMEP; BPN; ChER; EV-5; FiP; GEPC; GTBS-D; PoEL-5
"O, let the solid ground," Pt. I, xi. BPN; GEPC
(Song: "O, let the solid ground.") HBV
O That 'Twere Possible, Pt. II, iv. AtBAP; BMEP; BPN, *abr.*; EG; EtPaEn; GEPC; HBV; HoPM; LEAP; LH; LoPo; LoPS; OBEV, *sts.* 1 *and* 3; OBVV; *sts.* 1 *and* 3; OQP; *sts.* 1 *and* 3; PoD; PoFS; QP-2, *sts.* 1 *and* 3
"Rivulet crossing my ground," Pt. I, xxi. BPN
"See what a lovely shell," Pt. II, ii. BPN; PoEL-5
(Shell, The.) BoTP; GN; SN; VA
Sleeping House, The, Pt. XIV, iv. FaBoEn
There Is None like Her, Pt. XVIII, iii. FaBoEn
Voice by the Cedar Tree, A, Pt. I, v. AtBAP; BPN; GEPC; HBV
(Voice, A.) BLV
Maud Muller. Whittier. AA; AnEnPo; AnNE; APW; BAP; BAV; BeLS; CoBA; FaBoBe; HBV; IAP; LEAP; LPS-1; MOAP; MW; OBAV; OHFP; OnSP; PIR; PTA-1; PYM; REAL; TCAP; TreF; WBLP
Saddest Words, The, 2 *ll.* NePA; SiTL
Maud Muller all that summer day. Mrs. Judge Jenkins, *parody.* Bret Harte. BAV; FiBHP; HBV; InP; LauV; WhC
Maud Muller Mutatur. Franklin P. Adams. HBMV
Maude Clare. Christina Rossetti. BeLS
Maudle—in Ballad, A. *Unknown.* BOHV; PA
Mauhee. *Unknown. See* Little Mohee, The.
Maul, The. Mary E. Nealy. GA; MC
Maumee Ruth. Sterling A. Brown. CDC
Maunder's Praise of his Strowling Mort, The. *Unknown.* OxBoLi
Maunding Soldier, The; or, The Fruits of Warre Is Beggery. Martin Parker. CoMu; WaaP
Maureen. John Todhunter. HBV; OBEV (1st ed.); OBVV
Maureen O'Reilly. Sister Mary Eugene. PraNu
Maurice de Guerin. Maurice Francis Egan. AA; JKCP; LEAP
Mavourneen, we'll go far away. The Beggar's Child. Padraic Colum. GTIV
Mavrone. Arthur Guiterman. BOHV; FiBHP; InMe
Mavrone, Mavrone! the wind among the reeds. The Wind among the Reeds. Nora Hopper. DiM; GTIV
Mawgan of Melhuach. Robert Stephen Hawker. EPN; VA
Max Ernst. Paul Eluard, *tr. fr. French by* George Reavey. MiFP
Max Schmitt in a Single Scull. Richmond Lattimore. NePoAm-2
Maxim: "If he play, being young and unskilful." Kipling. *Fr.* Certain Maxims of Hafiz. OtMeF
Maxim Revised, A. *Unknown.* BLPA; NeHB; WBLP
Maximian Elegy V. Kenneth Rexroth. CrMA
Maxims. George Herbert. *Fr.* The Church Porch. CBE
Maxims (Cotton MS). *Unknown, tr. fr. Anglo-Saxon by* Charles W. Kennedy. AnOE
Maxims (Exeter Book). *Unknown, tr. fr. Anglo-Saxon by* Charles W. Kennedy. AnOE
(Gnomic Lines.) LiTW
Maximus, to Himself. Charles Olson. NeAP
Maxwel[l]ton braes [*or* banks] are bonnie. Annie Laurie. William Douglas, *revised by* Lady John Scott. BTP; EBSV; EtPaEn; FaBoBe; FaFP; GN; GTBS-W; HBV; InP; LiTG; LiTL; LPS-1; MCCG; OIF; OTPC; PECK; PYM; SiTL; TreF; WBLP
May. William Barnes. GTBS-D; RO
"Mother o' blossoms, and or all," 4 *ll.* ChTr
May. Stephan Moylan Bird. HBMV
May. Struthers Burt. *See* Resurgam.
May. Henry Sylvester Cornwell. HBV
May. Thomas Dekker. *See* O, the Month of May.
May. Richard Edwards. *See* M. Edwards' May.
May. Edward Hovell-Thurlow. EV-4; HBV; LEAP; OBEV; OBRV
May. George Macdonald. OTPC (1946 ed.)
May. John Shaw Neilson. NeLNL
May, *sel.* John Francis O'Donnell.
"Open, sweet flowers, your eyes." IrPN
May. J. G. Percival. BAV; BoTP; LPS-2
May. Christina Rossetti. BPN; EmBrPo; VLEP
("I cannot tell you how it was.") EG
May. Folgore da San Geminiano, *tr. fr. Italian by* Dante Gabriel Rossetti. *Fr.* Sonnets of the Months. LyMA
("I give you horses for your games in May.") AWP; LyPI
May. C. R. Saunders. CAG
May. Frank Dempster Sherman. PRWS
May. Laura Simmons. LPS-1
May. Spenser. *Fr.* The Faerie Queene, VII, 7. GN; PoRL
May ("May comes laughing, crowned with daffodils"). *Unknown.* PA; PEOR
May ("May's the merriest time of all"). *Unknown, tr. fr. Old Irish by* Frank O'Connor. AnIL; KiLC; LyMA
May afternoon with birds in every bush. Poem in May. John Hewitt. NeIP
May all-disposing Zeus ne'er set. Folly of Obstinacy. Aeschylus. *Fr.* Prometheus Bound. GrR
May Allah pardon us. Fate. Ibn Abdun. MooP
May and Death. Robert Browning. GEPC; GTML
May and June. James Russell Lowell. *Fr.* Under the Willows. APW
May, and the wall was warm again. W. R. Rodgers. Winter's Cold. EnLoPo
May Basket, The. Dora Read Goodale. PCH
May Basket, A. Lilian Bayne West. GFA
May, be thou never graced with birds that sing. Epitaph [*or* In Obitum M. S., X Maii, 1614]. William Browne. ElL; ElSeCe; EPP; OBEV; OBS; PCD; SeCeV; SeEP
"May be true what I had heard." Berrying. Emerson. AtBAP
May Burden, A. Francis Thompson. HBV
May Carols, *sels.* Aubrey Thomas De Vere.
Divine Presence, The, I, 3. BMEP; GoBC; MaRV
Fest. Puritatis, II, 1. PoVP
Festum Nativitatis, I, 12. IrPN
Implicit Faith, II, 64. GoBC
"In vain thy altars do they heap," III, 4.
(May Carol.) CAW
Mater Christi, I, 30. PoVP
"Night through yonder cloudy cleft, The," II, 20. IrPN
Turris Eburnea, II, 5. PoVP
"Who feels not, when the Spring once more," I, 1. IrPN
May Collin. Lady Isabel and the Elf-Knight (H *vers.*). *Unknown.* ESPB
May Colvin. *Unknown.* BLV; EBSV; MaC; OBB; StPo; TrGrPo
May come up with bird-din. Nuts in May. Louis MacNeice. MoAB; MoBrPo (1950 ed.)
May comes laughing, crowned with daffodils. May. *Unknown.* PA; PEOR
May-Day, *sel.* Emerson.
April and May. GN; OHIP
May Day. Sara Teasdale. *Fr.* The Dark Cup. CP; MM
May Day ("Good morning lords and ladies"). *Unknown.* MeMeAg; RIS
May Day ("May day!"). *Unknown, tr. fr. Old Irish by* T. W. Rolleston. SiB
(In Praise of May, *at. to* Fionn MacCumhaill, *tr. by* T. W. Rolleston.) AnIV
(Song of Finn, The, *tr. by* John O'Donovan.) OnYI
May Day, A. Sir Henry Wotton. *See* On a Bank as I Sat a-Fishing.
May-Day at Sea. John F. Finerty. EtS
May-Day! delightful day!/ Bright colours play the vale along. May Day [*or* In Praise of May]. *Unknown, tr. by* T. W. Rolleston. AnIV; SiB
May-day, delightful time! How beautiful the color! The Song of Finn. *Unknown, tr. by* John O'Donovan. OnYI
May Day Garland, The. Edmund Blunden. HBMV
May-Day on Magdalen Tower. Thomas Herbert Warren. OBVV
May-Day Song. *Unknown.* GoTP
May de Lord—He will be glad of me. Bright Sparkles in the Churchyard. *Unknown.* AA
May earth, O Acanthis, procuress, cover your grave. Propertius. Elegies, IV, 5. LaP
May, 1840. Hartley Coleridge. OBVV
May Evening. Eileen Brennan. NeIP
May every soul that touches mine. Making Life Worth While. "George Eliot." OQP; QP-2
May Flowers. Theodosia Garrison. VOD
May Garden. John Drinkwater. HBMV
May God be praised for woman. On Woman. W. B. Yeats. TwP
May God be praised! I have an equal skill. The Duel. Theodore Maynard. CAW
May God bless the bark of Clan-Ranald. The Bark of Clanranald. Alexander MacDonald, *tr. by* Alexander Nicolson. EBSV
May God Give Strength. Peter Van Wynen. BLRP
May has come from out the showers. The Jewish May. Morris Rosenfeld. TrJP
May he fall in with beasts that scatter fire. Ballad against the Enemies of France. Villon, *tr. by* Swinburne. AWP; PoFr
May His counsels sweet uphold you. God Be with You. *Unknown.* PoToHe (new ed.)
May I be, dear love, no more a caution so glowing. To Cerinthus. Sulpicia. LaP
May I Drink the Blood of My Enemies. Theognis, *tr. fr. Greek by* T. F. Higham. GrL; OxBG
May I Feel Said He. E. E. Cummings. LiTA

May I find a woman fair. True Beauty. Francis Beaumont. ElL; HBV
May I for my own self song's truth reckon. The Seafarer. *Unknown, tr. by* Ezra Pound. AmP; AnAmPo; EnL; ExPo; FaBoTw; KN; LA; LiTA; LiTW; LyMA; OxBA; PoE
"May I print a kiss on your lips?" I asked. A Full Edition. Joseph Lilienthal. CAG
May I, when at the end of this cruel insight. The Tenth Duino Elegy. Rainer Maria Rilke. *Fr.* The Duino Elegies. AnGP
May I Woo the Lassie? *with music. Unknown, tr. fr. German by* Janet E. Tobitt. SaSa
May in the Green-Wood. *Unknown. See* In Summer.
May is a pious fraud of the almanac. May and June. James Russell Lowell. *Fr.* Under the Willows. APW
May is blond and Madge is brown. Battledores. Fitz James O'Brien. PR
May Is Building Her House. Richard Le Gallienne. HBVY; LBMV; OHIP; POT; PoTo; YeAr; YT
May is Mary's month, and I. The May Magnificat. Gerard Manley Hopkins. AtBAP; ISi; PoLi; TriL
May is the month when "the white throat builds." The Merry Month. "Miss X *and* Miss Y." InMe
May It Be. Boris Pasternak, *tr. fr. Russian by* C. M. Bowra. BoRS; TrJP
May it for ever live to be. Stalingrad. Huw Menai. MoWP
May it not be that we at last shall win. Urbs Beata. Thomas S. Jones, Jr. UnW
May–June, 1940. Robinson Jeffers. AmPP (3d ed.); LiTA; LiTM (rev. ed.); MoAB; MoAmPo; NePA; WaP
(Battle.) AmPP (4th ed.)
May-Lure. Richard Burton. NLK
May Magnificat, The. Gerard Manley Hopkins. AtBAP; ISi; PoLi; TriL
May Margaret. Théophile Marzials. HBV; VA
May Margaret [*or* Margret] sits [*or* stood] in her bower [*or* bouer] door. Hind [*or* Hynd] Etin. ESPB (B *vers.*); OBB
May moon rises bright and clear, The. Tom Pringle. Louis Simpson. NePoAm-2
May-Morn and Cupid. Alexander Montgomerie. *Fr.* The Cherry and the Slae. EBSV
("About ane bank, where birdis on bewis.") GoTS
May Morning. Marjorie Barrows. GFA
May Morning. Chaucer. *Fr.* The Book of the Duchesse. WHA
May Morning. Milton. *See* Song on May Morning.
May Morning. Celia Thaxter. AA; OBAV
May Mornings. Ivy O. Eastwick. BrR; SiSoSe
May-Music. Rachel Annand Taylor. HBV
May my heart always be open to little. E. E. Cummings. AmPP
May my life and family. Patronage. Ibn al-Labbana. MooP
May never lady press his lips. *Unknown.* LauV
May Night. Afanasi Afanasievich Fet, *tr. fr. Russian by* Sir Cecil Kisch. WaL
May Night. William Ellery Leonard. AOAH
May nothing evil cross this door. Prayer for This [*or* a New] House. Louis Untermeyer. FaPON; MaRV; PoToHe; TrPWD; TSW; TSWC
May one kind grave unite each hapless name. Eloisa's Prayer for Abelard. Pope. *Fr.* Eloïsa to Abelard. GoBC
May one who fought in honor for the South. At Lincoln's Grave. Maurice Thompson. *Fr.* Lincoln's Grave. GA
May passing years send happiness. Prayer for Any Bride and Groom. J. Shenton Lodge. PraP
May Queen, The. Tennyson. BPN; LPS; OTPC (1923 ed.); PoRL
Sels.
Conclusion to the May Queen and New Year's Eve. OTPC (1923 ed.)
"He taught me all the mercy, for he show'd me all the sin," *2 ll.* ChIP
New Year's Eve. OTPC (1923 ed.)
"You must wake and call me early, call me early, mother dear," *first pt.* DD, *3 sts.*; MPB; OTPC
May! queen of blossoms. May. Edward Hovell-Thurlow. EV-4; HBV; LEAP; OBEV; OBRV
May rain clouds never burst. To the Sacred Battalion. Andreas Calvos. MoGP
May shall make the world anew. May. Frank Dempster Sherman. PRWS
May Song, A. "Violet Fane." DiM; OBVV; VA
May Song ("Spring is coming"). *Unknown.* HH
(Oxfordshire Children's May Song.) MeMeAg; OTPC
("Spring is coming, spring is coming.") BoTP
May Sun Sheds an Amber Light, The. AA; BAV
May Sunday, A. Thomas Caulfield Irwin. IrPN
May the Ambitious Ever Find. *At. to* the Earl of Rochester *and to* Charles Sackville. SeCL
May the Babylonish curse. A Farewell to Tobacco. Charles Lamb. BOHV; LPS-2; NBE; OBRV; OxBoLi
May the Cross and courteous Christ aid this beginning. Piers the Plowman's Creed. *Unknown.* MeEV
May the gates of Heaven be opened wide! The Senior Arbiter of Fate. Chu Yuan. *Fr.* The Nine Songs. WhP
May the glad dawn. An Easter Wish. *Unknown.* OQP; QP-1
May the Lord bless thee/ and keep thee. The Blessing of Saint Francis. St. Francis of Assisi. SaFP
May the men who are born. Hitomaro. *Fr.* Manyo Shu. AWP
May the Sweet Name of Jesus. *Unknown, tr. fr. Irish by* Eleanor Hull. JKCP (1926 ed.)
(Communion Hymn of the Ancient Irish Church.) CAW
May the will come from Thee. Annul Wars. Nahman of Bratzlav. TrJP
May the will of God be done by us. A Night Prayer. *Unknown.* JKCP (1926 ed.)
May the wrath of the heart of my god be pacified! Penitential Psalm to the Goddess Anunit. *Unknown.* WGRP
May they come, may they come. Song of the Highest Tower. Arthur Rimbaud. AWP; JAWP; WBP
May they wander [*or* stumble] stage by stage. The Traveler's [*or* Traveller's] Curse after Misdirection. Robert Graves. ExPo; FiBHP; HoPM; LiTM; MBP; MoAB; MoBrPo; NeMA; SiTL
May 30, 1893. John Kendrick Bangs. AA
May those who are born after me. Kakinomoto no Hitomaro. *Fr.* Manyo Shu. LiTW; OnPJ
May Time. *See* Maytime.
May Tree, The. William Barnes. LiTB; LoBV; POTE; TCPD
May 26, 1828. Pushkin, *tr. fr. Russian by* C. M. Bowra. BoR
May upon Ictis. Thomas S. Jones, Jr. TBM
May walks the earth again. Perennial May. T. A. Daly. CP; NV
May was a wonderful country. Wonderful Country. Miriam Waddington. PeCV
May we have leave to ask, illustrious Mother. Purification of the Blessed Virgin. Joseph Beaumont. ISi
May winds gently lift the willow leaves, The. Bathing. John Keble. OTPC (1923 ed.)
May you walk a little surer. My Easter Prayer. *Unknown.* PraP
May your wellknown mercy, Persephone, remain steadfast. Propertius. Elegies, II, 28 C. LaP
Mayakovsky Memory. Vera Inber, *tr. fr. Russian by* Jack Lindsay. *Fr.* Diary of a Journey. RuPo
Maybe a twelvemonth since/ Suddenly I began. Dark under Froth. W. B. Yeats. *Fr.* The Fisherman. LiA
Maybe again the organ-music blaring. "Anna Akhmatova," *tr. fr. Russian by* C. M. Bowra. BoRS
Maybe now you remember my solemn warning given. "And Left the Thorn." Thymocles. GrPE
Maybe that's mirabells ringing there. Epos. Julian Tuwim. LiTW
Maybe you ranted in the Grove. Ezry. Archibald MacLeish. MoVE
Mayblossom, The. John Masefield. AlDL
Maybrick trial is over now, The. Penal Servitude for Mrs. Maybrick. *Unknown.* OxBoLi; SiTL
Mayde Cristes me bit yorne, A. A Luve Ron. Thomas of Hales. EPP
Mayde ther ben, a wordy one and wyse, A. The Poets at a House-Party. Carolyn Wells. PA
Maydens Came, The. *Unknown. See* Maidens Came, The.
Maydens of London's Brave Adventures, The. *Unknown.* SG
Mayde's [*or* Maid's] Metamorphosis, The, *sels. Unknown, at. to* John Lyly *and to* Thomas Ravenscroft.
By the Moon We Sport and Play. OTPC; TuPP
(By the Moon.) CH
(Fairy Dances, 1.) ElL
(Fairy Frolic, The.) LEAP; PCH, *longer sel.*
(Urchins' Dance, The.) BoTP
Elves' Dance, The. CH; FaPON; HH; MPB; PoRh
(Fairy Dances, 2.) ElL
("Round about in a fair ring-a.") BoTP
Mayflower, The. Erastus Wolcott Ellsworth. AA; DDA; FaBoBe; HH; MC; PAH
Mayflower. John Boyle O'Reilly. AA; PAH
Mayflower once filled this shore, The. Epigram. Robert Haven Schauffler. ADAH
Mayhap when you are old and grey. When You Are Old. John McClure. LS
Mayombe—bombe—mayombé! Sensemaya; Chant for Killing a Snake. Nicolas Guillén. TwSpPo
Mayonette River, The. *Unknown.* CAG
Mayor, The. Luis Carlos López, *tr. fr. Spanish by* H. R. Hays. TwSpPo
Mayor Marston. Edgar Lee Masters. *Fr.* The New Spoon River. ChMo; CMP
Mayor of Scuttleton, The. Mary Mapes Dodge. GaP; NA
Mayors, The. Blake. *See* Good English Hospitality.

May's the merriest time of all. May. *Unknown.* AnIL; KiLC; LyMA
Mayster Sackvilles Induction. Thomas Sackville. *See* Mirror for Magistrates, A.
Maystress Jane Scroupe. John Skelton. *Fr.* Phyllyp Sparowe. NBE
(Commendations of Mistress Jane Scrope, The.) OBSC
("How shall I report," *abr.*) EG; ViBoPo
Maytime. Thomas Dekker. *See* O, the Month of May.
May-Time. Margaret Gant. PCH
May-Time. Christina Rossetti. BoTP
("There is but one May in the year.") TiPo
Maytime. *Unknown, tr. fr. Chinese by* L. Crammer-Byng. *Fr.* Shi King. AWP
May Time. Sir Thomas Wyatt. *See* Sonnet: "You that in love find luck . . ."
Maze. Richard Eberhart. AnAmPo
Mazeppa. Byron. EmBrPo; EnRP
"Up rose the sun; the mists were curl'd," *sel.* OBRV
Mazeppa. Roy Campbell. AnFE
Mazilla and Mazura. *Unknown.* ChTr
Mazing around my mind like moths at a shaded candle. Ghosts. Robert Bridges. FaBoTw
Mazzini. Laura Catherine Redden Searing. LPS-3
Me. Walter de la Mare. FaPON; TiPo (1959 ed.)
Me. Hughes Mearns. *Fr.* Later Antigonishes. InMe
Me Alone. Lula Lowe Weeden. CDC
Me an' My Doney-Gal (*diff. vers. of* Doney Gal). *Unknown.* CoSo
Me an' my pardner an' my pardner's frien'. Long Summer Day. *Unknown.* OuSiCo
Me and my wife live all alone. Little Brown Jug. *Unknown.* ABF
Me and Prunes. Rupe Sherwood. PoOW
Me clairvoyant. Variations on an Air: After Walt Whitman. G. K. Chesterton. InP
Me Cupid made a happy slave. Song. Sir Richard Steele. OBEC
Me father was the keeper of the Eddystone Light. The Eddystone Light. *Unknown.* StPo
Me, go to Florida! This Is Pioneer Weather. William Carlos Williams. NePoAm-2
Me Happy Night, Night Full of Brightness. Ezra Pound. *Fr.* Homage to Sextus Propertius. InvP
Me have ye gaoled and chained and burned. Song of the Old Man in Chains. Anatoli Vasilyevich Lunacharsky. *Fr.* Faust and the City. PoFr
Me Heart. G. K. Chesterton. OtMeF
Me, Hermes, near this breezy garden see! Spring for Travelers. *Unknown.* OnPM
Me hither from moonlight. Lines Written in a Nunnery Chapel. James Clarence Mangan. PraNu; TIP
Me Imperturbe. Walt Whitman. APW; CoBA; IAP; TCAP
Me Johnny Mitchell Man, *with music. Unknown.* TrAS
Me let the world disparage and despise. Honour. Ada Cambridge. BoAu
Me list no more to sing. Sir Thomas Wyatt. SiPS
Me Lord? can'st Thou mispend. Phineas Fletcher. *Fr.* The Divine Wooer. TrPWD
"Me loving subjects," sez she. Percy French. *Fr.* The Queen's Afterdinner Speech. OxBI
Me, Me, and None but Me. *Unknown.* ReIE
Me, me suffer this. Aeschylus. *Fr.* Eumenides. GrPo
Me Quoque Vatem. Thomas Freeman. SiCE; TuPP
Me so oft my fancy drew. The Choice. George Wither. OBEV
Me that 'ave been what I've been. Chant-Pagan [*or* English Irregular, '99-02]. Kipling. BPN; CBE; CBOV; OAEP (2d ed.)
Me the gods turned to stone, but turned in vain. Niobe in Living Stone. *Unknown.* OnPM
Mea Culpa. "Ethna Carbery." CAW; JKCP; TrPWD
Mea Culpa. Edward Sandford Martin. PR
Meadow, The. Manuel Altolaguirre, *tr. fr. Spanish by* Eleanor L. Turnbull. CoSP
Meadow and My Lady, A. Reinmar von Hagenau, *tr. fr. German by* F. C. Nicholson. LyMA
Meadow Brook Runs Over, The. Howard McKinley Corning. MAP; MoAmPo (1942 ed.)
Meadow for the little lambs, A. The Sweetest Place. Mary Frances Butts. PPL
Meadow Lark, The. Hamlin Garland. AA
Meadow Lark. Marion Mitchell Walker. GFA
Meadow Lark Sang, A. Charles Commerford. BLA
Meadow larks rejoice, The, as the bright sun. The Prairie Schooner. Edwin Ford Piper. StVeCh (1940 ed.)
Meadow Talk. Nora Archibald Smith. PPL
Meadows, The. Ann *or* Jane Taylor. BoTP
Meadows in Spring, The. Edward Fitzgerald. *See* Old Song.
Meadows with yellow cowslips all aglow. The Wood-Dove's Note. Emily Huntington Miller. BLA; HBV
Meagre soil, arid and harsh and rude, A. Bright Stars and Dark. Victor Hugo. *Fr.* Les Contemplations. LiA
Meaner than a brothel. Butcher Shop. Jorge Luis Borges. OnPM; TwSpPo
Meanes to Attain Happy Life. Martial. *See* Means to Attain Happy Life, The.
Meaning of a Letter, The. *Unknown.* PoToHe (new ed.)
Meaning of Prayer, The. *Unknown.* PraP
Meaning of the Look, The. Elizabeth Barrett Browning. ChIP; MaRV
Meaning of Violence, The. John Williams. NePoAm-2
Means, therefore, which unto us is lent, The. Spenser. *Fr.* An Hymne of Heavenly Beauty. EPP
Means to Attain [a] Happy Life, The. Martial, *tr. fr. Latin by* the Earl of Surrey. AEV; BCEP; CBOV; EIL; EM-1; EnLi-1 (1949 ed.); EnLit; EPP; EV-1; HBV; LPS-1; OBEV; SiCE; ViBoPo; WoL, *tr. by* Sir Richard Fanshawe
(Happy Life, The.) OnPM; SiPS
("Martial, the things for to attain.") ReEn
(Martial's Quiet Life.) OBSC
(Things That Cause a Quiet Life, The.) ElSeCe; TrGrPo; TuPP
(What Makes a Happy Life, *tr. by* Goldwin Smith.) AWP; JAWP; WBP
Meantime, at distance from the scene of blood. Homer. *Fr.* The Iliad, XVII. GrPo
Meantime the goddess-born in secret pin'd. Homer. *Fr.* The Iliad, I. GrPo
Meantime, the moist malignity to shun. Building a Home. John Armstrong. *Fr.* The Art of Preserving Health. LPS-2
Meantime the sunlight melted from the shore. Victory at Salamis [*or* The Battle of Salamis]. Aeschylus. *Fr.* Persians. GrR; PoFr
Meanwhile Achilles, plung'd. Homer. *Fr.* The Iliad, I. GrPo
Meanwhile, as chilly night gave way to dawn. The Stoic's Wedding. Lucan. *Fr.* Pharsalia, II. LaP
Meanwhile in other realms big tears were shed. Keats. *Fr.* Hyperion; a Fragment. NBE
Meanwhile Patroclus stood beside his friend. Homer. *Fr.* The Iliad, XVI. GrPo
Mean while the Adversary of God and Man. The Flight of Satan. Milton. *Fr.* Paradise Lost, II. PoF
Meanwhile the choleric Captain strode wrathful away to the council. The War-Token. Longfellow. *Fr.* The Courtship of Miles Standish. PAH
Meanwhile the Invaders fared as they deserved. Wordsworth. *Fr.* The Prelude, X. NBE
. . . Meanwhile the Moon. Moonlight. James Thomson. *Fr.* The Seasons: Autumn. BeR
Meanwhile the Queen with many piteous drops. Titania. Thomas Hood. *Fr.* The Plea of the Midsummer Fairies. OBRV
Meanwhile the Son/ On his great expedition now appear'd. The Creation of the World. Milton. *Fr.* Paradise Lost, VII. MaPo
Meanwhile the Steed's deep caverns, op'ning wide. Tryphiodorus. *Fr.* The Taking of Troy. GrPo
Meanwhile the Tuscan army. The Fight at the Bridge. Macaulay. *Fr.* Lays of Ancient Rome: Horatius. MaC; OtMeF
Meanwhile the two in the hut, Odysseus and the goodly swineherd. The Sound of Footsteps. Homer. *Fr.* The Odyssey, XVI. LiA
Meanwhile Ulysses at the palace waits. The Palace of Alcinous. Homer. *Fr.* The Odyssey, VII. GrR
Meare's milk and deer's milk. A Witch's Spell. *Unknown.* ChTr
Measure. Thomas Traherne. BLV
("All music, sauces, feasts, delights and pleasures.") UnS
Measure for Measure, *sels.* Shakespeare.
"Aye, but to die, and go we know not where," *fr.* III, i. BCEP; BrBE; PoD; TrEV
(Fear of Death, 2.) CoEV
(Let Me Live, *longer sel.*) LiA
(Life and Death.) UnPo (1st ed.)
(On Death.) FiP
"Be absolute for death," *fr.* III, i. NBE
(Fear of Death, 1.) CoEV
(Life and Death.) KN; UnPo
But Man, Proud Man, *fr.* II, ii. WHA
(Man.) BCEP
Doubts ("Our doubts are traitors"), *fr.* I, iv. MaRV
Man New Made, *fr.* II, ii. GoBC
Mercy ("Your brother is a forfeit of the law"), *fr.* II, ii. EV-1
Not Thine Own, *fr.* I, i. MaRV
Novice, A, *fr.* I, iv. PraNu
Take, O Take Those Lips Away, *fr.* IV, i (*also given, with add. st., in* The Bloody Brother, *by* John Fletcher, *and others*). AnFE; AtBAP; BCEP; BEL; BrBE; EIL; ElSeCe; EM-1; EnLi-1; EnLit; EPP; EnLoPo, 2 *sts.;* EtPaEn; EV-1; ExPo; HBV, 2 *sts.;* InPo; LEAP, 2 *sts.;*

LiTB; LiTG; LiTL; LO; LPS-1 (*2 sts.*); OAEP; OBEV; OnPM; OuHeWo; ReaPo; SeCeV; SiCE; TCEP; TOP; TwP; ViBoPo; WHA
(Boy's Song to Mariana.) BoLiVe
(Frustra.) GTSL
(Love Forsworn.) MCCG
(Madrigal.) GTBS; GTBS-D; GTBS-W; GTSE
(Sealed in Vain.) WoL
(Seals of Love.) BLV; TrGrPo
(Song: "Take, O take those lips away.") FiP; LoPS; PoEL-2 (*2 sts.*); REAL; UnPo (1st ed.)
(Song at the Moated Grange, A.) OBSC
(Song for Mariana.) EG
(Songs from the Plays.) AWP; JAWP; WBP
"Well; come to me to-morrow," *fr.* II, ii. LO
Measure Me, Sky. Leonora Speyer. BAP; FaPON; HBMV; MPB; NP; PC; PG (1945 ed.); TSW; TSWC
Measure thy life by loss instead of gain. Love's Strength. Harriet Eleanor Hamilton King. MaRV; OQP; QP-2
Measured blood beats out the year's delay, The. Simple Autumnal. Louise Bogan. MAP; MoAB; MoAmPo; MOAP
Measureless time or ever thy years, O man, were reckon'd. Time. Leonidas of Tarentum. GrL; GrPo; OxBG
Measurement. A. M. Sullivan. WaKn
Measuring out my life in flagons. Familiar Daemon. Roy Campbell. JKCP (1955 ed.)
Measuring worm with a hump on his back, A. Pedagogical Principles. Harry Amoss. CaP
Meat is high, The. Disgruntled Guest. *Unknown.* PIAE
Mechanical Optimist, The. Wallace Stevens. NAMP
Mecklenburg Declaration, The. William C. Elam. PAH
Medal, The; a Satire against Sedition. Dryden. CEP; EiPP
Vox Populi, *sel.* OBS
Medallion. Ezra Pound. *Fr.* Hugh Selwyn Mauberley. CoBMV; CoV; LiTA; LiTM (rev. ed.); MoPo
Medallion of Saint Francis. Harry Elmore Hurd. SaFP
Meddlesome Matty. Ann Taylor. EV-4; HBV; HBVY; OTPC (1946 ed.)
Meddow Verse, The; or, Anniversary to Mistris Bridget Lowman. Robert Herrick. SeCV-1
Medea, *sel.* Lord De Tabley.
Chorus: "Sweet are the ways of death to weary feet." OBEV (new ed.); OBVV
Medea, *sels.* Euripides, *tr. fr. Greek.*
Chorus: "When love has passed its limits," *tr. by* Frederic Prokosch. LiTW
Dawn of Woman's Day, The, *tr. by* R. C. Trevelyan. GrR
(Chorus: "Upward and back to their fountains the sacred rivers are stealing," *tr. by* Arthur S. Way.) PoFr
(Shifting Fortune, *tr. by* F. L. Lucas.) OxBG
If Music Might but Assuage! *tr. by* R. C. Trevelyan. GrR
Interlude, *tr. by* Gilbert Murray. GrR
Medea's Resolve, *tr. by* F. L. Lucas. OxBG
(Heart, Steel Thyself! *tr. by* Gilbert Murray.) GrR
"Of old are Erechtheus' folk favored of heaven," *tr. by* Moses Hadas *and* J. H. McLean. GrPo
"Rotten, heart-rotten, that is the word for you," *tr. by* Moses Hadas *and* J. H. McLean. GrPo
Sweetest in Measure, Each Pleasure, *tr. by* R. C. Trevelyan. GrR
Vengeance, *tr. by* F. L. Lucas. OxBG
Medea, *sel.* Bengt Lidner, *tr. fr. Swedish by* Charles W. Stork.
Song of the Battle-Skald. AnSL
Medea, *sel.* Seneca, *tr. fr. Latin by* John Studley.
Chorus: "What sharpe assaultes of cruell Cupids flame." LaP
Medea. *Unknown. Fr.* Gest Historiale of the Destruction of Troy. NBE
Medea Betrayed. Apollonius Rhodius, *tr. fr. Greek by* George Allen *and* T. F. Higham. *Fr.* Argonautica, IV. OxBG
Medea Goes to Gather Herbs for Her Incantations. John Gower. *Fr.* Confessio Amantis, V. LiA
Medea's Dream. Apollonius Rhodius, *tr. fr. Greek by* George Allen. *Fr.* Argonautica, III. OxBG
Medea's Hesitation. Apollonius Rhodius, *tr. fr. Greek by* George Allen. *Fr.* Argonautica, III. OxBG
Medea's Parting Words. Apollonius Rhodius, *tr. fr. Greek by* George Allen. *Fr.* Argonautica, III. OxBG
Medea's Passion. Apollonius Rhodius, *tr. fr. Greek by* Arthur S. Way. *Fr.* Argonautica, III. GrR
Medea's Resolve. Euripides, *tr. fr. Greek by* F. L. Lucas. *Fr.* Medea. OxBG
(Heart, Steel Thyself! *tr. by* Gilbert Murray.) GrR
Medelwold and Sidselille. *Unknown. See* Leesome Brand.
Media Vita. Notker Balbulus, *tr. fr. Latin by* Frederick Rowland Marvin. CAW
Mediator, The. Elizabeth Barrett Browning. TrPWD
Mediatrix of Grace, The. Francis Burke. ISi
Medical Aid. Walter Hard. WhC
Medical Corps, The. Beatrice Barry. PEDC
Medieval Appreciations. William M. T. Gamble. CAW
Medieval Mirth. *Unknown. Fr.* The Squire of Low Degree. ACP
Medieval Norman Songs. *Unknown, tr. fr. French by* John Addington Symonds. AWP; JAWP; WBP
Mediocracy. Caryll Houselander. JKCP (1955 ed.)
Mediocrity [*or* Mediocritie] in Love Rejected. Thomas Carew. ALV; ATP; BCEP; CaAE; ElSeCe; EnLit; EPS; HBV; MeLP; MePo; SeCL; SeCV-1; SeEP
(Give Me More Love or More Disdain.) LPS-1
(More Love or More Disdain.) TrGrPo
(Song: "Give me more love or more disdain.") LiTL; ViBoPo
Meditating in silence after the last note. J. C. Beaglehole. *Fr.* Considerations on Certain Music of J. S. Bach. AnNZ
Meditating on the glory of illustrious lineage. The Bitter Purple Willows. Allen Upward. *Fr.* Scented Leaves from a Chinese Jar. NP
Meditatio. Ezra Pound. FaBoCh; LoGBV
Meditation. Baudelaire, *tr. fr. French by* Dwight Durling. AnFP
Meditation. Donald Cox. MaRV
Meditation, A. Richard Eberhart. FiMAP; LiTA
Meditation. Roy Fuller. FaBoMo
Meditation. Paul Géraldy, *tr. fr. French by* Joseph T. Shipley. ALV
Meditation. Antoinette Goetschius. MaRV
Meditation. Dorothy Hobson. MuM
Meditation. Toyohiko Kagawa. MaRV
Meditation, A. Samuel Walter Kelly. PoP
Meditation. Li Ho, *tr. fr. Chinese by* Ho Chih-yuan. WhP
Meditation. Li Yu, *tr. fr. Chinese by* Hsiung Ting. WhP
(Girl's Yearning, A.) ChLP
Meditation. Blanaid Salkeld. OnYI
Meditation. Wang Wei, *tr. fr. Chinese by* Li Fu-ning. WhP
Meditation at Kew. Anna Wickham. AnEnPo; FaBoTw; MBP; MoBrPo
Meditation at Red Cliff. Su T'ung-po, *tr. fr. Chinese by* Yu Min-chuan. WhP
Meditation by Mascoma Lake. Donald C. Babcock. NePoAm-2
Meditation Eight ("I kenning through astronomy divine"). Edward Taylor. *Fr.* Sacramental Meditations. AmP; AmPP (3d ed.); AtBAP; LiTA
(I Kenning through Astronomy.) AmPP (4th ed.); OxBA; PoEL-3
Meditation Fifty-six ("Should I with silver tooles delve through the hill"). Edward Taylor. *Fr.* Sacramental Meditations. CoV
("Should I with silver tooles delve through the hill.") OxBA
Meditation for Christmas, A. Selwyn Image. OBEV (new ed.)
Meditation for His Mistress, A. Robert Herrick. EV-2; OBEV; OBS; PIAE; TyEnPo
Meditation in a Grove. Isaac Watts. *See* Sweet Muse.
Meditation in St. Mary's. Gertrude du Bois. ChIP
Meditation in Winter. William Dunbar. BSV; EBSV
(Meditatioun in Wyntir.) SeCePo
Meditation in Winter. Leonard Mann. BoAV
Meditation of a Patriot. G. S. Fraser. LiTM (rev. ed.)
Meditation on a March Wind. Sister Mary Gilbert. JKCP (1955 ed.)
Meditation on a Quiet Night. Li Po, *tr. fr. Chinese.* WhP
Meditation on Communion with God. Judah Halevi, *tr. fr. Hebrew by* Solomon Solis-Cohen. TrJP
Meditation on Jesus Christ. Johanna Rachel Branigan. QS
Meditation on Saviours. Robinson Jeffers. ChMo; CMP
Meditation on Time. Sister Mary Athanasius. JKCP (1955 ed.)
Meditation Seven ("Thy human frame, my glorious Lord, I spy"). Edward Taylor. *Fr.* Sacramental Meditations. LiTA
Meditation Six ("Am I thy Gold?"). Edward Taylor. *See* Am I Thy Gold.
Meditation Ten ("Stupendious Love! All Saints Astonishment"). Edward Taylor. *Fr.* Sacramental Meditations. CoV
("Stupendious Love!") OxBA
Meditation Thirty ("Prest down with sorrow, Lord, not for my sin"). Edward Taylor. *Fr.* Sacramental Meditations. CoV
Meditation Thirty-eight ("Oh! What a thing is Man?"). Edward Taylor. *See* Oh! What a Thing Is Man.
Meditation Thirty-three ("My Lord, my Life, can Envy ever bee"). Edward Taylor. *Fr.* Sacramental Meditations. AtBAP; PoEL-3
Meditation under Stars. George Meredith. EmBrPo; OAEP; POTT; ViP; VLEP
Meditations. Solomon ibn Gabirol, *tr. fr. Hebrew by* Emma Lazarus. TrJP
Meditations. Edward Taylor. *See* Sacramental Meditations.
Meditations in a Museum Cloister. Sister Maryanna. JKCP (1955 ed.)

Meditations in Time of Civil War. W. B. Yeats.
Ancestral Houses, I. ChMP; LiTB; MoVE
I See Phantoms of Hatred and of the Heart's Fullness and of the Coming Emptiness, VII. LiTB
My Descendants, IV. LiTB
My House, II. LiTB
My Table, III. LiTB
Road at My Door, The, V. LiTB; SoV
Stare's Nest by My Window, The, VI. LiTB
Meditations of a Gull. Sir John Davies. SiCE
Meditations of a Hindu Prince. Sir Alfred Comyn Lyall. VA; WGRP
Meditations of a Tortoise Dozing under a Rosetree near a Beehive at Noon While a Dog Scampers About and a Cuckoo Calls from a Distant Wood. E. V. Rieu. FiBHP
Meditations on a Landscape. Maxwell Bodenheim. MOAP
Meditations pure were ours. The Friendly Wood. Paul Valéry. AnFP
Meditatioun in Wyntir. William Dunbar. *See* Meditation in Winter.
Mediterranean, The. Allen Tate. AmP; ExPo; FaBoMo; InPo; LiTA; LiTG; LiTM; MAP; MoAB; MoAmPo; MoVE; NePA; PoFS; ReMP; SeCeV
Medusa. Louise Bogan. HoPM; InPo; MAP; MoAB; MoAmPo; MOAP; MoPo; MoVE; PoeMoYo; TCPD
Medusa. Robert Kelley Weeks. AA
Meek and the Proud, The. Abraham ibn Chasdai, *tr. fr. Hebrew by* Joseph Chotzner. TrJP
Meek Candidates for Grave Space. Leo Kennedy. BoCaPo
Meek dew shone, the grass lay prostrate, The. The Tree. Ilya Ehrenburg. TrJP; TrRV
Meek dwellers mid yon terror-stricken cliffs! The Alpine Flowers. Lydia Huntley Sigourney. AnAmPo; LA
Meek-ey'd Morn appears, Mother of Dews, The. Summer Morning. James Thomson. *Fr.* The Seasons: Summer. OBEC
Meek Shall Inherit, The. Donald F. Drummond. PtPa
Mee-ow, mee-ow,/ Here's a little pussy-cat. Pussy-Cat and Puppy-Dog. Lilian McCrea. BoTP
Meet Me in the Green Glen. John Clare. GTBS-D
Meet Me in the Primrose Lane. John Clare. AtBAP
Meet me my love, meet me my love. The Juniper Tree. Wilfred Watson. PeCV
Meet me tonight as usual at nine. Love Poem—1940. Miriam Hershenson. GoYe
Meet me to-night, lover, meet me. Moonlight. *Unknown.* AS
Meet-on-the-Road. *Unknown.* PoMS
Meet We No Angels, Pansie? Thomas Ashe. HBV; OBEV (1st ed.); OBVV
Meeting, The. Apollonius Rhodius. *See* Meeting of Medea and Jason, The.
Meeting. Matthew Arnold. Switzerland, I. OAEP; ViPP
Meeting. Olga Berggolts, *tr. fr Russian by* Jack Lindsay. Songs of the Spanish Children, II. RuPo
Meeting, The. Louise Bogan. NePoAm-2
Meeting. Robert Browning. *See* Meeting at Night.
Meeting, The. Arthur Hugh Clough. *See* Some Future Day . . .
Meeting. George Crabbe. HBV; OBEV
"My Damon was the first to wake," *sel.* LO
Meeting. Robert Desnos, *tr. fr. French by* Wallace Fowlie. MiCF
Meeting. Joseph Rodman Drake. UnW
Meeting, The. Georges Duhamel, *tr. fr. French by* Elizabeth Selden. BoFr
Meeting. Charles Eglington. BoSA
Meeting. Arthur Davison Ficke. NP
Meeting. Sam Harrison. NeIP
Meeting, A. Heine, *tr. fr. German by* Louis Untermeyer. PoMS
Meeting, A. Li Po, *tr. fr. Chinese.* WhP
Meeting, The. Katherine Mansfield. AV; LoPS
Meeting. Josephine Miles. FiMAP
Meeting, The. Harriet Monroe. PoTo
Meeting ("If we shall live, we live"). Christina Rossetti. LO
Meeting ("They made the chamber sweet"). Christina Rossetti. *See* Pause, A.
Meeting, The. Muriel Rukeyser. MoAmPo; TrJP
Meeting. William Saphier. AnAmPo; LA
Meeting, The. Arthur Stringer. CPG
Meeting, A. Tu Fu, *tr. fr. Chinese.* WhP
Meeting, The. Whittier. AmPP (3d ed.); IAP; LPS-2
Meeting a monster of mourning wherever I go. Epistle to Dylan Thomas. George Barker. LiTM
Meeting after Long Absence. Lilla Cabot Perry. AA; OBAV
Meeting and a Memory, A. Habberton Lulham. PoP
Meeting and Passing. Robert Frost. CoV; MaPo; OxBA
Meeting at Night. Robert Browning. AWP; BEL; BLV; BMEP; BoLiVe; BPN; CaAE; EM-2; EmBrPo; EnL; EnLi-2; EnLit; EPN; EtPaEn; FaBoEn; FiP; GBV (1952 ed.); GEPC; GTBS-D; GTBS-W; GTML; GTSL; HBV; InPo; InvP; JAWP; LiTL; LoPo; LoPS; MCCG; OAEP; OBEV; PCD; PFE; PG (1955 ed.); PIAE; PIR; PoeMoYo; PoFS; PoRA; PoVP; PreP; PYM; SeCePo; ShBV-3; TOP; TrGrPo; TwP; TyEnPo; UnPo (3d ed.); VA; ViBoPo; ViPo; ViPP; VLEP; WBP
(Meeting.) LPS-1
Meeting by the Gjulika Meadow. Geoffrey Grigson. WaP
Meeting his mother makes him lose ten years. Between the Porch and the Altar. Robert Lowell. FiMAP; MiAP; NePoEA
Meeting-House Hill. Amy Lowell. AmPP (3d ed.); LoGBV; MAP; MoAmPo; NeMA; NP; OxBA; PFY; TCAP
Meeting in the Road. *Unknown, tr. fr. Chinese by* Arthur Waley. TrCh
Meeting in Winter. William Morris. EnLi-2 (1949 ed.)
Meeting of a Poetry Society. Henry Rago. AnAmPo
Meeting of Medea and Jason, The. Apollonius Rhodius, *tr. fr. Greek by* Arthur S. Way. *Fr.* Argonautica, III. GrR
("But Medea—her thoughts unto nought else turned," *longer sel., tr. by* Arthur S. Way.) GrL
(Meeting, The, *tr. by* George Allen.) OxBG
Meeting of Orion and Artemis. Richard Henry Horne. *Fr.* Orion. VA
Meeting of Phantoms. Anders Österling, *tr. fr. Swedish by* Charles W. Stork. AnSL
Meeting of Priam and Achilles, The. Homer, *tr. fr. Greek by* F. L. Lucas. *Fr.* The Iliad, XXIV. GrPE
Meeting of Sighs, The. Blanche Edith Baughan. BoAu
Meeting of the Clabberhuses, The. Sam Walter Foss. BOHV
Meeting of the Ships, The. Thomas Moore. EtS
Meeting of the Waters, The. Thomas Moore. AnIL; ERP; OxBoLi; PoEL-4
(Vale of Avoca, The.) LPS-1
Meeting Point. Louis MacNeice. ChMP; POTE
Meeting the Easter Bunny. Rowena Bastin Bennett. GFA; MeMeAg; SiSoSe; SUS; TiPo; UTS
Meeting Together of Poles & Latitudes; in Prospect. Margaret Avison. PeCV
Meeting with Time, "Slack thing," said I. Time. George Herbert. SeCL
Meeting's in order, The. What's coming? What's to come? Town Meeting. John Hay. NePoAm
Meetings of the Ships, The. Felicia Dorothea Hemans. LPS-1
Meg Merrilies. Keats. AlDL; BLV; BoLiVe; BoTP; CBE; EmBrPo; ERP; EV-4; FaBoCh; FaPON; FiP; GaP; GBV (1952 ed.); HOAH; LoGBV; MuP; OnPP; OTPC; PCH; PoRL; PRWS; RG; RIS; StVeCh; TiPo
(Old Meg.) ThWaDe
Meganom. Osip Mandelstam, *tr. fr. Russian by* C. M. Bowra. BoRS
Mehitabel Sings a Song. Don Marquis. *Fr.* Archy and Mehitabel. InMe
Mein Herz, mein Herz ist traurig. Heine, *tr. fr. German by* James Thomson. AWP
Mein Kind, wir waren Kinder. Heine, *tr. fr. German by* Elizabeth Barrett Browning. AWP; JAWP; TrJP; WBP
Mein Liebchen, wir sassen zusammen. Heine, *tr. fr. German by* James Thomson. AWP; JAWP; WBP
(Forlornly.) OnPM
Melampus. George Meredith. EmBrPo; EnLi-2; OBVV; PoEL-5; ViP
Melampus, when will love be void of fears? Song of Coridon and Melampus [*or* Coridon and Melampus' Song]. George Peele. *Fr.* The Hunting of Cupid. OBSC; TuPP
Melancholetta, *sel.* "Lewis Carroll."
"My dismal sister! Couldst thou know." FiBHP
Melancholia. Robert Bridges. ChMo; CMP; EPN
Melancholia. Louis J. Karnosh. PoP
Melancholia ("Anear the centre"). James Thomson. The City of Dreadful Night, XXI. AnEnPo, 7 *sts.*; MBP, 7 *sts.*
("Anear the centre of that northern crest.") BMEP; FaBoEn; NBE; OAEP; POTT
(Melancholia: "Baffled and beaten back," 5 *sts.*) CoEV
(Melencolia: "Anear the centre.") VA
Melancholia. *Unknown.* NA
Melancholy. John Fletcher *and (at.)* Thomas Middleton. *Fr.* The Nice Valour. BCEP; EnLit; EV-2; GTBS; GTBS-D; GTBS-W; GTSE; GTSL; HBV; LEAP; OBEV
(Hence All You Vain Delights.) AtBAP; CenL; ElSeCe; LPS-1; OAEP; SeCL; TuPP; ViBoPo
(O Sweetest Melancholy.) TrGrPo
(Passionate Man's Song, The.) OBS; SiCE
(Song: "Hence all you vain delights.") CaAE; PoEL-2
(Sweetest Melancholy.) BEL; EPP; LiA
Melancholy. William Habington. *Fr.* Castara, II. LoBV
Melancholy. Li Shang-yin, *tr. fr. Chinese by* Soame Jenyns. ChLP
Melancholy. Liu Hsiao Hsien, *tr. fr. Chinese by* Henry H. Hart. PoHN
Melancholy. Li Yu, *tr. fr. Chinese by* Hsiung Ting. WhP
Melancholy. Thomas Lodge. *See* Earth, Late Choked with Showers, The.

Melancholy. August Straum, *tr. fr. German by* Glauco Cambon. OnPM
Melancholy. Edward Thomas. MoVE
Melancholy Cowboy, The. *Unknown.* CoSo; CSF
(Old Time Cowboy, *sl. diff.*) CSF
Melancholy days are come, the saddest of the year, The. The Death of the Flowers. Bryant. AA; AnAmPo; AnNE; APW; CoBA; DD; GN; HBV; IAP; LA; LBAP; LPS-2; OBAV; OTPC; PTA-2; PYM; TCAP; TreF; TVSH; WBLP
Melancholy face Charles Carville had, A. Charles Carville's Eyes. E. A. Robinson. MaPo; NePA; OxBA
Melancholy, hence! go get. James Shirley. *Fr.* Changes; or, Love in a Maze. TuPP
Melancholy Knight, The, *sels.* Samuel Rowlands.
Poetaster, The. ElL
Sir Eglamour. ElL; FaBoCh; InvP; LoGBV; WaKn
Melancholy Lay, A. Marjory Fleming. FaBoCh; FiBHP; LoGBV; SiTL
(Three Turkeys.) ThWaDe
Melancholy lieth dolorously ill. Arabs. Alfred Kreymborg. MAPA; TwAmPo
Melancholy little man was seated on the ground, A. Home. *Unknown.* HBV
Melancholy Pig, The. "Lewis Carroll." *Fr.* Sylvie and Bruno, *ch.* 10. FaPON; OTPC (1946 ed.); PPL; RAR
(Pig-Tale, The, *longer vers. in* Sylvie and Bruno Concluded.) BoN
Melancholy slackening that ensued, The. Cambridge and the Alps. Wordsworth. *Fr.* The Prelude. PoEL-4
Melancholy's Curse of Feasts. Edward Coote Pinkney. APW; SPP
Melancthon. Marianne Moore. AtBAP; CrMA
Melbourne and Memory, *sel.* Frank Wilmot.
Towers at Evening, The. NeLNL
Melbourne Ode, A; the Agricultural Show, Flemington, Victoria. Frank Wilmot. BoAu
Melchior, Gaspar, and Balthazar. The Legend of the Saintfoin. Pamela Tennant. GBV (1922 ed.)
Melchior, Gaspar, Balthazar. The Ballad of the Cross. Theodosia Garrison. HBMV; HBVY; NV
Melchizedek. Cardinal Newman. TriL
Melencolia. James Thomson. *See* Melancholia.
Melfort Dalton, I knew you well. To an Old Tenor. Oliver St. John Gogarty. WhC
Melicertus' Description of His Mistress. Robert Greene. *Fr.* Menaphon. ReIE
(Of His Mistress.) ElL
Melilot. Muna Lee. LoPS; NP
(Behind the House Is the Millet Plot.) SBMV
Melincourt, *sels.* Thomas Love Peacock.
Flower of Love, The. EV-4
Glee—the Ghosts. ViBoPo
Quintetto upon the Christmas Pie.
"My share of pie to win, I will dash through thick and thin." MyFE
Sun-Dial, The. OBRV
Melinda, who had never been. The Coquette. Aphra Behn. TrGrPo; ViBoPo
Melisea, Her Song in Scorn of Her Shepherd Narcissus. Jorge de Montemayor, *tr. fr. Spanish by* Bartholomew Young. *Fr.* Diana. TuPP
Melité, your eyes are Hera's. To Melité. Rufinus Domesticus. LiTW
Mellow October. October. Gerald Bullett. AlDL
Mellow the moonlight to shine is beginning. The Spinning Wheel [*or* The Spinning-Wheel Song]. John Francis Waller. AnIV; ChTr; LPS-1; StPo; TIP; VA
Mellow touch of musick most doth wound, The. Soft Musick. Robert Herrick. SeEP
Mellow year is hasting to its close, The. November. Hartley Coleridge. Sonnets on the Seasons, XII. LoBV; OBRV; PEOR; PoRL
Melodie Grotesque. Persis Greely Anderson. WhC
Melodies of Morn. The. James Beattie. *See* But Who the Melodies of Morn Can Tell?
Melody, from treble tones, The, VII. Frances Crawford. PtPa
Melon Girl. Mei Yao Ch'en, *tr. fr. Chinese by* Kenneth Rexroth. OnPC
Melons. Mary Mapes Dodge. GaP; TiPo
Melpomene among her livid people. The Two Masks. George Meredith. VA
Melpomene, the Muse of tragic songs. Oenone's Complaint. George Peele. *Fr.* The Arraignment of Paris. ElL; OBSC
Melrose Abbey. Sir Walter Scott. *Fr.* The Lay of the Last Minstrel, II. SeCePo
("If thou wouldst view fair Melrose aright.") EV-4; OBRV
Melt the Bells. F. V. Rockett. BlG
Melting Ice. Sophocles, *tr. fr. Greek by* J. S. Phillimore. OxBG
Melting of the Earl's Plate. George Walter Thornbury. VA
Melton Mowbray Pork-Pie, A. Richard Le Gallienne. BOHV; PA
Melville and Coghill. Andrew Lang. EBSV; VA
Members, Don't Git Weary, *with music.* *Unknown.* BoAN-2
Memento. Federico García Lorca, *tr. fr. Spanish by* Eleanor L. Turnbull. CoSP; OnPM
Memento. Winfield Townley Scott. FiMAP
Memento. Stephen Spender. AtBAP
Memento for Mortality [*or* Mortalitie], A. *At. to* Francis Beaumont *and to* William Basse. *See* On the Tombs in Westminster Abbey.
Memento Mori. George Herbert. *See* Virtue.
Memling's Virgin with Apple. Adèle Naudé. BoSA
Memnon. Leslie Holdsworth Allen. BoAu
Memnon. Clinton Scollard. AA; BAP; OBAV
Memo. Kenneth Fearing. ChMo
Memorabilia. Robert Browning. BEL; BMEP; BoLiVe; BPN; EmBrPo; EnLi-2; EnLit; EPN; FaBoEn; FiP; GEPC; GTBS-W; HBV; LEAP; LoBV; OAEP; PIR; PoeMoYo; PoVP; PtP; PYM; SeCePo; TCEP; TOP; TwP; VA; ViPo; ViPP; VLEP; WHA
(Something to Remember.) CBPC
Memorabilia. E. E. Cummings. OnHM
Memorandum on My Martinique, *sel.* Aimé Césaire, *tr. fr. French by* Lionel Able *and* Yvan Goll.
"Neither the teacher of the class nor the priest." PoNe
Memorandum to Saint Francis—April 16. Sister Mary Francis. SaFP
Memorial. Mae Winkler Goodman. PGD
Memorial Day. William E. Brooks. GrCo-2; HH; MaRV; OQP; PEDC; PGD; PoRL; PSO; QP-2
Memorial Day. Wallace Bruce. MDAH
Memorial Day. Emerette H. Dunning. OQP; PSO; QP-1
Memorial Day. Theodosia Garrison. DD; MPB; OHIP; PEDC
Memorial Day. Richard Watson Gilder. *See* Decoration Day.
Memorial Day. Louise Imogen Guiney. DD; MDAH
Memorial Day. Joyce Kilmer. MaRV
Memorial Day. Samuel Ellsworth Kiser. *See* Memorial Day, 1889.
Memorial Day. Emma A. Lent. OQP; PSO; QP-1; WBLP
Memorial Day. Rose Florence Levy. MeMeAg
Memorial Day. Clinton Scollard. *See* For Our Dead.
Memorial Day. "Margaret Sidney." PEOR
Memorial Day. Samuel F. Smith. *Fr.* Our Honored Heroes. OQP; QP-2
Memorial Day. Cy Warman. DD; HH
Memorial Day. Alma Adams Wiley. PEDC
Memorial Day. McLandburgh Wilson. DD; MaRV
Memorial Day. Annette Wynne. MaRV; OHIP
Memorial Day, 1889. S. E. Kiser. DD; HH; MDAH; PEDC
Memorial Day, 1898. Reginald Wright Kauffman. MDAH
Memorial (For Two Young Seamen Lost Overboard in a Storm in Mid-Pacific, January, 1940). George Barker. LiTG; LiTM
Memorial for a Young Seaman, I. ReMP
Memorial, The; 1914–1918. Edmund Blunden. SoV
Memorial of Africa, A, *sel.* George Macdonald.
This Infant World. EPN
(Sonnet: "This infant world.") OBVV
(World and Soul.) VA
Memorial Rain. Archibald MacLeish. AnFE; BLV; BoLiVe; CoAnAm; CoBA; LiTA; MAP; MoAB; MoAmPo; PoLFOT; TwAmPo; TwCV; TwHP
Memorial Sonnet. Marjorie Meeker. AnAmPo; LA
Memorial Tablet, A. Florence Wilkinson Evans. LBMV
Memorial Thresholds. Dante Gabriel Rossetti. The House of Life, LXXXI. BPN; EmBrPo; PoVP; ReaPo; ViPo
Memorial to D. C., *sels.* Edna St. Vincent Millay.
Chorus: "Give away her gowns," III. NP
Elegy: "Let them bury your big eyes," V. AnNE; BAP; HBMV; InP; MAP; MoAB; MoAmPo; NeMA; NePA; OxBA; PoRA
Epitaph: "Heap not on this mound," I. NP
"O, loveliest throat of all sweet throats." OxBA
Prayer to Persephone, II. BAP; NP; PoeMoYo
Memorial to the Great Big Beautiful Self-sacrificing Advertisers. Frederick Ebright. WaP
Memorial Trees. Juvenal, *tr. fr. Latin by* George Lamb. OnPM
Memorial Verses. Matthew Arnold. BMEP; BPN; EM-2; EmBrPo; EPN; FiP; GEPC; HBV; OAEP; PoVP; PtP; TCEP; TriL; TwHP; VA; ViPo; ViPP; VLEP
Memorials on the Slain at Chickamauga. Herman Melville. AA; MDAH
(On the Slain at Chickamauga.) APW
Memories. Thomas Bailey Aldrich. AA
Memories. Friedrich Hölderlin, *tr. fr. German by* Vernon Watkins. AnGP
Memories. Alexander Hay Japp. VA
Memories. Louise Labé, *tr. fr. French by* Alan Conder. TrFP
Memories. Claire Morris. CAG

Memories. George Denison Prentice. AA
Memories. Shen Yo, *tr. fr. Chinese by* Henry H. Hart. ChLP
Memories. Arthur Stringer. HBV
Memories. Charles Hanson Towne. OQP; QP-2
Memories. Mark Van Doren. MOAP
Memories. Whittier. CoBA; IAP; OBVV; TCAP
Memories of a Lost War. Louis Simpson. NePoAm
Memories of Childhood. Wu Tsung Ai, *tr. fr. Chinese by* Henry H. Hart. OnPM; PoHN
Memories of President Lincoln. Walt Whitman. *See* When Lilacs Last in the Dooryard Bloom'd *and* O Captain! My Captain! *and* Hush'd Be the Camps To-day *and* This Dust Was Once the Man.
Memory. Thomas Bailey Aldrich. AA; AnFE; AnNE; APA; BAP; CBOV; CoAnAm; LEAP; MAP; MCCG; NeHB; OBAV; OQP; PoeMoYo; PoMa; QP-2; TreFS; VOD (1935 ed.)
Memory, A. William Allingham. *See* Four Ducks on a Pond.
Memory ("Marina's gone, and now sit I"). William Browne. *Fr.* Britannia's Pastorals, III, Song 1. HBV
(Celadyne's Song.) OBS
(So Shuts the Marigold Her Leaves, *shorter sel.*) ChTr
Memory ("So shuts the marigold her leaves"). William Browne. *Fr.* Britannia's Pastorals, III, Song 1. CBOV; EV-2; OBEV
(Since She Is Gone.) LiTL
("So shuts the marigold her leaves.") EG; ViBoPo
Memory, A. Ina Donna Coolbrith. BAP
Memory, The. Lord Dunsany. OxBI
Memory. Francis Erskine, Earl of Rosslyn. VA
Memory. Oliver Goldsmith. *Fr.* The Captivity, I. OBEC, *sl. diff. vers.;* OBEV; PoP
(Song: "O memory, thou fond deceiver.") ViBoPo
Memory. Nikolai Gumilev, *tr. fr. Russian by* Y. Hornstein. BoRS
Memory. Helen Hoyt. NP
Memory. Victor Hugo, *tr. fr. French by* Alan Conder. TrFP
Memory, A. Frederic Lawrence Knowles. HBV
Memory. Walter Savage Landor. EmBrPo; VA
Memory. Abraham Lincoln. BLPA; FaBoBe; NeHB; WBLP
Memory, A. H. P. Lovecraft. UnW
Memory, A. D. MacAleese. TIP
Memory, A. Lola Ridge. AV
Memory. Arthur Rimbaud, *tr. fr. French.* AnFP, *tr. by* Louise Varèse; LiA, *tr. by* Wallace Fowlie; LiTW, *tr. by* Norman Cameron; ReMP, *tr. by* Wallace Fowlie
Memory. Christina Rossetti. CoEV
Memory. Siegfried Sassoon. ChMo; CMP; NLK (1947 ed.)
Memory. Duncan Campbell Scott. BoCaPo (1948 ed.)
Memory. Shakespeare. *See* Sonnets, XXX.
Memory. Edward Shanks. MM
Memory. Shelley. *See* Music, When Soft Voices Die.
Memory. Erik Johan Stagnelius, *tr. fr. Swedish by* Sir Edmund Gosse. AWP
Memory, A. L. A. G. Strong. SiTL; WhC
Memory. Arthur Symons. LBBV
Memory, A. Katharine Tynan. OxBI
Memory. Wordsworth. BPN
Memory cannot linger long. So Wags the World. Ellen M. H. Cortissoz. AA
Memory carries my fancy back. The Little Golden Ring. *Unknown.* ShS
Memory Green. Archibald MacLeish. Po
Memory, Hither Come. Blake. *See* Song: "Memory, hither come."
Memory is a watery flower, when watered. In the Garden. Richard Eberhart. NePoAm-2
Memory of a Witch. Iku Takenaka, *tr. fr. Japanese by* Takamichi Ninomiya *and* D. J. Enright. PoLJ
Memory of Brother Michael. Patrick Kavanagh. MoAB; OnYI; OxBI
Memory of Earth, The. "Æ." BMEP; LEAP; OBVV; PoVP; TIP
Memory of England. Edna St. Vincent Millay. NeTW
Memory of Kent, The. Edmund Blunden. HBMV
Memory of Lake Superior. George Dillon. MAP; MoAmPo (1942 ed.)
(In Memory of Lake Superior.) PoTo
Memory of one day, The. A Discovery of No Importance. Willard Wattles. PR
Memory of one particular hour, The. Wordsworth. *Fr.* The Prelude, IV. EV-3
Memory of the Dead, The. John Kelly Ingram. AnIV; GTIV; HBV; OnYI; OxBI; PoFr; TIP; VA
Memory of the Heart, The. Daniel Webster. LPS-1
Memory of the Players in a Mirror at Midnight, A. James Joyce. InvP; TIP; ViBoPo
Memory of time is here imprisoned, The. In a Strange House. Stanley J. Kunitz. NP
Memory, out of the mist, in a long slow ripple. Seagulls on the Serpentine. Alfred Noyes. EtS
Memphis and Karnak, Luxor, Thebes, the Nile. The Only Way. Louis V. Ledoux. LBMV
Memphis Blues. Sterling A. Brown. BANP
Memphis, the snub-nosed dancer, danced Daphne and Niobe. Ballet. Palladas. GrPE
Men, The. Maurice Bell. BIG
Men. Archibald MacLeish. ChMo; CMP; CoV; MoAB; NP; PoLFOT; ReaPo; YaD
Men. Dorothy E. Reid. DDA; NeMA; StaSt
Men and beasts of the zodiac, The. Winter Dawn. Tu Fu. OnPC
Men and Boys. Karl Theodor Körner, *tr. fr. German by* Charles T. Brooks. LPS-2
Men and brothers, who after us shall be. Ballade of the Hanged Men. Villon. LiTW; LyMA
Men and Man. George Meredith. EPN
Men are brethren of each other. Fur and Feather. Christina Rossetti. CBPC
Men Are Children of this World. Moses ibn Ezra, *tr. fr. Hebrew by* Solomon Solis-Cohen. TrJP
Men Are Made Human by the Mighty Fall. John Masefield. *Fr.* Sonnets ("Long, long ago"). EPN
Men Are the Devil. Mary Carolyn Davies. HBMV; YaD
Men at the Council Tables. Master Surgeon. Lucia Trent. ChIP
Men behind the Guns, The. John Jerome Rooney. AA; BLPA; EtS; FaBoBe; HBV; JKCP; MC; PaA; PAH; YaD
Men, brother men, that after us yet live. The Epitaph in Form of a Ballad. Villon, *tr. by* Swinburne. EnLi-2; LiA; OuHeWo
Men call you beautiful, and I suppose you are. A Question. C. L. Jones. CAG
Men call you fair [*or* fayre], and you do[e] credit it. Amoretti, LXXIX. Spenser. ATP; AWP; BEL; CBOV; EnLi-1; FaBoBe; HBV; JAWP; LiTL; PeBoSo; PoFS; ReIE; SiCE; TOP; WBP
Men cannot guess the things they do. The Little Things. Elizabeth Isler. PoToHe (new ed.)
Men do not long endure the light. Fleur de Lys. Rayner Heppenstall. WaP
Men, dying, make their wills; but wives. Woman's Will. John Godfrey Saxe. BOHV; FaFP; HBV; InP; LauV; LPS-3; SiTL
Men Fade like Rocks. W. J. Turner. OBMV; POTE
Men Follow Simon. Raymond Kresensky. ChIP; OQP; QP-1
Men found you subtle, master, blending skeins. Newman. George N. Shuster. JKCP (1926 ed.)
Men go out from the places where they dwelled. When Abraham Went Out of Ur. Nancy Byrd Turner. QS
Men go to their garden for pleasure. In the Garden. *Unknown.* MaRV
Men go to women mutely for their peace. Everyday Alchemy. Genevieve Taggard. PoeMoYo
Men grew sae cauld, maids sae unkind. The Blind Boy's Pranks. William Thom. EBSV; EV-4; OBEV
Men Have Forged. Jay G. Sigmund. OQP; QP-2
Men have made them gods of love. Pain. "Æ." MoBrPo
Men have their alien sons and love them. Son. Josephine Miles. FiMAP
Men heard this roar of parleying starlings, saw. February Afternoon. Edward Thomas. MoPW
Men if you love us, play no more. In the Person of Woman Kind. Ben Jonson. SeCV-1
Men Improve with the Years. W. B. Yeats. CoEV
Men in Green. David Campbell. BoAV; MoAuPo; NeLNL
Men in New Mexico. D. H. Lawrence. BrBE
Men know that the birch-tree always. Second Growth. Winifred Welles. BAP
Men lied to them and so they went to die. Thermopylae [*or* Thermopylae and Golgotha]. Robert Hillyer. AnAmPo; BAP; LA; MaRV
Men long have fought for their flying flags. The Flag of Peace. Charlotte Perkins Gilman. NeHB; OQP; QP-2
Men Loved Wholly beyond Wisdom. Louise Bogan. AnAmPo; AV; HBMV; InPo; LA; LiTA; LiTL; LiTM; MOAP; NePA; PG (1955 ed.); TBM; TCPD
Men Made Out of Words. Wallace Stevens. MoAB
Men march to war and come back on their shields. One Immortality. Norbert Engels. CAW
Men may leave [*or* leve] all games [*or* gamys]. The Sailing of the Pilgrims from Sandwich towards St. James of Compostella [*or* Pilgrims at Sea]. *Unknown.* SG; TMEV
Men moving in a trench, in the clear noon. These Men. Leon Gellert. BoAV; MoAuPo
Men, my brothers, men the workers, ever reaping something new. The Federation of the World. Tennyson. *Fr.* Locksley Hall. MaRV
Men never know. The Radical. Waring Cuney. CDC
Men of Affairs. Ch'en Tzu-ang. *See* Business Men.
Men of America, Answering the Call. Hal Borland. PoFr
Men of Andalus, to horse! Toledo Captured by the Franks. Al-Assal. MooP
Men of England. Thomas Campbell. BHV; EV-4; PoFr
Men of England. Shelley. *See* Song to the Men of England.

Men of "Forty-eight," The. Gerald Massey. PoFr
Men of Good Works. Michael Wigglesworth. *Fr.* The Day of Doom. AmPP
Men of Gotham, The. Thomas Love Peacock. *See* Three Men of Gotham.
Men of Harlan. William Aspenwall Bradley. POT; SBMV
Men of Harlech. *Unknown, tr. fr. Welsh by* John Oxenford. PoFr
(March of the Men of Harlech, *tr. by* William Duthie.) OlF
Men of learning say she must, The. Given Over. Thomas Woolner. VA
Men of Old, The. Richard Monckton Milnes. EV-5; GTBS; GTSL; LPS-3; OBEV (new ed.); OBVV
Men of Oyster Bay, The. *Unknown.* DDA
Men of Religion. Molière, *tr. fr. French by* Curtis Hidden Page. *Fr.* Tartuffe, I, vi. GrCo-2
Men of sin prevail, The. The Covenanter's Lament for Bothwell Brigg. Winthrop Mackworth Praed. OBRV
Men of the Alamo, The. James Jeffrey Roche. BoHiPo; PAH
Men of the earth, The, said: "We must war." Peace on Earth [*or* Why]. Robert Freeman. PGD; PSO
Men of the *Maine,* The. Clinton Scollard. MC; PAH
Men of the *Merrimac,* The. Clinton Scollard. PAH
Men of the North. John Neal. AA; MDAH
Men of the North and West. Richard Henry Stoddard. PAH
Men of the 21st. The Guards Came Through. Sir Arthur Conan Doyle. BoHiPo
Men of thought! be up and stirring. Song. Charles Mackay. PoFr
Men of valor, The. Tanka. Akahito. *Fr.* Manyo Shu. AWP; InP; LiTW; PFE
Men of wealthie Sestos, everie yeare, The. Christopher Marlowe. *Fr.* Hero and Leander, First Sestiad. BrBE
Men on Islands. Padraic Colum. TIP
Men once were surnamed for their shape and estate. Surnames. James Smith. BOHV
Men proffer presents here to my people. Wulf and Eadwacer. *Unknown.* TrGrPo
Men, remember the marches and the halts. Apoem I. Henri Pichette. LiTW
Men said at vespers: "All is well!" Chicago. Whittier. BAV; MC; PAH; PoRL
Men said he saw strange visions. Macaulay. *Fr.* Lays of Ancient Rome: The Battle of Lake Regillus. UnW
Men saw no portents on that [winter] night. Young Lincoln. Edwin Markham. DD; GA; OHIP; OQP; PEDC; QP-2
Men say, Columbia, we shall hear thy guns. America. Sydney Dobell. EPN; EPP; OBVV; ShGoBo
Men say the sullen instrument. In the Twilight. James Russell Lowell. AA; HBV; IAP
Men Say They Know Many Things. Henry David Thoreau. AnNE; ImOP
Men say unfriendly words of you, poor birds! To Some Philadelphia Sparrows. Jeannette Marks. MW
Men seldom make passes. News Item [*or* Some Beautiful Letters]. Dorothy Parker. InMe; SiTL; TreF; YaD
Men share perceptions. The Switch Blade; or, John's Other Wife. Jonathan Williams. NeAP
Men talk of those the fields that till. Ballad of Poor Chimney Sweeps. Villon. WoL
Men that are men again; who goes home? G. K. Chesterton. *Fr.* Who Goes Home? OtMeF
Men that are safe, and sure, in all they do[e]. An Epistle Answering to One That Asked to Be Sealed of the Tribe of Ben. Ben Jonson. OAEP; SeCV-1; TuPP
Men that delight to multiply desire. Caelica, XCIV [XCV]. Fulke Greville. OBS; SiCE
Men That Don't Fit In. Robert W. Service. BLPA
Men that worked for England, The. Elegy in a Country Churchyard. G. K. Chesterton. HBMV; LBBV; MBP; MoBrPo; NeMA; SoV; TCEP; TrGrPo; ViBoPo; WhC
Men the Angels eyed. Men and Man. George Meredith. EPN
Men Told Me, Lord! David Starr Jordan. MaRV; OQP; QP-1; WGRP
Men took the skyscraper. Crucifixion of the Skyscraper. John Gould Fletcher. MM
Men travel far and far away. Two Old Men. Louise Driscoll. NLK
Men Walked To and Fro. Blanaid Salkeld. NeIP
Men who have loved the ships they took to sea. Mariners. David Morton. EtS; PoMa; VOD
Men who here in harness died, The. On the Home Guards. Herman Melville. SoV
Men who made Texas, The. Song of the Forerunners. Karle Wilson Baker. HiLiAm
Men Who March Away ("We be the King's men"). Thomas Hardy. *Fr.* The Dynasts, Pt. I, Act I, sc. i. CH
Men Who March Away ("What of the faith and fire within us"). Thomas Hardy. BEL; EPP; PoFr; SoV
Men Who Turn from God. T. S. Eliot. *Fr.* The Rock. MaRV
Men! whose boast it is that ye. Stanzas on Freedom [*or* Freedom]. James Russell Lowell. AOAH; CoBA; GN; IAP; MaRV; MC; OHIP; PEOR; PGD; PoFr; PoNe
"Men will grow weary," said the Lord. Fishing. Edgar A. Guest. NLK
Men, women, call thee so or so. Complaint. John Gray. CaAE
Men wondered why I loved you, and none guessed. Lady Hamilton. Muriel Stuart. DiM
Men wrap themselves in smug cocoons. Conventionality. Eloise Hackett. MaRV
Menace. Katharine Tynan. AV
Menace of the Flower, The. Alfonso Reyes, *tr. fr. Spanish by* Samuel Beckett. AnMP
Menacing machine turns on and off, The. Terror Conduction. Philip Lamantia. NeAP
Menagerie, The. William Vaughn Moody. AmPP (3d ed.); OnAP; PFY; TCAP; TCPD; TOP; YaD
Menaion, *sel.* St. Cosmas, *tr. fr. Greek.*
Purification, The. ISi
Menaphon, *sels.* Robert Greene.
Doron's Jig [*or* Jigge]. AtBAP; ElSeCe; PoEL-2; TuPP
(Jig, A.) ElL
Melicertus' Description of His Mistress. ReIE
(Of His Mistress.) ElL
Menaphon's Ditty ("Fair fields"). OBSC
Menaphon's Roundelay ("When tender ewes"). WP
Menaphon's Song ("Some say love"). ElSeCe; LoBV; OBSC; ReIE
Samela. ElL; HBV; OBEV; OBSC; ViBoPo
(Doron's Description of Samela.) AtBAP; ElSeCe; EV-1; LoBV; PoEL-2; ReIE; SiCE; TuPP
Sephestia's Song to Her Child. AtBAP; BOL; CoBE; ElSeCe; EnLi-1 (1949 ed.); EnLit; EPP; EV-1; GTSL; LoBV; OBSC; PoEL-2; ReEn; ReIE; SiCE; TrGrPo; TuPP
(Sephestia's Lullaby.) HBV; LEAP; OBEV
(Weep Not, My Wanton.) ElL; SeCePo; ViBoPo
Mend my broken mood. Prayer for Song. Fay Lewis Noble. TrPWD
Mendacity. A. E. Coppard. GTBS-W; LiTL; LiTM; OBMV
Mendax. Gotthold Ephraim Lessing, *tr. fr. German.* BOHV
Mendelian Theory. *Unknown.* LiTM; SiTL
(Limerick: "There was a young lady called Starky.") CenHV
Mendicant, The. Enid Dinnis. SaFP
Mendicants, The. Bliss Carman. HBV; NLK, *abr.;* VA
Mending Sump. Kenneth Koch. NeAP
Mending the Bridge. Douglas Stewart. AnNZ
Mending Wall. Robert Frost. AmP; AmPP; AnNE; BAP; BoFr; CBOV; ChMo; CMP; CoBA; CoBMV; CP; ExPo; FaFP; GTBS-W; HBV; IAP; InP; InPo; LaNeLa; LiTA; LiTM; MAP; MCCG; MoAB; MoAmPo; MOAP; MoPW; MoVE; NeMA; NePA; NP; OHFP; OtMeF; OxBA; PFE; PFY; PoE; PoeMoYo; PoLFOT; PoMa; POT; PoTo; PreP; PYM; ReaPo; SeCeV; TCAP; TCPD; TOP; TwP; ViBoPo; WHA
"Something there is that doesn't love a wall," *sel.* MaRV
Mendip Hills over Wells, The. Henry Alford. EnSW
"Mene, Mene, Tekel, Upharsin." Madison Cawein. PAH
Menelaos; Blasphemy under Duress. Homer, *tr. fr. Greek by* William Cowper. *Fr.* The Iliad, XIII. GrR
Menelaus. Clarence Day. BOHV
Menelaus Abandoned. Aeschylus, *tr. fr. Greek by* E. D. A. Morshead. *Fr.* Agamemnon. LiA
Menelaus and Helen. Rupert Brooke. SeCePo
Menelaus and Helen at Troy. Walter Savage Landor. BPN
Menelaus and Odysseus. Homer, *tr. fr. Greek by* William Cowper. *Fr.* The Iliad, III. OxBG
Menelaus, Menelaus. Menelaus. Clarence Day. BOHV
Menelaus; What Price Earthly Splendor! Homer, *pr. tr. fr. Greek by* S. H. Butcher *and* Andrew Lang. *Fr.* The Odyssey, IV. GrR
Menodotis ("Menodotis's portrait here is kept"). Leonidas of Alexandria, *tr. fr. Greek by* Richard Garnett. AWP; JAWP; LiTW; WBP
Mens Creatrix. Stanley J. Kunitz. NP
Men's hearts love gold and jade. Lodging with the Old Man of the Stream. Po Chü-i. AWP; JAWP; TrCh; WBP
Mental Cases. Wilfred Owen. FaBoMo; LiTM (rev. ed.); WaP
Mental tapestry I spin, A. General Paresis. Louis J. Karnosh. PoP
Mental Traveller, The. Blake. EnRP; PoEL-4
Mentis Trist. Robert Hillyer. HBMV; TBM
Mentors. Gwendolyn Brooks. PoNe
"Mentrechè il Vento, Come Fa, Si Tace." Delmore Schwartz. The Repetitive Heart, II. AnFE; CoAnAm; LoPS; TwAmPo
(Will You Perhaps.) FiMAP
Menu, The. Thomas Bailey Aldrich. HBV
Mephibosheth. Nathaniel Parker Willis. MOAH
Mercator, *sel.* Plautus, *tr. fr. Latin by* Gilbert Highet.
"As soon as I passed out of my first youth" LaP

Mercedes, *sel.* Thomas Bailey Aldrich.
Andalusian Cradle-Song. BOL
Mercedes. Elizabeth Stoddard. AA; LBAP
Mercenary Muse, The. Pindar, *tr. fr. Greek by* F. L. Lucas. *Fr.* Isthmian Odes, II. GrPE
Merchandise. Seán Jennett. NeIP
Merchandise. Amy Lowell. LaNeLa; MAPA
Merchant, The. Rabindranath Tagore. MOAH
Merchant and scholar who have left me blood. Waters of the Boyne. W. B. Yeats. *Fr.* Responsibilities. LiA
Merchant and the Fidler's Wife, The. *Unknown.* CoMu
Merchant, as crafty a man is he, The. Do You Plan to Speak Bantu? or, Abbreviation Is the Thief of Sanity. Ogden Nash. FiBHP
Merchant of Venice, The, *sels.* Shakespeare.
Good Deeds, *fr.* V, i. BLP
"How sweet the moonlight sleeps upon this bank!" *fr.* V, i. CBE; MeRV; PIR; TreFS; TrGrPo
(From "The Merchant of Venice.") LEAP
(In Tune with the Infinite.) MaRV
(Moonlight.) OHFP; SN
(Moonlight and Music.) BCEP
(Moonlight Music.) EV-1
(Music.) LPS-3
In Such a Night, *fr.* V, i. ChTr; FiP; LiA; WHA
(Divine Harmony.) GoBC
Let Me Play the Fool, *fr.* I, i. TrGrPo
(Why Should a Man.) BLP
Portia's Picture, *fr.* III, ii. LPS-1
Power of Music, The, *fr.* V, i. GN
Quality of Mercy [Is Not Strain'd], The, *fr.* IV, i. EV-1; FaFP; LiTB; LiTG; OnHT; PIR; PTA-1
(From "The Merchant of Venice.") LEAP
(Mercy.) BBV; BCEP; BTP; CBE; MaRV; OHFP; OQP; OTPC; PC; PECK; QP-1; TrGrPo; TVSH; WBLP
(Portia's Appeal for Mercy.) PYM
(Portia's Plea for Mercy.) TreF
(When Mercy Seasons Justice.) GrCo-1
Shylock's Defense, *fr.* III, i. TreFS
"Tell me where is fancy bred," *fr.* III, ii. AnFE; AtBAP; BEL; CBE; CH; EG; ElL; ElSeCe; EM-1; EnLi-1; EnLit; EPP; EV-1; InPo; LiTB; LiTG; LO; OAEP; PIR; PoEL-2; ReaPo; RiBV; SeCeV; SiCE; TOP; TwP; TyEnPo; ViBoPo; WHA
(Casket Song, A.) OBSC
(Fancy.) BLV; CBPC; FaPON; TreFS; TrGrPo
(Love.) LPS-1; OBEV
(Madrigal.) GTBS; GTBS-D; GTBS-W; GTSE
(Song, A.) BoLiVe; BrBE
(Where Is Fancy Bred.) PC
"There's not the smallest orb which thou behold'st," *fr.* V, i. LO
"Well; tell me now, what lady is the same," *fr.* I, i. BoFr
Merchant, that dost endeavor all thy days. Miserable Merchant. Samuel Rowlands. SiCE
Merchant, to Secure His Treasure, The. Matthew Prior. *See* Ode, An: "Merchant, to secure . . ."
Merchantman, The. John Davidson. OBVV
(Eclogue: The Merchantman.) PoVP
Merchants from Cathay. William Rose Benét. CV; HBMV; MAP; MoAmPo; NeMA; NV
Merciful God, who readst my inmost mind. Prayer. Willem Bilderdijk. LiTW
Merciful Medusa. Winifred Welles. PIAE
Merciles Beaute. Chaucer. CaAE; EnLi-1 (1949 ed.); EnLoPo; LEAP; OBEV (1st ed.)
Sels.
Captivity, I. AEV; LiA
(Merciles Beaute, I.) AtBAP; CoEV
(Merciless Beauty, I, *mod. vers.*) ACP
(Rondel of Merciles Beautè [*or* Merciless Beauty], A, *orig. and mod. vers. by* Louis Untermeyer.) TrGrPo
(Roundel: "Your eyen two will slay me suddenly," *mod. vers.*) OnPM
Escape, III. LoPS
Mercury. Josephine Miles. FiMAP
Mercury Bay Eclogue, *sel.* M. K. Joseph.
"Child's castle crumbles, The; hot air shimmers." AnNZ
Mercury's Song to Phaedra. Dryden. *See* Song: "Fair Iris I love."
Mercutio Describes Queen Mab. Shakespeare. *See* Queen Mab.
Mercutio's Queen Mab Speech. Shakespeare. *See* Queen Mab.
Mercy ("The quality of mercy is not strained"). Shakespeare. *See* Quality of Mercy, The.
Mercy ("Your brother is a forfeit of the law"). Shakespeare. *Fr.* Measure for Measure, II, ii. EV-1
Mercy. *Unknown.* TMEV
Mercy and Love. Robert Herrick. SeCV-1
"Mercy, child, how young you are." Miriam's Unsaid Speech. Judith Stern. CAG
Mercy Is Most in My Mind. *Unknown.* CoBE
Mercy Passeth All Things. *Unknown.* TMEV
Mere dark is not so night-like as it seems. The Day's No Rounder than Its Angles Are. Peter Viereck. AmP
Mère Michel. *Unknown, tr. fr. French.* CIV
Merely the landscape of a vanished whim. Versailles. Adrienne Cecile Rich. NePoEA
Merely to say: "The hill is green." Poetry. William Soutar. HaMV
Merideth. *Unknown.* WhC
(On a Man Named Merideth.) GoTP
Merie Sungen the Muneches. *Unknown. See* Merrily Sang the Monkes in Ely.
Merit of True Passion, The. Sir Walter Ralegh. *See* Silent Lover, The.
Merlin, I ("Thy trivial harp will never please"). Emerson. AA; AmP; AmPo; AmPP (4th ed.); AnNE; CoV; IAP; LEAP; MOAP; OxBA; TCAP
"Thy trivial harp . . . ," *sel.* APW
(Poet, The.) BLV; BoLiVe
Merlin, II ("The rhyme of the poet"). Emerson. AmP; AmPo; AmPP (4th ed.); AnNE; IAP; PoEL-4
Merlin. Edwin Muir. FaBoTw; MoPW
Merlin and the Gleam. Tennyson. BEL; BPN; EM-2; EmBrPo; EPP; GEPC; OAEP; PoVP; REAL; VLEP
Follow the Gleam, IX. BBV; MaRV; OTPC (1946 ed.); PoRL
Merlin and Vivien. Tennyson. *See* Idylls of the King.
Merlin Enthralled. Richard Wilbur. NePoEA
Merlin in the Cave; He Speculates without a Book. Thom Gunn. NePoEA
Merlin's Apple-Trees. Thomas Love Peacock. *Fr.* The Misfortunes of Elphin. OBRV
Merlin's Riddle. Tennyson. *Fr.* Idylls of the King: The Coming of Arthur. BPN
Mermaid, The. A. J. M. Smith. TwCaPo
Mermaid, The. Tennyson. BPN; FaPON; GN; GoTP; MPB; OTPC (1946 ed.); PCH; PoMS; TSW
"Who would be/ A mermaid fair," *sel.* BoTP
Mermaid, The ("One [*or* 'Twas a] Friday morn"). *Unknown.* BaBo, *sl. diff. vers.*; ESPB (A *and* B *vers.*); LiTG; OuSiCo, *sl. diff. vers., with music;* SG; SiTL; TreF; ViBoFo (A *vers.*; B *vers., with music*)
(One Friday Morn.) CH; OnSP; OTPC (1946 ed.)
Mermaid, The ("To yon fause stream"). *Unknown.* CH
Mermaid, The. Allen Upward. *Fr.* Scented Leaves from a Chinese Jar. NP
Mermaid, The. W. B. Yeats. A Man Young and Old, III. TwP
Mermaid at Zennor, The. John Heath-Stubbs. FaBoMo
Mermaid found a swimming lad, A. The Mermaid. W. B. Yeats. A Man Young and Old, III. TwP
Mermaid of Margate, The. Thomas Hood. ERP
Mermaid Tavern, The. Keats. *See* Lines on the Mermaid Tavern.
Mermaiden, A. Thomas Hennell. FaBoTw
Mermaidens, The. Heine. *See* Mond ist aufgegangen, Der.
Mermaidens, The. Laura E. Richards. BrR; StVeCh (1955 ed.)
Mermaidens' [*or* Mermaids'] Vesper-Hymn, The. George Darley. Syren Songs, VI. BLV; FaBoEn; KN; LoBV; OBRV; PoEL-4; RO
(Siren Chorus.) GTIV; OxBI; ViBoPo
(Song of the Mermaids.) ChTr
Mermaids. Kenneth Slessor. NeLNL
Mermaids, The. Spenser. *Fr.* The Faerie Queene, II, 12. ChTr
Mermaids and Mermen. Sir Walter Scott. *Fr.* The Pirate, *ch.* 16. EtS
Mermaid's not a human thing, A. Lost and Given Over. E. J. Brady. BoAu
Mermaid's Pap, The. Christopher Smart. *Fr.* A Song to David. BeR
(Adoration.) FaBoEn
Mermaid's Spaeing, The. *Unknown, tr. fr. Danish by* E. M. Smith-Dampier. BoDaBa
Merman, The. Tennyson. BPN; FaPON; GN; GoTP; OTPC (1946 ed.); PCD; PCH; PoMS
"Who would be/ A merman bold," *sel.* BoTP
Mer-Man and Marstig's Daughter, The. *Unknown, tr. fr. Danish by* Robert Jamieson. AWP; JAWP; WBP
Merman Rosmer. *Unknown.* SG
Merops. Emerson. AnFE; APA; CoAnAm; FaBoEn; IAP; MOAP; OxBA
Merrill's Brook. Winfield Townley Scott. FiMAP
Merrill's Garden. John Freeman. MM
Merrily, merrily,/ All the spring. Merry Birds. Rodney Bennett. BoTP
Merrily Sang the Monkes in Ely. *Unknown, wr. at. to* King Canute. LEAP
(Merie Sungen the Muneches.) AtBAP
("Merie sungen the muneches binnen Ely.") NBE
(Monks of Ely, The, *mod.*) ACP; CAW
Merrily swim we, the moon shines bright. On Tweed River. Sir Walter Scott. *Fr.* The Monastery. EV-4

Merrily swinging on briar and weed. Robert of Lincoln. Bryant. AnNE; APW; BLA; BoChLi; DD; EV-4; FaBoBe; FaPON; GFA; HBV; HBVY; HH; IAP; LPS-2; MPB; MW; OTPC (1946 ed.); PCH; PECK; PIR; PRWS; PTA-1; TCAP; WBLP; WhBS
Merrimac Side, and Agiochook. Edward Everett Hale. From Potomac to Merrimac, III. PAH
Merritt Parkway. Denise Levertov. NeAP
Merry Are the Bells. *Unknown.* CBPC; HBV; HBVY; LiL; MoShBr; OTPC; PPL, *abr.;* TiPo (1959 ed.)
Merry Autumn Days. Charles Dickens. PCH
Merry Bagpipes, The. *Unknown.* CoMu
Merry Ballad of Vintners, A. John Payne. ALV
Merry Bee, A. Joseph Skipsey. OBVV
Merry Birds. Rodney Bennett. BoTP
Merry Boys of the Times. *Unknown. See* Courtier's Health, The.
Merry brown hares came leaping, The. A Rough Rhyme on a Rough Matter [*or* The Bad Squire]. Charles Kingsley. *Fr.* Yeast. BMEP; EV-5; LPS-1; PIR
Merry Christmas ("In the rush"). *Unknown.* COAH
Merry Christmas and a Glad New Year, A. George Cooper. PEOR
Merry Christmas Time, The. George Arnold. PEOR
Merry Country Lad, The. Nicholas Breton. *Fr.* The Passionate Shepherd. ElL; LoBV
(Happy Countryman, *shorter sel.*) CH
(Pastoral III: "Who can live in heart so glad.") ElSeCe; ReEn; TuPP
(Shepherd and Shepherdess.) OBSC
(Third Pastor's Song, The.) EV-1
("Who can live in heart so glad.") SiCE; ViBoPo
Merry Couple Madly Met, A. *Unknown. See* Roaring Lad and the Ranting Lass, The.
Merry Cuckold, The. *Unknown.* CoMu
Merry cuckoo [*or* cuckow] messenger [*or* messinger] of spring, The. Amoretti, XIX. Spenser. ES; EV-1; OBSC; PeBoSo; ReEn; ReIE; RiBV
Merry Drollery, *sel. Unknown.*
Old Souldier of the Queens, An. SoV
Merry-go-round. Dorothy Walter Baruch. BrR; MPB (1956 ed.); StVeCh; SUS; TiPo
Merry-go-round. Rachel Field. UTS
Merry-go-round. Langston Hughes. PoNe
Merry-go-round. Oliver Jenkins. GoYe
Merry-go-round, The. Roden Noel. VA
Merry-go-round, The. June. Mary Carolyn Davies. SiSoSe; TiPo (1959 ed.)
Merry Green Fields of England, *with music. Unknown.* FTB
Merry Guide, The. A. E. Housman. A Shropshire Lad, XLII. OAEP (2d ed.); PoeMoYo; PoTo; PoVP; ViPo
Merry have we met. A Party Song. *Unknown.* BoTP
Merry Hay-Makers, The; or, Pleasant Pastime between the Young-men and Maids, in the Pleasant Meadows. *Unknown.* CoMu
Merry Heart, A. Proverbs, Bible, *O.T. See* Lips of the Wise, The.
Merry Heart, The. Henry Hart Milman. TVSH
Merry Heart, The. Shakespeare. *See* Jog On, Jog On.
Merry Hoastess, The. *Unknown.* CoMu
Merry it is in May morning. By a Chapel as I Came. *Unknown.* ChTr
Merry it is in the good greenwood. Alice Brand [*or* Ballad: Alice Brand]. Sir Walter Scott. *Fr.* The Lady of The Lake. BeLS; EmBrPo; EV-4; HBV; HBVY; OTPC (1946 ed.); TVSH
Merry it is on a summer's day. A Swinging Song. Mary Howitt. OTPC (1923 ed.)
Merry Lark, The. Charles Kingsley. LPS-1; PIR
Merry Little Men. Kathleen M. Chaplin. BoTP
Merry Man of Paris, The. Stella Mead. SUS
Merry March wind is a boisterous fellow, The. The March Wind. E. H. Henderson. BoTP
Merry [*or* Mirry] Margaret,/ As midsummer flower. To Mistress Margaret Hussey [*wr.,* To Mistress Margery Wentworth]. John Skelton. *Fr.* The Garlande of Laurell. ACP; AnFE; AtBAP; CoEV; EnLoPo; EV-1; FaBoCh; GN; GoBC; GoTP; HBV; HoPM; InPo; KN; LEAP; LiTL; LoBV; LoGBV; LPS-1; OAEP; OBEV; OBSC; OTPC (1923 ed.); PG (1955 ed.); PoEL-1; PoRA; ReEn; RIS; SeCeV; SiCE; ThWaDe; TrGrPo; TuPP; ViBoPo
Merry May the Keel Row. *Unknown.* EBSV
Merry may the maid be. The Miller. Sir John Clerk of Penicuik. ChTr; EBSV
Merry, merry lark was up and singing, The. The Merry Lark. Charles Kingsley. LPS-1; PIR
Merry, merry, merry, cheery, cheery, cheery! Harvest. Thomas Nashe. *Fr.* Summer's Last Will and Testament. OBSC
Merry, merry sparrow! The Blossom. Blake. OTPC (1923 ed.); ThWaDe
Merry Miner, The. *Unknown.* IHA; StVeCh
Merry Month, The. "Miss X *and* Miss Y." InMe
Merry Month of March, The. Wordsworth. *See* Written in March.
Merry Old Souls. Morris Bishop. WhC
Merry Pieman's Song, The. John Bennett. LiL
Merry, rollicking, frolicking May. May. George Macdonald. OTPC (1946 ed.)
Merry sang the monks who in Ely fare. The Monks of Ely. *Unknown.* ACP; CAW. *See also* Merrily Sang the Monkes in Ely.
Merry Shanty Boys, The. *Unknown.* IHA
Merry Shepherdess, The. *Unknown. See* Amintas and Claudia.
Merry Sherwood, *sel.* John O'Keeffe.
Friar of Orders Gray, The. BOHV; OnYI; OxBI
(I Am a Friar of Orders Gray.) LPS-3
Merry Sunshine. *Unknown.* MPB; RAR
Merry voices chatterin'. Two-an'-six. Claude McKay. BANP; GoSl
Merry waves dance up and down, and play, The. Sport [*or* Song]. Abraham Cowley. *Fr.* Love's Riddle. AlDL; EPS (1942 ed.); SeCL
Merry wind danced over the hill, A. Such a Blustery Day! Elizabeth Gould. BoTP
Merry Wives of Windsor, The, *sels.* Shakespeare.
Fie on Sinful Fantasy, *fr.* V, v. ViBoPo
"What, have I 'scaped love-letters," *fr.* II, ii. LO
What I Am, I Cannot Avoide, *fr.* III, v. LiA
Merry [*or* Merrie] World did on a day, The. The Quip. George Herbert. AnFE; ATP; BEL; CenL; ElSeCe; EnLit; EPS; EV-2; LiTB; MaPo; MeRV; OAEP; OBS; OxBoCh; SeCV-1; SeEP
Merrythought's Song ("For Jillian of Berry"). Beaumont *and* Fletcher. *See* Jillian of Berry.
Merrythought's Song ("I would not be a servingman"). Beaumont *and* Fletcher. *Fr.* The Knight of the Burning Pestle. OBS
Mersa. Keith Douglas. FaBoMo
Merthe of alle this londe, The. Song of Ploughing. *Unknown.* LyMA
Merthymawr. George Woodcock. NeBP
(Merthyrmawr.) MoWP
Merthyr. Glyn Jones. PrWP
Mervail no more, although. *See* Marvel No More.
Mery it was in the grene foreste. Adam Bell, Clim of the Clough, and William of Cloudesley. *Unknown.* ESPB; OBB
Mesa Trail, *sel.* W. E. Bard.
"Up this beaten pathway." HiLiAm
Mesdames, never dare to deem those lovers yours. The Man Within. Annemarie Ewing. NePoAm-2
Meseemed There Called. Johannes Jørgensen, *tr. fr. Danish by* Charles W. Stork. BoDS
Meseemeth I heard cry and groan. The Complaint of the Fair Armoress. Villon, *tr. by* Swinburne. AWP; WoL
Mesnevi. Sadi, *tr. fr. Persian by* L. Cranmer-Byng. *Fr.* The Gulistan. AWP; JAWP; LiTW; WPB
Mesopotamia 1917. Kipling. SoV
Mess Deck Casualty. Alan Ross. WaP
Mess is all asleep, my candle burns, The. A Wry Smile. Roy Fuller. WaaP; WaP
Mess of Clams, A. Robert P. Tristram Coffin. DDA
Mess-tent is full, and the glasses are set, The. The Battle Eve of the Irish Brigade. Thomas Osborne Davis. AnIV; OnYI
Message, The. John Donne. ATP (1935 ed.); EIL; EnLit; EPS; GTBS-W; HBV; LiTG; MeLP; OBS; TuPP; ViBoPo; WHA
Message. Allen Ginsberg. NeAP
Message, The. Heine, *tr. fr. German by* Kate Freilgrath Kroeker. AWP; JAWP; WBP
Message, The. *At. to* Thomas Heywood. *See* Ye Little Birds That Sit and Sing.
Message, The. Meleager, *tr. fr. Greek by* Dudley Fitts. LiTW
Message. Nasir-i Khusrau, *tr. fr. Persian by* E. G. Browne. PeP
Message, A. Anna Nelson Reed. OQP; QP-1
Message, The. Lady Margaret Sackville. AV
Message. Sara Teasdale. SBMV
Message, A. Elizabeth Stuart Phelps Ward. PAH
Message for the Nations of the World, A. Bertrand Russell. SiTL
Message for the Year, A. Elizabeth Clarke Hardy. PTA-2
Message from a Little Ghost. Muriel Whitehead Jarvis. DDA
Message from her set his brain aflame, A. Modern Love, V. George Meredith. ViPo
Message from Home. Kathleen Raine. ImOP
Message of Hermes to Calypso, The. Homer, *tr. fr. Greek by* F. L. Lucas. *Fr.* The Odyssey, V. GrPE
Message of Peace, The. Julia Ward Howe. PGD; PSO
Message of Peace, A. Longfellow. *See* When War Shall Be No More.

Message of Peace, A. John Boyle O'Reilly. OnYI
Message of the Bells, The. Thomas Curtis Clark. PGD
Message of the March Wind, The. William Morris. EmBrPo; OBVV
"Fair now is the springtide, now earth lies beholding," *sel.* GTBS-D
Message of the New Year, The. *Unknown.* OQP; QP-1
Message of the Snowdrop, The. *Unknown.* PEOR
Message of Victory, The. Augusta Webster. *See* **News to the King.**
Message Received. Sonia Raiziss. PoF
Message to America, A. Alan Seeger. LPS-1
Message to General Montgomery. H. F. Ellis. WhC
Message to Meng Hao-jan, A. Li Po, *tr. fr. Chinese by* Witter Bynner. BoFr
Message to Siberia. Pushkin, *tr. fr. Russian by* Max Eastman. AWP; JAWP; PoFr; TrRV; WBP; WoL; BoR, *tr. by* C. M. Bowra
Message to the Bard. William Livingston, *tr. fr. Gaelic.* GoTS
Messages, The. W. W. Gibson. ChMo; CMP; InP; MCCG; NV; OHIP
Messages. Alfred Noyes. *Fr.* The Last Voyage. GoBC
Messages. Francis Thompson. CH; OtMeF; PoeT; UnW
Messalina Speaks. Charles Pelham Mulvany. TIP
Messe of Nonsense, A. *Unknown.* OBS
Messed Damozel, The. Charles Hanson Towne. BOHV
Messenger, The. Jacob Glatstein, *tr. fr. Yiddish by* Sarah Zweig Betsky. OnCuPl
Messenger, The. H. P. Lovecraft. DaM
Messenger, The. Alfred Noyes. GoBC
Messenger dispatch'd, again she view'd, The. Ave atque Vale. Dryden. *Fr.* Sigismonda and Guiscardo. OBS
Messenger of Sympathy and Love. The Meaning of a Letter. *Unknown.* PoToHe (new ed.)
Messenger Song, The. *At. to* John Calhoun. ShS
Messengers. Charles Hanson Towne. CAW
Messiah, The. Isaiah, VII: 14-25, Bible, *O.T.* AWP
Messiah, The. David Frishman, *tr. fr. Hebrew by* Maurice Samuel. LiTW
Messiah, The. Milton. *Fr.* Paradise Regained, I. OBS
Messiah. Pope. OxBoCh
Sels.
Rise, Crowned with Light [Imperial Salem, Rise], *sel., sl. diff.* GoBC; OlF; WGRP
(Hymn: "Rise, crowned with light . . .") NeHB
Vision of the Future, A. MuP
Messiah, The. Virgil, *tr. fr. Latin by* Dryden. Eclogues, IV. AWP; JAWP; OuHeWo; WBP
Sibylline Prophecy, The, *sel., tr. by* Roderick Gill. CAW
Messias. Thomas Merton. JKCP (1955 ed.)
Messidor. Swinburne. ViPo
Messire Geoffrey Chaucer to His Editor. Arthur Guiterman. PoeMoYo
Messmates. W. E. Henley. LBBV
Messmates. Sir Henry Newbolt. CH; HBV; LEAP; MCCG; SG; ShBV-2; TVSH
Met ye my love? Voices of Women. Frank Prewett. MBP
Metal Checks, The. Louise Driscoll. NP
Metamorphosed Gipsies, The. Ben Jonson. *See* **Gypsies Metamorphosed, The.**
Metamorphoses. "Lewis Carroll." *See* **Gardener's Song, The.**
Metamorphoses, The. Randall Jarrell. FiMAP
Metamorphoses, *sels.* Ovid, *tr. fr. Latin.*
Apollo and Daphne, *fr.* I, *tr. by* Gilbert Highet. LaP
"At length my chariot wheel about the mark hath found the way," *introductory poem by* Arthur Golding. ReIE
Baucis and Philemon, *fr.* VIII, *tr. by* Dryden. AWP; JAWP; RoL; WBP; WoL
(Philemon and Baucis, *tr. by* Arthur Golding.) OBSC
Creation of the World, The, *fr.* I, *tr. by* John E. Hankins. LaP
Daedalus and Icarus, *fr.* VIII, *tr. by* Samuel Croxall. RoL
Flood, The, *fr.* I, *tr. by* Dryden. ChTr
I Heard the Ruffian-Shepherd Rudely Blow, *fr.* XIII, *tr. by* Dryden. AtBAP
Narcissus, *fr.* III, *tr. by* Addison. RoL
Niobe, *fr.* VI, *tr. by* Samuel Croxall. RoL
Orpheus and Eurydice, *fr.* X, *tr. by* Congreve. RoL
Phoenix Self-born, The, *fr.* XV, *tr. by* Dryden. ChTr
Pygmalion and Galatea, *fr.* X, *tr. by* Gilbert Highet. LaP
Pyramus and Thisbe, *fr.* IV. LaP, *tr. by* Zechariah Chafee, Jr.; LiTW, *tr. by* Arthur Golding; OuHeWo, *tr. by* Laurence Eusden
Pyrrha and Deucalion, *fr.* I, *tr. by* Dryden. RoL
Story of Phaeton, The, *fr.* II, *tr. by* Zechariah Chafee, Jr. LaP
"Within the town (of whose huge walls so monstrous high and thick)," *fr.* IV, *tr. by* Arthur Golding. ReIE
Metamorphoses of a Vampire, The. Baudelaire, *tr. fr. French by* Donald Justice. ReMP
Metaphor for My Son. John Holmes. MiAP
Metaphysic Sphynx that preys on us, The. Epigram. John Swanwick Drennan. IrPN
Metaphysical Poem. Maxwell Bodenheim. AnAmPo; LA
Metaphysical Sectarian, The. Samuel Butler. *See* **Presbyterian Knight.**
Metaphysician, The. Schiller, *tr. fr. German by* J. H. Merivale. RO
Metaphysics. Franklin P. Adams. LHV
Metaphysics. Oliver Herford. NA
Mete Me Out My Loneliness. "Michael Field." MBP
Metempsychosis, The. Thomas Bailey Aldrich. UnW
Metempsychosis. Louella C. Poole. CIV
Metempsychosis. Kenneth Slessor. ViBoPo (1958 ed.)
Meteor. Al-Haitham, *tr. fr. Arabic by* A. J. Arberry. MooP
Meteorite, The. Arthur Guiterman. MuM
Meteor's arc of quiet, The; a voiceless rain. Faint Music. Walter de la Mare. FaBoCh; LoGBV
Methinks all things have travelled since you shined. On the Sun Coming Out in the Afternoon. Henry David Thoreau. PoEL-4
Methinks already, from this Chymick flame. The New London [*or* London]. Dryden. *Fr.* Annus Mirabilis. FaBoCh; OBS; SeCePo
Methinks heroick poesie till now. To Sir William Davenant upon His Two First Books of Gondibert. Abraham Cowley. CEP; SeCV-1
Methinks I am a prophet new inspir'd. John of Gaunt's Dying Speech [*or* This Royal Throne of Kings]. Shakespeare. King Richard II, *fr.* II, i. EV-1; FiP
Methinks I draw but sickly breath. The Farewell. *Unknown.* OxBoCh
Methinks I see great Diocletian walk. Great Diocletian. Abraham Cowley. *Fr.* The Garden. ChTr
Methinks, I see our mighty Monarch stand. Earl of Rochester. *Fr.* The Royal Angler. BeR
Methinks I see some crooked mimic jeer. Sonnet: To the Critic. Michael Drayton. Idea, XXXI. LoBV; SiCE; TuPP
Me thinks, I see, with what a busy haste. On Zacheus. Francis Quarles. LoBV; MePo; OBS
Methinks I'm now surrounded by despair. The Linnet on the Bough. John Gay. *Fr.* Dione; a Pastoral Tragedy. BeR
Methinks in Him there dwells alway. Risus Dei. Thomas Edward Brown. PoVP
Methinks it were no pain to die. To Death. Johann Christoph von Gluck. LPS-1
Methinks my tenderness the grass must be. *Unknown.* Yoshiki. OnPM
Methinks ofttimes my heart is like some bee. Sonnet. Ella Wheeler Wilcox. LBAP
Methinks some curious reader, I hear say. Ad Curiosum Lectorem. Thomas Bastard. SiCE
Methinks the little wit I had is lost. Francis Beaumont. *Fr.* Master Francis Beaumont's Letter to Ben Jonson. LEAP
Methinks the Measure. Percy Adams Hutchison. AA
Methinks the poor town has been troubled too long. Bonny Black Bess [*or* Song]. Charles Sackville, Earl of Dorset. CEP; SeCL; SeCV-2
Methinks the soul within the body held. Birth and Death. Thomas Wade. VA
Methinks the swooning air. Storm. Ibn al-Bain. MooP
Methinks the world is oddly made. The Atheist and the Acorn. Countess of Winchilsea. WP
Me thinkes this draught such vertue does infuse. The Office of Poetry. Nathaniel Whiting. *Fr.* Il Insonio Insonnado. OBS
Methinks 'Tis Pretty Sport [to Hear a Child]. Thomas Bastard. ElL; InvP
Methought. Ernst von der Recke, *tr. fr. Danish by* Charles W. Stork. BoDS
Methought, as I beheld the rookery pass. The Rookery. Charles Tennyson Turner. VA
Methought I heard a butterfly. The Butterfly and the Bee. William Lisle Bowles. HBV; HBVY; PECK
Methought I heard a voice cry, "Sleep no more!" Sleep—Innocent Sleep [*or* Conscience]. Shakespeare. *Fr.* Macbeth, II, ii. EV-1; MaRV; TreFS
Methought I met a Lady yester even. William Alexander. *Fr.* A Vision of Oxford. OBVV
Methought I saw/ Life swiftly treading. The Sea of Death. Thomas Hood. FaBoEn; LiTB; LoBV; PoEL-4; RO; UnW
Methought I Saw a Thousand Fearful Wrecks. Shakespeare. *See* **Dream of Clarence, The.**
Methought I saw a wondrous throng. To My Nun Sister. E. P. Tivnan. PraNu
Methought I saw him, but I knew him not. The Captain's Dream. Anne Brontë. UnW
Methought I saw how wealthy men. Popular Song. *Unknown.* PoFr
Methought I saw my late espousèd saint. On His Deceased [*or* Late] Wife [*or* Sonnet]. Milton. ATP; BEL; CBOV; EM-1; EnLi-1; EnLoPo; EPS; ES; EV-2; ExPo; FaBoEn; FaFP; GEPC; GTBS-W; InPo; LEAP; LiTB;

LiTG; LiTL; LoBV; MaPo; OBEV; OBS; PeBoSo; PoEL-3; PoFS; ReaPo; SeCeV; SeCL; SeEP; TOP; TreFS; TriL; TwHP; TyEnPo; UnW
Methought I saw the grave where Laura lay. **A Vision upon This Conceit of the Faerie Queene** [*or* The Faery Queen]. Sir Walter Ralegh. BCEP; BEL; CoBE; ElSeCe; EnLi-1 (1949 ed.); EnLit; ES; LEAP; OBSC; PoFS; PtP; ReEn; SiCE; SiPS; TOP; TuPP; ViBoPo
Methought I stood where trees of every clime. Keats. *Fr.* The Fall of Hyperion, I. OBRV
Methought in fancy I did hear complain. The Lament of "La Belle Heaulmière." Villon. LiTW
Methought on two Jews meeting I did chance. Moses and Jesus. Israel Zangwill. QS
Methought that in a solemn church I stood. The Sweeper of the Floor. George Macdonald. BMEP; MaRV
Me thought the spirit. George Chapman. *Fr.* Bussy d'Ambois, V, iii. NBE
Methought the stars were blinking bright. Sailing beyond Seas. Jean Ingelow. UnW; VA
Methought you stood at my bedside. Methought. Ernst von der Recke. BoDS
Methoughte thus:—that hit was May. The Dream. Chaucer. *Fr.* The Book of the Duchesse. FiP
Methuselah ("Methuselah ate what he found on his plate"). *Unknown.* BLPA; DDA; FaBoBe; NeHB; TreFS
Methuselah! Don Marquis. *Fr.* Song of a Thousand Years. BAP
Meticulous, past midnight in clear rime. Voyages, V. Hart Crane. ChMo; MoPo; MoVE
"Metis" Song of the Buffalo Hunters, The. Robindeau. CSF
Metric Figure. William Carlos Williams. MAP; MoAB; MoAmPo; MOAP; NeMA; NP
Metrical Feet. Samuel Taylor Coleridge. HBV; LPS-3
(Lessons for a Boy.) PCD
("Trochee trips from long to short.") ExPo
Metrodorus' Mind to the Contrary. Metrodorus, *tr. fr. Greek by* Nicholas Grimald. SiCE; TuPP
("In every way of life true pleasure flows," *tr. by* John Beaumont.) GrPo
Metropolis. John Hall. NeTW
Metropolitan Nightmare. Stephen Vincent Benét. DaM; ImOP
Metropolitan Tower, The. Sara Teasdale. ChMo; CMP
Metrum V. Henry Vaughan. EPS
Metrum Parhemiacum Tragicum. Eugenius Vulgarius, *tr. fr. Latin by* Helen Waddell. WaaP
Meuse and Marne have little waves, The. A Girl's Song. Katharine Tynan. OnYI
Mevrouw von Weber was brisk though fat. Tubby Hook. Arthur Guiterman. TSWC
Mews Flat Mona. William Plomer. FaBoTw
Mexican Jo and Mexican Jane. Raking Walnuts in the Rain. Monica Shannon. BrR; SiSoSe
Mexican Lullaby, A. Grace Hazard Conkling. BOL
Mexican Market Woman. Langston Hughes. GaP; TiPo (1952 ed.)
Mexican Quarter. John Gould Fletcher. Arizona Poems, II. ChMo; CMP; NP; TCPD
Mexican Serenade. Arthur Guiterman. BOHV; FiBHP
Mexican Soldiers. Rafael Estrada, *tr. fr. Spanish by* Donald Devenish Walsh. AnCL
Mexico City Blues, *sels.* Jack Kerouac. NeAP
Chorus: "Big Engines, The," 146.
Chorus: "Essence of Existence, The," 182.
Chorus: "Glenn Miller and I were heroes," 179.
Chorus: "Got up and dressed up," 113.
Chorus: "Love's multitudinous boneyard," 230.
Chorus: "Nobody knows the other side," 127.
Chorus: "Old Man Mose," 221.
Chorus: "Only awake to Universal Mind," 183.
Chorus: "Praised be man, he is existing in milk," 228.
Chorus: "Saints, I give myself up to thee," 219.
Chorus: "Void that's highly embraceable, The," 225.
Chorus: "Wheel of the quivering meat, The," 211.
Mexico Is a Foreign Country, *sels.* Robert Penn Warren. FiMAP
Small Soldiers with Drum in Large Landscape, IV.
World Comes Galloping, The; a True Story, III.
Mezzo Cammin. Longfellow. AmPP (3d ed.); CoBA; IAP; TCAP
Mia Carlotta. T. A. Daly. BAP; InMe; LEAP; MAP; MoAmPo (1942 ed.); NeMA; PCN; PoeMoYo; PYM; ShBV-3; TreFS; WhC
Micah, *sels.* Bible, *O.T.*
Acceptable Sacrifice, The, VI: 6-8. GrCo-1
(What Doth the Lord Require?) MaRV
And They Shall Beat Their Swords into Plowshares, IV: 1-5. TreF
Prince of Peace, The, V: 2. ChrBoLe
Woe Is Me! VII: 1-6. TrJP
Mice. Rose Fyleman. BoTP; FaPON; GoBP; MoSiPe; MPB; StVeCh; SUS; TiPo
Mice, The. Richard R. Kirk. LS
Mice. *Unknown, tr. fr. Greek by* A. J. Butler. RAR
Mice at the Door, The. Vincent McHugh. NePoAm-2
Mice masticate from crumb to tooth. Repast. Gertrude Tiemer-Wille. CoYe
Mice of Spain, The. Elizabeth J. Coatsworth. LiL
Mice That Ate Iron, The. *Unknown, tr. fr. Sanskrit by* Arthur W. Ryder. *Fr.* The Panchatantra. OuHeWo
Mice were not impressed by that great house, The. The Mice. Richard R. Kirk. LS
Michael. Kostas Kariotakis, *tr. fr. Modern Greek by* Rae Dalven. MoGP
Michael. Val Vallis. NeLNL
Michael. Wordsworth. AEV; BEL; BPN; EM-2; EmBrPo; EnL; EnLi-2; EnLit; EnLP; EnRP; EPN; ERP; EV-3; GEPC; GoTL; OAEP; PoE; ShBV-3; TOP; TyEnPo; UnPo (1st ed.); WHA
Michael and Christine. Arthur Rimbaud, *tr. fr. French by* Louise Varèse. AnFP
Michael, as much good hap unto thy state. To Master Michael Drayton. Thomas Lodge. ReIE
Michael bid sound. Battle between the Angels and the Anarchs. Milton. *Fr.* Paradise Lost, VI. BCEP
Michael Hayd'n and Patrick Buggy one night got very druggy. The Scow on Cowden Shore, *vers.* III. Larry Gorman. ShS
Michael Met a White Duck. J. Dupuy. BoTP
Michael Robartes Remembers Forgotten Beauty. W. B. Yeats. TIP
(He Remembers Forgotten Beauty.) PoVP; TyEnPo
Michael the Archangel. Katharine Tynan. JKCP
Michael the Archangel. Michael Williams. JKCP (1955 ed.)
Michael Walked in the Wood. Robert Greacen. NeIP
Michaelmas. Norman Nicholson. FaBoTw; MoBrPo (1950 ed.)
Michael's Song. W. W. Gibson. BoTP
Michelangelo, *sel.* Franklin McDuffee.
"He spoke, and death . . ." BAP
Michelangelo's Kiss. Dante Gabriel Rossetti. The House of Life, XCIV. BPN; PoVP; ViPo
Michié Préval, *with music. Unknown, pr. tr. fr. French.* ABF
Michigan, My Michigan! Mrs. Henry F. Lyster. PoRL
Mickey Free's Song. Charles James Lever. *See* It's Little for Glory I Care.
Mickleham Way. Ivy O. Eastwick. BrR
Microbe, The. Hilaire Belloc. BOHV; StaSt
Microbiblion, *sel.* Simon Wastell.
Man's Mortality. AlDL; FaBoCh; HBV; LoGBV; LPS-1; SeCL; WBLP. *See also* Hos Ego Versiculos, *sl. diff. vers. by* Francis Quarles, *fr.* Argalus and Parthenia.
(Like as the Damask Rose.) LoBV
(Of Man's Mortalitie.) EV-1
(Verses of Man's Mortality [*or* Mortalitie].) OBS; SeEP
Microcosm, The, *sel.* Abraham Coles.
Physician's Character and Aims: Science Progressive. PoP
Microcosm. Bertram Dobell. OBVV
Microcosm, The. Walt Whitman. *See* Miracles ("I believe a leaf of grass").
Microcosmos, *abr.* Nigel Heseltine. NeBP
Microcosmus, *sel.* Thomas Nabbes.
Love Sets Order in the Elements. UnS
Microphone, The. Gertrude Van Winkle. GFA
Microscopic Trout and the Machiavelian Fisherman, The. Guy Wetmore Carryl. WhC
'Mid all the ceaseless rush of life. Refuge. Mabel E. McCartney. BLRP
'Mid all the traffic of the ways. John Oxenham. *Fr.* The Vision Splendid. MaRV
Mid April seemed like some November day. San Terenzo. Andrew Lang. VA
Mid clamour and clang. Song of the Trip-Hammer. C. H. Collester. CAG
'Mid dewy pastures girdled with blue air. Saint Brigid. Rosa Mulholland. PraNu; TIP
'Mid glad green miles of tillage. The Poet's Town. John G. Neihardt. LBMV
'Mid Greenland's polar ice and snow. An Eskimelodrama; or, the Eskapade of an Eskamaid. *Unknown.* CAG
Mid just such a song hymenaean. Chorus Hymeneal. Aristophanes. *Fr.* The Birds. GrR
'Mid lava rock and glaring sand. The Bandit's Grave. Charles Pitt. SCC
'Mid letters heaped upon the floor. Feodor Ivanovich Tyutchev, *tr. fr. Russian by* Sir Cecil Kisch. WaL
Mid pleasures and palaces though we may roam. Home, Sweet Home. John Howard Payne. *Fr.* Clari, the Maid of Milan. AA; APW; BAV; BLPA; BoHiPo; FaBoBe; FaFP; HBV; LEAP; LPS-1; MaRV; NeHB; OBAV; OlF; OnHT; OTPC; PECK; TCAP; TreF; WBLP
'Mid pleasures and palaces though we may roam. Home, Sweet Home, with Variations, I. H. C. Bunner. BOHV; InMe; PA

'Mid roaring brooks and dark moss-vales. On the Death of a Recluse. George Darley. GTIV; OBVV
Mid seaweed on a sultry strand, ten thousand years ago. The First Story. Nathalia Crane. TSWC
Mid the flower-wreathed tombs I stand. Decoration. Thomas Wentworth Higginson. AA; OBAV; OHIP
'Mid the mountains Euganean. Shelley. *Fr.* Lines Written among the Euganean Hills. ViBoPo
Mid the squander'd [*or* squandered] colour. Cheddar Pinks. Robert Bridges. ChMP; MoVE; POTE; SeCePo
Mid the white spouses of the Sacred Heart. To St. Mary Magdalen. Benjamin Dionysius Hill. AA
Midas, *sels.* John Lyly.
Daphne. ElL
(Apollo's Song.) HBV
("My Daphne's hair is twisted gold.") SiCE
(Song of Daphne to the Lute, A.) OBSC
Pan's Song. AtBAP; BCEP; CoEV; EV-1; OBSC
(Pan's Syrinx Was a Girl.) ViBoPo
("Pan's Syrinx was a girl indeed.") SiCE
(Syrinx.) ElL; LoBV; SeCePo; WHA
"Sing to Apollo, god of day." ElSeCe
(Song to Apollo.) AtBAP; OBSC
Midas' Tomb. *At. to* Cleobulus of Lindus, *tr. fr. Greek by* F. L. Lucas. GrPE
Midas, we are in story told. The Fable of Midas. Swift. EV-3
Mid-August. Louise Driscoll. MW; YeAr
Midautumn at Huang-chou. Su T'ung-po, *tr. fr. Chinese by* Yu Min-chuan. WhP
Midautumn Festival, The. Li Ch'ing-chao, *tr. fr. Chinese by* Sophia H. Chen. WhP
Mid-Century. Mary Elizabeth Osborn. NePoAm
Midcentury Love Letter. Phyllis McGinley. ViBoPo (1958 ed.)
Mid-Day. Hilda Doolittle ("H. D.") ViBoPo (1941 ed.)
Midday half-moon slopes in heaven, A. Gold. Glyn Jones. NeBP
Midden of rotting bodies of men, A. Corpses in the Wood. Ernst Toller. TrJP
Middle-Age. E. B. C. Jones. HBMV
Middle Age. Rudolph Chambers Lehmann. HBV
Middle-aged Quixote. Louise Crenshaw Ray. JKCP (1955 ed.)
Middle Ages, The; Two Views. Leah Bodine Drake. NePoAm-2
Middle Ages sleep in alabaster, The. The Last Abbot of Gloucester. Wilfred Rowland Childe. CAW
Middle Kingdom, The. Allen Upward. *Fr.* Scented Leaves from a Chinese Jar. NP
Middleness of the Road, The. Robert Frost. CrMA; LiTA
Mid-Forest Fear. Roderic Quinn. BoAu
Midges Dance aboon the Burn, The. Robert Tannahill. EBSV; HBV; LPS-2
Mid-July Twilight, Eight o'Clock. Jules Laforgue, *tr. fr. French by* William Jay Smith. AnFP
Mid-morning of mid-June: her sudden whim. William Ellery Leonard. *Fr.* Two Lives, Pt. I. BAP; PFE
Midnight. Chao Tz'u, *tr. fr. Chinese by* Henry H. Hart. PoHN
Midnight. Dryden. ACP
Midnight. Archibald Lampman. BoCaPo; PeCV; TwCV
Midnight. Thomas Middleton. *Fr.* Blurt, Master Constable. ElL; SeCePo
Midnight. Eduard Mörike, *tr. fr. German by* Mabel Cotterell. AnGP
Midnight. Michael Roberts. OBMV; POTE
Midnight. Thomas Sackville. CH
Midnight ("The locks between her chamber"). Shakespeare. *Fr.* The Rape of Lucrece. OBSC
("Locks between her chamber and his will, The.") SiCE
Midnight. Henry Vaughan. OAEP
Midnight at Mestre. Alfonso Gatto, *tr. fr. Italian by* Glauco Cambon. OnPM
Midnight black with clouds is in the sky, A. Earth. Bryant. CoV
Midnight Court, The. Brian Merriman, *tr. fr. Modern Irish by* Frank O'Connor. AnIL; KiLC; OnYI, *tr. by* Arland Ussher
Maiden's Complaint, The, *sel., tr. by* Arland Ussher. LiTW
Midnight cry appalls the gloom, A. Johnny Appleseed. William Henry Venable. PaA; PAH
Midnight, December Thirty-first. Song for December Thirty-first. Frances Frost. YeAr
Midnight has come, and the great Christ Church Bell. All Souls' Night. W. B. Yeats. *Fr.* A Vision. MoVE; ReMP
Midnight is past, and it is time to go. The Last Dance. May Riley Smith. BAP
Midnight Lamentation. Harold Monro. BSV; ChMo; ChMP; CMP; LO; ViBoPo
Midnight Mass. Sister Mary Madeleva. Christmas in Provence, II. WHL
Midnight Mass for the Dying Year. Longfellow. APW; GoBC; PoRL
Midnight on the Great Western. Thomas Hardy. CH; CoBMV
Midnight past! not a sound of aught. The Portrait. "Owen Meredith." *Fr.* The Wanderer. HBV; LPS-1
Midnight Patrol. Eric Irvin. BoAV
Midnight Performance, A. Helen Wing. GFA
Midnight plane with its riding lights, The. Night Plane. Frances Frost. FaPON; TiPo (1959 ed.)
Midnight Prayer. Hayyim Nahman Bialik, *tr. fr. Hebrew by* Helena Frank. TrJP
Midnight—September 19, 1881. John Boyle O'Reilly. PAH
Midnight Show. Karl Shapiro. OxBA
Midnight Skaters, The. Edmund Blunden. CoEV; ExPo; FaBoTw; GTBS-D; MBP; MoBrPo; PoD; POTE
Midnight Song. Shakespeare. *See* Now the Hungry Lion Roars.
Midnight Special, The [*or* De] ("If you evah go to Houston"), *with music.* *Unknown.* ABF, *diff. vers., with music;* AS; SoAF
Midnight Special ("Yonder come Roberta!"), *with music.* *Unknown.* AS
Midnight! Spring! Two passionate arms of youthful. Lalage. "S. W. D. M." CAG
Midnight streets as I walk back, The. Letter I. Randall Swingler. WaP
Midnight—the black, dead vast of night. The Coming of Dawn. Grace Atherton Dennen. NLK
Midnight, the moving stars. In Praesepio. Charles L. O'Donnell. MM
Midnight the years last day the last. New Year's Eve, 1938. John Frederick Nims. MiAP
Midnight Train, The, *with music.* *Unknown.* AS
Midnight was come, when every vital thing. Midnight. Thomas Sackville. CH
Midnight's bell goes ting, ting, ting, ting, ting. Midnight. Thomas Middleton. *Fr.* Blurt, Master Constable. ElL; SeCePo
Midocean like a pale blue morning-glory. Calm Morning at Sea. Sara Teasdale. EtS
Mid-Rapture. Dante Gabriel Rossetti. The House of Life, XXVI. BEL; BPN; EPP; FaBoBe; HBV; LEAP; OAEP; PoE; PoVP; TOP; TyEnPo; ViPo
Midst the opacous gloom. Feast by the Manzanares. Juan Ruiz de Alarcón. *Fr.* The Suspicious Truth, I. AnMP
Midstream they met. Challenger and champion. The Swans. Clifford Dyment. MoVE
Midsummer. William Allingham. IrPN
Midsummer. Sybil Horatia Calverley. DiM
Midsummer. Hermann Hesse, *tr. fr. German by* Herman Salinger. LiTW
Midsummer. Oliver Wendell Holmes. SN
Midsummer. Sydney King Russell. BLPA; FaBoBe; NeHB
Midsummer. Stephen Spender. AtBAP
Midsummer. John Townsend Trowbridge. AA; DD; HBV; HBVY; OBAV
Midsummer. Ella Wheeler Wilcox. HBV
Midsummer Courtship. James Thomson. Richard Forest's Midsummer Night, VIII. OBVV
("Oh, how the nights are short.") POTT
Midsummer Eve, a year ago, my mother she commanded. Midsummer Magic. Ivy O. Eastwick. BrR; TiPo
Midsummer Frost. Isaac Rosenberg. MoBrPo (1950 ed.); MoPo
Midsummer Holiday, A, *sels.* Swinburne.
In the Water, II. BPN; PoVP; VLEP
On a Country Road, I. BPN; PoVP; TOP; VLEP
On the Verge, III. BPN; PoVP; VLEP
Midsummer Invitation. Myron B. Benton. SN
Midsummer Jingle. Newman Levy. WhC
Midsummer Lullaby. *Unknown, tr. fr. German.* BOL
Midsummer Madness. *Unknown.* BOHV
Midsummer Magic. Ivy O. Eastwick. BrR; TiPo
Midsummer Meadow, The. E. J. Scovell. PoN
Midsummer Midnight Skies. W. E. Henley. PoVP
Midsummer Moon. "E. M. G. R." BoTP
Midsummer Morn. Frank Marshall Davis. GoSl
Midsummer music in the grass. Golden-Rod. Lucy Larcom. PEOR
Midsummer Night. Marion Edey. YeAr
Midsummer Night. Elizabeth Gould. BoTP
Midsummer Night. Archibald Lampman. PC
Midsummer Night's Dream, A, *sels.* Shakespeare.
"Asleep, my love," *fr.* V, i. LBN
Compliment to Queen Elizabeth, *fr.* II, i. LPS-3
Course of True Love, The, *fr.* I, i. LPS-1; TreFS; WHA
Helen and Hermia, *fr.* III, ii. GN
I Know a Bank, *fr.* II, i. ADAH
(Titania's Bower.) PCH
(Violet Bank, A.) FaPON; OTPC (1946 ed.); PRWS
(Where the Wild Thyme Blows.) TrGrPo
"If we offend it is with our good will," *fr.* V, i. BoN
"If we shadows have offended," *fr.* V, ii. OBSC
Love-in-Idleness, *fr.* II, i. TrGrPo

Lunatic, the Lover, and the Poet, The, *fr.* V, i. FiP; InP; PIR
(Imagination.) EV-1; GTBS-W; LiTB; LiTG
(Inspiration, *sl. longer sel.*) CoEV
(Poet Greatly Pictured, The, *sl. longer sel.*) BCEP
(" 'Tis strange, my Theseus," *sl. longer sel.*) NBE
(Tricks of Imagination, The.) TreFS
Music of Hounds, The, *fr.* IV, i. EV-1
(Theseus and Hippolyta.) AlBD
Now the Hungry Lion Roars, *fr.* V, ii. AnFE; AtBAP; BLV; CH; ChTr; EG; EIL; LiTB; LiTG; OBSC; SeCeV; SiCE; ViBoPo
(Approach of the Fairies, The.) CG
(Epilogue.) BCEP; KN; LoBV
(Fairy Blessing, The.) OxBoLi
(Fairy Songs: "Now the hungry lion roars.") TrGrPo
(Midnight Song.) MuP
(Puck Speaks.) ThWaDe
(Puck's Song.) BoLiVe; MoShBr
(Song of Robin Goodfellow, A.) BoW
"Now, until the break of day," *fr.* V, ii.
(Fairy Songs.) TrGrPo
Oberon and Titania to the Fairy Train, *fr.* V, ii. GN
("Through the house give glimmering light.") SiCE
Ousel Cock, The, *fr.* III, i. ViBoPo
Over Hill, over Dale, *fr.* II, i. AnFE; BEL; EG; EIL; EM-1; EPP; EV-1; InvP; KN; OBSC; PoRh; SiCE; ThWaDe; ViBoPo; WP
(Fairy Land.) BCEP; GBV; OBEV
(Fairy Queen, The.) OTPC (1946 ed.)
(Fairy Song, A.) BoTP; CBE
(Fairy Songs: "Over hill, over dale."). BLV; HBV; HBVY; PCD; TrGrPo
(Fairy to Puck, The.) HOAH
(Fairy's Song.) BoLiVe
(Fairy's Wander-Song.) FaPON; RIS
("How now spirit, whether wander you?") AtBAP
(Puck and the Fairy.) GN
(Puck's Song.) RAR
(Shakespeare's Fairies.) CBPC
(Song of the Fairy.) PCH
(Songs: "Over hill, over dale.") EnLi-1
(Songs from "A Midsummer Night's Dream.") LEAP
Seasons Alter, The, *fr.* II, i. BoW
"Set your heart at rest," *fr.* II, i.
(Selections from the Works of William Shakespeare.) MotAn
Sunrise on the Sea, *fr.* III, ii. ChTr
"These are the forgeries of jealousie," *fr.* II, i. NBE
You Spotted Snakes [with Double Tongue], *fr.* II, ii. AnFE; BoTP; CBE; EG; InvP; KN; LiTB; LiTG; OBSC; OTPC (1923 ed.); PoRA; ShBV-1; SiCE; ViBoPo
(Fairies' Lullaby, The.) EIL; WHA
(Fairies' Song, The.) EV-1; LoBV
(Fairy Land, 2.) OBEV
(Fairy Lullaby.) FaPON; GoTP; RIS
(Fairy Lullaby: "Come, now a roundel," *longer sel.*) LPS-3
(Fairy Songs: "You spotted snakes with double tongue.") BLV; HBV; TrGrPo
(Lullaby for Titania.) BOL; CG; GN; RG
(Shakespeare's Fairies; They Sing Their Queen to Sleep.) CBPC
(Song: "You spotted snakes with double tongue.") FiP
(Song of the Fairies.) BoLiVe
(Songs from "A Midsummer Night's Dream.") LEAP
Midsummer Night's Dream. Byron Vazakas. NePA
Midsummer['s] Noon in the Australian Forest, A. Charles Harpur. BoAu; BoAV; NeLNL; VA
Midsummer Song, A. Richard Watson Gilder. HBV; LHV; OTPC (1946 ed.); POT; PRWS
Midsummer's Noon in the Australian Forest, A. Charles Harpur. *See* Midsummer Noon in the Australian Forest, A.
Midway the Journey. Dante, *tr. fr. Italian by* Laurence Binyon. *Fr.* Divina Commedia: Inferno, I. ExPo
Midways of a walled garden. Golden Wings [*or* Ladies' Gard]. William Morris. BMEP; ChTr; LiA; SeCePo; WHA
Midwest. John Frederick Nims. MoVE
Midwife laid her hand on his thick skull, The. Thomas Shadwell the Poet. Dryden. *Fr.* Absalom and Achitophel, Pt. II. ChTr
Midwinter. Margaret E. Bruner. PoToHe
Mid-Winter. Alun Lewis. MoWP
Midwinter. John Townsend Trowbridge. AA; AnAmPo; AnFE; APA; CoAnAm; GN; HBV; LA; LBAP; LEAP; OBAV; OTPC
Midwinter. Oscar Wilde. *Fr.* Humanitad. PCH
Midwinter Monochrome. Stanley E. Babb. HiLiAm
Midwinter spring is its own season. Little Gidding. T. S. Eliot. *Fr.* Four Quartets. AmPo; ExPo; FaBoEn; OAEP (2d ed.)
Midwinter Thaw. Lenore Pratt. CaP
Mid-Winter Waking. Robert Graves. CoEV; MoAB
Might and Right. Clarence Day. InMe
Might and Right. Hesiod, *tr. fr. Greek by* Sir William Marris. *Fr.* Works and Days. OxBG
Might and right are always fighting. Might and Right. Clarence Day. InMe
Might as well bury her. Maumee Ruth. Sterling A. Brown. CDC
"Might Is Right." Israel Zangwill. TrJP
Might of One Fair Face, The. Michelangelo, *tr. fr. Italian by* J. E. Taylor. LPS-1
Might these be thrushes climbing through almost. E. E. Cummings. CrMA
Mightie God, even the Lord hath spoken, The. A Psalme of Asaph. Psalm L, Bible, *O.T.* LiA
Mightier Church, A. Henry B. Carpenter. OQP; QP-1
Mighty, changeless God above! Prayer to Jesus. Mossén Tallante. OnPM
Mighty creature is the germ, A. The Germ. Ogden Nash. CenHV; MoShBr
Mighty Denier, The. Sir William Watson. LBBV
Mighty Fortress, A. Psalms, XCI, Bible, *O.T.* *See* God Our Refuge.
Mighty Fortress Is Our God, A. Martin Luther, *tr. fr. German by* Frederic H. Hedge. AWP; HBV; LPS-2; MaRV; OIF; PoFr; PreP, *with music;* TreFS
(Hymn: "Mighty fortress is our God, A.") WGRP
(Paraphrase of Luther's Hymn.) AA
Mighty God Poseidon, thee I sing. Hymn to Poseidon. *At. to* Arion. OxBG
Mighty growth, A! The county side. The Old Oak Tree at Hatfield Broadoak. Frederick Locker-Lampson. EV-5
Mighty hand from an exhaustless urn, A. The Flood of Years. Bryant. AA; IAP; LPS-3; MOAP
Mighty Harp, The. *Unknown, tr. fr. Danish by* E. M. Smith-Dampier. BoDaBa
Mighty Heart, The. Emerson. *Fr.* Woodnotes, II. AA
Mighty Lak' a Rose. Frank L. Stanton. OIF
(Sweetes' Li'l' Feller.) FaFP; TreFS
Mighty Love. John Fletcher. *See* Hear, Ye Ladies.
Mighty mass of brick, and smoke, and shipping, A. London Town. Byron. *Fr.* Don Juan, X. GEPC
Mighty master of the ocean! *At. to* Arion, *tr. fr. Greek by* Sir Edwin Arnold. GrPo
Mighty morn strode laughing up the land, The. Isabella Valancy Crawford. *Fr.* Malcolm's Katie. CPG
Mighty mother, and her son, who brings, The. Pope. *Fr.* The Dunciad, I. AtBAP; EiPP
Mighty Mountain Plains, The. Aubrey Thomas De Vere. IrPN
Mighty Must, The. W. S. Gilbert. *Fr.* Princess Ida. BOHV
Mighty Ocean Rolls and Raves, The. Arthur Hugh Clough. Songs in Absence, VIII. EmBrPo; EPN
Mighty, praised beyond compare. Rock of My Salvation. Mordecai ben Isaac. TrJP
Mighty river flows as when thine eyes, The. Out of Egypt Have I Called My Son. Caroline Hazard. StJW
Mighty Runner, A. E. A. Robinson, *after the Greek of* Nicarchus.
(Variations of Greek Themes, 2.) MOAP
Mighty Sea! Cameleon-like Thou Changest. Thomas Campbell. EtS
Mighty Sheep, The. *Unknown.* *See* Derby Ram, The.
Mighty soul that is ambition's mate, The. Disenchantment. Charles Leonard Moore. AA
Mighty Thoughts of an Old World, The. Thomas Lovell Beddoes. *Fr.* The Ivory Gate. CoEV; EG; NBE
(Song of Thanatos, The.) CaAE
(Stanzas: "Mighty thought of an old world, The.") ERP; TrGrPo
(Stanzas from "The Ivory Gate.") EnRP
Mighty waste of moaning waters lay, The. The Deep Dark Night. Tennyson. *Fr.* The Devil and the Lady. SeCePo
Mighty world's, The/ Eternity. Dedication. Piet Hein. BoDS
Mignon. Goethe, *tr. fr. German. Fr.* Wilhelm Meister's Apprenticeship, *Bk.* III, *ch.* 1. LiA, *tr. by* Edgar A. Bowring; LiTW, *tr. by* Anthony Hecht; LPS-3, *tr. by* Felicia Dorothea Hemans
(Mignon's Song, *tr. by* James Elroy Flecker.) AWP; JAWP; WBP
Mignonette. Erik Gustaf Geijer, *tr. fr. Swedish by* Charles W. Stork. AnSL
Mignon's Song. Goethe. *See* Mignon.
Migrant, The. Donald C. Babcock. NePoAm
Migrants. Ethel Anderson. BoAV
Migrants. Dudley G. Davies. NeTW
Migration. Clifford Bax. PtOT
Miguel de Cervantes. E. C. Bentley. *Fr.* Biography for Beginners. LauV
("People of Spain think Cervantes, The.") CenHV; FiBHP
Mihailovich. Roy McFadden. NeIP
Mihi Adhaerere Deo Bonum Est. *Unknown.* *See* God Be in My Head.
Mikado, The, *sels.* W. S. Gilbert.

Mikado, The *(continued)*
Humane Mikado, The. ALV; SiTL
(Let the Punishment Fit the Crime.) PoVP
(Mikado's Song, The.) LiTB
Ko-Ko's Song ("As some day it may happen"). LiTB; SiTL
(They'll None of 'em Be Missed.) EnLi-2 (1949 ed.); PoVP
Ko-Ko's Song ("There is beauty in the bellow of the blast"), 8 *ll.* PCD
Suicide's Grave, The. ALV; LiTG; LiTL; TreF; WhC
(Ko-Ko's Song.) FaFP
(Ko-Ko's Winning Song.) LiTB
(Tit-Willow.) OIF; SiTL
(Willow, Titwillow.) PoVP
Three Little Maids from School. PoVP
To Sit in Solemn Silence. FiBHP; SiTL; WhC
Wand'ring Minstrel, A. OIF; TreFS
Mike. F. C. W. Hiley. PoC
Mike. *Unknown.* ABF
Mike O'Day. *Unknown.* LiTG; LiTM (rev. ed.); SiTL; WhC
Mild-eyed oxen and the gentle ass, The. Attendants. David Morton. SDH
Mild hearts! and modest as the evening bell. The Wartons. Edmund Blunden. PtP
Mild Is the Parting Year. Walter Savage Landor. EmBrPo
(Autumn.) BLV; BoLiVe; OBEV (1st ed.)
(Ianthe.) TrGrPo
(Lament.) BCEP
(Lyrics and Epigrams.) CBOV
("Mild is the parting year, and sweet.") BPN; CaAE; EnLoPo; ERP; OBRV; PG
Mild, melancholy, and sedate, he stands. The Hottentot. Thomas Pringle. OBRV
Mild offspring of a dark and sullen sire! To an Early Primrose [*or* The Early Primrose]. Henry Kirke White. HBV; LPS-2; OBRV; OTPC (1923 ed.)
Mild Rebuke, A. Margaret L. Sullivan. CAG
Mild yoke of Christ, most harsh to me not bearing. Paradox. Vassar Miller. NePoEA
Mile an' a Bittock, A. Robert Louis Stevenson. EBSV; SeCePo
Mile behind is Gloucester town, A. Gloucester Moors. William Vaughn Moody. AmPP; ATP; BAP; HBV; IAP; LBMV; MAP; MoAmPo (1942 ed.); OBAV; OxBA; PFY; PIAE; TCPD; TOP; WHA
Mile from Eden, A. Anne Ridler. MoPo
Mile with Me, A. Henry van Dyke. BLPA; PFE; POT; PoTo
Miles and miles of quiet houses, every house a harbour. The Suburbs. Enid Derham. BoAu
Miles Gloriosus, *sel.* Plautus, *tr. fr. Latin by* Gilbert Highet. LaP
"Acroteleutium, I told you all our plan within."
"See that upon my shield the sheen is brighter."
Miles Keogh's Horse. John Hay. PAH; PoOW
Miles of pram in the wind and Pam in the gorse track. Potpourri from a Surrey Garden. John Betjeman. CenHV; FiBHP
Miles Standish ban having a courtship. The Courtship of Miles Standish. William F. Kirk. PoMa
Miles thick with torpor nauseate the gardens. Three Variations, II. Boris Pasternak. TrJP; TrRV
Militarism. Joseph Eliyia, *tr. fr. Modern Greek by* Rae Dalven. MoGP
Military Harpist, The. Ruth Pitter. FaBoTw; MoVE
Milk at the Bottom of the Sea. Oscar Williams. GTBS-W; LiTA; MoPo
Milk Below. *Unknown.* PCH
Milk-Cart Pony, The. Eleanor Farjeon. SUS; UTS
Milk for the Cat. Harold Monro. BoTP; FaBoBe; FaFP; GoTP; HBVY; MBP; MoBrPo; OBMV; PoC; ShBV-1; SiTL; ThWaDe; TwCV; VOD; YT
"Milk, in God's name," the gypsy pled. The Mirror. Robert Haven Schauffler. HOAH
Milk Jug, The. Oliver Herford. HBMV; HBVY; PCH; RAR; TSW; TSWC; UTS
Milk White Doe, The. *Unknown, tr. fr. French by* Andrew Lang. AWP
Milk-White Dove, The. *Unknown.* ChTr
Milk-white Hind, immortal and unchanged, A. The Churches of Rome and of England. Dryden. *Fr.* The Hind and the Panther. ACP; CEP; CoBE; EiPP; GEPC; NBE; SeCV-2; SeEP
Milk-white Moon, Put the Cows to Sleep. Carl Sandburg. FaPON; StVeCh
Milker, The. Eileen Duggan. CoBE
Milking before Dawn. Ruth Dallas. AnNZ
Milking Kraal. F. C. Slater. BoSA
Milking-Maid, The. Christina Rossetti. BeLS; LPS-1
Milking Pails ("Mary's gone a-milking"). *Unknown.* CH
Milking Time. Elizabeth Madox Roberts. BoChLi; FaPON; LS; OTPC (1946 ed.); RIS; SUS; UTS
Milking Time. Christina Rossetti. *See* When the Cows Come Home.
Milkmaid, The. William Allingham. IrPN
Milkmaid, The. Austin Dobson. HBV
Milkmaid, The. Thomas Hardy. SiTL
Milkmaid. Laurie Lee. ChMP; FaBoTw
Milkmaid, The. Robert Lloyd. CG
Milkmaid, The. Jefferys Taylor. LPS-3; OTPC (1923 ed.)
Milkmaid and the Milk-Jar, The. La Fontaine, *tr. fr. French by* Alan Conder. TrFP
Milkmaid singing leaves her bed, The. John Clare. *Fr.* The Shepherd's Calendar: February. OBRV
Milkmaid's Life, The. Martin Parker. TuPP
Milkmaid's Song, The. Sydney Dobell. LPS-1
Milkmaid's Song, The. Christopher Marlowe. *See* Passionate Shepherd to His Love, The.
Milkmaid's Song. Tennyson. *Fr.* Queen Mary. BPN; EPN
(Song of the Milkmaid.) HBV; LPS-1
Milkman, The. Leonard Feeney. MoSiPe
Milkman, The. Isabella Gardner. NePA
Milkman, The. Christopher Morley. GaP; MPB
Milkman, The. "Seumas O'Sullivan." GaP; SUS
Milkman, The. *Unknown.* BoTP
"Milkweed, and a buttercup, and cow-slip, A." Her Dairy. Peter Newell. NA; PCH
Milk-Wort and Bog Cotton. "Hugh MacDiarmid." NeBP
Milky Way, The. Zakarias Topelius, *tr. fr. Swedish by* Charles W. Stork. AnSL
Milky Way, The. Allen Upward. *Fr.* Scented Leaves from a Chinese Jar. NP
Milky Way revolves at night among the floating stars, The. A Song of Heaven. Li Ho. WhP
Mill, A [*or* The]. William Allingham. ChTr; IrPN; SeCePo
Mill, The. E. A. Robinson. AmP; ChMo; CMP; MaPo; MOAP; MoVE; NePA; PoLFOT; TwP
Mill, The. Emile Verhaeren, *tr. fr. French by* Ludwig Lewisohn. WoL
Mill Girl. James K. Baxter. AnNZ
Mill goes toiling slowly around, The. Nightfall in Dordrecht. Eugene Field. AA; OBAV; PRWS
Mill-Pond, The. Edward Thomas. POTE
Mill-stream, now that noises cease, The. More Poems, XIX. A. E. Housman. EmBrPo
Milla the glorie of whose bewteous rayes. *Unknown.* SeCSL
Millenium. James Kenneth Stephen. *See* To R. K.
Millennial Hymn of Iceland, The. Matthias Jochumsson, *tr. fr. Icelandic by* Jakobina Johnson. IcP
Millennium, The. Shelley. *Fr.* Prometheus Unbound, IV. BHV
("Thrones, altars, judgement-seats, and prisons.") NBE
Millennium, The—To a Ranting Field Orator. Philip Freneau. MOAP
Miller, A. Chaucer, *mod. by* Louis Untermeyer. *Fr.* The Canterbury Tales: Prologue. GoTP
Miller, The. Sir John Clerk of Penicuik. ChTr; EBSV
Miller, The. John Cunningham. CEP; OBEC
Miller, Miller. Ivy O. Eastwick. BoTP
Miller of the Dee, The. Charles Mackay. BTP; HBV; OTPC; PTA-1; TVSH
Miller, stout and sturdy as the stones, The. A Miller. Chaucer, *mod. by* Louis Untermeyer. *Fr.* The Canterbury Tales: Prologue. GoTP
Miller was a stout carl, for the nones, The. Seven Pilgrims. Chaucer. *Fr.* The Canterbury Tales: Prologue. TrGrPo
Milleres Tale, The. Chaucer. *See* Miller's Tale, The.
Miller's Daughter. John Crowe Ransom. MOAP
Miller's Daughter, The. Tennyson. VLEP
"It is the miller's daughter," *sel.* BLV; EG; GTBS; GTBS-W; LiTG; LiTL; OBEV; OBVV; PIR; RiBV; TrGrPo
(Song: "It is the miller's daughter.") GTSL; HBV; LPS-1
(Song: Miller's Daughter, The.) BPN
Miller's daughter, The/ Combs her hair. Spinning Song. Edith Sitwell. MBP; MoAB; MoBrPo
Miller's mill-dog lay at the mill-door, The. Bingo [*or* Bobby Bingo]. *Unknown.* CH; OTPC (1946 ed.); RIS
Miller's [*or* Milleres] Tale, The. Chaucer. *Fr.* The Canterbury Tales. OxBoLi
Sels.
Alisoun. CoEV
Carpenter's Young Wife, The. ExPo
Young Woman. BoW
Miller's wife had waited long, The. The Mill. E. A. Robinson. AmP; ChMo; CMP; MaPo; MOAP; MoVE; NePA; PoLFOT; TwP
Millery, millery, dustipole. *Unknown.* OxNR
Million butterflies rose up from South America, A. Annual Legend. Winfield Townley Scott. GTBS-W; LiTA; LiTM; WaP
Million Little Diamonds, A. Mary Frances Butts. AA; MeMeAg; TVC; TVSH
(Water Jewels.) OTPC (1946 ed.)

Million million spermatozoa, A. Fifth Philosopher's Song. Aldous Huxley. MBP; MoBrPo (1942 ed.); SiTL
Millionaires, presidents—even kings. Everyday Things. Jean Ayer. BoTP
Millions Are Learning How. James Agee. NAMP
Millions of cradles up in the trees. Waking Up. *Unknown.* TVC
Millions of Strawberries. Genevieve Taggard. FaPON; GoTP; MoShBr; MPB; TiPo
Millions who pass you see/ But incongruity. To a Blue Hippopotamus. Ellen de Young Kay. NePoEA
Millman Song, The, *with music.* *Unknown.* ShS
Millom Old Quarry. Norman Nicholson. ChMP; HaMV
Mills of Lancashire grind very small, The. Sir Leo Money. *Fr.* King Cotton. MaRV; OQP; QP-2
Mills of the Gods, The. *Unknown.* BLPA
Milord Saint Francis wed today. The Wagon of the Little Sisters. Hugh Francis Blunt. SaFP
Milton. William Edmonstoune Aytoun. BHV
Milton, *sels.* Blake.
And Did Those Feet in Ancient Time, *fr.* Preface. AEV; AtBAP; ATP; AWP; BCEP; BEL; CaAE; EG; EiPP; EM-1; EnRP; FaBoCh; InPo; JAWP; LEAP; LoBV; LoGBV; MaRV; OAEP; OBRV; PG (1945 ed.); PIR; PoE; PoEL-4; PoFS; PoRA; PreP; ReaPo; SeCeV; StJW; TOP; TyEnPo; UnPo (1st ed.); ViBoPo; WBP; WGRP; WP
(Building of Jerusalem, The.) TVSH
(Building of the New Jerusalem, The.) MuP
(Chariot of Fire.) OnPM
(Jerusalem.) BBV (1951 ed.); BoTP; CoEV; GTBS-W; OBEV (new ed.); OtMeF; ShBV-2; WaaP
(New Jerusalem, A [*or* The].) BLV; BoLiVe; CBE; EV-3; FaBoEn; LiTB; LiTG; PIAE; RiBV; TrGrPo
(Preface to "Milton.") AnFE; CEP; NeHB
(Song: "And did those feet in ancient time.") WoL
(Stanzas from "Milton.") EnLi-2; EnLit
(Till We Have Built Jerusalem.) OQP; QP-2
"But others of the sons of Los," *fr.* I. NBE
"Los is by mortals nam'd Time," *fr.* I. OBRV
Reason and Imagination, *fr.* II. EnRP
"Sky is an immortal tent, The," *fr.* I.
(Fragments from the Old Masters: Immortal Tent.) PoF
"Thou hearest the nightingale," *fr.* II. NBE; OBRV
(Birdsong.) FaBoEn
(Choir of Day, The.) EnRP
(Joy in the Flowers, *shorter sel.*) RO
(Nightingale and Flowers.) LoBV
(Vision of Beulah.) EV-3
Wine-Press of Los, The, *fr.* I. EnRP
Milton. Dryden. *See* Lines Printed under the Engraved Portrait of Milton.
Milton. Walter Savage Landor. NBE; RO
Milton. Longfellow. AA; AmP; AmPP; APW; AWP; BLV; IAP; InPo; MOAP; NePA; PeBoSo; PtP; TOP; TrGrPo
Milton. Lloyd Mifflin. AA
Milton. Tennyson. BPN; EM-2; EmBrPo; EnLi-2; EnLit; EPN; GEPC; InP; OAEP; PoFS; PoVP; PtP; TCEP; TOP; VLEP
Milton. Wordsworth. *See* London, 1802.
Milton Abbas Rhyme, The. *Unknown.* SiTL
Milton, I think thy spirit has passed away. To Milton. Oscar Wilde. BMEP
Milton! Thou Shouldst Be Living at This Hour. Wordsworth. *See* London, 1802.
Milton, you did them wrong the hour you sang. The Lord of All. Edwin Markham. BCEP; CAW
Milton's Prayer [of Patience]. Elizabeth Lloyd Howell. AA; MaRV; WGRP
Milwaukee Fire, The. *Unknown.* ABS
Mimi, do you remember. Biftek aux Champignons. Henry Augustin Beers. AA; HBV; PR
Mimma Bella, *sels.* Eugene Lee-Hamilton. HBV
"Have dark Egyptians stolen thee away," I.
"Oh, bless the law that veils the future's face," VI.
"Oh, rosy as the lining of a shell," IV.
"One day, I mind me, now that she is dead," VIII.
"Two springs she saw—two radiant Tuscan springs," II.
"What essences from Idumean palm," XX.
Mimnermus in Church. William Johnson Cory. EPN; GTBS; GTML; GTSE; HBV; LO; OBEV; VA
Mimnermus Incert. Walter Savage Landor. PoEL-4
Mimshi Maiden, The. Hugh McCrae. MoAuPo; NeLNL
Minaret Bells, The. Thackeray. RIS
Minarets wave on the plains of Stamboul, The. Eastern Serenade. William E. Aytoun *and* Sir Theodore Martin. InMe
Mincemeat. Elizabeth Gould. BoTP
Mind. Paul C. Boomer. PoP
Mind, The, *sel.* James Gates Percival.
"Of mind, and its mysterious agencies." PoP
Mind. Richard Wilbur. NePA; NePoEA
Mind and Matter. Sir Arthur Conan Doyle. PoP
Mind and Matter. *Unknown. See* Limerick: "There was a faith-healer of Deal."
Mind Content, A. Robert Greene. *See* Sweet Are the Thoughts That Savor of Content.
Mind Diseased, A. Shakespeare. *Fr.* Macbeth, V, iii. BCEP
(Remorse.) MaRV
Mind drowned in the sun may dream of birds, The. A Balcony with Birds. Howard Moss. NePoEA
Mind from nature, divorced by love, The. Around the Fish; after Paul Klee. Howard Moss. MoPo
Mind goes out in silver, submarine, The. Note for Navigators. Sherman Conrad. CAG
Mind has shown itself at times, The. For the Marriage of Faustus and Helen. Hart Crane. NePA
Mind in its purest play is like some bat. Mind. Richard Wilbur. NePA; NePoEA
Mind Is an Enchanting Thing, The. Marianne Moore. CoBMV; CrMA; InvP; MoAB; MoAmPo (1950 ed.); MoPo; OnAP; OxBA; Po; ReMP
Mind is its own place, and in itself, The. Myself Am Hell. Milton. *Fr.* Paradise Lost, I. MaRV
Mind of the people is like mud, The. Talking with Soldiers. W. J. Turner. ChMP; FaBoTw; GTBS-D; MBP; MoBrPo; SoV
Mind, with its own eyes and ears, The. The Mind's Liberty. W. H. Davies. MBP; MoBrPo
Minds awake in bodies that were asleep. Pandora and the Moon. Merrill Moore. MAP; MoAmPo
Mind's eye sees as the heart mirrors, The. To Sleep. Robert Graves. MoVE
Mind's Liberty, The. W. H. Davies. MBP; MoBrPo
Mine are the night and morning. Song of Nature. Emerson. AnNE; HBV; SN
Mine Argosy from Alexandria. Christopher Marlowe. *Fr.* The Jew of Malta, I, i. ChTr
("Give me the merchants of the Indian mines.") LO
Mine be a cot beside a hill. A Wish. Samuel Rogers. BoTP; BPP; CBPC; EnSW; EPN; ERP; EV-3; GTBS; GTBS-D; GTBS-W; GTSE; GTSL; HBV; LPS-1; MCCG; OBEC; OBEV (new ed.); OBVV; OTPC (1923 ed.); PECK; RIS; TreFS; WP
"Mine be a cot," for the hours of play. Household Art. Austin Dobson. VLEP
Mine ears have heard your distant moan. Lines. J. C. Squire. WhC
Mine eye and heart are at a mortal war. Sonnets, XLVI. Shakespeare. PeBoSo
Mine eye bewrays. Love Cannot Live. *Unknown.* EIL
Mine eye hath played the painter and hath steeled. Sonnets, XXIV. Shakespeare. PeBoSo
Mine eye with all the deadly sins is fraught. Henry Constable. *Fr.* Diana. SiCE; TuPP
Mine eyes are filled today with old amaze. Old Amaze. Mahlon Leonard Fisher. SBMV
Mine Eyes Beheld the Blessed Pity. Dante, *tr. fr. Italian by* Dante Gabriel Rossetti. La Vita Nuova, XXIII. LiTW
("Mine eyes beheld the blessed pity spring.") AWP
(Sonnet.) LyMA
Mine eyes fill, and I know not why at all. In Autumn. George Sterling. MOAP; UnW
Mine eyes have seen the glory of the coming of the Lord. Battle Hymn of the [American] Republic. Julia Ward Howe. AA; AnAmPo; AnFE; APA; APW; BAP; BAV; BBV (1923 ed.); BLPA; BoHiPo; CBPC; CH; CoAnAm; CoBA; DD; DDA; FaBoBe; FaFP; FaPON; GN; GoTP; HBV; HBVY; IAP; InP; LA; LBAP; LEAP; LiTG; LPS-2; MaRV; MC; MDAH; NeHB; NePA; OBAV; OBVV; OHIP; OIF; OnAP; OQP; OtMeF; OTPC; PaA; PAH; PAP; PIR; PoFr; PYM; QP-1; RG; TCAP; TOP; TrAS; TreF; TVSH; WBLP; WGRP; YaD
Mine eyes he closed, but open left the cell. Adam Describing Eve. Milton. *Fr.* Paradise Lost, VIII. LPS-1
Mine Host. *Unknown, tr. fr. Chinese by* Alun Lewis. AlDL
Mine Host of "The Golden Apple." Thomas Westwood. DD; GN; OHIP; OTPC
Mine is a wild strange story—the strangest you ever heard. The Old Actor's Story. George R. Sims. PTA-2
Mine is Cyllene's mountain steep. Hermes of the Playground. Nicias. OxBG
Mine is the spirit of mystery. Song of the Moon-Spirit. Mary Josephine Benson. CPG
Mine No. 6. Malcolm Cowley. *Fr.* Blue Juniata, I. InP; MAP; MoAmPo (1942 ed.)
Mine old dear enemy, my froward master. Translation from Petrarch. *Tr. by* Sir Thomas Wyatt. SiPS
Mine [*or* Myne] own John Poynz [*or* Poins], since ye delight to know. Of the Courtier's Life. Sir Thomas Wyatt. Satires, I. CoBE; GoTL; OBSC; PoEL-1; ReEn; ReIE; SiCE; SiPS; TuPP
Mine own zweet Jone, let me not moan. Jack Shows His Qualities and Great Good Will to Jone. Thomas Howell. ReIE; TuPP
Mine Sweepers. Kipling. ShBV-4

Mine to the core of the heart, my beauty! Plighted. Dinah Maria Mulock Craik. HBV
Mine was a Midwest home—you can keep your world. One Home. William Stafford. NePA
Mine was the book, Fidentine, till you ravished it for your recital. Martial, *tr. fr. Latin by* Robert R. Schnorr. Epigrams, I, 38. LaP
Miner, The. Maxwell Bodenheim. NP
Miner, The. Ibsen, *tr. fr. Norwegian by* Charles W. Stork. AnNoLy
Miner, The. Alfred Castner King. PoOW
Mineral Collection. Abbie Huston Evans. NP
Miners. Wilfred Owen. GTBS-D; MBP; MoAB; MoBrPo
Miners, The. César Vallejo, *tr. fr. Spanish by* H. R. Hays. TwSpPo
Miner's Protégée, The. *Unknown.* IHA
Miner's Song, The. Charles E. Winter. CSF; IHA
Miners went forth from the mine, The. The Miners. César Vallejo. TwSpPo
Mines. E. Serebrovskaya, *tr. fr. Russian by* Babette Deutsch. TrRV
Mingle your sighs with mine, ye dales, thou Dorian water. *At. to* Moschus, *tr. fr. Greek by* L. P. Chamberlayne. GrPo
Mingled aye with fragrant yearnings. Blue Moonshine. Francis G. Stokes. NA
Mingling a potion for his thirst the sun. Languor. Stéphane Mallarmé. MiFP
Mingling my prayer. Saigyo Hoshi, *tr. fr. Japanese by* Arthur Waley. AWP
Mingo. Juan del Encina, *tr. fr. Spanish by* George Ticknor. AnSpL-1
Minguillo's Kiss. *Unknown, tr. fr. Spanish by* Sir John Bowring. BOHV
(Kiss, The.) AnSpL-1
Miniature. Archilochus, *tr. fr. Greek by* H. Rushton Fairclough. GrR
(Girl, A, *tr. by* J. A. Symonds.) OxBG
(Girlhood, *tr. by* F. L. Lucas.) GrPE
Minion Wife, A. Nicholas Udall. *Fr.* Ralph Roister Doister. ElL
Minister, The. Fenton Johnson. AnAmPo; LA
Minister, New Style, A. Timothy Dwight. *Fr.* The Triumph of Infidelity. AmPP (3d ed.)
Minister of Wine, The. Omar Khayyám, *tr. fr. Persian by* Edward Fitzgerald. *Fr.* The Rubáiyát. OnPM
Minister said it wald dee, The. Last Lauch. Douglas Young. SeCePo
Minister, why do you direct your artillery against my nets? A Fisher's Apology. Arthur Johnstone. GoTS
Ministering Angels. Spenser. *Fr.* The Faerie Queene, II, 8. CBE
("And is there care in heaven?") OxBoCh
(Bright Squadrons, The.) GoBC
(Guardian Angels.) OBSC
(Heavenly Aid.) MaRV
(Ministering Spirits, The.) PC
(Ministry of Angels, The, *longer sel.*) LPS-2
Minister's Prayer, A. J. M. Bemiss. PraP
Ministers! you, most serious. The Prodigals. *Unknown.* PA
Ministration. Wordsworth. ES
Ministry of Angels, The. Spenser. *See* Ministering Angels.
Miniver Cheevy. E. A. Robinson. AmPP; AnNE; AWP; BAP; BAV; BOHV; ChMo; ChTr; CMP; CoBA; CoBMV; DDA; FaBoCh; FaFP; HBV; InMe; InPo; JAWP; LBMV; LEAP; LHV; LiTA; LiTM; LoGBV; MaC; MAP; MaPo; MCCG; MoAB; MoAmPo; MOAP; NAMP; NeMA; NePA; NP; NV; OBAV; OnPP; OxBA; PCN; PFE; PFY; Po; PoEL-5; PoRA; PYM; ReaPo; RiBV; SeCeV; ShBV-4; TCAP; TOP; TreF; TrGrPo; TwP; VOD (1935 ed.); WBP; WHA; WhC; YaD
Miniver Cheevy, Jr., *parody.* David Fisher Parry. InMe; WhC
Minna. Maxwell Bodenheim. MAPA
Minnesota, hail to thee! Hail! Minnesota! Truman E. Rickard *and* Arthur Upson. PoRL
Minnie. Eleanor Farjeon. GoTP
Minnie. Thomas Caulfield Irwin. IrPN
Minnie and Mattie. Christina Rossetti. *Fr.* Sing-Song. BoTP; GaP; InvP; SUS; TiPo
(Minnie, Mattie and May.) RAR; TSW
Minnie and Mrs. Hoyne. Kenneth Fearing. AnEnPo; PoRA
Minnie and Winnie. Tennyson. BPN; HBV; HBVY; NA; OTPC; PPL
Minnie can't make her mind up. Minnie. Eleanor Farjeon. GoTP
Minnie, Mattie and May. Christina Rossetti. *See* Minnie and Mattie.
Minnows. Keats. *Fr.* I Stood Tiptoe upon a Little Hill. FaPON; GN; GoTP; RIS
(I Stood Tiptoe.) MyFE
Minor Bird, A. Robert Frost. AlDL; BLA; ChMo; CMP
Minor Poet, A. John Richard Moreland. LS
Minor Poet, A. Alexander Smith. *Fr.* A Life-Drama. VA
Minor Prophet, A, *sels.* "George Eliot."
Life's Purpose. MaRV
Tides of Faith, The. GrCo-1
Minora Sidera. Sir Henry Newbolt. PoeT; TCPD
Minotaur, The. Eldon Grier. PeCV
Minotaur. Elinor Wylie. TwAmPo
Minot's Beacon. Alexander C. Corkum. DDA
Minot's Ledge. Fitz-James O'Brien. OnYI
Minott, Lee, Willard, Hosmer, Meriam, Flint. Hamatreya. Emerson. AnNE; FaBoEn. *See also* Bulkeley, Hunt, Willard, Hosmer . . .
Minstrel, The, *sels.* James Beattie.
"Ah! who can tell how hard it is to climb," I. CEP; EiPP
"And oft he traced the uplands, to survey," *fr.* I. EnSW
But Who the Melodies of Morn Can Tell, *2 sts., fr.* I. EBSV; ViBoPo
(Melodies of Morn, The, *3 sts.*) EV-3
(Morning, *2 sts.*) LPS-2
(Nature and the Poets.) OBEC, *5 sts.;* SeCePo, *3 sts.*
Edwin, the Minstrel, *fr.* I. EV-3
Nature's Charms, *fr.* I. OBEC
Minstrel, The. Goethe, *tr. fr. German by* James Clarence Mangan. AWP
Minstrel, The. Sir Walter Scott. *See* Last Minstrel, The.
Minstrel Boy, The. Thomas Moore. ACP; AnIL; BBV (1923 ed.); BHV; CBE; CoBE; ERP; EV-4; FaBoBe; FaFP; GN; GoBC; GoTP; HBV; OAEP; OlF; OnYI; OTPC; PIR; PoFr; PTA-2; RG; StaSt; TCEP; TreF
Minstrel came once more to view, The. The Battle of Beal' an Duine. Sir Walter Scott. LPS-2; TCEP
Minstrel of God, The, *sel.* Clement Wood.
"O sweet strange minstrel of the joyous singing." SaFP
Minstrel Worthy of His Hire, The. Homer, *tr. fr. Greek by* William Cowper. *Fr.* The Odyssey, VIII. GrR
Minstrels and Maids. William Morris. *See* Outlanders, Whence Come Ye Last?
Minstrel's Lowly Bower, The. Sir Walter Scott. *Fr.* The Lay of the Last Minstrel. EV-4
Minstrels played their Christmas tune, The. The Christmas Carol. Wordsworth. COAH
Minstrel's Song. Thomas Chatterton. *Fr.* Aella. BLV; CG; HBV; LEAP; LoBV; LPS-1; TrGrPo, *sl. abr.;* WHA
(Minstrel's Roundelay, The, *sl. abr.*) BCEP
(Mynstrelles Songe.) AnFE; BEL; CEP; EiPP; EnLi-2; EnLoPo; EV-3; OBEC
(O, Sing unto My Roundelay.) CH, *abr.;* GTBS-W; LiTB
(Roundelay.) CBOV; WP
(Song: "O sing unto my roundelay.") ATP (1935 ed.), *sl. abr.;* LiTL; LO, *abr.*
(Song from "Aella.") LiA; LiTG; OBEV; TOP
Mint by Night. Alfred Barrett. JKCP (1955 ed.)
Mint Julep, The. Charles Fenno Hoffman. AA
Minuet, The. Mary Mapes Dodge. BAP; OHFP; PTA-2
Minuet, The. Dorothy Leonard. VOD
Minuet on Reaching the Age of Fifty, A. George Santayana. FaFP; HBMV; LiTM; NePA; TriL
Minute, A. Innokenti Annenski, *tr. fr. Russian by* C. M. Bowra. BoR
Minute, The. Karl Shapiro. ATP (1953 ed.); MiAP; MoVE; UnPo (3d ed.)
Minute before Meeting, The. Thomas Hardy. NBE
Minute-Gun, The. R. S. Sharpe. LPS-2
Minute made visible and heard. The Earth. Leonard Mann. BoAV; MoAuPo; NeLNL
Minute-Men of North-Boro', The. Wallace Rice. PAH
Minutes are numbered by the fall of sands. John Ford. *Fr.* The Lover's Melancholy. PoD; PoEL-2
Minutes of Gold. *Unknown.* PoToHe
Minx in khaki struts the limelit boards, A. Ragtime. W. W. Gibson. POTT
Mir träumte von einem Königskind. Heine, *tr. fr. German by* Richard Garnett. AWP
Mir träumte wieder der alte Traum. Heine, *tr. fr. German by* James Thomson. AWP; JAWP; WBP
(Superfluous Bite.) OnPM
Mirabeau Bridge, The. Guillaume Apollinaire, *tr. fr. French by* W. S. Merwin. AnFP
(Pont Mirabeau, *tr. by* W. J. Strachan.) MiFP
Mirabile Dictu, *in mod. Eng. Unknown.* TMEV
Mirabile Misterium!/ The Son of God Is Man Become. *Unknown.* AnEC
Miracle. Liberty Hyde Bailey. OHIP; OQP; QP-2; YeAr
Miracle. Edith Daley. BAP; MaRV
Miracle, The. Walter de la Mare. CoBE; GTML; LiTB; UnPo (3d ed.)
Miracle, A. "George Klingle." OQP; QP-2
Miracle. Edith Mirick. ChIP
Miracle. Lizette Woodworth Reese. MAP; MoAmPo
Miracle, The. Caelius Sedulius, *tr. fr. Latin by* H. T. Henry. *Fr.* Carmen Paschale. CAW
Miracle, The. *Unknown. See* Behold a Wonder Here.
Miracle Dreams, The. Susie M. Best. QS

Miracle for Breakfast, A. Elizabeth Bishop. AmP; FiMAP; LiTA; MiAP
Miracle Indeed, A. Purohit. OBMV
Miracle, A? Is it more strange than nature's common way? A Miracle. "George Klingle." OQP; QP-2
Miracle of Spring, The. Bahar, *tr. fr. Persian by* A. J. Arberry. PeP
Miracle of the Dawn, The. Madison Cawein. HBV
Miracle of the world, I never will deny. To His Mistress. Henry Constable. *Fr.* Diana. OBSC; ReEn; TuPP
Miracle Songs of Jesus, The. Wilson MacDonald. CPG
Miracle-Workers, The. Elizabeth Akers Allen. SN
Miracles. Conrad Aiken. HBMV; MAP; MoAmPo; NeMA
Miracles. Arna Bontemps. GoSl; PoNe
Miracles. Roy Helton. MaRV
Miracles. E. Merrill Root. TBM
Miracles ("I believe a leaf of grass"). Walt Whitman. Song of Myself, XXXI. CBOV; MaRV; PoeMoYo
(Leaf of Grass, A.) OQP; QP-2
(Leaves of Grass.) YT
(Microcosm, The.) SN
(Poem XXXI.) SeCeV
(Song of Myself, XXXI.) AmPP; AnFE; BLV; BoLiVe; CoAnAm; CoBA; CoV; LiTA; MAP; MoAmPo; NeMA; OxBA; PG (1955 ed.); TrGrPo
Miracles ("Why, who makes much of a miracle?"). Walt Whitman. APW; BBV (1951 ed.), *abr.*; CaAE; CoBA; GoTP; GrCo-1; HBVY; LaNeLa; NeMA; OQP; PoMa; QP-2; StVeCh; VOD (1935 ed.); WaKn; YT
Miracles of Our Lady, The, *sels.* Gonzalo de Berceo, *tr. fr. Spanish by* Longfellow.
"I, Gonzalo de Berceo, in the gentle summertide." AnSpL-1
(Praise of Spring, The.) TeCS
San Miguel de la Tumba. CAW; TeCS
Miraculous morning! Frost and sun! Winter Morning. Pushkin. BoR
Miraculous silver-work in stone. At Burgos. Arthur Symons. VLEP
Mirage. R. P. Blackmur. *Fr.* Sea Island Miscellany. GTBS-W; LiTM; MoVE
Mirage. Richard Church. AlDL
Mirage. Walter de la Mare. MM
Mirage. Christina Rossetti. BLV; BrBE; EnLi-2; KN; MBP; PoRA
Mirage, *sel.* V. Sackville-West.
Song: "I know a room where tulips tall." AlDL
Mirage, The. Oscar Williams. CrMA; LiTL; LiTM; NePA
Miramichi Lightning. Alfred G. Bailey. TwCaPo
Miranda's lover sees himself. Two Lovers. Aline Kilmer. AV
Miranda's Song. W. H. Auden. *Fr.* The Sea and the Mirror. FaBoMo
Miranda's Supper. Elinor Wylie. TCPD
Mirèio, The, *sels.* Frédéric Mistral, *tr. fr. French.*
Cocooning, The, *tr. by* Harriet Waters Preston. AWP; JAWP; WBP; WoL
Mares of the Camargue, The, *tr. by* George Meredith. AWP
Mirelle of the Good Bed. Tom MacInnes. CPG
Miriam, *sel.* Whittier.
Bible, The. MaRV; NeHB; OQP; QP-1
(Book Our Mothers Read, The.) BLRP
(Knowledge.) PoToHe (new ed.)
Miriam, Mary, Maria, Marie. Mary. Fray Angelico Chavez. ISi
Miriam, strike your cymbal. Jerusalem Delivered. Louis Untermeyer. MAP
Miriam's Unsaid Speech. Judith Stern. CAG
Mirie it is while sumer ilast. Now Comes the Blast of Winter. *Unknown.* SeCePo
Mirror, The. W. H. Davies. MoSiPe
Mirror, The. Judah Halevi, *tr. fr. Hebrew by* Emma Lazarus. TrJP
Mirror, The. M. Whitcomb Hess. JKCP (1955 ed.)
Mirror, The. Ibn al-Sabuni, *tr. fr. Arabic by* A. J. Arberry. MooP
Mirror, The. Blanche Mary Kelly. GoBC; TrPWD
Mirror, The. Li Po, *tr. fr. Chinese by* Florence Ayscough *and* Amy Lowell. ChLP
Mirror, The. Li Sui Ch'u, *tr. fr. Chinese by* Henry H. Hart. PoHN
Mirror, The. Po Chü-i, *tr. fr. Chinese by* Ching Ti. WhP
Mirror, The. Dante Gabriel Rossetti. EmBrPo
Mirror, The. Robert Haven Schauffler. HOAH
Mirror. John Updike. WaKn
Mirror for Magistrates, A [*or* The], *sels.* William Baldwin, *and others.*
How Jacke Cade Traiterously Rebelling agaynst His Kyng, Was for His Treasons and Cruell Doinges Wurthely Punyshed. *At. to* William Baldwin. SiCE
How Shore's Wife, Edward the Fourth's Concubine, Was by King Richard Despoiled of All Her Goods and Forced to Do Open Penance. Thomas Churchyard. ReIE
How Thomas Wolsey Did Arise unto Great Authority and Government, His Maner of Life, Pompe, and Dignity, and How Hee Fell Downe into Great Disgrace, and Was Arested of High Treason. Thomas Churchyard. SiCE
Induction to "The Mirror for Magistrates." Thomas Sackville, Earl of Dorset. BEL; OBSC; Po, *abr.*; ReEn; ReIE; TuPP
(Complaint of Henrie Duke of Buckinghame, The.) PoEL-1
(Mayster Sackvilles Induction.) SiCE
Sels.
Approach of Winter, The ("The wrathful winter . . ."). CoEV
(Winter.) EIL; SeCePo
"Flat down I fell." EPP
Old Age ("And next in order sad Old Age"), *abr.* BCEP
Porch of Hell, The ("And first, within the porch . . ."). EV-1
Sleep ("Body's rest, the quiet of the heart, The"). CBOV
Sleep ("By him lay heavy Sleep . . ."). WHA
Troy ("But Troy, alas . . ."). SeCePo
Vision of Sorrow ('But how can I describe . . ."). LoBV
Vision of War, A ("Lastlie stode warre . . ."). FaBoEn
Mirror for Poets, A. Thom Gunn. NePoEA
Mirror, let us through the glass. The Flight into Egypt. W. H. Auden. *Fr.* For the Time Being. OAEP (2d ed.); OxBA
Mirror, Mirror. Robert Graves. HBMV
"Mirror, mirror, on the wall." Five Epigrams, 5. Donald Hall. NePoAm-2
Mirror, mirror, tell me. *Unknown.* GoTP
Mirror of Knighthood, The, *sels.* *At. to* Robert Parry.
Except I Love, *fr.* II. EIL
Song: "Fond affection, hence, and leave me!" *fr.* III. EIL
Mirror of men's eyes delights me less, The. Laus Virginitatis. Arthur Symons. EnLoPo
Mirror of Mortality, A. Thomas Proctor. ReIE
Mirror of poets, mirror of our age. Upon Ben Jonson. Edmund Waller. SeCV-1
Mirror of the pond gleams, The. Thoughts while Reading. Chu Hsi. OnPC
Mirror of those true brown eyes, The. Peregrina. Eduard Mörike. AnGP
Mirror-still the bay, no breeze molesting. Sabbath Eve. August Strindberg. AnSL
Mirrored in distant lakes, and gleaming. The Voice. Vissarion Sayanov. BoRS
Mirrors. Elizabeth Jennings. NePoEA
Mirrors. Toyohiko Kagawa, *tr. fr. Japanese by* Lois J. Erickson. SoLD
Mirrors: never yet has anyone described. Four Sonnets to Orpheus. Rainer Maria Rilke. *Fr.* Sonnets to Orpheus. LiTW
Mirrors of All Ages, The. Robert Hillyer. MuM
Mirry Margaret,/ As midsomer flowre. *See* Merry Margaret.
Mirth ("'Tis mirth that fills the veins with blood"). Beaumont *and* Fletcher. *Fr.* The Knight of the Burning Pestle. BLV; EIL; SiCE
(Laugh and Sing.) TrGrPo
Mirth. Robert Herrick. LiTB
Mirth. *Unknown.* SeCL
Mirth and Melancholy. Margaret Cavendish, Duchess of Newcastle. DiM
Mirth, now dead, that once was madly bubbling, The. Elegy. Pushkin. TrRV
Mis' Smith. Albert Bigelow Paine. BOHV
Misacmos, of Himself, Who Loves to Be Worst in the Company. Sir John Harington. SiCE
Misadventures at Margate. "Thomas Ingoldsby." *Fr.* The Ingoldsby Legends. BOHV; HBV; LPS-3
Misanthrope, The. Callimachus, *tr. fr. Greek by* F. L. Lucas. GrPE
Miscegeneous Zebra, The. Roland Young. BOHV
Misconceptions. Robert Browning. AtBAP; BPN; EmBrPo; EnLi-2 (1949 ed.); EPN; EtPaEn; GEPC; GTBS; OBEV; OBVV; PIAE; PoVP; TOP; VA; VLEP
Miscreant Angel, The. Lew Sarett. FAOV
Misdeeming eye! that stoopest to the lure. Lewd Love Is Loss. Robert Southwell. ACP; EV-1
Misdirection. Eleanor Slater. MoSiPe
Miser, The. Laura Bell Everett. OQP; QP-2
Miser, The. Ibn Sa'id of Alcala la Real, *tr. fr. Arabic by* A. J. Arberry. MooP
Miser. Gordon LeClaire. CaP
Miser. Harold Vinal. MCCG
Miser till his last quick breath, A. To One Who Worshipped Gods of Gold. John Richard Moreland. MaRV; MuM
Miser, traversing his house, A. Lucilius, *tr. fr. Greek by* William Cowper. GrPo
Miser with an eager face, A. The World's Miser. Theodore Maynard. CAW; JKCP; MBP; MoBrPo (1942 ed.); QS
Miserable Catullus, stop being foolish. Catullus, *tr. fr. Latin by* Louis Zukofsky. LaP
Miserable Merchant. Samuel Rowlands. SiCE

Miseremini mei, ye that be my friends! On the Death of the Noble Prince King Edward the Fourth. John Skelton. ReIE
Miserere. David Gascoyne. FaBoMo; NeBP
Sels.
Ecce Homo. ChMP; FaBoTw; LiTM (rev. ed.); OnHM
Lachrymae. AtBAP; BoW; POTE
Pieta. POTE
Miserere. Gaspar Núñez de Arce, *tr. fr. Spanish by* Thomas Walsh. CAW
Miserere. Herman Scheffauer. BAP
Miserere my maker. *Unknown.* SeCSL
Miserie. George Herbert. PoEL-2
Miserly Patron, A. *Unknown, tr. fr. Old Irish by* Myles Dillon. AnIL
Miser's Entertainment, The. Lucilius, *tr. fr. Greek by* F. L. Lucas. GrPE
Misery. Shao Ch'ang Heng, *tr. fr. Chinese by* Henry H. Hart. OnPM
"Misery," he said, "to have no chin." Soles Occidere et Redire Possunt, VIII. Aldous Huxley. ViBoPo (1941 ed.)
Misery is greater, as I live, The. Modern Love, XXIV. George Meredith. ViPo
Misery of Jerusalem, The. Lamentations, I, Bible, *O.T.* AWP
(Lamentation for the Fall of Jerusalem.) LiTW
Misery of Man, The. Alexander Craig. SeCL
Misery of the Beggars at the Gate of Zenkoji, The. Issa, *tr. fr. Japanese by* Max Bickerton. PoFr
Misfortune. Ralph Bergengren. FAOV
Misfortune to have lived not knowing thee! Emerson. Amos Bronson Alcott. AA; GA; OBAV
Misfortunes Never Come Singly. Harry Graham. FaFP; NA; SiTL
(Nurse.) MaC
Misfortunes of Elphin, The, *sels.* Thomas Love Peacock.
Merlin's Apple-Trees. OBRV
Not Drunk Is He, 4 *ll.* LEAP; ViBoPo
(Who Is Drunk? 4 *ll.*) OnPM
Song of Gwyntho. OBRV
Song of the Four Winds, The. OBRV
War-Song of Dinas Vawr, The, *fr. ch.* 11. ALV; AWP; BCEP; CBOV; EnRP; ERP; ExPo; FaBoCh; GTBS; InvP; JAWP; KN; LEAP, *abr.*; LiA; LiTG; LoBV; MuP; MyFE; OBRV; OtMeF; PIAE; ShBV-2; SoV; StPo; TOP; TVSH; ViBoPo, 4 *ll.*; WaaP; WBP; WhC
Misgiving. Robert Frost. TBM
Misgivings. Herman Melville. AmP; GTBS-D; NePA; OxBA
Misjudged Fiddler, The. Erik Axel Karlfeldt, *tr. fr. Swedish by* Charles W. Stork. AnSL
Misogonus, *sel. Unknown.*
"Sing care away with sport and play." ReEn
(Song to the Tune of Heart's Ease, A.) TuPP
Misogynist, The. L. F. Gerlach. PtPa
Misogynist. Hipponax, *tr. fr. Greek by* F. L. Lucas. GrPE
Misplaced? *Unknown, tr. fr. Spanish by* Havelock Ellis. OnPM
Miss April's come and I have found. Golden Tacks. Mildred D. Shacklett. GFA
Miss Bailey's Ghost. George Colman, the Younger. *See* Unfortunate Miss Bailey.
Miss Brown, before these walls unquote. Notation in Haste. Elias Lieberman. GoYe
Miss Buss and Miss Beale. *Unknown.* CenHV
Miss Caroline Cricket. Caroline Cricket. C. Lindsay McCoy. GFA
Miss Danae, when fair and young. An English Padlock. Matthew Prior. CEP; EiPP; FaBoEn; OBEC
Miss Euphemia. John Crowe Ransom. ChMo
Miss Foggerty's Cake. *Unknown.* BLPA
Miss Helen Slingsby was my maiden aunt. Aunt Helen. T. S. Eliot. TwP
Miss Hen. Booth Lowrey. IHA
Miss J. Hunter Dunn, Miss J. Hunter Dunn. A Subaltern's Love Song. John Betjeman. ChMP; ShBV-4
Miss James. A. A. Milne. MoShBr; MPB
("Diana Fitzpatrick Mauleverer James.") TiPo
Miss Kilmansegg and Her Precious Leg, *sels.* Thomas Hood.
Gold. OQP; QP-2; WBLP
(Her Moral.) VA
Her Death. VA
Miss Kilmansegg's Birth. OxBoLi
Miss Loo. Walter de la Mare. ChMo; CMP; EPP; NV; TVSH; VOD
(Miss Lou.) HBV
Miss Lucy she is handsome. Take Yo' Time, Miss Lucy. *Unknown.* GoSl
Miss Lucy she is slender, Miss Lucy she is stout. I Am Fur from My Sweetheart. *Unknown.* CoSo
Miss Lydia Banks, though very young. The Good Girl. Elizabeth Turner. Mrs. Turner's Object-Lessons, VIII. OTPC (1923 ed.)
Miss Mallarmé's Fan. Stéphane Mallarmé. *See* Another Fan.
Miss Melerlee. John Wesley Holloway. BANP; PoNe
Miss Minnie McFinney of Bute. Limerick. *At. to* Carolyn Wells. LiBL; WhC
Miss Nancy Ellicott. Cousin Nancy. T. S. Eliot. TwP
Miss Nancy's Gown. Zitella Cocke. AA
Miss One, Two, and Three. *Unknown.* OxNR
Miss Penelope Leith. Walter C. Smith. EBSV
Miss Pixie. Lloyd Roberts. CPG
Miss Rafferty wore taffeta. The Private Dining Room. Ogden Nash. ExPo
Miss Sophia. Elizabeth Turner. OTPC (1923 ed.)
Miss T. Walter de la Mare. CenHV; FaBoBe; GFA; GoBP; MoShBr; MPB (1956 ed.); PoRh; RAR; SUS; TiPo; TSW; TSWC
Miss Thompson Goes Shopping. Martin Armstrong. ShBV-2
Miss Twye. Gavin Ewart. FiBHP; LiTM; NeBP; SiTL
"Miss Ulalume, there are questions that linger here." Abbreviated Interviews with a Few Disgruntled Literary Celebrities. Reed Whittemore. FiBHP
Miss Wagnalls, when I brought you here. The Girl I Took to the Cocktail Party. Trevor Williams. FiBHP
Miss You. David Cory. BLPA; FaBoBe; NeHB; TreFS
Miss You. *Unknown.* PoToHe (new ed.)
Missa Papae Marcelli. J. P. McAuley. BoAV
Missa Vocis. R. P. Blackmur. ReMP
Missal, The. Rosemary Dobson. BoAV; MoAuPo
Missal, A. Charles Lamb. ES
Missal, The. Ruth Pitter. CAW
Missal of the Gothic age. To a Missal of the Thirteenth Century. Austin Dobson. POTT
Missed Again. John T. Durward. JKCP (1926 ed.)
Missed Train, The. Thomas Hardy. MaPo
Misses Poar Drive to Church, The. Josephine Pinckney. AnAmPo; InP; LA; LS
Misshapen, black, unlovely to the sight. A Bulb. Richard Kendall Munkittrick. AA
Missing. Irene Rutherford McLeod. BMEP
Missing. A. A. Milne. MoShBr
Missing. John Pudney. HaMV
Missing. John Banister Tabb. QS; TrPWD
Missing ("In the cool, sweet hush"). *Unknown.* BIG
Missing ("When the anxious hearts"). *Unknown.* WGRP
Missing Dates. William Empson. ChMP; CoBMV; FaBoEn; FaBoMo; LiTB; LiTM; MoAB; MoPo; ViBoPo (1958 ed.)
Missing Link, The. Oliver Herford. CenHV
Missing My Daughter. Stephen Spender. AtBAP
Mission Graves, The. Nora May French. BAP
Mission of Sister Seraphine, The, a Sister of Charity. "Owen Meredith." *Fr.* Lucile. PraNu
Missionary, The. Sister Mary Eleanore. WHL
Missionary, The. *Unknown.* PraP
Mississippi Girls. *Unknown. See* Kansas Boys.
Missive, The. Sir Edmund Gosse. HBV
Missouri Maiden's Farewell to Alabama, A. "Mark Twain." *Fr.* The Adventures of Tom Sawyer, *ch.* 21. InMe
Missouri she's a mighty river. Shenandoah. *Unknown.* ABF
Missouri Traveller Writes Home, A; 1830. Robert Bly. NePoEA
"Missy Sick." *Unknown.* CoMu
Mist. Arthur Davison Ficke. MuM
Mist. Georgie Starbuck Galbraith. MuM
Mist. Ibn Bassam, *tr. fr. Arabic by* A. J. Arberry. MooP
Mist. Li Ch'ing-chao, *tr. fr. Chinese by* Kenneth Rexroth. OnPC
Mist, The. Nellie Burget Miller. GFA
Mist. Henry David Thoreau. *Fr.* A Week on the Concord and Merrimack Rivers. AA; AmPP (4th ed.); AWP; DDA; HBMV; InPo; JAWP; LEAP; LPS-2; MOAP; OxBA; SN; WBP
(Low-anchored Cloud.) ImOP; ViBoPo
Mist, The. *Unknown, formerly at. to* Dafydd ap Gwilym, *tr. fr. Welsh by* George Borrow. PrWP
Mist and All, The. Dixie Willson. BrR; FaPON; MPB; YeAr
Mist and cold descend from the hills of Wales. Evening in Camp. Patricia Ledward. WaP
Mist came from an unknown place, The. Mist. Arthur Davison Ficke. MuM
Mist clogs the sunshine. Consolation. Matthew Arnold. GEPC; ViPo
Mist floats on the spring meadow. Otomo no Yakamochi, *tr. fr. Japanese by* Kenneth Rexroth. OnPJ
Mist Forms. Carl Sandburg. ChMo; CMP
Mist is a soft white pussy-cat, The. The Mist. Nellie Burget Miller. GFA
Mist is thick, The. On the wide river, the water-plants float smoothly. The Lonely Wife. Li Po. ChLP
Mist lay still on Heartbreak Hill, The. Ipswich Bar. Esther Willard Bates *and* Brainard L. Bates. HBMV
Mist Opening in the Hills. Wordsworth. *Fr.* The Excursion. UnW

Mist was driving down the British Channel, A. The Warden of the Cinque Ports. Longfellow. AA; AmPP (3d ed.); HBV; IAP; TCAP; WHA
Mistake, The. Theodore Roethke. NePoAm-2
Mistaken fair, lay Sherlock by. Verses Written in a Lady's Sherlock "Upon Death." Earl of Chesterfield. CEP; OBEC
Mistakes. Ella Wheeler Wilcox. PoToHe
Mistaking brains praise Norgus' wit for great. In Norgum. *Unknown.* TuPP
Mr. A. E. Housman on the Olympic Games, *parody.* E. V. Knox. WhC
Mr. and Mrs. Alonzo Sidney. Merrill Moore. MOAP
Mr. and Mrs. Discobbolos. Edward Lear. SiTL
Mr. and Mrs. Spikky Sparrow. Edward Lear. SAS
Mister Angleworm. —— Manchester. GFA
Mr. Apollinax. T. S. Eliot. OnHM
Mr. Attila. Carl Sandburg. ImOP
Mr. Barney Maguire's Account of the Coronation. "Thomas Ingoldsby." *Fr.* The Ingoldsby Legends. VA
Mister Beers. Hugh Lofting. FaPON; GaP
Mr. Beetle. Emily Hover. BoTP
Mr. Bernard Shaw. E. C. Bentley. *Fr.* Biography for Beginners. CenHV
Mr. Blake was a regular out-and-out hardened sinner. The Lost Mr. Blake. W. S. Gilbert. EnLi-2 (1949 ed.); InMe; ViP
Mr. Bourne and His Wife, *with music.* *Unknown.* FTB
Mr. Brown. Rodney Bennett. BoTP
Mister Carrot. Dorothy Aldis. GFA
Mister chairman and ladies and gentlemen. The Eyes Have It. William Stephens. NAMP
Mr. Coggs. E. V. Lucas. BoTP; GaP; GFA; HBV; HBVY (Mr. Coggs, Watchmaker.) FaPON; MPB
Mr. Cooper says these red men. The Power of the Pen. Mortimer Neal Thompson. LauV
Mr. Cowslip polished his coffins. The French Polisher. Constance Davies. MoWP
Mr. Cromek. Blake. ChTr
Mr. Cypress's Song. Thomas Love Peacock. *See* There Is a Fever of the Spirit.
Mr. Diaper Wants Advancement. William Diaper. *Fr.* An Imitation of the Seventeenth Epistle of the First Book of Horace. BeR
Mr. East gave a feast. Mother Goose. OTPC; OxNR; SiTL
Mister Eddyter—Our Hosea wuz down to Boston last week. Letter from Mr. Ezekiel Biglow to the Hon. Joseph T. Buckingham. James Russell Lowell. The Biglow Papers, 1st Series, No. I. TCAP
Mr. Edwards and the Spider. Robert Lowell. AmP; MoAB; MoPo; MoVE; NePoEA; ReMP; SeCeV
Mr. Eliot's Sunday Morning Service. T. S. Eliot. MaPo; PoFS
Mr. Finney's Turnip. *Unknown.* BOHV; GFA; HBV; HBVY; LiL; NA; OnHT; PTA-1
Mr. Flint goes up the West. Martial, *tr. fr. Latin by* "T. W. M." Epigrams, IX, 59. LaP
Mr. Flood's Party. E. A. Robinson. AmP; AmPP; AnAmPo; AnEnPo; AnNE; AWP; BLV; BoLiVe; ChMo; CMP; CoBMV; CrMA; FaFP; HoPM; IAP; InP; InPo; JAWP; LA; LiTA; LiTM (rev. ed.); MAP; MaPo; MoAB; MoAmPo; MOAP; NePA; NP; OxBA; PCN; PoE; PoLFOT; PoRA; PreP; ReaPo; ReMP; RiBV; SeCeV; TrGrPo; TwP; UnPo (3d ed.); ViBoPo; WBP
Mister Fly. Thomas Miller. OTPC (1923 ed.)
Mr. Francis Beaumont's Letter to Ben Jonson. Francis Beaumont. *See* Master Francis Beaumont's Letter to Ben Jonson.
Mister Frog Went a-Courting. *Unknown.* *See* Frog Went a-Courting.
Mr. Grumble. *Unknown.* *See* Father Grumble.
Mr. Heath-Stubbs as you must understand. Epitaph. John Heath-Stubbs. NePoEA; PoN
Mr. Hecatomb Styrax, the owner of a large estate and of large muscles. Moeurs Contemporaines. Ezra Pound. OnHM
Mr. Hilaire Belloc. E. C. Bentley. *Fr.* Biography for Beginners. CenHV
Mister Hop-Toad. James Whitcomb Riley. CV
Mr. Hosea Biglow Speaks. James Russell Lowell. *See* Letter from Mr. Ezekiel Biglow of Jaalam to the Hon. Joseph T. Buckingham, A.
Mr. Hosea Biglow to the Editor of the Atlantic Monthly. James Russell Lowell. *Fr.* The Biglow Papers, 2d Series, No. X. AA, *abr.;* IAP; PoEL-5 (Hosea Biglow's Lament, *abr.*) PFY
Mr. Ibister, and Betsy his sister. *Unknown.* OxNR
Mr. Johnson's Policy of Reconstruction. Charles Graham Halpine. PAH
Mr. Jones. Harry Graham. FaFP; LiTG; SiTL
(Common Sense.) FiBHP; OtMeF
(Four Ruthless Rhymes.) MaC
(Some Ruthless Rhymes, VIII.) CenHV
Mr. Le Strange His Verses in the Prison at Linn. Sir Roger L'Estrange. *See* Loyalty Confin'd.
Mr. Leach made a speech. Forensic Jocularities. *Unknown.* OxBoLi
Mr. Lear. Edward Lear. *See* How Pleasant to Know Mr. Lear.
Mr. Lear, I'm the Akond of Swat. A Reply from the Akond of Swat. Ethel Talbot Scheffauer. FiBHP
Mr. Macklin's Jack o'Lantern ("Mr. Macklin takes his knife"). David McCord. FaPON
Mr. Meant-To. *Unknown.* WBLP
Mr. Merry's Lament for "Long Tom." John Gardiner Calkins Brainard. AA
Mr. Minnitt. Rose Fyleman. GaP; HBVY; PCH
Mr. Molony's Account of the Ball. Thackeray. HBV; LPS-3
Mr. Moon. Bliss Carman. FaPON; GaP; SUS
Mr. Nigger. John Charles McNeill. NoCaPo
Mr. Nixon. Ezra Pound. *Fr.* Hugh Selwyn Mauberley. CoBMV; CoV; LiTA; LiTM (rev. ed.); MoPo
Mr. Nobody. *Unknown.* BoTP; DDA; FaPON; GaP; GoBP; HBVY; MPB (1956 ed.); OnHT; OTPC; PoMS; RAR, *abr.;* StVeCh
Mr. Ody met a body. Edith Nesbit. CenHV
Mr. Orator Puff had two tones in his voice. Orator Puff. Thomas Moore. *Fr.* M. P.; or, The Blue Stockings. LPS-3
Mr. Pennycomequick. P. M. Stone. BoTP
Mr. Pollington Remembers a Poet. Hyam Plutzik. FiMAP
Mr. Pope. Allen Tate. MAP; MoAB; MoAmPo; MOAP; PtP; ReaPo; SPP; TBM
Mr. Pope's Welcome from Greece. John Gay. OBEC, *abr.;* OxBoLi, *abr.;* PoEL-3; PtP, *abr.*
Mr. Pyme. Harry Behn. LiL; TiPo
Mr. Rabbit. Dixie Willson. GoBP
Mr. Rand and Mr. McNally. I Wonder What Became of Rand, McNally. Newman Levy. InMe; WhC
Mister Robin and his wife have started south once more. Traveling Light. Minnie Leona Upton. PCH
Mr. Scarecrow. Sheila Braine. BoTP
Mr. Sludge, "The Medium," *br. sel.* Robert Browning. Religion. MaRV
Mr. Smith. William Jay Smith. FiBHP
Mister Socrates Snooks, a lord of creation. Socrates Snooks. Fitz Hugh Ludlow. BLPA
Mr. Speeds will clean his auto. Some Who Do Not Go to Church. *Unknown.* WBLP
Mr. Squirrel. V. M. Julian. BoTP
Mr. Symons at Richmond, Mr. Pope at Twickenham. Julian Symons. WaP
Mr. T/ bareheaded. The Artist. William Carlos Williams. HoPM
Mr. Thomas had an old gray mule. The Old Gray Mule. *Unknown.* ABS
Mr. U Will Not Be Missed. E. E. Cummings. SiTL
Mr. Walter de la Mare Makes the Little Ones Dizzy. Samuel Hoffenstein. SiTL
Mr. Wells. Elizabeth Madox Roberts. FaPON; GaP; HBMV; HBVY; LS; TSW; TSWC
Mr. Whittier. Winfield Townley Scott. CrMA; OnHM
Mister William. W. S. Gilbert. TOP
Mr. Wright went out to fish. The Right Way to Fish. *Unknown.* WhC
Misther Denis's Return. Jane Barlow. *Fr.* Th' Ould Master. TIP
Mistletoe Bough, The. Thomas Haynes Bayly. BLPA; HBV; LPS-3; NeHB; TreFS
Mistletoe Sprites. Solveig Paulson Russell. ChBR
Mistress, The, *sels.* Abraham Cowley.
Against Hope. GTBS-W; LiTB; LiTG; LoBV; MeLP; MePo; OBS; SeCV-1
All-over Love. LiTL; SeCL
Change, The. BEL; CoBE; FaBoEn; LO; MeLP; MePo; OBS; ReEn; SeCV-1
Clad All in White. SeCV-1
Love and Life. SeEP
My Diet. LiTL; LO; SeCL; SeEP
Platonic[k] Love. SeCV-1; SeEP
Resolved to Be Beloved. CaAE
Spring, The. ElSeCe; EPS (1942 ed.); EV-2; LO; MeLP; OBS; ReEn; SeEP
(Love's Absence in the Spring.) LiTL
Thief, The. BEL; ElSeCe; EnLi-1; EnLit; OAEP; SeCL; WHA
Thraldome, The. SeCV-1
Welcome, The. SeCV-1
Wish, The. BEL; BLV; CBOV; CoBE; ElSeCe; EnLi-1; EnLit; EPP; EPS; EV-2; GTBS-W; HBV; LEAP; LiTB; LiTG; OAEP; OBEV; OBS; SeCL; SeCV-1; SeEP; TOP; TrGrPo; ViBoPo; WHA
Written in Juice of Lemmon. SeCV-1
Mistress, The. S. G. Leonard. MoWP
Mistress, The; a Song. Earl of Rochester. EPS; MePo; NBE; OBS
(His Mistress.) OnPM

Mistress, The; a Song (*continued*)
"Age in her embraces past, An," *sel.* AtBAP; ViBoPo
Mrs. Alfred Uruguay. Wallace Stevens. MoPo; NePA
Mrs. Ambrose watched the iridescence. Water-Images. Mary Elizabeth Osborn. NePoAm-2
Mrs. Barks. Rose Fyleman. BrR
Mistress, behold in this true-speaking glass. Barnabe Barnes. Parthenophil and Parthenophe, I. TuPP
Mrs. Brown. Rose Fyleman. BoTP; GaP; TiPo
Mrs. Brown and the Famous Author. Stoddard King. ATP
Mrs. Bubb was gay and free, fair, fat, and forty-three. The One Horse Chay. *Unknown.* OxBoLi
Mrs. C. (Or Any Other Too Practical Person). Rowena Bastin Bennett. GaP
Mrs. Caribou. William Jay Smith. PoMS
Mistress Comfort. Elizabeth Gould. BoTP
Mrs. Crudeman. Sir Osbert Sitwell. HaMV
Mrs. Frances Harris's Petition. Swift. *See* To Their Excellencies the Lords Justices of Ireland, the Humble Petition of Frances Harris.
Mrs. Golightly. Gertrude Hall. AA; PR
Mrs. Hague. Sir Osbert Sitwell. MM
Mistress Hale of Beverly. Lucy Larcom. PAH
Mrs. Harris's Petition to Their Excellencies the Lords Justices of Ireland. Swift. *See* To Their Excellencies the Lords Justices of Ireland, the Humble Petition of Frances Harris.
Mrs. Indiarubber Duck. D. Carter. BoTP
Mrs. Jenny Wren. Rodney Bennett. BoTP
Mrs. Judge Jenkins, *parody.* Bret Harte. BAV; FiBHP; HBV; InP; LauV; WhC
Mrs. June's Prospectus. "Susan Coolidge." ADAH
Mrs. Loewinsohn &c. Ron Loewinsohn. NeAP
Mrs. McGrath. *Unknown.* OnYI
Mrs. MacQueen. Walter de la Mare. BoTP
Mrs. Malone. Eleanor Farjeon. AIDL; PoMS
Mrs. Malooly. Agnes Lee. NP
Mistress Margaret Hussey. John Skelton. *See* To Mistress Margaret Hussey.
Mrs. Marmaduke Moore, at the age of ten. The Seven Spiritual Ages of Mrs. Marmaduke Moore. Ogden Nash. MoAmPo (1950 ed.)
Mrs. Mary Blaize. Goldsmith. *See* Elegy, An, on That Glory of Her Sex, Mrs. Mary Blaize.
Mistress Mary, quite contrary. *See* Mary, Mary, quite contrary.
Mrs. Mason bought a basin. *Unknown.* OxNR
Mrs. Meyers. Edgar Lee Masters. *Fr.* Spoon River Anthology. ChMo; CMP
Mistress Mine. Shakespeare. *See* O Mistress Mine, Where Are You Roaming?
Mrs. Mother Has a Nose. James Broughton. SiTL
Mrs. Ocean takes in washing. Washday. Elizabeth F. Upson. GFA
"Mistress of gods and men! I have been thine." Pygmalion. William Bell Scott. EPN; VA
Mistress of the House, The. "Anna Akhmatova," *tr. fr. Russian by* Babette Deutsch. TrRV
Mistress of the Manse, The, *sel.* Josiah Gilbert Holland.
Lullaby: "Rockaby, lullaby, bees in the clover." AA; HBV (Rockaby, Lullaby.) BOL; PRWS, *abr.*
Mistress of the Matchless Mine. Clyde Robertson. PoOW
Mistress of the roses, The. Unguarded. Ada Foster Murray. HBV
Mistress of Vision, The. Francis Thompson. CH, *abr.;* OBVV
Mrs. Peck-Pigeon. Eleanor Farjeon. StVeCh (1955 ed.); SUS; TiPo; UTS
Mrs. Reece Laughs. Martin Armstrong. POTE
Mrs. Severin. Winfield Townley Scott. FiMAP; NePoAm
Mrs. Seymour Fentolin. Oliver Herford. HBMV
Mrs. Smith. Frederick Locker-Lampson. BOHV; HBV
Mrs. Snipkin and Mrs. Wobblechin. Laura E. Richards. PoRh; StVeCh (1955 ed.); TiPo
Mrs. Southern's Enemy. Sir Osbert Sitwell. AtBAP; ViBoPo
Mrs. Thomas Willow seems very glum. Mrs. Willow. John Drinkwater. WP
Mrs. Throckmorton's bull-finch sang a song. Homage to William Cowper. Donald Davie. NePoEA
Mrs. Turner's Object-Lessons, *sels.* Elizabeth Turner.
Good Girl, The, VIII. OTPC (1923 ed.)
Letter, The, IX. OTPC (1923 ed.)
Mrs. Williams. Edgar Lee Masters. *Fr.* Spoon River Anthology. NAMP
Mrs. Willow. John Drinkwater. WP
Mrs. Winkelsteiner. Dorothy E. Reid. MotAn; NeMA; StaSt
Mistresses. *Unknown, tr. fr. Irish by* Frank O'Connor. KiLC
Mistrust me, when, distraught by grief's unreason. Aleksey Konstantinovich Tolstoy, *tr. fr. Russian by* Sir Cecil Kisch. WaL
Mistrust To-Morrow. Horace. *See* To Leuconoë.
Mistrustful minds be movèd. Sir Thomas Wyatt. SiPS
Mists and Rain. Baudelaire, *tr. fr. French by* Arthur Symons. OnPM
Mists Are Rising Now, The. Hasye Cooperman. GoYe
Mists have erased and smudged every road, every town, The. Driving the Rafts. Moyshe Kulbak. OnCuPl
Mists of Daybreak. Buson, *tr. fr. Japanese by* William N. Porter. MPB
Mists of Easter morning, The/ Roll slowly o'er the hills. An Easter Song. T. W. Handford. MeMeAg
Mists of thirty years, The. An Old Garden. Chien T'ang. PoHN
Mists on the mountain, mists far down the vale. Sonnet. Arthur Davison Ficke. MuM
Mists rise over, The/ The still pools at Asuka. Three Poems from the Japanese, II. Yamabe no Akahito, *tr. fr. Japanese by* Kenneth Rexroth. HoPM; LiTW; OnPJ
Misty-moisty was the morn. How Do You Do? *Unknown.* ChTr
Misty rain is falling, A. Evening at Chung Shan. Wang An Shih. PoHN
Misunderstanding, A. Martial, *tr. fr. Latin by* Paul Nixon. RoL
Mitherless Bairn, The. William Thom. EV-4; HBV; LPS-1; VA
Mithraic Emblems, *sel.* Roy Campbell.
"Oh let your shining orb grow dim." MeRV (To the Sun.) FaBoTw
Mithridates. Emerson. OnAP; TCAP
Mithridates, King of Pontus, *br. sel.* Nathaniel Lee.
Semandra's Death. BeR
Mitten Song, The. Marie Louise Allen. BrR; SUS; TiPo
Mix a Pancake. Christina Rossetti. *Fr.* Sing-Song. GFA; MeMeAg; OTPC (1946 ed.); PoRh; RAR; SUS; TiPo (1952 ed.)
(Pancake, The.) BoTP; HBVY; PCH
Mixed Beasts. Kenyon Cox. RIS
Sels.
Bumblebeaver, The. TiPo
Kangarooster, The. TiPo
Octopussycat, The. FaPON; RIS; TiPo
Mixed flower fragrance hung about. Kitten and Firefly. Marie Grimes. CIV
Mixer, The. Louis MacNeice. FaBoTw
Mixture of chloroform and oil of cloves. The Place of Pain in the Universe. Anthony Hecht. CrMA
Mixtures of this garden, The. In the Garden; Villa Cleobolus. Lawrence Durrell. ChMP
Miyoko San. Mary McNeil Fenollosa. AA
Mizpah. Julia A. Baker. BLPA; FaBoBe; NeHB; OQP; PTA-2; QP-2
Mnemosyne. Trumbull Stickney. AnFE; CoAnAm; CrMA; LiTA; MOAP; OxBA; TwAmPo; ViBoPo (1958 ed.)
Mo cheann ban beag, lie still and rest. A Lullaby. Mary Anne O'Reilly. BOL
Mo Craoibhin Cno. Edward Walsh. IrPN; TIP
Mo-Lennav-a-Chree. "Fiona Macleod." LEAP
Moan in the Form of a Ballade. Maurice Baring. WhC
Moan, Moan, Ye Dying Gales. Henry Neele. HBV; LPS-1
Moanin', *with music.* *Unknown.* ABF
Moanish Lady! *with music.* *Unknown.* AS
Moans the bay. The Dirge of Cael. *Unknown.* TIP
Moat, The. Oliffe Richmond. NeTW
Mob, The. Pope. *Fr.* The First Satire of the Second Book of Horace Imitated. BeR
Mob of Mountains. José Varallanos, *tr. fr. Spanish by* Muna Lee. AnCL
Mobile Bay, *with music.* *Unknown.* SoAmSa
Moby Dick, *sel.* Herman Melville.
Father Mapple's Hymn, *fr. ch.* 9. EtS; OnAP
(Ribs and Terrors, The.) ViBoPo
(Song: "Ribs and terrors in the whale, The.") MeRV
(Whale, The.) TrGrPo
Mock-bird in a village, A. The Mocking Bird and the Donkey. José Rosas. PCD
Mock Caliph, The. *Unknown, tr. fr. Arabic by* Richard F. Burton. *Fr.* The Thousand and One Nights. EnLi-1
Mock Epitaph, A. Simonides. *See* Timocreon.
Mock On, Mock On, Voltaire, Rousseau. Blake. AtBAP; CaAE; EiPP; EM-1; EnRP; NBE; OAEP; OBRV; OxBoCh; PoEL-4; PoFS
(Mockery, 2 *sts.*) TrGrPo
(Scoffers, The.) LiTB; OnPM; RiBV; SeCeV; UnPo
Mock Song, A. Alexander Brome. SeCL
Mock Trial. Aristophanes, *tr. fr. Greek by* Benjamin Bickley Rogers. *Fr.* The Wasps. GrR
(Trial of the Dog, The, *tr. by* George Allen.) OxBG
Mock Turtle's Song, The. "Lewis Carroll." *See* Lobster Quadrille, The.
Mockery. Blake. *See* Mock On, Mock On, Voltaire, Rousseau.
Mockery. Katherine Dixon Riggs. BrR; MPB; RAR; SP
Mockery. Louis Untermeyer. LBMV; QS
Mocking Bird, The. Irving Bacheller. BLA
Mocking Bird. Witter Bynner. VOD; WhBS

Mocking-Bird, The. Ednah Proctor Clarke. AA
Mocking-Bird, The. Paul Hamilton Hayne. AmPP (3d ed.); BAV
Mocking Bird, The. Richard Hovey. BLA; TSW; TSWC
Mocking Bird, The. Sidney Lanier. AA; AmPP (3d ed.); BLA; HiLiAm; IAP; TCAP
Mocking-Bird, The. Frank Lebby Stanton. AA; POT; PoTo
Mocking-Bird, The. Henry Jerome Stockard. AA; NoCaPo (1941 ed.)
Mocking Bird, The. Walt Whitman. *Fr.* Out of the Cradle Endlessly Rocking. BAP; LPS-2
Mocking Bird and the Donkey, The. José Rosas, *tr. fr. Spanish by* Bryant. PCD
Mocking bird is music-mad tonight, The. Music-mad. Grace Noll Crowell. LS
Mocking-Bird, Misnamed, The. Percy MacKaye. BAP
Mocking-Birds, The. Paul Hamilton Hayne. TCAP
Mocking Fairy, The. Walter de la Mare. GBV; MBP; MoBrPo; MoShBr
Mocking the water with their wings. To One Older. Marian Margaret Boyd. HBMV
Mocking your slow sepulchral horns. Song for a Proud Relation. Patrick MacDonogh. OnYI
Mode Atmospheric, The. Claire Wallis. DDA
Mode of the person becomes the mode of the world, The. Conversation with Three Women of New England. Wallace Stevens. NePA
Model, A. Dollie Radford. VA
Model and the Statue, The. Michelangelo, *tr. fr. Italian by* John Addington Symonds. OnPM
Moderate tasks and moderate leisure. The Second Best. Matthew Arnold. BPN; EM-2; EmBrPo; EPN; GEPC
Moderation. Horace, *tr. fr. Latin by* William Cowper. *Fr.* Odes. PoToHe (new ed.)
Moderation. Pindar, *tr. fr. Greek by* F. L. Lucas. *Fr.* Nemean Odes, XI. GrPE
Modereen Rue. Katharine Tynan. MW; TVSH
Modern Baby, The. William Croswell Doane. BLPA; YaD
(Hand That Rocks the Cradle, The, *st.* 1, *wr. at. to* Wilson Stewart Ross.) MotAn
Modern Ballad, A; the Ups and Downs of the Elevator Car. Caroline D. Emerson. BrR
Modern Beauty. Arthur Symons. EnLit; HBV; MBP; MoBrPo; POTT; PoVP
Modern Columbus, A. Eleanor Robbins Wilson. PoMa
Modern daub it was, perchance, A. The Academy at Venice. Arthur Hugh Clough. BHV
Modern Dragon, A. Rowena Bastin Bennett. GFA; TiPo; UTS
Modern Endymion, A. Marjorie Pickthall. TwCV
Modern Hiawatha, The, *parody.* George A. Strong. *Fr.* The Song of Milkanwatha. BBV (1951 ed.); BOHV; FaFP; FaPON; FiBHP; HBV; InMe; LiTG; MoShBr; NA; PA; PIAE; SiTL; TreFS; WhC; YaD
(Hiawatha's Mittens.) ShBV-1
Modern House That Jack Built, The. *Unknown, sometimes at. to* Pope. *See* Domicile of John, The.
Modern house, with great glass eye, The. Anecdote of the Sparrow. Robert Pack. NePA
Modern Improvements. John Hookham Frere. EnSW
Modern Jonas, The. *Unknown.* PAH
Modern Language Association, The. A Salute to the Modern Language Association, Convening in the Hotel Pennsylvania, December 28th–30th. Morris Bishop. WhC
Modern Lochinvar, A. George S. Bryan. PR
Modern Love. George Meredith. PoVP; ViPo; ViPP
Sels.
"All other joys of life he strove to warm," IV. EmBrPo; GTBS-D; OAEP; VA
Kinship with the Stars, 6 *ll.* GTBS-W; LiA
"Am I failing? For no longer can I cast," XXIX. EmBrPo; OAEP; POTT
"At dinner, she is hostess, I am host," XVII. EnLit; OAEP; POTT; ViP
(Hiding the Skeleton.) VA
"At last we parley: we so strangely dumb," XLVI. EmBrPo; EnLit; OAEP; POTT; VLEP
"But where began the change; and what's my crime?" X. EnLit; PoEL-5
"By this he knew she wept with waking eyes," I. AnEnPo; BEL; BMEP; EmBrPo; EnLi-2; EnLit; EnLoPo; HBV; LEAP; OAEP; Po; PoEL-5; POTT; TyEnPo; ViP; VLEP
(End of Love, The.) HoPM
"He felt the wild beast in him betweenwhiles," IX. EmBrPo; POTT
"He found her by the ocean's moaning verge," XLIX. BEL; BMEP; EmBrPo; EnLi-2; HBV; LEAP; OAEP; PoE; POTT; ViP
"Here Jack and Tom are paired with Moll and Meg," XVIII. InvP; PoEL-5; ViPo
"How many a thing which we cast to the ground," XLI. EnLit; HBV; LEAP
"I am not of those miserable males," XX. EmBrPo; EnLit; POTT; VLEP
"I am to follow her. There is much grace," XLII. ViBoPo
"I play for seasons, not eternities!" XIII. EmBrPo; EPN; FaBoEn; ViP
"In our old shipwrecked days there was an hour," XVI. BEL; BMEP; EnLi-2; GTBS; GTBS-D; GTML; HBV; LO; PIAE; PoFS; WHA
(Love Dies.) SeCePo
(Tragic Memory.) CBOV
"In Paris, at the Louvre, there have I seen," XXXIII. ViP
"It chanced his lips did meet her forehead cool," VI. ViBoPo
"It ended, and the morrow brought the task," II. BEL; EmBrPo; EnLi-2; HBV; OAEP; POTT; VLEP
"It is the season of the sweet wild rose," XLV. EmBrPo; PoEL-5
"Love ere he bleeds, an eagle in high skies," XXVI. HBV; VLEP
"Madam would speak with me. So, now it comes," XXXIV. POTT; VLEP
"Mark where the pressing wind shoots javelin-like," XLIII. AnFE; BEL; CaAE; CoEV; EnLi-2; EnLoPo; FaBoEn; GTBS-D; GTML; HBV; InPo; OAEP; PoEL-5; RiBV; SeCeV; ViP; ViPo
(Love's Grave.) OBEV
"Not solely that the future she destroys," XII. EmBrPo; EnLit; ViBoPo
"Out in the yellow meadows, where the bee," XI. EmBrPo
"Their sense is with their senses all mixed in," XLVIII. BEL; EmBrPo; EnLi-2; OAEP; ViP
"They say that Pity in Love's service dwells," XLIV. (Coin of Pity, The.) VA
"This was the woman; what now of the man?" III. EmBrPo; HBV
"Thus piteously Love closed what he begat," L. AnFE; BEL; BMEP; CaAE; EmBrPo; EnLi-2; EnLit; EnLoPo; EtPaEn; FaBoEn; GTBS-D; GTML; GTSL; HBV; InPo; LEAP; LoBV; LoPo; OAEP; PoE; PoEL-5; POTT; SeCeV; TrGrPo; UnPo (1st ed.); ViBoPo; ViP; WHA
(Dusty Answer, A.) SeCePo
" 'Tis Christmas weather, and a country house," XXIII. EmBrPo; ViP
"We saw the swallows gathering in the sky," XLVII. AnFE; BEL; BMEP; BoLiVe; CaAE; CoEV; EmBrPo; EnLi-2; EnLoPo; EtPaEn; FaBoEn; GTBS-D; GTML; GTSL; LEAP; POTT; SeCeV; TyEnPo; ViBoPo; WHA
(One Twilight Hour.) VA
(This Little Moment.) LiA
"We three are on the cedar-shadowed lawn," XXI. EmBrPo; OAEP; POTT
"What are we first? First, animals; and next," XXX. AnEnPo; OAEP; PoEL-5; ViBoPo; ViP
"What may the woman labor to confess?" XXII. EmBrPo; POTT; VLEP
"What soul would bargain for a cure that brings," XIV. HBV; POTT
"Yet it was plain she struggled, and that salt," VIII. EnLit; GTBS-D; OAEP; POTT
Modern Major-General, The. W. S. Gilbert. *Fr.* The Pirates of Penzance. InMe; PCD, *abr.*; SoV
(Major-General, The.) OnPP
(Major-General's Song.) CoBE
Modern malady of love is nerves, The. Nerves. Arthur Symons. FaBoTw; MBP; MoBrPo
Modern Mother, The. Alice Meynell. GTML
Modern Ode to the Modern School. John Erskine. YaD
Modern Orchard, A. David O'Neil. AnAmPo; LA
Modern Poet, The. Alice Meynell. *See* Song of Derivations, A.
Modern Romans, The. Charles Frederick Johnson. AA; LHV
Modern Rubaiyat, The. Kate Masterson. PA
Modern Saint, The. Richard Burton. OQP; QP-1
Modern Sappho, A. Matthew Arnold. VLEP
Modern Sonnet. Grace Hazard Conkling. BAP
Modern Traveller, The, *sel.* Hilaire Belloc.
"And yet I really must complain." OtMeF
Modern Woman to Her Lover, The. Margaret Widdemer. BAP; HBMV; PR; TCAP
Modernist married a fundamentalist wife, A. Marital Tragedy. Keith Preston. WhC
Modernists, The. Tom MacInnes. CaP
Modernity. F. L. Lucas. LO
Modest Blush. Ibn Abd Rabbihi, *tr. fr. Arabic by* A. J. Arberry. MooP
Modest front of this small floore, The. An Epitaph upon Mr. Ashton a Conformable Citizen. Richard Crashaw. OBS
Modest Girl, The. *Unknown, tr. fr. Chinese by* E. D. Edwards. ChLP
Modest Love, A. Sir Edward Dyer. *See* Lowest Trees Have Tops, The.

Modest Poet, The. *Unknown.* CAG
Modest Wit, A. Selleck Osborn. BLPA; BOHV; HBV; PECK
Modestly we violets cower. Violets. P. A. Ropes. BoTP
Modo and Alciphron. Sylvia Townsend Warner. MBP; MoBrPo
Modred was in Cornwall, and summoned many knights. Arthur's Last Fight. Layamon. *Fr.* The Brut. MeEV
Modryb Marya. Robert Stephen Hawker. *See* Aunt Mary.
Modyr Whyt as Lyly Flowr. *Unknown.* *See* Mother, White as Lily Flower.
Moeurs Contemporaines. Ezra Pound. OnHM
Mofaddaliyat. *See* Mufaddaliyat.
Mog the Brunette. *Unknown.* CoMu
Moggy and Me. James Hogg. HBV
Mohammed and Seid. Harrison Smith Morris. AA
Moira Dhu. Mary Brennan. CAG
Moist and soft and crinkled like a baby's fingers. A Song of Green. Phyllis Reid. DiM
Moist Moon People. Carl Sandburg. MAP; MoAmPo
Moistened osier of the hoary willow, The. The Coracle. Lucan. ChTr
Mokie's Madrigal. Ronald McCuaig. NeLNL
Molded to the owl is what the owl spits out. Natural Architecture. John Hay. NePoAm
Mole, The. Al-Munfatil, *tr. fr. Arabic by* A. J. Arberry. MooP
Mole, The. John Clare. SeCeV
Mole, The. Frederick William Harvey. MM
Mole. Aldous Huxley. LBBV
Mole, The. Edith King. GFA
Mole, The. E. L. Mayo. WaKn
Mole, The. P. K. Page. BoCaPo
Mole Catcher. Edmund Blunden. CaAE; OBMV
Molecatcher. Albert D. Mackie. GoTS
Mole goes down the slow dark personal passage, The. The Mole. P. K. Page. BoCaPo
Mole Talk. Leo Kennedy. PeCV
Mole, which sleeps beneath the woven peat, The. Sonnet. W. Wesley Trimpi. PtPa
Moles. Ibn Haiyun. *tr. fr. Arabic by* A. J. Arberry. MooP
Moll-in-the-wad and I fell out. *Unknown.* OxNR
Mollesse. Josephine Jacobsen. NePoAm-2
Mollie Bond. *Unknown.* *See* Molly Bawn.
Mollie [*or* Ollie] McGee. Edgar Lee Masters. *Fr.* Spoon River Anthology. BAP; NP
Mollis Abuti. Swift. BoN; ChTr
Mollusk, The. James J. Montague. PoMa
Mollusks. Henry Jerome Stockard. NoCaPo (1941 ed.)
Molly. *Unknown.* *See* When Molly Smiles.
Molly Asthore. *Unknown, tr. fr. Irish by* Sir Samuel Ferguson. IrPN
Molly Bawn. *Unknown.* BaBo; ViBoFo
(Mollie Bond.) ABS
(Shooting of His Dear.) OxBoLi
Molly Bawn and Brian Oge. *Unknown.* OnYI
Molly Maguire at Monmouth. William Collins. IDAH; OTPC; PaA; PAP
Molly Malone. *Unknown.* *See* Cockles and Mussels.
Molly Means. Margaret Walker. PoNe; StPo
Molly Mog; or, The Fair Maid of the Inn. John Gay. CEP; CoMu
Molly Odell on Her Birthday. Jonathan Odell. IAP
Molly Pitcher. Laura E. Richards. GA; MC; PAH; YaD
Molly Pitcher. Kate Brownlee Sherwood. GA; GoTP; MC; OTPC (1946 ed.); PAH
Moly. Edith M. Thomas. HBV; PECK
Moment, A. Stopford Brooke. IrPN
Moment, A. Mary Elizabeth Coleridge. BMEP; PoVP
Moment, The. Germán Pardo García, *tr. fr. Spanish by* Rolfe Humphries. AnCL
Moment, The. Kathleen Raine. MoPW
Moment, The. David Rowbotham. BoAV
Moment, The. Kendrick Smithyman. AnNZ
Moment, A. L. A. G. Strong. NeMA
Moment, A. John Todhunter. GTIV
Moment by Moment. Daniel W. Whittle. BLRP
Moment I glanced at the mirk-windowed mansion, The. The Spectre. Walter de la Mare. WhC
Moment I recall entrancing, A. To A. P. Kern. Pushkin. WaL
Moment in Ostia. Sister Mary Thérèse. JKCP (1955 ed.)
Moment in the Morning, A. *Unknown, at. to* Arthur Lewis Tubbs. PraP
(To Begin the Day.) BLRP
Moment Inexpressible, The. Jens Peter Jacobsen, *tr. fr. Danish by* Charles W. Stork. BoDS
Moment Musicale. Bliss Carman. HBMV; TCAP
Moment Musicale. Wallace Gould. AnAmPo; LA
Moment of the Rose, The. Dunstan Thompson. LiTA
Moment the wild swallows like a flight, A. A Thunderstorm. Archibald Lampman. CaP; OCL
Moment then Lord Marmion stayed, A. Flodden Field. Sir Walter Scott. *Fr.* Marmion, VI. LPS-2
Moment when the world is sunk in space, A. Inspiration. Hilda Mary Hooke. CPG
Momentous to himself as I to me. Epigram. Sir William Watson. AnEnPo; BMEP; LEAP
Moments. Hervey Allen. HBMV
Moments. Marcel Schwob, *tr. fr. French by* William Brown Meloney. TrJP
Moment's halt, A—a momentary taste. Omar Khayyám, *tr. by* Edward Fitzgerald. *Fr.* The Rubáiyát. PoFr
Moment's Interlude, A. Richard Aldington. POTE
Moment's patience, gentle Mistris Anne, A. William Shakespeare to Mrs. Anne, Regular Servant to the Rev. Mr. Precentor of York. Thomas Gray. CEP
Moments there are when heart and brain ring clear. Moments. Hervey Allen. HBMV
Momist. Amy Groesbeck. GoYe
Momotara. Rose Fyleman. TiPo
Momus. E. A. Robinson. ViBoPo
Mona Lisa. *See also* Monna Lisa.
Mona Lisa. John Kendrick Bangs. BOHV
Mona Lisa. Edward Dowden. OnYI
(Leonardo's "Monna Lisa.") VA
Mona Lisa, A. Angelina Weld Grimké. CDC
Mona Lisa. Walter Pater. OBMV
Monadnoc, *sels.* Emerson.
"Thousand minstrels woke me," OBAV
"World-soul knows his own affair, The." BAV
Monadnock through the Trees. E. A. Robinson. InP; TOP
Monaghan. Shane Leslie. OnYI
Monaltri. *Unknown, tr. fr. Gaelic by* Thomas Pattison. EBSV
Monarch, The. William Cowper. *See* Verses Supposed to Be Written by Alexander Selkirk . . .
Monarch oak, the patriarch of the trees, The. The Oak. Dryden. ADAH; OHIP
Monarch of Gods and Daemons, and all Spirits. Prometheus Unbound. Shelley. BEL; BHV; BPN; CoBE; EM-2; EmBrPo; EnLi-2; EnRP; EPN; ERP; FiP; GEPC
Monarch sat on his judgment-seat, The. The Fay's Sentence. Joseph Rodman Drake. *Fr.* The Culprit Fay. LEAP
Monarch who wears a shrieking crown, The. George Barker. Holy Poems, III. MoPo
Monaro, The. David Campbell. BoAV
Monasteries. Charles David Webb. NePoAm-2
Monastery, The, *sels.* Sir Walter Scott.
Book of Books, The ("Within this ample [*or* awful] volume lies"), *fr. ch.* 12. MaRV; NeHB; OQP; QP-1
(Bible, The.) BLRP
(Sir Walter Scott's Tribute.) WBLP
Border Ballad, *fr. ch.* 25. BHV; BPN; EmBrPo; EnLit; EPN; EV-4; GN; HBV; PCD
(Border March.) EBSV; EnRP; PCN
(March, March.) ViBoPo
(March, March, Ettrick and Teviotdale.) BSV
On Tweed River, *fr. ch.* 5. EV-4
Monastery on Kazbek [*or* Kasbek]. Pushkin, *tr. fr. Russian by* Sir Cecil Kisch. BoRS; WaL
Monastic Scribe, The. Thomas Bailey Aldrich. MOB
Monasticism. Aubrey Thomas De Vere. PraNu
Mond ist aufgegangen, Der. Heine, *tr. fr. German by* James Thomson. AWP; OuHeWo
(Mermaidens, The.) OnPM
Monday I was 'rested, Tuesday I was fined. Lookin' for the Bully of the Town. *Unknown.* BaBo
Monday is a good day. The Days of the Week. John Farrar. GFA
Monday Morning. Helen Wing. GFA; MeMeAg
Monday morning back to school. David McCord. TiPo (1959 ed.)
Monday's child is fair of [*or* in] face. Mother Goose [*or* Old Wives' Sayings *or* Old Superstitions]. BLPA; BoChLi; BoTP; FaBoBe; FaBoCh; GoTP; HBV; HBVY; LiTG; LoGBV; MoShBr; NeHB; OTPC; OxNR; PPL; SiTL; StaSt; StVeCh; TreF
Mone, Member, Mone. *Unknown.* ABF
Money. Richard Armour. FaFP; TreFS; WaKn; WhC
Money. Byron. *Fr.* Don Juan, XII. GEPC
Money. W. H. Davies. OBEV (new ed.); OBMV; OBVV
Money. Jehan du Pontalais, *tr. fr. French by* Henry Carrington. BOHV
Money, *with music.* *Unknown.* AS
Money abides not in the palm. The Sieve. Sadi. LiTW
Money and a Friend. *Unknown.* BLPA; NeHB
Money Makes the Man. Alcaeus, *tr. fr. Greek by* James S. Easby-Smith. GrR
Money, thou bane of bliss and source of woe. Avarice. George Herbert. GTBS-W; LiTB; PeBoSo
Money was once well known, like a townhall or the sky. Behaviour of Money. Bernard Spencer. LiTB
Moneyless Man, The. Henry Thompson Stanton. BLPA
Mongol. Dana Kneeland Akers. UnW
Mongolian Horse, The. Tu Fu, *tr. fr. Chinese by* Chi Hwang Chu *and* Edna Worthley Underwood. OnPM
Mongolian Idiot. Karl Shapiro. FiMAP

Mon-goos, The. Oliver Herford. *Fr.* Child's Natural History. AA; HBV; LEAP
Mongrel, The. Thomas Hardy. AlBD
Mongrel bred of every strain. Epitaph for Tristan-Joachim-Edouard Corbière, Philosopher, Stray, Stillborn. Tristan Corbière. LiTW
Mongrel Pup, A. Nancy Byrd Turner. PoMa
Mongst all the palaces in Hells command. Richard Crashaw. *Fr.* Sospetto d'Herode. SeCV-1
'Mongst the world's wonders, there doth yet remain. Female Glory. Richard Lovelace. MyFE
Mongst whom, some there were bards, that in their sacred rage. The Fourth Song. Michael Drayton. *Fr.* Polyolbion. PrWP
Monica. Oscar Levertin, *tr. fr. Swedish by* Charles W. Stork. AnSL
Monica, St. Augustine's Mother. *Unknown.* MOAH
Monica's Last Prayer. Matthew Arnold. MeRV
Monition. Sir Charles G. D. Roberts. CPG
Monk, The. Blake. *See* I Saw a Monk of Charlemain.
Monk, The, *sel.* Matthew Gregory Lewis.
Alonzo the Brave and Fair Imogine. LPS-3
Monk, The. "Seumas O'Sullivan." GTIV
Monk and His Pet Cat, The. *Unknown, tr. fr. Old Irish.* CH, *tr. by* Kuno Meyer; OnYI, *tr. by* Whitley Stokes, John Strachan, *and* Kuno Meyer, *arr. by* Kathleen Hoagland
(Monk and His Cat, The, *tr. by* Seán O'Faoláin.) SiB
(Pangur Ban, *tr. by* Robin Flower.) AnIL; FaBoCh; LoGBV; LyMA; OnYI; OxBI; PoC
(Scholar and the Cat, The, *tr. by* Frank O'Connor.) KiLC
(White Cat and the Student, The, *tr. by* Robin Flower.) RIS
Monk and the Peasant, The. Margaret E. Bruner. PoToHe
Monk Arnulphus uncork'd his ink, The. The Court Historian. George Walter Thornbury. HBV; OBVV
Monk in the Garden, The. Adelaide Crapsey. VOD (1935 ed.)
Monk in the Kitchen, The. Anna Hempstead Branch. AnFE; APA; BAP; CoAnAm; CP; LEAP; MAP; MAPA; MoAmPo; MOAP; OBAV; QS; SBMV; TwAmPo
"There is no small work unto God," *sel.* MaRV
Monk of Casal-Maggiore, The. Longfellow. *Fr.* Tales of a Wayside Inn: The Sicilian's Tale, Pt. III. AmPP (4th ed.); OxBA
Monk of Great Renown, The. *Unknown.* CoMu
Monk of Szechuan on the heights of Mount Omei, The. Listening to the Monk of Szechuan Playing on His Lute. Li Po. WhP
Monk sat in his den, The. The Weak Monk. Stevie Smith. FaBoTw
Monk there was, a monk of mastery, A. Seven [*or* Five] Pilgrims. Chaucer. *Fr.* The Canterbury Tales: Prologue. BLV; TrGrPo
Monk was preaching, The: strong his earnest word. A Legend. Adelaide Anne Procter. GoBC; JKCP
Monk, A, when his rites sacerdotal were o'er. The Philosopher's Scales. Jane Taylor. BCEP; HBV; LPS-3
Monkey, The. Nancy Campbell. NP; POT
Monkey, The. Mary Howitt. GN
Monkey, The. Vladislav Felitsyanovich Khodasevich, *tr. fr. Russian by* Babette Deutsch. TrRV
Monkey. Josephine Miles. FiMAP
Monkey. William Jay Smith. TiPo (1959 ed.)
Monkey and the Cat, The. La Fontaine, *tr. fr. French.* CIV
Monkey and the organ man, The. The Organ-Grinder. Jimmy Garthwaite. BrR
Monkey and the Pard, The. La Fontaine, *tr. fr. French by* Alan Conder. TrFP
Monkey, little merry fellow. The Monkey. Mary Howitt. GN
Monkey married the baboon's sister, The. The Monkey's Wedding. *Unknown.* AS; BLPA; NA
Monkey, monkey, bottle of beer. *Unknown.* RIS
Monkey Monkey Moo! So Many Monkeys. Marion Edey. TiPo
Monkey was a-settin' on a railroad track. *Unknown.* GoTP
Monkeys. Padraic Colum. AnFE; PoeMoYo
Monkeys. Joaquin Miller. *Fr.* Walker in Nicaragua. PCH
Monkeys, The. Marianne Moore. LiTA; NAMP; OxBA; SeCeV; TwAmPo
(My Apish Cousins.) AnFE; APA; CoAnAm
Monkeys, The. Edith Osborne Thompson. TiPo; UTS
Monkeys and the Crocodile, The. Laura E. Richards. BoChLi; FaPON; SUS; TiPo; UTS
Monkey's Carol, The. Winifred M. Letts. CV
Monkey's Glue, The. Goldwin Goldsmith. NA
Monkey's Wedding, The. *Unknown.* AS, *with music;* BLPA; NA
Monkeys winked [*or* Winked] too much and were afraid of snakes, The. The Monkeys [*or* My Apish Cousins]. Marianne Moore. AnFE; APA; CoAnAm; LiTA; NAMP; OxBA; SeCeV; TwAmPo
Monks. Cardinal Newman. GoBC
Monks at Ards, The. Patrick Maybin. NeIP
Monk's Day, The. Arthur L. Phelps. CPG
Monks of Bangor's March, The. Sir Walter Scott. CAW
Monks of Ely, The. *Unknown. See* Merrily Sang the Monkes in Ely.
Monk's Song. Sydney Dobell. *Fr.* The Roman. BMEP
Monk's Tale, The, *sels.* Chaucer. *Fr.* The Canterbury Tales.
Croesus. MyFE
Tale of Hugelin, Count of Pisa, The. MyFE
Monk's Vision, The. *Unknown.* PEOR
Monna Innominata. Christina Rossetti. EmBrPo; ViPo
Sels.
Abnegation, XII. VA
(If There Be Anyone.) MBP
"Come back to me, who wait and watch for you," I. AV; TCEP
(Come Back to Me.) MBP
"I wish I could remember that first day," II. TCEP
(First Day, The.) EnLi-2; EPP; FaBoBe; HBV; LO
"Many in aftertimes will say of you," XI. AV; PoVP; TCEP; ViBoPo
O My Heart's Heart, V. VLEP
Trust ("If I could trust mine own self with your fate"), XIII. HiLiEn; VA
"Youth gone, and beauty gone if ever there," XIV. ViBoPo
Monna Lisa. *See also* Mona Lisa.
Monna Lisa. James Russell Lowell. MOAP
Monoceros, beast that's born. The Unicorn. Philippe de Thaon. LyMA
Monochord, The. Dante Gabriel Rossetti. The House of Life, LXXIX. CaAE; PoVP; TCEP; ViPo
Monochrome. Louise Imogen Guiney. AnAmPo; LA
Monody. Herman Melville. AnFE; CoAnAm; GTBS-W; LiTA; PoEL-5; TriL
Monody on a Century. Earle Birney. CaP
Monody on the Death of Chatterton. Samuel Taylor Coleridge. PtP
Monody on the Death of Wendell Phillips. Thomas Bailey Aldrich. GA
Monody on the Demolition of Devonshire House. Siegfried Sassoon. FaBoTw
Monody to the Memory of a Young Lady, *sel.* Cuthbert Shaw.
Time's Balm, *abr.* OBEC
Monogamy. Euripides, *tr. fr. Greek by* M. Wodhull. *Fr.* Andromache. GrR
Monologue. Mikhail Yurevich Lermontov, *tr. fr. Russian by* Sir Cecil Kisch. WaL
Monologue at Midnight. Robert Penn Warren. PreP
Monologue of a Deaf Man. David Wright. POTE (1959 ed.)
Monotone. Carl Sandburg. CBOV; ChMo; CMP; CP; NV; POT; PoTo
Monotonous evil clock, The. A Round Number. Keith Douglas. NeBP
Monseigneur Plays. Theodosia Garrison. HBMV
Monserrat. William Edwin Collin. CaP
Monsieur Gaston. A. M. Klein. BoCaPo (1948 ed.)
Monsieur Pipereau. James Whaler. MAP; MoAmPo (1942 ed.)
Monsieur the Curé down the street. The Curé's Progress. Austin Dobson. HBV; MW; PoVP; VA
Monsieur Yousouf forgot his umbrella. Rain. Max Jacob. MiCF
Monsignore,/ Right Reverend Bishop Valentinus. A Blue Valentine. Joyce Kilmer. ISi; JKCP; LHV
Monsoon. Kenneth Slade Alling. NePoAm
Monster, The. Henry Rago. SiTL
Monsters. Quillevic, *tr. fr. French by* Patricia Terry. OnPM
Monstrous Marriage, The. William Carlos Williams. MoPo
Monstrous, uncouth, their vast leaves amply spread. Palm House, Botanic Gardens. George Hetherington. NeIP
Mont Blanc. Shelley. BPN; EmBrPo; EnRP; MaPo
Montana. Charles C. Cohan. PoRL
Montanus' Sonnet. Thomas Lodge. *Fr.* Rosalynde; or, Euphues' Golden Legacy. AtBAP; PoEL-2; TuPP
("Phoebe sat/ Sweet she sat.") SiCE
Montefiore. Ambrose Bierce. AA; AnAmPo; BAP; LA; PFY
Montenegro. Tennyson. BPN; PoVP
Monterey. Charles Fenno Hoffman. AA; FaBoBe; HBV; LBAP; LEAP; LPS-2; MC; OTPC (1923 ed.); PaA; PAH; PAP; PTA-2
Monterrey Sun. Alfonso Reyes, *tr. fr. Spanish by* Samuel Beckett. AnMP
Montesinos and Durandarte. *Unknown. See* Death of Durandarte.
Montezuma. D. F. Alderson. BoN
Montezuma. Witter Bynner. *Fr.* Chapala Poems. NP
Montgomery. J. C. Hall. ChMP
Montgomery at Quebec. Clinton Scollard. GA; PAH
Month after month the gathered rains descend. To the Nile. Shelley. OBRV

Month can never forget the year, The. Carol. John McClure. HBMV
Month of Falling Stars, The. Ella Higginson. YeAr
Month of gold, A: gold flowers, gold sun. The Golden Month. Marion Doyle. YeAr
Month of leaves,/ Month of roses. June. Irene F. Pawsey. BoTP
Month of May, The. Beaumont *and* Fletcher. *Fr.* The Knight of the Burning Pestle. ChTr
Month of the Thunder Moon, The. Marion Doyle. YeAr
Month, A, sweet little-ones. is past. The Mother's Return. Dorothy Wordsworth. MOAH; OTPC (1923 ed.)
Month was June, the day was hot, The. The Orange. Charles *and* Mary Lamb. OTPC (1923 ed.)
Months, The. Sara Coleridge. *See* Garden Year, The.
Months, The ("January cold"). Christina Rossetti. *Fr.* Sing-Song. FaPON; RIS
Months, The; a Pageant, *sel.* Christina Rossetti.
October: "I've brought you nuts and hops." BoTP
Months, The. Sheridan. PCH
Months, The. *Unknown.* ChTr
Montoro's Song against Count Alvaro de Luna, High Constable of Castile. Eduardo Marquina, *tr. fr. Spanish by* Dorothea Mackellar. MoAuPo
Montreal. A. M. Klein. CaP
Montreal. William Douw Lighthall. VA
Montrose to His Mistress. James Graham, Marquess of Montrose. *See* My Dear and Only Love.
Montross. Charles Cotton. SeCL
Montserrat. Arthur Symons. PoeT
Monument, The. Elizabeth Bishop. LiTA; MoPo
Monument, A. Charles Madge. FaBoMo
Monument. Pushkin. *See* Unto Myself I Reared a Monument.
Monument. A. M. Sullivan. GoYe
Monument for the Soldiers, A. James Whitcomb Riley. AOAH; DD; MDAH; PoRL
Monument girdled/ in a time so remote from your death. Strophes to a Statue. Eugenio Florit. AnCL
Monument Mountain. Bryant. BeLS; IAP; MOAP; PIAE; REAL
Monument of Cleita, The. Edward Cracroft Lefroy. *Fr.* Echoes from Theocritus. AWP; JAWP; WBP
Monument of Concord Fight, The. Emerson. EV-4
Monument outlasting bronze, The. The Ancient and Modern Muses. Francis Turner Palgrave. VA
Monumental Human Expressions. Emerson. *See* Problem, The.
Monuments Perish. Simonides, *tr. fr. Greek by* T. F. Higham. GrL; OxBG
(Sic Transit, *tr. by* John Addington Symonds.) GrR
Mony ane talks [*or* speaks] o' the grass, the grass. Willie and Earl Richard's Daughter (B *and* C *vers.*). *Unknown.* ESPB
Moo! Robert Hillyer. WhC
Moo-Cow-Moo, The. Edmund Vance Cooke. DDA; FaFP; MoShBr; PTA-1
Mood. Raymond Peckham Holden. CAG
Mood, A. Winifred Howells. AA
Mood. Winifred Kohn. CAG
Mood, A. Amélie Rives. AA
Mood and Figure Bride, A. Juvenal, *tr. fr. Latin by* Dryden. *Fr.* Satires, VI. BeR
Mood from 3000 B.C. Genevieve Taggard. OTPC (1946 ed.)
Moods, The. Fannie Stearns Davis. DDA; HBV
Moods. Leib Kwitko, *tr. fr. Yiddish by* Joseph Leftwich. TrJP
Moods. Edward Rowland Sill. BTP
Moods. Sara Teasdale. SBMV
Moods have laid their hands across my hair, The. The Moods. Fannie Stearns Davis. DDA; HBV
Moody child and wildly wise, A. The Poet. Emerson. AmPo
Moon, The. Azumamaro, *tr. fr. Japanese by* Asataro Miyamori. OnPM
Moon, The. Charles Best. *See* Sonnet of the Moon, A.
Moon, The. Bhasa, *tr. fr. Sanskrit by* A. Berriedale Keith. LiTW
Moon, The. W. H. Davies. AEV; MBP; MoVE; NeMA; POTE; PtOT; StaSt; TCPD; WP
Moon, The. Emily Dickinson. *See* Moon was but a chin of gold, The.
Moon, The. Camilla Doyle. MBP
Moon, The. Eliza Lee Follen. CBPC; HBV; HBVY; MPB; RIS
(Oh, Look at the Moon.) BoTP; OTPC; SAS
Moon, The. Louise Ayres Garnett. SiSoSe
Moon, The. Robert Beverly Hale. SiTL
Moon, The. Oliver Herford. GFA
Moon. Langston Hughes. *Fr.* A House in Taos. CDC
Moon, The. Kotomichi, *tr. fr. Japanese by* Asataro Miyamori. OnPM
Moon. Henry Rowe. OBEV
Moon, The. Sappho, *tr. fr. Greek by* T. F. Higham. GrL; OxBG
Moon, The ("And like a dying lady"). Shelley. BLV; BoLiVe; FaBoCh; LoGBV; OBEV; PIAE
(Waning Moon, The.) AnFE; CBE; CH; ChER; TrGrPo
Moon, The ("Art thou pale for weariness"). Shelley. BLV; BoLiVe; OBEV; PIAE
(Fragment: To the Moon.) EmBrPo; EnRP
(To the Moon.) AnFE; BPN; ChER; EPN; EV-4; GTBS; GTBS-D; GTBS-W; GTSE; GTSL; LoBV; MCCG; OnPM; TrGrPo; ViBoPo
Moon, The. Sir Philip Sidney. *See* Astrophel and Stella: Sonnets, XXXI.
Moon, The. Edith Södergran, *tr. fr. Finnish by* Erik Wahlgren *and* Martin S. Allwood. LiTW
Moon, The. *Unknown.* PCH
("I see the moon.") GoTP; OxNR; TiPo
Moon, The/ Casts the shadow of the plum. Memories of Childhood. Wu Tsung Ai. OnPM; PoHN
Moon a light-hung world of gold, The. Shadows. William Sloane Kennedy. SN
Moon, a sweeping scimitar, dipped in the stormy straits, The. Winged Man. Stephen Vincent Benét. MAP; MoAmPo; VOD
Moon above the milky field, The. Night-Piece. Léonie Adams. MAP; MoAB; MoAmPo
Moon and seven Pleiades have set, The. Alone. Sappho, *tr. by* William Ellery Leonard. AWP
Moon and the Dewdrop, The. *Unknown, tr. fr. Japanese by* Lois J. Erickson. SoLD
Moon and the Night and the Men, The. John Berryman. NeTW; WaP
Moon and the Nightingale, The. Milton. *See* Evening in Paradise.
Moon and Venus. Abul Mughira, *tr. fr. Arabic by* A. J. Arberry. MooP
Moon at full, A: indeed. The Beard. Ibn al-Hajj. MooP
Moon at the Fortified Pass, The. Li Po, *tr. fr. Chinese by* Witter Bynner *and* Kiang Kang-hu. LiTW; WaaP
(Moon over the Mountain Pass, The, *tr. by several hands.*) WhP
Moon-Bathers. John Freeman. TCPD
Moon behind High Tranquil Leaves, The. Robert Nichols. OBMV
Moon between the clouds shines down, The. The Moon and the Dewdrop. *Unknown.* SoLD
Moon-Child, The. "Fiona Macleod." CH; EtS; VLEP
Moon-Children. Michael Lewis. TSW
Moon-Come-Out. Eleanor Farjeon. TiPo
Moon comes every night to peep, The. The White Window. James Stephens. StVeCh; SUS; TiPo
Moon Compasses. Robert Frost. CoV; MoVE
Moon controls her horses, The. Tides. Josephine Williams. PCD
Moon-cradle's rocking and rocking, The. The Ballad of Downal Baun. Padraic Colum. SUS
Moon Daisies. Jacquetta Hawkes. PoN
Moon Festival. Tu Fu, *tr. fr. Chinese by* Kenneth Rexroth. OnPC
Moon fills up its hollow bowl of milk, The. The Postures of Love, V. Alex Comfort. NeBP
Moon, Flowers, Man. Su T'ung-po, *tr. fr. Chinese by* Kenneth Rexroth. OnPC
Moon Folly. Fannie Stearns Davis. *Fr.* Songs of Conn the Fool. CP; NV; RG; SP
Moon Goddess. Ben Jonson. *See* Hymn to Diana.
Moon, grown full now over the sea, The. Looking at the Moon and Thinking of One Far Away. Chang Chiu-ling. ChLP
Moon had climbed the highest hill, The. Mary's Dream. John Lowe. EBSV
Moon had long since sunk behind the mists, The. Dawn. "P. S. M." MCCG
Moon has a halo, there will be wind, The. I Remember the Blue River. Mei Yao Ch'en. OnPC
Moon has gone to her rest, The. A Nocturne. Wilfrid Scawen Blunt. OBMV
Moon has left the sky, The. A Night in Lesbos. George Horton. AA
Moon has made me weary, The. Folly. Vivian Yeiser Laramore. NLK
Moon Has Set, The. Sappho. *See* Night.
Moon has set fire, The. Moon Spell. Elise Aylen. TwCV
Moon hath left the sky, The. Sappho, *tr. fr. Greek by* John Addington Symonds. GrPo
Moon hung naked in a firmament, The. Conclusion. Wordsworth. *Fr.* The Prelude, XIV. ERP
Moon in Eclipse. Ibn Hamdis, *tr. fr. Arabic by* A. J. Arberry. MooP
Moon in heaven's garden, among the clouds that wander. Spinning in April. Josephine Preston Peabody. HBV
Moon, in her pride, once glanced aside, The. The Moon Sings [*or* The Moon's Love]. *Unknown.* OxBoLi; SeCL

Moon in Mist. Ibn Burd, *tr. fr. Arabic by* A. J. Arberry. MooP
Moon, The, is a roustabout! The Roustabout Moon. Dorothy Marie Davis. DDA
Moon is able to command the valley tonight, The. Moist Moon People. Carl Sandburg. MAP; MoAmPo
Moon is as complacent as a frog, The. Autumn Night. Evelyn Scott. AnAmPo; LA
Moon is bright, and the winds are laid, and the river is roaring by, The. In the Moonlight. David McKee Wright. AnNZ; BoAu
Moon is dead, I saw her die, The. The Moon's Funeral. Hilaire Belloc. MoSiPe
Moon is fully risen, The. Der Mond ist aufgegangen [*or* The Mermaidens]. Heine. AWP; OnPM; OuHeWo
Moon is gone, The. Night [*or* Vae Soli]. Sappho. GrL; GrR; OxBG
Moon Is Hiding In, The. E. E. Cummings. AtBAP
Moon is like a big round cheese, The. The Moon. Oliver Herford. GFA
Moon is like a lamp, The. The Weathercock. Rose Fyleman. BoTP
Moon is red through horizon's fog, The. The Shepherd's Hour. Paul Verlaine. AnFP
Moon Is Rising, The. *Unknown, tr. fr. Chinese.* WhP
Moon is round as a jack-o'-lantern, The. Hallowe'en. Frances Frost. TiPo (1959 ed.)
Moon is so high it is, The. I Walk Out into the Country at Night. Lu Yu. OnPC
Moon is soft arising, The. Nightfall. Antonio de Trueba. CAW
Moon is the tongue, The. Sergei Aleksandrovich Yesenin. *Fr.* The Jordan Dove. TrRV
Moon Is to Blood. Richard Duerden. NeAP
Moon Is Up, The. Alfred Noyes. PoeT; ShBV-1
Moon Is Up, The. *Unknown.* NA
Moon is up, and yet it is not night, The. Byron. *Fr.* Childe Harold's Pilgrimage. AnFE
Moon is weaving in the street, The. The Weaving. Harold Lewis Cook. MoSiPe
Moon, The? It is a griffin's egg. Yet Gentle Will the Griffin Be. Vachel Lindsay. MAPA; SP; StVeCh; TSW; TSWC; TwAmPo
Moon It Shines, The. *Unknown, tr. fr. German.* SAS
Moon, like a round device, The. Snow. Madison Cawein. MAP; PFY; SPP
Moon Looked into My Window, The. E. E. Cummings. MOAP
Moon looks down on the forest dim, The. The Cup Reversed. Johan Sebastian Cammermeyer Welhaven. AnNoLy
Moon-Madness. Victor Starbuck. HBMV
Moon Magic. Viscountess Grey of Fallodon. PCH
Moon Magic. Leigh Hanes. StaSt
Moon Mockery. Robert Ervin Howard. DaM
Moon, moon,/ Mak' me a pair o' shoon. *Unknown.* OxNR
Moon, moon shining bright. *Unknown. Fr.* Two Songs. LyMA
Moon, mother of the Sabbath, transfuse your loving. Prayer. César Tiempo. AnCL
Moon-Night. Joseph von Eichendorff, *tr. fr. German by* Mabel Cotterell. AnGP
Moon Now Rises [to Her Absolute Rule], The. Henry David Thoreau. FaBoEn; PoEL-4
Moon of Beauty. Ibn al-Faras, *tr. fr. Arabic by* A. J. Arberry. MooP
Moon of Brooklyn, The. Nathalia Crane. AnAmPo; LA
Moon of Grace. Al-Jazzar, *tr. fr. Arabic by* A. J. Arberry. MooP
Moon of her brow, it is beaming, The. Two Songs in Praise of Steingerd, 1. Cormac Ogmundarson. LiTW
Moon of Loveliness. Mu'tamid, King of Seville, *tr. fr. Arabic by* A. J. Arberry. MooP
Moon of the April night. Advent. Jorge Guillén. CoSP
Moon on the one hand, the dawn on the other, The. The Early Morning. Hilaire Belloc. BMEP; BoTP; GTBS-D; HBMV; HBVY; JKCP; LEAP; POTE; RIS; WaKn
Moon on the Ruined Castle, The. Bansui Tsuchii, *tr. fr. Japanese by* Takamichi Ninomiya *and* D. J. Enright. PoLJ
Moon over the Mountain Pass, The. Li Po. *See* Moon at the Fortified Pass, The.
Moon over the Pass, The. Lu Yu, *tr. fr. Chinese by* Pai Chwen-yu. WhP
Moon resumed all heaven now, The. The Arctic Moon. Joaquin Miller. *Fr.* The Yukon. MAP; MoAmPo (1942 ed.)
Moon, The, revolves outside; possibly, black air. Study in a Late Subway. Muriel Rukeyser. OnHM
Moon Rider. William Rose Benét. YT
Moon rises, The. The red cubs rolling. The Breath of Night. Randall Jarrell. CrMA
Moon seems like a docile sheep, The. The Moon-Sheep. Christopher Morley. UTS
Moon Shadows. Adelaide Crapsey. AnAmPo; LA; NeMA; PFE
Moon shall be a darkness, The. *Unknown.* LO
Moon shears up on Tahoe now, The. The Panther. Edwin Markham. TBM
Moon-Sheep, The. Christopher Morley. UTS
Moon shines bright, The. *Unknown.* OxNR
Moon shines bright, The: in such a night as this. In Such a Night [*or* The Divine Harmony]. Shakespeare. *Fr.* The Merchant of Venice, V, i. ChTr; FiP; GoBC; LiA; WHA
Moon shines bright, The; the stars give a light. May-Day Song. *Unknown.* GoTP
Moon shines clear as silver, The. Sun and Moon. Charlotte Druitt Cole. BoTP
Moon shines down on Flanders' Fields, The. Crosses. Mabel Hicks. PEDC
Moon shines in my body, but my blind eyes cannot see it, The. Songs of Kabir [*or* Two Songs]. Kabir. LiTW; WGRP
Moon shines on the Isle of Inishtrahull, The. Dawn in Inishtrahull. D. J. O'Sullivan. OnYI
Moon Ship, The. *Unknown, tr. fr. Japanese.* GFA
Moon Shone Bright, The; or, The Bellman. *Unknown.* AnEC
Moon silvers the bay, she waxes, she wanes, The. The Eternal Kinship. Maurice E. Peloubet. GoYe
Moon Sings, The. *Unknown.* OxBoLi
(Moon's Love, The.) SeCL
Moon, So Round and Yellow. Matthias Barr. GFA; HBV; HBVY; OTPC
Moon Solo. Jules Laforgue, *tr. fr. French by* William Jay Smith. AnFP
Moon Song. Hilda Conkling. SP; TiPo
Moon Song. Claude McKay. *See* Song of the Moon, A.
Moon Song. Mildred Plew Meigs. GoBP
Moon Spell. Elise Aylen. TwCV
Moon, that mirror bright, The. Moon in Mist. Ibn Burd. MooP
Moon . . . the moon . . . the moon . . . the moon, The. The Old Coon-Dog Dreams. Kenneth Porter. GoTP
Moon, thou with thy light. *Unknown, tr. fr. Spanish by* Eleanor L. Turnbull. TeCS
Moon was but a chin of gold, The. The Moon. Emily Dickinson. BoChLi; BoTP
Moon was languishing, The. Dreamy Seraphim. Apparition. Stéphane Mallarmé. AnFP
Moon was like a boat one night, The. Three Hours. Vachel Lindsay. ATP
Moon was round, The. The Whisperer. James Stephens. WGRP
Moon was shady, and soft airs, The. The Dog and the Water-Lily. William Cowper. CG; EV-3; OAEP
Moon was shining silver bright, The. Old Dan Tucker. *Unknown.* TrAS
Moon was up, the lake was shining clear, The. Wordsworth. *Fr.* The Prelude. FaBoEn
Moon wedded the Sun, The. Sun, Moon and Thunder. *Unknown.* OnPM
Moon, which earthward turns her radiant face, The. Man's Hidden Side. Nathan Haskell Dole. BAP
Moon-white waters wash and leap, The. The Coves of Crail. "Fiona Macleod." VA
Moon will run all consciences to cover, The. Ditty. Allen Tate. MOAP
Moon with sharpen'd horns looks coldly bright, The. The Frost at Sea. William Diaper. *Fr.* Nereides; or, Sea-Eclogues. BeR
Moon, worn thin to the width of a quill. Moon's Ending. Sara Teasdale. ChMo; CMP
Moon Worshippers, The. Eric Robertson Dodds. GTIV; POTE
Moonbeam. Hilda Conkling. BrR
Moonbeam floateth from the skies, A. Orkney Lullaby. Eugene Field. GoTP
Moonbeams. Carl David af Wirsén, *tr. fr. Swedish by* Charles W. Stork. AnSL
Moonbeams kelter i the lift, The. The Man in the Moon. "Hugh MacDiarmid." NeBP
Moonbeams over Arno's vale in silvery flood were pouring, The. The Veery. Henry van Dyke. AA; BLA; LBAP; OBAV
Moone-Calfe, The, *sel.* Michael Drayton.
"It was not long e're he perceiv'd the skies." PoEL-2
Mooni. Henry Clarence Kendall. BoAu; OBEV; OBVV
Moonless night—a friendly one, A. Running the Batteries. Herman Melville. PaA; PAH
Moonlight. Walter de la Mare. EnLoPo
Moonlight, The. Ann Hawkshaw. BoTP
Moonlight. Verner von Heidenstam, *tr. fr. Swedish by* Charles W. Stork. AnSL
Moonlight. Edward Moxon. OBRV
Moonlight. Philodemus of Gadara, *tr. fr. Greek by* Walter Headlam. OxBG
(Moonlit Love, *tr. by* F. L. Lucas.) GrPE
("Shine, twy-horned Lady of the Night, shine on!" *tr. by* the Earl of Cromer.) GrPo

Moonlight. Shakespeare. *See* How Sweet the Moonlight Sleeps upon This Bank.
Moonlight. Jacques Tahureau, *tr. fr. French by* Andrew Lang. AWP
Moonlight. James Thomson. *Fr.* The Seasons: Autumn. BeR
Moonlight, *with music. Unknown.* AS
Moonlight. Maud E. Uschold. StVeCh (1955 ed.)
Moonlight. Lord Vansittart. NeTW
Moonlight. Paul Verlaine. *See* Clair de lune.
Moonlight. Nils Collett Vogt, *tr. fr. Norwegian by* Charles W. Stork. AnNoLy
Moonlight and Music. Shakespeare. *See* How Sweet the Moonlight Sleeps upon This Bank.
Moonlight bends over black silence. Minna. Maxwell Bodenheim. MAPA
Moonlight breaks upon the city's domes [*or* city towers], The. A Song of the Moon [*or* Moon Song]. Claude McKay. PoNe; TSW
Moonlight filled them both with sundry glamors, The. Et Sa Pauvre Chair. Alec Brock Stevenson. HBMV
Moonlight in Autumn. James Thomson. *Fr.* The Seasons: Autumn. OBEC
Moonlight in Italy. Elizabeth Clementine Kinney. AA
Moonlight in Summer. Robert Bloomfield. LPS-2
Moonlight is a gentle thing, The. The Moonlight. Ann Hawkshaw. BoTP
Moonlight is shining, The. Mother Moon. Amelia Josephine Burr. TVC; TVSH; WHL
Moonlight Music. Shakespeare. *See* How Sweet the Moonlight Sleeps upon This Bank.
Moonlight Night on the Port. Sidney Keyes. PoD
Moonlight North and South. Robert Fuller Murray. BSV; EBSV
Moonlight on Lake Sydenham. Wilson MacDonald. CaP
Moonlight on the Han River. Su T'ung-po, *tr. fr. Chinese by* Henry H. Hart. PoHN
Moonlight on the Prairie. Longfellow. *Fr.* Evangeline, I. LPS-2
Moonlight on the West Tower. Pao Ssu Hsien, *tr. fr. Chinese by* Henry H. Hart. PoHN
Moonlight silvers the [shaken] tops of trees. Nocturne of Remembered Spring. Conrad Aiken. ChMo; CMP; HBMV
Moonlight Song of the Mocking-Bird. William Hamilton Hayne. AA
Moonlight, Waterlight and Opal. Norman Cameron. MoP
Moonlit Apples. John Drinkwater. BoTP; OBMV; PoRA; TCPD
Moonlit Doorway, The. Kenneth Mackenzie. MoAuPo
Moonlit Love. Philodemus of Gadara. *See* Moonlight.
Moonlit Night. Vladimir Mayakovsky, *tr. fr. Russian by* Babette Deutsch. TrRV
Moonpoison, mullock of sacrifice. Joseph Gordon Macleod. *Fr.* The Ecliptic: Cancer, or, The Crab. NeBP
Moonrise. John Cunningham. *Fr.* Contemplation; a Night Piece. RO
Moonrise. Hilda Doolittle ("H. D."). NP
Moonrise. Annette von Droste-Hülshoff, *tr. fr. German by* Herman Salinger. AnGP
Moonrise. Abbie Huston Evans. NP
Moonrise. Gerard Manley Hopkins. MBP; MoAB; MoBrPo; SeCePo
Moonrise. D. H. Lawrence. GTBS-W; LiTM; NP; TriL
Moonrise. Frank Dempster Sherman. AA
Moonrise in City Park. Josephine Miles. FiMAP
Moonrise in the Rockies. Ella Higginson. AA
Moons. David Morton. MuM
Moon's a devil jester, A. The Traveler. Vachel Lindsay. MoAmPo; NeMA
Moon's a holy owl-queen, The. What Grandpa Mouse Said. Vachel Lindsay. UTS
Moon's a little arch, The. A Classic Case. Gilbert Sorrentino. NeAP
Moon's a little prairie-dog, The. What the Rattlesnake Said. Vachel Lindsay. TSW; TSWC
Moon's a peck of corn, The. The Old Horse in the City. Vachel Lindsay. UTS
Moon's a steaming chalice, The. What Semiramis Said. Vachel Lindsay. MAPA; TwAmPo
Moon's Ending. Sara Teasdale. ChMo; CMP
Moon's Funeral, The. Hilaire Belloc. MoSiPe
Moon's glow by seven fold multiplied, turned red. After Reading St. John the Divine. Gene Derwood. LiTM; NePA
Moon's greygolden [*or* soft golden] meshes make, The. Alone. James Joyce. InvP; NP
Moon's Love, The. *Unknown. See* Moon Sings, The.
Moon's my constant mistress, The. Tom o' Bedlam ['s Song]. *Unknown.* CH; FaBoCh; LO; LoGBV; ShBV-4; WaKn
Moon's on the lake, and the mist's on the brae, The. MacGregor's Gathering. Sir Walter Scott. AnFE; BrBE; EBSV; EmBrPo; PoFr
Moon's Orchestra, The. John Gould Fletcher. Down the Mississippi, IV. ChMo; LaNeLa; LiTA
Moon's set, and Pleiads. Forsaken. Sappho. GrPE
Moon's Ship, The. Hitomaro, *tr. fr. Japanese by* Ishii *and* Obata. OnPM
Moon's soft golden meshes make, The. *See* Moon's greygolden meshes make, The.
Moon's the North Wind's Cooky, The. Vachel Lindsay. BoChLi; BrR; ChMo; CMP; FaFP; FaPON; GoTP; PoRh; SP; StVeCh; SUS; TSW; TSWC
Moonshine. Walter de la Mare. FiBHP
Moonshiner, The. Madison Cawein. *Fr.* The Mountain Still. SPP
Moonspath. Don Carlos Pamplin. CAG
Moonstar, The. Dante Gabriel Rossetti. The House of Life, XXIX. PoVP; ViPo
Moony Thin Desolation, A. Sergei Aleksandrovich Yesenin, *tr. fr. Russian by* Babette Deutsch. TrRV
Moor, The. Ralph Hodgson. MBP; MoBrPo
Moorish King rides up and down, The. Alhama [*or* Ay de mi Alhama *or* The Moorish King Who Lost Alhama]. *Unknown, tr. by* Byron. AnSpL-1; LH; LyMA; TeCS
Moorland Night. Charlotte Mew. BrBE; ChMP; MM; TwCV; ViBoPo
Moorland waste lay hushed in the dusk of the second day, The. Le Mauvais Larron. Rosamund Marriott Watson. VA
Moorlands of the Not. *Unknown.* NA
Moors, Angels, Civil Wars. Keith Sinclair. AnNZ
Moors, the Ethiops, and the Arabs then, The. Tasso. *Fr.* Jerusalem Delivered, XX. PrPoCR
Moosehead Lake, *with music. Unknown.* OuSiCo
Mopoke. Louis Lavater. NeLNL
Moppsikon Floppsikon Bear, The. Edward Lear. *See* Limerick: "There was an old person of Ware."
Moraima. *Unknown, tr. fr. Spanish by* George Ticknor. AnSpL-1
Moral, The. Robert Kelley Weeks. PR
Moral Alphabet, A. *sel.* Hilaire Belloc.
Gnu, The. BMEP
Moral Bully, The. Oliver Wendell Holmes. AnAmPo; AnNE; LA
Moral Cosmetics. Horace Smith. LPS-2
Moral Essays, *sels.* Pope.
"As hags hold sabbaths, not for joy but spite," *fr.* Epistle II. ExPo
As the Twig Is Bent, *2 ll., fr.* Epistle I. TreF
Characters of Women; Flavia, Atossa, and Cloe, *fr.* Epistle II. OBEC
Chloe, *fr.* Epistle II. AWP; JAWP; WBP
(Characters from the Satires: Chloe.) InPo
Coxcomb Bird, The, *fr.* Epistle I. LiTB; RiBV; SiTL
Death of Buckingham, The, *fr.* Epistle III. FiP
(Death of the Duke of Buckingham, The.) ExPo
(Duke of Buckingham, The.) OBEC
(Second Duke of Buckingham, The.) CoEV
Gem and the Flower, The, *fr.* Epistle I. OBEC
Heaven's Last Best Work, *fr.* Epistle II. OBEC
Man of Ross, The, *fr.* Epistle III. CoBE
Of the Use of Riches, Epistle IV. EiPP; PoEL-3
(On Riches.) TwP
Reverend Sire, A, *fr.* Epistle I. BeR
Ruling Passion, The, *fr.* Epistle I. BOHV, *br. sel.*; LPS-3, *abr.*
("Search then the Ruling Passion.") ViBoPo
Sir Balaam. *fr.* Epistle III. MaPo
Timon's Villa, *fr.* Epistle IV. CoEV; MaPo; OBEC
(At Timon's Villa.) ExPo
(Satire on Riches.) PoLi
To a Lady; of the Characters of Women, *fr.* Epistle II. OxBoLi; SiTL
("Nothing so true as what you once let fall," *longer sel.*) FaBoEn
(Of the Characters of Women, *longer sel.*) PoFS
Wharton, *fr.* Epistle I. AWP; JAWP; WBP
(Characters from the Satires: Wharton.) InPo
Woman's Ruling Passions, *fr.* Epistle II. OBEC
"Yes, you despise the man to books confin'd," Epistle I. CEP
Moral in Sèvres, A. Mildred Howells. AA; HBV; PR
Moral Responsibility. Dante, *tr. fr. Italian by* Jefferson Butler Fletcher. *Fr.* Divina Commedia: Purgatorio. XVI. GrCo-2
Moral Song. John Farrar. RAR
Moral Story II. David Wright. ChMP
Moral Tetrastich, A. Sir William Jones. *See* Baby, The.
Moral to "The Grumbling Hive," The. Bernard Mandeville. *Fr.* The Grumbling Hive; or, Knaves Turn'd Honest. BeR
Moral Warfare, The. Whittier. AnNE; CoV; IAP; PEOR; PoFr
Morality. Matthew Arnold. BMEP; BPN; EM-2; EmBrPo; EPN; EPP; GEPC; GTBS; GTSL; HBV; LEAP; PoVP; TOP; ViPo; ViPP; VLEP
"We cannot kindle when we will," *st.* 1. BLP; MaRV, *sts.* 1-2; OQP; QP-2
(Tasks in Hours of Insight Willed.) GrCo-1

Morando, the Tritameron of Love, *sel.* Robert Greene.
Fickle Seat Whereon Proud Fortune Sits, The. ReIE
More about People. Ogden Nash. Po
More Advice. Earl of Roscommon. *Fr.* An Essay on Translated Verse. BeR
More Ancient Mariner, A. Bliss Carman. NLK; SN; VA
More Animals. Oliver Herford.
Cow, The. NA
Hen, The. LBN; NA
More ballads! here's a spick and span new supplication. A Free Parliament Litany. *Unknown.* OxBoLi
More beautiful and soft than any moth. The Landscape near an Aerodrome. Stephen Spender. AnEnPo; AnFE; CoBMV; EnLit; LiTM; MBP; MoAB; MoBrPo; MoVE; OAEP (2d ed.); PoLFOT; ReMP; ShBV-4; WoL
More beautiful than any gift you gave. The Token. F. T. Prince. FaBoTw
More bleakly stricken, when I'm gone, she'll bend. My Mother. Nikolai Tikhonov. RuPo
More brightly must my spirit shine. The Spirit's Grace. Janie Screven Heyward. HBMV
More closely than the clinging vine. Pierre de Ronsard. *Fr.* Les Amours Diverses. PrPoCR
More Cruel Than War. W. S. Hawkins. PTA-2
(Your Letter, Lady, Came Too Late.) BlG
More discontents I never had. Discontents in Devon. Robert Herrick. EM-1; EPS; OAEP; ReEn; SeCV-1; SeEP
More Dissemblers besides Women, *sel.* Thomas Middleton. "Come, my dainty doxies," *fr.* IV, i. ElSeCe; TuPP
More Dullness. Earl of Rochester. *Fr.* Julian. BeR
More famed than Rome, as splendid as old Greece. My America. Thomas Curtis Clark. OQP; PEDC; QP-1
More Gold than Gold. "Michael Field." *See* Gold.
More Hair. Samuel Hoffenstein. SiTL
More haughty than the rest, the wolfish race. The Presbyterians. Dryden. *Fr.* The Hind and the Panther, I. OBS
More he strives to injure me, The. Clemency. Ibn al-Hajj. MooP
More humane Mikado never, A. The Humane Mikado [*or* The Mikado's Song]. W. S. Gilbert. *Fr.* The Mikado. ALV; LiTB; PoVP; SiTL
More ill at ease was never man than Walbach, that Lord's day. The Legend of Walbach Tower. George Houghton. PAH
More Impressions. "Oscuro Wildgoose." PA
More Letters Found near a Suicide. Frank Horne. *See* To James.
More Life . . . More! Lee Wilson Dodd. PC
More Light Shall Break from Out Thy Word. Allen Eastman Cross. MaRV
More Love or More Disdain. Thomas Carew. *See* Mediocrity in Love Rejected.
More Love or More Disdain. Charles Webbe. *See* Against Indifference.
More Lovely Grows the Earth. Helena Coleman. CaP; CPG; OCL
More lovely than the rose. Christmas Night. Marion Lochhead. MaRV
More marvels have occurred in Britain than in any other country that I know of. Sir Gawain and the Green Knight. *Unknown.* EnL
More my own poor wishes would commend me, The. Sonnet. Petrarch. Sonnets to Laura: To Laura in Life, CVIII. PoFr
More of Thee. Horatius Bonar. BLRP
More oft than once Death whispered in mine ear. Redeem Time Past. William Drummond of Hawthornden. EV-2
More out of dearest duty now than joy. Breviary on the Subway. Leonard McCarthy. JKCP (1955 ed.)
More paper blackened with more signatures. The Night There Was Dancing in the Streets. Elder Olson. NePA
More pleasing were these sweet delights. Francis Beaumont. *Fr.* The Masque of the Inner-Temple and Gray's Inne. OBS
More Power to Cromwell. Egan O'Rahilly, *tr. fr. Modern Irish by* P. S. Dinneen *and* T. O'Donoghue. OnYI
More rain has fallen this winter. Weather. Mary Ursula Bethell. AnNZ
More rapid than hail. Yosano Akiko, *tr. fr. Japanese by* Kenneth Rexroth. LiTW
More shower than shine. Valentines to My Mother, 1880. Christina Rossetti. DD; MOAH
More shy than the shy violet. Quaker Ladies. Ellen Mackay Hutchinson Cortissoz. AA
More soft than press of baby lips. Pussy-Willows. Arthur Guiterman. OTPC (1946 ed.); VOD
More Sonnets at Christmas. Allen Tate. LiTA; LiTM; NePA; WaP
Again the Native Hour Lets Down the Locks, *sel.* PeBoSo; PreP
More Stately Mansions. Oliver Wendell Holmes. *See* Chambered Nautilus, The.
More Strong than Time. Victor Hugo, *tr. fr. French by* Andrew Lang. AWP; JAWP; WBP
(Vase, The, *tr. by* Alan Conder.) TrFP
More than a Hundred. Tien Ch'ien, *tr. fr. Chinese by* Chu Chun-i. WhP
More than a year has passed. Good News. Lin I Ning. ChLP; PoHN
More than Flowers We Have Brought. Nancy Byrd Turner. SiSoSe
More than half beaten, but fearless. Battle Cry. John G. Neihardt. BAP; HBMV
More than honey the words you speak are sweet. Popular Sicilian Love Songs, 2. *Unknown.* LyPI
More than Most Fair. Fulke Greville. Caelica, III. ElL; SiCE
(To His Lady.) OBSC
More than most fair[e], full of the living fire. Amoretti, VIII. Spenser. BLV; BoLiVe; EPP; HBV; OAEP; PeBoSo; TrGrPo
"More than my brothers are to me." In Memoriam A. H. H., LXXIX. Tennyson. EM-2; EmBrPo; EnLi-2; EPN; GEPC; OAEP; ViPo; VLEP
More than Quit. Martial. *See* Epigram: "To John I owed great obligation."
More than the Moment. Sister Claude of Jesus. JKCP (1955 ed.)
More than the soul of ancient song is given. The Poet of To-Day. "Grace Greenwood." LPS-3
More than those. Rosa Nascosa. Maurice Hewlett. OBVV
More than two crosses stand on either side. Ave Crux, Spes Unica! Edward Shillito. ChIP; MaRV; OQP; QP-2
More than We Ask. Faith Wells. BLRP
More things are wrought by prayer. Prayer. Tennyson. *Fr.* Idylls of the King *and* Morte d'Arthur. BLRP; OQP; PraP; QP-1; TreF; WGRP
More throughly human nature. Friendship. Simon Dach. BoFr
"More to instruct thee, when five years shall end." *Unknown. Fr.* Homeric Hymns. GrPo
More Walks. "Thomas Ingoldsby." BOHV
More Ways to Kill. James Shirley. *See* Victorious Men of Earth.
More we live, more brief appear, The. The River of Life. Thomas Campbell. BSV; EBSV; FaFP; GTBS; GTBS-D; GTBS-W; GTSE; GTSL; HBV; LiTB; LiTG; LPS-3
More white than whitest lilies far. To Electra. Robert Herrick. ExPo
More years ago than I can state. My Last Illusion. John Kendall. FiBHP; WhC
Moreover, brethren, I declare unto you the gospel. Death and the Resurrection of the Dead. First Corinthians, Bible, *N.T.* EM-1
Moreton Miles, *sel.* William Baylebridge.
"Wherever I go, I do no wrong," LIV. BoAV
Morgan. Edmund Clarence Stedman. AA; HBV; OBAV
Morgan Oakley. Edgar Lee Masters. *Fr.* The New Spoon River. LEAP
Morgan Stanwood. Hiram Rich. PAH
Morgana. Gabriele d'Annunzio, *tr. fr. Italian by* L. R. Lind. LiTW
Morgan's Country. Francis Webb. BoAV
Morgante maggiore, Il, *sels.* Luigi Pulci, *tr. fr. Italian.*
Appeal for Illumination, *fr.* I, *tr. by* Byron. ISi
Prophecy. BoHiPo; PAH
Morgunok listened. His grand-dad said. Aleksandr Tvardovsky. *Fr.* The Land of Muravia. RuPo
Morisco, A. Jasper Fisher. *Fr.* Fuimus Troes. SeCL; TuPP
(Song; a Morisko.) SeEP
Moritura. Margaret Gilman Davidson. AA
Morituri Salutamus. Longfellow. CoBA; IAP
"For age is opportunity no less," *sel.* PoToHe (new ed.)
(Age Is Opportunity.) QP-2
Moriturus. Edna St. Vincent Millay. AnAmPo; GTBS-W; LA; LiTA; NAMP
Mormon Bishop's Lament, The. *Unknown.* CoSo; CSF
Mormon Immigrant Song, A. *At. to* George A. Hicks. CoSo
(Mormon Song, A.) CSF
Morn. Helen Hunt Jackson. AA
Morn, all beauteous to behold, The. Aeschylus. *Fr.* Persians. GrPo
Morn and noon of day and even, human ebb and flow. The Grave of Lawrence. Clinton Scollard. GA
Morn comes freshly from the east, The. John Francis O'Donnell. *Fr.* Adare. IrPN
Morn follows morn, and day succeeds to day. Ammianus, *tr. fr. Greek by* the Earl of Cromer. GrPo
Morn is cold, The. A whiteness newly-brought. Frost-Morning. William Alexander. IrPN
Morn of life is past, The. My Old Dog Tray. Stephen Collins Foster. OlF
Morn of the year, of day and May the prime! May-Day on Magdalen Tower. Thomas Herbert Warren. OBVV

Morn of winds and swaying trees, A. Song of the Summer Days. George Macdonald. BSV
Morn offers him her flasked light. The Poet's Bread. Charles L. O'Donnell. LEAP
Morn was cloudy and dark and gray, The. The Battle of Morris' Island. *Unknown.* PAH
Morn was fresh, and pure the gale, The. Mary Will Smile. William Cliffton. BAV
Morn when first it thunders in March, The. Old Pictures in Florence. Robert Browning. BPN; EmBrPo; GEPC; PoVP; VLEP
Morna's Hill, *sel.* James Stuart.
Distant Prospect of the City of Armagh, A. IrPN
Morning. Konstantin Balmont, *tr. fr. Russian by* C. M. Bowra. BoRS
Morning. James Beattie. *See* But Who the Melodies of Morn Can Tell?
Morning. Blake. BLV; BoLiVe; EG; FaBoCh; LoBV; LoGBV; OBRV
(Spirit's Warfare, The.) CBE
Morning. Charles Stuart Calverley. FiBHP
Morning. Chu Shu Chen, *tr. fr. Chinese by* Kenneth Rexroth. OnPC
Morning. John Clare. RO
Morning. Hilda Conkling. NP
Morning. John Cunningham. LPS-2
Morning. Sir William Davenant. *See* Lark Now Leaves His Wat'ry Nest, The.
Morning. Emily Dickinson. *See* Will there really be a morning?
Morning. Ivy O. Eastwick. BoTP
Morning. Dorothy Hamilton Gallagher. SiSoSe
Morning, A. Theodosia Garrison. NLK
Morning, The. John Gay. *See* On Walking the Streets by Day.
Morning. Thomas Heywood. *See* Pack, Clouds, Away.
Morning. Keats. *Fr.* Imitation of Spenser. GN
Morning. John Keble. OBRV
Morning. Mikhail Lukonin, *tr. fr. Russian by* Jack Lindsay. RuPo
Morning. Hugh McCrae. BoAV
Morning. José Manuel Martínez de Navarrete, *tr. fr. Spanish by* Samuel Beckett. AnMP
Morning. Thomas Otway. *Fr.* The Orphan. EV-3
Morning. John Crowe Ransom. LS
Morning. Henry Reed. MoVE; NeBP
Morning. Arthur Rimbaud, *tr. fr. French by* William M. Davis. AnFP
Morning. Johan Ludvig Runeberg, *tr. fr. Swedish by* Charles W. Stork. AnSL
Morning. Philip Henry Savage. AA
Morning. Shelley. *Fr.* Prometheus Unbound. ShBV-3
Morning. Viggo Stuckenberg, *tr. fr. Danish by* Charles W. Stork. BoDS
Morning. Jane Taylor. HBV
Morning. Sara Teasdale. NP
Morning. Haroutune Toumanian, *tr. fr. Armenian by* Zabelle C. Boyajian. ArmLP
Morning. Jones Very. AnNE; APW
Morning. Samuel Waddington. OBVV
Morning. Wang Wei, *tr. fr. Chinese.* WhP
Morning After, The. Dorothy Wellesley. OBMV
Morning again, nothing has to be done. Second Poem. Peter Orlovsky. NeAP
Morning Air. Jami, *tr. fr. Persian by* Sir William Jones. PeP
Morning and Evening. Philip P. Frost. CAG
Morning and evening. Goblin Market. Christina Rossetti. AnFE; AtBAP; BoTP; DaM; EmBrPo; EV-5; GoTL; OAEP; OnSP; PCN; PoVP; TCEP; ViP; ViPo; VLEP
Morning and Evening. Antoni Slonimski, *tr. fr. Polish by* Watson Kirkconnell. TrJP
Morning and evening, sleep she drove away. The Spinning Woman. Leonidas of Tarentum. AWP; JAWP; WBP
Morning and Evening Star. Plato, *tr. fr. Greek by* Shelley. AWP; JAWP; WBP
(Aster.) LiA; LiTW; OxBG
(Star.) OnPM; WoL
("Thou wert the morning star among the living.") GrPo
(To Aster.) GrL
(To Stella.) EnLoPo; InPo; ViBoPo
Morning, and streaks of heavenly blue. London Spring. Antoni Slonimski. TrJP
Morning at Arnheim. William Jay Smith. NePoEA
Morning at Chien-wei River. Tu Mu, *tr. fr. Chinese by* Yuan K'o-chia. WhP
Morning at the Beach. John Farrar. RIS
Morning at the Window. T. S. Eliot. AmPP; AnEnPo; ChMo; CMP; CoBA; InPo; JAWP; MAP; MoAmPo (1942 ed.); MOAP; NeMA; NePA; OnPM; WBP
Morning Bell of Fang T'a, The. Hsi P'ei Lan, *tr. fr. Chinese by* Henry H. Hart. OnPM; PoHN; WoL
Morning Bells. Georges Rodenbach, *tr. fr. French by* Alan Conder. TrFP
Morning Bird. Louis Untermeyer. BLA
Morning Breaks, The. John Oxenham. OQP; QP-1
(Coming Day, The.) MaRV
Morning breaks like a pomegranate, The. Wedding Morn. D. H. Lawrence. MBP; MoAB; MoBrPo
Morning Bus. John Coulter. CaP
Morning came at me like a flung snowball. Puerto Rican Side-Street. Louis Dudek. TwCaPo
Morning came up as other mornings came. Grubber's Day. Jay G. Sigmund. AnAmPo; LA
Morning Clouds. Nellie Burget Miller. GFA
Morning Comes, The. Blake. *Fr.* America. RO
(Empire Is No More.) EnRP
Morning comes to consciousness, The. Preludes, II. T. S. Eliot. AnAmPo; BAV; BoLiVe (1945 ed.); CoBA; InP; LA; LiTA; LiTM; OBMV; ReMP; UnPo; VOD (1935 ed.)
Morning Concert—Nantucket. Isabel Harriss Barr. JKCP (1955 ed.)
Morning Dreams. Mary Elizabeth Coleridge. AlDL
Morning Drum-Call [on My Eager Ear], The. Robert Louis Stevenson. EPN; TCEP
Morning, evening, noon and night. The Boy and the Angel. Robert Browning. BMEP; EmBrPo; EOAH; EV-5; GEPC; MW; OTPC; PoVP; TCEP; VLEP
Morning Express. Siegfried Sassoon. HaMV; ShBV-3
Morning Fancy. Mary McNeil Fenollosa. AA
Morning-Glories. Basho, *tr. fr. Japanese by* H. G. Henderson. OnPM
Morning-Glory, The. Florence Earle Coates. BAP; HBV
Morning-Glory, The. Maria White Lowell. AA; HBV; LPS-1
Morning Glory. Siegfried Sassoon. ChMo; CMP; TwCV
Morning Glory, The. *Unknown, tr. fr. Chinese by* Helen Waddell. *Fr.* Shi King. AWP; JAWP; WBP
Morning-glory, climbing the morning long, The. Indiana. Hart Crane. *Fr.* The Bridge: Powhatan's Daughter. AnFE; CoAnAm; LiTA; TwAmPo
Morning glory climbs above my head, The. The Morning Glory. *Unknown. Fr.* Shi King. AWP; JAWP; WBP
Morning glow creeps over, The. The Call of Spring. Shih Ch'eng Le. PoHN
Morning Hair. *Unknown, tr. fr. Japanese by* Ishii *and* Obata. OnPM
Morning has broken. A Morning Song. Eleanor Farjeon. AlDL
Morning Hymn, *abr.* Cecil Frances Alexander. OTPC
Morning Hymn. Joseph Beaumont. OxBoCh; TrPWD
Morning Hymn. St. Gregory the Great, *tr. fr. Latin by* Edward Caswall. CAW; WGRP
Morning Hymn. Thomas Ken. FaFP; MaRV; OBS, *abr.;* OTPC; TreFS
(Awake, My Soul.) OxBoCh
Morning Hymn, A. Charles Wesley. CEP; CoEV; OBEC; PoEL-3; TrPWD
(Christ, Whose Glory Fills the Skies.) OxBoCh
(Hymn: "Christ, whose glory fills the skies.") OlF
Morning Hymn in Paradise. Milton. *See* Adam's Morning Hymn.
Morning Hymn of Adam and Eve. Milton. *See* Adam's Morning Hymn.
Morning in Camp. Herbert Bashford. AA; BAP; POT
Morning in May. Chaucer. *Fr.* The Canterbury Tales: The Knight's Tale. LPS-2
(Dawn, 6 *ll.*) CBOV
Morning in Spring. Louis Ginsberg. GoYe
Morning in the Bay of Naples. John Todhunter. *Fr.* Laurella. TIP
Morning in the Market. Nora Archibald Smith. VOD
Morning in the North-West. Arthur Stringer. CaP; OCL
Morning in the Park. John Ciardi. MiAP
Morning is bright and sunlit, and the west wind running smoothly, The. Message to the Bard. William Livingston. GoTS
Morning is cheery, my boys, arouse, The! Reveille. Michael O'Connor. AA; HBV; MDAH
Morning is clean and blue, and the wind blows up the clouds, The. Irradiations, XXII. John Gould Fletcher. LA; MAP; NePA; NP
Morning is the gate of day, The. The Sentinel. Annie Johnson Flint. BLRP; MaRV; OQP; PraP; QP-2
Morning Light. Mary Effie Lee Newsome. CDC; PoNe
Morning light falls gently on the eyes, The. The Daily Task. "Marianne Farningham." PEOR
Morning Light for One with Too Much Luck, The. Delmore Schwartz. FiMAP
Morning Light Is Breaking, The. Samuel F. Smith. OlF; WGRP
(Daybreak.) BLRP
Morning Light Song. Philip Lamantia. NeAP
Morning Lullaby, A. J. A. Coll. BOL
Morning Meditations. Thomas Hood. LPS-3
Morning Mist, The. Robert Southey. OTPC

Morning mists still haunt the stony street, The. Enter Patient. W. E. Henley. *Fr.* In Hospital. BPN; PoVP
Morning now right earlily in dew, The. Morning. John Clare. RO
Morning of a cold month, The. The International Brigade Arrives at Madrid. "Pablo Neruda." WaaP
Morning of May, A. *Unknown. See* In Summer.
Morning of the winter's, The. Leaping Falls. Galway Kinnell. NePoAm-2
Morning, on a beach. A man & woman sitting by fire. Moon Is to Blood. Richard Duerden. NeAP
Morning on the Lievre. Archibald Lampman. CPG; MM
Morning on the misty highlands. Sandpipers. Helen Merrill Egerton. CaP; CPG; OCL
Morning Overture; Chorus of Dogs. Pearl Strachan. GoTP
Morning Porches, The. Donald Hall. NePoAm-2
Morning Prayer. Ch'eng Tsung Lo, *tr. fr. Chinese by* Henry H. Hart. PoHN
Morning Prayer ("A lowly woman"). Utako Hayashi, *tr. fr. Japanese by* Lois J. Erickson. SoLD
Morning Prayer ("I waken in the early dawn"). Utako Hayashi, *tr. fr. Japanese by* Lois J. Erickson. SoLD
Morning Prayer. Calvin W. Laufer. PraP
Morning Prayer. *Unknown.* PoToHe
Morning Prayer. *At. to* Rebecca J. Weston. *See* Prayer, A: "Father, we thank Thee for the night."
Morning Prayer, A. Ella Wheeler Wilcox. MaRV; OQP; PoToHe; QP-2
Morning Prayers. *Unknown.* PraP
Morning Purples All the Sky, The. Roman Breviary, *tr. fr. Latin.* BePJ
Morning rain of Wei city wets the white dust, The. A Song for Wei City. Wang Wei. WhP
Morning Sea. C. P. Cavafy, *tr. fr. Modern Greek by* Rae Dalven. MoGP
Morning Serenade. Madison Cawein. *See* Aubade.
Morning Shower, A. J. S. Ling, *tr. fr. Chinese by* E. Powys Mathers. ChLP
Morning sits outside afraid, The. Night and Morning. Dorothy Aldis. YeAr
Morning Song. Joanna Baillie. *See* Good Morning.
Morning Song. Karle Wilson Baker. BAP; HBMV; PCD
Morning-Song. George Darley. *Fr.* Sylvia; or, The May Queen. VA
(Serenade: "Awake thee, my lady-love.") HBV
Morning Song. Sir William Davenant. *See* Lark Now Leaves His Wat'ry Nest, The.
Morning Song, A. Eleanor Farjeon. AlDL
Morning Song. Afanasi Afanasievich Fet, *tr. fr. Russian by* Max Eastman. AWP
Morning Song. John Fletcher. *Fr.* The Faithful Shepherdess, V, i. EV-2
Morning Song. Solomon ibn Gabirol, *tr. fr. Hebrew by* Nina Davis Salaman. TrJP
Morning Song. Lancaster Pollard. NLK
Morning Song, A. Shakespeare. *See* Hark! Hark! the Lark.
Morning Song. Johan Skjoldborg, *tr. fr. Danish by* Charles W. Stork. BoDS
Morning Song. Kurt M. Stein. FiBHP
Morning Song for Imogen, A. Shakespeare. *See* Hark! Hark! the Lark.
Morning Song of Senlin. Conrad Aiken. *Fr.* Senlin; a Biography, Pt. II, ii. AmP; CBOV; ChMo; CMP; HBMV; LiTA; LiTM; MOAP; NV; OxBA; PoTo; ReMP; SBMV
(Morning Song.) InP; MAP; MoAB; MoAmPo; NeMA; NP; PIAE; TrGrPo; WoL
(Senlin; a Biography.) PoMa
Morning Sprite, The. Clinton H. Collester. CAG
Morning Star, The. Emily Brontë. ChTr
Morning Star. James J. Galvin. ISi
Morning Star, The. John Hall. SeCL
Morning Star. Reginald Heber. *See* Brightest and Best of the Sons of the Morning.
Morning star is paling, The. Song of the Texas Rangers. *Unknown.* BIG
Morning Sun. Louis MacNeice. MBP; MoAB; MoBrPo; NeMA
Morning sun shines from the east, The. Ode on Science. Jezaniah Sumner. TrAS
Morning Thanksgiving. John Drinkwater. BoTP
Morning that he drowned the white ship came, The. At the Discharge of Cannon Rise the Drowned. Hubert Witheford. AnNZ
Morning that my baby came, The. The Swallow. Ralph Hodgson. CMP; LBBV
Morning Thought, A. Edward Rowland Sill. UnW
Morning Twilight. Baudelaire, *tr. fr. French by* Barbara Gibbs. AnFP
Morning Visit, The, *sel.* Oliver Wendell Holmes.
"Morning visit—not till sickness falls, The." PoP
Morning! Wake up! Awaken! All the boughs. Week-End, VI. Harold Monro. CP; YT
Morning-Watch, The Henry Vaughan. BrBE; LiTB; LoBV; MaPo; MePo; OBS; OxBoCh; ReEn; SeCePo; ViBoPo
Morning Work. D. H. Lawrence. MoAB; MoBrPo (1950 ed.)
Morning Workout. Babette Deutsch. NePoAm-2
Morning Worship. Mark Van Doren. NePoAm-2
Morning Worship. Henrik Wergeland, *tr. fr. Norwegian by* Charles W. Stork. AnNoLy
Morning's dim twilight. Night Train. Sakutaro Hagiwara. PoLJ
Morning's fair, the lusty sun, The. The Country Walk. John Dyer. PrWP; RO
Morning's moist and fog-veiled, The. Elegies, V. Philippe Thoby-Marcelin. PoNe
Mornin's Mornin', The. Gerald Brennan. BLPA
Morns are meeker than they were, The. Emily Dickinson. OBAV; TiPo
(Autumn.) AA; AnNE; FaPON; HBV; LHV; MPB; NLK; PCH; TCAP; TOP; TSW; TSWC; YeAr
Morocco. R. N. Currey. BoSA
Moron. S. G. Leonard. MoWP
Moron, The. *Unknown.* DDA; YaD
("See the happy moron.") CenHV
Morpheus, *sel.* Hilda Doolittle ("H. D.").
Choros: "Give me your poppies." FaBoMo
Morpheus, the lively son of deadly sleep. Astrophel and Stella, XXXII. Sir Philip Sidney. ReEn; SiPS
Morrissey and the Russian Sailor, *with music. Unknown.* AS
Morrow's Message, The. Dante Gabriel Rossetti. The House of Life, XXXVIII. GTSE; PoVP; ViPo; VLEP
Mors Benefica. Edmund Clarence Stedman. AA; BLP; LEAP
Mors et Vita. Richard Henry Stoddard. AA
Mors et Vita. Samuel Waddington. HBV
Mors Iabrochii. *Unknown.* NA
Mors, Morituri Te Salutamus. Francis Burdett Money-Coutts. OBVV
Mortal Cage, The. John Oldham. *Fr.* To the Memory of Mr. Charles Morwent. BeR
Mortal Combat. Alice Fay di Castagnola. GoYe
Mortal Combat. Mary Elizabeth Coleridge. DiM; MBP; OBVV
Mortal, dost thou dare to say. Wingèd Change. Simonides. GrR
Mortal Grief. Francisco de Figueroa, *tr. fr. Spanish by* Sir John Bowring. OnPM
Mortal Love. Basil Dowling. AnNZ
Mortal my mate, bearing my rock-a-heart. To His Watch. Gerard Manley Hopkins. MBP; MoAB; MoBrPo
Mortal never won to view thee. The Beloved. Hafiz. PeP
Mortal, Sneer Not at the Devil. Heine, *tr. fr. German by* Emma Lazarus. *Fr.* Homeward Bound. TrJP
Mortal though I be. Immortality [*or* Starry Heavens Without]. Ptolemy, *tr. by* Robert Bridges. GrCo-1; OxBG
Mortal waves of sound are carried. A Singer's Prayer. Johan Sebastian Cammermeyer Welhaven. AnNoLy
Mortality. James Devaney. BoAV
Mortality. Gerald Gould. MBP; MoBrPo (1942 ed.)
Mortality. William Knox. *See* Oh! Why Should the Spirit of Mortal Be Proud?
Mortality. Pindar, *tr. fr. Greek by* F. L. Lucas. *Fr.* Nemean Odes, XI. GrPE
Mortality. Shakespeare. King Henry IV, Pt. II, *fr.* III, ii. LiA
Mortality, behold and fear. On [*or* Lines on] the Tombs in Westminster Abbey [*or* A Memento for Mortality]. *Unknown, at. to* Francis Beaumont, *also to* William Basse. ACP; BCEP; BEL; BLV; CH; CoEV; EIL; ElSeCe; EV-2; FaBoCh; GoBC; GTBS; GTBS-D; GTBS-W; GTSE; HBV; InP; LH; LoBV; LoGBV; MaRV; OBEV; OBS; SeEP; ShBV-3; TOP; TrGrPo; ViBoPo
Mortally. James Kirkup. NeBP
Mortals, that behold a Woman. Assumpta Maria. Francis Thompson. ISi
Morte Arthure [*or* Arthur] (*Alliterative*), *sels. Unknown, tr. fr. Middle English.*
"Arthur turns into Tuscany when the time is favorable," *mod.* MeEV
Sir Gawain Encounters Sir Priamus. PoEL-1
Morte d'Arthur, The. Wilfrid Scawen Blunt. VLEP
Morte d'Arthur. Tennyson. *Incorporated in* Idylls of the King, *with changes, as* The Passing of Arthur. AnEnPo; ATP; BBV; BEL; BMEP; BoLiVe; BPN; CBOV; EmBrPo, *with add. ll.* 324-354; EnL; EnLi-2; EPP; EV-5; FaBoBe; FiP; GEPC; HBV; OAEP; OnSP; PIR; PoE; PoEL-5; PoVP; ScCeV; ShBV-3; TCEP; TOP; TwCrTr; UnPo (1st ed.); ViPo; ViPP; VLEP; WHA
(Mort d'Arthur.) LPS-2
Sels.
"And answer made King Arthur, breathing hard." ReTS
"And slowly answered Arthur from the barge." FaBoEn; GTSL

Morte d'Arthur (*continued*)
Epic, The (Introduction). EmBrPo; VLEP
Prayer ("More things are wrought by prayer"). BLRP; OQP; PraP; QP-1; TreF; WGRP
Prayer ("The old order changeth, yielding place to new"). MaRV
(Prayer for the Dead.) GoBC
"Then saw they how there hove a dusky barge." VA
Mortgage on the Farm, The. *Unknown.* PTA-2
Mortification. George Herbert. MePo; OAEP; PoD; PoFS; ViBoPo
Mortifying Mistake, A. Anna Maria Pratt. AA; DDA; HBV; HBVY; OnHT
(Little Mistake, A.) RIS
Mortimeriados, *sels.* Michael Drayton.
Death of Edward, The. ReIE
"Low'ring heaven had mask'd her in a cloud, The." ReIE
To the Excellent and Most Accomplish'd Lady, Lucy, Countess of Bedford. ReIE
Mortis Dignitas. Richard Burton. BAP
Mortuary Parlors. Stephen Vincent Benét. NV
Morwe com, and goostly for to speke, The. Chaucer. *Fr.* Troilus and Criseyde. EPP
Morwennae Statio. Robert Stephen Hawker. GoBC
Mos' Done Toilin' Here, *with music. Unknown.* BoAN-2
Mosaic Worker, The. Arthur Wallace Peach. BLRP
Mosby at Hamilton. Madison Cawein. PAH
Moschatel. Daniel James O'Sullivan. NeIP
Moschatel. A. J. Young. MM
Moses; a Play, *sel.* Isaac Rosenberg.
"Yesterday as I lay nigh dead with toil." FaBoMo
Moses and Jesus. Israel Zangwill. QS; TrJP
Moses, from whose loins I sprung. The Jew. Isaac Rosenberg. MBP; MoBrPo; PoFr
Moses supposes his toeses are roses. *Unknown.* OxNR
Moses was keeping the flock of Jethro his father-in-law. The Burning Bush. Exodus, Bible, *O.T.* GrCo-1
Mosquito, The. D. H. Lawrence. SiTL
Mosquito Net. Fuyuji Tanaka, *tr. fr. Japanese by* Takamichi Ninomiya *and* D. J. Enright. PoLJ
Mosquito Turned Messenger, The. Meleager, *tr. fr. Greek by* R. A. Furness. OxBG
(Love-Messenger.) GrR
Mosquitoes. Al-Sumaisir, *tr. fr. Arabic by* A. J. Arberry. MooP
Moss-covered rock crowned with squirrels, A. Some One Attains to a Glimpse of Paradise. Jorge Guillén. CoSP
Moss-gathering. Theodore Roethke. CoBMV; FiMAP
Moss-grey mansion of my father stands, The. Apethorpe. Julian Fane. EnSW
Moss Rose, The. Friedrich Adolph Krummacher, *tr. fr. German.* LPS-2
Moss-Rose, The. Sir Henry Newbolt. HBV
Moss Supplicateth for the Poet, The. Richard Henry Dana. AA
Most Acceptable Gift, The. Matthias Claudius, *tr. fr. German by* J. M. Campbell. BLRP
Most Blessed Lady, Comfort to such as call. Dedication of the Chronicles of England and France. Robert Fabyan. ISi
Most every meal, when he's at home, my father says. Her Great Secret. Strickland Gillilan. PEDC
Most Excellent Song Which Was Salomon's, The. Michael Drayton. *Fr.* The Harmony of the Church. ReIE
Most Extraordinary Adventure, A. Vladimir Mayakovsky, *tr. fr. Russian by* Babette Deutsch. TrRV
Most fair and lovely maid, look from the shore. To Delia, XLIII. Samuel Daniel. TuPP
Most fragile of all is the cherry-bloom. Ki no Tsurayuki, *tr. fr. Japanese by* I. W. Furukami. LiTW
Most glorious Lord of life [*or* lyfe]! that on this day. Amoretti, LXVIII [*or* Easter *or* Easter Morning]. Spenser. ATP; BLV; BrBE; CAW; CoEV; DD; EIL; EOAH; ES; EV-1; HBV; LiTB; MaRV; MeRV; OBEV; OHIP; OxBoCh; PeBoSo; PoE; ReEn; ReIE; SeCeV; SiCE; StJW; TrPWD
Most glorious of all the Undying, many-named, girt round with awe! Hymn to Zeus. Cleanthes, *tr. by* Edward Hayes Plumptre. WGRP
Most glorious of immortals, Zeus all powerful. Hymn to Zeus. Cleanthes, *tr. by* Michael Balkwill. OxBG
Most glorious of the immortals. Hymn to Zeus. Cleanthes, *tr. by* James G. Frazer. GrCo-2
Most happy letters! framed by skilful trade. Amoretti, LXXIV. Spenser. PeBoSo
Most high, omnipotent, good Lord. The Canticle of the Sun [*or* The Canticle of Creatures]. St. Francis of Assisi. MeRV; ReTS; SaFP; WHL
Most holy Night, that still dost keep. The Night. Hilaire Belloc. AIDL; HBV; OBEV (new ed.); OBVV; PC; TCPD
Most holy Satyr. Holy Satyr. Hilda Doolittle ("H. D."). MAP; MoAmPo

Most Honored Guest. Walter Shea. ChIP
Most like some agèd king it seemed to me. Recollections of Burgos. Richard Chenevix Trench. OBRV
Most Lovely Shade. Edith Sitwell. AtBAP; FaBoTw; POTE
Most Men Know Love But as a Part of Life. Henry Timrod. *See* Quatorzain.
Most near, most dear, most loved and most far. Sonnet to My Mother [*or* To My Mother]. George Barker. FaBoMo; FaFP; GTBS-D; GTBS-W; LiTB; LiTM; MoAB; MoPW; PeBoSo; PG (1955 ed.); SeCePo; ViBoPo (1958 ed.); WaP
Most needy aren oure neighebores, The. The Poor. William Langland. *Fr.* The Vision of Piers Plowman. PoEL-1
Most noble Eteocles, Cadmean King. Gathering War Clouds. Aeschylus. *Fr.* Seven against Thebes. GrR
Most noble Excellence. The Introduction. Al-Dhahabi. MooP
Most of It, The. Robert Frost. CoV; CrMA; MaPo; MoPo; NePA
Most of my days are passed away, yet my heart is still impure. The Worthless Heart. Immanuel di Roma. TrJP
Most of you in Spoon River. Julius Brink. Edgar Lee Masters. ChMo; CMP
Most pines that fight their way to upper light. Dance of Death. Kimball Flaccus. AnAmPo
Most Pithy and Pleasant History of Glaucus and Scylla, The. Thomas Lodge. *Fr.* Scylla's Metamorphosis. ReIE
Most poets to a muse that is stone-deaf cry. On the Oxford Book of Victorian Verse. "Hugh MacDiarmid." MoBrPo
Most Quietly at Times. Cäsar Flaischlen, *tr. fr. German by* Jethro Bithell. AWP; JAWP; WBP
Most respected/ comrades heirs and descendants. At the Top of My Voice. Vladimir Mayakovsky. OnHM
Most-sacred Mountain, The. Eunice Tietjens. BAP; CP; HBMV; NLK (1947 ed.); NV; PoTo; QS; SBMV
Most souls, 'tis true, but peep out once an age. Dull, Sullen Prisoners. Pope. *Fr.* Elegy to the Memory of an Unfortunate Lady. BeR; CH; PoD
Most strenuous form of consecration, The. *Unknown.* *Fr.* Penitentes. SiB
Most stupendous show they ever gave, The. In Memory of the Circus Ship *Euzkera.* Walker Gibson. FiBHP; NePoAm
Most Sweet and Pleasing Are Thy Ways. Thomas Campion. TriL
Most Sweet It Is [with Unuplifted Eyes]. Wordsworth. *See* Inner Vision, The.
Most unlikely rebel, he, A. The Unlikely Rebel. Franklin D. Elmer, Jr. ChIP
Most Unloving One, The. Samuel Daniel. *See* To Delia: "My spotless love . . ."
Most valiant and noble Odysseus, seeing Atrides. Homer. *Fr.* The Iliad, IX. GrPo
Most Vital Thing in Life, The. Grenville Kleiser. PoToHe (new ed.)
Most worthy of praise were the virtuous ways. Little Red Riding Hood. Guy Wetmore Carryl. FiBHP; HBV; YaD
Most worthy she is in town, The. Ivy Chief of Trees It Is. *Unknown.* AnEC
Most wounds can Time repair. At Ease. Walter de la Mare. ChMP
Most wretched heart, most miserable. Sir Thomas Wyatt. SiPS
Mostellaria, *sel.* Plautus, *tr. fr. Latin by* F. A. Wright.
"I often have pondered and puzzled and wondered." LaP
Mostly Are We Mostless. José Garcia Villa. TwAmPo
Mot eran dous miei cossir. Arnaut Daniel, *tr. fr. French by* Harriet Waters Preston. AWP
Motect, A. *Unknown.* *See* Stranger Here, A.
Moth, The. Abu Yahya, *tr. fr. Arabic by* A. J. Arberry. MooP
Moth, The. Walter de la Mare. FaBoEn; MoVE; ShBV-3; TwCV
Moth, The/ Enraged. Of China and Her Wisdom. Paul Eldridge. PoeMoYo
Moth and the Flame, The. George Taggert. TreF
Moth ate a word, A. The [*or* A] Book-Worm [*or* Book-Moth]. *Unknown.* *Fr.* Riddles. AnOE; CoBE; EnLi-1; EnLit
Moth belated, sun and zephyr-kist, A. To a Moth That Drinketh of the Ripe October. Emily Pfeiffer. VA
Moth Miller. Aileen Fisher. UTS
Moth-Song. Ellen Mackay Hutchinson Cortissoz. AA
Moth-Terror. Benjamin De Casseres. BAP; SBMV; TrJP
Mother, The. Sarah Louise Arnold. PEDC
Mother, The. Wilfred Campbell. CPG; OCL
Mother. Thomas Curtis Clark. PGD
Mother, The. Sara Coleridge. DiM; OBVV
Mother. George Cooper. *See* Our Mother.
Mother. Ethel Barnett de Vito. MotAn
Mother. Mary Mapes Dodge. MeMeAg; OTPC (1946 ed.)
(Birdies with Broken Wings.) PRWS

Mother. Max Ehrmann. PoToHe
Mother. Sister M. Eulalia. WHL
Mother. Thomas W. Fessenden. *See* To Mother.
Mother. Helen Frazee-Bower. MuM
Mother. Rose Fyleman. DD; HH; MPB; SiSoSe
Mother. Hermann Hagedorn. *See* Mother in the House, The.
Mother. Theresa Helburn. FaPON; HBV; LBMV; MOAH; OHIP; TSW
Mother. Iraj, *tr. fr. Persian by* A. J. Arberry. PeP
Mother. Daniel Lawrence Kelleher. NeIP
Mother, The. George Newell Lovejoy. DD
(Gift, The.) PGD
Mother, The. Isabel Ecclestone Mackay. CPG
Mother, The. Catulle Mendès, *tr. fr. French by* W. J. Robertson. TrJP
Mother. Alice Meynell. *See* Maternity.
Mother, The. Kadie Molodowsky, *tr. fr. Yiddish by* Sarah Zweig Betsky. OnCuPl
Mother, The. Nikolai Alekseyevich Nekrasov, *tr. fr. Russian by* Sir Cecil Kisch. WaL
Mother, *sel.* Kathleen Norris.
Dedication: "As years [*or* long] ago we carried to your knees." MOAH; PoToHe
Mother. Carlos Oquendo de Amat, *tr. fr. Spanish by* H. R. Hays. AnCL
Mother, The. Nettie Palmer. BoAu
Mother, The. Padraic Pearse. OnYI
Mother, The. Beatrice Redpath. CPG
Mother. Lola Ridge. NV
Mother, The. Kathryn White Ryan. CAW
Mother. Keith Sinclair. AnNZ
Mother, The. Raymond Souster. PeCV
Mother. Emily Taylor. PGD
Mother, The. Tsung Wan Sheng, *tr. fr. Chinese by* Henry H. Hart. PoHN
Mother ("Each day to her a miracle"). *Unknown.* PGD; PSO
Mother, The ("From out the south the genial breezes sigh"). *Unknown, tr. fr. Chinese by* George Barrow. MOAH; OHIP
Mother ("Whenever I look in her kind eyes"). *Unknown.* DD
Mother. Percy Waxman. PEDC
Mother. Whittier. *Fr.* Snow-bound. AA; MW; OHIP; PFY
Mother—a Portrait. Ethel Romig Fuller. PGD; PSO
Mother and Child. Ivy O. Eastwick. SiSoSe
Mother and Child. William Gilmore Simms. LPS-1; MOAH
Mother and Child, The. Vernon Watkins. NeBP
Mother and Her Seven Sons, A. Second Maccabees, VII: 1-14, Bible, Apocrypha. BHV
Mother and Home. John Jarvis Holden. MOAH
Mother and I. Eugene Field. *See* Child and Mother.
Mother and maid and soldier, bearing best. A Portrait. Brian Hooker. HBV
Mother and Maiden. *Unknown. See* I Sing of a Maiden.
Mother and maker of us all. Earth Song. David McKee Wright. AOAH
Mother and Poet. Elizabeth Barrett Browning. HBV; LPS-1; MOAH; MotAn; VA; VLEP
Mother and sire, to you do I commend. Martial, *tr. fr. Latin by* Robert Louis Stevenson. Epigrams, V, 34. LaP
Mother and Son. Phoebe Cary. MOAH
Mother and Son. William Morris. EmBrPo; GTML
Mother and Son. Robert Louis Stevenson. *See* It Is Not Yours, O Mother, to Complain.
Mother and Son. Allen Tate. LiTA; MAP; MoAB; MoAmPo; MoVE
Mother at home quietly placing the dishes on the supper-table, The. Walt Whitman. *Fr.* There Was a Child Went Forth. MotAn
Mother, at that word your eloquent body spoke. The Poet Prays Her. Daniel Berrigan. JKCP (1955 ed.)
Mother, at the portal a little child is standing. The Christmas Child. *Unknown.* PCH
Mother before a Soldier's Monument, A. Winnie Lynch Rockett. PGD
Mother Bombie, *sel.* John Lyly.
O Cupid! Monarch over Kings. EIL; SiCE
(Fools in Love's College.) TrGrPo
(Love's Schooling.) BLV
(Song of Accius and Silena.) OBSC
Mother bore this child in the white moon. Sebastian in Dream. Georg Trakl. AnGP
Mother came when stars were paling, A. The Fairy Boy. Samuel Lover. OTPC (1923 ed.)
Mother Carey. John Masefield. FaBoTw
Mother Carey's Chicken. Theodore Watts-Dunton. OBVV
(Ode to Mother Carey's Chicken, *sl. diff.*) VA
Mother Church. Walter Freeman. PoP
Mother Country, The. Benjamin Franklin. PAH
Mother Country. Christina Rossetti. OxBoCh
"Mother, dear mother, come riddle to me." The Brown Girl, or Fair Ellender. *Unknown.* SPP
Mother Duck. Ann Hawkshaw. *See* Dame Duck's First Lecture on Education.
Mother Earth. Harriet Monroe. NP
Mother Earth, are the heroes dead? Heroes. Edna Dean Proctor. GA; HBV; TVSH
Mother England. Edith M. Thomas. AA; HBV
Mother Fear. Tove Ditlevsen, *tr. fr. Danish by* Charles W. Stork. BoDS
Mother, for love of grace. Shakespeare. *Fr.* Hamlet, III, iv. MotAn
Mother fragrant in her dust and grace, The. Celestine. Robert Fitzgerald. MoVE
Mother Goose. *Rhymes indexed by first lines.*
Mother Goose (circa 2054). Irene Sekula. SiTL
Mother Goose for Grown Folks, *sels.* Adeline D. T. Whitney.
Humpty Dumpty. HBV
Jack Horner. LPS-3
Mother Goose Sonnets, *sels.* Harriet S. Morgridge. AA
Jack and Jill.
Simple Simon.
Mother Goose Up-to-Date, *parodies.* Louis Untermeyer. MoAmPo
Edgar A. Guest Syndicates [*or* Considers] "The Old Woman Who Lived in a Shoe." MoAmPo; PreP; WhC
(Just Home.) StaSt
Mother-heart doth yearn at eventide, The. When Even Cometh On. Lucy Evangeline Tilley. AA
Mother, Home, Heaven. William Goldsmith Brown. DD; FaBoBe; HBV
Mother! Home!—that blest refrain. Mother and Home. John Jarvis Holden. MOAH
Mother Hubberd's Tale. Spenser. *See* Prosopopoia; or, Mother Hubberd's Tale.
Mother, I Cannot Mind My Wheel. Walter Savage Landor, *First st. par. fr. the Greek of* Sappho. AWP, *st.* 1; BLV; BoLiVe; BPN; EG; EnLi-1, *st.* 1; EnRP; EV-4; HBV; JAWP, *st.* 1; LiTL; OAEP; OBEV; OBRV; PG; TOP; TrGrPo; WBP
(Lyrics and Epigrams, XI.) ERP
(Margaret.) VA
(No Longer Could I Doubt Him True.) CBOV
Mother, I Cannot Mind My Wheel. Sappho, *tr. fr. Greek by* T. F. Higham. GrL; OxBG
Mother, I come from the aspen trees. *Unknown, tr. fr. Spanish by* Eleanor L. Turnbull. TeCS
Mother, I went to China this morning. Who Can Say. Alastair Reid. NePoEA
Mother in Egypt, A. Marjorie Pickthall. CaP; CPG; HBV; MOAH; OCL; PCN
Mother in gladness, Mother in sorrow. W. Dayton Wedgefarth. PoToHe
Mother in her office holds the key, The. Queen of the World. *Unknown.* PGD
Mother, in some sad evening long ago. The First Food. George Sterling. SBMV
Mother in the House, The. Hermann Hagedorn. DD; HBMV; MotAn; OHIP; PoRL
(Mother.) PoToHe
"Mother! is that the passing bell?" The Dark Girl by the Holy Well. John Keegan. TIP
Mother, is this [*or* this is] the darkness of the end. For "Our Lady of the Rocks." Dante Gabriel Rossetti. MeRV; NBE; OxBoCh
Mother likes the frocks and hats. Shop Windows. Rose Fyleman. TiPo; UTS
Mother Love. Janie Alford. PGD; PSO
Mother, Make Me a Cambric Shirt. *Unknown. See* Elfin Knight, The.
Mother Marie Therese. Robert Lowell. FiMAP
Mother Mary, thee I see. Communion. Caroline Giltinan. CAW; JKCP
Mother Mary Xavier. Francis P. Donnelly. PraNu
Mother Mary Xavier. Benjamin Dionysius Hill. PraNu
Mother Mary's mind. Mary Pondered All These Things. Edwin McNeill Poteat. ChIP
Mother Maudlin the Witch. Ben Jonson. *Fr.* The Sad Shepherd. ChTr
Mother, may I go out [*or* in] to [*or* and] swim? *Unknown.* FaPON; OTPC; OxNR; RIS; SAS; SiTL
Mother mine. Valentine to My Mother. Christina Rossetti. BoChLi
Mother mine, Mother mine, what do you see? Ballad. Annemarie Ewing. NePoAm
Mother Moon. Amelia Josephine Burr. TVC; TVSH; WHL
Mother Most Powerful. Giovanni Dominici, *tr. fr. Italian by* Thomas Walsh. CAW
Mother, mother. The One Who Struggles. Ernst Toller. TrJP
"Mother, mother, what is that." *Unknown.* ExPo
Mother Nature had a wash day. Nature's Wash Day. Marguerite Gode. GFA
Mother, Nurse, and Fairy. John Gay. MOAH
Mother, the Nurse, and the Fairy, The, *2 ll.* MotAn

Mother o' blossoms, and ov all. William Barnes. *Fr.* May. ChTr
Mother o' Mine. Kipling. The Light That Failed: Dedication. FaFP; MaRV; MotAn; NeHB; OQP; PSO; PTA-2; QP-1; WBLP
(Dedication: "If I were hanged on the highest hill.") MOAH
Mother o' mine, in the afterglow. In the Afterglow. Flora S. Rivola. MotAn
"Mother, O mother, go riddle my sport." The Brown Girl. *Unknown.* BaBo
Mother of a Daughter. Louis Johnson. AnNZ
Mother of Aeneas and his race, darling of men and gods. Invocation; the Bondage of Religion. Lucretius. *Fr.* De Rerum Natura. RoL
Mother of balms and soothings manifold. Midsummer Night. Archibald Lampman. PC
Mother of Christ, The. Kostas Varnalis, *tr. fr. Modern Greek by* Rae Dalven. MoGP
Mother of Christ, hear Thou Thy people's cry. Alma Redemptoris. *Unknown.* WHL
Mother of Christ long slain, forth glided she. Motherhood. Agnes Lee. BAP; BLPA; HBMV; MOAH; NP; NV
Mother, The, of Christ the Priest and of His/ royal and priestly people. The Mediatrix of Grace. Francis Burke. ISi
Mother of England, and sweet nurse of all. Ad Reginam Elizabetham. Thomas Bastard. SiCE
Mother of God. Lord Gorell. NeTW
Mother of God, The. *Unknown, tr. fr. Greek by* G. R. Woodward. *Fr.* Horologium. ISi
Mother of God, The. W. B. Yeats. EnLP; MeRV
Mother of God, all tenderness and truth. Mother of God. Lord Gorell. NeTW
Mother of God, mother of man reborn. Invocation. Arthur J. Little *Fr.* Christ Unconquered. ISi
Mother of God! no lady thou. Our Lady. Mary Elizabeth Coleridge. CAW; GTML; MBP; OBEV (new ed.); OBMV; OBVV; TCPD; TOP
Mother of God that's Lady of the Heavens. Two Translations from Villon [*or* A Translation from Villon]. *Pr. tr. by* J. M. Synge. MoBrPo; NeMA
Mother of God, whose burly love. On the Eve of the Feast of the Immaculate Conception, 1942. Robert Lowell. WaaP
"Mother of heaven, regina of the clouds." Le Monocle de Mon Oncle. Wallace Stevens. AnAmPo; AnFE; APA; CoAnAm; CoBMV; LA; LiTM; MAPA; MoAB; NP; TwAmPo
Mother of Hermes! and still youthful Maia. Fragment of an Ode to Maia, Written on May Day, 1818 [*or* To Maia]. Keats. BCEP; EM-2; EmBrPo; EnRP; EPN; LEAP; OAEP; OBEV; OBRV; PoEL-4; TwCrTr
Mother of Judas, The. Amelia Josephine Burr. WHL
Mother of life indulges all our wandering, The. Return to Ritual. Mark Van Doren. MoVE
Mother of light! how fairly dost thou go. Ode to the Moon. Thomas Hood. OBVV
Mother of man's time-traveling generations. Mater Triumphalis. Swinburne. EmBrPo; POTT; VLEP
Mother of memories! O mistress-queen! Le Balcon. Baudelaire. AWP
Mother of Men. Brian Hooker. HBMV
Mother of Men. Stephen Southwold. HBMV
Mother of Men, grown strong in giving. Mother of Men. Brian Hooker. HBMV
Mother of musings, Contemplation sage. The Pleasures of Melancholy. Thomas Warton, the Younger. CEP; EiPP; EnRP
Mother of nations, of them eldest we. America to England. George Edward Woodberry. AA
Mother of power, my soul goes out to you. Elsa Barker. *Fr.* Breshkovskaya. BAP
Mother of revolutions, stern and sweet. To France. Ralph Chaplin. HBMV
Mother of the Fair Delight. Ave. Dante Gabriel Rossetti. EmBrPo; GoBC; ISi; OxBoCh; POTT; ViPo; VLEP
Mother of the House, The. Proverbs, XXXI: 25-29, Bible, *O.T.* GoTP; OQP; PGD; PSO; QP-1
Mother of the Muses, we are taught, The. Memory. Walter Savage Landor. EmBrPo; VA
Mother of the Roman games and Greek pleasures. Lesbos. Baudelaire. AnFP
Mother of the Rose, The. James M. Hayes. JKCP
Mother of Us All, The, *sel.* Gertrude Stein.
"We cannot retrace our steps." CrMA
Mother on Her Daughter's Wedding Day, A. Faith V. Vilas. MotAn
Mother plays a march. Away We Go. Aileen Fisher. TiPo (1959 ed.)
Mother-Prayer. Margaret Widdemer. HBMV; PraP
Mother said to call her if the H bomb exploded. Belief. Josephine Miles. FiMAP
Mother Saint Urban. James M. Hayes. PraNu
Mother Sarah's Lullaby. Itzig Manger, *tr. fr. Yiddish by* Jacob Sonntag. TrJP
Mother sent me on the holy quest, The. The Living Chalice. Susan Mitchell. HBMV
Mother shake the cherry-tree. Let's Be Merry. Christina Rossetti. *Fr.* Sing-Song. FaPON; PoVP; TiPo
Mother Shipton's Prophecies. *At. to* Charles Hindley. BLPA
Mother sings a song of youth and May, The. A Very Happy Family. Joseph G. Francis. CIV
Mother-Song. Alfred Austin. *Fr.* Prince Lucifer. BOL; HBV; MOAH; VA
Mother-Song, A. Julia C. R. Dorr. BOL
Mother-Song, A. Harriet Prescott Spofford. BOL
Mother Speaks, A. Margaret E. Sangster. *See* Mother's Prayer, A.
Mother Tabbyskins. Elizabeth Anna Hart. CenHV; CIV
(Old Mother Tabbyskins, *with music.*) FTB
Mother, the Nurse, and the Fairy, The. John Gay. *See* Mother, Nurse, and Fairy.
"Mother, the poplars cross the moon." Refugees. Grace Hazard Conkling. NP
Mother, this is the darkness of the end. *See* Mother, is this the darkness of the end.
Mother Thought, A. Edgar A. Guest. PEDC
Mother to a Baby. Mary Elizabeth Coleridge. GTML
Mother to Her Infant, The. Thomas Miller. BOL; OTPC (1923 ed.)
Mother to Her Sick Child, A. W. H. Davies. BOL
Mother to her son did say, The. The Maiden Hind. *Unknown.* BoDaBa; LiTW; LyMA
Mother,—to my word/ Hearken ye! For Hellas! Euripides. *Fr.* Iphigenia in Aulis. GrR
Mother to Son. Langston Hughes. BoChLi (1950 ed.); CDC; FAOV; GoSl; IHA; PoNe; StVeCh
Mother to whose valiant will. Dedication. Archibald Lampman. *Fr.* Lyrics of Earth. MOAH
Mother under the Mould, The. *Unknown, tr. fr. Danish by* E. M. Smith-Dampier. BoDaBa
Mother Understands, A. Geoffrey Anketell Studdert-Kennedy. OQP; QP-2
Mother Wept. Joseph Skipsey. HBV; OBVV; VA
Mother wept, A: where were You, God. Calvary. Libby Stopple. GoYe
Mother, White as Lily Flower. *Unknown.* AnEC
(Modyr Whyt as Lyly Flowr, *abr.*) AtBAP
Mother Who Died Too, The. Edith M. Thomas. AA
Mother, who knew/ what hardship shakes. Our Lady of the Refugees. Sister Mary Maura. ISi
Mother! whose virgin bosom was uncrossed. The Virgin [*or* Sonnet to the Virgin]. Wordsworth. CAW; CoBE; GoBC; ISi
Mother, why weepest thou, before thine eyes. Aethra's Intercession. Euripides. *Fr.* Suppliants. GrR
Mother will not turn, who thinks she hears, The. Broken Music. Dante Gabriel Rossetti. The House of Life, XLVII. PoVP; VA; ViPo; VLEP
Mother with the life-giving power now comes. To Mother Corn. *Unknown, tr. fr. Pawnee Indian.* GrCo-1
Mother with Young Kittens, A. Richard Hart. CIV
Mother with your nine sons and your only daughter. The Vampire. *Unknown.* MoGP
Mother, your faithful child writes to you. Hoc, Genitrix, Scriptum Proles Tibi Sedula Mittit. George Herbert. LaP
Motherhood. Josephine Dodge Daskam Bacon. HBV
Motherhood. Charles Stuart Calverley. LPS-3
Motherhood. Karl M. Chworowsky. PGD
Motherhood. Agnes Lee. BAP; BLPA; HBMV; MOAH; NP; NV
Motherhood. William L. Stidger. PGD
Mothering. Mazie V. Caruthers. CIV
Motherland, The. Wordsworth. LH
Motherless. Elizabeth Barrett Browning. *Fr.* Aurora Leigh, I. MOAH; VA
Motherless. Mary Mapes Dodge. FAOV
Motherless Child, The. William Barnes. BCEP
Motherless Soft Lambkin. Christina Rossetti. *Fr.* Sing-Song. RIS
Mothers, The. John Peale Bishop. SPP
Mothers. Edwin L. Sabin. PEDC
Mothers. *Unknown.* PGD
Mothers,/ That hope of yours, your joyful burden. To the Mothers. Ernst Toller. TrJP
Mothers and Children. Orrick Johns. AnAmPo; HBMV; LA
Mothers and fathers of sons, what will you be saying. It Is Not Too Late. Lucia Trent. PGD
Mothers—and Others. Amos R. Wells. WBLP
Mothers are the queerest things! Mothers. Edwin L. Sabin. PEDC
Mother's Birthday, A. Henry van Dyke. MaRV; OHIP
Mother's Boy. Patrick Anderson. BoCaPo (1948 ed.)
Mother's Choice, The. *Unknown.* OxBoLi
Mother's Day. Edna Tucker Muth. PEDC

Mother's Diary. Elsie Duncan Sanders. DDA
Mother's Dream, The. William Barnes. *See* Mater Dolorosa.
Mother's Evening Hymn, A. Martin Luther, *tr. fr. German by* John Christian Jacobi. BOL; MOAH
Mother's Fool. *Unknown.* PTA-1
Mother's gift to her country's cause is a story yet untold, A. The Blue and the Gray. *Unknown.* ABS
Mother's gone a-visitin' to spend a month er two. Lonesome. Paul Laurence Dunbar. MPB; PoRL
Mother's Hands. W. Dayton Wedgefarth. PoToHe
Mother's Heart, The. Caroline Elizabeth Sarah Norton. LPS-1; MOAH
Mother's Heritage. Helen C. Smith. MotAn
Mother's Hope, The. Laman Blanchard. LPS-1; MOAH
Mother's Hymn, The. Bryant. DD; MaRV; MOAH; MotAn; OHIP
Mother's Idol Broken, The, *sel.* Gerald Massey.
 Our Wee White Rose. HBV; LPS-1
Mother's Knee. Edgar A. Guest. MotAn
Mothers' Lament at the Slaughter of the Innocents, The. *Unknown, tr. fr. Middle Irish by* Kuno Meyer. OnYI
Mother's Lament for the Death of Her Son, A. Burns. HoPM
Mother's Love. Thomas Burbidge. MOAH; VA
Mother's Love. Ross B. Clapp. WBLP
Mother's Love, A. James Montgomery. MotAn; PGD, *st.* 1
Mother's Love ("Her love is like an island"). *Unknown.* OQP; PSO; QP-1
Mother's love, A—how sweet the name! A Mother's Love. James Montgomery. MotAn; PGD
Mother's Malison, The; or, Clyde's Waters. *Unknown.* BaBo; ESPB (A *and* B vers.)
 (Clyde Water, *longer, diff. vers.*) OBB
 (Clyde's Waters, *abr.*) BSV
Mother's Name, A. *Unknown.* PGD; PSO
Mothers of Men. Amelia Josephine Burr. OQP; QP-2
Mothers of Men, The. Joaquin Miller. BPP; PGD; PTA-1; PTA-2
 (Bravest Battle, The.) WBLP, *sl. abr.*
Mothers of our Forest-Land, The. The Mothers of the West. William D. Gallagher. MC; PAH
Mothers of the Earth, The. Grace Noll Crowell. PEDC
Mothers of the West, The. William D. Gallagher. MC; PAH
Mother's Petition, in Wartime. Helen M. Burgess. ChIP
Mother's Picture, A. Alice Cary. MotAn
Mother's Picture, A. Edmund Clarence Stedman. MOAH; OHIP
Mother's Prayer, The. Elizabeth Barrett Browning. MotAn
Mother's Prayer, The. Cora A. McDermoth. DDA
Mother's Prayer, A. Margaret E. Sangster. MaRV; TrPWD
 (Mother Speaks, A.) PraP
Mother's Prayer, The. Dora Sigerson Shorter. HBV
Mother's Return, The. Dorothy Wordsworth. MOAH; OTPC (1923 ed.)
Mother's Reward, A. Ona Freeman Lathrop. MaRV
Mother's Sacrifice, The. Seba Smith. *See* Snow Storm, The.
Mother's Secret. Oliver Wendell Holmes. *Fr.* The Professor at the Breakfast Table, *ch.* 4. MotAn
 "Youth fades; love droops," 2 *ll.* PoToHe
Mother's Song, The. Virginia Woodward Cloud. AA
Mother's Song, A. Sydney Dobell. *Fr.* Balder. BOL
Mother's Song, A. Francis Ledwidge. EtS
Mother's Song, The. William P. M'Kenzie. BOL
Mother's Song, A. Christina Rossetti. *See* Love Me—I Love You.
Mother's Song ("Don't grow old too fast, my sweet!"). *Unknown.* BOL
Mother's Song ("My heart is like a fountain true"). *Unknown.* GN; HBV
 (Love and Protection of Mother and Father, The.) BOL
Mother's Soul, The. Isabella Valancy Crawford. CPG
Mother's Trust, The. *Unknown.* PraP
Mothers who have seen him die—your first child, your only one. Fourth Station. Paul Claudel. ISi
Mothers who raise/ A child by the book. Double Duty. W. E. Farbstein. WhC
Moths, The. Julian Bell. POTE
Moths. David Morton. MuM
Moth's Kiss, First, The. Robert Browning. *Fr.* In a Gondola. AtBAP; GTSL; LPS-1; OBEV; OBVV; PIR
 (Song: "Moth's kiss, first, The!") BoLiVe; HBV; TrGrPo
 (Song from "In a Gondola.") LEAP
Motif for Mary's Dolors. Sister Mary Madeleva. ISi
Motif from the Second Shepherd's Play. Sister Mary Maura. JKCP (1955 ed.)
Motion of gathering loops of water, The. The Glass Bubbles. Samuel Greenberg. LiTA; NePA
Motion of the Earth, The. Norman Nicholson. ImOP
Motion Picture Show. Ralph Cheyney. MuM
Motionless, gentle as it always was. And Then Her Burial. Merrill Moore. MAP; MoAmPo (1942 ed.)
Motionless, in a dark, cold cell in Rome. Epicharis. Arthur Palmer. TIP
Motive for Metaphor, The. Wallace Stevens. MoAB; MoAmPo (1950 ed.)
Motive of All of It, The. Muriel Rukeyser. MiAP
Motley's the Only Wear. Shakespeare. *Fr.* As You Like It, II, vii. TrGrPo
 ("Fool, A, a fool! I met a fool i' the forest.") PIR
Motor Bus, The. A. D. Godley. OtMeF
Motor Cars. Rowena Bastin Bennett. FaPON; GFA; PoMa; TiPo
Motorcycle. Benjamin Sturgis Pray. GoYe
Motto. *Unknown, ad. fr. German by* Louis Untermeyer. TiPo
Motto for a Dog House. Arthur Guiterman. AlBD
Motto for a Tree-planting. Richard Watson Gilder. PoRL
Motto from "Old Mortality." Thomas O. Mordaunt. *See* Sound, Sound the Clarion.
Mould, The. Gladys Cromwell. AnAmPo; BAP; LA; MAP; NP; NV; SBMV
Mould of clouds inflamed the skin of the sky, A. Illusion. Ján Rak. LiTW
Mould sprouts in old shoes and empty heads, XIV. Frances Crawford. PtPa
Mound by the Lake, The. Herman Melville. APW; MotAn
Mount, The. Léonie Adams. MAP; MoAB; MoAmPo; MoVE; NP
Mount Alvernia. H. E. G. Rope. SaFP
Mount Badon. Charles Williams. FaBoTw
Mount Holyoke. Phyllis Merrill. CAG
Mt. [*or* Mount] Lykaion. Trumbull Stickney. *Fr.* Sonnets from Greece. AnAmPo; AnFE; APA; CoAnAm; LA; MOAP; MoVE; NePA; OxBA; TrGrPo
 (Alone on Lykaion.) MAP; MoAmPo (1942 ed.)
Mount! mount! and away o'er the green prairie wide. The Ranger's Song. James T. Lytle. HiLiAm
Mount, mount for the chase! let your lassoes be strong. The White Steed of the Prairies. *Unknown.* CoSo
Mount of Olives ("Sweet sacred hill! on whose fair brow"). Henry Vaughan. Po; ReaPo
Mount Rainier. Herbert Bashford. AA
Mount Rhodope. Yiannis Griparis, *tr. fr. Modern Greek by* Rae Dalven. MoGP
Mount Vernon, the Home of Washington. William Day. OHIP; PoRL; WOAH
 (Mount Vernon.) DD; GA
Mount Vernon's Bells. M. B. C. Slade. PTA-1
Mount Wu lies southeast of Lushan. Looking toward Mount Wu. Li Po. WhP
Mountain, The. Al-Liss, *tr. fr. Arabic by* A. J. Arberry. MooP
Mountain, The, *sel.* William Ellery Channing.
 "In this sweet solitude." PFY
Mountain, The. Emily Dickinson. *See* Mountain sat upon the plain, The.
Mountain, The. Geoffrey Dutton. MoAuPo
Mountain, The. Robert Finch. CaP
Mountain, The. Robert Frost. AmPo; AmPP (3d ed.); CoBA; MOAP
Mountain, The. Mikhail Yurevich Lermontov, *tr. fr. Russian by* Max Eastman. AWP; JAWP; WBP
Mountain Air. John Galsworthy. OQP; QP-2
Mountain and Hillock. Steingrímur Thorsteinsson, *tr. fr. Icelandic by* Jakobina Johnson. *Fr.* Epigrams. IcP
Mountain and River. Louis Ginsberg. PFE
Mountain and the Squirrel, The. Emerson. *See* Fable: "Mountain and the squirrel had a quarrel, The."
Mountain brows, the rocks, the peaks are sleeping, The. Alcman, *tr. fr. Greek by* Sir Edwin Arnold. GrPo
Mountain Cemetery, The. Edgar Bowers. NePoEA; PtPa
Mountain Chant. *Tr. fr. Navajo Indian by* Washington Matthews. APW
Mountain Climber, The. Antonia Pozzi, *tr. fr. Italian by* Glauco Cambon. OnPM
Mountain Comes to Mahomet, The. Helene Mullins. MuM
Mountain Convent. Laura Benét. GoYe
Mountain Courtyard, The. Ch'üan Shen, *tr. fr. Chinese by* Henry H. Hart. PoHN
Mountain Creed. Medora Addison Nutter. GoYe
Mountain Dawn. Gene Boardman Hoover. StaSt
Mountain Evenings. Jamie Sexton Holme. PoOW
Mountain Gateway, A. Bliss Carman. CPG
Mountain Girl, The. DuBose Heyward. BLP; LS; MuM; NV
Mountain Glen, A. *Unknown, tr. fr. Greek by* T. F. Higham. OxBG
Mountain gorses, ever-golden. Lessons from the Gorse. Elizabeth Barrett Browning. HBV
Mountain Hamlet. Lew Sarett. PoMa
Mountain he flew over did not want him, The. The Mountain. Geoffrey Dutton. MoAuPo
Mountain Heart's-Ease, The. Bret Harte. HBV
Mountain heights are sleeping. After Goethe. Mikhail Yurevich Lermontov. WaL
Mountain held the town as in a shadow, The. The Mountain. Robert Frost. AmPo; AmPP (3d ed.); CoBA; MOAP

Mountain in Labor, The. Aesop, *rhymed tr. fr. Greek by* William Ellery Leonard. AWP
Mountain in the Sky, The. Howard McKinley Corning. MuM; NP
Mountain Interval. Robert Nathan. MuM
Mountain is so high—so high, The. So High. John Russell McCarthy. UnW
Mountain Lake, The. Richard Church. AtBAP; POTE
Mountain Laurel. Alfred Noyes. EPP; POTT; TCPD
Mountain Liars. Ann Woodbury Hafen. PoOW
Mountain Liberty. Ernest Rhys. *Fr.* The Ballads of the Last Prince. PoFr
Mountain like a beast, A. Dunedin Revisited. Denis Glover. AnNZ
Mountain Lion. D. H. Lawrence. AtBAP; HaMV; MoP; ShBV-2
Mountain Night. Ralph Cheyney. TBM
Mountain night is shining, Jim of Tellico, The. In the Blue Ridge. Olive Tilford Dargan. NoCaPo
Mountain Norther, The. Olav Aukrust, *tr. fr. Norwegian by* Charles W. Stork. AnNoLy
Mountain of stupendous height there stands, A. Pyrrha and Deucalion. Ovid. *Fr.* Metamorphoses, I. RoL
Mountain of the Lovers, The, *sel.* Paul Hamilton Hayne.
Love Scorns Degrees. LPS-1
Mountain over Aberdare, The. Alun Lewis. MoWP
Mountain path, The. Climbing Tung Kuan Mountain. Tai Ping. PoHN
Mountain peaks put on their hoods, The. Twilight Song. John Hunter-Duvar. *Fr.* De Roberval. VA
Mountain pine is a man at arms, The. The Elm. Odell Shepard. HBMV
Mountain Revery. Stanton A. Coblentz. MuM
Mountain Road, The. Enid Derham. BoAu
Mountain road ends here, The. Lyell's Hypothesis Again. Kenneth Rexroth. MoVE; OnHM
Mountain sat upon the plain, The. Emily Dickinson. NLK (1947 ed.)
(Mountain, The.) NeMA; OnPM; YT
Mountain sheep are sweeter, The. The War Song of Dinas Vawr. Thomas Love Peacock. *Fr.* The Misfortunes of Elphin. ALV; AWP; BCEP; CBOV; EnRP; ERP; ExPo; FaBoCh; GTBS; InvP; JAWP; KN; LEAP; LiA; LiTG; LoBV; MuP; MyFE; OBRV; OtMeF; PIAE; ShBV-2; SoV; StPo; TOP; TVSH; ViBoPo; WaaP; WBP; WhC
Mountain Song. Harriet Monroe. HBV; NP; NV
Mountain Song. Juan Ruiz, Archpriest of Hita, *tr. fr. Spanish by* Hubert Creekmore. LyMA
Mountain Speed. Geoffrey Winthrop Young. PoTo
Mountain Sprite, The. Thomas Moore. OTPC (1923 ed.)
Mountain Still, The. Madison Cawein. SPP
Moonshiner, The, I.
Sheriff, The, II.
Mountain Stream, A. *Unknown.* CAG
Mountain summits sleep, The: glens, cliffs, and caves. Sleep upon the World [*or* Fragment]. Alcman. AWP; ChTr; JAWP; RO; WBP
Mountain to the Pine, The. Clarence Hawkes. AA
Mountain Top, The. Hitomaro, *tr. fr. Japanese by* Mabel Lorenz Ives. PFE
Mountain Top. *Unknown. See* Liza Jane.
Mountain Top Blues. Spencer Williams. APW
Mountain tops, The. A Song of Parting. Chang Yung. PoHN
Mountain Tree, The. Hugh Connell. NeIP
Mountain Trolls. Gustaf Fröding, *tr. fr. Swedish by* Charles W. Stork. AnSL
Mountain was in great distress and loud, A. The Mountain in Labor. Aesop. AWP
Mountain Whippoorwill, The. Stephen Vincent Benét. HiLiAm; IHA; MOAP; OnAP; PoeMoYo; StPo; TBM; TrGrPo; YaD; YT
Mountain Wind, A. "Æ." AWP; JAWP; WBP
Mountain Woman, The. DuBose Heyward. AnAmPo; LA; LS; MuM; NP; OnPP; TBM; TCAP
Mountain Wreath, The, *sel.* Petar Petrovic Njegos, *tr. fr. Serbian by* James William Wiles.
Speech of Abbot Stephen. PoFr
Mountaineer, The. Robert Nathan. BAP; TrJP
Mountaineer is working with his Bible, The. Quatrina. Joseph Bennett. LiTA
Mountains. Ann Nolan Clark. StVeCh (1955 ed.)
Mountains, The. Louis Dudek. CaP
Mountains. Hesiod, *tr. fr. Greek by* F. L. Lucas. *Fr.* Theogony. GrPE
Mountains. Lucy Larcom. WBLP
Mountains. John Richard Moreland. LS
Mountains. Henry David Thoreau. MOAP
Mountains and Man ("Mountains and ocean waves"). *Unknown, tr. fr. Japanese by* Basil Hall Chamberlain. OnPM
Mountains and plains. Winter. Joso. OnPM; WoL
Mountains and rivers lie in the opening sun. Spring. Tu Fu. WhP
Mountains, The, and the lonely death at last. To a Traveler. Lionel Johnson. AnEnPo; MBP; MoBrPo; TriL
Mountains Are a Lonely Folk, The. Hamlin Garland. BAP; PoMa; POT; PoTo; VOD
Mountains are the high places. Mountains. Ann Nolan Clark. StVeCh (1955 ed.)
Mountains: blackness, silence, and snow. Birth. Georg Trakl. AnGP
Mountains blanket-wrapped. Men in New Mexico. D. H. Lawrence. BrBE
Mountain's giddy height I sought, A. The Lay of the Trilobite. May Kendall. CenHV
Mountains grow unnoticed, The. Emily Dickinson. MoAB; MoAmPo; TrGrPo
Mountains lie in curves so tender, The. Twilight. Olive Tilford Dargan. LS; NoCaPo
Mountains loom upon the path we take. Song to the Mountains. *Unknown.* AWP; JAWP; WBP
Mountains, stand again. Company Gone. Mark Van Doren. MOAP
Mountains that upwards to the clouds arise. A Nun's Beloved. Mother Francis Raphael. PraNu
Mountains they are [*or* Mountains are a] silent folk, The. The Mountains Are a Lonely Folk. Hamlin Garland. BAP; PoMa; POT; PoTo; VOD
Mountains waver through my tears, The. Lullaby for a Man-Child. Jean Starr Untermeyer. BOL; YT
Mountainy Childer, The. Elizabeth Shane. HBMV
Mountebanks, The. Charles Henry Luders. AA
Mountebank's Mask, The, *sel.* Thomas Campion.
Hours of Sleepy Night, The. ElL
(Dismissal.) OBSC
Mounted on Kyrat strong and fleet. The Leap of Roushan Beg. Longfellow. MW; PTA-1; StVeCh
Mounting on high I begin to realize the smallness of man's domain. Climbing the Ling Ying Terrace and Looking North. Po Chü-i. TrCh
Mounting the High Balcony. Li Ch'ing-chao, *tr. fr. Chinese by* Sophia H. Chen. WhP
Mountown! Thou Sweet Retreat. William King. *Fr.* Mully of Mountown. BeR
Mourn, hapless Caledonia, mourn. The Tears of Scotland. Tobias Smollett. CEP; EBSV; OBEC
Mourn her in the valleys, you young lovers, and throughout your gloom. W. H. Oliver. *Fr.* Death and the Maiden. AnNZ
Mourn No More. John Fletcher, *and others. See* Weep No More.
Mourn not for man, speeding to lay waste. Of Mourners. Dorothy Livesay. PECV
Mourn not my loss; tears change not destiny. *Unknown. Fr.* Carmina Epigraphica. LaP
Mourn Not the Dead. Ralph Chaplin. BAP; HBMV; MaRV; OQP; PoFr; QP-2; ViBoPo
Mourne no more faire widdow. The Widow's Solace. Thomas Deloney. SiCE
Mourner, The. W. H. Davies. POTE
Mourner à la Mode, The. John Godfrey Saxe. LHV
Mourner's Bench, The. Edgar Lee Masters. ChMo; CMP
Mourners Came at Break of Day, The. Sarah Flower Adams. HBV
Mourners slowly bring Him through the gloom, The. He Is Buried. William A. Donaghy. *Fr.* The Stations of the Cross. JKCP (1955 ed.)
Mournful Madonnas with pathetic smiles. Meditations in a Museum Cloister. Sister Maryanna. JKCP (1955 ed.)
Mournful majesty of human greatness, The. Diaduminius. Pierre Benoit. CAW
Mournful my tale to tell. Elegy: On a Pet Dove. Alexander MacDonald, *tr. by* Alexander Stewart. EBSV
Mournful Numbers. Morris Bishop. WhC
Mournful Nut-Tree, The. Antipater, *tr. fr. Greek by* Lord Neaves. OnPM
Mournfully answer my groan, dark vales and Dorian water. Epitaph of Bion. Moschus. WoL
Mourning. Victor Hugo, *tr. fr. French by* Alan Conder. TrFP
Mourning Bride, The, *sels.* Congreve.
Aisle of a Temple, The, *fr.* II, i. EV-3
Among the Dead, *fr.* II, iii. BeR
(Temple, The.) LiA
"Heaven hath no rage like love to hatred turned," *fr.* III, viii. TreF
Music, *fr.* I, i. EV-3
("Music hath charms to sooth a savage breast.") BCEP; LEAP; ViBoPo
Mourning Conquest, The. *Unknown.* CoMu
Mourning Dove, The. W. W. Christman. BLA
Mourning for Li San. Po Chü-i, *tr. fr. Chinese by* Henry H. Hart. PoHN

Mourning Garment, The. Robert Greene. *See* Greene's Mourning Garment.
Mourning in Spring, 1943. Kathleen Raine. DiM
Mourning Mother, The. Elizabeth Barrett Browning. MOAH
Mourning Muse of Alexis, The, *sel.* Congreve.
Death of a Queen, The. BeR
Mourning your dearest friends, be wise in grief. Not Dead, But Gone Before. Antiphanes. OxBG
Mouse, The. Elizabeth J. Coatsworth. BoTP; FaPON; MoShBr; MoSiPe; OTPC (1946 ed.); PCD; RIS; SUS; TiPo; UTS
Mouse. Hilda Conkling. GoBP; StVeCh; TiPo
Mouse, The. *Unknown, tr. fr. Chinese by* Isaac Taylor Headland. PCH
Mouse, The. Thirza Wakley. BoTP
Mouse, a Cat, and an Irish Bull, A. John Banister Tabb. CIV
Mouse and the Cake, The. Eliza Cook. OTPC (1923 ed.)
Mouse That Gnawed the Oak-Tree Down, The. Vachel Lindsay. ChMo; CMP; PCN; PoeMoYo; StaSt
Mouse, the Frog and the Little Red Hen, The. *Unknown.* BoTP
Mouse's Lullaby, The. Palmer Cox. PCH
Mouse's Nest. John Clare. ChTr; ExPo; LiTB; LoBV; SeCeV
Mouse's Petition, The, *sl. abr.* Anna Letitia Barbauld. CG
Mousetrap, The. Christian Morgenstern, *tr. fr. German by* W. D. Snodgrass. AnGP
Mousie, mousie,/ Where is your little wee housie? Conversation. Rose Fyleman. BoTP
Mouth and Eyes. *Unknown, tr. fr. Spanish by* Havelock Ellis. OnPM
Mouth and the Ears, The. Shem-Tob ben Joseph Palquera, *tr. fr. Hebrew by* Joseph Chotzner. TrJP
Mouth down in the timothy. Grass. John Holmes. MiAP
Mouth like old silk soft with use, A. A Leaving. William Plomer. OBMV
Mouth to mouth joined we lie, her naked breasts. Tantalus [*or* Tantalos]. Paulus Silentiarius. LiTW; LyMA
Mouths. Louis Dudek. PeCV
Mouths half-open, in their shrouds. Rain and Lightning. Ibn Shuhaid. MooP
Move Eastward, Happy Earth. Tennyson. PreP; ViPP; VLEP
Move him into the sun. Futility. Wilfred Owen. AtBAP; ChMP; CoBMV; FaBoMo; GTBS-D; HiLiEn; LiTM; LO; MBP; MoAB; MoBrPo; MoP; MoPW; NeMA; OAEP (2d ed.); PoE; SeCePo; SoV; TrGrPo
Move me that jasmine further from the bed. The Deaths of Myron and Klydone. Augusta Davies Webster. *Fr.* In a Day. VA
"Move my arm-chair, faithful Pompey." On the Shores of Tennessee. Ethel Lynn Beers. PTA-1
Move on with a will, nor dream thou back. At Dawn of the Year. "George Klingle." PGD; PSO
Move over, Ali Baba! Now there comes. Autosonic Door. Dorothy Brown Thompson. GoYe
Moved by Her Music. Richard Gillman. NePoAm-2
Movement. Paul Eluard, *tr. fr. French by* Wallace Fowlie. MiCF
(Our Movement, *tr. by* Stephen Spender *and* Frances Cornford.) LiTW
Movies, The. Florence Kiper Frank. MW; NP; POT; PoTo
Movies in the Fire. Mildred D. Shacklett. GFA
Moving. Eunice Tietjens. GaP; TiPo
Moving Day. Helen M. Hartman. PoRL
Moving Finger, The. Omar Khayyám, *tr. fr. Persian by* Edward Fitzgerald. *Fr.* The Rubáiyát. OnPM
("Moving Finger writes, and having writ, The.") EG; GTBS-W
Moving form or rigid mass, A. Song of the Screw. *Unknown.* NA
Moving from left to left, the light. View of the Capitol from the Library of Congress. Elizabeth Bishop. FiMAP
Moving House. Tao Yuan-ming, *tr. fr. Chinese.* TrCh, *tr. by* Arthur Waley; WhP, *tr. by* Yang Yeh-tzu
Moving In. C. Day Lewis. ReaPo
Moving is all over, The. Moving Day. Helen M. Hartman. PoRL
Moving Moon went up the sky, The. Samuel Taylor Coleridge. *Fr.* The Rime of the Ancient Mariner. LO
Moving Rocks, The. Apollonius Rhodius, *tr. fr. Greek by* George Allen *and* C. M. Bowra. *Fr.* Argonautica, IV. OxBG
Moving sun-shapes on the spray, The. Going and Staying. Thomas Hardy. ChMo; CMP; EPP
Moving through the Silent Crowd. Stephen Spender. EnLi-2 (1949 ed.)
Moving with you. Poet to Dancer. Bernice Kavinoky. UnS
Mow the grass in the cemetery, darkies. Two at Norfolk. Wallace Stevens. FaBoMo
Mower, The. *Unknown.* CoMu
Mower against Gardens, The. Andrew Marvell. LiTB; OAEP; PoEL-2; ReEn; SeCV-1; SeEP; UTS
Mower in Ohio, The. John James Piatt. AA
Mower to [*or* of] the Glow-Worms [*or* Glowworms], The. Andrew Marvell. ALV; AtBAP; AWP; EG; ElSeCe; EPS; InPo; InvP; OnPM; OxBoLi; ReaPo; SeCL; TrGrPo
(Mower to Glow-Worms, The.) ReEn
(Mower to the Glo-Worms, The.) BrBE; EnLoPo; KN; MePo; OBS; PoEL-2
(To Glow-Worms.) RIS
Mowers, The. William Allingham. IrPN
Mowers, The. Myron B. Benton. LPS-2; YeAr
Mowers, The. Christopher Smart. *Fr.* A Noon Piece; or, The Mowers at Dinner. RO
Mowers in the Line of Fire. Valery Bryusov, *tr. fr. Russian by* Jack Lindsay. RuPo
Mower's Song, The. Andrew Marvell. ElSeCe; EnL; EPS; LiTL; LoBV; PoEL-2; ReEn; SeCL; SeCV-1
Mowers, weary and brown and blithe. Scythe Song. Andrew Lang. BLP; GN; HBV; PCD; PoeMoYo; POTT; PoVP; SN; VA
Mowing. Robert Frost. AmPo; AmPP; AnFE; AnNE; APA; CoAnAm; CoV; ExPo; HBMV; HoPM; LiTA; MM; MOAP; NeMA; NP; OxBA; PeBoSo; ShBV-3; TwAmPo; UnPo (3d ed.); YT
Mowing, The. Sir Charles G. D. Roberts. BoCaPo; ExPo
Moxford Book of English Verse, The, *sels.* Archibald Stodart-Walker. CenHV
Counsel to Girls.
Early Bacon.
Inflictis.
Moy Castle. *Unknown.* GoTP; OnSP
Moyst with one drop of thy blood, my dry soule. Resurrection. John Donne. OBS
Moytura, *sel.* William Larminie.
Sword of Tethra, The. OnYI; TIP
Mozarabic Songs. *Unknown, tr. fr. Spanish by* Eleanor L. Turnbull. TeCS
"Easter is coming, and I without him!"
"My heart, my heart goes from me, Lord."
"So much loving, so much loving."
"What shall I do, my mother?"
"What shall I do, what will become of me?"
Mozart, a lorgnette's target, child without toys. Some Prodigies. Charles Fisher. MoWP
Mozart in Heaven. Manuel Bandeira, *tr. fr. Portuguese by* Dudley Poore. AnCL
Mozart, 1935. Wallace Stevens. AmP; UnS
Mozart Perhaps. John Hall Wheelock. UnS
Mozart's Grave. Paul Scott Mowrer. GoYe
Mu'allaqát, The, *sels. Tr. fr. Arabic.*
Abla. Antara, *tr. by* E. Powys Mathers. AWP; JAWP; LiTW; WBP
Ode: "Weep, ah weep love's losing." Imr el Kais, *tr. by* Lady Anne Blount. AWP
(Weep Love's Losing.) LiTW
Pour Us Wine. Ibn Kolthúm, *tr. by* E. Powys Mathers. AWP
Much Ado about Nothing, *sels.* Shakespeare.
Beauty Is a Witch, *fr.* II, i. TrGrPo
Hero's Epitaph, *fr.* V, iii. TriL
("Done to death by slanderous tongues.") OBSC
Pardon, Goddess of the Night, *fr.* V, iii. OBSC; SiCE; ViBoPo
Patience and Sorrow, *fr.* V, i. EV-1
Sigh No More, Ladies [Sigh No More], *fr.* II, iii. AnFE; AWP; CenL; EG; ElL; EM-1; EnLi-1 (1949 ed.); EnLit; EPP; EV-1; ExPo; HBV; InMe; InPo; JAWP; LiTB; LiTG; LiTL; LoPo; MCCG; OAEP; PoEL-2; SeCeV; SiCE; SiTL; TOP; TreFS; TrGrPo; TwP; TyEnPo; ViBoPo; WBP
(Balthasar's Song.) ALV; BoLiVe; OBSC
(Fraud of Men, The.) BLV
(Song: "Sigh no more, ladies, sigh no more.") FiP
(Song from "Much Ado about Nothing.") LEAP
Much as he left it when he went from us. Why He Was There. E. A. Robinson. ChMo; CMP
Much as I own I owe. Closed for Good. Robert Frost. MoAmPo (1950 ed.)
Much, beauty, is, less, than, the, face, of. José Garcia Villa. Divine Poems, 102. POTE (1959 ed.)
Much did I rage when young. Youth and Age. W. B. Yeats. TwP
Much-discerning Public hold, A. La Nuit Blanche. Kipling. MBP; MoBrPo
Much doth it task me. The Loss of My Sons. Egill Skallagrimsson. PaOS
Much Has Been Said . . . *Unknown.* CoMu
Much have I labored, much read o'er. Alas for Youth. Firdausi. AWP; JAWP; LiTW; WBP
Much have I spoken of the faded leaf. November. Elizabeth Stoddard. AA

Much have I travail'd in the realms of gold. On First Looking into the Dark Future. Roger Lancelyn Green. CenHV
Much have I travell'd [or travelled or traveled] in the realms of gold. On First Looking into Chapman's Homer. Keats. AEV; AnFE; ATP; BCEP; BEL; BLV; BoLiVe; BPN; BTP; CaAE; CBE; CBOV; CH; ChER; ChTr; CoBE; CoEV; DD; EG; EM-2; EmBrPo; EnL; EnLi-2; EnLit; EnLP; EnRP; EPN; EPP; ERP; ES; EV-4; ExPo; FaBoBe; FaBoCh; FaBoEn; FaFP; FiP; GEPC; GN; GTBS; GTBS-D; GTBS-W; GTSE; GTSL; HBV; HBVY; HiLiEn; HoPM; InP; InPo; KN; LEAP; LH; LiTB; LiTG; LoBV; LoGBV; MaPo; MCCG; MOB; NeHB; OAEP; OBEV; OBRV; OTPC; OuHeWo; PeBoSo; PECK; PFE; PIAE; PIR; PoEL-4; PoeMoYo; PoFS; PreP; PtP; PYM; ReaPo; ReTS; SeCeV; ShBV-3; TCEP; TOP; TreF; TrGrPo; TVSH; TwCrTr; TwHP; TwP; TyEnPo; UnPo (1st ed.); ViBoPo; WHA
Much have we heard the peevish world complain. On Friendship. William Whitehead. OBEC
Much honoured were my humble home. Challenge. Sir Walter Scott. *Fr.* Marmion. OtMeF
Much I guzzled, much I tippled, and of slander many loads. The Backbiter. Simonides. GrPE
Much I remember of the death of men. The Tomb of Michael Collins. Denis Devlin. OxBI
Much in Bithynia I pondered on. Ideal Passion, XXXII. George Edward Woodberry. MOAP
Much Knowledge, Little Reason. Sir John Davies. *Fr.* Nosce Teipsum. ChTr
(Knowledge and Reason.) OBSC
Much Love. *Unknown, tr. fr. Bohemian folk song.* PCH
Much madness is divinest sense. Emily Dickinson. AmPo; AmPP; CoBA; CoV; LiTA; LiTM (rev. ed.); OxBA; PFY; PoFr; PoLFOT
(Divinest Sense.) OnPM
Much of my native scenery appears. Robert Pollok. *Fr.* The Course of Time. EnSW
Much of transfiguration that we hear. The Interlude. Karl Shapiro. MoVE
Much power, indeed, Sir Money has and much for him we dabble. The Power of Money. Juan Ruiz, Archpriest of Hita. *Fr.* The Book of Good Love. AnSpL-1
Much spake the angel of presumption, thought. Satan's Presumption and Fall. Cædmon(?). *Fr.* Genesis. EPP
Much they reproached me and reviled. The Weaver's Apprentice. Al-Rusafi. MooP
Much vexes me; you'll hear my recital? Vexational. The Monk of Montaudon. LyMA
Much Virtue in If. T. Sturge Moore. TCPD
Mucilla dyes her locks, 'tis said. *See* Mycilla dyes her locks, 'tis said.
Muckish Mountain (The Pig's Back). Shane Leslie. AnIV
Muckle-mou'd Meg. James Ballantine. HBV; VA
Muckle-Mouth Meg. Robert Browning. BPN; HBV; OtMeF; PoVP; VA; VLEP
Mud. Polly Chase Boyden. GoBP; MPB; TiPo
Mud. Richard Church. MoBrPo (1942 ed.); MoP
Mud. Marty Hale. AlBD
Mud Cakes. Mildred D. Shacklett. GFA
Mud in a river flown in a bill to your eaves, The. The History of Communications and a Running Account. Pien Chih-lin. LiTW
Mud is very nice to feel. Mud. Polly Chase Boyden. GoBP; MPB; TiPo
Mud-stained and torn upon the sidewalk lying. The Queen of Hearts. Marc Cook. PR
Mud through my toes I'm from this land. Testimony to an Inquisitor. William Stafford. NePoAm-2
Mudarra and Rodrigo. *Unknown, tr. fr. Spanish by* James Young Gibson. LyMA; TeCS
Muddled Metaphors. Tom Hood. NA
Muddy Rat, The. Horiguchi Daigaku, *tr. fr. Japanese by* Kenneth Rexroth. LiTW
Mufaddaliyat, The, *sels. Tr. fr. Arabic by* Sir Charles Lyall.
Gone Is Youth. Salamah, Son of Jandal. AWP
His Camel. Alqamah. AWP; JAWP; WBP
Old Age. Al-Aswad, Son of Ya'fur. AWP
Muffin Man, The. Anne Croasdell. BoTP
Muffin-Man, The. Madeleine Nightingale. GaP
Muffin man walked down our street, The. The Muffin Man. Anne Croasdell. BoTP
Muffin-Man's Bell, The. Ann Hawkshaw. BoTP; OTPC
Muffled and faint the whispering begins. African Night. Jessie Lemont. MuM
Muffled drum is beating, The. Stonewall's Requiem. M. Deeves. BlG
Muffled drum's sad roll has beat, The. The Bivouac of the Dead. Theodore O'Hara. AA; AnAmPo; AOAH; BlG; BLPA; BoHiPo; DD; GA; HBV; HH; LA; LBAP; MC; MDAH; NeHB; OBAV; PaA; PAH; PAP; PoRL; PTA-2; SPP; TCAP; TreF
Mugford's Victory. John White Chadwick. PAH
Mugger's Song, The. W. W. Gibson. ChMo; CMP
Muiopotmos, *sel.* Spenser.
Butterfly, The. EV-1
Mulberry Garden, The, *sel.* Sir Charles Sedley.
Child and Maiden, *fr.* III, ii. GTBS; GTBS-D; GTBS-W; GTSE; GTSL; LiTL; TOP
("Ah Cloris! that I now could sit.") OAEP; OBS
(Song: "Ah Cloris! that I now could sit.") SeCV-2; ViBoPo
(Song: To Chloris.) EV-3
(To a Very Young Lady.) LPS-1
(To Chloris.) HBV; OBEV; SeCL
Mulberry is a double tree, The. Banjo Boomer. Wallace Stevens. WaKn
Mulberry Trees, The. *Unknown, tr. fr. Chinese by* Bernhard Karlgren. *Fr.* Shi King. ChLP
Mule, The. *Unknown.* LauV
Mule in the Mines, The. *Unknown.* ChTr
(Campfire and Bunkhouse.) CoSo
Mule Skinner's Song, The, *with music. Unknown.* AS
Mules, I think, will not be here this hour, The. Empedocles on Etna. Matthew Arnold. ViPP
Mulford. Whittier. AA
Mulier Amicta Sole. Fray Angelico Chavez. ISi
Mullet and the Hook, The. Oppian, *tr. fr. Greek by* F. L. Lucas. *Fr.* Halieuticks. GrPE
Mulligan Stew, The. *Unknown.* DDA
Mully of Mountown, *sel.* William King.
Mountown! Thou Sweet Retreat. BeR
Multicoloured mushroom seems, The. Haiku of the Flower-pot. José Juan Tablada. AnMP
Multiplication. Joyce Kilmer. WHL
Multiplication is vexation. Arithmetic. Mother Goose. BrR; GoTP; MeMeAg; OTPC; RIS; TreFS
Multitude of the skies, gold riddle of millions of stars. Dain do Eimhir, XVII. Sorley Maclean. NeBP
Multitudes thronged, The. Into a Mountain Apart. Alice E. Sherwood. PraP
Multitudinous Seas Incarnadine. Shakespeare. *See* Murder, The.
"Multum Dilexit." Hartley Coleridge. EnRP; ERP; EV-4; HBV; VA
Mumbo, Jumbo. Food for Thought. Michael Lewis. RIS
Mumford. Ina M. Porter. PAH
Mummer, The. Anna Wickham. TwCV
Mummy, The. Vernon Watkins. MoPo; NeBP
Mumps. Elizabeth Madox Roberts. FaPON; GaP; MPB; LiL; TSW
Munch's Scream. Donald Hall. NePoEA
Mundus et Infans. W. H. Auden. LiTB; LiTM; MoAB; MoBrPo (1950 ed.)
Mundus Morosus. Frederick William Faber. ACP; CAW
(World Morose, The.) OBVV
Munestruck. "Hugh MacDiarmid." NeBP
Munich Elegy No. 1. George Barker. LiTG; LiTM; SeCePo; WaP
Municipal. Kipling. WhC
Muncipal Gallery Revisited, The. W. B. Yeats. BoFr, *abr.*; LiTB
Munition-Maker. Laura Simmons. PIAE
Munitions Expert. W. H. Auden. *Fr.* On This Island, XVIII. MaRV
Munitions Plant. Louis Untermeyer. *See* Steel Mill.
Munster War-Song, The. Richard D'Alton Williams. TIP
Muppim and Huppim! Strike blows on your drums! The Dance of Despair. Hayyim Nahman Bialik. TrJP
Murat. Byron. *Fr.* The Ode from the French. LPS-3
Murder, The. Shakespeare. Macbeth, II, ii. CBOV; LPS-3
(Deed, The, *fr.* ii.) EV-1
(Macbeth Does Murder Sleep, *fr.* ii.) FiP
(Multitudinous Seas Incarnadine, *fr.* ii.) LiA
(Murderers, The.) WHA
("That which hath made them drunk hath made me bold.") AtBAP; MyFE
Murder, The. Bertram Warr. BoCaPo (1948 ed.)
Murder of Julius Caesar. Shakespeare. *Fr.* Julius Caesar, II, i. EV-1
Murder of Maria Marten, The. W. Corder. CoMu
Murder of Neoptolemus, The. Euripides, *tr. fr. Greek by* Hugh Owen Meredith. *Fr.* Andromache. GrR
Murder of Saint Thomas of Kent, The. *Unknown.* ACP
Murder of the Tsarevich Dimitri by Boris Godunov, The. *Unknown, tr. fr. Russian by* N. Kershaw Chadwick. LiTW
Murder Pact, The. Shakespeare. *See* Duncan's Murder.
Murder Will Out. Chaucer. *Fr.* The Canterbury Tales: The Nun's Priest's Tale. MyFE
Murdered eye is not dead, The. Blind Man's Cries. Tristan Corbière. AnFP
Murdered Little Bird. *Unknown.* FiBHP
Murdered Traveller, The. Bryant. CoBA
Murderers, The. Shakespeare. *See* Murder, The.
Murdering Beauty. Thomas Carew. OAEP

Murmur from the Stable, The. Rubén Darío, *tr. fr. Spanish by* Agnes Blake Poor. CAW
Murmur in the Grass, A. "Æ." ChMo; CMP
Murmer of a bee, The. Mysteries. Emily Dickinson. AnFE; APA; CBOV; CoAnAm; MAP; MoAmPo; NeMA
(Why?) OnPM
Murmur of the mourning ghost, The. The Ballad of Keith of Ravelston [*or* Keith of Ravelston]. Sydney Thompson Dobell. *Fr.* The Nuptial Eve. BMEP; CH; DaM; EV-5; GTBS; HBV; LEAP; OBEV; OBVV; TOP; UnW
Murmuring in empty shells, A. The Relic. Robert Hillyer. GoYe; UnS
Murmuring of Pine Trees, The. Ryokwan, *tr. fr. Japanese by* Asataro Miyamori. OnPM
Murning Maiden, The. *Unknown.* EBSV
Murrough Defeats the Danes, 994. *Unknown. See* On the Defeat of Ragnall . . .
Musa of the sea-blue eyes. On a Singing Girl. Elinor Wylie. TOP
Muscles flex, contract, The. Spring Poem. Julian Symons. NeBP
Musco, that always kept with policy. Henry Parrot. SiCE
Muse, The. "Anna Akhmatova," *tr. fr. Russian by* C. M. Bowra. BoRS
Muse, The. Thomas Blackburn. PoN
Muse, The. Abraham Cowley. BEL; Po
Muse and Poet. Robert Bridges. OBMV
Muse, bid the morne awake. To His Valentine. Michael Drayton. AtBAP; PoEL-2
Muse, disgusted at an age and clime, The. On the Prospect of Planting Arts and Learning in America [*or* Verses on . . .]. George Berkeley. CEP; CoBE; EiPP; FaFP; HBV; LPS-2; OBEC; OnYI; Po; PoE; SeCePo; SeCeV; TreF; TrGrPo; ViBoPo
Muse in Late November. Jonathan Henderson Brooks. PoNe
Muse in the New World, The. Walt Whitman. Song of the Exposition, II, III, *abr.* APW; MAP; MoAmPo
(Come Muse Migrate from Greece and Ionia.) OnAP
Muse, my sister, gave me a look, The. The Muse. "Anna Akhmatova." BoRS
Muse of Burns, The. Burns. *Fr.* The Vision. RO
Muse of Fire, A. Shakespeare. *Fr.* King Henry V, Prologue to Act I. ChTr
("O for a Muse of fire, that would ascend," *longer sel.*) BHV; EV-1
Muse of my native land! loftiest Muse! Keats. Endymion, IV. EnRP
Muse of Nonsense, The. Gelett Burgess. PIAE
Muse on Death. Palladas, *tr. fr. Greek by* Robert Guthrie MacGregor. OnPM
Muse Reviving, The. Sir John Davies. SiPS
Muse should be sprightly, The. A Skeltoniad. Michael Drayton. PoEL-2
Muse, tell of Pan, the dear seed of Hermes, that shows. To Pan. *Unknown. Fr.* Homeric Hymns. OxBG
Muse to an Unknown Poet, The. Paul Potts. FaBoTw
Muse with the hero's brave deeds being fired, The. Captain Death. *Unknown.* CoMu
Muse, you who cherish the comely white shore of Sirmio. To the Muse of Sirmio. Marc-Antonio Flaminio. LaP
Musée des Beaux Arts. W. H. Auden. ChMo; ChMP; CoBMV; EnL; ExPo; FaFP; LiTB; LiTG; LiTM; MaPo; MoAB; MoPo; NePA; OAEP (2d ed.); PG (1955 ed.); PoFS; PoLFOT; PoRA; SeCePo; SeCeV; TrGrPo (rev. ed.); TwHP
Muses, The. Edith M. Thomas. HBV
Muses/ Muses of Sicily. The Fourth Eclogue [*or* Dawn of the Golden Age]. Virgil. *Fr.* Eclogues. LaP; LiTW; RoL
Muses' Elysium, The, *sels.* Michael Drayton.
Cloris and Mertilla. LoBV
Description of Elysium, The. TuPP
Ferryman, Venus, and Cupid, The. CG
Fine Day, A. BoTP; CG; GN; OTPC; PCH
(Lines: "Clear had the day been from the dawn.") LoBV
(Sixt Nimphall, The.) OBS
(Sixth Nymphal, The.) TuPP
Nymphs' Song, The. SeCL
Second Nimphall, The.
"With full-leav'd lillies I will stick." AtBAP
Muse's fairest light in no dark time, The. To the Memory of Ben Jonson. John Cleveland. LPS-3
Muses' Gift, The. Hesiod, *tr. fr. Greek by* Jack Lindsay. *Fr.* Theogony. OxBG
(Gift of the Muses, *tr. by* Arthur S. Way.) GrR
Muses, I oft invoked your holy aid. Astrophel and Stella, LV. Sir Philip Sidney. SiPS; TuPP
Muses Love Me, The. Horace, *tr. fr. Latin by* John Coningtor. OnPM
Muses of Australia, The. Victor Daley. BoAu
Muses of Pieria, join one and all to sing. In Praise of Bombyca. Theocritus. *Fr.* Idylls. OxBG
Muses of Pieria who give glory through song, come hither Hesiod. *Fr.* Works and Days. GrL
Muses of Sicily, loftier be our song! The Sibylline Prophecy Virgil. *Fr.* The Fourth Eclogue. CAW; ISi
Muses that Fame's loose feathers beautify. George Chapman. *Fr.* A Coronet for His Mistress Philosophy. ReIE
Muses that sing love's sensual empery [*or* emperie]. Sonnet [*or* Love and Philosophy]. George Chapman. A Coronet for His Mistress Philosophy, I. BrBE; CoBE; ElL; ElSeCe; LoBV; LPS-1; OBSC; PoE; RiBV; SeCePo; TuPP
Muses took the vote and told, The. Helicon and Cithaeron. Corinna. OxBG
Muses weave a brightness for his head, The. Strepsiades of Thebes. Pindar. *Fr.* Isthmian Odes. OxBG
Muses wrapped in mysteries of light, The. The Whirlwind Road. Edwin Markham. AA
Museum, The. William Abrahams. WaP
Museum Meteorite. Ruby T. Scott. MuM
Museum-Piece. Audrey Alexandra Brown. CaP
Museum Piece. Lawrence P. Spingarn. GoYe
Museum Piece. Richard Wilbur. MiAP; NePA
Museum Portico. H. L. R. Edwards. MoWP
Museums. Louis MacNeice. ChMo; MBP; MoBrPo; NAMP
Mushroom is the elf of plants, The. Emily Dickinson. NePA
Mushrooms pert and pink. Sunday Morning. Isidor Schneider. AnAmPo; LA
Music. Baudelaire, *tr. fr. French by* Robert Fitzgerald. AnFP
Music. Ecclesiasticus, XXXII: 5–6, Bible, Apocrypha. TrJP
Music. Robert Browning. *Fr.* Abt Vogler. GrCo-1
Music. Thomas Carlyle. WBLP
Music. G. K. Chesterton. JKCP (1955 ed.)
Music. Congreve. *Fr.* The Mourning Bride, I. EV-3
("Music hath charms.") BCEP; LEAP; ViBoPo
Music. Hilda Conkling. HH; MPB
Music. Alice Corbin. NP
Music. Abraham Cowley. *See* Supplication, A.
Music. Walter de la Mare. AlDL; HH; PoRL; VOD
Music. George Du Maurier, *after the French of* Sully-Prudhomme. OBEV (new ed.); OBVV
Music. Emerson. AnNE; GoTP; MaRV; MOAP; WGRP
(Fragments.) OQP; QP-1
(Let Me Go Where'er I Will.) NLK
(Singing World, The.) MW
Music. Eleanor Farjeon. TiPo (1959 ed.)
Music. John Fletcher. LoGBV
Music ("Orpheus with his lute"). *At. to* John Fletcher, *also to* Shakespeare. *See* Orpheus with His Lute.
Music. Otto Freund. MuM
Music. Erik Gustaf Geijer, *tr. fr. Swedish by* Charles W. Stork. AnSL
Music. W. E. Henley. In Hospital, XXIII. BPN
Music. Amy Lowell. AnAmPo; LA; YaD
Music. Charles Phillips. CAW; JKCP
Music. Agnes Mary Frances Robinson. UnW
Music. Anne Ryan. CAW
Music. Daniel Sargent. SaFP
Music ("How sweet the moonlight sleeps"). Shakespeare. *See* How Sweet the Moonlight Sleeps upon This Bank.
Music ("If music be the food of love"). Shakespeare. *See* If Music Be the Food of Love.
Music ("Orpheus with his lute"). *At. to* Shakespeare, *also to* John Fletcher. *See* Orpheus with His Lute.
Music ("I pant for the music which is divine"). Shelley. CBE; ERP
(Fragment: Music.) EmBrPo
Music ("Music, when soft voices die"). Shelley. *See* Music. When Soft Voices Die.
Music ("Silver key of the fountain of tears"). Shelley. *See* Fragment, A: To Music.
Music. Edith M. Thomas. *See* God of Music.
Music. *Unknown.* MaRV
Music and Memory. John Albee. AA
Music and Words. Elizabeth Jennings. UnS
Music as of the winds when they awake. Beethoven. John Todhunter. TIP
Music at the Bower of Bliss, The. Spenser. *Fr.* The Faerie Queene, II, 12. MyFE
Music at Twilight. George Sterling. HBV
Music Box, A. Abbie Farwell Brown. PPL
Music can not stay. Pediment: Ballet. Louise Townsend Nicholl. UnS
Music can paint no pictures, speak no words. Music. Otto Freund. MuM
Music Comes. John Freeman. TwCV
Music first and foremost of all! Art poétique. Paul Verlaine. AWP
"Music for a while." Song at Night. Norman Nicholson. FaBoTw
Music God. Mark Van Doren. UnS
Music Grinders, The. Oliver Wendell Holmes. WhC
Music had the heat of blood, The. During Music. Arthur Symons. MBP; MoBrPo; VA

Music-Hall, The. Theodore Wratislaw. VA
Music has charms to soothe a savage breast. Music. Congreve. *Fr.* The Mourning Bride, I. BCEP; EV-3; LEAP; ViBoPo
Music I Heard [with You]. Conrad Aiken. Discordants, I. AWP; ChMo; CMP; FaFP; GTBS-W; HBV; LEAP; LiTA; LiTL; LiTM; LoPo; LoPS; MOAP; OxBA; PG; PoeMoYo; PoMa; PoRA; SBMV; TwCV
(Bread and Music.) MAP; MoAB; MoAmPo; NeMA; YT
Music in Camp. John R. Thompson. AA; BLPA; HBV; IAP; PaA; PAP; TCAP
Music in the Night. Harriet Prescott Spofford. AA
Music in the Rec Hut. Hubert Creekmore. WaP
Music in the Street. *Unknown.* TIP
Music is well said to be the speech of angels. Music. Thomas Carlyle. WBLP
Music is writ by the deaf. Replying to the Many Kind Friends Who Ask Me if I No Longer Write Poetry. Shaemas O'Sheel. TBM
Music Lesson, A. Alexander Hay Japp. VA
Music-mad. Grace Noll Crowell. LS
Music Magic. Edmund Leamy. JKCP
Music-Makers, The. Arthur O'Shaughnessy. *See* Ode: "We are the music-makers."
Music met Leviathan returning, A. Peter Quennell. *Fr.* Leviathan. MBP; MoBrPo
Music, murmur me to slumber. Evensong. Ruth Schaumann. CAW
Music, music hath its sway. The Flight of Malzah. Charles Heavysege. *Fr.* Saul. VA
Music, music with throb and swing. The Songster. E. Pauline Johnson. CPG
Music must be paramount. The Art of Poetry. Paul Verlaine. AnFP
Music of a Friend, The. Louis V. Ledoux. OQP; QP-2
Music of a Tree, The. W. J. Turner. MBP; MoBrPo
Music of Colours: The Blossom Scattered. Vernon Watkins. LiTB; PoN
Music of Colours—White Blossom. Vernon Watkins. FaBoMo; LiTM; WaP
Music of Hounds, The. Shakespeare. *Fr.* A Midsummer Night's Dream, IV, i. EV-1
(Theseus and Hippolyta.) AlBD
Music of Hungary. Anne Reeve Aldrich. AA
Music of the autumn winds sings low, The. Autumn. Edwin Curran. HBMV; TSW
Music of the Dawn. Virginia Bioren Harrison. HBV
Music of the dignity of souls, The. Crass Times Redeemed by Dignity of Souls. Peter Viereck. MiAP
Music of the Future, The. Oliver Herford. CenHV; PoMa
Music of the muted winds, The. A Voice before April. Briton Niven Busch, Jr. CAG
Music of the Night. John Neal. AA; APW
Music of the Spheres, The. Alfred Noyes. *Fr.* Watchers of the Sky. GrCo-1
Music of the star-shine shimmering o'er the sea. Haunted in Old Japan. Alfred Noyes. LEAP
Music of the World and of the Soul, The. Arthur Hugh Clough. VLEP
Music-stand of crimson lacquer, long since brought, A. The Red Lacquer Music-Stand. Amy Lowell. TCPD
Music, The! the/ music! as when Casals struck. William Carlos Williams. *Fr.* The Desert Music. UnS
Music to hear, why hear'st thou music sadly? Sonnets, VIII. Shakespeare. PeBoSo; PoEL-2; ViBoPo
Music, When Soft Voices Die. Shelley. BCEP; BoLiVe; CBE; EmBrPo; EV-4; GTBS; GTBS-D; GTBS-W; GTSE; GTSL; LEAP; LiTB; LiTG; LiTL; MCCG; OBEV; OBRV; OTPC (1946 ed.); PCD; ReaPo; TrGrPo; TyEnPo; WHA
(Love Slumbers On.) BLP
(Memory.) MaRV
(Music.) CH
(To——.) AtBAP; ATP; AWP; BEL; BLV; BPN; CaAE; EM-2; EnL; EnLi-2 (1949 ed.); EnLit; EnRP; EPN; ERP; ExPo; FiP; GEPC; InPo; JAWP; KN; LoBV; LPS-3; OAEP; PFE; PIAE; PoE; PoEL-4; PreP; REAL; SeCePo; TCEP; TOP; ViBoPo; WBP
Musica No. 3. Richard Duerden. NeAP
Musical Ass, The. Tomás de Iriarte, *tr. fr. Spanish.* BOHV
Musical Box, A. William Wetmore Story. PR
Musical Critic Anticipates Eternity, A. Siegfried Sassoon. UnS
Musical Duel, The. John Ford. *Fr.* The Lover's Melancholy, I, i. LPS-2
Musical Evening, A. Joseph G. Francis. CIV
Musical Instrument, A. Elizabeth Barrett Browning. BCEP; BEL; BPN; EmBrPo; EnLi-2; EPP; EV-4; FaBoBe; FaPON; GBV; GoTP; GTBS; GTML; GTSL; HBV; HBVY; HiLiEn; LEAP; LPS-3; MCCG; OAEP; OBEV; OBVV; OTPC (1946 ed.); PECK; PFE; PIR; PoRL; PoVP; ReTS; ShBV-3; TOP; TVSH; TwCrTr; TyEnPo; VA; ViPo; VLEP; YT
Musical Pitch, The. *Unknown.* PA
Musician. Clifford Bax. TCPD
Musician. Louise Bogan. UnS
Musician, The. R. P. Lister. UnS
Musicians wrestle everywhere. Emily Dickinson. UnS
Musick in time. *Unknown.* SeCSL
Musick, thou Queen of Heaven, care-charming-spel. To Musick. Robert Herrick. UnS
Musick to heare, why hear'st thou musick sadly. *See* Music to hear . . .
Musicks Duell. Richard Crashaw. *See* Music's Duel.
Musick's Empire. Andrew Marvell. NBE
Music's Anodyne. Pindar, *tr. fr. Greek by* C. J. Billson. *Fr.* Nemean Odes, IV. GrR
Music's Duel. Richard Crashaw. CoBE; GoTL; LPS-3; SeEP
(Musicks Duell.) OBS; SeCV-1
Nightingale's Song, The, *sel.* LPS-3
Music's Mastery. *Unknown, tr. fr. Greek by* Shelley. *Fr.* Homeric Hymns. GrR
Music's Silver Sound. Shakespeare. *Fr.* Romeo and Juliet, IV, v. GN; HH
Musing, between the sunset and the dark. Kindred. George Sterling. MuM; NP; OBAV
Musing I met in no strange land. The Three Witnesses. Coventry Patmore. MeRV
Musing, I sit on my cushioned settle. Firelight. Heine. CIV
Musing Maiden, The. Thomas Hardy. BEL
Musing on a Great Soldier. Herbert Trench. PoeT
Musing upon the restles bisinesse. Prologue. Thomas Hoccleve. *Fr.* De Regimine Principum. PoEL-1
Musings. Longfellow. PEOR
Musings on Man's Sad Estate. Sophocles, *tr. fr. Greek by* Lewis Campbell. *Fr.* Ajax. GrR
Musketaquid. Emerson. CoBA; IAP; MOAP
Musmee, The. Sir Edwin Arnold. VA
Musophilus, or Defence of All Learning, *abr.* Samuel Daniel. ReEn
Sels.
English Poetry. OBSC
(Poetry of England, The.) CoBE
(Treasure of Our Tongue, The, *abr.*) EV-1
"Fond man, Musophilus, that thus dost spend." ReIE; SiCE; TuPP
(Poet and Critic.) OBSC
To the Right Worthy and Judicious Favorer of Virtue, Master Fulke Greville. ReIE; SiCE
Musselburgh Field. *Unknown.* ESPB
Mussolini's pet Marshal, Graziani. Limerick. T. R. Ybarra. LiBL
Must ever the morning return? Hymns to the Night, II. "Novalis." AnGP; LiTW
Must hapless man, in ignorance sedate. Celestial Wisdom. Juvenal. Satires, X. AWP; JAWP; WBP
Must I be always merely a listener? Never reply. On Poets Who Recite in Public—and Other Sinners. Juvenal. Satires, I. LaP
Must I in my most hopefull yeares. *Unknown.* SeCSL
Must I love again, knowing that love grows cold? Bondage. Joan Lamburn. DiM
"Must I submissive bow to earth my head?" Faith. Theodore Maynard. OQP; QP-2
Must I take. Friday Night. Evelyn Underhill. PraNu
Must I then see, alas! eternal night. Elegy over a Tomb. Lord Herbert of Cherbury. AtBAP; ElL; FaBoEn; MeLP; MePo; OBEV (new ed.); OBS; PoEL-2; SeEP; TriL; ViBoPo
Must it be always so whenever rain. Revenants. Joseph Auslander. NP
Must Jesus bear the cross alone. Thomas Shepherd. OlF
Must noble Hastings immaturely die. Upon the Death of the Lord Hastings. Dryden. CEP; ReEn; SeCV-2
Must the poetry of everything vanish. Lightless Suburb. "Pablo Neruda." TwSpPo
Must we be devyded now. *Unknown.* SeCSL
Must we part. Von Hügel, though much alike, for we. W. B. Yeats. *Fr.* Vacillation. OBMV
Must you frown so? To My Son. John V. A. Weaver. FAOV
Mustang Gray. *Unknown.* ABF, *with music*; CoSo, *with music*; CSF
Mustapha, *sels.* Fulke Greville.
Chorus Primus: Wise Counsellors. OBS
Chorus Quintus: Tartarorum. OBS
Chorus Sacerdotum. ATP; BrBE; CoEV; FaBoEn; InvP; MePo; NBE; OBS; PoEL-1; RiBV; SeCePo; SiCE; TuPP
(Chorus: "O wearisome condition.") ViBoPo
(Chorus of Priests.) EV-1
(O Wearisome Condition of Humanity.) EG; LiTB; SeCeV
Chorus Tertius: Of Time; Eternitie. OBS
Justice and Mercy. EV-1

Mustard and Cress. Norman Gale. TVC; TVSH
Muster of the North, The. Sir Charles Gavan Duffy. TIP
Muster Out the Ranger[s]. *Unknown.* CoSo; CSF
Musterer, The. Eileen Duggan. CoBE
Mustering the Hosts of Hell. Milton. Paradise Lost, *Bk.* I, *ll.* 522–604. BCEP, *abr.*
("All these and more came flocking," *ll.* 522–571.) MyFE
Musty tomes, The. The Bookworm. Su T'ung-po. PoHN
Mutabilitie. Spenser. *See* Mutability.
Mutability. Rupert Brooke. POTT
Mutability. John Gould Fletcher. ChMo; CMP
Mutability. Ibn Hazm, *tr. fr. Arabic by* A. J. Arberry. MooP
Mutability. Shelley. BCEP; BEL; BoLiVe; BPN; CoBE; EM-2; EmBrPo; EnLi-2; EnLit; EnRP; EPN; ERP; FaBoEn; HBV; TOP; ViBoPo
Mutability [*or* Mutabilitie]. Spenser. *Fr.* The Faerie Queene, VII, *7 and* 8. CoEV (*fr.* 8); FaBoEn (*fr.* 7); OxBoCh (*fr.* 8); PoEL-1; TwCrTr (*fr.* 8)
("When I bethinke me on that speech whyleare," *fr.* 8.) ReEn
Mutability. Wordsworth. Ecclesiastical Sonnets, Pt. III, Sonnet XXXIV. BPN; EmBrPo; EnLi-2; EnLP; EnRP; EPN; ExPo; GEPC; LiTB; OBRV; OQP; PC; PoE; PoEL-4; QP-2; REAL; RiBV; SeCeV
("From low to high doth dissolution climb.") EG
(Sonnet: "From low to high doth dissolution climb.") CoEV
Mutans Nomen Evae. Eric Gill. CAW
Mutation. Bryant. AmPP (3d ed.); BAV
Mutations of the Phoenix. Sir Herbert Read. BrBE
"Phoenix, bird of terrible pride," *sel.* FaBoTw
Mute bird sidles through soft valleys of air, A. Afternoon in Anglo-Ireland. Bruce Williamson. NeIP
Mute figures with bowed heads. The Refugees. Sir Herbert Read. MBP; MoBrPo (1942 ed.)
Mute fishes, too, with eyes of gold inlaid. Golden Fish. Titanomachia. OxBG
Mute he sat in the saddle—mute 'midst our full acclaim. A Christopher of the Shenandoah. Edith M. Thomas. PAH
Mute is the final hour, and all that lives. Dies Irae. Inger Hagerup. LiTW
Mute Opinion. Thomas Hardy. ChMo; CMP; ViPo
Mute, sightless visitant. Helen Keller. Edmund Clarence Stedman. AA
Muted. Paul Verlaine, *tr. fr. French by* Alan Conder. TrFP
Mutes in Life's Chorus, The. Menander, *tr. fr. Greek by* Sir William Marris. OxBG
Mutilated choir boys, The. The Choir Boys. Heine. *Fr.* Die Heimkehr. AWP; LiTW
Mutiny. "Æ." ChMo; CMP; SoV
Mutis Mutandis. *Unknown.* TMEV
Mutter, Die, sagt, "Nau Lieschen listen here." Mama's Advice. Kurt M. Stein. InMe
Muttering at the crowd, indifferent. The Death of an Old Man. Michael Hamburger. NePoEA
Mutton. *Unknown.* PA
Mutton and Leather. *Unknown.* CoMu
Mutual forgiveness of each vice. For the Sexes; the Gates of Paradise. Blake. LiTB; PoEL-4
Muvver was barfin' 'er biby one night, A. "Biby's" Epitaph. *Unknown.* FiBHP
Muy Vieja Mexicana. Alice Corbin. OBAV; SBMV
(Una Anciana Mexicana.) NP
My absent daughter—gentle, gentle maid. A Living Memory. William Augustus Croffut. AA
My Aim. George Linnaeus Banks. *See* What I Live For.
My Ain Countree. Mary Augusta Demarest. HBV; WGRP
My Ain Fireside. Elizabeth Hamilton. FaBoBe; HBV; LPS-1
My Ain Kind Dearie, O. Burns. *See* Lea Rig.
My Ain Wife. Alexander Laing. HBV; VA
My Airedale Dog. W. L. Mason. GFA; UTS
My All. Takamoto, *tr. fr. Japanese by* Lois J. Erickson. SoLD
My Alma Mater. "T. M. M." CAG
My Altar. John H. Styles, Jr. MaRV
My Amaryllis was not made. When Amaryllis Bowls. John Farrar. LEAP; PR
My America. Thomas Curtis Clark. OQP; PEDC; QP-1
My Angel. Jonathan Henderson Brooks. PoNe
My Angeline. Harry B. Smith. *Fr.* The Wizard of the Nile. BOHV; InMe
My Anguish. Innokenti Annenski, *tr. fr. Russian by* C. M. Bowra. BoR
My answered prayer came up to me. The Prayer. Sara Teasdale. ChMo; CMP
My—anything but beautiful, that standest "knock-knee'd" by. The Horse and His Master. Philip F. Allen. PA
My Apish Cousins. Marianne Moore. *See* Monkeys, The.
My April Lady. Henry van Dyke. HBV
My ardors [*or* ardours] for emprize nigh lost. On an Invitation to the United States. Thomas Hardy. AWP; InPo; JAWP; WBP
My arms are round you, and I lean. To the Oaks of Glencree. J. M. Synge. GTIV; MBP; MoBrPo; OxBI
My arms were always quiet. Gesture. Winifred Welles. BAP; HBMV; MaRV
My aspens dear, whose airy cages quelled. Binsey Poplars (Felled 1879). Gerard Manley Hopkins. CoBMV; EG; MoVE; TwCV; UnPo (3d ed.)
My attire is noiseless when I tread the earth. Wild Swan. *Unknown. Fr.* Riddles. AnOE
My Auld Breeks. Alexander Rodger. CBOV; EBSV
My Aunt. Oliver Wendell Holmes. AmP; AmPP; AnNE; CoBA; DDA; HBV; HiLiAm; IAP; MCCG; MOAP; PR; TCAP; TreFS
My aunt she died a month ago. Death of My Aunt. *Unknown.* OxBoLi; SiTL
My aunties on each side of me are kneeling in a line. The Fly in Church. Jocelyn C. Lea. DDA
My Aunt's Spectre. Mortimer Collins. BOHV
My Autumn Walk. Bryant. AA; IAP; LPS-2
My Aviary. Oliver Wendell Holmes. SN
My Babes in the Wood. Sarah Morgan Bryan Piatt. AA
My baby boy, I sing of thee. Fatherhood. Patterson DuBois. FAOV
My Baby Dear. Samuel Abbott. BOL
My baby has a father and a mother. Christina Rossetti. *Fr.* Sing-Song. EmBrPo
My baby is sleeping. The Baby's Charms. *Unknown.* BOL
My baby, wouldst thou treasure hoard? The Treasure. Dorothy Frances McCrae. BoAu
My ball flew over in a Jew's garden. The Jew Lady. *Unknown.* ABS
My bands of silk and miniver. Full Moon. Elinor Wylie. CrMA; MAP; MoAB; MoAmPo
My banks they are furnish'd with bees. Hope [*or* The Shepherd's Home]. William Shenstone. *Fr.* A Pastoral Ballad. CG; GN; KN; OBEC; RO
My Barbaric Yawp. Walt Whitman. *Fr.* Song of Myself. NePA
("Spotted hawk swoops by and accuses me, The.") CoBA; CoV; PoLFOT; TrGrPo
My bark is wafted to the strand. My Pilot. Washington Gladden. OQP; QP-1
My Barrow. Elizabeth Fleming. GFA
My Bath. John Stuart Blackie. VA
My beak is bent downward, I burrow below. Plow. *Unknown. Fr.* Riddles. AnOE
My beasts, go feed upon the plain. Egloga Secunda. Barnabe Googe. ReIE
"My beautiful dog, my dear dog." Prose Poem: The Dog and the Flask. Baudelaire. OnPM
My Beautiful Lady. Thomas Woolner. OBVV; VA
My beautiful! my beautiful! that standest meekly by. The Arab to His Favorite Steed [*or* Arab's Farewell to His Horse]. Caroline Norton. BeLS; BLPA; LPS-2; TreFS
My beauty is not wine to me. The Song of the Narcissus. *Unknown. Fr.* The Thousand and One Nights. AWP
My Bed Is a Boat. Robert Louis Stevenson. GFA; HBV; HBVY; OnHT; OTPC; PCH; StVeCh; TreFS
My bed is so empty that I keep [on] waking up. Winter Night. Emperor Ch'ien Wen-ti. AtBAP; BoW; OnPM; TrCh
My bed will fold up where I fold. Convalescence, III. David McCord. WhC
My begging has exhausted not. Generosity. Al-Liss. MooP
My Belief. Albert Teodor Gellerstedt, *tr. fr. Swedish by* Charles W. Stork. AnSL
My beloved brother, my heart burneth for thy love. The Lovely Delightful Song of Thy Sister. *Unknown.* LiTW
My Beloved Is Mine, and I Am His; He Feedeth among the Lilies. Francis Quarles. *Fr.* Emblems. CaAE; MePo; OBS; TrGrPo, *abr.*
(Canticle.) FaBoEn
(Divine Rapture, A, 3 *sts.*) HBV; LO; OBEV
(Even [*or* Ev'n] like Two Little Bank-dividing Brooks.) ElSeCe; EPS (1942 ed.); MeLP; TriL
(He Is Mine, 3 *sts.*) LiTL
(Mystical Ecstasy, A, 3 *sts.*) GTSL
My beloved spake, and said unto me. For, Lo, the Winter Is Past. The Song of Solomon, Bible, *O.T.* LO; TreF
My Bess. Raymond W. Walker. CAG
My best of friends! what needs a chain to tie. An Acknowledgment (of a Locket Received). Henry King. CoEV
My Betsey-Jane, it would not do. To Betsey-Jane, on Her Desiring to Go Incontinently to Heaven. Helen Parry Eden. HBMV
My Bible. Edgar A. Guest. *Fr.* My Books and I. MaRV
My Bird. "Fanny Forester." AA; MOAH
My bird has a note of joy today. My Country Lies Wounded. Einar Hjörleifsson Kvaran. *Fr.* Governor Lenhard. IeP
My Bird-wrung Youth. Patrick Anderson. PeCV
My Birth. Minot Judson Savage. AA; WGRP
My Birthday. Thomas Moore. HBV; TIP
"'My birthday!' What a different sound," 4 *ll.* PoRL

"My birthday, Nelly, and your wedding day!" Washington's Last Birthday. Alfred Noyes. PoMa
My Birthday! O beloved mother! Absence. Nathaniel Parker Willis. MOAH
"My birthday"—what a different sound. My Birthday. Thomas Moore. HBV; PoRL; TIP
My birthplace was of Syria. On Himself. Meleager. GrR; OxBG
My Bishop's Eyes. *Unknown.* WhC
(Praying and Preaching.) GoTP
My black hills have never seen the sun rising. Shancoduff. Patrick Kavanagh. OxBI
My blessed mother dozing in her chair. Valentines [*or* A Valentine] to My Mother, 1882. Christina Rossetti. MOAH; MotAn; OHIP
My Blessing Be on Waterford. Winifred M. Letts. HBMV; VOD
My blood hath been too cold and temperate. Hotspur. Shakespeare. King Henry IV, Pt. I, *fr.* I, iii. BHV
My blood so red. The Call. *Unknown.* OBEV
My Blue-eyed Boy. *Unknown.* ABS
My boat is of ebony. Song of the River. Li Po. ChLP
My Boat Is on the Shore. Byron. *See* To Thomas Moore.
My boat lies waiting where the willow stirs. William Ellery Leonard. *Fr.* Two Lives, Pt. I. BAP
My body answers you, my blood. Music of Hungary. Anne Reeve Aldrich. AA
My body being dead, my limbs unknown. The Preparative. Thomas Traherne. OxBoCh; PoEL-2
My body, eh? Friend Death, how now? Habeas Corpus. Helen Hunt Jackson. AA; AnAmPo; BAP; LA; LEAP; OBAV; WGRP
My Body in the Walls Captived. Sir Walter Ralegh. ReIE; SeCePo; SiPS
My body is a poem. Anatomy Lesson. Ilo Orleans. RIS
My body is weary to death of my mischievous brain. Nebuchadnezzar. Elinor Wylie. MAP; MoAmPo; NeMA
My body seems to me to-day. Manuel Altolaguirre, *tr. fr. Spanish by* Eleanor L. Turnbull. CoSP
My body sleeps: my heart awakes. Indian Love-Song. "Owen Meredith." VA
My Bohemia. Arthur Rimbaud, *tr. fr. French.* AnFP, *tr. by* Louise Varèse; ReMP, *tr. by* R. G. Stern
(Gipsying, *tr. by* Alan Conder.) TrFP
My Bonie Mary. Burns. *See* My Bonnie Mary.
My Bonnie. H. J. Fuller. OlF
My bonnie blithe fisher-maiden. Du schönes Fischer-Mädchen. Heine. OuHeWo
My Bonnie lies over the ocean. My Bonnie. H. J. Fuller. OlF
My Bonnie [*or* Bonie] Mary. Burns. BSV; HBV; LEAP; OBEV; ViBoPo
(Before Parting.) LH
(Farewell, A: "Go fetch to me a pint o' wine.") GTBS; GTBS-D; GTBS-W; GTSE; GTSL
(Go Fetch to Me a Pint o' Wine.) BEL; EiPP; EnRP; PoE
(Silver Tassie, The.) EBSV; OBEC
My bonnie wean; my darlin' bairn! Baloo, My Bairnie, Fa' Asleep. James Smith. BOL
My Bonny Black Bess. *Unknown.* ABS; CoMu; ViBoFo
(Bonnie Black Bess.) CoSo, *with music;* CSF
My Bonny Lass, Thine Eye. Thomas Lodge. ReIE
(Love's Witchery.) ElL
My Book Holds Many Stories. Annette Wynne. HH
My Books. Austin Dobson. BPN; MOB
My Books. Longfellow. AA
My Books. *Unknown.* DDA
My Books and I, *sel.* Edgar A. Guest.
My Bible. MaRV
My Books I'd Fain Cast Off, I Cannot Read. Henry David Thoreau. *See* Summer Rain, The.
My Bosom Grac'd. Hafiz, *tr. fr. Persian by* Thomas Law. PeP
My Boy. James Whitcomb Riley. FAOV
My boy, be cool, do things by rule. Nimble Dick. Adelaide O'Keeffe. OTPC (1923 ed.)
My boy, do you know the boy I love? The Boy I Love. John Townsend Trowbridge. FAOV
My Boy Jack. Kipling. OtMeF
My boy Kree? Kree. A. C. Gordon. AA
My Boy Tammy. Hector MacNeill. CH
("Whar hae ye been a'day—my boy Tammy?") LO
My boy was scarcely ten years auld. Leesome Brand. *Unknown.* BaBo (A *vers.*); ESPB
My boyhood went: it went where went the trace. Lost Years. Eugene Lee-Hamilton. OBVV
My Boy's Come Home. Stefan George, *tr. fr. German by* Kate Flores. AnGP
(My Child Came Home, *tr. by* Carol North Valhope *and* Ernst Morwitz.) LiTW
My brain is like the ravaged shores—the sand. At Night. Frances Cornford. MBP; MoBrPo
My brave lad sleeps in his faded coat of blue. The Faded Coat of Blue. J. H. McNaughton. BlG
My brave, you of the golden stave. Wood-Thrush. Clinton Scollard. BLA
My brethren all attend. The Zealous Puritan. *Unknown.* OBS; SeEP
"My brethren . . ." And a bland, elastic smile. The Evangelist. Donald Davie. NePoEA
My briar that smelledst sweet. Upon a Sweet-Briar. Walter Savage Landor. *Fr.* Citation and Examination of William Shakespeare. BPN
"My bride is not coming, alas!" says the groom. At the Altar-Rail. Thomas Hardy. *Fr.* Satires of Circumstance. MBP; MoAB; MoBrPo; PoVP
My Brigantine. James Fenimore Cooper. *Fr.* The Water Witch, *ch.* 15. AA; EtS; LEAP; LPS-2
My Brother. Dorothy Aldis. TiPo
My Brother. Tu Fu, *tr. fr. Chinese by* Nee Wen-yei. WhP
My brother Cain, the wounded, liked to sit. Abel. Demetrios Capetanakis. AtBAP; WaaP
My brother has a little flute. The Fairy Flute. Rose Fyleman. BoTP
My brother Jack was nine in May. The Baby's Debut. Horace Smith *and* James Smith. ALV; BOHV; EV-4; OBRV
My brother, man, shapes him a plan. The Chant of the Colorado. Cale Young Rice. SBMV
My Brother Played. Charles Ballard. MuM
My brother, the god, and I grow sick. The Loom. Edgar Lee Masters. TBM
My brother, want to get religion? Lonesome Valley. *Unknown.* OlF
My brother was a year older than I. My Brother. Tu Fu. WhP
My Brothers, when the north wind bites us sharply. *Unknown. Fr.* Saint Francis' Lesson to His Brothers. SaFP
My brow with pain is often coryougated. Take Nothing for Granite. Nate Salsbury. InMe
My brudder sittin' on de tree of life. Roll, Jordan, Roll. *Unknown.* AA
My button gloves are very white. Easter Parade. Marchette Chute. BrR; SiSoSe
My cabinets are oyster-shells. The Sea-Goddess. Duchess of Newcastle. *Fr.* The Convent of Pleasure. SeCL
My calm and herculean dad. Gaiety of Descendants. Douglas Newton. NeBP
My Camping Ground. Morris Rosenfeld, *tr. fr. Yiddish by* Aaron Kramer. TrJP
My Canary's Rhapsody. Zöe Ackerman. VOD
My Candidate. Norman H. Crowell. YaD
My Candle Burns at Both Ends. Edna St. Vincent Millay. *See* First Fig.
My Captain. Dorothea Day. BePJ; BLPA
(Captain, The.) MaRV
My cares draw on mine everlasting night. To Delia, XXX. Samuel Daniel. AtBAP; OBSC
My cart jolts over. The Drunkard. Mao Kuang Sheng. PoHN
My cartridge belt is empty. The Huntsman. John Wheelwright. CrMA
My case is this: I love Zepheria bright. Gulling Sonnets, VIII. Sir John Davies. TuPP
My Cat. Baudelaire, *tr. fr. French.* CIV
My Cat and I. Edna Gearhart. CIV
My cat is quiet. Cat. Dorothy Baruch. SUS; TiPo; UTS
My Cat Jeoffry [*or* Jeoffrey]. Christopher Smart. *Fr.* Jubilate Agno. ChTr; FaBoCh; GoTP; LiTB; SeCePo; SiTL
(Cat, The.) BoW, *abr.;* PoC; RO
(For I Will Consider My Cat Jeoffry.) AtBAP; EiPP; PoEL-3; SeCeV
(Rejoice in the Lamb, *br. sel.*) PoD
My cat, Matilda, sits upon the floor. Matilda's Manners. Mazie V. Caruthers. CIV
My cat Timothy who has such lovely eyes. Timothy. Rose Fyleman. UTS
My Catbird. William Henry Venable. AA; BAP; BLA, *much abr.;* HBV; PFY
My Cathedral. Longfellow. BAV
My ceiling shows not brave. The Vanity of Riches. Horace. Odes, II, 18. RoL; WoL
My chant must enclose hell. The Tusks of Blood. Samuel Greenberg. MoPo
My Charge. Leslie Pinckney Hill. MaRV
My charioteer hastens to yoke my carriage. The Campaign against Wu, I. Wei Wen-ti. TrCh
My cheek is faded sair, love. Song of the Forsaken. William Thom. EBSV
My cherrystones! I prize them. Precious Stones. Charles Stuart Calverley. InMe
My chick, my pretty one. In Absence. Avenzoar. MooP
My Child. John Pierpont. AA; BAV; HBV; LBAP; LPS-1; OBAV

My child, ah, my child; thou art weary tonight. An Answer to "Rock Me to Sleep." *Unknown.* PTA-1
My Child Came Home. Stefan George. *See* My Boy's Come Home.
My child came to me with the equinox. The Storm-Child. May Byron. HBV
My child is lying on my knees. The Father's Hymn for the Mother to Sing. George Macdonald. BSV
My child, my sister, dream. Invitation to the Voyage. Baudelaire. AnFP
My child, ob-serve the use-ful Ant. The Ant. Oliver Herford. LBN
My child, the Duck-billed Plat-y-pus. The Platypus. Oliver Herford. FiBHP; NA
My child, thou seest, I am content to wait. To My Daughter. Victor Hugo. FAOV
My child, we were two children. Mein Kind, wir waren Kinder. Heine. AWP; JAWP; TrJP; WBP
My child, what painful vistas are before you! To a Very Young Gentleman. Christopher Morley. PoMa
My childhood is a sphere. Childhood. Thomas Traherne. TrGrPo
My childhood's home I see again. Memory. Abraham Lincoln. BLPA; FaBoBe; NeHB; WBLP
My children, know love is not love alone. The Power of Love. Sophocles. OxBG
My children! speak not ill of one another. To Poets. Walter Savage Landor. ViBoPo
My chile? Lord, no, she's none o' mine. The Borrowed Child. Howard Weeden. AA
My Choice. William Browne. *See* Shall I Tell You Whom I Love?
My Choice. Grace B. Renfrow. BePJ
My choice, a slim, fair, comely girl. Ode to a Chosen Girl. Hywel ab Owain Gwynedd, *tr. by* Gwyn Williams. PrWP
My chosen she is, my bright, dainty darling. A Love Poem. Hywel ab Owain Gwynedd, *tr. by* H. Idris Bell. LyMA
My chosen sweetheart wears a veil. Love Song. Björnstjerne Björnson. AnNoLy
My Christ Ever Faithful. *Unknown, tr. fr. Irish by* Robin Flower. GTIV
My Christ is the sweep of the lofty elm. "What Think Ye of Christ?" Geraldine Farrar. StJW
My Christmas gifts were few: to one. To a Lady. Thomas William Parsons. AA
My Church ("My church has but one temple"). "E. O. G." BLPA
My Church ("On me nor Priest nor Presbyter nor Pope"). *Unknown.* MaRV; OQP; QP-2
My City. James Weldon Johnson. BANP; CDC; PoNe
My city, my beloved, my white. N. Y. Ezra Pound. NP
My Clarion Call. Alberto Ghiraldo, *tr. fr. Spanish.* PoFr
My closest and dearest! Dirge on the Death of Art O'Leary. *Tr. by* Eleanor Hull. AnIV
My clothing was once of the linsey wolsey fine. Poor Old Horse. *Unknown.* CH; KN
My clumsiest dear, whose hands shipwreck vases. Love Poem. John Frederick Nims. HoPM; MiAP
My clumsy poem on the inn-wall none cared to see. The Poem on the Wall. Po Chü-i. TrCh
My coachman, in the moonlight there. Without and Within. James Russell Lowell. BOHV; HBV; PR; TOP
My cock pheasant is flying away. The Cock Pheasant. *Unknown.* WhP
My communioned figment impales the moon. Eventual Birth of Thought. B. J. Morse. MoWP
My Companion. Joyce Ramage. BePJ
My Company. Sir Herbert Read. FaBoMo
My Comrade. Edwin Markham. AA
My Comrade. James Jeffrey Roche. AA
My comrade is dead. Elegy. Salomón de la Selva. AnCL
My Constantine, why sleep in bronze? A Charioteer. *Unknown.* OxBG
My Contemporary. Pierre Jean de Béranger, *tr. fr. French by* Alan Conder. TrFP
My counterpane is soft as silk. A Child's Song of Christmas. Marjorie Pickthall. BOL; BoTP; HBV; HBVY; YeAr
My Country. Mikhail Yurevich Lermontov, *tr. fr. Russian.* BoR, *tr. by* J. S. Phillimore; LiTW, *tr. by* Frances Cornford *and* E. P. Salaman; TrRV, *tr. by* Babette Deutsch
My Country. James Russell Lowell. Ode Recited at the Harvard Commemoration, July 21, 1865, XII. GDAH
My Country. Dorothea Mackellar. BoAu
My Country. James Montgomery. *See* There Is a Land.
My Country. Robert Whitaker. OQP; QP-2
My Country, *sels.* George Edward Woodberry.
"For thou art founded in the eternal fact." PoFr
"O destined Land." AA
O Land Beloved. PAH
My Country Is the World. *Unknown, at. to* Robert Whitaker. PGD
(World-Brotherhood.) MaRV
My country is the world; I count/ No son of man my foe. My Country. Robert Whitaker. OQP; QP-2
My Country Lies Wounded. Einar Hjörleifsson Kvaran, *tr. fr. Icelandic by* Jakobina Johnson. *Fr.* Governor Lenhard. IcP
My country, O my land, my friends. Purgatorio. Hart Crane. NAMP
My Country, Right! Thomas Curtis Clark. PGD
My country 'tis of thee./ Sweet land of felony. Ambrose Bierce. YaD
My country, 'tis of thee. America. Samuel Francis Smith. AA; BoHiPo; BoPo; DD; FaBoBe; FaFP; FaPON; GFA; HBV; HBVY; HH; IDAH; LEAP; MaRV; MC; OlF; OnHT; OTPC; PaA; PECK; PEDC; PoFr; PoRL; TCAP; TreF; WBLP; YaD
"My country, 'tis of thee." Assembly; Harlem School. Eugene T. Maleska. GoYe
My country, 'tis of thee/ Land where things used to be. New National Anthem. *Unknown.* CoSo; CSF
My countrymen, though we are young as yet. The Circling Hearths. Roderic Quinn. BoAu
My Country's Flag. Juniata Stafford. HH
My coursers are fed with the lightning. The Charioteer. Shelley. *Fr.* Prometheus Unbound. OBRV; ShBV-3
My Cousin Agueda. Ramón López Velarde, *tr. fr. Spanish.* AnMP, *tr. by* Samuel Beckett; TwSpPo, *tr. by* H. R. Hays
My Cousin German came from France. *Unknown.* FaBoCh; LoGBV
My Cousins, on Sundays. Francisco López Merino, *tr. fr. Spanish by* Richard O'Connell. AnCL
My cousin's wife, the diabetic. Upon Differences of Opinion. Hy Sobiloff. SiTL
My Creed. Alice Cary. WGRP
My Creed. Jeannette L. Gilder. BPP; WGRP
My Creed. Edgar A. Guest. MaRV
My Creed. S. E. Kiser. PoToHe
My Creed. Howard Arnold Walter. BLP; FaFP; OQP; POT; PoTo; QP-1; WBLP
(I Would Be True.) MaRV; PoToHe (new ed.)
My Critic. Pushkin, *tr. fr. Russian by* Babette Deutsch. TrRV
My Cross. Zitella Cocke. HBV
My crown is in my heart, not on my head. Content. Shakespeare. King Henry VI, Pt. III, *fr.* III, i. MaRV; PoToHe (new ed.)
My curse be on the day when first I saw. Sonnet: To the Lady Pietra [degli Scrovigni]. Dante. AWP; LyMA
My curse upon thy [*or* your] venom'd stang. Address to the Toothache. Burns. BCEP; BOHV; LPS-3
My dad sometimes some little trip. When Dad Takes Me. Douglas Malloch. FAOV
My dad was a soldier and fought in the wars. The Hero. Leroy F. Jackson. SiSoSe
My daddie is a cankert carle. Low Doun in the Broom. *Unknown.* BSV; GoTS
My daddy, he lived in a wonderful house, and he played with such wonderful boys. My Wonderful Dad. James W. Foley. FAOV
My daddy is an engineer. Wanderin'. *Unknown.* AS
My daddy smells like tobacco and books. Smells (Junior). Christopher Morley. BoChLi; GFA; MPB; TiPo
My daddy went a-huntin'. The Grey Goose. *Unknown.* WaKn
My Dad's Dinner Pail. Edward Harrigan. BLPA
My Daily Creed. *Unknown.* BLP; MaRV
My Daily Prayer. Grenville Kleiser. BLRP; MaRV; PraP
My dame hath a lame tame crane. *Unknown.* OxNR
My Damon was the first to wake. Meeting. George Crabbe. HBV; LO; OBEV
My Dancing Day. *Unknown.* *See* To-Morrow Shall Be My Dancing Day.
My Daphne's hair is twisted gold. Daphne [*or* Apollo's Song]. John Lyly. *Fr.* Midas. EIL; HBV; OBSC; SiCE
My Darkness. Rose O'Neill. TBM
My darling, be brave. Aleksandr Blok, *tr. fr. Russian by* V. de S. Pinto. BoRS
My darling boy, so early snatched away. Of Such Is the Kingdom. Francis Greenwood Peabody. MaRV
My darling little fishing rods. A Song of Satisfaction on Completing an Overhauling of Fishing Tackle. Leslie P. Thompson. WhC
My darling, thou art flowerlike. A Prayer. Heine. OnPM
My darling, we sat together. Mein Liebchen, wir sassen zusammen [*or* Forlornly]. Heine. AWP; JAWP; OnPM; WBP
My Daughter Louise. Homer Greene. HBV
My dawn? my dawn? How if it never break? Psalm of the West. Sidney Lanier. PeBoSo
My Day and Night. John Payne. PIAE
(Rondeau Redoublé.) HBV
My Days among the Dead Are Past [*or* Passed]. Robert

My Days among the Dead Are Past (*continued*) Southey. EnRP; ERP; HBV; LEAP; MaRV; OBRV; TOP
(Among His Books.) EV-4
(His Books.) BCEP; OBEV
(Scholar, The.) GTBS; GTBS-D; GTBS-W; GTSE; GTSL
My days are full of pleasant memories. Phantoms. Thomas Ashe. VA
My days are in the yellow leaf. Remorse. Byron. *Fr.* On This Day I Complete My Thirty-sixth Year. MaRV
My days' delights, my springtime joys fordone. A Poem Entreating of Sorrow. Sir Walter Ralegh. SiPS
My Days Have Been So Wondrous Free, *with music.* Thomas Parnell. TrAS
(Song: "My days have been so wond'rous free.") CEP; EiPP
My Days of Love Are Over. Byron. *See* Disillusion.
My days were lighter. Epitaph. Lady Margaret Sackville. MM
My Dead. Frederick Lucian Hosmer. GrCo-2; WGRP
(Friends Beyond.) MaRV
(Their Silent Ministry.) GrCo-1
My dead [*or* dear] love came to me, and said. The Apparition [*or* A Dream]. Stephen Phillips. BMEP; GTML; LBBV; MaRV; MBP; OBEV (new ed.); OBVV; PoeMoYo
"My dear, adieu! my sweet love, farewell!" *sel. Unknown.* "Wilt thou forsake me? and wilt thou leave me." LO
My Dear and Only Love. James Graham, Marquess of Montrose. AEV; BSV; CoEV; LPS-1; OBS; SeCL
(Heroic Love.) LH, *abr.*; EV-2
(I'll Never Love Thee More.) EBSV; HBV; OBEV
(Montrose to His Mistress.) LoBV; ViBoPo
(Proper New Ballad, A.) LO
(Touch, The, 4 *ll.*) OtMeF
My dear brother Ned. The *South Carolina. Unknown.* PAH
My dear Castara, t'other day. Pastoral Dialogue, Castara and Parthenia. Thomas Flatman. CEP
My dear cockadoodle, my jewel, my joy. *Unknown.* BOL
My Dear Comes Down to Meet Me. Irene Rutherford McLeod. VOD
My dear companion, and my faithful friend! An Address to His Elbow-Chair, New Cloath'd. William Somervile. CEP; OBEC
My dear daddie bought a mansion. The Little Bird. Walter de la Mare. BrR
My dear, darkened in sleep, turned from the moon. To Judith Asleep. John Ciardi. LiTL; MiAP
My dear, do you [*or* you must] know. The Babes in the Wood. *Unknown.* ABS; OTPC (1946 ed.); PPL; RIS
My dear dumb friend, low lying there. To My Dog Blanco. Josiah Gilbert Holland. AlBD
My dear friend Davies, some against us partial. To Mr. [*or* Master] John Davies. Sir John Harington. SiCE; TuPP
My dear George, my end is nearing. A Legacy. Karl Gustaf af Leopold. AnSL
My dear, I cannot tell. The Goodwife Relents. Gwen Clear. MM
My dear, I do fear that this fiery love. Englynion to His Love. David Jones. PrWP
My Dear Lady. *Unknown. Fr.* The Trial of Treasure. EIL
("Am not I in blessed case.") TuPP
My dear little crane. A Pet Crane. *Unknown.* AnIL
My dear love came to me, and said. *See* My dead love came to me
My Dear Mistress. Earl of Rochester. *See* Song: "My dear mistress has a heart."
My dear, my dear, I know. To a Young Girl. W. B. Yeats. TwP
My dear, naïve, ingenuous child. Don't Say You Like Tchaikowsky. Paul Rosner. FiBHP
My dear, observe the rose! though she desire it. Elegy IX. William Bell. NePoEA
My Dear One is mine as mirrors are lonely. Miranda's Song. W. H. Auden. *Fr.* The Sea and the Mirror. FaBoMo
My dear Redeemer and my Lord. Isaac Watts. OlF
My dear, the time has come to say. A Song of Parting. Compton Mackenzie. HBV; OBVV
My Dear was a mason. The Man with a Hammer. Anna Wickham. AV
My dear! When I leave you. To My Dog. John Galsworthy. AlBD
My dear, when I was very young. To a Lady on Her Marriage. William Bell. NePoEA
My dear you must know that a long time ago. *See* My dear, do you know.
My dear young friend, whose shining wit. Comic Miseries. John Godfrey Saxe. BOHV
My Dearest Baby, Go to Sleep. Thomas Miller. BOL; OTPC
My dearest Betty, my more lovèd heart. Elisa, or an Elegy upon the Unripe Decease of Sir Antony Irby. Phineas Fletcher. ViBoPo
My dearest boy, become a fool. The Art of Succeeding. Johan Henrik Kellgren. AnSL
My dearest dear, my honey love. Winter-Night Song. Ford Madox Ford. NP
My dearest dear, the time draws near. The Lover's Lament. *Unknown.* AS
My dearest dust, could not thy hasty day. Epitaph on the Monument of Sir William Dyer at Colmworth, 1641. Lady Catherine Dyer. EnLoPo
My dearest Mary, wherefore hast thou gone. To Mary Shelley. Shelley. MotAn
My dearest Rival, least our love. Sir John Suckling. MeLP
"My Dearling." Elizabeth Akers Allen. AA; LBAP
My dearly loved friend, how oft have we. To My Most Dearly-loved [Friend] Henry Reynolds. Michael Drayton. OAEP; OBS; PtP; ReEn; SeEP; TuPP
My dears, 'tis said in days of old. The Bee, the Ant, and the Sparrow. Charles Cotton. RIS
My Death. Bedros Tourian, *tr. fr. Armenian by* Zabelle C. Boyajian. ArmLP
My Death. Carl Zuckmayer, *tr. fr. German by* E. B. Ashton. TrJP
My death must come; but when, I do not know. Waiting for Death. Michelangelo. OnPM
My debt to you, Belovèd. Debt [*or* Debts]. Jessie B. Rittenhouse. AV; BAP; HBMV; LEAP; LoPS
My Delight. Gamaliel Bradford. HBMV
My Delight and Thy Delight. Robert Bridges. AnFE; ChMo; CMP; GTML; GTSL; HBV; LiTL; LoPo; OAEP; OBEV; PoEL-5; POTT; PoVP; TOP; TyEnPo; ViP
My des Autels, whose true. Odes, II, 13. Pierre de Ronsard. PrPoCR
My Descendants. W. B. Yeats. Meditations in Time of Civil War, IV. LiTB
My desire springs upward in the pallid air. The Fountain. Luis Cernuda. CoSP
My Desk. Humbert Wolfe. YT
My desolation does begin to make. Shakespeare. *Fr.* Antony and Cleopatra, V, ii. NBE
My Diet. Abraham Cowley. *Fr.* The Mistress. LiTL; LO; SeCL; SeEP
My dismal sister! Couldst thou know. "Lewis Carroll." *Fr.* Melancholetta. FiBHP
My Dog. John Kendrick Bangs. BLPA; FaBoBe; MPB; OTPC (1946 ed.); StVeCh; UTS
My Dog. Marchette Chute. FaPON; MoSiPe; TiPo
My Dog. Marty Hale. AlBD
My Dog and I. Genevieve W. Mason. AlBD
My Dog and I. Isla Paschal Richardson. AlBD
My dog and I are both grown old. The Shepherd and His Dog. William Lisle Bowles. EnSW
My Dog I was ever well pleased to see. My Dog Tray. John Byrom. SeCePo
My dog lay dead five days without a grave. The Pardon. Richard Wilbur. NePoEA
My Dog, Spot. Rodney Bennett. BoTP
My Dog Tray. John Byrom. SeCePo
My Dog Tray. Thomas Campbell. *See* Harper, The.
My Doggie. C. Nurton. BoTP
My dog's so furry I've not seen. The Hairy Dog. Herbert Asquith. AlBD; BoChLi; FaPON; StVeCh; SUS; TiPo; UTS
My Dog's Tail. Arthur Wallace Peach. AlBD
My dolly hung her stocking up. *Unknown.* GFA
My dolly would not play with me. Self-Control. Polly Chase Boyden. GoBP
My Donkey. Rose Fyleman. TiPo
My donkey has a bridle. The Donkey. Rose Fyleman. BoTP
My donkey, my dear. My Donkey. Rose Fyleman. TiPo
My dove, my beautiful one. James Joyce. *Fr.* Chamber Music. TIP
My Doves. Elizabeth Barrett Browning. OTPC
My Dream. *Unknown.* BOHV; LauV; NA; SiTL
("I dreamed a dream next Tuesday week.") GoTP
My Dreams Are of a Field Afar. A. E. Housman. TwP
My dreams have boded all too right. The Flight of Fondest Hopes. Thomas Moore. *Fr.* Lalla Rookh. BCEP
My dreams wear thinner as the years go by. The Years. John Hall Wheelock. CrMA
My dreams were crumbled, and my house. Friendship. Marty Hale. AlBD
My dreams were doleful and drear. Song. Thomas Caulfield Irwin. IrPN
My Drinking Song. Richard Dehmel, *tr. fr. German by* Ludwig Lewisohn. AWP
My driver came this morning on the run. A Battle-Plane in France. O. C. A. Child. PaA
My Drowsy Little Queen. Samuel Minturn Peck. BOL
(My Little Girl.) AA
My Early Home. John Clare. BoTP; HBV; OTPC (1923 ed.)

"My ear-rings! my ear-rings! they've dropped into the well." Zara's Ear-Rings. *Unknown.* LPS-1
My Easter Prayer. *Unknown.* PraP
My Education. James Kenneth Stephen. WhC
My Enemy. Alice Williams Brotherton. AA
My Enemy. Edwin L. Sabin. OQP; QP-2
My enemy, by a wild bee gored. Bees. Richard R. Kirk. PIAE
My enemy came nigh. Hate. James Stephens. BMEP; BoFr; ChMo; CMP; MBP; MoAB; MoBrPo; NP; OBVV; PoeMoYo; PtOT; TCEP; TSW; TSWC; TwCV
My Epitaph. David Gray. MaRV; OBVV; VA
My Estate. John Drinkwater. HBMV
My Evening Prayer. *At. to* C. Maud Battersby, *also to* Charles H. Gabriel. *See* Evening Prayer.
My every waking hour. To J. S. Robert J. Misch. ALV
My existence in the world has been. The Wake. Tsurayuki. WoL
My eye descending from the hill surveys. The Thames from Cooper's Hill [*or* Praise of the Thames]. Sir John Denham. *Fr.* Cooper's Hill. CoEV; EPP; EV-2; OBS; ReEn; SeCePo; ViBoPo
My eye is not on Calvary, nor on Bethlehem the Blessed. Sorley Maclean. *Fr.* Dain Eile. NeBP
My eyelids red and heavy are. A Poor Scholar of the 'Forties. Padraic Colum. AnIL; GTIV; OxBI
My eyes already touch that hill, sun-gold. Walk. Rainer Maria Rilke. TwGV
My eyes and heart. Eye and Heart. Ibn al-Batti. MooP
My eyes are filmed, my beard is gray. The Time of the Barmecides. James Clarence Mangan. EnRP; TIP
My eyes are meet and right. Ransom. Ibn Ammar. MooP
My eyes are sick, I dare not open books. Lines Written in a Small Inn While Staying in the Capital in the Late Spring. Yang W'an-li. WhP
My eyes are tired of brick, of steel and stone. Nostalgia. Elizabeth Virginia Raplee. BLP
My eyes are turned aside from this vile race. From out the Glow the Wrath of Heaven Spoke. Stefan George. OnPM
My eyes dyed by the green of the leaves. The Bored Mirror. Syuichi Nagayasu. LiTW
My Eyes for Beauty Pine. Robert Bridges. VLEP
My Eyes! How I Love You. John Godfrey Saxe. LPS-1
(How I Love You.) NeHB
My Eyes That Hurry to See. Bilhana, *formerly at. to* Chauras, *tr. fr. Sanskrit by* E. Powys Mathers. *Fr.* Black Marigolds. OnPM
My eyes were all too wary. The Kerry Lads. Theodosia Garrison. HBMV
My eyes will never see the light. Street Song. Juan Ruiz, Archpriest of Hita. LyMA
My Fabio, the courtier's hopes are chains. Epistle to Fabio. *At. to* Andrés Fernández de Andrada. TeCS
My Face. Anthony Euwer. *See* Limerick: "As a beauty I'm not a great star."
My face is [*or* is wet] against the grass—the moorland grass is wet. Moorland Night. Charlotte Mew. BrBE; ChMP; MM; TwCV; ViBoPo
My face is wet with the rain. Walking at Night. Amory Hare. NLK
My Faggot and My Pipe. Sir Robert Aytoun. PeBoSo
My faint spirit was sitting in the light. Shelley. *See* From the Arabic.
My fair and rare one, my faithful fond one. My Faithful Fond One. *Unknown.* EBSV
My fair, look from those turrets of thine eyes. Idea's Mirrour, XXXIV. Michael Drayton. OBSC; SiCE
My Fair, no beauty of thine will last. Song. Alice Meynell. VA
My fair says, she no spouse but me. Inconsistency of Women's Love. Catullus. OnPM
My fairest child, I have no song to give you. A Farewell. Charles Kingsley. BLP; BLPA; BMEP; BoTP; DD; FAOV; GN; HBV; HBVY; LPS-1; NeHB; OTPC; PECK; PIR; PoVP; TreF; VA
My Fairy Lover. Donald A. MacKenzie. EBSV
My Faith. Ananda Acharya. WGRP
My Faith. Frederic Lawrence Knowles. OQP; QP-1
My faith is all a doubtful thing. Symbol. David Morton. HBMV; MaRV; OQP; POT; PoTo; QP-1; SBMV; StJW; VOD
My Faith Looks Up to Thee. Ray Palmer. BPP; OlF; WGRP
(Faith.) AA; HBV
My Faithful Fond One. *Unknown, tr. fr. Gaelic by* John Stuart Blackie. EBSV
My Familiar. John Godfrey Saxe. AnNE; APW; HBV; PR; TreFS
My Familiar Dream. Paul Verlaine, *tr. fr. French by* Alan Conder. TrFP
(My Recurring Dream, *tr. by* Muriel Kittel.) AnFP
My fancy loves to play with clouds. Clouds. W. H. Davies. TCEP
My Far-off Home. Li Po. *See* On a Quiet Night.
My Father. Rae Dalven. GoYe
My Father. William Drennan. TIP
My Father. Virginia Moore. FAOV
My Father. Jessie B. Rittenhouse. FAOV; MuM
My father/ Gave me in wedlock. Wedded to a Tartar. Liu Hsi Chün. PoHN
My Father,/ Here for a moment in your light I stand. Prayer to the Sun. John Hall Wheelock. BAP; FAOV
My Father above, beholding the meekness. The Child Jesus to Mary the Rose. John Lydgate. CAW; GoBC; ISi
My father and mother were Irish. The Ninepenny Fidil. Joseph Campbell. HBMV
My father and mother were Irish. Irish. Edward J. O'Brien. MoSiPe; SiSoSe
My father and my mother died and left me young and poor. The Orphan. *Unknown.* KiLC
My father bequeathed me no wide estates. Heirloom. A. M. Klein. BoCaPo; PeCV; TrJP
My father bought an undershirt. Song of the All-Wool Shirt. Eugene Field. StPo
My father bound me to a trade in Waterford's fair town. The *Flying Cloud. Unknown.* AmSS
My father carries a pearl-handled knife. A Wonderful Man. Aileen Fisher. SiSoSe
My father dear, so far from here. My Father Gave Me a Lump of Gold. *Unknown.* OuSiCo
My father died a month ago. *Unknown.* OxNR; SiTL
My father died when I was all too young. Sestina of Youth and Age. Gelett Burgess. PIAE
My Father Gave Me a Lump of Gold, *with music. Unknown.* OuSiCo
My father got me strong and straight and slim. The End. Marguerite Wilkinson. *Fr.* Songs of an Empty House. HBMV; SBMV
My father has a pair of shoes. Shoes. Tom Robinson. TiPo
My father he died, but I never knew how [*or* can't tell you how]. The Swapping Song. *Unknown.* OxNR; RIS
My father, he gave me a bantam man. Le Petit Mari. *Unknown.* OuSiCo
My father he left me three acres of land. Mad Farmer's Song [*or* Sing Ivy]. *Unknown.* BoTP; BrR; NA; OxNR; RIS
My father, he was a mountaineer. The Ballad of William Sycamore. Stephen Vincent Benét. AnAmPo; BLV; BoLiVe; HBMV; LA; MAP; MoAmPo; MOAP; MPB; OnSP; PFY; PoRA; PoTo; PreP; TBM; TCAP
My father he's at the kiln away. The Charcoal-Burner's Son. Erik Gustaf Geijer. AnSL; WoL
My father is a quiet man. Fruit of the Flower. Countee Cullen. PoNe
My father is happy or we should be poor. From the Day-Book of a Forgotten Prince. Jean Starr Untermeyer. HBMV; TSW; TSWC
My Father is rich in houses and lands. Hattie E. Buell. OlF
My father is the nightingale. *Unknown.* LO
My Father Knows. Wilbur Fisk Tillett. BLRP
My father knows the proper way. What Father Knows. *Unknown, at. to* Edgar A. Guest. BAP
My father left me three acres of land. *See* My father he left me.
My father mounted his horse and rode away into the country. Childhood. Carlos Drummond de Andrade. AnCL
My Father Moved through Dooms of Love. E. E. Cummings. AmP; AnFE; AtBAP; ChMo; CoAnAm; CoBMV; CrMA; LiTA; MoAB; MoPo; MoVE; OxBA; TriL; TwAmPo; UnPo (3d ed.)
(My Father Moved.) FaBoMo
My father owns the butcher shop. *Unknown.* FaFP; SiTL
My father puzzles me. The Farm Boy. Katharine Atherton Grimes. PoMa
My father sleeps. His august face. Distant Footsteps. César Vallejo. TwSpPo
My father smiled this morning when. Keep Smiling. *Unknown.* WBLP
My father thought that fact was dull. Garland for a Storyteller. Jessie Farnham. GoYe
My father tore out his native roots. My Father. Rae Dalven. GoYe
My father used to say. Silence. Marianne Moore. FaBoEn; FaBoMo; LiTA; MoP; PG (1955 ed.); ViBoPo
My father was a Frenchman. *Unknown.* OxNR
My father was a gambler, he learnt me how to play. The Gambler. *Unknown.* ABS; ViBoFo
My father was a mountaineer. *See* My father, he was a mountaineer.
My father was a sailor. Sailors [*or* Folk Songs]. *Unknown.* AWP; LiTW; OnPM
My father was a scholar and knew Greek. Development. Robert Browning. BPN; PoVP; VLEP
My father was a soldier young, the finest you might see. The Soldier Boy. Johan Ludvig Runeberg. AnSL; WoL

My father was a tall man, and yet the ripened rye. My Father. Jessie B. Rittenhouse. FAOV; MuM
My Fatherland. William Cranston Lawton. AA
My fatherland, O my Troy! Troy. Euripides. *Fr.* Hecuba. OxBG
My "Fatherlands." Kadie Molodowsky, *tr. fr. Yiddish by* Sarah Zweig Betsky. OnCuPl
My Father's at the Helm. *Unknown.* BePJ
My Fathers Came from Kentucky. Vachel Lindsay. *Fr.* Alexander Campbell. HBMV
My Father's Chair. Kipling. FAOV
My Father's Child. "Stuart Sterne." AA
My Father's Close. *Unknown, tr. fr. Old French by* Dante Gabriel Rossetti. AWP; PoVP
My father's face is brown with sun. Father. Frances Frost. FaPON; SiSoSe; StVeCh (1955 ed.); TiPo (1959 ed.)
My father's father's father and he who fathered him. Family History. John Maher Murphy. JKCP (1955 ed.)
My father's friend came once to tea. A Recollection. Frances Cornford. TSW; TSWC
My Father's Gray Mare. *Unknown.* ABS
My Father's House. James Oppenheim. *See* Priest, The.
My fathers long ago. Truce with a Southern Neighbor. Helen Bevington. NoCaPo (rev. ed.)
My Father's Voice in Prayer. May Hastings Nottage. BLRP
My Father's Watch. John Ciardi. ImOP
My Father's Watch. John Gould Fletcher. TriL
My Father's World. Maltbie D. Babcock. *See* This Is My Father's World.
My favorite dress. Her Favorites. Mattie Lee Hausgen. PCH
My Favorite Tree. Margarete Münsterberg. GFA
My Feet. Gelett Burgess. BOHV; MeMeAg; NA; PCH
(Nonsense Verses.) HBV
(Queer Quatrains.) RIS
My feet strike an apex of the apices of the stairs. Infinity. Walt Whitman. *Fr.* Song of Myself, XLIV–XLV. AA
My female friends, whose tender hearts. Swift. *Fr.* Verses on the Death of Dr. Swift. SeCePo; ViBoPo
My fifthe housbonde, god his soule blesse! Chaucer. *Fr.* The Canterbury Tales: The Wife of Bath's Prologue. FiP
My first half century was done. Per Quinquennia Iam Decem. Prudentius. LaP
My First Love. Harry Graham. FiBHP
My first love sighed for brooches. Prices. Louis Ginsberg. TrJP
My first small book was nourished in the dark. Karl Shapiro. Recapitulations, V. FiMAP
My first thought was, he lied in every word. Childe Roland to the Dark Tower Came. Robert Browning. AnFE; ATP; BEL; BHV; BMEP; BPN; EM-2; EmBrPo; EnL; EPP; GEPC; OAEP; OtMeF; Po; PoD; PoVP; SeCeV; TCEP; TOP; TwP; VA; ViPo; ViPP; VLEP
My flattering fortune, look thou never so fair. To Fortune. Sir Thomas More. ACP
My flesh is out of fashion for eternity. A Synonym for God. John Fandel. JKCP (1955 ed.)
My flesh is sad, alas, and I have read the books. Sea Breeze. Stéphane Mallarmé. ReMP
My flesh was water and my spirit foam. Epitaph. Lady Margaret Sackville. MM
My flocks feed [*or* flock feeds] not, my ewes breed [*or* breeds] not. The Unknown Shepherd's Complaint [*or* A Shepherd's Complaint]. Richard Barnfield. EIL; ElSeCe; OBSC; TuPP
My flower, my honor, my honey, my joy. Englynion. *Unknown.* PrWP
My Flowers. Shizumoki, *tr. fr. Japanese by* Lois J. Erickson. SoLD
My flowery and green age was passing away. He Understands the Great Cruelty of Death. Petrarch, *pr. tr. by* J. M. Synge. Sonnets to Laura: To Laura in Death, XLVII. OBMV; TwCV
My Foe. *Unknown.* BOHV; PA
My foe was dark, and stern, and grim. My Enemy. Alice Williams Brotherton. AA
My food is but spare. The Cottager's Hymn. Patrick Brontë. MaRV
My foot in the stirrup, my pony won't stan'. Good-by, Old Paint. *Unknown.* ABF; CoSo; CSF
My footsteps press where, centuries ago. The Red Men. Charles Sangster. CaP
My Forefathers. Erik Axel Karlfeldt, *tr. fr. Swedish by* Charles W. Stork. *Fr.* Songs of Nature and Love. AnSL
My forehead is weary as a river. Emilio Prados, *tr. fr. Spanish by* Eleanor L. Turnbull. CoSP
My form was wrapped in the slumber. The Phantom Host. Peronnean D. Hay. BlG
My Former Hopes Are Fled. William Cowper. OxBoCh
My Fortune. Francisco de Quevedo y Villegas, *tr. fr. Spanish by* Thomas Roscoe. AnSpL-1
My foster-children were not slack. Lament for Corc and Niall of the Nine Hostages. *At. to* Torna. OnYI
My Frail and Earthly Bark, by Reason's Guide. Thomas Lodge. ReIE
My Free Country. Rabindranath Tagore. *See* Where the Mind Is without Fear.
My friend and I have built a wall. Wall. Elizabeth Morrow. MaRV
My friend and neighbor through the year. The Crow. John Burroughs. BLA
My friend bade farewell at the Yellow Crane House. On Seeing Off Meng Hao-jan. Li Po. BoFr
My friend conceived the soul hereafter dwells. Aspiration. Edward William Thomson. OBVV
My friend Cornificus, your friend Catullus. Catullus, *tr. fr. Latin by* Horace Gregory. RoL
My friend from Asia has powers and magic. Credo. Robinson Jeffers. AnEnPo; MAP; MoAB; MoAmPo
My friend has gone. On My Dog's Death. George Herbert Clarke. OCL
My friend, have you heard of the town of Nogood. The Town of Nogood. William Edward Penney. BLPA
My friend, if thou wilt credit me in aught. Who Minds to Bring His Ship to Happy Shore. Jasper Heywood. SiCE
My friend is dwelling [*or* lodging high] in the eastern mountain [*or* range]. To Tan Ch'iu. Li Po. AWP; TrCh; WhP
My friend must be a bird. Emily Dickinson. BoFr
My friend, my bonny friend, when we are old. The Word. John Masefield. MaRV
My friend, speak always once, but listen twice. The Mouth and the Ears. Shem-Tob ben Joseph Palquera. TrJP
My Friend, the Cat. Carrie W. Stryker. CIV
My friend [*or* friends], the things that do attain. *See* Martial, the things that do attain.
My friend thy beauty seemeth good. The Penurious Quaker; or, The High Priz'd Harlot. *Unknown.* CoMu
My Friends. Mikhail Lukonin, *tr. fr. Russian by* Jack Lindsay. RuPo
My friends are borne to one another. Martin Buber in the Pub. Max Harris. BoAV
My Friends Are Little Lamps to Me. Elizabeth Whittemore. PoToHe (new ed.)
My friends, reproach not me. Changefulness. Abu Ishaq. MooP
My friends, the deed's resolved—that with all haste. Medea's Resolve. Euripides. *Fr.* Medea. OxBG
My friends, the leaves, who used to entertain me. In Coventry. James J. Daly. CAW
My friends [*or* friend], the things that do attain. *See* Martial, the things that do attain.
My friends will never be able to say. The Hidden Sorrow. Georgios Vizinos. MoGP
My funeral-shaft, and marble shapes that dwell. Baucis. Erinna. AWP
My Funny Umbrella. Alice Wilkins. GFA
My future will not copy fair my past. Sonnets from the Portuguese, XLII. Elizabeth Barrett Browning. BPN
My gal don' wear button-up shoes. Georgia Land. *Unknown.* OuSiCo
My Galilees. Belle Chapman Morrill. MaRV
My galleon of adventure. San Francisco. Walter Adolphe Roberts. PoNe
My Galley, Charged with Forgetfulness. Sir Thomas Wyatt. *See* Lover Compareth His State to a Ship, The.
My garage is a structure of excessive plainness. Detail. Mary Ursula Bethell. AnNZ
My Garden. Thomas Edward Brown. BMEP; DD; DDA; EnLit; GBV; GrCo-1; GTML; GTSL; HBV; HBVY; LEAP; MaRV; MBP; NeHB; NLK; OBEV; OBVV; OQP; OTPC (1946 ed.); PC; PIR; PoFS; POTT; PoVP; QP-1; TOP; TreF; VLEP; VOD; WBLP; WGRP; YT
(Garden, A.) GoTP
My Garden. Emerson. IAP
Words of the Gods, *sel.* OQP; QP-2
My Garden. Roger Lancelyn Green. BoN
My Garden. Norah Hussey. BoTP
My Garden. Janice Appleby Succorsa. HoPM
My Garden. Frederic E. Weatherly. OTPC (1946 ed.)
My garden bears testimony to divinity. Testimony. Eva Moad Turner. OQP; QP-1
My garden-ground of grief, where self-will's seeds are sown. A Strange Description of a Rare Garden-Plot. Nicholas Breton. ReIE
My Garden Is a Pleasant Place. Louise Driscoll. BLPA; FaBoBe; NeHB
My garden is daily more blighted. Swallows. Apollon Nikolayevich Maikov. WaL
My gen'rous heart disdains. Song. Francis Hopkinson. PreP
My gentle child, behold this horse. The Racing-Man. A. P. Herbert. FiBHP; WhC

My gentle Puck, come hither. Compliment to Queen Elizabeth. Shakespeare. *Fr.* A Midsummer Night's Dream, II, ii. LPS-3

My ghost pets are like shadows on the wall. Ghost Pet. Horatio Colony. GoYe

My ghostly father [*or* gostly fader], I me confess. Confession [*or* The Kiss]. Charles d'Orléans. ACP; ChTr; EG; EnLoPo

My Gift. Christina Rossetti. *Fr.* A Christmas Carol: "In the bleak mid-winter." BrR; ChBR; FaPON; MaRV; MeMeAg; OTPC (1946 ed.); SiSoSe

My girl hath violet eyes and yellow hair. The Little Milliner. Robert Buchanan. BeLS; LPS-1

My girl I say be on your guard. Death and the Maiden. *Unknown.* KiLC

My girl is waiting for me. Kakinomoto no Hitomaro, *tr. fr. Japanese by* Kenneth Rexroth. OnPJ

My Girl, Thou Gazest Much. *At. to* Plato, *tr. by* George Turberville. *See* Lover to His Lady, The.

My Glass Is Half Unspent. Francis Quarles. OxBoCh

My glass shall not persuade me I am old. Sonnets, XXII. Shakespeare. EG; EM-1; OBSC; PeBoSo

My glittering sky, high, clear, profound. The Lovers. Marya Zaturenska. MoAmPo

My glory, honor, all depend. The Gentleman. Menahem ben Judah Lonzano. TrJP

My gloves and cravat! Chaplin's Sad Speech. Rafael Alberti. LiTW

My God. Solomon ibn Gabirol, *tr. fr. Hebrew by* Alice Lucas. *Fr.* The Royal Crown. TrJP

My God, a verse is not a crown. The Quidditie. George Herbert. PoEL-2

My God Has Spoken. Paul Verlaine, *tr. fr. French by* John Gray. CAW

My God, How Wonderful Thou Art. Frederick William Faber. GoBC; TrPWD

My God, I heard this day. Man. George Herbert. BLV; BoLiVe; GrCo-2; InPo; MaPo; MePo; OAEP; PoEL-2; SeCV-1; TrGrPo; TrPWD

My God, I know that those who plead. My God. Solomon ibn Gabirol. *Fr.* The Royal Crown. TrJP

My God, I Love Thee. St. Francis Xavier, *tr. fr. Latin by* Edward Caswall. CAW; LPS-2; MaRV; OIF (Hymn: "My God, I love thee, not because.") WGRP

My God, I thank Thee that my course is set. After Hearing the Prime Minister, April 27th, 1941. Richard Elwes. NeTW

My God, I thank Thee who hast made. Thankfulness. Adelaide Anne Procter. MaRV; PraP; TrPWD

My God, is any hour so sweet. Prayer. Charlotte Elliott. PraP

My God is not a chiselled stone. True Knowledge. Panatattu. WGRP

My God! looke on me with thine eye. His Ejaculation to God. Robert Herrick. SeCV-1

My God, my Father, while I stray. "Thy Will Be Done." Charlotte Elliott. PraP

My God, my God, let me for once look on thee. Robert Browning. *Fr.* Pauline. TrPWD

My God, my God, why hast thou forsaken me? A Cry in Distress. Psalm XXII, Bible, *O.T.* TrGrPo

My God (oh, let me call Thee mine). A Prayer. Anne Brontë. TrPWD; VA

My God said: "Love me, son! Dost thou not see." Mystical Dialogue. Paul Verlaine. LO

My God, the bitter-tasting mouth was me. Homage (Diptych, 2). R. J. Schoeck. GoYe

My God, when I walk[e] in those groves. Religion. Henry Vaughan. OBS; OxBoCh

My God, where is that ancient heat towards Thee. To His Mother [*or* The Resolve]. George Herbert. ElSeCe; EPS; PoFS; SeEP

My godmother invited my cousin. My Cousin Agueda. Ramón López Velarde, *tr. by* Samuel Beckett. AnMP

My godmother used to invite my cousin Agueda. My Cousin Agueda. Ramón López Velarde, *tr. by* H. R. Hays. TwSpPo

My golden comrade, since I could not save. Tony's Grave. "Seumas O'Sullivan." PoC

My golden eagle, from a small, unnoticed fledgling. To the Imperial Eagle. Kostas Krystallis. MoGP

My Golden Helen. Pierre de Ronsard, *tr. fr. French by* Humbert Wolfe. LiA

My golden hoard is spear and sword. The Freelance. Hybrias. GrPE

My golden locks time hath to silver turned [*or* turnd]. George Peele. *Fr.* Polyhymnia. BrBE; CenL. *See also* His Golden Locks . . .

My good blade carves the casques of men. Sir Galahad. Tennyson. BEL; BHV; BMEP; BPN; EM-2; EmBrPo; EPN; EPP; GTBS; HBV; LiTG; MaRV; OBVV; OnPP; OTPC; PECK; PoVP; TCEP; TreF; TVSH; VA; ViPo; ViPP; VLEP

My good man is a clever man, which no one will gainsay. Never Trouble Trouble. Fannie Windsor. PTA-1

My good old father tucked his head. Noonday Grace. John Crowe Ransom. LS

My goodness, my goodness,/ It's Christmas again. Christmas. Marchette Chute. BrR; ChBR; SiSoSe

My gostly fader, I me confess. *See* My ghostly father, I me confess.

"My Grace Is Sufficient for Thee." *Unknown.* BePJ; BLRP; PraP

My gracious friend, whose arts are all refining. Confessed. Josephine Miles. FiMAP

My gracious lord! if you, indeed, complain. To the Duke Alphonso. Tasso. BoFr

My grandam was a gay wife, but a fair-made friend. The Ballad of Kind Kittok. William Dunbar. TMEV

My granddad [*or* grandpa] viewing earth's [*or* notes the world's] worn cogs. Going to the Dogs. *Unknown.* DDA; TreFS

My grandfather had two very fine hens. Merry Green Fields of England. *Unknown.* FTB

My grandfather said with a toss of his head. Fishing. Edgar A. Guest. NLK

My grandfather's beard. On the Photograph of a Man I Never Saw. Hyam Plutzik. FiMAP

My grandfather's clock was too large for the shelf. Grandfather's Clock. Henry Clay Work. FaFP; NeHB; PTA-2; TreF

My grandfather's hands were wise and hard. Rivets. N. S. Olds. EtS

My grandmother lived on yonder green. Grandma's Advice. *Unknown.* APW

My grandmother sent me a new-fashioned three-cornered cambric country-cut handkerchief. *Unknown.* OxNR

My grandmother, she, at the age of eighty-three. Grandmother's Old Armchair. *Unknown.* BLPA

My grandmother tells me. The Ballad of the Jabberwock. Leah Bodine Drake. DaM

My Grandmother's Love Letters. Hart Crane. ChMo; FaBoBe; MoAB; MOAP; PG (1945 ed.)

My Grandmother's Turkey-Tail Fan. Samuel Minturn Peck. PR

My grandpa is the finest man. Grandpa. Edgar A. Guest. OnHT

My grandpa notes the world's worn cogs. *See* My granddad, viewing earth's worn cogs.

My Grandser was a fearsome man! Grandser. Abbie Farwell Brown. BAP; HBMV

My grandsire sailed three years from home. The Master Mariner. George Sterling. HBV; MAP; MoAmPo (1942 ed.); PoTo; TCAP

My Granny she often says to me. Says She. Winifred M. Letts. MW

My Grave. Thomas Osborne Davis. OnYI

My Greaty-great Grannie is terribly small. Greaty-great Grannie. Lysbeth Boyd Borie. GaP

My Greenup Friends. Jesse Stuart. *Fr.* Man with a Bull-Tongue Plow. BoFr

My grief, my grief, maid without sin. The Body's Speech. Donal MacCarthy, First Earl Clancarty. KiLC

My Grief on Fál's Proud Plain, *sel.* Geoffrey Keating, *tr. fr. Late Middle Irish by* Padraic Pearse.
"From my grief on Fál's proud plain I sleep." OnYI

My Grief on the Sea. *Unknown, tr. fr. Modern Irish by* Douglas Hyde. AnIL; GTIV; LBBV; LiTW; MBP; OBEV; OBVV; OnYI; OxBI; TIP

My grief! that they have laid you in the town. Synge's Grave. Winifred M. Letts. AnIV; LBBV

My gudame wes a gay wif, bot scho wes ryght [*or* rycht] gend. The Ballad of Kynd Kittok. William Dunbar. GoTS; OxBoLi

My Guide. Robert Jones Burdette. MaRV
Christ, *sel.* BePJ

My Guide. George Francis Savage-Armstrong. VA

My Guide and I on that obscure road entered. Affinity with the Stars. Dante. *Fr.* Divina Commedia: Inferno. GrCo-2

My hair all ruffled and unkempt, I tramp. Confession of a Hooligan. Sergei Yesenin. RuPo

My hair bristles in my helmet. Full River Red. Yo Fei. WhP

My hair could hardly cover my forehead. A Song of Chang-kan. Li Po. WhP

My hair is gray [*or* grey], but not with years. The Prisoner of Chillon. Byron. BEL; BPN; EmBrPo; EnLi-2; EnLit; EnRP; EPN; EPP; EV-4; GEPC; HBV; HeT; HiLiEn; LPS-2; MaC; OnSP; PCN; PIAE; TCEP; TyEnPo

My hand cannot reach heaven's height. The Poet Meets Venus and Her Priest. John Gower. *Fr.* Confessio Amantis. MeEV

My hand cannot smooth your sigh. Microcosmos, III. Nigel Heseltine. NeBP

My hand is lonely for your clasping, dear. You and I. Henry Alford. BLPA; FaBoBe; NeHB

My hand is weary with writing. St. Columcille the Scribe. *At. to* St. Columcille. AnIL; OnYI

My hand waving from the window. Platform Goodbye. H. B. Mallalieu. WaP

My hands are numb and broken. My Violets. *Unknown.* SoLD

My hands lie on her shoulders. Stone Staircase Overlooking the Sea. Fuyuji Tanaka. PoLJ

My hands that guide a needle. Instruction. Hazel Hall. NP

My hands within your hand. To a Nun-Stigmatist. Sister Mary Thérèse. PraNu

My Handsome Gilderoy. *Unknown.* AtBAP; CH

My handsome gipsy, lover mine. The Bells. Guillaume Apollinaire. TrFP

My happier state. Of Middle Life. *Unknown.* SeCL

My hart is fled from mee yet live I doe. *Unknown.* SeCSL

My harvest has passed the reaping. 'Tis Growing So Hushed around Me. Karl August Tavaststjerna. AnSL

My hateful birthday is coming, and dismally I must spend it. To Cerinthus. Sulpicia. LaP

My hat's off—my jersey's torn. Robin Hood. Patience Adrian Ross. PCH

My head is like lead, and my temples they bulge. Hangover. Philip H. Rhinelander. WhC

My Head on My Shoulders. Jeremy Ingalls. GoYe

My Heart. Tove Ditlevsen, *tr. fr. Danish by* Charles W. Stork. BoDS

My Heart. Elizabeth Madox Roberts. NP

My Heart. Albert Samain, *tr. fr. French by* Alan Conder. TrFP

My heart,/ The sun hath set. All's Well. William A. Quayle. MaRV

My heart aches, and a drowsy numbness pains. Ode to a Nightingale [*or* To a Nightingale]. Keats. AEV; AnEnPo; AnFE; AtBAP; ATP; AWP; BCEP; BEL; BLA; BLV; BoLiVe; BPN; CaAE; CBE; CBOV; ChER; ChTr; CoBE; CoEV; EM-2; EmBrPo; EnL; EnLi-2; EnLit; EnLP; EnRP; EPN; EPP; ERP; EV-4; ExPo; FaBoBe; FaBoEn; FaFP; FiP; GBV; GEPC; GTBS; GTBS-D; GTBS-W; GTSE; GTSL; HBV; HBVY; HiLiEn; InP; InPo; JAWP; LEAP; LiA; LiTB; LiTG; LoBV; LPS-1; MaPo; MCCG; OAEP; OBEV; OBRV; OtMeF; OuHeWo; PC; PFE; PIAE; PIR; Po; PoE; PoEL-4; PoeMoYo; PoFS; PoRA; PreP; PYM; REAL; ReaPo; RiBV; SeCeV; ShBV-3; SN; TCEP; TOP; TreF; TrGrPo; TVSH; TwHP; TwP; TyEnPo; UnPo; ViBoPo; WBP; WHA; WoL

My heart and body would fain part company. Civil War. Friedrich von Hausen. LyMA

My Heart and I. Elizabeth Barrett Browning. HBV; VA

My heart and I were not so very well acquent. Upon Discovering One's Own Intolerance. Sara Henderson Hay. MaRV

My Heart Atones. Ramón López Velarde, *tr. fr. Spanish by* Samuel Beckett. AnMP

My heart, being hungry, feeds on food. The Hungry Heart. Edna St. Vincent Millay. TSW; TSWC

My heart, complaining like a bird. Burning Bush. Karle Wilson Baker. HBMV

My heart cried like a beaten child. Song Making. Sara Teasdale. WGRP

My heart doth fly. *Unknown, tr. fr. Arabic by* A. J. Arberry. MooP

My heart felt need to die. The Scourge. Stanley Kunitz. CrMA

My heart has become as hard as a city street. Discordants, II. Conrad Aiken. MOAP

My heart has fed today. Completion. Eunice Tietjens. HBMV; LEAP; LoPS; NP

My heart has gotten lost, it seems. My Heart. Tove Ditlevsen. BoDS

My heart has grown rich with the passing of years. The Solitary. Sara Teasdale. MAP; MoAmPo; NeMA; WHA

My heart has thank'd thee, Bowles! for those soft strains. To the Reverend W. L. Bowles. Samuel Taylor Coleridge. EmBrPo; EnRP; ERP

My heart, I cannot still it. Auspex. James Russell Lowell. AmPP (3d ed.); AnFE; AnNE; APA; APW; BLV; CBOV; CoAnAm; GTBS-W; HBV; IAP; LBAP; MOAP; NePA; OBVV; PoEL-5

My heart, imprisoned in a hopeless isle. Idea's Mirrour, XXII. Michael Drayton. OBSC; SiCE

My heart in middle age found the Way. My Retreat at Mount Chung-nan. Wang Wei. PoP

My Heart Is a Lute. *At. to* Lady Anne Lindsay, *also to* Lady Blanche Elizabeth Lindsay. HBV; VA

My heart is a-breaking, dear tittie. Tam Glen. Burns. ALV; AWP; BEL; BSV; CEP; EBSV; EM-1; EV-3; InPo; JAWP; OAEP; OBEC; TOP; WBP

My heart is as a freeborn bird. A Nun. Christina Rossetti. PraNu

My heart is bare to God who knows no wrong. Ode—Imitated from the Psalms. Nicolas Joseph Laurent Gilbert. CAW

My heart is beating up and down. My Heart. Elizabeth Madox Roberts. NP

My heart is chilled and my pulse is slow. Lost Light. Elizabeth Akers Allen. HBV

My heart is cold and weather-worn. Nameless Song. Elinor Wylie. CoBA

My heart is far from Liffey's tide. Mo Craoibhin Cno. Edward Walsh. IrPN; TIP

My heart is gray with bird-wings going south on the north wind. Gray. Frederick R. McCreary. TBM

My Heart Is Heavy. Sara Teasdale. NP

My Heart Is High [*or* Heich] Above. *Unknown.* EBSV; GoTS; LO; OBEV

My Heart Is in the East. Judah Halevi, *tr. fr. Hebrew.* TrJP

My heart is in woe. The Downfall of the Gael. Fearflatha O'Gnive, *tr. by* Sir Samuel Ferguson. AnIV; AWP; JAWP; OnYI; WBP

My heart is just a small red book. A Mild Rebuke. Margaret L. Sullivan. CAG

My heart is lighter than the poll. The New-slain Knight. *Unknown.* ESPB

My heart is like a city of the gay. The Buried City. George Sylvester Viereck. LBMV

My heart is like a fountain true. Mother's Song. *Unknown.* BOL; GN; HBV

My heart is like a ship on Neptune's back. Emaricdulfe, XXIX. "E. C." ElSeCe; TuPP

My heart is like a singing bird. A Birthday. Christina Rossetti. AV; AWP; BLV; BMEP; BoLiVe; BPN; CBOV; CH; CoBE; EG; EmBrPo; EnLi-2; EPP; EtPaEn; EV-5; FaFP; GTBS; GTSE; GTSL; HiLiEn; InvP; JAWP; LEAP; LiTB; LiTG; LiTL; LoBV; LoPS; MBP; OAEP; OBEV; OBVV; OuHeWo; PCD; PFE; PIAE; PoE; POTT; PoVP; ShBV-4; ThWaDe; TOP; TreFS; TrGrPo; TSW; TSWC; TyEnPo; ViBoPo; ViP; ViPo; VLEP; WBP; WHA; YT

My heart is rich as a brimming cup. Drink. Bertel Gripenberg. AnSL

My heart is sair—I dare na tell. For the Sake o' [*or* of] Somebody [*or* Somebody]. Burns. AtBAP; BSV; EV-3

My heart is set him down, twixt hope and fears. Thomas Watson. *Fr.* Hecatompathia. ReIE

My heart is set upon a lusty pin. I pray to Venus. Elizabeth of York. DiM

My heart is stirred to its depths. A Song of Cherry-Time. Tzu Yeh. ChLP; PoHN

My Heart is Turned into a Wailing Child. Nahabed Kouchak, *tr. fr. Armenian by* Zabelle C. Boyajian. ArmLP

My heart is wasted with my woe. The Ballad of Oriana. Tennyson. EmBrPo

My heart is withered and my health is gone! The Wave of Cliona. James Stephens, *after* Egan O'Rahilly. ChMo

My heart is yearning to thee, O Skye. Skye. Alexander Nicolson. EBSV

My heart is young—the breath of blowing trees. Certainties. Helen Frazee-Bower. *Fr.* Two Married. HBMV

My heart is yours now; keep it fast. I Promise You. *Unknown.* TMEV

My heart it was a cup of gold. The Prince. Josephine Dodge Daskam Bacon. BAP; LBMV

My Heart Leaps Up [When I Behold]. Wordsworth. AtBAP; ATP; BEL; BLV; BoLiVe; BPN; CaAE; CoBE; EG; EM-2; EmBrPo; EnLi-2; EnLit; EnRP; EPN; EPP; ERP; ExPo; FaBoEn; FaFP; GEPC; GTBS; GTBS-D; GTBS-W; GTSE; GTSL; HiLiEn; InPo; LoBV; LPS-2; MCCG; NLK; OAEP; OBRV; OTPC; OuHeWo; PCD; REAL; TCEP; TiPo; TOP; TreF; TrGrPo; TVSH; TwHP; TwP; TyEnPo; ViBoPo; WP; YT
(Rainbow, The.) BCEP; BLPA; BPP; CBE; CBOV; CG; DD; EV-3; HBV; HBVY; LEAP; LiTB; LiTG; NeHB; OBEV; PECK; PIR; PYM
(Rainbow in the Sky.) RIS

My heart leaps up when I behold. Song to be Sung by the Father of Infant Female Children. Ogden Nash. MoAmPo

My heart lies light in my own breast. The Wind Bloweth Where It Listeth. Susan L. Mitchell. AnIV

My heart, like a bird, ahover joyously. A Voyage to Cythera. Baudelaire, *tr. by* Frederick Morgan. AnFP

My heart, like a bird, veered up in joyous flight. A Voyage to Cythera. Baudelaire, *tr. by* Hubert Creekmore. LiTW

My heart, loyal, atones in the darkness. My Heart Atones. Ramón López Velarde. AnMP

My heart makes mock at the long day's harms. Lullaby. Nannie Fitzhugh Maclean. BOL

My heart, my heart goes from me, Lord. Mozarabic Songs, 1. *Unknown.* TeCS

My heart, my heart is mournful. Mein Herz, mein Herz ist traurig. Heine. AWP

My Heart of Gold. *Unknown.* AnEC
(My Lady Went to Canterbury.) KN

(Nonsense Carol, A.) OxBoLi
"Nine mile to Michaelmas," *sel.* BoN
My heart rebels against my generation. Odes, II. George Santayana. AnFE; ATP; CoAnAm; PoFr; TwAmPo; ViBoPo
My heart rejoiceth in the Lord, mine horn is exalted. The Song of Hannah [*or* Hannah's Song of Thanksgiving]. First Samuel, Bible, *O.T.* AWP; LiTW
My heart rose when I looked on Sampford. Walking Sampford Way. Paul L. Grano. BoAu
My Heart Shall Be Thy Garden. Alice Meynell. HBV
My heart that was so passionless. Rencontre. Jessie Fauset. CDC
My heart the anvil where my thoughts do beat. Idea, XL (*also given as XLIV in* Idea's Mirrour). Michael Drayton. HBV; ReIE
My heart, thinking. "Lady of Sakanoye." *Fr.* Manyo Shu. AWP; JAWP; LiTW; PFE; WBP
My heart was fired, as from his sight it turned. The Dream of Dakiki. Firdausi. WGRP
My heart was heavy, for its trust had been. Forgiveness. Whittier. AmPP (3d ed.); IAP; MaRV
My Heart Was Wandering [in the Sands]. Christopher J. Brennan. BoAu; BoAV
My heart was winter-bound until. Love's Springtide. Frank Dempster Sherman. LBMV
My heart, where have we been? Gerard Manley Hopkins. *Fr.* St. Winefred's Well. NBE
My heart, why think upon the birth of kings. Kings. Victor Hugo. TrFP
My heart will break—I'm sure it will. False Love and True Logic. Laman Blanchard. BOHV
My heart's a lovely lake, lonely and trembling. My Heart. Albert Samain. TrFP
My heart's best! Uncourtly Love. Walther von der Vogelweide. LiTW
My heart's delight and grief are not a bait. Noli Me Tangere. Carl Snoilsky. AnSL
My heart's delight, I must for love forget you! Felo de Se. Elinor Wylie. LoPS
My heart's desire is that the Muses fair. Virgil. *Fr.* Georgics, II. LaP
My heart's despair. Isabel. Sydney Dobell. OBVV
My Heart's in the Highlands. Burns. AnEnPo; AWP; BBV (1923 ed.); BEL; BHV; CBE; CEP; CoBE; EBSV; EM-1; EnRP; EV-3; FaBoBe; FaFP; FaPON; GN; HBV; InPo; JAWP; LiTG; LiTL; LPS-2; NeHB; OTPC; REAL; RIS; ShBV-2; StaSt; TCEP; TOP; TVSH; WBP; WaKn
My heart's joy, the whole of all my pleasure. This Little Bill. *Unknown.* TMEV
My heart's so heavy with a hundred things. Sonnet: In Absence from Becchina. Cecco Angiolieri da Siena. AWP; JAWP; WBP
My heavy hammer rang in the light air. The Vase. Henri de Régnier. LiA
My Heid Is Like to Rend, Willie. William Motherwell. LPS-1
My help, my hope, my strength shall be. The Law. Abraham ibn Ezra. TrJP
My Hereafter. Juanita De Long. WGRP
My heritage lost through disorder and famine. To My Brothers and Sisters Adrift in Troubled Times This Poem of the Moon. Po Chü-i. BoFr
My hero is na deck'd wi' gowd. The Hero. Robert Nicoll. HBV; VA
My Hero; to Robert Gould Shaw. Benjamin Brawley. BANP; PoNe
My highway is unfeatured air. Hymn of the Earth. William Ellery Channing. AA; AnNE; APW; IAP
My history extends/ Where moved my tourist hands. Abroad Thoughts from Home. Donald Hall. NePoEA
My hoary locks I dye with care. Self-Defense. Santob de Carrion. TrJP
My Home. Mikhail Yurevich Lermontov, *tr. fr. Russian by* Sir Cecil Kisch. WaL
My Home. *Unknown.* NA
My Home. Christian Winther, *tr. fr. Danish by* Charles W. Stork. BoDS
My home is a house/ Near a wood. The Country Child. Irene Thompson. BoTP
My home is in Meng Chin village. No News. Wang Wei. PoHN
My home is on the rolling deep. My Home. *Unknown.* NA
My home is surrounded by a clear stream. The Village and the River. Tu Fu. WhP
My home is where the warm sun shines on the Cicada River. Home Thoughts. Kyukin Susukida. PoLJ
My home was on the beach near the sea-shore. A Love-Letter. *Unknown, tr. by* Francis A. Blackburn. EPP
My home's in Montana, I wear a bandanna. Cowboy's Lament (C *vers.*). *Unknown.* CoSo
My homeward course led up a long ascent. The Demobilized Soldier. Wordsworth. *Fr.* The Prelude, IV. RO

My Honey, My Love. Joel Chandler Harris. *Fr.* Uncle Remus and His Friends. AA; FaBoBe
My Honeyed Languor. "Eduard Bagritzky," *tr. fr. Russian by* Babette Deutsch. TrJP; TrRV
My honoured lord, forgive the unruly tongue. Elinor Wylie. *Fr.* One Person. NP
My hope, alas, hath me abused. Sir Thomas Wyatt. SiPS
My hope and heart is with thee—thou wilt be. To J. M. K. Tennyson. PoVP; ViPo; VLEP
My Hope, My Love. *Unknown, tr. fr. Irish by* Edward Walsh. GTIV
My Hopes Retire [My Wishes as Before]. Walter Savage Landor. BPN; EmBrPo (Persistence.) VA
My Horses Ain't Hungry. *Unknown.* See Rebel Soldier, The.
My horse's feet beside the lake. A Farewell. Matthew Arnold. *Fr.* Switzerland. OAEP; ViPP
My houn' dog's gettin' anxious. Ol' Hound Dog. "Beau Justi." AlBD
My House. Joachim du Bellay. See Heureux qui, comme Ulysse, a fait un beau voyage.
My House. Helen H. Hall. DDA
My House. Claude McKay. CDC
My House. Harry Noyes Pratt. PoTo
My House. Robert Louis Stevenson. VLEP
My House. May Williams Ward. PC
My House. W. B. Yeats. Meditations in Time of Civil War, II. LiTB
My house has crickets. Crickets and Mice. Joseph Joel Keith. StVeCh (1955 ed.)
My House Has Windows. Anna Blake Mezquida. OQP; QP-2
My house, I say. But hark to the sunny doves. My House. Robert Louis Stevenson. VLEP
My house is little, but warm enough. My Little House. May Byron. OQP; QP-2
My house is made of graham bread. Queer Quatrains. Gelett Burgess. RIS
My house is not quiet, I am not loud. Fish in River. *Unknown. Fr.* Riddles. AnOE
My house is poor; those that I love have left me. Winter Night. Po Chü-i. TrCh
My house is red—a little house. A Happy Child. Kate Greenaway. BoTP; PPL; OTPC
My house is small. My House. May Williams Ward. PC
My house is small and white and trim. My House. Helen H. Hall. DDA
My house, my fairy/ palace. Jeronimo's House. Elizabeth Bishop. MiAP
My house stands high. The Harp of the Wind. Frances Shaw. NP
My hovering thoughts would fly to heaven, and quiet nestle in the sky. Man's Civil War. Robert Southwell. SiCE
My hungry eyes, through greedy covetise. Amoretti, XXXV. Spenser. PeBoSo
My Husband ("Heiho, my husband is brave"). *Unknown, tr. fr. Chinese.* WhP
My Husband ("My husband's a jockey"). *Unknown.* CoMu
My husband is far, far away. The Wife. *Unknown. Fr.* Shi King. OnPM; PoHN; WoL
My husband's a jockey, a jockey, a jockey. My Husband. *Unknown.* CoMu
My husband's a saucy foretopman. Eight Bells. *Unknown.* SaSa
My Hut. E. Mathias. BoTP
My hut, in spring! Spring in My Hut. Sodo. OnPM
My Infelice's face, her brow, her eye. A Portrait. Thomas Dekker. EV-2
My Inmost Hope. Sarah Copia Sullam, *tr. fr. Italian.* TrJP
My Inside-Self. Rachel Field. FaPON
My Instant. Mary Sinton Leitch. LS
My Irish great-grandfather, Patrick O'Flyng. Homer C. House. DDA
My Jack. John Francis O'Donnell. IrPN
My Jean. Burns. *See* Of A' the Airts.
My Jesus, as Thou Wilt. Benjamin Schmolke [*or* Schmolck], *tr. fr. German.* BePJ; PraP, *st.* 1 (Consecration, *abr.*) BLRP
My Jewels. Mary Dixon Thayer. TBM
My Johnny is left me and gone to the sea. The Answer. Isobel Pagan. DiM
My jowl's gone gray, gone bare my head. Labuntur Anni. Anacreon. GrR
My Joy, My Jockey, My Gabriel. George Barker. First Cycle of Love Poems, V. MoAB; MoBrPo (1950 ed.); MoPo; MoPW (Love Poem.) NeBP
My joy, my life, my crown! A True Hymn. George Herbert. GrCo-2; InvP; OxBoCh
My joyous youth has passed away. Adieu. Pierre de Ronsard. TrFP
My Kate. Elizabeth Barrett Browning. OBVV; OHFP; WBLP
My Kingdom. Louisa May Alcott. MaRV

My Kingdom. Robert Louis Stevenson. OnHT
My Kite. Beatrice Brown. GFA
My kite grabbed on a gusty gale. Kite Tales. Rose Waldo. GFA
My kitten slept in a cushioned chair. Change. Lalia Mitchell Thornton. CIV
My kitten walks on velvet feet. Night. Lois Weakley McKay. SiSoSe
My Laddie. Amélie Rives. HBV
My Laddie's Hounds. Marguerite Elizabeth Easter. AA
My Lady. Philip James Bailey. *Fr.* Festus. OBVV
("I loved her for that she was beautiful.") LO
My Lady April. Ernest Dowson. VLEP
My Lady Carries Love. Dante, *tr. fr. Italian by* Dante Gabriel Rossetti. La Vita Nuova, XII. AWP; JAWP; OnPM; WBP
(Sonnet: "My lady carries love within her eyes.") LyPI
(Within Her Eyes.) LiTW
My Lady Esther, beautiful. Esther. Fray Angelico Chavez. GoBC
My Lady Fair. Martha Day Fenner. MeMeAg
My Lady Goes to the Play. Arthur Ketchum. PR
My Lady Greensleeves. *Unknown.* EV-2; WP
(Lady [*or* Ladie] Greensleeves.) AtBAP; PoEL-2
(New Courtly Sonnet of the Lady Greensleeves, A.) CenL; ElL; FaBoCh, *abr.*; LoGBV; NBE; OAEP; OBSC; ReEn; ReIE; SiCE; TuPP
My Lady Has the Grace of Death. Joseph Plunkett. OxBI
My Lady Is a Pretty One. *Unknown.* OxBoLi
My Lady Is Compared to a Young Tree. Vachel Lindsay. ChMo; CMP
My lady looks so gentle and so pure. Sonnet. Dante. *Fr.* La Vita Nuova. AWP; JAWP; LyPI; WBP
My lady mine, I send. Canzonetta: Of His Lady and of His Making Her Likeness. Jacopo da Lentino. AWP; LyMA
My Lady Nature and Her Daughters. Cardinal Newman. GoBC
My lady ne'er hath given herself to me. Ideal Passion, I. George Edward Woodberry. MOAP; NV
"My lady of Rhodes, how did you gain entrance?" Noble Parentage. Lorenzo Mavilis. MoGP
My lady seems of ivory. Praise of My Lady. William Morris. HBV; PoVP; ViPo; VLEP
My lady sighs, and I am far away. Sonnet. George Henry Boker. MOAP
My Lady Springs. *Unknown.* BoTP
My Lady Takes the Sunlight for Her Gown. Thomas Cole. NePoAm
My Lady unto Madam makes her bow. Modern Love, XXXVI. George Meredith. ViPo
My lady walks her morning round. The Henchman. Whittier. HBV; OBEV (new ed.); OBVV; PR
My Lady Went to Canterbury. *Unknown. See* My Heart of Gold.
My Lady Wind. *Unknown.* HBV; HBVY; OTPC (1923 ed.); PCH
("My Lady Wind, my Lady Wind.") PPL
My Lady Wine-Pot. *Unknown, tr. fr. Greek by* F. L. Lucas. GrPE
My lady woke upon a morning fair. On His Lady's Waking. Pierre de Ronsard. AWP
My lady, you are of all beauty shrine. To Rosemound; a Balade. Chaucer. PoLi
My Lady's birthday crowns the growing year. In February. Henry Simpson. HBV
My lady's eyes are fire and jet. A Regretful Rondeau. Michael Lewis. PIAE
My Lady's face it is they worship there. Sonnet. Guido Cavalcanti. LyPI
My Lady's Grave. Emily Brontë. *See* Song: "Linnet in the rocky dells, The."
My lady's presence makes the roses red. Sonnet. Henry Constable. *Fr.* Diana. CoBE; ElL; HBV; LEAP; OBSC; ReIE; SiCE
My Lady's Slipper. *Unknown. See* Lass of Lochroyan, The.
My Lady's Tears. *Unknown. See* I Saw My Lady Weep.
My lamp, full charged with its sweet oil, still burns. Hero Entombed, I. Peter Quennell. FaBoMo; LiTB
My Land. Thomas Osborne Davis. DD; HBV; MPB (1956 ed.); OTPC
(This Native Land.) BoTP
My Land. James Oppenheim. TBM
My Land Is Fair for Any Eyes to See. Jesse Stuart. FaPON; TiPo (1959 ed.)
My land was the west land; my home was on the hill. The Homeland. Dana Burnet. BLP; SBMV
My Language. Heinz Politzer, *tr. fr. German by* Heinz Politzer. LiTW
My lank limp lily, my long lithe lily. A Maudle-in Ballad. *Unknown.* BOHV; PA
My Last Duchess. Robert Browning. ATP; AWP; BEL; BeLS; BLV; BMEP; BoLiVe; BPN; CaAE; CBOV; CoBE; CoEV; EM-2; EmBrPo; EnL; EnLi-2; EnLit; EPN; EPP; EV-5; ExPo; FaBoEn; FaFP; FiP; GEPC; HBV; HiLiEn; HoPM; InP; InPo; JAWP; LiTB; MCCG; OAEP; OnPP; OtMeF; OuHeWo; PFE; PIAE; PIR; PoE; PoEL-5; PoFS; PoVP; PYM; REAL; ReaPo; RiBV; SeCeV; ShBV-4; TCEP; TOP; TreFS; TrGrPo; TwHP; TwP; TyEnPo; UnPo (1st ed.); VA; ViPo; ViPP; VLEP; WBP; WHA
My Last Illusion. John Kendall. FiBHP; WhC
My Last Terrier. John Halsham. HBV
My Last Thought. José Rizal, *tr. fr. Spanish by* Murat Halstead. PoFr
My Last Will. Sir Walter Raleigh. MM
My least height flowers late with buds. Where Unimaginably Bright. Oliver Hale. GoYe
My Legacy. Helen Hunt Jackson. HBV; LPS-3
My Legs Are So Weary. Gelett Burgess. LBN
My Lesbia, I will not deny. Upon Lesbia—Arguing. Alfred Cochrane. HBV
My Letter. Grace Denio Litchfield. AA
My letters all dead paper, mute and white! Sonnets from the Portuguese, XXVIII. Elizabeth Barrett Browning. BPN; CoBE; EmBrPo; EnLi-2; EnLit; EPP; EV-4; HBV; LPS-1; ViBoPo; ViPo
My Library. Henry Jerome Stockard. NoCaPo
My liege,/ They are not yet come back. Shakespeare. *Fr.* Macbeth, I, iv. PIR
My Liege, I Did Deny No Prisoners. Shakespeare. King Henry IV, Pt. I, *fr.* I, iii. WaaP
("But I remember, when the fight was done.") PIR
(Hotspur.) BHV; ShGoBo
(Hotspur's Description of a Fop: "But I remember . . .") LPS-2
(Staff Officer, The: "But I remember . . .") OtMeF
My Life. Verner von Heidenstam, *tr. fr. Swedish by* Charles W. Stork. AnSL
My life closed twice before its close. Emily Dickinson. AmPP (4th ed.); AnAmPo; AnNE; AtBAP; BLV; BoLiVe; EG; FaBoEn; LA; LO; MAP; MoAB; MoAmPo; MoVE; NePA; OBAV; OxBA; PoLFOT; TrGrPo; TwP; ViBoPo; WHA
(Parting.) AA; AnFE; APA; AV; BAP; CoAnAm; GTBS-D; GTBS-W; LBAP; LEAP; LiTA; LiTL; LiTM; LoPo; LoPS; MAPA; OBEV (new ed.); OBVV; PFY; TCAP; TwAmPo
My life ebbs from me—I must die. First or Last. Margaret Veley. VA
My life had stood a loaded gun. Emily Dickinson. PoE; TwP
My Life Is a Bowl. May Riley Smith. BLPA
My life is a wearisome journey. The End of the Way. Harriet Cole. BLRP
My life is bitter with thy love. Anactoria. Swinburne. EmBrPo
My life is but an instant, a fleeting hour above me. My Song of Today. St. Thérèse of Lisieux. CAW
My life is cast. Sifting. Victor E. Beck. GoYe
My life is crowned by three consummate things. Reality. Robert Haven Schauffler. TBM
My Life is Full of Weary Days. Tennyson. PoVP
My life is legends of the yellow haired. Nor Mars His Sword. Dunstan Thompson. NePA
My life is like a dream. From Disciple to Master. Monk Gibbon. AnIV
My life is like a stroll upon the beach. The Fisher's Boy. Henry David Thoreau. AA; AnAmPo; AnNE; ChTr; LA; MOAP; OBAV; TCAP
My life is like daytime. The Wife's Lament. Nikolai Nekrasov. *Fr.* Who Can Be Happy and Free in Russia? BoR
My Life Is like the Summer Rose. Richard Henry Wilde. HBV; IAP; TCAP
(Life.) LPS-3
(Stanzas.) AA; APW; BAV; SPP
My life is measur'd by this glasse, this glasse. On an Hour[e]-Glasse. John Hall. MeLP; MePo
My life is now a burthen growne. *Unknown.* SeCSL
My life more civil is and free. Independence. Henry David Thoreau. AmPP (3d ed.); AnNE; CoBA; PoFr; TreFS
My life must touch a million lives in some way ere I go. My Prayer. *Unknown.* BLRP
My life seems dull and flat. Epitaph on a Pet Cat. Joachim du Bellay. FoS; PoC
My life shall touch a dozen lives before this day is done. As I Go on My Way. Strickland Gillilan. MaRV
My Life's Delight. Thomas Campion. *See* Come, Oh, Come, My Life's Delight.
My life's on the wane and I'm spent with work. A Poor Monk of Skara. Gustaf Fröding. AnSL
My Light and My Salvation. Psalms, XXVII, Bible, *O.T.* (*Moulton, Modern Reader's Bible*). MaRV
(Deliverance of Jehovah, The, *Moulton, Modern Reader's Bible.*) WGRP
(Serenity of Faith, The, 7-14, *tr. by* J. E. McFayden.) BLRP

My Light! My Way! Count von Zinzendorf, *tr. fr. German by* John Wesley. MaRV
My light thou art, without thy glorious sight. Earl of Rochester. *Fr.* To His Mistress. LiTL; PG
My Light with Yours. Edgar Lee Masters. ChMo; CMP; LoPS; NP; NV; TBM
My Li'l John Henry, *with music. Unknown.* ABF
My limbs I will fling. Song. William Strode. *Fr.* The Floating Island. CenL; SeCL
My lips apart. The Soul in the Kiss. *Unknown. Fr.* Attic Nights (*by* Aulus Gellius). LaP
My Lips Would Sing. Edmund Leamy. JKCP
My Little Almond Tree. Aleksey Konstantinovich Tolstoy, *tr. fr. Russian by* Babette Deutsch. TrRV
My little bed is wide enough. The White Dream. May Doney. HBMV
My Little Bird. Bunyan. *See* Of the Child with the Bird at the Bush.
My Little Birds. *Unknown, tr. fr. Arabic by* Henrietta Sisek-Su'ad. FaPON
My Little Boat. Sarah Jane S. Harrington. RAR
My Little Bo-Peep. S. B. McManus. BOL
My little boy at Christmas-tide. The Toy Cross. Roden Noel. VA
My little boy was not yet four years old. The Journey. Walter de la Mare. InP
My little breath, under the willows by the water-side we used to sit. A Lover's Lament. *Tr. by* H. J. Spinden. AWP; JAWP; WBP
My Little Brother. Mary Lundie Duncan. OTPC (1923 ed.)
My little brother is—oh, so funny! What My Little Brother Thinks! *Unknown.* MeMeAg
My little daughter is a tea-rose. Apple and Rose. Karle Wilson Baker. FAOV
My little daughter leans upon my arms. Guidance. Harriet B. Williams. PraP
My little daughter's eyes are blue. To Suzette. Arthur S. Bourinot. CPG
My Little Dear. Dollie Radford. BOL; VA
My little dears, who learn to read, pray early learn to shun. Cautionary Verses [to Youth of Both Sexes]. Theodore Hook. BOHV; HBV
My Little Dog. Pearl Forbes MacEwen. BoTP
My little dog lies curled asleep. Quality. Marty Hale. AlBD
My little doves have left a nest. My Doves. Elizabeth Barrett Browning. OTPC
My Little Dreams. Georgia Douglas Johnson. BANP; CDC; GoSl; PoNe
My Little Fool. *Unknown.* TuPP
My Little Girl. Samuel Minturn Peck. *See* My Drowsy Little Queen.
My Little House. May Byron. OQP; QP-2
My Little House. Hazel Harper Harris. DDA
My Little House. J. M. Westrup. BoTP
My little kitty has soft, white fur. My Pets. Sarah Jane S. Harrington. RAR
My little lady I may not leave behind. To My Lady Mirriel Howard. John Skelton. *Fr.* The Garlande of Laurell. LoBV
My Little Lodge. *Unknown, tr. fr. Old Irish by* Fred Norris Robinson. OnYI
My little lord, methinks 'tis strange. A Prognostication on Will Laud, Late Archbishop of Canterbury. *Unknown.* OxBoLi
My Little Love. Charles B. Hawley. HBV
My little love, do you remember. The Chess-Board. "Owen Meredith." HBV; LPS-1; OBVV; VA
My Little Lover. Cécile Sauvage, *tr. fr. French by* Alan Conder. LO
My little Mädchen found one day. A Chrysalis. Mary Emily Bradley. AA; HBV; PECK; SN
My little maiden two years old, just able. The Eternal Search. Sir William Watson. PoVP
My little milliner has slipp'd. A Machine Hand. Thomas Ashe. OBVV
My Little Neighbor. Mary Augusta Mason. AA; GFA
My little old dog. A Lyrical Epigram. Edith Wharton. PC
My little old man and I fell out. *Unknown.* OxNR
My little one begins his feet to try. The First Step. Andrew Bice Saxton. AA
My little one, sleep softly. Lullaby. Harriet Monroe. BOL; NP
My Little Pony. *Unknown.* SAS
My Little Pretty One, *in mod. Eng. Unknown.* LO, *st.* 1; TMEV, *sl. diff.*
My Little Saint. John Norris. LPS-1
My Little Sister. *Unknown.* OTPC (1923 ed.)
My little sisters, the birds, much bounden are ye unto God. Sermon to the Birds. St. Francis of Assisi. TreF
My little son. The Hostess. Wang Mou Fang. PoHN
My little son! I hold you to my heart. To My Son, Four Days Old. Leila Sprague Learned. MotAn
My little son, I wish you well, your mother's comfort when in grief. *Unknown.* BOL
My little son, who look'd from thoughtful eyes. The Toys. Coventry Patmore. ACP; AnFE; BeLS; BLV; BMEP; BPP; CAW; EnLit; EPN; EPP; FAOV; FaFP; GoBC; GTBS; GTBS-W; GTML; GTSL; HBV; JKCP; LEAP; MaRV; OBEV; OBVV; PC; PG; PoToHe (new ed.); POTT; PoVP; ReaPo; ReTS; TreFS; TrGrPo; TrPWD; VA; ViBoPo; ViP; VLEP; WP; YT
My little soul I never saw. Little Gray Songs from St. Joseph's, XLVII. Grace Fallow Norton. HBV; LBMV
My little stone/ Sinks quickly. Letters Found near a Suicide. Frank Horne. CDC; PoNe
My little white kitten's asleep on my knee. The White Kitten. "Marian Douglas." SAS
My Lode-Star. Robert Browning. *Fr.* Pauline. MaRV
My Lodge at Wang-ch'uan after a Long Rain. Wang Wei, *tr. fr. Chinese by* Witter Bynner. LiTW
My lodging it is on the cold ground. Song. Sir William Davenant. *Fr.* The Rivals. SeCL
My lonely ramble yester-eve I took. Caroline Anne Bowles. *Fr.* The Evening Walk. EnSW
My long poem, the "Eternal Grief," is a beautiful and moving work. The Fifteenth Volume. Po Chü-i. TrCh
My long two-pointed ladder's sticking through a tree. After Apple-picking. Robert Frost. AmP; AmPo; AnAmPo; AnNE; BrBE; CoBMV; CoV; LA; LEAP; LiTA; MAP; MoAB; MoAmPo; MoPo; MoVE; NP; OnAP; OxBA; ReaPo; ReMP; RiBV; SBMV; UnPo; ViBoPo; WoL
My lop eared pup looking up at me. Pup in the Snowstorm. Frances Frost. AlBD
My Lord. Martha Snell Nicholson. BePJ
My Lord and King. Tennyson. *See* In Memoriam A. H. H.: "Love is and was my lord and king."
My Lord came to me once a King. A Ballad of Wonder. Eleanor Slater. MaRV
My Lord Hides Himself. Kabir, *tr. fr. Hindi.* MaRV
My Lord, how full of sweet content. Since God Is There. Mme Guyon, *tr. by* William Cowper. MaRV
My Lord, I do not ask to stand. The Teacher's Prayer. Norman E. Richardson. PraP
My Lord, I have no clothes to come to thee. I Need Thee. George Macdonald. MaRV
My lord is all a-glow. Wedding Song. *Unknown. Fr.* Shi King. LiTW
My Lord Is Full of Delight. *Unknown, tr. fr. Chinese.* WhP
My Lord, my Life, can Envy ever bee. Meditation Thirty-three. Edward Taylor. *Fr.* Sacramental Meditations. AtBAP; PoEL-3
My Lord, my Saviour, and my God. Written by the Authoress on Her Death Bed. Laetitia Pilkington. MeRV
My lord said to my lady. Lamkin (K *vers.*). *Unknown.* ESPB
My Lord Says He's Gwineter Rain Down Fire, *with music. Unknown.* BoAN-2
My Lord Tomnoddy. Robert Barnabas Brough. FiBHP; VA
My Lord Tomnoddy got up one day. Hon. Mr. Sucklethumbkin's Story. "Thomas Ingoldsby." *Fr.* The Ingoldsby Legends. OBRV
My Lord Tomnoddy's the son of an Earl. My Lord Tomnoddy. Robert Barnabas Brough. FiBHP; VA
My Lord, What a Mornin', *with music. Unknown.* BoAN-1
My Lord, when he went back. Legacy. Ruth Winant Wheeler. ChIP
My lord will soon be here! Home from the Wars. Hsüeh T'ao. OnPM; PoHN
My lord, within thy halls I've stayed. Complaint of the Minstrel's Life. Colin Muset. LyMA
My Lord would make a cross for me. My Cross. Zitella Cocke. HBV
My lord, you know that I am married and have a husband. Song of a Modest Woman. Chang Chi. WhP
My Lord's a-Writin' All de Time, *with music. Unknown.* BoAN-1
My Lord's Motoring. Vincent Starrett. CIV
My Lords, my Lord of Warwick. Joan of Arc to the Tribunal. Anthony Frisch. CaP
My Lords, we heard you speak: you told us all. The Third of February, 1852. Tennyson. PoFr
My lords, with your leave. A New War Song by Sir Peter Parker. *Unknown.* PAH
My lore, my thoughts, and what the Muse hath given. Reliquiae. Crates. GrR
My Lost Youth. Longfellow. AA; AmPP; AnFE; AnNE; APA; APW; AWP; BAP, *abr.*; BLV, *abr.*; CoAnAm; CoBA; DDA; EtS; EV-5; ExPo; FaBoBe; FaFP; GTBS-D; GTBS-W; GTSE; HBV; IAP; InPo; JAWP; LaNeLa, *abr.*; LBAP; LEAP; LiTA; MCCG; MOAP; NePA; OBAV; OBEV; OTPC; OxBA; PCD; PFY; Po; PoEL-5; PoeMoYo; PoRA; PYM; RG; SeCeV; TCAP; TOP; TreF; ViBoPo; WBP
Sea Memories, *sel.* CBPC; FaPON; MPB
("Often I think of the beautiful town.") AlDL
My Love. E. E. Cummings. LiTL; LiTM

My Love. Bartholomew Griffin. *See* Sonnet: "Fair is my love that feeds among the lilies."
My Love. Kai Holdberg, *tr. fr. Danish by* Charles W. Stork. BoDS
My Love. James Russell Lowell. FaBoBe; HBV; IAP; LBAP; TVSH
My Love ("I only knew"). *Unknown. Fr. various poems.* LPS-3
My Love ("My love hath gone and hid from me"). *Unknown, tr. fr. French by* Alan Conder. TrFP
My love/ Is like the grasses. Ono no Yoshiki. *Fr.* Kokin Shu. AWP; LiTW; PFE
My Love and I. Arthur Davison Ficke. CAG
My love and I among the mountains strayed. A Pastoral. J. B. B. Nichols. VA
My love and I for kisses play'd. Kisses. William Strode. LPS-1; NeHB
My love and I, the other day. The Snake. Thomas Moore. HBV
My Love and I went maying. My Love and I. Arthur Davison Ficke. CAG
My love and my delight. The Lament for Art O'Leary. Eileen O'Leary. AnIL; KiLC
My Love and My Heart. Henry S. Leigh. BOHV; CIV
My Love Bound Me. *At. to* Thomas Campion. *See* Kisses.
My love came back to me. All Souls' Night. Frances Cornford. Two Poems, II. EnLoPo
My love came to me, when night. Night Visitor. Ibn Hamdis. MooP
My love came up from Barnegat. A [*or* The] Puritan's Ballad. Elinor Wylie. BAP; HBMV; LiTL; LoPo; OnAP; PFY; PoRA; TSW; TSWC
My love comes down from the mountain. Love on the mountain. Thomas Boyd. AnIV; GTIV; HBV; OxBI
My Love Could Walk. W. H. Davies. ChMo; CMP; LO; LoPS
My love dwelt in a northern land. Romance. Andrew Lang. BSV; HBV; PCD; VA
My love for her at first was like the smoke that drifts. Changing Love. John Gould Fletcher. ChMo; CMP
My love for him shall be. Medieval Norman Songs, XII. *Unknown, tr. by* John Addington Symonds. AWP; JAWP; WBP
My Love for Thee. Richard Watson Gilder. HBV
My love for thee doth take me unaware. The Thought of Her. Richard Hovey. LBMV
My love for you. Constancy. Tzu Yeh. PoHN
My love for you is like a lissome palm tree. My Love. Kai Holberg. BoDS
My Love for you, Mother. Eva Ingersoll Swasey. BAP
My love gave me a king's robe. Wardrobe. Sister Mary Madeleva. GoBC
My love gave me a passion-flower. The Passion-Flower. Margaret Witter Fuller. HBV
My love has been in London city. The Sailor Laddie. *Unknown.* SG
My love has built a bonny ship, and set her on the sea. *See* My love he's built . . .
My love has sicklied unto loath. Select Passages from a Coming Poet. "F. Anstey." BOHV
My love has talk'd with rocks and trees. In Memoriam A. H. H., XCVII. Tennyson. BPN; EmBrPo; EPN; GEPC; ViPo; VLEP
My love hath gone and hid from me. My Love. *Unknown.* TrFP
My love he built a bonny ship, and set her on the sea. *See* My love he's built . . .
My love he built me a bonnie bower. The Lament of the Border Widow [*or* Bonnie Bower *or* Border Widow's Lament]. *Unknown.* BSV; CBOV; CH; HBV; LO; LPS-2; OBB; OTPC (1923 ed.)
My love he was as fine a fellow. The Gallows Tree. *Unknown.* BaBo
My love he went to Burdon Fair. Memories. Alexander Hay Japp. VA
My love he's [*or* he *or* has] built a bonny ship, and set her on the sea. The Lowlands [*or* Lawlands] o' [*or* of] Holland. *Unknown.* BSV; CBOV; CH; EBSV; OBB; SG
My Love, I Cannot Thy Rare Beauties Place. William Smith. *Fr.* Chloris. InvP
(Sonnet.) ElL
My Love, I Have No Fear That Thou Shouldst Die. James Russell Lowell. *See* Sonnet: "My Love, I have no fear that thou shouldst die."
My love, I wish thee well; so lullaby! *Unknown.* BOL
My Love in Her Attire. *Unknown.* LiTB; SiTL
(Beauty's Self.) BLV; TrGrPo
(Madrigal: "My Love in her attire doth show her wit.") BCEP; CoEV; ElL; ElSeCe; HBV; LiTG; LiTL; OBEV; OBSC; PG; ReEn; TuPP
("My Love in her attire doth show her wit.") EG; GTSE; GTSL; ViBoPo
(Poetry of Dress, The, 3.) GTBS; GTBS-D; GTBS-W
My love is a rider and [*or* wild] broncos he breaks. Bucking Bronco [*or* The Cowgirl]. *Unknown.* ABF; CoSo; CSF
My Love Is a Tower. C. Day Lewis. AtBAP
My Love Is Always Near. Frederick Locker-Lampson. *See* Unrealized Ideal.
My love is as a fever, longing still. Sonnets, CXLVII. Shakespeare. HoPM; LO; PeBoSo; PoEL-2; ReEn; ReIE; TwP
My love is fallen upon a may. Love's Adventure. *Unknown.* TMEV
My Love Is like a Myrtle. Moses ibn Ezra, *tr. fr. Hebrew by* Solomon Solis-Cohen. TrJP
My Love Is like a Red Red Rose. Burns. *See* Red, Red Rose, A.
My Love Is like the Sun. *Unknown.* AnIV
My love is like [*or* lyke] to ice [*or* yse], and I to fire [*or* fyre]. Amoretti, XXX. Spenser. ATP; BLV; BoLiVe; LiTB; LiTG; LiTL; PeBoSo; PG (1955 ed.); TrGrPo
My love is living. South of the Great Sea. *Unknown.* ChLP; TrCh
My love is male and proper-man. The Contemplative Quarry. Anna Wickham. BMEP; HBMV; NP
My Love is neither young nor old. *Unknown.* OBSC
My Love is o' comely height an' straight. White an' Blue. William Barnes. RO
My love is of a birth as rare. The Definition of Love. Andrew Marvell. AnFE; BLV; BoLiVe; CoEV; ElSeCe; EPS; FaBoEn; GTBS-W; LiTB; LiTG; LiTL; LoBV; MaPo; MeLP; MePo; NBE; OAEP; OBEV (new ed.); OBS; Po; PoE; PoEL-2; PoFS; ReEn; SeCePo; SeCeV; SeCL; SeCV-1; SeEP; TrGrPo; UnPo; WHA
My Love Is Past. Thomas Watson. *Fr.* Hecatompathia. ElSeCe; ReIE; TuPP
(Here Lieth Love.) ElL
(Love's Grave.) OBSC
My love is sleeping; but her body seems. Sonnet. Kenneth Leslie. *Fr.* By Stubborn Stars. BoCaPo
My love is strengthen'd though more weak in seeming. Sonnets, CII. Shakespeare. AWP; CaAE; CoEV; ElL; ES; LiTG; LiTL; LoPS; OAEP; OBEV; OBSC; PeBoSo; SiCE; TOP; ViBoPo
My love is the flaming Sword. Sunday up the River, XVI. James Thomson. EmBrPo; OBVV
My love is the maid ov all maidens. In the Spring. William Barnes. RO
My love it should be silent, being deep. A Love Song. Theodosia Garrison. OBAV; SBMV
My love leads the white bulls to sacrifice. Processional. Alice Archer James. AA
My Love, let us see if the rose. To Cassandra. Pierre de Ronsard. FoS
My love lies in the gates of foam. The Churchyard on the Sands. Lord De Tabley. CBOV; CH; GTBS-D; HBV; LoBV
My love lies underground. Hymn to Priapus. D. H. Lawrence. CoBMV; MoAB; OBMV
My love must be as free. Free Love. Henry David Thoreau. MOAP
My love, my lord,/ hearken to my weary plaints awhile. Verses Expressing the Feelings of a Lover. Sister Juana Inés de la Cruz. AnMP
My love, my love, the golden hours. Love Endures. John Nichol. EBSV
My love, my love, thus spoke my love to me. Thus Spoke My Love. Pieter Corneliszoon Hooft. LiTW
My Love, Oh, She Is My Love. *Tr. fr. Irish by* Douglas Hyde. AnIV; GTIV; TIP
My Love o'er the water bends dreaming. Sunday up the River, XII [*or* Reflection]. James Thomson. EBSV; EnLit; OBEV (1st ed.)
My love on Wednesday letting fall her body. In a Time of Crisis. Lawrence Durrell. LiTM
My love sent me a chicken without e'er a bone. *Unknown.* OxNR
My love she is a gentlewoman. Auld Matrons. *Unknown.* BaBo; ESPB
My love she leans from the window. Imitation. H. C. Bunner. PA
My love she was born in the North counterie. Fair Maidens' Beauty Will Soon Fade Away. Robert Dwyer Joyce. GTIV
My love she went a-sailing. A Ballad of the Lakes. Laura E. McCully. CPG
My Love, She's But a Lassie Yet. Burns. EBSV; ViBoPo
My Love She's But a Lassie Yet. James Hogg. HBV
(She's But a Lassie Yet.) LiTL
My Love Ship. Ella Wheeler Wilcox. PTA-1
My love, sister mine. Invitation to Travel. Baudelaire. TrFP
My Love-Song. Else Lasker-Schüler, *tr. fr. German by* Jethro Bithell. TrJP
My love, still I think that I see her once more. Kathleen O'More. George Nugent Reynolds. TIP
My love stood by me at the dawn of day. Union of Love. Jami. OnPM

My Love Sways, Dancing. Moses ibn Ezra, *tr. fr. Hebrew by* Emma Lazarus. LiTW
My Love That Mourneth for Me. John Gwynneth. AnEC
My love, this is the bitterest, that thou. Any Wife to Any Husband. Robert Browning. BPN; EmBrPo; EtPaEn; FaBoEn; GEPC; OtMeF; PoVP
My love to fight the Saxon goes. The [*or* A] Spinning Song. John Francis O'Donnell. IrPN; TIP
My love to shew her cold desire. *Unknown.* SeCSL
My Love too stately is to be but fair. Electra. Francis Howard Williams. AA
My love took scorn my service to retain. Sonnets, VIII. Sir Thomas Wyatt. SiPS
My love was mask'd and armed with a fan. Licia, XXIII. Giles Fletcher. ReIE
My Love Who Loves Me Not. Hitomaro, *tr. fr. Japanese by* Mabel Lorenz Ives. PFE
My love within a forest walked alone. Love in Moonlight. Bhartrihari. LiTW
"My love, you are timely come, let me lie by your heart." The Door and the Window. Henry Reed. NeBP
My love, you know that I have never used. Unfinished Portrait. Elinor Wylie. CoBA
My loved [*or* lov'd], my honored [*or* honor'd], much-respected friend. The Cotter's Saturday Night. Burns. BEL; BeLS; BPP; CEP; EiPP; EM-1; EnL; EnLi-2; EnLit; EnRP; EPP; EV-3; FaBoBe; HBV; LPS-2; MCCG; OAEP; OBEC; TCEP; TOP
My lovely dark one, when thy life is spent. Remorse of the Dead. Baudelaire. TrFP
My lover has gone to Flanders. The Unremembered. Hermann Hagedorn. CAG
My lover he is a cowboy. The Jolly Cowboy. *Unknown.* CoSo
My lover is a fool more wise. Riddles. Sister Mary Madeleva. JKCP (1955 ed.)
My lover is but a small man. Fruit. *Unknown.* OnPM
My lover is like the tree-peony of Lo Yang. The Blossoms of Lo Yang. Ting Liu Niang. ChLP
My Loves. John Stuart Blackie. EBSV; OBVV
My loves as vertuous as yours is when you sware affection. *Unknown.* SeCSL
My Love's Guardian Angel. William Barnes. AtBAP; PoEL-4; RO
My love's manners in bed. The Way. Robert Creeley. NeAP
My Lucy was charming and fair. The Shepherd's Despair. Thomas Dermody. OnYI
My Lulu. *Unknown. See* Lulu.
My lute, awake and praise the Lord. A Song of the Lute in the Praise of God and Dispraise of Idolatry. John Hall. ReIE
My lute, awake! perform the last. The Lover Complaineth the Unkindness of His Love [*or* To His Lute]. Sir Thomas Wyatt. AEV; AtBAP; BoW; BrBE; CaAE; CenL; CoBE; CoEV; EG; ElL; ElSeCe; EM-1; EnL; EnLit; EPP; FaBoEn; LEAP; OAEP; OBEV; OBSC; PG; PoE; PoEL-1; PoFS; ReEn; ReIE, *2 vers.;* SiCE; SiPS; TCEP; TrGrPo; TriL; TuPP; TyEnPo; ViBoPo
My lute, be as thou wast [*or* wert] when thou didst grow. Sonnet [*or* To His Lute]. William Drummond of Hawthornden. BSV; EBSV; EG; ElL; ElSeCe; EPS; EV-2; GTBS; GTBS-D; GTBS-W; GTSE; GTSL; LoBV; OBS; UnS; ViBoPo
My Luve [Is like a Red, Red Rose]. Burns. *See* Red, Red Rose, A.
"My luve she lives in Lincolnshire." Alison and Willie. *Unknown.* BaBo; ESPB
My Luve's in Germany. *Unknown.* CH
My Luve's like a Red, Red Rose. Burns. *See* Red, Red Rose, A.
My Madeline. Walter Parke. BOHV
My Madonna. Robert W. Service. BLPA
My maid Mary,/ She minds her [*or* the] dairy. Mother Goose. CBPC; OxNR; PCH; PPL; RIS
My Maiden Aunt. Charles Henry Luders. PR
My maisters all attend you. Turners Dish of Lentten Stuffe; or, A Galymaufery. William Turner. CoMu
My Maker shunneth me. Spiritual Isolation. Isaac Rosenberg. TrJP
My Mammy Was a Wall-eyed Goat. *Unknown.* ChTr
My mammy's in the cold, cold ground. Po' Boy. *Unknown.* AS
My man is a bone ringèd with weed. First Woman's Lament [*or* Lament]. Brenda Chamberlain. NeBP; NeIP
My Man John, *with music. Unknown.* SaSa
My man Thomas. John Fletcher. EnLoPo
My man's a gypsy. Gypsy Man. Langston Hughes. TCPD
My Man's up the Rivuh, *with music. Unknown.* StDa
My margin is a fault of leaves. Seasonal Moraine. L. F. Gerlach. PtPa
My Mary. William Cowper. *See* To Mary.
My Maryland. James Ryder Randall. AA; AnAmPo; APA; BAP; CoBA; FaBoBe; FaFP; HBV; JKCP; LA; LBAP; LEAP, *abr.;* MC; OBAV; PaA; PAH; PoFr; TreF
(Maryland.) IAP
(Maryland, My Maryland.) PoRL; SPP
"Thou wilt not cower in the dust," *sel.* OIF
My Master. Harry Lee. ChIP; MaRV
My Master and Dame, I Well Perceive. *Unknown.* AnEC
My Master and I. *Unknown.* CoMu
My master bade me watch the flock by night. The Shepherd Who Stayed. Theodosia Garrison. MW; OHIP; SDH
My master Bukton, when of Christ our king. Counsel upon Marriage. Chaucer. PoLi
My Master Hath a Garden. *Unknown.* AtBAP; CH; GBV (1952 ed.); MeRV
My Master was a man who knew. The Outdoor Son of God. William L. Stidger. ChIP
My Master was a worker. The Master's Man. William G. Tarrant. MaRV; OQP; PSO; QP-1
My Master was so very poor. My Master. Harry Lee. ChIP; MaRV
My Master's Face. William Hurd Hillyer. ChIP; MaRV
My masters, I thank you, it's time to pack home. Thomas Deloney. *Fr.* Jack of Newbury. ReIE
My masters twain made me a bed. The Canoe. Isabella Valancy Crawford. BoCaPo; OnYI; VA
My May-Day Bride. Vilhelm Krag, *tr. fr. Norwegian by* Charles W. Stork. AnNoLy
My meaning is to work what woundes love hath wrought. Of the Mighty Power of Love. Edward de Vere, Earl of Oxford. TuPP
My memory fears. Three Love Poems, II. Stepan Petrovich Shchipachev. RuPo
My memory in the dark sky. Recollection of Love. Efrain Huerta. AnCL
My memory of Heaven awakes. Coventry Patmore. *Fr.* The Angel in the House. EG
My memory of the garden of our house. Natural Flow of Memory. Jorge Luis Borges. TwSpPo
My merry-hearted comrade on a day. A Faithful Dog. Richard Burton. POT
My Midnight Meditation. *At. to* Henry King, *also to* John King. MePo; OBS; SeCL
My mill grinds pepper and spice. *Unknown.* OxNR
My Mind and I. Hilda Conkling. NP
My mind has thunderstorms. Thunderstorms. W. H. Davies. GTML; HBV; POTE; PtOT; TSW; TSWC
My mind intensely strained. A Lunatic. Mokichi Saito. PoP
My mind is sad and weary thinking how. Odell. James Stephens. MBP; MoAB; MoBrPo
My mind is worn out, my features grown sharp and gaunt. Sitting at Night with My Nephew Who Has Just Come from Afar. Su T'ung-po. WhP
My mind lets go a thousand things. Memory. Thomas Bailey Aldrich. AA; AnFE; AnNE; APA; BAP; CBOV; CoAnAm; LEAP; MAP; MCCG; NeHB; OBAV; OQP; PoeMoYo; PoMa; QP-2; TreFS; VOD (1935 ed.)
My mind! prophetic of my coming fate. Petrarch. Sonnets to Laura: To Laura in Death, XLVI. PrPoCR
My Mind to Me a Kingdom Is. Sir Edward Dyer. BCEP; BEL; BHV; BPP, *abr.;* CoBE; ElL; ElSeCe; EM-1; EnLi-1; EnLit; EPP; EV-1; FaBoBe; HBV; LiTB; LiTG; LPS-3; MaRV, *3 sts.;* MCCG; NeHB; OuHeWo; PG, *sl. abr.;* PoE; PoFS; ReEn; SiCE; TreFS; TrGrPo; TuPP; TVSH, *abr.;* TyEnPo; ViBoPo; WGRP
(Contentment, *abr.*) OTPC; PECK
(Kingdom.) LoBV; OBSC
(My Mynde to Me a Kyngdome Is.) AEV; AtBAP; PoEL-1
My mind was once the true survey. The Mower's Song. Andrew Marvell. ElSeCe; EnL; EPS; LiTL; LoBV; PoEL-2; ReEn; SeCL; SeCV-1
My Mirror. Aline Kilmer. AnAmPo; LA; NP; NV
My mirth and merriment, soft and sweet art thou. The Fairies' Lullaby. *Unknown.* BOL
My Mistress. Richard Brathwaite. *Fr.* The English Gentlewoman. SeCL
My Mistress. Thomas Lodge. *See* My Mistress When She Goes.
My Mistress. William Warner. ElL
My mistress' eyes are nothing like the sun. Sonnets, CXXX. Shakespeare. ATP; AWP; BEL; CoBE; ElSeCe; EM-1; EnL; EnLi-1 (1949 ed.); EnLit; ExPo; HBV; HoPM; InvP; JAWP; LiTB; LiTL; OAEP; OtMeF; PeBoSo; PIAE; PoE; ReEn; ReIE; SeCeV; SiCE; TOP; TwP; TyEnPo; WBP
My mistress frowns when she should play. Fa La La [*or* Madrigals, 7]. *At. to* John Hilton. CH; OxBoLi; SiTL
My mistress is a paragon. My Mistress. William Warner. ElL
My mistress is as fair as fine. Madrigals, 6. *At. to* Thomas Ravenscroft. CH; OxBoLi; SiTL
My mistress loves noe woodcokes. *Unknown.* SeCSL
My Mistress When She Goes. Thomas Lodge. *Fr.* The Life and Death of William Longbeard. EG; SiCE; TuPP

My Mistress When She Goes (*continued*)
(Her Rambling.) LoBV; OBSC
(My Mistress.) TrGrPo
My Mistress's Boots. Frederick Locker-Lampson. BOHV; HBV; InP; PIAE; TOP
My mither men't my auld breeks. My Auld Breeks. Alexander Rodger. CBOV; EBSV
My mither's ay glowran o'er me. Katy's Answer. Allan Ramsay. CEP; EiPP
My monarch's generosity. Royal Bounty. Ibn Hani. MooP
My Moon. Gordon Bottomley. *Fr.* Night and Morning Songs. NP
My mortal love's a rabbit skin. Apology. Vassar Miller. NePoEA
My Most. My Most. O My Lost! José Garcia Villa. Divine Poems, 57. BoW; POTE (1959 ed.)
My Mother. George W. Bethune. MotAn
My Mother. Amelia Josephine Burr. DD; HBMV
My Mother. Josephine Rice Creelman. DD; MOAH; OHIP
My Mother. Mahlon Leonard Fisher. NV
My Mother. Francis Ledwidge. HBMV; OHIP
My Mother. Claude McKay. AnEnPo
My Mother. Bertha Nolan. PGD
My Mother. William Bell Scott. MOAH; VA
My Mother. Viggo Stuckenberg, *tr. fr. Danish by* Charles W. Stork. BoDS
My Mother. Ann Taylor. BLPA, *abr.*; DD, *much abr.*; MaRV, *abr.*; MOAH; MotAn; OHIP; PEDC; PTA-1; TreF, *sl. abr.*
"When sleep forsook my open eye," *sel.* MeMeAg
My Mother. Nikolai Tikhonov, *tr. fr. Russian by* Jack Lindsay. RuPo
My Mother. Zakarias Topelius, *tr. fr. Swedish by* Charles W. Stork. AnSL
My Mother. Samuel N. Wilson. PEDC
My mother and your mother. *Unknown.* OxNR; SAS
My Mother Bids Me Bind My Hair. Anne Hunter. EBSV; HBV; OBEC
My mother bore me in an island town. Sea Born. Harold Vinal. HBMV; TBM
My mother bore me in the southern wild. The Little Black Boy. Blake. *Fr.* Songs of Innocence. AnFE; AtBAP; AWP; BCEP; BEL; CEP; CH; CoEV; EiPP; EM-1; EnL; EnLi-2; EnLit; EnRP; EV-3; HBV; InPo; LoGBV; MotAn; MyFE; OAEP; OBEC; OBEV; OxBoCh; PoEL-4; PoFr; PoNe; RiBV; SeCeV; TOP; TreFS; TrGrPo
My mother called me to her deathbed side, these words she said to me. Coon Can. *Unknown.* AS
My mother died when I was young. As in a Picture-Book. Fannie Stearns Davis. TBM
My mother groaned, my father wept. Infant Sorrow. Blake. *Fr.* Songs of Experience. BLV; BoLiVe; EiPP; EnL; FaBoEn; PoEL-4; PoFS
My mother has the prettiest tricks. Songs [*or* A Song] for My Mother—Her Words. Anna Hempstead Branch. BoChLi; CV; FaPON; HH; LBMV; MOAH; NV; OBAV; OHIP; OnPP; POT; PoTo; SiSoSe; TiPo (1959 ed.); YeAr; YT
My mother is sensible, that's what they say. The Uncuddled Baby. Elsie Duncan Yale. DDA
My mother let me go with her. Iris Flowers. Mary McNeil Fenollosa. RAR
My mother, living by the sea. First Aid. Peter Hopegood. NeLNL
My mother said that I never should. Gypsies in the Wood. *Unknown.* BoTP; FaBoCh; LoGBV; OxBoLi; OxNR; SiTL
My mother said to me. Admonitions. Margaret Bell Houston. MoSiPe
"My mother says I must not pass." The Witch in the Glass. Sarah Morgan Bryan Piatt. AA; LEAP; PR
My mother sends our neighbors things. Neighborly. Violet Alleyn Storey. GaP; TiPo
My mother she's so good to me. A Boy's Mother. James Whitcomb Riley. DD; HBVY; HH; OHIP; OTPC; PoRL; PPL
My mother taught me. The Milky Way. Allen Upward. *Fr.* Scented Leaves from a Chinese Jar. NP
My mother taught me to be good. Poem for Mother's Day. Margaret Fishback. InMe; LauV
My mother the queen is dead. The Princess on the Headland. George Sterling. MOAP
My mother twines me roses wet with dew. The Child's Quest. Frances Shaw. NP
My Mother Was a Lady; or, If Jack Were Only Here. Edward B. Marks. TreF; YaD
(Two Drummers, The.) ABS
My mother was a singing wind I never knew. The Christmas Tree. Mary E. Wilkins Freeman. PEDC
"My mother was an ill woman." The Laird of Wariston (B *vers.*). *Unknown.* BaBo
My mother was embroidering, bent, by the window. To My Mother. "Petros Vlastos." MoGP
My mother whistled softly. The Little Whistler. Frances M. Frost. StVeCh (1955 ed.); TiPo
My mother, who has a hide. The Hide of My Mother. Edward Dorn. NeAP
My Mother's Bible. George Pope Morris. AA; BLRP; LPS-1; MOAH; MotAn; WBLP
My Mother's Clothes. Anna Hempstead Branch. MotAn
My Mother's Faith. Eugene Field. *See* In the Firelight.
My Mother's Garden. Alice E. Allen. BLPA; FaBoBe; NeHB
My Mother's Hands. Anna Hempstead Branch. *See* Her Hands.
My Mother's Hands. *Unknown.* TreFS
My mother's hands are cool and fair. Songs [*or* A Song] for My Mother—Her Hands. Anna Hempstead Branch. DD; HH; LBMV; MOAH; MPB; MW; OBAV; OHIP; OnPP; PoRL; POT; PoTo; RG; YT
My Mother's House. Eunice Tietjens. HBMV; NP; TBM
My mother's maids when they do sew and spin. Of the Mean and Sure Estate. Sir Thomas Wyatt. Satires, II. BEL; EPP; ReIE; SiCE; SiPS; TuPP
My Mother's Picture. William Cowper. *See* On the Receipt of My Mother's Picture Out of Norfolk.
My Mother's Prayer. T. C. O'Kane. BLPA; FaBoBe
My Mother's Table. Hy Sobiloff. NePA
My mother's voice! Fond memory can no richer treasure bring. Mother's Heritage. Helen C. Smith. MotAn
My Mother's Words. Anna Hempstead Branch. *See* Her Words.
My mouth doth water, and my breast doth swell. Astrophel and Stella, XXXVII. Sir Philip Sidney. ReEn; ReIE; SiPS; TuPP
My Mouth Is Very Quiet. José Garcia Villa. AnFE; CoAnAm; TwAmPo
My mouth to thy mouth. Never—Ever. Richard Le Gallienne. BMEP
My mouth will flame the sulphurs of the pit. Company Commander. Guillaume Apollinaire. AnFP
My mug is broken, my heart is sad! The Broken Mug. John Esten Cooke. BlG
My mule refreshed, his bells. The Descent. Samuel Rogers. *Fr.* Italy. LPS-2
My muse, by thee restor'd to life. An Altar and Sacrifice to Disdain for Freeing Him from Love. *Unknown.* ReIE; SiCE
My muse dwelleth not on Parnassus. Prelude. Erik Axel Karlfeldt. *Fr.* Fridolin's Pleasure-Garden. AnSL
My muse may well grudge at my heavenly joy. Astrophel and Stella, LXX. Sir Philip Sidney. ReEn; SiPS
My muse, though airy, glides softly along. The Song of the Pen. Judah Al-Harizi. TrJP
My music-loving self this afternoon. Sheldonian Soliloquy. Siegfried Sassoon. UnS
My Mynde to Me a Kingdome Is. Sir Edward Dyer. *See* My Mind to Me a Kingdom Is.
My Naked Aunt. Archibald MacLeish. NePA
My naked simple life was I. My Spirit. Thomas Traherne. SeCV-2
My name is Colin Clout [*or* Colyn Cloute]. The Prelates. John Skelton. *Fr.* Colyn Cloute. BLV; EPP; TrGrPo
My name is Edward Hollander [*or* Gilbert Howelding *or* Henry Hollinder], as you may understand. The *Flying Cloud. Unknown.* ABF; BaBo; IHA; ShS (*vers.* II); SoAmSa; ViBoFo
My name is Frank Bolar, 'n ol' [*or* lone *or* 'nole] bachelor [*or* bach'lor] I am. The Lane County Bachelor [*or* Starving to Death on a Government Claim]. *Unknown.* AS; IHA; SoAF
My name is Joe Bowers. *See* My name it is Joe Bowers.
My Name Is John Wellington Wells. W. S. Gilbert. *Fr.* The Sorcerer. PoMS
("Oh! my name is John Wellington Wells.") PIAE
My name is Juan Murray, and sad for my fate. Juan Murray. *Unknown.* CoSo; CSF
My name is Larry Gorman, to you I mean no harm. The Scow on Cowden Shore, *vers.* I. Larry Gorman. ShS
My Name Is Legion. Edward Sandford Martin. MaRV
(Which Is Me?) OQP; QP-2
My name is O'Kelley, I've heard the Revelly. Shillin' a Day. Kipling. OAEP (2d ed.); ViBoPo
My name is Parrot, a bird of paradise. Parrot's Soliloquy [*or* The Parrot]. John Skelton. *Fr.* Speak, Parrot. ACP; OxBoLi; PoEL-1
My name is Peter Emberly [*or* Embley]. Peter Emberley (*diff. versions*). John Calhoun. ShS
My name is Sam, an' I don't give a damn. A Cowboy Dance Song. *Unknown.* CoSo
My name is Stanford [*or* Stamford] Barnes. The State of Arkansas. *Unknown.* CoSo; CSF; TrAS
My name is Tommy, an' I hates. So Was I. Joseph Bert Smiley. PTA-1
My name is William Edwards, I live down Cove Creek way. The T.V.A. *Unknown.* TrAS

My name is young Davie and listen ye well. Young Davie's Song. Paul Green. NoCaPo
My name it is Bill Stafford; I was born in Buffalo town. The Arkansaw Traveler. *Unknown.* ViBoFo
My name it is Donald Macdonald. Donald Macdonald. James Hogg. PoFr
My name it is Hugh Reynolds, I come of honest parents. The Lamentation of Hugh Reynolds. *Unknown.* TIP
My name it is [*or* is] Joe Bowers. Joe Bowers. *Unknown.* ABF; ABS; APW; ATP; BaBo; BoHiPo; CoSo; CSF; TrAS; TreFS; ViBoFo
My name it is Nell, right [*or* quite] candid I tell. Nell Flaherty's Drake. *Unknown.* AnIV; OnYI
My name, my country—what are they to thee? No Matter [*or* Vanities]. Paulus Silentiarius. AWP; EnLi-1; GrPo; JAWP; OuHeWo; OxBG; WBP
"My name was—" "Does it matter?" "My country—" "Can it profit?" "The Rest Is Silence." Paulus Silentiarius, *tr. by* F. L. Lucas. GrPE
My name was William Kidd, when I sailed, when I sailed. The Ballad of Captain Kidd. *Unknown.* AmSS
My name's Mister Benjamin Bunny. Limerick. Frederic Edward Weatherly. CenHV
My Nanie, O. Burns. EBSV; EnLi-2 (1949 ed.)
(Song: My Nanie, O.) EnLi-2 (1939 ed.)
My Nanie, O. Allan Cunningham. EBSV
My Nannie's Awa'. Burns. GN; HBV; OTPC (1923 ed.)
(My Nanie's Awa'.) EBSV
My native country then, which so brave spirits hast bred. The Forest of Arden. Michael Drayton. *Fr.* Polyolbion: The Thirteenth Song. SeEP
My Native Land. John Boyle O'Reilly. LPS-2
My Native Land. Sir Walter Scott. *See* Breathes There the Man.
My native land is up there. At Gold Hill Monastery. Su T'ung-po. OnPC
My Native Land, thy Puritanic stock. The Rejected "National Hymns," II. "Orpheus C. Kerr." BOHV; InMe; PA
My native place. Native Place. Rofu Miki. PoLJ
My Native Village, *sel.* Noel T. Carrington.
"Touched by the sunlight of the evening hour." EnSW
My Nebraska. Theodore C. Diers. PoRL
My Needle Says. Hazel Hall. NP
My Neighbor. Virginia Eaton. BPP
My Neighbor. Seigniora Laune. DDA
My neighbor has a herd, my neighbor has a flock. Cock-a-doodle-doo! Richard R. Kirk. LS; TSWC
My neighbor Hunk's house and mine. Near Neighbors. Swift, *after* Martial. AWP
My neighbor lives on the hill. Differences. Paul Laurence Dunbar. TreFS
My neighbor shooed him out because. Mud. Marty Hale. AlBD
My neighbor to the East has. Rain in the Aspens. Su T'ung-po. OnPC
My neighbor's books sit primly in a row. Books. Florence Van Cleve. DDA; HH
My neighbors on the right. Next Door. Mai Yao Ch'en. OnPC
My Neighbor's Reply. *Unknown.* PoToHe
My Neighbor's Roses. Abraham L. Gruber. BLPA; NeHB; OQP; PoToHe; QP-2
My neighbor's willow sways its frail. The Willow. Tu Fu. OnPC
My net/ Is heavy with weed. The Disappointed Shrimper. P. A. Ropes. BoTP
My New-cut Ashlar. Kipling. *See* Dedication, A: "My new-cut ashlar . . ."
My new province is a land of bamboo-groves. Eating Bamboo-Shoots. Po Chü-i. TrCh
My New Rabbit. Elizabeth Gould. BoTP
My New Umbrella. M. M. Hutchinson. BoTP
My New World. Irving Browne. AA; LEAP
My next door neighbor's life to me. The Point of View. Margaret Prescott Montague. DDA
My niece, who is six years old, is called "Miss Tortoise." Children. Po Chü-i. TrCh
My noble king goes forth to ride. Two Seas. Abus Salt. MooP
My noble, lovely, little Peggy. A Letter to the Hon. Lady Miss Margaret Cavendish-Holles-Harley [*or* To a Child of Noble Birth]. Matthew Prior. CEP; LoBV; OBEC; OBEV; OTPC (1923 ed.); PRWS; SeCePo; WP
My nosegays are for captives. Emily Dickinson. PC
My November Guest. Robert Frost. AnFE; APA; BLV; BoLiVe; CoAnAm; HBMV; MoVE; NP; OBAV; OxBA; TwAmPo; ViBoPo
My oak has lost its choirs. Winter Oak. Mary Sinton Leitch. MuM
My Occupation. Henri Michaux, *tr. fr. French by* Wallace Fowlie. MiCF
My occupation is river man, as you may well know. Jack Haggerty. Dan McGinnis. ShS
My ocean-soul was free, without mistrust. The Last Boats. Endre Ady. LiTW
My Old Bible. *Unknown.* BLRP
My Old Books Closed. Stéphane Mallarmé, *tr. fr. French by* Frederick Morgan. AnFP
My Old Counselor. Gertrude Hall. AA; OBAV
My Old Dawg. Courtney Ryley Cooper. AlBD
My old desire to live in the Southern Village. Moving House. T'ao Ch'ien. Twelve Poems, 8. TrCh
My Old Dog Tray. Stephen Collins Foster. OlF
My old gardener leans on his hoe. The Naturalist on a June Sunday. Leonora Speyer. NLK
My Old Hammah, *with music. Unknown.* AS
(Rocks in de Mountens, *diff. vers., with music.*) SoAmSa
My Old Home. Ellen O'Leary. TIP
My Old Hound Pack. Archibald Rutledge. AlBD
My Old Kentucky Home. Stephen Collins Foster. AnAmPo; AnFE; APA; APW; CoAnAm; FaBoBe; FaFP; HBV; IAP; LA; LPS-1; OlF; OTPC; PECK; PoeMoYo; PoRL; PYM; StaSt; TrAS, *with music;* TreF; TrGrPo
(My Old Kentucky Home, Good-Night.) AA; LEAP; OBAV
My old love for the water has come back again. Sea Call. Margaret Widdemer. NLK; TSW
My old man's a white old man. Cross. Langston Hughes. AnAmPo; BANP; LA; PoNe; TBM
My old self. Translations from Modern Japanese Poetry. Akiko Yosano. PFE
My Old True Love, *with music. Unknown.* OuSiCo
My oldest friend, mine from the hour. Guardian Angel. Cardinal Newman. GoBC
My ole massa promised me. Shine On. Luke Schoolcraft. TrAS
My once dear love! hapless that I no more. The Surrender. Henry King. BLV; CoEV; ElSeCe; LO; MePo; TrGrPo
My Only Jo and Dearie, O. Richard Gall. EBSV
My only love is always near. Unrealized Ideal [*or* My Love Is Always Near]. Frederick Locker-Lampson. BMEP; EPP; LEAP; TSW
My Only Plea. Walter J. Kuhn. PraP
My Only Star. Francis Davison. ElL
My Orders. Ethelwyn Wetherald. MaRV
My Ornaments Are Arms. *Unknown. See* Wandering Knight's Song, The.
My Other Me. Grace Denio Litchfield. AA; HBV
My Owen. Ellen Mary Patrick Downing. HBV; TIP
My own! The Jester and His Daughter. Tom Taylor. *Fr.* The Fool's Revenge. VA
My own belovèd, who hast lifted me. Sonnets from the Portuguese, XXVII. Elizabeth Barrett Browning. BPN
My Own Cáilin Donn. George Sigerson. FaBoBe; HBV
My own darling little dove. To Cassandra. Pierre de Ronsard. TrFP
My own dear love, he is strong and bold. Love Song. Dorothy Parker. InMe; NeMA
My own dim life should teach me this. In Memoriam A. H. H., XXXIV. Tennyson. CoBE; EmBrPo; EnL; EPN; GEPC; MaPo; MaRV; OQP; QP-2; SeCePo; ViPo; VLEP
My Own Epitaph. John Gay. PIAE; SeCePo; SeCeV; TOP
(Epigram: "Life is a jest . . .") ALV; HBV
(Epitaph: "Life is a jest . . .") InP
(His Epitaph.) OnPM
(His Own Epitaph.) PreP; ViBoPo
My Own Heart Let Me More Have Pity On. Gerard Manley Hopkins. CoBMV; FaBoMo; LiTM; MoAB; MoBrPo (1950 ed.); ViPP
My Own Hereafter. Eugene Lee-Hamilton. WGRP
My own hope is, a sun will pierce. It's Wiser Being Good than Bad. Robert Browning. *Fr.* Apparent Failure. BMEP; PC
My own in a foreign land. The Jewish Conscript. Florence Kiper Frank. TrJP
My Own, My Native Land. Menander, *tr. fr. Greek by* C. M. Bowra. OxBG
My Own, My Native Land. Sir Walter Scott. *See* Breathes There the Man.
"My own necessity." Homer, *tr. by* Bryant. *Fr.* The Odyssey, II. GrPo
My Own Shall Come to Me. John Burroughs. *See* Waiting.
My Own Simplified Spelling. E. V. Knox. SiTL
My Own Song. Harriet Prescott Spofford. BPP
My pa he didn't go to town. Getting Information out of Pa. *Unknown.* FAOV
My Pa held me up to the moo-cow-moo. The Moo-Cow-Moo. Edmund Vance Cooke. DDA; FaFP; MoShBr; PTA-1
My Pa says that he used to be. Forgetful Pa. Edgar A. Guest. IHA; PoRL
My papa, he's the bestest man. A Boy's King. S. E. Kiser. FAOV
My papa sometimes scolds and says. A Speech. *Unknown.* MeMeAg
My Papa's Waltz. Theodore Roethke. AmP; CrMA; HoPM; MiAP; MoAB

My Parents Kept Me from Children Who Were Rough. Stephen Spender. MoPW; OAEP (2d ed.)
My parents raised me tenderly; they had no child but me. The Maid I Left Behind. *Unknown.* ShS
"My parents taught me well, as I sailed, as I sailed." Captain Kidd. *Unknown.* ABS; IHA
My Part of the City. Léon Paul Fargue, *tr. fr. French by* Wallace Fowlie. MiCF
My Party. Queenie Scott-Hopper. BoTP
My passion is as mustard strong. A New Song of New Similies. John Gay. BOHV; InMe; SiTL
My passport says I'm five feet and eleven. Letter to Lord Byron, IV. W. H. Auden. ChMo
My Past Has Gone to Bed. Siegfried Sassoon. AtBAP
My "Patch of Blue." Mary Newland Carson. BLPA; NeHB
My patron saint, St. Valentine. Valentine Verses. Thomas Nelson Page. DD
My Paw Said So. Edgar A. Guest. OnHT
My Peace I Give unto You. St. John, XIV: 1-31, Bible, *N.T.* WoL
(Peace of Christ, The, XIV: 1-27.) TreFS
My Peace I Give unto You. G. A. Studdert-Kennedy. MaRV
My peace is broken, my white gentle sleep. The April Earth. Max Eastman. AnEnPo
My Peggy. Allan Ramsay. *Fr.* The Gentle Shepherd. BSV; CoBE; GN, *abr.*; HBV; OTPC (1923 ed.), *abr.*
(Peggy.) EV-3; OBEV; ViBoPo
(Sang: "My Peggy is a young thing.") CEP; EiPP; LoBV; OBEC
(Waukin' o' the Fauld, The.) EBSV
My pen, obey my will a while. A Ditty of the Pen Inveighing against Usury and False Dealing. John Hall. ReIE
My pen, take pain a little space. To His Pen. Sir Thomas Wyatt. OBSC; SiPS
My Penguin Playmate. Donald E. Cooke. MPB (1956 ed.)
My pensioners who daily. Pensioners. Winifred M. Letts. BoTP
My pensive public, wherefore look you sad. Playhouse Musings. Horace Smith *and* James Smith. *Fr.* Rejected Addresses. EV-4
My pensive Sara! thy soft cheek reclined. The Eolian Harp. Samuel Taylor Coleridge. EmBrPo; EnRP; ERP; RO
My people have married me. Lament of Hsi-chün. Hsi-chün. TrCh
My people, hearken, 'tis the drum. Dare to Be Free. Georg Herwegh. PoFr
My people, what have I done to thee? The Reproaches. *Unknown.* WHL
My people? Who are they? Who Are My People? Rosa Zagnoni Marinoni. BLPA; PoToHe
My Pets. Sarah Jane S. Harrington. RAR
My Phyllis [*or* Phillis] hath the morning sun. Phyllis, XV. Thomas Lodge. ACP; CaAE; CBOV; EIL; ElSeCe; LoBV; OBEV; OBSC; SiCE; TuPP; ViBoPo
My Picture, Left in Scotland. Ben Jonson. LiTL; MePo; PoEL-2; SeCV-1
My pictures blacken in their frames. Death of the Day. Walter Savage Landor. TriL
My Pilgrimage. Sir Walter Ralegh. *See* Passionate Man's Pilgrimage, The.
My Pilot. Washington Gladden. OQP; QP-1
My Pipe. Christopher Morley. FAOV; LHV
My pipe is lit, my grog is mixed. The Bachelor's Dream. Thomas Hood. BOHV
My pipe is old. My Pipe. Christopher Morley. FAOV; LHV
My plaid awa, my plaid awa. The Elfin Knight. *Unknown.* BaBo (A *vers.*); CH; ViBoFo (A *vers.*)
My plaid is on my shoulder and my boat is on the shore. John o' Lorn. Neil Munro. EBSV
My Plan. Marchette Chute. BrR; FaPON
My Playmate. Mary I. Osborn. BoTP
My Playmate. Whittier. AnFE; APA; CoAnAm; CoBA; HBV; IAP; LBAP; MOAP; OBVV; PCD; PG (1945 ed.); TCAP
My Poem to the Children Killed in the War in Spain. José Ramón Heredia, *tr. fr. Spanish by* Dudley Fitts. AnCL
My Poems. Victor Hugo, *tr. fr. French by* Alan Conder. TrFP
My Poet, thou canst touch on all the notes. Sonnets from the Portuguese, XVII. Elizabeth Barrett Browning. BPN; EmBrPo; EPP; HBV; PtP; WHA
My poetic fancy wanders into thoughts of measured rhyme. The Family Man as a Poet. Joseph Schuyler Long. FAOV
My Poetry. Kotaro Takamura, *tr. fr. Japanese by* Takamichi Ninomiya *and* D. J. Enright. PoLJ
My Policeman. Rose Fyleman. BoChLi; TiPo
My Political Faith. George Frederick Cameron. BoCaPo; PeCV
My Pompous Friend. Lawrence Emerson Nelson. DDA; PoMa
My Pony. "A." GFA; PRWS
My poor body is alas unworthy. Ch'in Chia's Wife's Reply. *Unknown.* ChLP; TrCh
My Poore Foole. Shakespeare. *See* Death of Lear.
My pop is always buying books. Book-Lover. Ralph Bergengren. FAOV
My poplars are like ladies trim. The Poplars. Theodosia Garrison. HBMV; OHIP; PoRL; StVeCh; VOD
My Portrait. Moishe-Leib Halpern, *tr. fr. Yiddish by* Joseph Leftwich. TrJP
My Prairies. Hamlin Garland. FaPON; PTA-2
My Prayer. Horatius Bonar. BLRP
My Prayer. Lucy Carruth. PraP
My Prayer. Elsie Janis. BLP
My Prayer. Mark Guy Pearse. OQP; PraP; QP-2
My Prayer. Henry David Thoreau. DD; HBV; HBVY; LBAP; MOAP; OQP; QP-1
(Great God, I Ask Thee for No Meaner Pelf.) CoV; TrPWD
(Prayer: "Great God, I ask thee for no meaner pelf.") AnNE; MaRV, *abr.*; TCAP
My Prayer ("Lord Jesus, make thyself to me"). *Unknown.* BePJ; BLRP; PraP
My Prayer ("My life must touch a million lives"). *Unknown.* BLRP
My precious life I spent considering. Take the Crust. Sadi. *Fr.* The Gulistan. AWP
My pretty cat to my heart I hold. My Cat. Baudelaire. CIV
My Pretty Little Pink, *with music.* *Unknown.* AS
My pride is not in that I cause to bloom. April Speaks. Lloyd Mifflin. POT; PoTo
My pride should effect your escape. Pride. Josephine Miles. FiMAP
My prime of youth is but a frost of cares Elegy [*or* On the Eve of His Execution *or* Written on the Eve of Execution]. Chidiock Tichborne. ACP; AnFE; CenL; ChTr; CoBE; EG; EIL; ElSeCe; EM-1; GoBC; GTBS-W; HBV; LiTB; LiTG; LoBV; LPS-3; OBSC; PG (1955 ed.); PoD; PoFS; ReEn; TrGrPo; TuPP; ViBoPo; WP
My prince in God gife thee guid grace. A New Year's Gift to the King. William Dunbar. EBSV
My prow is tending toward the west. My New World. Irving Browne. AA; LEAP
My Puritan grandmother! I see her now. Sea Lavender. Louise Morey Bowman. BoCaPo (1943 ed.); CaP; CPG; OCL
My Queen. *Unknown.* HBV
My Queen. William Winter. AA
My quiet kin, must I affront you. Preliminary to Classroom Lecture. Josephine Miles. FiMAP
My quietness has a man in it, he is transparent. In Memory of My Feelings. Frank O'Hara. NeAP
My quill is charged with fire. Song of Hate. Jacob ben David Frances. TrJP
My Radio. Gertrude Van Winkle. GFA
My Ratclif [*or* Ratcliffe], when thy reckless youth offends. Exhortation to Learn by Others' Trouble [*or* Lines to Ratcliff]. Earl of Surrey. SiCE; SiPS; TuPP
My ravist spreit in that desart terribill. Nightmare. Gawin Douglas. *Fr.* The Palace of Honor. PoEL-1
My Recollectest Thoughts. Charles Edward Carryl. *Fr.* Davy and the Goblin, *ch.* 7. HBV; HBVY; NA
My Record ends: But hark! e'en now I hear. George Crabbe. *Fr.* The Parish Register. OBRV
My Recurring Dream. Paul Verlaine. *See* My Familiar Dream.
My red engine goes chuff-chuff-choo! chuff-chuff-choo! My Toys. Lilian McCrea. BoTP
My Retreat at Mount Chung-nan. Wang Wei, *tr. fr. Chinese by* Witter Bynner. PoP
My revelry is this: to scan. The Lyre and the Crown. Marcus Argentarius. OxBG
My reverend Elders, worthy citizens. Welcome to Agamemnon. Aeschylus. *Fr.* Agamemnon. LiA; OxBG
My Risen Lord. *Unknown.* OQP; PraP; QP-1
My Rival. Kipling. OnPP
My River. Eduard Mörike, *tr. fr. German by* William R. Hughes. AnGP
My Road. Handa, *tr. fr. Japanese by* Lois J. Erickson. SoLD
My Road. Oliver Opdyke. HBV
My road is a by-road, with big trees reaching high. The Road That Leads to Home. Ethel E. Mannin. NLK
My road is fenced with the bleached, white bones. Drought. Will H. Ogilvie. BoAu
My roads stretch out. Marshall Lyautey. R. N. Currey. BoSA
My robe is noiseless when I roam [*or* while I tread] the earth. A [*or* The] Swan. *Unknown.* EPP; OuHeWo
My roof is hardly picturesque. An Autumn Flitting. George Cotterell. VA
My room as usual a disorder of books. Crisis. G. S. Fraser. NeBP

My room is at the back of the courtyard. Visitation. Max Jacob. MiCF
My room's a square and candle-lighted boat. The Country Bedroom. Frances Cornford. MBP; MoBrPo
My Rose. Hildegarde Hawthorne. AA
My Sabine Farm. Eugene Field. InMe
My sad great Piers that met a small field flower. The Plowman. Max Harris. BoAV
My sad heart drivels at the poop. The Stolen Heart. Arthur Rimbaud. MiFP
My Saint. Johan Sebastian Cammermeyer Welhaven, *tr. fr. Norwegian by* Charles W. Stork. AnNoLy
My salamander in a world of flame. Cherry Tree. Sacheverell Sitwell. AtBAP
My Sanctuary. Meng Shu Ch'ing, *tr. fr. Chinese by* Henry H. Hart. GrCo-2; PoHN
My saul [*or* saull] and life [*or* lyfe], stand up and see. Ane Sang of the Birth of Christ. John Wedderburn, *after* Martin Luther. BSV; ChTr
My Saviour. Mary Hallet. ChIP
My Saxon shrine! the only ground. Morwennae Statio. Robert Stephen Hawker. GoBC
My scaffolde was the bedd where ease I fownde. On the Execution of Mary, Queen of Scots. Robert Southwell. *Fr.* At Fotheringay. MeRV
My Secret. John Banister Tabb. SPP; WaKn
My secrets cry aloud. Open House. Theodore Roethke. CoBMV
My Sense of Sight. Oliver Herford. HBMV; HBVY
My Serious Son. Walter Savage Landor. FAOV
My Servant Wakes Me. Po Chü-i, *tr. fr. Chinese by* Arthur Waley. TrCh
My sexual feats. Fred Apollus at Fava's. Nicholas Moore. NeBP
My shade, O Clytie, biddeth thee good-bye. Clytie. André Chénier. TrFP
My Shadow. Robert Louis Stevenson. FaBoBe; FaPON; GFA; GoBP; HBV; HBVY; LiTG; MPB; NeHB; OnHT; OTPC; PCH; PECK; PoVP; RIS; StVeCh; TiPo; TreF; VLEP
My shag-hair Cyclops, come let's ply. The [*or* A] Song in Making of the Arrows [*or* Vulcan's Song]. John Lyly. *Fr.* Sapho and Phao. ElL; ElSeCe; LoBV; OBSC; TuPP
My share of pie to win, I will dash through thick and thin. Quintetto upon the Christmas Pie. Thomas Love Peacock. *Fr.* Melincourt. MyFE
My Share of the World. Alice Furlong. HBV; OBVV
My Sheep Are Thoughts. Sir Philip Sidney. *Fr.* Arcadia. SiCE; SiPS
(Dorus His Comparisons.) CaAE; ReIE
My Sheep I Neglected. Sir Gilbert Elliot. *See* Amynta.
My shepherd's unkind; alas, what shall I do? The Lamentation of Chloris. *Unknown.* CoMu
My Ship. Elizabeth Akers Allen. LPS-1
My Ship. Edmund Leamy. JKCP; SUS
My Ship and I. Robert Louis Stevenson. BoChLi; PPL
My ship is an old ship and her sails are grey and torn. My Ship. Edmund Leamy. JKCP; SUS
My Ship Is on de Ocean, *with music. Unknown.* BoAN-2
My shoes fall on the house-top that is so far beneath me. Climb. Winifred Welles. BAP; NLK (1947 ed.); NV; PoeMoYo; TSW; TSWC; VOD
My short and happy day is done. The Stirrup-Cup. John Hay. AA; HBV; LBAP
My shoulders ache beneath my pack. Prayer of a Soldier in France. Joyce Kilmer. CAW; GoBC; SBMV
My Silent Guest. Benjamin Sledd. NoCaPo
My Silks and Fine Array. Blake. *See* Song: "My silks and fine array."
My silver cat with burning eyes. The Shrine. Ethna MacCarthy. PoC
My silver lamp. The Lamp and the Moon. Shan Ho Yü. PoHN
My silver stag is fallen—on the grass. The Silver Stag. Kathleen Raine. FaBoMo
My simple heart, bred in provincial tenderness. Sonnet. G. S. Fraser. NeBP
My simple system shall suppose. Matthew Prior. *Fr.* Alma; or, The Progress of the Mind. NBE
My single constancy is love of life. Epithalamium and Elegy. Witter Bynner. NBE
My sinnes are like the haires upon my head. The Authour's Dreame. Francis Quarles. *Fr.* Argalus and Parthenia. OBS
My sins, my sins, my Savior! In the Garden. John S. B. Monsell. OQP; QP-1
My Sister. Hyam Plutzik. FiMAP
My sister/ only you/ are left me. Yiannis Ritsos. *Fr.* To My Sister. MoGP
My sister and I when we were close together. Sisters. Dorothy Roberts. CaP
My Sister Helen. Drummond Allison. FaBoTw
My sister is not so defenseless left. Milton. *Fr.* Comus. NBE
My sister! my sweet sister! if a name. Epistle to Augusta [*or* To Augusta]. Byron. AnEnPo; BPN; EmBrPo; EnRP; EPN; ERP; GEPC; LPS-1
My Sister She Works in a Laundry, *with music. Unknown.* AS
My sister's best feller is 'most six-foot three. Sister's Best Feller. Joseph C. Lincoln. PTA-1
My sisters played beyond the doorway. Detail from an Annunciation by Crivelli. Rosemary Dobson. NeLNL
My Sister's Sleep. Dante Gabriel Rossetti. BPN; EmBrPo; EnL; EPN; ExPo; LoBV; MyFE; OAEP; POTT; PoVP; SeCeV; ViP; ViPo; ViPP; VLEP
My Six Toothbrushes. Phyllis McGinley. GoYe
My skirt is cut out of peacock silk. Song of the Courtesans. Ting Liu Niang. ChLP
My slain! Oh silver-hoof! Oh clover breath! Unbridled Now. Laura Lourene LeGear. GoYe
My slumber wholly forsook me. Longing. Christian Winther. BoDS
My Son. James D. Hughes. BLPA
My Son. Douglas Malloch. FAOV; MaRV
My son, despise not the chastening of the Lord. Happy Is the Man That Findeth Wisdom. Proverbs, Bible, *O.T.* TreF
My son, forsake your art. A Mhic, ná Meabhraigh Eigse. *Unknown, tr. by* Máire MacEntee. OxBI
My son, keep my words. Proverbs, Bible, *O.T.* LO
My Son, My Executioner. Donald Hall. NePoEA
My son Polynices, now you have first word. Eteocles and Polynices. Euripides. *Fr.* Phoenician Maidens. OxBG
My Son Stands Alone. John V. A. Weaver. FAOV
My son, these maxims make a rule. Address to the Unco Guid, or the Rigidly Righteous. Burns. AnFE; BoLiVe; EM-1; HBV; LoBV; LPS-3; OAEP; PIR; TreFS. *See also* O ye wha are sae guid yoursel.
My son, this is the very world I knew. Saint Francis of Assisi Talks with a Priest. Jay G. Sigmund. SaFP
My son, thou wast my heart's delight. On the Death of My Son Charles. Daniel Webster. AA; LEAP
My son was killed while laughing at some jest. A Son. Kipling. *Fr.* Epitaphs of the War. ChMP; PoVP
"My son!" What simple, beautiful words! To My Unborn Son. Cyril Morton Horne. BLPA
My son, why are you weeping? Thetis to Achilles. Homer. *Fr.* The Iliad, I. LiA
My son, you do not see. This Defileth a Man. Menander. OxBG
My Song. Eunice K. Biddle. PSO
My Song. Hazel Hall. HBMV; TBM
My Song. Rabindranath Tagore. MOAH; OHIP
My Song, I fear that thou wilt find but few. Epipsychidion. Shelley. EnRP
My song in your little bones. Ghetto Song. Jacob Glatstein. OnCuPl
My Song of Today. St. Thérèse of Lisieux, *tr. fr. French by* Prioress Augustine of the Mother of God. CAW
My song that was a sword is still. My Song. Hazel Hall. HBMV; TBM
My song, thus now in thy conclusions. The Visions of Petrarch. *Tr. by* Spenser. EnLi-1
My Song to the Jewish People. Leib Olitski, *tr. fr. Yiddish by* Jacob Sonntag. TrJP
My Songs. George Sterling. MuM
My Songs Are Poisoned! Heine, *tr. fr. German by* Louis Untermeyer. AWP; JAWP; WBP
My songs have run away from me. Good-bye! Fannie Stearns Davis. BAP
My songs, they say, are poisoned. My Songs Are Poisoned. Heine. AWP; JAWP; WBP
My songs to sell, good sir! Vendor's Song. Adelaide Crapsey. AnFE; APA; CoAnAm; HBV; MAP; MoAmPo (1942 ed.); OBAV
My Sons. Ron Loewinsohn. NeAP
My sons, and ye the children of my sons. Jacob. Arthur Hugh Clough. BHV; ViPP
My sons, behold what portion I do give. The Contents of the Scedule Which Sir John of Bordeaux Gave to His Sons. Thomas Lodge. *Fr.* Rosalynde. ReIE; SiCE
My Sore Thumb. Burges Johnson. HBVY
My Sorrow. "Seumas O'Sullivan." *See* Starling Lake, The.
My sorrow diligent would sweep. The Confessional. Helen Parry Eden. JKCP
My sorrow that I am not by the little dún. The Starling Lake [*or* My Sorrow *or* The Rosses]. "Seumas O'Sullivan." AnIV; AWP; HBV; JAWP; LBBV; NP; WBP
My sorrow, when she's here with me. My November Guest. Robert Frost. AnFE; APA; BLV; BoLiVe; CoAnAm; HBMV; MoVE; NP; OBAV; OxBA; TwAmPo; ViBoPo
My Soul. Emil Bønnelycke, *tr. fr. Danish by* Charles W. Stork. BoDS
My Soul and I. Charles Buxton Going. MaRV

My soul, asleep between its body-throes. The Soul Stithy. James Chapman Woods. VA
My soul, be not disturbed. Address to My Soul. Elinor Wylie. AnFE; APA; AWP; CoAnAm; LiTM; MOAP; OxBA; PoFr
My soul before Thee prostrate lies. Hope Springing Up. John Wesley. BePJ
My soul, calm sister, towards thy brow doth mount. A Sigh. Stéphane Mallarmé. AWP; JAWP; OnPM; TrFP; WBP
My soul doth magnify the Lord. The Magnificat [*or* Hymn of the Blessed Virgin]. St. Luke, Bible, *N.T.* CAW; MaRV; WGRP; WHL
My Soul Doth Pant towards Thee. Jeremy Taylor. *See* Prayer, The: "My soul doth pant towards thee."
My soul goes clad in gorgeous things. Souls. Fannie Stearns Davis. HBMV; LBMV
My soul has solitudes. Loneliness. Father Edwin Essex. JKCP (1926 ed.); TrPWD
My soul in reverence now prays. Mother's Day. Edna Tucker Muth. PEDC
My Soul in the Bundle of Life. *Unknown, tr. fr. French by* E. Margaret Rowley. *Fr.* The Dead Sea Scrolls. TrJP
My soul is a lifeless Venice. The Song of the Vanquished. Nicholas Karvounis. MoGP
My soul is a rhythm in fetters. My Soul. Emil Bønnelycke. BoDS
My soul is a ship adventuring day and night. A Masque of Souls. "Richard Scrace." CPG
My soul is a witness for my Lord. Who'll Be a Witness for My Lord? *Unknown.* BoAN-1; OlF
My Soul Is an Enchanted Boat. Shelley. *See* Asia.
My soul is awakened, my spirit is soaring. Lines Composed in a Wood on a Windy Day. Anne Brontë. DiM
My soul is ever alien to the earth. Alien to the Earth. Lilith Lorraine. UnW
My Soul Is like a Garden-Close. Thomas S. Jones, Jr. PR; VOD
My soul is like a well of dead, deep water. The Well. Luis Palés Matos. AnCL
My soul is like the oar that momently. Struggle. Sidney Lanier. LiTA; OxBA
My soul is like this cloudy, flaming opal ring. Opals. Arthur Symons. POTT; PoVP
My Soul Is Robbed. Isaac Rosenberg. MoPo
My soul is sad and much dismay'd. The Valley of the Shadow of Death. William Cowper. TriL
My soul is sailing through the sea. Barnacles. Sidney Lanier. IAP; OQP; PECK; QP-1; TCAP
My soul is the veil of his love. Revelaton. Hafiz. PeP
My soul leans toward Him; stretches out its arms. George Macdonald. *Fr.* Within and Without. WGRP
My soul lives in my body's house. Doubt. Sara Teasdale. ChMo; CMP; LO
My soul looked down from a vague height with Death. The Show. Wilfred Owen. LiTB; LiTG; LiTM (rev. ed.); MoAB; MoBrPo (1950 ed.); NAMP; WaaP; WaP
My soul, praise thou the Lord always! Lauda Anima Mea. Psalm CXLVI, Bible, *O.T.*, *tr. by* John Hopkins. ReIE
My Soul Shall Cling to Thee. Charlotte Elliott. BePJ
My soul, sit thou a patient looker-on. Epigram: Respice Finem [*or* The Human Touch]. Francis Quarles. MaRV; OBEV; PoToHe
My soul stands at the window of my room. Nostalgia. Karl Shapiro. AnFE; CoAnAm; CoBMV; LiTM; NePA; TrJP; TwAmPo; WaaP
My soul surcharged with grief now loud complains. Sonnet. Rachel Morpurgo. TrJP
My soul, there is a country. Peace. Henry Vaughan. AEV; AnFE; AWP; BEL; CaAE; CenL; ChTr; EG; ElSeCe; EnLit; EPS; EV-2; FaBoCh; GN; HBV; InPo; LoGBV; MePo; OAEP; OBEV; OBS; Po; PoD; PoFS; ReEn; SeCL; SeCV-1; SeEP; TriL; UnPo (1st ed.); WGRP; WHA; WP
My Soul Thirsteth for God. Psalms, XLII, Bible, *O.T.* TrGrPo
(Psalm XLII.) AWP; JAWP; TrJP; WoL
(Search, The, *Moulton, Modern Reader's Bible.*) WGRP
My Soul Thirsteth for God. William Cowper. MeRV
My soul today. Drifting. Thomas Buchanan Read. AA; GN; HBV; LBAP; LEAP; LPS-1; OBAV
My soul was an old horse. Pegasus [*or* A Glut on the Market]. Patrick Kavanagh. FaBoTw; MoAB; OnYI; OxBI
My soul's a new-fledged bird: it tries to fly. Even as the Bird. E. Merrill Root. ChIP
My Soul's Been Anchored in de Lord. *Unknown.* BoAN-2, *with music;* OlF
My South. Don West. PoNe
My spear wins bread, my spear wins Thracian wine. The Poet's Spear. Archilochus. OxBG
My Specialty Is Living Said. E. E. Cummings. MoVE
My Spectre around Me Night and Day. Blake. OxBoCh
(Seven of My Sweet Loves.) LiA
My Spirit. Thomas Traherne. SeCV-2
My spirit has pass'd in compassion and determination around the whole earth. Walt Whitman. *Fr.* Salut au Monde. AtBAP
My spirit is a pestilential city. Desolate. Claude McKay. CDC
My spirit is too weak—mortality. On Seeing the Elgin Marbles [*or* On the Elgin Marbles *or* Sonnet]. Keats. BEL; BLV; BoLiVe; BPN; CoBE; EmBrPo; EnLi-2; EnLit; EnRP; ERP; GEPC; GTBS-W; LiTB; PeBoSo; PIAE; Po; REAL; SeCeV; TCEP; TrGrPo; TwCrTr; TwHP; WHA
My spirit like a shepherd boy. Song. V. Sackville-West. HBMV
My Spirit Longeth for Thee. John Byrom. *See* Desponding Soul's Wish, The.
My Spirit, Sore from Marching. Edna St. Vincent Millay. ChMo; CMP
My spirit to yours, dear brother. To Him That Was Crucified. Walt Whitman. AnEnPo; BoFr; IAP; MaRV; StJW
My Spirit Will Grow Up. Ruth Evelyn Henderson. OQP; QP-2
My Spirit Will Not Haunt the Mound. Thomas Hardy. BrBE; MBP; MoBrPo; TOP
My spirit's on the mountains, where the birds. Sonnet Written during His Residence in College. Charles Wolfe. TIP
My spotless love hovers with purest wings. Beauty, Time and Love [*or* The Moth *or* Sonnets to Delia]. Samuel Daniel. To Delia, XII. ES; HBV; OBEV; OBSC; SeCePo; SiCE
My Springs. Sidney Lanier. UnPo
My Star. Robert Browning. BEL; BMEP; BoLiVe; EmBrPo; EPN; EPP; FaPON; GEPC; HBV; OAEP; OTPC (1946 ed.); OuHeWo; PC; PIAE; PoVP; StaSt; TOP; TrGrPo; UnPo (1st ed.); ViPo; ViPP
My Star. Plato, *tr. fr. Greek by* Alexander Lothian. EnLi-1; OuHeWo
My Star. John Banister Tabb. BPN; VLEP
My Step-Grandfather. Harold Lenoir Davis. NP
My stock lies dead, and no increase. Grace. George Herbert. SeCV-1
"My strength is failing fast." The Sea-King's Burial. Charles Mackay. PCN
My Study. Paul Hamilton Hayne. AmPP (3d ed.); SPP
My study's ornament, thou shell of death. Cyril Tourneur. *Fr.* The Revenger's Tragedy. ViBoPo
My Subtle and Proclamant Song. Seán Jennett. NeIP
My suffering public, take it not amiss. The Problem of the Poles. John Kendall. WhC
My sun has set, I dwell. Despised and Rejected. Christina Rossetti. MaRV; StJW
My Sun-killed Tree. Marguerite Harris. GoYe
My Sun Sets to Rise Again. Robert Browning. *Fr.* At the Mermaid. MaRV
My supercilious soul. Triumph. Kathryn White Ryan. TBM
My swan mysterious. A Swan. Ibsen. AnNoLy
My sweet did sweetly sleep. Stolen Pleasure. William Drummond of Hawthornden. EnLoPo
My Sweet Gazelle! Immanuel di Roma, *tr. fr. Italian.* TrJP
My sweet little Baby [*or* Babie], what meanest Thou to cry? The King in the Cradle [*or* An Old Carol, with Lullaby]. *Unknown.* AnEC; BOL
My sweet love is faire to see. *Unknown.* SeCSL
My Sweet Old Etcetera. E. E. Cummings. *Fr.* Is 5. AnAmPo; LA; NAMP; NePA; OxBA; WaaP; WaP
(Two XI.) MM
My Sweet Sweeting. *Unknown.* CH, *sl. abr.*; LoPS; LPS-1
("Ah, my sweet sweeting.") LO
My Sweetest Lesbia. Thomas Campion, *after the Latin of* Catullus. AnEnPo; AtBAP; AWP; ElSeCe; EnLi-1; JAWP; LoBV; PoD; PoFS; PoRA; ReIE; TrGrPo; TuPP; WBP
(My Sweetest Lesbia, Let Us Live and Love.) EIL; EnL; NBE; OBSC; ReEn; SiCE
(To Lesbia.) HBV
(Vivamus Mea Lesbia atque Amemus.) EG; SeCeV
My sweetheart has faults in plenty. Her Faults. Harry B. Smith. PR
My sweetheart's a mule in the mines. *See* My sweetheart's the mule in the mines.
My sweetheart's a sailor. Sailor. Eleanor Farjeon. BrR; PoRh
My Sweetheart's Dainty Lips. Judah Halevi, *tr. fr. Hebrew by* Emma Lazarus. TrJP
My sweetheart's the [*or* a] mule in the mines. The Mule in the Mines [*or* Campfire and Bunkhouse]. *Unknown.* ChTr; CoSo
My swing is my airship. The Swing Ship. Mildred D. Shacklett. GFA
My Swinging Shadow. Grace Wilson Coplen. GFA
My sword I shook. The Sword. Abu Bakr. MooP
My sword in a myrtle-spray I'll tie. The Harmodius Song. Callistratus. GrR

My Table. W. B. Yeats. Meditations in Time of Civil War, III. LiTB

My table shows the tracks of tiny feet. Souvenirs. Margaret E. Bruner. CIV

My tail is not impressive. Ode to the Pig: His Tail. Walter R. Brooks. LiL

My tall sunflowers love the sun. Sunflowers. Clinton Scollard. HBMV; MPB; NLK; VOD

My tameless will doth recklessly pursue. Of His Foolish Passion for Laura. Petrarch. Sonnets to Laura: To Laura in Life, VI. EnLi-1; OuHeWo

My Task. Hayashi, tr. fr. Japanese by Lois J. Erickson. SoLD

My Task. Maude Louise Ray. MaRV

My Task. Robert Louis Stevenson. BLP; MaRV

My tawny spear is hoar of head. The Spear. Abu Zakariya. MooP

My Taxicab. James S. Tippett. GFA; MPB

My tea is nearly ready and the sun has left the sky. The Lamplighter. Robert Louis Stevenson. FaPP; GaP; MPB; OTPC; PCH; PoVP; TreF; TVC; TVSH

My tears are true, though others be divine. Henry Constable. Fr. Diana. OBSC

My tears were Orion's splendour with sextuple suns and the million. Tears. Edith Sitwell. MoPo

My temples throb, my pulses boil. To Minerva [or Fewer Books, More Salad]. Thomas Hood. BCEP; BOHV; ChTr; FiBHP; HBV; InMe; OnPM; OxBoLi; PIAE; SiTL; TOP; WhC

My tender parents brought me up, providing me full well. The Lexington Murder. Unknown. BaBo

My tender parents who brought me here. The Lexington Murder. Unknown. OuSiCo

My tent stands in a garden. An Autumn Garden. Bliss Carman. HBV; NLK

My terminus near,/ The clouds already closing in upon me. Walt Whitman. Fr. Prayer of Columbus. MaRV

My thanks for all Thou gavest through the years. Gratitude. Mikhail Lermontov. LiTW; OnPM; TrRV

My thanks, friends of the County Scientific Association. Perry Zoll. Edgar Lee Masters. Fr. Spoon River Anthology. CrMA; NP

My Thing Is My Own. Unknown. CoMu

My thirsty soul desires her drought. A Prisoner's Song of Jerusalem. Unknown. ACP

My thought awaked me with Thy Name. Meditation on Communion with God. Judah Halevi. TrJP

My Thought Was on a Maid So Bright. Unknown. ISi (Alma Redemptoris Mater.) AnEC

My thought was thus—that it was May. May Morning. Chaucer. Fr. The Book of the Duchess. WHA

My thoughts are all in yonder town. The Friend's Burial. Whittier. OBVV

My thoughts are as a garden-plot, that knows. Thy Garden. Mu'tamid, King of Seville. AWP

My thoughts are fixed in contemplation. John Marston. Fr. Antonio and Mellida. ViBoPo

My Thoughts Are Not Your Thoughts. Isaiah, LV: 8–13, Bible, O.T. TrJP

My Thoughts Are Winged with Hopes. George Clifford. ElL (To Cynthia.) OBSC

My thoughts by night are often filled. Castles in the Air. Thomas Love Peacock. HBV

My thoughts go out like spider-threads. Immanence. Unknown. BPP

My thoughts grew dull, my eyelids slowly closed, the scene. Flight. Edwin Wiley Fuller. Fr. The Angel in the Cloud. NoCaPo

My Thoughts Hold Mortal Strife. William Drummond of Hawthornden. See Madrigal: "My thoughts . . ."

My thoughts impelled me to the resting-place. Elegy. Moses ibn Ezra. TrJP

My thoughts, like sailors becalmed in Cape Town harbor. Sailor's Harbor. Henry Reed. MoAB

My thoughts, my grief! are without strength. A Poem Written in Time of Trouble by an Irish Priest Who Had Taken Orders in France. Tr. by Lady Gregory. OBMV

My Thread. David Hofstein, tr. fr. Yiddish by Joseph Leftwich. TrJP

My throat is of gold, with a pretty black crescent. Meadow Lark. Marion Mitchell Walker. GFA

My Thrush. Mortimer Collins. BLA, abr.; HBV; OTPC (1923 ed.)

My tidings for you: the stag bells. Summer Is Gone. Unknown. FaBoCh; LoGBV; OnYI

My time, O ye Muses, was happily spent. A Pastoral [or Colin and Phebe]. John Byrom. EV-3; LPS-1; OBEC

My times are drawing in. The Musterer. Eileen Duggan. CoBE

My Times Are in Thy Hand. Christopher Newman Hall. VA

My Times Are in Thy Hand. William F. Lloyd. PraP

My Times Are in Thy Hand. Anna Laetitia Waring. PraP

My Tommy's gone, what shall I do? Tommy's Gone to Hilo. Unknown. ShS

My tongue-tied muse in manners holds her still. Sonnets, LXXXV. Shakespeare. EM-1; PeBoSo

My top is blue and silver, with a belt of emerald green. Hidden. ffrida Wolfe. TVC; TVSH

My Torn Heart. Alfred de Vigny, pr. tr. fr. French by A. W. Evans. LiA

My towers at last! These rovings end. L'Envoi: The Return of the Sire de Nesle. Herman Melville. AnFE; APA; CoAnAm; ViBoPo

My townspeople, beyond in the great world. Gulls. William Carlos Williams. FaBoEn; MOAP; OxBA

My Toys. Lilian McCrea. BoTP

My Treasure. Egi, tr. fr. Japanese by Lois J. Erickson. SoLD

My Treasures. Robert Louis Stevenson. SAS

My Trewest Tresowre. Richard Rolle of Hampole. See Song of the Passion, A.

My tricycle's a camel. The Race. Aileen Fisher. UTS

My Triumph. Whittier. AnNE; BHV; IAP; TCAP

My triumph lasted till the drums. Emily Dickinson. WaaP

My Troop. Björnstjerne Björnson, tr. fr. Norwegian by Charles W. Stork. AnNoLy

My True Love. Ivy O. Eastwick. SiSoSe

My true love from her pillow rose. Departure. Hermann Hagedorn. LBAP; LEAP

My true love has gone to France. Shoo, Shoo, Shoo-Lye. Unknown. ABF

My true love has my heart and I would be. Formal Lyric. W. J. Turner. FaBoTw

My True Love Hath My Heart [and I Have His]. Sir Philip Sidney. Fr. Arcadia. AtBAP; BLV; BoLiVe; CH; CoBE; EG; FaBoBe; HBV; LiTG; LiTL; LoPo; LoPS; MaPo; OAEP; OnPM; PeBoSo; PoE; PoEL-1; ReEn; SeCeV; SiCE; TrGrPo; ViBoPo
    (Arcadian Duologue.) SiPS
    (Bargain, The.) CBE; EV-1; OBEV; OtMeF; PG; TreFS
    (Ditty, A.) AWP; ElSeCe; GTBS; GTBS-D; GTBS-W; GTSE; GTSL; InPo; JAWP; PoRL; TOP
    (Ditty: Heart Exchange.) EnLit
    (Friendship.) ES
    (From "The Arcadia.") LEAP
    (Heart Exchange.) LiTB; LoBV
    (Just Exchange.) FaBoEn
    (Shepherdess' Song.) CaAE
    (Song: "My true love hath my heart.") EnLi-1
    (Sonnet: "My true love hath my heart.") ElL; WHA
    (True Love.) ALV; ChTr; OBSC

My Truest Treasure. Richard Rolle of Hampole. See Song of the Passion, A.

My Trundle Bed. J. G. Baker. BLPA; FaBoBe

My Trust, sel. Whittier.
    "Picture memory brings to me, A," first 3 sts. OHIP; PGD; PoRL

My tub is an aquarium. The Tub. George S. Chappell. DDA

My Twelve Oxen. Unknown. See I Have Twelve Oxen.

My Two Daughters. Victor Hugo, tr. fr. French by Alan Conder. LO; TrFP

My two white rabbits. Rabbits. Dorothy W. Baruch. SUS; TiPo; UTS

My Uncle Ben, who's been. Kiph. Walter de la Mare. AlDL; TiPo (1959 ed.)

My uncle Jack is a preacher. Pansies. Tom Robinson. BoChLi (1950 ed.)

My Uncle John he visits us. Hinkelmedunk, Ohio. Unknown. DDA

My Uninvited Guest. May Riley Smith. AA; WGRP

My Valentine. Mary Catherine Parsons. TiPo (1952 ed.)

My Valentine. Robert Louis Stevenson. See Romance.

My verse will reach you. Vladimir Mayakovsky. Fr. At the Top of My Voice. LiTW; TrRV

My Verses! Nikolai Alekseyevich Nekrasov, tr. fr. Russian by Babette Deutsch. TrRV

My verses dream-rich and tender you've read. Poet of Farewell. Christian Werleigh. PoNe

My verses, hope ye that posterity. Immortality. Joachim du Bellay. Antiquities of Rome, XXXII. TrFP

My verses! Living witnesses of tears. My Verses! Nikolai Alekseyevich Nekrasov. TrRV

My vessel, cargoed with oblivion, cleaves. Petrarch. Sonnets to Laura: To Laura in Life, CLVI. PrPoCR

My Violets. Unknown, tr. fr. Japanese by Lois J. Erickson. SoLD

My violin was in Cremona wrought. Riches. Derrick N. Lehmer. BAP

My Voice. "Demyan Bedny," tr. fr. Russian by Jack Lindsay. RuPo

My voice is still war. Sempronius's Speech for War. Addison. Fr. Cato. LPS-2; PoFr

My Wage. Jessie Belle Rittenhouse. BLP; BLPA; NeHB; PC; PoMa; PoToHe (new ed.)

My walls outside must have some flowers. Truly Great. W. H. Davies. ChMo; CMP; HBV; OBMV; OBVV; PCN; POTT

My wand strikes me no joy till loosened weeping. Third Madrigal. Gene Derwood. NePA

My wand'ring thoughts awake to love anew. Chanson. Chatelain of Coucy. LyMA
My wandringe thoughts have travelde rounde. *Unknown.* SeCSL
My Warrior Boy. *Unknown.* BlG
My Way's Cloudy, *with music.* *Unknown.* BoAN-1
My wealth's a burly spear and brand. A Soldier's Riches [*or* Song of a Legionnaire]. Hybrias. GrPo; GrR; OxBG
My Week. *Unknown.* MeMeAg
My weeping and the starlight. Nocturne. Juan Ramón Jiménez. OnPM
My Wellington boots go/ Thump-thump, thump-thump. Boots and Shoes. Lilian McCrea. BoTP
My What-is-it. Robert Frost. RIS
My whiskey is/ a tough way of life. Drink. William Carlos Williams. OxBA
My white charger rode to war. The White Charger. Abus Salt. MooP
My white, my shining girl. Moles. Ibn Haiyun. MooP
My white tiger bounding in the west! Welcome My World. Denis Devlin. AnIV
My Wife. Robert Louis Stevenson. BMEP; CP; EPP; LBBV; PoeT; POTT
(To My Wife.) MaRV
(Trusty, Dusky, Vivid, True.) HBV
My Wife and Child. Henry R. Jackson. LPS-2
My wife and I live [*or* lived] all alone. Little Brown Jug. *Unknown.* FaFP; TrAS; TreF; YaD
My wife and I lived all alone. Ballad of the Despairing Husband. Robert Creeley. NeAP
My wife broke a dollar tube of perfume. The Problem. Paul Blackburn. NeAP
My wife is left-handed. For Hettie. LeRoi Jones. NeAP
My Wife with Her Wood-Fire Hair. André Breton, *tr. fr. French by* Wallace Fowlie. MiCF
My Wife's a Wanton Wee Thing. *Unknown.* CoMu
My Wife's a Winsome Wee Thing. Burns. HBV; LiTL; LPS-1
My Wife's a Winsome Wee Thing. Robert Jamieson. EBSV
My Wife's Return. Henrik Wergeland, *tr. fr. Norwegian by* Charles W. Stork. AnNoLy
My will lies there, my hope, and all my life. Thomas Lovell Beddoes. *Fr.* Death's Jest Book. LO; NBE
My William was a soldier, and he says to me, says he. An Eastern Question. H. M. Paull. BOHV
My Wind Is Turned to Bitter North. Arthur Hugh Clough. OAEP
(Song of Autumn, A.) VLEP
My window is the open sky. Immortality. Arthur Sherburne Hardy. AA
My window looks upon a world grown gray. Midwinter. Margaret E. Bruner. PoToHe
My window opens out into the trees. Solace. Clarissa Scott Delany. CDC; PoNe
My window opens upon the sea. The Wistful One. Abigail Cresson. MW
My windows open to the autumn night. Cadgwith [*or* Song]. Lionel Johnson. CoBE; GTBS; JKCP; MeRV; OBVV; PoVP
My Winsome Dear. Robert Fergusson. *Fr.* Leith Races. SeCePo
My Wishes. Patrick Healy, *tr. fr. Modern Irish by* John D'Alton. OnYI
My Woe Must Ever Last. Sir Walter Ralegh. EIL
My woman says she wants no other lover. Catullus, *tr. fr. Latin by* Gilbert Highet. LaP
My woman says that she would rather wear the wedding-veil for me. Catullus, *tr. fr. Latin by* Horace Gregory. RoL
My Wonderful Dad. James W. Foley. FAOV
My Woodcock. Patrick Reginald Chalmers. CenHV
My words flash over you. Poppies. Henry Bellamann. TBM
My words for you. The Words of Finn. *Unknown.* ChTr
My words I know do well set forth my mind. Astrophel and Stella, LXIV. Sir Philip Sidney. SiPS
My words were delicately breathed. To Claudia Homonoea. Elinor Wylie. TOP
My Work. *Unknown.* MaRV
My work is done. Angel. Cardinal Newman. *Fr.* The Dream of Gerontius. GoBC
My work is finished; I am strong. Longfellow. *Fr.* Christus. ChIP
My World. Chauncey R. Piety. MaRV; OQP; QP-1
My world is a painted fresco, where coloured shapes. Dreams Old and Nascent. D. H. Lawrence. WGRP
My Worthy Lord, I Pray You. George Gascoigne. PoEL-1
My Yallow Gal, *with music.* *Unknown.* ABF
My Yoke Is Easy. St. Matthew, Bible, *N.T. See* Come Unto Me.
My Yoke Is Easy. Gladys Latchaw. ChIP; MaRV
My young love said to me, "My brothers won't mind." She Moved through the Fair. Padraic Colum. GTBS-D; InvP; TwCV
My young Mary do's mind the dairy. The Happy Husbandman; or, Country Innocence. *Unknown.* CoMu
My younger years I did employ. A Reflection on the Course of Human Life. William Lloyd. PrWP
My Youth It Was Free. *Unknown.* SeCL
My youth was no more than a dark, looming storm. The Enemy. Baudelaire, *tr. by* Vernon Watkins. AnFP
My youth was nothing but a storm, tenebrous, savage. The Enemy. Baudelaire, *tr. by* Arthur Symons. OnPM
My Zipper Suit. Marie Louise Allen. BrR; SUS; TiPo
My Zoölogical Flame. Edna E. Linsley. CAG
Myall in Prison, The. Mary Gilmore. BoAV
Mycenae Fallen. Alpheus, *tr. fr. Greek by* F. L. Lucas. GrPE
(Mycenae, *tr. by* Anne Hyde Greet.) OnPM
Mycenae Fallen. Pompeius, *tr. fr. Greek by* F. L. Lucas. GrPE
(Mycenae, *tr. by* Walter Leaf.) OxBG
Mycerinus. Matthew Arnold. EmBrPo; PoVP; ViPo; VLEP
Mycilla [*or* Mucilla *or* Nycilla] dyes her locks, 'tis said. On an Old Woman. Lucillius. AWP; GrPo; LiTW; OnPM
Mydas. John Lyly. *See* Midas.
Myles O'Hea. Charles J. Kickham. TIP
Myne owne John Poynz . . . *See* Mine own John Poynz . . .
Mynstrelles Songe: "Angelles bee wrogte to bee of neidher kynde." Thomas Chatterton. *Fr.* Aella. EnLoPo
Mynstrelles Songe: "Boddynge flourettes bloshes atte the lyghte, The." Thomas Chatterton. *Fr.* Aella. *See* Song of the Three Minstrels.
Mynstrelles Songe: "O! synge untoe mie roundelaie." Thomas Chatterton. *Fr.* Aella. *See* Minstrel's Song.
Myra. Fulke Greville. *See* I, with Whose Colors Myra Dressed Her Head.
Myriad roots of the entwining grass, The. Epitaphs, II. Lady Margaret Sackville. MM
Myriad singers pour their treasures. The Songs We Need. Bernard Freeman Trotter. MaRV
Myriads and myriads plumed their glittering wings. Leaves. Katharine Tynan. BoTP
Myriads of motley molecules through space. Soul and Sense. Hannah Parker Kimball. AA
Myrmidones, *sel.* Aeschylus, *tr. fr. Greek by* C. M. Bowra. Wounded Eagle, The. OxBG
Myrrh, *sel.* Joaquin Miller.
"Life knows no dead so beautiful." BAP
Myrtho. Gérard de Nerval, *tr. fr. French.* AnFP, *tr. by* Joseph Bennett; TrFP, *tr. by* Alan Conder
Myrtilla, to-night. A Corsage Bouquet. Charles Henry Luders. HBV; PR
Myrtis. Walter Savage Landor. *Fr.* Pericles and Aspasia. OBRV; VA
Myrtle, and eglantine. The Flower-Seller. William Young. *Fr.* Wishmakers' Town. AA
Myrtle and the Vine, The, *sel.* George Colman.
Gluggity Glug. HBV; LPS-3
Myrtle, as I lie here, wrapped in. Reflections in a Hospital. Emanuel Eisenberg. ALV
Myrtle bush grew shady, The. Jealousy. Mary Elizabeth Coleridge. CH; EnLoPo; PoVP
Myself. Edgar A. Guest. BLP; BLPA; MaRV; NeHB; OQP; QP-1
Myself. Po Chü-i, *tr. fr. Chinese by* Ching Ti. WhP
Myself. *Unknown.* OQP; QP-1
Myself. Walt Whitman. Song of Myself, I. AA; FaBoBe
(I Celebrate Myself.) NePA
("I celebrate myself, and sing myself.") OBAV (I *and* VI); PoFS (I-XLVIII, *much abr.*); TCAP; TrGrPo
Myself am Hang, the buccaneer. The Flying Fish. John Gray. SG
Myself Am Hell. Milton. *Fr.* Paradise Lost, I *and* IV. MaRV
Myself and Mine. Walt Whitman. APW; IAP
Myself grown old do fearfully frequent. Case History. Arthur W. Bell. WhC
Myself unto myself will give. The Holy Office. James Joyce. FaBoTw; SiTL
Myself when young did eagerly frequent. Worldly Wisdom [*or* Great Argument]. Omar Khayyám, *tr. by* Edward Fitzgerald. *Fr.* The Rubáiyát. EG; MaRV; OnPM; WGRP
Myselves/ The grievers. Ceremony after a Fire Raid. Dylan Thomas. CoBMV; ExPo; MoPo; WaP
Mysteries. Emily Dickinson. *See* Murmur of a bee, The.
Mysteries, The. L. A. G. Strong. HaMV
Mysteries: if a nymph naked and golden. Microcosmos, XX. Nigel Heseltine. NeBP
Mysterious barcarolles. Kindred Harmonies. Paul Verlaine. TrFP
Mysterious Biography. Carl Sandburg. SiSoCe
Mysterious Cat, The. Vachel Lindsay. ChTr; FaPON; MPB; PoRh; RAR; SP; StVeCh; TiPo; UTS
Mysterious death! who in a single hour. Transfiguration. Louisa May Alcott. MOAH
Mysterious flood—that through the silent sands. To the Nile. Bayard Taylor. TCAP
Mysterious guest! Hymn to Spring. Theodor Caspari. AnNoLy
Mysterious Landscape. Hans Carossa, *tr. fr. German by* R. F. C. Hull. LiTW
Mysterious Music of Ocean, The. *Unknown.* EtS
Mysterious Night. Joseph Blanco White. *See* To Night.
Mysterious night! Spread wide thy silvery plume. Night. John Addington Symonds. HBV

Mysterious Night, when our first parent knew. To Night [*or* Night *or* Night and Death]. Joseph Blanco White. AnFE; AnIV; BCEP; EG; EPN; ES; EV-4; GoBC; GTBS-W; GTIV; HBV; JKCP (1926 ed.); LiA; LPS-2; MaRV; OBEV (new ed.); OBRV; PoeMoYo; SN; TreFS; TVSH; ViBoPo; WGRP
Mysterious Nothing! how shall I define. Nothing. Richard Porson. BOHV
Mystery, The. *At. to* Amergin, *tr. fr. Old Irish by* Douglas Hyde. OnYI
Mystery. Jerome B. Bell. MaRV
Mystery. Elizabeth Barrett Browning. OBVV; UnPo
Mystery. John Drinkwater. TCPD
Mystery, The. Ralph Hodgson. BLV; BMEP; BoLiVe; CAW; CH; ChMo; CMP; HBV; LEAP; MaRV; MBP; MoAB; MoBrPo; NeMA; NP; OQP; QP-1; QS; WGRP
Mystery. Scudder Middleton. NV
Mystery, The. George Francis Savage-Armstrong. VA
Mystery, A. "Gabriel Setoun." PPL
Mystery. George Sterling. MuM
Mystery, The. Sara Teasdale. HBMV
Mystery, The. *Unknown, tr. fr. Irish by* Douglas Hyde. OxBI
Mystery, The. Lilian Whiting. AA
Mystery, A. Whittier. IAP; UnW
Mystery. "Yehoash," *tr. fr. Yiddish by* Marie Syrkin. TrJP
Mystery: lo! betwixt the sun and moon. Astarte Syriaca. Dante Gabriel Rossetti. PoVP
Mystery of Cro-a-tàn, The. Margaret Junkin Preston. PAH
Mystery of Dawn, ere yet the glory streams. Laurence Binyon. The Sirens, III, 3. GoTL (1949 ed.)
Mystery of Death, The. First Corinthians, XV: 51-58, Bible, *N.T.* BBV (1951 ed.)
Mystery of Pain. Emily Dickinson. *See* Pain has an element of blank.
Mystery of the Innocent Saints, The, *sel.* Charles Péguy, *tr. fr. French by* Joseph T. Shipley.
"I have often played with man, saith the Lord." CAW
Mystic, The. Gertrude Bone. QS
Mystic, The. Witter Bynner. HBV; LBMV; LEAP
Mystic, The. Don Marquis. UnW
Mystic, The. Cale Young Rice. BLP; LBMV; LS; MaRV; MuM; QS; WGRP
"I have ridden the wind," *sel.* NLK
Mystic, The. Tennyson. OAEP
Mystic and Cavalier. Lionel Johnson. CaAE; GTIV; MBP; MoBrPo; SeCePo; ViPP
Mystic as Soldier, A. Siegfried Sassoon. CP; LBBV; NP; WGRP
Mystic Borderland, The. Helen Field Fischer. OQP; QP-2; WBLP
(There Is a Mystic Borderland.) PoToHe
Mystic Cups. Iraqi, *tr. fr. Persian by* E. G. Browne. PeP
Mystic Magi, The. Robert Stephen Hawker. ChTr
(Southern Cross, The.) OxBoCh
Mystic River. John Ciardi. AmP
Mystic Song, A. *Unknown. See* Chanson mystique.
Mystic Trumpeter, The. Walt Whitman. IAP; TCAP
Mystic Union, The. *Unknown, tr. fr. Punjabi by* Puran Singh. OnPM
Mystic Weaver, The. *Unknown.* PTA-2
Mystical Ballad, A, *sel.* James Russell Lowell.
"One step beyond life's work-day things." UnW
Mystical Dialogue. Paul Verlaine, *tr. fr. French by* Alan Conder. LO
Mystical Ecstacy, A. Francis Quarles. *See* My Beloved Is Mine, and I Am His.
Mystical Poets. Amado Nervo, *tr. fr. Spanish by* Thomas Walsh. CAW
Mystical, sorrowful, stiff and still. The Discoverer. Nathalia Crane. PoMa; YT
Mystical strains unheard. Clymène. Paul Verlaine. AWP; JAWP; WBP
"Mysticism Has Not the Patience to Wait for God's Revelation." Richard Eberhart. MoPo
Mystic's Prayer, The. "Fiona Macleod." HBV; MaRV; TrPWD; WGRP
Mystic's Prayer. *Unknown.* MaRV
Myth, A. Charles Kingsley. *See* Night Bird, The.
Myth of Arthur, The. G. K. Chesterton. HBMV
Mythos. Ralph Gustafson. BoCaPo (1948 ed.); PeCV
Myths. Guy Butler. BoSA
Myths & Texts, *sel.* Gary Snyder.
Burning, III, *abr.* NeAP

N

N. B., Symmetrians. Gene Derwood. LiTA; NePA
N. Y. Ezra Pound. NP
Na Audiart. Ezra Pound. ReaPo
Naaman's Song. Kipling. OtMeF
Nabara, The. C. Day Lewis. HaMV
Nada. Pierre Emmanuel, *tr. fr. French by* Wallace Fowlie. MiCF
Nae shoon to hide her tiny taes. The Babie. Jeremiah Eames Rankin. AA; HBV; LPS-1; PECK; PTA-2
Naiad for Grecian waters! Queen Guennivar's Round. Robert Stephen Hawker. CoBE
Naiad, hid beneath the bank. Anteros [*or* A Dirge]. William Johnson Cory. BMEP; OBVV
Naiads, and ye pastures cold. Telling the Bees. Andrew Lang. VA
Nail-torn God, The. Edwin Markham. MaRV; QS
Nails. Leonard Feeney. WHL
Nails, The. Charles Wharton Stork. StJW
Naked and Alone. Phyllis Reid. DiM
Naked and brave thou goest. A Memorial Tablet. Florence Wilkinson Evans. LBMV
Naked and the Nude, The. Robert Graves. SiTL
Naked before the glass she said. Young Woman. Howard Nemerov. FiMAP
Naked Boughs. Harrison Smith Morris. PR
Naked earth is warm with Spring, The. Into Battle. Julian Grenfell. HBV; KN; LBBV; LoBV; MM; OBEV (new ed.); OBMV; OtMeF; POTE; ShBV-3; ShGoBo; TwCV; WaaP
Naked house, a naked moor, A. The House Beautiful. Robert Louis Stevenson. BSV; CaAE; CBE; EV-5; GTML; PoeT; PoVP
Naked I Came. Palladas, *tr. fr. Greek by* A. J. Butler. GrL; OxBG
(Vanity of Vanities, *tr. by* William M. Hardinge.) AWP; JAWP; WBP; GrPE, *tr. by* F. L. Lucas
Naked I lie in the green forest of summer. A Summer Day. Li Po. OnPM
Naked I saw thee. Ideal. Padraic Pearse. AnIV; AWP; CAW; JAWP; JKCP; LBBV; LiTW; NP; OnYI; TIP; WBP
Naked is the earth. Poems, 3. Antonio Machado. AWP; LiTW
Naked the flagstaff rises. We Shall Come Back. Nordahl Grieg. AnNoLy
Naked Things, The. Thomas Traherne. *Fr.* The Person. MeRV
Naked to earth was I brought—naked to earth I descend. Vanity of Vanities. Palladas. AWP; JAWP; WBP
Naked World, The. Sully-Prudhomme, *tr. fr. French by* William Dock. ImOP
Nam Semen Est Verbum Dei. Louise Imogen Guiney. CAW; QS
Namaqualand after Rain. William Plomer. BoSA
Namby Pamby. Henry Carey. EV-3
"Namby Pamby's doubly mild," *sel.* BoN
Name, The. Anna Hempstead Branch. SBMV
Name, The. Eileen Duggan. ISi
Name, The. Don Marquis. HBV; LEAP; OBAV
Name, The. Williamina Parrish. AV
Name, Cromac, makes us speak, A. Home. Léon Paul Fargue. MiCF
Name for My Love, A. W. K. Welsh. PR
Name-giving Aurora, The. Rafael Alberti, *tr. fr. Spanish by* Eleanor L. Turnbull. CoSP
Name in the Sand, A. Hannah Flagg Gould. AA; PECK
Name like a River, The. W. S. Graham. FaBoTw
Name me no names for my disease. Hills of Home. Witter Bynner. BAP; OBAV; SBMV
Name No Names. Pope. *Fr.* Epilogue to the Satires, Dialogue II. BeR
Name of Christ is Wonderful, for wonderful is He, The. The Glorious Name. Amos R. Wells. BePJ
Name of commonwealth is past and gone, The. Byron. *Fr.* Ode on Venice. PoFr
Name of her I dare adore, The. Fortunio's Song. Alfred de Musset. *Fr.* Le Chandelier. TrFP
Name of Jesus, The. Annie Johnson Flint. BePJ
Name of Jesus, The. John Newton. MaRV; OBEC
(How Sweet the Name of Jesus Sounds.) OxBoCh
(Hymn: "How sweet the name of Jesus sounds.") OIF
(Precious Name, The.) BePJ
"Jesus! my Shepherd, Husband, Friend," *sel.* TrPWD
Name of Mary. John Boyle O'Reilly. JKCP
Name of Mother, The. George Griffith Fetter. PGD
Name of Old Glory, The. James Whitcomb Riley. DD, *abr.;* FOAH; GN
Name of Osmund Toulmin, the Gentleman-Jockey, The. Osmund Toulmin. Sir Osbert Sitwell. AtBAP
Name of Washington, The. Arthur Gordon Field. PGD
Name of Washington, The. George Parsons Lathrop. DD; HH
Name the leaves on all the trees. My Loves. John Stuart Blackie. EBSV; OBVV
Name thou wearest does thee grievous wrong, The. The Mocking-Bird. Henry Jerome Stockard. AA; NoCaPo (1941 ed.)
Nameless and Immortal. Verner von Heidenstam, *tr. fr. Swedish by* Charles W. Stork. AnSL

Nameless as meadows on another star. Thoughts. Arthur L. Phelps. CPG
Nameless Doon [or Dun], The. William Larminie. AnIL; GTIV; IrPN; OxBI
(Nameless Ruin, The.) OnYI
Nameless Grave, A. Longfellow. IAP
Nameless Islands. Jorge Carrera Andrade, *tr. fr. Spanish by* H. R. Hays. TwSpPo
Nameless One, The James Clarence Mangan. ACP; BCEP; CBOV; EnRP; EPN; EV-4; GoBC; GTBS; GTIV; GTSE; HBV; IrPN; OBEV; OnYI; OxBI; TIP
Nameless Ones, The. Conrad Aiken. NePA; OxBA
Nameless Ruin, The. William Larminie. *See* Nameless Doon, The.
Nameless Saints, The. Edward Everett Hale. MaRV; OQP; QP-1; WGRP
Nameless Song. Elinor Wylie. CoBA
Names. Dorothy Aldis. BoChLi; SUS
Names. Abbie Farwell Brown. POT; PoTo
Names, The. Robert Browning. PtP
Names. Jorge Guillén, *tr. fr. Spanish by* Eleanor L. Turnbull. AnSpL-2; CoSP; LiTW
Names, The. Charles Lamb. OTPC (1923 ed.)
Names. Gotthold Ephraim Lessing. *See* I Asked My Fair, One Happy Day.
Names. Edwin McNeill Poteat. NoCaPo (rev. ed.)
Names and Order of the Books of the Old Testament. Thomas Russell. *See* Old Testament, The.
Names (for Mother). Elwyn Chauncey West. DD
Names of the trees, The. Nature-Hater. Tosaburo Ono. PoLJ
Naming of Parts. Henry Reed. Lessons of the War, I. HoPM; LiTB; LiTM (rev. ed.); MoAB; MoVE; SeCePo; ShBV-3; SiTL; ViBoPo (1958 ed.); WaP
("Today we have naming of parts.") TrGrPo (rev. ed.)
Namkwin Pul. Bernard Gutteridge. WaP
Nanak and the Sikhs, *sel. Unknown, tr. fr. Hindustani.* "How shall I address thee?" WGRP
Nancy Dawson. Herbert P. Horne. HBV; VA
Nancy Hanks. Rosemary Benét *and* Stephen Vincent Benét. BAP; FaPON; GBV (1952 ed.); LaNeLa; NeMA; SiSoSe; StVeCh (1955 ed.); TiPo
Nancy Hanks. Harriet Monroe. BAP; OHIP
Nancy Hanks dreams by the fire. Fire-Logs. Carl Sandburg. BAP; NP
Nancy Hanks, Mother of Abraham Lincoln. Vachel Lindsay. ATP (1935 ed.); ChMo; CMP; MAP; MoAmPo
Nancy Lee. Frederic E. Weatherly. AmSS, *with music;* OIF; VA
Nancy's Hair. Walter Savage Landor. TriL
Nancy's to the greenwood gane. Scornfu' Nancy. *Unknown.* EBSV
Ñáñigo to Heaven. Luis Palés Matos, *tr. fr. Spanish by* Dudley Fitts. AnCL
Nanking. Wei Chuang, *tr. fr. Chinese by* Henry H. Hart. PoHN
Nannette. Matthew Prior. AEV
Nanny. Francis Davis. HBV
Nanny-goat who felt the need, A. The Wolf, the Goat, and the Kid. La Fontaine. TrFP
Nanny's Sailor Lad. William Allingham. IrPN
Nano's Song. Ben Jonson. *Fr.* Volpone; or, The Fox, I, ii. BoLiVe; LoBV; TrGrPo
(Fools.) EIL; TuPP
("Fools, they are the only nation.") CenL; InvP
(Fortunate Fool.) BLV
Nantasket, *sel.* Mary Clemmer Ames. "Fair is thy face, Nantasket." SN
Nantucket. William Carlos Williams. OxBA
Nantucket Skipper, The. James Thomas Fields. *See* Alarmed Skipper, The.
Nantucket Whalers. Daniel Henderson. EtS
Naomi and Ruth. Ruth, I: 8-17, Bible, *O.T.* TrJP
Naomi (Omie) Wise. *Unknown.* BaBo (A *and* B *vers.*); ViBoFo, *with music*
(Poor Omie.) ABS
Naples. Samuel Rogers. *Fr.* Italy. LPS-2
Napoleon. Byron. *Fr.* Childe Harold's Pilgrimage, III. LPS-3; OBRV
Napoleon. Walter de la Mare. FaBoCh; FaBoTw; LoGBV; MoVE; OtMeF; SoV
Napoleon and the British Sailor. Thomas Campbell. BeLS; LPS-2
(Napoleon and the Sailor, *abr.*) CG
(Soldier and Sailor.) LH; ShGoBo
Napoleon II. Lydia Schuyler. BoHiPo
Napoleon took many captures and is dead. Epitaph. John Crowe Ransom. MOAP
"Napoleon was great, I know." For a Little Pupil. *Unknown.* WOAH
Napoleon writes me:/ "The school is very big." The Departed Friend. Salvador Novo. AnCL; WoL
Napoleon's banners at Boulogne. Napoleon and the Sailor. Thomas Campbell. CG
Napoleon's Farewell. Byron. CBE
Nappy, springer spaniel, leads a busy life. A Dog's Life. "Casual." AIBD
Narcissa. Edward Young. *Fr.* Night Thoughts, V. LPS-1
Narcissus. Alistair Campbell. AnNZ
Narcissus. William Cowper. OTPC
Narcissus. Charles Gullans. NePoEA
Narcissus. Ovid, *tr. fr. Latin by* Joseph Addison. *Fr.* Metamorphoses, III. RoL
Narcissus. Paul Valéry, *tr. fr. French by* Joseph T. Shipley. AWP
Narcissus; a Pompeian Bronze. Vyacheslav Ivanovich Ivanov, *tr. fr. Russian by* Babette Deutsch. TrRV
Narcissus Fields. Eleanor Farjeon. AlDL
Narcissus in a Cocktail Glass. Frances Minturn Howard. GoYe
Narrative. Louis Dudek. CaP
Narrative, A. Theodore Spencer. NeMA; WaKn; WhC
Narrow Doors, The. Fannie Stearns Davis. HBMV; SBMV
Narrow fellow in the grass, A. Emily Dickinson. AlDL; AmPo; AmPP (4th ed.); AtBAP; ExPo; FaFP; GTBS-D; HoPM; MOAP; MoPW; OxBA; PoE; PoEL-5; SeCeV; TwP
(Snake, The.) ATP (1953 ed.); BLV; BoLiVe; CoBA; GoTP; LiTA; LiTM (rev. ed.); MAPA; MCCG; MoAB; PIAE; TwAmPo; YT
Narrow paths beside the flower-beds run, The. The Moths. Julian Bell. POTE
Narrow Street, The. Menotti del Picchia, *tr. fr. Portuguese by* Dudley Poore. AnCL
Narrow Window, A. Florence Earle Coates. OQP; QP-2
Narrower bands were filled with unmixed Fire, The. Parmenides, *tr. fr. Greek by* Charles H. Kahn. GrPo
Narrowing of knowledge to one window to a door, A. Elegy for William Soutar. William Montgomerie. NeBP
Narva and Mored, *sel.* Thomas Chatterton. Flowers and Spice. RO
Nasal whine of power whips a new universe, The. Power. Hart Crane. *Fr.* The Bridge: Cape Hatteras. MAP; MoAB; MoAmPo; VOD (1935 ed.)
Naseby. Macaulay. *See* Battle of Naseby, The.
Naseby; Late Autumn. Basil Dowling. AnNZ
Nashe's old queens who bartered young and fair. Lament. Richard Wilbur. FiMAP
Nasturtiums, The. *Unknown.* GFA
Nat Lee's Images. Dryden. *Fr.* To Mr. Lee, on His Alexander. BeR
Natchul-born Easman. *Unknown. See* Casey Jones.
Nathan Hale. Francis Miles Finch. DD; GA; MC; PAH; PAP; PoFr, *abr.;* PTA-1
Nathan Hale. William Ordway Partridge. GA
Nathan Hale. *Unknown.* GA; IAP; PAH
(Hale in the Bush.) TCAP
Nathan, no thought today. The Bratzlav Rabbi to His Scribe. Jacob Glatstein. TrJP
Nathan Suffrin. Edgar Lee Masters. *Fr.* The New Spoon River. ChMo; CMP
Nation by the great, admired, carest, The. Rome a Greek City. Juvenal. *Fr.* Satires, III. RoL
Nation of trees, drab green and desolate grey, A. Australia. A. D. Hope. BoAV; MoAuPo; OnHM
"Nation Shall Speak Peace . . ." William Soutar. POTE
National Anthem, A. Lamprocles, *tr. fr. Greek by* C. M. Bowra. OxBG
National Anthem [Finnish], *abr.* Johan Ludvig Runeberg, *tr. fr. Swedish by* Elias Gordon. PoFr
National Hymn: "God of our fathers, whose almighty hand." Daniel C. Roberts. PaA
National Hymns, The. "Orpheus C. Kerr." *See* Rejected "National Hymns," The.
National Ode, Read at the Celebration in Independence Hall, Philadelphia, July 4, 1876. Bayard Taylor. PAH
America. *sel., fr.* III. AA; FOAH; HiLiAm; PoFr
(Liberty's Latest Daughter.) IDAH
National Paintings, The. Fitz-Greene Halleck *and* Joseph Rodman Drake. *Fr.* The Croaker Papers. AA
National Presage. John Kells Ingram. OnYI
National Song: "America, my own!" William Henry Venable. DD, *abr.;* MC; PAH
National Song: "Rise, Magyar." Alexander Petofi, *tr. fr. Hungarian by* William N. Loew. PoFr
National Song: "This our land." Björnstjerne Björnson. *See* Fatherland Song.
National Winter Garden. Hart Crane. *Fr.* The Bridge: Three Songs. AmP; LiTA; LiTM (rev. ed.); OxBA
Nationality. Thomas Osborne Davis. TIP
Nationality. Mary Gilmore. BoAV; NeLNL
Nationality. John Kells Ingram. TIP
Nationality in Drinks, *sel.* Robert Browning. "Here's to Nelson's memory," III. ViPo
Nation's Birthday, The. Mary E. Vandyne. DD; HH; IDAH; PEOR
Nation's Dead, The. *Unknown.* MDAH
Nation's Shrine, The. Alma Adams Wiley. PEDC
Nation's Strength, A. Emerson. FaPON; MaRV; PGD

Nation's voice, a nation's voice, A. Nationality. Thomas Osborne Davis. TIP
Nation's Wealth, A. John Dyer. *Fr.* The Fleece, III. OBEC
Nations, years and every creature. Viktor Khlebnikov, *tr. fr. Russian by* C. M. Bowra. BoRS
Native-born. Eve Langley. BoAV; NeLNL
Native Companions Dancing. John Shaw Neilson. NeLNL
Native drama's sick and dying, The. The Ballade of Adaptation. Brander Matthews. PC
Native Inhabitant. Douglas Stewart. NeLNL
Native Irishman, The. *Unknown.* OnYI
Native Land. Gina Ballantyne. BoAu
Native Land. "Andrei Bely," *tr. fr. Russian by* Jack Lindsay. RuPo
Native Land. Li Yu, *tr. fr. Chinese by* Hsiung Ting. WhP
Native Land. Sir Walter Scott. *See* Breathes There the Man.
Native Moments. Walt Whitman. IAP; NePA; OxBA
Native Place. Rofu Miki, *tr. fr. Japanese by* Takamichi Ninomiya *and* D. J. Enright. PoLJ
Native Son. Gertrude Callaghan. JKCP (1955 ed.)
Native Working on the Aerodrome. Roy Fuller. NeBP
Nativitie. John Donne. OBS
Nativitie, The. William Drummond of Hawthornden. *See* Angels, The.
Nativity. "Martín Adán," *tr. fr. Spanish by* Muna Lee. AnCL
Nativity, The. Richard Crashaw. *See* In the Holy Nativity of Our Lord God.
Nativity. Gladys May Casely Hayford (Aquah Laluah). CDC; PoNe
Nativity, The. Louisa Parsons Hopkins. PEOR
Nativity, The. James Montgomery. *See* Angels, from the Realms of Glory.
Nativity. W. R. Rodgers. NeBP
Nativity, The. E. Merrill Root. ChIP
Nativity. May Sarton. NePoAm-2
Nativity. Theognis, *tr. fr. Greek by* F. L. Lucas. GrPE
Nativity, The. Henry van Dyke. *Fr.* To the Child Jesus. MaRV
("Could every time-worn heart but see Thee once again.") TrPWD
Nativity, The. Charles Wesley. *See* Hark! the Herald Angels Sing.
Nativity Carol. James, John, *and* Robert Wedderburn. *See* Balulalow.
Nativity Chant, The. Sir Walter Scott. *Fr.* Guy Mannering. ChTr; FaBoCh; LoGBV
Nativity Ode. St. Cosmas, *tr. fr. Greek by* John Mason Neale. CAW
Nativity of Christ, The. Luis de Góngora, *tr. fr. Spanish by* Longfellow. CAW; TeCS
Nativity of Our Lord, The. Christopher Smart. LoBV; PoEL-3; RO
Nativity Song. Jacopone da Todi, *ad. fr. Latin by* Sophie Jewett. OHIP
Natura in Urbe. E. B. White. WaKn
Natura Maligna. Theodore Watts-Dunton. MeRV
Natura Naturans. Arthur Hugh Clough. ViP
Natura Naturata. Sir John Denham. CEP
Natural and Spiritual. First Corinthians, XV: 44-49, Bible, *N.T.* GrCo-1
Natural Architecture. John Hay. NePoAm
Natural Causes. Winfield Townley Scott. LiTL
Natural Flow of Memory. Jorge Luis Borges, *tr. fr. Spanish by* H. R. Hays. TwSpPo
Natural History, The, *sel.* Harold Monro.
"Vixen woman, The." OBMV
Natural History of Pliny, The. Vincent McHugh. NePoAm-2
Natural History of Selborne, The, *sel.* Gilbert White.
"While deepening shades obscure the face of day." LO
Natural Magic. "Æ." BEL
Natural Magic. Robert Browning. BPN; PoVP; VLEP
Natural Selection. David Brock. TwCaPo
Natural silence of a tree, The. Fortune. Charles Madge. MoPW
Natural Tears. Thomas Hood. *See* Epigram: "After such years of dissension and strife."
Naturalist on a June Sunday, The. Leonora Speyer. NLK
Nature. Mark Akenside. *Fr.* The Pleasures of Imagination, IV. LoBV
Nature. Laurence Binyon. BMEP; CBE
Nature. Byron. *See* Ocean, The.
Nature. H. D. Carberry. PoNe
Nature ("The rounded world"). Emerson. IAP; MOAP
Nature ("She is gamesome and good"). Emerson. MOAP
Nature ("A subtle chain of countless rings"). Emerson. AmPP; AWP; IAP; InPo; MOAP
Nature ("Winters know"). Emerson. GBV (1952 ed.); MOAP
Nature. Nikolai Gumilev, *tr. fr. Russian by* Y. Hornstein. BoRS
Nature. George Herbert. OAEP
Nature. Longfellow. AA; AmPP (3d ed.); AnNE; APW; BLP; BLV; CBOV; CoBA; CoV; ES; FaBoBe; HBV; IAP; InP; LEAP; MaRV; MotAn; OBAV; PFE; PIAE; PoeMoYo; PoMa; TOP; TrGrPo; WHA
Nature. Spenser. *Fr.* The Faerie Queene, VII, 7. NBE
Nature. Swinburne. *Fr.* Atalanta in Calydon. BPN; EmBrPo
Nature. Henry David Thoreau. ADAH; FaBoBe; HBV; OTPC
Nature. Jones Very. AnAmPo; HBV; LA; LPS-2; SN
Nature. Alfred de Vigny, *tr. fr. French by* Margaret Jourdain. AWP; JAWP; WBP
Nature ("I have learned"). Wordsworth. *Fr.* Lines Composed a Few Miles above Tintern Abbey. GrCo-1
("For I have learned/ To look on nature.") OQP; PC; QP-2
("I have learned/ To look on nature.") CBE; SN
(Lines Written above Tintern Abbey.) BBV
Nature ("The world is too much with us"). Wordsworth. *See* World Is Too Much with Us, The.
Nature, a jealous mistress, laid him low. Epigram on the Death of Edward Forbes. Sydney Dobell. VA
Nature Adorned Cassandra. Pierre de Ronsard, *tr. fr. French by* Alan Conder. *Fr.* Amours de Cassandre. TrFP
("When Nature formed Cassandra, who should move," *tr. by* Curtis Hidden Page.) PrPoCR
Nature and God. William Cowper. *Fr.* The Task. CoBE
Nature and he went ever hand in hand. A Priest. Norman Gale. VA
Nature and Life. George Meredith. Po; ViP; VLEP
Nature and Man. Wang Wei, *tr. fr. Chinese by* Henry Hersch Hart. PoP
Nature and nature's laws lay hid in night. Epitaph [*or* Epitaph on Sir Isaac Newton *or* Intended for Sir Isaac Newton]. Pope. CEP; ExPo; FaBoEn; FiP; ImOP; InP; MaRV; OAEP; PIAE; SeCeV; TOP; ViBoPo
Nature and Religion. Sam Walter Foss. *Fr.* The Higher Catechism. OQP; QP-2
Nature and the Child. John Lancaster Spalding. *Fr.* God and the Soul. AA
Nature and the Poet. Swift. *Fr.* Ode to Sir William Temple. BeR
Nature and the Poet. Wordsworth. *See* Elegiac Stanzas Suggested by a Picture of Peele Castle, in a Storm.
Nature and the Poets. James Beattie. *See* But Who the Melodies of Morn Can Tell?
Nature centres into balls. Circles. Emerson. APW
Nature, continuous me! An American, One of the Roughs, a Kosmos. *Unknown.* PA
Nature Cure. Jean Starr Untermeyer. PC
Nature doth have her dawn each day. Stanzas. Henry David Thoreau. MOAP
Nature gave horns to cattle. Beauty's Power. *Unknown. Fr.* Anacreontea. GrPE
Nature! great parent! whose unceasing hand. Winter Winds. James Thomson. *Fr.* The Seasons: Winter. UnPo (1st ed.)
Nature had long a treasure made. The Match. Andrew Marvell. NBE
Nature had made them hide in crevices. New Hampshire, February. Richard Eberhart. FiMAP
Nature has perpetual tears. Sir Herbert Read. *Fr.* The Analysis of Love. MBP; MoBrPo (1942 ed.)
Nature-Hater. Tosaburo Ono, *tr. fr. Japanese by* Takamichi Ninomiya *and* D. J. Enright. PoLJ
Nature hath giv'n no outward mark to note. What Makes the Man. Euripides. *Fr.* Electra. GrR
Nature, in thy largess, grant. To Mother Nature. Frederic Lawrence Knowles. HBV
Nature in War-Time. Herbert Palmer. HaMV
Nature is a temple from whose living columns. Correspondences. Baudelaire, *tr. by* Kate Flores. AnFP
Nature is a temple from whose living pillars. Correspondences. Baudelaire, *tr. by* R. G. Stern. ReMP
Nature. Love, and Man. Wordsworth. *Fr.* The Prelude, IV. RO
Nature, Man, Eternity. Henry Vaughan. *See* Bird, The, *and* Man *and* World, The.
Nature Morte. Louis MacNeice. ChMo
Nature needs [*or* requires] five; custom takes [*or* gives] seven. Hours of Sleep. *Unknown.* GoTP; PFE
Nature Note. Arthur Guiterman. SUS
Nature, nothing in you moves me, not the fruitful. Anguish. Paul Verlaine. AnFP
Nature nothing shows more rare. Shells. T. Sturge Moore. SeCePo
Nature of an Action, The. Thom Gunn. NePoEA
Nature of the Cat, The, *sel.* E. V. Lucas.
Cat's Conscience, The. CIV
Nature of Women, The, *sel.* Earl of Rochester.
Woman. BeR
Nature Poem. Ruth Herschberger. OnHM
Nature reads not our labels, "great" and "small." The Man with the Hoe; a Reply. John Vance Cheney. AA; BAP; DD; HBV

Nature requires five; custom gives seven. *See* Nature needs five; custom takes seven.
Nature selects the longest way. A Northern Suburb. John Davidson. BMEP
Nature That Framed [*or* Fram'd] Us of Four Elements. Christopher Marlowe. *Fr.* Tamburlaine the Great, Pt. I, Act II, sc. vii. MyFE; PoEL-2; TrGrPo (Climbing after Knowledge.) EV-I (Perfect Bliss and Sole Felicity.) SeCePo
Nature, That Washed Her Hands [in Milk]. Sir Walter Ralegh. ReEn; ReIE; TuPP (Love and Time.) SiPS
Nature the Artist. Empedocles, *tr. fr. Greek by* T. F. Higham. OxBG
Nature, the Artist. Frederic Lawrence Knowles. AA
Nature the False Goddess. James Jeffrey Roche. JKCP
Nature, they say, doth dote. The Martyr Chief [*or* Lincoln]. James Russell Lowell. *Fr.* Ode Recited at the Harvard Commemoration. DD; OQP; PEOR; PGD; PSO; QP-I
Nature! thou may'st fume and fret. To Miss Arundell. Walter Savage Landor. OBVV
Nature vive. Vicente Huidobro, *tr. fr. Spanish.* AnCL, *tr. by* Dudley Fitts; TwSpPo, *tr. by* H. R. Hays
Nature withheld Cassandra in the skies. Fragment of a Sonnet. Pierre de Ronsard. AWP; JAWP; OuHeWo; WBP
Nature's a fane where living pillars stand. Affinities. Baudelaire. TrFP
Nature's Chain. Pope. *Fr.* An Essay on Man, Epistle III. BCEP; LPS-2
Nature's Charms. James Beattie. *Fr.* The Minstrel, I. OBEC
Nature's Colours. Countess of Winchilsea. *Fr.* An Invitation to Daphnis. BeR
Natures compendium, th' worlds epitome. Man a Microcosm. John Collop. PoP
Nature's confectioner, the bee. Fuscara; or, The Bee Errant. John Cleveland. EPS
Nature's Creed. *Unknown.* MaRV; OHIP
Nature's decorations glisten. Christmas Day. Christopher Smart. Hymns and Spiritual Songs, Hymn XXXII. ChTr
Nature's Easter Music. Lucy Larcom. EOAH; OHIP
Nature's Embassy, *sel.* Richard Brathwaite. Nightingale, The. EIL
Nature's first green is gold. Nothing Gold Can Stay. Robert Frost. BoLiVe; MAP; MoAB; MoAmPo; NeMA; TwHP; WHA
Nature's Friend. W. H. Davies. BMEP; CP; LBBV; NV; PoRL; POT; PoTo; RG; TSW; TSWC
Nature's Gentleman. W. James Linton. BHV
Nature's Gifts to Lucy. Wordsworth. *Fr.* Three Years She Grew in Sun and Shower. LiA
Nature's Healing. Wordsworth. *Fr.* The Prelude, XII. EPN
Nature's Influence on Man. Mark Akenside. *Fr.* The Pleasures of Imagination, III. OBEC (Created Universe, The.) LoBV ("Oh! blest of heav'n, whom not the languid songs.") CEP
Nature's Key-Notes. Thomas Caulfield Irwin. IrPN
Nature's Lineaments. Robert Graves. FaBoTw
Nature's Ministry. Wordsworth. *See* Influence of Natural Objects.
Nature's Miracle. David Fallon. POT; PoTo
Natures Naked Jem. George Chapman. *See* Corinna Bathes.
Nature's Questioning. Thomas Hardy. BEL; CoBMV; EPN; InPo; MoPo; PoFS; ViP; ViPo
Nature's Sorrow Cure. Catherine Cate Coblentz. OQP; QP-2
Nature's Sympathy with the Poet. Sir Walter Scott. *Fr.* The Lay of the Last Minstrel, V. EV-4
Nature's Travail. *Unknown, tr. fr. Greek by* Goldwin Smith. AWP
Nature's Wash Day. Marguerite Gode. GFA
Naught disturbed my tranquil mood. The Dove. Abul Hasan of Seville. MooP
Naught, now, can pass belief; in Nature's ways. Archilochus, *tr. fr. Greek by* C. A. Elton. GrPo
Naughty Blackbird, The. Kate Greenaway. *See* Child's Song.
Naughty Boy, The. Keats. *See* Song about Myself, A.
Naughty Darkey Boy, The. *Unknown.* BOHV
Naughty Lord & the Gay Young Lady, The. *Unknown.* CoMu
Naughty Preposition, The. Morris Bishop. FiBHP
Nausea. Catherine Davis. NePoEA
Nausea. E. L. Mayo. MiAP
Nausicaa ("Having thus fulfilled her purpose Athene went away"). Homer, *pr. tr. fr. Greek by* T. E. Lawrence. *Fr.* The Odyssey, VI. OxBG (Olympus, *br. sel.*) LiA
Nausicaa ("Now when at last they arrived at the beautiful stream of the river"). Homer, *tr. fr. Greek by* H. B. Cotterill. *Fr.* The Odyssey, VI. OxBG
Nausicaa ("Now when they came to the bright running river"). Homer, *tr. fr. Greek by* Sir William Marris. *Fr.* The Odyssey, VI. LiTW

Nausicaa ("The servants then"). Homer, *tr. fr. Greek by* George Chapman. *Fr.* The Odyssey, VI. OBS
Nausicaa ("So flashing-eyed Athene spoke"). Homer, *tr. fr. Greek by* F. L. Lucas. *Fr.* The Odyssey, VI. GrPE
Nausicaa and Odysseus; the Meeting. Homer, *tr. fr. Greek by* George Chapman. *Fr.* The Odyssey, VI. GrR
Nausicaa; the Ingenue. Homer, *tr. fr. Greek by* H. B. Cotterill. *Fr.* The Odyssey, VI. GrR
Nautical Ballad, A. Charles Edward Carryl. *Fr.* Davy and the Goblin, *ch.* 8. FaPON; GFA; HBV; LauV; MPB; OTPC (1946 ed.); StVeCh (Walloping Window-Blind, The.) GoTP; InMe; LBN; LiL; MoShBr; NA; TreFS; WhC
Nautical Extravagance [*or* Extravaganza], A. Wallace Irwin. MW; StPo; StVeCh
Nautilus, The. Charlotte Smith. OTPC (1923 ed.)
Nautilus and the Ammonite, The. *Unknown.* PECK
Nauty Pauty Jack-a-Dandy. *Unknown.* OxNR
Navaho [*or* Navajo] Prayer. *Unknown. See* Prayer to the Mountain Spirit.
Navajo, The. Elizabeth J. Coatsworth. *Fr.* The Painted Desert. PoeMoYo
Navajo Hunting-Song. *Unknown. See* Hunting-Song.
Navies nor armies can exalt the state. Richard Watson Gilder. InP
Navigators, The. W. J. Turner. OBMV
Nay, a mother:/ Why not a mother? Shakespeare. *Fr.* All's Well That Ends Well, I, iii. MotAn
Nay, be you pardoner or cheat. Villon's Ballade. Andrew Lang, *after* Villon. HBV
Nay, blame me not; I might have asked. To My Readers. Oliver Wendell Holmes. AmPP (3d ed.); IAP; TCAP
Nay, but he is so helpless and so sweet. The Tears of Mary. Theodosia Garrison. BPP
Nay, but you, who do not love her. Song. Robert Browning. AnFE; BLV; BoLiVe; BPN; EmBrPo; EPN; EPP; GTBS-W; HBV; LiTL; LoPS; MaPo; OBEV (1st ed.); PIAE; PoVP; TrGrPo; ViBoPo; VLEP
Nay, Death, thou art a shadow! Even as light. Lux Est Umbra Dei. John Addington Symonds. VA
Nay, do not grieve tho' life be full of sadness. Transience. Sarojini Naidu. MCCG
Nay, do not think I flatter. Shakespeare. *Fr.* Hamlet, III, ii. PIR
Nay, enough, enough, my champion! Sin and Satiety. Aeschylus. *Fr.* Agamemnon. GrR
Nay, give me no more counsel. Bid me not. Blindness. Sophocles. *Fr.* Oedipus Rex. OxBG
"Nay, grieve not that ye can no honour give." The Dying of Père Pierre. John McCrae. BoCaPo
Nay, hold me not—I must be going. Duet. Charles Lotin Hildreth. PR
Nay, I cannot come into the garden just now. Maud. Henry S. Leigh. BOHV
Nay, I have loved thee! Theseus and Ariadne. Lloyd Mifflin. AA
Nay, I have ne'er forgotten yet. The Palanquins. Ibn Sa'id of Alcala la Real. MooP
Nay! if you will not sit upon my knee. Pan in Love. William Wetmore Story. LPS-2
Nay, I'll not chip and scratch them line by line. The Fatal Oil-Flask. Aristophanes. *Fr.* The Frogs. OxBG
Nay, in a poet put no trust. Feodor Tyutchev, *tr. fr. Russian after* J. S. Phillimore. BoR
Nay, Ivy, Nay. *Unknown.* CH (Song on the Ivy and the Holly, A.) AnEC
Nay, lady, one frown is enough. To Helen in a Huff. Nathaniel Parker Willis. PR
Nay, Lord, not thus! white lilies in the spring. Sonnet on Hearing the *Dies Irae* Sung in the Sistine Chapel. Oscar Wilde. TrPWD
Nay, Nay, Ivy! *Unknown. See* Holly and Ivy.
Nay, nay, sweet England, do not grieve! "How Sleep the Brave." Walter de la Mare. TOP
Nay, prethee Dear, draw nigher. A Loose Saraband. Richard Lovelace. PoEL-3
Nay prithee tell me, Love, when I behold. The Transfiguration of Beauty. Michelangelo. AWP
Nay, still the ancient Glory slumbers fast. To a Nation's Hero. Pindar. *Fr.* Isthmian Odes, VII. GrR
Nay, tell me now in what strange air. Ballade of Dead Ladies. Villon, *tr. by* Andrew Lang. HBV; LEAP; PIAE
Nay, tempt me not, my Corydon; I tell you once again. Football and Rowing—an Eclogue. Alfred Denis Godley. CenHV
Nay then, by Zeus, no longer line by line. The Tell-Tale Tag. Aristophanes. *Fr.* The Frogs. GrR
Nay then, farewell, if this be so. To Avisa. *At.* to Henry Willoby. *Fr.* Willobie His Avisa. EIL
"Nay then," quoth Adon, "you will fall again." Venus Abandoned. Shakespeare. *Fr.* Venus and Adonis. LO; OBSC
Nay, thou art my eternal attribute. Whym Chow. "Michael Field." BoFr

Nay, Traveller! rest. This lonely yew-tree stands. Lines Left upon a Seat in a Yew-Tree. Wordsworth. BPN; EM-2; EmBrPo; EPN; ERP; GEPC; MCCG
Nay, why should I fear Death. Laus Mortis. Frederic Lawrence Knowles. HBV
"Nay, with my goodwill." The Hell-Ride of Brynhild. *Unknown. Fr.* The Elder Edda. OuHeWo
Nay, Xanthias, feel unashamed. Ad Xanthiam Phoceum. Franklin P. Adams, *after* Horace. AWP; JAWP; WBP
Nay, you shall see mine orchard. Shakespeare. King Henry IV, Pt. II, Act V, sc. iii. MyFE
Nay, you wrong her, my friend, she's not fickle; her love she has simply outgrown. Outgrown. Julia C. R. Dorr. HBV; LPS-1
Nazareth. Thomas Curtis Clark. ChIP
Nazareth Shop, The. Robert McIntyre. StJW
(In the Carpenter Shop, *st.* 1.) ChIP; GoTP; OQP; QP-2
Nazim Hikmet. Yaroslav Smelyakov, *tr. fr. Russian by* Jack Lindsay. RuPo
Ne Plus Ultra. Samuel Taylor Coleridge. NBE
Neap-Tide. Swinburne. EmBrPo; PoVP; ViPo
Near a field overflowing. Roy Kloof Went Riding. Sydney Clouts. BoSA
Near a shady wall a rose once grew. The Rose Still Grows beyond the Wall. A. L. Frink. BLPA
Near an Old Prison. Frances Cornford. OBMV
Near Avalon. William Morris. BPN; PoVP
Near Barbizon. Galway Kinnell. NePoAm-2
Near Dover, September, 1802. Wordsworth. BPN; EM-2; EmBrPo; EnLi-2; EnRP; ES; REAL; TOP
(September, 1802; near Dover.) EPP; ERP; GEPC; MaPo; OAEP
(Sonnet: September, 1802.) ChER
Near down th' etherial steep. Sunset and Landscape. Richard Savage. *Fr.* The Wanderer. BeR
Near Dusk. Joseph Auslander. FaPON; OTPC (1946 ed.)
Near Helikon. Trumbull Stickney. *Fr.* Sonnets from Greece. AnFE; CoAnAm; LiTA; MOAP; TwAmPo
Near him she stole, rank after rank. The Woman Who Came behind Him in the Crowd. George Macdonald. StJW
Near is God. Patmos. Friedrich Hölderlin. AnGP
Near Lanivet, 1872. Thomas Hardy. AWP; LoBV
Near Neighbors. Swift, *after the Latin of* Martial. AWP
Near Périgord. Ezra Pound. FaBoMo; LiTA; LiTM (rev. ed.)
"I loved a woman," III. NP
Near Punjab and Pab, in Sutlej and Sind. Hasheesh. Victor Robinson. PoP
Near Springfield Mountain there did dwell. Springfield Mountain (D *vers.*). *Unknown.* ABS
Near strange, weird temples, where the Ganges' tide. The Bayadere. Francis Saltus Saltus. AA; OBAV
Near the Base Line. Samuel L. Albert. NePoAm-2
Near the Cross. *At. to* Jacopone da Todi. *See* Stabat Mater Dolorosa.
Near the dawn Mary went. Dawn. Miriam LeFevre Crouse. ChIP
Near the edge, as on a shelf. Cat on the Porch at Dusk. Dorothy Harriman. GoYe
Near the great pyramid, unshadowed, white. Oblivion. W. W. Gibson. NP
Near the Lake. George Pope Morris. AA
Near the mountain's summit, when the bells. The Fox. R. Williams Parry. PrWP
Near the river with white waves, we probed. Apology of the Young Scientists. Celia Dimmette. GoYe
Near the road brim. Pittsburgh. Hy Sobiloff. NePA
Near the Spring of the Hermitage. Wordsworth. BPN
Near this spot. Epitaph to a [Newfoundland] Dog. Byron. AlBD; BLPA; TreFS
Near Time's white dawn the cities stood. The Dreamer in the Desert. Francis Flagg. DaM
Near to a bank with roses set about. The Shepherd's Anthem. Michael Drayton. ReIE
Near [*or* Neare] to the silver Trent. Sirena [*or* Song to Sirena *or* The Jovial Shepheard's Song]. Michael Drayton. *Fr.* The Shepherd's Sirena. AtBAP; EV-1; OBEV; PoEL-2; SeCL; SeEP; TuPP
Near where I live there is a lake. Fringed Gentians. Amy Lowell. BrR; FaPON; MPB; SP
Near where the riotous Atlantic surge. Fragment. William Allingham. IrPN
Near where yonder evening star. Cockayne Country. Agnes Mary F. Robinson. OBVV; VA
Near Woodville Mound there did dwell. Woodville Mound. *Unknown.* ABS
Near yonder copse, where once the garden smiled. The Village Preacher [*or* Parson]. Goldsmith. *Fr.* The Deserted Village. CBOV; CoEV; GrCo-1; MaRV; OBEC; OTPC (1923 ed.); WGRP
Nearer. Robert Nichols. LBBV; MBP; NP; NV
Nearer Home Phoebe Cary. AA; AnAmPo; BLP; BLRP; FaFP; HBV; LA; LBAP; LPS-2; NeHB; OQP; PTA-2; QP-1; TreF; WBLP; WGRP
Nearer I approach that final day, The. Petrarch. Sonnets to Laura: To Laura in Life, XXV. PrPoCR
Nearer, My God, to Thee. Sarah Flower Adams. BLRP; FaBoBe; FaFP; LPS-2; MaRV; NeHB; OlF; TreF; WBLP; WGRP
(Nearer to Thee.) HBV; VA
Nearest Friend, The. Frederick W. Faber. TreFS
Nearest in blood to gods. The Gods' Children. Aeschylus. *Fr.* Niobe OxBG
Nearest the Dearest. Coventry Patmore. The Angel in the House, II, i, 4. HBV
Nearest Way to God, The. "Angelus Silesius," *tr. fr. German by* Paul Carus. OnPM
Nearest weedlands wore a misty veil, The. Autumn. Lloyd Mifflin. *Fr.* The Fields of Dawn. SN
Nearing Again the Legendary Isle. C. Day Lewis. *Fr.* The Magnetic Mountain. CoBMV; FaBoTw; GTBS-W; LiTB; MBP; MoAB; MoBrPo; MoPW; NeMA; PeBoSo; ReMP
Nearing Cold-Dale. Hannes Hafstein, *tr. fr. Icelandic by* Jakobina Johnson. IcP
Nearing the Ford. Dwight Edwards Marvin. PraP
Nearly any child will share. Generosity. Virginia Brasier. StVeCh (1955 ed.)
Nearly Ready. Mary Mapes Dodge. PRWS
Nearly right, The. To the Tune of the Coventry Carol. Stevie Smith. FaBoTw
Nearness of Death. Georg Trakl, *tr. fr. German by* Kate Flores. *Fr.* Rosary Songs. AnGP
Neat little book, full of pictures, was bought, A. The New Book. Elizabeth Turner. OTPC (1923 ed.)
Neat young lady at work in the garden, A. A Sweetheart in the Army (B *vers.*). *Unknown.* BaBo
'Neath Blue-Bell or Streamer. Poe. *See* Song: "Neath blue-bell or streamer."
'Neath leafy hawthorn in a garden gay. Troubadour Alba. *Unknown.* EnLi-1
'Neath northern skies thou hid'st thy punctual nest. The Loon. Theodore Harding Rand. CaP; OCL
Neath the hood and cape. Moon of Grace. Al-Jazzar. MooP
'Neath the spiring of spruces. God's Acre. Blanche Edith Baughan. BoAu
Neatherd's Lament, The. Theocritus, *pr. tr. fr. Greek by* Andrew Lang. Idylls, XX. GrL
Neatly labeled, it lies at last. Museum Meteorite. Ruby T. Scott. MuM
Neatness in Apparel. Charles *and* Mary Lamb. OTPC (1923 ed.)
Nebuchadnezzar. Irwin Russell. HBV; HiLiAm; IHA
Nebuchadnezzar. *Unknown.* SiTL
Nebuchadnezzar. Elinor Wylie. MAP; MoAmPo; NeMA
Nec Odi Nec Amo. Theognis, *tr. fr. Greek by* A. C. Benson. GrR
Necessity. Euripides, *tr. fr. Greek by* Gilbert Murray. *Fr.* Alcestis. GrR
Necessity. Letitia E. Landon. BCEP
Necessity of Religion, The. Walt Whitman. *Fr.* Starting from Paumanok. MaRV
(For Religion's Sake.) GrCo-1
Necessity, the impact of whose sidelong course. An Old Actor Addresses Julius Caesar. Decimus Laberius. LaP
Necho, The. Samuel Ellsworth Kiser. DDA
Neckan, The. Matthew Arnold. GBV (1952 ed.); TVSH
Necrological. John Crowe Ransom. MOAP
Necropolis. Karl Shapiro. MoAB
Ned Braddock. John Williamson Palmer. MC; PAH
Ned Bratts. Robert Browning. VLEP
Nedjé. Roussan Camille, *tr. fr. French by* Mercer Cook. PoNe
Neece the Rapparee. "Ethna Carbery." BOL
Need, The. Siegfried Sassoon. TrPWD
Need of an Angel. Raymond Souster. CaP
Need of Being Versed in Country Things, The. Robert Frost. FaBoEn; OxBA
Need of Loving. Strickland Gillilan. *See* Folks Need a Lot of Loving.
Need of the Hour, The. Edwin Markham. PaA
Needed Word, The. Jorge Guillén, *tr. fr. Spanish by* Eleanor L. Turnbull. CoSP
Needle, The. Grace Cornell Tall. GoYe
Needle, The. Samuel Woodworth. APW; GN; HBV
Needle Travel. Margaret French Patton. HBMV
Needles and pins, needles and pins. Mother Goose. BoChLi; FaBoBe; GoTP; HBV; OTPC; SiTL
Needless to catalogue heroes. No Man Knows War. Edwin Rolfe. TrJP; WaP
Needs. Elizabeth Rendall. HBMV
Needs. Charles Hanson Towne. DDA
Needs Must I Leave, and Yet Needs Must I Love. Henry Constable. *Fr.* Diana. InvP; OBSC; SiCE
Needy are our neighbours, if we note rightly, The. The Sufferings of the Poor. William Langland. *Fr.* The Vision of Piers Plowman. PoFr; PoLi

"Needy Knife-grinder! whither are you going?" The Friend of Humanity and the Knife-Grinder [*or* The Knife-Grinder *or* Sapphics]. George Canning *and* John Hookham Frere. BCEP; BOHV; CEP; CoEV; HBV; InMe; LPS-3; OBEC; TOP
Ne'er Shall I Forget. William Goldsmith Brown. MotAn
Ne'er to the son, in whom her age is blest. Petrarch. Sonnets to Laura: To Laura in Death, XVII. PrPoCR
Ne'er trouble thyself at the times or their turnings. A Catch. *Unknown.* SeCL
Ne'er was the sky so deep a hue. The Inn by the Road. C. E. Warner. OQP; QP-1
Ne'er yet from the root of a squill did rose or hyacinth wave. Race. Theognis. GrPE
Néère. André Chénier, *tr. fr. French by* Charles Richard Cammell. Bucoliques, XIII. LiA
Nefarious War, The. Li Po. *See* Fighting on the South Frontier.
Negation is the spectre, the reasoning power in man, The. Reason and Imagination. Blake. *Fr.* Milton. EnRP
Negative Love. John Donne. ReEn
Neglected long had been my useless lyre. On the Defeat at Ticonderoga or Carilong. *Unknown.* PAH
Neglected now it lies, a cold clay form. On a Broken Pipe. James Thomson. PIAE
Neglectful Edward. Robert Graves. MBP; MoBrPo; NeMA
Negro, The. Langston Hughes. *See* Proem: "I am a negro."
Negro/ in the cane fields. Cane. Nicolás Guillén. PoNe
Negro holds firmly the reins of his four horses, The. The Drayman. Walt Whitman. *Fr.* Song of Myself, XIII. PoNe
Negro Love Song, A. Paul Laurence Dunbar. BANP; PoNe
Negro Poets. Charles Bertram Johnson. BANP
Negro Reel, *with music.* *Unknown.* AS
Negro Serenade. James Edwin Campbell. BANP
Negro Sermon, A; Simon Legree. Vachel Lindsay. *See* Simon Legree—a Negro Sermon.
Negro Singer, The. James David Corrothers. BANP
Negro Sings, A. Normil Sylvain, *tr. fr. French by* Edna Worthley Underwood. PoNe
Negro Soldiers, The. Roscoe Conkling Jamison. BANP
Negro Speaks of Rivers, The. Langston Hughes. BANP; CaAE; CDC; GoSl; PoeMoYo; PoNe
Negro Spiritual ("Sable is my throat"). Perient Trott. PoNe
Negro Spiritual: "Swing low, sweet chariot." *Unknown.* *See* Swing Low, Sweet Chariot.
Negro Spirituals. Rosemary Benét *and* Stephen Vincent Benét. FaPON
Negro Student, The. Marguerite Steffan. MuM
Negro Woman. Lewis Alexander. CDC
Negroes. Maxwell Bodenheim. PoNe
Neighbour. J. R. Hervey. AnNZ
Neighbor, The. Rainer Maria Rilke, *tr. fr. German by* Jessie Lemont. OnPM
Neighbour mine not long ago there was, A. A Tale for Husbands. Sir Philip Sidney. *Fr.* Arcadia. SiPS
Neighbour of the near domain. To Austin Dobson. Sir Edmund Gosse. LEAP
Neighbour, The, sits in his window and plays the flute. Music. Amy Lowell. AnAmPo; LA; YaD
Neighbor thought that they, A. The Planetary Arc-Light. August Derleth. GoYe
Neighborhood of Saint-Merri, The. Robert Desnos, *tr. fr. French by* Wallace Fowlie. MiCF
Neighboring. Christina Rossetti. *Fr.* Sing-Song. GaP; PCH
Neighborly. Violet Alleyn Storey. GaP; TiPo
Neighbors. Marilyn Francis. GoYe
Neighbors, The. Theodosia Garrison. HBMV; UnW
Neighbors. "Lennox." InMe
Neighbors. Anne Blackwell Payne. GFA
Neighbors. E. A. Robinson. ChMo: CMP; CP; NV
Neighbors. Anne Spencer. CDC
Neighbors. Helen Wing. GFA
Neighbours and Kinsfolk. Hesiod, *tr. fr. Greek by* Sir William Marris. *Fr.* Works and Days. OxBG
Neighbor's Dog. Georgie Starbuck Galbraith. AlBD
Neighbors Help Him Build His House, The. *Unknown, tr. fr. Japanese by* Witter Bynner. LiTW
Neighbors of Bethlehem, The. *Unknown, tr. fr. French.* OHIP; SDH
Neighbors of the Christ Night. Nora Archibald Smith. ChrBoLe; CLS; COAH; PRWS
Neighing North, The. Annie Charlotte Dalton. CaP
Neither did the keen-sighted archer goddess assail me. Odysseus' Mother Speaks to Him in Hades. Homer. *Fr.* The Odyssey, XI. LiA
Neither Do I Condemn Thee. St. John, VIII: 1–11, Bible, *N.T.* GrCo-1
Neither Faith nor Beauty Can Remain. Edgar Lee Masters. ChMo; CMP
Neither her voice, her name. The Night Dream. Archibald MacLeish. TwHP
Neither Here nor There. W. R. Rodgers. FaBoMo; GTBS-W; LiTB; LiTM; MoAB; MoBrPo (1950 ed.); NeBP; ViBoPo (1958 ed.)
"Neither Maid nor Wife." Praxilla, *tr. fr. Greek by* F. L. Lucas. GrPE
Neither malt nor Milton can. In Humbleness. Daniel G. Hoffman. NePA
Neither of Earth nor Heaven here she lies. Epitaph. Lady Margaret Sackville. MM
Neither of them was better than the other. From Plane to Plane. Robert Frost. MoAmPo (1950 ed.)
Neither Out Far nor in Deep. Robert Frost. AmP; ChTr; CoBMV; CrMA; LiTA; MoAB; PoLFOT; TiPo (1952 ed.); TwP
Neither Poverty nor Riches. Proverbs, XXX: 7–9, Bible, *O.T.* TrJP
Neither sighs, nor tears, nor mourning. Song. *Unknown.* SeCL
Neither Spirit nor Bird. *Tr. fr. Shoshone Indian by* Mary Austin. AWP; JAWP; PG; WBP
Neither the intimacy of your forehead, fair as a feast-day. Love's Priority. Jorge Luis Borges. AnCL
Neither the teacher of the class nor the priest with his catechism. Aimé Césaire. *Fr.* Memorandum on My Martinique. PoNe
Neither tribal nor trivial he shouts. Newsboy. Irving Layton. CaP
Neither war, nor cyclones, nor earthquakes. Antipater of Thessalonica. Kenneth Rexroth. CrMA
Neither will I put myself forward as others may do. Eternal Masculine. William Rose Benét. AWP; InPo; MAP; MoAmPo; MoAP
Nekros. John Banister Tabb. AmP
Nell Flaherty's Drake. *Unknown.* AnIV; OnYI
Nell Gwynne's Looking-Glass. Laman Blanchard. HBV; VA
Nell scolded in so loud a din. A Quiet Life and a Good Name. Swift. EV-3
Nelly. Nikolai Tikhonov, *tr. fr. Russian by* Jack Lindsay. RuPo
Nelly Bly. Stephen Collins Foster. OlF
Nelly Trim. Sylvia Townsend Warner. MBP; MoAB; MoBrPo
Nelly Was a Lady. Stephen Collins Foster. BAV
Nelson. Archibald T. Strong. *Fr.* Sonnets of the Empire. BoAu
Nelson, Pitt, [and] Fox. Sir Walter Scott. *See* To William Stewart Rose, Esq.
Nelson Street. "Seumas O'Sullivan." GTIV; OxBI
Nelson's on a column. Trafalgar Square. Rose Fyleman. UTS
Nemea. Lawrence Durrell. ChMP; FaBoTw
Nemean Odes. Pindar. *See* Odes.
Nemesis. Emerson. AtBAP; MOAP
Nemesis. James William Foley. BOHV
Nemo Nascitur Artifex. Henry Parrot. SiCE
Neo-classical Poem. William Jay Smith. WaP
Neoplatonic Soliloquy. Donald C. Babcock. NePoAm
Nepenthe, *sels.* George Darley.
"As from the moist and gelid sleep." OnYI
Declivities of Heaven, 6 *ll.* RO
"List no more the ominous din." OBRV
"Lo! in the mute, mid wilderness." NBE; OBRV
(Unicorn, The.) ChTr; FaBoEn; PoEL-4
O Blest Unfabled Incense Tree. AnIV; ChER; EG; FaBoCh; GTBS-D; GTIV; NBE; OBRV
(Phenix, The, *longer sel.*) RO
(Phoenix, The.) BLV; ChTr; GTML; LoBV; OBVV; TriL
(Song of the Phoenix, A.) CBOV
"O fast her amber blood doth flow." OBRV
(Phoenix, The.) OBEV (new ed.)
"Over a bloomy land, untrod." OBRV
"Over hills and uplands high." TIP
Sea, The. BLV
(Lines: "Hurry me Nymphs! O, hurry me.") HoPM
"Solitary wayfarer!" OBRV
"Thou whose thrilling hand in mine." OBRV
Nephelidia. Swinburne. *Fr.* The Heptalogia. ALV; BOHV; EnLi-2 (1949 ed.); HBV; InMe; NA; OAEP; PA; PoFS; PoVP; ViP; ViPo; VLEP
"From the depth of the dreamy decline of the dawn," *sel.* HoPM
Nephews and nieces,—love your leaden statues. Paul and Virginia. John Wheelwright. CrMA
Nephon's Song. George Darley. *Fr.* Sylvia; or, The May Queen. VA
(Elfin Pedlar, The.) BoTP
(From "Sylvia.") LEAP
Nephree-ti-ta. Stanton A. Coblentz. UnW
Nepman. "Demyan Bedny," *tr. fr. Russian by* Babette Deutsch. TrRV
Neptune. Thomas Campion. *See* Hymn in Praise of Neptune, A.

Neptune and Mars in council safe. Louisburg. *Unknown.* PAH

Neptune, the mighty Marine God, I sing. Homeric Hymn to Neptune. George Chapman. EtS

Neptune's Raging Fury, or, The Gallant Seaman's Sufferings. Martyn Parker. SG

You Gentlemen of England, *st.* 1, *with music.* SoAmSa

Neptune's Triumph, *sel.* Ben Jonson.
Chorus: "Spring all the Graces of the age," *also given in* The Fortunate Isles and Their Union. OBS; SeCL

Nereid, A. Pushkin, *tr. fr. Russian by* Babette Deutsch. TrRV

Nereid, Grand Turk, Good Intent. Waterfront. Oliver Jenkins. EtS

Nereides; or, Sea-Eclogues, *sels.* William Diaper.
Eclogue: "Lycon begin—begin the mournful tale." SeCePo
Edges of the Sea. BeR
Frost at Sea. **BeR**
Prawn and Pearl. BeR
Roses and Lilies. BeR
Sea Eclogue: "Otys, begin." LoBV
Submarine Landscape. BeR
Two Sea Nymphs. BeR

Nereids Rise Out of the Sea and Sing, Tritons Dance. Dryden. *Fr.* Albion and Albanius. BeR

Nero, *sel.* Clark Ashton Smith.
"I would I were a god." BAP

Nerves. Arthur Symons. FaBoTw; MBP; MoBrPo

Nervous Prostration. Anna Wickham. DiM

Nest, The. Mary Elliott. OTPC (1923 ed.)

Nest, The. Andrew Young. AIDL

Nest Eggs. Robert Louis Stevenson. EBSV

Nest is built, the song hath ceas'd, The. The Silenced Singer. William James Linton. VA

Nest of Love, The. Shelley. *Fr.* Lines: "When the Lamp is shattered." RO

Nest of the Magpie, The. *Unknown, tr. fr. Chinese.* WhP

Nested. Habberton Lulham. HBV

Nesting Time. Archibald Lampman. CPG

Nesting-Time. Christina Rossetti. PCH

Nestling Church at Ovingdean, The. Alfred Noyes. SaFP

Nestor's Doubt, Homer, *tr. fr. Greek by* F. L. Lucas. *Fr.* The Iliad, XIV. GrPE

Nestor's Speech to Achilles and Agamemnon. Homer, *tr. fr. Greek by* George Chapman. *Fr.* The Iliad, I. ReEn

Nests are in the hedgerows, The. To a Child of Fancy. Lewis Morris. HBV

Nests in Elms. "Michael Field." BLA

Nests well hidden. Secret Places. Irene Thompson. BoTP

Net, The. W. R. Rogers. AnIL; OxBI; PoN

Net, The. Sara Teasdale. MOAP

Net-Braiders, The. Thomas Wade. VA

Net-Menders, The. Brian Vrepont. BoAV

Net of Law, The. James Jeffrey Roche. HBV; LEAP

Net to Snare the Moonlight, A. Vachel Lindsay. ChMo; CMP

Nets are real, The—heroin (sniffed) clears them. For Artaud. Michael McClure. NeAP

Nets to Catch the Wind. John Webster. *See* All the Flowers of the Spring.

Netted Strawberries. Gordon Bottomley. AtBAP; WP

Nettle, The. Bayard Taylor. PA

Nettle, the Flower, The. Morton Dauwen Zabel. NP

Network, The. Robert Finch. CaP

Neutral, The. Wrenne Jarman. DiM

Neutral Argos. Delphic Oracle, *tr. fr. Greek by* A. D. Godley. OxBG

Neutral island facing the Atlantic, The. Neutrality. Louis MacNeice. CoBMV

Neutral Tones. Thomas Hardy. ChMo; CMP; CoBMV; CoEV; LiTL; LoPo; MaPo; MBP; MoBrPo; PoFS; PoVP; RiBV; ViPP; VLEP

Neutrality. Sidney Keyes. MoAB

Neutrality. Louis MacNeice. CoBMV

Neutrality Loathsome. Robert Herrick. LiTB
("Ye cannot Serve God and Mammon.") PoFr

Nevada. Lawrence Gurney. GoYe

Nevada Cowpuncher to His Beloved, A. *Unknown.* SCC

Nevadaville upon a hill/ The home of Cousin Jack and Jill. The Fight at Nevadaville. *Unknown.* PoOW

Never. Afanasi Fet, *tr. fr. Russian by* C. M. Bowra. BoR

Never a beak has my white bird. Thistle-Down. Clara Doty Bates. AA

Never a careworn wife but shows. Wives in the Sere. Thomas Hardy. TyEnPo; VLEP

Never a mother spoke advice so wise. Sonnets on the Death of Laura, III. Petrarch. *Fr.* Sonnets to Laura. UnW

Never a mouse. Geometry. Alfred Kreymborg. AnAmPo; LA

Never a trial that is not there. Moment by Moment. Daniel W. Whittle. BLRP

Never Admit the Pain. Mary Gilmore. NeLNL

Never Again. Hugh McCrae. BoAu; UnW

Never again, beneath some fern or flower. To a Dead Cricket. Mnasalcas. RIS

Never again, oh city of my joy. Ilion Overthrown. Euripides. *Fr.* Hecuba. GrR

Never again rejoicing in the surges that I sunder. The Dolphin's Tomb. Anyte. GrPE

Never again shall we beat out to sea. Fiddler's Green. Theodore Goodridge Roberts. CaP; CPG; OCL

Never Again Will I Say. Moishe-Leib Halpern, *tr. fr. Yiddish by* Sarah Zweig Betsky. OnCuPl

Never Again Would Birds' Song Be the Same. Robert Frost. CrMA

Never and never, my girl riding far and near. In Country Sleep. Dylan Thomas. LiTB; LiTM (rev. ed.)

Never any more,/ While I live. In a Year. Robert Browning. AtBAP; BMEP; EPN; LPS-1; PIR; VLEP

Never any more shall the golden sun. The Fallen Poplar. Mary Webb. InP

Never Ask Me Why. Silvia Margolis. GoYe

Never ask of money spent. The Hardship of Accounting. Robert Frost. FaBoCh; FaFP; LoGBV; SiTL; WhC

Never be disenchanted of. Through Nightmare. Robert Graves. Po

Never Being, but Always at the Edge. Stephen Spender. ChMo

Never, being damned, see Paradise. Those Not Elect. Léonie Adams. MOAP; MoVE

"Never burn witchwood," my old Granny said. Witchwood. May Justus. SiSoSe

Never can I forget my woe. The Crusade. Rinaldo d'Aquino. CAW

Never-dying Fire. Thomas Carew. *See* Disdain Returned.

Never Enough of Living. Léonie Adams. MOAP

Never, even in a dream. The Wanderer: Abroad. William Carlos Williams. TwAmPo

Never—Ever. Richard Le Gallienne. BMEP

Never fear the phantom bird. Mentis Trist. Robert Hillyer. HBMV; TBM

Never for common signs dispraise or praise. To Young Imaginaries in Knowledge. Petrarch. *Fr.* Seven Penitential Psalms. ReEn

Never forget this when the talk is clever. The Sacred Order. May Sarton. ImOP

Never Get a Lickin' till I Go Down to Bimini, *with music. Unknown.* OuSiCo

Never Get Out! John Galsworthy. OtMeF

Never Give All the Heart. W. B. Yeats. ChMo; CMP; EnL; EnLit; GTML; GTSL; HBV

Never go to France. French and English. Thomas Hood. ERP

Never had child a more adventurous life. Iulus. Eleanor Glenn Wallis. NePoAm-2

Never has ship sailed on that sea. The Stone-Age Sea. Helen Hoyt. NP

Never have I found a place, or a season, without beauty. The Desert. C. E. S. Wood. *Fr.* The Poet in the Desert. AnEnPo

Never heard happier laughter. Long View. Genevieve Taggard. MoAmPo

Never held marble in its trust. Pitt and Fox. Sir Walter Scott. *Fr.* Marmion. BCEP

Never Hurt the Proud. Marguerite Wilkinson. BoFr; TBM

Never in a costly palace did I rest on golden bed. Henry van Dyke. *Fr.* The Toiling of Felix. ChIP

Never lived a Yankee yet. In the Catacombs. Harlan Hoge Ballard. BOHV

Never Love Unless You Can. Thomas Campion. *See* Advice to a Girl.

Never man again may swear, things shall be as once they were. There Is Nothing Strange. Archilochus. GrL; OxBG

Never May the Fruit Be Plucked. Edna St. Vincent Millay. CrMA

Never mind how the pedagogue proses. To Fanny. Thomas Moore. HBV

Never mind me, Uncle Jared, never mind my bleeding breast! The Ensign Bearer. *Unknown.* PTA-2

Never mind, old fellow, we'll just wait. A Hunter. Ray Ellis. CAG

Never mind the clouds which gather. I Have Always Found It So. Birdie Bell. BLRP

Never mind the day we left, or the way the women clung to us. The Klondike. E. A. Robinson. PaA; PAH

Never More. *See* Nevermore.

Never, my heart, is there enough of living. Never Enough of Living. Léonie Adams. MOAP

Never, Never Can Nothingness Come. Norma Keating. GoYe

Never, never did I see. Modest Blush. Ibn Abd Rabbihi. MooP

Never, never may the fruit be plucked from the bough. Never May the Fruit Be Plucked. Edna St. Vincent Millay. CrMA

Never Night Again. Lilian Cox. ChIP; MaRV

Never No More. James K. Baxter. AnNZ
Never on earth. Wings. Joseph Easton McDougall. MM
Never on this side of the grave again. A Life's Parallels. Christina Rossetti. PoEL-5; TriL
Never once—since the world began. God's Sunshine. John Oxenham. WBLP
Never Pharaoh's Night. In the Desert. Herman Melville. MeRV
Never presume that in this marble stable. The Brass Horse. Drummond Allison. FaBoTw
Never-resting Sun, The. Mimnermus, *tr. fr. Greek by* Gilbert Murray. OxBG
Never return in August to what you love. Return. Bernice Kenyon. NV
Never Said a Mumbalin' Word, *with music. Unknown.* ABF; TrAS
Never say die. Well-packed Wisdom. Benjamin Franklin. *Fr.* Poor Richard's Almanac. StaSt
Never Seek to Tell Thy Love. Blake. *See* Love's Secret.
"Never shall a young man." For Anne Gregory. W. B. Yeats. EnLP; ExPo; FaBoMo; FaFP; GTBS-W; InPo; LiTL; LiTM; LoBV; LoPo; RiBV; SeCeV; SiTL
Never shall I forget the wondrous night. The Departure. Carl Christian Bagger. BoDS
Never since our bad earth became one sea. Tennyson. *Fr.* Aylmer's Field. VLEP
Never sings a city-robin on the gray-stone window-ledges. Returning. Ruth Guthrie Harding. HBV
Never stoops the soaring vulture. The Ghosts. Longfellow. *Fr.* The Song of Hiawatha. DaM; HOAH; LoBV
Never Such Love. Robert Graves. FaBoEn
Never, surely, was holier man. Ambrose. James Russell Lowell. TCAP
Never talk to me of waltzing it. Waltzing It. William Thomas Moncrieff. UnS
Never tell a young thing. The Little Gift of Laughter. Kathleen Millay. BAP
Never the nightingale. Dirge. Adelaide Crapsey. AV; BAP; HBV; NP; OBAV; VOD
Never the spirit was born; the spirit shall cease to be never. *Unknown. Fr.* Bhagavad-Gita. MaRV
Never the Time and the Place. Robert Browning. AnFE; BMEP; BPN; EmBrPo; EnLoPo; EPN; EPP; EtPaEn; GEPC; HBV; LoPo; PoVP; ViPo; VLEP
Never the tramp of foot or horse. Farewell to Anactoria. Sappho. AWP; LiTW
Never think she loves him wholly. Appraisal. Sara Teasdale. MAP; MoAmPo
Never to see a nation born. The Great Virginian. James Russell Lowell. *Fr.* Under the Old Elm. PGD; PSO
Never Too Late, *sels.* Robert Greene.
 Description of a Shepherd and His Wife, The. EV-1
 Infida's Song. AtBAP; OBSC
 ("Sweet Adon', dar'st not glance thine eye?") LO
 Palmer's Ode, The. EV-1; OBSC; SiCE; TuPP
Never Trouble Trouble. Fannie Windsor. PTA-1
Never until our souls are strong enough. Sonnet. E. A. Robinson. PoLFOT
Never until the mankind making. A Refusal to Mourn the Death, by Fire, of a Child in London. Dylan Thomas. AtBAP; ChMP; CoBMV; FaBoEn; FaFP; GTBS-W; InPo; LiTB; LiTG; LiTM; MaPo; MoAB; MoPo; MoVE; NeBP; OAEP (2d ed.); Po; SeCePo; UnPo (3d ed.); WaaP
Never was I less alone than being alone. To His Posterity. Henry Parker, Baron Morley. TuPP
Never was there a man much uglier. Vain Gratuities. E. A. Robinson. MaPo; NePA
Never was there path our childhood used to roam. New Horizons. Sidney Royse Lysaght. HBMV
Never we needed Thee so sore. In Time of Need. Katharine Tynan. TrPWD
Never Weather-beaten Sail [More Willing Bent to Shore]. Thomas Campion. ChTr; CoEV; EG; ElL; GoBC; OBSC; OxBoCh; PoEL-2; SiCE; TriL; TuPP
 (O Come Quickly!) GTSE; MaRV; OBEV
Never wedding, ever wooing. The Maid's Remonstrance. Thomas Campbell. LPS-1
Never Will You Hold Me. Charles Divine. HBMV; PR; TBM
Never will you know his fabulous head. Torso of an Archaic Apollo. Rainer Maria Rilke. MeRV
Never would I lose thee! Love. Zuleika. Goethe. BoFr
Never yet was a springtime. Awakening. Margaret E. Sangster. AA; PTA-2
Nevermore, The. Dante Gabriel Rossetti. *See* Superscription, A.
Nevermore/ Shall the shepherds of Arcady follow. The God-Maker, Man. Don Marquis. HBV; OBAV; QS; WGRP
Nevermore Alone. Elizabeth Barrett Browning. *See* Sonnets from the Portuguese: "Go from me."
Never More, Sailor. Walter de la Mare. EtS
Nevermore, singing will you go now. Francis Ledwidge [*or* Elegy for the Irish Poet Francis Ledwidge]. Grace Hazard Conkling. SBMV; VOD
Never more will I protest. The Indifferent. Francis Beaumont. ElL; ElSeCe; EnLit; HBV
Never More Will the Wind. Hilda Doolittle ("H. D."). *Fr.* Hymen. TrGrPo
 (Hymen.) ViBoPo
Never more with flapping wing. To a Dead Cockerel. Anyte. GrR
Neverness; or, The One Ship Beached on One Far Distant Shore. Margaret Avison. BoCaPo
Nevertheless. Gustav Davidson. GoYe
Nevertheless. Marianne Moore. MoAB; OxBA; SeCeV
New Age, The. Frederic Lawrence Knowles. MaRV
 (Victory Which Is Peace, The.) BoHiPo; OQP; QP-1
New America, The. Aleksandr Blok, *tr. fr. Russian by* V. de S. Pinto. BoRS
New and Old. Austin Dobson. VLEP
New Arrival, The. George Washington Cable. AA; HBV; PA; PECK
New Art of Making Plays, The. Lope de Vega, *tr. fr. Spanish by* Lord Holland. AnSpL-1
New Baby Calf, The. Edith H. Newlin. TiPo
New Ballad, A. *Unknown.* PAH
New Ballade of the Marigolde, A. William Forrest. CoMu
 (Marigold, The.) PoLi
New Balow, The. *Unknown. See* Balow.
New Banner, The. Katrina Trask. PEDC
New Bath Guide, The, *sels.* Christopher Anstey.
 Letter Containing a Panegyric on Bath, VI, *abr.* OBEC
 Taste and Spirit, X. CEP
New beauties push her from the stage. The Aging Coquette. John Trumbull. *Fr.* The Progress of Dulness. AnNE
New Bedford and Nantucket launched the traders and the whalers. The Clipper Ships. Edgar Lee Masters. TCAP
New Birth, The. Jones Very. EOAH
New Book, The. Elizabeth Turner. OTPC (1923 ed.)
New-born. *See* Newborn.
New Brooms. Robert Wilson. *Fr.* The Three Ladies of London. ElL; EM-1
 (Conscience's Song.) OBSC
New Carol of Our Lady, A. *Unknown.* AnEC
New Castalia, The. William Hayes Ward. AA
New Challenge, The. Whittier. MaRV
New Charon, The. Robert Herrick. ReEn
New Chitons for Old Gods, *sel.* David McCord.
 Euterpe; a Symmetric. UnS
New Church, The. Ivan Alekseyevich Bunin, *tr. fr. Russian by* Babette Deutsch. TrRV
New Church Organ, The. Will M. Carleton. BOHV; LPS-3
New City, The. Marguerite Wilkinson. MaRV, *abr.*; OQP; PEDC; QP-2
New Colossus, The. Emma Lazarus. FaFP; FaPON; MaRV; PGD; TreFS
 "Give me your tired, your poor," *sel.* PoFr
 (Inscription on the Statue of Liberty.) PaA; PoRL
New-come. *See* Newcome.
New Commandment, The ("He riseth from supper"). St. John, XIII: 4–38, Bible, *N.T.* BoFr
New Commandment, The ("This is my commandment, That ye love one another"). St. John, XV: 12–13, 15, Bible, *N.T.* BoFr
New Construction; Bath Iron Works. G. Stanley Koehler. NePoAm-2
New Corn. T'ao Ch'ien, *tr. fr. Chinese by* Arthur Waley. Twelve Poems, 9. TrCh
New Courtly Sonnet of the Lady Greensleeves, A. *Unknown. See* My Lady Greensleeves.
New Covenant, A. Jeremiah, XXXI: 31–34, Bible, *O.T.* GrCo-2
New Crucifixion. Earl Bigelow Brown. ChIP
New Crucifixion. Thomas Curtis Clark. ChIP
New Crusade, The. Katharine Lee Bates. CV; MC
New-dated from the terms that reappear. To Oxford. Gerard Manley Hopkins. *Fr.* Low Sunday and Monday. NBE
New Day, The, *sels.* Richard Watson Gilder.
 After-Song. AA; LBAP
 Prelude: "Night was dark, though sometimes a faint star, The." HBV
 (Dawn.) LPS-2; SN
 Song: "Not from the whole wide world I chose thee," Pt. IV, Song IV.
 (Songs, 1.) AA; LBAP
 Song: "Years have flown since I knew thee first," Pt. IV, Song VII. BAP
 (Songs, 2.) AA; LBAP
New Day, The. Fenton Johnson. BANP
New Day. Mikhail Lukonin, *tr. fr. Russian by* Jack Lindsay. RuPo
New Day. Harold Monro. ChMo; CMP
New Day, The. Elizabeth Selden. BoFr
New Dixie, The. Maria Louisa Eve. BlG
New doth the sun appear. Change Should Breed Change.

William Drummond of Hawthornden. *Fr.* Flowers of Sion. BSV; EBSV; MeRV; OBEV; OxBoCh
New Dreams for Old. Thomas Curtis Clark. OQP; QP-2
New Dreams for Old. Cale Young Rice. HBV; SBMV
New Duckling, The. Alfred Noyes. *Fr.* Touchstone on a Bus. BoTP; FaPON; MPB
New Dummy, The. Geoffrey Grigson. LiTM (rev. ed.)
New Dynamo. Gerald Raftery. PoMa
New Earth, A. John Oxenham. MaRV
New England. James Gates Percival. AA; APW
New England. George Denison Prentice. AA
New England. E. A. Robinson. AmP; CoV; FaBoEn; InPo; MAP; MoAB; MoAmPo; MOAP; MoVE; OxBA; PoeMoYo; WhC
New England. Philip Henry Savage. OBAV
New England Church, A. Wilson Agnew Barrett. WGRP
New England Fog. Gertrude Callaghan. JKCP (1955 ed.)
New England Gentleman's Epitaph, A. Thomas Dudley. BAV
New England Gothic. Rachel Field. QS
New England in Winter. Whittier. *Fr.* Snow-bound. LPS-2
New England Is New England Is New England. Brenda Heloise Green. GoYe
New England Primer, The. *Unknown.* HiLiAm
New England Steeple. Frances Frost. QS
New Englanders Are Maples. Robert P. Tristram Coffin. AnNE
New England's Annoyances. *Unknown.* AnAmPo, *abr.*; BoHiPo, *abr.*; DDA; LA, *abr.*; PAH
(Forefathers' Song.) *Unknown.* AnNE; APW
New England's Chevy Chase. Edward Everett Hale. DDA; HBV; HBVY; PAH; PoRL; YaD
New England's Crisis, *sels.* Benjamin Tompson.
"Not ink, but bloud [*or* blood] and tears." AnAmPo; LA
Prologue: "Times wherein old Pompion, The." APW; IAP, *abr.*; TCAP
(Alarming Progress of Luxury in New England, The.) BAV
New England's Dead. Isaac McLellan, Jr. AA; PEDC
New England's Growth. William Bradford. PAH
New England's poet, rich in love as years. To Whittier [*or* To John G. Whittier]. James Russell Lowell. CoBA; PEOR
New English Canaan, *sel.* Thomas Morton.
Song[e], The: "Drink[e] and be merry, merry, merry boy[e]s." AmPP; IAP
New Every Morning. "Susan Coolidge." *See* Begin Again.
New every morning now the clerk docks off. Summer Holidays. W. R. Rodgers. LiTB
New Excavations. Leonora Speyer. InP
New Ezekiel, The. Emma Lazarus. AA; AnAmPo; LA
New Faces, The. W. B. Yeats. MoVE
New Farm Tractor. Carl Sandburg. FaPON
New Fern, A. "A." PRWS
New Freedom, The. Olive Tilford Dargan. HBMV
New Friends and Old Friends. Joseph Parry. *See* Friends Old and New.
New friends are no friends; how can that be true? Of Friendship. Sir John Harington. SiCE
New George Washington, The. *Unknown.* WOAH
New Gethsemane. Hazel M. Kerr. ChIP
New Ghost, The. Fredegond Shove. ChMP; HBMV; MoVE; NV; OxBoCh; TwCV
New God, The. Witter Bynner. *Fr.* The New World. WGRP
New God, The. James Oppenheim. SBMV; WGRP
New God, The; a Miracle, *sel.* Lascelles Abercrombie.
Margaret's Song. GTBS; LBBV; PoeT
New Guinea Lament. J. P. McAuley. BoAV
New Hampshire. T. S. Eliot. Landscapes, I. FaBoCh; KN; LoBV; LoGBV; ThWaDe
New Hampshire. Robert Frost. AmPP (4th ed.); CoV
New Hampshire Boy, A. Morris Bishop. HBMV
New Hampshire Farm Woman. Rachel Graham. GoYe
New Hampshire, February. Richard Eberhart. FiMAP
New Hampshire Sexton. James A. Notopoulos. CAG
New Haven. Frederick Scheetz Jones. *See* On the Democracy of Yale.
New Heart, The. *Unknown, tr. fr. Chinese.* WGRP
New Heaven, A. John Gould Fletcher. MAP; MoAmPo
New Heaven, New War [*or* Warre]. Robert Southwell. *See* Come to Your Heaven, You Heavenly Choirs.
New Hellas, The. Irwin Edman. InMe
New Horizons. Sidney Royse Lysaght. HBMV
New House, The. Joseph Easton McDougall. CaP
New House, The. Edward Thomas. GTML; HBMV; MoAB; MoBrPo; OBEV (new ed.); POTE; PrWP; TwCV
New House a-Gettèn Wold, The. William Barnes. RO
New Household, A. Longfellow. *Fr.* The Hanging of the Crane, Pt. I. GN
New Houses. Grace Noll Crowell. PEDC
New Hunting Song, A. *Unknown.* CoMu
New Hymns for Solitude, *sel.* Edward Dowden.
"I found Thee in my heart, O Lord." TrPWD
New Idol, A. Laurence Binyon. PoFr
New Inn, The, *sels.* Ben Jonson.
It Was a Beauty That I Saw, *fr.* IV, iv. OBS; ReEn; SeCL; SeEP
(Lovel's Song.) TrGrPo
(Vision of Beauty, A.) LPS-1
"What else/ Is love, but the most noble, pure affection," *fr.* III, ii. LO
New Interlude of Vice, Containing the History of Horestes, A. John Pickering. *See* Horestes.
New Jersey city where I did dwell. The Butcher Boy. *Unknown.* BaBo
New Jerusalem, The. Revelation, XXI, Bible, *N.T.* EM-1 (1–14, 22–27); TrGrPo (1–6, 10–12, 21, 23–25)
New Jerusalem, A [*or* The]. Blake. *See* And Did Those Feet in Ancient Time.
New Jerusalem, The. *Unknown, at. to* "F. B. P.," *after the Latin* Urbs Beata Hierusalem. EV-1, *longer vers.*; HBV; LPS-2, *diff. vers., at. to* David Dickson; OBEV; OxBoCh; ViBoPo, *longer vers.*
(Heavenly City, The.) CBOV; GoBC
(Hierusalem.) OBSC
(Hierusalem, My Happie Home.) AtBAP; PoEL-2
(Jerusalem.) CoEV; FaBoCh; LoGBV
(Jerusalem My Happy Home.) EIL, *longer vers.*; MaRV, *shorter vers.*; SiCE, *longer vers.*; WGRP
(Mater Hierusalem Civitas Sancta Dei.) MeRV
(O Mother Dear, Jerusalem.) OlF, *at. to* David Dickson; WGRP
(Song Made by F. B. P., A.) CoMu
New Jewish Hospital at Hamburg, The. Heine, *tr. fr. German by* Charles Godfrey Leland. TrJP
"New King Arrives in His Capital by Air . . ."—Daily Newspaper. John Betjeman. OxBoLi; WhC
New Law, The. Blake. *See* Jesus Was Sitting in Moses' Chair.
New Leaf, A. Carrie Shaw Rice. PTA-2
New Leaf, The [*or* A]. Kathleen Wheeler, *wr. at. to* Helen Field Fischer. BLRP; MaRV; OQP; PGD; PoToHe; PSO; QP-1; WBLP
New Legends. Robert Graves. AtBAP
New Liberty Bell, The. "H. B. C." PEOR
New Life. Amelia Josephine Burr. HBV
New Life, The. Witter Bynner. LBMV; VOD
New Life, The. Dante. *See* Vita Nuova, La.
New Limericks. *Unknown.* StaSt
New London, The. Dryden. *Fr.* Annus Mirabilis. FaBoCh; OBS
(London.) SeCePo
New Love. Richard Aldington. *Fr.* Epigrams. PFE
New Love and the Old, The. Arthur O'Shaughnessy. *See* Song: "I made another garden, yea."
New Love, New Life. Amy Levy. OBVV
New Married Couple, The; or, A Friendly Debate between the Country Farmer and His Buxome Wife. *Unknown.* CoMu
New Mars, The. Florence Earle Coates. PGD
New Memorial Day, The. Albert Bigelow Paine. DD; HH; MDAH; OQP; PEDC; PSO; QP-1
New mercies, new blessings, new light on the way. A New Year Wish. Frances Ridley Havergal. BLRP
New Mexico. Polly Chase Boyden. TiPo
New Mexico and Arizona. George Canterbury. PoOW
New Mistress, The. A. E. Housman. A Shropshire Lad, XXXIV. MoBrPo (1950 ed.); PoVP
New Moon, The. Bryant. OTPC
New Moon, The. Eliza Lee Follen. BoChLi; PPL; RAR; TVC; TVSH
New Moon. Tu Fu, *tr. fr. Chinese by* Kenneth Rexroth. OnPC
New moon, The. Autumn Moon. Wang I. PoHN
New moon hangs like an ivory bugle, The. The Penny Whistle. Edward Thomas. MBP; MoAB; MoBrPo
New moon hung in the sky, The. Prescience. Thomas Bailey Aldrich. AA; OBVV
New moon in the sky. Haiku. Basho. Po
New moony light. Said of the Earth and the Moon. Léonie Adams. TCPD
New Morality. George Canning, John Hookham Frere, *and others.* CEP
New Moses, The. M. K. Joseph. AnNZ
New Mother. Anita Laurie Cushing. MotAn
New-mown hay smell and wind of the plain. Population Drifts. Carl Sandburg. OxBA
New National Anthem. *Unknown.* CoSo; CSF
New National Hymn, A. F. Marion Crawford. HH; IDAH; PAH; PEOR
New Negro, The. James Edward McCall. CDC
New Neighbor, The. Rose Fyleman. GaP; TiPo
New neighbors came to the corner house. Clean Curtains. Carl Sandburg. TCAP; WoL
New Order of Chivalry, A. Thomas Love Peacock. CenHV
New Orleans. Lola Ridge. MAP; MoAmPo (1942 ed.); TBM

New Orleans Balcony, A. Dorothy Haight. CAW
New Orleans jail, no jail at all. Po' Boy. *Unknown.* ABF
New Pastoral, The, *sel.* Thomas Buchanan Read.
Blennerhasset's Island. PAH
New Patriotism, A. Chauncey R. Piety. PGD
New Philosophy, The. John Donne. *Fr.* An Anatomy of the World: The First Anniversary. ExPo
New Physician, The. Stephen Chalmers. HBMV
New Poet, A. William Canton. BMEP; HBV; VA
New Prince, New Pomp. Robert Southwell. AnEC; CenL; COAH; EV-1; GN; MaRV; OBSC; OHIP; ReIE; SDH; SiCE; StJW; ThWaDe; TriL; TuPP
("Behold, a silly tender babe.") EG
(Humble Pomp.) GoTP
New Roof, The. Francis Hopkinson. PAH
New season brought sure the visible good. Restoration. Woodridge Spears. GoYe
New Shakespeare, A. Andrew Lang. CenHV
New Shoes. Marjorie Seymour Watts. PCH
New Shoes. Alice Wilkins. GFA; SUS; TiPo
New shoes, new shoes. Choosing Shoes. ffrida Wolfe. BrR; GoBP; SUS; TiPo
New Shoots Scatter Their Scent Far Away, The. August, Graf von Platen, *tr. fr. German by* Edwin Morgan. AnGP
New Sights. *Unknown.* BoTP
New Sinai, The. Arthur Hugh Clough. BPN; PoVP; ViPo; VLEP
New-slain Knight, The. *Unknown.* ESPB
New Snow. Catharine Bryant Rowles. YeAr
New Song, The. Arthur Gordon Field. PGD; PSO
New Song, A. John Gay. BOHV; InMe
(New Song of New Similes, A.) SiTL
New Song, A. Joseph Stansbury. PAH
New Song, A ("As near beauteous Boston lying"). *Unknown.* PAH
New Song Called the Curling of the Hair, A. *Unknown.* CoMu
New Song Called the Gaspee, A. *Unknown.* PAH
New Song Composed on the Death of Lord Nelson, A. *Unknown. See* Death of Nelson, The.
New Song Entitled the Warming Pan, A. *Unknown.* CoMu
New Song of an Orange, A. *Unknown.* CoMu
New Song of New Similes, A. John Gay. *See* New Song, A.
New Song of Wood's Halfpence, A. Swift. OxBoLi
New Song on Lord Nelson's Victory at Copenhagen, A. *Unknown.* SG
New Song on Parker the Delegate, A. *Unknown.* SG
New Song on the Birth of the Prince of Wales, A. *Unknown.* CoMu
New Song, A; or, Lilliburlero. Thomas, Lord Wharton. *See* Lilli Burlero.
New Song to an Old Air. Victor Hugo, *tr. fr. French by* Harry Curwen. LiA
New Song to an Old Tune, A. *Unknown.* PAH
New Spoon River, The, *sels.* Edgar Lee Masters.
Arielle Grierson. ChMo; CMP
Benjamin Franklin Hazard. TCAP
Bertrand Hume. LEAP
Chandler Nicholas. NAMP
Cleanthus Trilling. LEAP
("Urge of the seed, The.") OQP; QP-1
D'Arcy Singer. ChMo; CMP
Euripides Alexopoulos. ChMo; CMP
Henry Cogdal. ChMo; CMP; TCAP
Henry Ditch. LEAP
Henry Zoll, the Miller. TCAP
Howard Lamson. LEAP; NAMP; ViBoPo
Jay Hawkins. ChMo; CMP
Julius Brink. ChMo; CMP
Levy Silver. ChMo; CMP
Linford Newman. GrCo-2
Lionel Grierson. ChMo; CMP
Louise Hedeen. LEAP
Mayor Marston. ChMo; CMP
Morgan Oakley. LEAP
Nathan Suffrin. ChMo; CMP
New Start, A. *Unknown.* OQP; QP-1
New Temples. Lexie Dean Robertson. OQP; QP-2
New Tenants, The. E. A. Robinson. NP
New Testament, The. Thomas Russell. TreFS
New Testament, Revised Edition. Sister Mary Catherine. ISi
New Theology, A. Euripides, *tr. fr. Greek by* Hugh Owen Meredith. *Fr.* Heracles. GrR
New Things and Old. Sister Mary Madeleva. GoBC
New Time. *Unknown.* BLRP
New Tower, The. *Unknown, tr. fr. Chinese.* WhP
New Triads. Constance Davies. MoWP
New Trinity, The. Edwin Markham. BoFr; PGD
New Version, The. William James Lampton. BOHV; PA
New Vestments, The. Edward Lear. BOHV; BoN; OnPP
New Victory, The. Margaret Widdemer. AOAH; WGRP
New View, The. John Holmes. MiAP
New War Song by Sir Peter Parker, A. *Unknown.* PAH
New-washed moon drew up from the sea's dark rim, The. Atlantic Moonrise. Vivian L. Virtue. PoNe
New Wife and the Old, The. Whittier. APW
New Wind a-Blowin', A, *with music.* Langston Hughes. TrAS
New Wine, Old Bottles. Colin Newbury. AnNZ
New Woman, The. Juvenal, *tr. fr. Latin by* William Gifford. *Fr.* Satires, VI. RoL
New Words for an Old Song. Babette Deutsch. NePoAm
"New words, new metres, new emotions—all." Modernity. F. L. Lucas. LO
New Words to the Tune of "O'Donnel Abu." Jim Connell. OnYI
New World, The, *sel.* Louis James Block.
Final Struggle, The. PAH
New World, The, *sels.* Witter Bynner.
"Celia was laughing. Hopefully I said." NV
Grieve Not for Beauty. NP
"Grieve not for the invisible, transported brow." LEAP; NV
New God, The. WGRP
"Somebody called Walt Whitman." InP
New World. Brewster Ghiselin. MoVE
New World, A. Shelley. *See* Chorus: "World's great age begins anew, The."
New World, The. Jones Very. AA; AnNE; APW
New world hath its wonders, The. Richard Henry Wilde. *Fr.* Hesperia. BAV
New Worlds. Milton. *Fr.* Paradise Lost, III. OBS
(Panorama, The, *shorter sel.*) WHA
("Satan from hence now on the lower stair.") BrBE
New World's sweetest singer, The. Time may lay. Longfellow. Craven Langstroth Betts. DD; GA
New Year, The. Augustus Henry Baldwin. *Fr.* On the Threshold. DD
New Year. Marie Barton. PraP
New Year, The. Donald E. Cooke. MPB (1956 ed.)
New Year, The. George Cooper. DD; PEDC; PEOR
New Year, The. Charles Cotton. CEP; GoTL; OBS
New Year, The. Dinah Maria Mulock Craik. BrR; DD; HH; MeMeAg; MPB; OTPC (1946 ed.); PCH; PTA-2; YeAr
New Year, A. Mary Carolyn Davies. OQP; QP-2; YeAr
New Year. Fujita, *tr. fr. Japanese by* Lois J. Erickson. SoLD
New Year, The. Lillian Gilchrist Gard. OQP; PSO; QP-1
New Year, The. Homera Homer-Dixon. BLRP; PraP
New Year, The. Frederick Lucian Hosmer. GrCo-2
New Year, The. Omar Khayyám, *tr. fr. Persian by* Edward Fitzgerald. *Fr.* The Rubáiyát. OnPM
New Year, The. Tsurue Miyauchi, *tr. fr. Japanese by* Lois J. Erickson. SoLD
New Year. John J. Moment. MaRV
New Year, The. Roy G. Pearce. PoP
New Year, The. Horatio Nelson Powers. OQP; PoRL; PoToHe; QP-1
New Year, A. Margaret E. Sangster. DD, *abr.*; PEDC; PEOR
New Year, A. Dora Sigerson Shorter. YeAr
New Year. Stephen Spender. AWP
New Year, The. J. D. Templeton. OQP; PGD; PSO; QP-1
New Year, The. Tennyson. *See* In Memoriam A. H. H.: "Ring out, wild bells . . ."
New Year ("Dear Master, for this coming year"). *Unknown.* PraP
New Year, The ("I am the little New Year, ho, ho!"). *Unknown.* BoTP
New Year, The ("Oh! I'm the New Year"). *Unknown.* BoTP
New Year ("Over the threshold a gallant newcomer"). *Unknown.* HH
New Year, The ("With gladness hail the dawning year"). *Unknown.* PEDC
New Year. Thomas Wearing. MaRV
New Year, a New Year, a Child Was Yborn, A. *Unknown.* AnEC
New Year Bride, A. Tamiko Yamamuro, *tr. fr. Japanese by* Lois J. Erickson. SoLD
New Year Carol, A: "Here we bring new water." *Unknown.* AtBAP; BoTP; CH; MeRV; OxBoLi; ThWaDe
New Year Ditty. Christina Rossetti. PoRL
New year [*or* yeare], forth looking out of Janus' [*or* Ianus] gate. Amoretti, IV. Spenser. PeBoSo; ReEn
New year hath come in sight, The. The Eighteenth Song. Hadewijch. LiTW; LyMA
New Year Is a Banner, The. Margaret E. Sangster. PEDC
New Year Is Begun, The. *Unknown.* AnEC
New Year Letter, *sel.* W. H. Auden.
"O Unicorn among the cedars." ChMo; FaBoEn
New Year met me somewhat sad. New Year Ditty. Christina Rossetti. PoRL
New Year Prayer. Edgar Daniel Kramer. PEDC; PraP

New Year Prayer, A. Theodore Parker. *See* Higher Good, The.
New Year Prayer, A. Laura Simmons. LPS-1
New Year Prayer, A. *Unknown. See* Good Creed, A.
New Year Song. Emily Huntington Miller. DD; HH; PoRL
New Year Wish, A. Frances Ridley Havergal. BLRP
New Year Wish, A. *Unknown.* BLRP
New Years and Old. Maud Frazer Jackson. PGD; PSO
New Year's Burden, A. Dante Gabriel Rossetti. AtBAP
New Year's Chimes. Francis Thompson. AlDL
New Year's Day. Richard Crashaw. SeEP
New Year's Day. Rachel Field. TiPo
New Year's Day. Robert Lowell. NePoEA
New Year's Day. *Unknown.* PEDC; PEOR
New Year's Days. Celia Standish. BoTP
New Year's Eve. F. A. Bartleson. PAP
New Year's Eve, *sel.* John Davidson.
Imagination. MBP; MoBrPo
New Year's Eve. Wyn Griffith. MoWP
New Year's Eve. Thomas Hardy. MBP; MoBrPo; POTT; PreP
New Year's Eve. Robinson Jeffers. CoV
New Year's Eve. H. B. Mallalieu. WaP
New Year's Eve ("If you're waking, call me early"). Tennyson. *Fr.* The May Queen. OTPC (1923 ed.)
New Year's Eve ("Ring out, wild bells"). Tennyson. *See* In Memoriam A. H. H.: "Ring out, wild bells, to the wild sky."
New Year's Eve, 1850. James Russell Lowell. MeRV
New Year's Eve—Midnight. Frederika Richardson Macdonald. VA
New Year's Eve, 1913. Gordon Bottomley. BMEP; LBBV
New Year's Eve, 1938. John Frederick Nims. MiAP
New Year's Gift to Brian Lord Bishop of Sarum, A. William Cartwright. EV-2; MePo
New Year's Gift to the King, A. William Dunbar. EBSV
New Year's Guest, A. Eliza F. Moriarty. PEOR
New Year's Hymn. Robert Browning. *See* All Service Ranks the Same with God.
New Year's Hymn. Matthías Jochumsson, *ad. fr. Icelandic by* Kemp Malone. IcP
New Year's Morning. *Unknown.* PraP
New Year's Promise, A. *Unknown.* BLRP
New Year's Resolve. Ella Wheeler Wilcox. PEOR
New Year's Thoughts. Lillian Gray. OQP; QP-2
New Year's Wish, A. "J. H. S." BLRP
New Year's Wishes. Frances Ridley Havergal. BLRP
New-Yeeres Gift, The, or Circumcisions Song, Sung to the King in the Presence at White Hall. Robert Herrick. SeCV-1
New York. "Æ." OBMV
New York. Richard Watson Gilder. BoHiPo
New York. Arthur Guiterman. PaA
New York City. George Abbe. GoYe
New York City. Maxwell Bodenheim. HBMV
New York—December, 1931. Babette Deutsch. ImOP
New York, it would be easy to revile. New York City. Maxwell Bodenheim. HBMV
New York Skyscraper, A, *sel.* James Oppenheim.
"O sprawling city! worlds in a world!" MaRV
New York, with your loud noise. Song of the Scarlet Banners over John Reed. Marya Zaturenska. *Fr.* Elegies over John Reed. BAP
New Zealand, *sel.* Hubert Church.
"Ye wandering winds that from your threshing floor." AnNZ
New Zealand. William Pember Reeves. BoAu
New Zealand Comforts. John Barr of Craigielee. AnNZ
New Zealand Regret, A. Eleanor Elizabeth Montgomery. VA
New-born, The. Helen Hoyt. BAP; NP
New-born Baby's Song, The. Frances Cornford. DiM
Newborn Death. Dante Gabriel Rossetti. The House of Life, XCIX–C. BPN; EmBrPo; PoVP; ViPo
New-born Year, The. Richard Hovey. GrCo-2
New-come Chief, The. James Russell Lowell. *See* Washington ("Beneath our consecrated elm").
Newcomer, you who look in Rome for Rome. Sonnet. Joachim du Bellay. FoS
Newcomer's Wife, The. Thomas Hardy. PoFS
Newer Vainglory, The. Alice Meynell. JKCP; MaRV; OQP; QP-2; QS
Newes from Virginia. Richard Rich. BAV; PAH
Newest moon is not so far, The. Neighbors. Anne Blackwell Payne. GFA
Newest Thing in Christmas Carols, The. *Unknown.* COAH; PA
Newfoundland. E. J. Pratt. TwCaPo
Newly Discovered "Homeric" Hymn, A. Charles Olson. NeAP
Newly-wedded, The. Winthrop Mackworth Praed. ERP; HBV; MaRV; VA
Newlyweds. Nikolai Alekseyevich Nekrasov, *tr. fr. Russian by* Babette Deutsch. TrRV
Newman. George N. Shuster. JKCP (1926 ed.)
Newport Beach. Henry T. Tuckerman. LPS-2
Newport Street, E. Douglas Goldring. HBMV
News. Godfrey Elton. ReTS
News, The. Charles Sprague. *Fr.* Curiosity. AA
News. Thomas Traherne. GTBS-W; MePo; OBEV; SeCV-2; SeEP
(On News.) EPS; FaBoEn
News for the Delphic Oracle. W. B. Yeats. CoBMV; LiTB; LiTM; MoPo; OAEP (2d ed.)
News frae Moidart cam' yestreen, The. Wha'll Be King but Charlie. Lady Nairne. EBSV; EV-3
News from a foreign [*or* forein *or* forrein] country came. News [*or* On News]. Thomas Traherne. EPS; FaBoEn; GTBS-W; MePo; OBEV; SeCV-2; SeEP
News from Home. Thad Stem, Jr. NoCaPo (rev. ed.)
News from Home? Wang Wei, *tr. fr. Chinese by* Henry H. Hart. PoHN
News from Plymouth, *sel.* Sir William Davenant.
"O thou that sleep'st like pig in straw," *fr.* III, i. CenL; EG; ElSeCe; InvP
(Song.) SeCL; SeEP
News from the Court. David Wagoner. NePoAm-2
News from the Heavens! Nicholas Breton. PeBoSo
(Rare News.) ReIE
News from Yorktown. Lewis Worthington Smith. MC; PAH
News is yellowing in the rain, The. The Paper in the Meadow. Oscar Williams. PG (1955 ed.)
News Item. Dorothy Parker. SiTL; TreF; YaD
(Some Beautiful Letters: News Item.) InMe
News lapped at us out of all, The. The Sirens. Donald Finkel. NePoEA
News! News! Eleanor Farjeon. SiSoSe
News of a Baby. Elizabeth Riddell. BoAV
News of the dead is heard through words of the living. The Speech of the Dead. Anne Ridler. ChMP
News of the Phoenix. A. J. M. Smith. BoCaPo
News of the World I ("Cold shuttered loveless star, skulker in clouds"). George Barker. FaBoMo; LiTB
News of the World II ("In the first year of the last disgrace"). George Barker. FaBoTw; LiTB
News of the World III ("Let her lie naked here, my hand resting"). George Barker. AtBAP; FaBoTw; LiTB; LiTM (rev. ed.)
News of War. Aeschylus. *See* Gathering War Clouds.
News, The! our morning, noon, and evening cry. The News. Charles Sprague. *Fr.* Curiosity. AA
News Reel. *See* Newsreel.
News to the King. Augusta Webster. VA
(Message of Victory, The.) BoHiPo
Newsboy, The. Mrs. E. T. Corbett. PTA-2
Newsboy. Irving Layton. CaP
Newspaper, A. Stephen Crane. War Is Kind, XII. AmP; TCAP
("Newspaper is a collection of half-injustices, A.") CoBA; ViBoPo
Newsreel. C. Day Lewis. MoAB; MoBrPo (1950 ed.); NeMA
News Reel. David Ross. GoYe
Newstead Abbey. Byron. ChER
Newt, The. David McCord. TiPo (1959 ed.)
Newton. Wordsworth. *Fr.* The Prelude, III. ImOP
Newton and Himself. Pope. *Fr.* An Essay on Man, Epistle II. BeR
Newton Fixes the Moon. James Thomson. *Fr.* A Poem Sacred to the Memory of Sir Isaac Newton. BeR
Newton on Light. James Thomson. *Fr.* A Poem Sacred to the Memory of Sir Isaac Newton. BeR
Newton to Einstein. Jeannette Chappell. GoYe
Next at our altar stood a luckless pair. George Crabbe. *Fr.* The Parish Register, II. OBRV
Next, bidding all draw near on bended knees. Pope. *Fr.* The Dunciad, IV. GEPC
Next came Covetousness; I cannot describe him. Avarice. William Langland. *Fr.* The Vision of Piers Plowman. PoLi
Next comes the dull disciple. Byron. *Fr.* English Bards and Scotch Reviewers. OBRV
Next Day, The. Charles Riviere Du Fresny, *tr. fr. French by* Alan Conder. TrFP
Next Day. Rachel Field. *Fr.* A Circus Garland. StVeCh
Next died the Lady who yon Hall possess'd. George Crabbe. *Fr.* The Parish Register: Burials. PoD
Next Door. Mei Yao Ch'en, *tr. fr. Chinese by* Kenneth Rexroth. OnPC
Next, for October, to some sheltered coign. Sonnets of the Months: October. Folgore da San Geminiano. AWP; LyPI
Next his chamber, beside his study. The Bishop's Harp. Robert Mannyng. ACP
Next Marlowe, bathed in the Thespian springs. Christopher Marlowe. Michael Drayton. *Fr.* To Henry Reynolds, of Poets and Poesy. ChTr

Next morn the Baron climbed the tower. Flodden; the March. Sir Walter Scott. *Fr.* Marmion, VI. LH
Next Next Shortest Poem in the World, The. Martha Salemme. SiTL
Next of Kin. H. B. Mallalieu. WaP
Next of Kin. Christina Rossetti. HBV
Next, Please. Philip Larkin. NePoEA
Next Shortest Poem in the World, The. *Unknown.* SiTL
Next these, a troop of buisy spirits press. *Fr.* Absalom and Achitophel, Pt. II. Dryden. CEP; SeCV-2
Next Time. Laura Simmons. PGD; PSO
Next, to a graver tribe we turn our view. Physic. George Crabbe. *Fr.* The Borough. PoP
Next, to a lady I must bid adieu. The Dean's Lady. George Crabbe. LoBV
Next to her chamber, closed by cedar doors. Charoba at Her Bath. Walter Savage Landor. *Fr.* Gebir. RO
Next to of Course God [America I]. E. E. Cummings. AmP; AnNE; ExPo; InPo; LiTM; MOAP; NePA; OxBA; SiTL; TwCV; WaaP; YaD
(147.) PoFr
Next to thee, O fair gazelle. The Arab to the Palm. Bayard Taylor. LPS-2
Next unto Him Was Neptune Pictured. Spenser. *Fr.* The Faerie Queene, III, 11. EtS
Next Voice You Hear, The. Thomas P. McDonnell. JKCP (1955 ed.)
Next War, The. Wilfred Owen. AnEnPo; WaP
Next week they're goin' to lay me off because I'm gettin' old. The Old Quartermaster. Gordon Grant. EtS
Next week will be publish'd (as "Lives" are the rage). "The Living Dog" and "The Dead Lion." Thomas Moore. OBRV
Next Year. Nora Perry. PEOR; PoToHe
Next year the grave grass will cover us. Street Corner College. Kenneth Patchen. MoAmPo
Niagara. Adelaide Crapsey. BAV; MAP; MoAmPo (1942 ed.)
Niagara. Edward F. Garesché. JKCP
Niagara. Nikolaus Lenau, *tr. fr. German by* Dwight Durling. AnGP
Niagara. J. C. Squire. PtOT
Nibble, nibble, little sheep. Sheep. Samuel Hoffenstein. AnAmPo; LA; TrJP
Nibelungenlied. *Unknown. See* Song of the Nibelungs, The.
Nice Correspondent, A. Frederick Locker-Lampson. HBV
Nice Day for a Lynching. Kenneth Patchen. PoNe
Nice Girls Don't Chase the Boys, *with music. Unknown, tr. fr. French by* Janet E. Tobitt. SaSa
Nice Leetle Canadienne, De. William Henry Drummond. CPG
Nice Mister Carrot. Mister Carrot. Dorothy Aldis. GFA
Nice old lady named Tweedle, A. Limerick. *Unknown.* LiBL
Nice to be God. The Convent. Jeanne D'Orge. AnAmPo; LA
Nice Valour, The, *sel.* John Fletcher *and (at.)* Thomas Middleton.
Melancholy, *fr.* III, iii. BCEP; EV-2; GTBS; GTBS-D; GTBS-W; GTSE; GTSL; HBV; LEAP; OBEV
(Hence All You Vain Delights.) AtBAP; CenL; ElSeCe; LPS-1; OAEP; SeCL; TuPP; ViBoPo
(O Sweetest Melancholy.) TrGrPo
(Passionate Man's Song, The.) OBS; SiCE
(Song: "Hence all you vain delights.") CaAE; PoEL-2
(Sweetest Melancholy.) BEL; EPP; LiA
Nice young man about the town, A. I've Got the Giggles Today. A. P. Herbert. FiBHP
Nice young ma-wa-wan, A. The Rattlesnake. *Unknown.* ABF; CoSo; CSF; IHA
Nicest child I ever knew, The. Charles Augustus Fortescue. Hilaire Belloc. OnPP
Nicest place in all the house. In the Study. Burges Johnson. FAOV
Nicest Story, The. Abbie Farwell Brown. HH
Nicholas Ned. Laura E. Richards. *Fr.* Nonsense Verses. RIS
Nicholas Nye. Walter de la Mare. BoChLi; BoTP; HBMV; WP
Nicht Is Neir Gone, The. Alexander Montgomerie. *See* Night Is Near Gone, The.
Nicodemus. Harry Kemp. OQP; QP-2
Nicodemus, *sel.* Andrew Young.
Conversion. MaRV
Nicolas Gatineau. Arthur S. Bourinot. CaP
Nicorn's Dower, The. Peter Hopegood. MoAuPo
Nicoteles. Callimachus, *tr. fr. Greek.* GrL, *tr. by* G. M. Young; GrR, *tr. by* Robert Allason Furness; OxBG, *tr. by* R. C. K. Ensor
(His Son, *tr. by* G. B. Grundy.) AWP; JAWP; WBP
Niels Ebbesen. Nikolai Frederik Severin Grundtvig, *tr. fr. Danish by* Charles W. Stork. BoDS
Niels Ebbeson (A *and* B *vers.*). *Unknown, tr. fr. Danish by* E. M. Smith-Dampier. BoDaBa
Niels Strangeson's Stone Tower. *Unknown, tr. fr. Danish by* E. M. Smith-Dampier. BoDaBa
Nievie nievie nick nack. *Unknown.* OxNR
Nigger. Frank Horne. BANP; CDC
Nigger. Karl Shapiro. OxBA
Nigger Demus. John Charles McNeill. NoCaPo
Nigger mighty happy w'en he layin' by co'n. The Plough-Hands' Song. Joel Chandler Harris. *Fr.* Uncle Remus, His Songs and His Sayings. AA; LHV
Nigh one year ago. Lucifer and Elissa. Philip James Bailey. *Fr.* Festus. VA
Nigh to a grave that was newly made. The Old Sexton. Park Benjamin. AA; HBV
Night. Alcman, *tr. fr. Greek by* H. T. Wade-Gery. GrL; OxBG
(Night and the Plain of Sparta.) GrR
Night. Al-Liss, *tr. fr. Arabic by* A. J. Arberry. MooP
Night, The. Hilaire Belloc. AlDL; HBV; OBEV (new ed.); OBVV; PC; TCPD
Night. William Rose Benét. MAP; MoAmPo; NeMA
Night. Hayyim Nahman Bialik, *tr. fr. Hebrew by* Maurice Samuel. AWP; LiTW
Night ("Still the faint harps"). Blake. *Fr.* The Four Zoas. BoW
Night ("The sun descending in the west"). Blake. *Fr.* Songs of Innocence. AlDL, *st.* 1; AnFE; AtBAP; BCEP; BoTP; BrBE; CaAE; CBE; CBOV; CEP; CH; CoBE; EnRP; EV-3; FaBoBe; FaPON; GoTP; GTBS-D; HBV; HBVY; MaPo; MyFE; OBEC; OBEV; OTPC (1923 ed.); OxBoCh; PoE; RAR, *st.* 1; RIS; SAS; ShBV-3; StaSt, *2 sts.;* WP
Night. Erik Blomberg, *tr. fr. Swedish by* Charles W. Stork. AnSL
Night. Francis William Bourdillon. *See* Night Has a Thousand Eyes, The.
Night. John Brown. OBEC
Night. William Browne. EV-2
Night. Christine Wood Bullwinkle. OTPC (1946 ed.); PCH
Night. Mary Frances Butts. BOL; OTPC (1946 ed.); PRWS
Night. Witter Bynner. *Fr.* To Celia. LoPo; LoPS; NP
Night ("It is the hush of night"). Byron. *See* It Is the Hush of Night.
Night ("'Tis night, when meditation bids us feel"). Byron. *Fr.* Childe Harold's Pilgrimage, II. LPS-2; SN
Night. George Chapman. *Fr.* The Shadow of Night. OBSC
Night. Charles Churchill. *See* Night; an Epistle to Robert Lloyd.
Night. Walter de la Mare. AlDL
Night, The. Lawrence Durrell. *Fr.* Eight Aspects of Melissa. NeBP
Night. Donald Jeffrey Hayes. CDC
Night. Charles Heavysege. BoCaPo
Night. Hermann Hesse, *tr. fr. German by* Ludwig Lewisohn. AWP; JAWP; WBP; TwGV, *tr. by* Herman Salinger
Night, The. Ralph Hodgson. ChMo; CMP
Night. Solomon ibn Gabirol, *tr. fr. Hebrew by* Emma Lazarus. TrJP
Night. Jami, *tr. fr. Persian by* Samuel Robinson. LiTW
Night. Robinson Jeffers. AmPP (3d ed.); AWP; CoBMV; InPo; JAWP; LiTA; MAP; MoAmPo; MOAP; MoPo; NP; OxBA; WBP; WHA
Night. Glyn Jones. NeBP
Night. Leconte de Lisle, *tr. fr. French by* Alan Conder. TrFP
Night, The. Helen Leuty. BoTP
Night. Longfellow. IAP
Night. Lois Weakley McKay. SiSoSe
Night. Sophus Michaëlis, *tr. fr. Danish by* Charles W. Stork. BoDS
Night. Michelangelo, *tr. fr. Italian by* Edwin Morgan. LyPI
Night. "Gabriela Mistral," *tr. fr. Spanish by* Alice Jane McVan. LiTW
Night. James Montgomery. HBV; LPS-2
Night, *sels.* James Oppenheim.
Priest, The. MaRV
(My Father's House.) QS
"When I consider Thy heavens." NV
Night, *sel.* Charles Péguy, *tr. fr. French by* Anne Green *and* Julian Green.
"Nights follow each other and are linked." LiTW
Night. Petrarch, *tr. by* the Earl of Surrey. *See* Complaint by Night of the Lover Not Beloved, A.
Night. Henri de Régnier, *tr. fr. French by* "Seumas O'Sullivan." AWP; JAWP; WBP
Night. Thomas William Rolleston. HBV
Night. Sappho, *tr. fr. Greek by* J. M. Edmonds. GrL; OxBG
(Alone, *tr. by* William Ellery Leonard.) AWP
(Forsaken, *tr. by* F. L. Lucas.) GrPE
(Lonely Night, *tr. by* H. De Vere Stacpoole.) LiTW
(Moon Has Set, The, *tr. unknown.*) ChTr; LiA
("Moon hath left the sky, The," *tr. by* John Addington Symonds.) GrPo

(Vae Soli, *tr. by* J. M. Edmonds.) GrR
Night. Shakespeare. *See* Dagger of the Mind, A.
Night ("How beautiful this night"). Shelley. *Fr.* Queen Mab, IV. LPS-2
Night ("Swiftly walk o'er the western wave"). Shelley. *See* To Night.
Night. Sir Philip Sidney. *Fr.* Arcadia. SiPS
("O Night, the ease of care.") NBE
Night. Robert Southey. *Fr.* Thalaba the Destroyer. GN
(Night in the Desert.) OTPC
Night, The. James Stephens. *See* Check.
Night. John Addington Symonds. HBV
Night. Arthur Symons. MBP; MoBrPo; PoVP
Night. Sara Teasdale. BrR; FaPON; MeMeAg; MoSiPe; SUS; TiPo
(It Is Not Far.) StVeCh
Night. *Unknown.* BoTP
Night, The ("Dear night, this world's defeat"). Henry Vaughan. *See* Dear Night, This World's Defeat.
Night, The ("Through that pure Virgin-shrine"). Henry Vaughan. EPS; EV-2; LiTB; MeLP; MePo; MeRV; NBE; OBEV (new ed.); OBS; OxBoCh; PoEL-2; PoFS; ReaPo; ReEn; RiBV; SeCeV; SeCL; SeCV-1; SeEP; TrGrPo; UnPo (1st ed.)
Night. Jones Very. APW
Night. Joseph Blanco White. *See* To Night.
Night. Tamiko Yamamuro, *tr. fr. Japanese by* Lois J. Erickson. SoLD
Night ("These thoughts, O Night!"). Edward Young. *Fr.* Night Thoughts, IX. EV-3
Night ("Tired Nature's sweet restorer"). Edward Young. *Fr.* Night Thoughts, I. CEP; EiPP; OBEC, *shorter sel.;* SeCePo, *br. sel.*
(Introduction.) EV-3
("Tir'd Nature's sweet restorer, balmy sleep!" *abr.*) EnRP
Night, A,/ a night all full of murmurs. Nocturne III. José Asunción Silva. LiTW
Night;/ And a doorway left ajar. Yakamochi, *tr. fr. Japanese by* Lois J. Erickson. SoLD
Night,/ And the yellow pleasure of candlelight. Song of the Rain. Hugh McCrae. BoAV; MoAuPo
Night, a gray sky, a ghostly sea. On the Beach. Arthur Symons. PoVP
Night a spongy dimness fill'd with moonshine, The. Three Fragments, II. William Allingham. IrPN
Night after Christmas, The. Anne P. L. Field. COAH
Night after Night. "Stuart Sterne." AA
Night after night I lie like this listening. Archibald MacLeish. *Fr.* The Hamlet of A. MacLeish. AnAmPo; LA; PoLFOT; PreP
Night air brings strange whisperings, The—vague scents. Columbus [*or* Great Master Dreamer]. Charles Buxton Going. HH; PEDC (1931 ed.); VOD
Night Airs and Moonshine. Walter Savage Landor. ChTr
Night Alert. Alison Boodson. NeBP
Night; an Epistle to Robert Lloyd, *sels.* Charles Churchill.
Nut, a World, a Squirrel, and a King, A. BeR
What Is't to Us? SeCePo
Night, and a bitter sky, and strange birds crying. The Pathfinders. Vance Palmer. BoAu
Night and Day. Asadi, *tr. fr. Persian by* E. G. Browne. PeP
Night and Day. Mary Mapes Dodge. PRWS
Night and Day. Michael Drayton. *See* Idea: "Dear, why should you . . ."
Night and Day. Ibn Darraj, *tr. fr. Arabic by* A. J. Arberry. MooP
Night and Day. Sidney Lanier. AA; AnAmPo; LA; MAP; MoAmPo (1942 ed.); MOAP
Night and Death. Joseph Blanco White. *See* To Night.
Night, and its muffled creakings, as the wheels. The Shako. Robert Lowell, *after* Rilke. OnHM
Night and Love. Sir Edward Bulwer-Lytton. *See* When Stars Are in the Quiet Skies.
Night and Morning. Dorothy Aldis. YeAr
Night and Morning. Robert Browning. *See* Meeting At Night *and* Parting at Morning.
Night and Morning. Austin Clarke. AnIL; MoAB; NeIP
Night and Morning Songs, *sels.* Gordon Bottomley.
Dawn. BoTP; MBP; MoBrPo; NP
Elegiac Mood. LBBV; NP
My Moon. NP
Night; and once again. Waiting. Masaoka Shiki. OnPM
Night and one single ridge of narrow path. Water and Air. Robert Browning. *Fr.* Pauline. OBRV
Night and Storm in the Alps. Byron. *See* Lake Leman ("Clear, placid Leman!").
Night and the Child. Judith Wright. SeCePo
Night and the distant rumbling; for the train. Last Evening. Rainer Maria Rilke. OnPM; WaaP
Night, and the down by the sea. Rain on the Down. Arthur Symons. OBVV; VLEP
Night, and the heavens beam serene with peace. Night. Solomon ibn Gabirol. TrJP
Night and the Madman. Kahlil Gibran. BAP
Night and the mountain road: a crag where burns. The Sheriff. Madison Cawein. *Fr.* The Mountain Still. SPP
Night and the Plain of Sparta. Alcman. *See* Night.
Night and the Soul, *sel.* Stanyan Bigg.
"I should be wretched as a cold lone house." BMEP
Night: and tired creatures over all the world. Virgil. *Fr.* The Aeneid, IV. LaP
Night and we heard heavy and cadenced hoofbeats. The Return. John Peale Bishop. LiTA; LiTM; MoPo; MoVE; OxBA; TwAmPo; UnPo (3d ed.); WaP
Night arches England, and the winds are still. Peace. Walter de la Mare. MoAB; MoBrPo; NeMA
Night as Well as Brightest Day. Thomas Campion. *Fr.* A Relation of the Late Royal Entertainment Given by the Lord Knowles. TuPP
Night at Gettysburg. Don C. Seitz. OHIP
Night at Yen Chou. Chou Shang Ju, *tr. fr. Chinese by* Henry H. Hart. PoHN
Night Attack. Donald M. Woodruff. TwCaPo
Night a-Zettèn In. William Barnes. RO
Night before and the Night after the Charge, The. Patrick MacGill. BMEP
Night before Christmas, The. Clement Clarke Moore. *See* Visit from St. Nicholas, A.
Night before Christmas, The. Christmas Snow. John Moore. StaSt
Night before Larry Was Stretched, The. *Unknown.* AnIV; GTIV; IrPN; OnYI; OxBoLi; TIP
Night before the Battle of Waterloo, The. Byron. *See* Waterloo ("There was a sound . . .").
Night before the Wedding, The; or, Ten Years After. Alexander Smith. LPS-1
Night before Waterloo. Byron. *See* Waterloo ("There was a sound . . .").
Night Bird, The. Charles Kingsley. OTPC (1946 ed.)
(Myth, A.) GN; VA
Night Blessing. *Unknown.* HBVY; PCH
(Good Night.) SAS
("Good-night,/ Sleep tight.") BOL
Night-blooming Cereus, The. Harriet Monroe. AA
Night Blossoms. Joseph von Eichendorff, *tr. fr. German by* Mabel Cotterell. AnGP
Night Boat. Audrey Alexandra Brown. CaP
Night Burial in the Forest. Duncan Campbell Scott. BoCaPo; CPG
Night by the River. Mu'tamid, King of Seville, *tr. fr. Arabic by* A. J. Arberry. MooP
Night by the Sea, A. Heine, *tr. fr. German by* Howard Mumford Jones. *Fr.* The North Sea. AWP
(Night on the Shore, *tr. by* Emma Lazarus.) LiTW
Night came, but without darkness or repose. The Fire of London. Dryden. *Fr.* Annus Mirabilis. BeR; FaBoEn
Night came to plunder, and with open fist. Night the Plunderer. Khanlari. PeP
Night Cat, The. W. E. Henley. *Fr.* London Voluntaries, II. BMEP
Night clos'd around the conqueror's way. After the Battle. Thomas Moore. ERP; TIP
Night closeth in. Cold, cold at Camelot. Guenevere at Almesbury. Margaret Potts. CAG
Night Clouds. Amy Lowell. BAP; MAP; MoAmPo; MoSiPe; NeMA; NP; PreP; WHA
Night comes again to bring us rest. Prayer at Eventide. R. B. Y. Scott. MaRV
Night comes, an angel stands. Nocturne. Kathleen Raine. ChMP
Night Comes Apace. Evan V. Shute. CaP
Night comes on, The. Nightfall. Hsiang Ssu. GrCo-2; PoHN
Night Cometh. Sidney Dyer. HH
Night Cometh, The. John McCrae. CPG; PoP
Night Coming Out of a Garden. Lord Alfred Douglas. MBP; MoBrPo (1942 ed.)
Night Concert. Virginia Earle. JKCP (1955 ed.)
Night Court, The. Ruth Comfort Mitchell. BAP; HBV
Night creeps in, The. Twilight. Ch'en Yün. LiTW
Night creeps over the city. Dawn Patrol; Chicago. Richard V. Durham. GoSl
Night Crow. Theodore Roethke. AmP; MoVE
Night Dancers. Thomas Kennedy. MoSiPe
Night Dirge. Elliott Coleman. NoCaPo (1941 ed.)
Night Don Juan came to pay his fees, The. Don Juan in Hell. Baudelaire. AWP; MiFP
Night Dream, The. Archibald MacLeish. TwHP
Night-driving. "A. E. M." VOD (1935 ed.)
Night Enchantment. Eleanor Muth. SiSoSe
Night-Errantry. Maurice Hewlett. BMEP; GTML
Night Express. MacKnight Black. NP
Night Express, The. Cosmo Monkhouse. OBVV
Night Falls on China. W. H. Auden. CoBMV
Night Falls on Eden. Milton. *See* Evening in Paradise.

Night falls, soothing to lascivious old men. The First Night. Jules Laforgue. AnFP
Night falls, the wild winds whistle more and more. The Pilgrim at St. Yuste. August, Graf von Platen. AnGP
Night Fears. Sophocles, *tr. fr. Greek by* John Addington Symonds. OxBG
Night Feeding. Muriel Rukeyser. MiAP
Night Flight. George Whalley. CaP
Night for Adventures. Victor Starbuck. HBV
Night Full of Nothing, A. Keith Sinclair. AnNZ
Night gathers itself into a ball of dark yarn. Carl Sandburg. *Fr.* The Windy City. PIAE
Night had pitched her tar-dark tent, The. Southwestern Night. Angelico Chavez. JKCP (1955 ed.)
Night Has a Thousand Eyes, The. Francis William Bourdillon. BMEP; BTP; CBE; FaFP; GTML; GTSL; HBV; LiTG; LiTL; LoPo; MCCG; OBEV (new ed.); OBVV; OHFP; OQP; OTPC; PoTo; PoToHe (new ed.); QP-1; TreF; VA; WBLP
(Light.) BLPA; FaBoBe; LPS-1; NeHB; TSW; TSWC
(Light and Love.) MaRV
(Night.) EtPaEn
Night has come truly now. The Oracle. A. E. Coppard. FaBoTw
Night-Hawk. Robert P. Tristram Coffin. BLA
Night he died, earth's images all came, The. Poet. Peter Viereck. HoPM; MiAP; MoAmPo (1950 ed.)
Night held me as I crawled and scrambled near. The Turkish Trench Dog. Geoffrey Dearmer. HiLiEn; LBBV; ShGoBo
Night-herding Song, The. Harry Stephens. CoSo, *with music;* CSF; SoAF, *with music;* TrAS, *with music*
(Cowboy Songs: "Oh, slow up, dogies, quit your roving round.") OuSiCo
Night Hunt, The. Thomas MacDonagh. OxBI
Night Hymns on Lake Nipigon. Duncan Campbell Scott. CoBE; MM
Night I brought the cows home, The. The Herd Boy. Haniel Long. HBMV
Night illuminated the night, The. The Forbidden Fire. Tristan Tzara. MiFP
Night in a Village, A. Ivan Savvich Nikitin, *tr. fr. Russian by* P. E. Matheson. AWP; JAWP; WBP
Night in Camp. Herbert Bashford. AA
Night in Italy, A, *sel.* "Owen Meredith."
"Sweet are the rosy memories." BMEP; OBEV (1st ed.)
Night in June, A. Wordsworth. *Fr.* The Sun Has Long Been Set. BoTP
Night in Lesbos, A. George Horton. AA
Night in Martindale. Kathleen Raine. NeBP
Night in October. Miriam Waddington. BoCaPo (1948 ed.)
Night in Spring, A. Wang An Shih, *tr. fr. Chinese by* Henry H. Hart. PoHN
Night in the bloodstained snow: the wind is chill. Hialmar Speaks to the Raven. Leconte de Lisle. AWP
Night in the Desert. Robert Southey. *See* Night.
Night in the far Judean land. A Christmas Carol. Mary A. O'Reilly. JKCP
Night in the Green Hill. Clara Platt Meadowcroft. BAP
Night in the House by the River. Tu Fu, *tr. fr. Chinese by* Kenneth Rexroth. OnPC
Night in the Villa by the River. Tu Fu, *tr. fr. Chinese by* Hsieh Wen Tung. WhP
Night in the Wood, A. Nancy M. Hayes. *See* At Night in the Wood.
Night is a cavalier dauntless and bold. Night. Christine Wood Bullwinkle. OTPC (1946 ed.); PCH
Night is an ancient sorceress, The. Song. Simeon S. Frug. LiTW
Night is beautiful, The. Poem. Langston Hughes. CDC
Night is calm, the cygnet's down, The. On a Calm Summer's Night. John Nicholson. EnLoPo
Night is come. The End [*or* Finis *or* Day's End]. Sir Henry Newbolt. GaP; MeMeAg; RIS; TiPo
Night is come, but not too soon, The. The Light of Stars [*or* The Little Moon]. Longfellow. BoTP; OTPC
Night is come like to the day, The. Evening Hymn [*or* A Colloquy with God]. Sir Thomas Browne. *Fr.* Religio Medici. EV-2; MaRV; OBS; OxBoCh; SeCL
Night is dark, The. And Yet. Errol B. Sloan. BLRP
Night is dark, the wind has dashed, The. The Midnight Prayer. Hayyim Nahman Bialik. TrJP
Night Is Darkening round Me, The. Emily Brontë. EmBrPo; PoEL-5
(Night Is Darkening, The.) EnLi-2 (1949 ed.)
Night Is Fallen. Mary Elizabeth Coleridge. POTE
Night Is Falling, The. James Clarence Mangan. IrPN
Night Is Freezing Fast, The. A. E. Housman. Last Poems, XX. AtBAP; EG; GTBS-D; LiTM; LoBV; MoPo; POTE; ReaPo; TriL; TwP
Night is full of stars, full of magnificence, The. Bagley Wood. Lionel Johnson. AnFE; VLEP
Night is full of the crying, The. Triolet. Alexander K. Laing. PIAE; YT
Night is late, the house is still, The. For Charlie's Sake. John Williamson Palmer. HBV; LPS-1
Night is like an ocean clear. Night Blossoms. Joseph von Eichendorff. AnGP
Night is like an old cat, The. Darkness. Peggy Bacon. BrR
Night is little by little, The. January Tenth. Emilio Prados. CoSP
Night is long, The. The Drums of Night. Tzu Yeh. PoHN
Night is long, the moor is bare, the hill is brown, The. Wisdom in Winter. *Unknown. Fr.* The Black Book of Carmarthen. PrWP
Night is measureless, The, no voice, no cry. The Letter. John Hall Wheelock. AnEnPo; LiTL
Night is my sister, and how deep in love. Sonnet. Edna St. Vincent Millay. LoPS
Night Is Near Gone, The. Alexander Montgomerie. EBSV; GoTS; OBEV
(Hey! Now the Day Dawns, *orig. and mod. vers.*) CH
(Nicht Is Neir Gone, The.) AtBAP; BSV
Night Is Nearing. James Clarence Mangan, *after the Persian.* IrPN
Night is not darkness. Avowal. A. M. Sullivan. JKCP (1926 ed.)
Night Is on the Downland. John Masefield. *See* Night on the Downland.
Night is over; through the clover globes of crystal shine. Lullaby for a Baby Fairy. Joyce Kilmer. BOL
Night is past, and shines the sun, The. The Storming of Corinth. Byron. *Fr.* The Siege of Corinth. LH
Night is soft with summer; yon faint arch, The. John Plummer Derwent Llwyd. *Fr.* The Vestal Virgin. CaP
Night is something watching. Song to Night. Elizabeth J. Coatsworth. WaKn
Night is soundless but its tide has turned, The. Knowing What Time It Is at Night. Louise Townsend Nicholl. PG (1955 ed.)
Night is still; the quarter moon slips down, The. The Warden's Watch, 2 A.M. Robert W. Cumberland. NeTW
Night is the time for rest. Night. James Montgomery. HBV; LPS-2
Night is the true democracy. Night's Mardi Gras. Edward J. Wheeler. HBV; LBMV; NV
Night is thick with storm and driving cloud, The. Australia, 1914. Archibald T. Strong. *Fr.* Sonnets of the Empire. BoAu
Night is white, The. Birch Trees. John Richard Moreland. DD; HBMV; HBVY; OHIP
Night it was a holy night, The. Godly Girzie. Burns. CoMu
Night it was, sweet as the morning of life, A. Night. Jami. LiTW
Night itself seems sad, The. Melancholy. Liu Hsiao Hsien. PoHN
Night Journey of a River, The. Bryant. PEOR
Night knows nothing of the chants of night, The. Restatement of Romance. Wallace Stevens. LiTL
Night-Labour. Quentin Stevenson. POTE (1959 ed.)
Night Landing. John Gould Fletcher. Down the Mississippi, VI. ChMo; CMP; LiTA; MOAP; NP; SPP; TCAP
Night Laughter. Leonard Bacon. BAP
Night Lies Silently. Kenetha Thomas. CAG
Night like a silver peacock in the sky. Poetry and Science. W. J. Turner. SeCePo
Night like purple flakes of snow. Night. Donald Jeffrey Hayes. CDC
Night Lilac. Mark Van Doren. MOAP
Night Litany. Ezra Pound. ChMo; CMP; MM; TwCV
Night Long, The. Imr el Kais, *tr. fr. Arabic by* Lady Anne Blunt *and* Wilfrid Scawen Blunt. LiTW
Night long I sigh, and soon as comes the day. The Swallows. Agathias Scholasticus. OxBG
Night Loves Us, The. Louis Adeane. NeBP
Night Ma Heard the Burglar, The. Douglas Malloch. OnHT
Night Magic. Amelia Josephine Burr. MPB; SP
Night Mail. W. H. Auden. AlDL; ChTr; MuP; ShBV-3
Night mantled earth in gloom, while mariners. Remorse. Apollonius Rhodius. *Fr.* Argonautica. OxBG
Night-March, The. Herman Melville. AnFE; CoAnAm; LiTA
Night Meeting, The. Adaline H. Tatman. DDA
Night Mists. William Hamilton Hayne. AA
Night Moths, The. Edwin Markham. HBMV
Night Musick for Thérèse. Dachine Rainer. NePoAm-2
Night my father got me, The. The Culprit. A. E. Housman. PG (1955 ed.); TwP
Night Mysteries. Milton. *See* Star That Bids the Shepherd Fold, The.
Night: mysterious, tender, quiet, deep, A. A Common Inference. Charlotte Perkins Gilman. AA; AnAmPo; LA; WGRP
Night Note. James Oppenheim. MAP; MoAmPo (1942 ed.)
Night Nurse Goes Her Round, The. John Gray. LoBV
Night of Bliss. Ibn al-Zaqqaq, *tr. fr. Arabic by* A. J. Arberry. MooP

Night of Forebeing, The. Francis Thompson. *See* From the Night of Forebeing.
Night of Gods, The. George Sterling. MAP; MoAmPo (1942 ed.); PFY; WHA
Night of Joy. Ibn Abi Ruh, *tr. fr. Arabic by* A. J. Arberry. MooP
Night of Marvels, The. Sister Violante do Ceo, *tr. fr. Portuguese by* Sir John Bowring. CAW
Night of nights drew to its tardy close, The. Love's Mortality. Richard Middleton. LBBV; WHA
Night of pleasure gay! Carousal. Ibn Khafaja. MooP
Night of Rain. Bernice Kenyon. HBMV
Night of Sorrow, The. Li Po, *tr. fr. Chinese by* Shigeyoshi Obata. WoL
Night of Spring. Thomas Westwood. AlDL; BoTP; OBVV; PIAE; TOP
Night of Stars. John Gould Fletcher. BAP
Night of Stars. Luis de León, *tr. fr. Spanish by* Aubrey F. G. Bell. TeCS
Night of the Immaculate Conception. Juan Maragall, *tr. fr. Spanish by* Thomas Walsh. CAW
Night of the Tomb! He has entered thy portal. Webster. Epes Sargent. GA
Night of Trafalgar, The. Thomas Hardy. *Fr.* The Dynasts, Pt. I, Act V, sc. vii. AlDL; ChTr; FaBoCh; MBP; MoBrPo; OBMV; PoVP; ReTS; ShBV-1
(Boatman's Song, The.) WaaP
(Trafalgar.) CH
Night of utter silences, A. Shadows. "Yehoash." TrJP
Night of Wind. Frances Frost. FaPON; TiPo
Night on earth and sky. A Terrible Thought. Eliezer Steinberg. TrJP
Night on Lake Leman. Byron. *See* Lake Leman ("Clear, placid Leman!").
Night on the Downland. John Masefield. Lollingdon Downs, XVIII. GTBS-W; LiTM; MBP; MoBrPo; MoPo
(Night Is on the Downland.) CP
("Night is on the downland, on the lonely moorland.") GoYe
Night on the Fields of Enna. Louis Golding. MBP
Night on the Prairie. Rufus B. Sage. PoOW
Night on the Prairies. Walt Whitman. IAP
Night on the Shore. Heine. *See* Night by the Sea, A.
Night on the West River. Po Chü-i, *tr. fr. Chinese by* Henry H. Hart. PoHN
Night-owl shrieked: a gibbous moon peered pallid o'er the yew, The. The Conscience-Curst. "F. Anstey." CenHV
Night passes. We are born day after day. Palladas, *tr. fr. Greek by* L. P. Chamberlayne. GrPo
Night-Piece. Léonie Adams. MAP; MoAB; MoAmPo
Night Piece. A. E. Coppard. POTE
Night-Piece, The. Robert Herrick. *See* Night Piece, to Julia.
Night Piece. Robert Hillyer. MAP; MoAmPo
Night Piece. John Manifold. MoBrPo (1950 ed.)
(Nightpiece.) LiTM; WaP
Night Piece. Pushkin. *See* Verses Written during a Sleepless Night.
Night Piece, A. Edward Shanks. HBMV
Night Piece. Edith Sitwell. NP
Night-Piece, A. *Unknown. See* O Night, O Jealous Night.
Night-Piece, A. Wordsworth. BPN; EmBrPo; EnRP; GEPC; SN
Night-Piece on Death, A. Thomas Parnell. AEV; CEP; EiPP; GTIV; OBEC; SeCePo
Sels.
"Death speaks:/ When men my scythe and darts supply." OnYI
"How deep yon azure dies the sky!" EV-3
Night Piece to Another Julia. Paul Fearon. CIV
Night-Piece, to Julia. Robert Herrick. AnFE; AtBAP; ATP; BCEP; BEL; CaAE; CBOV; CenL; CoBE; CoEV; EG; ElSeCe; EM-1; EnLi-1 (1949 ed.); EnLit; EPS; EV-2; HBV; InvP; LEAP; LiTB; LiTL; LoBV; MaPo; NeHB; OAEP; OBEV; OBS; PCD; PoEL-3; PoFS; PoRA; ReEn; RiBV; SeCeV; SeCL; SeCV-1; SeEP; ShBV-2; TOP; TwHP; TyEnPo; WHA
(Night-Piece, The.) OTPC
On a Dark Road, *sel.* BoTP
Night Plane. Frances Frost. FaPON; TiPo (1959 ed.)
Night Prayer, A. *Unknown, tr. fr. Irish by* Eleanor Hull. JKCP (1926 ed.)
Night Pulse. Ruth Guthrie Harding. MuM
Night Quarters. Henry Howard Brownell. GN
Night Rain. Ch'eng Wang, *tr. fr. Chinese by* Henry H. Hart. PoHN
Night Rain, The. Lu Yu, *tr. fr. Chinese by* Pai Chwen-yu. WhP
Night Reverie. Ling Ju Jung, *tr. fr. Chinese by* Henry H. Hart. PoHN
Night Rhapsody. Robert Nichols. PtOT
Night-Ride, The. Kenneth Slessor. NeLNL
Night Road. Robert A. Donaldson. VOD
Night saw the crew like pedlers with their packs. Lunar Stanzas. Henry Coggswell Knight. BOHV; NA
Night, say all, was made for rest, The. Upon Visiting His Lady by Moonlight. "A. W." OBSC; ReIE; TuPP
Night Serene, The. Luis de León, *tr. fr. Spanish by* Thomas Walsh. CAW; TrJP; WoL
Night Shower. Brock Milton. PoMa
Night showers cleared at dawn. Lotus. *Unknown.* SoLD
Night skies grow white. O Skylarks, Teach Japan to Sing. Toyohiko Kagawa. SoLD
Night Sky, The. Sir Charles G. D. Roberts. VA
Night Sky, The. *Unknown.* BoTP
Night sleeps, but the chill, The. The Harp of David. Jacob Cohen. TrJP
Night Song. A. R. D. Fairburn. AnNZ
Night Song. Wallace Gould. AnAmPo; LA
Night Song. Charles Williams. *See* Night Song for a Child.
Night Song at Amalfi. Sara Teasdale. ChMo; CMP; MAP; MoAmPo; SBMV
(Night Song of Amalfi.) NeMA
Night Song for a Child! Charles Williams. OBEV (new ed.)
(Night Song.) AlDL
Night Song for Two Mystics. Paul Blackburn. NeAP
Night-Song in the Jungle. Kipling. AlDL
Night Song of the Fish. Christian Morgenstern. AnGP
Night Sowing. David Campbell. BoAV
Night, Stars, Glow-Worms. H. Leivick, *tr. fr. Yiddish by* Jacob Sloan. LiTW
Night stilled the field, and every golden stook. Cornfield. Leo Cox. CaP
Night stirs but wakens not, her breathings climb. Animula Vagula. A. Y. Campbell. HBMV
Night Storm. Al-Lama'i, *tr. fr. Arabic by* A. J. Arberry. MooP
Night Storm. William Gilmore Simms. EtS
Night Stuff. Carl Sandburg. ChMo; CMP; NP; TSW
Night that has no star lit up by God, The. The New World. Jones Very. AA; AnNE; APW
Night that smells of sailor's tar, A. Lounge Bar. James K. Baxter. Cressida, XII. AnNZ
Night the green moth came for me, The. Green Moth. Winifred Welles. BoChLi (1950 ed.); FaPON; StVeCh; TiPo; UTS
Night the Plunderer. Khanlari, *tr. fr. Persian by* A. J. Arberry. PeP
Night: the street, a foolish lamp giving. Aleksandr Blok, *tr. fr. Russian by* V. de S. Pinto. BoRS
Night There Was Dancing in the Streets, The. Elder Olson. NePA
Night They Kept Vigil in the South, The. Jorge Luis Borges, *tr. fr. Spanish by* Robert Stuart Fitzgerald. AnCL
Night Thought of a Tortoise Suffering from Insomnia on a Lawn. E. V. Rieu. FiBHP
Night-Thoughts. Solomon ibn Gabirol, *tr. fr. Hebrew by* Emma Lazarus. TrJP
Night Thoughts. Lu Yu, *tr. fr. Chinese by* Kenneth Rexroth. OnPC
Night Thoughts, *sel.* Johan Sebastian Cammermeyer Welhaven, *tr. fr. Norwegian by* Charles W. Stork.
"I watch the shore of gladness," II. AnNoLy
Night Thoughts, *sels.* Edward Young.
Art Thou Dejected? *fr.* Night VIII. GrCo-1
At Home among the Stars ("This prospect vast, what is it?"), *fr.* Night IX. GrCo-1
Happiness an Art, *fr.* Night VIII. OBEC
"How populous, how vital is the grave!" PoD
"Know'st thou, Lorenzo! what a friend contains," *fr.* Night II. BoFr
(Fruits of Friendship, The.) GrCo-1
"Live ever here, Lorenzo?—shocking thought!" *fr.* Night III. EnRP
Man ("How poor, how rich, how abject"), *fr.* Night I. BCEP; EPP; LPS-3; MaRV
Narcissa, *fr.* Night V. LPS-1
Night ("These thoughts, O Night!"), *fr.* Night IX. EV-3
"On nature's Alps I stand," *fr.* Night IX. MaRV
Procrastination ("Be wise today; 'tis madness to defer"), *fr.* Night I. AnEnPo; BCEP, *abr.*; EV-3, *abr.*; LPS-3; OBEC, *abr.*
(Procrastination: "By Nature's law.") EPP
This Life and the Next ("A truth it is few doubt but fewer trust"), *fr.* Night III. GrCo-1
Time, *fr.* Nights I *and* II. LPS-3
(Lapse of Time, The, *longer sel.*) BCEP
"Tir'd Nature's sweet restorer, balmy sleep!" Night I. EnRP, *abr.*
(Introduction: "Tired Nature's sweet restorer, balmy sleep!") EV-3
(Night I.) CEP; EiPP; OBEC; SeCePo, *br. sel.*
Night Thoughts in Age. John Hall Wheelock. MoVE
Night Thoughts while Travelling. Tu Fu, *tr. fr. Chinese by* Kenneth Rexroth. OnPC
Night throbs on, The; O, let me pray, dear Lord! Motherhood. Josephine Dodge Daskam Bacon. HBV
Night through yonder cloudy cleft, The. Aubrey Thomas De Vere. *Fr.* May Carols. IrPN

Night, too long illumined, comes a stranger, The. In the Proscenium [*or* War's Clown in the Proscenium]. Gene Derwood. GTBS-W; LiTA; LiTM (rev. ed.); NePA
Night too quickly passes, The. The Roaring Days. Henry Lawson. BoAV; NeLNL
Night Train. Sakutaro Hagiwara, *tr. fr. Japanese by* Takamichi Ninomiya *and* D. J. Enright. PoLJ
Night Traveller, The. Ibn Atiya, *tr. fr. Arabic by* A. J. Arberry. MooP
Night unto Night. Inez Barclay Kirby. MuM
Night Vigil in the Left Court of the Palace, A. Tu Fu. *See* Staying at the Official Residence on a Spring Night.
Night Visitor. Ibn Hamdis, *tr. fr. Arabic by* A. J. Arberry. MooP
Night walked down the sky, The. A Memory. Frederic Lawrence Knowles. HBV
Night-Walker, The; or, The Little Thief, *sel.* John Fletcher.
"I've walked through all the lodgings," *fr.* II, i. MyFE
Night Walkers, The. Kendrick Smithyman. AnNZ
Night was coming very fast, The. The Hens. Elizabeth Madox Roberts. FaPON; GoTP; HBMV; MPB; PoeMoYo; PoRh; SP; StVeCh; SUS; TiPo; TSW; TSWC; UTS; VOD
Night Was Creeping. James Stephens. *See* Check.
Night was dark and fearful, The. The Watcher. Sarah Josepha Hale. AA
Night was dark, though sometimes a faint star, The. Prelude [*or* Dawn]. Richard Watson Gilder. *Fr.* The New Day. HBV; LPS-2; SN
Night was dark when Sam set out, The. Rustic Courtship. *Unknown.* PTA-2
Night was dark when she went away, and they slept, The. The Recall. Rabindranath Tagore. MOAH
Night was dark with indignation, The. Feodor Tyutchev, *tr. fr. Russian.* BoR
Night was done; we rose and after. This Summer's Love. Mikhail Alekseyevich Kuzmin. OnPM; TrRV
Night was drawing in, and the fire was low. Nikolai Gumilev, *tr. fr. Russian by* Y. Hornstein. BoRS
Night Was Going, The. Raúl Otero Reiche, *tr. fr. Spanish by* Rolfe Humphries. AnCL
Night was growing old, The. In the Night. *Unknown.* NA
Night, The, was made for beauty, and for shame. Night Dirge. Elliott Coleman. NoCaPo (1941 ed.)
Night was made for cooling shade, The. At Sea. John T. Trowbridge. EtS
Night was made for rest and sleep. Interim. Clarissa Scott Delany. CDC; PoNe
Night was thick and hazy, The. Robinson Crusoe's Story. Charles Edward Carryl. *Fr.* Davy and the Goblin. AA; BeLS; BHP; BoChLi; BOHV; FiBHP; HBV; HBVY; InMe; LEAP; LHV; MCCG; MPB; OnPP; OTPC (1946 ed.); PCD; PCN; PoRA; PoRh; TSW; TSWC
Night was time, The. The Three Stars of Prophecy. David Gascoyne. POTE
Night was winter in his roughest mood, The. William Cowper. *Fr.* The Task, VI. BrBE; EnRP; EnSW; EV-3; LPS-2; NBE; OBEC
Night Watch. Euripides, *tr. fr. Greek by* Gilbert Murray. *Fr.* Rhesus. OxBG
(Watch before Dawn, The.) GrR
Night Watch, A. *Unknown.* The Passionate Pilgrim, XIV. OBSC
Night Watch, The. William Winter. AA
Night-Watch Prayer. Henry van Dyke. PraP
Night Watchmen. Jimmy Garthwaite. BrR
Night-watchmen think of dawn and things auroral. Blindman's Buff. Peter Viereck. MiAP; MoAmPo (1950 ed.)
Night when last I saw my lad, The. Forgettin'. "Moira O'Neill." HBV
Night Will Never Stay, The. Eleanor Farjeon. AlDL; BoTP; CH; FaPON; HBMV; MW; PoRh; SiSoSe; StVeCh; TSW; TSWC
Night Wind, The. Emily Brontë. ChER; ChTr; OAEP
Night Wind, The. Eugene Field. FaPON
Night-Wind. Beatrix Demarest Lloyd. AA
Night Wind. Feodor Tyutchev, *tr. fr. Russian by* C. M. Bowra. LiTW
("Night wind, what cry you on your way?") BoRS
Night wind comes, The. A Night in Spring. Wang An Shih. PoHN
Nightwind sings and rustles through the reeds, The. Nocturne in G Minor. Karl Gustav Vollmoeller. AWP; LiTW
Night Winds. Adelaide Crapsey. NV; SBMV
Night with a Wolf, A. Bayard Taylor. *See* Story for a Child, A.
Night with her ebon hair and starry crown. The Eve of Ascension Day. Derenik Demirjian. ArmLP
Nightfall. Herbert Asquith. MoP
Nightfall. Hsiang Ssu, *tr. fr. Chinese by* Henry H. Hart. GrCo-2; PoHN
Nightfall. Kalidasa, *tr. fr. Sanskrit by* Arthur W. Ryder. LiTW
Nightfall. Una Marson. PoNe
Nightfall. Siraj, *tr. fr. Arabic by* A. J. Arberry. MooP
Nightfall. Charles Hanson Towne. *See* At Nightfall.
Nightfall. Antonio de Trueba, *tr. fr. Spanish by* Thomas Walsh. CAW
Nightfall. Feodor Tyutchev, *tr. fr. Russian by* Vladimir Nabokov. LiTW
Nightfall;/ And I all lone. *Unknown, tr. fr. Japanese by* Lois J. Erickson. SoLD
Nightfall; a Picture. Alfred B. Street. LPS-2
Nightfall before Syracuse. Walter Hauk. CAG
Nightfall. Clouds scatter and vanish. The Turning Year. Su T'ung-po. OnPC
Nightfall. I return from a/ Journey. Homecoming—Late at Night. Tu Fu. OnPC
Nightfall in Dordrecht. Eugene Field. AA; OBAV; PRWS
Nightfall in Inishtrahull. Daniel James O'Sullivan. NeIP
Nightfall, that saw the morning-glories float. On the Skeleton of a Hound. James Wright. NePoEA
Nightflight and Sunrise. Geoffrey Dutton. BoAV
Nightingale, The. Mark Akenside. *See* Ode to the Evening Star.
Nightingale, The. Richard Barnfield. *Fr.* The Passionate Pilgrim. AWP; BLA; BLV; CG; EV-2; GTBS; GTBS-D; GTBS-W; GTSE; JAWP; OTPC (1923 ed.); TOP; TVSH; WBP
(As It Fell upon a Day.) EG; EPP; ReEn; ViBoPo
(Ode, An: "As it fell upon a day.") ElL; ElSeCe; EM-1; LoBV; OBSC; ReIE; SiCE; TuPP
(Philomel.) BCEP; CH; GTSL; HBV; LEAP; OBEV
(To the Nightingale.) LiTG; LPS-2
Nightingale, The. Elizabeth Belloc. JKCP (1955 ed.)
Nightingale, The. Richard Brathwaite. *Fr.* Nature's Embassy. ElL
Nightingale. Eleanor Alletta Chaffee. MuM
Nightingale, The. Samuel Taylor Coleridge. EmBrPo; EnRP; ERP; EV-4; NBE
("'Tis the merry nightingale.") OBRV
Nightingales, *sel.* ChTr
Nightingale, The. Ferid ed-Din Attar, *tr. fr. Persian by* Edward Fitzgerald. *Fr.* The Bird-Parliament. PeP
Nightingale, The. Gerald Griffin. CAW; JKCP
(To the Blessed Virgin Mary.) OnYI
Nightingale, The. Jorge Guillén, *tr. fr. Spanish by* Eleanor L. Turnbull. CoSP
Nightingale, The. Keats. *See* Ode to a Nightingale.
Nightingale, The. Aleksey Koltsov, *tr. fr. Russian by* Maud F. Jerrold. BoR
Nightingale, The. Edward Moxon. OBRV
Nightingale, The. Petrarch, *tr. fr. Italian by* Thomas LeMesurier. Sonnets to Laura: To Laura in Death, XLIII. LiTW; LyMA
Nightingale, The. Sappho, *tr. fr. Greek by* Ben Jonson. GrL; OxBG
Nightingale, The. Sir Philip Sidney. AtBAP; ElL; EnLi-1; EPP; GTBS-W; LiTB; LoBV; OBSC; RiBV; SiPS; TuPP; UnPo (1st ed.); WHA
(Nightingale, as Soon as April Bringeth, The.) GTSL; LiTG; MaPo; ReEn; SiCE
(Philomela.) EV-1; HBV; OBEV; PreP
Nightingale, The. John Addington Symonds. VA
Nightingale, The. Katharine Tynan. BoTP
Nightingale, The ("Both old and young, I pray lend an ear"), *with music. Unknown.* ShS
Nightingale, The ("The little pretty nightingale"). *Unknown.* BLV; TrGrPo
("Little pretty nightingale, The.") EG; LO
("Lytyll prety nyghtyngale, The.") EPP; LyMA; OAEP
Nightingale, The ("One morning, one morning, one morning in May"). *Unknown. See* One Morning in May.
Nightingale, The. Sir John Vanbrugh. *Fr.* Aesop. SeCL
Nightingale, The. Paul Verlaine, *tr. fr. French by* Muriel Kittel. AnFP
Nightingale, The. Gil Vicente, *tr. fr. Portuguese by* Sir John Bowring. LPS-2
Nightingale, The. Maria Tesselschade Visscher, *tr. fr. Dutch by* Sir John Bowring. LPS-2
Nightingale, The. Wordsworth. DD; SN
(O Nightingale.) AtBAP
(O Nightingale! Thou Surely Art.) BLV; HBV
Nightingale and Flowers. Blake. *Fr.* Milton, II. LoBV
(Birdsong.) FaBoEn
(Choir of Day, The.) EnRP
(Joy in the Flowers, *shorter sel.*) RO
("Thou hearest the nightingale.") NBE; OBRV
(Vision of Beulah.) EV-3
Nightingale and [the] Glow-Worm, The. William Cowper. BoChLi; CG; GoTP; HBV; LPS-3; NeHB; OTPC; PECK; PRWS; RIS
Nightingale and the Lark, The. Ernest Whitney. ATP (1935 ed.)
Nightingale, as Soon as April Bringeth. Sir Philip Sidney. *See* Nightingale, The.
Nightingale Bereaved, The. James Thomson. *Fr.* The Seasons: Spring. BCEP

Nightingale, fluent songster, The. The Nightingale. Jorge Guillén. CoSP
Nightingale has a lyre of gold, The. The Blackbird [*or* To A. D.]. W. E. Henley. AnFE; BEL; BLA; BPN; BTP; EPP; HBV; HoPM; LoPo; LoPS; MBP; MoBrPo; NeMA; OuHeWo; PoeMoYo; POTT; PoVP; TOP; TrGrPo; TSW; TSWC; ViBoPo; VOD
Nightingale I never heard. My Catbird. William Henry Venable. AA; BAP; BLA; HBV; PFY
Nightingale in the Study, The. James Russell Lowell. IAP
Nightingale made a mistake, A. The Singing Lesson. Jean Ingelow. DD; HBV; OTPC (1946 ed.)
Nightingale near the House, The. Harold Monro. BMEP; EPP; HBMV; MBP; MM; MoBrPo; TwCV; VOD
Nightingale, oh, leave our garden. Cradle Song. Raphael Patkanian. ArmLP
Nightingale of Avarair, The. Leo Alishan, *tr. fr. Armenian by* Zabelle C. Boyajian. ArmLP
Nightingale on the flowering plum, The. Peasant and Geisha Songs. *Unknown.* LiTW
Nightingale, A, once lost his voice from too much love. Youth and Age. Ridgely Torrence. *Fr.* The House of a Hundred Lights. AA
Nightingale sat singing out his heart, A. Torin, *tr. fr. Japanese by* Lois J. Erickson. SoLD
Nightingale, A, that all day long. The Nightingale and [the] Glow-Worm. William Cowper. BoChLi; CG; GoTP; HBV; LPS-3; NeHB; OTPC; PECK; PRWS; RIS
Nightingale, the organ of delight, The. The Rivals. *Unknown.* PIAE
Nightingale, the rose's lover, The. The Nightingale. Aleksey Koltsov. BoR
Nightingale Unheard, The. Josephine Preston Peabody. BLA; LBMV
Nightingale Weather. Andrew Lang. BSV; POTT
Nightingales. Robert Bridges. AtBAP; BLA; BLV; CaAE; ChMo; CMP; CoBMV; EnLi-2 (1949 ed.); ExPo; FaBoEn; GTBS; GTML; HBMV; LEAP; LiTB; LiTM; MBP; MoAB; MoBrPo; MoPo; OBEV; OBMV; OBVV; Po; PoeMoYo; PoVP; ReaPo; RiBV; SeCeV; TrGrPo; TwCV; UnPo; ViP; VLEP; VOD
Nightingales. Samuel Taylor Coleridge. *Fr.* The Nightingale. ChTr
Nightingales. Grace Hazard Conkling. HBMV
Nightingales, The. Tu Mu, *tr. fr. Chinese by* Yuan K'o-chia. WhP
Nightingales at Fairford sing, The. Fairford Nightingales. John Drinkwater. BLA
Nightingales of Flanders, The. Grace Hazard Conkling. AOAH
Nightingales of Surrey, The. Jessie B. Rittenhouse. MaRV; MuM
Nightingale's Song, The. Richard Crashaw. *Fr.* Music's Duel. LPS-3
Nightingales warble about it. The Secret. George Edward Woodberry. *Fr.* Wild Eden. AA; BAP; HBV; LBMV
Nightingales warbled without. In the Garden at Swainston [*or* Valedictory]. Tennyson. GoBC; OBEV (new ed.); OBVV; PoVP; TCEP; ViPo; VLEP
Nightjar, The. Sir Henry Newbolt. MBP
Nightlong the water labored breathlessly. Roosters. Boris Pasternak. TrRV
Nightly Deed, A. Charles Madge. NeBP
Nightly I mark and praise, or great or small. Retractions, XV. James Branch Cabell. HBMV
Nightly, near Cosenza, by the deep Busento, ghostly singing. The Grave in the Busento. August, Graf von Platen. AnGP
Nightly tormented by returning doubt. The Struggle. Sully-Prudhomme. AWP
Nightmare. Gawin Douglas. *Fr.* The Palace of Honor. PoEL-1
Nightmare. W. S. Gilbert. *See* Lord Chancellor's Song.
Nightmare, The. Sorley Maclean. NeBP
Nightmare. Clark Ashton Smith. DaM
Nightmare. James Thomson. *See* As I Came through the Desert.
Nightmare Abbey, *sels.* Thomas Love Peacock.
There Is a Fever of the Spirit, *fr. ch.* 11. EPN; GTSE
(Mr. Cypress's Song.) LO
(Song, by Mr. Cypress.) OBRV
Three Men of Gotham, *fr. ch.* 11. CoEV; EV-4; FaBoCh; GTBS; GTBS-D; GTSL; LiTG; MuP; MyFE, *st.* 1; OBEV; SiTL; TOP
(Catch, A: "Seamen three!") AlDL; ViBoPo
(Men of Gotham, The.) CH; OTPC (1946 ed.)
(Seamen Three.) CaAE; OBRV
("Seamen three, what men be ye?") EG
(Wise Men of Gotham, The.) LoBV
Nightmare at Noon. Stephen Vincent Benét. OxBA
Nightmare leaves fatigue. Louis MacNeice. *Fr.* Autumn Journal. AnIL
Nightmare Number Three. Stephen Vincent Benét. DaM; MaC; MoAmPo (1950 ed.)
Nightmare of a Cook. Chester Kallman. CrMA
Nightmare (Written during Apparent Imminence of War). Sir William Watson. LEAP
Nightpiece. John Manifold. *See* Night Piece.
Night's Ancient Cloud. Thomas Keohler. AnIV
Nights are cold, the nights are long, The. The Cottager to Her Infant [*or* The Cottager's Lullaby]. Dorothy Wordsworth. BOL; CH; EV-3; HBV; MOAH; OTPC (1923 ed.); PRWS
Nights are warm again, The. St. Kilda. Barrie Reid. BoAV
Night's come—I've lost my path. A Warrior at Nightfall. *Unknown.* GaP
Night's diadem around thy head. Fairest of Freedom's Daughters. Jeremiah Eames Rankin. PAH
Night's Fall Unlocks the Dirge of the Sea. W. S. Graham. FaBoMo
(Night's Fall.) NeBP
Night's first sweet silence fell, and on my bed. The Malady of Love Is Nerves. Petronius Arbiter. AWP
Nights follow each other and are linked. Charles Péguy. *Fr.* Night. LiTW
Night's held breath, The. Night. Arthur Symons. MBP; MoBrPo; PoVP
Night's Mardi Gras. Edward J. Wheeler. HBV; LBMV; NV
Nights long unending oppress me. After Heine. Nikolai Alekseyevich Nekrasov. WaL
Nights on the Indian Ocean. Cale Young Rice. EtS
Nights Remember, The. Harold Vinal. HBMV
Night's soft armor welds me into thought. Poem. Dorothy Livesay. BoCaPo
Night's Song. *At. to* Sir William Davenant. *Fr.* Luminalia. SeCL
Nights, the railway-arches, the bad sky, The. Rimbaud. W. H. Auden. PtP
Night's wing is on the east—the clouds repose. Approach of Evening. George Croly. IrPN
Nihil Humani Alienum. Titus Munson Coan. AA
Nijinsky. Doris Ferne. CaP
Nijinsky's ashes here in peace repose. For Nijinsky's Tomb. Frances Cornford. UnS
Nikolina. Celia Thaxter. GN; HBV; OTPC (1946 ed.)
Nil Admirari. Congreve. OBEC
Nil Perdunt Mendici. Henry Parrot. SiCE
Nile, The. Leigh Hunt. EnRP; ES; OBRV; PeBoSo; ViBoPo
(River Nile, The.) EV-4
Nile Chantey, A. *Unknown, tr. fr. Greek by* Gilbert Highet. OxBG
Nilotic Elegy. G. S. Fraser. WaP
Nilus and Hillelille. *Unknown, tr. fr. Danish by* E. M. Smith-Dampier. BoDaBa
Nima, The. Jorge Isaacs, *tr. fr. Spanish by* Alice Jane McVan. TrJP
Nimble Dick. Adelaide O'Keeffe. OTPC (1923 ed.)
Nimble sigh, on thy warm wings. To Amoret. Henry Vaughan. EnLoPo
Nimble Stag, The. Edmund G. V. Knox. HBMV
Nimbus, The. Douglas Le Pan. PeCV
Niminy, piminy. Food for Thought. Michael Lewis. RIS
Nimium Fortunatus. Robert Bridges. *See* Fortunatus Nimium.
Nimmers, The, *abr.* John Byrom. EV-3
Nimmo. E. A. Robinson. HBMV
Nimphidia. Michael Drayton. *See* Nymphidia.
Nimrod, *sels.* Anna Hempstead Branch.
"And Nimrod cried aloud," *fr.* II. BAP
Babel Falls, *fr.* V. TCPD
Nimrod Wars with the Angels, *fr.* II. TCPD
Nimrud and the Gnat. *Unknown, tr. fr. Arabic by* Sir Edwin Arnold. OnPM
Nine are we who enter, each maiden votaress. Maidens' Song. *Unknown.* OxBG
Nine Declarations, The, *sel.* Chu Yuan, *tr. fr. Chinese by* Yu Min-chuan.
"This is the beautiful dress." WhP
Nine grenadiers, with bayonets in their guns. The Dream of a Little Boy Who Lived at Nine-Elms. William Brighty Rands. GaP; PPL; RIS
Nine Herbs Charm. *Unknown, tr. fr. Anglo-Saxon by* William O. Stevens. EPP
Nine mile to Michaelmas. *Unknown.* *Fr.* My Heart of Gold. BoN
Nine Monsters, The. César Vallejo, *tr. fr. Spanish by* H. R. Hays. TwSpPo
Nine months I waited in the dark beneath. Pro Sua Vita. Robert Penn Warren. MAP; MM; MoAmPo
Nine Nectarines and Other Porcelain. Marianne Moore. OxBA
Nine o'clock. Louis Simpson. PoNe
Nine-o'clock bell! School-Bell. Eleanor Farjeon. BrR; FaPON; SiSoSe
Nine Songs, The [Chu K'o]. Chu Yuan, *tr. fr. Chinese by* Shen Yu-ting. WhP
Nine times the space that measures day and night. Milton. *Fr.* Paradise Lost, I. NBE

Nine times the span of an old old man. Length of Life. Hesiod. *Fr.* Precepts of Chiron. OxBG
Nine Variations in a Chinese Winter Setting. Charles Tomlinson. PoN
Nine white chickens come. A Black November Turkey. Richard Wilbur. FiMAP; MoAB
Nine years ago I was diggin' up the land. The True Paddy's Song. *Unknown.* OuSiCo
Ninepenny Fidil, The. Joseph Campbell. HBMV
1918–1941. Robert D. Fitzgerald. BoAV
1905, *sel.* Boris Pasternak, *tr. fr. Russian by* Jack Lindsay.
Childhood. RuPo
1944—on the Invasion Coast. Jack Beeching. WaP
1904's Sundial at Wells College. Henry van Dyke. DDA
1914. Rupert Brooke. HBV; NP
Sels.
Dead, The ("Blow out, you bugles"), III. AOAH; BEL; GrCo-1; GTML; LBBV; LEAP; MCCG; NV; OQP; PoFr; QP-1; TCEP; TreF; VOD; WGRP
Dead, The ("These hearts were woven"), IV. AnFE; ATP; CH; CP; EnLit; ES; GTBS-W; GTSL; HiLiEn; LiTB; LiTG; MCCG; NV; OtMeF; PFE; PIAE; PoeMoYo; PoeT; PoRL; POTE; SeCeV; ShBV-4; TOP; TwCV; VOD; YT
(All This Is Ended.) AOAH
Peace, I. AOAH; EPN; LBBV; LEAP; MaRV; POTE; POTT; WGRP
("Now, God be thank'd Who has match'd us with His hour.") CBE
Safety, II. EnLoPo; LoPo; PoFr; VOD
Soldier, The, V. AEV; AnFE; AOAH; BBV; BEL; BLV; BMEP; BoLiVe; BTP; CaAE; CBOV; CP; EnLit; EPN; EPP; ES; EV-5; ExPo; FaBoEn; FaFP; GTBS; GTBS-W; GTML; GTSL; HiLiEn; InP; LBBV; LEAP; LiTB; LiTM; MaC; MaRV; MBP; MCCG; MoBrPo; MoVE; NeHB; NeMA; OBEV (new ed.); OTPC (1946 ed.); PIAE; PoeT; PoMa; PoRA; POT; POTE; PoTo; POTT; PreP; PYM; ShBV-3; TCEP; TCPD; TOP; TreF; TrGrPo; TVSH; TwCV; ViBoPo; VOD; WaP; WHA; WP; YT
1914. Frank Wilmot. BoAu; MoAuPo
1914—and After, *sel.* James Oppenheim.
Would You End War, IV. GrCo-1 (19 *ll.*); PSO (17 *ll.*)
(Create Great Peace, 17 *ll.*) MaRV
1914 Autumn and Winter. Maurice Hewlett. *Fr.* The Song of the Plow. PoFr
Nineteen Han Poems, The, *sels.* (I–XV). *Unknown, tr. fr. Chinese.* WhP
(Seventeen Old Poems, *tr. by* Arthur Waley.) TrCh
Nineteen Hundred and Nineteen. W. B. Yeats. LiTB; MoAB; MoPo; OnHM
Nineteen! of years a pleasant number. Aetate XIX. Herman Charles Merivale. OBVV; VA
1917–1919. Henry Martyn Hoyt. HBMV
1967. Thomas Hardy. PG (1945 ed.)
1938. Ruth Pitter. DiM; LO
1935. Stephen Vincent Benét. MAP; MoAmPo; NeMA
1934. Richard Eberhart. TwAmPo
Nineteen Thirty-nine, *sel.* Charles Brasch.
Poland, October. AnNZ
1933. Archibald MacLeish. TwCV
Nineteen Twenty-six. Wilson MacDonald. MaRV
1923. Archibald MacLeish. *Fr.* The Farm. CMP
Nineteenth of April (1861), The. Lucy Larcom. MC; MDAH; PAH
Nineteenth Psalm, The. Bible, *O.T.* *See* Heavens Declare the Glory of God, The.
Nineteenth Song, The: "Great good fortune ere it is had." Hadewijch, *tr. fr. Dutch by* A. J. Barnouw. LyMA
Ninetieth Psalm. Isaac Watts. *See* O God, Our Help in Ages Past.
Ninetta's Tom-Cat. Christian Richardt, *tr. fr. Danish by* Charles W. Stork. BoDS
Ninety and Nine, The. Elizabeth Cecilia Clephane. *See* There Were Ninety and Nine.
Ninety-nine. Carolyn Hancock. RIS
Ninety-nine in the Shade. Rossiter Johnson. BOHV
90 North. Randall Jarrell. CoBMV; FiMAP; MoAB; MoPo; MoVE
Nineveh. Robert Eyres Landor. *Fr.* The Impious Feast. OBRV
Nineveh, Tyre. Memphis Blues. Sterling A. Brown. BANP
Ninth Duino Elegy, The. Rainer Maria Rilke, *tr. fr. German by* R. F. C. Hull. *Fr.* The Duino Elegies. AnGP
Ninth Eclogue, The ("Gorbo, as thou camest this way"). Michael Drayton. *See* Gorbo and Batte.
Ninth Eglog, The ("What time the weatherbeaten flocks"). Michael Drayton. *Fr.* The Shepherd's Garland. ReIE
Ninth Elegy, *sel.* Muriel Rukeyser.
Antagonists, The. FiMAP
Ninth Hour, The. Caroline Hazard. ChIP; OQP; QP-1
Ninth, The; last half; the score was tied. Dorlan's Home-Walk. Arthur Guiterman. PFE
Ninth Moon. Li Ho, *tr. fr. Chinese by* Ho Chih-yuan. LiTW
Ninth of April, The. Otto Gelsted, *tr. fr. Danish.* BoDS, *tr. by* Charles W. Stork; PoFr, *tr. by* Joy Davidman
Ninth Philosopher's Song. Aldous Huxley. ViBoPo
Niobe, *sels.* Aeschylus, *tr. fr. Greek by* C. M. Bowra.
Gods' Children, The. OxBG
Inexorable Death. OxBG
Niobe. Alfred Noyes. MOAH
Niobe. Ovid, *tr. fr. Latin by* Samuel Croxall. *Fr.* Metamorphoses, VI. RoL
Niobe, *sel.* Frederick Tennyson.
"I too remember, in the after years." MOAH; VA
Niobe in Living Stone. *Unknown, tr. fr. Greek by* Lord Neaves. OnPM
Niobe on Phrygian sands. The Wish. Thomas Stanley. AWP; JAWP; WBP
Nipper and the Nanny-Goat. Off to Yakima. Leroy F. Jackson. GaP
Nipper's Lullaby, The. M. B. Spurr. BOL
Nirvana. Sir Edwin Arnold. *Fr.* The Light of Asia, VIII. VA
Nirvana. Sidney Lanier. BAV
Nirvana. Tom MacInnes. CPG
Nirvana. Dmitry Sergeyevich Merezhkovsky, *tr. fr. Russian by* Babette Deutsch. TrRV
Nirvana. *Unknown.* BOHV
(Clam, A.) StaSt
Nirvana. John Hall Wheelock. HBMV; MAP; MoAmPo; NP; NV; SBMV; TSW
Nisé. Juan Meléndez Valdés. *See* Sum of Kisses, A.
Nisus writes epigrams and so do I. Thomas Bastard. SiCE
Nix, The. Richard Garnett. CG
Nixie, The. Erik Johan Stagnelius, *tr. fr. Swedish by* Charles W. Stork. AnSL
Nixie, The. Johan Sebastian Cammermeyer Welhaven, *tr. fr. Norwegian by* Charles W. Stork. AnNoLy
No! Eliza Cook. PoToHe (new ed.)
No! Thomas Hood. BOHV; ChTr; FiBHP; GoTP; HBV; LPS-2; PFE; PoeMoYo
(November.) BBV; GN; OTPC (1946 ed.); RIS
(November in England.) NLK; SN
No./ The crystalline light that wounds the fire. Total Love. Vicente Aleixandre. CoSP
No Amalthea's horn for me! The Golden Mean. Anacreon. GrL; OxBG
No and Yes. Thomas Ashe. HBV
No and Yes. Theodore Tilton. PR
No angel is so high. Angelic Service. Winifred M. Letts. CV
No Angel Led. James Jeffrey Roche. *Fr.* Washington. DD
No angel's son am I, I own. Villon. *Fr.* The Testament. TrFP
No Answer. Laurence Whistler. MoVE
No answer comes to those who pray. Prayer and Deeds. *Unknown.* PraP
No answer, yet I called her name. The Trick. W. H. Davies. ChMP
No Appeasement. Kaj Munk, *tr. fr. Danish by* Charles W. Stork. BoDS
No Armistice in Love's War. Ralph Cheyney. PGD
No Baby in the House. Clara Dolliver. DDA; HBV; LPS-1
No beauty spot should ladies wear. Upon a Patch Face. Thomas, Lord Fairfax. SeCL
No Bed. Walter de la Mare. AlDL
No bees, no honey. Well-packed Wisdom. Benjamin Franklin. *Fr.* Poor Richard's Almanac. StaSt
No beggar she in the mighty hall where her bay-crowned sisters wait. Arizona. Sharlot Mabridth Hall. PAH
No berserk thirst of blood had they. Lexington. Whittier. MC; PAH
No Bird Can Reach the Mountain's Crest. Hovhannes Costaniantz, *tr. fr. Armenian by* Zabelle C. Boyajian. ArmLP
No bird has ever uttered note. Originality. Thomas Bailey Aldrich. AnNE
No bird hath ever lifted note so clear. "Love That Never Told Can Be." John Erskine. CAG
No bitterness: our ancestors did it. Ave Caesar. Robinson Jeffers. MoVE; OxBA
No Bread for the Poor. *Unknown.* *See* Orphan Girl, The ("No home, no home").
No breath of a wind rose then. Stillness and Sound. Simonides. GrL; OxBG
No bridal, but Death for bridegroom Clearista found her. The Bride of Death. Meleager. GrPE; GrR
No Buyers; a Street Scene. Thomas Hardy. LiTB
No ceaseless vigil with hard toil we keep. Compensation. Thomas Stevens Collier. AA
No Cherub's heart or hand for us might ache. Good Friday Evening. Christina Rossetti. PGD
No Child. Padraic Colum. AnFE; GTIV; OBMV; POTE
No Child. Victor Hugo, *tr. fr. French by* Alan Conder. TrFP
No, children, my trips are over. The Engineer's Story. *Unknown.* BeLS

No Chuck, you were wrong. To Chuck—Concerning a Rendezvous in Siam. Jack Charles. WaKn

No city shall I call my own. R. Ellsworth Larsson. *Fr.* O City, Cities! AnAmPo; LA

No Clock with Numbered Eyes. Christopher Hassall. POTE

No Clothes. *Unknown, tr. fr. Chinese.* WhP
(Ode I/XI/8: "How shall it be said that you have no clothes?" *tr. by* James Legge.) BoFr

No cloud can hide the glow of living faith. The Light of Faith. Edgar Dupree. BLRP

No cloud, no relic [*or* relique] of the sunken day. The Nightingale. Samuel Taylor Coleridge. EmBrPo; EnRP; ERP; EV-4; NBE

No cloud of smoke, from Tegea thrown. A Cenotaph. Simonides. GrL; OxBG

No clouds are in the morning sky. Autumn Song [*or* Going a-Nutting]. Edmund Clarence Stedman. BBV (1923 ed.); DD; GN

No Coaching. Christopher Morley. QS

No Cock Crows at Morning. Horace Gregory. ChMo

No Coming to God without Christ. Robert Herrick. OxBoCh

No, comrades, I thank you—not any for me. I Have Drank My Last Glass. *Unknown.* PTA-2

No corn, no wheat, and no barley. Song of the Times. Jacob Adler. OnCuPl

No corpus hangs upon the cross I wear. Victim Invisible. Sister Miriam. PraNu

No courtier this, and naught to courts he owed. Thomas Hood. Sir William Watson. PoVP

No Coward Soul Is Mine. Emily Brontë. *See* Last Lines: "No coward soul is mine."

No cradle years can I recall. Biography. Aleksey Nedogonov. RuPo

No creature's so unlucky as a fish! Antiphanes, *tr. fr. Greek by* F. A. Paley. GrPo

No Credit. Kenneth Fearing. ChMo; PoLFOT

No dandelions tell the time. Sing-Song Verses. Christina Rossetti. *Fr.* Sing-Song. BoN

No day has met another day. Separation. Charles Dalmon. TCPD

No day released from labour to the Sun-god's self is given. The Labours of the Sun. Mimnermus. GrPE

No Death. Philip Bourke Marston. BMEP; VA

No decent man will cross a field. Evelyn Ray. Amy Lowell. MAP; MoAmPo; MOAP

No dip and dart of swallows wakes the black. The Canal. Aldous Huxley. HBMV

No Distant Lord. Maltbie D. Babcock. MaRV

No Doctors Today, Thank You. Ogden Nash. ShBV-4

No doubt but ye are the People—your throne is above the King's. The Islanders. Kipling. BPN

No doubt left. Enough deceiving. James Agee. *Fr.* Lyrics. MAP; MoAmPo

No doubt on the hills of Nazareth. Hilltops. Leslie Savage Clark. ChIP

No doubt: the sun/ dogged me when a child. Monterrey Sun. Alfonso Reyes. AnMP

No doubt this active will. The Mould. Gladys Cromwell. AnAmPo; BAP; LA; MAP; NP; NV; SBMV

No dragon's blood breaking in crimson flowers. Landscape with Figures, I. A. R. D. Fairburn. AnNZ

No dream of mortal joy. Love and Lust. Isaac Rosenberg. ChMP; TrJP

No dust have I to cover me. An Inscription by the Sea [*or* Variations of Greek Themes, XI]. E. A. Robinson, *after* Glaucus. AWP; ChTr; InP; JAWP; MOAP; TOP; WBP

No ear hath heard, no tongue can tell. The Joy Awaiting. James Henry Darlington. BAP

No early buds of early spring. Valentine. "C. W. T." YeAr

No East or West. John Oxenham. *See* Brothers of the Faith.

No, editors don't care a button. Thoughts on Editors. Thomas Moore. WhC

No egg on Friday Alph will eat. Of Alphus. John Parkhurst, *tr. by* Timothe Kendall. TuPP

No end to this marching, forever and ever. The Nineteen Han Poems, I. *Unknown, tr. fr. Chinese.* WhP

No Enemies. Charles Mackay. BLP; GoTP; MaRV

No Envy, John Carter. Merrill Moore. NeMA

No Escape. Harriet L. Delafield. GoYe

No eye shall see the poem that I write. Early Love. V. Sackville-West. DiM

No fairies left? You need not tell me so. Frost Work. Mary Emily Bradley. PEOR

No Faith. Mark Van Doren. AnFE; CoAnAm; TwAmPo

No "fan is in his hand" for these. The Threshing Machine. Alice Meynell. SeCePo

No Fault in Women. Robert Herrick. BOHV; HBV

No fawn-tinged hospital pajamas could cheat him of his austerity. The Old Jew. Maxwell Bodenheim. BAP; LEAP; NP

No feathered bird can weave. Skywriting. Mary Maxtone. BrR

No fence will keep a growing boy outside. Father of the Man. Elizabeth Mabel Bryan. GoYe

No fish stir in our heaving net. Fisherman's Song. Joanna Braillie. *Fr.* The Beacon. EBSV; EV-3

No flattring pellow pon my beed. *Unknown.* SeCSL

No flaunting banners o'er them wave. Captives Going Home. *Unknown.* BIG

No fledgling feeds the fatherbird. Child Labor. Charlotte Perkins Gilman. BAP

No flocks that roam the valleys free. The Pitying Heart. Goldsmith. PCH

No Flowers. *Unknown.* PEOR

No foam;/ A trippling shallow tread. Too Near the Sea. Harold Monro. CoEV

No, for I'll save it! Seven years since. Apparent Failure. Robert Browning. PoVP; VLEP

No freeman, saith the wise, thinks much on death. The End. Wallace Rice. AA

No Friend like Music. Daniel Whitehead Hicky. PoToHe

No Funeral Gloom. William Allingham, *wr. at. to* Ellen Terry. BLPA; MaRV; NeHB

No Furlough. Stephen Stepanchev. WaP

No further, fathering logos, withering son. The Worm in the Whirling Cross. John Malcolm Brinnin. MoPo

"No gables are burning." The Attack on Finnsburg. *Unknown.* BEL

No gilt or tinsel taints the dress. The President. Charles H. L. Johnston. PTA-2

No girl among the much-loved few. Under a Spell. Catullus. OnPM

No Goddess is thy parent, nor th'art of Dardanus offspring. Dido to Aeneas. Virgil, *tr. by* Richard Stanyhurst. *Fr.* The Aeneid, IV. AnIV

No grave for woe, yet earth my watery tears devours. Yet Still I Live. Thomas Campion. PoP

No, great Dome of Agrippa, thou art not Christian! The Pantheon. Arthur Hugh Clough. *Fr.* Amours de Voyage, I. BPN

No Great, No Small. Emerson. *See* Informing Spirit, The.

No grief for the great ones whose labor is ended. Edgar Lee Masters. *Fr.* Lee. ChMo; CMP

No grim last judge recording on a slate. Last Judgment. Stanton A. Coblentz. MaRV

No Gull's Wings. Paul Engle. PoMa

No Harm to Lovers. Albius Tibullus, *tr. fr. Latin by* Hubert Creekmore. LiTW
(Plea and Counsel.) LaP

No heap of dust and petty stones. Cenotaph. Glaucus. OxBG

No heavier lies the everlasting snow. Truth. Cecil Francis Lloyd. CaP; OCL

No Hint of Stain. William Vaughn Moody. *Fr.* An Ode in Time of Hesitation. AA

No hint upon the hilltop shows. Inspiration. John Banister Tabb. WGRP

No, his exit by the gate. Exit. William Stanley Braithwaite. Sandy Starr and Willie Gee, III. BANP

No holy pointer, no unchanging Light. In Our Time. Huw Menai. MaRV

"No home, no home," cried an orphan girl. The Orphan Girl. *Unknown.* AS

No hope has man to live. Prison Song. *Unknown.* TMEV

No house of stone. The Elements. W. H. Davies. MBP; MoBrPo; OBVV; POTT; WaKn; YT

No human figure stirr'd, to go or come. Thomas Hood. *Fr.* The Haunted House. MyFE

No human lips caress. The Flute of Krishna. James B. Thomas. BLA

No human singing can. Music and Words. Elizabeth Jennings. UnS

No, I Am Not as Others Are. Villon, *tr. fr. French by* Arthur Symons. AWP; JAWP; WBP

No, I am through and you can call in vain. Admonition. Philip Stack. BLPA

No, I have never found. Places, Loved Ones. Philip Larkin. NePoEA

"No, I have tempered haste." The Mount. Léonie Adams. MAP; MoAB; MoAmPo; NP

No, I never, till life and its shadows shall end. The Bells of Ostend. William Lisle Bowles. PTA-2

No, I shall never climb above the hill. The Hesitant Heart. Winifred Welles. VOD

No. I'll have no bawds. Ben Jonson. *Fr.* The Alchemist. ViBoPo

No. I'm not an Englishman with a partisan religion. Tragic Guilt. Keidrych Rhys. MoWP; WaP

No image carved with cunning hand, no cloth of purple dye. To His Familar Friend. Nicholas Grimald. TuPP

No Images. Waring Cuney. BANP; CDC; GoSl; PoNe

No Immortality. Frances Cornford. DiM

No Jewel so Worthy. Jacopo da Lentino, *tr. fr. Italian by* Dante Gabriel Rossetti. OnPM

No King. Arthur Guiterman. MuM

No Labor-saving Machine. Walt Whitman. BoFr

No, lady, 'tis not you makes earth a heaven. Chinese Caprice. Théophile Gautier. TrFP
No Land like Ours. J. R. Barrick. BIG
No lapidary's heaven, no brazier's hell for me. Earth-born. Odell Shepard. OBAV
No Laws. Brian Allwood. WaP
No leaf is left unmoistened by the dew. Prayer by Moonlight. Roberta Teale Swartz. TrPWD
No learned discussion. Death. Etna Doop-Smith. PSO
No letters to the frontier come. Homeward. Li Pin. OuHeWo
No life in earth, or air, or sky. Crotalus. Bret Harte. AA; PFY
No lifeless thing of iron and stone. Brooklyn Bridge. Sir Charles G. D. Roberts. PAH
No lilies all for milk. Wild Blossoms. W. H. Davies. MeRV
No, little worm, you need not slip. The Worm. Ann Taylor. PCH; PPL; SAS
No longer am I what I was. Of Himself. Clément Marot. OnPM; TrFP
No longer, borne down insensible rivers. The Drunken Boat. Arthur Rimbaud. ReMP
No longer by the oak, O blackbird, sing. A Blackbird. Marcus Argentarius. LiTW; OxBG
No longer casual hand to lip. Blind, I Speak to the Cigarette. Joanne de Longchamps. GoYe
No Longer Could I Doubt Him True. Walter Savage Landor. *See* Mother, I Cannot Mind My Wheel.
No longer heed we war and strife. Thus Speak the Slain. Carl Holliday. PGD
No longer homes are flame against. Litany for Peace. Leslie Savage Clark. PGD
"No longer I avoid thee as of late." Homer. *Fr.* The Iliad, XXII. GrPo
No longer, mother dear, can I. Adolescence. Sappho. GrR
No longer mourn for me, when I am dead. Sonnets, LXXI. Shakespeare. AWP; BEL; BoLiVe; CoBE; EIL; ElSeCe; EM-1; EnL; EnLi-1; EnLit; EPP; EV-1; GTBS; GTBS-D; GTBS-W; GTSE; GTSL; HBV; InPo; JAWP; LiTB; LO; OAEP; OBSC; OuHeWo; PeBoSo; PIAE; PoE; PoRA; ReaPo; ReEn; ReIE; SeCeV; SiCE; TOP; TrGrPo; ViBoPo; WBP; WHA
No Longer Now. Marina Ivanovna Tzvetayeva, *tr. fr. Russian by* Babette Deutsch. TrRV
No longer, O scholars, shall Plautus. Future of the Classics. *Unknown.* BOHV
No longer of Him be it said. Citizen of the World. Joyce Kilmer. OQP; QP-1; StJW
No longer soiled with stain of earth, what seemed his mantle shone. Simile. Sir Samuel Ferguson. *Fr.* Congal. IrPN
No longer that gray visage fix. The Little Shade. Edwina Stanton Babcock. BAP
No longer the wife of the hero. The Vamp Passes. James J. Montague. HBMV
No longer torn by what she knows. The Poor Relation. E. A. Robinson. AnAmPo; LA; MAPA; TwP
No longer will the machine gun decide for liberty. Child of the Wind with the Harmonica. Nicephorus Vrettakos. MoGP
No Love, to Love of Man and Wife. Richard Eedes. InvP (Of Man and Wife.) EIL
No lover saith, I love, nor any other. The Paradox. John Donne. OAEP
No luck, there's no room here. A Word for the Innkeeper. Paul Grano. MoAuPo
No lullaby is older than the rain. Small Rain. Alice Lawry Gould. MoSiPe
No McTavish. Genealogical Reflection. Ogden Nash. ALV
No maiden dream, nor fancy theme. The Soldiers of the Plough. Charles Sangster. BoCaPo (1943 ed.); CPG
No man can bid a fool or sage. The Power of Thought. Süsskind von Trimberg. TrJP
No man can choose what coming hours may bring. What Man May Choose. Priscilla Leonard. MaRV
No man e'er found a happy life by chance. Happiness an Art. Edward Young. *Fr.* Night Thoughts, VIII. OBEC
No man has felt the cold that I have felt. Unemployment. Richard X. Evans. CAG
No man hath dared to write this thing as yet. Histrion. Ezra Pound. ChMo; CMP
No Man, If Men Are Gods. E. E. Cummings. InvP; MoPo; NePA
No man is born into the world whose work. Labor [*or* Work]. James Russell Lowell. *Fr.* A Glance behind the Curtain. MaRV; PEDC
No man knew whence the strange bird came. The Bird. Jorge de Lima. AnCL; LiTW
No man knows his father till he sees. The Way to Know a Father. Robert P. Tristram Coffin. PoRL
No Man Knows War. Edwin Rolfe. TrJP; WaP
"No man may him hyde." Sun! Marianne Moore. MeRV; NP
No man outlives the grief of war. The Permanence of the Young Men. William Soutar. NeBP
No man should stand before the moon. A Sense of Humour. Vachel Lindsay. MAPA; TwAmPo
No Man's Land. James H. Knight-Adkin. MCCG
No map shows my Jerusalem. The Burning-Glass. Walter de la Mare. QS; StJW
No Marvel Is It. Bernard de Ventadour, *tr. fr. Provençal by* Harriet Waters Preston. AWP; LiTW; LyMA; OuHeWo
No massive locks. The Wolf of Gubbio. Hyacinth Blocker. SaFP
No Master. W. H. Davies. PoFr; POTT
No Master. William Morris. BPN; EmBrPo; PoFr; PoVP
No Matter. Paulus Silentiarius, *tr. fr. Greek by* William Cowper. AWP; EnLi-1; JAWP; OuHeWo; WBP ("My name, my country—what are they to thee?" *tr. by* William Cowper.) GrPo ("Rest Is Silence, The," *tr. by* F. L. Lucas.) GrPE (Vanities, *tr. by* William Cowper.) OxBG
No matter how far from the right she hath strayed. Some Mother's Child. Frances L. Keeler. MotAn
No matter how grouchy you're feeling. Limerick [*or* The Smile]. Anthony Euwer. *Fr.* The Limeratomy. HBMV; LiBL; TSWC; WhC
No matter how the chances are. Jerry an' Me. Hiram Rich. HBV
No matter how you love me. Guadalupe. Grace Hazard Conkling. NP
No matter where they lived the same dream came. The Castaways. Marya Zaturenska. TrGrPo (1942 ed.)
No middle course fits love's extremity. Love Indivisible. Pierre de Ronsard. TrFP
No Miracle. Daniel Corkery. AnIV
No monuments or landmarks guide the stranger. A Country without a Mythology. Douglas Le Pan. BoCaPo (1948 ed.)
No moon. Night on the West River. Po Chü-i. PoHN
No More! Praxilla, *tr. fr. Greek by* Walter Headlam. GrR
No more be grieved at that which thou hast done. Sonnets, XXXV. Shakespeare. PeBoSo; UnPo
No More Booze. *Unknown.* AS, *with music;* TrAS, *with music;* TreF
No more, but in a woman, and commanded. Shakespeare. *Fr.* Antony and Cleopatra, IV, xiii. NBE
No more, Clarinda, shall thy charms. To Clarinda. *Unknown.* SeCL
No More Dams I'll Make. Shakespeare. *Fr.* The Tempest, II, ii. ViBoPo
No More Destructive Flame. Francis X. Connolly. ISi
No more for them shall Evening's rose unclose. Epicedium. J. Corson Miller. DD; HBMV; PAH
No more for us the little sighing. Threnos. Ezra Pound. MOAP
No more from out the sunset. Onus Probandi [*or* Sandy Star]. William Stanley Braithwaite. Sandy Star and Willie Gee, V. BANP; BAP; HBMV
No more, gaily humming, the lover. Love. Herman Wildenvey. AnNoLy
No more in any house can I be at peace. A Dream. Charles Williams. OBEV (new ed.)
No more in dreams as once it draws me there. A House of the Eighties. Edmund Wilson. AnFE; CoAnAm; TwAmPo
No more lewd lays of lighter loves I sing. Barnabe Barnes. *Fr.* A Divine Century of Spiritual Sonnets. TuPP
No more, my dear, no more these counsels try. Astrophel and Stella, LXIV. Sir Philip Sidney. BEL; CoBE; ElSeCe; HBV; NBE; OBSC; ReEn; SiCE; SiPS; TOP; TuPP
No more, my Stella, to the sighing shades. To Stella. Hester Chapone. OBEC
No more my visionary soul shall dwell. Pantisocracy. Samuel Taylor Coleridge. EnRP
No more, no more. The Riddle. Alexander Brome. OBS
No more—no more in Cashel town. The Roving Worker. *Unknown.* OnYI
No more—no more—Oh! never more on me. Disillusion [*or* My Days of Love Are Over]. Byron. *Fr.* Don Juan, I. FaBoEn; GEPC
No more, O maiden voices, sweet as honey. The Halcyons [*or* To His Maiden Quire]. Alcman. GrL; GrR; OxBG
No more, O maidens, with honey-dew voices that waken desire. No More, O Maidens. Alcman, *tr. by* Olga Marx *and* Ernst Morwitz. LiTW
No More, O My Spirit. Euripides, *tr. fr. Greek by* Hilda Doolittle ("H. D."). *Fr.* Hippolytus. AWP
No more of my Harriot, of Polly no more. The Lass with the Golden Locks. Christopher Smart. RO
No more of talk where God or Angel Guest. The Subject of Heroic Song. Milton. *Fr.* Paradise Lost, IX. OBS; SeEP
"No more of this, for goddes dignitee." Prologue to Melibeus. Chaucer. *Fr.* The Canterbury Tales. EM-1
No more of your titled acquaintances boast. Epigram. Burns. ALV
No more peck of corn for me, no more, no more. Many T'ousand Go. *Unknown.* ABF

No more, poor partridge, taught to lure. A Decoy Partridge. Simmias. OxBG
"No more shall I see." Frithiof's Farewell. Esaias Tegnér. *Fr.* Frithiof's Saga. AWP; JAWP; WBP
No more shall I, since I am driven hence. To Larr. Robert Herrick. BoW; SeCV-1
No more shall I work in the factory. The Factory Girl. *Unknown.* ABF
No more shall meads be decked with flowers. The Protestation. Thomas Carew. OuHeWo
No more shall nation against nation rise. A Vision of the Future. Pope. MuP
No more shall stones nor oakwoods on thy sweet music follow. Orpheus. Antipater of Sidon. GrPE
No more shall walls, no more shall walls confine. Hosanna. Thomas Traherne. PoEL-2; SeCV-2
No More than a Dream. Jens Peter Jacobsen, *tr. fr. Danish by* Charles W. Stork. BoDS
No more the battle or the chase. Indian Summer. John Banister Tabb. AA; DD
No more the English girls may go. High Germany. Edward Shanks. OBMV
No more the jousts and tourneys. Toledo. José Zorrilla. CAW
No more the road shall turn. The Way Back. Thomas S. Jones, Jr. VOD
No More the Slow Stream. Floris Clark McLaren. BoCaPo
No more the smoke-wisp signal climbs; no more. Rex Ingamells. *Fr.* Forgotten People. BoAu
No more the stream is gilded. Stratford upon Avon. Ivor Brown. NeTW
No more the swanboat on the artificial lake. Blind Date. Conrad Aiken. MoVE; ViBoPo (1958 ed.)
No More the Thunder of Cannon. Julia C. R. Dorr. OHIP
No more the white refulgent streets. Elegy. Allen Tate. TriL
No more these simple flowers belong. Burns. Whittier. CoBA; IAP; LPS-3; PtP; TCAP
No more upon my bosom rest thee. Woman's Song. Edward Shanks. LO
No More We'll to the Wood. Théodore de Banville, *tr. fr. French by* Alan Conder. TrFP
No more wine? then we'll push back chairs and talk. Bishop Blougram's Apology. Robert Browning. BrBE; OtMeF; PoEL-5; ViPo; ViPP
No more with candied words infect mine ears. Tell Me No More. William Drummond of Hawthornden. TrGrPo
No more with overflowing light. For a Dead Lady. E. A. Robinson. AmPP (4th ed.); AnFE; AnNE; APA; ChMo; CMP; CoAnAm; CoBMV; FaBoEn; GTBS-D; GTBS-W; IAP; InP; InvP; LiTA; LiTM; MAP; MAPA; MoAB; MoAmPo; MOAP; MotAn; OxBA; PoEL-5; PoeMoYo; PoRA; ReMP; RiBV; TCPD; TwAmPo; TwP; ViBoPo; WHA
No more with rocks and trees shalt thou prevail. Orpheus. Antipater of Sidon. OxBG
No More Words. Franklin Lushington. PAH
No more words,/ no vain, threadbare words used in epics! Kleisoura. Angelos Sikelianos. MoGP
No more work and no more play. Good Night. Ruth Ainsworth. BoTP
No mortal object did these eyes behold. Sonnet LII. Michelangelo, *tr. by* Wordsworth. BoFr; LyPI; RO
No mortal thing enthralled these longing eyes. Celestial Love. Michelangelo, *tr. by* John Addington Symonds. AWP; JAWP; WBP
No music He heard, and no angels He saw. The Welcome. Leonard Feeney. WHL
No! my desires are limited; nor expand. The Wish. John Dancer. SeCL
No, My Own Love of Other Years. Walter Savage Landor. *See* In After Time.
No myrtle can obliterate a name. Your Glory, Lincoln. Mae Winkler Goodman. PGD
No Names. *Unknown, tr. fr. Irish by* Frank O'Connor. KiLC
(Abusive Snatches. *diff. tr.*) SiB
No Nation Liveth unto Itself. *Unknown.* MaRV
No nearer home than Nassau Bay. Rondeau in Wartime. James Bertram. AnNZ
No need to hush the children for her sake. Out of Hearing. Jane Barlow. HBV
No! never such a draught was poured. A Ballad of the Boston Tea-Party. Oliver Wendell Holmes. MC; PaA; PAH; PoFr
No, Never Think. Pushkin, *tr. fr. Russian by* Babette Deutsch. TrRV
No new poems his brush will trace. On Hearing Someone Sing a Poem by Yüan Chen. Po Chü-i. TrCh
No News. Wang Wei, *tr. fr. Chinese by* Henry H. Hart. PoHN
No Nice Girl's Song. Robert Herring. MoWP
No night is there! Heaven. Clarence A. Vincent. OQP; QP-1
No! No! Bird in the darkness singing. The Tsigane's Canzonet. Edward King. AA
No, no, fair heretic[k], it needs must be. Song. Sir John Suckling. *Fr.* Aglaura. AtBAP; LiTL; LoBV; OBS; ReEn; RiBV; SeEP
No, no; for my virginity. A True Maid. Matthew Prior. ALV; LiTG
No, no! Go from me. I have left her lately. A Virginal. Ezra Pound. AmPP; APA; ChMo; CMP; CoAnAm; CoBMV; MAP; MoAB; MoAmPo; MOAP; NeMA; NePA; OxBA; PR; TCPD; TwAmPo
No, no, go not to Lethe, neither twist. Ode on Melancholy [*or* On Melancholy]. Keats. AnFE; AtBAP; ATP; BCEP; BEL; BLV; BoLiVe; BPN; CaAE; CoBE; EG; EM-2; EmBrPo; EnL; EnLi-2; EnLit; EnLP; EnRP; EPN; ERP; EV-4; ExPo; FaBoEn; FiP; GEPC; GTBS-W; HBV; LEAP; LiTB; LO; MaPo; OAEP; OBEV; PoE; PoEL-4; PoFS; PoRA; PreP; ReaPo; RiBV; SeCeV; TCEP; TOP; TreFS; TrGrPo; TwHP; TwP; TyEnPo; ViBoPo
No, no, guard thee. Get thee gone. Not That Way. Walter de la Mare. TriL
No, no I did not bargain for so much. Too Much. Edwin Muir. LiTB
No, no, I did not love you. "Anna Akhmatova," *tr. fr. Russian by* C. M. Bowra. BoR
No, No! I Ne'er Shall Love Thee Less. Henry Cromwell. SeCL
No, no. I well remember—proofs, you said. The Demon-Lover. James Abraham Hillhouse. *Fr.* Hadad. AA
No, no! It is not that which fills my eyes! Cold Confession. Vladimir Benediktov. BoRS
No, no, no, no! Come, let's away to prison. Shakespeare. *Fr.* King Lear, V, iii. NBE
No, no, no, no, I cannot hate my foe. Song. Sir Philip Sidney. SiPS
No, no, no, resistance is but vain. Song. Anthony Henly. SeCL
No, No, Poor Suffering [*or* Suff'ring] Heart. Dryden. *Fr.* Cleomenes, II, ii. AtBAP; GTBS-W; LiTB; LiTG; LiTL; LoBV; ViBoPo
(One Happy Moment.) OBEV (new ed.)
(Song: "No, no, poor suff'ring heart, no change endeavour.") CEP; SeCV-2; TCEP
No, no, the falling blossom is no sign. Song. George Meredith. EnLit
No, no, the utmost share. Robert Herrick. *Fr.* To Electra. LO
No noise is here, or none that hinders thought. The Robin in Winter. William Cowper. *Fr.* The Task, VI. RO
No, not cold beneath the grasses. In My Father's House. Robert Freeman. OQP; QP-1
No! not for those of women born. From a Hint in the Minor Poets. Samuel Wesley. OBEC
No, not for you, for you, does my love flame. Mikhail Lermontov, *tr. fr. Russian by* C. M. Bowra. BoR
No, not in the halls of the noble and proud. The Quakeress Bride. Elizabeth Clementine Kinney. AA
No, Not More Welcome. Thomas Moore. TIP
No, Not the Owl. T. I. Moore. MoAuPo
No not this old whalehall can whelm us. Mappemounde. Earle Birney. BoCaPo (1948 ed.); PeCV
No, nothing is asleep in this demesne. The Sleeping Beauty. Robert Layzer. NePoEA
No notice in the papers. Tombstone with Cherubim. Horace Gregory. NAMP
No, now I wish the sunshine would stop. "And Oh!—That the Man I Am Might Cease to Be." D. H. Lawrence. BrBE
Noone and a Star Stand, Am to Am. E. E. Cummings. NePoAm-2
"Noone" autumnal this great lady's gaze. E. E. Cummings. CrMA
No one can tell you why. W. D. Snodgrass. Heart's Needle, IV. NePoEA
No One Cares Less Than I. Edward Thomas. MoVE
No one could tell me where my soul might be. The Search. Ernest Crosby. AA; BAP; OQP; QP-1
No one dies cleanly now. Eclogue. Frederic Prokosch. ViBoPo
No one ever plucked. Robert Browning. *Fr.* The Ring and the Book. ChIP
No one goes there now. The Tune of Seven Towers. William Morris. PoVP; ViPP; VLEP
No one in the garden. Laughter. Olive Enoch. BoTP
No One Knew. "Demyan Bedny," *tr. fr. Russian by* Babette Deutsch. TrRV
(None Knew, *tr. by* Jack Lindsay.) RuPo
No One Knows the Countryside. Struthers Burt. TBM
No one knows what it is I say. Alone. Itzik Manger. OnCuPl
No one knows where the road may take us. As We Grow Older. Grantland Rice. DDA
No one of us can keep him in his stall. Old Major. Bianca Bradbury. MuM

No one sees me. The All-seeing Gods. Longfellow. *Fr.* The Masque of Pandora. OOP; QP-2
No One So Much as You. Edward Thomas. ChMP
No one spoke. Haiku. Ryota. LiTW; OnPJ
No one walks when the guardian drum sounds. Thinking of My Brothers on a Moonlit Night. Tu Fu. WhP
No one was in the fields. Tom's Angel. Walter de la Mare. POTE
No one was looking at his lonely case. Any Size We Please. Robert Frost. CoV
No one was with me there. Estranged. Walter de la Mare. FaBoEn
No one will ever really know. Vigil. Mabel Simpson. BAP
"No one will milk a cow within." Forbidden Drink. Robert Lovett. WhC
No one will remember. Child of the Long Grass. Roy Macnab. BoSA
No one would notice that gap between two fields. A Road in the Weald. Richard Church. HaMV
No Other Choice. *Unknown. See* Fain Would I Change That Note.
No other god is implicated here. A New Theology. Euripides. *Fr.* Heracles. GrR
No other man, unless it was Doc Hill. Doctor Meyers. Edgar Lee Masters. *Fr.* Spoon River Anthology. ChMo; CMP
No Other Slave. Pierre de Ronsard, *tr. fr. French by* Alan Conder. *Fr.* Sonnets pour Hélène. TrFP
("Cruel, farewell, since I do but annoy thee," *tr. by* Humbert Wolfe.) PrPoCR
No other torch save what my dreams discover. Pierre de Ronsard. *Fr.* Sonnets pour Hélène. PrPoCR
No Pains Comparable to His Attempt. William Hunnis. ReIE; TuPP
(Shipmen, The.) OBSC
No painter's brush, nor poet's pen. A Mother's Name. *Unknown.* PGD; PSO
No paltry promptings of unglutted hate. Jefferson Davis. Harry Thurston Peck. GA
No passenger was known to flee. Emily Dickinson. MoVE
No path at all goes somewhere. Woodlore. Kim Kurt. NePoAm-2
No Peace. *Unknown, tr. fr. Sanskrit by* Joseph Nadin Rawson. *Fr.* The Upanishads. OnPM
No permanent possession of the sky. To the Greatest City in the World. Rolfe Humphries. PoMa
No pictured likeness of my Lord have I. My Master's Face. William Hurd Hillyer. ChIP; MaRV
No place is safe, no temple yields defence. The Times. Marcus Manilius. LiTW
No Platonic Love. William Cartwright. ElSeCe; InvP; LiTB; SiTL
(No Platonique Love.) PoEL-2
No Pleasure without Some Pain. Thomas, Lord Vaux. ElL; SiCE; TuPP
(Death in Life.) OBSC
No poor Dutch peasant winged with all his fear. Prologue and Epilogue to the University of Oxford. Dryden. EV-3
No Possum, No Sop, No Taters. Wallace Stevens. AmP; MoVE; OxBA; PoFS
No price is set on [*or* in] the lavish summer. June [*or* What Is So Rare as a Day in June?]. James Russell Lowell. *Fr.* The Vision of Sir Launfal: Prelude to Pt. I. NePA; PTA-1
No pride hath he who sings of escape from love. James Stephens. *Fr.* Theme with Variations. POTE
No prisoner can tell his honest thought. Prison Song. Richard Cœur de Lion, *tr. by* Henry Adams. LiA; LiTW
No Prisoner of Time. William H. Hudnut, Jr. ChIP
No puppet master pulls the strings on high. Slaves. George Sylvester Viereck. LPS-3
No purple mars the chalice; not a bird. The Exquisite Sonnet. J. C. Squire. HBMV
No quarrel ever stirred. Of Quarrels. Arthur Guiterman. TiPo
No rack can torture me. Emily Dickinson. MaPo; MoAB; MoPo
No Reason Why. Thomas Brown. *See* I Do Not Love Thee, Doctor Fell.
No rock along the road but knows. Poet. Donald Jeffrey Hayes. PoNe
No roofs of gold o'er riotous tables shining. Description of a Convent. Richard Crashaw. PraNu
No Room. Robert Whitaker. ChIP
No room for mourning: he's gone out. William Wordsworth. Sidney Keyes. ChMP; GTBS-D; POTE; SeCePo
"No," said Patience patiently, and pulled from his wallet. Providence. William Langland. *Fr.* The Vision of Piers Plowman. PoLi
No sculptor I of forms whose feet stand clinging. The Poet's Praise. Pindar. *Fr.* Nemean Odes, V. GrPE
No Season for Our Season. Willard Maas. AnAmPo
No season frontiers here: the snow-white foam. Atlantic. George Rostrevor Hamilton. NeTW

No second love shall e'er my heart surprise. Elegy: to Delia. James Hammond. Love Elegies, XII. CEP
No Second Troy. W. B. Yeats. ChMo; EnLoPo; MaPo; NP; PoE; PoEL-5; SeCePo
Courage Equal to Desire, *sel.* LiA
No Sects [*or* Sect] in Heaven. Elizabeth H. Jocelyn Cleaveland. BLPA; PTA-2; TreFS
No secular sound—this is the house of prayer. Woodland. Sister Margaret Teresa. JKCP (1926 ed.)
No, she does not falter. Epithalamium. Helene Mullins. PraNu
No sheep in the folds. Christmas. Betty Scott Stam. BePJ
No shield against our crying griefs. We Ask No Shield. William Rose Benét. MOAP
No show of bolts and bars. Love. Henry David Thoreau. OBVV; OQP; QP-2
No sickness of the flesh is ours to-day. Feodor Tyutchev, *tr. fr. Russian by* R. Christie. BoR
No sight earth yields our eyes is lovelier than. The Deed. T. Sturge Moore. PtOT
No sight of it, only the song. Hark! Hark! Leonora Speyer. BAP; NLK (1947 ed.)
No sign is made while empires pass. Continuity. "Æ." ChMo; MBP; MoBrPo; NeMA; PoVP
No Single Thing Abides. Lucretius, *tr. fr. Latin by* W. H. Mallock. *Fr.* De Rerum Natura. AWP; ImOP, *abr.*; JAWP; PG (1945 ed.); WBP
No sky at all. Loneliness. Hanshin. WoL
No Slave beneath the Flag. George Lansing Taylor. DD, *abr.*; PEOR
No sleep! I rise and burn the night away. The Protagonist. Peter Hopegood. MoAuPo
No sleep like hers, no rest. White Roses. Ernest Rhys. VA
No sleep. The sultriness pervades the air. The House-Top. Herman Melville. APW; LiTA
No sleepy poison is more strong to kill. Choice. Anna Wickham. QS
No slightest golden rhyme he wrote. A Hint from Herrick. Thomas Bailey Aldrich. HBV
No sly usurping dream defeats the will. The Settled Men. George M. Brady. NeIP
No Snake in Springtime. Elizabeth J. Coatsworth. AnAmPo; LA
No soldier, statesman, hierophant, or king. To the Memory of Fletcher Harper. Dinah Maria Mulock Craik. LPS-3
No song of a soldier riding down. The Ride of Colin [*or* Collins] Graves. John Boyle O'Reilly. GA; PAH; TVSH
No Songs in Winter. Thomas Bailey Aldrich. OBAV
No sooner had th' Almighty ceas't, but all. Heaven. Milton. *Fr.* Paradise Lost, III. OBS
No sound is heard here where the grey cliffs rise. The Isle of the Dead. Otto Freund. MuM
No sound of any storm that shakes. Hillcrest. E. A. Robinson. CoBMV; CoV; FaBoEn; MoAB; MOAP; OxBA
No Spare Time. Ishikawa Kimiko, *tr. fr. Japanese by* Ishii *and* Obata. OnPM
No splendor 'neath the sky's proud dome. The Tribute. Coventry Patmore. *Fr.* The Angel in the House, I. LPS-1
No spot of earth where men have so fiercely for ages of time. Antrim. Robinson Jeffers. CoV
No spring nor summer beauty hath such grace. The Autumnal[1]. John Donne. Elegies, IX. AtBAP; EnL; EnLP; EPS (1942 ed.); NBE; OAEP; PoEL-2; ReFn; SeCV-1; SeEP; TuPP; ViBoPo
No spur or whiplash needed now. To My Mouse-colored Mare. Tristan Corbière. AnFP
No Star Is Ever Lost. Adelaide Anne Procter. *Fr.* A Legend of Provence. MaRV
No stars her eyes, to clear the wandering night. Phyllis, VIII. Thomas Lodge. TuPP
No state is enviable. To the luck alone. Modern Love, XIX. George Meredith. ViPo
No stately column marks the hallowed place. Alamance. Seymour W. Whiting. PAH
No stir in the air, no stir in the sea. The Inchcape Rock. Robert Southey. BeLS; CaAE; CG; ChTr; DaBS; EV-4; FaBoBe; GN; GoTP; HBV; HBVY; LPS-2; MW; OBRV; OnSP; OTPC; PECK; TreFS; TVSH
No stranger pilgrims wear the shepherd's way. To Mary at Christmas. John Gilland Brunini. ISi
No Sudden Thing of Glory. Alice Meynell. StJW
No Sufferer for Her Love. *Unknown, tr. fr. Late Middle Irish by* Robin Flower. AnIL
No sun-kissed golden-hearted flower. The Waterfall. Kristján Jónsson. IcP
No sun—no moon! No! [*or* November or November in England]. Thomas Hood. BBV; BOHV; ChTr; FiBHP; GN; GoTP; HBV; LPS-2; NLK; OTPC (1946 ed.); PFE; PoeMoYo; RIS; SN
No sunny ray, no silver night. Threnody. Thomas Lovell Beddoes. EnRP; ERP; TriL
No Swan So Fine. Marianne Moore. CoBMV; OxBA
No Sweeter Thing. Adelaide Love. PGD

No syllables that lightliest dance. April. Mary Sinton Leitch. LS
No syrup or perfume. Nox. Salvador Díaz Mirón. AnMP
No teacher I of boys or smaller fry. Allen Beville Ramsay. CenHV
No tears, no sorrowing farewells. When I Go Home. Milton Lee. OQP; QP-2
No, the human heart/ Is unknowable. Ki no Tsurayuki, *tr. fr. Japanese by* Kenneth Rexroth. OnPJ
No, they are come; their horn is lifted up. Gerard Manley Hopkins. *Fr.* Six Epigrams. SeCePo
No, they cannot touch me for coyning. I am the king himselfe. Shakespeare. *Fr.* King Lear, IV, vi. AtBAP
No things, my Laches, are so close akin. Marriage—Two Views. Menander. OxBG
No Thoroughfare. Ruth Holmes. BoTP
No! those days are gone away. Robin Hood. Keats. AWP; BEL; BPN; EM-2; EmBrPo; EnLi-2; EnLit; EnRP; EPN; EV-4; GEPC; InPo; OTPC (1946 ed.); PCD; PCN
No thought to complain, as atop the train. Supai Hill Patrol. Jack O'Brien. HiLiAm
No threat was ever yet sincerely made. Threats. Menander. OxBG
No thyng ys [*or* is] to man so dere. Praise of Women [*or* Woman's Love]. Robert Mannyng. BCEP; LO; LyMA; OBEV
No Time. Terence Tiller. NeBP
No Time for God. Norman L. Trott. BLRP
No time, no time, to sing my songs. The Spinner's Song. Kathleen Millay. BAP
No, Time, thou shalt not boast that I do change. Sonnets, CXXIII. Shakespeare. BLV; BoLiVe; OAEP; OBSC; PeBoSo: SiCE; TrGrPo
No Time to Hate. Emily Dickinson. *See* I had no time to hate, because.
"No time to pray!" Prayerlessness. *Unknown.* PraP
No, 'tis in vain to seek for bliss. Felicity. Isaac Watts. OxBoCh
No Title ("So difficult the meeting"). Li Shang-yin, *tr. fr. Chinese.* WhP
No tomb can hold the familiar voice interred. Mayakovsky Memory. Vera Inber. *Fr.* Diary of a Journey. RuPo
No tongue can tell, no pen describe. Stanzas. Philip Freneau. CoBA
No trace of verdant hillside, nor of meadow. A Steppe in the Nazas Country. Manuel José Othón. AnMP
No tranquil ordered day of ours. In Memoriam. Ada Jackson. PGD
No Truer Word. Walter Savage Landor. *See* Epigram: "No truer word, save God's . . ."
No trumpet blared the word that he was born. Abraham Lincoln. Virginia Fraser Boyle. BAP
No Trust in Men. *Unknown, tr. fr. Spanish by* Havelock Ellis. OnPM
No Trust in Time. William Drummond of Hawthornden. BSV; LoBV
(Look How the Flower.) EPS (1942 ed.); EV-2
(Sonnet: "Look how the flower which ling'ringly doth fade.") SeCL
(Thy Sun Posts Westward.) SeCePo
No Trust in Women. *Unknown, tr. fr. Spanish by* Havelock Ellis. OnPM
No, 'twasn't here dat tree firs' grew. The Woman's Tongue Tree. Arthur Guiterman. PoMS
No two eyes gaze alike. Janus. Madeline Mason. GoYe
No Uneasy Refuge. Blanaid Salkeld. AnIV
No use to speak, no good to tell you that. Communication. Elizabeth Jennings. NePoEA
No usual words can bear the woe I feel. For I Am Sad. Don Marquis. BOHV
No vainer thing there can be found amid this vale of strife. The Uncertainty of Life. Barnabe Googe. SiCE
No victor when in battle spent. The Dream. Sir William Davenant. EV-2
No village dames and maidens now are seen. Samuel Jackson Pratt. *Fr.* Cottage Pictures. EnSW
No vision and you perish. Some Faith at Any Cost. Harriet Du Autermont. MaRV
No walls confine! Can nothing hold my mind? Insatiableness. Thomas Traherne. OxBoCh
No wandering any more where the feet stumble. Marriage. Mark Van Doren. BAP
No warm, downy pillow His sweet head pressed. The Heavenly Stranger. Ada Blenkhorn. BLRP
No wasting sickness, but long years of peace. Dionysius, *tr. fr. Greek by* Walter Leaf. GrPo
No water so still as the/ dead fountains of Versailles. No Swan So Fine. Marianne Moore. CoBMV; OxBA
No waterfalls and no ravines. Earth. Sergei Smirnov. RuPo
No Way Is Good. Poseidippus, *tr. fr. Greek by* William Hay. OnPM
No way too long—no path too steep. Stefan George. *Fr.* Das Jahr der Seele. AWP
No wealth of silver or of gold. Nor Gold Nor Silver. Solon. GrR
No wind-wakeness here. A cricket's creed. Sunday in the Country. May Swenson. NePoAm-2
No wine is pledg'd me now; nigh my sweet Nell. The Usurper. Theognis. GrR
No Woman Born. Robert Farren. OxBI
No wonder the birds make whittlings of sound, that the hemlock. Sun-up in March. Abbie Huston Evans. NePoAm
No wonder you so oft have wept. Francis Burdett Money-Coutts. *Fr.* A Little Sequence. OBVV
No Word of Fear. Walter Savage Landor. *See* Death Stands above Me.
No word that is not flesh, he said. A Reason for Writing. Theodore Spencer. TwAmPo
No Words Are Lost. Margaret Widdemer. PoMa
No Worst, There Is None. Gerard Manley Hopkins. ChMo; EnL; EnLi-2 (1949 ed.); FaBoMo; LiTB; LiTM; LoBV; MaPo; MoAB; MoBrPo (1950 ed.); MoP; PeBoSo; PoEL-5; ReMP; ViP; ViPP; VLEP
(Abyss.) ES
(Life Death Does End.) SeCePo
(Sonnet: "No worst, there is none.") CoEV; FaBoEn; MoVE
(Terrible Sonnets, The, II.) MoPo
Noah. Roy Campbell. *Fr.* The Flaming Terrapin. BoSA
Noah an' Jonah an' Cap'n John Smith. Don Marquis. LHV; LoGBV
Noah and the Flood. Genesis, VI: 5–VIII: 22, Bible, *O.T.* OuHeWo
Noah and the Waters, *sel.* C. Day Lewis.
Chorus: "Since you have come thus far." OAEP (2d ed.)
Noah's Ark. *Unknown.* APW
Noah's Ark. Marguerite Young. MoPo
Noah's Flood. *Unknown, tr. fr. Anglo-Saxon. Fr.* Genesis. AnOE, *tr. by* Charles W. Kennedy; BEL
Noah's Floud, *sel.* Michael Drayton.
"Eternall and all-working God, which wast." PoEL-2
Nobilis, Precor. *Unknown, tr. fr. Latin by* Basil Blackett. *Fr.* Carmina Burana. LaP
Nobility. Alice Cary. OHFP; OQP; PTA-1; QP-2; WBLP
(Noble Life, The.) MaRV
Nobility. Tennyson. *Fr.* Lady Clara Vere de Vere. OTPC (1946 ed.)
Noble, The. Wordsworth. *Fr.* The Prelude, IX. ChTr
Noble Art of Murdering, The. Thackeray. BMEP
Noble Balm, The. Ben Jonson. *See* Ode, An: "High-spirited friend."
Noble be man,/ Helpful and good! The Godlike. Goethe. LiA
Noble Fisherman, The; or, Robin Hood's Preferment. *Unknown.* ESPB; OBB
Noble Friar, that worthy beggar, The. The Friar's Tale. Chaucer, *mod. by* Edwin M. Everett. *Fr.* The Canterbury Tales. EnLi-1 (1949 ed.)
Noble Friendship, A, Hamlet and Horatio. Shakespeare. *See* Friendship ("Horatio, thou art e'en as just a man").
Noble heart [*or* hart], that harbours virtuous [*or* vertuous] thought, The. The Fight of the Red Cross Knight and the Heathen Sansjoy. Spenser. *Fr.* The Faerie Queene, I, 5. FiP; ViBoPo
Noble horse with courage in his eye, The. Aristocrats. Keith Douglas. NePoEA
Noble is he who falls in front of battle. How Can Man Die Better. Tyrtaeus. GrL; OxBG; WaaP
Noble Kinsmen, The. Fletcher *and* Shakespeare. *See* Two Noble Kinsmen, The.
Noble Lay of Aillinn, The. Stopford Brooke. TIP
Noble Life, The. Alice Cary. *See* Nobility.
Noble Love. Richard Flecknoe. ACP
Noble mayd, still standing, all this vewd, The. The Masque of Cupid. Spenser. *Fr.* The Faerie Queene, III. PoEL-1
Noble, nasty course he ran, A. Epitaph on the Late King of the Sandwich Isles. Winthrop Mackworth Praed. FiBHP
Noble Nature, The. Ben Jonson. *See* It Is Not Growing like a Tree.
Noble nature is the essence of nobility. Plebeian Song. "Markos Avgeris." MoGP
Noble nurse who roused your jealousy, The. What Answer? Baudelaire. TrFP
Noble Old Pine Tree, Ye. *Unknown.* APW
Noble Parentage. Lorenzo Mavilis, *tr. fr. Modern Greek by* Rae Dalven. MoGP
Noble range it was, of many a rood, A. Places of Nestling Green. Leigh Hunt. *Fr.* The Story of Rimini. EnRP; OBRV
Noble Ritter Hugo, Der. Ballad of the Mermaid [*or* Ballad by Hans Breitmann *or* Ritter Hugo]. Charles Godfrey Leland. BOHV; CenHV; FiBHP; LauV; LPS-3
Noble Sisters. Christina Rossetti. CoBE
Noble Soldier, The, *sel.* Thomas Dekker, Samuel Rowley, *and* John Day.
O Sorrow, Sorrow. CenL; SeCL

Noble spot of my ancestors. To My Native City. Luis Carlos López. TwSpPo
Noble Tuck-Man, The. Jean Ingelow. NA
Noble Voyage, The. Earl of Surrey. PoLi
Noble Wood Displays, The. *Unknown, tr. fr. Latin by* Jack Lindsay. *Fr.* Carmina Burana. LaP
Noble Work. Charles Mackay. PSO
Nobleman and the Pensioner, The. Gottlieb Konrad Pfeffel, *tr. fr. German by* Charles T. Brooks. LPS-2
Nobleman's Wedding, The. William Allingham. IrPN
Nobleman's Wedding, The. *Unknown.* AnIV
Noblemen. Miles M. Dawson. BAP
Nobler Lesson, The. Don Marquis. OBAV
Nobles and heralds, by your leave. Epitaph on Himself [*or* Prior's Epitaph]. Matthew Prior. HBV; LEAP; TreFS; TrGrPo
Noblesse Oblige. Jessie Fauset. CDC
Noblesse Oblige. Ibn Sa'id of Alcala la Real, *tr. fr. Arabic by* A. J. Arberry. MooP
Noblest bodies are but gilded clay. Of Death. Samuel Harding. *Fr.* Sicily and Naples. SeCL
Noblest Roman, The. Shakespeare. *See* Portrait of Brutus.
Noblest thoughts my soul can claim, The. The Name of Mother. George Griffith Fetter. PGD
Nobly, nobly Cape Saint Vincent to the North-west died away. Home-Thoughts, from the Sea. Robert Browning. AWP; BEL; BPN; CBPC; EM-2; EnLi-2 (1949 ed.); EV-5; FaBoCh; FiP; GEPC; GTBS; GTSL; InP; InPo; JAWP; LH; OAEP; OBEV; OBVV; OTPC; PoVP; ShBV-2; TOP; ViPo; ViPP; VLEP; WBP
Nobody. Burns. LiTL
Nobody, A. Emily Dickinson. *See* I'm nobody! Who are you?
Nobody. Robert Graves. POTE
Nobody believes in Fate any more, nobody listens to the Norns. Waiting and Peeking. V. R. Lang. NePA
Nobody Comes. Thomas Hardy. MoVE; PoFS; ViPP
Nobody comes to the graveyard on the hill. The Hill above the Mine. Malcolm Cowley. NAMP
Nobody ever galloped on this road. The Dead Ride Fast. R. P. Blackmur. MoPo
Nobody ever stops to see. The Empty Little House. Ann Sutherland. DDA
Nobody Knows. Helen Coale Crew. GFA
Nobody knows. The Need. Siegfried Sassoon. TrPWD
Nobody Knows but Mother. Mary Morrison. BLPA
Nobody Knows—but Mother. *Unknown.* PEDC
Nobody Knows de Trouble I See [*or* I've Seen]. *Unknown.* APW; BoAN-1, *rare vers., with music;* BoAN-2, *familiar vers., with music;* OIF
Nobody knows of the work it makes. Nobody Knows—but Mother. *Unknown.* PEDC
Nobody knows the other side. Chorus. Jack Kerouac. *Fr.* Mexico City Blues. NeAP
Nobody lives in the cottage now. Fairy Feet. Phyllis L. Garlick. BoTP
Nobody Loses All the Time. E. E. Cummings. AnNE; ChMo; LiTM; PoLFOT
Nobody noogers the shaff of a sloo. On a Flimmering Floom You Shall Ride. Carl Sandburg. GoYe
Nobody stays here long. Not in the Guide-Books. Elizabeth Jennings. NePoEA
Nobody stuffs the world in at your eyes. Snow. Margaret Avison. PeCV
Nobody took any notice of her as she stood on the causey curb [*or* kerb]. The Market-Girl. Thomas Hardy. At Casterbridge Fair, IV. BEL; EmBrPo; EnLi-2 (1949 ed.); EnLit; PoVP
Nobody's but Mine, *with music. Unknown.* SoAF
Nobody's Child. Phila H. Case. PTA-2; TreF
Noctambule. A. J. M. Smith. BoCaPo (1948 ed.)
Noctiflora. Maurice Lesemann. NP
Nocturn. W. E. Henley. In Hospital, XXVII. BPN
Nocturn. Francis Thompson. POTE; TCPD
Nocturnal. Os Marron. NeBP
Nocturnal Collection. "Pablo Neruda," *tr. fr. Spanish by* Angel Flores. AnCL
Nocturnal Eclogue, The, *sel.* Moses Browne.
"Hark! the shrill cock, the rising morn proclaims." EnSW
Nocturnal Reverie, A. Countess of Winchilsea. BCEP; CEP; EiPP; EnSW; EPP; EV-3; FaBoEn; GoTL; LoBV; OBEC; PoEL-3; SeCePo
Nocturnal Sketch, A. Thomas Hood. BOHV; FiBHP; LPS-3; SiTL
Nocturnal upon Saint Lucy's Day, A. John Donne. CaAE; GTBS-W; LiTB; LiTG; MaPo; PoE; ReaPo; ReIE; TwP
(Nocturnal[l] upon S. Lucies Day.) AtBAP; BoW; EnLP; FaBoEn; MeLP; MePo; OBS; PoEL-2; SeCV-1; SeEP
Nocturne: "All the earth a hush of white." Amelia Josephine Burr. HBV
Nocturne: "Be thou at peace this night." Edward Davison. CH; SoV
Nocturne: "Beneath the stars a man alone." Georg Trakl, *tr. fr. German by* Herman Salinger. TwGV
Nocturne: "Blue water . . . a clear moon." Li Po, *tr. fr. Chinese by* Shigeyoshi Obata. OnPM
Nocturne: "Forest falls asleep and dreams, The." Conrado Nalé Roxlo, *tr. fr. Spanish by* Milton Ben Davis. AnCL
Nocturne: "Heart of my nights." Eugenio Florit, *tr. fr. Spanish by* H. R. Hays. TwSpPo
Nocturne: "How have you managed to enter so, like a mist." Xavier Abril, *tr. fr. Spanish by* H. R. Hays. AnCL
Nocturne: "I walked beside the deep, one night of stars." Victor Hugo, *tr. fr. French.* CAW
Nocturne: "I wander through the silent night." Joseph von Eichendorff, *tr. fr. German by* Herman Salinger. AnGP
Nocturne: "If the deep wood is haunted, it is I." Robert Hillyer. UnW
Nocturne: "Infold us with thy peace, dear moon-lit night." Virna Sheard. OCL
Nocturne: "Keen winds of cloud and vaporous drift." Richard Garnett. OBVV
Nocturne, A: "Moon has gone to her rest, The." Wilfrid Scawen Blunt. OBMV
Nocturne: "My weeping and the starlight." Juan Ramón Jiménez. *tr. fr. Spanish by* Thomas Walsh. OnPM
Nocturne III: "Night, A,/ a night all full of murmurs." José Asunción Silva, *tr. fr. Spanish by* Lloyd Watson. LiTW
(Nocturne: "One night." José Asunción Silva, *tr. by* Thomas Walsh.) WoL
Nocturne: "Night comes, an angel stands." Kathleen Raine. ChMP
Nocturne: " 'Nothin' or everythin' it's got to be.' " John V. A. Weaver. AnAmPo; HBMV; LA; NP
Nocturne: "One night." José Asunción Silva. *See* Nocturne III: "Night, A."
Nocturne: "Red flame flowers bloom and die, The." Crosbie Garstin. CH
Nocturne: "See how the dying west puts forth her song." Richard Church. ChMP
Nocturne: "Sleep that like the couched dove." Gerald Griffin. VA
(Sleep That like the Couchèd Dove.) OnYI
Nocturne: "Softly blow lightly." Donald Jeffrey Hayes. CDC
Nocturne: "There is a stillness in the heart of night." Minnie Markham Kerr. MuM
Nocturne: "This cool night is strange." Gwendolyn Bennett. BANP
Nocturne: "Up to her chamber window." Thomas Bailey Aldrich. HBV; PR
Nocturne: "When I am alone, to dream." Shahriyar, *tr. fr. Persian by* A. J. Arberry. PeP
Nocturne: "Wind is blowing from the hill, The." H. A. Vaughan. PoNe
Nocturne: "Wings of the windmill rustle no longer." Sigbjörn Obstfelder, *tr. fr. Norwegian by* Charles W. Stork. AnNoLy
Nocturne at Bethesda. Arna Bontemps. BANP; CDC; PoNe
Nocturne in a Deserted Brickyard. Carl Sandburg. AmPP; CoBA; MAP; MoAmPo; NP; PFE; TCPD
Nocturne in a Library. Arthur Davison Ficke. AOAH
Nocturne in G Minor. Karl Gustave Vollmoeller, *tr. fr. German by* Ludwig Lewisohn. AWP; LiTW
Nocturne in Which Death Speaks. Xavier Villaurrutia, *tr. fr. Spanish by* Dudley Fitts. AnCL
Nocturne of Remembered Spring. Conrad Aiken. ChMo; CMP; HBMV
Nocturne of Sin and Its Accusation. José Miguel Ferrer, *tr. fr. Spanish by* Richard O'Connell. AnCL
Nocturne of the Wharves. Arna Bontemps. BANP
Nocturne Varial. Lewis Alexander. PoNe
Nod. Walter de la Mare. AtBAP; BLV; BoTP; CaAE; CV; EnLit; GoTP; HBMV; MBP; MM; MoAB; PoeMoYo; PoeT; TCEP; ThWaDe; TSW; TSWC; TwCV; VOD
Nodding, its great head rattling like a gourd. Original Sin; a Short Story. Robert Penn Warren. AmP; CrMA; FiMAP; GTBS-W; LiTA; LiTM; MoVE; ReMP
Nodding oxeye bends before the wind, The. The Fear of Flowers. John Clare. AnFE; EG; OBRV; SeCeV
Nodes. Alice Corbin. NP; WGRP
Noe falce, noe faithles Lindamor. *Unknown.* SeCSL
Noe more of teares I have not left in store. *Unknown.* SeCSL
Noe more unto my thoughts appeare. Song [*or* Quatrains]. Sidney Godolphin. MeLP; MePo; OBS
Noe, noe I never was in love. *Unknown.* SeCSL
Noe, she ne're lov'de, 'twas the excess. *Unknown.* SeCSL
Noe, twas her eyes. *Unknown.* SeCSL
Noel. Hilaire Belloc. HBMV; JKCP; TSW
Noël. Robert Bridges. *See* Noel; Christmas Eve, 1913.
Noel. Gail Brook Burket. PGD
Noel. Leonard Feeney. OS
Noël. Richard Watson Gilder. AA
Noel! *in mod. Eng. Unknown.* TMEV

Noel; Christmas Eve, 1913. Robert Bridges. CAW; LiTB; MeRV; MoVE
(Noël.) GTML
Noel Dark. W. W. Gibson. *Fr.* Casualties. VOD
Noël de Thevet. *Unknown, tr. fr. French by* Edward Bliss Reed. ChrBoLe
Noel! Noel! Laura Simmons. PGD; PSO
Noel! Noel? I hear the bells in the night. Skeptic Christmas. Jules Laforgue. AnFP
Noise Grimaced. Larry Eigner. NeAP
Noise of hammers once I heard. The Hammers. Ralph Hodgson. CMP; MBP; MoBrPo; PoMa; POTE
Noise of Leaves, The. George Dillon. NLK (1947 ed.)
Noise of the Cabarets, The. Paul Verlaine, *tr. fr. French by* Kate Flores. AnFP
Noise of trampling, the wind of trumpets, The. Blake. *Fr.* The French Revolution. ChER
Noise of water teased his literal ears, The. Persistent Explorer. John Crowe Ransom. OxBA
Noise of Waters, The. James Joyce. *See* All Day I Hear.
Noise Protection. Christian Morgenstern, *tr. fr. German by* Lola Gruenthal. AnGP
Noise That Time Makes, The. Merrill Moore. NP; PoP; SPP; TrGrPo (rev. ed.); YaD
Noiseless Patient Spider, A. Walt Whitman. AmPP; AnFE; APA; APW; ATP (1935 ed.); AWP; BLP; CoAnAm; ExPo; GTBS-W; IAP; InPo; JAWP; LBAP; LiTA; LiTG; MAP; MaRV; MoAmPo; MOAP; NeMA; NePA; OnPM; OxBA; TCAP; TrGrPo; WBP
Noises in the Night. Lilian McCrea. BoTP
Noises of the street come up subdued, The. An Upper Room. Daniel Lawrence Kelleher. NeIP
Noises that strive to tear. The Inner Silence. Harriet Monroe. HBMV; NP
Noisette on my garden path, A. The Shadow Rose. Robert Cameron Rogers. AA
Noisy now are the sparring sparrows, but noisier. All Over the World. Geoffrey Johnson. HaMV
Noisy pearls noisy pearl coat. Gertrude Stein. *Fr.* Sacred Emily. AtBAP
Noisy sparrows in our clematis, The. George Levison. William Allingham. IrPN
Noli Aemulari. Arthur Hugh Clough. *See* In Controversial Foul Impureness.
Noli Me Tangere. Robert Lowell. *See* Death of the Sheriff, The.
Noli Me Tangere. Carl Snoilsky, *tr. fr. Swedish by* Charles W. Stork. AnSL
Nomad Exquisite. Wallace Stevens. AtBAP
Nomads of Beauty. Vyacheslav Ivanovich Ivanov, *tr. fr. Russian by* Babette Deutsch. TrRV
Noman and the Cyclops; a Tale Told over Cups. Homer, *tr. fr. Greek by* George Chapman. *Fr.* The Odyssey, IX. GrR
(Of Noman and Cyclops, *tr. by* William Morris.) OxBG
Non Amo Te. Thomas Brown. *See* I Do Not Love Thee, Doctor Fell.
Non Dolet. Oliver St. John Gogarty. BMEP; GTIV; JKCP (1926 ed.); OBMV; OnYI; OxBI
(Our Friends Go with Us.) POTE
Non Dolet. Swinburne. BPN; PoVP; ViPP
"Non ego hoc ferrem calida [*or* calidus] juventa." At Thirty Years [*or* Labuntur Anni]. Byron. *Fr.* Don Juan, I. BPN; FiP
Non Nobis. Henry Cust. EtPaEn; OBEV; OBVV
Non Nobis. L. A. MacKay. TwCV
Non Omnis Moriar. Manuel Gutiérrez Nájera, *tr. fr. Spanish by* Samuel Beckett. AnMP
Non Pax—Expectatio. Francis Thompson. PeBoSo; PreP
Non Sum Qualis Eram Bonae sub Regno Cynarae. Ernest Dowson. AnFE; AWP; BLPA; CaAE; EnLi-2; EnLit; EnLoPo; EPP; FaBoBe; GTBS-D; GTBS-W; GTML; HBV; InPo; LBBV; LEAP; LiTG; LiTL; LiTM (rev. ed.); LO; LoPo; MBP; MoBrPo; NeHB; OBEV (new ed.); OBMV; OBVV; PG; PoFS; POTT; PoVP; PreP; TreF; TrGrPo; ViBoPo; ViPP; VLEP
(Cynara.) AnEnPo; BeLS; BLV; BMEP; FaFP; LiTB; OtMeF; PoRA; UnPo
(To Cynara.) NeMA
Nona poured oil on the water and saw the eye. The Evil Eye. John Ciardi. AtBAP
Non-being then existed not nor being. Hymn of Creation. *Unknown. Fr.* The Rigveda. LiTW
Non-Combatant, The. Sir Henry Newbolt. SoV
Nonconformist, A. Emyr Humphreys. MoWP
None Are Wise That Savor to the Last. Stefan George, *tr. fr. German by* David Luke. AnGP
None await thy smiling rays. Spring. Hovhannes Hovhannessian. ArmLP
None but a Tuscan hand could fix ye here. On the Picture of the Three Fates in the Palazzo Pitti, at Florence. Arthur Henry Hallam. OBRV
None but one can harm you. The Foe Within. Longfellow. MaRV
None but Your Subtle Ear. Stefan George, *tr. fr. German by* David Luke. AnGP
None call thee flower! . . . I will not so malign. To the Milkweed. Lloyd Mifflin. AA
"None can usurp this height," return'd that shade. Ars Gratia Artis. Keats. *Fr.* The Fall of Hyperion. LiA; OBRV
None could ever say that she. True or False [*or* Love's Madness]. Catullus. AWP; JAWP; LiA; OuHeWo; WBP
None could more gracious nor more courtly be. Philip the Fourth. Manuel Machado. AnSpL-2
None ere drunke the Thespian spring. George Wither. *Fr.* The Shepherd's Hunting. NBE
None ever climbed to mountain height of song. A Woman's Hand. Sir Gilbert Parker. *Fr.* A Lover's Diary. VA
None Is Happy. Hartmann von Aue, *tr. fr. German by* Jethro Bithell. AWP
None Knew. "Demyan Bedny." *See* No One Knew.
None like Him, of the sons of men. The Fairest He. Horatius Bonar. BePJ
None of Self and All of Thee. Theodore Monod. BLRP
None of Us Cared for Kate. Shakespeare. *See* Master, the Swabber, The.
None other fame mine unambitious muse. To Delia, XLVIII [LV]. Samuel Daniel. ReEn; SiCE; TuPP
None Other Lamb, None Other Name. Christina Rossetti. OxBoCh; TrPWD
None other saw them when they came. The Envoys. Clark Ashton Smith. DaM
None phrased a song or sang a minstrel lay. To John Charles McNeill. Stewart Atkins. NoCaPo
None shall know it but the wise. Trance and Transformation. Goethe. LiTW
None should outlive his power. . . . Who kills. John Davidson. *Fr.* The Testament of John Davidson. LEAP
None spake when Wilson stood before. Catherine Kinrade. Thomas Edward Brown. OBVV
None walked behind that shoddy rain-swept hearse. Mozart's Grave. Paul Scott Mowrer. GoYe
Nones. W. H. Auden. CoBMV; PoLFOT
Non-Euclidean Elegy. John Frederick Nims. MoVE
Nongtongpaw. Charles Dibdin. BOHV; CG; HBV
Nonne Preestes Tale, The. Chaucer. *See* Nun's Priest's Tale, The.
Nonpareil. Matthew Prior. EnLoPo
Nonpareil of All Mortality, The. Joachim du Bellay, *tr. fr. French by* Alan Conder. Olive, II. TrFP
Non-Resistance. Oliver Wendell Holmes. TCAP
Non-returnable. Carolyn Wells. DDA
Nonsense! Samuel Goodrich. *See* Higglety, Pigglety, Pop!
Nonsense. Thomas Moore. *See* If You Have Seen.
Nonsense. Robert Haven Schauffler. HBMV
Nonsense. *Unknown. See* Odd but True.
Nonsense Alphabet ("A was an ape"). Edward Lear. SAS
Nonsense Alphabet, A ("A was once an apple-pie"). Edward Lear. SUS
(A. Apple Pie.) PPL
("A was once an apple-pie.") TiPo
Nonsense Carol, A. *Unknown. See* My Heart of Gold.
Nonsense Limericks. Edward Lear. *See* Nonsense Verses.
Nonsense Pictures in Rhyme. Edward Lear. MPB
Nonsense Quatrains: "Ah, yes! I wrote the 'Purple Cow.'" Gelett Burgess. *See* Cinq Ans Après.
Nonsense Quatrains: "I never saw a Purple Cow." Gelett Burgess. *See* Purple Cow, The.
Nonsense Quatrains: "I sent my Collie to the wash." Gelett Burgess. CenHV
Nonsense Quatrains: "Many people seem to think." Gelett Burgess. CenHV
Nonsense Quatrains: "Proper way to leave a room, The." Gelett Burgess. CenHV
Nonsense Rhymes. Gelett Burgess. *See* Nonsense Verses.
Nonsense Rimes for the Maids. *Unknown.*
(Hallowe'en Party, The.) HOAH
Nonsense Rimes for the Men. *Unknown.*
(Hallowe'en Party, The.) HOAH
Nonsense Song. *Unknown, ad. fr. German by* Michael Lewis. RIS
Nonsense Verses. Gelett Burgess. HBV
(Nonsense Rhymes.) TSW; TSWC
Nonsense Verses. Charles Lamb. BOHV; NA
Nonsense Verses. Edward Lear. HBV; OTPC; StVeCh
(Lear's Limericks.) OTPC; OxBoLi; RIS
(Limericks.) BoChLi; BOHV; LBN; NA; StaSt
(Nonsense Limericks.) TSW; TSWC
Nonsense Verses. Laura E. Richards. RIS
Nonsun Blob A. E. E. Cummings. PoE
Nooked underneath steep, sterile hills that rise. An Old Seaport. *Unknown.* EtS
Noon. John Clare. ERP; EV-4, *abr.*; OBRV; SeCePo
Noon. Robinson Jeffers. MAP; MoAmPo; TCPD
Noon. Richard Le Gallienne. CV
Noon. Jaime Torres Bodet, *tr. fr. Spanish by* Rolfe Humphries. AnCL

Noon. Whittier. *Fr.* Summer by the Lakeside. IAP
Noon: and the gentle air. A swallow's wing. The Dead. John Williams. NePoAm-2
Noon—and the north-west sweeps the empty road. February. William Morris. *Fr.* The Earthly Paradise. ViPo
Noon-enameled bees, The. Garden Incident. George O'Neil. TCPD
Noon in the park . . . A tropic sun. Brothers. Elias Lieberman. PFE; PoMa
Noon is hot, The. When we have crossed the stream. Matthew Arnold. *Fr.* Empedocles on Etna, I, ii. EPN; PoVP
Noon Is on the Cattle-Track, The. Rex Ingamells. BoAu
Noon like a naked sword lies on the grass. Noon. Richard Le Gallienne. CV
Noon on Alameda Street. Hildegarde Flanner. LiTM
Noon Piece, A; or, The Mowers at Dinner, *sel.* Christopher Smart.
Mowers, The. RO
Noon Quatrains. Charles Cotton. LoBV
Noon sun beats down the leaf; the noon. Grapes Making. Léonie Adams. MoVE; NePA; UnPo (3d ed.)
Noon was shady, and soft airs, The. The Dog and the Water-Lily. William Cowper. AlBD; CG; EV-3; OAEP
Noonday. Fan Tseng Hsiang, *tr. fr. Chinese by* Henry H. Hart. ChLP; PoHN
Noonday Ghosts. Geoffrey Johnson. UnW
Noonday Grace. John Crowe Ransom. LS
Noonday on de Ribber, *with music.* *Unknown.* SoAF
Noonday Sun. Kathryn Jackson *and* Byron Jackson. FaPON; TiPo
Noon-Tide. Thomas S. Jones, Jr. VOD
Noontide. John Keble. OTPC (1923 ed.)
Noontide. John Leyden. LPS-2
Noontide Rest. Antiphilus of Byzantium, *tr. fr. Greek by* Sir William Marris. OxBG
Nor a Lender Be. Martial, *tr. fr. Latin by* Paul Nixon. RoL
Nor can I not believe but that hereby. Personal Talk, IV. Wordsworth. EM-2; EmBrPo; PeBoSo
Nor do I fear the satire's venim'd bite. De Se. John Weever. ReIE
Nor dread nor hope attend. Death. W. B. Yeats. ChMP; GTBS-D; PoD; POTE; ShBV-4
Nor exults he nor complains he; silent bears whate'er befalls him. Ever Watchful. Ta' Abbata Sharra. AWP; JAWP; WBP
Nor force nor fraud shall sunder us! America, II. Sydney Dobell. BMEP; EPN; EPP; ES; HBV; OBVV; PaA; ShGoBo
Nor Gold nor Silver. Solon, *tr. fr. Greek by* J. M. Edmonds. GrR
Nor had great Hector and his friends the rampire overrun. Homer. *Fr.* The Iliad, XII. AtBAP
Nor happiness, nor majesty, nor fame. Political Greatness [*or* Sonnet: Political Greatness]. Shelley. BPN; EM-2; EmBrPo; EnRP; EPN; PeBoSo
Nor hath He given these blessings for a day. That the Soul Is Immortal, and Cannot Die. Sir John Davies. *Fr.* Nosce Teipsum. TuPP
Nor have the lips of poets sung in vain. Achilles. Pindar. *Fr.* Isthmian Odes, VIII. GrR
Nor House nor Heart. Elinor Lennen. PGD
Nor ice nor fire shall harm you now. Admonition. John L. Bonn. JKCP (1955 ed.)
Nor Is It Written. Laura Riding. Three Sermons to the Dead, III. FaBoMo; LiTA
Nor lady's wanton love, nor wandering knight. Satire I. Joseph Hall. *Fr.* Virgidemiarum. SiCE; TuPP
Nor less do I remember to have felt. Nature, Love, Man. Wordsworth. *Fr.* The Prelude. RO
Nor less meant Promus when that vow he made. Perdat Qui Caveat Emptor. Henry Parrot. SiCE
Nor less when spring had warmed the cultured vale. The Raven's Nest. Wordsworth. *Fr.* The Prelude. ShBV-3
Nor Mars His Sword. Dunstan Thompson. NePA
Nor may his flesh-house, when the spirit leaves it. The Hour of Death. *Unknown.* *Fr.* The Seafarer. PoLi
Nor mine own fears, nor the prophetic soul. *See* Not mine own . . .
Nor raging flames, O Rome, that burned thee down. Destruction. Joachim du Bellay. Antiquities of Rome, XIII. TrFP
Nor rose nor archangel had come into being. Three Memories of Heaven. Rafael Alberti. CoSP
Nor rural sights alone, but rural sounds. William Cowper. *Fr.* The Task, I. BrBE
Nor sea, nor land, nor heaven's lucid stretch. The Creation of the Infinite Universe; How It Is Maintained. Lucretius. *Fr.* De Rerum Natura, I. LaP
Nor should this, perchance. Wordsworth. *Fr.* The Prelude, II. ERP
Nor skin nor hide nor fleece. Lethe. Hilda Doolittle ("H. D."). BLV; CBOV; ChMo; CMP; MAP; MoAmPo; NeMA; PG (1945 ed.); PoRA; ReaPo; TCPD; TrGrPo; ViBoPo
Nor sleep, nor journey, nor affray. A Child's Game. Karle Wilson Baker. PCD
Nor were the courts divine. The Marriage of Thetis. Pindar. *Fr.* Isthmian Odes. OxBG
Nor Will These Tears Be the Last. Goethe, *tr. fr. German by* Stephen Spender. LiTW
Nor yet did it please the spirit of high-hearted Aias. Ajax on the Decks. Homer. *Fr.* The Iliad, XV. OxBG
Nor yet had Hector and his host prevail'd. Sarpedon and Glaucus; the Equation of Duty and Privilege. Homer. *Fr.* The Iliad, XII. GrR
Nora. Dora Sigerson Shorter. HBMV
Norah. Zoë Akins. AV; HBV
Nora's Vow. Sir Walter Scott. BOHV; EmBrPo; EV-4
Nor'easter. Bianca Bradbury. EtS
Norembega. Whittier. PAH
Norfolk. John Betjeman. ChMP
Norfolk Girls, The, *with music.* *Unknown.* AmSS
Norfolk Memorials. Coman Leavenworth. LiTA
Norfolk sprung thee, Lambeth holds thee dead. Epitaph on Thomas Clere. Earl of Surrey. SiPS
Norham Castle. Sir Walter Scott. *Fr.* Marmion, I. LPS-2
Norman Abbey. Byron. *Fr.* Don Juan, XIII. OBRV
Norman Cradle-Song. Vincent O'Sullivan. BOL
Normandy markets, The. In Normandy. E. V. Lucas. GaP
Norns Watering Yggdrasill, The. William Bell Scott. VA
Norris Dam. Selden Rodman. PoNe
Norse am I when the first snow falls. The Song of the Ski. Wilson MacDonald. CaP; PCN
Norse Lullaby. Eugene Field. BOL; BoTP; MPB; SUS
Norse Sailor's Joy. Wilfrid Thorley. EtS
Norsemen, The. Whittier. PAH
North. Philip Booth. NePoEA
North, The. Stephen Spender. *See* Polar Exploration.
North and South. Claude McKay. GoSl
North and South. Florida Watts Smyth. StaSt
North and the South, The. Elizabeth Barrett Browning. OBVV
North and west along the coast among the misty islands. The Trail Makers. H. H. Knibbs. OBAV
North Country, The. Robert Browning. *Fr.* The Flight of the Duchess. PCH
North Country, The. D. H. Lawrence. OAEP (2d ed.)
North Country Collier, The. *Unknown.* SG
North-country maid up to London had stray'd, A. The Oak and the Ash. *Unknown.* FaBoCh; LoGBV
North Dakota Hymn. James W. Foley. PoRL
North-east. *See* Northeast.
North East/ behold ye. *Unknown.* *Fr.* Sea Snatches. SiB
North, East, South, and West. *Unknown.* BOHV
North Garden, The. Po Chü-i, *tr. fr. Chinese by* Ching Ti. WhP
North is weather, Winter, and change. North. Philip Booth. NePoEA
North Labrador. Hart Crane. ChMo; FaBoMo
North of Wales, The. Herbert Morris. NePoAm-2
North Pickenham. Coman Leavenworth. *Fr.* Norfolk Memorials. LiTA
North Sea, The, *sels.* Heine, *tr. fr. German.*
Epilog, *tr. by* Louis Untermeyer. AWP; JAWP; WBP
(Epilogue, *tr. by* Emma Lazarus.) TrJP
Evening Twilight, *tr. by* John Todhunter. AWP; JAWP; WBP
Night by the Sea, A, *tr. by* Howard Mumford Jones. AWP
(Night on the Shore, *tr. by* Emma Lazarus.) LiTW
North Sea Undertaker's Complaint, The. Robert Lowell. NePoEA
North Star. Zona Gale. BAP; LEAP
North Star West. Earle Birney. TwCaPo
North to the South. Richard Watson Gilder. MDAH
North-west. *See* Northwest.
North Wind, The. Dorothy Gradon. BoTP
North Wind, The. Lincoln Reis. PCH
North Wind, The. *Unknown, tr. fr. Chinese.* WhP
North Wind and the Child, The. *Unknown, tr. fr. Greek.* PCH
North Wind Came Up Yesternight, The. Robert Bridges. SeCeV
North wind came whistling through the wood. Friends. L. G. Warner. OTPC (1946 ed.)
North wind clanged on the sharp hill-side, The. The Dirge of Kildare. Aubrey Thomas De Vere. IrPN
North wind doth blow, The. Mother Goose. BoTP; CBPC; GFA; HBV; OlF; OTPC; OxNR; PCH; PPL; RIS; SAS; StVeCh; WP
North-wind fall'n, in the new-starréd night, The. The Hesperides. Tennyson. ViPP
North Wind in October. Robert Bridges. BrBE; TCEP
North wind is a beggar, The. Winds a-Blowing. May Justus. BrR
"North Wind, North Wind—oh, whither so fast?" *Unknown.* GFA

North wind rolls the white grasses and breaks them, The. A Song of White Snow. Ts'en Ts'an, *tr. by* Witter Bynner. LiTW
North wind shakes the shivering moon, The. The North Wind. Lincoln Reis. PCH
North wind sweeps over the land, twisting and breaking off the hoary grass, The. Farewell. Ts'en Ts'an, *tr. by* Yuan Chia-hua. WhP
North winds send hail, south winds bring rain. A Description of the Properties of Winds All the [*or* at All] Times of the Year. Thomas Tusser. ReIE; SiCE; TuPP
Northboun'. Ariel Williams Holloway. BANP; CDC; GoSl; PoNe
Northeast blows, The. Memories. Friedrich Hölderlin. AnGP
North-east spends his rage, The. Prelude. James Thomson. *Fr.* The Seasons: Spring. CoEV
North-east Wind, The. Charles Kingsley. *See* Ode to the North-east Wind.
Northeast wind was the wind off the lake, The. Cook County [*or* Weather]. Archibald MacLeish. CrMA; MAP; MoAmPo; NLK (1947 ed.); PIAE
Northern Boulevard. Edwin Denby. CrMA
Northern Farmer: New Style. Tennyson. BLP; BOHV; BoLiVe; BPN; EM-2; EmBrPo; EPN; EV-5; PoVP; ShBV-4; ViPo; VLEP
Northern Farmer: Old Style. Tennyson. BEL; BPN; EM-2; EmBrPo; EPN; EV-5; GEPC; OAEP; PoVP; TCEP; VA; ViPo; VLEP
Northern Graveyards. "Katherine Hale." BoCaPo (1943 ed.); CPG
Northern Lass, The, *sels.* Richard Brome.
"Bonny, bonny bird I had, A." TuPP
Song: "Peace, wayward barne! O cease thy moan!" SeCL
Northern Legion, A. Sir Herbert Read. FaBoMo; SeCePo
Northern Light. L. A. G. Strong. POTE
Northern Lights. Einar Benediktsson, *tr. fr. Icelandic by* Jakobina Johnson. IcP
Northern Lights, The. Richard Savage. *Fr.* The Wanderer, III. BeR
Northern Lights, The. Benjamin Franklin Taylor. LPS-2
Northern Lights. Carlos Wilcox. *See* Sights and Sounds of the Night.
Northern Lights are flashing, The. Canadian Hunter's Song. Susanna Strickland Moodie. VA
Northern Seas. William Howitt. GN; OTPC (1923 ed.); TVSH
Northern sky, The. Bulletin of Bad Weather. Jorge Carrera Andrade. TwSpPo
Northern Soldier, The. Philip Freneau. AmPP (3d ed.)
Northern Star, The. *Unknown.* HBV
Northern Suburb, A. John Davidson. BMEP
Northern Vigil, A. Bliss Carman. BoCaPo; OBEV (new ed.); OBVV; PeCV; TwCV
Northman. Emerson. APW
Northumberland. Swinburne. VLEP
Northumberland Betrayed by Douglas. *Unknown.* ESPB; OBB
Northward in Thy Sir Skammel dwelt. Ebbé Skammelson. *Unknown.* BaBo
North-west Passage, *sel.* Robert Louis Stevenson.
Shadow March. HOAH
Norval. John Home. *Fr.* Douglas, II, i. LPS-2
Norway in Our Hearts. Nordahl Grieg, *tr. fr. Norwegian by* Charles W. Stork. AnNoLy
Norway's Highlands. Johan Sebastian Cammermeyer Welhaven, *tr. fr. Norwegian by* Charles W. Stork. AnNoLy
Norwegian Cradle-Song. Natanaël Fransen, *tr. fr. Norwegian by* Alma Strettell. BOL
Nor'-West Courier, The. John E. Logan. VA
Nosce Teipsum. Sir John Davies. SiPS
Sels.
Acclamation, An. OxBoCh; TuPP
Affliction. CoEV; OBSC
Dedication: "Strongest and the noblest argument, The," II. SiPS
Dedication: "To that clear majesty which in the north," I. OBSC; SiPS
(To My Most Gracious Dread Sovereign.) ReIE; SiCE
Immortality of the Soul, The ("All moving things to other things do move"). EV-2
Immortality of the Soul, The ("For why should we the busy soul believe"). ViBoPo
In What Manner the Soul[e] Is United to the Body. LiTB; PoEL-2
(Soul and the Body, The.) OBSC
Knowledge and Reason. OBSC
(Much Knowledge, Little Reason.) ChTr
Man, *3 sts.* BCEP, *2 sts.*; EIL; EM-1; OBEV, *2 sts.*
(I Know Myself a Man.) ChTr
(Vanity of Human Learning, The, *2 sts.*) MaRV
(Which Is a Proud, and Yet a Wretched Thing.) WHA
Of Human Knowledge. EV-2; ReIE; SiCE; TuPP
Of the Soul of Man and the Immortality Thereof. ReIE
That the Soul Is Immortal, and Cannot Die. TuPP
"We seek to know the moving of each sphere." MyFE
Nose and the Eyes, The. William Cowper. LPS-3; MPB
(Dispute between Nose and Eyes.) OTPC
(Report of an Adjudged Case; Not to Be Found in Any of the Books.) BOHV
Nose, nose, jolly red nose. Mother Goose (*also appears in* Beaumont *and* Fletcher's "The Knight of the Burning Pestle," I, iii). BrR; FaBoCh; LoGBV; OxNR
Nosegay, A. John Reynolds. OBEV
(Garden's Queen, The.) SeCL
Nosegay Always Sweet, A, for Lovers to Send for Tokens of Love at New Year's Tide, or for Fairings. *At. to* William Hunnis. EIL; ReIE
Nosegay for a Young Goat. Winifred Welles. PoeMoYo
Nosegay, lacking flowers fresh, A. A Nosegay Always Sweet, for Lovers to Send for Tokens of Love at New Year's Tide, or for Fairings. *At. to* William Hunnis. EIL; ReIE
Nostalgia. Mary Elizabeth Counselman. DaM
Nostalgia. Walter de la Mare. CoBMV
Nostalgia. D. H. Lawrence. LBBV; NP
Nostalgia. Louis MacNeice. GTBS-D; OnYI
Nostalgia. Tatsuji Miyoshi, *tr. fr. Japanese by* Takamichi Ninomiya *and* D. J. Enright. PoLJ
Nostalgia. Elizabeth Virginia Raplee. BLP
Nostalgia. Karl Shapiro. AnFE; CoAnAm; CoBMV; LiTM; NePA; TrJP; TwAmPo; WaaP
Nostalgia. Theognis, *tr. fr. Greek by* A. C. Benson. GrR
Nostalgie d'Automne. Leslie Daiken. NeIP
Not a bark was heard, not a warning note. The Lay of the Vigilantes. *Unknown.* PoOW
Not a cabin in the Glen shuts its door to-night. Christmas Eve in Ireland. Katharine Tynan. ChrBoLe
Not a care hath Marien Lee. Marien Lee. Mary Howitt. OTPC (1923 ed.)
Not a Child. Swinburne. FAOV
Not a Cloud in the Sky. Richard Armour. WhC
Not a drum was heard, not a funeral note. The Burial of Sir John Moore after [*or* at] Corunna. Charles Wolfe. AnIV; BBV; BCEP; BEL; BHV; BTP; CaAE; CBE; CBPC; ChTr; EnRP; EPN; EPP; ERP; EV-4; FaFP; GN; GTBS; GTBS-D; GTBS-W; GTIV; GTSE; GTSL; HBV; HBVY; InP; LEAP; LH; LiA; LiTG; LPS-3; MaC; MCCG; MW; NeHB; OBEV; OBRV; OnSP; OnYI; OTPC (1923 ed.); OxBI; PCD; PECK; PIR; PoRA; PTA-1; PYM; TCEP; TIP; TOP; TreF; TVSH; WaaP; WBLP; WHA
Not a hand has lifted the latchet. The House of Death. Louise Chandler Moulton. BAP; OBAV
Not a kiss in life; but one kiss, at life's end. To a Dead Woman. H. C. Bunner. OBAV
Not a leaf stirs in the rubbery looking trees. Pernambuco in May. Theodore Goodridge Roberts. BoCaPo (1948 ed.)
Not a line of her writing have I. Thoughts of Phena at News of Her Death. Thomas Hardy. BrBE
Not a man is stirring. Riding at Daybreak. Sun Yün Feng. PoHN
Not a melon can I eat. Recollections of My Children. *Unknown.* OnPM
Not a sigh was heard, not a funeral tone. The Marriage of Sir John Smith. Phoebe Cary. PA
Not a sign of life we rouse. Battery Moving Up to a New Position from Rest Camp: Dawn. Robert Nichols. QS
Not a sod hath Erasippus to entomb him, not a boulder. On the Cenotaph of One Lost at Sea. Glaucus. GrPE
Not a Sou Had He Got. "Thomas Ingoldsby." *Fr.* The Ingoldsby Legends: The Cynotaph. HBV; PA
Not a sound disturbs the air. A Midsummer Noon in the Australian Forest. Charles Harpur. BoAu; BoAV; NeLNL; VA
Not a thing on the river McCluskey did fear. The Little Brown Bulls. *Unknown.* BaBo; OuSiCo
Not a word, not a word. Water. Christian Morgenstern. AnGP
Not After nor Before. "Angelus Silesius," *tr. fr. German by* Paul Carus. OnPM
Not All Immaculate. Laura Riding. *Fr.* Three Sermons to the Dead. LiTA
Not All Sweet Nightingales. Luis de Góngora, *tr. fr. Spanish by* Sir John Bowring. CAW
(Roundelay: "They are not only nightingales," *tr. by* Alice Jane McVan.) TeCS
Not all the chorus sing: to swell their number. The Mutes in Life's Chorus. Menander. OxBG
Not All the Crosses. Lucile Kendrick. ChIP
Not all the Isle of Pelops, nor King's treasures past appraising. "And Thou Beside Me Singing in the Wilderness." Theocritus. *Fr.* Idylls, VIII. GrPE
Not Alone. Hayashi, *tr. fr. Japanese by* Lois J. Erickson. SoLD
Not Alone. Princess Ki, *tr. fr. Japanese by* Ishii *and* Obata. OnPM
Not Alone. Thad Stem, Jr. NoCaPo (rev. ed.)

Not Alone for Mighty Empire. William Pierson Merrill. TrPWD
(People's Thanksgiving, The.) MaRV

Not alone for the rich and great. The People's Holidays. "Marianne Farningham." PEOR

Not alone in Palestine those blessed feet have trod. Where the Blessed Feet Have Trod. "Michael Field." OxBoCh; StJW

Not alone those camps of white, old comrades of the wars. Camps of Green. Walt Whitman. PoE

Not Always. E. A. Robinson. CoV

Not always to the swift the race. The Law of Averages. "Troubadour." FiBHP; InMe

Not an epic, being not loosely architectured. King John's Castle. Thomas Kinsella. OxBI

Not another bite, not another cigarette. Search. Raymond Souster. BoCaPo (1948 ed.)

Not Any More. Dorothy Aldis. BoChLi

Not any more, nor ever while I live. Marriage. Babette Deutsch. AV

Not any sunny tone. Emily Dickinson. AnFE; APA; CoAnAm; MAPA; TwAmPo

Not as all other women are. My Love. James Russell Lowell. FaBoBe; HBV; IAP; LBAP; TVSH

Not as I am, nor as I wish to be. The Strange Pangs of a Poor Passionate Lover. *Unknown.* TuPP

Not As I Will. Helen Hunt Jackson. OQP; QP-2

Not as in time past, mountainy spaces. Looking Down on Mesopotamia. Mary Ursula Bethell. AnNZ

Not as the songs of other lands. An Australian Symphony. G. Essex Evans. BoAu

Not as the white nations know thee. The Black Madonna. Albert Rice. CDC

Not as These. Dante Gabriel Rossetti. The House of Life, LXXV. BPN; PoVP; ViPo

Not as they planned it or will plan again. The Day. Witter Bynner. PGD; PoFr

Not as when some great captain falls. Abraham Lincoln [*or* An Horatian Ode]. Richard Henry Stoddard. AA; FaBoBe; GDAH; LBAH; PAH

Not as with Sundering of the Earth. Swinburne. *Fr.* Atalanta in Calydon. PoVP; VLEP
(Fate.) BPN; EmBrPo

Not as you had dreamed was the battle's issue. To a Young Leader of the First World War. Stefan George. WaaP

Not as you meant, O learnèd man, and good! Hopefully Waiting. Anson D. F. Randolph. LPS-2

Not at midnight, not at morning, O sweet city. Caryatid. Léonie Adams. MoVE

Not at [the] first sight, nor yet with a dribbed shot. Astrophel and Stella, II. Sir Philip Sidney. ElSeCe; MaPo; ReEn; ReIE; SiCE; SiPS; TuPP

Not Baal, but Christus-Jingo! Heir. The Image in the Forum. Robert Buchanan. ChIP

Not baser than his own homekeeping kind. The Journeyman. Ralph Hodgson. AtBAP

Not beauty which men gaze on with a smile. Gougane Barra. Sir Aubrey De Vere. TIP

Not because of victories. Te Deum. Charles Reznikoff. TrJP

Not-Being was not, Being was not then. Brahma, the World Idea. *Unknown. Fr.* Rig-Veda. WGRP

Not born to the forest are we. Song of the Camels [*or* Twelfth Night]. Elizabeth J. Coatsworth. ChBR; FaPON; RIS

Not by Bread Alone. James Terry White. OQP; QP-1

Not by Gold Alone. *Unknown, tr. fr. Greek by* Thomas Girdlestone. GrR

Not by Hands Created. Piotr Vasilyevich Oreshin, *tr. fr. Russian by* Babette Deutsch. TrRV
(Not Made by Hands, *tr. by* Jack Lindsay.) RuPo

Not by instruction may this Self be gained. The Self. *Unknown. Fr.* The Upanishads. OnPM

Not by me these feet were led. Resurrection. "Æ." ChMo; CMP

Not by one measure mayst thou mete our love. Equal Troth. Dante Gabriel Rossetti. The House of Life, XXXII. BPN; PoVP; ViPo

Not by the ball or brand. Vanquished. Francis Fisher Browne. AA; DD; HBV; MDAH

Not by the city bells that chime the hours. A Summer Day. Florence Harrison. BoTP

"Not by the justice that my father spurned." Mycerinus. Matthew Arnold. EmBrPo; PoVP; ViPo; VLEP

Not by the poets. Discovery of This Time. Archibald MacLeish. LiTA; NeTW; WaP

Not by the Sea. Sara Teasdale. MuM

Not Celia That I Juster Am. Sir Charles Sedley. *See* To Celia.

Not costly domes, nor marble towers. Memorial Day. Samuel F. Smith. *Fr.* Our Honored Heroes. OQP; QP-2

Not Dead. Robert Graves. HBMV; LBBV; LEAP

Not Dead, but Gone Before. Antiphanes, *tr. fr. Greek by* T. F. Higham. OxBG

Not drowsihood and dreams and mere idleness. In Sleep. Richard Burton. AA

Not Drunk Is He. Thomas Love Peacock. *Fr.* The Misfortunes of Elphin. LEAP, 4 *ll.*; ViBoPo
(Who Is Drunk? 4 *ll.*) OnPM

Not entirely enviable, however envied. The Master. W. S. Merwin. NePoEA

Not even her slenderness of perfect weight, lying here. Above a Snow. Juan Ramón Jiménez. TeCS

Not even if with a wizard force I might. Caput Mortuum. E. A. Robinson. NP

Not even the remnant that remains behind. The Ghost of Dareius. Aeschylus. *Fr.* Persians. GrR

Not even when the early birds. The Rabbit. W. H. Davies. GFA

Not Every Day Fit for Verse. Robert Herrick. PoRA; SeEP

Not every ghost has died before it haunts. Perfumes. Terence Tiller. FaBoMo

Not every man has gentians in his house. Bavarian Gentians. D. H. Lawrence. AtBAP; CaAE; FaBoCh; FaBoMo; LiTB; LoGBV; OAEP (2d ed.); PoE; SeCeV; TriL; TwCV; UnPo (3d ed.); ViBoPo

Not every thought can find its words. Undeveloped Lives. W. E. H. Lecky. TIP

Not far above me in the boughs he sat, a solemn thing. The Whistling Jack. John Shaw Neilson. NeLNL

Not far advanced [*or* advanc'd] was morning day. Marmion and Douglas [*or* The Battle]. Sir Walter Scott. *Fr.* Marmion, VI. EnRP; LPS-2; OHFP; PTA-2; WHA

Not far from Ghúr once stood a city tall. The Blind Men and the Elephant. Sana'i. PeP

Not far from old Kinvara, in the merry month of May. The Ould Plaid Shawl. Francis A. Fahy. HBV; JKCP (1926 ed.); TIP

Not far from Paris, in fair Fontainebleau. The Angelus. Florence Earle Coates. HBV

Not far from that most famous theatre. Sir Samuel Garth. *Fr.* The Dispensary. CEP

Not far from these Phoenician Dido stood. Dido among the Shades. Virgil, *tr. by* Dryden. *Fr.* The Aeneid, VI. OBS

Not faster yonder rowers' might. Song. Sir Walter Scott. *Fr.* The Lady of the Lake, II. EV-4

Not fighting only. Love Means Adventure. Toyohiko Kagawa. SoLD

Not Flesh of Brass. Job, VI: 1-13, Bible, *O.T.* TrJP

Not for Its Own Sake. Hazel Littlefield. GoYe

Not for long can I be angry with the most beautiful. My Land. James Oppenheim. TBM

Not for me the general renowned nor the well-groomed dandy. The Ideal General. Archilochus. OxBG

Not for My Tears. Humbert Wolfe. TCPD

Not for one hour; so much the daily task. "Could Ye Not Watch One Hour?" Godfrey Fox Bradby. MaRV

Not for one year. Nazim Hikmet. Yaroslav Smelyakov. RuPo

Not for our lands, our wide-flung prairie wealth. We Thank Thee. Thomas Curtis Clark. OQP; PEDC; PGD; PoToHe (1941 ed.); QP-1

Not for our sake your life was ended thus. Non Nobis. L. A. MacKay. TwCV

Not for That City. Charlotte Mew. MoBrPo

Not for the broken bodies. Broken Bodies. Louis Golding. HBMV

Not for the child that wanders home. Benvenuto's Valentine. Elinor Wylie. AV

Not for the dead who fell that dreams may stand. Requiem. Glenn Ward Dresbach. MuM

Not for the eyes of men. Unto Thee. Thomas Curtis Clark. PraP

Not for the lakes of glancing blue. For Dominion Day. Jesse Edgar Middleton. CPG

Not for you/ Is mourning. To the Living. Ernst Toller. PoFr

Not from a vain or shallow thought. Monumental Human Expressions. Emerson. *Fr.* The Problem. BAV; GrCo-2; OQP; QP-1

Not from my reverent sires hath come. Poet's Prayer. Adelaide Love. TrPWD

Not from successful love alone. Halcyon Days. Walt Whitman. NePA; OxBA

Not from the earth, or skies. Health of Body Dependent on Soul. Jones Very. WGRP

Not from the glory of the cloud's pile and rift. Elegy on the Eve. George Barker. WaaP

Not from the ranks of those we call. Henry Fielding. Austin Dobson. BPN

Not from the stars do I my judgment pluck. Sonnets, XIV. Shakespeare. PeBoSo; SiCE

Not from the whole wide world I chose thee. Song. Richard Watson Gilder. *Fr.* The New Day. AA; LBAP

Not from This Anger. Dylan Thomas. LiTB

Not from two who supped with You. Reality. Amelia Josephine Burr. ChIP; PSO

Not gold, but only man can make. A Nation's Strength. Emerson. FaPON
Not Gone Yet. John Swanwick Drennan. IrPN
Not great ambitions gone astray. Spectres. Samuel Minturn Peck. BAP
Not greatly moved with awe am I. The Two Deserts. Coventry Patmore. The Unknown Eros, I, xviii. PoVP; VA
Not He That Knows. Thomas May. *Fr.* The Tragedy of Cleopatra. SeCL
("Not he that knows how to acquire.") TuPP
(Song, A.) SeEP
Not Heat Flames Up and Consumes. Walt Whitman. NePA
Not Heaving from My Ribb'd Breast Only. Walt Whitman. NePA
Not her own sorrow only that hath place. An Irish Face. "Æ." ChMo; CMP
Not Here. D. S. Leonard. UnW
Not here! the white North has thy bones; and thou. Sir John Franklin; On the Cenotaph in Westminster Abbey. Tennyson. EPP; InP; LiA
Not hers the young nun's quest to ride. Elderly Nun. Benjamin Francis Musser. PraNu
Not Honey. Hilda Doolittle ("H. D."). AnFE; APA; CoAnAm; MAPA; MoPo; TwAmPo
(Fragment 113.) LiTA; MOAP
Not I. Robert Louis Stevenson. BoN; NA
Not I. *Unknown.* BLRP
Not I myself know all my love for thee. The Dark Glass. Dante Gabriel Rossetti. The House of Life, XXXIV. BMEP; BPN; EmBrPo; EPN; HBV; LEAP; PoVP; TOP; VA; ViPo; VLEP
Not I, not I, but the wind that blows through me! Song of a Man Who Has Come Through. D. H. Lawrence. ChMP; CoBMV; FaBoMo; LiTM; MoPo; SeCeV; ViBoPo
Not Ideas about the Thing but the Thing Itself. Wallace Stevens. ViBoPo (1958 ed.)
Not if men's tongues and angels' all in one. William Shakespeare. Swinburne. *Fr.* Sonnets on English Dramatic Poets. BMEP; BPN; PIAE; PoVP; TrGrPo; VLEP
Not, I'll not, carrion comfort, Despair, not feast on thee. Carrion Comfort [*or* Sonnet]. Gerard Manley Hopkins. AnFE; AtBAP; CoBE; CoEV; EmBrPo; EnLi-2; FaBoEn; LiTB; LiTG; MaPo; MoP; MoPo; MoVE; NBE; OAEP; OxBoCh; PoEL-5; PoLi; POTT; PoVP; ViP; ViPo; ViPP
Not in a Silver Casket Cool with Pearls. Edna St. Vincent Millay. AnEnPo; ChMo; CMP
Not in a valley ivoried with grain. Winter Apples. Winifred Welles. AnAmPo; LA
Not in city nor town shall our banquet be strown. Samoan Revel. Nicaenetus. GrR
Not in Dumb Resignation. John Hay. MaRV; WGRP
(Thy Will Be Done.) WBLP
Not in every generation do virtues long-descended. Moderation. Pindar. *Fr.* Nemean Odes, XI. GrPE
Not in Narrow Seas, *sels.* Allen Curnow. AnNZ
Bishop Boundary-rides His Diocese, The.
Water is Burred with Rain, The.
Not in our time, America light-hearted. Our Time. Leonard Bacon. NeTW
Not in palaces of marble. Pedro Salinas, *tr. fr. Spanish by* Eleanor L. Turnbull. CoSP
Not in sleep I saw it, but in daylight. Kindly Vision. Otto Julius Bierbaum. AWP; JAWP; WBP
Not in Solitude. F. W. H. Myers. *Fr.* St. Paul. OQP; QP-2
Not in the ancient abbey. Threnody for a Poet. Bliss Carman. CaP; OCL
Not in the cosmic vast alone. Life of Our Life. Henry Burke Robins. MaRV
Not in the crises of events. The Spirit's Epochs. Coventry Patmore. *Fr.* The Angel in the House, I, i, 6. EG; EPP; GoBC
Not in the crystal air of a Greek glen. Upon a Drawing. Lionel Johnson. VLEP
Not in the dire, ensanguined front of war. The Men of the *Maine.* Clinton Scollard. MC; PAH
Not in the field of vision stands His form. Inner Vision. *Unknown. Fr.* The Upanishads. OnPM
Not in the Guide-Books. Elizabeth Jennings. NePoEA
Not in the laughing bowers. The Dreamer. *Unknown.* LPS-1
Not in the Lucid Intervals of Life. Wordsworth. EPN
Not in the morning vigor, Lord, am I. Strength in Weakness. Richard Burton. MaRV
Not in the rustle of water, the air's noise. Night in Martindale. Kathleen Raine. NeBP
Not in the sepulchre Thou art. Passiontide Communion. Katharine Tynan. TrPWD
Not in the silence only. My Prayer. Horatius Bonar. BLRP
Not in the sky. The Last Pleiad. William Gilmore Simms. AA; APW; OBAV; SPP
Not in the solitude. Hymn of the City. Bryant. BAV; IAP; MOAP
Not in the time of pleasure. The Rainbow. John Vance Cheney. OQP; QP-1
Not in the wind-hushed isles and gardens Elysian. The City of God. Anna Louise Strong. MaRV
Not in the world of light alone. The Living Temple. Oliver Wendell Holmes. *Fr.* The Autocrat of the Breakfast-Table. AA; AmPP (3d ed.)
Not in those climes where I have late been straying. To Ianthe. Byron. *Fr.* Childe Harold's Pilgrimage. FaBoEn
Not in thy body is thy life at all. Life-in-Love. Dante Gabriel Rossetti. The House of Life, XXXVI. PoVP; ViPo; VLEP
Not in Vain. Emily Dickinson. *See* If I can stop one heart from breaking.
Not in Vain. *Unknown.* BLRP
Not ink, but bloud [*or* blood] and tears now serve the turn. Benjamin Tompson. *Fr.* New England's Crisis. AnAmPo; LA
Not Iris in Her Pride. George Peele. *Fr.* The Arraignment of Paris. ViBoPo
(Peeping Flowers.) EV-1
Not Jerusalem—lowly Bethlehem. Lowly Bethlehem. Count Zinzendorf. TrAS
Not just folklore, or. Fast Ball. Jonathan Williams. NeAP
Not Just for the Ride. *Unknown. See* Limerick: "There was a young lady of Niger."
Not Kings. Kenneth W. Porter. PSO
Not Knowing. Mary Gardiner Brainard. AA
Faith and Sight, *sel.* MaRV
Not knowing he rose from earth, not having seen him rise. On First Having Heard the Skylark. Edna St. Vincent Millay. BLA
Not least, 'tis ever my delight. Morning. Philip Henry Savage. AA
Not less because in purple I descended. Tea at the Palaz of Hoon. Wallace Stevens. FaBoMo; NP
Not light of love, lady! The Lover Exhorteth His Lady to Be Constant. *Unknown.* OBSC; TuPP
Not like Beauty were you born. Truth. Erik Blomberg. AnSL
Not like the brazen giant of Greek fame. The New Colossus. Emma Lazarus. FaFP; FaPON; MaRV; PGD; TreFS
Not like the tombs where sleep Egyptian kings. Grant at Rest. John James Meehan. GA
Not lips of mine have ever said. In Youth. Evaleen Stein. AA
Not long ago from hence I went. The Lusty Fryer of Flanders. *Unknown.* CoMu
Not long ago I fell in love. Love at First Sight. Christopher Morley. FAOV
Not long ago it was a bird. A Volunteer's Grave. William Alexander Percy. HBMV
Not long ago the rain walked through this clearing. Lyubka. Boris Pasternak. TrRV
Not long it was her fate among the flowers. Moschus, *tr. fr. Greek by* H. H. Chamberlin. GrPo
Not long since lived a farmer plain. The Farmer's Advice to the Villagers. Timothy Dwight. *Fr.* Greenfield Hill, VI. IAP
Not long we basked in the illusions. To Chaadayev. Pushkin. TrRV
Not Lost, but Gone Before. Caroline Elizabeth Sarah Norton. BLRP; WBLP
Not lost or won but above all endeavour. Fidelity. Trumbull Stickney. AnFE; CoAnAm; LiTA; TwAmPo
Not Love, Not War, nor the Tumultuous Swell. Wordsworth. PeBoSo
Not Made by Hands. Piotr Vasilyevich Oreshin. *See* Not by Hands Created.
Not Made with Hands. Lilith Lorraine. ChIP
"Not Marble nor the Gilded Monuments." Archibald MacLeish. AmPP (3d ed.); ChMo; CMP; CoBMV; CoV; LiTL; MoAB; PoeMoYo; PoRA; TwHP; ViBoPo
Not marble, nor the gilded monuments. Sonnets, LV. Shakespeare. AEV; AnEnPo; AnFE; ATP; AWP; BEL; CoBE; CoEV; EG; EM-1; EnL; EnLi-1; EnLit; EPP; ExPo; FaBoEn; FaFP; GTBS-W; InPo; JAWP; LEAP; LiTB; LiTG; LiTL; LoBV; OAEP; OBSC; OuHeWo; PeBoSo; PoE; PoEL-2; PoRA; REAL; ReEn; ReIE; SeCeV; SiCE; TOP; TrGrPo; TwHP; TwP; TyEnPo; ViBoPo; WBP
Not marching now in fields of Thrasimene [*or* Thrasymene]. The Tragical History of Doctor Faustus. Christopher Marlowe. CoBE; EnLi-1; EnLit; TwCrTr
Not merely for our pleasure, but to purge. "Ej Blot til Lyst." William Morton Payne. AA
Not merely in matters material, but in things of the spirit. America First! G. Ashton Oldham. PGD
Not met and marred with the year's whole turn of grief. James Agee. *Fr.* Lyrics. MAP; MoAmPo
Not 'mid the thunder of the battle guns. The Birth of Australia. Percy Russell. VA

Not midst the lightning of the stormy fight. Stonewall Jackson. Henry Lynden Flash. AA; DD; GA; PAH
Not [*or* Nor] mine own fears, nor the prophetic soul. Sonnets, CVII [*or* I'll Live in This Poor Rime]. Shakespeare. AWP; EG; EM-1; EnLi-1; EPP; ES; EV-1; FiP; InPo; JAWP; LiTB; LiTG; LoBV; MaPo; OAEP; OBSC; OuHeWo; PeBoSo; PoFr; ReaPo; ReEn; ReIE; SeCeV; SiCE; TOP; WBP
Not mine to draw the cloth-yard shaft. The Satirist. Harry Lyman Koopman. AA
Not more blue at the dawn of the world. Autumn on the Beaches. Sara Teasdale. PoTo
Not more of light I ask, O God. A Prayer. Florence Holbrook. PraP
Not more of light I ask, O God. Understanding. *Unknown.* PoToHe (new ed.)
Not My Will. "Green Forest." PraP
Not, Nicias, as we dreamed once, for us alone was Love. Hylas. Theocritus. Idylls, XIII. GrPE
Not noisily, but solemnly and pale. Irradiations, XXI. John Gould Fletcher. LA; NP
Not now, but in the coming years. Some Time We'll Understand. Maxwell N. Cornelius. BLRP; WBLP
Not now expecting to live forever. Dublin Bay. Ewart Milne. NeIP
Not of Itself but Thee. *Unknown, tr. fr. Greek by* Richard Garnett. AWP
Not of ladies, love, or graces. La Araucana. Alonso de Ercilla y Zúñiga. OuHeWo
Not of my choosing, traveller, this desert eminence. Hermes of the Lonely Hill. *Unknown.* OxBG
Not of silver nor of coral. He Made This Screen. Marianne Moore. TCPD
Not of the princes and prelates with periwigged charioteers. A Consecration. John Masefield. BEL; BMEP; ChMo; CMP; CP; EnLit; GrCo-2; HBMV; HiLiEn; InP; MBP; MCCG; MoAB; MoBrPo; NeMA; NV; OtMeF; PCN; PoFr; POT; PoTo; POTT; PYM; VOD; WHA
Not of the sunlight. Follow the Gleam. Tennyson. Merlin and the Gleam, IX. BBV; MaRV; OTPC (1946 ed.); PoRL
Not of This World. Bartolomé Leonardo de Argensola, *tr. fr. Spanish by* Sir John Bowring. OnPM
Not oft such marvel the years reveal. The People's King. Lyman Whitney Allen. PGD
Not often, when the carnal dance is mad. The Final Faith. George Sterling. CAW
Not on a prayerless bed, not on a prayerless bed. Exhortation to Prayer. Margaret Mercer. AA
Not on an altar shall mine eyes behold thee. Real Presence. Ivan Adair. OQP; QP-1; WGRP
Not on sad Stygian shore, nor in clear sheen. Samuel Butler. GTML
Not on the Battle-Field. John Pierpont. LPS-2
Not on the neck of prince or hound. The Splendid Spur. Sir Arthur Quiller-Couch. BMEP; HBV; HBVY; LBBV; LEAP; VA
Not one blithe leap of welcome? To Sigurd. Katharine Lee Bates. CV
Not One Thing Alone. Marius Bohun-Greene. PoP
Not One to Spare. Ethel Lynn Beers. *See* Which Shall It Be?
Not Only around Our Infancy. James Russell Lowell. *Fr.* The Vision of Sir Launfal. FaFP; GTBS-W; NePA (Prelude.) BLV
Not only by day, but by night the image obedient I see. Lines from a Ghazel. Mir Alishir. BoFr
Not only heads are haloed, nor are faces. Golden Outline. Winifred Welles. MuM
Not only how far away, but the way that you say it. Judging Distances. Henry Reed. Lessons of the War, II. ChMP; FaBoMo; LiTB; MoAB
Not only in the Christmas-Tide. Mary Mapes Dodge. ChBR
Not only once, and long ago. Christ Is Crucified Anew. John Richard Moreland. ChIP; MaRV; PGD
Not only once, when to His feet there came. The Great Refusal. Thomas S. Jones, Jr. QS
Not only sands and gravels. One Step Backward Taken. Robert Frost. OnHM
Not only that thy puissant arm could bind. Wellington. Disraeli. EPN; OBVV; VA
Not only the soot from the city air. The Floor Is Dirty. Edward Field. NeAP
Not only there where jewelled vestments blaze. The Poor Man's Daily Bread. Denis A. McCarthy. JKCP
Not only we, the latest seed of time. Godiva. Tennyson. BeLS; LPS-2
Not Our Good Luck. Robinson Jeffers. PC
"Not ours," say some, "the thought of death to dread." The Great Misgiving. Sir William Watson. HBV; OBEV (1st ed.); OBVV
Not Ours the Vows. Bernard Barton. HBV; LPS-1; MaRV
Not out of the East but the West. The Star of Sangamon [*or* The Great American]. Lyman Whitney Allen. PGD; PSO
Not Overlooked. James Oppenheim. NP
Not Palaces [an Era's Crown]. Stephen Spender. BoLiVe (1939 ed.); ChMo; EnLi-2 (1949 ed.); LiTB; LiTM; MoAB; MoBrPo; NeMA; PoLFOT; ReaPo; WaP
Not Peace at Any Price. Euripides, *tr. fr. Greek by* M. Wodhull. *Fr.* Children of Heracles. GrR
Not picnics or pageants or the improbable. Terror. Robert Penn Warren. MoPo; NePA; WaP
Not Poppy, nor Mandragora. Shakespeare. *See* Jealousy.
Not Quite Fair. H. S. Leigh. InMe
Not quite sixteen. Nedjé. Roussan Camille. PoNe
Not Quite Social. Robert Frost. CoV
Not Ragged-and-tough. *Unknown.* ChTr
Not Revenge . . . but These. Emmanuel Litvinoff. NeTW
Not roses flaming in the dawning light. Many Joys. Pierre de Ronsard. TrFP
Not Seldom, Clad in Radiant Vest. Wordsworth. BPN
Not serried ranks with flags unfurled. What Makes a Nation Great? Alexander Blackburn. OQP; QP-2; WBLP
Not she for whom proud Troy did fall and burn. The Lover in the Praise of His Beloved and Comparison of Her Beauty. *Unknown.* ReIE; TuPP
Not she. Not Freedom. Of Old Sat Freedom on the Heights. Hildegarde Flanner. PoFr
Not she with traitorous kiss her Saviour stung. Woman. Eaton Stannard Barrett. HBV; OnYI; OxBI; PIAE
Not skies serene, with glittering stars inlaid. Petrarch. Sonnets to Laura: To Laura in Death, XLIV. PrPoCR
Not so, for living yet are those. A Dead Past. *At. to* C. C. Munson. BLRP; WBLP
Not So Impossible. *Unknown. See* I Saw a Peacock.
Not So in Haste, My Heart. Bradford Torrey. MaRV
Not solely that the future she destroys. Modern Love, XII. George Meredith. EmBrPo; EnLit; ViBoPo; ViPo
Not solitarily in fields we find. Earth's Secret. George Meredith. EmBrPo; EPN; PoVP
Not songs of loyalty alone are these. Walt Whitman. *Fr.* To a Foil'd European Revolutionaire. PoFr
Not soon shall I forget. Farewell. Katharine Tynan. CH; LBBV; NLK; PoeT; VOD
Not Spring. James Rorty. MOAP
Not Spring's/ Thou art. Arbutus. Adelaide Crapsey. MoAmPo (1942 ed.)
Not Such Your Burden. Agathias Scholasticus, *tr. fr. Greek by* William M. Hardinge. AWP; JAWP; WBP ("Not such your burden, happy youths, as ours.") GrPo
Not that by this disdain. The Repulse. Thomas Stanley. CaAE; LO; MeLP; MePo; OBS
Not that her blooms are mark'd with beauty's hue. To Mr. Gray. Thomas Warton, the Younger. PtP
Not that I care for ceremonies—no. After Browning. *Unknown.* PA
Not that I have cause for celebration. New Year's Eve. H. B. Mallalieu. WaP
Not that I love thy children, whose dull eyes. Sonnet to Liberty. Oscar Wilde. BMEP; LBBV; LEAP; PoFr
Not that in colour it was like thy haire. Elegie XI: The Bracelet. John Donne. *Fr.* Elegies. EnLP
Not that, in sooth, o'er mortal urn. Nature's Sympathy with the Poet. Sir Walter Scott. *Fr.* The Lay of the Last Minstrel, V. EV-4
Not that the earth is changing, O my God! On Refusal of Aid between Nations. Dante Gabriel Rossetti. BPN; CoBE; EmBrPo; EPN; EPP; ES; LoBV; PeBoSo; PoVP; TOP; VLEP
Not that the pines were darker there. The Long Voyage. Malcolm Cowley. AnFE; CoAnAm; GBV (1952 ed.); NePA; TwAmPo; WaKn
Not that thy hand is soft, is sweet, is white. Henry Constable. *Fr.* Diana. OBSC
Not That Way. Walter de la Mare. TriL
Not the angelic host of Moors were the foe. Moors, Angels, Civil Wars. Keith Sinclair. AnNZ
Not the Circean wine. The Dread of Height. Francis Thompson. JKCP; VLEP
Not the cougar leaping to myth. Man Is a Snow. Earle Birney. PeCV
Not the last struggles of the sun. On the Death of Southey. Walter Savage Landor. OBVV; TriL
Not the Pilot. Walt Whitman. AmPo; CoV
Not the setting of the Pleiades so fearful is to me. The Terrifying Tell-Tale. Antipater. OnPM
Not thee, O world's desire. Helen and Thetis. Alcaeus. GrL; OxBG
Not theirs the vain, tumultuous bliss. Husband and Wife. Edward Harry William Meyerstein. LO; LoPS
Not then/ Withal had doughty Hektor and his men. Sarpedon and Glaucus. Homer. *Fr.* The Iliad, XII. OxBG
Not there, my dear, not there. Bargain Basement. F. T. Macartney. MoAuPo
Not these appal. Faith's Difficulty. Theodore Maynard. TrPWD

Not Thine Own. Shakespeare. *Fr.* Measure for Measure, I, i. MaRV
Not this dark stand of pines that house/ Quick deer. World, Defined. Edward Weismiller. AnAmPo
Not this spring shall return again. Aftermath. Margaret McCulloch. PGD
Not those elate upon the mountain height. Test. Helen Pursell Roads. OQP; QP-1
Not those patient men who knocked and were unheeded. 1918–1941. Robert D. Fitzgerald. BoAV
Not Thou but I. Philip Bourke Marston. BLPA
("It must have been for one of us, my own.") LEAP
Not Thou from Us! Richard Chenevix Trench. ChIP
Not though I grow old and gray. Island Tea. Aspenwall Bradley. PR
Not though I know she, fondly, lies. Song: The Hopeless Comfort. Robert Gould. CEP
Not Three—but One. Esther Lilian Duff. HBMV
Not tiring round the shores his rigid shadow, prompt. Gull. Glyn Jones. MoWP
Not to arrive since faring forth there is no road. Cancelled Itinerary. Frederick Mortimer Clapp. LiTM (rev. ed.)
Not to be believed, this blunt savage wind. Paper Mill. Joseph Kalar. AnAmPo
Not to be born at all is the happiest lot for mortal. Despair [*or* The Better Part]. Theognis. GrPE; GrR
Not to Be Ministered To. Maltbie D. Babcock. *See* Today, O Lord.
"Not to be tuneless in old age!" Henry Wadsworth Longfellow. Austin Dobson. DD; GA; HBV
Not to dance with her. A Triviality. Waring Cuney. CDC
Not to Die. Simonides, *tr. fr. Greek by* Lord Neaves. OnPM
Not to exclude or demarcate, or pick out evils. "Leaves of Grass's" Purport. Walt Whitman. CaAE; IAP
Not to Forget Miss Dickinson. Marshall Schacht. LiTM
Not to Keep. Robert Frost. AmPP; AnAmPo; LA; OxBA; TCAP
Not to know vice at all, and keepe true state. Epode. Ben Jonson. SeCV-1
Not to Love. Robert Herrick. OAEP
Not to scatter bread and gold. Love's Nobility. Emerson. *Fr.* Celestial Love. TreF
Not to sigh and to be tender. Song. Aphra Behn. *Fr.* Lycidus. CaAE
Not to the hills where cedars move. The Wish. Thomas Flatman. SeCL
Not to the staring day. Rhymes and Rhythms, XXIII. W. E. Henley. POTT
Not to the swift, the race. Reliance. Henry van Dyke. FaFP
Not to the twelve alone. Communion. Phoebe Smith Bachelder. ChIP
Not to the weak alone. The Call to the Strong. William Pierson Merrill. BLRP
Not Too Deeply in Love. Cecco Angiolieri da Siena. *See* Sonnet: He Will Not Be Too Deeply in Love.
Not-too-near slip softly by, The. Convalescence, I. David McCord. WhC
Not trust you, dear? Nay, tis not true. One Way of Trusting. Hannah Parker Kimball. AA
Not twice a twelve-month you appear in print. One Thousand Seven Hundred and Thirty Eight; a Dialogue Something like Horace. Pope. CEP
Not Understood. Thomas Bracken. BLPA; NeHB; PTA-1
Not unremembering we pass our exile from the starry ways. Aphrodite. "Æ." LBBV
Not unto the Forest. Margaret Widdemer. *See* Remembrance; a Greek Folk-Song.
Not unto us, not unto us. America Prays. Arthur Gordon Field. PGD
Not unto us, O Lord. Non Nobis. Henry Cust. EtPaEn; OBEV; OBVV
Not upon earth, as you suppose. "Tu Non Se' in Terra, Si Come Tu Credi . . ." Kathleen Raine. NeBP
Not Vain the Winds. Sergei Yesenin, *tr. fr. Russian by* Jack Lindsay. RuPo
Not weaned yet, without comprehension loving. Love's Immaturity. E. J. Scovell. LiTB
Not what, but Whom, I do believe. Credo. John Oxenham. BLRP; ChIP; MaRV; OQP; QP-1; StJW
Not what I am, O Lord, but what Thou art. More of Thee. Horatius Bonar. BLRP
Not what men see. Beauty of the World. Frank Wilmot. MM; MoAuPo
Not what we did shall be the test. Emily Dickinson. CoBA
Not What We Give. James Russell Lowell. *Fr.* The Vision of Sir Launfal. GrCo-1
Not what you get, but what you give. Of Giving. Arthur Guiterman. TiPo
Not when the buxom form which nature wears. George Henry Boker. *Fr.* Sonnets. MOAP
Not when, with self dissatisfied. With Self Dissatisfied. Frederick L. Hosmer. TrPWD
Not when your banners sweep the sky. Sanctuary. Kendall Banning. MuM
Not where the battle red. On the Death of Jackson. *Unknown.* PAH
Not white and shining like an ardent flame. The Ten Lepers. Katharine Tynan. MaRV; StJW
Not who you are, but what you are. A Message for the Year. Elizabeth Clark Hardy. PTA-2
Not with a clamor of golden deeds. Gandhi. Angela Morgan. BAP
Not with a club the heart is broken. Emily Dickinson. LiTA; WHA
Not with an outcry to Allah nor any complaining. The Captive. Kipling. VLEP
Not with Deserters. "Anna Akhmatova," *tr. fr. Russian by* Babette Deutsch. TrRV
Not with Libations. Edna St. Vincent Millay. *See* Sonnet: "Not with libations . . ."
Not with more glories, in th' etherial plain. Pope. *Fr.* The Rape of the Lock. FaBoEn; ViBoPo; WHA
Not with my hands. Benediction. Donald Jeffrey Hayes. PoNe
Not with old masters, rich on crowded walls. Madonna. Pushkin. TrRV
Not with slow, funereal sound. An Ode: On the Unveiling of the Shaw Memorial on Boston Common, May 31, 1897. Thomas Bailey Aldrich. AA; HBV; MDAH; PAH
Not with the cheer of battle in the throat. Sir Henry Yule. *Fr.* The *Birkenhead.* OtMeF
Not with the high-voiced fife. Peace. Clinton Scollard. BPP; OQP; PoRL; PSO; QP-1
Not with the Mind. Feodor Ivanovich Tyutchev, *tr. fr. Russian by* Babette Deutsch. TrRV
Not with vain tears, when we're beyond the sun. Sonnet. Rupert Brooke. BrBE
Not within a granite pass. Philomel in London. Sir Edmund Gosse. PoeT
Not without Beauty. John A. B. McLeish. CaP
Not without fortitude I wait. Francis Thompson. *Fr.* From the Night of Forebeing. VLEP
Not without heavy grief of heart did he. Epitaphs, VIII. Gabriello Chiabrera. AWP; JAWP; WBP
Not without sorrow did she watch the sod. Cotton Mill Funeral. Stewart Atkins. NoCaPo
Not woman-faced and sweet, as look. Michael the Archangel. Katharine Tynan. JKCP
Not worlds on worlds in phalanx deep. The Daisy. John Mason Good. PEOR
Not writ in water, nor in mist. For John Keats, Apostle of Beauty [*or* Four Epitaphs, 2]. Countee Cullen. CDC; PFE
Not Wrongly Moved. William Empson. *See* Sonnet: "Not wrongly moved by this dismaying scene."
"Not ye who have stoned, not ye who have smitten us," cry. Arraignment. Helen Gray Cone. AA
Not yesterday did the blacksmith hammer. Nikolai Tikhonov, *tr. fr. Russian by* C. M. Bowra. BoRS
Not yesterday, nor yet a day. The Annunciation. Margaret Devereaux Conway. ISi
Not Yet. Mary Elizabeth Coleridge. BoFr
Not yet, dear love, not yet: the sun is high. The Parting Hour. Olive Custance. HBV; VA
Not yet! Do not yet touch. The Turning of the Leaves. Vernon Watkins. FaBoMo; NeBP
Not yet had Nessus crossed the narrow ford. Inferno. Dante. *Fr.* Divina Commedia. EnLi-1
Not yet, not yet; it's hardly four. One More Quadrille. Winthrop Mackworth Praed. OBRV
"Not yet, not yet; steady, steady!" Bunker Hill. George Henry Calvert. BeLS; DD; FaBoBe; GA; MC
"Not yet, the flowers are in my path." Death and the Youth. Letitia E. Landon. LPS-1
Not yet trodden under wholly. Enthusiasm. James Clarence Mangan. IrPN
Not young, I think. The Cap That Fits. Austin Dobson. TSW; TSWC
Not Yours but You. Christina Rossetti. ChIP; MaRV
Not Youth Pertains to Me. Walt Whitman. IAP
Nota Bene, A. Karl Mikael Bellman, *tr. fr. Swedish by* Charles W. Stork. AnSL
(Note Bene, A.) OnPM
Nota: man is the intelligence of his soil. The Comedian as the Letter C. Wallace Stevens. NePA; OxBA
Notable Description of the World, A. *At. to* William Smith. ReIE
Notably fond of music, I dote on a sweeter tone. The Clink of the Ice. Eugene Field. InMe
Notation in Haste. Elias Lieberman. GoYe
Notation on Immortality. Nancy Byrd Turner. AlBD
Note-Book of a European Tramp, The, *sel.* Michael Hamburger.
"Townsman on his yielding bed, The," XI. NePoEA
Note for Navigators. Sherman Conrad. CAG
Note from an Intimate Diary. Emanuel Litvinov. NeBP

Note from the Pipes, A. Leonora Speyer. HBMV; OBAV; SBMV
Note of Humility, A. Arna Bontemps. PoNe
Note on Intellectuals. W. H. Auden. FiBHP; SiTL
Note on Local Flora. William Empson. AtBAP; FaBoMo; MoVE
Note on the Continuity of Life, A. John Ransom Palmer. PoP
Note on the Latin Gerunds, A. Richard Porson. *See* Dido.
Note to Gongyla. Sappho, *tr. fr. Greek by* D. L. Feldstone. LiTW
Notes after Blacking Out. Gregory Corso. NeAP
Notes by a Foreigner. Bernard Spencer. PoN
Notes for a Bestiary. Terence Heywood. LiTM
Notes for a Movie Script. M. Carl Holman. PoNe
Notes for My Son. Alex Comfort. The Song of Lazarus, VI. MoBrPo (1950 ed.); NeBP; SeCePo
Notes toward a Supreme Fiction, *sels.* Wallace Stevens.
"Bethou me, said sparrow, to the crackled blade." LiTM (rev. ed.); MoPo; NePA
(Bethou Me, Said Sparrow.) CrMA
"It feels good as it is without the giant." MoPo; NePA
"It is the celestial ennui of apartments." MoPo; NePA
"Lion roars at the enraging desert, The." MoPo; NePA
"President ordains the bee to be, The." AtBAP; LiTA
Soldier, There Is a War [between the Mind]. LiTM (rev. ed.); NePA
We Reason of These Things. CrMA
Nothin' Done. Sam S. Stinson. LHV
"Nothin' or everythin' it's got to be." Nocturne. John V. A. Weaver. AnAmPo; HBMV; LA; NP
Nothing. Richard Porson. BOHV
Nothing. Barrie Reid. BoAV
Nothing adds to your fond fire. The Answer. Earl of Rochester. EPS
Nothing and the Soul. Bhartrihari, *tr. fr. Sanskrit by* Paul Elmer More. OnPM
Nothing Belongs to Us. Jorge Carrera Andrade, *tr. fr. Spanish by* H. R. Hays. TwSpPo
Nothing Between. C. A. Tindley. BePJ
Nothing but darkness enters in this room. Return at Night. Sara Teasdale. PIAE
Nothing but Flags. Moses Owen. FOAH
Nothing but Flight. José Moreno Villa, *tr. fr. Spanish by* Eleanor L. Turnbull. CoSP
Nothing but Leaves. Lucy E. Akerman. LPS-2
Nothing but No and I, and I and No. Idea, V. Michael Drayton. PoEL-2
Nothing can be more delightful than the having wings to wear! Aristophanes. *Fr.* The Birds. GrPo
Nothing can match you, Rome. Roman Elegy. Hildebert of Lavardin. LiA
Nothing could make me sooner to confesse. Of the Progress of the Soule: The Second Anniversary. John Donne. PoD; ReEn; SeEP
Nothing endures but personal qualities. What Endures? Walt Whitman. *Fr.* Song of the Broad-Axe. BHV
Nothing ever grips me. To My Father. "Philardee." FAOV
Nothing Fair on Earth I See. "Angelus Silesius," *tr. fr. German by* Catherine Winkworth. BePJ
Nothing from you at all. Your being seems. Remoteness. Germán Pardo García. AnCL
Nothing Gold Can Stay. Robert Frost. BoLiVe; MAP; MoAB; MoAmPo; NeMA; TwHP; WHA
Nothing has been quite the same. After Reading the Reviews of "Finnegans Wake." Melville Cane. WhC
Nothing here is bitter. Wisdom. Phyllis Hanson. GoYe
Nothing I have is worth a tear. Song. E. N. da Costa Andrade. POTE
Nothing is better, I well think. The Leper. Swinburne. LO; VLEP
Nothing is easy! Pity then. James Stephens. LO
Nothing Is Enough. Laurence Binyon. AlDL; LBBV; MBP; MoBrPo; POTE
Nothing is ever really lost, or can be lost. Continuities. Walt Whitman. EOAH
Nothing Is Given: We Must Find Our Law. W. H. Auden. Po
Nothing is gone, not time, when death is done. Too Early Death. L. F. Gerlach. PtPa
"Nothing Is Here to Wail." Philetas, *tr. fr. Greek by* F. L. Lucas. GrPE
Nothing is judged according to its size. Quatrain V. Thomas S. Jones, Jr. PFE
Nothing is new; I have seen the spring too often. I Have Seen the Spring. Sara Teasdale. ChMo; CMP
Nothing is quite so quiet and clean. Snow in Town. Rickman Mark. BoTP; TVC; TVSH
Nothing is real. The world has lost its edges. Scarcely Spring. Louis Untermeyer. GoTP; MAP; MoAmPo (1942 ed.)
Nothing is so beautiful as spring. Spring. Gerard Manley Hopkins. AlDL; BLV; BoLiVe; EG; FaBoEn; InvP; JKCP; LiTM; LO; MaPo; MBP; MoAB; MoBrPo; MoVE; OAEP (2d ed.); OBMV; OnHM; OxBoCh; PoLi; TwCV; ViP; ViPP; VLEP
Nothing more. The Tray. Gerardo Diego. CoSP
"Nothing much here!" they say. With careless glance. Auction Sale—Household Furnishings. Adele de Leeuw. PoToHe (new ed.)
Nothing now to mark the spot. A Circus Garland. Rachel Field. StVeCh
Nothing older than stone but the soil and the sea and the sky. The Mason. Robert Farren. JKCP (1955 ed.); OnYI; OxBI
Nothing Small. Elizabeth Barrett Browning. BCEP
Nothing so difficult as a beginning. The Author's Purpose [*or* Romantic to Burlesque]. Byron. *Fr.* Don Juan, IV. BEL; BPN; CoBE; EM-2; EnRP; EPN; FiP; PoFS
Nothing so sharply reminds a man he is mortal. Departure in the Dark. C. Day Lewis. ChMP; CoBMV; MoPo
Nothing so true as what you once let fall. Of the Characters of Women [*or* To a Lady]. Pope. *Fr.* Moral Essays, II. FaBoEn; OxBoLi; PoFS; SiTL
Nothing! thou elder brother ev'n to shade. Upon Nothing. Earl of Rochester. AtBAP; BLV; MePo; NBE; OBS; Po; PoEL-3; SeEP; TrGrPo; ViBoPo
Nothing to do but work. The Pessimist. Ben King. ALV; BLPA; BOHV; FaFP; InMe; LiTG; NA; NeHB; WaKn
Nothing to Say, You Say? Conrad Aiken. Preludes to Attitude, IX. LiTA; TwAmPo
Nothing to Wear. William Allen Butler. BOHV; HBV; LPS-3; PR, *abr.*
Nothing to Wish or to Fear. John Newton. BePJ
Nothing wild. Inertia. Audrey McGaffin. NePoAm
Nothing will ever change beside this river. Changeless Shore. Sarah Leeds Ash. GoYe
Nothing will give delight. Nausea. Catherine Davis. NePoEA
Nothing would sleep in that cellar, dank as a ditch. Root Cellar. Theodore Roethke. FiMAP
Nothing you give while alive; but you promise a legacy, Maro. Martial, *tr. fr. Latin by* Robert R. Schnorr. Epigrams, XI, 67. LaP
Nothinge one earth remaines to show so right. *Unknown.* SeCSL
Nothingness, nothingness,/ Ye Children of Man. "Vanity of Vanities; All Is Vanity." Sophocles. *Fr.* Oedipus Rex. GrR
Nothing's wholly mine on earth. Poet-Hearts. Count Joseph von Eichendorff. CAW
Notice Given. Berton Braley. AlBD
Notice the convulsed orange inch of moon. Sonnets—Actualities. E. E. Cummings. AnAmPo; LA
Notice with what careful nonchalance. Portrait. Hyam Plutzik. FiMAP
Notre Dame des Petits. Louis Mercier, *tr. fr. French by* Liam Brophy. ISi
Nottamun Town. *Unknown.* OxBoLi; SiTL
Nou goth sonne under wod. Sunset on Calvary. *Unknown.* AtBAP
Nought have I to bring. November. Christina Rossetti. YeAr
"Nought loves another as itself." A Little Boy Lost. Blake. *Fr.* Songs of Experience. CEP; EM-1; EnLi-2; EnLit; EnRP; OAEP; ViBoPo
Nought of the bridal will I tell. Hymn for the Dead. Sir Walter Scott. *Fr.* The Lay of the Last Minstrel, VI. BSV; OBRV
Nought to the far-off Hades but an empty echo cries. The Eternal Silence. Erinna. GrPE
Noureddin, the Son of the Shah. Clinton Scollard. BOHV
Nova. Robinson Jeffers. ChMo
Nova, Nova: Ave Fit ex Eva. *Unknown.* AnEC
Novel. Arthur Rimbaud, *tr. fr. French by* Alan Conder. TrFP
Novel, The. Wallace Stevens. ReMP
Novel of High Life, A. Thomas Haynes Bayly. EV-4
Novelettes, *sel.* Louis MacNeice.
Gardener, The. AlDL
Novelty, A. G. K. Chesterton. AlDL
November. Robert Bridges. PoEL-5
November. Alice Cary. PTA-1
November. John Clare. GoTP
November. C. L. Cleaveland. DD; HBV; SN
November. Elizabeth J. Coatsworth. YeAr
November. Hartley Coleridge. Sonnets on the Seasons, XII. LoBV; OBRV; PEOR; PoRL
November, *sel.* John Davidson.
Epping Forest. CP; GTSL
November. Richard Watson Dixon. *See* Song: "Feathers of the willow, The."
November. Aileen Fisher. SiSoSe; TiPo (1959 ed.)
November. Mahlon Leonard Fisher. BAP; HBV; PFY
November. Patricia Flinn. CAG
November. Thomas Hood. *See* No!
November. John Keble. OBEV (new ed.); OBVV
November. Richard Le Gallienne. LBBV

November. Samuel Longfellow. SN
November. Hilda Morris. *See* November Wears a Paisley Shawl.
November. William Morris. *Fr.* The Earthly Paradise. EmBrPo; EPN; GTML; GTSL; ViPo; ViPP
November. Margaret Rose. BoTP
November. Christina Rossetti. YeAr
November. Spenser. *Fr.* The Shepheardes Calender. MaPo; PoEL-1
"Up then Melpomene thou mournefulst Muse of nyne," *sel.* AtBAP
(Dido My Dear, Alas, Is Dead.) ChTr
November. Elizabeth Stoddard. AA
November. Edward Thomas. TCPD
November. Emile Verhaeren, *tr. fr. French by* Ludwig Lewisohn. WoL
November Afternoons. Sister Mary Madeleva. GoBC
November Blue. Alice Meynell. AlDL; MBP; MM; MoBrPo; PoeMoYo; PoeT; VOD; YT
November chill blaws loud wi' angry sugh. November Evening. Burns. *Fr.* The Cotter's Saturday Night. OBEC; UnPo (1st ed.)
November comes. November. Elizabeth J. Coatsworth. YeAr
November Cotton Flower. Jean Toomer. CDC
November Dusk. Arthur Davison Ficke. UnW
(Sonnet: "There are strange shadows fostered of the moon.") MAP
November, 1806 ("Another year!"). Wordsworth. BPN; OBRV; PoFr; SoV
November Eleventh. Katherine Burton. PoRL
November 11th, 1942. Lawrence Toynbee. NeTW
November Evening. Burns. *Fr.* The Cotter's Saturday Night. UnPo (1st ed.)
November Eves. James Elroy Flecker. MoVE; VOD
November 1 ("How clear, how keen"). Wordsworth. BPN; EPN
November Fugitive. Henry Morton Robinson. *See* December Fugitive.
November Furrow. Ruth Kennon. CAG
November Garden. Louise Driscoll. YeAr
November in England. Thomas Hood. *See* No!
November in Ettrick Forest. Sir Walter Scott. *See* To William Stewart Rose, Esq.
November is a spinner. November. Margaret Rose. BoTP
November Morning. Evaleen Stein. YeAr
November Night. Adelaide Crapsey. AnAmPo; BAP; BLV; FaPON; LA; MAP; MoAmPo (1942 ed.); MPB; NeMA; NP; NV; PFE; PFY; PIAE; VOD (1935 ed.)
November, 1941. Roy Fuller. MoPo
November Rain. Maud E. Uschold. YeAr
November 7; Ode to a Day of Victories. "Pablo Neruda," *tr. fr. Spanish by* Dudley Fitts. AnCL
(November 7th, *tr. by* Lloyd Mallan.) PoFr
November should be cold and grey. Weather Vanes. Frances Frost. SiSoSe
November Sunshine. Albert E. S. Smythe. CPG
November Surf. Robinson Jeffers. CrMA; MoPo; OxBA
November 24, 1918. Vincent Starrett. MuM
November 2 A.M. Conspiracy. Sara Bard Field. AnEnPo
November Wears a Paisley Shawl. Hilda Morris. YeAr
(November.) PCH
November woods are bare and still. Down to Sleep. Helen Hunt Jackson. GN
November's Cadence. James Carnegie. EBSV
November's days are thirty. November. Edward Thomas. TCPD
November's sky is chill and drear. To William Stewart Rose, Esq. Sir Walter Scott. Marmion, *Introd. to* I. BSV; EBSV; OBRV
Novice, A. Shakespeare. *Fr.* Measure for Measure, I, iv. PraNu
Novice when I came beneath thy gaze, A. Stanzas concerning Love. Stefan George. AWP; JAWP; WBP
Novus Sol de Virgine. *Unknown.* AnEC
Now. Robert Browning. EnLi-2 (1949 ed.); GEPC; PoVP; VLEP
Now. Mary Barker Dodge. AA
Now. Thomas Ken. OxBoCh
Now. Harriet Monroe. HBV
Now!/ Not now!/ Give me them again. In a Balcony. Robert Browning. EnLi-2 (1949 ed.); PoVP; ViPP
Now a certain man was sick, named Lazarus. Jesus and Lazarus. St. John, Bible, *N.T.* BoFr
Now a knightlier sort you'll never find. Medieval Appreciations. William M. T. Gamble. CAW
Now Aage sat with proud Ellen. The Slaying of Thord Iverson. *Unknown.* BoDaBa
Now after David had lived seventy years. The Death of David. Hayyim Nahman Bialik. TrJP
Now after the maids had bathed him and anointed him. Farewell to Nausicaa. Homer. *Fr.* The Odyssey, VIII. GrR
Now after the ship had left the stream of the river Oceanus. Homer. *Fr.* The Odyssey, XII. GrL
Now after twenty years have passed; again he's here. After Twenty Years. Ramón de Campoamor. *Fr.* Doloras. AnSpL-2
Now al is done; bring home the bride againe. Spenser. *Fr.* Epithalamion. FiP
Now Alf dwells up in Odderskerry. Alf of Odderskerry. *Unknown.* BoDaBa
Now all away to Tir na N'Og are many roads that run. The King of Ireland's Son. Nora Hopper. GTIV
Now all day long the man who is not dead. Mother and Son. Allen Tate. LiTA; MAP; MoAB; MoAmPo; MoVE
Now all good fellows, fill the bowl, fill the bowl. Drinking Song for Present-Day Gatherings. Morris Bishop. ALV
Now All Is Sold. "Anna Akhmatova." *See* All Is Sold.
Now all of change. Sir Thomas Wyatt. SiPS
Now all sat down. Thersites. Homer. *Fr.* The Iliad, II. OxBG
Now all the cloudy shapes that float and lie. "Such Stuff as Dreams Are Made Of." Thomas Wentworth Higginson. AA
Now all the flowers that ornament the grass. Unreturning. Elizabeth Stoddard. AA
Now all the hosts are marching to the grave. Resurrection. D. H. Lawrence. NP
Now all the peacefull regents of the night. *See* Now all ye peacefull ...
Now all the truth is out. To a Friend Whose Work Has Come to Nothing. W. B. Yeats. AnFE; AWP; CP; EnLP; GTBS-W; InPo; JAWP; LiTG; LiTM (rev. ed.); MoAB; MoBrPo; NP; OBMV; PC; TCPD; TwP; WBP
Now all the ways are open. The New Freedom. Olive Tilford Dargan. HBMV
Now all the youth of England are on fire. Shakespeare. King Henry V, Prologue to Act II. BHV; EV-1; LH
Now all things melt and shift. Archibald Fleming MacLiesh. *Fr.* The Destroyers. NAMP
"Now, all ye Nymphs, tell me truly of Daphnis—where shall I find him?" Pan the Lover. Glaucus. GrPE
Now all ye [*or* yee *or* the] peacefull regents of the night. George Chapman. *Fr.* Bussy d'Ambois, II, ii. LO; NBE; PoEL-2
Now along the solemn heights. Recessional. Sir Charles G. D. Roberts. HBV; LBMP; LEAP
Now am I a tin whistle. A Fresh Morning. J. C. Squire. MBP; WhC
Now am I happy, snug and warm! Old Friends. R. W. Waddy. TVSH
Now am I nought—abandoned: oftentimes. Sophocles, *tr. fr. Greek by* John Addington Symonds. GrPo
Now Am I Orson to Your Valentine. Elinor Wylie. ChMo
Now among good harvests. Harvests. Marie de L. Welch. PoFr
Now and Afterwards. Dinah Maria Mulock Craik. LPS-1; WGRP
Now and again I like to see. The Complete Hen. Elizabeth J. Coatsworth. GoTP
Now and, I fear, again. Table Talk. Donald Mattam. FiBHP
Now and Then. Jane Taylor. OTPC (1923 ed.)
Now Antoninus, in a smiling age. Martial, *tr. fr. Latin by* Robert Louis Stevenson. Epigrams, X, 23. LaP
Now Apollo have mercy, and Artemis be thou kind. The Blind Old Man. *Unknown.* *Fr.* Homeric Hymns. OxBG
Now apprehension, with terrible dragon-eyes. The Annual Solution. Edwin Meade Robinson. InMe
Now are our prayers divided, now. At the "Ye That Do Truly." Charles Williams. OxBoCh
Now are the bells unlimbered from their spires. Pilgrimage. Eileen Duggan. AnNZ
Now are the forests dark and the ways full. Southern Summer. Francis Stuart. NeIP
Now are the Tritons heard, to Loving-land to call. Song. Michael Drayton. *Fr.* Polyolbion. AtBAP
Now are the winds about us in their glee. Song in March. William Gilmore Simms. AA; BPP; DD; HBV
Now are those peaks unscalable sierras. On Having Grown Old. E. G. Moll. BoAV
Now, aren't men asses. Second News Item. *Unknown.* SiTL
Now, around the world, the mills. New Crucifixion. Earl Bigelow Brown. ChIP
Now, a-roving, a-roving. A-Roving, *vers.* II. *Unknown.* ShS
Now as at all times I can see in the mind's eye. The Magi. W. B. Yeats. CoBMV; MaPo; NP; TwHP
Now as even's warning bell. Solitude. John Clare. EnRP; ERP
Now as fame does report, a young duke keeps a court. The Frolicsome Duke; or, The Tinker's Good Fortune. *Unknown.* EV-2
Now as I go between sands red and yellow as poppies. Journey from New Zealand. "Robin Hyde." AnNZ
Now as I was young and easy under the apple boughs. Fern Hill. Dylan Thomas. AtBAP; ChMP; CoBMV; EnL;

Now as I was young and easy under the apple boughs (*cont.*) FaBoEn; GTBS-D; LiTB; LiTM; LoGBV; MaPo; MoAB; MoBrPo (1950 ed.); MoPo; MoPW; MoVE; NeMA; OAEP (2d ed.); Po; PoRA; PrWP; ShBV-4; TrGrPo (rev. ed.); ThWaDe; ViBoPo (1958 ed.); WaKn
Now, as Never. Ramón López Velarde, *tr. fr. Spanish by* Samuel Beckett. AnMP
Now as she lay upon her couch awhile. Apollonius Rhodius. *Fr.* Argonautica, III. GrPo
Now as the night treads softly on its way. Midnight Patrol. Eric Irvin. BoAV
Now as the twilight's doubtful interval. The Eldritch Dark. Clark Ashton Smith. DaM
Now as the year closes and turns. Josephine W. Johnson. *Fr.* Year's End. QS
Now as Then. Anne Ridler. WaP
Now as these slaughtered seven hundreds hear. On the Struma Massacre. Ralph Gustafson. BoCaPo (1948 ed.)
Now, at a particular spot on the radio dial, "—in this corner, wearing purple trunks." Reception Good. Kenneth Fearing. PoLFOT
Now at his hour Love rises, while all the earth is springing. The False One. Theognis. GrPE
Now at the end of summer stands the oak. Only the Arrogant Heart. Winifred Gray Stewart. MuM
Now at the hour when brightest shone on high. Home-coming. Homer. *Fr.* The Odyssey, XIII. OxBG
Now at the lowest ebb of night. At the Lowest Ebb of Night. Robert P. Tristram Coffin. MuM
Now at thy soft recalling voice I rise. Acknowledgment. Sidney Lanier. CBOV; PeBoSo
Now austere lips are laid. The Hard Lovers. George Dillon. AnAmPo; LA; TCPD
Now Autumn comes, the wise fool of the year. Autumn. Frances Winwar. GoYe
Now Autumn comes to me. Shiko, *tr. fr. Japanese by* Lois J. Erickson. SoLD
Now baby-talk for babies is taboo. The Safety-Valve. Ruth Pitter. PoC
Now backward the founts of the sacred streams are driven. Shifting Fortune. Euripides. *Fr.* Medea. OxBG
Now Bar the Door. Eva Byson. QS
Now be glad. Noel! *Unknown.* TMEV
Now Be We Glad, and Not Too Sad. *Unknown.* AnEC
Now before the feast of the passover. The Last Supper. St. John, Bible, *N.T.* OuHeWo
Now begin wailing notes; the flesh is thrilled. Paolo and Francesca. Dante. *Fr.* Divina Commedia: Inferno, V. ExPo
Now beginneth Glutton for to go to shrift. The Glutton. William Langland. *Fr.* The Vision of Piers Plowman. ACP
Now begins the cry. The Guitar. Federico García Lorca. AnSpL-2
Now behold: hither comes the ray of our father sun. To Father Sun. *Tr. fr. Pawnee Indian.* GrCo-1
Now bid thy soul man's busy scenes exclude. Books. George Crabbe. *Fr.* The Library. EV-3; OBEC
Now blessed be Thou, Christ Jesu. Of the Birth of Christ. Miles Coverdale. AnEC
Now blest be the Briton, his beef and his beer. Bacon and Eggs. A. P. Herbert. WhC
Now blow the daffodils on slender stalks. Sweet Weather. Lizette Woodworth Reese. LS
Now blows the white rose round our garden pales. The Spring. John Francis O'Donnell. IrPN
Now bold Robin Hood to the north would go. Robin Hood and the Scotchman. *Unknown.* ESPB
Now, boys, if you will listen, I will sing to you a song. The Lumber Camp Song. *Unknown.* ShS
Now boys, we're on the steamer *Natchez.* Roustabout Holler. *Unknown.* OuSiCo
Now breaks the sheath and spreads the leaf! Hazel Buds. Mary Webb. AlDL
Now Brigham Young is a Mormon bold. Brigham Young (B *vers.*). *Unknown.* CoSo; CSF
Now bring we sweet flowers, bring lilies and roses. The Silent Grand Army. "E. M. H. C." PEOR
Now, brother Walter, brother mine. Orrm. *Fr.* The Orrmulum. EPP
Now burst above the city's cold twilight. Six o'Clock. Trumbull Stickney. MOAP; OxBA
Now bursting on his head with thundering sound. Homer. *Fr.* The Iliad, XXI. GrPo
"Now, by Columba!" Con exclaimed. Denis Florence MacCarthy. *Fr.* The Foray of Con O'Donnell A.D. 1495. OnYI
Now, by her troth, she hath been, Phædra says. In Phædram. Thomas Freeman. TuPP
Now, by my love, the greatest oath that is. My Diet. Abraham Cowley. *Fr.* The Mistress. LiTL; LO; SeCL; SeEP
"Now, by our Lady, here is master speech!" Shakespeare Reads the King James Version. Richard Burton. PoeMoYo
Now, by the blessed Paphian queen. The Dilemma. Oliver Wendell Holmes. PR
Now by this lake, this fallen thunderstorm. Four Poems for April. Louis Adeane. NeBP
Now by this was the harvest of Earth-born men over all that field. The Slaying of the Earth-born. Apollonius Rhodius. *Fr.* Argonautica. GrR
Now bylow, baby, and slumber sweet and soundly. Lullaby. *Unknown.* BOL
Now came jolly Summer, being dight. Summer. Spenser. *Fr.* The Faerie Queene, VII. GN
Now came still evening on and twilight gray. Evening in Paradise [*or* Night Falls on Eden]. Milton. *Fr.* Paradise Lost, IV. BCEP; ChTr; FaBoEn; GN; LoBV; LPS-2; PoFS; SeEP; TCEP; TreFS
Now Camilla's fair fingers are plucking in rapture the pulsating strings. Camilla. Charles Augustus Keeler. AA
Now can you see the monument? It is of wood. The Monument. Elizabeth Bishop. LiTA; MoPo
Now Cana sees a wonder new. The Miracle. Caelius Sedulius. *Fr.* Carmen Paschale. CAW
Now Cease, My Wandering Eyes. *Unknown.* ReIE; TuPP
Now cease, ye damsels, your delights forepast. Spenser. *Fr.* Epithalamion. CoEV
Now chant me a dirge for the Isles of the Sea. The Beaufort Exile's Lament. *Unknown.* BIG
Now, Charles Gustavus Anderson is my right and proper name. Charles Gustavus Anderson, *vers.* I. *Unknown.* ShS
Now Charlotte lived on the mountain side. Young Charlotte. *Unknown.* APW
Now cheer our hearts this eventide. At Eventide. *Unknown, tr. by* Robert Bridges. MaRV
Now Christendom bids her cathedrals call. Elegy X. William Bell. NePoEA
Now Christmas comes again, to find my heart. Christmas, 1943. Vera Bax. DiM
Now Christmas Draweth Near. Nicholas Breton. AnEC
Now Clear the Triple Region of the Air. Christopher Marlowe. *Fr.* Tamburlaine the Great, Pt. I, Act IV, sc. ii. TrGrPo
Now coil up your nonsense 'bout England's great Navy. Charge the Can Cheerily. *Unknown.* AmSS
Now, come all you young sailors and listen to me,/ Sure I'll tell you a story. As I Went a-Walking down Ratcliffe Highway, *vers.* I. *Unknown.* ShS
Now, come all you young sailors and listen to me,/ With your way, hay, blow the man down. Blow the Man Down, *vers.* I. *Unknown.* ShS
Now come, my boon companions. Thomas Randolph. EG
Now come the rosy dogwoods. In October. Bliss Carman. YeAr
Now come to me all men. Experience Evoked. Richard Eberhart. TwAmPo
Now come, ye Naiads, to the fountains lead. The Home of the Naiads. John Armstrong. *Fr.* The Art of Preserving Health. OBEC
Now come, young men, and list to me. Macaffie's Confession. *Unknown.* BeLS; CoSo; CSF
Now comes Fourth Month and the early buds on the trees. Ode to Walt Whitman. Stephen Vincent Benét. PtP
Now comes my lover tripping like the roe. George Peele. *Fr.* David and Bethsabe. ViBoPo
Now Comes the Blast of Winter. *Unknown.* SeCePo
Now comes the graybeard of the north. Winter Days. Henry Abbey. AA; SN
Now comes the Paschal Victim bringing. Victimae Paschali Laudes. Wipo. CAW
Now cometh the fearful hour of the Passion. A Sequence, with Strophes in Paraphrase Thereof. Francis Burke. CAW
Now concerning spiritual gifts, brethren. Spiritual Gifts. First Corinthians, Bible, *N.T.* WoL
Now condescend, Almighty King. An Evening Hymn for a Little Family. Ann *or* Jane Taylor. BOL; OTPC (1946 ed.)
Now cracking grass encrusts the yard. For My Students, Returning to College. John Williams. NePoAm-2
Now crouch, ye kings of greatest Asia. Emperor of the Threefold World [*or* The Bloody Conquests of Mighty Tamburlaine]. Christopher Marlowe. *Fr.* Tamburlaine the Great, Pt. II, Act IV, sc. iii. ChTr; TrGrPo
Now dandelions in the short, new grass. Dandelions. John Albee. AA
Now, dearest, lend a heedful ear. Autumn. Kalidasa. *Fr.* The Seasons. AWP; JAWP; WBP
Now death at last had taken her. Her Death. W. W. Gibson. ChMo; CMP
Now Delia breathes in woods the fragrant air. Elegy: On Delia's Being in the Country. James Hammond. *Fr.* Love Elegies. CEP
Now did they stretch forth hands to the food that was lying

before them. Demodocus Sings a Song of Troy. Homer. *Fr.* The Odyssey, VIII. GrR

"Now did you mark a falcon." Noble Sisters. Christina Rossetti. CoBE

Now do I hear thee weep and groan. Ale. W. H. Davies. PC

Now do our eyes behold. Lament for the Two Brothers Slain by Each Other's Hand. Aeschylus. *Fr.* The Seven against Thebes. AWP; JAWP; WBP

Now do the birds in their warbling words. Song. Patrick Hannay. SeCL

Now does Spain's fleet her spacious wings unfold. On the Victory Obtained by Admiral Blake. Andrew Marvell. SG

Now don't overindulge grief for your lost coquette. Horace. Odes, I, 33. LaP

Now, don't you want to know something concernin'. The Ballad of Davy Crockett. *Unknown.* ABF

Now dost Thou dismiss Thy servant, O Lord. Nunc Dimittis. St. Luke, Bible, *N.T.* WGRP; WHL

Now Dreary Dawns the Eastern Light. A. E. Housman. Last Poems, XXVIII. ChMo; CMP; EmBrPo

Now Dry Thy Eyes. Mikhail Alekseyevich Kuzmin, *tr. fr. Russian by* Babette Deutsch. OnPM; TrRV

Now dumb is he who waked the world to speak. On Hearing the News from Venice. George Meredith. PoVP

Now each creature joys the other. An Ode. Samuel Daniel. *Fr.* To Delia. ElL; ElSeCe; LoBV; OBSC; SiCE; TuPP

Now early sink away the starry Twins. Midsummer. William Allingham. IrPN

Now earth and sky melt into one. Plaza Square. Louis Untermeyer. VOD

Now, Earth, to thy keeping we send him. For the Burial of the Dead. Prudentius. LaP

Now Empress Fame had publisht the renown. The Poet Shadwell's Coronation. Dryden. *Fr.* MacFlecknoe. BeR

Now England lessens on my sight. To England. Charles Leonard Moore. AA

Now English eyes the cancerous sun behold! Charles Madge. *Fr.* The Hours of the Planets. BoSA

Now Entertain Conjecture of a Time. Shakespeare. King Henry V, Prologue to IV. NBE; WaaP
(Eve of Agincourt, The.) ShBV-3

Now Europe balanced [*or* Europe's balanc'd], neither side prevails. The Balance of Europe. Pope. SeCeV; TOP

Now, even now, I yield, I yield. Now Is the Accepted Time. Charles Wesley. BePJ

Now evening comes. Now stirs my discontent. When Plaintively and Near the Cricket Sings. Nora May French. AV

Now evermore, lest some one hope might ease. The Portents. Lucan, *tr. by* Christopher Marlowe. *Fr.* Pharsalia. OBSC

Now Every Child. Eleanor Farjeon. SUS
(Our Brother Is Born.) ChrBoLe

Now every leaf, though colorless, burns bright. Sonnet to the Moon. Yvor Winters. TwAmPo

Now everything that shadowy thought. In Festubert. Edmund Blunden. OBMV

Now fades the last long streak of snow. In Memoriam A. H. H., CXV [*or* Spring]. Tennyson. ADAH; AlDL; BEL; BPN; BrBE; CaAE; CoBE; DD; EM-2; EmBrPo; EOAH; EPN; FaBoEn; GEPC; GTBS-D; HBV; LPS-2; MaPo; OAEP; OBEV (1st ed.); PoE; SeCeV; ShBV-4; SN; TCEP; ViBoPo; ViPo; VLEP; YT

Now faintly the falling sun. Chengtu. Tu Fu. WhP

Now, fair beneath his view, the important age. Vision of Columbus. Joel Barlow. *Fr.* The Columbiad, IX. APW

Now Fair, Fairest of Every Fair. William Dunbar. EBSV
(Welcome to Margaret Tudor.) BoHiPo

Now fall the height of Heaven in headlong ruin above me. An Eye for an Eye. Theognis. GrPE

Now falleth star-dew out of dusky space. Night. Erik Blomberg. AnSL

Now falling drops like shining pearls are seen. Evening and Night and Meteors. William Diaper. *Fr.* Dryades; or, The Nymphs Prophecy. BeR

Now fare-you-well! my bonny ship. Nanny's Sailor Lad. William Allingham. IrPN

Now Father Autumn heaps the vat. Ecce Autem Dulces Labris Pater Ingerit Uvas. Politian. LaP

Now, fathers, now our meeting's over. Now Our Meeting's Over. *Unknown.* ABF

Now fayre, fayrest off every fayre. Welcome to Margaret Tudor. William Dunbar. BoHiPo

Now fear no more the enemy spear of Argos. Macaria and Iolaus. Euripides. *Fr.* Heraclidae. OxBG

Now felt the Queen the sharp, slow-gathering pangs. Aeneas and Dido. Virgil. The Aeneid, IV. RoL

Now ferkes to the firthe thees fresche men of armes. Sir Gawain Encounters Sir Priamus. *Unknown.* *Fr.* Morte Arthure. PoEL-1

Now fie on foolish love, it not befits. Fie on Love. Francis Beaumont. AnEnPo

Now fields are striped in green and brown. The Busy Body. Rachel Field. InMe

Now find I true that hath been often told. He Declares That Albeit He Were Imprisoned in Russia, Yet His Mind Was at Liberty and Did Daily Repair to His Friend. George Turberville. TuPP

Now first, as I shut the door. The New House. Edward Thomas. GTML; HBMV; MoAB; MoBrPo; OBEV (new ed.); POTE; PrWP; TwCV

Now flower the oldest seeds. Doom in Bloom. Laura Riding. MoP

Now folded back across the changing earth. Lines to the Unborn. Patrick D. Waddington. TwCaPo

"Now for a brisk and cheerful fight!" The Fight at [the] San Jacinto. John Williamson Palmer. AA; DD; LEAP; PaA

Now for all time I am absolved of haste. On Coming to an End. George Meason Whicher. BAP

Now for one day, from sun to sun. The Star of Bethlehem. Alice Corbin Henderson. ChrBoLe

Now for the broken bodies. Broken Bodies. Louis Golding. MaRV

Now for the Chorus, the Graces, the minstrelsy. Hymn of Peace [*or* Rejoicings for Peace]. Aristophanes. *Fr.* Lysistrata. GrR; OxBG

Now for the crown and throne of Israel. George Peele. *Fr.* David and Bethsabe. ViBoPo

Now for to tell you will I turn. "Scots Wha' Hae!" Reversed. *Unknown.* TMEV

Now friends if you'll listen to a horrible tale. The Dreary Black Hills. *Unknown.* ABS; IHA

Now from reveille till dark, on work-days, holidays. The Market Place. Lucilius. LaP

Now from the dark, a deeper dark. Calling In the Cat. Elizabeth J. Coatsworth. AnAmPo; LA; NeMA

Now from the darkness of myself. Escape and Return. Elizabeth Jennings. NePoEA

Now from the fresh soft lap and twilight bower. Tasso. *Fr.* Jerusalem Delivered, XIV. PrPoCR

Now from the topmost boughs resounds the song of the cuckoo. To the Cuckoo. Alcuin. LaP

Now from the World the Light of God Is Gone. Robert Nathan. MaRV
(Sonnet VI: "Now from the world.") QS

Now from their slumber waking. Comrades. Henry R. Dorr. MC; PAH

Now, from yon range of rocks, strong rays rebound. King-Cups and a Stream. Richard Savage. *Fr.* The Wanderer. BeR

Now, gentle friend, if thou be kind. The Author's Life. Thomas Tusser. ReIE

Now gentle sleep hath closèd up those eyes. A Stolen Kiss [*or* Sonnet upon a Stolen Kiss]. George Wither. *Fr.* Fair Virtue. HBV; LiTL; LPS-1; PeBoSo; SeCL

Now get thee back, retreat, depart, O Serpent. He Overcometh the Serpent of Evil in the Name of Ra. *Unknown.* *Fr.* Book of the Dead. AWP

Now, Gibbon has told the story of old. Fighting McGuire. William Percy French. CenHV

Now, Gilbert, you know you're our man. To G. K. Chesterton. Joseph Mary Plunkett. OnYI

Now ginnes [*or* gins] this goodly frame of Temperaunce [*or* Temperance]. The Legend of Sir Guyon [*or* The Bower of Bliss]. Spenser. *Fr.* The Faerie Queene, II. PoEL-1; WHA

"Now, give us a wrap." Baby Lapp's Ride. *Unknown.* SAS

"Now give us lands where the olives grow." The North and the South. Elizabeth Barrett Browning. OBVV

Now glorious Leto's child goes up with the sound. The Choirs of Heaven. *Unknown.* *Fr.* Homeric Hymns. OxBG

Now glory to the Lord of Hosts. Ivry [*or* The Battle of Ivry]. Macaulay. BHV; GN; HBV; HBVY; OBRV; OTPC; PECK; RG; TVSH; VA; WBLP

Now glowing Venus wakes. New Guinea Lament. J. P. McAuley. BoAV

Now go I quietly. Song. Garcilaso de la Vega. TeCS

Now God alone that made all things. The Leather Bottel. John Wade. SeCL

Now God be praised that I have known. Free Men. Struthers Burt. PoFr

Now God be thanked that roads are long and wide. Forgiveness. Charles L. O'Donnell. LEAP; TBM

Now, God be thanked Who has matched us with His hour. Peace. Rupert Brooke. 1914, I. AOAH; CBE; EPN; HBV; LBBV; LEAP; MaRV; NP; POTE; POTT; WGRP

Now God preserve, as you well do deserve. The Masque of Christmas. Ben Jonson. OxBoLi

"Now Goldborg, hear what I ask of thee." Ribold and Goldborg. *Unknown.* BoDaBa

Now good-bye, my friend, good-bye, my darling. Last Lines. Sergei Yesenin. BoRS

Now gowans sprout and lavrocks sing. An Ode to Mr. F——. Allan Ramsay. CEP

Now gracious plenty rules the board. Thanksgiving. Florence Earle Coates. PEDC; TrPWD
Now grapes are plush upon the vines. Contrary Theses, I. Wallace Stevens. OxBA
Now green, now burning, I make a way for peace. Tenth Elegy: Elegy in Joy. Muriel Rukeyser. MiAP
Now had night measured with her shadowy cone. Then When I Am Thy Captive, Talk of Chains. Milton. *Fr.* Paradise Lost, IV. WHA
Now had the Almighty Father from above. The Scheme of Redemption. Milton. *Fr.* Paradise Lost, III. StJW
"Now half a hundred years had I been born." His Statement of the Case. James Herbert Morse. AA
Now Hamlet, where's Polonius? Shakespeare. *Fr.* Hamlet, IV, iii. AtBAP
Now hand in hand, you little maidens, walk. Spring. André Spire. AWP
Now hands to seed-sheet, boys! Sower's Song. Thomas Carlyle. DDA; OBVV; VA
Now hardly here and there a hackney-coach. A Description of the Morning. Swift. BeR; CEP; EiPP; ExPo; FaBoEn; PoFS; SeCeV; ViBoPo
Now has ended the battle of Saul. Saul. Nathan Alterman. TrJP
Now has the blue-eyed spring. A Catch for Spring. Robert Nichols. GBV
Now has the lingering month at last gone by. Atalanta's Defeat. William Morris. *Fr.* The Earthly Paradise. VA
Now has the third day's red sail come. The Road to Emmaus. Vyacheslav Ivanov. BoR
Now hath a wonder lit the saddened eyes. Brookfield. William E. Marshall. CPG
Now Hath Flora Robbed Her Bowers. Thomas Campion. *See* Roses.
Now hath my life across a stormy sea. On the Brink of Death [*or* His Great Love on High]. Michelangelo. AWP; JAWP; OnPM; WBP
Now hath the cast been made, and the net wide-spread is waiting. The Capture of Athens. Oracle. OxBG
Now hath the summer reached her golden close. September. Archibald Lampman. PeCV
Now haud your tongue, baith wife and carle. Harlaw. Sir Walter Scott. *Fr.* The Antiquary, *ch.* 40. EnLi-2
Now Have Good Day, Now Have Good Day! *Unknown. See* Here Have I Dwelt.
Now have I lived, O Rome, enough for me. Theodore Beza, *tr. by* Nicholas Grimald. *Fr.* Marcus Tullius Cicero's Death. TuPP
Now have I reared a monument more durable than brass. Title to Fame. Horace. *Fr.* Odes. RoL
Now have the cries of bombed and drowned. A Pastoral for Poland. Clark Mills. NeTW
Now Having Proved Thy Fond Delays. Edward Howard. SeCL
Now he begins: his fingers feel. The Surgeon. W. J. Funk. PoMa
"Now, he belongs to the ages." The Soul of Lincoln. Chauncey R. Piety. PGD
Now He Is Dead. Alistair Campbell. AnNZ
Now he was coming voluntary home. Return of the Prodigal. A. E. Johnson. JKCP (1955 ed.)
Now, he who knows old Christmas. Old Christmas. Mary Howitt. GN; OTPC
Now he will close the book, walk toward the window. The Hammer-Throw. Reuel Denney. PreP
Now heap the branchy barriers up. The Keepers of the Pass. Sir Charles G. D. Roberts. VA
Now hear the old Rule. The Old Education. Aristophanes. *Fr.* The Clouds. OxBG
Now heaven be thanked, I am out of love again! Freedom. "Jan Struther." LoPS; POTE
Now heed and hearken, gentle folk. Bethlehem. Arthur Ketchum. ChrBoLe
Now here I think needful a pause for to make. A Digression from Husbandry to a Point or Two of Huswifery. Thomas Tusser. ReIE
Now here, now there, lightheaded, crazed with grief. A Psalm of the Early Buddhist Sisters. *Unknown.* WGRP
Now Hermes of Cyllene called to the world beyond. Odysseus and His Father. Homer. *Fr.* The Odyssey, XXIV. GrPE
Now hid from sight are great Mount Fusi's fires. Hidden Fires. *Unknown.* OnPM
Now high and low, where leaves renew. Canzo of Bird-Songs and Love. Arnaut Daniel. LiTW
Now Hollow Fires Burn Out to Black. A. E. Housman. A Shropshire Lad, LX. ChMo; CMP; EmBrPo; PoVP; VLEP
Now how I came to get this hat 'tis very strange and funny. Where Did You Get That Hat? Joseph J. Sullivan. TreF
Now hue and cry I make for Love! Love the Rascal. Meleager. OxBG
Now I am dead, be earth devoured of hell. Après Moi le Déluge. *Unknown.* OxBG
Now I am left on this lonely island to die. Wabanaki Song. *Tr. by* Charles G. Leland. BoCaPo
Now I am slow and placid, fond of sun. With Child. Genevieve Taggard. AnAmPo; AnEnPo; LA; MAP; MoAmPo
Now I am thankful this unbroken flesh. Fisherman's Son. Charles Bruce. CaP
Now I am tired of being Japanese. Picture of a Castle. William Meredith. NePoEA
Now I am young and credulous. Wisdom Cometh with the Years. Countee Cullen. TBM
Now I can see what Helen was. A Lovely Woman. W. H. Davies. FaBoTw
Now, I confess, I am in Love. A Rhapsody. *Unknown.* SeCL
Now I find [*or* see] thy looks were feigned. An Ode [*or* Song]. Thomas Lodge. *Fr.* Phyllis. EIL; LoBV; OBSC; SiCE; TuPP
Now I go grieving for the days on earth. Sonnet. Petrarch. Sonnets to Laura: To Laura in Death, LXXXVI. LyPI
Now I have climbed the hillside to discover. Maine Woods in Winter. Grace Hazard Conkling. CP
Now I Have Found a Friend. Henry Hope. BePJ
Now I have found the reasons why. *Unknown.* SeCSL
Now I have found thee I will evermore. Upon the Crucifix. William Alabaster. PoEL-2
Now I have lost you, I must scatter. Farewell, Sweet Dust. Elinor Wylie. AnAmPo; LA; LiTA
Now I have tempered haste. The Mount. Léonie Adams. MoVE
Now I have touched you near the grated bone. Postscript. Mary Mills. NePoAm
Now I have touched your soil I will go back. Frank Wilmot. *Fr.* The Gully. NeLNL
"Now I Lay Me Down to Sleep." Eugene Henry Pullen. AA; FaBoBe
"Now I lay me down to sleep. . . ." A Foxhole for the Night. John Quinn. BoAV
Now I Lay Me Down to Take My Sleep ("Now I lay me . . ."). *Unknown.* TreF
(Children's Prayers.) BLRP
(Evening Prayer, An.) MaRV; PraP
(Now I Lay Me Down to Sleep.) FaFP; OxNR; SiTL
(Prayer: "Now I lay me down to sleep.") RAR
Now I must betray myself. Prothalamion. Delmore Schwartz. OxBA
Now I must these three praise. Friends. W. B. Yeats. BoFr
Now I pray the man who may love this lay. Cynewulf. *Fr.* Fates of the Apostles. AnOE
Now I remember a dream of rage and of wind. City. Jaime Torres Bodet. AnCL
Now I see the leaves tilting. Variations on a Still Morning. Thomas Cole. NePoAm
Now I see thy looks were feigned. *See* Now I find thy looks
Now I shall reach over. With Lilacs in My Eye. Lucile Coleman. GoYe
Now I tell what my mother told me to-day as we sat at dinner together. The Indian Woman. Walt Whitman. *Fr.* The Sleepers. PCD; PCH
Now I, the sinless saint, aiming at honour. Charisius Rebukes Himself. Menander. *Fr.* Epitrepontes. OxBG
Now I understand. Valentine. Mary H. Blodgett. CAG
Now I wake and see the light. Morning Prayers [*or* Children's Prayers]. *Unknown, at. to* Eugene Henry Pullen. BLRP; PraP
Now I want/ Spirits to enforce, art to enchant. Shakespeare. *Fr.* The Tempest: Epilogue. MyFE
Now I was born on the Rio Grande. Rio Grande, *vers.* II. *Unknown.* ShS
Now I Who Saw. John Russell McCarthy. MuM
Now I will do nothing but listen. Song of Myself, XXVI. Walt Whitman. HoPM; MaPo
Now I will fashion the tale of a fish. The Whale. *Unknown.* *Fr.* Physiologus. AnOE
Now if a man shall show him in speed of foot the faster. Athleticism. Xenophanes. GrPE
Now, if any one has an easy time. Plea for Boys. *Unknown.* FAOV
Now if ever it is time to cleanse Helicon. Homage to Sextus Propertius, V. Ezra Pound. CrMA
Now, if ever, let poets sing. Let Dreamers Wake. Lilith Lorraine. PGD
Now if the dull and thankless heart declare. Malediction upon Myself. Elinor Wylie. AnAmPo; LA
"Now, if the fish will only bite, we'll have some royal fun." Timid Hortense. Peter Newell. NA
Now, if to be an April fool. The First of April. Mortimer Collins. ADAH
Now, If You Will Look in My Brain. José Garcia Villa. AnFE; CoAnAm; TwAmPo

Now I'll put on your nice little evening coat. A Sleepy Song. Carrie Jacobs Bond. BOL
Now, I'm a good Rebel, now that's just what I am. I'm a Good Old Rebel. Innes Randolph. ABF; CSF; SPP
Now, I'm leaving old England, the land that I love. The First of the Emigrants. *Unknown.* ShS
Now I'm Resolved to Love No More. Alexander Brome. ALV
Now in a thought, now in a shadowed word. L'Envoi. E. A. Robinson. GrCo-2; MeRV; TwP
Now in her green mantle blythe Nature arrays. My Nannie's Awa. Burns. EBSV; GN; HBV; OTPC (1923 ed.)
Now, in his joy. The Wind. John Banister Tabb. AnAmPo; LA
Now in midsummer come and all fools slaughtered. Credences of Summer. Wallace Stevens. CoBMV
Now in myself I notice take. The Soldier. George Wither. BHV
Now in the Bloom. Florence Kiper Frank. GoYe
Now in the circulating torrent of the stars. In Conjunction. Charles Madge. FaBoMo; NeBP
Now in the Days of Youth. Walter J. Mathams. PraP
Now, in the evenings, when the light. The Generations. George M. Brady. OnYI
Now in the Mayday twilight. Evening in May. Gabriele d'Annunzio. WoL
Now, in the name of Justice thou hurl'st down. A Case for the Defense. Aeschylus. *Fr.* Agamemnon. GrR
Now in the night where the nameless crickets make. Letter to the Night. Lloyd Frankenberg. AnAmPo
Now in the oak the sap of life is welling. Spring in the South. Henry van Dyke. ADAH
Now in the Palace Gardens. Trumbull Stickney. Eride, V. AnFE; CoAnAm; LiTA; TwAmPo
Now in the red and opalescent sun. On the Eve of Departure. Juan Ramón Jiménez. TeCS
Now in the sad declenshion of thy tyme. *Unknown.* SeCSL
Now in the sad, leaf-haunted autumn weather. To Lorna. Eric Wilson Barker. MuM
Now in the Time of This Mortal Life. Norman Nicholson. NeBP
Now, in the twilight, after rain. The Shining Streets of London. Alfred Noyes. AlDL
Now in this quiet love-illumined night. Christmas in Carmel. Sister Mary Thérèse. PraNu
Now in this while gan Daedalus a wearinesse to take. The Fall of Icarus. Ovid. PoF
Now, innocent, within the deep. M., Singing. Louise Bogan. CrMA; LiTA; NePA
Now is a great and shining company. Resurgam [*or* May]. Struthers Burt. BAP; HBMV
Now is Christ risen from the dead. Death's Conqueror. First Corinthians, Bible, *N.T.* MaRV
Now Is Christmas Ycome. *Unknown. See* Three Kings, The.
Now is come Midsummer Night. Song for Midsummer Night. Elizabeth J. Coatsworth. YeAr
Now is Death merciful. He calls me hence. Two Sonnets, II. Hans Zinsser. LoPS
Now is earth visibly gone over to spirit. Jones's Pasture. Abbie Huston Evans. NP
Now Is Farewell. Blanaid Salkeld. NeIP
Now is it most like as if on ocean. The Voyage of Life. Cynewulf. *Fr.* Christ 2. AnOE
Now is it pleasant in the summer-eve. Amusements. George Crabbe. *Fr.* The Borough. OBRV
Now is Light, sweet mother, down the west. Evening Songs, III. John Vance Cheney. AA
Now is my Chloris fresh as May. *Unknown.* OBSC
Now Is the Accepted Time. Charles Wesley. BePJ
Now is the autumn of the Tree of Life. Progress of Unbelief. Cardinal Newman. GoBC
Now is the bright morning star, Day's harbinger. Song on a May Morning. Milton. PoRL
Now Is the Cherry in Blossom. Mary E. Wilkins Freeman. AA
Now Is the High-Tide of the Year. James Russell Lowell. *Fr.* The Vision of Sir Launfal: Prelude to Part First. TreFS
Now is the hour of sorrow unreproved. Horace. Odes, I, 24. LaP
Now is the hour of the bell, now am I caught. John Donne's Defiance. J. R. Hervey. AnNZ
Now is the hour when, swinging in the breeze [*or* trembling to and fro]. Harmonie du Soir. Baudelaire. AWP; JAWP; WBP
Now is the month of maying. Song. *Unknown.* EG; OBSC
Now is the night, foreshadowed of our fears. Edwin Booth. Alice Brown. HBV
Now is the pause between asleep and awake. The Spring Equinox. Anne Ridler. NeBP
Now is the poet dead. Let honor claim. The Poet's Death. Mikhail Yurevich Lermontov. TrRV
Now is the sailing time. Soft blows the breeze. Spring Sailing. Leonidas. OnPM
Now is the time for mirth. To Live Merrily and to Trust to Good Verses. Robert Herrick. AWP; BEL; EPS (1942 ed.); InPo; InvP; LoBV; MyFE; OBS; ReEn; SeCV-1; SeEP
Now is the time for the burning of the leaves. The Burning of the Leaves. Laurence Binyon. ChMP; GTBS-D; MoVE; POTE
Now is the time in valiant days. Epithalamium in Time of War. Ralph Gustafson. BoCaPo
Now is the time that hills put on. Spring Signs. Rachel Field. InMe
Now is the time to surrender our hearts to merry-making. "Vive Hodie." Theognis. GrPE
Now is the time, when all the lights wax dim. To Anthea. Robert Herrick. NBE; OAEP; OBS; PoEL-3; SeEP
Now is the time when cheery crickets. Autumn! Nancy Byrd Turner. YeAr
Now is the Twelfth Day ycome. Reges de Saba Venient. *Unknown.* AnEC
Now is the winter of our discontent. Winter of Our Discontent [*or* Evil Designs *or* Hate the Idle Pleasures]. Shakespeare. King Richard III, *fr.* I, i. LiA; TreF; TrGrPo
Now Is Well and All Things Aright. *Unknown.* AnEC (All's Well!) TMEV
Now is woven in my dark tresses. "Anna Akhmatova," *tr. fr. Russian by* C. M. Bowra. BoRS
Now Isabel the young afflicted queen. Richard II as Captive. Samuel Daniel. *Fr.* The Civil Wars. SiCE
Now Israel loved Joseph more than all his children. Joseph and His Brethren. Genesis, Bible, *O.T.* OuHeWo
Now it begins. Now the subaqueous evening. A Is for Alpha; Alpha Is for A. Conrad Aiken. NePA
Now it came to pass in the days when the judges ruled. Ruth, Bible, *O.T.* BoFr; EM-1; EnLi-1; OuHeWo; WoL
Now it grows dark. Hymn to Night. Melville Cane. MAP; MoAmPo
Now it grows late—the angel has passed by. *Unknown, tr. fr. French by* Alma Strettell. BOL
Now it is as thou didst promise. The Incorporation. Stefan George. AnGP
Now it is autumn and the falling fruit. The Ship of Death. D. H. Lawrence. FaBoTw; LiTB; LoBV; OAEP (2d ed.)
Now it is fifteen years you have lain in the meadow. Lines for an Interment. Archibald MacLeish. ChMo; CMP; InP; MaRV; ReaPo
Now it is seven years since you were the Queen. The Decay of Vanity. Ted Hughes. POTE (1959 ed.)
Now, it takes all 'ands to man the capstan. Rolling Home. *vers.* II. *Unknown.* ShS
Now it was Spring. Grant at Appomattox. Gertrude Claytor. GoYe
Now, it's blow, you winds, 'ow I long to hear you. Blow, Boys, Blow, *vers.* III. *Unknown.* ShS
Now, it's one cold and dreary morning in December. Mainsail Haul, *vers.* I. *Unknown.* ShS
Now, I've got no use for the women. Bury Me Out on the Prairie. *Unknown.* CoSo
Now Ixion's wheel is stilled. Missa Papae Marcelli. J. P. McAuley. BoAV
Now Jesus knew that they were desirous to ask him. Be of Good Cheer; I Have Overcome the World. St. John, Bible, *N.T.* TreFS
Now. Jesus, Mary's Son, be unto Thee. A Wish. *Unknown.* CAW
Now Jones had left his new-wed bride to keep his house in order. A Code of Morals. Kipling. OnSP
Now joy be to the Trinity. Wassail, Wassail, Wassail, Sing We. *Unknown.* AnEC
Now, Joy is born of parents poor. Joy and Pleasure. W. H. Davies. OBMV
Now joy, the flower of heaven. The Splendid Flower. Etta May Van Tassel. JKCP (1955 ed.)
Now keep that long revolver at your side. Sonnet. George Hetherington. NeIP
Now Kindness. Peter Viereck. LiTA
Now know I when the last morning will be. Hymns to the Night, IV. "Novalis." AnGP
Now, ladies, if you'll listen, a story I'll relate. Pearl Bryan. *Unknown.* BaBo
Now, lads and lassies, cease your mirth. On a Pet Cat. George A. Persell. CAG
Now, lamb, no longer naughty be. The Lamb. Kate Greenaway. OTPC (1923 ed.); PPL; SAS
Now lamp-lit gardens in the blue dusk shine. Princeton. Alfred Noyes. POT; PoTo; POTT
Now, landsmen, list! There is no sight more fair. Norse Sailor's Joy. Wilfrid Thorley. EtS
Now late/ I follow Time's Necessity. The Scholar Recruit. Pao Chao. SoV; TrCh
Now lay me in a cushioned chair. The Ballad of the Foxhunter. W. B. Yeats. CMP

Now lay up thy barley land, dry as ye can. October's Husbandry. Thomas Tusser. CoBE
Now leif thy mirth, now leif thy haill plesance. War Summons the Lover. Henry the Minstrel. *Fr.* The Wallace, VI. EBSV
Now Lent is come, let us refrain. Stanzas for Lent. James Howell. PrWP
Now let each common and heroic man. Lidice. Charles Schiff. NeTW
Now let every tongue adore Thee! Johann Sebastian Bach. *Fr.* Sleepers, Wake! OlF
Now let me alone, though I know you won't. Barney O'Hea. Samuel Lover. OnYI; TIP
Now Let Me Lay the Pearl Away. Elizabeth Prentiss. BOL; MOAH
Now let no charitable hope. Let No Charitable Hope. Elinor Wylie. AnAmPo; ChMo; HBMV; LA; LEAP; LiTA; LiTM; MAP; MoAB; MoAmPo; MOAP; NePA; NV; OxBA; TBM; TrGrPo
Now let the coward be dragged out to die. I. H. S. Sean Jennett. MeRV
Now let the drums roll muffled; let the bells'. Charles Heavysege. *Fr.* Count Filippo. PeCV
Now let the garden sleep. Winter Revery. Sara Bard Field. BAP; PoeMoYo
Now let the heart that gazed, remember. Colour of October. Leila Jones. MuM
Now, let us down to Hell: we've seen the last. Hell's Road. Charles Heavysege. *Fr.* Saul. BMEP
Now Let Us Sing, Both More and Less. *Unknown.* AnEC
Now Let Us Sing with Joy and Mirth. John Wedderburn. AnEC
Now let us sing with mirth and joy. In Dulci Iubilo. John Wedderburn. AnEC
Now let us take the measure of the man. Ave. Ada Foster Murray. GA
Now let us turn to the people. Male Inconsistency. Aristophanes. *Fr.* The Thesmophoriazusae. GrR
Now Liddesdale has ridden a raid. Jock o' the Side. *Unknown.* ESPB (B *vers.*); OBB
Now Liddisdale has lain long in. Dick o the Cow. *Unknown.* BaBo; ESPB; OBB
Now lies the Lord in a most quiet bed. Now Sleeps the Lord. Margaret L. Woods. StJW
Now life is whirled like a delirious dancer. The Question. William Rose Benét. BoFr
Now, like a magpie, he collects the bright. "Trade" Rat. Eleanor Glenn Wallis. NePoAm
Now list and lithe, you gentlemen. Northumberland Betrayed by Douglas. *Unknown.* ESPB; OBB
Now list to my song, it will not take me long. The U.S.A. Recruit. *Unknown.* CSF
Now list you, lithe you, gentlemen. Robin Hood and Queen Katherine. *Unknown.* ESPB
Now listen to boasting which leaves the heart dazed. Al-Samau'al ibn Adiya. *Fr.* Are We Not the People. TrJP
"Now lithe and list, thou handsome squire." The Game of Dice. *Unknown.* BoDaBa
Now, Lord, I give myself to Thee. A Covenant. Frances Ridley Havergal. PraP
Now, Lord, or never they'll believe on Thee. On the Miracle of Loaves. Richard Crashaw. ACP
Now, Lord, upon Thy Sea of Air. Mary Louisa Anderson. MaRV
Now Love Dies. John Ford. *See* Song: "Oh, no more, no more, too late."
Now love has bound me, trembling, hands and feet. The Captive. Sappho. GrR
Now lufferis comis with largesse loud. The Petition of the Grey Horse, Auld Dunbar. William Dunbar. EBSV
Now Make We Merry, All and Some. *Unknown.* AnEC
Now many are the stately ships that northward steam away. The Lover Thinks of His Lady in the North. Shaemas O'Sheel. HBV
Now Maria came out to fill. Maria's Prayer. Dionysios Solomos. *Fr.* Lambros. MoGP
Now Mars showers down a fiery sleet, and winds. Lycophron. *Fr.* Alexandra. GrPo
Now marshall'd all beneath their several chiefs. The Advance of the Trojans. Homer. *Fr.* The Iliad, III. OxBG
Now Marstig woke at the mirk midnight. Marsk Stig Made an Outlaw. *Unknown.* BoDaBa
Now may I see the time hath beene in vaine. *Unknown.* SeCSL
Now may I very worthy be. Lines for a Girl's Study. Nancy Byrd Turner. MOB
Now may we mirthes make. Alleluia, Alleluia. *Unknown.* AnEC
Now may we singen as it is. This Babe to Us That Now Is Born. *Unknown.* AnEC
Now may we turn aside and dry our tears. Inis Fal. *Tr. by* James Stephens. GTIV; OBMV
Now may'st thou take sweet sleep, my babe, now may'st thou go to sleep. *Unknown, tr. fr. Greek by* A. N. Jannaris. BOL
Now Memory, false, spendthrift Memory. Lough Bray. Standish James O'Grady. IrPN; TIP
Now mighty pyramids the sight surprise. The Egyptian Dead. Elizabeth Rowe. *Fr.* The History of Joseph. BeR
Now milkmaids' pails are deckt with flowers. Stool Ball. *Unknown.* CH
Now, miners, if you'll listen, I'll tell you quite a tale. Coming around the Horn. *Unknown.* ABF
Now mirk December's dowie face. The Daft Days. Robert Fergusson. BSV; CEP; EV-3
"Now, Miss Clara, point your toe." The Dancing Lesson. Eliza Grove. OTPC (1923 ed.)
Now Mrs. Eberle early had been told. La Donna E Perpetuum Mobile. Irwin Edman. FiBHP
Now Morn her rosie steps in th' eastern clime. Adam and Eve. Milton. *Fr.* Paradise Lost, V. LiA
Now Morning from her orient chamber came. Imitation of Spenser [*or* Morning]. Keats. ATP; BPN; EmBrPo; EnRP; ERP; GN
Now, most noble Brutus. A Farewell. Shakespeare. *Fr.* Julius Caesar, V, i. BHV
Now must all satisfaction. Certain Mercies. Robert Graves. CoBMV
Now must I learn to live at rest. Sir Thomas Wyatt. SiPS
Now must I wait. The Blank Book Letter. Samuel Greenberg. LiTA
Now must the storied Potomac. Lincoln. Edna Dean Proctor. LBAH
Now must we hymn the Maker of heaven. The Hymn of the World's Creator. Cædmon. CAW
Now must we praise heaven's Keeper. The Creation. Cædmon. PoLi
Now my boys if you will listen, I'll sing you a little song. The Cruise of the *Bigler*. *Unknown.* SoAmSa
Now my charms are all o'erthrown. Prospero's Epilogue. Shakespeare. *Fr.* The Tempest: Epilogue. KN; NBE
Now, my co-mates and brothers in exile. The Uses of Adversity [*or* The Banished Duke Speaks to His Retainers *or* Sermons in Stones]. Shakespeare. *Fr.* As You Like It, II, i. CBE; GrCo-1; LiTB; LiTG; PIR; TreFS; TrGrPo
Now, my fair'st friend. Some Flowers o' the Spring. Shakespeare. *Fr.* The Winter's Tale, IV, iii. ChTr; NBE
Now, my name is Samuel Hall, Sam Hall. Sam Hall. *Unknown.* ViBoFo
Now, my son, is life for you. Wishes for My Son. Thomas MacDonagh. AnIV; CP; FAOV; GoBC; HBMV; JKCP; LBBV; MBP; NV; TSW
Now my thick years bend your back. The Turn of the Road. Fannie Stearns Davis. HBMV
Now Nature cleeds the flowery lea. Lassie wi' the Lint-white Locks. Burns. EV-3
Now Nature hangs her mantle green. Mary Queen of Scots [*or* Lament of Mary Queen of Scots]. Burns. BHV; BoHiPo
Now near the burning domes the squadrons stood. The Battle of Ai. Timothy Dwight. *Fr.* The Conquest of Canaan. BAV
Now, night; and once again. Avalon. Audrey McGaffin. NePoAm
Now night comes on, your first night in the grave. The First Night. Isolde Kurz. TwGV
Now night drew darkness over earth; far out at sea. The Heart-Searchings of Medea. Apollonius Rhodius. *Fr.* Argonautica, III. GrPE
Now not a window small or big. For Christmas. Rachel Field. ChBR; GaP
Now, now the sun is fled. Drinking Song. William Cartwright. *Fr.* The Royal Slave. SeCL
Now, O Bacchus, I turn humbly to your shrine. Propertius. Elegies, III, 17. LaP
Now, O Lord, please lend me thine ear. The Cowman's Prayer. *Unknown.* CoSo; CSF
Now, O now, in this brown land. Chamber Music, XXXIII. James Joyce. ReaPo
Now o'er the one half world. Shakespeare. *Fr.* Macbeth, II, i. NBE
Now o'er the topmost pine. Morning. Samuel Waddington. OBVV
Now of all fashions, she thinks change the best. Rhodon and Iris. Ralph Knevet. BoHiPo
Now, of all the trees by the king's highway. Aunt Mary [*or* Modryb Marya]. Robert Stephen Hawker. AnEC; JKCP; OHIP
Now of my life each gay and greener year. The Jealous Enemy. Petrarch. Sonnets to Laura: To Laura in Death, XLVII. LiTW
Now of that vision I, bereaven. Grace of the Way. Francis Thompson. MBP; MoAB; MoBrPo
Now of the conqueror this isle had Brutain unto name. William Warner. *Fr.* Albion's England. ReIE
Now, of the ways of dolphins, this wonder too I hear. The Dolphin's Death. Oppian. *Fr.* Halieuticks. GrPE

Now, on a sudden, I know it, the secret, the secret of life. Revealed. Harry Lyman Koopman. AA

Now on the shining/ back breaking water. Icarus. Kendrick Smithyman. AnNZ

Now on the verge of spring the icy silver leaf. Return to Spring. Florence Ripley Mastin. GoYe

Now on you is the hungry equinox. Rebuke of the Rocks. Robert Penn Warren. Kentucky Mountain Farm, I. SPP

Now once again the Christ keeps watch beside. New Gethsemane. Hazel M. Kerr. ChIP

Now once again the gloomy scene explore. The Pauper's Funeral. George Crabbe. *Fr.* The Village. FaBoEn

Now once more the hunt commences. An Old Print. Edwin Morgan. PFE

Now once there was a wooden fence. The Wooden Fence. Christian Morgenstern. LiTW

Now once upon a time the King of Astrakhan, at that. The Lacquer Liquor Locker. David McCord. FiBHP; InMe

Now Once Your Garden in the Early Haze. Stefan George, *tr. fr. German by* David Luke. AnGP

Now one and all, you roses. A Wood Song. Ralph Hodgson. HBV; TCPD

Now orange blossoms filigree. Ain't Nature Commonplace! Arthur Guiterman. FiBHP; InMe

Now ore the sea from her old Love comes she. Ovid. Amores, I, 13. LaP

Now Our Meetings Over, *with music. Unknown.* ABF

Now over earth was spread the veil of night. Apollonius Rhodius. *Fr.* Argonautica, III. GrPo

Now over most of living kind. At the Moon's Eclipse. Robert P. Tristram Coffin. NeTW

Now peace, and be still! Demos Rejuvenated. Aristophanes. *Fr.* The Knights. OxBG

Now perish, Baia, root and stock and name. Boccaccio. *Fr.* Sonnets. LyMA; LyPI

Now Philippa Is Gone. Anne Ridler. FaBoTw

Now, Polemo, if the matter really is. Advice to a Lover. Menander. *Fr.* Perikeiromene. OxBG

Now ponder well, you parents dear. The Babes [*or* Children] in the Wood[s]. *Unknown.* CG; EnSB; EV-2; HBV; HBVY; OBB; OnSP; OTPC (1923 ed.)

Now, poor Rufus he has come to town. Rufus's Mare. George Calhoun. ShS

Now poor Tom Dunstan's cold. Tom Dunstan; or, The Politician. Robert Buchanan. HBV; PoFr

"Now, pray, where are you going, child?" said Meet-on-the-Road. Meet-on-the-Road. *Unknown.* PoMS

Now prompts the Muse poetic lays. Monody on the Death of Chatterton. Samuel Taylor Coleridge. PtP

Now quietly the evening tends. Upon Reading an Old Book. Pearce Young. PtPa

Now Rann the Kite brings home the night. Night-Song in the Jungle. Kipling. AIDL

Now rede me, dear mither, a sonsy rede. The Mer-Man and Marstig's Daughter. *Unknown.* AWP; JAWP; WBP

Now rest for evermore, my weary heart! A sè stesso. Giacomo Leopardi. AWP; JAWP; WBP

Now rest in abeyance. Hands. Geoffrey Dearmer. AIDL

Now riseth up on either hand. Persia Prostrated. Aeschylus. *Fr.* Persians. GrR

Now Robin Hood, Will Scadlock and Little John. Robin Hood and the Prince of Aragon. *Unknown.* ESPB

Now, rocking horse! rocking horse! where shall we go? Through Nurseryland. *Unknown.* BoTP

Now roves the eye. William Cowper. *Fr.* The Task, I. EnSW

Now St. Joseph's cottage stood. A Legend of Cherries. Charles Dalmon. HBMV; TSW

"Now say," he said, "were it not worse indeed." Dante. *Fr.* Divina Commedia: Paradiso. PoFr

Now science is a dandy thing—explaining, as it can. Folks, I Give You Science! Al Graham. WhC

Now seven days from land the gulls still wheel. Transport. William Meredith. WaP

Now shall I tell a tale to kings. Might and Right. Hesiod. *Fr.* Works and Days. OxBG

Now shall I walk. The Best Friend. W. H. Davies. OBMV

Now shall my song remember Apollo, Lord of the Bow. Hymn to the Delian Apollo. *Unknown. Fr.* Homeric Hymns. GrPE

Now shall the body. The Cloud of Unknowing. Philip Murray. NePoAm-2

Now shall we drink our fill. After the Tyrant's Death. Alcaeus. GrR

Now shall we see, that nature hath no end. George Chapman. *Fr.* Bussy d'Ambois, V, ii. PoEL-2

Now shame can hurt men mightily. Shame. Hesiod. *Fr.* Works and Days. OxBG

Now She Is like the White Tree-Rose. C. Day Lewis. *Fr.* From Feathers to Iron. ChMo; FaBoTw; MBP; MoBrPo

Now she who never lived is dead. Futility. Louise Driscoll. DDA

Now shout into my dream. These trumpets snored. Farewell in a Dream. Stephen Spender. MBP; MoAB; MoBrPo

Now silent are the forests old, amid whose cool retreats. One Land, One Flag, One Brotherhood. Thomas S. Collier. FOAH

"Now since mine even is come at last." The Ride to the Lady. Helen Gray Cone. AA; LBMV

Now Sing We, Both All and Some. *Unknown.* AnEC

Now Sing We, Sing We: Gloria Tibi, Domine. *Unknown.* AnEC

Now Sing We with Angelis. *Unknown.* AnEC

Now Sing We with Joy and Bliss. *Unknown.* AnEC

Now sinks another day to rest. The Bull. V. Sackville-West. DiM

Now, sirs and ladies, bold and blythe. Against My Will I Take My Leave. *Unknown.* TMEV

Now sit thee down, Melpomene. A Sonnet upon the Pitiful Burning of the Globe Playhouse in London. *Unknown.* TuPP

Now, sitting by her side, worn out with weeping. The Dream of the World without Death. Robert Buchanan. *Fr.* The Book of Orm. VA

Now, skulls, rise from the hills, your hour is come. The Last Day. Daniel Sargent. CAW

Now Sleep and Take Thy Rest. Fernando de Rojas, *tr. fr. Spanish by* James Mabbe. *Fr.* Celestina. SeCL

Now, Sleep, Bind Fast. George Chapman. *Fr.* The Masque of the Middle Temple and Lincoln's Inn. TuPP
(Bridal Song.) EIL
("Now sleep, bind fast the flood of air.") LO

Now sleep, my baby, sweetly sleep. *Unknown.* BOL

Now sleep the mountain-summits, sleep the glens. Vesper. Alcman. GrPE

Now Sleeps the Crimson Petal [Now the White]. Tennyson. *Fr.* The Princess, Pt. VII. AnFE; AtBAP; BoLiVe; BrBE; ChER; ChTr; EnL; EnLi-2; EPN; EV-5; FiP; GEPC; GTBS-D; KN; LEAP; LoPS; MaPo; OBVV; PoE; PoEL-5; PoFS; PoVP; ReaPo; ShBV-3; TrGrPo; ViBoPo; ViPo; ViPP; VLEP
(Song: "Now sleeps the crimson petal.") CaAE; ExPo; FaBoBe; LoBV; NeHB
(Songs from "The Princess.") EmBrPo; MotAn; OAEP; SeCeV
(Summer Night.) EtPaEn; OBEV; SeCePo; UnPo (1st ed.)

Now Sleeps the Gorge. Alistair Campbell. AnNZ

Now sleeps the land of houses, and dead night holds the street. Mother and Son. William Morris. EmBrPo; GTML

Now Sleeps the Lord. Margaret L. Woods. StJW

Now so high,/ Now so low. The Swing. Mary I. Osborn. BoTP

Now, solitary, and in pensive guise. James Thomson. *Fr.* The Seasons: Winter. FaBoEn

Now some may drink old vintage wine. Early Morning Meadow Song. Charles Dalmon. ALV; CH; HBMV

Now, sometimes in my sorrow shut. In Memoriam A. H. H., XXIII. Tennyson. BPN; EmBrPo; EnLi-2; EPN; GEPC; LPS-1; OBEV (1st ed.); TOP; ViPo; VLEP

Now south and south and south the mallard heads. The North Sea Undertaker's Complaint. Robert Lowell. NePoEA

Now speech is very curious. Words. Nancy Byrd Turner. TSW

Now spring brings back the tepid breeze. Catullus, *tr. fr. Latin by* L. R. Lind. LaP

Now spring is far behind with its pink mist of overflowing blossoms. Fair Japan. Bansui Tsuchii. PoLJ

Now spring returns: but not to me returns. Elegy: In Spring. Michael Bruce. BSV

Now Springs the Spray. *Unknown.* MeEV, *mod. vers. by* Mabel Van Duzee; TMEV, *mod. vers.*
(Now Sprinkes the Spray, *middle English vers.*) AtBAP; PoEL-1

Now stamp the Lord's Prayer on a grain of rice. Sonnets, VII. Dylan Thomas. GTBS-W; LiTM

Now stands our love on that still verge of day. Sonnets, XX. James Agee. MAP; MoAmPo

Now Stina and Matts went to Stockholm, and he. The Sun-Parasol. Fredrik August Dahlgren. AnSL

Now stir the fire, and close the shutters fast. William Cowper. *Fr.* The Task, IV. LEAP

Now stoops the sun, and dies day's cheerful light. The Gauls Sacrifice Their Prisoners. C. M. Doughty. *Fr.* The Dawn in Britain. FaBoTw

Now stop your noses, readers, all and some. Og and Doeg. Dryden. *Fr.* Absalom and Achitophel, Pt. II. FiP

Now storming fury rose. The War in Heaven. Milton. *Fr.* Paradise Lost, VI. PoF

Now Strike Your Sailes Ye Jolly Mariners! Spenser. *Fr.* The Faerie Queene, I, 12, *and* II, 6. EtS

Now summer finds her perfect prime. Heaven, O Lord, I Cannot Lose. Edna Dean Proctor. AA

Now sunk the sun, now twilight sunk, and night. Night. John Brown. OBEC

Now supposing the French or the Neapolitan soldier. Arthur Hugh Clough. *Fr.* Amours de Voyage, II. SoV
Now sure, within this twelve-month past. Love and Life. Abraham Cowley. *Fr.* The Mistress. SeEP
Now take your fill of love and glee. A Double Ballad of Good Counsel. Villon. AWP
Now tatters of denuded clouds. Three Variations, III. Boris Pasternak. TrJP; TrRV
Now tell I a fable for princes, who know what meaneth the tale. Quoth a Hawk to a Nightingale. Hesiod. *Fr.* Works and Days. GrR
Now tell us what 'twas all about. Robert Southey. *Fr.* The Battle of Blenheim. OQP; QP-2
Now Thank We All Our God. Martin Rinkart, *tr. fr. German by* Catherine Winkworth. OlF; TreFS
Now That Can Never Be Done. Sister Maris Stella. GoBC
Now that Fate is dead and gone. Song. Edith Sitwell. MoAB; MoBrPo (1950 ed.); NeMA
Now that I am dressed I'll go. Peadar Og Goes Courting. James Stephens. WhC
Now that I am lame. The Gift. Rose O'Neill. BAP
Now that I have cooled to you. Postlude. William Carlos Williams. AnAmPo; LA; NP
Now that I have decided I must go. The Missionary. Sister Mary Eleanore. WHL
Now that I have your face by heart, I look. Song for the Last Act. Louise Bogan. NePoAm
Now that I know how passion. Knowledge. Louise Bogan. HBMV
Now that I know that what I am must be. Prayer. Edwin Morgan. PFE
Now that I leave for foreign lands. Greek Earth. Georgios Drossinis. MoGP
Now that I, tying thy glass mask tightly. The Laboratory; Ancien Régime. Robert Browning. ATP; BLV; BoLiVe; CBOV; GTML; OBEV (new ed.); OBVV; PoFS; PoVP; REAL; ReTS; ShBV-3; ViPo; ViPP; VLEP; YT
Now that I'm old. Winter. Issa. OnPM
Now that I'm old I do not venture far. An Old Cat Meditates. Margaret E. Bruner. CIV
Now that it doesn't matter so much any longer. This Way Out. Margaret Fishback. ALV
Now that it is moonlight, I must be mournful. Trinket. Winifred Welles. NP
Now that my little dog is dead. Lugete O Veneres Cupidinesque. Godfrey Elton. ReTS
Now that nature has put an end at last. On the Death of the Emperor Henry VII. Cino da Pistoia. LyPI
Now that no shrill hunting horn. An Old Dog. Celia Duffin. AlBD; PCD
Now that of absence the most irksome night. Astrophel and Stella, LXXXIX. Sir Philip Sidney. SiPS
Now that our love has drifted. Finis. Waring Cuney. BANP; PoNe
Now that Paris, her stones, her statues too. At Villequier. Victor Hugo. TrFP
Now that summer's ripen'd bloom. A Landscape. John Cunningham. CEP; EnSW; RO
Now That the April of Your Youth. Lord Herbert of Cherbury. *See* Ditty in Imitation of the Spanish, A.
Now that the ashen rain of gummy April. A Hyacinth for Edith. A. J. M. Smith. BoCaPo; TwCaPo
Now that the barbarians have got as far as Picra. Translation. Roy Fuller. ChMP
Now that the day is done. Centaur Song. Hilda Doolittle ("H. D."). MOAP
Now that the flesh is gone there but remains. The Dream Is Not Enough. Zoe Kincaid Brockman. NoCaPo
Now That the Flowers. Cullen Jones. GoYe
Now that the flush of summer is gone. The Kernel. Frank Kendon. MBP; MoBrPo (1942 ed.)
Now that the giant sunflowers rise. Goldfinches. Elisabeth Scollard. BLA; WhBS
Now that the gods are gone. Full-Circle. Maxwell Anderson. QS
Now that the green hill-side has quite. In May. Robert Kelly Weeks. SN
Now that the hills are all a-glow. Detour—Gypsy Trail Closed. Sara Henderson Hay *and* Raymond Holden. StaSt
Now that the others are gone, all of them, forever. Tomorrow. Kenneth Fearing. ChMo
Now that the seas are lined. Crisis. Mark Van Doren. NeTW
Now that the shutter of the dusk. Last Supper. Elinor Wylie. ChMo
Now that the spring hath filled our veins. A Round. William Browne. ElSeCe; ViBoPo
Now That the Time Has Come Wherein. *Unknown.* SDH
Now that the tower is standing. The Tower. Agnes Lee. NP
Now that the Truth Is Tried. Thomas Whythorne. ElL
Now that the twilight slants the curled edges of wheat. Berceuse for Birds. Joseph Auslander. BLA
Now that the Village-Reverence doth lye hid. A New-Years-Gift to Brian Lord Bishop of Sarum. William Cartwright. MePo
Now That the Winter's Gone. Thomas Carew. BoTP; EG; EV-2; OTPC; WP
(Spring, The.) ElSeCe; EPS; FaBoEn; GN; PoE; PoEL-3; PoFS; RIS; SeCV-1; TrGrPo; TyEnPo
Now that the world is all in a maze. The Unconcerned. Thomas Flatman. CEP; FaBoCh
Now that the young buds are tipped with a falling sun. Early Spring. Sidney Keyes. FaBoMo
Now That These Two. James Rorty. MOAP; TBM
Now that these wings to speed my wish ascend. Sonnet: The Philosophic Flight [*or* Spurning the Earth]. Giordano Bruno. AWP; LyPI; OnPM; PoFr
Now that they've got it settled whose I be. The Pauper Witch of Grafton. Robert Frost. CrMA
Now that we're almost settled in our house. In Memory of Major Robert Gregory. W. B. Yeats. AnIL; OAEP (2d ed.); PoFS; TriL
Now that we've done our best and worst, and parted. The Busy Heart. Rupert Brooke. HBV; LoPo; MBP; MoBrPo
Now that winter has gone hence. Spring Song. Jean Antoine de Baïf. TrFP
Now That You Are Gone. J. Patrick Walsh. JKCP (1955 ed.)
Now that you lie. Before Sleep. Anne Ridler. NeBP
Now that you would leave me. Love-Faith. Harry Kemp. HBMV
Now that your fingers, talented and fleet. To a Jazz Pianist, Dead. Stewart Atkins. NoCaPo
Now that your soul has fallen. To a Dead Poet (Armando Más Leite). Augusto Frederico Schmidt. BoFr
Now the ambassadors have gone, refusing. Meditation. Roy Fuller. FaBoMo
Now the autumn shudders. Autumn Chant. Edna St. Vincent Millay. BAP; CP
Now the beautiful business of summer is over. Birthday. Jean Starr Untermeyer. MAP; MoAmPo (1942 ed.)
Now the blackout of frontiers. To My Son. Babette Deutsch. NeTW
Now, the boys and the girls went out huckleberry hunting. Huckleberry Hunting. *Unknown.* ShS
Now the bright crocus flames, and now. In the Spring [*or* Spring]. Meleager, *tr. by* Andrew Lang. ADAH; AWP; JAWP; VOD; WBP
Now the bright morning-star, Day's harbinger. Song on May Morning [*or* On May Morning]. Milton. ADAH; BCEP; BLV; BoLiVe; CBE; CBOV; CG; CH; DD; ElSeCe; EPS; ExPo; GN; HBV; HBVY; LPS-2; OTPC; PIAE; PoRL; RG; TrGrPo; TyEnPo; WP; YeAr
Now the *Chesapeake* so bold. The *Shannon* and the *Chesapeake*. *Unknown.* AmSS
Now the cool twilight, glowing. Evening. Harold Monro. FaBoTw
Now the cormorants are coming in to roost. Shag Rookery. William Hart-Smith. AnNZ
Now the Dawn arose from her couch. Homer. *Fr.* The Odyssey, V. GrL
Now the Day Is Over. Sabine Baring-Gould. BTP; MaRV; OlF; OTPC; PCH, *5 sts.*
(Child's Evening Hymn.) VA; WGRP
(Evening Hymn.) BOL
Now the day slips away. Day's End. Hermann Hagedorn. *Fr.* Songs from the Rockies. VOD
Now the dead past seems vividly alive. Heritage. Claude McKay. PoNe
Now the descending triumph stops its flight. The Day of Judgement. David Young. OxBoCh
Now the dreary night is done. Morning Hymn. Cecil Frances Alexander. OTPC
Now the dreary winter's over. Spring Song. Nahum. TrJP
Now the drowsy sunshine. Evening. Harry Behn. TiPo (1959 ed.)
Now the ears, so I always had thunk. The Ears. Anthony Euwer. *Fr.* The Limeratomy. HBMV
Now the Earth, the Skies, the Air. *Unknown.* ElL
Now the first silly bastard he got in an aeroplane. Ops in a Wimpey. *Unknown.* CoMu
Now the floor is clean, and our hands. Xenophanes, *tr. fr. Greek by* Emily Ann Wolff. GrPo
Now the Four-Way Lodge is opened, now the Hunting Winds are loose. The Feet of the Young Men. Kipling. GBV; LBBV; OtMeF; PoRL
Now the frosty stars are gone. Ariel in the Cloven Pine. Bayard Taylor. AA; TCAP
Now the full-throated daffodils. From Feathers to Iron. C. Day Lewis. ViBoPo
Now the furnaces are out. Piper, Play. John Davidson. BMEP; TOP
Now the golden day is ending. Slumber Song. Mary H. Poynter. BOL
Now the golden fields of sunset rose on rose to me-ward fall.

Day and dark. George Cabot Lodge. AnAmPo; AnFE; APA; CoAnAm; LA
Now the golden leafage is beggared. Vyacheslav Ivanov, *tr. by* Babette Deutsch. *Fr.* Vespers, V. TrRV
Now the golden leaves have been beggared. Vyacheslav Ivanov, *tr. by* C. M. Bowra. *Fr.* Vespers, V. BoRS
Now the golden Morn aloft. Ode on the Pleasure Arising from Vicissitude. Thomas Gray. CEP; EV-3; GTBS; GTBS-D; GTBS-W; GTSE; GTSL; OBEC
Now the good man's away from home. Sally Sweetbread. Henry Carey. CoMu
Now the holy hour is nigh. Walk to Church. John Keble. EnSW
Now the Hungry Lion Roars. Shakespeare. *Fr.* A Midsummer Night's Dream, V, ii. AnFE; AtBAP; BLV; CH; ChTr; EG; ElL; LiTB; LiTG; OBSC; SeCeV; ViBoPo
(Approach of the Fairies, The.) CG
(Epilogue.) BCEP; KN; LoBV
(Fairy Blessing, The.) OxBoLi
(Fairy Songs.) TrGrPo
(Midnight Song.) MuP
(Puck Speaks.) ThWaDe
(Puck's Song.) BoLiVe; MoShBr; SiCE
(Song of Robin Goodfellow, A.) BoW
Now the joys of the road are chiefly these. The Joys of the Road. Bliss Carman. DDA; HBV; HBVY; NLK; OBVV; PCN; PIR; SN; TCAP; TSW; TSWC
Now the Laborer's Task Is O'er. John Lodge Ellerton. BLPA; HBV; MaRV, *abr.;* OlF; TreFS; WGRP
Now the last day of many days. The Recollection [*or* To Jane]. Shelley. CBE; ChER; EmBrPo; EPN; EV-4; GTBS; GTBS-D; GTBS-W; GTSE; GTSL; OBRV; SN
Now the last drop, both sweet and fierce. Middle-Age. Emily B. C. Jones. HBMV
Now the last light of amber day is dying. Adoration. David Morton. MaRV
Now the Leaves Are Falling Fast. W. H. Auden. ChMo; CoBMV
Now the light o' the west is a-turn'd to gloom. Evenen in the Village. William Barnes. CaAE; GTSE
Now the little rivers go. Winter Streams. Bliss Carman. YeAr
Now the little white sheep. Baby's Evening-Song. Edith M. Thomas. BOL
Now the long blade of the sun, lying. Thebes of the Seven Gates. Sophocles. *Fr.* Antigone. WaaP
Now, the Lord made the bee and the bee did make the honey. Swansea Town. *Unknown.* ShS
Now the lusty spring is seen. Love's Emblems [*or* Love Song]. John Fletcher. *Fr.* The Tragedy of Valentinian. EG; ElL; ElSeCe; FaBoEn; HBV; LEAP; OBEV; SeEP; ViBoPo
Now the means of subsistence from men do the Gods keep hidden away. Creation of Pandora. Hesiod. *Fr.* Works and Days. GrR
Now the moisty wood discloses. Spring Morning. Frances Cornford. BoTP
Now the New Year reviving old Desires. The New Year. Omar Khayyám, *tr. by* Edward Fitzgerald. *Fr.* The Rubáiyát. OnPM
Now the night came on stormy and very dark. Eumaeus the Swineherd. Homer. *Fr.* The Odyssey, XIV *and* XV. OxBG
Now the Noisy Winds Are Still. Mary Mapes Dodge. PRWS; YeAr
Now the North wind ceases. Tardy Spring. George Meredith. EV-5; OBEV (1st ed.)
Now the plains come to adore the mountain wall. Colorado. Robert Fitzgerald. MoPo
Now the purple night is past. Song. Alfred Noyes. *Fr.* Drake. ChMo; CMP
Now the quietude of earth. The Hermit. "Æ." BEL; CaAE; PoVP
Now the renowned minstrel was singing to the wooers. A Passing Glimpse of Penelope. Homer. *Fr.* The Odyssey, I. GrR
Now the rich cherry whose sleek wood. Country Summer. Léonie Adams. AnEnPo; ATP (1953 ed.); BLV; BoLiVe (1939 ed.); LiTM; MAP; MoAB; MoAmPo; MoPo; MoVE; TCPD; TrGrPo; TwAmPo; ViBoPo (1958 ed.)
Now the rite is duly done. The Newly-wedded. Winthrop Mackworth Praed. ERP; HBV; MaRV; VA
Now the rites are over, the drums are joined. The Sacrifice. Chu Yuan. *Fr.* The Nine Songs. WhP
Now the shiades o' the elems da stratch muore an muore. Evening, and Maidens. William Barnes. OBEV (new ed.); OBVV
Now the Sky. Mark Van Doren. MOAP
Now the small birds come to feast. Winter Feast. Frances Frost. YeAr
Now the sneeze is a joy-vent, I s'pose. The Sneeze. Anthony Euwer. *Fr.* The Limeratomy. HBMV
Now the starry day is ended. The Stars' Song. Greville MacDonald. BOL
Now the stealthy sunrise hoverer. Pendulum. Joseph Auslander. BAP
Now the stone house on the lake front is finished. A Fence. Carl Sandburg. AmP; InP
Now the storm begins to lower. The Fatal Sisters. Thomas Gray. BEL; CEP; CoBE; EiPP; EM-1; EnRP; EPP; OAEP; RO
Now the sun again, like a bloody convict. The Rising Sun. Lawrence Durrell. *Fr.* Eight Aspects of Melissa. NeBP
Now the sun begins to sprinkle. Morning. Johan Ludvig Runeberg. AnSL
Now the sun has passed away. Evening Hymn. *Unknown.* BOL
Now the sun's gane out o' sight. Up in the Air. Allan Ramsay. BSV; CEP
Now the sweet-voiced nightingale. The Beginning of Day. Euripides. OxBG
Now the swift rot of the flesh is over. My Sister. Hyam Plutzik. FiMAP
Now the third and fatal conflict for the Persian throne was done. Harmosan. Richard Chenevix Trench. TVSH
Now the time comes when you are bored with Antiquity. Zone. Guillaume Apollinaire. OnHM
Now, the times are hard and the wages low. Time for Us to Leave Her. *Unknown.* ShS
Now the trouble with setting down a: written calypso. Calypsomania. Anthony Brode. FiBHP
Now the violet blooms again. Persuasion's Rose [*or* Love in Spring]. Meleager. GrR; OxBG
Now the white violet's blooming, and that lover of the showers. "Lenten Ys Come with Love to Toune." Meleager. GrPE
Now the Widow McGee and Larrie O'Dee. Larrie O'Dee. William W. Fink. BOHV; HBV; OTPC (1946 ed.)
Now the wild bees that hive in the rocks. The Brown Bear. Mary Austin. FaPON; MPB; OTPC (1946 ed.); UTS; WaKn
Now the winds are all composure. Spring. Christopher Smart. *Fr.* St. Philip and St. James. LoBV; OBEC
Now the Winter's Come to Stay. *Unknown.* IHA
Now the wood, in sun and leisure. The Bargain. Neidhart von Reuental. LiTW
Now, the wry Rosenbloom is dead. Cortège for Rosenbloom. Wallace Stevens. TwAmPo
Now the zephyrs diminish the cold, and the year being ended. Ovid. Tristia, III, 12. LaP
Now then, shipmates, come gather and join in my ditty. The *Cumberland*'s Crew. *Unknown.* ShS
Now there is frost upon the hill. Where It Is Winter. George O'Neil. HBMV
Now there is none of the living who can remember. Epitaph for a Concord Boy. Stanley Young. WaKn
Now There Is Nothing Left. L. A. MacKay. CaP; PeCV
Now there is prescience everywhere. March. Raymond Holden. CAG
Now there shall be a new song and a new star. To Mother—in Heaven. Bennett Weaver. OQP; QP-1
Now therefore, while the youthful hue. Andrew Marvell. *Fr.* To His Coy Mistress. AlDL
Now they are gone with all their songs and sins. Sonnet. John Masefield. *Fr.* Sonnets ("Like bones"). InP
Now they are resting. Fine Work with Pitch and Copper. William Carlos Williams. OxBA
Now they call me Hanging Johnny. Hanging Johnny. *Unknown.* ShS
Now they have come, those afternoons in November. November Afternoons. Sister Mary Madeleva. GoBC
Now they have two cars to clean. Do It Yrself. Larry Eigner. NeAP
Now, think you, Life, I am defeated quite? One Fight More. Theodosia Garrison. BLP; PC
Now this is my first counsel. Counsels of Sigrdrifa. *Unknown.* *Fr.* The Elder Edda. AWP
Now this is new: that I (habitué). First Day of Teaching. Bonaro W. Overstreet. TrPWD
Now this is the Law of the Jungle—as old and as true as the sky. The Law of the Jungle. Kipling. *Fr.* The Second Jungle Book. BoChLi; LiTB; PoEL-5; PoVP; ShBV-1; VA
Now this is the strangest thing since the world began. Diagonals. Aline Kilmer. AV
Now this Ophelia was a wiser woman. Spouse. Witter Bynner. AnFE; CoAnAm
Now, this, to my notion, is pleasant cheer. The Beggar's Soliloquy. George Meredith. EmBrPo
Now, Thomas, know thy sin. It was not fear. The Sale of St. Thomas. Lascelles Abercrombie. LBBV
Now those that are low spirited I hope won't think it wrong. A New Hunting Song. *Unknown.* CoMu
Now thou hast loved [*or* lov'd] me one whole day. Woman's Constancy. John Donne. ElSeCe; EnLit; EnLP; EPS; LiTL; PoE; PoFS; ReIE; SeCV-1; SeEP; TuPP

Now thought seeks shelter, lest the heart melt. Recovery. F. R. Scott. CaP
Now Thrice Welcome Christmas. *Unknown.* AnEC; OHIP (Thrice Welcome Christmas.) SDH
Now Through Night's Caressing Grip. W. H. Auden. PoLFOT; PoRA
Now, through the dusk. The World of Dream. Walter de la Mare. GaP
Now through the greying darkness, while you're sleeping. Last Hour of Leave. Arthur Gordon. LoPo
Now through the stifling air, thick with the murk. The Known Soldier. Mark Antony De Wolfe Howe. AOAH
Now Time throws off his cloak again. Return of Spring. Charles d'Orléans, *tr. by* Longfellow. ADAH
Now Time's Andromeda on this rock rude. Andromeda. Gerard Manley Hopkins. FaBoMo; LiTB
Now to be clean he must abandon himself. The Swan Bathing. Ruth Pitter. MoBrPo
Now to great Britain we must make our way. Of England, and of Its Marvels. Fazio degli Uberti. AWP; JAWP; WBP
Now to his restless sea-bed wends. Sunset. George Darley. *Fr.* Harvest Home. RO
Now to meet only in dreams. Otomo no Yakamochi, *tr. fr. Japanese by* Kenneth Rexroth. OnPJ
Now to mid-heav'n the whiten'd moon inclines. The Northern Lights. Richard Savage. *Fr.* The Wanderer. BeR
Now to my prayer in season, O Zeus of Olympus, hearken! Against the Demos. Theognis. GrPE
Now to th'ascent of that steep savage hill. Satan Journeys to the Garden of Eden. Milton. *Fr.* Paradise Lost, IV. ChTr
Now to the church behold the mourners come. The Pauper's Funeral. George Crabbe. *Fr.* The Village. CoEV
Now to the right, now to the left I turn. Crinagoras, *tr. fr. Greek by* F. A. Wright. GrPo
Now to the spring he came. Hylas. Apollonius Rhodius. *Fr.* Argonautica. OxBG
Now to the World. Frank Kendon. PtOT
Now Tomlinson gave up the ghost in his house in Berkeley Square. Tomlinson. Kipling. BeLS; ChMo; OtMeF; PIR; PoVP; VLEP
Now Tom's translated, not a mouse. Cat of Cats. Vivien Bulkley. PoC
Now touch the air softly. A Pavane for the Nursery. William Jay Smith. NePoAm-2
Now toward the *Hunter's* gloomy sides we came. The Hospital Prison Ship. Philip Freneau. *Fr.* The British Prison Ship. IAP
Now trees are weedy mazes, upright, still. Larch Hill. Leslie Daiken. OnYI
Now Turnus rolls aloof o'er empty plains. The Death of Turnus. Virgil. *Fr.* The Aeneid, XII. WoL
Now twenty springs had cloath'd the Park with green. The Toilette; a Town Eclogue. John Gay. CEP
Now twenty years ago/ This day we found the thing. The Anniversary. Sir Ronald Ross. PoP
Now two have met, now two have met. The Great Grey Water. E. J. Brady. BoAu
Now, until the break of day. Fairy Songs. Shakespeare. *Fr.* A Midsummer Night's Dream, V, ii. TrGrPo
Now unto Him who brought His people forth. Benediction. Stephen Phillips. *Fr.* Herod. MaRV
Now, upon Syria's land of roses. Syria. Thomas Moore. *Fr.* Lalla Rookh. LPS-2
Now upon this piteous year. The Stranger. Jean Garrigue. LiTA; LiTM
Now very quietly, and rather mournfully. A House. J. C. Squire. MBP; NV
Now wait till I put on my gospel shoes. If I Got My Ticket, Can I Ride? *Unknown.* OuSiCo
Now Walks the Devil Up and Down. Grace Buchanan Sherwood. MuM
Now wanderer in hostile forests, exile. Flower of Exile. Max Dunn. BoAV
Now War Is All the World About. Sir Richard Fanshawe. *Fr.* Il Pastor Fido. LoBV
(Ode, An, upon Occasion of His Majesties Proclamation in the Year 1630.) MePo; OBS
Now warm with ministerial ire. The Liberty Pole. John Trumbull. *Fr.* M'Fingal, III. AmPP (3d ed.); APW; TCAP
Now was the Lord and Lady of the May. William Browne. *Fr.* Britannia's Pastorals, II. EPP
Now was the welkin all inveloped. Richard Barnfield. *Fr.* Cynthia. ReIE
Now wat ye wha I met yestreen. The Young Laird and Edinburgh Katy. Allan Ramsay. CEP; EiPP
Now watch this autumn that arrives. Song at the Beginning of Autumn. Elizabeth Jennings. PoN
Now We Are Back to Normal. Louis MacNeice. *Fr.* Autumn Journal. ChMo
Now we are civilized, the old men die. Old Men's Ward. Elma Dean. GoYe
Now we are suddenly afraid. Man Returns to the Gates of Eden. Dorothy Hobson. MuM
Now we begin another day together. Prayer at Dawn. Edwin McNeill Poteat. TrPWD
Now we know well how each can bear the shock. "Anna Akhmatova," *tr. fr. Russian by* V. de S. Pinto. BoRS
Now We Should Sing and Say Nowell. *Unknown.* AnEC
Now weave the winds to music of June's lyre. June. Theodore Harding Rand. CaP; OCL
Now Welcome Summer [*or* Welcom Somer]. Chaucer. *See* Roundel, A: "Now welcom, somer . . ."
Now welcome, welcome, baby-boy, unto a mother's fears. The Irish Mother in the Penal Days. John Banim. AnIV; TIP
Now wend we to the Palmalle. Domine, Quo Vadis? *Unknown.* ACP; CAW
Now went forth the morn. Battle of the Angels. Milton. *Fr.* Paradise Lost, VI. BCEP; LPS-2
Now we're afloat upon the tropic sea. Tropical Weather. Epes Sargent. EtS
Now we're warping her into the docks. Galloping Randy Dandy O! *Unknown.* SoAmSa
Now westward Sol had spent the richest beams. Music's Duel [*or* The Nightingale's Song]. Richard Crashaw. CoBE; GoTL; LPS-3; OBS; SeCV-1; SeEP
Now what can he want. The Vagrant. John Crowe Ransom. NV
Now what do you think. *Unknown.* OxNR; SiTL
Now what in the world shall we dioux. The Sioux. Eugene Field. FiBHP
Now What Is Love. Sir Walter Ralegh. *See* Description of Love, A.
Now what is love I will thee tell. Thomas Heywood. *Fr.* The Rape of Lucrece. LO
Now, what news on the Rialto? Shylock's Defense. Shakespeare. *Fr.* The Merchant of Venice, III, i. TreFS
Now what you all know about this? Stagolee (A *vers.*). *Unknown.* ViBoFo
Now when at last they arrived at the beautiful stream of the river. Nausicaa. Homer. *Fr.* The Odyssey, VI. OxBG
Now, when declining from the noon of day. Evening in the Capital. Pope. *Fr.* The Rape of the Lock. BeR
Now when drowning imagination clutches. Word over All. C. Day Lewis. CaAE; OAEP (2d ed.)
Now when I could not find the road. The Shepherd's Hut. Andrew Young. ThWaDe
Now when I sleep the thrush breaks through my dreams. A Dream in Early Spring. Fredegond Shove. MoVE; TwCV
Now when I stand upon the stair alone. The Child upon the Stair. Carolyn Hall. TSW
Now when Jesus was born in Bethlehem of Judea. The Visit of the Wise Men. St. Matthew, Bible, *N.T.* ChrBoLe; CLS
Now, when my life is more than half consumed. Gruach. Gordon Bottomley. TCPD
Now When So Much Has Passed. George Seferis, *tr. fr. Modern Greek by* Bernard Spencer *and* Nanos Valaoritis. LiTW
Now, when the cheerless empire of the sky. James Thomson. *Fr.* The Seasons: Winter. BSV
Now when the first foul torrent of the brooks. Angling. James Thomson. *Fr.* The Seasons: Spring. LPS-2
Now when the giant in us wakes and broods. Symbolism. "Æ." TIP
Now when the goddess, white-armed Hera. Homer. *Fr.* The Iliad, V. GrPo
Now, when the joy of Jove had its fulfilling. The Birth of Hermes. *Unknown.* *Fr.* Homeric Hymns. GrR
Now, when the kindling Spring breathes life and joy. Hymn on the Seasons. Anna Maria Porter. DiM
Now when the lumber camp is done. Send Her On Along. *Unknown.* IHA
Now, when the Master left us. To Don Francisco Giner de los Rios. Antonio Machado. AnSpL-2; TeCS
Now when the time of fruit and grain is come. Autumn. Bliss Carman. VOD
Now when they both had fortified their hands. The Two Boxers. Theocritus. *Fr.* Idylls. GrR
Now when they came to the bright running river. Nausicaa. Homer. *Fr.* The Odyssey, VI. LiTW
Now when they had put from them the desire of meat and drink. Menelaus; What Price Earthly Splendor! Homer. *Fr.* The Odyssey, IV. GrR
Now when they were about to move for home. Homer. *Fr.* The Odyssey, VI. GrPo
Now when we had gone down to the ship. Homer. *Fr.* The Odyssey, XI. GrL
Now where are all the gay raftsmen? The Raftsmen. *Unknown.* IHA
"Now where are ye goin'," ses I, "wid the shawl." The Road. Patrick R. Chalmers. HBV
"Now, where are you going this beautiful day?" The Baby in the Basket. Emily Carter. SAS

"Now where have you been, Johnny Randall, my son?" Johnny Randall. *Unknown.* PIAE
Now Where To? Heine, *tr. fr. German by* Lola Gruenthal. AnGP
Now where's a song for our small dear. The Unwritten Song. Ford Madox Ford. BoTP
Now whether folks are Methodists. That Radio Religion. William Ludlum. WBLP
Now, while amid those dainty downs and dales. To His Pandora, from England. Alexander Craig. TuPP
Now, while our money is piping hot. The Merchantman [*or* Eclogue: The Merchantman]. John Davidson. OBVV; PoVP
Now while rest the happy herds. A Lullaby. Helen Gray Cone. BOL
Now while Rogero learns the arms and name. Angelica and the Ork. Ariosto. *Fr.* Orlando Furioso, X. OBSC
"Now, while she's changing," said the Dean. The Wedding Sermon. Coventry Patmore. *Fr.* The Angel in the House. PoVP
Now, while the long delaying ash assumes. To a Friend. David Gray. EnSW
Now while the night her sable veil hath spread. William Drummond of Hawthornden. EG
Now while the solemn evening shadows sail. Swans. Wordsworth. *Fr.* An Evening Walk. OBEC
Now while the sun was going about mid-heaven. Homer. *Fr.* The Iliad, XVI. GrPo
Now while the sunset offers. Santa Barbara Beach. Ridgely Torrence. HBMV; NV; TBM
Now while the wind and earth and heavens rest. Sonnet. Petrarch. Sonnets to Laura: To Laura in Life, CXXXI. LyPI
Now while the wind is up, I hear. Ghostly Reaper. Harold Vinal. TBM; UnW
Now, while thou hast the wondrous power of word. The Gift of Speech. Sadi. *Fr.* The Gulistan. AWP; LiTW
"Now whither go ye?" Would that we did know. Our Poets' Breed. Luis Montoto y Rautenstrauch. CAW
Now who is he on earth that lives. Medieval Norman Songs, X. *Unknown, tr. by* John Addington Symonds. AWP
Now who will rise. A Question. P. T. Forsyth. OQP; QP-2
Now why should I, who sneer and frown. He Visits a Hospital. Rolfe Humphries. AnAmPo; LA; TBM
Now will I a lover be. The Combat. Thomas Stanley. AWP
Now will you please observe our doctors of the law. Concerning Lawyers. Pero López de Ayala. *Fr.* Palace Rhymes. AnSpL-1
Now will you stand for me, in this cool light. Love in the Museum. Adrienne Cecile Rich. NePoEA
Now wilt me take for Jesus sake. A Prayer. Katharine Tynan. OBVV
Now winds of winter glue. Upon New Year's Eve. Sir Arthur Quiller-Couch. OBVV
Now winter downs the dying of the year. At Year's-End [*or* Years-End]. Richard Wilbur. FiMAP; LiTM (rev. ed.); MiAP; NePA; NePoEA
Now Winter melts beneath. Solvitur Acris Hiems. Francis Sylvester Mahony. IrPN
Now Winter Nights Enlarge. Thomas Campion. AnFE; AtBAP; BEL; CenL; ElL; ElSeCe; EnLi-1 (1949 ed.); EV-2; KN; LoBV; OBSC; PG (1955 ed.); PoRA; SeCePo; SiCE; TuPP; ViBoPo; WoL
(Song: "Now winter nights enlarge.") BrBE
(Winter Nights.) LEAP; OBEV
Now, winter's dolorous days are o'er, and through. Sonnet. Thomas Caulfield Irwin. IrPN
Now winter's winds are banished from the sky. Spring. Meleager. AWP; JAWP
Now with a clean thread. The Spider. David McCord. MAP
Now with a general peace the world was blest. Dryden. *Fr.* Astraea Redux. CEP
Now with a sigh November comes to the brooding land. Autumn in Carmel. George Sterling. TBM
Now with earth riven and a bloodied sun. We Shall Say. Miriam Allen deFord. GoYe
Now with gray hair begins defeat. Farewell to Town. Laurence Housman. HBMV
Now with swift thought I range from pole to pole. The Godlike Brute. John Arbuthnot. *Fr.* Know Yourself. BeR
Now with the coming in of the spring the days will stretch a bit. The County Mayo. Anthony Raftery, *tr. by* James Stephens. AnIL; GTIV
Now with the Moon. Louise Liebhardt. MuM
Now with the slow revolving year. Two Old Lenten Rhymes, II. *Unknown.* WHL
Now with the springtime the days will grow longer. County Mayo. Anthony Raftery, *tr. by* Frank O'Connor. KiLC
Now with your head thrown back. I Tell of Another Young Death. Cesar Tiempo. TrJP
Now wither rose and lily flower. Autumn. *Unknown.* TMEV
Now Wolde. A. Godwhen. *See* Now Would I Fain.
"Now, woman, why without your veil?" The King of the Crocodiles. Robert Southey. CG
Now worlds on worlds in phalanx deep. The Daisy. James Mason Good. PEOR
Now Would I Fain. A. Godwhen. TMEV
(Now Wolde, *abr.*) CH
("Now wolde [*or* would] I fain[e] some merthes make.") EG, *abr.*; LO
(Song for My Lady.) OxBoLi
Now would I weave her portrait out of all dim splendour. Portrait. Ezra Pound. OBVV
Now would to God swift ships had ne'er been made! Sopolis. Callimachus. AWP; GrPo
Now Wu Tao-tzu, continuing his stroll. A Flight of Wild Geese. Harold Stewart. MoAuPo
Now you are among us, you really exist. The Baby Girl. Eugenio Florit. AnCL
"Now you are buried, Timon, is the darkness worse, or the light?" The Misanthrope. Callimachus. GrPE
Now you are holding my skull in your hand. A Meditation. Richard Eberhart. FiMAP; LiTA
Now You Are in Your Country. Frank Kendon. POTE
Now you are nodding in every well-bred garden. Daffodils. Gina Ballantyne. BoAu
Now you are one with us, you know our tears. To America, on Her First Sons Fallen in the Great War. E. M. Walker. PAH
Now, you great stanza, you heroic mould. Single Sonnet. Louise Bogan. AnEnPo
Now you have freely given me leave to love. To a Lady That Desired I Would Love Her. Thomas Carew. CoEV; LiTL; LoBV; MeLP; MePo; OBS; SeCL; SeCV-1; SeEP
Now you may have Him, Mary, they are done. Thirteenth Station. William A. Donaghy. *Fr.* The Stations of the Cross. ISi
Now You're Content. André Spire, *tr. fr. French by* Stanley Burnshaw. TrJP
Now you're married you must obey. *Unknown.* GoTP; RIS
Now zebras are a kind of horse. Zebras. S. H. Stackpole. CAG
Nowel. Théophile Gautier, *tr. fr. French by* Alan Conder. TrFP
Nowell, el, el, el, el ("The first day when Christ was born"). *Unknown.* AnEC
Nowell, ell, both old and ying. Nowell, ell, ell, ell . . . *Unknown.* AnEC
Nowell, ell, ell, ell ("A Babe is born all of a may"). *Unknown.* AnEC
(Three Christmas Carols, 1.) ACP
Nowell, ell, ell, ell, ell . . . ("Mary mother, meek and mild"). *Unknown.* AnEC
Nowell, ell, ell, ell, ell . . . ("Nowell, ell, both old and ying"). *Unknown.* AnEC
Nowell, Nowell. Robert Finch. TwCaPo
Nowell, Nowell, Nowell, Nowell ("Tidings true, there be come new"). *Unknown.* AnEC
Nowell, nowell, nowell, nowell,/ Tidings good I think to tell. In Die Nativitatis. *Unknown.* AnEC
"Nowell, nowell, nowell, nowell."/ "Who is there that singeth so nowell." In Die Nativitatis. *Unknown.* AnEC
Nowell, nowell, nowell, nowell, nowell, nowell. Out of Your Sleep Arise and Wake. *Unknown.* AnEC
Nowell, nowell, nowell, sing we with mirth. A Song upon "Now Must I Sing." *Unknown.* AnEC
Nowell Sing We. *Unknown.* ChTr
Nowell sing we, both all and some. *Exortum Est* in Love and Lysse. *Unknown.* AnEC
Nowell sing we now all and some. Nowell Sing We. *Unknown.* ChTr
Nowhere is one alone. Wood and Hill. Andrew Young. HaMV
Nowise beautiful/ Was Marian Erle. Elizabeth Barrett Browning. *Fr.* Aurora Leigh, III. VLEP
Now's the time for mirth and play. A Lark's Nest. Christopher Smart. *Fr.* Hymns for the Amusement of Children. FaBoCh; LoGBV
Nox. Salvador Díaz Mirón, *tr. fr. Spanish by* Samuel Beckett. AnMP
Nox Benigna. William Pember Reeves. AnNZ
Nox Est Perpetua. Marion Lochhead. LO
Nox Est Perpetua una Dormienda. *Unknown, tr. fr. Greek by* E. J. Myers. *Fr.* Lament for Bion. OxBG
Nox Ignatiana. James J. Daly. CAW; JKCP
Nox Mortis. Paul Bewsher. PtOT
Nox Nocti Indicat Scientiam. William Habington. *Fr.* Castara, III. ACP; CAW; CoEV; ElSeCe; EV-2; GoBC; GTSL; HBV; LoBV; MeLP; MePo; MeRV; OBEV; OBS; PoFr; PoLi; SeCL; TriL
(When I Survey the Bright.) OxBoCh
Nox was lit by lux of Luna, The. Carmen Possum. *Unknown.* BLPA
Nu brotherr Wallterr, brotherr min. Orrm. *Fr.* The Ormulum. EPP

Nuances of a Theme by Williams. Wallace Stevens. LiTA
Nubia. Bayard Taylor. HBV
Nuclear wind, when wilt thou blow. Paul Dehn. *Fr.* A Leaden Treasury of English Verse. FiBHP
Nude nymph, when from Neuberg's I led her. The Maid of the Meerschaum. Kipling. PA
Nudging and thrusting to the light. Gideon at the Well. Geoffrey Hill. NePoEA
Nudities. André Spire, *tr. fr. French.* AWP, *tr. by* Jethro Bithell; TrJP, *tr. by* Stanley Burnshaw
Nudity is everywhere. The Satyr; or, The Song of Nudity. Kostes Palamas. MoGP
Nugatory. E. B. White. BOHV
Nugly Little Man, The. Marion St. John Webb. TVC; TVSH
Nuit Blanche. Amy Lowell. TBM
Nuit Blanche; North End. Conrad Aiken. OxBA
Nulla Fides. Patrick Carey. SeEP
Nullum Stimulum Ignavis. Henry Parrot. SiCE
Number Five. John Crowe Ransom. TCPD
No. XVII. "Pablo Neruda," *tr. fr. Spanish by* H. R. Hays. *Fr.* Twenty Poems of Love. TwSpPo
No. 6 of Choruses from "The Rock." T. S. Eliot. LiTM
Numberless are the world's wonders, but none. Choral Ode. Sophocles. *Fr.* Antigone. LiTW
Numbers, *sels.* Bible, *O.T.*
Balaam's Blessing, XXIV: 5–9. TrGrPo
Benediction, VI: 24–26. TrGrPo
(Blessing of the Priests.) TrJP
Song of the Well, XXI: 17–18. TrJP
Numbers. Agnes Lee. NP
Numbers, *sels.* Constantino Suasnavar, *tr. fr. Spanish.*
"I have lost my shoes," XXVI, *tr. by* Muna Lee. AnCL; FaPON
"I like the boss' daughter," XVII, *tr. by* Dudley Fitts. AnCL
"I look up hotels," XXX, *tr. by* Muna Lee. AnCL; OnPM
"Sown fields./ Herds," XXI, *tr. by* Dudley Fitts. AnCL
"These are the three principles, friend," XLIII, *tr. by* Dudley Fitts. AnCL
"What a thin life the girl," IX, *tr. by* Muna Lee. AnCL
Numbers and Faces, *sel.* W. H. Auden.
"Kingdom of Number is all boundaries, The." ImOP
Numerous host of dreaming saints succeed, A. The Duke of Buckingham [*or* The Crowd and Buckingham]. Dryden. *Fr.* Absalom and Achitophel. EPP; FaBoEn; NBE
Nun, A. J. O. Austin. PraNu
Nun, The. Leigh Hunt. ALV; BOHV; HBV; InMe; OBRV; OBVV
(If You Be a Nun.) PG (1945 ed.)
Nun, The. Shiel MacDara. PraNu
Nun, A. Christina Rossetti. PraNu
Nun, The. Odell Shepard. PraNu; SBMV
Nun, A, green-girdled in a forest tower. The Blind Nun. Thomas S. Jones, Jr. PraNu
Nun has no nation, A. A Sister of Charity Comforts a Wounded Soldier. "Owen Meredith." *Fr.* Lucile. PraNu
Nun is a city builded, A. Sister and Nun. "A. Page." PraNu
Nun of Nidaros, The. Longfellow. Tales of a Wayside Inn: The Musician's Tale, Pt. I, xxii. PraNu
Nun Snow. Alfred Kreymborg. AnFE; APA; CoAnAm; MAPA; TwAmPo
Nun Speaks to Mary, A. Sister Mary Madeleva. ISi; PraNu
Nun to Mary, Virgin, A. Sister Mary St. Virginia. ISi
Nunc Dimittis, The. St. Luke, II: 29–32. Bible, *N.T.* WGRP; WHL
Nunc Est Bibendum. Anacreon, *tr. fr. Greek by* T. F. Higham. GrL; OxBG
Nunc Gaudet Maria. *Unknown.* ISi
(A, A, A, A,/ Nunc Gaudet Maria.) AnEC
Nunc Scio, Quid Sit Amor. L. A. MacKay. BoCaPo
Nuns, The. Edward F. Garesché. PraNu
Nuns at Eve. John Malcolm Brinnin. MoAB
Nun's Beloved, A. Mother Francis Raphael. PraNu
Nun's Diamond Jubilee, A. Gertrude Jane Codd. PraNu
Nuns Fret Not at Their Convent's Narrow Room. Wordsworth. BEL; BPN; EM-2; EmBrPo; EnL; EnRP; EPN; OAEP; PeBoSo; PFE; PreP; TOP; TyEnPo
(Nuns Fret Not.) CoBE; ERP
(Of the Sonnet.) ES
(Prefatory Sonnet.) OBRV
(Sonnet: "Nuns fret not at their convent's narrow room.") OBEV; ViBoPo
(Sonnet-Prison, The.) LEAP
Nun's Heart, The. *Unknown.* PraNu
Nun's Hobby, A. Sister Mary of the Angels. PraNu
Nuns in the Wind. Muriel Rukeyser. FiMAP
Nun's Lament for Philip Sparrow, The. John Skelton. *Fr.* Phyllyp Sparowe. CG
Nun's Lot, The. Pope. *Fr.* Eloisa to Abelard. PraNu
(Vestal, The.) ACP; CAW
Nuns of the Perpetual Adoration. Ernest Dowson. BrBE; CaAE; PoVP; PraNu; TOP; TriL; ViPP
Nun's Priest's Tale, The. Chaucer. *Fr.* The Canterbury Tales. AnFE; AtBAP; BEL; CoBE; EnL, *mod. by* Theodore Morrison; EnLi-1; GEPC; MaPo; OAEP; OuHeWo, *mod. by* J. U. Nicolson; PoEL-1; SeCeV; TOP, *abr.*; TrGrPo, *orig., with mod. vers. by* Frank Ernest Hill
(Cock and the Fox, The.) LiA
(Nonne Preestes Tale, The.) EM-1; EV-1; PIAE; TCEP, *sl. abr.*; TyEnPo
Sels.
Chasing the Fox. CoEV
Murder Will Out. MyFE
Poor Widow's Cock, The, 6 *ll.* MyFE
"This Chauntecleer stood hye up-on his toos." FiP
Nun's Vow, The. Sister Mary Wilfrid. PraNu
Nuptiae post Nummos. Henry Parrot. SiCE; TuPP
Nuptial. Mary Fabyan Windeatt. JKCP (1955 ed.)
Nuptial Eve, A. Sydney Dobell. VA
Sels.
Ballad of Keith of Ravelston, The. BMEP; HBV; LEAP; OBEV; OBVV; TOP; UnW
(Keith of Ravelston.) CH; DaM; EV-5; GTBS
"Ravelston, Ravelston." LO
Nuptial Hymn. Henry Peacham. *Fr.* The Period of Mourning. ElL
Nuptial Sleep. Dante Gabriel Rossetti. The House of Life, VI(A). BrBE; LoBV; PeBoSo; ViPo; ViPP
Nuptial Song. Lord de Tabley. OBVV
Nuptiall Song, or Epithalamie, on Sir Clipseby Crew and His Lady, A. Robert Herrick. AtBAP; PoEL-3; SeCV-1
Nuptials, The. Ibn Sa'id of Alcala la Real, *tr. fr. Arabic by* A. J. Arberry. MooP
Nuptials of Haemon and Antigone, The. Sophocles, *tr. fr. Greek by* Gilbert Murray. *Fr.* Antigone. GrR
Nuremberg. Longfellow. AmPP; CoBA; HBV; IAP; LPS-2
Nurse. Harry Graham. *See* Misfortunes Never Come Singly.
Nurse, The. Iosif Utkin, *tr. fr. Russian by* Jack Lindsay. RuPo
Nurse Edith Cavell. Alice Meynell. BoHiPo; CP
Nurse-Life Wheat within His Green Husk Growing, The. Fulke Greville. Caelica, XL. PeBoSo
(Youth and Maturity.) ES; OBSC; RiBV
Nurse looks round my clinic screen, The. Convalescence, IV. David McCord. WhC
Nurse not one changeless humour in thy breast. Omniscience Granted to No Man. Sophocles. *Fr.* Antigone. GrR
Nursery, The. Mrs. Motherly. SAS
Nursery Hour, A. Lady Anne Lindsay. BOL
Nursery Legend, A. Henry S. Leigh. BOHV
Nursery Nonsense, *sels.* D'Arcy Wentworth Thompson. BoN
"In London-town Dame Trottypeg."
"Inquisitive Cock Sparrow, An."
"There lived an old man in a garret."
"Two little dogs went out for a walk."
Nursery Rhyme, A: "Hushy baby, my doll." *Unknown.* BOL
Nursery Rhymes à la Mode. *Unknown.* BOHV; PA
Nursery Rhymes for the Tender-hearted, *sels.* Christopher Morley.
"I knew a black beetle, who lived down a drain," IV. HBMV; TCAP; YaD
"Scuttle, scuttle, little roach," I. FaFP; HBMV; SiTL; TCAP; YaD
Nursery Song, A. Ann A. G. Carter. BOL; MOAH; OTPC (1923 ed.); PPL; RAR; SAS
Nursery Song, A. Laura E. Richards. BoChLi; HBV; HBVY; RAR; TVC
Nursery Song in Pidgin English. *Unknown.* BOHV; PA; WhC
Nursery Tales: "There was an old man/ And he had a calf." *Unknown.* *See* There Was an Old Man and He Had a Calf.
Nurse's Prayer, A. Ruth Winant Wheeler. PraP
Nurse's Song ("When the voices of children are heard on the green/ And laughing"). Blake. *Fr.* Songs of Innocence. AWP; BoChLi; BOL; CBE; CEP; CH; EiPP; EnRP; EV-3; FaBoBe; GaP; GoTP; HBV; HBVY; InPo; KN; MPB; OBEC; OnPM; OTPC (1923 ed.); RG; ThWaDe; TiPo (1952 ed.); WoL; WP
(Play Time.) FaPON
Nurse's Song ("When the voices of children are heard on the green/ And whisp'rings"). Blake. *Fr.* Songs of Experience. CEP; EnLi-2 (1949 ed.); PoFS; TOP
Nurse's Song. *Unknown, tr. fr. German.* ThWaDe
Nusaib. *Unknown, tr. fr. Arabic by* C. J. Lyall. MOAH
Nut, a World, a Squirrel, and a King, A. Charles Churchill. *Fr.* Night; an Epistle to Robert Lloyd. BeR
Nut-brown Ale, The. *At. to* John Marston. ElL
Nut-brown Bride, The. *Unknown.* *See* Lord Thomas and Fair Annet.
Nut-brown Maid, The. *Unknown.* EV-1; LiTL; MeEV; OBB; OBEV; OBSC
(Nutbrown Mayde, The.) TCEP

(Nutbrowne Maide.) EPP
Nutcrackers and the Sugar-Tongs, The. Edward Lear. ALV; BoN; RAR
Nuts in May. Louis MacNeice. MoAB; MoBrPo (1950 ed.)
Nutting. Wordsworth. BPN; EM-2; EmBrPo; EnRP; EnSW; ERP; GEPC
Nutting Time. Emilie Poulsson. BrR
Nycilla dyes her locks, 'tis said. *See* Mycilla dyes her locks, 'tis said.
Nyctalops. Clark Ashton Smith. DaM
Nydia's Song. Sir Edward Bulwer-Lytton. *Fr.* The Last Days of Pompeii, III, *ch.* 2. OBVV
Nymph, The. Walter Savage Landor. *Fr.* Gebir. RO
(Tamar and the Nymph.) VA
(Tamar's Wrestling.) EnRP
("'Twas evening, though not sunset, and the tide.") NBE
Nymph and a Swain, A. William Congreve. *Fr.* Love for Love. ALV; SeCL
(Song; Set by Mr. John Eccles.) SeEP
Nymph Complaining for the Death of Her Fawn, The. Andrew Marvell. AtBAP; BrBE; CH; EPS; EV-2; GoTL; HBV; LoBV; MePo; OBS; PoEL-2; ReEn; SeCV-1
(Death of the White Fawn, The.) LPS-1
Sels.
"It is a wond'rous thing how fleet."
(Maiden Lamenting for Her Fawn, A.) BCEP
"With sweetest milk and sugar first."
(Girl and Her Fawn, The.) BoTP; OTPC (1923 ed.)
(Girl Describes Her Fawn, The.) GTSL
(Nymph and Her Fawn, The.) FaBoCh; LoGBV
Nymph Diana's Song, The. Jorge de Montemayor, *tr. fr. Spanish by* Bartholomew Young. *Fr.* Diana. ReIE
Nymph I come once more awooing. Ay or Nay? Ralph Schomberg. *Fr.* The Judgment of Paris. TrJP
Nymph, nymph, what are your beads? Overheard on a Saltmarsh. Harold Monro. BoTP; CH; FaPON; HiLiEn; HOAH; MoShBr; PCD; PCH; PoMS; SP; ThWaDe; TiPo; WP
Nymph [*or* Nymphs] of the downward smile and sidelong glance. To G. A. W. Keats. ERP; PIR
Nymph of the Garden Where All Beauties Be. Sir Philip Sidney. Astrophel and Stella, LXXXII. InvP; SiPS
Nymph of the Severn, The. Milton. *Fr.* Comus. LPS-3
(Sabrina.) OBS
("There is a gentle nymph not far from hence.") MyFE; SeEP
Nymph, roving the shadowy wood by night, The. The Satyr. André Chénier. TrFP
Nymph Selvagia, The, Her Song. Jorge de Montemayor, *tr. fr. Spanish by* Bartholomew Young. *Fr.* Diana. ElSeCe; TuPP
("Shepherd, who can pass such wrong.") SiCE
(Song.) ElL
Nymph that undoes me is fair and unkind, The. Silvia. Sir George Etherege. SeCL
Nymph there was in Arcadie, A. Alpheus and Arethusa. Eugene Howell Daly. AA
Nymphidia; or, The Court of Fairy. Michael Drayton. NBE; OAEP; ReEn; TuPP
(Nimphidia, the Court Fayrie.) SeEP
Sels.
Arming of Pigwiggen, The. GN; OTPC
(Pigwiggen.) BoTP
(Pigwiggen Arms Himself.) MoShBr
(Pigwiggen Prepares for the Fight with King Oberon.) EV-1
Court of Fairy, The. EPP
("Pigwiggen was this fairy knight," *longer sel.*) ViBoPo
(Queen Mab Visits Pigwiggen, the Fairy Knight, *abr.*) EV-1
(Queen Mab's Chariot.) OTPC
(Queen Mab's Journey to Pigwiggen.) PCH
(Queen's Chariot.) OBS
Nympholept, A. Swinburne. VLEP
Nymphs, The, *sel.* Leigh Hunt.
"There are the fair-limbed nymphs." OBRV
Nymphs and Graces Dancing to a Shepherd's Pipe, The. Spenser. *Fr.* The Faerie Queene, VI, 10. BCEP
Nymphs and shepherds, dance no more. Song [*or* Third Song]. Milton. *Fr.* Arcades. AtBAP; ElSeCe; FiP; SeCL; ViBoPo
Nymph's Disdain of Love, A. *Unknown.* ElL; EPP; SiCE; TuPP
Nymphs of sea and land, away. Nuptial Hymn. Henry Peacham. *Fr.* The Period of Mourning. ElL
Nymphs of the downward smile and sidelong glance. *See* Nymph of the downward smile
Nymph's Passion, A. Ben Jonson. ElSeCe; EnLit
(Nymph's Secret, A.) OBEV (new ed.)
Nymph's Reply to the Shepherd, The. Sir Walter Ralegh. ATP; BLV; CBOV; CenL; CoBE; ElL; EM-1; EnL; EnLi-1; EPP; ExPo; GTBS-W; HoPM; LiTB; LiTG; LiTL; LoBV; OAEP; OuHeWo; PoE; PoFS; ReaPo; ReEn; ReIE; RiBV; SeCePo; SeCeV; SiCE; SiPS; SiTL; TCEP; TOP; TreFS; TrGrPo; TuPP; WHA
(Answer to Marlowe.) OBSC; UnPo (1st ed.)
(Her Reply.) OBEV
(Nymph's Reply, The.) ElSeCe; LPS-1; PG (1945 ed.); Po
(Nymph's Reply to Marlowe's Passionate Shepherd, The.) EV-1
(Nymph's Reply to the Passionate Shepherd, The.) HBV; LEAP
(Reply.) ViBoPo
Nymph's Secret, A. Ben Jonson. *See* Nymph's Passion, A.
Nymphs' Song, The. Michael Drayton. *Fr.* The Muses' Elysium. SeCL
Nymph's Song to Hylas, The. William Morris. *See* I Know a Little Garden Close.
Nymphs, wanton out your hour. To the Nymphs Pursuing Hylas. Ausonius. LaP
Nymphs, who dwell among the waters of the Rhine. Thyrsis. Antonio Mario. LaP
Nyum-nyum, The. *Unknown.* NA

O

O. Richard Wilbur. LiTA; MoPo
O/ Out of a bed of love. Holy Spring. Dylan Thomas. MeRV; WaP
Oh, a capital ship for an ocean trip. The Walloping Window Blind. Charles Edward Carryl. *Fr.* Davy and the Goblin. MoShBr. *See also* Capital ship for an ocean trip, A.
Oh, a dainty plant is the ivy green. The Ivy Green. Charles Dickens. *Fr.* Pickwick Papers, *ch.* 6. BPP; HBV; HBVY; LPS-2; OTPC (1946 ed.); PECK; PIR; RIS; TVSH; VA
O, a gallant set were they. A Huguenot. Mary Elizabeth Coleridge. OBVV; PoeT; PoVP; TVSH
Oh, a grand old time has the earth. Mother Earth. Harriet Monroe. SP
Oh, a leper must be a terrible thing to see. The Vocation of St. Francis. Sister Mary Eleanore. CAW; SaFP; WHL
Oh, a little Dutch soldier from over the Rhine. Snapoo. *Unknown.* SoAmSa
O, a little talk wid Jesus, makes it right. A Little Talk wid Jesus Makes It Right. *Unknown.* BoAN-2
Oh, a long, long time and a very long time. A Long Time Ago, *vers.* IV. *Unknown.* ShS
Oh, a lush green English meadow—it's there that I would lie. The Poplars. Bernard Freeman Trotter. CaP; CPG; OCL
Oh, a man there lives on the western plains. The Cowboy. *Unknown.* CoSo
Oh, a pearl is a thing of much value. A Student's Kiss. *Unknown.* OnPM
Oh! a private buffoon is a light-hearted loon. The Family Fool. W. S. Gilbert. *Fr.* The Yeomen of the Guard. ALV; InMe; SiTL
Oh, a raftsman's life is a wearisome one. The Pinery Boy. *Unknown.* IHA
Oh, a sailor's life is the life for me. The Warrior's Lament. Sir Owen Seaman. FiBHP
Oh, a shantyman's life is a wearisome life [*or* drearisome one]. A Shantyman's Life. *Unknown.* AS; ShS (*vers.* I); TrAS
Oh, a wonderful horse is the Fly-away Horse. The Fly-away Horse. Eugene Field. GoTP
O, a wonderful stream is the river [of] Time. The Isle of [the] Long Ago [*or* The Long Ago]. Benjamin Franklin Taylor. BLPA; FaFP; HBV; NeHB; PTA-2; TreFS; WBLP
Oh, a Yankee ship came down the river. Blow, Boys, Blow, *vers.* II. *Unknown.* ShS
"O, Aaron Burr, what have you done?" Aaron Burr. Stephen Vincent Benét. InMe
O Abishag, my little serving-maid. Abishag. André Spire. TrJP
O absent presence! Stella is not here. Astrophel and Stella, CVI. Sir Philip Sidney. SiPS
O Abu Talib, rise. Invitation. Al-Mutawakkil. MooP
Oh, aged Time! how far, and long. The Roman Legions. John Mitford. VA
O ah drove three mules foh Gawge McVane. The Mule Skinner's Song. *Unknown.* AS
Oh! Alas, Earth! Apollo, Apollo! The Death of Agamemnon. Aeschylus. *Fr.* Agamemnon. LiA
O Alison [*or* Allison] Gross, that lives in yon towr [*or* tow'r]. Alison [*or* Allison] Gross. *Unknown.* BaBo; CH; ESPB; FaBoCh; OBB

Oh, all day long they flood with song. The Mocking-Birds. Paul Hamilton Hayne. TCAP
Oh, all the ladies of the world. Broom. John Farrar. GFA
Oh all ye, who passe by, whose eyes and minde. The Sacrifice. George Herbert. AtBAP; PoEL-2; ReEn
O all you little blackey tops. Scaring Crows. *Unknown.* BoTP; OxNR
O Altitudo! Sarah N. Cleghorn. PC
O Amber Day, amid the Autumn Gloom. William Talbot Allison. CaP; OCL
Oh, an I were where Gadie rins. Where Gadie Rins. John Park. EBSV
Oh, ancient sin, oh, bathtub gin. Bathtub Gin. Philip H. Rhinelander. WhC
O angel bird, O winged word whom I. The Burden of Everyday. Buddhadeva Bose. LiTW
Oh, Annie, Oh! *with music.* *Unknown.* StDa
O, answer me a question, Love, I pray. The Sweetest Story Ever Told. R. M. Stults. TreFS
O Apple Betty fiend, attend. Lines to a Man Who Thinks That Apple Betty with Hard Sauce Is Food for a Human Being. George S. Kaufman. InMe
O apple blossoms. Japanese Hokku. Lewis Alexander. CDC
O Are Ye Sleeping, Maggie? Robert Tannahill. EBSV; OBRV
Oh, as I walked down the Landing Stage. We're All Bound to Go. *Unknown.* AmSS
Oh, as I went a-walkin' down Ratcliffe 'Ighway,/ I stepped into Paddy West's house. Paddy West. *Unknown.* ShS
Oh, as I went a-walking down Ratcliffe 'Ighway,/ I spied a flash packet. As I Went a-Walking down Ratcliffe Highway, *vers.* II. *Unknown.* ShS
"Oh, Ask Me Not." John Charles McNeill. NoCaPo
O Autumn! Thou hast strewn and heaped our garden bare. Aleksey Konstantinovich Tolstoy, *tr. fr. Russian by* Sir Cecil Kisch. WaL
O babbling spring, than glass more clear. The Fountain of Bandusia [*or* O Fons Bandusiae]. Horace, *tr. by* Austin Dobson. OuHeWo; VA
Oh, Baby Christ, so dear to me. Saint Bride's Lullaby. "Fiona Macleod." BOL; PraNu
O baby, where you been so long? Lord, Lord, Lord, Lord! Levee Moan. *Unknown.* AS
Oh, back in the fall of nineteen-two. "Haec Olim Meminisse Iuvabit." Deems Taylor. InMe
Oh, bad the march, the weary march. Fontenoy, 1745. Emily Lawless. AnIV; PoFr
Oh, band in the pine-wood, cease! The Band in the Pines. John Esten Cooke. AA; SPP
O banner blazoned in the sky. The Flag. Henry C. Potter. FOAH
O-Bar Cowboy. *At. to* Bill Wagon. CoSo
O barber, spare those hairs. Barber, Spare Those Hairs. John Love, Jr. YaD
Oh, be not ether-borne, poet of earth. Poet of Earth. Stephen Henry Thayer. AA
O be swift. The Helmsman. Hilda Doolittle ("H. D."). AnAmPo; LA; MOAP; OxBA
Oh be thou blest with all that Heav'n can send. To Mrs. M. B. on Her Birthday. Pope. CEP; EnLoPo; FaBoEn; MeRV; OBEC
O bear him where the rain can fall. Elegy on William Cobbett. Ebenezer Elliott. VA
O bear me to the paths of fair Pell Mell. The Pell Mell Celebrated. John Gay. *Fr.* Trivia; or, The Art of Walking the Streets of London, II. EnLi-1 (1949 ed.)
O bear me where the streamlets stray. The Wish of the Aged Bard. *Unknown.* EBSV
O beauteous God! uncircumscribèd treasure. Heaven. Jeremy Taylor. LPS-2
O beautiful Amaryllis, why no longer from your cave. Rustic Serenade. Theocritus. *Fr.* Idylls. GrR; OxBG
Oh, beautiful are the flowers of your garden. The Lover Sings of a Garden. Helen Hoyt. NP
O beautiful beneath the magic moon. In the Piazza at Night. Arthur Hugh Clough. *Fr.* At Venice. ViPo
O beautiful for spacious skies. America, the Beautiful. Katharine Lee Bates. AOAH; BLP; BLPA; CP; CV; DD; FaBoBe; FaFP; FaPON; GrCo-1; HBMV; HBVY; HiLiAm; MaRV; MC; MCCG; MPB; MW; NeHB; OBAV; OlF; OQP; OTPC (1946 ed.); PaA; PCH; PEDC; PoRL; POT; PoTo; PSO; QP-1; TreF; WBLP; WGRP; YaD
O Beautiful Forever! I Saw Eternity. Louise Bogan. LiTA; MOAP
O Beautiful, My Country. Frederick L. Hosmer. MaRV; MC; PGD
(Our Country.) PSO
O beautiful my country! Ours once more. My Country. James Russell Lowell. *Fr.* Ode Recited at the Harvard Commemoration. GDAH
O beautiful vision of peace. The Vision of Peace. Nathan Haskell Dole. PSO
O beautiful young dead! Soldier-Dead. Gilbert Emery. PEDC
O Beauty (beams, nay, flame). A Description of Beauty. Giambattista Marini. OBSC
Oh, because you never tried. Because. Sara Teasdale. ChMo; CMP
O bed in my mother's house. Travel's End. May Folwell Hoisington. TBM
O beech, unbind your yellow leaf, for deep. Ghostly Tree. Léonie Adams. MAP; MoAB; MoAmPo; MOAP
Oh, believe I wish you well! Can't You. Gamaliel Bradford. PR
O Bells in the Steeple. May Riley Smith. PCH
Oh, bells that chime your sweetest! A Merry Christmas and a Glad New Year. George Cooper. PEOR
O Bessie Bell and Mary Gray. Bessie [*or* Bessy] Bell and Mary Gray. *Unknown.* BSV; CBOV; EBSV; ESPB; LO; OBB; ViBoFo. *For Mother Goose vers., see* Bessy Bell and Mary Gray.
O, Bethlem town to-night is cold. A Carol for Christmas Day before Dawn. Gordon Bottomley. QS
"O Billie, billie, bonny billie." Bothwell Bridge. *Unknown.* BaBo; ESPB
O Billy Riley, *with music.* *Unknown.* SoAmSa
O Bird at night, who, hearing, could forget. Bird at Night. Marion Ethel Hamilton. GoYe
O Bird, So Lovely. Louis Golding. TrJP
O bird that somewhere yonder sings. To a Bird at Dawn. Richard Le Gallienne. BLA; BMEP
O bird, thou dartest to the sun. Song. Maria White Lowell. AA; LBAP
O birds and stones, rejoice and pray. Saint Francis Weds the Three Maidens. Helene Mullins. SaFP
Oh, Bisham Banks are fresh and fair. A Marlow Madrigal. Joseph Ashby-Sterry. VA
O bitter herb, Forgetfulness. The Bitter Herb. Jeanne Robert Foster. SBMV
O bitter moon, O cold and bitter moon. Eagle Sonnets, IX. Clement Wood. HBMV; NV
O Bitter Sea. William Morris. *Fr.* The Life and Death of Jason, IV. EmBrPo; PoVP
(Song of the Argonauts.) EtS
(To the Sea.) BPN
O bitter wind toward the sunset blowing. The Only Son. Sir Henry Newbolt. HBV
O bitterness never spoken, the death mask etched in silver. Salvos for Randolph Bourne. Horace Gregory. ChMo; NAMP
O Black and Unknown Bards. James Weldon Johnson. BANP; PoNe; StJW; UnS
O blackbird! sing me something well. The Blackbird. Tennyson. OTPC; SN
O Blackbird, what a boy you are! Vespers. T. E. Brown. BLV; BMEP; BoTP; EnLit; MBP; PIAE; VLEP; YT
Oh, blackbird with the shining yellow beak. Secrets. Luisa Hewitt. PCH
Oh, blame me not if I express but ill. Soul, Mind, and Body. Lillah A. Ashley. MuM
Oh Blame Not the Bard. Thomas Moore. OnYI
Oh, Blank Confusion. Wordsworth. *Fr.* The Prelude. AtBAP
Oh, bless the law that veils the future's face. Mimma Bella, VI. Eugene Lee-Hamilton. HBV
Oh! bless'd of Heaven, whom not the languid songs. *See* Oh! blest of heav'n . . .
O blessed Dead! beyond all earthly pains. A Threnody: In Memory of Albert Darasz. William James Linton. VA
Oh blessed drums of Aldershot! The South Wind. Charles Kingsley. EV-5
O blessed freedom of the press! Gentle Reminders. Goethe. PoFr
O blessed God in Trinity. Te Laudamus, Te Dominum. *Unknown.* AnEC
O Blessèd House, That Cheerfully Receiveth. Karl Johann Philipp Spitta, *tr. fr. German by* Charles William Schaeffer. TrPWD
Oh blessed ray. The Joys of the Virgin Mary. Juan Ruiz, Archpriest of Hita. *Fr.* The Book of Good Love. AnSpL-1
O blessedful bird, full of grace. Salve Regina, Mater Misericordie. *Unknown.* AnEC
O blest of all the scattered spots that lie. Home to Sermio. Catullus. OnPM
Oh! blest [*or* bless'd] of heav'n [*or* heaven], whom not the languid songs. Nature's Influence on Man [*or* The Created Universe]. Mark Akenside. *Fr.* The Pleasures of Imagination. CEP; LoBV; OBEC
O Blest Unfabled Incense Tree. George Darley. *See* Phoenix, The.
O Blisful Light. Chaucer. *See* Wooing of Criseide, The.
Oh, blithe and bonny is fair Scotland, where the bluebells gently grow. The Paisley Officer, *vers.* I. *Unknown.* ShS

O blithe new-comer! I have heard. To the Cuckoo. Wordsworth. BCEP; BEL; BLA; BLV; BoLiVe; BoTP; BPN; CoBE; EM-2; EmBrPo; EnLit; EnRP; EPN; EPP; ERP; EV-3; FaFP; FiP; GEPC; GoTP; GTBS; GTBS-D; GTBS-W; GTSE; GTSL; LEAP; LiTG; LoBV; LPS-2; MCCG; OBRV; OTPC; OuHeWo; PIR; ShBV-2; SN; TCEP; TOP; TrGrPo; TVSH; TwHP; WP

Oh blithely [*or* blythely] shines the bonny [*or* bonnie] sun. We'll Go to Sea No More. *Unknown.* ChTr; EtS

O blood-root and hepatica. Blue Hepatica. "John Crichton." CPG

Oh, blow away, I long to hear you. Blow, Boys, Blow, *vers.* I. *Unknown.* ShS

Oh, blow the man down, boys [*or* bullies], blow the man down. Blow the Man Down. *Unknown.* AmSS; PYM; SG; SoAmSa; TrAS

Oh, blow the man down, Johnny, blow him right down. Blow the Man Down, *vers.* III. *Unknown.* ShS

O blue eyes close in slumber. Cradle Song. Caris Brooke. BOL

O Blue Jay up in the maple tree. The Blue Jay. Susan Hartley Swett. PRWS

O blue poplars are in Picardy. Terrae Illuminatae. Robert P. Tristram Coffin. CAG

O blush not so! O blush not so! Sharing Eve's Apple [*or* Eve's Sweet Pippen]. Keats. ChER; RO

Oh blythely shines the bonnie sun. *See* Oh blithely shines the bonny sun.

O bold, majestic downs, smooth, fair and lonely. The Downs. Robert Bridges. EPP; ReTS

Oh, Boney was a warrior. Boney, *vers.* II. *Unknown.* ShS

Oh Boney's on the sea. The Shan Van Vocht. *Unknown.* OxBoLi

O bonnie bird, that in the brake, exultant, dost prepare thee. The Waking of the Lark. Eric Mackay. VA

O bonnie Toshie Norrie. Toshie Norrie. Alexander Anderson. EBSV

O bonny Baby Livingston. Bonny Baby Livingston. *Unknown.* BaBo; ESPB

O bonny, bonny sang the bird. The Unquiet Grave. *Unknown.* EnSB

O born in days when wits were fresh and clear. Flee fro' the Press. Matthew Arnold. *Fr.* The Scholar Gipsy. LH

O bosomed earth, O altar of my prayer. O Zeus, Our Spirit Fails [*or* Prayer for Deliverance]. Aeschylus. *Fr.* Suppliants. GrR; OxBG

Oh, Boston! late with ev'ry pleasure crown'd. Elegy on the Times. John Trumbull. APW

Oh, Boston's a fine town, with ships in the bay. Home, Dearie, Home. *Unknown.* AmSS; SoAmSa

Oh, both my shoes are shiny new. Autobiography. Dorothy Parker. WhC

Oh, bow your head, Tom Dooley. Tom Dooley. *Unknown.* ViBoFo

O bowl that held the hot imprisoned fire. The Skull. Mary E. Fullerton. BoAu

O boy cutting grass. Hitomaro. *Fr.* Manyo Shu. AWP

O Boys! O Boys! Oliver St. John Gogarty. OBMV

O boys, we're goin' for to fight. Way Down in Mexico. *Unknown.* CoSo; CSF

O brant, brant, One is waiting for you. Eskimo String-Figure Chant. E. Hope Kerr, *tr. fr. Eskimo song.* TwCaPo

O Brazil, the Isle of the Blest. Gerald Griffin. ACP (Hy-Brasail, the Isle of the Blest.) BLPA; GTIV

O, breath is sweet, here in this mountain land! Sonnet. Eunice Tietjens. BAP

Oh, Breathe Not His Name. Thomas Moore. AnIL; BEL; CoBE; EnLi-2; EnRP; ERP; HBV; LPS-3; PIR; TreFS

Oh! breathe upon this hapless world. Ode to Peace. *Unknown.* PAH

"O brent's your brow, my Lady Elspat." Lady Elspat. *Unknown.* ESPB; OBB

O bretheren, my way. My Way's Cloudy. *Unknown.* BoAN-1

O briar-scents, on yon wet wing. Breath of the Briar. George Meredith. EG; POTT

O brief and breathing creature, wilt thou cease. Stephen Phillips. *Fr.* Marpessa. BMEP; LEAP

O brightness of my bright eyes, how art thou? On the Death of His Child. Faydi. LiTW

O, Brignall banks are wild and fair. Brignall Banks [*or* The Outlaw *or* Edmund's Song *or* Song]. Sir Walter Scott. *Fr.* Rokeby, III. BCEP; BEL; BPN; EBSV; EmBrPo; EnLi-2; EnRP; EPN; ERP; EV-4; GTBS; GTBS-D; GTBS-W; GTSE; GTSL; HBV; LH; OAEP; OBEV; OBRV; OtMeF; PCN; PoRA; TOP; TyEnPo

O bring a gift along. A Song of Cash. *Unknown.* LyMA

Oh, Bring Not Gold! Violet Alleyn Storey. SDH

O broad-breasted Queen among nations! Boston. John Boyle O'Reilly. PAH

O Brooding Spirit. Sir William Rowan Hamilton. *See* Spirit of Wisdom and of Love.

O brother, brother! are men always men? The Corruption of Power. Walter Savage Landor. *Fr.* Antony and Octavius. RO

Oh, Brother Christ, come play with me. The Christ-Child [*or* The Christ Child's Christmas]. Laura Spencer Portor. PEDC; StJW

O brother, lift a cry, a long world cry. Peace. Edwin Markham. PGD; WBLP

O Brother Man. Whittier. MaRV

O brother men, who live on after us. Villon's Epitaph in Ballade Form. Villon. FoS

O Brother Planets, unto whom I cry. Isolation. Josephine Preston Peabody. AA; AnAmPo; LA

O Brother Tree. Max Michelson. NP; TrJP

O brother, what is there to say. Ernest Dowson. John Hall Wheelock. HBMV

O brothers mine, take care! Take care! The White Witch. James Weldon Johnson. BANP; CDC

O brothers mine, today we stand. Fifty Years, 1863–1913. James Weldon Johnson. BANP; PoFr; PoNe

O brothers who live on while we be dead. The Epitaph in the Form of a Ballade That Villon Made for Himself and His Fellows, Expecting to Be Hanged with Them. Villon. TrFP

O brothers, who must ache and stoop. To My Brothers. Norman Gale. VA

O brown brook, O blithe brook, what will you say to me. Water Fantasy. Fannie Stearns Davis. LBMV

O Bruadair. James Stephens. *See* O'Bruidar.

Oh, bubbles of the vanished wine. L'Envoi. *Unknown.* DDA

O Bury Me Beneath the Willow, *with music.* *Unknown.* AS

Oh, bury me beside my knife and six-shooter. Dodge City, the End of the Trail. *Unknown.* CoSo

"Oh, bury me not in the deep, deep sea." The Ocean Burial. Edwin H. Chapin. ShS; ViBoFo

O Bury Me Not on the Lone Prairie. *Unknown.* *See* Dying Cowboy, The ("Oh, bury me not . . .").

O, but how white is white, white from shadows come. Music of Colours: The Blossom Scattered. Vernon Watkins. LiTB; PoN

Oh, but life went gayly, gayly. In the House of Idiedaily. Bliss Carman. BoCaPo; OBVV; PFY

Oh, but my husband, Matthew. Splendid Isolation. Katharine Lee Bates. LHV

Oh! but my mind is weary! The Summer's Revel. Pierre de Ronsard. Odes, II, 18. PrPoCR; WoL

Oh but, says one, tradition set aside. Tradition. Dryden. *Fr.* Religio Laici. OBS; PoLi

Oh, but she was dark and shrill. Nursery Rhymes à la Mode. *Unknown.* BOHV; PA

O but there is wisdom. Consolation. W. B. Yeats. TwP

O, by an' by, by an' by. By an' By. *Unknown.* BoAN-1

O By the By. E. E. Cummings. OxBA

Oh, by Thy cross and passion, by Thy pain. Litany. Marie LeNart. ChIP

"O Caesar, we who are about to die." Morituri Salutamus. Longfellow. CoBA; IAP

O Caledonia! stern and wild. Scotland. Sir Walter Scott. *Fr.* The Lay of the Last Minstrel, VI. BSV; LPS-2

Oh, call my brother back to me. The [Child's] First Grief. Felicia Dorothea Hemans. BLPA; CH; NeHB

O call not me to justify the wrong. Sonnets, CXXXIX. Shakespeare. PeBoSo; ReIE

O calm, yellow-haired girl, all gold is the burden on thy head. A Reproach to Morvyth. Dafydd ab Gwilym. LiTW

O cam ye in by the House o Rodes. John Thomson and the Turk (B *vers.*). *Unknown.* ESPB

"Oh, came ye ower by the Yoke-burn Ford." Jock Johnstone, the Tinkler. James Hogg. BCEP; LPS-2

O camel in the zoo. Camel. Mary Britton Miller. TiPo (1959 ed.); UTS

O camp of flowers, with poplars girded round. Memory. Erik Johan Stagnelius. AWP

O, can ye sew cushions? Can Ye Sew Cushions? *Unknown.* BOL; FaBoCh; LoGBV

Oh, Cape Cod girls are very fine girls. Cape Cod Girls. *Unknown.* TrAS

Oh, Cape Cod girls they have no combs. Cape Cod Girls. *Unknown.* AmSS

O Captain! My Captain! Walt Whitman. *Fr.* Memories of President Lincoln. AA; AmPP (3d ed.); AnFE; APA; APW; BAP; BAV; BBV (1923 ed.); BIG; BoLiVe; BTP; CBOV; CBE; CoAnAm; CoBA; CV; DD; DDA; EV-5; FaBoBe; FaBoCh; FaFP; FaPON; GA; GN; GTBS; GTBS-W; HBV; HBVY; HH; HiLiAm; IAP; InP; LaNeLa; LBAH; LEAP; LiTA; LiTG; LoGBV; MAP; MaRV; MC; MDAH; MoAmPo; MOAP; MPB; NeHB; NeMA; NePA; OBAV; OBEV; OHFP; OHIP; OQP; OTPC; OuHeWo; PaA; PAH; PAP; PCD; PCN; PECK; PEDC; PG (1945 ed.); PIR; Po; PoeMoYo; PoFr; PoRL; PTA-1; PYM; QP-1; REAL; RG; SG; StaSt; StVeCh; TCAP; TOP; TreF; TrGrPo; TSW; TSWC; TVSH; WP; YT (To Abraham Lincoln.) CBE

O Captain of the wars, whence won Ye so great scars? The Veteran of Heaven. Francis Thompson. ChIP; HBV; MaRV; PoLi
Oh, Captain of wide western seas. San Gloria. "Tom Redcam." PoNe
O Carib Isle! Hart Crane. MoPo; NePA; OnHM
O Carpenter of Nazareth. Upon This Rock. Robert Whitaker. ChIP
O carrion-eaters, O presumptuous ones. To Certain Men of Science. Kimball Flaccus. CAG
O Cartmel bells ring soft tonight. New Year's Eve, 1913. Gordon Bottomley. BMEP; LBBV
O Cat of Carlish Kind. John Skelton. *See* Tragedy of the Sparrow and the Cursing of the Cat, The.
O Catch Miss Daisy Pinks. Alistair Campbell. AnNZ
O caves, and you, O springs. Odes, IV, 4. Pierre de Ronsard. PrPoCR
O caves of the Nymphs fresh-flowing, that scatter from your fountains. Hunter's Thanksgiving. Crinagoras. GrPE
Oh, cease, my wandering soul. Fulfillment. William A. Muhlenberg. WGRP
O Cedar-tree, Cedar, my mother. Song of Basket-weaving. Constance Lindsay Skinner. AnAmPo; LA
O Celius! think, our Lesbia, once your pride. Lesbia's Disgrace. Catullus. OnPM
O chansons foregoing. Epilogue. Ezra Pound. OxBA
Oh, Charley, he's a nice [*or* fine] young man. Weevily Wheat. *Unknown.* ABF; AS
O Charmian, I will never go from hence. The Deaths of Antony and Cleopatra. Shakespeare. *Fr.* Antony and Cleopatra, IV, xiii. CBOV
O Chatterton! how very sad thy fate! To Chatterton. Keats. PtP
O child, had I thy lease of time! such unimagined things. A Child of To-Day. James Buckham. AA
O Child of Beauty Rare. Goethe, *tr. fr. German by* William E. Aytoun. ISi
O child of nations, giant-limbed. Canada. Sir Charles G. D. Roberts. BoCaPo; PeCV; PoFr; VA
O children of men, O sons and daughters of sorrow. Song for Tomorrow. Lucia Trent. PGD
O chillen, run, de Conjuh man. De Conjuh Man. James Edwin Campbell. BANP
O Chloe, why wish you that your years. To Chloe. William Cartwright. OBEV
O Christ, great Lover of all souls. Thy Kingdom Come! Thomas Curtis Clark. ChIP
O Christ my Lord and King. Thy Kingdom Come. A. B. Simpson. BePJ
O Christ, my Lord, which for my sins didst hang upon a tree. Though Here in Flesh I Be [*or* Through Thy Cross and Passion]. Philip Howard. CoBE; PoLi
O Christ of Calvary, This Lent. Alice Mortenson. BePJ
O Christ of God! whose life and death. Vesta. Whittier. OBEV (1st ed.); TrPWD; WHA
O Christ of Olivet, you hushed the wars. Edwin Markham. *Fr.* The Christ of the Andes. TrPWD
O Christ, the glorious Crown. Hymn. Philip Howard. ACP; CAW
O Christ, the Way. George L. Squier. MaRV
O Christ, they took Your living words. Walls. Myriam Page. ChIP
O Christ Thou Art within Me like a Sea. Edith Lovejoy Pierce. MaRV; TrPWD
O Christ, Who Died. John Calvin Slemp. ChIP; TrPWD
O Christ who holds the open gate. The Ploughman. John Masefield. *Fr.* The Everlasting Mercy. AtBAP; TreFS
O Christ, who mountest up the sky. Ascension Hymn. Jean Batiste de Santeuil. CAW
Oh, Christmas is a jolly time. A Christmas Song. Florence Evelyn Dratt. MaRV; SDH
Oh! Christmas is coming again, you say. A Christmas Thought. Lucy Larcom. PEOR
O Christmas, merry Christmas! Bells across the Snow. Frances Ridley Havergal. COAH
Oh Christmas, that your Gift of Gifts might be. Noel! Noel! Laura Simmons. PGD; PSO
Oh! Christmas time is coming again. Emily Jane. Laura E. Richards. RIS
O Church of God. Rolland W. Schloerb. MaRV
O Church of God triumphant, above the world's dark fears. Church Triumphant. S. Ralph Harlow. MaRV
O Chu-tzu! Spring returns, and we are still separated. To My Youngest Son. Tu Fu. WhP
O cities of Euphrates! Ages. Friedrich Hölderlin. OnPM
O cities, you have nudged at their velvet flanks. The Deer Come Down, II. Edward Weismiller. MuM
O City, Cities! *sel.* R. Ellsworth Larsson. "No city shall I call my own." AnAmPo; LA
O City, Look the Eastward Way. Enid Derham. BoAu
O city metropole, isle riverain! Montreal. A. M. Klein. CaP
O city of light and song, town of the violet crown. Athens. Pindar. GrPE
O city of the world, with sacred splendor blest. Longing for Jerusalem. Judah Halevi. TrJP
O clinging hands, and eyes where sleep has set. Mater Dolorosa. Louis V. Ledoux. BAP; SBMV
O clipper ships! where are, where are ye now? Clipper Ships. John Anderson. EtS
O close your bright eyes, brown child of the forest. Hazeleye's Lullaby. Chief Simon Pokagon. BOL
O cloud, the parching spirit stirs thy pity. Kalidasa. *Fr.* The Cloud-Messenger. LiTW
O Columbia, the gem of the ocean. Columbia, the Gem of the Ocean [*or* Red, White and Blue]. David T. Shaw. FaBoBe; FOAH; OlF; WBLP
Oh, come again to Astolat! Elaine. Edna St. Vincent Millay. AV; BAP; LEAP; PoeMoYo; TBM
O come, all my young lovers. The Unconstant Lover. *Unknown.* TrAS
O Come, All Ye Faithful. *Unknown, at. to* St. Bonaventure, *tr. fr. Latin by* Frederick Oakeley. FaFP; OlF; SDH; TreFS; YaCaBo
(Adeste Fideles.) CAW; MaRV; WGRP; WHL, *2 sts.*
Oh, come all ye true bold raftsmen, and friends both far and near. Whalen's Fate. *Unknown.* ShS
"O come and be my mate!" said the eagle to the hen. Wedded Bliss. Charlotte Perkins Gilman. HBV
Oh, come and go, you almost child, entrancing. Rainer Maria Rilke. *Fr.* Sonnets to Orpheus. UnS
O come and take thou me/ Beneath thy wing. Beneath Thy Wing. Hayyim Nahman Bialik. TrJP
Oh, come, cowboys, and listen to my song! The U-S-U Range. *At. to* G. W. Barr. CoSo; CSF
O come, let us sing unto the Lord. Psalm XCV, Bible, *O.T.* AWP; BLRP; BoChLi (1950 ed.); JAWP; OHIP; OnPM; OuHeWo; PC
Oh, come let us welcome sweet Sabbath the Queen! Welcome, Queen Sabbath. Zalman Schneour. TrJP
O, come, list awhile, and you soon shall hear. The Female Smuggler. *Unknown.* AmSS
Oh come, my darkness. My Darkness. Rose O'Neill. TBM
Oh, come my joy, my soldier boy. Ballad. Henry Treece. WaP
Oh, come, my lad, or go, my lad. The Betrothal. Edna St. Vincent Millay. NP; PG
O Come, O Come, Emmanuel, *with music.* *Unknown.* YaCaBo
O come, our Lord and Saviour. Table Graces, or Prayers. *Unknown.* BLRP
O Come Out of the Lily. Ruth Pitter. AnFE
(Come Out of the Lily.) MeRV
O Come Quickly! Thomas Campion. *See* Never Weather-beaten Sail.
O come, soft rest of cares! come, Night! Bridal Song [*or* Song *or* Come, Night]. George Chapman. BCEP; EG; OBEV; OnPM; ViBoPo
O come sweet death, sang Bach. Horn. James Hayford. NePoAm-2
O come to Masonborough's grove. Piece upon Masonborough. Thomas Godfrey. NoCaPo
Oh, Come to Me When Daylight Sets. Thomas Moore. EnRP
O come to the garden, dear brother, and see. Snow. Jane Taylor. OTPC (1923 ed.); PCH; PPL
O! Come to the Greenwood Shade. Alexander McLachlan. PeCV
Oh come! unseen a flute sighs. The Song That Lovers Sing. Victor Hugo. TrFP
Oh, come where the cyanides silently flow. The Chemist to His Love. *Unknown.* BOHV
Oh, come with me in my little canoe. Ossian's Serenade [*or* The Burman Lover]. Calder Campbell. BLPA; NeHB; TrAS
O Comes Amoris, Dolor. *Unknown, tr. fr. Latin by* George F. Whicher. *Fr.* Carmina Burana. LaP
O comrades. Poem for the Living. Harold Andrew. TwCaPo
O comrades, on each lonely grave we place one flower to-day. The Red, the White, the Blue. Kate B. Sherwood. PEOR
Oh, concerning of some gentlemen who lived down below. Hog Rogues on the Harricane. *Unknown.* OuSiCo
O Contemporaries. Louis Dudek. TwCaPo
O cool in the summer is salad. Salad. Mortimer Collins. ALV; BOHV
O cork that stoppered the strong iodine. The Cork. Vladislav Felitsyanovich Khodasevich. TrRV
Oh! could I acquire my fullest desire. My Wishes. Patrick Healy. OnYI
Oh! could I hope the wise and pure in heart. Hymn to Death. Bryant. IAP
O could I tell ye surely would believe it! Experience. Frederic W. H. Myers. *Fr.* Saint Paul. MaRV
Oh, could I worship aught beneath the skies. Address to Liberty. William Cowper. IDAH
Oh, could we know with disencumbered eyes. Ideal Passion, XX. George Edward Woodberry. MOAP

Oh country, fair and grand. The Patriot Hymn. Nathan Haskell Dole. PaA
O courteous Christ—kind guest, most gracious host. To a Crucifix. Anna Wickham. MBP; MoBrPo
O cricket, from your cheery cry. Basho, *tr. fr. Japanese by* Curtis Hidden Page. AWP; JAWP; LiTW; PFE; WBP
"O crikey, Bill!" she ses to me, she ses. Culture in the Slums. W. E. Henley. BOHV; CenHV; HBV; InMe; PA
O crucified Son of God, I pray. An Easter Prayer. Chester M. Davis. PraP
O Crudelis Amor. Thomas Campion. *See* When Thou Must Home.
O cruel Alexis, don't you care for my songs? Corydon. Virgil. Eclogues, II. RoL
O cruel cloudless space. Nativity. May Sarton. NePoAm-2
"O cruel Death, give three things back." Three Things. W. B. Yeats. AtBAP; FaBoEn; OBMV
O cruel Love! on thee I lay. Sapho's Song. John Lyly. *Fr.* Sapho and Phao. OBSC
O cruel manger, how bleak, how bleak! The Babe of Bethlehem. Condé Benoist Pallen. JKCP
Oh, cruel off St. Andrews Bay. For Scotland. Robert Fuller Murray. BSV
O Cruel Still. Horace, *tr. fr. Latin by* Philip Francis. OnPM
Oh! cruel were my parents as tore my love from me. *Unknown.* LO
O crystal Well. Minnie. Thomas Caulfield Irwin. IrPN
O cuckoo. *Unknown. Fr.* Kokin Shu. AWP
O cuckoo, once your song was loud and gay. To a Run-away Pupil. Alcuin. LyMA
O Cuckoo! shall I call thee bird. To the Cuckoo. F. H. Townsend. ChTr
O cuckoo troubling yonder hill. The Cuckoo. Richard Le Gallienne. BLA; LBBV
O cunning thief, to rifle. The Stolen Penknife. Ibn Sa'id of Alcala la Real. MooP
O Cupid! Monarch over Kings. John Lyly. *Fr.* Mother Bombie. ElL; SiCE
(Fools in Love's College.) TrGrPo
(Love's Schooling.) BLV
(Song of Accius and Silena.) OBSC
O curfew of the setting sun! O Bells of Lynn! The Bells of Lynn. Longfellow. AA
Oh curves, meanderings. Insinuation. Paul Valéry. AnFP
Oh, cut me reeds to blow upon. Tampico. Grace Hazard Conkling. HBMV; NV; SBMV
ODV. *Unknown.* BOHV
O Daedalus Fly Away Home. Robert E. Hayden. PoNe
O daffodils, come out, I pray. Daffodils. *Unknown.* SUS
O dainty gland, whose lobulated grace. To the Parotid Gland. —— Schlesinger. WhC
Oh Danaan brethren. At My Whisper. Lyle Donaghy. AnIV
O Dandelion. *Unknown. See* Dandelion, The ("O dandelion").
O dandelion, rich and haughty. The Dandelion. Vachel Lindsay. BrR
"O dandelion, yellow as gold." The [*or* O] Dandelion. *Unknown.* BoTP; PCH
O dappled throat of white! Shy, hidden bird! The Lonely-Bird. Harrison Smith Morris. AA; SN
O Dark, Dark, Dark, *abr.* Milton. *Fr.* Samson Agonistes. WHA
("O wherefore was my birth from heaven foretold.") AnFE
"O Dark, Dark, Dark amid the Blaze of Noon." Sophocles, *tr. fr. Greek by* John Swinnerton Phillimore. *Fr.* Oedipus Rex. GrR
O dark-haired girl, let us now. From an Irish-Latin Macaronic. Geoffrey Taylor. NeIP
O dark of the earth, O God. Guilt! Euripides. *Fr.* Electra. GrR
O darkling river! Through the night I hear. The Night Journey of a River. Bryant. PEOR
Oh! "darkly, deeply, beautifully blue." Learned Ladies. Byron. *Fr.* Don Juan, IV. GEPC
O darlin', you can't love but one. Darlin'. *Unknown.* ABF
"O daughter of Helios, Moon of many turnings, nurse of all!" Nonnos. *Fr.* Dionysiaca. GrPo
O daughter of Pelias. To Alcestis. Euripides. *Fr.* Alcestis. OxBG
O daughters of Renata. To the Princesses of Ferrara. Tasso. LyPI
O David, highest in the list. Christopher Smart. *Fr.* A Song to David. OxBoCh
O David, if I had/ Your power. That Harp You Play so Well. Marianne Moore. HBMV; MAP; MoAB; MoAmPo; NP; NV; TBM; TCPD
O dawn upon me slowly, paradise! Come Slowly, Paradise. James Benjamin Kenyon. AA
"O day! he cannot die." A Death-Scene. Emily Brontë. EmBrPo; EV-5
O day most calm, most bright. Sunday. George Herbert. EPS; OBSC; SeCV-1; SeEP
O day of days! shall hearts set free. Easter Day. John Keble. EOAH
O day of gladness, O feast of glory. The New America. Aleksandr Blok. BoRS
O Day of Rest and Gladness. Christopher Wordsworth. MaRV; OlF; WGRP
O day of roses and regret. Memorial Day. Louise Imogen Guiney. DD; MDAH
O day of woe!/ They have left the camp. Hour of National Emergency. Aeschylus. *Fr.* Seven against Thebes. GrR
O! day thrice lovely! when at length the soldier. The Soldier's Return. Samuel Taylor Coleridge. BHV
O days and hours, your work is this. In Memoriam A. H. H., CXVII. Tennyson. BEL; EmBrPo; EnLi-2; EPN; GEPC; HBV; LPS-1; MaPo; OAEP; TCEP; ViPo; VLEP
Oh, days of beauty standing veiled apart. Prevision. Ada Foster Murray. HBV; LBAP
Oh, de band o' Gideon. De Band o' Gideon. *Unknown.* BoAN-1
O, de birds ar' sweetly singin'. 'Weh down Souf. Daniel Webster Davis. BANP
O de black cat cotch old Sambo Lee. De Black Cat Crossed His Luck. James D. Corrothers. CIV
O, de blin' man stood on de road an' cried. De Blin' Man Stood on de Road an' Cried. *Unknown.* BoAN-1
Oh, de boats on de ribber. Alabama Bound. *Unknown.* SoAF
Oh, de boll weevil am a li'l [*or* little] black bug. The Boll Weevil Song [*or* The Ballad of the Boll Weevil]. *Unknown.* APW; AS; SoAF; SPP; TrAS
O de Glory Road! O de Glory Road! De Glory Road. Clement Wood. BAP; HBMV; IHA; PFY; YaD
Oh, de good ole chariot swing so low. Swing Low, Sweet Chariot. *Unknown.* AA
Oh, de grubbin' hoe's a-rustin' in de co'nah. The Deserted Plantation. Paul Laurence Dunbar. IHA
Oh, de hearse keep a-rollin'. I Feel Like My Time Ain't Long. *Unknown.* OuSiCo
O, de light-bugs glimmer down de lane. Negro Serenade. James Edwin Campbell. BANP
Oh, de Lo'd says to Noah. Climb to Glory. *Unknown.* SoAF
O, de ol' ark's a-moverin. De Ol' Ark's a-Moverin' an' I'm Goin' Home. *Unknown.* BoAN-2
Oh, de ol' sheep done know de road. De Ol' Sheep Done Know de Road. *Unknown.* BoAN-2
O! de sun quit a-shinin' fo' dis arternoon. A Dixie Lullaby. T. A. Daly. BOL
Oh, de weathah it is balmy an' de breeze is sighin' low. Li'l' Gal. Paul Laurence Dunbar. GoSl
Oh, de white gal ride in a automobile. De Black Gal. *Unknown.* ABF
O' de wurl' ain't flat. Northboun'. Ariel Williams Holloway. BANP; CDC; GoSl; PoNe
Oh, de yaller, muddy, lazy, ol' Savannah. Savannah River. Roselle Mercier Montgomery. LS
Oh! Dear! *Unknown. See* Oh! Dear! What Can the Matter Be?
O dear and loving God. Prayer for Living and Dying. Christopher La Farge. TrPWD
Oh, dear beyond our dearest dreams. Outland Fare. "Lewis Carroll." *Fr.* Sylvie and Bruno. BoN
O Dear Dark Head, bowed low in death-black sorrow. Dear Dark Head. William Rooney. JKCP (1926 ed.)
O Dear Life, When Shall It Be? Sir Philip Sidney. *Fr.* Astrophel and Stella: Tenth Song. SiPS
Oh dear love tokens that did work me harm. Sonnet. Garcilaso de la Vega. TeCS
O Dear Me! Walter de la Mare. TiPo
Oh! Dear! What Can the Matter Be? *Unknown.* LiTL; LO; OlF; OTPC; OxNR
("Dear, dear! what can the matter be?") PPL
(Oh! Dear!) CH; PCD
O dearer far than light and life are dear. To ——. Wordsworth. ERP
O dearest, canst thou tell me why. Warum sind denn die Rosen so blass. Heine. AWP; JAWP; WBP
O dearest maidens, tread with feet of wool. Euripides. *Fr.* Orestes. GrPo
O dearly-bought revenge, yet glorious! Heroic Vengeance. Milton. *Fr.* Samson Agonistes. OBS; TwHP
O dearly loved land. The Lover of His Country. Andreas Calvos. MoGP
O Death. Ecclesiasticus, XLI: 1-4, Bible, Apocrypha (*Moulton, Modern Reader's Bible*). TrJP
(On Death—a Sonnet.) MaRV
O Death, *with music. Unknown.* TrAS
O Death,/ How bitter is the remembrance of thee. O Death [*or* On Death—a Sonnet]. Ecclesiasticus, Bible, Apocrypha (*Moulton, Modern Reader's Bible*). MaRV; TrJP
O Death, Rock Me Asleep. *At. to* George Boleyn, *also to* Anne Boleyn. EG; ElL; ElSeCe; TrGrPo; TuPP

O Death, Rock Me Asleep (*continued*)
(Death.) OBSC
(O Death, Rock Me on Sleep.) ChTr
O Death, That Maketh Life So Sweet. William Morris. *Fr.* The Life and Death of Jason, XII. EmBrPo; PoVP; ViPo; VLEP
(Orpheus' Song of Triumph.) BPN
O Death! thou victor of the human frame! Elegy to the Memory of My Beloved Friend, Mr. Thomas Godfrey. Nathaniel Evans. IAP
O Death, when thou shalt come to me. Strong as Death. H. C. Bunner. HBV; LBAP; OBAV
Oh! Death Will Find Me. Rupert Brooke. *See* Sonnet: "Oh, Death will find me, long before I tire."
O deep, creating Light. Eagle Song. Gordon Bottomley. *Fr.* Suilven and the Eagle. MBP; MoBrPo
O Deep of Heaven, 'tis thou alone art boundless. The Night Sky. Sir Charles G. D. Roberts. VA
O deep unlovely brooklet, moaning slow. The Brooklet. David Gray. EnSW
O Deirdré, terrible child. The Druid Song of Cathvah. John Todhunter. TIP
Oh, delicate white apple-bloom. Apple Blossoms. Ludvig Holstein. BoDS
Oh! Dem Golden Slippers. James A. Bland. GoSl; OlF
O Desolate Eves [along the Way, How Oft]. Christopher Brennan. BoAV; CoBE; MM
O destined Land, unto thy citadel. George Edward Woodberry. *Fr.* My Country. AA
O Deus, Ego Amo Te. *Unknown, at. to* St. Francis Xavier, *tr. fr. Latin by* Gerard Manley Hopkins. LaP; PoLi; TrPWD
Oh, dewy was the morning, upon the first of May. Manila. Eugene Fitch Ware. BOHV; FiBHP; InMe; YaD
Oh, dey whupped him up de hill. Never Said a Mumbalin' Word. *Unknown.* ABF; TrAS
O did ye ever hear o' brave Earl Brand? Earl Brand. *Unknown.* OBB
Oh did you go to see the show. The Orange Lily O. *Unknown.* IrPN
Oh! did you ne'er hear of Kate Kearney? Kate Kearney. Lady Morgan. BLPA; FaBoBe; NeHB
O did you see a troop go by. The Camp within the West. Roderic Quinn. BoAu
O did you see him in the street, dressed up in army-blue. Re-enlisted. Lucy Larcom. MDAH
Oh, did you see him riding down. Riding Down. Nora Perry. AA; HBV; OBAV
O Dieu, purifiez nos coeurs! Night Litany. Ezra Pound. ChMo; CMP; MM; TwCV
O dim delicious heaven of dreams. John Francis O'Donnell. *Fr.* Reminiscences of a Day. IrPN
Oh! Dinna Ask Me Gin I Lo'e Thee. John Dunlop. *See* Dinna Ask Me.
Oh, dip some 'taters down in grease. 'Possum Time Again. John Charles McNeill. NoCaPo
Oh, dis is de day we pick on de banjo. Gimme de Banjo. *Unknown.* ShS
O distaff, thou the spinner's friend, grey-eyed Athene's gift to dames. Gift-Card Enclosed. Theocritus. *Fr.* Idylls. GrR
O distant Christ, the crowded, darkening years. Doubt. Margaret Deland. MaRV; PraP; TrPWD
O divine air! Breezes on swift bird-wings. Aeschylus. *Fr.* Prometheus Bound. OxBG
O diviner air. Song. Tennyson. *Fr.* The Sisters. BPN
O divinest star of heaven! Prayer to Venus. John Fletcher. *Fr.* The Mad Lover. SeCL
Oh, do, my Johnny Boker. Johnny Boker. *Unknown.* AmSS
Oh do [*or* doe] not die, for I shall hate. A Fever [*or* Feaver]. John Donne. EnLP; EPS
O do not grieve, Dear Heart, nor shed a tear. Margaret Cavendish, Duchess of Newcastle. EnLoPo
O Do Not Prize Thy Beauty. *Unknown.* *See* Do Not, Oh, Do Not Prize.
O do not use me/ After my sinnes. Sighs and Grones. George Herbert. AtBAP; PoEL-2
O, Do Not Wanton [with Those Eyes]. Ben Jonson. EV-2; LPS-1
(Song: "O, do not wanton . . .") EPS; HBV; OBS; ReEn
O! Do You Hear the Rain. Olive Custance. LEAP
O do you know old Reuben Ranzo? Reuben Ranzo. *Unknown.* SG
Oh, do you remember Sweet Betsy from Pike. *See* Oh, don't you remember . . .
O doe not goe from us and bring. *Unknown.* SeCSL
O doe not melt thyselfe in vaine. *Unknown.* SeCSL
O dog-wood tree. Incantations. Annie Charlotte Dalton. CPG
O Domine Deus! Speravi in te. Prayer before Execution. Mary, Queen of Scots. CAW; WGRP
O Donall Oge, if you go across the sea. Donall Oge; Grief of a Girl's Heart. *Unknown.* OnYI; OxBI
O don't be sorrowful, darling! Don't Be Sorrowful, Darling [*or* Faith and Hope]. Rembrandt Peale. HBV; LPS-1
Oh! Don't You Remember Sweet Alice. Thomas Dunn English. *See* Ben Bolt.
Oh, don't you [*or* do you] remember sweet Betsy from Pike. Betsy [*or* Sweet Betsy] from Pike. *Unknown.* AmPP (4th ed.); AS; BaBo; CSF; OxBoLi; SoAF; TrAS; ViBoFo
Oh! don't you see the turtle-dove. The Turtle Dove. *Unknown.* LO; OxBoLi
O dotards both, most easily seduced from wisdom's train. Aristophanes. *Fr.* Plutus. GrPo
O down in the orchard. Apple Harvest. Helen Leuty. BoTP
Oh dragon,/ you who rule the shoreless sea of death. The Shoreless Sea. Li Hung-chang. ChLP
O Dreams, O Destinations. C. Day Lewis. MoPo
Sonnet: "To travel like a bird, lightly to view," *sel.* ChMP
"Oh, dreamy autumn days!" An Autumn Change. Charles Sangster. *Fr.* The Happy Harvesters. BoCaPo
O Dreamy, Gloomy, Friendly Trees! Herbert Trench. ADAH; BMEP; GTIV; NLK; PoeT
(Trees, The.) POTE
O dreamy one, that I may plunge. Another Fan (of Mademoiselle Mallarmé). Stéphane Mallarmé. AnFP
"O dreary life," we cry, "O dreary life!" Patience Taught by Nature. Elizabeth Barrett Browning. OxBoCh
Oh! *drimin donn dilis!* the landlord has come. Drimin Donn Dilis. John Walsh. TIP
Oh drinking deep of slumber's holy wine. To an Infant Sleeping. Richard Chenevix Trench. BOL
Oh, Duke see the tie pile an' Duke git mad. Duke See the Tie Pile. *Unknown.* StDa
O Duty,/ Why hast thou not the visage of a sweetie or a cutie? Kind of an Ode to Duty. Ogden Nash. TrGrPo; UnPo (3d ed.); WhC
O d'you hear the seas complainin', and complainin', while it's rainin'? The Doom-Bar. Alice E. Gillington. ReTS; VA
"O Earl Rothes, an thou wert mine." Earl Rothes. *Unknown.* BaBo; ESPB
Oh, Earlier Shall the Rosebuds Blow. William Johnson Cory. HBV
O early one morning I walked out like Agag. The Streets of Laredo. Louis MacNeice. ChTr
O Earth! Richard Realf. *See* World, The.
O earth-and-autumn of the setting sun. Indian Summer. William Ellery Leonard. *Fr.* Two Lives, Pt. III. AnAmPo; HBMV; LA; MOAP; MuM; NP; NV; PG (1945 ed.); SBMV
O Earth! Art Thou Not Weary? Julia C. R. Dorr. AA
O Earth, How Like to Heav'n. Milton. *Fr.* Paradise Lost, IX. MaPo
O earth, I count the praises. Praise of Earth. Elizabeth Barrett Browning. OBVV
O Earth, I will have none of thee. The Heart's Low Door. Susan Mitchell. HBMV
Oh Earth, I wonder if your trees and flowers. The Dreamers of Death. Julia Cooley Altrocchi. MuM
O Earth, Lie Heavily upon Her Eyes. Christina Rossetti. *See* Rest.
O Earth, O dewy mother, breathe on us. A Prayer. Archibald Lampman. TrPWD
O Earth, Sufficing All Our Needs. Sir Charles G. D. Roberts. CaP; CPG; OCL
O Earth! thou hast not any wind that blows. The World [*or* The Ever-Present Spirit *or* The Word]. Richard Realf. *Fr.* Symbolisms. AA; AnEnPo; GrCo-1; MaRV; OBAV; UnW; WGRP
O Earth! throughout thy borders. Easter Carol. George Newell Lovejoy. ChIP; DD; EOAH; OHIP; OQP; PGD; PSO; QP-1
O Earth, unhappy planet born to die. Epitaph for the Race of Man, IV. Edna St. Vincent Millay. AmP
O Earth, who daily kissed His feet. Holy Saturday. John Banister Tabb. MaRV; StJW
Oh, East is East, and West is West, and never the twain shall meet. The Ballad of East and West. Kipling. AnFE; BBV (1951 ed.); BEL; BeLS; BoFr; BPN; ChMo; CP; FaBoBe; HBV; HiLiEn; LBBV; LH; MaC; MaRV; PIR; POT; PoTo; PoVP; PTA-2; PYM; ShGoBo; TCEP; TSW; TSWC; VA
Oh, Easter anthems gladly sing. Easter Day. Josephine Rice Creelman. EOAH
Oh ecstasy of bliss! Ecstasy of Bliss. Jorge Guillén. CoSP
O ecstasy of the remembering heart. Ideal Passion, XXXIV. George Edward Woodberry. MOAP
O Einisheen O Dhua, your woman's voice is calling me. The Nun. Shiel MacDara. PraNu
Oh, Eleazar Wheelock was a very pious man. Eleazar Wheelock. Richard Hovey. LauV; WhC
O embittered joy. Fiend's Weather. Louise Bogan. MoVE
O Empress high, celestial Queen most rare. Ballad of Our Lady. William Dunbar. ISi

O empty cross, portentous against the sky. In Him Ye Are Made Full. William H. Hudnut, Sr. ChIP
Oh, England!/ Sick in head and sick in heart. England. *Unknown.* SeCL
O England, Country of My Heart's Desire. E. V. Lucas. BoTP
Oh, England is a pleasant place for them that's rich and high. The Last [*or* Old] Buccaneer [*or* The Pleasant Isle of Aves]. Charles Kingsley. BeLS; CBPC; EtS; EV-5; FaBoBe; GoTP; HBV; LH; MCCG; MoShBr; PoVP; SG; ShBV-1; VA
O English mother, in the ruddy glow. In Snow. William Allingham. IrPN
Oh Erasistratus forbear. George L. Walton. *Fr.* Erasistratus Forbear. PoP
O Eros, all-subduing. To Eros. Anacreon, *tr. by* John Ounsted. LiTW
O Eros, conqueror of hearts, with whom. To Eros. Anacreon, *tr. by* Judson France Davidson. GrR
O erth! on erth it is a wonders case. The Epitaph of Graunde Amour. Stephen Hawes. *Fr.* The Pastime of Pleasure. OBSC
O Eternal, in thy majesty ride. Jewish Arabic Liturgies. *Unknown.* TrJP
"Oh, Eve, where is Adam?" Adam in the Garden Pinnin' Leaves. *Unknown.* OuSiCo
O ever beauteous, ever friendly, tell. Elegy to the Memory of an Unfortunate Lady. Pope. ACP; EV-3; HBV; OBEC; OBEV
O, ever from the deeps. The Soul's Cry. Ray Palmer. LPS-2
Oh, ever skill'd to wear the form we love! To Hope. Helen Maria Williams. *Fr.* Julia, a Novel. OBEC
Oh, ever thus from childhood's hour, I've seen my fondest hopes recede. Muddled Metaphors. Tom Hood. NA
O everie living warldly wight. Of God's Omnipotencie. Alexander Hume. EV-1
O everlasting kingdom of the scepter. He Maketh Himself One with the Only God Whose Limbs Are the Many Gods. *Unknown.* *Fr.* Book of the Dead. AWP; JAWP; WBP
O Everlasting Light! Christ Is All. Horatius Bonar. BePJ
Oh, every fall the chestnut men. Chestnut Stands. Rachel Field. SiSoSe
Oh, everything is far. Lament. Rainer Maria Rilke. TrJP
O Evil man, with passions fraught. Concerning Death. Hovhannes Tulkourantzi. ArmLP
O eyes which do the spheres of beauty move. Astrophel and Stella, XLII. Sir Philip Sidney. SiPS
O eyes, you mortal stars. Dream of His Lady. Giovanni Battista Guarini. LyPI
Oh, face to face with trouble. Margaret E. Sangster. *Fr.* Face to Face with Trouble. PoToHe
O, fain would I, before I die. *Unknown.* LO
O faint, delicious, spring-time violet! The Violet. William Wetmore Story. HBV; LPS-2
O fair Acoka-tree, with love's own red. The Sign. Bhartrihari. LiTW
O fair and stately maid, whose eyes. To Eva. Emerson. EV-4; GTBS
Oh Fair Enough Are Sky and Plain. A. E. Housman. A Shropshire Lad, XX. MCCG; PoVP
(Look into Water.) BMEP
(Shropshire Lad, A.) YT
O fair face at the window, looking down alone. "Neither Maid nor Wife." Praxilla. GrPE
Oh, fair immaculate rose of the world, rose of my dream, my Rose! The Rose of Flame. "Fiona Macleod." PoVP
O, Fair New Mexico. Elizabeth Garrett. PoRL
O fair! O sweet! when I do look on thee. Song. Sir Philip Sidney. SiPS
O fair [*or* faire] sweet face, O eyes celestial[l] bright. Song. John Fletcher. *Fr.* Women Pleas'd. OBS; PoEL-2
Oh, Fair to See. Christina Rossetti. *Fr.* Sing-Song. DD; FaPON; MPB; OHIP; OTPC (1946 ed.); RAR; TiPo; YeAr
O faire content where do'st thou dwell. *Unknown.* SeCSL
O Faire! O Sweete! Sir Philip Sidney. *See* Song: "O fair! O sweet!"
Oh! fairer than the lily tall, and sweeter than the rose. Irish Molly O. Francis A. Fahy. TIP
O fairest of creation, last and best. Adam to Eve. Milton. *Fr.* Paradise Lost, IX. LPS-1
O Fairest of the Rural Maids. Bryant. AA; AmPP; AnAmPo; AnFE; AnNE; APA; BAP; CoAnAm; CoBA; IAP; LA; LaNeLa; LPS-1; MOAP; OBAV; TCAP; ViBoPo
"O fairest rose, with rosebud mouth," I sighed. God behind the Veil. Jami. OnPM
Oh, fairies love a holly tree. Holly Fairies. Aileen Fisher. ChBR
O faithless world, and thy most faithless part. An Elegy. Sir Henry Wotton. ElSeCe
O Fall of the leaf, I am tired. Leaf. John Hewitt. NeIP
O, Falmouth Is a Fine Town. W. E. Henley. POT; PoTo; VLEP
(Falmouth.) MBP; MoBrPo
(Home.) GN; HBV
O false and treacherous probability. Caelica, CIII [CIV]. Fulke Greville. OBS; OxBoCh; RiBV
O famed Phocaean city, with this last cry despairing. The Last Word. Damagetus. GrPE
O far away, and far away. The Happy Islands. Isabel Maud Peacocke. BoAu
O far-off darling in the South. Coeur de Lion to Berengaria. Theodore Tilton. AA
O far-off rose of long ago. A Far-off Rose. Josephine Preston Peabody. AA
O far withdrawn into the lonely West. To K. H. Thomas Edward Brown. VLEP
Oh, fare you well, I wish you well [*or* we're homeward bound]. Good-bye, Fare You Well. *Unknown.* AmSS; SoAmSa
O, fare you well, my Polly dear, since you and I must part. The Bold Privateer. *Unknown.* SG
Oh, fare you well, we're homeward bound. *See* Oh, fare you well, I wish you well.
Oh farmer have you a daughter fair, parlay-voo. Hinky Dinky. *Unknown.* TrAS
O fast her amber blood doth flow. The Phoenix. George Darley. *Fr.* Nepenthe. OBEV (new ed.); OBRV
O, fastidious mind, gorging on absolutes, remember. Promises. Ruth Forbes Sherry. GoYe
O Fate, implacable in my pursuit. Sonnet. Garcilaso de la Vega. TeCS
O fate, O fault, O curse, child of my bliss! Astrophel and Stella, XCIII. Sir Philip Sidney. SiPS
O Father Abram, I can never rest. Lazarus. Wilfred Campbell. BoCaPo
"Oh Father," cried the boy, "Oh come!" The Priest and the Pirate. Hervey Allen. LS
O father, father of our woe! "Dies Irae" [*or* Invocation of Agamemnon's Ghost]. Aeschylus. *Fr.* Choephoroe. GrR; OxBG
Oh Father—if Thou wouldst indeed. Father. Arthur Davison Ficke. QS; TrPWD
Oh, Father Jove! Thee wisest we account. Menelaos; Blasphemy under Duress. Homer. *Fr.* The Iliad, XIII. GrR
O Father, let me not die young! A Prayer for Life. George S. Burleigh. LPS-2
O Father, Thou Who Givest All. John Haynes Holmes. MaRV
O Father, we approach Thy throne. Adam's Hymn in Paradise [*or* The Hymn of Adam]. Joost van den Vondel. CAW; WGRP
O father Zeus, if ever among the Gods I gave. Homer. *Fr.* The Iliad, I. GrPE
O Fatherland, whose memory. A March, November Sixth, 1832. Erik Gustaf Geijer. AnSL
Oh, father's gone to market-town: he was up before the day. A Midsummer Song. Richard Watson Gilder. HBV; LHV; OTPC (1946 ed.); PRWS
O fayre Astrea, whyther, whyther art thou gone. *Unknown.* SeCSL
O Fearfull, Frowning Nemesis. Samuel Daniel. *Fr.* Cleopatra. PoEL-2
"O Felix Culpa!" *Unknown.* *See* Adam Lay I-bowndyn.
O fellow-citizens of storm-tossed lands. The New Banner. Katrina Trask. PEDC
O fickle as the heart of May. Gorse. Helen Foley. POTE
O fields of corn, O fields of corn. Sergei Yesenin, *tr. fr. Russian by* R. M. Hewitt. BoR
O Fiery Fervence, inflamed with all grace. To the Holy Ghost. John Skelton. TriL
"Oh, fill me flagons full and fair." Ballad of a Bridal. Edith Nesbit. VA
O Fir-tree green! O Fir-tree green! To the Fir-Tree. *Unknown.* COAH
O fire of light divine. To the Virgin. Rodríguez del Padrón. OnPM
O first created and creating source. Ode to the Sea. Howard Baker. OxBA; UnPo (1st ed.)
O first of human blessings, and supreme! War for the Sake of Peace. James Thomson. *Fr.* Britannia. LPS-2
Oh, flag of a resolute nation. Our Cherished Flag. James Montgomery. PEOR
O flame and horror, masterpiece of evil. The Stolen Bow. Sophocles. *Fr.* Philoctetes. OxBG
Oh, flame and pain that sweeps me once again! Cassandra's Lament. Aeschylus. *Fr.* Agamemnon. LiTW
O Flame of Living Love. St. John of the Cross. *See* Living Flame of Love, The.
O flavorless white hour. Winter among the Days. Raymond Holden. MAP; MoAmPo (1942 ed.)
O fleece that foams upon those shoulders bare! Tresses. Baudelaire. TrFP
O flesh now putrefied,—I'm spirit in agony. Dialogue of the

O flesh now putrefied (*continued*)
    Body with the Soul, [Which Is] Leading It to Judgment. Jacopone da Todi. LyMA; LyPI
O Flos de Jesse Virgula. *Unknown.* AnEC
O flower of all that springs from gentle blood. Epitaphs, VII. Gabriello Chiabrera. AWP
O Flower of flowers, our Lady of the May! Our Lady of the May. Lionel Johnson. ISi
O flower of passion, rocked by balmy gales. Gold-of-Ophir Roses. Grace Atherton Dennen. AA
Oh flowers, oh flowers of the tall green pine-tree. Cossante. Dinis, King of Portugal. LyMA
O Fly My Soul. James Shirley. *Fr.* The Imposture, II, ii. AtBAP; EG; OBS; OxBoCh
    (Hymn, A: "O fly, my soul!") GoBC; OBEV (1st ed.)
    (Song of Nuns, A.) ACP; CAW; PraNu
Oh fly not, pleasure, pleasant-hearted pleasure. Song. Wilfrid Scawen Blunt. JKCP; OBEV (1st ed.); OBVV; ViBoPo
O Fons Bandusiae. Horace. *See* To the Fountain of Bandusia.
O Foole, I Shall Go Mad. Shakespeare. *Fr.* King Lear, II, iv. LiA
    ("Good morrow to you both.") AtBAP
O foolish builders!/ Not as the Architect Eternal planned. Danger. Theodora L. Paine. PGD
O Foolishnes of Men. Milton. *Fr.* Comus. AtBAP
    (Comus Tempts the Lady.) CoEV
    (Comus's Praise of Nature.) PoEL-3
    ("O foolishness of men! that lend their ears.") ViBoPo
O for a Booke [*or* Book]. *Unknown.* CH; MOB; PCH; SiSoSe
    (Open Sesame.) BoTP
O for a Bowl of Fat Canary. John Lyly. *See* Serving Men's Song, A.
Oh! for a Closer Walk with God. William Cowper. *See* Walking with God.
O for a day at the Hint o' Hairst. The Hint o' Hairst. Charles Murray. EBSV
Oh, for a day in the white wind's cheek. With the Mallard Drake. *Unknown.* BLA
O for a faith that will not shrink. Unshrinking Faith. William Hiley Bathurst. BLRP
O for a ferryman to steer my yearning. Home-Sickness. Hedwig Lachmann. TrJP
O for a heart to praise my God. Charles Wesley. OIF
O for a lodge in a garden of cucumbers! Ninety-nine in the Shade. Rossiter Johnson. BOHV
Oh for a lodge in some vast wilderness. Slavery. William Cowper. *Fr.* The Task. CoBE; EnRP; EPP; LPS-2; OAEP
Oh, for a man to take me out. Wanted: One Cave Man with Club. Margaret Fishback. WhC
O for a Moon to Light Me Home. Walter de la Mare. OTPC
O for a Muse of fire, that would ascend. A Muse of Fire. Shakespeare. *Fr.* King Henry V, Prologue to Act I. BHV; ChTr; EV-1
Oh, for a Pentecost ("Oh, for a passionate passion for souls"). *Unknown.* BLRP
Oh for a Poet—for a Beacon Bright. E. A. Robinson. NePA; OxBA
Oh! for a Steed. Thomas Osborne Davis. IrPN
O, for a thousand tongues to sing. Triumph of His Grace. Charles Wesley. BePJ; OIF
Oh, for an hour when the day is breaking. Nanny. Francis Davis. HBV
O for an hour with Robin Hood, deep deep in the forest green. Robin Hood. W. J. Linton. BHV
O, for Ane-and-twenty. Burns. BSV
O for Cyprus. Bacchanal. Euripides. *Fr.* Bacchae. OxBG
O for Doors to Be Open and an Invite with Gilded Edges. W. H. Auden. OAEP (2d ed.); ViBoPo
    (O for Doors to Be Open.) AtBAP; CoBMV
Oh, for 'is heart is like the sea. They All Love Jack. *Unknown.* ShS
Oh, for me a horse and saddle. Just a-Ridin'! Badger Clark. SCC
O for my sake do you with Fortune chide. Sonnets, CXI. Shakespeare. EM-1; EPP; EV-1; PeBoSo; SiCE; TOP
O for one hour of youthful joy! The Old Man Dreams. Oliver Wendell Holmes. HBV; IAP; LPS-3; PTA-2; TCAP
O for one minute hark what we are saying! A Prayer. Frederic W. H. Myers. TrPWD
O for our upland meads. Shepherd and Shepherdess. Thomas Hennell. FaBoTw
Oh! for some honest lover's ghost. A Doubt of Martyrdom [*or* Actuality *or* Sonnet]. Sir John Suckling. ATP; BEL; BrBE; EnL; EnLi-1; EPS; FaBoEn; HBV; LoBV; MeLP; MePo; OBEV; PoEL-3; ReEn; SeCV-1; SeEP; TyEnPo
O, for some sunny spell. Keats. *Fr.* Lines to Fanny. LoPS
O, for that long littleness. We only know. Without Syncopation. Joyce Rowe. DiM

O for that warning voice, which he who saw. The Prospect of Eden. Milton. *Fr.* Paradise Lost, IV. PoEL-3
Oh, for the day when Polish armies sweeping. Waiting for Sunrise. Zygmunt Krasinski. PoFr
Oh, for the dull and muffled roar. Landlocked. Charles Buxton Going. VOD
Oh for the good old times! When all was new. The Della Cruscans. William Gifford. *Fr.* The Baviad. OBEC
O for the mighty wakening that aroused. The Half-asleep. Thomas Wade. OBEV (1st ed.)
Oh, for the Time When I Shall Sleep. Emily Brontë. *Fr.* The Philosopher. ATP; BLV; PoD
O for the times which were (if any). Tempora Acta. "Owen Meredith." OBVV; VA
Oh, for the veils of my far away youth. Lost Illusions. Georgia Douglas Johnson. BANP
O for the voice of that wild horn. The Black Prince. Sir Walter Scott. *Fr.* Rob Roy, II. CBPC
O for the Wings of a Dove. Euripides. *tr. fr. Greek by* Gilbert Murray. *Fr.* Hippolytus. AWP; JAWP; WBP
    (Birds of God, The.) OxBG
    (Chorus: "Could I take me to some cavern for mine hiding.") ShBV-4
    (Escape.) GrR
    (Longing.) PCD
    ("Would that I were under the cliffs, in the secret hiding-places of the rocks," *tr. by* David Grene.) GrPo
O, formed by nature, and refined by art. To a Lady before Marriage. Thomas Tickell. LPS-1
O fortunate, O happy day. A New Household. Longfellow. *Fr.* The Hanging of the Crane, I. GN
Oh Fortune suffers me not to clasp my sweetheart to my breast. Shiraz. Sadi. PeP
O Fortune, thou'rt not worth my least exclaim. John Donne. *Fr.* Elegies, XII: His Parting from Her. CoBE
O fountain-mouth, O giving, O mouth that speaks. Four Sonnets to Orpheus. Rainer Maria Rilke. *Fr.* Sonnets to Orpheus. LiTW
O fountain of Bandusia! To the Fountain of Bandusia. Horace, *tr. by* Eugene Field. AA; AWP; JAWP; WBP
O frail Adam. Epitaph for Mr. Moses Levy. *Unknown.* TrJP
Oh frame some little word for me. The Clue. Charlotte Fiske Bates. AA
O France, Mother of Arts. Joachim du Bellay, *tr. fr. French by* Alan Conder. Regrets, IX. TrFP
O France, though deep is thy slumber. Luna. Victor Hugo. TrFP
O France When Thou Art Prone and Bound. Victor Hugo, *tr. fr. French by* Wilfrid Thorley. PoFr
O France, with what a shamed and sorry smile. An American to France. Alice Duer Miller. HBMV
O Francis, doer of lovely things. To Saint Francis. Edwin Markham. SaFP
Oh Freedom! thou art not, as poets dream. Bryant. *Fr.* The Antiquity of Freedom. PoFr
O Friend, hope in Him while thou livest. Hope in Him While Thou Livest. Kabir. MaRV
O Friend, I know not which way I must look. Written in London, September, 1802 [*or* England, 1802]. Wordsworth. BCEP; BLV; BoLiVe; BPN; ChER; EM-2; EmBrPo; EnLi-2; EnRP; EPN; ERP; ES; GEPC; GTBS; GTBS-D; GTBS-W; GTSL; HBV; LEAP; MaRV; OBEV; PeBoSo; PoeMoYo; ReaPo; TrGrPo
O friend, like some cold wind to-day. To a Desolate Friend. William James Dawson. VA
O Friend of souls! how blest the time. Friend of Souls. *Unknown.* BePJ
O Friend—see the lightning there! The Storm. Imr el Kais. LiTW
O friends! with whom my feet have trod. The Eternal Goodness. Whittier. AA; AmPP (3d ed.); AnAmPo; AnFE; AnNE; APA; APW; BLP; CoAnAm; CoBA; CoV; GrCo-1; IAP; LA; LBAP; LEAP; MaRV; OBAV; OHFP; PTA-1; TCAP; WGRP
O frivolous mind of man. Fragment of Chorus of a "Dejaneira." Matthew Arnold. ViPP
Oh frog went a-courtin' and he did ride, uh-huh, uh-huh. Frog Went a-Courtin'. *Unknown.* TrAS
O from what power hast thou this powerful might. Sonnets, CL. Shakespeare. NBE; PeBoSo
Oh, full and soft, upon the orange trees. Tropic Sunset. Walter Adolphe Roberts. *Fr.* Boyhood Etchings. PoNe
O! Full of Scorpions. Shakespeare. *Fr.* Macbeth, III, ii. FiP
O furrowed plaintive face. The Hurrier. Harold Monro. MBP; MoBrPo
Oh! fye upon care. The Ranting Wanton's Resolution; 1672. *Unknown.* CoMu
Oh, gaily sings the bird! and the wattle-boughs are stirred. Whisperings in Wattle-Boughs. Adam Lindsay Gordon. BoAu; OBVV
O gain that lurk'st ungained in all gain! Desiderium Indesideratum. Francis Thompson. StJW; TriL
O Galatea faire, why dost thou shun thy lover true? Poly-

phemus to Galatea. Theocritus. *Fr.* Idylls. GrPo; OxBG
O gallant brothers of the generous South. Henry Peterson. *Fr.* Ode for Decoration Day. AA; FaBoBe
Oh, gallant was our galley from her carven steering-wheel. The Galley-Slave. Kipling. BEL
Oh, gallantly they fared forth in khaki and in blue. America's Welcome Home. Henry van Dyke. AOAH; MC
Oh Galuppi, Baldassaro, this is very sad to find! A Toccata of Galuppi's. Robert Browning. AnFE; ATP (1935 ed.); BPN; EmBrPo; EnLi-2 (1949 ed.); GEPC; HBV; LEAP; LiTB; LoBV; OAEP; OtMeF; PIAE; PoE; PoFS; PoVP; REAL; ReaPo; ViPo; ViPP; VLEP; WHA
O, Gambler, Git Up off o' Yo' Knees, *with music.* *Unknown.* BoAN-1
O Gather Me the Rose. W. E. Henley. Echoes, III. BEL; BPN; MBP; MoBrPo
(Collige Rosas.) OBVV; PG
Oh gather the thoughts of your early years. Early Thoughts. William Edward Hartpole Lecky. OnYI
Oh, gay are the king and his merry men all. Young Svend Dyre. *Unknown.* BoDaBa
Oh! gay pretty valentines gladly we send. The Valentine's Message. Mildred J. Hill. GFA
O generation of the thoroughly smug and thoroughly uncomfortable. Salutation. Ezra Pound. LoGBV; MoAB; MoAmPo (1950 ed.); MoPW; OxBA
O Genevieve, I'd give this world. Sweet Genevieve. George Cooper. OlF; TreFS
Oh, Gentle Beauty. Thibaut of Champagne, *tr. fr. Old French by* Henry Adams. LiA
(Chanson: "There is no comfort to be found for pain.") LyMA
O gentle, gentle land. Night Sowing. David Campbell. BoAV
O gentle, gentle summer rain. Invocation to Rain in Summer [*or* Summer Invocation]. William C. Bennett. GN; HBV; LPS-2; OTPC
O Gentle Love. George Peele. *Fr.* The Arraignment of Paris. ElL
(Colin, the Enamored Shepherd, Singeth This Passion of Love.) ReIE
(Colin's Passion of Love.) OBSC
O gentle queen of the afternoon. Poem. W. S. Graham. NeBP
O Gentle Ships. Meleager, *tr. fr. Greek by* Andrew Lang. AWP
O gentle sleep, that teachest man to die. To Sleep. Jan Kochanowski. LiTW
O gentle sleep, whose lenient power thus soothes. In the Furies' Grasp. Euripides. *Fr.* Orestes. GrR
O gentle Zephyr! if o'er Samarcand. The Tears of Khorassan. Anvari. PeP
Oh, gentlemen, listen, I pray. The Rover's Apology. W. S. Gilbert. *Fr.* Trial by Jury. ALV
O gie the lass her fairin', lad. Gie the Lass Her Fairin'. Burns. CoMu
O gift of God! O perfect day! A Day of Sunshine. Longfellow. TCAP
O, gimme yo' han'. Gimme Yo' Han'. *Unknown.* BoAN-2
Oh, Gingilee, my aching heart. Gingilee. Moishe-Leib Halpern. TrJP
Oh, gipsy hearts are many enough, but gipsy feet are few. Gipsy Feet. Fannie Stearns Davis. NLK
O girl among the roses, O pressure of doves. Ode with a Lament. "Pablo Neruda." TwSpPo
Oh, git around, Jinny, git around. Jinny Git Around. *Unknown.* OuSiCo
Oh, Give Me a Home Where the Buffalo Roam. *Unknown.* *See* Home on the Range, A.
Oh give me a pup. Poetic Tale. Grace Maddock Miller. AlBD
O give me back my rigorous English Sunday. The Fresh Start. Anna Wickham. ViBoPo
O give me gilliflowers. Gilliflower. Ibn al-Abbar. MooP
O Give Me Joys That Are Not Bound. Christian Morgenstern, *tr. fr. German by* Eileen Hutchins *and* Ursula Grahl. AnGP
O give me the Pole Star overhead. The Deep Water Man. James Stuart Montgomery. NLK
Oh! give thanks for the summer and winter. Thanksgiving. *Unknown.* PEOR
O give thanks unto the Lord, for He is good. O Give Thanks. Psalm CXVIII, Bible, *O.T.* TrJP
O give thanks unto [*or* to] the Lord; for he is good [*or* gracious]. Thanksgiving. Psalm CXXXVI, Bible, *O.T.* AWP; BoChLi (1950 ed.); OHIP
Oh, give us pleasure in the flowers today. A Prayer in Spring. Robert Frost. AlDL; MaRV; OTPC (1946 ed.); QS; TrPWD; YeAr; YT
Oh, glad am I that I was born! My Own Song. Harriet Prescott Spofford. BPP
O glad New Year! O glad New Year! New Year's Day. *Unknown.* PEDC; PEOR
O Glass-Blower of time. Invocation. Clara Shanafelt. SBMV
O gloom of night. Aristophanes. *Fr.* The Frogs. GrPo
Oh gloomy and dreary! and no one to stretch out a hand. Mikhail Lermontov, *tr. fr. Russian by* C. M. Bowra. BoR
O Glorious Childbearer. Joseph Campbell. OnYI
O Glorious Immensity. Deus Immensa Trinitas. *Unknown.* CAW
O glorious Lady of the Light. Death-Bed Hymn of Saint Anthony of Padua. St. Anthony of Padua. CAW
Oh glorious spirits, who after all your bands. To All Angels and Saints. George Herbert. SeCV-1
O glory of the lighted mind. The Everlasting Mercy. John Masefield. StJW
O Glory of Virgins. Fortunatus, *tr. fr. Latin by* Sister Maura. ISi
"O go again," said the King. King Arthur's Death. *Unknown.* ACP
O, go not yet, my love. Hero to Leander. Tennyson. LPS-1
O god above, relent. Here Followeth the Songe of the Death of Mr. Thewlis. *Unknown.* CoMu
O God, beneath Thy guiding hand. The Pilgrim Fathers. Leonard Bacon. MaRV; WGRP
O God creator, in whose hand. The Airmen's Hymn. Harry Webb Farrington. MaRV
O God, from whom all good gifts come. Table Blessing. Julia Budd Shafer. MeMeAg
O God! Have Mercy, in This Dreadful Hour. Robert Southey. TrPWD
O God, Hear Thou the Nation's Prayer. Irving Maurer. MaRV
O God, help me proclaim Thy truth. A Minister's Prayer. J. M. Bemiss. PraP
O God, How Many Years Ago. Frederic William Henry Myers. HBMV
O God, I am in Your hand a blackened slate. The Road of Suffering. Chaim Grade. OnCuPl
O God! I have been too slack, too slack. Tennyson. *Fr.* Queen Mary. ReTS
O God, I have to stretch my thoughts to think of You. I Stretch My Thoughts. Jeanette E. Perkins. PraP
O God, I love thee, I love thee. O Deus, Ego Amo Te. *Unknown, tr. by* Gerard Manley Hopkins. LaP; PoLi; TrPWD
O God, I love Thee in the stars at night. Prayer. Nadejda de Bragança. MaRV
O God! if this indeed be all. If This Be All. Anne Brontë. TrPWD
O God, in Restless Living. Harry Emerson Fosdick. MaRV; TrPWD
O God, in the dream the terrible horse began. The Dream. Louise Bogan. LiTA; LiTM; MoAB; MoAmPo (1950 ed.)
O God, in whom my deepest being dwells. A Psalm. Edmund Blunden. QS; TrPWD
Oh God, in your highest glory. A Prayer for the Dogs in War. Mrs. E. Worthing. AlBD
O God, inasmuch as without Thee. Limerick. *Unknown.* LiBL
O God, keep not Thou silence. Keep Not Thou Silence. Psalm LXXXIII, Bible, *O.T.* TrJP
Oh, God, let me be beautiful in death. Last Plea. Jean Starr Untermeyer. TrPWD
O God-like Achilles, thy father call to remembrance. Priam's Prayer to Achilles. Homer. *Fr.* The Iliad, XXIV. LiA
O God, make it rain! Prayer for Rain. Herbert E. Palmer. HaMV; POTE
O God! methinks it were a happy life. King Henry VI Yearns for a Simple Life. Shakespeare. King Henry VI, Pt. III, *fr.* II, v. TreFS
O God most glorious, called by many a name. Hymn to Zeus. Cleanthes. GrL; GrPo; MaRV
O God! my God! have mercy now. Supposed Confessions of a Second-rate Sensitive Mind. Tennyson. ViPP
O God, my master God, look down and see. The Artisan. Alice Brown. TrPWD
O God, no more Thy miracle withhold. Prayer for Miracle. Anna Wickham. GoTP; OQP; QP-2; YT
O God! O Montreal! Samuel Butler. OxBoLi
O God, O Venus, O Mercury, patron of thieves. The Lake Isle. Ezra Pound. CrMA; SiTL
O God of Battles, who art still. On the Eve of War. Danske Dandridge. BoHiPo; PAH
O God of Calvary and Bethlehem. The Hem of His Garment. Anna Elizabeth Hamilton. TrPWD
Oh, God of dust and rainbows, help us see. Two Somewhat Different Epigrams, I. Langston Hughes. NePoAm-2
O God of Earth and Altar. G. K. Chesterton. *See* Hymn, A: "O God of earth and altar."
O God of Field and City. John Haynes Holmes. MaRV
O God of Goodness, Forwardness, and Fulness. Prayer. Doris Hedges. GoYe
O God of hosts, whose mighty hand. In Days Like These. Thomas H. Stacy. MDAH

O God of Light. R. B. Y. Scott. MaRV
O God of love, O King of peace. Christ the Consoler. Henry W. Baker. BePJ; OlF
O God of Love, to Thee We Bow. William Vaughan Jenkins. MaRV
O God of love unbounded! Lord supreme! Prayer to God. "Plácido." CAW
O God of righteousness and truth. Reproaches. "Frik." ArmLP
O God, our Father, if we had but truth! A Prayer. Edward Rowland Sill. AA
O [*or* Our] God, Our Help in Ages Past. Isaac Watts. BPP; GrCo-1; HBV; LEAP; MaRV; NeHB; OlF; OxBoCh; Po; TOP; TriL; WGRP
(Hymn: "Our God, our help in ages past.") CoEV
(Man Frail and God Eternal.) EiPP; NBE; OBEC; PoE; PoEL-3
(Ninetieth Psalm.) BLRP
(Recessional.) TreF; WGRP
O God that I. The Provinces. Francis Carlin. SBMV
O God that madest earth and sky. Prologue to "The Lost Colony." Paul Green. NoCaPo
O God, the cleanest offering. Father Damien. John Banister Tabb. ACP; AmP; JKCP
O God, the heathen are come into Thine inheritance. The Heathen Are Come into Thine Inheritance. Psalm LXXIX, Bible, *O.T.* TrJP
O God, the Rock of Ages. Edward H. Bickersteth. BLPA; OlF
Oh God, this night of the mournful winter. Prayer to God to Rest All the Unfortunate. "Kostes Ouranis." MoGP
O God, thou art my right wiseness. Cum Invocarem. Psalm IV, Bible, *O.T.*, *tr. by* Thomas Sternhold. SiCE
O God, Thou art the object of my love. Hymn of Love. St. Francis Xavier. WHL
O God! though sorrow be my fate. Prayer. Mary, Queen of Hungary. LPS-2
O God, Thy heavens, in the hush of night. The City of God. Henry B. Robins. MaRV
O God, thy moon is on the hills. Kelpius's Hymn. Arthur Peterson. AA
O God, thy ways are dark. Edward Bliss Reed. *Fr.* Prayer: "She cannot tell my name." MaRV
O God, 'tis not for laurel wreaths I pray. The Armenian Poet's Prayer. Alexander Dzadourian. ArmLP
O God to Thee I Yield. Thomas Edward Brown. POTT; PoVP; VLEP
O God, unknown, invisible, secure. John Addington Symonds. *Fr.* An Invocation. MaRV; TrPWD
O God, when You send for me, let it be. Prayer to Go to Paradise with the Asses. Francis Jammes. AWP; JAWP; WBP
O God, where do they tend—these struggling aims? Robert Browning. *Fr.* Pauline. WGRP
O God, who comest with the dawn. Morning Prayer. Calvin W. Laufer. PraP
O God, Who guid'st the fate of nations. Hymn. Gunnar Wennerberg. AnSL; PoFr
O God, who has three eyes. Song of the Young Girls. *Unknown.* OnPM
O God, whose daylight leadeth down. George Macdonald. *Fr.* Evening Hymn. TrPWD
O God Whose Love Is over All. John Haynes Holmes. MaRV
O God, Whose Smile Is in the Sky. John Haynes Holmes. MaRV
O God, whose will is life and peace. Prayer for Peace. Rolland W. Schloerb. MaRV
O God, within whose sight. Prayer for the Churches. John Oxenham. OQP; QP-1
O goddess! give me back the ready laughter. To the Frivolous Muse. George Meason Whicher. InMe
O Goddess! hear these tuneless numbers, wrung. Ode to Psyche. Keats. BCEP; BPN; BrBE; CaAE; ChER; EM-2; EnLP; EmBrPo; EnRP; EPN; ERP; EV-4; GEPC; GTBS-W; HBV; LEAP; LiA; LiTB; LoBV; MaPo; OAEP; OBEV; OBRV; PoEL-4; TwHP; TyEnPo; ViBoPo; WHA
O Goddess! sing the wrath of Peleus' son. Homer, *tr. by* Bryant. *Fr.* The Iliad, I. EnLi-1
O Godhead hid, devoutly I adore Thee. Adoro Te Devote. St. Thomas Aquinas. CAW
O gods of all enchanting lies. Prayer after Youth. Maxwell Anderson. TBM
O gold Hyperion, love-lorn Porphyro. Keats. William Wilberforce Lord. *Fr.* Ode to England. AA
O Golden Fleece. George Barker. LiTM; MoAB; MoBrPo (1950 ed.)
(Love Poem.) LiTL
("O Golden Fleece she is where she lies tonight.") NeBP
Oh, golden-lilied Queen—immortal France! France. Elliott Napier. BoAu
O Golden Love, what life, what joy but thine? Sine Amore Nil Est Jucundum. Mimnermus. GrL; OxBG
O Golden Lyre! Pindar, *tr. fr. Greek by* H. T. Wade-Gery *and* C. M. Bowra. *Fr.* Pythian Odes, I. GrR
(First Pythian Ode of Pindar, The, *tr. by* Arthur S. Way.) WoL
(Magic of Melody, The, *tr. by* F. L. Lucas.) GrPE
(Power of Music, The, *tr. by* H. T. Wade-Gery *and* C. M. Bowra.) OxBG; UnS, *shorter sel.*
O golden-red and tall chrysanthemums. Chrysanthemums. F. S. Flint. MBP; MoBrPo (1942 ed.)
Oh, Golden-Rod. W. L. Jaquith. PEOR
O golden-tongued Romance, with serene lute! On Sitting Down to Read "King Lear" Once Again. Keats. ATP; EnRP; PeBoSo; PtP
Oh, good gigantic smile o' the brown old earth. Among the Rocks [*or* The Ancient Doctrine]. Robert Browning. *Fr.* James Lee's Wife. BLV; BoLiVe; BPN; EPN; OBVV; VLEP; YT
"O good Lord Judge, and sweet Lord Judge." The Maid Freed from the Gallows. *Unknown.* AnFE; BaBo (A *vers.*); ESPB; InPo; TOP; ViBoFo (A *vers.*)
O good New Year! we clasp. Address to the New Year. Dinah Maria Mulock Craik. PEDC; PEOR
O good painter, tell me true. An Order for a Picture. Alice Cary. BLPA; OBAV; PTA-1
O good Sun/ Look thou down upon us. Song for Fine Weather. *Tr. by* Constance Lindsay Skinner. AWP; JAWP; WBP
O Goodly Hand. Sir Thomas Wyatt. InvP; SiPS
(His Lady's Hand.) OBSC
O Goody, it's coming, the circus parade. The Circus Parade. Olive Beaupré Miller. TiPo
O graceful balcony, where now is she that with her gleam. Sonnet: To a Balcony. Matteo Maria Boiardo. LyPI
O gracious city well-beloved. The Laud of Saint Catherine. Swinburne. *Fr.* Siena. CAW
O gracious God, O Saviour sweet. O That I Had Wings like a Dove. *Unknown.* OxBoCh
O Gracious Shepherd. Henry Constable. OxBoCh
O grammar-rules, O now your virtues show. Astrophel and Stella, LXIII. Sir Philip Sidney. PeBoSo; SiPS; TuPP
O grandest of the Angels, and most wise. Litany to Satan. Baudelaire. AWP
Oh, grant me, Satan, a soul simple and complex. To Satan. Luis Carlos López. TwSpPo
O grasses wet with dew, yellow fallen leaves. A Glimpse. Frances Cornford. OBMV
O grave, O bridal chamber; O thou deep. Antigone Entombed Alive. Sophocles. *Fr.* Antigone. GrR
O graveyard. Lay Dis Body Down. *Unknown.* ABF
O Great Creator. *At. to* Zoroaster. *See* Zoroaster Devoutly Questions Ormazd.
O Great Mary. The Gaelic Litany to Our Lady. *Unknown.* CAW; ISi
O great outdoors, without floors. The Great Outdoors. Maud Russell. NLK
O great, rebellious and ferocious sea! Against the Hope of Reconstruction. F. T. Marinetti. OnHM
O Great Spirit! A Voyager's Prayer. *Unknown.* WGRP
O great sun of heaven, harm not my love. An Incantation. Marguerite Wilkinson. AV; NP
Oh, greata game ees basaball. Da Greata Basaball. T. A. Daly. TSWC
Oh, green curved the hill road and beckoned to my feet. The Sea Road. Martha Haskell Clarke. NLK
Oh! greenly and fair in the land of the sun. The Pumpkin. Whittier. DD; LPS-2; OHIP; TOAH
O Grief! *Unknown.* EIL
Oh, grieve not, ladies, if at night. Grieve Not, Ladies. Anna Hempstead Branch. AnAmPo; BAP; FaFP; HBV; LA; LBMV; LEAP; PR
O grip the earth, ye forest trees. The Storm. Frederick George Scott. CPG
Oh guard, dear Pan, so great and wise. Prayer for Little Beasts. Beulah May. DDA
O guns, fall silent till the dead men hear. The Anxious Dead. John McCrae. BTP; CPG; OCL; OHIP; PoP
Oh, had it been in autumn, when all is spent and sere. Frost in Spring. Jessie B. Rittenhouse. NV
Oh, had it been mine, that upper room. The Upper Room. Belle F. Owens. ChIP
O had she not been fair and thus unkind. To Delia, VII. Samuel Daniel. ReIE
O had truth power, the guiltless could not fall. His Petition to Queen Anne of Denmark (1618). Sir Walter Ralegh. SiPS
Oh! had you eyes, but eyes that move. Formosae Puellae. Herbert P. Horne. VA
O [*or* Ah,] had you seen the Coolun. The Coolun. Maurice O'Dugan. AnIV; OnYI; OxBI
O Hades, death's inexorable king. A Child. *Unknown.* OxBG
O Halcyon Bird. Euripides. *See* Bird of the Sea.

"Oh handsome love, are you still asleep?" Dawn Song. Dietmar von Aist. LyMA
Oh, hapless sire, distraught with cares. The Yoke. Kalonymos ben Kalonymos. *Fr.* The Touchstone. TrJP
O happie Tems, that didst my Stella beare. *See* O happy Thames . . .
O happiest village! how I turned to you. Old Homes. Edmund Blunden. MoVE
Oh, happiness! he said, and took his life. Five Epigrams, 2. Donald Hall. NePoAm-2
Oh Happiness! our being's end and aim! Happiness. Pope. *Fr.* An Essay on Man, Epistle IV. ATP; LEAP; LPS-3
O happy age of gold; happy hours. The Golden Age. Tasso. *Fr.* Aminta. LyPI
O happy dames, that may embrace. Complaint of the Absence of Her Lover Being upon the Sea [*or* A Lady Complains *or* The Seafarer]. Earl of Surrey. CoEV; ElL; ElSeCe; OBEV; OBSC; ReEn; RiBV; SiCE; SiPS
Oh, happy folk, contented folk, and ye that go with gold. The Red Cross Christmas Seal. Theodosia Garrison. PEDC
O happy golden Age. A Pastoral[l]. Tasso, *tr. by* Samuel Daniel. *Fr.* Aminta. OBSC; PoEL-2; ReEn; ReIE
O, happy, happy he, who flies. Ode to Retirement. Luis de León. AnSpL-1
Oh, happy, happy maid. A Nuptial Eve. Sydney Dobell. VA
O Happy Home. Karl J. P. Spitta, *tr. fr. German.* MaRV; PraP
O happy life, whose love is found! Queen and Slave. Mortimer Collins. OBVV
O happy living things! no tongue. Samuel Taylor Coleridge. *Fr.* The Rime of the Ancient Mariner. PC
O happy seafarers are ye. Songs of Orpheus and the Sirens. William Morris. *Fr.* The Life and Death of Jason. BPN; ViBoPo
Oh happy shades! to me unblest. The Shrubbery. William Cowper. CEP; FaBoEn; GTSL; NBE; OBEC; TwHP
O happy Sleep! thou bear'st upon thy breast. Sleep. Ada Louise Martin. HBV
O Happy Soul. Washington Gladden. MaRV
O happy soul, forget thy self! Renaissance. T. Sturge Moore. PoeT
O happy Thames [*or* happie Tems] that didst my Stella bear. Astrophel and Stella, CIII. Sir Philip Sidney. EV-1; HBV; ReEn; SiPS
O happy the huntsman returns to his native wood. Ode. Frederic Prokosch. ViBoPo (1941 ed.)
O happy Tithon! if thou know'st thy hap. Earl of Stirling. *Fr.* Aurora, Song IX. OBEV
O happy trees that we plant today. Tree Planting. *Unknown.* OHIP
Oh, happy wind, how sweet. Happy Wind. W. H. Davies. NLK; OTPC (1946 ed.); PCH; RIS; StaSt; TSW; TSWC
O happy world to-day if we could know. Thought for Easter. Mary E. McCullough. MaRV
Oh, hark the pulses of the night. The Reason. James Oppenheim. HBV
O hark! 'tis the note of the Schmaltztenor! Schmaltztenor. M. W. Branch. FiBHP
Oh, hark to the brown thrush! hear how he sings! Joy-Month. David Atwood Wasson. HBV; SN
O Hark to the Herald. Eleazar ben Kalir, *tr. fr. Hebrew by* Israel Zangwill. TrJP
Oh, hark to the story of Willie the Weeper. Willie the Weeper. *Unknown.* SoAF
O harmless feast. Song. Barten Holyday. *Fr.* Technogamia. ElL
O harp of Cnoc I Cosgair. In Praise of a Harp. *Unknown.* SiB
O, hate me not for my grey hair. To His Mistress, Who Said She Hated Him for His Grey Hairs [*or* A Song: In the Name of a Lover]. William Wycherley. SeCL; SeCV-2
O hateful harm! condicion of poverte! Prologue to the Man of Law's Tale. Chaucer. *Fr.* The Canterbury Tales. FiP
Oh, haul away the bowline, the packet ship's a-rollin'! Haul Away, Joe, *vers.* II. *Unknown.* ShS
Oh, haul pulley, yoe! Cheer'ly, O! *Unknown.* AmSS
Oh, Haunting Spirit of the Ever True. Allan Knight Chalmers. MaRV
O, have ye been in love, me boys. I Met Her in the Garden Where the Praties Grow. *Unknown.* AS
O have ye na heard o' the fause Sakelde? Kinmont Willie. *Unknown.* BaBo; BEL; BSV; CBOV; EBSV; ESPB; EV-2; LH; OBB
O, have you been in Gudbrand's dale, where Laagen's mighty flood. Thoralf and Synnöv. Hjalmar Hjorth Boyesen. AA
Oh, have you heard the news, my Johnny? One More Day. *Unknown.* SoAmSa
"Oh, have you not a message, you who come over the sea?" The Message. Lady Margaret Sackville. AV
Oh, have you seen Aastrid? She lives on The Spur. Aastrid. Kristofer Janson. AnNoLy
O have you seen my fairy steed? "She Wandered after Strange Gods." Laura Benét. HBMV
O, have you seen the leper healed. The Healing of the Leper. Vernon Watkins. FaBoTw
"O have you seen the Stratton flood." Stratton Water. Dante Gabriel Rossetti. EmBrPo
Oh, He who walked with fishermen. A Fisherman Speaks. Scharmel Iris. ChIP
O healer Death, spurn not to come to me. Philoctetes Calls for Death. Aeschylus. *Fr.* Philoctetes. OxBG
Oh, hear a pensive prisoner's prayer. The Mouse's Petition. Anna Letitia Barbauld. CG
Oh, Hear Me Prayin', *with music. Unknown.* BoAN-2
O hear ye that foul and fiendish laughter. War. J. Gilchrist Lawson. WBLP
O heard ye na o' the silly blind Harper. The Lochmaben Harper. *Unknown.* OBB
O heard ye of a bloody knight. Lady Isabel and the Elf-Knight (B *vers.*). *Unknown.* BaBo
O heard ye of Sir James the Rose. Sir James the Rose. *Unknown.* ESPB
O heard ye yon pibroch sound sad in the gale. Glenara. Thomas Campbell. HBV; UnW
O hearken, all ye little weeds. Candlemas. Alice Brown. AA; LBMV; PoRL
O hearken and hear, and I will you tell. The Friar in the Well (B *vers.*). *Unknown.* ESPB
Oh hearken, spring, from whom I drank. To Bellerie Spring. Pierre de Ronsard. TrFP
Oh, hearken to my story, hearken gentles all. The Prodigal Son. *Unknown.* SaSa
O Heart. Maurice Rowntree. OQP; QP-2
O heart, be at peace, because. Against Unworthy Praise. W. B. Yeats. AnFE
Oh Heart, keep faith with Him! tho scant and poor. Vigil. Laura Simmons. LPS-1
O heart of hearts, the chalice of love's fire. Cor Cordium. Swinburne. ATP (1935 ed.); BMEP; BPN; EmBrPo; EPN; PoVP; TOP; ViPo; VLEP
O heart of mine, we shouldn't worry so. Just Be Glad. James Whitcomb Riley. WBLP
O Heart of Spring! Shaw Neilson. BoAu
Oh heart rejoice! For I Have Done a Good and Kindly Deed. Franz Werfel. TrJP
O Heart, Small Urn. Hilda Doolittle ("H. D."). AtBAP
O heart submissive in this martyrdom. The Assumption. John Gilland Brunini. ISi
O Heart, that beats with every human heart. O Heart. Maurice Rowntree. OQP; QP-2
O heart that gave its first sweet love. Song. Joseph William Holden. NoCaPo (rev. ed.)
O heart, the equal poise of love's both parts. Richard Crashaw. *Fr.* The Flaming Heart. EG; ElSeCe; KN; ReEn; TrGrPo; TwHP
O heart, when a time of sorrow overtakes thee. A Kind Friend. Jami. BoFr
O heart, why dost thou sigh, and wilt not break? When He Thought Himself Contemned. Thomas Howell. ElL; ReIE; TuPP
O hearts that never cease to yearn! Grief for the Dead. *Unknown.* LPS-1
O heavenly colour [*or* color], London town. November Blue. Alice Meynell. AlDL; MBP; MM; MoBrPo; PoeMoYo; PoeT; VOD; YT
O heavenly fool! thy most kiss-worthy face. Anna Wickham. LO
O heavens. Lear's Prayer. Shakespeare. *Fr.* King Lear, II, iv. BCEP
Oh! heavens—while thus hoarse Codrus perseveres. A Fair Field for Satire. Juvenal. *Fr.* Satires, I. RoL
"O Heav'n! the veriest child might plainly see." Homer. *Fr.* The Iliad, XVII. GrPo
O Heavy Step of Slow Monotony. Ernst Toller, *tr. fr. German by* Ashley Dukes. TrJP
O Hector, blood of Ares, can you hear beneath. Troy Restored. Hadrianus. OxBG
Oh heere's my mother: I ha strange newes for you. John Webster. *Fr.* The Devil's Law-Case, III, iii. AtBAP
O helpless few in my country. The Rest. Ezra Pound. AmP; MAP; MoAB; MoAmPo; OxBA
O herdsman, driving your slow twilight flock. The Herdsman. "Seumas O'Sullivan." TIP
O here/ Will I set up my everlasting rest. Shakespeare. *Fr.* Romeo and Juliet, V, iii. EtPaEn
Oh, here's a jolly lark. The Old Marquis and His Blooming Wife. *Unknown.* CoMu
O Hero, Hero, thus he cry'de full oft. Christopher Marlowe. *Fr.* Hero and Leander. AtBAP

Oh, hero of our younger race! Washington. Harriet Monroe. *Fr.* Commemoration Ode. AA; OQP; PoRL; QP-1; WOAH
O he's a ranting roving blade. The White Cockade. *Unknown.* EBSV
O Hesperus! thou bringest all good things. Evening [*or* Hesperus *or* Hesperus the Bringer]. Byron. *Fr.* Don Juan, III. AWP; BoLiVe; JAWP; OnPM; OuHeWo; TOP; TrGrPo; WBP
O Hesperus! Thou bringest all things home. Sappho, *tr. fr. Greek by* W. H. Appleton. GrPo
O hideous little bat, the size of snot. The Fly. Karl Shapiro. CoBA; LiTM; MiAP; MoVE; NePA; TwAmPo
O high and mighty king. The Hawk. Ibn al-Qabturnu. MooP
Oh, his horse went dead, and his mule went lame. Tough Luck. *Unknown.* LauV
Oh ho! oh ho! Pray, who can I be? Guessing Song. Henry Johnstone. OTPC (1946 ed.); PRWS
"Oh, hold your hand, butcher!" this fair one she cried. The Silk Merchant's Daughter, *vers.* I. *Unknown.* ShS
"Oh, Hollow! Hollow! Hollow!" W. S. Gilbert. *Fr.* Patience. PoVP
Oh! holly branch and mistletoe. December. Harriet F. Blodgett. COAH
O holy Aether, and swift-winged Winds. The Wail of Prometheus Bound. Aeschylus. *Fr.* Prometheus Bound. GrPo; WGRP
Oh, holy cause. Sung on a Sunny Morning. Jean Starr Untermeyer. TrPWD
O Holy City seen of John. The Holy City. W. Russell Bowie. MaRV
O holy ensign! symbol fair. The Free Flag. *Unknown.* FOAH
O Holy Ghost, Arise. A. J. Gordon. PraP
O holy Jerusalem, Vision of peace. Advent Lyrics, III. *Unknown. Fr.* Christ I. AnOE
O Holy Light! Thou who art strength! Dawn. Ernest Fewster. NeTW
O holy Love, religious saint! Ditty. Sir Robert Chester. *Fr.* Love's Martyr. ElL
O Holy Mother, thou who still dost send. At the Tomb of Rachel. "Yehoash." TrJP
O holy Saviour! Friend unseen! My Soul Shall Cling to Thee. Charlotte Elliott. BePJ
O holy virgin! clad in purest white. To Morning. Blake. EnRP
O Holy Water. Margot Ruddock. OBMV
O homeless dust, within this green field hidden. Children of Earth. Josephine Johnson. MuM
"O hone a rie'! O hone a rie'!" Glenfinlas. Sir Walter Scott. EmBrPo; GoTL
O honest face, which all men knew! Abraham Lincoln [*or* An Horatian Ode]. Richard Henry Stoddard. AA; GDAH; LBAH; PAH
Oh, honey, li'l honey, come and lay yo' wooly head. Lullaby. Edmund S. Leamy. BOL; GBV (1922 ed.)
O! Honour! Honour! Honour! Oh! the Gain! God's Selecting Love in the Decree. Edward Taylor. *Fr.* God's Determinations. PoEL-3
O hotspur torrent, crested high in air. A Freshet. Antiphilus of Byzantium. LiTW; OxBG
O hour of all hours, the most blest upon the earth. The Dinner Hour. "Owen Meredith." *Fr.* Lucile. VA
O hour of incest! Cyril Tourneur. *Fr.* The Revenger's Tragedy, I, iii. AtBAP
Oh house with two doors that is mine. House with Two Doors. Enrique González Martínez. AnMP
O how came I that loved stars, moon, and flame. The Image of Delight. William Ellery Leonard. AnFE; APA; CoAnAm; HBMV; MAP; MoAmPo (1942 ed.)
O how canst thou renounce the boundless store. Nature's Charms. James Beattie. *Fr.* The Minstrel, I. OBEV
O, how comely it is, and how reviving. The Deliverer [*or* Out of Adversity]. Milton. *Fr.* Samson Agonistes. LH; OBEV; OBS; SeCeV
O how feeble is man's power. John Donne. *Fr.* Song: "Sweetest love, I do not go." LO
Oh, How Good. "Anna Akhmatova," *tr. fr. Russian by* Babette Deutsch. TrRV
O how I faint when I of you do write. Sonnets, LXXX. Shakespeare. PeBoSo; ReEn; SiCE
O! how I long to be at rest! Aspiration. William Drennan. IrPN
Oh, how I love Humanity. The World State. G. K. Chesterton. CoBE
Oh! how I love, on a fair summer's eve. Keats. EV-4
Oh, how I love to skip alone. Skipping Along Alone. Winifred Welles. TiPo
O how I wish, blind Money-God. The Evil Genius. Simonides. GrR
Oh! how many gallant captains and brave hands. Oceano Nox. Victor Hugo. TrFP
Oh, how may I/ Call this a lightning? With a Kiss I Die. Shakespeare. *Fr.* Romeo and Juliet, V, iii. LiTL
O, how much more doth beauty beauteous seem. Sonnets, LIV. Shakespeare. AWP; ElL; EnLi-1 (1949 ed.); EV-1; JAWP; LiTG; OBEV; OBSC; PeBoSo; ReEn; ReIE; SiCE; TOP; ViBoPo; WBP
Oh, how my pulse pipes to go riding, go riding. Riding. Harry Amoss. CaP
O! how my thoughts do beat me. *Unknown.* OBSC
Oh how oft I wake and find. To My God. George Macdonald. TrPWD
O how oft shalt thou complain. Richard Crashaw. *Fr.* A Hymn to the Name and Honor of the Admirable Saint Teresa. PoLi
O how one ugly trick has spoiled. Meddlesome Matty. Ann Taylor. EV-4; HBV; HBVY
Oh! how shall I get it, how shall I get it? The Egg. Laura E. Richards. MPB; RAR; TiPo (1952 ed.)
Oh, how she plough'd the ocean, the good ship *Castle Down.* The Good Ship *Castle Down.* William B. McBurney. TIP
O How Sweet Are Thy Words! Anne Steele. BLRP
Oh, how the nights are short. Midsummer Courtship. James Thomson. *Fr.* Richard Forest's Midsummer Night. OBVV; POTT
O how the pleasant airs of true love be. Astrophel and Stella, LXXVIII. Sir Philip Sidney. SiPS
O, How the Thought of God Attracts. Frederick William Faber. LPS-2
Oh! how they murdered poor Bob White to-day! The Last Bob White. Whitney Montgomery. BLA
O, how this spring of love resembleth. This Spring of Love. Shakespeare. *Fr.* The Two Gentlemen of Verona, I, iii. ChTr
O how thy worth with manners may I sing. Sonnets, XXXIX. Shakespeare. PeBoSo
Oh how widely wandereth he. Francesco Redi. *Fr.* Bacchus in Tuscany. PoP
Oh, how with brightness hath Love filled my way. Ideal Passion, XXX. George Edward Woodberry. HBMV; MOAP
O human hearts,/ Beating through fear, through jealousy. Prepare. Witter Bynner. PGD
Oh, Huntsman, when will the hunting stop. To Charlotte Corday. Sir Osbert Sitwell. ChMP
O hurry where by water among trees. The Ragged Wood. W. B. Yeats. LO; VLEP
Oh, hush, my heart, and take thine ease. April Weather. Lizette Woodworth Reese. DD; HBMV; LS; NLK; PoTo; SPP; VOD
Oh, hush thee, here in the hollow. Mary's Lullaby. Elizabeth J. Coatsworth. ChrBoLe
Oh hush thee, little Dear-my-Soul. Christmas Eve. Eugene Field. BOL; OHIP
O, hush thee, my babie [*or* baby], thy sire was a knight. Lullaby of an Infant Chief [*or* Cradle Song]. Sir Walter Scott. BHV; BOL; CBE; CBPC; EmBrPo; EnRP; ERP; EV-4; FaPON; GoTP; HBV; MPB; OTPC; PCH; PoRh; PRWS; RIS; TVC; TVSH
Oh! hush thee, my baby, the night is behind us. Seal Lullaby [*or* The White Seal's Lullaby]. Kipling. *Fr.* The Jungle Book: The White Seal. CaAE; FaPON; NV; PoRA; PRWS; RAR; TiPo (1959 ed.)
O hush thee, my child. *Unknown.* BOL
O hush thee, my child! thy mother bends o'er thee. Danaë's Cradle-Song. *Unknown.* BOL
O! hush thee, my darling, sleep soundly my son. Lullaby. *Unknown.* TrJP
Oh! hush Thee, oh! hush Thee, my Baby so small. Cradle Song at Bethlehem. E. J. Falconer. BoTP
O hushaby, baby! Why weepest thou? A Lullaby. Owen Roe O'Sullivan. BOL
O hushed October morning mild. October. Robert Frost. AIDL; MaPo
Oh, I am a brave desperado. A Song of the Movie Mexican. Edwin Meade Robinson. LHV
Oh, I am a rusty cowboy. The Drifter. Dave Hughes. CoSo
Oh, I am a Texas cowboy, far away from home. The Texas Cowboy. *Unknown.* CoSo; CSF
Oh, I am engaged to be married now. Ballade of the Engaged Young Man. Richard K. Munkittrick. PR
O, I am green and fair. Sycamore. Vernon Watkins. MoWP
O I am sick, I am sick to death, tis soe. *At. to* Henry Hughes. SeCSL
Oh I am the King of Siam, I am! Dynastic Tiff. Geoffrey Hellman. ALV
Oh, I am weary of a heart that brings. Helios. Joel Elias Spingarn. AA
Oh I am weary of tongues a-clacking. My Dog and I. Genevieve W. Mason. AIBD
Oh, I be vun of the useful troibe. A Rustic Song. Anthony C. Deane. FiBHP; InMe
O I C. *Unknown.* SiTL; WhC

Oh, I can hear you, God, above the cry. Wind in the Pine. Lew Sarett. BAP; MaRV; MW; OTPC (1946 ed.); QS; TrPWD
Oh, I come from the world below. Rise Me Up from Down Below. *Unknown.* ShS
O, I could wish, most richly yellowing. Sonnet. Pierre de Ronsard. FoS
O I do love, then kiss me. Madrigal. Robert Jones. OxBoLi; SiTL
Oh, I don't want to be a gambler. I Don't Want to Be a Gambler. *Unknown.* AS
O I feel like the kinks in the paws of the Sphinx. Hotel Continental. William Jay Smith. WaP
O I followed down the highway. Old Love Should Not Be Ruptured. *Unknown.* BoFr
"O I forbid you, maidens a'." Tam Lin. *Unknown.* BaBo; BSV; EBSV; ESPB; OBB; OBEV (new ed.); ViBoFo
Oh, I had a horse and his name was Bill. The Horse Named Bill. *Unknown.* AS
O I hae come from far away. The Witch's Ballad. William Bell Scott. AnFE; BMEP; BSV; CH; EBSV; OBEV; OBVV
O, I have been in the land where you were born. Song. Olga Berggolts. *Fr.* Parting. RuPo
Oh! I have been North, and I have been South, and the East hath seen me pass. North, East, South, and West. *Unknown.* BOHV
Oh, I have drained the cups of ecstasy! Flute of God. John Daniel Logan. CPG
Oh I have grown so shrivelled and sere. Body of John. R. A. K. Mason. AnNZ
Oh, I have lived to be so glad. The Radiant Loss. Jessie B. Rittenhouse. LEAP
Oh! I have loved thee fondly, ever. Stanzas to Pale Ale. *Unknown.* BOHV
O, I have passed a miserable night. The Dream of Clarence. Shakespeare. King Richard III, *fr.* I, iv. UnW
Oh, I have slipped the surly bonds of earth. High Flight. John Gillespie Magee, Jr. BBV (1951 ed.); FaFP; FaPON; MaC; MaRV; NeTW; PGD; POTE; PreP; QS; TreFS; TwCV; WaKn
Oh, I have sown my love so wide. After Parting. Sara Teasdale. TOP
Oh, I have swept the hearth clean. The Witch-Wife. Mary Eleanor Roberts. BAP
Oh, I have walked in Kansas. Kansas. Vachel Lindsay. TOP
Oh, I know a certain woman who is reckoned with the good. A Pin. Ella Wheeler Wilcox. BOHV
O, I know de Lord. I Know de Lord's Laid His Hands on Me. *Unknown.* BoAN-2
Oh! I know why the alder trees. I Know. Elsa Barker. AV; HBMV; VOD
Oh! I love to travel far and near throughout my native land. Wizard Oil. *Unknown.* AS
Oh, I must be in Darley Dale before the sun dips low. Darley Dale. Clinton Scollard. PR
Oh, I once was a lad. To Browning, the Music Master. Robert Haven Schauffler. BAP
O I say my Mammy Dinah,/ What is the matter? Sing Sally O! *Unknown.* SoAmSa
O I see now/ Your purpose is to fright me. Tennyson. *Fr.* Becket. ReTS
O I shall be as dead, mother. *Unknown.* *Fr.* The Cherry Tree Carol. PoD
O, I shall run mad! John Webster. *Fr.* The Devil's Law Case. LO
Oh, I should like to ride the seas. Song of Perfect Propriety. Dorothy Parker. InMe
Oh, I should love to be like one of those. The Youth Dreams. Rainer Maria Rilke. AWP; JAWP; TrJP; WBP
Oh I suppose I should/ wash the walls of my office. Le Médecin Malgré Lui. William Carlos Williams. PoP
Oh I thought I heard the *Kate Adams* when she blowed. The *Kate Adams.* *Unknown.* StDa
Oh, I used to sing a song. The Endless Song. Ruth McEnery Stuart. BOHV
Oh! I vu'st knew o' my true love. Heedless o' My Love. William Barnes. RO
Oh, I wad like to ken—to the beggar-wife says I. The Spaewife. Robert Louis Stevenson. POTT; PoVP; VA
Oh, I want to win me hame. Lament of the Scotch-Irish Exile. James Jeffrey Roche. BOHV
Oh! I was harsh to say that I could part. The Recantation. Albius Tibullus. LiTW
Oh, I was honest in the womb. Scarabs for the Living, VI. R. P. Blackmur. TwAmPo
Oh, I was hungry from head to foot. Old Bill. *Unknown.* ABF
Oh, I went down South for to see my Sal. Polly Wolly Doodle. *Unknown.* TreF; YaD
Oh, I went down to Framingham. Spooks. Nathalia Crane. StaSt
O I went into the stable. Our Goodman. *Unknown.* ESPB
Oh, I will go with carefree laugh. Inexperience. June Breining. PoMa
Oh, I will have me a heart's-beloved. Yes, I Will Have Me a Heart's-beloved. Claus Pavels Riis. AnNoLy
"Oh, I will put my ship in order." The Drowsy Sleeper (B *vers.*). *Unknown.* BaBo
O I will sing to you a sang. The Clerk's Twa Sons o Owsenford. *Unknown.* BaBo; ESPB
Oh! I will take the match. The Wife's Song. Elizabeth J. Coatsworth. DDA
Oh! I wish I were a tiny brown bird from out the south. Valentine's Day. Charles Kingsley. BoTP
O! I wish the sun was bright in the sky. The Terrible Robber Men. Padraic Colum. HBMV; RG
Oh, I wonder they break not in blossom. Stones and Blossoms. *Unknown.* OnPM
O I Won't Lead a Homely Life. Thomas Hardy. UnS
Oh, I worried a lot (and what father has not?). A Daddy Like Mine. Douglas Malloch. FAOV
Oh, I woud I wee a cose, cose fiend. Sim Ines. Jane Stubbs. FiBHP
Oh, I would be a cowboy and with the cowboys stand. Up the Trail. *Unknown.* CoSo
O I would be as clear as air. A Song of Light. Marguerite Wilkinson. MeRV
Oh, I would like to be a ghoul. Desire. Nathalia Crane. MAP; MoAmPo (1942 ed.)
Oh! I would the world were all mine own. I Would the World Were Mine. Caroline E. S. Norton. DiM
O Iacchus! power excelling. Initiates. Aristophanes. *Fr.* The Frogs. GrR
O Icarus, incarnate soul of flight. Icarus. Alfred Raymond Bellinger. LPS-1
O Idleness, too fond of me. Idleness [*or* To Idleness]. T. Sturge Moore. PoeT; TCPD
Oh, if ever I get married, it will be in June. The Banks of the Roses. *Unknown.* ShS
Oh, if I could only make you see. Her Mother. Alice Cary. OHIP
O if love were had for asking. The Sailor's Sweetheart. Duncan Campbell Scott. PeCV
Oh, if my love offended me. Pet's Punishment. Joseph Ashby-Sterry. BOHV
O, if poor sinners did but know. The Preacher's Legacy. *Unknown.* ABS
Oh, if the world were mine, Love. If. James Jeffrey Roche. HBV; PR
Oh if They Only Knew! Edith L. Mapes. BLRP; WBLP
Oh, if thou knew'st how thou thyself dost harm. Sonnet [*or* To Aurora *or* Two in One]. Earl of Stirling. Aurora, XXXIII. EBSV; ElL; ES; EV-2; FaFP; GTBS; GTBS-D; GTBS-W; GTSE; GTSL
Oh, if you love her. Advice to a Lover. S. Charles Jellicoe. HBV
Oh, if you were a little boy. Wishes. Kate Greenaway. BoChLi (1950 ed.)
Oh! ignorant boy, it is the secret hour. Phraxanor to Joseph. Charles Jeremiah Wells. *Fr.* Joseph and His Brethren. VA
O ignorant poor man, what dost thou bear. An Acclamation. Sir John Davies. *Fr.* Nosce Teipsum. OxBoCh; TuPP
Oh, I'm a good old rebel, that's what I am. The Rebel [*or* Good Old Rebel *or* I'm a Good Old Rebel]. Innes Randolph. ABF; CSF; KN; OxBoLi; SPP
Oh, I'm a gwinter sing, gwinter sing. Gwinter Sing All along de Way. *Unknown.* BoAN-1
Oh, I'm a little Tuchman. The Little Dutchman. Mary Mapes Dodge. GaP
Oh, I'm a Texas cowboy. The Texas Cowboy. *Unknown.* CSF
Oh, I'm a-gwine to leave you, Shallo. Shallo Brown. *Unknown.* SoAmSa
Oh I'm in love with the janitor's boy. The Janitor's Boy. Nathalia Crane. GoTP; NeMA; StaSt; TSWC
Oh, I'm mad for Don Juan. How to Tell Juan Don from Another. Gardner E. Lewis. FiBHP
Oh, I'm the man that kin raise so long. I'm the Man That Kin Raise So Long. *Unknown.* StDa
Oh! I'm the New Year. The New Year. *Unknown.* BoTP
Oh, in Byrontown of high renown. Byrontown. Larry Gorman. ShS
Oh, in eighteen hundred and forty-one [*or* sixty-one]. Paddy Works on the Railway [*or* Poor Paddy . . .]. *Unknown.* AmSS; AS; SoAmSa
Oh, in mah dyin' hour. Jesus Goin' to Make Up Mah Dyin' Bed. *Unknown.* SoAF
Oh, in South Australia where I was born. South Australia. *Unknown.* ShS
Oh! in the quiet haven, safe for aye. Inscription. William Alexander. TIP
Oh in whose grove have we wakened, the bees. Two Horses. W. S. Merwin. NePA
O, Inexpressible as Sweet. George Edward Woodberry. Wild Eden, VII. AA; BAP; HBV; PFY

O, Inexpressible as Sweet (*continued*)
(Song: "O, inexpressible as sweet.") InMe
O Inverey came down Deeside, whistling and playing. The Baron o' Brackley. *Unknown.* EBSV
Oh! is it bale-fire in thy brazen hand. To the Goddess of Liberty. George Sterling. PoFr
O is it death or life. Requies. Arthur Symons. POTT
Oh Is It the Jar of Nations. A. E. Housman. MaPo
(Jar of Nations, The.) LiTB
Oh, Is It Wrought. Ernst von der Recke, *tr. fr. Danish by* Charles W. Stork. BoDS
O, is not this a holy spot? On Laying the Cornerstone of the Bunker Hill Monument. John Pierpont. AnNE; PAH
O Islay! sweet Islay! Dear Islay! Thomas Pattison. EBSV
Oh, isn't it fun—when the rain comes down? My Funny Umbrella. Alice Wilkins. GFA
O it fell out upon a day. The Laird o Drum. *Unknown.* ESPB
Oh, it is good to camp with the spirit! Courage, Mon Ami [*or* The Devil Is Dying]. Willard Wattles. PC; PR
O, it is great for our country to die, where ranks are contending! Elegiac. James Gates Percival. AA; HBV; LBAP; LEAP; MDAH
O it is hard to work for God. Right Must Win. Frederick William Faber. JKCP; LPS-2; MaRV; VA
O it is well, that ye have hearts to feel. Physician's Character and Aims: Science Progressive. Abraham Coles. *Fr.* The Microcosm. PoP
Oh, it was a musical old Beetle! The Concert Rehearsal. Wolstan Dixey. PEOR
Oh, it was not a pheasant cock. The Drowned Lady. *Unknown.* ChTr
O, it was out by Donnycarney. Song. James Joyce. Chamber Music, XXXI. MBP; MoBrPo; OBVV
O Italy, how beautiful thou art! Samuel Rogers. *Fr.* Italy. LPS-2
O Italy, I see the lonely towers. To Italy. Giacomo Leopardi. AWP; WoL
Oh, it's a southerly wind and a cloudy sky. Southerly Wind. *Unknown.* ShS
Oh, it's H-A-P-P-Y I am, and it's F-R-double-E. The Bells. *Unknown.* BOHV; FiBHP
Oh, it's hell to sit in a side car when the trucks are crashing by. Ode to a Side Car. "J. P. H." PaA
O it's hippity hop to bed! Hippity Hop to Bed. Leroy F. Jackson. GFA; TiPo
"Oh, it's Hynde Horn fair, and it's Hynde Horn free." Hynde Horn. *Unknown.* GN
O it's I that am the captain of a tidy little ship. My Ship and I. Robert Louis Stevenson. BoChLi; PPL
Oh, it's move along, you dogies, don't be driftin' by th' way. Cowboy's Salvation Song. Robert V. Carr. PoOW
Oh, it's Sinbad the sailor and Robinson Crusoe. Sinbad. *Unknown.* SoAmSa
Oh, it's spring once more in France, and it's spring in gay Algiers. The Vagabond at Home. Ruth Wright Kauffman. NLK
Oh, it's treat the cook with a pleasant look. Campfire and Bunkhouse. *Unknown.* CoSo
Oh, it's twenty gallant gentlemen. The Last Hunt. William Roscoe Thayer. AA; FaBoBe; HBV
O it's up in the Highlands. Bonnie James Campbell. *Unknown.* BaBo (A *vers.*); ESPB
"Oh! I've got a plum-cake, and a fine feast I'll make." The Plum-Cake [*or* Another Plum-Cake]. Ann Taylor. HBVY; OTPC (1923 ed.)
Oh, I've ridden plenty of horses. Noonday Sun. Kathryn Jackson *and* Byron Jackson. FaPON; TiPo
Oh, Jack St. James can always cut a dash. Anthony Delius. *Fr.* The Great Divide. BoSA
Oh, Jack's come home from sea today. Our Jack's Come Home Today. *Unknown.* ShS
O Jan Vermeer of Delft, descend, come near. She Lives with the Furies of Hope and Despair. Delmore Schwartz. FiMAP
Oh, Jane was a neighbor for six months or more. Jane Was a Neighbor. *Unknown.* BaBo
O Janitor bound with hard iron—a truly unworthy fate! To a Janitor. Ovid. Amores, I, 6. RoL
O Jean Baptiste, pourquoi. Pourquoi You Greased. *Unknown.* ChTr
O Jean, my Jean, when the bell ca's the congregation. Tam i' the Kirk. Violet Jacob. GoTS; HBMV; MM; POTE
O Jehanne, with the trumpets in your name. Prayer to Jehanne of France. Joseph Auslander. NeTW
O Jellon Grame sat in Silver Wood. Jellon Grame. *Unknown.* BaBo; ESPB; OBB
Oh! Jesse was the man, he traveled through the land. Jesse James (C *vers.*). *Unknown.* CoSo
O Jesu. Jean Jacques Olier. WHL
O Jesu Parvule. *Unknown, at. to* John Brackley. *See* I Saw a Sweet and Silly Sight.
O Jesus! at Thy feet we wait. Come, Lord Jesus. Charles Wesley. BePJ
O Jesus, hidden God, I cry to thee. Veni, Domine Jesu! Henry Augustus Rawes. WHL
O Jesus, I have promised. To the End. John E. Bode. BLRP
O Jesus! Jesus! dearest Lord! Jesus, My God and My All. Frederick William Faber. BePJ
O Jesus, King most wonderful. The Conqueror Renowned. St. Bernard of Clairvaux. BePJ
O Jesus, little King. Gifts. Sister Mary of the Visitation. WHL
O Jesus, living in Mary. O Jesu. Jean Jacques Olier. WHL
Oh Jesus nevuh come in the mornin'. Jesus Nevuh Come in the Mornin'. *Unknown.* StDa
O Jesus! Sweet the Tears I Shed. Ray Palmer. BePJ
O Jesus, thou art standing. William Walsham How. OIF
O Jesus, Thou the beauty art. The King in His Beauty. St. Bernard of Clairvaux. BePJ
O Jesus! When I Think of Thee. George W. Bethune. BePJ
O Job, Job (uh-huh). Job. *Unknown.* OuSiCo
O Johney was as brave a knight. Johnie Scot. *Unknown.* BaBo (A *vers.*); ESPB
Oh, Johnny Bull! you know, John. The Red and the Blue. H. A. Roby. FOAH
Oh, Johnny came over the other day. The Rio Grande. *Unknown.* ABF
O Johnny Dear, Why Did You Go? *Unknown. See* Springfield Mountain.
Oh, Johnny Fife and Johnny's wife. Johnny Fife and Johnny's Wife. Mildred Plew Meigs. GaP; TiPo
O Joseph, of the holy family least. The Father. Dorothy Scott Ballard. ChIP
O joy of creation. What the Bullet Sang. Bret Harte. AA; BAV; LEAP; LH; MAP; MDAH; MoAmPo (1942 ed.); OBEV; OBVV; PFY
O Joy of Love's Renewing. Andrew Lang. BSV
O joy of suffering! Walt Whitman. *Fr.* The Poem of Joys. PC
O joy! that in our embers. Wordsworth. *Fr.* Ode: Intimations of Immortality. OQP; QP-2
O joy, too high for my low style to show! Astrophel and Stella, LXIX. Sir Philip Sidney. BLV; BoLiVe; MaPo; PoFS; ReEn; SiCE; SiPS; TrGrPo; TuPP
O joys! infinite sweetness! with what flowers. The Morning Watch. Henry Vaughan. BrBE; LiTB; LoBV; MaPo; MePo; OBS; OxBoCh; ReEn; SeSePo; ViBoPo
O joys of love and joys of fame. The Last Hour. Ethel Clifford. HBV; NLK
Oh, Juley, you're a lady. Juley. *Unknown.* SoAmSa
O Julie Ann Johnson. Julie Ann Johnson. *Unknown.* ABF
O June has her diamonds, her diamonds of sheen. October in New Zealand. Jessie Mackay. BoAu
O June, O June, that we desired so. June. William Morris. *Fr.* The Earthly Paradise. BPN; POTT; PoVP; ViBoPo; ViPo; VLEP
O kangaroo, O kangaroo. The Kangaroo. Ogden Nash. WhC
"O Katie, what I suffer'd for your sake!" Tennyson. *Fr.* The Brook. EnSW
O keen pellucid air! nothing can lurk. A Brilliant Day. Charles Tennyson Turner. EnSW
Oh, keep your kisses, young provoking girl! The Kiss. *Unknown.* OnYI; OxBI
O keeper of the Sacred Key. In State. Forceythe Willson. AA; BlG; LPS-2
O ken ye Wullie Broon, Jeanie. Bonnie Jeanie. J. B. Morton. ShBV-4
O Kia-Kunae, praise! The Chief's Prayer after the Salmon Catch. Constance Lindsay Skinner. BoCaPo; NP
Oh, kind folks, listen to my song. Abraham's Daughter. Septimus Winner. TrAS
O kindly house, where time my soul endows. The Old House. George Edward Woodberry. HBMV
"O King Amasis, hail!" Amasis. Laurence Binyon. OBVV
Oh King of Stars! Hospitality in Ancient Ireland. *Unknown.* OnYI
O king of Terrors! whose unbounded sway. To Death. Countess of Winchilsea. HBV
O King of the Friday. *Unknown, tr. fr. Irish by* Douglas Hyde. GTIV; MeRV
O King of the starry sky. Starry Sky. *Unknown.* AnIL; SiB
Oh! King who hast the key. Exspecto Resurrectionem. Charlotte Mew. LO
O kiss, which dost those ruddy gems impart. Astrophel and Stella, LXXXI. Sir Philip Sidney. SiPS
Oh, kneel to that God force of love. Prayer. Lucia Trent. ChIP
O knight of silent hour and silent soul. Sonnet on the Death of Paul Ehrlich, Discoverer of Salvarsan. Jerome Meyers. PoP
Oh, la, Willie, I'll tell your mamma. Going to Boston. *Unknown.* ABF

Oh! ladies and gentlemen, please to draw near; I'll sing of a man who lived in Hartfordshire. Down, Down Derry Down. *Unknown.* AS
O lady amorous. Canzonetta: A Bitter Song to His Lady. Pier Moronelli di Fiorenza. AWP; JAWP; WBP
O Lady leal and lovesomest. To Our Lady. Robert Henryson. ACP; CAW
O lady, leave thy silken thread. Song. Thomas Hood. HoPM
O Lady Moon. Christina Rossetti. *Fr.* Sing-Song. PRWS (Lady Moon.) PCH
O Lady o'er the skies, Regent Terrene. Ballade That Villon Made at the Request of His Mother to Intercede with Our Lady. Villon. TrFP
O Lady of all the poems in the world! Complaint to the Moon. Henry Longan Stuart. GTIV
O Lady of the Passion, dost thou weep? Our Lady of the Passion. John Mauropus. ISi
O Lady, rock never your young son young. Young Hunting. *Unknown.* BaBo (A *vers.*); ESPB; OBB; ViBoFo
O Lady, together with the Child you take. Cry from the Battlefield. Robert Menth. ISi
O, Lady, twine no wreath for me. The Cypress Wreath. Sir Walter Scott. *Fr.* Rokeby, V. ERP
Oh, lady, wake! the azure moon. Ballad of Bedlam. *Unknown.* NA
O Lady! we receive but what we give. The Life of Nature. Samuel Taylor Coleridge. *Fr.* Dejection; an Ode. RO
O lady with the luminous sombre eyes. Sister Mary Conceptia. Helene Mullins. PraNu
O Lamb of God, O little infant lying. Agnus Dei. Victor Kinon. CAW
Oh, Lamkin was a mason. Lamkin (C *vers.*). *Unknown.* BaBo
O Land Beloved. George Edward Woodberry. *Fr.* My Country. PAH
Oh, land of Castile, you do raise me up. Castile. Miguel de Unamuno. TeCS
O Land, of every land the best. Peace. Phoebe Cary. LPS-2; PAH
O land of gold, I sing to thee. Alaska. *Unknown.* PoRL
O land without guilt, strong city, safe built in a marvellous place. Bernard of Cluny. *Fr.* De Contemptu Mundi. LaP
Oh, landlord, have you a daughter fair, parley-voo? Hinky Dinky, Parley Voo? *Unknown.* ABF
O Lapwing! Blake. ChTr (Lapwing, The.) RO
Oh, larch tree with scarlet berries. Larch Tree. Laurie Lee. NeBP
Oh lark, lark of my silence. Longings. José Moreno Villa. CoSP; OnPM
O lark! sweet lark! The Singer. Edmund Clarence Stedman. PRWS
Oh! Larry M'Hale he had little to fear. Larry M'Hale. Charles James Lever. *Fr.* Charles O'Malley, the Irish Dragoon. OnYI; TIP
Oh last and best of Scots! who did'st maintain. Upon the Death of the Viscount [*or* Earl] of Dundee. Dryden. ACP; OBS; PoFr
O late and sweet, too sweet, too late! The Rose in October. Mary Townley. SN
O Lawd, Black Betty, Bambalam. Black Betty. *Unknown.* ABF
Oh, Lawd, How Long? *with music.* *Unknown.* ABF
Oh Lawd I Went Up on the Mountain, *with music.* *Unknown.* OuSiCo
Oh, Lawd. Shot my pistol in de heart o' town. Shot My Pistol in de Heart of Town. *Unknown.* ABF
Oh, lay my ashes on the wind. The Curse. Edna St. Vincent Millay. NP
Oh! lay the burden care aside. A New Year's Guest. Eliza F. Moriarty. PEOR
O, Lay Thy Hand in Mine, Dear! Gerald Massey. HBV; LPS-1
O Le Lupe, Gelett Burgess, this is very sad to find. A Staccato to O Le Lupe. Bliss Carman. PA
Oh, lead me to a quiet cell. Portrait of the Artist. Dorothy Parker. PFE; PoeMoYo; WhC
O League of Kindness, woven in all lands. The League of Love in Action. Edwin Markham. PEDC
O learned man who never learned to learn. The Myth of Arthur. G. K. Chesterton. HBMV
Oh leave his body broken on the rocks. On a Dying Boy. William Bell. NePoEA
Oh, leave me to my own. Leave Me to My Own. Lew Sarett. LEAP
Oh! leave the past to bury its own dead. To One Who Would Make Confession. Wilfrid Scawen Blunt. The Love Sonnets of Proteus, LXII. HBV; LEAP; ViBoPo
O leave them, Muse! O leave them to their woes. Keats. *Fr.* Hyperion. ViBoPo
O leave this barren spot to me! The Beech Tree's Petition. Thomas Campbell. ADAH; GTSL; HBV; SN
O leave your hand where it lies cool. Song and Music. Dante Gabriel Rossetti. EmBrPo
O leeze me on my spinning-wheel. Bess and Her Spinning-Wheel. Burns. BSV
O lend to me, sweet nightingale. The Daughter of Mendoza. Mirabeau Bonaparte Lamar. AA; HBV; HiLiAm
"O Lente, Lente." Meleager, *tr. fr. Greek by* F. L. Lucas. GrPE
O Lente, Lente, Curite Noctis Equi. Christopher Marlowe. *See* End of Dr. Faustus, The.
O lest the world should task you to recite. Sonnets, LXXII. Shakespeare. PeBoSo
O, lest your true love may seem false in this. Shakespeare. *Fr.* Sonnets, LXXII. LO
Oh, let a father's curse be on thy soul. To the Lord Chancellor. Shelley. ViBoPo
O let me be in loving nice. Punctilio. Mary Elizabeth Coleridge. OBEV (new ed.); OBVV; TOP
O let me breathe what all men pray! Asclepius. Pindar. *Fr.* Pythian Odes, III. GrR; OxBG
O let me die a-singing! Morning Fancy. Mary McNeil Fenollosa. AA
Oh let me die at dawn. The Soul's Departure. James Smetham. RO
O, Let Me Kiss. Karl Gjellerup, *tr. fr. Danish by* Charles W. Stork. BoDS
Oh, let me know. For Easter [*or* Easter Prayer]. Frances Ridley Havergal. OQP; PraP; QP-1
O let me, Lady, silence calumny. Protestation. Bertrans de Born. LiTW
Oh, let me lay my head tonight upon your breast. I Am Your Wife. *Unknown.* PoToHe (new ed.)
O let me leave the plains behind. Shakespeare. Sir William Watson. HBV
O Let Me Love My Love unto Myself Alone. Arthur Hugh Clough. *Fr.* Dipsychus. OAEP, *abr.*; ViPP, *sl. diff.* (Hidden Love, The.) BPN
O, let me reverently kiss thine eye. O, Let Me Kiss. Karl Gjellerup. BoDS
Oh, let me run and hide. Spring Ecstasy. Lizette Woodworth Reese. MAP; MoAmPo
Oh, let mee not serve so, as those men serve. Elegie VI. John Donne. *Fr.* Elegies. EnLP
O let mee still and silente lye. *Unknown.* SeCSL
O let not a word of ill omen be heard. Demus; a Return to His Better Self. Aristophanes. *Fr.* The Knights. GrR
O let sweete slumber dreames. *Unknown.* SeCSL
Oh let the magpie blow. Heart of Light. David Campbell. BoAV
O let the solid ground. Song. Tennyson. *Fr.* Maud. BPN; GEPC; HBV
O, let the soul her slumbers break! Ode on the Death of His Father [*or* Coplas on the Death of His Father]. Jorge Manrique. AnSpL-1; LyMA; TeCS; WoL
Oh, Let Thy Teachings. Immanuel di Roma, *tr. fr. Hebrew by* Joseph Chotzner. TrJP
Oh, Let Us Howl Some Heavy Note. John Webster. *Fr.* The Duchess of Malfi, IV, ii. InvP; SiCE (Madman's Song, The.) ElL
O, let us pay the time but needful woe. Shakespeare. *Fr.* King John, V, vii. PoFr
Oh let your shining orb grow dim. To the Sun. Roy Campbell. *Fr.* Mithraic Emblems. FaBoTw; MeRV
Oh let-n me ride, oh let-n me ride. Low Down Chariot. *Unknown.* OuSiCo
Oh, let's fix us a julep and kick us a houn'. Boogie-woogie Ballads. St. Clair McKelway. PoNe
Oh, let's go up the hill and scare ourselves. The Bonfire. Robert Frost. InvP
O Liberty, proud inspiration! Nikolai Yazykov, *formerly at. to* Kondrati Ryleyev, *tr. fr. Russian by* C. M. Bowra. BoRS
O Liberty, thou child of Law. Law and Liberty. E. J. Cutler. PTA-2
O Liberty, thou goddess heavenly bright. Addison. *Fr.* A Letter from Italy. PoFr
Oh, life in the Lab. is a frolic. Life in the Chem. Lab. Henry W. Eliot, Jr. CAG
Oh, life is a glorious cycle of song. Some Beautiful Letters: Comment. Dorothy Parker. ALV; InMe
O Life! that mystery that no man knows. Life. Lizzie M. Little. VA
Oh Life, thou Nothing's younger brother! Life and Fame. Abraham Cowley. AnEnPo; LiTG
O life! what lets thee from a quick decease? I Die [*or* Dye] Alive. Robert Southwell. MeRV; ReIE; SiCE
O Life, what refuge have we fleeing thee. Aesop, *tr. fr. Greek by* Lilla Cabot Perry. GrPo
O Life with the sad seared face. To Life. Thomas Hardy. ChMo; CMP; EmBrPo; TOP
O! lift me as a wave, a leaf, a cloud! Shelley. *Fr.* Ode to the West Wind. PC
O, Lift One Thought. Samuel Taylor Coleridge. *See* Epitaph: "Stop, Christian passerby!"

O lift with reverent hand that tarnished flower. The Missal. Charles Lamb. ES

O lifted face of mute appeal! Come Love or Death. Will Henry Thompson. AA

O Light. Kay Smith. BoCaPo (1948 ed.)

O Light Invisible, we praise Thee! T. S. Eliot. *Fr.* The Rock. OxBoCh; TrPWD; TwCV

O Light serene! present in one [*or* him] who breathes. Ideal Beauty. Fernando de Herrera. CAW; TeCS

O light that grows in eyes purged with the tears of agony. O Light. Kay Smith. BoCaPo (1948 ed.)

Oh Light Was My Head. C. Day Lewis. *Fr.* Two Songs (Written to Irish Airs). OAEP (2d ed.)

O, like a queen's her happy tread. Song. Sir William Watson. HBV

Oh, like a tree. The Tree. John Freeman. BoTP

O l'il' lamb out in de col'. Hymn. Paul Laurence Dunbar. AA; BAP; VOD

O-o-o-oh, lil' man. Chahcoal Man. *Unknown.* AS

O lilac. Lilac. F. S. Flint. HBMV

O Lily of the King, low lies thy silver wing. Lilium Regis. Francis Thompson. HBMV; JKCP; WGRP

O limerick, Learest of lyrics. Lessons in Limericks, III. David McCord. InMe

Oh, limpid stream of Tyrus, now I hear. A Classic Ode. Charles Battell Loomis. NA

O Linos, pure music was given. Linos. *Unknown.* OxBG

O Lionel has the itch to etch. The Itch to Etch. Harold A. Larrabee. WhC

Oh! list to the lay of a poor Irish harper. Bold Phelim Brady, the Bard of Armagh. *Unknown.* OnYI

Oh, list to this incredible tale. Thomson Green and Harriet Hale. W. S. Gilbert. TSWC

Oh, Listen. Sergei Aleksandrovich Yesenin, *tr. fr. Russian by* Babette Deutsch. TrRV

O listen, gude peopell, to my tale. The Laird o Logie (B *vers.*) *Unknown.* ESPB

Oh listen, listen, ladies gay! Rosabelle [*or* Harold's Song]. Sir Walter Scott. *Fr.* The Lay of the Last Minstrel, VI. BeLS; BSV; CG; EBSV; EmBrPo; EnLi-2; EnRP; EPP; ERP; EV-4; GTBS; GTBS-D; GTBS-W; GTSE; GTSL; HBV; OTPC

Oh! listen, little children, to a proper little song. A Nursery Legend. Henry S. Leigh. BOHV

Oh! listen, man! Immortality. Richard Henry Dana. AA; WGRP

Oh, listen—the sleigh's rushing on. Oh, Listen. Sergei Aleksandrovich Yesenin. TrRV

Oh, listen to the tale of Mister William, if you please. Mister William. W. S. Gilbert. TOP

Oh! listen to the water-mill, through all the live-long day. The Water Mill. Sarah Doudney. *Fr.* The Man o' Airlie. PTA-2. *See also* Listen to the water mill.

O Listen You to Whom I Meaning Much. Michael Strange. BoFr

O little bird, I'd be. To a Songster. John Banister Tabb. InP

O little bird, you sing. The Secret. Arthur Wallace Peach. HBMV

O little breeze, how fresh and sweet. Spring. Muggurdich Beshigtashlian. ArmLP

O little buds all bourgeoning with spring. A Song in Spring [*or* Two Songs in Spring]. Thomas S. Jones, Jr. LBMV; POT; PoTo; VOD

O little buds, break not so fast! Budding-Time Too Brief. Evaleen Stein. AA

Oh, little cat beside my stool. Cinderella's Song. Elizabeth Madox Roberts. PoRh

O Little Child of Bethlehem. The Silent Stars Go By. Harriet Hartridge Tompkins. MaRV

O little child, our first-born. For Virginia Dare. Lucy Cherry Crisp. NoCaPo (rev. ed.)

Oh, little Christ, why do you sigh. Christmas Eve in France. Jessie Redmond Fauset. BANP

O little city-gals, don't never go it. Spring. James Russell Lowell. *Fr.* The Biglow Papers, 2d Series, No. VI. MCCG

Oh, little Dame Crump with her little hair broom. Little Dame Crump. *Unknown.* FTB

O little feet! that such long years. Weariness. Longfellow. IAP

O little fleet! that on thy quest divine. Columbus and the *Mayflower.* Richard Monckton Milnes. MC; PAH

O little flower, you love me so. A Child's Fancy. "A." PRWS

O little friend, I wait on you with praise. The Resurrection and the Life. Robert Norwood. MaRV

O little friend, your nose is ready: you sniff. Dog[s]. Harold Monro. GoTP; MBP; MoBrPo; TCEP

O little frozen peach blossoms. April Fools. Katherine Brégy. JKCP (1955 ed.)

Oh! Little Girl! A Negro Sings. Normil Sylvain. PoNe

O little head of gold! O candle of my house! Lullaby of a [*or* the] Woman of the Mountain. Padraic Pearse. BOL; NP; OnYI

O little hearts, beat home, beat home. Swallow Song. Marjorie Pickthall. CaP; OCL

O little house, O dear and sweet my dwelling. Lament for Alcuin. Fredugis, *tr. by* Helen Waddell. TriL

O little insects in my autumn garden. Miyamori, *tr. fr. Japanese by* Lois J. Erickson. SoLD

O little lambs! the month is cold. Lambs in the Meadow. Laurence Alma-Tadema. PRWS

O little land of lapping seas. The Promised Land. Jessie E. Sampter. TrJP

O little lark, you need not fly. In the Heart. Anna Bunston de Bary. MaRV

Oh, little loveliest lady mine! A Valentine. Laura E. Richards. AA; DD; HH; MPB; YeAr

O little mouse, so frightened of each sound. O Pity Our Small Size. Benjamin Rosenbaum. TrJP

O little one, daughter, my dearest. To My Daughter. Archibald Lampman. CPG

O little room, my harbor from the sea. Sonnet. Petrarch. Sonnets to Laura: To Laura in Life, CXCVIII. LyPI

O little self, within whose smallness lies. Sonnet. John Masefield. *Fr.* Sonnets ("Long long ago"). GTML; HBV; PoeMoYo; POTE; WGRP

O little soldier with the golden helmet. Dandelion. Hilda Conkling. BoChLi; FaPON; GFA; MPB; PoRh; TiPo; TSW; TSWC; TVC; TVSH

"O little Son, upon your brow." Young Jesus. Leslie Savage Clark. ChIP

O little stag, thou little bleating one. *Unknown.* *Fr.* Sweeney the Mad. SiB

O little town, O little town. The Little Town [*or* Bethlehem]. Clinton Scollard. MaRV; SDH

O Little Town of Bethlehem. Phillips Brooks. AA; BLRP; COAH; FaFP; FaPON; GN; HBV; HH; MaRV; NeHB; OHIP; OlF; OTPC; PCH; PTA-1; SDH; TreF; WBLP; WGRP; YaCaBo

Oh! little town of Bethlehem, how still we see thee lie. Carol with Variations. Phyllis McGinley. QS

O lively, O most charming pug. *See* O lovely O most charming pug.

Oh! lives there, Heaven! beneath thy dread expanse. The Pilgrim of a Day. Thomas Campbell. OBRV

O living flame of love. The Living Flame of Love. St. John of the Cross. LiTW; TeCS

O living image of eternal youth! Trilby. Alice Brown. AA

O living pictures of the dead. The War Films. Sir Henry Newbolt. MaRV; MM

O living will that shalt endure. In Memoriam A. H. H., CXXXI [*or* Prayer *or* The Truths That Never Can Be Proved]. Tennyson. BEL; BoLiVe; BPN; CBE; CoBE; EM-2; EmBrPo; EnL; EnLi-2; EnLit; EPN; FaBoBe; GEPC; HBV; MaRV; OAEP; PIAE; TOP; ViPo; VLEP; WGRP

O loathsome place! where I. Earl of Surrey. SiPS

O Logan, sweetly didst thou glide. Logan Braes. Burns. RO

O Logie o' Buchan, O Logie the laird. Logie o' Buchan. George Halket. EBSV; EV-3

O London is a dainty place. London Is a Fine Town. *Unknown.* CoMu

Oh! London town, you are grim and grey. London. T. P. Cameron Wilson. HBMV; VOD

Oh, London Town's a fine town, and London sights are rare. London Town. John Masefield. ChMo; CMP; OtMeF

O lonely bay of Trinity. The Cable Hymn. Whittier. PAH

Oh! lonely is our old green fort. Old Fort Meigs. *Unknown.* MC; PAH

O lonely trumpeter, coasting down the sky. To a Wild Goose over Decoys. Lew Sarett. BLA; MAP; NP; PoeMoYo; PoTo

"O lonely workman, standing there." In the Moonlight. Thomas Hardy. BMEP; LEAP; NP

O lonesome sea-gull, floating far. Sea-Birds. Elizabeth Akers Allen. AA; BLA; FaBoBe; HBV; LBAP

O long ago, when Faery-land. Prince Riquet's Song. Stopford Brooke. *Fr.* Riquet of the Tuft. VA

Oh, long long. The Grass on the Mountain. *Tr. by* Mary Austin. AWP; FaPON; JAWP; WBP

Oh! Look at the Moon. Eliza Lee Follen. *See* Moon, The.

Oh, look down upon Long Lance. Death-Song. Chief Long Lance. APW

O look how the loops and balloons of bloom. Stormy Day. W. R. Rodgers. AlDL; LiTB

Oh, look up and down that long, lonesome road. Long, Lonesome Road. *Unknown.* OuSiCo

Oh, loosen the snood that you wear, Janette. Janette's Hair. Charles Graham Halpine. HBV

O Lord!/ Thou hast given me a body. Thanksgiving for the Body. Thomas Traherne. ImOP

O Lord, as You lay so soft and white. A Christmas Song. Teresa Brayton. JKCP

O Lord, at Joseph's humble bench. The Carpenter. George Macdonald. TrPWD
O Lord, dear Lord, behold me at Thy feet. The Nun's Vow. Sister Mary Wilfrid. PraNu
O Lord, for all I done today. The Telephone Girl's Prayer. Oliver Herford. LauV
O Lord, fulfil Thy will. Fulfil Thy Will. Christina Rossetti. PraP
Oh Lord, give me a plane. Queen of Horizons. Joseph Dever. ISi; JKCP (1955 ed.)
O Lord God of my salvation, I have cried day and night before thee. Psalms, LXXXVIII, Bible, *O.T.* TriL
O Lord, How Excellent Is Thy Name. Psalms, VIII, Bible, *O.T.* TreFS
O Lord, How Long Shall I Cry? Habakkuk, I: 2–II: 20, Bible, *O.T.* LiTW
O Lord, how many do increase. Domine Quid Multiplicati Sunt. Psalm III, Bible, *O.T., tr. by* Thomas Sternhold. SiCE
O Lord, I Come Pleading. James Gilchrist Lawson. BLRP
O Lord, I have heard Thy speech, and was afraid. The Prayer of Habakkuk. Habakkuk, Bible, *O.T.* BHV
O Lord, I pray. Today, O Lord [*or* Not to Be Ministered To]. Maltbie D. Babcock. OQP; PraP; QP-2; TrPWD
O Lord, I pray: that for each happiness. Petition. John Drinkwater. TrPWD
O Lord, I wonder at thy lov. Thomas Traherne. *Fr.* The Approach. TrPWD
O Lord, I would be great. I Would Be Great. Hattie B. McCracken. OQP; QP-2
O Lord, in me there lieth nought. Psalm CXXXIX. Countess of Pembroke. OBSC; OxBoCh
O Lord, in your courtesy. Praise of Diseases. Jacopone da Todi. LyPI
Oh Lord, I've never lived where churches grow. A Cowboy's Prayer. Badger Clark. DDA
O Lord Jesus, let me know myself, let me know Thee. Petitions of Saint Augustine. *Unknown.* WHL
Oh Lord! methought, what pain it was to drown! A Dream of Wrecks. Shakespeare. King Richard III, *fr.* I, iv. ChTr
O Lord, My Best Desire Fulfil. William Cowper. OxBoCh
O Lord My God, Let Flesh and Blood. *Unknown.* ReIE
O Lord! My Hiding Place. Thomas Raffles. BePJ
O Lord! O Lord!—how are the seas of thought. In the Depths of Night. Manuel Gutiérrez Nájera. CAW
Oh, Lord, Oh, my Lord! Keep Me f'om Sinkin' Down. *Unknown.* BoAN-1
O Lord of all compassionate control. The Portrait. Dante Gabriel Rossetti. The House of Life, X. BPN; EmBrPo; OAEP; PoVP; ViPo; VLEP
O Lord of heaven, and earth, and sea! Giver of All [*or* Giving to God]. Christopher Wordsworth. MaRV; VA
O Lord of Hosts! Almighty King! Oliver Wendell Holmes. OlF
O Lord of Life and God of Love. The Teacher's Prayer. Nancy Byrd Turner. PraP
O Lord of Life, Thy Kingdom Is at Hand. Marion Franklin Ham. MaRV
O Lord, our Lord, how excellent is thy name. Psalm VIII, Bible, *O.T.* AWP; CBOV; EM-1; EnLi-1; JAWP; MaRV; OnPM; OTPC (1946 ed.); OuHeWo; PFE; PG (1955 ed.); TreFS; TrGrPo; TrJP
O Lord, our Lord! how wondrously (quoth she). The Prioress' Tale. Chaucer, *mod. by* Wordsworth. *Fr.* The Canterbury Tales. GoBC
O Lord, our Lord, thy name how merveillous. The Prioress's Prologue [*or* The Prioress's Tale *or* Prologe of the Prioresses Tale]. Chaucer. *Fr.* The Canterbury Tales. AtBAP; EM-1; OAEP; OxBoCh
O Lord, permit us here to raise our voice. The Holy Angels. *Unknown. Fr.* The Little Office of the Holy Angels. WHL
O Lord, please lend me now Thine ear. The Cowman's Prayer. *Unknown.* SoAF
O Lord, Save We Beseech Thee. *Unknown.* TrJP
O Lord, seek us, O Lord, find us. Lord, Save Us, We Perish. Christina Rossetti. TrPWD
O Lord, the children of my people are Thy peculiar treasures. The Rapture. Thomas Traherne. EPS (1942 ed.)
O Lord, the Giver of my days. A Heathen Hymn. Sir Lewis Morris. MaRV
O Lord, the hard-won miles. A Prayer. Paul Laurence Dunbar. TrPWD
O Lord, the sun is low. Evening. Robert J. Craig. PraP
O Lord, the whistling sword is beauty. Headsong. Joseph Bennett. LiTM (rev. ed.); NePA
O Lord, there sit apart in lonely places. For Christmas Eve—a Prayer. *Unknown.* PraP
O Lord, Thou Hast Enticed Me. Jeremiah, XX: 7–10, Bible, *O.T.* TrJP
Oh Lord! thou hast known me, and searched me out. An Hymn on the Omnipresence. John Byrom. CEP; TrPWD
O Lord, thou hast searched me, and known me. The Searcher of Hearts. Psalm CXXXIX, Bible, *O.T.* CBOV; GrCo-1; WGRP
O Lord, thou hast to Poland lent thy might. Polish National Hymn. Aloizy Felsinki. PoFr
O Lord, Thy Wing Outspread. William John Blew. VA
O Lord, we come this morning. Listen, Lord. James Weldon Johnson. BANP
Oh Lord, when all our bones are thrust. Supplication. Edgar Lee Masters. ChMo; CMP; TrPWD
O Lord, who didst create all things. Plaint of an Humble Servant. Robert Nichols. WP
O Lord, who knowest every need of mine. A Woman's Prayer. *Unknown.* PraP
O Lord! who seest from yon starry height. The Image of God. Francisco Aldana. CAW; WGRP
O Lord, Who, when Thy cross was nigh. The Child's Evening Hymn. Francis Turner Palgrave. BOL
O Lord whose mercy never fails. Pro Libra Mea. Joseph I. C. Clarke. TrPWD
"O Lord, why grievest Thou?" By the Earth's Corpse. Thomas Hardy. ChMo; CMP; ViPo
O Lord, why must thy poets peak and pine. Priest or Poet. Shane Leslie. CAW; WGRP
O Lord, wilt thou not look upon our sore afflictions. Blake. *Fr.* Vala; or, The Four Zoas. ViBoPo
O Lord, with good the people dower! Hymn. Nikolai Nekrasov. WaL
O Lord, you know my inmost hope and thought. My Inmost Hope. Sarah Copia Sullam. TrJP
O Lords! O rulers of the nation! The People's Petition. Wathen Mark Wilks Call. OBVV; PoFr; VA
O Lordy, jes' give me a long white robe! Choose You a Seat 'n Set Down. *Unknown.* OuSiCo
Oh! lose the winter from thine heart, the darkness from thine eyes. May-Music. Rachel Annand Taylor. HBV
O loss of sight, of thee I most complain! The Blindness of Samson [*or* Samson on His Blindness]. Milton. *Fr.* Samson Agonistes. LiTB; LPS-1; UnPo
Oh! lost! forever lost!—no more. Hymn of a Virgin of Delphi at the Tomb of Her Mother. Thomas Moore. MOAH
Oh, Love and Death go ever hand in hand. Love and Life. Winfred Ernest Garrison. OQP; QP-2
O Love, Answer. Anne Ridler. SeCePo
O love, are all those arrowes gone. *Unknown.* SeCSL
O Love, be fed with apples while you may. Sick Love [*or* O Love in Me]. Robert Graves. CoEV; FaBoMo; POTE
Oh, Love builds on the azure sea. Love's Land. Isabella Valancy Crawford. CaP; OCL
O love divine, that stooped to share. Hymn of Trust. Oliver Wendell Holmes. *Fr.* The Professor at the Breakfast Table. AA; IAP; MaRV; NeHB; OlF; PraP; TrPWD
O Love, give me a passionate heart. A Prayer. Irene Rutherford McLeod. TrPWD
O Love! how cold and slow to take my part. Love, as a Warrior Lord. Ovid. LiTW
O Love, how deadly beats thy measure. Feodor Ivanovich Tyutchev, *tr. fr. Russian by* Sir Cecil Kisch. WaL
O Love, How Strangely Sweet. John Marston. *Fr.* The Dutch Courtesan. AtBAP; ElSeCe; TuPP (Song.) ElL; LO
O Love, how thou art [*or* Love, how thou'rt] tired out with rhyme! Margaret Cavendish, Duchess of Newcastle. EnLoPo; LO
O love, how utterly am I bereaved. Sonnets from "One Person." Elinor Wylie. NP
O Love, I never, never thought. Cancion. Juan II of Castile. AWP; JAWP; WBP
O Love, if you were here. If You Were Here. Philip Bourke Marston. HBV; VA
O Love, in every battle victor owned. Sophocles. *Fr.* Antigone. GrPo
O Love in Me. Robert Graves. *See* Sick Love.
"Oh love is fair, and love is rare;" my dear one she said. There's Wisdom in Women. Rupert Brooke. HBV
O, Love Is Not a Summer Mood. Richard Watson Gilder. HBV
O Love, king of this ample earth, behold. Beauty's Paradigm. Pierre de Ronsard. *Fr.* Sonnets pour Hélène. TrFP
O Love, Love, Love! O withering might! Fatima. Tennyson. LO; NBE; PIR; SeCePo
O Love, more fond in life's decline. Last Love. Feodor Ivanovich Tyutchev. WaL
O Love, my love, and perfect bliss. Medieval Norman Songs, VIII. *Unknown, tr. by* John Addington Symonds. AWP; JAWP; WBP
O Love, My Muse. Robert Bridges. ChMo; CMP
Oh Love! no habitant of earth thou art. Bitter Meditation [*or* Love *or* Love Unseen]. Byron. *Fr.* Childe Harold's Pilgrimage, IV. EPP; ERP; RO; ViBoPo
Oh, Love—no, Love! All the noise below, Love. Epilogue. Robert Browning. *Fr.* Ferishtah's Fancies. ViPP

O Love! O Glory! what are ye who fly. Vanitas Vanitatum [or The Siege of Ismail]. Byron. *Fr.* Don Juan, VII *and* VIII. GEPC; WoL
O Love, O thou that, for my fealty. Sonnet: To Love, in Great Bitterness [or In Great Bitterness]. Cino da Pistoia. AWP; OnPM
O Love of God incarnate. Incarnate Love. Wilbur Fisk Tillett. BLRP
Oh, love of woman, you are known to be. Sonnet. Alan Seeger. BAP
O love, so sweet at first. Disarmed. Laura Catherine Redden Searing. AA
O Love that casts out fear. Horatius Bonar. OlF
O Love, That Dost with Goodness Crown. John W. Chadwick. TrPWD
O love that is not love, but dear, so dear! There's Rosemary. Olive Tilford Dargan. LBMV
O Love That Lights the Evening Sky. Louis FitzGerald Benson. BPP
O Love! that stronger art than wine. Song [or Of Love]. *At. to* Aphra Behn *and to* —— Ousley. *Fr.* The Lucky Chance (*by* Aphra Behn). BrBE; LO; SeCL
O Love That Triumphs over Loss. Walter Russell Bowie. MaRV
O Love, That Wilt Not Let Me Go. George Matheson. BPP; GrCo-1; MaRV; OlF; TreFS; TrPWD; WGRP
O Love, the Interest Itself in Thoughtless Heaven. W. H. Auden. *See* Perhaps.
O Love, There Is No Beauty. Austin Clarke. GTIV
"Oh! Love," they said [or cried], "is King of Kings." Song. Rupert Brooke. HBV; TSW; TSWC
Oh, love this house, and make of it a home. For a New Home. Rosa Zagnoni Marinoni. PoToHe
O love, this morn when the sweet nightingale. William Morris. *Fr.* The Earthly Paradise. EG
O Love, thou art—so runs tradition. Predestination. Feodor Ivanovich Tyutchev. WaL
O Love, thou knowest well how that this lady. Canzone [or Sestina]: To the Lady Pietra, of Sienna [or Siena]. Dante. LiTW; LyPI
O Love! thou makest all things even. Love. Sarah Flower Adams. VA
O Love, Thy Hair! Kamal ud-Din of Isfahan, *tr. fr. Persian by* Ethel Watts Mumford *and* Louis H. Gray. LiTW
O Love triumphant over guilt and sin. L'Envoi [or Life]. Frederic Lawrence Knowles. ChIP; MaRV; OQP; QP-1; TrPWD
O love, turn from the unchanging sea, and gaze. October. William Morris. *Fr.* The Earthly Paradise. EPN; FaBoEn; POTT; ViPP; VLEP
O love, what hours were thine and mine. The Daisy. Tennyson. EnLoPo; OBVV; PoEL-5; VA; VLEP
O Love, when in my day of doom. The Gardener. Laurence Housman. TrPWD
O Love, who all this while hast urged me on. Canzone: To Love and to His Lady. Guido delle Colonne. AWP; LyPI
O Love, whose patient pilgrim feet. The Golden Wedding. David Gray. FaBoBe; HBV
O loved. . . I lost. . . . "The very world." Fickleness. Harry Kemp. PR
O, loveliest throat of all sweet throats. Edna St. Vincent Millay. *Fr.* Memorial to D. C. OxBA
O lovely age of gold! The Golden Age. Tasso. *Fr.* Aminta. AWP; WoL
Oh, Lovely Appearance of Death, *with music.* George Whitefield. OuSiCo
O lovely April, rich and bright. Song. Gustave Kahn. TrJP
O lovely Bellerie. To a Fountain. Pierre de Ronsard. FoS
O lovely chance, what can I do. Lovely Chance. Sara Teasdale. CP
Oh lovely day, oh happy day! Romance. Anton Delvieg. BoRS
Oh Lovely Fishermaiden. Heine. *See* Thou Lovely Fishermaiden.
O lovely Galatea, sweeter than. The Love Song of Polyphemus. Luis de Góngora. *Fr.* Polyphemus and Galatea. LiTW
O lovely little bird, I watch you fly. Sonnet. Petrarch. Sonnets to Laura: To Laura in Death, XC. LyPI
O lovely maiden, thou hast drawn my heart. The Unhappy Lover. Judah Al-Harizi. TrJP
Oh, lovely Mary Donnelly, my joy, my only best. Lovely Mary Donnelly. William Allingham. AnIV; GTSE; HBV; IrPN; LPS-1; VA
O lovely [or lively] O most charming pug. A Sonnet on a Monkey [or To a Monkey]. Marjory Fleming. ALV; FaFP; FiBHP; GoTP; LiTG; SiTL
Oh, Lovely Rock. Robinson Jeffers. Po
O lovely smile, O glint and glow. The Smile. Sophus Michaëlis. BoDS
Oh! lovely voices of the sky. Hymn for Christmas. Felicia Dorothea Hemans. COAH; GN; OTPC
Oh, lovers' eyes are sharp to see. The Maid of Neidpath. Sir Walter Scott. BeLS; BPN; EBSV; EmBrPo; EnRP; ERP; GTBS; GTBS-D; GTBS-W; GTSE; GTSL
O lovers, this song I give to you. Song. A. R. D. Fairburn. *Fr.* To Daphnis and Chloe in the Park. AnNZ
O loyal to the royal in thyself. To the Queen. Tennyson. *Fr.* Idylls of the King. PoVP
Oh Lucky Jim! *Unknown.* ChTr
O lucky prison, blithe captivity. The Lover's Prison. Ariosto. OnPM
Oh lucky you, cicada. Cicada. *Unknown. Fr.* Anacreontea. GrPE
O luely, luely, cam she in. The Tryst. William Soutar. GoTS; GTBS-D; NeBP
O lullaby, my baby. The bee has gone to sleep. Cradle Song. Eben E. Rexford. BOL
O Lusty May. *Unknown.* EBSV
(Lusty May.) OBEV
O Lydia, tell me why it is, by all the gods above. The Slump in Sybaris. Franklin P. Adams. PoeMoYo
Oh Lydia, when I hear you rave. To the Polyandrous Lydia. Franklin P. Adams. HBMV
O Lynx, wake Silenus and Casey. Ezra Pound. *Fr.* Canto LXXIX. AtBAP; POTE (1959 ed.)
O lyre of gold, Apollo's/ Treasure. O Golden Lyre! [or The Power of Music]. Pindar. *Fr.* Pythian Odes, I. GrR; OxBG; UnS
O Lyric Love. Robert Browning. *Fr.* The Ring and the Book, I. EPN; EtPaEn; EV-5; FiP; OAEP
(Dedication: "O lyric Love . . .") BPN; CoBE
(Lyric Love.) GEPC; OBVV; TOP
("O lyric Love, half angel and half bird.") PoVP
O. M. B. Ford Madox Brown. VA
O Mad Spring, One Waits. Merrill Moore. AnAmPo; LA
O Mademoiselle from gay Paree, parley voo? Mademoiselle from Armentières. *Unknown.* BoHiPo
O Maecenas, of kings boasting your ancestry. Horace. Odes, I, 1. LaP
O magic music of the Spring. Bluebirds. Helen Merrill Egerton. CPG
O magic sleep! O comfortable bird. Sleep [or Life Again]. Keats. *Fr.* Endymion. BCEP; SeCePo
O magical word, may it never die from the lips that love to speak it. Our Mothers. *Unknown.* OQP; PSO; QP-1
O Magnet-South. Walt Whitman. IAP; LaNeLa; MOAP
O Mahsr! let dis gath'rin fin' a blessin' in yo' sight! Blessing [on] the Dance. Irwin Russell. *Fr.* Christmas Night in the Quarters. AnAmPo; LA; SPP
O maister deere and fadir reverent. On Chaucer. Thomas Hoccleve. *Fr.* De Regimine Principum. EPP
Oh, make me not as other men. Prayer of the Satirist. "O. L." CAG
Oh, make me see thy face in every place! Sonnet. Michelangelo. LyPI
Oh, make my heart so still, so still. Prayer. Utsunomiya. SoLD
O Maker of the Mighty Deep. Voyagers [or Thy Sea Is Great, Our Boats Are Small]. Henry van Dyke. MaRV; OQP; PraP; QP-1
O Mally's Meek, Mally's Sweet. Burns. GN; HBV; OTPC
O man, keep in remembrance how thy father first begot thee. Yahoo. Palladas. GrPE
"O man of little wit." The Pine to the Mariner. George Turberville. EtS
O Man of my [or mine] own people, I alone. The Jew to Jesus. Florence Kiper Frank. BPP; ChIP; GrCo-1; HBMV; MaRV; NP; NV; StJW; WGRP
O man, on thyself have mercy. What madness bids ye follow. Ill Merchandise. *At. to* Automedon of Aetolia *and to* Theocritus. GrPE
O Man, Remember. Palladas, *tr. fr. Greek by* D. L. Feldstone. LyMA
(Yahoo, *tr. by* F. L. Lucas.) GrPE
O man that for Fergus of the feasts dost kindle fire. Song of the Forest Trees [or Wood to Burn and Not to Burn]. *Unknown.* OnYI; SiB
O Man, who walked by Galilee. Man of Galilee. Mary Louise Deissler. BePJ
Oh, man's capacity/ For spiritual sorrow. The Crucifixion. Alice Meynell. MeRV; OxBoCh; PoLi
Oh, many a day have I made good ale in the glen. The Outlaw of Loch Lene. *Unknown, tr. by* Jeremiah Joseph Callanan. AnIV; CH; GTIV; IrPN; OBEV; OBRV; OnYI; OxBI; RO; TIP
Oh, many a leaf will fall to-night. The Dear Old Toiling One. David Gray. MOAH; VA
Oh! many a tear from hearts by anguish torn. Many a Tear. Paulus Silentiarius. LiA
O, many are the poets that are sown. Unknown Poets. Wordsworth. *Fr.* The Excursion, I. LPS-3
Oh, many have told of the monkeys of old. A Darwinian Ballad. *Unknown.* BOHV
O many the tents that gave their riches to me of old! The Assignation. Imr el Kais. LiTW

Oh, many's the time in the evening. The Childless Mother's Lullaby. Ella Higginson. BOL
O Marcius, Marcius! Martial Friendship. Shakespeare. *Fr.* Coriolanus, IV, v. LPS-1
O Marduk, lord of countries, terrible one. *Unknown. Fr.* Hymn to Marduk. WGRP
O Mariners! Archibald Rutledge. EtS
O mark yon rose-tree! When the west. Love's Likeness. George Darley. OBVV
O Martyred Spirit. George Santayana. TrPWD
O Martyrs Numberless. *Unknown.* PEOR
O Mary, at thy window be. Mary Morison [*or* Devotion *or* Song]. Burns. AnFE; AWP; BEL; BLV; BoLiVe; CEP; CoBE; EBSV; EG; EM-1; EnLi-2; EnLit; EnRP; EV-3; GTBS; GTBS-D; GTBS-W; GTSE; HBV; InPo; JAWP; LH; LPS-1; MCCG; OAEP; OBEC; OBEV; OuHeWo; REAL; TOP; TrGrPo; TyEnPo; WBP; WHA
Oh, Mary, dear, oh, Mary, fair. Molly Asthore. *Unknown.* IrPN
O Mary, Go and Call the Cattle Home. Charles Kingsley. *See* Sands of Dee, The.
Oh, Mary had a little lamb, regarding whose cuticular. The Original Lamb. *Unknown.* BOHV; InMe
O Mary, in thy clear young eyes. The Madonna of the Carpenter Shop. Ruth Guthrie Harding. SDH
O Mary, mother, if the day we trod. Lullaby. Arthur Sherburne Hardy. BOL
O Mary Pierced with Sorrow. Kipling. *Fr.* Song before Action. ISi
Oh, Mary's lovelier than anything that grows. Prisoner's Song. Horace Gregory. NP
O Master, Let Me Walk with Thee. Washington Gladden. MaRV; MOB; OIF; PraP; WGRP
(Service.) BLRP
O Master Masons. Ernst Toller, *tr. fr. German by* Ashley Dukes. TrJP
O Master, O thou great of heart and tongue. L'Envoi. William Morris. *Fr.* The Earthly Paradise. BPN
"O master of fortunes and of poverties." Antonio Machado. *Fr.* Iberian God. PoFr
O Master of the common weal. The Master of Laborers. George Edward Day. PGD; PSO
O Master of the Galilean Way. A Prayer for Christian Unity. Molly Anderson Haley. ChIP; OQP; QP-1
O Master of the loving heart. A Prayer Poem. Calvin W. Laufer. PraP
O Master of the modern day. A Hymn for the New Age. William Steward Gordon. MaRV; OQP; QP-1
O Master of the waking world. The Waking World. Frank Mason North. MaRV
O Master Scribe, in all your manuscript. Palimpsest. LeGarde S. Doughty. MuM
O Master Workman of the Race. Jay T. Stocking. MaRV
Oh, Masters, you who rule the world. The Masters. "Laurence Hope." HBV
O matchless honor, all unsought. The Missionary. *Unknown.* PraP
O May I Join the Choir Invisible. "George Eliot." BMEP; BPP; EPN; GTBS; GTBS-W; GTSL; HBV; LEAP; LPS-3; MaRV; TOP; TreFS; VA; WGRP
(Choir Invisible, The.) DiM; GrCo-1, *abr.;* NeHB; OBVV; OHFP; OQP; PECK; QP-1; WBLP
O may I with myself agree. John Dyer. *Fr.* Grongar Hill. TrGrPo
O may my constant feet not fail. God and Man [*or* Chorus *or* The People Pray]. Sophocles. *Fr.* Oedipus Rex. GrR; OxBG; WGRP
O may she comes and may she goes. The Bonny Hind. *Unknown.* ESPB; ViBoFo
Oh! may those ravish'd beauties fall to earth. Semandra's Death. Nathaniel Lee. *Fr.* Mithridates, King of Pontus. BeR
Oh, maybe it was yesterday, or fifty years ago! Cuttin' Rushes. "Moira O'Neill." AV
Oh, Mayflower, made of filigree gold. Virginia. Vachel Lindsay. ATP (1935 ed.)
O me! what eyes hath love put in my head. Sonnets, CXLVIII [*or* Blind Love]. Shakespeare. EV-1; GTBS; GTBS-D; GTBS-W; GTSE; GTSL; PeBoSo
O! Meary, when the zun went down. Woone Smile Mwore. William Barnes. VA
O melancholy bird, a winter's day. The Heron [*or* To a Bird]. Edward Hovell-Thurlow. BLA; HBV; LPS-2
O Melancholy, linger here awhile! Keats. *Fr.* Isabella or the Pot of Basil. ViBoPo
"O, 'Melia, my dear, this does everything crown!" The Ruined Maid. Thomas Hardy. FiBHP; LiTB; MaPo; SeCeV; SiTL; ViP
O mellow moonlight warm. James Thomson. Sunday at Hampstead, XII. EmBrPo
O Memory! celestial maid! Ode to Memory. William Shenstone. Po
O memory, thou fond deceiver. Memory [*or* Song]. Goldsmith. *Fr.* The Captivity. OBEC; OBEV; PoP; ViBoPo
O men from the fields! A Cradle Song. Padraic Colum. AS; BOL; CaAE; GoBC; ISi; MM; OnYI; OxBI; PoeT; StJW; WHL
O men, grown sick with toil and care. Thanksgiving. Phoebe Cary. TOAH
O men or rustic gods, you who were born. The Welcome of the Young Cacique. Alonso de Ercilla y Zúñiga. *Fr.* La Araucana. BoFr
O men, walk on the hills. Poem. Maxwell Bodenheim. MOAP; TrJP
O Men, with sisters dear! Sweated Labor. Thomas Hood. *Fr.* The Song of the Shirt. MaRV
Oh Menelaus,/ Oh my poor friend. On Hearing the First Cuckoo. Richard Church. MoBrPo (1942 ed.); OBMV
O merciful Father, my hope is in thee! Prayer before Execution. Mary Queen of Scots. CAW; MaRV; WGRP
O Merlin in your crystal cave. Merlin. Edwin Muir. FaBoTw; MoPW
O Meropé!/ And where art thou. Distraught for Meropé. Richard Henry Horne. *Fr.* Orion. VA
O Merry Hae I Been Teethin' a Heckle. Burns. BSV
O Merry May the Maid Be. Sir John Clerk. HBV
O Metaphysical Tobacco. *Unknown.* TuPP
Oh, Mexico, my Mexico. Santy Anna, *vers.* II. *Unknown.* ShS
O mice! if here you come for food, you'd better go elsewhere. A Poor Scholar to Mice. *Unknown.* OnPM
O Michael, you are at once the enemy. Garden-Lion. "Evelyn Hayes." ChTr
O mickle yeuks the keckle doup. Justice to Scotland. *Unknown.* BOHV; InMe
O might those sighs and tears return again. Holy Sonnets, III. John Donne. AnEnPo; OBS; PeBoSo; SeEP
O might we know beyond all doubt. The World's Harmonious Plan. Aeschylus. *Fr.* Suppliants. LiA
O mighty Caesar! does thou lie so low? Mark Antony's Lament [*or* Antony's Oration]. Shakespeare. *Fr.* Julius Caesar, III, i. BHV; LPS-3; TreFS
O mighty God, Which for us men. A Prayer. Humphrey Gifford. OxBoCh
O Mighty Lady, *in mod. Eng. Unknown.* TMEV
O Mighty, Melancholy Wind. John Todhunter. *See* Song: "Bring from the craggy haunts of birch and pine."
O mighty mind, in whose deep stream this age. To Byron. Shelley. PtP
O mighty-mouth'd inventor of harmonies. Milton. Tennyson. BPN; EM-2; EmBrPo; EnLi-2; EnLit; EPN; GEPC; InP; OAEP; PoFS; PoVP; PtP; TCEP; TOP; VLEP
O Mighty Nothing! unto thee. And He Answered Them Nothing. Richard Crashaw. MePo
O mighty, powerful, dark-dispelling sun. Prayer at Sunrise. James Weldon Johnson. QS
O mighty, powerful, strong one of Ashur. *Unknown. Fr.* Hymn to Marduk. WGRP
O mighty river! strong, eternal will. The Great River. Henry van Dyke. TrPWD
O Mind of God, Broad as the Sky. Oliver Huckel. TrPWD
O mine own sweet heart. Simon and Susan. *Unknown.* OxBoLi
O Minister of War. *Unknown, tr. fr. Chinese.* WhP
Oh, minstrel of these borean hills. Golden Crown Sparrow of Alaska. John Burroughs. SN
O miserable sorrow, withouten cure. Sir Thomas Wyatt. SiPS
Oh Mr. Froude, how wise and good. Killarney. Charles Kingsley. WhC
"Oh Mrs. McGrath!" the sergeant said. Mrs. McGrath. *Unknown.* OnYI
O Mistress Mine ("O Mistress mine, till you I me commend"). *Unknown.* GoTS
O Mistress Mine, Where Are You Roaming? Shakespeare. *Fr.* Twelfth Night, II, iii. AnFE; BEL; BLV; EG; EIL; ElSeCe; EM-1; EnL; EnLi-1; EnLit; EPP; EV-1; ExPo; FaFP; InMe; InPo; KN; LiA; LiTB; LoBV; LoPo; LPS-1; MCCG; OAEP; OBSC; OtMeF; OuHeWo; PIR; PoE; PoFS; PoRA; PreP, *with music;* SeCeV; ShBV-2; SiCE; TOP; TrGrPo; TwHP; TyEnPo; ViBoPo; WHA
(Carpe Diem.) GTBS; GTBS-D; GTBS-W; GTSE; GTSL
(Clown's Song.) FaBoEn
(Feste's Song[s].) ALV; CoEV
(Mistress Mine.) CBOV
(Song: "O mistress mine, where are you roaming?") CaAE; FiP; HBV; PG (1945 ed.)
(Song from "Twelfth Night.") LEAP
(Songs from the Plays.) AWP; JAWP; WBP
(Sweet-and-twenty.) LiTG; LiTL; OBEV
(Two of Feste's Songs.) BoLiVe
O mitsch mein inkum stinkum buckerroom. Ja, Ja, Ja! *Unknown.* ShS
O Mollie, O Mollie, 'tis [*or* it is] for your sake alone. Jack o' Diamonds. *Unknown.* CoSo; CSF

O money is the meat in the cocoanut. Money. *Unknown.* AS

"O monstrous, dead, unprofitable world." Written in Emerson's Essays. Matthew Arnold. EmBrPo; GEPC; VA; VLEP

O month of fairer, rarer days. September Days. Helen L. Smith. PTA-2

O Monument of shame to this our time! Rousseau. Schiller. PoFr

O Mooder Mayde. Chaucer. *See* Invocation: "O mother-maid! O maiden-mother free!"

O Moon, Mr. Moon. Mr. Moon. Bliss Carman. FaPON; GaP; SUS

O moon, O hide thy golden light. O World, Be Not So Fair. Maria Jäger. HBV

O Moon! the oldest shades 'mong oldest trees. Keats. *Fr.* Endymion, III. EnRP

Oh Moon! when I look on thy beautiful face. Poetic Thought. *Unknown.* FiBHP; SiTL

O Morning-Maker, deign that ray. Plea for Hope. Francis Carlin. TrPWD

O Mors Aeterna. Horace Gregory. ChMo

O Mors! Quam Amara Est Memoria Tua Homini Pacem Habenti in Substantiis Suis. Ernest Dowson. GTSL; LoPS; OBMV; PG; POTT; ViPP; VLEP

O mortal folk, you may behold and see. An Epitaph [*or* His Epitaph]. Stephen Hawes. *Fr.* The Pastime of Pleasure. ACP; BCEP; BLV; CBOV; ChTr; GoBC; LEAP; MyFE; OBEV; OBSC; OtMeF; SeCeV; TrGrPo; TriL; ViBoPo

O mortal man, that lives by bread. Sally Birkett's Ale. *Unknown.* ChTr

O mortal man, who livest here by toil. The Castle of Indolence. James Thomson. BEL; CEP; EiPP; EM-1; EnLi-2 (1949 ed.); EV-3; LPS-3; TCEP

O mortall man how longe wilte thow remaine. *Unknown.* SeCSL

O most high, almighty, good Lord God. The Canticle of the Sun [*or* The Song of the Creatures]. St. Francis of Assisi, *tr. by* Matthew Arnold. CAW; GoBC; LiTW; MaRV; OuHeWo; TreFS

O Most High, Omnipotent, Good Lord. Canticle of the Sun [*or* The Canticle of the Creatures]. St. Francis of Assisi, *tr. by* Eleanor L. Turnbull. LyPI; WoL

O most just Vizier, send away. The Sick King in Bokhara. Matthew Arnold. EmBrPo; PoVP; VLEP

O Mother dear, didst thou but hear. Dialogue at the Cross. Frederick Spee. CAW

O Mother Dear, Jerusalem. *Unknown. See* New Jerusalem, The.

O Mother Earth! upon thy lap. Randolph of Roanoke. Whittier. GA

O Mother Eve, I do believe that after all you're glad you ate. Ode to Eve. Edwin Meade Robinson. InMe

Oh, mother, I shall be married to Mr. Punchinello. *Unknown.* OxNR

O Mother, lay your hand on my brow. The Sick Child. Robert Louis Stevenson. CH

O mother-maid! O maiden-mother free! Invocation [*or* Prayer to the Blessed Virgin]. Chaucer. *Fr.* The Canterbury Tales: Prologue of the Prioress's Tale. ACP; CAW; ISi

O Mother Mary, Flower of all womankind. Ballade to Our Lady. Sebastian Brant, *tr. by* Alexander Barclay. *Fr.* The Ship of Fools. ISi

O Mother mine, 'tis Cupid. Wily Cupid. *Unknown.* TeCS

O mother, mother, I swept the hearth, I set his chair and the white board spread. All Souls' Night. Dora Sigerson Shorter. DaM; TIP; VA

"O mother, mother! I'm so cold!" Chickens in Trouble. *Tr. by* Emilie Poulsson. PPL

O mother-my-love, if you'll give me your hand. Child and Mother [*or* Mother and I]. Eugene Field. CBPC; HH; MOAH; MotAn; MPB

O Mother of a Mighty Race. Bryant. CoBA; DD, *sl. abr.;* FaBoBe; GA; GDAH, *sl. abr.;* HBV; HBVY, *sl. abr.;* IAP; MC; PaA; PAH; *sl. abr.;* PoFr, *abr.* (America.) AA; APW; IDAH; LPS-2

O Mother of Fair Love, it was not alone. Cause of Our Joy. Sister Maris Stella. ISi

O Mother State. James Russell Lowell. *Fr.* To John Gorham Palfrey. BHV

O Mother State! the winds of March. Sumner. Whittier. GA

O Mothers of the Human Race. Robert Whitaker. PGD

Oh, mountains loom the grandest in Montana. In Montana. Washington Jay McCormick. SiTL; WhC

Oh mourn, oh mourn, ye Lowlands. The Bonny Earl of Murray (B *vers.*). *Unknown.* BaBo

O move in me, my darling. Woman's Song. Judith Wright. BoAV

Oh, move, thou Cottage, from behind that oak! Wordsworth. *Fr.* 'Tis Said That Some Have Died for Love. EnSW

O much-enduring heart and hand of mine! Death the Enemy. Euripides. *Fr.* Alcestis. GrPo; OxBG

"Oh, murder! What was that, Papa?" Hildebrand. Hilaire Belloc. BoN

O Muse! by thee conducted down, I dare. The Court of Neptune. John Hughes. EtS

O Muse! relate (for you can tell alone). The Triumph of Dulness. Pope. *Fr.* The Dunciad. CoEV; EPP; EV-3; OBEC

O muse that swayest the sad Northern Song. To the Muse of the North. William Morris. BPN; EmBrPo; PoVP; ViP; VLEP

O my aged Uncle Arly! Incidents in the Life of My Uncle Arly. Edward Lear. AlDL; MoShBr; NA; OxBoLi; SiTL;TrGrPo; WhC

Oh my Beauty of Night!—close, close quick your robe. Belle-de-nuit. Ignace Nau. PoNe

Oh, my beloved, have you thought of this. Unnamed Sonnets, X. Edna St. Vincent Millay. HBMV

Oh my black[e] Soul[e]! now thou art summonèd. Holy Sonnets, IV. John Donne. MePo; MyFE; OBS

. . . Oh! my countrymen!/ We have offended very grievously. Samuel Taylor Coleridge. *Fr.* Fears in Solitude. PreP

Oh! my daddy was a fool about a yellow gal. My Yellow Gal. *Unknown.* ABF

O my dark Rosaleen. Dark Rosaleen. *Unknown, at. to* Hugh O'Donnell, *tr. by* James Clarence Mangan. ACP; AnFE; AnIL; AnIV; AWP; BCEP; CH; CoBE; EnRP; ERP; EV-4; GTIV; GTML; GTSL; HBV; IrPN; JAWP; JKCP; LEAP; LiTW; LO; OBEV; OBVV; OnYI; OxBI; PoFr; TIP; VA; ViBoPo; WBP

Oh, My Darling Clementine. Percy Montross. FaBoBe; FaFP; OlF; TreF

"O my daughter! lead me forth to the bastion of the north." The Siege of Derry. Cecil Frances Alexander. TIP

O my deir hert, young Jesus sweit. Balulalow [*or* Cradle Song *or* Nativity Carol]. James, John, *and* Robert Wedderburn. BOL; LoBV; OBEV; OxBoCh

O my earliest love, who, ere I number'd. First Love. Charles Stuart Calverley. BOHV; FiBHP; InMe; LauV

Oh, my fair Pastheen is my heart's delight. Pastheen Finn [*or* Páistín Fionn]. *Unknown.* IrPN; OxBI

O my fine, my honeycoloured Duke of Marmalade! Elegy of the Duke of Marmalade. Luis Palés Matos. AnCL; LiTW

O my friends! I drew. Betrayal. Ibn Sa'id of Alcala la Real. MooP

O my garden! lying whitely in the moonlight and the dew. Homesick. Julia C. R. Dorr. NLK

Oh, my Geraldine. F. C. Burnand. BOHV; NA

O my God, my God. By Solitary Fires. Elizabeth Barrett Browning. *Fr.* Aurora Leigh, V. VA

O my God, Thou hast wounded me with love. A Confession. Paul Verlaine. CAW; WGRP

Oh, my golden slippers am laid [*or* a-laid] away. Oh, Dem Golden Slippers. James A. Bland. GoSl; OlF

Oh, My Good Lord, Show Me de Way, *with music.* *Unknown.* BoAN-2

Oh, my hammer. The Hammer Song. *Unknown.* ABF

O My Harte Is Wo. *Unknown.* AtBAP

O my heart is the unlucky heir of the ages. Personal History; for My Son. Ruthven Todd. NeBP

O my Heart, my Mother, my Heart, my Mother. He Approacheth the Hall of Judgment. *Unknown. Fr.* Book of the Dead. AWP; JAWP; WBP

O My Heart's Heart. Christina Rossetti. Monna Innominata, V. CoBE; EmBrPo; ViPo; VLEP

O My Honey, Take Me Back, *with music.* *Unknown.* AS

Oh, my laddie, my laddie. My Laddie. Amélie Rives. HBV

Oh, my laddie! Oh, my laddie! A Mother Thought. Edgar A. Guest. PEDC

O my land! O my love! Lament for Banba. Egan O'Rahilly, *tr. by* James Clarence Mangan. AnIV; AWP; JAWP; WBP

O my little almost island, little island Sirmio. Return to Sirmio. Catullus. LaP; LiTW; RoL

Oh, My Liver and My Lungs, *with music.* *Unknown.* OuSiCo

O my lord Ajax, of all things most hard. Tecmessa's Fruitless Plea. Sophocles. *Fr.* Ajax. GrR

O my love! my wife! Everlasting Rest. Shakespeare. *Fr.* Romeo and Juliet, V, iii. WHA

Oh, my love was more hot. Song. Aleksey Koltsov. BoRS

O my Lover, blind me. The Tired Woman. Anna Wickham. AV; MBP; MoBrPo

O my love's like the steadfast sun. The Poet's Bridal-Day Song. Allan Cunningham. LPS-1

O my Lucasia, let us speak our love. To My Lucasia, in Defence of Declared Friendship. Katherine Philips. MeLP

O My Luve Is like a Red, Red Rose. Burns. *See* Red, Red Rose, A.

Oh my mother! What a fool I be! *Unknown.* BoN

Oh, my mother's moaning by the river. The Lonely Mother. Fenton Johnson. GoSl; NP; PoNe

Oh! my name is John Wellington Wells. My Name Is John Wellington Wells. W. S. Gilbert. *Fr.* The Sorcerer. PIAE; PoMS

Oh, my name is Larry Gorman, to you I mean no harm. The Scow on Cowden Shore, *vers.* II. Larry Gorman. ShS

Oh, my name is Peter Emberley. Peter Emberley, *vers.* I. John Calhoun. ShS

Oh, my name it is Sam Hall [*or* is Samuel Hall]. Sam [*or* Samuel] Hall. *Unknown.* ABF; ChTr; CoSo

Oh, my name was Robert Kidd, as I sailed, as I sailed. Captain Kidd. *Unknown.* BBV (1923 ed.); MoShBr; TrAS; ViBoFo

O my own Italy! though words are vain. Canzone 128. Petrarch. LyPI

O My Poor Darling. Wilfred Watson. EnLoPo

O my poor son, O Anticles, and poor me, who beheld. An Only Son. Leonides of Tarentum. OxBG

O my pretty cock and my pretty crowing cock. Mother Goose. PCH

Oh! my Saint Francis of the gentle eyes. In Memoriam. Dorothy Frances Gurney. SaFP

O My Saviour and Redeemer. Alice Mortenson. BePJ

O, my soul is a witness for my Lord. Who'll Be a Witness for My Lord? *Unknown.* APW

O my Soul, let us go unto our hills. The Hills. Theodosia Garrison. NLK

O My Swallows! Ernst Toller, *tr. fr. German by* Ashley Dukes. TrJP

Oh, my sweet mother, 'tis in vain. Sappho, *tr. fr. Greek by* Thomas Moore. GrPo

O my true love's a smuggler and sails upon the sea. The Smuggler. *Unknown.* CBPC; SG; WhC

O my worshipful lord, an't please your grace. Shakespeare. King Henry IV, Pt. II, *fr.* II, i. LO

O my young brothers. Children's Festival. Tien Ch'ien. WhP

O Mystery and Longing and Defeat. Requiem. Alice Hunt Bartlett. BAP

Oh! Mystery of Man. Wordsworth. *Fr.* The Prelude, XII. FiP

O Mystic Rose, in God's fair garden growing. Rosa Mystica. Denis A. McCarthy. JKCP

Oh, Nancy Dawson, hio! Cheer'ly, Man. *Unknown.* AmSS

O Nancy, Wilt Thou Go with Me? Thomas Percy. HBV
(O Nanny, Wilt Thou Gang wi' Me?) LPS-1
(Song: "O Nancy, wilt thou go with me?") CEP

O native Britain! O my Mother Isle! England. Samuel Taylor Coleridge. *Fr.* Fears in Solitude. EV-4

O nature! I do not aspire. Nature. Henry David Thoreau. ADAH; FaBoBe; HBV; OTPC

O Navis. Austin Dobson. VA

O Nectar! O Delicious Stream! Love. Thomas Traherne. SeCV-2

Oh, Never Ask! Daniel Fallström, *tr. fr. Swedish by* Charles W. Stork. AnSL

Oh never call it waste of wishing. Aspiration. Eileen Duggan. JKCP (1955 ed.)

Oh never marry Ishmael! Song for Unbound Hair. Genevieve Taggard. AV; PG; PoRA; TBM

Oh, never, never more will I go to Cashel. The Journeyman. *Unknown.* KiLC

Oh, Never! No, Never! Caroline Oliphant, the Younger. EBSV

Oh, never say that I was false of heart. Sonnets, CIX [*or* The Unchangeable]. Shakespeare. BEL; ElL; EM-1; EPP; ES; EtPaEn; EV-1; GTBS; GTBS-D; GTBS-W; GTSE; GTSL; HBV; LiTG; LiTL; LO; LoPo; OBEV; OBSC; PeBoSo; ReaPo; SiCE; TwP; WoL

Oh, never say that you have reached the very end. We Survive! Hirsch Glick. TrJP

O never star/ Was lost. Faith. Robert Browning. OQP; QP-1

O Night, Be Long. Nahabed Kouchak, *tr. fr. Armenian by* Zabelle C. Boyajian. ArmLP

O Night here stay! I want no morning light. The Mock Caliph. *Unknown. Fr.* The Thousand and One Nights. EnLi-1

O night, O eyes of love! Drinking Song. *Unknown. Fr.* The Thousand and One Nights. LiTW

O Night, O Jealous Night [Repugnant to My Pleasures]. *Unknown.* EG; LO; ReIE; TuPP
(Night-Piece, A.) ElL
(To Night.) OBSC

O night, O sweet though sombre span of time! The Defence of Night. Michelangelo. CAW; OnPM

O Night O Trembling Night. Stephen Spender. NeBP

O Night, send up the harvest moon. Songs of the Autumn Night, I. George Macdonald. EBSV

O Night, the ease of care, the pledge of pleasure. Night. Sir Philip Sidney. *Fr.* Arcadia. NBE; SiPS

O Night, Thou Starry River! Christian Morgenstern, *tr. fr. German by* Eileen Hutchins. AnGP

O Nightingale. Milton. *See* To the Nightingale.

O nightingale. Nakatsukasa, *tr. fr. Japanese by* Arthur Waley. LiTW

O Nightingale. Wordsworth. *See* Nightingale, The.

O nightingale of woodland gay. Medieval Norman Songs, XVI. *Unknown, tr. by* John Addington Symonds. AWP

O Nightingale That on Yon Bloomy Spray. Milton. *See* To the Nightingale.

O nightingale, the poet's bird. A Song about Singing. Anne Reeve Aldrich. AA

O Nightingale! Thou Surely Art. Wordsworth. *See* Nightingale, The.

Oh! ninna and anninia! Sardinian Lullaby [*or* Sleep, Baby Boy]. *Unknown.* BOL; FaPON; RIS

O no, beloved, I am most sure. An Ode upon a Question Moved, Whether Love Should Continue for Ever? Lord Herbert of Cherbury. LiTL; OBS; ViBoPo

Oh, No Cross That I May Carry! Alice Mortenson. BePJ

Oh, No, He'll Not Need Them Again. *Unknown.* BlG

Oh No More, No More, Too Late. John Ford. *See* Song: "Oh, no more, no more, too late."

O no, no—let me lie. Not on the Battle-Field. John Pierpont. LPS-2

"O no," said It: "her lifedoings." The Absolute Explains. Thomas Hardy. MM

O noble brow, so wise in thought! Washington [*or* When Shall We See Thy Like Again?]. Mary Wingate. HH; OHIP; PGD; PSO; WOAH

O noble Chaucer whos pullisshyd eloquence. John Skelton. *Fr.* The Garlande of Laurell. PtP

O Noble England. A Joyfull New Ballad. Thomas Deloney. CoMu; ViBoPo

O noble, gracious English tongue. A Grub Street Recessional. Christopher Morley. InMe

O noble heart, Sabinus, of the great love we cherished. On a Stone at Corinth. *Unknown.* GrPE

"O noble knight of France." Popular Lament. *Unknown.* TrFP

O noble Oisin, son of the king. Oisin in the Land of Youth. Michael Comyn. AnIL

O Noble Virgin. Prudentius, *tr. fr. Latin by* Raymond F. Roseliep. *Fr.* Cathemerinon. ISi

Oh, none of your boarding-school misses. Widow-ology. Charles Graham Halpine. PR

Oh, north and east from Conran. Southerly. E. J. Brady. NeLNL

Oh, Northern men—true hearts and bold. Cast Down, but Not Destroyed. *Unknown.* PAH

Oh not alone the eager South. The Flag of Stars. Grace Ellery Channing. FOAH

O not by Phidias' art alone. The Mirror. M. Whitcomb Hess. JKCP (1955 ed.)

O not by this old tune. Guitar. Iosif Utkin. RuPo

Oh, not for more or longer days, dear Lord. A Prayer. B. Y. Williams. MaRV; PraP

Oh, not more subtly silence strays. To the Beloved. Alice Meynell. PoeT; TCPD

O not till the time when flight. A Sonnet to Orpheus. Rainer Maria Rilke. Sonnets to Orpheus, Pt. I, XXIII. PoF

O! Nothing earthly save the ray. Al Aaraaf. Poe. AmP

O nothing, in this corporal earth of man. The Heart [*or* All's Vast *or* Correlated Greatness]. Francis Thompson. AnFE; BLV; BoLiVe; GTML; MBP; MoAB; MoBrPo; OBMV; PeBoSo; PIAE; VLEP

O, now, for ever/ Farewell the tranquil mind. Farewell Content. Shakespeare. *Fr.* Othello, III, iii. TrGrPo

O now I know: a smile. Rest O Sun I Cannot. Joseph Tusiani. GoYe

Oh, now that it's vacation time. Vacation Time. Rowena Bennett. SiSoSe

O! now the summer woods! and O! the joy. Thomas Aird. *Fr.* Frank Sylvan. EnSW

O Nymph, compar'd with whose young bloom. To Lady Anne Fitzpatrick, when about Five Years Old, with a Present of Shells. Horace Walpole. CEP; OBEC

O nymph with the nicest of noses. Foam and Fangs. Walter Parke. BOHV; PA

Oh, oh, how the wild winds blow! Wild Winds. Mary Frances Butts. OTPC; PRWS

Oh, Oh, where shall I lament. *Unknown.* SeCSL

O of our every fortune, thou, the fateful symbol! Funeral Toast. Stéphane Mallarmé. LiTW

O ole Zip Coon he is a larned skoler [*or* skolar]. Zip Coon [*or* Old Zip Coon]. *Unknown, at. to* Bob Farrell. TrAS; YaD

O once fair earth. Wales—a Mourning. Walter Dowding. MoWP

O, Once I lov'd a Bonie Lass, *sel.* Burns.
"She dresses aye so clean and neat."
(From His First Song.) BLP

O once I was happy but now I'm forlorn. The Flying Trapeze. George Lebourne. TreF

O, one I need to love me. Friends—with a Difference. Mary Elizabeth Coleridge. BoFr

O only Source of all our light and life. Qui Laborat, Orat. Arthur Hugh Clough. BEL; BPN; EmBrPo; EnLi-2; EPN; PoVP; TrPWD; ViPo; ViPP; VLEP

O, Open the Door to me, O! Burns. FaBoCh; LoGBV
(Open the Door to Me, O.) AtBAP; PoEL-4

O, Opportunity, thy guilt is great. Opportunity. Shakespeare. *Fr.* The Rape of Lucrece. LiTB; OBSC; PoEL-2

Oh, our hired man is the funniest chap. Funny and Wise. Jack Lowell. DDA

Oh, our manhood's prime vigor! No spirit feels waste. The Wild Joys of Living [*or* David's Song]. Robert Browning. *Fr.* Saul. BLV; BoLiVe; OtMeF. *See also* Oh, the wild joys of living.

Oh, out in the West where the riders are ready. Roll a Rock Down. Henry Herbert Knibbs. AnAmPo; PFY

O Paddy dear, an' did ye hear the news that's goin' round? The Wearin' o' [*or* Wearing of] the Green. *Unknown.* AnIL; AnIV; AWP; DD; FaFP; HBV; HH; JAWP; OlF; OnYI; OxBoLi; PoFr; SiTL; TIP; TreF; WBP

O, Pain, Love's mystery. Pain. Coventry Patmore. PoLi

O pale art thou, my lamp, and faint. Fragment. Henry Kirke White. ERP

O pale-lipped blossom. A Murmur in the Grass. "Æ." ChMo; CMP

O pale! O vivid! dear! Conquered. Zoë Akins. HBMV

"O paleys, whylom croune of houses alle." The Complaint of Troilus. Chaucer. OBEV (new ed.)

O pallid student! leave thy dim alcove. Midsummer Invitation. Myron B. Benton. SN

Oh, paltry miracles. Miracle. Edith Mirick. ChIP

"O Pan, O Pan, where'er thou rangest now." The Passing of Daphnis. Theocritus. *Fr.* Idylls. OxBG

O pansy-eye, O polished face. Debutantrum. William Rose Benét. InMe; LHV

O Paradise! O Paradise! Frederick William Faber. *See* Paradise.

O, pardon me, thou bleeding piece of earth. Shakespeare. *Fr.* Julius Caesar, III, i. PIR

O Parent of each lovely Muse. Ode to Fancy. Joseph Warton. CEP; EiPP

Oh, pass around your bottle, we'll all take a drink. Pass Around Your Bottle. *Unknown.* OuSiCo

O pass not on, but stay. Syren's Song. Dryden. *Fr.* King Arthur, IV, i. BeR

Oh, Passage town is of great renown. The Town of Passage. *Unknown.* OxBoLi

O pastoral heart of England! like a psalm. Upon Eckington Bridge, River Avon. Sir Arthur Quiller-Couch. OBVV; PoeT; POTE

O patience, that dost wait eternally! Sonnet. Pedro Malon de Chaide. CAW

O patron saints of all my friends! Friends. Lionel Johnson. GoBC

O Paulus! vex my grave with tears no more. A Roman Matron to Her Husband. Propertius. Elegies, IV, 11. RoL

O Peace, O Dove, O shape of the Holy Ghost. To Peace. Richard Watson Dixon. EV-5

O pearl, for prince's pleasure wrought. The Pearl. *Unknown.* TCEP

Oh, peasant who seemed quite simple. The Peasant. *Unknown.* ChLP

O pensive, tender maid, downcast and shy. Song from the "Story of Cupid and Psyche" [*or* Song: To Psyche]. William Morris. *Fr.* The Earthly Paradise: May. BPN; POTT; VA; VLEP

O peony, O pink inverted bell. A Peony for Apollo. Charles Edward Eaton. GoYe

O people-chosen! are ye not. To the Thirty-ninth Congress. Whittier. PAH

O perfect Light, which shaid [*or* whilk shed] away. A Summer Day [*or* Of the Day Estivall]. Alexander Hume. BSV; EBSV; EV-1; LoBV; LPS-2; OBEV (1st ed.)

O Perfect Love. Dorothy F. Gurney. MaRV; OlF

Oh, Peter, go ring dem bells. Peter, Go Ring Dem Bells. *Unknown.* BoAN-1

"O Peter, O Apostle, hast thou seen my bright love?" The Keening of Mary. *Unknown.* ISi

Oh, Peterkin Pout and Gregory Grout. A Nursery Song. Laura E. Richards. BoChLi; HBV; HBVY; RAR; TVC

O Petrarch, head and prince of poets all. A Praise of Petrarch and of Laura, His Lady. *Unknown.* ReIE

O petty blood-nobility of ours! Dante. *Fr.* Divina Commedia: Paradiso. PoFr

O Phoebus embattling the high wall of Ilium. Chorus: The Kings of Troy. Euripides, *tr. by* George Allen. *Fr.* Andromache. OxBG; WaaP

O Phoebus, who gavest to Ilium a glory. Gone Are Ilium's Kings. Euripides, *tr. by* Arthur S. Way. *Fr.* Andromache. GrR

"Oh, Piggy, what was in your trough." The Greedy Piggy That Ate Too Fast. Eliza Grove. OTPC (1923 ed.)

Oh, Pillykin, Willykin Winky Wee! Punkydoodle and Jollapin. Laura E. Richards. DDA

O pine-tree standing. Hakutsu. *Fr.* Manyo Shu. AWP; JAWP; PFE; WBP

O piteous race! Judaism. Cardinal Newman. ACP

O Pittie. Thomas Dekker. *See* Priest's Song, A.

O Pity Our Small Size. Benjamin Rosenbaum. TrJP

Oh pity poor Reuben Ranzo. Reuben Ranzo. *Unknown.* SoAmSa

"O pitying angel, pause, and say." In Paradise. Arlo Bates. AA

O placid nun!/ That lov'st, immured within thy sparry cell. To My Egeria. George Darley. RO

O Plaguy Spring. Pierre Jean de Béranger, *tr. fr. French by* Alan Conder. TrFP

Oh pleasant eventide! Twilight Calm. Christina Rossetti. AlDL; GTSE

O pleasant exercise of hope and joy. The French Revolution [*or* Residence in France, Continued]. Wordsworth. *Fr.* The Prelude, XI. BPN; EnLi-2; ERP; EV-3; FiP; OBRV; PoEL-4; RO; TOP

Oh, Please Don't Get Up! Ogden Nash. NePA; SiTL

O Pleasing Thoughts. Thomas Lodge. Phyllis, I. PeBoSo ("O pleasing thoughts, apprentices of love.") SiCE; TuPP

O plovers flying over the evening waves. The Plovers. Hitomaro. OnPM

Oh-h-h-h, po' roustabout don't have no home. Roustabout Holler. *Unknown.* OuSiCo

O, po' sinner, O, now is yo' time. What Yo' Gwine to Do When Yo' Lamp Burn Down? *Unknown.* BoAN-1

O Poesy! for thee I grasp my pen. Keats. *Fr.* Sleep and Poetry. ERP

O poet, come you haunting here. At a House in Hampstead. Thomas Hardy. EmBrPo

O poet of the future! The Future. George Frederick Cameron. BoCaPo

O poet, prize not thou the people's love. To the Poet. Pushkin. WaL

O poet rare and old! Astraea. Whittier. AA; IAP

O Poet, then, forbear. Austin Dobson, *after* Théophile Gautier. *Fr.* Ars Victrix. InP

O poet, what do you do? I praise. Praise. Rainer Maria Rilke. ChTr

O Polish mother, if the radiant eyes. To a Polish Mother. Adam Mickiewicz, *tr. by* Jewell Parish *and* George R. Noyes. CAW

O Polish mother, if the radiant light. To a Polish Mother. Adam Mickiewicz, *tr. by* Watson Kirkconnell. LiTW

"Oh Polly love, Oh Polly, the rout has now begun." High Germany. *Unknown.* WaaP

"O Polly, you might have toy'd and kist." John Gay. *Fr.* The Beggar's Opera. EnLoPo

Oh, poor old Reuben Ranzo. Reuben Ranzo. *Unknown.* AmSS; ShS, *vers.* I *and* II

"Oh, poor Reuben Ranzo." Poor Reuben Ranzo. Arthur H. Clark. IHA

O Pope! the sweetest of the tuneful race. William Thompson. *Fr.* On Laurel Hill. EnSW

"O poppy Death!—sweet poisoner of sleep!" Scylla's Lament. Thomas Hood. *Fr.* Hero and Leander. EnRP

Oh Portes, it was not any vulgar tie. To Philippe Desportes. Jean Antoine de Baïf. BoFr

O Possible and Probable. Adventure. Grace Fallow Norton. HBMV

O potent Earth, and Heaven god-built. Earth and Sky. Euripides. OxBG

O, pour upon my soul again. Rosalie. Washington Allston. AA; LPS-1

Oh! poverty is a weary thing, 'tis full of grief and pain. The Sale of the Pet Lamb. Mary Howitt. CH

O power of Love, O wondrous mystery! Love. Katrina Trask. AA

O Power to whom this earthly clime. Peccavi, Domine. Archibald Lampman. MaRV

O Powers Celestial, with what sophistry. Barnabe Barnes. *Fr.* Parthenophil and Parthenophe. EnLoPo

O prairie mother, I am one of your boys. Carl Sandburg. *Fr.* Prairie. BAP; NP

O, praise an' tanks! De Lord he come. Song of the Negro Boatman. Whittier. *Fr.* At Port Royal. GN

O praise God in his holiness: praise him in the firmament of his power. Laudate Dominum. Psalm CL, Bible, *O.T.* ChTr

Oh, praise me not the silent folk. The Silent Folk. Charles W. Stork. SBMV

O pray for our peace, sweet Virgin Mary. Ballade for Peace. Charles d'Orléans. FoS

O praying one, who long has prayed. Ask and Ye Shall Receive. Mrs. Havens. BLRP

O precious codex, volume, tome. To a Thesaurus. Franklin P. Adams. BOHV; SiTL; WhC

Oh! precious, holy altar. The Bulwark of Home. Grace B. Palmer. PraP

O precious locket, found by luckless me. Sonnet X. Garcilaso de la Vega. AnSpL-1

O Prince of Life, Thy life hath tuned. The Prince of Life. John Oxenham. TrPWD

O Prince of Peace, who came to bless. Forgive. Lalia Mitchell Thornton. BePJ

Oh Promise Me. Clement Scott. FaFP; OlF; TreF
O Prophets and Redeemers! Stanton A. Coblentz. ChIP
O Proserpina!/ For the flowers now. Flowers. Shakespeare. *Fr.* The Winter's Tale, IV, iii. ADAH; BCEP; CBPC; EV-1; LEAP; SN; WHA
Oh, Prue she has a patient man. She Is Overheard Singing. Edna St. Vincent Millay. InMe
O pulsing earth with heart athrill. A Prayer at Bethlehem. Anne P. L. Field. COAH
O pulsing heart with voice attuned. Giotto's Campanile. Thomas O'Hagan. JKCP
O Purblind Race. Tennyson. *Fr.* Idylls of the King: Geraint and Enid. OQP; QP-2
Oh, pure and gentle ones, within your ark. To the Ursulines. Caroline Gilman. PraNu
O pure of soul, and fond and deep of heart. To His Wife. Daniel Henry Deniehy. BoAV
O pure reformers! not in vain. The Reformers. Whittier. MaRV
Oh, put no trust in women! No Trust in Women. *Unknown.* OnPM
Oh, put not your trust in men, dear! No Trust in Men. *Unknown.* OnPM
O Queen, awake to thy renown. Honor and Desert. Coventry Patmore. *Fr.* The Angel in the House. HBV
O queen of heaven, be joyful, alleluia. Regina Coeli. *Unknown, tr. by* Winfred Douglas. ISi
O queen of heaven, rejoice. Regina Coeli. *Unknown.* WHL
O queen of heaven, thou sittest in thy see. Sing We to This Merry Company. *Unknown.* AnEC
O Queen, we are loyal: shall sad ones forget? The Devotion of the Flowers to Their Lady. Herman Melville. MeRV
O Qui Perpetua Mundum Ratione Gubernas. Boethius, *tr. fr. Latin by* Samuel Johnson. MeRV; TriL
(O Thou Whose Pow'r.) TrPWD
O quick quick quick, quick hear the song-sparrow. Cape Ann. T. S. Eliot. Landscapes, V. KN; LoGBV; ThWaDe
Oh, quiet peoples sleeping bed by bed. A Solis Ortus Cardine. Ford Madox Ford. ViBoPo
Oh, rabbit, rabbit, rabbit, rabbit a-hash. Rabbit Hash. *Unknown.* ABF
O Rachel, crying and lamenting loud. Rachel Laments. Marion Ethel Hamilton. MuM
O radiant city of the Violet Crown. To Athens. Pindar. GrR
O radiant luminary of light interminable. A Prayer to the Father of Heaven. John Skelton. SiCE; TrPWD; TuPP
O ragged, ragged sailors! Ragged Sailors. *Unknown.* PEOR
O raging seas, and mighty Neptune's reign! Coming Homeward Out of Spain. Barnabe Googe. EIL; MeRV; ReIE; SiCE; TuPP
O rain at seven. Virginia. Hart Crane. *Fr.* The Bridge: Three Songs. LiTA
O rain, depart with blessings. Song of the Dew. *Unknown.* TrJP
O! raise the woeful Pillalu. An Irish Lamentation. Goethe. AWP
Oh, rare Harry Parry. *Unknown.* OxNR; SiTL
O Reader! hast thou ever stood to see. The Holly Tree. Robert Southey. ADAH; EnRP; ERP; HBV; LPS-2; TVSH
O reason not the need: our basest beggars. Shakespeare. *Fr.* King Lear, II, iv. NBE
Oh, religion is a fortune, I really do believe. Religion Is a Fortune I Really Do Believe. *Unknown.* BoAN-2; OlF
O remnant of that perished host. Army of the Potomac. Joaquin Miller. PEOR
Oh! rest, my baby, rest! The Song of Eve to Cain. John Sterling. BOL
O restless, caressing eyes. Petronius, *tr. fr. Latin by* Kenneth Rexroth. LaP
O reverend Chaucer! rose of rhetoris all. William Dunbar. LEAP
O reverend sir, I do declare. Widow Bedott to Elder Sniffles. Frances Miriam Whitcher. BOHV; LPS-3
O rich and happy flowers forever apart. Petrarch. Sonnets to Laura: To Laura in Life, CXXIX. PrPoCR
O rich young lord, thou ridest by. Compensation. James Edwin Campbell. BANP
Oh, Riley, with your home folks you've won my heart entire. Home Folks. *Unknown.* LPS-1
O Ring the Bells. Kate Greenaway. SAS
O, rise up now away from it all, rise up fiercely hearts. The End of the World. Bertram Warr. BoCaPo (1948 ed.)
"O, rise up, Willy Reilly [*or* Willie Riley], and come along with me." Willy Reilly [*or* Willie Riley]. *Unknown.* BaBo (A *vers.*); HBV; OnYI; OuSiCo; TIP
O Risen Saviour, when the daylight wanes. When the Daylight Wanes. Thomas Tiplady. MaRV
Oh, rock-a-by, baby mouse, rock-a-by, so! The Mouse's Lullaby. Palmer Cox. PCH
O, Rocks Don't Fall on Me, *with music.* *Unknown.* BoAN-1
Oh, Roll on Babe, *with music.* *Unknown.* OuSiCo
Oh, roll the cotton, roll me, boys. Roll the Cotton Down, *vers.* I. *Unknown.* ShS
Oh Rome! my country! City of the soul! Rome [*or* On Rome]. Byron. *Fr.* Childe Harold's Pilgrimage, IV. BEL; CBOV; EPN; EPP; ERP; InP; MaPo; ShBV-3; TCEP
O Romeo, Romeo! wherefore art thou Romeo? Shakespeare. *Fr.* Romeo and Juliet, II, ii. WHA
O Rosamond, thou fair and good. Dreams and Realities. Phoebe Cary. LPS-1
O Rose, O Rainbow. Nicholas Moore. NeBP
O rose the red and white lily. Rose the Red and White Lily. *Unknown.* ESPB; OBB
O rose, thou art sick! The Sick Rose. Blake. *Fr.* Songs of Experience. AtBAP; AWP; BEL; BLV; BoLiVe; BoW; BrBE; ChER; ChTr; EG; EiPP; EnL; EnLoPo; EPP; ExPo; FaBoEn; GTBS-D; InPo; JAWP; LoBV; MaPo; OAEP; OnPM; PoEL-4; PoFS; SeCeV; ShBV-4; TOP; TrGrPo; TwHP; ViBoPo; WBP
O rose, who dares to name thee. A Dead Rose. Elizabeth Barrett Browning. EV-4
O Rose with Two Hearts. Sacheverell Sitwell. Rosario d'Arabeschi; Poems and Rose Portraits, II. POTE (1959 ed.)
Oh roses for the flush of youth. Song. Christina Rossetti. BMEP; BPN; EmBrPo; GTBS; LoBV; ViBoPo; ViPo
Oh, rosy as the lining of a shell. Mimma Bella, IV. Eugene Lee-Hamilton. HBV
Oh, round the corner we will go. Round the Corner. *Unknown.* SoAmSa
Oh, rouse you, rouse you, men at arms. Great Swamp Fight. Caroline Hazard. PAH
O roving muse, recall that wondrous year. The Great Frost. John Gay. *Fr.* Trivia; or, The Art of Walking the Streets of London. OBEC; SeCePo
O rowan tree, O rowan tree! thou'lt aye be dear to me! The Rowan Tree. Lady Nairne. HBV
O Ruddier than the Cherry. John Gay. *Fr.* Acis and Galatea. LiTL; ViBoPo
(Song: "O ruddier than the cherry.") CaAE; EiPP; EV-3; HBV; OBEC; OBEV (1st ed.)
O ruddy Lover. The Clover. Margaret Deland. AA; PR
O ruined father dead, long sweetly rotten. For the Word Is Flesh. Stanley J. Kunitz. AnAmPo; LA; NP
O ruinous morning, unjustifiable. Crash at Leithfield. Allen Curnow. AnNZ
O sacred friendship, Heaven's delight. Friendship. Cervantes. OnPM
O Sacred Head, Now Wounded. *Unknown, at. to* St. Bernard of Clairvaux *and to* Arnulf von Loewen, *tr. fr. Latin into German by* Paul Gerhardt, *tr. fr. German by* James W. Alexander. BePJ; MaRV, *abr.*
(Dying Saviour, The.) LPS-2
O sacred lance that heals the wound it makes. The Damascus Road. Daniel Hughes. ChIP
O Sacred Love, and thou, O Love Profane. Ideal Passion, XIX. George Edward Woodberry. MOAP
O sacred poesie, thou spirit of [Romane] artes. Ben Jonson. *Fr.* The Poetaster. NBE; PoEL-2
O sad memorial of the life I priz'd. A Burial Urn. Sophocles. *Fr.* Electra. OxBG
Oh Sad, Sad Was My Soul. Paul Verlaine, *tr. fr. French by* Muriel Kittel. AnFP
(Exile, *tr. by* Alan Conder.) LO
O sad, sad world, O world that knows not love. Dirge. Edith Lovejoy Pierce. MaRV; MuM
O, sad when grass is green. Sad! Sad! Thomas Edward Brown. VLEP
O saftly sleep, my bonnie bairn! A Lullaby. Alexander A. Ritchie. BOL; EBSV
O Sailor, Come Ashore. Christina Rossetti. *Fr.* Sing-Song. BoTP; BrR; GaP
(Coral.) GFA
O sailor sailor tell me why. Scarabs for the Living, I. R. P. Blackmur. AnFE; CoAnAm; TwAmPo
Oh! St. Patrick was a gentleman. St. Patrick Was a Gentleman. Henry Bennett. DD; LPS-3; PoRL; SiSoSe
O sairly may I rue the day. The Women Folk. James Hogg. HBV; LPS-3
Oh, Sally Brown, of New York City. Sally Brown. *Unknown.* AmSS; SG
Oh, Sally Racket, hi-oh! Cheerly, Man. *Unknown.* SoAmSa
O Salutaris Hostia. *Unknown, tr. fr. Latin.* WHL
Oh, Santa [*or* Santy] Anna fought for fame [*or* gained the day]. Santa [*or* Santy] Anna. *Unknown.* AmSS; SoAmSa
O saving Victim opening wide. O Salutaris Hostia. *Unknown.* WHL
O Saviour, precious Saviour. Frances Ridley Havergal. OlF
O Saviour, welcome to my heart. Welcome to My Heart. *Unknown.* BePJ
O Saviour, when we have no work. Hymn of the Unemployed. Thomas Tiplady. MaRV
O Saw Ye Bonnie Lesley. Burns. *See* Bonnie Lesley.

"O saw ye my father? or saw ye my mother?" The Grey Cock. *Unknown.* BaBo (B *vers.*); ESPB
O saw ye not fair Ines? Fair Ines. Thomas Hood. BCEP; EnRP; ERP; EV-4; HBV; LEAP; OBEV; OBRV; OBVV; PG (1945 ed.); TOP; UnPo (1st ed.); VA
O, Saw Ye the Lass. Richard Ryan. FaBoBe; HBV; LPS-1
Oh, say, can you see, by the dawn's early light. The Star-spangled Banner. Francis Scott Key. AA; APW; BAV; BBV; BlG; BLPA; BoHiPo; DD; FaBoBe; FaFP; FaPON; FOAH; HBV; HBVY; HH; InP; LEAP; LPS-2; MaRV; MC; NeHB; NePA; OlF; OnHT; OTPC; PaA; PAH; PAP; PECK; PEDC; PoFr; PoRL; PSO; SPP; TCAP; TreF; TVSH; WBLP; YaD
Oh! say can you see, through the gloom and the storm. The Southern Cross. St. George Tucker. FOAH
O say, dear life, when shall these twinborn berries. *Unknown.* EG
O say, have you seen at the Willows so green. The Ballad of the Emeu. Bret Harte. BOHV
Oh say, little dogies, quit your rovin' around. The Night-herding Song. Harry Stephens. SoAF
O Say, My Brown Drimin. *Unknown, tr. fr. Modern Irish by* James Joseph Callanan. OnYI
O say, my flattering heart. Loves She like Me? Samuel Woodworth. AA
O say not he is dead! What messenger. Dedication. Marian Osborne. CPG
Oh say not that my heart is cold. Song. Charles Wolfe. EV-4
Oh! say not woman's love [*or* heart] is bought. Song. Isaac Pocock, *wr. at. to* Thomas Love Peacock. *Fr.* The Heir of Vironi. HBV
O say were [*or* was] you ever in Rio Grande. Rio Grande. *Unknown.* LO; SoAmSa; TrAS
O say what is that thing call'd Light. The Blind Boy. Colley Cibber. CEP; CG; GTBS; GTBS-D; GTBS-W; GTSE; GTSL; HBV; LPS-1; NeHB; OBEC; PRWS; TreFS; TVSH
Oh, say, what is this fearful, wild. The Hippopotamus. Oliver Herford. NA
Oh, say, who comes to town today. "Who Ride?" Stella Kobrin. GA
Oh! say you so, bold sailor. The Herald Crane. Hamlin Garland. BLA; HBV; SN
Oh, says the linnet, if I sing. Birds' Lament. John Clare. PoEL-4
Oh, scarlet hurts like some strange lust. Colors. Weir Vernon. DDA
O Scotia! my dear, my native soil! Prayer for My Native Land. Burns. *Fr.* The Cotter's Saturday Night. MaRV
Oh, 'scusa, lady, 'scusa, pleass'. W'en Spreeng Ees Com'. T. A. Daly. CV
O Sea of Dust, I stand upon your shore. The Poet Dreams of the Wings of Death. Edwin Justus Mayer. LEAP
O, sea of many songs, whoever hears. Bright Delusion. Inez Barclay Kirby. MuM
O search the heart and belly you may find. Forebears. Elizabeth Riddell. BoAV
O searchlights, pierce the night with swords and drive the stars in ruin thence. Searchlights. Edward Shanks. NV
O season of repetition and return. Spring 1940. W. H. Auden. OAEP (2d ed.)
O Season supposed of all free flowers. Song of the Springtide. *Unknown.* BOHV
O see how narrow are our days. Prayer of the Maidens to Mary. Rainer Maria Rilke. AWP
Oh, See How Thick the Goldcup Flowers. A. E. Housman. A Shropshire Lad, V. EnLi-2; MBP; MoBrPo; PoVP; TwCV; VLEP
(Good-by, Young Man, Good-by.) EnLit
O seeded grass, you army of little men. Irradiations, IX [XV]. John Gould Fletcher. AnAmPo; LA; MAP; MAPA; MoAmPo; NeMA; NePA; PFE; TwAmPo
Oh, seek me not within a tomb. Envoi. John G. Neihardt. HBV; NP; OQP; QP-1; WGRP. *See also* Seek not for me . . .
O seeker of the Greater Light. The Circle. Carol Coates. CaP
Oh! send Lewie Gordon hame. Lewie Gordon. Alexander Geddes. EBSV
Oh send to me an apple that hasn't any kernel. *Unknown, tr. fr. Welsh by* Gwyn Williams. FaBoCh; LoGBV
O servant of God's holiest charge. Christopher Smart. *Fr.* A Song to David. ViBoPo; WoL
Oh, setting sun, had you no aureole? February 12, 1809. Gail Brook Burket. PGD
Oh, Seventy-seven. *Unknown, tr. fr. Danish by* E. M. Smith-Dampier. BoDaBa
O sextant of the meetin house, which sweeps. To the "Sextant" [*or* A Appeal for Are]. Arabella M. Willson. BOHV; LPS-3
O Shadow. Shadow Dance. Ivy O. Eastwick. TiPo
O Shady Vales! O Fair Enrichèd Meads! Thomas Lodge. *See* Sonnet: "O shady vales . . ."
O! shairly ye hae seen my love. Ballad. William Soutar. NeBP
Oh shall I never never be home again? Brumana. James Elroy Flecker. LBBV; PoeT; POTT
O shame to men! Devil with devil damned. Satan on War. Milton. *Fr.* Paradise Lost, II. MaRV
O Shannadore, I love your daughter. The Wide Mizzoura. *Unknown.* AS
Oh, she is fair: fair as the eastern morn. Seeing a Lady. John Tatham. *Fr.* Ostella. LO; SeCL
Oh! she is good, the little rain! and well she knows our need. The Little Rain. Tu Fu. FaPON
O she looked out of the window. The Two Magicians. *Unknown.* ChTr; OxBoLi
O, she walked unaware of her own increasing beauty. She Walked Unaware. Patrick MacDonogh. FaBoTw; NeIP; OnYI; OxBI
O she was playing with her cat. Femme et Chatte. Paul Verlaine, *tr. by* Ashmore Wingate. CIV
Oh, Shenandoah, I long to hear you. Shenandoah. *Unknown.* SoAmSa; TrAS
Oh, Shenandoah, I love your daughter. Shenandoah. *Unknown.* AmSS
O Shepherd, dost Thou leave. The Ascension. Luis de León. TeCS
O shepherd, out upon the snow. In January. Golden Bottomley. MM; TCPD
O Shepherd with the bleeding feet. The Good Shepherd. Christina Rossetti. ChIP
O shepherds! take my crook from me. Adieu. Eleanor Elizabeth Montgomery. VA
O shield me from his rage, celestial Powers! Esther Johnson. LO
O ship incoming from the sea. Off Rivière du Loup. Duncan Campbell Scott. EtS; HBV; MCCG; SG
O Ship! new billows sweep thee out. The Ship of State. Horace. Odes, I, 14. AWP; JAWP; RoL; WBP
O Ship of State. Longfellow. *See* Ship of State, The.
O Ship, Ship, Ship. Arthur Hugh Clough. Songs in Absence, XIV. BPN; EmBrPo; PoVP; VLEP
O Sicily, O Tuscany, where I. Easter Sunday, 1945. G. A. Borgese. NePoAm
"Oh, sick I am to see you, will you never let me be?" The New Mistress. A. E. Housman. A Shropshire Lad, XXXIV. MoBrPo (1950 ed.); PoVP
O sigh of the sea, O soft lone-wandering sound. The Calling. George Sigerson. JKCP (1926 ed.); TIP
O sight of pity, shame and dole! The Singer in the Prison. Walt Whitman. BeLS
Oh, sight too dearly bought! Sleeping Beauty. William Drummond of Hawthornden. LiTL
Oh, silence, silence! now, when night is near. The Lines around Petersburg. Samuel Davis. BlG
O Silent God, Thou whose voice afar. A Litany at [*or* of] Atlanta. W. E. B. DuBois. BANP; CDC; PoNe
O silver-throated swan. The Dying Swan. T. Sturge Moore. GTBS-D; MBP; OBMV; SeCePo
Oh, silver tree! Jazzonia. Langston Hughes. BANP
Oh silvery streamlet of the fields. The Stream of Life. Bryant. AnNE
O sing a song of Bethlehem. Songs of Jesus. Louis F. Benson. MaRV
Oh, sing a song of phosphates. Boston Nursery Rhymes. Joseph Cook. BOHV; PA
O sing, in heart of silence hiding near. Philomel. Paul Fort. MiFP
Oh, sing of our glorious Southland. Song of Our Glorious Southland. Mary Ware. BlG
O sing the glories of our Lord. A Psalm for Sunday Night. Thomas Pestel. OxBoCh
Oh sing unto Jehovah a new song. *See* O sing unto the Lord a new song.
O, Sing unto My Roundelay. Thomas Chatterton. *See* Minstrel's Song.
O sing unto the Lord [*or* Jehovah] a new song. The Floods Clap Their Hands. Psalm XCVIII, Bible, *O.T.* BLRP; StaSt; TrGrPo; TriL; TrJP
O singer of Persephone! Theocritus. Oscar Wilde. BMEP; EV-5; HBV; LBBV; OxBI; PIAE; ShBV-4; VLEP
O singer of the field and fold. For a Copy of Theocritus. Austin Dobson. HBV; LPS-2; PtP; VA; VLEP
O singing wind. The Fir-Tree. Edith M. Thomas. OHIP
O, sinner, sinner, you better pray. Death's Gwineter Lay His Cold Icy Hands on Me. *Unknown.* BoAN-2
"O sister, O sister, come go with me." The Two Sisters. *Unknown.* ABS
O sister take the vase of sallow clay. Anniversary. Stefan George. AnGP
Oh, sister, there are midnight dreams. The Dowie Dens o' Yarrow. Henry Scott Riddell. EBSV
Oh Sky, you look so drear! Earth and Sky. Eleanor Farjeon. BoChLi; MeMeAg; SUS
O skylark! I see thee and call thee joy! To a Skylark. George Meredith. EnLit

O Skylarks, Teach Japan to Sing. Toyohiko Kagawa, *tr. fr.*
Japanese by Lois J. Erickson. SoLD
O Slavery! thou frost of the world's prime. Chorus. Shelley.
Fr. Hellas. PoFr
O Sleep. Grace Fallow Norton. HBV; LEAP
Oh, Sleep, Fond Fancy. *Unknown.* EiL
Oh, Sleep Forever in the Latmian Cave. Edna St. Vincent
Millay. ExPo; LiTM; MAP; MoAmPo; MOAP; MoVE;
PIAE; SeCeV; ViBoPo
(Endymion.) AnEnPo
Oh! sleep in peace where poppies grow. Reply to "In Flan-
ders Fields." John Mitchell. BLPA
O Sleep, My Babe. Sara Coleridge. *Fr.* Phantasmion.
BOL; MotAn; OBEV (1st ed.); OBRV
O Sleep, O Sleep, O thou beguiler. *Unknown.* BOL
O Sleep, O tranquil son of noiseless Night. To Sleep.
Giovanni della Casa. AWP; JAWP; WBP
O sleep, sweet infant, for we all must sleep. Lullaby. Hart-
ley Coleridge. BOL
Oh, sleep this night is difficult to woo. Lines for Insomnia.
Anne Mary Lawler. DDA
O sleep unlearned of sorrow, painless sleep. Sleep! Sopho-
cles. *Fr.* Philoctetes. GrR
O Sleep, who takest little ones. *Unknown.* BOL
Oh, slow to smite and swift to spare. Abraham Lincoln [*or*
The Death of Lincoln]. Bryant. AmP; BAV; BlG;
BoHiPo; CoBA; DD; GA; GDAH; HH; IAP; InP;
LBAH; MC; OHIP; PaA; PAH; RiBV
Oh, slow up, dogies, quit your roving round. Night-herd-
ing Song [*or* Cowboy Songs]. Harry Stephens. CoSo;
CSF; OuSiCo; TrAS
Oh Slumber, hold him softly, and you, Sleep. For That
Pale God of Silence Men Call Death. Lois Carver.
CAG
O slumber; washed on Saturday. *Unknown.* BOL
O small black puppy with angel eyes. Neighbor's Dog.
Georgie Starbuck Galbraith. AlBD
"O smile, maiden, smile, if you care to be wise." A Misun-
derstanding. Martial. RoL
O smitten mouth! O forehead crowned with thorn! For Our
Sakes. Oscar Wilde. PGD
O smoother me to death. *Unknown.* SeCSL
Oh! Snatch'd Away in Beauty's Bloom. Byron. BCEP;
BPN; CBE; EM-2; EmBrPo; EnRP; ERP; EV-2; FiP;
HBV; InP; LoBV; LPS-1; OBRV; TOP
(Elegy: "Oh! snatch'd away.") GTBS; GTBS-D;
GTBS-W; GTSE; GTSL
O snow! oft called the beautiful. Ode to City Snow. Arthur
H. Folwell. LauV
O So Dear from Far Away, So Near and White. Stéphane
Mallarmé, *tr. fr. French by* Vernon Watkins. AnFP
Oh, so good. Moral Song. John Farrar. RAR
O soft embalmer of the still midnight. To Sleep [*or* Sonnet to
Sleep]. Keats. AIDL; AtBAP; BoLiVe; BPN; BrBE;
ChTr; EM-2; EmBrPo; EnLi-2; EnRP; EPN; EPP; ES;
EV-4; GTBS-W; LoBV; OAEP; OBEV; OBRV; PC;
PeBoSo; PoE; PoEL-4; ReaPo; ViBoPo; WHA
Oh soft flowing rivers. My South. Don West. PoNe
O Softly Singing Lute. Francis Pilkington. OAEP
O Solitary of the Austere Sky. Sir Charles G. D. Roberts.
CaP; OCL
O solitary pine, how many. Solitary Pine. Prince Ichihara.
OnPM
O Solitude! If I Must with Thee Dwell. Keats. *See* To
Solitude.
O solitude, romantic maid! Solitude [*or* Ode to Solitude].
James Grainger. CEP; OBEC; ViBoPo
Oh, solitude! thou wonder-working fay. The Imaginative
Crisis. *Unknown.* BOHV
Oh some are fond of red wine, and some are fond of white.
Captain Stratton's Fancy. John Masefield. MBP;
MoBrPo; OBEV (new ed.); OnPP
Oh something just now must be happening there! Home
Thoughts. Claude McKay. GoSl
O sometimes in the street, or in the Paris Metro. Remem-
brance. Antoni Slonimski. TrJP
O somewhere, somewhere, God unknown. A Last Appeal.
Frederic W. H. Myers. MaRV; VA
O Son of God! Thy children we. Light of the World.
Sylvester Judd. BePJ
O Son of Man. Frank Fletcher. MaRV
O Son of Man, Thou Madest Known. Milton S. Littlefield.
TrPWD
O son of man, when thou findest wine. Five Arabic Verses
in Praise of Wine, V. *Unknown.* TrJP
O Son of Man, who walked each day. The Fellowship of
Prayer. Nancy Byrd Turner. BePJ; PraP
O Son of mine, when dusk shall find thee bending.
From Generation to Generation. Sir Henry Newbolt.
FaBoTw
O son of Virginia, thy mem'ry divine. Our Washington.
Eliza W. Durbin. HH; PEDC; PEOR
O song as yet unsung! A Song as Yet Unsung. "Yehoash."
TrJP

O sons of men, that toil, and love with tears! The Fair Maid
and the Sun. Arthur O'Shaughnessy. BeLS; VA
O soothing sleep, dear friend, best nurse of sickness! Orestes
and Electra. Euripides. *Fr.* Orestes. OxBG
O Sorrow! Keats. *See* Song of the Indian Maid.
O Sorrow, cruel fellowship. In Memoriam A. H. H., III.
Tennyson. BPN; EM-2; EmBrPo; EnL; EnLi-2; EPN;
GEPC; MaPo; OAEP; TOP; ViPo; VLEP
O Sorrow, Sorrow. Thomas Dekker, Samuel Rowley, *and*
John Day. *Fr.* The Noble Soldier. CenL; SeCL
Oh! Sorrow, Sorrow, scarce I knew. Song. Charlotte Mew.
BrBE; MM
O Sorrow, wilt thou live with me. In Memoriam A. H. H.,
LIX. Tennyson. EmBrPo; EPN; GEPC; GTSL; ViPo;
VLEP
O sorrowful and ancient days. Metrum Parhemiacum Tra-
gicum. Eugenius Vulgarius. WaaP
O soul, canst thou not understand. Aridity. "Michael Field."
OBMV; OxBoCh
O soul, O God, O glory of liberty. Swinburne. *Fr.* The Eve
of Revolution. PoFr
O Soul of Nature! excellent and fair! Imagination and Taste,
How Impaired and Restored. Wordsworth. *Fr.* The
Prelude, XII *and* XIII. ERP
O soul, what hast thou seen. The Dryad. Alexander M.
Stephen. CPG
O Soul, with Storms Beset. Solomon ibn Gabirol, *tr. fr.*
Hebrew by Alice Lucas. TrJP
O sovereign power of love! O grief! O balm! Invocation to
the Power of Love. Keats. *Fr.* Endymion, II. BPN;
EnRP; ERP; ViBoPo
O Sower of Sorrow. Joseph Plunkett. *See* Poppies.
Oh, Spanish composers may seem quite *castizo.* Iberia. Leo
Kirschenbaum. UnS
O Spark, you winged from secret woodland forges. To a
Scarlet Tanager. Glenn Ward Dresbach. BAP; BLA
"O spheral, spheral!" he seems to say. A Hermit Thrush in
the Catskills. William Griffith. BLA
O spirit of the summertime! Song. William Allingham.
IrPN
O Spirit, that dost prefer. A Poet-Preacher's Prayer. Mil-
ton. *Fr.* Paradise Lost, I. MaRV
O spiteful bitter thought. Assurance. George Herbert.
OxBoCh
O splendid, glowing clouds. Song of the Splendid Clouds.
Unknown. Fr. The Fountain of Old Poems. WhP
O sprawling city! worlds in a world! James Oppenheim.
Fr. A New York Skyscraper. MaRV
O spread agen [*or* ageàn] your leaves an' flow'rs. The Wood-
lands. William Barnes. GTBS-D; LEAP; OBVV;
PoVP
O Spring, Come Prettily In. Adolf Strodtmann. CAW
O Spring, I know thee! Seek for sweet surprise. In Early
Spring. Alice Meynell. AnFE; HBV
O Spring, thou youthful beauty of the year. Spring. Gio-
vanni Battista Guarini. AWP; JAWP; OnPM; WBP
O spring, upon your bank I lean. Beside a Spring. Johan
Ludvig Runeberg. AnSL
O Spring's a pleasant time. Aye Waukin' O! *Unknown.*
BSV; EBSV; GoTS
O springtime, springtime, save me! To Spring. Henrik
Wergeland. AnNoLy
O sprinting of the wind over land. Invocation to the Wind.
Joseph Kalar. AnEnPo
Oh, Stack in the rivuh. Stacker Lee. *Unknown.* StDa
O star of evening, harbinger whose face. The Evening Star.
Alfred de Musset. TrFP
O Star of France. Walt Whitman. IAP; PoFr
O Star of Galilee. Savonarola, *tr. fr. Latin by* R. R. Mad-
den. ISi
O star of morning and of liberty! Divina Commedia, VI.
Longfellow. AmP; AmPP; AnAmPo; AnFE; AnNE;
APA; APW; CoAnAm; CoBA; CoV; ES; GoBC; IAP;
LA; LPS-2; MOAP; NePA; OBAV; OxBA; PIAE;
PtP; ReaPo; TCAP; TOP
O star-spangled banner! the flag of our pride. The Stripes and
the Stars. Edna Dean Proctor. FOAH
O Star that led the Wise Men from the East. Star of Beth-
lehem. Florence Van Cleve. OQP; QP-2
O Star (the fairest one in sight). Choose Something like a
Star. Robert Frost. AnNE; MoAB; MoAmPo (1950
ed.); NeMA
Oh, stately though we walk. The Wall. Isidor Schneider.
PG (1933 ed.)
Oh Stay at Home, My Lad. A. E. Housman. Last Poems,
XXXVIII. EmBrPo; TwP
O stay, Madonna! stay. Song. Macaulay. FtPaFn
O Stay, Sweet Love. *Unknown.* EG; TrGrPo
O stay, sweet warbling wood-lark, stay. Address to the
Woodlark. Burns. BCEP
O steadfast trees that know. Man and Nature. Robert
Kelley Weeks. AA
O, stealthy beauty, crouching in my tree. The Black Leopard.
Frances Crawford. PtPa

O stiffly shapen houses that change not. Suburbs on a Hazy Day. D. H. Lawrence. OBMV
O! still my child, Orange. *Unknown.* BOL
O still, still, still. Reapers. Frederic Prokosch. NeTW
O still, white face of perfect peace. Ripe Grain. Dora Read Goodale. HBV
O stolid granite hills, that tower serene. Granite. Lew Sarett. BAP
O stoodent A has gone and spent. Ballad with an Ancient Refrain. *Unknown.* NA
Oh, Stop Being Thankful All over the Place. Ogden Nash. NePA; SiTL
Oh stormy, stormy world. Happiness Makes Up in Height for What It Lacks in Length. Robert Frost. MoAB; MoAmPo; MoPo
Oh, Stormy's gone, that good old man. Stormalong. *Unknown.* AmSS
O strange and lovely sight. The Inky Mouth. Al-Barraq. MooP
O Strassburg. *Unknown, tr. fr. German by* C. F. MacIntyre. WaaP
O stream descending to the sea. The Stream of Life. Arthur Hugh Clough. BPN
O stream, my morning-sunlit stream. My River. Eduard Mörike. AnGP
O, strew the way with rosy flowers. Song. James Clarence Mangan. IrPN
Oh, strong and faithful and enduring. The Return. Martha Ostenso. CaP; OCL
Oh strong ridged and deeply hollowed. Smell. William Carlos Williams. MoAB; MoAmPo
O strong sun of heaven, harm not my love. An Incantation. Marguerite Wilkinson. AV; NP
O strong was the wood in the ashen oar. Lament for Seán. D. J. O'Sullivan. NeIP
O, Struck beneath the Laurel. George Edward Woodberry. Wild Eden, XXXIII. AA; PFY; TCPD
O such a commotion under the ground. Flower Chorus [*or* A Laughing Chorus]. *Unknown, wr. at. to* Emerson. BoTP; NLK; PCH; PTA-2
Oh! such a funny thing I found. A Discovery. Arthur A. Knipe. GFA
Oh such a tiny colony. Helmet Orchid. Douglas Stewart. BoAV
O sug'red talk, wherewith my thoughts do live. Licia, LII. Giles Fletcher. ReIE
O Suibhne from lofty Sliabh na nEach. *Unknown. Fr.* Sweeney the Mad. SiB
O suitably-attired-in-leather-boots. Fragment of a Greek Tragedy. A. E. Housman. CenHV
Oh, summer has the roses. A Winter Song. *Unknown.* PEOR
O Summer Sun. Laurence Binyon. PoeT
Oh, Summer's on the mountain. The Call. Edwin Markham. PoTo
O sun and skies and clouds of June. *See* O suns and skies and clouds of June.
O sun! instigator of cocks! Salute. Archibald MacLeish. ChMo
Oh sun, oh good comrade, good friend. Riding Song. Isidor Schneider. PG (1933 ed.)
O Sun of Life. Thomas Curtis Clark. ChIP
O Sun, when I stand in my green leaves. To the Sun from a Flower. Guido Gezelle. FaPON; LiTW
Oh Sunne,/ Burne the great sphere thou mov'st in. Shakespeare. *Fr.* Antony and Cleopatra, IV, xv. AtBAP
O suns [*or* sun] and skies and clouds of June. October's Bright Blue Weather. Helen Hunt Jackson. BBV (1923 ed.); BLPA; BoChLi; CV; DD; FaBoBe; GN; HBVY; MW; NeHB; OTPC (1946 ed.); PTA-1
O supreme Light, who dost thy glory assert. The Vision of God. Dante. *Fr.* Divina Commedia: Paradiso, XXXIII. ExPo
O surely now the fisherman. Song of Orpheus. William Morris. *Fr.* The Life and Death of Jason. LEAP
O surely, surely life is fair. Fiorentina. Ernest Myers. OBVV
O surely with terrible wrath. The Rivals. Aristophanes. *Fr.* The Frogs. GrR
Oh, Susan Blue. Susan Blue. Kate Greenaway. MPB; OTPC (1946 ed.); RAR; TiPo
Oh, Susan Van Dusan. Susan Van Dusan. *Unknown.* ABF
Oh! Susanna. Stephen Collins Foster. FaFP; OlF; PaA; RIS; StaSt; TrAS, *with music;* TreF
O swallow, gentle swallow. The Wandering Armenian to the Swallow. C. A. Dodochian. ArmLP
O Swallow, Swallow, Flying, Flying South. Tennyson. *Fr.* The Princess, Pt. IV. AtBAP; BMEP; BPN; EV-5; GTBS; GTSL; HBV; LPS-1; PoVP
(From "The Princess.") LEAP
(Songs from "The Princess.") MotAn; ViPo; VLEP
O swan of slenderness. The Little Red Lark. Alfred Perceval Graves. HBV
Oh swearing and telling. Cockcrow. Eithne Wilkins. NeBP
O Sweden, Sweden, Sweden, native land. Sweden. Verner von Heidenstam. AnSL
O sweet and luminous Bird. Celestial Bird. Jessica Powers. JKCP (1955 ed.)
O Sweet Anne Page. William Shenstone. SeCePo
(Slender's Ghost.) EiPP
O sweet are tropic lands for waking dreams! North and South. Claude McKay. GoSl
O Sweet Athens. Sotiris Skipis, *tr. fr. Modern Greek by* Rae Dalven. MoGP
Oh, Sweet Content. W. H. Davies. CH
O Sweet Content. Thomas Dekker. *See* Happy Heart, The.
O Sweet Delight. Thomas Campion. EV-2; GTSE
("O sweet delight, O more than human bliss.") EG
(Song: "O sweet delight . . .") HBV
O sweet everlasting Voices, be still. The Everlasting Voices. W. B. Yeats. AWP; BrBE; JAWP; WBP
O sweet incendiary! show here thy art. Richard Crashaw. *Fr.* The Flaming Heart. EPS; PoFS; SeEP
O sweet is Love, and sweet is Lack! Francis Thompson. EG
O sweet is snow to June-parched lips; when winter's over. Joy's Crown of Joy. Asclepiades. GrPE
O, sweet is the vale where the Mohawk gently glides. Bonny Eloise. C. W. Elliott. BlG
Oh, sweet it is, in academic groves. Residence in France. Wordsworth. *Fr.* The Prelude, IX. ERP
O sweet Queen-city of the golden South. Patrick Moloney. Sonnets—Ad Innuptam, VII. BoAu
O sweet September! thy first breezes bring. Sweet September. George Arnold. GN
O sweet severity, repulses mild. Petrarch. Sonnets to Laura: To Laura in Death, LXXXVII. PrPoCR
O Sweet Spontaneous. E. E. Cummings. AnNE; BoLiVe (1945 ed.); PoLFOT
(La Guerre.) MAP; MoAB; MoAmPo
(O Sweet Spontaneous Earth.) OxBA; TrGrPo
O sweet strange minstrel of the joyous singing. Clement Wood. *Fr.* The Minstrel of God. SaFP
O sweet the time, when neither folly might. Truth's Complaint over England. Thomas Lodge. ACP (1952 ed.)
Oh, sweet Virginia hills! George Washington. Francesca Falk Miller. PEDC
O sweet wild April. Sweet Wild April. William Force Stead. HBV; HBVY
O Sweet Woods (*three sonnets*). Sir Philip Sidney. *Fr.* Arcadia. AtBAP; CoBE, *first sonnet;* KN, 16 *ll., diff.;* PeBoSo, *second sonnet;* PoEL-1; TuPP
(Delight of Solitariness, The.) LiTB
(Dorus's Song.) LoBV
(Solitariness.) OBSC; SiPS
("O sweet woods, the delight of solitariness!") SiCE
O sweete and bitter monuments of paine. Upon the Ensignes of Christes Crucifyinge. William Alabaster. MePo
O sweeter than the marriage-feast. He Prayeth Best. Samuel Taylor Coleridge. *Fr.* The Rime of the Ancient Mariner, VII. GrCo-1; MaRV
O Sweetest Melancholy. John Fletcher *and (at.)* Thomas Middleton. *See* Melancholy.
O sweetest sleep, come now at last to stay. Sonnet. Lorenzo de' Medici. LyPI
O Sweetheart, Hear You. James Joyce. Chamber Music, XVIII. HBMV; LBBV; MBP; MoBrPo; ReaPo
O swift forerunners, rosy with the race. Sunrise on Mansfield Mountain. Alice Brown. HBV
O swiftness of the swallow and strength. Robinson Jeffers. *Fr.* Tamar. TCPD
O swinging sword of Carroll hail! Carroll's Sword. *At. to* Dallan MacMore. KiLC
O sylvan prophet, whose eternal fame. Hymn for St. John's Eve. *Unknown.* AWP
O! synge untoe mie roundelaie. Mynstrelles Songe. Thomas Chatterton. *Fr.* Aella. AnFE; BEL; CEP; EiPP; EnLi-2; EnLoPo; EnRP; EV-3; OBEC. *See also* O. Sing unto My Roundelay.
O Syrian dancing-girl with the filleted hair. Copa; the Barmaid. Virgil. LaP
O, Tabby of the yellow eyes. To a Cat. Fanny Elizabeth Perkins. CIV
O take my hand, Walt Whitman! Salut au Monde. Walt Whitman. BoFr
O Talk Not to Me. Byron. *See* Stanzas Written on the Road between Florence and Pisa.
Oh, tamp 'em up solid. Tie-tamping Chant. *Unknown.* ABF
O Tan-faced Prairie-Boy. Walt Whitman. FaPON; LO; OxBA; TCAP
O tardy plane-tree. Plane-Tree. F. S. Flint. MBP; MoBrPo (1942 ed.)
O, tears, no tears, but rain from Beauty's skies. Astrophel and Stella, C. Sir Philip Sidney. ReIE; SiPS
O tell me, drayman, who quietly descend. The Drayman. Giovanni Pascoli. OnPM
Oh! tell me have you ever seen a red, long-leg'd flamingo? The Flamingo. Lewis Gaylord Clark. BOHV; NA

O Tell Me How to Woo Thee. Robert Graham. *See* If Doughty Deeds.
Oh, tell me less or tell me more. The Petition. James Russell Lowell. PR
Oh, tell me, little children, have you seen her. Nikolina. Celia Thaxter. GN; HBV; OTPC (1946 ed.)
O tell me not that he is dead—for yet he lives. Semyon Yakovlevich Nadson, *tr. fr. Russian by* Sir Cecil Kisch. WaL
"Oh tell me, sailor, tell me true." The Gray Swan. Alice Cary. BeLS; BLPA; GN; PTA-2
Oh, tell me what you see. Nonsense Song. *Ad. by* Michael Lewis. RIS
O tell me whence that joy doth spring. The Queer. Henry Vaughan. MaPo; NBE; PoEL-2
O tell me where and to what land. Ballade of the Women of the Past. Villon. FoS
O Tell Us, Poet. Rainer Maria Rilke, *tr. fr. German by* Herman Salinger. TwGV
(I Praise, *tr. by* Jessie Lemont.) OnPM
O, Tempora! O, Mores! John Dickson Bruns [Burns, *wr.*]. BIG
O Tempora! O Mores! Thomas Freeman. SiCE
O tender dove, sweet circling in the blue. Vale! Roden Noel. OBVV
O tender shade! To a Photograph. John Banister Tabb. AmP
O tender time that love thinks long to see. A Vision of Spring in Winter. Swinburne. PoVP; VLEP
O Tender under Her Right Breast. George Barker. *Fr.* Second Cycle of Love Poems. MoAB; MoBrPo (1950 ed.); NeMA
(Love Poem.) NeBP
O tenderly the haughty day. Ode [Sung in the Town Hall, Concord, July 4, 1857]. Emerson. AA; AnNE; APW; BAP; DD; GN; IAP; IDAH; LEAP; MPB; PaA; PoRL; TCAP
O, terribly proud was Miss MacBride. The Proud Miss MacBride. John Godfrey Saxe. LPS-3
"O than the fairest day thrice fairer night!" The Shepherds [*or* For the Nativity of Our Lord]. William Drummond of Hawthornden. COAH; StJW
O thank you for giving me the chance. Thank You. Kenneth Koch. NeAP
Oh! thank you, good Dobbin, you've been a long track. Good Dobbin. Ann *or* Jane Taylor. SAS
Oh, thanks for all since the days long past. Synnöve's Song. Björnstjerne Björnson. AnNoLy; LiTW
O that a lovely lyre were I. Wishes. *Unknown.* OxBG
Oh that bright impossible beast of the mind. Virgin and Unicorn. John Heath-Stubbs. NeBP
Oh, that day there was a great demand for sailors. Mainsail Haul, *vers.* II. *Unknown.* ShS
Oh, that fate had let me see. Matthew Arnold. *Fr.* Empedocles on Etna. NBE
Oh! that I always breath'd in such an air. The Experience. Edward Taylor. *Fr.* Sacramental Meditations. AmPP (4th ed.); CoV
O that I could my Lord receive. The Conquering Love of Jesus. Charles Wesley. BePJ
O That I Had Wings like a Dove. *Unknown.* OxBoCh
Oh that I had wings like a dove! Wings. *Fr.* Psalm LV, Bible, *O.T.* AWP; FaPON; PCD; PCH
Oh That I Knew Where I Might Find Him. Job, XXIII: 3, 8-10, Bible, *O.T.* MaRV
O that I knew whether Sulayma is dwelling in the valley of the demesne. Remembrance. Ibnu'l-Farid. LiTW
O that I might believe that time. Device. Sir Herbert Read. MBP; MoBrPo (1942 ed.)
O that I now, I too were. Nature. Swinburne. *Fr.* Atalanta in Calydon. BPN; EmBrPo
O that I were. English Hills. John Freeman. MM
Oh, that I were a lovely flower. The Flower. *At. to* Samuel Speed. OxBoCh; SeCL
Oh! that I were a poet now in grain! Urian Oakes. *Fr.* Elegy on the Death of Thomas Shepard. BAV
Oh that I were an orange-tree. Employment. George Herbert. EV-2; OBS
"O that I were as sure to live, immortal, and sustain." Homer. *Fr.* The Iliad, VIII. AtBAP
Oh That I Were in the Wilderness. Jeremiah, IX: 1-10, Bible, *O.T.* TrJP
O that I were lying under the olives. March Thoughts from England. Margaret L. Woods. LBBV; OBVV
O that it were possible we might. The Heart-Cry of the Duchess. John Webster. *Fr.* The Duchess of Malfi, IV, ii. BCEP; PoD
Oh that I were where I would be. *Unknown.* OxNR; SiTL
Oh, That Joy So Soon Should Waste. Ben Jonson. *See* Song: "Oh, that joy . . ."
Oh! that last day in Lucknow fort. The Relief of Lucknow. Robert T. S. Lowell. HBV; LPS-2; StPo
O that mine armes were wings, that I might flie. George Chapman. *Fr.* The Conspiracy of Charles, Duke of Byron, III, i. NBE
O that mine eyes might closèd be. A Prayer. Thomas Ellwood. PraP; WGRP
Oh! that my life were a lasting dream! *See* Oh! that my young life were a lasting dream.
Oh, that my load of sin were gone. The Light Yoke and Easy Burden. Charles Wesley. BePJ
Oh that my lungs could bleat like butter'd peas [*or* buttered pease]. Odd but True [*or* Nonsense]. *Unknown.* NA; SiTL
Oh that my soul a marrow-bone might seize! Sonnet Found in a Deserted Madhouse. *Unknown.* BOHV; InvP; NA; SiTL
Oh! that my young life were a lasting dream. Dreams. Poe. AmPP (4th ed.); IAP; OxBA
O that our dreamings all, of sleep or wake. On Imagination. Keats. *Fr.* Epistle to Reynolds. EPN
O that of thus much that return was made. An Idea of Wealth. Christopher Marlowe. *Fr.* The Jew of Malta. BCEP
O that the chemist's magic art. On a Tear [*or* A Tear]. Samuel Rogers. HBV; LPS-3
Oh! that the desert were my dwelling-place. The Ocean [*or* Man and Nature]. Byron. *Fr.* Childe Harold's Pilgrimage, IV. BEL; EPP; ERP; PoEL-4
O that the pines which crown yon steep. Evening Melody. Aubrey Thomas De Vere. GoBC; HBV
O that this last farewell. *Unknown.* LO; SeCSL
O! That This Too Too Solid Flesh Would Melt. Shakespeare. *Fr.* Hamlet, I, ii. BCEP; PIR
(Frailty, Thy Name Is Woman.) LiA; TrGrPo
(Hamlet Broods over the Death of His Father.) TreFS
"O that this too, too solid flesh would melt." On a Young Lady's Going into a Shower Bath. Francis Scott Key. YaD
Oh that those lips had language! Life has passed. On the Receipt of My Mother's Picture Out of Norfolk [*or* My Mother's Picture]. William Cowper. AEV; BCEP; BEL; CEP; CH; CoBE; EiPP; EM-1; EnLi-2 (1949 ed.); EnLit; EnRP; EPP; EV-3; FiP; HBV; LPS-1; MOAH; MotAn; OAEP; OBEC; OHIP; PoE; ShGoBo; TCEP; TOP
O that torment should not be confin'd. Milton. *Fr.* Samson Agonistes. BrBE
O That 'Twere Possible. Tennyson. *Fr.* Maud, Pt. II, iv. AtBAP; BMEP; BPN, *longer sel.;* EG; EtPaEn, *longer sel.;* GEPC; HBV; HoPM; LEAP; LH; LoPo; LoPS; OBEV; OBVV; OQP; PoD; PoFS; QP-2
O that we now had here. England at War. Shakespeare. King Henry V, *fr.* IV, iii. EV-1
Oh! that we two were maying. Song. Charles Kingsley. *Fr.* The Saint's Tragedy. HBV; VA
O that you were yourself! but, love, you are. Sonnets, XIII. Shakespeare. OAEP; PeBoSo; SiCE
Oh, the agony of having too much power! The Interne. Maxwell Bodenheim. NP
Oh, the anchor's aweigh, the anchor's aweigh. The Anchor's Aweigh. *Unknown.* ShS
Oh, the auld house, the auld house. The Auld House. Lady Nairne. HBV; MotAn; OTPC (1923 ed.)
Oh, the banks of May are fair. To a Carmelite Postulant. Michael Earls. CAW; JKCP
O the barberry bright, the barberry bright. Song against Children. Aline Kilmer. CP; FAOV; SP; TSW; TSWC
Oh, the beautiful maiden has gone away. A Garland of Recital Programs. Franklin P. Adams. InMe
Oh, the beauty of the Christ Child. Offertory. Mary Mapes Dodge. COAH; HH; PRWS
O the birds of bonnie Scotland. The Birds of Scotland. Hugh Macdonald. SN
Oh, the bitter shame and sorrow. None of Self and All of Thee. Theodore Monod. BLRP
O the black angel who softly stepped from the heart of the tree. To One Who Died Young. Georg Trakl. AnGP
Oh, the blue blue bloom. Pansy. Mary Effie Lee Newsome. CDC
O the bonny Christ Church bells! Christ Church Bells. *At. to* Henry Aldrich. SeCL
Oh, the boys and the girls went a-huckleberry hunting. Huckleberry Hunting. *Unknown.* SoAmSa
Oh, the brave old Duke of York. *Unknown.* OxNR
O the broom, the bonnie, bonnie broom. The Broom of Cowdenknowes. *Unknown.* EBSV
O the broom, the yellow broom. The Broom Flower. Mary Howitt. HBV
Oh, the Burden, the Burden of Love Ungiven. Grace Fallow Norton. AV; LoPS
O, the captain went below. The Captain Went Below. *Unknown.* AmSS
O the charge at Balaklava. Balaklava. Alexander Beaufort Meek. LPS-2

Oh, the comfort—the inexpressible comfort of feeling safe with a person. Friendship. Dinah Maria Mulock Craik. BLPA; NeHB; PoToHe (new ed.)
Oh, the cow-puncher loves the whistle of the rope. From the Chuck Wagon [*or* Tail Piece]. *Unknown.* ABF; CSF
O the crossbones of Galway. Galway. Louis MacNeice. OxBI
Oh! the days are gone, when beauty bright. Love's Young Dream. Thomas Moore. HBV; LPS-1; OlF; PIR; WBLP
Oh, the days gone by! Oh, the days gone by! The Days Gone By. James Whitcomb Riley. TreF
Oh, the days of the Kerry dancing! The Kerry Dance. James Lyman Molloy. OlF; OnYI
O the days of the Messiah are at hand, are at hand! Ballad of the Days of the Messiah. A. M. Klein. TrJP
Oh, the days were ever shiny. My Love and My Heart. Henry S. Leigh. BOHV; CIV
Oh, the Days When I Was Young. Sheridan. *Fr.* The Duenna, III, ii. EV-3
Oh, the Devil in hell they say he was chained. Hell in Texas. *Unknown.* ABF; BLPA; CoSo; CSF
Oh! the dew-wet grass of the meadow in North Carolina. John Wasson. Edgar Lee Masters. *Fr.* Spoon River Anthology. LaNeLa
Oh! the downs high to the cool sky. The Downs. John Galsworthy. MM
Oh the enormous avenues of the holy land. Lives. Arthur Rimbaud. AnFP
O the evening, far in the shadowy country of childhood. Nearness of Death. Georg Trakl. *Fr.* Rosary Songs. AnGP
O the evening's for the fair, bonny lassie O! Bonny Lassie O! John Clare. CH
Oh the falling snow! For Snow. Eleanor Farjeon. CH; RAR; TiPo
O, the Fickle State of Lovers. Francis Quarles. ElSeCe
(Song: "Oh, the fickle state of lovers.") SeCL
O the Fierce Delight. Hamlin Garland. BAP
Oh, the fisherman is a happy wight! The Fisherman's Chant. F C. Burnand. BOHV
Oh, the four walls of the cell! Trilce, XVIII. César Vallejo. TwSpPo
Oh, the fox went out one winter's night. The Fox Went through the Town, Oh! *Unknown.* SoAF
Oh! the French are on the sea [*or* say]. The Shan Van Vocht. *Unknown.* AnIL; AnIV; OnYI; PoFr; TIP
O the gallant fisher's life. The Angler. John Chalkhill. HBV; LPS-2
Oh, the gen'ral raised the devil with the kernel, so 'tis said. Bugs. Will Stokes. BBV (1923 ed.); MoShBr
Oh, the girl that I loved she was handsome. The Man on the Flying Trapeze. George Leybourne. ABF; FaFP; LiTG; LoGBV; OxBoLi; SiTL
O the girl with the eyes. True Romance. Edwin Honig. SiTL
Oh, the glorious Thanksgivings. Thanksgivings of Old. E. A. Smuller. PEOR
Oh, the gold hills of Ireland. They Who Wait. Charles Buxton Going. HBMV
Oh, the good ole chariot swing so low. Swing Low, Sweet Chariot. *Unknown.* AA
O the green glimmer of apples in the orchard. Ballad of Another Ophelia. D. H. Lawrence. ChTr; CoBMV; MoVE
O the green things growing, the green things growing. Green Things Growing. Dinah Maria Mulock Craik. ADAH; DD; FaFP; GN; HBV; HBVY; OHIP; OTPC; SN
O the grey, grey company. The Grey Company. Jessie Mackay. BoAu
O the heart in her breast oft fainted, whenever in fancy she heard. The Meeting of Medea and Jason. Apollonius Rhodius. *Fr.* Argonautica. GrR
Oh, the hearts of men, they are rovers, all! Ulysses Returns, IV. Roselle Mercier Montgomery. BAP; HBMV; LPS-1; LS; TBM
Oh the hills of dear New Castle. Our Delaware. George B. Hynson. PoRL
Oh, the hog-eye man is the man for me [*or* men are all the go]. The Hog-Eye Man. *Unknown.* AS; SoAmSa
Oh, the joy of a woolless pate. A Phantasy. *Unknown.* CAG
O the joy of my spirit! it is uncaged! it darts like lightning! Walt Whitman. *Fr.* The Poem of Joys. PC
Oh, the last steer has been branded. A Cowboy's Love Song. *Unknown.* SCC
Oh, the little birds are singing in the budding willow trees. The Gardener. Lucy Fitch Perkins. PCH
Oh, the little birds sang east, and the little birds sang west. Round Our Restlessness. Elizabeth Barrett Browning. *Fr.* Rhyme of the Duchess May. MaRV
Oh, the little brown bull came down from the mountain. Tearin' Out-a Wilderness. *Unknown.* ABF
Oh, the little flax flower! The Flax Flower. Mary Howitt. PRWS
O the little rusty dusty miller. *Unknown.* OxNR
Oh, the littles that remain! After. Lizette Woodworth Reese. HBV; LS
Oh, the lives of men, lives of men. Bindlestiff. Edwin Ford Piper. HBMV; MAP
O the long and dreary winter! The Famine. Longfellow. The Song of Hiawatha, XX. BAV; IAP
O, the lovely rivers and lakes of Maine! The Lovely Rivers and Lakes of Maine. George B. Wallis. BLPA
O the Man in the Moon has a crick in his back. The Man in the Moon. James Whitcomb Riley. BOHV; HBV; HBVY; NA; OTPC; YT
O, the Marriage! Thomas Osborne Davis. OBVV
Oh, the meadow grass was high. In the Meadow. Charles Campbell Washburn. CAG
Oh, the men who laughed the American laughter. American Laughter. Kenneth Allan Robinson. PaA; TreFS
O the merry bells of Chester, ancient Chester on the Dee! Trafalgar. William Canton. TVSH
Oh the miller, the dusty, musty miller. A Ballad of All the Trades. *Unknown.* CoMu
Oh, the Month of May! Thomas Dekker. *Fr.* The Shoemaker's Holiday, III, v. EIL; ViBoPo
(First Three-Man's Song, The.) EV-2
(May.) OBSC
(Maytime.) TrGrPo
Oh, the moon shines bright, and we sail to-night. Bound for Sourabaya! Charles Henry Souter. BoAu
Oh! the night that I struck New York. The Bowery. Charles Hale Hoyt. TreF; YaD
Oh the North Countree is a hard countree. The Ballad of Yukon Jake. Edward E. Paramore, Jr. BeLS; BLPA; NeHB
Oh, the old gray mare, she ain't what she used to be. Old Gray Mare. *Unknown.* AS
Oh! the old swimmin'-hole! whare the crick so still and deep. The Old Swimmin'-Hole. James Whitcomb Riley. BeLS; FaFP; HBV; POT; PoTo
Oh, the opal and the sapphire of that wandering western sea. Beeny Cliff. Thomas Hardy. PoVP; TwHP
O, the Pleasant Days of Old! Frances Brown. LPS-2
O the Ploughboy was a-ploughing. The Simple Ploughboy. *Unknown.* FaBoCh; LoGBV; OBB
O, the postman's is as pleasant a life. Edward Capern. *Fr.* The Rural Postman. AlDL
Oh, the prairie dogs are screaming. A Cow Camp on the Range. *Unknown.* CoSo; CSF
Oh! the pride of Portsmouth water. The Lost War-Sloop. Edna Dean Proctor. PAH
O the quietest home in earth had I. The Bald-headed Tyrant. Mary E. Vandyne. BOHV
O the Raggedy Man! He works fer Pa. The Raggedy Man. James Whitcomb Riley. BoChLi; FaPON; GoBP; GoTP; HBV; HBVY; MPB; OTPC; PTA-1; StVeCh; TiPo; TreFS
O, the rain, the weary, dreary rain. Twenty Golden Years Ago. James Clarence Mangan. IrPN; OnYI
Oh, the raven flies at fall of day. The Wood-Raven. *Unknown.* BoDaBa
Oh, the Roman was a rogue. Lay of Ancient Rome. Thomas R. Ybarra. BOHV; CAG; HBV; InMe; LauV; LHV; WhC
Oh, the roses we plucked for the blue. The New Memorial Day. Albert Bigelow Paine. DD; HH; MDAH; OQP; PEDC; PSO; QP-1
Oh, the sad day! The Sad Day [*or* Death]. Thomas Flatman. OBEV; SeCL
Oh, the salt wind in my nostrils! Short Beach. Richard Hovey. NLK
Oh, the shambling sea is a sexton old. The Gravedigger. Bliss Carman. CP; LBAP; MAP; MoAmPo (1942 ed.); OCL
O the shepherds in Judea. The Shepherds in Judea. Mary Austin. ChrBoLe; COAH; DD; SDH
Oh, the ships will come and the ships will go. Get up, Jack! John, Sit Down! *Unknown.* ABF
Oh, the sky is so blue. Child's Evensong. Ethel Robb. GFA
Oh, the smartest clipper you can find. Clear the Track. *Unknown.* SoAmSa
Oh! the snow, the beautiful snow/ (This is a parody, please, you know). Beautiful Snow. *Unknown.* PA
Oh! the snow, the beautiful snow. The Beautiful Snow. John Whittaker Watson. BLPA; LPS-1; TreF; WBLP
Oh the summer's afloat on spindrift beaches. Never No More. James K. Baxter. AnNZ
Oh, the sun sets red, the moon shines white. The *Armstrong* at Fayal. Wallace Rice. PAH
Oh, the sweet contentment. Coridon's Song. John Chalkhill. EV-2; HBV; ViBoPo
O, the sweet melancholy of the time. David Gray. *Fr.* October. EnSW
Oh, the sweet pleasure full of sweet thought. Loves. Jean Antoine de Baïf. LiA
Oh, the swift plunge into the cool, green dark. Louis Untermeyer. *Fr.* Swimmers. PFY; TCPD

Oh, the times are hard and the wages low. Across the Western Ocean. *Unknown.* AmSS; AS; SoAmSa
Oh, the times are hard and the wages low. Leave Her Johnny [*or* Leave Her, Bullies, Leave Her]. *Unknown.* AS; SoAmSa (B *vers.*)
Oh! the tragedy. A Modern Orchard. David O'Neil. AnAmPo; LA
O the vines were golden, the birds were loud. Fable. Frederic Prokosch. LiTM; WaP
O the way sometimes is low. The Tryst. Lauchlan MacLean Watt. MaRV
Oh, the West Virginia hills! The West Virginia Hills. Ellen King *and* H. E. Engle. PoRL
Oh, the white sea-gull, the wild sea-gull. The Sea-Gull. Mary Howitt. BoTP
Oh, the wide world's ways! The Way of the World. Ryota. OnPM
Oh the wild engine! Every time I sit. Harold Monro. *Fr.* Journey. AlDL
Oh, the wild joys [*or* joy] of living; the leaping from rock up to rock. The Wild Joys of Living [*or* Youth *or* David Sings to Saul]. Robert Browning. *Fr.* Saul. BoTP; GTML; MuP; PC; ShBV-2. *See also* Oh, our manhood's prime vigor.
O the wild trees of my home. The Wild Trees. Laurie Lee. GTBS-D
Oh, the wind blow east. The Wind Blow East. *Unknown.* OuSiCo
Oh, the wind from the desert blew in!—Khamsin. Khamsin. Clinton Scollard. AA; LBAP; PFY
Oh, the wind is brisk and biting. Christmas Shoppers. Aileen Fisher. ChBR
Oh, the wings of the ephemera. The Ephemera. *Unknown.* ChLP
Oh, the winter joy of the flying of feet over snow-clad hill. Mountain Speed. Geoffrey Winthrop Young. PoTo
Oh, the work was hard and the wages low. Time to Leave Her. *Unknown.* AmSS
Oh, the world is all too rude for thee, with much ado and care. A World for Love. John Clare. PG
Oh, them days on Red Hoss Mountain, when the skies was fair 'nd blue. Casey's Table d'Hote. Eugene Field. PoOW
O! then, I see, Queen[e] Mab hath been[e] with you. Queen Mab [*or* Mercutio's Queen Mab Speech]. Shakespeare. *Fr.* Romeo and Juliet, I, iv. BCEP; BoW; CG; EV-1; FaPON; FiP; HOAH; LEAP; LiTB; LPS-3; MPB; OTPC; PC; TreF
"Oh, then tell me, Shawn O'Ferrall." The Rising of the Moon. John Keegan Casey. AnIV; GTIV; IrPN; OnYI; TIP
O Theophilus. Margaret Allonby. BoSA
Oh! There Are Spirits. Shelley. EmBrPo (To Coleridge.) BPN
Oh, there are those, a sordid clan. The Child's Heritage. John G. Neihardt. FAOV; HBV; NV
O, there are times/ When all this fret. Daily Trials. Oliver Wendell Holmes. PoEL-5
Oh, there be many candles bright. The Gift. Laura Spencer Portor. PEDC
O, there be many things. Many Things. Oliver Wendell Holmes. PoToHe (new ed.)
O there is a little artist. The Fairy Artist. Nellie M. Garabrant. PCH
Oh there is blessing in this gentle breeze. The Prelude: Introduction—Childhood and School-Time. Wordsworth. BEL; EM-1; EmBrPo; EnLit; EnLP; EnRP; ERP
Oh! there is never sorrow of heart. Wordsworth. *Fr.* The Force of Prayer. MaRV
Oh, there once was a lady, and so I've been told. Fable. Dorothy Parker. ALV
Oh, there once was a puffin. There Once Was [*or* Was Once] a Puffin. Florence Page Jaques. GoBP; TiPo
Oh! there once was a swagman camped in a Billabong. Waltzing Matilda. A. B. Paterson. WhC
Oh! there was a moanish lady. Moanish Lady. *Unknown.* AS
O there was a woman, and she was a widow. Flowers in the Valley. *Unknown.* AtBAP; OxBoLi
Oh! there was an old soldier. There Was an Old Soldier. *Unknown.* AS; TrAS, *with* Old Zip Coon
Oh, there were fifteen men in green. Men in Green. David Campbell. BoAV; MoAuPo; NeLNL
O there were lights and laughter. Voices. Witter Bynner. MAP; MoAmPo (1942 ed.); PCH; PoeMoYo; TSW; TSWC
O there were three jolly hunters. The Three Jolly Hunters. James Whitcomb Riley. WaKn
Oh, there's mony a gate eawt ov eawr teawn-end. Th' Sweetheart Gate. Edwin Waugh. VA
Oh, these precipitous rocks! The Precipitous Rocks. *Unknown.* WhP
Oh, these spring days! Spring Days. Basho. OnPM
O these wakeful wounds of thine! On the Wounds of Our Crucified Lord. Richard Crashaw. SeEP
Oh, they call me Hanging Johnny. Hanging Johnny. *Unknown.* SoAmSa
Oh, they told me love was laughter. Fancy. Paul D. Page, Jr. CAG
Oh! they've swept the parlor carpet. When the Minister Comes to Tea. Joseph C. Lincoln. DDA; PTA-1
Oh, think how hard it is to die when young! Charles Heavysege. *Fr.* Jephthah's Daughter. CaP
Oh, Think Not I Am Faithful to a Vow! Edna St. Vincent Millay. ChMo; CMP (Sonnets.) NP
O, this is a sin-tryin' world. This Is a Sin-tryin' World. *Unknown.* TrAS
O this is no my ain house. This Is No My Ain House. *Unknown.* EBSV
O this is the beast that does not have being! Rainer Maria Rilke. Sonnets to Orpheus, Pt. II, IV. ReMP
Oh, this is the joy of the rose. In Rose Time. Willa Cather. OBAV
Oh, this is the tale of Jack Monroe. The Ballad of Jack Monroe. Jesse Edgar Middleton. CPG
O thorn-crowned sorrow, pitiless and stern. Sorrow. Katrina Trask. AA
O, those little, those little blue shoes! Baby's Shoes. William Cox Bennett. LPS-1
Oh those were happy days, heaped up with wineskins. Silenus in Proteus. Thomas Lovell Beddoes. EnRP; ERP
O Thou/ God of all long desirous roaming. Rupert Brooke. *Fr.* The Song of the Pilgrims. TrPWD
O thou afflicted, drunken not with wine! Dirge for the Ninth of Ab. *Unknown.* TrJP
O Thou almighty will. Strength, Love, Light. Robert II, King of France. WGRP
Oh, thou alphabetic row. A. B. C. Eliza Cook. OTPC (1923 ed.)
O thou art such, that I could be. Henry Vaughan. LO
O Thou, as represented here to me. Our Known Unknown [*or* From the Pope's Speech]. Robert Browning. *Fr.* The Ring and the Book, X. EV-5; OQP; QP-2
O Thou best gift from heaven. Send Me. *Unknown.* MaRV
O thou, brave ruin of the passed time. On Beholding Bodiam Castle. Lord Thurlow. EnSW
O thou, by nature taught. Ode to Simplicity. William Collins. BEL; CEP; EiPP; EnLi-2 (1949 ed.); EnRP; EV-3; GTSL; OBEC; OBEV; PoFS; UnPo (1st ed.)
O Thou, Creator from original chaos. Invocation. George Rostrevor Hamilton. BoFr; NeTW; QS
Oh, thou day o' the world. Shakespeare. *Fr.* Antony and Cleopatra, IV, viii. EtPaEn
O Thou Eternal One! Gavril Romanovich Derzhavin. *See* God.
O Thou Eternal One, may I commune. A Prayer. Theodore Parker. GrCo-1
O Thou Eternal Source of Life. Rolland W. Schloerb. TrPWD
O thou exalted mightily. Poor Lodgings. Ibn Abdun. MooP
O thou fair silver Thames, O clearest crystal flood! Song to Beta. Michael Drayton. *Fr.* The Shepherd's Garland: Third Eclogue. OBSC
O thou fire!/ Thou universal horror! Philoctetes Robbed of His Bow. Sophocles. *Fr.* Philoctetes. GrR
O Thou? for whom no name is bad ynough. I Was the Man. Cyril Tourneur. *Fr.* The Revenger's Tragedy. LiA
O Thou, from whom all goodness flows. Remember Me! Thomas Haweis. BePJ
O thou glory of the Lord! Guardian of heaven's hosts. *At. to* Cædmon. *Fr.* Christ and Satan. LiA
O Thou God who at creation. Sound Thy Trumpet, God of Action. Arthur B. Dale. PraP
O Thou good giver of all gifts. Peace on Earth. Marie Barton. PraP
Oh, Thou, grand builder of the universe! A Thanksgiving Prayer. *Unknown.* PEOR
O Thou great author of the world. A Prayer. Sister Albertus Magnus. WHL
"O, thou great Babel—out of nothing reared." Babel Falls. Anna Hempstead Branch. *Fr.* Nimrod, V. TCPD
O Thou Great Being! what Thou art. Prayer under the Pressure of Violent Anguish. Burns. TrPWD
O thou great Friend to all the sons of men. The Way, the Truth, and the Life. Theodore Parker. ChIP; TrPWD
O thou great movement of the universe. Bryant. *Fr.* An Evening Revery. AA
O thou great Power, in whom I move. A Hymn to My God in a Night of My Late Sicknesse [*or* It Is Finished]. Sir Henry Wotton. BePJ; MeLP; MePo; OBS
O thou great wrong, that, through the slow-paced years. The Death of Slavery. Bryant. AA; DD; MDAH; PoFr
O Thou Immortal Deity. Shelley. TrPWD
O thou in heaven and earth the only peace. The Plan of Salvation. Milton. *Fr.* Paradise Lost, III. WGRP

Oh, thou! in Hellas deem'd of heavenly birth. The Farewell. Byron. *Fr.* Childe Harold's Pilgrimage, I. EPP
O Thou, in whom we live and move. A Poet's Grace. Burns. TrPWD
O thou Moor of Morería. Abenamar, Abenamar. *Unknown.* AnSpL-1; AWP; OuHeWo
O thou, my lovely boy, who in thy power. Sonnets, CXXVI. Shakespeare. MyFE; PeBoSo; ReIE
Oh, Thou, My Lover. Victor Hugo, *tr. fr. French by* Mrs. Newton Crosland. *Fr.* Hernani, V, iii. LiA
O thou newcomer who seek'st Rome in Rome. Rome. Joachim du Bellay. AWP; JAWP; WBP
Oh, thou northland bobolink. To the Lapland Longspur. John Burroughs. BLA; SN
O Thou not made with hands. The City of God. Francis Turner Palgrave. MaRV; WGRP
O thou of angels the most wise and fair. The Litanies of Satan. Baudelaire. EnLi-2
O thou of home the guardian Lar. A Winter Evening Hymn to My Fire. James Russell Lowell. LPS-1
O thou of little faith. Hitherto Hath the Lord Helped. *Unknown.* BLRP
O thou of soul and sense and breath. Hymn. Oliver Wendell Holmes. LBAH
O Thou, our Saviour, brother, friend. For the Peace of Jerusalem. Charles Wesley. BePJ
O thou pale form. Robert Browning. *Fr.* Pauline. ChIP
O Thou pure fountain of pure love, my Lord! To Our Lord. Francisco Galvam. CAW
O thou so fair in summers gone. Freedom. Tennyson. PoVP; VLEP
O thou soft naturall death, thou art joint-twin. John Webster. *Fr.* The White Devil, V, iii. AtBAP
O thou that after toil and storm. In Memoriam A. H. H., XXXIII. Tennyson. BPN; EmBrPo; EPN; GEPC; TOP; ViPo; VLEP
O thou that cleavest heaven. Bird's Song at Morning. William James Dawson. VA
Oh thou, that dear and happy isle. Andrew Marvell. *Fr.* Upon Appleton House. OxBoLi
O Thou, that dost cover the heavens. Song of the Wind and the Rain. Solomon ibn Gabirol. TrJP
O thou that from the green vales of the West. To Spring [on the Banks of the Cam]. William Stanley Roscoe. OBVV; UnPo (1st ed.)
O thou, that from the seven-toned strings. The Divine Betrayal. Euripides. *Fr.* Ion. GrR
O thou that from thy mansion. For My Funeral. A. E. Housman. ChMo; ReaPo; TrPWD; ViBoPo
O thou that hauntest Cyprus, and Miletus, and Cythera. The Courtesan to Aphrodite. Poseidippus. GrPE
O thou that held'st the blessed Veda dry. Hymn to Vishnu. Jayadeva. *Fr.* Gita Govinda. AWP
O Thou, that in the heavens dost dwell. *See* O Thou, wha in the heavens . . .
O thou that often hast within thine eyes. Sonnet: He Speaks of a Third Love. Guido Cavalcanti. AWP
O thou that rollest above, round as the shield. Ossian's Address to the Sun. James Macpherson. *Fr.* Carthon. BEL
O thou, that sendest out the man. England and America in 1782. Tennyson. BPN; EPN; MC; OTPC (1946 ed.); PaA; PAH; PoFr; PoVP; VLEP
O Thou, that sitt'st [*or* sit'st] upon a throne. A Song to David. Christopher Smart. AtBAP; CEP; ChTr; EiPP; EV-3; GoTL; LaA; LiA; LoBV; OBEC; OBEV; PoEL-3; PtP; TrGrPo; TriL; UnS
O Thou That Sleep'st like Pig in Straw. Sir William Davenant. *See* Song: "O thou that sleep'st . . ."
Oh thou that swing'st upon the waving hair [*or* haire *or* eare]. The [*or* To the] Grasshopper [*or* Ode]. Richard Lovelace. AtBAP; EPP; EPS; EV-2; FaBoEn; LoBV; MeLP; MePo; OBEV; OBS; PIAE; Po; ReEn; SeCePo; SeCL; SeCV-1; SeEP
O thou that with surpassing glory crown'd [*or* crowned]. Satan Reflects [*or* Satan's Soliloquy *or* Satan Speaks]. Milton. *Fr.* Paradise Lost, IV. CoEV; EV-2; LiTB; NBE; OBS; PIAE
O Thou! the first fruits of the dead. Buriall. Henry Vaughan. SeCV-1
O thou, the friend of man, assigned [*or* assign'd]. Ode to Pity. William Collins. CEP; EiPP
O thou, the wonder of all dayes! The Dirge of Jephthah's Daughter; Sung by the Virgins. Robert Herrick. MeRV
O thou to whom, athwart the perished days. Mary Arden. Eric Mackay. VA
O Thou to Whom the Musical White Spring. E. E. Cummings. InPo; MOAP
(Sonnet: "O thou to whom . . .") NP
O Thou to whom, without reserve. Thy Will Be Done in Me. Fanny Crosby. MaRV
O Thou, to whose all-searching sight. My Light! My Way! Count von Zinzendorf. MaRV
O thou undaunted daughter of desires! Upon the Book and Picture of the Seraphical Saint Teresa. Richard Crashaw. *Fr.* The Flaming Heart. BCEP; BLV; CoBE; OBEV; PtP; WHA
O Thou unknown, Almighty Cause. A Prayer in the Prospect of Death. Burns. BCEP; HBV; MaRV; TrPWD; WGRP
O thou vast ocean! ever-sounding sea! Address to the Ocean. "Barry Cornwall." LPS-2
O Thou, wha [*or* that] in the heavens [*or* heav'ns] does dwell. Holy Willie's Prayer. Burns. BEL; BOHV; CEP; EBSV; EiPP; EM-1; EnL; EnRP; GoTS; KN; LiA; OxBoLi; PIAE; PIR; PoE; PoEL-4; TOP; TyEnPo; ViBoPo
O Thou! whatever title suit thee. Address to the Deil. Burns. BCEP; CEP; DaM; EBSV; EiPP; EM-1; EnRP; EPP; EV-3; GoTS; OAEP; PoE; PoEL-4; REAL; TCEP; TyEnPo; UnPo (1st ed.)
O Thou who all-things hast of nothing made. Deo Opt. Max. George Sandys. *Fr.* Paraphrase on the Psalms. OBS
O thou who art of all that is. Through Unknown Paths. Frederick L. Hosmer. TrPWD
O thou who at Love's hour ecstatically. Love's Testament. Dante Gabriel Rossetti. The House of Life, III. BPN; PoVP; ViPo
O Thou who bidst the torrent flow. Whittier. *Fr.* Hymn from the French of Lamartine. TrPWD
O Thou Who Camest from Above. Charles Wesley. *See* Hymn: "O Thou who camest from above."
O thou who clothest thyself in mystic form. Ideal Passion, XXXVIII. George Edward Woodberry. MOAP
O thou, who didst furnish. Hymn to Moloch. Ralph Hodgson. HBMV
Oh Thou, who didst with pitfall and with gin. There Is No Sin. Omar Khayyám, *tr. by* Edward Fitzgerald. *Fr.* The Rubáiyát. OnPM
Oh, Thou! Who Dry'st the Mourner's Tear. Thomas Moore. TrPWD
O thou who giving helm and sword. The Dreamer. Walter de la Mare. ChMo; CMP; OTPC (1923 ed.)
O, Thou, who hast comforted me in the night watches. A Thanksgiving Prayer. Ruth G. Winant. PSO
O Thou, who kindly dost provide. A Poet's Grace. Burns. TrPWD
O Thou, who love in mercy hast created. Thomas Tiplady. *Fr.* A Wedding Hymn. MaRV
O Thou who lovest not alone. The Aim. Sir Charles G. D. Roberts. MaRV; PeCV
Oh Thou, who Man of baser Earth didst make. Equity with God. Omar Khayyám. *Fr.* The Rubáiyát. OnPM; SeCeV
O thou who movest onward with a mind. Epitaphs, III. Gabriello Chiabrera. AWP; JAWP; WBP
O thou, who passest thro' our vallies in. To Summer. Blake. CEP
O thou, who plumed with strong desire. The Two Spirits. Shelley. CH; EmBrPo; EPN; ERP
O Thou who seekest me. A Prayer. Laurence Binyon. QS
O Thou who speedest time's advancing wing. He Asketh Absolution of God. *Unknown.* *Fr.* Book of the Dead. AWP
O Thou whom sacred duty hither calls. "Cease to Do Evil—Learn to Do Well." Denis Florence MacCarthy. TIP
O thou whose ancient, all-disclosing light. Kepler. Albert Durrant Watson. CPG; OCL
O thou whose cheeks are the Pleiades and whose lips are coral. To a Young Lover. Amur Mu'izzi. LiTW
O Thou whose equal purpose runs. Invocation. Wendell Phillips Stafford. MaRV; TrPWD
O thou, whose eye of love. Thanksgiving Hymn. *Unknown.* TOAH
O Thou whose face. Goddess. Amir Khusrau. PeP
O thou, whose face hath felt the winter's wind. What the Thrush Said. Keats. PIR
O thou! whose fancies from afar are brought. To H. C. Wordsworth. BPN; ChER; EmBrPo; EnRP; GEPC; HBV; LiA; NBE; OBRV; PoEL-4; RO
O Thou Whose Feet Have Climbed Life's Hill. Louis F. Benson. MaRV
O Thou, whose glorious orbs on high. Hymn of [*or* to] the West. Edmund Clarence Stedman. HBV; PaA; PAH; TrPWD
O Thou Whose Gracious Presence Blest. Louis F. Benson. *See* Dedication: "O thou . . ."
O Thou Whose Image. Arthur Hugh Clough. *See* Hymnos Ahymnos.
O thou, whose mighty palace roof doth hang. Hymn to Pan. Keats. *Fr.* Endymion. AtBAP; BCEP; BPN; ChER; EPN; NBE; OBRV; PoEL-4
O thou, whose potent genius (like the sun). To Longfellow. Paul Hamilton Hayne. SPP
O Thou Whose Pow'r. Boethius. *See* O Qui Perpetua Mundum Ratione Gubernas.
O Thou, whose Spirit through this universe. Preliminary Invocation. Jami. *Fr.* Salámán and Absál. PeP

O thou whose wisdom is the rule of kings. Man's Prime Desire. Jami. OnPM

O thou wild fancy, check thy wing! No more. Lines on an Autumnal Evening. Samuel Taylor Coleridge. BPN

O thou with dewy locks, who lookest down. To Spring. Blake. ATP; BoTP; CEP; EG; EnRP; EV-3; HBV; MuP; OBEC; OBEV; PoEL-4; UnPo

O Thought! Süsskind von Trimberg, *tr. fr. Middle High German.* TrJP

O thought, fly to her when the end of day. Old Memory. W. B. Yeats. Po

O Thought, free gift to humankind! O Thought! Süsskind von Trimberg. TrJP

Oh, threats of Hell and Hopes of Paradise! This Life Flies. Omar Khayyám, *tr. by* Edward Fitzgerald. *Fr.* The Rubáiyát. OnPM

O thy bright eyes must answer now. Plead for Me [*or* God of Visions *or* Speak, God of Visions]. Emily Brontë. EmBrPo; EnLi-2 (1949 ed.); GTML; PoEL-5; TrGrPo; ViP

O thy bright looks! thy glance of love. The Favour. Henry Vaughan. EV-2

Oh Tiber's banks where scarlet jas'mines bloom. Tygers. Thomas Chatterton. *Fr.* The Death of Nicou. RO

O tide-enwreathed and time-tormented Man. The Gatineaus. James Wreford Watson. CaP

O time and change! with hair as gray. Whittier. *Fr.* Snow-bound. BPP

Oh, time keeps steadily on and on. Thanksgiving Exercise. Lizzie M. Hadley. TOAH

"O Time, whence comes the mother's moody look amid her labours." The Lacking Sense. Thomas Hardy. PoEL-5

O Time! who know'st a lenient hand to lay. Time and Grief [*or* Healing *or* Sonnet]. William Lisle Bowles. ATP; BCEP; CEP; EnRP; ES; EV-3; FaBoEn; HBV; LO; OBEC; OBEV; ReTS

Oh, Timely Happy, Timely Wise. John Keble. BHV
  As We Pray, *last st.* MaRV; PraP

O tired heart, too full of sorrows. A Dolefull Passion. Nicholas Breton. CaAE

Oh, 'tis little Mary Cassidy's the cause of all my misery. Little Mary Cassidy. Francis A. Fahy. HBV

Oh, 'tis May, the month of May. The Prisoner. *Unknown.* AnSpL-1

Oh! 'tis of a bold major a tale I'll relate. A Longford Legend. *Unknown.* OnYI; StPo

"Oh, 'tis time I should talk to your mother." Ask and Have [*or* How to Ask and Have]. Samuel Lover. BOHV; HBV; PFE; TreFS

Oh, to be a cricket. The Cricket. Sir Charles G. D. Roberts. LEAP

O to Be a Dragon. Marianne Moore. GoYe

O to be blind! The Blind Man at the Fair. Joseph Campbell. AnIV; AWP; JAWP; TIP; WBP

Oh, to be breathing and hearing and feeling and singing! April Theology. John G. Neihardt. LEAP

Oh, to be in England. Home-Thoughts from Abroad. Robert Browning. ADAH; AnEnPo; AnFE; AWP; BBV; BEL; BLV; BMEP; BoLiVe; BoTP; BPN; BTP; CaAE; CBE; CBOV; CBPC; CG; CoBE; EG; EM-2; EmBrPo; EnLi-2 (1949 ed.); EnLit; EPN; EPP; EV-5; FaBoBe; FaBoEn; FaFP; FaPON; FiP; GBV (1922 ed.); GEPC; GN; GTBS; GTBS-W; GTML; GTSL; HBV; HBVY; HiLiEn; InPo; JAWP; LEAP; LiTB; LiTG; MCCG; NeHB; OAEP; OBEV; OBVV; OtMeF; OTPC; PCH; PFE; PIAE; PIR; PoeMoYo; PoFS; PoRA; PoVP; PYM; SeCeV; ShBV-2; SN; TCEP; TOP; TreF; TrGrPo; TyEnPo; VA; ViPo; ViPP; VLEP; WBP; WHA; WP; YT

Oh! to be in England. Home Truths from Abroad, *parody. Unknown.* PA

Oh, to Be in England Now the Weather's There! *Unknown.* SiTL

Oh, to be "kept for Jesus!" Kept for Jesus. Edith E. Cherry. BePJ

Oh! to be wafted away. Quatrain. *Unknown.* NA

Oh, to come home once more, when the dusk is falling. A Song of Twilight. *Unknown.* HBV

Oh, to feel the fresh breeze blowing. The Song of the Forest Ranger. Herbert Bashford. HBV; OHIP

Oh, to feel the tremble of a ship beneath my feet again. Sea Urge. *Unknown.* NLK; PoMa

Oh, to go forth at last. Departure. Jorge Guillén. CoSP

O, to have a little house! An [*or* The] Old Woman of the Roads. Padraic Colum. BLV; BMEP; BoTP; CAW; CH; CP; EPP; FaBoBe; FaPON; GaP; GBV (1952 ed.); GoBC; GTSL; HBMV; HiLiEn; JKCP; LBBV; MBP; MM; MoBrPo; MPB; NP; NV; OBEV (new ed.); OnPP; OTPC (1946 ed.); PG; PoRA; PoTo; SP; StVeCh; TreFS; TVSH; TwCV; VOD; YT

O to have known him, looked into his eyes. Charles Dickens. Louella C. Poole. POT; PoTo

O to lie in long grasses! In the Grass. Hamlin Garland. LBAP; POT; PoTo

O to make the most jubilant song. A Song of Joys. Walt Whitman. *Fr.* A Poem of Joys. LEAP

Oh, to part now, and, parting now. After Love. Arthur Symons. NeHB

O to scuttle from the battle and to settle on an atoll far from brutal mortal neath a wattle portal! Titles [*or* What'll Be the Title?] Justin Richardson. FiBHP; ShBV-3

O to think, O to think as I see her stand there. A Love-Song. Norman Gale. LEAP

Oh, to vex me, contraries [*or* contraryes] meet in one. Inconstancy [*or* Devout Fits]. John Donne. Holy Sonnets, XIX. EPS (1942 ed.); MaRV; NBE; PeBoSo; PoEL-2; SeCePo

Oh, to what purpose dost thou hoard thy words. Shakespeare. King Richard II, *fr.* II, iii. CBE

O tomb! O nuptial chamber! Buried Alive. Sophocles. *Fr.* Antigone. OxBG

Oh, Tommy's gone, what shall I do? Tommy's [*or* Tom's] Gone to Hilo. *Unknown.* AmSS; SG; SoAmSa

O touch me not unless thy soul. Unless. Ella Maria Dietz Glynes. AA

"O Trade! O Trade! would thou wert dead!" The Symphony. Sidney Lanier. AmPP; ATP (1935 ed.); CoBA; CoV; LiTA; SPP

O tragic hours when lovers leave each other. Partings. Charles Guérin. AWP

Oh tread not the road. Nikolai Nekrasov, *tr. fr. Russian by* Juliet M. Soskice. *Fr.* Who Can Be Happy and Free in Russia? BoR

Oh tree nursed by freedom! Song of the Mound. Wincenty Pol. PoFr

O tree of many branches! One thou hast. To W. M. Francis Thompson. VLEP

O trees, to whom the darkness is a child. Advice to a Forest. Maxwell Bodenheim. TrJP

O Trivia, Goddess, leave these low abodes. John Gay. *Fr.* Trivia; or, The Art of Walking the Streets of London, III. EnLi-1 (1949 ed.)

"O Troy Muir, my lily-flower." The Queen of Scotland. *Unknown.* ESPB

O truant muse, what shall be thy amends. Sonnets, CI. Shakespeare. PeBoSo

O true and tried, so well and long. In Memoriam A. H. H., Epilogue. Tennyson. EmBrPo; EPN; GEPC; ViPo; VLEP

Oh! true was his heart while he breathèd. The King of Thule. Goethe. *Fr.* Faust. AWP; JAWP; WBP

O trusty of the trusty, compeers of my youth. The Ghost of Darius. Aeschylus. *Fr.* Persians. LiA

O, Tuomy! you boast yourself handy. Andrew Magrath's Reply to John O'Tuomy. Andrew Magrath. OnYI

O turn away those cruel eyes. The Relapse. Thomas Stanley. EV-2; OBEV; SeCL

O Turn Once More. Duncan Campbell Scott. CoBE; MM

Oh 'twas a poor country, in Autumn it was bare. The Poor, Poor Country. John Shaw Neilson. NeLNL

Oh, 'twas bitter cold/ As our steamboat rolled. The Red-Breast of Aquitania. Francis S. Mahony. OnYI

Oh! 'twas Dermot O'Nowlan McFigg. The Humours of Donnybrook Fair [*or* the Donnybrook Jig]. Charles O'Flaherty, *wr. at. to* Viscount Dillon. BOHV; OnYI

O 'twas on a bright mornin' in summer. Who's the Pretty Girl Milkin' the Cow? *Unknown.* AS

O twilight, twilight! evermore to hear. Music at Twilight. George Sterling. HBV

"O tyrant, armed with insolence and pride!" Homer. *Fr.* The Iliad, I. PoFr

O Ubi? Nusquam. R. W. Dixon. LO

O Unas, watch out for pitfalls. Inscription on the Pyramid of Unas. *Unknown.* LiTW

Oh, Uncle Bud goin' down the road. Uncle Bud. *Unknown.* StDa

O undistinguished Dead! Rank and File. Austin Dobson. PoVP

O unexpected stroke, worse than of death! Eve's Lament. Milton. *Fr.* Paradise Lost, XI. LPS-1

O unforgiving thoughts, I pray you: Peace! Sonnet. Petrarch. Sonnets to Laura: To Laura in Death, VI. LyPI

O unhatch'd bird, so high preferr'd. Ode: To the Roc. William John Courthope. *Fr.* The Paradise of Birds. VA

O Unicorn among the Cedars. W. H. Auden. *Fr.* New Year Letter. ChMo; FaBoEn

O universal Mother, who dost keep. Hymn to Earth the Mother of All [*or* Earth, Universal Mother]. *Unknown. Fr.* Homeric Hymns. AWP; GrPo; GrR; JAWP; OuHeWo; OxBG; WBP

O unknown belov'd one! to the perfect season. Therania. William Allingham. TIP

O unseen spirit! now a calm divine. On a Beautiful Day. John Sterling. LPS-2

Oh, up aloft this yard must go. So Handy. *Unknown.* SoAmSa

Oh, up the brae, and up and up, beyont the fairy thorn. Out in the Dark. Stephen Lucius Gwynn. TIP

"O Urizen! Creator of men! mistaken Demon of heaven!" Take Thy Bliss, O Man. Blake. *Fr.* Visions of the Daughters of Albion. EnRP
O valiant Hearts, who to your glory came. The Supreme Sacrifice. John Stanhope Arkwright. POT; WGRP
O valiant leader of the little band. Brock; Valiant Leader. John Daniel Logan. CPG
O valley of waving broom. In the Rangitaki Valley. Katherine Mansfield. DiM
O vast earth-apple, waiting to be fried. To a Sinister Potato. Peter Viereck. OnHM
Oh Venice! Venice! when thy marble walls. Ode on Venice. Byron. EmBrPo; EPP
O, very gloomy is the House of Woe. The Haunted House. Thomas Hood. SeCePo
Oh, Vicksburg is in the bend. Vicksburg 'round the Bend. *Unknown.* StDa
O Victory, whose feet are shod with triumph sweet. For Alexidamus of Metapontum. Bacchylides. GrL
O vile ingrateful me. Βιοθάνατος (Biothanatos). Joseph Beaumont. OBS
O violet-tressed Sappho chaste. To Sappho. Alcaeus. GrR
Oh, Virgin Joy of all the world art thou. Mary, Virgin and Mother. Elizabeth Seton. JKCP
O virgin mother, daughter of thy Son. Saint Bernard's Prayer to Our Lady. Dante. *Fr.* Divina Commedia: Paradiso. ISi
Oh virgin queen of mountain-side and woodland. The Pine Tree for Diana. Horace. AWP
O virgin-rose, no blushes. Pushkin, *tr. fr. Russian by* Maud F. Jerrold. BoR
"O virgins, very lovely in your troop." Too Late. "Michael Field." MBP
O Virtuous Light. Elinor Wylie. AnAmPo; LA; LiTG; MAP; MoAB; MoAmPo; MoP; MoPo; NePA; ReaPo; TwAmPo
O Vocables of Love. Laura Riding. TCPD
O Voice That Calls to Me. R. B. Y. Scott. MaRV
O votary of earthly idol's fane. One Heart, One Love. Jami. OnPM
O wad some power the giftie gie us. As Others See Us. Burns. *Fr.* To a Louse. MaRV
O wad that my time were owre but. The Rustic Lad's Lament in the Town. David Macbeth Moir. LPS-1
O Wahkonda (Master of Life) pity me! A Dance Chant. *Tr. by* D. G. Brinton. WGRP
O wailing and sorrow, O wailing and woe! Aeschylus. *Fr.* Seven against Thebes. GrPo
Oh, Wake Dat Girl! *Unknown. See* Johnny Come Down to Hilo.
Oh, wake her, oh, shake her. Johnny Walk Along to Hilo. *Unknown.* ShS
O Wall-flower! or ever thy bright leaves fade. The Wall-Flower. Henrik Wergeland. AWP; JAWP; WBP
"O waly, waly, my gay goss-hawk." The Gay Goshawk. *Unknown.* ESPB
O waly, waly up the bank. Waly, Waly [*or* Forsaken *or* Jamie Douglas]. *Unknown.* BaBo; BCEP; BSV; CBOV; CoEV; EBSV; EG; EnLoPo; EnSB; EV-2; GoTS; GTBS; GTBS-D; GTBS-W; GTSE; GTSL; HBV; LEAP; LO; LPS-1; OBB; OBEV; OBS; ViBoFo; ViBoPo; WHA
O wanderer from an antique shore. Rider on the Sands. Douglas Le Pan. BoCaPo (1948 ed.)
O wanderer in the southern weather. An Indian Song. W. B. Yeats. VA
O, wandering dim on the extremest edge. Si Descendero in Infernum, Ades. James Russell Lowell. BAV
"Oh Washington! I thought thee great and good." Execution of Major André. Anna Seward. BoHiPo
Oh, Wasn't Dat a Wide River? *with music. Unknown.* BoAN-1
"Oh, wasn't he hard on poor sinners this mornin'?" The Fret of Father Carty. Joseph I. C. Clarke. JKCP (1926 ed.)
Oh, wast thou with me, dearest, then. In Memoriam A. H. H., CXXII. Tennyson. EmBrPo; EPN; GEPC; TOP; ViPo; VLEP
O, water for me! Bright water for me! The Water-Drinker. Edward Johnson. LPS-2
O water, voice of my heart, crying in the sand. The Crying of Water. Arthur Symons. AnEnPo; BLV; MBP; MoBrPo
O waves gigantic that roaring break. Rima LII. Gustavo Adolfo Bécquer. *Fr.* Rimas. AnSpL-2
Oh, we come on the sloop *John B.* The *John B.* Sails. *Unknown.* AS
Oh, we don't get no justice here in Atlanta. We Don't Get No Justice Here in Atlanta. *Unknown.* OuSiCo
Oh, we had an old hen and she had a wooden leg. Another Little Drink. *Unknown.* TrAS, *with* Old Zip Coon
O we have made a vow to study, Lords. Shakespeare. *Fr.* Love's Labour's Lost, IV, iii. NBE
Oh, we sail'd to Virginia, and thence to Fyal. Admiral Benbow. *Unknown.* SG
"O we were sisters seven, Maisry." Fair Mary of Wallington (C *vers.*). *Unknown.* ESPB
O we were sisters, sisters seven. Earl Crawford. *Unknown.* BaBo; ESPB
O weariness of men who turn from God. Men Who Turn from God. T. S. Eliot. *Fr.* The Rock. MaRV
O Wearisome Condition of Humanity. Fulke Greville. *See* Chorus Sacerdotum.
O weary fa' the east wind. The Winds. Swinburne. POTT; TOP; VLEP
Oh! Weary Mother. Barry Pain. *Fr.* The Poets at Tea. NA
O Weary Pilgrims, Chanting of Your Woe. Robert Bridges. The Growth of Love, XXIII. ChMo; CMP; MBP; MoAB; MoBrPo; PoVP
O wedding-guest! this soul hath been. He Prayeth Best. Samuel Taylor Coleridge. *Fr.* The Rime of the Ancient Mariner. BPP; PECK
O weel may the boatie row. The Boatie Row. John Ewen. EBSV
Oh, weep for Mr. and Mrs. Bryan! The Lion. Ogden Nash. CenHV
Oh! Weep for Those. Byron. AnEnPo
Oh welcome, bat and owlet gray. Song. Joanna Baillie. EV-3
O Welcome! Gentle Death. Sophocles. *See* Ajax's Death.
Oh well done Lord E[ldo]n! and better done R[yde]r! An Ode to the Framers of the Frame Bill. Byron. CoMu
Oh, well for him who breaks his dream. George Macdonald. *Fr.* Phantastes. UnW
O well for him whose will is strong! Will. Tennyson. BHV; BPN; EmBrPo; EPN
O well I love the spring. A Wife's Song. William Cox Bennett. HBV
Oh, well I wot where the greenwood grows. The Maiden in Bird's Plumage. *Unknown.* BoDaBa
"O well is me, my gay [*or* jolly] goshawk." The Gay Goshawk. *Unknown.* EBSV; EV-2; GN; HBV; RG
O well, whose waters are as glass to shine. Fountain of Bandusia. Horace. Odes, III, 13. RoL
Oh, Wellington! (or "Villainton") for Fame. Wellington [*or* On Wellington]. Byron. *Fr.* Don Juan, IX. FiP; GEPC; OBRV; OxBoLi
"O well's me o my gay goss-hawk." The Gay Goshawk [*or* Goss-Hawk]. *Unknown.* BaBo; EnLit; ESPB; OBB; TOP
O, Were My Love. Burns. HBV; OBEV
(O Were My Love Yon Lilac Fair.) BSV; ChTr
Oh, we're up in the morning ere breaking of day. The Railroad Corral. *Unknown.* CoSo; CSF
O Wert Thou in the Cauld Blast. Burns. BCEP; BEL; BLV; BoLiVe; CBOV; EBSV; EiPP; EM-1; EnL; EnLi-2; EnLit; EnRP; GBV; LoPo; OAEP; OBEC; OlF; OuHeWo; PFE; ReaPo; TCEP; TOP; TrGrPo; TyEnPo; UnPo (3d ed.); WHA
(Address to a Lady.) CEP
O Western Wind. *Unknown. See* Western Wind, When Wilt Thou Blow?
Oh wha are sae happy as me an' my Moggy? Moggy and Me. James Hogg. HBV
"Oh wha [*or* what] hae ye brought us hame now, my brave lord." Muckle-mou'd Meg. James Ballantine. HBV; VA
O wha my babie-clouts will buy? The Rantin' Dog, the Daddie o't. Burns. OxBoLi
"O wha will bake my bridal bread." Fair Annie (E *vers.*). *Unknown.* ESPB
"O wha will lace my shoes sae small?" The Lass of Roch Royal (A *vers.*). *Unknown.* ViBoFo
"O wha [*or* who] will shoe my bonnie [*or* bonny] foot?" The Lass of Lochroyan. *Unknown.* EBSV; HBV; OBB; OBEV (1st ed.); SG
O wha woud wish the win to blaw. Brown Adam. *Unknown.* ESPB; OBB
Oh, whar shill [*or* shall] we go w'en de great day comes. Revival Hymn. Joel Chandler Harris. *Fr.* Uncle Remus; His Songs and His Sayings. HBV; MCCG
"O whare [*or* where] are ye gaun?" The False Knight [*or* Fause Knicht] upon [*or* on] the Road [*or* The False Knight and the Wee Boy]. *Unknown.* AtBAP; CH; EnSB; ESPB; FaBoCh; OxBoLi
"O whare hae ye been a' day, Lord Donald, my son?" Lord Randal (B *vers.*) *Unknown.* BaBo; ESPB
"O whare hae ye been a' day, my bonnie wee croodlin dow?" Lord Randal. *Unknown.* BaBo (C *vers.*); ESPB (J *vers.*); ViBoFo (C *vers.*)
"O whare hae ye been, my dearest dear." James Harris (D *vers.*). *Unknown.* ESPB
"O whare hae ye been, Peggy?" Young Peggy. *Unknown.* BaBo; ESPB
O Wha's Been Here afore Me, Lass. "Hugh MacDiarmid." AtBAP; FaBoTw; NeBP; OBMV, *abr.*
Oh what a cunning guest. Confession. George Herbert. ReEn

Oh, what a dawn of day! A Lovers' Quarrel. Robert Browning. EtPaEn
Oh, what a fund of joy jocund lies hid in harmless hoaxes! The Practical Joker. W. S. Gilbert. *Fr.* His Excellency. BOHV
O what a happy soul am I! Blind but Happy. Fanny Crosby. MaRV
Oh, what a kiss. The Modern Mother. Alice Meynell. GTML
O what a loud and fearful shriek was there. Koskiusko. Samuel Taylor Coleridge. EnRP
O what a midnight curse has he, whose side. A Mood and Figure Bride. Juvenal, *tr. by* Dryden. *Fr.* Satires. BeR
Oh, what a night for a soul to go! Iter Supremum. Arthur Sherburne Hardy. AA; LBAP
Oh, what a night! The hoarfrost flies. On the Boulevard. Stepan Petrovich Shchipachev. TrRV
O, what a noble mind is here o'erthrown! A Shakespeare Gallery: Hamlet. Shakespeare. *Fr.* Hamlet, III, i. MaC
Oh! what a plague [*or* pain] is love. Phillada [*or* Phyllida] Flouts Me [*or* The Disdainful Shepherdess]. *Unknown.* BCEP; BLV; BrBE; CBOV; CoMu; EIL; ElSeCe; EM-1; HBV; InvP; LEAP; OBEV; OBSC; ReEn; TrGrPo; ViBoPo
O, what a rogue and peasant slave am I. Shakespeare. *Fr.* Hamlet, II, ii. PIR; PreP
Oh, what a set of vagabundos. Morgan. Edmund Clarence Stedman. AA; HBV; OBAV
O what a tangled web we weave. A Word of Encouragement. J. R. Pope. FiBHP; SiTL
Oh! What a Thing Is Man. Edward Taylor. *Fr.* Sacramental Meditations. AnNE; OxBA (Meditation Thirty-eight.) CoV
Oh, what a you say, seekers. Die in de Fiel'. *Unknown.* BoAN-1
O what an eve was that which ushered in. Sonnets—Ad Innuptam, VI. Patrick Moloney. BoAu
O what are heroes, prophets, men. Pan. Emerson. IAP; MOAP
Oh, What Are You Waiting For. James Thomson. Sunday up the River, II. VLEP (Bridge, The.) OBVV; TOP ("Oh, what are you waiting for here, young man?") EmBrPo; PoVP
O what avails the sceptred race. Rose Aylmer. Walter Savage Landor. FaBoEn. *See also* Ah! What Avails the Sceptred Race.
O [*or* Ah,] what can ail thee, knight-at-arms [*or* wretched wight]. La Belle Dame sans Merci. Keats. AEV; AnFE; AtBAP; ATP; AWP; BBV; BCEP; BEL; BeLS; BLV; BoLiVe; BPN; CaAE; CBE; CBOV; CG; CH; ChTr; CoBE; CoEV; DaM; EM-2; EmBrPo; EnL; EnLi-2; EnLit; EnRP; EPP; ERP; EtPaEn; EV-4; ExPo; FaBoBe; FaBoCh; FaFP; FiP; GBV; GEPC; GoTP; GTBS; GTBS-D; GTBS-W; GTSE; GTSL; HBV; HOAH; HoPM; InP; InPo; InvP; JAWP; KN; LEAP; LiA; LiTB; LiTG; LO; LoBV; LoEn; LoGBV; MaC; MCCG; MyFE; OAEP; OBEV; OBMV; OBRV; OnSP; OtMeF; OTPC (1923 ed.); PFE; PG; PIAE; PoE; PoEL-4; PoFS; PoRA; PreP; REAL; ReaPo; RG; RiBV; SeCeV; ShBV-3; ShGoBo; StPo; TCEP; TOP; TrGrPo; TVSH; TwHP; TwP; UnPo; ViBoPo; WaKn; WHA; WoL; WP
O what can you give me? Idris Davies. Gwalia Deserta, XV. MoWP
Oh, what delirious fun this is. Ego's Dream. Alfred Kreymborg. MAPA
Oh, what do the sea shells murmur. Sea Shells. Clinton Scollard. BrR
Oh, what fun. Betsinda's Bun. Thackeray. *Fr.* The Rose and the Ring. BoN
O what had my youth with ambition to do? My Sheep I Neglected. Sir Gilbert Elliot. EBSV
"Oh, what hae ye brought us hame now, my brave lord." *See* "Oh, wha hae ye brought us hame now, my brave lord."
O what harper could worthily harp it. The Schoolmaster. Charles Stuart Calverley. BOHV
Oh, what have you got for dinner, Mrs. Bond? *Unknown.* OxNR
O What If the Fowler. Charles Dalmon. CH
Oh, what is abroad in the marsh and the terminal sea? Sidney Lanier. *Fr.* The Marshes of Glynn. EtS
"Oh, what is longer than the way?" *Unknown.* LO
"Oh, what is love?" the fair maid sighed. What Is Love? "A. J. T." CAG
"Oh! what is that comes gliding in." Sally Simpkin's Lament. Thomas Hood. BOHV; EnRP; ERP
Oh what is that country. Mother Country. Christina Rossetti. OxBoCh
O What Is That Sound Which So Thrills the Ear. W. H. Auden. *See* Ballad: "O what is that sound . . ."
Oh, what is the use of such pretty wings. Sweet Peas. *Unknown.* PEOR
O What Is This Moaning So Faint and Low? Robert Buchanan. UnW
Oh, what is this which shines so bright. The Glow-Worm. William Lisle Bowles. EnSW
Oh, what know they of harbo[u]rs. Plymouth Harbo[u]r. Ernest Radford, *wr. at. to* Dollie Maitland Radford. HBV; PoeT
Oh, what sadness! To the Tune of "The South River Song." Li Yu. WhP
Oh, what shall be the burden of our rhyme. Cadences: Major. John Payne. VA
"Oh! what shall I do?" sobbed a tiny mole. Who'll Help a Fairy? *Unknown.* BoTP
Oh, what shall my blue eyes go see. To Baby. Kate Greenaway. MPB
Oh, what shall we do with a drunken sailor. The Drunken Sailor; or, Early in the Morning. *Unknown.* ShS
O what to me the little room. The Heart of the Woman. W. B. Yeats. GTML; GTSL; LoPo; LoPS; POTE
Oh, what was your name in the States? What Was Your Name in the States? *Unknown.* AS
O, what would people say if you. Lizard. Agnes Maxwell-Hall. PoNe
Oh, what's de use of workin' so hard. In de Mornin'. *Unknown.* SoAmSa
Oh! what's the matter? what's the matter? Goody Blake and Harry Gill. Wordsworth. BEL; CG; EmBrPo; GEPC
Oh, what's the matter wi' you, my lass. Jimmy's Enlisted; or, The Recruited Collier. *Unknown.* CoMu
Oh, what's the way to Arcady. The Way to Arcady. H. C. Bunner. AA; BOHV; InMe; OBAV; PFY
Oh, when a mother meets on high. Robert Southey. *Fr.* The Curse of Kehama. MotAn
O when afield the waves of yellow corn are swaying. Mikhail Yurevich Lermontov, *tr. fr. Russian by* Sir Cecil Kisch. WaL
Oh, when I am safe in my sylvan home. In the Woods. Emerson. *Fr.* Good-bye. OQP; QP-2
Oh, when I come to die. Give Me Jesus. *Unknown.* BoAN-1
Oh, When I Git My New House Done, *with music. Unknown.* StDa
Oh, when I go down to Bimini. Never Get a Lickin' Till I Go Down to Bimini. *Unknown.* OuSiCo
O, when I hear at sea. Wind and Wave. Charles Warren Stoddard. AA; BAP
Oh, when I reach the shores of misty Lethe. Wilhelm Küchelbecker. *Fr.* To Alexander Griboyedow. BoFr
Oh, when I saw your eyes. Found. Josephine Preston Peabody. AV
"Oh, when I was a little ghost." Ghost's Confession. "Lewis Carroll." *Fr.* Phantasmagoria. HOAH
Oh, When I Was in Love with You. A. E. Housman. A Shropshire Lad, XVIII. BLV; BoLiVe; EmBrPo; InP; LiTB; LiTL; LoPo; MBP; MoBrPo; NeMA; OAEP; PoeMoYo; PoVP; TwP; ViPo (Then and Now.) YT
Oh! when my friend and I. Friendship. Robert Blair. *Fr.* The Grave. OBEC
O when our clergie, at the dreadfull day. On Those That Deserve It. Francis Quarles. MePo; OBS
O, when she cam ben, she bobbèd fu' law! When She Cam Ben, She Bobbed. Burns. EBSV
Oh! when that humble, slowly-pealing bell. The Village Bell. Alphonse de Lamartine. TrFP
Oh when the early morning at the seaside. East Anglian Bathe. John Betjeman. AIDL; GTBS-D
O when the half-light weaves. The Sad Mother. Katharine Tynan. MOAH; VA
Oh, when the ripe acorns. Acorns. Edith King. GFA; RAR
Oh! when thy fingers touch the notes, I think. To Sheila Playing Haydn. Sylvia Lynd. LO
O, when 'tis summer weather. The Greenwood. William Lisle Bowles. LPS-2
O when will life taste clean again? For the air. There Is Still Splendour. Laurence Binyon. NeTW
O when will they let them love. 1938. Ruth Pitter. DiM; LO
Oh, when you see them flying. The Little Flags. John Clair Minot. DD; HH; PEDC
Oh, whenever I went away, the story I'd like to tell. The *Campañero. Unknown.* ShS
Oh Where and Oh Where Is My Little Wee Dog? *Unknown.* OTPC
Oh where! and oh where [*or* tell me where] is your Highland laddie gone? The Bluebells of Scotland. *Unknown.* EBSV; HBV; OlF; OTPC (1946 ed.); PECK; TreFS
O Where Are Kings and Empires Now. Arthur Cleveland Coxe. MaRV
"O where are ye gaun?" *See* "O, whare are ye gaun?"

O Where Are You Going. W. H. Auden. *Fr.* The Orators. CoEV; LiTB; MoVE; Po; UnPo (3d ed.)
(Epilogue: "'O where are you going?' said reader to rider.") ChMo; EnLit; FaBoCh; LoGBV; ShBV-3; SiTL
(Song.) EnL
"O where are you going, Lord Lover," said she. Lord Lover. *Unknown.* ABS
O, where are you going, says Milder to Malder. The Cutty Wren. *Unknown.* GTBS-W; LiTG; OxBoLi; SiTL
"O where are you going?" said reader to rider. O Where Are You Going [*or* Epilogue *or* Song]. W. H. Auden. *Fr.* The Orators. ChMo; CoEV; EnL; EnLit; FaBoCh; LiTB; LoGBV; MoVE; Po; ShBV-3; SiTL; UnPo (3d ed.)
O where are you going so early? he said. The Milkmaid. William Allingham. IrPN
O where are you going to, my pretty little dear. Dabbling in the Dew. *Unknown.* CH
"O where are you going to, my pretty maid." The Pretty Milkmaid. *Unknown.* ABS. *See also* "Where are you going, my pretty maid?"
"Oh where are you going with your love-locks flowing." Amor Mundi. Christina Rossetti. EmBrPo; MeRV; PoEL-5; POTT; PoVP; ViP; ViPo; VLEP
Oh, where are you, Huns, who are coming? The Coming Huns. Valery Yakovlevich Bryusov. BoR
Oh! Where Do Fairies Hide Their Heads. Thomas Haynes Bayly. HBV; HBVY; OTPC; VA
(Till Green Leaves Come Again.) EV-4
Oh, where [*or* Where] do you come from. Little Raindrops. *At. to* Ann Hawkshaw. BoTP; HBV; HBVY; OTPC (1923 ed.)
O where do you go, and what's your will. London Feast. Ernest Rhys. VA
"O where hae ye been a' day, Lord Donald, my son?" Lord Donald. *Unknown.* BrBE
"O where hae [*or* ha *or* have] ye [*or* you] been, Lord Randal, my son?" Lord Randal. *Unknown.* AtBAP; ATP; AWP; BaBo (A *vers.*); BEL; BLV; BoLiVe; BSV; CaAE; CBOV; CG; CoBE; EM-1; EnL; EnRP; EnSB; EPP; ESPB; GBV (1952 ed.); HBV; HoPM; InP; InPo; JAWP; LiTB; LiTG; LiTL; LoBV; OBB; OnSP; OuHeWo; PCN; PFE; PIAE; PreP; RiBV; SeCeV; ShBV-1; TOP; TreF; TrGrPo; TwHP; UnPo; ViBoFo (A *and* B *vers.*); WBP; WP
"O where hae ye been, my long, long love." *See* "O where have you been, my long, long love."
Oh, where has my honey gone? The Lost Love. Fenton Johnson. NP
"O where have ye been, my dearest dear." *See* "O where have you been, my long, long love."
Oh where have you been all the day. In the Woods. Dorothy Baker. BoTP
"Oh, where have you been, Billy boy, Billy boy." Billy Boy. *Unknown.* ABS; BLPA; IHA
"O where have you been, Lord Randal, my son?" *See* "O where hae ye been, Lord Randal, my son?"
"O where have you [*or* hae ye] been, my long long love [*or* dearest dear *or* dear, dear love]." The Daemon [*or* Demon] Lover [*or* James Harris]. *Unknown.* BaBo (C *vers.*); CG; EBSV; EnL; EnLi-1; EnLit; EnSB; ESPB; LiTB; OBB; PoMS; SG; TOP; UnPo; ViBoFo (A *vers.*)
"Oh, where have you been to-day, Terence, my son?" Lord Randal (D *vers.*). *Unknown.* BaBo
Oh, where is the boy dressed in jacket of gray. Lost—Three Little Robins. *Unknown.* DD; PEDC
Oh, where is the doctor who treated our ills. The Old-Time Family Doctor. Spencer Michael Free. PoP
"Oh, where is the sea?" the fishes cried. Where Is God? Minot J. Savage. OQP; QP-2
O where is tiny Hewe? The Goblin's Song. James Telfer. ChTr
Oh, where, Kincora! is Brian the Great? Kincora [*or* Lamentation of Mac Liag for Kincora]. *Unknown.* AnIL; AnIV; GTIV; OnYI; OxBI
Oh where, oh where has my little dog gone? *Unknown.* OxNR
O Where, Tell Me Where. *Unknown.* *See* Bluebells of Scotland, The.
Oh, where the white quince blossom swings. Japanesque. Oliver Herford. FiBHP
"O where were ye, my milk-white steed." The Broomfield Hill. *Unknown.* CH
Oh, where will be the birds that sing. A Hundred Years to Come. William Goldsmith Brown, *wr.* [Hiram Ladd Spencer]. HBV
"O where will ye gang to, and where will ye sleep." The Witch-Mother. Swinburne. TOP
Oh, where wuz you las' night? Where Wuz You Las' Night. *Unknown.* StDa
"Oh, where'd you git yo' learnin'? Please tell it to me." My Li'l John Henry. *Unknown.* ABF
Oh! wherefore come ye forth, in triumph from the North. The Battle of Naseby. Macaulay. BHV; EV-4; GTBS; HBV; LPS-2; OBRV; ShBV-3; TVSH; VA
O wherefore was my birth from Heaven foretold. O Dark, Dark, Dark. Milton. *Fr.* Samson Agonistes. AnFE; WHA
Oh, where's that girl that will go with me. Campfire and Bunkhouse. *Unknown.* CoSo
"Oh, whet your saws and shine your knives." Crawford Long and William Morton. Rosemary Benét *and* Stephen Vincent Benét. PoMa
"O which is the last rose?" The Last Rose. John Davidson. OBEV (1st ed.)
Oh, whiffaree an' a-whiffo-rye. Honey, Take a Whiff on Me. *Unknown.* LiTM; OxBoLi; SiTL
O while within a Jewish breast. Hatikvah—a Song of Hope. Naphtali Herz Imber. TrJP
Oh, whiskey is the life of man. Whiskey! Johnny [*or* Whiskey for My Johnny]. *Unknown.* AmSS; SG; ShS (*vers.* II)
O whisper, O my soul! The afternoon. The Tired Worker. Claude McKay. BANP
O Whistle an' I'll Come to Ye, My Lad. Burns. *See* Whistle an' I'll Come to Ye, My Lad.
O white and midnight sky! O starry bath! The Celestial Passion. Richard Watson Gilder. AA; AnAmPo; LA; LEAP; OBAV
O white clay, O fine clay of the earth cold. Fine Clay. Winifred Shaw. MoAuPo
O white priest of eternity. Kinchinjunga. Cale Young Rice. AnAmPo; HBV; LA; LBMV
O white, white, light moon, that sailst in the sky. Donald. Henry Abbey. AA
O White Wind. Christopher Brennan. MoAuPo; OnPM
(O White Wind, Numbing the World.) BoAu
Oh, whither am I rapt beyond myself? Thomas Dekker. *Fr.* Old Fortunatus. ViBoPo
O whither goest thou, pale student. Ye Laye of Ye Woodpeckore. Henry A. Beers. NA
Oh whither, oh why, and oh wherefore. Goosey Goosey Gander —by Various Authors (Swinburne's Version). William Percy French. CenHV
O, whither sail you, Sir John Franklin? A Ballad of Sir John Franklin. George Henry Boker. AA; HBV
O Whither Shall I Fly? Francis Quarles. OxBoCh; TriL
O who are thou with that queenly brow. Roisin Dubh. Aubrey Thomas De Vere. AnIV
O Who Can Ever Gaze His Fill. W. H. Auden. ChMo
Oh, who can sleep/ On a summer night. Night Enchantment. Eleanor Muth. SiSoSe
Oh who can speak, what numbers can reveal. Pompey and Cornelia. Lucan. *Fr.* Pharsalia. OBEC
Oh, who could have such fortune. Count Arnaldos. *Unknown.* AnSpL-1
O, who dat a-comin' ovah yondah. Who Dat a-Comin' ovah Yondah? *Unknown.* BoAN-1
Oh, who has not heard of the Northmen of yore. America. Arthur Cleveland Coxe. *Fr.* England and America. MC; PAH
"O who is at my bedroom window." Willie and Mary. *Unknown.* ABS
Oh, who is so merry, so merry, heigh ho! The Light-hearted Fairy [*or* The Fairy]. *Unknown.* BoChLi; BoTP; FaPON; GaP; MeMeAg; MPB (1956 ed.); OTPC; PCH; PPL; SUS; TiPo (1952 ed.); TVSH
Oh! who is that poor foreigner that lately came to town. Irish Molly O. *Unknown.* HBV; TIP
Oh Who Is That Young Sinner. A. E. Housman. AtBAP; ChMP; FaBoTw
"O, who is this that seeks at night." A Legend of Gethsemane. Teresa Hooley. StJW
Oh! who on the mountain, the plain, or the wave. The Song of the Micmac. Joseph Howe. BoCaPo; CaP
Oh, Who Regards. *Unknown.* EIL
Oh! who rides by night thro' the woodland so wild? The Erl-King. Goethe, *tr. by* Sir Walter Scott. AWP; HOAH; JAWP; OTPC (1946 ed.); WBP
O who shall, from this dungeon, raise. A Dialogue between the Soul and Body. Andrew Marvell. CoEV; MeLP; MePo; NBE; OBS; OxBoCh; PoEL-2; PoFS; ReEn; SeCV-1; SeEP
Oh who that ever lived and loved. Our Friend the Egg. Clarence Day. BOHV
O, who will drive the chariot when she comes? She'll Be Comin' round the Mountain. *Unknown.* AS
Oh, who will find a lover for Death and for her only? A Lover for Death. Ralph Cheyney. TBM
Oh, who will follow old Ben Milam into San Antonio? The Valor of Ben Milam. Clinton Scollard. HBV; MC; PAH
Oh, who will lodge at my inn tonight? A la Belle Etoile. Sara Hamilton Birchall. NLK
"O who will shoe my bonny foot?" *See* "O wha will shoe my bonnie foot?"

"O who will shoe my fair foot." Fair Annie of Lochyran. *Unknown.* AS
"Oh, who will shoe your foot, my dear?" The Lass of Roch Royal (B *vers.*). *Unknown.* ViBoFo
O who will shoe your pretty little foot. Who Will Shoe Your Pretty Little Foot. *Unknown.* AS
O, who will show me those delights on high? Heaven. George Herbert. BLV; BoLiVe; TrGrPo
"O, who will speak from a womb or cloud," and cloud. To George Barker. Gene Derwood. NePA
O who will walk a mile with me. A Mile with Me. Henry van Dyke. BLPA; PFE; POT; PoTo
Oh! who would keep a little bird confined? The Bird in a Cage. William Lisle Bowles. TVC
Oh, who would stay indoor, indoor. Hunting Song. Richard Hovey. *Fr.* King Arthur. HBV; NLK
O, why?—/ Only a dove can venture that reply. Elm Angel. Harold Monro. FaBoMo
Oh, why can't things stay as they were? The Old Man. Beatrice Herford. PEDC
Oh, why did e'er my thoughts aspire. Song. Charles Sackville. SeCL
O why do you walk through the fields in gloves. To a [Fat] Lady Seen from the Train. Frances Cornford. BLPA; LBBV; LiTM; MBP; MoBrPo; NeMA; OBMV; OnPP; PoeMoYo; PoeT; SiTL; TCPD; TwCV; YT
Oh, why does New York go to France for its fun. Come to Britain; a Humble Contribution to the Movement. A. P. Herbert. WhC
Oh, why does the white man follow my path. The Indian Hunter. Eliza Cook. BLPA
Oh, why don't you [*or* I] work like other men do? Hallelujah, I'm a Bum [*or* Hallelujah, Bum Again]. *Unknown.* ABF; APW; AS; TrAS
Oh why is heaven built so far. De Profundis. Christina Rossetti. BPN; CoBE; OuHeWo; PoVP; VLEP
O Why Left I My Hame? Robert Gilfillan. *See* Exile's Song, The.
Oh, why, my brother-mariners, so near the boisterous wave. Too Near the Waves. Poseidippus. OnPM
O why should our dull retrospective addresses. The Living Lustres. Horace Smith. EV-4
Oh, why should the sight of your cloth cap. The Cloth Cap. *Unknown.* WhP
Oh! Why Should the Spirit of Mortal Be Proud? William Knox. BCEP; BLPA; FaFP; HBV; LPS-1; NeHB; OQP; QP-2; TreF; WBLP; WGRP
(Mortality.) MaRV; PECK
(Why Should the Spirit of Mortal Be Proud?) PTA-1
O wide and shining, miles on miles. Far Distances. Henry W. Clark. OQP; QP-2
Oh! wide and winding river. Tweedmouth Bar. Will H. Ogilvie. TVSH
O wielder of the lance. The Army. Abu Zaid. MooP
O wife of Hector, Phrygia's mightiest once. Andromache Learns of Her Son's Fate. Euripides. *Fr.* Trojan Women. LiA
O wild heart, track the land's perfume. The Flight. George Edward Woodberry. NV
O wild West Wind, thou breath of Autumn's being. Ode to the West Wind. Shelley. AEV; AnEnPo; AnFE; ATP; AWP; BCEP; BEL; BLV; BoLiVe; BPN; CaAE; CBE; CBOV; CBPC; CH; CoBE; CoEV; EM-2; EmBrPo; EnL; EnLi-2; EnLit; EnRP; EPN; EPP; ERP; EV-4; ExPo; FaBoBe; FaBoEn; FaFP; FiP; GEPC; GTBS; GTBS-D; GTBS-W; GTSE; GTSL; HBV; HiLiEn; InP; InPo; JAWP; LEAP; LiTB; LiTG; LoBV; MaPo; MCCG; OAEP; OBEV; OBRV; OHFP; OTPC (1946 ed.); OuHeWo; PFE; PIAE; PoE; PoEL-4; PoeMoYo; PoFS; PoMa; PoRA; PreP; PYM; REAL; ReaPo; RiBV; SeCeV; ShBV-4; TCEP; TOP; TreFS; TrGrPo; TwHP; TyEnPo; UnPo; ViBoPo; WBP; WHA
Oh will this lively, lovely, virgin day. The Swan. Stéphane Mallarmé. TrFP
O will ye choose to hear the news? Mr. Molony's Account of the Ball. Thackeray. HBV; LPS-3
O, Willie Brew'd a Peck o' Maut. Burns. *See* Willie Brew'd a Peck o' Maut.
"O Willie my son, what makes you sae sad?" Willie's Lyke-Wake. *Unknown.* BaBo
Oh, Willie was a plowboy. The Banks of Dundee. *Unknown.* BaBo
O Willie's gane to Melville Castle. Willie's Gane to Melville Castle. *Unknown.* SaSa
O Willie's large o' limb and lith. The Birth of Robin Hood [*or* Willie and Earl Richard's Daughter]. *Unknown.* ESPB; OBB
O Willy was as brave a lord. Willie o' Douglas Dale. *Unknown.* BaBo; ESPB
Oh, wilt thou have my hand, Dear, to lie along in thine? Inclusions. Elizabeth Barrett Browning. BPN; EmBrPo; HBV; OBVV; TOP
O wind from the sea! O wind from the sea! Sea-Song. Irene Rutherford McLeod. YT
O Wind from the Westward! O West wind wild! Ode to the West Wind. Edwin Christmas. ReTS
O Wind of the Mountain! Thomas Westwood. VA
O wind, rend open the heat. Heat. Hilda Doolittle ("H. D."). *Fr.* The Garden. BAP; BLV; MAP; MoAmPo; NeMA; OxBA; PIAE; SBMV; TSW; UnPo; WHA
O wind, thou hast thy kindom in the trees. Wind of Summer. "Michael Field." VA
O Wind, Where Have You Been? Christina Rossetti. *Fr.* Sing-Song. BoTP
O wind, why do you never rest. Christina Rossetti. *Fr.* Sing-Song. TiPo
Oh, winds blow cool! Oh, young leaves, sift! Ruth Goes By. Edna Tucker Muth. PEDC
O winds of heaven, pray. Poppies. *Unknown.* MPB
O winds that blow across the sea. The Wind's Song. "Gabriel Setoun." HBV; HBVY; OTPC; PPL
Oh, Wing Tee Wee. Wing Tee Wee. J. P. Denison. BOHV
O Winter! bar thine adamantine doors. To Winter. Blake. AnEnPo; EM-1; TyEnPo
Oh Winter! ruler of th' inverted year. Winter. William Cowper. *Fr.* The Task, IV. OBEC; TyEnPo
O Winter! Wilt Thou Never Go? David Gray. LPS-2
O Winter's a beautiful time of the year. Winter. Enid Blyton. BoTP
O! wither'd is the garland of the war. Lament. Shakespeare. *Fr.* Antony and Cleopatra, IV, xiii. KN
Oh, Wizard Soul. Feodor Ivanovich Tyutchev, *tr. fr. Russian by* Babette Deutsch. TrRV
O, Woman! Sir Walter Scott. *See* O, Woman! In Our Hours of Ease.
O Woman Full of Wile. *At. to* Geoffrey Keating, *tr. fr. Late Middle Irish by* Padraic Pearse. OnYI
O, Woman! In Our Hours of Ease. Sir Walter Scott. *Fr.* Marmion, VI. BCEP
(O, Woman!) TreFS
O woman in the pantry. The Cad. *Unknown.* SiB
O woman, let thy heart not cleave. Forepledged. John Lancaster Spalding. AA
O Woman! Lovely Woman! Thomas Otway. *Fr.* Venice Preserved. EV-3
O woman of my love, I am walking with you on the sand. Love Song. Arthur Symons. GTML; PoVP
O woman of the piercing wail. A Lament for the Princes of Tyrone and Tyrconnel [*or* Tir-Owen and Tirconnell]. *Tr. by* James Clarence Mangan. AnIV; TIP
O Woman of Three Cows, agra! The Woman of Three Cows. *Unknown, tr. by* James Clarence Mangan. AnIL; EnRP; GTIV; IrPN; OnYI; OxBI; TIP
O woman very unhappy and very wise. Cassandra Prepares to Die. Aeschylus. *Fr.* Agamemnon. OxBG
O woman, washing by the river! Fairy Lullaby. *Unknown.* BOL
O, wonder!/ How many goodly creatures are there here! Brave New World. Shakespeare. *Fr.* The Tempest, V, i. TrGrPo
O wonderful nonsense of lotions of Lucky Tiger. Haircut. Karl Shapiro. FiMAP; MoPo; MoVE
Oh, wonderful story of deathless love. He Cares. "Susan Coolidge." MaRV
O wondrous changes of a fatal scene. Dryden. *Fr.* Threnodia Augustalis. NBE
O wondrous night of star and song. Prayer on Christmas Eve. Nancy Byrd Turner. MaRV; PraP
O wondrous scene is Meeker. Lines on Mountain Villages. "Sunset Joe." PoOW
O wood, burn bright; O flame, be quick. A Charm. Christopher Morley. POT; PoTo
O Woodland Cool. Clemens Brentano, *tr. fr. German by* Mabel Cotterell. AnGP
O Word of God Incarnate. William Walsham How. MaRV
"O Words are lightly spoken." The Rose Tree. W. B. Yeats. EnLP; GTBS-D; OBMV; PoFr
O words, O words, and shall you rule. Words. Stella Benson. MBP; MoBrPo (1942 ed.)
O words, which fall like summer dew on me! Rural Poesy. Sir Philip Sidney. *Fr.* Arcadia. ElL; ElSeCe; MaPo
O World. Alice Corbin. NP
O World. George Santayana. Sonnets, III. HBMV; MaRV; TrGrPo
(Faith.) OQP; PoeMoYo; QP-1; WGRP
(Light of Faith, The.) GrCo-1
("O world, thou choosest not the better part!") ATP; MAP; MoAmPo; PFE; TreFS
O World, Be Nobler. Laurence Binyon. BMEP; GTSL; HBV; LEAP; LoPS; MBP; MoBrPo; OBEV; PtOT; TOP
O World, Be Not So Fair. Maria Jäger, *tr. fr. German by* Grace Fallow Norton. HBV
"Oh, World-God, give me wealth!" the Egyptian cried. Gifts. Emma Lazarus. TrJP; WGRP
O world, I cannot hold thee close enough! God's World. Edna St. Vincent Millay. BAP; BTP; ChMo; CoBA; FaBoBe; GoTP; HBV; MAP; MCCG; MoAmPo; NLK;

O world, I cannot hold thee close enough (*continued*) NP; PoTo; PYM; SBMV; TCAP; TSW; **TSWC; YT**

O world, in very truth thou art too young. Written at Florence. Wilfrid Scawen Blunt. OBEV (1st ed.); OBVV

O world invisible, we view thee. In No Strange Land [*or* The Kingdom of God]. Francis Thompson. AnFE; AtBAP; BLV; BMEP; BoLiVe; ChIP; CoBE; CoEV; CP; EmBrPo; EPN; GoBC; GTBS; GTML; HBMV; LBBV; LiTB; LiTG; MaRV; MBP; MoAB; OBEV (new ed.); OQP; OxBoCh; Po; PoeT; PoLi; POTE; POTT; PoVP; QP-2; ReaPo; RiBV; SeCeV; ShBV-4; TCEP; TrGrPo; TriL; TwCrTr; VLEP; WGRP; WoL

O world! O life! O time! A Lament. Shelley. AtBAP; BCEP; BLV; BoLiVe; BPN; BrBE; CBE; CBOV; ChER; ChTr; EG; EmBrPo; EnLi-2 (1949 ed.); EnLit; EnRP; EPN; ERP; EV-4; GEPC; GTBS; GTBS-D; GTBS-W; GTSE; GTSL; KN; LoBV; LPS-1; OAEP; OBRV; PIR; PoRA; TCEP; TOP; TrGrPo; WHA

O world of love and beauty. Hymn. George Edward Hoffman. MaRV

O world that changes under my hand. O World. Alice Corbin. NP

O world that turneth as a vane that veers! Heliodore. John Daniel Logan. CaP; OCL

O World, Thou Choosest Not the Better Part. George Santayana. *See* O World.

O worship the King, all glorious above! The Majesty and Mercy of God. Sir Robert Grant. OHIP; OlF; WGRP

O worthy Lord and most of might. Into This World Now Is Come/ Christe Redemptor Omnium. *Unknown.* AnEC

Oh would I were a politician. Yes and No. Ogden Nash. MaRV

Oh, would I were the golden light. Watching and Wishing. Charlotte Brontë. DiM

O would I were the salt sea-wind. Would I Were the Wind. *Unknown.* OxBG

O would I were where I would be! Suspiria. *Unknown.* OBEV (new ed.)

Oh, Would That I Knew. Al-Samau'al Ibn Adiya, *tr. fr. Arabic.* TrJP

O would that in the world there were no night. On His Love. Dakiki. LiTW

Oh, would that working I might shun. Ode to Work in Springtime. Thomas R. Ybarra. BOHV; HBMV

Oh would you know why Henry sleeps. Inhuman Henry. A. E. Housman. FiBHP

O, woven in one wide loom thro' the throbbing weft of the whole. Alfred Noyes. *Fr.* The Loom of Years. MaRV

O Wretch, Beware. William Dunbar. BSV

O wretched dog. To a Dog. Luis Carlos López. TwSpPo

O write it up above your hearth. A Dublin Ballad; 1916. "Dermot O'Byrne." AnIV; OxBI

O, write my name. De Angels in Heab'n Gwineter Write My Name. *Unknown.* BoAN-2

O Yankee Doodle went to town. Yankee Doodle. *Unknown.* OlF

O ye, all ye that walk in Willowwood. Willowwood, 3. Dante Gabriel Rossetti. The House of Life, LI. BPN; BrBE; EmBrPo; OAEP; POTT; PoVP; ReaPo; TCEP; ViP; ViPo; ViPP; VLEP

Oh, Ye Censurers. Al-Samau'al Ibn Adiya, *tr. fr. Arabic by* Hartwig Hirschfeld. TrJP

O ye dales. Nature. Mark Akenside. *Fr.* The Pleasures of Imagination, IV. LoBV

O ye dead poets, who are living still. The Poets. Longfellow. APW; IAP

O ye inhabitants of Sparta, the whole human race loathes you. Euripides. *Fr.* Andromache. GrPo

O ye Northumbrian shades, which overlook. Early Influences. Mark Akenside. *Fr.* The Pleasures of Imagination, IV. OBEC

O ye splendid children of Memory and Zeus the Olympian. Solon, *tr. fr. Greek by* N. H. Dole. GrPo

O Ye Sweet Heavens! Thomas William Parsons. AA

O ye that look on Ecstasy. Ecstasy. Rachel Annand Taylor. GoTS

O ye that put your trust and confidence. A Rueful [*or* Ruful] Lamentation on the Death [*or* Deth] of Queen Elizabeth. Sir Thomas More. LiTB; LiTG; NBE; OBSC

O Ye That Would Swallow the Needy. Amos, VIII: 4-10, Bible, *O.T.* TrJP

O [*or* A] ye wha are sae guid yoursel. Address to the Unco Guid, or the Rigidly Righteous. Burns. AnFE; BEL; BoLiVe; CBOV; CEP; CoBE; EiPP; EM-1; EnLit; EnRP; EPP; HBV; LoBV; LPS-3; OAEP; OBEC; PIR; PoFr; SeCeV; TCEP; TOP; TreFS; TrGrPo; ViBoPo

O ye who gaze in wonder at the old. Ruined Glories. Joachim du Bellay. Antiquities of Rome, XXVII. TrFP

O ye who see with other eyes than ours. Life and Death. Lilla Cabot Perry. AA

Oh ye! who so lately were blithesome and gay. The Butterfly's Funeral. *Unknown.* OTPC (1923 ed.)

Oh, ye who taste that love is sweet. Ye Who Taste That Love Is Sweet. William Michael Rossetti. OQP; QP-2

Oh ye! who teach the ingenuous youth of nations. Don Juan, II. Byron. EmBrPo; EnRP; ERP; GEPC

O ye, who thoughtlessly repose. Envoi. Nizami. *Fr.* Laili and Majnún. PeP

Oh ye who tread the Narrow Way. The Buddha at Kamakura. Kipling. LoBV

O ye, whose cheek the tear of pity stains. Epitaph on My Father. Burns. FAOV; MaRV

"O ye whose end was happy, O spirits already chosen." Marvel Ye Not. Dante. *Fr.* Divina Commedia: Purgatorio. LiA

"Oh, ye whose hearts are resonant, and ring to war's romance." Jean Desprez. Robert W. Service. CV

Oh, ye wild waves, shoreward dashing. The Song of the Wild Storm-Waves. Percy F. Sinnett. VA

O ye youngster gods! Aeschylus. *Fr.* Eumenides. GrPo

O Year, grow slowly. Exquisite, holy. Slow Spring. Katharine Tynan. BLV; BoTP; MBP

O year that is going, take with you. A Prayer for the New Year. Laura F. Armitage. OQP; QP-2

O years, and age, farewell! Eternity. Robert Herrick. SeCL; TriL; WHA

O Years Unborn. John Richard Moreland. PGD

O ye'll tak the high road, and I'll tak the low road. The Bonnie Banks of Loch Lomond. *Unknown.* EBSV

O yellow bird, yellow bird. The Yellow Bird. *Unknown.* WhP

O yellow flowers that Herrick sung! To Daffodils. Austin Dobson. InP

Oh, yes, I'm gwine up, gwine up. Gwine Up. *Unknown.* BoAN-1

"Oh, yes, Mrs. Proctor, for months I've been ailing." Organ Recital. Arthur L. Lippmann. PFE

Oh, yes, my lads, we'll roll alee. Come Down, You Bunch of Roses, Come Down. *Unknown.* ShS

O yes, O yes! if any maid. Cupid's Indictment [*or* A Song of Diana's Nymphs]. John Lyly. *Fr.* Galathea. EIL; OBSC

O yes! O yes! O yes! I have lost him, Love the gipsy. Hue and Cry after Love. Meleager. GrPE

O yes! O yes! the farmers all may go. Once More the Simple Things. Aristophanes. *Fr.* The Peace. GrR

Oh, Yes! Oh, Yes! Wait 'til I Git on My Robe, *with music.* *Unknown.* BoAN-2

Oh, yes, we've be'n fixin' up some sence we sold that piece o' groun'. Sary "Fixes Up" Things. Albert Bigelow Paine. BOHV

Oh yesterday the cutting edge drank thirstily and deep. Tomorrow. John Masefield. MBP; MoBrPo; NeMA; OtMeF; POTE; StaSt; TrGrPo; YT

Oh, yesterday was the merry Yuletide. On the Day after Christmas. Franklin P. Adams. PIAE

Oh! yet a few short years of useful life. Wordsworth. *Fr.* The Prelude, XIV. EV-3; NBE; OBRV

Oh yet we trust that somehow good. In Memoriam A. H. H., LIV [*or* The Larger Hope]. Tennyson. AnFE; AtBAP; BEL; BoLiVe; BPN; BPP; EM-2; EmBrPo; EnL; EnLi-2; EnLit; EPN; EPP; ExPo; GEPC; GrCo-1; GTBS-W; GTSL; HBV; LEAP; LiTB; LiTG; LoBV; LPS-2; MaPo; MaRV; OAEP; OQP; OuHeWo; PIAE; PoE; PoFS; QP-1; ReaPo; RiBV; SeCeV; TCEP; TOP; TreFS; TrGrPo; TyEnPo; UnPo; ViPo; VLEP; WGRP

Oh Yield, Fair Lids. Sheridan. OnYI

O yonge freshe folkes, he or she. *See* O younge freshe folkes, he and she.

O you, all life, and you, the primal cause. Holiday. Edith Sitwell. CoEV

Oh, you and I, wild thrush—we share. Articulate Thrush. Lew Sarett. BLA

O you are a rajah in your rage. Courage for the Pusillanimous. Paul Roche. GoYe

O you away high there. Au Jardin. Ezra Pound. MOAP

O you fortunate swans, who sentinel. Sonnet: The Death of Virgil. Angelo di Costanzo. LyPI

O you girls, girl friends, you who have also loved. Mourning in Spring, 1943. Kathleen Raine. DiM

Oh, you hear sweet music. Song. John McClure. LS

O you High Gods, have pity, and let me find. Six Sonnets. Mary, Queen of Scots. DiM

Oh, you know Joe Silovatsky. Me Johnny Mitchell Man. *Unknown.* TrAS

O you liar tell me this. The Liar. *Unknown.* KiLC

Oh, you may drive a horse to water. *Unknown.* SiTL

Oh, you may sing your gypsy songs. The Little Gods. Abigail Cresson. PoMa

Oh, you may take a highway. Highways and Byways. John Vanderbilt. PCD

O you not only worshipful but dear. Credo. Zona Gale. TrPWD

O, you plant the pain in my heart with your wistful eyes. Maureen. John Todhunter. HBV; OBEV; OBVV

O you that from some southern land. Ode to the Nightingale. John Kendall. InMe
O You That Hear[e] This Voice. Sir Philip Sidney. Astrophel and Stella, Sixth Song. NBE; OBSC; SiPS
O you that still have rain and sun. The Dead to the Living. Laurence Binyon. POT
O you, who chide my passion. The Garden. Al-Nashshar. MooP
Oh, you who love me not, tell me some way. Tell Me Some Way. Lizette Woodworth Reese. PG
O you, who on your cheek. Favourites. Ibn Abd Rabbihi. MooP
Oh, You Wholly Rectangular. E. R. Cole. GoYe
O you whom God hath called and set apart. The Ideal City. Washington Gladden. OQP; QP-2
O you, with whom I used to learn of God. To One in Heaven. Nagata. SoLD
O you would house me in silken frocks. The Wild Goat. Claude McKay. CDC
O You Young Eagles! Edgar Lee Masters. PoFr
O you youths, Western youths. Pioneers! O Pioneers. Walt Whitman. GrCo-1
O young and brave, it is not sweet to die. Dulce et Decorum. T. P. Cameron Wilson. HBMV; VOD (1931 ed.)
O Young and Fearless Prophet. S. Ralph Harlow. MaRV; TrPWD
O young John Talbot! I did send for thee. Father and Son. Shakespeare. King Henry VI, Pt. I, *fr.* IV, v *and* vii. BHV
Oh! young Lochinvar has [*or* is] come out of the West. Young Lochinvar, *parody. Unknown, at. to* J. J. Fay. BOHV; FiBHP; InMe
Oh, young Lochinvar is come out of the west. Lochinvar [*or* Lady Heron's Song]. Sir Walter Scott. *Fr.* Marmion. ATP; BBV; BCEP; BEL; BeLS; BHV; BoChLi; BoTP; BSV; CaAE; CBOV; CBPC; CG; CoBE; EBSV; EmBrPo; EnLi-2 (1949 ed.); EnLit; EnRP; EPN; ERP; EV-4; FaBoBe; FaFP; FaPON; GN; GoTP; GoTS; HBV; HBVY; HiLiEn; InP; LH; LoEn; LoPo; LPS-1; MaC; MCCG; MW; NeHB; OAEP; OBRV; OnHT; OnSP; OtMeF; OTPC; PCD; PECK; PFE; PIAE; PIR; PoE; PoRA; PYM; RG; ShBV-1; StPo; StVeCh; TCEP; TOP; TreF; TVSH; WHA
O young Mariner/ You from the haven. Merlin and the Gleam. Tennyson. BEL; BPN; EM-2; EmBrPo; EPP; GEPC; OAEP; PoVP; REAL; VLEP
Oh Young Men Oh Young Comrades. Stephen Spender. NAMP; PreP; ReaPo
O, young New Year—take not these things from me. A New Year Prayer. Laura Simmons. LPS-1
O young people, hark while I relate. Wicked Polly (B *vers.*). *Unknown.* ABS
O younge freshe [*or* yonge fresshe] folkes, he or [*or* and] she. Exhortation to Youth [*or* The Love Unfeigned]. Chaucer. *Fr.* Troilus and Criseyde. CAW; ExPo; LO; OBEV; PoLi
O youngest, best-loved daughter of Hsieh. An Elegy. Yüan Chen. ChLP; LiTW
O, you're braw wi' your pearls and your diamonds. Lassie, What Mair Wad You Hae? Heine. GoTS
"Oh, you're welcome home again," said the young man to his love. The Grey Cock (A *vers.*). *Unknown.* BaBo
Oh youth, beware! that laurel-rose. Larissa. Thomas Love Peacock. *Fr.* Rhododaphne. OBRV
O youth, if thou but have the heart. Song of the Battle-Skald. Bengt Lidner. *Fr.* Medea. AnSL
O Youth of the Bound Black Hair. *Unknown, tr. fr. Irish by* Douglas Hyde. GTIV
O Youth Whose Hope Is High. Robert Bridges. VA
O Youth with Blossoms Laden. Arthur Wallace Peach. HBMV
O Zeus, I look upon this form laid low. Sophocles. *Fr.* Electra. LiA
O Zeus, O Zeus-born justice, O bright sun. Vengeance. Euripides. *Fr.* Medea. OxBG
O Zeus our king and Night our friend. Chorus. Aeschylus. *Fr.* Agamemnon. LiTW
O Zeus, Our Spirit Fails. Aeschylus. *See* Prayer for Deliverance.
O Zozima, your soul was ever free. A Slave Girl. Damascius. OxBG
O zummer clote! when the brook's a-glidèn [*or* a-sliden]. The Clote (Water-Lily). William Barnes. GTBS-D; PoEL-4
O' zummer night, as day did gleam. The Lost Little Sister. William Barnes. PoEL-4
Oak. Philip Child. CaP
Oak, The. Dryden. ADAH; OHIP
Oak, The. Mary Elliott. OTPC (1923 ed.)
Oak, The. George Hill. *See* Fall of the Oak, The.
Oak, The. John Keble. EnSW
Oak, The. James Russell Lowell. ADAH
Oak, The. Tennyson. BPN; EmBrPo; EPN; FaPON; MPB; PoVP; YT
Oak and Lily. Ben Jonson. *See* It Is Not Growing like a Tree.
Oak and Olive. James Elroy Flecker. HBMV; POTT
Oak and the Ash, The. *Unknown.* FaBoCh; LoGBV
Oak and the Beech, The. Thomas Love Peacock. *See* Song: "For the tender beech and the sapling oak."
Oak and the Brere, The. Spenser. *Fr.* The Shepheardes Calender: Februarie. OBSC
Oak and the Reed, The. La Fontaine, *tr. fr. French by* Elizur Wright. OuHeWo
Oak, fern, ivy and pine. Little Epithalamium. Chester Kallman. CrMA
Oak Grove, The. Nikolaus Lenau, *tr. fr. German by* Dwight Durling. AnGP
Oak is called the king of trees, The. Trees. Sara Coleridge. BoTP; DD; MeMeAg; MPB; OHIP; PCH; RAR; TVC
Oak Leaves. Elizabeth J. Coatsworth. StVeCh
Oak leaves are big as the mouse's ear. Every One to His Own Way. John Vance Cheney. AA
Oak of State, The. Dryden. *Fr.* Don Sebastian. BeR
Oak one day addressed the reed, The. The Oak and the Reed. La Fontaine. OuHeWo
Oak-Tree, The. William Barnes. *See* Girt Woak Tree That's in the Dell, The.
Oakeley, whenas the bass you beat. To E. M. O. Thomas Edward Brown. WhC
Oak's Farewell, The. George H. Stover. CAG
Oaks, how subtle and marine, The. Bearded Oaks. Robert Penn Warren. AmP; AnFE; CoAnAm; FiMAP; LiTM; MoAmPo (1950 ed.); MoVE; OnHM; ReMP
Oars fell from our hands, The. The Island. George Woodcock. NeBP
Oarsmen, The, *sel.* Rabindranath Tagore.
"We have known sins and evils every day." MaRV
Oasis. Edward Dowden. OxBI; TIP
Oath, The. Allen Tate. LiTM; OxBA
Oath, An. Theognis, *tr. fr. Greek by* A. E. Crawley. OxBG
Oath of Freedom, The. James Barron Hope. MDAH
Oath of Friendship ("If you were riding in a coach"). *Unknown, tr. fr. Chinese by* Arthur Waley. BoFr
(Oaths of Friendship.) TrCh
Oath of Friendship ("Shang Ya!"). *Unknown, tr. fr. Chinese by* Arthur Waley. BoFr
Oats, The. Jeppe Aakjaer, *tr. fr. Danish by* Charles W. Stork. BoDS
Oats, peas, beans and barley grow. *Unknown.* RIS
Obedience. Phoebe Cary. PCH
Obedience. Robert Herrick. PoFr
Obedience. George Macdonald. BePJ; BLRP; MaRV; WGRP
(What Christ Said.) ChIP; HBV; OQP; OTPC; QP-1
Oberammergau. Leonora Speyer. AnAmPo; HBMV; LA
Obermann Once More. Matthew Arnold. BPN; EPN; GEPC; PoEL-5; PoVP; VLEP
Sels.
East, The. OtMeF
Pagan World, The. GTML
(West and East, *abr.*) CBPC
Oberon and Titania to the Fairy Train. Shakespeare. *Fr.* A Midsummer Night's Dream, V, ii. GN
("Through the house give glimmering light.") SiCE
Oberon, the Fairy Prince. Ben Jonson. EPS
Buz, Quoth the Blue Fly, *sel.* NA; TuPP
("Buzz, quoth the blue fly," *sl. diff.*) OxNR
(Catch, A.) EIL
(Sylvan Catch.) BoN
Oberon's Feast. Robert Herrick. BLV; BoLiVe; EPS; OAEP; OTPC (1923 ed.); SeCV-1; TrGrPo
"Little mushroom table spread, A," *sel.* ViBoPo
Obit on Parnassus. F. Scott Fitzgerald. InMe; WhC
Obituary. Anthony Brode. FiBHP
Obituary. Thomas William Parsons. AA; HBV; HBVY
Obituary. Louis Untermeyer. MAP
Obituary; In Mem. S. B. V. 1834–1909. Allen Tate. MOAP
Object among dreams, you sit here with your shoes off, An. A Girl in a Library. Randall Jarrell. FiMAP
Objects. W. H. Auden. NePoAm-2
Objects are disposed: the sky is suitable, The. November, 1941. Roy Fuller. MoPo
Objects of the Summer Scene, The. Thomas Caulfield Irwin. IrPN
Oblation. A. Newberry Choyce. HBMV
Oblation, The. Swinburne. BPN; EmBrPo; EnLit; EtPaEn; HBV; LEAP; POTT; PoVP; VLEP
Obliged by frequent visits of this man. Fleckno, an English Priest at Rome. Andrew Marvell. SeEP
Oblivion. Jessie Redmond Fauset, *fr. the French of* Massillon Coicou. BANP; PoNe
Oblivion. W. W. Gibson. NP
Oblivion. John Marston. *See* To Everlasting Oblivion.
Oblivion. Octavio Paz, *tr. fr. Spanish by* Dudley Fitts. AnCL
Oblivion. *Unknown.* MM
Obmittamus Studia. *Unknown, tr. fr. Latin by* Helen Waddell. *Fr.* Carmina Burana. LaP

O'Bruidar. James Stephens, *after the Irish of* David O'Bruaidar. GTIV
(O Bruadair.) OxBI
Obscure and Dark Is All the Gloomy Air. Robert Greene. *Fr.* Perimedes the Blacksmith. ReIE
Obscure Night of the Soul, The. St. John of the Cross, *tr. fr. Spanish by* Arthur Symons. AWP; CAW; MeRV; OBMV; OuHeWo; TriL; VLEP
(Dark Night of the Soul, The, *tr. by* E. Allison Peers.) LiTW; TeCS
(Songs of the Soul, *tr. by* E. Allison Peers.) AnSpL-1
(Upon a Gloomy Night, *tr. by* Roy Campbell.) AtBAP
Obscure Writer, An. John Donne. ReIE
Obscurest night involv'd [*or* involved] the sky. The Castaway. William Cowper. AtBAP; BEL; CEP; CoBE; CoEV; EiPP; EnLi-2; EnLit; EnRP; EV-3; FaBoEn; FiP; GTSL; InPo; NBE; OAEP; OBEC; PoE; PoEL-3; PoFS; TCEP; TOP; TriL; TwHP
Obscurity ("Obscurity becomes the final peace"). Jessica Powers. JKCP (1955 ed.)
Obsequies of Stuart. John Reuben Thompson. BlG; GA; PAH
Obsequies of [*or* to] the Lord Harrington, The, *sel.* John Donne.
"Thou seest me here at midnight, now all rest." MeRV; MyFE
Observation. Samuel Hoffenstein. PoMa
Observation. Dorothy Parker. FiBHP
(Some Beautiful Letters.) InMe
Observe, beloved, the increasing years. The Upward Pass. Henry Bellamann. LS
Observe, dear George, this nut so small. The Oak. Mary Elliott. OTPC (1923 ed.)
Observe how he negotiates his way. Swimmer. Robert Francis. CrMA; NePoAm
Observe. I myself will proceed/ To put him in his place. Cyrano de Bergerac Discusses His Nose. Edmond Rostand. *Fr.* Cyrano de Bergerac. TreFS
Observe. Ridged, raised, tactile, the horror. Munch's Scream. Donald Hall. NePoEA
Observe the gentle murmurs of that dove. The Birds and Plants of Love. Tasso, *tr. by the* Countess of Winchilsea. *Fr.* Aminta. BeR
Observe the Hellespont a while. *Unknown.* SeCSL
Observe the weary birds ere night be done. Orinda to Lucasia. Katherine Philips. LO; SeCL
Observe this song, which is both neat and pretty. The Gallant Seaman's Return from the Indies. *Unknown.* SG
Observing point by point mere instances. On a Baltimore Bus. Charles G. Bell. NePoAm
Obstacle, An. Charlotte Perkins Gilman. DDA; OBAV
Occasion of Sin. Maurice James Craig. *Fr.* Three Cat Poems. PoC
Occasional mornings when an early fog. Housewife. Josephine Miles. FiMAP
Occasioned by General Washington's Arrival in Philadelphia, on His Way to His Residence in Virginia. Philip Freneau. GA, *abr.;* PAH
Occasions drew me early to this city. Samson at Gaza. Milton. *Fr.* Samson Agonistes. BHV; EV-2; ShGoBo
Ocean, The. Psalms, CVII: 23–32, Bible, *O.T. See* They That Go Down to the Sea in Ships.
Ocean, The ("Roll on thou deep and dark blue ocean, roll"). Byron. *Fr.* Childe Harold's Pilgrimage, IV, *sts.* 179–183. BCEP; BLV; BoLiVe; CoEV; PIAE; TrGrPo; UnPo (1st ed.)
(Address to the Ocean.) TreFS
(Apostrophe to the Ocean.) EtS; GDAH; OHFP; WBLP
(Roll On, Thou Dark Blue Ocean.) FaPON
(Roll On, Thou Deep and Dark Blue Ocean.) AtBAP
(To the Ocean.) GN; LEAP; WGRP
"There is a pleasure in the pathless woods," *sts.* 178–183. CBE; EPN; EV-4; InP; MaPo; MaRV, 9 *ll.;* MCCG; NLK; OBRV; PreP; ShBV-3; TCEP; ViBoPo
(And I Have Loved Thee, Ocean!) WHA
(Communion with Nature, 9 *ll.*) GrCo-1
(Deep and Dark Blue Ocean.) ChTr
(Man and Nature: "Oh, that the desert.") EPP
(Nature.) BEL
("Oh, that the desert were my dwelling-place.") ERP; PoEL-4
(Roll On, Thou Deep and Dark Blue Ocean.) FiP
(Sea, The.) FaBoBe; HBV; LiTB; LiTG; LPS-2; PYM; SG
(Solitude, *shorter sel.*) SN
(There Is Pleasure in the Pathless Woods, 9 *ll.*) TreF
("Thou glorious mirror, where the Almighty's form," 9 *ll.*) MW
(Where None Intrudes, 9 *ll.*) PC
Ocean, The. Andreas Calvos, *tr. fr. Modern Greek by* Rae Dalven. MoGP
Ocean. Robinson Jeffers. CoBMV; CoV; MOAP
Ocean. Louis Lavater. BoAu
Ocean, The. James Montgomery. LPS-2
Ocean, The. Moschus, *tr. fr. Greek by* Shelley. AWP; JAWP; WBP
(Gleaming Sea, The.) CBE
(Landsman, The.) OxBG
Ocean. Robert Pollok. *Fr.* The Course of Time. EtS; LPS-2
Ocean, The. George D. Prentice. EtS
Ocean, The. Florence Wilson Roper. MuM
Ocean, The. John Augustus Shea. EtS
Ocean, The. Charles Tennyson Turner. LPS-2
Ocean, an Ode, *sel.* Edward Young.
Ocean and Stars. BeR
Ocean at the bidding of the moon, The. The Ocean. Charles Tennyson Turner. LPS-2
Ocean Burial, The. Edwin H. Chapin. ShS, *with music;* ViBoFo
Ocean does not shrink or vaster grow, The. The Hidden Truth. Jami. LiTW; OnPM
Ocean-fight, The. *Unknown.* PAH
Ocean has not been so quiet for a long while, The. Evening Ebb. Robinson Jeffers. AmPP (3d ed.); OTPC (1946 ed.)
Ocean—I yearn toward it. Ha! the ocean. The Sea. Björnstjerne Björnson. AnNoLy
Ocean laughs, The. Gerasimos Markoras. *Fr.* Spring Nights. MoGP
Ocean Lullaby, An. Charles Keeler. EtS
Ocean of Ice, The. Ambrose Philips. *Fr.* A Winter Piece. BeR
Ocean Spills, The. Samuel Hoffenstein. ALV
Ocean stood like crystal, The. The soft air. The Birth of Venus. *Unknown.* EtS
Ocean thunders in the caverned sky, The. Homecoming in Storm. Bernice L. Kenyon. EtS
Ocean to Cynthia, The. Sir Walter Ralegh. OBSC, *sl. abr.;* ReIE
(Ocean's Love to Cynthia, The.) SiPS
Sels.
"But stay, my thoughts, make end, give fortune way." TuPP
"To seeke new worlds, for golde, for prayse, for glory." FaBoEn
"With youth, is deade the hopes of loves returne." FaBoEn
Ocean Wanderer, The. *Unknown.* BOHV; NA
Ocean, with a calm sardonic titter, The. Anthony Delius. *Fr.* The Great Divide. BoSA
Oceano Nox. Victor Hugo, *tr. fr. French by* Alan Conder. TrFP
Ocean's Love to Cynthia, The. Sir Walter Ralegh. *See* Ocean to Cynthia, The.
Och, here I am wid arms and legs. Caoch O'Lynn. Arthur Stringer. CPG
Och hey! for the splendour of tartans! The Return. Pittendrigh Macgillivray. GoTS
Och hon for somebody! Somebody. *Unknown.* CBOV; EBSV
Och, hush ye then, och hush ye. Hush Song. Elizabeth Shane. BOL; LBBV; MoSiPe
Och, Modereen Rue, you little red rover. Modereen Rue. Katharine Tynan. MW; TVSH
Och! the Coronation! what celebration. Mr. Barney Maguire's Account of the Coronation. "Thomas Ingoldsby." VA
Och, what's the good o' spinnin' words. The Shepherd to the Poet. Agnes Kendrick Gray. BAP; POT; PoTo
Och, when we lived in ould Glenann. A Song of Glenann. "Moira O'Neill." HBV; LBBV
Ochagon! here is the head. Conall's Head. *Unknown.* SiB
Ochil Farmer, An. James Logie Robertson. EBSV
(Farmer of Westerha', The.) POT
Ock Gurney and old Pete were there. The Countrymen. John Masefield. *Fr.* Reynard the Fox. ChMo; CMP
Octaves, *sels.* E. A. Robinson. CoV
"Like a white wall whereon forever breaks," XVIII.
"Still through the dusk of dead, blank-legended," XI.
"To me the groaning of world-worshippers," III.
"Tumultuously void of a clean scheme," II.
October. Richard Aldington. *Fr.* Epigrams. PFE
October. Thomas Bailey Aldrich. *See* Maple Leaves.
October. John Bayliss. NeBP
October. Nancy Birckhead. StaSt
October. Bryant. IAP; PEOR
October. Gerald Bullett. AlDL
October. T. A. Daly. JKCP
October. Robert Frost. AlDL; MaPo
October. Rose Fyleman. SiSoSe; TiPo (1959 ed.)
October, *sel.* David Gray.
"O, the sweet melancholy of the time." EnSW
October. Teresa Hooley. SaFP
October. Helen Hunt Jackson. TCAP
October. Helen McMahan. DDA; PoRL

October. John Charles McNeill. NoCaPo
October. Anatoly Borisovich Marienhof, *tr. fr. Russian by* Babette Deutsch. TrRV
October. William Morris. *Fr.* The Earthly Paradise. EPN; POTT; ViPP; VLEP
"O love, turn from the unchanging sea, and gaze," *sel.* FaBoEn
October. Dollie Radford. VA
October. Christina Rossetti. *Fr.* The Months; a Pageant. BoTP
October. Spenser. *Fr.* The Shepheardes Calender. NBE; ReEn; ReIE; SiCE
(Contempt of Poetry, The.) OBSC
"But, ah! Maecenas is yclad in clay[e]," *sel.* MyFE; PoD
October. Dylan Thomas. *Fr.* Poem in October. YeAr
October. Edward Thomas. BrBE; ChMP; MoVE; POTE
October. Jones Very. AnNE
October. S. W. Whitman. BoTP
October—an Etching. Edna St. Vincent Millay. CaAE
October, and a rain-blurred face. At the Fishing Settlement. Alistair Campbell. AnNZ
October and a rainbow. The Difference. Anne Blackwell Payne. NoCaPo
October,—and the skies are cool and grey. Late Autumn. William Allingham. IrPN
October at last has come! The thicket has shaken. Autumn. Pushkin. AnEnPo; AWP
October Birthday. Sister Mary Madeleva. JKCP (1955 ed.)
October Boy. Virginia Graham. AlDL
October! Can I stand it one more year? The Game. Walker Gibson. NePoAm-2
October chestnuts showered their perishing gold. Rupert Brooke, IV. W. W. Gibson. PtP
October 1803 ("These times strike monied worldlings with dismay"). Wordsworth. EmBrPo
October 1803 ("When, looking on the present face of things"). Wordsworth. BPN; EmBrPo; EnRP; PeBoSo
October Ending. Price Day. CAG
October 1. Karl Shapiro. FiMAP; MoAB; MoAmPo (1950 ed.)
October Garden. Pearce Young. PtPa
October gave a party. October's Party. George Cooper. BoChLi; BoTP; BrR; HBV; HBVY; MeMeAg; OTPC; RIS; SiSoSe
October has arrived. The grove is shaking. Autumn. Pushkin. TrRV
October in New England. Home Thoughts. Odell Shepard. HBMV
October in New Zealand. Jessie Mackay. BoAu
October in Tennessee. Walter Malone. AA
October is a piper. Autumn Song. Margaret Rose. BoTP
October Journey. Margaret Walker. PoNe
October Morning. John James Piatt. YeAr
October Myth. Innokenti Annensky, *tr. fr. Russian by* C. M. Bowra. BoRS
October Night. Agnes Louise Dean. YeAr
October, 1942. Roy Fuller. WaP
October of the Angels. James J. Daly. WHL
October Prelude. "Joseph Upper." MuM
October Redbreast, The. Alice Meynell. MBP; MoBrPo
October turned my maple's leaves to gold. Maple Leaves [*or* October]. Thomas Bailey Aldrich. AnNE; GN; GoTP; TOP
October XXIX, 1795 (Keats' Birthday). William Stanley Braithwaite. CDC
October Winds. Virginia D. Randall. YeAr
October's bellowing anger breaks and cleaves. Autumn. Siegfried Sassoon. NP
October's Bright Blue Weather. Helen Hunt Jackson. BBV (1923 ed.); BLPA; BoChLi; CV; DD; FaBoBe; GN; HBVY; MW; NeHB; OTPC (1946 ed.); PTA-1
October's gold is dim—the forests rot. Sonnet. David Gray. EV-5
October's Husbandry. Thomas Tusser. CoBE
October's hush is on the trees. Witch's Moon. Eleanor Osborn Scheier. CAG
October's lap holds patches. October. Helen McMahan. DDA; PoRL
October's Party. George Cooper. BoChLi; BoTP; BrR; HBV; HBVY; MeMeAg; OTPC; RIS; SiSoSe
October's Song. Eleanor Farjeon. AlDL
Octopus. Arthur Clement Hilton. CenHV
Octopus, The. Ogden Nash. NePA; TiPo
Octopussycat, The. Kenyon Cox. *Fr.* Mixed Beasts. FaPON; RIS; TiPo
Oculi Augent Dolorem. Barnabe Googe. *See* Out of Sight, Out of Mind.
Oculist prescribes me spectacles, The. On Oculists. J. C. Squire. WhC
Odcomb's Complaint, *sel.* John Taylor.
Sonnet: "Sweet semi-circled Cynthia played at maw." ElL
Odd but True. *Unknown.* SiTL
(Nonsense.) NA
Odd Conceit, An. Nicholas Breton. ElL; OBSC; SiCE; TuPP
(Song: "Lovely kind, and kindly loving.") LO
Odd Ones, The. Ruth Suckow. MCCG
Odd to a Krokis. *Unknown.* NA
Oddities composed the sum of the news. For the Lost Generation. Galway Kinnell. NePoAm
Oddity Land, *sels.* Edward Anthony. TiPo (1959 ed.)
"I know a barber."
"I know seven mice."
Ode, *sel.* Alessandro Manzoni, *tr. fr. Italian by* William Dean Howells.
Fifth of May, The—Napoleon. CAW
Ode: "Absence, hear thou my protestation." John Hoskins. *See* Absence.
Ode: Allusion to Horace. Mark Akenside. CEP
Ode, An: "As it fell upon a day." Richard Barnfield. *See* Nightingale, The.
Ode: "As late I sought the spangled bowers." Anacreon, *tr. fr. Greek by* Thomas Moore. OuHeWo
Ode: "Astronomers should treat of stars and comets." "Peter Pindar." PoP
Ode: "At her fair hands." Walter Davison. *See* How Can the Heart Forget Her.
Ode: Autumn. Thomas Hood. *See* Autumn ("I saw old Autumn").
Ode, An: "Awake fair Muse for I intend." William Browne. OBS; SeEP
Ode: "Bards of Passion and of Mirth." Keats. BEL; BPN; ChER; EM-1; EnRP; EPN; EPP; ERP; GEPC; GTBS; GTSE; GTSL; OAEP; OBRV; PreP; TOP
(Bards of Passion and of Mirth.) BCEP; EmBrPo; EnLi-2; EnLit; OBEV; PtP
(Ode on the Poets.) ATP (1935 ed.); GTBS-D; GTBS-W
(Ode to the Poets.) EV-4
(To the Poets.) HBV; ViBoPo
Ode: "Come leave the loathed stage." Ben Jonson. *See* Ode to Himself ("Come leave . . .").
Ode: "Day is set did earth adorn, The." Charles Cotton. ElSeCe
Ode II: Dialogue between Him and His Heart, A. Walter Davison. *See* How Can the Heart Forget Her.
Ode: Dying Christian to His Soul, The. Pope. *See* Dying Christian to His Soul, The.
Ode: Eumenides, The. A. J. M. Smith. BoCaPo (1948 ed.)
Ode: "Gathering the echoes of forgotten wisdom." George Santayana. Odes, III. AnAmPo; AnFE; APA; CoAnAm; LA; TwAmPo
Ode: "Give me the harp of epic song." Anacreon, *tr. fr. Greek by* Thomas Moore. OuHeWo
Ode: "God save the Rights of Man!" Philip Freneau. AmPP (3d ed.); CoBA; HiLiAm; IAP; PoFr
Ode: "Good night, my Love." Charles Cotton. ViBoPo
Ode: Grasshopper, The. Richard Lovelace. *See* Grasshopper, The.
Ode: "Here where a new life stirs and broods." Elise Aylen. BoCaPo (1943 ed.)
Ode, An: "High-spirited friend." Ben Jonson. EV-2
(Noble Balm.) OBEV
(True Balm.) LH
Ode V: His Farewell to His Unkind and Unconstant Mistress. Francis Davison. ReIE
Ode: "How are thy servants blest, O Lord!" Addison. *See* How Are Thy Servants Blest.
Ode I/XI/8: "How shall it be said that you have no clothes?" *Unknown, tr. fr. Chinese by* James Legge. *See* No Clothes.
Ode: "How sleep the brave, who sink to rest." William Collins. *See* How Sleep the Brave.
Ode: "I am the spirit of the morning sea." Richard Watson Gilder. AA; OBAV
Ode II: "I cannot thank you, Lord—because." Gerald Gould. QS
Ode: "I care not for the idle state." Anacreon, *tr. fr. Greek by* Thomas Moore. OuHeWo
Ode: "I saw the smiling bard of pleasure." Anacreon, *tr. fr. Greek by* Thomas Moore. OuHeWo
Ode, An: "I sing a song of sixpence." Anthony C. Deane. PA
Ode: "Idea of justice may be precious, An." Frank O'Hara. NeAP
Ode, An: "I'm going to write a novel, hey." John Updike. FiBHP
Ode: Intimations of Immortality from Recollections of Early Childhood. Wordsworth. AnFE; AWP; BCEP; BEL; BLV, *abr.*; BoLiVe; BPN; BrBE; CaAE; CBOV; ChER; CoBE; EnL; EnLi-2; EnLit; EnRP; EPN; EPP; ERP; EV-3; ExPo; FiP; GEPC; InP; InPo; InvP; JAWP; LiA; LiTB; LiTG; LoBV; LPS-3; MaPo; MCCG; OAEP; OBEV; OBRV; OuHeWo; PIAE; Po; PoEL-4;

Ode: Intimations of Immortality (*continued*)
PoFS; PreP; REAL; ReaPo; RiBV; SeCeV; TCEP;
TOP; TrGrPo; TwHP; TyEnPo; ViBoPo; WBP
(Intimations of Immortality from Recollections of Early
Childhood.) ATP; TVSH, *abr.;* WoL
(Ode on Intimations of Immortality from Recollections of
Early Childhood.) EM-2; EmBrPo; EnLP; FaFP;
GTBS; GTBS-D; GTBS-W; GTSE; GTSL; HiLiEn;
MaRV, *abr.;* OHFP; PIR; ShBV-4; TreF, *abr.;* UnW;
WHA
(Ode on the Intimations of Immortality from Recollections
of Early Childhood.) AtBAP; HBV; LEAP
Sels.
"O joy that in our embers."
(Ode on Intimations of Immortality, *st.* 9.) OQP; QP-2
"Our birth is but a sleep and a forgetting." WGRP
(Intimations of Immortality.) BLP; ChTr, *sts.* 5 *and* 6;
FaBoEn, *st.* 5; GrCo-1, *sts.* 5, 9, *and* 10, *abr.;* OQP, *st.*
5; QP-1, *st.* 5
"There was a time when meadow, grove, and stream."
(Ode on Intimations of Immortality, *sts.* 1-2.) OQP;
QP-2
(Recollections of Early Childhood, *sts.* 1-5.) CBPC
"Thou, whose exterior semblance doth belie."
(Trailing Clouds of Glory, *st.* 8.) GrCo-2
Ode I/X/7: "Lamb's wool and leopard's cuffs." *Unknown,
tr. fr. Chinese by* James Legge. BoFr
Ode: "Listen to the Muse's lyre." Anacreon, *tr. fr. Greek by*
Thomas Moore. OuHeWo
Ode: "Love thy country, wish it well." George Bubb Doding-
ton. CEP; OBEC
(Shorten Sail.) OBEV (1st ed.)
Ode, An: "Merchant, to secure his treasure, The." Matthew
Prior. AWP; CEP; EiPP; ElSeCe; EnLoPo; InPo;
JAWP; LiA; PoE; PoRA; SeCL; TCEP; ViBoPo;
WBP
(Merchant to Secure His Treasure, The.) GTBS;
GTBS-D; GTBS-W; GTSE; GTSL; OnPM
(Song: "Merchant to secure his treasure, The.") AnFE;
BLV; EV-3; HBV; LiTL; OBEV; TrGrPo
Ode: "My heart rebels against my generation." George
Santayana. Odes, II. AnFE; APA; ATP; CoAnAm;
PoFr; TwAmPo; ViBoPo
Ode, An: "Now each creature joys the other." Samuel Daniel.
EIL; ElSeCe; LoBV; OBSC; SiCE; TuPP
Ode, An: "Now I find thy looks were feigned." Thomas
Lodge. *Fr.* Phyllis. EIL; OBSC; SiCE; TuPP
(Song: "Now I see thy looks were feigned.") LoBV
Ode: "O happy the huntsman . . .," V. Frederic Prokosch.
ViBoPo (1941 ed.)
Ode: "O tenderly the haughty day." Emerson. AA; DD,
abr.; IDAH; MPB; PaA; TCAP
(Ode Sung in the Town Hall, Concord, July 4, 1857.)
AnNE; APW; BAP; GN; IAP; LEAP; PoRL
Ode: "Oh Venice! Venice! when thy marble walls." Byron.
See Ode on Venice.
Ode: Of Cynthia. *Unknown.* SiCE
(Of Cynthia.) OBSC
Ode: "Of thee the Northman by his beachèd [*or* bleachèd]
galley." George Santayana. Odes, V. AnAmPo; AnFE;
APA; CoAnAm; LA; TwAmPo
(Ode to the Mediterranean.) EtS
Ode: Of Wit. Abraham Cowley. CEP; MeLP; MePo;
OAEP; SeCV-1; SeEP
(Of Wit.) OBS; ReEn
Ode: On the Death of W. B. Yeats. A. J. M. Smith.
BoCaPo; PeCV; TwCV
Ode II/I/5: "On the trees go the blows." *st.* 1. *Unknown,
tr. fr. Chinese by* James Legge. *See* Woodman's Ax, The.
Ode, An: On the Unveiling of the Shaw Memorial on Boston
Common. Thomas Bailey Aldrich. AA; HBV; MDAH;
PAH
Ode: "On yonder verdant hillock laid." Mark Akenside.
EV-3
Ode: "Once more the country calls." Allen Tate. *See* Ode
to Our Young Pro-Consuls of the Air.
Ode: "Peer of gods he seemeth to me, the blissful." Sappho.
See To a Bride.
Ode: Salute to the French Negro Poets. Frank O'Hara.
NeAP
Ode: "Sculptor, wouldst thou glad my soul." Anacreon, *tr.
fr. Greek by* Thomas Moore. OuHeWo
Ode: "See, Mignonne, hath not the rose." Pierre de Ronsard.
See Rose, The.
Ode, An: "Sire of the rising day." Lord De Tabley. OBVV;
PoVP
Ode: "Sleep sweetly in your humble graves." Henry Timrod.
See At Magnolia Cemetery.
Ode: "Slowly the black earth gains upon the yellow." George
Santayana. Odes, IV. AnFE; APA; CoAnAm; TwAmPo
Ode: Solitude, at an Inn. Thomas Warton, the Younger.
CEP
Ode: "Spacious firmament on high, The." Addison. *See*
Spacious Firmament on High, The.

Ode: Sung in the Town Hall, Concord, July 4, 1857. Emer-
son. *See* Ode: "O tenderly the haughty day."
Ode: "Tell me, thou soul of her I love." James Thomson.
See Tell Me, Thou Soul of Her I Love.
Ode VIII: That All Other Creatures Have Their Abiding in
Heaven, Hell, Earth, Air, Water, or Fire; but He in All
of Them. Francis Davison. ReIE
Ode I/VI/10: "There is a solitary russet pear tree." *Un-
known, tr. fr. Chinese by* James Legge. BoFr
Ode I/X/10: "There is a solitary russet pear tree." *Un-
known, tr. fr. Chinese by* James Legge. BoFr
Ode: "They journeyed." Ibn al-Arabi, *tr. fr. Arabic by* R. A.
Nicholson. AWP; LiTW
Ode, An: To Himself ("Come leave the loathed stage").
Ben Jonson. *See* Ode to Himself ("Come leave . . .").
Ode, An: To Himself ("Where do'st thou careless lie").
Ben Jonson. *See* Ode to Himself, An ("Where do'st
thou . . .").
Ode: To My Pupils. W. H. Auden. *See* Which Side Am I
Supposed to Be On?
Ode: To the Cuckoo. Michael Bruce, *revised by* John Logan.
See To the Cuckoo.
Ode: To the Roc. William J. Courthope. *Fr.* The Paradise
of Birds. VA
Ode: "Tonight is so coarse with chocolate." Louis MacNeice.
ChMo
Ode: "Until thine hands clasp girdlewise." Sadi, *tr. fr. Per-
sian by* R. A. Nicholson. AWP
Ode: "Vulcan! hear your glorious task." Anacreon, *tr. fr.
Greek by* Thomas Moore. OuHeWo
Ode: "We are the music-makers," 3 *sts.* Arthur O'Shaugh-
nessy. BLV; CBOV; EnLi-2; EnLit; GBV (1952 ed.);
GTBS; GTBS-D; GTIV; GTSE; GTSL; HBV, 9 *sts.;*
InP; LEAP; LiTG; MaRV; MBP; MoBrPo (1942 ed.);
NeHB; NeMA; OBEV; OBVV; OnYI; OxBI, 2 *sts.;*
PoFr; PoFS; PoRL, 6 *sts.;* PoVP, 9 *sts.;* PreP; TCEP;
TOP; TreF; TrGrPo; TSW; TSWC; TVSH; ViBoPo;
VLEP; WHA
(Music-Makers, The.) BMEP; OtMeF
(Poets, The.) PIAE; YT
(We Are the Music-Makers.) GTBS-W; OQP; QP-2
Ode: "Weep, ah weep love's losing." Imr el Kais. *See*
Weep Love's Losing.
Ode: "What god will choose me from this labouring nation."
George Santayana. Odes, I. AnFE; APA; CoAnAm;
TwAmPo
Ode, An: "When Britain first, at heaven's command." James
Thomson. *See* Rule, Britannia!
Ode: "When I walk forth into the woods." Barnabe Barnes.
Fr. Parthenophil and Parthenophe. TuPP
Ode: "Where do'st thou careless lie." Ben Jonson. *See* Ode
to Himself, An ("Where do'st thou . . .").
Ode: "Who can Support the anguish of Love?" Ibn al-Arabi,
tr. fr. Arabic by R. A. Nicholson. AWP; LiTW
Ode, An: "Why doth heaven bear a sun." Barnabe Barnes.
Fr. Parthenophil and Parthenophe. EIL; OBSC
Ode: "Why will they never sleep." John Peale Bishop.
LiTA; LiTM; MoPo; MoVE; NePA
Ode: "Without the evening dew and showers," 6 *sts.* Charles
Cotton. ViBoPo
Ode: "Women tell me every day, The." Anacreon, *tr. fr.
Greek by* Thomas Moore. LoBV; OuHeWo
Ode I/X/12: "Would you gather the liquorice." *Unknown,
tr. fr. Chinese by* James Legge. BoFr
Ode: Written during the Battle of Dunkirk, May, 1940. Sir
Herbert Read. *See* Ode Written during the Battle of
Dunkirk . . .
Ode: Written in the Beginning of the Year 1746. William
Collins. *See* How Sleep the Brave.
Ode for a Master Mariner Ashore. Louise Imogen Guiney.
AA; GoBC; JKCP
Ode for a Social Meeting. Oliver Wendell Holmes. APW;
BOHV; LPS-3; PIR
Ode for Ben Jonson, An. Robert Herrick. AWP; BEL;
CBOV; CoBE; EG; ElSeCe; EM-1; EnLi-1; EnLit;
EV-2; InPo; InvP; JAWP; LoBV; PIR; PoE; PoFS;
PreP; PtP; RiBV; SeEP; TOP; TrGrPo; TwHP;
UnPo; WBP
(Ode for Him, An.) EPS; OAEP; OBS; SeCV-1
(Ode for Him [Ben Jonson], An.) MaPo
(Ode to Ben Jonson.) LPS-3
(To Ben Jonson.) BCEP; LEAP, *abr.*
Ode for Decoration Day. Theodore P. Cook. MDAH
Ode for Decoration Day. Henry Peterson. MDAH; OHIP;
PEOR
"O gallant brothers of the generous South," *sel.* AA;
FaBoBe
Ode for Decoration Day. Henry Timrod. PoRL
Ode for Him, An. Robert Herrick. *See* Ode for Ben Jonson,
An.
Ode for Memorial Day. Paul Laurence Dunbar. MDAH
Ode for Music on St. Cecilia's Day. Pope. CEP
(Ode on St. Cecilia's Day.) TCEP
Descend, Ye Nine, *sel.* GN

Ode for Soft Voice. Michael McClure. NeAP
Ode for the American Dead in Korea. Thomas McGrath. NePoEA
Ode for the Burial of a Citizen. John Ciardi. MiAP
Ode for the Diamond Jubilee of Queen Victoria, 1897, *sel.* Francis Thompson.
"First went the holy poets, two on two." PtP
Ode for the Fourth of July, 1876, An. James Russell Lowell. CoBA
Flawless His Heart, *sel.* MC; PAH
Ode for the New Year, An. *At. to* John Gay. OxBoLi
Ode for Washington's Birthday. Oliver Wendell Holmes. DD; GA; PSO, *abr.*
(Washington's Birthday.) PEDC; WOAH, *abr.*
Ode from the French, *sel.* Byron.
"There, where death's brief pang was quickest."
(Murat.) LPS-3
Ode—Imitated from the Psalms. Nicolas Joseph Laurent Gilbert, *tr. fr. French by* Thomas Walsh. CAW
Ode in a Night of Overhanging Weather. Vincent McHugh. WaKn
Ode in Honor of St. Cecilia's Day, An. Dryden. *See* Alexander's Feast.
Ode in Imitation of Alcaeus, An. Sir William Jones. *See* What Constitutes a State?
Ode, in Imitation of Pastor Fido. George Lyttelton. CEP
Ode in May. Sir William Watson. BMEP; CBOV; GTML; MBP; MoBrPo (1942 ed.); OBEV; OBVV; PC; PoeT; PoVP; WGRP
Ode in Memory of the American Volunteers Fallen for France. Alan Seeger. PAH
Ode in the Praise of Sack, An. *Unknown.* OBS
Ode in Time of Hesitation, An. William Vaughn Moody. AmPP; AnFE; APA; ATP; CoAnAm; HBV; LBMV; OxBA; PaA; PAH; TOP
Sels.
No Hint of Stain, *st.* 9. AA
Robert Gould Shaw, *sts.* 5 *and* 6. AA; MDAH
Ode Inscribed to the Earl of Sunderland at Windsor, An. Thomas Tickell. OBEC
Ode Inscribed to W. H. Channing. Emerson. AmP; AmPo; AmPP; AnNE; APW; CoBA; CoV; IAP; MOAP; OnAP; OxBA; PoLFOT; TOP; WoL
"God who made New Hampshire, The," *sel.* ViBoPo
Ode of Johannes Secundus, An. Johannes Secundus, *tr. fr. Latin by* Charles Cotton. BoFr
Ode of Lament. Randolph Jeck. WhC
Ode of the Birth of Our Saviour, An. Robert Herrick. *See* Ode on the Birth of Our Saviour, An.
Ode of the Sun to the People's Army. "Pablo Neruda," *tr. fr. Spanish by* H. R. Hays. TwSpPo
Ode on a Distant Prospect of Eton College. Thomas Gray. ATP (1935 ed.); BCEP; BEL; CaAE; CEP; CoBE; EiPP; EM-1; EnLi-2 (1949 ed.); EnLit; EPP; EV-3; ExPo; GTBS; GTBS-D; GTBS-W; GTSE; GTSL; LiTB; LiTG; OAEP; OBEC; OuHeWo; PoE; PoEL-3; SeCeV; TOP; TwHP; ViBoPo
(On a Distant Prospect of Eton College.) HBV
Where Ignorance Is Bliss, *sel.* TreF
Ode on a Grecian Urn. Keats. AnEnPo; AnFE; AtBAP; ATP; AWP; BCEP; BEL; BLV; BoLiVe; BPN; CaAE; CBE; CBOV; ChER; CoBE; CoEV; EM-2; EmBrPo; EnL; EnLi-2; EnLit; EnLP; EnRP; EPN; EPP; ERP; EV-4; ExPo; FaBoBe; FaBoEn; FaFP; FiP; GEPC; GTBS-W; GTSL; HBV; HBVY; HiLiEn; HoPM; InP; InPo; JAWP; KN; LEAP; LiA; LiTB; LiTG; LoBV; LPS-2; MaPo; MCCG; OAEP; OBEV; OBRV; OHFP; OuHeWo; PFE; PIAE; PIR; Po; PoE; PoEL-4; PoeMoYo; PoFS; PoMa; PreP; PYM; REAL; ReaPo; RiBV; SeCeV; ShBV-4; TCEP; TOP; TreF; TrGrPo; TVSH; TwHP; TwP; TyEnPo; UnPo; WBP; WHA
(Ode to a Grecian Urn.) PC
(On a Grecian Urn.) AEV; TwCrTr; ViBoPo
Ode on a Jar of Pickles. Bayard Taylor. PA
Ode, on a Sermon against Glory. Mark Akenside. CEP
Ode on Advancing Age. Richard Watson Dixon. GTML
Ode on Christmas. J. E. Clinton. PEOR
Ode on Conflicting Claims. Richard Watson Dixon. VA
Ode on Indolence. Keats. BPN; EmBrPo; EnRP; GTBS-W; LiTB; TwHP
(Ode to Indolence.) GEPC
Ode on Intimations of Immortality from Recollections of Early Childhood. Wordsworth. *See* Ode: Intimations of Immortality . . .
Ode on Leaving the Great Town. Thomas Randolph. *See* Ode to Mr. Anthony Stafford to Hasten Him into the Country, An.
Ode on Lyric Poetry. Sir James Marriott. Po
Ode on Melancholy. Keats. AnFE; AtBAP; ATP; BCEP; BEL; BLV; BoLiVe; BPN; CaAE; CoBE; EM-2; EmBrPo; EnL; EnLi-2; EnLit; EnLP; EnRP; EPN; ERP; EV-4; ExPo; FaBoEn; FiP; GEPC; GTBS-W; LiTB; LO; MaPo; OAEP; OBEV; PoE; PoEL-4; PoFS; PoRA; PreP; ReaPo; RiBV; SeCeV; TCEP; TOP; TreFS; TrGrPo; TwHP; TwP; TyEnPo
("No, no, go not to Lethe, neither twist.") EG
(On Melancholy.) HBV; LEAP; ViBoPo
Ode on Miss Harriet Hanbury at Six Years Old, An. Sir Charles Hanbury Williams. OBEC
Ode on Nothing. Edward Harry William Meyerstein. MM
Ode on St. Cecelia's Day. Pope. *See* Ode for Music on St. Cecilia's Day.
Ode on Science, *with music.* Jezaniah Sumner. TrAS
Ode on Solitude. Pope. ATP; AWP; CEP; EV-3; ExPo; FiP; GoBC; HBV; HBVY; InPo; JAWP; OAEP; OBEC; OnPP; OTPC (1923 ed.); PoE; PoFS; PoRA; SeCeV; SeCL; SN; TreFS; ViBoPo; WBP
(Contented Man, The.) InMe
(Happy the Man.) MaRV
("Happy the man whose wish and care.") EG
(Ode to Solitude.) InvP; LPS-1
(Quiet Life, The.) ALV; BPP; GTBS; GTBS-D; GTBS-W; PoToHe; WP
(Solitude.) BLV; BoLiVe; FaFP; GTSE; GTSL; MCCG; NeHB; PECK; PG (1955 ed.); TrGrPo
Ode on Superstition, *sel.* Vincenzo Monti, *tr. fr. Italian by* William Dean Howells.
"Tyrant has fallen, The." PoFr
Ode on the Birth of Our Saviour, An. Robert Herrick. AnEC; COAH; GN, *sts.* 1–3; OTPC (1923 ed.)
Instead of Neat Inclosures, *sel.* ChTr
Ode on the Celebration of the Battle of Bunker Hill, June 17, 1825, *sel.* Grenville Mellen.
Lonely Bugle Grieves, The. AA; BAP; IDAH; LEAP
Ode on the Death of a Favorite [*or* Favourite] Cat, Drowned in a Tub [*or* Bowl] of Goldfishes. Thomas Gray. ATP; BEL; CaAE; CEP; EM-1; EnLi-2 (1949 ed.); EnLit; FaBoBe; HoPM; KN; NeHB; OAEP; OBEC; OTPC (1923 ed.); PoE; PoEL-3; TOP; TyEnPo
(On a Favorite [*or* Favourite] Cat, Drowned in a Tub of Goldfishes.) BeLS; CG; EV-3; GBV (1952 ed.); GN; GTBS; GTBS-D; GTBS-W; GTSE; GTSL; InvP; LiTB; LiTG; MCCG; OBEV; OnSP; ShBV-2; WP
(On the Death of a Favourite [*or* Favorite] Cat, Drowned in a Tub of Goldfishes.) BOHV; CIV; ExPo; HBV; InMe; PoC; PoRA; SeCeV
Ode on the Death of Don Sebastian. Fernando de Herrera, *tr. fr. Spanish.* AnSpL-1, *tr. by* W. Herbert; TeCS, *tr. by* Eleanor L. Turnbull
Ode on the Death of His Father. Jorge Manrique, *tr. fr. Spanish by* Longfellow. AnSpL-1, *abr.;* TeCS; WoL, *abr.*
(Coplas on the Death of His Father.) LyMA
(Coplas on the Death of His Father, the Grandmaster of Santiago, *tr. by* Thomas Walsh.) CAW
Ode on the Death of Mr. Thomson. William Collins. EiPP; EV-3; OBEC; PtP
(Ode on the Death of Thomson.) SeCePo
Ode on the Death of the Duke of Wellington. Tennyson. BEL; BHV; BPN; EM-2; EmBrPo; GEPC; HBV; OBVV; PCD; PoVP; ShGoBo, *abr.;* TOP; TVSH; TyEnPo; UnPo (1st ed.); VA; ViPo; ViPP; VLEP
Sels.
"Bury the Great Duke." BMEP
"Thank him who isled us here, and roughly set." PoFr
What Know We Greater than the Soul? *br. sel.* MaRV
Ode on the Death of Thomson. William Collins. *See* Ode on the Death of Mr. Thomson.
Ode on the Despoilers of Learning in an American University (1947), An. Yvor Winters. ExPo
Ode on the Intimations of Immortality from Recollections of Early Childhood. Wordsworth. *See* Ode: Intimations of Immortality . . .
Ode on the Morning of Christ's Nativity. Milton. *See* On the Morning of Christ's Nativity.
Ode on the Pleasure Arising from Vicissitude. Thomas Gray. CEP, *abr.;* EV-3; GTBS; GTBS-D; GTBS-W; GTSE; GTSL; OBEC
Ode on the Poetical Character. William Collins. CEP; EiPP; EnRP; OAEP; PoEL-3; PoFS
Ode on the Poets. Keats. *See* Ode: "Bards of Passion and of Mirth."
Ode, An, on the Popular Superstitions of the Highlands of Scotland [Considered as the Subject of Poetry]. William Collins. CEP; EiPP; EnRP; EV-3; OAEP; OBEC
Sels.
St. Kilda. FaBoEn
"Unbounded is thy range." BCEP
Ode on the Spring. Thomas Gray. BrBE; CEP; EV-3; GTBS; GTBS-D; GTBS-W; GTSE; GTSL; HBV
(Spring.) LPS-2
Ode on Venice. Byron. EmBrPo
(Ode: "Oh Venice! Venice! when thy marble walls.") EPP
Sels.
"Name of Commonwealth is past and gone, The," *fr.* IV. PoFr
Race with Death, The, *fr.* I. LH

Ode on Vicissitude, *sel.* William Julius Mickle.
Seasons, The. RO
Ode pour l'Election de Son Sepulchre. Ezra Pound. *See* E. P. Ode pour l'Election de Son Sepulchre.
Ode Recited at the Harvard Commemoration, July 21, 1865. James Russell Lowell. AA; AmPP; BlG; CoBA; HBV; IAP; PaA; PAH; REAL; TCAP; TOP
(Commemoration Ode, The.) AnAmPo; LA
Sels.
Abraham Lincoln, VI. GDAH; LPS-3 (*fr.* V *and* VI); PAP
(Lincoln.) AnNE
(Martyr Chief, The, *fr.* V *and* VI.) LBAH
(Our Martyr-Chief.) OHIP; PEDC, *abr.*
("Such was he, our Martyr-Chief.") InP
Bow Down, Dear Land, XI, *abr.*, *and* XII. DD
"I, with uncovered head," *fr.* VIII *and* XII. OHIP
"Many loved Truth, and lavished life's best oil," III, VIII, *and* XII. PoFr
(Harvard Commemoration Ode, III *and* IV.) PFY
Martyr Chief, The, *abr.*, *fr.* VI. OQP; PSO; QP-1
(Abraham Lincoln.) PEOR
(Commemoration Ode, The.) PGD
(Lincoln.) DD
My Country, XII. GDAH
Our Country Saved, *fr.* XI *and* XII. IDAH
"Weak-winged is song," I-IV, VI, *and* IX. LEAP
"Whither leads the path," V.
(Harvard Commemoration Ode.) MDAH
Ode, Sacred to the Memory of Mrs. Oswald of Auchencruive. Burns. EM-1
Ode Sung in the Town Hall, Concord, July 4, 1857. Emerson. *See* Ode: "O tenderly the haughty day."
Ode Sung on the Occasion of Decorating the Graves of the Confederate Dead, at Magnolia Cemetery, Charleston, S.C. Henry Timrod. *See* At Magnolia Cemetery.
Ode to a Bobtailed Cat. *Unknown.* BOHV; CIV
Ode to a Butterfly. Thomas Wentworth Higginson. AA; FaBoBe; HBV
Ode to a Chosen Girl. Hywel ab Owain Gwynedd. *See* Love Poem, A.
Ode to a Cud-chewing Cow. *Unknown.* DDA
Ode to a Dawg. Eloise Burtis. AlBD
Ode to a Dental Hygienist. Earnest A. Hooton. FiBHP; WhC
Ode to a Friend. William Mason. OBEC
Ode to a Friend on His Leaving a Favourite Village in Hampshire, *sel.* Thomas Warton, the Younger.
"Ah, mourn, thou loved retreat!" EnSW
Ode to a Frog. George O'Neil. PFE
Ode to a Garden. Annie Charlotte Dalton. OCL
Ode to a Grecian Urn. Keats. *See* Ode on a Grecian Urn.
Ode to a London Fog. *Unknown.* PA
Ode to a Monk on the Tai-pei Mountains. Ts'en Ts'an, *tr. fr. Chinese by* Yuan Chia-hua. WhP
Ode to a Nightingale. Keats. AEV; AnEnPo; AnFE; AtBAP; ATP; AWP; BCEP; BEL; BLA; BLV; BoLiVe; BPN; CaAE; CBE; CBOV; ChER; CoBE; CoEV; EM-2; EmBrPo; EnL; EnLi-2; EnLit; EnLP; EnRP; EPN; EPP; ERP; EV-4; ExPo; FaBoBe; FaBoEn; FaFP; FiP; GBV; GEPC; GTBS; GTBS-D; GTBS-W; GTSE; GTSL; HBV; HBVY; HiLiEn; InP; InPo; JAWP; LEAP; LiA; LiTB; LiTG; LoBV; LPS-1; MaPo; MCCG; OAEP; OBEV; OBRV; OtMeF; OuHeWo; PC; PFE; PIAE; PIR; Po; PoE; PoEL-4; PoeMoYo; PoFS; PoRA; PreP; PYM; REAL; ReaPo; RiBV; SeCeV; ShBV-3; SN; TCEP; TOP; TreF; TrGrPo; TVSH; TwHP; TwP; TyEnPo; UnPo; WBP; WoL
(Ode to the Nightingale.) WHA
(To a Nightingale.) ChTr; ViBoPo
Nightingale, The, *st.* 7. DD
Ode to a Side Car. "J. P. H." PaA
Ode to a Skylark. Shelley. *See* To a Skylark.
Ode to a Water Nymph. William Mason. Po
Ode to a Young Lady, Somewhat Too Sollicitous about Her Manner of Expression. William Shenstone. CEP
Ode to Anactoria. Sappho. *See* To a Bride.
Ode to Aphrodite. Sappho, *tr. fr. Greek.* AWP, *tr. by* William Ellery Leonard; EnLi-1, *tr. by* Sir Edwin Arnold; LiA, *tr. by* John Addington Symonds; OuHeWo, *tr. by* Sir Edwin Arnold, *wr. at. to* John Addington Symonds
(Hymn to Aphrodite, *tr. by* John Addington Symonds.) GrR
(Immortal Aphrodite, *tr. by* Lindley W. Hubbell.) LiTW
("Throned in splendor, deathless, O Aphrodite," *tr. by* Richmond Lattimore.) GrPo
(To Aphrodite, *tr. by* Sir William Marris.) GrL; OxBG; GrPE, *tr. by* F. L. Lucas
Ode to Autumn. Thomas Hood. *See* Autumn ("I saw old Autumn").
Ode to Autumn. Keats. *See* To Autumn.
Ode to Beauty. Emerson. IAP; MOAP; PoEL-4
Ode to Ben Jonson. Robert Herrick. *See* Ode for Ben Jonson, An.
Ode to Bolívar, *sel.* Joaquín de Olmedo, *tr. fr. Spanish by* Elizabeth Selden.
"Held by a federal bond from pole to pole." BoFr
Ode to City Snow. Arthur H. Folwell. LauV
Ode to Creation. Addison. *See* Spacious Firmament on High, The.
Ode to Discord. *Unknown.* PC
Ode to Dr. William Sancroft, *sel.* Swift.
Pleased with an Empty Swelling. BeR
Ode to Duty. Wordsworth. AWP; BCEP; BEL; EM-2; EmBrPo; EnLit; EnLP; EnRP; EPN; EPP; ERP; EV-3; GEPC; GrCo-1, *abr.*; GTBS; GTBS-D; GTBS-W; GTSE; GTSL; HBV; InPo; JAWP; MaRV; OBEV; OBRV; PIAE; PoFS; REAL; TCEP; TOP; TreFS; TyEnPo; WBP; WGRP
(To Duty.) LH
Stern Daughter of the Voice of God, *sel.* HBVY
Ode, An, to Eight Cats Belonging to Israel Mendez, a Jew, *abr.* "Peter Pindar." PoC
Ode to England, *sels.* William Wilberforce Lord. AA
Keats.
Wordsworth.
Ode to Eve. Edwin Meade Robinson. InMe
Ode to Evening. William Collins. AEV; AnEnPo; AnFE; ATP; AWP; BCEP; BEL; BLV; BrBE; CaAE; CBOV; CEP; CoBE; CoEV; EiPP; EM-1; EnL; EnLi-2; EnRP; EnSW; EPP; EV-3; ExPo; FaBoBe; FaBoEn; GTSL; HBV; InP; InPo; JAWP; KN; LEAP; LiTB; LiTG; LoBV; OAEP; OBEC; OBEV; OuHeWo; PIAE; Po; PoE; PoEL-3; PoFS; PreP; ReaPo; RiBV; SeCePo; SeCeV; TCEP; TOP; TrGrPo; TwHP; TyEnPo; UnPo (1st ed.); ViBoPo; WBP; WHA
("If aught of oaten stop, or pastoral song.") EG
(To Evening.) AtBAP; GTBS; GTBS-D; GTBS-W; GTSE; ShBV-4
Ode to Evening. Joseph Warton, *wr. at. to* Thomas Warton, the Younger. ATP; UnPo (1st ed.)
Ode to Fancy. Joseph Warton. CEP; EiPP
Invocation to Fancy, *sel.* OBEC
Ode to Fanny, *sel.* Keats.
"Ah! dearest love, sweet home of all my fears." ChER
Ode to Fear. William Collins. BrBE; CEP; EiPP; OAEP; PIAE; Po; TrGrPo, *abr.*
Ode to Fear. Allen Tate. BLV; MM
Ode to Felipe Ruiz. Luis de León, *tr. fr. Spanish by* Aubrey F. G. Bell. TeCS
Ode to Fortune. Fitz-Greene Halleck *and* Joseph Rodman Drake. *Fr.* The Croaker Papers. AA
Ode to Francisco Salinas, *abr.* Luis de León, *tr. fr. Spanish by* Ida Farnell. AnSpL-1
(Ode to Salinas, *tr. by* Aubrey F. G. Bell.) TeCS
Ode to Freedom. Thomas of Strengnaes, *tr. fr. Swedish by* Elias Gordon. PoFr
Ode to Himself ("Come leave the loathed stage"). Ben Jonson. CoEV; SeEP
(Ode, An: To Himself.) EPS; EV-2; OBS; ReEn
Ode to Himself, An ("Where do'st thou careless lie"). Ben Jonson. AtBAP; EV-2; ExPo; FaBoEn; LiTB; NBE; OAEP; OBS; PoEL-2; PoFr; SeCePo; SeCeV; SeCV-1; SeEP; TuPP
(To Himself.) SeCL
Ode to Himself. Sir Walter Raleigh. WhC
Ode to His Mistress. Abraham Cowley. *See* To His Mistress.
Ode to Independence, *sel.* Tobias Smollett.
Independence. OBEC
("Thy spirit, Independence, let me share!") PoFr
Ode to Indolence. Keats. *See* Ode on Indolence.
Ode to Jamestown. James Kirke Paulding. PAH
Ode to Joy. Frank O'Hara. NeAP
Ode to Joy. Schiller, *tr. fr. German by* Norman Macleod. LiA; LiTW
(Hymn to Joy, *abr.*, *tr. by* Edgar A. Bowring.) GrCo-2
Ode to Leven Water. Tobias Smollett. CEP; EBSV; EV-3; OBEV
Ode to Liberty. Thomas Chatterton. *See* Freedom's War Song.
Ode to Liberty. Shelley. BEL; GEPC
Sels.
"Sun and the serenest moon, The." NBE
"Thou huntress swifter than the moon!" PoFr
Ode to Lowell House. Frederick Bertolet. CAG
Ode to Machines. Louis Ginsberg. PoMa
Ode to Maia, Written on May Day. Keats. *See* Fragment of an Ode to Maia.
Ode to Memory. William Shenstone. Po
Ode to Michael Goldberg's Birth and Other Births. Frank O'Hara. NeAP
Ode to Mr. [*or* Master] Anthony Stafford to Hasten Him into the Country, An. Thomas Randolph. ElSeCe; EV-2; FaBoEn; HBV; LEAP; OBEV; OBS; SeCL; SeEP; ViBoPo

("Come, spur away.") EG; NLK, *2 sts.*
(Ode on Leaving the Great Town.) GoTL
Ode to Mr. F——, An. Allan Ramsay. CEP
Ode to Mother Carey's Chicken. Theodore Watts-Dunton. *See* Mother Carey's Chicken.
Ode to Music, *sels.* Robert Bridges. TwCV
Dirge: "Man born of desire," VII.
"Love to love calleth," V.
Ode to My Ingenious Friend, Mr. Thomas Godfrey. Nathaniel Evans. IAP
Ode to Myself, An. Thomas Dermody. OnYI
Ode to Naples. Shelley. ATP (1935 ed.)
"I stood within the city disinterred," *sel.* EPN
Ode to Napoleon Buonaparte. Byron. BCEP; BPN; EV-4
Sels.
Cincinnatus of the West, The. PoRL
Washington, *st.* 19. BoHiPo; DD; GA; MC; OHIP; PaA; PAH
Ode to New Jersey. Elias F. Carr. PoRL
Ode to Our Young Pro-Consuls of the Air. Allen Tate. AmPP (3d ed.)
(Ode: "Once more the country calls.") WaP
Ode to Peace. William Tennant. LPS-2
Ode to Peace. *Unknown.* PAH
Ode to Pity. William Collins. CEP; EiPP
Ode to Psyche. Keats. BCEP; BPN; BrBE; CaAE; ChER; EM-2; EmBrPo; EnLP; EnRP; EPN; ERP; EV-4; GEPC; GTBS-W; HBV; LEAP; LiA; LiTB; LoBV; MaPo; OAEP; OBEV; OBRV; PoEL-4; TwHP; TyEnPo; WHA
(To Psyche.) TwCrTr; ViBoPo
"Surely I dreamt to-day, or did I see," *sel.* LO
Ode to Quinbus Flestrin. Pope. OAEP
Ode to Rain. *Unknown, tr. fr. Russian.* PCH
Ode to Retirement. Luis de León, *tr. fr. Spanish.* AnSpL-1
Ode to Rhys ap Maredudd of Tywyn. Dafydd Nanmor, *tr. fr. Welsh by* Sir Idris Bell. PrWP
Ode to Salinas. Luis de León. *See* Ode to Francisco Salinas.
Ode to Simplicity. William Collins. BEL; CEP; EiPP; EnLi-2 (1949 ed.); EnRP; EV-3; GTSL; OBEC; OBEV; PoFS; UnPo (1st ed.)
Ode to Sir William Temple, *sels.* Swift.
Nature and the Poet. BeR
Our Knowledge. BeR
Ode to Slavdom, *sel.* Petar Preradovic, *tr. fr. Croatian by* Paul Selver.
"But so long as/ This prison-planet." PoFr
Ode to Sleep. Paul Hamilton Hayne. TCAP
Ode to Sleep. Fernando de Herrera, *tr. fr. Spanish by* Eleanor L. Turnbull. TeCS
Ode to Sleep. Tobias Smollett. PoP
Ode to Solitude. James Grainger. *See* Solitude.
Ode to Solitude. Pope. *See* Ode on Solitude.
Ode to Spain—after the Revolution of March. Manuel José Quintana, *tr. fr. Spanish by* Thomas Walsh. AnSpL-2
"Swear, 'Rather death than tyrants in the land!'" *sel.* PoFr
Ode to Spring. Anna Letitia Barbauld. EV-3
Ode to Spring in the Metropolis, An. Sir Owen Seaman. FiBHP; WhC
Ode to Stephen Dowling Bots, Dec'd. "Mark Twain." *Fr.* The Adventures of Huckleberry Finn. FiBHP
Ode to Thaliarchus. Horace. *See* To Thaliarchus.
Ode to the American Flag. Joseph Rodman Drake. *See* American Flag, The.
Ode to the Cambro-Britons [*or* -Britains] and Their Harp, His Ballad of Agincourt. Michael Drayton. *See* Agincourt.
Ode to the Chinese Paper Snake. Richard Eberhart. CrMA
Ode to the Confederate Dead. Allen Tate. AnFE; ATP (1953 ed.); CoAnAm; FaBoMo; InPo; LiTA; LiTM; MAP; MoAB; MoAmPo; MOAP; MoPo; MoVE; NP; OxBA; ReMP; SeCeV; SPP; TwAmPo; UnPo; ViBoPo (1958 ed.)
Ode to the Country Gentlemen of England, An, *sel.* Mark Akenside.
England, Unprepared for War. OBEC
Ode to the Cuckoo. Michael Bruce. EiPP
Ode to the Departing Year. Samuel Taylor Coleridge. EmBrPo; EnRP
Ode to the Earl of Northumberland. *sel.* Christopher Smart.
On a Bed of Guernsey Lilies. OBEC
Ode to the Evening Star. Mark Akenside. CEP; OBEC
(Nightingale, The.) EV-3; HBV, *sl. abr.*; OBEV, *sl. abr.*
(To the Evening Star.) PoEL-3
Nightingale, The, *sel.* RO
Ode to the Fatherland, *sel.* Manuel María Flores, *tr. fr. Spanish by* Alice Stone Blackwell.
"We lift our standard to the mountain top." PoFr
Ode to the Flag. Charles C. Crellin. PEDC
Ode to the Fourth of July, *with music.* Daniel George. TrAS
Ode to the Framers of the Frame Bill, An. Byron. CoMu
Ode to the Germans. Thomas Campbell. PoFr
Ode to the Hayden Planetarium. Arthur Guiterman. ImOP
Ode to the Human Heart. Laman Blanchard. BOHV; InMe; NA
Ode to the Inhabitants of Pennsylvania. *Unknown.* PAH
Ode to the Lighthouse at Malta. Duque de Rivas, *tr. fr. Spanish.* AnSpL-2
Ode to the Maguire. *At. to* Eochadh O'Hussey. *See* O'Hussey's Ode to the Maguire.
Ode to the Mediterranean. George Santayana. *See* Ode: "Of thee the Northman . . ."
Ode to the Moon. Thomas Hood. OBVV
Ode to the Nightingale. Keats. *See* Ode to a Nightingale.
Ode to the Nightingale, *parody.* John Kendall. InMe
Ode to the North-east Wind. Charles Kingsley. EV-5; GN; GTBS; TVSH
(North-east Wind, The, *much abr.*) OTPC
(Welcome, A.) LH
Ode to the Pig: His Tail. Walter R. Brooks. LiL
Ode to the Pious Memory of the Accomplished Young Lady, Mrs. Anne Killigrew. Dryden. *See* To the Pious Memory of the Accomplished Young Lady, Mrs. Anne Killigrew.
Ode to the Poets. Keats. *See* Ode: "Bards of Passion and of Mirth."
Ode to the Present Century. Thomas Merton. JKCP (1955 ed.)
Ode to the Sea. Howard Baker. OxBA; UnPo (1st ed.)
Ode to the Setting Sun. Francis Thompson. EmBrPo; GoBC
Sels.
"And now, O shaken from thine antique throne." VLEP
"If with exultant tread." OHIP
Prelude: "Wailful sweetness of the violin, The." VLEP
Sun, The. MBP; MoAB; MoBrPo
Ode to the Sky of the New Atlantis. Emilio Oribe. *See* Song to the Glory of the Sky of America.
Ode to the Spirit of Earth in Autumn. George Meredith. EmBrPo
"Great Mother Nature! teach me, like thee," *sel.* EPN
Ode to the Spirit of Life. James Harold Manning. CPG
Ode to the Spleen, An. Countess of Winchilsea. *See* Spleen, The.
Ode to the Virgin. Petrarch. *See* To the Virgin Mary.
Ode to the Virginian Voyage. Michael Drayton. *See* To the Virginian Voyage.
Ode to the West Wind. Edwin Christmas. ReTS
Ode to the West Wind. Shelley. AEV; AnEnPo; AnFE; ATP; AWP; BCEP; BEL; BLV; BoLiVe; BPN; CaAE; CBE; CBOV; CBPC; CH; CoBE; CoEV; EM-2; EmBrPo; EnL; EnLi-2; EnLit; EnRP; EPN; EPP; ERP; EV-4; ExPo; FaBoBe; FaBoEn; FaFP; FiP; GEPC; GTBS; GTBS-D; GTBS-W; GTSE; GTSL; HBV; HiLiEn; InP; InPo; JAWP; LEAP; LiTB; LiTG; LoBV; MaPo; MCCG; OAEP; OBEV; OBRV; OHFP; OTPC (1946 ed.); OuHeWo; PFE; PIAE; PoE; PoEL-4; PoeMoYo; PoFS; PoMa; PoRA; PreP; PYM; REAL; ReaPo; RiBV; SeCeV; ShBV-4; TCEP; TOP; TreFS; TrGrPo; TwHP; TyEnPo; UnPo; ViBoPo; WBP; WHA
Sels.
"Make me thy lyre, even as the forest is." MaRV
"O lift me as a wave, a leaf, a cloud!" PC
West Wind, The, *2 ll.* PCH
Ode to Tobacco. Charles Stuart Calverley. ALV; BOHV, FiBHP; HBV; InMe; LPS-3; PIR; TOP; WhC
Ode to Tranquillity. Samuel Taylor Coleridge. BPN; EmBrPo
Ode to Walt Whitman. Stephen Vincent Benét. PtP
Ode to Walt Whitman. Federico García Lorca, *tr. fr. Spanish by* Stephen Spender *and* J. L. Gili. KN
Ode to Winter. Thomas Campbell. BSV; EBSV; EV-4; GTBS; GTBS-D; GTBS-W; GTSE; GTSL
Ode to Wisdom. Elizabeth Carter. OBEC
Ode to Work in Springtime. Thomas R. Ybarra. BOHV; HBMV
Ode to Zion. Judah Halevi, *tr. fr. Hebrew by* Nina Davis Salaman. TrJP
Ode, An, upon a Question Moved, Whether Love Should Continue for Ever? Lord Herbert of Cherbury. CoEV; LiTL; MeLP; MePo; OBS; SeEP
Sels.
"Long, their fixed eyes to heaven bent." LO
"O no, beloved, I am most sure." ViBoPo
Ode upon Doctor Harvey. Abraham Cowley. PoEL-2
Ode upon Liberty, *sels.* Abraham Cowley.
Liberty. GrCo-1
"'Tis morning; well; I fain would yet sleep on." PoFr
Ode, An, upon Occasion of His Majesties Proclamation in the Year 1630. Sir Richard Fanshawe. *See* Now War Is All the World About.
Ode with a Lament. "Pablo Neruda," *tr. fr. Spanish by* H. R. Hays. TwSpPo
Ode Written at Vale-Royal Abbey in Cheshire. Thomas Warton, the Younger. CoBE

Ode Written during the Battle of Dunkirk, May, 1940, *sel.* Sir Herbert Read.
"Happy are those who can relieve/ suffering with prayer," V. MaRV; QS
Ode, Written during the Negociations with Buonaparte, in January, 1814. Robert Southey. LiA
Ode Written during the War with America, 1814, *sel.* Robert Southey.
Bower of Peace, The. MC; PAH
Ode Written for the Completion and Opening of the New Buildings, Marischal College, Aberdeen. Ronald Campbell Macfie. EBSV
Ode Written in the Beginning of the Year [*or* Ode Written in] 1746. William Collins. *See* How Sleep the Brave.
Ode Written in the Peak[e], An. Michael Drayton. OBS; ReIE
Odell. James Stephens. MBP; MoAB; MoBrPo
Odes, *sels.* Anacreon, *tr. fr. Greek by* Thomas Moore.
"As late I sought the spangled bowers." OuHeWo
"Give me the harp of epic song." OuHeWo
"I care not for the idle state." OuHeWo
"I saw the smiling bard of pleasure." OuHeWo
"Listen to the Muse's lyre." OuHeWo
"Sculptor, wouldst thou glad my soul." OuHeWo
"Vulcan! hear your glorious task." OuHeWo
"Women tell me every day, The." GrPo; LoBV; OuHeWo
Odes, *sels.* Hafiz, *tr. fr. Persian.*
"Comrades, the morning breaks," II, *tr. by* Richard Le Gallienne. AWP
"Days, The, of spring are here! the eglantine," X, *tr. by* Gertrude Lowthian Bell. AWP; JAWP; WBP
"Grievous folly shames my sixtieth year, A," IV, *tr. by* Richard Le Gallienne. AWP
"I cease not from desire," IX, *tr. by* Gertrude Lowthian Bell. AWP; WoL
"I have borne the anguish of love," XI, *tr. by* John Hindley. AWP; JAWP; OuHeWo; WBP
"I said to heaven that glowed above," XII, *tr. by* Emerson. AWP; OuHeWo
"Jewel of the secret treasury, The," VI, *tr. by* Gertrude Lowthian Bell. AWP; JAWP; LiTW; WBP
"Lady that hast my heart within thy hand," VIII, *tr. by* Gertrude Lowthian Bell. AWP; LiTW
"Oft have I said, I say it once more," XIII, *tr. by* Emerson. AWP; OuHeWo
"Rose is not the rose unless thou see, The," III, *tr. by* Richard Le Gallienne. AWP; LiTW
"Saki, for God's love, come and fill my glass," I, *tr. by* Richard Le Gallienne. AWP
"Where is my ruined life, and where the fame," V, *tr. by* Gertrude Lowthian Bell. AWP
"Wind from the east, oh, lapwing of the day," VII, *tr. by* Gertrude Lowthian Bell. AWP
Odes, *sels.* Horace, *tr. fr. Latin.*
I, 1. "O Maecenas, of kings boasting your ancestry" ("Maecenas atavis edite regibus"), *tr. by* Leonard Albert. LaP
I, 2. "Surely enough of rain and rattling showers" ("Iam satis terris"), *tr. by* Jack Lindsay. LaP
I, 3. To the Ship in Which Virgil Sailed to Athens ("Sic te diva potens Cypri"), *tr. by* Dryden. AWP
("Wave-born Queen of the Cyprian foam," *tr. by* Alfred Noyes.) LaP
I, 4. To Lucius Sestius ("Solvitur acris hiems"), *tr. by* Sir Theodore Martin. OuHeWo
(Spring, *tr. by* J. O. Sargent.) RoL
("Winter to Spring: the west wind melts the frozen rancour," *tr. by* Louis MacNeice.) LaP
I, 5. To Pyrrha ("Quis multa gracilis"), *tr. by* Milton. AWP; JAWP; WBP
(Fifth Ode of Horace, *tr. by* Milton.) EnLoPo; LiA; PoEL-3
(For Whom, Pyrrha? *tr. by* Milton.) LiTW
(Horace to Pyrrha, *tr. by* Eugene Field.) LHV
(To a Flirt, *tr. by* Milton.) RoL
(To Mistress Pyrrha, *tr. by* Eugene Field.) PR
(To Pyrrha, *tr. by* Goldwin Smith.) EnLi-1; OuHeWo
(What slim elegant youth, drenched in effusive scent," *tr. by* Gilbert Highet.) LaP
("What slim youth, moistened with liquid perfumes," *tr. by* Joseph Bennett.) LaP
I, 8. Questioning Lydia ("Lydia, dic, per omnes"), *tr. by* Louis Untermeyer. InP
(Slump in Sybaris, The, *par. by* Franklin P. Adams.) PoeMoYo
I, 9. To Thaliarchus ("Vides ut alta"), *tr. by* Dryden. AWP; JAWP; PreP; WBP
("Look up at Mount Soracte's dazzling snow," *tr. by* Muriel Spark.) LaP
(Ode to Thaliarchus, *tr. by* Dryden.) LiTW
(Winter, *tr. by* Dryden.) RoL
I, 11. To Leuconöe ("Tu ne quaesieris"). AA, *tr.* I *by* Roswell Martin Field, *tr.* II *by* Eugene Field; ALV, *tr. by* Eugene Field; LoBV, *tr. by* Charles Stuart Calverley (Ad Leuconoen, *par. by* **Franklin P.** Adams.) AWP; JAWP; WBP
(Carpe Diem, *tr. by* Thomas Hawkins.) RoL
("I pray you not, Leuconöe, to pore," *tr. by* E. A. Robinson.) LaP
(Mistrust To-Morrow, *tr. by* Charles Stuart Calverley.) OnPM
I, 13. Tell Me, Lydia ("Cum tu, Lydia"), *tr. by* William Boscawen. OnPM
(To the Polyandrous Lydia, *par. by* Franklin P. Adams.) HBMV
("When you to Telephus devote," *tr. by* George F. Whicher.) LaP
I, 14. The Ship of State ("O navis, referent"), *tr. by* William Ewart Gladstone. AWP; JAWP; WBP; OuHeWo, *tr. by* Sir Stephen E. De Vere
(Seek a Haven, *tr. by* Charles Stuart Calverley.) OnPM
(Ship of State, The, *tr. by* William Ewart Gladstone.) RoL
I, 17. To Tyndaris ("Velox amoenum").
(Paraphrase of Horace. Genaro Estrada, *tr. fr. Spanish by* Donald Devenish Walsh.) AnCl
I, 18. "Plant no tree, O my friend" ("Nullam, Vare"), *tr. by* Barbara J. Hodge. LaP
I, 21. Invocation: "Maidens young and virgins tender" ("Dianam tenerae dicite virgines"), *tr. by* Louis Untermeyer. AWP; JAWP; WBP
("Virgins, sing the Virgin Huntress," *tr. by* Patrick Branwell Brontë.) LaP
I, 22. Integer Vitae, *tr. by* Sir Theodore Martin. EnLi-1
("He who is innocent and pure," *tr. by* W. S. Marris.) LaP
(Purity, *tr. by* Sir Theodore Martin.) RoL
(To Aristius Fuscus.) OuHeWo
I, 23. To Chloe ("Vitas hinnuleo"), *tr. by* Austin Dobson. AWP; JAWP; WBP; LiTW, *tr. by* Patrick Branwell Brontë; OuHeWo, *tr. by* Goldwin Smith
(Time to Choose a Lover, *tr. by* Patrick Branwell Brontë.) OnPM
("Young deer lost on the mountain, A," *tr. by* Robert Fitzgerald.) LaP
I, 24. "Now is the hour of sorrow unreproved" ("Quis desiderio sit pudor aut modus"), *tr. by* William J. Philbin. LaP
I, 25. "Less and less often now, the horny young men" ("Parcius iunctas quatiunt fenestras"), *tr. by* Rolfe Humphries. LaP
("Ribauld romeos less and less berattle," *tr. by* John Frederick Nims.) LaP
("Young men come less often, The—isn't it so?" *tr. by* Robert Fitzgerald.) LaP
I, 27. "It is a Thracian trick to brawl in wine" ("Natis in usum"), *tr. by* Lucius Beebe. LaP
I, 31. "And now before the new-built shrine" ("Quid dedicatum"), *tr. by* Edmund Blunden. LaP
I, 33. Albi, Ne Doreas, *wr.* ("Albi, ne doleas"), *tr. by* Austin Dobson. AWP
("Now don't overindulge grief for your lost coquette," *tr. by* Gilbert Highet.) LaP
I, 37. The Death of Cleopatra ("Nunc est bibendum"), *tr. by* Sir Stephen E. De Vere. EnLi-1; OuHeWo
(Fall of Cleopatra, The, *tr. by* the Earl of Derby.) RoL
I, 38. Persian Fopperies ("Persicos odi"), *tr. by* William Cowper. AWP; JAWP; WBP; WoL
(Frippery, *tr. by* L. R. Lind.) LiTW
("I condemn all luxury Oriental," *tr. by* Gilbert Highet.) LaP
(I Hate Their Empty Shows, *tr. by* William Cowper.) OnPM
(Persian Luxury, *tr. by* William Cowper.) RoL
(Persian Pomp, *tr. by* William Cowper.) EnLi-1
(Persicos Odi, *par. by* Franklin P. Adams.) HBMV; PoeMoYo
(Simplicity, *diff. par. by* Franklin P. Adams.) PoeMoYo
(To His Cup-Bearer, *tr. by* Sir Theodore Martin.) OuHeWo
II, 1. "Strife in Metellus' year first stirred" ("Motum ex Metello"), *tr. by* G. S. Fraser. LaP
II, 3. To Quintus Dellius ("Aequam memento"), *tr. by* John Herman Merivale. OuHeWo
(Life Is Short, *tr. by* J. H. Deazeley.) RoL
("Remember, Dellius, when times are bad," *tr. by* Lord Dunsany.) LaP
II, 4. Ad Xanthium Phoceum ("Ne sit ancillae"), *par. by* Franklin P. Adams. AWP; JAWP; WBP
("Xanthias Phoceus, never mind your loving," *tr. by* Lord Dunsany.) LaP
II, 5. "Unschooled as yet the yoke to wear" ("Nondum subacta"), *tr. by* J. S. Blake-Reed. LaP
II, 7. "Pompeius, best of all my comrades, you and I" ("O saepe mecum"), *tr. by* John Wight. LaP; WaaP
(Returned Warrior, *tr. by* John Wight.) LiTW
II, 8. "If for all the promises you regard so lightly" ("Ulla si iuris"), *tr. by* John Frederick Nims. LaP

II, 10. To Licinius ("Rectius vives"), *tr. by* William Cowper. AWP; JAWP; WBP
(Golden Mean, The.) HBV, *tr. by* William Cowper; RoL, *tr. by* Sir Philip Sidney
(To Licinius Murena, *tr. by* William Cowper.) EnLi-1; OuHeWo
(Translated out of Horace Which Begins Rectius Vives, *tr. by* Sir Philip Sidney.) ReIE
Moderation, *br. sel., tr. by* William Cowper. PoToHe (new ed.)
II, 11. To an Ambitious Friend ("Quid bellicosus"), *tr. by* Matthew Arnold. AWP
("Thoughtful Quinctius, cease to ask," *tr. by* Gilbert Highet.) LaP
II, 14. To Postumus ("Eheu, fugaces"), *tr. by* Sir Stephen Edward De Vere. LiTW; OuHeWo
(Death Inevitable, *tr. by* Thomas Creech.) RoL
("Postumus, Postumus, the years glide by us," *tr. by* Lord Lytton.) LaP
II, 15. On Luxury ("Iam pauca aratro"), *tr. by* W. E. Gladstone. RoL
II, 18. Vanity of Riches ("Non ebur neque aureum"), *tr. by* T. Rutherford Clark. RoL; WoL
("With no wrought roof of ivory and gold," *tr. by* J. S. Blake-Reed.) LaP
III, 1. The Profane ("Odi profanum vulgus"), *par. by* Abraham Cowley. AWP
(Simplicity, *tr. by* T. R. Clark.) RoL
("Tread back—and back, the lewd and lay!" *tr. by* Gerard Manley Hopkins.) LaP
III, 2. "Let the youth hardened by a sharp soldier's life" ("Angustam amice"), *tr. by* Gardner Taplin *and* Richard Eberhart. LaP; WaaP
(Endurance and Faithfulness, *tr. by* Swift.) RoL
III, 5. Coelo Tonantem ("Caelo tonantem"), *tr. by* Sir Edward Marsh. SoV
III, 9. The Reconciliation ("Donec gratus eram"). OuHeWo, *tr. by* Sir Theodore Martin; RoL, *tr. by* Ben Jonson
(February 14, 22 B.C., *par. by* Franklin P. Adams.) InMe
(Reconciliation of Lovers, *tr. by* Ben Jonson.) LiA
III, 10. Extremum Tanain, *tr. by* Austin Dobson. AWP; JAWP; WBP
III, 13. To the Fountain of Bandusia ("O fons Bandusiae"), *tr. by* Eugene Field. AA; AWP; JAWP; WBP
(Bandusia, Stainless Mirror, *tr. by* Charles Stuart Calverley.) OnPM
(Fountain of Bandusia, The.) OuHeWo, *tr. by* Austin Dobson; RoL, *tr. by* M. Jourdain
("Hail, Bandusian spring, clearer than crystal pure," *tr. by* Gilbert Highet.) LaP
(O Fons Bandusiae, *tr. by* Austin Dobson.) VA
III, 18. To Faunus ("Faune, Nympharum"), *tr. by* Alfred Noyes. LiTW
("Faunus, fleet-foot lover of flying wood-nymphs.") LaP
III, 22. The Pine Tree for Diana ("Montium custos nemorumque"), *tr. by* Louis Untermeyer. AWP
III, 23. To Phidyle ("Caelo supinas si tuleris"), *tr. by* Austin Dobson. AWP
("If suppliant palms, upraised at the sacrifice," *tr. by* Alfred Noyes.) LaP
III, 28. Holiday ("Festo quid potius die"), *tr. by* Louis Untermeyer. AWP; JAWP; WBP
(Celebration for Neptune, *tr. by* Roselle M. Montgomery.) LiA
III, 29. To Maecenas ("Tyrrhena regum progenies"), *par. by* Dryden. AWP; JAWP; PoFr, *sel.*; WBP
(Horat. Ode 29. Book 3.) CEP; SeCV-2
(Twenty-ninth Ode of the Third Book of Horace.) LiA
Enjoy the Hour, *sel.* BeR
Happy the Man, *br. sel.* MaRV
(Happiness, *4 ll.*) TreF
III, 30. Title to Fame ("Exegi monumentum aere perennius"), *tr. by* W. E. Gladstone. RoL
IV, 1. To Venus ("Intermissa, Venus"), *tr. by* Ben Jonson. AWP
IV, 3. This Is Thy Gift, O Muse ("Quem tu, Melpomene, semel"), *tr. by* Christopher Smart. LiA
(Gift of Song, The.) LiTW
IV, 7. Spring's Return ("Diffugere nives"), *tr. by* Samuel Johnson. LiA
("Snows are fled away, leaves on the shaws, The," *tr. by* A. E. Housman.) LaP
(Translation of Horace, *tr. by* Samuel Johnson.) TriL
IV, 11. To Phyllis ("Est mihi nonum"), *tr. by* Eugene Field. InMe
Flaming Torches, *br. sel., tr. by* Thomas Creech. BeR
IV, 13. Revenge ("Audivere, Lyce"), *tr. by* Louis Untermeyer. AWP; WoL
IV, 15. The Restorer ("Phoebus volentem"), *tr. by* J. O. Sargent. RoL
Odes, *sels.* Pindar, *tr. fr. Greek.*
Isthmian Odes.
Achilles, *fr.* VIII, *tr. by* C. J. Billson. GrR
Before the Laureate's Day, *fr.* II, *tr. by* C. J. Billson. GrR
Marriage of Thetis, The, *fr.* VIII, *tr. by* C. J. Billson. OxBG
Mercenary Muse, The, *fr.* II, *tr. by* F. L. Lucas. GrPE
Poet's Power, The, *fr.* IV, *tr. by* F. L. Lucas. GrPE
Sons of Aeacus, The, *fr.* V, *tr. by* C. J. Billson. OxBG
Strepsiades of Thebes, *fr.* VII, *tr. by* C. J. Billson. OxBG
(To a Nation's Hero, *longer sel.*) GrR
"Thebes of the golden shield, my mother, I will put," I, *tr. by* Richmond Lattimore. GrPo
To Melissus of Thebes, Victor in the Horse-Race, III, *tr. by* Abraham Moore. PreP
Nemean Odes.
Castor and Polydeuces, *fr.* X, *tr. by* C. J. Billson. OxBG
(Twin Brothers.) GrR
Childhood of Achilles, The, *fr.* III, *tr. by* C. J. Billson. OxBG
God and Man, *fr.* VI, *tr. by* F. L. Lucas. GrPE
Hearken! O Eileithyia, *fr.* VII, *tr. by* C. J. Billson. GrR
Infant Heracles, The, *fr.* I, *tr. by* C. J. Billson. OxBG
Moderation, *fr.* XI, *tr. by* F. L. Lucas. GrPE
Mortality, *fr.* XI, *tr. by* F. L. Lucas. GrPE
Music's Anodyne, *fr.* IV, *tr. by* C. J. Billson. GrR
Nemean Ode, VI, *tr. by* Richmond Lattimore. LiTW
Of Gods and Men, *fr.* VI, *tr. by* C. J. Billson. GrR
Poet's Praise, The, *fr.* V, *tr. by* F. L. Lucas. GrPE
Olympian Odes.
Evadne and Her Son, *fr.* VI, *tr. by* C. J. Billson. OxBG
(Evadné, *br. sel.*) GrR
For Asopichus of Orchomenus, XIV, *pr. tr. by* Sir John Sandys. LiA
For Hiero, Tyrant of Syracuse, I, *tr. by* Arthur S. Way. GrL
("Best of all things is water; but gold, like a gleaming fire," *tr. by* Richmond Lattimore.) GrPo
(First Olympionique to Hiero of Syracus, Victorious in the Horse-Race, The, *tr. by* Ambrose Philips.) ATP
(For Hieron of Syracuse, *pr. tr. by* Sir John Sandys.) LiA
(Olympian Ode I: To Hiero the Syracusan, *tr. by* Abraham Moore.) EnLi-2; OuHeWo
For Theron, Tyrant of Akragas, II, *tr. by* Arthur S. Way. GrL
Fortune's Tides, *fr.* II, *tr. by* C. J. Billson. GrR
Island of the Blest, The, *fr.* II. OBEC, *tr. by* Gilbert West; OxBG, *tr. by* C. J. Billson
(Islands of the Blest, The, *tr. by* C. J. Billson.) GrR
Olympian Ode, VI, *tr. by* Richmond Lattimore. LiTW
Pathless Briars, *fr.* VI, *tr. by* Abraham Moore. LiA
Pelops, *fr.* I, *tr. by* H. T. Wade-Gery *and* C. M. Bowra. OxBG
(Bride to the Victor, A, *tr. by* C. J. Billson.) GrR
Taming of Pegasus, The, *fr.* XIII, *tr. by* C. J. Billson. GrR
(Bellerophon.) OxBG
To Goddess Luck, *fr.* XII, *tr. by* C. J. Billson. GrR
Pythian Odes.
Aetna, *fr.* I, *tr. by* H. T. Wade-Gery *and* C. M. Bowra. GrR
Asclepius, *fr.* III, *tr. by* C. J. Billson. GrR; OxBG
Coming of Jason to Iolcus, The, *fr.* IV, *tr. by* F. L. Lucas. GrPE
Courage in Exile, *fr.* IV, *tr. by* F. L. Lucas. GrPE
For Arkesilas of Kyrene, IV, *tr. by* H. T. Wade-Gery *and* C. M. Bowra. GrL
Great Heart, *fr.* IV, *tr. by* C. J. Billson. GrR
Hyperboreans, The, *fr.* X, *tr. by* C. J. Billson. GrR; OxBG
Jason's Father Sees His Returning Son, *fr.* IV, *pr. tr. by* Sir John Sandys. LiA
O Golden Lyre, *fr.* I, *tr. by* H. T. Wade-Gery *and* C. M. Bowra. GrR
(First Pythian Ode, *tr. by* Arthur S. Way.) WoL
(Magic of Melody, The, *tr. by* F. L. Lucas.) GrPE
(Power of Music, The.) OxBG; UnS, *sel.*
Only a Dream-Shadow, *fr.* VIII, *tr. by* H. T. Wade-Gery *and* C. M. Bowra. GrR
(Human Life.) OxBG
Orestes, *fr.* XI, *tr. by* H. T. Wade-Gery *and* C. M. Bowra. OxBG
Prize, The, *fr.* IX, *pr. tr. by* Sir John Sandys. LiA
Quest of the Golden Fleece, The, *fr.* IV, *tr. by* C. J. Billson. OxBG
(Argonauts, The, *abr., tr. by* C. J. Billson.) GrR
(Tale of the Golden Fleece, The, *tr. by* H. T. Wade-Gery *and* C. M. Bowra.) GrL
Wooing of Cyrene, The, *fr.* IX, *tr. by* C. J. Billson. GrR
(Cyrene, *shorter sel., tr. by* H. T. Wade-Gery *and* C. M. Bowra.) OxBG
Odes, *sels.* Pierre de Ronsard, *tr. fr. French.*
I, 17. "Sweet-heart, come see if the rose," *tr. by* Curtis Hidden Page. PrPoCR

Odes (*continued*)
(Spring, *tr. by* Alan Conder.) TrFP
II, 13. "My des Autels, whose true," *tr. by* Curtis Hidden Page. PrPoCR
II, 18. "Oh! but my mind is weary!" *tr. by* Curtis Hidden Page. PrPoCR
(Summer's Revel, The.) WoL
III, 20. "Calmly to wait whatever Chance may give," *tr. by* Curtis Hidden Page. PrPoCR
IV, 4. "O caves, and you, O springs," *tr. by* Curtis Hidden Page. PrPoCR
(Of the Choice of His Burial-Place, *tr. by* John Payne.) LiA
(On the Choice of His Sepulchre, *tr. by* Alan Conder.) TrFP
IV, 21. "God guard you, and greet you well," *tr. by* Curtis Hidden Page. PrPoCR
(Spring Song, *tr. by* Alan Conder.) TrFP
IV, 22. "Hawthorn fair, whose burgeoning," *tr. by* Curtis Hidden Page. PrPoCR
IV, 38. "Pour we roses into wine!" *tr. by* Curtis Hidden Page. PrPoCR
V, 16. "We hold not in our power," *tr. by* Curtis Hidden Page. PrPoCR
Odes, I–V. George Santayana.
"Gathering the echoes of forgotten wisdom," III. AnAmPo; AnFE; APA; CoAnAm; LA; TwAmPo
"My heart rebels against my generation," II. AnFE; APA; ATP; CoAnAm; PoFr; TwAmPo; ViBoPo
"Of thee the Northman by his beachèd [*or* bleachèd] galley," V. AnAmPo; AnFE; APA; CoAnAm; LA; TwAmPo
(Ode to the Mediterranean.) EtS
"Slowly the black earth gains upon the yellow," IV. AnFE; APA; CoAnAm; TwAmPo
"What god will choose me from this labouring nation," I. AnFE; APA; CoAnAm; TwAmPo
Odes of Ching, *sel.* Ching, *tr. fr. Chinese.*
Shuh's Hunting. RAR
Odi et Amo. Ibn al-Hajj, *tr. fr. Arabic by* A. J. Arberry. MooP
Odi Profanum Vulgus. Callimachus. *See* Fastidious!
O'Donnell Aboo. Michael Joseph McCann. OnYI
Odour, The. George Herbert. EV-2; OBS
Odor [*or* Odour] from the flower is gone, The. On a Faded Violet. Shelley. BPN
Odor of a rose, The: light of a star. Shelley. Alexander Hay Japp. VA
Odor of Blood, The. Thomas McGrath. NePoEA
Odorous air, morn's messenger, now spread, The. The Crusaders Behold Jerusalem. Tasso. CAW; PrPoCR
Odorous shade lingers the fair day's ghost, An. Night. Henri de Regnier. AWP; JAWP; WBP
O'Driscoll drove with a song. The Host [*or* Folk] of the Air. W. B. Yeats. CBOV; CH; GTIV; LoEn; OnYI; PoVP; SeCeV; VA
O'Duffy's Ironsides. "Tom Moore, Jr." OnYI
Odysseus and Demodocus. Homer, *tr. fr. Greek by* F. L. Lucas. *Fr.* The Odyssey, VIII. GrPE
Odysseus and Eurycleia. Homer, *tr. fr. Greek by* F. L. Lucas. *Fr.* The Odyssey, XIX. GrPE
Odysseus and His Father. Homer, *tr. fr. Greek by* F. L. Lucas. *Fr.* The Odyssey, XXIV. GrPE
Odysseus and His Son. Homer. *See* Reunion of Ulysses and Telemachus.
Odysseus and Penelope Meet. Homer, *pr. tr. fr. Greek by* A. T. Murray. *Fr.* The Odyssey, XXIII. LiA
Odysseus Dying. Sheila Wingfield. OxBI
Odysseus has come home, to the gully farm. The Homecoming. James K. Baxter. AnNZ
Odysseus heard the sirens; they were singing. The Sirens. John Manifold. LiTB; LiTM; WaP
Odysseus in Hades. Homer, *tr. fr. Greek by* William Cowper. *Fr.* The Odyssey, XI. GrR
Odysseus' Mother Speaks to Him in Hades. Homer, *pr. tr. fr. Greek by* A. T. Murray. *Fr.* The Odyssey, XI. LiA
Odysseus Puts to Sea. Homer, *tr. fr. Greek by* J. W. Mackail. *Fr.* The Odyssey, V. OxBG
(Odysseus; the Shores of Scheria at Last, *tr. by* H. B. Cotterill.) GrR
Odysseus' Return to Ithaca. Homer, *tr. fr. Greek by* F. L. Lucas. *Fr.* The Odyssey, XIII. GrPE
Odysseus Spurns Calypso. Homer, *pr. tr. fr. Greek by* S. H. Butcher *and* Andrew Lang. *Fr.* The Odyssey, V. GrR
Odyssey, The, *sels.* Homer, *tr. fr. Greek.*
"Afterward, soon as the chaste Persephone hither and thither," *fr.* XI, *tr. by* Edmund C. Stedman. GrPo
"And now arriving at the isle, he springs," *fr.* V, *tr. by* Leigh Hunt. GrPo
"And Odysseus of many counsels answered him saying," IX, *pr. tr. by* S. H. Butcher *and* Andrew Lang. GrL
Arete; Portrait of a High-born Matron, *fr.* VII, *tr. by* Pope. GrR
At-Home in Sparta, An, *fr.* IV, *pr. tr. by* Samuel Butler. GrR
At Pylos, *fr.* III, *tr. by* J. W. Mackail. OxBG
At Sparta; Menelaus and Proteus, *fr.* IV, *pr. tr. by* S. H. Butcher *and* Andrew Lang. OxBG
Blame Not the Gods, *fr.* I, *pr. tr. by* Butcher *and* Lang. GrR
"But Minerva fetch'd/ The winds from sea," *fr.* V, *tr. by* George Chapman. EnLi-1
Calypso's Island, *fr.* V, *tr. by* George Chapman. GrR; OxBG
Circe, *fr.* X, *tr. by* F. L. Lucas. GrPE
(Of Circe, *shorter sel., tr. by* William Morris.) OxBG
Debate in Ithaca, The, *fr.* II, *tr. by* F. L. Lucas. GrPE
Demodocus Sings a Song of Troy, *fr.* VIII, *tr. by* H. B. Cotterill. GrR
(Phaeacian Nights—Demodocus, *pr. tr. by* T. E. Lawrence.) OxBG
End of the Suitors, The, *fr.* XXII, *tr. by* George Chapman. OBS
Escape from Cyclop, The, *fr.* IX, *tr. by* George Chapman. LiTW
Eumaeus Plays Host to His Master, *fr.* XIV, *pr. tr. by* Samuel Butler. GrR
Eumaeus Tells the Story of His Life, *fr.* XV, *pr. tr. by* Samuel Butler. GrR
(Tale of Eumaeus, The, *tr. by* F. L. Lucas.) GrPE
Eumaeus the Swineherd, *fr.* XIV *and* XV, *pr. tr. by* Samuel Butler. OxBG
Farewell to Kind Hosts and a Godspeed, *fr.* XIII, *tr. by* William Morris. GrR
Farewell to Nausicaa, *fr.* VIII, *pr. tr. by* Butcher *and* Lang. GrR
"He spake, to whom I, answ'ring, thus replied," *fr.* XI, *tr. by* William Cowper. GrPo
Helen, Menelaos, and Memories of Troy, *fr.* IV, *tr. by* George Chapman. GrR
(At Sparta; Helen and Menelaus, *pr. tr. by* Samuel Butler.) OxBG
Heroic Answer to the Servant Problem, An, *fr.* XV, *pr. tr. by* Samuel Butler. GrR
Home-coming, *fr.* XIII, *tr. by* J. W. Mackail. OxBG
"In mean time flew our ships, and straight we fetched," *fr.* XII, *tr. by* George Chapman. TuPP
Kingdom of Death, The, *fr.* XI, *tr. by* F. L. Lucas. GrPE
Laertes, *fr.* XXIV. GrR, *tr. by* William Morris; OxBG, *longer sel., tr. by* Sir William Marris
Last Journey of the Wooers, The, *fr.* XXIV, *tr. by* William Cowper. OxBG
(Limbo; the Shades of the Suitors.) GrR
"Lo, Helen came from her chamber fragrant, high-vaulted of old," *fr.* IV, *tr. by* William Morris. GrPo
Lotus-Land and the Cyclops' Cave, *fr.* IX, *tr. by* F. L. Lucas. GrPE
Man of Many Devices, The, *fr.* I, *pr. tr. by* A. T. Murray. LiA
Man, the Feeblest of Earth's Creatures, *fr.* XVIII, *tr. by* William Cowper. GrR
Menelaus; What Price Earthly Splendor, *fr.* IV, *pr. tr. by* Butcher *and* Lang. GrR
Message of Hermes to Calypso, The, *fr.* V, *tr. by* F. L. Lucas. GrPE
Minstrel Worthy of His Hire, The, *fr.* VIII, *tr. by* William Cowper. GrR
"My own necessity," *fr.* II, *tr. by* Bryant. GrPo
Nausicaa ("Having thus fulfilled her purpose Athene went away"), *fr.* VI, *pr. tr. by* T. E. Lawrence. OxBG
(Olympus, *br. sel.*) LiA
Nausicaa ("Now when at last they arrived at the beautiful stream of the river"), *fr.* VI, *tr. by* H. B. Cotterill. OxBG
Nausicaa ("Now when they came to the bright running river"), *fr.* VI, *tr. by* Sir William Marris. LiTW
Nausicaa ("The servants then"), *fr.* VI, *tr. by* George Chapman. OBS
Nausicaa ("So flashing-eyed Athene spoke"), *fr.* VI, *tr. by* F. L. Lucas. GrPE
Nausicaa and Odysseus; the Meeting, *fr.* VI, *tr. by* George Chapman. GrR
Nausicaa; the Ingenue, *fr.* VI, *tr. by* H. B. Cotterill. GrR
Noman and the Cyclops, *fr.* IX, *tr. by* George Chapman. GrR
(Of Noman and Cyclops, *tr. by* William Morris.) OxBG
"Now after the ship had left the stream of the river Oceanus," XII, *pr. tr. by* Butcher *and* Lang. GrL
"Now the Dawn arose from her couch," V, *pr. tr. by* Butcher *and* Lang. GrL
"Now when they were about to move for home," *fr.* VI, *tr. by* Bryant. GrPo
"Now when we had gone down to the ship," XI, *pr. tr. by* Butcher *and* Lang. GrL
Odysseus and Demodocus, *fr.* VIII, *tr. by* F. L. Lucas. GrPE
Odysseus and Eurycleia, *fr.* XIX, *tr. by* F. L. Lucas. GrPE
Odysseus and His Father, *fr.* XXIV, *tr. by* F. L. Lucas. GrPE

Odysseus and Penelope Meet, *fr.* XXIII, *pr. tr. by* A. T. Murray. LiA
Odysseus in Hades, *fr.* XI, *tr. by* William Cowper. GrR
Odysseus' Mother Speaks to Him in Hades, *br. sel. fr.* XI, *pr. tr. by* A. T. Murray. LiA
Odysseus Puts to Sea, *fr.* V, *tr. by* J. W. Mackail. OxBG
(Odysseus; the Shores of Scheria at Last, *tr. by* H. B. Cotterill.) GrR
Odysseus' Return to Ithaca, *fr.* XIII, *tr. by* F. L. Lucas. GrPE
Odysseus Spurns Calypso, *fr.* V, *pr. tr. by* Butcher *and* Lang. GrR
Of Cyclops and the Ram, *fr.* IX, *tr. by* William Morris. OxBG
Of His Mother's Shade, *fr.* XI, *tr. by* J. W. Mackail. OxBG
Of the Laestrygones, *fr.* X, *tr. by* Sir William Marris. OxBG
Of the Shade of Achilles, *fr.* XI, *tr. by* William Cowper. OxBG
Old Man of the Sea, The, *fr.* IV, *tr. by* F. L. Lucas. GrPE
"Our ship now pass'd the streights of th' ocean flood," *fr.* XII, *tr. by* George Chapman. ReIE
Palace of Alcinous, The, *fr.* VII, *tr. by* Pope. GrR
Passing Glimpse of Penelope, A, *fr.* I, *pr. tr. by* Butcher *and* Lang. GrR
Penelope Dreams ("But when her heart had had its fill of weeping"), *fr.* XX, *tr. by* Sir William Marris. OxBG
Penelope Dreams ("So said he and the crone went down the hall"), *fr.* XIX, *tr. by* J. W. Mackail. OxBG
(Penelope's Dream: "Then went the ancient matron forth," *tr. by* William Cowper.) GrR
Penelope Forlorn, *fr.* IV, *tr. by* J. W. Mackail. OxBG
(Penelope; New Woes on Old, *tr. by* H. B. Cotterill.) GrR
Penelope's Constancy Rewarded, *fr.* XXIII, *tr. by* William Cowper. GrR
(Penelope Makes Trial of Odysseus, *shorter sel., pr. tr. by* Samuel Butler.) OxBG
"Perhaps, like thee, poor guest! in wanton pride," *fr.* XIX, *tr. by* Pope. GrPo
Return of Ulysses, The, *abr., fr.* XXI, *tr. by* Bryant. BBV (1923 ed.)
Reunion of Odysseus and Penelope, The, *fr.* XXIII, *tr. by* F. L. Lucas. GrPE
Reunion of Ulysses and Telemachus, *fr.* XVI, *tr. by* William Cowper. GrR
(Odysseus and His Son, *tr. by* F. L. Lucas.) GrPE
(Telemachus Finds His Father, *tr. by* William Cowper.) OxBG
("Zeus-born son of Laertes, thou wise and wileful Odysseus," *tr. by* H. B. Cotterill.) GrPo
Sacrifice, The, *fr.* III, *tr. by* George Chapman. OBS
Sailing of Odysseus from Ogygia, The, *fr.* V, *tr. by* F. L. Lucas. GrPE
Scylla and Charybdis, *fr.* XII, *tr. by* George Chapman. OBS
Silence of Ajax, The, *fr.* XI, *pr. tr. by* T. E. Lawrence. LiA
(Of the Shade of Ajax, *tr. by* T. F. Higham.) OxBG
"Sing, O Muse, of the man so wary and wise, who in far lands," *fr.* I, *tr. by* H. B. Cotterill. GrPo
Sirens, The; Scylla and Charybdis, *fr.* XII. GrPE, *tr. by* F. L. Lucas; LiTW, *tr. by* Pope
(Sirens' Song, The, *shorter sel., tr. by* George Chapman.) EV-1
(Ulysses and the Sirens, *shorter sel., tr. by* George Chapman.) ReEn
Slaying, The, *fr.* XXI *and* XXII, *tr. by* William Morris. OxBG
Slaying of the Suitors, The, *fr.* XXI *and* XXII. GrPE, *tr. by* F. L. Lucas; GrR, *fr.* XXII, *tr. by* William Morris
"So he spake, and fell to cleaving the logs with the ruthless brass," *fr.* XIV, *tr. by* William Morris. GrPo
"So he spake; but the Grey-eyed, the Goddess Athene, smiled and now," *fr.* XIII, *tr. by* William Morris. GrPo
"So there he lay asleep, the steadfast goodly Odysseus," VI, *pr. tr. by* Butcher *and* Lang. GrL
Sound of Footsteps, The, *fr.* XVI, *pr. tr. by* A. T. Murray. LiA
"Tell me, Muse, of that man, so ready at need, who wandered far and wide," *fr.* I, *pr. tr. by* Butcher *and* Lang. GrL
Test of the Bow, The, *fr.* XXI, *tr. by* William Morris. GrR
"That moment, fainting as he touch'd the shore," *fr.* V, *tr. by* Pope. PreP
"Then answered him Antinoüs and said: 'What god has brought to us this pest,'" *fr.* XVII, *pr. tr. by* George H. Palmer. GrPo
"Then did Ulysses cast his rags aside," *fr.* XXII, *tr. by* Bryant. GrPo
"Then Eurycleia, the dear nurse, rejoined," *fr.* XXIII, *tr. by* Bryant. GrPo
"Then in two several bands I did portion and number my comrades," *fr.* X, *tr. by* L. P. Chamberlayne. GrPo
"Then Odysseus of many counsels stripped him of his rags," XXII, *pr. tr. by* Butcher *and* Lang. GrL
"Then we came to the isle Aeolian," X, *pr. tr. by* Butcher *and* Lang. GrL
"Then with the rich harp came Pontonous," *fr.* VIII, *tr. by* George Chapman. GrPo
"There are stranger guests come hither, Menelaus God-bred king," *fr.* IV, *tr. by* William Morris. GrPo
"This now seemed to my mind to be counsel the best and the wisest," *fr.* IX, *tr. by* H. B. Cotterill. GrPo
"This said, the golden-throned Aurora," *fr.* XII, *tr. by* George Chapman. EPP
"This spoke, a huge wave took him by the head," *fr.* V, *tr. by* George Chapman. PreP
Ulysses and His Dog, *fr.* XVII, *tr. by* Pope. FiP; OBEC
("And a dog, lying there, lifted its head," *pr. tr. by* Martin Johnson.) LO
(Death of Argus, The, *tr. by* F. L. Lucas.) GrPE
(Dog Argos, The, *pr. tr. by* T. E. Lawrence.) OxBG
("Dog lying near lifted his head and ears, A," *pr. tr. by* George H. Palmer.) GrPo
(Old Hound Argos, The, *pr. tr. by* Samuel Butler.) GrR
Ulysses Hears the Prophecies of Tiresias, *fr.* XI, *tr. by* George Chapman. LoBV
Ulysses in the Waves, *fr.* V, *tr. by* George Chapman. OBS
"'Ulysses!' (with a sigh she thus began;)," *fr.* V, *tr. by* Pope. GrPo
Vision of Theoclymenus, The, *fr.* XX. GrPE, *tr. by* F. L. Lucas; OxBG, *pr. tr. by* T. E. Lawrence
Web, The, *fr.* II, *tr. by* Sir Wiliam Marris. OxBG
Wise Penelope, *fr.* XIX, *pr. tr. by* A. T. Murray. LiA
Odyssey, The, *sel.* Nicholas Kazantzakis, *tr. fr. Modern Greek by* Rae Dalven.
"When he had cut down the ardent youth in his spacious courts." MoGP
Odyssey, The. Andrew Lang. BMEP; ES; GTBS-D; HBV; InP; LEAP; LoBV; OBEV; OBVV; OtMeF; PC; PFE; PoeMoYo; PoRA; POTT; PoVP; PtP; TOP; VA; ViBoPo; VOD; WHA; YT
Odyssey of Big Boy. Sterling A. Brown. BANP; CDC
Oedipus. Thomas Blackburn. FaBoTw
Oedipus, *sels.* Dryden.
Incantation: "Choose the darkest part o' the grove," *fr.* III, i. TriL
Song: "Hear, ye sullen Pow'rs below." PoD
Oedipus. Robert Garnier, *pr. tr. fr. French. Fr.* Antigone, I, i. LiA
Oedipus at Colonus, *sels.* Sophocles, *tr. fr. Greek.*
Choral Poem: "Land beloved of horsemen, fair, The," *tr. by* Robert Fitzgerald. LiTW
Decay, Earth's Universal Law, *tr. by* Lewis Campbell. GrR
(Everything Decays, *tr. by* C. M. Bowra.) OxBG
(Triumph of Time, The, *tr. by* F. Storr.) LiA
Grove of Colonus, The, *tr. by* Walter Headlam. OxBG; WoL
(Glories of Athens, The, *pr. tr. by* R. C. Jebb.) LiA
(Lovely Colonus, *tr. by* Lewis Campbell.) GrR
He Sins Not Who Sins Unwittingly, *tr. by* Robert Whitelaw. GrR
Oedipus' Last Hour, *tr. by* Robert Whitelaw. GrR
(Passing of Oedipus, The, *tr. by* C. M. Bowra.) OxBG
Old Age, *tr. by* A. E. Housman. LiTW; OxBG
(Chorus: "What man is he that yearneth," *tr. by* A. E. Housman.) AWP; JAWP; WBP
("Endure what life God gives and ask no longer span," *tr. by* W. B. Yeats.) OBMV; PoD
(Old Age the Friendless, *tr. by* Robert Whitelaw.) GrR
Out of Suffering, Tolerance, *tr. by* Lewis Campbell. GrR
"To a land rich in goodly horses," *tr. by* H. N. Couch. GrPo
Oedipus, King-Saviour. Sophocles, *tr. fr. Greek by* Robert Whitelaw. *Fr.* Oedipus Rex. GrR
Oedipus' Last Hour. Sophocles, *tr. fr. Greek by* Robert Whitelaw. *Fr.* Oedipus at Colonus. GrR
(Passing of Oedipus, The, *tr. by* C. M. Bowra.) OxBG
Oedipus Rex [*or* Oedipus Tyrannus], *sels.* Sophocles, *tr. fr. Greek.*
Blindness, *tr. by* J. T. Sheppard. OxBG
Chorus from "King Oedipus" ("For this one thing above all I would be praised as a man"), *tr. by* W. B. Yeats. LiTW
Creon, *tr. by* F. Storr. PoFr
Fatal Discovery, *tr. by* Gilbert Murray. GrR
God and Man, *tr. by* Robert Whitelaw. OxBG
(Chorus: "Oh, may my constant feet not fail.") WGRP
(People Pray, The.) GrR
In Time of Pestilence, *tr. by* J. T. Sheppard. OxBG
Jocasta's Death, *tr. by* J. T. Sheppard. LiA; OxBG
(Death of Jocasta, The, *tr. by* Gilbert Murray.) GrR
"Lord of the Pythian treasure," *tr. by* A. W. Verrall. GrPo
"O Dark, Dark, Dark Amid the Blaze of Noon," *tr. by* John S. Phillimore. GrR
Oedipus, King-Saviour, *tr. by* Robert Whitelaw. GrR
Outlaw, The, *tr. by* Gilbert Murray. GrR

Oedipus Rex (*continued*)
"Vanity of Vanities; All Is Vanity," *tr. by* Gilbert Murray. GrR
When Pestilence Strikes, *tr. by* Gilbert Murray. GrR
Oedipus to the Oracle. Wesley Trimpi. NePoEA
Oenone. Tennyson. BEL; BPN; BrBE; EM-2; EmBrPo; EnLi-2; EnLit; EPN; GEPC; OAEP; OBRV; PoVP; TCEP; TwCrTr; ViBoPo; ViPo; ViPP; VLEP
Way to Power, The, *br. sel.* MaRV; OQP; QP-2
Oenone sat within the cave from out. The Death of Oenone. Tennyson. PreP
Oenone's Complaint. George Peele. *Fr.* The Arraignment of Paris. ElL; OBSC
O'er a dark field I held my dubious way. Philip Freneau. *Fr.* The House of Night. APW
O'er a low couch the setting sun. The Baron's Last Banquet. Albert Gorton Greene. AA; BeLS; LPS-1
O'er all my songs the image of a face. The Negro Singer. James David Corrothers. BANP
O'er all the hill-tops. Wanderer's Night-Songs, II. Goethe, *tr. by* Longfellow. AWP; InP; JAWP; LiA; OnPM; WBP; WoL
O'er better waves to speed her rapid course. Purgatory. Dante, *tr. by* Henry F. Cary. *Fr.* Divina Commedia. OuHeWo
O'er books the mind inactive lies. Conversation. Hannah More. *Fr.* Bas Bleu. OBEC
O'er Cambridge set the yeoman's mark. Lexington. Sidney Lanier. *Fr.* The Psalm of the West. PaA; PAH
O'er Carmel fields in the springtime the sea-gulls follow the plow. Spring in Carmel. George Sterling. SBMV
O'er Desert Plains and Rushy Meers. William Shenstone. AEV
(Song.) FaBoEn
O'er faded heath-flowers spun or thorny furze. The Gossamer. Charlotte Smith. ViBoPo
O'er golden sands my waters flow. The Enchanted Spring. George Darley. RO
O'er Huron's wave the sun was low. The Battle of Bridgewater. *Unknown.* PAH
O'er many a sea, through many a tribe and nation. World without End. Catullus. LiTW
O'er me alas! thou dost too much prevail. Countess of Winchilsea. *Fr.* The Spleen. BeR
O'er Provence breathing, nimble air. Gay Provence. George Francis Savage-Armstrong. TIP
O'er sapphire seas the white mist bleaches. The Sail. Mikhail Yurevich Lermontov. WaL
O'er sleepy fields a vulture broods. Vulture. Aleksandr Blok. BoR
O'er sunbaked plains he winds his way. The Rattlesnake. Robert V. Carr. PoOW
O'er the bare woods, whose outstretched hands. The Last Walk in Autumn. Whittier. IAP
O'er the glad waters of the dark-blue sea. The Corsair's Life [*or* Song of the Corsairs]. Byron. *Fr.* The Corsair, I. EtS; EV-4; LPS-2
O'er the haycocks comes the moon. Lullaby. Alice Archer Sewall James. BOL
O'er the heath the heifer strays. Evening. John Cunningham. *Fr.* Day; a Pastoral. EnSW
O'er the high and o'er the lowly. Our National Banner. Dexter Smith. PAH
O'er the hills far away, at the birth of the morn. Song. Francis Hopkinson. IAP
O'er the level plains, where mountains greet me as I go. Time's Song. Winthrop Mackworth Praed. EnRP
O'er the men of Ethiopia she would pour her cornucopia. Husband and Heathen. Sam Walter Foss. BOHV
O'er the mountain slopes reign quietude and peace. Night. Leconte de Lisle. TrFP
O'er the Mountains High He Went. *Unknown, tr. fr. Armenian by* Zabelle C. Boyajian. ArmLP
O'er the rough main with flowing sheet. The *Bonhomme Richard* and *Serapis* [*or* On the Memorable Victory by Captain Paul Jones]. Philip Freneau. GA; IAP; PAH
O'er the rugged mountain's brow. Some Ruthless Rhymes, VI. Harry Graham. CenHV
O'er the Smooth Enamelled Green. Milton. *See* Song: "O'er the smooth . . ."
O'er the warrior gauntlet grim. Parricide. Julia Ward Howe. PAH
O'er the waste of waters cruising. Song: On Captain Barney's Victory over the Ship *General Monk.* Philip Freneau. PAH
O'er the Water to Charlie. Burns. EBSV; FaBoCh
O'er the wet sands an insect crept. An Autograph. James Russell Lowell. AA
O'er the wide-spreading plains rolled the emigrant trains. The Dust of the Overland Trail. James Barton Adams. PoOW
O'er the Wild Gannet's Bath. George Darley. *Fr.* Ethelstan. ChTr; PoEL-4
(Runilda's Chant.) OnYI
O'er the world's plain that stretches vastly, sadly. Three Springs. Pushkin. BoR
O'er the yellow crocus on the lawn. A Russian Fantasy. Nathan Haskell Dole. AA
O'er town and cottage, vale and height. Valley Forge. Thomas Buchanan Read. *Fr.* The Wagoner of the Alleghanies. MC; PAH
Of a Cat's Look. John Heywood. SiCE; TuPP
Of a Certain Green-eyed Monster. Esther Lilian Duff. *See* Charles Gave Elizabeth a Dodo.
Of a Certain [*or* Certaine] Man. Sir John Harington. BOHV; LPS-3; SiCE
Of a Child That Had Fever. Christopher Morley. PFY; PoeMoYo; PR; TBM
Of a Contented Mind. Thomas, Lord Vaux. CoBE; ElL; EV-1; GoBC; MaRV; ReIE; SiCE; TuPP
(Content.) OBSC
(On a Contented Mind.) HBV
Of a Cozener. John Hoskins. TuPP
Of a Dead Poet. Lord Alfred Douglas. JKCP (1926 ed.)
Of a Death in Winter ("The ravenous earth that now wooes her"). John Donne. *Fr.* Elegie: Death. BoW
Of a Death in Winter ("Manshape, that shone"). Gerard Manley Hopkins. *Fr.* That Nature Is a Heraclitean Fire and of the Comfort of the Resurrection. BoW
Of a Fair Lady Playing with a Snake. Edmund Waller. *See* To a Fair Lady Playing with a Snake.
Of a Fair Shrew. Sir John Harington. *See* Fair, Rich, and Young.
Of a Flatterer. John Davies of Hereford. SiCE
Of a Gull. Sir John Davies, *after the Latin of* Martial. SiCE; TuPP
Of a Husband Hang'd. John Heywood. ReIE
Of a little take a little. *Unknown.* OxNR
Of a lovely maid I tell. Lovely Maid. Ibn Khafaja. MooP
Of a Mistress. Sir Aston Cokayne. SeCL
Of a New-married Student. *Unknown.* SiCE; TuPP
Of a Poet Patriot. Thomas MacDonagh. CAW; HBMV; LBBV; MBP; OnYI; OxBI; PoFr
(On a Poet Patriot.) AnIV; TSW
Of a Precise Tailor. Sir John Harington. BOHV
Of a Rose, a Lovely Rose. *Unknown.* AnEC; AtBAP; BoW; OBEV; OxBoCh
Of a rose singe we. This Rose Is Railed on a Ryse. *Unknown.* AnEC
Of a Sheep's Eye. John Heywood. SiCE; TuPP
Of a Small Daughter Walking Outdoors. Frances Frost. DDA; FAOV
Of a Spider. Wilfrid Thorley. BrR; FaPON
Of a steady winking beat between. Paraphrase. Hart Crane. MOAP; MoVE; TwAmPo
Of A' the Airts [the Wind Can Blaw]. Burns. AWP; BEL; CoBE; EBSV; EiPP; EM-1; EnLi-2; EnRP; EV-3; GoTS; InPo; JAWP; LoBV; OAEP; OBEC; PFE; REAL; TOP; TyEnPo; ViBoPo
(I Love My Jean.) CaAE; CEP; EnLit; GN; HBV, *with 2 add. sts. by* John Hamilton; LPS-1; OTPC (1923 ed.)
(Jean.) BTP; GTBS; GTBS-D; GTBS-W; GTSE; GTSL; HiLiEn; LEAP; MCCG; OBEV; PoMa; TreFS; TrGrPo
(My Jean.) OuHeWo
Of a' the festivals we hear. Hallowe'en. John Mayne. HBV
Of a' the maids o fair Scotland. Young Benjie. *Unknown.* BaBo; EBSV; ESPB; OBB
Of a Vision of Hell, Which a Monk Had. Richard Watson Dixon. *Fr.* Mano; a Poetical History. VA
Of a Woman, Dead Young. Dorothy Parker. DDA
Of a Woman's Heart. Sir Henry Wotton. EV-2
Of Adam's first wife, Lilith, it is told. Body's Beauty. Dante Gabriel Rossetti. The House of Life, LXXVIII. ATP (1953 ed.); BMEP; BPN; EmBrPo; EnL; HBV; LEAP; PoEL-5; POTT; PoVP; TrGrPo; ViP; ViPo; ViPP; VLEP
Of Albion's glorious ile the wonders whilst I write. The First Song. Michael Drayton. *Fr.* Polyolbion. ReIE
Of Alice in Wonderland. "Lewis Carroll." Alice's Adventures in Wonderland, *introd.* VA
Of all among the fallen from on high. Doctor of Billiards. E. A. Robinson. TwP
Of all beasts he learned the language. Hiawatha's Brothers. Longfellow. *Fr.* The Song of Hiawatha, III. PCH
Of all chaste birds the phoenix doth excel. Of Rosalind [*or* Rosalynd]. Thomas Lodge. *Fr.* Rosalynde. GoBC; PoLi; ReIE; SiCE
Of all dear days is Christmas Day. Christmas Day. Margaret E. Sangster. PEDC
Of all Earth's varied, lovely moods. Indian Summer. Helena Coleman. CPG
Of all great Nature's tones that sweep. Implicit Faith. Aubrey Thomas De Vere. *Fr.* May Carols. GoBC; MaRV
Of All He Would Do. Cecco Angiolieri da Siena. *See* Sonnet: Of All He Would Do.

Of all life's plagues I recommend to no man. On a Deaf Housekeeper. *Unknown.* BOHV
Of all mad creatures, if the learn'd are right. Why Did I Write? Pope. *Fr.* Epistle to Dr. Arbuthnot. OBEC
Of all men, saving Sylla the man-slayer. Daniel Boone. Byron. *Fr.* Don Juan, VIII. LPS-3
Of all my epigrams, reader, read not one. Ad Lectorem. John Weever. ReIE
Of all of the gruesome attempts at a twosome. Owen Seaman [*or* Spratt vs. Spratt]. Louis Untermeyer. ALV; PC. *See also* Of all the mismated pairs ever created.
Of all our antic [*or* antick] sights and pageantry. The Medal; a Satire against Sedition. Dryden. CEP; EiPP
Of all sad words of tongue or pen. The Saddest Words. Whittier. *Fr.* Maud Muller. NePA; SiTL
Of all sounds out of the soul of sorrow. Sounds Out of Sorrow. Edgar Lee Masters. ChMo; CMP
Of all that world of woe on woe. L'Inferno. Benjamin Sledd. NoCaPo
Of all the animals on earth. Christmas Song. Elizabeth-Ellen Long. ChBR; SiSoSe
Of all the beasts that live, we must. Cats and Humans—All the Same. Anthony Euwer. CIV
Of all the beasts which we for our veneriall name. Michael Drayton. *Fr.* Polyolbion. OBS
Of All the Birds. George Gascoigne. *See* Praise of Philip Sparrow, The.
Of all the birds from East to West. Chanticleer. Katharine Tynan. HBV; HBVY; MPB; MW; OTPC; TiPo; TSW; TSWC; TVSH
Of all the birds that ever I see. *Unknown.* SeCSL
Of all the birds that I do know. The Praise of Philip Sparrow. George Gascoigne. CH; ViBoPo
Of all the birds upon the wing. The Blackbird. William Barnes. EV-4; GTSE; HBV
Of all the causes which [*or* that] conspire to blind. Pope. An Essay on Criticism, Pt. II. CoBE; EnL; FaBoEn; NBE
Of all the cities in Romanian lands. Theodore and Honoria. Dryden. GEPC; SeEP
Of all the fated company who passed. Valedictory. Wrenne Jarman. DiM
Of all the floures in the mede. The Daisy. Chaucer. *Fr.* The Legend of Good Women: Prologue. LO; LPS-2
Of all the flowers rising now. Maritae Suae. William Philpot. OBEV; OBVV
Of all the fonts from which man's heart has drawn. The Guerdon of the Sun. George Sterling. HBMV
Of all the forest trees that grow. The Fir Tree. *Unknown.* COAH
Of all the fruits I ever pluck. Hunger and Thirst. Louis Ginsberg. PFE
Of all the gay places the world can afford. Letter Containing a Panegyric on Bath. Christopher Anstey. *Fr.* The New Bath Guide. OBEC
Of all the gentle tenants of the place. Sons of Indolence. James Thomson. *Fr.* The Castle of Indolence, I. OBEC
Of all the girls that are so smart. Sally in our Alley. Henry Carey. AWP; BOHV; BTP; CBOV; CEP; CoMu; EiPP; EV-3; FaBoBe; FaFP; GTBS; GTBS-D; GTBS-W; GTSE; GTSL; HBV; InMe; JAWP; KN; LEAP; LiTG; LiTL; LO; LPS-1; NeHB; OBEC; OBEV; OlF; PG (1945 ed.); PoE; RIS; SiTL; TiPo (1952 ed.); TOP; TreF; ViBoPo; WBP
Of all the girls that e'er were seen. Ballad. John Gay. CoMu
Of all the gruesome attempts at a twosome. *See* Of all of the gruesome . . .
Of all the heavenly gifts that mortal men commend. Of Friendship. Nicholas Grimald. SiCE
Of all the kings that ever here did reign. Astrophel and Stella, LXXV. Sir Philip Sidney. SiPS
Of all the Lombards, by their trophies knowne. Sir William Davenant. *Fr.* Gondibert. SeCV-1
Of all the many trees there are. My Favorite Tree. Margarete Münsterberg. GFA
Of all the meals you can buy for money. A Song of Bread and Honey. Richard Le Gallienne. PCH
Of All the Men. Thomas Moore. BOHV; FiBHP
Of all the mismated pairs ever created. Owen Seaman. Louis Untermeyer. BOHV. *See also* Of all of the gruesome attempts at a twosome.
Of all the nuns no heart was half so light. A Legend of Provence. Adelaide Anne Procter. PraNu
Of all the places on the map. In Philistia. Bliss Carman. ALV
Of all the pleasant ways. Driving in the Park. *Unknown.* OxBoLi
Of all the prizes/ That earth can give. True Riches. *Unknown.* MaRV
Of all the rides since the birth of time. Skipper Ireson's Ride. Whittier. AmP; AmPP; AnNE; APW; BeLS; BOHV; CoBA; DDA; GA; GBV; HBV; HiLiAm; IAP; InMe; InP; MOAP; OBAV; OnHT; OnSP; OTPC; OxBA; PAH; PFE; PFY; PIAE; StPo; StVeCh (1940 ed.); TCAP; TreFS; YaD; YT
Of all the sad sights in this old world of sin. The Expectant Father. E. O. Laughlin. LauV
Of all the sayings in this world. *Unknown.* OxNR
Of all the seasons in the year. The Bonny Harvest Moon. John Barr of Craigielee. AnNZ
Of all the shafts to Cupid's bow. The Three Arrows. Edward Fitzgerald. OBVV
Of all the ships upon the blue. Captain Reece. W. S. Gilbert. CenHV; FiBHP; GN; HBV; LPS-3; MaC; OTPC
Of all the sons of Romulus who walk the earth. Catullus, *tr. fr. Latin by* Horace Gregory. RoL
Of all the souls that stand create. Emily Dickinson. AnNE; BAV; GTBS-D; MaPo; NePA; OBAV; TrGrPo (Choice.) AA; AnFE; APA; AV; CoAnAm; LBAP; LoPS; PIAE; TOP
Of all the sounds despatched abroad. The Wind. Emily Dickinson. AnFE; CoAnAm; MAPA; TwAmPo
Of all the stars that bathe the heavens in glory. La Donna e Mobile. "A. K." FiBHP; InMe
Of all the theocratic beasts. Ubasti. Gelett Burgess. CIV
Of all the thoughts of God that are. The Sleep. Elizabeth Barrett Browning. AlDL; BPP; EV-4; HBV; LPS-3; MaRV; VA; WGRP
Of all the torments, all the cares. Rivals [*or* Song]. William Walsh. EV-3; HBV; LiTL; LoPo; LPS-1; OBEC; OBEV; ViBoPo
Of all the treasures on this pilgrimage. Duet. Elizabeth Selden. BoFr
Of all the trees in England. Trees. Walter de la Mare. GTBS; OHIP
Of all the tyrannies of human kind. Dryden. *Fr.* The Hind and the Panther, I. PoFr
Of all the wild deeds upon murder's black list. Verses on Daniel Good. *Unknown.* CoMu
Of all the wimming doubly blest. A Grain of Salt. Wallace Irwin. BOHV; HBV; WhC
Of all the wives as e'er you know. Nancy Lee. Frederic E. Weatherly. AmSS; OlF; VA
Of all the woodland creatures. The Flying Squirrel. Mary E. Burt. PECK
Of all the world's enjoyments. The Fisherman's Song. Thomas D'Urfey. ALV
Of all thes kene conquerours to carpe it were kynde. The Tournament of Tottenham. *Unknown.* OxBoLi
Of all things beautiful and good. Brotherhood. Edwin Markham. OQP; POT; PoTo; QP-1
Of all things human which are strange and wild. James Thomson. *Fr.* The City of Dreadful Night. LoBV; ViBoPo
Of all trades agoing, begging it is my delight. The Happy Beggarman. *Unknown.* OnYI
Of all who went to the woods of Hate. Fox Hunters of Hell. Byron Herbert Reece. DaM
Of all women that ever were born. A Lamentation of the Virgin. *Unknown.* TMEV
Of Alphus. John Parkhurst, *tr. fr. Latin by* Timothe Kendall. TuPP
Of an Ancient Spaniel in Her Fifteenth Year. Christopher Morley. WaKn
Of an old King in a story. Variations on an Air: After W. B. Yeats. G. K. Chesterton. InP
Of an Old Song. William E. H. Lecky. WGRP
Of an old Souldier of the Queens. An Old Souldier of the Queens. *Unknown.* OBS; SoV
Of an Orchard. Katharine Tynan. GoBC; HBV; OBVV; WGRP
Of Armenye, I rede thus. The Tale of Rosiphelee. John Gower. *Fr.* Confessio Amantis. ArmLP
Of Astraea. Sir John Davies. *Fr.* Hymns of Astraea. SiCE; TrGrPo; TuPP
(Virgin Queen, The; an Anagram.) BLV
Of Baiting the Lion. Sir Owen Seaman. BOHV; NA
Of Ballad-Singers. John Gay. *Fr.* Trivia; or, The Art of Walking the Streets of London, III: Of Walking the Streets by Night. EnLi-1 (1949 ed.)
Of beasts am I, of men was he most brave. The Lion over the Tomb of Leonidas. *Unknown.* AWP; JAWP; WBP
Of Beauty. Sir Richard Fanshawe. *See* Of Time.
Of Beauty, *sel.* John Hall.
"What do I here! what's beauty? 'las." LO
Of beauty yet she passeth all. What Would She More? *Unknown.* TMEV
Of Birds and Birders. John Heywood. SiCE
Of Black Beauty. Lord Herbert of Cherbury. *See* Sonnet of Black Beauty.
Of Blue China. Andrew Lang. *See* Ballade of Blue China.
Of Books. John Florio. *See* Concerning the Honour of Books.
Of bronze and blaze. Emily Dickinson. MoPo
(Aurora.) MAPA; TwAmPo
Of caterpillars Fabre tells how day after day. Caterpillars. John Freeman. ChMP

Of Caution. Francesco da Barberino, *tr. fr. Italian by* Dante Gabriel Rossetti. AWP; JAWP; LyPI; OnPM; WBP
Of Ceaseless Thoughts My Mind Hath Fram'd His Wings. Thomas Lodge. ReIE
Of Charity. Arthur Symons. VLEP
Of children nine and twenty that I bore. A Joyful Mother of Children. *Unknown.* OxBG
Of China and Her Wisdom. Paul Eldridge. PoeMoYo
Of Cinna's Election. Sir John Harington. SiCE
Of Circe. Homer, *tr. fr. Greek by* William Morris. *Fr.* The Odyssey, X. OxBG
Of Clementina. Walter Savage Landor. EV-4; HBV; OBEV (In Clementina's Artless Mien.) OBRV; ViBoPo (Lyrics and Epigrams, II.) ERP
Of Clergymen and Their Livings. Sir John Harington. TuPP
Of comfort no man speak. Sad Stories of the Death of Kings. Shakespeare. King Richard II, *fr.* III, ii. BCEP; PIR
Of Common Devotion. Francis Quarles. PIAE
Of Common Meddlers. John Heywood. SiCE
Of Content. William Dunbar. EBSV
Of cool sweet dew and radiance mild. Simples. James Joyce. CaAE; HBMV; NP
Of cord and cassia-wood is the harp compounded. The Old Harp. Po Chü-i. TrCh
Of Corinna's Singing. Thomas Campion. *See* When to Her Lute Corinna Sings.
Of Cornelius. Everard Guilpin. *Fr.* Skialetheia. SiCE; TuPP
Of course I prayed. Emily Dickinson. MAP; MoAmPo; ReaPo
Of course, I thought I'd never let him stay. Silhouette. Violet Alleyn Storey. CIV
Of course I tried to tell him. Poets Hitchhiking on the Highway. Gregory Corso. NeAP
Of course, the entire effort is to put myself. Thoughts during an Air Raid. Stephen Spender. MoBrPo (1950 ed.); NeMA; ViBoPo
Of course this little pencil sketch/ resembles him. Of the Ship. C. P. Cavafy. MoGP
Of course you have read of the wicked ways. The Ballad of Chicken Bill. F. E. Vaughn. PoOW
Of Courtesy. Arthur Guiterman. TiPo
Of courtesy, it is much less. Courtesy. Hilaire Belloc. ACP (1952 ed.); BMEP; HBMV; JKCP; LBBV; OtMeF; PoeT; SDH
Of Crossing the Street. John Gay. *Fr.* Trivia; or, The Art of Walking the Streets of London, III: Of Walking the Streets by Night. EnLi-1 (1949 ed.)
Of Cruelty to Animals. Martin Farquhar Tupper. *Fr.* Proverbial Philosophy. LPS-3
Of Cyclops and the Ram. Homer, *tr. fr. Greek by* William Morris. *Fr.* The Odyssey, IX. OxBG
Of Cynthia. *Unknown. See* Ode: Of Cynthia.
Of dames, of knights, of arms, of love's delight. Ariosto. *Fr.* Orlando Furioso, I. ReIE
Of Darts from Lattices Beware. Charles d'Orléans, *tr. fr. French by* Alan Conder. TrFP
Of Death. Robert Garnier. *See* Chorus: "Alas, with what tormenting fire."
Of Death. Samuel Harding. *Fr.* Sicily and Naples. SeCL
Of Death. Samuel Sheppard. SeCL
Of Death. James Shirley. *See* Death the Leveller.
Of deepest blue of summer skies. Alice. Herbert Bashford. HBV
Of Demeter the bright-haired, worshipful Goddess, beginneth my lay. The Rape of Persephone. *Unknown. Fr.* Homeric Hymns. GrR
Of De Witt Williams on His Way to Lincoln Cemetery. Gwendolyn Brooks. PoNe
Of Difference between Wise Men and Fools. John Heywood. ReIE
Of Disdainful Daphne. M. H. Nowell. ElL
Of Dissembling Words. Sir Thomas Wyatt. *See* Honesty.
Of Don Pedro and His Poetry. Sir John Harington, *after the Latin of* Martial. SiCE
Of Drinking. Abraham Cowley. *See* Drinking.
Of Drunkenness. George Turberville. TuPP
Of Eden lost, in ancient days. Rondeau, Humbly Inscribed to the Right Hon. William Eden. *At. to* George Ellis. OBEC
Of Edenhall, the youthful Lord. The Luck of Edenhall. Ludwig Uhland, *tr. by* Longfellow. AWP; StPo
Of Edwards of the Chapel. Barnabe Googe. ReIE
Of Enclosing a Common. Sir John Harington. SiCE
Of England and of Its Marvels. Fazio degli Uberti, *tr. fr. Italian by* Dante Gabriel Rossetti. AWP; JAWP; WBP
Of English Verse. Edmund Waller. OBS
Of Enough and a Feast. John Heywood. SiCE; TuPP
Of evenings now above the restaurants. The Stranger. Aleksandr Blok. TrRV
Of every step I took in pain. The Recompense. Anna Wickham. NP; PC
Of everykune tre. The Hawthorn. *Unknown.* ChTr
Of evident invisibles. Portrait II. E. E. Cummings. TCPD
Of famed Megistias here behold the tomb. Prophetic Death. Simonides. OnPM
Of Faustus, a Stealer of Verses. Sir John Harington. SiCE; TuPP
Of [*or* Off] Februar[y] the fifteen nicht. The Dance of the Seven Deadly Sins [*or* Sevin Deidly Sinnis *or* Synnis]. William Dunbar. BCEP; BSV; EBSV; GoTS
Of few words, Sir, you seem to be. *Unknown.* SiPS
Of Fiammetta Singing. Boccaccio, *tr. fr. Italian by* Dante Gabriel Rossetti. *Fr.* Sonnets. AWP (Fiammetta.) GoBC
Of Fishing. Karl Mikael Bellman, *tr. fr. Swedish by* Charles W. Stork. AnSL
Of Fortune, *abr.* Thomas Kyd. *Fr.* Cornelia. ElL
Of Fortune. Sir Thomas More. CoBE
Of Fortune's Power. Richard Edwards. ReIE
Of fret, of dark, of thorn, of chill. Opposition. Sidney Lanier. AmPP (3d ed.); AnFE; APA; CoAnAm; LiTA; OBAV
Of Friendship. Charles Stuart Calverley. PA
Of Friendship. Nicholas Grimald. SiCE
Of Friendship. Sir John Harington, *after the Latin of* Martial. SiCE
Of funerals the saddest. Funeral [*or* Funerals]. Vyacheslav Ivanov. BoRS; OnPM; TrRV
Of Fuscus, a Drunkard. Sir Thomas More, *tr. fr. Latin by* Timothe Kendall. TuPP
Of Galla's Goodly Periwig. Sir John Harington. SiCE
Of Giving. Arthur Guiterman. TiPo
Of gladde things there be four, ay four. Gladde Things. *Unknown.* TiPo (1952 ed.)
Of God to thy doings, a time there is sent. A Description of Time, and the Year. Thomas Tusser. SiCE
Of Gods and Men. Pindar, *tr. fr. Greek by* C. J. Billson. *Fr.* Nemean Odes, VI. GrR
Of God's Omnipotencie. Alexander Hume. EV-1
Of Good and Evil, *sel.* Erasmus Darwin.
"Each pregnant oak ten thousand acorns forms." PoP
Of Good Sauce. Sir John Harington. SiCE
Of grass, insurgent bud aware. Final Spring. Ralph Gustafson. BoCaPo
Of great Demeter here begins my lay. The Rape of Persephone. *Unknown. Fr.* Homeric Hymns. OxBG
Of Greatness in Teaching. Leslie Pinckney Hill. MaRV
Of green and hexagonal glass. The Bottle. Walter de la Mare. MoPo; POTE
Of Haga. Karl Mikael Bellman, *tr. fr. Swedish by* Charles W. Stork. AnSL
Of Heaven Considered as a Tomb. Wallace Stevens. AnFE; AnNE; APA; CoAnAm
Of Heaven or Hell I have no power to sing. An Apology [*or* Prologue]. William Morris. *Fr.* The Earthly Paradise. AWP; BEL; BLPA; BMEP; BPN; BrBE; CoBE; EmBrPo; EnLi-2; EnLit; EPN; EPP; FaBoEn; GTBS-W; GTSL; HBV; InP; LEAP; LiTB; LoBV; OAEP; OtMeF; POTT; PoVP; TCEP; TOP; VA; ViBoPo; ViP; ViPo; ViPP; VLEP
Of heavenly stature, but most human smile. Written in the Visitors' Book at the Birthplace of Robert Burns. George Washington Cable. AA
Of Her Breath. Robert Herrick. EG
Of Hermes sing, O Muse. To Hermes. *Unknown. Fr.* Homeric Hymns. GrL
Of heroes and statesmen I'll just mention four. Paul Jones—a New Song. *Unknown.* PAH
Of Heywood. John Heywood. ReIE; SiCE; TuPP
Of high Honour should be her hood. The Garment of Good Ladies. Robert Henryson. ACP
Of highway dust the Buddha made his throne. Gautama. Thomas S. Jones, Jr. AnAmPo; LA
Of Him I Love Day and Night. Walt Whitman. MOAP
Of him that had for mother the glorious Semele. Hymn to Dionysus. *Unknown. Fr.* Homeric Hymns. GrPE
Of Himself. Clément Marot, *tr. fr. French by* Alan Conder. OnPM; TrFP
Of Himself. Meleager, *tr. fr. Greek by* Richard Garnett. AWP
Of His Choice of a Sepulchre. Andrew Lang. *See* Ballade of His Choice of a Sepulchre.
Of His Cynthia. Fulke Greville. Caelica, LII. ElL; ElSeCe (Another of His Cynthia.) TuPP ("Away with these self-loving lads.") AtBAP; SiCE (Cynthia.) OBSC; RiBV (Song to His Cynthia.) ViBoPo (Sonnet.) ReIE
Of His Daughter Catherine Dead Long Since. Wordsworth. *See* Surprised by Joy . . .
Of His Dear Son, Gervase. Sir John Beaumont. *Fr.* Of My Dear Son Gervase Beaumont. OBEV ("Dear Lord, receive my son, whose winning love.") GoBC
Of His Death. Meleager, *tr. fr. Greek by* Andrew Lang. AWP

Of His Divine Poems. Edmund Waller. *See* Of the Last Verses in the Book.
Of His Foolish Passion for Laura. Petrarch, *tr. fr. Italian by* Susan Wollaston. Sonnets to Laura: To Laura in Life, VI. EnLi-1; OuHeWo
Of His Lady. Chaucer. *See* Balade: "Hyd, Absolon, thy gilte tresses clere."
Of His Lady. *Unknown.* ElL
Of His Lady's Face. Jacopo da Lentino, *tr. fr. Italian by* Dante Gabriel Rossetti. OnPM
(Sonnet: Of His Lady's Face.) AWP
Of His Lady's Old Age. Pierre de Ronsard, *tr. fr. French by* Andrew Lang. AWP; JAWP; POTT; WBP
(To Helen.) OuHeWo
Of His Last Sight of Fiammetta. Boccaccio, *tr. fr. Italian by* Dante Gabriel Rossetti. *Fr.* Sonnets. AWP; JAWP; OnPM; WBP
(Fiammetta.) GoBC
Of His Love Called Anna. Sir Thomas Wyatt. ElSeCe; ReIE; TuPP
Of His Love That Pricked Her Finger with a Needle. Sir Thomas Wyatt. ReIE; TCEP
Of His Majesties Receiving the News of the Duke of Buckingham's Death. Edmund Waller. SeCV-1
Of His Mistress. Robert Greene. *See* Melicertus' Description of His Mistress.
Of His Mistress. Peter Hausted. *Fr.* The Rival Friends. EG; SeCL
Of His Mistress Grown Old. William Hicks. SeCL
Of His Mother's Shade. Homer, *tr. fr. Greek by* J. W. Mackail. *Fr.* The Odyssey, XI. OxBG
Of His Muse. Sir John Harington. SiCE
Of His Return[e] from Spain[e]. Sir Thomas Wyatt. FaBoEn; ReIE; TuPP
(In Spain.) OBSC; SeCePo
("Tagus, farewell, that westward with thy streams.") ReEn; SiCE
Of Holding of a Nose. John Heywood. ReIE
Of Holy Poverty. Jacopone da Todi, *tr. fr. Italian by* Mrs. Theodore Beck. SaFP
Of Homer's Odyssey. Sir John Davies. *Fr.* Orchestra. EG
Of Honest Theft. To My Good Friend Master Samuel Daniel. Sir John Harington. SiCE
Of honey and heat and weed and wheat. Love and a Day. Madison Cawein. PR
Of Howard's stem a glorious branch is dead. Elegy for Margaret Howard, Lady Buckhurst. Robert Southwell. CoBE
Of Human Knowledge. Sir John Davies. *Fr.* Nosce Teipsum. EV-2; ReIE; SiCE; SiPS; TuPP
Of Human Life. Henry King. *See* Sic Vita.
Of Human Progress. Lucretius, *tr. fr. Latin by* William Ellery Leonard. *Fr.* Of the Nature of Things (De Rerum Natura). WoL
Of Humane Learning, *sel.* Fulke Greville.
"Chiefe use then in man, The." OBS; SiCE
(Man's Service, 1 *st.*) PoFr
Of Impatience Which Brings All Our Gains to Nothing. Jacopone da Todi, *tr. fr. Italian by* Mrs. Theodore Beck. CAW
Of Improving the Present Time, *sel.* Congreve.
Nil Admirari. OBEC
Of Joan's Youth. Louise Imogen Guiney. AA; HBV; LBMV; LEAP
Of Jolly Good Ale and Old. *At. to* William Stevenson. *See* Back and Side Go Bare, Go Bare.
Of Jonathan Chapman/ Two things are known. Johnny Appleseed. Rosemary Benét *and* Stephen Vincent Benét. BoChLi (1950 ed.); MPB; OTPC (1946 ed.); TrAS
Of Labienus. John Owen, *tr. fr. Latin by* Thomas Harvey. *Fr.* Four Epigrams. PrWP
Of late/ Since I parted from Liadin. Liadin and Curither. *Unknown.* OnYI
Of late a noble steamer, the *Cedar Grove* by name. The Loss of the *Cedar Grove*. *Unknown.* ShS
Of Late and Never. John Heywood. TuPP
Of late, in one of those most weary hours. The Garden of Boccaccio. Samuel Taylor Coleridge. BPN; EmBrPo; EPN
Of late our friend has bought a purple-dyed toga. Martial, *tr. fr. Latin by* Robert R. Schnorr. Epigrams, VIII, 10. LaP
Of Leinster, famed for maidens fair. Colin and Lucy [*or* Lucy and Colin]. Thomas Tickell. CEP; CG; EiPP; EV-3; OBEC; OTPC (1923 ed.)
Of Liberty; an Essay, *sel.* Abraham Cowley.
Portrait of a Freeman. PoFr
Of Liberty and Charity, *sel.* Richard Realf.
Holy Nation, A. PoFr
Of Liddesdale [*or* Liddisdale] the common thievis. Against the Thieves of Liddesdale [*or* Aganis the Thievis of Liddisdale]. Sir Richard Maitland. BSV; EBSV; GoTS
Of Life. Andrew Lang. VA
Of Life and Death. Ben Jonson. PreP; ReIE
"Of like race with the leaves is human kind." Thus Sang the Chian Singer. Simonides. GrR
Of Little Faith. Harold Trowbridge Pulsifer. EtS
Of little use the man you may suppose. The Poet's Use. Pope. *Fr.* The First Epistle of the Second Book of Horace. EV-3; OBEC
Of living creatures most I prize. Butterfly. William Jay Smith. TiPo (1959 ed.)
Of London Bridge, and the Stupendous Sight, and Structure Thereof. James Howell. ChTr
Of Love. *At. to* Aphra Behn. *See* Song: "Oh Love! that stronger art than wine."
Of Love. Robert Herrick. EV-2
Of Love. James Sandford. ElL
Of Love ("Long annoys and short contentings"). *Unknown.* SeCL
Of Love and Time. John Henderson. BoAV
Of love he sang, full hearted one. A Forced Music. Robert Graves. MBP; MoBrPo
Of Love of Silence and of Solitude. Thomas à Kempis. *Fr.* Imitation of Christ. TreF
Of loves and ladies, knights and arms, I sing. Orlando Furioso, I. Ariosto. EnLi-1; PrPoCR
Of Love's Awakening. Juan Meléndez Valdés, *tr. fr. Spanish by* James Kennedy. TeCS
(Juvenilities.) AnSpL-2
Of love's designed joys. Stay, O Stay. A. E. Coppard. MBP; MoBrPo (1942 ed.)
Of Loving a Dog. John Heywood. SiCE; TuPP
Of Lynus, Borrowing. Sir John Harington. SiCE
Of Madame Bergström's Portrait at the Inn of Lilya in Torshälla. Karl Mikael Bellman, *tr. fr. Swedish by* Charles W. Stork. AnSL
Of Maids' Inconstancy. Richard Brathwaite. *Fr.* A Strappado for the Devil. ElL
(Wooer's Song, The.) ElSeCe
Of Man and Wife. Richard Eedes. *See* No Love, to Love of Man and Wife.
Of Manly Disposition. Aneirin, *tr. fr. Welsh by* D. S. Evans. LyMA
Of manners gentle, of affections mild. On Mr. Gay; in Westminster Abbey, 1732 [*or* Epitaph XI]. Pope. CEP; FiP; PtP
Of Man's first disobedience, and the fruit. Invocation to the Heavenly Muse [*or* The Fallen Angels *or* The Opening Argument]. Milton. Paradise Lost, I. ATP; BCEP; BEL; BoLiVe; CBE; CoBE; EM-1; EnL; EnLi-1; EnLit; EPP; EV-2; FaBoEn; FiP; GEPC; OAEP; OuHeWo; PoEL-3; PoFS; REAL; SeEP; TCEP; TOP; TreFS; TyEnPo; WoL
Of Man's Mortalitie. *At. to* Simon Wastell. *See* Man's Mortality.
Of many marvels in my time. A Description of a Strange (and Miraculous) Fish. Martin Parker. CoMu
Of many things adulterate. Epitaph; for Himself. Tristan Corbière. AWP
Of Mariners. Harold Vinal. BAP
Of marsh-mallows my boat is made. The Ferry. Emperor Ch'ien Wen-ti. ChLP; TrCh
Of Mary's pains may now learn whoso will. The Holy Mother at the Cross. Richard Watson Dixon. ViP
Of me ye may say many a bitter thing. Worth Remembrance. Philip Bourke Marston. LBBV
Of Melodies Unheard. Mahlon Leonard Fisher. MuM
Of men, nay beasts; worse, monsters; worst of all. Phineas Fletcher. The Locusts, or Apollyonists, I. EPS; SeCV-1; SeEP
Of Middle Life. *Unknown.* SeCL
Of mind, and its mysterious agencies. James Gates Percival. *Fr.* The Mind. PoP
Of mine acquaintance a certain young man. John Heywood. *Fr.* A Dialogue Containing the Number of the Effectual Proverbs in the English Tongue. ReIE
Of Misery. Thomas Howell. ElL; TuPP
Of Modern Poetry. Wallace Stevens. AmP; AmPP (4th ed.); CoV; InvP; NePA; OxBA
Of Money. Barnabe Googe. ElL
Of mortal blessings here the first is health. The Four Blessings. *Unknown.* OnPM
Of Mountains, *sel.* Leonora Speyer.
"Who is the pioneer?" PC
Of Mourners. Dorothy Livesay. PeCV
Of my city the worst that men will ever say is this. They Will Say. Carl Sandburg. PC
Of My Dear Son [*or* Sonne], Gervase Beaumont. Sir John Beaumont. OBS; SeCL; SeEP; ViBoPo, *abr.*
(On My Dear Son, Gervase Beaumont.) EV-2
"Dear Lord, receive my son, whose winning love," *sel.* GoBC
(Of His Dear Son, Gervase.) OBEV
Of my deep hunger. S. Funaroff. *Fr.* Dusk of the Gods. NAMP
Of My Lady Isabella Playing on the Lute. Edmund Waller. MePo

Of my lady, wel me rejoise I may. Hoccleve's Humorous Praise of His Lady. Thomas Hoccleve. OAEP
Of my ould loves, of their ould ways. Memories. Arthur Stringer. HBV
Of Myself. Abraham Cowley. *Fr.* A Vote. ElSeCe; LPS-3; OAEP; OBS; SeCL
("This only grant me.") SeEP
(Wish, A.) ReTS; WP
Of myself a true tale can I tell and speak. The Seafarer, Pt. I. *Unknown.* REAL
Of myself I can tell a true song-tale. Afar on the Floodways. *Unknown.* The Seafarer, Pt. I. PoLi
Of myself, my dear joy, if you wish to be told. An Irishman's Christening. *Unknown.* OnYI
Of Narrow Streets. John Gay. *Fr.* Trivia; or, The Art of Walking the Streets of London, II: Of Walking the Streets by Day. EnLi-1 (1949 ed.)
Of Nature broad and free. Arbor Day Song. Mary A. Heermans. ADAH; HH
Of Nelson and the North. The Battle of the Baltic. Thomas Campbell. BHV; CoBE; EBSV; EnRP; EPP; ERP; EV-4; GN; GTBS; GTBS-D; GTBS-W; GTSE; GTSL; HBV; LH; OBEV; OTPC (1923 ed.); TVSH
Of Neptune's empire let us sing. A Hymn in Praise of Neptune. Thomas Campion. EtS; GTSL; OBEV; OBSC; TVSH
Of Nicolette. E. E. Cummings. HBMV
Of Noman and Cyclops. Homer. *See* Noman and the Cyclops.
Of Nothing and Althing. John Heywood. SiCE
Of old, a man who died. Immortal Flowers. Wallace Rice. AA
Of old, all invitations ended. Thoughts on Being Invited to Dinner. Christopher Morley. HBMV
Of old are Erechtheus' folk favored of heaven. Euripides. *Fr.* Medea. GrPo
Of old it went forth to Euchenor, pronounced of his sire, Euchenor Chorus. Arthur Upson. *Fr.* The City. LBMV
Of old our fathers' God was real. Exit God. Gamaliel Bradford. HBMV; InMe; MaRV; QS
Of old sailors, the song you would hear. Old Sailors. *Unknown.* SG
Of Old Sat Freedom on the Heights. Hildegarde Flanner. PoFr
Of Old Sat Freedom on the Heights. Tennyson. BEL; BHV; EmBrPo; HBV; OAEP; PoFr; PoVP; TCEP; ViPo; VLEP
(Freedom.) MaRV
Of old the Muses sat on high. The Muses. Edith M. Thomas. HBV
Of old the Winds came romping down. The Bridge Builder. Isabel Ecclestone Mackay. CPG
Of old when folk lay sick and sorely tried. On Hygiene. Hilaire Belloc. MBP; MoBrPo
Of old, when Scarron his companions invited. Retaliation. Goldsmith. CEP; EiPP; LaA; OAEP; OxBoLi; TCEP; TOP
Of On [*or* One] That Is So Fayr and Bright. *Unknown.* *See* Hymn to the Virgin.
Of One Blood Hath God Created. Henry B. Robins. MaRV
Of One Dead. Leo Kennedy. PeCV
Of One Dead. Tennyson. In Memoriam A. H. H., XIV. LiTB; LiTG
Of One Hanged. John Heywood. ReIE
Of One Self-slain. Charles Hanson Towne. BAP; LEAP; SBMV; WGRP
(To One Self-slain.) BPP
Of One That Is So Fair and Bright. *Unknown.* *See* Hymn to the Virgin, A.
Of One Who neither Sees nor Hears. Richard Watson Gilder. AA
Of One Who Seemed to Have Failed. S. Weir Mitchell. AA; LBAP; OBAV
Of Order in Our Lord Christ. *At. to* St. Francis of Assisi. *See* Cantica: Our Lord Christ.
Of Our Lord's Passion, *sel.* St. Bernard of Clairvaux, *tr. fr.* Latin.
"In Thine hour of holy sadness." ChIP
Of Pan we sing, the best of singers, Pan. Ben Jonson. *Fr.* Pan's Anniversary; or, The Shepherd's Holiday. ElSeCe
Of Pansa. Everard Guilpin. *Fr.* Skialetheia. ReIE
Of Peleus' son, Achilles, sing, O Muse. Sing, O Muse. Homer. *Fr.* The Iliad, I. LiA
Of Perfect Friendship. *At. to* Henry Cheke. *See* Plain Description of Perfect Friendship, A.
Of Phyllis. William Drummond of Hawthornden. *See* Phyllis.
Of Pick-Pockets. John Gay. *Fr.* Trivia; or, The Art of Walking the Streets of London, III: Of Walking the Streets by Night. EnLi-1 (1949 ed.)
Of praise then, and of honourable report. He Sins Not Who Sins Unwittingly. Sophocles. *Fr.* Oedipus at Colonus. GrR
Of priests we can offer a charmin' variety. Father O'Flynn. Alfred Perceval Graves. BOHV; HBV; OnYI
Of Pyramus and Thisbe I will sing. Pyramus and Thisbe. Ovid. *Fr.* Metamorphoses. LaP
Of Quarrels. Arthur Guiterman. TiPo
Of quiet things, of things at rest. Beside Lilia Dead. Sister Mary Catherine. JKCP (1955 ed.)
Of Rama. Herman Melville. AnFE; CoAnAm; LiTA
Of Reading. Charles Stuart Calverley. PA
Of Rebellion. John Heywood. ReIE
Of Red in Spring. David McCord. MAP; MoAmPo (1942 ed.)
Of Religion. Kahlil Gibran. *Fr.* The Prophet. GrCo-2
Of Rome. Herman Melville. *Fr.* Clarel. OxBA
Of Rosalind. Thomas Lodge. *Fr.* Rosalynde. GoBC
(Of Rosalynd.) PoLi
(Sonetto: "Of all chaste birds the phoenix doth excel.") ReIE; SiCE
Of Roses. Mary Carolyn Davies. PR
Of Silence and the Air. Ruth Pitter. MeRV
Of Sir Philip Sidney. Sir John Beaumont. GoBC
Of Snow. Norman Brick. WaP
Of so divine a loss. Emily Dickinson. BoFr
Of Solitude. Abraham Cowley. EPS; OBS; SeCL; SeEP
(On Solitude.) EV-2
Essay on Solitude ("Hail, old patrician trees, so great and good"), *sel.* ViBoPo
Of Sorrow, 'tis as Saints have said. Sorrow. Helen Parry Eden. JKCP
Of souls departed, if our minds were strong. The Dead. Semonides. OxBG
Of speckled eggs the birdie sings. Singing. Robert Louis Stevenson. GaP; GFA; MeMeAg; OnHT; PCH; SUS
Of Spenser's Faerie Queene [*or* Fairy Queen]. Thomas Freeman. SiCE; TuPP
Of Spenser's Faery Queen. Sir Walter Ralegh. *See* Vision upon This Conceit of the Faerie Queene, A.
Of spring water,—thirty or forty miles. How I Sailed on the Lake till I Came to the Eastern Stream. Lu Yu. TrCh
Of Such as Had Forsaken Him. Sir Thomas Wyatt. TuPP
(Epigram: "Lux, my fair falcon, and your fellows all.") SiPS
("Lux, my fair falcon, and your fellows all.") SiCE
Of Such Is the Kingdom. Francis Greenwood Peabody. MaRV
Of Such Is the Kingdom of Heaven. Swinburne. *See* Children.
Of Summum Bonum. Sir John Harington. SiCE
Of Tabacco. Sir John Davies. ReIE
Of Tact. Arthur Guiterman. MoShBr
(How Are You?) WhC
Of Taking Things Wrong. John Heywood. ReIE
Of Tears. *Unknown.* LoPS
Of Temperance in Fortune. Richard Watson Dixon. *Fr.* Mano; a Poetical History. VA
Of th' Atrides I would sing. *Unknown, tr. fr. Greek by* Thomas Stanley. GrPo
Of that wherein thou art a questioner. Sonnet: To Dante Alighieri (He Interprets Dante Alighieri's Dream). Dante da Maiano. AWP
Of that world's conquest and the fortunate wars. The Argument. Archibald MacLeish. *Fr.* Conquistador. AtBAP
Of the Abbot and His Valet. Clément Marot, *tr. fr. French by* Wilfrid Thorley. LiA
Of the beast . . . an angel. The Everlasting Contenders. Kenneth Patchen. CrMA
Of the beauty of kindness I speak. Kindness. T. Sturge Moore. GTML; OBMV
Of the birds that fly in the farthest sea. The Flying Fish. John Gray. ChTr; LoBV
Of the Birth and Bringing Up of Desire. Edward de Vere, Earl of Oxford. OBSC; ReIE; SiCE; TuPP
Of the Birth of Christ. Miles Coverdale. AnEC
Of the Blessèd Sacrament of the Altar. Robert Southwell. GoBC; OBEV (new ed.)
Of the Book-Hunter. Andrew Lang. VA
Of the Changes of Life. William Dunbar. EBSV
Of the Characters of Women. Pope. Moral Essays, Epistle II. PoFS
To a Lady, *sel.* OxBoLi; SiTL
("Nothing so true as what you once let fall," *longer sel.*) FaBoEn
Of the Child with the Bird at the Bush. Bunyan. SeCL; SeEP
(My Little Bird.) OBS
Of the Choice of His Burial-Place. Pierre de Ronsard. *See* On the Choice of His Sepulchre.
Of the Courtier's Life. Sir Thomas Wyatt. Satires, I. CoBE; GoTL; OBSC; ReIE; SiCE; TuPP
(Satire I: "Mine [*or* Myne] own John Poynz.") PoEL-1; ReEn; SiPS
Of the dark past. Ecce Puer. James Joyce. MeRV; ReaPo
Of the Day Estivall. Alexander Hume. *See* Summer Day.
Of the dear son of Hermes, O Muse, sing now to me. Hymn to Pan. *Unknown.* *Fr.* Homeric Hymns. GrPE

Of the Death of Kings. Shakespeare. King Richard II, *fr.* III. ii. ChTr
("For heaven's [*or* God's] sake, let us sit upon the ground.") HoPM; PoFr
Of the Death of Sir Thomas Wyatt [the Elder]. Earl of Surrey. *See* On the Death of Sir Thomas Wyatt.
Of the divine and human thought. A Spinozaism. John Swanwick Drennan. IrPN
Of the Dust in an Hour-Glass. Girolamo Amaltheo, *pr. tr. fr. Latin by* Richard Aldington. LaP
Of the erl Hugelyn of Pyse the langour. The Tale of Hugelin, Count of Pisa. Chaucer. *Fr.* The Canterbury Tales: The Monk's Tale. MyFE
Of the Father's Love Begotten. Prudentius, *tr. fr. Latin.* BePJ
Of the first Paradice there's nothing found. On St. James's Park, as Lately Improved by His Majesty. Edmund Waller. CEP
Of the Gentle Heart. Guido Guinicelli. *See* Canzone: Of the Gentle Heart.
Of the glorious body telling. Hymn for Corpus Christi Day. St. Thomas Aquinas. LiA
Of the Gods and these other matters none knows the verity. The Agnostic. Xenophanes. GrPE
Of the Going Down of the Sun. Bunyan. CH
Of the Golden Aphrodite tell to me, Muse, the ways. Hymn to Aphrodite. *Unknown. Fr.* Homeric Hymns. GrPE
Of the Golden World. Thomas Howell. SiCE; TuPP
Of the Great and Famous [Sir Francis Drake]. Robert Hayman. CH; FaBoCh
Of the Great Marriage between Grand Amour and La Belle Pucelle. Stephen Hawes. The Pastime of Pleasure, XXXIX. ReIE
(Of the Great Mariage betwene Graunde Amour and Labell Pucell.) EPP
Of the Holy Eucharist. *Unknown.* ACP (1952 ed.)
Of the Laestrygones. Homer, *tr. fr. Greek by* Sir William Marris. *Fr.* The Odyssey, X. OxBG
Of the Last Verses in the Book. Edmund Waller. BEL; CEP; CoBE; ElSeCe; EPS; FaBoEn; HBV; MePo; OAEP; OBS; PoD; PoE; PoFS; SeCL; SeCV-1; SeEP; ViBoPo
(Of His Divine Poems.) LoBV
(On the Last Verses in His Book of Poems.) TriL
Sels.
Old Age ("The seas are quiet"). BCEP; CBOV; MaRV; OBEV
(From "Divine Poems.") EV-2
(Last Verses.) OxBoCh
(Old Age and Death.) LEAP; LPS-3
Soul's Dark Cottage, The. ChTr
Of the light of the dawn let none be silent. On a Papyrus of Oxyrhynchus. *Unknown.* CAW
Of the Lost Ship. Eugene Richard White. AA; DDA; OBAV
Of the Manner of Addressing Clouds. Wallace Stevens. AnFE; APA; CoAnAm
Of the Mathematician. Alice Clear Matthews. GoYe
Of the Mean and Sure Estate. Seneca, *tr. fr. Latin by* Sir Thomas Wyatt. *See* Stond Who So List upon the Slipper Toppe.
Of the Mean and Sure Estate [Written to John Poins]. Sir Thomas Wyatt. Satires, II. BEL; EPP; ReIE; SiCE; TuPP
("My mother's maids, when they did sew and spin.") SiPS
Of the Mean Estate. Thomas, Lord Vaux. SiCE
Of the Mighty Power of Love. Edward de Vere, Earl of Oxford. TuPP
Of the million or two, more or less. Instans Tyrannus. Robert Browning. PoFr; VLEP
Of the Months. Folgore da San Geminiano. *See* Sonnets of the Months.
Of the Moon. Charles Best. *See* Sonnet of the Moon, A.
Of the myriad afflictions that beset Hellas. Euripides, *tr. fr. Greek by* Moses Hadas. GrPo
Of the Nativity of the Lady Rich's Daughter. Henry Constable. OBSC
Of the Nature of Things. Lucretius. *See* De Rerum Natura.
Of the New Prosody. Brewster Ghiselin. MoVE
Of the old house, only a few crumbled. The House That Was. Laurence Binyon. MBP; MoBrPo
Of the onset, fear-inspiring, and the firing and the pillage. The Sack of Deerfield. Thomas Dunn English. PAH
Of the Passing Away of Brynhild. William Morris. *Fr.* The Story of Sigurd the Volsung. PoVP; TCEP; VA; VLEP
Of the Pillars of the Church. Sir John Harington. SiCE
Of the Progress[e] of the Soul[e]; the Second Anniversary. John Donne. SeEP
Sels.
Contemplation of Our State in Our Deathbed. OBS
("Think then, my soul, that death is but a groom.") CoEV; OxBoCh, *longer sel.*
"Forget this rotten world; and unto thee." FaBoEn
"Nothing could make me sooner to confesse." PoD, *abr.;* ReEn, *longer sel.*
Our Companie in the Next World. OBS
"She of whose soul, if we may say 'twas gold." TuPP
Soules Ignorance in This Life and Knowledge in the Next, The. OBS
Of the pursuit of beauty and the husk that remains. Sir Walter Raleigh. William Carlos Williams. *Fr.* In the American Grain. OnHM
Of the Resurrection of Christ. William Dunbar. OxBoCh; PoLi
(Done Is a Battle on the Dragon Black.) BSV
(On the Resurrection of Christ.) PoEL-1; TMEV
Of the Sad Lot of the Humanists in Paris. George Buchanan, *pr. tr. fr. Latin.* GoTS
Of the Senses. John Heywood. ReIE
Of the Shade of Achilles. Homer, *tr. fr. Greek by* William Cowper. *Fr.* The Odyssey, XI. OxBG
("He spake, to whom I, answ'ring, thus replied.") GrPo
Of the Shade of Ajax. Homer. *See* Silence of Ajax, The.
Of the Ship. C. P. Cavafy, *tr. fr. Modern Greek by* Rae Dalven. MoGP
Of the Small Respect Had of Learned Men in General. John Davies of Hereford. SiCE
Of the Sonnet. Wordsworth. *See* Nuns Fret Not at Their Convent's Narrow Room.
Of the Soul of Man and the Immortality Thereof. Sir John Davies. *Fr.* Nosce Teipsum. ReIE
Of the Stalking of the Stag. Sir Owen Seaman. CenHV
Of the Surface of Things. Wallace Stevens. NP
Of the Terrible Doubt of Appearances. Walt Whitman. EV-5; NePA
Of the Unscathing Fire. Anne Ridler. *See* Phoenix Answered, The.
Of the Use of Riches. Pope. Moral Essays, Epistle IV. EiPP; PoEL-3
(On Riches.) TwP
Of the Vanity of Man's Life. *Unknown.* SiCE; TuPP
(On the Vanity of Man's Life.) OBSC
("Vain is the fleeting wealth.") EG
Of the Virgin and Child. *Unknown. See* Lullay, Mine Liking.
Of the Warres in Ireland. Sir John Harington. LPS-2
Of the white purity. The House of Sorrows. Francis Thompson. MeRV
Of the wrath of the son of Peleus—of Achilles—Goddess, sing. The Wrath of Achilles. Homer. *Fr.* The Iliad, I. GrPE
Of thee I dream now, Myrtho, witch divine. Myrtho. Gérard de Nerval. TrFP
Of Thee, Kind Boy. Sir John Suckling. *See* Sonnet: "Of thee (kind boy) I ask no red and white."
Of thee the Northman by his beachèd [*or* bleachèd] galley. Odes, V [*or* Ode to the Mediterranean]. George Santayana. AnAmPo; AnFE; APA; CoAnAm; EtS; LA; TwAmPo
Of their lament white-armed Andromache. The Lamentations. Homer. *Fr.* The Iliad, XXIV. LiTW; OxBG
Of these houses. San Martino del Carso. Giuseppe Ungaretti. OnPM
Of these the false Achitophel was first. Achitophel [*or* The False Achitophel *or* Shaftesbury]. Dryden. *Fr.* Absalom and Achitophel, Pt. I. AtBAP; AWP, *br. sel.;* BCEP, *br. sel.;* EPP; EV-3; FiP; InPo; JAWP; NBE; OBS; PoEL-3; SeCePo; ViBoPo; WBP
Of these two spitefull Rocks, the one doth shove. Scylla and Charybdis. Homer. *Fr.* The Odyssey, XII. OBS
Of thick and thin, light, heavy, dark, and clear. A Notable Description of the World. *At. to* William Smith. ReIE
Of Things Not Seen. Leslie Savage Clark. ChIP
Of this bad world the loveliest and the best. On a Dead Hostess. Hilaire Belloc. MBP; MoBrPo; MoVE; PIAE
Of this day's glorious feast and revel. *At. to* Mei Sheng, *tr. fr. Chinese by* Arthur Waley. Seventeen Old Poems, 4. TrCh
Of This Fair Volume. William Drummond of Hawthornden. *See* Book of the World, The.
Of this my life, which never has been mine. To the Marquesa Mancera. Sister Juana Inés de la Cruz. BoFr
Of this world's theatre in which we stay. Amoretti, LIV. Spenser. PeBoSo; ReEn; ReIE
Of Thomas Traherne and the Pebble Outside. Sydney Clouts. BoSA
Of those at famed Thermopylae who lie. Thermopylae. Simonides, *tr. by* Lord Neaves. OnPM
Of those who at Thermopylae were slain. Simonides, *tr. by* John Sterling. GrPo
Of Those Who Walk Alone. Richard Burton. HBV
Of those whom I have known, the few and fatal friends. Largo. Dunstan Thompson. LiTA; LiTM; MoPo; WaP
Of Three Damsels in a Meadow. John Payne. OBVV

Of Three Girls and [of] Their Talk. Boccaccio, *tr. fr. Italian by* Dante Gabriel Rossetti. *Fr.* Sonnets. AWP; JAWP; OnPM; WBP
Of thy life, Thomas, this compass well mark. The Golden Mean. Earl of Surrey. SiPS
Of Time. Sir Richard Fanshawe. *Fr.* Il Pastor Fido. SeCL (Of Beauty.) InMe
Of Titus. Everard Guilpin. *Fr.* Skialetheia. ReIE; SiCE; TuPP
Of Treason. Sir John Harington. ALV; BCEP; ExPo; OxBoLi; SiCE; TuPP
(Epigram: "Treason doth never prosper.") HBV; OtMeF
(On Treason.) FiBHP
(Treason.) LiTG; SiTL
(Treason Never Prospers, *sl. diff., at. to* James Harrington.) InvP
Of True Liberty. Sir John Beaumont. OBS; PoFr
Of two fair virgins, modest, though admired. On a Nun [*or* Sonnet]. Jacopo Vittorelli. AWP; CAW; JAWP; LiTW; WBP
Of Two Religions. Sir John Harington. SiCE
Of votive lights there were only seven. Ash Wednesday. Rosa Zagnoni Marinoni. PoRL; WHL
Of W. W. (Americanus). James Kenneth Stephen. *See* Imitation of Walt Whitman.
Of Walking the Streets by Day. John Gay. *Fr.* Trivia; or, The Art of Walking the Streets of London. EiPP
Sels.
Dangers of Football, The. EnLi-1 (1949 ed.)
Morning, The. EnLi-1 (1949 ed.)
(On Walking the Streets by Day.) TOP
Of Narrow Streets. EnLi-1 (1949 ed.)
Pell Mell Celebrated, The. EnLi-1 (1949 ed.)
Pleasure of Walking through an Alley, The. EnLi-1 (1949 ed.)
"Thus far the muse has traced in useful lays." CEP; EnLi-1 (1949 ed.)
Of Walking the Streets by Night, *sels.* John Gay. *Fr.* Trivia; or, The Art of Walking the Streets of London, III. EnLi-1 (1949 ed.)
"Consider, reader, what fatigues I've known."
Evening, The.
"O Trivia, Goddess, leave these low abodes."
Of Ballad-Singers.
Of Crossing the Street.
Of Pick-Pockets.
Of Watchmen.
Of wealthy lustre was the banquet-room. The Banquet. Keats. *Fr.* Lamia. SeCePo
Of wedded bliss. Pair'd, Not Match'd. Thomas Hood. ERP
Of what an easie quick accesse. Prayer. George Herbert. AtBAP
Of what are Thou thinking, oh my dead Christ? Miguel de Unamuno. *Fr.* The Christ of Velázquez, Pt. I. TeCS
"Of what are you afraid, my child?" inquired the kindly teacher. Wild Flowers. Peter Newell. NA
Of What Are Your Clothes Made? Ann *or* Jane Taylor. OTPC (1923 ed.)
Of what avail are any words to tell. Communion. T. Turner. LO
Of what avail these willing finite minds. Descent of the Holy Ghost. John Gilland Brunini. JKCP (1955 ed.)
Of what good can Paradise be. Paradise. Immanuel di Roma. TrJP
Of What Use Are You, Days? Yevgeny Abramovich Boratynsky, *tr. fr. Russian by* Babette Deutsch. TrRV
Of white and tawny, black as ink. Variation on a Sentence. Louise Bogan. ImOP
Of Wit. Abraham Cowley. *See* Ode: Of Wit.
Of woman and wine, of woods and spring. Inexhaustible. Israel Zangwill. TrJP
Of Women. Richard Edwards. ElL
Of Women No More Evil. *Unknown, tr. fr. Late Middle Irish by* Robin Flower. AnIL
Of Wonder. Mary Gilmore. BoAV; NeLNL
Of Work. Kahlil Gibran. *Fr.* The Prophet. GrCo-2
(On Work, *abr.*) PoToHe (new ed.)
Of world-admired Drake (for of his worth what argues more). William Warner. *Fr.* Albion's England. SG
Of worthy Captain Lovewell, I purpose now to sing. Lovewell's Fight. *Unknown.* BaBo; HBV; PAH
Of Wounds. Sister Mary Madeleva. ISi
Of wounds and sore defeat. Pandora's Song [*or* Lyric]. William Vaughn Moody. *Fr.* The Fire-Bringer. BAP; BAV; BBV; GBV; HBV; LBAP; MOAP; NV; PC; PFY; PoeMoYo; TCPD
Of "Yea" and "Nay." Clément Marot. *See* Yes and No.
Of your trouble, Ben, to ease me. Her Man Described by Her Own Dictamen. Ben Jonson. *Fr.* A Celebration of Charis. AtBAP; NBE
Of Youth He Singeth. R. Wever. *See* In Youth Is Pleasure.
Of Zeno. Everard Guilpin. *Fr.* Skialetheia. SiCE
Off a Puritane. *Unknown.* CoMu
Off all the lords in faire Scotland. The Heir of Linne. *Unknown.* ESPB
Off an ancient story I'll tell you anon. King John and the Bishop. *Unknown.* BaBo; ESPB
Off Banks Peninsula. Denis Glover. AnNZ
Off Broadway, where they sell those photographs. Manhattan Menagerie. Joseph Cherwinski. GoYe
Off Duty. George Herbert Clarke. NeTW
Off Februar the fyiftene nycht. *See* Of Februar the fifteen nicht.
Off from Boston. *Unknown.* MC; PAH
Off from the shore at last he took his way. The Discoverer. Arthur Gordon Field. PGD
Off in the twilight hung the lowfull moon. Full Moon. Sappho. AWP; JAWP; WBP
Off Manilly. Edmund Vance Cooke. PAH
Off Portland: wind east, visibility eight. Hydrographic Report. Frances Frost. EtS
Off Rivière du Loup. Duncan Campbell Scott. EtS; HBV; MCCG; SG
Off the coast of Ireland. Seascape. Langston Hughes. BrR
Off the Ground. Walter de la Mare. CBPC; MuP; RG; StaSt; StPo; YT
Off the long headland, threshed about by round-backed breakers. The Black Rock. John Gould Fletcher. SPP; TCPD
Off to Sea Once More, *2 vers., with music.* *Unknown.* ShS (Jack Wrack, *with music.*) ABF
Off to the Fishing Ground. L. M. Montgomery. CaP; CPG
Off to Yakima. Leroy F. Jackson. GaP
Off we go into the wild blue yonder. The U. S. Air Force. Robert Crawford. PoRL
Off We Go to Market. Gwen A. Smith. BoTP
Off with sleep, love, up from bed. Love in May. Jean Passerat. AWP
Off with the fetters. Vagabondia. Richard Hovey. PC
Off with the ruffle! Washington. Robert Haven Schauffler. PaA
Off with your hat! along the street. The Marquis of Carabas. Robert Brough. HBV
Off with your hat as the flag goes by! The Old Flag [*or* Salute the Flag]. H. C. Bunner. PGD; PSO
Offensive, The. Keith Douglas. NeBP
Offer, An. Arthur Guiterman. TrJP
Offering. Leslie Savage Clark. ChIP
Offering, The. Olive Cecilia Jacks. MaRV
Offering to Zeus was making at the hearth. The Madness of Heracles. Euripides. *Fr.* Heracles. GrR
Offertory. Mary Mapes Dodge. COAH; HH; PRWS
Office building treads the marble dark, The. The Minute. Karl Shapiro. ATP (1953 ed.); MiAP; MoVE; UnPo (3d ed.)
Office of Poetry, The. Nathaniel Whiting. *Fr.* Il Insonio Insonnado. OBS
Officer Brady. Robert W. Chambers. BOHV; DDA; InMe
Officers get all the steak, The. World War I. *Unknown.* FaFP; SiTL
Officers' Prison Camp Seen from a Troop-Train, An. Randall Jarell. WaP
Off'rings of the Eastern[e] kings of old, The. Royal[l] Presents. Nathaniel Wanley. MaRV; OBS; OxBoCh
Offspring, The, *sel.* Thomas Francis.
"Hard on the high road side, midway between." EnSW
Offspring of Zeus, the shepherd Ganymede. Ganymede. Johan Sebastian Cammermeyer Welhaven. AnNoLy
Oft am I by the women told. Age. Abraham Cowley. AWP; JAWP; OnPM; WBP
Oft and often I sang it, I will cry it yet from the tomb. On Anacreon. Julianus. GrPE
Oft, as we run the weary way. Courage. Stopford Brooke. WGRP
Oft did I hear our eyes the passage were. Sir John Davies. *Fr.* Sonnets to Philomel. SiPS
Oft had I heard of Lucy Gray. *See* Oft I had heard of Lucy Gray.
Oft happening on some halting paraphrase. Of a Dead Poet. Lord Alfred Douglas. JKCP (1926 ed.)
Oft has it been my lot to mark. The Chameleon. James Merrick. HBV
Oft has our poet wisht, this happy seat. Epilogue Spoken at Oxford by Mrs. Marshall [*or* Epilogue Spoken by Mrs. Boutell]. Dryden. ATP; CEP; FaBoEn; SeCV-2
Oft have I heard my lief[e] Corydon report on a love-day. Hexametra Alexis in Laudem Rosamundi [*or* In Praise of Rosamund]. Robert Greene. *Fr.* Greene's Mourning Garment. AtBAP; ElL; PoEL-2; TuPP
Oft have I heard of Lucy Gray. *See* Oft I had heard of Lucy Gray.
Oft have I heard the nightingale and thrush. Wordsworth. *Fr.* The Cuckoo at Laverna. SaFP
Oft have I mused, but now at length I find. A Farewell. Sir Philip Sidney. ElL; EnLi-1; OBSC; ReIE; SiCE; SiPS
Oft have I mused the cause to find. Ladies' Eyes Serve Cupid Both for Darts and Fire. "A. W." OBSC

Oft have I said, I say it once more. Odes. Hafiz, *tr. by* Emerson. AWP; OuHeWo
Oft have I searcht both court and towne. *Unknown.* SeCSL
Oft Have I Seen at Some Cathedral Door. Longfellow. Divina Commedia, I. TreF
(Dante.) OBEV (new ed.)
(Divina Commedia, I.) AmP; AmPP; AnAmPo; AnFE; AnNE; APA; APW; ATP; BPP; CoAnAm; CoBA; CoV; ES; GoBC; HBV; LA; LBAP; LPS-2; MOAP; NePA; OBAV; OQP; OxBA; PIAE; PoE; PtP; QP-1; ReaPo; TCAP; TOP; TwCrTr; ViBoPo
(On Dante's "Divine Comedy.") AnEnPo
(On Translating the "Divina Commedia.") OuHeWo
(Peace through Prayer.) MaRV
(Three Sonnets on the Divina Commedia, I.) SeCeV
(With the Ages.) GrCo-2
Oft have I sigh'd for him that heares me not. Thomas Campion. FaBoEn
Oft Have I Stood by Thee. Robert Browning. *Fr.* Pauline. MaRV
Oft have I stood upon the foaming strand. Darkness. James Naumburg Rosenberg. AA
Oft have I thought and troubled not my head. To the Moon. Henry Longan Stuart. GTIV
Oft have I wakened ere the spring of day. Will It Be So? Edith M. Thomas. *Fr.* The Inverted Torch. AA
Oft have I walked these [*or* the] woodland paths. Under the Leaves. Albert Laighton. HBV; OHIP; SN
Oft have you seen a swan superbly frowning. Epistle to Charles Cowden Clarke [*or* To Charles Cowden Clarke]. Keats. EmBrPo; EnRP; GEPC
Oft I had heard of Lucy Gray. Lucy Gray; or, Solitude. Wordsworth. BEL; BeLS; BPN; CBOV; CG; CH; EM-2; EmBrPo; EnRP; EPN; EPP; ERP; EV-3; FiP; GEPC; GTSL; HBV; HiLiEn; OAEP; OBRV; OnSP; OTPC; PoFS; PRWS; PYM; REAL; SeCeV; TCEP; TOP; TreFS; TVSH; TwP; UnPo (1st ed.)
Oft I must strive with wind and wave. Anchor. *Unknown. Fr.* Riddles. AnOE
Oft in midnight visions. The Childless Mother. Francis Turner Palgrave. MotAn
Oft in my laughing rhymes I name a gull. Of a Gull. Sir John Davies. SiCE; TuPP
Oft in the after days, when thou and I. Ad Matrem. Julian Fane. HBV
Oft in the pleasant summer years. Theology in Extremis. Sir Alfred Comyn Lyall. LH
Oft in the Silent Night. Otto Julius Bierbaum, *tr. fr. German by* Ludwig Lewisohn. AWP; JAWP; WBP
Oft in the Stilly Night. Thomas Moore. AnFE; BCEP; BEL; BLV; CoBE; EnLit; EnRP; EPN; EPP; ERP; FaBoBe; GoBC; GTIV; LiTB; LiTG; LoBV; LPS-1; MCCG; NeHB; OAEP; OBRV; OIF; OTPC; OxBI; PIR; PoEL-4; TCEP; WHA
(Light of Other Days, The.) BTP; CBE; EV-4; FaFP; GTBS; GTBS-D; GTBS-W; GTSE; GTSL; HBV; MaRV; OBEV; PECK; PoeMoYo; TIP; TreF
(Scotch Air.) PoE
Oft it befalls by the grace of God. Fates of Men. *Unknown.* AnOE
Oft I've implored the Gods in vain. A Prayer for Indifference. Fanny Greville. LoBV; OBEC
Oft o'er my brain does that strange fancy roll. Sonnet: Oft o'er My Brain. Samuel Taylor Coleridge. ChER
Oft on a plat of rising ground. Milton. *Fr.* Il Penseroso. PC
Oft on some evening, sunny, soft, and still. Gilbert White. *Fr.* The Invitation to Selborne. EnSW
Oft-repeated Dream, The. Robert Frost. *Fr.* The Hill Wife. ChMo; CMP; IAP; MOAP; NP; PG (1945 ed.); SBMV
Oft shall the soldier think of thee. Ben Milam. William H. Wharton. PAH
Oft since thine earthly eyes have closed on mine. Sarah Helen Whitman. Sonnets from the Series Relating to Edgar Allan Poe, III. AA
Oft Thou Hast. *Unknown.* TuPP
Oft times I get to thinkin' of the changes times has wrought. A Veteran Cowboy's Ruminations. John M. Kuykendall. PoOW
Oft to the Wanderer, weary of exile. The Wanderer. *Unknown.* AnOE; EnL; LiTW
Oft upon the twilight plain. Ode, Solitude, at an Inn. Thomas Warton, the Younger. CEP
Oft when my spirit doth spre[a]d her bolder wing[e]s. Amoretti, LXXII. Spenser. EG; EnLi-1; LEAP; OAEP; OBSC; PeBoSo; RiBV; SiCE
Oft when, returning with her loaded bill. The Nightingale Bereaved. James Thomson. *Fr.* The Seasons: Spring. BCEP
Oft when the fires of sunset were sinking and dying. The Wood-Gatherers. F. C. Slater. BoSA
Oft with true sighs, oft with uncallèd tears. Astrophel and Stella, LXI. Sir Philip Sidney. SiPS
Often,/ Stepping so delicately through the shrubbery of learning. Salt. Monk Gibbon. OxBI
Often as I strain and stew. To a Pomeranian Puppy Valued at 2500 Dollars. Louis Untermeyer. AlBD
Often beneath the wave, wide from this ledge. At Melville's Tomb. Hart Crane. ATP (1953 ed.); CaAE; CoBMV; InPo; MOAP; NePA; OnAP; Po; ReMP; TriL; UnPo
Often has it crossed my fancy. Symptoms of an Ailing Democracy. Aristophanes. *Fr.* The Frogs. GrR
Often I have heard it said. Her Lips [*or* Song]. Walter Savage Landor. HBV; NeHB
Often I have this strange and penetrating dream. My Recurring Dream. Paul Verlaine. AnFP
Often I looked at you—stood at the window I had started. The Great Night. Rainer Maria Rilke. AnGP
Often I talk to men, on this or that. Talk. Philip A. Stalker. FiBHP
Often I think of the beautiful town. My Lost Youth [*or* Sea Memories]. Longfellow. AA; AlDL; AmPP; AnFE; AnNE; APA; APW; AWP; BAP; BLV; CBPC; CoAnAm; CoBA; DDA; EtS; EV-5; ExPo; FaBoBe; FaFP; FaPON; GTBS-D; GTBS-W; GTSE; HBV; IAP; InPo; JAWP; LaNeLa; LBAP; LEAP; LiTA; MCCG; MOAP; MPB; NePA; OBAV; OBEV; OTPC; OxBA; PCD; PFY; Po; PoEL-5; PoeMoYo; PoRA; PYM; RG; SeCeV; TCAP; TOP; TreF; ViBoPo; WBP
Often I watch the walkers on the street. On the Street. Hazel Hall. NP
Often in summer on a tarred bridge plank standing. Wild Bees. James K. Baxter. AnNZ
Often in the morning the fog is thick over Jersey. A View of Jersey. Edward Field. NeAP
Often in times before. A Death. W. W. E. Ross. BoCaPo
Often Rebuked, Yet Always Back Returning. *At. to* Emily Brontë. *See* Stanzas: "Often rebuked, yet always back returning."
Often the birds of mere or main, with ceaseless dives. Signs of Rain. Aratus. *Fr.* Phaenomena. GrPE
Often the lone man waits for mercy. The Lone Man. *Unknown. Fr.* Widsith. PoLi
Often the lonely one longs for honors. The Wanderer. *Unknown.* EnLi-1 (1949 ed.)
Often the pain of living have I met. The Pain of Living. Eugenio Montale. OnPM
Often the road-menders gather. Fever. "Klabund." OnPM
Often the western wind has sung to me. A Prayer. Lord Alfred Douglas. CAW; JKCP (1926 ed.); TrPWD
Often the woodman scares them as he comes. Wood-Pigeons. John Masefield. ChMP
Often this thought wakens me unawares. Night. Hermann Hesse. AWP; JAWP; WBP
Often we spent an intimate night. The Room and the Windows. Feng Chih. LiTW
Often, when I would sit, a dreamy, straight-haired child. A Man. Jean Starr Untermeyer. FAOV
Often, when o'er tree and turret. "Hic Vir, Hic Est." Charles Stuart Calverley. OxBoLi
Often when the night is come. To a Maid Demure. Edward Rowland Sill. PR
Often with heavy burdens freighted. The Coach of Time. Pushkin. BoRS; LiTW
Oftener Seen, the More I Lust, The. Barnabe Googe. *See* Out of Sight, Out of Mind.
Oftener than he'd like it known. Soldier's Dog. Ethel Barnett de Vito. AlBD
Oftimes I pray with words. Prayer. Gertie Stewart Phillips. BPP
Oft'ner seen, the more I lust, The. *See* Oftener seen . . .
Ofttimes, for diversion, the men of the crew. The Albatross. Baudelaire, *tr. by* Kate Flores. AnFP
Ofttimes for sport the mariners will take. The Albatross. Baudelaire, *tr. by* Frances Winwar. EnLi-2
Ofttimes have I heard you speak of one who commits a wrong. Crime and Punishment. Kahlil Gibran. *Fr.* The Prophet. PoToHe (new ed.)
Ofttimes I get to thinking of the changes time has wrought. The Old-Time Cowboy. *Unknown.* CoSo
Oft-times it has been told. *Constitution* and *Guerrière*. *Unknown.* ABF
Og and Doeg. Dryden. *Fr.* Absalom and Achitophel, Pt. II. AWP; BeR; FiP, *shorter sel.;* JAWP; WBP
(Characters from the Satires: Og and Doeg.) InPo
("Doeg though without knowing.") PoEL-3
Ogier the Dane. William Morris. *See* Song from "Ogier the Dane."
O'Grady's Goat. Will S. Hays. PTA-2
Ogre leaps with massing hands, The. Uncrowned. Alfred G. Bailey. BoCaPo
Ogres and Pygmies. Robert Graves. FaBoMo; LiTB; LiTM; SeCePo; SeCeV
Ohio Farmstead. Minnie Hite Moody. MuM
Ohio Rivuh, She's So Deep an' Wide, *with music. Unknown.* StDa
Ohnáwa. John Hunter-Duvar. *Fr.* De Roberval. VA

Oho for the woods where I used to grow. The Song of the Christmas Tree. Blanche Elizabeth Wade. OHIP; SDH
Oho! have you seen the Frost-King. The Frost-King. Mary Mapes Dodge. DD
Oho, my love, oho, my love, and ho, the bough that shows. A Pastoral. Lizette Woodworth Reese. LS
Oho, why don't you blow? Come Roll Him Over. *Unknown.* SG
Ohone! my Highlandman. Lewie Gordon. Alexander Geddes. EBSV
O'Hussey's Ode to the Maguire. *At. to* Eochadh O'Hussey, *tr. fr. Late Middle Irish by* James Clarence Mangan. AnIV; ERP; GTIV; IrPN; SeCePo; TIP
(Hugh Maguire, *tr. by* Frank O'Connor.) AnIL; KiLC
(Ode to the Maguire, *tr. by* James Clarence Mangan.) OnYI; OxBI
Oi! beneath the wooden hill-top. The Widow. *Tr. by* Florence Randal Livesay. CPG
Oil Painting of the Artist as the Artist. Archibald MacLeish. Frescoes for Mr. Rockefeller's City, IV. NAMP; OnHM; ReaPo; UnPo
Oisin. *Unknown, tr. fr. Irish by* Frank O'Connor. KiLC
Oisin in the Land of Youth. Michael Comyn, *tr. fr. Modern Irish by* Tomás O'Flannghaile. AnIL
Ojibwa War Songs. *Unknown, tr. fr. Ojibwa Indian by* H. R. Schoolcraft. AWP; JAWP; WBP
OK, it's imperishable or a world as Will. The Same Old Jazz. Philip Whalen. NeAP
Okaru and Kampei. Hakushu Kitahara, *tr. fr. Japanese by* Takamichi Ninomiya *and* D. J. Enright. PoLJ
Oklahoma. Harriet Parker Camden. PoRL
Ol' Ark's a-Moverin' an' I'm Goin' Home, De, *with music. Unknown.* BoAN-2
Ol' Clothes. *Unknown.* PoToHe (new ed.)
Ol' Cow Hawse, The. Earl Alonzo Brininstool. SCC
Ol' Dan Tucker clomb a tree. Old Dan Tucker. *Unknown.* ABF
Ol' Doc' Hyar. James Edwin Campbell. BANP
Ol' Hag, You See Mammy? *with music. Unknown.* OuSiCo
Ol' Hound Dog. "Beau Justi." AlBD
Ol' Jinny Mine, The. Daisy L. Detrick. PoOW
Ol' John Brown. *Unknown.* ABF
Ol' mammy gwine to tell yo'. De Li'l Road to Res'. Leigh Richmond Miner. BOL
Ol' Man, De. Alonzo W. Combs. IHA
Ol' man Adam were de fus' man invented. Live a-Humble. *Unknown.* SoAF
Ol' Mother Hare, *with music. Unknown.* ABF
Ol' Rattler, *with music. Unknown.* ABF
Ol' Sheep Done Know de Road, De, *with music. Unknown.* BoAN-2
Olaf Trygveson. Björnstjerne Björnson, *tr. fr. Norwegian by* Charles W. Stork. AnNoLy
Old. Ralph Hoyt. AA; LPS-1
Old, The. Roden Noel. OBEV (1st ed.); OBVV; YT
(Dying.) VA
Old. John V. A. Weaver. DDA
Old, The,/ Old winds that blew. Night Winds. Adelaide Crapsey. NV; SBMV
Old Abe Lincoln [Came Out of the Wilderness], *with music. Unknown.* AS; TrAS
Old Abram Brown. *Unknown.* RIS
("Old Abram Brown is dead and gone.") OxNR
Old Actor Addresses Julius Caesar, An. Decimus Laberius, *tr. fr. Latin by* J. V. Cunningham. LaP
Old Actor's Story, The. George R. Sims. PTA-2
Old Adam. Margaret Avison. *See* Simple Horizontal, The.
Old Adam, The. William Rose Benét. MOAP; YaD
Old Adam, *with music. Unknown.* AS
Old Adam, the Carrion Crow. Thomas Lovell Beddoes. *See* Song: "Old Adam, the carrion crow."
Old Adam, with his fist-full of plump earth. Neverness. Margaret Avison. BoCaPo
Old Admiral, The. Edmund Clarence Stedman. GA, *abr.*; LPS-3
Old Age. Al-Aswad, Son of Ya'fur, *tr. fr. Arabic by* Sir Charles Lyall. *Fr.* The Mufaddaliyat. AWP
Old Age. Anacreon, *tr. fr. Greek by* T. F. Higham. GrL; OxBG
Old Age. Maxwell Bodenheim. MAP; MoAmPo (1942 ed.)
Old Age. Joseph von Eichendorff, *tr. fr. German by* Vernon Watkins. AnGP
Old Age. Euripides, *tr. fr. Greek by* C. M. Bowra. OxBG
Old Age ("Irrigate the high wasteland and the slopes for plowing"). Lu Yu, *tr. fr. Chinese by* Pai Chwen-yu. WhP
Old Age ("Unbearable is the sickness that invades old age"). Lu Yu, *tr. fr. Chinese by* Pai Chwen-Yu. WhP
Old Age. Percy MacKaye. NV
Old Age. Ou-yang Hsiu, *tr. fr. Chinese by* Kenneth Rexroth. OnPC
Old Age. Po Chü-i, *tr. fr. Chinese by* Arthur Waley. TrCh
Old Age. Cale Young Rice. NLK (1947 ed.); SBMV
Old Age, *abr.* Thomas Sackville. *Fr.* Induction to "The Mirror for Magistrates." BCEP
Old Age. Sir Philip Sidney. *Fr.* Arcadia. SiPS
Old Age. Sophocles, *tr. fr. Greek by* A. E. Housman. *Fr.* Oedipus at Colonus. LiTW
(Chorus: "What man is he that yearneth," *tr. by* A. E. Housman.) AWP; JAWP; WBP
("Endure what life God gives and ask no longer span," *tr. by* W. B. Yeats.) OBMV; PoD
(Old Age the Friendless, *tr. by* Robert Whitelaw.) GrR
Old Age. Edmund Waller. *Fr.* Of the Last Verses in the Book. BCEP; CBOV; MaRV; OBEV
(From "Divine Poems.") EV-2
(Last Verses.) OxBoCh
(Old Age and Death.) LEAP; LPS-3
Old Age am I, with lockes thin and hoar. Age. Sir Thomas More. TuPP
Old age has scattered disbelief. The Rational Man. Pearce Young. PtPa
Old age hath yet his honor and his toil. Tennyson. *Fr.* Ulysses. BLP
Old age is. To Waken an Old Lady. William Carlos Williams. InPo
Old Age of Temperance. Shakespeare. *Fr.* As You Like It, II, iii. LPS-2
Old Age, on tiptoe, lays her jewelled hand. A Minuet on Reaching the Age of Fifty. George Santayana. FaFP; HBMV; LiTM; NePA; TriL
Old Age Pensioner, The. Joseph Campbell. AnIL
Old Age the Friendless. Sophocles. *See* Old Age.
Old Age, the irrigator. Old Age. Percy MacKaye. NV
Old Air, An. F. R. Higgins. AnIL
Old Amati, The. Oliver Wendell Holmes. BPP
Old Amaze. Mahlon Leonard Fisher. SBMV
Old anatomies, The. Shelley. *Fr.* The Triumph of Life. CoEV
Old Anchor Chanty. Herbert Trench. AnFE
Old, and abandon'd by each venal friend. Impromptu, Suggested by a View, in 1766, of the Seat and Ruins of a Nobleman, at Kingsgate, Kent. Thomas Gray. CoEV; HoPM; MyFE; SeCePo; SeCeV
Old and alone sit we. The Old Men. Walter de la Mare. MBP; MoAB; MoBrPo
Old and Blind. Josiah Gilbert Holland. PoP
Old and crippled veteran to the War Department came, An. Scott and the Veteran. Bayard Taylor. PaA; PAP
Old and New ("Farewell, Old Year!"). *Unknown.* BLRP
Old and New ("She went up the mountain"). *Unknown, tr. fr. Chinese by* Arthur Waley. AWP; LiTW; TrCh
Old and New Art. Dante Gabriel Rossetti. The House of Life, LXXIV-LXXVI.
Husbandman, The. BPN; PoVP; ViPo
Not as These. BPN; PoVP; ViPo
St. Luke the Painter. BPN; GoBC; PoVP; ViPo
Old and New Year Ditties, *sel.* Christina Rossetti.
Passing Away [Saith the World], III. EmBrPo; EPN; GoBC; GTBS-W; LiA; MBP; OBEV (1st ed.); OBVV; PoD; POTT; TOP; ViP; ViPo
Old and quiet house set down, An. Possessions. Lizette Woodworth Reese. HBMV; VOD
Old and Young. Francis William Bourdillon. VA
Old and Young Courtier, The. *Unknown, at. to* Thomas Dekker. EV-2; LEAP, *abr.*; ViBoPo
(Old and the New Courtier, The.) CoMu
(Old Courtier, *abr.*) CG
Old Angler, The. Walter de la Mare. GoTL (1949 ed.); OAEP (2d ed.); POTT
Old Anguish, The. Chu Shu Chen, *tr. fr. Chinese by* Kenneth Rexroth. OnPC
Old Apis, old sacred bull. A Song for Old Apis. James Schevill. FiMAP
Old Apothecary, The. Lu Yu, *tr. fr. Chinese by* Pai Chwen-yu. WhP
Old April. Virginia Lyne Tunstall. Sonnets of an Old Town, II. LS
Old Are Sleepy, The. Harold Lenoir Davis. NP
Old Arm-Chair, The. Eliza Cook. ATP; LPS-1; MotAn; OTPC (1923 ed.); WBLP
Contrast in Styles, A, *sel.* ShGoBo, *st.* 1
Old as a coat on a chair; and his crushed hand. Beggar. Terence Tiller. PoN
Old as I am, for ladies' love unfit. Apology for Love. Boccaccio. LiTW; LyMA
Old Astronomer to His Pupil, The. Sarah Williams. BLPA; BoHiPo
"Though my soul may set in darkness," *2 ll.* MaRV
Old Bachelor, The, *sel.* Congreve.
"Thus grief still treads upon the heels of pleasure," *2 ll. fr.* V, iii. TreF
Old Bachelor, An. Tudor Jenks. BOHV; LHV
Old Bachelor, The ("I am a stern old bachelor"), *with music. Unknown.* ABF
Old Balaam. *Unknown.* PoOW
Old Bangum. *Unknown. See* Sir Lionel.
Old Barbarossa. Sleeping Heroes. Edward Shanks. OBMV

Old Bard Speaks, The. Joseph R. N. Maxwell. JKCP (1955 ed.)
Old Baron, The. Thomas Miller. VA
Old Battlefield, The. Li Hua, *tr. fr. Chinese.* WhP
Old Battle-Field, An. Frank L. Stanton. OQP; QP-2
Old battle field, fresh with spring flowers again. All That Is Left. Basho. AWP; LiTW; PFE; WaaP
Old Bayou, The. Madison Cawein. PFY; PoeMoYo
Old Beau, The. Edgar Fawcett. OBAV; PR
Old Beau, An. Richard Kendall Munkittrick. PR
Old Bed, The. W. W. Gibson. NV
Old Bee-Master, The. *Unknown, tr. fr. Greek by* F. L. Lucas. GrPE
Old bellwether, The. Lamb. Humbert Wolfe. MBP; MoBrPo; TwCV
Old Ben Franklin was a merry old soul. Merry Old Souls. Morris Bishop. WhC
Old Bill (*2 vers.*), *with music. Unknown.* ABF
(Dis Mornin', Dis Evenin', So Soon, *sl. diff.*) AS
Old Bill Barnacle sticks to his ship. The Barnacle. A. P. Herbert. RIS
Old Bill's Memory Book. William Rose Benét. InMe
Old Birch, who taught the village school. The Retort. George Pope Morris. BOHV; HBV; LPS-3; PR
Old Black Billy an' Me, The. Louis Esson. BoAu; NeLNL
Old Black Joe. Stephen Collins Foster. FaFP; IHA; OlF; TreFS
Old Black Men. Georgia Douglas Johnson. CDC; PoNe
Old Blue, *with music. Unknown.* OuSiCo
Old Boat, The. Lenore Pratt. CaP
"Old Bob"—"Friend." Marty Hale. AlBD
Old Boniface he loved good cheer. *Unknown.* OxNR
Old Books. Margaret Widdemer. DDA
Old Books Are Best. Beverly Chew. HBV
Old Books for New. Edwin Francis Edgett. POT; PoTo
Old Boys, The. Arthur Guiterman. FAOV
Old Brass Wagon, *with music. Unknown.* AS
Old Bridge, The. Hilda Conkling. MPB; SP
Old Bridge at Florence, The. Longfellow. BAV
Old bridge has a wrinkled face, The. The Old Bridge. Hilda Conkling. MPB; SP
Old Brother Ass stands mumchance in the sun. Brother Ass. Eric Irvin. BoAV
Old brown hen and the old blue sky, The. Continual Conversation with a Silent Man. Wallace Stevens. LiTM (rev. ed.); NePA
Old Brown Horse, The. W. K. Holmes. BoTP
Old Brown Schoolhouse, The. *Unknown.* TreF
Old brown thorn-trees break in two high over Cummen Strand, The. Red Hanrahan's Song about Ireland. W. B. Yeats. *Fr.* Hanrahan and Cathleen the Daughter of Hoolihan. BEL; ChMo; CMP; FaBoCh; FaBoMo; GTIV; LoGBV; OnYI; OxBI
Old Buccaneer, The. Charles Kingsley. *See* Last Buccaneer, The.
Old Buck's Ghost. Frank Benton. PoOW
Old Buffer, An. Frederick Locker-Lampson. CenHV
Old Burden, An. Amado Nervo, *tr. fr. Spanish by* Samuel Beckett. AnMP
Old Canada; or Gee Buck Gee. Alexander McLachlan. BoCaPo (1943 ed.)
Old Carol, with Lullaby, An. *Unknown. See* King in the Cradle, The.
Old Carthusian cloisters still enclose, The. The Insane in the Garden. Rainer Maria Rilke. AnGP
Old castle towers o'er the billow, An. Fineen the Rover. Robert Dwyer Joyce. JKCP (1926 ed.); TIP
Old castles on the cliff arise. John Dyer. *Fr.* Grongar Hill. ViBoPo
Old Cat and the Young Mouse, The. La Fontaine, *tr. fr. French.* CIV
Old Cat Care. Richard Hughes. AlDL; OBMV; ShBV-1; ThWaDe
Old Cat Meditates, An. Margaret E. Bruner. CIV
Old Cavalier, The. Sir Francis Hastings Doyle. VA
Old Cellar. Robert P. Tristram Coffin. DDA
Old Chang died after three years' sickness. Death. Lu Yu. WhP
Old Chang, the Crab. *Unknown, tr. fr. Chinese by* Isaac Taylor Headland. PCH
Old charcoal-seller, An. The Charcoal-Seller. Po Chü-i. TrCh; WoL
Old Chartist, The. George Meredith. EmBrPo
"Whate'er I be, old England is my dam!" *sts.* 1–5. PoFr
Old Chaucer doth of Thopas [*or* Topas] tell. Nymphidia; or, The Court of Fairy. Michael Drayton. NBE; OAEP; ReEn; SeEP; TuPP
Old Chaucer, like the morning star. On Mr. Abraham Cowley, His Death and Burial amongst the Ancient Poets. Sir John Denham. OBS; PtP; SeCV-1
Old Chief, feeling now well-nigh his end, The. A Chippewa Legend. James Russell Lowell. BAV; MPB
Old China. Carl Snoilsky, *tr. fr. Swedish by* Charles W. Stork. AnSL
Old Chinese Poem: "At the beginning of winter." *Unknown, tr. fr. Chinese by* Arthur Waley. BoFr
(Seventeen Old Poems, 16.) TrCh
Old Chinese Poem: "Bright moon illumines the night-prospect, A." *Unknown, tr. fr. Chinese by* Arthur Waley. BoFr
(Seventeen Old Poems, 7.) TrCh
Old Chinese Poem: "Cold, cold the year draws to its end." *Unknown, tr. fr. Chinese by* Arthur Waley. BoFr
(Old Poem.) AWP
(Seventeen Old Poems, 15.) TrCh
Old Chisholm Trail, The. *Unknown.* ABS; BeLS; CoSo, *add. sts., with music;* CSF; FaBoBe; PreP, *with music*
(Chisholm Trail, The, *diff. vers., with music.*) TrAS
(Old Chizzum Trail, The, *diff. vers., with music.*) ABF
Old Christmas. Roy Helton. *See* Old Christmas Morning.
Old Christmas. Mary Howitt. GN; OTPC
Old Christmas ("Those Christmas bells as sweetly chime"). *Unknown.* PEOR
Old Christmas. George Wither. *See* Christmas Carol, A: "So now is come our joyfullest feast."
Old Christmas Carol, An ("Joseph was an old man"). *Unknown. See* Cherry-Tree Carol, The.
Old Christmas Greeting, An. *Unknown. See* Christmas Greeting ("Sing hey! Sing hey!").
Old Christmas Morning. Roy Helton. MAP; MoAmPo; NeMA
(Old Christmas.) DaM; MaC; PoMS
Old Christmas Returned. *Unknown.* COAH; GN; OHIP
Old Christmastide. Sir Walter Scott. *See* Christmas in the Olden Time.
Old Church at Lismore, The. Ellen Mary Patrick Downing. TIP
Old Church Cock, The. Eduard Mörike, *tr. fr. German by* William R. Hughes. AnGP
Old Churchyard of Bonchurch, The. Philip Bourke Marston. HBV; OBVV; VA
Old City, The. Ruth Manning-Sanders. CH
Old Cloak, The. *Unknown.* BLV; CBOV; OBB; OBEV; OBSC; TrGrPo
(Bell My Wife.) EV-1
(Tak Your Auld Cloak about Ye, *sl. diff.*) EBSV
(This Winter's Weather It Waxeth Cold.) InvP
Old Clock, The. John Charles McNeill. NoCaPo
Old Clock on the Stairs, The. Longfellow. BLP; CoBA; HBV; IAP; OTPC, *sl. abr.;* PTA-1; TCAP; WBLP
Old-Clothes Woman. Stéphane Mallarmé, *tr. fr. French.* AnFP, *tr. by* Kate Flores; MiFP, *tr. by* Ithell Colquhoun
Old Coach Road, The. Rachel Field. GFA
Old coat, for some three or four seasons. Le Dernier Jour d'un Condamné. George Baker. PR
Old Collector, The. Beatrice Hanscom. PR
Old Collier, An. Ken Etheridge. MoWP
Old Conservative, The. L. Frank Tooker. EtS
Old Continentals, The. Guy Humphreys McMaster. *See* Carmen Bellicosum.
Old Convict, The. H. A. Vaughan. PoNe
Old Coon-Dog Dreams, The. Kenneth Porter. GoTP
Old Cottagers, The. John Clare. OBRV
Old Countryside. Louise Bogan. LiTA; MOAP; NePA; NP; TwAmPo
Old Couple, The, *sel.* Thomas May.
"Dear, do not your fair beauty wrong," III, i. EG; ElSeCe; TuPP; ViBoPo
(Love's Prime.) SeCL
Old Courtier, The. *Unknown. See* Old and Young Courtier, The.
Old Cove, The. Henry Howard Brownell. PAH
Old Cowboy, The. *Unknown.* CoSo
Old Cowboy's Lament, The. Robert V. Carr. PoOW
Old Cowman, The. Badger Clark. SCC
Old Cowman, The/ cross-legged, sat before the fire. Eighteen-ninety. E. Richard Shipp. PoOW
Old Crabbed Men. James Reeves. ChMP
Old cradle of an infant world. Ode to Jamestown. James Kirke Paulding. PAH
Old creeping time, with silent tread. On the Birthday of a Young Lady. William Whitehead. OTPC (1923 ed.)
Old Crow. John Drinkwater. WP
Old Crow, The, *with music. Unknown.* FTB
Old Crow, upon the tall tree-top. The Crow. Mrs. Alexander. BoTP; OTPC (1946 ed.); PCH
Old Crummles, *with music. Unknown.* FTB
Old Cumberland Beggar, The. Wordsworth. EnRP; ERP; GEPC; LaA; PoE
Old Cyniras to the Nymphs this net: no more. Old Fisherman. Julian. OnPM
Old cypresses. The sailor wind works into deep-sea knots. A California Vignette. Robinson Jeffers. *Fr.* Tamar. PC
Old Dad Morton has got us in jail, 'tis hard. The Cryderville Jail. *Unknown.* ABF
Old Daddy Darkness. James Ferguson, *ad. fr. Scotch.* RIS
Old Daddy Witch. *Unknown.* ExPo

Old Dafydd, eyes like bloodhound's red with age. Mid-Winter. Alun Lewis. MoWP
Old Dame Cricket. *Unknown.* GFA
Old Damon's Pastoral. Thomas Lodge. OBSC; SiCE
Old Dan Tucker. Daniel Decatur Emmett. ABF; APW; SoAF, *with music;* TrAS, *with music*
Old Dan Tucker. *Unknown.* ABF, *with music;* TrAS, *with music*
Old Dan'l. L. A. G. Strong. MBP; MoBrPo; NeMA; WhC
Old Dan'l Hanks he says this town. The Village Oracle. *Unknown.* DDA
Old Diamond Joe was a rich old jay. Diamond Joe. *Unknown.* CoSo; OuSiCo
Old Dick Johnson, gentleman, adventurer. The Dick Johnson Reel. "Jake Falstaff." WhC
Old Doc Higgins shot a mermaid. Ballad of Old Doc Higgins. Leonora Speyer. PFE
Old Doctor, The. Habberton Lulham. PoP
Old Doctor Foster. *Unknown.* OxNR
Old Dog, An. Celia Duffin. AlBD; PCD
Old Dog, The. Robert Frost. *See* Span of Life, The.
Old Dog. Leonard Twynham. StaSt
Old dog barks backward without getting up, The. The Span of Life [*or* The Old Dog]. Robert Frost. HoPM; LiTM; RIS; SiTL
Old Dog lay in the summer sun. Sunning. James S. Tippett. AlBD; SiSoSe; SUS; TiPo
Old Dogs. William Sydney Thayer. PoP
Old Doll, The. Wilhelmina Seegmiller. MPB
Old draught-ox, worn in the furrowed field, The. The Draught-Ox. Addoeus. OnPM
Old dream comes again to me, The. Mir träumte wieder der alte Traum [*or* Superfluous Bite]. Heine. AWP; JAWP; OnPM; WBP
Old Eagle, The. E. J. Pratt. BoCaPo (1943 ed.)
Old Earth-Mother calls us, The. A Song of the Open Road. Louis J. McQuilland. NLK
Old Earthworks. Thomas Sweeney. OQP; QP-2
Old Eben Flood, climbing alone one night. Mr. Flood's Party. E. A. Robinson. AmP; AmPP; AnAmPo; AnEnPo; AnNE; AWP; BLV; BoLiVe; ChMo; CMP; CoBMV; CrMA; FaFP; HoPM; IAP; InP; InPo; JAWP; LA; LiTA; LiTM (rev. ed.); MAP; MaPo; MoAB; MoAmPo; MOAP; NePA; NP; OxBA; PCN; PoE; PoLFOT; PoRA; PreP; ReaPo; ReMP; RiBV; SeCeV; TrGrPo; TwP; UnPo (3d ed.); ViBoPo; WBP
Old Education, The. Aristophanes, *tr. fr. Greek by* George Allen *and* T. F. Higham. *Fr.* The Clouds. OxBG
(Education vs. Fads, *longer sel., tr. by* Benjamin Bickley Rogers.) GrR
Old Ellen Sullivan. Winifred Welles. FaPON; GaP; MPB; TiPo
Old Emily. Hyacinthe Hill. GoYe
Old enchantment reigns again, The. Lost Eden. Kendall Banning. MuM
Old Enemy, The. Sara Teasdale. MaRV
Old England is eaten by knaves. Song. Alexander McLachlan. *Fr.* The Emigrant. BoCaPo
Old England's sons are English yet. Ready, Ay, Ready. Herman Charles Merivale. HBV; OTPC; VA
Old English Carol: "All you that in this house be here." *Unknown. See* All You That in This House Be Here.
Old English Charm Song. *Unknown.* CAW
Old Essex Door. Agnes MacCarthy Hickey. GoYe
Old eternal spring once more, The. The Unreturning. Bliss Carman. LBMV
Old Euclid drew a circle. Euclid. Vachel Lindsay. ImOP; MAPA; NAMP; TSW; TSWC; TwAmPo; YaD
Old Face, An. Francesca Falk Miller. PEDC
Old face of the mother of many children, The. Whitman's Mother [*or* The Justified Mother of Men]. Walt Whitman. *Fr.* Faces. APW; OHIP
Old faces in a gambling hall. Impression at Reno. C. R. Holmes. PtPa
Old Familiar Faces, The. Charles Lamb. AWP; BCEP; BLPA; BoFr; EnLit; EnRP; EPN; EPP; ERP; EV-4; FaBoBe; FaFP; GTBS; GTBS-D; GTBS-W; GTSE; GTSL, *sl. abr.;* HBV; JAWP; LEAP; LiTG; LPS-1; NeHB; OBEV; OBRV; PCD; PG; PIAE; PoeMoYo; PYM; TCEP; TOP; TreF; ViBoPo; WBP
("I have had playmates, I have had companions.") EG
Old Farmer Alone. Robert P. Tristram Coffin. PoTo
Old Farmer Giles. *Unknown.* OxNR
Old Farmer Oats and his son Ned. Song. John Jay Chapman. PoEL-5
Old farm-house with meadows wide, An. Two Pictures. "Marian Douglas." LPS-1
Old Fashioned Fun. Thackeray. BOHV; InMe; PA
Old-fashioned Garden, The. John Russell Hayes. AA
Old-fashioned Love. *Unknown.* MaC
Old-fashioned Poet, An. Ada Foster Murray. HBV
Old Father Annum. Leroy F. Jackson. GaP; SiSoSe
Old Father Greybeard. *Unknown.* OxNR
Old Father Ocean calls my tide [*or* tyde]. Song of Thamesis [*or* A Song of the River Thames]. Dryden. *Fr.* Albion and Albanius. FaBoEn; TCEP
Old Fence Post. Leigh Hanes. GoYe
Old Ferryman, The. Antiphilus of Byzantium, *tr. fr. Greek by* Sir William Marris. OxBG
Old Figurehead Carver, The. H. A. Cody. EtS
Old Fisherman. Julianus. *See* Old Fishing Net.
Old Fisherman, The. *Unknown, tr. fr. Chinese by* C. W. Luh. OnPM
Old Fishing Net, An. Julianus, *tr. fr. Greek by* A. J. Butler. OxBG
(Old Fisherman, *tr. by* Lord Neaves.) OnPM
Old Fitz, who from your suburb grange. To Edward Fitzgerald. Tennyson. LoBV; PoEL-5; PtP
Old Flag, The. H. C. Bunner. PGD
(Salute the Flag.) PSO
Old Flag. Hubbard Parker. DD; FOAH; HH; OTPC (1946 ed.); PoRL
Old Flag Forever, The. Frank L. Stanton. DD; FOAH; HH; PSO; PTA-2
(Our Flag Forever.) PGD
Old flag is a-doin' of her very level best, The. Regiment Song. Frank L. Stanton. FOAH
Old Flagman, The. Carl Sandburg. MOAP; YaD
Old Flemish Lace. Amelia Walstien Carpenter. AA
Old Flood Ireson, all too long. A Plea for Flood Ireson. Charles Timothy Brooks. PAH
Old Folks at Home. Stephen Collins Foster. AA; APW; BAV; FaBoBe; FaFP; HBV; IAP; InP, *with music;* LEAP; MotAn; OBAV; OlF; PECK; TreF; WBLP
(Swanee River.) PoRL
Old Forge, The. Clinton Scollard. PoTo
Old forgetting, An. After Pain. Marjorie Meeker. NP
Old Fort Meigs. *Unknown.* MC; PAH
Old Fortunatus, *sels.* Thomas Dekker.
"Behold you not this globe, this golden bowl." ViBoPo
Fortune and Virtue. GoTL
(Fortune.) OBSC
(Fortune Smiles.) AtBAP
(Song: "Fortune smiles: cry holiday.") EPP
O Pittie. AtBAP
"Oh, whither am I rapt beyond myself?" ViBoPo
Song: "Virtue's branches wither, virtue pines." ElL
(Priest's Song, A.) OBSC
("Virtue's branches wither, virtue pines.") SiCE
"Stay, Fortunatus, once more hear me speak." ViBoPo
Old friend, bidding farewell to Yellow Crane Tower from the west. On Seeing Off Meng Hao-jan. Li Po. WhP
Old friend, dear friend. A. R. D. Fairburn. *Fr.* To a Friend in the Wilderness. AnNZ
Old friend, I greet you! you are still the same. To One Who Denies the Possibility of a Permanent Peace. Lady Margaret Sackville. HBMV; MaRV
Old friend, where you and I were once at home. He Thinks of the Friend of His Youth, and of His Rooms at College. Robert Nathan. *Fr.* Youth Grows Old. BoFr
Old Friends. Hsü Chi, *tr. fr. Chinese by* Henry H. Hart. BoFr; PoHN
Old Friends. R. W. Waddy. TVSH
Old friends are best! And so to you. To Richard Watson Gilder. Austin Dobson. BoFr
Old Friendship. Eunice Tietjens. NP
Old Furniture. Thomas Hardy. MoVE
Old Gaelic Cradle-Song [*or* Lullaby], An. *Unknown. See* Gaelic Lullaby.
Old Garden, An. Chien T'ang, *tr. fr. Chinese by* Henry H. Hart. PoHN
Old Garden, The. Joseph von Eichendorff, *tr. fr. German.* AnGP, *tr. by* Mabel Cotterell; LiTW, *tr. by* Werner Heider
Old Garden, The. Arthur Stringer. CPG
Old Gardener Time. Rachel Field. GBV (1952 ed.)
Old Gardens. Frances Beatrice Taylor. CPG
Old Gardens. Arthur Upson. HBV
Old gardens have a language of their own. The Garden. Gertrude Huntington McGiffert. VOD
Old Garrets. Morris Abel Beer. LEAP
Old General, The. Sir Charles Hanbury Williams. *Fr.* Isabella. OBEC
Old Gentleman of Seventy-seven, An. *Unknown, tr. fr. Latin by* F. L. Lucas. *Fr.* Carmina Epigraphica. LaP
Old German Mottos. *Ad. by* Louis Untermeyer. StaSt
Old gilt vane and spire receive, The. The Late, Last Rook. Ralph Hodgson. MBP; MoBrPo
Old Glory! say, who. The Name of Old Glory. James Whitcomb Riley. FOAH; GN
Old god who has taken mortal guise, An. Leonardo da Vinci, II. Thomas S. Jones, Jr. MuM
Old Gods, The. Edwin Muir. FaBoMo; POTE
Old gods, avaunt! The rosy East is waking. Courage, All. Edwin Markham. HBMV
Old Grahame he is to Carlisle gone. Bewick and Graham. *Unknown.* BaBo; ESPB

Old Gray [or Grey] Goose, The. *Unknown.* ABF, *with music;* ChTr; FTB, *with music*
("Go tell old Nancy.") LaNeLa
Old gray hoss come tearin' out-a wilderness, De. Tearin' Out-a Wilderness. *Unknown.* ABF
Old Gray Mare, *with music. Unknown.* AS
Old Gray Mule, The ("I am an old man"). *Unknown.* CSF
Old Gray Mule, The ("Mr. Thomas had an old gray mule"). *Unknown.* ABS
Old Gray Squirrel. Alfred Noyes. *See* Old Grey Squirrel.
Old Grenadier's Story, The. George Walter Thornbury. VA
Old Grey Goose, The. *Unknown. See* Old Gray Goose, The.
Old Grey Hearse goes rolling by, The. The Hearse Song. *Unknown.* ABF; AS; OxBoLi
Old grey shade of the mountain, The. In the Selkirks. Duncan Campbell Scott. CaP; OCL
Old Grey [or Gray] Squirrel. Alfred Noyes. PoMa; POT; PoTo
Old Grey Wall, The. Bliss Carman. CaP; OCL
Old Grimes. Albert Gorton Greene. AnAmPo; BeLS; BOHV; HBV; HBVY; InMe; LA; LEAP; LPS-3; OnPP; OTPC; PECK; PIR; StaSt; TreFS
Old Gumbie Cat, The. T. S. Eliot. GoTP
Old guy put down his beer, The. Do the Dead Know What Time It Is? Kenneth Patchen. MoAmPo
Old Habitant, An. Frank Oliver Call. *Fr.* A Sonnet Series of French Canada. CaP; CPG; OCL
Old hamlets with your fragrant flowers. Far East. Edmund Blunden. PtOT
Old Harp, The. Po Chü-i, *tr. fr. Chinese by* Arthur Waley. TrCh
Old Hercynian Forest sent, The. The Village Stork. Bayard Taylor. BLA; PFY
Old Heywood, have with thee, in his odd vein. To Old John Heywood the Epigrammatist, Wheresoever. John Davies of Hereford. SiCE
Old Hickory. Clinton Scollard. GA
Old Hokum Buncombe, The. Robert E. Sherwood. InMe
Old Home, The. Madison Cawein. HBV; POT
Old Home Calls, The. L. M. Montgomery. CPG
Old Homes. Edmund Blunden. MoVE
Old Horace on a summer afternoon. Classical Criticism. George Lynde Richardson. AA
Old Horn to All Atlantic said. Frankie's Trade. Kipling. EtS
Old Horse in the City, The. Vachel Lindsay. UTS
Old horse, old horse, what brought [or how came] you here? The Sailor's Grace [or Blow the Man Down, *vers.* V]. *Unknown.* ShS; SoAmSa
Old Hound. Florence Ripley Mastin. DDA; PoMa
Old Hound Argos, The. Homer. *See* Ulysses and His Dog.
Old House, The. William Barnes. OBVV
Old House, The. Tristan Klingsor, *tr. fr. French by* Alan Conder. TrFP
Old House, The. George Edward Woodberry. HBMV
Old house leans upon a tree, The. Deserted. Madison Cawein. MAP; MCCG; PFE; SPP
Old Houses. Struthers Burt. NoCaPo (1941 ed.)
Old Houses. Homer D'Lettuso. PoToHe (new ed.)
Old Houses. Jennie Romano. PoToHe (new ed.)
Old Houses of Flanders, The. Ford Madox Ford. NV; PoeMoYo; VOD
Old Hundred. Mark Van Doren. UnS
Old Hundredth. Thomas Ken. UnS
("Praise God, from whom all blessings flow!") OlF
Old Hundredth. William Kethe. *See* Hundredth Psalm, The.
Old Huntsman, The, *abr.* Siegfried Sassoon. ChMo; CMP
Old husband and young wife never agree. Crabbed Age and Youth. Theophilus. OxBG
Old hymn-book, sure I thought I'd lost you. On a Hymn-Book. William J. Henderson. PR
Old Hymns, The. Frank L. Stanton. BLRP
Old I Am. Thomas Stanley, *after the Greek of* Anacreon. AWP; OnPM
Old, indeed, as his people go—three score years and ten. The Councillor. Cullen Gouldsbury. BoSA
Old infirmity has left its traces, An. To a Giant Sequoia, Fallen and Enshrined in Calaveras County, California. Pearce Young. PtPa
Old Inn, The. Karle Wilson Baker. VOD
Old inn glimmered like a glowworm eye, The. The Arrival. William Rose Benét. QS
Old Inn on the Eastern Shore. William H. Matchett. NePoEA
Old Inn-Sign, The. Wilfrid Thorley. BrR
Old inventive poets, had they seen, The. The Plain of Donnerdale. Wordsworth. The River Duddon, XX. EnLi-2; PeBoSo
Old Iron. Douglas Stewart. BoAV
Old Ironsides. Oliver Wendell Holmes. AA; AmPP (3d ed.); AnNE; APW; BBV; BLPA; BTP; CoBA; DD; EtS; FaBoBe; FaFP; FaPON; GA; GDAH; GN; HBV; HBVY; IAP; LPS-2; MaC; MC; MCCG; MOAP; NeHB; OnHT; OTPC; OuHeWo; PaA; PAH; PAP; PECK; PIR; PoRL; PTA-1; PYM; TCAP; TreF; TVSH; YaD
Old Ironsides at anchor lay. The Main Truck; or, A Leap for Life. George Pope Morris. PTA-1
Old Jack-o'-lantern lay on the ground, An. Judging by Appearances. Emilie Poulsson. MPB
Old Jan Smuts, who was numbered with the foe. Jan. G. D. Martineau. NeTW
Old January. Spenser. *Fr.* The Faerie Queene, VII, 7. YeAr
Old Jew, The. Maxwell Bodenheim. BAP; LEAP; NP
Old Jim Finley had a little pig. Jim Finley's Pig. *Unknown.* FTB
Old Joan. Kathleen Conyngham Greene. PCH
Old Jockey, The. F. R. Higgins. AnIV; GTBS-D; OBMV; OxBI
Old Joe. *Unknown.* OxBoLi
(Poor Old Joe.) SG
Old Joe Brown, he had a wife. *Unknown.* GoTP
Old Joe Clark[e], *with music. Unknown.* ABF; TrAS, *diff. vers.*
Old Joe Digger, Sam and Dave. Groun' Hog. *Unknown.* ABF
Old Joe is dead, and gone to hell. Old Joe [or Poor Old Joe]. *Unknown.* OxBoLi; SG
Old John Henry. James Whitcomb Riley. OBAV; OnPP
Old Joyce. Seán Jennett. NeIP
Old King, The. John Heath-Stubbs. NePoEA
Old King Cole. E. A. Robinson. HBV; MOAP; SBMV
Old King Cole was a merry old soul. Mother Goose. BoChLi; ExPo; FaBoBe; FaFP; GaP; HBV; HBVY; MOAP; OlF; OnHT; OTPC; OuSiCo; OxNR; PPL; RIS; SBMV; SiTL; StVeCh (1940 ed.); WP
Old King Cole was a merry old soul. Variations on an Air. G. K. Chesterton. InP
Old Kitchen Clock, The. Ann Hawkshaw. BoTP; OTPC (1923 ed.)
Old Kitchen Floor, The. *Unknown.* PTA-2
Old Knight, The. George Peele. *See* His Golden Locks Time Hath to Silver Turned.
Old Knight Phoenix, The. Homer. *See* Appeal of Phoenix, The.
Old Labourer, An. Margaret Willy. DiM
Old Lady, An. "Katherine Hale." CPG
Old Lady, The. Humbert Wolfe. InP; OnPP; TCPD; TSW; TSWC
Old lady sat in her old arm-chair, An. Prayer and Potatoes. J. T. Pettee. PTA-2
Old Lambro pass'd unseen a private gate. Byron. *Fr.* Don Juan, III. EnRP
Old lame Bridget doesn't hear. The Shadow People. Francis Ledwidge. GaP; HOAH; MCCG; MPB; PCH; POT; PoTo; RAR; SP; TSW; TSWC; VOD
Old Landmarks, *sel.* Sidney Royse Lysaght.
Home. GrCo-2
Old lane, an old gate, an old house by a tree, An. The Old Home. Madison Cawein. HBV; POT
Old Leadville was booming in eighty-eight. The Little Johnny Mine. Daisy L. Detrick. PoOW
Old Lem. Sterling A. Brown. PoNe
Old Liberals, The. John Betjeman. ChMP
Old Line Fence, The. A. W. Bellaw. BOHV
Old Lines; a Fragment. Dino Campana, *tr. fr. Italian by* Glauco Cambon. OnPM
Old lions/ be with us now. Ode in a Night of Overhanging Weather. Vincent McHugh. WaKn
Old Lizette on Sleep. Agnes Lee. HBMV
Old Log House. James S. Tippett. BrR; FaPON
Old London's time-encrusted walls. London, 1940. A. A. Milne. MaRV
Old-long syne. *Unknown.* OBS
Old looking glass grows darker, it is true. Color Alone Can Speak. Louise Townsend Nicholl. NePoAm
Old Looney of Rhyme, An. *Unknown.* SiTL
Old Love. William Morris. GTBS; ViPo; ViPP; VLEP
Old Love, The. Katharine Tynan. HBMV; PoeT
Old Love Should Not Be Ruptured. *Unknown, tr. fr. Chinese by* William Jennings. BoFr
Old lover of the sun, who thus made moan. Lines. Leconte de Lisle. UnW
Old Lover to a Young Gentlewoman, An. *Unknown.* TuPP
Old Loves. Henry Murger, *tr. fr. French by* Andrew Lang. AWP
Old Mackenzie Trail, The. John A. Lomax. SCC
Old, mad, blind, despised, and dying king, An. England in 1819 [or Sonnet: England in 1819]. Shelley. BPN; CoEV; EM-2; EmBrPo; EnL; EnLi-2 (1949 ed.); EnRP; EPN; FiP; OAEP; OBRV; PeBoSo; PoFS; PreP; SeCePo; SeCeV; TrGrPo
Old Maid, The. George Barlow. VA
Old Maid, The. La Fontaine, *tr. fr. French by* Alan Conder. TrFP
Old Maid. J. U. Nicholson. HBMV
Old Maid, The. Amelia B. Welby. LPS-3

Old maid, an old maid, An. *Unknown.* OxNR
Old Maids. Luis Carlos López, *tr. fr. Spanish by* H. R. Hays. TwSpPo
Old Major. Bianca Bradbury. MuM
Old Man, The. Beatrice Herford. PEDC
Old Man. Edward Thomas. ChMP; CoEV; MoP; MoVE; SeCeV
Old Man, An. Wordsworth. FaBoCh; LoGBV
(Animal Tranquillity and Decay.) ERP
Old Man and Jim, The. James Whitcomb Riley. AA; BOHV; CV; LBAP; LHV; OBAV; StPo
Old Man and the Ass, The. La Fontaine, *tr. fr. French by* Elizur Wright. OnPM
Old Man and Young Wife, The. *Unknown.* CoMu
Old Man at a Cricket Match. Norman Nicholson. HaMV
Old Man at the Crossing, The. L. A. G. Strong. OBMV
Old man bending I come among new faces, An. The Wound-Dresser [*or* The Dresser]. Walt Whitman. AmPo; CoBA; IAP; LEAP; TCAP; ViBoPo
Old Man Dreams, The. Oliver Wendell Holmes. HBV; IAP; LPS-3; PTA-2; TCAP
Old Man from Peru, An. *Unknown.* *See* Limerick: "There was an old man from Peru."
"Old man, God bless you! does your pipe taste sweetly?" The Nobleman and the Pensioner. Gottlieb Konrad Pfeffel. LPS-2
Old man, going [*or* traveling] a lone highway, An. The Bridge Builder [*or* Building the Bridge for Him]. Will Allen Dromgoole. BLP; FAOV; MaRV; NeHB; OQP; PoToHe; PTA-2; QP-2; TreFS
Old man had been listless, but he perked, The. End of Steel. Thomas Saunders. CaP
Old man had his box and wheel, The. The Scissors-Grinder. Vachel Lindsay. MAPA; TwAmPo
Old man in a lodge within a park, An. Chaucer. Longfellow. AA; AmP; AmPP; APW; ATP (1935 ed.); AWP; BLV; ES; IAP; InPo; InvP; JAWP; LEAP; MOAP; NePA; OBAV; OBEV (new ed.); OBVV; OnPP; OxBA; PeBoSo; PFE; PoRA; PtP; TOP; TrGrPo; WBP
Old Man in the Model Church, The. John H. Yates. PTA-2
Old Man in the Moon, The. *Unknown.* PCH
Old Man in the Park. Mary Elizabeth Osborn. NePoAm-2
Old Man Jobling. W. W. Gibson. CV
Old Man Long Ago. Nancy Byrd Turner. GaP
Old Man Mose. Chorus. Jack Kerouac. *Fr.* Mexico City Blues. NeAP
Old Man Mountain. Alfred Noyes. GoBC
Old Man near Verona Who Never Left His Farm, The. Ausonius, *tr. fr. Latin by* Jack Lindsay. LaP
Old man never had much to say. The Old Man and Jim. James Whitcomb Riley. AA; BOHV; CV; LBAP; LHV; OBAV; StPo
Old Man of Boulogne, An. *Unknown.* *See* Limerick: "There was an old man of Boulogne."
Old Man of St. Bees. W. S. Gilbert. *See* Limerick: "There was a young man of St. Bees."
Old Man of Tennessee. John Hay. NePoAm-2
Old Man of the Sea, The. Homer, *tr. fr. Greek by* F. L. Lucas. *Fr.* The Odyssey, IV. GrPE
Old man of the sea, briny bell. Now Is Farewell. Blanaid Salkeld. NeIP
Old Man of Verona, The. Claudian, *tr. fr. Latin by* Abraham Cowley. AWP; JAWP; LyMA; WBP; WoL
Old man, old man, whither are you hobbling? Old Man Jobling. W. W. Gibson. CV
Old Man, or Lad's-Love—in the name there's nothing. Old Man. Edward Thomas. ChMP; CoEV; MoP; MoVE; SeCeV
Old Man Playing with Children. John Crowe Ransom. MoPW
Old Man Pondered. John Crowe Ransom. MAP; MoAmPo
Old Man Pot. Lyon Sharman. CaP; OCL
Old Man Rain. Madison Cawein. GaP
Old man, riding on his ass, An. The Old Man and the Ass. La Fontaine. OnPM
Old Man Said, An. Padraic Colum. *See* Deer of Ireland, The.
Old Man Sees Himself, An. Conrad Aiken. NV
Old man selling charms in a cranny of the town wall, An. The Pedlar of Spells. Lu Yu. TrCh
Old man sits, An/ In the shadow of a pine tree. Six Significant Landscapes. Wallace Stevens. CoV
Old man speaking of poetry, An. Denbigh Eisteddfod. Nigel Heseltine. MoWP
Old man takes his tobacco, An. A Poor Little Conscience. José Gorostiza. AnCL
Old Man to His Scythe, The. Denis Wrafter. NeIP
Old Man to the Lizard, The. Archibald MacLeish. CoV
Old man traveling a lone highway, An. *See* Old man, going a lone highway, An.
Old Man under the Hill, The. *Unknown.* CSF
Old man went to meetin', for the day was bright and fair, The. The Preacher's Vacation. *Unknown.* BLPA
Old Man Who Lived in a Wood, The. *Unknown.* MoShBr; MPB
("There was an old man who lived in a wood.") StVeCh
Old Man with a Beard. Edward Lear. *See* Limerick: "There was an old man with a beard,/ Who said, 'It is just as I feared!'"
Old Man with a Mowing Machine. May Carleton Lord. GoYe
Old Man with the Broken Arm, The. Po Chü-i, *tr. fr. Chinese by* Arthur Waley. TrCh
Old Mandarin, The. Persis Greely Anderson. DDA
Old Mandarin, The/ Always perplexes his friend the Adjuster. Unearned Increment. Christopher Morley. SiTL; WhC
Old mandarin loves his quiet pleasures in later life, The. The Old Mandarin. Persis Greely Anderson. DDA
Old Mandarin was always pleased, The. Psychoanalysts. Christopher Morley. WhC
Old Man's Carousal, The. James Kirke Paulding. AA; LEAP
Old Man's Cold, The. *Unknown.* PA
Old Man's Comforts [and How He Gained Them], The. Robert Southey. CG; HBV; HoPM; LPS-2
(Father William.) OTPC
Old Man's Dream after He Died, The. Robinson Jeffers. *Fr.* Cawdor. CoV
Old Man's Dreams, An. Eliza M. Sherman. PTA-2
Old man's fair-haired consort, whose dewy axle-tree, The. Slowly, Slowly [*or* Lente, Lente]. Ovid. AWP; LiTW; WoL
Old Man's Grave, The. L. M. Montgomery. CPG
Old Man's Idyl, An. Richard Realf. AA; HBV; OBAV
Old Man's Motto, The. John Godfrey Saxe. BPP
Old Man's Song, An. Aleksey Vasilyevich Koltsov, *tr. fr. Russian.* BoR, *tr. by* C. M. Bowra; TrRV, *tr. by* Babette Deutsch
Old Man's Song, An. Richard Le Gallienne. HBV; VA
Old Man's Toes, The. Eleanor Farjeon. PoRh
Old Man's Weariness, An. Arthur L. Phelps. CPG
Old Man's Winter Night, An. Robert Frost. AmPP; AnAmPo; AnEnPo; AnNE; AWP; BLV; BoLiVe; CoBA; HBMV; JAWP; LA; MAP; MoAB; MoAmPo; MOAP; MoVE; NP; NV; OnPP; OxBA; PoMA; WBP
Old Man's Wish, The. Walter Pope. CoMu, 9 *sts.*; OBS, 5 *sts.*; PoP, 13 *sts.*; SeEP, 5 *sts.*
(Wish, The, 5 *sts.*) SeCL
Old Mansion. John Crowe Ransom. OxBA
(Southern Mansion, *abr.*) MoP
Old Mansion, The, *sel.* Robert Southey.
"Aye, master! fine old trees!" EnSW
Old Manuscript. Alfred Kreymborg. BAP; CP; LEAP; MAP; NeMA; NP; NV; PFE; SBMV
Old Maps. Eunice Tietjens. BrR
Old Mare, The. Elizabeth J. Coatsworth. MAP; MoAmPo
Old Marlborough Road, The. Henry David Thoreau. PoEL-4
Old Marquis and His Blooming Wife, The. *Unknown.* CoMu
Old-Marrieds, The. Gwendolyn Brooks. PoNe
Old Master Brown brought his ferule down. Old-School Punishment. *Unknown.* LPS-1
Old Masters, The. Emile Verhaeren, *tr. fr. French by* Jethro Bithell. AnEnPo
Old May Song. *Unknown.* AtBAP; BoTP; CH; HH
Old Mayor climbed the belfry tower, The. The High-Tide on the Coast of Lincolnshire (1571). Jean Ingelow. BeLS; BMEP; EV-5; GBV; GN; GTBS; GTBS-D; GTSL; HBV; LPS-1; OBVV; OtMeF; PIR; PTA-2; ShBV-3; TOP; VA
Old Meg ("Old Meg she was a gipsy"). Keats. *See* Meg Merrilies.
Old memories waken old desires. Lovers Parted. Lesbia Harford. BoAu
Old Memory. W. B. Yeats. Po
Old Men, The. Walter de la Mare. MBP; MoAB; MoBrPo
Old Men, The. Euripides, *tr. fr. Greek by* C. M. Bowra. *Fr.* Aeolus. OxBG
Old Men, The. Alexander Javitz. TrJP
Old Men. Nancy Keesing. BoAV
Old Men. Merrill Moore. MOAP
Old Men, The. Ernest Rhys. POTE
Old Men Admiring Themselves in the Water, The. W. B. Yeats. BMEP; FaBoCh; LoGBV; VLEP
Old Men and Old Women Going Home on the Street Car. Merrill Moore. MAP; MoAmPo
Old Men and the Young Men, The. Clement Wood. BAP
Old Men and Young Men. John Holmes. WaKn
Old Men Are Facts. Vivian Smith. NeLNL
Old men are full of zest and information. Old Men and Young Men. John Holmes. WaKn
Old Men on the Blue. Thomas Hornsby Ferril. PoOW
Old men sat with hats pull'd down, The. The White Rose over the Water. George Walter Thornbury. VA
Old men sit by the chimney piece and drink the good red wine, The. The Green Estaminet. A. P. Herbert. HBMV

Old men sit here, quietly lost, The. Hotel Lobby. C. R. Holmes. PtPa
Old men, white-haired, beside the ancestral graves. Basho, *tr. fr. Japanese by* Curtis Hidden Page. AWP; JAWP; PFE; WBP
Old Men's Ward. Elma Dean. GoYe
Old Menalcas on a day. The Palmer's Ode. Robert Greene. *Fr.* Never Too Late. EV-1; OBSC; SiCE; TuPP
Old Mexican tamale man. The Hot Tamale Man. Hazel Harper Harris. HiLiAm
Old Michael. George M. Brady. NeIP
Old Mike Clancy went out for a stroll. Two Days. T. A. Daly. LHV
Old Mill, The. Thomas Dunn English. AA
Old Miss Flipper Flopper. *Unknown. See* Fox, The.
Old Mr. Chang, I've oft heard it said. Old Chang, the Crab. *Unknown, tr. by* Isaac Taylor Headland. PCH
Old Mr. So-and-So. Malville Haller. NV
Old Mr. Tatterlock. Irene Cheyne. MoAuPo
Old Mrs. Caribou lives by a lake. Mrs. Caribou. William Jay Smith. PoMS
Old Mrs. Hague. Mrs. Hague. Sir Osbert Sitwell. MM
Old Mrs. Jarvis. Elizabeth Fleming. BoTP
Old Mrs. Tressider. The Scarf. Ivy O. Eastwick. BoTP
Old Molly Means was a hag and a witch. Molly Means. Margaret Walker. PoNe; StPo
Old Montague. M. K. Joseph. *Fr.* The Lovers and the City. AnNZ
Old moon is tarnished, The. Sea Lullaby. Elinor Wylie. NeMA
Old Morgan. G. D. Roberts. BoTP
Old Mortality, *sels.* Sir Walter Scott.
And What Though Winter Will Pinch Severe, *fr. ch.* 19. EnRP
(Cavalier Song.) BPN
Sound, Sound the Clarion, *fr. ch.* 34. Thomas O. Mordaunt, *formerly at. to* Scott. AnFE; BCEP; BHV; EBSV; EV-4; InP; OAEP; OQP; QP-2; TOP
(Answer.) OBEV (1st ed.)
(Call, The.) GTBS-W; OBEV (new ed.)
(Clarion.) BEL; BPN; EmBrPo
(Motto from "Old Mortality.") CaAE
(One Crowded Hour.) CBOV; MaRV; TrGrPo
(Sound the Clarion.) ERP; TreFS
Old Mother, The. *Unknown.* PoToHe
Old Mother Duck has hatched a brood. Dame Duck's [First] Lecture [*or* Mother Duck]. Ann Hawkshaw. BoTP; DDA; OTPC (1923 ed.); SAS
Old Mother Earth woke up from her sleep. A Spring Song. *Unknown.* ADAH
Old Mother Goose when/ She wanted to wander. Mother Goose. BoTP; OTPC (1923 ed.); OxNR; PPL; RIS
Old Mother Hubbard. Sarah Catherine Martin. BoChLi; BoTP; FaBoBe; GoTP; HBV; HBVY; OnHT; OTPC; OxNR; RIS; SAS; SiTL; StVeCh; TiPo (1959 ed.)
(Old Mother Hubbard and Her Dog.) BoN
Old Mother Niddity Nod. *Unknown.* OxNR
Old Mother Shuttle. *Unknown.* BoN; OxNR
Old Mother Tabbyskins. Elizabeth Anna Hart. *See* Mother Tabbyskins.
Old Mother Twitchett has [*or* had] but one eye. Mother Goose. HBV; HBVY; OTPC; OxNR; RIS; SiTL; TiPo
Old Mother Wind. *Unknown, tr. fr. Chinese by* Isaac Taylor Headland. PCH
Old Mother Witch. *Unknown.* RIS
Old Mothers. Charles S. Ross. *See* Dear Old Mothers.
Old Mountain Troll, The. Gustaf Fröding, *tr. fr. Swedish by* Charles W. Stork. AnSL
Old Mountains, The. Ivar Aasen, *tr. fr. Norwegian by* Charles W. Stork. AnNoLy
Old Music Box, The. Rachel Field. BoChLi
Old Name, The. Katherine Drayton Mayrant Simons. LS
Old Navy, The. Frederick Marryat. *See* Captain Stood on the Carronade, The.
Old Nevada prospector, An. The Dyeing Prospector. Dan Foley. DDA
Old New Hampshire. John F. Holmes. PoRL
Old New-Year's Song, An. Oscar Levertin, *tr. fr. Swedish by* Charles W. Stork. AnSL
Old Nick in Sorel. Standish O'Grady. *Fr.* The Emigrant. BoCaPo
Old Nick, who taught the village school. The Retort. George Pope Morris. BOHV; HBV; LauV; LPS-3; PR
Old Noah he had an ostrich farm and fowls on the largest scale. Wine and Water. G. K. Chesterton. *Fr.* The Flying Inn. ACP (1952 ed.); CenHV; FiBHP; GoBC; HBMV; InMe; LiTM; MBP; MoBrPo; ShBV-4; ViBoPo
Old Noah once he built the Ark. One More River. *Unknown.* TreFS
Old North State, The. William Gaston. NoCaPo; PoRL, *abr.*
Old Nuns. James M. Hayes. JKCP; PraNu
Old Nürnberg. Grace Hazard Conkling. PoeMoYo; VOD
Old Nurse, The. Frances Cornford. TCPD
Old Nurse Winter. Jean Starr Untermeyer. TSW
Old Nurse's Song, The. Edith Sitwell. NeMA; TSW
Old Oak Tree, The, *with music. Unknown.* ShS
Old Oak Tree at Hatfield Broadoak, The, *sl. abr.* Frederick Locker-Lampson. EV-5
Old Oaken Bucket, The, *parody. Unknown.* BLPA; FaFP; WBLP
Old Oaken Bucket, The. Samuel Woodworth. APW; BLPA; FaBoBe; FaFP; LEAP; LPS-1; NeHB; OlF; OTPC (1946 ed.); PECK; PIR; PYM; TreF; WBLP
(Bucket, The.) AA; BAV; HBV; OBAV; TCAP
"How dear to this heart are the scenes of my childhood," *sel.* FaPON
Old ocean was/ Infinity of ages ere we breathed. The Beatific Sea. Thomas Campbell. EtS
Old October. Thomas Constable. HBV
Old, old is the sea to-day. Sea Variations. E. J. Pratt. CPG
Old, old lady, The. The Old Lady. Humbert Wolfe. InP; OnPP; TCPD; TSW; TSWC
Old Old Old Andrew Jackson. Vachel Lindsay. *See* Oration, Entitled "Old, Old, Old, Old Andrew Jackson," An.
Old, Old Song, The. Charles Kingsley. *See* Young and Old.
Old Olives at Bordighera. Duncan Campbell Scott. TwCV
"Old order changeth, yielding place to new, The." Prayer [*or* Prayer for the Dead]. Tennyson. *Fr.* Morte d' Arthur. GoBC; MaRV
Old Paint. *Unknown. See* Good-by, Old Paint.
Old Pal. Marty Hale. AlBD
Old papers yellow on the porch. Return. Queena Davidson Miller. DDA
Old Parish Church, Whitby, The. Hardwicke Drummond Rawnsley. OBVV
Old Pastor, The. John Banister Tabb. AmP
Old Patient, The. Jerome Meyers. PoP
Old Peasant in the Billiard Saloon, The. Huw Menai. MoWP
Old Pedhar Carthy from Clonmore. Patrick Joseph McCall. TIP
Old People. Richard R. Kirk. LS
Old Peter Grimes made fishing his employ. Peter Grimes. George Crabbe. *Fr.* The Borough. EnRP; PoEL-4
Old Peter led a wretched life. The Perils of Invisibility. W. S. Gilbert. StPo
Old Peter Prairie-Dog. Prairie-Dog Town. Mary Austin. FaPON; StVeCh (1955 ed.); TiPo
Old Pictures in Florence. Robert Browning. BPN; EmBrPo; GEPC; PoVP; VLEP
Old Pilot Tunnels under the English Channel, The. James Schevill. FiMAP
Old pine, you whisper like the waves. The Whispering Pine Tree. Mariana Griswold Van Rensselaer. PCH
Old Pioneer, The. Theodore O'Hara. SPP
Old Place, The (New Zealand). Blanche Edith Baughan. AnNZ; BoAu
Old Poem: "At fifteen I went with the army." *Unknown, tr. fr. Chinese by* Arthur Waley. TrCh
(Return.) LiTW
Old Poem: "Cold, cold the year." *Unknown. See* Old Chinese Poem: "Cold, cold the year."
Old Poet to His Love, An. Maxwell Bodenheim. *See* Poet to His Love, The.
Old Poet to His Maiden Choir, The. Alcman. *See* Halcyons, The.
Old Poets. Joyce Kilmer. LEAP
Old pond, An. Haiku. Basho. LiTW; OnPJ
Old Pond, An. Bocho Yamamura, *tr. fr. Japanese by* Takamichi Ninomiya *and* D. J. Enright. PoLJ
Old pride and consequence, where lodge they now? Mais où est le preux Charlemagne? *Unknown.* OxBG
Old priest, Peter Gilligan, The. The Ballad of Father Gilligan [*or* Father Gilligan]. W. B. Yeats. AnIV; CV; EnLit; HBV; InP; InPo; MBP; MoBrPo; NeMA; OnYI; PCN; PoRA; POTT; TSW; TSWC; TVSH; TwP; WaKn; WHL
Old Print, An. Edwin Morgan. PFE
Old Prison, The. Judith Wright. NeLNL
Old professor of zoology, The. The Parrot. James Elroy Flecker. BLA; FaBoTw
Old Quartermaster, The. Gordon Grant. EtS
Old Quin Queeribus. Nancy Byrd Turner. GaP; TiPo
Old Rat's Tale, An. *Unknown.* GFA
(What Became of Them?) BoTP
Old Red Cradle, The. Annie J. Granniss. PTA-1
Old Red Hoss Mountain. Cy Warman. PoOW
Old Reveller, The. *Unknown, tr. fr. Greek by* F. L. Lucas. *Fr.* Anacreontea. GrPE
Old Rhyme ("Here comes a lusty wooer"). *Unknown. See* Here Comes a Lusty Wooer.
Old Rhyme, An ("I went to market and bought me a cat"). *Unknown.* BoTP
Old River Road. Blanche Whiting Keysner. GoYe
Old Road, The. Jones Very. AA
Old Road to Paradise, The. Margaret Widdemer. HBMV
Old Robin-a-thrush he married a wife. Robin-a-Thrush. *Unknown.* PreP

Old Robin of Portingale. *Unknown.* ESPB, *abr.;* OBB
Old Rodilard, a certain cat. The Council Held by the Rats. La Fontaine. CIV; OuHeWo
Old Roger. *Unknown.* OxBoLi
Old Room, An. Gustaf Fröding, *tr. fr. Swedish by* Charles W. Stork. AnSL
Old Rosin, the Beau. *Unknown. See* Rosin the Bow.
Old Ross, Cockburn, and Cochrane too. The Battle of Baltimore. *Unknown.* PAH
Old rude church, with bare, bald tower, is here, The. Wordsworth's Grave. Sir William Watson. BMEP; EnLit; GoTL; HBV; LEAP; PoVP
Old Russian Song. Ippolit Bogdanovich, *tr. fr. Russian by* Sir John Bowring. BoRS
Old, sad man who catches moles, An. The Lament of the Mole-Catcher. Sir Osbert Sitwell. LBBV
Old Sailor, The. Glenn Ward Dresbach. EtS
Old Sailor, The. A. A. Milne. CenHV
Old Sailor, The. Elizabeth Riddell. MoAuPo
Old Sailors. *Unknown.* SG
Old Sailor's Song. *Unknown.* SoAmSa
Old Saint, The. Muriel Stuart. HBMV
Old St. David's at Radnor. Longfellow. MeRV
Old Sam was black and long of limb. Ancestry. William A. Donaghy. JKCP (1955 ed.)
Old Sam's Wife. *Unknown.* ChTr
Old Sandhills, Hobart, The. Hubert Church. MM
Old Santa Claus puts on his cap. Santa Claus. *Unknown.* GFA
Old Santa Fé Trail, The. Richard Burton. PAH
Old Santa Is an Active Man. Lois Lenski. ChBR
Old Saul. Lizette Woodworth Reese. LS; MAP; MoAmPo; SPP; TCAP
Old Saying, An. Swinburne. MeRV
Old Scent of the Plum Tree. Fujiwara Ietaka, *tr. fr. Japanese by* E. Powys Mathers. AWP
Old Sceptic, The. Alfred Noyes. QS
Old School List, The. James Kenneth Stephen. CenHV
Old-School Punishment. *Unknown.* LPS-1
Old School Tie-up, The. Laurence McKinney. WhC
Old Scottish Cavalier, The. William Edmondstoune Aytoun. GN; HBV; PoVP
Old Scout's Lament, The. William F. Drannan. CoSo; CSF; PoOW
Old scythe in the hedge. The Old Man to His Scythe. Denis Wrafter. NeIP
Old sea captains, when their work, The. Between Brielle and Manasquan. Oliver St. John Gogarty. OnYI
Old sea-dog on a sailor's log, An. The Powerful Eyes o' Jeremy Tait. Wallace Irwin. FiBHP; StPo
Old Seaport, An. *Unknown.* EtS
Old Seawoman. Gordon LeClaire. CaP
Old Sergeant, The. Forceythe Willson. BlG
"Come a little nearer, doctor," *sel.* AA; BeLS; PaA
Old Sexton, The. Park Benjamin. AA; HBV
Old Shawnee, The. *Unknown.* ABS
Old Sheepskin, The. *Unknown. See* Wife Wrapt in Wether's Skin, The.
Old Shellover. Walter de la Mare. AtBAP; BoTP; UTS
Old Shepherd, The. Zacharias Papondoniou, *tr. fr. Modern Greek by* Rae Dalven. MoGP
Old Shepherds, The. Eleanor Farjeon. AlDL
Old Shepherd's Prayer. Charlotte Mew. MBP; MoAB; MoBrPo
Old Ship Riggers. H. A. Cody. EtS
Old Ships, The. James Elroy Flecker. AnFE; CaAE; CBE; CH; EnLit; EPP; EtS; GTBS-D; GTML; GTSL; MBP; MoBrPo; MoVE; OBMV; OtMeF; PC; PoeMoYo; PoRA; POTE; POTT; ShBV-3; TCPD; TwCV; WHA
Old Ships. Louis Ginsberg. HBMV
Old Ships. David Morton. BAP; BBV; EtS; OBAV; PoTo; PYM; SBMV; StVeCh; TSW; TSWC
Old ships are tired sailing into port. The Invalid. Virginia J. Foley. PFE
Old Shoes. Gertrude Ryder Bennett. DDA
Old Shoes and Leggin's, *with music.* *Unknown.* OuSiCo
Old Silenus came, lolling in the sunshine, The. Matthew Arnold. *Fr.* The Strayed Reveller. VLEP
Old silver church in a forest, An. Poet [*or* The Old Poet] to His Love. Maxwell Bodenheim. BAP; MAP; MoAmPo (1942 ed.)
Old Sir Simon the king. *Unknown.* OxNR
Old sisters at our Maris Stella House. Mother Marie Therese. Robert Lowell. FiMAP
Old Skinflint. W. W. Gibson. OBMV
Old Slave, The. Dioscorides. *See* Faithful Servant, A.
Old Smoky. *Unknown. See* Wagoner's Lad, The.
Old Sodos no longer makes saddles. Lola Ridge. *Fr.* The Ghetto. MAP; MoAmPo (1942 ed.)
Old Soldier. Padraic Colum. OBMV; POTE
Old Soldier, The. Walter de la Mare. SoV
Old Soldier, The. Katharine Tynan. AOAH
Old Soldier Dead. Annette Kohn. HH
Old Soldiers. Crosbie Garstin. ReTS
Old soldiers true, ah, them all men can trust. At Lincoln's Grave. Maurice Thompson. *Fr.* Lincoln's Grave. GA
Old Song, The. G. K. Chesterton. FaBoTw
Old Song. Hart Crane. ChMo
Old Song, An. Fannie Stearns Davis. AV
Old Song. Edward Fitzgerald. EV-5; GN, *abr.;* OBEV; OBVV
(Meadows in Spring.) HBV
Old Song, An. Thomas S. Jones, Jr. POT; PoTo
Old Song, The. Charles Kingsley. *See* Young and Old.
Old Song. F. R. Scott. PeCV
Old Song ("Haste thee, Winter, haste away!"). *Unknown.* PCH
Old Song ("She went up the mountain"). *Unknown, tr. fr. Chinese.* WhP
Old Song, An. "Yehoash," *tr. fr. Yiddish by* Marie Syrkin. AWP; JAWP; LiTW; WBP
Old Song by New Singers, An. A. C. Wilkie. BOHV; PA
Old Song Ended, An. Dante Gabriel Rossetti. *See* Friar of Orders Grey, The.
Old song made by an old aged [*or* agéd old] pate, An. The Old and Young [*or* the New] Courtier. *Unknown.* CG; CoMu; EV-2; LEAP; ViBoPo
Old Song of Fairies, An. *Unknown. See* Fairy Queen, The.
Old Song Resung, An. Charles Larcom Graves. CenHV
Old Song Re-sung, An. John Masefield. AlDL; ExPo; LiTB; PtOT
Old Song Re-sung, An. Katharine Tynan. QS
Old Song Resung, An. W. B. Yeats. *See* Down by the Salley Gardens.
Old Song Reversed, An. Richard Henry Stoddard. AA; LEAP
Old Song Written during Washington's Life. *Unknown.* OHIP
Old Songs, The. Sir Owen Seaman. InMe
Old songs die, The. Music. Alice Corbin. NP
Old songs I will not sing. A Manifesto. Timotheus. OxBG
Old Sorrow I shall meet again. Childhood. John Banister Tabb. HBV
Old Soul, The. Edith M. Thomas. LBAP
Old Souldier of the Queens, An. *Unknown.* OBS; SoV
Old Souls. Thomas Gordon Hake. VA
Old Squaw, The. Indian Sky. Alfred Kreymborg. NP
Old Squire, The. Wilfrid Scawen Blunt. HBV; OBEV (new ed.); OBVV; VA
Old Stoic, The. Emily Brontë. BLV; BPP; EmBrPo; EnLi-2; EnLit; EV-5; GTML; OAEP; OBEV (new ed.); OBVV; OxBI; PC; PIAE; PoFr; PoVP; TrGrPo; VA; ViBoPo; YT
Old Stone Basin, The. "Susan Coolidge." PEOR
Old Stone God, An. Olivia Freeman. UnW
Old stories tell how Hercules. The Dragon of Wantley. *Unknown.* CG
Old Stormy [*or* Stormalong] was [*or* he was] a fine [*or* good *or* gay] old man. Stormalong [*or* Storm Along]. *Unknown.* SG; ShS; SoAmSa
Old Story, The. John O'Hagan. TIP
Old Story, The ("Like many a one"). E. A. Robinson, *par. fr. the Greek of* Marcus Argentarius. AWP; JAWP; LiTW; WBP
(Variations of Greek Themes, VIII.) MOAP
Old Story, An ("Strange that I did not know him then"). E. A. Robinson. AnNE; BTP; HBMV; MAP; MaRV; MoAmPo; NeMA; TreFS
Old Story Over Again, The. James Kenney. OnYI
Old Street, An. Virginia Woodward Cloud. AA
Old Stuff. Bert Leston Taylor. BOHV; HBMV; LHV
Old Summerhouse, The. Walter de la Mare. ChMo; MoPo
Old sun, the gold sun, The. Sun and Wind. Eleanor Farjeon. OTPC (1946 ed.)
Old *Superb,* The. Sir Henry Newbolt. BBV (1923 ed.)
Old Susan. Walter de la Mare. ChMo; CMP; InP; MBP; MoBrPo; NeMA; OnPP; PoeMoYo; PoRL; POT; PoTo; TCEP; TreFS; TwCV; VOD
Old Sweetheart of Mine, An. James Whitcomb Riley. BeLS; BLPA; NeHB
(Old Sweetheart, An, *abr.*) OBAV
"As one who cons at evening o'er an album all alone," *sel* TreFS
Old Swimmin'-Hole, The. James Whitcomb Riley. BeLS; FaFP; HBV; POT; PoTo
Old Tale, An. Marya Zaturenska. NP; TBM
Old tales were told of Sigemund's daring. The Tale of Sigemund. *Unknown. Fr.* Beowulf. AnOE
Old Talk. Winfield Townley Scott. FiMAP
Old Teacher. Gerald Raftery. BPP
Old Temple in Mountains. Chang Chi, *tr. fr. Chinese by* Arthur Christy. OnPM
Old Testament, The. Thomas Russell. TreFS
(Names and Order of the Books of the Old Testament.) BLPA
Old Testament Contents. *Unknown.* BLPA
Old Thad Stevens. Kenneth Porter. NePoAm-2
Old Thanksgiving Days, The. Ernest W. Shurtleff. PEOR

Old Things Need Not Be Therefore True. Arthur Hugh Clough. *See* Ah! Yet Consider It Again.
Old thorn tree in a stony place, An. Ode: On the Death of W. B. Yeats. A. J. M. Smith. BoCaPo; PeCV; TwCV
Old Thought, An, *abr.* Maurice Hewlett. *Fr.* The Song of the Plow. PoFr
Old Thought, An. Charles Henry Luders. AA
Old Tillie Turveycombe. Tillie. Walter de la Mare. PoMS; TiPo
Old Time Cowboy ("Come all you melancholy folks"). *Unknown. See* Melancholy Cowboy, The.
Old-Time Cowboy, The ("Ofttimes I get to thinking"). *Unknown.* CoSo
Old-Time Family Doctor, The. Spencer Michael Free. PoP
Old Time is lame and halt. Wie langsam kriechet sie dahin. Heine. AWP
Old-Time Love. Clément Marot, *tr. fr. French.* LiA
Old-Time Sea-Fight, An. Walt Whitman. *See* Sea-Fight, A.
Old-Time Service. Thomas Churchyard. *Fr.* A Fayned Fancye betweene the Spider and the Gowte. OBSC
Old-Time Virtues. Aristophanes, *tr. fr. Greek by* Benjamin Bickley Rogers. *Fr.* The Knights. GrR
Old Timers. Carl Sandburg. AnAmPo; BAP; CoV; LA; NP; TBM; YaD
Old Times Were the Best, The. James Whitcomb Riley. FaFP
Old Tippecanoe. *Unknown.* GA; PAH
Old tips come out as good as new. John William Mackail. *Fr.* The Masque of Balliol. CenHV
Old Tithon must forsake his dear. *Unknown. Fr.* Wily Beguiled. TuPP
Old Tityrus to Eugenia, *sel.* Charles Cotton.
"Eugenia, young and fair and sweet." ViBoPo
Old Tom's Song. Paul Green. *Fr.* The Lost Colony. NoCaPo
Old Toper, The. Ibn Sa'id of Alcala la Real, *tr. fr. Arabic by* A. J. Arberry. MooP
Old town lies afar, An. There Is an Old City. Karl Bulcke. AWP; JAWP; WBP
Old Traveller, The. Homer, *tr. fr. Greek by* F. L. Lucas. *Fr.* The Iliad, XV. GrPE
Old Trouper, The. Don Marquis. *Fr.* Archy and Mehitabel. MoP
Old Tubal Cain was a man of might. Tubal Cain. Charles Mackay. BMEP; GTBS; LPS-2; MPB; PIR; TVSH; WBLP
Old Tune, An. Gérard de Nerval, *tr. fr. French by* Andrew Lang. AWP; HBV; JAWP; WBP
(Fantasia, *tr. by* Alan Conder.) TrFP
(Fantasy, *tr. by* Anthony Bower.) AnFP; LiTW
Old Tup, The. *Unknown. See* Derby Ram, The.
Old Uncle Jim was as blind as a mole. Uncle Jim. Alice Corbin. *Fr.* Echoes of Childhood. PoNe
Old Uncle Ned. Stephen Collins Foster. APW; OlF
Old Venice grappled with the Turk. Captain Loredan. Edward King. PFY
Old Vicarage, Grantchester, The. Rupert Brooke. GoTL (1949 ed.); MBP; MoBrPo; MoVE; PoeT; PoRA; POTT; ShBV-3; TCPD; TOP
Old Violin, The. Maurice Francis Egan. AA; JKCP
Old Voyager. Walter Blackstock. GoYe
Old waggon drudges through the miry lane, The. The Waggoner. Edmund Blunden. AnFE; MM
Old War-Dreams. Walt Whitman. DDA
Old warder of these buried bones. In Memoriam A. H. H., XXXIX. Tennyson. EmBrPo; EPN; GEPC; OAEP; PoEL-5; ViPo; VLEP
Old was Iamblichus, the whole world's friend. Picture of a Physician. Leontius. OxBG
Old Waterford Woman, An. Mary Devenport O'Neill. NeIP
Old West, the old time, The. Spanish Johnny. Willa Cather. ABF; BAP; FaPON; HBMV; MPB; MW; NP; PFY; WaKn
Old Wichet. *Unknown.* StPo
Old Wife and the Ghost, The. James Reeves. PoMS
Old wife sat by her bright fireside, An. There's but One Pair of Stockings to Mend To-Night. *Unknown.* PTA-1
Old Wife's Tale, The. George Peele. *See* Old Wives' Tale, The.
Old Willie Gray will sit and stare. The Monaro. David Campbell. BoAV
Old wind stirs the hawthorn tree, The. The Road of Remembrance. Lizette Woodworth Reese. HBV
Old wine filled him, and he saw, with eyes, The. Maurice de Guérin. Maurice Francis Egan. AA; JKCP; LEAP
Old wine to drink! A Winter Wish [*or* Give Me the Old]. Robert Hinckley Messinger. AA; HBV; LEAP; LPS-1; ViBoPo
Old Winter. Thomas Noel. DD, *abr.*; GN; HBV; OTPC (1923 ed.)
Old Winter is a sturdy one. Winter. *Unknown.* DD
Old Winter sad, [is] in snow yclad. Old Winter. Thomas Noel. DD; GN; HBV; OTPC (1923 ed.)
Old Winter with an angry frown. Putting Winter to Bed. E. J. Pratt. PCN
Old Witch in the Copse, The. Frances Cornford. TCPD
Old witch-wife beside her door, The. A Lowland Witch Ballad. William Bell Scott. DaM
Old Wives Prayer, The. Robert Herrick. SeCV-1
Old Wives' Sayings, *sels.* *Unknown.* StaSt
When to Be Born.
When to Cut Your Nails.
When to Sneeze.
Old Wives' [*or* Wife's] Tale, The, *sels.* George Peele.
Harvester's Song ("All ye that lovely lovers be"). BLV; TrGrPo
(Harvestmen a-Singing.) EPP
"Lo! here we come a-reaping, a-reaping," 4 *ll.* OBSC
Song at the Well, The. AtBAP; ExPo; SeCeV
(Celanta at the Well of Life.) LoBV; ThWaDe
(Fair Maiden.) PoEL-2
(Voice from the Well [of Life Speaks to the Maiden], The.) ChTr; FaBoEn
(Voice Speaks from the Well, A.) FaBoCh; LoGBV; OBSC; OxBoLi; RiBV; SiTL
Spell, A. ChTr
"Whenas [*or* When as] the rye reach to the chin." ElSeCe; EM-1; EnLoPo; FaBoCh; InvP; LO; LoGBV; OBSC; SiTL; TuPP; ViBoPo
(Song.) ALV; AtBAP; ElL; FaBoEn; LoBV; OxBoLi; PoEL-2
(Summer Song, A.) OBEV (new ed.)
(When as the Rye.) SeCePo
Old Woman, The. John Bunker. CAW
Old Woman, The. Joseph Campbell. AWP; BMEP; CBOV; CP; EPP; GoBC; GTIV; HBMV; JAWP; LBBV; MBP; MCCG; MoBrPo; MotAn; NeHB; NeMA; NP; NV; OnYI; OxBI; POTE; PoToHe (new ed.); TIP; ViBoPo; WBP; YT
Old woman, The. One. Andrew Hewitt. NoCaPo (rev. ed.)
Old Woman, The. Marjorie Allen Seiffert. AnAmPo; NP
Old Woman, An. Edith Sitwell. CoBMV; MoPo
Old Woman, The ("Untidy, squat, and soft old body slack"). *Unknown.* DDA
Old Woman All Skin and Bone, *with music. Unknown.* TrAS
Old Woman and Her Cats, The. John Gay. BeR
Old woman has forgotten her face, The. Evasion. Blanaid Salkeld. NeIP
Old Woman Laments in Springtime, An. Edith Sitwell. LO; ViBoPo
Old woman must stand, The. *Unknown.* OxNR
Old Woman of Beare [Regrets Lost Youth], The. *Unknown. See* Woman of Beare, The.
Old Woman of Berkeley, The. Robert Southey. OBRV
Old Woman of the Roads, An [*or* The]. Padraic Colum. BLV; BMEP; BoTP; CAW; CH; CP; EPP; FaBoBe; FaPON; GaP; GBV (1952 ed.); GoBC; GTSL; HBMV; HiLiEn; JKCP; LBBV; MBP; MM; MoBrPo; MPB; NP; NV; OBEV (new ed.); OnPP; OTPC (1946 ed.); PG; PoRA; PoTo; SP; StVeCh; TreFS; TVSH; TwCV; VOD; WHA; YT
Old woman, old and bent and worn. Morning Bus. John Coulter. CaP
Old woman, old woman, are you fond of smoking? The Deaf Woman's Courtship. *Unknown.* SaSa
"Old woman, old woman, shall we go a-shearing?" Mother Goose. BoChLi; OTPC; OxNR; RIS; TiPo (1952 ed.)
Old Woman, outside the Abbey Theater, An. L. A. G. Strong. FiBHP; MBP; MoBrPo
Old Woman Rain. Louise Driscoll. MW
Old Woman Remembers, The. Lady Gregory. OnYI
Old woman sits on a bench before the door and quarrels, The. Fawn's Foster-Mother. Robinson Jeffers. AmPP (3d ed.); MOAP
Old woman went to market and bought a pig, An. *Unknown.* OxNR
Old Woman Who Lived in a Shoe, The. *Unknown.* LiTG; OxBoLi. *For* Mother Goose *vers., see* There was an old woman who lived in a shoe.
Old Woman Who Lives in the Town, The. Pringle Barret. PCH
Old Woman with Flowers, An. Agnes Lee. NP
Old Woman's Answer to a Letter from Her Girlhood, An. Susan L. Emory. CAW
Old Woman's Lamentations, An. Villon, *pr. tr. fr. French by* J. M. Synge. OBMV; TwCV
(Complaint of the Fair Armoress, The, *tr. by* Swinburne.) AWP; WoL
(Two Translations from Villon, *pr. tr. by* J. M. Synge.) MoBrPo
Old Woman's Song. Thomas Cole. NePoAm-2
Old Women. Frances Alexander. HiLiAm
Old Women. Babette Deutsch. BAP; HBMV; TBM
Old Women, The. Arthur Symons. PoVP
Old women do not know this piercing song. Desdemona. Sister Mary Jeremy. JKCP (1955 ed.)

Old women sit at Willowsleigh and spin, The. Spinners at Willowsleigh. Marya Zaturenska. HBMV; TBM
Old women sit, stiffly, mosaics of pain. Old Women. Babette Deutsch. BAP; HBMV; TBM
Old wood, stands uncut of long yeares space, An. Ovid. Amores, III, 1. LaP
Old-World Effect, An. Siegfried Sassoon. ChMo; CMP
Old world staggers, The, but a young, triumphant world is born. Toward a True Peace [*or* A True Peace]. Lucia Trent *and* Ralph Cheyney. *Fr.* Ten Years After. PGD; PSO
Old World to the New, The. Florence Ellenwood Allen. CAG
Old, worn harp that had been played, An. The Master-Player. Paul Laurence Dunbar. MaRV
Old Year, The. John Clare. PG
Old Year, The. Clarence Urmy. OQP; PGD; PoToHe; PSO; QP-1
Old Year and the New, The. Annie Johnson Flint. BLRP
Old Year, going, take with you. Farewell and Hail! Thomas Curtis Clark. PGD
Old Year is a diary where is set, The. Diaries [*or* Diary]. Ethel Romig Fuller. PGD; PSO
Old Year's gone away, The. The Old Year. John Clare. PG
Old Year's Prayer, The. Minna Irving. PGD; PSO
Old yellow stucco, The. Winter Nightfall. J. C. Squire. GTML; ShBV-3
Old Yew, which graspest at the stones. In Memoriam A. H. H., II. Tennyson. CoEV; EmBrPo; EnLi-2; EPN; FaBoEn; GEPC; GTBS-D; MaPo; OAEP; PoEL-5; ReaPo; SeCeV; TyEnPo; UnPo (3d ed.); ViPo; VLEP
Old Zip Coon. *Unknown, at. to* Bob Farrell. *See* Zip Coon.
Olde Menalcas on a day. The Palmer's Ode. Robert Greene. *Fr.* Never Too Late. EV-1; OBSC
Olden Days, The. Joseph Hall. *Fr.* Virgidemiarum. OBSC ("Time was, and that was termed the time of gold.") SiCE
Olden Love-making. Nicholas Breton. ElSeCe; OBSC
Older I grow, The. Triolet on a Downhill Road. Margaret Fishback. WhC
Older than anything else in the world. The Sound of Rain. Cale Young Rice. MuM
Older than I are the houses. Migration. Clifford Bax. PtOT
Oldest of friends, the trees! Trees. Thomas Curtis Clark. OQP; PGD; QP-2
Ole Ark's a-Moverin', De. *Unknown.* APW
Ole Billy William ("Ole Mistah Billy William Goat"). Booth Lowrey. IHA
O'Leary, from Chicago, and a first-class fightin' man. Yanks. James W. Foley. PaA
Olger the Dane and Desiderio. Charlemagne. Longfellow. AnAmPo; FaFP; LA
Olim Haec Meminisse Juvabit. Henry Parrot. SiCE
Olim Meminisse Juvabit. Aline Kilmer. JKCP
O'Lincoln Family, The. Wilson Flagg. HBVY; LPS-2; OTPC; SN
(O'Lincon Family, The.) HBV
Olive, *sels.* Joachim du Bellay, *tr. fr. French.*
Autumn Fruits, XXXII, *tr. by* Alan Conder. TrFP
Home, CXIII, *tr. by* Alan Conder. TrFP
(Sonnet: "If life on earth be less than is a day," *tr. by* Armel O'Conner.) CAW
(Sonnet: "If of our life the span be not a day," *tr. by* Eleanor L. Turnbull.) WoL
(Sonnet to Heavenly Beauty, *tr. by* Andrew Lang.) AWP; JAWP; WBP
Nonpareil of All Mortality, The, II, *tr. by* Alan Conder. TrFP
Ye Huntsmen Who Halloo and Wind the Horn, LXXXII, *tr. by* Alan Conder. TrFP
Olive, The. A. E. Housman. MaPo
Olive. Swinburne. GTBS
Olive Branch, The. Robert Herrick. OnPM
Olive Grove. James Merrill. NePoAm
Olive in its orchard, The. The Olive. A. E. Housman. MaPo
Olive Tree, The. Sabine Baring-Gould. GN; OTPC (1946 ed.)
Olive Tree. Lorenzo Mavilis, *tr. fr. Modern Greek by* Rae Dalven. MoGP
Olive Trees. Padraic Colum. NePoAm
Olive Trees. Bernard Spencer. FaBoMo
Oliver Wendell Holmes. William Hamilton Hayne. GA; DD
Oliver Wiggins. "Stanley Vestal." IHA
Olivia. Elijah Fenton. AEV
Olivia. Edward Pollock. AA
Olivia. Shakespeare. *Fr.* Twelfth Night, I, v. LPS-1
Olivia. Tennyson. *Fr.* The Talking Oak. GN
Olivia's lewd, but looks devout. Olivia. Elijah Fenton. AEV
Olivier Metra's Waltz of Roses. La Mélinite; Moulin-Rouge. Arthur Symons. POTT
Ollie McGee. Edgar Lee Masters. *Fr.* Spoon River Anthology.
(Mollie McGee.) BAP; NP
Olrig Grange, *sel.* Walter C. Smith.
Daughters of Philistia. VA
Oluf and Peter sat at the board. Sir Oluf and His Gilded Horn. *Unknown.* BoDaBa
Olympia, *sl. abr.* Boccaccio, *tr. fr. Latin by* Sir Israel Gollancz. WoL
Olympian Odes. Pindar. *See* Odes.
Olympian sunlight is the Poet's sphere. The Crystal. Titus Munson Coan. AA
Olympian Zeus, a timely prayer fulfill. May I Drink the Blood of My Enemies. Theognis. GrL; OxBG
Olympias' matchless son, whenas he knew. To Samuel Daniel, Prince of English Poets. Francis Davison. ReIE
Olympio's Sadness. Victor Hugo, *tr. fr. French by* Alan Conder. TrFP
Olympus. Homer. *See* Nausicaa ("Having thus fulfilled her purpose").
Om. "Æ." VA
Omar and Death, *abr.* Omar Khayyám, *tr. fr. Persian by* Edward Fitzgerald. *Fr.* The Rubáiyát. GTSE
("Ah, with the Grape my fading life provide," *abr.*) GTBS-W; OBEV; OBVV
(Ritual of the Grape.) OnPM
Omar and the Persian. Sarah Williams. VA
Omar, dear Sultan of the Persian Song. To Omar Khayyám. Justin Huntly M'Carthy. LEAP
Omar for Ladies, An. Josephine Dodge Daskam Bacon. HBV; PA
Omar Meets a Toy. Burges Johnson. AlBD
Omar's the fad! Well then, let us indite. The Baby's Omar. Carolyn Wells. PA
Ombre at Hampton Court. Pope. *Fr.* The Rape of the Lock, III. OBEC
("Close by those meads, for ever crowned with flowers.") FiP; OxBoLi; WHA
Ombre Chinoise. Amy Lowell. NP
Omens. James H. Cousins. OnYI
Omit, omit, my simple friend. To an Ambitious Friend. Horace. AWP
Omnes Eodem Cogimur. Ammianus, *tr. fr. Greek by* Sir William Marris. OxBG
Omnes Gentes Plaudite. *Unknown.* AnEC
Omnia Exeunt in Mysterium. George Sterling. AnAmPo; LA; LEAP; NP; TBM; WGRP
(Omnium Exeunt in Mysterium.) BAP; SBMV
Omnia Somnia. Joshua Sylvester. OBS
(Go, Silly Worm.) EIL
Omnia Somnia. Rosamund Marriott Watson. HBV
Omnia Tempus Habent. "The Archpoet of Cologne," *tr. fr. Latin by* George F. Whicher. LaP
Omnia Vanitas. Dugald Buchanan, *tr. fr. Gaelic.* GoTS
Omnia Vincit. Alfred Cochrane. HBV
Omnia Vincit. *Unknown. See* Fain Would I Change That Note.
Omnibus across the bridge, An. Symphony in Yellow. Oscar Wilde. MBP; MoBrPo; OTPC (1946 ed.); PCH; ViP
"Omnipotence Divine," I pray in awe. I Turn the Key. Winifred Corrigan. JKCP (1955 ed.)
Omnipotent, The. Sir Walter Scott. *See* Time.
Omnipotent and steadfast God. John Brown's Prayer. Stephen Vincent Benét. *Fr.* John Brown's Body. AtBAP; NP; PoNe
Omnipotent confederate of all good. Prayer. Amos N. Wilder. TrPWD
Omnipresence. Stanton A. Coblentz. MaRV
Omnipresence. Edward Everett Hale. WGRP
Omnipresent Self. *Unknown, tr. fr. Sanskrit by* Joseph Nadin Rawson. *Fr.* The Upanishads. OnPM
Omniscience. Blanche Mary Kelly. TrPWD
Omniscience Granted to No Man. Sophocles, *tr. fr. Greek by* Lewis Campbell. *Fr.* Antigone. GrR
Omnium Exeunt in Mysterium. George Sterling. *See* Omnia Exeunt in Mysterium.
Omphalos; the Well. Seán Jennett. NeIP
On a Bad Singer. Samuel Taylor Coleridge. BOHV; TreF
(Desired Swan-Song, The.) UnS; WhC
(Swan Song.) GoTP
On a Baltimore Bus. Charles G. Bell. NePoAm
On a [*or* the] Bank as I Sat [*or* Sate] a-Fishing. Sir Henry Wotton. EV-2; LoBV; MyFE; OBS
(Description of the Spring, A.) ElSeCe; SeCL; WP
(May Day, A.) CH
On a bank, beside a willow. The Tears of Amynta, for the Death of Damon. Dryden. MaPo
On a Bas-Relief. Wesley Trimpi. NePoEA
On a battle-trumpet's blast. Shelley. *Fr.* Prometheus Unbound. OBRV
On a Beautiful Day. John Sterling. LPS-2
On a Beautiful Virgin. *Unknown.* TriL
On a Beautiful Youth Struck Blind with Lightning. Goldsmith, *after the Spanish.* OAEP

On a Bed of Guernsey Lilies. Christopher Smart. *Fr.* Ode to the Earl of Northumberland. OBEC
On a Bereaved Girl. Alun Lewis. SoV
On a Birthday. J. M. Synge. ChTr; OBMV
On a Blind Girl. Baha Ad-din Zuhayr, *tr. fr. Arabic by* E. H. Palmer. AWP
On a board of bright mosaic wrought in many a quaint design. College "Oil Cans." Will Victor McGuire. PTA-1
On a Book by John Milton, Annotated. Donald F. Drummond. PtPa
On a Book Called Unitarian Theology. Philip Freneau. CoV
On a bough a bird pipes a cheery note. The Blackbird. Théophile Gautier. TrFP
On a Box Containing His Own Works. Po Chü-i, *tr. fr. Chinese by* Arthur Waley. TrCh
On a Boy's First Reading of "King Henry V." S. Weir Mitchell. AA; LEAP
On a Broken Pipe. James Thomson. PIAE
On a brown isle of Lough Corrib. Celibacy. Austin Clarke. JKCP (1926 ed.)
On a bull's hollow horn. Reaping the Barley. Jorge Carrera Andrade. AnCL; WoL
On a Bust of Dante. Thomas William Parsons. AA; AnAmPo; APW; BAP; CBOV; HBV; LBAP; LEAP; LPS-3; OBAV
On a Bust of General Grant. James Russell Lowell. GA
On a Bust of Lincoln. Clinton Scollard. PEDC
On a Calm Summer's Night. John Nicholson. EnLoPo
On a Cast from an Antique. George Pellew. AA
On a Cat, Ageing. Alexander Gray. PoC
On a center staff and on two cross bars. The Mother. Kathryn White Ryan. CAW
On a Certain Lady at Court. Pope. ALV; BCEP; BLV; BoLiVe; CaAE; CEP; CoBE; EnLit; HBV; OAEP; OBEC; OBEV; TrGrPo
On a Certain Nun. Sister Mary Ignatius. PraNu
On a Certain Scholar. W. Craddle. SiTL; WhC
On a Child. Walter Savage Landor. *See* Child of a Day.
On a Child. Lucian, *tr. fr. Greek by* F. L. Lucas. GrPE
On a Child with a Wooden Leg. Bertram Warr. BoCaPo (1948 ed.)
On a Christ in Jesuit Robes. Voltaire, *tr. fr. French by* J. G. Legge. LiA
On a cleere morne as Phoebus run his race. *Unknown.* SeCSL
On a clear day in Paris, walking where. In the Place de la Bastille. Richard Burton. BAP
On a Clergyman's Horse [Biting Him]. *Unknown.* GoTP; LiTG; OxBoLi; SiTL; WhC
On a Cock at Rochester. Sir Charles Sedley. BeR
On a Cock Which Was Stolen from a Good Priest. Egan O'Rahilly, *tr. fr. Modern Irish by* P. S. Dinneen *and* T. O'Donoghue. OnYI
On a cold winter day the snow came down. Proud Little Spruce Fir. Jeannie Kirby. BoTP
On a Colonial Picture. Lizette Woodworth Reese. PR
On a Contented Mind. Thomas, Lord Vaux. *See* Of a Contented Mind.
On a Country Road. Swinburne. *Fr.* A Midsummer Holiday. BPN; PoVP; TOP; VLEP
On a Curate's Complaint of Hard Duty. Swift. GTIV
On a dark and stormy night, as the train rolled [*or* rattled] on. The Baggage Coach Ahead [*or* In the Baggage Coach Ahead]. Gussie L. Davis. ABS; TreFS
On a Dark Road. Robert Herrick. *Fr.* Night-Piece to Julia. BoTP
On a dark stormy mornin' when the snow was a-fallin'. The Wreck on the Somerset Road. *Unknown.* OuSiCo
On a Day—Alack the Day! Shakespeare. *Fr.* Love's Labour's Lost, IV, iii. EIL; ElSeCe; EV-1; ViBoPo
(Blossom, The.) OBEV
(Dumain's Rhymes.) OBSC
(Love's Perjuries.) GTBS; GTBS-D; GTBS-W; GTSE; GTSL; HBV
(Passionate Shepherd's Song, The.) ReIE
On a Dead Child. Robert Bridges. ChMo; CMP; EnLi-2 (1949 ed.); GTML; GTSL; LiTB; LiTG; LiTM (rev. ed.); OAEP; OBEV (1st ed.); OBMV; PoeT; PoP; ViBoPo
On a Dead Child. Richard Middleton. OBVV
On a Dead Cripple. Ronald Allison Kells Mason. MM
On a Dead Hostess. Hilaire Belloc. MBP; MoBrPo; MoVE; PIAE
On a Dead Lady. Alfred De Musset, *tr. fr. French by* Germaine Loir. EnLi-2 (1949 ed.)
On a Dead Poet. Frances Sargent Osgood. AA
On a Dead Scholar, *sel.* St. Columcille, *tr. fr. Old Irish by* Robin Flower.
"Lon's away/ Cill Garad is sad today." AnIL
On a Dead Teacher. Gerald Raftery. JKCP (1926 ed.)
On a Deaf Housekeeper. *Unknown.* BOHV
On a Dentist. *Unknown.* *See* Epitaph on a Dentist.
On a Detractor, *sel.* Mellin de Saint-Gelais, *tr. fr. French by* Ralph N. Currey.
"I pray for poverty for you." FoS
On a Discovery Made Too Late. Samuel Taylor Coleridge. EnRP
On a Distant Prospect of Eton College. Thomas Gray. *See* Ode on a Distant Prospect of Eton College.
On a Doctor Named Isaac Letsome. *Unknown.* *See* On Dr. Isaac Letsome.
On a Dog. Simonides, *tr. fr. Greek by* Walter Leaf. GrR
On a Dream. Keats. *See* Dream, after Reading Dante's Episode of Paolo and Francesca, A.
On a Drop of Dew. Andrew Marvell. EnLi-1; EV-2; GoBC; GTBS-W; LiTB; LiTG; MeLP; MePo; OBS; OuHeWo; OxBoCh; PoFS; ReEn; SeCV-1; SeEP; UnPo (1st ed.)
(Drop of Dew, A.) LPS-2; WoL
On a Dying Boy. William Bell. NePoEA
On a Faded Violet. Shelley. BPN
On a Fair Beggar. Philip Ayres. ElSeCe; EnLoPo; LO; OBS; SeCL; SeEP
On a Fair Morning. *Unknown.* ViBoPo
On a fair summer's morning of soft recreation. The Blackbird. *Unknown.* OnYI
On a Fair Woman. Francis Burdett Money-Coutts. OBVV
On a Fan That Belonged to the Marquise de Pompadour. Austin Dobson. ALV; BPN; OBVV; PoVP; ViBoPo
(On a Fan.) HBV; LPS-3; VA
(Ballade of the Pompadour's Fan.) PFE
On a Favorite Cat, Drowned in a Tub of Goldfishes. Thomas Gray. *See* Ode on the Death of a Favorite Cat, Drowned in a Tub of Goldfishes.
On a Favorite Poet. Sister Mary Thérèse. PraNu
On a Ferry Boat. Richard Burton. AA
On a fine Sunday morning I mounted my steed. Sabbath-Day Chace. Philip Freneau. WoL
On a flat road runs the well-train'd runner. The Runner. Walt Whitman. APW; MOAP; PCH; TSW; TSWC
On a Flimmering Floom You Shall Ride. Carl Sandburg. GoYe
On a Fly Drinking out of [*or* from] His Cup. William Oldys. EG; EV-3; FaFP; GoTP; GTBS-W; LEAP; LiTG; OBEV; PoeMoYo; TrGrPo; ViBoPo
(Fly, The.) BoHiPo; OBEC
(To a Fly.) OTPC (1923 ed.)
On a Fly-Leaf of a Book of Old Plays. Walter Learned. PR
(On the Fly-Leaf of a Book of Old Plays.) HBV
On a Flyleaf of Burns's Songs. Frederic Lawrence Knowles. HBV; LBMV; PoMa
On a Fly-Leaf of Longfellow's Poems, *sel.* Whittier.
Undying Soul, The. MaRV
On a Fly-Leaf of Schopenhauer's "Immortality." Ruth Guthrie Harding. MaRV; MuM
On a Fly-Leaf of Theocritus. Maurice Thompson. OBAV
On a Fortification at Boston Begun by Women. Benjamin Tompson. PAH; TCAP
On a Fountain. Anyte, *tr. fr. Greek by* Walter Leaf. GrR
(By the Fountain, *tr. by* Lord Neaves.) OnPM
(Shepherd's Gift, A, *tr. by* John William Burgon.) AWP
On a Fowler. Isidorus, *tr. fr. Greek by* William Cowper. AWP
On a Full-Length Portrait of Beau Marsh, *wr.* [Nash]. Earl of Chesterfield. *See* Immortal Newton Never Spoke.
On a gaunt and shattered tree. Osprey and Eagle. Jessie B. Rittenhouse. BLA
On a General Election. Hilaire Belloc. *See* On a Great Election.
On a Gentleman in a Late Engagement against the Turks, Was Slain and Thrown Overboard, and She Since Mad. *Unknown.* SeCL
On a Gentlewoman Walking in the Snow[e]. William Strode. *See* On Chloris Walking in the Snow.
On a German Tour. Richard Porson. *See* Epigram on an Academic Visit to the Continent.
On a Girdle. Edmund Waller. ALV; AWP; BEL; BLV; CEP; ElSeCe; EM-1; EnLi-1; EnLit; EPP; EPS; EV-2; GTBS; GTBS-D; GTBS-W; GTSE; GTSL; HBV; InMe; InPo; JAWP; LEAP; LiTB; LiTG; LiTL; LoBV; LPS-1; OAEP; OBEV; OBS; PG (1945 ed.); PoFS; PoRA; SeCePo; SeCL; SeCV-1; SeEP; TCEP; TOP; TreFS; TrGrPo; ViBoPo; WBP; WHA
("That which her slender waist confined.") EG
On a Gloomy Easter. Alice Freeman Palmer. MaRV; OHIP
On a Goldfinch, Starved to Death in His Cage. William Cowper. CaAE
On a grassy pillow. Happy Myrtillo. Henry Carey. SeCePo
On a Grave at Grindelwald. Frederic William Henry Myers. VA
On a Grave in Christ-Church, Hants. Oscar Fay Adams. AA
On a Gravestone. *Unknown.* PCD
On a Great Election. Hilaire Belloc. OxBoLi; WhC
(On a General Election.) MoVE
On a Great Man Whose Mind Is Clouding. Edmund Clarence Stedman. AA
On a Grecian Urn. Keats. *See* Ode on a Grecian Urn.

On a Greek Vase. Frank Dempster Sherman. AA; LBAP; OBAV
On a Green Hillock. Howard Ramsden. MuM
On a green island in the Main Street traffic. Pro Patria. Constance Carrier. NePoAm
On a green slope, most fragrant with the spring. My Rose. Hildegarde Hawthorne. AA
On a Hessian Debarkation. Philip Freneau. MOAP
On a Hill. Irene Rutherford McLeod. NLK; VOD
On a hill far away stood an old rugged cross. George Bennard. OlF
On a hill that grac'd the plain. Thyrsis' Praise of His Mistress. William Browne. ReIE
On a hill there blooms a palm. Hayyim Nahman Bialik. *Fr.* Songs of the People. AWP; JAWP; WBP
On a hill there grows a flower. A Pastoral of Phillis and Corydon [*or* Phillis the Fair *or* Phyllida and Corydon *or* Ipsa Quae]. Nicholas Breton. BLV; CBOV; CoBE; EIL; EV-1; LO; LPS-1; OBSC; SiCE; TrGrPo; TuPP
On a Historic Landmark. Tu Fu, *tr. fr. Chinese by* Hsieh Wen Tung. WhP
On a holy day when sails were blowing southward. The Straying Student. Austin Clarke. AnIL; MoAB; NeIP; OxBI
On a Honey Bee [Drinking from a Glass of Wine and Drowned Therein]. Philip Freneau. AmPP; CoBA; IAP; TCAP
(Honey Bee, The.) HiLiAm
(To a Honey Bee.) AA; BAP; LEAP; YaD
On a Hymn-Book. William L. Henderson. PR
On a Journey. Basho, *tr. fr. Japanese by* H. G. Henderson. OnPM
On a Journey. Li Po, *tr. fr. Chinese.* WhP
On a Lady Singing. Isaac Rosenberg. FaBoTw
On a Lady Sleeping. *Unknown.* SeCL
On a Lady Who Beat Her Husband. *Unknown.* FiBHP
On a Lady Who Fancied Herself a Beauty. Charles Sackville. *See* Song: "Dorinda's sparkling wit, and eyes."
On a Lady with Foul Breath. Thomas Parnell. PoE
On a Lamp. Eduard Mörike, *tr. fr. German by* Kate Flores. AnGP
On a Lane in Spring. John Clare. EnSW
On a Little Bird. Martin Armstrong. CH
(Bird's Epitaph, A.) POTE
On a Little Dog. Martial, *tr. fr. Latin by* J. A. Pott *and* F. A. Wright. AlBD
On a little green knoll. Old Log House. James S. Tippett. BrR; FaPON
On a little piece of wood. Mr. and Mrs. Spikky Sparrow. Edward Lear. SAS
On a lonely road quite long ago. The Arkansas Traveler. *At. to* Sanford C. Faulkner. PoRL
On a Lonely Spray. James Stephens. AnFE; ChMo; CMP; OnYI
On a Lord. Samuel Taylor Coleridge. FiBHP
On a Lost Opportunity. Wilfrid Scawen Blunt. The Love Sonnets of Proteus, LVII. EtPaEn
On a Lover's Dust, Made Sand for an Hour-Glass. Ben Jonson. *See* Hour Glass, The.
On a Lute Found in a Sarcophagus. Sir Edmund Gosse. GTML; GTSL; VA
On a Magazine Sonnet. Russell Hilliard Loines. AA; BOHV; InP; PC; SiTL
On a magical morning with twinkling feet. To Keats. Lord Dunsany. BMEP
On a Maide of Honour Seene by a Schollar in Sommerset Garden. Thomas Randolph. MePo
On a Man Named Merideth. *Unknown.* *See* Merideth.
On a mandolin with slender. Serenade. Vilhelm Krag. AnNoLy
On a May morning. Milton. *See* Song on May Morning.
On a Memory of Beauty. G. S. Fraser. FaBoMo; NeBP
On a Midsummer['s] Eve. Thomas Hardy. FaBoTw; GTML; GTSL; VLEP
On a midsummer night, on a night that was eerie with stars. August Night. Sara Teasdale. MAP; MoAmPo; NV; TBM
On a Midsummer's Eve. Thomas Hardy. *See* On a Midsummer Eve.
On a Miniature. Henry Augustin Beers. AA
On a Miscellany of Poems [to Bernard Lintott]. John Gay. CEP; EiPP
On a Mistress of Whose Affections He Was Doubtful. Thomas Nabbes. *Fr.* The Spring's Glory. SeCL
On a Monday morning it began to rain. Jay Gould's Daughter. *Unknown.* AS
On a Monument to Marti. Walter Adolphe Roberts. PoNe
On a Moonlight Night. Tu Fu, *tr. fr. Chinese by* Witter Bynner. ChLP
On a mountain of sugar-candy. Phantasus, I-8. Arno Holz. LiTW
On a Nankin Plate. Austin Dobson. PoVP
On a Newcastle Architect. *Unknown.* WhC
On a Night of Snow. Elizabeth J. Coatsworth. CIV; GoTP; MAP; MoAmPo; MoShBr; MW; PoTo
On a Night of Stars. Leah Bodine Drake. UnW
On a night the sun and the earth and the weather. The Pepper Tree. Sister Mary Madeleva. RIS
On a Nightingale in April. "Fiona Macleod." HBV; OBVV; PoVP
On a Note of Triumph, *sel.* Norman Corwin.
"Lord God of trajectory and blast." QS
(Man unto His Fellow Man.) TrJP
On a Nun. Jacopo Vittorelli, *tr. fr. Italian by* Byron. AWP; CAW; JAWP; WBP
(Sonnet: Addressed by a Father Mourning His Recently Deceased Married Daughter to the Father Whose Daughter Had Entered a Convent.) LiTW
On a Painted Woman. Shelley. SiTL
On a Pair of Garters. Sir John Davies. EG; SiPS
On a Pair of Shoes Presented to Him, *sel.* Egan O'Rahilly, *tr. fr. Modern Irish by* P. S. Dinneen *and* T. O'Donoghue.
"I have received jewels of conspicuous beauty." OnYI
On a Papyrus of Oxyrhynchus. *Unknown.* CAW
On a Parisian Boulevard. James Kenneth Stephen. England and America, II. InMe
On a Pet Cat. George A. Persell. CAG
On a Photo of Sgt. Ciardi a Year Later. John Ciardi. MiAP
On a Picture. Anne C. Lynch Botta. LPS-1
On a Picture by Michele da Verona. Anne Ridler. PoN
On a Picture by Pippin, Called "The Den." Selden Rodman. PoNe
On a Picture by Poussin Representing Shepherds in Arcadia. John Addington Symonds. FaBoBe; HBV
On a Picture of an Infant Playing near a Precipice. Leonidas of Alexandria, *tr. fr. Greek by* Samuel Rogers. MOAH
(On the Picture of an Infant . . .) LPS-1
On a Picture of Leander. Keats. BPN; ERP; PeBoSo; TOP
(Sonnet: On a Picture of Leander.) EnRP; GEPC
On a Picture of Lincoln. John Vance Cheney. PGD
On a Piece of Music. Gerard Manley Hopkins. UnS
On a Piece of Tapestry. George Santayana. AA; OBAV
On a Pine Tree Shown to Me by the Taoist Scholar Li. Tu Fu, *tr. fr. Chinese by* Pu Hsiang-hsing. WhP
On a Poet Patriot. Thomas MacDonagh. *See* Of a Poet Patriot.
On a Poet's Lips I Slept. Shelley. *See* Poet's Dream, The.
On a Political Prisoner. W. B. Yeats. OBMV; PoE
On a Politician. Hilaire Belloc. *See* Epitaph on the Politician.
On a Portrait. Erinna, *tr. fr. Greek by* Walter Leaf. GrR
On a Portrait of Columbus. George Edward Woodberry. AA
On a Portrait of Dr. Samuel Johnson, LL.D. Christopher Morley. PoeMoYo
On a Portrait of Wordsworth. Elizabeth Barrett Browning. DiM; LPS-3; PtP
On a Prayer Book Sent to Mrs. M. R. Richard Crashaw. BCEP; BrBE
(Prayer: "Lo, here a little volume, but great book.") HBV
(Prayer; an Ode.) SeEP
"Lo here a little volume, but large book," *sel.* MeRV
On a Pretty Madwoman. Matthew Prior. CEP
On a Prohibitionist Poem. G. K. Chesterton. ViBoPo
On a Puppy. Feng Chih, *tr. fr. Chinese by* Chu K'an. LiTW
On a Puritanicall Lock-Smith. William Camden. WhC
(On a Thieving Locksmith, *sl. diff. vers.*) GoTP
On a Quiet Conscience. Charles I, King of England. CH; PCD
On a Quiet Night. Li Po, *tr. fr. Chinese by* Shigeyoshi Obata. WoL
(My Far-off Home.) OnPM
On a Replica of the Parthenon. Donald Davidson. MoVE
On a Return from Egypt. Keith Douglas. NeBP; NePoEA
On a Rhine Steamer. James Kenneth Stephen. England and America, I. InMe
On a rock, whose haughty brow. Thomas Gray. *Fr.* The Bard. SeCePo
On a Roman Helmet. Will H. Ogilvie. EBSV
On a Rosebud Sent to Her Lover. *Unknown.* AtBAP; SeCL
("Tender bud within herself doth close, The.") LO
On a Royal Demise. Thomas Hood. FiBHP
On a Schoolmaster. *Unknown, tr. fr. Greek by* Lord Neaves. OnPM
On a Sculptured Head of the Christ. Mahlon Leonard Fisher. HBV
On a Seal. Plato, *tr. fr. Greek by* Thomas Stanley. AWP; JAWP; WBP; WoL
On a Sense of Humor. Frederick Locker-Lampson. BOHV; InP
On a Seventeenth Birthday. Anne P. L. Field. MOAH
On a Ship at Sea. Ann Stanford. MuM
On a ship's poop I'd like to lie, if I could have my way. Once in a Way. Antiphilus ofByzantium. GrPo; OxBG

On a Shipwrecked Sailor. Theodoridas, *tr. fr. Greek by* F. L. Lucas. GrPE
On a showery night and still. The Dandelions. Helen Gray Cone. ADAH; DD; GFA; HBV; NLK; PRWS; SN
On a Singing Girl. Elinor Wylie. TOP
On a Slain Warrior. Anacreon, *tr. fr. Greek by* Hugh Macnaghten. GrL
On a Sleeping Friend. Hilaire Belloc. *See* Dawn Shall over Lethe Break.
On a small six-acre farm dwelt John Grist the miller. Under the Drooping Willow Tree. *Unknown.* OxBoLi
On a Snow Storm. Edward Capern. AlDL
On a snug evening I shall watch her fingers. Piano after War. Gwendolyn Brooks. PoNe
On a Soldier Fallen in the Philippines. William Vaughn Moody. AmPP (3d ed.); HBV; LBAP; MAP; MC; MoAmPo (1942 ed.); PaA; PAH
On a Spaniel Called Beau Killing a Young Bird. William Cowper. AlBD; FaBoCh; PRWS
On a Spark of Fire Fixing on a Gentlewoman's Breast. Thomas Philipott. ElSeCe; SeCL
On a Spring Board. Edward Cracroft Lefroy. OBVV; ShGoBo
On a Squirrel Crossing the Road in Autumn, in New England. Richard Eberhart. NePA
On a starred night Prince Lucifer uprose. Lucifer in Starlight. George Meredith. AnEnPo; AnFE; ATP; BEL; BLV; BMEP; BoLiVe; CBOV; CH; CoBE; EmBrPo; EnL; EnLi-2; EnLit; EPN; EPP; ES; ExPo; GTML; HBV; HoPM; InP; InPo; LEAP; LiTB; LiTG; LoBV; OAEP; OBEV; OBVV; PG (1955 ed.); PIAE; PoEL-5; PoeT; PoFS; POTT; PoVP; ReaPo; RiBV; SeCeV; ShBV-4; TCEP; TOP; TrGrPo; TwCV; UnPo; VA; ViBoPo; ViP; ViPo; ViPP; VLEP
On a Steamer. Dorothy W. Baruch. FaPON
On a Steamship. Upton Sinclair. MaRV
On a Stone at Corinth. *Unknown, tr. fr. Greek.* GrPE, *tr. by* F. L. Lucas; OxBG, *tr. by* R. A. Furness
On a Stone at Salonica. *Unknown, tr. fr. Greek by* Sir William Marris. OxBG
On a strange land we have the light now, we are banked. Transcontinental Bus. Daniel Smythe. NeTW
On a street in Knoxville. Street Scene—1946. Kenneth Porter. PoNe
On a Subway Express. Chester Firkins. BAP; LBMV; PC; PFY; QS; VOD (1935 ed.); YaD
On a summer's day when the sea was rippled. The Ship That Never Returned. Henry Clay Work. BLPA
On a summer's day while the waves were rippling, with a quiet and a gentle breeze. The Ship That Never Returned. *Unknown.* AS
On a Sunbeam. Thomas Heyrick. MePo
On a Sunday morn sat a maid forlorn. Wait till the Sun Shines, Nellie. Andrew B. Sterling. TreFS
On a Sunday mornin' it begins to rain. Casey Jones. *Unknown.* ABF; ViBoFo (C *vers.*)
On a Sundial. Hilaire Belloc. MoVE
On a sunny brae alone I lay. A Day Dream. Emily Brontë. UnW
On a Tear. Samuel Rogers. HBV
(Tear, A.) LPS-3
On a Thieving Locksmith. William Camden. *See* On a Puritanicall Lock-Smith.
On a throne of new gold the Son of the Sky. The Emperor. Tu Fu. AWP
On a Thrush Singing in Autumn. Sir Lewis Morris. OBVV; VA
On a Time. *Unknown.* ElSeCe; TuPP
(On a Time the Amorous Silvy.) LO; SeEP; ViBoPo
(Silvy.) SeCL
(Wakening, The.) OBEV
On a train in Texas German prisoners eat. Defeat. Witter Bynner. PoNe
On a Travelling Speculator. Philip Freneau. AA
On a tree by a river a little tom-tit. The Suicide's Grave [*or* Tit-Willow]. W. S. Gilbert. *Fr.* The Mikado. ALV; FaFP; LiTB; LiTG; LiTL; OlF; PoVP; SiTL; TreF; WhC
On a Tree Fallen across the Road. Robert Frost. TwP
On a True Friend. William Cowper. BoFr
On a Valetudinarian. Ibn al-Rumi, *tr. fr. Arabic by* J. D. Carlyle. LiTW
On a Very Young, Very Dead Soldier. Richard Gillman. NePoAm
On a Violet in Her Breast. Thomas Stanley. OBS
On a Virtuous Young Gentlewoman That Died Suddenly. William Cartwright. OBEV
On a Wag in Mauchline. Burns. FiBHP
(Epitaph for James Smith.) ALV
On a Waiter. David McCord. WhC
On a Watchman Asleep at Midnight. James Thomas Fields. CenHV
On a Wet Summer. John Codrington Bampfylde. EnSW; ES
On a white field. The Sower. R. Olivares Figueroa. AnCL; FaPON; OnPM
On a wide-open, windless Autumn morning. The Plough-Horse. Rhoda Coghill. OnYI
On a Wife. Francis Burdett Money-Coutts. OBVV
On a winter evening, by a winter fire. A Hymn to No One Body. James Palmer Wade. NAMP
On a winter night/ When the moon is low. Christmas Eve. Marion Edey. YeAr
On a winter's night. The Two Foxes. *Unknown.* FTB
On a winter's night long time ago. Noël. Hilaire Belloc. HBMV; JKCP; TSW
On a withered bough. A Crow. Basho. OnPM
On a Woman's Inconstancy. Sir Robert Ayton. *See* I Loved Thee Once.
On a World War Battlefield. Thomas Curtis Clark. PGD
On a wrinkled rock, in a distant sea. The Three Gannets. Fitz-James O'Brien. DaM
On a Young Lady's Going into a Shower Bath. Francis Scott Key. YaD
On a Young Married Couple. Richard Crashaw. *See* Epitaph upon Husband and Wife Which Died and Were Buried Together, An.
On a Young Poetess's Grave. Robert Buchanan. VA
On Again Meeting a Lady. Otomo Miyori, *tr. fr. Japanese by* Asataro Miyamori. OnPM
On Alexis. Plato, *tr. fr. Greek by* Thomas Stanley. AWP
On alien ground, breathing an alien air. Where a Roman Villa Stood, above Freiburg. Mary Elizabeth Coleridge. BoHiPo; PoeT; PoMa; TCPD
On all the upland pastures the strong winds gallop free. The Madness of Winds. Lloyd Roberts. CPG
On Alpine heights the love of God is shed. Alpine Heights. Friedrich Adolph Krummacher. LPS-2
On an American Soldier of Fortune Slain in France. Clinton Scollard. MC
On an Ancient Tomb East of the Village. Po Chü-i, *tr. fr. Chinese by* Ching Ti. WhP
On an Anniversary. J. M. Synge. OBMV
On an early Sunday in April, a feeble day. An Extract from Addresses to the Academy of Fine Ideas. Wallace Stevens. GTBS-W; LiTA; LiTM (rev. ed.)
On an eve that May. Song on Beholding an Enlightenment. Matías de Bocanegra. AnMP
On an Hour-Glass [*or* Houre-Glasse]. John Hall. MeLP; MePo
"This gapes for marriage, yet his fickle head," *br. sel.* LO
On an Icelandic Skald. Henry Adams Bellows. PaOS
On an Ill-managed House. Swift. AnIV
On an Infant Dying as Soon as Born. Charles Lamb. BCEP; EV-4; GTBS; GTBS-D; GTBS-W; GTSE; GTSL; MotAn; OBEV; OBRV
On an Infant Eight Months Old. *Unknown.* SiTL; WhC
On an Intaglio Head of Minerva. Thomas Bailey Aldrich. HBV; InMe; LPS-3; PR
On an Invitation to the United States. Thomas Hardy. AWP; InPo; JAWP; WBP
On an Island. J. M. Synge. MBP; MoBrPo; OBVV
On an Old Horn. Wallace Stevens. LiTA
On an Old Muff. Frederick Locker-Lampson. CenHV; LPS-3; VA
On an Old Song. William Edward Hartpole Lecky. HBV
On an Old Tippleress. *Unknown, tr. fr. Greek by* F. L. Lucas. GrPE
On an Old Woman. Lucillius, *tr. fr. Greek by* William Cowper. AWP; LiTW; OnPM
("Nycilla dyes her locks, 'tis said.") GrPo
On an olive-crested steep. Virgil's Tomb. Robert Cameron Rogers. AA
On an Unpleasant Woman. Catullus, *tr. fr. Latin by* George Lamb. OnPM
On an Upright Judge. Swift. ALV
On an Urn. Richard Garnett. VA
On Anacreon. Julianus, *tr. fr. Greek by* F. L. Lucas. GrPE
On and on,/ O white brother! The Sea Bird to the Wave. Padraic Colum. BMEP; EtS; LEAP; SUS
On and on, always on and on. *Unknown, tr. fr. Chinese by* Arthur Waley. Seventeen Old Poems, 1. TrCh
On Angels. W. W. E. Ross. BoCaPo
On Another's Sorrow. Blake. *Fr.* Songs of Innocence. AWP; CEP; EnRP; EV-4; LiTG; MaRV; OTPC (1923 ed.); PoEL-4; ViBoPo
On Archaeanassa. Plato, *tr. fr. Greek by* Thomas Stanley. AWP
On Aristophanes. Plato. *See* To Aristophanes.
On Ascending a Hill Leading to a Convent. Francisco Manuel de Mello, *tr. fr. Spanish by* Felicia Dorothea Hemans. CAW
On August Thirteenth, at the Mount, Marsden, Bucks. Frances Cornford. MoP
On Bathing. Thomas Warton, the Younger. ES
On Beau Nash's Picture, Which Once Stood between the Busts of Newton and Pope. Jane Brereton. InP
On Beauty; a Riddle. Matthew Prior. CEP

On bed of flowers Endymion sleeping lay. Endymion and Diana. Philip Ayres. AEV
On Behalf of Some Irishmen Not Followers of Tradition. "Æ." AnIL; MM; PoFr
Charge to Youth, A, *sel.* GrCo-2
On Beholding Bodiam Castle. Lord Thurlow. EnSW
On Being a Woman. Dorothy Parker. BOHV
On Being Asked for a War Poem. W. B. Yeats. MoVE; TwP
On Being Good. John Kendrick Bangs. PR
On Being Invited to a Testimonial Dinner. William Stafford. NePoAm-2
On Being Removed from Hsün-yang and Sent to Chung-chou. Po Chü-i, *tr. fr. Chinese by* Arthur Waley. TrCh
On Being Sixty. Po Chü-i, *tr. fr. Chinese by* Arthur Waley. AWP; TrCh
On Being Stricken with Paralysis. Po Chü-i, *tr. fr. Chinese by* Henry H. Hart. PoHN
On Being Told That One's Ideas Are Victorian. Sara Henderson Hay. InMe
On Bellosguardo, when the year was young. To Vernon Lee. Amy Levy. VA
On Ben Jonson. *At. to* John Cleveland, *also at. to* James Clayton. *See* Elegy on Ben Jonson, An.
On Bertrand Russell's "Portraits from Memory." Donald Davie. PoN
On black bare trees a stale cream moon. Eauforte. F. S. Flint. TwCV
On Blenheim. Swift, *after the Latin of* Martial. OnPM
(Verses on Blenheim.) AWP
On Blenheim House. Abel Evans. OBEC
On blessed youths, for Jove doth pause. Francis Beaumont. *Fr.* The Masque of the Inner-Temple and Gray's Inne. OBS
On blood, smoke, rain and the dead. Who Knows Where. Detlev von Liliencron. AWP
On bluish inlets bristling. The Painter. Robert Fitzgerald. MoVE
On Board Ship; Reading Yüan Chen's Poems. Po Chü-i, *tr. fr. Chinese by* Arthur Waley. TrCh
On Board the *Cumberland* (March 7, 1862). George Henry Boker. IAP; PAH
On brick and stone and trees all stark and bare. To the City in the Snow. Agnes O'Gara Ruggeri. MoSiPe
On bridle-paths, and pricked by golden wheat. Feeling. Arthur Rimbaud. TrFP
On broad plains of bright sound. The White Peacock. Mary Mills. NePoAm
On Broadway. W. W. Gibson. ChMo; CMP; CP
On Broadway. George Sylvester Viereck. OQP; QP-2
On Buena Vista battlefield. Buena Vista Battlefield. *Unknown.* CSF
On Burns. Dante Gabriel Rossetti. BPN
On Burns. Wordsworth. BoHiPo
On Butler's Monument. Samuel Wesley. *See* On the Setting Up Mr. Butler's Monument . . .
On Calais Sands. Andrew Lang. PoVP; VA
On Calvary's Lonely Hill. Herbert Clark Johnson. PoNe
On Calvert's plains new faction reigns. Maryland Resolves. *Unknown.* PAH
On came the whirlwind—like the last. The Charge at Waterloo. Sir Walter Scott. *Fr.* The Field of Waterloo. PEOR
On Carrigdhoun the heath is brown. The Lament of the Irish Maiden. Denny Lane. TIP
On Catullus. Walter Savage Landor. EV-4; OBEV; PtP; TOP; ViBoPo
On Censure. Swift. EV-3
On Charles II. Earl of Rochester. *See* Epitaph on Charles II.
On charts they fall like lace. Delos. Lawrence Durrell. NeBP
On Chaucer. Thomas Hoccleve. *See* Hoccleve's Lament for Chaucer and Gower.
On Cherubs. Arthur Guiterman. LauV
On Children. Kahlil Gibran. *Fr.* The Prophet. PoToHe (new ed.)
On Chillon. Byron. *See* Sonnet on Chillon.
On China Blue. Sir Stephen Gaselee. WhC
On Chloris Walking in the Snow. William Strode. ElSeCe; HBV (8th ed.); SeCL
(Chloris in the Snow.) EV-2; GTBS-W; HBV (6th ed.); OBEV
("I saw fair Chloris walk alone.") EG
(On a Gentlewoman Walking in the Snow[e].) OBS; SeEP
On Choosing Friends. Theognis, *tr. fr. Greek by* C. T. Murphy. GrL
(Choosing Friends, *tr. by* A. E. Crawley.) OxBG
On Christës day, I understand. A Blessed Bird, as I You Say. *Unknown.* AnEC
On Christians, Mercy Will Fall. *Unknown, tr. fr. Welsh by* D. M. Lloyd. *Fr.* The Black Book of Carmarthen. PrWP
On Christmas Day. Clement Paman. AlDL; MeRV; OxBoCh; SeCL
(On Christmas Day to My Heart.) OBS
On Christmas-Day. Thomas Traherne. OBS; PoEL-2
"Shake off thy sloth, my drowsy soul, awake," *sel.*, 8 *sts.* OxBoCh
On Christmas day I dined with Brown. A Christmas Wail. *Unknown.* PA
On Christmas day in seventy-six. Battle of Trenton. *Unknown.* IDAH; MC; PAH; PAP
On Christmas Day to My Heart. Clement Paman. *See* On Christmas Day.
On Christmas Eve I lay abed. Christmas Eve. John Drinkwater. HBMV
On Christmas Eve I turned the spit. *Unknown.* BoN; OxNR
On Christmas Eve my mother read. Christmas Eve. Edna Kingsley Wallace. BoTP
On Christmas-eve the bells were rung. Christmas in the Olden Time. Sir Walter Scott. *Fr.* Marmion. COAH
On Christmas Eve the little stars. Christmas Eve. Charlotte Druitt Cole. BoTP
On Christmas eve they filled the house, some fifty guests all told. Christmas at Babbitt's. Henry Hallam Tweedy. MaRV
On Christmas Eve while hamlets sleep. Legends of Christmas. Aileen Fisher. ChBR
On Christmas Eve, would you believe, the forest gave a party. A Christmas Party. Carolyn Sherwin Bailey. PCH
On Christmas Morn. *Unknown.* *See* Words from an Old Spanish Carol.
On Cithaeron. Euripides, *tr. fr. Greek by* Gilbert Murray. *Fr.* Bacchae. OxBG
On City Streets. Margaret E. Bruner. PoToHe
On Clarastella Singing. Robert Heath. OBS
On Clarastella, Walking in Her Garden. Robert Heath. OBS; SeCL
On Clergymen Preaching Politics. John Byrom. SeCePo
On Climbing the Heights on the Ninth Day of the Ninth Moon. Tu Fu, *tr. fr. Chinese.* WhP
On Climbing the Phoenix Tower at Chin-ling. Li Po, *tr. fr. Chinese.* WhP
On Clingman Dome. Olive Tilford Dargan. LS; NoCaPo; VOD
On Coming to an End. George Meason Whicher. BAP
On Common Ground. R. P. Blackmur. Scarabs for the Living, III. CrMA
On Compassion ("And as ye would that men should do to you"). St. Luke, VI: 31-32, 36, Bible, *N.T.* BoFr
On Compassion ("He, willing to justify himself"). St. Luke, X: 29-37, Bible, *N.T.* BoFr
On Corinth Fallen. Antipater of Sidon. *See* Ruins of Corinth, The.
On Count M. S. Vorontzov. Pushkin, *tr. fr. Russian by* Babette Deutsch. TrRV
On Critics. Matthew Prior. *See* In Imitation of Anacreon.
On crystal rims, they wheel in space. Snowflakes. Alice Behrend. GoYe
On Cupid's bow how are my heart-strings bent. Astrophel and Stella, XIX. Sir Philip Sidney. SiPS
On Dante Alighieri. Michelangelo. *See* Soul of Dante, The.
On Dante's "Divine Comedy." Longfellow. *See* Oft Have I Seen . . .
On Dean Inge. Humbert Wolfe. ChTr
On Death. Walter Savage Landor. *See* Death Stands above Me.
On Death. Shakespeare. *Fr.* Measure for Measure, III, i. FiP
(Let Me Live, *longer sel.*) LiA
On Death, *sel.* Angelos Sikelianos, *tr. fr. Modern Greek by* Kimon Friar.
"Listen to the roar of your liberation!" LiTW
On Death—a Sonnet. Ecclesiasticus, Bible, Apocrypha. *See* O Death.
On December, the sixth. Trenton and Princeton. *Unknown.* PAH
On Deck. Robert Browning. James Lee's Wife, IX. EtPaEn
On Degree. Shakespeare. *Fr.* Troilus and Cressida, I, iii. ExPo
("Heavens themselves, the planets and this center, The.") ImOP
(Ulysses; on Degree.) EV-1
On Dido's famous image, friend, you stare. A Painting of Dido. *Unknown.* OxBG
On Digital Extremities. Gelett Burgess. *See* I'd Rather Have Fingers than Toes.
On Dirphys' wrinkled side [*or* slope] we fell. The Athenian Dead. Simonides. GrL; OxBG; WoL
On Disbanding the Army. David Humphreys. PAH
On Dives. Richard Crashaw. *See* Dives Asking a Drop.
On Dr. Isaac Letsome. *Unknown.* LiTG
(On a Doctor Named Isaac Letsome.) GoTP
(Self-composed Epitaph on a Doctor by the Name of I. Letsome.) WhC

On Donne's Poetry. Samuel Taylor Coleridge. InvP; OAEP; PtP; SeCePo
On Douglas Bridge I met a man. Ballad of Douglas Bridge. Francis Carlin. AnIV; BoFr; GTIV; HBMV; OxBI
On Drinking. Abraham Cowley. *See* Drinking.
On dry land. Pedro Salinas, *tr. fr. Spanish by* Eleanor L. Turnbull. CoSP
On Dulcina. *At. to* Sir Walter Ralegh. *See* Dulcina.
On Dürer's "Melencolia." Sir William Watson. *See* Dürer's "Melancholia."
On dusty benches in the park. Reflections in a Little Park. Babette Deutsch. NePoAm
On Dwelling. Robert Graves. MoPW; MoVE
On eagle, lamb, and peacock. Song of Life. Hugo von Hofmannsthal. AnGP
On ear and ear two noises too old to end. The Sea and the Skylark. Gerard Manley Hopkins. LiTB; OBMV; POTT; PoVP
On Easter Day. Celia Thaxter. FaPON; YeAr
On Easter Morn. Edith M. Thomas. EOAH
On Easter morn,/ On Easter morn. Easter. Elizabeth J. Coatsworth. YeAr
On Easter morn/ Up the faint cloudy sky. Easter. Hilda Conkling. HH; TiPo (1952 ed.)
On Easter morn at early dawn. Meeting the Easter Bunny. Rowena Bastin Bennett. GFA; MeMeAg; SiSoSe; SUS; TiPo; UTS
On Easter Morning. Eben E. Rexford. BLRP
On Eastnor Knoll. John Masefield. CH; MCCG; ShBV-3; VOD
On Echo and Silence. Sir Samuel Egerton Brydges. ES
On Editing Scott Fitzgerald's Papers. Edmund Wilson. CrMA
On Edward Seymour, Duke of Somerset. *Unknown. See* Poor Estate to Be Holden for Best, The.
On either side. The Lover's Journey. George Crabbe. Tales, X. EPP
On either side the river lie. The Lady of Shalott. Tennyson. AnFE; ATP; BEL; BeLS; BMEP; BoLiVe; BPN; CBE; CBOV; CBPC; EM-2; EmBrPo; EnL; EnLi-2; EnLit; EPN; EPP; EV-5; FaFP; FiP; GBV; GEPC; GN; GTML; GTSL; HBV; InP; LEAP; LiTG; MaC; MCCG; MW; OAEP; OBEV; OBRV; OBVV; OnSP; OTPC; PIAE; PoE; PoVP; ReaPo; RG; SeCeV; ShBV-1; TCEP; TOP; TreF; TyEnPo; ViPo; ViPP; VLEP; WHA
On Eleanor Freeman, Who Died 1650, Aged 21. *Unknown.* OBEV (new ed.)
On Elizabeth L. H. Ben Jonson. *See* Epitaph on Elizabeth, L. H.
On Entering a Chapel. John Davidson. MaRV; OQP; QP-2
On Entering a Forest. Elinor Lennen. PGD
On Ettrick Banks in a summer's night. Ettrick Banks. *Unknown.* EBSV
On Euripides. *Unknown, tr. fr. Greek by* Lord Neaves. OnPM
On Euripides' plays we debated. The Blind Student. Edmund John Armstrong. TIP
On Even Keel [with Gentle Gale]. Matthew Green. *Fr.* The Spleen. BeR; CoEV; OBEC
(Voyage of Life, The.) LPS-3
On every schoolhouse, ship, and staff. Half-Mast. Lloyd Mifflin. PAH
On Every Still Suburban Street. Osip Emilyevich Mandelstamm, *tr. fr. Russian by* Babette Deutsch. TrRV
On every wind there comes the dolorous cry. Ballade of the Unchanging Beauty. Richard Le Gallienne. InP; PFE
On Exodus III, 14, I Am That I Am. Matthew Prior. CEP
On faith's mysterious heights you stand. Pray for Me. Amos R. Wells. PraP
On Fame. Keats. *See* Two Sonnets on Fame.
On Fanny Godwin. Shelley. ChER; FaBoEn; LoPS
On feet of steel the waves are lapping there. The Man Seven Years Standing. Vladimir Mayakovsky. *Fr.* About This. RuPo
On File. John Kendrick Bangs. PoToHe (new ed.); WBLP
On First Entering Westminster Abbey. Louise Imogen Guiney. AA
On First Having Heard the Skylark. Edna St. Vincent Millay. BLA
On First Hearing Beethoven. George Barker. UnS
On First Looking into a Circular for a Student's Around-the-World-Cruise. "B. A. D." CAG
On First Looking into Chapman's Homer. Keats. AEV; AnFE; ATP; BCEP; BEL; BLV; BoLiVe; BPN; BTP; CaAE; CBE; CBOV; CH; ChTr; CoBE; CoEV; DD; EM-2; EnL; EnLi-2; EnLit; EnLP; EnRP; EPN; EPP; ERP; ES; EV-4; ExPo; FaBoBe; FaBoCh; FaBoEn; FaFP; FiP; GN; GTBS; GTBS-D; GTBS-W; GTSE; GTSL; HBV; HBVY; HiLiEn; HoPM; InP; InPo; KN; LEAP; LiTB; LiTG; LoBV; LoGBV; MaPo; MCCG; MOB; NeHB; OAEP; OBEV; OBRV; OTPC; OuHeWo; PeBoSo; PECK; PIAE; PIR; PoEL-4; PoeMoYo; PoFS; PreP; PtP; PYM; ReaPo; ReTS; SeCeV; ShBV-3; TCEP; TOP; TreF; TrGrPo; TVSH; TwCrTr; TwHP; TwP; TyEnPo; UnPo (1st ed.); ViBoPo; WHA
(Lines on First Looking into Chapman's Homer.) PFE
(On Looking into Chapman's Homer.) EG
(Sonnet: On First Looking into Chapman's Homer.) ChER; EmBrPo; GEPC
(To the Adventurous.) LH
On First Looking into the Dark Future. Roger Lancelyn Green. CenHV
On Fleas. Augustus De Morgan. *See* Great Fleas.
On Fleas. Swift. TreFS
On fog days, early mornings wet at the mirror. The Old Pilot Tunnels under the English Channel. James Schevill. FiMAP
On Fort Sumter. *Unknown, ad. fr.* Where There's a Will There's a Way *by* John Godfrey Saxe. MC; PAH
On Francis Drake. *Unknown. See* Epigram: On Sir Francis Drake.
On Friday morning as we set sail. *See* One Friday morn when we set sail.
On Friendship. Kahlil Gibran. *Fr.* The Prophet. BoFr
On Friendship. Marqués de Santillana, *tr. fr. Spanish by* Elizabeth Selden. BoFr
On Friendship. William Whitehead. OBEC
On Fujiyama/ Under the midsummer moon. Yamabe no Akahito, *tr. fr. Japanese by* Kenneth Rexroth. OnPJ
On Garland Sunday, the weaver told me. Garland Sunday. Padraic Colum. GoYe
On Gay Wallpaper. William Carlos Williams. MAP; MoAB; MoAmPo
On George Herbert's "The Temple" Sent to a Gentlewoman. Richard Crashaw. *See* On Mr. G. Herbert's Book.
On Giving. Kahlil Gibran. *Fr.* The Prophet. BoFr; MaRV
On Going Away. Wang Wei, *tr. fr. Chinese.* WhP
On Going Home. Marjorie L. Agnew. GoYe
On Going to a Tavern. Wang Chi, *tr. fr. Chinese by* Arthur Waley. OnPM; TrCh
On Going to the Wars. Earle Birney. NeTW; WaP
On golden seas of drink, so the Greek poet said. Alcohol. Louis MacNeice. LiTM
On gossamer nights when the moon is low. The Fairy Thrall. May Byron. HBV; HBVY; VA
On Great Sugarloaf. George Arthur Greene. TIP
On Gredos. Miguel de Unamuno, *tr. fr. Spanish by* Eleanor L. Turnbull. TeCS
On Growing Old. John Masefield. BEL; BMEP; ChMo; CMP; CoBE; FaFP; HBMV; LBBV; LiTB; LiTM; MBP; MoAB; MoBrPo; PG; PoRA; ReaPo; TreFS; ViBoPo; VOD; WHA
"Be with me, Beauty, for the fire is dying," *sel.* InP
On Hallow-Mass Eve, ere you boune ye to rest. St. Swithin's Chair. Sir Walter Scott. *Fr.* Waverley. HOAH
On Hampstead Heath. W. W. Gibson. EPN, HBV; NP
On, happy shades—to me unblessed! The Shrubbery. William Cowper. EiPP
On Having Arrived at the Age of Twenty-three. Milton. *See* On His Having Arrived at the Age of Twenty-three.
On Having Grown Old. E. G. Moll. BoAV
On he goes, the little one. Tortoise Family Connections. D. H. Lawrence. ChMP; HaMV
On Hearing a Bird Sing at Night. David Morton. BLA
On Hearing a Blackbird at Ch'ang An. Wei Ting, *tr. fr. Chinese by* Henry H. Hart. PoHN
On Hearing a Broadcast of Ceremonies in Connection with Conferring of Cardinals' Hats. Denis Wrafter. NeIP
On Hearing a Flute at Night from the Wall of Shou-hsiang. Li Yi, *tr. fr. Chinese by* Witter Bynner. UnS
On Hearing a Lady Praise a Certain Rev. Doctor's Eyes. George Outram. BOHV; LauV
On Hearing a Symphony of Beethoven. Edna St. Vincent Millay. GTBS-W; InP; LiTA; LiTM; MAP; MoAB; MoAmPo; NeMA; NePA; NP; TrGrPo; TwAmPo; UnS
On Hearing al-Mutanabbi Praised. Ibn Wahbun, *tr. fr. Arabic by* A. J. Arberry. MooP
On Hearing Her Play the Harp. Li Tüan, *tr. fr. Chinese by* Witter Bynner. ChLP
On Hearing Jazz. Alice Phelps-Rider. PoMa
On Hearing Miss Thrale Deliberate about Her Hat. Samuel Johnson. BeR
On Hearing Someone Sing a Poem by Yüan Chen. Po Chü-i, *tr. fr. Chinese by* Arthur Waley. TrCh
On Hearing that Our Arms Have Captured Honan and Hupeh. Tu Fu, *tr. fr. Chinese.* WhP
On Hearing That the Students of Our New University Have Joined the Agitation against Immoral Literature. W. B. Yeats. FaBoTw
On Hearing the First Cuckoo. Richard Church. MoBrPo (1942 ed.); OBMV
On Hearing the Flute. Lu Yu, *tr. fr. Chinese by* Pai Chwen-yu. WhP
On Hearing the News from Venice. George Meredith. PoVP
On Hearing the Sound of Flutes at Loyang on a Spring Night. Li Po, *tr. fr. Chinese.* WhP

On Heaven, *sel.* Ford Madox Ford.
"And my dear one sat in the shadows." ViBoPo
On Heaven, *sel.* Elizabeth Rowe.
Seraphs in Heaven, The. BeR
On Helen's heart the day were night! The First Kiss. Norman Gale. VA
On Hellespont, guilty of true love's blood. Hero and Leander. Christopher Marlowe. AnFE; AtBAP; BCEP; EPP; LoBV; OAEP; OBSC; PoEL-2; ReaPo; ReEn; ReIE; SeCePo; SiCE; TuPP
On Her Absence. Thomas Rymer. SeCL
On Her Child's Death. Kaga no Chiyo, *tr. fr. Japanese by* Curtis Hidden Page. LiTW
On Her Coming to London. Edmund Waller. HBV
On her great venture, man. Earth and Man. George Meredith. EmBrPo; EPN; ViPo
On Her Laugh. Clément Marot. *See* Madam d'Albert's Laugh.
On her side, reclining on her elbow. So-and-So Reclining on Her Couch. Wallace Stevens. LiTM; SiTL
On her still lake the city sits. At Venice. Arthur Hugh Clough. ViPo
On Her Twenty-fifth Birthday. Louis Hasley. JKCP (1955 ed.)
On her white breast a sparkling cross she wore. Belinda. Pope. *Fr.* The Rape of the Lock. ACP; LPS-1
On high by the sea sat a beautiful maid. Ballad. Mikhail Yurevich Lermontov. WaL
On hill and plain, in the islands of the sea. Englyn. *Unknown. Fr.* The Black Book of Carmarthen. PrWP
On hills too harsh for firs to climb. The Singer of High State. Louis Golding. MBP
On him the unpetitioned heavens descend. A Counsel of Moderation. Francis Thompson. MBP; MoBrPo
On Himself. Charles Churchill. *Fr.* The Prophecy of Famine. OBEC
On Himself. Robert Herrick. ChTr; TriL
(On Himselfe.) SeCV-1
On Himself. Walter Savage Landor. *See* On His Seventy-fifth Birthday.
On Himself. James Russell Lowell. *See* Lowell.
On Himself. Meleager, *tr. fr. Greek by* Walter Leaf. GrR; OxBG
On Himself. Richard Savage. *Fr.* The Bastard. BeR
On Himself. Swift. AnIV
On Himself, upon Hearing What Was His Sentence. James Graham, Marquess of Montrose. *See* Verses Composed on the Eve of His Execution.
On his arms he wears. Tattooed. William Plomer. ChMP
On His Baldness. Po Chü-i, *tr. fr. Chinese by* Arthur Waley. TrCh
On His Baptismal Birthday. Samuel Taylor Coleridge. MaRV
On His Being Arrived at the Age of Twenty-three. Milton. *See* On His Having Arrived at the Age of Twenty-three.
On His Birthday. Milton. *See* On His Having Arrived at the Age of Twenty-three.
On His Blindness. Milton. ATP; AWP; BCEP; BEL; BLV; BoLiVe; CBE; ChTr; CBOV; CoBE; CoEV; ElSeCe; EM-1; EnLi-1; EnLit; EPP; EPS; ES; EV-2; FaBoEn; FaFP; FiP; GBV (1952 ed.); GEPC; GN; GrCo-1; GTBS; GTBS-D; GTBS-W; GTSE; GTSL; HBV; HBVY; InPo; JAWP; LEAP; LH; LiA; LiTB; LPS-2; MaRV; MCCG; OBEV; OuHeWo; OxBoCh; PC; PCD; PeBoSo; PECK; PFE; PG (1945 ed.); PIAE; PoEL-3; PoeMoYo; PoFS; PoMa; PoRA; PreP; PTA-1; PYM; RiBV; ShBV-4; TCEP; TOP; TreF; TrGrPo; TVSH; TwCrTr; UnPo; WBP; WHA
(Sonnet: "When I consider how my light is spent.") AnFE; LoBV; OBS; Po; SeCL; SeEP
(Sonnet on His Blindness.) AEV; BBV; BLP; FaBoBe; NeHB; OHFP; OQP; OTPC (1946 ed.); PIR; QP-1; WGRP
(When I Consider How My Light Is Spent.) CaAE; EnL; ExPo; InP; LiTG; MaPo; OAEP; ReaPo; SeCeV; TwHP; TyEnPo; ViBoPo
On His Books. Hilaire Belloc. ACP (1952 ed.); MBP; MoBrPo; OxBoLi; SiTL; WhC
(Epigram: "When I am dead I hope it may be said.") OtMeF
On His Deafness. Joachim du Bellay, *tr. fr. French by* Alan Conder. Les Amours, XXVI. TrFP
On his death-bed poor Lubin lies. A Reasonable Affliction. Matthew Prior. ALV; BLV; HBV; PIAE; TrGrPo; WhC
On His Deceased Wife. Milton. ATP; BEL; CBOV; EM-1; EnLi-1; EPS; ES; EV-2; ExPo; FaFP; GEPC; GTBS-W; InPo; LEAP; LiTB; LiTG; LiTL; OBEV; PeBoSo; PoFS; ReaPo; SeCeV; TOP; TreFS; TyEnPo; UnW
(Katherine Milton: Died MDCLVIII.) FaBoEn
(Methought I Saw My Late Espoused Saint.) EnLoPo; MaPo; TwHP
(On His Late Wife.) PoEL-3
(Sonnet: "Methought I saw my late espousèd saint.") OBS; SeCL; SeEP; TriL
(Sonnet on His Deceased Wife.) LoBV
On His Departed Wife. Hitomaro, *tr. fr. Japanese.* UnW
On His Dog. John Gay. ALV
On His Exile to Iona. St. Columcille, *tr. fr. Old Irish by* Douglas Hyde. CAW; LiTW
On His First Sonne. Ben Jonson. *See* On My First Son.
On His Friend, Joseph Rodman Drake. Fitz-Greene Halleck. *See* On the Death of Joseph Rodman Drake.
On His Having Arrived at the Age of Twenty-three. Milton. ATP; AWP; BEL; CoBE; EnLi-1; EPP; ES; JAWP; MCCG; OuHeWo; PeBoSo; PIAE; TOP; TrGrPo; WBP
(How Soon Hath Time.) EG; InPo; LEAP; OAEP; ReaPo; RiBV; SeCePo; SeCeV; TwHP; TyEnPo
("How soon hath time, the subtle thief of youth.") EnL; ExPo; GTBS-W; LiTB
(On Having Arrived at the Age of Twenty-three.) PFE
(On His Being Arrived at His Twenty-third Year.) EnLit
(On His Being Arrived at [*or* to] the Age of Twenty-three.) CBOV; ElSeCe; EM-1; GEPC; MaRV; PoeMoYo; PreP
(On His Birthday.) EPS
(On His 24th Birthday.) FaBoEn
(On His Twenty-third Birthday.) FiP
(Sonnet: "How soon hath Time, the subtle thief of youth.") AEV; CaAE; LiTG; LoBV; OBS; SeCL; SeEP; ViBoPo
(Sonnet: On His Being Arrived at the Age of Twenty-three.) HBV
On His Lady's Waking. Pierre de Ronsard, *tr. fr. French by* Andrew Lang. AWP
On His Late Espoused Saint. Sir Kenelm Digby. ACP
On His Late Wife. Milton. *See* On His Deceased Wife.
On His Love. Dakiki, *tr. fr. Persian by* R. A. Nicholson. LiTW
On His Mistress. John Donne. Elegies, XVI. EPS; LiTB; LiTG; MyFE; NBE; ReaPo; ReEn; TriL; TuPP; TwP; ViBoPo
(Elegie: On His Mistris.) MePo; SeCV-1
(Elegy on His Mistress.) LoBV; SeCeV; SeEP
(On His Mistris.) MeLP; PoEL-2
On His Mistress. *Unknown, at. to* Henry Noel *and to* William Strode. *See* Beauty Extoll'd.
On His Mistress Crossing the Sea. Thomas Cary. SeCL
(On His Mistresse Going to Sea.) OBS
On His Mistress Drowned. Thomas Sprat. ATP; EnLoPo; SeCL
On His Mistress' Garden of Herbs. *Unknown.* SeCL
On His Mistress Going from Home. *Unknown.* OBS
On His Mistress [*or* Mistris], the Queen of Bohemia. Sir Henry Wotton. AEV; CaAE; CoEV; ElL; ElSeCe; EnLoPo; LoBV; MeLP; MePo; MyFE; OBS; ReEn; SeEP; TrGrPo; ViBoPo
(Elizabeth of Bohemia.) BCEP; EV-2; FaBoCh; GTBS; GTBS-D; GTBS-W; GTSE; GTSL; HBV; LEAP; OBEV; PIAE; TOP
(To His Mistress, Elizabeth Queen of Bohemia.) LPS-1
("You meaner beauties of the night.") EG
Elizabeth of Bohemia, *sel., st.* 1. OtMeF
On His Mistresse Going to Sea. Thomas Cary. *See* On His Mistress Crossing the Sea.
On His Mistris. John Donne. *See* On His Mistress.
On His Mistris That Lov'd Hunting. *Unknown.* OBS
On His Mistris, the Queen of Bohemia. Sir Henry Wotton. *See* On His Mistress . . .
On his morning rounds the master. Incident Characteristic of a Favourite Dog. Wordsworth. CG
On His Ninth Decade. Walter Savage Landor. *See* To My Ninth Decade.
On His Own Agamemnon and Iphigeneia. Walter Savage Landor. EmBrPo; OBRV
(On His Own Iphegeneia and Agamemnon.) BPN
On His Own Blindness. Milton. *See* To Cyriack Skinner ("Cyriack, this three years' day").
On His Own Deafness. Swift. BeR
On His Own Death. Walter Savage Landor. *See* Death Stands above Me.
On His Own Iphegeneia and Agamemnon. Walter Savage Landor. *See* On His Own Agamemnon and Iphigeneia.
On His Portrait between Two Others. Voltaire, *tr. fr. French by* J. G. Legge. LiA
On His Seventy-fifth Birthday. Walter Savage Landor. *Fr.* The Last Fruit off an Old Tree. AEV; AnEnPo; AnFE; BEL; BLV; BoLiVe; BPN; CaAE; CoEV; EmBrPo; EPN; EPP; InP; InPo; LiTB; MaRV; OAEP; PFE; PIAE; PIR; PoE; PreP; SeCeV; TOP; TreF; TrGrPo; TyEnPo; WHA; WP
(Dying Speech of an Old Philosopher.) ViBoPo
(End, The.) EV-4; SeCePo
(Envoi.) FaBoEn

(Finis.) BCEP; BTP; GTBS-W; OBEV; OBVV; OnPP; PC
(I Strove with None.) ChTr; EG; EnRP; GTBS; GTML; GTSL; HBV; LEAP; MCCG
(Introduction to "The Last Fruit off an Old Tree.") EnLi-2
(Lyrics and Epigrams.) CBOV; ERP
(On Himself.) VA
On His "Sonnets of the Wingless Hours." Eugene Lee-Hamilton. VA
On His Twenty-third Birthday. Milton. *See* On His Having Arrived at the Age of Twenty-three.
On His Wife's Death. Henry King. *See* Exequy, The.
On history's page their names do not shine. My Forefathers. Erik Axel Karlfeldt. *Fr.* Songs of Nature and Love. AnSL
On hoary Conway's battlemented height. With a Rose from Conway Castle. Julia C. R. Dorr. AA
On Honour, *sel.* Bernard Mandeville.
Honour. BeR
On hooks beneath his arm-pits. *Unknown. Fr.* Penitentes. SiB
On Hope, by Way of Question and Answer, betweene A. Cowley, and R. Crashaw. Abraham Cowley *and* Richard Crashaw. MePo. *See also* Against Hope *and* For Hope.
On Human Ambitions. Lucretius, *tr. fr. Latin by* Jack Lindsay. *Fr.* De Rerum Natura, III. LaP
On Hygiene. Hilaire Belloc. MBP; MoBrPo
On Imagination. Keats. *Fr.* Epistle to Reynolds. EPN
On Imagination. Phillis Wheatley. APW; PoNe
On Inclosures. *Unknown.* OxBoLi
On Independence. Jonathan Mitchell Sewall. PAH
On Ithaca Standing. Lawrence Durrell. FaBoTw
On its straight iron pathway the long train was rushing. Beside the Railway Track. *Unknown.* PEOR
On Izumo Cliff. Basho, *tr. fr. Japanese by* H. G. Henderson. OnPM
On J. W. Ward. Samuel Rogers. ALV
On Jean Fréron. Voltaire, *tr. fr. French by* Alan Conder. OnPM; TrFP
On Jefferson. Bryant. BoHiPo
On Joe. P. Dodd. *See* Epigram: "Joe hates a sycophant. It shows."
On John Bun. *Unknown.* GoTP
(John Bun.) WhC
On John Donne's Book of Poems. John Marriott. CH
On John Grubb. *Unknown.* WhC
On Jordan's Bank. Byron. ChER
On Jordan's bank the Baptist's cry. Glad Tidings from the King of Kings. Charles Coffin. BePJ
On Jordan's banks the Arab's camels stray. On Jordan's Bank. Byron. ChER
On Jordan's stormy banks I stand. The Promised Land. Samuel Stennett. OlF; TrAS
On Julia's Death. Vasili Kapnist, *tr. fr. Russian by* Sir John Bowring. BoRS
On July 5 the Associated Press gave the news to the world. Harangue on the Death of Hayyim Nahman [*or* Chayim Nachman] Bialik. César Tiempo. AnCL; TrJP
On June 15, 1215, King John met the barons. Magna Charta. *Unknown.* OHFP; WBLP
On Kiley's Run. Andrew Barton Paterson. BoAu
On Kingston Bridge. Ellen M. H. Cortissoz. AA; UnW
On Knighthood. Folgore da San Geminiano, *tr. fr. Italian by* John Addington Symonds. AWP; JAWP; WBP
On Knowing When to Stop. L. J. Bridgman. BOHV
On Lady Poltagrue, a Public Peril. Hilaire Belloc. ALV; MBP; MoBrPo; WhC
On Lake Llanquihue. Wilberto L. Cantón, *tr. fr. Spanish by* Donald Devenish Walsh. AnCL
On Lamb's Specimens of Dramatic Poets. Swinburne. EPP
On land and sea I strove with anxious care. Bombed in London. Kipling. *Fr.* Epitaphs of the War. PoVP
On Laurel Hill, *sel.* William Thompson.
"O Pope! the sweetest of the tuneful race." EnSW
On Laying the Cornerstone of the Bunker Hill Monument. John Pierpont. AnNE; PAH
On Laying Up Treasure. Lois Smith Hiers. GoYe
On Leaping over the Moon. Thomas Traherne. AtBAP; LiTB; LoBV; SeCV-2
"As if it had ev'n twenty thousand faces," *sel.* AlDL
On Leaving Prison. Luis de León, *tr. fr. Spanish by* Aubrey F. G. Bell. AnSpL-1
On Leaving the Tomb of Premier Fang. Tu Fu, *tr. fr. Chinese by* Witter Bynner. BoFr
On Leaving Ullswater. Kathleen Raine. NeBP
On Lebanon. David Gray. AA
On Lending a Punch-Bowl. Oliver Wendell Holmes. AA; CoBA; IAP; TCAP
On Leslie Moore. *Unknown.* GoTP
On Leven's banks, while free to rove. Ode to Leven Water. Tobias Smollett. CEP; EBSV; EV-3; OBEV
On Liberty and Slavery. George Moses Horton. PoNe
On Life's Way. Charles F. Deems. OQP; QP-2
(Worry.) MaRV
On Limited Warfare. *Unknown.* SiTL
On Lincoln's Birthday. John Kendrick Bangs. HH
On Linden, when the sun was low. Hohenlinden [*or* The Battle of Hohenlinden]. Thomas Campbell. BCEP; BeLS; BHV; BTP; CBOV; CH; ChTr; EBSV; EnRP; ERP; EV-4; FaBoCh; GN; GTBS; GTBS-D; GTBS-W; GTSE; GTSL; HBV; LiA; LPS-2; MuP; OBRV; OTPC (1923 ed.); PECK; TCEP; TreF; TVSH; WaaP; WBLP; WHA
On Lisa's Golden Hair. Francisco de Quevedo y Villegas. *See* Lisa's Golden Hair.
On Living Too Long. Walter Savage Landor. *See* Is It Not Better at an Early Hour.
On London fell a clearer light. Summer in England 1914. Alice Meynell. SoV
On long, serene midsummer days. Wild Roses. Edgar Fawcett. HBV
On Looking at a Copy of Alice Meynell's Poems, Given Me, Years Ago, by a Friend. Amy Lowell. BoFr, *abr.*; NP; PtP
On Looking at the School War Memorial. Joseph Manton. ShGoBo
On Looking Backward. Ernestine Mercer. MaRV
On Looking into Chapman's Homer. Keats. *See* On First Looking into Chapman's Homer.
On Looking Up by Chance at the Constellations. Robert Frost. ChMo; CMP; NePA; NP
On Lord Holland's Seat near Margate, Kent. Thomas Gray. *See* Impromptu, Suggested by a View . . .
On lotus-leaves and myrtles fine. Let's Drink and Love. *Unknown.* GrL
On Love. Sir Robert Ayton. LPS-1
On Love. Countess of Winchilsea. SeCL
(Song, A: "Love, thou art best of human joys.") DiM; SeEP
On Lucretia Borgia's Hair. Walter Savage Landor. AnFE; BCEP; BPN; EnRP; TOP; UnPo (1st ed.); VA
(On Seeing a Hair of Lucretia Borgia.) OAEP; ReaPo; RiBV
On Lucy, Countess[e] of Bedford. Ben Jonson. EPS; OAEP; OBS; SeCV-1; SeEP; TuPP
On Luxury. Horace, *tr. fr. Latin by* W. E. Gladstone. Odes, II, 15. RoL
On Lydia Distracted. Philip Ayres. EnLoPo
On Lynn Terrace. Thomas Bailey Aldrich. IAP
On Lyric Poetry, *sel.* Mark Akenside.
"Once more I join the Thespian choir." PtP
On Ma Journey. *Unknown.* APW
On Malvern Hill. John Masefield. TCPD; WP
On Mammon. Herman Melville. *Fr.* Clarel. OxBA
On Man. Walter Savage Landor. OBRV; TriL
(Man.) VA
On Man, on Nature, and on Human Life. Wordsworth. *Fr.* The Recluse. EnRP; EPN; EPP; KN; NBE; OBRV
On many a gallant battle-field. The Sword and the Skewer. Tomás de Iriarte. AnSpL-2
On many a lazy river, in many a sparkling bay. The Little Boats of Britain. Sara E. Carsley. CaP
On many and many a soft, still summer's night. Towards the North Star. John Gould Fletcher. LaNeLa
On Maou Dying at the Age of Six Months. Frances Cornford. PoC
On Marcus the Physician. Nicarchos, *tr. fr. Greek by* Dudley Fitts. LiTW
On Margaret Ratcliffe. Ben Jonson. ReIE; TriL
On Margate beach, where the sick one roams. The Mermaid of Margate. Thomas Hood. ERP
On market days we always call. Mrs. Barks. Rose Fyleman. BrR
On Marriage. Richard Crashaw. ReEn
On Marriage. Thomas Flatman. FiBHP; WhC
(Bachelor's Song, The.) EnLoPo
On Martha Snell. *Unknown.* GoTP
("Poor Martha Snell, she's gone away.") WhC
On Mary, Duchess of Richmond. Richard Flecknoe. SeCL
On Maurus the Rhetor. Palladas of Alexandria, *tr. fr. Greek by* Dudley Fitts. LiTW
On Mayday we dance. *Unknown.* BoTP
On May-day, when the lark began to ryse. *Unknown.* LO
On May Morning. Milton. *See* Song on May Morning.
On me and on my children! Cromwell and Henrietta Maria. William Gorman Wills. *Fr.* Charles the First. VA
On me he shall ne'er put a ring. Feminine Arithmetic. Charles Graham Halpine. BOHV; PR
On me nor Priests nor Presbyter nor Pope. My Church. *Unknown.* MaRV; OQP; QP-2
On me to rest, my bird, my bird. Rest. "Æ." POTE
On Meesh-e-gan, *with music.* *Unknown.* ABF; TrAS
On Meeting a Lady. Charles L. O'Donnell. MM
On Meeting a Messenger to the Capital. Ts'en Ts'an, *tr. fr. Chinese by* Yuan Chia-hua. WhP

On Meeting a Sick Soldier. Lu Lun, *tr. fr. Chinese.* WhP
On Meeting a Stranger in a Bookshop. Oscar Williams. LoPo; NePA
On Meeting Li Kuei-nien down the River. Tu Fu, *tr. fr. Chinese by* Witter Bynner. LiTW
On Melancholy. Keats. *See* Ode on Melancholy.
On Midas' grave, a maid of bronze, I lie. Homeric Epigram: Midas' Tomb. *Unknown.* OxBG
On Middleton Edge. Andrew Young. POTE
On Milton's "Paradise Lost." Andrew Marvell. OAEP
(On Mr. Milton's "Paradise Lost.") PtP
(On Paradise Lost.) SeEP
On Mr. Abraham Cowley, His Death and Burial amongst the Ancient Poets. Sir John Denham. PtP
(On Mr. Abraham Cowley.) SeCV-1
"Old Chaucer, like the morning star," *sel.* OBS
On Mr. Francis Beaumont (Then Newly Dead). Richard Corbet. OBS
On Mr. G. Herbert's Book. Richard Crashaw. OxBoCh; PtP; SeCV-1
(On George Herbert's "The Temple" Sent to a Gentlewoman.) EV-2
On Mr. Gay; in Westminster Abbey, 1732. Pope. FiP; PtP
(Epitaph: "Of manners gentle.") CEP
On Mr. Hobbs, and His Writings. John Sheffield, Duke of Buckingham and Normanby. PoEL-3
On Mr. Milton's "Paradise Lost." Andrew Marvell. *See* On Milton's "Paradise Lost."
On Mr. Paine's "Rights of Man." Philip Freneau. PoFr
On Mr. Partridge. *Unknown.* WhC
On Mr. Wm. Shakespeare. William Basse. *See* Elegy on Shakespeare.
On Mrs. Biddy Floyd. Swift. CEP
On Mrs. Corbet. Pope. BCEP
(Epitaph V: On Mrs. Corbet, Who Dyed of a Cancer in Her Breast.) CEP
On Mistress Nicely, a Pattern for Housekeepers. Thomas Hood. OBRV
(Sonnet on Mistress Nicely, a Pattern for Housekeepers.) NBE
On Mrs. W——. Nicolas Bentley. FiBHP
On Monday I wash my dollies' clothes. My Week. *Unknown.* MeMeAg
On Monday, Monday. My True Love. Ivy O. Eastwick. SiSoSe
On Monday, when the sun is hot. Hums of Pooh. A. A. Milne. *Fr.* Winnie the Pooh. BoN
On Monsieur Coué. Charles Inge. FaFP; SiTL
On Montorio's Height. Arthur Hugh Clough. Amours de Voyage, Canto III, xi. BPN
On moonlight bushes. Nightingales. Samuel Taylor Coleridge. *Fr.* The Nightingale. ChTr
On Moonlit Heath and Lonesome Bank. A. E. Housman. A Shropshire Lad, IX. BPN; ChMo; CMP; EmBrPo; OAEP; POTT; PoVP; ReaPo; TCEP; TwP; VLEP
On moony nights the dogs bark shrill. At Night. Frances Cornford. StaSt; TSW; TSWC
On Morpheus. *Unknown.* SeCL
On Mt. Iron. Charles Brasch. AnNZ
On Mount Tsukuba. Mushimaro, *tr. fr. Japanese by* Basil Hall Chamberlain. OnPM
On mountains cold and bold and high. The Whistling Marmot. Hamlin Garland. SN
On Moving into a Skylight Room. Sister Rita Agnes. JKCP (1926 ed.)
On mules we find two legs behind. The Mule. *Unknown.* LauV
On Mundane Acquaintances. Hilaire Belloc. FiBHP; MoVE
On Music. Walter Savage Landor. BPN; HBV; TriL; VA
On Music. Thomas Moore. TIP
On music drawn away, a sea-borne mariner. Music. Baudelaire. AnFP
On My Bed I Sought Him. The Song of Solomon, III: 1–5, Bible, *O.T.* TrJP
On My Birthday July 21. Matthew Prior. OBEV
On my charger golden-bright. A Yellow Horse with a Blaze and a Black Mane. Ibn Sa'id of Alcala la Real. MooP
On my cornice linger the ripe, black grapes ungathered. The Third of November. Bryant. PEOR
On My Dear Son, Gervase Beaumont. Sir John Beaumont. *See* Of My Dear Son, Gervase Beaumont.
On My Dog's Death. George Herbert Clarke. OCL
On My First Daughter. Ben Jonson. EPS; LoBV; OBS; PoFS; ReIE; SeCV-1; SeEP
On My First Son [*or* Sonne]. Ben Jonson. AtBAP; AWP; CoBE; EIL; ElSeCe; EnL; EPS; ExPo; FaBoEn; InPo; LiTB; LoBV; MaPo; OAEP; OnPM; PoD; PoE; PoEL-2; PoFS; ReEn; ReIE; SeCV-1; SeEP; TriL; TuPP; UnPo (3d ed.); WoL
(On His First Sonne.) OBS
On my flute of ebony I played to you the most impassioned. The Jewel. Wan Tse. ChLP
On my flute, tipped with jade, I sang a song to mortals. Prose Poem: Sages' Dance. Judith Gautier. OnPM
On My Joyful Departure from the City of Cologne. Samuel Taylor Coleridge. InvP
(On My Joyful Departure from the Same [City].) WhC
On my knees do I entreat thee, O Pheraean. Prayer to Artemis. Anacreon. GrR
On my little magic whistle I will play to you all day. The Magic Whistle. Margaret Rose. BoTP
On my perambulator. Perambulator Poems, I. David McCord. WhC
On my return (I think of it with dread!). Cold Kisses. Pierre de Ronsard. TrFP
On My Sorrowful Life. Moses ibn Ezra, *tr. fr. Hebrew by* Solomon Solis-Cohen. TrJP
On My Thirty-third Birthday. Byron. OBRV
On my torn heart come and place thy pure hand. My Torn Heart. Alfred de Vigny. LiA
On my wall to eastward. Casements. Isabel Fisk Conant. BAP
On My Wander Flute. Abraham Sutskever, *tr. fr. Yiddish by* Sarah Zweig Betsky. OnCuPl
On Myself. Countess of Winchilsea. TrGrPo
On National Vanity. J. E. Clare McFarlane. PoNe
On nature ever idly spying. Swallows. Afanasi Fet. BoR
On nature's Alps I stand. Edward Young. *Fr.* Night Thoughts. MaRV
On Nebo's lonely mountain. *See* By Nebo's lonely mountain.
On New Year's Day, as I heard say. Dicky of Ballyman. *Unknown.* OTPC (1946 ed.)
On New-Years Day 1640. To the King. Sir John Suckling. SeCV-1
On Newblown Roses. Ausonius, *tr. fr. Latin by* Helen Waddell. LaP
On News. Thomas Traherne. *See* News.
On No Work of Words Now. Dylan Thomas. FaBoTw; LiTB; PoLFOT
(Poem.) MoWP
On Not Hearing the Birds Sing in Ireland. Padraic Colum. NePoAm
On Nova Zembla's peaks, in vales of parched Ceylon. Introduction to "Spastara's Death." Bengt Lidner. AnSL
On Oculists. J. C. Squire. WhC
On old Cold Crendon's windy tops. The Fox Awakes. John Masefield. *Fr.* Reynard the Fox. MoVE
On Old Rome. Philip Ayres. AEV
On. On compassion shall never enter heere, tis tyme. *Unknown.* SeCSL
On, On, Forever. Harriet Martineau. VA
On, on, my brown Arab, away, away! The Arab. Charles Stuart Calverley. LPS-3
On, on, on, with never a doubt nor a turning. Song of the Grail Seekers. Hermann Hagedorn. VOD
On one fix'd point all nature moves. On the Uniformity and Perfection of Nature. Philip Freneau. AmPP; CoBA; CoV
On One Ignorant and Arrogant. John Owen, *tr. fr. Latin by* William Cowper. PC
On one of those days with the Legion. A Day with the Foreign Legion. Reed Whittemore. NePoEA
On one Saturday evenin'. Harvey Logan. *Unknown.* OuSiCo
On One Who Died Discovering Her Kindness. John Sheffield, Duke of Buckingham and Normanby. LO; OBEV
On One Who Died in May. Clarence Chatham Cook. AA; LEAP
On One Who Made Long Epitaphs. Pope. ALV
On opal Aprilian mornings like this. Life-drunk. Arthur Stringer. PC
On Opening a New Book. Abbie Farwell Brown. YeAr
On other fields and other scenes the morn. Burnt Lands. Sir Charles G. D. Roberts. VA
On Our Crucified Lord Naked, and Bloody. Richard Crashaw. *See* Upon the Body of Our Blessed Lord, Naked and Bloody.
On Our Farm. Esther Antin. RIS
On Our Lady of Blachernae. *Unknown, tr. fr. Greek by* Shane Leslie. ISi
On our last night together. The Sluggard. A. E. Coppard. MBP; MoBrPo (1942 ed.)
On our lone pathway bloomed no earthly hopes. Sonnet to Edgar Allan Poe. Sarah Helen Whitman. Sonnets from the Series Relating to Edgar Allan Poe, V. AA; AnAmPo; BAP; LA; LEAP
On Our Thirty-ninth Wedding Day. Jonathan Odell. CaP
On our way rejoicing. John S. B. Monsell. OIF
On Paradise Lost. Andrew Marvell. *See* On Milton's "Paradise Lost."
On Parent Knees, a Naked New-born Child. Sir William Jones. *See* Baby, The.
On Parting. Edward Coote Pinkney. APW; SPP
On Parting with Moses ibn Ezra. Judah Halevi, *tr. fr. Hebrew by* Solomon Solis-Cohen. TrJP
On Parting with Spot. Helen Welshimer. AlBD

On Passing a Friend's House. Wang Wei, *tr. fr. Chinese by* Arthur Christy. OnPM
On Passing the New Menin Gate. Siegfried Sassoon. AnEnPo; OBMV
On Passing through the Haymarket. Nikolai Nekrasov, *tr. fr. Russian by* Babette Deutsch. OnPM; TrRV
On Peace. *At. to* Samuel Speed. *See* Peace.
On peaks where the clouds have sifted. Edelweiss. Carl Snoilsky. AnSL
On Peter Robertson. John Gibson Lockhart. SiTL
On Peter Robinson. Francis Jeffrey. OxBoLi; WhC
On Philiphaugh a fray began. The Battle of Philiphaugh. *Unknown.* ESPB
On Poetry. Louis Dudek. BoCaPo (1948 ed.)
On Poetry; a Rhapsody, *sels.* Swift.
"All human race wou'd fain be wits." BeR; PoEL-3
Critics. CoEV; OBEC; SeCePo
(Rhapsody on Poetry, A.) BCEP
On Poets Who Recite in Public—and Other Sinners. Juvenal, *tr. fr. Latin by* L. R. Lind. Satires, I. LaP
On Portents. Robert Graves. FaBoMo
On Praxiteles' Statue of Aphrodite at Cnidus. Plato, *tr. fr. Greek by* J. M. Edmonds. GrR
On Presenting to a Lady a White Rose and a Red on the Tenth of June. William Somervile. *See* Presenting to a Lady a White Rose . . .
On primal rocks she wrote her name. Our Country. Julia Ward Howe. DD; MC; PaA; PAH
On Primrose Hill in the early spring. Primrose Hill. Rose Fyleman. BoTP
On Prince Frederick. *Unknown.* GoTP; OxBoLi; TreFS; WhC
On Professor Drennan's Verse. Roy Campbell. WhC
On Psalm CXIX, 5. Francis Quarles. EV-2
On quarry walls the spleenwort spreads. Rockferns. Norman Nicholson. MoBrPo (1950 ed.); NeMA
On Queen Anne's Death. *Unknown.* ElL
On rainy days alone I dine. On Himself. Swift. AnIV
On Reading. Thomas Bailey Aldrich. AA
On Reading a Poet's First Book. H. C. Bunner. AA
On Reading Arthur Machen. Frank Belknap Long. DaM
On Reading Gene Derwood's "The Innocent." Willard Maas. NePA
On Reading Keats in Wartime. Karl Shapiro. MuM; PtP
On Reading the *Metamorphoses.* George Garrett. NePoAm-2
On Reading the War Diary of a Defunct Ambassador. Siegfried Sassoon. ChMo; CMP; PoeMoYo; TwCV
"World will find no pity in your pages, The," *sel.* PoFr
On Receiving News of the War. Isaac Rosenberg. MoBrPo
On Recrossing the Rocky Mountains after Many Years. John Charles Frémont. PoOW
On Reformed Gamester. Ben Jonson. ReIE
On Refusal of Aid between Nations. Dante Gabriel Rossetti. BPN; CoBE; EmBrPo; EPN; EPP; LoBV; PeBoSo; PoVP; TOP; VLEP
(Refusal of Aid between Nations.) ES
On Rereading Shelley. Bryllion Fagin. MuM
On Rereading Télémaque. James Jeffrey Roche. PR
On Retirement. Philip Freneau. CoV; IAP
(Retirement.) OBAV
On Revisiting Cintra after the Death of Catarina. Luís de Camões, *tr. fr. Portuguese by* Richard Garnett. AWP
On Revisiting Dunolly Castle. Wordsworth. PeBoSo
On Richard Dent, Landlord. *Unknown.* GoTP
On Richard, Duke of Cornwall, Brother to Henry III. *Unknown.* *See* Song of Lewes, The.
On Riches. Pope. *See* Of the Use of Riches.
On Richmond Hill there lives a lass. The Lass of Richmond Hill. James Upton. HBV; LPS-1
On Rome. Byron. *See* Rome.
On Rome in the Pontificate of Julius II. Michelangelo, *tr. fr. Italian by* John Addington Symonds. PoFr
"On royal crowns and purples, I." Long John. Padraic Fallon. NeIP
On St. James's Park, as Lately Improved by His Majesty. Edmund Waller. CEP
On St. Martin's evening green. Nuns at Eve. John Malcolm Brinnin. MoAB
On Saturday Morning Early. Rudolph Chambers Lehmann. TVSH
On Saturday morning there was a great battle. The Battle of Argoed Llwyfain. Taliesin. PrWP
On Saturday night. Mother Goose. OTPC (1923 ed.); OxNR
On Saturday sailed from Bremen. Gerard Manley Hopkins. *Fr.* The Wreck of the *Deutschland.* SeCePo
On scent of game from town to town he flew. On a Travelling Speculator. Philip Freneau. AA
On Scotia's plains, in days of yore. Elegy on the Death of Scots Music. Robert Fergusson. TCEP
On Scotland. John Cleveland. BOHV
On Scott's [Poem] "The Field of Waterloo." Thomas, Lord Erskine. FiBHP; WhC
On Scratchbury Camp. Siegfried Sassoon. HaMV
On Scribe Pergamus, a Slave Who Vainly Fled. Ausonius, *tr. fr. Latin by* Jack Lindsay. LaP
On Seeing a Beautiful Woman Ride By in a Cart. Hsüan Ti, *tr. fr. Chinese by* Henry H. Hart. PoHN
On Seeing a Dead Man. Prince Shotoku, *tr. fr. Japanese by* Ishii *and* Obata. OnPM
On Seeing a Hair of Lucretia Borgia. Walter Savage Landor. *See* On Lucretia Borgia's Hair.
On Seeing a Piece of Our Artillery Brought into Action. Wilfred Owen. LiTM (1946 ed.)
On Seeing a Poet of the First World War on the Station at Abbeville. Charles Causley. ChMP
On Seeing a Wounded Hare [Limp by Me]. Burns. BPP; SN
(Wounded Hare.) OTPC
On Seeing Ch'ang-an in Spring. Lu Lun, *tr. fr. Chinese.* WhP
On seeing me, he, frightened, stopped. Robinson Finds Friday. Maria Louise Weissmann. *Fr.* Robinson. BoFr
On Seeing Off Meng Hao-jan. Li Po, *tr. fr. Chinese.* BoFr, *tr. by* Shigeyoshi Obata; WhP
On Seeing Swift in Laracor. Brinsley MacNamara. AnIV; OxBI
On Seeing the Elgin Marbles. Keats. BEL; BoLiVe; BPN; CoBE; EmBrPo; EnLi-2; EnLit; EnRP; ERP; GTBS-W; LiTB; PeBoSo; Po; SeCeV; TCEP; TrGrPo; TwCrTr; TwHP; WHA
(On the Elgin Marbles.) BLV; PIAE
(Sonnet on Seeing the Elgin Marbles.) GEPC; REAL
On Seeing Two Brown Boys in a Catholic Church. Frank Horne. BANP; CDC; PoNe
On Seeing Weather-beaten Trees. Adelaide Crapsey. BLV; CBOV; InP; MAP; MCCG; MoAmPo (1942 ed.); NeMA; PIAE
On Seeming to Presume. Lawrence Durrell. LiTM (rev. ed.)
On Shakespeare. Milton. BEL; BLV; BoLiVe; CaAE; CoBE; EM-1; EnLit; GTBS-W; InvP; LoBV; MeLP; MePo; OAEP; PG (1945 ed. *and* 1955 ed.); PoRA; PtP; SeCePo; SeCL; SeEP; TCEP; TOP; TrGrPo; TyEnPo; WHA
(Epitaph, An, on the Admirable Dramatic Poet, William [*or* W.] Shakespeare.) BCEP; ElSeCe; HBV; LEAP; LPS-3; PIR; ViBoPo
On "Shep," a Pet Dog. Stanton A. Coblentz. AIBD
On Shooting Particles beyond the World. Richard Eberhart. GTBS-W; LiTA; LiTM (rev. ed.)
On shores of Sicily a shape of Greece! A Shepherd Maiden. Edward Cracroft Lefroy. *Fr.* Echoes from Theocritus. VA
On siege and battlefield I mused. The Restorer. Horace. Odes, IV, 15. RoL
On Sight of a Gentlewomans Face in the Water. Thomas Carew. SeCV-1
On Sir Francis Drake, *abr.* Charles Fitzgeffrey. *Fr.* Sir Francis Drake. SG
On Sir Henry Clinton's Recall. *Unknown.* PAH
On Sir John Vanbrugh. Abel Evans. *See* Epitaph on Sir John Vanbrugh.
On Sir Philip Sidney. Henry Constable. *See* On the Death of Sir Philip Sidney.
On Sir Philip Sidney. Matthew Royden. *Fr.* An Elegy, or Friend's Passion for His Astrophil. ElL
(Sir Philip Sidney, 4 *sts.*) LPS-3
On Sitting Down to Read "King Lear" Once Again. Keats. ATP; EnRP; PeBoSo; PtP
On Sivori's Violin. Frances Sargent Osgood. AA
On Skugg. Benjamin Franklin. *See* Here Skugg Lies Snug.
On Snowflakes Melting on His Lady's Breast. William Martin Johnson. AA; BAV
On softest pillows my dim eyes unclose. Vita Benefica. Alice Wellington Rollins. AA
On Solitude. Abraham Cowley. *See* Of Solitude.
On Some Buttercups. Frank Dempster Sherman. AA
On some days I'm domestic. Vesta. Sarah Trousdale Mallory. DDA
On Some Shells Found Inland. Trumbull Stickney. AnFE; APA; CoAnAm; LiTA; LiTG; NePA; TwAmPo
On Some South African Novelists. Roy Campbell. AnFE; BoSA; ChMP; CoBE; MBP; MoBrPo; MoPW; MoVE; PIAE; SiTL; WhC
On Some Verses of Virgil. Virgil, *tr. fr. Latin by* James Rhoades. *Fr.* The Aeneid, VIII. LiA
On Someone's Death. Eugenio Florit, *tr. fr. Spanish by* Muna Lee. AnCL
On Something That Walk[e]s Somewhere. Ben Jonson. CoBE; SeCV-1; TuPP
On Sophocles. Simmias. *See* Sophocles' Tomb.
On Southey's Death. Walter Savage Landor. BPN; EmBrPo; TOP
(Lyrics and Epigrams, X: "Friends, hear the words.") CBOV
On Springfield Mountain there did dwell. Springfield Moun-

On Springfield Mountain there did dwell (*continued*) tain. *Unknown.* BaBo; Po; SoAF; TrAS; ViBoFo (A, B, C, *and* D *vers.*)
On Stella's Birthday. Swift. *See* Stella's Birthday, Written in the Year 1718.
On stifling summer days. Old Inn on the Eastern Shore. William H. Matchett. NePoEA
On still black waters where the stars lie sleeping. Ophelia. Arthur Rimbaud. ChTr
On stormy days. Brooms. Dorothy Aldis. GFA
On stormy seas we six years sailed. Sept ans sur mer. *Unknown.* OuSiCo
On Strymon built and Hellespontus wide. Amphipolis. Antipater of Thessalonica. OxBG
On Stubborn Michael Shay. *Unknown.* GoTP
On Sturminster Foot-Bridge. Thomas Hardy. OAEP
On Such a Day. Mary Elizabeth Coleridge. GTBS-D; LO; MoVE
On such a day as this I think. An April Day. Joseph S. Cotter, Jr. CDC
On such a day St. Francis walked. Return. Mary S. Hawling. PoMa
On Such a Wet and Blustery Night. Ralph Gustafson. PeCV
On summer afternoons I sit. La Vie C'est la Vie. Jessie Redmond Fauset. BANP; CDC; PoNe
On summer evenings blue, pricked by the heat. Sensation. Arthur Rimbaud. AWP; JAWP; WBP
On summer nights when moonbeams flow. The Worked-out Mine. Edward Dyson. BoAu; WoL
On Sunday in the Sunlight. William Rose Benét. HBMV
On Sunday Morning. William Alexander Percy. *Fr.* In New York. QS; SPP
On Sunday morning, then he comes. Mr. Wells. Elizabeth Madox Roberts. FaPON; GaP; HBMV; HBVY; LS; TSW; TSWC
On Sunday Morning Well I Knew. *Unknown, tr. fr. Italian by* John Addington Symonds. OnPM
(Popular Songs of Tuscany.) AWP
On Sundays see his saintly look. The Lettergae. Charles Murray. EBSV
On sunny slope and beechen swell. Burial of the Minnisink. Longfellow. DDA; LaNeLa; MOAP
On sword and gun the shadows reel and riot. The Night before and the Night after the Charge. Patrick MacGill. BMEP
On Syrian Hills. Richard Burton. ChIP
On Taine. Alfred Ainger. ALV
On Taking a Wife. Thomas Moore. BOHV; LauV; TreF
("Come, Come," Said Tom's Father.) WhC
(Epigram: " 'Come, come,' said Tom's father, 'at your time of life.' ") ALV; HBV
(Joke Versified. A.) LiTG; SiTL
On Taking Up a Humble Place at Court. Ibn Adha, *tr. fr. Arabic by* A. J. Arberry. MooP
On Tappan Zee a shroud of grey. The Flying Dutchman of the Tappan Zee. Arthur Guiterman. CP
On taut air—bells; lifted, adoring eyes. Immolation. Robert Farren. OnYI
On th' other side, Adam, soon as he heard. Milton. *Fr.* Paradise Lost, IX. NBE
On that first day so singular. The Secret. John Richard Moreland. NLK; OQP; QP-2
On that gray night of mournful drone. A Man Was Drawing Near to Me. Thomas Hardy. InPo
On that last night before we went. In Memoriam A. H. H., CIII. Tennyson. EmBrPo; EnLi-2; EPN; GEPC; OAEP; PoEL-5; UnW; ViPo; VLEP
On that side of the street a woman passes. This Side and That Side. Mokutaro Kinoshita. PoLJ
On that wild verge in the late light he stood. Preludes to Definition, II. Conrad Aiken. TwAmPo
On the Acequia Madre. Alice Corbin. NP
On the Advantages of Travel. *Unknown.* CAG
On the Altai. Aleksandr Yashin, *tr. fr. Russian by* Jack Lindsay. RuPo
On the Anniversary of the Storming of the Bastille, at Paris, July 14th, 1789. Philip Freneau. AmPP (3d ed.); CoBA; IAP
On the Annunciation. *Unknown, tr. fr. Greek by* Shane Leslie. ISi
On the Annunciation of Fra Angelico. Manuel Machado, *tr. fr. Spanish by* Thomas Walsh. CAW
On the Antiquity of Microbes. Strickland Gillilan. PIAE; WhC
(Lines on the Antiquity of Microbes.) InP; PreP
On the Approach of Summer, *sel.* Thomas Warton, the Younger.
Sunshine after a Shower. OTPC
On the Aristocracy of Harvard ("Here's to good old Boston"). John Collins Bossidy. *See* Boston Toast, A.
On the Aristocracy of Harvard ("I come from good olde Boston"). *At. to* Samuel C. Bushnell. BOHV. *See also* Boston Toast, A.
On the Army of Spartans, Who Died at Thermopylae. Simonides. *See* Thermopylae.
On the Assumption [of the Virgin Mary]. Richard Crashaw. *See* On the Glorious Assumption of Our Blessed Lady.
On the Asylum Road. Charlotte Mew. MoBrPo (1950 ed.)
On the Atchafalaya. Longfellow. *Fr.* Evangeline, Pt. II. AA
On the Bad Government of Toledo. Gómez Manrique, *tr. fr. Spanish by* Thomas Walsh. WoL
On the Banisters. Margaret E. Gibbs. BoTP
On the Bank as I Sat a-Fishing. Sir Henry Wotton. *See* On a Bank as I Sat a-Fishing.
On the bank of a clear spring. Ballad of Our Lady. *Tr. by* Mary Austin. APW
On the bank the maiden sat. Trouble Not the Maiden's Soul. Johan Ludvig Runeberg. AnSL; LiTW
On the bank worn bare. Summer—Noon. Thomas Gisborne. *Fr.* Walks in a Forest. EnSW
On the banks of Allan Water. Allan Water. Matthew Gregory Lewis. HBV; OTPC (1923 ed.)
On the banks of Shannon when Sheelah was nigh. *See* On the green banks . . .
On the Banks of the Old Pedee. *Unknown.* ABS
On the Banks of the Wabash, Far Away. Paul Dresser. PoRL
On the banks of the Xenil the dark Spanish maiden. The Pumpkin. Whittier. DD; LPS-2; OHIP; TOAH
On the Banks uv the Ole Tennessee, *with music. Unknown.* StDa
On the Baptized Ethiopian [*or* Aethiopian]. Richard Crashaw. SeCV-1; SeEP
On the barren south hill. The Cow-Feeders' Song. *Unknown. Fr.* The Fountain of Old Poems. WhP
On the Beach. Manuel Altolaguirre, *tr. fr. Spanish by* Eleanor L. Turnbull. CoSP
On the Beach. Charles Stuart Calverley. ALV; FiBHP
On the Beach. Cale Young Rice. VOD
On the Beach. Emilie Blackmore Stapp. GFA
On the Beach. Arthur Symons. PoVP
On the Beach at Calais. Wordsworth. *See* It Is a Beauteous Evening, Calm and Free.
On the Beach at Fontana. James Joyce. AnEnPo; LO; MBP; MoBrPo; NP; OBMV; TwCV
On the Beach at Night. Walt Whitman. AmPo; AmPP (4th ed.); APW; AWP; BLV; BoLiVe; ChTr; InPo; MAP; MoAmPo; MOAP; NeMA; NePA; OBVV; OxBA
On the beryl-rimmed rebecs of Ruby. Lily Adair. Thomas Holley Chivers. SPP
On the Big Horn. Whittier. PAH
On the Birth of a Child. Louis Untermeyer. CP; NeMA
On the Birth of His Son. Su T'ung-po, *tr. fr. Chinese by* Arthur Waley. AWP; FAOV; JAWP; LiTW; OnPM; TrCh; WBP; WoL
On the Birthday of a Young Lady. William Whitehead. OTPC (1923 ed.)
On the black and one-armed gibbet flaunt. Gibbet Dance. Arthur Rimbaud. TrFP
On the Bleeding Wounds of Our Crucified Lord. Richard Crashaw. SeCV-1
(Upon the Bleeding Crucifix, *later vers.*)
"Jesu, no more! It is full tide," *sel.* TrGrPo
On the Blessed Virgin's Bashfulness. Richard Crashaw. EnLi-1; ISi; OAEP
On the bloody field of Monmouth. Molly Maguire at Monmouth. William Collins. IDAH; OTPC; PaA; PAP
On the blue plains in wintry days. Native Companions Dancing. John Shaw Neilson. NeLNL
On the bluff of the Little Big Horn. Miles Keogh's Horse. John Hay. PAH; PoOW
On the Boulevard. Stepan Petrovich Shchipachev, *tr. fr. Russian by* Babette Deutsch. TrRV
On the Breaking-up of a School. Tadhg O'g O'Huiginn, *tr. fr. Late Middle Irish by* Osborn Bergin. AnIL; SiB
On the Bridge. Kate Greenaway. MCCG; MPB; RAR; SAS
On the Bridge. Arthur Reed Ropes. VA
On the Bridge of Athlone; a Prophecy. Donagh MacDonagh. OxBI
On the Brink. Charles Stuart Calverley. VA
On the Brink of Death. Michelangelo, *tr. fr. Italian by* John Addington Symonds. AWP; JAWP; WBP
(His Great Love on High.) OnPM
On the British Invasion. Philip Freneau. PAH
On the British King's Speech. Philip Freneau. PAH
On the Building of Springfield. Vachel Lindsay. AmPP (3d ed.); InP; LBMV; MOAP; NAMP; OHFP; PaA; TOP; WHA
On the Burial of His Brother. Catullus, *tr. fr. Latin by* Aubrey Beardsley. AWP; EnLi-1; JAWP; OuHeWo; WBP
(Hail and Farewell.) LiA
On the Bust of Helen by Canova. Byron. EmBrPo
On the calm black wave where the stars sleep. Ophelia. Arthur Rimbaud. AnFP

On the Campagna. Elizabeth Stoddard. AA
On the Capture of the *Guerrière*. Philip Freneau. GA; PAH
On the Castle of Chillon. Byron. *See* Sonnet on Chillon.
On the Cenotaph of One Lost at Sea. Glaucus, *tr. fr. Greek by* F. L. Lucas. GrPE
On the Charlie So Long, *with music*. *Unknown*. AS
On the charred earth of Psara. The Destruction of Psara. Dionysios Solomos. MoGP
On the Choice of His Sepulchre. Pierre de Ronsard, *tr. fr. French by* Alan Conder. Odes, IV, 4. TrFP
("O caves, and you, O springs," *tr. by* Curtis Hidden Page.) PrPoCR
(Of the Choice of His Burial-Place, *tr. by* John Payne.) LiA
On the Cliff. Hal Summers. ChMP
On the Cliffs. Swinburne. BPN; EmBrPo
Sappho, *sel*. GTML; VA
On the Coast of Coromandel. Sir Osbert Sitwell. MoBrPo; MoP; SeCePo
On the Coast of Coromandel. The Courtship of the Yonghy-Bonghy-Bo [*or* The Yonghy-Bonghy Bo]. Edward Lear. BOHV; BoN; EnLoPo; GoTP; HBV; LBN; NA; OTPC
On the Coincidence of the Feasts of the Annunciation and the Resurrection in 1627. Sir John Beaumont. ACP (1926 ed.)
On the Collar of a Dog [Presented by Mr. Pope to the Prince of Wales]. Pope. *See* Epigram: "I am his Highness' dog at Kew."
On the Coming of Age of a Rich, Extravagant Young Man. Samuel Johnson. *See* One-and-twenty.
On the Couch. Oscar Williams. WaP
On the Countess Dowager of Pembroke. William Browne, *wr. at. to* Ben Jonson. BEL, *abr.*; CaAE; EG, *abr.*; EnLi-1; EPP, *abr.*; EV-2; InvP; PoEL-2; SeCeV; SeEP; TriL; UnPo (1st ed.)
(Epitaph: "Underneath this sable hearse," *abr.*) OBEV
(Epitaph of the Countess Dowager of Pembroke.) LEAP
(Epitaph on the Countess Dowager of Pembroke.) BoFr; CenL, *abr.*; CoEV, *abr.*; HBV; LoBV, *abr.*; OBS, *abr.*
(Epitaph on the Countess of Pembroke.) BCEP; LPS-3; MyFE, *abr.*
(On the Countess of Pembroke.) AWP; ElSeCe; JAWP; TOP; TreFS, *abr.*; WBP; WoL
(On the Death of Marie, Countess of Pembroke.) OnPP; ReEn; SeCL; WHA
(On the Dowager Countess of Pembroke.) ViBoPo
("Underneath this sable hearse.") InP
On the craggy mountain-top the mist. Majuba Hill. Roy Macnab. BoSA
On the Creation and Ontogony. *Unknown*, *tr. fr. Lenape Indian by* C. S. Rafinesque. *Fr.* Wallam Olum. LiTA
On the crimson edge of the eve. A Damascus Nightingale. Stephen Crombie. BLA
On the crooked arm of Columbus, on his cloak. Pigeons. Alastair Reid. NePoEA; SiTL
On the cross-beams, under the Old South bell. The Belfry Pigeon. N. P. Willis. LPS-2
On the Crucifix. Michelangelo, *tr. fr. Italian by* Longfellow. CAW
On the Crucifixion. Giles Fletcher. *Fr.* Christ's Victory and Triumph. OxBoCh
On the Danger of War. George Meredith. CoBE; EmBrPo; EPN
On the dark hill's western side. Evening Hymn. Cecil Frances Alexander. OTPC (1923 ed.)
On the dark wings of the cutting blast. In the Wet Shadows. Ramón López Velarde. AnMP
On the Daughter of Hippias, Son of Pisistratus. Simonides. *See* Archedike.
On the Day after Christmas. Franklin P. Adams. PIAE
On the day of cold food. Spring Sun. Chu Hsi. OnPC
On the Day of Judgement. Swift. *See* Day of Judgement, The.
On the Day of Judgement. Thomas of Celano. *See* Dies Irae.
On the day that Christ ascended. The Anger of Christ. Richard Watson Gilder. StJW
On the day when I stopped begging at the heels of life. The Bell. James Rorty. BLP; PC
On the day when the lotus bloomed. Rabindranath Tagore. Gitanjali, XX. NP; NV
On the Dead. Walter Savage Landor. TriL
On the Death of a Cat, a Friend of Mine Aged Ten Years and a Half. Christina Rossetti. CIV; PoC
On the Death of a Certain Journal. Charles Kingsley. BMEP
On the Death of a Child. Edward Silvera. PoNe
On the Death of a Favorite Canary. Matthew Arnold. *Fr.* Poor Matthias. BLA; PC
(Atossa.) PoC
("Poor Matthias! Wouldst thou have.") CIV
On the Death of a Favorite Cat. *Unknown*. CIV
On the Death of a Favorite Cat, Drowned in a Tub of Gold-fishes. Thomas Gray. *See* Ode on the Death of a Favorite Cat . . .
On the Death of a Friend's Child, *sel*. James Russell Lowell.
" 'Tis sorrow builds the shining ladder up." MaRV
On the Death of a Journalist. Roy Campbell. CoBE
On the Death of a Kinsman. James Matthew Legaré. SPP
On the Death of a Lady's Owl. Moses Mendes. TrJP
On the Death of a Metaphysician. George Santayana. AA; AnFE; APA; CoAnAm; LEAP; MAP; MoAmPo; OBAV; ViBoPo
On the Death of a Monkey. Thomas Heyrick. MePo
On the Death of a New Born Child. Mei Yao Ch'en, *tr. fr. Chinese by* Kenneth Rexroth. OnPC
On the Death of a Particular Friend. James Thomson. *See* Verses Occasioned by the Death of Dr. Aikman.
On the Death of a Pious Lady. Olof Wexionius, *tr. fr. Swedish by* Sir Edmund Gosse. AWP; JAWP; WBP
On the Death of a Recluse. George Darley. GTIV; OBVV; OxBI; TriL
On the Death of a Young and Favorite Slave. Martial, *tr. fr. Latin by* Goldwin Smith. AWP; JAWP; LiTW; WBP
On the Death of a Young Girl. Evariste de Parny, *tr. fr. French by* Alan Conder. TrFP
On the Death of Amalia Riznich. Pushkin. *See* Beneath Her Native Skies.
On the Death of an Acquaintance. Oscar Williams. Variations on a Theme, I. LiTA; NePA
On the Death of an Aged Friend. Roselle Mercier Montgomery. MaRV
On the Death of Anne Brontë. Charlotte Brontë. ViBoPo
On the Death of Arnold Toynbee. John William Mackail. PoeT
On the Death of Beatrice. Dante, *tr. fr. Italian by* Dante Gabriel Rossetti. *Fr.* La Vita Nuova. MeRV
("Weep, lovers, sith Love's very self doth weep.") AWP
On the Death of Beatrice: The Dream. Dante, *tr. fr. Italian by* Dante Gabriel Rossetti. *Fr.* La Vita Nuova. MeRV
On the Death of Benjamin Franklin. Philip Freneau. *See* On the Death of Dr. Benjamin Franklin.
On the Death of Captain Nicholas Biddle. Philip Freneau. PAH
On the Death of Catarina de Attayda. Luís de Camões, *tr. fr. Portuguese by* R. F. Burton. AWP; JAWP; WBP
On the Death of Charles I. James Graham, Marquess of Montrose. *See* Epitaph on King Charles I.
On the Death of Commodore Oliver H. Perry. John Gardiner Calkins Brainard. GA; PAH
On the Death of Crashaw. Abraham Cowley. *See* On the Death of Mr. Crashaw.
On the Death of Decatur, *abr.* William Crafts. GA
On the Death of Dr. Benjamin Franklin. Philip Freneau. BAV; BoHiPo; MOAP
(On the Death of Benjamin Franklin.) DD; GA; PAH
On the Death of Dr. Robert Levett. Samuel Johnson. *See* On the Death of Mr. Robert Levet, a Practiser in Physic.
On the Death of Doctor Swift. Swift. *See* Verses on the Death of Dr. Swift.
On the Death of Francis Thompson. Alfred Noyes. OBVV
On the Death of Garcilaso. Juan Boscán Almogáver, *tr. fr. Spanish by* J. H. Wiffen. BoFr
On the Death of His Baby Son. Su T'ung-po, *tr. fr. Chinese by* Kenneth Rexroth. OnPC
On the Death of His Child. Faydi, *tr. fr. Persian by* Edward G. Browne. LiTW
On the Death of His Child. Okura, *tr. fr. Japanese by* Mabel Lorenz Ives. PFE
On the Death of His Father. Wei Wen-ti, *tr. fr. Chinese by* Arthur Waley. TrCh
On the Death of His Son. Lewis Glyn Cothi, *tr. fr. Welsh by* Gwyn Williams. LyMA
On the Death of His Son Vincent. Leigh Hunt. ERP
On the Death of His Wife. Ibn al-Hammara, *tr. fr. Arabic by* A. J. Arberry. MooP
On the Death of His Wife. Mei Yao Ch'en, *tr. fr. Chinese by* Kenneth Rexroth. OnPC
On the Death of Jackson. *Unknown*. PAH
On the Death of Joseph Rodman Drake. Fitz-Greene Halleck. AA; AnAmPo; BAP; BAV; DD; DDA; GA; HBV; IAP; LA; LBAP; MaRV; OBAV; PAH; PoEL-4; TCAP; TreFS
(Elegy in Memory of Joseph Rodman Drake.) BoHiPo
(Joseph Rodman Drake.) BLPA; LPS-3
(On His Friend, Joseph Rodman Drake, *st.* 1.) OBVV
On the Death of King Charles I. James Graham, Marquess of Montrose. *See* Epitaph on King Charles I.
On the Death of Little Mahala Ashcraft. James Whitcomb Riley. AA; OBAV
On the Death of Mlle de Conty. François de Malherbe, *tr. fr. French by* J. G. Legge. LiA
On the Death of M. d'Ossoli and His Wife, Margaret Fuller. Walter Savage Landor. PAH; VA

On the Death of Marie, Countess of Pembroke. William Browne. *See* On the Countess Dowager of Pembroke.
On the Death of Mary. Rainer Maria Rilke, *tr. fr. German by* M. D. Herter Norton. ISi
On the Death of Mr. Crashaw. Abraham Cowley. AEV; EPS; MeLP; MePo; NBE; OBS; PtP; SeCV-1; SeEP; ViBoPo
(On the Death of Crashaw.) GoBC
On the Death of Mr. Purcell. Dryden. UnS
On the Death of Mr. Richard West. Thomas Gray. *See* Sonnet on the Death of Richard West.
On the Death of Mr. Robert Levet [*or* Levett], a Practiser in Physic. Samuel Johnson. BCEP; CBOV; CEP; EiPP; EV-3; HBV; OBEC; OBEV; PoE; PoFS
(Dr. Levett.) BHV
(Lines on the Death of Mr. Levett.) FaBoEn
(On the Death of Dr. Robert Levet.) PoEL-3; TriL
(Quiet Life, The.) LH
"In Misery's darkest cavern known," *sel.* ViBoPo
On the Death of Mr. William Aikman the Painter, *sel.* James Thomson.
Verses Occasioned by the Death of Dr. Aikman. CoEV; OBEC
(Finis: "As those we love decay.") BSV
(On the Death of a Particular Friend.) OBEV
On the Death of Mr. William Hervey. Abraham Cowley. BoFr; CoEV; EPS; EV-2; GTSL; OBEV, *abr.*; OBS, *abr.*; SeCV-1; SeEP
"It was a dismal and a fearful night," *sel.* ViBoPo
On the Death of Mrs. Browning. Sydney Dobell. VA
On the Death of Mrs. Elizabeth Filmer, *abr.* Richard Lovelace. EV-2
On the Death of Mrs. (now Lady) Throckmorton's Bullfinch. William Cowper. EV-3; HBV
On the Death of My Child. Joseph von Eichendorff, *tr. fr. German.* AnGP, *tr. by* Kate Flores; UnW, *tr. by* Karl Vogel
On the Death of My Son Charles. Daniel Webster. AA; LEAP
On the Death of Phillips. *Unknown.* OBSC
On the Death of President Garfield. Oliver Wendell Holmes. GA, *abr.*; PAH
On the Death of Pushkin. Mikhail Yurevich Lermontov, *tr. fr. Russian by* Martha Dickinson Bianchi. PoFr
On the Death of Pym. William Drummond of Hawthornden. ALV
On the Death of Richard West. Thomas Gray. *See* Sonnet on the Death of Richard West.
On the Death of Robert Browning. Swinburne. A Sequence of Sonnets on the Death of Robert Browning, VII. EmBrPo; EnLit; EPN; PoVP; VLEP
("He held no dream worth waking: so he said.") BPN
On the Death of Roger Casement. Padraic Colum. PoFr
On the Death of Sir Albert Morton's Wife. Sir Henry Wotton. *See* Upon the Death . . .
On the Death of Sir Philip Sidney. Henry Constable. GoBC; OBEV; PtP
(On Sir Philip Sidney.) OBSC
(To Sir Philip Sidney's Soul.) ElL; ES; SeCePo
On the Death of Sir Thomas Wyatt [the Elder]. Earl of Surrey. BEL; EnLi-1 (1949 ed.); GoTL; PtP
(Of the Death of Sir Thomas Wyatt [the Elder].) FaBoEn; ReIE; SiCE; TuPP
(Tribute to Wyatt, A.) EnLit; SiPS
("Wyatt resteth here, that quick could never rest.") ReEn
On the Death of Southey ("It was a dream"). Walter Savage Landor. BPN
On the Death of Southey ("Not the last struggles of the Sun"). Walter Savage Landor. OBVV; TriL
On the Death of the Emperor Henry VII. Cino da Pistoia, *tr. fr. Italian by* L. R. Lind. LyPI
On the Death of the Noble Prince King Edward the Fourth. John Skelton. ReIE
On the Death of Tibullus. Domitius Marsus, *tr. fr. Latin by* Hubert Creekmore. LaP
On the Deaths of Thomas Carlyle and George Eliot. Swinburne. BEL; BMEP; BPN; EmBrPo; HBV; PoVP; TOP; VA; VLEP
On the Deception of Appearances. Sadi, *tr. fr. Persian by* L. Cranmer-Byng. *Fr.* The Gulistan. AWP; LiTW
On the deck of Patrick Lynch's boat I sat in woeful plight. The County of Mayo. *At. to* Thomas Flavell [*or* Lavelle], *tr. by* George Fox. AnIV; GTIV; IrPN; OBEV; OnYI; OxBI; TIP
On the Defeat at Ticonderoga or Carilong. *Unknown.* PAH
On the Defeat of Henry Clay. William Wilberforce Lord. GA; PAH
(On the Defeat of a Great Man.) AA
On the Defeat of Ragnall by Murrough King of Leinster A.D. 994. *Unknown, tr. fr. Middle Irish by* Kuno Meyer. OnYI
(Murrough Defeats the Danes, 994, *tr. by* Frank O'Connor. KiLC
On the Democracy of Yale. Frederick Scheetz Jones. BOHV; HBV; WhC; YaD
(New Haven.) BoHiPo
(To New Haven.) TreFS
On the Departure of Sir Walter Scott from Abbotsford, for Naples. Wordsworth. EnRP
On the Departure of the British from Charleston. Philip Freneau. PAH
On the Departure Platform. Thomas Hardy. ChMo; CMP; LO
On the desert, between pale mountains, our cries. Two Songs of Advent. Yvor Winters. NP
On the Detraction Which Followed upon My Writing Certain Treatises ("A book was writ of late"). Milton. EM-1; SeCeV
On the Detraction Which Followed upon My Writing Certain Treatises ("I did but prompt the age"). Milton. ATP; CaAE; ExPo; MaPo; PeBoSo; TOP
(On the Same.) EM-1; SeCeV
(Second Sonnet on "Tetrachordon.") PoFr
On the Discoveries of Captain Lewis. Joel Barlow. GA; MC; PAH
On the door a thick and heavy curtain. The Steps of the Commander. Aleksandr Blok. BoR
On the Doorstep. Thomas Hardy. MoVE
On the Dowager Countess of Pembroke. William Browne. *See* On the Countess Dowager of Pembroke.
On the Downtown Side of an Uptown Street. William Johnston. BOHV
On the Dunes. Sara Teasdale. NP; TCAP
On the dusty earth-drum. Rain Music. Joseph S. Cotter, Jr. BANP; BrR; CDC; PCH
On the dyke there are magpies' nests. Forsworn. *Unknown. Fr.* Shi King. ChLP
On the Earl of Strafford's Trial and Death. John Denham. LoBV
On the Eastern Way at the city of Lo-yang. Song. Sung Tzu-hou. TrCh
On the edge of a lawn where weeds. The Death of a Dove. James Schevill. FiMAP
On the Edge of the Copper Pit. Pauline Henson. GoYe
On the Edge of the Pacific. Theodore Maynard. CAW
On the 18th of April in '28. Happy Lifetime to You. Franklin P. Adams. InMe
On the eighteenth of September in eighteen seventy three. The Winter of '73. Larry Gorman. ShS
On the eighth day God died: his bearded mouth. The Worms of History. Robert Graves. MoPo
On the eighth day of March it was, some people say. The Birth of Saint Patrick. Samuel Lover. BOHV; DD; HBV; LPS-3; PoRL
On the Elgin Marbles. Keats. *See* On Seeing the Elgin Marbles.
On the Embankment. W. W. Gibson. PoFr; POTT
On the Emigration to America. Philip Freneau. AmPP (3d ed.); CoV; MOAP; PAH
On the Emperor's Departure, December 7, 1812. Gavril Derzhavin, *tr. fr. Russian by* Babette Deutsch. TrRV
On the Eta, the Untouchables. Issa, *tr. fr. Japanese by* Max Bickerton. PoFr
On the Eve of All Hallows. Arthur L. Phelps. CPG
On the Eve of Bunker Hill. Clinton Scollard. *See* Eve of Bunker Hill, The.
On the Eve of Departure. Juan Ramón Jiménez, *tr. fr. Spanish by* Eleanor L. Turnbull. TeCS
On the Eve of His Execution. Chidiock Tichborne. *See* Elegy: "My prime of youth . . ."
On the Eve of New Wars. Louis Untermeyer. MAP
On the Eve of the Feast of the Immaculate Conception, 1942. Robert Lowell. WaaP
On the Eve of War. Danske Dandridge. BoHiPo; PAH
On the evening of a day on the threshold of summer. The Unattained. David Gascoyne. MoP
On the Execution of Mary, Queen of Scots. Robert Southwell. *Fr.* At Fotheringay. MeRV
On the Extinction of the Venetian Republic. Wordsworth. BEL; BoLiVe; BPN; CaAE; CBOV; EM-2; EmBrPo; EnL; EnLi-2; EnLit; EnLP; EnRP; EPN; EPP; ERP; ES; EV-3; GEPC; GTBS; GTBS-D; GTBS-W; GTSE; GTSL; HBV; LoBV; MCCG; OAEP; OBEV; OBRV; OuHeWo; PeBoSo; PoFr; ReaPo; TCEP; TOP; TrGrPo; ViBoPo
(Venice.) LH
On the far reef the breakers. The Tide Will Win. Priscilla Leonard. MaRV
On the farm it never mattered. The Assistance. Paul Blackburn. NeAP
On the Fasting Monk Chu Chuan. Po Chü-i, *tr. fr. Chinese by* Ching Ti. WhP
On the Feast of the Assumption. Eleanor Downing. JKCP
On the Ferry. Douglas V. Kane. MuM
On the fifth day after the rise of Spring. Parting from the Winter Stove. Po Chü-i. TrCh
On the Firs. Nikolai Alekseyevich Kluyev, *tr. fr. Russian by* Babette Deutsch. TrRV

On the first day of snow, my train. Letter VIII. Randall Swingler. WaP
On the first day of the week cometh Mary Magdalene. St. John, Bible, *N.T.* LO
On the first day, the lifted siege at last. A Death in Hospital. John Lehmann. AtBAP; ChMP
On the first Easter, ere the harbinger. Mary. Nellie Knight. ChIP
On the first hour of my first day. The Beginner. Kipling. *Fr.* Epitaphs of the War. FaBoTw; LiA
On the first of March. The Crows. *Unknown.* OxNR; RIS
On the first of the feast of feasts. Epilogue. Robert Browning. ViPo
On the first summer day I lay in the valley. On the Third Day. Stephen Spender. NeBP
On the Fitness of Seasons. Enzo, King of Sardinia, *tr. fr. Italian by* Dante Gabriel Rossetti. OnPM
On the Flightiness of Thought. *Unknown, tr. fr. Middle Irish by* Kuno Meyer. OnYI
On the floor of the low, white-clouded seas. Glints of the Year—from a Window. Thomas Caulfield Irwin. IrPN
On the Fly-Leaf of a Book of Old Plays. Walter Learned. *See* On a Fly-Leaf of a Book of Old Plays.
On the Fly-Leaf of Manon Lescaut. Walter Learned. AA
On the forest laces morning's pink is shed. A Russian Song. "Igor Severyanin." TrRV
On the fourteenth of April we sailed from England. The Fair *Princess Royal. Unknown.* SoAmSa
On the fourteenth of April we sailed from the strand. The Bold *Princess Royal, vers.* I. *Unknown.* ShS
On the Frontier. Nathaniel Micklem. NeTW
On the Frozen Lake. Wordsworth. *Fr.* The Prelude, I. FaBoCh; LoGBV
("And in the frosty season, when the sun.") InP; MyFE; PoMa
(Skating.) CH; GN; GoTP; ShBV-3
On the Future of Poetry. Austin Dobson. PoVP; VLEP
On the Gift of a Cloak. Hugo Primas of Orléans, *tr. fr. Latin by* George F. Whicher. LaP
On the Glorious Assumption of Our Blessed Lady. Richard Crashaw. ISi; OBS; PoLi
(In the Glorious Assumption of Our Blessed Lady.) LoBV
(On the Assumption [of the Virgin Mary].) AEV; ElSeCe
On the Goodness of the Supreme Being, *sel.* Christopher Smart.
Kneel to the Lord. BeR
On the Gout. Guillaume de Chaulieu, *tr. fr. French by* Alan Conder. TrFP
On the Grand Canal. David Gascoyne. SeCePo
On the Grasshopper and Cricket. Leigh Hunt. *See* To the Grasshopper and the Cricket.
On the Grasshopper and Cricket. Keats. BLV; BoLiVe; BPN; EmBrPo; EnL; EnLi-2; EnLit; EnRP; EPN; ERP; ES; EV-4; ExPo; FaBoBe; GN; GoTP; HBV; HiLiEn; InP; InPo; LiTB; OuHeWo; PIAE; PIR; SeCeV; TCEP; TrGrPo
(Grasshopper and the Cricket, The.) BCEP; BoTP; EPP; LPS-2; OTPC; TVSH
(Poetry of Earth [Is Never Dead], The.) GTBS-W; LiTG
(Sonnet: On the Grasshopper and Cricket.) GEPC
On the Grassy Banks. Christina Rossetti. *Fr.* Sing-Song. RAR; UTS
(Lambs at Play.) BoTP
(Woolly Lambkins.) StVeCh
On the Great Plateau. Edith Franklin Wyatt. HBMV; NP; NV
On the green banks [*or* the banks] of Shannon when Sheelah was nigh. The Harper [*or* Poor Dog Tray *or* The Irish Harper and His Dog]. Thomas Campbell. AlBD; CG; CH; ERP; GoTP; MPB
On the green hills a herd of horses strays. The Herd of Horses. Sergei Yesenin. BoR
On the greening grasses. Cantiga de Amigo. Pero Meogo. LyMA
On the grey sand beside the shallow stream. Ego Dominus Tuus. W. B. Yeats. ChMo; CMP; NP
On the Head of a Stag. Edmund Waller. Po
On the Hearth-Rug. Mary Elizabeth Coleridge. CBE
On the Heart's Beginning to Cloud the Mind. Robert Frost. ChMo
On the Height. Eunice Tietjens. HBMV; NP
On the Heights. Basho, *tr. fr. Japanese by* H. G. Henderson. OnPM
On the Heights. Edward Dowden. TIP
On the Heights. Lucius Harwood Foote. AA
On the heights of great endeavor. Attainment. Madison Cawein. WGRP
On the heights of Killiecrankie. The Battle of Killiecrankie. William E. Aytoun. TVSH
On the Heights of Mission Ridge. J. Augustine Signaigo. BlG
On the Hellenics. Walter Savage Landor. *Fr.* The Hellenics. BEL; BPN; EmBrPo; EnRP; EPN; ERP
(Proem to Hellenics.) ViBoPo
On the helpless Flemish village. How the Ransom Was Paid. *Unknown.* PEOR
On the High Cost of Dairy Products. James McIntyre. FiBHP
On the high hill pastures. Wild Thyme. Joyce Sambrook. BoTP
On the hill of weeping. The Two Mothers. Shane Leslie. ISi
On the hill to the south of the city. The Charcoal-Burner. Po Chü-i. WhP
On the holiest day of the holy seven. Good Friday's Hoopoe. Douglas Ainslie. EBSV
On the Home Guards. Herman Melville. SoV
On the Hon. Simon Harcourt. Pope. OnPM; WoL
On the horizon rises holy night. Feodor Tyutchev, *tr. fr. Russian by* C. M. Bowra. BoR
On the horizon the peaks assembled. Stephen Crane. The Black Riders, XXXVII. MOAP
On the horses of desire. The Rider. John Cowper Powys. BAP
On the hottest day of the year I rode the mail. The Insult. Robert Layzer. NePoEA
On the Hurry of This Time. Austin Dobson. HBV; PoVP
On the Idle Hill of Summer. A. E. Housman. A Shropshire Lad, XXXV. BPN; MBP; MoBrPo; NeMA; OAEP (2d ed.); OuHeWo; PoVP
On the Infancy of our Saviour. Francis Quarles. AnEC; ElSeCe; OBS; OxBoCh; SeCePo; SeCL
(Child Jesus, The.) StJW
On the Ingenious Mr. Jones's Elegant Translations and Imitations of Eastern Poetry, and His Resolution to Decline Translating the Persian Poets. John Scott of Amwell. PtP
On the island of Skip-scoop-anellie. Skip-Scoop-Anellie. Tom Prideaux. FiBHP
On the isle of Pago Pago, land of palm trees, rice and sago. Rain. Newman Levy. BOHV
On the isle of Penikese. The Prayer of Agassiz. Whittier. IAP; LPS-3
On the itching back. Teemothy Hatch. Wilson MacDonald. WhC
On the Just and the Unjust. Blanche Edith Baughan. BoAu
On the Lacadaemonian Dead at Plataea. Simonides. *See* Spartan Monument, The.
On the Lake. V. Sackville-West. ChMP; MoVE; OBMV
On the large highway of the awful air that flows. The Fish-Hawk. John Hall Wheelock. AnAmPo; BLA; BLV; EtS; HBMV; LA; NV; PoeMoYo
On the Last Verses in His Book of Poems. Edmund Waller. *See* Of the Last Verses in the Book.
On the Late Massacre in Piedmont [*or* Piemont]. Milton. ATP; AWP; BEL; CBOV; CoEV; EM-1; EnL; EnLi-1; EnLit; EPP; EPS; ES; EV-2; ExPo; GEPC; GTBS; GTBS-D; GTBS-W; GTSE; GTSL; HBV; InP; InPo; JAWP; LEAP; LiTB; LoBV; MaPo; OAEP; OnPM; OuHeWo; PeBoSo; PIAE; Po; PoFS; ReaPo; RiBV; SeCeV; ShBV-3; TCEP; TOP; TwCrTr; TwHP; UnPo; ViBoPo; WaaP; WBP; WoL
(Avenge, O Lord.) BHV
(Late Massacre in Piedmont.) LH
(On the Late Massacher in Piemont.) KN; PoEL-3
(On the Massacre in Piedmont.) WHA
(Sonnet: Avenge, O Lord Thy Slaughtered Saints.) AEV
(Sonnet: On the Late Massacre in Piedmont.) OBS; SeCL; SeEP
On the Late S. T. Coleridge. Washington Allston. AA
On the Late Successful Expedition against Louisbourg. Francis Hopkinson. PAH
On the Latin Gerunds. Richard Porson. *See* Dido.
On the Lawn. Cametas, *tr. fr. Greek by* Anne Hyde Greet. OnPM
On the Lido. Arthur Hugh Clough. *Fr.* At Venice. ViPo
On the Life-Mask of Abraham Lincoln. Richard Watson Gilder. AA; HBV; LBAH; OBAV; PoRL
On the Life of Man. Francis Bacon. *See* Life.
On the Life of Man. Henry King. *See* Sic Vita.
On the Life of Man. Sir Walter Ralegh. OAEP
(All the World's a Stage.) OBSC
(What Is Our Life?) MePo; RiBV
("What is our life? A play of passion.") CenL; EG; ReEn; SiPS
On the lone bleak moor,/ At the midnight hour. The Hand of Glory. "Thomas Ingoldsby." DaM
On the long dusty ribbon of the long city street. "All Ye That Pass By." John Masefield. ChMo; CMP
On the long shore, lit by the moon. The Goose Fish. Howard Nemerov. FiMAP; NePoEA
On the Lord General Fairfax at the Siege of Colchester. Milton. *See* Fairfax, Whose Name in Arms through Europe Rings.
On the Lord Mayor and Court of Aldermen, Presenting the

On the Lord Mayor and Court of Aldermen (*continued*)
Late King and Duke of York Each with a Copy of Their Freedoms, Anno Dom. 1674. Andrew Marvell. CoMu
On the Loss of His Shield. Archilochus. *See* Poet's Shield, The.
On the Loss of the *Royal George*. William Cowper. AnFE; BEL; CBOV; EPP; EtS; FiP; GN; HBV; InPo; LEAP; LPS-2; MyFE; OAEP; OBEC; SG; TCEP; TrGrPo
(Loss of the *Royal George*, The.) CBE; CG; EV-3; GTBS; GTBS-D; GTBS-W; GTSE; GTSL; MuP; TVSH; WHA
(*Royal George*, The.) LH
(Toll for the Brave.) BHV
On the low wall of my garden. My Sanctuary. Meng Shu Ch'ing. GrCo-2; PoHN
On the marches of Pamplona—out to sun and wind and star. La Preciosa. Thomas Walsh. ISi
On the Margin Wrought. William Drummond of Hawthornden. *See* Book of the World, The.
On the Marriage of a Beauteous Young Gentlewoman with an Ancient Man. Francis Beaumont. LiTL; ViBoPo
On the Marriage of a Virgin. Dylan Thomas. *See* Marriage of a Virgin, The.
On the Massacre in Piedmont. Milton. *See* On the Late Massacre in Piedmont.
On the Memorable Victory by Captain Paul Jones. Philip Freneau. *See Bonhomme Richard* and *Serapis*, The.
On the Memory of Mr. Edward King [Drowned in the Irish Seas]. John Cleveland. EPS (1942 ed.); OBS; SeEP
On the Miracle of Loaves. Richard Crashaw. ACP
On the Mississippi. Hamlin Garland. BAP
On the Mönchsberg. Georg Trakl, *tr. fr. German by* David Luke. AnGP
On the Monument Erected to Mazzini at Genoa. Swinburne. *See* Lines on the Monument of Giuseppe Mazzini.
On the Moor. Cale Young Rice. HBV
On the moor of Kasuga. Hitomaro. *Fr.* Manyo Shu. AWP
On the morning/ sky a stone of sun. The Idol in the Porch. José Juan Tablada. AnMP
On the Morning of Christ's Nativity. Milton. AnFE; AtBAP; BEL; CaAE; CoBE; EPP; ExPo; GEPC; GoTL; HBV; LoGBV; MeLP; OBS; OxBoCh; PoE; PoEL-3; ReaPo; SeCeV; SeEP; TCEP; TOP; TwCrTr; TwHP; UnPo (1st ed.); WGRP
(Ode on the Morning of Christ's Nativity.) GBV, *without hymn;* GTBS; GTBS-D; GTBS-W; GTSL; LiTB; LiTG; MaRV, *abr.;* PoFS
Sels.
Hymn on the Morning of Christ's Nativity. CBE; CBOV; EV-2; MotAn; OBEV; OtMeF, *abr.;* StJW
(Hymn on the Nativity.) COAH
(On the Morning of Christ's Nativity.) FiP; KN
"But peaceful was the night," *sts.* 5–13. FaBoCh
(Peaceful Night, The, *sts.* 5–7.) ChrBoLe; CLS
Hymn: "It was the winter wild," *sts.* 1–23. WHA
(Christmas Hymn, *sts.* 1–13, *abr.*) BCEP
Magi, The, 2 *ll.* ChTr
On the morning of thy birth. Birthday Song. Nahabed Kouchak. ArmLP
On the motionless pond waters. Sedge Songs, III. Nikolaus Lenau. AnGP
On the Mountain. Olive Tilford Dargan. NoCaPo
On the Mountain. M. K. Joseph. AnNZ
On the Mountain. Neidhart von Reuental, *tr. fr. German by* Jethro Bithell. AWP; JAWP; LiTW; LyMA; WBP
On the Mountain of Boiled Rice I met Tu Fu. To Tu Fu. Li Po. WhP
On the mountain peak, called "Going-to-the-Sun." The Apple-Barrel of Johnny Appleseed. Vachel Lindsay. MAP; MoAmPo; NeMA; OxBA
On the mountain peak, called "Going-to-the-Sun." The Comet of Going-to-the-Sun. Vachel Lindsay. ChMo; CMP
On the mountain peak, called "Going-to-the-Sun." Johnny Appleseed Still Further West. Vachel Lindsay. HiLiAm
On the Mountains. Alcman, *tr. fr. Greek by* C. M. Bowra. GrL; LiTW; OxBG
On the mountain's blind and rugged ridge. The Crag. Joaquín Arcadio Pagaza. AnMP
On the mountains of Judea. The Expectation. Frederick William Faber. *Fr.* Our Lady's Expectation. ACP
On the mountains of the prairie. The Peace-Pipe. Longfellow. *Fr.* The Song of Hiawatha. AnNE; IAP
On the Move. Thom Gunn. ShBV-4; UnPo (3d ed.)
On the Muse of Poetry. George Wither. *Fr.* The Shepherd's Hunting. EV-2
On the Nativity of Christ. William Dunbar. *See* Rorate Coeli Desuper.
On the Nativity of Christ Our Lord. Joseph Bennett. NePA
On the Nature of Love. Wilfrid Scawen Blunt. The Love Sonnets of Proteus, XXII. ViBoPo
On the Nature of Things. Lucretius. *See* De Rerum Natura.
On the Needle of a Sundial. Francis Quarles. OBS; TrGrPo
On the New Forcers of Conscience under the Long Parliament. Milton. PoFr
On the night of the Belgian surrender the moon rose. The Moon and the Night and the Men. John Berryman. NeTW; WaP
On the north and south of the house—spring tide. An Unexpected Visit. Tu Fu. OnPM
On the Occident she shed her light. Beauty on a Western Balcony. Luis de Sandoval y Zapata. AnMP
On the ocean that hollows the rocks where ye dwell. O Brazil [*or* Hy-Brasail], the Isle of the Blest. Gerald Griffin. ACP; BLPA; GTIV
On the one hand the steel works. Joliet. Carl Sandburg. CoV
On the Other Train; a Clock's Story. Isaac Hinton Brown. MOAH
On the outermost far-flung ridge of ice and snow. Inspiration. W. W. Gibson. WGRP
On the outside grows the furside. The Sleeping-Bag. Herbert George Ponting. CenHV
On the outskirts of a great city. The Triumph of Civilization. Edward Carpenter. EPP
On the Oxford Book of Victorian Verse. "Hugh MacDiarmid." MoBrPo
On the Oxford Carrier. Milton. BOHV; NA
On the Palisades. Louis Untermeyer. POT; PoTo
On the Parapet of Notre Dame. Charles J. Quirk. *Fr.* Quatrains. CAW
On the Park Bench. Kenneth Slade Alling. NePoAm
On the Passing of My Little Daughter. Joost van den Vondel, *tr. fr. Dutch by* Herbert J. Grierson. EBSV
On the Passing of the Last Fire Horse from Manhattan Island. Kenneth Slade Alling. TBM
On the pavements the sexless toys run down. Fête Champêtre. Kenneth Allott. POTE
On the Photograph of a Lynching. Wendell Phillips Stafford. PoFr
On the Photograph of a Man I Never Saw. Hyam Plutzik. FiMAP
On the Phrase, "To Kill Time." Voltaire, *tr. fr. French.* ALV
On the Picture of a "Child Tired of Play." Nathaniel Parker Willis. HBV
On the Picture of an Infant. Leonidas of Alexandria. *See* On a Picture of an Infant . . .
On the Picture of the Three Fates in the Palazzo Pitti, at Florence. Arthur Henry Hallam. OBRV
On the Pilots Who Destroyed Germany in the Spring of 1945. Stephen Spender. NeBP; Po
On the plain there is the dead hind. The Dead Hind. *Unknown.* ChLP
On the Plains. Francis Brooks. *Fr.* Intaglios. AA
On the Plough-Man. Francis Quarles. OBS
On the Poet O'Shaughnessy. Dante Gabriel Rossetti. *See* Limerick: "There's an Irishman, Arthur O'Shaughnssy."
On the poplars and oaks. The Bard's Song. Sir Robert Stapylton. SeCePo
On the Porch. Harriet Monroe. BAP; NP
On the porch a trooper marvels. The Starling. Aleksandr Trifonovich Tvardovsky. TrRV
On the porch of the three-storied flat. The Next Voice You Hear. Thomas P. McDonnell. JKCP (1955 ed.)
On the Portrait of a Woman About to Be Hanged. Thomas Hardy. ChMo; CMP
On the Portrait of Shakespeare Prefixed to the First Folio Edition, 1623. Ben Jonson. HBV; LEAP; OTPC (1923 ed.)
(On the Portrait of Shakespeare.) EV-2
On the Princess Mary. John Heywood. *See* Praise of His Lady, A.
On the Proposal to Erect a Monument in England to Lord Byron. Emma Lazarus. AA; LBAP
On the Prospect of a Revolution in France. Philip Freneau. IAP
On the Prospect of Planting Arts and Learning in America. George Berkeley. FaFP; HBS; LPS-2; OnYI; SeCeV; TreF; TrGrPo
(Verses on the Prospect of Planting Arts and Learning in America.) CEP; CoBE; EiPP; OBEC; Po; PoE; SeCePo; ViBoPo
Sels.
America. BeR
"Westward the course of empire takes its way." BCEP
On the Quay. John Jay Bell. HBV
On the Queen's Return from the Low Countries. William Cartwright. MePo; OBEV
On the Receipt of My Mother's Picture Out of Norfolk. William Cowper. AEV; BCEP; BEL; CEP; CoBE; EiPP; EM-1; EnLi-2 (1949 ed.); EnLit; EnRP; EPP; EV-3; FiP; HBV; MotAn; OAEP; OBEC; PoE; TCEP; TOP
(Lines on Receiving His Mother's Picture, *abr.*) CH; OHIP
(My Mother's Picture.) LPS-1; MOAH
Sels.
Contrast in Styles, A, 10 *ll.* ShGoBo
"Could Time, his flight reversed, restore the hours." WHA

On the Recent Sale by Auction of Keats's Love-Letters. Oscar Wilde. BMEP; LBBV; LEAP
(On the Sale by Auction of Keats' Love Letters.) AnEnPo
On the Reed of Our Lord's Passion. William Alabaster. PoEL-2
On the Relative Merit of Friend and Foe, Being Dead. Donald Thompson. WaP
On the Religion of Nature. Philip Freneau. AmPP; CoBA; Po
On the Religious Memory of Mrs. Catherine Thomson. Milton. ES; PeBoSo
(Sonnet XIV: On the Religious Memorie of Mrs. Catherine Thomason My Christian Friend Deceas'd Decem. 1646.) OBS
On the Reported New Outbreak of Christianity. James H. McCabe. JKCP (1955 ed.)
On the Resurrection of Christ. William Dunbar. *See* Of the Resurrection of Christ.
On the Reverend Jonathan Doe. *Unknown.* ChTr
On the Rhine. Matthew Arnold. LO
On the Rhine. William Lisle Bowles. LPS-2
On the Rising Generation. Howard Dietz. ALV
On the Road. Paul Laurence Dunbar. AA
On the Road. W. W. Gibson. HiLiEn
On the Road. Tudor Jenks. NA
On the Road. John Oxenham. StJW
On the Road. Sir Charles G. D. Roberts. CPG
On the Road. Ivan Sergeyevich Turgenev, *tr. fr. Russian by* Sir Cecil Kisch. WaL
On the road over head. An Old Waterford Woman. Mary Devenport O'Neill. NeIP
On the road, the lonely road. The Stab. Will Wallace Harney. AA; BTP
On the Road to Anster Fair. William Tennant. *Fr.* Anster Fair. OBRV
On the Road to Arden. T. A. Daly. LHV
On the Road to Chorrera. Arlo Bates. AA
On the Road to Emmaus. St. Luke, XXIV: 13–36, Bible, *N.T.* TreFS
On the Road to Mandalay. Kipling. *See* Mandalay.
On the road to Raffydiddle. The Road to Raffydiddle. Mildred Plew Meigs. GoBP; TiPo (1952 ed.)
On the Road to the Sovkoz. Stepan Shchipachev, *tr. fr. Russian by* Jack Lindsay. RuPo
On the Road to Vicenza. Ralph Gustafson. CaP
On the Road to Woodlawn. Theodore Roethke. FiMAP
On the roads at night I saw the glitter of eyes. Eyes of Night-Time. Muriel Rukeyser. MiAP; NePA
On the roof of a coach at night I lie. Moon Solo. Jules Laforgue. AnFP
On the Ruins of a Country Inn. Philip Freneau. *See* Stanzas Occasioned by the Ruins of a Country Inn . . .
On the Sabbath-day. Barbara. Alexander Smith. BMEP; BSV; GoTS; GTBS; HBV; OBEV (1st ed.); OBVV
On the sacred flame, O Mighty Mystery. Chant for the Moon-of-Flowers. Lew Sarett. NV
On the Safe Side. Lord Dunsany. OxBI
On the Sale by Auction of Keats' Love Letters. Oscar Wilde. *See* On the Recent Sale . . .
On the salt water streets. Venice Recalled. Bruce Boyd. NeAP
On the Same. Roy Campbell. BoSA
On the Same. Milton. *See* On the Detraction Which Followed upon My Writing Certain Treatises ("I did but prompt").
On the school platform, draping the folding seats. Political Meeting. A. M. Klein. BoCaPo (1948 ed.)
On the Sea. Keats. ATP (1935 ed.); BLV; BoLiVe; BPN; CoBE; EM-2; EmBrPo; EnL; EnRP; EPN; EPP; ERP; EV-4; ExPo; GTBS-W; HBV; KN; LiTB; MaPo; MCCG; PeBoSo; PIAE; PreP; SeCeV; TCEP; TrGrPo; TwHP
(Sea, The.) CBE
(Sonnet on the Sea.) EtS; GEPC; SeCePo; SG; ViBoPo
On the sea and at the Hogue, sixteen hundred ninety-two. Hervé Riel. Robert Browning. BEL; BeLS; BPN; FaBoBe; GN; HBV; LH; LPS-2; MCCG; OtMeF; OTPC (1946 ed.); PECK; PoVP; PIR; TCEP; TOP
On the Sea Wall. C. Day Lewis. SeCePo
On the Sea-Shore near Calais. Wordsworth. *See* It Is a Beauteous Evening, Calm and Free.
On the second of October, a Monday at noon. Walter Lesly. *Unknown.* BaBo; ESPB
On the Setting Sun. Sir Walter Scott. MaRV
On the Setting Up [of] Mr. Butler's Monument in Westminster Abbey. Samuel Wesley. ALV; CoEV; InvP; OBEC; WhC
(On Butler's Monument.) BOHV
On the Seventh Anniversary of the Death of My Father. Robert Pack. NePoEA
On the seventh day the storm lay dead. The Dyke-Builder. Henry Treece. LiTB; LiTM; WaP
On the shingle/ Beaten by the waves. Hitomaro, *tr. fr. Japanese by* Kenneth Rexroth. OnPJ
On the shore I watch. Marginal. José María Eguren. AnCL
On the shore of Nawa. Hioki no Ko-Okima. *Fr.* Manyo Shu. AWP
On the shores of Lake Michigan. Children of the Wind. Carl Sandburg. *Fr.* The People, Yes. StVeCh
On the Shores of Tennessee. Ethel Lynn Beers. PTA-1
On the Shortness of Time. Wilfrid Scawen Blunt. The Love Sonnets of Proteus, XCVI. MBP; MoBrPo (1942 ed.)
On the Sicilian strand a hare well wrought. Epigrams. Ausonius. LaP
On the sightless seas of ether. Mikhail Lermontov. *Fr.* The Demon. AWP
On the silk curtain the slanting sun suggests approaching evening. The Silk Curtain. Tu Mu. WhP
On the Siu Cheng Road. Su T'ung-po, *tr. fr. Chinese by* Kenneth Rexroth. OnPC
On the Skeleton of a Hound. James Wright. NePoEA
On the skim of the wharf where the planks split. Bucket of Sea-Serpents. Howard Ant. GoYe
On the Skull of Shakespeare. George Sterling.
"Here an immortal river had its rise," II. PFE
(Skull of Shakespeare, The.) BAP
"Without how small, within how strangely vast," I. PFE
On the Slain at Chickamauga. Herman Melville. *See* Memorials on the Slain at Chickamauga.
On the Sleep of Plants. Philip Freneau. IAP
On the Slope of the Desolate River. Rabindranath Tagore. Gitanjali, LXIV. OBMV
On the small marble-paved platform. Margrave. Robinson Jeffers. ChMo; CMP
On the Smooth Brow and Clustering Hair. Walter Savage Landor. BPN; EmBrPo; EPN
On the Snake. *Unknown.* PAH
On the Snuff of a Candle. Sir Walter Ralegh. SiPS
On the Sonnet. Keats. ERP
(Sonnet Claims More Freedom, The.) ES
On the Soul. Emperor Hadrian. *See* To His Soul.
On the South Coast. Swinburne. EmBrPo
On the South Downs. Sara Teasdale. MAP; MoAmPo; YT
(On the Sussex Downs.) NP
On the Spartans Who Fell at Thermopylae. Simonides. *See* Thermopylae.
On the Speech of Robert Emmet. Robert Southey. *See* Written Immediately after Reading the Speech of Robert Emmet.
On the Stair. Annie Campbell Huestis. UnW
On the Staircase. Eleanor Farjeon. SiSoSe
On the steps, in the corners. The Women Will Soon Knit Again. Roger Burlingame. NeTW
On the Street. Hazel Hall. NP
On the Struma Massacre. Ralph Gustafson. BoCaPo (1948 ed.)
On the Subjugation of Switzerland. Wordsworth. *See* Thought of a Briton on the Subjugation of Switzerland.
On the Sultan Mahmúd. Firdausi, *tr. fr. Persian by* R. A. Nicholson. LiTW
On the Sun Coming Out in the Afternoon. Henry David Thoreau. PoEL-4
On the sun your eyes be closing. The Mountain. Al-Liss. MooP
On the Sunday morning, just at the hour of ten. The *Bigler.* *Unknown.* AmSS
On the sunny hillside sleeping. Beneath the Flag. *Unknown.* FOAH; HH
On the Supernatural. W. W. E. Ross. BoCaPo
On the Sussex Downs. Sara Teasdale. *See* On the South Downs.
On the Swag. R. A. K. Mason. AnNZ
On the Swiss. Wordsworth. *See* Swiss Peasant, The.
On the tallest day in time, the dead came back. V-J Day. John Ciardi. MiAP
On the taut silk-spun strings of high autumn. To the Harp Player. Li Ho. WhP
On the Telescopic Moon. John Swanwick Drennan. IrPN
On the tenth day of December. Musselburgh Field. *Unknown.* ESPB
On the Texas coast. Annie. Guillaume Apollinaire. AnFP
On the Third Day. Stephen Spender. NeBP
On the third day from this (Saint Brendan said). The Burial of Saint Brendan. Padraic Colum. OxBI
On the Thread of the Pale Hour. Léon Paul Fargue, *tr. fr. French by* W. J. Strachan. MiFP
On the Threshold. Augustus Henry Baldwin. HH; PEDC; PEOR
New Year, The, *sel.* DD
On the Threshold. Karl Kraus, *tr. fr. German by* Albert Bloch. TrJP
On the Threshold *Unknown.* BLPA
On the Toilet Table of Queen Marie-Antoinette. J. B. B. Nichols. PoeT
On the Tomb of Bliss Carman. Bliss Carman. *See* Envoy: "Have little care that life is brief."
On the Tomb of Crethis. Callimachus. *See* Crethis.

On the Tomb of Sophocles. Simmias, *tr. fr. Greek.* OnPM
("Wind, gentle evergreen, to form a shade.") GrPo
On the Tombs in Westminster Abbey. *At. to* Francis Beaumont, *also to* William Basse. ACP; BCEP; BEL; CH; EV-2; GTBS; GTBS-D; GTBS-W; GTSE; InP; LoBV; OBEV; ShBV-3; TOP; TrGrPo; ViBoPo
(In Westminster Abbey.) LH
(Lines on the Tombs in Westminster.) GoBC; MaRV
(Memento for Mortality [*or* Mortalitie], A, *diff. vers., longer.*) CoEV; EIL; ElSeCe; FaBoCh; LoGBV; OBS; SeEP
(On the Tombs in Westminster.) BLV; HBV
On the top of old Smoky all covered in snow. Old Smoky. *Unknown.* BaBo
On the top of the Crumpetty Tree. The Quangle Wangle's Hat. Edward Lear. BoChLi; BoN; GFA; PoRh; PTA-2; RIS; SAS; StaSt
On the top of the mount. The Bald Old Woman. *Tr. by* I. T. Headland. GaP
On the Tower. Annette von Droste-Hülshoff, *tr. fr. German by* James Edward Tobin. AnGP
On the Tower of Gathering Remoteness. Su T'ung-po, *tr. fr. Chinese by* Yu Min-chuan. WhP
On the tower of Little Saling. Little Saling. Olaf Baker. HBMV
On the Tower Overlooking the River. Po Chü-i, *tr. fr. Chinese by* Ching Ti. WhP
On the Trail to Idaho. *Unknown.* CoSo; PoRL
On the Translation of the Iliad. Pushkin, *tr. fr. Russian by* Babette Deutsch. TrRV
On the trees go the blows, chang-chang. Ode II/I/5. *Unknown.* BoFr
On the twenty-second of June. *At. to* Ben Jonson. WhC
On the Twenty-third Psalm. *Unknown. See* He Leadeth Me.
On the unbreathing sides of hills. Squatter's Children. Elizabeth Bishop. NePoAm-2
On the Uniformity and Perfection of Nature. Philip Freneau. AmPP; CoBA; CoV
On the Universality and Other Attributes of the God of Nature. Philip Freneau. AmP
On the University Carrier ("Here lieth one who did most truly prove"). Milton. *See* On the Oxford Carrier.
On the University Carrier (Who Sickn'd in the Time of His Vacancy) ("Here lies old Hobson"). Milton. FaBoCh; LoGBV; MePo
On the Unusual Cold and Rainie Weather in the Summer, 1648. Robert Heath. OBS
On the Upright Judge, Who Condemned the "Drapier's" Printer. Swift. SiTL
On the Vanity of Earthly Greatness. Arthur Guiterman. HoPM; NAMP; TrJP; WhC
On the Vanity of Man's Life. *Unknown. See* Of the Vanity of Man's Life.
On the vast aerial ocean. Mikhail Lermontov. *Fr.* The Demon. OnPM; TrRV
On the Verge. Swinburne. A Midsummer Holiday, III. BPN; PoVP; VLEP
On the Verge. William Winter. AA
On the Victory Obtained by Admiral Blake. Andrew Marvell. SG
On the Victory of Poland and Her Allies over the Sultan Osman, 1621. Casimir Sarbiewski, *tr. fr. Latin by* Francis Sylvester Mahony. CAW
On the Virgin. *Unknown. See* I Sing of a Maiden.
On the "Vita Nuova" of Dante. Dante Gabriel Rossetti. EmBrPo; PoVP
On the volcanic hill. Precarious Ground. Leah Bodine Drake. GoYe
On the voyage where/ the Black Horseman leads you. Kostes Palamas. *Fr.* The Grave. MoGP
On the Wall. Immanuel di Roma, *tr. fr. Hebrew by* Solomon Solis-Cohen. TrJP
On the wan sea-strand. Evening Twilight. Heine. *Fr.* The North Sea. AWP; JAWP; WBP
On the warm Sunday afternoons. A Side Street. Louis Untermeyer. CBOV
On the Water of Our Lord's Baptism. Richard Crashaw. SeEP
On the Way. Georg Trakl, *tr. fr. German by* Ernst Sigler. LiTW
On the Way to Hang-chow; Anchored on the River at Night. Po Chü-i, *tr fr. Chinese by* Arthur Waley. TrCh
On the Way to Kew. W. E. Henley. Echoes, XXXVIII. BPN; LBBV; LoPo; OBVV; PoVP; ViBoPo; VLEP
On the way to my daily occupation. Life. Franklin P. Adams. InMe
On the Way to the Island. David Ferry. NePoAm-2
On the Way to the Mission. Duncan Campbell Scott. CaP; OCL
On the way up from Steep I met some children. To Edward Thomas. Alun Lewis. MoWP; WaP
On the white throat of the useless passion. Ad Finem. Ella Wheeler Wilcox. BLPA
On the Wide Heath. Edna St. Vincent Millay. ChMo; CMP
On the wide level of a mountain's head. Time, Real and Imaginary. Samuel Taylor Coleridge. BPN; EmBrPo; EnRP; EV-4; OBEV; OBRV
On the wide veranda white. A Corn-Song. Paul Laurence Dunbar. AA; OBAV
On the wind of January. A Year's Windfalls. Christina Rossetti. BoTP; OTPC (1923 ed.); PRWS; YeAr
On the Winter Solstice, 1740, *abr.* Mark Akenside. EV-3
On the World. Swift. *See* Day of Judgement, The.
On the Wounds of Our Crucified Lord. Richard Crashaw. SeEP
On the yard shines white the autumnal moon. The Rats. Georg Trakl. LiTW
On these electric branches. Miracles. Roy Helton. MaRV
On these occasions, the feelings surprise. Father and Son. Delmore Schwartz. LiTA
On these salt acres glittering in the sun. Driftwood Fires. John Richard Moreland. MuM
On these swift waters borne along. Thomas Moore at St. Anne's. Thomas D'Arcy McGee. BoCaPo (1943 ed.)
On these white cliffs, that calm above the flood. Dover Cliffs [*or* At Dover Cliffs]. William Lisle Bowles. CEP; EnRP; EV-5; HBV; OBEC; ViBoPo
On this auspicious day, at the felicitous hour. The Great Unity, the Sovereign of the East. Chu Yuan. *Fr.* The Nine Songs. WhP
On This Day I Complete My Thirty-sixth Year. Byron. AnFE; BEL; BPN; CoBE; EM-2; EmBrPo; EnL; EnLi-2; EnLit; EnRP; EPN; ERP; EV-4; FiP; GEPC; HBV; MaPo; MCCG; OAEP; OnPP; ViBoPo
(Byron's Farewell.) LEAP
(Byron's Latest Verses.) LPS-1; PIR
(Hail and Farewell.) LH
Remorse, *sel.* MaRV
On this day man's disgust is known. On Shooting Particles beyond the World. Richard Eberhart. GTBS-W; LiTA; LiTM (rev. ed.)
On this feast day, O cursèd day and hour. Christopher Marlowe. *Fr.* Hero and Leander, First Sestiad. ViBoPo
On this great day a child of time and fate. Inauguration Day. Richard Watson Gilder. PoRL
On this great day I must drink and eat. Riding in a Boat on the Day before the Spring Festival. Tu Fu. WhP
On this great plain the eye. Canterbury. Basil Dowling. AnNZ
On this lone isle, whose rugged rocks affright. Sonnet: Suppos'd to be Written at Lemnos [*or* Philoctetes]. Thomas Russell. CEP; ES; FaBoEn; LoBV; OBEC
On This My Sick-Bed Beats the World. Jiri Wolker, *tr. fr. Czech by* Karl W. Deutsch. WaaP
On this night that is cold. Otomo no Yakamochi, *tr. fr. Japanese by* Arthur Waley. LiTW
On this resemblance—where we find. Elizabeth Tollet. LO
On this road. Haiku. Basho. LiTW; OnPJ
On this shattered sky, on these panes of sweet water. Death Is Dead. Paul Eluard. OnPM
On this side, and on that, men see their friends. All Impelled Onward Alike. Robert Blair. *Fr.* The Grave. EV-3
On this sweet bank your head thrice sweet and dear. Youth's Spring-Tribute. Dante Gabriel Rossetti. The House of Life, XIV. BPN; PoVP; REAL; ViPo; VLEP
On this tomb shed no tears, O passer-by. Epitaph for Elizabeth Ranquet. Corneille. TrFP
On this wondrous sea. Eternity. Emily Dickinson. AA; LEAP; TCAP
On Thomas Moore's Poems. *Unknown.* FiBHP; SiTL
On Thomas Woodcock. *Unknown.* WhC
On those great waters now I am. When We Are upon the Seas. George Wither. *Fr.* Hallelujah. BEL
On those islands. The Hebrides. Louis MacNeice. ReaPo
On Those That Deserve It. Francis Quarles. MePo; OBS
On Those Who Fell. Simonides, the Younger, *tr. fr. Greek by* John Herman Merivale. OnPM
On Those Who Fell at Plataea. Simonides. *See* Athenian Monument, The.
On Those Who Fell at Thermopylae. Simonides. *See* Greek Dead at Thermopylae, The.
On through the Libyan sand. Gordon. Ernest Myers. VA
On, through the lovely archipelago. Charles Sangster. *Fr.* The St. Lawrence and the Saguenay. PeCV
On thy fair bosom, silver lake. To Seneca Lake [*or* Seneca Lake]. James Gates Percival. AnNE; BAV; BoTP; LPS-2; SN
On thy waters, thy sweet valley waters. Georgia Waters [*or* Song]. Thomas Holley Chivers. MOAP; SPP
On thy wild and windy upland, Tornamona. Shane O'Neill. Seumas MacManus. OnYI
On tidings of the wreck of Vrishni's race. The Great Journey. *Unknown. Fr.* Mahabharata. BoFr
On Time. Richard Hughes. MBP; MoBrPo
On Time. Milton. BLV; GTBS-W; KN; LiTB; LiTG; LoBV; MaPo; MePo; MeRV; OBEV; OBS; OxBoCh; PoE; SeCeV; TyEnPo

On Timely Death. Walter Savage Landor. *See* Is It Not Better at an Early Hour.
On tip-toe comes the gentle dark. Good Night. Dorothy Mason Pierce. BrR; SiSoSe; TiPo (1952 ed.)
On to Richmond. John R. Thompson. PAH
On to the Morgue, *with music.* *Unknown.* AS
On Tobacco. Thomas Pestel. ElL
On tongues uncurbed by reverent awe. Euripides. *Fr.* Bacchae. GrPo
On Top of Old Smoky. *Unknown.* FaFP; SiTL
On Top of Troubled Waters. Dorothy J. Langford. BePJ
On Translating the "Divina Commedia." Longfellow. Divina Commedia, I, II, III, V. OuHeWo
On Treason. Sir John Harington. *See* Of Treason.
On Troy. Oliver St. John Gogarty. WhC
On True Worth. Sadi, *tr. fr. Persian by* L. S. Costello. LiTW
On Tsukuda-Isle in July. Munetake, *tr. fr. Japanese by* Asataro Miyamori. OnPM
On Tweed River. Sir Walter Scott. *Fr.* The Monastery, *ch.* 5. EV-4
On Two Brothers. Simonides, *tr. fr. Greek by* W. H. D. Rouse. AWP
On Uvedale Price's Essay, *sel.* Lord Leigh.
"Master mind, that taste and genius grace, A." EnSW
On Viewing a Florist's Whimsy at Fifty-ninth and Madison. Margaret Fishback. WhC
On Volga Banks. Bronislav Kezhyn, *tr. fr. Russian by* Jack Lindsay. RuPo
On Waking. Joseph Campbell. AnIV; NP
On Waking. Alida Carey Gulick. GoYe
On Waking from a Dreamless Sleep. Annie Fields. AA
On Walking the Streets by Day. John Gay. *See* Of Walking the Streets by Day.
On wan dark night on Lac St. Pierre. The Wreck of the *Julie Plante* [*or* The *Julie Plante*]. William Henry Drummond. BeLS; BLPA; BoCaPo; BOHV; CaP; CP; CPG; FaBoBe; FaPON; HBV; IHA; InMe; MM; NA; OCL; PeCV; StaSt; TreFS; WhC
On Waterloo's ensanguined plain. On Scott's [Poem] "The Field of Waterloo." Thomas, Lord Erskine. FiBHP; WhC
On Wellington. Byron. *See* Wellington.
On Wenlock Edge [the Wood's in Trouble]. A. E. Housman. A Shropshire Lad, XXXI. BLV; BoLiVe; CBE; CoBMV; HBV; LiTB; MaPo; MBP; MoAB; MoBrPo; OAEP (2d ed.); OuHeWo; PoE; PoEL-5; PoRA; POTT; PoVP; RiBV; ShBV-4; ViP; ViPo (Wenlock Edge.) CoEV; OBEV (new ed.)
On Westwall Downes. William Strode. FaBoEn; PoEL-2 (On Westwell Down[e]s.) SeCL; SeEP
On what a brave and curious whim. Clocks. Louis Ginsberg. PIAE; TrJP
On what divine adventure has he gone? Pilot and Prophet [*or* Theodore Roosevelt—Pilot and Prophet!]. Charles Hanson Towne. DD; GA; PEDC
On what foundation stands the warrior's pride? Charles XII of Sweden. Samuel Johnson. *Fr.* The Vanity of Human Wishes. BCEP; CoEV; LPS-3; OBEC; PIR; ViBoPo
On what long tides. Fires of Driftwood. Isabel Ecclestone Mackay. CaP; CPG; OCL
On Will Smith. *Unknown.* SiTL
On William Shakespeare. William Basse. *See* Elegy on Shakespeare.
On Willy's birthday, as you see. A Party. Laura E. Richards. SiSoSe
On windy days the mill. The Unfortunate Miller. A. E. Coppard. FaBoTw; POTE
On Wings of Song. Bacchylides, *tr. fr. Greek by* Arthur S. Way. GrR
On with another new love. Two Songs, 2. Abraham Reisen. LiTW
On with the hosts that toil, and on with the young and strong. A March for Youth. K. G. Ossian-Nilsson. AnSL; PoFr
On with thine embassy! To Gabriel of the Annunciation. Peter Abelard. CAW
On Wodin's day, sixth of December, thirty-nine. *In re* Solomon Warshawer. A. M. Klein. BoCaPo
On Woman. Goldsmith. *See* Song: "When lovely woman stoops to folly."
On Woman. W. B. Yeats. TwP
On Women. Simonides. *See* Some Women.
On woodlands ruddy with autumn. My Autumn Walk. Bryant. AA; IAP; LPS-2
On Wordsworth. Hartley Coleridge. FiBHP; PA (He Lived amidst th' Untrodden Ways.) SiTL
On Work. Kahlil Gibran. *See* Of Work.
On Worship. George Herbert. *Fr.* The Church Porch. MaRV
On, ye glory of Sparta's youth! Marching Song. Tyrtaeus. GrR
On Yes Tor. Sir Edmund Gosse. AlDL; CH
On yon hill's top which this sweet plain commands. Invites His Nymph to His Cottage. Philip Ayres. EnLoPo
On yonder hill there is a red deer. Riddle. *Unknown.* ChTr
On yonder hill there stands a creature. The One Answer. *Unknown.* GoTP
On yonder hill there stands a tree. Tree on the Hill. *Unknown.* OTPC; PPL
On yonder taut aerial wire. Birds on a Telegraph Wire. Carl Snoilsky. AnSL
On yonder verdant hillock laid. Ode. Mark Akenside. EV-3
On your altars I have spent my incense. Envoy. Manuel José Othón. AnMP
On your bald, dirty head you wear. To an Old Fraud. Martial. LaP; LiTW
On your bare rocks, O barren moors. The Barren Moors. William Ellery Channing. AA
On your midnight pallet lying. A. E. Housman. A Shropshire Lad, XI. PoVP
On your verdant throne elate. The Cicada. *Unknown.* OuHeWo
On Zacheus. Francis Quarles. LoBV; MePo; OBS
Once. Eric N. Batterham. CH
Once. Trumbull Stickney. LBMV
Once. *Unknown.* CH
Once/ I went for an ocean trip. On a Steamer. Dorothy W. Baruch. FaPON
Once a Big Molicepan. *Unknown.* FaPON
Once a boy beheld a bright. The Rose. Goethe. AWP; JAWP; WBP
Once a boy espied a rose. Briar-Rose. *Unknown.* RIS
Once a Child ("It troubled me as once I was"). Emily Dickinson. ImOP
Once a dream did weave a shade. A Dream. Blake. *Fr.* Songs of Innocence. CH; EnRP; EV-3; MPB; NBE; PECK; PoRh; RAR; TVC; TVSH
Once a fair city, courted then by kings. Masar. Walter Savage Landor. *Fr.* Gebir. LoBV; OBRV
Once a Frenchman who'd promptly said "Oui." *Unknown.* SiTL
Once a gay wit, subsequently a wretched instructor. The Father. Richmond Lattimore. NePoAm-2
Once a hawk said this to a nightingale. Hesiod. *Fr.* Works and Days. GrPo
Once a jolly swagman camped by a billabong. Waltzing Matilda. Andrew Barton Paterson. ChTr; StPo; WaKn; WhC
Once a little baby lay. The First Christmas. Emilie Poulsson. MW; OHIP; PCH; SDH
Once a little baby, on a sunny day. The Story of Baby's Blanket. Emilie Poulsson. PPL
Once a little sugar ant made up his mind to roam. The Ant Explorer. C. J. Dennis. NeLNL
Once a mouse, a frog, and a little red hen. The Mouse, the Frog and the Little Red Hen. *Unknown.* BoTP
Once a pallid vestal. The Vestal. Nathalia Crane. AnAmPo; LA; MAP; MoAmPo (1942 ed.); TrJP
Once a poor widow, aging year by year. The Nun's Priest's Tale. Chaucer. *Fr.* The Canterbury Tales. EnL
Once a rover of the sea, captain of a barkentine. The Captain of St. Kitts. Beulah May. EtS
Once a surgeon, Dr. Baker. Martial, *tr. fr. Latin by* "T. W. M." Epigrams, I, 30. LaP
Once a wife in Bethlehem. A Prayer for a Sleeping Child. Mary Carolyn Davies. OHIP
Once Achaemenides, Menippus now. Tenancy. *Unknown.* OxBG
Once again the flowers we gather. Flowers for the Fallen Heroes. E. W. Chapman. PEOR
Once again the scurry of feet—those myriads. The Face of the Waters. Robert D. Fitzgerald. BoAV; MoAuPo
Once again the storm-clouds hover. Foreboding. Pushkin. BoR
Once again thou flamest heavenward, once again we see thee rise. Hymn. Tennyson. *Fr.* Akbar's Dream. PoVP
Once Alien Here. John Hewitt. NeIP
Once all this mighty continent was ours. Tecumseh to General Harrison. Charles Mair. *Fr.* Tecumseh. BoCaPo; CPG
Once along the high way. The High Road. *Unknown.* WhP
Once an archdeacon dwelt within my land. The Friar's Tale. Chaucer. *Fr.* The Canterbury Tales. BLV
Once April grew. Prematurity. Constance Mercer Klugh. CAG
Once and Upon. Madeline Gleason. NeAP
Once as a child I loved to hop. Adam's Footprint. Vassar Miller. NePoEA
Once, as a lad, alone in bed. And Left Me Stranded on a Hush. Doyle Hennessy. JKCP (1955 ed.)
Once as I lay upon a winter night. The Debate of the Body and the Soul. *Unknown.* MeEV
Once, as I shed bitter tears. Hymns to the Night, III. "Novalis." AnGP
Once, as methought, fortune me kiss'd [*or* kist]. The Lover Rejoiceth the Enjoying of His Love [*or* A Promise]. Sir Thomas Wyatt. FaBoEn; OBSC; ReIE; SiPS

Once, as old Lord Gorbals motored. Lord Gorbals. Harry Graham. ShBV-2
Once as we were sitting by. Spring 1942. Roy Fuller. LiTM; NeBP; WaaP
Once at a simple turning of the way. William Vaughn Moody. *Fr.* Jetsam. MAP; MoAmPo (1942 ed.)
Once at Isola Bella. White Peacocks. Jessie B. Rittenhouse. BLA
Once Before. Mary Mapes Dodge. AA
Once, before I came, a witch. The Mistress of the House. "Anna Akhmatova." TrRV
Once before, this self-same air. Once Before. Mary Mapes Dodge. AA
Once between us the Atlantic. Sundered. Israel Zangwill. TrJP
Once, bright Sylviola! in days not far. A Child's Kiss. Francis Thompson. GTML
Once—but no matter when. A Chronicle. *Unknown.* NA; SiTL
Once by mishap two poets fell a-squaring. Comparison of the Sonnet and the Epigram. Sir John Harington. SiCE; TuPP
Once by the Pacific. Robert Frost. AmPP; AnFE; CoAnAm; CoBMV; GTBS-W; InPo; LiTA; LiTM; MAP; MoAB; MoAmPo; MOAP; NePA; NP; PoFS; PreP; TwP
Once came an exile, longing to be free. Blennerhassett's Island. Thomas Buchanan Read. *Fr.* The New Pastoral. PAH
Once Daedalus in distant Crete. Mythos. Ralph Gustafson. BoCaPo (1948 ed.); PeCV
Once did I love and yet I live. *Unknown.* LO; OBSC; SiCE
Once did my Philomel reflect on me. Sir John Davies. *Fr.* Sonnets to Philomel. SiPS
Once Did My Thoughts. *Unknown.* ElSeCe; TuPP
("Once did my thoughts both ebb and flow.") LO
Once did she hold the gorgeous east in fee. On the Extinction of the Venetian Republic. Wordsworth. BEL; BoLiVe; BPN; CaAE; CBOV; EM-2; EmBrPo; EnL; EnLi-2; EnLit; EnLP; EnRP; EPN; EPP; ERP; ES; EV-3; GEPC; GTBS; GTBS-D; GTBS-W; GTSE; GTSL; HBV; LH; LoBV; MCCG; OAEP; OBEV; OBRV; OuHeWo; PeBoSo; PoFr; ReaPo; TCEP; TOP; TrGrPo; ViBoPo
Once, ere God was crucified. The Abdication of Fergus Mac Roy. Sir Samuel Ferguson. AnIL
Once, ere the gold-hair'd sun shot the new ray. Thomas Chatterton. *Fr.* Elegy: "Why blooms the radiance of the morning sky?" RO
Once for our consolation it seemed, O Lord. No More Destructive Flame. Francis X. Connolly. ISi
Once, from the parapet of gems and glow. A Flight from Glory. Eugene Lee-Hamilton. BMEP; VA
Once git a smell o' musk into a draw. Sunthin' in the Pastoral Line. James Russell Lowell. *Fr.* The Biglow Papers. AmPP (3d ed.); APW; CoBA; IAP; MCCG; PFY, SN
Once grandma quavered out a tale. The Trance. Konstantin Simonov. RuPo
Once hairy scenter did transgress. *Unknown.* *Fr.* Riddles. CoBE
Once he was passing by an ill-used pup. Pythagoras and the Dog. Xenophanes. OxBG
Once he will miss, twice he will miss. Death. *Unknown.* *Fr.* The Thousand and One Nights. AWP; JAWP; WBP
Once hoary winter chanced—alas! Why Ye Blossome Cometh before Ye Leafe. Oliver Herford. AA; ADAH
Once I am dead, let earth go up in flame. "Après Moi le Déluge." *Unknown.* GrPE
Once I am sure there's nothing going on. Church Going. Philip Larkin. HaMV; NePoEA; UnPo (3d ed.)
Once I came to Siena. The Daisies. George Edward Woodberry. LBAP
Once I cried for new songs to sing. I Sing No New Songs. Frank Marshall Davis. PoNe
Once I followed horses. Thistledown. Denis Glover. AnNZ
Once I fought a shadow. The Duel. Harold Trowbridge Pulsifer. HBMV
Once I found riches here. The Discovery. Stanley Snaith. LO; POTE
Once I gave away my heart. For All Fathers. Stella Weston. FAOV
Once I had passed the shortened autumn day. The Suire. Thomas Caulfield Irwin. IrPN
Once I heard a hobo, singing by the tie-trail. The Long Road West. H. H. Knibbs. IHA
Once I knelt in my shining mail. Vigils. Aline Kilmer. PFE; PoTo
Once I knew a fine song. 'Scaped. Stephen Crane. The Black Riders, LXV. AA
Once I knew a little girl, and I loved her as my life. Do Come Back Again. *Unknown.* OuSiCo
Once I knew for every rain. The Stranger. Richard Sullivan. JKCP (1955 ed.)
Once I knowed old lady. The Rich Old Lady. *Unknown.* OuSiCo
Once I learnt in wilful hour. On a Wife. Francis Burdett Money-Coutts. OBVV
Once I Pass'd through a Populous City. Walt Whitman. AmPP (4th ed.); LoPo; MOAP; NePA; OxBA
Once I prayed to the Lord of Battles. Repentance. Thomas Curtis Clark. ChIP
Once, I remember well the day. The Enthusiast; an Ode. William Whitehead. OBEC
Once I saw a little bird going hop, hop, hop. The Little Bird. Mother Goose. BoTP; GFA; GoBP; MeMeAg; OxNR; SAS; StVeCh
Once I saw Death go sporting through a plain. Death's Apology. Francisco Manuel de Mello. CAW
Once I saw it with uncaring eyes. This Hill. Otomo Yakamochi. OnPM
Once I saw mountains angry. Ancestry. Stephen Crane. The Black Riders, XXII. AA; LEAP; MOAP
Once I saw thee idly rocking. Stephen Crane. Intrigue, IV. MOAP
Once I saw white swallows flying. Bird Omens. Stefan George. AnGP
Once I stood on a rugged cliff. A Phantasy of the Sea. Antoinette Miller. CAG
Once I Thought to Die for Love. *Unknown.* ElL; ElSeCe
Once I took a fancy to the ship's lamp, lighted on a night voyage. A Gyroscopic Lamp. Kaoru Maruyama. PoLJ
Once I used to be called to join your parties. Martial, *tr. fr. Latin by* Robert R. Schnorr. Epigrams, VII, 86. LaP
Once I was a brakeman on the E-r-i-e Canal. The Erie Canal Ballad. *Unknown.* ABF
Once I was a monarch's daughter. Once. *Unknown.* CH
Once I was a tiny tad [*or* lad]. Innocence. George S. Chappell. DDA; YaD
Once I was Achaemenides's field. The Good Earth. *Unknown.* OnPM
Once I was at a nobleman's wedding. The Nobleman's Wedding. *Unknown.* AnIV
Once I was common wood, a shapeless log. Words from a Wooden Image. John Oldham. *Fr.* Satyrs upon the Jesuits. BeR
Once I was good like the Virgin Mary and the minister's wife. The Scarlet Woman. Fenton Johnson. BANP; PoNe
Once I was happy, but now I'm forlorn. The Man on the Flying Trapeze. George Leybourne. BeLS; BLPA; FaBoBe; NeHB; YaD
Once I was part of the music I heard. Youth in Age. George Meredith. EmBrPo; PoVP; VLEP
Once I went to Fairyland—but it's years and years ago. When You Go to Fairyland. *Unknown.* PCD
Once I wished I might rehearse. Freedom. Emerson. PoFr
Once in a dream I saw the flowers. Paradise; in a Dream. Christina Rossetti. HBV; OxBoCh; PoVP; ViPo; WGRP
Once in a golden hour. The Flower. Tennyson. BPN; EmBrPo; EPN; EV-2; HBV; InP; PoVP; VA; VLEP
Once in a hundred years the lemmings come. The Lemmings. John Masefield. ChMo; CMP
Once in a lifetime, we may see the veil. Midnight—September 19, 1881. John Boyle O'Reilly. PAH
Once in a lonely hamlet I sojourned. The Emigrant Mother. Wordsworth. BPN
Once in a Lonely Hour. John Hall Wheelock. LoPS; NP
Once, in a night as black as ink. How Samson Bore Away the Gates of Gaza. Vachel Lindsay. NP
Once, in a roostery. The Hen and the Carp. Ian Serraillier. AlDL
Once in a Saintly Passion. James Thomson. BBV (1951 ed.); PoVP; TreFS; VLEP
Once in a season past we left the town. Bound for the Harvest-Home. Theocritus. *Fr.* Idylls. OxBG
Once in a simple quest. Through a Fog of Stars. John Nixon, Jr. MaRV
Once in a Way. Antiphilus of Byzantium, *tr. fr. Greek by* "J. E. B." OxBG
("On a ship's poop I'd like to lie, if I could have my way.") GrPo
Once in a while/ we'd find a patch. The Children. William Carlos Williams. NePoAm-2
Once in a while a curious weed unknown to me. William Jones. Edgar Lee Masters. *Fr.* Spoon River Anthology. ImOP
Once in a wood at winter's end. Winter's End. Howard Moss. NePoEA
Once in an arbor was my mistress sleeping. Madrigal. Barnabe Barnes. *Fr.* Parthenophil and Parthenophe. TuPP
Once, in finesse of fiddles found I ectasy. The Embankment [*or* Fantasia of a Fallen Gentleman]. T. E. Hulme. FaBoMo; MBP; MoBrPo (1942 ed.); SeCePo
Once in good hour there came in company. Sonnet. Matteo Maria Boiardo. LyPI

Once in his shop a workman wrought. The Camel's Nose. Lydia Huntley Sigourney. OTPC (1923 ed.); PRWS
Once, in my darkest hour, in some dim place. Lux in Tenebris. *Unknown.* GoBC
Once in my garret—you being far away. Rupert Brooke, II. W. W. Gibson. ChMo; CMP; HBMV; LBBV; PoeMoYo; POTT; PtOT; PtP; TwCV; VOD
Once in our land there lived a maid. The Knight in the Feather-Fell. *Unknown.* BoDaBa
Once in our lives. A Farewell to Wives. *Unknown.* SeCL
Once in Persia reigned [*or* ruled] a king. Even This Shall Pass Away [*or* The King's Ring]. Theodore Tilton. BLPA; HBV; MaRV; NeHB; PTA-2; TreFS; WGRP
Once in Royal David's City. Cecil Frances Alexander. MaRV; MeMeAg; OlF; OTPC; YaCaBo, *with music*
(Christmas.) COAH
(Christmas Hymn, A.) OHIP
Once in the dear dead days beyond recall. Love's Old Sweet Song. G. Clifton Bingham. FaBoBe; OlF; TreF
Once in the ear of Apollo said Envy, privily. The Parnassian. Callimachus. GrPE
Once, in the flight of ages past. The Common Lot. James Montgomery. BCEP; EBSV; LPS-1
Once in the hours of midnight. Love's Stratagem. *Unknown. Fr.* Anacreontea. GrPE
Once in the misty dawn with timid foot. Vladimir Soloviev. *See* With Wavering Feet I Walked.
Once in the Phoenix Tower the phoenix made her nest. On Climbing the Phoenix Tower at Chin-ling. Li Po. WhP
Once in the wind of morning. The Merry Guide. A. E. Housman. A Shropshire Lad, XLII. OAEP (2d ed.); PoeMoYo; PoTo; PoVP; ViPo
Once in the winter. The Forsaken. Duncan Campbell Scott. CaP; MM; OCL; TwCaPo; TwCV
Once in winter shone the ground and full sped. On the Nativity of Christ Our Lord. Joseph Bennett. NePA
Once it happened I'd been dining, on my couch I slept reclining. The Goblin Goose. *Unknown.* PA
Once it smiled a silent dell. The Valley of Unrest. Poe. AmPo; AmPP; APW; IAP; KN; LBAP; MOAP; PoEL-4; TriL; ViBoPo
Once it was difficult to keep to roads. Roads. Ruth Dallas. AnNZ
Once it was packed like a box with the toys of childhood. History. Babette Deutsch. NeTW
Once it was the blessing. Jesus Only. A. B. Simpson. BePJ
Once it was the colour of saying. Poem. Dylan Thomas. MoWP
Once, long ago, a friend gave me a book. The Gift. Margaret E. Bruner. PoToHe
Once, long ago—if I remember rightly—my life was a sumptuous feast. Arthur Rimbaud. *Fr.* A Season in Hell. AnFP
Once, long ago, set close beside a wood. The Nun's Priest's Tale. Chaucer. *Fr.* The Canterbury Tales. TrGrPo
Once Love among the roses. Love and the Bee. *Unknown. Fr.* Anacreontea. GrPE
Once, Man entirely free, alone and wild. The Swiss Peasant [*or* On the Swiss]. Wordsworth. OBEC; PoFr
Once, measuring his height, he stood. The Boy Jesus. John Banister Tabb. StJW
Once mermaids mocked your ships. Mermaids. Kenneth Slessor NeLNL
Once more/ Through the near door. A Mother on Her Daughter's Wedding Day. Faith V. Vilas. MotAn
Once more are we met for a season of pleasure. Cattle Round-up. H. D. C. McLachlan. SCC
Once more around should do it, the man confided. Flight of the Roller-Coaster. Raymond Souster. PeCV
Once more at dusk the gentle ghosts must know. Spring Dusk in Williamsburg. Virginia Lyle Tunstall. Sonnets of an Old Town, I. LS
Once more fictitious joy is spread. Nowell, Nowell. Robert Finch. TwCaPo
Once More Fields and Gardens. Tao Yuan-ming. *See* Return to the Country.
Once more following blue grief of evening. In Hellbrunn. Georg Trakl. LiTW
Once more God hither moves their course. The Arrival of the Crusaders. St. Nerses. ArmLP
Once more I came to Sarum Close. Coventry Patmore. *Fr.* The Angel in the House, I, i. EnSW
Once more I hear the everlasting sea. Resurrection. Alfred Noyes. EOAH
Once more I join the Thespian choir. Mark Akenside. *Fr.* On Lyric Poetry. PtP
Once More I Pray. "Andrei Bely," *tr. fr. Russian by* Babette Deutsch. TrRV
Once more in man's frail world! which I had left. The Prophecy of Dante, I. Byron. EmBrPo
Once more in misted April. An April Morning. Bliss Carman. CV; DD; GBV; HBMV; HBVY; NV; VOD
Once More into the Breach. Shakespeare. *See* Once More unto the Breach . . .
Once More It Is the Springtime. Adam Oehlenschläger, *tr. fr. Danish by* Charles W. Stork. BoDS
Once more, listening to the wind and rain. The Return. Arna Bontemps. CDC; PoNe
Once more on the morrow-morning fair shineth the glorious sun. Of the Passing Away of Brynhild. William Morris. *Fr.* The Story of Sigurd the Volsung. PoVP; TCEP; VA; VLEP
Once more, once more, my Mary dear. Memories. George Denison Prentice. AA
Once more Orion and the sister Seven. A Welcome to Dr. Benjamin Apthorp Gould. Oliver Wendell Holmes. ImOP
Once more the ancient [*or* northbound] wonder. Easter, 1923 [*or* Easter]. John G. Neihardt. AnAmPo; HBMV; LA; OHIP
Once more the changed year's turning wheel returns. Barren Spring. Dante Gabriel Rossetti. *Fr.* The House of Life, LXXXIII. BPN; FaBoEn; NBE; PoEL-5; PoVP; ViPo; VLEP
Once more the country calls. Ode to Our Young Pro-Consuls of the Air. Allen Tate. AmPP (3d ed.); WaP
Once more the crimson rumor. Autumn Song. William Griffith. BAP
Once more the favoring breezes blow. Paul Jones. William A. Phelon. GA
Once more the Flower of Essex is marching to the wars. Essex Regiment March. George Edward Woodberry. GA
Once more the gipsy aster. The Gipsy Wedding. Sara Hamilton Birchall. NLK
Once more, the head, O Lord, we bow. Blessings at Table. *Unknown.* PraP
Once more the Heavenly Power/ Makes all things new. Early Spring. Tennyson. DD; GTML; HBV; HBVY; LiA; NLK; SN
Once more the lad with golden hair. Love. Anacreon. GrL; OxBG
Once more the liberal year laughs out. Harvest Hymn [*or* Thanksgiving Ode]. Whittier. *Fr.* For an Autumnal Festival. OHIP; PEOR; PGD; PoRL; PSO; TOAH
Once more the lumbering earth heaves its chill flank. Intempestiva. Henry Longan Stuart. JKCP (1926 ed.)
Once more the northbound wonder. *See* Once more the ancient wonder.
Once More the Simple Things. Aristophanes, *tr. fr. Greek by* Benjamin Bickley Rogers. *Fr.* The Peace. GrR
Once more the stars of love cross. Excerpts from a "Gothic Notebook." Mario Luzi. *Fr.* Gothic Notebook. LiTW
Once more the storm is howling, and half hid. A Prayer for My Daughter. W. B. Yeats. ChMo; CMP; CoBMV; EnL; EnLP; GTBS-W; LiTB; LiTG; LiTM (rev. ed.); LoBV; MoAB; PoLFOT; VLEP
Once more the windless days are here. Anniversaries. Aldous Huxley. LBBV
Once more the woodlands ring with birds—but not to the birds men hearken. Spring-Song, 1939. F. L. Lucas. NeTW
Once more this Autumn-earth is ripe. The Australian. Arthur Adams. BoAu
Once more, through God's high will and grace. Spring. Aubrey Thomas De Vere. *Fr.* The Year of Sorrow: Ireland—1849. IrPN; TIP
Once more to distant ages of the world. Wordsworth. *Fr.* The Excursion. InP
Once more today you ride your city round. To the King. Kaj Munk. BoDS
Once More unto the Breach, Dear Friends, Once More. Shakespeare. King Henry V, *fr.* III, i. WaaP
(Blast of War, The.) TrGrPo
(England at War; Harfleur, England, and St. George.) EV-1
(Henry V at Harfleur.) TreF
(Henry V before Harfleur.) ShBV-2; TVSH
(Henry V to His Soldiers.) PoFS
(Henry Fifth's Address to His Soldiers.) WHA
(King Henry before Harfleur.) PC
(King to His Soldiers before Harfleur, The.) LPS-2
Once more we gather under skies of May. O Martyrs Numberless. *Unknown.* PEOR
Once more we sail with a favoring gale. Rolling Down to Old Maui. *Unknown.* SoAmSa
Once more with the blue grief of evening. In Hellbrunn. Georg Trakl. AnGP
Once, morn by morn, when snowy mountains flamed. Picture of a Bull. Joaquin Miller. AmPP (3d ed.)
Once Musing as I Sat. Barnabe Googe. LO; TuPP
(Fly, The.) CH
("Once musing as I sat, and candle burning by.") SiCE
Once my feet trod Nineveh. The Babe. Monk Gibbon. OxBI
Once my heart was a summer rose. Song. Edith Sitwell. ChMP; GTBS-D
Once (O wonderful). The Swimmer. Ibn Khafaja. MooP
Once, on a cliff, I saw perfection happen. The Heart of Light. Winifred Welles. NP
Once, on a golden afternoon. The Telltale. *Unknown.* LPS-2

Once on a Time. Kendall Banning. BAP; HBV; PR
Once on a Time. Margaret Benson. HBV
Once on a time, a monarch, tir'd with whooping. Apple Dumplings and a King. "Peter Pindar." OBEC
Once on a time, a nightingale. The Nightingale. Sir John Vanbrugh. *Fr.* Aesop. SeCL
Once on a time a rustic dame. The Milkmaid. Robert Lloyd. CG
Once on a time an old red hen. Contentment. Eugene Field. CBPC
Once, on a time and in a place. The Arrogant Frog and the Superior Bull. Guy Wetmore Carryl. StPo
Once on a time did Eucritus and I. Harvest-Home. Theocritus. *Fr.* Idylls. AWP; GrPo; GrR
Once on a time from all the Circles seven. Prelude. Ferid ed-Din Attar. *Fr.* The Bird-Parliament. PeP
Once on a time I used to be. Harlots' Catch. Robert Nichols. FaBoTw
Once on a time I used to dream. Once on a Time. Margaret Benson. HBV
Once on a time, in rainy weather. The Dog and the Cat, and the Duck and the Rat. Eliza Lee Follen. CIV
Once on a time it came to pass. The Piece of Glass and the Piece of Ice. John Hookham Frere. OTPC (1923 ed.)
Once on a time it came to pass. The Song of Mary-of-the-Angels. Jean Richepin. TrFP
Once on a time it happened that a knight. Too Late, My Love. Conon de Béthune. LyMA
Once on a time old Johnny Bull flew in a raging fury. Yankee Doodle. George Pope Morris. PaA
Once on a time, once on a time. Once on a Time. Kendall Banning. BAP; HBV; PR
Once on a time (so runs the fable). The Two Mice. Pope. *Fr.* An Imitation of the Sixth Satire of the Second Book of Horace. BeR
Once on a time, some centuries ago. The Monk of Casal-Maggiore. Longfellow. *Fr.* Tales of a Wayside Inn. AmPP (4th ed.); OxBA
Once on a time there lived a man. Peter Gray. *Unknown.* OuSiCo
Once on a time—'twas long ago. The Youth and the North-wind. John Godfrey Saxe. StPo
"Once . . . once upon a time . . ." Martha. Walter de la Mare. GBV; MBP; MoBrPo; OTPC (1946 ed.); PoeT; TreFS; TwCV
Once Only. Ato Tobira, *tr. fr. Japanese by* Ishii *and* Obata. OnPM
Once only by the garden gate. Youth and Love. Robert Louis Stevenson. BMEP
Once or twice this side of death. Crystal Moment. Robert P. Tristram Coffin. PIAE; PoeMoYo
Once-over, The. Paul Blackburn. NeAP
Once, Paumanok. The Mocking Bird. Walt Whitman. *Fr.* Out of the Cradle Endlessly Rocking. LPS-2
Once ran my prayer as runs the brook. Be Merciful. John T. McFarland. OQP; PraP; QP-2
Once riding in Old Baltimore. Incident. Countee Cullen. BoChLi (1950 ed.); CDC; GoSl; MoSiPe; OQP; PoNe; QP-2
Once Saint Francis of Assisi saw a crowd of little birds. Saint Francis and the Birds. Robert Hugh Benson. SaFP
Once she, the Lesbian,—lyric heart of Greece. Again, Sappho. Mary Brent Whiteside. LS
Once Switzerland was free! With what a pride. Switzerland. James Sheridan Knowles. *Fr.* William Tell. LPS-2; PoFr
Once the Days. Denis Glover. AnNZ
Once the Emperor Charles of Spain. The Emperor's Bird's-Nest. Longfellow. MPB
Once the great Sibyl, as I passed her cave. The Immortal Panoply. Wallace B. Nichols. *Fr.* Prometheus in Piccadilly. ReTS
Once the head is gray. A Catch. Richard Henry Stoddard. AA; LEAP
Once the orioles sang in chorus. Ballade of Big Plans. Dorothy Parker. InMe
Once the sacker of towns, men say. Heracles and the Wraith of Meleager. Bacchylides. GrPE
Once there came a man. Four Poems, II. Stephen Crane. CrMA
Once there dwelt a king aforetime. Irmeline Rose. Jens Peter Jacobsen. BoDS
Once there lived a little man. The Little Disaster. *Unknown.* BoTP; SAS
Once there lived in a land. Playing the Lyre. Apostolos Melachrinos. *Fr.* Apollonius. MoGP
Once there was a cabin here, and once there was a man. Stafford's Cabin. E. A. Robinson. CV; DDA; TCAP
Once there was a fence here. Former Barn Lot. Mark Van Doren. MAP; MoAmPo; MOAP
Once there was a King of Thule. Complaint of the King of Thule. Jules Laforgue. AnFP
Once there was a little boy. The Boy Who Never Told a Lie. *Unknown.* PECK
Once there was a little boy. The Perfect Child. Monica Shannon. BoChLi
Once there was a little boy, whose name was Robert Reece. An Overworked Elocutionist. Carolyn Wells. BLPA; PTA-1
Once there was a little Kitty. Long Time Ago [*or* Kitty *or* Little Kitty]. Elizabeth Prentiss. BoTP; CBPC; CIV; GFA; MoShBr; MPB; SAS; TVC; TVSH
Once there was a snowman. *Unknown.* GFA
Once there was a spaniel. Bed-Time Story. Melville Cane. GoTP
Once there was an elephant. Eletelephony. Laura E. Richards. BoChLi; FaPON; LiL; MPB; TiPo; YaD
Once there was neither heaven nor earth. The Two Pigeons. *Unknown.* OnPM
Once they minted Our Lady in multiple golden medallions. Ox-Bone Madonna. James J. Galvin. ISi
Once this soft turf, this rivulet's sands. The Battlefield. Bryant. AA; CoBA; CBOV; IAP; LPS-2; MOAH; TCAP
Once—though a lethargy oppressed my brain. Dreams in Hades. Gustaf Fröding. AnSL
Once to Europa sweetly came a dream. Moschus, *tr. fr. Greek by* H. H. Chamberlin. GrPo
Once to Every Man and Nation. James Russell Lowell. *Fr.* The Present Crisis. APW; OlF
Once to his master a disciple cried. The Ways of Love. Jami. OnPM
Once to life I said, yes! To Life I Said Yes. Chaim Grade. TrJP
Once to the verge of yon steep barrier came. The Recluse. Wordsworth. BEL
Once, twice, thrice. *Unknown.* OxNR
Once upon a midnight dreary, eerie, scary. Ravin's of Piute Poet Poe. Charles L. Edson. PoeMoYo
Once upon a midnight dreary, while I pondered, weak and weary. The Raven. Poe. AA; AmP; AmPo; AmPP; AnFE; APA; APW; BAP; BAV; BBV (1923 ed.); BeLS; BLPA; CG; CH; CoAnAm; CoBA; DaM; EV-5; FaBoBe; FaBoCh; FaFP; GN; HBV; HiLiAm; IAP; LEAP; LiTA; LiTG; LoGBV; LPS-3; MCCG; MOAP; NeHB; NePA; OBAV; OHFP; OnSP; OTPC; OxBA; PCD; PCN; PECK; PFE; PFY; PG (1945 ed.); PIR; PoeMoYo; PoRA; PreP; PYM; SPP; TCAP; TOP; TreF; TVSH; ViBoPo; WBLP; WHA
Once upon a night like this. Even on a Night like This. Ralph Friedrich. MuM
Once upon a Time. Elizabeth Thomas. DDA
Once upon a Time. D'Arcy W. Thompson. GaP (Funny Old Man and His Wife.) SUS
Once upon a time,/ When the pigs were swine. *Unknown.* BoN
Once upon a time. All. Cyril G. Taylor. ReTS
Once upon a time. Mr. Pyme. Harry Behn. LiL; TiPo
Once upon a time, I planned to be. Once upon a Time. Elizabeth Thomas. DDA
Once upon a time, in a little wee house. Once upon a Time [*or* Funny Old Man and His Wife]. D'Arcy W. Thompson. GaP; SUS
Once upon a time there were three little foxes. The Three Foxes. A. A. Milne. MoShBr; StVeCh (1955 ed.)
Once upon Iceland's solitary strand. The Broken Oar. Longfellow. LiA
Once upon the earth at the midnight hour. The Wooing Lady. William Jay Smith. NePoEA
Once, walking home, I passed beneath a tree. The Music of a Tree. W. J Turner. MBP; MoBrPo
Once was a fiddler. Play could he. A Fiddler. Walter de la Mare. UnS
Once was a grave slow gentleman. The Grave Gentleman. Andrew Hewitt. NoCaPo
Once was every woman the witch. Witches. Ted Hughes. GoYe
Once we read Tennyson aloud. Reading Aloud. Christopher Morley. PoeMoYo
Once we were strong. Charles Mair. *Fr.* Tecumseh. PeCV
Once when a child I ran to pick. Bitter-sweet. Elisabeth Scollard. TBM
Once when I looked at willows, I would say. Actual Willow. Winifred Welles. MAP
Once, when I wandered in the woods alone. Amaryllis. E. A. Robinson. TwP
Once, when I was little, as the summer night was falling. The Wastrel. Reginald Wright Kauffman. HBV
Once when my heart was passion-free. Communion. John Banister Tabb. MaRV; WGRP
Once when she was very small. Biography. Mavor Moore. TwCaPo
Once, when the days were ages. Brahma's Answer. Richard Henry Stoddard. LPS-3
Once when the snow of the year was beginning to fall. The Runaway. Robert Frost. AlDL; AnNE; AWP; BBV (1951 ed.); BoChLi; CH; DDA; FaBoCh; FaPON; GoTP; GTBS-D; HaMV; InPo; JAWP; LoGBV; MAP;

MCCG; MoAB; MoAmPo; MOAP; MPB; NeMA; NLK; NV; PIAE; PoRL; PoTo; ShBV-3; StVeCh; TiPo; TSW; TSWC; TwP; WBP

Once when the wind was on the roof. Beyond. Hannah Parker Kimball. AA

Once when they gathered long ago. No Room. Robert Whitaker. ChIP

Once When You Were Walking. Annette Wynne. SUS

Once, with a whirl of thought oppressed. The Day of Judgment. Swift. EiPP

Once with his sling Ariston, poor weapon of the lowly. The Dead Fowler. *Unknown.* GrPE

Once ye were happy, once by many a shore. The Loons. Archibald Lampman. VA

Once You Git the Habit. *At. to* Berton Braley. *See* Habit, The.

Once you journeyed with Him, Mary. The Thirteenth Station. Caroline Giltinan. LS

Oncet in the museum. Two Ways. John V. A. Weaver. HBMV; LoPS; NP

One, The. Everard Jack Appleton. MaRV

One. Marion Monks Chase. EOAH

One. John Vance Cheney. LBAP

One. Andrew Hewitt. NoCaPo (rev. ed.)

One Aeschylus, Athenian born. His Own Epitaph. Aeschylus. OxBG

One Almost Might. A. S. J. Tessimond. ChMP

One alone, a sister without her peer. A Love Song. *Unknown.* LiTW

One and His Mistress a-Dying. *Unknown.* SeCL

One and One. C. Day Lewis. OAEP (2d ed.); UnS

One and One. Mary Mapes Dodge. HBV; HBVY; PPL

One and one only is the splendid Lover. The Splendid Lover. John Richard Moreland. ChIP; PGD

One-and-twenty. Samuel Johnson. BCEP; LEAP; OBEV; TyEnPo
(Short Song of Congratulation, A.) BeR; InvP; LoBV; OBEC; PoEL-3
(To a Young Heir.) UnPo (3d ed.)
"Wealth, my lad, was made to wander," *sel.* OtMeF
(On the Coming of Age of a Rich Extravagant Young Man.) ViBoPo

One Answer, The. *Unknown.* GoTP

One April Day. John Richard Moreland. ChIP

One April day/ Green glitter. Diakos. Kostas Kariotakis. MoGP

One April when the harrowed fields were dark. A Deserted Farm. George Sterling. LPS-1

One asked a sign from God; and day by day. The Seekers. Victor Starbuck. BPP; MaRV; WGRP

One asked [*or* ask'd] me where the roses grow [*or* grew]. The Rosary [*or* Rosarie]. Robert Herrick. EPS (1942 ed.); InMe

One asked of regret. Regret. Richard Le Gallienne. BMEP; MBP; VA

One autumn night, in Sudbury town. The Wayside Inn. Longfellow. *Fr.* Tales of a Wayside Inn. CoBA; TCAP

One Beauty Still. George Dillon. MAP; MoAmPo (1942 ed.)

One before the Last, The. Rupert Brooke. OBVV

One Beneath Old Glory. *Unknown.* MDAH

One black horse standing by the gate. The Farmyard. A. A. Attwood. BoTP

One Blackbird. Harold Monro. *Fr.* Strange Meetings. BoTP; NLK; RIS; StaSt
("Stars must make an awful noise, The.") WP

One bland elipse in cornflower blue. Rigor Viris. Margaret Avison. BoCaPo (1948 ed.); CaP

One blessing had I, than the rest. Emily Dickinson. LiTA

One bliss for which. Taboo to Boot. Ogden Nash. FiBHP

One brought me the news of your death, O Herakleitos my friend. Elegy on Herakleitos. Callimachus. LiTW

One by his father kept long time to school. Of Two Religions. Sir John Harington. SiCE

One by One. Hazel Hall. NP

One by One. Adelaide Anne Procter. GN; HBV

One by one. A Bowl of Wine. Ming Ti. PoHN

One by one, as harvesters, all heavy laden. Sacheverell Sitwell. *Fr.* Agamemnon's Tomb. MoBrPo

One by one, like leaves from a tree. Leaves. Sara Teasdale. HBV; NP; NV

One by one, one by one. One by One. Hazel Hall. NP

One by one the pale stars die before the day now. Sailing at Dawn. Sir Henry Newbolt. CP; EtS

One by one the sands are flowing. One by One. Adelaide Anne Procter. GN; HBV

One by one they go. Monody on the Death of Wendell Phillips. Thomas Bailey Aldrich. GA

One calm and cloudless winter night. Medusa. Robert Kelley Weeks. AA

One came to me in the night. A Song of Dreams. "Fiona Macleod." VLEP

One cannot have enough. Soliloquy of a Tortoise on Revisiting the Lettuce Beds after an Interval of One Hour While Supposed to Be Sleeping in a Clump of Blue Hollyhocks. E. V. Rieu. FiBHP

One Careless Look. John Clare. LiTL
("One gloomy eve I roam'd about.") AnFE; EG

One Certainty. Christina Rossetti. EmBrPo

One chestnut, only one. Baby's Hands. Gomei. MPB

One chilly autumn evening when the day was nearly spent. The Sigh of the Forest. Bernhard Elis Malmström. AnSL

One Christmas eve, when Santa Claus. Santa Claus and the Mouse. Emilie Poulsson. ChBR; GFA; UTS

One Christmas night in the long ago. God's Unspeakable Gift. Mrs. Macey P. Sealey. BePJ

"One ciarog knows another ciarog." The Tinkers. Joseph Campbell. OnYI

One City Only. Alice Corbin. NP

One Consciousness. Albert Durrant Watson. CPG

One Country. Frank Lebby Stanton. AA; PaA

One Crowded Hour. Thomas O. Mordaunt. *See* Sound, Sound The Clarion.

One crown not any seek. Emily Dickinson. MaRV

One crucifixion is recorded only. Emily Dickinson. AnNE

One dark December day, the text-books teach. The Phoenix Liberty. Helen Parry Eden. PoFr

One day. Clown. Henri Michaux. MiCF

One day a statistician great. Doomed. *Unknown.* CIV

One day as I sat and suffered. The Heretic. Bliss Carman. WGRP

One day as I unwarily did gaze. Amoretti, XVI. Spenser. PeBoSo; ReEn

One day, as I was going by. The Lost Heir. Thomas Hood. LPS-1

One day, at dusk, we pass, after the rain. On the Thread of the Pale Hour. Léon Paul Fargue. MiFP

One Day at Rouen. Sister Mary Bernetta. JKCP (1955 ed.)

One day between the Lip and Heart. The Lip and the Heart. John Quincy Adams. AA; LHV; PR

One day, from beyond the foliage. Prose Poem: Mysterious Flute. Judith Gautier. OnPM

One day, Good-bye Met How-D'-Y'-Do. How D'-Y-Do and Good-bye. William Robert Spencer. OTPC (1923 ed.)

One day I asked my heart. Ballade. Charles d'Orléans. FoS

One day I could not read or play. Clouds. Norman Ault. HBVY

One day I heard a clear untremorous reed. Earth Melody. Christy MacKaye. PIAE

One day I made a taxicab. My Taxicab. James S. Tippett. GFA; MPB

One day, I mind me, now that she is dead. Mimma Bella, VIII. Eugene Lee-Hamilton. HBV

One day I observed a grey hair in my head. The Grey Hair. Judah Halevi. TrJP

One day I saw a downy duck. Good Morning. Muriel Sipe. SUS; TiPo

One day I saw a ship upon the sands. Sea Irony. John Langdon Heaton. AA

One day I sought with her heart-thrilling eyes. Amoretti, XII. Spenser. PeBoSo

One day I thought I'd have some fun. The Horse Wrangler. D. J. O'Malley. CoSo

One day I thought I'd have some fun. The Tenderfoot. *Unknown.* AS

One day I wandered where the salt sea-tide. The Seaside Well. *Unknown.* LPS-3

One day I was walking out on the mountain. The Cowboy's Lament (B *vers.*). *Unknown.* ViBoFo

One day I wrote her name upon the strand. Amoretti, LXXV. Spenser. AnFE; ATP; AWP; BEL; BoLiVe; CoBE; ElL; ElSeCe; EnLi-1; EnLit; ES; FiP; HBV; JAWP; LEAP; LiTB; LiTG; LiTL; OAEP; PeBoSo; PG (1955 ed.); PoE; PoFS; PreP; REAL; ReaPo; ReEn; ReIE; SeCePo; SeCeV; SiCE; TOP; ViBoPo; WBP

One day in a dream as I lay at the edge of a cliff. Dream. William Jay Smith. MoVE

One day in a lonesome grove. The Lonesome Grove. *Unknown.* TrAS

One day in the blue month of September. In Memory of Marie A. Bertolt Brecht. LiTW

One day into the sea I cast. The Lost Wine. Paul Valéry. AnFP

One day, it matters not to know. St. Romuald. Robert Southey. CG

One day, it thundered and lightened. Adam, Lilith, and Eve. Robert Browning. BPN; HBV; PoVP; ViPP; VLEP

One day, Mamma said: "Conrad dear." The Story of Little Suck-a-Thumb. Heinrich Hoffmann. BoN; HBV; HBVY

One Day More, *with music.* *Unknown.* AmSS

One day more/ These muttering shoalbrains leave the helm to me. James Russell Lowell. *Fr.* Columbus. PGD

One day my life will end. Biography. "Jan Struther." InMe

One day, nigh weary of the irksome way. Una and the Lion. Spenser. *Fr.* The Faerie Queene, I, 3. LPS-3

One day, not here, you will find a hand. Again. Charlotte Mew. MBP; MoAB; MoBrPo; NeMA

One day one young Creole Candio. Criole Candjo. *Unknown.* ABF
One day, or no, one night. The Salt and Pepper Dance. Jimmy Garthwaite. GFA
One day people will touch and talk perhaps easily. Daydream. A. S. J. Tessimond. SeCePo
One day that black and shining angel who. Black Angel. Lewis Thompson. AtBAP
"One day that we mustered on Sliabh Truim." *Unknown. Fr.* The Hunt of Sliabh Truim. OnYI
One day the dreary old King of Death. Death's Ramble. Thomas Hood. BOHV
One day the Earth will be only. Prophecy. Jules Supervielle. MiCF
One day the god of fond desire. Song. James Thomson. EnLoPo
One day the letters went to school. The Letters at School. *Unknown.* OTPC (1923 ed.)
One day, the vine. The Rebellious Vine. Harold Monro. WaKn
One day there came with glowing soul. The Story of Macha. *Unknown. Fr.* Dinnshenchas. OnYI
One day there entered at my chamber door. My Uninvited Guest. May Riley Smith. AA; WGRP
One day there reached me from the street. The Goatherd. Grace Hazard Conkling. GaP; TiPo
One day there wandered on a river bank. The Heron. La Fontaine. TrFP
One day thou didst desert me—then I learned. To Imagination. Edith M. Thomas. AA
One day through the primeval wood. The Calf-Path [*or* Boston]. Sam Walter Foss. BoHiPo; CV; DDA; HBV; HBVY
One day,—'twas on a gentle, autumn noon. Leigh Hunt. *Fr.* The Story of Rimini, III. ERP
One day we built a snowman. Snowman. *Unknown.* GFA
One day we took a journey. Pop-Corn Land. Elsie F. Kartack. GFA
One day when Father and I had been. Moon Magic. Viscountess Grey of Fallodon. PCH
One day when I went visiting. I Held a Lamb. Kim Worthington. TiPo (1959 ed.)
One Day When We Went Walking. Valine Hobbs. BrR
One day, while still the dawn denied the call. Dawn in the Everglades. Halle W. Warlow. BLA
One died upon a lonely Cross. The Atonement. Gerald Gould. POTE
One dignity delays for all. Emily Dickinson. AnAmPo; LA
One Distant April. Gertrude Hall. LBAP
One does such work as one will not. In the Matter of Two Men. James David Corrothers. BANP
One Down. Richard Armour. WhC
One Driveth Out Another. John Heywood. ReIE
One dwelt in darkness and sang within his dwelling. The Banquet. Louise Driscoll. MaRV
One effort more, my altar this bleak sand. Walt Whitman. *Fr.* The Prayer of Columbus. OQP; PGD; PoRL; QP-1
One elf, I trow, is diving now. Song of the Elfin Steersman. George Hill. AA; APW
One End of Love. James Branch Cabell. SPP
One-erum, two-erum. *Unknown.* OxNR
One-ery, ore-ery [*or* two-ery], ickery, Ann. *Unknown.* FaPON; OxNR; RIS; SiTL
One-ery, two-ery, tickery, seven. *Unknown.* OxNR
One eve of beauty, when the sun. Constancy. *Unknown.* LPS-2
One eve, when St. Columba strode. The Cross of the Dumb. "Fiona Macleod." ChrBoLe; CLS
One evening above all I remember. The Moment Inexpressible. Jens Peter Jacobsen. BoDS
One evening as a maid did walk. The Trooper and Maid. *Unknown.* BaBo
One evening as I chanced to stray along the banks of Clyde. The *Lady of the Lake. Unknown.* ShS
One evening as the sun went down [*or* when the sun was low]. The Big Rock Candy Mountains. *Unknown.* APW; ChTr
One evening fair when Venus bright her radiant beams displayed. The Irish Girl's Lament. *Unknown.* ShS
One evening last June as I rambled. The Little Eau Pleine. *Unknown.* IHA
One evening late I chanced to stray. MacKenna's Dream. *Unknown.* OnYI
One evening (surely I was led by her). Wordsworth. *Fr.* The Prelude, I. OBRV
One evening walking out, I o'ertook a modest colleen. Among the Heather. William Allingham. IrPN
One evening when the sun was low. *See* One evening as the sun went down.
One evening while reclining. Accepted and Will Appear. "Parmenas Mix." BOHV
One evening, while the cooler shade she sought. Dryden. *Fr.* The Hind and the Panther, I. PoEL-3
One eye screwed up, cheek out of joint. The Biologic Face. "L. B." CAG
One-eyed Calendar, The. Conrad Aiken. Preludes for Memnon, LII. BLV
(Prelude LII.) LiTM
One Face Alone. Sara Coleridge. *Fr.* Phantasmion. VA
One face looks out from all his canvases. In an Artist's Studio. Christina Rossetti. EnLi-2; OAEP; POTT; VLEP
One fantee wave. Edith Sitwell. *Fr.* Gold Coast Customs. OBMV
One Fight More. Theodosia Garrison. BLP; PC
One figure flitting through my dreamland ways. November Sunshine. Albert E. S. Smythe. CPG
One fine day in the middle of the night. *Unknown.* BoN; CenHV
One fine morning, in a land full of mild-mannered folk. Royalty. Arthur Rimbaud. AnFP
One fine October morning. *Unknown.* BoN
One flame-winged brought a white-winged harp-player. Passion and Worship. Dante Gabriel Rossetti. The House of Life, IX. BPN; EmBrPo; PoVP; ViPo
One for All Time, The. Paul Eluard, *tr. fr. French by* Wallace Fowlie. MiCF
One for her Club and her own Latch-key fights. An Omar for Ladies. Josephine Dodge Daskam Bacon. HBV; PA
One for [the] money. Mother Goose. OxNR; StVeCh (1955 ed.)
One for sorrow, two for joy. *Unknown.* OxNR
One Forgotten, The. Dora Sigerson Shorter. PoRL; TIP
One Friday morn when [*or* On Friday morning as] we set sail. The Mermaid [*or* One Friday Morn]. *Unknown.* CH; ESPB; OnSP; OTPC (1946 ed.); SG; ViBoFo (A *vers.*).
One Generation to Another. Carla Lanyon Lanyon. ReTS
One Gift I Ask. Virginia Bioren Harrison. HBV
One Girl. Sappho, *tr. fr. Greek by* Dante Gabriel Rossetti. AWP; BMEP; EnLi-1; JAWP; LEAP; OuHeWo; WBP
(Beauty.) ViBoPo
("Like the sweet apple which reddens upon the topmost bough.") GrPo
(Young Bride, A [*or* The]). GrL; LiTW; OxBG
One glance and I had lost her in the riot. The Nun. Odell Shepard. PraNu; SBMV
One gloomy eve I roam'd about. One Careless Look. John Clare. AnFE; EG; LiTL
One God, The. *Unknown, tr. fr. Egyptian by* E. A. Wallis Budge. MaRV
One good thing my mother done. This Ole Worl' Ain't Goin' to Stan' Much Longer. *Unknown.* StDa
One great truth in life I've found. Those We Love the Best. Ella Wheeler Wilcox. PoToHe
One grey and foaming day. R. P. Blackmur. Sea Island Miscellany, V. MoVE
One Grey Hair, The. Walter Savage Landor. *See* One White Hair, The.
One had grown almost affluent: one had. Elegy for an Estrangement. John Holloway. NePoEA
One half of me was up and dressed. The Gentle Check. Joseph Beaumont. SeCL
One Happy Moment. Dryden. *See* No, No, Poor Suffering Heart.
One Hard Look. Robert Graves. LoPo
(Song: One Hard Look.) MBP; MoBrPo
One Haunted Night. John Irvine. UnW
One Heart, One Love. Jami, *tr. fr. Persian by* F. Hadland Davis. OnPM
One heifer and one fleecy sheep. Aristeides. Antipater of Sidon. AWP
One hero dies,—a thousand new ones rise. Nathan Hale. William Ordway Partridge. GA
One holy Church of God appears. The Church Universal. Samuel Longfellow. GrCo-1; MaRV; OlF; WGRP
One Home. William Stafford. NePA
One honest John Tomkins, a hedger and ditcher. Contented John. Jane Taylor. HBV; HBVY
One Hope, The. Dante Gabriel Rossetti. The House of Life, CI. BEL; BPN; EmBrPo; EnLi-2; EnLit; EPN; EPP; HBV; NBE; POTT; PoVP; REAL; ViPo; ViPP
One Horse Chay. *Unknown.* OxBoLi
"One-Hoss Shay," The; or, The Deacon's Masterpiece. Oliver Wendell Holmes. *See* Deacon's Masterpiece, The.
One Hour to Madness and Joy. Walt Whitman. AnAmPo; LA
One hue of our flag is taken. The Rejected "National Hymns," VI. "Orpheus C. Kerr." BOHV; InMe; LPS-3; PA
One hundred dead, hanging in a cellar. For Dissection. Jerome Meyers. PoP
111. E. E. Cummings. AnEnPo
One Hundred Fifty-first Psalm, A. Henry B. Robins. MaRV
147. E. E. Cummings. *See* Next to Of Course God.
104° Fahrenheit. Francis Brett Young. PoP
One I love. *Unknown.* OxNR

One Immortality. Norbert Engels. CAW
One in a Thousand of Years of the Night. Delmore Schwartz. FiMAP
One in herself not rent by schism, but sound. The Catholic Church. Dryden. *Fr.* The Hind and the Panther, II. OBS; SeEP
One in the boat cried out. The Door. L. A. G. Strong. MBP; MoBrPo
One in the Infinite. George Francis Savage-Armstrong. PC; VA
One in thy thousand statues we salute thee. The Black Virgin. G. K. Chesterton. ISi
One is the race of Gods and men; and yet, though Earth. God and Man. Pindar. *Fr.* Nemean Odes, VI. GrPE
One Kind of Humility. Jean Starr Untermeyer. MAP; MoAmPo (1942 ed.); NLK (1947 ed.)
One Kingfisher and One Yellow Rose. Eileen Brennan. NeIP
One king's daughter said to anither. Sheath and Knife. *Unknown.* CH; ESPB; LO
One-l lama, The. The Lama. Ogden Nash. FaBoCh; FaPON; FiBHP; LiL; LoGBV; SiTL
One Land, One Flag, One Brotherhood. Thomas S. Collier. FOAH
One lay lit by the moon, breast white and bare. Maidens at Rest. Chaeremon. GrL; OxBG
One leaf and then another. Impression of Autumn. Rachel Annand Taylor. EBSV
One lesson, Nature, let me learn of [*or* from] thee. Quiet Work. Matthew Arnold. BPN; CBE; EM-2; EmBrPo; EnL; EnLit; EPN; FaBoBe; GEPC; GrCo-2; HBV; LEAP; MCCG; NeHB; OAEP; OQP; PoRL; PoVP; QP-1; ReTS; TrGrPo; TVSH; ViPP; VLEP; YT
One little dicky-bird/ Hopped on my shoe. Ten Little Dicky-Birds. A. W. I. Baldwin. BoTP
One little Indian boy making a canoe. Ten Little Indian Boys. M. M. Hutchinson. BoTP
One little minute more, Maud. Darling, Tell Me Yes. John Godfrey Saxe. HBV
One London night in a half fog. The Song of the Ill-Beloved. Guillaume Apollinaire. AnFP
One Long Nuptial Day. Dryden. *Fr.* Secret Love. BeR
One looks from the train. The Orient Express. Randall Jarrell. AmP; CoBMV; FiMAP
One Lost, The. Isaac Rosenberg. MBP; MoBrPo
One Love. Edward Shillito. *See* I Am the Last.
One love I; One: within His bridal bower. Aubrey Thomas De Vere. *Fr.* Saint Frideswida. PraNu
"One lump or two? It's comforting to think." Conversation. Berenice C. Dewey. InMe
One man craves a scarf or glove. Civilization. Stanton A. Coblentz. OQP; QP-2
One man in a thousand, Solomon says. The Thousandth Man. Kipling. BoFr
One man's shoulder, another man's thigh. The Unknown Soldier. Charles A. Wagner. AnAmPo; LA
One March Day. *Unknown.* PCH
One midnight, deep in starlight still. Bankrupt. Cortlandt W. Sayres. PoToHe (new ed.)
One misty moisty morning. Mother Goose. BoTP; FaBoBe; HBV; HBVY; MeMeAg; OTPC; OxNR; PPL; RIS; SAS; StVeCh (1955 ed.); TiPo
One moment the boy, as he wander'd by night. The Sea-Maids' Music. Ernest Myers. VA
One More Day, *with music.* *Unknown.* SoAmSa
One more little spirit to Heaven has flown. Little Libbie. Julia A. Moore. ATP
One More Quadrille. Winthrop Mackworth Praed. OBRV
One More River. *Unknown.* SiTL; TreFS
One more Unfortunate. The Bridge of Sighs. Thomas Hood. BCEP; BEL; BeLS; CBOV; EnLi-2; EnLit; EnRP; ERP; EV-4; GTBS; GTBS-D; GTBS-W; GTSE; GTSL; HBV; HoPM; LEAP; LiTG; LPS-2; OBEV; OBVV; PC; PFE; PG; PYM; TreF; VA; WBLP; WHA
One More Year. A. Norton. PEOR
One morn an angel stopped beside my door. The Angel of Dawn. Julian S. Cutler. PEOR
One morn before me were three figures seen. Ode on [*or* to] Indolence. Keats. BPN; EnRP; GEPC; GTBS-W; LiTB; TwHP
One morn I rose and looked upon the world. The Dawn. *Unknown.* PoToHe (new ed.)
One morning a weasel came swimming. The Weasel. *Unknown.* ChTr
One morning as I was traversing. Mountain Song. Juan Ruiz, Archpriest of Hita. LyMA
One morning before Titan thought of stirring his feet. Reverie at Dawn [*or* The Reverie]. Egan O'Rahilly. AnIL; KiLC
One Morning in May (The Nightingale). *Unknown.* AS, *with music;* BaBo
One morning in spring/ We marched from Devizes. Fife Tune. John Manifold. BoAV; ExPo; FaFP; GTBS-W; LiTB; LiTL; LiTM; LoGBV; ShBV-3; SiTL; WaaP; WaP
One morning in the month of June. The Royal Fisherman. *Unknown.* ChTr
One Morning, Oh! So Early. Jean Ingelow. HBV
One morning, one morning, one morning in May. One Morning in May (The Nightingale). *Unknown.* AS; BaBo
One morning, one morning, one morning in May. The Rebel Soldier. *Unknown.* LoGBV; OxBoLi
One morning, one morning, the weather being fine. I Must and I Will Get Married. *Unknown.* TrAS
One morning (raw it was and wet). The Sailor's Mother. Wordsworth. CG
One Morning the World Woke up. Oscar Williams. FaFP; NeTW; WaaP; WaP
One morning when I went downtown. Morning in Spring. Louis Ginsberg. GoYe
One morning, when Spring was in her teens. Two Fishers. *Unknown.* BOHV
One Morning When the Rain-Birds Call. Lloyd Roberts. CaP; OCL
One motionless, yet swift as thought. The All. *Unknown.* *Fr.* The Upanishads. OnPM
One must have a mind of winter. The Snow Man. Wallace Stevens. AnEnPo; CoBMV; CoV; CrMA; NP; Po; PoFS; ReMP
One nail driveth out another with strokes so stout. One Driveth Out Another. John Heywood. ReIE
One nears with Harvard-man expression. Crossing Boston Common. Louise Dyer Harris. WhC
One Need, The. Ella Wheeler Wilcox. BAP
One Night. Marchette Chute. ChBR
One Night. W. W. Gibson. POTE
One Night. Juan Ramón Jiménez, *tr. fr. Spanish by* Thomas Walsh. AnSpL-2
One night,/ One night all full of murmurs. Nocturne. José Asunción Silva. WoL
One night a score of Erris men. Danny. J. M. Synge. AnEnPo
One night all tired with the weary day. The Gnat. Joseph Beaumont. LoBV; OBS
One night as Dick lay fast asleep. Full Moon. Walter de la Mare. AtBAP; TiPo
One night, as dreaming on my bed I lay. There Was No Place Found. Mary Elizabeth Coleridge. OxBoCh
One night as I lay on the prairie. Cowboy Song. *Unknown.* ABS
One night as they was sitting courting. The Bamboo Briars. *Unknown.* ABS
One night came on a hurricane. The Sailor's Consolation. William Pitt [*wr. at. to* Charles Dibdin]. BBV; BeLS; CBOV; EtS; HBV; LBN; LPS-2; OTPC (1946 ed.); PYM; StVeCh (1955 ed.); TreFS; TVSH
One night came Winter noiselessly and leaned. The Frosted Pane. Sir Charles G. D. Roberts. HBV; LEAP; SN
One night he lay on my breast. One Night. W. W. Gibson. POTE
One night I dreamed I was locked in my Father's watch. My Father's Watch. John Ciardi. ImOP
One night I held all Europe in my arms. The Enemy. John Waller. NeBP
One night I lay asleep in Africa. Bookra. Charles Dudley Warner. AA; HBV; LBAP
One night I met when stepping out. Frustrated Male. Hughes Mearns. *Fr.* Later Antigonishes. InMe; SiTL
One night I reached a cave: I slept, my head. Incident on a Journey. Thom Gunn. NePoEA
One night i' th' year[e] my dearest beauties, come. To His Lovely Mistresses. Robert Herrick. OAEP; TriL
One night I wandered alone from my comrades' huts. A Moment's Interlude. Richard Aldington. POTE
One night in late October. Judged by the Company One Keeps. *Unknown.* BLPA; NeHB; YaD
One night of the two bad years. The Nightmare. Sorley Maclean. NeBP
One night on the fall beef round-up. The Cowboy's Fate. Wallace D. Coburn. PoOW
One night Polly Oliver lay musing in bed. Polly Oliver's Rambles. *Unknown.* ViBoFo
One night quite bang up to the mark. Johnny Raw and Polly Clark. *Unknown.* CoMu
One night returning from my twilight walk. A Ballad of Past Meridian. George Meredith. EmBrPo
One Night Stand. LeRoi Jones. NeAP
One night the wind it blew cold. Mary of the Wild Moor. *Unknown.* BaBo
One night upon the southern sea. The Silence of God. Sir Osbert Sitwell. WaKn
One night we were together, you and I. Lion and Lioness. Edwin Markham. LBAP
One night when I got frisky. I'll Never Get Drunk Any More. *Unknown.* OnYI

One night when I went down. The Heap of Rags. W. H. Davies. EPP
One noble heart, one only, grieved in sincerity. The Death of Oenone. Quintus Smyrnaeus. *Fr.* Posthomerica, X. GrPE
One noonday, at my window in the town. Ball's Bluff. Herman Melville. BAV; SoV
One No. 7. John Frederick Frank. GoYe
One o'clock in the letter-box. The Meeting. Muriel Rukeyser. MoAmPo; TrJP
One of her hands, one of her cheeks lay under. A Supplement of an Imperfect Copy of Verses of Mr. Wil. Shakespeare. Sir John Suckling. SeEP
One of my foes deprived me of life. *Unknown. Fr.* Riddles. EnLit
One of my wishes is that those dark trees. Into My Own. Robert Frost. TwP
One of Our Presidents. Wendell Phillips Stafford. GrCo-2
One of the days when one's a martyr. Sad September Sentiments. Edwin Meade Robinson. YT
One of the Jews (50 A.D.). C. P. Cavafy, *tr. fr. Modern Greek by* Rae Dalven. MoGP; TrJP
One of the Kings of Scanderoon. The Jester Condemned to Death. Horace Smith. BOHV; PoeMoYo
One of the Pharisees desired [Jesus] that he would eat with him. St. Luke, Bible, *N.T.* LO
One of the Regiment. Douglas Le Pan. CaP
One of the two according to your choice. Haidee. Byron. *Fr.* Don Juan. SeCePo
One of these men will find my skeleton. Sequence. Elinor Wylie. AV
One of those queer, artistic dives. The Women of the Better Class. Oliver Herford. HBMV
One of us in the compartment stares. Two Travelers. C. Day Lewis. EnLit
One of Us Two. Ella Wheeler Wilcox. PoToHe
One Old Ox ("One old ox opening oysters"). *Unknown.* ChTr
(One Old Oxford Ox.) OTPC (1923 ed.)
One on another against the wall. The Blackbird. Alice Cary. BLA; LBAP
One only rose our village maiden wore. Flos Florum. Arthur Joseph Munby. VA
One other bitter drop to drink. The Rubicon. William Winter. HBV; LBAP
One ought not to have to care. Loneliness. Robert Frost. *Fr.* The Hill Wife. AmPo; BAP; ChMo; CMP; FaBoEn; IAP; MOAP; NP; SBMV; TwP
One Paddy Doyle lived near Killarney. Doran's Ass. *Unknown.* OnYI
One pale November day. Affaire d'Amour. Margaret Deland. HBV
One Perfect Rose. Dorothy Parker. ALV; FiBHP; PFE
One Person, *sels.* Elinor Wylie.
"I hereby swear that to uphold your house." LoPS; NePA; ReaPo
(House Sonnet.) LiTL
(Sonnet from "One Person.") LiTA; MAP; MoAB; MoAmPo
(Sonnets from "One Person.") NP; OxBA
"Let us leave talking of angelic hosts."
(Sonnets from "One Person.") OxBA
"My honored lord, forgive the unruly tongue."
(Sonnets from "One Person.") NP
"O love, how utterly I am bereaved."
(Sonnets from "One Person.") NP
"Upon your heart, which is the heart of all."
(Sonnets from "One Person.") NP
"When I perceive the sable of your hair." ChMo; PeBoSo
(Sonnet: "When I perceive the sable of your hair.") LoPS
(Sonnets from "One Person.") NP
One petal of a blood-red tulip pressed. Hallucination, I. Arthur Symons. VLEP
One phrase of these plain country people. Getting Through. Robert P. Tristram Coffin. AnNE
One Piecee Thing. *Unknown, quoted by* "Lewis Carroll" *in* A Tangled Tale, VI. WhC
One pleasant summer morning [*or* day] it came a storm of snow. The Crooked Gun [*or* A Deer Hunt]. *Unknown.* CSF; OuSiCo
One Poet Visits Another. W. H. Davies. FaBoTw
One potato, two potato. Counting-out Rhymes. *Unknown.* FaPON
One race are men and gods, for all and each. Of Gods and Men. Pindar. *Fr.* Nemean Odes, VI. GrR
One Race, One Flag. A. R. D. Fairburn. AnNZ
One range of mountains. Meditation [*or* A Girl's Yearning]. Li Yu. ChLP; WhP
One remains, the many change and pass, The. Lumen de Lumine. Shelley. *Fr.* Adonais. GoBC; InP
One Remembering the Marshes. Loren C. Eiseley. CAG
One righteous word for Law—the common will. The Pilgrim Fathers. John Boyle O'Reilly. PEDC
One road leads to London. Roadways. John Masefield. BEL; BoTP; GTSL; MCCG
One room I'll have that's full of shelves. Frank Sidgwick, *wr. at. to* Robert Jones Burdette. *Fr.* When My Ship Comes In. DDA
One Rose. Mary Sinton Leitch. PR
One, round the candytuft. I Spy. N. E. Hussey. BoTP
One rule of life there is, one path that leads to happiness. The Way of Happiness. Bacchylides. GrR
One sat within a hung and lighted room. Love and Poverty. Elisabeth Cavazza Pullen. AA
One Saturday. "Marian Douglas." AA
One sees her brougham still. At Eighty. "Katherine Hale." OCL
1 September 1939. John Berryman. NeTW
One shadow glides from the dumb shore. Gloucester Harbor. Elizabeth Stuart Phelps Ward. AA
One Shall Be Taken and the Other Left. Aline Kilmer. LEAP; NP; TBM
One Ship Drives East. Ella Wheeler Wilcox. *See* Winds of Fate, The.
One shoulder up, the other down. The Scarecrow. H. L. Doak. OnYI
One side of the coin has a vicious monarch's face. Render unto Caesar. Rolfe Humphries. CrMA
One side of the potato-pits was white with frost. A Christmas Childhood. Patrick Kavanagh. AnIL; OxBI
One silent night of late. The Cheat of Cupid; or, The Ungentle Guest. Robert Herrick. AWP; PG (1945 ed.); SeCeV
One single Nymph all other Nymphs above. The Blinding [*or* Sacrilege] of Tiresias. Callimachus. GrR; OxBG
One single summer grant me, you mighty ones. To the Fates. Friedrich Hölderlin. AnGP
One sister have I in our house. Emily Dickinson. BoFr
One small life in God's great plan. God's Plan. "Susan Coolidge." *Fr.* Commonplace. MaRV
One soft June night Nettie Blaine rode in. The Coquette. Muriel Earley Sheppard. IHA
One sole baptismal sign. George Robinson. OIF
One solitary bird melodiously. Evening. Charles Sangster. CaP
One son was a jewel to me. On the Death of His Son. Lewis Glyn Cothi. LyMA
One song leads on to another. The Empty Purse. W. W. Gibson. ChMo; CMP
One Song More. Clinton Scollard. MuM
One standing on the empty beach. Ballykinlar, May, 1940. Patrick Maybin. NeIP
One star/ Is better far. Thomas Traherne. *Fr.* The Apostasy. CoBE
One Star Fell and Another. Conrad Aiken. Preludes for Memnon, LVII. MAP; MoAmPo; PreP
One steed I have of common clay. Comrades. Henry Ames Blood. AA
One Step at a Time. *Unknown.* WBLP
One Step Backward Taken. Robert Frost. OnHM
One step beyond life's work-day things. James Russell Lowell. *Fr.* A Mystical Ballad. UnW
One stormy day in winter. The Splinter. James Kenneth Stephen. CenHV
One stormy morn I chanced to meet. A Kiss in the Rain. Samuel Minturn Peck. BOHV
One Stormy Night. *Unknown. See* Two Little Kittens.
One summer evening (led by her) I found. Wordsworth. *Fr.* The Prelude, I. EV-3; FiP; MyFE; ShBV-3; ViBoPo
One summer I stayed/ On a farm, and I saw. The Two Families. Joyce L. Brisley. BoTP
One summer morn my lady fair did rise. Helen's Bosom. Pierre de Ronsard. TrFP
One summer morning a daring band. The Ballad of Ishmael Day. *Unknown.* PAH
One summer's day a fox was passing through. The Fox and the Grapes. Joseph Lauren. GoTP; RIS
One summer's day in the month of May. The Big Rock Candy Mountain. *Unknown.* MaC
One Sunday after dark, I went to take the air. Youpe! Youpe! River Along. *Unknown.* IHA
One Sunday morning, into Youghall walking. Youghall Harbor. *Unknown.* OnYI
One Sunday morning soft and fine. Brigadier. *Unknown.* BoCaPo (1948 ed.)
One sweet of hands, one starred for grace. A Woman of Words. Amanda B. Hall. HBMV
One sweetly solemn thought. Nearer Home. Phoebe Cary. AA; AnAmPo; BLP; BLRP; FaFP; HBV; LA; LBAP; LPS-2; NeHB; OQP; PTA-2; QP-1; TreF; WBLP; WGRP
One tawny paw is all it takes to squash. Some Lines in Three Parts. Peter Viereck. MiAP; MoAmPo (1950 ed.)
One that I cherished. Falstaff's Lament over Prince Hal Become Henry V. Herman Melville. ViBoPo

One that is ever kind said yesterday. The Folly of Being Comforted. W. B. Yeats. AnIL; AnIV; GTBS; GTMS; GTSL; LoPS; Po; PoE; PoeT

One there lived on the east side of the city. Meeting. Josephine Miles. FiMAP

One There Was. Stella Fisher Burgess. ChIP; StJW

One they hunt by night, The. I Am Ham Melanite. William Millett. GoYe

One Thing. "Owen Meredith." OQP; QP-2; WBLP

One Thing at a Time. M. A. Stodart. PoToHe (new ed.)

One thing at a time. *Unknown.* OxNR

One thing has a shelving bank. A Drumlin Woodchuck. Robert Frost. GoYe; PoLFOT; WaKn

One thing in all things have I seen. The Secret [*or* Unity]. "Æ." MBP; MoBrPo; PoVP

One thing is sure. The Pulse. Mark Van Doren. MAP; MoAmPo

One Thing Needful, The. Max Isaac Reich. BLRP

One thing that literature would be greatly the better for. Very like a Whale. Ogden Nash. ShBV-3; TrGrPo

One thing they say displeases me. Deduction. Reinmar von Hagenau. LyMA

One thing to sing the beloved, another, alas! The Third Duino Elegy. Rainer Maria Rilke. LiTW

One thought I have, my ample creed. The Thought of God. Frederick Lucian Hosmer. GrCo-1

One Thousand Seven Hundred and Thirty-eight. Pope. *See* Epilogue to the Satires.

One time I heard a tender story told. Going Blind. Ella Higginson. MOAH

One time, in Alexandria, in wicked Alexandria. Thais. Newman Levy. BoHV; FiBHP; InMe

One time when I sat talking to a friend. Something Sorto' Healing. Margaret E. Bruner. AlBD

One time when I was sick. Clouds and Sky. Lancaster Pollard. NLK

One to All Men. Plato, *tr. fr. Greek by* Lord Neaves. OnPM

One to destroy is murder by the law. The Criminality of War. Edward Young. PGD

One to make ready. A Line-up. *Unknown.* OxNR; PCH

One Token. W. H. Davies. ChMo; CMP; MM

One told me, Heraclitus, you were dead. Heraclitus [*or* The Dead Poet]. Callimachus. GrL; GrPE

One touch there is of magic white. Very Far Away. William Alexander. TIP

One Twilight Hour. George Meredith. *See* Modern Love: "We saw the swallows . . ."

One, two,/ Buckle my shoe. Mother Goose. BoChLi; BoTP; GoTP; HBV; HBVY; OTPC; OxNR; PCH; PPL; RIS; SAS; SiTL; StVeCh; TiPo

One-two, is one to you. Ball. Kate Greenaway. PCH

One, Two, Three. Samuel L. Albert. NePoAm-2

One, Two, Three! H. C. Bunner. FaPON; HBV; InP; MPB; OTPC; PCH; PRWS; PTA-2; RAR; TSW; TSWC; TVC; TVSH

One, Two, Three. "Robin Christopher." RIS

One, two, three,/ The bumble-bee. *Unknown.* RIS

One, two, three,/ I love coffee. *Unknown.* OxNR

One! two! three!/ Outside the school. Sing-Song Rhyme. *Unknown.* BoTP; SiSoSe

One, two, three,/ Caroline, what is the matter with you, my dear? Un, Deux, Trois. *Unknown.* ABF

One, two, three, four,/ Mary at the cottage door. Mother Goose. OxNR; PCH

1, 2, 3, 4, 5!/ I caught a hare alive. Mother Goose. TiPo

One, two, three, four, five,/ Once I caught a fish alive. *Unknown.* OxNR

One, two, three, four, five, six, seven,/ All good children go to heaven. *Unknown.* RIS

One, two, three, four; it's four o'clock. Snow-bound. Edward Sandford Martin. PR

1-2-3 was the number he played but today the number came 3-2-1. Dirge. Kenneth Fearing. AmP; HoPM; LiTM; NAMP; PoRA; TrJP

One, two, whatever you do. *Unknown.* OxNR

One ugly trick has often spoiled. Meddlesome Matty. Ann Taylor. EV-4; HBV; HBVY; OTPC (1946 ed.)

One unkind word in the early morn. The Boomerang. Carrie May Nichols. PoToHe

One used his pinions eagle-like. De Gustibus. John Erskine. TBM

One Version. Leonora Speyer. *See* Mary Magdalene.

One very earnest prayer is mine today. Thank Thee. Egi. SoLD

One Voice. Winifred Welles. VOD

One voice, one people, one in heart. Brock. Charles Sangster. BoCaPo; CPG

One wading a Fall meadow finds on all sides. The Beautiful Changes. Richard Wilbur. FiMAP

One was fire and fickleness, a child, The. Voltaire and Gibbon. Byron. *Fr.* Childe Harold's Pilgrimage, III. CoEV; OBRV

One Was God. *Unknown.* HiLiAm

One watch had passed, and still sweet slumber shed. Sohráb Is Born. Firdausi. *Fr.* Shah Namah. PeP

One Way of Love. Robert Browning. BPN; EmBrPo; GEPC; HBV; OtMeF; PoVP; TOP; VA; VLEP

One Way of Trusting. Hannah Parker Kimball. AA

One-Way Song, *sel.* Wyndham Lewis.
"In any medium except that of verse," XXIV. SiTL

One weapon I would keep. Preparedness. Jean Grigsby Paxton. PGD

One Week. Carolyn Wells. LBN; PFE; PoeMoYo

One well might say the town was very dull. Revelation. David Morton. PoTo

One Wept Whose Only Child Was Dead. Alice Meynell. *See* Maternity.

One White Hair, The. Walter Savage Landor. HBV; VA
(One Grey Hair, The.) LPS-3

One whitest lily, reddest rose. One. John Vance Cheney. LBAP

One Who Dared to Die. Thomas Curtis Clark. ChIP

One who has loved the hills and died. Pony Rock. Archibald MacLeish. ChMo; CMP

One who hath betrayed/ His own bliss. The Void of a Joyless Heart. Sophocles. *Fr.* Antigone. GrR

One, who is not, we see; but one, whom we see not, is. The Higher Pantheism in a Nutshell. Swinburne. *Fr.* Heptalogia. ALV; BOHV; EmBrPo; HBV; NA; PA; PoVP; SiTL; ViP; ViPo; ViPP; VLEP

One who lets down Cassiopeia's hair, The. Constellation. Merrill Moore. TrGrPo (1942 ed.)

One Who Never Turned His Back. Robert Browning. *Fr.* The Epilogue to "Asolando." GrCo-2

One who sees giant Orion, the torches of winter midnight. Flight of Swans. Robinson Jeffers. CoV

One Who Stayed, The. Ada Foster Murray. LEAP

One Who Struggles, The. Ernst Toller, *tr. fr. German by* E. Ellis Roberts. TrJP

One Who Watches. Siegfried Sassoon. TrJP

One whom I knew, a student and a poet. Epitaph [*or* Poem]. Alex Comfort. MoBrPo (1950 ed.); SeCePo

One whom I loved and never can forget. The Ghost. Hermann Hagedorn. UnW

One will be close beside you as you stare. At Palomar. Sister Mary Edwardine. JKCP (1955 ed.)

One with eyes the fairest. Chorus: Love Song. Euripides. *Fr.* Cyclops. AWP; GrPo; JAWP; WBP

One with Nature. Shelley. *Fr.* Adonais. MaRV

One with the turf, one with the tree. Epitaph for Us. Edgar Lee Masters. ChMo; CMP

One with the Universe. Toyohiko Kagawa, *tr. fr. Japanese by* Lois J. Erickson. SoLD

One without looks in to-night. The Fallow Deer at the Lonely House. Thomas Hardy. AWP; CH; ChMo; CMP; InPo; MoVE

One Woman. Zoë Akins. BLP; LEAP

One word! Robert Norwood. *Fr.* The Witch of Endor. CPG

One word beyond all rules. Love. Gordon LeClaire. CaP

One Word Is Too Often Profaned. Shelley. EmBrPo; EV-4; GTBS; GTBS-D; GTBS-W; GTSE; LiTB; LiTG; LiTL; MCCG; NeHB; OBRV; TyEnPo; WHA
(Desire of the Moth, The.) BLV; BoLiVe
(Love.) FiP
(To ——: "One word is too often profaned.") ATP; BCEP; BEL; BPN; CaAE; EM-2; EnL; EnLi-2; EnRP; EPN; EPP; ERP; ExPo; FaBoEn; GEPC; GTSL; HBV; LEAP; LoBV; LoPo; OAEP; OBEV; PC; PG; PoE; ShBV-4; TCEP; TOP; TrGrPo; ViBoPo

Worship, *sel.* MaRV

One Word More. Robert Browning. BMEP; BPN; EPP; EtPaEn; FiP; GEPC; HBV; OtMeF; PoEL-5; PoVP; REAL; VA; ViBoPo, *abr.*; ViPP; VLEP

Phases of the Moon, *sel.* ChTr

One word of well directed wit. David and Goliath. John Banister Tabb. PoMa

"One World." Brent Dow Allinson. MaRV

One World. Dante. *Fr.* Divina Commedia. MaRV

One would be in less danger. Family Court. Ogden Nash. FiBHP

One would not hope to meet. Thoughts at the Museum. Eileen Brennan. OnYI

One writes, that "other friends remain." In Memoriam A. H. H., VI. Tennyson. BEL; BPN; EM-2; EmBrPo; EnLi-2; EPN; GEPC; OAEP; PoEL-5; ViPo; VLEP

One X. E. E. Cummings. FaBoMo

One Year Ago [My Path Was Green]. Walter Savage Landor. EnLi-2
(Lyrics and Epigrams, XII.) ERP
(Lyrics to Ianthe.) BPN

One year ago—a ringing voice. Only a Year. Harriet Beecher Stowe. LPS-1

One year, asleep already. The Good Angel. Rafael Alberti. CoSP

One Year to Live. Mary Davis Reed. PoToHe (new ed.)

O'Neill's War Song. Michael Hogan. OnYI

Onely a little more. *See* Only a little more.
Onely Joy, Now Here You Are. Sir Philip Sidney. *See* Only Joy, Now Here You Are.
Oneness with Him. George Macdonald. MaRV
One's feet are baking, one can feel the arteries throbbing in one's ankles. A Hot Stagnant Evening. Jules Laforgue. AnFP
One's grand flights, one's Sunday baths. The Sense of the Sleight-of-Hand Man. Wallace Stevens. CoBMV; LiTM (rev. ed.); MoAB; MoAmPo (1950 ed.); MoPo
One's none. *Unknown.* OxNR
One's-Self I Sing. Walt Whitman. AmPP (4th ed.); AnAmPo; COBA; CoV; IAP; LA; LEAP; MOAP; OxBA; PoLFOT; TCAP
Ongoing, The. Mary Siegrist. BAP
Onion, The. C. C. Ward. PCH
Onion Skin in Barn. Kenneth Slade Alling. NePoAm
Onions. Swift. *Fr.* Verses for Fruitwomen. AnIV; OnYI
Only. Harriet Prescott Spofford. HBV
Only a baby, fair and small. George Washington. *At. to* Eliza Cook. GA; MPB; OHIP; PEDC; PEOR
Only a Baby Small. Matthias Barr. HBV; HBVY; OTPC (1923 ed.); TVSH
Only a bit of color. Our Flag. Frances Crosby Hamlet. PGD; PSO
Only a boy. Willow Whistle. Ethel Romig Fuller. DDA
Only a cabin, old and poor. The Cabin Where Lincoln Was Born. Robert Morris. GA
Only a Cowboy. *Unknown.* CoSo; CSF
Only a Dad. Edgar A. Guest. FAOV
Only a Dog. Marty Hale. AlBD
Only a Dog. Grenville Kleiser. AlBD
Only a Dream, *sel.* Gerald Massey.
Around Me Rose the Phantoms of the Dark. UnW
Only a Dream-Shadow. Pindar, *tr. fr. Greek by* H. T. Wade-Gery *and* C. M. Bowra. *Fr.* Pythian Odes, VIII. GrR (Human Life.) OxBG
Only a few could understand his ways and his outfit queer. The Lost Range. Henry Herbert Knibbs. DDA
Only a Flower. Toyohiko Kagawa. MaRV
Only a fool would eat his heart out so. Ballad of the Bushman. Eileen Duggan. CoBE
Only a Gambler Loves Peace. Eunice de Chazeau. OnPM
"Only a housemaid!" She looked from the kitchen. Unsatisfied. Oliver Wendell Holmes. AnNE; APW
Only a Little. Dora Read Goodale. PEOR
Only [*or* Onely] a little more. His Poetry [*or* Poetrie] His Pillar. Robert Herrick. CenL; CoEV; EG; EM-1; EnL; EnLit; FaBoEn; LoBV; MyFE; OBS; SeCL; SeEP
Only a Little Thing. Mrs. M. P. Handy. PEOR; PoToHe
Only a little while since first we met. Song. Brian Hooker. HBMV
Only a man harrowing clods. In Time of "The Breaking of Nations." Thomas Hardy. AnEnPo; BMEP; CaAE; CBOV; ChMo; CMP; CoBMV; EnLi-2 (1949 ed.); EnLit; EPP; EV-5; ExPo; GTBS-W; GTML; GTSL; InP; LiTB; LiTM; LoBV; MBP; MM; MoAB; MoBrPo; NeMA; NP; OAEP (2d ed.); OBEV (new ed.); POTE; PoVP; SeCeV; ShBV-3; TreF; TwCV; ViP; VLEP
Only a manger, cold and bare. The Christmas Symbol. *Unknown.* OQP; QP-1
Only a night forlorn will ever know. Etching. Dennis Murphy. BAP
Only a Private. "F. W. D." BIG
Only a Soldier's Grave. S. A. Jonas. BIG; MDAH
Only a tender little thing. A Snowdrop. Harriet Prescott Spofford. GN
Only a touch, and nothing more. Kate Temple's Song. Mortimer Collins. HBV; VA
Only a Woman. Dinah Maria Mulock Craik. LPS-1
Only a Year. Harriet Beecher Stowe. LPS-1
Only an exile, a Japanese. Fabre, the Bughunter. James Schevill. FiMAP
Only awake to Universal Mind. Chorus. Jack Kerouac. *Fr.* Mexico City Blues. NeAP
Only because she said. Sosei Hoshi, *tr. fr. Japanese by* I. W. Furukami. LiTW
Only begotten Son, seest thou what rage. Free Will and God's Foreknowledge. Milton. *Fr.* Paradise Lost, III. ExPo
Only blossoms of the plains are black, The. The Plains. Roy Fuller. BoSA; MoPo
Only by sorrows' ladder shall we rise. Sorrows' Ladder. Gertrude Callaghan. CAW
Only cows can loll at ease. Pastorale. Mildred Weston. PoMa
Only Five. *Unknown.* MeMeAg
Only for love of love. Emblem. Michael Hamburger. PoN
Only for these I pray. Two Prayers. Charlotte Perkins Gilman. OQP; QP-2; WGRP
Only for this I grieve for you. *Unknown, tr. fr. Modern Greek by* Rae Dalven. MoGP
Only from chaos/ Is creation. Song for These Days. Patrick F. Kirby. GoBC
Only from day to day. To-Day. John Boyle O'Reilly. OnYI
Only ghost I ever saw, The. Emily Dickinson. NePA
Only Heaven Is Given Away. Rose Darrough. MaRV
Only in Dreams. Josiah Gilbert Holland. PEOR
Only in my deep heart I love you, sweetest heart. A Farewell. "Æ." OBVV
Only in spring do the quince-flowers quiver. Passion without Respite. Ibycus. GrPE
Only in the evening does my part of the city. My Part of the City. Léon Paul Fargue. MiCF
Only Jealousy of Emer, The, *sel.* W. B. Yeats.
Song: "Woman's beauty, A, is like a white/ frail bird." MoAB
Only Jesus Will I Know. Charles Wesley. BePJ
Only Joy, Now Here You Are. Sir Philip Sidney. Astrophel and Stella: Fourth Song. EIL; InvP; OBSC; SiPS (Fourth Song.) AtBAP; ReEn; ReIE; SiCE; TuPP (Song from "Astrophel and Stella.") LEAP
Only kid, An! an only kid. Had Gadya—a Kid, a Kid. *Unknown.* TrJP
Only last week, walking the hushed fields. Father and Son. F. R. Higgins. LiTM; OBMV; OxBI; PG (1955 ed.); POTE
Only leaf upon its tree of blood, The. The Red Heart. James Reaney. CaP
Only loneliness is the wind's, The. Submergence. Hazel Hall. NP
Only look at this nosegay of pretty wild flowers. The Wild Wreath. *Unknown.* OTPC (1923 ed.)
Only My Opinion. Monica Shannon. FaPON; MPB; StVeCh (1955 ed.); TiPo
Only Name Given under Heaven, The. Anne Steele. BePJ
Only news I know, The. Emily Dickinson. BLV; BoLiVe
Only, O Lord, in Thy dear love. John Keble. *Fr.* As We Pray. MaRV; PraP
Only of Thee and Me. Louis Untermeyer. HBV; LBMV
Only once more and not again—the larches. In Ampezzo. Trumbull Stickney. AnFE; APA; CoAnAm; CrMA; TwAmPo
Only One. George Cooper. *See* Our Mother.
Only One, The. Jo Gardner. BePJ
Only One Killed. Julia L. Keyes. BIG
Only One King. John Richard Moreland. ChIP; PGD
Only one more day, my Johnny. One Day More. *Unknown.* AmSS
Only One Mother. George Cooper. *See* Our Mother.
Only one who has lifted the lyre. Four Sonnets to Orpheus. Rainer Maria Rilke. *Fr.* Sonnets to Orpheus. LiTW
Only our love hath no decay. John Donne. *Fr.* The Anniversary. LO
Only Pretty Ringtime, The. A. V. Bowen. POTE
Only quiet death. Threnody. Waring Cuney. BANP
Only real airship, The. The Dirigible. Ralph Bergengren. FaPON
Only Rose, The. Juan Ramón Jiménez, *tr. fr. Spanish by* John Crow. OnPM
Only serpents change their outward skin. Memory. Nikolai Gumilev. BoRS
Only Seven. Henry S. Leigh. BOHV; HBV; LPS-3; PA
Only Silence. Arthur S. Bourinot. CaP
Only Son, An ("I have slain none"). Kipling. LiA
Only Son, The ("She dropped the bar"). Kipling. *Fr.* All the Mowgli Stories. VLEP
Only Son, An. Leonidas of Tarentum, *tr. fr. Greek by* E. R. Bevan. OxBG
Only Son, The. Sir Henry Newbolt. HBV
Only stand high a long enough time your lightning will come. The Summit Redwood. Robinson Jeffers. AmPP (3d ed.); MOAP
Only, sweet Love, afford me but thy heart. For Her Heart Only. *Unknown.* EIL; LO
Only Tell Her That I Love. Lord Cutts. *See* Song: "Only tell her that I love."
Only that which made us, meant us to be mightier by and by. That Which Made Us. Tennyson. *Fr.* Locksley Hall Sixty Years After. OQP; QP-2
Only the Arab stallion will I. To a Man on His Horse. F. T. Prince. MoPW
Only the Arrogant Heart. Winifred Gray Stewart. MuM
Only the Clothes She Wore. Nathaniel Graham Shepherd. LPS-1
Only the creaking murmur of the wheel. Twelve o'Clock Boat. J. A. R. McKellar. BoAV; MoAuPo
Only the diamond and the diamond's dust. Epitaph for the Race of Man, II. Edna St. Vincent Millay. MoPo
Only the Dream Is Real. Anderson M. Scruggs. OQP; QP-2
Only the fair day's fragrant darkness is ours. Light and Darkness. Henri de Régnier. TrFP
Only the hands are living; to the wheel attracted. Casino. W. H. Auden. MoPo; PoLFOT

Only the Heart. Marjorie Freeman Campbell. CaP
Only the human dead may lie. With Regard to Dogs. Nancy Byrd Turner. AlBD
Only the Lion and the Cock. After Galen. Oliver St. John Gogarty. OBMV; PoRA
Only the living are concerned with living. The Dead. Selma Robinson. PIAE
Only the nest of spices. The Body. Rachel Annand Taylor. GTML
Only the nicorn knows. The Nicorn's Dower. Peter Hopegood. MoAuPo
Only the prism's obstruction shows aright. Deaf and Dumb. Robert Browning. MaRV
Only the shock/ Of earthquake. The Fish-Cart. J. Redwood Anderson. PoTo; TCPD
Only the snowshoes whisper. Snow Forest. Frank Ernest Hill. PoTo
Only the wholesomest foods you eat. Poems in Praise of Practically Nothing, II. Samuel Hoffenstein. BOHV; InMe; SiTL; TrJP
Only the Wind Says Spring. Helen Janet Miller. GoTP
Only Then. Frances Revett Wallace. MuM
Only Thing That Is Left to Do, The. Aasmund Olafsson Vinje, *tr. fr. Norwegian by* Charles W. Stork. AnNoLy
Only thing to cheer me, The. Nature's Sorrow Cure. Catherine Cate Coblentz. OQP; QP-2
Only this evening I saw again low in the sky. Martial Cadenza. Wallace Stevens. NePA; NeTW; OxBA
Only thorns for the Master. Crowns. Louise Upham Brooks. ChIP
Only those coral insects live. The Builders. Judith Wright. SeCePo
"Only through Me!" . . . The clear, high call comes pealing. Dies Irae—Dies Pacis. John Oxenham. MaRV
Only Thy Dust. Don Marquis. LoPo
Only to find Forever, blest. Heaven. Martha Dickinson Bianchi. AA; HBV
Only to those who have climbed the dusky hill. The Swans. Randall Swingler. POTE
Only track now visible was one, The. Crossing the Alps. Wordsworth. *Fr.* The Prelude, VI. CoBE
Only true God, betwixt whom and me, The. Ad Deum. George Chapman. ReIE
Only twice is womankind. Praise of Women. Palladas of Alexandria. LiTW; LyMA
Only two patient eyes to stare. Faded Pictures. William Vaughn Moody. OBAV
Only Waiting. Frances Laughton Mace. BLPA; LPS-2
Only walls. No grass, nor glass. Factory Street in Daylight. Paul Zech. WoL
Only Way, The. Louis V. Ledoux. LBMV
Only Way to Have a Friend, The. *Unknown.* PoToHe (new ed.)
Only Way to Win, The. *Unknown.* WBLP
Only what is heroic and courageious moves our blood. Michael McClure. The Flowers of Politics, II. NeAP
Only when he was old enough, and silent. His Trees. Mark Van Doren. AnFE; CoAnAm; TwAmPo
Only when heaven is unaffronted can we make friends with stars. Heaven and Earth. Frederic Thompson. CAW
Only your arm, and nothing more, I found. Pierre de Ronsard. *Fr.* Sonnets pour Hélène. PrPoCR
Onondaga Madonna, The. Duncan Campbell Scott. PeCV
Onset, The. Robert Frost. AmP; AnNE; ChMo; CMP; CoBMV; CP; IAP; MoAB; MoAmPo; NeMA; OBAV; OxBA; TBM
Onset, The. Jessie B. Rittenhouse. BLA
Onus Probandi. William Stanley Braithwaite. Sandy Star and Willie Gee, V. BANP
(Sandy Star.) BAP; HBMV
Onward and Upward. John Charles Earle. MaRV
Onward, Christian Soldiers. Sabine Baring-Gould. BPP; FaBoBe; HBV; MaRV; NeHB; OlF; OTPC; PCH; TreF; WGRP
Onward flies the rushing train. The Engine Driver. "G. S. O." BoTP
Onward he goeth harping, renownèd Leto's son. The Immortal Choirs. *Unknown. Fr.* Homeric Hymns. GrR
Onward led the road again. Hell Gate. A. E. Housman. ReaPo; UnPo
Onward! Onward! —'neath curse and blow. The Way of the Cross. Joseph I. C. Clarke. CAW
Onwardness. Doris Hedges. CaP
Oocuck, The. Justin Richardson. FiBHP
Oom-pah. Hugh Lofting. GaP
Oon of the greatest authors that men rede. Murder Will Out. Chaucer. *Fr.* The Canterbury Tales: The Nun's Priest's Tale. MyFE
Opal. Josephine Miles. FiMAP
Opal ring and a holly tree, An. Sailor's Woman. Annette Patton Cornell. GoYe
Opals. Arthur Symons. POTT; PoVP
Ope your doors and take me in. The House of the Trees. Ethelwyn Wetherald. CaP; CPG; NLK; OCL; OQP; QP-2; VA
Open. Larry Eigner. NeAP
Open a window on the world. The Puppet Dreams. Conrad Aiken. *Fr.* Punch; the Immortal Liar. MAP
Open afresh your round of starry folds. Marigolds. Keats. *Fr.* I Stood Tiptoe upon a Little Hill. ADAH
Open Air Performance of "As You Like It," An. E. J. Scovell. ChMP
Open-Air Scriptorium, The. *Unknown. See* Over My Head the Forest Wall.
Open Door, The. Grace Coolidge. DDA; MaRV
Open Door, The. Ida Norton Munson. ChIP
Open Door, The. *Unknown, tr. fr. Irish by* Frank O'Connor. KiLC
Open foe may prove a curse, An. Poor Richard's Wisdom. Benjamin Franklin. GoTP
Open Gate, The. John Masefield. *Fr.* The Everlasting Mercy. GrCo-2
Open Grave, An. Walter Savage Landor. TriL
Open House. Theodore Roethke. CoBMV
Open Letter. Rafael Alberti, *tr. fr. Spanish by* Eleanor L. Turnbull. CoSP
Open My Eyes. Bertha Gerneaux Woods. PraP
Open Range. Kathryn Jackson *and* Byron Jackson. FaPON; TiPo
Open Road, The. Walt Whitman. *See* Song of the Open Road.
Open road and a wide road, An. Road Song. Margaret E. Sangster. PoMa
Open Sea, The. Dorothea Mackellar. BoAu
Open Sea, The. William Meredith. NePoEA; UnPo (3d ed.)
Open Secret, An. Caroline Atherton Mason. AA
Open Secret, An. *Unknown.* BoChLi
Open Sesame. *Unknown. See* O for a Booke.
Open, sweet flowers, your eyes. John Francis O'Donnell. *Fr.* May. IrPN
Open the breast. The Signature of Pain. Alan Porter. POTE
Open the Door. Marion Edey. SiSoSe; TiPo
Open the Door. *Unknown.* EIL; ElSeCe; LO
Open the door and who'll come in? Open the Door. Marion Edey. SiSoSe; TiPo
"Open the door, some pity to show!" The Palmer. Sir Walter Scott. CG; OTPC (1923 ed.)
Open the Door to Me, O. Burns. *See* O, Open the Door to Me, O!
"Open the door! Who's there within?" Open the Door. *Unknown.* EIL; ElSeCe; LO
Open the garden gate, walk in, my heart. Written in a Volume of "The Imitation of Christ." Marya Zaturenska. NV
Open the Gates. *Unknown, tr. fr. Hebrew by* Israel Zangwill. TrJP
Open the gates. The Bonny Earl of Murray. *Unknown.* ESPB
Open the old cigar-box, give me a Cuba stout. The Betrothed. Kipling. HBV
"Open the window, and let me in." The Rain. *Unknown.* GFA
Open Thy Doors, O Lebanon. Zechariah, XI: 1-14, Bible, *O.T.* AWP
Open, Time. Louise Imogen Guiney. OBAV
Open to Me! He Commandeth a Fair Wind. *Unknown. Fr.* Book of the Dead. AWP
Open wide all shutters and doors. The Saviour. Piotr Vasilievich Oreshin. BoFr
Open Windows. Sara Teasdale. OBAV; SBMV
Open wound which has been healed anew, An. Sonnet. Richard Chenevix Trench. TrPWD
Open Your Eyes. Emma Boge Whisenand. PoToHe (new ed.)
Open your gates for him. Harold at Two Years Old. Frederic W. H. Myers. HBMV
Open your gates, ye everlasting Piles! Cathedrals, etc. Wordsworth. PeBoSo
Open Your Heart. William James Price. LPS-1
Opened like a big new colored-picture book. Indian Summer —Buffalo Summer. Winfield Townley Scott. FiMAP
Opening Address ("Kind friends, we welcome you today"). *Unknown.* MeMeAg
Opening Argument, The. Milton. *See* Invocation to the Heavenly Muse.
Opening of the Tomb of Charlemagne, The. Sir Aubrey De Vere. HBV
Opening our windows toward Jerusalem. Toward Jerusalem. Amy Carmichael. MaRV
Opening Poem. Boethius, *tr. fr. Latin at. to* Alfred, King of England. *Fr.* Consolation of Philosophy. LaP
Opening Year, The. *Unknown, tr. fr. Latin by* F. Pott. BLRP

Openly, yes,/ with the naturalness. Melancthon. Marianne Moore. AtBAP; CrMA
Opera House, An. Amy Lowell. CV
Opera in English? Benjamin M. Steigman. WhC
Opera singer softly sang, The. Essence. Samuel Greenberg. MoPo; NePA
Opera star named Maria, An. *Unknown.* GoTP
Operatic Note. Melville Cane. UnS
Operation, The. W. W. Gibson. CP
Operation. W. E. Henley. *Fr.* In Hospital. EPP; LEAP; PoVP; ViP
Ophelia. Arthur Rimbaud, *tr. fr. French.* AnFP, *tr. by* Daisy Aldan; ChTr, *tr. by* Brian Hill; TrFP, *tr. by* Alan Conder
Ophelia. Vernon Watkins. MOVE
Ophelia's Death. Shakespeare. *Fr.* Hamlet, V, i. ChTr
Ophelia's Songs. Shakespeare. *Fr.* Hamlet, IV, v.
And Will He [*or* A'] Not Come Again? EG; InPo; PoEL-2; ViBoPo
(Ophelia's Songs, 2.) AnFE; TrGrPo
He Is Dead and Gone, Lady. LO
How Should I Your True Love Know. CBOV; ChTr; EG; EPP; EV-1; InPo; LiTB; LiTG; LiTL; TCEP; ViBoPo
(Friar of Orders Grey, The.) GoBC
(Ophelia's Song.) CBE; OBSC
(Ophelia's Songs, 1.) AnFE; TrGrPo
(Song.) CH
(Song from "Hamlet.") LEAP
Tommorrow Is [*or* Good Morrow, 'Tis] Saint Valentine's Day. InPo; ViBoPo
(Saint Valentine's Day.) LiTB; LiTG
(Song.) HH; MPB
Ophra. Judah Halevi, *tr. fr. Hebrew by* Nina Salaman. LiTW; TrJP
Opifex. Thomas Edward Brown. OBVV; PoVP
Opinions of the New Chinese Student. Regino Pedroso, *tr. fr. Spanish by* Langston Hughes. PoNe
(Opinions of the New Student.) AnCL
Opium Clippers. Daniel Henderson. EtS
Opium Dream. George Crabbe. *Fr.* The World of Dreams. RO
Opium Fantasy, An. Maria White Lowell. AnFE; APA; CoAnAm
Opium Jottings. Samuel Taylor Coleridge. RO
Opossum. William Jay Smith. GoTP; TiPo (1959 ed.)
Opponent Charm Sustained, The. Samuel Greenberg. MoPo
Opportunity. Berton Braley. FAOV; WBLP
Opportunity. Madison Cawein. AA
Opportunity. Paul Laurence Dunbar. MW
Opportunity. John James Ingalls. AA; BAP; BTP; FaFP; HBV; HBVY; LBAP; MaRV; OHFP; OQP; PTA-1; QP-1; TreF; WBLP; YaD
Opportunity. Machiavelli, *tr. fr. Italian by* James Elroy Flecker. AWP; JAWP; WBP
Opportunity. Walter Malone. BLP; BLPA; DDA; FaBoBe; HBV; LBAP; MaRV; NeHB; OQP; PTA-1; QP-1; SPP; WBLP; YaD
Opportunity. Edwin Markham. OQP; QP-2
Opportunity. Shakespeare. *Fr.* The Rape of Lucrece. LiTB; OBSC
("O opportunity thy guilt is great.") PoEL-2
Opportunity. Edward Rowland Sill. AnNE; BAP; BBV; BLPA; BLV; BTP; GN; GoTP; HBV; HBVY; IAP; LBAP; MAP; MaRV; MCCG; MoAmPo (1942 ed.); NeHB; NeMA; OBAV; OHFP; PCD; PoeMoYo; PoMa; PYM; TCAP; TreFS; TSW; TSWC; WGRP; YaD
(Broken Sword, The.) PoToHe
Opposites. José Moreno Villa, *tr. fr. Spanish by* Eleanor L. Turnbull. CoSP; OnPM
Opposition. Sidney Lanier. AmPP (3d ed.); AnFE; APA; CoAnAm; LiTA; OBAV
Oppressed and few, but freemen yet. The Mecklenberg Declaration. William C. Elam. PAH
Oppressed with grief, in heavy strains I mourn. Elegy by Green for Byles's Cat. Joseph Green. CIV
Ops in a Wimpey. *Unknown.* CoMu
Optimism. Newton Mackintosh. BOHV
Optimism. Blanaid Salkeld. NeIP
Optimism. Ella Wheeler Wilcox. *See* Talk Happiness.
Optimist, The. Sheila Kaye-Smith. ReTS
Optimist, The. D. H. Lawrence. MoPW
Optimist, The. "G. O. R." CAG
Optimist. James Stephens. ChMo; CMP
Optimist, The. *Unknown.* BLPA; GoTP; NeHB; YaD
Optimist, The. Rosamund Marriott Watson. PC
Optimist builds himself safe inside a cell, The. The Optimist. D. H. Lawrence. MoPW
Optimist fell ten stories, The. The Optimist. *Unknown.* BLPA; GoTP; NeHB; YaD
Options. "O. Henry." FiBHP
Opus rises to fortissimo, The. Lengthy Symphony. Persis Greely Anderson. WhC
Opusculum paedagogum. Study of Two Pears. Wallace Stevens. AmPP (4th ed.); OxBA
Or else I sat on in my chamber green. Reading. Elizabeth Barrett Browning. *Fr.* Aurora Leigh. GN; HH
Or else, in an afternoon of minor reflection. Time in the Rock, XCIII. Conrad Aiken. MoVE
Or ever a lick of Art was done. Bygones. Bert Leston Taylor. BOHV; HBMV
Or Ever the Earth Was. Charles Leonard Moore. AA
Or ever the knightly years were gone. To W. A. [*or* I Was a King in Babylon]. W. E. Henley. Echoes, XXXVII. BLPA; BMEP; BPN; EnLi-2; HBV; LoPo; OuHeWo; PoVP; TreF; VLEP
"Or from what spring doth your opinion rise." Sir John Davies. *Fr.* Orchestra. UnS
Or higher, holier, saintlier, when as now. Francis Thompson. *Fr.* A Corymbus for Autumn. VLEP
Or I shall live your epitaph to make. Sonnets, LXXXI. Shakespeare. OAEP; OBSC; PeBoSo
Or I will burst/ Damnation's iron egg, my tomb. Fragment. Thomas Lovell Beddoes. RO
Or is it all illusion? Do the years. David P. Berenberg. *Fr.* Two Sonnets. HBMV
Or love me less [*or* mee lesse] or love me [*or* mee] more. Song. Sidney Godolphin. ElSeCe; MePo; OBS; SeCL; SeEP
Or, Pyrrha, tell me who's the guy. Horace the Wise. Morrie Ryskind. HBMV
Or rushing thence, in one diffusive band. The Sheep-washing. James Thomson. *Fr.* The Seasons: Summer. EnLi-2; EPP
Or scorn [*or* scorne] or pity [*or* pittie] on me take. The Dream [*or* The Dreame]. Ben Jonson. ElSeCe; PoEL-2
Or shall I say, Vain word, false thought. Alteram Partem. Arthur Hugh Clough. BPN; PoVP; VLEP
Or the black centaurs, statuesquely still. Ambuscade. Hugh McCrae. BoAV
Or to the beach descending, with joined hands. Alfred Domett. *Fr.* Ranolf and Amohia. AnNZ
Or what is closer to the truth. When I Buy Pictures. Marianne Moore. OxBA
Or whether doth my mind, being crowned with you. Sonnets, CXIV. Shakespeare. PeBoSo
Or you, or I, Nature did wronge! *Unknown.* SeCSL
Oracle, The. A. E. Coppard. FaBoTw
Oracle, The. Arthur Davison Ficke. HBV; OBAV
Oracle. E. L. Mayo. MiAP
Oracle, The. Walther von der Vogelweide, *tr. fr. German by* Margarete Münsterberg. LyMA
Oracle at Delphi. Robert Bagg. NePoAm-2
Oracle of Delphi, The. Adèle Naudé. BoSA
Oracles, The. A. E. Housman. Last Poems, XXV. AnFE; PoFr; POTT
Oracles. Lionel Johnson. VLEP
I. "Let not any withering Fate."
II. "And yet, what of the sorrowing years."
Oracular Portcullis, The. James Reaney. PeCV
Orange, The. Frank Kendon. PtOT
Orange, The. Charles *and* Mary Lamb. OTPC (1923 ed.)
Orange air grows fetid with smoke, The. Mess Deck Casualty. Alan Ross. WaP
Orange Lily O, The. *Unknown.* IrPN
Orange Tree, The. John Shaw Neilson. BoAV; MoAuPo; NeLNL
Orange Tree by Day. Sacheverell Sitwell. *Fr.* The Red-gold Rain. AtBAP
(Red-gold Rain, The.) MBP; MoBrPo
Orange Tree by Night. Sacheverell Sitwell. *Fr.* The Red-gold Rain. AtBAP
Oranges, The. Abu Dharr, *tr. fr. Arabic by* A. J. Arberry. MooP
Oranges. Ibn Sara, *tr. fr. Arabic by* A. J. Arberry. MooP
Oranges at Jaffa gate, The. Gates. Sister Mary Madeleva. GoBC
Orara. Henry C. Kendall. BoAu
Oratio ad Dominum. Hildebert of Lavardin, *tr. fr. Latin by* Thomas Holley Chivers. LaP
Oration, An, *sel.* Kenneth Porter. *Fr.* To the Younger Old-Americans.
"Too long we have cheated our bellies with crumbs of tradition." PoFr
Oration, An, Entitled "Old, Old, Old, Old Andrew Jackson," *abr.* Vachel Lindsay. ATP (1935 ed.); YaD
(Old Old Old Andrew Jackson, *much abr.*) GA
Orator. Emerson. *Fr.* Quatrains. AnNE; OxBA
Orator, The. Roy McFadden. OnYI
Orator Puff. Thomas Moore. *Fr.* M. P.; or, The Blue Stockings. LPS-3
Orators, The, *sel.* W. H. Auden.
O Where Are You Going. CoEV; LiTB; MoVE; Po; UnPo (3d ed.)
(Epilogue: "'O where are you going?' said reader to rider.") ChMo; EnLit; FaBoCh; LoGBV; ShBV-3; SiTL
(Song.) EnL

Orb I like is not the one, The. The Quiet Eye. Eliza Cook. VA
Orbits. Richard Le Gallienne. VA
Orchard. Hilda Doolittle ("H. D."). AnFE; APA; AtBAP; CoAnAm; CoBA; ExPo; LiTA; MAP; MoAmPo; OxBA; PoTo; SBMV
(Keeper of the Orchards.) BAP
(Priapus.) LEAP
Orchard. Kenji Miyazawa, *tr. fr. Japanese by* Takamichi Ninomiya *and* D. J. Enright. PoLJ
Orchard, The. Sir Herbert Read. *Fr.* Eclogues. BrBE
Orchard at Avignon, An. Agnes Mary Frances Robinson. HBV
Orchard by the Shore, The; a Pastoral. Elinor Sweetman. OBVV
Orchard Ghost, The. Mark Van Doren. DaM
Orchard-Pit, The. Dante Gabriel Rossetti. EnLoPo; PoEL-5; RO; ViP
Orchard Song. Sappho, *tr. fr. Greek by* Edwin M. Cox. LiTW
Orchard will be planted here, you say, An. Mines. E. Serebrovskaya. TrRV
Orchards half the way, The. The First of May. A. E. Housman. TCPD
"Orchards," said Johnny Appleseed. Johnny Appleseed. Arthur S. Bourinot. CaP
Orchards, we linger here because. For a Second Marriage. James Merrill. NePoEA
Orchestra; or, A Poem of [*or* on] Dancing. Sir John Davies. OBSC; ReIE, *abr.*; SiPS; TuPP
Sels.
Dance of Love, The. ElL; SeCePo
Dancing of the Air, The. LPS-2
Dancing Sea, The. ChTr
(Sea Danceth, The.) EtS
"Dauncing (bright Lady) then began to bee." AtBAP; FaBoEn; PoEL-2
Dedications, I: To His Very Friend, Master Richard Martin. SiPS
Dedications, II: To the Prince. SiPS
Of Homer's Odyssey. EG
"Or from what spring doth your opinion rise." UnS
"Yet, once again, Antinous did reply." LO
Orchid, The. Tao Yuan-ming, *tr. fr. Chinese by* Yang Yeh-tzu. WhP
Orchids blossomed beneath the window. Friendship. Tao Yuan-ming. WhP
Ordeal by Fire, The, *sel.* Edmund Clarence Stedman.
"Thou who dost feel Life's vessel strand." WGRP
Ordeal's fatal trumpet sounded, The. Adelgitha. Thomas Campbell. CG
Order. *At. to* St. Francis of Assisi. *See* Cantica: Our Lord Christ.
Order for a Picture, An. Alice Cary. BLPA; OBAV; PTA-1
Order, The, goes; what if we rush ahead. Next Time. Laura Simmons. PGD; PSO
Order is a lovely thing. The Monk in the Kitchen. Anna Hempstead Branch. AnFE; APA; BAP; CoAnAm; CP; LEAP; MAP; MAPA; MoAmPo; MOAP; OBAV; QS; SBMV; TwAmPo
Ordinary, The, *sel.* William Cartwright.
Good Eating Song, A. SeCL
Ordinary Dog, The. Nancy Byrd Turner. AlBD; TiPo
Ordinary Evening in New Haven, An, *sel.* Wallace Stevens.
"Inescapable romance, inescapable choice." ReMP
Ordinary people are peculiar too. Conversation. Louis MacNeice. FaBoMo
Ordinary valour only works, The. "F. Anstey." CenHV
Ordinary Women, The. Wallace Stevens. OxBA
Ordination. Sister Mary Immaculate. GoBC
Ore in the crucible is pungent, smelling like acrid wine, The. Iron Wine. Lola Ridge. NP
O're the Smooth Enameld Green. Milton. *See* Song: "O'er the smooth . . ."
Oread. Hilda Doolittle ("H. D."). AWP; BLV; ExPo; InP; JAWP; MAP; MoAmPo; MOAP; MoVE; NeMA; OxBA; PoeMoYo; PoTo; TCPD; TSW; WBP
Oregon State Song. J. A. Buchanan. PoRL
Oregon Trail, The. William Rose Benét. PaA
Oregon Trail, The. Arthur Guiterman. FaPON; MPB
Oregon Trail, 1851. James Marshall. IHA; PaA; StVeCh
Orestes, *sel.* Lord De Tabley.
"Let us go up and look him in the face." BMEP; LEAP
Orestes, *sels.* Euripides, *tr. fr. Greek.*
In the Furies' Grasp, *tr. by* R. Potter. GrR
(Orestes and Electra, *tr. by* J. A. Symonds.) OxBG
"O dearest maidens, tread with feet of wool," *tr. by* J. A. Symonds. GrPo
Powers of Darkness, *tr. by* Hugh Owen Meredith. GrR
(Furies, The, *tr. by* George Allen.) OxBG
Voice of Hypocrisy, The, *tr. by* Hugh Owen Meredith. GrR
Orestes. Pindar, *tr. fr. Greek by* H. T. Wade-Gery *and* C. M. Bowra. *Fr* Pythian Odes, XI. OxBG
Orestes and Electra. Euripides. *See* In the Furies' Grasp.
Orestes Goes Mad. Aeschylus, *tr. fr. Greek by* G. M. Cookson. *Fr.* Choephoroe. OxBG
Orestes, I am tender of your person. The Voice of Hypocrisy. Euripides. *Fr.* Orestes. GrR
Orestes Pursued. Charles David Webb. NePoAm-2
Orfeo, *sel.* Angelo Poliziano, *tr. fr. Italian by* Hubert Creekmore.
Sacrifice of the Bacchantes in Honor of Bacchus. LyPI
Organ Cactus, The. Dorothy Scarborough. HiLiAm
Organ-Grinder, The. Jimmy Garthwaite. BrR
Organ Grinders' Garden, The. Mildred Plew Meigs. GaP
Organ Recital. Arthur L. Lippmann. PFE
Organist, The. George W. Stevens. BLPA
Organist, The. *Unknown.* BLPA
Organist in Heaven, The. Thomas Edward Brown. LoBV (1949 ed.); OBVV; POTT
Orgy of stone! Death Wedding. Pierre Emmanuel. MiCF
Orient, The. Byron. *See* Bride of Abydos, The.
Orient Express, The. Randall Jarrell. AmP; CoBMV; FiMAP
Orient Ode. Francis Thompson. CoBE
Orient Wheat. Adrienne Cecile Rich. NePoEA
Oriental. José Zorrilla, *tr. fr. Spanish by* Elizabeth du Gué Trapier. AnSpL-2
Oriental Apologue, An. James Russell Lowell. PoEL-5
Orientale. E. E. Cummings. NP; PG; TBM
Orientale. W. E. Henley. BPN
Oriflamme. Jessie Fauset. BANP; MotAn
(I Think I See Her.) GoSl
Origin of Baseball, The. Kenneth Patchen. Po
Origin of Centaurs, The. Anthony Hecht. NePoEA
Origin of Didactic Poetry, The. James Russell Lowell. IAP; PoEL-5
Origin of Ireland, The. *Unknown.* BOHV
Origin of Pattens, The. John Gay. *Fr.* Trivia; or, The Art of Walking the Streets of London. BeR
Origin of the Harp, The. Thomas Moore. LPS-3
Origin of the Opal. *Unknown.* LPS-3
Original Cuss, An. Keith Preston. ALV; WhC
Original Lamb, The, *parody. Unknown.* BOHV; InMe
Original Sin. Robinson Jeffers. MoAB; MoAmPo (1950 ed.); MoVE
Original Sin; a Short Story. Robert Penn Warren. AmP; CrMA; FiMAP; GTBS-W; LiTA; LiTM; MoVE; ReMP
Originality. Thomas Bailey Aldrich. AnNE
Origins and Savage Period of Mankind. Lucretius, *tr. fr. Latin by* William Ellery Leonard. *Fr.* Of the Nature of Things (De Rerum Natura). OuHeWo
Origins of Vegetable and Animal Life. Lucretius, *tr. fr. Latin by* William Ellery Leonard. *Fr.* Of the Nature of Things (De Rerum Natura). OuHeWo
(Origins of Life, The.) LiTW
Orinda to Lucasia. Katherine Philips. LO; SeCL
Orinda to Lucasia Parting, October, 1661, at London. Katherine Philips. OBS
Orinoco, give me a romance. The Complaint. Jacinto Fombona Pachano. TwSpPo
Oriole. Edgar Fawcett. *See* To an Oriole.
Oriole. Marion Mitchell Walker. GFA
Oriole—athlete of the air. Spring's Torch-Bearer. Maurice Thompson. BLA
Orion. Paul Engle. AnAmPo
Orion. Charles Tennyson Turner. VA
Orion; an Epic Poem, *sels.* Richard Henry Horne.
Akinetos. VA
Distraught for Meropé. VA
Eos. VA
In Forest Depths. VA
Meeting of Orion and Artemis. VA
"Scene in front two sloping mountain sides, The." BCEP
Orion Seeks the Goddess Diana. Sacheverell Sitwell. *Fr.* Landscape with the Giant Orion. MoVE
Orion swung southward aslant. Before Marching, and After. Thomas Hardy. AOAH
Orion, tonight forsake your distant walking. Orion. Paul Engle. AnAmPo
Orisons. Edwin McNeill Poteat. NoCaPo (rev. ed.); OQP; QP-2
Orkney Lullaby. Eugene Field. GoTP
Orlando Furioso, *sels.* Ariosto, *tr. fr. Italian.*
"All night the maid reposes in the cave," *fr.* III, *tr. by* William Stewart Rose. PrPoCR
Angelica and the Ork, *fr.* X, *tr. by* Sir John Harington. OBSC
"Angelica, when she had won again," *fr.* XIX, *tr. by* William Stewart Rose. PrPoCR
"Course in pathless woods, which, without rein, The," *fr.* XXIII, *tr. by* William Stewart Rose. PrPoCR
"He stretched his arms, and would embrace the knight," *fr.* XXXIX, *tr. by* William Stewart Rose. PrPoCR
Her Matchless Person, *fr.* VII, *tr. by* John Hoole. LiA
"I speak of that famed damsel, by whose spear," *fr.* II, *tr. by* William Stewart Rose. PrPoCR

Orlando Furioso (*continued*)
"Just as those swans are, poets must be rare," *fr.* XXXV, *tr. by* Edwin Morgan. LyPI
"Little virgin is like unto a rose, A," *fr.* I, *tr. by* L. R. Lind. LyPI
Lunar Valley of Lost Things, The, *fr.* XXXIV, *tr. by* Sir John Harington. LiTW
"Of loves and ladies, knights and arms, I sing," *fr.* I, *tr. by* William Stewart Rose. EnLi-1; PrPoCR
("Of dames, of knights, of arms, of love's delight," *tr. by* Sir John Harington.) ReIE
"Rogero heard the call in joyous vein," *fr.* XXXVI, *tr. by* William Stewart Rose. PrPoCR
Rose, The, *fr.* I, *tr. by* John Hoole. LiA
"Soone after he a christall streame espying," *fr.* XXXIV, *tr. by* Sir John Harington. SiCE
"Then backed the griffin-horse, and soared a flight," *fr.* XXXIV, *tr. by* William Stewart Rose. PrPoCR
"This while does good duke Aymon's daughter mourn," *fr.* XXXII, *tr. by* William Stewart Rose. PrPoCR
"Though an ill mind appear in simulation," *fr.* IV, *tr. by* William Stewart Rose. EnLi-1; PrPoCR
"'Twere frenzy of his every frantic feat," *fr.* XXIX, *tr. by* William Stewart Rose. PrPoCR
"When Reason, giving way to heat of blood," *fr.* XXX, *tr. by* William Stewart Rose. PrPoCR
"When she in other writing had displayed," *fr.* XXXV, *tr. by* William Stewart Rose. PrPoCR
Orlando's Rhymes. Shakespeare. *Fr.* As You Like It, III, ii. OBSC
Orlo's Valediction. Jon Manchip White. NePoEA
Ornamental Water. Louise Townsend Nicholl. NePoAm
Ornithology in Florida. Arthur Guiterman. InMe
Oro Stage, The. H. H. Knibbs. IHA
Oro, the islandmen. The Waistcoat. Padraic Fallon. OxBI
O'Rourk's Frolic. Hugh MacGowran. *See* Description of an Irish Feast, The.
Orphan, The, *sels.* Thomas Otway.
Come, All Ye Youths. OAEP
Morning. EV-3
Orphan, The. *Unknown, tr. fr. Irish by* Frank O'Connor. KiLC
Orphan, The. *Unknown, tr. fr. Chinese by* Arthur Waley. TrCh
Orphan Born. Robert J. Burdette. BOHV
Orphan Girl, The ("No home, no home"). *Unknown.* AS
(Coal Miner's Child, The, *diff. vers., with music.*) OuSiCo
(Mag's Song, *diff. vers., with music.*) AS
"Orphan Hours, the Year is dead." Dirge for the Year. Shelley. DD; GN; HBV; HBVY
Orphans, The. W. W. Gibson. CP
Orphan's Song, The. Sydney Dobell. CH; GTBS-D; LEAP; OTPC; PPL
Orpheus. Antipater of Sidon, *tr. fr. Greek.* GrPE, *tr. by* F. L. Lucas; GrR, *tr. by* Walter Leaf; OxBG, *tr. by* A. J. Butler
Orpheus. *At. to* John Fletcher, *also to* Shakespeare. *See* Orpheus with His Lute.
Orpheus. J. F. Hendry. NeBP
Orpheus. Phanocles, *tr. fr. Greek by* George Allen. OxBG
Orpheus. Elizabeth Madox Roberts. MAP; MoAmPo
Orpheus. Simonides, *tr. fr. Greek by* John Sterling. GrL; OxBG
Orpheus. Yvor Winters. MoVE
Orpheus and Eurydice. Valery Yakovlevich Bryusov, *tr. fr. Russian by* C. M. Bowra. BoR
Orpheus and Eurydice. Ovid, *tr. fr. Latin by* Congreve. *Fr.* Metamorphoses, X. RoL
Orpheus by his magic tones. In the Album of a Composer. Ibsen. AnNoLy
Orpheus, Eurydice, and Hermes. Rainer Maria Rilke, *ad. fr. German by* Robert Lowell. AnGP
Orpheus I Am, Come from the Deeps Below. John Fletcher. TriL
Orpheus in the Underworld. David Gascoyne. FaBoTw; MoP
Orpheus, no more the charmed oaks. Orpheus. Antipater of Sidon. GrR
Orpheus, O Orpheus, gently touch thy Lesbyan lyre. *Unknown.* SeCSL
Orpheus' Song of Triumph. William Morris. *See* O Death, That Maketh Life So Sweet.
Orpheus, whom Oeagrus begot in Thrace. Orpheus. Phanocles. OxBG
Orpheus with His Lute. *At. to* John Fletcher, *also to* Shakespeare. King Henry VIII, *fr.* III, i. CBE; GN; KN; OAEP; TrGrPo; ViBoPo
(Music.) BLV; FaBoCh; LoGBV
(Orpheus.) CoEV; ElL; EV-1; OBEV; OTPC; PoRL; TVSH; UnS
("Orpheus with his lute made trees.") AtBAP; ChTr; SiCE; TuPP
(Song: "Orpheus with his lute made trees.") OBS; PoEL-2
(Sweet Music.) PIAE
Orphic Interior. Leonardo Sinisgalli, *tr. fr. Italian by* Creighton Gilbert. LiTW
Orra, *sel.* Joanna Baillie.
Outlaw's Song, The, *fr.* III. EBSV; EV-3; OBEV; OTPC (1923 ed.); PoFr; TVSH
(Song of the Outlaws.) OBRV
Orrmulum, The, *sel.* Orrm.
"Nu, brotherr Wallterr brotherr min," *Mid. and mod. Eng.* EPP
Orsames' Song. Sir John Suckling. *See* Why So Pale and Wan?
Orson of the Muse, An. George Meredith. EPN
Orthodox. Mark Guy Pearse. MaRV
Orthodox, orthodox, wha believe in John Knox. The Kirk's Alarm. Burns. OxBoLi
Orthopedic elephants at the beginning will constantly turn into apples, The. Surrealist Poem of the Elephant and the Song. Carlos Oquendo de Amat. AnCL
Ortiz. Hezekiah Butterworth. PAH
Ortus. Ezra Pound. LEAP; LiTA; NePA; NP
Ortus Novus Urbe Britannus. Henry Parrot. TuPP
Ortygia. Jessie Mackey. BoAu
O'Ryan was a man of might. Irish Astronomy. Charles G. Halpine. HBV
Oscar was a radish. Vegetable Fantasies. Helen Hoyt. RIS
Oscar Wilde. *At. to* Swinburne. SiTL
Oscar Wilde and Aubrey Beardsley. John Waller. PoN
Osculation. Henry Sydnor Harrison. InMe
Osler. William Sydney Thayer. PoP
Osmund Toulmin. Sir Osbert Sitwell. AtBAP
Osorio. Samuel Taylor Coleridge. *See* Remorse.
Osprey and Eagle. Jessie B. Rittenhouse. BLA
Osprey sails about the sound, The. The Fisherman's Hymn. Alexander Wilson. AA; EtS; LEAP
Ossawatomie. Carl Sandburg. OxBA; PFY; TCPD
Ossian, *sel.* John Francis O'Donnell.
"Spoke my heart in the dearth of the night." IrPN
Ossian's Address to the Sun. James MacPherson. *Fr.* Carthon. BEL
Ossian's Serenade. Calder Campbell. BLPA; NeHB
(Burman Lover, The, *with music.*) TrAS
Ostella, *sel.* John Tatham.
Seeing a Lady. SeCL
("Oh, she is fair: fair as the eastern morn.") LO
Ostend, on Hearing the Bells at Sea. William Lisle Bowles. *See* Sonnet: At Ostend, July 22, 1787.
Ostera! spirit of spring-time. Easter Morning. Frances Laughton Mace. EOAH
Ostia Antica. Anthony Hecht. NePA
Ostler, The. Hyam Plutzik. Horatio, II. FiMAP
'Ostler Joe. George R. Sims. BeLS; BLPA; HBV; TreF
Ostrava. Petr Bezruc, *tr. fr. Czech by* David Daiches. LiTW
Ostrich Is a Silly Bird, The. Mary E. Wilkins Freeman. FaPON; LBN; LiL; MeMeAg; OTPC (1946 ed.); TiPo (1959 ed.); WaKn
Ostriches & Grandmothers! LeRoi Jones. NeAP
Othello. Newman Levy. PIAE
Othello, *sels.* Shakespeare.
"And let the canakin clink, [clink]," *fr.* II, iii. LiBL
Desdemona's Song, *fr.* IV, iii. BCEP; KN; LoBV
"Dost thou in conscience think—tell me, Emilia," *fr.* IV, iii. MyFE
Farewell Content, *fr.* III, iii. TrGrPo
Good Name, A, *fr.* III, iii. BCEP; BTP; FaFP; OTPC (1946 ed.); TreFS
"Had it pleas'd Heaven, *fr.* IV, ii. NBE
"I have laied these sheetes you bad me on the bed," *fr.* IV, iii. AtBAP
"It is the cause, it is the cause, my soule," *fr.* V, ii. AtBAP
(Othello and Desdemona.) FiP
"It is the very error of the moon," *fr.* V, ii. MyFE
Not Poppy, nor Mandragora, *fr.* III, iii. WHA
(Jealousy.) LiA
Othello's Death, *fr.* V, ii. LiA
(Death of Othello.) FiP
("I pray you, in your letters.") InP
(Othello Reviews His Career.) BCEP
(Othello's Farewell.) TreFS
Othello's Defense, *fr.* I, iii. LPS-1; TreF
(Othello. How He Won the Love of Desdemona.) EV-1
(Othello's Wooing.) BCEP
Othello's Remorse, *fr.* V, ii. LPS-3
"Perdition catch my soul," *br. sel. fr.* III, iii. LO
"What did thy song boad Lady?" *fr.* V, ii. AtBAP
Othello: Tomcat. Laura Simmons. CIV; DDA
Other. *See also* T'other.
Other, The. "Ethna Carbery." AV
Other, An ("The purest soul that e're was sent"). Thomas Carew. SeCV-1; SeEP

Other, An ("This little vault, this narrow roome"). Thomas Carew. *See* Epitaph, An: "This little vault, this narrow room."
Other Children. Helen Wing. GFA; OTPC (1946 ed.)
Other countries, far and near. Our Native Land. Charles Phillips. MeMeAg
Other day a partridge, The. The Talk of the Town. Ed Fisher. FiBHP
Other day, as I was twining roses for a crown to dine in, The. Cupid Swallowed [*or* Cupid Drowned]. Leigh Hunt. BCEP; HBV; LPS-1; PECK
Other day by hedge-row seated, The. Pastorela. Marcabrun. LyMA
Other day I went upstairs, The. Elizabeth Ann Peabody. Ivy O. Eastwick. BrR
Other day to my surprise, The. The Beetle. Edith King. GFA
Other day, when I looked at a tree, The. Roots. Louis Ginsberg. TrJP
Other Days. Fu Yüan, *tr. fr. Chinese by* Henry H. Hart. PoHN
Other Fellow's Job, The. Strickland W. Gillilan. WBLP
Other Journey, The. Katherine Garrison Chapin. MoVE
Other loves may sink and settle. The Strange Music. G. K. Chesterton. OtMeF
Other night, The. A Christmas Carol. *Unknown.* BLV
Other night before the storm, The. Concerning a Storm [*or* The Storm]. Richard *and* Louis Untermeyer. FAOV; RIS
Other One, The. Harry Thurston Peck. AA
Other People, The. Lilith Lorraine. MuM
Other people—innocents or lunatics. In the Woods. Paul Verlaine. AnFP
Other Room, The. *Unknown.* PraP
. . . Other shape, The,/ If shape it might be call'd that shape had none. Death [*or* The Challenge of Death]. Milton. *Fr.* Paradise Lost, II. BCEP; LiA
Other Sheep I Have, Which Are Not at This Fold. Bryant. TrPWD
(Home Mission Prayer, A.) PraP
Other Shepherd, The. Margaret Widdemer. SDH
Other Shore, The, *with music. Unknown.* ABF
Other Side of the Sky, The. W. Graham Robertson. PPL
Other Side of the Valley, The. *Unknown, tr. fr. Chinese by* Arthur Waley. TrCh
Other states were carved or born. Cattle. Berta Hart Nance. HiLiAm
Other stones the aera tell. Inscription. William Cowper. MeRV
Other two, slight air and purging fire, The. Sonnets, XLV. Shakespeare. PeBoSo
Other World, The. Harriet Beecher Stowe. AA; HBV; LPS-2; WGRP
Other World, The. *Unknown, tr. fr. Egyptian by* Robert Hillyer. *Fr.* Book of the Dead. AWP; JAWP; WBP
Othere, the old sea-captain. The Discoverer of the North Cape. Longfellow. AnNE; APW; AtBAP; DDA; LH; ShBV-1; StVeCh (1940 ed.); TCAP
Others. Harry Behn. TiPo (1959 ed.)
Others. Charles D. Meigs. MaRV; OQP; QP-1; WBLP
Others, The. "Seumas O'Sullivan." AnIV; GBV; GTIV; HBMV; NP; OxBI; TIP
Others abide our question. Thou art free. Shakespeare. Matthew Arnold. AEV; AnFE; ATP; BEL; BLV; BMEP; BoLiVe; BPN; CaAE; CoBE; EM-2; EmBrPo; EnLi-2; EnLit; EPN; EPP; ES; EV-5; FiP; GEPC; GTBS; GTSE; GTSL; HBV; InP; InvP; LEAP; OAEP; OBEV; OBVV; OnPP; OTPC (1923 ed.); OuHeWo; PFE; PIAE; PoeMoYo; PoRL; PoVP; PtP; REAL; ReTS; TCEP; TOP; TrGrPo; TyEnPo; ViBoPo; ViPo; ViPP; VLEP; WHA
Others apart sat on a hill retired. The Fallen Angels. Milton. *Fr.* Paradise Lost, II. CBE
Others as Fair, but Not So Faithful. George Turberville. *See* That He Findeth Others as Fair, but Not So Faithful as His Friend.
Others because you did not keep. A Deep-sworn Vow. W. B. Yeats. GTIV; ReMP; TwP; UnPo
Others endure man's rule: he therefore deems. The Unconquered Air. Florence Earle Coates. LBMV; PoMa
Others for language all their care express. Pope. *Fr.* An Essay on Criticism. NBE
Others, I Am Not the First. A. E. Housman. A Shropshire Lad, XXX. LiTB; MoBrPo; NAMP; PoVP; TwP
Others make verses of grace. Ardor. Gamaliel Bradford. HBMV
Others march in freedom's van. Marching Song. Ebenezer Elliott. BCEP
Others may forget you, but not I. The Empress Yamatohime, *tr. fr. Japanese by* Kenneth Rexroth. OnPJ
Others May Fuss and May Worry, The. Ivar Aasen, *tr. fr. Norwegian by* Charles W. Stork. AnNoLy
Others may need new life in Heaven. Speculative. Robert Browning. EPN; PoVP
Others May Praise What They Like. Walt Whitman. IAP
. . . Others more mild,/ Retreated in a silent valley, sing. Milton. *Fr.* Paradise Lost, II. MyFE
Others taunt me with having knelt at well-curbs. For Once, Then, Something. Robert Frost. AnFE; CoAnAm; IAP; PoFS
Others weary of the noise. Mothers—and Others. Amos R. Wells. WBLP
Otherwise. Aileen Fisher. GoBP; SUS
Otsuta. Toson Shimazaki, *tr. fr. Japanese by* Takamichi Ninomiya *and* D. J. Enright. PoLJ
Ottawa. Duncan Campbell Scott. VA
Ottima and Sebald, Two Lovers. Robert Browning. *Fr.* Pippa Passes. BMEP
O'Tuomy's Drinking Song. John O'Tuomy, *tr. fr. Modern Irish by* John O'Daly, *vers. by* James Clarence Mangan. OnYI
Otys, begin. Sea Eclogue. William Diaper. *Fr.* Nereides; or, Sea-Eclogues. LoBV
Ou Phrontis. Charles Causley. AtBAP; NePoEA; PoN
Ou Som Sourroucou, *with music. Unknown, tr. fr. French.* ABF
Oubit, The. Charles Kingsley. BOHV; PoVP
O-u-g-h. Charles B. Loomis. BOHV
Oui, oui, Monsieur, Timagami. Pierre of Timagami in New York. Wilson MacDonald. WhC
Oul' Grey Mare, The. *Unknown.* AnIV
Ould Apple Woman, The. T. A. Daly. CV
Ould Doctor Mack. Alfred Perceval Graves. BOHV
Ould Kilkinny. James B. Dollard. CPG
Ould Master, Th', *sel.* Jane Barlow.
Misther Denis's Return. TIP
Ould Orange Flute, The. *Unknown.* OxBoLi
Ould Plaid Shawl, The. Francis A. Fahy. HBV; JKCP (1926 ed.); TIP
Ouphe and goblin! imp and sprite! Elfin Song. Joseph Rodman Drake. *Fr.* The Culprit Fay. AA; OBAV; PoMS
Our age bereft of nobility. A Poem for Painters. John Wieners. NeAP
Our Airmen. Gertrude Robinson Dugan. PraP
Our anchors drag and our cables surge. The Cheer of the *Trenton.* Walter Mitchell. EtS
Our Anglo-Saxon Tongue. James Barron Hope. SPP; TCAP
Our author by experience finds it true. Prologue to "Aureng-Zebe." Dryden. ATP; CEP; EiPP; FiP; OBS; OxBoLi; SeCeV; SeCV-2; SeEP; SiTL
Our Autocrat. Whittier. PEOR
Our Baby's Rabbits. *Unknown.* SAS
Our backyards touched somewhere upon the hill. Neighbors. Marilyn Francis. GoYe
Our Ball. Winthrop Mackworth Praed. *Fr.* Letters from Teignmouth. EnRP; TCEP
Our balloon man has balloons. The Balloon Man. Dorothy Aldis. TiPo
Our band is few, but true and tried. Song of Marion's Men. Bryant. AnNE; APW; BoHiPo; CoBA; DD; DDA; GA; HBV; HBVY; HiLiAm; IAP; IDAH; LPS-2; MC; MOAP; PAH; PAP; PTA-2; TCAP; TreF
Our bark is on the waters: wide around. "Pater Vester Pascit Illa." Robert Stephen Hawker. CAW; CoBE; VA
Our bark was [out] far, far from [the] land. The Sailor's Grave. *Unknown, at. to* Eliza Cook. BLPA; ShS; SoAmSa
Our barn roof has three lovely holes. Three Lovely Holes. Winifred Welles. StVeCh
Our bells ring to all the earth. A Christmas Hymn for Children. Josephine Dodge Daskam Bacon. SDH
Our Bias. W. H. Auden. *See* Hour Glass Whispers, The.
Our birches yellowing and from each. To General Hamley. Tennyson. SoV
Our birth is but a sleep and a forgetting. Intimations of Immortality. Wordsworth. *Fr.* Ode: Intimations of Immortality from Recollections of Early Childhood. BLP; ChTr; FaBoEn; GrCo-1; OQP; QP-1; WGRP
Our Birthday. Marion Edey. SiSoSe
Our Blessed Lady's Lullaby. Richard Verstegan. *See* Lullaby: "Upon my lap . . ."
Our blest Redeemer, ere He breathed. The Holy Spirit. Harriet Auber. MaRV
Our Blood and State. James Shirley. *See* Death the Leveller.
Our boat thrusts steadily through the blue water. The Viking Ship. Norreys Jephson O'Conor. NeTW
Our Boat to the Waves. William Ellery Channing. LPS-2
Our body is our doom, a place of death. Prison-House of Flesh. *Unknown.* OxBG
Our Boy. Oliver Herford. GA
Our brains ache, in the merciless iced east winds that knive us. Exposure. Wilfred Owen. FaBoMo; LiTM (rev. ed.); MoVE; OnHM; WaP
Our broken cries of shame dispute. Hymn to Sophia; the Wisdom of God. "Hugh MacDiarmid." TriL

Our Brother Christ. Ozora Stearns Davis. MaRV

Our brother Clarence goes to school. Big Brother. Elizabeth Madox Roberts. FaPON; GaP; MPB

Our Brother Is Born. Eleanor Farjeon. *See* Now Every Child.

Our brows are wreathed with spindrift and the weed is on our knees. The Coastwise Lights. Kipling. EtS

Our bugles sang truce—for the night-cloud had lowered. The Soldier's Dream. Thomas Campbell. BeLS; BHV; BTP; CBE; CG; EnRP; EV-4; GTBS; GTBS-D; GTBS-W; GTSE; GTSL; HBV; LPS-2; MCCG; TreFS

Our Burden Bearer. Phillips Brooks. MaRV; PraP (Unfailing One, The.) BLRP

Our Calvary. Constance Holm. OQP; QP-1

Our camp-fires shone bright on the mountains. Sherman's March to the Sea [*or* Song of Sherman's . . .]. Samuel H. M. Byers. DD; GA; HBV; MC; OTPC; PAH; PAP

Our Casuarina Tree. Toru Dutt. VA

Our Cat. Janet Vaughn. PCD

Our Cause. William James Linton. VA

Our Chariots Are Strong. *Unknown, tr. fr. Chinese.* WhP

Our chariots are strong. *Unknown, tr. fr. Chinese by* Yu Min-chuan. The Stone Drums, I. WhP

Our chariots so strong. Our Chariots Are Strong. *Unknown.* WhP

Our Cherished Flag. James Montgomery. PEOR

Our Children's Children Will Marvel. Ilya Ehrenburg, *tr. fr. Russian by* Jeannette Eyre. WaaP

Our Chloe, fresh from London town. A Theme with Variations, II. Barry Pain. PA

Our Christ. Harry Webb Farrington. BePJ; MaRV; OQP; QP-1; QS

Our Christ. Lucy Larcom. MaRV; OQP; QP-1; StJW

Our Christmas Hymn. John Dickson Bruns [Burns, *wr.*]. BIG

Our Christmas pudding was made in November. Pudding Charms. Charlotte Druitt Cole. BoTP

Our Circus. Laura Lee Randall. GFA; TiPo (1952 ed.); UTS

Our city, by the immortal gods' intent. The Protectress of Athens. Solon. OxBG

Our city's sons and daughters. School Days in New Amsterdam. Arthur Guiterman. FaPON

Our Clock. Florence Eakman. SiSoSe

Our coffee cups contain the litter. Eight o'Clock. Richard K. Arnold. PtPa

Our Colonel. Arthur Guiterman. DD; GA; HH; PoRL

Our Colors. Laura E. Richards. FOAH

Our Companie in the Next World. John Donne. *Fr.* Of the Progresse of the Soule. OBS

Our Comrades. *Unknown.* PEOR

Our Confederate Dead. Henry Marvin Wharton. BIG

Our Country. Frederick L. Hosmer. *See* O Beautiful, My Country.

Our Country. Julia Ward Howe. DD; MC; PaA; PAH

Our Country. Anna Louise Strong. MaRV; OQP; QP-2

Our Country. *Unknown.* PraP

Our country hath a gospel of her own. America's Gospel. James Russell Lowell. MaRV; PGD

Our Country Saved. James Russell Lowell. *Fr.* Ode Recited at the Harvard Commemoration, July 21, 1865, XI *and* XII. IDAH

Our Country's Call. Bryant. AnNE; MC; PaA; PAH

Our Country's Emblem. *Unknown.* WBLP

Our country's God! Our country's God! The Millennial Hymn of Iceland. Matthias Jochumsson. IcP

Our courage is an old legend. The Defeated; for Wales. Alun Lewis. MoWP; PrWP

Our course will seem too bloody, Caius Cassius. Shakespeare. *Fr.* Julius Caesar, II, i. PIR

Our crosses are hewn from different trees. Golgotha. Frederic L. Knowles. OQP; QP-1

Our Daily Bread. Maltbie D. Babcock. BPP; OQP; QP-1 ("Give Us This Day Our Daily Bread.") MaRV

Our Daily Bread. Adelaide Anne Procter. JKCP

Our darkness stays, the only dark we know. Degrees of Shade. H. A. Pinkerton. NePoAm

Our Dead. Victor Hugo, *tr. fr. French by* Alan Conder. TrFP

Our Dead. Edwin Markham. OQP; QP-2 (Epitaph, An: "Let us not think of our departed dead.") MaRV

Our Dead. Robert Nichols. WGRP

Our Dead Heroes. Rose Terry Cooke. HH

Our Dead Heroes. Morton Bryan Wharton. BIG

Our Dead, Overseas. Edwin Markham. DD; MC

Our dear Lord now is taken from the cross. Easter Even. Margaret French Patton. EOAH

Our death implicit in our birth. The Paradox. Ruth Pitter. MaRV; QS

Our Delaware. George B. Hynson. PoRL

Our Departed Comrades. J. Marion Shirer. BIG

Our Dim Eyes Seek a Beacon. *Unknown.* OQP; QP-1

Our Dinah is a Persian cat. Dinah. Norman Gale. MW; OTPC (1946 ed.)

Our doctor had called in another. In the Children's Hospital. Tennyson. HBV; PoVP

Our Dog. Janet Vaughn. PCD

Our doom is in our being. We began. Sonnets, II. James Agee. MAP; MoAmPo

Our door was shut to the noon-day heat. Cézanne. Alfred Kreymborg. BAP; NP

Our doubts are traitors. Doubts. Shakespeare. *Fr.* Measure for Measure, I, iv. MaRV

Our Echoes Roll from Soul to Soul. Tennyson. *See* Bugle Song, The.

Our efforts are those of the ill-fated. Trojans. C. P. Cavafy. MoGP

Our Enemies Have Fallen. Tennyson. *Fr.* The Princess, Pt. VI. BHV; PoVP (Songs from "The Princess.") MotAn; VLEP

Our England is a garden that is full of stately views. The Glory of the Garden. Kipling. VLEP

Our England's heart is sound as oak. Heart and Will. William James Linton. VA

Our English critics their dull wits keep straining. On Taine. Alfred Ainger. ALV

Our epoch takes a voluptuous satisfaction. Hypocrite Auteur. Archibald MacLeish. CoV; MoVE; NePA

Our Euripides, the human. Elizabeth Barrett Browning. *Fr.* Wine of Cyprus. PtP

Our Ever-present Guide. *Unknown.* BePJ

Our eyeless bark sails free. The Earth. Emerson. AA

Our eyes are holden that we do not see. Faith and Sight. Anna M. King. BLRP

Our eyes have viewed the burnished vineyards. Letter to a Friend. Robert Penn Warren. MAP; MoAmPo

Our fairest garland, made of Beauty's flowers. Contention between Four Maids Concerning That Which Addeth Most Perfection to That Sex. Sir John Davies. SiPS

Our faith is in the Christ who walks. Thomas Curtis Clark. *Fr.* The Faith of Christ's Freemen. ChIP

Our faith is not in dead saints' bones. The Faith of Christ's Freemen. Thomas Curtis Clark. OQP; QP-1

Our Father, As We Start the Day. Agnes Smyth Kelsey. PraP

Our Father, fill our hearts, we pray. Thanksgiving Day Grace. Luther B. Cross. PraP

Our Father, grant us to lie down in peace. Evening Prayer. *Unknown.* TrJP

Our Father in heaven hallowed be Thy name. The Poem of the Our Father. St. Matthew, Bible, *N.T.* CAW

Our Father Land! and wouldst thou know. Father Land and Mother Tongue. Samuel Lover. HBV; LPS-3

Our Father our all-wielding is. The "Pater Noster." *Unknown.* ACP; CAW

Our Father, Our King. *Unknown, tr. fr. Hebrew.* TrJP

Our Father which [*or* who] art in heaven. The Lord's Prayer. St. Matthew, Bible, *N.T.* MaRV; TrGrPo

"Our Father Who Art." Virginia French. QS

Our Father, whose creative Will. Chorale. W. H. Auden. *Fr.* For the Time Being. QS; TrPWD

Our Fathers. Ecclesiasticus, Bible, Apocrypha. *See* Let Us Now Praise Famous Men.

Our fathers did but use the world before. Thomas Bastard. SiCE

Our Father's Door. Oliver Wendell Holmes. *Fr.* The Professor at the Breakfast Table. OQP; QP-2

Our fathers fought for Liberty. Fourth of July Ode. James Russell Lowell. HH; PoRL; TSW; TSWC

Our fathers' God! from out whose hand. The Centennial Hymn. Whittier. AA; APW; FOAH; HiLiAm; IDAH; MC; PaA; PAH; TOP

Our Father's Hand. Anne Johnson Flint. BLRP

Our fathers in their books and speech. Orient Wheat. Adrienne Cecile Rich. NePoEA

Our fathers to creed and tradition were tied. Commercial Candour. G. K. Chesterton. ALV; WhC

Our fathers to their graves have gone. The New Challenge. Whittier. MaRV

Our fathers were fellows of substance and weight. Commissary Report. Stoddard King. ALV

Our Father's World. Margaret E. Sangster. MaRV

Our fathers wrung their bread from stocks and stones. Children of Light. Robert Lowell. FiMAP; MoAB; OxBA

Our feet have wandered from Thy path. Wanderers. Thomas Curtis Clark. ChIP; OQP; QP-1; TrPWD

Our fellow-countrymen in chains! Expostulation. Whittier. IAP

Our first ancestor (Abram) alone received his religion from Heaven. Therefore We Preserve Life. Shen Ch'üan. TrJP

Our First Century. George Edward Woodberry. PAH

Our Flag. Frances Crosby Hamlet. PGD; PSO

Our Flag. Mary H. Howliston. GFA

Our Flag. Margaret E. Sangster. PEDC; PTA-2

Our Flag Forever. Frank L. Stanton. *See* Old Flag Forever, The.
Our Flag Is There. *Unknown.* FOAH
Our flesh that was a battle-ground. Litany of the Dark [*or* Black] People. Countee Cullen. MaRV; NV; QS; SDH; StJW; TrPWD
Our floods' queen, Thames, for ships and swans is crowned. To the River Anker. Michael Drayton. Idea, XXXII. SiCE; TuPP
Our Folks. Ethel Lynn Beers. PTA-1
Our forty-gun frigate from Baltimore came. Paul Jones. *Unknown.* BaBo
Our friend has gone—the one who sat in front. Lament of the Players. Roland Burke Hennessy. LPS-1
Our Friend the Egg. Clarence Day. BOHV
Our Friends Go with Us. Oliver St. John Gogarty. *See* Non Dolet.
Our friendship, Robert, firm through twenty years. A Letter to Robert Frost. Robert Hillyer. MoAmPo; PtP
Our gaieties, our luxuries. Arthur Hugh Clough. *Fr.* Dipsychus, Pt. II, sc. ii. BPN; EPN
Our garden's very near the trains. Trains. Hope Shepherd. BoTP
Our God and Father surely knows. The Father Knows. "F. L. H." BLRP
Our God and God of our fathers. Prayer for Dew. Eleazar ben Kalir. TrJP
Our God and soldiers we alike adore. Of Common Devotion. Francis Quarles. PIAE
Our God, Our Help in Ages Past. Isaac Watts. *See* O God, Our Help in Ages Past.
Our good steeds sniff the evening air. Cavalry Song. Edmund Clarence Stedman. *Fr.* Alice of Monmouth. LPS-2; PEOR
Our Goodman. *Unknown.* BaBo; EnLi-1; ESPB (A *and* B *vers.*); ViBoFo (A *and* B *vers.*)
(Three Nights Drunk, *diff. vers., with music.*) OuSiCo
Our great-great-grandpapas had schooled. Witchcraft. Edmund Clarence Stedman. PR
Our happiest earthly comradeships hold a foretaste. Robert Bridges. *Fr.* The Testament of Beauty, IV. MaRV
Our Hasty Life. *Unknown.* TuPP
Our hearth has been lighted! First Grandchild. M. Whitcomb Hess. JKCP (1955 ed.)
Our hearths are gone out, and our hearts are broken. The Raven Days. Sidney Lanier. NePA; OxBA
Our hearts beat quicker, we lift our voices. The Dawn. Robert Buchanan. GTSE
Our Heavenly Father, *sel.* Frederick William Faber. "My God! how wonderful Thou art." GoBC; TrPWD
Our herded kine were moving in the dawn. On Cithaeron. Euripides. *Fr.* Bacchae. OxBG
Our Heritage. Joseph Mary Plunkett. *See* This Heritage to the Race of Kings.
Our hero is a man of peace. Theodore Roosevelt. McLandburgh Wilson. BoHiPo
Our Heroes. Phoebe Cary. BLPA
Our Heroes' Graves. *Unknown.* PEOR
Our Heroic Times, *sel.* George Henry Boker. Lincoln. DD; GA; LBAH; MC; OHIP
Our High Priest. Annie Johnson Flint. PraP
Our Hired Girl. James Whitcomb Riley. HBV; HBVY; OTPC
Our Hired Man (and His Daughter, Too). Monica Shannon. FaPON
Our History. Catherine Cate Coblentz. BrR; FaPON
Our history is exalted tragic. Hunting Horns. Guillaume Apollinaire, *tr. by* Dudley Fitts. AnFP
Our history is grave, noble, and tragic. Men. Archibald MacLeish. ChMo; CMP; CoV; MoAB; NP; PoLFOT; ReaPo; YaD
Our history is the noble tragic. Hunting Horns. Guillaume Apollinaire, *tr. by* W. J. Strachan. MiFP
Our history sings of centuries. Our History. Catherine Cate Coblentz. BrR; FaPON
Our Hold on the Planet. Robert Frost. PreP
Our Homestead. Phoebe Cary. PTA-2
Our Honored Heroes. Samuel F. Smith. PEOR
Memorial Day, *sel.* OQP; QP-2
Our hopes, like towering falcons aim. To the Hon. Charles Montague. Matthew Prior. LPS-3
Our horse fell down the well around behind the stable. Good-by Liza Jane. *Unknown.* AS
Our Hoste sey wel that the brighte sonne. Introduction to the Man of Law's Prologue. Chaucer. *Fr.* The Canterbury Tales. FiP
Our House. Nellie Burget Miller. GFA
Our House. Dorothy Brown Thompson. BrR
Our house had wings for children, chandeliers. The Exile. Larry Rubin. GoYe
Our Hunting Fathers Told the Story. W. H. Auden. PoE
Our Hymn. Oliver Wendell Holmes. BOHV
Our images withdraw, the rose returns. Beyond Possession. Elizabeth Jennings. NePoEA
Our indolence was despair. We were still at times struck. An Interlude. John Peale Bishop. LiTA
Our Insufficiency to Praise God Suitably for His Mercy. Edward Taylor. *Fr.* God's Determinations. LiTA
Our isolated units could be brought. The City of Dreadful Night, XII. James Thomson. ViP
Our Jack's Come Home Today, *with music.* *Unknown.* ShS
Our journey had advanced. Emily Dickinson. AtBAP; LiTA; LiTM (rev. ed.); MoAB; PoEL-5
Our Joyful Feast. George Wither. *See* Christmas Carol, A: "So now is come our joyful'st feast."
Our keels are furred with tropic weed that clogs the crawling tides. The Captive Ships at Manila. Dorothy Paul. PAH
Our king has wrote a lang letter. Lord Derwentwater. *Unknown.* BaBo; ESPB
Our king he has a secret to tell. The Bonny Lass of Anglesey. *Unknown.* ESPB
Our king he kept a false steward. Sir Aldingar. *Unknown.* BaBo (A *vers.*); ESPB; OBB
Our king lay at Westminster. Hugh Spencer's Feats in France. *Unknown.* ESPB
Our king went forth to Normandy. Agincourt Song of Victory. *Unknown.* MuP
Our King went up upon a hill high. Henry before Agincourt: October 25, 1415. John Lydgate. CH
Our kinship is with flower, vine leaf, fruit. Sonnets to Orpheus, Pt. I, XIV. Rainer Maria Rilke. AnGP
Our kites seem. The Two Kites. James Reaney. TwCaPo
Our Knowledge. Swift. *Fr.* Ode to Sir William Temple. BeR
Our Known Unknown. Robert Browning. *Fr.* The Ring and the Book, X. OQP; QP-2
(From the Pope's Speech, *longer sel.*) EV-5
Our Lady. Robert Bridges. ISi; QS
Our Lady. Mary Elizabeth Coleridge. CAW; GTML; MBP; OBEV (new ed.); OBMV; OBVV; TCPD; TOP
Our Lady, Help of Christians. Paul Claudel, *tr. fr. French by* Sister Mary David. ISi
Our Lady in the Middle Ages. Frederick William Faber. ACP; CAW; ISi
Our Lady is my fear. Family Portrait. Leonard Feeney. ISi
Our Lady of France. Lionel Johnson. ISi
Our Lady of Good Voyage. Lucy A. K. Adee. ISi
Our Lady of Idleness. Florence Wilkinson Evans. BAP
Our Lady of Mercy. Sister Mary Bertrand. ISi
Our Lady of the Apocalypse. Sister Mary Bertrand. JKCP (1955 ed.)
Our Lady of the Libraries. Sister Mary Ignatius. ISi
Our Lady of the May. Lionel Johnson. ISi
Our Lady of the Passion. John Mauropus, *tr. fr. Greek by* Elizabeth Barrett Browning. ISi
Our Lady of the Refugees. Sister Mary Maura. ISi
Our Lady of the Rocks. Dante Gabriel Rossetti. *See* For "Our Lady of the Rocks."
Our Lady of the Rosary. Francis A. Gaffney. JKCP
Our Lady of the Sea. Alfred Noyes. OBVV
Our Lady of the Skies. James M. Hayes. ISi
Our Lady of the Snows. Lionel Johnson. JKCP
Our Lady of Walsingham. Robert Lowell. *Fr.* The Quaker Graveyard in Nantucket. MeRV
Our Lady on Calvary. Sister Michael Marie. ISi
Our Lady Peace. Mark Van Doren. WaP
Our Lady smiles on youthful nuns. Old Nuns. James M. Hayes. JKCP; PraNu
Our Lady walks the desolated lands. Mater Misericordiae. Sister St. Miriam of the Temple. JKCP (1955 ed.)
Our Lady walks the parapets of heaven. Our Lady of Mercy. Sister Mary Bertrand. ISi
Our Lady went forth pondering. The Annunciation. *Unknown, tr. fr. German.* ISi
Our Lady went into a strange country. Regina Angelorum. G. K. Chesterton. ISi
Our Lady with Two Angels. Wilfred Rowland Childe. ISi
Our Lady's Assumption. Sister Agnes. JKCP (1955 ed.)
Our Lady's Death. Benjamin Dionysius Hill. JKCP
Our Lady's Expectation, *sel.* Frederick William Faber. Expectation, The. ACP
Our Lady's Labor. John Duffy. ISi
Our Lady's Lullaby. Richard Verstegan. *See* Lullaby: "Upon my lap . . ."
Our Lady's Salutation. Robert Southwell. ISi
Our Lady's Song. *Unknown.* OBEV (new ed.)
(Christmas Night.) TMEV
(Cradle Song of the Virgin.) ISi
(Jesu, Swetē Sonē Derē.) EnL
(Virgin's Song, The.) AtBAP
Our Land. Johan Ludvig Runeberg, *tr. fr. Swedish by* Charles W. Stork. AnSL
Our Last Toast. Bartholomew Dowling. *See* Revel, The.
Our Left. Francis Orrery Ticknor. MC; PAH
Our Lesser Kindred. Blake. *See* Robin Redbreast, A.

Our life in the world is only a great dream. Awakening from Drunkenness on a Spring Day. Li Po. WhP
Our life is but a summer's day. A Churchyard in Wales. *Unknown.* SiTL; WhC
Our life is likest a long sea-voyage. The Christ. Cynewulf. EnLi-1
Our life is not life, save in the fleeting. Responding Voice. Francisco A. de Icaza. AnMP
Our life is twofold: sleep hath its own world. The Dream. Byron. BCEP; BeLS; ChER; GEPC; LPS-3
Our Light Afflictions. *Unknown.* BLRP
Our Lips and Ears. *Unknown.* BLPA; NeHB; TreF; WBLP
(Caution, A.) PFE
(Rhymes to Remember.) StaSt
"Our little babe," each said, "shall be." The Wonder-Child. Richard Le Gallienne. VA
Our little baby fell asleep. Christina Rossetti. *Fr.* Sing-Song. EmBrPo
Our little bird in his full day of health. The Vacant Cage. Charles Tennyson Turner. VA
Our Little Calf. Dorothy Aldis. TiPo (1959 ed.)
Our Little Cowgirl. *Unknown.* SCC
Our Little House. Thomas Walsh. SBMV
Our little kinsmen after rain. Emily Dickinson. FaPON; ImOP
Our Little Life. Shakespeare. *See* Our Revels Now Are Ended.
Our Little Sister. Laura E. McCully. CPG
Our Lives Are Pendulums. Ramón López Velarde, *tr. fr. Spanish by* H. R. Hays. TwSpPo
Our Lives Are Rivers. Luis G. Urbina, *tr. fr. Spanish by* Samuel Beckett. AnMP
Our lives float on quiet waters. Quiet Waters. Blanche Shoemaker Wagstaff. BLPA
Our Lombard country-girls along the coast. A Last Confession. Dante Gabriel Rossetti. ViPP
Our Lord and Our Lady. Hilaire Belloc. AlDL; GoBC; HBMV; ISi; JKCP; WHL
Our Love Is Not a Fading Earthly Flower. James Russell Lowell. IAP
(Sonnet: "Our love is not a fading earthly flower.") LPS-1
Our Love Shall Be the Brightness. James Wreford Watson. CaP
Our Love Was a Grim Citadel. R. A. K. Mason. AnNZ
Our love was conceived in silence and must live silently. At the Dark Hour. Paul Dehn. WaP
Our love was like most other loves. The Belle of the Ball-Room. Winthrop Mackworth Praed. ViBoPo
Our love was pure. Song of Snow-white Heads. Cho Wen-chün. ChLP; TrCh
Our Madonna at Home. Rafael Pombo. CAW
Our many years are made of clay and cloud. Destiny. Harrison Smith Morris. AA
Our March. Vladimir Mayakovsky, *tr. fr. Russian by* Babette Deutsch *and* Avrahm Yarmolinsky. AWP; PoFr; BoR, *tr. by* C. M. Bowra; TrRV, *rev. tr. by* Babette Deutsch
Our Martyr-Chief. James Russell Lowell. *See* Abraham Lincoln.
Our Master. Whittier. BLRP; IAP; StJW; WBLP
Sels.
"Immortal Love, forever full," *sts.* 1-16, *abr.* MaRV; WGRP
"We may not climb the heavenly steeps," *sts.* 5-16, *abr.* BePJ; ChIP; OQP; QP-1
Our Master lies asleep and is at rest. Mary Magdalene and the Other Mary. Christina Rossetti. StJW
Our Master toiled, a carpenter. Song of Christian Working-men. Thomas Curtis Clark. OQP; PSO; QP-1
Our masters of satire are vigorous gents. Wasted Ammunition. Stoddard King. InMe
Our millions rose in arms, one fateful day. Armistice Day Vow. Dorothy Gould. PGD
Our Missionaries. Margaret E. Sangster. MaRV; PraP
Our Mr. Toad. David McCord. TiPo (1959 ed.)
Our Modest Doughboys. Charlton Andrews. PAH
Our Mother. George Cooper. BoTP; BTP; HH; OHIP; OTPC; PPL
(Mother.) PCH
(Only One.) AA
(Only One Mother.) FaPON; MeMeAg; MPB; SiSoSe
Our Mother. "George Eliot." MotAn
Our Mother. *Unknown.* PEDC
Our Mother, loved of all thy sons. Sea and Shore. Harry Lyman Koopman. AA
Our mother sang tunes. Our Mother's Tunes. Eleanor Farjeon. MPB
Our mother, the pride of us all. Mugford's Victory. John White Chadwick. PAH
Our Mother Tongue. Richard Monckton Milnes. GN; OTPC
(Envoy to an American Lady, An.) VA
Our mother, while she turned her wheel. Mother. Whittier. *Fr.* Snow-bound. AA; MotAn; MW; OHIP; PFY
Our Mothers. *Unknown.* OQP; PSO; QP-1
Our Mother's Tunes. Eleanor Farjeon. MPB
Our motion on the soft still misty river. Coming to Port. Max Eastman. NV
Our motors pierce the clouds. They penetrate. These Times. Gertrude Ryder Bennett. MaRV; OQP; QP-2
Our Movement. Paul Eluard. *See* Movement.
Our Nation Forever. Wallace Bruce. OHIP; PEDC
Our National Banner. Dexter Smith. PAH
Our Nation's birth gave history your name. Washington. John A. Prentice. OHIP
Our nation's movies, foolish, false, erotic. Essay in Defense of the Movies. Walker Gibson. NePoAm
Our Native Birds. Nathan Haskell Dole. BOHV
Our native cactus closes. Good Night. Bernard Isaac Durward. JKCP (1926 ed.)
Our Native Land. Kalakaua, King of the Hawaiian Islands, *tr. fr. Hawaiian by* Henry L. Sheldon. PoRL
Our Native Land. Siegfried A. Mahlmann *and* William E. Hickson. *See* God Bless Our Native Land!
Our Native Land. Charles Phillips. MeMeAg
"Our native land—our native vale." The Emigrant's Farewell. Thomas Pringle. EBSV
Our neighbor, Mrs. Waters' only son. Casualty. Edwin McNeill Poteat. MaRV
Our night repast was ended: quietness. Youth and Age. William Bell Scott. VA
Our old brown homestead reared its walls. Our Homestead. Phoebe Cary. PTA-2
Our Orders. Julia Ward Howe. AA; APW
Our orisons are heard, the gods are merciful. Royall Lady. John Ford. *Fr.* The Broken Heart. LiA
Our Own. Margaret E. Sangster. BLPA; NeHB; PoToHe; PTA-2
Our party scattered at yellow dusk and I came home to bed. After Getting Drunk Becoming Sober in the Night. Po Chü-i. TrCh
Our passions are most like to floods and streams. The Silent Lover [*or* To the Queen]. Sir Walter Ralegh. CaAE; ElL; ElSeCe; OAEP; OBSC; SiPS; TuPP. *See also* Passions are liken'd best to floods and streams.
Our pennant glitters in the breeze. The Mariner's Adieu. George Hill. APW
Our Pets. Esther Antin. *Fr.* On Our Farm. RIS
Our Photographs. Frederick Locker-Lampson. ALV
Our plot is small, but sunny limes. Bubble-blowing. William Canton. TVSH
Our Poets' Breed. Luis Montoto y Rautenstrauch, *tr. fr. Spanish by* Thomas Walsh. CAW
Our poor, doubting souls refresh! At His Table. Bertha Gerneaux Woods. PraP
Our Prayer. George Herbert. MaRV; PGD; PraP; PSO
Our Prayer of Thanks. Carl Sandburg. NP
Our Presidents. *Unknown.* BLPA
Our Presidents—a Memory Rhyme. Isabel Ambler Gilman. PTA-2
Our quin's seek, an very seek. Queen Eleanor's Confession. *Unknown.* ESPB
Our Refuge. Psalms, XLVI, Bible, *O.T.* (*Moulton, Modern Reader's Bible*). MaRV
(From Psalm XLVI, *abr.*) PC
(Psalm XLVI: "God is our refuge . . .") AWP; OnPM
(Refuge, The, *Moulton, Modern Reader's Bible.*) WGRP
(Though the Earth Be Removed.) TrGrPo
Our Refuge and Strength. Grenville Kleiser. PraP
Our Revels Now Are Ended. Shakespeare. *Fr.* The Tempest, IV, i. GTBS-W; LiTB; LiTG; MaRV; PG; PIR; ShBV-3; WHA
(Airy Nothings.) LPS-3
(Finale.) BCEP
(From "The Tempest.") LEAP
(Grand Style, The.) LiA
(Our Little Life.) OQP; QP-1
(Prospero.) FiP
(Prospero Ends the Revels.) TreF
(Such Stuff as Dreams Are Made On.) EV-1, *sl. abr.;* PC; TrGrPo
Our river is wide; our river is deep. The River Bridge. James S. Tippett. GFA
Our Rock. Francis Scott Key. BePJ
Our Rock with loving care. Grace after Meals. *Unknown.* TrJP
Our Rooms. Nikolai Tikhonov, *tr. fr. Russian by* Babette Deutsch. TrRV
Our rural ancestors, with little blest. The Ideals of Satire. Pope. *Fr.* First Epistle of the Second Book of Horace. FiP
"Our saints are poets, Milton and Blake." Encounter. Denis Devlin. OnYI
Our sardine fishermen work at night in the dark of the moon. The Purse-Seine. Robinson Jeffers. ChMo; OxBA; PoLFOT
Our Saviour/ (Paterne of true holinesse). Ensamples of Our Saviour. Robert Southwell. PoEL-2

Our Saviour's cross, begilt with guiltless blood. The Cross. Thomas Bancroft. StJW
Our second Eve puts on her mortal shroud. The Virgin Mary's Conception. Robert Southwell. ReIE
Our servant girl Marigo. Marigo. Zacharias Papondoniou. MoGP
Our share of night to bear. Emily Dickinson. OBAV; OQP; QP-1; TCAP
(Life.) AA; LEAP
Our shepherds all as pilgrims have departed. Boots and Saddles. Nicolas Saboly. OHIP; SDH
Our ship is a cradle on ocean's blue billow. An Ocean Lullaby. Charles Keeler. EtS
Our ship now pass'd the streights of th' ocean flood. Homer. *Fr.* The Odyssey, XII. ReIE
Our shops and farms wide open lie. The Invader. Norman Cameron. POTE
Our Silly Little Sister. Dorothy Aldis. FaPON
Our Singing Strength. Robert Frost. AnAmPo; AtBAP; CoBA; InP; LA
Our single purpose was to walk through snow. Polar Exploration [*or* The North]. Stephen Spender. ChMP; FaBoMo; MoAB; MoPo
Our Sister. Horatio Nelson Powers. HBV
Our Skater Belle. *Unknown.* LPS-2
Our songs are dead, and dead in vain. The Flower. Lee Wilson Dodd. HBMV; TBM
Our sorrow sends its shadow round the earth. J. A. G. Julia Ward Howe. GA; PAH
Our steps again are homed. Io. Aeschylus. *Fr.* Suppliants. OxBG
Our steps are scattered far. In the Wilderness. Edith Lovejoy Pierce. TrPWD
Our storm is past, and that storm's tyrannous rage. The Calm. John Donne. LoBV; MePo; ReEn; ReIE; SeEP; SG; TuPP; TwP
Our Sun Hath Gone Down. Phoebe Cary. LBAH
Our Sweetest Songs. Shelley. *Fr.* To a Skylark. MaRV
Our tears have fallen for this world of stone. My Subtle and Proclamant Song. Seán Jennett. NeIP
Our Thanks. Nan F. Weeks. PraP
Our Thanksgiving Accept. William Dean Howells. *See* Undiscovered Country, The.
Our thirteenth love returns . . . She's still the first. Artemis. Gérard de Nerval. TrFP
Our Thirty Pieces. Harry Kemp. TBM
Our thoughts are torpid as an ice-locked stream. Though Your Words Be Messengers of Hate. Sophie Himmell. MuM
Our Thrones Decay. "Æ." TIP
Our Time. Leonard Bacon. NeTW
Our time is a strife-time, a battle-time. Youth. Bertel Gripenberg. AnSL
Our top-sails reef'd and filled away. The Norfolk Girls. Unknown. AmSS
Our Torah. Joseph Eliyia, *tr. fr. Modern Greek by* Rae Dalven. MoGP
Our Traveller. Henry Cholmondeley-Pennell. BOHV; InMe
Our Treasure in Heaven. Francis Orray Ticknor. PoP
Our tree breaks in this earth, a fallow life. Korea. Vincent Buckley. BoAV
Our True Beginnings. Wrey Gardiner. NeBP
Our trust is now in thee. Beauregard. Catherine Anne Warfield. GA; MC; PaA; PAH
Our Two Gardens. Richard Kirk. TSWC
Our Two Opinions. Eugene Field. AA; CP; IHA; MAP; MoAmPo (1942 ed.); PFY
Our two small sons and one I love. Defense against the Dark. Louis Ginsberg. UnW
Our Two Worthies. John Crowe Ransom. LS; SPP
Our uncle called us on the phone. Surprise. Harry Behn. TiPo (1959 ed.)
Our uncle, innocent of books. The Uncle. Whittier. *Fr.* Snow-bound. GoTP
Our vicar still preaches that Peter and Poule. Soldier's Song. Sir Walter Scott. *Fr.* The Lady of the Lake, VI. ViBoPo
Our Village—by a Villager. Thomas Hood. EV-4; InMe; PoEL-4
Our Village Eleven. W. L. Donaldson. ShGoBo
Our walk was far among the ancient trees. To M. H. Wordsworth. *Fr.* Poems on the Naming of Places. ERP
Our wandering eyes are sated with the dancer's skill. The Cock-Fight. Ts'ao Chih. TrCh
Our Wars Are Wars of Life. Robert Browning. *Fr.* Before. StJW
("Our wars are wars of life, and wounds of love.") ChIP
Our Washington. Eliza W. Durbin. HH; PEDC; PEOR
Our waters are clean. *Unknown, tr. fr. Chinese by* Yu Minchuan. The Stone Drums, III. WhP
Our Wee White Rose. Gerald Massey. *Fr.* The Mother's Idol Broken. HBV; LPS-1
Our Whippings. Eugene Field. FAOV
Our Willie's away to Jeddart. Rob Rool and Rattlin Willie. Allan Cunningham. EBSV
Our window is a magic frame. The Magic Window. Eleanor Hammond. MPB
Our window is stained. Alfred Kreymborg. *Fr.* Berceuse Ariettes. PG (1955 ed.)
Our youth began with tears and sighs. Ballade of Middle Age. Andrew Lang. HBV; LEAP
Our youth is like a rustic at the play. The Rustic at the Play. George Santayana. HBV; MAP; MoAmPo; OBVV, ReaPo
Ours all are marble halls. Song of the Kings of Gold. Ebenezer Jones. VA
Ours, and All Men's. James Russell Lowell. *See* Washington ("Soldier and statesman . . .").
Ours is a dark Eastertide, and a scarlet spring. The Old Road to Paradise. Margaret Widdemer. HBMV
Ours is a great, wild country. The North Country. Robert Browning. *Fr.* The Flight of the Duchess. PCH
Ours is no venal pomp to-day—we seek no vain parade. Scotland's Tribute to Wallace. James MacFarlan. PoFr
Ours Is the Land. Henry Scott Riddell. EBSV
Ours is the storm and stress. Sonnets to Orpheus, Pt. I, XXII. Rainer Maria Rilke. AnGP
Ours not to sleep in shady bowers. The Northern Soldier. Philip Freneau. AmPP (3d ed.)
Ours was a happy lot. Chorus of Batavian Women. Joost van den Vondel. WoL
Ourselves, *sel.* Percy MacKaye.
Trail, The. AOAH
Ourselves Alone. John O'Hagan. TIP
Ousel Cock, The. Shakespeare. *Fr.* A Midsummer Night's Dream, III, i. ViBoPo
Out. Ernest Radford. PIAE
Out, alas!/ You'd be so lean. Flowers. Shakespeare. *Fr.* The Winter's Tale, IV, iii. UnPo (1st ed.)
Out and Fight. Charles Godfrey Leland. PAH
Out beyond the sunset, could I but find the way. The Golden City of St. Mary. John Masefield. GTSL; MCCG
Out by the front walk—have you seen? St. Patrick's Day. Eleanor Hammond. GFA
Out come the leaves. The Neighbors Help Him Build His House. *Unknown.* LiTW
Out for a walk the other day. Chanson Mystique [*or* Mystic Song]. *Unknown.* CAW; WGRP
Out for my evening stroll. The Power-House. Christopher Morley. MaRV
Out forever and forever. The Children of the Foam. Wilfred Campbell. CPG
Out from Gloucester. Harlan Trott. EtS
Out from his bed the breaking seas. A Dream Observed. Anne Ridler. NeBP
Out from the City's dust and roar. The Forgotten Grave. Austin Dobson. VA
Out from the harbor of Amsterdam. Henry Hudson's Quest. Burton Egbert Stevenson. HBV; MC; PAH
"Out from the horror of infernal deeps." The Complaint of Rosamund. Samuel Daniel. OBSC; ReEn; ReIE; SiCE; TuPP
Out from the tall plantation gate. The Misses Poar Drive to Church. Josephine Pinckney. AnAmPo; InP; LA; LS
Out from the whirl of factional unrest. The Escape. Lee Wilson Dodd. PC
Out from the wrought-iron gate. Beyond Debate. Hervey Allen. LS
Out from this fluted shell the muffled roar. Sea Shell. Elizabeth Stanton Hardy. MaRV; MuM
Out goes the rat. Counting-out Rhymes. *Unknown.* FaPON
Out I came from the dancing-place. Ashore. "Laurence Hope." BMEP; HBV; LEAP
Out in a dark, lost kingdom of their own. Nor'easter. Bianca Bradbury. EtS
Out in a world of death, far to the northward lying. The Winter Lakes. W. W. Campbell. BoCaPo
Out in the Dark. Stephen Lucius Gwynn. TIP
Out in the Dark. Edward Thomas. CaAE; CH; FaBoEn; LiTM; MBP; MoAB; MoBrPo; MoVE; ShBV-3; TwCV
Out in the dark it throbs and glows. On the Verge. William Winter. AA
Out in the dark night long. Countersign. Arthur Ketchum. *Fr.* Legends for Trees. HBMV
Out in the dark something complains. Cradle Song. F. R. Higgins. POTE
Out in the dark that is bitter with fear. Norway in Our Hearts. Nordahl Grieg. AnNoLy
Out in the dark the train passes. Whistle-Fantasy. Margaret Widdemer. VOD
Out in the desert spaces, edged by a hazy blue. The Valley That God Forgot. Henry Herbert Knibbs. PCD; PFE
Out in the Fields. *Unknown.* *See* Out in the Fields with God.
Out in the fields which were green last May. A Child's Thought of Harvest. "Susan Coolidge." BoChLi (1939 ed.); DD; OHIP; OTPC (1946 ed.)

Out in the Fields with God. *Unknown, at. to* Louise Imogen Guiney *and to* Elizabeth Barrett Browning. BLRP; DD; GoTP; HBV; HBVY; MaRV; MPB; NLK; OQP; OTPC (1946 ed.); QP-2; WBLP; WGRP
(Cares.) BLP
(In the Fields.) MW
(Out in the Fields.) NeHB; PTA-1; TreFS
(Song from "Sylvan," A.) BLPA
Out in the garden,/ Up in a tree. The Blackbird. Phyllis Drayson. BoTP
Out in the garden/ When school was done. Bubbles. L. Nicholson. BoTP
Out in the garden,/ Out in the sun. The Pigeons. Rodney Bennett. BoTP
Out in the garden, sunny and still. Freedom. Joan Agnew. BoTP
Out in the lake a lotus flower, full-blown. The Lotus. Johan Sebastian Cammermayer Welhaven. AnNoLy
Out in the late amber afternoon. In Shadow. Hart Crane. TwAmPo
Out in the marsh reeds. Ki no Tsurayuki, *tr. fr. Japanese by* Kenneth Rexroth. OnPJ
Out in the misty moonlight. Ghosts. R. K. Munkittrick. AA; YT
Out in the night thou art the sun. Star of Ethiopia. Lucian B. Watkins. BANP
Out in the sky the great dark clouds are massing. Ships That Pass in the Night. Paul Laurence Dunbar. BANP; CDC
Out in the Snow. Louise Chandler Moulton. PTA-2
Out in the south, when the day is done. The Song of the Spanish Main. John Bennett. HBV
Out in the waving meadow grass. Fairy Umbrellas. Lucy Diamond. GFA
Out in the Wood. Clinton Scollard. MoSiPe
Out in the yellow meadows, where the bee. Modern Love, XI. George Meredith. EmBrPo; ViPo
Out it spake Lizee Linzee. Lizie Lindsay. *Unknown.* ESPB
Out of a cavern on Parnassus' side. The New Castalia. William Hayes Ward. AA
Out of a Dust. Alban A. Levy. MoWP
Out of a fired ship, which, by no way. A Burnt Ship. John Donne. WaaP
Out of a Northern city's bay. The Cruise of the *Monitor.* George Henry Boker. MC; PAH
Out of a silence. In Memoriam A. M. W. Gordon Bottomly. LEAP
Out of Adversity. Milton. *See* Deliverer, The.
Out of an empty sky, the dust of hours. Towers of Song. Malcolm Cowley. NP
Out of autumn like a blade. Autumn Journey. Denise Levertov. NeBP
Out of Babylon. Clinton Scollard. TBM
Out of Bounds. John Banister Tabb. JKCP; MaRV
Out of childhood into manhood. Hiawatha and Mudjekeewis. Longfellow. *Fr.* The Song of Hiawatha. AnNE; EV-1; IAP; TCAP
Out of Darkness. Sister Maris Stella. JKCP (1955 ed.)
Out of Doors. Walter Conrad Arensberg. AnAmPo; BAP; LA; PoeMoYo
Out-of-Doors. Ethel E. Mannin. NLK
Out of Doors. E. North. BoTP
Out-of-Doors. Robert Whitaker. TrPWD
Out of Egypt Have I Called My Son. Caroline Hazard. StJW
Out of God's Word clear, living waters roll. God's Word. Takayoshi Matsuyama. SoLD
Out of Hearing. Jane Barlow. HBV
Out of her house she crept. Miss Euphemia. John Crowe Ransom. ChMo
Out of her lattice gazing on the leas. Pierre de Ronsard. *Fr.* Sonnets pour Hélène. PrPoCR
Out of his body grows revolving steel. The Significance of John Brown. Stephen Vincent Benét. *Fr.* John Brown's Body. PaA; VOD (1935 ed.)
Out of his cottage to the sun. Old Dan'l. L. A. G. Strong. MBP; MoBrPo; NeMA; WhC
Out of John Brown's Strong Sinews. Stephen Vincent Benét. *Fr.* John Brown's Body. WHA
Out of Luck. Abraham ibn Ezra, *tr. fr. Hebrew by* Solomon Solis-Cohen. TrJP
Out of Lycophron ("What shall become of Man so wise"). Lycophron, *tr. fr. Greek by* Sir Charles Sedley. *Fr.* Alexandra. BeR
Out of me unworthy and unknown. Anne [*or* Ann] Rutledge. Edgar Lee Masters. *Fr.* Spoon River Anthology. AmP; BAP; ChMo; CMP; CP; FaFP; InPo; LiTA; LiTM (rev. ed.); LoPo; MAP; MoAmPo; MoVE; NeHB; NeMA; NePA; NP; NV; OHFP; OxBA; PaA; PG (1945 ed.); PYM; SBMV; TCAP; TrGrPo; VoD
Out of midnight smile on me. Barrier. John Frederick Nims. JKCP (1955 ed.)
Out of my birth. Horoscope. J. V. Cunningham. NePoAm
Out of my door I step into. The Old Love. Katharine Tynan. HBMV; PoeT
Out of my longing, dusk-aware. Candle Song. Anna Elizabeth Bennett. GoYe
Out of my need you come to me, O Father. Recognition. Margaret E. Sangster. MaRV
Out of my own great woe. Proem. Heine. AWP
Out of my sorrow. Duet. Leonora Speyer. BAP; HBMV; PC
Out of My Soul's Depth. Thomas Campion. OxBoCh
Out of My Want. Gertrude MacGregor Moffat. CPG
Out of my way! Off! or my sword may smite thee. Menelaus and Helen at Troy. Walter Savage Landor. BPN
Out of my window late at night I gape. In the Night. Elizabeth Jennings. NePoEA
Out of November; Speaking for One. David McCord. MAP
Out of one golden breath. Love-Song. Else Lasker-Schüler. TrJP
Out of Our Shame. Norman Rosten. TrJP
Out of Sight, Out of Mind. Barnabe Googe. BOHV; ElL; ReEn; TuPP
(Oculi Augent Dolorem.) SiCE
(Oftener Seen, the More I Lust, The.) InvP
Out of Sleep. Allen Curnow. AnNZ
Out of Sorts. W. S. Gilbert. *Fr.* The Grand Duke. ALV
Out of Soundings. Padraic Fallon. NeIP
Out of Suffering, Tolerance. Sophocles, *tr. fr. Greek by* Lewis Campbell. *Fr.* Oedipus at Colonus. GrR
Out of Superstition. Boris Pasternak, *tr. fr. Russian by* Babette Deutsch. LiTW; TrRV
Out of That Sea. David Ferry. NePoAm-2
Out of the air a time of quiet came. The Clipper Loitered South. John Masefield. *Fr.* Dauber. EtS
Out of the Ark's grim hold. Roy Campbell. *Fr.* The Flaming Terrapin. AlDL
Out of the base, insensate clod. The Luminous Hands of God. Eleanor Kenly Bacon. OQP; QP-1
Out of the Beast. Solomon Solis-Cohen. PoP
Out of the black fog comes a rider. Aristotelis Valaoritis. *Fr.* Photinos the Plowman. MoGP
Out of the blackthorn edges. The Love Song. Ivor Gurney. EnLoPo
Out of the Blossom Sprang a Thorn. *Unknown.* AnEC
Out of the bosom of the Air. Snow-Flakes [*or* Snow]. Longfellow. AnNE; BBV (1951 ed.); BoTP; ChTr; LPS-2; PCH; PoEL-5
Out of the boundless firmament there whirled. The Circle. Katharine Welles Wheeler. MuM
Out of the chaos of sunset, the one white star and silence. Flight of Crows. William Ellery Leonard. FAOV
Out of the church she follow'd them. Maude Clare. Christina Rossetti. BeLS
Out of the cleansing night of stars and tides. Brooklyn Bridge at Dawn. Richard Le Gallienne. HBMV; PoeMoYo; PoTo; VOD
Out of the clod of earth. The Cypress Tree. Grace Blackburn. CPG
Out of the clothes that cover me. Inspect Us. Edith Daniell. BOHV
Out of the cloud-chambers this sevenfold ray is thrown. The Rainbow. Edward Shanks. TCPD
Out of the cloud-world sweeps thy awful form. To an Alaskan Glacier. Charles Keeler. SN
Out of the clover and blue-eyed grass. Driving Home the Cows. Kate Putnam Osgood. AA; BeLS; BTP; HBV; LEAP; LPS-2; MDAH; PAH; PECK; PTA-1; TreFS
Out of the complicated house, come I. The Hills. Frances Cornford. MBP; MoBrPo; TwCV
Out of the conquered past. After a Dolmetsch Concert. Arthur Upson. LBMV; PFY; PoeMoYo
Out of the Cradle Endlessly Rocking. Walt Whitman. AA; AmPo; AmPP; AnAmPo; AnFE; APA; APW; ATP (1935 ed.), *orig.*; AWP; BAV; BLA; CoAnAm; CoBA; CoV; ExPo; HiLiAm; InPo; KN; LA; LBAP; MAP, *abr.*; MoAmPo; MOAP; NePA; OBAV; OxBA; PFY, *abr.*; PoEL-5; REAL; SeCeV; TCAP; TOP; TreFS; ViBoPo, *abr.*; WBP; WHA
(Brown Bird, The.) OBVV
Mocking Bird, The, *sel.* BAP; LPS-2
Out of the damp black night. The End of a Leave. Roy Fuller. NeBP
Out of the dark. Tracks in the Snow. Elizabeth J. Coatsworth. BoChLi (1950 ed.)
Out of the dark a shadow. *See* Out of the dusk a shadow.
Out of the darkness of time and the stress of an impulse unending. The Wave. John Curtis Underwood. EtS
Out of the dear dark years. Akiko Yosano, *tr. fr. Japanese by* Glenn Hughes *and* Yozan T. Iwasaki. *Fr.* Translations from Modern Japanese Poetry. PFE
Out of the deep and the dark. The Poet. Yone Noguchi. NP; WGRP
Out of the deep, my child, out of the deep. De Profundis. Tennyson. BPN; VLEP

Out of the deeps I cry to thee, O God! A Prayer. Richard Le Gallienne. TrPWD

Out of the Depths. Frederic Lawrence Knowles. TrPWD

Out of the depths, from cleft to cleft. Vinco. Elliot Field. ChIP

Out of the depths [*or* deep] have I cried [*or* called] unto thee, O Lord. De Profundis. Psalm CXXX, Bible, *O.T.* BLRP; EnLi-1; LiTW; MaRV; OnPM; TreF; TrGrPo; TrJP; WGRP; WHL

Out of the depths of darkling life where sin. Thomas Decker. Swinburne. *Fr.* Sonnets on English Dramatic Poets. PtP; VLEP

Out of the dusk a shadow. Evolution. John Banister Tabb. AA; AmP; BAP; InP; LA; LEAP; MaRV; OBAV; OQP; PFY; PoeMoYo; QP-1; QS; TreF; VOD

Out of the dusk into whose gloom you went. Sonnets of a Portrait Painter, L. Arthur Davison Ficke. AnAmPo; LA

Out of the dusk stepped down. On a Colonial Picture. Lizette Woodworth Reese. PR

Out of the Earth. Mary Carolyn Davies. HBMV

Out of the earth come good things. One, Two, Three. "Robin Christopher." RIS

Out of the earth to rest or range. The Passing Strange. John Masefield. AnFE; BLV; BoLiVe; LiTB; MBP; MoAB; MoBrPo; MoPo; NP; OBEV (new ed.); TwCV

Out of the East a star shone bright. Be Merry All That Be Present. *Unknown.* AnEC

Out of the east the hero came. The Hero. George Woodcock. TwCaPo

Out of the East the plane spun; over rolling. Selden Rodman. *Fr.* Lawrence; the Last Crusade. NAMP

Out of the East we have followed a star. The Carol of Three Kings. Nora Hopper Chesson. ChrBoLe

Out of the Eden of my love. Discovery. Hermann Hagedorn. PC

Out of the fat lands. Man-Child. Michael Breathnach. JKCP (1926 ed.)

Out of the focal and foremost fire. Little Giffen. Francis Orrery Ticknor. AA; BlG; BoHiPo; CoBA; DD; GA; HBV; IAP; MaC; MC; OBAV; PaA; PAH; PCD; PoP; SPP; TCAP; TreFS

Out of the fog and the gloom. The True Story of Skipper Ireson. Charles Buxton Going. YT

Out of the four and twenty hours. An Air of Coolness Plays upon His Face. Sarah N. Cleghorn. PC

Out of the frozen earth below. The Crocus. Harriet Eleanor Hamilton King. SN; VA

Out of the garden in the gathering gloom. Shrine in Nazareth. Sister Mary St. Virginia. ISi

Out of the ghetto streets where a Jewboy. Autobiographical. A. M. Klein. BoCaPo

Out of the golden [remote] wild west where the sea without shore is. Hesperia. Swinburne. EmBrPo; OBVV; VA

Out of the Goodness of His Heart. José Martí, *tr. fr. Spanish by* Elizabeth Selden. BoFr

Out of the grey [*or* gray] air grew snow and more snow. Snow. W. R. Rodgers. AlDL; LiTG; LiTM (rev. ed.)

Out of the heart there flew a little singing bird. Youth. Virginia Woodward Cloud. AA

Out of the highest agonies of pain. The Poet. Grace Noll Crowell. InP

Out of the hills of Habersham. Song of the Chattahoochee. Sidney Lanier. AA; AmP; AmPP; AnAmPo; AnEnPo; BBV (1923 ed.); CoBA; FaBoBe; HBV; IAP; InP; LA; LaNeLa; LEAP; LiTA; MAP; MCCG; MoAmPo (1942 ed.); MOAP; NePA; OBAV; OHFP; OTPC (1946 ed.); PCD; PFE; PoeMoYo; PTA-2; PYM; RG; SPP; TCAP; TreF; YaD; YT

Out of the Hitherwhere. James Whitcomb Riley. BLPA

Out of the horror of the deepe. *Unknown.* SeCSL

Out of the Hurly-Burly. "Max Adeler." CenHV

Out of the icy storms the white hare came. Ecclesiastes. Joseph Langland. NePoEA

Out of the Italian. Joel Elias Spingarn. BAP

Out of the Italian; a Song. Richard Crashaw. SeCV-1

Out of the jug we drank; there was no cup. Economy. Hipponax. GrPE

Out of the land of the burning sun. Song of Hannibal; Rome. Marcus B. Christian. GoSl

Out of the light that dazzles me. My [*or* The] Captain. Dorothea Day. BePJ; BLPA; MaRV

Out of the lights and roar of cities. Harmon Whitney. Edgar Lee Masters. *Fr.* Spoon River Anthology. SBMV

Out of the lofty cavern wandering. The Tortoise-Shell [*or* The Singing Tortoise]. *Unknown.* *Fr.* Homeric Hymns. GrR; OxBG

Out of the matrix of the sky and sea. Father Point in August. Leo Cox. TwCaPo

Out of the midnight sky a great dawn broke. The Shepherd Speaks. John Erskine. ChIP; MaRV; OQP; QP-1

Out of the mighty Yule log came. The Yule Log. William Hamilton Hayne. AA

Out of the mill and mine. The Bridge. Henry Dumont. PoTo

Out of the mist I have visioned you. Something. Beth Lacy. CAG

Out of the mists of childhood. Fairy Faces. *Unknown.* COAH

Out of the mud two strangers came. Two Tramps in Mud Time. Robert Frost. AmPo; AmPP; AnNE; BoLiVe; ChMo; CoBA; CoBMV; CoV; LiTA; LiTM; MAP; MoAB; MoAmPo; NAMP; NePA; PoFS; PoLFOT; TrGrPo; TwP; UnPo (3d ed.)

Out of the mud which covers me. Inflictis. Archibald Stodart-Walker. *Fr.* The Moxford Book of English Verse. CenHV

Out of the Night. W. E. Henley. *See* Invictus.

Out of the Night. Frank Prewett. MBP

Out of the night and the north. The Train Dogs. E. Pauline Johnson. OCL; TwCaPo

Out of the night of the sea. At Carbis Bay. Arthur Symons. PoVP

Out of the night they drop with troubled cries. Out of the Night. Frank Prewett. MBP

Out of the night to my leafy porch they came. The Night Moths. Edwin Markham. HBMV

Out of the north on a Christmas tree. The Coming of Mary Louise. Gertrude Boughton Urquhart. PCH

Out of the North the wild news came. The Rising. Thomas Buchanan Read. *Fr.* The Wagoner of the Alleghanies. PAH; TreFS

Out of the northeast/ A white horse galloped. War. Tu Fu, *tr. by* Henry H. Hart. PoHN

Out of the northeast/ galloped a white charger. The White Horse. Tu Fu, *tr. by* Rewi Alley. ChTr

Out of the Old House, Nancy. Will Carleton. AA; IHA; LEAP

Out of the Orient, Crystal Skies. *Unknown.* AnEC

Out of the pillaged dark that makes no moan. While Life Sits Idly. Cullen Jones. *Fr.* Sonnets in Wartime. MuM

Out of the purple drifts. Witchery. Frank Dempster Sherman. LBMV

Out of the rich and deep-bosomed earth. A Hymn to Democracy. Paul Green. *Fr.* The Highland Call. NoCaPo

Out of the rocked cradle. Out of the Cradle Endlessly Rocking. Walt Whitman. ATP (1935 ed.)

Out of the Rolling Ocean the Crowd. Walt Whitman. IAP; MOAP; TCAP; ViBoPo

Out of the scabbard of the night. Dawn. Frank Dempster Sherman. MAP

Out of the Shadow. Michael Fairless. SDH

Out of the silence song. Genesis. Arthur Wallace Peach. LPS-1

Out of the silence, the wind. Requiem. William Thomas Walsh. JKCP (1955 ed.)

Out of the sparkling sea. Battle: Hit. W. W. Gibson. HiLiEn; MCCG; NP; TCEP

Out of the storm that muffles shining night. Garden under Lightning. Leonora Speyer. PFY

Out of the table endlessly rocking. Just Friends. Robert Creeley. NeAP

Out of the tense awed darkness, my Frangepani comes. Rainy Season Love Song. Gladys May Casely Hayford. CDC

Out of the terra cotta still a voice. Etruscan Warrior's Head. Helen Rowe Henze. GoYe

Out of the tomb we bring Badroulbadour. The Worms at Heaven's Gate. Wallace Stevens. NP; TCPD

Out of the utmost pitch of wilderment. De Profundis. Amos N. Wilder. TrPWD

Out of the uttermost ridge of dusk, where the dark and the day are mingled. The Tryst of the Night. May C. G. Byron. VA

Out of the Vast. Augustus Wright Bamberger. MaRV; OQP; QP-1

(Each a Part of All.) WBLP

Out of the vastness that is God. A Litany for Latter-Day Mystics. Cale Young Rice. WGRP

Out of the way, there!—in plumes arrayed the provost flashes. Concerning Mollberg's Parade to Corporal Boman's Grave. Karl Mikael Bellman. AnSL

Out of the Whirlwind. Job, Bible, *O.T.* *See* Voice Out of the Whirlwind, The.

Out of the wild sweet grape, I have trampled a wine. On Laying Up Treasure. Lois Smith Hiers. GoYe

Out of the Wilderness. Ulrich Troubetzkoy. GoYe

Out of the wind and the wind's image. To My Wife. John Bayliss. POTE

Out of the Window. Aldous Huxley. AlDL

Out of the window a sea of green trees. Open Windows. Sara Teasdale. OBAV; SBMV

Out of the window the trees in the Square. Red May. Agnes Mary Frances Robinson. AV; HBMV; VOD

Out of the winds' and the waves' riot. Ebb Tide. Marjorie Pickthall. CaP; OCL

Out of the wood of thoughts that grows by night. Cock-Crow. Edward Thomas. EPP; MBP; MoAB; MoBrPo; PoeMoYo; NeMA; TCPD
Out of their slumber Europeans spun. Snow in Europe. David Gascoyne. MoPW
Out of these depths. De Profundis. David Gascoyne. *Fr.* Miserere. NeBP
Out of this anteroom whose light is broken. The Anteroom. Denise Levertov. NeBP
Out of this cloud, O see: so wildly hiding. The Spanish Trilogy. Rainer Maria Rilke. AnGP
Out of this seemliness, this solid order. On August Thirteenth, at the Mount, Marsden, Bucks. Frances Cornford. MoP
Out of this town there riseth a high hill. Of a Vision of Hell, Which a Monk Had. Richard Watson Dixon. *Fr.* Mano; a Poetical History. VA
Out of this wilderness, this stony time. What Sanguine Beast? LeRoy Smith, Jr. NePoAm
Out of this world's imperial terror. Sonnet. Peter Johnson. PoN
Out of Trenches; the Barn, Twilight. Robert Nichols. NV
Out of Tune. W. E. Henley. Echoes, XL. MBP; MoBrPo ("Spring, my dear, The.") BPN
Out of what ancient summer of soft airs. On Hearing a Bird Sing at Night. David Morton. BLA
Out of what calms and pools the cool shell grows. The Atoll in the Mind. Alex Comfort. FaBoMo; GTBS-W; LiTB; LiTM; POTE; SeCePo
Out of Your Sleep Arise and Wake. *Unknown.* AnEC
Out of your whole life give but a moment! Now. Robert Browning. EnLi-2 (1949 ed.); GEPC; PoVP; VLEP
Out on a limb and frantically sawing. Martyrdom of Two Pagans. Philip Whalen. NeAP
Out on a ranch way out West. Sun of a Gun. *Unknown.* CoSo
Out on the breeze. Flag Song [*or* A Song for Flag Day]. Lydia Avery Coonley Ward. HH; MPB; OTPC (1946 ed.); PEDC; PoRL; YeAr
Out on the endless purple hills, deep in the clasp of somber night. The Little Gray Lamb. Archibald Beresford Sullivan. ChrBoLe; CLS; SDH
Out on the furthest tether let it run. The Undiscovered Planet. Norman Nicholson. ChMP; FaBoMo; PoN
Out on the margin of moonshine land. The Lugubrious Whing-Whang. James Whitcomb Riley. BOHV; NA; YaD
Out on the roads of sky the moon stands poised. Elegy. Roy McFadden. NeIP
Out on the wastes of the Never Never. Where the Dead Men Lie. Barcroft Henry Boake. BoAu; BoAV; NeLNL
Out on the water was the same display. E. J. Pratt. *Fr.* The *Titanic.* PeCV
Out, Out. Robert Frost. AmPP (4th ed.); CoV; InP; OxBA; PreP; TCPD; TwP; UnPo
Out, Out, Brief Candle! Shakespeare. *See* Tomorrow and Tomorrow and Tomorrow.
Out, out, harrow! Into bale am I brought. Satan and Pilate's Wife. *Unknown.* ACP
Out rode from his wild, dark castle. The Legend of Heinz von Stein. Charles Godfrey Leland. BOHV; HBV
Out shopping, little Julia spied. The Coconut. "Ande." FiBHP
Out There Somewhere. H. H. Knibbs. BLPA
Out there, we've walked quite friendly up to Death. The Next War. Wilfred Owen. AnEnPo; WaP
Out they came from Liberty, out across the plains. Oregon Trail, 1851. James Marshall. IHA; PaA; StVeCh
Out through the fields and the woods. Reluctance. Robert Frost. AmPP; ChMo; ExPo; GTBS-D; LoPo; LoPS; MAP; MoAB; MoAmPo; OxBA; Po; PoFS
Out to Old Aunt Mary's. James Whitcomb Riley. BPP; FaFP; OHFP
Out to Sea. Richard Henry Stoddard. TCAP
Out to the world's dim boundary line. "Gone West." Geoffrey Anketell Studdert-Kennedy. OQP; QP-1
Out, traitor Absence, darest thou counsel me. Astrophel and Stella, LXXXVIII. Sir Philip Sidney. SiPS
Out upon It! I Have Loved. Sir John Suckling. *See* Constant Lover, The.
Out upon the four winds blow. Flag Sound. Harriet Prescott Spofford. FOAH
Out upon the round-up boys, tell you what you get. Campfire and Bunkhouse. *Unknown.* CoSo
Out upon the sand-dunes thrive the coarse long grasses. The Children of Lir. Katharine Tynan. GTIV
Out walking in the frozen swamp one gray day. The Wood-Pile. Robert Frost. AmP; BrBE; CoBMV; LiTA; MAPA; MOAP; SeCeV; TwAmPo; YT
Out went the taper as she hurried in. Keats. *Fr.* The Eve of St. Agnes. ViBoPo
Out West is windy. New Mexico. Polly Chase Boyden. TiPo
Out West, they say, a man's a man. Etude Géographique. Stoddard King. IHA; WhC
Out West, where the stars are brightest. The Great Grey Plain. Henry Lawson. BoAu
Out where the handclasp's a little stronger. Out Where the West Begins. Arthur Chapman. BAP; BLPA; FaBoBe; FaFP; HBV; NeHB; PaA; PoOW; SCC; TreF
Out where the line of battle cleaves. The Red Cross Nurses. Thomas L. Masson. PEDC
Out where the sky and the sky-blue sea. Flying Fish. Mary McNeill Fenollosa. AA; OBAV
Out where the waves of the Ocean. Minot's Beacon. Alexander C. Corkum. DDA
Out Where the West Begins. Arthur Chapman. BAP; BLPA; FaBoBe; FaFP; HBV; NeHB; PaA; PoOW; SCC; TreF
Out where the white clouds slowly drift. Adventure. Henry Holcomb Bennett. BoHiPo
Out where the white waves whisper. Out from Gloucester. Harlan Trott. EtS
Out with the tide, beneath the morning sun. The Lightship. Josephine Winslow Johnson. MoSiPe
Outcast, The. "Æ." GTIV; LO; OxBI; POTE
Outcast, The. John Davidson. MBP; MoBrPo (1942 ed.)
Outcast, The. James Stephens. MBP; MoBrPo
Outcast, a horror to his kind. On the Just and the Unjust. Blanche Edith Baughan. BoAu
Outcast bones from a thousand biers. Ballade. Don Marquis. *Fr.* Archy and Mehitabel. WhC
Outcast in Hell, An. *Unknown.* AlBD
Outcast Mother, The ("I've seen this dell in July's shine"); *known also as* A Farewell to Alexandria. Emily Brontë. EmBrPo
Outcast on the Mountains of the Heart. Rainer Maria Rilke, *tr. fr. German by* Kate Flores. AnGP
Outclassed. Martial, *tr. fr. Latin by* Paul Nixon. RoL
Outdoor Christmas Tree, The. Aileen Fisher. SiSoSe
Outdoor Litany, An. Louise Imogen Guiney. TrPWD
Outdoor Son of God, The. William L. Stidger. ChIP
Outdoor Theatre, The. Anne Goodwin Winslow. LS
Outer and Inner. George Meredith. PrWP
Outer and the Inner Man, The. Shakespeare. *See* Sonnets, CXLVI.
Outer Gate, The. Nora May French. LBMV
Outgoing Sabbath. *Unknown, tr. fr. Yiddish by* Joseph Leftwich. TrJP
Outgrown. Julia C. R. Dorr. HBV; LPS-1
Outland Fare. "Lewis Carroll." *Fr.* Sylvie and Bruno. BoN
Outland Piper, An. Donald Davidson. LS
Outlanders. Clark Ashton Smith. DaM
Outlanders, Whence Come Ye Last? William Morris. *Fr.* The Earthly Paradise. AnEC; OxBoCh; StJW (Minstrels and Maids.) COAH; GN (Song from "The Land East of the Sun and West of the Moon.") POTT
Outlandish Knight, The. *Unknown.* CG; GoTP; RIS; StaSt
Outlaw, The. Badger Clark. SCC
Outlaw, The. Alfred Noyes. BMEP
Outlaw, The. Sir Walter Scott. *See* Brignall Banks.
Outlaw, The. Robert W. Service. AlBD; CV
Outlaw, The. Sophocles, *tr. fr. Greek by* Gilbert Murray. *Fr.* Oedipus Rex. GrR
Outlaw Murray, The. *Unknown.* ESPB; OBB, *sl. diff.*
Outlaw of Loch Lene, The. *Unknown, tr. fr. Modern Irish by* Jeremiah Joseph Callanan. AnIV; CH; GTIV; IrPN; OBEV; OBRV; OnYI; OxBI; RO; TIP
Outlaw's Song, The. Joanna Baillie. *Fr.* Orra, III. EBSV; EV-3; OBEV; OTPC (1923 ed.); PoFr; TVSH (Song of the Outlaws.) OBRV
Outlet, The. Eleanor Farjeon. DiM
Outlined black in the fog and snow. A Vision. Arthur Rimbaud. TrFP
Outlined in fire against primeval night. Zarathustra. Thomas S. Jones, Jr. AnAmPo; LA
Outlived are all my aspirations. Elegy. Pushkin. WaL
Outlook wasn't brilliant for the Mudville nine that day, The. Casey at the Bat. Ernest Lawrence Thayer. BLPA; BOHV; FaPON; HBV; IHA; LHV; PTA-1; PYM
Outlook wasn't brilliant for the Mudvillettes, it seems, The. Casey's Daughter at the Bat. Al Graham. InMe
Outside. Hugh Chesterman. BoTP
Outside. William Stafford. NePoAm-2
Outside Dunsandle. Sacheverell Sitwell. ChMP
Outside here in the city the burning pavements lie. A City Voice. Theodosia Garrison. NLK; VOD
Outside hove Shasta, snowy height on height. Train-Mates. Witter Bynner. MAP; MoAmPo (1942 ed.); PFY; TCAP
Outside it is blowing and raining. Aleksey Konstantinovich Tolstoy, *tr. fr. Russian by* Maurice Baring. BoR
Outside Kimberley. N. H. Brettell. BoSA
Outside the barracks now the bugle called, and woke. Dawn. Baudelaire. WoL
Outside the Bureau all the trams and trains. Laid Off. Francis Webb. BoAV

Outside, the cubist fells are drawn again. Cockley Moor, Dockray, Penrith. Norman Nicholson. NeBP
Outside the Door. Annette Wynne. SUS
Outside the east gate. Village Loves Outside the Gate. *Unknown.* ChLP
Outside the house an ash-tree hung its terrible whips. Discord in Childhood. D. H. Lawrence. MoPW
Outside the palace windows. Sleepless. Meng Hao-jan. PoHN
Outside the village, by the public road. The Dried-up Fountain. Robert Leighton. VA
Outside the world crackles like a daily. A Room I Once Knew. Henry Birnbaum. GoYe
Outside—wind heavy and wet. Elegies, I. Philippe Thoby-Marcelin. PoNe
Outspoken buttocks in pink beads. National Winter Garden. Hart Crane. *Fr.* The Bridge: Three Songs. AmP; LiTA; LiTM (rev. ed.); OxBA
Outspread world to span, The. Empedocles' Song [*or* Lyric Stanzas]. Matthew Arnold. *Fr.* Empedocles on Etna, I, ii. BPN; EmBrPo; PIAE; TOP
Outstretched at ease his furry form. My Friend, the Cat. Carrie W. Stryker. CIV
Outstretched beneath the leafy shade. The Greenwood Shrift. Robert *and* Caroline Southey. LPS-2
Outward. John G. Neihardt. HBV
Outward Bound. Thomas Bailey Aldrich. AA; EtS
Outward Bound. Edward Sydney Tylee. GA; PAH
Outward from the planets are blown the fumes of thought. The Awakening. Don Marquis. HBMV
Outward looks are not enough. Petronius, *tr. fr. Latin by* Jack Lindsay. LaP
Outward Man Accused, The. Edward Taylor. *Fr.* God's Determinations. LiTA
Outwardly splendid as of old. The Church Today. Sir William Watson. MaRV; QS; WGRP
Outwards. *Unknown.* SG
Outwards and Homewards. Francis William Bourdillon. BTP
Outweighing all, heavy out of the souvenir bundle. Three American Women and a German Bayonet. Winfield Townley Scott. FiMAP; OnHM
Outwit me, Lord, if ever hence. Security. Charles L. O'Donnell. TrPWD
Outwitted. Edwin Markham. AnAmPo; BAP; BLPA; BLV; DDA; GrCo-1; LA; MAP; MaRV; MCCG; MoAmPo; NeMA; OQP; PC; PIAE; PoeMoYo; PoToHe; PreP; PYM; QP-1
Out-worn heart, in a time out-worn. Into the Twilight. W. B. Yeats. BEL; ChMo; CMP; EPN; EV-4; HBV; PC; PoeT; POTT; PoVP
Ov all the birds upon the wing. The Blackbird. William Barnes. EV-4; GTSE; HBV
Ovanuna Believed. André Salmon, *tr. fr. French by* W. J. Strachan. MiFP
Oven, The. Frank Oliver Call. CPG; OCL
Oven-Bird, The. Frank Bolles. SN
Oven Bird, The. Robert Frost. AmPP (4th ed.); AWP; BLA; CoBMV; CrMA; InPo; JAWP; MAPA; MaPo; MOAP; OxBA; Po; RiBV; TwAmPo; UnS
Over. Robert Finch. BoCaPo
Over/ the angular lily. The Tear. Ramón López Velarde. AnMP
Over a bloomy land, untrod. George Darley. *Fr.* Nepenthe OBRV
Over a corner of the wall. The Plum Tree. Wang An Shih. PoHN
Over a crystal table. Etchers of Eld. Donald Wing Hathaway. MuM
Over a ground of slate and light gravel. The Sanctuary. Howard Nemerov. NePoEA
Over a lost orchard I have strayed. Edgar Lee Masters. *Fr.* The Lost Orchard. LaNeLa
Over a pipe the Angel of Conversation. Inter Sodales. W. E. Henley. HBV
Over a scarred and war-torn world. The Bethlehem Star Shines On! Alice Mortenson. BePJ
Over a wild and stormy sea. Mother Shipton's Prophecies. *At. to* Charles Hindley. BLPA
Over against the treasury. His Gift and Mine. Edith B. Gurley. BLRP
Over against the triumph and the close. A Sunset. Aldous Huxley. MBP; MoBrPo (1942 ed.)
Over All the Face of Earth Main Ocean Flowed. Milton. *Fr.* Paradise Lost, VII. EtS
Over All the Roof Tops. Reuben Iceland, *tr. fr. Yiddish by* Sarah Zweig Betsky. OnCuPl
Over and back. At Ithaca. Hilda Doolittle ("H. D."). AnAmPo; LA; MM
Over and over I tell the sky. Free. Mary Carolyn Davies. *Fr.* A Girl's Songs. SBMV
Over and over, when the wayside dust has grayed us. To Be Said at the Seder. Karl Wolfskehl. TrJP
Over and Under. William Jay Smith. TiPo (1959 ed.)
Over and under/ The shaking sky. Iron-Wind Dances. Lew Sarett. Thunderdrums, V. MAP
Over back where they speak of life as staying. The Investment. Robert Frost. ChMo; OxBA
Over by Peppard. Country Song. Elinor Wylie. BAV
Over crag, over dale. The Three Valkyries. Johannes Ewald. BoDS
Over crimson clover-seas. The Quest. Clinton Scollard. BrR
Over dead craters, hushed with snows. *See* After volcanoes husht . . .
Over deep drifts of snow. The Ox. Sara Maynard. ChrBoLe
Over Guiana, Clouds, *sel.* A. J. Seymour. PoNe
"Over Guiana, clouds./ Little curled feathers."
Over-Heart, The. Whittier. OQP, *abr.;* QP-2, *abr.;* WGRP
"World sits at the feet of Christ, The," *sel.* ChIP; MaRV
Over here in England I'm helpin' wi' the hay. Corrymeela. "Moira O'Neill." AnIV; AWP; BMEP; HBV; JAWP; LBBV; TIP; WBP
Over Hill, over Dale. Shakespeare. *Fr.* A Midsummer Night's Dream, II, i. AnFE; BEL; EG; EIL; EM-1; EPP; InvP; KN; OBSC; PoRh; SiCE; ThWaDe; ViBoPo; WP
(Fairy Land.) BCEP; GBV; OBEV
(Fairy Queen, The.) OTPC (1946 ed.)
(Fairy Song, A.) BoTP; CBE
(Fairy Songs: "Over hill, over dale.") BLV; HBV; HBVY; PCD; TrGrPo
(Fairy to Puck, The.) HOAH
(Fairy's Song.) BoLiVe
(Fairy's Wander-Song.) FaPON; RIS
("How now spirit, whether wander you?") AtBAP
(Puck and the Fairy.) GN
(Puck's Song.) RAR
(Shakespeare's Fairies.) CBPC
(Song of the Fairy.) PCH
(Songs: "Over hill, over dale.") EnLi-1
(Songs from "A Midsummer-Night's Dream.") LEAP
Over hill, over dale,/ As we hit the dusty trail. Caisson Song. Edmund L. Gruber. OlF; TreF
Over hills and high mountains. The Wandering Maiden; or, True Love at Length United. *Unknown.* CoMu
Over hills and uplands high. George Darley. *Fr.* Nepenthe. TIP
Over his face his gray hair drifting hides his labor-glory in smoke. Pittsburgh. James Oppenheim. PoeMoYo; StaSt
Over his keys the musing organist. The Vision of Sir Launfal. James Russell Lowell. APW; AnNE; BAP; HBV; IAP; LiTA; LiTG; MCCG; PoRL; TCAP
Over his millions Death has lawful power. On the Death of M. d'Ossoli and His Wife, Margaret Fuller. Walter Savage Landor. PAH; VA
Over in the Meadow. "Olive A. Wadsworth." GFA; MoShBr; OTPC (1946 ed.); PoRh; SAS; WhBS, 1 *st.*
(Wonderful Meadows, The.) RAR; UTS
Over Jordan. *Unknown.* *See* Poor Wayfaring Stranger.
Over kings and priests and scholars. The Lord of Dollars [*or* Letrilla]. Francisco de Quevedo y Villegas. AnSpL-1; TeCS; WoL
Over lava beds. Thorvaldur Thoroddsen. Thorsteinn Gislason. IcP
Over meadows purple-flowered. The Riding to the Tournament. George Walter Thornbury. CBPC
Over mountains, pride. The Praise of Ben Dorain. Duncan Ban MacIntyre. GoTS
Over my garden. Indifference. Louise Driscoll. MW; PoMa
Over My Head the Forest Wall. *Unknown, tr. fr. Irish by* Robin Flower. GTIV
(Open-Air Scriptorium, The.) SiB
Over my ledger I can see. From a Downtown Skyscraper. Wilfred J. Funk. DDA
Over my shaded doorway. A Bird's Nest. Elizabeth Akers Allen. PEDC (1931 ed.)
Over Night, a Rose. Caroline Giltinan. *See* Overnight, a Rose.
Over Northumbria's lone, gray lands. How Oswald Dined with God. Edwin Markham. CV
Over our cups of wine. A Visit. Wang Chien. PoHN
Over our head the branches made. The Mountebanks. Charles Henry Luders. AA
Over, Over. Thomas Love Peacock. *Fr.* Maid Marian. EV-4
Over rock and wrinkled ground. Beagles. W. R. Rodgers. FaBoTw; OnYI
Over Salève. George Herbert Clarke. CaP; OCL
Over Sir John's Hill. Dylan Thomas. LiTB; LiTM (rev. ed.); MoAB
Over Sixth Avenue the sun. Sunset on Sixth Avenue. J. C. Cadden. CAG
Over-Song of Niagara, The. John Daniel Logan. CPG
Over swamps and alligators I'm on my weary way. The Creole Girl. *Unknown.* ABS
Over that morn hung heaviness, until. Seascape. Francis Brett Young. PtOT
Over the ball of it. Pisgah-Sights. Robert Browning. PoVP

Over the Beautiful River no bird is crying. Song of the Cossack Girl. Ilya Selvinsky. RuPo
Over the bleak and barren snow. Tony O! Colin Francis. CH
Over the borders, a sin without pardon. Keepsake Mill. Robert Louis Stevenson. TSW; TSWC
Over the Bridge. Li Kwang-t'ien, *tr. fr. Chinese by* Harold Acton *and* Ch'en Shih-hsiang. LiTW
Over the bridge, mile-long it whistled. The Bridge. Nikolai Tikhonov. RuPo
Over the briny wave I go. The Kayak. *Unknown.* FaPON; GFA; OTPC (1946 ed.); PCH
Over the Carnage Rose Prophetic a Voice. Walt Whitman. AmPo; AmPP (3d ed.); IAP
Over the chimney the night wind sang. What the Chimney Sang. Bret Harte. BTP
Over the City. The First Zeppelin. James S. Tippett. GFA
Over the city,/ from infinite heights. Snow at Midnight; the Elevated. Frederick Mortimer Clapp. VOD (1935 ed.)
Over the climbing meadows. Dandelions. Frances M. Frost. TiPo
Over the conquered countries. Migrants. Dudley G. Davies. NeTW
Over the cradle the mother hung. Where Shall the Baby's Dimple Be? Josiah Gilbert Holland. BLPA; BOL
Over the dark water. A Kayak Song. Lucy Diamond. BoTP
Over the dim blue hills. Maire My Girl. John Keegan Casey. AnIV; IrPN; JKCP (1926 ed.); OnYI; TIP
Over the dim blue rim of the sea. Outwards. *Unknown.* SG
Over the dim confessional cried. A Priest's Prayer. Martha Dickinson Bianchi. AA
Over the Door at the Entrance into the Apollo. Ben Jonson. *See* Verses Placed over the Door . . .
Over the downs there were birds flying. On the Sussex [*or* South] Downs. Sara Teasdale. MAP; MoAmPo; NP; YT
Over the dumb campagna-sea. A View across the Roman Campagna. Elizabeth Barrett Browning. LPS-2
Over the empty fields a black hawk hovers. The Hawk. Aleksandr Aleksandrovich Blok. TrRV
Over the far faint slope of wistful trees. Diana. Audrey Alexandra Brown. OCL
Over the far-flung purple moor. Lines from an Elegy on the Death of His Wife. Kakinomoto no Asomi Hitomaro. LiTW
Over the Fields. Adeline White. BoTP
Over the fields the autumn mist had begun to stray. Hay Mowing. Moyshe Kulbak. OnCuPl
Over the fields the daisies lie. A Summer Day. *Unknown.* PEOR
Over the fields to Shottery, fresh with a wet-green scent. The Path to Shottery. Cornelia Otis Skinner. MoSiPe
Over the fields where the cornflowers grow. Over the Fields. Adeline White. BoTP
Over, the four long years! And now there rings. Oxford. Lionel Johnson. OBVV
Over the frozen plains snow-white. Waiting for the Kings. Richard Lawson Gales. SDH
Over the Garden Wall. Eleanor Farjeon. StVeCh
Over the gate the willow. Spring Scene at River Town. *Unknown.* OnPM
Over the Georgian hills the night her mantle throws. Pushkin, *tr. fr. Russian by* V. de S. Pinto. BoR
Over the Great City. Edward Carpenter. WGRP
Over the great windy waters, and over the clear-crested summits. En Route. Arthur Hugh Clough. *Fr.* Amours de Voyage, I. BPN; EPN; ViPP
Over the green and yellow rice-fields sweep the shadows of the autumn clouds. Rabindranath Tagore. *Fr.* The Gardener. AlDL; NP
Over the green lies the white. Snow. Jorge Guillén. CoSP
Over the gulf and soaring of the city. Diretro al Sol. Charles G. Bell. NePoAm
Over the Heather [the Wet Wind Blows]. W. H. Auden. EnLi-2 (1949 ed.); PoRA
Over the Hill. George Macdonald. GaP
Over the Hill from the Poor-House. Will Carleton. PTA-2
Over the hill the clouds race by. Clouds. Helen Wing. GFA
Over the hill the farm-boy goes. Evening at [*or* on] the Farm [*or* Farm-Yard Song]. John Townsend Trowbridge. BBV (1923 ed.); BTP; FaPON; GN; MPB; MoShBr; PECK; RIS; StVeCh (1940 ed.)
Over the hill to feed my sheep. Weevily Wheat (B *vers.*). *Unknown.* ABF
Over the Hill to the Poor-House. Will Carleton. ATP (1935 ed.); BeLS; BLPA; FaFP; LPS-1; PTA-1; TreF
Over the Hills and Far Away. John Gay. *See* Song: "Were I laid on Greenland's coast."
Over the Hills and Far Away. W. E. Henley. HBVY; TreF; TSW
(Stanzas: "Where forlorn sunsets flare and fade.") HBV
(Where Forlorn Sunsets [Flare and Fade].) PoVP; ViP; VLEP
Over the Hills and Far Away. *Unknown.* GaP; GoBP; RIS
("Tom he was a piper's son.") OxNR; TiPo (1952 ed.)
(Tom, He Was the Piper's Son.) OTPC; PPL
(Tom, the Piper's Son.) OnHT; PCH
Over the hills comes the call of the hounds. The Hunt. Sheldon Christian. CAG
Over the hills of April. Spring's Saraband. Bliss Carman. TwCV
Over the hills where the pine-trees grow. You and I. Thomas S. Jones, Jr. PR
Over the Hills with Nancy, *abr.* Gelett Burgess. WhC
Over the Kokonor the long clouds darken the snow mountains. Recruiting Song. Wang Ts'ang-ling. WhP
Over the land freckled with snow half-thawed. Thaw. Edward Thomas. FaBoTw; HaMV; MBP; MoAB; MoBrPo; NeMA
Over the leagues of lifeless Sea. Before Ararat. J. Redwood Anderson. QS
Over the lids of thine eyes. Images. Richard Schaukal. AWP
Over the Lofty Mountains. Björnstjerne Björnson, *tr. fr. Norwegian by* Charles W. Stork. AnNoLy
Over the long-shut house. Greek Excavations. Bernard Spencer. ChMP
Over the lotus leaves. Lotus Leaves. Mitsukuni. OnPM
Over the melancholy river thousands of peaks are folded. A Poem Written on a Painting Called "The Smoky River and the Folding Peaks" Possessed by Wang Ting-kuo. Su T'ung-po. WhP
Over the mists of a century they come, and their tramping feet. Independence Day To-Day. Margaret E. Sangster. PEDC
Over the monstrous shambling sea. Marsh Song—at Sunset. Sidney Lanier. CoBA; MOAP; SPP; TOP
Over the mountains/ And over the waves. Love Will Find Out the Way [*or* The Great Adventurer *or* Truth's Integrity]. *Unknown.* BLV; CBOV; FaBoCh; FaFP; GN; GTBS; GTBS-D; GTBS-W; GTSE; GTSL; HBV; LiTG; LiTL; LO; LoGBV; OBEV; OTPC (1923 ed.); PCD; SeCL; SeEP; TreFS; TuPP
Over the mountains,/ Over the plains. Trains. James S. Tippett. FaPON; GFA; OTPC (1946 ed.); SUS; TiPo
Over the mountains we trample, the troop of us. The Vagabonds. John Albert Macy. CAG
Over the mountains will the hunter go. Love's Chase. Callimachus. GrL
Over the multiple terrors of Mars. T. Inglis Moore. *Fr.* Kookaburra. NeLNL
Over the plain two dark. The Triumph of Chastity. Barbara Howes. NePoAm-2
Over the plains where Persian hosts. The Cyclamen. Arlo Bates. AA; HBV
Over the pond and down the road. Half Past Tears. Edith Ogden. AlBD
Over the rim of glory. After Reading Twenty Years of Grantland Rice. Don Skene. InMe
Over the River. Jane T. H. Cross. BlG
Over the River. Nancy Woodbury Priest. HBV; LPS-1
Over the river and through the wood. Thanksgiving Day. Lydia Maria Child. DD; DDA; FaPON; GFA; GoTP; HH; MeMcAg; MPB; OHIP; OTPC; PCH; PEDC; PRWS; PTA-1; SAS; SiSoSe; StVeCh; TOAH; TreFS
Over the river on the hill. The Two Villages. Rose Terry Cooke. HBV
Over the river, over the bay. Ferry-Boats. James S. Tippett. GFA; SUS; TiPo
Over the river they beckon to me. Over the River. Nancy Woodbury Priest. HBV; LPS-1
Over the rocks, steadily, steadily. The St. Kilda Maid's Song. *Tr. by* Alexander Stewart. EBSV
Over the roof-tops race the shadows of clouds. Irradiations, III [V]. John Gould Fletcher. AnAmPo; AnFE; APA; LA; LaNeLa; MAP; MAPA; MoAmPo; NeMA; NePA; NP; PFE; PFY; TwAmPo
Over the Roofs. Sara Teasdale. BAP; NP; OBAV
Over the rounded sides of the Rockies, the aspens of autumn. Autumn at Taos. D. H. Lawrence. BrBE
Over the Sea Our Galleys Went. Robert Browning. *See* Song: "Over the sea . . ."
Over the sea the stork flies. St. Gregory's Day. *Unknown, tr. fr. Czech* PCH
Over the Sea to Skye. Robert Louis Stevenson. *See* Sing Me a Song.
Over the seas tonight, love. Sea Lyric. William Stanley Braithwaite. GoSl
Over the shining pavement of the sea. The Ship. Louise A. Doran. EtS
Over the Shoulders and Slopes of the Dune. Bliss Carman. *See* Daisies.
Over the snow at night. The Winter Lightning for Paul. Howard Nemerov. FiMAP; MoVE
Over the Snows. The Snows. Charles Sangster. LPS-2

Over the spikes of the ripened corn. Lightfooted Iphiclus. Hesiod. *Fr.* Eoiae. OxBG
Over the threshold a gallant new-comer. New Year. *Unknown.* PEDC (1931 ed.)
Over the turret, shut in his ironclad tower. Craven. Sir Henry Newbolt. BBV (1923 ed.); GA; HBV; HBVY; PAH; PoeMoYo
Over the vast field of mustard flowers. Haiku. Buson. OnPJ
Over the village, on the hill. The Two Villages. Rose Terry Cooke. HBV
Over the water and over the sea [*or* lea]. Mother Goose. OTPC (1923 ed.); OxNR; RIS
Over the waters but a single bough. Robert Hillyer. Sonnets, XXIII. HBMV
Over the wave-patterned sea-floor. Greeting. Ella Young. AnIV
Over the Way. Mary Mapes Dodge. BOHV
Over the white pool. Desolation. Georg Trakl. AnGP
Over the wide reach of emerald rushes. Flamingoes. Harriet Sennett. BLA
Over the widespread race. Hymns to the Night, V. "Novalis." AnGP
Over the wilds of Sugano. The Tempest. Mabuchi. OnPM
Over the Wintry Threshold. Bliss Carman. HBV
Over their edge of earth. The Little Clan. F. R. Higgins. OBMV
Over Their Graves. Henry Jerome Stockard. AA; MDAH; OHIP
Over them all, we sit aloft and sing. Shadows of Sails. John Anderson. EtS
Over this battered track. Express Train. Karl Kraus. TrJP
Over this hearth—my father's seat. The Returned Volunteer to His Rifle. Herman Melville. TriL
Over this huge escarpment, valiant heart. In the Fourth Year. Lord Gorell. NeTW
Over three thousand li. A Letter from Home. Yüan K'ai. PoHN
Over 2000 Illustrations and a Complete Concordance. Elizabeth Bishop. FiMAP
Over Yonder's a Park ("He bare him up, he bare him down"). *Unknown. See* Falcon, The.
Over Yonder's a Park ("Over yonder's a park which is newly begun") (B *vers.*). *Unknown.* BaBo
(All Bells in Paradise.) AnEC
Over you falls the sea-light, festive yet pale. Ireland. Francis Stuart. NeIP
Over you the battle's breeze. Victory. Ibn Hani. MooP
Over your dead heart I'll lift. I'll Be Your Epitaph. Leonora Speyer. HBMV
Over your grave we pronounce our name. Elegy on the Grave of a Small Fighter. Nicephorus Vrettakos. MoGP
Overdose of beautiful words, An. 12th Raga: For John Wieners. David Meltzer. NeAP
Overflow. John Banister Tabb. CAW; HBV
Overgrown Back Yard, The. John Holmes. CrMA; NePoAm
Overhead at sunset all heard the choir. The Singers in a Cloud. Ridgely Torrence. AnAmPo; CP; HBMV; LA; LEAP; UnS
Overhead, in a tranquil sky, out of the sunset glow. The Last Pilot. Duncan Tovey. POT
Overhead in the Paris sky. Hills. Guillaume Apollinaire. AnFP
Overheard at a Sculpture Show at a Museum. *Unknown.* SiTL
Overheard in an Orchard. Elizabeth Cheney. BLRP; MaRV
Overheard in Arcady, *sel.* Robert Bridges.
Dedication: "Long years you've kept the door ajar." MOAH
Overheard on a Saltmarsh. Harold Monro. BoTP; CH; FaPON; HiLiEn; HOAH; MoShBr; PCD; PCH; PoMS; SP; ThWaDe; TiPo; WP
Overland Mail, The. Kipling. CV; PECK
Overloaded, undermanned. The Coasters. Thomas Fleming Day. AA; OBAV; PFY
Over-logical fell for the witch, The. The Useful. W. H. Auden. ChMo
Overlooking the Desert. Tu Fu, *tr. fr. Chinese by* Kenneth Rexroth. OnPC
Overlord. Bliss Carman. CaP; OCL
(Veni Creator: "Lord of the grass and hill.") WGRP
Overnight, a Rose. Caroline Giltinan. HBMV; SBMV
(Over Night a Rose.) LS
Overnight in the Apartment by the River. Tu Fu, *tr. fr. Chinese.* ChTr
Over-proud young girl once sought, An. The Old Maid. La Fontaine. TrFP
Overripe Fruit. Kasmuneh, *tr. fr. Arabic.* TrJP
Overseer of the Poor. James Hayford. NePoAm-2
Oversoul. "Æ." ChMo; CMP; MaRV; PoVP
(Krishna.) VA
Overthrow of Lucifer, The. Phineas Fletcher. *Fr.* The Purple Island, XII. OBS
Overthrow of Zeus, The. Aeschylus, *tr. fr. Greek by* G. M. Cookson. *Fr.* Prometheus Bound. OxBG
Overtones. William Alexander Percy. BAP; BLA; DD; HBMV; HBVY; LS; MaRV; NLK; SBMV; SPP
Overture. Walter Savage Landor. *Fr.* Thrasymedes and Eunoë. VA
Overtures to Death. C. Day Lewis. ChMo
Overworked Elocutionist, An. Carolyn Wells. BLPA; PTA-1, *abr.*
Overworked Horse, The. Gerald Gould. MoBrPo (1942 ed.)
Overworld, The. Thomas Hardy. The Dynasts, Pt. III, After Scene. WoL
Ovibos, The. Robert Hale. FiBHP
Ovid's Banquet of Sense, *sels.* George Chapman.
Corinna Bathes. OBSC
(Natures Naked Jem.) FaBoEn
"Earth from heavenly light conceived heat, The." ReIE
Owd Pinder. Edwin Waugh. VA
Owed to Dickens, 1956. Jan Burroway. NePoAm-2
Owed to New York. Byron Rufus Newton. BLPA; NeHB; TreFS
Owen, not to use flattery (as they). In Owenni Epigrammata. Thomas Freeman. SiCE
Owen Seaman. Louis Untermeyer. ALV; BOHV
(Spratt vs. Spratt.) PC
Owen's praise demands my song. The Triumphs of Owen. Thomas Gray, *after* Meilir ap Gwalchmai. CEP; EnRP; EV-3; LiTW; PoEL-3; PrWP
Owl, The. "Barry Cornwall." BCEP; CG; LPS-2; SN
(Horned Owl, The.) BLA; OTPC; TVSH
Owl, The. Walter de la Mare. BrBE
Owl, The. Hildegarde Flanner. BLA
Owl, The. Tennyson. AlDL; BLA; BoTP; DD; FaBoCh; GBV (1952 ed.); GoTP; LoGBV; MoShBr; MuP; MW; MyFE; OnHT; OTPC; PCH; PRWS; RAR; RIS; StaSt; WP; UTS
(Song: Owl, The.) FaPON; HBV; HBVY; MPB; OBRV; PTA-1; SUS; ThWaDe
(When Cats Run Home.) CH; EG
(White Owl, The.) WhBS
Owl, The. Edward Thomas. ChTr; FaBoTw; LiTB; MoP; UnPo (3d ed.)
Owl, The. *Unknown, tr. fr. German.* SAS
Owl, The. Robert Penn Warren. MAP; MoAmPo
Owl, The. Roland Young. BOHV
Owl against Robin, *abr.* Sidney Lanier. LaNeLa
Owl and the Eel and the Warming-Pan, The. Laura E. Richards. HBV; HBVY; PPL
Owl and the Fox, The. *Unknown.* BLPA
(Tragic Tale of Hooty the Owl, The, *sl. diff.*) FTB
Owl and the Nightingale, The, *abr. Unknown, at. to* Nicholas de Guildford, *tr. fr. Middle English.* EPP, *Mid. and mod. Eng.;* MeEV
Owl and the Pussy-Cat, The. Edward Lear. BeLS; BoChLi; BOHV; BoN; BoTP; BTP; CIV; EnLi-2 (1949 ed.); FaBoBe; FaBoCh; FaFP; FaPON; GFA; GoBP; GoTP; HBV; HBVY; KN; LBN; LEAP; LiTG; LoGBV; MeMeAg; MoShBr; MPB; NA; NeHB; OnHT; OnSP; OtMeF; OTPC; OxBoLi; PCD; PCH; PECK; PIR; PoRA; PoRh; PoVP; PRWS; PTA-1; RAR; RIS; SAS; ShBV-1; SiTL; StVeCh; SUS; TiPo; TreFS; TrGrPo; TSW; TSWC; TVC; TVSH; UTS; WhC
Owl-Critic, The. James Thomas Fields. BLPA; BOHV; CenHV; GoTP; HBV; MW; PoeMoYo; PTA-1; RIS; StPo; TreFS; WBLP; YaD
Owl expires, The! Death gave the dreadful word. On the Death of a Lady's Owl. Moses Mendes. TrJP
Owl, horned wizard of the night, An. Three Nocturns. Sir Osbert Sitwell. POTE
Owl is abroad, the bat and the toad, The. Witches' Charm [*or* Charm]. Ben Jonson. *Fr.* The Masque of Queens. FaBoCh; KN; LoBV; LoGBV; ReEn
Owl Is an Only Bird of Poetry, An. Robert Duncan. NeAP
Owl is hooting in the grove, An. Winter Night. Roy Fuller. NeBP
Owl is very very wise, The. The Owl. Roland Young. BOHV
Owl Sinister. Rose O'Neill. BLA
Owl, the Eel and the Warming-Pan, The. Laura E. Richards. *See* Owl and the Eel . . ., The.
Owl to her mate is calling, The. The Fate of the Oak. "Barry Cornwall." OHIP; OTPC
Owls, The. Timeus Gaylord. DaM
Owls have feathers lined with down, The. The Hedgehog and His Coat. Elizabeth Fleming. BoTP
Ownership. Lizette Woodworth Reese. MAP; MoAmPo
Ownership. Isla Paschal Richardson. AlBD
Owning. Wilmot B. Lane. CaP
Owre the Muir amang the Heather. Jean Glover. EBSV; HBV
Owt of thise blake wawes for to sayle. Troilus and Criseyde. Chaucer. EnLi-1
Ox, The. Giosuè Carducci, *tr. fr. Italian.* OnPM, *tr. by* Glauco Cambon; WoL, *tr. by* Lorna de' Lucchi
Ox, The. John Gray. GBV (1952 ed.)
Ox, The. Sara Maynard. ChrBoLe

Ox and the Ass, The. Five Carols for Christmastide, V. Louise Imogen Guiney. ISi
Ox and Donkey's Carol. Sister Maris Stella. PoRL
Ox-Bone Madonna. John Duffy. ISi
Ox-Bone Madonna. James J. Galvin. ISi
Ox-driving Song, *with music*. *Unknown*. OuSiCo
Ox he openeth wide the Doore, The. Tryste Noël [*or* Five Carols for Christmastide, I]. Louise Imogen Guiney. HBV; ISi; JKCP; LBMV; LEAP; OBVV; SDH
Ox Past Service, An. Addaeus. *See* Pensioned Ox, The.
Ox, rewarded for his pains, The. Addaeus, *tr. fr. Greek by* the Earl of Cromer. GrPo
Ox-Tamer, The. Walt Whitman. MOAP
Ox-team and the automobile, The. The Meeting. Harriet Monroe. PoTo
Ox with horned head, The. Pan Ježišku. *Unknown*. ChrBoLe
Oxen, The. Thomas Hardy. BLV; BoLiVe; BoTP; CaAE; CBOV; ChMo; ChrBoLe; CMP; CoBMV; EnL; GTBS-W; GTML; GTSL; HBMV; LiTM; MaPo; MaRV; MBP; MoAB; MoBrPo; OAEP; OTPC (1946 ed.); Po; PoLFOT; POT; PoTo; POTT; PoVP; QS; RiBV; SDH; ShBV-2; StJW; TCPD; TSW; TVSH; TwCV; TwHP; VLEP; WP; ViPP
Oxen. Ralph Mortimer Jones. BAP
Oxen That Rattle the Yoke and Chain. Walt Whitman. *Fr.* Song of Myself, XIII. SN
Oxford. Keith Douglas. NePoEA
Oxford. Gerald Gould. PoeT
Oxford. Lionel Johnson. OBVV
Oxford. Archibald T. Strong. *Fr.* Sonnets of the Empire. BoAu
Oxford & Cambridge. Sir William Browne. WhC
(Epigram: "King to Oxford sent a troop of horse, The.") ALV
Oxford Bells. Sister Maris Stella. GoBC
Oxford Idyll, An. Thomas Edward Brown. PoVP; VLEP
Oxford Is a Stage. Edward Nolan. CenHV
Oxford Nights. Lionel Johnson. EnLit
Oxford, since late I left thy peaceful shore. Sonnet: To Oxford. Thomas Russell. ATP; CEP; OBEC; PeBoSo
Oxfordshire Children's May Song. *Unknown*. *See* May Song ("Spring is coming").
Oxus. Matthew Arnold. *Fr.* Sohrab and Rustum. NBE; VA, *shorter sel.*
Oyster, The. Ogden Nash. ALV
Oyster, The. Sir Walter Scott. *See* Harlaw.
Oyster and the Litigants, The. La Fontaine, *tr. fr. French by* Elizur Wright. WoL
Oyster Crabs. Carolyn Wells. PA
Oyster Shell, The ("An oyster in his shell"). Ariake Kambara, *tr. fr. Japanese by* Takamichi Ninomiya *and* D. J. Enright. PoLJ
Oyster shuts his gates to form the pearl, The. The Precious Pearl. Pat Wilson. AnNZ
Oyster's a confusing suitor, The. The Oyster. Ogden Nash. ALV
Ozark Song. Dennis Murphy. BAP
Ozymandias. Shelley. ATP; AWP; BEL; BLV; BoLiVe; BPN; CaAE; CBE; CBOV; CoBE; EM-2; EmBrPo; EnL; EnLi-2; EnLit; EnRP; EPN; EPP; ERP; ES; EV-4; ExPo; FaBoBe; FaBoCh; FaBoEn; FaFP; FiP; GEPC; GoTP; HoPM; InP; InPo; JAWP; LoBV; LoGBV; MaPo; MaRV; MCCG; MyFE; NeHB; OAEP; OuHeWo; PeBoSo; PFE; PG (1955 ed.); PIAE; PIR; Po; PoE; PoeMoYo; PoFS; PoRA; PreP; PYM; REAL; RiBV; RO; SeCeV; ShBV-3; TCEP; TOP; TrGrPo; TyEnPo; UnPo (1st ed.); WaKn; WBP; WHA
(Ozymandias of Egypt.) Shelley. BCEP; BeLS; BLP; CH; GTBS; GTBS-D; GTBS-W; GTSE; GTSL; HBV; HBVY; LPS-2; OTPC (1946 ed.); PC; PECK; TreF
Ozymandias Revisited. Morris Bishop. ALV

P

P-51. John Ciardi. PreP
P Is for Paleontology. Milton Bracker. FiBHP; InMe; WhC
P.R.B., The. Christina Rossetti. ViP
Pa followed the pair to Pawtucket. Limerick. *Unknown*. LiBL. *See also* But he followed the pair . . .
Pa lays around 'n' loafs all day. Options. "O. Henry." FiBHP
Pablo. Grace Hazard Conkling. GaP
Pace, pace, go the ladies, oh! *Unknown*. SAS
Pacific Door. Earle Birney. PeCV; TwCaPo
Pacific Engagement, The. *Unknown*. *Fr.* Bungiana. WhC
Pacific Railway, The. C. R. Ballard. PAH
Pacific Winter. Hildegarde Flanner. NP
Pacifist, The. Hilaire Belloc. MoVE; SoV
Pacifists. M. A. De Wolfe Howe. AOAH
Pacing with leisured tread the echoing nave. The Cathedral Verger. Margaret Willy. DiM
Pack, Clouds, Away. Thomas Heywood. *Fr.* The Rape of Lucrece, IV, vi. BLA; BoTP; EIL; EM-1; GTBS; GTSE; KN; LPS-2; OTPC; SN; ThWaDe; ViBoPo; WHA; WP
(Good-Morrow.) ALV; CBOV; CH; TOP
(Matin Song.) EV-2; GTSL; HBV; OBEV; ShBV-1
(Morning.) TVSH
("Pack, clouds, away! and welcome day!") CaAE; EG; ElSeCe; GTBS-D; GTBS-W
(Waking Song.) RIS
(Welcome to Day.) BLV; PIAE
Pack is too hard on the shoulders, The. The Silver Canoe. Arthur Guiterman. TBM
Packed in my mind lie all the clothes. The Inward Morning. Henry David Thoreau. AMP; AmPP (3d ed.); MOAP
Packet of Letters. Louise Bogan. LiTL
Packing a Photograph from Firenze. William H. Matchett. NePoEA
Packs are on, the cinches tight, The. Line Up, Brave Boys. Hamlin Garland. SN
Pact. Kenneth Fearing. ChMo
Pact, The. Alfred Noyes. MaRV
Pact, A. Ezra Pound. CoV; LiTA; MoPW; NePA; OxBA; Po
Paddle Your Own Canoe. Sarah K. Bolton. FaFP
Paddling Pool, The. E. M. Adams. BoTP
Paddy Doyle, *with music*. *Unknown*. AmSS; SG; ShS; SoAmSa
Paddy Get Back, *with music*. *Unknown*. AmSS; ShS; SoAmSa
Paddy, in want of a dinner one day. Paddy O'Rafther. Samuel Lover. BOHV; HBV; StPo
Paddy McCabe was dying one day. Father Molloy. Samuel Lover. BOHV; HBV
Paddy O'Flynn. *Unknown*. MuP
Paddy O'Rafther. Samuel Lover. BOHV; HBV; StPo
Paddy West, *with music*. *Unknown*. ShS
Paddy Works on the Railway, *with music*. *Unknown*. AmSS; SoAmSa
(Paddy Works on the Erie, *with music*.) ABF
(Pat Works on the Railway.) TrAS
(Poor Paddy Works on the Railway, *with music*.) AS
Paddy's Metamorphosis. Thomas Moore. OnYI
Padraic O'Conaire, Gaelic Storyteller. F. R. Higgens. OBMV; OnYI; OxBI; PtP
Padstow Night Song, The. *Unknown*. ChTr
Paean. Jonathan Henderson Brooks. CDC
Paean of Dawn in May. Herbert Trench. GTIV
Paean of Joy. Sophocles, *tr. fr. Greek by* Lewis Campbell. *Fr.* Trachiniae. GrR
Pagan, The. Mary Sinton Leitch. LS
Pagan Epitaph. Richard Middleton. BMEP; OBVV; TOP
Pagan gods of force reclaim their altars, The. Today. Thomas Curtis Clark. ChIP
Pagan Hymn, A. John Runcie. NLK
Pagan king tormented fiercely all, A. Life through Death. Richard Chenevix Trench. EOAH
Pagan Prayer. Alice Brown. WGRP
Pagan Reinvokes the Twenty-third Psalm, A. Robert L. Wolf. HBMV; NV; TBM; TrPWD
Pagan World, The. Matthew Arnold. *Fr.* Obermann Once More. GTML
(West and East, *abr.*) CBPC
Pagani's, November 8. Ezra Pound. ReaPo
Pagan's Baptism, A. A. S. Cripps. BoSA
Page-eater thou, the Muses' bitterest foe. Evenus, *tr. fr. Greek by* Norman Douglas. GrPo
Page from America's Psalter, A. Willard Wattles. *See* Thy Kingdom Come!
Page IX. Gertrude Stein. WaKn
Page of Lancelot, The. May Kendall. VA
Pageant. Margaret Widdemer. AV; TBM
Pageant of Man, The, *sel.* Stanton A. Coblentz.
Patient Is Time. MaRV; MuM
Pageant of Seamen, The. May Byron. HBV
Pageant of the Seasons and the Months, The. Spenser. *Fr.* The Faerie Queene, VII, 7. EV-1
(Mask of Mutability, The.) OBSC
(Procession of Times and Seasons, The.) NBE
(Seasons, *abr.*) GN
Page's Road Song, A. William Alexander Percy. LS; TrPWD; YeAr
Pages' Song, The. Shakespeare. *See* It Was a Lover and His Lass.
Pagget, a school-boy, got a sword, and then. Upon Pagget. Robert Herrick. FaBoCh; LoGBV
Paging Mr. McGregor. Edgar A. Guest. OnHT
Paid on Both Sides, *sels.* W. H. Auden.
Chorus: "Though he believe it, no man is strong." CoEV
Chorus: "To throw away the key and walk away." MBP; MoBrPo; PIAE

(To Throw Away the Key.) ChMo
Pain. "Æ." MoBrPo
Pain. Enrique González Martínez, *tr. fr. Spanish by* Samuel Beckett. AnMP
Pain. St. John Lucas. HBV
Pain. Harriet Monroe. NP
Pain. Coventry Patmore. PoLi
Pain. Elsie Robinson. PoToHe (new ed.)
Pain. Leonora Speyer. HBMV
Pain. *Unknown. See* Lord, Take Away Pain.
Pain has an element of blank. Emily Dickinson. CoV; LiTA; LiTM (rev. ed.); MoAB; MoAmPo (1950 ed.); TwP (Mystery of Pain.) OnPM
Pain is a beckoning hand. Pain. Leonora Speyer. HBMV
Pain is a blacksmith. Blacksmith Pain. Otto Julius Bierbaum. AWP; JAWP; WBP
Pain of Living, The. Eugenio Montale, *tr. fr. Italian by* Glauco Cambon. OnPM
Pain of loving you, The. A Young Wife. D. H. Lawrence. ChMP; MBP; MoBrPo
Pain of Stone, The. Sophie Himmell. MuM
Pain of too poignant beauty fills the heart. The World's Desire. William Rose Benét. TrPWD
Painful smith with force of fervent heat, The. Amoretti, XXXII. Spenser. PeBoSo
Painfully writhed the few last weeds upon those houseless uplands. An Infantryman. Edmund Blunden. ViBoPo
Pains and Gains. Edward de Vere, Earl of Oxford. EIL
Pains of Education, The. Charles Churchill. SiTL
Pains of saints and saints' rewards are twins, The. Paulinus. Versus Apud Epist. XXXII. 17. Henry Vaughan. TriL
Pains of Sleep, The. Samuel Taylor Coleridge. BPN; EmBrPo; EnRP; EPN; ERP; OAEP; OBRV; SeCePo (Child's Evening Prayer, A.) BOL; OTPC (1923 ed.); TrPWD
Pains of the Virgin Mary, The. Kostas Varnalis, *tr. fr. Modern Greek by* Rae Dalven. MoGP
Pains, reading, study, are their just pretence. Verbal Critics. Pope. *Fr.* Epistle to Dr. Arbuthnot. CoEV; OBEC
Pains the sharp sentence the heart in whose wrath it was uttered. Pardon. Julia Ward Howe. GA; PAH
Paint a whitelimbed girl for me. Painted Passion. *At. to* Octavianus. LaP
Paint last the King, and a dead shade of Night. Andrew Marvell. *Fr.* Last Instructions to a Painter. OBS
Paint me a cavernous waste shore. Sweeney Erect. T. S. Eliot. TwP
Painted Desert, The. Elizabeth J. Coatsworth. PoeMoYo
Ceremonial Hunt.
In Walpi.
Navajo, The.
Painted Fan, A. Louise Chandler Moulton. AA
Painted Head. John Crowe Ransom. CoBMV; CrMA; LiTA; LiTG; LiTM (rev. ed.); MoPo; MoVE; OxBA; ReMP
(Painting; a Head.) MAP; MoAB; MoAmPo
Painted Hills of Arizona, The. Edwin Curran. BAP; HBMV; MW; PFY
Painted Indian rides no more, The. *Unknown.* WhC
Painted Passion. *At. to* Octavianus, *tr. fr. Latin by* Howard Mumford Jones. LaP
Painter, The. Robert Fitzgerald. MoVE
Painter and poet, runner and disk-thrower. One of the Jews (50 A.D.). C. P. Cavafy. MoGP; TrJP
Painter, by unmatch'd desert. The Picture. Thomas Stanley. AWP; GrPo; JAWP; WBP
Painter in New England, A. Charles Wharton Stork. HBMV
Painter on Silk, The. Amy Lowell. CV
Painter Who Pleased Nobody and Everybody, The. John Gay. BeLS; CEP
Painter, you're come, but may be gone. The Picture of Her Mind. Ben Jonson. GoBC
Painting; a Head. John Crowe Ransom. *See* Painted Head.
Painting of a Lobster by Picasso. Hy Sobiloff. NePA
Painting of an Eagle, The. Tu Fu, *tr. fr. Chinese.* WhP
Painting of Dido, A. *Unknown, tr. fr. Greek by* George Allen. OxBG
Pair, A. Karl Gjellerup, *tr. fr. Danish by* Charles W. Stork. BoDS; OnPM
Pair of golden orioles, A. Far Up the River. Tu Fu. OnPC
Pair of Lovers, A. Jeanne Robert Foster. HBMV
Pair of Lovers in the Street, A. Arthur Adams. BoAu
Pair of steady Rooks, A. The Death of Master Tommy Rook. Eliza Cook. OTPC (1923 ed.)
Pair'd, Not Match'd. Thomas Hood. ERP
Pairing-Time Anticipated. William Cowper. BOHV
"It chanced upon a winter's day," *sel.* CG
Paisley Officer, The, *2 vers., with music. Unknown.* ShS
Paisley Shawl, The. W. W. Gibson. ChMo; CMP; VOD
Páistín Fionn. *Unknown. See* Pastheen Finn.
Palabras Cariñosas. Thomas Bailey Aldrich. AA; HBV; InP; LBAP; OBAV; PR
Palabras Grandiosas. Bayard Taylor. *Fr.* The Echo Club. BOHV
Palace. Dorothy Vena Johnson. GoSl
Palace, The. Humbert Wolfe. HOAH
Palace of Alcinous, The. Homer, *tr. fr. Greek by* Pope. *Fr.* The Odyssey, VII. GrR
Palace of Art, The. Tennyson. BEL; BPN; EM-2; EmBrPo; EnLi-2; GEPC; NBE; OAEP; PoVP; UnPo (1st ed.); ViPo; ViPP; VLEP
To ——: "I send you here a sort of allegory," *introd.* ViPo
Palace of Honor, The, *sel.* Gawin Douglas.
Nightmare. PoEL-1
Palace of the Fairies, The. Michael Drayton. OTPC
Palace of the Gnomes. Maria Gowen Brooks. *Fr.* Zophiel; or, The Bride of Seven. AA
("He sat upon a car," *longer sel.*) BAP
Palace of the Sun stood, reared above, The. The Story of Phaeton. Ovid. *Fr.* Metamorphoses. LaP
Palace of Truth, The. William Langland. *Fr.* The Vision of Piers Plowman. ACP
Palace Poem, A. Hsüeh Feng, *tr. fr. Chinese by* Witter Bynner. LiTW
Palace Rhymes, *sel.* Pero López de Ayala, *tr. fr. Spanish by* S. Griswold Morley.
Concerning Lawyers. AnSpL-1
Palaces are sombre cliffs by night, The. On the Grand Canal. David Gascoyne. SeCePo
Palacio, dear friend. To José María Palacio. Antonio Machado. TeCS
Palanquin Bearers. Sarojini Naidu. MoSiPe
Palanquins, The. Ibn Sa'id of Alcala la Real, *tr. fr. Arabic by* A. J. Arberry. MooP
Palatine, The. Willa Cather. BAP; HBMV; InP; LEAP; NP
Palatine, The. Whittier. EtS
Pale and by the hand and like two friends. Autumn Twilight. Henri de Régnier. LiTW
Pale and soul-sick woman with wan eyes, A. The Age. Herbert Edwin Clarke. VA
Pale and still with bent head standing there. To Sorrow. Steen Steensen Blicher. BoDS
Pale autumn daisies turn to face pale sun. Furlough. Ann Louise Hayes. PtPa
Pale beech and pine so blue. In a Wood. Thomas Hardy. *Fr.* The Woodlanders. InP; OAEP; POTT; ViP
Pale beryl sky, with clouds. A Winter Twilight. Arlo Bates. AA
Pale, beyond porch and portal. Proserpine. Swinburne. *Fr.* The Garden of Proserpine. ChTr; FaBoEn
Pale brows, still hands and dim hair. The Lover Mourns for the Loss of Love. W. B. Yeats. Po
Pale, climbing disk, who dost lone vigil keep. To the Moonflower. Craven Langstroth Betts. AA
Pale Conquerors, The. "Pablo de Rokha," *tr. fr. Spanish by* H. R. Hays. TwSpPo
Pale dressed evening star, The. Twinkling Gown. Dorothy Vena Johnson. GoSl
Pale Ebenezer thought it wrong to fight. The Pacifist. Hilaire Belloc. MoVE; SoV
Pale, fugitive, wind-driven, frail and sere. Prophecy. Mellie Burget Miller. BAP
Pale, funeral flowers. Melancholy's Curse. Edward Coote Pinkney. APW; SPP
Pale genius roves alone. Emerson. *Fr.* Fragments on the Poet and the Poetic Gift. TOP
Pale green of the *English Hymnal!* Yattendon hymns. The Old Liberals. John Betjeman. ChMP
Pale green-white in a gallop across the sky. The Gale. John Gould Fletcher. *Fr.* Sand and Spray; a Sea Symphony. PIAE
Pale grey sea crawls stealthily, The. Twilight. Arthur Symons. POTT
Pale hands I loved beside the Shalimar. Kashmiri Song. "Laurence Hope." BLPA; FaBoBe; FaFP; LBBV; NeHB; OlF; TreF
Pale Heinrich he came sauntering by. The Window-Glance. Heine. AWP
Pale inke, thou art not black enough of hew. *Unknown.* SeCSL
Pale is Death. Joachim du Bellay, *tr. fr. French by* Hubert Creekmore. LiTW
Pale is the February sky. The Twenty-second of February. Bryant. DD; GA; HH; MPB; OTPC (1946 ed.); PEOR; PoRL
Pale Italian peasant, A. At the Shrine. Richard Kendall Munkittrick. AA; OBAV
Pale moon was rising above the green mountain, The. The Rose of Tralee. William Pembroke Mulchinock. OnYI
Pale primrose her petals fain would hide, The. Oh, Golden-Rod. W. L. Jaquith. PEOR
Pale road winds faintly upward into the dark skies, The. The Glow-Worm. Edward Shanks. WHA
Pale rose is a smell that has no fountain, A. Gertrude Stein. *Fr.* Scenes. AtBAP
Pale sand edges England's Old/ Dominion. Virginia Britannia. Marianne Moore. MoVE

Pale stars are gone, The! Shelley. Prometheus Unbound, IV. EnLi-2 (1949 ed.)
Pale Sun, The. John Clare. NBE
Pale transparent Autumn mists, The. The Yard in December. Arthur Davison Ficke. CAG
Pale Woman, The. Arthur Symons. FaBoTw
Palely intent, he urged his keel. At the Cannon's Mouth. Herman Melville. PAH
Palermo. Harriet Eleanor Hamilton King. *Fr.* The Disciples. VA
Palestine. Whittier. WBLP
Palimpsest. LeGarde S. Doughty. MuM
Palimpsest. Hyman Edelstein. CaP
Palimpsest; a Deceitful Portrait. Conrad Aiken. *Fr.* The House of Dust, Pt. IV, iii. ChMo; CMP
Palinode, A. Edmund Bolton. ElL; ElSeCe; InvP; OBSC; PoEL-2; SiCE; TuPP
Palinode. Oliver St. John Gogarty. OBMV; PG (1955 ed.); PoP
Palinode, A. Robert Greene. *Fr.* Greene's Groatsworth of Wit. OBSC
("Deceiving world, that with alluring toys.") SiCE
Palinode. James Russell Lowell. AA; IAP
Palinode on Helen. Stesichorus, *tr. fr. Greek by* C. M. Bowra. OxBG
Palinurus. George Cronyn. BAP
Palladium. Matthew Arnold. BPN; EPN; FaBoEn; OAEP; PoVP; TwCrTr; ViPP; VLEP
Pallas, born by Triton side. To Athena. *Unknown.* OxBG
Pallas has not been able to soften the lord of Olympus. Delphian Oracle, *tr. fr. Greek by* George Rawlinson. GrPo
Pallas' home contenteth me. The Transformation of the Furies [*or* The Eumenides]. Aeschylus. *Fr.* Eumenides. GrR; OxBG
Pallas in Olympus. Charles Kingsley. *Fr.* Andromeda. CBOV
Pallid cuckoo, The. Late Winter. J. P. McAuley. NeLNL
Pallid, mis-shapen he stands. The World's grimed thumb. In the Dock. Walter de la Mare. ChMP
Pallid rout stepping like phantoms, A. Tourists in a Sacred Place. Sir Herbert Read. MBP; MoBrPo (1942 ed.)
Pallid taper its long prayer recites, A. Sursum. Guillermo Valencia. CAW
Pallid with too much longing. Laus Veneris. Louise Chandler Moulton. AA; HBV; OBAV; VLEP
Pallidly sleeping, the Ocean's mysterious daughter. Elegy on a Dead Mermaid Washed Ashore at Plymouth Rock. Robert Hillyer. EtS
Palm, The. Roy Campbell. MBP; MoBrPo
Palm. Paul Valéry, *tr. fr. French.* AnFP, *tr. by* Barbara Gibbs; TrFP; *tr. by* Alan Conder
Palm House, Botanic Gardens. George Hetherington. NeIP
Palm of the Hand. Rainer Maria Rilke, *tr. fr. German by* Jessie Lemont. OnPM
Palm, Palm, Palm Sunday. Palm Sunday. *Unknown.* PCH
Palm Sunday. Francis Jammes, *tr. fr. French by* Theodore Yung. CAW
Palm Sunday. John J. Moment. MaRV
Palm Sunday. *Unknown, tr. fr. Greek.* PCH
Palm-Sunday. Henry Vaughan. AtBAP
Triumphant Entry, The, *sel.* MaRV; StJW
Palm Sunday and Monday. Edwin McNeill Poteat. ChIP; MaRV
Palm Sunday Hymn. George Klingle. ChIP; PSO
Palm-Tree, The. Abd-ar-Rahman I, *tr. fr. Arabic by* J. B. Trend. AWP; JAWP; WBP
Palm Tree, The. Felicia Dorothea Hemans. ERP
Palm-Tree, The. Whittier. LPS-2
Palm-Tree and the Pine, The. Richard Monckton Milnes. EV-5; HBV
Palmer, The. John Heywood. *Fr.* The Four P's. ACP; CAW
Palmer, The. William Langland. *Fr.* The Vision of Piers Plowman. ACP; CAW
Palmer, The. Sir Walter Scott. CG, *sl. abr.;* OTPC
Palmer bent, with locks of silver gray, The. Petrarch. Sonnets to Laura: To Laura in Life, XIV. PrPoCR
Palmer's Ode, The. Robert Greene. *Fr.* Never Too Late. EV-1; OBSC; SiCE; TuPP
Palmetto and the Pine, The. Lucy Virginia Smith French. BIG
Palmetto Town. Hervey Allen. LS
Palms and Myrtles. Eleazar ben Kalir, *tr. fr. Hebrew by* Alice Lucas. TrJP
Palms of Mammon have ordained, The. The Revealer. E. A. Robinson. DD
Palmström got a fine Exlibris. Ex Libris. Christian Morgenstern. AnGP
Palmström hasn't a crumb in the house. The Mousetrap. Christian Morgenstern. AnGP
Palmström likes to wrap himself in noises. Noise Protection. Christian Morgenstern. AnGP
Palmström, now no longer so/ young. The Impossible Fact. Christian Morgenstern. TwGV
Palmström sets a bunch of candles. The Dreamer. Christian Morgenstern. AnGP
Palmström to a Nightingale Who Kept Him from Sleeping. Christian Morgenstern, *tr. fr. German by* Lola Gruenthal. AnGP
Palos, Spain, 1492. Annette Wynne. HH
Palpable Silence. Leonora Clawson Stryker. MuM
Pals. John E. Donovan. AlBD
Paltry Nude Starts on a Spring Voyage, The. Wallace Stevens. NP
Pambo. Robert Browning. VLEP
Pamela in Town. Ellen Mackay Hutchinson Cortissoz. AA; HBV
Pamphlet. Luis Muñoz Marin, *tr. fr. Spanish by* Muna Lee. AnCL; PoFr; WoL
Pan. Emerson. IAP; MOAP
Pan. John Fletcher. *See* Hymn to Pan.
Pan. Leconte de Lisle, *tr. fr. French by* Alan Conder. TrFP
Pan. Francis Ledwidge. TCPD
Pan. Apollon Maikov, *tr. fr. Russian by* J. S. Phillimore. BoR
Pan. *Unknown, tr. fr. Greek by* A. J. Butler. RAR
Pan and Daphnis. Glaucus, *tr. fr. Greek by* Walter Leaf. OxBG
Pan and the Cherries. Paul Fort, *tr. fr. French by* Jethro Bithell. AWP; PoMS
Pan, blow your pipes and I will be. A Note from the Pipes. Leonora Speyer. HBMV; OBAV; SBMV
Pan came out of the woods one day. Pan with Us. Robert Frost. GBV (1952 ed.); OxBA
Pan Crucified. Leonora Speyer. BAP
Pan—did you say he was dead, that he'd gone, and for good. Pan-Pipes. Patrick Chalmers. HBMV; VOD
Pan-imbued/ Tempe wood. Pastoral. Francis Thompson. PoLi
Pan in Love. William Wetmore Story. LPS-2
Pan in Pandemonium. Berton Braley. LHV
Pan in Vermont. Kipling. ViP; WhC
Pan in Wall Street. Edmund Clarence Stedman. AA; AnAmPo; BAP; HBV; IAP; LA; LEAP; PFY
Pan is not dead, but sleeping in the brake. Villanelle of the Living Pan. Walter Adolphe Roberts. LEAP; PoNe
Pan Ježišku. *Unknown, tr. fr. Slovakian by* Leclaire Alger. ChrPoLe
Pan Learns Music. Henry van Dyke. PCH
Pan leave piping, the gods have done feasting. The Green-Gown. *Unknown.* CoMu
Pan loved his neighbour, Echo. Love's Lesson [*or* A Lesson to Lovers *or* The Love-Chain]. Moschus. AWP; GrR; OxBG
Pan-Pipes. Patrick Chalmers. HBMV; VOD
Pan Pipes. *Unknown.* VOD (1935 ed.)
Pan, stay awhile. On the Lawn. Cametas. OnPM
Pan, the horned goat-foot of Arcady. Pan. Leconte de Lisle. TrFP
Pan the Lover. Glaucus, *tr. fr. Greek by* F. L. Lucas. GrPE
Pan-thrilled saplings swayed in sportive bliss, The. May. Stephen Moylan Bird. HBMV
Pan went dancing up and down the city. Pan in Pandemonium. Berton Braley. LHV
Pan, who hast to thy command. To Pan. *Unknown.* OxBG
Pan with Us. Robert Frost. GBV (1952 ed.); OxBA
Panacea. Georgia B. Gierasch. MuM
Panama. Amanda Theodosia Jones. PAH
Panama. James Jeffrey Roche. MC; PAH; PoRL
Pancake, The. Christina Rossetti. *See* Mix a Pancake.
Panchatantra, The, *sels. Unknown, tr. fr. Sanskrit by* Arthur W. Ryder.
Fool and False. AWP; JAWP; WBP
Heron That Liked Crab-Meat, The. OuHeWo
How the Crow-Hen Killed the Black Snake. OuHeWo
"In houses where no snakes are found. LiTW
"In sensuous coil." LiTW
(Kings). AWP; PoFr
Leap and Creep. OuHeWo
Mice That Ate Iron, The. OuHeWo
Penalty of Virtue, The. AWP; PoFr
Poverty. AWP; PoFr
"Some eat the countries; these are kings." LiTW
"Some things a man should tell his wife." LiTW
"'Tis hard to find in life." LiTW
(True Friendship.) AWP; JAWP; WBP
"'Tis only saints in youth." LiTW
Pandemonium and Its Architect. Milton. *Fr.* Paradise Lost, I. PoFS; TreFS
Pandora. Hesiod, *tr. fr. Greek. Fr.* Works and Days. LiA, *pr. tr. by* H. G. Evelyn-White; OxBG, *tr. by* Jack Lindsay
Pandora. Absolution. Martha Lindstedt. CAG
Pandora and the Moon. Merrill Moore. MAP; MoAmPo
Pandora's Songs. William Vaughn Moody. *Fr.* The Fire-Bringer.
"Along the earth and up the sky." GBV; MOAP
"Because one creature of his breath." MOAP

"I stood within the heart of God." AnFE; APA; BAP; CBOV; CoAnAm; GBV; IAP; LBAP; MAP; MoAmPo (1942 ed.); MOAP; OQP; QP-1; QS; WGRP
"Of wounds and sore defeat." BAP; BBV; GBV; HBV; LBAP; MOAP; NV; PC; PFY; PoeMoYo; TCPD
(Lyric from "The Fire-Bringer.") BAV
"Thousand aeons, A, nailed in pain." MOAP
"Too far, too far, though hidden in thine arms." MOAP
Pandosto, *sel.* Robert Greene.
Fawnia. HBV; OBEV; OBSC
("Ah, were she pitiful as she is fair.") EG; ElSeCe; ES; PeBoSo, *abr.;* TrGrPo, *abr.;* ViBoPo
(In Praise of His Loving and Best-beloved Fawnia.) AtBAP; PoEL-2
Panegyric. Abu Bakr Muhammad, *tr. fr. Arabic by* A. J. Arberry. MooP
Panegyric on Geese, A. Francis Sylvester Mahony. OnYI
Panegyric on the Ladies. *Unknown.* BOHV
Panegyrick to My Lord Protector, A [*or* Panegyrick upon O. Cromwell]. Edmund Waller. OBS
"Whilst [*or* While] with a strong and yet a gentle hand," *sel.* EV-2; SeCV-1
Pang of the long century of rains, The. The Lament of Edward Blastock. Edith Sitwell. OBMV
Pange Lingua Gloriosa. St. Thomas Aquinas. *See* Hymn for Corpus Christi Day.
Pangloss' Song. Richard Wilbur. NePoAm-2
Pangolin, The. Marianne Moore. CoBMV; CrMA
Pangs that Guard the Gates of Joy, The. Christopher J. Brennan. BoAu
Pangur Ban. *Unknown.* *See* Monk and His Pet Cat, The.
Panhandle Cob. *At. to* H. D. Maclachan. CoSo
Panic, *sels.* Archibald MacLeish. MAP; MoAmPo
Final Chorus.
Panic ("Slowly the thing comes").
Panic. Rosamond Dargan Thomson. NeTW
Pannyra of the Golden Heel. Albert Samain. AWP
Panope. Edith Sitwell. MBP; MoAB; MoBrPo; NP
Panorama, The. Milton. *See* New Worlds.
Pan's Anniversary; or, The Shepherd's Holiday, *sels.* Ben Jonson.
"Of Pan we sing, the best of singers, Pan." ElSeCe
Thus, Thus Begin. TuPP
(Song: "Thus, thus begin the yearly rites.") EPS (1942 ed.)
("Thus, thus begin the yearly rites.") OBS
Pan's Piping. Plato, *tr. fr. Greek by* F. L. Lucas. GrPE
Pan's Song. John Lyly. *Fr.* Midas, IV, i. AtBAP; BCEP; CoEV; EV-1; OBSC
(Pan's Syrinx Was a Girl.) ViBoPo
("Pan's Syrinx was a girl indeed.") SiCE
(Syrinx.) ElL; LoBV; SeCePo; WHA
Pansies. Tom Robinson. BoChLi (1950 ed.)
Pansies, lilies, kingcups, daisies. To the Small Celandine. Wordsworth. AlDL; BPN; EmBrPo; EnRP; ERP; GEPC; HBV; OBRV; OTPC; SN
Pansy. Mary Effie Lee Newsome. CDC
Pansy and the Prayer-Book, The. Matilda Barbara Betham-Edwards. OBVV
Pansy-face and raspberry-paws. To a Cat Purring. Florence Small Edsall. CIV
Pantheist's Song of Immortality, The. Constance Caroline Woodhill Naden. VA
Pantheon, The. Byron. *Fr.* Childe Harold's Pilgrimage, IV. LPS-2
Pantheon, The. Arthur Hugh Clough. Amours de Voyage, Canto I, viii. BPN
Panther, The. Edwin Markham. TBM
Panther, The. Ogden Nash. FaPON; LiL; MoShBr; TiPo (1959 ed.)
Panther, The. Rainer Maria Rilke, *tr. fr. German.* AnGP, *tr. by* Kate Flores; LiTV; *tr. by* C. F. MacIntyre; OnPM, *tr. by* Jessie Lemont; ReMP, *tr. by* Paul Engle
Panther, The. *Unknown.* NA
(Kindly Advice.) BOHV
Panther is like a leopard, The. The Panther. Ogden Nash. FaPON; LiL; MoShBr; TiPo (1959 ed.)
Panther, knowing that his spotted hide, The. Amoretti, LIII. Spenser. PeBoSo
Panther sure the noblest, next the Hind, The. The Church of England. Dryden. *Fr.* The Hind and the Panther, I. OBS
Panting City cried to the Sea, The. The City and the Sea. Longfellow. PEOR
Pantisocracy. Samuel Taylor Coleridge. EnRP
Pantomime. Paul Verlaine. AWP; JAWP; WBP
Paola and Francesca. Frances Anne Kemble. DiM
Paolo and Francesca. Dante, *tr. fr. Italian.* *Fr.* Divina Commedia: Inferno, V. ExPo, *tr. by* Laurence Binyon; LiA, *tr. by* Byron
Paolo and Francesca, *sel.* Stephen Phillips.
"What is that book you read?" ReTS
Papa's Letter. *Unknown.* PTA-2
Paper. Benjamin Franklin. LHV; LPS-3; MOB
Paper Boats. Rabindranath Tagore. FaPON; MCCG; PCH; RAR; SP
"Day by day I float my paper boats one by one down the running stream," *sel.* AlDL
Paper in the Gate-legged Table, The. Amy Lowell. DaM
Paper in the Meadow, The. Oscar Williams. PG (1955 ed.)
Paper, little sticks and a cord. The Kite. José Moreno Villa. CoSP; OnPM
Paper Mill. Joseph Kalar. AnAmPo
Paper Nautilus, The. Marianne Moore. FaBoMo
Paper of Pins, A. *Unknown.* ABF, *with music;* ABS
(Keys of Heaven, The, *sl. diff., with music.*) FTB
Paper Roses. Dana Burnet. NV
Paper that my dad received, The. The Way of a Man. Lois Halderman. FAOV
Paper Windmill, The. Amy Lowell. CP
Pap's got his pattent-right, and rich as all creation. Back to Griggsby's Station. James Whitcomb Riley. BLPA
Parable, A. James Russell Lowell. ChIP; MaRV, *sl. abr.;* PGD, *abr.*
Parable. William Soutar. HaMV
Parable for Poetasters, A. Oliver St. John Gogarty. WhC
Parable of Generosity. Antonio Spinetti Dini, *tr. fr. Spanish by* Muna Lee. BoFr
Parable of the Mustard Weed, The. Dora Hagemeyer. StaSt
Parable of the Old Men and the Young, The. Wilfred Owen. TwCV
Parable of the Pharisee and the Publican. St. Luke, XVIII: 10–14, Bible, *N.T.* GrCo-1
Parable of the Spirit, A. John Arthur Goodchild. VA
Parable of the Talents, The. St. Matthew, XXV: 14–30, Bible, *N.T.* EnLi-1
Parables from Nature. St. Mark, IV: 3–9, 26–29, Bible, *N.T.* GrCo-1
Parabola, The. Hooper Reynolds Goodwin. PoMa
Parabolas of grief, the hills are never. In Africa. Roy Fuller. BoSA
Paracelsus, *sels.* Robert Browning.
Awakening of Man, The, *fr.* V. WGRP
Development of Man, *fr.* V. EPN
Heap Cassia, Sandal Buds and Stripes, *fr.* IV. BPN; EmBrPo; EV-5; GTML; GTSL; MyFE; OBRV; PoVP
(Song: "Heap cassia, sandal-buds and stripes.") AnFE; OBEV; WHA
In His Good Time, *br. sel.* OQP; QP-1
(Guidance.) BPP
(I Go to Prove My Soul.) MaRV
Lost, Lost! Yet Come, *fr.* II. EmBrPo
Paracelsus Attains, *fr.* V. EmBrPo
"Progress is the law of life," *fr.* V. OQP; QP-2
(Man's Destiny.) MaRV
Scene in a Garden, *fr.* I. PCH
Song: "Over the sea our galleys went," *fr.* IV. BPN; OBRV; VA
(Over the Sea Our Galleys Went.) EmBrPo; EV-5; PoVP
(Song from "Paracelsus.") SG
(Wanderers, The.) OBEV; OBVV
Song: "Thus the Mayne glideth," *fr.* V. OBRV
(Thus the Mayne Glideth.) PoVP
Truth Is Within, *fr.* I. MaRV
Parachute. Stanley Snaith. HaMV
Parachute Descent. David Bourne. WaP
Parachutes, My Love, Could Carry Us Higher. Barbara Guest. NeAP
Paraclete. Jorge de Lima, *tr. fr. Portuguese by* Dudley Poore. AnCL; PoFr
Paraclete. Alfred Noyes. LBBV
Parade, The. Mary Esther Badley. PEDC
Parade. Harry Brown. TwAmPo
Parade. Rachel Field. *Fr.* A Circus Garland. StVeCh; UTS
Parade, The. Ashton Greene. NePoAm
Parade, The. Marjorie Seymour Watts. PCH
Paradigm. Babette Deutsch. TrJP
Paradigm, The. Allen Tate. MOAP
Parading near Saint Peter's flood. The Battle of Lake Champlain. Philip Freneau. PAH
Paradise. George Birdseye. BOHV
(Paradise; a Hindoo Legend.) HBV
Paradise. Charles G. Blanden. OQP; QP-1
Paradise. Dante. *See* Paradiso.
Paradise. Dryden. *Fr.* The State of Innocence and the Fall of Man. BeR
Paradise. Frederick William Faber. HBV; VA
(O Paradise, O Paradise.) OIF; WGRP
Paradise. George Herbert. BLV; BoLiVe; TrGrPo
Paradise. Omar Khayyám. *See* Rubáiyát of Omar Khayyám of Naishápúr.
Paradise. Milton. *Fr.* Paradise Lost, IV. OBS
Paradise. Immanuel di Roma, *tr. fr. Hebrew by* Joseph Chotzner. TrJP
Paradise. Christina Rossetti. HBV; OxBoCh; PoVP; WGRP
(Paradise; in a Dream.) ViPo
Paradise. Christopher Smart. RO
Paradise; a Hindoo Legend. George Birdseye. *See* Paradise.

Paradise Lost, *sels.* Milton.
Adam and Eve ("Now Morn her rosie steps"), *Bk.* V, *ll.* 1–25. LiA
Adam and Eve ("So passed they naked on"), *Bk.* IV, *ll.* 319–355. SeCePo
Adam and Eve in the Garden, *Bk.* IV, *ll.* 288–351, 598–688. EV-2
(Adam and Eve, *ll.* 288–355, *sl. abr.*) LPS-2
(Man and Woman Made One Unity, *ll.* 288–299, *abr.*) BCEP
(Satan Looks upon Adam and Eve in Paradise, *ll.* 288–324.) TreFS
Adam Describing Eve, *Bk.* VIII, *ll.* 460–606, *abr.* LPS-1
Adam, First Man of Men, *Bk.* VIII, *ll.* 250–299. MaPo
Adam to Eve, *Bk.* IX, *ll.* 896–959, *abr.* LPS-1
"All these and more came flocking; but with looks," *Bk.* I, *ll.* 522–571. MyFE
(Mustering the Hosts of Hell, *ll.* 522–604, *abr.*) BCEP
And God Created the Great Whales, *Bk.* VII, *ll.* 391–416. EtS
"And Uriel to his charge," *Bk.* IV, *ll.* 589–609. BrBE
Ark, The, *Bk.* XI, *ll.* 710–753. EtS
"As when a vulture on Imaus bred," *Bk.* III, *ll.* 431–443. HoPM
"At last his sail-broad vannes," *Bk.* II, *ll.* 927–967. BrBE
Atonement, The, *Bk.* III, *ll.* 227–265. OBS
Battle of the Angels, *Bk.* VI, *ll.* 12–669, *much abr.* LPS-2
(Battle between the Angels and Anarchs, *ll.* 202–669, *much abr.*) BCEP
(Beginning of the Battle of the Angels, *ll.* 12–110, *much abr.*) BCEP
Beëlzebub Rises to Speak, *Bk.* II, *ll.* 284–309. UnPo (1 st. ed.)
"But now at last the sacred influence," *Bk.* II, *ll.* 1034–1055. BrBE
Council of Satan, The, *Bk.* I, *ll.* 271–669. PoEL-3
Death, *Bk.* II, *ll.* 666–673. LiA
(Challenge of Death, The, *ll.* 666–726.) BCEP
"Descend from Heav'n Urania, by that name," *Bk.* VII, *ll.* 1–39. BrBE; NBE; TCEP
(Invocation to Urania.) FiP; OBS
Eve, *Bk.* IX, *ll.* 417–466. OBS
Eve and the Serpent, *Bk.* IX, *ll.* 445–526, *sl. abr.* BLV
(Satan Beholds Eve, *ll.* 445–472.) PoFS
Eve Penitent, *Bk.* X, *ll.* 914–946. OBS
Eve to Adam, *Bk.* XII, *ll.* 613–623. LPS-1
Eve's Lament, *Bk.* XI, *ll.* 268–285. LPS-1
Faithful Angel, The, *Bk.* V, *ll.* 896–907. LPS-2
Fall, The, *Bk.* IX, *ll.* 385–1189. PoEL-3
Fallen Angels, The, *Bk.* II, *ll.* 557–628. CBE
First Day of Creation, The, *Bk.* VII, *ll.* 192–260. OxBoCh
(Creation of the World, The, *ll.* 192–242.) MaPo
Flight of Satan, The, *Bk.* II, *ll.* 629–635, 1011–1055. PoF
"For now, and since first break of dawne the Fiend," *Bk.* IX, *ll.* 412–433. BrBE
Fragments from the Old Masters: Formation Flight, *Bk.* VII, *ll.* 425–432. PoF
Free Will and God's Foreknowledge, *Bk.* III, *ll.* 80–134. ExPo
Gabriel Meets Satan, *Bk.* IV, *ll.* 823–1015. LoBV
"God made thee perfet, not immutable," *Bk.* V, *ll.* 524–540. PoFr
"Hail, holy light, offspring of Heaven first-born!" *Bk.* III, *ll.* 1–55. AtBAP; ATP, *ll.* 1–137; BrBE; EM-1; ExPo; FiP; GTBS-W; InP; LiA; LoBV; OAEP; SeEP; ShBV-4; ViBoPo; WHA
(Hymn to Light.) FaBoEn, *ll.* 1–50; GrCo-2
(Invocation to Light.) CoEV; EV-2; LPS-2
(Light.) LiTB; OBEV; OBS; RiBV
"He, above the rest/ In shape and gesture proudly eminent," *Bk.* I, *ll.* 589–604. InP
"He ended, and they both descend the hill," *Bk.* XII, *ll.* 606–649. ATP; NBE; SeEP; TCEP
(Banishment, The, *ll.* 624–649.) OBS
(Banishment from Paradise, *ll.* 607–649.) TreFS
(Departure from Paradise, The, *ll.* 637–649.) LPS-1
(Expulsion from Paradise, The.) BEL, *ll.* 606–649; ChTr, *ll.* 633–649
(". . . For now too nigh/ Th' Archangel stood," *ll.* 625–649.) BrBE
(Leave Taking, *ll.* 610–649.) FaBoEn
(Their Banishment, *ll.* 625–649.) SeCePo
"He ended; and thus Adam last replied," *Bk.* XII, *ll.* 552–649. CoBE; MyFE
(Retreat from Paradise, The.) PoEL-3
"He sayde, and on his Son with rayes direct," *Bk.* VI, *ll.* 719–741. NBE
Heaven, *Bk.* III, *ll.* 344–371. OBS
Hell, *Bk.* II, *ll.* 475–628. OBS
"High on a throne of royal state, which far," *Bk.* II, *complete.* AtBAP, *ll.* 1–505, 506–628; CoBE, *ll.* 1–505; EM-1; EnL, *ll.* 1–889, *abr.;* EnLi-1; EnLit; GEPC; OAEP; REAL; SeEP, *ll.* 1–505; TCEP; TOP
"Him the Almighty Power/ Hurld headlong flaming," *fr. Bk.* I. AnFE, *ll.* 44–109, 283–330; MyFE, *ll.* 44–191
(Fallen Angels, The, *ll.* 44–74.) FaBoEn
(Satan Defiant, *ll.* 44–109.) WHA
Inner Light, *Bk.* III, *ll.* 40–55. MaRV
"Is this the region, this the soil, the clime," *Bk.* I, *ll.* 242–270. MyFE; NBE
(Fall of the Angels, The, *ll.* 242–363.) FiP
(Satan Greets Hell, *ll.* 249–263.) LiA
(Satan Ponders His Fallen State, *ll.* 242–263.) TreFS
(Satan's Kingdom, *ll.* 242–270.) CBE
Lucifer, *Bk.* I, *ll.* 594–615. UnPo (1st ed.)
Mammon, *Bk.* I, *ll.* 679–684. MaRV
Myself Am Hell ("The mind is its own place"), *Bk.* I, *ll.* 254–255, *Bk.* IV, *ll.* 73–80. MaRV
"Nine times the space that measures day and night," *Bk.* I, *ll.* 50–126. NBE
"No more of talk where God or Angel Guest," *Bk.* IX, *ll.* 1–47. SeEP
(Subject of Heroic Song, The.) OBS
"Now came still evening on and twlight gray," *fr. Bk.* IV. BCEP, *ll.* 598–609; SeEP, *ll.* 598–775
(Evening in Paradise.) FaBoEn, *ll.* 598–609; GN, *ll.* 598–609; LoBV, *ll.* 598–688; LPS-2, *ll.* 598–609; TCEP, *ll.* 598–633
(Moon and the Nightingale, The, *ll.* 598–609.) ChTr
(Night Falls on Eden, *ll.* 598–609.) PoFS; TreFS
O Earth, How Like to Heav'n, *Bk.* IX, *ll.* 99–178. MaPo
"O thou that with surpassing glory crown'd," *Bk.* IV, *ll.* 32–113. NBE
(Satan Reflects, *ll.* 32–78.) CoEV
(Satan Speaks, *ll.* 32–78, *abr.*) PIAE
(Satan's Address to the Sun, *ll.* 32–113.) EV-2
(Satan's Soliloquy, *ll.* 32–113.) LiTB; OBS
"Of Man's first disobedience, and the fruit," *Bk.* I, *complete.* ATP; BEL; BoLiVe; CBE, *ll.* 1–191; CoBE; EM-1; EnL; EnLi-1; EnLit; EPP; EV-2; FiP, *ll.* 1–26; GEPC; OAEP; OuHeWo; REAL; SeEP; *ll.* 1–26; TCEP; TOP; TyEnPo
(Fallen Angels, The, *ll.* 1–363.) WoL
(Invocation.) FaBoEn, *ll.* 1–26; PoEL-3, *ll.* 1–26; PoFS, *ll.* 1–49
(Invocation to the Heavenly Muse, *ll.* 1–26.) TreFS
(Opening Argument, The, *ll.* 1–69.) BCEP
"On th' other side, Adam, soon as he heard," *Bk.* IX, *ll.* 888–997. NBE
"Others more mild,/ Retreated in a silent valley, sing," *Bk.* II, *ll.* 546–627. MyFE
Over All the Face of Earth Main Ocean Flowed, *Bk.* VII, *ll.* 278–308. EtS
Pandemonium and Its Architect, *fr. Bk.* I. PoFS, *ll.* 710–751; TreFS, *ll.* 710–746
Paradise, *Bk.* IV, *ll.* 257–294. OBS
Place of the Damned, The, *Bk.* II, *ll.* 582–603. FaBoEn
Plan of Salvation, The, *Bk.* III, *ll.* 274–343. WGRP
Poet-Preacher's Prayer, A, *Bk.* I, *ll.* 17–19, 22–26. MaRV
Prospect of Eden, The, *Bk.* IV, *ll.* 1–775. PoEL-3
Satan, *fr. Bk.* I. BLV, *ll.* 36–543, *abr.;* CBOV, *ll.* 64–75; LiA, *ll.* 589–599; SeCePo, *Bk.* I, *ll.* 283–313, *and Bk.* II, *ll.* 1010–1055; TrGrPo, *ll.* 36–543, *abr.*
Satan and His Host, *Bk.* I, *ll.* 527–669. OBS
Satan and the Fallen Angels, *Bk.* I, *ll.* 283–313. CoEV; LiTB; OBS
(Satan Rallies the Fallen Angels, *ll.* 283–330, *abr.*) BCEP
(Superior Fiend, The, *ll.* 283–330.) MaPo
"Satan from hence now on the lower stair," *Bk.* III, *ll.* 540–571. BrBE
(New Worlds, *ll.* 543–571.) OBS
(Panorama, The, *ll.* 540–565.) WHA
Satan in Sight of Eden, *Bk.* IV, *ll.* 27–113. TCEP
Satan Journeys to the Garden of Eden, *Bk.* IV, *ll.* 172–201. ChTr
Satan on War, *Bk.* II, *ll.* 496–505. MaRV
Satan Views the World, *Bk.* II, *ll.* 1010–1055. WHA
Satan's Adjuration, *Bk.* I, *ll.* 105–124. FaBoEn
Satan's First Meeting with Death, *Bk.* II, *ll.* 681–703. CBE
Satan's Pride ("Is there no place"), *Bk.* IV, *ll.* 79–110. MaRV
Scene in Paradise, A, *Bk.* IV, *ll.* 23–55, *abr.* GN
Scheme of Redemption, The, *Bk.* III, *ll.* 56–343. StJW
"She, as a veil down to the slender waist," *Bk.* IV, *ll.* 304–311. LoPS
"Silent, and in face/ Confounded, long they sat, as stricken mute," *Bk.* IX, *ll.* 1064–1189. EnL
"So on he fares, and to the border comes," *Bk.* IV, *ll.* 131–268, *abr.* PreP
(Garden of Eden, *ll.* 131–165.) EV-2
(Satan Discovers Eden, *ll.* 131–196, *abr.*) ExPo
"So spake the archangel Michael; then paused," *Bk.* XII, *ll.* 466–649. EnL
"So spake the false Arch-Angel, and infus'd," *Bk.* V, *ll.* 691–734. NBE
"So spake the Son, and into the terrour chang'd," *Bk.* VI, *ll.* 824–912. NBE
(Victor, The, *ll.* 824–866.) BCEP

"So talked the spirited sly snake; and Eve," *Bk.* IX, *ll.* 613–833. EnL
"So threaten'd hee, but Satan to no threats," *Bk.* IV, *ll.* 968–1015. BrBE
"Southward through Eden went a river large," *Bk.* IV, *ll.* 223–311. ViBoPo
Standing on Earth, *Bk.* VII, *ll.* 23–39. ChTr
Sum of Wisdom, The, *Bk.* XII, *ll.* 557–587. MaPo
Summons, The, *Bk.* I, *ll.* 299–587, *abr.* WHA
Sweet Is the Breath of Morn, *Bk.* IV, *ll.* 641–656. TyEnPo
(World Beautiful, The, *ll.* 641–649.) GN
Then, When I Am Thy Captive, Talk of Chains, *Bk.* IV, *ll.* 970–1015. WHA
"These are thy glorious works Parent of good," *fr. Bk.* V. BrBE, *ll.* 153–208; MaRV, *ll.* 153–159; TCEP, *ll.* 153–208
(Adam's Morning Hymn, *ll.* 153–210.) WGRP
(Adam's Morning Hymn in Paradise, *ll.* 153–212.) LPS-2
(Morning Hymn in Paradise, *ll.* 153–208.) GrCo-1
(Morning Hymn of Adam, *ll.* 153–165, 195–208.) TrPWD
(Morning Hymn of Adam and Eve, *ll.* 153–208.) OxBoCh; TCEP
"Thus saying, from her side the fatal key," *Bk.* II, *ll.* 871–967. NBE
"Thus was this place/ A happy rural seat of various view," *Bk.* IV, *ll.* 246–268, 285–527. ATP
(Eden, *ll.* 246–268.) FaBoEn
"To him she hasted; in her face excuse," *Bk.* IX, *ll.* 853–1033. EnL
"To whom the angel; Son of Heav'n and Earth," *Bk.* V, *ll.* 519–540. NBE
(Free to Serve, *ll.* 519–543.) GrCo-2
"To whom thus also th' angel last replied," *Bk.* XII, *ll.* 574–649. FiP
Universe of Death, A, *Bk.* II, *ll.* 614–628. CoEV
War in Heaven, The, *Bk.* VI, *ll.* 207–274. PoF
War in Heaven (The First Battle), *Bk.* VI, *ll.* 44–405, *abr.* ExPo
Wedded Love, *fr. Bk.* IV. OBS, *ll.* 750–755; PoFS; *ll.* 736–775
(Their Wedded Love, *ll.* 750–775.) SeCePo
"With grave/ Aspect he rose," *Bk.* II, *ll.* 300–389, 629–648, 879–1055. ATP
"With thee conversing I forget all time," *Bk.* IV, *ll.* 639–656. BrBE; LoPS
(Eve Speaks to Adam.) ChTr
(Eve to Adam.) CBE; FaBoEn; TreFS; TrGrPo, *ll.* 639–658
Yonder Nether World, *Bk.* XI, *ll.* 315–333. LiA
Paradise, my heavenly home. White and Black. Ibn al-Attar. MooP
Paradise of Birds, The, *sels.* William John Courthope.
Birdcatcher's Song. VA
Dodoism, *br. sel.* OtMeF
In Praise of Gilbert White. VA
Ode: To the Roc. VA
Paradise on earth is found, A. The Description of Elysium. Michael Drayton. *Fr.* The Muses' Elysium. TuPP
Paradise Regained, *sels.* Milton.
Athens, *Bk.* IV, *ll.* 236–364. OBS
(Athens the Eye of Greece, *ll.* 221–284.) TwCrTr
("Look once more e're we leave this specular Mount," *ll.* 236–284.) SeEP; ViBoPo
(Satan's Survey of Greece, *ll.* 237–284.) EV-2
(Vision of Athens, *ll.* 237–284.) TOP
But to His Mother Mary, *Bk.* II, *ll.* 60–108. ISi
Calm and Sinless Peace, *Bk.* IV, *ll.* 409–425. LiA
First Temptation, The, *Bk.* I, *ll.* 303–502. OxBoCh
Messiah, The, *Bk.* I, *ll.* 182–293. OBS
Parthians, The, *Bk.* III, *ll.* 310–343. OBS
Rome, *Bk.* IV, *ll.* 44–108. OBS
Satan's Guile, *Bk.* I, *ll.* 357–405. LiTB; OBS
Son of God in the Wilderness, The; His Dream, *Bk.* II, *ll.* 260–284. EV-2
Table Richly Spread, A, *Bk.* II. *ll.* 340–365. FaBoCh; LoGBV
"They err who count it glorious to subdue," *Bk.* III, *ll.* 71–107. PoFr
"To whom the Tempter inly rackt reply'd," *Bk.* III, *ll.* 203–222. NBE
True and False Glory, *Bk.* III, *ll.* 43–107. LiTB; OBS
"With that (such power was given him then), he took," *Bk.* III, *ll.* 250–443, *Bk.* IV, *ll.* 449–639. StJW
Paradisi Gloria. Thomas William Parsons. AA; APW; OBAV; OQP; QP-1
Paradiso, *sels.* Dante, *tr. fr. Italian. Fr.* Divina Commedia.
Affinity with the Stars, *br. sel. fr.* XXXIII, *tr. by* Wendell Phillips Stafford. GrCo-2
Being Underived, *fr.* I, *tr. by* Longfellow. CAW
Freedom of the Will: Beatrice to Dante, *br. sel., fr.* V, *tr. by* M. B. Anderson. GrCo-1
His Will Is Our Peace, *br. sel. fr.* III, *tr. by* GrCo-2
Incommunicable Glory, The. 12 *ll., fr.* I, *tr. by* Wendell Phillips Stafford. GrCo-2
"Into the justice of eternity," *fr.* XIX, *tr. by* Jefferson Butler Fletcher. PoFr
Love, XXXIII, *tr. by* Philip Henry Wicksteed. LiA
"'Now say,' he said, 'were it not worse indeed,'" *fr.* VIII, *tr. by* Jefferson Butler Fletcher. PoFr
"O petty blood-nobility of ours!" *fr.* XVI, *tr. by* Jefferson Butler Fletcher. PoFr
One World, 4 *ll.* MaRV
Paradise, *abr., tr. by* Henry F. Cary. OuHeWo
Paradise: Cacciaguida's Prophecy to Dante, *fr.* XVII, *tr. by* Frances Winwar. EnLi-1
Primal Cause, The, *fr.* XXVIII, *tr. by* Longfellow. CAW
Saint Bernard's Prayer to Our Lady, *fr.* XXXIII, *tr. by* Louis How. ISi
(St. Bernard's Prayer to the Virgin Mary, *tr. by* Laurence Binyon.) MeRV
("Thou Virgin Mother, daughter of thy Son," *tr. by* Longfellow.) CAW
Saints in Glory, The, *fr.* XXXI, *tr. by* Henry F. Cary. WGRP
Paradox, The. John Donne. OAEP
Paradox, The. Michael Drayton. Idea, LXII, *also in* Idea's Mirrour, L. BLV; PIAE
("When first I ended, then I first began.") TrGrPo
Paradox. Angelina Weld Grimké. CDC
Paradox, A. Richard Lovelace. Po
Paradox. Sister Maryanna. SaFP
Paradox. Huw Menai. MaRV
Paradox. Vassar Miller. NePoEA
Paradox, A. Earl of Pembroke. ElL
Paradox, The. Ruth Pitter. MaRV; QS
Paradox. Jessie B. Rittenhouse. PR; TBM
Paradox of Time, The. Austin Dobson, *after the French of* Pierre de Ronsard. AWP; HBV; JAWP; PG (1945 ed.); VLEP; WBP
Paradox: That Fruition Destroys Love, *sel.* Henry King. "Since lovers' joys then leave so sick a taste." LO
Paradox; the Birds. Karl Shapiro. CrMA
Paradoxes. Lao-tse, *tr. fr. Chinese by* Walter Gorn Old. *Fr.* The Simple Way. GrCo-2
Paradoxes. Christina Rossetti. *Fr.* Sing-Song. OTPC (1946 ed.)
(Pin Has a Head, A.) RIS
Paradoxical December afternoon, A. The Plane. Sidney Alexander. PoF
Paragon of Animals, The. Pope. *See* Know Then Thyself.
Paramours, to those who would accuse, The. Sirventes. Peire Cardenal. LyMA
Paranoia. Louis J. Karnosh. PoP
Paranoia in Crete. Gregory Corso. NeAP
Paraphrase. Hart Crane. MOAP; MoVE; TwAmPo
Paraphrase from the French, A. Matthew Prior. OxBoLi
Paraphrase of Horace. Genaro Estrada, *tr. fr. Spanish by* Donald Devenish Walsh. AnCL
Paraphrase of the Scriptures, The. Cædmon (?). *See* Exodus; Genesis.
Paraphrase on Part of the Book of Job, A, *sels.* Edward Young. BeR
Chambers of Death, The.
Leviathan.
Paraphrase on the Psalms of David, A, *sels.* George Sandys.
Deo Opt. Max. Psalm CIV. OBS
Psalme CXXXVII. OBS
Paraphrase on Thomas à Kempis, A. Pope. GoBC; OBEC
"Speak, Gracious Lord, oh speak; thy Servant hears," *sel.* TrPWD
Parasite, The. Ben Jonson. *Fr.* Volpone. CoEV
Parasite. Alfred Kreymborg. NP
Pardners. Berton Braley. SCC
Pardon. Julia Ward Howe. GA; PAH
Pardon, The. Richard Wilbur. NePoEA
Pardon, goddess of the night. Shakespeare. *Fr.* Much Ado about Nothing, V, iii. OBSC; SiCE; ViBoPo
Pardon, great enemy. Her Friends Bring Her a Christmas Tree. W. B. Yeats. Upon a Dying Lady, VII. LiTB
Pardon if I ravel rhyme. Ballade of Youth Remaining. Tom MacInnes. CPG
Pardon, Lord, the lips that dare. Whittier. *Fr.* Andrew Rykman's Prayer. TrPWD
Pardon me, lady, but I wanta ast you. Drug Store. John V. A. Weaver. HBMV; NP; PoeMoYo; YaD
Pardon mine ears, both I and they do pray. Astrophel and Stella, LI. Sir Philip Sidney. SiPS
Pardon, Old Fathers. W. B. Yeats. *Fr.* Responsibilities. OAEP (2d ed.)
("Pardon, old fathers, if you still remain.") PoEL-5
Pardon our visit to this place. The Framework-Knitters Petition. C. Briggs. CoMu
Pardon the faults in me. Wife to Husband. Christina Rossetti. VA; ViPo
Pardoner's Tale, The. Chaucer. *Fr.* The Canterbury Tales. BEL; CoBE; EM-1, *sl. abr.;* EnL, *mod. by* Theodore

Pardoner's Tale, The (*continued*)
Morrison; EnLi-1; EnLit; EV-1; FiP, *abr.;* LiA; OAEP; PoEL-1; RiBV, *mod. by* Frank Ernest Hill
(Death and the Ruffians, *abr., mod. by* Leigh Hunt.) BCEP
"Thise ryotoures three, of which I tell," *sel.* MyFE
(Quest for Death.) CoEV
("These rioters, of whom I make my rime.") WHA
Pards. Hugh J. Hughes. POT; PoTo
Parent of all, omnipotent. The American Patriot's Prayer. *Unknown.* PAH
Parent of blooming flowers and gay desires. Ode: In Imitation of Pastor Fido. George Lyttelton. CEP
Parental Ode to My Son, Aged Three Years and Five Months, A. Thomas Hood. BOHV; FAOV; HBV; LauV
(To My Infant Son.) LPS-1
(To My Son.) RIS
(To My Son, Aged Three Years and Five Months.) FaPON
"Thou happy, happy elf!" *sel.* FiBHP
Parental Recollections. Mary Lamb. FAOV; OBRV
(Child, A.) EV-4; OBEV
(In Memoriam.) GTSL
Parenthood. John Farrar. FAOV; MPB; OHIP
Parents are sinful now, for they must whisper. Marriage. Austin Clarke. OxBI
Parfum exotique. Baudelaire. *See* Exotic Perfume.
Paris. Elizabeth Barrett Browning. *Fr.* Aurora Leigh, VI. ViP
Paris Again. *Unknown.* AOAH
Paris-am-Seine. Jean Malaquais, *tr. fr. French by* Dwight Macdonald. MiFP
Paris, Anchises, and Adonis—three. Praxiteles. *Unknown.* LPS-3
Paris and Oenone, *sel.* Laurence Binyon.
"Who in this desert calls on Paris?" ReTS
Paris at dawn; Egypt beneath the stars. After All Splendors. Mary Brent Whiteside. LS
Paris at Night. Tristan Corbière, *tr. fr. French by* Kenneth Koch *and* Georges Guy. AnFP
Paris gutter of the good old times, A. Baudelaire. Eugene Lee-Hamilton. BMEP; LEAP
Paris in 1815, *sel.* George Croly.
A Fauxbourg. Pt. I, xx. OBRV
Paris Is Dead. Quintus Smyrnaeus, *tr. fr. Greek. Fr.* Posthomerica, X. OxBG
Paris Is Worsted by Menelaus and Returns to Helen. Homer, *tr. fr. Greek by* F. L. Lucas. *Fr.* The Iliad, III. GrPE
Paris lay hushed beneath the midday sun. On the Parapet of Notre Dame. Charles J. Quirk. CAW
Paris Rescued by Aphrodite. Homer, *tr. fr. Greek by* Maurice Hewlett. *Fr.* The Iliad, III. GrR
Paris; the Seine at Night. Charles Divine. HBMV
Paris: This April Sunset Completely Utters. E. E. Cummings. NAMP
Paris Twin-Galleys. Charles Péguy, *tr. fr. French by* W. J. Strachan. MiFP
(Paris Two-banked Galley, *tr. by* Alan Conder.) TrFP
Parish Church, The. Julio Herrera y Reissig, *tr. fr. Spanish by* Thomas Walsh. CAW
Parish Poor-House, The. George Crabbe. *See* Parish Workhouse, The.
Parish Priest, The. Chaucer. *See* Parson, The.
Parish priest, The/ of Austerity. The Preacher's Mistake. Brewer Mattocks, *sometimes at. to* William Croswell Doane. BLPA; MaRV; PoToHe; StaSt
Parish Register, The, *sels.* George Crabbe.
"Behold the cot!" *fr.* Pt. I: Baptisms. OBRV
"My record ends," *fr.* Pt. III: Burials. OBRV
"Next at our altar," *fr.* Pt. II: Marriages. OBRV
"Next died the Lady who yon Hall possess'd," *fr.* Pt. III: Burials. PoD
"There was, 'tis said, and I believe, a time," *fr.* Pt. III: Burials. EiPP
Parish Workhouse, The. George Crabbe. *Fr.* The Village. BCEP, *br. sel.;* LEAP
(Parish Poor-House, The, *longer sel.*) OBEC
Park. Glyn Jones. MoWP
Park, The. James S. Tippett. BrR; SUS; TiPo
Park Avenue Cat. Frances M. Frost. CIV
Park is filled with night and fog, The. Spring Night. Sara Teasdale. ChMo; CMP; FaBoBe; HBMV; LiTA; LiTL; LiTM (1946 ed.); MAP; MoAmPo; NeMa; PG (1945 ed.)
Parked among benches of oak, in the nooks of the church. The Poor in Church. Arthur Rimbaud. LiTW
Parks and Ponds. Emerson. PoEL-4
Parlement of Foules, The, *sels.* Chaucer.
Dream Garden, A. CBOV
Proem: "Lyf so short, the craft so long to lerne, The." FiP; MyFE; NBE
(Parliament of Fowls, The.) ViBoPo
Roundel: "Now welcom somer, with thy sonnë softe." ATP; CBOV; EPP
(Foules Rondel, *orig., with mod. vers.* [The Birds' Rondel] *by* Louis Untermeyer.) TrGrPo
(Now Welcom[e] Somer.) SeCePo; TyEnPo
(Now Welcome Summer.) PoLi
(Qui Bien Aime à Tard Oublie.) AEV; EnLoPo
(Rondel: "Now welcome, somer . . .") LyMA
(St. Valentine Rondel, A, *mod. by* Edwin Markham.) BCEP
Parley of Beasts. "Hugh MacDiarmid." LO; MoBrPo; OBMV
Parley with His Empty Purse, A. Thomas Randolph. OBS
Parleyings with Certain People of Importance, *sel.* Robert Browning.
With Christopher Smart. PtP
Parliament Hill. Henry Howarth Bashford. BrR; MPB; SP; VOD
Parliament Hill Fields. John Betjeman. FaBoTw; HaMV
Parliament of Bees, The, *sels.* John Day. ViBoPo
"High steward of thy vines."
"I will have one built/ Like Pompey's theatre."
"This baseness follows your profession."
Parliament of England, Ye, *with music. Unknown.* SoAmSa
Parliament of Fowls, The. Chaucer. *See* Parlement of Foules, The.
Parlor Car. Dorothy Brown Thompson. PoMa
Parlor Cat, A. Louella C. Poole. CIV
Parnassian, The. Callimachus, *tr. fr. Greek by* F. L. Lucas. GrPE
Parnell. Lionel Johnson. POTT
Parnell's Memory. Thomas Michael Kettle. ACP; JKCP (1926 ed.)
(Parnell.) AnIV
Parochial Theme. Wallace Stevens. LiTA
Parodie, A: "Soul's joy, when thou art gone." George Herbert. OBS
Parody, A: "Farewell! A long farewell to all our school days!" Edith Putnam Painton. PEDC
Parody on "A Psalm of Life." *Unknown, sometimes at. to* Oliver Wendell Holmes. BLPA
Parody on Thomas Hood's "The Bridge of Sighs." *Unknown.* FiBHP
Paroles sur la dune, *sel.* Victor Hugo, *tr. fr. French by* Henry Carrington.
"At times I lie stretched out, and never rise." LiA
Parrhasius. Nathaniel Parker Willis. AA
"Parrhasius stood, gazing forgetfully," *sel.* LPS-3, *abr.*
Parricide. Julia Ward Howe. PAH
Parrot, The. Thomas Campbell. CG; OTPC
Parrot, The. Ferid ed-Din Attar, *tr. fr. Persian by* Edward Fitzgerald. *Fr.* The Bird-Parliament. PeP
Parrot, The. James Elroy Flecker. BLA; FaBoTw
Parrot, The ("Long since I'd ceased to care"). W. W. Gibson. OBMV
Parrot, The. John Skelton. *See* Parrot's Soliloquy.
Parrot, The. José Juan Tablada, *tr. fr. Spanish by* Samuel Beckett. AnMP
Parrot, The. Tu Fu, *tr. fr. Chinese by* Henry H. Hart. PoHN
Parrot, bird that can, A. Crinagoras, *tr. fr. Greek by* Norman Douglas. GrPo
Parrot from the Spanish main, A. The Parrot. Thomas Campbell. CG
Parrot identical with that. The Parrot. José Juan Tablada. AnMP
"Parrot, if I had your wings." The Boy and the Parrot. John Hookham Frere. OTPC (1923 ed.)
Parrot of Bagdad, The. Jalal ed-Din Rumi, *tr. fr. Persian by* E. H. Palmer. PeP
Parrot sits, The. The Parrot. Tu Fu. PoHN
Parrots, The ("Somewhere, somewhen I've seen"). W. W. Gibson. CH
Parrots in the birdhouse of the zoölogical garden, The. For Shame! Kaj Munk. BoDS
Parrot's Soliloquy. John Skelton. *Fr.* Speak, Parrot. PoEL-1
(Parrot, The.) ACP
(Speke, Parrot.) OxBoLi
Parrot's Song, The. Raffi, *tr. fr. Armenian by* Zabelle C. Boyajian. ArmLP
Parrot's voice snaps out, The. "Psittacus Eois Imitatrix Ales ab Indis." Sacheverell Sitwell. AtBAP; MBP; MoBrPo
Parry, of all my friends the best. The Invitation. Goronwy Owen. LiTW; PrWP
Parsifal. Paul Verlaine, *tr. fr. French by* Denis Devlin. *Fr.* Amour. LiA
Parsley, parsley, everywhere. Sprig Fever. Margaret Fishback. BOHV
Parsnip, The. Ogden Nash. NePA
Parson, The. Chaucer. *Fr.* The Canterbury Tales: Prologue. CBOV; GrCo-1, *abr., with mod. vers.*
(Good Parson, The, *mod. by* H. C. Leonard.) MaRV; WGRP
(Parish Priest, The.) PoLi
(Poor Parson, The.) ACP; CAW
(Poure Persoun, The.) GoBC
Parson Allen's Ride. Wallace Bruce. GA; MC; PAH

Parson Avery. Whittier. BHV
(Swan Song of Parson Avery, The.) AA
Parson Gray. Goldsmith. BOHV; NA
Parson Grocer, The. *Unknown.* CoMu
Parson, having a tithe pig or two, A. John Heath. SiCE
Parson, The, him answered, "Bendicite!" The Shipman. Chaucer. *Fr.* The Canterbury Tales: Prologue. ACP; SG
Parson of a country town was he, The. The Parson [*or* The Good Parson *or* The Poor Parson]. Chaucer. *Fr.* The Canterbury Tales: Prologue. ACP; CAW; CBOV; MaRV; WGRP
Parsonage, The. Wordsworth. *Fr.* The Excursion, VIII. ERP
Parson's Looks, The. Burns. OxBoLi
Parson's Prayer, The. Ralph Spaulding Cushman. MaRV; PraP
Part more wise/ In common. Fragments from the Old Masters: Formation Flight. Milton. *Fr.* Paradise Lost, VII. PoF
Part of a Novel, Part of a Poem, Part of a Play, *sel.* Marianne Moore.
Steeple-Jack, The. AmPP; CoBMV; CrMA; ExPo; FaBoMo; MoPo; OnHM; OxBA
Part of Mandevil's Travels. William Empson. AtBAP
Part of Plenty. Bernard Spencer. LiTB; LiTL; LiTM
Parta Quies. A. E. Housman. More Poems, XLVIII. TriL; TwP
(Alta Quies.) EmBrPo; ReaPo; SeCeV
Partaking of the miraculous. Apparition of Splendor. Marianne Moore. NePoAm
Parted. Alice Meynell. PoeT
Parted Friends. James Montgomery. LPS-1
Parted Love. Dante Gabriel Rossetti. The House of Life, XLVI. PoVP; ViPo
Parted Lovers. Judah Halevi, *tr. fr. Hebrew by* Nina Salaman. LiTW
Parterre, The. E. H. Palmer. BOHV; NA
Parthenia. Phineas Fletcher. *Fr.* The Purple Island. EV-2
Parthenophil and Parthenophe, *sels.* Barnabe Barnes.
"Ah, sweet Content, where is thy mild abode?" LXVI. ReEn; TuPP
(Content.) ES; OBSC
(Sonnet: "Ah, sweet Content, where is thy mild abode?") ElL; ElSeCe; PeBoSo
"Burn on, sweet fire, for I live by that fuel," LXXXVII. TuPP
"Jove for Europa's love took shape of bull," LXIII. ReEn
Madrigal I: "O Powers Celestial, with what sophistry." EnLoPo
Madrigal: "Once in an arbor was my mistress sleeping." TuPP
Madrigal XIII: "Soft, lovely, rose-like lips, conjoined with mine." EnLoPo
"Mistress, behold in this true-speaking glass," I. TuPP
Ode: "When I walk forth into the woods." TuPP
Ode, An: "Why doth heaven bear a sun." ElL; OBSC
"This careful head, with divers thoughts distressed," XCIX. TuPP
Parthenophil is lost, and I would see him. John Ford. *Fr.* The Lover's Melancholy. PoD
Parthians, The. Milton. *Fr.* Paradise Regained, III. OBS
Particles invisible of air, The. Rima X. Gustavo Adolfo Bécquer. *Fr.* Rimas. AnSpL-2
Particular Entertainment of the Queen and Prince at Althrope, 1603. Ben Jonson. *See* Satyr, The.
Parting. "Æ." GTIV; PoVP
Parting. Matthew Arnold. *fr.* Switzerland. ViPP
Parting, The. James K. Baxter. Cressida, VI. AnNZ
Parting, *sels.* Olga Berggolts, *tr. fr. Russian by* Jack Lindsay. RuPo
Endpiece.
Letter.
Song: "O, I have been in the land where you were born."
Parting. William Johnson Cory. EV-5
Parting. Emily Dickinson. *See* My life closed twice before its close.
Parting, The. Michael Drayton. *See* Idea: "Since there's no help . . ."
Parting. Robert Gittings. ES
Parting. Judah Halevi, *tr. fr. Hebrew by* Nina Davis Salaman. AWP; TrJP
Parting. Gerald Massey. HBV
Parting. Thomas Middleton. *Fr.* A Chaste Maid in Cheapside. ElL
("Weep eyes, break heart!") TuPP
Parting, The. John Norris. NBE
Parting. Alice Freeman Palmer. AV
Parting. Coventry Patmore. PoToHe
Parting. Kathleen Raine. LiTL
Parting. William Caldwell Roscoe. OBVV
(For Ever.) HBV
Parting. Sappho, *tr. fr. Greek by* C. M. Bowra. GrL; OxBG; LiTW, *tr. by* Olga Marx *and* Ernst Morwitz
Parting, A. Wang Wei, *tr. fr. Chinese.* LiTW, *tr. by* Witter Bynner; OnPM, *tr. by* W. J. B. Fletcher
Parting. W. B. Yeats. FaBoTw
Parting after a Quarrel. Eunice Tietjens. AV; HBMV; LEAP; LoPS; NP
Parting and Meeting. Kao Shih, *tr. fr. Chinese by* Henry H. Hart. ChLP
Parting as Descent. John Berryman. LiTA; MoAmPo (1950 ed.)
Parting at Dawn. John Crowe Ransom. AnAmPo; LA
Parting at Morning. Robert Browning. AWP; BEL; BMEP; BPN; CaAE; EM-2; EmBrPo; EnL; EnLi-2; EnLit; EPN; EtPaEn; FaBoEn; FiP; GBV (1952 ed.); GEPC; GTML; GTSL; HBV; JAWP; LEAP; MCCG; OAEP; OBEV; OBVV; PCD; PIR; PoVP; PreP; ShBV-3; TOP; TwP; UnPo (3d ed.); VA; ViPo; ViPP; VLEP; WBP
Parting at Morning. Dietmar von Aist, *tr. fr. German by* F. C. Nicholson. AWP
Parting Friends, *with music. Unknown.* ABF
Parting friends put me the query. Anglo-Eire Vignette. Patric Stevenson. NeIP
Parting from My Old Wife. Tu Fu, *tr. fr. Chinese.* WhP
Parting from the Winter Stove. Po Chü-i, *tr. fr. Chinese by* Arthur Waley. TrCh
Parting Gift. Elinor Wylie. BAP; OxBA
Parting Glass, The. Philip Freneau. AA; AmP; IAP; LEAP; LHV; TCAP
Parting Guest, A. James Whitcomb Riley. BLP; CP; HBV; IAP; LBMV; LEAP; MAP; MoAmPo (1942 ed.); NeMA; PoMa; POT; PoTo; VA
Parting Hour, The. Olive Custance. HBV; VA
Parting in Autumn. Holger Drachmann, *tr. fr. Danish by* Charles W. Stork. BoDS
Parting in the Rain. Ts'ui Shu, *tr. fr. Chinese by* Henry H. Hart. PoHN
Parting love, far-fled content. Illimitable. Gamaliel Bradford. TBM
Parting Lovers. Elizabeth Barrett Browning. LPS-1
Parting Lovers, The. *Unknown, tr. fr. Chinese by* William R. Alger. LPS-1
Parting of Hector and Andromache, The. Homer, *tr. fr. Greek. Fr.* The Iliad, VI. SeEP, *tr. by* George Chapman; TreFS, *tr. by* William B. Smith *and* Walter Miller
(Hector and Andromache, *shorter sel.*) GrPE, *tr. by* F. L. Lucas; GrR, *tr. by* William Cowper; OBEC, *tr. by* Pope
("Hector left in haste," *br. sel., tr. by* Bryant.) GrPo
(Hektor and Andromache, *tr. by* Maurice Hewlett.) LiTW; OxBG, *shorter sel.*
(Hektor [*or* Hector] to Andromache, *shorter sel.*) ReEn, *tr. by* George Chapman; WaaP, *tr. by* Richmond Lattimore
("I myself will now go home and see," *tr. by* George Chapman.) ReIE
(Last Parting of Hector and Andromache, The, *tr. by* Dryden.) SeEP
("She with his sight made breathless haste to meet him," *shorter sel., tr. by* George Chapman.) ViBoPo
Parting of King Philip and Marie, The. John Westland Marston. *Fr.* Marie de Meranie. VA
Parting of Launcelot and Guinevere, The. Stephen Phillips. BMEP; ReTS
Parting of Marmion and Douglas, The. Sir Walter Scott. *See* Marmion: Marmion and Douglas.
Parting of the Red Sea, The. *Unknown, tr. fr. Anglo-Saxon by* Charles W. Kennedy. *Fr.* Exodus. AnOE
Parting of the Ways, The. Joseph B. Gilder, *wr. at. to* Jeannette L. Gilder. AA; HBV; PAH
"Be thou guardian of the weak," *sel.* MaRV
(Will to Serve, The.) OQP; QP-2
Parting of Venus and Old Age, The. John Gower. *Fr.* Confessio Amantis, VIII. PoEL-1
Parting Song. *Tr. fr. Kootenay Indian by* Constance Lindsay Skinner.
(Two Lyrics from the Kootenay.) BAP
Parting Verse, the Feast There Ended, The. Robert Herrick. SeCV-1
Parting with Li Po on the Tung-ting Lake. Chia Chi, *tr. fr. Chinese by* Shigeyoshi Obata. BoFr
Parting, without a Sequel. John Crowe Ransom. BLV; LiTL; MAP; MoAB; MoAmPo; MoVE; NP; OxBA
Partings. Charles Guérin, *tr. fr. French by* Jethro Bithell. AWP
Partner, The. Theodore Roethke. Four for Sir John Davies, II. NePA; NePoAm
Partner, remember the hills? The Hills. Berton Braley. MCCG; POT; PoTo
Partners. Jaime Castiello. WaKn
Partnership. E. A. Robinson. ChMo; CMP
Partridge berry, bittersweet. Counting-out Rhyme for March. Frances Frost. YeAr
Partridge-breasted Gypsy. Love. Kostes Palamas. *Fr.* The Twelve Songs of the Gypsy. MoGP
Partridge is a mighty pretty fowl, The. Birds, Beasts and Bugs. *Unknown.* APW

Parts of Speech. *Unknown. See* Grammar in a Nutshell.
Party. Constance Carrier. NePoAm-2
Party, The. Ibn al-Qabturnu, *tr. fr. Arabic by* A. J. Arberry. MooP
Party, A. Laura E. Richards. SiSoSe
Party finished early, 'twas on the stroke of nine, The. The Keyhole in the Door. *Unknown.* CoMu
Party Knee. John Updike. FiBHP
Party Song, A ("Merry have we met"). *Unknown.* BoTP
Parvenant. Arthur Hugh Clough. Spectator ab Extra, III. OxBoLi
Parvuli Ejus. Aubrey Thomas De Vere. IrPN
Parzival, *sel.* Eithne Wilkins.
Dreamers and the Sea, The. NeBP
Pa's Chickens. Homer Roberts. IHA
Pa's Soft Spot. D. A. Ellsworth. FAOV
Pasa Thalassa Thalassa. E. A. Robinson. EtS; LaNeLa, *abr.*
Pascal had his gulf, wandering with him. The Gulf. Baudelaire. AnFP
Paseo de la Castellana. John Dos Passos. *Fr.* Winter in Castile. VOD (1935 ed.)
Pass Around Your Bottle, *with music. Unknown.* OuSiCo
Pass forth, my wonted cries. Sir Thomas Wyatt. SiPS
Pass It On. Henry Burton. BLRP; MaRV
Pass me not, O gentle Saviour. Fanny Crosby. OIF
Pass not too near these outcast sons of men. The Way. Laura Simmons. ChIP
Pass of Kirkstone, The. Wordsworth. HBV
Pass On. Theodorides, *tr. fr. Greek by* W. H. D. Rouse. OxBG; WoL
Pass On the Torch. Allen Eastman Cross. OQP; QP-2
Pass round the bowl; the breeze of morn. In Praise of the King. Ibn Ammar. MooP
Pass the accordion quickly. He Saw Her Home. Mikhail Isakovsky. RuPo
Pass the cups upon the lawn. Star Flowers. Ibn al-Zaqqaq. MooP
Pass the winecup; in the east. Dawn Song. Ibn Sa'id of Alcala la Real. MooP
Pass, thou wild light. Leavetaking. Sir William Watson. AEV; HBV; PoVP; TCPD
Pass we the ills, which each man feels or dreads. Power. Matthew Prior. *Fr.* Solomon. LoBV; PoEL-3
Pass with all men's approval through life to Hades' portals. Critics. Theognis. GrPE
Pass within/ A maze of corridors contrived for sin. A Vault inside the Castle at Goito. Robert Browning. *Fr.* Sordello. MyFE
Passage. Elliott Coleman. NoCaPo (1941 ed.)
Passage. Hart Crane. ExPo; MoVE
Passage, The. Ludwig Uhland, *tr. fr. German by* Sarah Austen. LPS-1
Passage, immediate passage! The blood burns in my veins! The Sea of Faith. Walt Whitman. *Fr.* Passage to India. OQP; QP-2
Passage in the Life of St. Augustine, A. *Unknown.* LPS-2
Passage Magnolia, The. Charles Edward Eaton. NoCaPo (rev. ed.)
Passage of a Year, The. *Unknown. Fr.* Sir Gawain and the Green Knight. PoEL-1
Passage of an August. Eithne Wilkins. NeBP
Passage On. Cedric Morris. PoC
Passage to India, *abr.* Luis de Camões, *tr. fr. Portuguese by* J. J. Aubertin. *Fr.* The Lusiads. WoL
Passage to India. Walt Whitman. AmPo; AmPP (4th ed.); CoBA; CoV; IAP; Po; PoEL-5
Sels.
"Ah, more than any priest," *fr.* XI–XIII. WGRP
"Bathe me O God in thee, mounting to thee," *fr.* XI. TrPWD
Brotherhood ("Lo, soul, seest thou not God's purpose"), *fr.* III. MW
("Passage to India!/ Lo soul!") PC
"Passage to more than India," *fr.* XIII. PC
(Sea of Faith, The.) OQP; QP-1
Passage to the End. Eduardo Anguita, *tr. fr. Spanish by* Lloyd Mallan. AnCL
Passages. Larry Eigner. NeAP
Passamquoddy's Apple Toddy. James W. Foley. LHV
Passed the end of a day in the provinces. The End of a Day in the Provinces. Jules Laforgue. AnFP
Passenger train stood in the shed. Ol' John Brown. *Unknown.* ABF
Passenjare, The. Isaac H. Bromley. FiBHP
Passer-by, A. Robert Bridges. AIDL; BLV; ChMo; CMP; CoBMV; CoEV; EnLit; EPP; EtS; EV-5; GTBS-W; GTML; GTSE; GTSL; HBV; LEAP; LiTB; LiTM; MBP; MoAB; MoBrPo; OAEP; OBVV; POTT; PoVP; SeCeV; SG; ShBV-3; TCEP; TwCV; TyEnPo; VA; VLEP
Passer-by, The. Edith M. Thomas. AV
Passer-by might just as well be blind, A. Walls. Robert Francis. CrMA
Passer Mortuus Est. Edna St. Vincent Millay. MAP; MoAmPo; OxBA; TBM
Passers By, The. Al-Radi Billah, *tr. fr. Arabic by* A. J. Arberry. MooP
Passetyme, The. Stephen Hawes. *See* Epitaph: "O mortal folk . . ."
Passing across the billowy sea. Popular Songs of Tuscany [*or* Giving a Heart]. *Unknown.* AWP; JAWP; OnPM; WBP
Passing and Glassing. Christina Rossetti. FaBoEn; VA
Passing Away. Lucian, *tr. fr. Greek by* Walter Leaf. OxBG; WoL
Passing Away [Saith the World]. Christina Rossetti. Old and New Year Ditties, III. EmBrPo; EPN; GoBC; GTBS-W; LiA; MBP; OBEV (1st ed.); OBVV; PoD; POTT; TOP; ViP; ViPo
Passing Bell, The. Thomas Heywood. *Fr.* The Rape of Lucrece. SeCL
Passing Bell, The. James Shirley. ACP
Passing-Bell, The. *Unknown.* ElSeCe; SeCL; SeEP
Passing Bell at Stratford, The. William Winter. AA
Passing between the stumbling generations. The Wandering Jew Comes to the Wall. Edmond Fleg. *Fr.* The Wall of Weeping. TrJP
Passing By. *Unknown. See* There Is a Lady Sweet and Kind.
Passing Christ, The. Richard Watson Gilder. *See* Passing of Christ, The.
Passing feet pause, as they pass. Marian. Thomas Ashe. VA
Passing Flower, The. Harry Kemp. HBMV
Passing from Italy to Greece the tales. The Musical Duel. John Ford. *Fr.* The Lover's Melancholy. LPS-2
Passing glance, a lightning long the skies, A. Sonnet. William Drummond of Hawthornden. EPP; ViBoPo
Passing Glimpse, A. Robert Frost. InP; NeMA
Passing Glimpse of Penelope, A. Homer, *pr. tr. fr. Greek by* S. H. Butcher *and* Andrew Lang. *Fr.* The Odyssey, I. GrR
Passing I saw her as she stood beside. The Gypsy Girl. Henry Alford. HBV; OTPC (1923 ed.)
Passing motorist glanced back, A. The Shack. Nellie Burget Miller. PoOW
Passing of Arthur, The. Tennyson. *Fr.* Idylls of the King. CoBE; EM-2; EPN; HeT; PCN; REAL. *See also* Morte d'Arthur.
Passing of Christ, The, *sel.* Richard Watson Gilder.
Real Christ, The. OQP; QP-1
("Behold Him now as He comes!") ChIP; MaRV
Passing of Daphnis, The. Theocritus, *tr. fr. Greek by* Sir William Marris. *Fr.* Idylls, I. OxBG
Passing of March, The. Robert Burns Wilson. HBV; SN
Passing of Oedipus, The. Sophocles. *See* Oedipus' Last Hour.
Passing of Richard Somers, The. Wallace Rice. GA
Passing of the Buffalo, The. Hamlin Garland. StVeCh
Passing of the Forest, The. William Pember Reeves. AnNZ
Passing of the Shee, The. J. M. Synge. OnYI; TIP
Passing of the Sidhe, The. James B. Dollard. CPG
Passing of the Unknown Soldier, The. Vilda Sauvage Owens. DD; MC
Passing out of the shadow. Just Passing. *Unknown.* BLRP
Passing policeman found a little child, A. The Little Lost Child. Edward B. Marks. TreFS
Passing Show, The. Menander, *tr. fr Greek by* John Addington Symonds. GrR
("Whom the gods love die young; that man is blest.") GrPo
Passing Strange, The. John Masefield. AnFE; BLV; BoLiVe; LiTB; MBP; MoAB; MoBrPo; MoPo; NP; OBEV (new ed.); TwCV
Passing the Cape. Otomo Tabito, *tr. fr. Japanese by* Ishii *and* Obata. OnPM
"Passing the Love of Women." Plato, *tr. fr. Greek by* F. L. Lucas. GrPE
Passing Through. Annie Johnson Flint. BLRP
Passing through huddled and ugly walls. The Harbor. Carl Sandburg. CoBA; NP; PreP
Passing T'ien-men Street in Ch'ang-an and Seeing a Distant View of Chung-nan Mountain. Po Chü-i, *tr. fr. Chinese by* Arthur Waley. TrCh
Passing today by a cottage, I shed tears. C. S. Lewis. LO
Passing traveller with wonder sees, The. Stone-Pit. John Clare. RO
Passing under the Ryogoku Bridge. Ryogoku. Mokutaro Kinoshita. PoLJ
Passing Year, The. *Unknown.* PEOR
Passion, A. Robert Devereux, Earl of Essex. *See* Happy Were He.
Passion. Galway Kinnell. NePoAm
Passion, The, *sel.* Milton.
"Ere-while of Musick, and Ethereal mirth." PoD
Passion: "If Jove himself be subject unto love." Thomas Watson. Hecatompathia, XXXVII. ElSeCe
Passion and Worship. Dante Gabriel Rossetti. The House of Life, IX. BPN; EmBrPo; PoVP; ViPo

"Passion o' me!" cried Sir Richard Tyrone. The Sally from Coventry. George Walter Thornbury. HBV
Passion of M'Phail, The, *sels.* Horace Gregory.
"Lunchroom bus boy, The, who looked like Orson Welles," IV. TwAmPo
This Is the Place to Wait, V. MoAmPo
Passion of Man, The: 1918–1938. J. C. Squire. QS
Passion of Our Lady, The, *sel.* Charles Péguy, *tr. fr. French by* Julian Green.
"For the past three days she had been wandering, and following." ISi
Passion the fathomless spring, and words the precipitate waters. The Lyrical Poem. Richard Garnett. VA
Passion without Respite. Ibycus, *tr. fr. Greek by* F. L. Lucas. GrPE
Passionate are palms that clasp in double fist. In the Wind's Eye. R. P. Blackmur. Scarabs for the Living, II. CrMA
Passionate Clerk to His Love, The. Ronald McCuaig. MoAuPo
Passionate Encyclopedia Britannica Reader to His Love. "Maggie." InMe
Passionate Man's Pilgrimage, The. Sir Walter Ralegh. AnFE; AtBAP; BLV; CaAE; CenL; ChTr; CoEV; ElL; ElSeCe; LiTB; LoBV; MePo; OAEP; OBSC; OxBoCh; PoE; PoEL-2; ReEn; SeCePo; SiCE; TrGrPo; TriL; TuPP
("Give me my scallop-shell of quiet.") AnFE; EG; PoRA
(His Pilgrimage.) BEL; CoBE; EnLit; HBV; KN; LEAP; OBEV; PC; PoFS; TOP; TyEnPo
(My Pilgrimage.) WGRP
(Pilgrimage, The.) BBV (1951 ed.); BCEP; CAW; LPS-2; SiPS; TreFS; ViBoPo, *abr.*
(Soul's Pilgrimage, The.) CBE
(Verses Made by Sir Walter Raleigh the Night before He Was Beheaded.) EV-1
Passionate Man's Song, The. John Fletcher. *See* Melancholy.
Passionate Pilgrim, The, *sels.* Shakespeare, *and others.*
Beauty ("Beauty is but a vain and doubtful good"), XIII. *Unknown.* OBSC
Crabbed Age and Youth, XII. Shakespeare. BCEP; BLV; CBOV; ElSeCe; EV-1; HBV; LEAP; LiA; LiTB; OBEV; ReEn; TreFS; ViBoPo
(Age and Youth.) ElL; FaBoEn
("Crabbed age and youth cannot live together.") SiCE
(Madrigal, A: "Crabbed age and youth.") GBV (1952 ed.); GTBS; GTBS-D; GTBS-W; GTSE; GTSL
(Youth and Age.) OBSC
Fair Is My Love, VII. *At. to* Shakespeare. ElL
If Music and Sweet Poetry, VIII. Richard Barnfield. ViBoPo
(In Praise of Music and Poetry.) ElSeCe
(To His Friend Master [*or* Maister] R. L., in Praise of Music and Poetry.) ElL; ES
It Was a Lording's Daughter. *Unknown, at. to* Shakespeare. ElL
(Contentions.) HBV
Night Watch, A ("Good night, good rest. Ah! neither be my share"), XIV. *Unknown.* OBSC
Nightingale, The. Richard Barnfield. AWP; BLA; BLV; CG; EV-2; GTBS; GTBS-D; GTBS-W; GTSE; JAWP; OTPC (1923 ed.); TOP; TVSH; WBP
(As It Fell upon a Day.) EG; EPP; ReEn; ViBoPo
(Ode, An: "As it fell upon a day.") ElL; ElSeCe; EM-1; LoBV; OBSC; ReIE; SiCE; TuPP
(Philomel.) BCEP; CH; GTSL; HBV; LEAP; OBEV
(To the Nightingale.) LiTG; LPS-2
Sweet Rose, Fair Flower, X. *At. to* Shakespeare. ElL
Venus, and [*or* with] Young Adonis Sitting by Her, XI. Bartholomew Griffin. PeBoSo; ViBoPo
Passionate Reader to His Poet, The. Richard Le Gallienne. HBV; VA
Passionate Shepherd, The, *sels.* Nicholas Breton.
Aglaia. OBSC
Merry Country Lad, The. ElL; LoBV
(Happy Countryman, *shorter sel.*) CH
(Pastoral II [III]: "Who can live in heart so glad.") ElSeCe; ReEn; TuPP
(Shepherd and Shepherdess.) OBSC
(Third Pastor's Song, The.) EV-1
(Who can live in heart so glad.") SiCE; ViBoPo
Pastoral I: "Flora hath been all about." TuPP
Pretty Twinkling Starry Eyes. ElL
Passionate Shepherd to His Love, The, 6 *sts.* Christopher Marlowe. AnEnPo; ATP; AWP; BEL; BLV, 7 *sts.;* BoLiVe; CaAE; CBOV; CenL; CoBE; ElL; ElSeCe; EM-1; EnL; EnLi-1; EnLit; EPP; EV-1; ExPo; FaBoBe; FaBoEn; FaFP; GBV (1952 ed.); GTBS, 7 *sts.;* GTBS-D, 7 *sts.;* GTBS-W, 7 *sts.;* GTSE, 7 *sts.;* GTSL, 7 *sts.;* HBV; HoPM; InPo; JAWP; KN, 7 *sts.;* LEAP; LiTB; LiTG; LiTL, 5 *sts.;* LoBV; LoPo; LPS-1, 22 *ll.;* NeHB; OAEP, OBEV; OBSC; OuHeWo; PG (1945 ed.); PIAE; PIR; Po; PoE; PoFS; PoRA, 7 *sts.;* ReaPo; ReEn; ReIE; RiBV; SeCePo; SeCeV; SiCE; SiTL; TCEP; ThWaDe; TOP; TreF; TrGrPo; TuPP; TVSH, 7 *sts.;* TwHP; UnPo (1st ed.); ViBoPo, 7 *sts.;* WBP; WHA; WP, 7 *sts.*
("Come live with me and be my love," 7 *sts.*) EG
(Milkmaid's Song, The, 7 *sts.*) AEV
(Shepherd to His Love, The.) BTP; CG, 7 *sts.;* GN, 7 *sts.;* OTPC (1923 ed.); 7 *sts.;* RG, 7 *sts.*
(Shepherd's Plea, The.) SiPS
Passionate Shepherd's Song, The. Shakespeare. *See* On a day—Alack the Day!
Passionate Sword, The. Jean Starr Untermeyer. BAP; GrCo-2; HBMV; MaRV; QS; TrJP; TrPWD
Passionately fierce the voice of God is pleading. The Christian Soldier. G. A. Studdert-Kennedy. MaRV
Passion Flower, The. Charles G. Blanden. ChIP; OQP; QP-1
Passion-Flower, The. Margaret Witter Fuller. HBV
Passions, The; an Ode to [*or* for] Music. William Collins. BCEP; BEL; CEP; CoBE; EiPP; EM-1; EnLi-2 (1949 ed.); EPP; EV-3; GoTL; GTBS; GTBS-D; GTBS-W; GTSE; GTSL; HBV; LoBV; LPS-3; OBEC
Passions are liken'd [*or* likened] best to floods and streams. The Silent Lover. Sir Walter Ralegh. BCEP; EPP; LiTB; OBEV; PG; ViBoPo. *See also* Our passions are most like to floods and streams.
Passion's Hounds. Thomas Lodge, *after the French of* Pierre de Ronsard. Phyllis, XXXI. OnPM
("Devoid of reason, thrall to foolish ire.") ReEn; SiCE
Passiontide Communion. Katharine Tynan. TrPWD
Passive I lie, looking up through leaves. Seventh Day. Kathleen Raine. ChMP
Passive within the heart. The Meaning of Violence. John Williams. NePoAm-2
Passivity. Mary Fullerton. BoAV
Passover. John Beauchamp Thompson. ChIP
Passover Eve. Fania Kruger. GoYe; QS
Passover in the Holy Family, The. Dante Gabriel Rossetti. GoBC
Passport beyond Tyranny. David Ross. PG (1945 ed.)
Passus II: Lady Meed. William Langland, *mod. by* Albert C. Baugh. *Fr.* The Vision of Piers Plowman. EnLit
Password, The. Reginald C. Eva. ChIP
Past, The. Bryant. AA; BAV; IAP; MOAP; OBAV; TCAP; TOP
(Thou Unrelenting Past, *much abr.*) BAP
Past, The. Emerson. AmP; FaBoCh; LiTA; LoGBV; PoEL-4; TCAP
Past. John Galsworthy. HBV
Past. Winifred Howells. AA
Past, The. Li Yu, *tr. fr. Chinese by* Hsiung Ting. WhP
Past and Present. Thomas Hood. *See* I Remember, I Remember.
Past and present wilt, The—I have fill'd them, emptied them. Song of Myself, LI. Walt Whitman. CoV
Past can be no more, The. Now. Thomas Ken. OxBoCh
Past comfort, all despairing. Lament for the Sailing of the Crusade. Rinaldo d'Aquino. LyPI
Past Help. Cecco Angiolieri da Siena, *tr. fr. Italian by* Dante Gabriel Rossetti. OnPM
(Sonnet: He Is Past All Help.) AWP
Past is fresh, dust is fresh, The. Ebb. John Lyle Donaghy. NeIP
Past is past, and if one. Salute. James Schuyler. NeAP
Past keeps watch above the present's sleep, The. Persephone the Queen. Robert Morse. MuM
Past love, past sorrow, lies this darkness. Requiem. Kathleen Raine. NeBP
Past my window runs a tree. The Changing Wind. Julian Orde. NeBP
Past only to be lamented, The. The Past. Li Yu. WhP
Past ploughed and fallow, at the top. Glenarm. John Lyle Donaghy. NeIP
Past Reason Hunted. Shakespeare. *See* Sonnets, CXXIX.
Past Ruin'd Ilion Helen Lives. Walter Savage Landor. *Fr.* Ianthe. AnFE; AWP; BoLiVe; CaAE; CBOV; EmBrPo; EnLoPo; EnRP; EPN; ExPo; FaBoEn; GTBS-D; InPo; JAWP; LiTL; LO; LoBV; OAEP; OBRV; OQP; Po; PoE; PoEL-4; QP-2; ReaPo; RiBV; TOP; TrGrPo; TyEnPo; UnPo (1st ed.); ViBoPo; WBP
(Ianthe.) LiTB
(Lyrics to Ianthe.) BPN
(Verse: "Past ruined Ilion Helen lives.") BCEP; BLV; HBV; OBEV
Past Song. Joyce Rowe. DiM
Past the closed portals of earthly kings. The Bethlehem Road. Ida Norton Munson. ChIP
Past the gibbet-stock all stuck with nails. John Masefield. *Fr.* Reynard the Fox. ViBoPo
Past them he strode. The Hinds of Kerry. William S. Wabnitz. GoYe
"Past two o'clock and Cornwallis is taken." News from Yorktown. Lewis Worthington Smith. MC; PAH
Past walks here, noiseless, unasked, alone, The. An Old Street. Virginia Woodward Cloud. AA
Pastel. Théophile Gautier, *tr. fr. French by* Alan Conder. TrFP
Pastel. Francis Saltus Saltus. AA; OBAV

Pastheen Finn. *Unknown, tr. fr. Irish by* Sir Samuel Ferguson. IrPN
(Páistín Fionn.) OxBI
Pastime. Henry VIII, King of England. *See* Pastime with Good Company.
Pastime of Pleasure, The, *sels.* Stephen Hawes.
"And as Dame Fame was in laudation," *fr. ch.* 44. ReIE
"And forasmuch that he made Nature," *fr. ch.* 23. ReIE
Dame Music *fr. ch.* 16. PoEL-1
Epitaph: "O mortal folk, you may behold and see," *fr. ch.* 42. ACP; BLV; OBEV; OtMeF; TrGrPo
(Epitaph of Graunde Amoure.) ChTr; OBSC; SeCeV
(His Epitaph.) BCEP; CBOV; GoBC; LEAP; TriL
("O mortal folk, you may behold and see.") MyFE
(Passetyme, The.) ViBoPo
Excusation of the Auctor, The, *fr. ch.* 46. ReIE
Here Begynneth the Passe Tyme of Pleasure. SiCE
How Grand Amour Walked in a Meadow and Met with Fame Environed with Tongues of Fire, *fr. ch.* 1. ReIE
Of the Great Mariage betwene Graunde Amoure and Labell Pucell, *fr. ch.* 39. EPP
(Of the Great Marriage between Grand Amour and La Belle Pucelle.) ReIE
Seven Deadly Sins, The, *fr. ch.* 42. PoEL-1
"Than forth I went into a meadow green," *fr. ch.* 22. ReIE
Time and Eternity, *fr. ch.* 44. PoEL-1
True Knight, The, *fr. ch.* 27. ACP; AnEnPo; OBEV
(True Knighthood.) TrGrPo
Pastime with Good Company. Henry VIII, King of England. CaAE; ElSeCe; PrWP; TuPP
(Good Company.) BLV; TrGrPo
(Pastime.) OBSC
Pastoral, A: "Along the lane beside the mead." Norman Gale. HBV
Pastoral, A: "By the side of a green stagnate pool." G. A. Stevens. CoMu
Pastoral: "Death./ The Death of a million." Ron Loewinsohn. NeAP
Pastoral: "Dove walks with sticky feet, The." Kenneth Patchen. AtBAP
Pastoral: "Farmer turns for home, The; his team's glad tread." Muriel Lewis. MoAuPo
Pastoral: "Farmhouse skyline, draped with trees, The." Alan Creighton. CaP
Pastoral I: "Flora hath been all about." Nicholas Breton. *Fr.* The Passionate Shepherd. TuPP
Pastoral, A: "Flower of the medlar." Théophile Marzials. HBV; VA
Pastoral: "For Chloris long I sigh'd in vain." Thomas Godfrey. NoCaPo
Pastoral, A: "From thence into the open fields he fled." Spenser. *Fr.* The Faerie Queene, VI, 9. OBSC
Pastoral: "Hark to the cowbells, hark how the singing." Gustaf Fröding, *tr. fr. Swedish by* Charles W. Stork. AnSL
Pastoral: "Hill was flowing with sheep, The." Marion Strobel. NP
Pastoral, A: "In the merry month of May." Nicholas Breton. *See* Phyllida and Corydon ("In the merry month of May").
Pastoral: "In the old days the white gates swung." Clifford Dyment. MoVE
Pastoral: "It's the Spring." W. E. Henley. In Hospital, XXII. Po
Pastoral: "Little Sparrows, The." William Carlos Williams. MOAP
Pastoral, A: "My love and I among the mountains strayed." J. B. B. Nichols. VA
Pastoral, A: "My time, O ye Muses was happily spent." John Byrom. LPS-1; OBEC
(Colin and Phebe—a Pastoral.) EV-3
Pastoral [*or* Pastorall], A: "Oh happy golden age." Tasso, *tr. fr. Italian by* Samuel Daniel. *Fr.* Aminta. PoEL-2; ReEn; ReIE
(Pastoral of Tasso, A.) OBSC
Pastoral, A: 'Oho, my love, oho, my love." Lizette Woodworth Reese. LS
Pastoral, A: "On a hill there grows a flower." Nicholas Breton. *See* Pastoral of Phillis and Corydon, A.
Pastoral: "Pan-imbued/ Tempe wood." Francis Thompson. PoLi
Pastoral: "So soft in the hemlock wood." Robert Hillyer. MAP; MoAmPo
Pastoral, A: "Sweet birds, that sit and sing amid the shady valleys." Nicholas Breton. CBOV; ElL; ReIE; SiCE
(Phyllis.) OBSC; TrGrPo
("Sweet birds! that sit and sing amid the shady valleys.") EG
Pastoral, A: "There went out in the dawning light." *Unknown, tr. fr. Latin by* John Addington Symonds. AWP
(Pastoral Dialogue.) OnPM
Pastoral: "When I was younger." William Carlos Williams. OxBA
Pastoral III: "Who can live in heart so glad." Nicholas Breton. *See* Merry Country Lad, The.
Pastoral Ballad, A. William Shenstone. CEP
Sels.
Absence, Pt. I. OBEC
Hope, Pt. II. KN, *sel.*; OBEC; RO
(Shepherd's Home, The.) CG; GN
Pastoral Courtship, A, *sel.* Thomas Randolph.
"Being set, let's sport a while." ViBoPo
Pastoral Courtship, A, *sel.* Earl of Rochester.
Within the Canopy of Leaves. BeR
Pastoral Dialogue, A. Thomas Carew. EV-2
Pastoral Dialogue. *Unknown. See* Pastoral, A. "There went out in the dawning light."
Pastoral Dialogue, Castara and Parthenia. Thomas Flatman. CEP
Pastoral Elegy, A. Albius Tibullus, *tr. fr. Latin by* Sir Charles Abraham Elton. AWP
(Elegy: "Let others pile their yellow ingots high.") LiTW
Pastoral Elegy. *Unknown.* ABS
Pastoral for Poland, A. Clark Mills. NeTW
Pastoral Hymn. Addison. OBEC
("Lord my pasture shall prepare, The.") OlF
(Trust in God.) EV-3
Pastoral[l] Hymn[e], A: "Happy choristers of air." John Hall. EG; MeLP; NBE; OBS; OxBoCh; SeCL; TriL; TrPWD
Pastoral in Imitation of Drayton's Second Nymphal, A, *sel.* Elizabeth Rowe.
Bright Offerings from Shepherds. BeR
Pastoral Landscape. Ambrose Philips. *See* Sixth Pastoral, The.
Pastoral of Phillis and Corydon, A. Nicholas Breton. CoBE; EV-1; SiCE; TuPP
(Ipsa Quae.) OBSC
("On a hill there grows a flower.") LO
(Pastoral, A: "On a hill there grows a flower.") BLV; CBOV; ElL
(Phillis the Fair.) LPS-1
(Phyllida and Corydon: "On a hill there grows a flower.") TrGrPo
Pastoral of Tasso, A. Tasso. *See* Pastoral, A: "Oh happy golden age."
Pastoral on the King's Death, The. Written in 1648. Alexander Brome. OBS
Pastoral Poem, *sel.* Edward Richard, *tr. fr. Welsh by* Evan Evans.
Poet's Welcome, The. PrWP
Pastoral Song, A. Henry Kirke White. ERP
Pastorale: "Only cows can loll at ease." Mildred Weston. PoMa
Pastorale: "Willow tree leans, A." Robert A. Davis. GoSl
Pastorall, A: "O happy golden age." Tasso. *See* Pastoral, A: "O happy golden age."
Pastorall Hymne, A. John Hall. *See* Pastoral Hymn: "Happy choristers of air."
Pastorals, *sel.* Ambrose Philips.
Sixth Pastoral, The ("How still the sea!"). CEP
(Pastoral Landscape, *abr.*) OBEC
Pastorals, *sel.* Pope.
Summer. CaAE; CEP; ReaPo
Pastorela. Marcabrun, *tr. fr. Provençal by* Hubert Creekmore. LyMA
Pastorella. *At. to* Sir Henry Sheers. SeCL
Pastor's Prayer, A. Grace E. Troy. PraP
Pastor's Prayer for His Congregation, A. Grace E. Troy. PraP
Pastourelle. *Unknown.* OBSC
("'Hey, troly, loly lo, maid, whither go you?'") LO
Pasts. Alfred Kreymborg. NP
Pasture, The. Robert Frost. AmPP; AnNE; ChMo; CMP; CoV; DDA; FaPON; LaNeLa; MAP; MoAB; MoAmPo; NeMA; MOAP; MoShBr; OxBA; Po; PoRh; RAR; SP; StVeCh; SUS; TiPo; TSW; TSWC; TwCV; TwP; UTS; ViBoPo
Pasture, A. Frederic Lawrence Knowles. AA
Pasture is a forest where we lie, The. Sonnet XXVI. Olive Tilford Dargan. NoCaPo
Pat-a-cake, pat-a-cake, baker's man. Mother Goose. OTPC; OxNR; PCH; PPL; RIS; SAS; StVeCh
"Pat-a-cake, pat-a-cake, in the bright sun." Sand Cooking. *Unknown.* PCH
Pat it, kiss it. When Baby Hurts Her Hand. *Unknown.* PPL; SAS
Pat pat! a little cake. *Unknown, tr. fr. German.* SAS
Pat Works on the Railway, *with music. Unknown. See* Paddy Works on the Railway.
Patapan. Bernard de la Monnoye. *See* Burgundian Carol.
Patch of Old Snow, A. Robert Frost. ChMo; CMP; PoFS; TwP
Patch-Shaneen. J. M. Synge. LoBV
Patchwork. Clinton Scollard. OQP; QP-2
Patchwork of snowy roofs and sombre walls. Steam. Frederick Mortimer Clapp. VOD
Patchwork Quilt, The. Elizabeth Fleming. BoTP
Patchwork Quilt, The. Dora Sigerson Shorter. HBMV

Patchwork sunshine nets the lea, The. John Davidson. *Fr.* Fleet Street Echoes: Good Friday. BSV
Pater and Credo, *in mod. Eng. Unknown.* TMEV
Pater Filio. Robert Bridges. ChMo; CMP; OBEV; OBVV; POTT; PoVP; ViBoPo; ViP; VLEP
Pater Noster. Euripides, *tr. fr. Greek by* Arthur S. Way. *Fr.* Helen. GrR
"Pater Noster," The. *Unknown.* ACP; CAW
"Pater Vester Pascit Illa." Robert Stephen Hawker. CAW; CoBE; VA
Paterson, *sels.* William Carlos Williams.
"Before the grass is out the people are out." ReMP
How Strange You Are. OnAP
Library, The. AtBAP
Paterson: Book One, Preface. CoBMV
Paterson: Episode 17. OxBA
Signs Everywhere of Birds Nesting, While. MoVE
Sunday in the Park. CrMA
Path, The. Bryant. SN
Path, The. Edward Thomas. MoVE
Path by which we twain did go, The. Tennyson. In Memoriam A. H. H., XXII. EmBrPo; EnLi-2; EPN; GEPC; LPS-1; TOP; TVSH; ViPo; VLEP
Path Flower. Olive Tilford Dargan. BAP; CP; HBMV; NV; SBMV
Path of the Old Spells, The. Donald Sinclair, *tr. fr. Gaelic.* GoTS
Path of the quiet fields! that oft of yore. Ebenezer Elliott. *Fr.* The Splendid Village. EnSW
Path of the Stars, The. Thomas S. Jones, Jr. Four Sonnets, IV. ChIP; NV; SBMV; WGRP
Path of Wisdom, The. Baruch, III: 9–IV: 4, Bible, Apocrypha. TrJP
Path ran out, The. The clouds, no longer fleecy. The Birds and Francis. Louis Untermeyer. SaFP
Path That Leads to Nowhere, The. Corinne Roosevelt Robinson. BLPA; HBMV; NeHB; NLK; SBMV
Path that runs to Paradise climbs up a stone-heaped hill, The. Fiddlers' Green. Margaret Widdemer. YT
Path through the Marsh, The. Leah Bodine Drake. DaM
Path through which that lovely twain, The. Shelley. *Fr.* Prometheus Unbound, II, ii. AtBAP; ViBoPo
Path to Shottery, The. Cornelia Otis Skinner. MoSiPe
Path to the Woods, The. Madison Cawein. LBMV
Path we have climbed has been steep and hard, The. Princess Daihaku, *tr. fr. Japanese by* Lois J. Erickson. SoLD
Path we planned beneath October's sky, The. The Path. Bryant. SN
Pathfinder—and Path-clincher! John Charles Frémont. Charles F. Lummis. PAH
Pathfinders, The. Vance Palmer. BoAu
Pathless Briars. Pindar, *tr. fr. Greek by* Abraham Moore. *Fr.* Olympian Odes, VI. LiA
Paths of my disquiet, The. John Landless beside the Road. Iwan Goll OnPM
Pathway to Paradise, The. Ozora Stearns Davis. OQP; QP-2
Patience, *sels.* W. S. Gilbert.
Bunthorne's Song [The Aesthete]. FiBHP; LiTB; SiTL; ViP
(Aesthete, The.) ALV; EnLi-2
(Song: Bunthorne.) PoVP
Fable of the Magnet and the Churn, The. FaPON; MPB
Heavy Dragoon, The. PC
"Oh, Hollow! Hollow! Hollow!" PoVP
Recitation and Song: "Am I alone." MBP; WoL
(Bunthorne's Recitative and Song.) CoBE
(Recitative and Song: Bunthorne.) PoVP
Song: Colonel. PoVP
Patience. Harry Graham. FiBHP; MoShBr; WhC
Patience. William James Linton. VA
Patience. E. E. Nott-Bower. WhC
Patience. Geoffrey Anketell Studdert-Kennedy. OQP; QP-2; TrPWD
Patience, *sel. Unknown.*
Jonah. ACP
Patience. Sir Thomas Wyatt. OBSC; SiPS; TrGrPo
(Patience, though I Have Not.) MaPo; SiCE
Patience and Sorrow. Shakespeare. *Fr.* Much Ado about Nothing, V, i. EV-1
Patience—but peace of heart we cannot choose. Wilson. Percy Mackaye. GA
Patience, for I have wrong. Sir Thomas Wyatt. SiPS
Patience for my device. Sir Thomas Wyatt. SiPS
Patience, Hard Thing! Gerard Manley Hopkins. *See* Sonnet: "Patience, hard thing! the hard thing but to pray."
Patience is a virtue. *Unknown.* OxNR
Patience, my lord! why, 'tis the soul of peace. *See* Patience, why 'tis the soul . . .
Patience of all my smart! Sir Thomas Wyatt. SiPS
Patience on a Monument. Shakespeare. *See* She Never Told Her Love.
Patience Taught by Nature. Elizabeth Barrett Browning. OxBoCh
Patience, Though I Have Not. Sir Thomas Wyatt. *See* Patience.
Patience! [*or* Patience, my lord!] why, 'tis the soul of peace. The First True Gentleman. Thomas Dekker. The Honest Whore. BCEP; LEAP; ViBoPo
Patience with the Living. Margaret Elizabeth Sangster. PoToHe
Patient above his tinted tiles he bent. The Mosaic Worker. Arthur Wallace Peach. BLRP
Patient and Meek Grissill. John Phillip. *See* Comedy of Patient and Meek Grissell.
Patient Church, The. Cardinal Newman. GoBC
Patient Griselda. Chaucer, *mod. by* Edward Hodnett. *Fr.* The Canterbury Tales: The Clerk's Tale. PoRA
Patient Grissill. Thomas Dekker. *See* Pleasant Comedy of Patient Grissill, The.
Patient Is Time. Stanton A. Coblentz. *Fr.* The Pageant of Man. MaRV; MuM
Patient Scientists, The. Bertha Gerneaux Woods. MaRV; OQP; QP-2
Patient she is—long suffering, our Land. America. Florence Earle Coates. PEDC
Patio. Jorge Luis Borges, *tr. fr. Spanish.* AnCL, *tr. by* Robert Stuart Fitzgerald; TwSpPo, *tr. by* H. R. Hays
Patio, The. Rose Henderson. VOD
Patmos. Friedrich Hölderlin, *tr. fr. German by* R. F. C. Hull. AnGP
Patmos. Edith M. Thomas. HBV
Patriarch, The. Burns. CoMu
Patriarchal Home, The. Charles Jeremiah Wells. *Fr.* Joseph and His Brethren. VA
Patrick Goes to School. Alicia Aspinwall. MPB
Patrick Sarsfield, Lord Lucan. *Unknown.* *See* Farewell, O Patrick Sarsfield.
Patrick you chatter too loud. The Praise of Fionn. *Unknown.* KiLC
Patrick's Breastplate. *At. to* St. Patrick. *See* Deer's Cry, The.
Patrico's Song. Ben Jonson. *See* Gipsy Song.
Patrins. Jessie B. Rittenhouse. NV
Patriot, The. Robert Browning. BHV; BPN; CBPC; EPN; EV-5; GTBS-D; MW; PCN; PoRA; PoVP; TCEP; TrGrPo; ViPP; VLEP
Patriot, The. Thomas Godfrey, *paraphrased from* Psalm I, Bible, *O.T.* PoFr
Patriot Hymn, The. Nathan Haskell Dole. PaA
Patriot I am, but in so strange a fashion. My Country. Mikhail Lermontov. BoR
Patriot Mother, The. *Unknown.* MOAH
Patriotic Band, The. *Unknown.* *Fr.* Washington, Lincoln, and the American Flag. FAOH
Patriotic Song ("I'll wreathe my sword in myrtle bough"). Callistratus, *tr. fr. Greek by* Henry Wellesley. PoFr
Patriotism. "Susan Coolidge." OQP; PSO; QP-1
Patriotism. Sir Walter Scott. *See* Breathes There the Man.
Patriotism at Squawville. *Unknown.* PAP
Patriots of Mankind. Christopher Smart. PoFr
Patriot's Pass-Word, The. James Montgomery. *See* Arnold von Winkelried.
Patriots Who Died in Battle, The. Chu Yuan, *tr. fr. Chinese by* Shen Yu-ting. *Fr.* The Nine Songs. WhP
Patroclus' Body Saved. Homer, *tr. fr. Greek by* E. R. Dodds. *Fr.* The Iliad, XVII. OxBG; WaaP
Patroclus Goes to Battle. Homer, *tr. fr. Greek by* F. L Lucas. *Fr.* The Iliad, XVI. GrPE
Patroclus Intercedes for the Achaeans. Homer, *tr. fr. Greek by* F. L. Lucas. *Fr.* The Iliad, XVI. GrPE
Patroclus lights, impatient for the fight. Homer, *tr. by* Pope. *Fr.* The Iliad, XVI. GrPo
Patroclus to Achilles. Homer. *See* Achilles and Patroclus.
Patrol, The. J. H. Knight-Adkin. MCCG
Patrol; Buonamary. Bernard Gutteridge. WaP
Patrolling Barnegat. Walt Whitman. GTSE; LoBV; NePA
Patron, The. George Crabbe. *Fr.* Tales. EnSW
Patron of true Holinesse, The. *Fr.* The Faerie Queene, I, 1. Spenser. TyEnPo
Patronage. Ibn al-Labbana, *tr. fr. Arabic by* A. J. Arberry. MooP
Patronage. Thomas Thornely. QS
Patter of the Rain, The. Coates Kinney. *See* Rain on the Roof.
Patter of the Shingle, The. *Unknown.* BLPA
Pattering rain on the empty steps quickens at night, The. The Night Rain. Lu Yu. WhP
Pattering rush like the rattle of hail, A. A Cowboy Race. J. C. Davis. SCC
Pattern of Saint Brendan. Francis MacManus. AnIV; OxBI
Patterne often drawne in minde, The. *Unknown.* SeCSL
Patterns. Amy Lowell. AmPP; AnFE; AnNE; APA; ATP; AWP; BAP; BAV; BLV; BoLiVe; ChMo; CMP; CoAnAm; CoBA; FaFP; HBV; IAP; JAWP; LiTA; MAP; MoAmPo; MOAP; NeMA; NePA; NP; NV; OBAV; OxBA; PFE; PoFr; POT; PoTo; PreP; ReaPo;

Patterns (*continued*)
SBMV; TCAP; TCPD; TOP; TreFS; TrGrPo; UnPo (1st ed.); WBP
Pattonio, the Pride of the Plain. *Unknown.* CoSo
Patty-Poem. Nick Kenny. PoToHe
Pau-Puk-Keewis. Longfellow. *Fr.* The Song of Hiawatha. CoBA
Paucitatem Dierum Meorum Nuncia Mihi. David. William Habington. MeRV
Paudeen. W. B. Yeats. MaPo; PoEL-5
Paul. Earl Marlatt. OQP; QP-1
Paul. James Wright. NePoEA
Paul and Silas, bound in jail. All Night Long. *Unknown.* AS
Paul and Virginia. John Wheelwright. CrMA
Paul Bunyan. Arthur S. Bourinot. TwCaPo
"He came,/ striding," *sel.* FaPON
Paul Faber, Surgeon, *sel.* George Macdonald.
That Holy Thing, *fr. ch.* 49. ChIP; HBV; MaRV; OBEV; OBVV; OQP; QP-1; SDH; StJW; TrPWD; WGRP
Paul Jannes was working very late. The Shadow. Amy Lowell. ChMo; CMP
Paul Jones. William A. Phelon. GA
Paul Jones ("An American [*or* A forty-gun] frigate from Baltimore came"). *Unknown.* BaBo; GA; PAH; ViBoFo
(Paul Jones' Victory, *with music.*) TrAS
Paul Jones ("A song unto Liberty's brave buccaneer"). *Unknown.* GA; PAH
Paul Jones—a New Song. *Unknown.* PAH
Paul Laurence Dunbar. James David Corrothers. BANP; PoNe; PtP
Paul, let thy faces from the canvas look. Paul Veronese: Three Sonnets, I. Sir Samuel Ferguson. IrPN
Paul on the Road to Damascus. The Acts, IX: 3–6, Bible, *N.T.* TreF
Paul Revere was a rider bold. The Ride of Jennie M'Neal. Will M. Carleton. PTA-1
Paul Revere's Ride. Longfellow. *Fr.* Tales of a Wayside Inn: The Landlord's Tale, Pt. I. AmPP (4th ed.); AnNE; APW; BAP; BAV; BBV; BeLS; BLPA; BoHiPo; CoBA; DD; EV-5; FaBoBe; FaFP; FaPON; GA; GoTP; HBV; HBVY; IAP; IDAH; LoGBV; LPS-2; MC; NeHB; OBAV; OHFP; OnHT; OnSP; PaA; PAH; PAP; PEDC; PIR; PoFr; PoRL; PTA-1; PYM; REAL; RIS; StPo; StVeCh; TCAP; TiPo (1952 ed.); TreF; TrGrPo; WBLP; YaD
Paul said and Peter said. Blondie Goes to Heaven. *Unknown.* OtMeF
Paul to Peter and John. Marjorie E. Johnson. UnW
Paul Veronese: Three Sonnets. Sir Samuel Ferguson. IrPN
Paul was the only man. The Living Christ. Toyohiko Kagawa. SoLD
Pauline, *sels.* Robert Browning.
Andromeda. OBRV
"I ne'er had ventured e'en to hope for this." PtP
"My God, my God, let me for once look on thee." TrPWD
My Lode-Star. MaRV
"O God, where do they tend—these struggling aims?" WGRP
"O thou pale form." ChIP
Oft Have I Stood by Thee. MaRV
Shelley. OBRV
"Stay we here/ With the wild hawks?" MyFE
Water and Air. OBRV
Pauline ("Pauline, Pauline/ I don' love nobody but you"), *with music.* *Unknown.* OuSiCo
Paulinus. Versus Apud Epist. XXXII. 17. Henry Vaughan. TriL
Paul's midnight voice prevail'd; his music's thunder. Epigram. Francis Quarles. *Fr.* Emblems. LoBV
Paul's Wife. Robert Frost. AnAmPo; LA
Paulus a pamphlet doth in prose present. Henry Parrot. TuPP
Pauper, A. Allen Tate. LiTM
Pauper Witch of Grafton, The. Robert Frost. CrMA
Pauper's Deathbed, The. Caroline Anne Bowles. LPS-1
Pauper's Drive, The. Thomas Noel. LPS-1
Pauper's Funeral, The. George Crabbe. *Fr.* The Village. CoEV; FaBoEn
Pausanias you may praise. Themistocles. Timocreon. OxBG
Pause. Henry Bellamann. LS
Pause. Mary Ursula Bethell. AnNZ
Pause. Ann Hamilton. HBMV
Pause, A. Christina Rossetti. CBOV; GTBS-D; NBE; POTT
(Meeting.) HBV
Pause a moment by this spot. Epitaph for a Scotch Terrier. Rachel Field. AlBD
Pause, courteous spirit!—Balbi supplicates. Epitaphs, IX. Gabriello Chiabrera. AWP
Pause en Route. Thomas Kinsella. OxBI
Pause not to dream of the future before us. To Labor Is to Pray. Francis Sargent Osgood. LPS-2
Pause not with lingering foot, O pilgrim, here. On Ascending a Hill Leading to a Convent. Francisco Manuel de Mello. CAW
Pause of Thought, A. Christina Rossetti. *See* Three Stages.
Pause on the March. Sergey Orlov, *tr. fr. Russian by* Babette Deutsch. TrRV
Pauses, II. José Gorostiza, *tr. fr. Spanish by* H. R. Hays. OnPM; TwSpPo
Pausing to let the hush of evening pass. The Angelus. Edwin Markham. GrCo-2
Pavane. Donald Davidson. BAP
Pavane for the Nursery, A. William Jay Smith. NePoAm-2
Pave the sky with stars for Punch. Conrad Aiken. *Fr.* Punch; the Immortal Liar. NP
Pavement Artist, The. James Kirkup. HaMV
Pavilion on the Pier, The. Byron Vazakas. NePA
Pawky auld carle came o'er the lea, The. The Gaberlunzie Man. *Unknown, at. to* James IV, King of Scotland. BSV; EBSV; EnSB; GoTS
Pawky Duke, The. David Rorie. GoTS
Pawnbrokers. Marguerite Wilkinson. HBMV
Pawning the Coffers of Sand. *Unknown, tr. fr. Spanish by* R. Selden Rose *and* Leonard Bacon. *Fr.* The Cid. LiTW
Pawns, The. Frank Betts. HBMV; QS
Pawns, The. William Young. *Fr.* Wishmakers' Town. AA
(Losers, The.) HBMV
Pawnshop Window. R. H. Grenville. GoYe
Pax. D. H. Lawrence. MaRV
Pax Anima, *sel.* Manuel Gutiérrez Nájera, *tr. fr. Spanish by* Samuel Beckett.
"To remember . . . to forgive . . . to have loved." AnMP
Pax Beata. Mary Rachel Norris. VOD
Pax Paganica. Louise Imogen Guiney. AA
Pay Day at Coal Creek, *with music.* *Unknown.* OuSiCo
Pay-off. Kenneth Fearing. ChMo
Paying a Debt. Chevalier de Boufflers, *tr. fr. French by* Leigh Hunt. OnPM
Paysage Moralisé. W. H. Auden. *See* Hearing of Harvests Rotting in the Valleys.
Paysage Moralisé. John Hollander. NePoEA
Pazons, The. Thomas Edward Brown. In the Coach, V. POTT
Pea-Fields, The. Sir Charles G. D. Roberts. *Fr.* Songs of the Common Day. PeCV
Peace, The, *sels.* Aristophanes, *tr. fr. Greek by* Benjamin Bickley Rogers.
"Ah, there's nothing half so sweet as when the seed is in the ground." GrPo
Once More the Simple Things. GrR
Sky-Riding on a Beetle. GrR
(To Heaven on a Beetle, *shorter sel., tr. by* T. F. Higham.) OxBG
Vignette of Ancient Peace. GrR
Peace. Bacchylides. *See* Blessings of Peace.
Peace. Bhartrihari, *tr. fr. Sanskrit by* Paul Elmer More. AWP
Peace. Rupert Brooke. 1914, I. AOAH; EPN; LBBV; LEAP; MaRV; POTE; POTT; WGRP
(1914, I.) HBV; NP; NV
("Now, God be thank'd Who has matched us with His hour.") CBE
Peace. Charles Stuart Calverley. ViP; WhC
Peace. Phoebe Cary. LPS-2; PAH
Peace. Charles De Kay. SN
Peace. Walter de la Mare. MoAB; MoBrPo; NeMA
Peace. Emily Dickinson. *See* I many times thought peace had come.
Peace. Irwin Edman. TrJP
Peace. Samuel Greenberg. CrMA
Peace. George Herbert. AWP; ChTr; EPS; ExPo; InPo; JAWP; OxBoCh; ReEn; SeCeV; SeEP; WBP
Peace. Gerard Manley Hopkins. AtBAP; GTBS-D; OAEP (2d ed.); POTT
Peace. Agnes Lee. BAP; SBMV
Peace. Longfellow. *See* When War Shall Be No More.
Peace, The. Henry Luttrell. *Fr.* Advice to Julia. OBRV
Peace. Edwin Markham. PGD; WBLP
Peace. John Oxenham. PraP
Peace. Beatrice Plumb. PraP
Peace. Adeline Pratt. CAG
Peace. Harold Trowbridge Pulsifer. AOAH; MC; PEDC
Peace. Clinton Scollard. OQP; PoRL; PSO; QP-1
Peace. James Shirley. *See* Piping Peace.
Peace. *At. to* Samuel Speed. OxBoCh; SeCL
(On Peace.) SeEP
Peace. Sara Teasdale. BAP; LoPo; NV
Peace. Henry van Dyke. MaRV
Peace. Henry Vaughan. AEV; AnFE; AWP; BEL; CaAE; CenL; ChTr; ElSeCe; EnLit; EPS; EV-2; FaBoCh; GN; HBV; InPo; LoGBV; MePo; OAEP; OBEV; OBS; Po; PoFS; ReEn; SeCL; SeCV-1; SeEP; TriL; UnPo (1st ed.); WGRP; WHA
("My soul, there is a country.") EG; PoD
(Sweet Peace.) WP
Peace. Brian Vrepont. BoAu
Peace. G. O. Warren. HH; PEDC
Peace. Adeline D. T. Whitney. PAH

Peace. Marguerite Wilkinson. BAP
Peace after Sorrow. Jessie Rose Gates. MaRV
Peace and Joy. G. A. Studdert-Kennedy. *Fr.* The Suffering God. MaRV; OQP; QP-2
Peace and Joy in Jesus Christ. Johann Franck. BePJ
Peace and Mercy and Jonathan. First Thanksgiving of All. Nancy Byrd Turner. FaPON; SiSoSe
Peace and Silence. Georg Trakl. *See* Rest and Silence.
Peace and silence be the guide. Francis Beaumont. *Fr.* The Masque of the Inner-Temple and Gray's Inne. GoBC; OBS
Peace! and There Is No Peace. Jeremiah, VIII: 1-22, Bible, *O.T.* WoL
Peace at Morning. Dana Burnet. AOAH
Peace, battle-worn and starved. Peace. G. O. Warren. HH; PEDC
Peace Be around Thee. Thomas Moore. OTPC (1923 ed.)
Peace, be at peace, O thou my heaviness. Sois sage o ma douleur. Baudelaire. AWP; JAWP; WBP
Peace! Be Still. *Unknown.* OQP; QP-1
Peace Be Thine. Winthrop Mackworth Praed. ERP
Peace be unto you. Shalom Aleichem. *Unknown.* TrJP
Peace be with you, gentle scrivener. Sholom Aleichem. Elias Lieberman. TrJP
Peace by Night. Sister Mary Madeleva. GoBC
Peace Call, The. Edgar Lloyd Hampton. PEDC
Peace, come away: the song of woe. In Memoriam A. H. H., LVII. Tennyson. BoFr; BPN; EM-2; EmBrPo; EPN; EPP; GEPC; OAEP; TCEP; TOP; ViPo; VLEP
Peace, deep and rich. Euripides, *tr. fr. Greek by* Moses Hadas. GrPo
Peace does not mean the end of all our striving. Peace and Joy. G. A. Studdert-Kennedy. *Fr.* The Suffering God. MaRV; OQP; QP-2
Peace flows into me. Peace. Sara Teasdale. BAP; LoPo; NV
Peace-Giver, The. Swinburne. *See* Christmas Antiphon, A.
Peace, Heart! No Cry! Clemens Brentano, *tr. fr. German by* Mabel Cotterell. AnGP
Peace Hymn for England and America. George Huntington. PaA
Peace in her chamber, wheresoe'er. First Love Remembered. Dante Gabriel Rossetti. BPN; POTT; PoVP; VLEP
Peace in our time, O Lord. Peace. John Oxenham. PraP
Peace in the Welsh Hills. Vernon Watkins. ChMP
Peace in the World. John Galsworthy. MaRV
Peace in thy hands. The Ghost. Walter de la Mare. OAEP (2d ed.); POTE
Peace is declared, and I return. The Return. Kipling. MBP; MoBrPo; NeMA
Peace Is Only an Interlude. Ruth Guthrie Harding. MuM
Peace is the heir of dead desire. Suicide's Stone. Robinson Jeffers. MM; PC; TwCV
Peace is the object of my dear delight. Not Peace at Any Price. Euripides. *Fr.* Children of Heracles. GrR
"Peace Is the Tranquillity of Order." Robert Wilberforce. GoBC; JKCP (1955 ed.)
Peace lies profound on these forgotten acres. Meditation by Mascoma Lake. Donald C. Babcock. NePoAm-2
Peace Message, The. Burton Egbert Stevenson. PAH
Peace Must Come As a Troubadour. Marie Drennan. OQP; QP-1
Peace now and ever on this gravestone be. At My Father's Grave. Matthias Claudius. WoL
Peace of Christ, The. St. John, Bible, *N.T.* *See* My Peace I Give unto You.
Peace of Christ, The. John Antes La Trobe. BePJ
Peace of great doors be for you, The. For You. Carl Sandburg. ChMo; CMP; MAP; MoAmPo; WaKn
Peace of Prayer, The. Nagata, *tr. fr. Japanese by* Lois J. Erickson. PraP
Peace of the Roses, The. Thomas Philipps. ACP
Peace on Earth. Anatolius, *tr. fr. Greek.* BePJ
Peace on Earth. Bacchylides, *tr. fr. Greek by* John Addington Symonds. AWP; JAWP; WBP
("To mortal men Peace giveth these good things.") GrPo
Peace on Earth. Marie Barton. PraP
Peace on Earth. Helen Wieand Cole. ChIP; OQP; QP-1
Peace on Earth. Robert Freeman. PSO
(Why.) PGD
Peace on Earth, *sel.* Gudmundur Gudmundsson, *tr. fr. Icelandic by* Jakobina Johnson.
Prologue. IcP
Peace on Earth. Samuel Longfellow. PGD
Peace on Earth. Edmund H. Sears. *See* It Came upon the Midnight Clear.
Peace on Earth. William Carlos Williams. LiTA, MAP; NP; PFY; TBM; TCPD; ViBoPo
Peace on New England, on the shingled white houses, on golden. Jehu. Louis MacNeice. LiTG; LiTM (rev. ed.); MoAB; WaP
Peace on the earth,/ Joyfully sang the angels long ago. Through the Ages. Margaret Hope. PGD
Peace! peace! A mighty Power, which is as darkness. Shelley. *Fr.* Prometheus Unbound. OAEP
Peace, peace be unto all the world. War and Peace. Alexander Petofi. PoFr
Peace! Peace! God of our fathers grant us Peace! A Prayer for Peace. S. Teackle Wallis. BIG
Peace, peace! he is not dead, he doth not sleep. He Is Not Dead [*or* Against Oblivion]. Shelley. *Fr.* Adonais. BoFr; FaBoEn; LEAP; LO; MaRV; TreFS; UnW
Peace! peace! It is not so. Thou does miscall. Affliction. Henry Vaughan. PoP
Peace, peace, my friend; these subjects fly. George Crabbe. *Fr.* Sir Eustace Grey. PoEL-4
Peace, Peace, my Hony, do not cry. Christ's Reply. Edward Taylor. *Fr.* God's Determinations. PoEL-3
Peace, peace on earth! the heart of man forever. Peace on Earth. Samuel Longfellow. PGD
Peace, peace, peace, make no noise. A Ditty. John Day. *Fr.* Humour Out of Breath. ElL
Peace, Perfect Peace. Edward H. Bickersteth. BePJ; BLRP; WGRP
Peace-Pipe, The. Longfellow. *Fr.* The Song of Hiawatha. AnNE; IAP
Peace pratler, do not lowre. Conscience. George Herbert. NBE
Peace, Shepherd, peace! What boots it singing on? Genius Loci. Margaret L. Woods. ES; HBV; OBEV; OBVV
Peace the End of the Good Man. Robert Blair. *Fr.* The Grave. EV-3
Peace, the one-time radiant goddess. The Child of Peace. Selma Lagerlöf. AnSL
Peace! The perfect word is sounding, like a universal hymn. In the Dawn. Odell Shepard. WGRP
Peace, the wild valley streaked with torrents. The Straw. Robert Graves. MoVE
Peace, there is peace in this awaking. Waking. Patrick MacDonogh. NeIP
Peace through Prayer. Longfellow. *See* Oft Have I Seen . . .
Peace to all such! but were there one whose fires. Atticus [*or* Characters from the Satires: Atticus *or* Addison *or* Portrait of Atticus]. Pope. *Fr.* Epistle to Dr. Arbuthnot. AWP; InPo; JAWP; LPS-3; MaPo; OBEC; PoFS; SeCePo; ShBV-4; UnPo (1st ed.); ViBoPo; WBP; WHA
Peace to the quiet dead. The Elegy of the Kremlin Bells. Marya Zaturenska *Fr.* Elegies over John Reed. BAP; NP
Peace to the Slumberers! Thomas Moore. HBV; OnYI
Peace to the Statue. *Unknown, tr. fr. Greek by* Lord Neaves. OnPM
Peace to the Tomb. *At. to* Theocritus *and to* Leonidas of Tarentum, *tr. fr. Greek by* "D. M. P." LiA
Peace to these little broken leaves. Leaves. W. H. Davies. MBP; MoBrPo
Peace to-night, heroic spirit! Requiem for a Young Soldier. Florence Earle Coates. OHIP
Peace Triumphant. Cale Young Rice. PEDC
Peace Universal. Anna H. Thorne. PEDC; PoRL
(Dawn of the Century.) PEOR
Peace upon earth/ Brings wealth and blossom of dulcet Song to birth. Blessings of Peace. Bacchylides. GrR; OxBG
Peace waits among the hills. Montserrat. Arthur Symons. PoeT
Peace, war, religion. This Tokyo. Gary Snyder. NeAP
Peace, wayward barne! O cease thy moan! Song. Richard Brome. *Fr.* The Northern Lass. SeCL
Peace! What Do Tears Avail? "Barry Cornwall." VA
Peaceable Kingdom, The. Isaiah, XI: 6-9, Bible, *O.T.* FaPON (XI: 6); LiTW
Peaceable Race, The. T. A. Daly. HBV
Peaceful, archangelic sun, A. The Ruined Farm. William Plomer. BoSA
Peaceful Death. Walt Whitman. OQP; QP-1
Peaceful life, A—just toil and rest. Lincoln. James Whitcomb Riley. DD; OHIP
Peaceful Man, A. Henri Michaux, *tr. fr. French by* Wallace Fowlie. MiCF
Peaceful Night, The. Milton. *Fr.* On the Morning of Christ's Nativity. ChrBoLe; CLS
("But peaceful was the night.") FaBoCh; LoGBV
Peaceful Shepherd, The. Robert Frost. *Fr.* A Sky Pair. MAP; MoAB; MoAmPo; QS
Peaceful Western Wind, The. Thomas Campion. LoBV
Peacemaker, The. Joyce Kilmer. CAW; MaRV; PoFr
Peach, The. Abbie Farwell Brown. GFA
Peach, The. Charles *and* Mary Lamb. OTPC (1923 ed.)
Peach blossom is redder because rain fell overnight, The. Morning. Wang Wei. WhP
Peachblossoms flutter like pink butterflies, The. Prose Poem: Indifference. Judith Gautier. OnPM
Peachtree. Archibald Rutledge. LS
Peach Tree, The. Edith Sitwell. NP
Peacock and the mocking-bird, The. Demon Lovers. Elinor Wylie. OnAP

Peacock-eye of the half-moon long since up, The. The Moonlit Doorway. Kenneth Mackenzie. MoAuPo
Peacock has a score of eyes, The. Sing-Song Verses. Christina Rossetti. *Fr.* Sing-Song. BoN
Peacock in Leucadia loved a maid, A. From Burton the Anatomist. Maurice James Craig. NeIP
Peacock moulted; soon a jay was seen, A. The Jay in the Feathers of the Peacock. La Fontaine. OnPM
Peacocks. Walter Adolphe Roberts. PoNe
Peadar Og Goes Courting. James Stephens. WhC
Peak, The. Mary Carolyn Davies. POT; PoTo
Peak and Puke. Walter de la Mare. BOL
Peaks, The. Stephen Crane. War Is Kind, XVIII. AA; AmP; HBV; TCAP; WGRP
Peaks, and the starlit skies, the deeps of the fathomless seas, The. God Within Yet Above. Sir Lewis Morris. MaRV
Peaks in a sea of light! Not moaningly. Main Range. James Picot. BoAu
Peaks of Life. Shelley. *See* Promethean Ideal, The.
Peanuts. *Unknown.* FaFP; SiTL
("Boy stood on the burning deck, The.") GoTP
Pear blossoms are pure, The. Spring. Su T'ung-po. OnPC
Pear Tree Hilda Doolittle ("H. D."). HBMV; MAP; MoAmPo; NeMA; UnPo
Pear-Tree, The. Iwan Goll, *tr. fr. German by* Babette Deutsch *and* Avram Yarmolinsky. TrJP
Pear Tree, The. E. Elizabeth Longwell. BrR
Pear Tree, The. Edna St. Vincent Millay. MAP; MoAmPo
Pear Tree, The. *Unknown, tr. fr. Chinese by* Allen Upward. AWP; JAWP; WBP
Pearl, The. Hans Christian Andersen, *tr. fr. Danish by* Charles Wharton Stork. BoDS; LiTW
Pearl, The. George Herbert. EPS; FaBoEn; MePo; OxBoCh; PoEL-2; ReEn; SeCV-1
Pearl, The. *Unknown.* EPP, *Middle English vers., much abr.*; MeEV, *mod. vers. by* Sophie Jewett; NBE, *Middle English vers., much abr.*
Sels.
"O Pearl, for princes' pleasure wrought," *mod. vers., much abr.* TCEP
Queen of Courtesy, The. ACP; CAW, *mod. vers.;* ISi, *mod. vers. by* Stanley Perkins Chase
Pearl, a Girl, A. Robert Browning. BPN; PoVP; VLEP
Pearl Bryan. *Unknown.* BaBo; ViBoFo
Pearl Diver. William Rose Benét. AnAmPo; BLV; LA
Pearl of the White Breast. *Tr. fr. Modern Irish by* George Petrie. AnIV; OnYI
Pearl that the Prince full well might prize. The Pearl. *Unknown.* MeEV
Pearls. Al-Mushafi, *tr. fr. Arabic by* A. J. Arberry. MooP
Pearls!/ Twin pearls. A Letter. Chang Chi. ChLP; PoHN
Pearls of a day hung in the topmost height, The. The Yorkshire Moors. Hal Summers. HaMV
Pearls of the Faith, *sel.* Sir Edwin Arnold.
After Death in Arabia, *abr.* BMEP; EOAH; HBV; VA; WGRP
"Farewell, friends! Yet not farewell." MaRV
Pearls Seen through Amber. *Unknown, tr. fr. Arabic by* E. Powys Mathers. *Fr.* The Thousand and One Nights. LiTW
Pearly Everlasting, The. Ernest Fewster. CaP; OCL
Peas. *Unknown.* FaPON; SiTL
("I eat my peas with honey.") BoN; CenHV
Peasant. Alfred Kreymborg. MAP
Peasant, A. R. S. Thomas. MoWP
Peasant, The. *Unknown, tr. fr. Chinese by* E. D. Edwards. ChLP
Peasant and Geisha Songs. *Unknown, tr. fr. Japanese by* Kenneth Rexroth. LiTW
"Cicada cries out, The."
"First time I saw you, The."
"In the open sea."
"In the summer, by the river."
"Nightingale on the flowering plum, The."
Peasant and the Sheep, The. Ivan Andreyevich Krylov, *tr. fr. Russian by* C. Fillingham Coxwell. AWP; JAWP; WBP
Peasant Declares His Love, The. Emile Roumer, *tr. fr. French by* John Peale Bishop. AnCL; LiTW; PoNe
Peasant haled a sheep to court, A. The Peasant and the Sheep. Ivan Andreyevich Krylov. AWP; JAWP; WBP
Peasant in form and face old Philippe stood. The Sugar-Maker. Frank Oliver Call. CPG
Peasant leaves his plough afield, The. Bernardo's March to Roncesvalles. *Unknown.* AnSpL-1
Peasant once unthinkingly, A. The Monk and the Peasant. Margaret E. Bruner. PoToHe
Peasant Poet, The. John Clare. WGRP
Peasant Song, A. *Unknown, tr. fr. Chinese by* Henry H. Hart. ChLP
Peasant stands, The. The Hungry One. Nikolai Nekrasov. *Fr.* Who Can Be Happy and Free in Russia? BoR
Peasant stood before a king and said, A. Ahab Mohammed. James Matthew Legaré. AA
Peasant sun went crushing grapes, The. Laurence Dakin. *Fr.* Tancred, I, i. CaP
Peasant to his lord paid yearly court, A. The Cottager and His Landlord. Milton. OTPC (1923 ed.)
Peasant Woman's Song, A. Dion Boucicault. *See* Exiled Mother, The.
Peasantry. Eileen Duggan. CoBE
Peasants, The. Alun Lewis. FaBoMo
Peasants in the fields have no calendar, The. The Cries of Birds. Lu Yu. WhP
Peasants my forebears were. Forebears. Monk Gibbon. NeIP
Peasant's shack, A, beside the/ Clear river. Country Cottage. Tu Fu. OnPC
Pease-porridge [*or*-pudding] hot. Mother Goose. BoChLi; FaFP; HBV; HBVY; OTPC; OxNR; PCH; PPL; RIS; SiTL; StVeCh (1940 ed.); TiPo
Peat-Cutters. Geoffrey Johnson. HaMV
Pebble, The. Elinor Wylie. BoFr; MAP; MoAmPo
Pebbles. May Brinkley. DDA
Pebbles. Edith King. BoTP; GFA; RAR
Peblis to the Play. *Unknown.* EBSV; GoTS
Peccavi, Domine. Archibald Lampman. MaRV
Peck of Gold, A. Robert Frost. LaNeLa
Pecos Puncher, The. *Unknown.* CoSo
Pecos Queen, The. *Unknown.* CSF
Peculiar ghost! great and immortal ghost! Epitaph for the Poet V., XVII. Arthur Davison Ficke. HBMV
Pedagogical Principles. Harry Amoss. CaP
Pedant dove, the poet who admires him, The. Literary Landscape with Dove and Poet. Phyllis McGinley. NePoAm-2
Pedantic Literalist. Marianne Moore. APA; CoAnAm
Peddler and the Reddleman, The. V. Sackville-West. *Fr.* The Land. TCPD
Peddler's Caravan, The. William Brighty Rands. *See* Pedlar's Caravan, The.
Pedestrian's Plaint, The. E. V. Lucas. CenHV
Pedigree. Emily Dickinson. *See* Pedigree of honey, The.
Pedigree, The. Thomas Hardy. CoBMV
Pedigree. Mary Mills. NePoAm
Pedigree. Pope. *See* Worth Makes the Man.
Pedigree of honey, The. Pedigree. Emily Dickinson. GoTP; NeMA; PoeMoYo; TSW; TSWC; YaD
Pediment: Ballet. Louise Townsend Nicholl. UnS
Pediment of Appearance, The. Wallace Stevens. Po
Pedlar, The. Charlotte Mew. TCPD
(Pedler, The.) HBMV
Pedlar, A. *Unknown.* *See* Fine Knacks for Ladies.
Pedlar Jim. Florence Hoare. BoTP
Pedlar of Spells, The. Lu Yu, *tr. fr. Chinese by* Arthur Waley. TrCh
Pedlar's [*or* Peddler's] Caravan, The. William Brighty Rands. BoChLi; BoTP; GaP; GFA; HBV; HBVY; MPB; OTPC; PCH; PRWS; RIS; StVeCh (1940 ed.); TVC; TVSH
Pedlar's Song, The ("Lawn as white . . ."). Shakespeare. *See* Lawn as White as Driven Snow.
Pedlar's Song, The ("When daffodils . . ."). Shakespeare. *See* When Daffodils Begin to Peer.
Pedler, The. Charlotte Mew. *See* Pedlar, The.
Pedra. John William Burgon. BLPA
(Petra.) NeHB
Pedro. Phoebe W. Hoffman. GoYe
Pedro Rojas. César Vallejo, *tr. fr. Spanish by* H. R. Hays. TwSpPo
Peedy, Peedy; Pally, Ludy; Lady Whistle. To Be Said to Baby's Fingers. *Unknown.* SAS
Peeler and the Goat, The. *Unknown.* AnIL
Peeler, hast thou found my treasure. I've Lost My ——. Harry Cholmondeley-Pennell. CenHV
Peeler's Lament, The. *Unknown.* CoSo
Peeny-Pen-Pone. Laura Campbell. MeMeAg
Peepin' through the knothole. Go Get the Axe. *Unknown.* AS; TrAS
Peeping Flowers. George Peele. *See* Not Iris in Her Pride.
Peer Gynt. Charles Hamilton Sorley. HBMV
Peer of gods he seemeth to me, the blissful. Peer of the Gods [*or* Ode]. Sappho, *tr. by* John Addington Symonds. EnLi-1; GrPo; LiTW
Peer of the Gods, the happiest man I seem. To a Bride. Sappho, *tr. by* Edwin Marion Cox. GrR
Peer of the golden gods is he to Sappho. Ode to Anactoria. Sappho, *tr. by* William Ellery Leonard. AWP
Peerless lass who gathered the lilies of the Graces, The. "In Fields Where Roses Fade." Pompeius. GrPE
Peerless yet hapless maid of Q! Dirge. *Unknown.* BOHV
Peers of heav'n kept a parliament, The. Ad Michaelem Drayton. John Weever. ReIE
Peeter a Whi[t]feild he hath slaine. Jock o' the Side. *Unknown.* ESPB; ViBoFo
Peewee. Alfred Kreymborg. TCPD
Peewee, The. John Townsend Trowbridge. *See* Pewee, The.
"Peg Away." Frederic E. Weatherly. TVSH
Peg-Leg's Fiddle. Bill Adams. BBV; EtS
(Billy Peg-Leg's Fiddle.) MW

Peg Nicholson was a gude bay mare. Elegy on the Death of Peg Nicholson. Burns. RO
Pegasus. C. Day Lewis. AtBAP
Pegasus. Patrick Kavanagh. FaBoTw; MoAB; OxBI
(Glut on the Market, A.) OnYI
Pegasus Lost. Elinor Wylie. MAP; MoAmPo; NeMA
Peggy. Allan Ramsay. *See* My Peggy.
Peggy. Blanaid Salkeld. OnYI
Peggy Considers Her Grandmothers. Josephine Pinckney. NP
Peggy Mitchell. Anthony Raftery, *tr. fr. Irish by* James Stephens. GTIV
Peggy's Wedding. Thomas Edward Brown. EnLit; VLEP
Pekes and the Pollicles, everyone knows, The. The Battle of the Pekes and the Pollicles, and the Intervention of the Great Rumpus Cat. T. S. Eliot. AlBD
Peking. Pien Chih-lin, *tr. fr. Chinese.* WhP
Peleus. Euripides, *tr. fr. Greek by* Hugh Owen Meredith. *Fr.* Andromache. GrR
Pelican, The. James Montgomery. *Fr.* The Pelican Island. LPS-2
Pelican, The. Philippe de Thaun, *tr. fr. French by* Richard Wilbur. WaKn
Pelican, The. *Unknown.* TreFS
Pelican Chorus, The. Edward Lear. LiL
Pelican Island, The, *sels.* James Montgomery. LPS-2
Birds.
Coral Reef, The, *abr.*
Pelican, The.
Sea Life.
Pelicans. Robinson Jeffers. MAP; MoAmPo; TCPD
Pelicans My Father Sees, The. Sister Maris Stella. GoBC
Pelides then set forth. The Wrestling Match. Homer. *Fr.* The Iliad, XXIII. GrR
Pell Mell Celebrated, The. John Gay. *Fr.* Trivia; or, The Art of Walking the Streets of London, II: Of Walking the Streets by Day. EnLi-1 (1949 ed.)
Pelleas and Ettarre. Tennyson. *See* Idylls of the King.
Pellicanus is the word. The Pelican. Philippe de Thaun. WaKn
Pelops. Pindar, *tr. fr. Greek by* H. T. Wade-Gery *and* C. M. Bowra. *Fr.* Olympian Odes, I. OxBG
(Bride to the Victor, A, *tr. by* C. J. Billson.) GrR
Pelops and Hippodamia, *sel.* Matthew Grove.
In Praise of His Lady. ElL
Pelters of Pyramids. Richard Henry Horne. VA
Pemmy Was a Pretty Girl. *Unknown.* OTPC
Pen, The. Al-Hajjam, *tr. fr. Arabic by* A. J. Arberry. MooP
Pen and the Album, The. Thackeray. VA
Pen stops in a phrase of a letter home, The. Music in the Rec Hut. Hubert Creekmore. WaP
Pen—to register; a key, A. Memory. Wordsworth. BPN
Penal Servitude for Mrs. Maybrick. *Unknown.* OxBoLi; SiTL
Penalties of Baldness, The. Sir Owen Seaman. FiBHP
Penalty of Virtue, The. *Unknown, tr. fr. Sanskrit by* Arthur W. Ryder. *Fr.* The Panchatantra. AWP; PoFr
Penance by Whipping. *Tr. fr. the Spanish of the* Penitentes *by* Mary Austin. APW
Pencil and paper first I found. Drawing. Sergei Mikhalkov. RuPo
Pendennis, *sel.* Thackeray.
At the Church Gate, *fr. ch.* 32. BMEP; EPN; HBV; LoPo; LPS-1; VA
Pendulous mouth, you flap in a wind. Mouths. Louis Dudek. PeCV
Pendulum. Joseph Auslander. BAP
Pendulum Rhyme. Selma Robinson. InMe
Penelope. Persis Greeley Anderson. DDA
Penelope. Ursula Wood. SoV
Penelope Dreams ("But when her heart had had its fill of weeping"). Homer, *tr. fr. Greek by* Sir William Marris. *Fr.* The Odyssey, XX. OxBG
Penelope Dreams ("So said he, and the crone went down the hall"). Homer, *tr. fr. Greek by* J. W. Mackail. *Fr.* The Odyssey, XIX. OxBG
(Penelope's Dream: "Then went the ancient matron forth," *tr. by* William Cowper.) GrR
Penelope, for her Ulysses' [*or* Ulisses] sake. Amoretti, XXIII. Spenser. CoBE; PeBoSo; ReaPo; ReEn; ReIE
Penelope Forlorn. Homer, *tr. fr. Greek by* J. W. Mackail. *Fr.* The Odyssey, IV. OxBG
(Penelope; New Woes on Old, *tr. by* H. B. Cotterill.) GrR
Penelope Makes Trial of Odysseus. Homer. *See* Penelope's Constancy Rewarded.
Penelope; New Woes on Old. Homer. *See* Penelope Forlorn.
Penelope's Constancy Rewarded. Homer, *tr. fr. Greek by* William Cowper. *Fr.* The Odyssey, XXIII. GrR
(Penelope Makes Trial of Odysseus, *pr. tr. by* Samuel Butler, *shorter sel.*) OxBG
Penelope's Dream. Homer. *See* Penelope Dreams ("So said he").
Penetralia. Madison Cawein. CP; NV
Penguin, A ("The pen-guin sits up-on the shore"). Oliver Herford. FiBHP
Peniny and the Silken Lady. Lucy Cherry Crisp. NoCaPo (rev. ed.)
Penitence. Pedro Soto de Rojas, *tr. fr. Spanish by* Sir John Bowring. OnPM
Penitent, The. Edna St. Vincent Millay. ALV; BOHV; DDA; YaD
Penitent, The. Jeremy Taylor. OBS; OxBoCh
Penitent Palmer's Ode, The. Robert Greene. *Fr.* Francesco's Fortunes. LoBV; OBSC
Penitentes. *Unknown, tr. fr. Old Irish by* Seán O'Faoláin. SiB
Penitential Psalm ("I, thy servant, full of sighs, cry unto thee"). *Unknown, tr. fr. Babylonian.* WGRP
Penitential Psalm to the Goddess Anunit ("May the wrath of my god be pacified"). *Unknown, tr. fr. Babylonian.* WGRP
Penitential Week, A. Carolyn Wells. PC
Penitentiary Blues, The, *with music. Unknown.* SoAF
Pennies. Joyce Kilmer. CAW
Penniless. Toyohiko Kagawa. MaRV
Pennsylvania. Helen Hall Bucher. PoRL
Penny, The. Laura Benét. PCH
Penny and penny. *Unknown.* OxNR
Penny for a ball of thread, A. Pop Goes the Weasel. *Unknown.* RIS
Penny is heavier than the shrew, A. The Masked Shrew. Isabella Gardner. ImOP
Penny Problem. John Farrar. GaP
Penny Whistle, The. Edward Thomas. MBP; MoAB; MoBrPo
Penny Whistle Blues. E. H. L. Island. InMe
Penny Wish, A. Irene Thompson. BoTP
Penny Ye Mean to Gi'e, The. *Unknown.* PTA-1
Pensées de Noël. A. D. Godley. BOHV; InMe
Pensioned Ox, The. Addaeus, *tr. fr. Greek.* GrPE, *tr. by* F. L. Lucas; GrR, *tr. by* Walter Leaf
(Draught-Ox, The, *tr. by* Lord Neaves.) OnPM
(Ox Past Service, An, *tr. by* Walter Leaf.) OxBG
("Ox, rewarded for his pains, The," *tr. by* the Earl of Cromer.) GrPo
Pensioners. Winifred M. Letts. BoTP
Pensive, I view'd a sacred pile, of late. Pulling Down St. Martin's Church. Aaron Hill. *Fr.* To Clelia, on the Pulling Down St. Martin's Church. BeR
Pensive nun with step demure and still, A. Peace. Adeline Pratt. CAG
Pensive on Her Dead Gazing. Walt Whitman. IAP; TCAP
Pensive photograph, A. To a Portrait. Arthur Symons. VA
Pensy Ant, right trig and clean, A. The Caterpillar and the Ant. Allan Ramsay. SeCePo
Pentecost. Adelbert Sumpter Coats. TrPWD
Pentecost. Laura Simmons. ChIP
Pentucket. Whittier. MC; PAH
Penumbra. Dante Gabriel Rossetti. PoVP; VLEP
Penurious Quaker, The; or, The High Priz'd Harlot. *Unknown.* CoMu
"Peona! ever have I long'd to slake." Wherein Lies Happiness. Keats. *Fr.* Endymion, I. ERP
Peonies. Liu Yü Shih, *tr. fr. Chinese by* Henry H. Hart. PoHN
Peonies of the temple. The Temple That Charged Admission. Issa. PoFr
Peon's Mother, The. Jewel Wurtzbaugh. HiLiAm
Peony for Apollo, A. Charles Edward Eaton. GoYe
People, The. Tommaso Campanella, *tr. fr. Italian by* John Addington Symonds. AWP; JAWP; OnPM; WBP; WoL
People, The, *sels.* "Robin Hyde." AnNZ
"After we'd left off loving, long after that," I.
"But letting go . . . hands, eyes, teeth, body, all ways," IV.
"How she grew old happened in fine-darned places," II.
People. D. H. Lawrence. EPP
People. Lois Lenski. FaPON
People, The. Elizabeth Madox Roberts. GoBP; TiPo
People, The. W. B. Yeats. ChMo
People along the sand, The. Neither Out Far nor in Deep. Robert Frost. AmP; ChTr; CoBMV; CrMA; LiTA; MoAB; PoLFOT; TiPo (1952 ed.); TwP
People and a Heron. Robinson Jeffers. ReMP
People—and a lot/ I don't care for. Perambulator Poems, IV. David McCord. WhC
People are of two kinds, and he. Tribute on the Passing of a Very Real Person. *Unknown.* PoToHe (new ed.)
People arrive to worship in their church. The Church. Jules Romain. WGRP
People as Flowers. Francis Maguire. JKCP (1955 ed.)
People at the Party, The. Lisel Mueller. NePoAM-2
People Buy a Lot of Things. Annette Wynne. UTS
People buying and selling, consuming pleasures, The. Reference to a Passage in Plutarch's Life of Sulla. Robinson Jeffers. CrMA
People from nooks and corners. The Avaricious Angel. Rafael Alberti. CoSP
People Going By. Elizabeth Madox Roberts. GaP

People Has No Obituary, The. Eunice Clark. NAMP
People have teased and vexed me. Two Songs. Heine. WoL
People Hide Their Love. Emperor Wu Ti, *tr. fr. Chinese by* Arthur Waley. ChLP; LiTW; TrCh
People in the Park, The. Léonie Adams. MoVE
People is a beast of muddy brain, The. The People. Tommaso Campanella. AWP; JAWP; OnPM; WBP; WoL
People, Look East, *with music*. Eleanor Farjeon. YaCaBo
People made a ring, The. The Hemorrhage. Stanley Kunitz. WaP
People of Ireland—I am an old woman; I am near my end. A Leitrim Woman. John Lyle Donaghy. OnYI; OxBI
People of Spain think Cervantes, The. Miguel de Cervantes. E. C. Bentley. *Fr.* Biography for Beginners. CenHV; FiBHP; LauV
People of Tao-chou, The. Po Chü-i, *tr. fr. Chinese by* Arthur Waley. ChTr; TrCh
People of that sort seem to attract each other. Mr. and Mrs. Alonzo Sidney. Merrill Moore. MOAP
People of the middle heaven. Rain-Songs from the Rio Grande Pueblos. *Tr. by* Mary Austin. APW
People Pray, The. Sophocles. *See* God and Man.
People simper and drawl. Gnat. Rosalie Moore. GoTP
People, The, that walked in darkness have seen a great light. The Prince of Peace. Isaiah, Bible, *O.T.* ChrBoLe
People up and down the world that talk and laugh and cry, The. Old Books. Margaret Widdemer. DDA
People vs. the People, The. Kenneth Fearing. MoAmPo (1950 ed.)
People waddle on the boat, The. Dolphins. Molly Michaels. RIS
People walk upon their heads, The. Topsy-turvy Land. H. E. Wilkinson. BoTP
People who have what they want are very fond of telling people. The Terrible People. Ogden Nash. NePA; SiTL
People who live in cities never know. Wide Front Porch. Leslie N. Jennings. DDA
People Who Must. Carl Sandburg. SAS
People whom I take to walk, The. A Dog's Eye View. Amelia Josephine Burr. AlBD
People Will Live On, The. Carl Sandburg. *Fr.* The People, Yes. AmPP; BoLiVe (1945 ed.); CoV; MoAmPo; NAMP; OxBA; TrGrPo
People Will Talk. Samuel Dodge. TreFS, *sl. diff.*; WBLP, *sl. abr.*
People with Proud Chins. Carl Sandburg. PFY
People wonder what Dan Wholebrook found. Star-Pudding. Robert P. Tristram Coffin. DDA
People, Yes, The, *sels.* Carl Sandburg.
Best, The, *fr.* Sec. 51. MaRV
Children of the Wind, *fr.* Sec. 13. StVeCh
"Father sees a son nearing manhood, A," Sec. 9. PoLFOT
"From Illinois and Indiana came a later myth," Sec. 2. CoV
"From the four corners of the earth," Sec. 1. CoV
Hope Is a Tattered Flag, Sec. 16. NAMP
"Lincoln?/ He was a mystery in smoke and flags," Sec. 57. PoLFOT
Man in the Street Is Fed, The, Sec. 99. AmPP (4th ed.); OxBA
People Will Live On, The, Sec. 107. AmPP; BoLiVe (1945 ed.); CoV; MoAB; MoAmPo; MoPo; NAMP; NePA; TrGrPo
People, Yes, The, Sec. 29. ChMo
"People, yes, the people, The," Sec. 86. BBV (1951 ed.); NAMP; PoFr
"Record is a scroll of many indecipherable scrawls, The," Sec. 76. CoV
Sleep Is a Suspension, Sec. 106. NAMP
They Have Yarns, Sec. 45. LiTA; MoAmPo; PreP
(American Yarns.) StVeCh (1955 ed.)
(Yarns.) GoTP
(Yarns of the People.) NeMA
"What the people learn out of lifting and hauling and waiting and losing and laughing," Sec. 32. CoV
"Who can make a poem of the depths of weariness," Sec. 83. MaRV; NAMP
"Who shall speak for the people?" Sec. 24. CoV
People's Anthem, The. Ebenezer Elliott. *See* When Wilt Thou Save the People?
People's Attorney, servant of the right! Wendell Phillips. Amos Bronson Alcott. AA, GA, LEAP; PoFr
People's Holidays, The. "Marianne Farningham." PEOR
Peoples in their peril and their pain, The. Plan. Richard Burton. POT
People's King, The. Lyman Whitney Allen. PGD
People's Petition, The. Wathen Mark Wilks Call. OBVV; PoFr; VA
People's Prayer, The. Amos R. Wells. PraP
People's Song, 1849. Charles Kingsley. *See* Alton Locke.
People's Song of Peace, The. Joaquin Miller. *Fr.* Song of the Centennial. LPS-2
People's Thanksgiving, The. William Pierson Merrill. *See* Not Alone for Mighty Empire.
"Pep." Grace G. Bostwick. WBLP
Pepita. Alfred de Musset, *tr. fr. French by* Alan Conder. TrFP
Pepper Tree, The. Sister Mary Madeleva. RIS
Peppered mud walls are yellow, The. Song of Returning to Kwei-chi. Li Ho. WhP
Peppertrees, the peppertrees, The! Scenes from the Life of the Peppertrees. Denise Levertov. NeAP
Peppery Man, The. Arthur Macy. FaPON; GaP
Per Amica Silentia Lunae. Ronald de Carvalho, *tr. fr. Portuguese by* Harold Morland. LiTW
Per Ardua. Simonides, *tr. fr. Greek by* J. M. Edmonds. GrR
Per Ardua ad Astra. John Oxenham. TrPWD
Per Aspera. Florence Earle Coates. BLP, HBMV; VOD
Per Contra. Mahlon Leonard Fisher. BAP; ChIP; MaRV
Per Diem et per Noctem. Mary Stanley. AnNZ
Per Iter Tenebricosum. Oliver St. John Gogarty. AnIL; OBMV; OxBI
Per Omnia Deus. Thomas Edward Brown. MBP
Per Pacem ad Lucem. Adelaide Anne Procter. MaRV; TrPWD; VA
Per Quinquennia Iam Decem. Prudentius, *tr. fr. Latin by* Asa M. Hughes. LaP
Perambulator Poems (I–VII). David McCord. WhC
"Perceived and taken things right thou hast long." Of Taking Things Wrong. John Heywood. ReIE
Perchance in days to come. Strange Love. Moses ibn Ezra. TrJP
Perchance in Dreams. Antonio Machado, *tr. fr. Spanish by* Eleanor L. Turnbull. TeCS
Perchance it was her eyes of blue. A Vague Story. Walter Parke. BOHV
Perchance it was the peace that stirless breasts. The Presence of the Spirit. Giulio Salvadori. CAW
Perchance that I might learn what pity is. Thou Alone Art Good [*or* A Prayer for Purification]. Michelangelo. AWP; OnPM
Perchance there where meet the earth and the sea? Where? José Moreno Villa. CoSP
Perch'd on a lofty oak. The Raven and the Fox. La Fontaine. OnPM
"Perchè Pensa? Pensando S'Invecchia." Arthur Hugh Clough. BPN; EmBrPo; EPP; PoVP; ViP; VLEP
(To Spend Uncounted Years of Pain.) ViPP
Perched in a tower of this ancestral Wall. At the Great Wall of China. Edmund Blunden. HaMV
Perched on a dead volcanic pile. The Witches' Brew. E. J. Pratt. BoCaPo (1948 ed.)
Perched on a great fall of air. Landscape with Figures. Keith Douglas. NePoEA
Perched on its yellow peak beneath a sky. Toledo. Antonio Gómez Restrepo. CAW
Perched on my city office-stool. The Ice-Cart. W. W. Gibson. POT; PoTo; PtOT; ShBV-2; TCPD; TwCV; WP
Perched upon a maple bough. Bird's Song in April. Clinton Scollard. PEOR
Percival Wilberforce Henderson Crane. The Scandalous Tale of Percival and Genevieve. Newman Levy. WhC
Percy Bysshe Shelley. Dante Gabriel Rossetti. Five English Poets, 5. BPN; EmBrPo; PoVP; PtP
Percy [*or* Persè] out of Northumberland, The. Chevy Chase [*or* The Ancient Ballad of Chevy Chase *or* The Hunting of the Cheviot]. *Unknown.* BaBo (*A vers.*); BEL; EnRP; ESPB; KN; LiA; OBB; TCEP; ViBoPo; WHA
Perdat Qui Caveat Emptor. Henry Parrot. SiCE
Perdie, I said it not. *See* Perdye I saide Yt Not.
Perdita. Florence Earle Coates. AA
Perdita. John Swanwick Drennan. IrPN
Perdita. James Hebblethwaite. BoAu
Perdita's Garden. Shakespeare. *See* Flowers ("O Proserpina!").
Perdition catch my soul. Shakespeare. *Fr.* Othello, III, iii. LO
Perdye I Saide Yt Not. Sir Thomas Wyatt. PoEL-1
(Constancy.) OBSC
("Perdie, I said it not.") SiPS
Père Lalement. Marjorie Pickthall. BoCaPo; CaP; MM; OCL; PeCV; TwCaPo; TwCV
Père Sévère, Le. *Unknown, tr. fr. French by* Andrew Lang. AWP; JAWP; WBP
Peregrina. Eduard Mörike, *tr. fr. German by* Mabel Cotterell. AnGP
Peregrine. Elinor Wylie. HBMV; LEAP; TCPD
Peregrine White and Virginia Dare. Rosemary Benét *and* Stephen Vincent Benét. PoRh
Perennial fluctuation,/ Interior lift of the sea. Cuvier Light. Pat Wilson. AnNZ
Perennial May. T. A. Daly. CP; NV
Perette, her milk-jar cushioned on her crown. The Milkmaid and the Milk-Jar. La Fontaine. TrFP
Perfect. "Hugh MacDiarmid." NeBP
Perfect and endles circls are. *Unknown.* SeCSL
Perfect Bliss and Sole Felicity. Christopher Marlowe. *See* Nature That Framed Us of Four Elements.
Perfect Child, The. Molly Michaels. RIS

Perfect Child. The. Monica Shannon. BoChLi
Perfect Day, A. Carrie Jacobs Bond. PTA-1; TreF; WBLP
Perfect Gift, The. Julia Benson Parker. BePJ; PraP
Perfect Greyhound, The. *Unknown.* PCH
Perfect Guest, The. *Unknown.* DDA
Perfect Life, The. Jorge Carrera Andrade, *tr. fr. Spanish by* Dudley Fitts. AnCL; LiTW; WoL
Perfect Life, The. Ben Jonson. *See* It Is Not Growing like a Tree.
Perfect Life, The. Charles Francis Richardson. BePJ
Perfect little body, without fault or stain on thee. On a Dead Child. Robert Bridges. ChMo; CMP; EnLi-2 (1949 ed.); GTML; GTSL; LiTB; LiTG; LiTM (rev. ed.); OAEP; OBEV (1st ed.); OBMV; PoeT; PoP; ViBoPo
Perfect Love. Sana'i, *tr. fr. Persian by* A. J. Arberry. PeP
Perfect Reactionary, The. Hughes Mearns. SiTL; WhC
Perfect Round, The. Hilda Mary Hooke. CPG
Perfect Sailor, The. Charles Dibdin. *See* Tom Bowling.
Perfect shield bedecks some Thracian now, A. The Poet's Shield. Archilochus. LiTW; OxBG
Perfect Sign, The. Marion Couthouy Smith. BAP
Perfect Tribute, The. Shakespeare. *Fr.* Julius Caesar, V, v. MaRV
Perfect Woman. Wordsworth. *See* She Was a Phantom of Delight.
Perfection. Francis Carlin. FaFP; HBMV
Perfection. Ruth Scofield Fargo. OQP; QP-2
Perfection. Oliver St. John Gogarty. GTIV
Perfection. Jorge Guillén, *tr. fr. Spanish by* Eleanor L. Turnbull. AnSpL-2; CoSP
Perfection-bright figure, daily with me sojourning. Hymn to the Guardian Angel. J. Corson Miller. JKCP (1926 ed.)
Perfection in Small Things. Ben Jonson. *See* It Is Not Growing like a Tree.
Perfectly happy now, he looked at his estate. Voltaire at Ferney. W. H. Auden. GTBS-W; LiTM; NePA; PoE
Perforated Spirit, The. Morris Bishop. FiBHP
Performances, assortments, résumés. The Tunnel. Hart Crane. *Fr.* The Bridge. AmP; LiTA; LiTG; MAP; MoAB; MoAmPo; MoVE; NePA; OxBA; PoFS; TCPD
Performing Seal, The. Rachel Field. *Fr.* A Circus Garland. StVeCh; TiPo (1959 ed.); UTS
Perfume blows from the kingfisher. Song of Liang Chou. Ou-yang Hsiu. OnPC
Perfume is the same, the same the hue, The. The Avenue of Trees. Tsurayuki. OnPM
Perfume of plum upon the air. Basho, *tr. fr. Japanese by* Lois J. Erickson. SoLD
Perfume of the red water lilies, The. To the Tune, "Plum Blossoms Fall and Scatter." Li Ch'ing-chao. OnPC
Perfumes. Terence Tiller. FaBoMo
Pergamon city of the Phrygians. The Aftermath. Euripides. *Fr.* Iphigenia in Aulis. WaaP
Perhaps. W. H. Auden. MoPo; NePA; OAEP (2d ed.); ReMP
(O Love, the Interest Itself in Thoughtless Heaven.) CoEV
(Prologue: "O love, the interest itself in thoughtless Heaven.") FaBoMo; NAMP
Perhaps. Pringle Barret. PCH
Perhaps a Prayer. James Schevill. FiMAP
Perhaps from out the thousands passing by. At the Stevenson Fountain. Wallace Irwin. POT; PoTo
Perhaps he plays with cherubs now. A Phantasy of Heaven. Harry Kemp. HBMV; TSW; TSWC
Perhaps he'll tell you "Once I brought a cargo." A Low Trade. Herodas. OxBG
"Perhaps I may allow the dean." Swift. *Fr.* Verses on the Death of Dr. Swift. FaBoEn; OnYI
Perhaps if Death is kind, and there can be returning. If Death Is Kind. Sara Teasdale. ChMo; CMP
Perhaps, if you/ Are very good. Hob the Elf. Norman M. Johnson. BoTP
Perhaps in mercy is the future masked. George Henry Boker. *Fr.* Sonnets; a Sequence of Profane Love. MOAP
Perhaps it is no matter that you died. To Hasekawa. Walter Conrad Arensberg. HBV
Perhaps it is well now. We Who Are Left. George Whalley. CaP
"Perhaps, like thee, poor guest! in wanton pride." Homer. *Fr.* The Odyssey, XIX. GrPo
Perhaps, long hence, when I have pass'd away. She, to Him. Thomas Hardy. OBEV (new ed.)
Perhaps one would be better off. The Simple Life. Toyohiko Kagawa. SoLD
Perhaps she hears the breath of kneelers here. Requiem. Nathalia Crane. *Fr.* The Death of Poetry. MoAmPo (1942 ed.)
Perhaps she watches where a silver bay. La Madonna di Lorenzetti. John Williams Andrews. HBMV
Perhaps some child was here. Island Battlefield. C. R. Holmes. PtPa
Perhaps some needful service of the state. Epitaphs, II. Gabriello Chiabrera. AWP
Perhaps the Best Time. William Meredith. NePoEA
Perhaps there is no magic in this dull old world of ours. Music Magic. Edmund Leamy. JKCP
Perhaps they laughed at Dante in his youth. The New Life. Witter Bynner. LBMV; VOD
Perhaps too far in these considerate days. Non-Resistance. Oliver Wendell Holmes. TCAP
Perhaps we did not know how much of God. Phillips Brooks. Harriet Prescott Spofford. GA
Perhaps you expected a face that was free from tears. Narcissus. Paul Valéry. AWP
Perhaps you find the angel most improbable? Poem for a Christmas Broadcast. Anne Ridler. NeBP
Perhaps you may a-noticed I been soht o' solemn lately. I Didn't Like Him. Harry B. Smith. BOHV
Pericles. Cratinus, *tr. fr. Greek by* T. F. Higham. OxBG
Pericles. Eupolis, *tr. fr. Greek by* T. F. Higham. OxBG
Pericles, *sel.* Shakespeare.
"Sinful father, The/ Seem'd not to strike," *fr.* I, ii. PoFr
Pericles and Aspasia, *sels.* Walter Savage Landor.
Behold, O Aspasia! I Send You Verses, *fr.* CXC. LoBV
("Beauty! thou art a wanderer on the earth.") ViBoPo
Cleone to Aspasia, *fr.* CXIX. BPN
Copy of Verses sent by Cleone to Aspasia, A, *fr.* CXXXI. LoBV
Corinna, from Athens, to Tanagra, *fr.* XLIV. OBEV (new ed.); OBVV
(Corinna to Tanagra.) OBRV; ViBoPo, *abr.*
(Corinna to Tanagra from Athens.) BPN; TOP
Death of Artemidora, The, *fr.* LXXXV. BEL; BPN; EnRP; EPN; ERP; InP; SeCeV; VA
("Artemidora! Gods invisible.") ViBoPo
Dirce, *fr.* CCXXX. AnFE; AWP; BCEP; BLV; BoLiVe; BPN; CoEV; EnRP; EV-4; ExPo; FaBoEn; InPo; JAWP; LEAP; LiA; LiTB; LoBV; OAEP; OBEV; OBRV; PoEL-4; PoRA; SeCeV; TOP; TrGrPo; VA; ViBoPo; WBP; WHA; WhC
(Epigram: Stand Close Around, Ye Stygian Set.) AEV
(Lyrics and Epigrams, IV.) CBOV
(Stand Close Around.) ChTr
("Stand close around, ye Stygian set.") EG; GTBS-D
Little Aglae, *fr.* CXIII. BPN; VA
Myrtis, *fr.* LIII. OBRV; VA
Sappho to Hesperus, *after the Greek of* Sappho, *fr.* CL. BPN
Pericles, Prince of Tyre. Shakespeare. *See* Pericles.
Perigoo's Horse. *At. to* George Calhoun *and to* John Calhoun. ShS
Perigot and Willie's [*or* Willy's] Roundelay. Spenser. *Fr.* The Shepheardes Calender: August. ElSeCe; EV-1
(It Fell upon a Holy Eve.) InvP; PoE
(Perigot and Willye.) LoBV
(Roundelay, A: "It fell upon a holy eve.") ElL
Perikeiromene, *sel.* Menander, *tr. fr. Greek.*
Advice to a Lover, *tr. by.* Gilbert Highet. OxBG
(Plight of a Forsaken Lover, *tr. by* Francis G. Allinson.) GrR
Perilla! to thy fates resign'd. A Copy of Verses sent by Cleone to Aspasia. Walter Savage Landor. *Fr.* Pericles and Aspasia. LoBV
Perilous Life, A ("A perilous life, and hard"). *Unknown.* EtS
Perilous life, and sad as lite may be, A. The Fisherman. "Barry Cornwall." CG
Perilous Light, The. Eva Gore-Booth. NLK
Perils and dangers of the voyage past, The. Jack Robinson. Thomas Hudson. SG
Perils of Invisibility, The. W. S. Gilbert. StPo
Perils of Obesity, The. Harry Graham. FiBHP
Perils of Thinking, The. Mrs. Edward Craster. *See* Centipede Was Happy Quite, A.
Perimedes, *sels.* Robert Greene.
Coridon and Phillis. OBSC
(Phillis and Corydon.) HBV
Fair Is My Love for April in [*or* Is *or* April's in] Her Face. ElSeCe; HBV; ReIE; ViBoPo
(Fair Is My Love.) ElL
Obscure and Dark Is All the Gloomy Air. ReIE
Period of Mourning, The, *sel.* Henry Peacham.
Nuptial Hymn. ElL
Perished. Mary Louise Ritter. LPS-1
Periwinkle Girl, The. W. S. Gilbert. MBP
Perjured, The. Albert E. Johnson. QS
Perle plesaunt[e] to prynces paye. The Pearl. *Unknown.* EPP; NBE
Permanence. Francis Meynell. HBV; LoPo, *diff.;* MBP; MoBrPo (1942 ed.)
Permanence of the Young Men, The. William Soutar. NeBP
Permanency of Life, The. William Drummond of Hawthornden. BSV
Permit Me Voyage. James Agee. MAP; MoAmPo; TriL
Pernambuco in May. Theodore Goodridge Roberts. BoCaPo (1948 ed.)
Pernicious Weed. William Cowper. InMe; WhC

Perpetual Christmas. Arthur Gordon Field. PGD
Perpetual Journey, The. Walt Whitman. *See* I Tramp a Perpetual Journey.
Perpetual Motion. Gerardo Diego, *tr. fr. Spanish by* Eleanor L. Turnbull. CoSP
Perpetual night and endless sleep. Nox Est Perpetua. Marion Lochhead. LO
Perpetual Vows. Sister Mary Angelita. PraNu
Perpetuum Mobile. Edith Sitwell. BMEP; HBMV
Perplex'd with trifles thro' the vale of life. A Nut, a World, a Squirrel, and a King. Charles Churchill. *Fr.* Night; an Epistle to Robert Lloyd. BeR
Perplext in faith, but pure in deeds. A Stronger Faith. Tennyson. *Fr.* In Memoriam A. H. H., XCVI. MaRV
Perplext no more with Human or Divine. The Minister of Wine. Omar Khayyám, *tr. by* Edward Fitzgerald. *Fr.* The Rubáiyát. OnPM
Perry Zoll. Edgar Lee Masters. *Fr.* Spoon River Anthology. CrMA; NP
Perry's Victory. *Unknown.* PAH
Perry's Victory—a Song. *Unknown.* PAH
(Perry's Victory.) GA
Perry's Victory on Lake Erie. James Gates Percival. PaA; PAP
Persae. Aeschylus. *See* Persians.
Persae, *sels.* Timotheus, *tr. fr. Greek.*
"Bold as thou art, ere now thou hast had thy boisterous throat," *pr. tr. by* R. C. Jebb. GrPo
Sea-Fight, A, *tr. by* Gilbert Highet. OxBG
Persè owt of Northombarlande, The. *See* Percy out of Northumberland, The.
Persephone (Singing). Louis V. Ledoux. BAP
Persephone the Queen. Robert Morse. MuM
Perseus. Louis MacNeice. CoBMV; GTBS-W; LiTM; ReMP
Perseverance. R. S. S. Andros. LPS-2
Perseverance. Leonardo da Vinci, *tr. fr. Italian by* William W. Story. LPS-3
Perseverance; or, Half a Coronet, *sel.* A. P. Herbert. Finale. InMe
Pershing at the Tomb of Lafayette. Amelia Josephine Burr. PAH
Persia Prostrated. Aeschylus, *tr. fr. Greek by* Gilbert Murray. *Fr.* Persians. GrR
(Xerxes Defeated, *tr. by* G. M. Cookson.) OxBG
Persian Eclogues, *sel.* William Collins.
Hassan; or, The Camel Driver, Eclogue II. EV-3
(Persian Eclogues—Eclogue the Second.) CEP
Persian fable, A, says; One day. Influence. *Unknown.* MaRV
Persian Fopperies ("Persicos odi"). Horace, *tr. fr. Latin by* William Cowper. Odes, I, 38. AWP; JAWP; WBP; WoL
(Frippery, *tr. by* L. R. Lind.) LiTW
(I Hate Their Empty Shows, *tr. by* William Cowper.) OnPM
(Persian Luxury, *tr. by* William Cowper.) RoL
(Persian Pomp, *tr. by* William Cowper.) EnLi-1
(Persicos Odi, *par. by* Franklin P. Adams.) HBMV; PoeMoYo
(Simplicity, *diff. par. by* Franklin P. Adams.) PoeMoYo
(To His Cup-Bearer, *tr. by* Sir Theodore Martin.) OuHeWo
Persian galleys plumed with warriors, The. Before Salamis. William Bedell Stanford. NeIP
Persian Luxury. Horace. *See* Persian Fopperies.
Persian Maxim ("The baneful company of friends I fear"). Sadi, *tr. fr. Persian by* L. Cranmer-Byng. BoFr
Persian Miniature. William Jay Smith. MoVE
Persian penman named Aziz, A. The Careful Penman. *Unknown.* BOHV
Persian Pomp. Horace. *See* Persian Fopperies.
Persian Song, A. Hafiz, *tr. fr. Persian by* Sir William Jones. AWP; OBEC; OuHeWo; PeP
(Persian Song of Hafiz, A.) PrWP
Persian Version, The. Robert Graves. LiTB; LiTM (rev. ed.); SiTL
Persians, *sels.* Aeschylus, *tr. fr. Greek.*
Ghost of Dareius [*or* Darius], The. GrR, *tr. by* Lewis Campbell; LiA, *longer sel., tr. by* Herbert Weir Smyth
"Morn, all beauteous to behold, The, *tr. by* Robert Potter. GrPo
Persia Prostrated, *tr. by* Gilbert Murray. GrR
(Xerxes Defeated, *tr. by* G. M. Cookson.) OxBG
Salamis, *tr. by* G. M. Cookson. OxBG; WaaP, *shorter sel.*
(Battle of Salamis, The, *tr. by* Gilbert Murray.) PoFr
(Victory at Salamis, *tr. by* Gilbert Murray.) GrR
Persia's Crew, The, *with music. Unknown.* SoAmSa
Persia's pomp, my boy, I hate. To His Cup-Bearer. Horace, *tr. by* Sir Theodore Martin. OuHeWo
Persicos Odi. Franklin P. Adams, *after* Horace. *See* Persian Fopperies.
Persicos Odi. Charles Edmund Merrill, Jr. AA
Persicos Odi. Thackeray. *See* Ad Ministram.
Persimmon, lo, The! To Her Husband, at the Wedding. Kaga no Chiyo. LiTW
Persistence. Walter Savage Landor. *See* My Hopes Retire.
Persistency of Poetry. Matthew Arnold. PoVP
Persistent Explorer. John Crowe Ransom. OxBA
Person, The, *sel.* Thomas Traherne.
"Naked things, The." MeRV
Person had become a master in the art of wrestling, A. The Wrestler. Sadi. *Fr.* The Gulistan. OuHeWo
Person is always self-conscious about his head, A. Thoughts on One's Head. William Meredith. SiTL
Personal. Langston Hughes. PoNe
Personal History; for My Son. Ruthven Todd. NeBP
Personal Poem. Kendrick Smithyman. AnNZ
Personal Talk. Wordsworth. BEL; BPN; EM-2; EmBrPo; EnRP; EPN; EPP; ERP; GEPC; InPo; PeBoSo
Sels.
Books a Substantial World, *fr.* III *and* IV. MOB
"I am not one who much or oft delight," I. MyFE
Wings Have We, III. CBOV
Personal Valour. V. Sackville-West. NeTW
Personality. Carl Sandburg. CrMA
Personally, I don't care whether a detective-story writer was educated in night school or day school. Don't Guess, Let Me Tell You. Ogden Nash. SiTL
Personified Sentimental, The. Bret Harte. NA
Perspective. Margaret Avison. BoCaPo (1948 ed.); PeCV
Perspective never withers from their eyes. Quaker Hill. Hart Crane. *Fr.* The Bridge. LiTA; LiTM (rev. ed.)
Perspective of Co-ordination. Arthur Davison Ficke. NP
Perspectives Are Precipices. John Peale Bishop. LiTA; LiTM; MoVE; NePA
Persuasion. Wordsworth. Ecclesiastical Sonnets, XVI. MaRV; OQP; QP-2
Persuasion's Rose. Meleager, *tr. fr. Greek by* Robert Allason Furness. GrR
(Love in Spring.) OxBG
Persuasions to Joy [a Song]. Thomas Carew. ElSeCe; EnLi-1; OBEV; RiBV
(Persuasions to Enjoy.) EPS; HBV; SeCL
(Perswasions to Enjoy.) MePo; SeCV-1
(Song: Perswasions to Enjoy.) BrBE
Persuasions to Love. Thomas Carew. LiTL
"For that lovely face will fail," *sel.* ViBoPo
Pert as any young page-boy, the small black cat. Le Petit Chat. Edmond Rostand. PoC
Perturbation at Dawn. Ibn Maatuk, *tr. fr. Arabic by* E. Powys Mathers. LiTW
Perugia. Amelia Josephine Burr. HBV
Perverse habit of cat-goddesses, A. Cat-Goddesses. Robert Graves. MoVE
Pesach Has Come to the Ghetto Again. Binem Heller, *tr. fr. Yiddish by* Max Rosenfeld. TrJP
Pescadero Pebbles. Charles Augustus Keeler. BAP
Peschiera. Arthur Hugh Clough. BPN; HBV; PoVP; VA; ViPo; VLEP
Pesci Misti. L. Aaronson. FaBoTw
Pessimism. Newton Mackintosh. BOHV
Pessimist, The. Ben King. ALV; BLPA; BOHV; FaFP; InMe; LiTG; NA; NeHB; WaKn
Pessimist, The. *Unknown.* PoToHe (new ed.)
Pessimist and Optimist. Thomas Bailey Aldrich. AnNe; PIAE; TOP
Pessimist's a cheerless man, The. The Pessimist. *Unknown.* PoToHe (new ed.)
Pet Crane, A. *Unknown, tr. fr. Old Irish by* Myles Dillon. AnIL
Pet Lamb, The. Wordsworth. OTPC; PRWS; SAS
Pet Name, The. Elizabeth Barrett Browning. HBV; LPS-1
Pet was never mourned as you. Last Words to a Dumb Friend. Thomas Hardy. PoC; PoFS; OAEP (2d ed.)
Petals of the bignonia, The. The Flowers of the Bignonia. *Unknown.* WhP
Pete at the Seashore. Don Marquis. AlBD
Peter. Laura Benét. HBMV
Peter. Marianne Moore. AnAmPo; LA; OxBA
Peter and James and John. Good Friday. Lizette Woodworth Reese. OQP; QP-1; QP-2
Peter and John. Elinor Wylie. HBMV; MaC; MAP; MoAB; MoAmPo; StJW
Peter and Michael were two little menikin. *Unknown.* BoTP
Peter and Polly. Esther Antin. *Fr.* On Our Farm. RIS
Peter at Fourteen. Constance Carrier. NePoAm
Peter at His Mirror. John Holmes. CAG
Peter Bell, *sels.* Wordsworth.
Among the Stars. GoTP
Crescent Boat, The. ThWaDe
Peter Bell; a Lyrical Ballad. John Hamilton Reynolds. OBRV
Peter Bell the Third, *sel.* Shelley.
"Among the guests who often stayed," Part the Fifth. ChER
Peter Cooper. Joaquin Miller. AA
Peter denied, but Jesus did not scold. The Focus of That Face. Edwin McNeill Poteat. ChIP
Peter Emberley, 3 *vers., with music.* John Calhoun. ShS

Peter, Go Ring Dem Bells, *with music. Unknown.* BoAN-1
Peter Gray, *with music. Unknown.* OuSiCo
Peter Grimes. George Crabbe. The Borough, Letter XXII. EnRP; PoEL-4
Sels.
"Alas, for Peter not a helping hand," *br. sel.* OBRV
Sea Marsh. RO
"Thus by himself compell'd to live each day." FaBoEn; SeCePo
(Foreshore, The.) CoEV
Peter hath lost his purse, but will conceal it. Henry Parrot. TuPP
Peter, in what pools of fear. Peter at His Mirror. John Holmes. CAG
Peter is a funny cat. Peter and Polly. Esther Antin. *Fr.* On Our Farm. RIS
Peter meanwhile perceived the time draw nigh. The Bandit Peter Mancino's Death. *Unknown.* CAW
Peter of the brothers three. Peter. Laura Benét. HBMV
Peter Ottawa, *sel.* Edward William Thomson.
"Count up the dead by fever, shot and shell." CPG
Peter Parasol. Wallace Stevens. NP
Peter, Peter, along the ground. Four Sides to a House. Amy Lowell. ChMo; CMP; MOAP; NP; PoRA
Peter, Peter, pumpkin-eater. Mother Goose. BoChLi; BoN; FaBoBe; FaFP; HBV; HBVY; OTPC; OxNR; PCH; PPL; RIS; SiTL; TiPo (1959 ed.)
Peter Piper picked a peck of pickled [*or* pickling] pepper[s]. Mother Goose. BoChLi; FaBoBe; FaFP; FaPON; HBV; HBVY; OTPC; OxNR; RIS; SiTL; StVeCh; TiPo (1959 ed.); TreFS
Peter Quince at the Clavier. Wallace Stevens. AmPP (4th ed.); AnFE; AnNE; APA; ATP (1953 ed.); BLV; CoAnAm; CoBMV; CoV; ExPo; HBMV; InPo; LiTM; MAP; MAPA; MM; MoAB; MoAmPo; MOAP; NAMP; NP; OxBA; PreP; ReaPo; ReMP; RiBV; TCPD; TrGrPo; TwAmPo; UnPo (3d ed.); ViBoPo; WoL
Peter Simson's Farm. Edward Dyson. BoAu
Peter Stuyvesant's New Year's Call. Edmund Clarence Stedman. PaA; PAH
Peter was a fisher boy. The First Christmas. Keith Preston. DDA
Peter White will never [*or* ne'er] go right. Mother Goose. OTPC; OxBoLi; OxNR; PPL; RIS
Pete's Holiday. Don Marquis. AlBD
Pete's Theology. Don Marquis. AlBD
Petit Chat, Le. Edmond Rostand, *tr. fr. French by* "Seumas O'Sullivan." PoC
Petit Mari, Le, *with music. Unknown.* OuSiCo
Petit Testament, Le. Villon, *tr. fr. French.*
(Lesser Testament, The, *abr., tr. by* John Payne.) WoL
(Little Testament, The, *tr. by* John Heron Lepper.) OuHeWo
Christmas Time, *br. sel., tr. by* John Payne. LiA
Petit, the Poet. Edgar Lee Masters. *Fr.* Spoon River Anthology. AnFE; APA; ChMo; CMP; CoAnAm; InPo; LaNeLa; LoGBV; MAP; MoAmPo; MoVE; NeMA; OxBA
Petite Madame, your smiling face. Porcelaine de Saxe. Virginia Lyne Tunstall. TBM
Petite Ste. Rosalie. S. Frances Harrison. *Fr.* Down the River. BoCaPo (1943 ed.); CPG
Petition. Abur Rabi, *tr. fr. Arabic by* A. J. Arberry. MooP
Petition, A. Thomas Bailey Aldrich. AA
Petition. W. H. Auden. *See* Sir, No Man's Enemy.
Petition. John Drinkwater. TrPWD
Petition, The. James Russell Lowell. PR
Petition. Clinton Scollard. BAP; MaRV
Petition. Eleanor Slater. TrPWD
Petition, A. Robert Ernest Vernède. InP
Petition for a Miracle. David Morton. *Fr.* Boke of Two Ladies. ISi
Petition for an Absolute Retreat, The. Countess of Winchilsea. BLV; OBEC, *abr.*; PoEL-3
"Give me, O indulgent fate!" *sel.* TrGrPo
Petition of the Grey Horse, Auld Dunbar, The. William Dunbar. EBSV
Petition of Tom Dermody to the Three Fates in Council Sitting, The. Thomas Dermody. AnIV
Petition of Youth before Battle. John Bunker. CAW
Petition to Have Her Leave to Die. "A. W." OBSC
(Give Me Leave.) TrGrPo
("When will the fountain of my tears be dry.") EG
Petition to Time, A. "Barry Cornwall." BCEP; VA
Petitions of Saint Augustine. *Unknown.* WHL
Petitions of the Maids of New-York. *Unknown.* LauV
Petra. John William Burgon. *See* Pedra.
Petrarch. Giosuè Carducci, *tr. fr. Italian by* William Dudley Foulke. AWP
Petrel nests far out on the shore, The. The Stormy Petrel. Ibsen. AnNoLy
Petrified Fern, The. Mary Lydia Bolles Branch. AA; CV; LPS-3; PTA-2
Petrillo, *parody.* "Gilbertulus." WhC

Petron, the Desert Father. Lawrence Durrell. *Fr.* Eight Aspects of Melissa. NeBP
Petronius Arbiter. *Tr. fr. Latin by* Helen Waddell. DiM
Pets, The. Robert Farren. CoBE; OxBI
Pet's Punishment. Joseph Ashby-Sterry. BOHV
Pettitoes are little feet, The. *Unknown.* OxNR
Petty Officers' Mess, The. Roy Fuller. ChMP
Petty sneaking knave I knew, A. Cromek. Blake. FiBHP; RO
Petunias in mass formation. Giardino Pubblico. Sir Osbert Sitwell. ChMP
Pew, pew. The Milk-white Dove. *Unknown.* ChTr
Pewee [*or* Peewee], The. John Townsend Trowbridge. HBV; OTPC; SN
Peyote Poem, *sel.* Michael McClure.
"Clear—the senses bright—sitting in the black chair—Rocker—," I. NeAP
Phaeacian Nights—Demodocus. Homer. *See* Demodocus Sings a Song of Troy.
Phaedra Declares Her Love for Her Stepson. Racine, *tr. fr. French by* Robert Henderson. *Fr.* Phèdre, II, v. LiA
Phaedra Jealous. Racine, *tr. fr. French by* Robert Henderson. *Fr.* Phèdre, IV, vi. LiA
Phaenomena, *sels.* Aratus, *tr. fr. Greek.*
"Below the Waggoner's feet," *tr. by* E. Poste. GrPo
"Let us begin with Zeus, the power we mortals never leave," *tr. by* E. Poste. GrPo
Proem, *tr. by* George Allen. OxBG
Signs of Rain, *tr. by* F. L. Lucas. GrPE
When Justice Dwelt on Earth, *tr. by* George Allen. OxBG
Phaleuciacs I: "Time nor place did I want; what held me tongue-tide?" *Unknown.* SiCE
Phaleuciacs II: "Wisdom warns me to shun that once I sought for." *Unknown.* SiCE
Phallic Symbol, The. Nicholas Moore. NeBP
Phanopoeia, *sel.* Ezra Pound.
Rose White, Yellow, Silver. CoV
Phantasmagoria, *sel.* "Lewis Carroll."
Ghost's Confession, The, *fr.* IV. HOAH
Phantasmion, *sels.* Sara Coleridge.
He Came Unlook'd For. OBRV; VA
(Song: "He came unlook'd for, undesir'd.") OBVV
I Was a Brook. OBRV
O Sleep, My Babe. BOL; MotAn; OBEV (1st ed.); OBRV
One Face Alone. VA
Phantastes, *sel.* George Macdonald.
"Oh, well for him who breaks his dream," *fr. ch.* 21. UnW
Phantasus ("Its roof among the stars projected"). Arno Holz, *tr. fr. German by* Ludwig Lewisohn. AWP; JAWP; WBP
Phantasus, I–8 ("On a mountain of sugar-candy"). Arno Holz, *tr. fr. German by* Babette Deutsch *and* Avrahm Yarmolinsky. LiTW
Phantasus, VI–14 ("I wish you were real!"). Arno Holz, *tr. fr. German by* Babette Deutsch *and* Avrahm Yarmolinsky. LiTW
Phantasy ("All is phantom that we mid fare"). *Unknown.* ACP
Phantasy, A ("Oh, the joy of a woolless pate"). *Unknown.* CAG
Phantasy of Heaven, A. Harry Kemp. HBMV; TSW; TSWC
Phantasy of the Sea, A. Antoinette Miller. CAG
Phantom. Samuel Taylor Coleridge. DaM; LO; NBE; PoEL-4; TriL; UnW
Phantom, The Salvador Díaz Mirón, *tr. fr. Spanish by* Samuel Beckett. AnMP
Phantom Bark, The. Hart Crane. ChMo
Phantom Horsewoman, The. Thomas Hardy. LO; PoEL-5
Phantom Host, The. Peronnean D. Hay. BIG
Phantom Light of the Baie des Chaleurs, The. Arthur Wentworth Hamilton Eaton. CaP; CPG; OCL; PoMS
Phantom-Lover, The. Thomas Lovell Beddoes. *See* Phantom-Wooer, The.
Phantom Mail Coach, The. L. O. Welcome. BoHiPo; PoMS
Phantom or Fact. Samuel Taylor Coleridge. BPN; EmBrPo; EnRP
Phantom Rose, The. Mary Sinton Leitch. MuM
Phantom Ship, The. J. W. De Forest. EtS
Phantom Ship, The. Longfellow. DaM; EtS
Phantom-Wooer, The. Thomas Lovell Beddoes. DaM; EnRP; ERP; NBE; OBRV; TrGrPo; ViBoPo
(Phantom-Lover, The.) LO
"Young soul, put off your flesh, and come," *sel.* PoD
Phantoms. Thomas Ashe. VA
Phantoms. Frances Kiely. CAG
Phantoms. Harry McGuire. CAW
Phantoms All. Harriet Prescott Spofford. AA; PFY
Phantoms and Spring. Gunnar Reiss-Andersen, *tr. fr. Norwegian by* Charles W. Stork. AnNoLy
Phaon to Sappho. Marian Osborne. CPG
Pharaoh Cheops lived to die, The. Cheops. James Schevill. FiMAP
Pharaoh's Army Got Drownded, *with music. Unknown.* AS

Pharmaceutria, The. Theocritus. *See* Incantation, The.
Pharonnida, *sel.* William Chamberlayne.
"Strong Prophetick dream, A." NBE
Pharsalia, *sels.* Lucan, *tr. fr. Latin.*
Cato's Address to His Troops in Lybia, *fr.* IX, *tr. by* Nicholas Rowe. OBEC
Pompey and Cornelia, *fr.* V, *tr. by* Nicholas Rowe. OBEC
Portents, The, *fr.* I, *tr. by* Christopher Marlowe. OBSC
Stoic's Wedding, The, *fr.* II, *tr. by* Gilbert Highet. LaP
"Wars worse then civil on Thessalian plains," *fr.* I, *tr. by* Christopher Marlowe. ReIE
Phases of the Moon. Robert Browning. *Fr.* One Word More. ChTr
Pheasant, The. Robert P. Tristram Coffin. TiPo
Pheasant. Sidney Keyes. HaMV
Pheasant, The. Pope. *Fr.* Windsor Forest. GoTP
(Flames of Death, The.) BeR
("See! from the brake the whirring pheasant springs.") FaBoEn; PoEL-3
Pheasant of the mountain, The. Kakinomoto no Hitomaro, *tr. fr. Japanese by* Kenneth Rexroth. OnPJ
Phèdre, *sels.* Racine, *tr. fr. French.*
Conquest of Love, The, *tr. by* Lacy Lockert. LiTW
Phaedra Declares Her Love for Her Stepson, *fr.* II, v. *tr. by* Robert Henderson. LiA
Phaedra Jealous, *fr.* IV, vi, *tr. by* Robert Henderson. LiA
Pheidippides. Robert Browning. MW; PoVP
Phenix, The. George Darley. *See* Phoenix, The.
Phenomena. Robinson Jeffers. OxBA
Phil, the Black Persian. Herbert Palmer. PoC
Philaenion is dark and small. Philodemus, *tr. fr. Greek by* Elsie Spoerl. GrPo
Philaenis weeps with just one eye. An Explanation. Martial. RoL
Philander was a jolly swain. A Jolly Swain. Aphra Behn. *Fr.* The City Heiress; or, Sir Timothy Treat-All. DiM
Philanderer, The. Moses Mendes. *Fr.* The Chaplet. TrJP
Philanderer, The. *Unknown, tr. fr. Chinese by* Henry H. Hart. *Fr.* Shi King. PoHN
Philander's a king, a dandy king. Phil, the Black Persian. Herbert Palmer. PoC
Philander's Song. Sir Charles G. D. Roberts. BoCaPo (1948 ed.)
Philaret on Willy cals. The Fourth Eglogue. George Wither. *Fr.* The Shepherd's Hunting. SeCV-1
Philarete Praises Poetry. George Wither. *Fr.* The Shepherd's Hunting. OBS
("Seest thou not in clearest dayes," *sl. longer.*) EPS
Philemon and Baucis. Ovid. *See* Baucis and Philemon.
Philip Dagg. W. W. Gibson. *Fr.* Casualties. VOD
Philip, foozling with his cleek. Some Ruthless Rhymes, VII. Harry Graham. CenHV
Philip, King of Macedon. Alcaeus of Messene, *tr. fr. Greek by* Sir William Marris. OxBG
Philip Massinger. Swinburne. *Fr.* Sonnets on English Dramatic Poets (1590-1650). EmBrPo; PtP; VLEP
Philip My King. Dinah Maria Mulock Craik. HBV; LPS-1; VA
Philip Sparrow. John Skelton. *See* Phyllyp Sparowe.
Philip the Fourth. Manuel Machado, *tr. fr. Spanish by* Beatrice Gilman Proske. AnSpL-2
Philip van Artevelde, *sels.* Sir Henry Taylor.
Elena's Song. LEAP; OBEV; OBRV; OBVV
(Song: "Quoth tongue of neither maid nor wife.") VA
Heart-Rest. LPS-1
John of Launoy. VA
Philip van Artevelde. VA
Revolutions. PoFr; VA
Song: "Down lay in a nook my lady's brach." VA
Wife, A. LPS-1
Philippians, *sel.* Bible, *N.T.*
Think on These Things, IV: 8. GrCo-1
("Whatsoever things are true.") TiPo (1952 ed.)
Philippine Madonna. Louise Crenshaw Ray. ISi
Philippines were drenched in sun, The. Portrait Philippines. Alfred A. Duckett. PoNe
Philip's Nicoteles, a twelve-year lad. Nicoteles. Callimachus. OxBG
Philips, whose touch harmonious could remove. *See* Phillips! whose touch harmonious . . .
Philira. Sir John Vanbrugh. *Fr.* The Provoked Wife. SeCL
(Song: "Fly, fly, you happy shepherds, fly.") SeEP
Philistines are forming fours, The. The War with the Weeds. Keith Sinclair. AnNZ
Phillada Flouts Me. *Unknown.* BCEP; BLV, *abr.;* BrBE; LEAP; OBEV; TrGrPo; ViBoPo
(Disdainful Shepherdess, The.) OBSC
(Oh, What a Plague Is Love!) InvP
(Phillida Flouts Me.) CoMu; HBV; ReEn
(Phyllida Flouts Me.) CBOV; ElL; ElSeCe; EM-1
Phillida and Coridon. Nicholas Breton. *See* Phyllida and Corydon ("In the merry month of May").
Phillida Flouts Me. *Unknown.* *See* Phillada Flouts Me.
Phillida [*or* Phyllida] was a fair [*or* fayer] maid. Harpalus' Complaint [of Phillida's Love]. *Unknown.* OBSC; TuPP; ViBoPo
Phillida's Love-Call to Her Corydon, and His Replying. *Unknown.* *See* Phyllida's Love-Call to Her Corydon . . .
Phillips Brooks. John Hall Ingham. GA
Phillips Brooks. Harriet Prescott Spofford. GA
Phillips! [*or* Philips] whose touch harmonious could remove. An Epitaph on [*or* upon the Celebrated] Claudy Phillips, a Musician. Samuel Johnson. OBEC; TriL; UnS
Phillis. Thomas Lodge. *See* Phyllis.
Phillis and Amintas. *Unknown.* *See* Coy Shepherdess, The.
Phillis and Corydon. Arthur Colton. HBV; PR
Phillis and Corydon. Robert Greene. *See* Coridon and Phillis.
Phillis for Shame Let Us Improve. Charles Sackville. *See* Song: "Phyllis, for shame, let us improve."
Phillis Is My Only Joy. Sir Charles Sedley. *See* Phyllis Is My Only Joy.
Phillis kept sheep along the western plains. Coridon and Phillis [*or* Phillis and Corydon]. Robert Greene. *Fr.* Perimedes. HBV; OBSC
Phillis Knotting. Sir Charles Sedley. *See* Hears Not My Phyllis.
Phillis, let's shun the common fate. Song. Sir Charles Sedley. LO; SeCV-2
Phillis on the new made hay. The Coy Shepherdess; or, Phillis and Amintas. *Unknown.* CoMu
Phillis; or, The Progress of Love. Swift. ExPo; PoEL-3
(Progress of Love, The.) BeR
Phillis the Fair. Nicholas Breton. *See* Pastoral of Phillis and Corydon, A.
Phillis the Fair. Burns. EV-3
Phillis took a red rose from the tangles of her hair. Phillis and Corydon. Arthur Colton. HBV; PR
Phillis, why should we delay. To Phillis. Edmund Waller. CEP; OAEP
Phillis's Age. Matthew Prior. *See* Phyllis's Age.
Philo begat Diophon, who was crowned at the Isthmus and Delphi. A Winner of the Pentathlon. Simonides. OxBG
Philo is richly 'rayed, and beareth high. In Philonem. Thomas Bastard. SiCE
Philo, with twelve years' study, hath been griev'd. An Obscure Writer. John Donne. ReIE
Philocles. Leonidas of Tarentum, *tr. fr. Greek by* F. A. Wright. AWP
Philoctetes, *sel.* Aeschylus, *tr. fr. Greek by* C. M. Bowra.
Philoctetes Calls for Death. OxBG
Philoctetes, *sel.* Lord De Tabley.
Chorus: "In wonder and time-mists." PoVP
Philoctetes. Thomas Russell. *See* Sonnet: Suppos'd to Be Written at Lemnos.
Philoctetes, *sels.* Sophocles, *tr. fr. Greek.*
Castaway, The, *tr. by* Robert Whitelaw. GrR
(Philoctetes Deserted, *tr. by* C. M. Bowra.) OxBG
Embittered Youth, *tr. by* Robert Whitelaw. GrR
Scruple, *tr. by* Lewis Campbell. GrR
Sleep! *tr. by* Robert Whitelaw. GrR
Stolen Bow, The, *tr. by* C. M. Bowra. OxBG
(Philoctetes Robbed of His Bow, *tr. by* Sir George Young.) GrR
"Thou fire, thou utter monster, thou hateful masterpiece of subtle villainy," *pr. tr. by* R. C. Jebb. GrPo
Philoctetes Calls for Death. Aeschylus, *tr. fr. Greek by* C. M. Bowra. *Fr.* Philoctetes. OxBG
Philomel. Richard Barnfield. *See* Nightingale, The.
Philomel. Paul Fort, *tr. fr. French by* James Elroy Flecker. MiFP
Philomel in London. Sir Edmund Gosse. PoeT
Philomel to Corydon. William Young. AA
Philomela. Matthew Arnold. AtBAP; BEL; BLA; BLV; BMEP; BoLiVe; BPN; CBOV; EM-2; EmBrPo; EnL; EnLi-2; EnLit; EPP; GEPC; GTBS; GTBS-D; GTSE; GTSL; HBV; InP; LPS-2; MaPo; MCCG; OAEP; OBEV; PIR; PoFS; PoVP; PreP; ReaPo; SeCeV; SN; TCEP; TOP; TwCrTr; TyEnPo; UnPo (1st ed.); VA; ViPo; ViPP; VLEP; WHA
Philomela. John Crowe Ransom. AmP; ChTr; MoVE; OnAP; OxBA; PoFS
Philomela. Sir Philip Sidney. *See* Nightingale, The.
Philomela, the Lady Fitzwater's Nightingale, *sels.* Robert Greene.
Philomela's Ode That She Sung in Her Arbor. ElSeCe; ReIE; SiCE; TuPP
(Philomela's Ode [in Her Arbour].) EPP; OBSC
("Sitting by a river's side.") LO
Philomela's Second Ode. OBSC; SiCE
Philon [the Shepherd]. *Unknown.* *See* Faithless Shepherdess, The.
Philosopher, A. John Kendrick Bangs. HBV; ShGoBo
Philosopher, The. Emily Brontë. EmBrPo; VLEP
"'Oh, for the time when I shall sleep,'" *sel.* ATP; BLV; PoD
Philosopher, A. Sam Walter Foss. BOHV
Philosopher, The. Edna St. Vincent Millay. ChMo; CMP; PR; TOP

Philosopher, The. Po Chü-i. *See* Lao-tzu.
Philosopher, The. Sara Teasdale. PoToHe
Philosopher and comrade, not for thee. A Cat. Jules Lemaitre. CIV
Philosopher and Her Father, The. Shirley Brooks. CenHV
Philosopher and the Birds, The. Richard Murphy PoN
Philosopher and the Lover, The; to a Mistress Dying. Sir William Davenant. *See* To a Mistress Dying.
Philosopher called Stesichore, A. Lucian, *tr. fr. Greek by* Norman Douglas. GrPo
Philosopher to His Mistress, The ("Because thou canst not see"). Robert Bridges. ChMo; CMP; LiTM (rev. ed.); OAEP; PoEL-5; POTT; VLEP
Philosopher Toad, The. Rebecca S. Nichols. LPS-2
Philosopher, whom dost thou most affect. Epigram. Richard Garnett. HBV
Philosophers, The. Po Chü-i. *See* Chuang-tzu, the Monist *and* Lao-tzu.
Philosophers, The. Schiller. PoP
Philosophers devoid of reason find. The Great Idealist. Jami. LiTW; OnPM
Philosopher's Devotion, The. Henry More. SeCL
Philosopher's Garden. John Oxenham. PoMa
Philosophers have measur'd mountains. The Agonie. George Herbert. MePo; NBE
Philosopher's Scales, The. Jane Taylor. BCEP; HBV; LPS-3
Philosophic Advice. *Unknown. See* Arabian Proverb.
Philosophic Apology, The. Samuel Greenberg. MoPo; NePA
Philosophic butterfly, The. Hotel of Sparks. André Breton. MiCF
Philosophic Flight, The. Giordano Bruno. *See* Sonnet: Philosophic Flight, The.
Philosophical Poem on Cats, A. Fillmore Hyde. CIV
Philosophy. John Kendrick Bangs. PoToHe (new ed.)
Philosophy. Heine, *tr. fr. German by* James Thomson. OnPM
(Zu fragmentarisch ist Welt und Leben, *tr. by* Charles G. Leland.) AWP
Philosophy. Milton. *Fr.* Comus. BCEP
Philosophy. Dorothy Parker. InMe
. . . Philosophy, baptiz'd/ In the pure fountain of eternal love. Science and Prayer. William Cowper. *Fr.* The Task, III. RO
Philosophy shows us 'twixt monkey and man. A "Caudal" Lecture. William Sawyer. BOHV
Philosophy the great and only Heir. To the Royal Society. Abraham Cowley. CEP; EPS; EV-2
Philotas. Samuel Daniel. *See* Tragedie of Philotas, The.
Phineas Pratt. Gloria MacArthur. GoeY
Phizzog. Carl Sandburg. TiPo (1952 ed.)
Phlebas the Phoenician, a fortnight dead. Death by Water. T. S. Eliot. *Fr.* The Waste Land. CaAE; PoD
Phlegm. W. Wesley Trimpi. PtPa
Phlox. Louise Driscoll. MW
Phoebe. *Unknown.* BLA
Phoebe Dawson. George Crabbe. GoTL
Phoebe on Latmus. Michael Drayton. *Fr.* Endimion and Phoebe. OBSC
("In Ionia whence sprang old poet's fame.") ReIE
Phoebe sate,/ Sweet she sate. Montanus' Sonnet. Thomas Lodge. *Fr.* Rosalynde. AtBAP; PoEL-2; SiCE; TuPP
Phoebe's Sonnet. Thomas Lodge. ElSeCe; ViBoPo
Phoebus, Arise! William Drummond of Hawthornden. BSV; ElL; GoTS
(Invocation: "Phoebus, arise!") EBSV; LEAP; OBEV
(Invocation to Love.) EV-2
(Song: "Phoebus arise/ And paint the sable skies.") BCEP; ElSeCe; EPS; HBV; LoBV; OBS; SeEP; ViBoPo
(Summons to Love.) GTBS; GTBS-D; GTBS-W; GTSE; GTSL
Phoebus, art thou a god, and canst not give. Funeral Elegy on the Death of His Very Good Friend, Mr. Michael Drayton. Sir Aston Cokayne. OBS
Phoebus, farewell! A sweeter saint I serve. A Sweeter Saint I Serve. Sir Philip Sidney. *Fr.* Arcadia. SiPS
Phoebus, lie still, and take thy rest. To Phoebus Seeing a Lady before Sunrise. Edmund Prestwich. SeCL
Phoebus, make haste, the day's too long, be gone. A Letter to Her Husband. Anne Bradstreet. AmP; AmPP; AnFE; APA; CoAnAm; LiTA; MOAP
Phoebus, sitting one day in a laurel-tree's shade. Daphne's Embarkation. James Russell Lowell. *Fr.* A Fable for Critics. APW
Phoebus, the car. He Inspects His Armory. Hyam Plutzik. FiMAP
Phoebus was judge between Jove, Mars, and Love. Astrophel and Stella, XIII. Sir Philip Sidney. SiPS
Phoebus with Admetus. George Meredith. EnLi-2; OBEV; OBVV; ViP
Phoenician Maidens, *sels.* Euripedes, *tr. fr. Greek.*
Epilogue to Fratricidal Folly, *tr. by* Arthur S. Way. GrR
Eteocles and Polynices, *tr. by* George Allen. OxBG
Jocasta, *tr. by* M. Woodhull. GrR
Refugee, *tr. by* Arthur S. Way. GrR
Phoenix, The. A. C. Benson. OBEV; OBVV; ShBV-4
Phoenix, The. Audrey Alexandra Brown. NeTW; TwCV
Phoenix, The ("O blest unfabled incense tree"). George Darley. *Fr.* Nepenthe. BLV; ChTr; GTML; LoBV; OBVV; TriL
(O Blest Unfabled Incense Tree.) AnIV; AtBAP; ChER; EG; FaBoCh; GTBS-D; GTIV; LoGBV; NBE; OBRV
(Phenix, The.) RO
(Song of the Phoenix, A.) CBOV
Phoenix, The ("O fast her amber blood doth flow"). George Darley. *Fr.* Nepenthe. OBEV (new ed.)
("O fast her amber blood doth flow.") OBRV
Phoenix. E. H. W. Meyerstein. NeTW
Phoenix, The. Ogden Nash. CenHV; NePA
Phoenix, The. Howard Nemerov. NePA
Phoenix, The. W. H. Oliver. AnNZ
Phoenix. E. Merrill Root. MuM
Phoenix, The. Siegfried Sassoon. ChTr
Phoenix, The. Theodore Spencer. CrMA
Phoenix, The, *sels. Unknown, tr. fr. Anglo-Saxon.*
"Lo! I have learned of the loveliest of lands," *tr. by* Charles W. Kennedy. AnOE
"'Tis a region calm of sunny groves," *shorter sel., tr. by* J. D. Spaeth. LiTW
Phoenix and the Turtle, The. Shakespeare. FaBoEn; GTBS-W; KN; LiTB; LiTG; LiTL; LoBV; MaPo; MePo; MyFE; OBEV; OBSC; PoEL-2; SeCePo; SeCeV; SiCE
(Phoenix and Turtle, The.) CaAE
Phoenix Answered, The. Anne Ridler. ChMP; POTE
(Of the Unscathing Fire.) LiTL
Phoenix, bird of terrible pride. Sir Herbert Read. *Fr.* Mutations of the Phoenix. FaBoTw
Phoenix comes of flame and dust, The. The Phoenix. Howard Nemerov. NePA
Phoenix Hairpins. Lu Yu, *tr. fr. Chinese by* Kenneth Rexroth. OnPC
Phoenix Liberty, The. Helen Parry Eden. PoFr
Phoenix Nest, The, *sel. Unknown.*
Grief's Ship. CoEV
Phoenix said to me, The. The Phoenix. Audrey Alexandra Brown. NeTW; TwCV
Phoenix Self-born, The. Ovid, *tr. fr. Latin by* Dryden. *Fr.* Metamorphoses, XV. ChTr
Phoenix' Throne, The. D. J. Enright. PoN
Phony War. Raymond Souster. BoCaPo (1948 ed.)
Phosphorescence. Rosamond Langbridge. ReTS
Photinos the Plowman, *sel.* Aristotelis Valaoritis, *tr. fr. Modern Greek by* Rae Dalven.
"Out of the black fog comes a rider." MoGP
Photograph. James J. Galvin. JKCP (1955 ed.)
Photograph of Isadora Duncan, A. Robert E. Hayden. PoN
Phraxanor to Joseph. Charles Jeremiah Wells. *Fr.* Joseph and His Brethern. VA
Phryges, *sel.* Aeschylus, *tr. fr. Greek by* C. M. Bowra.
Justice Protects the Dead. OxBG
Phryne. John Donne. TuPP
Phyllida. Yevgeny Abramovich Boratynsky, *tr. fr. Russian by* Babette Deutsch. TrRV
Phyllida and Corydon ("In the merry month of May"). Nicholas Breton. *Fr.* The Honourable Entertainment Given to the Queen's Majesty in Progress at Elvetham. 1591. ElL; ElSeCe; EM-1; EPP; OAEP; OBSC; ReIE; SeCePo
("In the merry month of May.") EG
(Pastoral, A.) TrGrPo
(Phillida and Corydon [*or* Coridon]. BCEP; BLV; EV-1; HBV; LPS-1; OBEV; ReEn; TuPP; ViBoPo
(Ploughman's [*or* Plowman's] Song, The.) ALV; CenL; FaBoEn; LiTL; OBSC; SiCE
Phyllida and Corydon ("On a hill there grows a flower"). Nicholas Breton. *See* Pastoral of Phillis and Coridon, A.
Phyllida, as the nights grow colder. Phyllida. Yevgeny Abramovich Boratynsky. TrRV
Phyllida Flouts Me. *Unknown. See* Phillada Flouts Me.
Phyllida was a fairmaid. *See* Phillida was a fair maid.
Phyllida's Love-Call [to Her Corydon, and His Replying] *Unknown.* AnFE; ElL; EPP; OBSC
(Corydon, Arise, My Corydon!) InvP
(Phillida's Love-Call [to Her Corydon, and His Replying].) EV-1; OBEV; TuPP
Phyllidula. Ezra Pound. FaBoTw
Phyllip Sparrow. John Skelton. *See* Phyllyp Sparowe.
Phyllis. Nicholas Breton. *See* Pastoral, A: "Sweet birds, that sit and sing . . ."
Phyllis. William Drummond of Hawthornden. ElSeCe; GN, OTPC
(Of Phyllis.) ElL; HBV; LiTL
Phyllis. Dryden. *See* Wherever I Am, and Whatever I Do
Phyllis, *sels.* Thomas Lodge.
"Devoid of reason, thrall to foolish ire," *after the French of* Pierre de Ronsard, XXXI. ReEn; SiCE
(Passion's Hounds.) OnPM

Phyllis (*continued*)
"Dewy, roseate morn had with her hairs, The," IX. SiCE
"I would in rich and golden-colored rain," XXXIV. ReEn
"I'll teach thee, lovely Phillis, what love is," XXVI. TuPP
"Love guards [*or* guides] the roses of thy lips," XIII. EG; ElL; ElSeCe; ReEn; SiCE; TuPP
(Fidelity.) OBSC
(Phillis, 2.) OBEV
(To Phyllis.) ViBoPo
"My Phyllis [*or* Phillis] hath the morning sun," XV. CaAE; ElL; ElSeCe; SiCE; TuPP
(Phillis.) LoBV; OBEV, 12 *ll.*; OBSC
(Phyllis.) ACP
(To Phyllis, the Fair Shepherdess.) CBOV; ViBoPo
"No stars her eyes, to clear the wandering night," VIII. TuPP
O Pleasing Thoughts, I. PeBoSo
("O pleasing thoughts, apprentices of love.") SiCE; TuPP
Ode, An: "Now I find thy looks were feigned." ElL; OBSC; SiCE; TuPP
(Song: "Now I see thy looks were feigned," *sl. diff.*) LoBV
Phyllis. Sir Charles Sedley. *See* Phyllis Is My Only Joy.
Phyllis. *Unknown.* SeCL
Phyllis and Damon. Nora Hopper. TIP
Phyllis and I fell out one day. The Reconciliation. James Benjamin Kenyon. PR
Phyllis and the Philosopher. Josephine Pinckney. NP
Phyllis [*or* Phillis], for shame, let us improve. Song [*or* The Advice]. Charles Sackville. BrBE; CEP; ElSeCe; EPS (1942 ed.); OBS; SeCL
Phyllis, I pray. To Phyllis. *Unknown.* SeCL
Phyllis, if I could paint you. The Poet's Proposal. Oliver Herford. PR
Phyllis Inamorata. Francis Andrewes. ElSeCe; SeCL
Phyllis [*or* Phillis] Is My Only Joy. Sir Charles Sedley. EG; ElSeCe; LPS-1
(Phyllis.) EPS (1942 ed.); SeCL
(Song: "Phyllis [*or* Phillis] is my only joy.") ATP; CEP; EnLoPo; EV-3; InMe; OBS; SeCV-2; SeEP
Phyllis Lee. Oliver Herford. BOHV
Phyllis, the grasping shepherdess. The Next Day. Charles Riviere Du Fresny. TrFP
Phyllis, though your all powerful charms. To His Mistress. *At.* to George Villiers, Duke of Buckingham. SeCL
Phyllis, why should we delay. To Phyllis [*or* Phillis]. Edmund Waller. CEP; ElSeCe; OAEP; TrGrPo
Phyllis's Age. Matthew Prior. CEP
(Phillis's Age.) BOHV; EnLoPo
Phyllyp Sparowe. John Skelton.
(Philip Sparrow.) PoEL-1; ReIE, *abr.*
Sels.
Dirge for Phyllip Sparowe, A. EPP
Funeral of Philip Sparrow, The, *abr.* ACP
Maystress Jane Scroupe. NBE
(Commendations of Mistress Jane Scrope, The.) OBSC
("Howe [*or* How] shall I report," *abr.*) EG; ViBoPo
Nun's Lament for Philip Sparrow, The, *abr.* CG
"Pla ce bo,/ Who is there, who?" CoBE, *abr.*; NBE; OxBoLi; *abr.*; ReEN; TuPP
(Placebo.) AtBAP
(Sparrow's Dirge, The.) OBSC
"That vengeance I ask and cry." SiCE
Tragedy of the Sparrow and the Cursing of the Cat, The. EV-1
(O Cat of Carlish Kind.) ChTr
"When I remember again." SeCePo
(Sparrow's Dirge, The.) FaBoCh; LoGBV
Physic, *abr.* George Crabbe. *Fr.* The Borough, Letter VII. PoP
Physical Geography. Louise Townsend Nicholl. ImOP
Physician's Advice. Augustus Peck Clarke. PoP
Physician's Character and Aims; Science Progressive. Abraham Coles. *Fr.* The Microcosm. PoP
Physics. William Whewell. LPS-3
Physiologus, *sel.* *Unknown, tr. fr. Anglo-Saxon by* Charles W. Kennedy.
Whale, The. AnOE
Piano. D. H. Lawrence. CoEV; InvP; LiTB; MBP; MoAB; MoBrPo; NeMA; OAEP (2d ed.); PoE; UnPo (3d ed.)
Piano, The. Paul Verlaine, *tr. fr. French by* Sir Edward Marsh. LiTW
Piano after War. Gwendolyn Brooks. PoNe
Piano, aquiver, will lick the foam its lips, The. Rupture. Boris Pasternak. TrRV
Piano Recital. Babette Deutsch. NePoAm
Piano Tuner, Untune Me That Tune. Ogden Nash. UnS
Piazza di Spagna. Willard M. Grimes. GoYe
Piazza Piece. John Crowe Ransom. BLV; CoBMV; InPo; MAP; MoAB; MoAmPo; MOAP; MoPW; MoVE; NeMA; OxBA; PG (1955 ed.); Po; TBM; TrGrPo
Piazza Tragedy, A. Eugene Field. FiBHP
Piazzas. Barbara Guest. NeAP
Pibroch of Donuil [*or* Donald] Dhu. Sir Walter Scott. BHV; BPN; EBSV; EmBrPo; EnLi-2; EnRP; EPN; EV-4; FaBoCh; HBV; InPo; LH; LPS-2; PoEL-4; ShBV-1
(Gathering Song of Donald Dhu [*or* Donuil Dhu], The.) GN; PECK; RG; TVSH
(Gathering Song of Donald the Black.) CBOV; GTBS; GTBS-D; GTBS-W; GTSE; GTSL; MuP
Picasso and Matisse. Robert Francis. NePoAm
Piccadilly. Thomas Burke. HBMV
Piccadilly. Erza Pound. BAP; LEAP
Picciola. "Orpheus C. Kerr." AA; PTA-2
Piccolomini, The, *sels.* Schiller, *tr. fr. German by* Samuel Taylor Coleridge.
Thekla's Song, *fr.* II, vi. AWP; JAWP; WBP
" 'Twas the first leisure of my life," *fr.* I, iv. SoV
Pick a Bale o' Cotton, *with music.* *Unknown.* ABF
Pick upon Pick. Alex Comfort. NeBP
Pickaninny, ninny, ninny,/ so tiny. Cradle Song to Put a Negro Baby to Sleep. Ildefonso Pereda Valdés. AnCL
Picket fence, The. Analogy. Edith Dorothea Morrell. DDA
Picket-Guard, The. Ethel Lynn Beers, *sometimes at. to* Lamar Fontaine. HBV; IAP; LBAP; LPS-2; MC; PaA; PAH; PAP
(All Quiet along [*or* on] the Potomac.) AA; BeLS; BlG; FaBoBe; FaFP; LEAP; MDAH; TCAP (*wr. at. to* Thaddeus Oliver); TrAS, *with* music; TreFS
Pickett's Charge. Stephen Vincent Benét. *Fr.* John Brown's Body. PoeMoYo
Pickety fence, The. David McCord. TiPo (1959 ed.)
Picking Up Sticks. Eleanor Farjeon. PCH
Pickwick Papers, *sel.* Charles Dickens.
Ivy Green, The, *fr. ch.* 6. OTPC (1946 ed.); PECK; BPP; HBV; HBVY; LPS-2; PIR; RIS; TVSH; VA
Picnic, The. Dorothy Aldis. TiPo (1952 ed.)
Picnic. Hugh Lofting. SUS
Picnic. Ray Mathew. BoAV
Picnic, The. Elizabeth Madox Roberts. GoBP; RIS
Picnic Boat, The. Carl Sandburg. WoL
Picnic Day. Rachel Field. SiSoSe; TiPo
Picnics. *Unknown.* BoTP
Pictor Ignotus. Robert Browning. BPN; EmBrPo; PoVP; ViPo; ViPP; VLEP
Picture, A. Charles Gamage Eastman. LPS-1
Picture, The. Heine, *tr. fr. German by* James Thomson. OnPM
Picture, The. *sel.* Philip Massinger.
Song: "Blushing rose and the purple flower, The." LiTL; ViBoPo
(Song of Pleasure, A.) SeCL
Picture, The. Thomas Stanley, *after the Greek of* Anacreon. AWP; JAWP; WBP
("Painter, by unmatch'd desert.") GrPo
Picture, The. Frederick O. Sylvester. NLK
Picture, A. *Unknown.* *See* Sweet Love, If Thou Wilt Gain a Monarch's Glory.
Picture and book remain. An Acre of Grass. W. B. Yeats. GTBS-D; POTE
Picture Drawn by a Boy. Shizuo Ito, *tr. fr. Japanese by* Takamichi Ninomiya *and* D. J. Enright. PoLJ
Picture memory brings to me, A. Whittier. *Fr.* My Trust. OHIP; PGD; PoRL
Picture of a Bull. Joaquin Miller. AmPP (3d ed.)
Picture of a Castle. William Meredith. NePoEA
Picture of a Physician. Leontius, *tr. fr. Greek by* T. F. Higham. OxBG
Picture of Death, A. Byron. *Fr.* The Giaour. LPS-1
Picture of Her Mind, The. Ben Jonson. GoBC
Picture of Little T. C. in a Prospect of Flowers, The. Andrew Marvell. CaAE; EPS; EV-2; ExPo; GTSL; HBV; LiTB; MeLP; MePo; OBEV; OBS; PoE; SeCeV; SeCV-1
Picture of Seneca Dying in a Bath. Matthew Prior. CEP
Picture People. Rowena Bennett. MPB (1956 ed.); YeAr
Picture-Show. Siegfried Sassoon. ChMo; CMP
Picture That Is Turned toward the Wall, The. Charles Graham. TreF
Picture the grave in his diabolical dream. Israfel. Karl Shapiro. PtP
Pictures. F. Ann Elliott. BoTP
Pictures. Cicely Fox Smith. EtS
Pictures at an Exhibition. Nathan Rosenbaum. GoYe
Pictures of Memory. Alice Cary. BLP; LPS-1
(Among the Beautiful Pictures.) BLPA
Pictures of the Gone World, *sels.* Lawrence Ferlinghetti. NeAP
"Dada would have liked a day like this," Sec. 23.
"Sarolla's women in their picture hats," Sec. 8.
Piece of Black Bread, A. "Eduard Bagritsky," *tr. fr. Russian by* C. M. Bowra. TrJP
(Black Bread, *tr. by* Babette Deutsch.) TrRV
("Piece of black bread and a faithful wife, A," *tr. by* C. M. Bowra.) BoRS
Piece of Clay, A. *Unknown.* OQP; QP-2

(Sculpture, The.) PoToHe (new ed.)
(Sculpture.) MaRV
Piece of colored cloud shines on the stone well, A. The Stone Well. Chien Hsu. WhP
Piece of Glass, and the Piece of Ice, The. John Hookham Frere. OTPC (1923 ed.)
Piece upon Masonborough. Thomas Godfrey. NoCaPo
Piecemeal the summer dies. Exeunt. Richard Wilbur. FiMAP
Pieces of animals, pieces of all my friends. The Antagonists. Muriel Rukeyser. *Fr.* Ninth Elegy. FiMAP
Pied Beauty. Gerard Manley Hopkins. AlDL; AnEnPo; AnFe; ATP (1953 ed.); AWP; BLV; BoLiVe; BrBE; CaAE; ChMo; CoBE; CoBMV; CoEV; EnL; EnLi-2 (1949 ed.); EnLit; FaBoEn; FaBoMo; FaFP; GoTP; GTBS; GTBS-D; GTBS-W; GTML; InPo; InvP; KN; LiTB; LiTG; LiTM; MaPo; MaRV; MBP; MoAB; MoBrPo; MoVE; MuP; NAMP; NeMA; OAEP (2d ed.); OBEV (new ed.); OBMV; PG (1955 ed.); PoRA; POTT; PoVP; ReaPo; ReMP; ShBV-3; ThWaDe; TreFS; TrGrPo; TriL; TwHP; ViBoPo; ViP; ViPo; ViPP; VLEP; VOD (1935 ed.); WaKn
("Glory be to God for dappled things.") EG
Pied Piper of Hamelin, The. Robert Browning. BBV; BeLS; BMEP; BoChLi; BOHV; BPN; CG; EmBrPo; EV-5; FaBoBe; FaBoCh; FaFP; GEPC; GN; GoTP; HBV; HBVY; HiLiEn; LoGBV; LPS-3; OnHT; OnSP; OtMeF; OTPC; PoE; PoVP; RG; RIS; ShBV-1; StVeCh; TCEP; TiPo (1952 ed.); TVSH; WP
"Into the street the Piper stept," *sel.* BoTP
Pier delle Vigne. Dante, *tr. fr. Italian by* John Ciardi. *Fr.* Divina Commedia: Inferno. HoPM
Pier-Glass, The. Robert Graves. CoBMV; MoAB
Pierce through my heart. My Road. Handa. SoLD
Pierced are Thy feet, O Lord, pierced are Thy hands. The Divine Passion. Paravicino y Arteaga. CAW
Piere Vidal Old. Ezra Pound. MoAB
Pierian Muses whose songs glorify, hither! Hesiod. *Fr.* Works and Days. GrPo
Piero della Francesca. Anne Ridler. FaBoMo; PoN
Pierre of Timagami in New York. Wilson MacDonald. WhC
Pierrette in Memory. William Griffith. *Fr.* Loves and Losses of Pierrot. BAP; HBV; SBMV
Pierrot. Sara Teasdale. ChMo; CMP; PFE; PR
Pierrot Makes a Song. William Griffith. *Fr.* Loves and Losses of Pierrot. PR
Pierrot, no sentimental swain. Pantomime. Paul Verlaine. AWP; JAWP; WBP
Pierrot stands in the garden. Pierrot. Sara Teasdale. ChMo; CMP; PFE; PR
Pierrots (One Has Principles). Jules Laforgue, *tr. fr. French by* Joseph Bennett. AnFP
Piers Plainness' Seven Years' Prenticeship, *sel.* Henry Chettle.
Wily Cupid. EG
(Aeliana's Ditty.) ALV; OBSC
(Of Cupid.) ElL
Piers Plowman. William Langland. *See* Vision of Piers Plowman, The.
Piers the Plowman's Creed, *sl. abr.* *Unknown, tr. fr. Middle English.* MeEV
Pieta. Guy Butler. BoSA
Pieta. David Gascoyne. *Fr.* Miserere. NeBP; POTE
Pietro Bernardone's son. The Rich Man of Assisi. Sister M. Benvenuta. SaFP
Piety. Morris Abel Beer. *See* Church in the Heart, The.
Pig, The. Ogden Nash. SiTL
Pig, The. Robert Southey. BOHV
Pig, if I am not mistaken, The. The Pig. Ogden Nash. SiTL
Pig-Tale, The. "Lewis Carroll." *See* Melancholy Pig, The.
Pigeon-Feeders in Battery Park, The. Julia Cooley Altrocchi. GoYe
Pigeon House, A. Wetenhall Wilkes. *Fr.* Bellville. BeR
Pigeons, The. Rodney Bennett. BoTP
Pigeons, The. Maud Burnham. PCH; PPL
Pigeons. George Dillon. BLA; WhBS
Pigeons. Alastair Reid. NePoEA; SiTL
Pigeons and Snow. Andrew Hewitt. NoCaPo
Pigeons in home flight swooping. The Autumn Rain. Hubbard Fulton Page. NoCaPo
Pigeons Just Awake. Hilda Conkling. YT
Pigeons on the grass alas. Gertrude Stein. *Fr.* Four Saints in Three Acts. CrMA
Pigeon's Story, The. Jeannie Kirby. BoTP
Piggy-Wig found he had four little feet. What Piggy-Wig Found. Enid Blyton. BoTP
Pig's Tail, The. Norman Ault. BoTP
Pigwiggen. Michael Drayton. *See* Arming of Pigwiggen, The
Pigwiggin Arms Himself. Michael Drayton. *See* Arming of Pigwiggen, The.
Pigwiggen Prepares for the Fight with King Oberon. Michael Drayton. *See* Arming of Pigwiggen, The.
Pigwiggen was this fairy knight. Michael Drayton. *Fr.* Nymphidia. ViBoPo
Pike, The. Edmund Blunden. AnFe; MoVE; ShBV-3
Pike, The. Christian Morgenstern, *tr. fr. German.* AnGP, *tr. by* R. F. C. Hull; TwGV, *tr. by* Herman Salinger
Pikes Peak. *Unknown.* PoOW
Pike's Peakers, The. Lawrence N. Greenleaf. PoOW
Pike's Peakers! All! From whatsoever climes. Grand Opening of the People's Theatre. O. J. Goldrick. PoOW
Pilaster, The. Elizabeth Madox Roberts. NP
Pilate and Caiaphas. The Black Christ. Arthur Shearly Cripps. BoSA
Pilate made report to Rome. Death of Christ. Arthur R. Macdougall, Jr. ChIP
Pilate must heed the public pulse and poll. He Is Condemned. William A. Donaghy. *Fr.* The Stations of the Cross. QS
Pilate, Pilate, wash your hands. Again the Story Is Told. Ada Jackson. MaRV
Pilate Remembers. Thomas Durley Landels. *Fr.* Pontius Pilate. MaRV
Pile high the hickory and the light. Winter Night. Edna St. Vincent Millay. BAP; PoRL
Pile on the soil; thrust on the soil. Song of the Fairies. *Unknown.* OnYI
Pile the bodies high at Austerlitz and Waterloo. Grass. Carl Sandburg. AmPP; AWP; BAV; BBV (1951 ed.); BLV; BoLiVe; CV; JAWP; MAP; MaRV; MCCG; MoAB; MoAmPo; MOAP; MoVE; NeMA; NP; OHFP; OxBA; PoeMoYo; PoMa; PSO; ReaPo; TBM; TCAP; TrGrPo; WaaP; WBP; WHA
Piled deep below the screening apple-branch. The Orchard-Pit. Dante Gabriel Rossetti. EnLoPo; PoEL-5; RO; ViP
Pilgrim, The. Bunyan. *Fr.* The Pilgrim's Progress. BoTP; EV-2; GN; HBV; MaRV; OtMeF; OTPC; PCH; RG; TiPo (1952 ed.)
("He who would valiant be.") OlF
(Pilgrim['s] Song, The.) CoMu; OBS; WaKn
Pilgrim, The. Eleanor Downing. JKCP
Pilgrim, The. "E. Foxton." AA
Pilgrim. Ibn al-Batti, *tr. fr. Arabic by* A. J. Arberry. MooP
Pilgrim, The. Edwin Markham. MaRV
Pilgrim, The. Robert Nichols. MBP
Pilgrim. A. M. Sullivan. JKCP (1955 ed.)
Pilgrim, The. Richard Wightman. WGRP
Pilgrim am I, on my way, A. The Pilgrim. "E. Foxton." AA
Pilgrim and the Herdboy, The. Robert Buchanan. OBVV
Little Herd-Boy's Song, The, *sel.* BoTP
Pilgrim at Rome, The. *Unknown, tr. fr. Old Irish by* Kuno Meyer. AnIL
(Word of Warning, A, *tr. by* Frank O'Connor.) KiLC
Pilgrim at St. Yuste, The. August, Graf von Platen, *tr. fr. German by* Edwin Morgan. AnGP
(Pilgrim before St. Just, The, *tr. by* Norman Macleod.) LiA
Pilgrim Fathers, The. Leonard Bacon. MaRV; WGRP
Pilgrim Fathers, The. Felicia Dorothea Hemans. *See* Landing of the Pilgrim Fathers, The.
Pilgrim Fathers, The. John Boyle O'Reilly. PEDC
Pilgrim Fathers, The. John Pierpont. AA; APW; DD; HBV; HH; MC; PAH
Pilgrim Fathers, The. Wordsworth. PAH; PoRL
Pilgrim Fathers, The—where are they? The Pilgrim Fathers. John Pierpont. AA; APW; DD; HBV; HH; MC; PAH
Pilgrim from the East, The. Gustave Kahn, *tr. fr. French by* Jethro Bithell. TrJP
Pilgrim hearts that sought a holy shrine, The. Land of Destiny. Catherine Parmenter. PEDC
Pilgrim of a Day, The. Thomas Campbell. OBRV
Pilgrim of the Night, The. In the Azure Night. Bartolomé Galindez. CAW
Pilgrim Song, The. Bunyan. *See* Pilgrim, The.
Pilgrim Song. Florence Earle Coates. OHIP
Pilgrim to Pilgrim. *Unknown, at. to* Sir Walter Ralegh. *See* As You Came from the Holy Land.
Pilgrim Way, The. John Oxenham. OQP; QP-1
"Pilgrim, you of the loosened latchet." The Bells of Christmas. Clinton Scollard. SDH
Pilgrimage, The. Albrecht von Johannsdorf, *tr. fr. German by* F. C. Nicholson. LiTW
Pilgrimage. Austin Clarke. OxBI
Pilgrimage. Eileen Duggan. AnNZ
Pilgrimage, The. George Herbert. ChTr; EPS (1942 ed.)
Pilgrimage. Elinor Lennen. PGD
Pilgrimage. Catherine Parmenter. PEDC
Pilgrimage, The. Sir Walter Ralegh. *See* Passionate Man's Pilgrimage, The.
Pilgrimage. Sydney King Russell. UnW
Pilgrimage, The. Louis Untermeyer. QS
Pilgrimage. Blanche Shoemaker Wagstaff. MaRV; MuM
Pilgrimage towards Loves Holy Land, A. Thomas Campion. *See* Love's Pilgrims.
Pilgrims, The. Anthony Delius. BoSA
Pilgrims, The. John McCrae. CPG
Pilgrims, The. Adelaide Anne Procter. UnPo
Pilgrims, The. Swinburne. BPN; PoVP; TCEP; VLEP

Pilgrims and the Peas, The. "Peter Pindar." BOHV; LPS-3
Pilgrims at Sea. *Unknown. See* Sailing of the Pilgrims from Sandwich towards St. James of Compostella, The.
Pilgrims Came The. Annette Wynne. GFA; MPB; OHIP
Pilgrims landed, worthy men, The. The Pilgrims' Thanksgiving Feast. Arthur Guiterman. WhC
Pilgrims of the trackless deep. Pilgrim Song. Florence Earle Coates. OHIP
Pilgrims of Thibet, The. Cale Young Rice. PFY
Pilgrim's Progress, The, *sels.* Bunyan.
Pilgrim, The. BoTP; EV-2; GN; HBV; MaRV; OtMeF; OTPC; PCH; RG; TiPo (1952 ed.)
("He who would valiant be.") OlF
(Pilgrim['s] Song, The.) CoMu; OBS; WaKn
Shepherd Boy's Song, The. BOL; BoTP; LEAP, *abr.;* MaRV; OTPC (1923 ed.); PCH, *st.* 1; TVSH
(Enough.) BLRP
("He that is down, needs fear no fall.") SeEP
(Shepherd Boy Sings [in the Valley of Humiliation], The.) EG; GBV; GN; HBV; HBVY; OBEV; OQP; QP-2; WGRP
(Shepherd Boy's Song in the Valley of Humiliation, The.) CaAE
(Shepherd's Song, The.) OxBoCh
(Song [of the Shepherd] in the Valley of Humiliation.) BCEP; EV-2; OBS
Pilgrim's Song. Psalms, CXXI, Bible, *O.T. See* I Will Lift Up Mine Eyes unto the Hills.
Pilgrim's Song. Bunyan. *See* Pilgrim, The.
Pilgrim's Song. Bernhard S. Ingemann, *tr. fr. Danish by* Sabine Baring-Gould. WGRP
Pilgrims' Thanksgiving Feast, The. Arthur Guiterman. WhC
Pilgrims throng to the market place, The. Vanity Fair. Victor Starbuck. LS
Pilk lauds the verse of Jobble to the skies. Perpetuum Mobile. Edith Sitwell. BMEP; HBMV
Pillar-Box, The. Jiri Wolker, *tr. fr. Czech by* Paul Selver. LiTW
Pillar of Fame, The. Robert Herrick. EPS
Pillar of fire by night, A. The Song of Sherman's Army. Charles Graham Halpine. GA; MC; PAH; PAP
Pillar of fire went before them by night, A. The New Moses. M. K. Joseph. AnNZ
Pillar of the Cloud, The. Cardinal Newman. ACP; AnEnPo; AWP; BEL; EnLi-2; EPN; FaFP; GoBC; GTML; HBV; JAWP; JKCP; LEAP; LPS-2; MaRV; PC; Po; PoEL-5; PoVP; PreP; TOP; TrPWD; TyEnPo; VA; WBP; WGRP
(Lead, Kindly Light.) BCEP; BTP; FaBoBe; HiLiEn; InP; MyFE; NeHB; OlF; PECK; PIR; TreF; UnPo (3d ed.)
(Light in the Darkness.) OBRV
Pillars of death! carved sirens [*or* syrens]! tearful urn[s]. Erinna to Her Friend. Erinna. GrPo; GrR; OnPM
Piller Fights. D. A. Ellsworth. PTA-2
Pillow Cases. Richard Armour. WhC
Pillowing their cheeks all night. Revenge. Avenzoar. MooP
Pills to Purge Melancholy, *sel.* Thomas d'Urfey.
Maid's Longing, The. SiTL
Pilot, The. George Chapman. *Fr.* Bussy d'Ambois, I, i. EtS
Pilot, The. E. A. Robinson. ChMo; CMP
Pilot and Prophet. Charles Hanson Towne. DD; GA
(Theodore Roosevelt—Pilot and Prophet!) PEDC
Pilot Cove. C. J. Dennis. WhC
Pilot-fish, who giv'st to sailors pleasant sailing. A Distaff. Erinna. OxBG
Pilot from the Carrier, A. Randall Jarrell. MoPo
Pilot, how far from home? The Lights of Home. Alfred Noyes. EOAH
Pilot in the Jungle, The. John Ciardi. MiAP
Pilot of the Plains, The. Emily Pauline Johnson. CPG; PCN
Pilots, Man Your Planes. Randall Jarrell. MoAB; MoAmPo (1950 ed.)
Pimpernel. Charlotte Druitt Cole. BoTP
Pin, The. Ann Taylor. HBV; HBVY
Pin, A. Ella Wheeler Wilcox. BOHV
Pin Has a Head, A. Christina Rossetti. *See* Paradoxes.
Pin-swin or spine-swine, The. His Shield. Marianne Moore. LiTM; NePA; TwAmPo
Pin-up Girl. Louis O. Coxe. WaP
Pin wheels whirling round. Fourth of July Night. Dorothy Aldis. SiSoSe; TiPo
Pinafore. W. S. Gilbert. *See* H.M.S. Pinafore
Pinch him, pinch him, black and blue. Song by Fairies. John Lyly. *Fr.* Endymion. EPP; OAEP; OBSC; ReEn; TuPP
Pinch of Salt, A. Robert Graves. HBMV; LBBV; MBP; MoBrPo; PtOT
Pindar. Antipater of Sidon, *tr. fr. Greek by* John Addington Symonds. AWP
Pindar is imitable by none. The Praise of Pindar. Abraham Cowley. CEP; EPS; PtP
Pindar Peel, of Passamquoddy. Passamquoddy's Apple Toddy. James W. Foley. LHV
Pindaric Ode, A: To the Immortal Memory and Friendship of That Noble Pair, Sir Lucius Cary and Sir Henry Morison. Ben Jonson.
(To the Immortal[l] Memorie [*or* Memory] and Friendship of That Noble Pair[e], Sir Lucius Cary and Sir H. Morison.) OBS; PoEL-2; PoFS; SeCV-1; SeEP; TuPP
Sels.
"He stood a soldier to the last right end." CoBE
It Is Not Growing like a Tree. BBV (1951 ed.); EnLi-1 (1949 ed.); LiTB; LiTG; OQP; QP-2; RiBV
(From "An Ode to Sir Lucius Cary and Sir H. Morrison.") LEAP
(Good Life, Long Life.) LPS-3
(Greatness in Littleness.) BCEP
(Honour in Bud.) LH
("It is not growing like a tree.") AnFE, 3 *sts.;* BEL; CBE; ChTr; CoBE; EPP; EPS; OBEV; TOP
(Noble Nature, The.) BTP; CG; EV-2; GN; GoBC; GTBS; GTBS-D; GTBS-W; GTSE; GTSL; HBV; HBVY; MaRV; MCCG; MW; OTPC; PECK; PG; TVSH
(Oak and Lily.) BoLiVe; TrGrPo
(Perfect Life.) WP
(Perfection in Small Things.) GrCo-1
(Proportion.) FaBoEn
(Short Measures.) BLV
Pindarum Quisquis. Corinna, *tr. fr. Greek by* C. M. Bowra. OxBG
Pine, The. Gertrude MacGregor Moffat. CPG
Pine, The. Augusta Davies Webster. DD; HBV; OHIP
Pine against the Blue, The. Victor Starbuck. NoCaPo
Pine at Timber-Line, The. Harriet Monroe. NP
Pine Bough, The. Richard Aldridge. NePoAM
Pine bough, pine bark. For My Fireplace. Henry Noyes Pratt. DDA
Pine branch is so wholesome and so sweet, A. Christmas Eve. Zoe Kincaid Brockman. NoCaPo
Pine-crowned hills against the sky. Christmas Eve. Catherine Parmenter. PEDC; PGD
Pine Music. Kate Louise Brown. BoTP
Pine needle carpets and crisp brown leaves. Fairy Carpets. Anne Blackwell Payne. GFA
Pine Needles, *sel.* William H. Hayne.
"If Mother Nature patches." ADAH; PCH
(Sewing.) GFA; MeMeAG; OTPC (1946 ed.)
Pine spirit! To a Tawny Thrush. Max Eastman. LEAP
Pine to the Mariner, The. George Turberville. EtS
Pine-trail [*or* Pinetrail]; and all the hours are white, are long. A Walk on Snow. Peter Viereck. MiAP; OnHM
Pine Tree, The. Heine. *See* Fichtenbaum steht einsam, Ein
Pine Tree, The. Pei Pao Yu Lan, *tr. fr. Chinese by* Henry H. Hart. PoHN
Pine Tree, The. *Unknown.* PEOR
Pine-Tree Buoy, A. Harrison Smith Morris. AA
Pine Tree for Diana, The ("Montium custos nemorumque"). Horace, *tr. fr. Latin by* Louis Untermeyer. Odes, III, 22. AWP
Pine tree standeth lonely, A. Ein Fichtenbaum steht einsam. Heine, *tr. by* James Thomson. AWP; JAWP; OuHeWo; WBP
Pine Trees and the Sky; Evening. Rupert Brooke. MCCG
Pine-Trees in the Courtyard, The Po Chü-i, *tr. fr. Chinese by* Arthur Waley. TrCh
Pine-trees lift their dark, bewildered eyes, The. The Snow-Messengers. Paul Hamilton Hayne. SPP
Pine Woods, The. John, Lord Hanmer. VA
Pinery Boy, The. *Unknown.* IHA
Pines, The. Julie Mathilde Lippmann. AA
Pines, Anderson M. Scruggs. PoMa
Pines, The. Harriet Prescott Spofford. AA
Pines, and a blur of lithe young grasses. From A Car-Window. Ruth Guthrie Harding. AV; HBMV; VOD
Pines and the Sea, The. Christopher Pearse Cranch. AA; AnAmPo; HBV; LA; LEAP
Pines are white-powdered, The. New Snow. Catharine Bryant Rowles. YeAr
Pines have gathered upon the hill, The. A Cradle Song of the Night Wind. Willis Boyd Allen. BOL
Pine's Mystery, The. Paul Hamilton Hayne. SPP; TCAP
Pines were dark on Ramoth hill, The. My Playmate. Whittier. AnFE; APA; CoAnAm; CoBA; HBV; IAP; LBAP; MOAP; OBVV; PCD; PG (1945 ed.); TCAP
Pinetrail; and all the hours are white, are long. *See* Pine-trail . . .
Pink Almond. Katharine Tynan. BoTP
Pink and white hands like roses and rice cake! Phoenix Hairpins. Lu Yu. OnPC
Pink Dominoes. Kipling. CenHV
Pinkletinks. Grace Elisabeth Allen. GoYe
Pinto. *Unknown.* CoSo; CSF
Pioneer, The. Eugene Field. PoOW
Pioneer, The. Arthur Guiterman. MPB; TiPo
Pioneer, The. Edna St. Vincent Millay. PoFr
Pioneer Mother, The. Ethel Romig Fuller. PGD

Pioneer of Monaro, A. Francis Webb. MoAuPo
Pioneer state built a College to share, A. Here We Have Idaho. Harry A. Powell. PoRL
Pioneer Woman. Vesta Pierce Crawford. PoOW
Pioneers. Badger Clark. FaBoBe
Pioneers. Hamlin Garland. AA
Pioneers. Gertrude B. Gunderson. DDA
Pioneers. Arthur W. Jose. BoAu
Pioneers. Frederick William Ophel. BoAu
Pioneers, The. Selden Rodman. PoF
Pioneers ("For the first man to climb the hill"). *Unknown.* MaRV
Pioneers ("We shall not travel by the road we make"). *Unknown, at. to* V. H. Friedlaender. BMEP; PoTo
(Road Makers.) MaRV
Pioneers! O Pioneers! Walt Whitman. AmPP; APW; ATP; CoBA; EV-5; FaBoBe; IAP; MOAP; MPB; PaA; PFE; PIAE; PoeMoYo; PYM; TCAP; TOP; UnPo (1st ed.); WHA
"O you youths, western youths," *sel., abr.* GrCo-1
Pioneers, The; or, Twenty Years After. William Plomer. BoSA
Pious Celinda. Congreve. *See* Pious Selinda.
Pious Editor's Creed, The. James Russell Lowell. The Biglow Papers, 1st Series, No. VI. AnNE; IAP; PIAE; REAL; TOP
(Candidate's Creed, The, *abr.*) BOHV; YaD
(From "The Biglow Papers.") MOAP
Pious Giant, The. Christian Morgenstern, *tr. fr. German by* Lola Gruenthal. AnGP
Pious Selinda. Congreve. HBV
(Pious Celinda.) ALV
(Song: "Pious Selinda goes to prayers.") InMe
Pious words are but a bubble. Poem on a Slippery Sidewalk. Kenneth Porter. WhC
Pip! pop! flippety flop! The Song of the Cornpopper. Laura E. Richards. BoChLi
Pipe and Can ("The Indian weed"). *At. to* Robert Wisdome. *See* Religious Use of Taking Tobacco, A.
Pipe and Can ("Whenas the chill sirocco blows"). *Unknown. See* In Praise of Ale.
Pipe, little minstrels of the waning year. The Crickets. Harriet McEwen Kimball. SN
Pipe of Pan, The. Elizabeth Akers Allen. SN
Pipe of Peace, The. F. L. Lucas. HaMV
Pipe of Tobacco, A, *sels.* Isaac Hawkins Browne. OBEC
In Imitation of Pope.
In Imitation of Young.
Pipe of Tobacco, The. *At. to* John Usher. HBV
Pipe-Player, The. Sir Edmund Gosse. VA
Pipe thee high and pipe thee low. Pipings. J. Paget-Fredericks. BrR
Pipe, with solemn interposing puff, The. Pernicious Weed. William Cowper. InMe; WhC
Piped a tiny voice hard by. The Chickadee. Emerson. *Fr.* The Titmouse. FaPON; GFA; OTPC (1946 ed.)
Piped the blackbird on the beechwood spray. Little Bell. Thomas Westwood. GN; HBV; LPS-1; OTPC (1946 ed.); TVC
Piper, The. Blake. *See* Piping down the Valleys Wild.
Piper, The. Donn Byrne. PoTo
Piper, The. Rachel Field. PoRh
Piper, A [*or* The]. "Seumas O'Sullivan." BoTP; CH; FaPON; GaP; MoShBr; MPB; OxBI; PoRh; TiPo
Piper, The. Josephine Preston Peabody. CV
Piper in the street[s] to-day, A. A Piper. "Seumas O'Sullivan." BoTP; CH; FaPON; GaP; MoShBr; MPB; OxBI; PoRh; TiPo
Piper o' Dundee, The. *Unknown.* EBSV
Piper of Arll, The. Duncan Campbell Scott. BoCaPo; OCL; PeCV; SG
Piper of the fields and woods. The Cricket. James B. Kenyon. LBAP
Piper on the Hill, The. Dora Sigerson Shorter. HBV; HBVY; OnYI; OTPC (1923 ed.)
Piper, Play. John Davidson. BMEP; TOP
"Piper, sit thee down and write." Blake. *Fr.* Songs of Innocence: Piping down the Valleys Wild. YT
"Piper, wherefore wilt thou roam?" The Piper. Josephine Preston Peabody. CV
Piper's Progress, The. Francis Sylvester Mahony. FiBHP
Pipes and Drums. Lilian Holmes. GFA
Pipes at Lucknow, The. Whittier. BHV; BoHiPo; GN; HBVY; ShGoBo; TVSH
Pipes in the Sty. John Kendall. WhC
Pipes o' Gordon's Men, The. J. Scott Glasgow. HBV
Pipes of the misty moorlands. The Pipes at Lucknow. Whittier. BHV; BoHiPo; GN; HBVY; ShGoBo; TVSH
Pipes on the bridge struck up to play. Åleksandr Blok, *tr. fr. Russian by* Oliver Elton. BoRS
Piping down the Valleys Wild (*Introd. to* Songs of Innocence). Blake. BTP; FaBoCh; GBV; HiLiEn; InvP; LoGBV; OBEC; PoRh; PRWS; TreFS; TVSH; TyEnPo; UnS
(Child and the Piper, The.) CG
(Happy Piper, The.) CBPC
(Happy Songs.) GoTP; MeMeAg; RIS
(Introduction: "Piping down the valleys wild.") AnFE; BEL; BrBe; CEP; EiPP; EnLit; EnRP; EV-3; OAEP; PoE; PoEL-4; SeCeV; ThWaDe
(Introduction to "Songs of Innocence.") CaAE; CoBE; EM-1; EnLi-2; ExPo; FaBoBe; KN; NeHB; OuHeWo; PG (1945 ed.); Po; TCEP; TiPo; TrGrPo; ViBoPo; WHA
(Piper, The.) AWP; BoChLi; BoTP; GaP; InPo; JAWP; LPS-1; MPB; OTPC; PIR; TOP; WBP
(Reeds of Innocence.) BCEP; GTBS-W; HBV; HBVY; LEAP; LiTB; LiTG; OBEV
(Songs of Innocence.) WP
(Songs of Innocence: Introduction.) EiPP; EPP; LoBV
"Piper, sit thee down and write," *last 2 sts.* YT
Piping hot, smoking hot. *Unknown.* OxNR
Piping Peace. James Shirley. *Fr.* The Imposture. I, ii. ACP; LoBV; OBEV (new ed.)
(Io.) OBS; SeCL; SeEP
(Peace.) EV-2
(Song: "You virgins that did late despair.") PoEL-2
(You Virgins.) ViBoPo
Pipings. J. Paget-Fredericks. BrR
Pipit sate upright in her chair. A Cooking Egg. T. S. Eliot. CaAE
Pipling. Theodore Roethke. NePA; SiTL
Pippa Passes. Robert Browning. BPN; EmBrPo; GEPC; PoVP; ViPP; VLEP
Sels.
All Service Ranks the Same with God, *fr.* Introduction. BEL; MaRV; OQP; QP-1
(New Year's Hymn.) BMEP; HiLiEn; TCEP
(Service.) TrGrPo; TSW
(Song: "All service ranks the same with God.") LoBV
"Day!/ Faster and more fast," *fr.* Introduction. AlDL; GTSL; SN
(Sunrise.) NLK; OQP; QP-2
"Give her but a least excuse to love me," *fr.* sc. ii. EPN; GTBS; GTSL; ViBoPo
"King lived long ago, A," *fr.* sc. iii. EV-5
Ottima and Sebald, Two Lovers, *fr.* sc. i. BMEP
Year's at the Spring, The, *fr.* sc. i. AEV; BEL; BLPA; BoChLi; DD; EPN; EV-5; FaBoBe; GTBS; GTSL; HiLiEn; InP; NeHB; PoRL; PoToHe (new ed.); StVeCh; TSW; TSWC; YeAr
(Good Morning.) OnHT; PRWS
(Pippa.) PECK
(Pippa's Song.) ADAH; BBV (1923 ed.); BoTP; BrR; BTP; CaAE; EnLi-2; FaFP; FaPON; GTBS-W; LiTB; LiTG; MeMeAg; MPB; NLK; OBEV; OBVV; OHIP; OQP; OTPC; PC; PCH; PTA-1; QP-1; RAR; SiTL; ShBV-1; TreF; UnPo (3d ed.)
(Song: "Year's at the spring, The.") ATP; EnLit; GBV; HBV; HBVY; MaRV; MCCG; MW; PIR; RG; TCEP; TOP; TrGrPo; VA; WGRP
(Song from "Pippa Passes.") LEAP; PFE; WP
(Spring Song.) GoTP
You'll Love Me Yet! *fr.* sc. iii. BMEP; EPN; EV-5; HoPM; LoPo; OBEV (1st ed.)
(Song: "You'll love me yet! and I can tarry.") HBV
Pirate, The, *sels.* Sir Walter Scott.
Claud Halcro's Song: "And you shall deal the funeral dole," *fr. ch.* 23. BHV; EBSV
(And You Shall Deal the Funeral Dole.) BSV
Cleveland's Song: "Farewell! Farewell! the voice you hear," *fr. ch.* 23. BSV
(Farewell.) LH
(Farewell! Farewell!) EBSV
Cleveland's Song: "Love wakes and weeps," *fr. ch.* 23. EmBrPo
Mermaids and Mermen, *fr. ch.* 16. EtS
Song of the Reim-Kennar, The, *fr. ch.* 6. OAEP
Pirate Don Durk of Dowdee. Mildred Plew Meigs. BoChLi; GaP; PCD; PoRh; TiPo
Pirate of High Barbary, The. *Unknown. See* Salcombe Seaman's Flaunt to the Proud Pirate, The.
Pirate of sea and sky. Rafael Alberti, *tr. fr. Spanish by* Eleanor L. Turnbull. CoSP
Pirate Story. Robert Louis Stevenson. BeLS; FaPON; GFA; GoTP; OTPC (1946 ed.); PoVP; TiPo; VA
Pirate Treasure. Abbie Farwell Brown. EtS; TBM
Pirate Wind. Mary Jane Carr. BrR; SiSoSe
Pirates. Elizabeth J. Coatsworth. DDA; EtS
Pirates. Alfred Noyes. MCCG; VOD
Pirates, after all, were usually. Pirates. Elizabeth J. Coatsworth. DDA; EtS
Pirates' Fight, The. Joseph Schull. *Fr.* The Legend of Ghost Lagoon. CaP
Pirates of Penzance, The, *sels.* W. S. Gilbert.
Modern Major-General, The. InMe; PCD, *much abr.*; SoV
(Major-General, The.) OnPP
(Major-General's Song.) CoBE
Policeman's Lot, The. ALV; NeHB; PoVP; TrGrPo

Pirate's Song. José de Espronceda, *tr. fr. Spanish by* Alice Jane McVan. AnSpL-2; TeCS
Pirates' Tea-Party, The. Dorothy Una Ratcliffe. BoTP
Pis-Aller. Matthew Arnold. BMEP; BPN; EmBrPo; EPN; PoVP; VLEP
Pisan Cantos, The. Ezra Pound. *See under* Canto.
Piscatores Vocat. Richard Crashaw, *tr. fr. Latin by* D. C. Allen. Epigrammata Sacra, I, 84. LaP
Piscatorie Eclogues, *sels.* Phineas Fletcher.
Chromis, IV. LoBV
"Fisher-lad, A (no higher dares he look)," III. SeCV-1
Pisces Multiplicati. Richard Crashaw, *tr. fr. Latin by* D. C. Allen. Epigrammata Sacra, II, 29. LaP
Pisgah. Willard Wattles. WGRP
Pisgah-Sights. Robert Browning. PoVP
Pit, The. Baudelaire, *tr. fr. French by* Alan Conder. TrFP
Pit of Bliss, The. James Stephens. AnFE; ChMo; CMP
Pit, pat, well-a-day. *Unknown.* OxNR
Pit yawned always before Pascal's sight, The. The Pit. Baudelaire. TrFP
Pitch-black road, and rain, A. Night Road. Robert A. Donaldson. VOD
Pitch here the tent, while the old horse grazes. Juggling Jerry [*or* The Last Words of Juggling Jerry]. George Meredith. BEL; BeLS; BoLiVe; EmBrPo; EnLit; EPN; EPP; HBV; HiLiEn; OAEP; OnPP; PoeT; POTT; SeCePo; TCEP; TOP; VA; ViPo; VLEP
Pitcher. Robert Francis. NePoAm
Pitcher, The. Yüan Chen, *tr. fr. Chinese by* Arthur Waley. AWP; JAWP; TrCh; WBP
Pitcher of Mignonette, A. H. C. Bunner. AA; ADAH; HBV; InP; LEAP; PC; PFE; PFY; PoeMoYo
Pitcher plant makes a living by, The. The Resident Worm. James Hayford. NePoAm-2
Pitcher the gunner is brisk and young. Molly Pitcher. Laura E. Richards. GA; MC; PAH
Pitee, that I have sought so yore agoo. The Complaint unto Pity. Chaucer. LyMA
Pith of faith is gone, The. And as there lie. Child of Loneliness. Norman Gale. WGRP
Pitiful in Your Bravery. Marion Strobel. BAP
Pitiful mouth, saith he, that living gavest. Henry's Lament. Samuel Daniel. *Fr.* The Complaint of Rosamond. OBSC
Pitiful the playing of the flood with dire destruction! Egan O'Rahilly. *Fr.* The Storm. OnYI
Pitiful these crying swans tonight. The Icebound Swans. *Unknown.* SiB
Pitiless Beauty. John Hall Wheelock. LEAP
Pitiless heat from heaven pours. Summer. Kalidasa. *Fr.* The Seasons. AWP
Pitt. Reginald Heber. BHV
Pitt and Fox. Sir Walter Scott. *See* To William Stewart Rose, Esq.
Pitted and pock-marked by a roving gun. Crucifix. Edith Lovejoy Pierce. ChIP
"Pitter patter!" falls the rain. The Umbrella Brigade. Laura E. Richards. SUS; TiPo
Pitter-patter, hear it raining? Rain. Lilian McCrea. BoTP
Pittsburgh. James Oppenheim. PoeMoYo; StaSt
Pittsburgh. Hy Sobiloff. NePA
Pitty Patty Polt! *Unknown.* BoTP
Pity. Babette Deutsch. TBM; WHA
Pity and Love. *Unknown.* ALV; SeCL
Pity beyond all telling, A. The Pity of Love. W. B. Yeats. AnIV; ChMo; CMP
Pity Me Not. Edna St. Vincent Millay. AnNE; LoPS; MAP; MoAB; MoAmPo; NeMA; NePA; PIAE; TrGrPo
(Pity Me Not because the Light of Day.) OxBA
Pity me on my pilgrimage to Loch Derg! At Saint Patrick's Purgatory. *At. to* Donnchadh mor O'Dala. AnIL; LiTW; LyMA; OnYI; SiB
Pity me, Stranger! shed one passing tear. Four Years Only. *Unknown.* OnPM
Pity! mourn in plaintive tone. The Death of Lesbia's Bird [*or* The Dead Starling]. Catullus. AWP; OnPM
Pity Not. William Haskell Simpson. *Fr.* In Arizona. HBMV; NP
Pity not! The Army gave. Ex-Clerk. Kipling. *Fr.* Epitaphs of the War. PoVP
Pity now poor Mary Ames. Mary Ames. *Unknown.* NA
Pity of beauty in distress. Pity and Love. *Unknown.* ALV; SeCL
Pity of It, The. Thomas Hardy. ChMo; CMP; InP; LiTM (rev. ed.); WaP
Pity of Love, The. W. B. Yeats. AnIV; ChMo; CMP
Pity of the Leaves, The. E. A. Robinson. AA; MoAmPo (1950 ed.)
Pity, oh pity! death had power. Thomas Freeman. SiCE; TuPP
Pity, pity, pity. A True Love Ditty. Thomas Middleton. *Fr.* Blurt, Master Constable. ElL
Pity reminds my tears. Fallen Flyer Aged 19. David Ross. PG (1955 ed.)
Pity, repulsion, love and anger. Poem. Roy Fuller. NeBP
Pity the Captive Maiden's Lot. Sophocles, *tr. fr. Greek by* Robert Whitelaw. *Fr.* Trachiniae. GrR
Pity the Great. Mary Sinton Leitch. LS
Pity the great with love, they are deaf, they are blind. A Cry on the Wind. "Fiona Macleod." LBBV
Pity the innocent. There are none innocent, none. Rend Your Heart and Not Your Garments. L. A. MacKay. TwCV
Pity the nameless, and the unknown, where. The Nameless Ones. Conrad Aiken. NePA; OxBA
Pity the sorrows of a poor old man! The Beggar. Thomas Moss. LPS-1
Pity the unicorn. The Unicorn and the Hippogrif. Martha Ostenso. BAP
Pity This Busy Monster, Manunkind. E. E. Cummings. AmP; CoBA; CoBMV; CrMA; LiTA; LiTM; MoVE; NePA; OxBA; PeBoSo
Pity this man who, slave to an affliction. The Ailing Parent. Lora Dunetz. NePoAm-2
Pity those men who from the start. A Song about Great Men. Michael Hamburger. NePoEA
Pity us not/ Because we tried to battle and to go. From Beyond. Lucia Trent. PGD
Pity would be no more. The Human Abstract. Blake. *Fr.* Songs of Experience. EiPP; EnRP; MaPo; PoEL-4
Pitying Heart, The. Goldsmith. PCH
Pius, the springtime rolls like a wave upon our land. To Blessed Pius X at Easter. John Hazard Wildman. JKCP (1955 ed.)
Pixie, kobold, elf, and sprite. Hallowe'en. Joel Benton. DD; HOAH; OTPC (1946 ed.); PoRL
Pixies, slipping, dipping, stealing. Cornish Magic. Ann Durell. FaPON
Pla ce bo. *Filed as* Placebo.
Place and the Person, The, *sel.* Henry Reed.
"From the far horizon, and breaking in triumph towards him." GTBS-D
Place for No Story, The. Robinson Jeffers. CoV
Place in Thy Memory, A. Gerald Griffin. HBV; VA
(Song: "Place in thy memory, dearest, A.") BLPA; NeHB
Place is palpable me, for here I was born, The. Nostalgia. D. H. Lawrence. LBBV; NP
Place Me in the Breach. Yehuda Karni, *tr. fr. Hebrew by* Sholom J. Kahn. TrJP
Place me once more, my daughter, where the sun. Milton. William Edmonstoune Aytoun. BHV
Place me where herb and flower the sun has dried. Petrarch. Sonnets to Laura: To Laura in Life, CXIII. PrPoCR
Place not your faith in blood. We are controlled. Heritage. Stanton A. Coblentz. AlBD
Place of His Rest, The. Sir Charles G. D. Roberts. CPG; OCL
Place of Pain in the Universe, The. Anthony Hecht. CrMA
Place of Peace, The. Edwin Markham. MaRV; OQP; QP-2
Place of Prayer, The. Annie Johnson Flint. PraP
Place of Rest, The. "Æ." CMP; PC; WGRP
Place of the Damn'd, The. Swift. BeR
Place of the Damned, The. Milton. *Fr.* Paradise Lost, II. FaBoEn
Place of the Solitaires, The. Wallace Stevens. NP
Place was dark and dusty and half-lost, The. Fungi from Yuggoth. H. P. Lovecraft. DaM
Place where a great city stands is not the place, The. The Great City. Walt Whitman. *Fr.* Song of the Broad-Axe. BAP
Place where our two gardens meet, The. The Wall. Henry Reed. LiTB
Place Where Soon, The. Walter Savage Landor. EmBrPo
(Wall-Flower, The.) OBVV
Pla ce bo./ Who is there, who? Phyllyp Sparowe [*or* Philip Sparrow *or* The Sparrow's Dirge]. John Skelton. AtBAP; CoBE; NBE; OBSC; OxBoLi; PoEL-1; ReEn; ReIE; TuPP
Placed in a country on a desert verging. Delusions VIII. Charles Madge. BoSA
Places. Carl Sandburg. NP
Places, Loved Ones. Philip Larkin. NePoEA
Places of Nestling Green. Leigh Hunt. *Fr.* The Story of Rimini. OBRV
("Noble range it was, of many a road, A.") EnRP
Places of Worship. Wordsworth. GEPC
Placid Man's Epitaph, A. Thomas Hardy. MBP; MoBrPo
Placid, rotted harbour has no voice, The. Arrival and Departure. Charles Eglington. BoSA
Plácido's Sonnet to His Mother. "Plácido," *tr. fr. Spanish.* (Farewell to My Mother.) BANP, *tr. by* Bryant; PoNe, *tr. by* James Weldon Johnson
(Plácido's Farewell to His Mother, *tr. by* James Weldon Johnson.) BANP
Plague is love, A, a plague! but yet. The Little Love-God. Meleager. AWP
Plague like this, a tempest big with fate, A. Lucretius. *Fr.* De Rerum Natura. PoP

Plague take all your pedants, say I! Sibrandus Schafnaburgensis. Robert Browning. Garden Fancies, II. EnLi-2 (1949 ed.); VLEP
Plague the Meddling Female, A! Euripides, *tr. fr. Greek by* Hugh Owen Meredith. *Fr.* Andromache. GrR
Plaidie, The. Charles Sibley. BOHV; HBV; LPS-1
Plain Bob and a Job. James W. Foley. PTA-1
Plain Chant for America. Katherine Garrison Chapin. PoFr
Plain Chant of the Hill Country. Sister Mary David. JKCP (1955 ed.)
Plain Dealing. Alexander Brome. OBS
Plain Description of Perfect Friendship, A. *At. to* Henry Cheke. TuPP
(Of Perfect Friendship.) ElL
Plain Direction, A. Thomas Hood. OTPC (1946 ed.); TVSH
Plain Golden Band, The, *2 vers., with music. At. to* Joe Scott. ShS
Plain Language from Truthful James. Bret Harte. AmPP; BAV; BeLS; BLPA; BOHV; CoBA; DD; DDA; FaBoBe; HBV; IAP; InMe; LEAP; LHV; LPS-3; MAP; MoAmPo (1942 ed.); OBAV; OnSP; PFY; PoE; PoeMoYo; PYM; TreF; WhC; YaD
(Heathen Chinee, The.) BAP; CenHV
(Plain Talk from Truthful James.) AnAmPo; LA
(That Heathen Chinee.) EV-5
Plain Living. Hesiod, *tr. fr. Greek by* Sir William Marris. *Fr.* Works and Days. OxBG
Plain Man's Dream, A. Frederick Keppel. AA
Plain of Donnerdale, The. Wordsworth. The River Duddon, XX. PeBoSo
("Old inventive poets, had they seen, The.") EnLi-2
Plain Sense of Things, The. Wallace Stevens. CoV
Plain-Song. Jean Cocteau, *tr. fr. French.* LiTW, *tr. by* W. J. Strachan; MiCF, *tr. by* Wallace Fowlie
Plain Tales from the Hills, *sel.* Kipling.
Predestination. LoBV
Plain Talk. William Jay Smith. FiBHP
Plain Talk from Truthful James. Bret Harte. *See* Plain Language from Truthful James.
Plain tilt-bonnet on her head, A. In the Days of Crinoline. Thomas Hardy. WhC
Plain was grassy, wild and bare, The. The Dying Swan. Tennyson. EmBrPo; GTSE; OTPC
Plain, when summer days withdraw their light, The. June Nights. Victor Hugo. TrFP
Plainest lodge room in the land was over Simpkins' store, The. The Lodge Room over Simpkins' Store. Lawrence N. Greenleaf. PoOW
Plainness and clearness without shadow of stain! Matthew Arnold. *Fr.* A Summer Night. PC
Plains. W. H. Auden. NePA
Plains, The. Roy Fuller. BoSA; MoPo
Plains of Abraham, The. Charles Sangster. CPG
Plaint. Chu Shu Chen, *tr. fr. Chinese by* Kenneth Rexroth. OnPC
Plaint. Ebenezer Elliott. MeRV; OBEV; OBVV; TriL
(Land Which No One Knows, The.) HBV
Plaint. Charles Henri Ford. AtBAP; MoVE
Plaint of an Humble Servant. Robert Nichols. WP
Plaint of Friendship by Death Broken. Robert Nichols. TCPD
Plaint of the Camel, The. Charles Edward Carryl. *Fr.* The Admiral's Caravan. AnAmPo; BoTP; FaPON; HBV; HBVY; LA; OTPC (1946 ed.); PCN; PoeMoYo; PoRh; SP; StVeCh; UTS
(Camel's Complaint, The.) GoBP
(Camel's Lament, The.) GoTP
Plaint of the Nightingale, The. Sophocles, *tr. fr. Greek by* Robert Whitelaw. *Fr.* Electra. GrR
Plaint of the Wife, The. *Unknown, tr. fr. Russian by* W. R. S. Ralston. AWP; JAWP; WBP
Plaint to Man, A. Thomas Hardy. ChMo; CMP
Plainte Eternelle. Lord Alfred Douglas. PoVP
Plaintive sonnet flow'd from Milton's pen, A. Sonnet: Anniversary, February 23, 1795. William Mason. OBEC
Plan, The. Richard Burton. POT
Plan, A. John Alden Carpenter. RIS
Plan for a Novel. Frederic Thompson. JKCP (1955 ed.)
Plan of Salvation, The. Milton. *Fr.* Paradise Lost, III. WGRP
Plane, The. Sidney Alexander. PoF
Plane Geometry. Emma Rounds. ImOP
Plane, released, its twin blades waving, The. The Aviator. Aleksandr Blok. OnHM; PoF
Plane-Tree. F. S. Flint. MBP; MoBrPo (1942 ed.)
Plane-Tree, The. Amy Levy. *See* London Plane-Tree, A.
Planet Moon, *sel.* Will Dyson.
"Planet moon and dancing star." MoAuPo
Planetary Arc-Light, The. August Derleth. GoYe
Planh for the Young English King. Bertrans de Born, *tr. fr. Provençal by* Ezra Pound. LiTW
Plans. Luisa Hewitt. PCH
Plant, The. Schiller, *tr. fr. German by* J. H. Merivale. RO
Plant a Tree. Lucy Larcom. ADAH; DD; HBVY; OHFP; OnHT; PEOR; PGD; WBLP
Plant cut down to the root, The. Elizabeth J. Coatsworth. TiPo (1952 ed.)
Plant here a willow, for one there was. For a Shakespearean Garden. Edna Davis Romig. PoTo
Plant no tree, O my friend. Horace. Odes, I, 18. LaP
Plant No Trees. Li Ho, *tr. fr. Chinese by* Ho Chih-yuan. WhP
Plant That Will Not Grow, A. Dryden. *Fr.* Aureng-Zebe: Prologue. BeR
Plantains, The. *Unknown, tr. fr. Chinese.* WhP
Plantation Ditty, A. Frank Lebby Stanton. AA; BAP; HBV; LHV; OBAV
Plantation Play-Song. Joel Chandler Harris. *Fr.* Uncle Remus, His Songs and His Sayings. MCCG
Planter's Charm. Fay M. Yauger. HiLiAm; InP
Planter's Daughter, The. Austin Clarke. OxBI
Planting a Lichi Tree. Po Chü-i, *tr. fr. Chinese by* Henry H. Hart. PoHN
Planting a Tree. Nancy Byrd Turner. YeAr
Planting Bamboos. Po Chü-i, *tr. fr. Chinese by* Arthur Waley. TrCh
Planting Beans. T'ao Ch'ien, *tr. fr. Chinese by* C. W. Luh. OnPM
Planting Bulbs. Katharine Tynan. JKCP
Planting Flowers on the Embankment. Po Chü-i, *tr. fr. Chinese by* Arthur Waley. TrCh
Planting of the Apple Tree, The. Bryant. AA; ADAH; AnNE; DD; *much abr.*; GN; HBV; HBVY; LaNeLa; LEAP; LPS-2; MPB (1956 ed.); OHIP; PECK; PTA-1; SN; StVeCh
Plants Decay, The. Shelley. *Fr.* The Sensitive Plant. RO
Plants in the Earth. Paul Green. *Fr.* Shroud My Body Down. NoCaPo
Plants Stand Silent Round Me, The. Johannes Jørgensen, *tr. fr. Danish by* Robert S. Hillyer. OnPM
Plaque. Bruce Ruddick. CaP
Plastic Airman. Wrenne Jarman. DiM
Plastic Glass, The. Josephine Miles. FiMAP
Plataea. Simonides, *tr. fr. Greek.* GrL; OxBG
Platelayer, The. W. W. Gibson. POTT
Platform Goodbye. H. B. Mallalieu. WaP
Plato, a Musician. Leontius, *tr. fr. Greek by* A. J. Butler. OxBG; UnS
Plato to Theon. Philip Freneau. AA
Plato Told. E. E. Cummings. CrMA; MoVE; OxBA; WaP
Platonic. Hildegarde Dolson. CAG
Platonic. William Terrett. LPS-1
Platonick Love. Abraham Cowley. *Fr.* The Mistress. SeCV-1
(Platonic Love.) SeEP
Platonick Love. Lord Herbert of Cherbury. OBS
(Platonic Love.) SeEP
Plato's Tomb. *Unknown. See* Spirit of Plato.
Plattsburg Bay! Plattsburg Bay! The Battle of Plattsburg Bay. Clinton Scollard. GA; MC; PAH
Platypus, The. Oliver Herford. FiBHP; NA
Play. Charles Stuart Calverley. PCD
Play, The. James B. Kenyon. HBV
Play-acting. Frances Barber. GoYe
Play, Beggars, Play! "A. W." *See* In Praise of a Beggar's Life.
Play is done; the curtain drops, The. The End of the Play. Thackeray. *Fr.* Dr. Birch and His Young Friends. BMEP; COAH; FaFP; GN; LEAP; LPS-1; TreF; VA
Play is ended, The? Be it so! The Moral. Robert Kelley Weeks. PR
Play is over, The. While the light. After the Curfew. Oliver Wendell Holmes. IAP
Play it once. Saturday Night. Langston Hughes. MAP; MoAmPo
Play me a march, low-toned and slow—a march for a silent tread. A Dead March. Cosmo Monkhouse. HBV; OBVV; VA
Play of "King Lear," The. Sir William Watson. VA
Play of the Four P's. John Heywood. *See* Four P's, The.
Play of the Weather, The, *sels.* John Heywood.
English Schoolboy, The. ACP
"Sir, I pray you, be you not master god?" CoBE
Play on the seashore. Shore. Mary Britton Miller. SUS; TiPo (1952 ed.)
Play on Words, A. Eugene Field. WhC
Play, play, while yet it is day. Play. Charles Stuart Calverley. PCD
Play-Song. *Unknown, tr. fr. Greek by* J. M. Edmonds. LiTW
Play that thing. Jazz Band in a Parisian Cabaret. Langston Hughes. BANP; MAP; MoAmPo
Play the Game. Sir Henry Newbolt. *See* Vitai Lampada.
Play their offensive and defensive parts. Good Christians. Robert Herrick. LiTB
Play Then and Sing! Swinburne. GTML
Play Time. Blake. *See* Nurse's Song ("When the voices of children are heard on the green/ And laughing").

Play was done, The. An Epilogue at Wallack's. John Elton Wayland. AA
Play was each, pleasure each. Cuchullain's Lament over Fardiad [*or* Cuchulainn's Lament for Ferdiad]. *Tr. by* George Sigerson. AnIL; AnIV; BoFr; SiB
Play with Proverbs, A. Michael Drayton. *See* Love's Proverbs.
Playboy of the dawn. Gone Boy. Langston Hughes. NePoAm-2
Playboy of the Demi-World, The, 1938. William Plomer. FaBoTw
Playbox, The. Nathalia Crane. TBM
Played-out Humorist, The. W. S. Gilbert. *Fr.* His Excellency. BOHV
Player Queen, The. Olga Katzin. DiM
Players Ask for a Blessing on the Psalteries and on Themselves, The. W. B. Yeats. UnS
Player's Christmas, The. William Lackaye. CAG
Playful Crickets, The. *Unknown. See* Game of Tag, A.
Playgrounds. Laurence Alma-Tadema. BoTP; HBV; HBVY; OTPC; PCH; PPL
Playhouse Key, The. Rachel Field. BoTP; FaPON; MPB
Playhouse Musings. James Smith. EV-4
Playing a phonograph record of a windy morning. From the Duck-Pond to the Carousel. Muriel Rukeyser. FiMAP
Playing Cards, The. Pope. *Fr.* The Rape of the Lock, III. ChTr
Playing on the virginals. Jean Ingelow. GTBS
Playing Robinson Crusoe. Kipling. *See* First Friend, The.
Playing, she puts her instrument to sleep. Improvising. Louise Townsend Nicholl. NePoAm-2
Playing the Game. *Unknown.* BLP, *st.* 2
Playing the Lyre. Apostolos Melachrinos, *tr. fr. Modern Greek by* Rae Dalven. *Fr.* Apollonius. MoGP
Playing upon the hill three centaurs were! The Centaurs. James Stephens. AnEnPo; MM
Playmates. Lillian Everts. GoYe
Playmates. Mary White Slater. FAOV
Playmates, The. Sir William Watson. PoVP
Plays. Walter Savage Landor. BCEP; BLP; HBV; OnPM; OxBoLi; VA
(Alas, How Soon [the Hours Are Over].) BPN; EmBrPo; EnRP; EPN; TOP
(Epigram.) ALV
(Lyrics and Epigrams, XVII.) ERP
Plaything. Asclepiades, *tr. fr. Greek by* Walter Leaf. GrR
Playthings. William Cowper. WaaP
Plaza Santa Ana. John Dos Passos. *Fr.* Winter in Castile. VOD (1935 ed.)
Plaza Square. Louis Untermeyer. VOD
Plea. Eileen Duggan. JKCP (1955 ed.)
Plea, A. Arthur Guiterman. PR
Plea, A. Hazel Miners. CAG
Plea and Counsel. Tibullus. *See* No Harm to Lovers.
Plea for a Cat. Jewell Bothwell Tull. CIV
Plea for a Plural, A. Rudolf Chambers Lehmann. CenHV
Plea for Alias, A. James Schevill. FiMAP
Plea for Flood Ireson, A. Charles Timothy Brooks. GA, *abr.*; PAH
Plea for Hope. Francis Carlin. TrPWD
Plea for the Animals. James Thomson. *Fr.* The Seasons: Spring. LPS-3
Plea for the Enemy, A. Aristophanes, *tr. fr. Greek by* B. B. Rogers. *Fr.* The Acharnians. OxBG
Plea for Tolerance. Margaret E. Bruner. PoToHe (new ed.)
Plea for Trigamy, A. Sir Owen Seaman. BOHV
Plea of Cornelia, The ("Guard, Paullus, guard"). Propertius, *tr. fr. Latin by* E. D. A. Morshead. *Fr.* Elegies, IV, 11. MOAH
Plea of the Midsummer Fairies, The, *sels.* Thomas Hood.
Shakespeare. OBRV
Tender Babes. OBRV
Titania. OBRV
Plead for Me. Emily Brontë. EmBrPo; EnLi-2 (1949 ed.); PoEL-5; ViP
(God of Visions.) TrGrPo
(Speak, God of Visions.) GTML
Pleasant above the city's din. Under the Eaves. Celia Thaxter. MW
Pleasant Comedie of Old Fortunatus, The. Thomas Dekker. *See* Old Fortunatus.
Pleasant Comedy of Patient Grissell [*or* Grissill], *sels.* Thomas Dekker *and others.*
Bridal Song: "Beauty, arise, show forth thy glorious shining," *fr.* V, ii. OBSC; TrGrPo
(Beauty, Arise!) EIL
("Beauty arise, show forth thy glorious shining.") TuPP
Golden Slumbers [Kiss Your Eyes], *fr.* IV, ii. CenL; CH; EV-2; HBV; OTPC; PoE; ReEn; ShBV-4; SiCE; TuPP; ViBoPo
(Cradle Song.) OBSC; TrGrPo
(Lullaby.) BLV; BOL; EIL; LoBV
Happy Heart, The, *fr.* I, i. GTBS; GTBS-D; GTBS-W; GTSE; GTSL; HBV; LEAP; LPS-2; WoL
("Art thou poor, yet hast thou golden slumbers?") EG; ElSeCe; OAEP; SiCE; TCEP; TOP; TuPP; ViBoPo
(Basket-Maker's Song, The.) CenL; OBSC; ThWaDe; TrGrPo
(Content.) BBV (1923 ed.); CBE; EnLi-1; EPP
(O Sweet Content.) AtBAP; BEL; BLV; CBOV; EV-2; ShBV-2
(Sweet Content.) CH; ElL; EnLit; LoBV; OBEV; OtMeF; PG; TVSH; WHA
Pleasant Historie of Albino and Bellama, The. Nathaniel Whiting. *See* Le Hore di Recreatione.
Pleasant is the theme that falls to my care. The Enchanted Fawn. *Unknown. Fr.* Dinnshenchas. OnYI
Pleasant Isle of Aves, The. Charles Kingsley. *See* Last Buccaneer, The.
Pleasant isle of Rügen looks the Baltic water o'er, The. The Brown Dwarf of Rügen. Whittier. PoMS
Pleasant it is, when over a great sea the winds trouble the waters. Introduction; Combinations of Atoms; Creation and Destruction of Worlds. Lucretius. *Fr.* De Rerum Natura. RoL
Pleasant journey, little book. To the Lady with a Book. *Unknown.* KiLC
Pleasant little villages that grace the Irish glynns, The. Song of the Little Villages. James B. Dollard. CAW; JKCP
Pleasant New Ballad of Two Lovers, A. *Unknown.* CoMu
Pleasant New Court Song, A. *Unknown.* CoMu
Pleasant Pastime between the Young-Men and Maids, in the Pleasant Meadows. *Unknown. See* Merry Hay-Makers, The.
Pleasant place I was at today, A. The Woodland Mass. Dafydd ap Gwilym. PrWP
Pleasant Things. Byron. *See* 'Tis Sweet.
Pleasantly rose next morn the sun on the village of Grand Pré. Longfellow. *Fr.* Evangeline, Pt. I. IAP
Please. Rose Fyleman. MPB
Please excuse this letter. The Letter. Beatrice M. Murphy PoNe
Please Excuse Typing. J. B. Boothroyd. FiBHP; SiTL
"Please give me a ride on your back." Edward Lear. *Fr.* The Duck and the Kangaroo. MeMeAg
Please to remember. *Unknown.* OTPC (1923 ed.); OxNR
Please to Ring the Belle. Thomas Hood. HBV
Please your grace, from out your store. The Beggar, to Mab the Fairy Queen. Robert Herrick. OTPC (1923 ed.)
Pleased Intimacy, The. Bilhana, *formerly at. to* Chauras, *tr. fr. Sanskrit by* E. Powys Mathers. *Fr.* Black Marigolds. OnPM
Pleased with an Empty Swelling. Swift. *Fr.* Ode to Dr. William Sancroft. BeR
Pleasing Constraint, The. Aristaenetus, *tr. fr. Greek by* Sheridan *and* Nathaniel Brassey Halhed. ALV
Pleasing land of drowsy-head it was, A. James Thomson. *Fr.* The Castle of Indolence. BCEP; LEAP
Pleasing 'tis, O modest moon! To the Harvest Moon. Henry Kirke White. LPS-2
Pleasure and Guilt. Arthur Hugh Clough. *Fr.* Dipsychus Continued. VLEP
Pleasure and Sorrow. Robert Browning Hamilton. *See* Along the Road.
Pleasure-Boat, The. Richard Henry Dana. LPS-2
Pleasure is not the one I love. The Rivals. W. H. Davies. ChMo; CMP
Pleasure Is Too Surely Found. Herbert A. Kenny. JKCP (1955 ed.)
Pleasure It Is. William Cornish. CH; TuPP
(God's Blessings.) CBOV
(Gratitude.) OBSC
(Spring.) ChTr
Pleasure of Hope, The. Pope. *See* Hope.
Pleasure of Walking through an Alley, The. John Gay. *Fr.* Trivia; or, The Art of Walking the Streets of London, II. EnLi-1 (1949 ed.)
Pleasure Reconciled to Virtue, *sel.* Ben Jonson.
Hymn to Comus. EIL; OAEP
(Hymn to the Belly.) SeCePo; SiTL
(Song: To Comus.) SeEP
Pleasure! Why Thus Desert [the Heart]. Walter Savage Landor. *Fr.* Ianthe. BPN; EmBrPo
Pleasures. Denise Levertov. NeAP
Pleasures, Beauty, Youth Attend Ye. John Ford. *Fr.* The Lady's Trial. LiTL; ViBoPo
Pleasures lie thickest where no pleasures seem. Hidden Joys. Laman Blanchard. VA
Pleasures newly found are sweet. To the Same Flower (Celandine). Wordsworth. BPN; EmBrPo; EnRP; GEPC
Pleasures of a poultry yard, The. The Swan and the Cook. La Fontaine. BoChLi
Pleasures of Hope, The, *sels.* Thomas Campbell.
"At summer eve, when Heaven's ethereal bow." EnRP
Hope ("Unfading hope!"). LPS-3
Poland. LPS-2
Pleasures of Imagination, The, *sels.* Mark Akenside.
Delights of Fancy, *fr.* I. LPS-3
Early Influences, *fr.* IV. OBEC

Invocation to the Genius of Greece, *fr.* I. OBEC
Nature, *fr.* IV. LoBV
Nature's Influence on Man, *fr.* III. OBEC
(Created Universe, The.) LoBV
("Oh! blest of heav'n, whom not the languid songs.") CEP
Poets, *fr.* IV. OBEC
That Delightful Time. SeCePo
"With what attractive charms this goodly frame," *fr.* I. EiPP; EnRP
Pleasures of Love, The. Wilfrid Scawen Blunt. HBV
Pleasures of love, and the joys of good wine, The. Song. Sir George Etherege. *Fr.* The Man of Mode. CEP
Pleasures of Melancholy, The. Thomas Warton, the Younger. CEP; EiPP
Sels.
Goodbye to Mr. Pope. BeR
"Mother of musings, Contemplation sage." EnRP
Solemn Noon of Night, The. OBEC; SeCePo
Wet Morning, The. BeR
Pleasures of Memory, The, *sel.* Samuel Rogers.
Inscription on a Grot. OBEC
Pleasures of Merely Circulating, The. Wallace Stevens. LiTA; OnHM
Pleasures that I most enviously sense. The Cat. Walter Adolphe Roberts. CIV; PFE
Plebeian Song. "Markos Avgeris," *tr. fr. Modern Greek by* Rae Dalven. MoGP
Pledge, The. Adelaide Crapsey. NP; TOP
Pledge of Cheerfulness, The. William Cowper. *Fr.* Retirement. BPP
Pleiades, The. Arthur Adams. BoAu
Pleiades, The. Elizabeth J. Coatsworth. ImOP
Pleiads, The. John Banister Tabb. UTS
Plenitude. Otto D'Sola, *tr. fr. Spanish by* Angel Flores. AnCL
Plenitude. A. M. Sullivan. JKCP (1926 ed.)
Plenteous place is Ireland for hospitable cheer, A. The Fair Hills of Ireland. *Unknown, tr. by* Sir Samuel Ferguson. AnIV; GTIV; IrPN; OBEV; OBVV; OnYI
Plentiful harvest is garnered in, The. Autumn. Meta E. B. Thorne. *Fr.* Songs of the Seasons. PEOR
Plight of a Forsaken Lover. Menander, *tr. fr. Greek by* Francis G. Allinson. *Fr.* Perikeiromene. GrR
(Advice to a Lover, *tr. by* Gilbert Highet.) OxBG
Plight of Wounded Aphrodite, The. Homer, *tr. fr. Greek by* George Chapman. *Fr.* The Iliad, V. GrR
Plighted. Dinah Maria Mulock Craik. HBV
Plot against Proteus, The. A. J. M. Smith. BoCaPo; PeCV
Plot against the Giant, The. Wallace Stevens. OxBA
Plot Improbable, Character Unsympathetic. Elder Olson. NePA
Plough, The. Richard Henry Horne. OBEV; OBVV; VA; WP
(Plow, The.) HBV
Plough-Hands' Song, The. Joel Chandler Harris. *Fr.* Uncle Remus, His Songs and His Sayings. AA; LHV
Plough-Horse, The. Rhoda Coghill. OnYI
Ploughboy, The. John Clare. PoEL-4
Plougher, The. Padraic Colum. AnFE; EPP; GoBC; GTIV; GTML; GTSL; HBMV; LBBV; OnYI; PFE; TwCV
(Plower, The.) MBP; MoBrPo;NeMA
Ploughing. V. Sackville-West. *Fr.* The Land. TCPD
Ploughing on Sunday. Wallace Stevens. FaPON; ThWaDe
Ploughman, The. Karle Wilson Baker. WGRP
Ploughman, The. Gordon Bottomley. POTE
Ploughman, The. Oliver Wendell Holmes. LPS-2
Ploughman, The. Raymond Knister. *See* Plowman, The.
Ploughman, The. John Masefield. *Fr.* The Everlasting Mercy. AtBAP
("O Christ who holds the open gate.") TreFS
Ploughman, The. Gilbert Thomas. HBMV
Ploughman, The. *Unknown.* CoMu
Ploughman at the Plough. Louis Golding. HBMV; OHIP
(Plowman at the Plow.) MBP
Ploughman he's a bonnie lad, The. The Ploughman. *Unknown.* CoMu
Ploughman, whose gnarly hand yet kindly wheeled. *See* Plowman, whose gnarly hand . . .
Ploughman's Song, The. Nicholas Breton. *See* Phyllida and Corydon ("In the merry month of May").
Plover. Luella Boynton. MuM
Plovers, The. Hitomaro, *tr. fr. Japanese by* Ishii *and* Obata. OnPM
("Plovers cry, The," *tr. by* Kenneth Rexroth.) LiTW
Plow, The. Max Barthel, *tr. fr. German by* Herman Salinger. TwGV
Plow, The. Richard Henry Horne. *See* Plough, The.
Plow. *Unknown, tr. fr. Anglo-Saxon by* Charles W. Kennedy. *Fr.* Riddles. AnOE
Plower, The. Padraic Colum. *See* Plougher, The.
Plowing; a Memory. Hamlin Garland. StVeCh
Plowman, The. Max Harris. BoAV
Plowman. Sidney Keyes. MoAB; PoRA
Plowman, The. Raymond Knister. BoCaPo; PeCV; TwCaPo
Plowman at the Plow. Louis Golding. *See* Ploughman at the Plough.
Plowman of Today, The. Hamlin Garland. StVeCh
Plowman [*or* Ploughman], whose gnarly hand yet kindly wheeled. The Waving of the Corn. Sidney Lanier. CoV; MOAP
Plowman's Song, The. Nicholas Breton. *See* Phillida and Coridon.
Plowman's Song. Raymond Knister. CaP
Pluck me ten berries from the juniper. Recipe, *parody.* A. P. Herbert. *Fr.* Two Gentlemen of Soho. WhC
Pluck the Fruit and Taste the Pleasure. Thomas Lodge. *Fr.* Robert, Second Duke of Normandy. ElL; EV-1
(Carpe Diem.) OBSC
Plucking the Rushes. *Unknown, tr. fr. Chinese by* Arthur Waley. ChLP; OnPM; ShBV-4; TrCh; WoL
Plum-blossom, The. Akahito. *Fr.* Manyo Shu. AWP
Plum Blossoms ("Far across hill and dale"). Basho, *tr. fr. Japanese.* SUS
Plum Blossoms ("So sweet the plum trees smell"). Ranko. *See* Plum Trees.
Plum blossoms, The. Regrets. Tzu Yeh. PoHN
Plum-Cake, The. Ann Taylor. HBVY
(Another Plum-Cake.) OTPC (1923 ed.)
Plum Tree, The. James Reaney. CaP
Plum Tree, The. Wang An Shih, *tr. fr. Chinese by* Henry H. Hart. PoHN
Plum Tree by the House, The. Oliver St. John Gogarty. OBEV (new ed.); PoRA
Plum Trees. Ranko, *tr. fr. Japanese.* FaPON; MPB
(Plum Blossoms: "So sweet the plum trees smell!") SUS
Plume Travelling. Henri Michaux, *tr. fr. French by* Wallace Fowlie. MiCF
Plummets of moonlight thinning through. The Farm, 1923. Archibald MacLeish. ChMo; CMP
Plump little baby clouds. Lullaby. *Unknown.* BOL
Plump Mr. Pl'f is washing his hands of America, The. Oil Painting of the Artist as the Artist. Archibald MacLeish. Frescoes for Mr. Rockefeller's City, IV. NAMP; OnHM; ReaPo; UnPo
Plumpuppets, The. Christopher Morley. FaPON; GaP; MPB; TiPo
Plums are like blue pendulums, The. The Plum Tree. James Reaney. CaP
Plunged in night, I sit alone. Samson. Frederick George Scott. CPG; VA
Plunger. Carl Sandburg. BLV; BoLiVe; NeMA
Plunging limbers over the shattered track, The. Dead Man's Dump. Isaac Rosenberg. FaBoMo; LiTM; MoPo; TrJP; WaP
Plutarch. Agathias Scholasticus, *tr. fr. Greek by* Dryden. AWP; JAWP; WBP
("Chaeronean Plutarch, to thy deathless praise.") GrPo
Pluto and Venus. *Unknown, tr. fr. Greek by* William Hay. OnPM
Plutocracy. Theognis, *tr. fr. Greek by* F. L. Lucas. GrPE
Pluto's Council. Tasso, *tr. fr. Italian by* Edward Fairfax. *Fr.* Godfrey of Bulloigne. OBSC
Plutus, *sels.* Aristophanes, *tr. fr. Greek.*
Bounteous Poverty, *tr. by* Benjamin Bickley Rogers. GrR
Gifts of Poverty, The, *pr. tr. by* Henry Fielding *and* William Young. OxBG
"O dotards both, most easily seduced from wisdom's train," *tr. by* W. R. Kennedy. GrPo
Pluviose. Julian Bell. ChMP
Plymouth Harbor [*or* Harbour]. Ernest Radford. HBV; PoeT
Plymouth Harvest, The. William Bradford. PCH
Po' Boy, *with music. Unknown.* AS; TrAS, *diff. vers.*
(As I Set Down to Play Tin-Can, *with music, diff. vers.*) OuSiCo
Po' Boy (*diff. ballad*). *Unknown. See* Cryderville Jail, The.
Po' Boy Blues. Langston Hughes. BANP
Po' Farmer, *with music. Unknown.* OuSiCo
Po' Laz'us, *with music. Unknown.* ABF; OuSiCo, *diff. vers.*
Po' lil' brack sheep dat strayed away. De Sheepfol' [*or* The Little Black Sheep]. *At. to* Paul Laurence Dunbar, *also to* Sarah Pratt McLean Greene. MaRV; WBLP
Po' Mourner's Got a Home at Las', *with music. Unknown.* BoAN-2
Po' Ole Slave, The, *with music. Unknown.* StDa
Po, Po, Po, Po/ [I] Love Brawn and So Do Mo. *Unknown.* AnEC
Po' Shine, *with music. Unknown.* StDa
Po, the unrivaled poet. To Li Po on a Spring Day. Tu Fu. WhP
Pobble Who Has No Toes, The. Edward Lear. BOHV; BoN; FaBoCh; GaP; GoTP; HBV; HBVY; InP; LBN; LiL; LiTG; LoGBV; MaC; MoShBr; MPB; NA; OnHT; OnSP; OTPC; PIAE; WhC; YT
Pocahontas. George Pope Morris. GA; MC; PAH
Pocahontas. Thackeray. DD; FaPON; GA; GN; GoTP; MC; MPB; OTPC; PAH; TVSH
Po Chü-i to Yüan Chen. PoChü-i, *tr. fr. Chinese by* Arthur Waley. BoFr
Pocket and Steeple. M. A. De Wolfe Howe. WhC

Pocket-Cattle-Thief. *Unknown. See* Hymn to Mercury.
Pocket Guide for Servicemen. Hubert Creekmore. WaP
Pocket Handkerchief to Hem, A. Christina Rossetti. *Fr.* Sing-Song. RIS; SAS
(Stitching.) OTPC (1946 ed.); PPL
Pockets. Susan Adger Williams. BrR; DDA
Poe and Longfellow. James Russell Lowell. *Fr.* A Fable for Critics. AnNE; APW; OxBA
("There comes Poe, with his raven, like Barnaby Rudge.") CoBA; PtP
Poe Cottage, The. Nathalia Crane. TCAP
Poe-'em of Passion, A. Charles Fletcher Lummis. BOHV
Poem: "Ah I know what happiness is!" Blanche Taylor Dickinson. CDC
Poem: "And when I pay death's duty." Robin Blaser. NeAP
Poem: "As rock to sun or storm." Niall Sheridan. OnYI
Poem: "As the cat." William Carlos Williams. FaPON; InvP; ThWaDe
Poem: "By the road to the contagious hospital." William Carlos Williams. *See* By the Road to the Contagious Hospital.
Poem: "Child—in all the flying sky." Josephine Strongin. AnAmPo; LA
Poem I: "Cotton-still spire cracks in chimes on the, The." David Evans. MoWP
Poem: "Death walks through the mind's dark woods." Henry Treece. NeBP
Poem, A: Dedication of the Pittsfield Cemetery, September 9, 1850, *sel.* Oliver Wendell Holmes.
"Father of all! in Death's relentless claim." TrPWD
Poem: "Distinction is in fire and division, The." José Garcia Villa. POTE (1959 ed.)
Poem: "Especially when the October wind." Dylan Thomas. *See* Especially When the October Wind.
Poem: "For years I've heard." Robin Blaser. NeAP
Poem: "Force that through the green fuse drives the flower, The." Dylan Thomas. *See* Force That Through the Green Fuse, The.
Poem: "Grecian tulip and the gothic rose, The." Terence Tiller. POTE
Poem: "Hate is only one of many responses." Frank O'Hara. NeAP
Poem: "He lying spilt like water from a bowl." Alison Boodson. NeBP
Poem: "Heart of the heartless world." John Cornford. *See* Huesca.
Poem: "Here poppies move beneath the sun." Ann Louise Hayes. PtPa
Poem: "High on a ridge of tiles." Maurice James Craig. *See* High on a Ridge of Tiles.
Poem: "I burn for England with a living flame." Gervase Stewart. *See* I Burn for England . . .
Poem: "I cannot tell, not I, why she." Walter Savage Landor. RO
(Lyrics and Epigrams, IX.) ERP
Poem: "I do not want to be your weeping woman." Alison Boodson. NeBP
Poem: "I knew a woman, lovely in her bones." Theodore Roethke. *See* I Knew a Woman, Lovely in Her Bones.
Poem: "I take four devils with me when I ride." Gervase Stewart. WaP
Poem: "'If there be time enough before the slaughter." Wyn Griffith. MoWP
Poem: "I'll tell you how the sun rose." Emily Dickinson. *See* I'll tell you how the sun rose.
Poem: "I'll write a poem, then sink to dreams." Guillem IX, Count of Poitou, *tr. fr. Provençal by* Hubert Creekmore. LyMA
Poem: "In fear of death do not neglect small bounty." John Prichard. MoWP
Poem: "In the dark caverns of the night." Henry Treece. NeBP
Poem: "Is there virtue in the sweet medium?" John Prichard. MoWP
Poem: "Is to love, this—to nurse a name." Rhoda Coghill. NeIP
Poem: "Khrushchev is coming on the right day!" Frank O'Hara. NeAP
Poem, A: "Like to an Hermit poore in place obscure." *At. to* Sir Walter Ralegh. *See* Like to a Hermit.
Poem: "Little brown boy." Helene Johnson. BANP; CDC
(Little Brown Boy.) GoSL
Poem: "Living, giant, all, in, little, pieces, A." José Garcia Villa. MeRV
Poem: "Night is beautiful, The." Langston Hughes. CDC
Poem: "Night's soft armor welds me into thought." Dorothy Livesay. BoCaPo
Poem: "O gentle queen of the afternoon." W. S. Graham. NeBP
Poem: "O men, walk on the hills." Maxwell Bodenheim. MOAP; TrJP
Poem: "On no work of words now for three lean months in the bloody." Dylan Thomas. *See* On No Work of Words Now.
Poem: "Once it was the colour ot saying." Dylan Thomas. MoWP
Poem: "One whom I knew, a student and a poet." Alex Comfort. *See* Epitaph: "One whom I knew, a student and a poet."
Poem, A: "Out upon it! I have loved." Sir John Suckling. *See* Constant Lover, The.
Poem: "Pity, repulsion, love and anger." Roy Fuller. NeBP
Poem: "Process in the weather of the heart, A." Dylan Thomas. *See* Process in the Weather of the Heart, A.
Poem: "Progress in the peaceable blue of a sky in summer." George Ewart Evans. MoWP
Poem II: "Screamlight streams of gleaming waterbreasts smiling." David Evans. MoWP
Poem: "So they begin. With two years gone." Boris Pasternak, *tr. fr. Russian by* C. M. Bowra. TrJP
("So they begin . . .") BoRS
Poem: "Some are too much at home in the role of wanderer." Denise Levertov. NeBP
Poem: "Spire cranes, The. Its statue is an aviary." Dylan Thomas. MoWP
Poem: "Supremest fictions grow with fungus speed." Arthur Boyars. PoN
Poem: "Take thy silent entity apart." Ann Louise Hayes. PtPa
Poem: "These grasses, ancient enemies." Keith Douglas. NeBP
Poem: "They will not, then, with victory return." Ann Louise Hayes. PtPa
Poem: "This room is very old and very wise." Sam Harrison. NeBP
Poem: "Through the dark aisles of the wood." Henry Treece. NeBP
Poem: "To go, to leave the classics and the buildings." Gavin Ewart. NeBP
Poem: "Upstood upstaffed passing sinuously away." Russell Atkins. PoNe
Poem: "We are such stuff as dreams are made of, and these." Hugo von Hofmannsthal, *tr. fr. German by* Jethro Bithell. LiTW
Poem: "We lying by seasand, watching yellow." Dylan Thomas. MoWP
Poem: "When birds and brittle leaves come down." John Prichard. MoWP
Poem: "Wisdom has no end and folly no ornament." Nathan Alterman, *tr. fr. Hebrew by* Herbert Howarth. LiTW
Poem: "You, who in April laughed, a green god in the sun." Brenda Chamberlain. *See* You, Who in April Laughed.
Poem about Love, A. G. S. Fraser. NeBP
Poem about Waking. David Ferry. NePoAm-2
Poem Beginning with a Line by Pindar, A. Robert Duncan. NeAP
Poem by a Perfectly Furious Academician. *Unknown.* FiBHP
Poem by Stages, *sels.* Charles Madge. BoSA
"Adventures of my separate bark, The," XIX.
"Among all the myths and masks and make-believes," XXXII.
"First, erected ironworks in a spiry hollow," XXIV.
"Flesh is sad but there are books unread, The," XXXI.
"To us, goddess, who are in barbary," I.
Poem by the Charles River. Robin Blaser. NeAP
Poem, Composed in Anticipation of Leaving School. Wordsworth. *See* Dear Native Regions.
Poem Containing Some Remarks on the Present War, A. *Unknown.* PAH
Poem Entreating of Sorrow, A. Sir Walter Ralegh. SiPS
Poem Five. Dylan Thomas. *See* Force That through the Green Fuse, The.
Poem for a Christmas Broadcast. Anne Ridler. NeBP
Poem for a Neighbour. Keidrych Rhys. MoWP
Poem for Caitlin. Dylan Thomas. MoWP
Poem for Christmas, A. C. A. Snodgrass. PoToHe (new ed.)
Poem for Combatants. Alan White. MaRV
Poem for D. Robert Griffiths. Davies Aberpennar. MoWP
Poem for Epiphany. Norman Nicholson. StJW
Poem for Gwyn and Käthe. Davies Aberpennar. MoWP
Poem for Keith Scott. Davies Aberpennar. MoWP
Poem for Little Dogs, A. Nancy Byrd Turner. AlBD
Poem for M. A. J. D. Davies Aberpennar. MoWP
Poem for Mother's Day. Margaret Fishback. InMe; LauV
Poem for Museum Goers, A. John Wieners. NeAP
Poem for My Thirty-second Birthday. John Ciardi. MiAP
Poem for Painters, A. John Wieners. NeAP
Poem for the Atomic Age. Emanuel Litvinov. NeBP
Poem for the Insane, A. John Wieners. NeAP
Poem for the Living. Harold Andrew. TwCaPo
Poem for the Meeting of the American Medical Association, A. Oliver Wendell Holmes. PoEL-5
Poem for the Old Man, A. John Wieners. NeAP
Poem for This Age. Stefan George, *tr. fr. German by* Reginald H. Phelps. AnGP

Poem for Trapped Things, A. John Wieners. NeAP
Poem for Wang Lung, A. Li Po, *tr. fr. Chinese.* ChLP; WhP
Poem for You. Robert Pack. NePoEA
Poem from Llanybri. Lynette Roberts. MoWP; NeBP
Poem from London, 1941. George Woodcock. NeBP
Poem from "The Year of Loss." Nicholas Moore. TriL
Poem I Should Like to Write, The. Margaret A. Windes. MaRV; OQP; QP-2
Poem, A, in Defence of the Decent Ornaments of Christ-Church, Oxon, Occasioned by a Banbury Brother, Who Called Them Idolatries, *sels. Unknown.*
Beauty in Worship. OBS
Church-Windows, The, *abr.* OBS
Poem in February. Ormond Thomas. MoWP
Poem in Karori. Louis Johnson. AnNZ
Poem in May. John Hewitt. NeIP
Poem in October ("Especially when the October wind"). Dylan Thomas. *See* Especially When the October Wind.
Poem in October ("It was my thirtieth year to heaven"). Dylan Thomas. CoBMV; EnL; GTBS-W; LiTB; LiTM (rev. ed.); MaPo; MoVE; NeBP; OAEP (2d ed.); PoLFOT; PoRA; SeCePo
October ("A springful of larks in a rolling"), *br. sel.* YeAr
Poem in Prose. Archibald MacLeish. LiTL; LoPS
Poem in the Matukituki Valley. James K. Baxter. AnNZ
Poem in Time of War. William Abrahams. WaP
Poem Intended to Incite the Utmost Depression, A. Samuel Hoffenstein. BOHV; SiTL
Poem must not charm us like a play, The. Against the False Magicians. Thomas McGrath. NePoEA
Poem, neither Hilláryous Norgay. Gardner E. Lewis. FiBHP
Poem of Any Virgin. Jorge de Lima, *tr. fr. Portuguese by* Dudley Poore. AnCL
Poem of Bunker Hill, The, *sel.* Harry Brown.
"Then once more men's ears were full of 'Yankee Doodle,'" *abr. fr.* Conclusion. PoFr
Poem of Circumstance. Jean Cocteau, *tr. fr. French by* Joseph T. Shipley. CAW
Poem of Holy Madness, *sel.* Ray Bremser.
"Let me lay it to you gently, Mr. Gone!" NeAP
Poem of Joys, A, *sels.* Walt Whitman.
"O Joy of suffering!" PC
"O the joy of my spirit!" PC
Song of Joys, A. LEAP
Poem of Margery Kempe, A. Howard Nemerov. FiMAP
Poem of Privacy, A. *Unknown, tr. by* John Addington Symonds. ALV
Poem of Quietness, *sels.* Robert Herring.
"Ache is easy, An. Longing's length," III. MoWP
"Through centuries of cyclists' traffic-blocks," II. MoWP
Poem of Ten "Ones," The. Ho P'ei Yü, *tr. fr. Chinese by* Henry H. Hart. PoHN
Poem of the Cid, The. *Unknown. See* Cid, The.
Poem of the mind in the act of finding, The. Of Modern Poetry. Wallace Stevens. AmP; AmPP (4th ed.); CoV; InvP; NePA; OxBA
Poem of the Our Father, The. St. Matthew, Bible, *N.T. See* Lord's Prayer, The.
Poem of the Universe, The. Charles Weldon. VA
Poem on a Slippery Sidewalk. Kenneth Porter. WhC
Poem on Canada, *sels.* Patrick Anderson.
Cold Colloquy, V. CaP; PeCV
"What are you . . . ? they ask," *shorter sel.* TwCaPo
Coming of the White Man, The, II. BoCaPo (1948 ed.); CaP
Poem on Hampstead Heath. Louis Adeane. NeBP
Poem on His Birthday. Dylan Thomas. PoLFOT
Poem on Spring, The. Arthur Guiterman. LHV
Poem on the Wall, The. Po Chü-i, *tr. fr. Chinese by* Arthur Waley. TrCh
Poem, or Beauty Hurts Mr. Vinal. E. E. Cummings. AmP; MoAB; MoAmPo; MoVE; OnAP; OxBA
Poem Put into My Lady Laiton's Pocket, A. Sir Walter Ralegh. SiPS
Poem Sacred to the Memory of Sir Isaac Newton, A. James Thomson. CEP; EiPP
Sels.
Newton Fixes the Moon. BeR
Newton on Light. BeR
Poem should be, as our best ever are, A. The Whole Duty of a Poem. Arthur Guiterman. PoToHe (new ed.)
Poem should be palpable and mute, A. Ars Poetica. Archibald MacLeish. AmP; AmPP; AWP; CoBMV; CoV; ExPo; HoPM; InP; InPo; LiTA; LiTM; MAP; MoAB; MoAmPo; MOAP; NAMP; NeMA; NP; OxBA; PreP; ReMP; SeCeV; TBM; TwHP
Poem to Be Said on Hearing the Birds Sing, A. *Tr. fr. Irish by* Douglas Hyde. AnIV; AWP; JAWP; WBP
Poem to Delight My Friends Who Laugh at Science-Fiction, A. Edwin Rolfe. NePA; NePoAm
Poem to Lou. Guillaume Apollinaire, *tr. fr. French by* Hubert Creekmore. LiTW
Poem to Negro and Whites. Maxwell Bodenheim. PoNe
Poem to the Mysterious Woman. Robert Desnos, *tr. fr. French by* Wallace Fowlie. MiCF
Poem upon the Death of His Late Highness the Lord Protector, A, *sels.* Andrew Marvell.
"He without noyse still travell'd to his end." PoD
"I saw him dead, a leaden slumber lies."
(Cromwell Dead.) ChTr
(Poem upon the Death of Oliver Cromwell, A.) OBS; ViBoPo
Poem, A, where we all perfections find. The Fantastick Mind. Nicolas Boileau-Despréaux. *Fr.* L'Art poétique. BeR
Poem Written in Time of Trouble by an Irish Priest Who Had Taken Orders in France, A. *Unknown, tr. fr. Irish by* Lady Gregory. OBMV
Poem, A, Written on a Painting Called "The Smoky River and the Folding Peaks" Possessed by Wang Ting-kuo. Su T'ung-po, *tr. fr. Chinese by* Yu Min-chuan. WhP
Poem, Written on the Eve of Execution. Chidiock Tichborne. *See* Elegy: "My prime of youth is but a frost of cares."
Poema Morale. Charles Gullans. NePoEA
Poema Morale, *sel. Unknown.*
"Ich aem eldre then Ich wes," *Middle English and mod. vers.* EPP
Poems: "Sir, no man's enemy, forgiving all." W. H. Auden. *See* Sir, No Man's Enemy.
Poems: "Who will endure," XXV. W. H. Auden. CaAE
Poems. Hilda Conkling. ExPo; NP
Poems. Léon Damas, *tr. fr. French by* Langston Hughes. PoNe
Poems. Antonio Machado, *tr. fr. Spanish by* John Dos Passos.
"Figures in the fields against the sky." AWP; JAWP; WBP
(Four Poems, 2.) LiTW
"Frail sound of a tunic trailing, A." AWP; JAWP; TeCS; WBP
(Four Poems, 1.) LiTW
"Naked is the earth." AWP
(Four Poems, 3.) LiTW
"We think to create festivals." AWP
(Four Poems, 4.) LiTW
Poems. Philip O'Connor. LiTM
Poems about the Moon. Vachel Lindsay. MAPA; TwAmPo
Poems by the Roadside. St. Luke, XII: 32–37; St. Matthew, V: 14–16, XVI: 17–19, Bible, *N.T.* CAW
Poems Come Easier, The. Ray Mathew. BoAV
Poems for My Brother Kenneth. Owen Dodson. PoNe
Poems for My Daughter. Horace Gregory.
(Stanzas for My Daughter.) MoVE; TriL
"Tell her I love she will remember me," *sel.* MAP; MoAmPo
Poems from MSS. Blake. *Poems indexed separately by titles and first lines.*
Poems in Depression, at Wei Village (*two poems*). Po Chü-i, *tr. fr. Chinese by* Arthur Waley. TrCh
"I hug my pillow and do not speak a word," 1.
"Turned to jade are the boy's rosy cheeks," 2.
Poems in Praise of Practically Nothing, *sels.* Samuel Hoffenstein.
"Only the wholesomest foods you eat." BOHV; InMe; SiTL; TrJP
"You buy some flowers for your table." BOHV; FiBHP; InMe; PFE; SiTL; TrJP
"You buy yourself a new suit of clothes." BOHV; InMe; SiTL
"You get a girl; and you say you love her." BOHV; InMe; SiTL
"You go to high school; even college." PFE
"You hire a cook, but she can't cook yet." InMe; WhC
"You leap out of bed; you start to get ready." BOHV; InMe; SiTL
"You meet a girl and you surrender." InMe
"You practise every possible virtue." BOHV; InMe
"You take a bath, and sit there bathing." InMe
"You work and work and keep on working." WhC
"You're a good girl; you're gray with virtue." InMe
"You're kind to women, children, worms." InMe
Poems of Our Climate, The. Wallace Stevens. AmP; CoV; MoPo; OxBA; TrGrPo (rev. ed.)
Poems of Passion, Carefully Restrained So as to Offend Nobody. Samuel Hoffenstein. InMe
Poems of the Machine Age. MacKnight Black. PoeMoYo
Poems of West Ham, The, *sel. Unknown.*
"From a high place I saw the city." BMEP; UnW
Poems on Dalecarlian Paintings, *sel.* Erik Axel Karlfeldt, *tr. fr. Swedish by* Charles W. Stork.
Virgin Mary, The. AnSL
Poems on the Naming of Places, *sels.* Wordsworth.
It Was an April Morning, I. BPN; EmBrPo; ERP
(April Morning, An, *abr.*) RO
There Is an Eminence, III. ERP

Poems on the Naming of Places (*continued*)
To M. H., V. ERP
Poems (Received in Response to an Advertised Call for a National Anthem). "Orpheus C. Kerr." *See* Rejected "National Hymns," The.
Poems to Thyrza. Byron. *Fr.* And Thou Art Dead, as Young and Fair. PoD
Poems Translated from the Chinese. *Unknown, tr. fr. Chinese by* John Francis Davis. RO
Poe's Cottage at Fordham. John Henry Boner. AA; GA; LBAP; NoCaPo; OBAV; PtP
Poe's Critics. John Banister Tabb. BAP
Poe's Mother. Beatrice Ravenel. LS
Poesy. Paul Valéry, *tr. fr. French by* Alan Conder. TrFP
Poet, The. Philip James Bailey. *Fr.* Festus. VA
Poet, The. Joel Benton. WGRP
Poet, The. H. C. Bosman. BoSA
Poet, The. Elizabeth Barrett Browning. WGRP
Poet, The. Bryant. AA; AmPP (3d ed.); CoBA; CoV; IAP; InP
Poet, The. Witter Bynner. *See* Poet Lived in Galilee, A.
Poet, The. Ina Donna Coolbrith. POT; PoTo
Poet, The. Grace Noll Crowell. InP
Poet, The. T. A. Daly. JKCP
Poet, The. C. Day Lewis. OxBI
Poet, The ("A moody child and wildly wise"). Emerson. AmPo
Poet, The ("Thy trivial harp"). Emerson. *Fr.* Merlin, I. BLV; BoLiVe
(Merlin.) APW
Poet ("To clothe the fiery thought"). Emerson. *Fr.* Quatrains. AnNE; APW; OnPM; OxBA
Poet, The. Padraic Fiacc. NeIP
Poet, The. Anita Grannis. HBMV
Poet, A. Thomas Hardy. VLEP
Poet. Donald Jeffrey Hayes. PoNe
Poet, A. Daniel Henderson. PFE
Poet. Nat Henry. PFE
Poet, The. Mary Sinton Leitch. BoHiPo; HBMV; LS; PoMa
Poet, The. Haniel Long. HBMV
Poet, The. Amy Lowell. WGRP
Poet, The. Edwin Markham. WGRP
Poet, The. Cornelius Mathews. AA
Poet. Merrill Moore. MOAP
Poet. John Richard Moreland. BoHiPo
Poet, The. Angela Morgan. WGRP
"Why hast thou breathed, O God, upon my thoughts," *sel.* TrPWD
Poet, The. Yone Noguchi. NP; WGRP
Poet, The. Seumas O'Brien. JKCP (1926 ed.)
Poet, The. Bernard O'Dowd. BoAu
Poet, The. Pushkin, *tr. fr. Russian by* C. M. Bowra. BoR
Poet, The. Rainer Maria Rilke, *tr. fr. German by* Selden Rodman. *Fr.* Sonnets to Orpheus. OnHM
Poet, The. William Rooney. JKCP (1926 ed.)
Poet. Karl Shapiro. AnFE; CoAnAm; MoAB; MoAmPo (1950 ed.); TwAmPo
Poet, The. Christopher Smart. *Fr.* The Blockhead and Beehive. BeR
Poet, The. Mildred I. McNeal Sweeney. LBMV
Poet, The. Tennyson. BPN; EM-2; EmBrPo; EnL; EnLit; OAEP; PoVP; ViPo; ViPP; VLEP
"And Freedom rear'd in that august sunrise," *sel.* PoFr
Poet. Peter Viereck. HoPM; MiAP; MoAmPo (1950 ed.)
Poet, The. Sir William Watson. *See* Epigram: "Poet gathers fruit from every tree, The."
Poet, The. Walt Whitman. By Blue Ontario's Shore, IX-XVII. MoAmPo (1950 ed.)
Poet and Critic. Samuel Daniel. *Fr.* Musophilus; or, Defence of All Learning. OBSC
("Fond man, Musophilus, that thou dost spend.") ReIE; SiCE; TuPP
Poet and His Book, The. Edna St. Vincent Millay. MAP; MoAmPo; NePA; TCPD
Poet and His Patron, The. Edward Moore. Fables for the Ladies, V. CEP
Poet and His Public, The. Aristophanes. *See* Poet and the People, The.
Poet and His Rivals, The. Aristophanes, *tr. fr. Greek by* Gilbert Murray. *Fr.* The Knights. OxBG
(To the Fickle Gallery, *tr. by* Benjamin Bickley Rogers.) GrR
Poet and His Song, The. Anna Hempstead Branch. MuM
Poet and His Song, The. Paul Laurence Dunbar. PoRL
Poet and Lark. "Madeline Bridges." AA; HBV
Poet and Saint! to thee alone are given. On the Death of [Mr.] Crashaw. Abraham Cowley. AEV; EPS; GoBC; MeLP; MePo; NBE; OBS; PtP; SeCV-1; SeEP; ViBoPo
Poet and the Bird, The. Elizabeth Barrett Browning. VLEP
Poet and the Child, The. Winifred Howells. AA
Poet and the French Revolution, The. Wordsworth. *Fr.* The Prelude, XI. EPN
Poet and the People, The. Aristophanes, *tr. fr. Greek by* Benjamin Bickley Rogers. *Fr.* The Acharnians. OxBG
(Poet and His Public, The.) GrR
Poet and the Rose, The. John Gay. TCEP
Poet and the Wood-Louse, The. Helen Parry Eden. HBV
Poet and the Woodlouse, The, *parody on* Walt Whitman. Swinburne. PA
Poet and the World, The. Byron. *See* Defiance.
Poet at Night-Fall, The. Glenway Wescott. LiTM (1946 ed.); NP
Poet at the Breakfast Table, The, *sels.* Oliver Wendell Holmes.
Epilogue to the Breakfast-Table Series. AA
Manhood. APW
Poet at the Court of Pan, A. Lady Margaret Sackville. ReTS
Poet, be deaf to popular acclaim. To the Poet. Pushkin. TrRV
Poet, be seated at the piano. Mozart, 1935. Wallace Stevens. AmP; UnS
Poet, The, Byron/ Was made of iron. Important People. Louis Untermeyer, *and others.* StaSt
Poet, cast your careful eye. On Seeing a Poet of the First World War on the Station at Abbeville. Charles Causley. ChMP
Poet Confides, The. Herbert T. J. Coleman. CaP
Poet Considers Perfection, The. Elizabeth Virginia Raplee. MaRV
Poet Describes His Love, The. Robert Nathan. HBMV
Poet Diodorus has left these lines that cover, The. The Gods Forget. Diodorus. GrPE
Poet Dreams of the Wings of Death, The. Edwin Justus Mayer. LEAP
Poet gathers fruit from every tree, The. Epigram [*or* The Poet]. Sir William Watson. CaAE; MBP; MoBrPo (1942 ed.); TrGrPo
Poet Greatly Pictured, The. Shakespeare. *See* Lunatic, the Lover, and the Poet, The.
Poet had a cat, A. How a Cat Was Annoyed and a Poet Was Booted. Guy Wetmore Carryl. CIV; MAP; MoAmPo (1942 ed.)
Poet hath the child's sight in his breast, The. The Poet. Elizabeth Barrett Browning. WGRP
Poet, having taken the bridle off his tongue, A. The Intoxicated Poet. Allen Upward. *Fr.* Scented Leaves from a Chinese Jar. NP
Poet, A!—He Hath Put His Heart to School. Wordsworth. BPN; EmBrPo; EnRP; ERP
Poet heard a skylark sing, A. The Super-Lark. R. H. Long. BoAu
Poet-Hearts. Joseph von Eichendorff, *tr. fr. German by* George N. Shuster. CAW
Poet honed, The. Lyric Barber. Liboria E. Romano. GoYe
Poet! I come to touch thy lance with mine. Wapentake. Longfellow. AA; PtP
Poet, I sing of Pope. A Dialogue to the Memory of Mr. Alexander Pope. Austin Dobson. BPN
Poet in a golden clime was born, The. The Poet. Tennyson. BPN; EM-2; EmBrPo; EnL; EnLit; OAEP; PoVP; ViPo; ViPP; VLEP
Poet in his lone yet genial hour, The. Apologia pro Vita Sua. Samuel Taylor Coleridge. EnRP
Poet in His Poverty, The. Nizami, *tr. fr. Persian by* Samuel Robinson. LiTW
Poet in Life and Death, The. *Unknown, tr. fr. Greek by* Lord Neaves. OnPM
Poet in the City, The. Catherine C. Liddell. VA
Poet in the Desert, The, *sels.* Charles E. S. Wood.
Desert, The ("Never have I found a place"). AnEnPo
Desert, The ("She is a nun"), *abr.* AnAmPo; LA; MAP
Desert, The ("She is a queen"), *abr.* BAP
"Desert murmurs to the sun a strange murmur, The." PoFr
"I have come into the desert," *abr.* NP
"Suddenly night flung wide the sapphire gate." PoFr
Sunrise ("The lean coyote, prowler of the night"). GoTP; MAP; PFY
"This is the pedigree of degradation." PoFr
Poet is a lazy man, The. Achievement. Morris Abel Beer. PFE; PoMa
Poet is, or ought to be, a hater of the city, The. Rural Bliss. Anthony C. Deane. InMe
Poet, Jesus, speak to me. The Poet of Palestine. William L. Stidger. ChIP
Poet, let passion sleep. Art, II. Alfred Noyes. OBEV (new ed.)
Poet Lived in Galilee, A. Witter Bynner. OQP; QP-1
(Poet, The.) BPP; WGRP
Poet Loosed a Wingèd Song, The. Joseph Campbell. OnYI
Poet loved a star, A. Possession. "Owen Meredith." LPS-1
Poet Loves a Mistress, but Not to Marry, The. Robert Herrick. ALV
Poet Meets Venus and Her Priest, The. John Gower, *tr. fr. Middle English by* Muriel Bowden. *Fr.* Confessio Amantis, I. MeEV
Poet Mourns His Japanese Friend, The. Li Po, *tr. fr. Chinese by* Shigeyoshi Obata. BoFr

Poet of Earth. Stephen Henry Thayer. AA
Poet of Farewell. Christian Werleigh, *tr. fr. French by* Edna Worthley Underwood. PoNe
Poet of Gardens, The. Daniel Henderson. HBMV
Poet of Nature, The. Philip James Bailey. *Fr.* Festus. LPS-3
Poet of Nature, thou hast wept to know. To Wordsworth. Shelley. EmBrPo; EnRP; EPN; ERP; FiP; MCCG; PoRL; PtP
Poet of One Mood, A. Alice Meynell. HBMV; POTT
Poet of Palestine, The. William L. Stidger. ChIP
Poet of the pulpit, whose full-chorded lyre. Bartol. Amos Bronson Alcott. AA
Poet of the tropics, your dining room. Interior. Ronald de Carvalho. AnCL
Poet of To-Day, The. "Grace Greenwood." LPS-3
Poet Prays, The. Grace Noll Crowell. TrPWD
Poet Prays Her, The. Daniel Berrigan. JKCP (1955 ed.)
Poet Prays to the Cross, The. *Unknown. Fr.* The Dream of the Rood. PoLi
Poet-Preacher's Prayer, A. Milton. *Fr.* Paradise Lost, I. MaRV
Poet seldom finds the way, A. Form 1040A. Phyllis Eleanor Armstrong. SiTL
Poet Shadwell, The. Dryden. *See* Shadwell.
Poet Shadwell's Coronation, The. Dryden. *Fr.* MacFlecknoe. BeR
Poet Songs (I–III). Karle Wilson Baker. HBMV
"Dropped feathers from the wings of God," III.
"I cast my nets in many streams," II.
"I shall not get my poem done," I.
Poet, starving in a garret, A. Poets and Poetasters. Swift. *Fr.* To Stella, Who Collected and Transcribed His Poems. BeR
Poet stood in the sombre town, The. The Poet in the City. Catherine C. Liddell. VA
Poet, take up your lyre. The New Song. Arthur Gordon Field. PGD; PSO
Poet Tells about Nature, The. Merrill Moore. NP
Poet Thinks, A. Lui Chi, *tr. fr. Chinese by* E. Powys Mathers. AWP; JAWP; LiTW; PG (1945 ed.); WBP
Poet to Bird. Ralph Cheyney. BLA
Poet to Dancer. Bernice Kavinoky. UnS
Poet to His Father, A. Mahlon Leonard Fisher. NV
Poet to His Love, The. Maxwell Bodenheim. MAP; MoAmPo (1942 ed.)
(Old Poet to His Love, The.) BAP
Poet to the Birds, The. Alice Meynell. NP
Poet wandering on, through Arabie, The. Shelley. *Fr.* Alastor. UnW
Poet who sleepest by this wandering wave! Sir William Watson. Wordsworth's Grave, II. BMEP; GoTL; HBV; LEAP
Poet writ a song of May, A. The First Song. Richard Burton. AA
Poeta Fit, Non Nascitur. "Lewis Carroll." PC
Poeta Nascitur. Thomas Ashe. VA
Poetaster, The, *sels.* Ben Jonson.
"If I freely may discover," *fr.* II, ii. EG; ElSeCe; ReEn; TuPP
(Song: "If I freely may discover.") ElL
"O sacred poesie, thou spirit of [Romane] artes," *fr.* I, ii. NBE; PoEL-2
Swell Me a Bowl, *fr.* III, i. TuPP
"There is no bountie to be shew'd to such," *fr.* III, vi. PoEL-2
Poetaster, The. Samuel Rowlands. *Fr.* The Melancholy Knight. ElL
Poetess Erinna, The. Antipater of Sidon, *tr. fr. Greek by* F. L. Lucas. GrPE
Poetic Land, The. William Caldwell Roscoe. OBVV
Poetic Pains. William Cowper. *Fr.* The Task, II. FiP
(Poetry; Satire and Pulpit.) CoBE
Poetic Responses. Amelia E. Barr. *See* Thanksgiving.
Poetic Tale. Grace Maddock Miller. AlBD
Poetic Thought. *Unknown.* FiBHP; SiTL
Poetical Commandments. Byron. *Fr.* Don Juan, I. BPN; FiP; GEPC; OBRV
("If ever I should condescend to prose.") OxBoLi
(Poet's Credo.) SeCePo
Poetical Economy. Harry Graham. CenHV; SiTL; TreFS
Poetical Numbers. Pope. *See* Art of Writing, The.
Poetics. Robert Browning. BPN; PoVP
Poetry. Lucius Harwood Foote. AA
Poetry. Ella Heath. HBV; WGRP
Poetry. Hesiod, *tr. fr. Greek by* F. L. Lucas. *Fr.* Theogony. GrPE
Poetry. Stéphane Mallarmé, *tr. fr. French by* Alan Conder. TrFP
Poetry. Edwin Markham. AA
Poetry. Marianne Moore. AmP; AnFE; APA; ATP (1953 ed.); CoAnAm; CoBMV; ExPo; InPo; LiTA; LiTM; MoAB; MoAmPo (1950 ed.); NePA; NP; OxBA; PreP; ReMP; SeCeV; TwAmPo; ViBoPo (1958 ed.)
"I too dislike it," *sel.* NAMP
Poetry. Salvador Novo, *tr. fr. Spanish by* Donald Devenish Walsh. AnCL
Poetry. William Soutar. HaMV
Poetry and Learning. George Chapman. *Fr.* The Epistle Dedicatory to Chapman's Translation of the Iliad. OBS
("Princes statue, A, or in marble carv'd.") AtBAP
Poetry and Philosophy. Thomas Randolph. *Fr.* An Eclogue to Mr. Johnson. OBS
Poetry and Science. W. J. Turner. SeCePo
Poetry and Thoughts on Same. Franklin P. Adams. HBMV
Poetry and Wine. Samuel Butler. BeR
Poetry, almost blind like a camera. Imaginary Elegies, I–IV. Jack Spicer. NeAP
Poetry Cure, The. Robert Haven Schauffler. MOB
Poetry Defined. Thomas Randolph. EV-2
Poetry, Emily. Brief History. Olga Hampel Briggs. GoYe
Poetry Is a Destructive Force. Wallace Stevens. CoV; OxBA
Poetry is a projection across silence. Ten Definitions of Poetry. Carl Sandburg. MAP; MoAmPo
Poetry Is Happiness. Wrey Gardiner. NeBP
Poetry is no uneasy refuge, stilly centred. No Uneasy Refuge. Blanaid Salkeld. AnIV
Poetry is the supreme fiction, madame. A High-toned Old Christian Woman. Wallace Stevens. CoBMV; CoV; MoVE; PoFS
Poetry itself is no more than a dream. No More than a Dream. Jens Peter Jacobsen. BoDS
Poetry of a Root Crop, The. Charles Kingsley. LoBV
Poetry of Departures. Philip Larkin. NePoEA
Poetry of Dress, The. Robert Herrick. *See* Delight in Disorder *and* Upon Julia's Clothes.
Poetry of Dress, The. *Unknown. See* My Love in Her Attire Doth Show Her Wit.
Poetry of Earth, The. Florence Earle Coates. BAP
Poetry of Earth Is Never Dead, The. Keats. *See* On the Grasshopper and Cricket.
Poetry of England, The. Samuel Daniel. *See* English Poetry.
Poetry; Satire and Pulpit. William Cowper. *See* Poetic Pains.
Poets. Mark Akenside. *Fr.* The Pleasures of Imagination, IV. OBEC
Poets, The, *sel.* Joseph Auslander.
"We who were prophets and priest-men." PoeMoYo
Poets, The ("I had found the secret of a garret-room"). Elizabeth Barrett Browning. *Fr.* Aurora Leigh, I. VA
Poets, The ("There, obedient to her praying"). Elizabeth Barrett Browning. *Fr.* Lady Geraldine's Courtship. BCEP
Poets. Hortense Flexner. BAP; HBMV
Poets, The. Robert Graves. MoPW
Poets, The. Leigh Hunt. *See* Dearest Poets, The.
Poets. Joyce Kilmer. AnAmPo; LA; NP; SBMV; WGRP
Poets, The. Longfellow. APW; IAP
Poets, The. Scudder Middleton. HBMV
Poets, The. Arthur O'Shaughnessy. *See* Ode: "We are the music-makers."
"Poet's age is sad, The; for why?" Prologue to "Asolando." Robert Browning. PoVP; ViPo; ViPP
Poets and Linnets. Tom Hood. CenHV; HBV
Poets and Poetasters. Swift. *Fr.* To Stella, Who Collected and Transcribed His Poems. BeR
Poets are singing the whole world over. Rus in Urbe. Clement Scott. HBV; VA
Poets at a House-Party, The. Carolyn Wells. PA
Poets at Tea, The. Barry Pain. BOHV; HBV; PA
(Macaulay at Tea.) CenHV
Oh! Weary Mother, *sel.* NA
Poet's Bread, The. Charles L. O'Donnell. LEAP
Poet's Bread. Sister Mary Philip. GoBC
Poet's Bread, The. *Unknown.* DDA
Poet's Bridal-Day Song, The. Allan Cunningham. LPS-1
Poet's Call, The. Thomas Curtis Clark. WGRP
Poet's cat, sedate and grave, A. The Retired Cat. William Cowper. BOHV; CIV; EV-3; OTPC (1923 ed.), *sl. abr.*; PoC
Poet's Confidence, The. Coventry Patmore. The Angel in the House, I, i, 3. POTT
Poet's Credo. Byron. *See* Poetical Commandments.
Poet's daily chore, The. Lens. Anne Wilkinson. PeCV
Poet's Death, The, *abr.* Mikhail Yurevich Lermontov, *tr. fr. Russian by* Robert Hillyer. TrRV
Poet's Dream, The. William Dunbar. *Fr.* The Golden Targe. PoEL-1
Poet's Dream, The. Shelley. *Fr.* Prometheus Unbound, I. GTBS; GTBS-D; GTBS-W; GTSE; GTSL; PC; ReTS; WP
("On a poet's lips I slept.") AnFE; AtBAP; ChER; FiP; ShBV-3; ViBoPo
(Poet's World, The, *sl. abr.*) EV-4
(Spirit's Song in "Prometheus.") CBE
Poets Easily Consoled. Christopher Morley. LHV
Poet's Epitaph, A. Ebenezer Elliott. BCEP; VA
(Burns.) LPS-3

Poet's Epitaph, A. Wordsworth. BPN; EmBrPo; EnRP; GEPC; OBRV; UnPo (1st ed.)
Poet's Eye-View, A. Anne Wilkinson. TwCaPo
Poet's Fate, The. Thomas Hood. FiBHP
Poet's Father, The. Callimachus, *tr. fr. Greek by* R. A. Furness. OxBG
Poet's Friend, The. Pope. *See* Literary Poet to His Patron, A.
Poet's Friend, The. Simonides, *tr. fr. Greek by* G. B. Grundy. GrL; OxBG
("This is the grave of famed Magistias, whom.") GrPo
Poet's Grace, A. Burns. TrPWD
Poet's Grave, A. Thomas Bailey Aldrich. GA
Poet's Harvesting, The. Charles J. O'Malley. CAW
Poets have muddied all the little fountains, The. Abla. Antara. *Fr.* The Mu'allaqát. AWP; JAWP; LiTW; WBP
Poets henceforth for pensions need not care. A Comfort for Poor Poets. Sir John Harington. SiCE
Poets Hitchhiking on the Highway. Gregory Corso. NeAP
Poet's Hope, A, *sel.* William Ellery Channing.
"Lady, there is a hope that all men have." AA; AnAmPo; IAP; LA; LEAP
Poet's Impulse, The. Byron. Childe Harold's Pilgrimage, III. LPS-3
Poets in Time of War. Bertram Warr. CaP
Poet's Inspiration, The. Cratinus, *tr. fr. Greek by* Thomas Moore. OxBG
Poet's Journal, The, *sel.* Bayard Taylor.
"God, to whom we look up blindly." TrPWD
Poets like shepherds on green hills. The Shepherds. Beren Van Slyke. GoYe
Poets loiter all their leisure. The Hour Glass. Edward Quillinan. OBRV
Poet's Lot, The. Oliver Wendell Holmes. PoEL-5
Poets make pets of pretty, docile words. Pretty Words. Elinor Wylie. HBMV; YaD; YT
Poets may boast (as safely vain). Of English Verse. Edmund Waller. OBS
Poets' May is dead and done, The. Summer. John Davidson. VLEP
Poets may sing of their Helicon streams. The Federal Constitution. William Milns. PAH
Poet's Mind, The. Tennyson. ViPP
Poet's Own Epitaph, The. Callimachus. *See* Epitaph on Himself.
Poets, Painters, Puddings. Richard Hughes. PtOT
Poet's Pen, The. Christopher Marlowe. *Fr.* Tamburlaine the Great, Pt. I, Act V, sc. ii. EV-1
(Beauty.) TrGrPo
(If All the Pens That Ever Poets Held.) ChTr
(Immortal Flowers of Poesy.) LiA
Poet's Portion, The, *sl. abr.* Thomas Hood. RO
"Poets pour us wine, The." Epilogue to the Pacchiarotto Volume. Robert Browning. BPN
Poet's Poverty, The. Rutebeuf, *tr. fr. French by* J. G. Legge. LyMA
Poet's Power, The. Pindar, *tr. fr. Greek by* F. L. Lucas. *Fr.* Isthmian Odes, IV. GrPE
Poet's Praise, The. Pindar, *tr. fr. Greek by* F. L. Lucas. *Fr.* Nemean Odes, V. GrPE
Poet's Prayer. Adelaide Love. TrPWD
Poet's Prayer, A [*or* The]. Stephen Phillips. CP; WGRP
Poet's Pride. Ibn Ammar, *tr. fr. Arabic by* A. J. Arberry. MooP
Poet's Progress, A. Michael Hamburger. NePoEA
Poet's Prophecy, A. Tennyson. *See* Prophecy.
Poet's Proposal, The. Oliver Herford. PR
Poet's Protest. Doris Hedges. CaP
Poet's Proverb, A. Arthur Guiterman. MaRV
Poet's Resurrection. Dryden. *Fr.* Ode to the Pious Memory of . . . Mrs. Anne Killigrew. WHA
(Last Day, The). BeR
Poet's Secret, The. Elizabeth Stoddard. AA
Poets Seven Years Old. Arthur Rimbaud. *See* Seven-year-old Poet.
Poet's Shield, The. Archilochus, *tr. fr. Greek.* GrL, *tr. by* Paul Shorey; LiTW, *tr. by* Sir William Marris; OxBG, *tr. by* Sir William Marris
(Better Part of Valour, The, *tr. by* F. L. Lucas.) GrPE
(On the Loss of His Shield, *tr. by* H. N. Coleridge.) GrR
("Some Thracian strutteth with my shield," *tr. by* Paul Shorey.) GrPo
Poet's Simple Faith, The. Victor Hugo, *tr. fr. French by* Edward Dowden. OQP; QP-1; WGRP
(Where Goest Thou?) MaRV
Poet's Song, The. Tennyson. AlDL; BPN; EmBrPo; FiP; GBV (1952 ed.); PoVP; TOP
Poet's song, the painter's art, The. A Treasure House. Mark Antony De Wolfe Howe. PC
Poet's Song to His Wife, The. "Barry Cornwall." HBV; LPS-1; VA
Poet's soul has sung its way to God, A. The Dead Singer. Mary Ashley Townsend. AA
Poet's Spear, The. Archilochus, *tr. fr. Greek by* C. M. Bowra. OxBG
Poets themselves must fall like those they sung. Pope. *Fr.* Elegy to the Memory of an Unfortunate Lady. PoD
Poet's Thought, A. "Barry Cornwall." VA
Poets to Come. Walt Whitman. AnAmPo; CoBA; IAP; LA; LiTA; MOAP; TCAP; TrGrPo; YaD
Poet's Town, The. John G. Neihardt. LBMV
"But still did the Mighty Makers," X–XII. OBAV
Poet's Use, The. Pope. *Fr.* The First Epistle of the Second Book of Horace. OBEC
("Of little use the man you may suppose," *longer sel.*) EV-3
Poet's Voice, The. Blake. *See* Hear the Voice of the Bard.
Poet's Vow, The, *sel.* Elizabeth Barrett Browning.
Rosalind's Scroll. HBV; OBEV (1st ed.)
Poet's Welcome, The. Edward Richard, *tr. fr. Welsh by* Evan Evans. *Fr.* Pastoral Poem. PrWP
Poet's Welcome to His Love-begotten Daughter, A. Burns. LiTB; OxBoLi; PoEL-4; SiTL; ViBoPo
Poets, who in time of war. Poets in Time of War. Bertram Warr. CaP
Poet's Wish, The; an Ode. Allan Ramsay. CEP; EBSV; EiPP; OBEC
Poet's words are winged with fire, The. The Poet. Joel Benton. WGRP
Poet's World, The. Shelley. *See* Poet's Dream, The.
Poets yeggs and thirsties. E. E. Cummings. *Fr.* Is 5. AnAmPo; LA
Poinsettia petal drops, A. The rain pastes twisted flowing drapery. Family Reunion. Hollis Summers. GoYe
Point beheld I, that was raying out, A. The Primal Cause. Dante. *Fr.* Divina Commedia: Paradiso. CAW
Point is turned, The; the twilight shadow fills. Between the Rapids. Archibald Lampman. VA
Point Lobos, California. Eric Wilson Barker. MuM
Point of Flame. Jules Supervielle, *tr. fr. French by* Alan Conder. TrFP
Point of honor has been deemed of use, The. Duelling. William Cowper. *Fr.* Conversation. LPS-3
Point of life between my parent's dust, A. In Sight of the Town of Cockermouth, Where the Author Was Born, and His Father's Remains Are Laid. Wordsworth. ES
Point of Noon, The. Christopher Brennan. MoAuPo
Point of one white star is quivering still, The. Morning. Shelley. *Fr.* Prometheus Unbound. ShBV-3
Point of View, The. Margaret Prescott Montague. DDA
Point of View. Virginia Lyne Tunstall. BAP
Point, the Line, the Surface and Sphere, The. Claude Bragdon. *Fr.* The Beautiful Necessity. ImOP
Point where beauty and intelligence meet, The. Sonnet. Gavin Ewart. WaP
Pointed houses lean so you would swear, The. Amsterdam. Francis Jammes. AWP; FaPON; JAWP; WBP
Pointed People, The. Rachel Field. FaPON; MBP
Pointillism. Joseph Bennett. SiTL
Pointless, without meaning. A Wish. Haruo Sato. PoLJ
Poise. Violet Alleyn Storey. BLP
Poised between its banks, the stream. The Stream. Al-Rusafi. MooP
Poised to plunge beneath the waves of sleep. Plain-Song. Jean Cocteau. LiTW
Poison Ivy! Katharine Gallagher. SiSoSe
Poison of insult and the bile of torment, The. Freedom. Georgi Efimovich Nechayev. PoFr
Poison Tree, A. Blake. *Fr.* Songs of Experience. AnFE; AWP; BoLiVe; CaAE; EM-1; EnL; EnLi-2; EnLit; EnRP; EPP; FaFP; HoPM; InPo; JAWP; LEAP; LiTB; LiTG; MaPo; OAEP; OtMeF; PoEL-4; PoFS; PoMS; PreP; TOP; TreFS; TrGrPo; TyEnPo; WBP
("I was angry with my friend.") EG; GTBS-W
Poisoned in Search of the Medicine of Immortality. Sheila Wingfield. PoN
Poker. *Unknown.* PA
Poland. Thomas Campbell. *Fr.* The Pleasures of Hope. LPS-2
Poland, France, Judea ran in her veins. An Electric Sign Goes Dark. Carl Sandburg. HBMV
Poland, October. Charles Brasch. *Fr.* Nineteen Thirty-nine. AnNZ
Polar Exploration. Stephen Spender. ChMP; MoAB; MoPo
(North, The.) FaBoMo
Polar Quest, The. Richard Burton. AA
Pole Star for This Year. Archibald MacLeish. AmPP; NAMP; NePA; OxBA
(Pole Star.) CoBMV
Pole, the Bear, and Cassiopeia, The. Night Piece. A. E. Coppard. POTE
'Poleon Dore. William Henry Drummond. BBV (1923 ed.)
Poles are flying where the two eyes set, The. Discoveries. Vernon Watkins. LiTM; WaP
Policeman, The. Marjorie Seymour Watts. PCH; TiPo
Policeman buys shoes slow and careful, The. Psalm of Those

Who Go Forth before Daylight. Carl Sandburg. AnAmPo; LA; MOAP; MoShBr; OxBA; StVeCh
Policeman, policeman, don't take me. I Stole Brass. *Unknown.* ChTr
Policeman walks with heavy tread, The. Action Rhyme. E. M. Adams. BoTP
Policeman's Lot, The. W. S. Gilbert. *Fr.* The Pirates of Penzance. ALV; NeHB; PoVP; TrGrPo
Policy. Carolyn Wells. WhC
Polifemo y Galatea. Luis de Góngora. *See* Polyphemus and Galatea.
Polish Boy, The. Ann S. Stephens. PTA-2
Polish National Hymn, *abr.* Aloizy Felsinki, *tr. fr. Polish by* Paul Soboleski. PoFr
Polite Petrarch Peck. Horatio Winslow. LauV
Politeness. Elizabeth Turner. HBV; HBVY
Politeness. *Unknown. See* Hearts, like Doors.
Politest musician that ever was seen, The. The Music of the Future. Oliver Herford. CenHV; PoMa
Politic Peter meets his friend ashore. Samuel Rowlands. SiCE
Political Balance, The. Philip Freneau. IAP
Political Cartoon. Aristophanes. *See* Demos and His Flatterer.
Political Chaos in Italy. Dante, *tr. fr. Italian by* Longfellow. *Fr.* Divina Comedia: Purgatorio, VI. WoL
Political Greatness. Shelley. EM-2; EnRP; EPN; PeBoSo
(Sonnet: Political Greatness.) BPN; EmBrPo
Political Litany, A. Philip Freneau. *See* Emancipation from British Dependence.
Political Meeting. A. M. Klein. BoCaPo (1948 ed.)
Politician, The. Ambrose Bierce. BAP
Politician, A. E. E. Cummings. LiTM
(Politician Is an Arse Upon, A.) SiTL
Politician, The. Po Chü-i, *tr. fr. Chinese by* Arthur Waley. TrCh
Politician and Mr. Gay, The. Swift. *Fr.* To Mr. Gay. BeR
Politician Is an Arse Upon, A. E. E. Cummings. *See* Politician, A.
Politics. Tennyson. CoBE; PoRL
Politics. W. B. Yeats. ChMo; POTE
Politics and Perquisites. Aristophanes, *tr. fr. Greek by* Benjamin Bickley Rogers. *Fr.* The Wasps. GrR
Polka Lyric, A. Gilbert Abbott à Beckett. *See* Holiday Task, A.
Poll Tax (1378). Maurice Hewlett. *Fr.* The Song of the Plow. PoFr
Pollie. Walter de la Mare. AlDL
Pollio; an Elegy, *sel.* William Julius Mickle.
Evening at the Abbey. RO
Polly, *sel.* John Gay.
"Sleep, O sleep," Air XXIII. ViBoPo
(Song.) FaBoEn
Polly. William Brighty Rands. GoTP; OTPC (1923 ed.); PRWS; VA
Polly, from me, tho' now a love-sick youth. To a Young Lady. Richard Savage. OBEC
Polly Oliver's Rambles, *with music. Unknown.* ViBoFo
Polly Pansy. William Brighty Rands. SAS
Polly, Peg, and Poppety. Kate Greenaway. SAS
Polly Perkins. *Unknown.* OxBoLi
Polly, put the kettle on. Mother Goose. BrR; OTPC; OxNR; PCH; SAS; StVeCh (1940 ed.)
Polly Williams, *with music. Unknown.* ABF
Polly Wolly Doodle. *Unknown.* TreF; YaD
Polly's, Peg's, and Poppety's. Polly, Peg, and Poppety. Kate Greenaway. SAS
Polo Grounds. Rolfe Humphries. HoPM; PreP
Polo Match. Sunday, 2 P.M. Josephine Miles. FiMAP
Polo Player. Daniel Whitehead Hicky. MoSiPe
Polonius. Walter de la Mare. AtBAP
Polonius' Advice to Laertes. Shakespeare. *Fr.* Hamlet, I, iii. BBV; FAOV; OQP; PoeMoYo; PTA-1; PYM; QP-1
(Be True, 3 *ll.*) PCD; PCH
(Counsel of Polonius, The.) TVSH
(Polonius' Advice to His Son.) BTP; MaRV; PECK; TreF
(Polonius Advises His Son.) BCEP
(Polonius to Laertes.) GN
(". . There; my blessing with thee.") PIR
(These Few Precepts.) EV-1
(This above All.) TrGrPo
(To Thine Own Self Be True.) FaFP; LiTB; LiTG
Polonius and the Ballad-Singers. Padraic Colum. NP
Polonius to Laertes. Shakespeare. *See* Polonius' Advice to Laertes.
Poltroon, The. Sarah N. Cleghorn. QS
Polwart on the Green. Allan Ramsay. CEP
Polycrates, whose passing hap caus'd him to lose his fate. Of Fortune's Power. Richard Edwards. ReIE
Polyhymnia, *sel.* George Peele.
His Golden Locks Time Hath to Silver Turned. AtBAP; EIL; ElSeCe; EM-1; LoBV; PoE; ReEn; ReIE; TuPP; ViBoPo; WHA
(Farewell to Arms, A.) AnFE; CBOV; CoBE; CoEV; EG; EnLi-1; EPP; EV-1; HBV; LEAP; OBEV; PoRA
("My golden locks time hath to silver turned.") BrBE; CenL
(Old Knight, The.) ChTr; OBSC; TrGrPo
(Sonet, A: "His golden lockes, Time hath to silver turn'd.") FaBoEn; PoEL-2; SiCE
(Sonnet: "His golden locks . . .") CaAE
Polyolbion, *sels.* Michael Drayton.
"Away yee barb'rous woods," *fr.* Third Song. OBS
Birds in the Fens, *fr.* Two and Twentieth Song. ChTr
"Earle Douglasse for this day," *fr.* Two and Twentieth Song. OBS
Fools Gaze at Painted Courts, *fr.* Eighteenth Song. ChTr
"Mongst whom, some there were bards, that in their sacred rage," *fr.* Fourth Song. PrWP
"Now are the Tritons heard, to loving-land to call," *fr.* Twentieth Song. AtBAP
"Of Albion's glorious ile the wonders whilst I write," *fr.* First Song. ReIE
Thirteenth Song, The, *abr.* ReEn
Sels.
Forest of Arden, The ("My native Country then, which so brave spirits hast bred"). SeEP
"Forest so much fallen from what she was before, The." SeCePo
"Of all the beasts." OBS
"Upon the midlands now th' industrious muse doth fall." ReIE; TuPP
"When Phoebus lifts his head." OBS
"To these, the gentle South," *fr.* Second Song. OBS
"World of mightie kings, A," *fr.* Twentieth Song. OBS
Polyphemus and Galatea, *sels.* Luis de Góngora, *tr. fr. Spanish.*
"Cyclops—terrific son of Ocean's God!" *tr. by* Thomas Roscoe. AnSpL-1
Love Song of Polyphemus, The, *tr. by* Frances Fletcher. LiTW
Polyphemus to Galatea. Theocritus, *tr. fr. Greek. Fr.* Idylls, XI. OxBG
(Giant's Wooing, The, *tr. by* C. S. Calverley.) GrR
("O Galatea faire, why dost thou shun thy lover true?") GrPo
Polyphiloprogenitive. Mr. Eliot's Sunday Morning Service. T. S. Eliot. MaPo; PoFS
Polyxena. Euripides, *tr. fr. Greek. Fr.* Hecuba. GrR, *tr. by* Hugh Owen Meredith; OxBG, *tr. by* George Allen
Pomegranate, The. Louis Dudek. PeCV
Pomegranates. Roy Campbell. AtBAP
Pomegranates. Paul Valéry, *tr. fr. French.* LiTW, *tr. by* Herman Salinger; TrFP, *tr. by* Alan Conder
Pomegranates come from red hot pearls. Fruits of Experience. James Broughton. SiTL
Pommier doux, Le. *Unknown, tr. fr. French-Canadian folk song by* William McLennan. BoCaPo
Pomp of the Persian I hold in aversion, The. Persicos Odi. Franklin P. Adams. HBMV; PoeMoYo
Pompadour, The. George Walter Thornbury. BeLS
Pompeius, best of all my comrades, you and I. Returned Warrior. Horace. *Fr.* Odes. LaP; LiTW; WaaP
Pompey and Cornelia. Lucan, *tr. fr. Latin by* Nicholas Rowe. *Fr.* Pharsalia, V. OBEC
Pompey's Ghost. Thomas Hood. DaM
Pompilia. Robert Browning. The Ring and the Book, VII. EM-2, *abr.;* OAEP; PoVP; ViPo; ViPP; VLEP
Ponce de Leon. Edith M. Thomas. PAH
Pond, The. W. H. Davies. ChMP
Pond, The. Annette von Droste-Hülshoff, *tr. fr. German by* Herman Salinger. AnGP
Pond, The. Howard Nemerov. FiMAP
Pond, The. Jane Taylor. OTPC (1923 ed.)
Pond, The. James Whaler. *Fr.* Runaway. MAP; MoAmPo (1942 ed.)
Ponder, Darling, These Busted Statues. E. E. Cummings. SiTL
Ponder It, O Soul! Eduard Mörike, *tr. fr. German by* Kate Flores. AnGP
Ponder the Tone; the Broken Theme. Robert Hillyer. BoFr
(Prelude: "Ponder the tone; the broken theme.") TBM
Ponder thy cares, and sum them all in one. Sonnet. Sir David Murray. *Fr.* Caelia. EIL
Ponder, ye Just, the scoffs that frequent go. Prophets Who Cannot Sing. Coventry Patmore. CoBE; PoVP
Pondy Woods. Robert Penn Warren. MAP; MoAmPo
Ponies, The. W W Gibson. WaKn
Ponsonby Perks. Laura E. Richards. Nonsense Verses, II. RIS
Pont du Carrousel. Rainer Maria Rilke, *tr. fr. German by* Jessie Lemont. OnPM
Pont Mirabeau. Guillaume Apollinaire. *See* Mirabeau Bridge, The.
Pontifical, that night in alien Rome. John Keats. T. A. Daly. PoeMoYo
Pontius Pilate, *sel.* Thomas Durley Landels.
Pilate Remembers. MaRV

Ponto the Fool. Beatrice Redpath. CPG
Pontoon Bridge Miracle, The. Vachel Lindsay. *Fr.* Every Soul Is a Circus, IV. LiTM (rev. ed.); LoBV; NePA
Pony, The. Rachel MacAndrew. BoTP
Pony Rock. Archibald MacLeish. ChMo; CMP
Pooh! Walter de la Mare. FiBHP
Pooh—men! Baby. Florence Kiper Frank. HBMV
Pooh! to those Caspar Milquetoasts who. The Big Boss Speaks. Nate Salsbury. LauV
Pool, The. Fritz S. Burnell. BoAu
Pool, The. Alice Corbin. NP
Pool, The. Hilda Doolittle ("H. D."). ExPo; NP
Pool, The. E. L. Mayo. MiAP
Pool, The. Marjorie Pickthall. CPG; MM; NLK (1947 ed.); OCL
Pool, The. Tsou Hao, *tr. fr. Chinese by* Henry H. Hart. PoHN
Pool in a garden green, A. The Other Side of the Sky. W. Graham Robertson. PPL
Pool in My Garden, The. Ku Shih, *tr. fr. Chinese by* Henry H. Hart. PoHN
Pool is radiant, The. The Pool. Tsou Hao. PoHN
Pool of Sleep, The. Arlo Bates. LBAP; PC
Poor, The. William Langland. *See* Sufferings of the Poor, The.
Poor, The. Carl Sandburg. *See* Masses.
Poor, The. Speer Strahan. CAW; JKCP
Poor, The. *Unknown. Quoted by* George Crabbe *in* The Borough, *at head of* Letter XVIII. AEV
Poor, The. Emile Verhaeren, *tr. fr. French by* Ludwig Lewisohn. AWP; JAWP; WBP; WoL
Poor, The. William Carlos Williams. MoAB; MoAmPo; NeMA
Poor are treated scurvily, The. Rich and Poor. Al-Haitham. MooP
Poor babe of France and captive of her foes. Napoleon II. Lydia Schuyler. BoHiPo
Poor benighted Hindoo, The. Limericks. Cosmo Monkhouse. HBV; PCD; TSW; TSWC
Poor bird! I do not envy thee. The Robin. George Daniel. UnPo (1st ed.)
Poor Boy. *Unknown. See* Coon Can.
Poor Brother. *Unknown.* NA
Poor but Honest. *Unknown.* KN; LiTG; OtMeF; OxBoLi (She Was Poor but She Was Honest.) FiBHP; SiTL
Poor Children. Victor Hugo, *tr. fr. French by* Swinburne. AWP; JAWP; WBP
Poor Copies. Jalal ed-Din Rumi, *tr. fr. Persian by* R. A. Nicholson. PeP
Poor creature, come!/ I should think shame to be afraid. The Coast Guard's Cottage. Elinor Wylie. BoFr
Poor Creature! nay, I'll not say poor. To a Moth. Charles Edward Thomas. AA
Poor damned Catullus, here's no time for nonsense. Catullus, *tr. fr. Latin by* Horace Gregory. RoL
Poor Dear Grandpapa. D'Arcy W. Thompson. BOHV; NA
Poor degenerate from the ape, A. The First Philosopher's Song. Aldous Huxley. AWP; HBMV; InPo; JAWP; WPB
Poor Doctor Blow went out of church. Queen Anne's Musicians. Thomas Hennell. FaBoTw
Poor Dog Bright. *Unknown.* SAS
Poor Dog Tray. Thomas Campbell. *See* Harper, The.
Poor drooping flowers and pallid violets. Sonnet. Matteo Maria Boiardo. LyPI
Poor Estate, The. Robert Greene. *See* Sweet Are the Thoughts That Savor of Content.
Poor Estate to Be Holden for Best, The. *Unknown, at. to* Edward Seymour, Duke of Somerset. SiCE; TuPP (On Edward Seymour, Duke of Somerset.) OBSC
Poor Farmer's Offering, The. Apollonides, *tr. fr. Greek by* Sir William Marris. OxBG
Poor Fool. Evan V. Shute. CaP
Poor for Our Sakes. Mary Brainerd Smith. BLRP
Poor French Sailor's Scottish Sweetheart, A. William Johnson Cory. VA
Poor Girl. Stephen Spender. FaBoMo ("Poor girl, inhabitant of a strange land.") GTBS-D
Poor girl! Our little home is haunted. Lacrimae Rerum. "Lambros Porphyras." MoGP
Poor Girl's Meditation, The. *Unknown, tr. fr. Irish by* Padraic Colum. GTIV; OBMV
Poor Goins. *Unknown.* ABS
Poor Grandma, I do hate to tell her. Grandma's Mistake. *Unknown.* DDA
Poor have childher and to spare, The. Quantity and Quality. Winifred M. Letts. CV; HBMV
Poor heart of mine, which in the days gone by. A Woman without Tears. Euripides. *Fr.* Iphigenia in Tauris. GrR
Poor Henry. Walter de la Mare. HBMV
Poor-House Nan. Lucy H. Blinn. PTA-1
Poor humble roach. To a Humble Bug. Linda Lyon Van Voorhis. GoYe
Poor I saw at the cloister gate, The. The Poor. Speer Strahan. CAW; JKCP
Poor in Church, The. Arthur Rimbaud, *tr. fr. French by* Gerard Previn Meyer. LiTW
Poor in my youth, and in life's later scenes. Riches. *Unknown.* AWP
Poor Is the Life That Misses. *Unknown.* EIL
Poor Jack. Charles Dibdin. BeLS; EV-3; HBV; LPS-2
Poor Johnny was bended well-nigh double. Apple-Seed John. Lydia Maria Child. DD; GA; OHIP; OTPC
Poor Kings. W. H. Davies. HBV
Poor Kitty Popcorn, *with music. Unknown.* AS
Poor lad once and a lad so trim, A. Jean Richepin's Song. Herbert Trench. LiTG; LiTM (rev. ed.); OBMV; OxBI; POTE
Poor Lady Dumpling. *Unknown.* FTB
Poor Lil' Brack Sheep. Ethel M. C. Brazelton. BLPA
Poor little bee, The. Ke-ni-ga Song. *Tr. by* Natalie Barnes. MPB
Poor Little Conscience, A. José Gorostiza, *tr. fr. Spanish by* Donald Devenish Walsh. AnCL
Poor little daws, hungry little daws. Daw's Dinner. Joyce Kilmer. CAW
Poor little foal of an oppressèd race! To a Young Ass. Samuel Taylor Coleridge. EmBrPo; EnRP; OBEC
Poor Little Joe. David Law Proudfit. PTA-2
Poor little Lucy. The Lost Shoe. Walter de la Mare. BoChLi (1939 ed.); BrR; TSW; TSWC
Poor little Nellie is weeping tonight. Why Did They Dig Ma's Grave So Deep? George Cooper. TreFS
Poor little, pretty, fluttering thing. To His Soul [*or* Adriani Morientis ad Animam Suam]. Emperor Hadrian, *tr. by* Matthew Prior. CEP; EPP; InP; SeCL
Poor Lodgings. Ibn Abdun, *tr. fr. Arabic by* A. J. Arberry. MooP
Poor lone Hannah. Hannah Binding Shoes. Lucy Larcom. GN; HBV
Poor, lonely clown, somersaulting horribly. The Clown. Tefcros Anthias. MoGP
Poor lonely willow tree. The Brook and the Willow Tree. *Unknown.* GFA
Poor Lonesome Cowboy. *Unknown.* ABF; AS; CoSo, *with music;* CSF; TiPo
Poor Lucy Lake was overgrown. Lucy Lake. Newton Mackintosh. BOHV; HBV; PA
Poor mad Poll, pretty Poll. Mad Poll. J. Corson Miller. JKCP (1955 ed.)
Poor Mailie's Elegy. Burns. EBSV
Poor Man, The. Francis Carlin. PR
Poor Man Is Not Loved, The. Marcus Argentarius, *tr. fr. Greek by* Sir William Marris. OxBG
Poor Man's Daily Bread, The. Denis A. McCarthy. JKCP
Poor Man's Epitaph, A. Simonides, *tr. fr. Greek by* Robert Allason Furness. GrR
Poor Man's Pig, The. Edmund Blunden. CoEV; MBP; MoBrPo
Poor man's sins are glaring, The. Rich and Poor; or, Saint and Sinner. Thomas Love Peacock. SiTL
Poor Martha Snell, she's gone away. On Martha Snell. *Unknown.* GoTP; WhC
Poor Mary Byrne is dead. Grandeur. Winifred M. Letts. BMEP
Poor Matthias. Matthew Arnold. PoEL-5; SN
On the Death of a Favorite Canary, *sel.* BLA; PC
(Atossa.) PoC
("Poor Matthias! Wouldst thou have.") CIV
Poor Me. *Unknown, tr. fr. French by* Richard Beaumont. LyMA
Poor men's God that gives them sleep, The. Overseer of the Poor. James Hayford. NePoAm-2
Poor Monk of Skara, A. Gustaf Fröding, *tr. fr. Swedish by* Charles W. Stork. AnSL
Poor mortals that are clog'd with earth below. Song of Aerial Spirits. Sir Robert Howard *and* John Dryden. *Fr.* The Indian Queen. AtBAP
Poor naked wretches, wheresoe'er you are. Take Physic, Pomp [*or* Discovery of Pity]. Shakespeare. *Fr.* King Lear, III, iv. TrGrPo; UnPo (1st ed.)
Poor Old Cannon, The. Elinor Wylie. LHV
Poor old Chi has died and gone. Lament for a Dead Wine-Maker. Li Po. PoHN
Poor old cottage tottering to its fall, A. My Old Home. Ellen O'Leary. TIP
Poor Old Horse. *Unknown.* CH; KN
Poor Old Joe. *Unknown. See* Old Joe.
Poor old Jonathan Bing. Jonathan Bing. Beatrice Curtis Brown. FaPON; GaP; LiL; PCD; RIS; TiPo
Poor old king with sorrow for my crown, A. Lear. Thomas Hood. VA
Poor Old Lady. *Unknown.* GoTP
Poor old lady, set her aside. The Old Mother. *Unknown.* PoToHe
Poor old lady, she swallowed a fly. Poor Old Lady. *Unknown.* GoTP

Poor Old Man, The. J. C. Squire. HBMV
(How They Do It.) InMe
Poor Old Man, *with music.* *Unknown.* ShS; SoAmSa
Poor Old Pilgrim Misery. Thomas Lovell Beddoes. *Fr.* The Bride's Tragedy. EnRP; NBE
(Hesperus Sings.) VA
Poor old Robinson Crusoe! Mother Goose. BoTP; OTPC; OxNR; RIS
Poor old widow in her weeds, A. A Widow's Weeds. Walter de la Mare. AtBAP
Poor old woman, A/ Four score and a day. Mickleham Way. Ivy O. Eastwick. BrR
Poor Omie Wise. *Unknown.* *See* Naomi Wise.
Poor Paddy Works on the Railway. *Unknown.* *See* Paddy Works on the Railway.
Poor painters oft with silly poets join. Cupid. Sir Philip Sidney. *Fr.* Arcadia. SiPS
Poor Parson, The. Chaucer. *See* Parson, The.
Poor Poet's Lullaby, The. John Huston Finley. BAP
Poor Poll. Robert Bridges. MoPo; OxBoLi
Poor Poncho, the gringos drove him nuts. Blood on a Stone. Francisco Méndez. AnCL
Poor, Poor Country, The. John Shaw Neilson. NeLNL
Poor Puss is gone! 'Tis fate's decree. To a Cat. Ibn Alalaf Alnaharwany. PoC
Poor pussy-cat mew. Mother Goose. *See* Pussy-cat Mew . . .
Poor Relation, A. Audrey McGaffin. NePoAm-2
Poor Relation, The. E. A. Robinson. AnAmPo; LA; MAPA; TwP
Poor Reuben Ranzo. Arthur H. Clark. IHA
Poor Richard's Almanac, *sels.* Benjamin Franklin.
Poor Richard's Wisdom. GoTP
Well-packed Wisdom. StaSt
Poor Robin. *Unknown.* ABS
Poor Rose! I lift you from the street. Romaunt of the Rose. Austin Dobson. LPS-1
Poor Scholar, The. Abraham ibn Chasdai, *tr. fr. Hebrew by* Joseph Chotzner. TrJP
Poor Scholar of the 'Forties, A. Padraic Colum. AnIL; GTIV; OxBI
Poor Scholar to Mice, A. *Unknown, tr. fr. Greek by* Lord Neaves. OnPM
Poor Scholars, The. Tao Yuan-ming, *tr. fr. Chinese by* Yang Yeh-tzu. WhP
Poor slaves, how terrible this Death is to them! George Chapman. *Fr.* Caesar and Pompey. ViBoPo
Poor Snail, The. J. M. Westrup. BoTP
Poor solitary bird, that pour'st thy lay. Petrarch. Sonnets to Laura: To Laura in Death, XC. PrPoCR
Poor Son of Mary, The. Spanish Lullaby. *Unknown, ad. by* Louis Untermeyer. RIS
Poor Soul. Shakespeare. *See* Sonnets, CXLVI.
Poor soul! God's goodness hath been great to thee. Gratitude. Shakespeare. King Henry VI, Pt. II, *fr.* II, i. MaRV
Poor soul sat sighing by a sycamore tree, The. Desdemona's Song. Shakespeare. *Fr.* Othello, IV, iii. BCEP; KN; LoBV
Poor [*or* Poore] soul sat sighing by a sycamore tree, The: Sing [*or* O] willow, willow, willow. The Green Willow [*or* The Complaint of a Lover Forsaken of His Love]. *Unknown.* CoMu; OBSC
Poor soul, the centre [*or* center] of my sinful earth. Sonnets, CXLVI [*or* Soul and Body *or* The Death of Death]. Shakespeare. AtBAP; ATP; AWP; BEL; BLV; BoLiVe; CAW; CoBE; EIL; EM-1; EnL; EnLi-1; EPP; ES; EV-1; ExPo; FaBoEn; GoBC; GTBS; GTBS-D; GTBS-W; GTSE; GTSL; HBV; InPo; JAWP; LEAP; LiTB; LiTG; LO; MaPo; MaRV; MyFE; OBEV; OBSC; OxBoCh; PeBoSo; PIAE; PoEL-2; ReaPo; ReEn; ReIE; RiBV; SeCeV; SiCE; TOP; TreFS; TrGrPo; TwP; UnPo (1st ed.); ViBoPo; WBP; WHA
Poor souls, who think that joy is bought. Joy. W. H. Davies. POTT
Poor South! Her books get fewer and fewer. J. Gordon Coogler. FiBHP
Poor Susan's Dream. Wordsworth. *See* Reverie of Poor Susan.
Poor tired Tim! It's sad for him. Tired Tim. Walter de la Mare. ALV; BMEP; BoTP; FaPON; GaP; MoShBr; MPB; OnPP; TiPo; TSW; TSWC
Poor Tom Bowling. Charles Dibdin. *See* Tom Bowling.
Poor Tom, or the Sailor's Epitaph. Charles Dibdin. *See* Tom Bowling.
Poor Uncle Joe. Sartorial Solecism. R. E. C. Stringer. FiBHP
Poor unpardonable length Snake. John Russell McCarthy. BAP
Poor Virtue, she's but words. Virtue. *Unknown.* OxBG
Poor Voter on Election Day, The. Whittier. PoRL; TCAP
"Poor wanderer," said the leaden sky. The Subalterns. Thomas Hardy. ChMo; MaPo; MBP; MoAB; MoBrPo
Poor Wat. Shakespeare. *Fr.* Venus and Adonis. OBSC; UnPo (1st ed.)
Poor wayfaring man of grief, A. The Stranger. James Montgomery. BCEP
Poor Wayfaring Stranger, *with music.* *Unknown.* TrAS
(Over Jordan, *with music.*) OuSiCo
Poor wayworn creature! Oh, sorely harried deer. Feud. Lew Sarett. AnAmPo; LA; MAP; TBM
Poor who begs with bated breath, The. The Price of Begging. Emmanuel ben David Frances. TrJP
Poor Widow's Cock, The. Chaucer. *Fr.* The Canterbury Tales: The Nun's Priest's Tale. MyFE
Poor Withered Rose. Robert Bridges. VA
Poor Working Girl, The, *with music.* *Unknown.* AS
Poor wretch with what calamity art thou joined. His Death. Euripides. *Fr.* Hippolytus. OxBG
Poore bird! I doe not envie thee. The Robin. George Daniel. OBS
Poore Man Payes for All, The. *Unknown.* CoMu
Poore pensive I o're chargde with woe. *At. to* Thomas Carew. SeCSL
Poore soule, in this thy flesh what dost thou know? The Soules Ignorance in This Life and Knowledge in the Next. John Donne. *Fr.* Of the Progresse of the Soule. OBS
Poore soule sate sighing by a sicamore tree, A. *See* Poor soul sat sighing by a sycamore tree, The.
Poore things be those vowes we boast on. *Unknown.* SeCSL
Pop. Elinor Maxwell. FAOV
Pop bottles pop-bottles. Song of the Pop-Bottlers. Morris Bishop. FaPON; FiBHP
Pop Goes the Weasel ("All around the cobbler's bench"). *Unknown.* OIF; RIS
Pop Goes the Weasel ("Up and down the City Road"). *Unknown.* BoN
("Up and down the City Road.") OxNR
Pop took me to the circus 'cause it disappoints me so. Story of Self-Sacrifice. James W. Foley. FAOV
Pop-Corn Land. Elsie F. Kartack. GFA
Popcorn Man, The. Edith D. Osborne. GFA
Popcorn man, The,/ At the park. The Popcorn-Popper. Dorothy Walter Baruch. BrR
Popcorn Party, The. "E. R. B." GFA
Popcorn-Popper, The. Dorothy Walter Baruch. BrR
Pop Corn Song, A. Nancy Byrd Turner. FaPON; GFA; MPB
Pope, The. Robert Browning. The Ring and the Book, X. ViPo; ViPP
Pope, The. Charles Lever. *Fr.* Harry Lorrequer. BOHV
(Pope He Leads a Happy Life, The.) HBV
Pope and Prelate notwithstanding, The. King Sverrir. Grímur Thomsen. IcP
Pope and the Net, The. Robert Browning. BOHV
Pope at Twickenham. Charles Kent. PtP; VA
Pope he is a happy man, The. Commanders of the Faithful. Thackeray. ALV
Pope He Leads a Happy Life, The. Charles Lever. *See* Pope, The.
Pope on Dryden. Pope. *Fr.* The First Epistle of the Second Book of Horace. BeR
Popish Plot, The. Dryden. *Fr.* Absalom and Achitophel, Pt. I. ACP
("Inhabitants of old Jerusalem, The.") TCEP
Poplar, The. Richard Aldington. HBMV; NP; PoTo
Poplar drops beside the way, The. In April [*or* Spring at the Capital]. Elizabeth Akers Allen. MDAH; OTPC (1946 ed.); PRWS
Poplar-Field, The. William Cowper. CH; ChTr; EiPP; EnSW; FiP; GTBS; GTBS-D; GTBS-W; GTSE; GTSL; HBV; InPo; OBEC; Po; PoEL-3; RiBV; SeCeV; ShBV-1; TrGrPo; UnPo (3d ed.)
Poplar is a lonely tree, The. Poplars. Edward Bliss Reed. DD; HBMV; HBVY; OHIP; PEDC; VOD
Poplar Tree. Padraic Colum. NePoAm
Poplars. Hilda Conkling. NP
Poplars, The. Theodosia Garrison. HBMV; OHIP; PoRL; StVeCh; VOD
Poplars. Helen Leuty. BoTP
Poplars, The. "Seumas O'Sullivan." GTIV
Poplars. Edward Bliss Reed. DD; HBMV; HBVY; OHIP; PEDC; VOD
Poplars, The. Bernard Freeman Trotter. CaP; CPG; OCL
Poplars and the ancient elms, The. Theocritus. Sir Edmund Gosse. PtP; VA
Poplars are fell'd [*or* felled], farewell to the shade, The. The Poplar-Field. William Cowper. CH; ChTr; EiPP; EnSW; FiP; GTBS; GTBS-D; GTBS-W; GTSE; GTSL; HBV; InPo; OBEC; Po; PoEL-3; RiBV; SeCeV; ShBV-1; TrGrPo; UnPo (3d ed.)
Poplars are standing there still as death. Southern Mansion. Arna Bontemps. BANP; PoNe
Poplars bow forward and back, The. Poplars. Hilda Conkling. NP
Poplars in the fields of France, The. In France. Frances Cornford. HBMV

Poppies. Innokenti Annensky, *tr. fr. Russian by* C. M. Bowra. BoRS
Poppies. Henry Bellamann. TBM
Poppies. Joseph Plunkett. LBBV; MBP
(O Sower of Sorrow.) CAW
Poppies. P. A. Ropes. BoTP
Poppies. Laura Livingston Speyers. CAG
Poppies. *Unknown. tr. fr. Japanese by* William N. Porter. MPB
Poppies. Charles Weekes. OnYI
Poppies. ffrida Wolfe. *See* Poppies in the Garden, The.
Poppies in Ludlow Castle. Willa Cather. OBAV
Poppies in the Garden, The. ffrida Wolfe. BoTP
(Poppies.) PCH
Poppies in the Wheat. Helen Hunt Jackson. AA; BAP; LEAP; OBAV; PFY
Poppies paramour the girls. Song. Haniel Long. HBMV; LEAP
Poppies, ye flaming blushes of July. Flanders Poppies. Ian Colvin. AOAH
Popping Corn Song ("Bring a yellow ear of corn, then rub, rub, rub"). *Unknown.* MeMeAg
Poppy, The. Jane Taylor. OTPC; TVC; TVSH
Poppy, The. Francis Thompson. EmBrPo; MBP; MoBrPo; OBEV (1st ed.); PoP; POTT; PoVP; VLEP
Poppy Fields. William Alexander Percy. LS
Poppy Grows upon the Shore, A. Robert Bridges. PoVP
Poppy-Land Limited Express, The. Edgar W. Abbott. BOL
Popular Ballad: "Never Forget Your Parents." Franklin P. Adams. BOHV
Popular Lament: "'O noble knight of France.'" *Unknown, tr. fr. French by* Alan Conder. TrFP
Popular Poplar Tree, The. Blanche Willis Howard. ADAH
Popular Recollections of Bonaparte. Pierre Jean de Béranger, *tr. fr. French by* Francis Sylvester Mahony. LPS-3
Popular Sicilian Love Songs. *Unknown, tr. fr. Italian.* LyPI
"More than honey the words you speak are sweet," *tr. by* L. R. Lind.
"Send me no messages, for they are lies," *tr. by* Cecil Clifford Palmer.
Popular Song: "Methought I saw how wealthy men." *Unknown.* PoFr
Popular Songs of Tuscany. *Unknown, tr. fr. Italian by* John Addington Symonds.
"I see the dawn e'en now begin to peer." AWP
"I would I were a bird so free." AWP
"It was the morning of the first of May." AWP; JAWP; WBP
"On Sunday morning well I knew." AWP; OnPM
"Passing across the billowy sea." AWP; JAWP; WBP
(Giving a Heart.) OnPM
"Sleeping or waking, thou sweet face." AWP; JAWP; WBP
"Strew me with blossoms when I die." AWP; JAWP; WBP
"What time I see you passing by." AWP
Popularity. Robert Browning. BPN; PoVP; PtP; TCEP
Population Drifts. Carl Sandburg. OxBA
Porcelain Factory, The. Carl Snoilsky, *tr. fr. Swedish by* Charles W. Stork. AnSL
Porcelain of the North. Rafael Méndez Dorich, *tr. fr. Spanish by* Donald Devenish Walsh. AnCL
Porcelaine de Saxe. Virginia Lyne Tunstall. TBM
Porch of Hell, The. Thomas Sackville. *Fr.* Induction to "The Mirror for Magistrates." EV-1
Porcus, that foul unsociable hog. In Porcum. John Heath. SiCE; TuPP
Porgy, Maria, and Bess. DuBose Heyward. PoNe
Porphyria's Lover. Robert Browning. AtBAP; AWP; BeLS; BoLiVe; BPN; CaAE; EM-2; EmBrPo; EV-5; GEPC; GTBS; GTML; GTSE; GTSL; HBV; InPo; JAWP; KN; LEAP; MaPo; OAEP; OBEV; OuHeWo; PoVP; REAL; ShBV-4; TOP; TrGrPo; TwHP; TwP; ViPo; ViPP; VLEP; WBP
Porpoise. Guillaume Apollinaire, *tr. fr. French by* Lillian White Spencer. OnPM
Port Admiral. Frederick Marryat. SG
Port after Stormie Seas. Spenser. *See* What if Some Little Paine the Passage Have.
Port Bou. Stephen Spender. MoPo
Port o' Heart's Desire, The. John S. McGroarty. HBV; NLK
Port-of-Call. Sister Mary Therese. PraNu
Port of Embarkation. Randall Jarrell. MiAP
Port of Holy Peter. John Masefield. AtBAP; OBMV; POTE; ShBV-2
Port of Many Ships. John Masefield. OBMV
Port of St. John, The. H. A. Cody. CPG
Portal as of shadowy adamant, A. An Allegory. Shelley. EmBrPo
Portent. Richard Church. MBP; MoBrPo (1942 ed.)
Portent, The. Ibn al-Zaqqaq, *tr. fr. Arabic by* A. J. Arberry. MooP
Portent, The. Herman Melville. AmPP; ExPo; OxBA; PoEL-5; PoFS
Portents, The. Lucan, *tr. fr. Latin by* Christopher Marlowe. *Fr.* Pharsalia, I. OBSC
Portents and Prodigies are [*or* have] grown so frequent. Wild Weather. Dryden. *Fr.* All for Love. AtBAP; BoW
Porter shouted, "Syracuse," The. Reveille. Hughes Mearns. *Fr.* Later Antigonishes. InMe; SiTL
Porter to th' infernall gate is Sin, The. Sin, Despair, and Lucifer. Phineas Fletcher. *Fr.* The Locusts, or Apollyonists. OBS
Portia's Appeal for Mercy. Shakespeare. *See* Quality of Mercy, The.
Portia's Picture. Shakespeare. *Fr.* The Merchant of Venice, III, ii. LPS-1
Portia's Plea for Mercy. Shakespeare. *See* Quality of Mercy, The.
Portico. Rubén Darío, *tr. fr. Spanish by* Thomas Walsh. CAW
Portion of this yew. Transformations. Thomas Hardy. ChMo; CMP; NV; TwCV
Portland County Jail, *with music. Unknown.* AS
Portly Roman Senator was sipping his Rock and Rye, A. A War Bird's Burlesque. *Unknown.* AS
Portly wood-louse, full of cares, A. The Poet and the Wood-Louse. Helen Parry Eden. HBV
Portoferraio. Alan Ross. PoN
Portrait. George Leonard Allen. CDC
Portrait, A. Joseph Ashby-Sterry. HBV; VA
Portrait. Francesco Berni, *tr. fr. Italian by* L. R. Lind. LyPI
Portrait. Louise Bogan. HBMV
Portrait, A. Elizabeth Barrett Browning. GN; HBV; LPS-1; OTPC
Portrait. Hal Chadwick. DDA
Portrait. Máire Cotter. SaFP
Portrait ("Buffalo Bill's/ defunct"). E. E. Cummings. AnNE; MAP; MoAB; MoAmPo; UnPo
(Buffalo Bill.) CoBA
(Buffalo Bill's.) LiTA; NePA
("Buffalo Bill's/ defunct.") AmPP
Portrait ("Here is little Effie's head"). E. E. Cummings. AnAmPo; LA
Portrait ("Of evident invisibles"). E. E. Cummings. TCPD
Portrait ("Somebody knew Lincoln Somebody Xerxes"). E. E. Cummings. TCPD
Portrait, A. Thomas Dekker. EV-2
Portrait. Jeanne D'Orge. AnAmPo; LA
Portrait, A. Caroline Duer. AA; OBAV
Portrait. Kenneth Fearing. MoAmPo; OnAP; PoLFOT
Portrait, The. John Gould Fletcher. MOAP
Portrait, The. John Heywood. *See* Praise of His Lady, A.
Portrait, A. Brian Hooker. HBV
Portrait, A. Keats. *See* Spenserian Stanzas on Charles Armitage Brown.
Portrait, The. "Owen Meredith." *Fr.* The Wanderer. HBV; LPS-1
Portrait. Hyam Plutzik. FiMAP
Portrait. Ezra Pound. OBVV
Portrait. Pushkin, *tr. fr. Russian by* Babette Deutsch. OnPM; TrRV
Portrait, A ("She gave up beauty"). Christina Rossetti. POTT; VLEP
Portrait, The ("O Lord of all compassionate control"). Dante Gabriel Rossetti. The House of Life, X. BPN; EmBrPo; OAEP; PoVP; ViPo; VLEP
Portrait, The ("This is her picture as she was"). Dante Gabriel Rossetti. BMEP; BPN; EmBrPo; EV-5; GTML; GTSE; OAEP; POTT; PoVP; TriL; VA; ViPo; VLEP
Portrait. Sydney King Russell. PoMa
Portrait, A. Robert Louis Stevenson. SeCePo
Portrait. Miriam Waddington. BoCaPo (1948 ed.)
Portrait, The. Countess of Winchilsea. *Fr.* The Birthday of Catharine Tufton. OBEV
Portrait by a Neighbor. Edna St. Vincent Millay. FaPON; GaP; MoShBr; MPB; SP; TiPo; TSW; TSWC
Portrait d'une Femme. Ezra Pound. AnAmPo; APA; CoAnAm; HBMV; LA; MAP; MoAB; MoAmPo; MoVE; PoFS; ReaPo; TwAmPo
Portrait in Winter. Katherine Garrison Chapin. GoYe
Portrait of a Boy. Stephen Vincent Benét. HBMV; MCCG; MW; NeMA; PC; PoMa; TCAP
Portrait of a Child. Louis Untermeyer. BAP; FAOV; HBMV
Portrait of a Cree. "Katherine Hale." CaP; CPG
Portrait of a Florentine Lady, The. Lizette Woodworth Reese. HBMV
Portrait of a Freeman. Abraham Cowley. *Fr.* Of Liberty; an Essay. PoFr
Portrait of a Girl. Conrad Aiken. *See* This Is the Shape of the Leaf.
Portrait of a Girl with Comic Book. Phyllis McGinley. CrMA
Portrait of a Lady. Sarah N. Cleghorn. CP
Portrait of a Lady. T. S. Eliot. AnAmPo; BAP; CoAnAm; HBMV; LA; LiTG; MAP; MAPA; MoAmPo (1942 ed.);

MOAP; NP; PoLFOT; ReaPo; TBM; TCPD; TwAmPo; TwHP
Portrait of a Lady. William Carlos Williams. OxBA
Portrait of a Lady in the Exhibition of the Royal Academy. Winthrop Mackworth Praed. *Fr.* Every-Day Characters. PoEL-4
Portrait of a Machine. Louis Untermeyer. ShBV-3
Portrait of a Poet. Edgar Lee Masters. *Fr.* Jack Kelso. ATP
Portrait of a Very Old Man. Sara E. Carsley. CaP
Portrait of a Vicar. George Crabbe. *Fr.* The Borough, Letter III. RO
Portrait of an Indian. R. E. Rashley. CaP
Portrait of an Old Cathedral. Louis Untermeyer. QS
Portrait of an Old Woman. Arthur Davison Ficke. BAP; MAP; NP; PC
Portrait of Atticus. Pope. *See* Atticus.
Portrait of Brutus. Shakespeare. *Fr.* Julius Caesar, V, v. TrGrPo
(Brutus.) BCEP; GoTP
(Fragment from Mark Antony's Speech.) PECK
(Man, A.) BHV
(Noblest Roman, The.) FaFP; TreFS
(Shakespeare Gallery, A: Brutus.) MaC
("This was the noblest Roman of them all.") PIR
Portrait of Caesar. Shakespeare. *Fr.* Julius Caesar, I, ii. TrGrPo
(Shakespeare Gallery, A: Caesar.) MaC
("Why, man, he doth bestride the narrow world.") PIR
Portrait of Cressida. Shakespeare. *Fr.* Troilus and Cressida, IV, v. TrGrPo
Portrait of Helen. Shakespeare. *Fr.* Troilus and Cressida, II, ii, *and* IV, i. TrGrPo
Portrait of Henry VIII, The. Earl of Surrey. *See* Sardanapalus.
Portrait of Hudibras. Samuel Butler. *See* Presbyterian Knight.
Portrait of Milton, The. Dryden. *See* Lines Printed under the Engraved Portrait of Milton.
Portrait of One Dead. Conrad Aiken. *Fr.* The House of Dust, Pt. III, vi. ChMo; CMP; HBMV; NP; WHA
Portrait of Several Selves. Charles Davies. MoWP
Portrait of Sidrophel. Samuel Butler. *Fr.* Hudibras, Pt. II, Canto III. PoEL-3
(Sir Sidrophel, the Conjuror.) FaBoEn
Portrait of the Artist. Dorothy Parker. PFE; PoeMoYo; WhC
Portrait of the Artist as a Prematurely Old Man. Ogden Nash. CrMA; FaFP; LiTA; LiTM; NePA; SiTL
Portrait Philippines. Alfred A. Duckett. PoNe
Portrait with Background. Oliver St. John Gogarty. OBMV
Portraitist, The. Lucillius, *tr. fr. Greek by* F. L. Lucas. GrPE
Portraits. Robert Fitzgerald. OnHM
Portraits, The. Anna Maria Lenngren, *tr. fr. Swedish by* Charles W. Stork. AnSL
Ports Astern. Joseph Singer. DDA
Ports of death are sins, The; of life, good deeds. Of Life and Death. Ben Jonson. PreP; ReIE
Portugal's ships in vain. Avarice. Luis de León. WoL
Posey-Boy. *Unknown.* APW
Posies for Thine Own Bedchamber. Thomas Tusser. SiCE
Positivists, The. Mortimer Collins. BOHV
Possession. Richard Aldington. MBP; MoBrPo
Possession. "Owen Meredith." LPS-1
Possession. Bayard Taylor. LPS-1
Possession ("Heaven above is softer blue"). *Unknown.* BLRP
Possession. Jean Starr Untermeyer. AV
Possessions. Lizette Woodworth Reese. HBMV; VOD
Possibility, A. Carolyn Wells. ALV; PR
Possibles we dare, The. Love's Progress. Theodore Roethke. FiMAP
Possibly. "Elspeth." PR
Possum and the Moon, The. David Campbell. MoAuPo; NeLNL
'Possum Time Again. John Charles McNeill. NoCaPo
Possum up de gum tree. Little Gal at Our House. *Unknown.* ABF
Post-Boy, The. William Cowper. *See* Winter Evening, The ("Hark! 'tis the twanging horn").
Post-boy drove with fierce career, The. Alice Fell. Wordsworth. BEL; BeLS; CG; OTPC
Post Captain, The. Charles Edward Carryl. BOHV; PCD
Post-Impressionism. Bert Leston Taylor. BAP; BOHV; HBMV; InMe; PoeMoYo; PYM
Post-Meridian. Wendell Phillips Garrison. AA
Afternoon.
Evening.
Post Mortem. Emily Dickinson. *See* Bustle in a house, The.
Post Mortem. Verna Loveday Harden. CaP
Post-Mortem. Richard Hoffman. PIAE
Post Mortem. Robinson Jeffers. MAP; MoAmPo; MoPo; TrGrPo
Post-Mortem. Fanny Parnell. *See* After Death.
Post Mortem. Shakespeare. *See* Sonnets, XXXII.
Post-Obits and the Poets. Martial, *tr. fr. Latin by* Byron. AWP; JAWP; OuHeWo; WBP
Post-Rail Song, *with music.* *Unknown.* AS
Post That Fitted, The. Kipling. CenHV; HBV
Post-War. Eileen Duggan. AnNZ
Post-War Roll Call. Nicholas Pappas, *tr. fr. Modern Greek by* Rae Dalven. MoGP
Postcard from the Volcano. A. Wallace Stevens. AmPP; LiTA
Poster Girl, The, *parody.* Carolyn Wells. HBV; InMe; PA
Posters shout, their glowing motley blares, The. Eventide. Valery Yakovlevich Bryusov. TrRV
Posters show my country blonde and green, The. Meditation of a Patriot. G. S. Fraser. LiTM (rev. ed.)
Posthomerica, *sels.* Quintus Smyrnaeus, *tr. fr. Greek.*
"But through the livelong night no sleep laid hold," *fr.* X, *tr. by* A. S. Way. GrPo
Death of Oenone, The, *fr.* X, *tr. by* F. L. Lucas. GrPE
"He spake; he swung up in his mighty hand," *fr.* I, *tr. by* A. S. Way. GrPo
Paris Is Dead, *fr.* X. OxBG
Return from Troy, The, *fr.* XIV. OxBG
"So cried she: but for him far less she mourned," *fr.* X, *tr. by* A. S. Way. GrPo
"Through mountain gorges so she won to where," *fr.* X, *tr. by* A. S. Way. GrPo
Posthumous. Henry Augustin Beers. AA
Posthumous Coquetry. Théophile Gautier, *tr. fr. French by* Arthur Symons. AWP
Posthumous Remorse. Baudelaire. *See* Remorse after Death.
Posthumous Tales, *sels.* George Crabbe.
Ancient Mansion, The, X. ChTr; EnSW; EV-3
Young Paris, XIX. OBRV
Posthumus, not the last of many more. Suum Cuique Pulchrum. Henry Parrot. TuPP
Postilion, The. Nikolaus Lenau, *tr. fr. German by* Dwight Durling. AnGP
Postlude. William Carlos Williams. AnAmPo; LA; NP
Postman, The. William Cowper. *See* Winter Evening, The ("Hark! 'tis the twanging horn").
Postman, The. Laura E. Richards. TiPo
Postman, The. Christina Rossetti. *Fr.* Sing-Song. GaP; GFA; PCH
("Eight o'clock.") EmBrPo; RIS; SAS
Postman, The. Clive Sansom. BoTP
Postman, The. Alice Todd. BoTP
Postman, The. *Unknown.* FaPON
Postman comes when I am still in bed, The. A Sick Child. Randall Jarrell. InvP
Postman's Bell Is Answered Everywhere, The. Horace Gregory. MoAmPo; MoVE
Postman's Knock. Rodney Bennett. BoTP
Postmen and milkmen. Beware Our Loving Dog. Lucretia Penny. AlBD
Postponement. Thomas Hardy. PoVP
Postscript. Thomas Hardy. NV
Postscript. Mary Mills. NePoAm
Postscript. Raymond Souster. PeCV
Postscript to a Letter on the Excise Laws. Burns. PIR
Postscript to "Retaliation," A. Austin Dobson. POTT; PoVP
Postumus, Postumus, the years glide by us. Horace. Odes, II, 14. LaP
Posture of the tree, The. Lovers in Winter. Robert Graves. Po
Postures of Love, The. Alex Comfort. NeBP
"There is a white mare that my love keeps," *sel.* FaBoMo
Posy, The. George Herbert. EPS (1942 ed.)
Posy Ring, The. Clément Marot, *tr. fr. French by* Ford Madox Ford. AWP; JAWP; WBP
Pot and Kettle. Robert Graves. HBMV
Pot of wine among flowers, A. Drinking Alone in the Moonlight. Li Po. AWP
Potato. Richard Wilbur. CrMA; LiTA; MoAB; TrGrPo (rev. ed.)
Potato Harvest, The. Sir Charles G. D. Roberts. CaP; OCL
Potatoes. E. V. Lucas. *Fr.* Counsel to Those That Eat. GaP
Potatoes' Dance, The. Vachel Lindsay. BoChLi; FaPON; MPB; SP; SUS
Potatoes on the table. Potatoes. E. V. Lucas. GaP
Potatores Exquisiti. *Unknown, tr. fr. Latin by* Basil Blackett. *Fr.* Carmina Burana. LaP
Potion, The. Winnie Lynch Rockett. ChIP
Potiphar Gubbins, C. E. Study of an Elevation, in Indian Ink. Kipling. BOHV; InMe
Potomac, The. Karl Shapiro. CoBMV
Potomac Side. Edward Everett Hale. *Fr.* From Potomac to Merrimac. PAH
Potomac Town in February. Carl Sandburg. WaKn
Pot-Pourri. Austin Dobson. POTT
Potpourri from a Surrey Garden. John Betjeman. CenHV; FiBHP

Potpourri in Rhyme. *Unknown.* SiTL
Potter and the Clay, The. Jeremiah, XVIII: 1-11, Bible, *O.T.* WoL
Potter's at odds with potter. Wholesome Strife. Hesiod. *Fr.* Works and Days. OxBG
Potter's Song, The. Longfellow. *See* Kéramos.
Poultries, The. Ogden Nash. AlDL; CenHV
Pound of flesh, a pound of gold, A. Epitaph for a Reno Woman. Donald F. Drummond. PtPa
Pounded spice both taste and scent doth please, The. At Fotheringay [*or* Decease, Release]. Robert Southwell. PoEL-2; SiCE
Pour a libation, stranger, as you pass. Anacreon's Tomb. *Unknown.* OxBG
Pour Down. John Holmes. NePoAm
Pour l'Election de Son Sepulchre. Ezra Pound. *See* E. P. Ode pour l'Election de Son Sepulchre.
Pour me wine: the dew. Wine at Morning. Ibn Safar. MooP
Pour, O pour that parting soul in song. Song of the Son. Jean Toomer. CDC; MAP; PoNe
Pour, O Rain! Ode to Rain. *Unknown, tr. fr. Russian.* PCH
Pour out those pearls. Stephen Phillips. *Fr.* Herod. LEAP
Pour the unhappiness out Another Weeping Woman. Wallace Stevens. MoVE; NP
Pour Us Wine. Ibn Kolthum, *tr. fr. Arabic by* E. Powys Mathers. *Fr.* The Mu'allaqát. AWP
Pour, varlet, pour the water. The Poets at Tea [*or* Macaulay at Tea]. Barry Pain. BOHV; CenHV; HBV; PA
Pour we roses into wine! Odes, IV, 38. Pierre de Ronsard. PrPoCR
Pour wine, and cry, again, again, again. Heliodore. Meleager, *tr. by* Andrew Lang. OBVV; POTT
Poure Persoun, The. Chaucer. *See* Parson, The.
Poure widwe [*or* wydwe], somdel stape in age, A. *See* Povre widwe, somdel stape in age, A.
Pouring music, soft and strong, The. A Song. Frederic William Henry Myers. VA
Pourquoi You Greased. *Unknown.* ChTr
Poussie, poussie, baudrons. *Unknown.* OxNR
Poverty. Theognis, *tr. fr. Greek by* John Hookham Frere. AWP; JAWP; OnPM; WBP; GrPE, *tr. by* F. L. Lucas
Poverty. Thomas Traherne. ElSeCe; OxBoCh
Poverty ("All poor men and humble"). *Unknown, tr. fr. Welsh by* K. E. Roberts. SDH
Poverty ("A beggar to the graveyard hied"). *Unknown, tr. fr. Sanskrit by* Arthur W. Ryder. *Fr.* The Panchatantra. AWP; PoFr
Poverty, Diophantus, wakes the Arts. Fisherman's Hut. Theocritus. *Fr.* Idylls. GrR; OxBG
Poverty in London. Samuel Johnson. *Fr.* London. BeR; ChTr; CoEV; OBEC
("By numbers here from shame or censure free.") EnLi-1 (1949 ed.); EPP; ViBoPo
Poverty, Kyrnos, breaks a gallant man. The Bane of Poverty. Theognis. GrL; OxBG
Poverty Not All Loss. William Langland, *mod. by* Henry W. Wells. *Fr.* The Vision of Piers Plowman. PoLi
Poverty, whose path is safe and clear. Of Holy Poverty. Jacopone da Todi. SaFP
Povre Ame Amoureuse. Louise Labé, *tr. fr. French by* Robert Bridges. AWP; EPP
Povre widwe, somdel stape in age, A. The Nun's Priest's [*or* Nonne Preestes] Tale [*or* The Cock and the Fox]. Chaucer. *Fr.* The Canterbury Tales. AnFE; AtBAP; BEL; CoBE; EM-1; EnLi-1; EV-1; GEPC; LiA; MaPo; OAEP; PIAE; PoEL-1; SeCeV; TCEP; TOP; TrGrPo
Powder of diamond. Deep Snow. Louise Morey Bowman. CPG
Power. Hart Crane. *Fr.* The Bridge: Cape Hatteras. MAP; MoAmPo; VOD (1935 ed.), *shorter sel.*
(Cape Hatteras, *longer sel.*) WoL
("Nasal whine of power whips a new universe, The.") MoAB
Power. Thomas Stephens Collier. AA
Power. Grace Noll Crowell. PoMa
Power. Edwin Markham. GrCo-2
Power, *sel.* Matthew Prior. *Fr.* Solomon.
"Pass we the ills, which each man feels." LoBV
Power. Sir Ronald Ross. TCPD
Power. Duncan Campbell Scott. TwCaPo
Power above powers, O heavenly Eloquence. English Poetry [*or* The Poetry of England *or* The Treasure of Our Tongue]. Samuel Daniel. *Fr.* Musophilus. CoBE; EV-1; OBSC
Power and the Glory, The. Siegfried Sassoon. GrCo-2; OBMV; QS
Power-driven. José Moreno Villa, *tr. fr. Spanish by* Eleanor L. Turnbull. CoSP
Power from the unknown God, A. Shelley. *Fr.* Hellas. StJW
Power-House, The. Christopher Morley. MaRV
Power-house, A. Classic Scene. William Carlos Williams. AmP; OxBA; WoL
Power lies in my hand. The Sibyl. Joan LaBombard. GoYe
Power of an Oath, The. Delphic Oracle, *tr. fr. Greek by* A. D. Godley. OxBG
Power of Armies is a visible thing, The. Sonnet: 1811. Wordsworth. SoV
Power of Beauty, The. James Herbert Morse. LBAP
Power of Custom, The. Pindar, *tr. fr. Greek by* C. M. Bowra. OxBG
Power of Fancy, The. Philip Freneau. AmPP; CoBA; IAP
Power of God, The. *Unknown, tr. fr. Greek by* T. F. Higham. OxBG
Power of Love, The. Asclepiades, *tr. fr. Greek.* GrL, *pr. tr. by* W. R. Paton; GrR, *tr. by* J. H. Merivale
Power of Love, The. Dryden. *Fr.* Cymon and Iphigenia. OBS
Power of Love. John Fletcher. *See* Hear, Ye Ladies.
Power of Love, The ("My children, know Love is not Love alone"). Sophocles, *tr. fr. Greek by* Sir Richard Livingstone. OxBG
Power of Love, The ("When Love disputes"). Sophocles. *Fr.* Antigone. *See* Love, Conquering and Unconquerable.
Power of Love, The. *Unknown, tr. fr. Arabic by* E. Powys Mathers. *Fr.* The Thousand and One Nights. LiTW
Power of Malt, The. A. E. Housman. *Fr.* A Shropshire Lad, LXII. HBV; LEAP
Power of Memory. Ibsen, *tr. fr. Norwegian by* Charles W. Stork. AnNoLy
Power of Money, The. Byron. *Fr.* Don Juan, XII. CoEV
Power of Money, The. Juan Ruiz, Archpriest of Hita, *tr. fr. Spanish by* Elisha K. Kane. *Fr.* The Book of Good Love. AnSpL-1
Power of Music, The. Dryden. *See* Alexander's Feast.
Power of Music, The. Pindar. *See* O, Golden Lyre!
Power of Music, The. Shakespeare. *Fr.* The Merchant of Venice, V, i. GN
Power of Music, The. *Unknown, tr. fr. Greek by* Shelley. *Fr.* Homeric Hymns. OxBG
Power of Numbers, The. Abraham Cowley. *Fr.* Davideis, I. OBS
Power of Poets, The. Ben Jonson. *Fr.* Epistle to Elizabeth, Countess of Rutland. WHA
Power of Prayer, The. Richard Chenevix Trench. *See* Prayer: "Lord, what a change . . ."
Power of Prayer, The. John Aikman Wallace. PraP
Power of princes rests in the consent, The. Obedience. Robert Herrick. PoFr
Power of raven be thine. Good Wish. *Unknown.* FaBoCh; LoGBV
Power of the Bards, The, *sel.* Philip Pendleton Cooke.
"And owe we not these visions." SPP
Power of the Dog, The. Kipling. AlBD; BLPA
Power of the Pen, The. Mortimer Neal Thompson. LauV
Power of Thought, The. Süsskind von Trimberg, *tr. fr. Middle High German.* TrJP
Power Station. T. W. Ramsey. HaMV
Power that gives with liberal hand, The. On the Religion of Nature. Philip Freneau. AmPP; CoBA; Po
Power that Moves to Good, The. Sir Edwin Arnold. *Fr.* The Light of Asia. GrCo-2
Power to the Faint. Isaiah, XL: 28-31, Bible, *O.T.* GrCo-1
Power to thine elbow, thou newest of sciences. Darwinity. Herman C. Merivale. BOHV; InMe; NA
Power was given at birth to me, The. One Token. W. H. Davies. ChMo; CMP; MM
Powerful Eyes o' Jeremy Tait, The. Wallace Irwin. FiBHP; StPo
Powers of Darkness. Euripides, *tr. fr. Greek by* Hugh Owen Meredith. *Fr.* Orestes. GrR
(Furies, The, *tr. by* George Allen.) OxBG
Powhatan's Daughter. Hart Crane. *Fr.* The Bridge. CoV; LiTA
Pox of this fooling, and plotting of late, A. The Careless Good Fellow. John Oldham. CEP; SeCV-2
Pox on pelfe why should we love it. *Unknown.* SeCSL
Practical Answer, A. Shirley Brooks. SiTL
Practical Joker, The. W. S. Gilbert. *Fr.* His Excellency. BOHV
Practical People. Robinson Jeffers. NAMP
Praesto. Thomas Edward Brown. ChIP
Praeterita ex Instantibus. William Douw Lighthall. VA
Praetorium Scene: Good Friday. Elinor Lennen. PGD
Prague Students' Song. Joseph von Eichendorff, *tr. fr. German by* James Edward Tobin. AnGP
Prairie. Herbert Bates. AA
Prairie. K. N. Llewellyn. YeAr
Prairie. Carl Sandburg. ChMo; CMP; HeT; IAP; LaNeLa; MM
Sels.
Look at Six Eggs. FaPON
"O prairie mother." BAP; NP
Prairie Birth. Grace Stone Coates. DDA; PaA
Prairie child. Nancy Hanks. Harriet Monroe. BAP; OHIP
Prairie-Dog Town. Mary Austin. FaPON; StVeCh (1955 ed.); TiPo

Prairie Fire, The. John G. Neihardt. *Fr.* The Song of Three Friends. TCPD
Prairie Fires. Hamlin Garland. BAP
Prairie goes to the mountain. Open Range. Kathryn Jackson *and* Byron Jackson. FaPON; TiPo
Prairie-Grass Dividing, The. Walt Whitman. Po
Prairie Graveyard. Anne Marriott. BoCaPo; CaP; PeCV
Prairie Mother's Lullaby, A. E. A. Brininstool. BOL
Prairie Ride, A. William Vaughn Moody. AnEnPo
Prairie School, The. Isabel Ecclestone Mackay. CPG
Prairie Schooner, The. Edward Everett Dale. HiLiAm
Prairie Schooner, The. Edwin Ford Piper. StVeCh (1940 ed.)
Prairie Spring. Edwina Fallis. SUS
Prairie Sunset, A. E. J. Pratt. MM; NLK (1947 ed.)
Prairie Sunset, A. Walt Whitman. CaAE; CoBA
Prairie Winds. Helena Coleman. CPG; OCL
Prairie Wolves. Robert V. Carr. PoOW
Prairies, The. Bryant. AmP; AmPP (3d ed.); AnAmPo; CoBA; CoV; IAP; LA; MOAP; OxBA; Po; PoE; PoEL-4; TCAP
"These are the gardens of the Desert, these," *sel.* InP
Praise. Mary Anderson. BoTP
Praise. R. H. Grenville. PoToHe (new ed.)
Praise. Guido Guinicelli. *See* Sonnet: He Will Praise His Lady.
Praise. George Herbert. LPS-2
Praise. "Seumas O'Sullivan." BMEP; HBV; LBBV; MBP
Praise. Rainer Maria Rilke, *tr. fr. German.* ChTr
Praise. Christopher Smart. RO
Praise. *Unknown.* PCH
Praise and Love. William Brighty Rands. OBVV
Praise and Prayer. Sir William Davenant. *Fr.* Gondibert. GoBC; OBEV
Praise be to God, the Designer, Builder of Earth and of Heaven! Allah, the Artificer. *Unknown.* OnPM
Praise Blindness, Eyes. *Unknown.* ReIE
Praise for an Urn. Hart Crane. AmP; AnFE; ATP (1953 ed.); AWP; ChMo; CoAnAm; CoBMV; InPo; LiTG; LiTM (rev. ed.); MAP; MoAB; MoAmPo; MOAP; MoVE; OxBA; PoE; ReMP; UnPo (3d ed.)
Praise for Sick Women. Gary Snyder. NeAP
Praise for the Fountain Opened. William Cowper. EiPP
(Olney Hymns.) CEP
Praise God. *Unknown.* PPL
Praise God from whom all blessings flow. Old Hundredth. Thomas Ken. OlF; UnS
"Praise God from whom all blessings flow," Praise him who sendeth. A Lancashire Doxology. Dinah Maria Mulock Craik. LPS-2
Praise God, ye peoples of the earth. Doxology for Peace. R. B. Y. Scott. MaRV
Praise, hard as that is in a world where fires. Sent Ahead. John Hay. NePoAm
Praise Him, all ye heights of heaven. Laudate for Christmas. Prudentius. CAW
Praise is a quiet and a gracious thing. Praise. R. H. Grenville. PoToHe (new ed.)
Praise is devotion fit for mighty minds. Praise and Prayer. Sir William Davenant. *Fr.* Gondibert. GoBC; OBEV
Praise is the thing! Like one destined for singing. Sonnets to Orpheus, Pt. I, VII. Rainer Maria Rilke. AnGP
Praise not the avaricious man. Fragment. Ibn al-Missisi. MooP
Praise, O my heart, with praise from depth and height. Adam's Song of the Visible World. Ridgely Torrence. TrPWD
Praise of a Heroine. Euripides. *See* To Alcestis.
Praise of Age, The. Robert Henryson. BSV; MeRV
Praise of Amen Ra! Hymn to Amen Ra, the Sun God. *Unknown.* WGRP
Praise of Ben Dorain, The Duncan Ban MacIntyre, *tr. fr. Gaelic by* "Hugh MacDiarmid." GoTS
Haunt of the Deer, The, *sel., tr. by* John Campbell Shairp. EBSV
Praise of Ceres. Thomas Heywood. *Fr.* The Silver Age. ElL
Praise of Created Things. St. Francis of Assisi. FaPON; GBV (1952 ed.)
Praise of Derry, The. St. Columcille, *tr. fr. Gaelic by* D. P. Conyngham. CAW
Praise of Diseases. Jacopone da Todi, *tr. fr. Italian by* L. R. Lind. LyPI
Praise of Dust, The. G. K. Chesterton. BLV; MBP; MoBrPo; OtMeF; PoeT; POTE
Praise of Earth. Elizabeth Barrett Browning. OBVV
Praise of Engineers. James J. Donohue. JKCP (1955 ed.)
Praise of Famous Men. Ecclesiasticus, Bible, Apocrypha. *See* Let Us Now Praise Famous Men.
Praise of Fionn, The. *Unknown, tr. fr. Irish by* Frank O'Connor. KiLC
Praise of His Lady, A. John Heywood, *wr. at. to* Thomas Heywood. BCEP; ElL; ElSeCe; HBV; OBEV; SiCE; TuPP; ViBoPo
(Description of a Most Noble Lady, A.) CoBE
(On the Princess Mary.) OBSC
(Portrait, The.) LPS-1
Praise of His Love, A. Earl of Surrey, *wr. at. to* Thomas Heywood. CenL; ElL; EV-1; TCEP; TuPP; WHA
(Give Place, Ye Lovers.) CoBE; LPS-1
("Give place, ye lovers, here before.") ReEn; SiPS
(His Incomparable Lady.) OBSC
Praise of Homer. George Chapman. *Fr.* The Dedication *to tr. of* The Odyssey. OBS
Praise of Husbandry, The. Thomas Tusser. TuPP
(As True as Thy Faith, This Riddle Thus Saith.) SiCE
Praise of Industry, The. James Thomson. *Fr.* The Castle of Indolence, II. OBEC
Praise of Little Women. Juan Ruiz, Archpriest of Hita, *tr. fr. Spanish by* Longfellow. *Fr.* The Book of Good Love. AnSpL-1; AWP
"In a little precious stone what splendor meets the eyes!" *sel.* TeCS
Praise of Mary. *Unknown, tr. fr. Old French by* Henry Sorg. ISi
Praise of meaner wits this work like profit brings, The. Another of the Same. Sir Walter Ralegh. SiPS
Praise of My Lady. William Morris. HBV; PoVP; ViPo; VLEP
Praise of New England. Thomas Caldecot Chubb. GoYe
Praise of New Netherland, The. Jacob Steendam. PAH
Praise of Our Soldiers, The Thomas Churchyard. TuPP
Praise of Petrarch and of Laura, His Lady, A. *Unknown.* ReIE
Praise of Philip Sparrow, The. George Gascoigne. ViBoPo
(Of All the Birds, *sl. abr.*) CH
Praise of Pindar, The. Abraham Cowley. CEP; EPS; PtP
Praise of Poets. William Browne. *Fr.* Britannia's Pastorals, II, Songs 1 *and* 2. OBS
Praise of Saccarello Street. Hipólito Sánchez Quell, *tr. fr. Spanish by* Dudley Fitts. AnCL
Praise of Spenser. William Browne. *Fr.* Brittania's Pastorals, II, Song 1. EV-2
Praise of Spring, The. Gonzalo de Berceo, *tr. fr. Spanish by* Longfellow. *Fr.* The Miracles of Our Lady. TeCS
("I, Gonzalo de Berceo, in the gentle summer tide.") AnSpL-1
Praise of the Pudding. Joel Barlow. *Fr.* The Hasty Pudding, I. AnNE
Praise of the Thames. Sir John Denham. *See* Thames from Cooper's Hill, The.
Praise of Women. Robert Mannyng. BCEP; OBEV
("No thyng ys to man so dere.") LO
(Woman's Love.) LyMA
Praise of Women. Palladas of Alexandria, *tr. fr. Greek by* Dudley Fitts. LiTW; LyMA
Praise the Lord. Milton. *See* Let Us with a Gladsome Mind.
Praise the Lord and Pass the Ammunition. Frank Loesser. YaD
Praise the Lord for all the seasons. Praise. Mary Anderson. BoTP
Praise, then, to Uriel, who in unlikely places. William Force Stead. *Fr.* Uriel, Pt. IV. OxBoCh
Praise Thou Sion, praise Thy Saviour. Lauda Sion. St. Thomas Aquinas. WHL
Praise thou the Mighty Mother for what is wrought, not me. Louise Imogen Guiney. Two Epitaphs, II. OBAV
Praise to Jesus! William Ball. BePJ
Praise to John Skelton. Horace Gregory. PtP
Praise to Light. Thomas Cole. NePoAm-2
Praise to the Holiest in the Height. Cardinal Newman. *Fr.* The Dream of Gerontius. PoEL-5
(Fifth Choir of Angelicals.) GoBC
Praise to the Lamb. *Unknown, tr. fr. Latin by* Robert Campbell. EOAH
Praise ye the Lord!/ For it is good to sing praises unto our God. Who Maketh the Grass to Grow. Psalm CXLVII, Bible, *O.T.* FaPON; TiPo (1952 ed.)
Praise ye the Lord./ Praise ye the Lord. A Song of Praise. Psalm CXLVIII, Bible, *O.T.* TrGrPo; TriL; TrJP
Praise ye the Lord for the avenging of Israel. The Song of Deborah [and Barak]. Judges, Bible, *O.T.* AWP; LiTW
Praise ye the Lord, O Nations! Psalm CLI. Alter Brody. QS
Praise ye the Lord. Praise God in His sanctuary. Psalm CL, Bible, *O.T.* OnPM; TiPo (1952 ed.); UnS
Praise ye the Lord. Praise, O ye servants of the Lord. Psalm CXIII, Bible, *O.T.* OnPM
"Praise ye the Lord!" The psalm to-day. Thanksgiving in Boston Harbor [*or* The First Boston Thanksgiving—July 1630]. Hezekiah Butterworth. AA; DD; MC; OHIP; PAH; PEOR; TOAH
Praise youth's hot blood, if you will. Age in Prospect. Robinson Jeffers. BLV; BoLiVe; MAP; MoAB; MoAmPo; NeMA
Praised and exalted. Alabado. *Unknown.* TrAS
Praised Be Diana's Fair and Harmless Light. Sir Walter Ralegh. SiCE; TuPP
(Diana.) OBSC
(Shepherd's Praise of Diana, The.) SiPS

Praised be man, he is existing in milk. Chorus. Jack Kerouac. *Fr.* Mexico City Blues. NeAP

Praised be my Lord for Brother October. October. Theresa Hooley. SaFP

Praised be our Lord for our brother the sun. Thanksgiving for the Earth. Elizabeth Goudge. YeAr

Praised be the art whose subtle power could stay. Upon the Sight of a Beautiful Picture. Wordsworth. BPN

Praised be the name of the Lord, who created the wine. Five Arabic Verses in Praise of Wine, III. *Unknown.* TrJP

Praised Be the Psalmist. David Ross. PG (1955 ed.)

Praise-God Barebones. Ellen Mackay Hutchinson Cortissoz. AA

Praisers of women in their proud and beautiful poems, The. "Not Marble nor the Gilded Monuments." Archibald MacLeish. AmPP (3d ed.), ChMo; CMP; CoBMV; CoV; LiTL; MoAB; PoeMoYo; PoRA; TwHP; ViBoPo

Praises of God, The. *Unknown, tr. fr. Middle Irish by* Kenneth Jackson. AnIL

Praises of Laura Transcend His Poetic Power, The ("Ashamed at times that I am silent"). Petrarch, *tr. fr. Italian by* Robert Guthrie MacGregor [Susan Wollaston, *wr.*]. Sonnets to Laura: To Laura in Life, XVIII. EnLi-1; OuHeWo

Praises to those who can wait. Zealots of Yearning. David Rokeah. TrJP

Praiseworthy are the Thracians, who lament. Best Not to Be Born. Archias. OnPM

Praising of Women, A. *Unknown. See* I Am as Light as Any Roe.

Prancing mounts and twinkling wheels, The. The King of Kings. Lon Woodrum. BePJ

Pranks that Padus play'd, The. The Second Egloge Entituled Fortunatus. Mantuan, *tr. by* George Turberville. *Fr.* The Eglogs of the Poet B. Mantuan Carmelitan. ReIE

Prattling Swallows. Nicostratus, *tr. fr. Greek by* Thomas Moore. OnPM

Prawn and Pearl. William Diaper. *Fr.* Nereides; or, Sea-Eclogues. BeR

Praxagora Rehearses [Her Speech]. Aristophanes, *tr. fr. Greek by* Benjamin Bickley Rogers. *Fr.* The Ecclesiazusae. GrR; OxBG

Praxinoa at home?/ Of course she is. Gorgo and Praxinoa. Theocritus, *tr. by* Jack Lindsay. *Fr.* Idylls. OxBG

Praxinoa at home?/ Dear Gorgo, at last! The Syracusan Women at the Adonis Festival. Theocritus, *tr. by* R. C. Trevelyan. *Fr.* Idylls. GrR

Praxinoa in?/ Yes, Gorgo dear! Theocritus, *tr. by* Leigh Hunt. *Fr.* Idylls. GrPo

Praxiteles. *Unknown, tr. fr. Greek.* LPS-3

Praxiteles and Phryne. William Wetmore Story. AA; BeLS; LBAP; OBAV

Pray! Irene Arnold. BLRP; PraP

Pray! Amos R. Wells. PraP

Pray but one prayer for me 'twixt thy closed lips. Summer Dawn. William Morris. AtBAP; BPN; EV-5; FaBoEn; GTBS; GTBS-D; GTSL; LoBV; OBEV; OBVV; PeBoSo; ViBoPo; ViPo; VLEP

Pray! for earth has many a need. Pray! Amos R. Wells. PraP

Pray for Me! Adelaide Anne Procter. PraP

Pray for Me. Amos R. Wells. PraP

Pray for the Dead. Arthur Dentworth Hamilton Eaton. AA; PoRL

Pray for Us that We Savëd Be. *Unknown.* AnEC

Pray for Us to the Prince of Peace. *Unknown.* AnEC

Pray for Us to the Trinity. *Unknown.* AnEC

Pray—Give—Go. Annie Johnson Flint. BLRP

Pray, how shall I, a little lad. A Speech. Thaddeus Mason Harris. MeMeAg

Pray in the early morning. Pray! Irene Arnold. BLRP; PraP

Pray list to me a modest while. Advice to Worriers. George S. Kaufman. ALV; PC

Pray One for Another. "Marianne Farningham" *and* James M. Gray. PraP

Pray Pity for Bill Smith. Paul L. Grano. BoAu

Pray thee, take care, that tak'st my book in hand. To the Reader. Ben Jonson. MaPo; OAEP; ReIE; SeCV-1; TuPP

Pray; though the gift you ask for. Strive, Wait and Pray. Adelaide Anne Procter. PraP

Pray to What Earth Does This Sweet Cold Belong. Henry David Thoreau. CoV

Pray, where are the little bluebells gone. About the Fairies. Jean Ingelow. BoTP

Pray why are you so bare, so bare. The Haunted Oak. Paul Laurence Dunbar. BANP

Pray with Faith. Joseph Hart. PraP

Pray without Ceasing. Ophelia Guyon Browning. *See* Sometime, Somewhere.

Prayer, A: "Angels, where you soar." Alfred Noyes. BMEP

Prayer, A: "As I lie in bed." Joseph Seamon Cotter, Jr. BANP

Prayer: "As I walk through the streets." F. S. Flint. CP; NV; TrPWD

Prayer: "Be not afraid to pray—to pray is right." Hartley Coleridge. ES; MaRV; OQP; QP-1; VA

Prayer, A: "Be Thou my vision, O Lord of my heart." *Unknown, tr. fr. Old Irish by* Eleanor Hull. OnYI

Prayer: "Bear with me, Master, when I turn from Thee." Edith Lovejoy Pierce. ChIP; TrPWD

Prayer: "Bless Thou this year, O Lord!" Andrew Stuart Currie Clarke. PGD; PSO
(Prayer for a Happy New Year, A.) BLRP

Prayer: "But since He heareth prayer at any time." *Unknown.* PraP

Prayer, A: "Clother of the lily, Feeder of the sparrow." Christina Rossetti. OBVV
(They Toil Not neither Do They Spin.) TrPWD

Prayer, A: "Crowned Caprice is god of this world, A." Grant Allen. BMEP; LEAP

Prayer: "Dawn of the everlasting day, The." E. F. Benson. *Fr.* The Image in the Sand. PC

Prayer: "Dear God, the light is come, our outgrown creeds." *Unknown.* OQP; QP-1

Prayer, A: "Dear, let me dream of love." Selwyn Image. VA

Prayer: "Dear Refuge of my weary soul." Anne Steele. PraP

Prayer, A: "Each day I walk with wonder." Clinton Scollard. TrPWD

Prayer, A: "Eternal God, our life is but." "Yehoash," *tr. fr. Yiddish by* Isidore Goldstick. TrJP

Prayer: "Eternal God, whose power upholds." Henry Hallam Tweedy. *See* Eternal God, Whose Power Upholds.

Prayer: "Father, I scarcely dare to pray." Helen Hunt Jackson. *See* Last Prayer, A.

Prayer, A: "Father in Heaven! from whom the simplest flower." Felicia Dorothea Hemans TrPWD

Prayer, A: "Father, we thank Thee for the night." *At. to* Rebecca J. Weston. MeMeAg; RAR; TVC; TVSH
(Child's Prayer, A.) BoTP
(Father, We Thank Thee.) MaRV; OTPC (1946 ed.); PraP
(Morning Prayer.) PCH

Prayer: "For the few hours of life allotted me." *Tr. fr. Latin by* Abraham Cowley. PoFr

Prayer, A: "From falsehood and error." Digby Mackworth Dolben. GoBC

Prayer: "From food when it is hash." Edward Shippen. LauV

Prayer, A: "Give me a good digestion, Lord." Thomas Harry Basil Webb, *after* A Prayer Found in Chester Cathedral. PoMa
(Ancient Prayer, An.) BBV (1951 ed.); BLPA; FaBoBe; NeHB
(Prayer Found in Chester Cathedral, A.) DDA; PoToHe (new ed.); TreFS

Prayer, A: "Give me the faith that asks not 'Why?'" *Unknown.* PraP

Prayer, A: "Give me work to do." *Unknown.* PGD; PSO

Prayer: "God, although this life is but a wraith." Louis Untermeyer. *See* Prayer: "God, though this life . . ."

Prayer: "God, I fain would pray with fervor." Joseph von Eichendorff, *tr. fr. German by* Mabel Cotterell. AnGP

Prayer, A: "God, is it sinful if I feel." Mary Dixon Thayer. HBMV; TrPWD

Prayer: "God, listen through my words to the beating of my heart." Margueritte Harmon Bro. TrPWD

Prayer: "God of light and blossom." James P. Mousley. GoYe

Prayer, A: "God of the Granite and the Rose!" Elizabeth Doten. *Fr.* Reconciliation. OQP; QP-1
("God of the Granite and the Rose.") TrPWD

Prayer: "God of the sunlight, God of the sea." Grenville Kleiser. PraP

Prayer: "God, though [*or* although] this life is but a wraith." Louis Untermeyer. BAP; GoTP; MAP; MaRV; MoAmPo; NeMA; OQP; PC; PoFr; PoMa; PYM; QP-2; StaSt; TOP; TrJP; VOD; WGRP; YT

Prayer, A: "Grant me, O Lord, this day to see." Edgar A. Guest. PraP

Prayer, A: "Grant us the will to fashion as we feel." John Drinkwater. BMEP

Prayer: "Great God! I ask thee for no meaner pelf." Henry David Thoreau. *See* My Prayer.

Prayer: "Have pity on us, Power just and severe." John Hall Wheelock. NePoAm

Prayer, A: "Hermits and blameless women full of grace." Pushkin. *See* Eremites of Old, The.

Prayer: "I am a garden of red tulips." Richard Aldington. PFE

Prayer: "I ask good things that I detest." Robert Louis Stevenson. TrPWD

Prayer: "I ask you this." Langston Hughes. CDC

Prayer: "I asked for bread; God gave a stone instead." *Unknown.* OQP; QP-1

Prayer: "I do not ask a truce." Peter Gething. OQP; QP-2

Prayer, A: "I kneel not now to pray that Thou." Harry Kemp. BAP, *abr.;* HBV; MaRV, *abr.;* WGRP

Prayer: "I know not by what methods rare." Eliza M. Hickok. *See* This I Know.
Prayer: "I often say my prayers." John Burton. MaRV
Prayer, A: "I pray for you, and yet I do not frame." Mary Dixon Thayer. MaRV
Prayer, A: "I pray not for the joy that knows." Marion Franklin Ham. TrPWD
Prayer, A: "I pray Thee O Lord." Juljan Tuwim, *tr. fr. Polish by* Wanda Dynowska. TrJP
Prayer: "I stood upon the threshold." George Sylvester Viereck. BAP; LPS-1
Prayer, A: "I would, dear Jesus, I could break." John D. Long. OQP; QP-1
Prayer, The: "If on a spring night I went by." John Galsworthy. *See* Courage.
Prayer: "If, when I kneel to pray." Charles Francis Richardson. AA
Prayer: "If you hear a prayer that moves you." *Unknown.* PraP
Prayer: "In the bright bay of your morning, O God." Claire Goll, *tr. fr. German by* Babette Deutsch *and* Avrahm Yarmolinsky. TrJP
Prayer: "In this hour of worship." *Unknown.* PraP
Prayer: "Incline, O Maiden." Goethe, *tr. fr. German by* Bayard Taylor. *Fr.* Faust. LiA
Prayer, A: "It is my joy in life to find." Frank Dempster Sherman. POT; PoTo; TreFS
Prayer: "Keep me from fretting, Lord, today." May Carleton Lord. PGD
Prayer: "King of Heaven, make me whole." Yevgeny Abramovich Boratynsky, *tr. fr. Russian by* Babette Deutsch. TrRV
Prayer: "Last night I crept across the snow." John Farrar. ChrBoLe; OTPC (1946 ed.); PoRL; SDH
Prayer, A: "Let me be like that lonely house, O Lord." André Lafon, *tr. fr. French by* Alan Conder. TrFP
Prayer, A: "Let me do my work each day." Max Ehrmann. BLPA; FaBoBe; MaRV; NeHB; PoToHe
Prayer: "Let me not know how sins and sorrows glide." James Elroy Flecker. TrPWD
Prayer: "Let me remember music." Sydney King Russell. MuM
Prayer, A: "Let me work and be glad." Theodosia Garrison. TrPWD
Prayer: "Lo, here a little volume, but great book!" Richard Crashaw. *See* On a Prayer Book Sent to Mrs. M. R.
Prayer: "Lord, as thou wilt, bestow." Eduard Mörike, *tr. fr. German by* John Drinkwater. TrPWD
Prayer, A: "Lord, for the erring thought." William Dean Howells. *See* Undiscovered Country, The.
Prayer: "Lord, forgive." Pauline Schroy. OQP; QP-2
Prayer, A: "Lord, give us more of faith." Nancy Byrd Turner. PraP
Prayer: "Lord God of the oak and the elm." George Villiers. TrPWD
Prayer: "Lord, grant us eyes to see, and ears to hear." Christina Rossetti. ChIP
Prayer, A: "Lord, in mercy pardon me." Frances Ridley Havergal. PraP
Prayer, A: "Lord, let me live like a regular man." Berton Braley. BLPA
Prayer, A: "Lord, let not my religion be." Clarence M. Burkholder. OQP; QP-2
Prayer: "Lord, make me an instrument of Thy Peace." St. Francis of Assisi. *See* Lord, Make Me an Instrument of Your Peace.
Prayer: "Lord, make me sensitive to the sight." Barbara Marr. TrPWD
Prayer, A: "Lord, make my childish soul stand straight." "William Laird." HBMV
Prayer, A: "Lord, not for light in darkness do we pray." John Drinkwater. HBV; MaRV; OBVV; QS; TrPWD; WGRP
Prayer: "Lord, the newness of this day." Henry van Dyke. PraP
Prayer: "Lord, what a change within us one short hour." Richard C. Trench. GrCo-1; MaRV; PraP; WBLP; WGRP
(Hour with Thee, An.) BePJ
(In Thy Presence.) OQP; QP-1
(Power of Prayer, The.) PoToHe
(Prevailing Prayer.) BLRP
(Sonnet: "Lord, what a change within us one short hour.") TrPWD
Prayer, A: "Lord, when on my bed I lie." John Oxenham. PraP
Prayer: "Make me feverish, sleepless, and breathless." "Anna Akhmatova," *tr. fr. Russian by* Babette Deutsch. OnPM; TrRV
Prayer: "Matthew, Mark, Luke, and John." *Unknown. See* Matthew, Mark, Luke, and John.
Prayer: "Merciful God, who readst my inmost mind." Willem Bilderdijk, *tr. fr. Dutch by* A. J. Barnouw. LiTW
Prayer: "Moon, mother of the Sabbath, transfuse your loving." César Tiempo, *tr. fr. Spanish by* Donald Devenish Walsh. AnCL
Prayer: "More things are wrought by prayer." Tennyson. *See* Morte d'Arthur.
Prayer, The: "My answered prayer came up to me." Sara Teasdale. ChMo; CMP
Prayer, A: "My darling, thou art flowerlike." Heine, *tr. fr. German by* James Thomson. OnPM
Prayer: "My God, is any hour so sweet." Charlotte Elliott. PraP
Prayer, A: "My God (oh, let me call Thee mine)." Anne Brontë. TrPWD; VA
Prayer, The: "My soul doth pant towards thee." Jeremy Taylor. SeCL
(My Soul Doth Pant towards Thee.) TrPWD
Prayer, A: "Not more of light I ask, O God." Florence Holbrook. PraP
Prayer: "Now I lay me down to sleep." *Unknown. See* Now I Lay Me Down to Take My Sleep.
Prayer: "Now that I know that what I am must be." Edwin Morgan. PFE
Prayer, A: "Now wilt me take for Jesus' sake." Katharine Tynan. OBVV
Prayer, A: "O brooding Spirit of Wisdom and of Love." Sir William Rowan Hamilton. *See* Spirit of Wisdom and of Love.
Prayer, A: "O Earth, O dewy mother, breathe on us." Archibald Lampman. TrPWD
Prayer, A: "O for one minute hark what we are saying!" Frederic W. H. Myers. TrPWD
Prayer: "O God, I love Thee in the stars at Night." Nadejda de Bragança. MaRV
Prayer: "O God of earth and altar." G. K. Chesterton. *See* Hymn, A: "O God of earth and altar."
Prayer: "O God of Goodness, Forwardness, and Fulness." Doris Hedges. GoYe
Prayer, A: "O God, our Father, if we had but truth." Edward Rowland Sill. AA
Prayer: "O God! though sorrow be my fate." Mary, Queen of Hungary, *tr. fr. Hungarian.* LPS-2
Prayer: "Oh, kneel to that God force of love." Lucia Trent. ChIP
Prayer, The: "O living will that shalt endure." Tennyson. *See* In Memoriam A. H H.: "O living will."
Prayer, A: "O Lord, the hard-won miles." Paul Laurence Dunbar. TrPWD
Prayer, A: "O Love, give me a passionate heart." Irene Rutherford McLeod. TrPWD
Prayer: "Oh, make my heart so still, so still." Utsunomiya, *tr. fr. Japanese by* Lois J. Erickson. SoLD
Prayer, A: "O mighty God, Which for us men." Humphrey Gifford. OxBoCh
Prayer, A: "Oh, not for more or longer days, dear Lord." B. Y. Williams. MaRV, PraP
Prayer, A: "O, that mine eyes might closèd be." Thomas Ellwood. PraP; WGRP
Prayer, A: "O Thou Eternal One, may I commune." Theodore Parker. GrCo-1
Prayer, A: "O Thou great Author of the World." Sister Albertus Magnus. WHL
Prayer, A: "O Thou who seekest me." Laurence Binyon. QS
Prayer: "Of what an easie quick accesse." George Herbert. AtBAP
Prayer: "Oft times I pray with words." Gertie Stewart Phillips. BPP
Prayer, A: "Often the western wind has sung to me." Lord Alfred Douglas. CAW; JKCP (1926 ed.); TrPWD
Prayer: "Old order changeth, yielding place to new, The." Tennyson. *See* Morte d'Arthur.
Prayer: "Omnipotent confederate of all good." Amos N. Wilder. TrPWD
Prayer, A: "Out of the deeps I cry to thee, O God!" Richard Le Gallienne. TrPWD
Prayer: "Pray for my soul." Tennyson. *See* Morte d'Arthur.
Prayer: "Prayer is the mightiest force that men can wield." *Unknown.* PraP
Prayer: "Prayer is the soul's sincere desire." James Montgomery. *See* What Is Prayer?
Prayer: "Prayer is work, dost thou believe it?" *Unknown.* PraP
Prayer: "Prayer, the church's banquet, angels' age." George Herbert. MaPo; MePo; OBS; OxBoCh; Po; PoEL-2; SeCV-1; SeEP
Prayer, A: "Purge me, O God." Wilbur Humphrey Fowler. MaRV
Prayer: "She cannot tell my name." Edward Bliss Reed. HBMV
"O God, thy ways are dark," *sel.* MaRV
Prayer: "Spirit of Christ my sanctification." *Unknown, tr. fr. Spanish by* Thomas Walsh. CAW
Prayer: "Take from the earth its tragic hunger, Lord." Hazel J. Fowler. TrPWD
Prayer, A: "Teach me, Father, how to go." Edwin Markham. BOL; BoTP; BPP; DD; HBMV; HBVY; MaRV; MW;

Prayer, A: "Teach me, Father, how to go" (*continued*)
NLK; OTPC (1946 ed.); PGD; PoRL; POT; PoTo; PraP; QS; RG; StVeCh; TrPWD; TSW; TSWC; WGRP
Prayer, A: "Tend me my birds, and bring again." Norman Gale. TrPWD
Prayer: "These are the gifts I ask of thee." Henry van Dyke. WGRP
Prayer: "This evening, our Father." *Unknown.* OuSiCo
Prayer, A: "Those who love Thee may they find." George F. Chawner. BLRP
Prayer, The: "Thou knowest, Lord, with what flaming boldness." "Gabriela Mistral," *tr. fr. Spanish by* Donald Devenish Walsh. AnCL
Prayer: "Thou who didst multiply, by Galilee." Frances Crosby Hamlet. ChIP
Prayer, A: "Through every minute of this day." John Oxenham. BLRP; PraP
Prayer: "Thy blessing on the boys—for time has come." Haim Guri, *tr. fr. Hebrew by* Ruth H. Lask. TrJP
Prayer, A: "To Thy continual Presence, in me wrought." William Ellery Channing. TrPWD
Prayer, A: "Until I lose my soul and lie." Sara Teasdale. HBMV; TrPWD
Prayer, A: "We know the paths wherein our feet should press." John Drinkwater. *See* Purpose.
Prayer: "What a commanding power." Thomas Washbourne. WGRP
Prayer, A: "What weight of ancient witness can prevail." Dryden. *See* Private Judgment Condemned.
Prayer, A: "When I look back upon my life nigh spent." George Macdonald. BSV; TrPWD
Prayer: "When in the morning hour you rise." W. T. Pearman. PraP
Prayer: "When life's oppressive hour is mine." Mikhail Lermontov, *tr. fr. Russian by* C. M. Bowra. BoR
Prayer: "When the last sea is sailed." John Masefield. GTSL; LEAP; VOD
(D'Avalos' Prayer.) POTT; TrPWD
Prayer: "Where then shall Hope and Fear their objects find?" Samuel Johnson. *Fr.* The Vanity of Human Wishes. CoEV; OBEC
("Where then shall Hope . . .") EnLi-1 (1949 ed.)
Prayer: "White Captain of my soul, lead on." Robert Freeman. ChIP; MaRV; OQP; QP-1
(Soldier's Prayer, A.) TrPWD
Prayer, The: "Wilt thou not visit me?" Jones Very. APW; MaRV; OxBA; TriL; TrPWD
Prayer: "With Him who sets the lily on the stem." Hildegarde Flanner. NV; VOD (1935 ed.)
Prayer after Illness, A. Violet Alleyn Storey. TrPWD
Prayer after Youth. Maxwell Anderson. TBM
Prayer against Indifference. Joy Davidman. AnAmPo; AnEnPo; TrPWD
Prayer against Love. Catullus, *tr. fr. Latin by* Jack Lindsay. LiTW
Prayer amid Flames. Verner von Heidenstam, *tr. fr. Swedish by* Charles W. Stork. AnSL
Prayer; an Ode. Richard Crashaw. *See* On a Prayer Book Sent to Mrs. M. R.
Prayer and Deeds. *Unknown.* PraP
Prayer and Potatoes. J. T. Pettee. PTA-2
Prayer at a Wedding. Charles Carroll Albertson. PraP
Prayer at a Wedding. Sidney Lanier. PraP
(Wedding-Hymn.) TrPWD
Prayer at Bethlehem, A. Anne P. L. Field. COAH
Prayer at Christmas Time, A. Nancy Byrd Turner. PraP
Prayer at Dawn. Diarmuid O'Shea, *tr. fr. Irish by* Frank O'Connor. KiLC
Prayer at Dawn. Edwin McNeill Poteat. TrPWD
Prayer at Eventide. R. B. Y. Scott. MaRV
Prayer at New Year's. Nancy Byrd Turner. PraP
Prayer at Sunrise. James Weldon Johnson. QS
Prayer at Thanksgiving Time. Nancy Byrd Turner. PraP
Prayer at the Close of a Marred Day. Elizabeth Stuart Phelps Ward. PraP
Prayer at Winter Thanksgiving, A. *Unknown, tr. fr. Chinese. Fr.* The Fountain of Old Poems. WhP
Prayer before Birth. Louis MacNeice. LiTB; OAEP (2d ed.)
Prayer before Execution. Mary Queen of Scots, *tr. fr. Latin by* John Fawcett. CAW; MaRV; WGRP
Prayer before Going to Sleep. *Unknown, tr. by* Eleanor Hull. JKCP (1926 ed.)
Prayer before Meat. Una W. Harsen. ChIP; TrPWD
Prayer before Poems. Anne Blackwell Payne. NLK
Prayer before Sleep. Alice Lucas. TrJP
Prayer before Sleeping. *Unknown. See* Matthew, Mark, Luke, and John.
Prayer before Study. Theodore Roethke. TrPWD
Prayer Brings Rain, A. Tasso, *tr. fr. Italian by* Edward Fairfax. *Fr.* Godfrey of Bulloigne. OBSC
Prayer by Moonlight. Roberta Teale Swartz. TrPWD
Prayer during Battle. Hermann Hagedorn. POT; SBMV; TrPWD
Prayer for a Bride. Helen Welshimer. PraP
Prayer for a Bride's House. Christie Lund. PraP
Prayer for a College Girl. Ella Broadus Robertson. PraP
Prayer for a Day's Walk. Grace Noll Crowell. PoToHe
Prayer for a Friend. Annie Johnson Flint. PraP
Prayer for a Happy New Year, A. Andrew Stewart Currie Clarke. *See* Prayer: "Bless Thou this year, O Lord!"
Prayer for a Little Home, A. Florence Bone. BLPA; FaBoBe; FaFP; MaRV; MW; NeHB; OQP; PCH; PraP; PTA-2; QP-2
Prayer for a Marriage, A. Mary Carolyn Davies. TrPWD
Prayer for a New House. Louis Untermeyer. *See* Prayer for This House.
Prayer for a New Mother. Dorothy Parker. QS
Prayer for a Pilot. Cecil Roberts. BBV; FaPON; OTPC (1946 ed.)
(Prayer for the Pilot.) TrPWD
Prayer for a Play House. Elinor Lennen. TrPWD
Prayer for a Preacher, A. Edward Shillito. TrPWD
Prayer for a Priest. *Unknown.* WHL
Prayer for a Silver Jubilee. Sister Mary Colman. PraNu
Prayer for a Sleeping Child, A. Mary Carolyn Davies. OHIP
Prayer for a Very New Angel. Violet Alleyn Storey. BLPA; DDA; MotAn; TreFS
Prayer for All Poets at This Time. Irwin Edman. TrPWD
Prayer for an Airman. Richard Zouche. ShGoBo
Prayer for Any Bride and Groom. J. Shenton Lodge. PraP
Prayer for Aviators, A. Norman E. Richardson. MaRV; PraP
Prayer for Broken Little Families, A. Violet Alleyn Storey. PoToHe
Prayer for Brotherhood, A. John S. Hoyland. MaRV
Prayer for Charity, A. Edwin O. Kennedy. TrPWD
Prayer for Christian Unity, A. Molly Anderson Haley. ChIP; OQP; QP-1
Prayer for Contentment. Edwin McNeill Poteat. NoCaPo (rev. ed.); TrPWD
Prayer for Courage, A. Grace Noll Crowell. PraP
Prayer for Courage, A. Joseph Morris. PraP
Prayer for Courage. Rabindranath Tagore. MaRV
Prayer for Courage. Louis Untermeyer. OQP; PraP; QP-1
Prayer for Deliverance. Aeschylus, *tr. fr. Greek by* Gilbert Murray. *Fr.* The Suppliants. OxBG
(O Zeus, Our Spirit Fails.) GrR
Prayer for Dew. Eleazar ben Kalir, *tr. fr. Hebrew by* Israel Zangwill. TrJP
Prayer for Dogs, A. Goldie Capers Smith. AlBD
Prayer for Dreadful Morning. E. Merrill Root. TrPWD
Prayer for Each Awakening. Luis Cané, *tr. fr. Spanish by* Dudley Fitts. AnCL
Prayer for Every Day, A. Mary Carolyn Davies. BLPA; FaBoBe; NeHB; PoToHe
Prayer for Faith, A. Michelangelo, *tr. fr. Italian by* John Addington Symonds. OnPM
Prayer for Faith, A. Alfred Norris. BLRP
Prayer for Faith, A. Margaret E. Sangster. PoToHe
Prayer for Faith in Peace. Bertha Gerneaux Woods. PraP
Prayer for Family Love, A. John S. Hoyland. MaRV
(For Family Love.) GrCo-2
Prayer for Forbearance. *Unknown.* LoBV
Prayer for Gentleness to All Creatures. John Galsworthy. BoTP
Prayer for Gentlewomen and Others to Use, A. Nicholas Breton. SiCE
Prayer for Help. *Unknown.* PraP
Prayer for Home-Coming. Julius Polyaenus, *tr. fr. Greek by* Walter Leaf. OxBG
Prayer for Indifference. Fanny Greville. LoBV; OBEC
"I ask no kind return of love," 3 *sts.* DiM; LO; OBEV
Prayer for Inspiration, A. Michelangelo. *See* For Inspiration.
Prayer for Life, A. George S. Burleigh. LPS-2
Prayer for Light. Stanton A. Coblentz. TrPWD
Prayer for Little Beasts. Beulah May. DDA
Prayer for Living and Dying. Christopher La Farge. TrPWD
Prayer for Love, A. Elsa Barker. OQP; QP-1
Prayer for Miracle. Anna Wickham. GoTP; OQP; QP-2; YT
Prayer for Mothers, A. John F. Todd. PraP
Prayer for My Daughter, A. W. B. Yeats. ChMo; CMP; CoBMV; EnL; EnLP; GTBS-W; LiTB; LiTG; LiTM (rev. ed.); LoBV; MoAB; PoLFOT; VLEP
"I have walked and prayed for this young child an hour," *sel.* ViBoPo; WoL
Prayer for My Native Land. Burns. *Fr.* The Cotter's Saturday Night. MaRV
Prayer for My Playmates, A. *Unknown.* PraP
Prayer for My Son, A. Yvor Winters. CrMA; TrPWD
Prayer for Old Age, A. W B. Yeats. BrBE
Prayer for One Dead. Julia C. R. Dorr. OQP; QP-1
Prayer for Our Home. John S. Hoyland. MaRV
Prayer for Pain. John G. Neihardt. HBV; NP; PFY; TBM; TrPWD; WGRP
Prayer for Peace, A. William Adams Brown. MaRV

Prayer for Peace. St. Francis of Assisi. *See* Lord, Make Me an Instrument of Your Peace.
Prayer for Peace, A. John Oxenham. PraP
Prayer for Peace. Johnstone G. Patrick. TrPWD
Prayer for Peace. Rolland W. Schloerb. MaRV
Prayer for Peace, A. Edward Rowland Sill. TrPWD
Prayer for Peace, A. S. Teackle Wallis. BlG
Prayer for Pentecost, A. Catherine Bernard Brown. BLRP
Prayer for Prince, A. Betsey Mann Collins. AlBD
Prayer for Purification, A. Michelangelo. *See* Thou Alone Art Good.
Prayer for Rain. Herbert E. Palmer. HaMV; POTE
Prayer for Rain. *Unknown, tr. fr. Finnish. Fr.* Kalevala. WGRP
Prayer for Recollection, A. *Unknown, tr. fr. Irish by* Frank O'Connor. KiLC
Prayer for Redemption. *Unknown.* TrJP
Prayer for St. Innocent's Day, A. Helen Parry Eden. CAW
Prayer for Shut-Ins. Ruth Winant Wheeler. PoToHe (new ed.)
Prayer for Singleness of Vision, A. Sherard Vines. QS
Prayer for Song. Fay Lewis Noble. TrPWD
Prayer for Sophistication. Mark Turbyfill. NP
Prayer for Strength. Margaret E. Bruner. MaRV; PoToHe
Prayer for Strength. Samuel Johnson. MaRV
(For Divine Strength, *sl. abr.*) PraP
Prayer for Strength, A. Michelangelo, *tr. fr. Italian by* John Addington Symonds. OnPM
Prayer for Strength. Rabindranath Tagore. Gitanjali, XXXVI. MaRV
Prayer for Teachers, A. Marguerite Emilio. OQP; PraP; QP-2
Prayer for Thanksgiving, A. Joseph Auslander. TrPWD
Prayer for the Age. Myron H. Broomell. TrPWD
Prayer for the Churches. John Oxenham. OQP; QP-1
Prayer for the Dead. Tennyson. *See* Morte d'Arthur.
Prayer for the Dogs in War, A. Mrs. E. Worthing. AlBD
Prayer for the Healing of the Wounds of Christ, A. Laurence Housman. MaRV
Prayer for the Home, *sel.* Edgar A. Guest.
"Lord, this humble house we'd keep." MaRV
Prayer for the Hunted. Daniel Henderson. SaFP
Prayer for the New Year, A. Laura F. Armitage. OQP; QP-2
Prayer for the New Year. Richard of Chichester. PraP
Prayer for the New Year, A. Violet Alleyn Storey. TrPWD
Prayer for the New Year, A. *Unknown.* BLRP
Prayer for the Old Courage, A. Charles Hanson Towne. PC; TrPWD
Prayer for the Pilot. Cecil Roberts. *See* Prayer for a Pilot.
Prayer for the Poor. William Langland, *mod. by* Henry W. Wells. *Fr.* The Vision of Piers Plowman. PoLi
Prayer for the Presence of Christ, A. Thomas Tiplady. ChIP; MaRV
(Grace, A.) TrPWD
Prayer for the President. Amos R. Wells. PraP
Prayer for the Speedy End of Three Great Misfortunes. *Tr. fr. Irish by* Frank O'Connor. OBMV
Prayer for the Useless Days. Edith Lovejoy Pierce. TrPWD
Prayer for This Day. Hildegarde Flanner. TrPWD
Prayer for this House. Louis Untermeyer. FaPON; MaRV; PoToHe; TSW; TSWC
(Prayer for a New House.) TrPWD
Prayer for This Our Time. Thomas Moult. QS
Prayer for Today, A. Charles Nelson Pace. MaRV; OQP; QP-2
Prayer for Violence. John Donne. *See* Holy Sonnets: "Batter my heart . . ."
Prayer for Wings. Dmitry Merezhkovsky, *tr. fr. Russian by* Babette Deutsch. OnPM; TrRV
Prayer Found in Chester Cathedral, A. T. H. B. Webb. *See* Prayer: "Give me a good digestion, Lord."
Prayer from 1936, A. Siegfried Sassoon. TrPWD
Prayer Hymn. "M. K. H." ChIP; OQP; QP-2
Prayer in a Country Church. Ruth B. Van Dusen. TrPWD
Prayer in Affliction. Violet Alleyn Storey. MaRV; TrPWD
Prayer in April. Sara Henderson Hay. MaRV; OQP; QP-2; TrPWD
Prayer in Darkness, A. G. K. Chesterton. BMEP; MBP; MoBrPo; TrGrPo
Prayer in Late Autumn, A. Violet Alleyn Storey. TrPWD
Prayer in Sorrow. Frederick L. Hosmer. *See* Father, to Thee.
Prayer in Spring, A. Robert Frost. AlDL; MaRV; OTPC (1946 ed.); QS; TrPWD; YeAr; YT
Prayer in the Bower, The. Leigh Hunt. ERP
Prayer in the Prospect of Death, A. Burns. BCEP; HBV; MaRV; TrPWD; WGRP
Prayer in the Trenches. Brent Dow Allinson. AOAH
De Profundis, II.
"Lord God of Hosts," I.
Prayer in Time of Blindness, A. Clement Wood. TrPWD
Prayer in Time of War. Henry Treece. WaP
Prayer is appointed to convey. Pray with Faith. Joseph Hart. PraP
Prayer is the mightiest force that men can wield. Prayer. *Unknown.* PraP
Prayer is the soul's sincere desire. What is Prayer? [*or* Prayer]. James Montgomery. BLRP; GrCo-1; MaRV; PraP; WGRP
Prayer is work, dost thou believe it? Prayer. *Unknown.* PraP
Prayer, Living and Dying, A. Augustus Montague Toplady. *See* Rock of Ages.
Prayer, Made in Ballat Form bi Villon for His Mither, The. Villon. *See* His Mother's Service to Our Lady.
Prayer-Meeting, The. Gustaf Fröding, *tr. fr. Swedish by* Charles W. Stork. AnSL
Prayer Meeting, The. Amos R. Wells. PraP
Prayer of a Beginning Teacher. Ouida Smith Dunnam. TrPWD
Prayer of a Modern Thomas. Edward Shillito. ChIP; MaRV; PGD
Prayer of a Patriot. Henry J. von Schlichten. BePJ
Prayer of a Soldier in France. Joyce Kilmer. CAW; GoBC; SBMV
Prayer of a Teacher. Dorothy Littlewort. TrPWD
Prayer of a Teacher, The. Elizabeth McE. Shields. PraP
Prayer of a Tired Woman. Mazie V. Caruthers. PraP
Prayer of Achilles, The. Homer. *See* Achilles' Prayer.
Prayer of Agassiz, The. Whittier. IAP; LPS-3
Prayer of an Unbeliever. Lizette Woodworth Reese. QS; TrPWD
Prayer of an Unemployed Man. W. C. Ackerly. MaRV; PoToHe
Prayer of Any Husband. Mazie V. Caruthers. MaRV; PoToHe
Prayer of Beaten Men, The. William Hervey Woods. *Fr.* The House of Broken Swords. HBV
Prayer of Busy Hands, A. B. Y. Williams. MaRV
Prayer of Calcas, The. *Unknown, tr. fr. Welsh by* Gwyn Williams. *Fr.* Troelus a Chresyd. PrWP
Prayer of Columbus. Walt Whitman. AmPP (4th ed.); APW; ATP; WGRP
Sels.
"My terminus near,/ The clouds already closing in upon me." MaRV
"One effort more, my altar this bleak sand." OQP; PGD; PoRL; QP-1
"Thou knowest my years entire, my life." TrPWD
Prayer of Cyrus Brown, The. Sam Walter Foss. BOHV; LHV; StaSt
Prayer of Habakkuk, The. Habakkuk, III, Bible, *O.T.* BHV
Prayer of Iphigenia, The. Euripides, *tr. fr. Greek by* Arthur S. Way. *Fr.* Iphigenia in Aulis. GrR
Prayer of Penitence, A. Robert Whitaker. PSO
Prayer of Praise to Mary, A. *Unknown.* WHL
Prayer of St. Francis Xavier. Pope. TrPWD
Prayer of Steel. Carl Sandburg. OQP; QP-1
Prayer of the Five Wounds, A, *sel.* *Unknown.*
"Jhesu cryst, myn leman swete." AtBAP
Prayer of the Homesteader. Gwendolen Haste. PoTo
Prayer of the Humble, The. Zacharias Papondoniou, *tr. fr. Modern Greek by* Rae Dalven. MoGP
Prayer of the Maidens to Mary. Rainer Maria Rilke, *tr. fr. German by* Jethro Bithell. AWP
Prayer of the Night Chant, A. *Unknown, tr. fr. Navajo Indian by* Washington Matthews. ExPo
Prayer of the Peoples, A. Percy MacKaye. TrPWD, 3 *sts.*; WGRP
Prayer of the Quest, The. Eleanor B. Stock. MaRV
Prayer of the Satirist. "O. L." CAG
Prayer of the Unemployed. Raymond Kresensky. OQP; QP-2
Prayer of the Unemployed. *Unknown.* MaRV
Prayer of the Young Stoic. Stephen P. Dunn. TrPWD
Prayer on Christmas Eve. Nancy Byrd Turner. MaRV; PraP
Prayer on Entering Church. Bertha Gerneaux Woods. PraP
Prayer on Fourth of July. Nancy Byrd Turner. YeAr
Prayer Perfect, The. James Whitcomb Riley. MaRV; OQP; PraP; QP-2
(Love's Prayer.) AA
Prayer-Poem, A. Mary S. Edgar. *See* Youth's Prayer, A.
Prayer Poem, A. Calvin W. Laufer. PraP
Prayer Reaches Him. Nagata, *tr. fr. Japanese by* Lois J. Erickson. SoLD
Prayer Rug, The. Sara Beaumont Kennedy. HBMV; VOD
Prayer That an Infant May Not Die. Francis Jammes, *tr. fr. French by* Joseph T. Shipley. CAW
Prayer the Church's [*or* churches] banquet, angels' age. Prayer. George Herbert. MePo; OBS; OxBoCh; Po; PoEL-2; SeEP
Prayer Time. Ruby Weyburn Tobias. PraP
Prayer to Artemis. Anacreon, *tr. fr. Greek by* Judson France Davidson. GrR

Prayer to Ben Jonson. Robert Herrick. *See* His Prayer to Ben Jonson.
Prayer to Christ Our Lord, *mod.* Cynewulf. PoLi
Prayer to Go to Paradise with the Asses. Francis Jammes, *tr. fr. French by* Jethro Bithell. AWP; JAWP; WBP; TrFP, *tr. by* Alan Conder
(Prayer to Go to Paradise with the Donkeys, *tr. by* Vernon Watkins.) LiTW; MiFP
("When You elect to call me, God, O call," *tr. by* Alan Conder.) LO
Prayer to God. "Plácido," *tr. fr. Spanish.* CAW
Prayer to God to Rest All the Unfortunate. "Kostes Ouranis," *tr. fr. Modern Greek by* Rae Dalven. MoGP
Prayer to Jehanne of France. Joseph Auslander. NeTW
Prayer to Jesus. Mossén Tallante, *tr. fr. Spanish by* Sir John Bowring. OnPM
Prayer to Persephone. Edna St. Vincent Millay. Memorial to D.C., II. BAP; NP; PoeMoYo
Prayer to Saint Anthony of Padua, A. Arthur Symons. VLEP
Prayer to St. Francis. Frances Frost. SaFP
Prayer to Saint Francis for Poverty. Liam Brophy. SaFP
Prayer to St. Patrick. Ninine, *tr. fr. Old Irish by* Whitley Stokes *and* John Strachan. OnYI
Prayer to Santa Maria del Vade. Juan Ruiz, Archpriest of Hita. CAW
Prayer to Sleep. Samuel Daniel. *See* Care-Charmer Sleep.
Prayer to the Blessed Virgin, A. Chaucer. *See* Invocation: "O mother-maid!"
Prayer to the Blessed Virgin. Rodríguez del Padrón, *tr. fr. Spanish by* Sir John Bowring. CAW
Prayer to the Crucifix. Mossén Juan Tallante, *tr. fr. Spanish by* Thomas Walsh. CAW
Prayer to the Father of [*or* in] Heaven, A. John Skelton. SiCE; TrPWD; TuPP
Prayer to the Giver. Charles Hanson Towne. OQP; PSO; QP-1
Prayer to the Holy Trinity, *sel.* Hildebert of Lavardin, *tr. fr. Latin by* William Crashaw.
"In Syon lodge me (Lord) for pitty." LiA
Prayer to the Holy Trinity, A. Richard Stanyhurst. *See* Prayer to the Trinity, A.
Prayer to the Mountain Spirit. *Tr. fr. Navaho Indian by* Mary Austin, *tr. wr. at. to* G. W. Cronyn *and to* Edward S. Yeomans. WGRP
(Navaho [*or* Navajo] Prayer.) PoRL; StVeCh
Prayer to the Sun. John Hall Wheelock. BAP; FAOV
Prayer to the Trinity. James Edmeston. HBV; VA
(Hymn: "Lead us, heavenly Father, lead us.") NeHB
("Lead us, heavenly Father, lead us.") OlF
Prayer to the Trinity, A. Richard Stanyhurst. CoBE; ElL; TuPP
(Prayer to the Holy Trinity, A.) PoEL-2
(To the Trinity.) OxBoCh
Prayer to the Virgin. *Unknown. See* Hymn to the Virgin.
Prayer to the Virgin. *Unknown, tr. fr. Middle Irish by* John Strachan *and* Kuno Meyer. OnYI
Prayer to the Virgin of Chartres. Henry Adams. CAW; GoBC; ISi
Prayer to Venus. Chaucer, *mod. vers. by* John Hall Wheelock. *Fr.* The Canterbury Tales: The Knight's Tale. LiTL
Prayer to Venus. John Fletcher. *Fr.* The Mad Lover. SeCL
Prayer to Venus. Lucretius, *tr. by* Spenser. *See* Address to Venus.
Prayer under the Pressure of Violent Anguish. Burns. TrPWD
Prayer unsaid, and mass unsung. The Sea Ritual [*or* Deadman's Dirge]. George Darley. Syren Songs, V. CH; OBRV; OnYI; OxBI; TriL
Prayerlessness. *Unknown.* PraP
Prayers. Henry Charles Beeching. BoTP; CP; LH; MaRV; OBVV; PoeT; TVSH; VA
(Boy's Prayer, A.) GN; OTPC (1946 ed.), *st.* 1; PoRL, *st.* 1
Prayers. Flora Hastings. OTPC (1923 ed.)
Prayers. *Unknown.* BOL
Prayers I make will then be sweet indeed, The. For Inspiration [*or* A Prayer for Inspiration *or* To the Supreme Being]. Michelangelo. AWP; CAW; GoBC; GrCo-1; JAWP; LiTW; OQP; QP-1; TrPWD; WBP; WGRP
Prayers in the whitewashed sitting-room. Afrikaans Homestead. Peter Jackson. BoSA
Prayers Must Have Poise. Robert Herrick. LiTB
Prayers of Steel. Carl Sandburg. AnAmPo; BAP; ChMo; CMP; CV; FaPON; IAP; LA; MAP; MoAmPo; MPB; NeMA; NP; PFY; PoMa; PoTo; TrPWD; YaD
Prayerwheel 2. David Meltzer. NeAP
Praying and Preaching. *Unknown. See* My Bishop's Eyes.
Praying-Mantis, The. Annie Charlotte Dalton. BoCaPo (1943 ed.); TwCaPo
Praying Mantis Visits a Penthouse, The. Oscar Williams. FaFP; LiTM; NePA; PreP
Preach about the old sins, Preacher! Charlotte Perkins Gilman. *Fr.* To the Preacher. MaRV
Preach wisdom unto him who understands! Che Sara Sara. Victor Plarr. HBV; LBBV
Preacher, The. Al-Mahdi, *tr. fr. Arabic by* A. J. Arberry. MooP
Preacher and the Slave, The, *with music. Unknown.* AS; TrAS
Preacher Sought to Find Out Acceptable Words, The. Richard Eberhart. WaP
Preachers, The. Norman Nicholson. NeBP
Preacher's Legacy, The. *Unknown.* ABS
Preacher's Mistake, The. Brewer Mattocks, *sometimes at. to* William Croswell Doane. BLPA; MaRV; PoToHe; StaSt
Preacher's Prayer, The. George Macdonald. MaRV
Preachers; the True vs. the Insincere. William Cowper. *Fr.* The Task, II. MaRV
Preacher's Urgency, A. Richard Baxter. MaRV
Preacher's Vacation, The. *Unknown.* BLPA
Preaching and Not Doing. William Langland, *mod. by* Henry W. Wells. *Fr.* The Vision of Piers Plowman. PoLi
Preachment for Preachers. Sebastian Brant, *tr. fr. German by* Alexander Barclay. *Fr.* The Ship of Fools. ACP; CAW
Pre-admonisheth the writer. The Flight of the Bucket. Kipling. PA
Preamble to a Great Adventure. Ronald Bottrall. MoP
Preamble to N[icholas] B[reton] His Garden-Plot, The. Nicholas Breton. ReIE
Precarious Ground. Leah Bodine Drake. GoYe
Precarious Life of Man. Euripides, *tr. fr. Greek by* F. W. Pember. *Fr.* Hippolytus. GrR
Precept of Silence, The. Lionel Johnson. ACP (1926 ed.); BMEP; CAW; HBV; LBBV; LEAP; MBP; MoBrPo; PoeT; PoToHe (1941 ed.); PoVP; ViBoPo; ViPP; VLEP
Precepts He Gave His Folk. Elijah ben Menahem Hazaken of Le Mans, *tr. fr. Hebrew by* Israel Zangwill. TrJP
Precepts of Chiron, *sel.* Hesiod, *tr. fr. Greek by* Sir William Marris.
Length of Life. OxBG
Precinct—Rochester, The. Amy Lowell. OBAV; VOD
"Precious in the Sight of the Lord." *Unknown.* BLRP
Precious jewel can I find none to sell. A Greeting on New Year's Morning. *Unknown.* TMEV
Precious Moments. Carl Sandburg. MAP; MoAmPo
Precious, mouldering [*or* moldering] pleasure 'tis, A. Emily Dickinson. TwP
(In a Library.) CV; MOB
Precious Music of Heresy, The. Hakushu Kitahara, *tr. fr. Japanese by* Takamichi Ninomiya *and* D. J. Enright. PoLJ
Precious Name, The. John Newton. *See* Name of Jesus, The.
Precious, oh how precious is that blessed sleep. "Precious in the Sight of the Lord." *Unknown.* BLRP
Precious Pearl, The. Pat Wilson. AnNZ
Precious Stones. Charles Stuart Calverley. InMe
Precious Stones. Christopher Marlowe. *Fr.* The Jew of Malta, I, i. EV-1
Precious Stones. Christina Rossetti. *See* Emerald Is as Green as Grass, An.
Precious Things. *Unknown.* GoSl
Precious thought, my Father knoweth. God Knoweth Best [*or* Your Father Knoweth]. *Unknown.* BLRP; WBLP
Precious treasure had I long possessed, A. Wordsworth's Early Reading. Wordsworth. *Fr.* The Prelude, V. MOB
Precious Words. Emily Dickinson. *See* He ate and drank the precious words.
Precipice, The. John Banister Tabb. AmP
Precipitous Rocks, The. *Unknown, tr. fr. Chinese.* WhP
Precocious fruits that Nature hath begot. Autumn Fruits. Joachim du Bellay. Olive, XXXII. TrFP
Precocious Piggy. Thomas Hood. MeMeAg
(Little Piggies, The.) BoTP
Predestination. Omar Khayyám, *tr. fr. Persian by* Edward Fitzgerald. *Fr.* The Rubáiyát. OnPM
Predestination. Kipling. *Fr.* Plain Tales from the Hills. LoBV
Predestination. Feodor Ivanovich Tyutchev, *tr. fr. Russian by* Sir Cecil Kisch. WaL
Pre-Existence. Frances Cornford. DiM; HBMV; PoeT; POTE; TwCV; WaKn
Pre-Existence. Empedocles, *tr. fr. Greek by* F. L. Lucas. GrPE
Pre-Existence. Paul Hamilton Hayne. HBV; LPS-3; UnW
Preface. W. H. Auden. *Fr.* The Sea and the Mirror. LiTA; SeCeV
Preface, A, *sel.* Winthrop Mackworth Praed.
Voltaire, Cobbett, and Gastronomy. RO
Preface. Michizo Tachihara, *tr. fr. Japanese by* Takamichi Ninomiya *and* D. J. Enright. PoLJ
Preface, The. Edward Taylor. *Fr.* God's Determinations. AmPP; CoV; OxBA
Preface ("To make a start"). William Carlos Williams. *Fr.* Paterson, I. CoBMV

Preface to Confessional. "C. H. W." CAG
Preface to Erinna's Poems. Antipater of Sidon. *See* Erinna.
Preface to Erinna's Poems. Asclepiades. *See* Erinna's Poems.
Preface to "Milton." Blake. *See* And Did Those Feet in Ancient Time.
Preface to the Book of Housewifery, The. Thomas Tusser. SiCE
Preface to the Buyer of This Book, A. Thomas Tusser. SiCE; TuPP
Prefatory Sonnet. Henry Kendall. BoAV
Prefatory Sonnet. Wordsworth. *See* Nuns Fret Not at Their Convent's Narrow Room.
Prefer the Cash. Omar Khayyám, *tr. fr. Persian by* Edward Fitzgerald. *Fr.* The Rubáiyát. OnPM
Preference. Berton Braley. AlBD
Preference, A. John Farrar. GFA
Preference. Daniel Sargent. ISi
Preferring "resemblance to beauty." An Esthetic of Imitation. Donald Finkel. NePoEA
Pregnant again with th' old twins Hope, and Feare. To Mr. T. W. John Donne. BoFr
Prehistoric Burials. Siegfried Sassoon. MBP; MoBrPo
Prehistoric Camp, A. Andrew Young. MoPW
Prehistoric Smith. David Law Proudfit. BOHV
Prejudice against the Past, The. Wallace Stevens. LiTM (rev. ed.)
Prelates, The. John Skelton. *Fr.* Colyn Cloute. BLV; TrGrPo
("My name is Colin Cloute.") EPP
Preliminary Invocation. Jami, *tr. fr. Persian by* Edward Fitzgerald. *Fr.* Salámán and Absál. PeP
Preliminary to Classroom Lecture. Josephine Miles. FiMAP
Prelude, The [or, Growth of a Poet's Mind]. Wordsworth. EmBrPo, *much abr.;* EnLP, *abr.;* EnRP, *much abr.;* OAEP, *much abr.*
Sels.
"Among that band of Officers was one," *fr.* IX, *Oxford ed., incl.* Vaudracour and Julia. ChER
"And in the frosty season, when the sun," *fr.* I. InP; MyFE; PoMa
(On the Frozen Lake.) FaBoCh; LoGBV
(Skating.) CH, *shorter sel.;* GN; GoTP; ShBV-3
As If Awakened, Summoned, *fr.* III. AtBAP
"As the black storm upon the mountain top," *fr.* VII. NBE
(Residence in London.) ERP; PoEL-4, *longer sel.*
Band of Military Officers, A, *fr.* IX. EnLi-2
"Beside the pleasant Mill of Trompington," *fr.* III. OBRV
Blest the Infant Babe, *fr.* II. AtBAP
Books, *fr.* V.
"When contemplation, like the night-calm felt." ERP
"Whereupon I told,/ That once in the stillness of a summer's noon." PoEL-4
Childhood ("When he had left the mountains"), *fr.* I. CoBE
Communion with Nature, *fr* II. TOP
("For I would walk alone," *sl. diff.*) OBRV
Conclusion, *fr.* XIV. FaBoEn
("It was a close, warm, breezeless summer night," *longer sel.*) PoEL-4
(Majestic Intellect.) RO
"Moon hung naked in a firmament, The." ERP
Crossing the Alps ("The only track now visible was one"), *fr.* VI.
Dedicated Spirit, A, *fr.* IV. SeCePo
Demobilized Soldier, The, *fr.* IV. RO
"Dust as we are, the immortal spirit grows," *fr.* I. CoEV
Enough of Humble Arguments, *fr.* VIII. AtBAP
"Fair seed-time had my soul, and I grew up," *fr.* I. EnL; EnLi-2; EV-3, *shorter sel.;* ExPo; NBE; OBRV, *shorter sel., sl. diff.;* PoEL-4; TyEnPo
(Childhood.) TCEP
(Childhood and School-Time.) FaBoEn
(Fair Seed-Time Had My Soul.) AtBAP; MaPo
(Presences of Nature in Boyhood.) EPN
"Far better never to have heard the name," *fr.* I. GEPC
"Favorite pleasure hath it been with me, A," *fr.* IV, *Oxford ed.* OBRV
France ("But indignation works"), *fr.* XI. ERP
French Revolution, The, *fr.* XI. BPN; ERP; FiP; RO; TOP
("O pleasant exercise of hope and joy!") EnLi-2; EV-3; OBRV
(Residence in France, Continued.) PoEL-4
Glow-Worm, The, *fr.* VII. RO
"Gracious spirit o'er this earth presides, A," *fr.* V. OBRV
"Grave teacher, stern preceptress," *fr.* VIII. NBE
He Remembers the Vista of a Towering Peak, *br. sel., fr.* I. LiA
"He, who in his youth/ A daily wanderer among woods and fields," *fr.* V. NBE
"Hitherto,/ In progress through this verse," *fr.* V. NBE
"How gracious, how benign, is solitude," *abr., fr.* IV. NBE
"I felt most deeply in what world I was," *fr.* X. NBE
"I, too, have been a wanderer; but, alas!" *fr.* VI. PtP
Imagination and Taste, How Impaired and Restored, *fr.* XII *and* XIII. ERP
"Imagination—here the power so called," *fr.* VI. NBE
(Cambridge and the Alps.) ERP
(Imagination, *longer sel.*) FiP
In Childhood and Youth ("I remember when the changeful earth"), *much abr., fr.* I *and* II. GrCo-2
In One of Those Excursions, *fr.* XIV. MaPo
Influence of Natural Objects, *fr.* I. AWP; BPN; InPo; JAWP; LoBV; MCCG; OBRV; RO; WBP
(Boyhood, *sl. longer sel.*) WHA
(Nature's Ministry.) GrCo-2
(Wisdom and Spirit of the Universe.) AtBAP; CoEV
Introduction—Childhood and School-Time, I. BEL; EM-2; EnLit; ERP
Love ("By love subsists"), *fr.* XIV. RO
"Meanwhile the invaders fared as they deserved," *fr.* X. NBE
"Memory of one particular hour, The," *fr.* IV. EV-3
("In a throng, a festal company," *sl. diff.*) OBRV
"Moon was up, the lake was shining clear, The," *fr.* I. FaBoEn
Nature, Love, and Man, *fr.* IV. RO
Nature's Healing, *fr.* XII. EPN
Newton, *fr.* III. ImOP
Noble, The, 3 *ll., fr.* IX. ChTr
"Nor should this, perchance," *fr.* II. ERP
Oh, Blank Confusion, *fr.* VII. AtBAP
Oh! Mystery of Man, *fr.* XII. FiP
"Oh! yet a few short years of useful life," *fr.* XIV. EV-3; NBE; OBRV, *sl. diff.*
"One summer evening (led by her) I found," *fr.* I. EV-3; FiP; MyFE; ViBoPo
("One evening—surely I was led by her," *Oxford ed.*) OBRV
(Stolen Boat, The.) ShBV-3
Poet and the French Revolution, The, *fr.* XI. EPN
Raven's Nest, The, *fr.* I. ShBV-3
Residence in France.
"Cheered with this hope," *fr.* X. BEL; PoEL-4
"France lured me forth," *much abr., fr.* IX. BEL
"I resolved/ How much the destiny of man," *fr.* X. ERP
"Oh, sweet it is, in academic groves," *fr.* IX. ERP
Retrospect—Love of Nature Leading to Love of Man, *fr.* VIII. ERP
School-Time, II. BEL; EM-2; GEPC
"Seasons came, The," *fr.* II. NBE
Simplon Pass, The, *fr.* VI. BPN; EM-2; ERP; InPo; PoFS
(Alpine Descent.) WHA
("Brook and road, The.") EV-2; OBRV
(Down the Simplon Pass.) EPN
("Melancholy slackening that ensued, The.") PoEL-4
"Single tree there was, A," *fr.* VI, *Oxford ed.* OBRV
Solitude ("The antechapel where the statue stood"), 4 *ll., fr.* III. LiA
"Stationary blasts of waterfalls, The," *fr.* VI. MeRV
Summer Vacation, *fr.* IV.
"When first I made/ Once more the circuit of our little lake." ERP; OBRV, *shorter sel.*
"Yet in spite/ Of pleasure won, and knowledge not withheld." PoEL-4
"There are in our existence spots of time," *fr.* XII. LO, *shorter sel., abr.;* NBE; PoEL-4
"There, 'tis the shepherd's task the winter long," *fr.* VIII. CoEV
There Was a Boy, *fr.* V. BoLiVe; BPN; ChER; CoEV; ERP; FaBoCh; FaBoEn; GEPC; LoGBV; MaPo; MCCG; MyFE; NBE; OBRV; PoEL-4; PTA-2; REAL; RO, *abr.;* SN; TCEP; TwP
(Winander Lake.) FiP
"This spiritual love acts not nor can exist," *fr.* XIV. NBE
"'Tis told by one whom stormy waters threw," *fr.* VI. ImOP
"Thus while the days flew by, and years passed on," *fr.* II, IV, *and* VI. UnW
'Twere Long to Tell, *fr.* II AtBAP
Universal Heart of Man, The, *fr.* XIII. TOP
"What, then, were my emotions, when in arms," *fr.* X. NBE
"With forehead bent/ Earthward, as if in opposition set," *fr.* XIV. NBE
Wordsworth's Early Reading, *fr.* V. MOB
Prelude: "Along the roadside, like the flowers of gold." Whittier. *Fr.* Among the Hills. CoBA; OxBA; PoEL-4
Prelude: "As one, at midnight, wakened by the call." W. W. Gibson. MBP; MoBrPo
(Proem.) LBBV
Prelude: "Between the green bud and the red." Swinburne. *See* Prelude to "Songs before Sunrise."
Prelude: "Dim, gradual thinning of the shapeless gloom." Siegfried Sassoon. *See* Troops, The.
Prelude: "Hush'd is each [busy] shout." A. C. Benson. LEAP; OBVV
Prelude: "I have eaten your bread and salt." Kipling. *Fr.* Departmental Ditties. BPN

Prelude: "I saw the constellated matin choir." Edmund Clarence Stedman. AA
Prelude: "Love, that is first and last of all things made." Swinburne. *See* Tristram and Iseult.
Prelude: "My muse dwelleth not on Parnassus. Erik Axel Karlfeldt, *tr. fr. Swedish by* Charles W. Stork. *Fr.* Fridolin's Pleasure-Garden. AnSL
Prelude: "Night was dark, though sometimes a faint star, The." Richard Watson Gilder. *See* Dawn.
Prelude: "North-east spends his rage, The." James Thomson. *Fr.* The Seasons: Spring. CoEV
Prelude: "Not only around our infancy." James Russell Lowell. *See* Not Only around Our Infancy.
Prelude: "Once on a time from all the Circles seven." Ferid ed-Din Attar, *tr. fr. Persian by* Edward Fitzgerald. *Fr.* The Bird-Parliament. PeP
Prelude: "Over his keys." James Russell Lowell. *Fr.* The Vision of Sir Launfal. APW; BAP; LiTA; LiTG
Prelude: "Ponder the tone, the broken theme." Robert Hillyer. *See* Ponder the Tone . . .
Prelude: "Rimbaud and Verlaine, precious pair of poets." Conrad Aiken. *Fr.* Preludes for Memnon, LVI. FaBoMo; NAMP; PtP
(Preludes to Attitude, V.) LiTA; TwAmPo
Prelude, A: "Spirit that moves the sap in spring." Maurice Thompson. HBV; LBAP
Prelude: "Still south I went and west and south again." J. M. Synge. AWP; ChTr; HBMV; JAWP; MBP; MoBrPo; NeMA; OBMV; PoFr; TSW; WBP
Prelude LII: "Stood, at the closed door, and remembered." Conrad Aiken. *See* One-eyed Calendar.
Prelude: "Tell us a story, old Robin Gray!" Robert Southey. ERP
Prelude: "That word which never appears." José Gorostiza, *tr. fr. Spanish by* H. R. Hays. TwSpPo
Prelude: "Thing long sought, A." Neil Tracy. BoCaPo
Prelude: "This fugitive between the earth and sky." Tu Fu, *tr. fr. Chinese by* Hsieh Wen Tung. WhP
Prelude: "This is not you?" Conrad Aiken. Preludes for Memnon, VI. MAP; MoAB; MoAmPo
Prelude: "This short straight sword." R. A. K. Mason. AnNZ
Prelude: "Though black the night, I know upon the sky." John Drinkwater. TCPD
Prelude: "Time draws nigh when I shall go forth, The," Steen Steensen Blicher, *tr. fr. Danish by* Charles W. Stork. *Fr.* Birds of Passage. BoDS
Prelude: Tristram and Iseult. Swinburne. *See* Tristram and Iseult.
Prelude: Troops, The. Siegfried Sassoon. *See* Troops, The.
Prelude: "Wailful sweetness of the violin, The." Francis Thompson. *Fr.* Ode to the Setting Sun. VLEP
(Ode to the Setting Sun.) EmBrPo; GoBC
Prelude XXIII: "We are those same children who amazed." Stefan George, *tr. fr. German by* C. F. MacIntyre. WaaP
Prelude: "What in these lines doth ripened stand." Clemens Brentano. *See* Prelude: "Whatever ripened in these lines."
Prelude: "What makes a plenteous harvest." Virgil, *tr. fr. Latin by* Dryden. *Fr.* Georgics. AWP
Prelude: "What shall we do—what shall we think—what shall we say?" Conrad Aiken. Preludes for Memnon, XXIX. FaBoMo
Prelude: "Whatever ripened in these lines." Clemens Brentano, *tr. fr. German by* Werner Heider. LiTW
(Prelude: "What in these lines doth ripened stand," *tr. by* Mabel Cotterell.) AnGP
Prelude: "When first we met, our souls stood up." Jamie Sexton Holme. LoPS
Prelude: "Winter evening settles down, The." T. S. Eliot. Preludes, I. AmPP; ExPo; GBV (1952 ed.); MAP; MoAmPo (1942 ed.); MoShBr; NeMA; ShBV-3; TiPo (1952 ed.)
(Preludes.) AnAmPo; BAV; BoLiVe (1945 ed.); CoBA; GTBS-W; InP; LA; LiTA; LiTM; OBMV; PoFS; ReMP; UnPo; VOD (1935 ed.)
Prelude: "Winter for a moment takes the mind." Conrad Aiken. Preludes for Memnon, I. LiTM; NP; OxBA
(Preludes to Attitude, IV.) LiTA; TwAmPo
Prelude: "Words, words, ye are like birds." Josephine Preston Peabody. AA
Prelude: "You went to the verge, you say, and came back safely?" Conrad Aiken. Preludes for Memnon, XIV. TwCV
(Preludes to Attitude, III.) LiTA; LiTG; TwAmPo
Prelude: "Youth was there, of quiet ways, A." Longfellow. *Fr.* Tales of a Wayside Inn: The Wayside Inn, Pt. I. LEAP; TCAP, *longer sel.*
Prelude for Spring. Dorothy Livesay. BoCaPo; PeCV; TwCV
Prelude from "The Vision of Sir Launfal." James Russell Lowell. *See* Prelude: "Over his keys."
Prelude of the New Testament ("Hail Mary full of grace!"). St. Luke, I: 28, 38, 42, II: 10–11, 14, Bible, *N.T.* (*Douay vers.*). CAW
Prelude to an Evening. John Crowe Ransom. CoBMV; MAP; MoAB; MoAmPo; MoPo; MoVE; NePA; OxBA
Prelude to Cricket. Thomas Moult. POTE
Prelude to "Departmental Ditties." Kipling. BPN
Prelude to Hope. Vicente Huidobro, *tr. fr. Spanish by* H. R. Hays. TwSpPo
Prelude to Objects. Wallace Stevens. CoV
Prelude to Revel. Euripides, *tr. fr. Greek by* H. H. Milman. *Fr.* Bacchae. GrR
Prelude to "Songs before Sunrise." Swinburne. EmBrPo; PoVP; TCPD; ViP; ViPo
Prelude to "The Earthly Paradise." William Morris. *See* Apology, An: "Of Heaven or Hell . . ."
Prelude to this smooth scene—mark well, The. After Jena. Thomas Hardy. *Fr.* The Dynasts. WaaP
Prelude to "Tristram of Lyonesse." Swinburne. *See* Tristram and Iseult.
Preludes (I–IV). T. S. Eliot. AmP; AnAmPo; BAV; BoLiVe (1945 ed.); CoBA; GTBS-W; InP; LA; LiTA; LiTM; MoVE; OBMV; PoFS; ReMP; SeCePo; TwP; UnPo
Sels.
"Morning comes to consciousness, The," II. VOD (1935 ed.)
"Winter evening settles down, The," I. MoShBr; TiPo (1952 ed.); VOD (1935 ed.)
(Prelude.) AmPP; ExPo; GBV (1952 ed.); MAP; MoAmPo (1942 ed.); NeMA; ShBV-3
Preludes. Coventry Patmore. *See* Attainment, The, *and* Unthrift.
Preludes for Memnon, *sels.* Conrad Aiken.
"Beloved, let us once more praise the rain," VII. *Also in* Preludes to Attitude, VIII. LiTA; TwAmPo
"First note, simple, The," XXI. *Also in* Preludes to Attitude, X. LiTA; TwAmPo
"Keep in the heart the journal nature keeps," XLII. ChMo; CMP; NePA; OxBA
"Nothing to say, you say?" LIII. *Also in* Preludes to Attitude, IX. LiTA; TwAmPo
"One star fell and another," LVII. MAP; MoAmPo; PreP
"Rimbaud and Verlaine, precious pair of poets," LVI. *Also in* Preludes to Attitude, V. FaBoMo; LiTA; LiTM (rev. ed.); MoPo; NAMP; NePA; PtP; TwAmPo
"Sleep; and between the closed eyelids," III. *Also in* Preludes to Attitude, II. LiTA; LiTG; TwAmPo
"So, in the evening, to the simple cloister," XX. *Also in* Preludes to Attitude, VI. LiTA; TwAmPo
(Cloister.) MAP; MoAB; MoAmPo
"Stood, at the closed door," LII. LiTM
(One-eyed Calendar.) BLV
"Then came I to the shoreless shore of silence," XXXIII. *Also in* Preludes to Attitude, VII. LiTA; NePA; OxBA; TwAmPo
"This is not you?" VI. MAP; MoAB; MoAmPo
"Time has come, the clock says time has come, The," XXVIII. NePA; OxBA
"Two coffees in the Espanol," II. *Also in* Preludes to Attitude, I. LiTA; LiTG; TwAmPo
"Watch long enough, and you will see the leaf," XIX. ChMo; CMP; NePA; OxBA
"What shall we do—what shall we think—what shall we say?" XXIX. FaBoMo
"Winter for a moment takes the mind," I. *Also in* Preludes to Attitude. IV. LiTA; LiTM; MoPo; MoVE; NP; OxBA; TwAmPo
"You went to the verge, you say," XIV. *Also in* Preludes to Attitude, III. LiTA; LiTG; TwAmPo; TwCV
Preludes to Attitude. Conrad Aiken. LiTA; TwAmPo
Sels.
"Rimbaud and Verlaine, precious pair of poets," V. *Also in* Preludes for Memnon, LVI. FaBoMo; LiTM; MoPo; NAMP; NePA; PtP
"Sleep; and between the closed eyelids," II. *Also in* Preludes for Memnon, III. LiTG
"So, in the evening, to the simple cloister," VI. *Also in* Preludes for Memnon, XX.
(Cloister.) MAP; MoAB; MoAmPo
"Then came I to the shoreless shore of silence," VII. *Also in* Preludes for Memnon, XXXIII. NePA; OxBA
"Two coffees in the Español," I. *Also in* Preludes for Memnon, II. LiTG
"Winter for a moment takes the mind," IV. *Also in* Preludes for Memnon, I. LiTM; MoPo; NP; OxBA
"You went to the verge you say," III. *Also in* Preludes for Memnon, XIV. LiTG; TwCV
Preludes to Definition. Conrad Aiken. *See* Time in the Rock.
Prematurity. Constance Mercer Klugh. CAG
Premonition. Laura Goodman Salverson. CaP
Prentice Boy, The. *Unknown.* ABS
Preoccupation with Death. Charles Fisher. MoWP
Preparation. Thomas Edward Brown. OBEV (new ed.); OBVV; TOP; VLEP

Preparation of the Pyre for Patroclus. Homer. *See* Pyre of Patroclus, The.
Preparations. *Unknown.* *See* Yet If His Majesty, Our Sovereign Lord.
Preparative, The. Thomas Traherne. OxBoCh; PoEL-2
Prepare. Witter Bynner. PGD
Prepare for songs; he's come, he's come. The New-Yeeres Gift, or Circumcisions Song, Sung to the King in the Presence at White Hall. Robert Herrick. SeCV-1
Prepare, prepare the iron helm of war. A War Song to Englishmen. Blake. *Fr.* King Edward the Third. BHV; CH; MeRV; OHIP; RO; WaaP
Prepared for a Soldiers' and Sailors' Monument in Boston. James Russell Lowell. TOP
("To those who died for her on land and sea.") InP
Preparedness. Edwin Markham. FaFP; MAP; MoAmPo; NeMA; OQP; PoeMoYo; PYM; QP-1; YT
Preparedness. Jean Grigsby Paxton. PGD
Preparing me chicken and rice, old friend. Stopping at a Friend's Farm-House. Meng Hao-jan. BoFr
Prepayre you, Parrot, bravely your passage to take. Salutation to Cardinal Wolsey. John Skelton. *Fr.* Speke, Parrot. CoEV
Pre-Raphaelite, A/ Had to have things right. Christopher Morley. WhC
Presage. Thomas Thornely. QS
Presage and caveat not only seem. The Window Sill. Robert Graves. AtBAP; EnLoPo
Presage of Storme. George Chapman. *Fr.* Eugenia. FaBoEn
Presaging. Rainer Maria Rilke, *tr. fr. German by* Jessie Lemont. AWP; JAWP; TrJP; WBP
Presbyterian Church Government. Samuel Butler. *Fr.* Hudibras, I, 3. OBS
Presbyterian Knight [and Independent Squire], *abr.* Samuel Butler. *Fr.* Hudibras, I, 1. CoEV; OBS
(Hudibras, the Presbyterian Knight, *abr.*) OxBoLi; SiTL
(Logic of Hudibras.) LPS-3
(Metaphysical Sectarian, The.) MeLP
(Portrait of Hudibras.) AtBAP; PoEL-3
Presbyterian Wedding, The. *Unknown.* CoMu
Presbyterians, The. Dryden. *Fr.* The Hind and the Panther, I. OBS
Prescience. Thomas Bailey Aldrich. AA; OBVV
Prescience. Donald Jeffrey Hayes. PoNe
Prescience. Harold Vinal. MuM
Prescience. Margaret Widdemer. HBMV
Prescott, press my Ascot waistcoat. Ascot Waistcoat. David McCord. FiBHP
Prescription for a Spring Morning, A. John Davidson. *Fr.* Fleet Street Eclogues. CBPC
(From "Fleet Street Eclogues.") LEAP
Prescription of Painful Ends. Robinson Jeffers. CoV; LiTA; MoAB; MoAmPo; OxBA
Presence, A. Kenneth Slade Alling. QS
Presence, The. Robert Graves. ChMP
Presence. Edith Willis Linn. UnW
Presence. Mary E. McCullough. MaRV
Presence of an External Master of Knowledge. Wallace Stevens. NePA
Presence of Mind. Harry Graham. WhC
Presence of Snow. Melville Cane. GoYe
Presence of the Spirit, The. Giulio Salvadori, *tr. fr. Spanish by* Thomas Walsh. CAW
Presences of Nature in Boyhood. Wordsworth. *See* Fair Seed-Time Had My Soul.
Presences Perfected. Siegfried Sassoon. MBP; MoBrPo
Present, The. Adelaide Anne Procter. WGRP
Present Age, The. Arthur Cleveland Coxe. BLPA; MaRV
Present Crisis, The. James Russell Lowell. BAP; CoBA; GrCo-1, *abr.*; IAP; MaRV; OHFP; OQP, *abr.*; QP-1, *abr.*
Sels.
"Count me o'er earth's chosen heroes." WGRP
"Once to every man and nation comes the moment to decide," *abr.* APW
(Once to Every Man and Nation.) OlF
"When a deed is done for freedom," *abr.* PSO
Present Evening, The. Eugenio Florit, *tr. fr. Spanish by* H. R. Hays. TwSpPo
Present Heaven, The. Jones Very. *See* Spirit-Land, The.
Present in Absence. John Hoskins. *See* Absence.
Presentiment. Ambrose Bierce. AA
Presentiment is that long shadow on the lawn. Emily Dickinson. CoV; FaBoEn; InPo; OxBA
(Presentiment.) AmPP; BAP; MOAP
Presenting to a Lady a White Rose and a Red, on the Tenth of June. William Somervile. AEV; CEP
(On Presenting to a Lady a White Rose and a Red on the Tenth of June.) OBEC
Presents. Marchette Chute. BrR; ChBR; SiSoSe; StVeCh
Preserve a respectful demeanor. To a Baked Fish. Carolyn Wells. FiBHP
Preserve that old kettle, so blackened and worn. My Dad's Dinner Pail. Edward Harrigan. BLPA
Preserve thy sighs, unthrifty girl [*or* girle]! The Soldier [*or* Souldier] Going to the Field. Sir William Davenant. EV-2; MePo
Preserve us, Lord, by thy dear Word. Turk and Pope. Robert Wisdom. ReIE
President, The. Charles H. L. Johnston. PTA-2
President Garfield. Longfellow. PAH
President Garfield, *parody. Unknown.* PA
President Lincoln's Grave. Caroline Atherton Briggs Mason. DD; GA; OHIP
President Ordains the Bee to Be, The. Wallace Stevens. *Fr.* Notes toward a Supreme Fiction. AtBAP; LiTA
Press close, bare-bosom'd night—press close magnetic nourishing night! Earth at Night [*or* Bare-Bosm'd Night]. Walt Whitman. *Fr.* Song of Myself. PIAE; SN
Press-Gang, The. *Unknown.* CBPC; ChTr; SG
Press [*or* Presse] me not to take more pleasure. The Rose. George Herbert. AtBAP; LiTB; PoEL-2
Press of the Spoon River *Clarion* was wrecked, The. Carl Hamblin. Edgar Lee Masters. *Fr.* Spoon River Anthology. AmP; ChMo; CMP; LiTA; LiTM (rev. ed.)
Press Onward. *Unknown.* FaFP
Presse me not to take more pleasure. *See* Press me not . . .
Pressed Gentian, The. Whittier. AnAmPo; LA
Prest by the load of life, the weary mind. Prologue. Samuel Johnson. *Fr.* The Good-natur'd Man (*by* Goldsmith). LoBV
Prest down with sorrow, Lord, not for my sin. Meditation Thirty. Edward Taylor. *Fr.* Sacramental Meditations. CoV
Presto Furioso. Sir Owen Seaman. BOHV
Presto, pronto! Two boys, two horses. Boy Riding Forward Backward. Robert Francis. NePoAm-2
Presumption. Eileen Duggan. CAW; SaFP
Presumptuous, The. W. H. Auden. *Fr.* The Quest. ChMo
Pretences. Ibn Rashiq, *tr. fr. Arabic by* A. J. Arberry. MooP
Pretender yields the crown, The. The Striking of the Tent. Ibn al-Khabbaza. MooP
Pretense. Helen Welshimer. PoMa
Pretext. Yakamochi, *tr. fr. Japanese by* Arthur Waley. *Fr.* Manyo Shu. WoL
("By way of pretext.") AWP; JAWP; LiTW; WBP
Prettiest girl that ever I saw, The. Sucking Cider through a Straw. *Unknown.* AS
Prettiest lady that ever I've seen, The. Pretty Lady. Rose Fyleman. BoTP
Prettiest Things, The. Camilla Doyle. YT
Pretty a Day, A. E. E. Cummings. ChMo
Pretty as a posy. Ritual. Ibn Abd Rabbihi. MooP
Pretty bright flags have we. Flag Play. *Unknown.* FOAH
Pretty brook was running at play, A. *Unknown.* GFA
Pretty Cow. Ann *or* Jane Taylor. *See* Cow, The.
Pretty Fair Maid, A. *Unknown.* *See* Sweetheart in the Army, A.
Pretty fair miss all in the garden, A. The Love Token. *Unknown.* BaBo
Pretty flowers, tell me why. The Flowers. *Unknown.* OTPC (1923 ed.)
Pretty Futility. Elizabeth J. Coatsworth. MAP
Pretty game, my girl, A. The Flirt. W. H. Davies. EnLoPo
Pretty Girl of Loch Dan, The. Sir Samuel Ferguson. HBV; LPS-1
Pretty good firm is "Watch & Waite," A. The Best Firm. Walter G. Doty. HBV; HBVY; RIS
Pretty John Watts. *Unknown.* OxNR
Pretty Lady. Rose Fyleman. BoTP
Pretty little boy and a pretty little girl, A. Courtesy. Mary Mapes Dodge. BrR
Pretty little crocus, in your cosy bed. Waking Up. *Unknown.* BoTP
Pretty Little Maiden, The. *Unknown.* MeMeAg
Pretty Maid, The. Paul Fort. *See* Ballade: "Pretty maid, she died, she died . . . , The."
Pretty Maid. *Unknown.* OTPC; OxNR
Pretty maid both kind and fair, A. The Very Pretty Maid of This Town, and the Amorous 'Squire Not One Hundred Miles from the Place. *Unknown.* CoMu
Pretty Maid Marion. Ivy O. Eastwick. BoTP
Pretty maid, pretty maid, where have you been? Pretty Maid. *Unknown.* OTPC; OxNR
Pretty maid she died, she died, in love-bed as she lay, The. Ballade [*or* The Pretty Maid]. Paul Fort. AWP; JAWP; OBMV; WBP
Pretty Maids Beware! *Unknown.* CoMu
Pretty Miss Apathy. Pooh! Walter de la Mare. FiBHP
Pretty Mohea [*or* Maumee], The. *Unknown.* *See* Little Mohee, The.
"Pretty Moo-cow, will you tell." The Cow. Mrs. Motherly. PPL; SAS
Pretty Nossis vows that she. Nossis, *tr. fr. Greek by* the Earl of Cromer. GrPo
Pretty Phoebe Lane and I. Dropping Corn. Maurice Thompson. PR
Pretty Polly. E. Merrill Root. BLA; MAP

Pretty Polly ("Go get me some of your father's gold"), *with music. Unknown.* AS
Pretty Polly ("I courted pretty Polly the livelong night"), *with music. Unknown.* OuSiCo
Pretty Polly Pansy. Polly Pansy. William Brighty Rands. SAS
"Pretty Polly, pretty Polly, come go 'long with me." The Gosport Tragedy (B *vers.*). *Unknown.* BaBo
Pretty rabbits are so tame, The. Our Baby's Rabbits. *Unknown.* SAS
Pretty red Squirrel lives up in a tree, The. The Squirrel. Mary Howitt. BoTP
Pretty Redhead, The. Guillaume Apollinaire, *tr. fr. French by* Kate Flores. AnFP
Pretty sneaking knave I knew, A. Mr. Cromek. Blake. ChTr
Pretty task, A; and so I told the Fool. Epilogue. Dryden. *Fr.* Aureng-Zebe. SeEP
Pretty task, Miss S——, to ask, A. I'm Not a Single Man [*or* Lines in a Young Lady's Album]. Thomas Hood. ALV; HBV
Pretty Twinkling Starry Eyes. Nicholas Breton. *Fr.* The Passionate Shepherd. ElL
Pretty Wantons. *Unknown.* ElL
Pretty Words. Elinor Wylie. HBMV; YaD; YT
Pretty young actress, a stammerer, A. Limerick. Eille Norwood. CenHV
Prevailing Prayer. Richard Chenevix Trench. *See* Prayer: "Lord, what a change . . ."
Prevailing Winds. Lee Anderson. TwAmPo
Prevalent Poetry. Charles Follen Adams. CenHV
Prevesa. Kostas Kariotakis, *tr. fr. Modern Greek by* Rae Dalven. MoGP
Prevision. Aline Kilmer. SBMV
Prevision. Ada Foster Murray. HBV; LBAP
Priam. Dudley Fitts. OnHM
Priam and Achilles. Homer, *tr. fr. Greek. Fr.* The Iliad, XXIV. OBEC, *tr. by* Pope; OBS, *tr. by* George Chapman; OxBG, *tr. by* Robert Bridges
(Priam at the Feet of Achilles, *tr. by* the Earl of Derby.) GrR
(Priam's Prayer to Achilles, *tr. by* Robert Bridges.) LiA
Priam and Helen on the Wall. Homer, *tr. fr. Greek by* F. L. Lucas. *Fr.* The Iliad, III. GrPE
("And then came Iris as a messenger," *shorter sel., tr. by* H. N. Couch.) GrPo
Priapus. Hilda Doolittle ("H. D."). *See* Orchard.
Priapus and the Pool, *sels.* Conrad Aiken.
And Already the Minutes, V [VI]. InPo; MOAP
Fade, Then, XVII [XX]. MOAP
See, as the Carver Carves a Rose, XVI [XIX]. AnAmPo; LA; MM; PFY
(Carver, The.) HBMV
There Is Nothing Moving There, IX [X]. ChMo; CMP; MOAP
"There was an island in the sea," XV [XVIII]. ChMo; CMP
This Is the Shape of the Leaf, IV [V]. AnAmPo; AtBAP; ChMo; CMP; HBMV; LA; MAPA; MOAP; NePA; OxBA; TBM; TrGrPo; WHA
(Portrait of a Girl.) MAP; MoAmPo; TSW
When Trout Swim down Great Ormond Street, III [IV]. AnAmPo; InPo; LA; MAPA; MOAP; PFY; TBM
(Whim.) TSW
Why Is It, VII [VIII]. MOAP
Priapus, with his god's virility. Design for a List of Pictures. Arthur Symons. FaBoTw
Price, The. John Davidson. CaAE
Price He Paid, The. Ella Wheeler Wilcox. WBLP
Price of Begging, The. Emmanuel ben David Frances, *tr. fr. Hebrew by* A. B. Rhine. TrJP
Price of Experience, The. Blake. *Fr.* Vala; or, The Four Zoas. EnRP; RO
Price of Wisdom, The. Job, XXVIII: 1-28, Bible, *O.T.* TrGrPo
Prices. Louis Ginsberg. TrJP
Prickly pears stick out their tongues at us, The. Journey. Salvador Novo. AnCL
Pride. Josephine Miles. FiMAP
Pride and ambition, and peevishness too. Song. *Unknown.* SeCL
Pride held my will. The Help-Givers. Laurence Housman. MaRV
Pride Is the Canker. *Unknown. See* Do Not, Oh, Do Not Prize.
Pride it was that laid Magnesia low. Pride of the Flesh. Theognis. GrL; OxBG
Pride of a Jew, The. Judah Halevi, *tr. fr. Hebrew by* Israel Cohen. TrJP
Pride of Battery B, The. Frank H. Gassaway. BlG; PTA-2
Pride of every grove I chose, The. The Garland. Matthew Prior. SeCL
Pride of the Flesh. Theognis, *tr. fr. Greek by* T. F. Higham. GrL; OxBG
Pride of Youth. Dante Gabriel Rossetti. The House of Life, XXIV. BPN; FaBoEn; PoVP; ViPo; ViPP
Pride of Youth, The. Sir Walter Scott. *See* Proud Maisie.
Priest, A. Norman Gale. VA
Priest, The. James Oppenheim. *Fr.* Night. MaRV
(My Father's House.) QS
Priest and Pagan. Albert Durrant Watson. CaP; CPG; OCL
Priest and the Mulberry Tree, The. Thomas Love Peacock. *Fr.* Crotchet Castle. BoTP; CG; EV-4; GN; OTPC; RIS; StPo; TVSH
Priest and the Pirate, The. Hervey Allen. LS
Priest Is Come and the Candles Burn, The. John Richard Moreland. PR
Priest of Coloony, The. W. B. Yeats. OnYI
Priest of God, unto thee I come. Absolution. Edward Willard Watson. AA
Priest of the springtime's Koran. Viktor Khlebnikov, *tr. fr. Russian by* C. M. Bowra. BoRS
Priest or Poet. Shane Leslie. CAW; WGRP
Priest performs rites: let there be silence during the rites, The. Propertius. Elegies, IV, 6. LaP
Priest Rediscovers His Psalm-Book, The. *Unknown, tr. fr. Irish by* Frank O'Connor. KiLC
Priestcraft and Private Judgement. Dryden. *Fr.* Religio Laici. OBS
Priesthood, The. Yvor Winters. NP
Priest-mannerly the mind. Missa Vocis. R. P. Blackmur. ReMP
Priests and Soldiers, The. *Unknown.* PSO
Priests and the Friars, The. *Unknown, tr. fr. Irish by* Douglas Hyde. GTIV; MeRV
Priest's Chant, The. John Fletcher. *See* Evening Song.
Priest's Lament, The. Robert Hugh Benson. ACP
Priests of Apollo, sacred be the Roome. The Sacrifice to Apollo. Michael Drayton. OBS; SeEP
Priest's Prayer, A. Martha Dickinson Bianchi. AA
Priest's Song, A. Thomas Dekker. *Fr.* Old Fortunatus. OBSC
(O Pittie.) AtBAP
(Song: "Virtue's branches wither, virtue pines.") ElL; SiCE
Prim old room where memories stir, A. In an Old Nursery. Patrick R. Chalmers. HBMV; VOD
Primacy of Dullness, The. Dryden. *See* Shadwell.
Primal Cause, The. Dante, *tr. fr. Italian by* Longfellow. *Fr.* Divina Commedia: Paradiso, XXVIII. CAW
Primaleon of Greece, *sel.* Anthony Munday.
To Colin Clout. CenL; ElSeCe; OAEP; OBSC; TuPP; ViBoPo
(Beauty Bathing.) EV-1; OBEV; PG (1955 ed.)
(Beauty Sat Bathing by a Spring.) ElL
(Colin.) GTBS; GTBS-D; GTBS-W; GTSE; GTSL
Prime. W. H. Auden. PoLFOT
Prime. Amy Lowell. VOD
Prime cantante! My Catbird. William Henry Venable. AA; BAP; BLA; HBV; PFY
Prime indignity of solitude. The Sandpiper. Ivan Swift. BLA
Prime of Life, The. Walter Learned. HBV
Primer. Samuel Hoffenstein. BOHV
Primer Lesson. Carl Sandburg. FaPON; MAP; MoAmPo; MoShBr; StVeCh; TSW; TSWC
Primer of Plato. Jean Garrigue. MoVE
Primeval Forest. Longfellow. *See* Prologue to "Evangeline."
Primeval night had repossessed. Festum Nativitatis. Aubrey Thomas De Vere. IrPN
Primitiae. William Drummond of Hawthornden. *See* Sonnet: "Alexis, here she stayed; among these pines."
Primitive Man. Moschion, *tr. fr. Greek by* George Allen. OxBG
Primo Vere. Giosuè Carducci, *tr. fr. Italian by* John Bailey. AWP; JAWP; WBP
Primrose, The. John Clare. *See* To a Primrose.
Primrose, The. Robert Herrick. EM-1; EV-2; HBV; OBEV; ViBoPo
Primrose by a river's brim, A. The Amateur Botanist. Franklin P. Adams. PreP
Primrose by the Wayside, A. Anna Bunston de Bary. MaRV
Primrose Dame, A. Gleeson White. HBV; VA
Primrose has her gentle root, The. Unity. Eva Gore-Booth. DiM
Primrose Hill. Olive Custance. JKCP
Primrose Hill. Rose Fyleman. BoTP
Primrose in the green forest, The. Song. Thomas Deloney. *Fr.* The Gentle Craft. AlDL; TiPo (1959 ed.); ViBoPo
Primrose in the sheade do blow, The. *See* Primrwose in the sheade do blow, The.
Primrose of the Rock, The. Wordsworth. BPN
Primroses. Alfred Austin. BMEP; OBVV
Primroses, The. W. Graham Robertson. ADAH
Primrwose [*or* Primrose] in the sheade do blow, The. Blackmwore Maidens. William Barnes. EPN; EV-4; GTBS; HBV; PoVP; ShBV-3; VA
Prince, The. Josephine Dodge Daskam Bacon. BAP; LBMV

Prince, The. Walter de la Mare. LiL
Prince Adeb. George Henry Boker. LPS-2
Prince Aladdin of the Lamp. Gustaf Fröding, *tr. fr. Swedish by* Charles W. Stork. AnSL
Prince and bishop and knight and dame. The Losers [*or* The Pawns]. William Young. *Fr.* Wishmakers' Town. AA; HBMV
Prince Arthur. Spenser. *Fr.* The Faerie Queene, I, 7. OBSC
Prince Athanese, *sel.* Shelley.
"'Twas at the season when the earth upsprings." CBE
Prince Bailè of Ulster rode out in the morn. The Noble Lay of Aillinn. Stopford Augustus Brooke. TIP
Prince Finikin. Kate Greenaway. SAS
Prince Heathen (A *and* B *vers.*). *Unknown.* ESPB
Prince Lucifer, *sels.* Alfred Austin.
Grave-Digger's Song. VA
(Elegy: "Crab, the bullace and the sloe, The.") BMEP
Mother-Song. BOL; MOAH; VA
(Mother-Song from "Prince Lucifer.") HBV
Prince of Life, The. John Oxenham. TrPWD
Prince of my People, Oedipus the king. Oedipus, King-Saviour. Sophocles. *Fr.* Oedipus Rex. GrR
Prince of Parthia, The, *sel.* Thomas Godfrey.
Evanthe's Invitation. NoCaPo
Prince of Peace, The. Micah, V: 2, Isaiah, IX: 2, Bible, *O.T.* ChrBoLe
Prince of Peace, The. Edward Henry Bickersteth. BePJ
Prince of Peace, The. Philip Doddridge. MaRV
Prince of Peace, The. Harry Emerson Fosdick. MaRV; TrPWD
Prince of Wales' Marriage. *Unknown.* CoMu
Prince Peter. Nancy Byrd Turner. GaP; RIS
Prince Riquet's Song. Stopford Augustus Brooke. *Fr.* Riquet of the Tuft. VA
Prince Robert. *Unknown.* ESPB (A *and* B *vers.*); LoEn; OBB, *sl. abr.*
Prince Rupert's drop, paper muslin ghost. Pedantic Literalist. Marianne Moore. APA; CoAnAm
Prince Tatters. Laura E. Richards. GaP; HBV; HBVY; MPB; TVSH
Prince William, of the Brunswick race. The Royal Adventurer. Philip Freneau. PAH
Princely Ditty in Praise of the English Rose, A. Thomas Deloney. BoTP
"Princes!—and you, most valorous." The Prodigals. Austin Dobson. InP
Prince's Progress, The. Christina Rossetti. EmBrPo; EV-5
"Too late for love, too late for joy," *sel.* ViBoPo
(Bride Song.) EPP; OBEV; OBVV; TOP
(Too Late for Love.) PoVP
Prince's Quest, The, *sel.* Sir William Watson.
"About him was a ruinous fair place." BMEP
Princes statue, A, or in marble carv'd. George Chapman. *Fr.* The Epistle Dedicatory to Chapman's Translation of the Iliad. AtBAP; OBS
Princes, what grief hath set the jaundice on your cheeks. Agamemnon and Nestor. Shakespeare. *Fr.* Troilus and Cressida, I, iii. EV-1
Princess, The. Björnstjerne Björnson, *tr. fr. Norwegian by* Charles W. Stork. AnNoLy
Princess, The. C. Ethel Evans. VOD
Princess, The, *sels.* Tennyson.
"As thro' [*or* through] the land at eve we went," *fr.* Pt. I. AnFE; AtBAP; BPN; EV-5; GTBS; GTBS-W; LiTB; LiTG; LiTL; MaRV; OBVV; PoVP; TreFS; VA
(Reconciliation, The.) HBV
(Songs from "The Princess.") MotAn; OAEP; ViPo; VLEP
(We Kiss'd Again with Tears.) PoToHe
"Ask me no more: the moon may draw the sea," *fr.* Pt. VI. AnFE; AtBAP; BoLiVe; BPN; EM-2; EnLi-2; EnLit; EPN; GEPC; GTBS-W; HBV; LiTB; MaPo; PIR; PoEL-5; PoVP; REAL; TrGrPo; VA; ViPP
(Songs from "The Princess.") EmBrPo; MotAn; OAEP; ViPo; VLEP
Bugle Song, *fr.* Pt. III. ATP; BEL; BoChLi; BTP; CBOV; EnLit; FaPON; GN; HBV; MCCG; MPB; MW; PCD; PECK; PFE; PG (1945 ed.); PTA-1; RG; StVeCh; TreF; VA
(Blow, Bugle, Blow.) BLV; BMEP; CBPC; ChTr; FaFP; GTBS-W; LiTB; LiTG; OBEV; TSW; TSWC; UnS
(Bugle, The.) LPS-2; ShBV-2
(From "The Princess.") LEAP
(Horns of Elfland, The.) GBV
(Lyrics from "The Princess.") OuHeWo
(Our Echoes Roll from Soul to Soul.) MaRV
(Song: "Splendor [*or* Splendour] falls on castle walls, The.") AlDL; CaAE; ExPo; LoBV; NeHB; ThWaDe; TOP
(Songs from "The Princess.") AWP; EmBrPo; GEPC; InPo; JAWP; OAEP; PIR; ViPo; WBP
(Splendor [*or* Splendour] Falls [on Castle Walls], The.) AnFE; AtBAP; BoLiVe; BPN; CH; CoBE; EM-2; EnL; EnLi-2; EPN; EV-5; FaBoCh; FiP; GTBS; GTBS-D; GTML; GTSL; InP; LoGBV; OBVV; OQP; OTPC; PoE; PoEL-5; PoVP; QP-2; REAL; TCEP; TrGrPo; TVSH; TyEnPo; ViBoPo; ViPP
Come Down, O Maid [from Yonder Mountain Height], *fr.* Pt. VII. AnEnPo; AnFE; ATBAP; BrBE; EG; EmBrPo; EnL; EV-5; GTBS; MaPo; OBEV; OBVV; PIR; PoE; PoVP; RiBV; TOP; ViBoPo; ViPo; ViPP; WHA
(From "The Princess.") LEAP
(Idyl, An.) TrGrPo
(Shepherd's Song.) LoBV
(Song.) FaBoEn
(Songs from "The Princess.") EnLi-2; MotAn; OAEP; SeCeV; VLEP
"'Come out,' he said," *fr.* Prologue. EnSW
"Deep in the night I woke: she, near me, held," *fr.* Pt. VII. ReTS
Home They Brought Her Warrior Dead, *fr.* Pt. V. BEL; BHV; BoLiVe; BPN; EM-2; EnLi-2; EPN; EV-5; HBV; LPS-1; MaRV; OTPC (1923 ed.); PoVP; PTA-2; TreFS; TrGrPo; ViPP
(From "The Princess.") LEAP
(Lyrics from "The Princess.") OuHeWo
(Songs from "The Princess.") EmBrPo; OAEP; ViPo; VLEP
(Widow and Child.) MOAH
"I loved her, one/ Not learned, save in gracious household ways," *fr.* Pt. VII. PGD
(Happy He with Such a Mother.) PSO
"Now sleeps the crimson petal, now the white," *fr.* Pt. VII. AnFE; AtBAP; BoLiVe; BrBE; ChER; ChTr; EnL; EnLi-2; EPN; EV-5; FiP; GEPC; GTBS-D; KN; LoPS; MaPo; OBVV; PoE; PoEL-5; PoFS; PoVP; ReaPo; ShBV-3; TrGrPo; ViBoPo; ViPP
(From "The Princess.") LEAP
(Song: "Now sleeps the crimson petal, now the white.") CaAE; ExPo; FaBoBe; LoBV; NeHB
(Songs from "The Princess.") EmBrPo; MotAn; OAEP; SeCeV; ViPo; VLEP
(Summer Night.) EtPaEn; OBEV; SeCePo; UnPo (1st ed.)
"O Swallow, Swallow, flying, flying south," *fr.* Pt. IV. AtBAP; BMEP; BPN; EV-5; GTBS; GTSL; HBV; LPS-1; PoVP
(From "The Princess.") LEAP
(Songs from "The Princess.") MotAn; ViPo; VLEP
"Our enemies have fallen, have fallen: the seed," *fr.* Pt. VI. BHV; PoVP
(Songs from "The Princess.") MotAn; VLEP
"Sweet and low, sweet and low," *fr.* Pt. II. BEL; BMEP; BoChLi; BoTP; BPN; BTP; CBPC; CoBE; EnLi-2; EnLit; EPN; EtS; EV-5; FaBoBe; FaPON; GEPC; GFA; GoTP; InP; MCCG; MPB; NeHB; OIF; OTPC; PC; PECK; PG (1945 ed.); PIR; PoE; PoVP; PRWS; PTA-1; REAL; ShBV-1; StVeCh; TCEP; TreF; TrGrPo; TSW; TSWC; VA; ViPP; WP
(Cradle Song.) CBE
(Lullaby: "Sweet and low, sweet and low.") GBV (1922 ed.); HBV; HBVY; LPS-1; MOAH; OnHT; PoRh; TVC
(Lyrics from "The Princess.") OuHeWo
(Song: "Sweet and low.") BOL; RAR; ThWaDe
(Songs from "The Princess.") EmBrPo; MotAn; ViPo; VLEP
"Tears, idle tears, I know not what they mean," *fr.* Pt. IV. AnFE; AtBAP; BEL; BLV; BMEP; BoLiVe; BPN; EG; EM-2; EnL; EnLi-2; EnLit; EPN; EV-5; FiP; GEPC; GTBS; GTBS-W; GTML; GTSL; HBV; LEAP; LiTB; LiTG; MaPo; MCCG; NeHB; OBVV; PC; PG (1945 ed.); PIR; PoE; PoEL-5; PoeMoYo; PoFS; PoVP; PYM; REAL; ShBV-4; TCEP; TreF; TrGrPo; TwHP; TyEnPo; UnPo; VA; ViBoPo; ViPP; WHA
(Days That Are No More, The.) LiA
(Lyrics from "The Princess.") OuHeWo
(Retrospection.) LPS 1
(Song: "Tears, idle tears, I know not what they mean.") CoEV; FaBoEn; TOP
(Songs from "The Princess.") AWP; EmBrPo; InPo; JAWP; MotAn; OAEP; SeCeV; ViPo; VLEP; WBP
"Ah, sad and strange, as in dark summer dawns," 2 *sts.* LoPS
"This world was once a fluid haze of light," 4 *ll.* ImOP
"Thy voice is heard thro' rolling drums," *fr.* Interlude. BHV; BPN; GEPC; OBVV; PoVP; TrGrPo; VA
(Songs from "The Princess.") MotAn; ViPo; VLEP
Woman and Man, *abr., fr.* Pt. VII. BMEP; OQP; QP-2
Princess, The. W. J. Turner. HBMV
Princess and the Gypsies, The. Frances Cornford. StPo
Princess Ida, *sels.* W. S. Gilbert.
Arac's Song. FiBHP; WhC
Disagreeable Man, The. ALV; FiBHP; MPB; PoVP
Mighty Must, The. BOHV

Princess is sad, The. What brings tears to her eyes? Sonatina. Rubén Darío. WoL
Princess of pretty pets. The Little Rebel. Joseph Ashby-Sterry. VA
Princess of Scotland, The. Rachel Annand Taylor. GoTS
Princess on the Headland, The. George Sterling. MOAP
Princess Sabbath. Heine, *tr fr. German by* Charles Godfrey Leland. TrJP
Princess sat high in her bower forlorn, The. The Princess. Björnstjerne Björnson. AnNoLy
Princess, the first beginner of all the woes. Salamis. Aeschylus. *Fr.* Persians. OxBG
Princess with her women-train without the fort he found, The. Sir Samuel Ferguson. *Fr.* Congal. TIP
Princeton. Alfred Noyes. POT; PoTo; POTT
Principes portas tollite. The Harrowing of Hell. *Unknown.* ACP; CAW
Printer to the Reader, The. *At. to* Richard Jones. EIL, *abr.;* ReIE
Printer's Error. P. G. Wodehouse. FiBHP
Prior to Miss Belle's Appearance. James Whitcomb Riley. BOHV
Prioress, The. Chaucer. *Fr.* The Canterbury Tales: Prologue. CBOV; PraNu, *shorter sel., mod.*
(Seven Pilgrims, *mod. by* Louis Untermeyer.) TrGrPo
(Three Canterbury Pilgrims, *mod. by* Louis Untermeyer.) MaC
Prioress's Tale, The. Chaucer. *Fr.* The Canterbury Tales. ACP, *mod.;* BEL; EM-1; GEPC; GoBC, *mod. vers. by* Wordsworth; ISi, *mod. vers. by* Frank Ernest Hill; LoBV; OAEP; OxBoCh
Prologe of the Prioresses Tale. AtBAP
Invocation: "O mother maid! O maiden-mother free," *sel., mod. by* Frank Ernest Hill. Isi
(O Mooder Mayde.) BoW
(Prayer to the Blessed Virgin, *7 ll., mod.*) CAW
(Two Invocations of the Virgin, 2, *mod.*) ACP
Prior's Epitaph. Matthew Prior. *See* Epitaph on Himself.
Priscilla and John Alden lie at rest. American History. Marguerite Janvrin Adams. PoRL
Prism, The. H. A. Pinkerton. NePoAm
Prism in sunlight. Hummingbird. Elizabeth Palmer. WhBS
Prison. *Unknown, tr. fr. Spanish by* Havelock Ellis. OnPM
Prison-House of Flesh. *Unknown, tr. fr. Greek by* F. A. Wright. OxBG
Prison Moan, *with music. Unknown.* OuSiCo
Prison Song. Richard Cœur de Lion, *tr. fr. Old French by* Henry Adams. LiA; LiTW
Prison Songs. *Unknown, tr. fr. Middle English.* TMEV
Prison Sonnet. Wilfrid Scawen Blunt. CAW
(Honour Dishonoured.) OBMV
Prisoned in Windsor, He Recounteth His Pleasure There Passed. Earl of Surrey. BEL; CoBE; FaBoEn; OAEP; PoE; ReIE; SiCE; TuPP
(In Windsor Castle.) OBSC; SeCePo
("So cruel prison how could betide, alas.") ReEn
Prisoner, A. "Æ." *See* Terence MacSwiney.
Prisoner, The. Emily Brontë. AnFE; BrBE; EmBrPo; EnLi-2 (1949 ed.); UnW; ViP
(Prisoner, The; a Fragment.) EV-5, *abr.;* OAEP
Sels.
"He comes with western winds, with evening's wandering airs." GTBS-D
"Still, let my tyrants know, I am not doomed to wear." ChER; EG; GTML; LEAP; OBEV; OBVV
Prisoner, The. Afanasi Fet, *tr. fr. Russian by* C. M. Bowra. BoR
Prisoner. Marguerite George. GoYe
Prisoner, The. William Plomer. ChMP
Prisoner, The. Po Chü-i, *tr. fr. Chinese by* Arthur Waley. PoFr; SoV; TrCh
Prisoner, The. Pushkin, *tr. fr. Russian by* C. M. Bowra. BoRS
Prisoner, The. *Unknown, tr. fr. Spanish.* AnSpL-1, *tr. by* William J. Entwistle; TeCS, *tr. by* Eleanor L. Turnbull
Prisoner, The; a Fragment. Emily Brontë. *See* Prisoner, The.
Prisoner for Life, A, *with music. Unknown.* CoSo; CSF
Prisoner Freed, A. Geoffrey Dutton. BoAV
Prisoner of Chillon, The. Byron. BEL; BeLS; BPN; EmBrPo; EnLi-2; EnLit; EnRP; EPN; EPP; EV-4; HBV; HeT; HiLiEn; LPS-2; MaC; OnSP; PCN; PIAE; TCEP; TyEnPo
(Prisoner of Chillon, The; a Fable.) GEPC; MCCG
Sels.
"I made a footing in the wall." OBRV
"Lake Leman lies by Chillon's walls." OBRV
"Light broke in upon my brain, A." OBRV
Sonnet on Chillon. AnEnPo; ATP; BEL; BLP; BoLiVe; BPN; EM-2; EmBrPo; EnLi-2; EnLit; EnRP; EPN; EPP; ExPo; FiP; GEPC; HiLiEn; InP; LEAP; LiTB; LoBV; OAEP; OBRV; PoFr; PoFS; REAL; SeCeV; TCEP; TOP; TreFS; TrGrPo
(Chillon.) BCEP; PFE
(Freedom's Hero.) MaRV
(On Chillon.) ES
(On the Castle of Chillon.) GTBS; GTBS-D; GTBS-W; GTSE; GTSL; PYM
(Prisoner of Chillon, The.) HBV; LPS-2; MCCG
Prisoner of Love. Blake. *See* Song: "How sweet I roamed from field to field."
Prisoner of the field, frenzied in agony. First in the World. Paul Eluard. MiCF
Prisoner of War. Gertrude May Lutz. GoYe
Prisoners. Randall Jarrell. OxBA; WaP
Prisoners. Helen M. Lehman. DDA
Prisoners. Nancy Barr Mavity. HBMV
Prisoners, The. Stephen Spender. FaBoMo; GTBS-D; MBP; MoAB; MoBrPo
Prisoners. *Unknown. See* Dainty Fine Bird.
Prisoners in the dark of wood. Flames. E. Merrill Root. PoMa
Prisoner's Song. Horace Gregory. NP
Prisoner's Song, A. Mme Guyon. *See* Little Bird I Am, A.
Prisoner's Song of Jerusalem, A. *Unknown.* ACP
Prissie was a turnip. Vegetable Fantasies. Helen Hoyt. RIS
Prithee, Chloe, Not So Fast. John Oldmixon. SeCL
Prithee, honey-sweet husband, let me bring thee to Staines. Shakespeare. King Henry V, Act II, sc. iii. MyFE
Prithee (lest maids should censure thee) but say. Robert Herrick. *Fr.* His Parting with Mrs. Dorothy Kennedy. MyFE
Prithee now, fond Fool, give o'er. A Dialogue between Strephon and Daphne. Earl of Rochester. SeCV-2
Prithee, say aye or no. The Resolute Courtier. Thomas Shipman. LO; SeCL
Prithee, Strive Not. Harry Kemp. LEAP; PR
Prithee tell me, Dimple-Chin. Toujours Amour. Edmund Clarence Stedman. HBV; OBAV; PR
Private, A. Edward Thomas. SoV
Private Blair of the Regulars. Clinton Scollard. PAH
Private Devotion. Phoebe Hinsdale Brown. *See* I Love to Steal Awhile Away.
Private Dining Room, The. Ogden Nash. ExPo
Private Enterprise. Christopher Morley. MaRV
Private Judgment Condemned. Dryden. *Fr.* The Hind and the Panther, I. OBS
(Prayer, A: "What weight of ancient witness can prevail.") FiP
Private madness has prevailed, A. O Virtuous Light. Elinor Wylie. AnAmPo; LA; LiTG; MAP; MoAB; MoAmPo; MoP; MoPo; NePA; ReaPo; TwAmPo
Private of the Buffs, The. Sir Francis Hastings Doyle. EV-5; GTBS; HBV; InP; LH; LPS-2; OBEV (new ed.); OBVV; PoVP; VA
(Private of the Buffs; or, The British Soldier in China, The.) BMEP
Private Smith of the Royals; the veldt and a slate-black sky. War. Herbert Cadett. BHV
Private Theatricals. Louise Imogen Guiney. PR
Private Worship. Mark Van Doren. LiTL; MoVE
Privately, your pencil makes. Snapshot of a Pedant. George Garrett. NePoAm-2
Prize, The. Pindar, *pr. tr. fr. Greek by* Sir John Sandys. *Fr.* Pythian Odes, IX. LiA
Prize Cat, The. E. J. Pratt. PeCV; TwCaPo; TwCV
Prize of the Margaretta, The. Will Carleton. PAH
Prize thou the nightingale. The Nightingale. Maria Tesselschade Visscher. LPS-2
Pro Libra Mea. Joseph I. C. Clarke. TrPWD
Pro Memoria. Ina M. Porter. BlG
Pro Mortuis. Francis Turner Palgrave. VA
Pro Patria. Constance Carrier. NePoAm
Pro Patria. Tyrtaeus, *tr. fr. Greek by* Thomas Campbell. GrR
(Young Hero, The.) BHV
Pro Patria Mori. Thomas Moore. EV-4; GTBS; GTBS-D; GTBS-W; GTSE; GTSL
(When He, Who Adores Thee.) HoPM; OBRV; TIP
Pro Rege Nostro. W. E. Henley. *See* England, My England.
Pro Sua Vita. Robert Penn Warren. MAP; MM; MoAmPo
Probe foramini a cat. Fabula. *Unknown.* CIV
Problem, The. Paul Blackburn. NeAP
Problem, The. Emerson. AA; AmP; AmPo; AmPP; AnAmPo; AnNE; AWP; BAP; CoBA; CoV; EV-4; HBV; IAP; JAWP; LA; LBAP; LiTA; LPS-3; MaRV; MOAP; NePA; OBAV; OuHeWo; OxBA; PECK; TCAP; TOP; WBP; WGRP
(Monumental Human Expressions, *abr.*) GrCo-2
"Not from a vain or shallow thought," *sel.* BAV; OQP; QP-1
Problem, The. Theognis, *tr. fr. Greek by* F. L. Lucas. GrPE
Problem in Logic. Phocylides. *See* Exception That Proves the Rule, The.
Problem of the Poles, The. John Kendall. WhC

Problem that confronts me here, The. Auditors In. Patrick Kavanagh. OxBI
Process. Charles L. O'Donnell. TrPWD
Process in the Weather of the Heart, A. Dylan Thomas. MoAB
(Poem.) NeBP
Process of time worketh such wonder. Sir Thomas Wyatt. SiPS
Processes of death abound, The. All Saints. Wyn Griffith. MoWP
Procession, The. Margaret Widdemer. YeAr
Procession, its back turned to us, The. Faces in the Procession. Fuyuhiko Kitagawa. PoLJ
Procession of Bacchus. Keats. *Fr.* Endymion, IV. TwCrTr
("Beneath my palm-trees, by the river side.") ViBoPo
Procession of Cupid, The. Spenser. *See* Masque of Cupid, The.
Procession of the Flowers, The. Sydney Dobell. *See* Chanted Calendar, A.
Procession of Times and Seasons. Spenser. *See* Pageant of the Seasons and the Months, The.
Procession with the Standard of a Faction, The; a Cantata, *sel.* *Unknown.*
Derry-Down. APW
(Liberty Pole, The.) PAH
Processional. Stanton A. Coblentz. UnW
Processional. Alice Archer James. AA
Processional. William Jay Smith. NePoAm
Processional. Stesichorus, *tr. fr. Greek by* John Herman Merivale. GrR
Processional for Demetrius Poliorcetes. Hermocles. *See* Demetrius Enters Athens.
Proclamation. *Arr. fr.* Isaiah, XLIX, Bible, *O.T.* StaSt
Proclamation, The. Longfellow. *Fr.* John Endicott. PAH
Proclamation, A. *Unknown.* PAH
Proclamation, The. Whittier. GA; LBAH; PAH
Proclos, a silvern gift I send. Crinagoras, *tr. fr. Greek by* W. C. Lawton. GrPo
Procne. Peter Quennell. ChMP; FaBoMo; GTBS-W; LiTB; LiTM; MBP; MoBrPo
Procne, Philomela, and Itylus. Philomela. John Crowe Ransom. AmP; ChTr; MoVE; OnAP; OxBA; PoFS
Proconsul of Bithynia. To Petronius Arbiter. Oliver St. John Gogarty. OBMV
Procrastination. Martial, *tr. fr. Latin by* Abraham Cowley. AWP; JAWP; LiTW; OuHeWo; WBP
(Tomorrow.) OnPM
Procrastination ("Be wise to-day"). Edward Young. *Fr.* Night Thoughts: Night I. AnEnPo; BCEP, *abr.;* EV-3, *abr.;* LPS-3; OBEC, *abr.*
Procrastination ("By Nature's law"). Edward Young. *Fr.* Night Thoughts: Night I. EPP
Prodigal, The. Elizabeth Bishop. FiMAP; InvP; MoAB
Prodigal. Ellen Gilbert. GoBC; MaRV
Prodigal, The. Sara Henderson Hay. StaSt
Prodigal. DuBose Heyward. SPP; TCAP
Prodigal Son, The. St. Luke, XV: 11–32, Bible, *N.T.* EM-1; TreF
(Gospel According to Saint Luke, The: "And Jesus said . . .") LO
Prodigal Son, The. A. E. Coppard. MBP; MoBrPo (1942 ed.)
Prodigal Son, The. James Weldon Johnson. StJW
Prodigal Son, The. E. A. Robinson. MAP; MoAmPo; TriL
Prodigal Son, The, *with music.* *Unknown, tr. fr. Flemish by* Alice M. G. White. SaSa
Prodigals, The. Austin Dobson. InP
Prodigals. Charles L. O'Donnell. HBMV
Prodigals, The, *parody.* *Unknown.* PA
Prodiggus reptile long and skaly kuss. Some Verses to Snaix. *Unknown.* NA
Prodjeckin' Son, De. Booth Lowrey. IHA
Proem: "As one, at midnight, wakened by the call." W. W. Gibson. *See* Prelude: "As one, at midnight."
Proem: City of Dreadful Night, The. James Thomson. *See* Proem: "Lo, thus, as prostrate, 'In the dust I write.'"
Proem: "From Zeus begin we." Aratus, *tr. fr. Greek by* George Allen. *Fr.* Phaenomena. OxBG
Proem: "I am a Negro." Langston Hughes. PreP
(Negro, The.) BAP
Proem: "I love the old melodious lays." Whittier. AA; AmPP; AnNE; CoBA; CoV; HBV; IAP; MOAP; NePA; OBAV; OxBA; TCAP
(Proem: Written to Introduce the First General Collection of His Poems.) LEAP
Proem: "If this little world to-night." Oliver Herford. *See* Earth.
Proem: "Lo, thus, as prostrate, 'In the dust I write.'" James Thomson. *Fr.* The City of Dreadful Night. EnLit; GoTS; OAEP; POTT; ViBoPo; ViP
Proem: "Lyf so short, the craft so long to lerne, The." Chaucer. *See* Proem to "The Parlement of Foules."
Proem: "Man grows up." Robert Nathan. DDA
Proem: "Out of my own great woe." Heine, *tr. fr. German by* Elizabeth Barrett Browning. AWP
Proem: "Snug in my easy ch ir." W. W. Gibson. *See* Snug in My Easy Chair.
Proem: "Strong Son of God, immortal Love." Tennyson. *See* In Memoriam A. H. H.: "Strong Son of God . . ."
Proem: "There is no rhyme that is half so sweet." Madison Cawein. AA
Proem: To Brooklyn Bridge. Hart Crane. *See* To Brooklyn Bridge.
Proem, A: "When in my walks I meet some ruddy lad." Samuel Ward. AA
Proem: Written to Introduce the First General Collection of His Poems. Whittier. *See* Proem: "I love the old melodious lays."
Proem to Hellenics. Walter Savage Landor. *See* On the Hellenics.
Proem to "The Kid." Conrad Aiken. *Fr.* The Kid. MoAB
Proem to "The Parlement of Foules." Chaucer. FiP; MyFE; NBE
(Parliament of Fowls, The.) ViBoPo
Proemium I: "As in the greatest of societies." Everard Guilpin. *Fr.* Skialetheia. ReIE
("As in the greatest of societies.") SiCE
Proemium in Librum Primum. John Marston. *Fr.* The Scourge of Villainy. ReIE
Proface. *Unknown.* AnEC
Profane, The. Abraham Cowley, *after the Latin of* Horace. AWP
Profession of Flattery, The. Antiphanes, *tr. fr. Greek by* T. F. Higham. OxBG
Profession Song. Sister Mary of the Visitation. PraNu
Professor at the Breakfast Table, The, *sels.* Oliver Wendell Holmes.
Crooked Footpath, The, *fr. ch.* 4. HBV; TreF
Hymn of Trust, *fr. ch.* 11. AA; IAP; MaRV; NeHB; PraP
("O Love divine, that stooped to share.") OlF
Mother's Secret, The, *fr. ch.* 5. MotAn
"Youth fades; love droops," *2 ll.* PoToHe
Our Father's Door, *fr. ch.* 4. OQP; QP-2
Sun-Day Hymn, A, *fr. ch.* 12. AnNE; APW; IAP; InP; MaRV; WGRP
(Lord of All Being.) GrCo-1; OlF
Two Streams, The, *fr. ch.* 6. PEOR
Under the Violets, *fr. ch.* 10. AA; IAP
Professor Burke's symphony, "Colorado Vistas." Cultural Notes. Kenneth Fearing. ChMo
Professor of Medieval Balladry. Sister Mary Maura. JKCP (1955 ed.)
Professor strolls at dusk in the college garden, The. Processional. William Jay Smith. NePoAm
Professor, you've convinced me a semester of astronomy. To Harold Jacoby. Irwin Edman. InMe
Professors. Harold A. Larrabee. InMe
Proffered Rose, The. Wenceslas, King of Bohemia, *tr. fr. German by* Jethro Bithell. LiTW
Proffered to sun and moon. The Condemned. Enrique González Martinez. AnMP
Profit and Loss ("Profit?—Loss?"). OQP; QP-2
Prognosis. Louis MacNeice. ChMo; OxBI
Prognostic. Samuel Yellen. NePoAm
Prognostication on Will Laud, Late Archbishop of Canterbury, A. *Unknown.* OxBoLi
Prognostication upon Cards and Dice, A. Sir Walter Ralegh. SiPS
Program Note on Sibelius. Donald Babcock. UnS
Progress. Matthew Arnold. EmBrPo; EPN; MaRV; StJW
"Master stood upon the Mount, and taught, The," *sel.* ChIP
Progress. David McCord. ImOP
Progress. Ella Wheeler Wilcox. BLPA
Windows of the Soul, *sel.* OQP; QP-1
Progress. Frank Wilmot. BoAu
Progress in the peaceable blue of a sky in summer. Poem. George Ewart Evans. MoWP
Progress is/ The law of life, man is not Man as yet. Man's Destiny [*or* The Awakening of Man]. Robert Browning. *Fr.* Paracelsus, V. MaRV; OQP; QP-2; WGRP
Progress of Balloons, The. Philip Freneau. IAP
Progress of Beauty, The. Swift. RiBV
"Three Colours, Black, and Red, and White," *sel.* BrBE
Progress of Dulness, The, *sels.* John Trumbull.
Aging Coquette, The. AnNE
Amorous Temper, An. AmPP (4th ed.)
Harriet Simper Has Her Day. AmPP (4th ed.)
Tom Brainless as Student and Preacher. AmPP (4th ed.)
Tom Brainless at College. AmPP (3d ed.); ATP (1935 ed.); IAP
Tom Brainless Seeks a Wife. AmPP (3d ed.)
Progress of Evening, *sel.* Walter Savage Landor.
"From yonder wood mark blue-eyed Eve proceed." EnSW
Progress of Faust, The. Karl Shapiro. MoAB; OnHM

Progress of Love, The. Swift. *See* Phillis; or, The Progress of Love.
Progress of Man, The, *sel.* George Canning *and* John Hookham Frere.
Canto Twenty-third, *abr.* CEP
Progress of Man, The. Jalal ed-Din Rumi, *tr. fr. Persian by* R. A. Nicholson. PeP
Progress of Photography, The. Byron Vazakas. MoPo
Progress of Poesy, The. Matthew Arnold. EnL; PoVP; VLEP
Progress of Poesy, The. Thomas Gray. ATP; AWP; BEL; CBOV; CEP; CoBE; EiPP; EM-1; EnLi-2 (1949 ed.); EnLit; EnRP; EPP; EV-3; GTBS; GTBS-D; GTBS-W; GTSE; GTSL; HBV; OAEP; OBEC; OBEV; PIAE; PoFS; TCEP; ViBoPo
Sels.
"Far from the sun and summer-gale." PtP
(From the "Progress of Poetry," *abr.*) LEAP
Supreme Dominion. LiA
"Woods that wave." BCEP
Progress of Poetry, The. Swift. BeR; InvP; OnYI
Progress of Poets, The. Wordsworth. *Fr.* Resolution and Independence. RO
("I thought of Chatterton, the marvellous boy.") PtP
Progress of Sir Jack Brag, The. *Unknown.* PAH
Progress of Spring, The, *sel.* Tennyson.
"Groundflame of the crocus breaks the mould, The." EnSW
Progress of the Soul, The ("I sing the progress of a deathless soul"), *sels.* John Donne.
"Great Destiny the commissary of God." OxBoCh
"It quickned next a toyfull ape." PoEL-2
Whale, The. ChTr
Progress of the Soul, The ("Nothing could make me sooner to confess"). John Donne. *See* Of the Progresse of the Soule; the Second Anniversary.
Progress of Unbelief. Cardinal Newman. GoBC
Progresse of the Soule, The. John Donne. *See* Progress of the Soul, The.
Progression. Francis Scarfe. NeBP
Progression. Inez Clark Thorson. MaRV
Prohibition, The. John Donne. ElL; MeLP; OBS; TuPP
Sels.
"Take heed of hating mee." BoFr
"Take heed of loving mee." EG
Prohibition. Don Marquis. WhC
Projected from the bilious Childe. Manfred. George Meredith. EPN
Projection, A. Reed Whittemore. NePoEA; WaKn
Proletaria. Bernard O'Dowd. BoAu
Proletarians. Luis Muñoz Marín, *tr. fr. Spanish by* Muna Lee. AnCL
Prolog: "Books composed before our day, The." John Gower, *tr. fr. Middle English by* Muriel Bowden. *Fr.* Confessio Amantis. MeEV
Prolog, The: "There was a priest in the land." Layamon, *tr. fr. Middle English. Fr.* The Brut. MeEV
Prologue: "Against time and the damages of the brain." James Agee. *Fr.* Let Us Now Praise Famous Men. OnAP
Prologue: "Ane doolie season to ane careful dyte." Robert Henryson. *Fr.* The Testament of Cresseid. BSV; GoTS
Prologue: Before the Curtain. Arthur Symons. POTT
Prologue, A: "Chain hangs down with golden fetters, A." Pushkin, *tr. fr. Russian by* Oliver Elton. BoRS
Prologue: "Delusions of the days that once have been." Longfellow. *Fr.* Giles Corey of the Salem Farms. PAH
Prologue, The: "Famous poets with the muses nine, The." Alexander Barclay. *Fr.* Certain Eclogues. ReIE
Prologue: "Fancy I had to-day, The." Robert Browning. *Fr.* Fifine at the Fair. BPN
(Amphibian.) AlDL
Prologue: "Father and founder of faith and felicity." Sir David Lindsay. *Fr.* The Satire of the Three Estates. TMEV
Prologue: "For who can longer hold? when every press." John Oldham. *Fr.* Satires upon the Jesuits. CEP; SeCV-2
Prologue: "Forget six counties overhung with smoke." William Morris. *Fr.* The Earthly Paradise. BEL; EmBrPo; EPN, *abr.*; EPP, *abr.*
(Earthly Paradise, The: Introduction.) ViPo
(Introduction.) ViPP
Prologue: "I first adventure, with foolhardy might." Joseph Hall. *Fr.* Virgidemiarum. ReEn; ReIE; SiCE; ViBoPo
Prologue: "I heard an angel speak last night." Elizabeth Barrett Browning. *See* Curse for a Nation, A.
Prologue: "If yet there be a few that take delight." Dryden. *Fr.* The Loyal General (*by* Nahum Tate). CEP; SeCV-2
Prologue: "In a somer sesun [*or* summer season], when softe [*or* soft] was the sonne [*or* sun *or* when the sun was softest]." William Langland. *Fr.* The Vision of Piers Plowman. BCEP, *much abr.*; BEL; CoBE; EnLi-1, *mod. by* W. A. Neilson *and* K. G. T. Webster; EnLit, *mod. by* Albert C. Baugh; EPP, *Middle English and mod. vers.*; TCEP, *abr.*
(Field Full of Folk, The, *mod. vers.*) MeEV
(Field of Folk, The.) PoEL-1
(Induction, The, *shorter sel., mod. by* Henry W. Wells.) PoLi
Prologue: In Darkness. J. C. Squire. MBP
Prologue, The: "In the moneth of May when the new tender green." *Unknown.* ReIE
Prologue: "In-to the calendis of Januarie." Sir David Lindsay. *Fr.* The Dreme. EBSV
Prologue: "Musing upon the restles bisinesse." Thomas Hoccleve. *Fr.* De Regimine Principum. PoEL-1
Prologue: "O love, the interest itself in thoughtless Heaven." W. H. Auden. *See* Perhaps.
Prologue: "Of Heaven or Hell I have no power to sing." William Morris. *See* Apology, An: "Of Heaven or Hell . . ."
Prologue: "Our author by experience finds it true." Dryden. *See* Prologue to "Aureng-Zebe."
Prologue: " 'Poet's age is sad, The: for why?' " Robert Browning. *See* Prologue to "Asolando."
Prologue: "Prest by the load of life, the weary mind." Samuel Johnson. *Fr.* The Good-natur'd Man (*by* Goldsmith). LoBV
Prologue: "Rawish dank of clumsy winter ramps, The." John Marston. *Fr.* Antonio's Revenge. CoEV; LoBV; NBE; ViBoPo
Prologue: "See my lov'd Britons, see your Shakespeare rise." Dryden. *Fr.* Troilus and Cressida. CEP; SeCV-2
Prologue: "So oft as I with state of present time." Spenser. *Fr.* The Faerie Queene, V. PoFS
Prologue: "Strong Son of God, immortal Love." Tennyson. *See* In Memoriam A. H. H.: "Strong Son of God . . ."
Prologue: "Such a starved bank of moss." Robert Browning. *See* Such a Starved Bank of Moss.
Prologue: "These alternate nights and days, these seasons." Archibald MacLeish. MAP; MoAmPo
Prologue: "This day winding down now." Dylan Thomas. GTBS-W
Prologue: "This worthy limitour, this noble frere." Chaucer. *Fr.* The Canterbury Tales: The Friar's Tale. EnLi-1 (1949 ed.)
Prologue, A: "Thou Speaker of all wisdom in a Word." Coventry Patmore. PoLi
Prologue, The: "Thousand tymes have I herd men tell, A." Chaucer. *Fr.* The Legend of Good Women. NBE
Prologue: "Times wherein old Pompion was a saint, The." Benjamin Tompson. *Fr.* New England's Crisis. APW; IAP, *abr.*; TCAP
(Alarming Progress of Luxury in New England, The.) BAV
Prologue, The. "To sing of wars, of captains, and of kings." Anne Bradstreet. AmPP (3d ed.); BAV; IAP; OxBA
Prologue: "Tonight we strive to read, as we may best." Longfellow. *Fr.* John Endicott. PAH
Prologue: "We who with songs." James Elroy Flecker. *Fr.* The Golden Journey to Samarkand. GTBS; MM; OBMV
Prologue: "Whan that Aprille with his shoures so[o]te." *See* Canterbury Tales, The.
Prologue and Epilogue to the University of Oxford (*spoken by Mr. Hart at the acting of* "The Silent Woman"). Dryden. EV-3
Prologue to the University of Oxford, 1673. OBS
Prologue and Epilogue to "Tyrannick Love; or, The Royal Martyr." Dryden. *Fr.* Tyrannick Love; or, The Royal Martyr. OAEP
Prologue, Each to the Other, *sel.* Christopher La Farge.
"Here is no tragedy." AnAmPo
Prologue for a Magician. Arthur Guiterman. PoMS
Prologue from "Peace on Earth." Gudmundur Gudmundsson, *tr. fr. Icelandic by* Jakobina Johnson. IcP
Prologue in Heaven. Goethe, *tr. fr. German by* Shelley. *Fr.* Faust. AWP; JAWP; WBP
Prologue of the Attendant Spirit in "Comus." Milton. *Fr.* Comus. CBE
Prologue of the Pardoner's Tale, The. Chaucer. *Fr.* The Canterbury Tales. BEL; EM-1; OAEP
(Prologue to the Pardoner's Tale.) CoBE; EnL, *mod. vers.* by Theodore Morrison; RiBV, *mod. vers. by* Frank Ernest Hill
Prologue of the Prioress's Tale, The. Chaucer. *See* Prioress's Tale, The.
Prologue Spoken by Mr. Garrick at the Opening of the Theatre Royal [*or* in Drury Lane], 1747. Samuel Johnson. CEP; EiPP; NBE; OBEC; PoFS; SeCeV
(Prologue Spoken at the Opening of the Drury Lane Theatre, 1747.) CBOV; EV-3
(Shakespeare.) LPS-3
(Shakespeare and Jonson.) BCEP
Sels.
"When Learning's triumph o'er her barb'rous foes." PtP
Wits, The. BeR
Prologue to a Saga. Dorothy Parker. InMe
Prologue to "Antonio's Revenge." John Marston. *See* Prologue: "Rawish dank of clumsy winter ramps, The."

Prologue to "Asolando." Robert Browning. PoVP; ViPo
(Prologue: "'Poet's age is sad, The: for why?'") ViPP
Prologue to "Aureng-Zebe." Dryden. ATP; CEP; EiPP; FiP; OBS; OxBoLi; SeCeV; SiTL
(Prologue: "Our author by experience finds it true.") SeCV-2; SeEP
Prologue to Eighteenth-Century Vignettes (Third Series). Austin Dobson. *Fr.* Eighteenth-Century Vignettes. BPN
Prologue to "Evangeline." Longfellow. CaAE
(In the Forest.) PCD
(Primeval Forest, *abr.*) LPS-2; WBLP
("This is the forest primeval.") AmPP; CoBA; IAP; InP; LEAP; OBAV; PIAE; TCAP; TreF
Prologue to "Fifine at the Fair." Robert Browning. *See* Prologue: "Fancy I had to-day, The."
Prologue to "La Saisiaz." Robert Browning. BPN; EmBrPo; PoVP
Prologue to "Love Triumphant." Dryden. OxBoLi; SiTL
Prologue to Melibeus, *abr.* Chaucer. *Fr.* The Canterbury Tales. EM-1
Prologue to Mr. Addison's Tragedy of Cato. Pope. CEP; EV-3
Prologue to Morning. Hermann Hagedorn. MaRV
Prologue to Nahum Tate's "The Loyal General," *sel.* Dryden.
Sippets of Gruel. BeR
Prologue to "Rhymes and Rhythms." W. E. Henley. BPN; PoVP
Prologue to "Rhymes to Be Traded for Bread." Vachel Lindsay. ChMo; CMP; LaNeLa
Prologue to "Secret Love; or, The Maiden-Queen." Dryden. SeCV-2; SeEP
Prologue to Sir Thopas. Chaucer. *Fr.* The Canterbury Tales. EM-1
Prologue to "The Canterbury Tales." Chaucer. *See* Canterbury Tales, The.
Prologue to "The Earthly Paradise." William Morris. *See* Prologue: "Forget six counties overhung with smoke."
Prologue to "The Earthly Paradise," *wr. title.* William Morris. *See* Apology, An: "Of Heaven or Hell . . ."
Prologue to the First Satire ("I never did"). Persius, *tr. fr. Latin by* Dryden. *Fr.* Satires. AWP
Prologue to "The Golden Journey to Samarkand." James Elroy Flecker. GTBS; MM; OBMV; ReTS; TwCV
Prologue to "The Good-natur'd Man." Samuel Johnson. *See* Prologue: "Prest by the load of life, the weary mind."
Prologue to "The Lost Colony." Paul Green. NoCaPo
Prologue to the Man of Law's Tale. Chaucer. *Fr.* The Canterbury Tales. FiP
Prologue to the Pardoner's Tale. Chaucer. *See* Prologue of the Pardoner's Tale.
Prologue to the Satires. Pope. *See* Epistle to Dr. Arbuthnot.
Prologue to the Second Nun's Tale, The. Chaucer. *See* Second Nun's Tale, The.
Prologue to "The Tempest." Dryden. EiPP; EnL; PoE; RiBV
Prologue to "The Two Poets of Croisic." Robert Browning. *See* Such a Starved Bank of Moss.
Prologue to the Wife of Bath's Tale, The. Chaucer. *See* Wife of Bath's Prologue, The.
Prologue to Towie Castle. Gordon Bottomley. MM
Prologue to "Tristram of Lyonesse." Swinburne. *See* Tristram and Iseult.
Prologue; Written for the Re-opening of the Theatre Royal, Richmond, Yorkshire, 1942. "Sagittarius" (Olga Katzin). DiM
Prologues are over, The. It is a question, now. Asides on the Oboe. Wallace Stevens. CoV; MoAB; MoAmPo
Prologues to Henry V. Shakespeare. *Fr.* King Henry V. BHV; EV-1; LH
Prologues to the Aeneid, *sels.* Gawin Douglas.
Difficulties of Translation, The, *abr., fr.* Prologue to Bk. I. GoTS
Evening and Morning in June, An, *abr., fr.* Prologue to Bk. XIII. BSV
Evening and Morning in Winter, An, *fr.* Prologue to Bk. VII. BSV
"Frend, farly nocht; na caus is to complene," *fr.* Prologue to Bk. X. OxBoCh
"Quhill schortly, with the blesand torch of day," *fr.* Prologue to Bk. XII. AtBAP
Winter, *fr.* Prologue to Bk. VII. EBSV; SeCePo
Prologues to What Is Possible. Wallace Stevens. NePoAm
Prolonged Sonnet: When the Troops Were Returning from Milan. Niccolò degli Albizzi, *tr. fr. Italian by* Dante Gabriel Rossetti. AWP; LyPI
(Troops Returning from Milan.) OnPM
(When the Troops Were Returning from Milan.) WaaP
Prolonged Sonnet. Simone dall' Antella, *tr. fr. Italian by* Dante Gabriel Rossetti. AWP
Promenade. David Ignatow. TrJP
Promenades and Interiors, *sel.* François Coppée, *tr. fr. French by* Joseph T. Shipley.
"I am writing near the lamp." CAW
Promethean culture here reveals such horrors. Charing Cross Road. Bernard Bergonzi. PoN
Promethean Ideal, The. Shelley. *Fr.* Prometheus Unbound, IV. GrCo-2
(Closing Lines of "Prometheus Unbound.") PC
(Peaks of Life.) BCEP
("To suffer woes which Hope thinks infinite.") LEAP
(Victory.) CBOV
Prometheus. Aeschylus. *See* Prometheus Bound.
Prometheus. Byron. BPN; EmBrPo; EnRP; EPN
Prometheus. W. W. Gibson. EPN
Prometheus. Goethe, *tr. fr. German by* John S. Dwight. AWP; JAWP; WBP; WoL
Prometheus ("Who reigns?"). Shelley. *Fr.* Prometheus Unbound, II, iv. BHV
Prometheus Bound. Aeschylus, *tr. fr. Greek by* Elizabeth Barrett Browning. EnLi-1 (1939 ed.)
Sels.
Answer to Defiance; the Earthquake, *tr. by* Gilbert Murray. GrR
Defiance, *tr. by* Lewis Campbell. GrR
Folly of Obstinacy, *tr. by* Lewis Campbell. GrR
"O holy Aether, and swift-winged Winds," *tr. by* Elizabeth Barrett Browning. GrPo
Overthrow of Zeus, The, *tr. by* G. M. Cookson. OxBG
Prometheus Bound ("O divine air!"), *tr. by* G. M. Cookson. OxBG
Prometheus Doomed, *tr. by* Gilbert Murray. GrR
Prometheus' Gifts to Man, *tr. by* Gilbert Murray. GrR
Prometheus in the Earthquake, *tr. by* G. M. Cookson. LiTW; OxBG
Prometheus the Teacher of Men, *tr. by* G. M. Cookson. LiTW; OxBG
Wail of Prometheus Bound, The, *tr. by* Elizabeth Barrett Browning. WGRP
Prometheus in Piccadilly, *sel.* Wallace B. Nichols.
Immortal Panoply, The. ReTS
Prometheus knew. The Fire-Bringers. Lawrence Lee. NeTW
Prometheus Liberatus. Aeschylus. *See* Prometheus Unbound.
Prometheus Unbound, *sel.* Aeschylus, *tr. fr. Greek by* C. M. Bowra.
Red Sea, The. OxBG
Prometheus Unbound. Sister Miriam. JKCP (1955 ed.)
Prometheus Unbound. Shelley. BEL; BPN; CoBE, *much abr.*; EM-2, *much abr.*; EmBrPo; EnLi-2; EnRP; ERP; GEPC
Sels.
Asia ("My soul is an enchanted boat"), *fr.* II, v. PoFS; ViBoPo
(Asia's Response.) TCEP
(Asia's Song.) ATP (1935 ed.); UnPo (1st ed.)
(My Soul Is an Enchanted Boat.) PC
(To a Singer.) CBPC
Chorus of Spirits: "From unremembered ages we," *fr.* I. LoBV
Curse, The, *fr.* I. PoFr
Day of Liberty, The, *fr.* III, iv. EPN
End of Tyranny, The, *fr.* III, iv. ShBV-3
"From all the blasts of heaven thou hast descended," *fr.* II, i. NBE
"I rise as from a bath of sparkling water," *fr.* IV. NBE
"I wandering went/ Among the haunts and dwellings of mankind," *fr.* III, iv. FiP
"Joy, the triumph, the delight, the madness, The!" *fr.* IV. AtBAP
Life of Life, *fr.* II, v. CH; FiP; ReTS
(Chorus: "Life of Life! thy lips enkindle.") LoBV
(Hymn to the Spirit of Nature.) GTBS; GTBS-D; GTBS-W; GTSE
("Life of Life! thy lips enkindle.") AnFE; AtBAP; LO; OBRV; PoEL-4; TCEP; ViBoPo
(Voice in the Air [Singing].) BCEP; LiA
"Loud deep calls me home even now to feed it, The," *fr.* III, ii. ChER
"Man, one harmonious soul of many a soul," *fr.* IV. CBE
"Monarch of Gods and Daemons, and all Spirits," I. EPN; FiP, *sel.*
(Defiance, *sel.*) BHV
Morning, *fr.* II, i. ShBV-3
"My coursers are fed with the lightning," *fr.* II, iv. OBRV
(Charioteer, The.) ShBV-3
"On a battle-trumpet's blast," *fr.* I. OBRV
"On a poet's lips I slept," *fr.* I. AnFE; AtBAP; ChER; FiP; ShBV-3; ViBoPo
(Poet's Dream, The.) GTBS; GTBS-D; GTBS-W; GTSE; GTSL; PC; ReTS; WP
(Poet's World, The, *sl. abr.*) EV-4
(Spirit's Song in "Prometheus.") CBE
"Pale stars are gone, The!" IV. EnLi-2 (1949 ed.)
"Path through which that lovely twain, The," *fr.* II, ii. AtBAP; ViBoPo
"Peace! Peace! A mighty power, which is as darkness," *fr.* IV. OAEP
Prometheus ("Who reigns?"), *fr.* II, iv. BHV

Prometheus Unbound (*continued*)
 (Who Reigns?) SeCePo
Rainbow's Arch, A, *fr.* I. ShBV-3
"Snow upon my lifeless mountains, The," *fr.* IV. NBE
 (Day of Love, The, *longer sel., abr.*) EPN
"Soon as the sound had ceased whose thunder filled," *fr.* III, iv. ChER
"Sphere, which is as many thousand spheres, A," fr. IV. ImOP
"This is the day which down the void abysm," *fr.* IV. EnLit; OQP; QP-2; SeCeV
 (Demogorgon's Last Words.) KN
 (Demogorgon's Speech.) LoBV
 (Epilogue of "Prometheus.") CBE
 (Final Victory, The.) ShBV-3
 (Ideal, The.) BHV
"Thou, Earth, calm empire of a happy soul," *fr.* IV. EV-4; OBRV
 (To Suffer Woes Which Hope Thinks Infinite.) RO
"Thrones, altars, judgement-seats, and prisons," *fr.* III, iv. NBE
 (Millennium, The.) BHV
"To suffer woes which Hope thinks infinite," *fr.* IV. LEAP
 (Closing Lines of "Prometheus Unbound.") PC
 (Peaks of Life.) BCEP
 (Promethean Ideal, The.) GrCo-2
 (Victory.) CBOV
"What veiled form sits on that ebon throne," *fr.* II, iv. NBE
"Ye congregated powers of heaven, who share," *fr.* III. EnLit
Prometheus Vinctus. Aeschylus. *See* Prometheus Bound.
Prometheus When First from Heaven. Sir Edward Dyer. TuPP
 (Shepherd's Conceit of Prometheus, The.) ES
Promiscuous tags and liberal lip I hate. Written in Flight from His Royal Patron. Al Mutanabbi. LiTW
Promise. "Æ." ChMo; CMP; POTE; TCEP; TwCV
Promise. Florence Lacey. BoTP
Promise, A. Sir Thomas Wyatt. *See* Lover Rejoiceth the Enjoying of His Love, The.
Promise Lan', De. John Richard Moreland. IHA
Promise Made, A. *Unknown.* FaFP; SiTL
Promise of a Constant Lover, The. *Unknown.* EIL; ReIE
Promise of our years was caught, The. Monody on a Century. Earle Birney. CaP
Promise of Peace. Robinson Jeffers. BLV; BoLiVe; CoBMV; GTBS-W; LiTA; LiTM (rev. ed.); MAP; MoAB; MoAmPo; NePA
Promise of these fragrant flowers, The. With a Spray of Apple Blossoms. Walter Learned. AA; ADAH
Promised Country, The. Speer Strahan. JKCP
Promised Land, The. Jessie E. Sampter. TrJP
Promised Land, The. Samuel Stennett. TrAS, *with music*
 ("On Jordan's stormy banks I stand.") OIF
Promised Landscape, The. Sidney Keyes. LoPS
Promises. Ruth Forbes Sherry. GoYe
Promises of the World, The. Moses ibn Ezra, *tr. fr. Hebrew by* Solomon Solis-Cohen. *Fr.* The World's Illusion. TrJP
Promissory Note, The. Bayard Taylor. BOHV; HBV; PA
Promotion. John Oxenham. MaRV
Promotion lately was bestow'd. *Unknown. Fr.* Riddles. CoBE
Prone in Gethsemane upon His face. Gethsemane. Annette von Droste-Hülshoff. CAW
Pronouns. Karle Wilson Baker. GrCo-2; LS; QS
Proof. Ethel Romig Fuller. DDA; MaRV; MoSiPe; PraP
 (God Hears Prayer.) OQP; QP-2; QS
Proof, The. Lucy Larcom. EOAH
Proofs of Buddha's Existence. *Unknown.* WGRP
Prop yer eyes wide open, Joey. Poor Little Joe. David Law Proudfit. PTA-2
Prope ripam fluvii solus. Malum Opus. James Appleton Morgan. NA
Proper Clay. Mark Van Doren. LoPS; PoRA; TrGrPo; UnW
Proper Ditty, A. *Unknown.* ReIE
Proper fathers behind their ashen faces, The. Poem in Karori. Louis Johnson. AnNZ
Proper New Ballad, A. James Graham, Marquess of Montrose. *See* My Dear and Only Love.
Proper New Ballad, A, Intituled The Fairies' Farewell or God-a-Mercy Will. Richard Corbet. *See* Fairies' Farewell, The.
Proper New Song Made by a Student in Cambridge, A. Thomas Richardson. TuPP
 Take Heed of Gazing Overmuch, *sel.* EIL
Proper scale would pat you on the head, The. The Scales. William Empson. LiTM (rev. ed.)
Proper Song, A, Entitled: Fain Would I Have a Pretty Thing to Give unto My Lady. *Unknown. See* Fain Would I Have a Pretty Thing.
Proper Sonnet, A, How Time Consumeth All Earthly Things. *Unknown, at. to* Thomas Proctor. OBSC; SiCE; TuPP
 (Ayme, Ayme, I Sigh to See the Scythe Afield.) PoD
 (How Time Consumeth All Earthly Things.) ChTr; EIL
 (Sic Transit.) BLV; TrGrPo
Proper Sonnet, A, Intituled: I Smile to See How You Devise. *Unknown.* ReIE
Proper Study of Man [*or* Mankind], The. Pope. *See* Know Then Thyself.
Proper way for a man to pray, The. The Prayer of Cyrus Brown. Sam Walter Foss. BOHV; LHV; StaSt
Proper way to leave a room, The. Nonsense Quatrains. Gelett Burgess. CenHV
Propertian. L. A. MacKay. *Fr.* Erotica Antiqua. PeCV
Propertius! nerve thy spirit for the fight. Cynthia, Cynthia. Propertius. LiTW
Prophecy, A. Walter Savage Landor. *See* Proud Word You Never Spoke.
Prophecy, A. *At. to* Arthur Lee. PAH
Prophecy. Marjorie Meeker. NP
Prophecy. Nellie Burget Miller. BAP
Prophecy. Luigi Pulci, *tr. fr. Italian. Fr.* Il Morgante maggiore. BoHiPo; PAH
Prophecy. Jules Supervielle, *tr. fr. French by* Wallace Fowlie. MiCF
Prophecy. Tennyson. *Fr.* Locksley Hall. CBE; GTBS-W; TreF; WBLP
 (Federation of the World.) MaRV; PoRL
 ("For I dipped [or dipt] into the future, far as human eye could see.") PGD; PYM
 (Poet's Prophecy, A.) PTA-1
 (Universal Peace, The.) AOAH
 (Vision, A.) BoHiPo
 (Vision of the World, The.) GrCo-1
Prophecy, A. Maurice Thompson. *See* He Is Not Dead.
Prophecy. *Unknown.* DDA
Prophecy. Gulian Verplanck. MC
Prophecy, The. Lon Woodrum. MaRV
Prophecy. Elinor Wylie. AnAmPo; LA; MOAP
Prophecy of Capys, The. Macaulay. BHV
Prophecy of Cuauhtémoc, *sel.* Ignacio Rodríguez Galván, *tr. fr. Spanish by* Samuel Beckett.
 "Space is azure and the mountains bathe." AnMP
Prophecy of Dante, The. Byron. EmBrPo
Prophecy of Diana, The. Layamon, *tr. fr. Middle English. Fr.* The Brut. MeEV
Prophecy of Famine, The; a Scots Pastoral. Charles Churchill. EiPP
 Scotland, *sel.* BeR
Prophecy of Taliesin, The. Taliesin, *tr. fr. Welsh by* George Borrow. PoFr
Prophecy Sublime, The. Frederick Lucian Hosmer. *See* Thy Kingdom Come, O Lord.
Prophet, The. Thomas Curtis Clark. HH; PEDC
Prophet, The. Abraham Cowley. BLV; TrGrPo
Prophet, The, *sels.* Kahlil Gibran.
 Crime and Punishment. PoToHe (new ed.)
 "In the depth of your hopes and desires." UnW
 Of Religion. GrCo-2
 Of Work. GrCo-2
 (On Work, *abr.*) PoToHe (new ed.)
 On Children. PoToHe (new ed.)
 On Friendship. BoFr
 On Giving. BoFr; MaRV
Prophet, The. Mikhail Lermontov, *tr. fr. Russian by* J. S. Phillimore. BoR
Prophet, The. Kostes Palamas, *tr. fr. Modern Greek by* Rae Dalven. Fr. The Twelve Songs of the Gypsy. MoGP
Prophet, The. George Matthews Perkins. CAG
Prophet, The. Pushkin, *tr. fr. Russian by* Babette Deutsch *and* Avrahm Yarmolinsky. AWP; JAWP; WBP; WGRP; BoR, *tr. by* Maurice Baring; LiTW, *rev. tr. by* Babette Deutsch; TrRV, *rev. tr. by* Babette Deutsch
Prophet, The. Sherard Vines. LBBV; QS
Prophet, The. "Yehoash," *tr. fr. Yiddish by* Isidore Goldstick. TrJP
Prophet and Fool. Louis Golding. HBMV
Prophet Jeremiah and the Personification of Israel, The. *At. to* Eleazar Ben Kalir, *tr. fr. Hebrew by* Nina Davis Salaman. TrJP
Prophet Lost in the Hills at Evening, The. Hilaire Belloc. JKCP; OxBoCh
Prophet of disaster ceased to shout, The. The Broken Drought. Robert Frost. CoV
Prophet of the body's roving. Walt Whitman. Edwin Honig. NePA
Prophet, scourged by his own hand, progressed, The. John the Baptist. Louis Simpson. NePoEA
Prophetess. Whittier. *Fr.* Snow-bound. AA
Prophetess, The; or, The History of Dioclesian, *sel. At. to* Dryden *and to* Thomas Betterton.
 What Shall I Do? SeCL
Prophetic Death. Simonides, *tr. fr. Greek by* Lord Neaves. OnPM
Prophetic Hour, The. Michael Thwaites. PoFr
Prophets Exposed. Euripides, *tr. fr. Greek by* M. Wodhull. *Fr.* Helen. GrR

Prophets, gazing toward the mountains. The Home Winner. Gene Lindberg. PoOW
Prophets in Their Time. Longfellow. *Fr.* Christus; a Mystery: Introitus. GrCo-2
(Fate of the Prophets, The.) WGRP
Prophets, preaching in new stars. The Pontoon Bridge Miracle. Vachel Lindsay. *Fr.* Every Soul Is a Circus. LiTM (rev. ed.); LoBV; NePA
Prophet's vision leaves me cold, The. City of God. R. H. Long. BoAu
Prophets Who Cannot Sing. Coventry Patmore. *Fr.* The Unknown Eros, II, xvi. CoBE; PoVP
Propinquity Needed. Charles Battell Loomis. BOHV; InMe; PA
Proportion. Ben Jonson. *See* It Is Not Growing like a Tree.
Proposal. Bayard Taylor. PR
Proposal. *Unknown.* TreFS
Proposed Barter. Grace Hazard Conkling. TBM
Proposition. Nicolás Guillén, *tr. fr. Spanish by* Langston Hughes. FaPON; PoNe
Propped on pillows, not attending to business. Sick Leave. Po Chü-i. TrCh
Propped on the bar. Sam. Arthur St. John Adcock. WhC
Propriety. Marianne Moore. UnS
Prosaic miles of streets stretch all round. Seder-Night. Israel Zangwill. TrJP
Prose and Poesy; a Rural Misadventure. Thomas R. Ybarra. WhC
Prose Poem: Angels, The. Théodore de Banville, *tr. fr. French by* Stuart Merrill. OnPM
Prose Poem: By the River. Judith Gautier, *tr. fr. French by* Stuart Merrill. OnPM
Prose Poem: Dog and the Flask, The. Baudelaire, *tr. fr. French by* Arthur Symons. OnPM
Prose Poem: Harlequin. Théodore de Banville, *tr. fr. French by* Stuart Merrill. OnPM
Prose Poem: House in the Heart. Judith Gautier, *tr. fr. French by* Stuart Merrill. OnPM
Prose Poem: Indifference. Judith Gautier, *tr. fr. French by* Stuart Merrill. OnPM
Prose Poem: Irremediable, The. Emile Hennequin, *tr. fr. French by* Stuart Merrill. OnPM
Prose Poem: Mysterious Flute. Judith Gautier, *tr. fr. French by* Stuart Merrill. OnPM
Prose Poem: Red Flower, The. Judith Gautier, *tr. fr. French by* Stuart Merrill. OnPM
Prose Poem: Sadness of the Husbandman. Judith Gautier, *tr. fr. French by* Stuart Merrill. OnPM
Prose Poem: Sages' Dance. Judith Gautier, *tr. fr. French by* Stuart Merrill. OnPM
Prose Poem: Stranger, The. Baudelaire, *tr. fr. French by* Stuart Merrill. OnPM
Prose Poem: Windows, The. Baudelaire, *tr. fr. French by* Stuart Merrill. OnPM
Prose Poem: Words. Emile Hennequin, *tr. fr. French by* Stuart Merrill. OnPM
Proserpina. Thomas Campion. *See* Hark, All You Ladies That Do Sleep!
Proserpine. Swinburne. *Fr.* The Garden of Proserpine. ChTr
("Pale, beyond porch and portal.") FaBoEn
Proserpine at Enna. Ronald Bottrall. SeCePo
Proserpine may pull her flowers. Song of the Stygian Naiades. Thomas Lovell Beddoes. EnRP; ERP; NBE
Prosit Neujahr. George Santayana. InMe
Prosopopoia; or, Mother Hubberd's Tale, *abr.* Spenser. ReIE
At Court, *sel.* PoFr
Prospect. Thomas Curtis Clark. PoRL
Prospect, The. Thomas Hardy. NeMA
Prospect is bare and white, The. Winter Dusk. Richard Kendall Munkittrick. BOHV
Prospect of Children, A. Lawrence Durrell. *Fr.* Eight Aspects of Melissa. NeBP
Prospect of Eden, The. Milton. *Fr.* Paradise Lost, IV. PoEL-3
Prospect of Heaven Makes Death Easy, A. Isaac Watts. *See* Heaven.
Prospectus. Wordsworth. *Fr.* The Recluse. ERP
("On Man, on Nature.") EPN; EPP; NBE; OBRV
Prospero [Ends the Revels]. Shakespeare. *See* Our Revels Now Are Ended.
Prospero's Epilogue. Shakespeare. *Fr.* The Tempest: Epilogue. KN
(Epilogue: "Now my charmes are all ore-throwne.") NBE
Prospice. Robert Browning. AEV; AnFE; BBV; BEL; BLP; BLV; BMEP; BoLiVe; BPN; CoBE; DD; EM-2; EmBrPo; EnL; EnLi-2; EnLit; EPN; EV-5; FaBoEn; FiP; GEPC; GTBS; GTBS-W; GTSL; HBV; HBVY; HiLiEn; InP; LEAP; LiTB; LiTL; MaRV; MCCG; NeHB; OAEP; OBEC; OBVV; OQP; OuHeWo; PC; PECK; PIAE; PoRA; PoVP; QP-1; REAL; RiBV; TreFS; SeCeV; TCEP; TOP; TrGrPo; TwP; TyEnPo; UnPo (1st ed.); VA; ViPo; ViPP; VLEP; WGRP; YT
Prostrate, self-scorning. Prayer for Wings. Dmitry Sergeyevich Merezhkovsky. OnPM; TrRV
Protagonist, The. Peter Hopegood. MoAuPo
Proté, thou art not dead; but thou hast passed. Immortality. *Unknown.* OnPM
Protecting Tree, The. William O'Kelly. James Stephens. BoFr
Protection of Jehovah, The. Psalms, XXIII, Bible, *O.T. See* Lord Is My Shepherd, The.
Protection of the Lord, The. Psalms, XCI, Bible, *O.T. See* God Our Refuge.
Protective Colouring. Theognis, *tr. fr. Greek by* F. L. Lucas. GrPE
Protector, The. Ibn Sharaf. *tr. fr. Arabic by* A. J. Arberry. MooP
Protector, The, *sel.* George Wither.
"This glorious title hath in it exprest." PoFr
Protectress of Athens, The. Solon, *tr. fr. Greek by* Gilbert Highet. OxBG
Protest, A. Arthur Hugh Clough. VA
Protest. Countee Cullen. CDC; PFE
Protest, The. James Russell Lowell. PR
Protest, A. Sir Thomas Wyatt. OBSC
Protest against the Ballot. Wordsworth. EPN
Protest in Passing. Leonora Speyer. BAP; HBMV; PC
Protest in the Sixth Year of Ch'ien Fu, A (A.D. 879). Ts'ao Sung, *tr. fr. Chinese by* Arthur Waley. LiTW; MoPW; OnPM; PoFr; TrCh
Protest of the Illiterate, The, *sel.* Gelett Burgess.
"I seen a dunce of a poet once, a-writin' a little book." FiBHP
Protestant Ascendency. John O'Hagan. TIP
Protestation. Bertrans de Born, *tr. fr. Provençal by* John Peale Bishop. LiTW
Protestation, The. Thomas Carew. OuHeWo
Protestation, The. Selwyn Image. VA
Proteus; or, The Shapes of Conscience. Rolfe Humphries. LiTM (1946 ed.)
Protevangelium of James, The, *sel. Unknown.*
Lament of Saint Ann, The. CAW
Prothalamion, *sel.* Robert Hillyer.
Second Section: "The hills turn hugely in their sleep." MAP; MoAmPo
Prothalamion. Delmore Schwartz. OxBA
Prothalamion. Spenser. AnFE; AtBAP; ATP; AWP; BEL; CaAE; CBOV; ChTr; CoBE; ElL; ElSeCe; EnL; EnLi-1; EnLit; EPP; EV-1; FaBoEn; GEPC; GoTL; GTBS; GTBS-D; GTBS-W; GTSE; GTSL; HBV; InPo; LEAP; LiTB; LiTG; LiTL; LoBV; MaPo; MCCG; OBEV; OBSC; OuHeWo; PoE; ReaPo; ReEn; ReIE; RiBV; SeCePo; ShBV-4; SiCE; TCEP; TOP; TwHP; TyEnPo; UnPo (1st ed.); ViBoPo; WHA
Prothalamion. Terence Tiller. NeBP
Prothalamion. Francis Brett Young. HBMV
Prothalamium. Donagh MacDonagh. NeIP
Prothalamium. May Sarton. NePoAm
Prothalamium. A. J. M. Smith. CaP
Protinus Extremo cum Jam Boreas Autumno. Politian, *tr. fr. Latin by* D. C. Allen. LaP
Protogenes and Apelles. Matthew Prior. GoTL
Proton, neutron, electron. This Age, This Faust. George Reavey. SiTL
Prototypes. Madison Cawein. SPP
Proud, The. Frances Frost. OQP; QP-2
Proud Aegyptian queen, her Roman guest, The. *See* Proud Egyptian queen . . .
Proud and lowly, beggar and lord. London Bridge. Frederic Edward Weatherly. VA
Proud and rest-ive Chim-pan-zee, The. Having a Wonderful Time. D. B. Wyndham Lewis. FiBHP
Proud as Apollo on his forked hill. Bufo. Pope. *Fr.* Epistle to Dr. Arbuthnot. OBEC
Proud Chloe's Heart. Horace, *tr. fr. Latin by* William Boscawen. OnPM
Proud Egyptian [*or* Aegyptian] queen, her Roman guest, The. And She Washed His Feet with Her Teares [*or* The Magdalen]. Sir Edward Sherburne. ACP; AEV; ChTr; GoBC; MeLP; MeRV; OBS; OxBoCh; SeCL; SeEP
Proud Ellensborg. *Unknown, tr. fr. Danish by* E. M. Smith-Dampier. BoDaBa
Proud Florentines, The. Keats. *Fr.* Isabella; or, The Pot of Basil. PoFr
Proud fountains, wave your plumes. Fountains. Sir Osbert Sitwell. MBP; MoBrPo
Proud Hollyhock. Marguerite Buller. BrR
Proud in thy love, how many have I cited. *Unknown. Fr.* Zepheria. ReIE; TuPP
Proud is Phasellus here, my friends, to tell. Catullus, *tr. fr. Latin by* James Elroy Flecker. LaP
Proud King, The. William Morris. *Fr.* The Earthly Paradise. EV-5
Proud Lady, A. Elinor Wylie. ChMo
Proud Lady Margaret. *Unknown.* BaBo; ESPB; OBB

Proud, languid lily of the sacred Nile. The Lotus of the Nile. Arthur W. H. Eaton. CPG
Proud Little Spruce Fir. Jeannie Kirby. BoTP
Proud Lover. Richard Henry Stoddard. PR
Proud Maisie. Sir Walter Scott. *Fr.* The Heart of Midlothian, *ch.* 38. AtBAP; BCEP; BLV; BPN; BSV; CaAE; CBOV; CH; ChTr; CoBE; CoEV; EBSV; EmBrPo; EnLi-2; EnLit; EnRP; EPN; ERP; EtPaEn; EV-4; GoTS; GTSL; HBV; InP; LEAP; LoBV; OAEP; OBEV; OBRV; OTPC (1923 ed.); PIAE; PoE; PoEL-4; SeCePo; SeCeV; ShBV-1; TCEP; TrGrPo; TyEnPo; UnPo
(Pride of Youth.) CG; GTBS; GTBS-D; GTBS-W
("Proud Maisie is in the wood.") EG; FaBoCh; LoGBV
Proud men/ Eternally/ Go about. The Kallyope Yell. Vachel Lindsay. BLV; BoLiVe
Proud Miss MacBride, The. John Godfrey Saxe. LPS-3
Proud New York. John Reed. HBMV; NP
Proud of my broken heart since thou didst break it. Emily Dickinson. ViBoPo
Proud of the war, all glorious went the son. Inscription for a Fountain. Stephen Gwynn. GTIV
Proud of you, fond of you, clinging so near to you. My Owen. Ellen Mary Patrick Downing. HBV; TIP
Proud Paulus, late my secrecies revealing. Of Honest Theft. To My Good Friend Master Samuel Daniel. Sir John Harington. SiCE
Proud Riders. Harold Lenoir Davis. AnAmPo; LA; NP
Proud Song, A. Marguerite Wilkinson. BAP; HBMV
Proud Trees, The. Walter H. Kerr. NePoAm-2
Proud, Unhoped-for Light. Raymond Holden. MAP; MoAmPo (1942 ed.)
Proud Vegetables, The. Mary McNeil Fenollosa. GFA
Proud with success, richly pleased. Alexander Jannai. C. P. Cavafy. TrJP
Proud Word You Never Spoke [but You Will Speak]. Walter Savage Landor. *Fr.* Ianthe. BPN; CaAE; CBOV; EmBrPo; EnLoPo; EPN; ERP; EV-4; GTBS; GTSL; OBEV; TOP; ViBoPo
(Prophecy, A.) VA
Proudest now is but my peer, The. The Poor Voter on Election Day. Whittier. PoRL; TCAP
Proudly the note of the trumpet is sounding. O'Donnell Aboo. Michael Joseph McCann. OnYI
Proudly, the sleek horseman tramples the fallen flowers. To a Beautiful Lady Encountered on the Road. Li Po. WhP
Provençal Lovers; Aucassin and Nicolette. Edmund Clarence Stedman. HBV; LBAP
Proverb reporteth, no man can deny, The. *Unknown. Fr.* Tom Tyler and His Wife. ElL; ElSeCe; SiCE; TuPP
Proverbial Philosophy, *sel.* Martin Farquhar Tupper.
Of Cruelty to Animals. LPS-3
Proverbial Wisdom. *Unknown, tr. fr. Sanskrit by* Sir Edwin Arnold. BoFr
Proverbs, *sels.* Bible, *O.T.*
Drunkard, The, XXIII: 29–35. TrJP
(Wine and Woe, *Moulton, Modern Reader's Bible.*) MaRV
Fear of the Lord, The, I: 7. TrJP
Foolish Woman, A, IX: 13–18. TrGrPo
Four Things, XXX: 24–28. FaPON; GoTP
Good Housewife, The, XXXI: 10–29. GrCo-2
(Good Wife, The, XXXI: 10–31.) TrGrPo
(Mother of the House, XXXI: 25–29.) GoTP; OQP; PGD; PSO; QP-1
(Virtuous Wife, The, XXXI: 10–31.) MaRV
(Virtuous Woman, The, XXXI: 10–31.) TrJP
Happy Is the Man That Findeth Wisdom, III: 11–18. TreF
(Happy Is the Man, III: 13–18.) TrJP
(Wisdom, III: 16–18.) BPP
"He that is slow to anger is better than the mighty," XVI: 32. FaPON; TiPo (1952 ed.)
House of Wisdom, The, IX. 1–6. TrGrPo
Legacy, The, IV: 1–13. TrJP
Lips of the Wise, The, XV: 1–5, 7–8, 15–17. TrGrPo
(Merry Heart, A, XV: 1, 13, 15–17.) StVeCh
("Soft answer turneth away wrath, A," XV: 1) TiPo (1952 ed.)
"Lord possessed me in the beginning of his ways, The," VIII: 22–31, *Douay vers.* ISi
"My son, keep my words," VII: 1, 4–10, 12–27. LO
Neither Poverty nor Riches, XXX: 7–9. TrJP
Reproof, A, VI: 6–11. TrGrPo
(Go to the Ant.) FaPON (6–8); LiTW
(Go to the Ant, Thou Sluggard.) TrJP
(Sluggard, The—a Sonnet, *Moulton, Modern Reader's Bible.*) MaRV
Seven Evils, VI: 16–19. TrGrPo
(Sower of Discord, A, *Moulton, Modern Reader's Bible.*) MaRV
She of the Impudent Face, VII: 6–27. TrJP
"Withhold not good from them to whom it is due," III: 27–29, VI: 1–4. BoFr
Word Fitly Spoken, A, XXV: 11. FaPON
Words of Agur, The, XXX: 4, 15–16, 18–19, 24–28. TrGrPo
(Too Wonderful, XXX: 18–19.) TrJP
Proverbs. Samuel ha-Nagid. *tr. fr. Hebrew by* Israel Abrahams. TrJP
Proverbs. *Unknown, ad. fr. German by* Louis Untermeyer. RIS
Proverbs of Hell. Blake. *Fr.* The Marriage of Heaven and Hell. AtBAP; EM-1; EnLi-2; RO
Proverbs of King Alfred, *sels. At. to* Alfred, King of England, *tr. fr. Middle English.* TCEP; WaKn
Provide, Provide. Robert Frost. AmP; AtBAP; MoAB
Providence. Addison. *See* When All Thy Mercies.
Providence. William Cowper. *See* Light Shining Out of Darkness.
Providence. Vincenzo da Filicaja, *tr. fr. Italian by* Leigh Hunt. CAW
Providence. Reginald Heber. GN; HBV; OHIP
(Lo, the Lilies of the Field.) OTPC (1923 ed.)
Providence. Matthias Jochumsson, *tr. fr. Icelandic by* Jakobina Johnson. IcP
Providence. William Langland, *mod. by* Henry W. Wells. *Fr.* The Vision of Piers Plowman. PoLi
Providence. Cale Young Rice. WGRP
Provident and wakeful fear, A. Walter Savage Landor. Lyrics and Epigrams, XX. ERP
Province I govern is humble and remote, The. To Li Chien. Po Chü-i. AWP; TrCh
Provinces, The. Francis Carlin. SBMV
Provincia Deserta. Ezra Pound. CrMA; OxBA; TCPD
Provincial old maids. Old Maids. Luis Carlos López. TwSpPo
Proving. Georgia Douglas Johnson. CDC
Provocation to Satire. Pope. *See* Satire: "Ask you what provocation I have had?"
Provoked Wife, The, *sel.* Sir John Vanbrugh.
Philira. SeCL
(Song: "Fly, fly, you happy shepherds, fly.") SeEP
Prowling wolf, whose shaggy skin, A. The Wolf and the Dog. La Fontaine, *wr. at. to* Félix María de Samaniego. AnSpL-2; LiA; LiTW; PoFr
Proximity to the sea is hereby abolished. Gulf of Mexico. Alfonso Reyes. OnHM
Prudence. Benjamin Franklin. LauV
Prudence. Sadi, *tr. fr. Persian by* Sir Edwin Arnold. PeP
Prudent chief with calm attention heard, The. After the Chariot-Race. Homer. *Fr.* The Iliad, XXIII. OxBG
Prue, my dearest maid, is sick. Upon Prudence Baldwin Her Sicknesse. Robert Herrick. OAEP; SeCV-1
Prune Flowers. Lu Yu, *tr. fr. Chinese by* Pai Chwen-yu. WhP
Prune thou thy words, the thoughts control. Flowers without Fruit. Cardinal Newman. EPN; LPS-3
Prune Trees. Lu Yu, *tr. fr. Chinese by* Pai Chwen-yu. WhP
Pruned Trees. Gloria Goddard. BAP
Pruners; Conca di Marini. Joseph Langland. NePoEA
Pruning Trees. Po Chü-i, *tr. fr. Chinese by* Arthur Waley. TrCh
Pruning Vines. Howard McKinley Corning. MAP; MoAmPo (1942 ed.)
P's and Q's. Rupert Sargent Holland. OTPC
P's the proud Policeman. Phyllis McGinley. *Fr.* All Around the Town. TiPo
Psallite Gaudentes. *Unknown.* AnEC
Psalm VI: "And on that day, upon the heavenly scarp." A. M. Klein. *Fr.* The Psalter of Avram Haktani. PeCV
(Upon the Heavenly Scarp.) BoCaPo
Psalm II: "Hail to the springtime of deathless creation." Björnstjerne Björnson, *tr. fr. Norwegian by* Charles W. Stork. AnNoLy
Psalm: "Happy is the man whom Thou hast set apart." "Yehoash," *tr. fr. Yiddish by* Isidore Goldstick. TrJP
Psalm CXLVIII: "Hosanna to the King." Christopher Smart, *paraphrased from* Bible, *O.T.* RO
Psalm LXXXIV: "How lovely are thy dwellings fair!" Milton, *paraphrased fr.* Bible, *O.T.* TrPWD
Psalm IX: "I am not of the saints, O Lord, to wear." A. M. Klein. QS
Psalm: "I proclaim Thee great and wonderful." Murilo Mendes, *tr. fr. Portuguese by* Dudley Poore. AnCL
Psalm XCI: "Make the great God thy fort, and dwell." Thomas Carew, *paraphrased fr.* Bible, *O.T.* MeRV
Psalm, A: "O God, in whom my deepest being dwells." Edmund Blunden. QS; TrPWD
Psalm CXXXIX: "O Lord, in me there lieth nought." Countess of Pembroke, *paraphrased fr.* Bible, *O.T.* OBSC; OxBoCh
Psalm VIII: "O Lord, our Lord," *sel.* Christopher Smart, *paraphrased fr.* Bible, *O.T.*
"Lord what is man, that he should find." TrPWD
Psalm XC: "Our God, our help in ages past." Isaac Watts. *See* O God, Our Help in Ages Past.
Psalm CLI: "Praise ye the Lord, O Nations!" Alter Brody. QS

Psalm: "Savior Eternal, night and day before Thee." Théodore Agrippa d'Aubigné, *pr. tr. fr. French, paraphrased fr.* Bible, *O.T.*
(Psalm Eighty-eight.) LiA
Psalm: "Show pity, Lord." R. A. Lapsley, *paraphrased fr.* Bible, *O.T.*
(Psalm Fifty-one.) PraP
Psalm XIX: "Spacious firmament on high, The." Addison. *See* "Spacious Firmament on High, The."
Psalm XII: "These were the ones who thanked their God." A. M. Klein. *Fr.* The Psalter of Avram Haktani. PeCV
Psalm: "They have burned to Thee many tapers." Jessie E. Sampter. NV; OQP; QP-1
Psalm XXXVII: "Trust in the Lord." Charles Frederic Sheldon, *paraphrased fr.* Bible, *O.T.* BLRP
Psalm, The: "While Northward the hot sun was sinking o'er the trees." Robert Bridges. FaBoTw; LiTB
Psalm against the Darkness. A. M. Sullivan. MaRV
Psalm Eighty-eight. Théodore Agrippa d'Aubigné. *See* Psalm: "Savior Eternal, night and day before Thee."
Psalm Fifty-one. R. A. Lapsley. *See* Psalm: "Show pity, Lord."
Psalm for Christmas Day. Thomas Pestel. OxBoCh
(For Christmas Day, *sl. abr.*) AnEC
Psalm for Moderns, A. Thomas P. McDonnell. JKCP (1955 ed.)
Psalm for Sunday Night, A. Thomas Pestel. OxBoCh
Psalm of Battle. *Unknown, tr. fr. Arabic by* E. Powys Mathers. *Fr.* The Thousand and One Nights. AWP; JAWP; WBP
Psalm of Confidence, A. Horace Westwood. MaRV
Psalm of David, A. Psalms, XXIII, Bible, *O.T. See* Lord Is My Shepherd, The.
Psalm of David, A. Psalms, VIII, Bible, *O.T. See* What Is Man?
Psalm of Life, A, *parody.* Phoebe Cary. PA
Psalm of Life, A, *parody.* Andrew Lang. CenHV
Psalm of Life, A. Longfellow. AA; AnNE; BAP; BAV; BHV; CoBA; FaBoBe; HBV; HBVY; IAP; LEAP; LPS-3; MaRV; NeHB; OHFP; PECK; PIR; PreP; PTA-1; PYM; TCAP; TreF; TSWC; TVSH; UnPo; WBLP; YaD
Life, *sel.* GN
(Lives of Great Men All Remind Us, *shorter sel.*) DD
Psalm of Praise, A. Psalms, VIII, Bible, *O.T. See* What Is Man?
Psalm of Praise. Psalms, C, Bible, *O.T. See* Thanksgiving.
Psalm of Silence, The. Konstantin Dmitreyevich Balmont, *tr. fr. Russian by* Babette Deutsch. OnPM; TrRV
Psalm of the Early Buddhist Sisters, A. *Unknown.* WGRP
Psalm of the Shepherd, The. Psalms, XXIII, Bible, *O.T. See* Lord Is My Shepherd, The.
Psalm of the Singing Grave. Alexander Janta, *tr. fr. Polish by* Gladys Anthony White *and* Alexander Janta. LiTW
Psalm of the West, The, *sels.* Sidney Lanier.
Land of the Wilful Gospel. PAH
Lexington. PaA; PAH
(Battle of Lexington, *shorter sel.*) PAP
"My Dawn? my Dawn? How if it never break?" *sonnet* II. PeBoSo
"Or haply how if this contrarious West," *sonnet* III. PeBoSo
Story of Vinland, The. PAH
Triumph, The. PAH
Psalm of Those Who Go Forth before Daylight. Carl Sandburg. AnAmPo; LA; MOAP; MoShBr; OxBA; StVeCh
Psalm to My Belovèd. Eunice Tietjens. LoPS
(Fulfillment.) PoToHe (new ed.)
Psalm to the Holy Spirit. A. M. Sullivan. TrPWD
Psalm to the Son, A. Marguerite Wilkinson. TrPWD
Psalme CXXXVII: "As on Euphrates shady banks we lay." George Sandys. *Fr.* A Paraphrase on the Psalms of David. OBS
Psalme of Asaph, A. Psalms, L, Bible, *O.T.* LiA
Psalms, *sels.* Bible, *O.T.*
Psalm I ("Blessed is the man . . ."). AWP; JAWP; WoL
(Beatus Vir, *tr. by* Thomas Sternhold.) ReIE; SiCE
(Blessed Is the Man.) EnLi-1; HiLiEn
(Godly and the Ungodly, The.) TreF
(Happy Is the Man.) TrJP
(Patriot, The, *paraphrased by* Thomas Godfrey.) PoFr
(Tree and the Chaff, The, *Moulton, Modern Reader's Bible.*) WGRP
Psalm III ("Lord, how are they increased that trouble me!").
(Domine Quid Multiplicati Sunt, *tr. by* Thomas Sternhold.) SiCE
Psalm IV ("Hear me when I call . . .").
(Cum Invocarem, *tr. by* Thomas Sternhold.) SiCE
Psalm VIII ("O Lord, our Lord . . ."). AWP; JAWP; OnPM; OuHeWo; PFE; PG (1955 ed.)
(How Glorious Is Thy Name.) TrJP
(O Lord, How Excellent Is Thy Name.) TreFS
(Psalm of David, A.) OTPC (1946 ed.)
(Psalm of Praise, A.) CBOV
(Song of Praise, A.) EnLi-1
(What Is Man?) EM-1; MaRV; TrGrPo
"Lord what is man, that he should find," 4-9, *paraphrased by* Christopher Smart. TrPWD
When I Consider Thy Heavens, 3-8. FaPON; ImOP; InP
Psalm IX ("I will praise thee, O Lord . . .").
I Will Sing Praise, 1-2. FaPON
Psalm XIV ("The fool hath said in his heart, There is no God"). OnPM
(Fool Hath Said in His Heart, The.) TrJP
Psalm XV ("Lord, who shall abide . . ."). OuHeWo
Psalm XVIII ("I will love thee, O Lord . . .").
(David Praiseth God for His Manifold and Marveilous Blessings.) LiA
Psalm XIX ("The heavens declare . . ."). AWP; InP (1-4); JAWP; OuHeWo; PC; WoL
(Glory of God, The.) TrJP
(God's Glory.) TrGrPo
(Heavens Above and the Law Within, The, *Moulton, Modern Reader's Bible.*) WGRP
(Heavens Declare the Glory of God, The.) FaPON (1-4); HiLiEn; MaRV (1-6); ShBV-1; TreF
(Nineteenth Psalm.) WBLP
God's Precepts Perfect, 7-9. BLRP
Heavens, The, 1-6. ChTr
Law Within, The, 7-14, *Moulton, Modern Reader's Bible.* MaRV
Psalm XXII ("My God, my God . . .").
(Cry in Distress, A, 1-15.) TrGrPo
Psalm XXIII ("The Lord is my shepherd . . ."). AWP; EM-1; EnLi-1; ExPo; JAWP; OHIP; OnPM; OuHeWo; PC; PG (1955 ed.); ReIE; TiPo (1952 ed.); WBLP; WoL
(Lord Is My Shepherd, The.) FaPON; HiLiEn; MaRV; StVeCh; TreF; TrJP
(Protection of Jehovah, The, *Moulton, Modern Reader's Bible.*) WGRP
(Psalm of David.) SUS
(Psalm of the Shepherd, The.) GrCo-1
(Shepherd's Psalm, The.) PCD; PCH
(Twenty-third Psalm, The.) FaBoBe; NeHB; OTPC (1946 ed.); PoeMoYo; PreP; PYM; StaSt; TrGrPo
Psalm XXIV ("The Earth is the Lord's . . ."). AWP; EnLi-1; JAWP; OHIP, OnPM; OuHeWo; TiPo (1952 ed.); WoL
(Antiphonal, An.) CBOV
(Earth Is the Lord's, The.) FaPON (1-4); TrJP
(Lift Up Your Heads [O Ye Gates].) PCD; PCH; TrGrPo
(Twenty-fourth Psalm, The.) PreP
Psalm XXVII ("The Lord is my light . . .").
(Deliverance of Jehovah, The, *Moulton, Modern Reader's Bible.*) WGRP
(My Light and My Salvation, *Moulton, Modern Reader's Bible.*) MaRV
Serenity of Faith, The, 7-14, *tr. by* McFadyen. BLRP
Psalm XXIX ("Give unto the Lord . . ."). AWP; OnPM; PFE
Psalm XXXVII ("Fret not thyself . . ."). WoL
(Psalm XXXVII: "Trust in the Lord," *paraphrased by* Charles Frederic Sheldon.) BLRP
Fret Not Thyself because of Evildoers, 1, 2, 35, 36, 3. TiPo (1952 ed.)
Psalm XXXIX ("I said: 'I will take heed to my ways' ").
(Lord, Make Me to Know Mine End.) TrJP
Psalm XLI ("Blessed is he . . ."), *sel.*
"All that hate me whisper together against me," 7, 9, 12. BoFr
Psalm XLII ("As the hart panteth . . ."). AWP; JAWP; WoL
(As the Hart Panteth.) TrJP
(My Soul Thirsteth for God.) TrGrPo
(Search, The, XLII *and* XLIII, *Moulton, Modern Reader's Bible.*) WGRP
(Where Is Thy God? *paraphrased by* J. Lewis Milligan.) MaRV
Psalm XLIII ("Judge me, O God . . ."). OnPM
(Search, The, XLII *and* XLIII, *Moulton, Modern Reader's Bible.*) WGRP
Psalm XLIV ("My heart hath uttered . . ."), *Douay vers., sel.*
"Queen stood on thy right hand, The," 10-16. ISi
Psalm XLVI ("God is our refuge . . ."). AWP; OnPM
(From Psalm XLVI, *abr.*) PC
(Our Refuge, *Moulton, Modern Reader's Bible.*) MaRV
(Refuge, The, *Moulton, Modern Reader's Bible.*) WGRP
(Though the Earth Be Removed.) TrGrPo
Psalm L ("The mighty God . . .").
(Psalme of Asaph, A.) LiA
Psalm LI ("Have mercy upon me, O God, after thy great goodness," *Book of Common Prayer*). LiTW
(Psalm Fifty-one: "Show pity, Lord," *paraphrased by* R. A. Lapsley.) PraP

Psalms (*continued*)
Psalm LV ("Give ear to my prayer . . ."). AWP
"And I said, Oh that I had wings like a dove!" 6–7, 12–14. 21–22. BoFr
(Wings, 6–7.) FaPON; PCD; PCH
Psalm LXII ("Truly my soul waiteth . . .").
(Leave It all Quietly to God, 1–8, *tr. by* James Moffatt.) MaRV
Psalm LXV ("Praise waiteth for thee . . ."), *sel.*
"Thou visiteth the earth," 9–13. OHIP
Psalm LXVII ("God be merciful unto us, and bless us"). OnPM
Let the Nations Be Glad, 1–5. FaPON
Psalm LXX ("Make haste, O God, to deliver me"). OnPM
Psalm LXXVII ("I cried unto God . . ."). AWP
Psalm LXXIX ("O God, the heathen are come into Thine inheritance").
(Heathen Are Come into Thine Inheritance, The.) TrJP
Psalm LXXX ("Give ear, O Shepherd of Israel . . ."), *sel.*
Vine Out of Egypt, A, 8–15. LiA
Psalm LXXXIII ("O God, keep not Thou silence").
(Keep Not Thou Silence.) TrJP
Psalm LXXXIV ("How amiable are thy tabernacles . . .").
(Psalm LXXXIV: "How lovely are thy dwellings fair!" *paraphrased by* Milton.) TrPWD
How Lovely Are Thy Tabernacles, 1–5. TrJP
Psalm LXXXVIII ("O Lord God of my salvation . . ."). TriL
(Psalm Eighty-eight: "Savior Eternal, night and day before Thee," *paraphrased by* Théodore Agrippa d'Aubigné, *pr. tr. fr. French.*) LiA
Psalm XC ("Lord, thou hast been our dwelling place . . ."). AWP
(God, Our Dwelling Place, *Moulton, Modern Reader's Bible.*) MaRV
(Span of Man, The.) EM-1
(Thou Art God, *abr.*) BPP
Psalm XCI ("He that dwelleth . . ."). AWP; PC; WoL
(Everlasting Arms, *Moulton, Modern Reader's Bible.*) WGRP
(God Our Refuge, *Moulton, Modern Reader's Bible.*) MaRV
(Mighty Fortress, A.) TrGrPo
(Protection of the Lord.) EM-1
(Psalm XCI: "Make the great God thy fort, and dwell," *paraphrased by* Thomas Carew.) MeRV
Psalm XCIII ("The Lord reigneth . . .").
(Jehovah's Immovable Throne, *Moulton, Modern Reader's Bible.*) WGRP
Psalm XCV ("O come, let us sing . . ."). AWP; BLRP, *abr.*; JAWP; OHIP, *abr.*; OnPM; OuHeWo; PC, *abr.*
(Thanksgiving, 1–7.) BoChLi (1950 ed.)
Psalm XCVIII ("O sing unto the Lord . . ."). TriL
(Floods Clap Their Hands, The.) TrGrPo
(O Sing unto the Lord a New Song.) TrJP
(Sing unto Jehovah.) BLRP
(Sing unto the Lord.) StaSt
Psalm C ("Make a joyful noise . . ."). MPB; OHIP; OnPM; PG (1955 ed.); TiPo (1952 ed.); UnS
(Be Thankful unto Him.) FaPON
(Hundredth Psalm, The, *metrical vers.* William Kethe.) OtMeF
(Old Hundredth, *metrical vers.* William Kethe.) MaRV
(Psalm of Praise, A.) SiSoSe; SUS
(Scotch Te Deum, *metrical vers.* William Kethe.) WGRP
(Thanksgiving.) BoChLi (1950 ed.); StVeCh
Psalm CIII ("Bless the Lord, O my soul . ."). AWP; JAWP; PC, *abr.*; TiPo (1952 ed.) (1–5)
(Hymn of the World Within, The, *Moulton, Modern Reader's Bible.*) WGRP
Psalm CIV ("Bless the Lord, O my soul . . ."). OHIP, *sel.*
(Bless the Lord, O My Soul.) TrJP
(Hymn of the World Without, 1–24, *Moulton, Modern Reader's Bible.*) WGRP
Rich Earth, The, 16–24. GoTP
Psalm CVII ("O give thanks . . ."), *sel.*
They That Go Down to the Sea in Ships. BBV (1951 ed.) (23–31); ChTr (23–31); EtS (23–30); FaPON (23–24); GaP (23–24); MuP (23–31)
(Ocean, The, 23–32, *Moulton, Modern Reader's Bible.*) WGRP
Psalm CXIII ("Praise ye the Lord . . ."). OnPM
Psalm CXIV ("When Israel came out of Egypt," *Book of Common Prayer*). LiTW
(When Israel Came Forth out of Egypt.) TrJP
Psalm CXVIII ("O give thanks unto the Lord, for He is good").
(O Give Thanks.) TrJP
Psalm CXXI ("I will lift up mine eyes . . ."). AWP; BBV (1951 ed.); EnLi-1; JAWP; OnPM; OuHeWo; PC
(I Will Lift Up Mine Eyes [unto the Hills].) BLP; FaPON; HiLiEn; TreF
(Pilgrim's Song, *Moulton, Modern Reader's Bible.*) WGRP
(Song of Safety, A.) PCH
(Song of Trust, A.) PCD; TrGrPo
(Unto the Hills, *paraphrased by* John Campbell.) MaRV
Psalm CXXIV ("If it had not been the Lord . . ."). OnPM
Psalm CXXVI ("When the Lord turned again the captivity of Zion"). OnPM
(Like unto Them That Dream.) TrJP
Psalm CXXVII ("Except the Lord build the house . . .). OnPM
(Except the Lord Build the House.) TrJP
Psalm CXXVIII ("Blessed is everyone that feareth the Lord").
(Beati Omnes, *tr. by* Thomas Sternhold.) ReIE; SiCE
Psalm CXXX ("Out of the depths . . ."). EnLi-1; LiTW (*Book of Common Prayer*); OnPM
(De Profundis.) BLRP; MaRV; TreF; WGRP; WHL
(Out of the Depths.) TrJP
(Song of Supplication, A.) TrGrPo
Psalm CXXXII ("Behold, how good and how pleasant it is").
(To Dwell Together in Unity.) TrJP
Psalm CXXXIII ("Behold, how good . . ."). AWP; JAWP; OnPM
Psalm CXXXVI ("O give thanks . . ."). AWP; OHIP
(Thanksgiving, 1–9, 26). BoChLi (1950 ed.)
"To him that smote Egypt in their firstborn," 10–24. PoFr
Psalm CXXXVII ("By the rivers of Babylon . . ."). AWP; ExPo; JAWP; LiTW; OnPM; PG (1955 ed.); StaSt (1–6, *ad.*)
(By the Rivers of Babylon.) TrJP
(Lament in Exile, A.) CBOV
(Psalme CXXXVII: "As on Euphrates shady banks," *paraphrased by* George Sandys.) OBS
(Song of Exile, A.) TrGrPo
Psalm CXXXIX ("O Lord, thou hast searched me . . .").
(Psalm CXXXIX: "O Lord, in me there lieth nought," *paraphrased by* the Countess of Pembroke. OBSC; OxBoCh
(Searcher of Hearts, The, 1–12, 23–24.) GrCo-1
(Searcher of Hearts Is Thy Maker, The, *Moulton, Modern Reader's Bible.*) CBOV; WGRP
Psalm CXLVI ("Hallelujah,/ Praise the Lord, O my soul").
(Hallelujah.) TrJP
(Lauda Anima Mea, *tr. by* John Hopkins.) ReIE
Psalm CXLVII ("Praise ye the Lord"). TiPo (1952 ed.), *abr.*
"Sing unto the Lord," *sel.* OHIP
"Sing unto the Lord with thanksgiving," 7–9, 12. PoRL
Who Maketh the Grass to Grow, 1, 5, 8–9, 16–18, 20. FaPON
Psalm CXLVIII ("Praise ye the Lord . . ."). TriL
(Hallelujah Chorus, A [Smith-Goodspeed *tr.*].) MaRV
(Praise Ye the Lord.) TrJP
(Psalm CXLVIII: "Hosanna to the King," *paraphrased by* Christopher Smart.) RO
(Song of Praise, A.) TrGrPo
(Universal Hallelujah, The, *paraphrased by* Isaac Watts.) BeR
Psalm CL ("Praise ye the Lord . . ."). OnPM; TiPo (1952 ed.); UnS
(Closing Doxology, The [Smith-Goodspeed *tr.*].) MaRV
(Laudate Dominum.) ChTr
Psalms of Love. Peter Baum, *tr. fr. German by* Jethro Bithell. AWP
Psalter of Avram Haktani, The, *sels.* A. M. Klein.
Psalm VI: "And on that day, upon the heavenly scarp." PeCV
(Upon the Heavenly Scarp.) BoCaPo
Psalm XII: "These were the ones who thanked their God." PeCV
Psalter of the Blessed Virgin Mary, *sels.* St. Bonaventure, *tr. fr. Latin by* Sister Mary Emmanuel. ISi
"Psittacus Eois Imitatrix Ales ab Indis." Sacheverell Sitwell. AtBAP; MBP; MoBrPo
Psyche. Viktor Rydberg, *tr. fr. Swedish by* Charles W. Stork. AnSL
Psyche hath found her Cupid out. Forewarned. Alice Brown. PR
Psyche's Lamp. Ada Foster Murray. BAP
Psychoanalysts. Christopher Morley. WhC
Psychology Class. Elizabeth K. Campbell. TwCaPo
Psycholophon. Gelett Burgess. CenHV; NA
Psychometrist. James Stephens. POTE
Psychopompos. H. P. Lovecraft. DaM
Ptolemy, poor Ptolemy. The Old Nurse's Song. Edith Sitwell. NeMA; TSW
Pub. Julian Symons. LiTB; LiTM; WaP
Public Acclaim. Friedrich Hölderlin, *tr. fr. German by* Kate Flores. AnGP
Public Aid for Niagara Falls. Morris Bishop. InMe

Public haunt they found her in, A. A Girl of Pompeii. Edward Sandford Martin. AA; HBV; OBAV
Public Holiday; Paris. Joyce Horner. GoYe
Public Library. Candace T. Stevenson. GoYe
Publication is the auction. Emily Dickinson. CoBA
Publisher to His Client, A. Byron. *See* Epistle from Mr. Murray to Dr. Polidori.
Puccini was Latin, and Wagner Teutonic. The Birds. Ogden Nash. *Fr.* The Carnival of Animals. UnS
Puck and the Fairy. Shakespeare. *See* Over Hill, over Dale.
Puck Goes to Court. Fenton Johnson. CDC; GoSl
Puck of Pook's Hill, *sels.* Kipling.
Cities and Thrones and Powers. CoEV; FaBoEn; GTBS-D; GTML; MoVE; PoEL-5; POTE; POTT; PoVP; SeCeV; ShBV-4; TwCV; ViPP
Land of Our Birth. BoTP; MaRV
(Children's Song, The.) MW; PoVP; TVSH
Puck's Song ("See you the ferny ride that steals"). FaBoCh; LoGBV; POTT
Smuggler's Song, A. ShBV-1
Puck Speaks. Shakespeare. *See* Now the Hungry Lion Roars.
Puck's Song ("Now the hungry lion"). Shakespeare. *See* Now the Hungry Lion Roars.
Puck's Song ("Over hill, over dale"). Shakespeare. *See* Over Hill, over Dale.
Pud-Wudjies. Patrick R. Chalmers. *See* Puk-Wudjies.
Pudden Tame. *Unknown.* ChTr
("What's your name?") GoTP
Pudding and Milk. *Unknown.* MeMeAg
Pudding and pie. Greedy Jane. *Unknown.* HBVY
Pudding Charms. Charlotte Druitt Cole. BoTP
Pudding Prepared and Eaten, The. Joel Barlow. *See* Husking, The.
Puddle, The. Morris Abel Beer. LEAP
Puddle, The. Jacinto Fombona Pachano, *tr. fr. Spanish by* H. R. Hays. TwSpPo
Puddle, The. Eden Phillpotts. BMEP; HBMV
Pudens to-day his Claudia doth claim. Marriage of Claudia. Martial. LiA
Puella Parvula. Wallace Stevens. PoFS
Puer ex Jersey. *Unknown* NA
Puer Nobis Natus Est. *Unknown.* AnEC
Puerto Rican Side-Street. Louis Dudek. TwCaPo
Puffed up with luring to her knees. The Flute. Joseph Russell Taylor. AA
Puffin, The. W. W. Gibson. ChMo; CMP
Pug-Dog and Spitz. F. Hey. SAS
Pugilist. Hipponax, *tr. fr. Greek by* F. L. Lucas. GrPE
Pugilistic Parody. *Unknown.* CAG
Puir Dash, thou'rt getting auld and frail. To My Auld Dog Dash. John Barr of Craigielee. AnNZ
Puk-Wudjies. Patrick R. Chalmers. BoTP; DD; HBVY
(Pud-Wudjies.) HOAH
Pulkovo Meridian, The, *sel.* Vera Inber, *tr. fr. Russian by* Dorothea Prall Radin *and* Alexander Kaun.
Leningrad: 1943. WaaP
Pull Down Thy Vanity. Ezra Pound. *Fr.* Canto LXXXI. MeRV
("Ant's a centaur in his dragon world, The.") FaBoEn
"Pull, men, for, lo, see there they blow!" Brand Fire New Whaling Song Right from the Pacific Ocean. *Unknown.* EtS
Pulled from our ruts by the made-to-order gale. Trans Canada. Francis Reginald Scott. BoCaPo (1948 ed.); PeCV
Pulley, The. George Herbert. AnFE; AtBAP; ATP; AWP; BCEP; BEL; BLV; BoLiVe; CaAE; CBOV; CenL; CoBE; CoEV; ElSeCe; EM-1; EnL; EnLi-1; EPS; ExPo; FaBoEn; HBV; InPo; LiTB; LiTG; MaRV; MePo; OAEP; OBEV; OBS; OtMeF; OuHeWo; OxBoCh; PoFS; PreP; ReaPo; ReEn; RiBV; SeCeV; SeCL; SeCV-1; SeEP; TCEP; TrGrPo; TwCrTr; TwHP; TyEnPo; UnPo (1st ed.); ViBoPo; WHA
(Gifts of God, The.) EV-2; GTBS; GTBS-D; GTBS-W; GTSE; GTSL; LPS-3
Pulling Down St. Martin's Church. Aaron Hill. *Fr.* To Clelia, on the Pulling Down St. Martin's Church. BeR
Pulling the dead sun's weight through County Meath. Cycling to Dublin. Robert Greacen. OnYI
Pulpit, therefore (and I name it filled), The. The True Preacher. William Cowper. *Fr.* The Task, II. MaRV
Pulse, The. Mark Van Doren. MAP; MoAmPo
Pulse of Darkness, The. John Fandel. JKCP (1955 ed.)
"Pulvis et Umbra." Callimachus, *tr. fr. Greek by* F. L. Lucas. GrPE
Pulvis et Umbra. Agnes Mary Frances Robinson. UnW
Pumas. George Sterling. BAP
Pumpkin, The. Robert Graves. PoMS
Pumpkin, The. Whittier DD; LPS-2; OHIP; PoRL; TOAH
Pumpkin Speaks, A. Amanda Barris. PCH
Punch and Judy. *Unknown.* OxNR
Punch, the Immortal Liar, *sels.* Conrad Aiken.
"Build a house of gold for Punch," Third Voice. NP
"Like a tower of brass is Punch," Fourth Voice. NP
"Look, he comes! how tall he is," Second Voice. NP
"Pave the sky with stars for Punch!" First Voice. NP
Puppet Dreams, The.
"Open a window on the world." MAP; MoAmPo
"Sheba, now let down your hair." MAP; MoAmPo
"There is a fountain in a wood." MAP; MoAmPo; NeMA
"Solomon, Clown, put by your crown," Fifth Voice. NP
Punchinello. Hugh de Burgh. CAW
Punching Clock, The. Milos Macourek, *tr. fr. Czech by* Michael Flach. LiTW
Punctilio. Mary Elizabeth Coleridge. OBEV (new ed.); OBVV; TOP
Punctually at Christmas the soft plush. White Christmas. W. R. Rodgers. ChMP; GTBS-W; LiTM; MoAB; MoBrPo (1950 ed.); SeCePo
Punishment. Emil Aarestrup, *tr. fr. Danish by* Charles W. Stork. BoDS
Punishment. John Charles McNeill. NoCaPo
Punkydoodle and Jollapin. Laura E. Richards. DDA
Puny child who knows he can have but little love, The. Our Lady, Help of Christians. Paul Claudel. ISi
Pup, The. Edgar A. Guest. AlBD
Pup Dog's Opinion of the Quick Tempered Man, The. Rowland C. Bowman. AlBD
Pup een da Snow, Da. T. A. Daly. AlBD; TSW
Pup in the Snowstorm. Frances Frost. AlBD
Pupil Returns to His Master. Fannie Stearns Davis. TBM
(Pupil to His Master, The.) PFY
Puppet Dreams, The. Conrad Aiken. *Fr.* Punch; the Immortal Liar. MAP; MoAmPo
"There is a fountain in a wood," *sel.* NeMA
Puppet Player, The. Angelina Weld Grimké. CDC
Puppets. Ming Huang, *tr. fr. Chinese by* Henry H. Hart. PoHN
Puppets. Patricia K. Page. BoCaPo (1948 ed.)
Puppy and I. A. A. Milne. BoTP; FaPON; TiPo
Puppy Problem, A. Emilie Poulsson. AlBD
(Puppy's Problem, A.) PPL
Pur. W. H. Auden. *See* This Lunar Beauty.
Pure air trembles, O pitiless God. Noon. Robinson Jeffers. MAP; MoAmPo; TCPD
Pure, and fragile and pale. Kiyowara, *tr. fr. Japanese by* Lois J. Erickson. SoLD
Pure are its waters—its shallows are bright. Green River. Bryant. IAP; PEOR; TCAP
"Pure as the snow," we say. Ah! never flake. Mary Immaculate. Eleanor C. Donnelly. CAW; JKCP
Pure blood domestic, guaranteed. The Prize Cat. E. J. Pratt. PeCV; TwCaPo; TwCV
Pure Cinna makes no question he's elect. Of Cinna's Election. Sir John Harington. SiCE
Pure, cold beyond the dream of death or birth. Stones of Greece. Stephen Gwynn. NeTW
Pure contralto sings in the organ loft, The. Song of Myself, XV. Walt Whitman. CoV; MaPo
Pure Death. Robert Graves. AWP; CoBMV; InPo; MoAB; MoPo; PoD
Pure founts of unapproachable fire. Aetna. Pindar. *Fr.* Pythian Odes, I. GrR
Pure Heart, The. Tennyson. *Fr.* Sir Galahad. MaRV; TreF
Pure Hypothesis, A. May Kendall. VA
Pure is the body on the Earth. He Singeth in the Underworld. *Unknown. Fr.* Book of the Dead. AWP; JAWP; WBP
Pure Is the Dewy Gem. Jeremiah Joseph Callanan. IrPN
Pure is the white pony. The White Pony. *Unknown.* ChLP; WhP
Pure Light, The. St. Matthew, V: 14-16, VI: 22-23, VII: 3-5, Bible, *N.T.* GrCo-1
Pure Love. Euripides, *tr. fr. Greek by* C. M. Bowra. OxBG
Pure Mathematician, A. Arthur Guiterman. PoMa
Pure Nails Brightly Flashing. Stéphane Mallarmé, *tr. fr. French by* Charles Glenn Wallis. LiTW
Pure of heart and therefore hungry. A Cicada. Li Shang-yin. OuHeWo
Pure pearl of silence brooding on the sky. Sonnet XV. Maximilian Aleksandrovich Voloshin. *Fr.* Lunaria. TrRV
Pure poetry, programme of the living heart. The Network. Robert Finch. CaP
Pure Products of America, The. William Carlos Williams. OnHM; OxBA
(Elsie.) AnAmPo; LA
(To Elsie.) CoBMV
Pure Spirit of the always-faithful God. Hymn for Pentecost. James Clarence Mangan. CAW; JKCP
Pure Spirit! that within a form of clay. The Disembodied Spirit. Fernando de Herrera. OnPM; TeCS
Pure stream, in whose transparent wave. To Leven Water. Tobias George Smollett. OBEV
Pure swan floating between air and wave, The. The Swan. Jorge Guillén. CoSP
Pure sweet spirit, generous and large, A. Henry Wadsworth Longfellow. William Wetmore Story. GA; PEOR

Pure, the bright, the beautiful, The. Things That Never Die. Charles Dickens. MaRV
Pure white mantle blotted out, A. Snow. Alfred Noyes. AlDL
Pure white the shields their arms upbear. The Fairy Host. *Tr. by* Alfred Perceval Graves. AnIV
Pure woman is to a man a crown. The Virtuous Wife. Süsskind von Trimberg. TrJP
Purest Soul[e] that e're was sent, The. An Other. Thomas Carew. SeCV-1; SeEP
Purgatorio. Hart Crane. NAMP
Purgatorio, *sels.* Dante. *Fr.* Divina Commedia.
  Buonconte Relates His Fate, *fr.* V, *pr. tr. by* Charles Eliot Norton. LiA
  Celestial Pilot, *fr.* II, *tr. by* Longfellow. WGRP
  Dante Sees Beatrice in Glory, *fr.* XXX, *tr. by* Thomas Okey. LiA
  Freedom of the Will, *fr.* XVIII, *tr. by* M. B. Anderson. GrCo-1
  "How haughty was thy mien," *fr.* VI, *tr. by* Jefferson Butler Fletcher. PoFr
  Marvel Ye Not, *fr.* III, *tr. by* Thomas Okey. LiA
  Moral Responsibility, *fr.* XVI, *tr. by* Jefferson Butler Fletcher. GrCo-2
  Political Chaos in Italy, *fr.* VI, *tr. by* Longfellow. WoL
  Purgatory, I, II, XXX-XXXIII, *with summaries of other cantos, tr. by* Henry F. Cary. OuHeWo
  Purgatory: Dante's Dream, *fr.* IX, *tr. by* Frances Winwar. EnLi-1
  Self-Guidance, *fr.* XXVII, *tr. by* Jefferson Butler Fletcher. GrCo-2
  " 'Twas now the hour that turneth back desire," *fr.* VIII, *tr. by* Longfellow. CAW
  "Veracious people, The," *fr.* XXX, *tr. by* Longfellow. CAW
Purgatory May Be Paradise. Sadi, *pr. tr. fr. Persian by* Sir Edwin Arnold. *Fr.* The Gulistan. OuHeWo
Purge me, O God. A Prayer. Wilbur Humphrey Fowler. MaRV
Purification, The. Richard Church. MBP; MoBrPo (1942 ed.); POTE
Purification, The. St. Cosmas, *tr. fr. Greek. Fr.* Menaion. ISi
Purification, The, *sel.* John Keble.
  Purity of Heart, *abr.* BLRP
Purification of the Blessed Virgin. Joseph Beaumont. ISi
Purist, The. Ogden Nash. FiBHP; MoAmPo (1950 ed.); MoShBr; NeMA; PreP
Purist to Her Love, The. Margaret Fishback. WhC
Puritan, The. Karl Shapiro. MoAmPo (1950 ed.)
Puritan Lady, A. Lizette Woodworth Reese. AnAmPo; InP; LA; MAP; MoAmPo; NP
Puritan on His Honeymoon, The. Robert Bly. NePoEA
Puritan Severus oft doth read, The. In Severum. Sir John Davies. ReIE
Puritan Sonnet. Elinor Wylie. Wild Peaches, IV. MAP; MoAB; MoAmPo; NeMA; TrGrPo
  (Sonnet: "Down to the Puritan marrow of my bones.") PoeMoYo
  (Wild Peaches, IV.) InP; PIAE
Puritan spring beauties stood freshly clad for church, The. The Spring Beauties. Helen Gray Cone. AA
Puritan's Ballad, A. Elinor Wylie. BAP; HBMV; LiTL; LoPo; OnAP; PFY; PoRA; TSW; TSWC
Purity. Horace. *See* Integer Vitae.
Purity of Heart. John Keble. *Fr.* Purification. BLRP
Purity of the moonlight, The. *Unknown, tr. fr. Japanese by* Kenneth Rexroth. OnPJ
Purple and white the crocus flowers. Crocuses in [the] Grass. John Gray. CaAE; CAW
Purple Autumn unloosed her tresses and flung them. Autumnal Love. Georgy Ivanovich Chulkov. TrRV
Purple Carpet, The. Aeschylus, *tr. fr. Greek by* Walter Headlam. *Fr.* Agamemnon. OxBG
Purple cloud hangs half-way down, A. Before Sunrise in Winter. Edward Rowland Sill. AA
Purple Clover. Emily Dickinson. MoAmPo (1950 ed.)
Purple Cow, The. Gelett Burgess. BOHV; FaFP; FaPON; FiBHP; HBV; HBVY; InP; LBN; LEAP; LiTM; MeMeAg; NA; NeHB; NePA; PIAE; PoeMoYo; SiTL; StaSt; TiPo; TreFS; YaD
  (I Never Saw a Purple Cow.) LiL
  (Nonsense Quatrains.) CenHV
  (Nonsense Rhymes.) TSW; TSWC
Purple Grackles. Frances Frost. BLA
Purple Grackles. Amy Lowell. BLA; ChMo; CMP; CP; CV; IAP; TwCV
Purple heather is the cloak, The. The Bog Lands. William A. Byrne. AnIV; JKCP (1926 ed.)
Purple hills of Kirkland, The. Ballad of the Thanksgiving Pilgrim. Clinton Scollard. TOAH
Purple horses with orange manes. Merry-Go-Round. Rachel Field. UTS
Purple Island, The, *sels.* Phineas Fletcher.
  "But ah! let me under some Kentish hill," *fr.* I. ViBoPo
  Desiderium, *fr.* I. OBS
  Overthrow of Lucifer, The, *fr.* XII. OBS
  Parthenia. EV-2
Purple morning left her crimson bed, The. The Crusaders Reach Jerusalem. Tasso. *Fr.* Jerusalem Delivered. EnLi-1
Purple Peach Tree, The. Su T'ung-po, *tr. fr. Chinese by* Kenneth Rexroth. OnPC
Purple peaks begin to flame with stranger brighter dyes, The. Dawn Song—Pachayachachi's Gate. A. S. Davis, Jr. CAG
Purple robed, with crownèd hair. The Pawns. Frank Betts. HBMV; QS
Purple, yellow, red, and green. *Unknown.* OxNR
Purpose. John Drinkwater. OQP; QP-1
  (Prayer, A: "We know the paths wherein our feet should press.") PraP
Purpose. Langdon Elwyn Mitchell. *Fr.* To a Writer of the Day. AA
Purpose. John James Piatt. AA
Purpose of Amendment, A. Helen Parry Eden. JKCP
Purpose of Fable-writing, The. Phaedrus, *tr. fr. Latin by* Christopher Smart. AWP
Purpose of its sex is obvious, The. Skyscraper. Byron Vazakas. OnHM
Purse-Seine, The. Robinson Jeffers. ChMo; OxBA; PoLFOT
Purse, who'll not know you have a Poet's been. A Parley with His Empty Purse. Thomas Randolph. OBS
Pursuer, eluder. While the Bells Ring. Lora Dunetz. NePoAm
Pursuing beauty, men descry. Song [*or* A Song in the Second Act]. Thomas Southerne. *Fr.* Sir Antony Love. SeCL; SeEP
Pursuit, The. Struthers Burt. MuM
Pursuit. Juljan Tuwim, *tr. fr. Polish by* Watson Kirkconnell. TrJP
Pursuit, The. Henry Vaughan. OAEP; TrPWD
Pursuit. Robert Penn Warren. CrMA; FiMAP; LiTA; MoPo; NePA; PoFS; ReMP; TwAmPo
Pursuit of Love. *Unknown. See* Art Thou Gone in Haste?
Pursuit round the Walls, The. Homer, *tr. fr. Greek by* William Cowper. *Fr.* The Iliad, XXII. OxBG
  ("Thus pondering he stood; meantime approached.") GrPo
Pursuits! alas, I now have none. Walter Savage Landor. Lyrics and Epigrams, III. ERP
Push about the brisk bowl, 'twill enliven the heart. The Ass. Moses Mendes. *Fr.* The Chaplet. TrJP
Push hard across the sand. A Song in Time of Order (1852). Swinburne. BPN; POTT; PoVP; VLEP
Pushan, God of Pasture. *Unknown, tr. fr. Sanskrit by* Romesh Dutt. *Fr.* The Rig-Veda. AWP; JAWP; WBP
Pushcart Row. Rachel Field. BrR
Puss came dancing out of a barn. *Unknown.* OxNR
Puss passer-by, within this simple tomb. Epitaph on the Duchess of Maine's Cat. François La Mothe le Vayer. PoC
Pussicat, Wussicat. *Unknown.* OTPC (1923 ed.)
  ("Pussicat, wussicat, with a white foot.") OxNR; PPL
Pussy. Jane Taylor. *See* I Like Little Pussy.
Pussy and the Mice. *Unknown.* MoShBr
Pussy can sit by the fire and sing. The First Friend [*or* Playing Robinson Crusoe]. Kipling. *Fr.* Just-so Stories. MPB; PECK
Pussy-Cat. Ann Hawkshaw. OTPC (1923 ed.)
Pussy-Cat and Puppy-Dog. Lilian McCrea. BoTP
Pussy cat ate the dumplings. *Unknown.* OxNR
Pussy-cat Mew [*or* Mole] jumped over a coal. Mother Goose. CBPC; GFA; OTPC; OxNR; PCH; PoC; SAS
Pussy-cat, Pussy-cat, where are you going? *Unknown.* PoC
Pussy-cat, pussy-cat, where have you been? Mother Goose. BoChLi; BoTP; FaBoBe; FaFP; HBV; HBVY; OTPC; OxNR; PCH; PoC; PPL; RIS; SAS; SiTL; StVeCh; TiPo
Pussycat, pussycat with a white foot. Pussicat Wussicat. *Unknown.* OTPC (1923 ed.); OxNR; PPL
Pussy-cat sits by the fire. *See* Pussy sits beside the fire.
Pussy-Cat Who Visited the Queen. Carolyn Wells. CIV
Pussy has a whiskered face. Four Pets. Christina Rossetti. *Fr.* Sing-Song. PPL; TiPo
Pussy in Bed. *Unknown. See* Why Is Pussy in Bed?
Pussy, Pussy, Do Not Mew. William Bourn Oliver Peabody. SAS
Pussy [*or* Pussy-cat] sits beside [*or* by] the fire. *Unknown.* OTPC; OxNR; PPL; RIS; SAS
Pussy that climbs to the top of the tree, The. The Cat. Helen Hay Whitney. GFA
Pussy Willow. Kate L. Brown. PCH; PPL
Pussy Willow had a secret. An Open Secret. *Unknown.* BoChLi
Pussy Willows. Rowena Bastin Bennett. GFA
Pussy-Willows. Arthur Guiterman. OTPC (1946 ed.); VOD
Pussy Willows. Mary E. Plummer. GFA; MPB; RAR
Pussy Willows. *Unknown.* GFA

Pussywillow's buds are soft, The. Spring Is in the Making. Nona Keen Duffy. YeAr
"Pussy, you lift your paws so high." The Cat in the Snow. F. Hey. SAS
Put away the Christ Child. After-Christmas Poem. Elizabeth-Ellen Long. ChBR
Put away the flutes. Song for War. W. R. Rodgers. NeBP
Put by the sun, my joyful soul. The Pilgrim. Robert Nichols. MBP
Put by thy days like withered flowers. Unregarding. Walter de la Mare. ChMo
Put down "Cook—forty pounds; Surgeon—a shilling." The Ledger. Crates. GrR
Put down my coat; I can get into it. Heard on Leaving the Opera. Phyllis Merrill. CAG
Put down your wrath, let your contention end. Sonnet: To the Emperor Charles V and to King Francis I of France. Veronica Gambara. LyPI
Put 'em up solid, they won't come down! Post-Rail Song. *Unknown.* AS
Put every tiny robe away! In Vain. Rose Terry Cooke. AA; LEAP
Put Forth, O God, Thy Spirit's Might. Howard Chandler Robbins. TrPWD
Put Forth Thy Leaf, Thou Lofty Plane. Arthur Hugh Clough. *See* In a London Square.
Put Grief Away. Robert K. Ekvall. *Fr.* Tibetan Comforter. MaRV
Put in the sickles and reap. Messidor. Swinburne. ViPo
Put It Through. Edward Everett Hale. MC; PAH
Put Money in Thy Purse. Theognis, *tr. fr. Greek by* T. F. Higham. GrL; OxBG
"Put Money in Thy Purse," *in. mod. Eng. Unknown.* TMEV
Put off Thy robe of purple then go on. Good Friday; Rex Tragicus, or Christ Going to His Cross. Robert Herrick. TriL
Put on thy ivy crown. Prelude to Revel. Euripides. *Fr.* Bacchae. GrR
Put Out My Eyes, and I Can See You Still. Rainer Maria Rilke, *tr. fr. German by* Babette Deutsch. MaRV
(Extinguish My Eyes, *tr. by* Jessie Lemont.) OnPM
Put out the candle, close the biting rose. The End of the Story. Terence Tiller. ChMP; NeBP
Put out the lights now! The Christmas Tree. C. Day Lewis. GTBS-D
Put out the mourners from your heart. To One of Little Faith. Hildegarde Flanner. HBMV
Put out the sun, and shroud those mocking stars. Heathcliffe Mourns for Cathy. Margaret Willy. DiM
Put out to sea, if wine thou wouldest make. Sent from Egypt with a Fair Robe of Tissue to a Sicilian Vinedresser. T. Sturge Moore. GTML; OBEV (new ed.); OBVV
Put the rubber mouse away. For a Dead Kitten. Sarah Henderson Hay. BAP; CIV; StaSt
Put them aside—I hate the sight of them! Relics. George Frederick Cameron. PeCV
Put them in print? Posthumous. Henry Augustin Beers. AA
Put to the door—the school's begun. The Country School. *Unknown.* APW
"Put up the sword!" The voice of Christ once more. Disarmament. Whittier. AOAH; BHV; PGD; ShGoBo
Put your finger in Foxy's hole. *Unknown.* OxNR; SiTL
Put your head, darling, darling, darling. Dear Dark Head [*or* Cean Dubh Deelish]. *Tr. by* Sir Samuel Ferguson. AnIV; GTIV; IrPN; LoPS; OBEV (1st ed.); OnYI; OxBI; SeCePo
Putney Hymn, *with music. Unknown.* TrAS
Putting God in the nation's life. God in the Nation's Life. *Unknown.* BLRP; WBLP
Putting in the Seed. Robert Frost. FaBoEn; OxBA
Putting the World to Bed. Esther W. Buxton. TVC; TVSH
Putting to Sea. Louise Bogan. LiTM
Putting Winter to Bed. E. J. Pratt. PCN
Puva . . puva . . puva. Lullaby. *Tr. by* Natalie Curtis. SUS
Puzzled Census-Taker, The. John Godfrey Saxe. HBV
Puzzled Centipede, The. Mrs. Edward Craster. *See* Centipede Was Happy Quite, A.
Puzzled Game-Birds, The. Thomas Hardy. VLEP
Puzzles. John Drinkwater. WaKn
Pwlldu—an eternal place! Ballad of the Equinox. Vernon Watkins. PrWP
Pygmalion. Hilda Doolittle ("H.D."). AnAmPo; LA; WGRP *abr.*
Pygmalion. Louis Johnson. AnNZ
Pygmalion. Albert G. Miller. InMe
Pygmalion. William Bell Scott. EPN; VA
Pygmalion. W. Wesley Trimpi. PtPa
Pygmalion and Galatea, *sel.* W. S. Gilbert.
"Thing is but a statue after all, The," *abr.* VA
Pygmalion and Galatea. Ovid, *tr. fr. Latin by* Gilbert Highet. *Fr.* Metamorphoses, X. LaP
Pygmalion thought that women were a great abomination. Pygmalion. Albert G. Miller. InMe
Pygmalion to Galatea. Robert Graves. PG
Pylades. Euripides, *tr. fr. Greek by* Gilbert Murray. *Fr.* Iphigenia in Tauris. OxBG
(By Friendship's Ties.) GrR
Pylons, The. Stephen Spender. AWP; ChMo; EnLi-2 (1949 ed.); EnLit
Pyms Anarchy, *abr. At. to* Thomas Jordan. OBS
Pyramids, The; those domes and spires and towers. Source. Lee Mitchell Hodges. LPS-1
Pyramus and Thisbe, *sel.* Laurence Dakin.
"How sweetly sings this stream," *fr.* III, iii. CaP
Pyramus and Thisbe. John Donne. ReIE
Pyramus and Thisbe. Ovid, *tr. fr. Latin. Fr.* Metamorphoses, IV. LaP, *tr. by* Zechariah Chafee, Jr.; LiTW, *tr. by* Arthur Golding; OuHeWo, *tr. by* Laurence Eusden
("Within the town, of whose huge walls so monstrous high and thick," *tr. by* Arthur Golding.) ReIE
Pyramus and Thisbe. John Godfrey Saxe. HBV
Pyre of Patroclus, The. Homer, *tr. fr. Greek by* Pope. *Fr.* The Iliad, XXIII. OBEC
(Preparation of the Pyre for Patroclus, *shorter sel.*) UnPo (1st. ed.)
Pyrrha and Deucalion. Ovid, *tr. fr. Latin by* Dryden. *Fr.* Metamorphoses, I. RoL
Pythagoras. Thomas S. Jones, Jr. AnAmPo; LA
Pythagoras and the Dog. Xenophanes, *tr. fr. Greek.* GrR, *tr. by* Humbert Wolfe; OxBG, *tr. by* Sir William Marris
Pythagoras planned it. Why did the people stare? The Statues. W. B. Yeats. AnIL
Pythagoras th'art right. *Unknown.* SeCSL
Pythian Odes. Pindar. *See* Odes.
Pythian Oracle, A. *Unknown, tr. fr. Greek by* A. J. Butler. OxBG
Python, The. Hilaire Belloc. HBVY; NA; StaSt
Python. Grace Hazard Conkling. NP; PoeMoYo; TCPD
Pythoness, The. Kathleen Raine. FaBoMo; ViBoPo (1958 ed.)
Pyxidanthera, The. Augusta Cooper Bristol. AA

Q

Qain, *sel.* Charles Marie Leconte de Lisle, *pr. tr. fr. French.*
"Thogorma in his imagination saw walls of iron arise." LiA
Qua Cursum Ventus. Arthur Hugh Clough. BEL; BPN; EmBrPo; EnLi-2; EnLit; EPN; EPP; EtS; EV-5; GTBS; GTML; HBV; LPS-1; OAEP; OBEV (new ed.); OBVV; PoVP; TCEP; TOP; VA; ViP; ViPo; ViPP; VLEP
Quack! Walter de la Mare. TiPo
Quack Medicines. George Crabbe. *Fr.* The Borough, Letter VII. LPS-3
"Quack! Quack!" Ducks at Dawn. James S. Tippett. SiSoSe; TiPo; UTS
Quack Vendor, The. Augustus Peck Clarke. PoP
Quadrille, A. "Lewis Carroll." *See* Lobster Quadrille, The.
Quadrille. Fiona Stewart. DiM
Quadroon mermaids, Afro angels, saints. A Ballad of Remembrance. Robert E. Hayden. PoNe
Quadrupedremian Song, A. Tom Hood. *Fr.* From Nowhere to the North Pole. BoN
Quaerit Jesum Suum Maria. Richard Crashaw. ACP; CAW
Quaeritur. Kipling. PA
Quail, The. Alcman, *tr. fr. Greek by* A. C. Benson. GrR
Quail. Bernard O'Dowd. BoAu
Quail and rabbit hunters with tawny hounds. Hunters in the Snow: Brueghel. Joseph Langland. NePoEA
Quail are still, The. Hawk Afield. Evelyn Scott. BLA
Quail Sky. Li Ch'ing-chao. *tr. fr. Chinese by* Kenneth Rexroth. OnPC
Quaint Character, A. Alexander Smith. *Fr.* A Life-Drama. BMEP
Quaint old house with brilliant tiles. Holland. Barbara Jane Provost. PCH
Quaint Rider. Francis Maguire. PraNu
Quaint stiff metres of olden France, The. At Ste. Thérèse. S. Frances Harrison. BoCaPo (1943 ed.)
Quaker Graveyard, The. Silas Weir Mitchell. AA; OBAV
Quaker Graveyard in Nantucket, The. Robert Lowell. CoBMV; FiMAP; MiAP; MoAB; MoPo; MoVE; NePA; OnAP; OxBA; ReMP; UnPo (3d ed.); ViBoPo (1958 ed.)
Our Lady of Walsingham, *sel.* MeRV
Quaker Hill. Hart Crane. *Fr.* The Bridge. LiTA; LiTM (rev. ed.)
Quaker Ladies. Ellen Mackay Hutchinson Cortissoz. AA
Quaker Meeting-House. William Ellery Leonard. PFY
Quaker of the Olden Time, The. Whittier. AnNE; APW
Quaker Widow, The. Bayard Taylor. AA; IAP
Quakerdom. Charles G. Halpine. LPS-1
Quakeress Bride, The. Elizabeth Clementine Kinney. AA

Quaker's Courtship, The. *Unknown.* ABS
(Quaker's Wooing, The, *with music.*) AS
Quaker's Meeting, The. Samuel Lover. BOHV; CenHV; OnYI
Quaker's Song, The. *Unknown.* CoMu
Quaker's wife got up to bake, The. *Unknown.* OxNR
Quality. Marty Hale. AlBD
Quality of life on earth, The. Life. W. H. Davies. ChMo
Quality of Mercy, The ("The quality of mercy is not strained."). Shakespeare. *Fr.* The Merchant of Venice, IV, i. EV-1; FaFP; LiTB; LiTG; OnHT; PIR; PTA-1
(From "The Merchant of Venice.") LEAP
(Mercy.) BBV; BCEP; BTP; CBE; MaRV; OHFP; OQP; OTPC; PC; PECK; QP-1; TrGrPo; TVSH; WBLP
(Portia's Appeal for Mercy.) PYM
(Portia's Plea for Mercy.) TreF
(When Mercy Seasons Justice.) GrCo-1
Quality of Mercy, The. Mary M. Walsh. CAG
Quan lo ruis de la fontana. Jaufré Rudel, *tr. fr. Provençal by* John Peale Bishop. LiTW
Quand Vous Serez Bien Vieille. Samuel Daniel. *See* To Delia: "When men shall find thy flower, thy glory pass."
"Quand Vous Serez Bien Vieille." Plato. *See* Dedication of a Mirror.
Quandary. Mrs. Edward Craster. *See* Centipede Was Happy Quite, A.
Quangle Wangle's Hat, The. Edward Lear. BoChLi; BoN; GFA; PoRh; PTA-2; RIS; SAS; StaSt
Quantity and Quality. Winifred M. Letts. CV; HBMV
Quantrell, *with music.* *Unknown.* ABF; CoSo (A *and* B *vers.*)
Quantum Est Quod Desit. Thomas Moore. *See* Did Not.
Quarrel, The. Conrad Aiken. LiTL; MAP; MoAB; MoAmPo
Quarrel, The. Eleanor Farjeon. FaPON
Quarrel, The. Homer. *See* Wrath of Achilles, The.
Quarrel. Jean McDougall. GoBC; JKCP (1955 ed.)
Quarrel, A. *Unknown.* MeMeAg
Quarrel of Friends, The. Samuel Taylor Coleridge. *Fr.* Christabel, Pt. II. BoFr; LPS-1
("Alas! they had been friends in youth.") CBE; LEAP; LO; OBRV
(Friendship, *abr.*) MCCG
Quarrel of the sparrows in the eaves, The. The Sorrow of Love. W. B. Yeats. LBBV; MBP; MoAB; MoBrPo; PoEL-5
Quarrel with Juventius. Catullus, *tr. fr. Latin by* George Lamb. OnPM
Quarrelling. Isaac Watts. *See* Let Dogs Delight to Bark and Bite.
Quarrelling winds perplex me, The. Storm at Sea. Alcaeus. GrL; OxBG
Quarrelsome Trio, The. "L. G." WBLP
Quarries in Syracuse. Louis Golding. TrJP
Quarry, The. Juan Boscán, *tr. fr. Spanish by* Grace Hardendorff Burr. LiTW
Quarry, The. William Vaughn Moody. AnAmPo; LA
Quarry whence thy form majestic sprung, The. Washington's Statue. Henry T. Tuckerman. AA; WOAH
Quarter Less Ta-wain [*or* Twain]. Soundings. *Unknown.* StDa
Quarter of pleasures where the rich are always waiting. The Capital. W. H. Auden. ChMo; MoPW
Quartz cut of diamond, rose and sea-wrack green. Twickenham Grotto. Robin Skelton. PoN
Quatorzain. Henry Timrod. AA; BAP; LBAP; LEAP; OBAV; PoeMoYo
(Love.) BTP
(Most Men Know Love but as a Part of Life.) AmP; IAP; TCAP
(Sonnet: "Most men know love but as a part of life.") HBV; SPP
Love and Life, *sel.* OQP; QP-2
Quatrain: "As I'm French born, I'm pained to say." Villon, *tr. fr. French by* Alan Conder. TrFP
Quatrain: "Before you praise spring's advent, note." Tu Fu, *tr. fr. Chinese by* Hsieh Wen Tung. WhP
Quatrain: "Christ bears a thousand crosses now." Charles G. Blanden. ChIP; PGD
Quatrain: "Golf links lie so near the mill, The." Sarah N. Cleghorn. *See* Golf Links, The.
Quatrain, A: "Hark at the lips of the pink whorl of shell." Frank Dempster Sherman. AA
Quatrain: "Here is the Truth in a little creed." Edwin Markham. MaRV; OQP; QP-1
(Creed, A.) ChIP
Quatrain: "Here upon earth eternity is won." Thomas S. Jones, Jr. PFE
Quatrain: "Jack eating rotten cheese, did say." Benjamin Franklin. *See* Jack and Roger.
Quatrain: "Nothing is judged according to its size." Thomas S. Jones, Jr. PFE
Quatrain: "Oh! to be wafted away." *Unknown.* NA
Quatrain: "Sarmèd, whom they intoxicated from the cup of love." Sarmèd the Yahud, *tr. fr. Persian by* David Shea. TrJP
Quatrain: "Squeak's heard in the orchestra, A." George T. Lanigan. WhC
Quatrain: "Teach me your mood, O patient stars!" Emerson. *Fr.* Fragments on the Poet and the Poetic Gift. CBOV
Quatrain: "This existence has, without the azure sphere, no reality." Sarmèd the Yahud, *tr. fr. Persian by* David Shea. TrJP
Quatrain: "Though love repine." Emerson. *See* Sacrifice.
Quatrain: "Young Apollo, golden-haired, A." Frances Cornford. WhC
Quatrains. Gwendolyn B. Bennett. CDC
"Brushes and paints are all I have," I.
"How strange that grass should sing," II.
Quatrains, *sels.* Emerson.
Gardener. APW; OxBA
Orator. AnNE; OxBA
Poet. AnNE; APW; OnPM; OxBA
Sacrifice. HBV; HBVY; MaRV
(Faith.) OtMeF
(Quatrain: "Though love repine.") OQP; QP-2
Quatrains. Sidney Godolphin. *See* Song: "Noe more unto my thoughts appeare."
Quatrains: "Dog Star now, negating all desires, The." John Heath-Stubbs. PoN
Quatrains. Omar Khayyam. *See* Rubáiyát of Omar Khayyám.
Quatrains for a Bank Cashier. Samuel A. De Witt. PG (1955 ed.)
Quatrina. Joseph Bennett. LiTA
Qu'avec-vous, oui, belle blonde, *with music.* *Unknown.* OuSiCo
Quaver'd plea of the fiddle, The; gardens glowing. The Swan. Yakov Polonsky. BoR
Quayside. Robert Graves. FaBoMo
Quebec. Eldon Grier PeCV
Quebec, the grey old city on the hill. At Quebec. Jean Blewett. CaP; OCL
Queen, The. William Winter. HBV
Queen,/ thou holdest in thine arms. To the Most Holy Mother of God. *Unknown.* ISi
Queen and Huntress, Chaste and Fair. Ben Jonson. *See* Hymn to Diana.
Queen and Slave. Mortimer Collins. OBVV
Queen Anne. *Unknown.* ChTr
Queen Anne's Lace. Georgia Benedict. CAG
Queen Anne's Lace. Mary Leslie Newton. BrR; FaPON; GFA; MoShBr; MPB; SP
Queen Anne's Musicians. Thomas Hennell. FaBoTw
Queen-Ann's-Lace. William Carlos Williams. MAP; MoAB; MoAmPo
Queen Athena, strong in war. To Athena. Alcaeus. OxBG
Queen Becomes an Abbess, A. Tennyson. *See* Guinevere.
Queen Bee, The. Mary K. Robinson. BoTP
Queen Bengerd. *Unknown, tr. fr. Danish by* E. M. Smith-Dampier. BoDaBa
Queen Bess was Harry's daughter. Stand forward partners all! The Looking Glass. Kipling. FaBoTw; GTSL; OBMV; OnPP
Queen Cleopatra. Conrad Aiken. Variations, X. HBMV
Queen Dagmar lay in Ribe sick. The Death of Queen Dagmar. *Unknown.* BoDaBa
Queen Djenira. Walter de la Mare. BMEP; LEAP
Queen Eleanor's Confession. *Unknown.* BaBo; ESPB (A *and* B *vers.*)
Queen Elizabeth at Tilbury. Thomas Deloney. SiCE
Queen, for whose house my fathers fought. Adieux à Marie Stuart. Swinburne. EmBrPo; PoVP
Queen Forgets, The. George Sterling. MOAP; TCPD; UnW
Queen Guennivar's Round. Robert Stephen Hawker. CoBE
Queen Guinevere had fled the court. Guinevere [*or* A Queen Becomes an Abbess]. Tennyson. *Fr.* Idylls of the King. BPN; EnLit; EPN; GEPC; PraNu; VLEP
Queen Hynde was in the rowan-wood with scarlet fruit aflame. The Tryst of Queen Hynde. "Fiona Macleod." BMEP
Queen in Parliament, 1941, The. A. P. Herbert. OnPP
Queen is gone a-hunting in the royal wood, The. A-Hunting. Jennie Dunbar. BoTP
Queen is taking a ride today, The. The Queen's Last Ride. Ella Wheeler Wilcox. BLPA
Queen Jane was in labour full six weeks and more. The Death of Queen Jane. *Unknown.* BaBo (A *vers.*); ESPB
Queen Jeanie, Queen Jeanie, travel'd six weeks and more. The Death of Queen Jane. *Unknown.* ESPB (B *vers.*); ViBoFo
Queen lived in the South, A. Dagonet's Canzonet. Ernest Rhys. BMEP; HBV; NV
Queen Mab. Thomas Hood. DD; EV-4; HBV; HBVY; HOAH; OTPC, *abr.*; PCH; PPL; RAR, *abr.*; StVeCh; TVC; TVSH
Dream Fairy, The, *sel.* BoTP
Queen Mab. Ben Jonson. *Fr.* The Satyr, sc. i. HBV; OTPC (1923 ed.)

(Particular Entertainment of the Queen and Prince at Althrope.) ElSeCe
(Mab the Mistress-Fairy.) ElL
("This is Mab the mistress-fairy.") SiCE
Queen Mab. Shakespeare. *Fr.* Romeo and Juliet, I, iv. BCEP, *abr.;* CG, *abr.;* EV-1; FaPON; FiP; GoTP; HOAH, *abr.;* LPS-3; MPB; OTPC, *abr.;* PC, *abr.;* PoFS
(From "Romeo and Juliet.") LEAP
(Mercutio Describes Queen Mab.) TrGrPo
(Mercutio's Queen Mab Speech.) LiTB; TreF
(Queene Mab.) BoW
(Shakespeare Gallery, A: Queen Mab.) MaC
Queen Mab, *sels.* Shelley.
Dedication: To Harriet —. EmBrPo; EPN
"How wonderful is Death," I, *complete.* EmBrPo
Magic Car Moved On, The, *fr.* I. GN
Night, *fr.* IV. LPS-2
Sunset, *fr.* II. LPS-2
To Ianthe, Sleeping, *fr.* I. LPS-2
War, *fr.* IV. LPS-2
Queen Mab's Chariot. Michael Drayton. *Fr.* Nymphidia. OTPC
(Court of Fairy, The.) EPP
(Queen Mab Visits Pigwiggen, the Fairy Knight, *abr.*) EV-1
(Queen Mab's Journey to Pigwiggen.) PCH
(Queen's Chariot, The.) OBS
Queen Mary, *sels.* Tennyson.
Hapless Doom of Woman. VLEP
(Low, Lute, Low.) BPN
Milkmaid's Song. BPN; EPN
(Song of the Milkmaid.) HBV; LPS-1
"O God! I have been too slack, too slack." ReTS
Queen, my lord, is dead, The. Macbeth on His Wife's Death. Shakespeare. *Fr.* Macbeth, V, v. CoEV
Queen of all Queens, oh! Wonder of the loveliness of women. Hymn to the Virgin Mary. Conal O'Riordan. ISi
Queen of all streets, Fifth Avenue. Thompson Street. Samuel McCoy. HBMV
Queen of all streets, you stand alway. Piccadilly. Thomas Burke. HBMV
Queen of Aragon, The, *sel.* William Habington.
"Fine young folly, though you were," *fr.* IV, i. ElSeCe; OBS
(Song.) FaBoEn; MePo
Queen of brave nations—Liberty! To Liberty. Casimir Sarbiewski. PoFr
Queen of Cheese. James McIntyre. FiBHP
Queen of Corinth, The, *sel.* John Fletcher, *and others.*
Weep No More, *fr.* III, ii, *at. to* Fletcher. AtBAP; BEL; CH; ElL; EPP; EV-2; LiTG; OBEV; OnPM; TOP; TriL; ViBoPo
(Mourn No More.) BLV; TrGrPo
("Weep no more, nor sigh, nor groan.") TuPP
Queen of Courtesy, The. *Unknown, tr. fr. Middle English. Fr.* The Pearl. ACP; CAW; ISi, *mod. vers. by* Stanley Perkins Chase
Queen of Crete, The. John Grimes. HBMV
Queen of Egypt yawned and frowned, The. Events. George O'Neil. HBMV
Queen of Eleusis, The. Robert Morse. MuM
Queen of Elfland, The. *Unknown. See* Thomas the Rhymer.
Queen of Elfland's Nourice, The. *Unknown.* OBB
(Queen of Elfan's Nourice, The.) ESPB
"I heard a cow low, a bonnie cow low," *sel.* FaBoCh
Queen of Fairies, The. *Unknown. See* Fairy Queen, The.
Queen of fragrance, lovely rose. The Rose-Bud. William Broome. CEP; LoBV; OBEC; OBEV
Queen of Hearts, The. Marc Cook. PR
Queen of Hearts, The,/ She made some tarts. Mother Goose. BoChLi; BoN; FaBoBe; HBV; HBVY; OTPC; OxNR; PCH; PPL; RIS; SiTL
Queen of heaven, blessed mav thou be. Virgo, Rosa Virginum. *Unknown.* AnEC
Queen of Heaven, of Hell eke Emperess. To the Virgin. John Lydgate. ACP; CAW; GoBC; PoLi
Queen of Horizons. Joseph Dever. ISi; JKCP (1955 ed.)
Queen of Paphos, Erycine, The. *Unknown.* ElL
Queen of Scotland, The. *Unknown.* ESPB
Queen of Seasons, The. Cardinal Newman. GoBC
Queen of the Angels, The. Boccaccio, *tr. fr. Italian by* Thomas Walsh. CAW; ISi
Queen of the double sea, beloved of him. To Corinth. Walter Savage Landor. ERP
Queen of the heavens, we hail thee. Ave Regina Coelorum. *Unknown.* ISi
Queen of the phantom faces that no smiles ever brighten. Laughter to the Last. Julianus. GrPE
Queen of the World. *Unknown.* PGD
Queen of the Year, The. Edna Dean Proctor. DD
Queen Rose. Christina Rossetti. BPN
Queen Sabbath. Hayyim Nahman Bialik, *tr. fr. Hebrew by* Jessie Sampter. TrJP
Queen sat in her balcony, The. Gil, the Toreador. Charles Henry Webb. AA
Queen she sent to look for me, The. Grenadier. A. E. Housman. Last Poems, V. EG; OBMV
Queen stood on thy right hand, The. Psalm XLIV, Bible, *O.T.* (*Douay vers.*). ISi
Queen Theodolind has built. The Song of Theodolinda. George Meredith. EmBrPo; NBE
Queen Venus wander'd away with a cry. Our Lady of the Sea. Alfred Noyes. OBVV
Queen Victoria. *Unknown.* CoMu
Queen Victoria. Humbert Wolfe. MBP; MoBrPo
Queen Virtue's court, which some call Stella's face. Astrophel and Stella, IX. Sir Philip Sidney. SiPS
Queen was beloved by a jester, A. The Cap and Bells. W. B. Yeats. BMEP; GTSL; LEAP; MBP; MoAB; MoBrPo; OBVV
Queen was in her chamber, and she was middling old, The. The Looking Glass. Kipling. GTSL; OBMV
Queen was sick for her hills, The. Mood from 3000 B.C. Genevieve Taggard. OTPC (1946 ed.)
Queen Wasp, A. Walter de la Mare. AtBAP
Queen! What is this that comes. "Victoria." Sir Arthur Quiller-Couch. SG
Queen Yang-se-fu. Yang-se-fu. "Yehoash," *tr. fr. Yiddish by* Isidore Goldstick. TrJP
Queene and Huntresse. Ben Jonson. *See* Hymn to Diana.
Queene Mab. Shakespeare. *See* Queen Mab.
Queene of Arragon, The. William Habington. *See* Queen of Aragon, The.
Queene of Corinth, The. John Fletcher, *and others. See* Queen of Corinth, The.
Queens. J. M. Synge. ChTr; MoBrPo; OBMV; OnYI; TIP
Queen's Afterdinner Speech, The, *sel.* Percy French.
" 'Me loving subjects,' sez she." OxBI
Queen's Chariot, The. Michael Drayton. *See* Queen Mab's Chariot.
Queen's Last Ride, The. Ella Wheeler Wilcox. BLPA
Queen's Marie, The. *Unknown. See* Mary Hamilton.
Queen's Men, The. Kipling. AtBAP
Queens of Hell had lissome necks to crane, The. The Tall Girl. John Crowe Ransom. PeBoSo
Queen's Song. Stopford Augustus Brooke. *Fr.* Riquet of the Tuft. VA
Queen's Song, The. James Elroy Flecker. HBV; POTT
Queen's Vespers, The. Aubrey Thomas De Vere. VA
Queen's Wake, The, *sels.* James Hogg.
Kilmeny, *fr.* Night II. CBPC; EBSV; EV-3; GBV (1922 ed.); HBV; LPS-3; OBEV; OBRV; OnSP; OtMeF
(Bonny Kilmeny Gaed up the Glen, *abr.*) BSV; GoTS
Witch of Fife, The, *fr.* Night I. BCEP; BSV
Queer, The. Henry Vaughan. MaPo; NBE; PoEL-2
Queer are the ways of a man I know. The Phantom Horsewoman. Thomas Hardy. LO; PoEL-5
Queer Habits. Corneille McCarn. GFA
Queer Quatrains. Gelett Burgess. RIS
Queer Things. James Reeves. PoMS
Quel Dommage. "Eleanor Putnam." PR
Quem Pastores Laudaverunt. *Unknown, tr. fr. Latin by* Barbara J. Hodge. LaP
Quem Tu, Melpomene. J. Logie Robertson. EBSV
Quentin Durward, *sel.* Sir Walter Scott.
County Guy, *fr. ch.* 4. BCEP; BEL; BPN; EBSV; EmBrPo; EPN; EtPaEn; EV-4; LPS-1; OAEP; OBRV; TCEP; TOP
(Serenade, A: "Ah! County Guy.") GTBS; GTBS-D; GTBS-W; GTSE; GTSL
(Song.) CH
Queroqué the Frog; an Autobiography. Shimpei Kusano, *tr. fr. Japanese by* Takamichi Ninomiya *and* D. J. Enright. PoLJ
Query. Ann Louise Hayes PtPa
Query. Virginia Lawrence. PR
Query. Lucia Trent. ChIP
Quest, The, *sels.* W. H. Auden.
Presumptuous, The. ChMo
Useful, The. ChMo
Vocation. ChMo
Quest, The. Ellen Mackay Hutchinson Cortissoz. HBV
Quest, The. Gladys Cromwell. HBMV
Quest, The. Chester B. Emerson. OQP; QP-1
Quest, The, *sel.* Edward Salisbury Field.
Dedication: "I've gone about for years I find." MOAH
Quest, The. Eva Gore-Booth. MaRV; OQP; QP-1
Quest, The. Agnes Lee. VOD
Quest, The, *sel.* John G. Neihardt.
Let Me Live Out My Years. GrCo-2
Quest, The. Clinton Scollard. BrR
Quest, The. Eliza Scudder. GrCo-1; MaRV; TrPWD
(Who by Searching Can Find Out God?) WGRP
Quest. Edmund Clarence Stedman. *Fr.* Corda Concordia. AA
Quest, The. Harold Vinal. GoYe
Quest Eternal, The. Alice M. Pullen. MaRV

Quest for Death. Chaucer. *Fr.* The Canterbury Tales: The Pardoner's Tale. CoEV
("These rioters, of whom I make my rime," *mod. vers.*) WHA
("Thise ryotoures three, of which I tell.") MyFE
Quest of Saint Truth, The, *in mod. Eng. Unknown.* TMEV
Quest of the Golden Fleece, The. Pindar, *tr. fr. Greek by* C. J. Billson. *Fr.* Pythian Odes, IV. OxBG
(Argonauts, The, *abr., tr. by* C. J. Billson.) GrR
(Tale of the Golden Fleece, The, *tr. by* H. T. Wade-Gery *and* C. M. Bowra.) GrL
Quest of the Grail, The. Tennyson. *Fr.* Idylls of the King: The Holy Grail. BHV
Quest of the Purple Cow, The. Hilda Johnson. BOHV
Quest of the Sangraal, The, *sel.* Robert Stephen Hawker.
"There the brown barrow curves its sullen breast." EnSW
Quester, The. Elizabeth Griswold King. CAG
Questing. Anne Spencer. CDC
Question, A. Matthew Arnold. VLEP
(To Fausta.) EmBrPo; PoVP
Question, The. William Rose Benét. BoFr
Question. Howard McKinley Corning. ChIP
Question, The. Robert Duncan. NeAP
Question, A. P. T. Forsyth. OQP; QP-2
Question, The. Norman Gale. FiBHP
Question, The. W. W. Gibson. BEL
Question, A. C. L. Jones. CAG
Question. Nikolaus Lenau, *tr. fr. German by* Dwight Durling. AnGP
Question, A. Edna Livingston. GoYe
Question, The. F. T. Prince. ChMP
Question, The ("I dreamed that, as I wandered by the way"). Shelley. BPN; CBE; CH; EmBrPo; EnRP; EPN; EV-4; FiP; HBV; MyFE; OBEV; OBRV; RO
(Dream of the Unknown, A.) GTBS; GTBS-D; GTBS-W; GTSE; GTSL
Question. May Swenson. NePoEA
Question, A. J. M. Synge. GTIV; MBP; MoBrPo; OBMV; OBVV; OxBI
Question, The. Rachel Annand Taylor. ChIP; HBV; MaRV
Question, The. R. S. Thomas. MoWP
Question, A ("I ask thee, whence those ashes were"). *Unknown.* SeCL
Question, A ("If I really, really trust him"). *Unknown.* BLRP
Question, The ("Were the whole world good as you"). *Unknown.* WBLP
Question and Answer. Elizabeth Barrett Browning. BPN
Question and Answer. Samuel Hoffenstein. FiBHP
Question & Answer. Edward Hersey Richards. *See* Wise Old Owl, A.
Question and answer. Dialogue, without End. Isabel Hariss Barr. JKCP (1955 ed.)
Question Answer'd, The. Blake. ViBoPo
Question in the Cobweb, The. Alastair Reid. WaKn
Question Is Proof, The. Elizabeth Bartlett. NePoAm-2
Question Mark, The. Persis Greely Anderson. PoMa; WhC
Question Not. Adam Lindsay Gordon. *Fr.* Ye Wearie Wayfarer, Fytte VIII. PoToHe
(Man's Testament.) OtMeF
Question of Gender, A. Palladas, *tr. fr. Greek by* Sir William Marris. OxBG
Question of Lovers, A. Sister Mary Madeleva. PraNu
Question of Sacrifice, A. Sister M. Eulalia. WHL
Question to Lisetta, The. Matthew Prior. OBEV
Question Whither, The. George Meredith. BMEP; EPN; HBV; OQP; POTT; QP-2; WGRP
Questioning. Grace Noll Crowell. DD
Questioning Lydia ("Lydia, dic, per omnes"). Horace, *tr. fr. Latin by* Louis Untermeyer. Odes, I, 8. InP
(Slump in Sybaris, The, *par. by* Franklin P. Adams.) PoeMoYo
Questioning Spirit, The. Arthur Hugh Clough. BPN; EmBrPo; PoVP; VLEP
Questionings. Frederic Henry Hedge. HBV
Questions. Lord Thomson of Cardington. OtMeF
Questions at Night. Louis Untermeyer. FaPON; GoTP; OTPC (1946 ed.); RIS
Questions on a Nun's Habit. Sister Mary Madeleva. PraNu
Questions with Answers. *Unknown.* BOHV
Questo di Verde. Thomas Watson. TuPP
Quhen Alysandyr Our King Was Dede. *Unknown.* *See* When Alexander Our King Was Dead.
Quhen Flora had o'erfret the firth. When Flora Had O'erfret the Firth. *Unknown.* EBSV; OBEV
Quhill schortly, with the blesand torch of day. Gawin Douglas. *Fr.* Prologues to the Aeneid. AtBAP
Quho is at my windou, quho? quho? *Unknown.* *See* Who Is at My Window.
Qui Bien Aime a Tard Oublie. Chaucer. *See* Roundel, A: "Now welcom, somer . . ."
Qui Laborat, Orat. Arthur Hugh Clough. BEL; BPN; EmBrPo; EnLi-2; EPN; PoVP; TrPWD; ViPo; ViPP; VLEP
Qui nunc dancere vult modo. A Polka Lyric [*or* A Holiday Task]. Barclay Philips. BOHV; NA
Qui Perdiderit Animam Suam. Richard Crashaw. ACP
Qui Vive! Anne Goodwin Winslow. LS
Quia Amore Langueo ("In a tabernacle"). *Unknown.* ACP; CoBE, *sts.* 1-3; ISi, *tr. fr. Middle English by* E. M. Clerke
Quia Amore Langueo ("In a valley [*or* vaile] of this restless mind [*or* restless mynd]"). *Unknown.* AtBAP; CoEV; EnLit; LiA; LiTG; LiTL; LO; OBEV; OxBoCh; PoEL-1; PoLi, *abr.;* WoL
"Quia Multum Amavi." Oscar Wilde. ACP (1926 ed.)
Quia Pulvis Es. Victor Hugo, *tr. fr. French by* Alan Conder. TrFP
Quick, The. Sean Jennett. NeBP
Quick, bind this dog-thief! Haul the rogue away. The Rogue. Aristophanes. *Fr.* The Frogs. LiA
Quick compunction cannot serve, The. The Selector's Wife. Mary Fullerton. MoAuPo
Quick-falling dew. Basho, *tr. fr. Japanese by* Curtis Hidden Page. AWP; JAWP; WBP
Quick, for the tide is sifting down the shore. Pause. Ann Hamilton. HBMV
Quick gleam, that ridest on the gossamer! To the Gossamer-Light. Charles Tennyson Turner. VA
Quick hoof-beats down a moonless country highway. Edmund Campion. Sister Mary St. Virginia. JKCP (1955 ed.)
Quick in spite I said unkind/ Words. Brazen Tongue. William Rose Benét. MAP; MoAmPo
Quick now—loose it—here at the stable door. Here at the Stable Door. Sister Mary Paulinus. JKCP (1955 ed.)
Quick, painter, quick, the moment seize. Currente Calamo. Arthur Hugh Clough. *Fr.* Mari Magno. LoBV
Quick return to me, come tonight, my budding. Note to Gongyla. Sappho. LiTW
Quick sea shone, The. Sunrise at Sea. Swinburne. *Fr.* Tristram of Lyonesse. EtS
Quick sparks on the gorse-bushes are leaping, The. The Wild Common. D. H. Lawrence. CoBMV
Quick, woman, in your net. The Net. W. R. Rodgers. AnIL; OxBI; PoN
Quickening. Christopher Morley. HBMV
Quickening, The. Stella Weston Tuttle. GoYe
Quickly and pleasantly the seasons blow. Sonnets, I. Robert Hillyer. HBMV; OBAV
Quickly, before the walls split, while they stand. Room under Bombardment. Phyllis Allfrey. NeTW
Quickness. Henry Vaughan. LoBV; MaPo; MeLP; MePo; OBS; OxBoCh; ReEn; SeCePo; SeCV-1; TriL
Quicksand Years. Walt Whitman. IAP; MaRV; TCAP
Quid Non Speremus, Amantes? Ernest Dowson. HBV
Quid Petis, O Fili [*or* Fily]? *Unknown.* AnEC; SeCeV
(Christmas Carols, 2, *abr.*) EPP
(Mater Dulcissima, *abr.*) CBOV
Quid Sit Futurum. *Unknown, tr. fr. Greek by* Sir William Marris. OxBG
Quidditie, The. George Herbert. PoEL-2
Quids, The. Laura Riding. MoP
Quién Sabe? Ruth Comfort Mitchell. PoMa; VOD
Quiet. Léonie Adams. MOAP
Quiet, The. W. W. Gibson. BEL
Quiet. Marjorie Pickthall. BoCaPo; PeCV; TwCaPo
Quiet. Ernest Radford. OBVV
Quiet. Yaha, *tr. fr. Japanese by* Harold Gould Henderson. WoL
Quiet as are the quiet skies. A Smiling Demon of Notre Dame. Sophie Jewett. AA
Quiet Days. Mildred T. Mey. PoToHe (new ed.)
Quiet Enemy, The. Walter de la Mare. ChMo; CMP
Quiet Eye, The. Eliza Cook. VA
Quiet form of silent nun. "Sœur Monique." Alice Meynell. PraNu
Quiet from Fear of Evil. "S. C. M'K." BLRP
Quiet home had Parson Gray, A. Parson Gray. Goldsmith. BOHV; NA
Quiet Hour, The. Louise Hollingsworth Bowman. BLRP
Quiet is what we need. By telephone. Private Enterprise. Christopher Morley. MaRV
Quiet Kingdom, The. Carl Busse, *tr. fr. German by* Ludwig Lewisohn. AWP; JAWP; WBP
Quiet Life, The. Samuel Johnson. *See* On the Death of Mr. Robert Levet, a Practiser in Physic.
Quiet Life, The. Pope. *See* Ode on Solitude.
Quiet Life, The. Seneca. *See* Chorus: "Climb at Court for me that will."
Quiet Life, The. *Unknown.* ElL; GoBC; HBV; OTPC
(Herdmen, The.) OBSC
(What Pleasure Have Great Princes.) CenL; ReIE; SiCE; WP
Quiet Life and a Good Name, A. Swift. EV-3
Quiet Mind, The. *Unknown.* OBSC
("I joy not in no earthly bliss.") SiCE
Quiet morning of an April day, The. Morning. Viggo Stuckenberg. BoDS

Quiet Night, The. Heine, *tr. fr. German by* Emma Lazarus. LiTW
Quiet Nights, The. Katharine Tynan. HBV
Quiet Persian seated at her loom, The. The Weaver. Eloise Hamilton. MuM
Quiet Pilgrim, The. Edith M. Thomas. AA; BAP, *abr.;* LEAP; OBAV
Quiet Place, The. George A. McCauliff. JKCP (1955 ed.)
Quiet Singer, The. Charles Hanson Towne. HBV; LBMV; VOD
Quiet, sleep! or I will make. A Charm. Thomas Randolph. *Fr.* The Jealous Lovers. SeCL
Quiet Soul, A. John Oldham. *See* Tranquil Soul, A.
Quiet Street, The. Nan McDonald. NeLNL
Quiet Streets. Victor Starbuck. NoCaPo
Quiet the self, and silence brims like spring. Scarabs for the Living, IX. R. P. Blackmur. TwAmPo
Quiet Things. "I. W." OQP; QP-2
Quiet Waters. Blanche Shoemaker Wagstaff. BLPA
Quiet Woman, The. Genevieve Taggard. AnEnPo; NP
Quiet woods in the hot Eastertide, The. Woods and Kestrel. Julian Bell. ChMP
Quiet Work. Matthew Arnold. BPN; CBE; EM-2; EnL; EnLit; EPN; FaBoBe; GEPC; GrCo-2; HBV; LEAP; MCCG; NeHB; OAEP; OQP; PoRL; PoVP; QP-1; ReTS; TrGrPo; TVSH; ViPP; VLEP; YT
(Sonnet: Quiet Work.) EmBrPo
Quietly and while at rest on the trim grass I have gazed. The Air of June Sings. Edward Dorn. NeAP
Quietly as rosebuds. Love's Coming. Shaw Neilson. BoAu; MoAuPo
Quietly I enter the closet. Communion. P. M. Snider. PoToHe (new ed.)
Quietly sipping rain that sucks the rose, The. Pacific Winter. Hildegarde Flanner. NP
Quietly the children wait. The Children. Clifford Dyment. ChMP
Quietude of a soft wind, The. The Creditor. Louis MacNeice. MoP; QS; ShBV-3
Quilt, The. Mary Effie Lee Newsome. CDC
Quilt. John Updike. WaKn
Quilting Party, The. Frances Kyle. OlF
Quince, The. Ibn Sara, *tr. fr. Arabic by* A. J. Arberry. MooP
Quince, The. *Unknown, tr. fr Chinese.* ChLP; WhP
Quinks, The. Don Marquis. YaD
Quinquireme of Nineveh from distant Ophir. Cargoes. John Masefield. AnEnPo; ATP; BEL; BMEP; CaAE; CBE; CBOV; ChMo; CMP; CP; EnLi-2 (1949 ed.); EnLit; ExPo; FaPON; GTBS-D; GTSL; LEAP; LiTM; MBP; MCCG; MoAB; MoBrPo; MuP; NP; NV; OBEV (new ed.); OBMV; OBVV; OtMeF; PCH; PCN; PIAE; PoeMoYo; PoRA; PtOT; SeCeV; ShBV-1; SP; TCEP; TCPD; TiPo (1952 ed.); TOP; TreF; TVSH; VOD; YT
Quintetto upon the Christmas Pie, *sel.* Thomas Love Peacock. *Fr.* Melincourt.
"My share of pie to win, I will dash through thick and thin." MyFE
Quintia is beautiful, many will tell you: to me. Catullus, *tr. fr. Latin by* Arthur Symons. LaP
Quintilia Dead. Catullus, *tr. fr. Latin by* George Lamb. OnPM
Quintius, if it's thy wish and will. To Quintius. Catullus. OnPM
Quip, The. George Herbert. AnFE; ATP; BEL; CenL; ElSeCe; EnLit; EPS; EV-2; LiTB; MaPo; MeRV; OAEP; OBS; OxBoCh; SeCV-1; SeEP
Quip to the Reader. Timothe Kendall. *See* To the Reader.
Quire of bright Beauties in spring did appear, A. The Lady's Song. Dryden. EV-3; LoBV
"Quis pro Domino?" Robert Browning. *Fr.* The Ring and the Book, X. OAEP
Quit yo' long-time talkin' 'bout yo' heavy hipted woman. The Heavy-hipted Woman. *Unknown.* ABF
Quit You like Men. William Herbert Hudnut. OQP; QP-1
Quite by Chance. Frederick Langbridge. BOHV
Quite gentle is a St. Bernard. Omar Meets a Toy. Burges Johnson. AlBD
Quite like a Stocking. Thomas Bailey Aldrich. *See* Kriss Kringle.
Quite, quite./ Oh I agree. Restricted. Eve Merriam. TrJP
Quite spent with thoughts, I left my cell and lay. Vanity of Spirit. Henry Vaughan. EPS; ReEn
Quite the Cheese. H. C. Waring. PA
Quite unexpectedly as Vasserot. The End of the World. Archibald MacLeish. AnEnPo; CoBMV; CoV; HoPM; LiTM; MAP; MoAB; MoAmPo; NeMA; NePA; NP; OxBA; PeBoSo; Po; TCPD; TrGrPo; TwHP
Quits. Thomas Bailey Aldrich. AA
Quits. Matthew Prior. *See* Epigram: "To John I ow'd great obligation."
Quitter, The. *Unknown.* BLPA; WBLP
Quitting my horse, a cup with you I drank. "So Farewell." Wang Wei. OnPM
Quiver of wings and the gulls dip into the sunset, A. Port-of-Call. Sister Mary Thérèse. PraNu
Quivering fears, heart-tearing cares. In Praise of Angling. Sir Henry Wotton. LPS-2
Quivering, unseen atoms of air, The. Love Passing By. Gustavo Adolfo Bécquer. Rimas, X. OnPM; TeCS
Quivira. Arthur Guiterman. PAH; PFY; PoeMoYo
Quixotic is his enterprise and hopeless his adventure is. The Played-out Humorist. W. S. Gilbert. *Fr.* His Excellency. BOHV
Quo Ruis ab Demens? Londons Progress. Thomas Freeman. SiCE
Quo Vadis? Myles E. Connolly. JKCP (1926 ed.); MaRV
Quod Dunbar to Kennedy. William Dunbar. OxBoLi
Quod Semper. Lucy Lyttelton. VOD
Quod Tegit Omnia. Yvor Winters. MoVE
Quoits. Mary Effie Lee Newsome. CDC; GoSl
Quoniam Ego in Flagella Paratus Sum. William Habington. ACP
Quorum Porum. Ruth Pitter. PoC
Quot Bipedes Aurum. Thomas Freeman. SiCE
Quotations from Pope. Pope. HiLiEn
Quoth a Hawk to a Nightingale. Hesiod, *tr. fr. Greek by* Arthur S. Way. *Fr.* Works and Days. GrR
Quoth John to Joan. *Unknown.* CH
(Clown's Courtship, The.) BOHV
Quoth Rab to Kate, My sonsy dear. Marriage and the Care o't. Robert Lochore. HBV
Quoth Satan to Arnold: "My worthy good fellow." Epigram. *Unknown.* PAH
Quoth she, "The matter's not so far gone." Samuel Butler. *Fr.* Hudibras, Pt. II, Canto I. NBE
Quoth the fir-tree, "Orange and vine." Carol of the Fir Tree. Alfred Noyes. SDH
Quoth tongue of neither maid nor wife. Elena's Song [*or* Song]. Sir Henry Taylor. *Fr.* Philip van Artevelde, II. LEAP; OBEV; OBRV; OBVV; VA
Qwhen Alexander [*or* Quhen Alysandyr] our kynge was dede. When Alexander Our King Was Dead [*or* Cantus]. *Unknown.* AtBAP; BSV; GoTS

R

R. I. P. "Jan Struther." InMe
R is for the Restaurant. Phyllis McGinley. *Fr.* All Around the Town. TiPo (1959 ed.)
R. S. S. Wendell Phillips Stafford. GrCo-2
R. T. Hamilton Bruce. W. E. Henley. *See* Invictus.
Ra has purified the heavens. Inscription on the Pyramid of Pepi I. *Unknown.* LiTW
Rabbi Ben Ezra. Robert Browning. ATP (1935 ed.); BBV (1951 ed.), *abr.;* BEL; BMEP, *much abr.;* BPN; CoBE; EM-2; EmBrPo; EnLi-2; EnLit; EPN; EPP; EV-5; FaFP; FiP; GEPC; GTBS; GTBS-W; GTSL; HBV; HiLiEn; LiTG; MaRV; OAEP; OBVV; OQP, *much abr.;* OuHeWo; PECK; PIAE; PoFS; PoVP; PreP, *abr.;* QP-1, *much abr.;* REAL; TCEP; TOP; TwP; TyEnPo; UnPo (1st ed.); ViPo; ViPP; VLEP; WGRP; YT, *cond.*
Sels.
"Grow old along with me!" 6 *ll.* MCCG; PoToHe
Youth and Age. GrCo-2
Rabbi Ben Levi, on the Sabbath, read. The Legend of Rabbi Ben Levi. Longfellow. *Fr.* Tales of a Wayside Inn. AnNE; BAV; DaM; EV-5; GBV (1952 ed.)
Rabbi Jehosha used to say. What Rabbi Jehosha Said. James Russell Lowell. BAP
Rabbi Nathan two score years and ten, The. The Two Rabbis. Whittier. EV-5
Rabbi, Where Dwellest Thou? Come and See. *Unknown.* BePJ
Rabbi Yom-Tob of Mayence Petitions His God. A. M. Klein. TrJP
Rabbi Yussel Luksh of Cheim. Jacob Glatstein, *tr. fr. Yiddish by* Nathan Halper. TrJP
Rabbi's Song, The. Kipling. GTML
Rabbit, The. W. H. Davies. GFA
Rabbit, The. Camilla Doyle. MBP; PIAE; StaSt
Rabbit, The. Georgia R. Durston. GFA
Rabbit, The. Edith King. BoTP; GFA; HBMV; StVeCh
Rabbit, The. John Lewisohn. PCD
Rabbit, The. Elizabeth Madox Roberts. BAP; BoChLi; GoTP; MPB; TiPo; TSW; TSWC; UTS
Rabbit. Tom Robinson. FaPON
Rabbit, The. *Unknown.* FiBHP; SiTL
Rabbit as King of the Ghosts, A. Wallace Stevens. ThWaDe
Rabbit has a charming face, The. The Rabbit. *Unknown.* FiBHP; SiTL

Rabbit has a habit, The. The Rabbit. Georgia R. Durston. GFA
Rabbit Hash, *with music.* *Unknown.* ABF
Rabbit in his burrow keeps. Haunted. Walter de la Mare. TwCV
Rabbit sits upon the green, The. Vice Versa. Christian Morgenstern. AnGP
Rabbit: timid brother! My teacher and philosopher! The Perfect Life. Jorge Carrera Andrade. AnCL; LiTW; WoL
Rabbit works its ears, and tries, A. The Rabbit. W. H. Davies. GFA
Rabbits. Dorothy W. Baruch. SUS; TiPo; UTS
Rabbits, The. *Unknown, tr. fr. German.* PCH; SAS
("Between the hill and the brook, ook, ook.") PPL
Rabbits and squirrels. The Reason. Dorothy Aldis. TiPo (1952 ed.)
Rabbits ate my tulips, The. Garden Visitor. Betsey Mann Collins. DDA
Rabbits' Song outside the Tavern, The. Elizabeth J. Coatsworth. *See* Song of the Rabbits outside the Tavern.
Rabble Soldier. *Unknown.* *See* Rebel Soldier, The.
Rabboni! Master! Mother Loyola. WHL
Rabia. *Unknown, tr. fr. Arabic by* James Freeman Clarke. HBV
Raccoon an' a possum. Cotton Field Song. *Unknown.* ABF
Raccoon on the Road. Joseph Payne Brennan. GoYe
Raccoon up a 'Simmon Tree. *Unknown.* HiLiAm
Race, The. Aileen Fisher. UTS
Race, A. Mrs. Molesworth. BoN
Race. Theognis. GrPE
Race of nobles may die out, A. Kossuth. James Russell Lowell. BHV
Race of the *Oregon,* The. John James Meehan. PAH
Race of Veterans. Walt Whitman. CoV
Race with Death, The. Byron. *Fr.* Ode on Venice. LH
Racer, The. John Masefield. PreP
Racers, The. James B. Kenyon. LBAP
Rachel. Ruth Gilbert. AnNZ
Rachel. Charles Jeremiah Wells. *Fr.* Joseph and His Brethren. VA
Rachel Laments. Marion Ethel Hamilton. MuM
Rachel, the beautiful (as she was call'd). Rachel. Charles Jeremiah Wells. *Fr.* Joseph and His Brethren. VA
Racing-Man, The. A. P. Herbert. FiBHP; WhC
Racing to conquer minutes, we whirl by. The Subway. Morris Abel Beer. VOD (1935 ed.)
Racing Water. Mary Bayard Clarke. NoCaPo
Rack upon rack of leaves all elbowing. Spring. W. R. Rodgers. OnYI
Rackheath. Coman Leavenworth. *Fr.* Norfolk Memorials. LiTA
Racoon ("The racoon wears a black mask"). Kenneth Rexroth. *Fr.* A Bestiary. FiBHP
(Advices from Rexroth's Bestiary.) SiTL
Radiance of that star that leans on me, The. Delay. Elizabeth Jennings. NePoEA
Radiant Loss, The. Jessie Rittenhouse. LEAP
Radiant Ranks of Seraphim. Valery Bryusov, *tr. fr. Russian by* Babette Deutsch *and* Avrahm Yarmolinsky. AWP; JAWP; WBP
(Radiant Ranks, *rev. tr. by* Babette Deutsch.) TrRV
Radiant ruler of the year, The. On the Winter Solstice, 1740. Mark Akenside. EV-3
Radiant Sister of the Day. Shelley. *Fr.* To Jane: The Invitation. ThWaDe
Radiator Lions. Dorothy Aldis. GoBP; MPB; UTS
Radical, The. Waring Cuney. CDC
Radical Song of 1786, A. St. John Honeywood. PAH
Radio, The. Edgar A. Guest. PEDC
Radio. Therese Lindsey. BAP; PoeMoYo; VOD (1935 ed.)
Radio. Harriet Monroe. PoeMoYo
Radio. A. S. J. Tessimond. HaMV
Radio Prayer. Lexie Dean Robertson. PraP
Radio waves coming over the air. Magic Waves. Gertrude Van Winkle. GFA
Radish, The. Ibn Quzman, *tr. fr. Arabic by* A. J. Arberry. MooP
Radium. Agnes Lee. PoMa
Rafael! It must be he; we only miss. Written under the Engraving of a Portrait of Rafael. Leigh Hunt. ERP
Raftsmen, The. *Unknown.* IHA
Rag Doll and Summer Birds. Owen Dodson. PoNe
Ragged-and-Tough. Not Ragged-and-Tough. *Unknown.* ChTr
Ragged Piper, The. Dana Burnet. OBAV
Ragged Regiment, The. Alice Williams Brotherton. NLK
Ragged Robin. Elizabeth Godley. BoTP
Ragged Robin and Bouncing Bet. Alice Reid. DD
Ragged Sailors. *Unknown* PEOR
Ragged Wood, The. W. B. Yeats. LO; VLEP
Raggedy Man, The. James Whitcomb Riley. BoChLi; FaPON; GoBP; GoTP; HBV; HBVY; MPB; OTPC; PTA-1; StVeCh; TiPo; TreFS
Raggle Taggle Gypsies, The. *Unknown.* *See* Wraggle Taggle Gipsies, The.
Raggles. Robert C. V. Meyers. AlBD
Raging and the ravenous, The. The Tigress. Ruth Pitter. FaBoTw; HaMV
Raging Canawl, *with music.* *Unknown.* AS
(Ragin' Can-all, *diff. vers.*) IHA
(Raging Can-all, *diff. vers.*) ABF
Raglan. Sir Edwin Arnold. VA
Ragman, The. *Unknown.* FTB
Ragpicker, The. Frances Shaw. BAP; NP
Rags. Edmund Vance Cooke. AlBD; BLPA
Rags and Bones. W. H. Davies. ChMo; CMP
Rags and tatters,/ Tatters and rags. Ragged Robin. Elizabeth Godley. BoTP
Ragtime. W. W. Gibson. POTT
Ragwort, The. John Clare. ChTr
Rahab. Robert Norwood. OCL
Ráhat, The. John Jerome Rooney. AA; BAP
Rahere. Kipling. VLEP
Raid, The. William Everson. OnHM
Raider, The. W. R. Rodgers. AnIL; MoBrPo (1950 ed.)
Raiders, The. Will H. Ogilvie. EBSV; ShBV-2
Rail not at grinding poverty, nor curse. Reproach No Man for Poverty. Theognis. GrL; OxBG
Railroad Bill, *with music.* *Unknown.* ABF; AS, *diff. vers.*
Railroad Blues. *Unknown.* APW
Railroad bridge's, De/ A sad song. Homesick Blues. Langston Hughes. CDC; MAP; MoAmPo; NeMA
Railroad Cars are Coming, The. *Unknown.* AS, *with music;* BrR; FaPON; MPB
Railroad Corral, The. *Unknown.* CoSo, *with music;* CSF; TrAS, *with music*
Railroad Crossing, The. Hezekiah Strong. PTA-2
Rail-road crossing. *Unknown.* RIS
Railroad Rhyme. John Godfrey Saxe. *See* Rhyme of the Rail.
Railroad track is miles away, The. Travel. Edna St. Vincent Millay. FaPON; InMe; LaNeLa; MoShBr; MoSiPe; MPB; NP; PFY; StVeCh; TCAP; TiPo
Railroad Train, The. Emily Dickinson. *See* I like to see it lap the miles.
Railway Junction, The. Walter de la Mare. ChMP
Railway Station. John Hay. WaP
Railway Station, The. Archibald Lampman. CPG
Railway Train, The. Emily Dickinson. *See* I like to see it lap the miles.
Railway Tunnel, The. Queenie Scott-Hopper. TVC; TVSH
Rain. Kenneth Slade Alling. HBMV; NLK
Rain. Einar Benediktsson, *tr. fr. Icelandic by* Watson Kirkconnell. IcP; LiTW
Rain, The. Lord Bowen. *See* Rain It Raineth, The.
Rain. *At. to* Mary Frances Butts, *also to* Lucy Larcom. NLK
Rain. Ch'en Fu Liang, *tr. fr. Chinese by* Henry H. Hart. PoHN
Rain. "Robin Christopher." RIS; StaSt
Rain. Elizabeth J. Coatsworth. CIV
Rain, The. W. H. Davies. BoTP; ChMo; CMP; EnLit; NV; PCH; POTE; RIS; TiPo
Rain. Frank Marshall Davis. GoSl
Rain. Sam Harrison. NeIP
Rain. Langston Hughes. *Fr.* A House in Taos. CDC
Rain. Max Jacob, *tr. fr. French by* Wallace Fowlie. MiCF
Rain. Patrick F. Kirby. GoBC
Rain. *At. to* Lucy Larcom, *also to* Mary Frances Butts. NLK
Rain. Newman Levy. BOHV
Rain. Vachel Lindsay. ChMo; CMP
Rain. Lilian McCrea. BoTP
Rain. Junzaburo Nishiwaki, *tr. fr. Japanese by* Takamichi Ninomiya *and* D. J. Enright. PoLJ
Rain. "Seumas O'Sullivan." OnYI
Rain. Po Chü-i, *tr. fr. Chinese by* Arthur Waley. TrCh
Rain. Frances Shaw. HBMV
Rain, The. Robert Louis Stevenson. BoChLi; GFA; MPB; NeHB; OnHT; OTPC (1946 ed.); PCH; PPL; RIS; StVeCh; SUS; TiPo
Rain. Bert Leston Taylor. RIS
Rain. Edward Thomas. POTE
Rain. Tu Fu, *tr. fr. Chinese by* Chi Hwang Chu *and* Edna Worthley Underwood. OnPM
Rain, The ("Open the window"). *Unknown.* GFA
Rain, The ("The rain came down"). *Unknown.* GFA
Rain, The ("Rain on the green grass"). *Unknown.* BoTP; TiPo
("Rain on the green grass.") OxNR
Rain. Jean Starr Untermeyer. AV
Rain. William Carlos Williams. CoBMV
Rain. Helen Wing. GFA
Rain. Ella Young. TiPo (1952 ed.)
Rain advances like a king, The. Rains. Kalidasa. *Fr.* The Seasons AWP
Rain after a Vaudeville Show. Stephen Vincent Benét. MAP; MoAmPo

Rain and Lightning. Ibn Shuhaid, *tr. fr. Arabic by* A. J. Arberry. MooP
Rain and Shine. Brander Matthews. PFE
Rain and wind, the rain and wind, raved endlessly, The. Melancholy. Edward Thomas. MoVE
Rain at Festival. Ibn Rashiq, *tr. fr. Arabic by* A. J. Arberry. MooP
Rain at Night. Helen Walker Homan. JKCP (1955 ed.)
Rain at Night. Helen Hoyt. LiTM; NP
Rain at Night. Lu Ying Su, *tr. fr. Chinese by* Henry H. Hart. PoHN
Rain at Night, The. Tu Fu, *tr. fr. Chinese.* WhP
Rain-beaten Cathedral, The. Kotaro Takamura, *tr. fr. Japanese by* Takamichi Ninomiya *and* D. J. Enright. PoLJ
Rain before seven. Weather Signs [*or* Signs and Charms *or* Rhymes about the Weather]. *Unknown.* FaBoBe; GoTP; HBV; HBVY; OTPC; OxNR; StaSt; TreF
Rain came down in torrents, The. The Rain. *Unknown.* GFA
Rain Clouds. Elizabeth-Ellen Long. BrR
Rain-Crow, The. Madison Cawein. AA; BAP; BLA; LBAP; LEAP
Rain does down in torrents pour, The. McKinley Brook. George Calhoun. ShS
Rain falls briskly on my worn shelter-half. Inner Brother. Stephen Stepanchev. WaP
Rain falls down upon the grass, The. April Puddle. Rowena Bennett. TiPo (1959 ed.)
Rain fire from Heaven down upon thy head. Sonnet. Petrarch. Sonnets to Laura: To Laura in Life, CV. LyPI
Rain, frost or snow, or hot or cold. Milk Below. *Unknown.* PCH
Rain had fallen, the poet arose. The Poet's Song. Tennyson. AlDL; BPN; EmBrPo; FiP; GBV (1952 ed.); PoVP; TOP
Rain, hail and brutal sun, the plow in the roots. Robinson Jeffers. *Fr.* The Broken Balance. PIAE
Rain has ceased, and in my room, The. After the Rain. Thomas Bailey Aldrich. LPS-2
Rain has silver sandals, The. Footwear. May Justus. YeAr
Rain has such fun in April. Rain in April. Eleanor Hammond. GFA
Rain has washed the sadness from the sky, The. Autumn. Nagata. SoLD
Rain imprinted the step's wet shine, The. On the Doorstep. Thomas Hardy. MoVE
Rain in April. Eleanor Hammond. GFA
Rain in my ears: impatiently there raps. Essay on Memory. Robert D. Fitzgerald. BoAV; MoAuPo
Rain in Spring. "Gabriel Setoun." PPL
Rain in Summer. Longfellow. BAV; BBV (1923 ed.), *sl. abr.*; CG, *sl. abr.*; GN, *sl. abr.*; LPS-2; MW; OTPC, *sl. abr.*; SN
"How beautiful is the rain!" *first* 15 *ll.* BoChLi; BoTP; PCH; RIS
Rain in the Aspens. Su T'ung-po, *tr. fr. Chinese by* Kenneth Rexroth. OnPC
Rain in the City ("All the streets"). Rachel Field. GFA
Rain in the city! City Rain. Rachel Field. TiPo
Rain in the Desert. John Gould Fletcher. Arizona Poems, VI. TCPD
(Rain in the Street.) NP
Rain in the Hills. Charles Buxton Going. VOD
Rain in the Night. Amelia Josephine Burr. MPB; SP; TiPo
Rain in the Street. John Gould Fletcher. *See* Rain in the Desert.
Rain Inters Maggiore. Alfred Kreymborg. AnAmPo; LA
Rain is clinging to the round rose-cheek, The. After Rain. Eleanor Farjeon. BoChLi
Rain is due to fall, The. A Poet Thinks. Lui Chi. AWP; JAWP; LiTW; PG (1945 ed.); WBP
Rain is plashing on my sill, The. The Unknown Dead. Henry Timrod. AmP; MDAH; MOAP; SPP
Rain is raining all around, The. The Rain. Robert Louis Stevenson. BoChLi; GFA; MPB; NeHB; OnHT; OTPC (1946 ed.); PCH; PPL; RIS; StVeCh; SUS; TiPo
Rain is raining all around, The. Rain. Bert Leston Taylor. RIS
Rain It Raineth, The. Lord Bowen. FiBHP
(Just & Unjust.) WhC
(Rain, The.) FaFP; LiTG; SiTL
("Rain it raineth on the just, The.") CenHV
Rain It Raineth Every Day, The. Shakespeare. *See* When That I Was and a Little Tiny Boy.
Rain, It Streams on Stone and Hillock, The. A. E. Housman. Last Poems, XVIII. ChMo; CMP; ReaPo
Rain, like a traveler, walks on the night. The Marginal Dark. John Malcolm Brinnin. TwAmPo
Rain, midnight rain, nothing but the wild rain. Rain. Edward Thomas. POTE
Rain Music. Joseph S. Cotter, Jr. BANP; BrR; CDC; PCH
Rain, Night, and Wine. Asclepiades, *tr. fr. Greek by* Charles Glenn Wallis. LiTW
Rain of Zeus descends, and from high heaven, The. Antidote. Alcaeus. GrR
Rain on a Cottage Roof. Freda Laughton. OnYI
Rain on a Grave. Thomas Hardy. CoBMV; EmBrPo; HBV; OAEP
Rain on Rahoon falls softly, softly falling. She Weeps over Rahoon. James Joyce. NP; TIP; ViBoPo
Rain on the Down. Arthur Symons. OBVV; VLEP
Rain on the face of the Sea. Commonplaces. Kipling. BOHV; HBV; PA
Rain on the green grass. The Rain. *Unknown.* BoTP; OxNR; TiPo
Rain on the River. Lu Yu, *tr. fr. Chinese by* Kenneth Rexroth. OnPC
Rain on the Roof. Coates Kinney. HBV; LPS-1; PTA-2
(Patter of the Rain, The.) BLP
Rain on the windows, creaking doors. The Division. Thomas Hardy. PG (1945 ed.)
Rain or Shine. *Unknown.* APW
Rain, Rain. Zoë Akins. AV; HBMV; NV
Rain, Rain! *Unknown, tr. fr. Russian by* W. R. S. Ralston. OnPM
Rain, rain,/ Are you there yet? Rain-Talk. Raelene Newell White. PCH
Rain, rain, and sun! a rainbow in the sky! Merlin's Riddle. Tennyson. *Fr.* Idylls of the King. BPN
Rain, rain—fall, fall. Rain, Rain. Zoë Akins. AV; HBMV; NV
Rain, rain, go away. Mother Goose. OxNR; RIS; SAS; SiTL; TiPo
Rain, rain, go to Spain. *Unknown.* OxNR
Rain, rain on Tyburn tree. To the English Martyrs. Francis Thompson. JKCP; MeRV
Rain Riders. Clinton Scollard. GaP; TiPo
Rain rins doun through Mirry-land toune, The. Sir Hugh; or, The Jew's Daughter (B *vers.*). *Unknown.* ESPB
Rain, said the first, as it falls in Venice. Song Tournement: New Style. Louis Untermeyer. CrMA
Rain set early in to-night, The. Porphyria's Lover. Robert Browning. AtBAP; AWP; BeLS; BoLiVe; BPN; CaAE; EM-2; EmBrPo; EV-5; GEPC; GTBS; GTML; GTSE; GTSL; HBV; InPo; JAWP; KN; LEAP; MaPo; OAEP; OBEV; OuHeWo; PoVP; REAL; ShBV-4; TOP; TrGrPo; TwHP; TwP; ViPo; ViPP; VLEP; WBP
Rain slants on an empty square. Plaza Santa Ana. John Dos Passos. *Fr.* Winter in Castile. VOD (1935 ed.)
Rain Song. Robert Loveman. *See* April Rain.
Rain Song, The. Alex Rogers. BANP
Rain-Songs from the Rio Grande Pueblos. *Tr. fr. Pueblo Indian by* Mary Austin. APW
Rain-sunken roof, grown green and thin. The Barn. Edmund Blunden. GTML; MBP; MoBrPo; SeCePo
Rain-Talk. Raelene Newell White. PCH
Rain, The! the Rain! Mad Girl's Song. L. E. F. Barry. ReTS
Rain to the wind said, The. Lodged. Robert Frost. BAP
Rain was over, and the brilliant air, The. Landscapes. Louis Untermeyer. HBV; LEAP
Rain was raining cheerfully, The. The Vulture and the Husbandman. Arthur Clement Hilton. CenHV; PA
Rain, with a silver flail. Whale. William Rose Benét. EtS MAP; MoAmPo; TBM
Rainbird, The. Bliss Carman. BLA
Rainbow, The. Thomas Campbell. *See* To the Rainbow.
Rainbow, The. John Vance Cheney. OQP; QP-1
Rainbow, The. Vine Colby. AV; HBMV
Rainbow, The. W. H. Davies. CMP; HiLiEn
Rainbow, The. Walter de la Mare. PtOT; TiPo
Rainbow, The, *abr.* John Keble. CG
Rainbow, The. David McCord. FaPON; RIS
Rainbow, The. Christina Rossetti. *See* Boats Sail on the Rivers.
Rainbow, The. Edward Shanks. TCPD
Rainbow, The. Konstantin Simonov, *tr. fr. Russian by* Jack Lindsay. RuPo
Rainbow, The. *Unknown, tr. fr. Chinese.* ChLP, *tr. by* E. D. Edwards; WhP
Rainbow, The. Wordsworth. *See* My Heart Leaps Up.
Rainbow. Xenophanes, *tr fr Greek by* F. L. Lucas. GrPE
Rainbow, The—a Riddle. Schiller, *tr. fr. German.* OTPC (1946 ed.)
Rainbow arches in the sky, The. The Rainbow. David McCord. FaPON; RIS
Rainbow at night. Weather Wisdom [*or* Rhymes about the Weather]. *Unknown.* FaBoBe; GoTP; HBV; HBVY; OTPC; PCH; PPL; RIS; TreF
Rainbow Fairies, The. Lizzie M. Hadley. BoTP; OTPC (1946 ed.); TVC; TVSH
"Two little clouds one April day," *sel., sl. diff.* GFA
Rainbow in the morning. Country Proverbs. *Unknown.* StaSt

Rainbow in the Sky. Wordsworth. *See* My Heart Leaps Up.
Rainbow is in the east, The. The Rainbow. *Unknown.* ChLP
Rainbow Lands. Howard McKinley Corning. NP
Rainbow o'er the sea of afternoon, The. Sonnet. Thomas Caulfield Irwin. IrPN
Rainbow on the ocean, The. So Slow to Die. George Edward Woodberry. *Fr.* Wild Eden. AA
Rainbows. Dixie Willson. GFA
Rainbows all lie crumpled on these hills, The. The Painted Hills of Arizona. Edwin Curran. BAP; HBMV; MW; PFY
Rainbow's Arch, A. Shelley. *Fr.* Prometheus Unbound. ShBV-3
Rainbows are lovely things. The Rainbow. W. H. Davies. CMP; HiLiEn
Raindrops. Isla Paschal Richardson. GFA
Raindrops. *Unknown.* PCH
Rainer,/ the man who was about to celebrate his 52nd birthday. The Death of Europe. Charles Olson. NeAP
Raining on earth/ Means weeping in heaven. Rain. "Robin Christopher." RIS; StaSt
Raining, raining. Rain in the Night. Amelia Josephine Burr. MPB; SP; TiPo
Rains, The. Kalidasa, *tr. fr. Sanskrit by* Arthur W. Ryder. *Fr.* The Seasons. AWP
Rain's lovely gray daughter has lost her tall lover. Fog. Kenneth Patchen. TwAmPo
Rains of Spring, The. Lady Ise, *arr. by* Olive Beaupré Miller. SUS; TiPo
Rainy country this, that I am monarch of, A. The King of the Rainy Country. Baudelaire. WoL
Rainy Day, The. Longfellow. AnNE; AWP; HBV; IAP; InPo; LPS-1; MaRV; MOAP; MW; NeHB; PTA-2
Rainy Day, A. Emilie Blackmore Stapp. GFA
Rainy Day in April, A. Francis Ledwidge. MBP
Rainy Day Song. Violet Alleyn Storey. YeAr
Rainy Morning. Jessica Nelson North. NP
Rainy Night. Juana de Ibarbourou, *tr. fr. Spanish by* Rolfe Humphries. AnCL
Rainy Night. James Rorty. MOAP
Rainy Night. Samuel Schrieber. CAG
Rainy Nights. Irene Thompson. BoTP
Rainy Season, The. William Meredith. NePoEA
Rainy Season Love Song. Gladys May Casely Hayford. CDC
Rainy Song. Max Eastman. FaBoBe; HBMV
Rainy Summer, The. Alice Meynell. AlDL; MoVE
Rainy Summer. Ruth Pitter. MoVE; UnPo (3d ed.)
Raise a Rukus Tonight, *with music.* *Unknown.* ABF
Raise Me Up, Lord. Miguel de Guevara, *tr. fr. Spanish by* Samuel Beckett. AnMP
Raise the Cromlech high! The Lament of Maev Leith-Dherg. *Unknown.* OnYI; TIP
Raise the light, my page! that I may see her. Iseult of Ireland. Matthew Arnold. Tristram and Iseult, II. PoVP; ReTS
Raise up, boys, raise up, raise up. Shack Bully Holler. *Unknown.* ABF
Raised are the dripping oars. The Youth of Nature. Matthew Arnold. BPN; EmBrPo; GEPC; PoVP; VLEP
Raised in a canebrake, and suckled by a lion. Cowboy Talks to a Pitching Horse. *Unknown.* CoSo
Raised on six-shooters till I get big enough to eat ground shotguns. The Boasting Drunk in Dodge. *Unknown.* CoSo
Raising of Tabitha, The, *sel.* Thomas Holly Chivers.
"He lifted up her hand from off her breast." PoP
Raising of the Flag, The. Condé Benoist Pallen. JKCP
Rake the embers, blow the coals. The King Is Cold. Robert Browning. LPS-3
Rakes of Mallow, The. *Unknown.* GTIV; IrPN; OnYI
Raking Walnuts in the Rain. Monica Shannon. BrR; SiSoSe
Rakob is dead, what is left of him travels. Funeral in Hungary. Kay Boyle. AnEnPo
Rally, The. Homer, *tr. fr. Greek by* Sir William Marris. *Fr.* The Iliad, V. OxBG
Rally round the flag, boys. The Stars and Stripes. James T. Fields. FOAH; HH
Rallying Hymn for the Church. Alexander Louis Fraser. PraP
Rallying Song. Callinus. *See* Call to Action, A.
Ralph Roister Doister, *sels.* Nicholas Udall.
I Mun Be Married a Sunday. ElL
Minion Wife, A. ElL
Ralph Straker. W. W. Gibson. *Fr.* Casualties. VOD
Ram, The. Robert P. Tristram Coffin. AnAmPo; LA
Ram, The. *Unknown.* *See* Derby Ram, The.
Ram, ass, and horse, my Kyrnos, we look over. Eugenics [*or* Advice to Kyrnos]. Theognis, *tr. by* T. F. Higham. GrL; LiTW; OxBG
Ram of Darby, The. *Unknown.* *See* Derby Ram, The.
Ram or a stallion, Cyrnus, of good stock each man chooses, A. Eugenics. Theognis, *tr. by* F. L. Lucas. GrPE
Ramadan. Al-Qalami, *tr. fr. Arabic by* A. J. Arberry. MooP
Rambling along the marshes. *See* Flight of the Wild Geese. William Ellery Channing. APW; PFY
Rambling Boy. *Unknown.* CSF
Rambling Cowboy, The. *Unknown.* CoSo, *with music;* CSF
Rambling Gambler, *with music.* *Unknown.* CoSo
Rambling I looked for an old abode. Life Laughs Onward. Thomas Hardy. TwCV
Rambling Sailor, The. Charlotte Mew. HBMV; PoRA
Rambunctious Brook. Frances Frost. BrR
Ramon. Bret Harte. BeLS; LPS-3
Ranchers. Maurice Lesemann. NP
Randolph of Roanoke, *abr.* Whittier. GA
Random Reflections on a Cloudless Sunday. John Hall Wheelock. NePoAm
Random Thoughts. Bahar, *tr. fr. Persian by* A. J. Arberry. PeP
Rang through the dim tavern a voice yesterday. Lawful Wine. Hafiz. PeP
Rang'd on the Line Opposed, Antonius Brings. Virgil, *tr. fr. Latin by* Dryden. *Fr.* The Aeneid, VIII. WaaP
Range-finding. Robert Frost. MaPo; SoV
Range Riders, The. *Unknown.* CoSo (A *and* B *vers.*); CSF
Range Rider's Soliloquy, The. Earl Alonzo Brininstool. PoOW
Ranger, A. Badger Clark. SCC
Ranger, The. *Unknown.* *See* Yankee Man-of-War, The.
Ranger's Song, The. James T. Lytle. HiLiAm
Range's filled up with farmers and there's fences ev'rywhere, The. The Old Cowboy's Lament. Robert V. Carr. PoOW
Ranil bade saddle his steed so free. The Wedding of Rane Jonson. *Unknown.* BoDaBa
Rank and File. Austin Dobson. PoVP
Rank and File. Marion Lee. MuM
Rank and File. Edith M. Thomas. OBAV
Rank offence that we have grown so free, The. Riding the Rims. James Wreford Watson. BoCaPo (1948 ed.)
Rann I Made. Padraic Pearse. NP
Rann of the Three, The. *Unknown, tr. fr. Irish by* Thomas Walsh. CAW; WHL
(Sacred Trinity, The, *tr. by* Eleanor Hull.) JKCP (1926 ed.)
Rannoch by Glencoe. T. S. Eliot. Landscapes, IV. FaBoEn; KN; LoGBV
Rano Raraku. André Breton, *tr. fr. French by* Wallace Fowlie. MiCF
Ranolf and Amohia, *sels.* Alfred Domett. AnNZ
"About the heights, soft clouds, a few."
"And near some river-mouth—shoal—marshy-wide."
"And Tangi and his tribe thus much had gained."
"But evening now."
"In deep blue sky the sun is bright."
"Or to the beach descending, with joined hands."
"So Ranolf felt when over wood and wild."
Ransom, The. Baudelaire, *tr. fr. French by* Alan Conder. LO
Ransom. Ibn Ammar, *tr. fr. Arabic by* A. J. Arberry. MooP
Rantin' Dog, the Daddie o't, The. Burns. OxBoLi
Rantin Laddie, The. *Unknown.* BaBo (A *and* B *vers.*); ESPB
Ranting Wanton's Resolution, The; 1672. *Unknown.* CoMu
Rap! Rap.—The watchman in Po Ti Town! Day Comes. Tu Fu. OnPM
Rapacious Spain follow'd her hero's triumphs o'er the main. The Lust of Gold. James Montgomery. *Fr.* The West Indies. PAH
Rape of Europa, The. R. P. Blackmur. CrMA
Rape of Helen, *sel.* Colluthus, *tr. fr. Greek by* H. Meen.
"At morning's dawn Hermione appears." GrPo
Rape of Helen, The. Thomas Gray. *Fr.* Agrippina. RO
Rape of Lucrece, The, *sels.* Thomas Heywood.
"Now what is love I will thee tell." LO
Pack, Clouds, Away [and Welcome Day]. BLA; BoTP; EG; ElL; ElSeCe; EM-1; GTBS; GTBS-D; GTBS-W; GTSE; KN; LPS-2; OTPC; SN; ThWaDe; ViBoPo; WHA; WP
(Good-Morrow.) ALV; CBOV; CH; TOP
(Matin Song.) EV-2; GTSL; HBV; OBEV; ShBV-1
(Morning.) TVSH
(Song: "Pack clouds away, and welcome day.") CaAE
(Waking Song.) RIS
(Welcome to Day.) BLV; PIAE
Passing Bell, The. SeCL
"Thus go the cries." NBE
Valerius on Women. HBV
("She that denies me, I would have.") LO
Rape of Lucrece, The Shakespeare. BeLS
Sels.
"For much imaginary work was there," 5 *ll.* MyFE
"Locks between her chamber and his will, The." SiCE
Midnight. OBSC
"O opportunity thy guilt is great." PoEL-2
(Opportunity.) LiTB; OBSC
Time's Glory. ChTr

Troy Depicted. OBSC
Rape of Persephone, The. *Unknown, tr. fr. Greek. Fr.* Homeric Hymns. GrR, *tr. by* Arthur S. Way; OxBG, *tr. by* W. M. W. Call *and* T. F. Higham
Rape of the Lock, The. Pope. AtBAP; ATP; BEL; BLV, *abr.;* BoLiVe, *abr.;* CEP; CoBE; EiPP; EM-1; EnL; EnLi-1; EnLit; EPP; EV-3; GEPC; LiA; MaPo; OAEP; OuHeWo; Po; PoE; PoEL-3; PoFS; REAL; ReaPo; RiBV; SeCeV; TCEP, *abr.;* TOP; TrGrPo, *sl. abr.;* TwHP; TwP; TyEnPo
Sels.
Belinda, *fr.* II. CBOV; LPS-1, *shorter sel.*
("On her white breast a sparkling cross she wore," *longer sel.*) ACP
"Close by those meads, for ever crown'd with flowers," III. FiP; OxBoLi, *sl. abr.;* WHA, *abr.*
(Ombre at Hampton Court, *shorter sel.*) OBEC
Evening in the Capital, *fr.* I. BeR
"Not with more glories, in th' etherial plain," *fr.* II. FaBoEn; ViBoPo; WHA
Playing Cards, The, *fr.* III. ChTr
"She said: then, raging to Sir Plume repairs," *fr.* IV. MyFE
Toilet, The, *fr.* I. CoEV; LPS-2; OBEC
("And now, unveil'd the toilet stands display'd.") BCEP, *longer sel.;* BrBE; LEAP
(Belinda's Morning.) ExPo
Raphael, *sel.* Whittier.
Destiny ("We shape ourselves the joy or fear.") MaRV
Raphael, they ask for some verses from you. For Ammonis Who Died at 29 in 610. C. P. Cavafy. MoGP
Raphael's San Sisto Madonna. George Henry Miles. CAW
Rapid, The. Charles Sangster. CaP; CPG; OCL
Rapid Transit. James Agee. AnAmPo; MoAmPo; NAMP
Rapidly cruising or lying on the air there is a bird. The Frigate Pelican. Marianne Moore. InvP; PoF
Rapids at Night. Duncan Campbell Scott. CaP; OCL
Rapier, lie there! and there, my hat and feather! The Poetaster. Samuel Rowlands. *Fr.* The Melancholy Knight. EIL
Rappahannock Army Song, The. John C. M'Lemore. BIG
Rapt with the rage of mine own ravisht thought. An Hymne of Heavenly Beautie. Spenser. TwCrTr
Rapture, A. Thomas Carew. *See* I Will Enjoy Thee Now.
Rapture. Stefan George, *tr. fr. German by* Ludwig Lewisohn. AWP; JAWP; WBP
(Transport, *tr. by* Carol North Valhope *and* Ernst Morwitz.) LiTW
Rapture, The ("O Lord, the children of my people are Thy peculiar treasures"). Thomas Traherne. EPS (1942 ed.)
Rapture, The ("Sweet Infancy!/ O heavenly fire!"). Thomas Traherne. OBS
Rapture; an Ode. Richard Watson Dixon. OxBoCh
Rapture on the Cornish Hills, A. Robert Stephen Hawker. EnSW
Raptures. W. H. Davies. CMP; EPP; WP
Rapunzel. William Morris. EmBrPo; PoVP
Rarae Aves. Franklin P. Adams. WhC
Rare Moments. Charles Henry Phelps. AA
Rare News. Nicholas Breton. *See* News from the Heavens!
Rare old bird is the Pelican, A. The Pelican. *Unknown.* TreFS
Rare Willy Drowned in Yarrow. *Unknown. See* Willy Drowned in Yarrow.
Rarely, Rarely, Comest Thou. Shelley. *See* Song: "Rarely, rarely, comest thou."
Rarest of ladies, all of all I have. To the Excellent and Most Accomplish'd Lady, Lucy, Countess of Bedford. Michael Drayton. *Fr.* Mortimeriados. ReIE
Rash author, 'tis a vain presumptuous crime. The Art of Poetry. Nicolas Boileau. EnLi-1
Rash virtue, whose ambitious wing. Hope. Sarah Wingate Taylor. JKCP (1955 ed.)
Rat-a-tat-tat. The Drummer. Anne Robinson. SUS
Rat-a-tat-tat, rat-a-tat-tat. The Postman. Clive Sansom. BoTP
Rat Who Withdrew from the World, The. La Fontaine, *tr. fr. French by* Alan Conder. TrFP
Ratcatcher and Cats, The. John Gay. CIV; EV-3; PoC
Ratcatcher's Daughter, The. *Unknown.* ChTr; OxBoLi
"Rather dead than spotted"; and/ believe it. Then the Ermine. Marianne Moore. NePoAm
Rather had we been ground. Lament of Granite. David Ross. PG (1945 ed.)
Rather than a first class hotel. Visit to a Tenement. Nicolás Guillén. AnCL
Rather than their Mount Lycaeus. Paraphrase of Horace. Genaro Estrada. AnCL
Rathers. Mary Austin. FaPON
Ration Party. John Manifold. WaP
Rational Man, The. Pearce Young. PtPa
Rats, The. Albrecht Haushofer, *tr. fr. German by* Herman Salinger. *Fr.* Sonnets from Moabite Prison. TwGV
Rats, The. Georg Trakl, *tr. fr. German by* Ernst Sigler. LiTW
Rats Away! *Unknown.* TMEV
Rats by night such mischief did, The. The Ratcatcher and Cats. John Gay. CIV; EV-3; PoC
Rats Hold Council, The. La Fontaine, *tr. fr. French by* Alan Conder. TrFP
Rattat! Rattat!/ There's the postman at the door. Postman's Knock. Rodney Bennett. BoTP
Rattle of musket and sword. The Woman on the Walls. H. A Cody. CPG
Rattlesnake, The. Robert V. Carr. PoOW
Rattlesnake, The [a Ranch Haying Song]. *Unknown.* CoSo, *with music;* CSF; IHA
(Rattle Snake, *with music.*) ABF
Ravaged Villa, The. Herman Melville. GTBS-D; PoEL-5
Ravelston, Ravelston. Sydney Dobell. *Fr.* The Ballad of Keith of Ravelston. LO
Raven, The. Samuel Taylor Coleridge. *See* Raven and the Oak, The.
Raven, The. Kuthaiyir, *tr. fr. Arabic by* A. J. Arberry. MooP
Raven, The. Poe. AA; AmP; AmPo; AmPP; AnFE; APA; APW; BAP; BAV; BBV (1923 ed.); BeLS; BLPA; CG; CH; CoAnAm; CoBA; DaM; EV-5; FaBoBe; FaBoCh; FaFP; GN; HBV; HiLiAm; IAP; LEAP; LiTA; LiTG; LoGBV; LPS-3; MCCG; MOAP; NeHB; NePA; OBAV; OHFP; OnSP; OTPC; OxBA; PCD; PCN; PECK; PFE; PFY; PG (1945 ed.); PIR; PoeMoYo; PoRA; PreP; PYM; SPP; TCAP; TOP; TreF; TVSH; ViBoPo; WBLP; WHA
Raven, The. E. A. Robinson, *after the Greek of* Nicarchus. AWP; JAWP; LiTW; UnS; WBP
(Variations of Greek Themes, III.) MOAP
Raven, The. Shinkichi Takahashi, *tr. fr. Japanese by* Takamichi Ninomiya *and* D. J. Enright. PoLJ
Raven and the Fox, The. La Fontaine, *tr. fr. French by* Elizur Wright. OnPM
Raven and the Oak, The. Samuel Taylor Coleridge. CG
(Raven, The.) OTPC (1923 ed.)
Raven croak'd as she sate at her meal, The. The Old Woman of Berkeley. The. Robert Southey. OBRV
Raven Days, The. Sidney Lanier. NePA; OxBA
Raven sat upon a tree, A. The Sycophantic Fox and the Gullible Raven. Guy Wetmore Carryl. AA; AnAmPo; BLPA; CenHV; FaFP; FiBHP; HBV; InMe; LA; LEAP; LHV; MAP; MoAmPo (1942 ed.); PoeMoYo; ShBV-3
Ravenna. Aleksandr Blok, *tr. fr. Russian by* Oliver Elton. BoRS
Ravenous earth that now wooes her to be, The. Of a Death in Winter, II. John Donne. *Fr.* Elegie: Death. BoW
Ravenous Time has flowers for his food. Time Eating. Keith Douglas. FaBoMo; NeBP; PoN
Ravens, The. Arthur Rimbaud, *tr. fr. French by* Alan Conder. TrFP
Raven's Nest, The. Wordsworth. *Fr.* The Prelude. ShBV-3
Ravens shall pick. *Unknown Fr.* The Combat of Ferdiad and Cuchulain. OnYI
Ravens, the Sexton, and the Earthworm, The. John Gay. NBE
Ravignan Street. Max Jacob, *tr. fr. French by* Wallace Fowlie. MiCF
Ravine of the Flowering Peach Tree, The. Chang Hsu, *tr. fr. Chinese.* WhP
Ravin's of Piute Poet Poe. Charles L. Edson. PoeMoYo
Ravish me in thine answere; art thou rare. Cyril Tourneur. *Fr.* The Revenger's Tragedy, II, ii. AtBAP
Ravished by all that to the eyes is fair. Madrigal 109 [*or* Poems]. Michelangelo. AWP; JAWP; LyPI; WBP
Ravngard and Memering. *Unknown. See* Sir Aldingar.
Rawish dank of clumsy winter ramps, The. Prologue. John Marston. *Fr.* Antonio's Revenge. CoEV; LoBV; NBE; ViBoPo
Ray of the sun, O fairest ray. Victory over Aggressors. Sophocles. *Fr.* Antigone. GrR
Rayons et les ombres, Les, *sel.* Victor Hugo, *tr. fr. French by* Sir George Young.
Sadness of Olympio, The. LiA
Razor Seller, The. "Peter Pindar." BCEP; BOHV; HBV; InMe; LPS-3
Razors pain you. Résumé [*or* Some Beautiful Letters]. Dorothy Parker. ALV; InMe; PoeMoYo; TCPD; TrJP; WhC
Reach down, O Steady Hand, enclose him fast. The Vision. Walter Greenough. DD; GA
Reach forth Thy hand! William Force Stead. *Fr.* Uriel, Pt. V, i. OxBoCh
Reach me a blue pencil of the moon. Ur Burial. Richard Eberhart. NePoAm
Reach me down my Tycho Brahe. The Old Astronomer to His Pupil. Sarah Williams. BLPA; BoHiPo
Reach with your whiter hands to me. To the Water Nymphs, Drinking at the Fountain. Robert Herrick. EG; EPS; PoFS; ViBoPo

Reaching down arm-deep into bright water. Shells. Kathleen Raine. ImOP
Reaching home, having retired from official service. Echoing Chang Tzu-yeh's "Spring Daylight." Su T'ung-po. WhP
Reactionary Critic. Martial, *tr. fr. Latin by* Thomas Fuller. OnPM
Read books of iron! See, below. For the Signboards. Vladimir Mayakovsky. RuPo
Read here,/ This is the story of Evarra—man. Evarra and His Gods. Kipling. MBP; MoBrPo
Read here (sweet maid) the story of my woe [*or* wo]. Idea's Mirrour, I. Michael Drayton. OBSC; ReIE
Read in these roses the sad story. Red and White Roses. Thomas Carew. ElSeCe
Read me no moral, priest, upon my life. The Condemned. Edward Howland. AA
Read no more of cantos Pisan. To a Young Poet. Harry M. Meacham. GoYe
Read not Milton, for he is dry; nor Shakespeare, for he wrote of common life. Of Reading. Charles Stuart Calverley. PA
"Read out the names!" and Burke sat back. The Fighting Race. Joseph Ignatius Constantine Clarke. AA; BAP; BLPA; DD; DDA; HBV; LHV; MC; OBAV; OnYI; PaA; PAH; PFY; YaD
Readen ov a Head-Stwone. William Barnes. CH; HBV (Head-Stone, The.) OBVV
Reader, behold! this monster wild. Infant Innocence. A. E. Housman. EnLi-2 (1949 ed.); WhC
Reader, could his limbs be found. Epitaph on a Bombing Victim. Roy Fuller. NeBP
Reader, my book flies low, and comes not near. Ad Lectorem. Thomas Bastard. SiCE
Reader, pass on—don't waste your time. *Unknown.* WhC
Reader placid and bucolic. Epigraph for a Condemned Book. Baudelaire. AnFP
Reader, preserve thy peace; those busy eyes. An Elegie upon the Death of the Lord Hastings. Sir John Denham. ReEn; SeCV-1
Reader, remember that I do forewarn thee. Lectori Quomodo Legat. Thomas Freeman. SiCE
Reader, there is no biting in my verse. Ad Lectorem. Thomas Bastard. SiCE
Reader, within this church Sir Philip Sidney lies. Epitaph on Sir Philip Sidney. Lord Herbert of Cherbury. SeEP
Reader Writes, The. Carl Crane. WhC
Readers and the hearers like my books, The. Critics and Cooks [*or* Against Writers That Carp at Other Men's Books]. Sir John Harington, *after the Latin of* Martial. ALV; AWP; OnPM; TuPP
Readers of riddles dark. The Spark. Helen Gray Cone. PC
Readers of the *Boston Evening Transcript,* The. The *Boston Evening Transcript.* T. S. Eliot. NePA; OnAP
Reading. Elizabeth Barrett Browning. *Fr.* Aurora Leigh, I. GN; HH ("Good from a Book.") PoRL
Reading a book of tales. The Emotion of Fiction. Roy Fuller. LiTM (1946 ed.)
Reading Aloud. Christopher Morley. PoeMoYo
Reading, at night, the shutter closed and barred. Air Raid. John Allan Wyeth. PoP
Reading Boy, The. Nathalia Crane. PoTo
Reading Giraldus Cambrensis. T. H. White. NeTW
Reading Hesiod. Marcus Argentarius, *tr. fr. Greek by* Humbert Wolfe. OxBG; WoL
Reading in Ovid the sorrowful story of Itys. Thomas Trevelyan. Edgar Lee Masters. *Fr.* Spoon River Anthology. AnFE; APA; CoAnAm; MoPo; SBMV
Reading in War Time. Edwin Muir. WaP
Reading Mother, The. Strickland Gillilan. BLPA; DDA
Reading "The Book of Strange Places and Seas." Tao Yuanming, *tr. fr. Chinese by* Yang Yeh-tzu. WhP (Reading the Book of Hills and Seas, *tr. by* Arthur Waley.) TrCh
Reading the headlines in the revolutionary. The Second Man. Julian Symons. WaP
Reading the List. *Unknown.* BlG; MDAH
Reading the Poems of an Absent Friend. Ou-yang Hsiu, *tr. fr. Chinese by* Kenneth Rexroth. OnPC
Reading them over and over. These Poems I Have So Loved. Leonora Speyer. PG (1955 ed.)
Reading Time: 1 Minute 26 Seconds. Muriel Rukeyser. MoPo; NePA
Reading Tolstoy. John Peter. BoSA
Readings, Forecasts, Personal Guidance. Kenneth Fearing. MoAmPo; PoLFOT
Ready. Phoebe Cary. PAH; PAP
Ready, Ay, Ready. Herman Charles Merivale. HBV; OTPC; VA
Ready for the Ride—1795. H. C. Bunner. PFE
Ready They Make Hauberks Sarrazinese. *Unknown, tr. fr. French by* C. K. Scott Moncrieff. *Fr.* The Song of Roland. WaaP
Ready to seek out death in my disgrace. Henry Constable. *Fr.* Diana. OBSC; SiCE
Ready with leaves and with buds stood the tree. The Tree. Björnstjerne Björnson. ADAH; DD; HH; MPB; OHIP; PRWS; PTA-1; RAR
Real. Emily Dickinson. *See* I like a look of agony.
Real Christ, The. Richard Watson Gilder. *Fr.* The Passing of Christ. OQP; QP-1
Real Estate. *Unknown.* SiTL
Real Happiness. Goldsmith. *Fr.* The Traveller. OBEC
Real Miracles. Max Jacob, *tr. fr. French by* Wallace Fowlie. MiCF
Real original, I think, A. An Original Cuss. Keith Preston. ALV; WhC
Real Presence. Ivan Adair. OQP; QP-1; WGRP
Real Property. Harold Monro. AlDL; ChMo; CMP; MoP; ReTS; TCEP; TCPD; WP
Real Question, The. Arthur Hugh Clough. *Fr.* Amours de Voyage, Canto V, ii. BPN
Real Riches, The. John Godfrey Saxe. PTA-2
Real Santa Claus, A. Frank Dempster Sherman. ChBR; GaP
Real was always something that came out of streets, The. The Epiphany. George Strong. GoYe
Real Woman, A. Keats. LiTL
Realism. Thomas Bailey Aldrich. AnNE
Realism. A. C. Benson. VA
Realism. Maxwell Bodenheim. MOAP
Realism. Ruth Samuels. CAG
Reality. Martha Dickinson Bianchi. AA
Reality. Amelia Josephine Burr. ChIP; PSO
Reality. Sir Aubrey De Vere. WGRP
Reality. John Drinkwater. BMEP
Reality. Frances Ridley Havergal. BePJ; WGRP
Reality. Herman Eugene Kittredge. UnW
Reality. Angela Morgan. WGRP
Reality. Robert Haven Schauffler. TBM
Reality. Raymond Souster. CaP
Reality and Appearance. Jalal ed-Din Rumi, *tr. fr. Persian by* R. A. Nicholson. PeP
Reality, reality,/ Lord Jesus Christ Thou art to me! Reality. Frances Ridley Havergal. BePJ; WGRP
Reality! Reality! What Is It? Richard Eberhart. FiMAP
Realization. Ananda Acharya. WGRP
Realization. Mahlon Leonard Fisher. AnAmPo; LA
Really I know. Poems. Léon Damas. PoNe
Really, what a shocking scene! A Man of Experience. Laoiseach Mac an Bhaird. KiLC
Realm is here of masquing light, A. Light at Equinox. Léonie Adams. CrMA
Realm of Fancy, The. Keats. *See* Fancy.
Realm of Love, The. George Tucker Bispham, Jr. CAG
Reaped is the harvest. Autumnal. Ann Louise Hayes. PtPa
Reaper, The. L. H. Allen. MoAuPo; NeLNL
Reaper, The. Robert Duncan. CrMA
Reaper, The. James Matthew Legaré. SPP
Reaper, The. John Banister Tabb. ACP
Reaper, The. Wordsworth. *See* Solitary Reaper, The.
Reaper and the Flowers, The. Longfellow. AnNE; HBV; IAP; LEAP; LPS-2; PIR; TCAP
Reapers, The. Frederic Prokosch. NeTW
Reapers. Jean Toomer. CDC
Reapers, The. Lauchlan MacLean Watt. PGD
Reapers' Song. Theocritus, *tr. fr. Greek. Fr.* Idylls, X. GrR, *tr. by* Henry Harmon Chamberlin; OxBG, *tr. by* T. F. Higham
Reapers that with whetted sickles stand, The. Poetry and Philosophy. Thomas Randolph. *Fr.* An Eclogue to Mr. Johnson. OBS
Reaping the Barley. Jorge Carrera Andrade, *tr. fr. Spanish by* Muna Lee. AnCL; WoL
Reappearing. Horatius Bonar. EOAH
Rear Guard, The. Irene Fowler Brown. BlG; PAH
Rear-Guard, The. Siegfried Sassoon. BLV; BMEP; BoLiVe; MBP; MCCG; MoBrPo; NeMA; TCEP; WaP
Rear Porches of an Apartment Building. Maxwell Bodenheim. AnAmPo; LA; NP
Reared within the mountains. Mountain Chant. *Tr. by* Washington Matthews. APW
Rearmament. Robinson Jeffers. CoV; OxBA
Rearrange a wife's affection? Emily Dickinson. AnNE; OnAP; PoEL-5
Reason, The. Dorothy Aldis. TiPo (1952 ed.)
Reason, The. Leonard Bacon. YaD
Reason. Marjory E. Cole. CAG
Reason. Ralph Hodgson. *See* Reason Has Moons.
Reason. Josephine Miles. FiMAP
Reason, The. James Oppenheim. HBV
Reason. *Unknown.* TreF
Reason and Imagination. Blake. *Fr.* Milton. EnRP
Reason and Imagination, *sel.* Christopher Smart. Imagination. BeR
Reason and Instinct. Pope. *Fr.* An Essay on Man, Epistle III. LPS-3

Reason and Revelation. Dryden. *Fr.* Religio Laici. CoEV; OBS, *longer sel.;* PoLi, *longer sel.*
("Dim as the borrow'd beams of moon and stars.") MeRV; OxBoCh; ViBoPo, *br. sel.*
(Finite Reason.) LoBV
(Reason and Religion.) FiP
(Reason and the Soul.) BeR
Reason Fair to Fill my Glass, A. Charles Morris. HBV
Reason for Not Writing Orthodox Nature Poetry. John Wain. HaMV
Reason for Writing, A. Theodore Spencer. TwAmPo
Reason Has Moons. Ralph Hodgson. MoVE, *9 ll.;* ShBV-4
(Reason.) MBP; MoBrPo
("Reason has moons, but moons not hers.") CaAE; FaBoCh; LoGBV; SiTL
Reason I Stay on Job So Long, *with music. Unknown.* ABF
Reason, in faith thou art well serv'd, that still. Astrophel and Stella, X. Sir Philip Sidney. MaPo; ReEn; SiCE; SiPS
Reason is our soul's left hand, faith her right. To the Countess of Bedford. John Donne. ATP (1953 ed.)
Reason, tell me thy mind, if here be reason. Love and Reason. Sir Philip Sidney. *Fr.* Arcadia. SiPS
Reason thus with life. Life and Death. Shakespeare. *Fr.* Measure for Measure, III, i. UnPo (1st ed.)
Reason Why, The. Thomas Lovell Beddoes. OBRV
Reason why our work is brittle, The. The Reason. Leonard Bacon. YaD
Reasonable Affliction, A. Matthew Prior. ALV; BLV; HBV; PIAE; TrGrPo; WhC
Reasons for Drinking. Henry Aldrich. BOHV; InMe; YaD
(Catch, A: "If all be true that I do think.") InvP; OBS; SeEP
(Five Reasons [for Drinking], The.) LiTG; SiTL
(If All Be True That I Do Think.) ElSeCe; SeCL
Reasons for Music. Archibald MacLeish. NePA
Rebecca. Hilaire Belloc. BoChLi (1939 ed.); RIS; StaSt
Rebecca and Abigail. Katharine Lee Bates. CV
Rebecca and Rowena, *sel.* Thackeray.
Age of Wisdom, The. ALV; BMEP, *sl. abr.;* HBV; LEAP; LPS-1; VA; WhC
(Love at Two Score.) PoVP
Rebecca's After-Thought. Elizabeth Turner. HBV; HBVY
Rebecca's Hymn. Sir Walter Scott. *Fr.* Ivanhoe, *ch.* 40. BPN; EmBrPo; EnRP; LPS-2
("When Israel, of the Lord beloved.") ViBoPo
Rebel, The. Baudelaire, *tr. fr. French by* Cosmo Monkhouse. LiA
Rebel, The. Hilaire Belloc. BMEP; CoBE; PoFr
Rebel, A. John Gould Fletcher. MAP; MoAmPo
Rebel. Irene Rutherford McLeod. BMEP; HBMV
"Beyond the murk," *sel.* WGRP
Rebel, The. Padraic Pearse. OnYI; PoFr
Rebel, The. Innes Randolph. KN; OxBoLi
(Good Old Rebel, A *and* B *vers., with music.*) ABF
(I'm a Good Old Rebel.) CSF; SPP
Rebel Mother's Lullaby. Shane Leslie. BOL
Rebel Scot, The. John Cleveland. EPS
"Come, keen iambics, with your badger's feet," *sel.* OBS; ViBoPo
Rebel Soldier, The. *Unknown.* LoGBV; OxBoLi
(Jack o' Diamonds; or, The Rabble Soldier, *diff. vers., with music.*) CoSo; CSF
(My Horses Ain't Hungry, *diff. vers.*) APW
(Rabble Soldier, *diff. vers., with music.*) AS
(Troubled Soldier, The, *diff. vers., with music.*) AS
"Rebel Soldier Killed in the Trenches before Petersburg, Va., April 15, 1865, A." *Unknown.* BlG
Rebellion. Stephen Chalmers. NLK
Rebellion. Samuel Taylor Coleridge. *Fr.* France; an Ode. RO
Rebellion against death, the old rebellion. The Old Enemy. Sara Teasdale. MaRV
Rebellion shook an ancient dust. April Mortality. Léonie Adams. AnAmPo; LA; MAP; MoAB; MoAmPo; MOAP
Rebellious, he studied. The Chiseler. Francis X. Maynard. JKCP (1955 ed.)
Rebellious heart, in the grip of fate. Soul Growth. Annerika Fries. OQP; QP-2
Rebellious Vine, The. Harold Monro. WaKn
Rebels. Ernest Crosby. MC; PAH
Rebirth. Margaret E. Bruner. PoToHe
Rebirth; 1914–18. Kipling. GTML; GTSL; LoBV
Re-Birth of Venus, The. Geoffrey Hill. NePoEA
Rebuff. Samuel L. Albert. NePoAm-2
Rebuke. Ambrose Bierce. BAP
Rebuke. Euripides, *tr. fr. Greek by* Gilbert Murray. *Fr.* Rhesus. GrR
Rebukeful reason, what words fall from thee? Ideal Passion, XXXV. George Edward Woodberry. MOAP
Recall, The. Kipling. POTE; PoVP
Recall, The. Rabindranath Tagore. MOAH
Recall how with frozen fingers December's clouds outspread. The Miracle of Spring. Bahar. PeP
Recalling War. Robert Graves. CoBMV; LiTM (rev. ed.); WaP
Recantation, The. Albius Tibullus, *tr. fr. Latin by* James Cranstoun. LiTW
Recapitulations, *sels.* Karl Shapiro.
"At one the Apocalypse had spoken," II. FiMAP
"I was born downtown on a wintry day," I. FiMAP
"My first small book was nourished in the dark," V. FiMAP
"We waged a war within a war," XI. PoNe
"When nuns were spitted and poets fell," XIII. FiMAP
Receipt to Restore Stella's Youth, A. Swift. Po
Receive, Beloved. Virginia Earle. JKCP (1955 ed.)
Receive, dear friend, the truths I teach. To Licinius [Murena]. Horace, *tr. by* William Cowper. AWP; EnLi-1; HBV; JAWP; OuHeWo; WBP
Receive me again, Father God. The Song of the Child. Anna Wickham. QS
Receive my body, pretty bed. Going to Bed at Night. Adelaide O'Keeffe. BOL; OTPC (1923 ed.)
Receive these writs, my sweet and dearest friend. Coelia, XX. William Percy. ReIE
Reception Good. Kenneth Fearing. PoLFOT
Recessional. Georgia Douglas Johnson. CDC; PoNe
Recessional. Kipling. AWP; BBV; BEL; BLPA; BLRP BLV; BMEP; BoLiVe; BPN; BTP; CaAE; ChMo; CP; CV; EnLi-2; EnLit; EPN; FaFP; GN; GrCo-1; GTBS; GTBS-W; GTSL; HBV; HBVY; InP; InPo; JAWP; LBBV; LEAP; LiA; LiTB; LiTM; LPS-1; MaRV; MBP; MCCG; MoBrPo; NeHB; NeMA; OAEP (2d ed.); OBEV; OBVV; OHFP; OlF; OQP; PECK; PFE; PIR; PoE; PoMa; POT; PoTo; PoVP; PraP; PTA-1; PYM; QP-1; TCEP; TCPD; TOP; TreF; TrGrPo; TSW; TSWC; TVSH; TwCV; ViBoPo; ViP; ViPP; VLEP; VOD; WBLP; WBP; WGRP; WHA
(Lest We Forget!) YT
Recessional, The. Sir Charles G. D. Roberts. HBV; LBMV; LEAP
Recessional. Isaac Watts. *See* O God, Our Help in Ages Past.
Recife/ Not the Venice of America. Salute to Recife. Manuel Bandeira. AnCL
Recipe. A. P. Herbert. *Fr.* Two Gentlemen of Soho. WhC
Recipe for a Happy Life. Margaret of Navarre. PoMa
Recipe for a Salad, A. Sydney Smith. *See* Salad, A.
Recipe for an Evening Musicale. Phyllis McGinley. UnS; WhC
Recipe for Living. Alfred Grant Walton. PoToHe (new ed.)
Recipes. *Unknown.* LPS-3
Reciprocity. John Drinkwater. EPP; NeMA; NP
Reciprocity. Vassar Miller. NePoEA
Recital, *sel.* Louise Townsend Nicholl.
"In the motionless haze of interior heat." UnS
Recitation and Song: "Am I alone." W. S. Gilbert. *Fr.* Patience. MBP; WoL
(Bunthorne's Recitative and Song.) CoBE
(Recitative and Song: Bunthorne.) PoVP
Recitative. Hart Crane. FaBoMo; MOAP
Reckless Devil-may-care. Nikolai Tikhonov, *tr. fr. Russian by* Jack Lindsay. RuPo
Reckon the days that Zeus ordains, and in due array. Good Days and Bad. Hesiod. *Fr.* Works and Days. OxBG
Recluse, The. Wordsworth. BEL; KN
Sels.
"Embrace me then, ye Hills, and close me in." EnSW
"On Man, on Nature." EnRP; EPN; EPP; NBE; OBRV
(Prospectus.) ERP
Recluses, The. Stuart Z. Perkoff. NeAP
Recogitabo Tibi Omnes Annos Meos. William Habington. *See* Time! Where Didst Thou Those Years Inter.
Recognition, A. Elizabeth Barrett Browning. *See* To George Sand; a Recognition.
Recognition. John White Chadwick. AA
Recognition. Margaret E. Sangster. MaRV
Recognition, The. William Sawyer. HBV; PA
Recognition. John Banister Tabb. ChIP; JKCP; OQP; QP-1
Recognition of Eve, The. Karl Shapiro. *Fr.* Adam and Eve. MoAB
Recoleta, The. Jorge Luis Borges, *tr. fr. Spanish by* H. R. Hayes. TwSpPo
Recollection. "Æ." NV
Recollection. Anne Reeve Aldrich. AA; BAP; LEAP
Recollection, A. John Peale Bishop. LiTA; TwAmPo
Recollection. Amelia Walstien Carpenter. AA
Recollection, A. Frances Cornford. TSW; TSWC
Recollection, The. Shelley. CBE, *abr.;* GTBS; GTBS-D; GTBS-W; GTSE; GTSL; SN
(To Jane; the Recollection.) ChER; EmBrPo; EPN; EV-4; OBRV
"We wandered to the Pine Forest," *sel.* CH
Recollection in Autumn. Valentin Iremonger. OnYI
(Elizabeth.) NeIP
(This Houre Her Vigill.) OxBI
Recollection of Love. Efrain Huerta, *tr. fr. Spanish by* Dudley Fitts. AnCL

Recollections. Aasmund Olafsson Vinje, *tr. fr. Norwegian by* Charles W. Stork. AnNoLy
Recollections after an Evening Walk. John Clare. ERP
Recollections of Burgos. Richard Chenevix Trench. OBRV
Recollections of Caoilte. *Unknown, tr. fr. Old Irish by* Seán O'Faoláin. SiB
Recollections of Early Childhood. Wordsworth. *Fr.* Ode: Intimations of Immortality from Recollections of Early Childhood. CBPC
Recollections of Love. Samuel Taylor Coleridge. ChER
Recollections of My Children. *Unknown, tr. fr. Japanese by* Basil Hall Chamberlain. OnPM
Recollections of Oisin. *Unknown, tr. fr. Old Irish by* Seán O'Faoláin. SiB
Recollections of the Arabian Nights. Tennyson. EV-5; PoVP; VLEP
Recommendation, The. Richard Crashaw. PoLi
Recompense. Grace Noll Crowell. PCD
Recompense. Agnes Aston Hill. NeTW
Recompense. Robert Ervin Howard. DaM
Recompense. John Richard Moreland. OQP; QP-2
Recompense. Wade Oliver. PoP
Recompense. Nixon Waterman. HBV
Recompense, The. Anna Wickham. NP; PC
Reconcilement, The. John Sheffield. CEP; LiTL; LO; LoPo; LoPS; OBEV
Reconciliation. "Æ." ChMo; CMP; LBBV; OBMV; OxBI; PoVP
Reconciliation, *sel.* Elizabeth Doten.
"God of the Granite and the Rose!" TrPWD
(Prayer, A: "God of the Granite and the Rose!") OQP; QP-1
Reconciliation, The ("Donec gratus eram"). Horace, *tr. fr. Latin.* Odes, III, 9. OuHeWo, *tr. by* Sir Theodore Martin; RoL, *tr. by* Ben Jonson
(February 14, 22 B.C., *par. by* Franklin P. Adams.) InMe
(Reconciliation of Lovers, *tr. by* Ben Jonson.) LiA
Reconciliation, The. James Benjamin Kenyon. PR
Reconciliation. Charles Mackay. *See* Under the Holly Bough.
Reconciliation, The. Archibald MacLeish. MoAmPo
Reconciliation. Caroline Atherton Briggs Mason. AA
Reconciliation. J. U. Nicolson. HBMV
Reconciliation, The. Tennyson. *See* As thro' the Land at Eve We Went.
Reconciliation. Frank M. Towne. PreP
Reconciliation. *Unknown, tr. fr. Late Middle Irish by* Kenneth Jackson. AnIL
Reconciliation. John Hall Wheelock. CrMA
Reconciliation. Walt Whitman. AnAmPo; AnEnPo; APW; BLV; BoLiVe; CBOV; CoBA; CoV; FaBoEn; GTBS-D; IAP; LA; MAP; MaRV; MoAmPo; MOAP; NeMA; OxBA; PoE; SoV; TCAP; TrGrPo; WaaP
Reconciliation. W. B. Yeats. TwP
Reconciliation of Achilles and Agamemnon, The. Homer, *tr. fr. Greek by* the Earl of Derby. *Fr.* The Iliad, XIX. GrR
Reconciliation of Lovers. Horace. *See* Reconciliation, The.
Reconsecration. Dorothy Gould. PGD
Record is a scroll of many indecipherable scrawls, The. Carl Sandburg. *Fr.* The People, Yes. CoV
Record Perpetual Loss. Mary Stanley. AnNZ
Record Stride, A. Robert Frost. NePA
Recorder, tax collector, landlord, friends. Ode for the Burial of a Citizen. John Ciardi. MiAP
Recorders Ages Hence. Walt Whitman. APW; BoFr; IAP; MAP; MoAmPo; NePA
Recorders in Italy. Adrienne Cecile Rich. UnS
Records, The, grow/ Unceasingly. Alfred Noyes. *Fr.* The Torch Bearers: Epilogue. GrCo-1
Recovery, The. Edmund Blunden. MBP; MoBrPo; MoPW
Recovery. F. R. Scott. CaP
Recovery, The. Thomas Traherne. EPS
Recovery from Mental Illness. H. C. Bosman. BoSA
Recreation. Jane Taylor. OBRV; OxBoLi
Recrimination. Euripides, *tr. fr. Greek by* R. Potter. *Fr.* Iphigenia in Aulis. GrR
Recrimination. Ella Wheeler Wilcox. AA
Recruit, The. Robert W. Chambers. AA; BOHV; HBV; LEAP; PFY
Recruit, The. A. E. Housman. A Shropshire Lad, III. PoVP
Recruited Collier, The. *Unknown. See* Jimmy's Enlisted.
Recruiting Drive. Charles Causley. NePoEA
Recruiting Officer, The. Tu Fu, *tr. fr. Chinese by* Chu Chun-i. WhP
Recruiting Song. Wang Ts'ang-ling, *tr. fr. Chinese by* Wang Sheng-chih. WhP
Recuerdo. Grace Hazard Conkling. TBM
Recuerdo. Edna St. Vincent Millay. FaFP; LiTA; LiTL; LiTM; NP; OxBA
Recurrence, The. Edwin Muir. MoPo
Red. Countee Cullen. GoSl
Red and fiery/ The dawn lights the sky. Harvest. Aleksey Koltsov. BoRS
Red and green neon lights, the jazz hysteria. Nuit Blanche; North End. Conrad Aiken. OxBA
Red and the Blue, The. H. A. Roby. FOAH
Red and White Roses. Thomas Carew. ElSeCe
Red and yellow of the Autumn salt-grass, The. At Tide Water. Sir Charles G. D. Roberts. PeCV
Red are the hands of the reapers. The Reapers. Lauchlan MacLean Watt. PGD
Red as a blow of autumn leaves. A Hawk from Cuckoo Tavern. Lawrence Lee. GA
Red as the lips of Rahab. The Scarlet Thread. Daniel Henderson. HBMV
Red as the sky. Song of the Four Colors. Wang Jung. PoHN
Red as your maple tree. Inspiration. "John Crichton." CPG
Red at night,/ Sailor's delight. Rules of the Road. *Unknown.* SoAmSa
Red beans grow in the south country. Meditation. Wang Wei. WhP
Red Book of Hergest, The, *sel. Unknown, tr. fr. Middle Welsh by* Ernest Rhys.
Lament for Urien, The. OBMV
Red Bow, The. *Unknown, tr. fr. Chinese.* WhP
Red bricks in the suburbs, white horse on the wall. Ballad to a Traditional Refrain. Maurice James Craig. SeCePo
Red Bridge, The. Tu Mu, *tr. fr. Chinese.* WhP
Red-Bud, the Kentucky Tree, The. Christmas in Freelands. James Stephens. ChMo; CMP
Red-cap sang in Bishop's wood, A. Path Flower. Olive Tilford Dargan. BAP; CP; HBMV; NV; SBMV
Red Carpet for Shelley, A. Elinor Wylie. PtP
Red Cliff, The. Su T'ung-po, *tr. fr. Chinese by* Kenneth Rexroth. OnPC
Red Cockatoo, The. Po Chü-i, *tr. fr. Chinese by* Arthur Waley. ChTr; LiTW; MoPW; OuHeWo; TrCh
Red Country, The. William Rose Benét. AOAH
Red Cross, The. John H. Finley. *See* Red Cross Spirit Speaks, The.
Red Cross, The. Edna Jacques. PoRL
Red Cross, The. Henry van Dyke. PEDC
Red Cross Christmas Seal, The. Theodosia Garrison. PEDC
Red-Cross Knight, The. Spenser. *See* Una and the Red Cross Knight.
Red Cross Nurse, The. Edith M. Thomas. PEDC
Red Cross Nurses, The. Thomas L. Masson. PEDC
Red Cross Nurses. Gervase Stewart. WaP
Red Cross Spirit Speaks, The. John H. Finley. BoHiPo; PEDC
(Red Cross, The.) LPS-1
Red dawn clouds coming up! the heavens proclaim you. Morning Light Song. Philip Lamantia. NeAP
Red deer loves the chaparral, The. The Rocky Mountain Sheep. Mary Austin. MPB
Red Eagle—the Mountain with Wings. Vachel Lindsay. NV
Red Earth. Grace Noll Crowell. HiLiAm
Red-edged/ Big blue crucifers. Picture Drawn by a Boy. Shizuo Ito. PoLJ
Red firelight on the Sioux tepees. Cottonwood Leaves. Badger Clark. TiPo
Red Fisherman, The. Winthrop Mackworth Praed. PCN
Red flame flowers bloom and die, The. Nocturne. Crosbie Garstin. CH
Red fool, my laughing comrade. To a Comrade in Arms. Alun Lewis. FaBoTw
Red for Santa's fur-lined cloak. All in Red. Eileen Mathias. BoTP
Red foxgloves against a yellow wall streaked with plum-colored shadows. Ombre Chinoise. Amy Lowell. NP
Red fruit of the lichi, The. Planting a Lichi Tree. Po Chü-i. PoHN
Red Geraniums. Martha Haskell Clark. BLPA; NeHB; VOD
Red Ghosts Chant, The. Lilian White Spencer. PoOW
Red gold of pools. Harvest Sunset. Carl Sandburg. TSW; TSWC
Red-gold Rain, The, *sels.* Sacheverell Sitwell.
Orange Tree by Day. AtBAP; MBP; MoBrPo
Orange Tree by Night. AtBAP
Red Gown, The. Ibn al-Sabuni, *tr. fr. Arabic by* A. J. Arberry. MooP
Red granite and black diorite, with the blue. The Skeleton of the Future. "Hugh MacDiarmid." GoTS; MoBrPo; OBMV; ShBV-4
Red-haired Man's Wife, The. James Stephens. HBMV; MBP; MoBrPo; OBVV
Red Hanrahan's Song about Ireland. W. B. Yeats. *Fr.* Hanrahan and Cathleen the Daughter of Hoolihan. BEL; ChMo; CMP; FaBoCh; FaBoMo; GTIV; LoGBV; OnYI; OxBI
Red Harlaw, The. Sir Walter Scott. *See* Harlaw.
Red has parted from the green, The. Traveling. Chu Tun-ru. ChLP; WhP
Red-headed Restaurant Cashier. Carl Sandburg. ChMo; CMP
Red Heart, The. James Reaney. CaP

Red Hills, The. Pao Chao, *tr. fr. Chinese by* Arthur Waley. TrCh
Red Hugh. Thomas McGreevy. *See* Aodh Ruadh O'Domhnaill.
Red in Autumn. Elizabeth Gould. BoTP
Red Iron Ore. *Unknown.* ABF, *with music;* AS, *with music;* IHA, *with music;* TiPo (1952 ed.), *abr.*
Red Jacket, The. George M. Baker. PTA-2
Red Jacket. Fitz-Greene Halleck. AA; IAP
Red-kerchiefed fruit man, The. The Fruit Vendor. Frances Beatrice Taylor. CPG; MW
Red Lacquer Music-Stand, The. Amy Lowell. TCPD
Red leaves fall upon the lake, The. Threnody. John Farrar. BrR; BoChLi; GFA; SUS
Red leaves flutter. Cover. Frances Frost. SUS
Red Light Saloon, The, *with music. Unknown.* ShS
Red lips are not so red. Greater Love. Wilfred Owen. AtBAP; BLV; BoLiVe; EnLi-2 (1949 ed.); EnLoPo; FaBoMo; FaFP; GTBS-W; LiTB; LiTG; LiTM; LO; MBP; MoAB; MoBrPo; NAMP; OAEP (2d ed.); SeCeV; ViBoPo; WaaP; WaP
Red Man's Wife, The. *Unknown, tr. fr. Modern Irish by* Douglas Hyde. GTIV; OnYI; OxBI; SeCePo
Red May. Agnes Mary Frances Robinson. AV; HBMV; VOD
Red Men, The. Charles Sangster. CaP
Red Moon. Norman Bethune. PoP
Red mountain, red forest. The Situation. Sydney Clouts. BoSA
Red o'er the Forest. John Keble. *See* November.
Red oxen/ in a field of gold. Federico García Lorca, *tr. fr. Spanish by* Eleanor L. Turnbull. CoSP
Red paths that wander through the gray, and cells. With God Conversing. Gene Derwood. LiTA; LiTM; NePA
Red Patrol, The. Sir Gilbert Parker. CPG
Red Poppies. "Fiona Macleod." *Fr.* Sospiri di Roma. VA
Red Poppies in the Corn. W. Campbell Galbraith. POT
Red rain spatter under the redhaw, The. Redhaw Rain. Carl Sandburg. Po
Red, Red Rose, A. Burns. AEV; AtBAP; AWP; BCEP; BEL; BSV; CaAE; CBE; CBOV; CBPC; CEP; ChTr; CoBE; EBSV; EiPP; EM-1; EnL; EnLi-2; EnLit; EtPaEn; EV-3; FaFP; HiLiEn; HBV; InPo; InvP; JAWP; LEAP; LoPS, *st.* 1; MCCG; OBEC; OBEV; OnPM; OtMeF; OuHeWo; PCD; PG; PIAE; PoE; PoEL-4; PoMa; PoRL; PreP; REAL; SeCeV; TOP; TVSH; ViBoPo; WBP; WP
(My Love Is [*or* Luve's] like a Red Red Rose.) AnFE; CoEV; EnRP; FaBoBe; LiTB; LiTG; NeHB; OAEP; PYM; ShBV-4; TyEnPo
(My Luve.) BLV; BoLiVe; HoPM; TrGrPo
(O My Luve's [*or* Luve Is *or* Love Is] like a Red, Red Rose.) ExPo; FaBoCh; GoTS; GTBS; GTBS-D; GTBS-W; GTSE; GTSL; LiTL; LoGBV; LoPo; LPS-1; PoeMoYo; ReaPo; TreF; WHA
(Song: "My luve is like a red, red rose.") LoBV
(Song: "O my luve's like a red, red rose.") PC
Red reins, O Goat, these boys have set about. The Goat. Anyte. OxBG
Red Riding Hood. Guy Wetmore Carryl. HBV; YaD
Red Right Returning. Louis O. Coxe. MoVE; WaP
Red River Shore, *with music. Unknown.* ABF; CoSo
Red River Valley. *Unknown.* AS *with music;* CoSo, *with music;* FaBoBe; FaFP; OIF; TrAS, *with music;* TreFS
Red-Rock, the Moose-Hunter. Lew Sarett. PFE
Red rock wilderness, The. The Wilderness. Sidney Keyes. LiTB; LiTM (rev. ed.); NeBP
Red Rooster, The. Hilda Conkling. TSW; TSWC
Red Rose. Hafiz, *tr. fr. Persian by* John Payne. PeP
Red Rose, The. Thomas Howell. *See* Rose, The.
Red Rose, proud Rose, sad Rose of all my days! To the Rose upon the Road of Time. W. B. Yeats. OAEP (2d ed.); Po
Red rose whispers of passion, The. A White Rose. John Boyle O'Reilly. AA; ACP; AnAmPo; HBV; LA; LBAP; LEAP; OBAV; OBEV; OBVV; OnYI; PR
Red rowes the Nith 'tween bank and brae. My Nanie, O. Allan Cunningham. EBSV
Red rust is on the blade. Rust. Virginia Moore. BAP
Red Sea, The. Aeschylus, *tr. fr. Greek by* C. M. Bowra. *Fr.* Prometheus Unbound. OxBG
Red Sea. James Agee. *Fr.* Two Songs on the Economy of Abundance. MAP; MoAmPo
Red Sea, *with music. Unknown.* StDa
Red Sea Place in Your Life, The. Annie Johnson Flint. *See* At the Place of the Sea.
Red Skins left their agency, the soldiers left their post, The. The Indian Ghost Dance and War. W. H. Prather. PoOW
Red Sky at Morning. Gilbert Thomas. LO; TreFS
Red sky at night. *Unknown.* OxNR
Red Slippers. Amy Lowell. NP
Red Square, The. Nikolai Poletayev, *tr. fr. Russian.* BoRS, *tr. by* V. de S. Pinto; TrRV, *tr. by* Babette Deutsch
Red stockings, blue stockings. *Unknown.* OxNR
Red sun, remember. On Mt. Iron. Charles Brasch. AnNZ
Red sun, that with thy taper shining bright. Sonnet. Fernando de Herrera. TeCS
Red the dust and brown the rock. Native Inhabitant. Douglas Stewart. NeLNL
Red, the White, the Blue, The. Kate B. Sherwood. PEOR
Red Thread of Honour, The. Sir Francis Hastings Doyle. BBV; LH; OtMeF; PoVP
Red-tiled towers of the old Chateau, The. Chateau Papineau. S. Frances Harrison. CaP; OCL; VA
Red-Top and Timothy. Lucy Larcom. BoChLi (1939 ed.); UTS
Red towers lofty and glowing, The. Old Lines; a Fragment. Dino Campana. OnPM
Red Trillium. "John Crichton." CPG
Red Wheelbarrow, The. William Carlos Williams. HoPM; LiTA; MoAB; MoAmPo; UnPo (3d ed.)
(Spring and All.) ThWaDe
Red, White, and Blue. David T. Shaw. *See* Columbia, the Gem of the Ocean.
Red Wig, The. *Unknown.* CoMu
Red Wind, The. Lionel Johnson. PoVP
Red Wine in a Black Glass. Ibn Mujbar, *tr. fr. Arabic by* A. J. Arberry. MooP
Redbirds. Sara Teasdale. BLA; MM; WhBS
Redbreast Chasing a Butterfly, The. Wordsworth. CG; OTPC
Red-Breast of Aquitania, The. Francis S. Mahony. OnYI
Reddened Road, The. H. M. Tickener. PSO
Rededication. Emanuel Litvinoff. WaP
Redeem Time Past. William Drummond of Hawthornden. EV-2
Redeemer, The. "Fiona Macleod." WGRP
Redeemer, The. Siegfried Sassoon. WGRP
Redeeming Mercy, The. Israel Zangwill. *Fr.* Jehovah. GrCo-2
Redemption. George Herbert. ElSeCe; ExPo; GTBS-W; LiTB; LiTG; MeLP; MePo; OBS; PeBoSo; PoE; SeCeV; SeCV-1; SeEP; StJW
Redemption of the Ridiculous. Donald F. Drummond. PtPa
Redeployment. Howard Nemerov. NePA; TrJP
Redesdale and Wise William *Unknown.* ESPB
Redhaw Rain. Carl Sandburg. Po
Rediscovery. Geoffrey Johnson. UnW
Redivivus. Donald Davidson. SPP
Redondillas. Sister Juana Inéz de la Cruz, *tr. fr. Spanish by* Garrett Strange. CAW
Redoubted knights, and honorable Dames. Malbecco and Hellenore. Spenser. *Fr.* The Faerie Queene, III, 9 *and* 10. MaPo
Redshanks, The. Julian Bell. LO; OBMV
Redwing, The. Patric Dickinson. HaMV
Reed, The. Abul Hajjaj, *tr. fr. Arabic by* A. J. Arberry. MooP
Reed, The. Audrey Alexandra Brown. BoCaPo
Reed, The. Henry Bernard Carpenter. AA
Reed, The. Caryll Houselander. ISi
Reed, The. Mikhail Yurevich Lermontov, *tr. fr. Russian by* J. J. Robbins. AWP; JAWP; WBP
Reed Call. Madison Cawein. PR
Reed-Player, The. Archibald MacLeish. HBMV
Reed-Player, The. Duncan Campbell Scott. OCL; VA
Reeds, The. Konstantin Dmitreyevich Balmont, *tr. fr. Russian by* C. M. Bowra. BoR
Reeds in the Loch Sayis, The. *Unknown.* GoTS
(Reeds in the Loch Say, The.) EBSV
Reeds of Innocence. Blake. *See* Piping down the Valleys Wild.
Reef Wrack. Clement B. Christesen. BoAu
Reefing Topsails. Walter Mitchell. EtS
Reek and the Rambling Blade, The, *with music. Unknown.* OuSiCo
Re-enlisted. Lucy Larcom. MDAH
Reeve's Tale, The, *sel.* Chaucer. *Fr.* The Canterbury Tales.
"At Trumpyngtoun nat fer from Cantebrigge." ViBoPo
Reference. *Unknown.* LauV
Reference to a Passage in Plutarch's Life of Sulla. Robinson Jeffers. CrMA
Referring to Flowers. *Unknown, tr. fr. Japanese by* Ishii *and* Obata. *Fr.* Manyo Shu. OnPM
Refined Gold. Theognis, *tr. fr. Greek by* T. F. Higham. GrL; OxBG
Refined Man, The. Kipling. *Fr.* Epitaphs of the War. FaBoTw
Refinement is itself refined. Noblesse Oblige. Ibn Sa'id of Alcala la Real. MooP
Refiner's Fire. *Unknown.* BLRP
Reflection. Margaret Allonby. BoSA
Reflection. Keats. *See* When I Have Fears.
Reflection. Lew Sarett. MoSiPe
Reflection. Kurt M. Stein. InMe
Reflection, The. Edward Taylor. AmPP; NePA
(Reflexion, The.) AtBAP; OxBA

Reflection. James Thomson. Sunday up the River, XII. EnLit
("My Love o'er the water bends dreaming.") EBSV; OBEV (1st ed.)
Reflection. W. J. Turner. OBMV
Reflection by a Mailbox. Stanley Kunitz. TrJP; WaP
Reflection for a Sunday Morning. Leo Kennedy. OCL
Reflection in Blue. David McCord. MoAmPo (1942 ed.)
Reflection in the Mirror, The. Annette von Droste-Hülshoff, *tr. fr. German by* Herman Salinger. AnGP
Reflection on the Course of Human Life, A. William Lloyd, Bishop of St. Asaph. PrWP
Reflections. Cyrus E. Albertson. MaRV
Reflections. Edna Becker. MaRV; OQP; QP-2
Reflections. George Crabbe. TriL
Late Wisdom, *sel.* EV-3; HBV, *abr.;* OBEV, *abr.;* TrGrPo
("We've trod the maze of error round.") OBRV
Reflections. Amy Lowell. *Fr.* Chinoiseries. AnAmPo; LA; NP
Reflections at Dawn. Phyllis McGinley. FiBHP
Reflections in a Hospital. Emanuel Eisenberg. ALV
Reflections in a Little Park. Babette Deutsch. NePoAm
Reflections in an Iron Works. "Hugh MacDiarmid." NAMP
Reflections in Bed. Julian Symons. LiTM; WaP
Reflections of Spring. Ibycus, *tr. fr. Greek by* John Addington Symonds. GrR
Reflections on an Ideal Existence. Sara Henderson Hay. CIV
Reflections on Cleopathera's Needle. Cormac O'Leary. BOHV
Reflections on Having Left a Place of Retirement. Samuel Taylor Coleridge. BPN; EmBrPo; EnRP; OBEC
Reflections on Ice-breaking. Ogden Nash. FaFP; LiTM; NePA; ShBV-4; SiTL
Reflections on the Fall of France, June, 1940. Eiluned Lewis. POTE
Reflexion, The. Edward Taylor. *See* Reflection, The.
Reformation of Godfrey Gore, The. William Brighty Rands. *See* Godfrey Gordon Gustavus Gore.
Reformation of Manners, *sels.* Defoe.
City Magistrate. BeR
Regenerate London. BeR
Reformed Wife, The, *sel. At. to* Charles Burnaby *and to* William Burnaby.
Upon a Sickly Lady. SeCL
Reformer, The ("All grim and soiled and brown with tan"). Whittier. CoV; LPS-2
Reformers, The ("O pure reformers!"). Whittier. MaRV
Refracted Lights. Celia Parker Wooley. WGRP
Refrain: "Come and kiss me, Mistress Beauty." Douglas Brooke Wheelton Sladen. *Fr.* Charles II. VA
Refrain, A: "Tell the tune his feet beat." Arthur Shearly Cripps. PoeT; TVSH
Refrain Refrain Refrain. Aesthetics. Gerardo Diego. CoSP
Refreshing rest, ecstatic dream. In the Grass. Annette von Droste-Hülshoff. AnGP
Refreshment. Anyte, *tr. fr. Greek by* F. A. Wright. GrR
Refreshment. George Edward Hoffman. ChIP
Refuge. "Æ." CaAE; ChMo; CMP; GTIV; HBV; OnYI; POTE
Refuge. Hervey Allen. HBMV
Refuge, The. Psalms, XLVI, Bible, *O.T. See* Our Refuge.
Refuge. Mable E. McCartney. BLRP
Refuge. Lew Sarett. HBMV; MaRV
Refuge. John Thompson. BoAu
Refuge. William Winter. HBV; LBAP
Refuge in Venice. Byron. *See* Venice.
Refugee, The. Lord Dunsany. NeTW
Refugee. Euripides, *tr. fr. Greek by* Arthur S. Way. *Fr.* Phoenician Maidens. GrR
Refugee, The. Helen Molyneaux Salisbury. PSO
Refugee, The. Theognis, *tr. fr. Greek by* F. L. Lucas. GrPE
Refugee. Naomi Long Witherspoon. PoNe
Refugee Blues. W. H. Auden. InPo; LiTA; LiTM; SoV
Refugee in America. Langston Hughes. WaKn
Refugee in New England. Frances Frost. BoFr; NeTW
Refugees. Grace Hazard Conkling. NP
Refugees, The. Randall Jarrell. MoAB; MoAmPo (1950 ed.)
Refugees. Louis MacNeice. LiTB; TwHP; WaP
Refugees, The. Sir Herbert Read. MBP; MoBrPo (1942 ed.)
Refusal, A. Thomas Hardy. LiTB
Refusal. Raymond Kresensky. OQP; QP-2
Refusal of Aid between Nations. Dante Gabriel Rossetti. *See* On Refusal of Aid between Nations.
Refusal of Charon, The. William E. Aytoun. EBSV
Refusal to Mourn the Death, by Fire, of a Child in London, A. Dylan Thomas. AtBAP; ChMP; CoBMV; FaBoEn; FaFP; GTBS-W; InPo; LiTB; LiTG; LiTM; MaPo; MoAB; MoPo; MoVE; NeBP; OAEP (2d ed.); Po; SeCePo; UnPo (3d ed.); WaaP
Reg wished me to go with him to the field. My Mother. Claude McKay. AnEnPo
Regard an American farm. Realism. Maxwell Bodenheim. MOAP
Regard, O reader, how it is with me. Look, in the Labyrinth of Memory. Delmore Schwartz. TrJP
Regard the capture here, O Janus-faced. Recitative. Hart Crane. FaBoMo; MOAP
Regard the little needle. The Needle. Grace Cornell Tall. GoYe
Regarding (1) the U. S. and (2) New York. Franklin P. Adams. HBMV
Regenerate London. Defoe. *Fr.* Reformation of Manners. BeR
Regeneration. Walter Savage Landor. BPN; ERP; ViBoPo, *abr.*
(Invocation, An: "We are what suns and winds and waters make us.") VA
Regeneration. Henry Vaughan. AEV; ExPo; KN; LoBV; MeLP; MePo; OBS; SeEP
Regent-Bird and Girl. Clem Christesen. MoAuPo
Regent of song! who bringest to our shore. To Rosina Pico. William Wilberforce Lord. AA
Reges de Saba Venient. *Unknown.* AnEC
Regiment of Princes, The. Thomas Hoccleve. *See* De Regimine Principum.
Regiment Song. Frank L. Stanton. FOAH
Regina Angelorum. G. K. Chesterton. ISi
Regina Celi, Letare. *Unknown* AnEC
Regina Coeli. Coventry Patmore. ISi; JKCP; MOAH; POTT; PoVP; VA; VLEP
Regina Coeli. *Unknown, tr. fr. Latin.* ISi, *tr. by* Winfred Douglas; WHL
Regina Confessorum. *Unknown.* GoBC
Region of life and light! The Life of the Blessed. Luis de León, *tr. by* Bryant. AnSpL-1; AWP
Region of light eterne. The Heavenly Home. Luis de León, *tr. by* Ida Farnell. TeCS
Regions of soft clear air, of cold green leaves. Sonnet. Thomas Caulfield Irwin. IrPN
Regret. William Drummond of Hawthornden. AtBAP
(Regrat.) PoEL-2
Regret. Benedikt Gröndal, *tr. fr. Icelandic by* Jakobina Johnson. IcP
Regret, A. Charles Harpur. BoAu
Regret. Winifred Kohn. CAG
Regret. Richard Le Gallienne. BMEP; MBP; VA
Regret. Yüan Chi, *tr. fr. Chinese by* Arthur Waley. TrCh
Regret Not Me. Thomas Hardy. GTBS-D; LO; MoVE; SeCeV
Regret, return, do not return, retreat. Cymbalum Mundi. Horace Gregory. ChMo
Regretful Rondeau, A. Michael Lewis. PIAE
Regrets, *sels.* Joachim du Bellay, *tr. fr. French.*
Exile in Rome, XXV, *tr. by* Alan Conder. TrFP
Heureux qui, comme Ulysse, a fait un beau voyage, XXXI, *tr. by* G. K. Chesterton. AWP
(Happy Ulysses, The, *tr. by* G. K. Chesterton.) WoL
(My House, *tr. by* Alan Conder.) TrFP
(Returning Home, *tr. by* William Stirling.) LiTW
(Sonnet: "Happy as Ulysses, his voyage done," *tr. by* Ralph N. Currey.) FoS
(Translation from Du Bellay: "Happy, who like Ulysses or that lord," *tr. by* G. K. Chesterton.) InP
I Hate, LXVIII, *tr. by* Alan Conder. TrFP
(Sonnet: "I hate the money-lending avarice," *tr. by* Ralph N. Currey.) FoS
O France, Mother of Arts, IX. TrFP
Slave I Languish, A, XXXIX. TrFP
Regrets. Tzu Yeh, *tr. fr. Chinese by* Henry H. Hart. PoHN
Regulation-skirted. Emergency. Isabel Fiske Conant. HBMV
Regulus, *sel.* John Crowne
To Many Deaths Decreed. SeCL
Reid at Fayal. John Williamson Palmer. PAH
Reign in my thoughts, fair hand, sweet eye, rare voice! To Delia, XXV. Samuel Daniel. ReIE
Reign of Chaos, The. Pope. *See* Conclusion: "In vain, in vain . . ."
Reign of Peace, The. Mary Starck. WBLP
Reign of Peace, The. Eliza Thornton. PEDC
Reign on, majestic Ville Marie! Montreal. William Douw Lighthall. VA
Reilly's Answer, Releasement, and Marriage with Coleen Bawn. *Unknown. See* Willy Reilly.
Reilly's Trial. *Unknown. See* Willy Reilly.
Reincarnation. Nikolai Gumilev, *tr. fr. Russian by* Y. Hornstein. BoRS
Reincarnation. Lloyd Frank Merrell. ChIP
Reincarnation. David Banks Sickels. AA
(It Cannot Be.) HBV
Reincarnation. E. Wyndham Tennant. UnW
Reine d'Amour. Francis Turner Palgrave. GBV (1952 ed.)
Reinforcements. Thomas Toke Lynch. OBVV
Reivers they stole Fair Annie, The. Fair Annie. *Unknown.* CH; EV-2; HBV; OBEV (1st ed.)
Reject the Burden. "Anna Akhmatova," *tr. fr. Russian by* Babette Deutsch. TrRV
Rejected. Wu Wen Ti, *tr. fr. Chinese by* Henry H. Hart. PoHN

Rejected "National Hymns," The. "Orpheus C. Kerr."
By Dr. Ol–v–r W–nd–l H–lmes, III. BOHV; InMe; PA
(Poems.) LPS-3
By H–y W. L–ngf–w, I. BOHV; InMe; PA
By J–hn Gr–nl–f Wh–t–r, II. BOHV; InMe; PA
By N. P. W–ll–is, VI. BOHV; InMe; PA
(Poems.) LPS-3
By R–lph W–ldo Em–r–n, IV. BOHV; InMe; PA
(Parodies.) ALV
By Th–m–s B–il–y Ald–ch, VII. BOHV; InMe; PA
(Poems.) LPS-3
By W–ll–m C–ll–n B–y–nt, V. BOHV; InMe; PA
(Poems.) LPS-3
Poems: National Anthem—by General George P. M. LPS-3
Rejected Odyssey. John Perrin. NeTW
Rejected Wife, The. Yüan Ti, *tr. fr. Chinese by* Arthur Waley. TrCh
Rejoice. Joaquin Miller. PAH
Rejoice,/ Ye woods and fountains. Epithalamium. *Unknown.* SeCL
Rejoice! Another revolutionist. The Imprisoned Revolutionist. Mihran Damadian. PoFr
Rejoice! He Liveth! Kathryn Blackburn Peck. BePJ
Rejoice in God. Christopher Smart. *Fr.* Jubilate Agno. AtBAP
("Rejoice in God, O ye Tongues.") EiPP
Rejoice in the Abyss. Stephen Spender. OnHM
Rejoice in the Lamb. Christopher Smart. *See* My Cat Jeoffry.
Rejoice, my heart, that the stars do not comprehend you. Confidants. William Alexander Percy. TBM
Rejoice, O Bridegroom! *Unknown, tr. fr. Hebrew by* Israel Abrahams. TrJP
Rejoice, O Youth, in the Lovely Hind. Moses ibn Ezra, *tr. fr. Hebrew by* Solomon Solis-Cohen. TrJP
Rejoice, rejoice, brave patriots, rejoice! Reparation or War. *Unknown.* PAH
Rejoice, rejoice, with heart and voice! For Christmas Day. Francis Kinwelmersh. AnEC
Rejoice, the Lord is King! Charles Wesley. OlF
Rejoice, ye nations, vindicate the sway. British Commerce. John Dyer. *Fr.* The Fleece. OBEC
Rejoice, ye pure in heart! Edward H. Plumptre. OlF
Rejoicing at the Arrival of Ch'en Hsiung. Po Chü-i, *tr. fr. Chinese by* Arthur Waley. AWP; TrCh
Rejoicing in Hope. Augustus Montague Toplady. BePJ
Rejoicings for Peace. Aristophanes. *See* Hymn of Peace.
Rejoyce whyle in thy youth thou art. *Unknown.* SeCSL
Relapse, The. John Sheffield, Duke of Buckingham and Normanby. NBE
Relapse, The. Thomas Stanley. EV-2; OBEV; SeCL
Relation of the Late Royal Entertainment Given by the Lord Knowles, A, *sels.* Thomas Campion.
"Can you the author of our joy." SiCE
Night as Well as Brightest Day. TuPP
"Welcome to this flowery place." SiCE
Relations. Alessandro Tassoni, *tr. fr. Italian by* Lorna de' Lucchi. WoL
Relativity. Kathleen Millay. PoMa
Relativity. *Unknown. See* Limerick: "There was a young lady named Bright."
Relativity that cloaks the Word, The. Two Morsels of Profundity from the Minor Pre-Socratics. John Simon. SiTL
Releas'd from the noise of the butcher and baker. Jinny the Just. Matthew Prior. CEP; OBEV (new ed.); PoEL-3
Release. Jean Grigsby Paxton. DDA; OQP; QP-2
Release. Margaret Tod Ritter. AV
Released. Olive Tilford Dargan. NoCaPo
Released. Anne Blackwell Payne. NoCaPo
Releasing a Migrant "Yen" (Wild Goose). Po Chü-i, *tr. fr. Chinese by* Arthur Waley. TrCh
Relent, my dear yet unkind Coelia. Coelia, XVII. William Percy. TuPP
Relentless press of little things. The Lien. Adelaide Love. MoSiPe
Reliance. Henry van Dyke. FaFP
Relic, The. John Donne. *See* Relique, The.
Relic, The. Robert Hillyer. GoYe; UnS
Relics. George Frederick Cameron. PeCV
Relics. Joachim du Bellay, *tr. fr. French by* Alan Conder. Antiquities of Rome, XXX. TrFP
Relics. Swinburne. POTT; VLEP
Relics of Saints. Cardinal Newman. JKCP
Relief of Lucknow, The. Robert Traill Spence Lowell. HBV; LPS-2; StPo
Relief on Easter Eve, The. Thomas Pestel. MeRV; OxBoCh; SeCL
Relief Worker Reflects on Suicide, A. Stewart Atkins. NoCaPo (rev. ed.)
(WPA Worker Reflects on Suicide, A.) NoCaPo (1941 ed.)
Relieving Guard. Bret Harte. BTP; LBAP
Religio Laici. Dryden. CEP; EiPP; LiA; SeCV-2; SeEP
Sels.
"Dim as the borrowed beam of moon and stars." MeRV; OxBoCh; ViBoPo, *br. sel.*
(Finite Reason.) LoBV
(Reason and Religion, *br. sel.*) FiP
(Reason and Revelation.) CoEV; OBS, *longer sel.*; PoLi, *longer sel.*
(Reason and the Soul.) BeR
Priestcraft and Private Judgement. OBS
Scriptures, The. OBS
"Thus man by his own strength." WGRP
Tradition. OBS; PoLi
Religio Medici, *sel.* Sir Thomas Browne.
Evening Hymn. EV-2; MaRV; OxBoCh
(Colloquy with God, A.) OBS; SeCL
Religio Novissima. Aubrey Thomas De Vere. IrPN
Religion. Ambrose Bierce. BAP
Religion. Robert Browning. *Fr.* Mr. Sludge, "The Medium." MaRV
Religion. Hildegarde Dolson. CAG
Religion. John Donne. *See* Satire III: "Kind pity chokes my spleen . . ."
Religion. Heine, *tr. fr. German by* Louis Untermeyer. LiTW
Religion. Hesiod, *tr. fr. Greek by* F. L. Lucas. *Fr.* Theogony. GrPE
Religion. Henry Vaughan. OBS; OxBoCh
Religion. Jean Vauquelin de la Fresnaye, *tr. fr. French.* CAW, *tr. by* Wilfrid Thorley; TrFP, *tr. by* Alan Conder
Religion and Doctrine. John Hay. MaRV; OBAV; StJW; WGRP
Religion Is a Fortune I Really Do Believe. *Unknown.* BoAN-2, *with music;* OlF
Religion is of faith indeed. Faith. Hugh O. Isbell. ChIP
Religion of Hudibras, The. Samuel Butler. *Fr.* Hudibras, I, 1. BOHV; InMe; LPS-2
(For All Fanatics.) PoFr
("For his religion it was fit.") LoBV; ViBoPo
("He was of that stubborn crew.") BPP
(Sir Hudibras's Religion.) FaBoEn
Religion's all or nothing; it's no mere smile. Religion. Robert Browning. *Fr.* Mr. Sludge, "The Medium." MaRV
Religious faith is a most filling vapor. Innate Helium. Robert Frost. ImOP
Religious Isolation. Matthew Arnold. EmBrPo; EPN
Religious Musings, *sels.* Samuel Taylor Coleridge.
"Believe, thou, O my soul." RO
Desultory Poem, A, Written on the Christmas Eve of 1794, *abr.* EmBrPo
("Lovely was the death.") EnRP; ERP
"There is one Mind, one omnipresent Mind." WGRP
"Toy-bewitched." WGRP
Religious Unity. Hartley Coleridge. MaRV
Religious Use of Taking Tobacco, A. *At. to* Robert Wisdome. CenL; ElL; HBV; OBS; SeEP
(Pipe and Can.) OBEV
Relinquishing. Theda Kenyon. AOAH
Relique, The. John Donne. AnFE; AtBAP; EPS; MeLP; MePo; OAEP; OBS; PoEL-2; ReIE; SeCV-1; SeEP; TyEnPo; ViBoPo
(Relic, The.) CaAE; ElL; ElSeCe; EtPaEn; LiTB; LiTG; LoBV; MaPo; MyFE; ReEn; SeCeV; TuPP; TwP; WHA
Reliques, *sel.* Edmund Blunden.
"And mathematics, fresh as May," 2 *ll.* ImOP
Reliquiae. Crates, *tr. fr. Greek by* J. M. Edmonds. GrR
Reluctance. Robert Frost. AmPP; ChMo; ExPo; GTBS-D; LoPo; LoPS; MAP; MoAB; MoAmPo; OxBA; Po; PoFS
Reluctantly I laid aside my smiles. The Journey. Mary Berri Hansbrough. AA
Relying on the disasters o' the war. March, 1941. Paul Goodman. LiTA
Remain, Ah Not in Youth Alone. Walter Savage Landor. *See* Appeal, The.
Remain, for me, chaste, unapproached, unstirred. To the Unimplored Beloved. Edward Shanks. TCPD
Remainder. Frederika Blankner. GoYe
Remarkable truly, is art! Limerick. Gelett Burgess. HBV
Remarks from the Pup. Burges Johnson. AlBD
Rembrandt alone could paint this mammoth shed. The Roundhouse. William Rose Benét. PoMa
Remedy, The. Harry Kemp. POT
Remedy Worse than the Disease, The. Matthew Prior. ALV; BOHV; EPP; HBV; TrGrPo
(I Sent for Ratcliffe.) TOP
Remember. William Johnson Cory. LEAP; OBVV; TOP
Remember. Georgia Douglas Johnson. PoNe
Remember [*parody on* Christina Rossetti]. "Judy." ALV; PA
Remember. Christina Rossetti. AnEnPo; AnFE; AWP; BLV; BMEP; BoFr; BoLiVe; BPN; CaAE; CH; DiM; EmBrPo; EnLi-2; EnLoPo; EPP; ES; EtPaEn; EV-5; FaBoEn; GTBS; GTBS-D; GTSL; HBV; JAWP; LEAP; LoPo; MaRV; MCCG; NeHB; OAEP; OBEV; OBVV; OQP; OuHeWo; PeBoSo; PIAE; PoRA; POTT; PoVP;

Remember (continued)
QP-2; ReaPo; TOP; TreFS; TrGrPo; VA; ViBoPo; ViPo; VLEP; WBP; WHA
(Remember Me When I Am Gone Away.) EG; MBP; PFE
(Sonnet: "Remember me when I am gone away.") LoBV
"But if the darkness and corruption leave," *sel.* LO
Remember Also Thy Creator. Ecclesiastes, Bible, *O.T. See* Remember Now Thy Creator.
Remember, Dellius, when times are bad. Horace. Odes, II, 3. LaP
Remember he was poor and country-bred. Abraham Lincoln. Mildred Plew Meigs. TiPo
Remember if this man is lost at sea. Sonnets from Camp, III. Jesse Stuart. MuM
Remember it, although you're far away. Remember. "Judy." ALV; PA
Remember man that passeth by. An Epitaph and a Reply. *Unknown.* TreFS
Remember March, the ides of March remember. Shakespeare. *Fr.* Julius Caesar, IV, iii. PIR
Remember May? Rhyme for Remembrance of May. Richard Burton. HBMV
Remember Me. Keith Douglas NeBP; OnHM
(Simplify Me When I'm Dead.) NePoEA
Remember Me! Thomas Haweis. BePJ
Remember Me. Winthrop Mackworth Praed. ERP
Remember Me, Gulls! Joseph Auslander. YT
Remember me when I am dead. Remember Me [*or* Simplify Me When I'm Dead]. Keith Douglas. NeBP; NePoEA; OnHM
Remember Me When I Am Gone Away. Christina Rossetti. *See* Remember.
Remember me you men in years to come. Vendémiaire. Guillaume Apollinaire. AnFP
Remember, Mother, when I said right here. Look, the Soldiers! Felix V. Ramos. PoFr
Remember Not. Helene Johnson. BANP; PoNe
Remember now, my Love, what piteous thing. A Carrion. Baudelaire. LiTW
Remember Now Thy Creator. Ecclesiastes, XII: 1–7, Bible, *O.T.* AWP; BLP; BrBE; CBOV; ChTr (1–8); EnLi-1 (1949 ed.) (1–8); HiLiEn; JAWP; LiTW; MaRV; NV; PoeMoYo; PYM; ShBV-1; TreF (1–14); WBP
(Remember Also Thy Creator.) ExPo
(Remember Then Thy Creator, 1–8.) TrJP
(Youth and Age.) OuHeWo (XI: 1–XII: 7); TrGrPo (XII: 1–8)
Remember, O man, how your father made you, his son! What Is Man? Palladas. OxBG
Remember, O Thou Man. *Unknown.* AnEC
Remember or Forget. Hamilton Aïdé. HBV; VA
"Remember Pearse," he said; "if we/ Lose Irish we lose Ireland." The Orator. Roy McFadden. OnYI
Remember, Phyllis. Honeymoon. Samuel L. Albert. GoYe
Remember Richard, lately king of price. The Tudor Rose. Sebastian Brant, *tr. by* Alexander Barclay. *Fr.* The Ship of Fools. ACP
Remember September. May Justus. SiSoSe; YeAr
Remember that Our Love Moves like the Snow. Elda Tanasso. MuM
Remember that we are dust. It is said. Camel. W. S. Merwin. NePA
Remember the blackness of that flesh. Memento. Stephen Spender. AtBAP
Remember the covenant of our youth. A Dying Wife to Her Husband. Moses ibn Ezra. TrJP
Remember the Promise, Dakotah. Robert V. Carr. PoOW
Remember the pure machine. Heart. MacKnight Black. AnAmPo; LA
Remember the spider/ Weaving a snare. Tanist. James Stephens. OnYI
Remember the sun in the autumn, its rays. Abraham Sutzkever. *Fr.* The Secret Town. TrJP
Remember Thee! Remember Thee! Byron. ViBoPo
Remember Then Thy Creator. Ecclesiastes, Bible, *O.T. See* Remember Now Thy Creator.
Remember three things come not back. Three Things Come Not Back. *Unknown.* MaRV; OQP; QP-2
Remember, though the Telescope Extend. George Dillon. ImOP
Remember, though we cannot write it, the delicate dream. Rainy Summer. Ruth Pitter. MoVE; UnPo (3d ed.)
Remember us poor Mayers all! The Song of the Mayers [*or* The Hitchen May-Day Song]. *Unknown.* CG; CH; PoD
Remember what I promised you. Way Out in Idyho. *Unknown.* CoSo
Remember when you hear them beginning to say Freedom. Notes for My Son. Alex Comfort. *Fr.* The Song of Lazarus. MoBrPo (1950 ed.); NeBP; SeCePo
Remember, Wormwood, what thou didst reveal. Nine Herbs Charm. *Tr. by* William O. Stevens. EPP
Remember Your Lovers. Sidney Keyes. WaP
Remember, youth will not last more. Advice to a Young Man (of Letters) Who Doesn't Know How to Take Care of Himself. Irwin Edman. InMe
Remember'd long, adown the far-stretch'd vale. William Holloway. *Fr.* Scenes of Youth. EnSW
Remembered Grace. Coventry Patmore. The Unknown Eros, I, xxiii. CoEV; OxBoCh
Remembered Music. Jalal ed-Din Rumi, *tr. fr. Persian by* R. A. Nicholson. PeP
Remembering. Alice Hartich. PoeMoYo
Remembering Calvary. Ethel Fanning Young. OQP; QP-2
Remembering Day. Mary Wright Saunders. DD; HH; MeMeAg; OTPC (1946 ed.); PEDC; YeAr
Remembering Golden Bells. Po Chü-i, *tr. fr. Chinese by* Arthur Waley. AtBAP; AWP; JAWP; TrCh; WBP
Remembering his taste for blood. Of Baiting the Lion. Sir Owen Seaman. BOHV; NA
Remembering Lincoln. Frank Mundorf. GoYe
Remembering Nat Turner. Sterling A. Brown. PoNe
Remembering now, my love, what piteous thing. A Carrion. Baudelaire. AWP
Remembering sunlight on the steepled square. Spring. David Morton. *Fr.* Sonnets from a Hospital. TBM
Remembering That Island. Thomas McGrath. NePoEA
Remembering the Ancient Farmstead. Tao Yuan-ming, *tr. fr. Chinese by* Yang Yeh-tzu. WhP
Remembering the past/ And gloating at it now. What the Bones Know. Carolyn Kizer. NePoAm-2
Remembering the Strait of Belle Isle or. Large Bad Picture. Elizabeth Bishop. MiAP
Remembering the 'Thirties. Donald Davie. NePoEA
Remembering the Winter. Rowena Bennett. SiSoSe
Remembering thy lip. Jalal ed-Din Rumi, *tr. fr. Persian by* A. J. Arberry. PeP
Remembering Thy sacrificial throne. The Litany of the Comfortable. Viola Chittenden White. QS
Remembering what passed. Old Scent of the Plum Tree. Fujiwara Ietaka. AWP
Remembrance. John Henry Boner. AA
Remembrance. Emily Brontë. AV; BMEP; CaAE; CH; CoEV; DiM; EmBrPo; EnLi-2; EnLit; EnLoPo; EtPaEn; EV-5; FaBoEn; FaFP; GTBS-D; GTBS-W; GTIV; GTML; GTSL; HBV; LiTB; LiTG; LiTL; LO; LoPo; LoPS; OAEP; OBEV (1st ed.); OxBI; PoD; PoEL-5; PoVP; RiBV; TrGrPo; ViP; VLEP
Remembrance. Margaret E. Bruner. PoToHe
Remembrance. John Bunker. JKCP (1955 ed.)
Remembrance. Francisco Castillo Nájera, *tr. fr. Spanish by* Margaret Allison. PoP
Remembrance. Leslie Savage Clark. ChIP
Remembrance, A. Willis Gaylord Clarke. AA
Remembrance. Walter de la Mare. ChMo; CMP
Remembrance. Hortense Flexner. VOD (1935 ed.)
Remembrance. Ibnu'l-Farid, *tr. fr. Arabic by* R. A. Nicholson. LiTW
Remembrance. Aline Kilmer. CAW
Remembrance. George Parsons Lathrop. AA; LEAP
Remembrance. John Richard Moreland. PR
Remembrance. Pushkin, *tr. fr. Russian by* Babette Deutsch. TrRV
(Remembrances, *tr. by* R. M. Hewitt.) BoR
Remembrance. Rainer Maria Rilke, *tr. fr. German by* Paul Engle. ReMP
Remembrance. Shakespeare. *See* Sonnets, XXX.
Remembrance. Shelley. EmBrPo; EV-4
Remembrance. Antoni Slonimski, *tr. fr. Polish by* Frances Notley. TrJP
Remembrance. Sir Thomas Wyatt. *See* Lover Showeth How He Is Forsaken of Such as He Sometime Enjoyed.
Remembrance. Vasily Zhukovsky, *tr. fr. Russian by* Babette Deutsch. TrRV
Remembrance; a Greek Folk-Song. Margaret Widdemer. LEAP; NV
(Not unto the Forest.) HBMV
Remembrance of Collins. Wordsworth. PtP
Remembrance of Some English Poets, A. Richard Barnfield. ReIE; SiCE; TuPP
Remembrance of Things Past. Shakespeare. *See* Sonnets, XXX.
Remembrance Sunday, Coombe Church, 1940. A. L. Rowse. NeTW
Remembrancer of joys long passed away. To a Golden Heart, Worn round His Neck. Goethe. AWP; JAWP; LiTW; WBP
Remembrances. Pushkin. *See* Remembrance.
Reminder, The. Léonie Adams. MoVE
Reminder. John Galsworthy. OQP; QP-1
Reminder, The. Thomas Hardy. ChMo; CMP
Reminder. Sherry Kane. BoHiPo
Reminder. *Unknown, tr. fr. German.* PIAE
Reminiscence. Thomas Bailey Aldrich. AA; AnAmPo; LA
Reminiscence. Jeanne Gidding. CAG
Reminiscence. Wallace Irwin. FiBHP
Reminiscence, A. Amy Levy. AV

Reminiscence of Early Love, A. Samuel Daniel. *Fr.* Hymen's Triumph. EV-1
Reminiscences of a Dancing Man. Thomas Hardy. MoVE
Reminiscences of a Day, *sel.* John Francis O'Donnell.
"O dim delicious heaven of dreams." IrPN
Reminiscences of a Landlord. Elizabeth J. Coatsworth. *See* After Christmas a Landlord Remembers.
Rémon, *with music. Unknown, tr. fr. French.* TrAS
Remonstrance. Philodemos the Epicurean, *tr. fr. Greek by* Dudley Fitts. LiTW
Remonstrance with the Snails. *Unknown.* BMEP; LPS-2
R-e-m-o-r-s-e. George Ade. ALV; FiBHP; LauV
Remorse. Apollonius Rhodius, *tr. fr. Greek by* George Allen. *Fr.* Argonautica, III. OxBG
(Vigil and Remorse, *tr. by* Arthur S. Way.) GrR
Remorse. Byron. *Fr.* On This Day I Complete My Thirty-sixth Year. MaRV
Remorse (Osorio), *sels.* Samuel Taylor Coleridge.
Alvar's Address to the Spirits of the Dead, *fr.* III, i. EmBrPo
Dungeon, The, *fr.* V, i. MCCG
Invocation, An: "Hear, sweet spirit," *fr.* III, i. EmBrPo; KN; OAEP
(Hear, Sweet Spirit.) ViBoPo
(Song: "Hear, sweet spirit.") MCCG; RO
(Song from "Osorio.") BPN; TOP
(Voice Sings, A.) CAW; CH
Lovely in Decay, *fr.* IV, iii. RO
Remorse. Sydney Dayre. DD
Remorse. Shakespeare. *See* Mind Diseased, A.
Remorse. Shelley. *See* Stanzas—April, 1814.
Remorse. Tennyson. *Fr.* Idylls of the King: Guinevere. MaRV
Remorse after Death. Baudelaire, *tr. fr. French by* Arthur Symons. OnPM
(Posthumous Remorse, *tr. by* Barbara Gibbs.) AnFP
(Remorse of the Dead, *tr. by* Alan Conder.) TrFP
Remorse for Intemperate Speech. W. B. Yeats. TwP
Remorse in Garb of Night. Luis Cernuda, *tr. fr. Spanish by* Eleanor L. Turnbull. CoSP
Remorse is memory awake. Emily Dickinson. TwP
Remorse of the Dead. Baudelaire. *See* Remorse after Death.
Remote and ineffectual Don. Lines to a Don. Hilaire Belloc. MBP; MoBrPo; OtMeF
Remote, beneath a sultry star. Stanzas to an Alien. Philip Freneau. CoV
Remote from cities liv'd a swain. The Shepherd and the Philosopher. John Gay. CEP
Remote from smoky cities, aged and grey. Sonnet. Thomas Caulfield Irwin. IrPN
Remote, in a Closed Space. Valery Bryusov, *tr. fr. Russian by* Jack Lindsay. RuPo
Remote, unfriended, melancholy, slow. The Traveller. Goldsmith. CEP; EiPP; EV-3; OAEP; ViBoPo
Remoteness. Germán Pardo García, *tr. fr. Spanish by* Rolfe Humphries. AnCL
Renaissance. Robert Avrett. GoYe
Renaissance. Idris Davies. MoWP
Renaissance. T. Sturge Moore. PoeT
Renascence. Muredach J. Dooher. OnYI
Renascence. Edna St. Vincent Millay. AmPP; BAV; ChMo; CMP; FaFP; HBV; LBMV; MAP; MoAB; MoAmPo; NeMA; NePA; NV; OHFP; PFY; TCPD; TwAmPo, *sl. abr.*
"World stands out on either side, The," *sel.* MaRV
Rencontre. Jessie Fauset. CDC
Rend America asunder. The Ship Canal From the Atlantic to the Pacific. Francis Lieber. PAH
Rend Your Heart and Not Your Garments. L. A. MacKay. TwCV
Render unto Caesar. Rolfe Humphries. CrMA
Rendezvous, The. Catullus, *tr. fr. Latin by* George Lamb. OnPM
Rendezvous. Mary Scott Fitzgerald. PoToHe (new ed.)
Rendezvous. Antonia Pozzi, *tr. fr. Italian by* Glauco Cambon. OnPM
Rendezvous, The. Alan Seeger. *See* I Have a Rendezvous with Death.
Rendition, The. Whittier. IAP
Renegado, The, *sel.* Philip Massinger.
"Yet there's one scruple with which I am much," *fr.* V, i. ACP (1952 ed.)
Renewal. Gladys Cromwell. AnAmPo; LA; NP
Renewal. "Michael Field." DiM; OBVV
Renewal. Charles Hanson Towne. CV; NLK
Renounce those threads of twisted gold that close. To a Beautiful but Heartless Coquette. Francisco de Terrazas. LiTW
Renouncement. Stéphane Mallarmé, *tr. fr. French by* Alan Conder. TrFP
Renouncement. Alice Meynell. AnFE; AV; BLV; BMEP; CAW; CBOV; EnLit; EPP; ES; EtPaEn; GTML; GTSL; HBV; LBBV; LEAP; LiTL; LO; LoPo; LoPS; MBP; MM; MoBrPo; OBEV; OBMV; OBVV; PIAE; POTT; PoVP; TCEP; TOP; VA; ViBoPo
Renouncing of Hardly Escaped Love, A. Sir Thomas Wyatt. ReIE
("Farewell the reign of cruelty.") SiPS
Renouncing of Love, A. Sir Thomas Wyatt. BEL; ElSeCe; EnLi-1 (1949 ed.); EnLit; FaBoEn; LiTL; OAEP; ReIE; TOP; TuPP
("Farewell, Love, and all thy laws for ever.") LiTB; ReEn; SiCE; SiPS
(Lover Renounceth Love, The.) TrGrPo
Renowned Generations, The. W. B. Yeats. OxBoLi
Renownèd Spencer lie [*or* lye] a thought more nigh. Elegy on Shakespeare [*or* Epitaph *or* On William Shakespeare]. William Basse. BCEP; BoFr; ElL; ElSeCe; LEAP; OBS; PtP; SeEP; ViBoPo
Rent Basket, The. *Unknown, tr. fr. Chinese.* WhP
Renunciants. Edward Dowden. GTIV; OBVV; VA
Renunciation. Wathen Mark Wilks Call. OBVV; WGRP
Renunciation, A. Thomas Campion. *See* Thou Art Not Fair.
Renunciation. Emily Dickinson. MoAmPo (1950 ed.); TCAP; TwP
Renunciation. Cathleen Keegan. *Fr.* Three Sonnets. MuM
Renunciation. Henry King. OBEV
Renunciation, A. Edward de Vere, Earl of Oxford. *See* If Women Could Be Fair.
Renunciation. Mary Brent Whiteside. LS
Reparation. Helen Hoyt. HBMV
Reparation or War. *Unknown.* PAH
Repast. Gertrude Tiemer-Wille. GoYe
Repeat that, repeat. The Cuckoo [*or* A Fragment]. Gerard Manley Hopkins. AlDL; MBP; MoAB; MoBrPo
Repeated Journey, The. Thomas McGrath. NePoEA
Repeated Pilgrimage. John Gilland Brunini. GoBC
Repent, O ye, predestinate to woe! The Conscience-Keeper. William Young. *Fr.* Wishmakers' Town. AA
Repentance. George Chapman. *Fr.* Hero and Leander, Third Sestiad. OBSC
Repentance. Thomas Curtis Clark. ChIP
Repentance. George Herbert. OAEP
Repetitions. Carl Sandburg. HBMV; NP
Repetitions of a Young Captain. Wallace Stevens. WaP
Repetitive Heart, The, *sels.* Delmore Schwartz.
All Clowns Are Masked, III. LiTA; OxBA; ViBoPo
All of Us Always Turning Away for Solace, I. OxBA
"Calmly we walk through this April's day," IV. MoVE
(For Rhoda.) MoAB; MoAmPo; OxBA
(Time Is the Fire.) LiTA; LiTM
Dog Named Ego [the Snowflakes as Kisses], A, X. AmP; LiTA; LiTM; MiAP
Heavy Bear Who Goes with Me, The, IX. MiAP; MoPo; MoVE; NePA; TrJP; UnPo (3d ed.)
(Heavy Bear, The.) AnAmPo; CrMA; FiMAP; LiTA; LiTG; LiTM; ReMP
Will You Perhaps, II. FiMAP
("Mentrechè il Vento, Come Fa, Si Tace.") AnFE; CoAnAm; LoPS; TwAmPo
Rephan. Robert Browning. VLEP
Repine not, Gray, that our weak dazzled eyes. To Mr. Gray. David Garrick. OBEC
Reply. Janet Norris Bangs. OQP; QP-1
Reply, A. Cecil Browne. SiTL
Reply. Hartley Coleridge. OBRV
Reply. Sidney Godolphin. OBS
Reply, The. Sister Monica. PraNu
Reply, A. Pope. *See* Epigram: "Sir, I admit your general rule."
Reply. Sir Walter Ralegh. *See* Nymph's Reply to the Shepherd, The.
Reply. Sir Ronald Ross. *See* Lines Written after the Discovery by the Author of the Germ of Yellow Fever.
Reply from the Akond of Swat, A. Ethel Talbot Scheffauer. FiBHP
Reply of Socrates, The. Edith M. Thomas. WGRP
Reply to "A Woman's Question." Nettie H. Pelham. PTA-2
Reply to an Imitation of the Second Ode in the Third Book of Horace, A. Richard Bentley. *See* Verses: "Who strives to mount Parnassus hill."
Reply to "In Flanders Fields." John Mitchell. BLPA
Reply to Lines by Thomas Moore, A, *sel.* Walter Savage Landor.
"Will you come to the bower I have shaded for you?" ChTr
Reply to Mr. Wordsworth, *sel.* Archibald MacLeish.
"Space-time, our scientists tell us, is impervious." ImOP
Reply to Nancy Hanks, A. Julius Silberger. TiPo
Reply to the Apparition. Max Jacob, *tr. fr. French by* Wallace Fowlie. MiCF
Replying to the Many Kind Friends Who Ask Me If I No Longer Write Poetry. Shaemas O'Sheel. TBM
Report. Robert Finch. TwCaPo
Report. Archibald Fleming MacLiesh. *Fr.* The Jungle. NAMP
Report of an Adjudged Case; Not to Be Found in Any of the Books. William Cowper. *See* Nose and the Eyes, The.
Report on Experience. Edmund Blunden. FaBoEn; FaBoTw; LO; MoPW; OBMV; POTE
Report on the Planet, Earth. James Oppenheim. PoMa

Report Song, A. Nicholas Breton. OBSC; SeCePo
(Country Song.) TrGrPo
"Reported Missing." Audrey Alexandra Brown. NeTW
Reporter. Ethel Louise Knox. DDA
Reporters, The. Newman Levy. InMe
Repose of Rivers. Hart Crane. AWP; CoBMV; ExPo; InPo; LiTM (rev. ed.); MM; MoAB; MoAmPo (1950 ed.); MOAP; NP; OxBA; SeCeV
Repository where the plane. On a Book by John Milton, Annotated. Donald F. Drummond. PtPa
Representing nothing on God's earth now. Lines on the Back of a Confederate Note [*or* The Confederate Note]. Samuel Alroy Jonas. BIG; BLPA; PaA
Repression. Timothy Corsellis. WaP
Reprieve. Barbara Villy Cormack. CaP
Reproach. Firdausi, *tr. fr. Persian by* E. G. Browne. LiTW
Reproach. Robert Graves. GTML; GTSL
Reproach No Man for Poverty. Theognis, *tr. fr. Greek by* T. F. Higham. GrL; OxBG
Reproach to Dead Poets. Archibald MacLeish. ChMo; CMP
Reproach to Morvyth, A. Dafydd ab Gwilym, *tr. fr. Welsh by* H. Idris Bell. LiTW
Reproaches. "Frik," *tr. fr. Armenian.* ArmLP
Reproaches, The. *Unknown.* WHL
Reproof, A. Proverbs, VI: 6-11, Bible, *O.T.* TrGrPo
(Go to the Ant [Thou Sluggard].) FaPON (6-8); TrJP
(Sluggard, The—a Sonnet, *Moulton, Modern Reader's Bible.*) MaRV
Reprove Gently. *Unknown.* FAOV
Reptilian green the wrinkled throat. Sir Gawaine and the Green Knight. Yvor Winters. AnFE; CoAnAm; MoVE; TwAmPo
Republic, The. Longfellow. *See* Ship of State, The.
Republic, forever, the land of the free. Hymn of the Soviet Union. Sergei Mikhalkov *and* El-Registan. PoFr
Republic of the West. England and America, I. James Kenneth Stephen. InMe
Republic of the World. Victor Hugo. *See* Universal Republic, The.
Republic to Republic. Witter Bynner. PAH
Republican Genius of Europe. The. Philip Freneau. AmPP (3d ed.)
Republics are ungrateful, but ours, its best-loved son. Washington's Name in the Hall of Fame. Margaret E. Sangster. WOAH
Repulse, The. Thomas Stanley. CaAE; LO; MeLP; MePo; OBS
Request. "Laurence Hope." BMEP
Request for a Song. Julian Tuwim, *tr. fr. Polish by* Jack Lindsay. LiTW
Request Number. G. N. Sprod. FiBHP
Requests. Digby Mackworth Dolben. *See* I Asked for Peace.
Requiem. Alice Hunt Bartlett. BAP
Requiem, *sel.* "Andrei Bely," *tr. fr. Russian by* Babette Deutsch.
"You sit on the bed there." TrRV
Requiem. Thomas Curtis Clark. PEDC
Requiem. Nathalia Crane. *Fr.* The Death of Poetry. MoAmPo (1942 ed.)
Requiem. Robert Davenport. *Fr.* King John and Matilda. SeCL
("Matilda, now go take thy bed.") TuPP
Requiem. Glenn Ward Dresbach. MuM
Requiem. Kenneth Fearing. ChMo; TriL
Requiem. Douglas V. Kane. UnW
Requiem. Joseph Lee. DD; OHIP
Requiem. George Lunt. AA; PaA
(Requiem for One Slain in Battle.) OBAV
Requiem. John Frederick Matheus. CDC
Requiem. Theodore Maynard. GoBC
Requiem, A. Herman Melville. *See* Requiem For Soldiers Lost in Ocean Transports, A.
Requiem. Ogden Nash. SiTL
Requiem. Conal O'Riordan. HBV
Requiem. Sir Joseph Noel Paton. VA
Requiem. Kathleen Raine. NeBP
Requiem. Robert Richardson, *ad. by* "Mark Twain." *See* Epitaph Placed on His Daughter's Tomb.
Requiem. Christina Rossetti. *See* Song: "When I am dead, my dearest."
Requiem. Archibald Rutledge. LS
Requiem. Robert Louis Stevenson. AnFE; ATP; BBV; BMEP; BTP; CaAE; CBE; CBOV; DD; EBSV; EPN; EPP; EV-5; GoTP; GoTS; GTML; GTSL; HBV; HBVY; HiLiEn; InP; LBBV; LEAP; LiTG; MaRV; MBP; MCCG; MoBrPo; MPB; NeHB; NeMA; OBEV; OBVV; OQP; OtMeF; OTPC; PCD; PFE; PIAE; PIR; PoeMoYo; PoeT; PoFS; PoRA; POTT; PoVP; PreP; PYM; QP-1; ReaPo; ShBV-2; TCEP; TOP; TreF; TrGrPo; TSW; TSWC; TVSH; VA; ViBoPo; VOD; WaKn; WGRP; WHA; WP; YT
Requiem, A. James Thomson. EnLit; HBV
Requiem. William Thomas Walsh. JKCP (1955 ed.)
Requiem. Hamilton Warren. GoYe
Requiem, *sels.* Humbert Wolfe.
"Feathers in a fan, The." POTE
High Song, The. MM; ReTS; TCPD
Man. MBP; MoBrPo
Saint, The ("Do you remember, Joan"). CAW; TwCV; VOD (1935 ed.)
Saint, The ("Saint Francis of Assisi, do you remember"). SaFP
Soldier, The ("Down some cold field"). TCPD
Soldier, The ("I do not ask God's purpose"). TCPD
Requiem for a Dead Warrior. Edgar McInnis. PEDC
Requiem for a Modern Croesus. Lew Sarett. MaRV
Requiem for a Young Soldier. Florence Earle Coates. OHIP
Requiem for One Slain in Battle. George Lunt. *See* Requiem.
Requiem for Soldiers Lost in Ocean Transports, A. Herman Melville. PoEL-5
(Requiem, A.) GTBS-D
Requiem—for the Death of a Boy. Rainer Maria Rilke, *tr. fr. German by* Randall Jarrell. AnGP
Requiem of Archangels for the World. Herbert Trench. MM
Requiem; to Paula Modersohn-Becker. Rainer Maria Rilke, *tr. fr. German by* "Hugh MacDiarmid." AnGP
Requies. Arthur Symons. POTT
Requiescat. Matthew Arnold. AWP; BEL; BLV; BMEP; BoLiVe; BPN; CaAE; CBOV; DD; EM-2; EmBrPo; EnLi-2; EnLit; EPN; EV-5; FiP; GEPC; GTBS; GTBS-D; GTBS-W; GTML; GTSL; HBV; InP; InPo; InvP; JAWP; LEAP; LiTB; LiTG; LiTL; OAEP; OBEV; OBVV; OHIP, OuHeWo; PG; PoFS; PoRA; PoVP; PYM; ReaPo; RiBV; TCEP; TOP; TreFS; TrGrPo; TyEnPo; ViBoPo; ViPo; ViPP; VLEP; WBP; WHA
Requiescat. Otto Freund. MuM
Requiescat. Katherine Anne Porter. HBMV
Requiescat. Frederick George Scott. DD; OHIP
Requiescat. Rosamund Marriott Watson. AV; BMEP; HBV; LBBV; LEAP
Requiescat. Oscar Wilde. BLV; BMEP; CaAE; EnLit; GTIV; GTSL; HBV; InvP; LEAP; MBP; MoBrPo; NeMA; OBVV; OnYI; OxBI; PIAE; PoVP; TreF; TrGrPo; ViPP; VLEP; WHA
Required Course. Frances Stoakley Lankford. GoYe
Requirement. Whittier. *See* We Live by Faith.
Requital. Adelaide Anne Procter. VA
Re-run. Winfield Townley Scott. FiMAP
Res Publica. J. A. R. McKellar. MoAuPo
Rescue. Olive Tilford Dargan. GoYe
Rescue the perishing, care for the dying. Fanny Crosby. OlF
Rescuing gate is wide, The. Like a Mourningless Child. Kenneth Patchen. MoAmPo
Resembles life what once was deem'd of light. What Is Life? Samuel Taylor Coleridge. FiP
Resentment. Li Po, *tr. fr. Chinese.* WhP
Reservation. David McCord. WhC
Reserve. Lizette Woodworth Reese. AA
Reserve. Mary Ashley Townsend. AA
Residence in France. Wordsworth. *See* Prelude, The.
Residence in France (Continued). Wordsworth. *Fr.* The Prelude. *See* French Revolution, The.
Residence in London. Wordsworth. *Fr.* The Prelude, VII. ERP; PoEL-4
("As the black storm upon the mountain-top.") NBE
Resident Worm, The. James Hayford. NePoAm-2
Resign the rhapsody, the dream. To the Muse. Robert Louis Stevenson. VLEP
Resignation. Matthew Arnold. EmBrPo; OAEP; PoVP; ViPP; VLEP
Resignation. Mother Francis d'Assisi. WHL
Resignation. Walter Savage Landor. *See* Why, Why Repine.
Resignation. Longfellow. CoBA; HBV; LPS-1; MaRV; TCAP
Resignation. Seumas MacManus. JKCP
Resignation. Julia Claire O'Connor. PraNu
Resignation. Po Chü-i, *tr. fr. Chinese by* Arthur Waley. TrCh
Resignation. Santob de Carrion, *tr. fr. Spanish by* George Ticknor. TrJP
Resignation. William L. Stidger. ChIP
Resignation. St. George Tucker. *See* Days of My Youth.
Resignation. *Unknown.* OBSC
Resignation. Sir Thomas Wyatt. OBSC
Resignation to God. John Donne. *See* Holy Sonnets: As due by many titles I resigne."
Resistance. Angelos Sikelianos, *tr. fr. Modern Greek by* Rae Dalven. MoGP
Resisted by the tangle. Walking in Bush. Basil Dowling. AnNZ
Resolute Cat, The. Nancy Byrd Turner. RIS
Resolute Courtier, The. Thomas Shipman. LO; SeCL
Resolution. Henry More. OxBoCh
Resolution. Charles L. O'Donnell. GoBC; TrPWD
Resolution. "Wiolar." InMe
Resolution, The. George Wither. *See* Shall I, Wasting in Despair.

Resolution and Independence. Wordsworth. AEV; BEL; BPN; ChER; EM-2; EmBrPo; EnL; EnLi-2; EnLit; EnLP; EnRP; EPN; ERP; EV-3; GEPC; LiTB; NBE; OAEP; OBRV; PoE; PoEL-4; ShBV-4; TriL; TwP
(Leech-Gatherer, The.) CBE
Progress of Poets, The, *sel.* RO
("I thought of Chatterton, the marvellous boy.") PtP
Resolution in Four Sonnets, of a Poetical Question Put to Me by a Friend, Concerning Four Rural Sisters. Charles Cotton. PoEL-3
(Concerning Four Rural Sisters.) PeBoSo
Sels.
Alice. TrGrPo
("Alice is tall and upright as a pine.") EG
(Two Rural Sisters.) EnLoPo
Margaret. TrGrPo
("Margaret of humbler stature by the head.") EG
(Two Rural Sisters.) EnLoPo
Resolution of Dependence. George Barker. FaBoTw; LiTB; LiTM (rev. ed.)
Resolution; the Song of Hylobaris Concerning Divine Providence. Henry More. OxBoCh
Resolutions for April. Anne Blackwell Payne. NoCaPo
Resolve, The. Alexander Brome. ElSeCe; LiTL; LO; OBEV; SeCL
("Tell me not of a face that's fair.") EG
Resolve, The. Mary, Lady Chudleigh. OBEC
Resolve. Charlotte Perkins Stetson Gilman. OQP; PoToHe; QP-2; WGRP
(I Resolve.) BLP
Resolve, The. George Herbert. *See* To His Mother.
Resolve me, Chloe, what is this. On Beauty; a Riddle. Matthew Prior. CEP
Resolve upon resolve to reach the height. Self-Guidance. Dante. *Fr.* Divina Commedia: Purgatorio. GrCo-2
Resolved in time, the sun's attractive force. Eadem Mutato Resurgo. Selden Rodman. OnHM
Resolved to Be Beloved. Abraham Cowley. *Fr.* The Mistress. CaAE
Resolved to dust, entombed here lieth Love. Love's Grave [*or* My Love Is Past *or* Here Lieth Love]. Thomas Watson. *Fr.* Hecatompathia. ElL; ElSeCe; OBSC; TuPP
Resolved to Love, *sel.* Abraham Cowley.
"If learned in other things you be." LO
Resound my voice, ye woods that hear me plain. Sir Thomas Wyatt. SiPS
Resounding booms. The surf. Sand. Jorge Guillén. CoSP
Respect for the Dead. Laura Riding. LiTA
Respect My Faith. Thomas Campion. TuPP
Respectability. Robert Browning. BPN; EmBrPo; EnLoPo; EPN; PoVP; VA; ViBoPo; ViPP; VLEP
Respectable Burgher, The. Thomas Hardy. ViP
Respectable Folks, The. Henry David Thoreau. DDA; MOAP
Respects. Alan Brownjohn. PoN
Respice Finem. Thomas Proctor. OBSC; ReIE; SiCE; TuPP
Respice Finem. Francis Quarles. *See* Epigram: Respice Finem.
Respite, The. Maria Gowen Brooks. *Fr.* Zophiel; or, The Bride of Seven. AA
Resplendent precinct of the skies. The Valley of the Heavens. Luis de León. CAW
Respondez! Walt Whitman. PoEL-5
Responding Voice. Francisco A. de Icaza, *tr. fr. Spanish by* Samuel Beckett. AnMP
Response. Struthers Burt. NoCaPo (1941 ed.)
Response to Rimbaud's Later Manner. T. Sturge Moore. OBMV
Responsibilities. J. C. Hall. HaMV
Responsibilities, *sels.* W. B. Yeats.
"Pardon, old fathers, if you still remain," Prologue. PoEL-5
(Pardon, Old Fathers.) OAEP (2d ed.)
Waters of the Boyne. LiA
Responsible William. Keith Preston. FAOV
Responsio Regis. William Dunbar. *Fr.* The Petition of the Grey Horse, Auld Dunbar. EBSV
Responsories. Carmen Alicia Cadilla, *tr. fr. Spanish by* Dudley Fitts. AnCL
Responsory for García Lorca. Oscar Castro Z., *tr. fr. Spanish by* Dudley Fitts. AnCL
Rest. "Æ." POTE
Rest. Mary Woolsey Howland. *See* In the Hospital.
Rest. George Macdonald. BSV
Rest. Irene Rutherford McLeod. AV
Rest. Cardinal Newman. OBRV; OBVV
Rest. Percy Somers Payne. TIP
Rest, The. Ezra Pound. AmP; MAP; MoAB; MoAmPo; OxBA
Rest. Christina Rossetti. BMEP; CoEV; EmBrPo; EnLi-2; EPN; EPP; ES; GTBS; HBV; LEAP; OBEV; OBVV; PeBoSo; PIAE; POTT; ReaPo; TOP; TrGrPo; ViP; VLEP
(O Earth, Lie Heavily upon Her Eyes.) MBP
Rest ("Are you very weary?"). *Unknown.* PoToHe
Rest. Margaret L. Woods. VA
Rest and Silence. Georg Trakl, *tr. fr. German by* Werner Heider. LiTW
(Peace and Silence, *tr. by* Glauco Cambon.) OnPM
Rest and Work. Anna Temple Whitney. *See* Kneeling Camel, The.
Rest asthoreen, down the boreen. Hush Song. Mary Anne O'Reilly. BOL
Rest friend, no tears for you. Life's Medley. Philetas. OxBG
Rest from Loving and Be Living. C. Day Lewis. CoBMV; MBP; MoBrPo; OBMV; POTE; ReaPo; ReMP
Rest here, at last. At Last. Philip Bourke Marston. VA
Rest here in peace the sacred dust. The Epitaph Acrostick on Robert Blake. George Harrison. SG
Rest Is Not Here. Lady Nairne. HBV
Rest is not quitting. Goethe. *Fr.* True Rest. MaRV; OQP; QP-2; WBLP
Rest Is Silence, The. Palladas, *tr. fr. Greek by* Walter Leaf. OxBG
"Rest Is Silence, The." Paulus Silentiarius. *See* No Matter.
Rest, little Guest. After Annunciation. Anna Wickham. MBP; MoBrPo
Rest, Master, for we be a-weary, weary. The Eyes. Ezra Pound. ChMo; CMP; PFE
Rest, my babe, rest! Lullaby. *Unknown.* BOL
Rest now took their seats and kept to their own several places, The. Homer. *Fr.* The Iliad, II. GrPo
Rest O Sun I Cannot. Joseph Tusiani. GoYe
Rest of the Weary. *Unknown.* BePJ
Rest on, O heroes! in your silent slumber! Our Dead Heroes. Rose Terry Cooke. HH
Rest on this shore, Aeneas, for a time. Dido, on the Departure of Aeneas. Helen Pinkerton. PtPa
Rest on your battle-fields, ye brave. A Dirge. Felicia Dorothea Hemans. BHV
Rest quietly—the world moves toward its end. Two Cats on the Hearth. Bernice Kenyon. CIV
Rest Remaineth. Robert Browning. *Fr.* Christmas-Eve and Easter-Day. OQP; PoRL; QP-1
Rest, rest; the troubled breast. The Dream. Christina Rossetti. EmBrPo
Rest Sad Eyes. *Unknown. See* Weep You No More, Sad Fountains.
Rest there awhile, my bearded lance. A Tale of Drury Lane. Horace Smith. LPS-3
Rest! This little fountain runs. For a Fountain [*or* Inscription for a Fountain]. "Barry Cornwall." OBEV (new ed.); OBRV; OBVV
Rest Where You Are. Charles Poole Cleaves. OQP; QP-2
Rest ye in peace, ye Flanders dead. America's Answer [*or* America's Reply]. R. W. Lillard. BLPA; HH; PEDC; POT
Restatement of Romance. Wallace Stevens. LiTL
Restful place, reviver [*or* renewer] of my smart, The. The Lover to His Bed, with Describing of His Unquiet State. Sir Thomas Wyatt. ReIE; SiPS; TuPP
Restles streame thy self persuinge. *Unknown.* SeCSL
Restless as a Wolf. Moishe-Leib Halpern, *tr. fr. Yiddish by* Jacob Sloan. TrJP
Restless clock is ticking out, The. The Christmas Lullaby. Arthur Weir. BOL
Restless Heart, The. Earl of Surrey. SiPS
Restless Heart, The. *Unknown, tr. fr. Marathi.* WGRP
Restless Night in Camp, A. Tu Fu, *tr. fr. Chinese by* Kenneth Rexroth. OnPC
Restless sea is calling, and I would be away, The. Voices. James S. Hearst. MoSiPe
Restless State of a Lover, The. Earl of Surrey. GoTL
("Sun hath twice brought forth the tender green, The.") SiPS
Restless, to-night, and ill at ease. In the Dark. Frances Louisa Bushnell. AA
Restoration. Woodridge Spears. GoYe
Restore thy tresses [*or* treasure] to the golden ore. To Delia, XVIII [XIX]. Samuel Daniel. ElSeCe; EPP
Restored to favour, he's allowed to look. The Book of Life. Maurice James Craig. *Fr.* Three Cat Poems. PoC
Restorer, The. Horace, *tr. fr. Latin by* J. O. Sargent. Odes, IV, 15. RoL
Restricted. Eve Merriam. TrJP
Restricted. Miriam Waddington. CaP
Rests Charidas beneath this tomb? Sinister Dialogue. Callimachus. GrPo; OnPM
Résumé. Dorothy Parker. ALV; PoeMoYo; TCPD; TrJP; WhC
(Some Beautiful Letters: Résumé.) InMe
Resurgam. W. Nelson Bitton. BLRP
Resurgam. Struthers Burt. HBMV
(May, *abr.*) BAP
Resurgam. Mary Bayard Clarke. NoCaPo
Resurgam. Emily Dickinson. WGRP
Resurgam. Theodosia Garrison. MaRV
Resurgam. John Richard Moreland. ChIP
Resurgam. Marjorie Pickthall. BoCaPo

Resurgam ("Alleluia! Alleluiah! finished is the battle now"). *Unknown, tr. fr. Latin by* John M. Neale. EOAH
Resurgam ("'I shall arise.' For centuries"). *Unknown.* WGRP
Resurgat. A. S. Cripps. BoSA
Resurge San Francisco. Joaquin Miller. PAH
Resurgence. John L. Bonn JKCP (1955 ed.)
Resurgence. Laura Bell Everett. PGD
Resurgence. Jalal ed-Din Rumi, *tr. fr. Persian by* E. G. Browne. LiTW
Resurgence. Margaret Tod Ritter. TBM
Resurgence. Robert Louis Stevenson. MaRV
(Though He That Ever Kind and True.) BBV
(Verses Written in 1872.) BLPA; NeHB
Resurgent. Richard Linn Edsall. JKCP (1955 ed.)
Resurrection. "Æ." ChMo; CMP
Resurrection. Sarah H. Bradford. EOAH
Resurrection, The. Jonathan Henderson Brooks. CDC; PoNe
Resurrection, The. John Gilland Brunini. MaRV
Resurrection. George Crabbe. OxBoCh
Resurrection. Blodwen Davies. PSO
Resurrection. John Donne. OBS; StJW
Resurrection. Kenneth Fearing. ChMo
Resurrection. Laurence Housman. *Fr.* Rue, III. MaRV
Resurrection. St. John of Damascus. *See* Day of Resurrection, The.
Resurrection. Harry Kemp. HBV
Resurrection, The. Friedrich Gottlieb Klopstock. EOAH
Resurrection. Sidney Lanier. PoEL-5
Resurrection. D. H. Lawrence. NP
Resurrection. Lloyd Frank Merrell. ChIP
Resurrection. Angela Morgan. OQP; QP-1
Resurrection. Ida Norton Munson. ChIP
Resurrection. Alfred Noyes. EOAH
Resurrection. Lady Margaret Sackville. HBMV
Resurrection. Clark Ashton Smith. DaM
Resurrection. Agnes W. Storer. ChIP; OQP; QP-1
Resurrection. *Unknown.* ChIP; MaRV
Resurrection, The. Nathaniel Wanley. LoBV
Resurrection, The, *sel.* W. B. Yeats.
Two Songs from a Play.
"I saw a staring virgin stand," I. CoBMV; EnLP; ExPo; FaBoTw; LiTB; MoPo; PoFS; RiBV; SeCeV; UnPo
(Song from a Play.) FaBoTw
"In pity for man's darkening thought," II. EnLP; ExPo; LiTB; MoPo; PoFS; RiBV; SeCeV; UnPo
Resurrection and Ascension. Earl D. Todd. ChIP
Resurrection and the Life, The. Robert Norwood. MaRV
Resurrection Hymn. Michael Weiss. BePJ
Resurrection, or Easter-Day, The. George Herbert. EOAH
Resurrection Song. Thomas Lovell Beddoes. PoE
Resurrexit. Henry Longan Stuart. CAW
Retaliation. Margaret E. Bruner. PoToHe
Retaliation. Goldsmith. CEP; EiPP; LaA; OAEP; OxBoLi; TCEP, *abr.;* TOP, *abr.*
Sels.
David Garrick ("Here lies David Garrick"). OBEC; SeCeV
Edmund Burke ("Here lies our good Edmund"). CoEV; InvP; OBEC; SeCeV
Sir Joshua Reynolds ("Here Reynolds is laid"). OBEC; SeCePo
Reticent Lover. Clinton Scollard. PR
Reticulations creep upon the slack stream's face. On Sturminster Foot-Bridge. Thomas Hardy. OAEP
Retired Business Man. Anderson M. Scruggs. DDA
Retired Cat, The. William Cowper. BOHV; CIV; EV-3; OTPC (1923 ed.), *sl. abr.;* PoC
Retired Pork-Butcher and the Spook, The. G. E. Farrow. BOHV
Retired thoughts enjoy their own delights. Look Home. Robert Southwell. TuPP
Retirement, *sel.* James Beattie.
Solitude, *abr.* OBEC
Retirement, The. Charles Cotton. CEP; HBV; LPS-3; NBE, *sts.* 1-5; OBS; SN
(To Mr. Izaak Walton, *abr.*) ViBoPo
Retirement, *sels.* William Cowper.
Absence of Occupation. OBEC
"I praise the Frenchman, his remark was shrewd," *br. sel.* BLPA; NeHB
Pledge of Cheerfulness, The. BPP
Statesman in Retirement. OBEC
Retirement. Philip Freneau. *See* On Retirement.
Retirement, The. John Norris. OBS
Retirement. Richard Chenevix Trench. EPN; OBVV
(Sonnet: "Wretched thing it were, to have our heart, A.") OQP; QP-2
Retirement ("In youth I served my time"). *Unknown, tr. fr. Irish by* Frank O'Connor. KiLC
Retirement, The ("'Tis weak and worldly to conclude"). *Unknown.* OBEC
Retirement. Henry Vaughan. EPS (1942 ed.)
Retirement. Thomas Warton, the Younger. LPS-2; SN
(Inscription in a Hermitage.) HBV
Retirement, an Ode, *sel.* Thomas Warton, the Elder.
"Joy, rose-lipped dryad, loves to dwell." ViBoPo
Retort. Paul Laurence Dunbar. AA
Retort, The. George Pope Morris. BOHV; HBV; LauV; LPS-3; PR
Retort Discourteous, The. Stephen Vincent Benét. HBMV
Retort on the Foregoing. John Scott of Amwell. *See* Drum, The.
Retractions, *sels.* James Branch Cabell. HBMV
"Although as yet my cure be incomplete," I.
"And therefore praise I even the most high," *closing st.*
"Cry Kismet! and take heart. Eros is gone," XII.
"I am contented by remembrances," II.
"It is in many ways made plain to us," V.
"Nightly I mark and praise, or great or small," XV.
"So, let us laugh—lest vain rememberings," XIV.
"With Love I garnered mirth and dreams, and shame," VI.
"You ask a sonnet? Well, it is your right," *introd. st.*
Retreat, The. Charles Cotton. SeCL
Retreat. Virginia Graham. NeTW
Retreat, The. Henry Vaughan. ATP; AWP; BCEP; BEL; BLV; BoLiVe; CaAE; CAW; CBOV; CenL; CoBE; CoEV; EM-1; EnL; EnL-1; EnLit; EPP; EPS; EV-2; ExPo; FaBoEn; GTBS; GTBS-D; GTBS-W; GTSE; GTSL; HBV; InPo; InvP JAWP; LEAP; LiTB; LiTG; LoBV; MaPo; MePo; OAEP; OBEV; PoFS; PoP; PoRA; PreP; ReEn; RiBV; SeCePo; SeCeV; SeCL; SeEP; TCEP; TOP; TrGrPo; TwCrTr; TwHP; TyEnPo; UnPo (1st ed.); UnW; ViBoPo; WBP; WHA
("Happy those early days when I.") EG; LO, 6 *ll.*
(Retreate, The.) AtBAP; EOAH; MeLP; OBS; PoEL-2; SeCV-1
Retreat from Heaven, The. J. A. R. McKellar. MoAuPo
Retreat from Paradise, The. Milton. *Fr.* Paradise Lost, XII. PoEL-3
("He ended; and thus Adam last replied.") CoBE; MyFE
Retreat in the Mountains, A. Chu Wan, *tr. fr. Chinese.* WhP
Retreate, The. Henry Vaughan. *See* Retreat, The.
Retribution. Friedrich von Logau, *tr. fr. German by* Longfellow. LPS-3; MaRV; PoToHe; TreF
Retrievers run through the meadow. Exercise in a Meadow. Jean Elliot. GoYe
"Retro Me, Sathana!" Dante Gabriel Rossetti. The House of Life, XC. BPN; EmBrPo; PoVP; ViPo
Retrospect. Rupert Brooke. NP
Retrospect. Roy Davis. WhC
Retrospect. "An Pilibin." OnYI
Retrospect. Agnes Mary Frances Robinson. OBVV
Retrospect. Tao Yuan-ming, *tr. fr. Chinese by* Yang Yeh-tzu. WhP
Retrospect. Chidiock Tichborne. *See* Elegy: "My prime of youth is but a frost of cares."
Retrospect—Love of Nature Leading to Love of Man. Wordsworth. *Fr.* The Prelude, VIII. ERP
Retrospection. Hubert Church. AnNZ
Retrospection. Sir Arthur Quiller-Couch. CenHV
Retrospection. Tennyson. *See* Tears, Idle Tears.
Return, The. Conrad Aiken. NePA
Return, The. John Peale Bishop. LiTA; LiTM; MoPo; MoVE; OxBA; TwAmPo; UnPo (3d ed.); WaP
Return, The. Arna Bontemps. CDC; PoNe
Return. Sterling A. Brown. CDC
Return, The. John Burroughs. MaRV
Return. H. D. Carberry. PoNe
Return. C. P. Cavafy, *tr. fr. Modern Greek by* Rae Dalven. MoGP
Return, The. Eleanor Rogers Cox. PAH
Return, The. Emily Dickinson. MoAmPo (1950 ed.); NeMA
Return! Sydney Dobell. LO; OBEV (1st ed.); OBVV
Return, The. Ethel Ashton Edwards. UnW
Return, The. Jessie Fauset. CDC
Return, The. Annie Fields. AA
Return, The. W. W. Gibson. BMEP; ChMo; CMP; TwCV
Return, The. George Arthur Greene. TIP
Return. Mary S. Hawling. PoMa
Return. Robinson Jeffers. GoYe
Return. Bernice Kenyon. NV
Return, The. Kipling. MBP; MoBrPo; NeMA
England, *br. sel.* OtMeF
Return, The. Pittendrigh Macgillivray. GoTS
Return. Sister Mary Madeleva. JKCP (1955 ed.)
Return, The. Edna St. Vincent Millay. GTBS-W; InP; LiTA; MAP; MoAB; MoAmPo; MoPo; OxBA
Return. Queena Davison Miller. DDA
Return, The. Edwin Muir MoPW
Return, The. Martha Ostenso. CaP; OCL
Return. Josephine Preston Peabody. CV
Return, The. Ezra Pound. AnEnPo; APA; CoAnAm; CoBMV; FaBoEn; MAP; MoAB; MoAmPo; MoP; MoPo; NAMP; NePA; NP; OxBA; TwAmPo; TwCV; ViBoPo

Return. Earl of Rochester. *See* Song, A: "Absent from thee, I languish still."
Return, The. Muriel Rukeyser. FiMAP
Return, The. L. A. G. Strong. HaMV
Return, The. Swinburne. *See* Sea, The.
Return, The. Arthur Symons. BMEP; HBMV; LoPS; VLEP
Return, The. Tao Yuan-ming, *tr. fr. Chinese.* WhP
Return, The. Tu Fu, *tr. fr. Chinese by* Robert Payne. LiTW; WhP
Return. *Unknown.* See Old Poem ("At fifteen I went with the army").
Return, The, *sels.* Margaret L. Woods.
Facing the Gulf. HBMV
"Father of Life, with songs of wonder." TrPWD
Return again, my forces late dismayed. Amoretti, XIV. Spenser. PeBoSo
Return and go again and yet return! Repeated Pilgrimage. John Gilland Brunini. GoBC
Return at Night. Sara Teasdale. PIAE
Return, Content! for fondly I pursued. The River Duddon, XXVI. Wordsworth. EnLi-2
Return from Egypt, The. Pope Leo XIII, *tr. fr. Latin by* H. T. Henry. CAW
Return from the Freudian Islands, The. A. D. Hope. MoAuPo
Return from Troy, The. Quintus Smyrnaeus, *tr. fr. Greek. Fr.* Posthomerica, XIV. OxBG
Return of a Reaper. Alan Creighton. CaP
Return of Autumn. "Pablo Neruda," *tr. fr. Spanish by* Lloyd Mallan. LiTW
Return of Belisarius, The; Mud Flat, 1860. Bret Harte. IHA
Return of Eve, The. G. K. Chesterton. ISi; PoLi
Return of Morgan and Fingal, The. E. A. Robinson. TOP
Return of Napoleon from St. Helena, The. Lydia Huntley Sigourney. AA
Return of Proserpine, *sel.* Florence Wilson Roper.
Sonnet: "I heard beneath the quiet stars last night." UnW
Return of Spring. Charles d'Orléans. *See* Spring.
Return of Spring. Pierre de Ronsard, *tr. fr. French.* LPS-2
Return of Spring, The. Sui Fu Jen, *tr. fr. Chinese by* Henry H. Hart. PoHN
Return of Spring, The. Bayard Taylor. ADAH
Return of the Fairy, The. Humbert Wolfe. PoMS
Return of the Golden Age, with the Birth of Pollio, The. Virgil, *tr. fr. Latin by* Dryden. *Fr.* Eclogues, IV. BeR
Return of the Heroes, The, *sel.* Walt Whitman.
Annual Drama, The. GrCo-1
Return of the Men, The. Luc Durtain, *tr. fr. French by* Elizabeth Selden. BoFr
Return of the Prodigal. A. E. Johnson. JKCP (1955 ed.)
Return of Ulysses, The. Homer, *tr. fr. Greek by* Bryant. *Fr.* The Odyssey, XXI. BBV (1923 ed.)
Return, return! all night my lamp is burning. Return! Sydney Dobell. LO; OBEV (1st ed.); OBVV
Return, Return, O Shulammite. The Song of Solomon, VII: 1-10, Bible, *O.T.* TrJP
Return, sad sister, Faith. Amen. A. C. Benson. OBVV
Return Thee, Heart. Alexander Scott. BSV
Return to Birds. Louis Untermeyer. BLA
Return to Life. Abbie Huston Evans. NePoAm
Return to me often and possess me. Return. C. P. Cavafy. MoGP
Return to Nature, The. William T. Allison. CPG
Return to Ritual. Mark Van Doren. MoVE
Return to Sirmio. Catullus. *See* Home to Sermio.
Return to Spring. Florence Ripley Mastin. GoYe
Return to the Country. Tao Yuan-ming, *tr. fr. Chinese.* WhP
(Once More Fields and Gardens, *tr. by* Florence Ayscough *and* Amy Lowell.) AWP
(Returning to the Fields, *tr. by* Arthur Waley.) LiTW; PoFr; TrCh
Return to the deep sources, nothing less. Santos; New Mexico. May Sarton. NeTW; QS
"Return," we dare not as we fain. In Time of Mourning. Swinburne. BPN; VLEP
Returned, a wraith from her defrauded tomb. Transformation Scene. Constance Carrier. GoYe
Returned from Mehiko he'll grab. A Hex on the Mexican X. David McCord. FiBHP
Returned Soldier, The. John Clare. SoV
Returned Soldier. E. G. Moll. MoAuPo
Returned Volunteer to His Rifle, The. Herman Melville. TriL
Returned Warrior ("O saepe mecum"). Horace, *tr. fr. Latin by* John Wight. Odes, II, 7. LiTW
("Pompeius, best of all my comrades, you and I.") LaP; WaaP
Returning. Ch'en Fu, *tr. fr. Chinese by* Henry H. Hart. PoHN
Returning. Olive Tilford Dargan. NoCaPo
Returning. Ruth Guthrie Harding. HBV
Returning at Night. Lu Yu, *tr. fr. Chinese by* Pai Chwen-yu. WhP
Returning each morning from a timeless world. Autumn 1940. W. H. Auden. LiTA
Returning from its daily quest, my Spirit. To Dante. Guido Cavalcanti. AWP; JAWP; LyMA; WBP
Returning Home. Joachim du Bellay. *See* Heureux qui, comme Ulysse, a fait un beau voyage.
Returning Home. Joseph von Eichendorff, *tr. fr. German by* Mabel Cotterell. AnGP
Returning Spring. Joseph von Eichendorff, *tr. fr. German by* George N. Shuster. CAW
Returning to Goleufryn ("Returning to my grandfather's house"). Vernon Watkins. MoWP
Returning to the Fields. Tao Yuan-ming. *See* Return to the Country.
Returning, We Hear the Larks. Isaac Rosenberg. FaBoMo; WaaP
Retyred thoughts enjoy their owne delights. Look Home. Robert Southwell. EV-1
Reuben. Phoebe Cary. BOHV
Reuben Bright. E. A. Robinson. AmP; AnNE; CoV; MAP; MaPo; MoAB; MoAmPo; NePA; TCAP; TrGrPo; TwP
Reuben James. James Jeffrey Roche. GA; PAH
Reuben Pantier. Edgar Lee Masters. *Fr.* Spoon River Anthology. BoFr
Reuben Ranzo. *Unknown.* AmSS, *with music;* SG, *abr.;* ShS, *2 vers., with music;* SoAmSa, *with music*
(Poor Reuben Ranzo, *diff. vers.*) IHA
Reunion of Odysseus and Penelope, The. Homer, *tr. fr. Greek by* F. L. Lucas. *Fr.* The Odyssey, XXIII. GrPE
Reunion of Ulysses and Telemachus. Homer, *tr. fr. Greek by* William Cowper. *Fr.* The Odyssey, XVI. GrR
(Odysseus and His Son, *tr. by* F. L. Lucas.) GrPE
(Telemachus Finds His Father, *tr. by* William Cowper.) OxBG
("Zeus-born son of Laertes, thou wise and wileful Odysseus," *tr. by* H. B. Cotterill.) GrPo
Reunited. Sir Gilbert Parker. *Fr.* A Lover's Diary. OBVV; OQP; QP-2
(Envoy: "When you and I have played the little hour.") VA
Reunited. Frank L. Stanton. MDAH
Rev Owl. A. M. Klein. TrJP
Rêve du Midi. Rose Terry Cooke. LPS-2
Reveal Thy Presence now, O Lord. A Prayer for the Presence of Christ [*or* A Grace]. Thomas Tiplady. ChIP; MaRV; TrPWD
Revealed. Harry Lyman Koopman. AA
Revealer, The. E. A. Robinson. DD
Revealment. John Richard Moreland. ChIP
Reveillé. Audrey Alexandra Brown. CaP
Reveille. W. W. Gibson. ChMo; CMP
Reveille, The. Bret Harte. BlG; EV-5; GN; HBV; LH; MC; OHIP; OtMeF; OTPC (1946 ed.); PaA; PAH; PoRL; TVSH
Reveille. A. E. Housman. A Shropshire Lad, IV. AlDL; BEL; BMEP; BPN; ChMo; CMP; CoBE; CP; EmBrPo; EnLi-2; EnLit; EPN; FaFP; GTBS-W; LiTB; LiTM (rev. ed.); MBP; MoAB; MoBrPo; NeMA; OAEP; OuHeWo; PG; PoeMoYo; PoLFOT; PoMa; PoTo; POTT; PoVP; PYM; TCEP; TreF; TwCV; TyEnPo; ViP; ViPo
Reveille. Hughes Mearns. *Fr.* Later Antigonishes. InMe; SiTL
Reveille. Ada Foster Murray. VOD
Reveille. Michael O'Connor. AA; HBV; MDAH
Reveillé. Eden Phillpotts. POT
Reveille. Lola Ridge. AnAmPo; HBMV; LA; PoFr; TCPD
Reveille. Louis Untermeyer. HBV; NLK (1947 ed.); OBAV; PaA; SBMV
Reveille at Daybreak. Nicolás Guillén, *tr. fr. Spanish by* H. R. Hays. TwSpPo
Reveille for the Dead. Yiannis Griparis, *tr. fr. Modern Greek by* Rae Dalven. MoGP
Reveille rang out in the barracks-courts. Morning Twilight. Baudelaire. AnFP
Revel. Abul Hasan of Santa Maria, *tr. fr. Arabic by* A. J. Arberry. MooP
Revel, The. Bartholomew Dowling. BLPA; HBV; OnYI; VA
(Our Last Toast.) YaD
(Revelry for the Dying.) AnIV
(Revelry of the Dying.) LPS-3; PIR
(Stand to Your Glasses.) TreF
Revel, The. Euripides, *tr. fr. Greek by* Gilbert Murray. *Fr.* Bacchae. GrR
Revel, A. Donagh MacDonagh. NeIP
Revel pauses and the room is still, The. Pannyra of the Golden Heel. Albert Samain. AWP
Revelation. William Baylebridge. *Fr.* Life's Testament. MM
("I worshipped, when my veins were fresh.") BoAV

Revelation, *sels.* Bible, *N.T.*
"And there appeared a great wonder in heaven," XII: 1–17. CAW
(Woman Clothed with the Sun, A. Apocalypse, XII: 1, 2, 5, 10, *Douay vers.*) ISi
Last Judgment, The, XX: 11–XXI: 7. TreF
New Jerusalem, The, XXI. EM-1 (1–14, 22–27); TrGrPo (1–6, 10–12, 21, 23–25)
There Shall Be No Night, XXII: 1–5. TrGrPo
Revelation. Verne Bright. BLRP; OQP; QP-1; WBLP
Revelation. Alice Brown. *Fr.* The Road to Castaly. WGRP
Revelation. Warren F. Cook. BLRP
Revelation. Blanche Taylor Dickinson. CDC
Revelation, The. Havelock Ellis. PoP
Revelation. Robert Frost. InPo; MOAP; TwP
Revelation. Sir Edmund Gosse. BMEP; OBEV; OBVV; TCPD
Revelation. Hafiz, *tr. fr. Persian by* R. A. Nicholson. PeP
Revelation, The. Max Jacob, *tr. fr. French by* Wallace Fowlie. MiCF
Revelation, The. Leslie Clare Manchester. OQP; QP-2
Revelation. Edwin Markham. MaRV; OQP; QP-1; WGRP
Revelation. John Masefield. *See* If I Could Come Again to That Dear Place.
Revelation. David Meltzer. NeAP
Revelation. Whitney Montgomery. PraP
Revelation. David Morton. PoTo
Revelation, The. Coventry Patmore. The Angel in the House, I, viii, 20. EnLoPo; EPP; POTT
("Idle poet, here and there, An.") EG; ViBoPo
"Love wakes men, once a life-time each," *sel.* LO
Revelation. John Jerome Rooney. JKCP
Revelation. William Soutar. HaMV
Revelation. *Unknown.* LauV
Revelation. Robert Penn Warren. AnFE; CoAnAm; FiMAP; LiTA; MoPo; NePA; TwAmPo
Revelry for [*or* of] the Dying. Bartholomew Dowling. *See* Revel, The.
Revenant. Ernest Rhys. UnW
Revenants. Joseph Auslander. NP
Revenants des Enfants. Frederic Manning. UnW
Revenge. Avenzoar, *tr. fr. Arabic by* A. J. Arberry. MooP
Revenge. Hamda, *tr. fr. Arabic by* A. J. Arberry. MooP
Revenge ("Audivere, Lyce"). Horace, *tr. fr. Latin by* Louis Untermeyer. Odes, IV, 13. AWP; WoL
Revenge, The. Pierre de Ronsard, *tr. fr. French by* Thomas Stanley. AWP
Revenge, The [a Ballad of the Fleet]. Tennyson. BBV; BEL; BeLS; BPN; EM-2; EmBrPo; EnLi-2; EnLit; EPN; FaBoCh; GDAH; GEPC; GTML; HBV; HiLiEn; HoPM; MaC; MCCG; OAEP; OnHT; OTPC; PCD; PCN; PECK; PoRA; PoVP; ShBV-1; TCEP; TOP; UnPo (1st. ed.); ViPo; VLEP
(Ballad of the Fleet, A.) LH
Revenge of Bussy d'Ambois, The, *sels.* George Chapman.
"Danger (the spurre of all great mindes) is ever," *fr.* V, i. NBE
"Good sir, beleeve that no perticular torture," *fr.* IV, i. NBE
(High and General Cause, The, *abr.*) EV-1
"I am engag'd both in my word, and hand," *fr.* III, iv. NBE
Revenge of Hamish, The. Sidney Lanier. AnEnPo; CoBA; HoPM; OnAP; PFE; PoEL-5; SPP; TCAP; TOP
Revenge of Injuries. Lady Elizabeth Carew. *Fr.* Mariam. LPS-3
Revenge of Rain-in-the-Face, The. Longfellow. BBV; GA; PaA; PAH
Revenge to Come. Propertius, *tr. fr. Latin by* Kirby Flower Smith. Elegies, III, 25. AWP; JAWP; LiTW; WBP
Revenger's Tragedy, The, *sels.* Cyril Tourneur.
"And now methinks I could e'en chide myself," *fr.* III, iv. PoD; ViBoPo
(To His Mistress' Skull.) CoEV
"Does every proud and selfe-affecting Dame," *fr.* III, iv. PoD
I Was the Man, *fr.* IV, iv. LiA
"Madame, his grace will not be absent long," III, iv. AtBAP; NBE; PoEL-2
"My study's ornament, thou shell of death," *fr.* I, i. ViBoPo
"O hour of incest!" *fr.* I, iii. AtBAP
"Ravish me in thine answere; art thou rare," *fr.* II, ii. AtBAP
Revered, beloved—O you that hold. To the Queen. Tennyson. BPN
Reverence to Prana. *Unknown, tr. fr. Vedic by* Maurice Blomfield. *Fr.* Vedic Hymns. GrCo-1
Reverend Dr. Harcourt, folk agree, The. This Side of Calvin. Phyllis McGinley. QS
Rev. Gabe Tucker's Remarks. *Unknown.* BOHV
Reverend Henry Ward Beecher, The. Limerick [*or* An Eggstravagance]. *At. to* Oliver Wendell Holmes. CenHV; ChTr; HBVY; PCD; TSWC
Reverend Sire, A. Pope. *Fr.* Moral Essays, Epistle I. BeR
Reverie. Fan Ch'eng Ta, *tr. fr. Chinese by* Henry H. Hart. PoHN
Reverie. "Laurence Hope." LoPo
Reverie, The. Egan O'Rahilly, *tr. fr. Modern Irish by* Frank O'Connor. AnIL
(Reverie at Dawn.) KiLC
Reverie. Edward Rowland Sill. UnW
Reverie at Dawn. Egan O'Rahilly. *See* Reverie, The.
Reverie of Poor Susan, The. Wordsworth. BPN; CBE; CH; EM-2; EmBrPo; EnRP; EV-3; GEPC; GTBS; GTBS-D; GTBS-W; GTSE; GTSL; HBV; MCCG; MW; OTPC (1923 ed.); OxBoLi; ShBV-1
(Poor Susan's Dream.) CBPC
Reverse English ("If I ever attain"). *Unknown.* CAG
Reverse English ("You may read in the papers"). *Unknown.* CAG
Reverse the flight of Lucifer. The Task. Ruth Pitter. MoBrPo; TrGrPo (1942 ed.)
Reverses. Cardinal Newman. VA
Reversible Metaphor, The. "Troubadour." InMe
Revery. Emily Dickinson. *See* To make a prairie it takes a clover.
Revery of a Business Man. Horace. *See* Country Life.
Review of a Cook Book. Louise Dyer Harris. WhC
Revisitants. Margaret Widdemer. TBM
Revisitation. Siegfried Sassoon. BoFr
Revival. Arthur Hugh Clough. VLEP
Revival, The. Tennyson. *Fr.* The Day-Dream. LPS-1
(Sleeping Beauty, The, II. The Fairy Prince's Arrival.) CG
Revival, The. Henry Vaughan. BLV; BoLiVe; MaPo; OBS; OxBoCh; PoEL-2; PrWP; SeCL; SeEP; TrGrPo; TriL
Revival Hymn. Joel Chandler Harris. *Fr.* Uncle Remus, His Songs and His Sayings. HBV; MCCG
Revocation, A. Sir Thomas Wyatt. *See* Farewell: "What should I say."
Revolt. Joachim du Bellay, *tr. fr. French by* Alan Conder. Antiquities of Rome, XII. TrFP
Revolt of Islam, The, *sels.* Shelley.
"And they, and all, in one loud symphony," *fr.* V. PoFr
"Can man be free if woman be a slave?" *fr.* II. PoFr
Child of Twelve, A, *fr.* II. GN
Ever as We Sailed, *fr.* XII. SeCePo
"I could not choose but gaze; a fascination," *fr.* I. ChER
"Islands and the mountains in the day, The," *fr.* III. ChER
Laon and Cythna, *sels. fr.* I, III, VIII, *and* XII. MyFE
"Lifting the thunder of their acclamation." *fr.* V. ChER
Spring, *fr.* IX. EV-4
To Mary; Dedication. BPN; EmBrPo; EnRP; EPN
(Dedication.) ERP
"Tyrants of the Golden City tremble, The," *fr.* IV. PoFr
Revolution. "Basil Dahl," *tr. fr. Yiddish by* Joseph Leftwich. PoFr
Revolution. Emily Dickinson. CoBA
Revolution. A. E. Housman. Last Poems, XXXVI. ImOP
("West and away the wheels of darkness roll.") CaAE
Revolution, The. Filip Stepanovich Shkulev, *tr. fr. Russian by* George Z. Patrick. PoFr
Revolution is the pod. Revolution. Emily Dickinson. CoBA
Revolutions. Matthew Arnold. EmBrPo; EPN; PoVP; VLEP
Revolutions. Shakespeare. *See* Sonnets, LX.
Revolutions. Sir Henry Taylor. *Fr.* Philip Van Artevelde. PoFr; VA
Revolving doors have trapped our nervous feet. Five o'Clock. Richard K. Arnold. PtPa
Revulsion. Thomas Hardy. EmBrPo
Reward, The. Grace G. Bostwick. MaRV
Reward. Bert Leston Taylor. RIS
Reward Doth Not Always Answer Desert. Thomas Howell. SiCE
Reward of Innocent Love, The. William Habington. *See* To Castara: Reward of Innocent Love, The.
Reward of Service. *St.* 1, *Unknown, at. to* Elizabeth Barrett Browning; *st.* 2, Elizabeth Barrett Browning, *fr.* A Drama of Exile. BLPA; FaBoBe; NeHB
(Duty.) PTA-2
(Sweetest Lives, The.) MaRV
Reward of Service. *Unknown, tr. fr. German by* F. C. Nicholson. LyMA
Reward of Virtue. Arthur Guiterman. InMe
Rex Mundi. David Gascoyne. ChMP
Reynard the Fox, *sels.* John Masefield.
"Cobbler bent at his wooden foot, The," *fr.* II. ViBoPo
Countrymen, The ("Ock Gurney and old Pete were there"), *fr.* I. ChMo; CMP
Fox Awakes, The, *fr.* II. MoVE
"Fox knew well that, before they tore him, The," *fr.* II. OtMeF
"From the Gallows Hill to the Tineton Copse," *fr.* II. NAMP
(Fox Hunt, The.) CoEV
"Past the gibbet-stock all stuck with nails," *fr.* II. ViBoPo

"They were a lovely pack for looks," *fr.* I. OtMeF
"Tom Dansey was a famous whip," *fr.* I. OtMeF
Reynard the Fox. *Unknown.* OnYI
Rhaiadr. Constance Davies. MoWP
Rhaicos was born amid the hills wherefrom. The Hamadryad. Walter Savage Landor. *Fr.* The Hellenics. BPN; CBOV; EmBrPo; EnRP; EPN; ERP; TOP; VA
Rhapsody. William Stanley Braithwaite. *See* I Am Glad Daylong.
Rhapsody. Florence Earle Coates. AV
Rhapsody, A. T. H. Gould. CAG
Rhapsody, A ("Now, I confess, I am in love"). *Unknown.* SeCL
Rhapsody, A. Henry Vaughan. ReEn
Rhapsody for the Mule. José Lezama Lima, *tr. fr. Spanish by* Donald Devenish Walsh, José Rodríguez Feo, *and* Dudley Fitts. AnCL
Rhapsody of the Deaf Man. Tristan Corbière, *tr. fr. French by* Walter McElroy. LiTW; OnHM; AnFP, *tr. by* Kate Flores
Rhapsody on a Windy Night. T. S. Eliot. AmP; ExPo; InPo; MAP; MoAmPo (1942 ed.); MOAP; TwP
Rhapsody on Poetry, A. Swift. *See* Critics.
Rheims Cathedral. Grace Hazard Conkling. AOAH
Rhenish Autumn. Guillaume Apollinaire, *tr. fr. French by* Daisy Aldan. AnFP
Rhesus, *sels.* Euripides, *tr. fr. Greek by* Gilbert Murray.
Death of Rhesus, The. OxBG
Night Watch. OxBG
(Watch before Dawn, The.) GrR
Rebuke. GrR
Solitary Mourner, The. GrR
Rheumatic old man in White Plains, A. Limerick. *Unknown.* LiBL
Rhine, The. Byron. *Fr.* Childe Harold's Pilgrimage, III. LPS-2
("Castled crag of Drachenfels, The.") ViBoPo
Rhine was red with human blood, The. Blake. *Fr.* Jerusalem. ViBoPo
Rhinoceros, The ("Rhinoceros, your hide looks all undone"). Hilaire Belloc. ChTr; FaPON; RIS
Rhinoceros, The ("The rhino is a homely beast"). Ogden Nash. CenHV; FiBHP; GoTP; MoAmPo; NeMA
Rhinocerostrich, The. Kenyon Cox. *Fr.* Mixed Beasts. RIS
Rhodanthe. Agathias Scholasticus, *tr. fr. Greek by* Andrew Lang. AWP
("Weeping and wakeful all the night I lie.") GrPo
Rhode Island. T. Clarke Brown. PoRL
Rhodian Swallow Song. *Unknown, tr. fr. Greek by* J. M. Edmonds. GrR
Rhodocleia, flowers of spring. The Rosy Wreath. Rufinus. OxBG
Rhododaphne, *sels.* Thomas Love Peacock.
Bacchus. OBRV
Larissa. OBRV
Rhodon and Iris, *br. sel.* Ralph Knevet.
"Now of all fashions, she thinks change the best." BoHiPo
Rhodora, The [on Being Asked, Whence Is the Flower]. Emerson. AA; ADAH; AmPo; AmPP; AnAmPo; AnEnPo; AnFE; AnNE; APA; APW; AWP; BAP; BAV; BLV; BoLiVe; BTP; CoAnAm; CoBA; DD; FaFP; GA; GN; GoTP; GTSE; HBV; HBVY; HiLiAm; IAP; InPo; JAWP; LA; LEAP; LiTA; LiTG; LPS-2; MCCG; MOAP; MPB; NeHB; NLK; OBAV; OHFP; OTPC; OxBA; PEOR; PFE; PIAE; PIR; PoLFOT; PTA-2; PYM; REAL; SeCeV; TCAP; TOP; TreFS; TrGrPo; TVSH; WBP; WHA; YT
Rhoecus. James Russell Lowell. IAP; MCCG; TCAP
"Hear now this fairy legend," *sel.* AA
Rhondda. Meurig Walters. MoWP
Rhotus on Arcadia. John Chalkhill. *Fr.* Thealma and Clearchus. OBS
Rhyme about an Electrical Advertising Sign, A. Vachel Lindsay. InP
Rhyme-beginning Fragment, A. *Unknown.* AnIL
Rhyme for a Phonetician. Frances Cornford. YT
Rhyme for All Zionists, A. Vachel Lindsay. MeRV
Rhyme for Francis, A; October 4th. Eleanor Farjeon. SaFP
Rhyme for Musicians, A. E. Lemke. BOHV
Rhyme for Remembrance of May. Richard Burton. HBMV
Rhyme for Thanksgiving Day, A. Edwin Markham. *See* Thanksgiving Rosary, A.
Rhyme for Washing Hands, A. *Unknown.* BoTP
Rhyme from Grandma Goose Annemarie Ewing. NePoAm
Rhyme o' The Raggedy Man's 'at's best, The. The Lugubrious Whing-Whang. James Whitcomb Riley. BOHV; NA
Rhyme of Death's Inn, A. Lizette Woodworth Reese. LBMV
Rhyme of Life, A. Charles Warren Stoddard. HBV; LBAP; MaRV
Rhyme of One, A. Frederick Locker-Lampson. HBV
Rhyme of Rain. John Holmes. WaKn
Rhyme of the Ancient Mariner, The. Samuel Taylor Coleridge. *See* Rime of the Ancient Mariner, The.
Rhyme of the Duchess May, The, *sel.* Elizabeth Barrett Browning.
Round Our Restlessness, *last st.* MaRV
Rhyme of the Kipperling, The. Sir Owen Seaman. CenHV
Rhyme of the poet, The. Merlin, II. Emerson. AmPo; AnNE; IAP; PoEL-4
Rhyme of the Rail. John Godfrey Saxe. APW; BOHV; InMe; MoShBr
(Railroad Rhyme.) LPS-3
(Riding on the Rail.) PTA-1
Rhyme of the Three Captains, The. Kipling. BeLS
Rhyme Out of Motley, A. Amy Lowell. TBM
Rhyme Sheet of Other Lands, A. Hugh Chesterman. BoTP
Rhyme [*or* Rime], the rack of finest wits. A Fit of Rhyme against Rhyme [*or* Rime against Rime]. Ben Jonson. InvP; NBE; PoEL-2; PoFS; SeCV-1; TuPP
Rhymed Dance Calls. *Unknown.* CoSo
Rhymeless. John Freeman. MoP
Rhymes: "Still, for all slips of hers." Thomas Hood. *Fr.* The Bridge of Sighs. LiA
Rhymes about a Little Woman. William Canton. PPL
Rhymes about the Weather. *Unknown.* *See* Weather Signs.
Rhymes and Rhythms, *sels.* W. E. Henley.
Epilogue: "These to you now, O, more than ever now." POTT; ViBoPo
Prologue: "Something is dead." BPN
"Trees and the menace of night," XXI. Po
Rhymes for a Modern Nursery, *sels.* Paul Dehn. FiBHP
"Hey diddle diddle."
"In a cavern, in a canyon."
"Jack and Jill went up the hill."
"Little Miss Muffet."
"Two blind mice."
Rhymes to Remember. *Unknown.* StaSt
Rhymester, A. Samuel Taylor Coleridge. BOHV
Rhyming Riddles, *sels.* Mary Austin. TiPo
"First I am frosted."
"I come more softly than a bird."
"I have no wings, but yet I fly."
"I never speak a word."
Rhythm. Emerson. OQP; QP-2; TOP
Rhythm ("Rhythm in the pulse of Time"). Jean Percival Waddell. CaP
Rhythm of His Life, The. Mary Hallet. ChIP
Rhythmus ad SS. Sacramentum. St. Thomas Aquinas, *tr. fr. Latin by* Gerard Manley Hopkins. LaP
Ribald romeos less and less berattle. Horace. Odes, I, 25. LaP
Ribbed breathing flesh, thrice often crucified. The Body of Man. Sir Charles Scott Sherrington. PoP
Ribbon Two Yards Wide, A. Alfred Kreymborg. HBMV
Ribold and Goldborg. *Unknown, tr. fr. Danish by* E. M. Smith-Dampier. BoDaBa
Ribs and Terrors, The. Herman Melville. *See* Father Mapple's Hymn.
Ribs of new moons, The. The Haymaker's Lullaby. Francis Carlin. BOL
Rice Fields. Basho, *tr. fr. Japanese by* H. G. Henderson. OnPM
Rice Seller, The. *Unknown. tr. fr. Chinese by* Isaac Taylor Headland. PCH
Rich. Aileen Fisher. GaP; MPB
Rich and Poor. Al-Haitham, *tr. fr. Arabic by* A. J. Arberry. MooP
Rich and Poor; or, Saint and Sinner. Thomas Love Peacock. SiTL
Rich and Rare Were the Gems She Wore. Thomas Moore. ERP
Rich and strange thy history. Dust. Sister Mary Angelita. JKCP (1926 ed.)
Rich arrived in pairs, The. The Garden Party. Hilaire Belloc. MoVE
Rich colours on the vellum cease to lay. Nature's Colours. Countess of Winchilsea. *Fr.* An Invitation to Daphnis. BeR
Rich damask roses in fair cheeks do bide. Robert Tofte. *Fr.* Laura. EIL
Rich Days. W. H. Davies. BoTP; TwCV
Rich Earth, The. Psalms, CIV: 16–24, Bible, *O.T.* GoTP
Rich folks 'cided to take a trip, De. De Titanic. *Unknown.* AS
Rich fools there be whose base and filthy heart. Astrophel and Stella, XXIV. Sir Philip Sidney. OAEP; ReEn; ReIE; SiCE; SiPS; TuPP
Rich, honored by my fellow citizens. Washington McNeely. Edgar Lee Masters. *Fr.* Spoon River Anthology. SBMV
Rich in her weeping country's spoils, Versailles. The Charms of Nature. Joseph Warton. *Fr.* The Enthusiast; or, The Lover of Nature. OBEC
Rich in the waning light she sat. Waiting. John Freeman. CH
Rich is thy soil, and merciful thy clime. Britannia. James Thomson. *Fr.* The Seasons: Summer. BeR

Rich Jew of Malta, The. Christopher Marlowe. *See* Jew of Malta, The.
Rich labor is the struggle to be wise. The Discipline of Wisdom. George Meredith. EmBrPo; EPN; TyEnPo
Rich Lazarus! richer in those gems, thy teares. Upon Lazarus His Teares. Richard Crashaw. SeCV-1
Rich Man, The. Franklin P. Adams. FiBHP; InMe; LEAP; MAP; MoAmPo (1942 ed.); PC; PoMa
Rich Man and the Kingdom of Heaven, The. St. Matthew, XIX: 13–30, Bible, *N.T.* TreF
Rich man bought a swan and goose, A. The Swan and the Goose. Aesop. AWP; FaPON; JAWP; LiTW; UnS; WBP
Rich man builds a house, but the wise a tomb, The. *Unknown. Fr.* Carmina Epigraphica. LaP
Rich man has his motorcar, The. The Rich Man. Franklin P. Adams. FiBHP; InMe; LEAP; MAP; MoAmPo (1942 ed.); PC; PoMa
Rich man lay on his velvet couch, The. Mag's Song. *Unknown.* AS
Rich Man of Assisi, The. Sister M. Benvenuta. SaFP
Rich man, poor man, beggar-man, thief. Oberammergau. Leonora Speyer. AnAmPo; HBMV; LA
Rich man's son inherits lands, The. The Heritage. James Russell Lowell. HBV; HBVY; OTPC; PTA-2
Rich men, trust not in wealth. Thomas Nashe. AnFE; EG
Rich Mine of Knowledge. George Chapman. SeCePo
Rich Old Lady, The, *with music. Unknown.* OuSiCo
Rich Statue, double-faced. To the New Yeere. Michael Drayton. AtBAP; PoEL-2
Rich the peace of the elements tonight on the Land-of-Joy. The Path of the Old Spells. Donald Sinclair. GoTS
Rich, voluptuous languor of dim pain, A. Vanitas Vanitatum. Israel Zangwill. TrJP
Rich Young Farmer, The. *Unknown.* ABS
Rich Young Man, The. Laura Simmons. BAP; ChIP
Richard and Robin were two pretty men. *See* Robin and Richard were two pretty men.
Richard Cory. E. A. Robinson. AmP; AmPP; AnNE; BAP; CaAE; ChMo; CMP; CoBA; CoV; ExPo; FaFP; GTBS-W; IAP; LiTA; LiTG; LiTM; LoGBV; MAP; MM; MoAB; MoAmPo; MoVE; NeMA; NePA; NP; NV; OnPP; OxBA; PFE; PFY; PoLFOT; PoMa; PoRA; ReaPo; SBMV; StPo; TCPD; TOP; TreF; TrGrPo; TwP
Richard Crashaw. Thomas S. Jones, Jr. PtP
Richard Crashaw's Answer; for Hope. Richard Crashaw. *See* For Hope.
Richard de Castre's Prayer to Jesus, *in mod. Eng. Unknown.* TMEV
Richard Dick upon a stick. *Unknown.* OxNR
Richard Forest's Midsummer Night, *sel.* James Thomson.
Midsummer Courtship, VIII. OBVV
("Oh, how the nights are short.") POTT
Richard Has Something to Say. Rose Fyleman. GaP
Richard II. Shakespeare. *See* King Richard II.
Richard II as Captive. Samuel Daniel. *Fr.* The Civil Wars. SiCE
Richard II Banishes Bolingbroke. Shakespeare. King Richard II, *fr.* I, iii. PoFS
Richard II's Dejection. Shakespeare. *See* Death of Kings, The.
Richard Somers. Barrett Eastman. AA
Richard the Second. Shakespeare. *See* King Richard II.
Richard the Third. Shakespeare. *See* King Richard III.
Richard Tolman's Universe. Leonard Bacon. ImOP
Richardson, Erik Follows, Reed and I. The Paper in the Gate-legged Table. Amy Lowell. DaM
Riche Croesus, whylom king of Lyde, The. Croesus. Chaucer. *Fr.* The Canterbury Tales: The Monk's Tale. MyFE
Richelieu; or, The Conspiracy, *sel.* Sir Edward Bulwer-Lytton.
Cardinal's Soliloquy, The, *fr.* III, i. VA
Riches. Blake. *Fr.* Gnomic Verses. BoLiVe; StaSt; TrGrPo
Riches. Derrick N. Lehmer. BAP
Riches. Robert Loveman. OQP; QP-2
Riches. *Unknown, tr. fr. Greek by* William Cowper. AWP
Riches I hold in light esteem. The Old Stoic. Emily Brontë. BLV; BPP; EmBrPo; EnLi-2; EnLit; EV-5; GTML; OAEP; OBEV (new ed.); OBVV; OxBI; PC; PIAE; PoFr; PoVP; TrGrPo; VA; ViBoPo; YT
Riches will serve for titles, too. That's a Lie! Luis de Góngora. AnSpL-1
Richest realm of all the earth, The. The Poet's Confidence. Coventry Patmore. *Fr.* The Angel in the House. POTT
Richest Woman, The. Elizabeth Madox Roberts. GaP
Richie Story. *Unknown.* BaBo; ESPB (A *and* B *vers.*)
Richly scattered temple ruins. Mysterious Landscape. Hans Carossa. LiTW
Rick of Green Wood, The. Edward Dorn. NeAP
Rid of the world's injustice, and his pain. The Grave of Keats. Oscar Wilde. PoVP
Riddle, A: Book, A. Hannah More. *See* Book, A.
Riddle: "As I went over London Bridge." *Unknown.* ChTr
Riddle: "As I went over Tipple Tyne." *Unknown.* ChTr
Riddle: "At the end of my yard there is a vat." *Unknown.* ChTr
Riddle, A: "Clothes make no sound when I tread ground." *Unknown, tr. fr. Anglo-Saxon.* ChTr
Riddle, A: "Four stiff-standers." *Unknown.* ChTr; OxNR
Riddle, The: "He told himself and he told his wife." Ralph Hodgson. WhC
Riddle: "Here is a riddle most abstruse." *Unknown.* SiTL
Riddle: "Highty, tighty, paradighty, clothed in green." *Unknown.* ChTr; OxNR
Riddle, A: "I am just two and two, I am warm, I am cold." William Cowper. HBV
Riddle: "I am within as white as snow." *Unknown.* ChTr
Riddle: "I washed my face in water." *Unknown.* ChTr
Riddle: "In Mornigan's park there is a deer." *Unknown.* ChTr
Riddle: "It is in the rock, but not in the stone." *Unknown.* ChTr
Riddle: "Land was white, The." *Unknown.* ChTr; OxNR
Riddle, A: Letter "H," The. Catherine Fanshawe. *See* Riddle, A: "'Twas whispered in heaven . . ."
Riddle: "Long white barn, A." *Unknown.* ChTr
Riddle, The: "No more, no more." Alexander Brome. OBS
Riddle: "On yonder hill there is a red deer." *Unknown.* ChTr
Riddle, A: "Though the goddess made you wonder, do believe the things she said." Sophocles, *tr. fr. Greek by* George Allen. OxBG
Riddle, A: "'Twas whispered in heaven [*or* in heaven pronounced], 'twas muttered in hell." Catherine Maria Fanshawe. BCEP; ChTr; OTPC
(Enigma.) LiTG; SiTL
(Enigma on the Letter H.) BOHV; GoTP
(Letter for You, A.) RIS
(Riddle, A: Letter "H," The.) GN; LPS-3
Riddle, The: "Underneath the leaves of life." W. H. Auden. EnLi-2 (1949 ed.)
Riddle, A: "We are little airy creatures." Swift. GN; OTPC
(A E I O U.) BoTP
(Five, The.) RIS
(Riddle, A; the Vowels.) OnYI
(Vowels, The; a Riddle.) MeMeAg
Riddle, The: "We were laying the road to a Riddle." Dana Burnet. OBAV
Riddle: "Wee man o' leather." *Unknown.* ChTr
Riddle, The: "Where's an old woman to go when the years." "H. E. H." PoToHe
Riddle: "White bird featherless." *Unknown.* ChTr
(Snow.) RIS
("White bird featherless.") OxNR
Riddle: "White bird floats down through the air, A." *Unknown.* ChTr
Riddle: "You are a riddle I would not unravel." Josephine Miles. FiMAP
Riddle, a riddle, as I suppose, A. Mother Goose. OxNR; TiPo
Riddle cum diddle cum doodle. Kindness to Animals. Laura E. Richards. TiPo
Riddle-me riddle-me riddle-me-ree. Mother Goose. BoChLi; OTPC (1946 ed.); OxNR; PPL
Riddle me, riddle me, what is that. *Unknown.* OTPC (1946 ed.)
Riddle of the World. Pope. *See* Know Then Thyself.
Riddle, A; the Vowels. Swift. *See* Riddle, A: "We are little airy creatures."
Riddlers, The. Walter de la Mare. TCPD
Riddles. Patrick F. Kirby. GoBC
Riddles. Sister Mary Madeleva. JKCP (1955 ed.)
Riddles, *sels. Unknown, formerly at. to* Cynewulf, *tr. fr. Anglo-Saxon.*
Anchor: "Oft I must strive with wind and wave," *tr. by* Charles W. Kennedy. AnOE
Bible, A: "A stern destroyer struck out my life," *tr. by* Stith Thompson. EnLi-1; OuHeWo
Bookworm, A: "A moth ate a word. To me that seemed," *tr. by* Stith Thompson. EnLi-1
(Book-Moth: "A moth ate a word. To me it seemed," *tr. by* Charles W. Kennedy.) AnOE
(Book-Worm, The: "A moth ate a word. Methought it.") CoBE
("Moth ate words, A. To me that seemed," *tr. by* Harold S. Stine.) EnLit
Cuckoo: "In former days my father and mother," *tr. by* Charles W. Kennedy. AnOE
Fish in River: "My house is not quiet, I am not loud," *tr. by* Charles W. Kennedy. AnOE
Honey-Mead: "I am valued by men, fetched from afar," *tr. by* Charles W. Kennedy. AnOE
Horn, A: "I was once an armed warrior," *tr. by* Stith Thompson. OuHeWo
(Horn: "Time was when I was weapon and warrior," *tr. by* Charles W. Kennedy.) AnOE

Ring soft across the dying day. The Angelus. Frances Laughton Mace. PEOR
Ring the bell! Baby at Play. *Unknown.* HBV; HBVY; OxNR; PPL
Ring the bells, nor ring them slowly. Cedar Mountain. Annie Fields. MC; PAH
Ring the bells, ring! *Unknown.* OxNR
Ring the Old Year, O ring it out! For the Old Year. Raymond Kresensky. PSO
Ring-ting! I wish I were a primrose. Wishing. William Allingham. BoChLi (1939 ed.); BoTP; CBPC; DD; FaPON; GFA; HBV; HBVY; MPB; NLK; OHIP; OTPC; PCH; PRWS; PTA-1; RAR; TVC; TVSH
Ringely, Ringely. Eliza Lee Follen. SAS
Ringleted Youth of My Love. *Unknown, tr. fr. Modern Irish by* Douglas Hyde. AnIL; AnIV; LBBV; OnYI; OxBI; TIP
Ringlets of slender silver, curled artlessly. Portrait. Francesco Berni. LyPI
Ringsend. Oliver St. John Gogarty. AnIL; LiTM; OBMV
Rintrah roars and shakes his fires in the burden'd [*or* burdened] air. The Marriage of Heaven and Hell. Blake. CEP; EiPP; EnRP; LoBV
Rio Bravo—a Mexican Lament. José de Saltillo, *tr. fr. Spanish by* Charles Fenno Hoffman. PAH
Rio de Janeiro, Rio de Enero. River of Oblivion. Alfonso Reyes. AnMP
Rio Grande, The. Sacheverell Sitwell. SeCePo
Rio Grande ("Heave away, Rio!"), *with music. Unknown.* ShS
Rio Grande, The ("Oh, Johnny came over"), *with music. Unknown.* ABF
Rio Grande ("Oh, say, were you ever in Rio Grande?"), *with music. Unknown.* SoAmSa; TrAS
("O say, were you ever in Rio Grande.") LO
Rio Grande, The ("Where are you going to"). *Unknown.* SG
Rioupéroux. James Elroy Flecker. OBEV (new ed.); OBVV
Rip up the sagebrush. Harvest of Dust. Carol M. Ritchie. MuM
Ripe and Bearded Barley, The. *Unknown.* ChTr
Ripe apple, the banana and the pear. Rainer Maria Rilke. Sonnets to Orpheus, Pt. I, XIII. OnPM
Ripe cherries and ripe maidens. Cherries. Zalman Schneour. TrJP
Ripe Grain. Dora Read Goodale. HBV
Ripe old age for her dog. Epicure. Ruth Lambert Jones. DDA
Ripe Plums. *Unknown, tr. fr. Chinese.* WhP
Ripe, the plums fall from the bough. Anxiety of a Young Lady to Get Married. *Unknown.* OuHeWo
Ripened the Fruit. Friedrich Hölderlin, *tr. fr. German by* Kate Flores. AnGP
Ripeness is all; her in her cooling planet. To an Old Lady. William Empson. AtBAP; CoBMV; CoEV; FaBoTw; MoAB; MoPW
Riposte. Nazhun, *tr. fr. Arabic by* A. J. Arberry. MooP
Ripping Trip, A. *Unknown.* CoSo; CSF
Ripple of dust panicked across, A. Ghosts. Ethna MacCarthy. NeIP
Rippling in the ocean of that darkening room. Woman at the Piano. Marya Zaturenska. MoAmPo
Rippling through thy branches goes the sunshine. The Birch-Tree. James Russell Lowell. BAV
Riprap. Gary Snyder. NeAP
Riquet of the Tuft, *sels.* Stopford Brooke. VA
Prince Riquet's Song.
Queen's Song.
Rise, A. Ernest McGaffey. AA
Rise and Fall, The. Samuel Johnson. *Fr.* The Vanity of Human Wishes. BeR
("Unnumbered suppliants crowd Preferment's gate.") PoFr
Rise and Fall of Creede, The. Cy Warman. PoOW
Rise and Fall of Valentines. Fairfax Downey. InMe
Rise and hold up the curved glass. Pour Us Wine. Ibn Kolthúm. *Fr.* The Mu'allaqát. AWP
Rise, and pour me rosy wine. Wine at Dawn. Ibn Sa'id of Alcala la Real. MooP
Rise, brothers, rise; the wakening [*or* waking] skies pray to the morning light. The Coromandel Fishers. Sarojini Naidu. BBV; EtS; MCCG; VOD
Rise, crowned with hope, O! prostrate South, arise! Resurgam. Mary Bayard Clarke. NoCaPo
Rise, Crowned with Light. Pope. *Fr.* Messiah. GoBC; OlF; WGRP
(Hymn: "Rise, crowned with light, imperial Salem, rise!") NeHB
Rise from the waves, my rivering one. Four Poems for April, II. Louis Adeane. NeBP
Rise from thyself, thou phoenix world. Phoenix. E. H. W. Meyerstein. NeTW
Rise, Glorious Conqueror! Rise. Matthew Bridges. BePJ
Rise, Happy Morn. Tennyson. *See* In Memoriam A. H. H.: "Time draws near the birth of Christ, The."
Rise, happy youth, this bright machine survey. John Gay. *Fr.* The Fan. ViBoPo
Rise heart; thy Lord is risen. Sing his praise. Easter. George Herbert. CaAE; EOAH; SeCV-1; SeEP; TriL
Rise, Heir of fresh Eternity. Easter Day. Richard Crashaw. MeRV; PoLi
Rise, Lady Mistress, Rise! Nathaniel Field. *Fr.* Amends for Ladies. ElL; TuPP
(Matin Song.) HBV
(Song: "Rise Lady Mistress, rise.") OBS
Rise Love and with my heart's. Venus on a Sea Horse. Maurice Carpenter. FaBoTw
Rise, Magyar; 'tis the country's call! National Song. Alexander Petofi. PoFr
Rise Me Up from Down Below, *with music. Unknown.* ShS
Rise, Mourner, Rise, *with music. Unknown.* BoAN-2
Rise my soul and break your prison. The Day of Victory. Rachel Capen Schauffler. EOAH
Rise, O earth from out thy slumber. Prayer for Rain. *Unknown. Fr.* Kalevala. WGRP
Rise, O My Soul! *Unknown, sometimes at. to* Sir Walter Ralegh. OxBoCh
(To Jesus.) MaRV
Rise of Dictatorship, The. Solon, *tr. fr. Greek by* F. L. Lucas. GrPE
Rise of Man, The. John White Chadwick. AA
Rise Oot Your Bed. John Barr of Craigielee. AnNZ
Rise, rise princely shepherd & bee arbiter. *Unknown.* SeCSL
"Rise," said the Master, "come unto the feast." The Bride [*or* Sonnet]. Henry Alford. LPS-1; OBEV (1st ed.)
Rise! Sleep no more! 'Tis a noble morn! The Hunter's Song. "Barry Cornwall." BBV (1923 ed.); GN; OTPC; VA
Rise, thou best and brightest morning! New Year's Day. Richard Crashaw. SeEP
Rise up and do begin the day's adorning. Sonnet. Hilaire Belloc. AlDL
Rise up, my song! stretch forth thy wings and fly. A Greeting. Philip Bourke Marston. VA
Rise Up, O Men of God! William Pierson Merrill. MaRV
(Festal Song.) WGRP
Rise up, rise up,/ And, as the trumpet blowing. The Trumpet. Edward Thomas. BLV; HBMV; MBP; MoBrPo; OHIP; POTE; TSW
Rise up, rise up in haste. Early Pleasure. Ibn Hamdis. MooP
"Rise up, rise up, my seven brave sons." Earl Brand (A *vers.*) *Unknown.* ViBoFo
"Rise up, rise up, now, Lord Douglas," she says. The Douglas Tragedy [*or* Earl Brand]. *Unknown.* BLV; BoLiVe; CaAE; EBSV; ESPB (B *vers.*); HBV; MaC; OBB; OnSP; PIAE; TrGrPo
Rise Up Shepherd an' Foller. *Unknown.* BoAN-2, *with music;* ChrBoLe
Rise up! You have my leave. Invitation. Ibn Sa'id of Seville. MooP
"Rise up, you seven bretherens." Earl Brand (B *vers.*). *Unknown.* BaBo
Rise you up, my dearest dear. Shoot the Buffalo. *Unknown.* TrAS
Risen with Healing in His Wings. St. John of Damascus, *tr. fr. Greek.* BePJ
Risest thou thus, dim dawn, again,/ And howlest, issuing out of night. In Memoriam A. H. H., LXXII. Tennyson. EM-2; EmBrPo; EPN; GEPC; GTBS-D; PoEL-5; ViPo; VLEP
Risest thou thus, dim dawn, again,/ So loud with voices of the birds. In Memoriam A. H. H., XCIX. Tennyson. BrBE; EM-2; EmBrPo; EnLi-2; EPN; GEPC; OAEP; ViPo; VLEP
Rising, The. Thomas Buchanan Read. *Fr.* The Wagoner of the Alleghanies. PAH; TreFS
Rising in the North, The. *Unknown.* ACP (1952 ed.); BaBo; ESPB
Rising moon has hid the stars, The. Endymion. Longfellow. AA; HBV; IAP; MOAP; TCAP
Rising of the Moon, The, A.D. 1798. John Keegan Casey. AnIV; GTIV; IrPN; OnYI; TIP
Rising Sun, The. Al-Haitham, *tr. fr. Arabic by* A. J. Arberry. MooP
Rising Sun, The. Lawrence Durrell. *Fr.* Eight Aspects of Melissa. NeBP
Rising Sun Blues, The, *with music. Unknown.* OuSiCo
Rising Sun! when you shall shine. Song of the House. *Tr. fr. Navajo Indian.* GrCo-1
Rising Village, The, *sels.* Oliver Goldsmith, the Younger.
"What noble courage must their hearts have fired." BoCaPo; PeCV
"While now the Rising Village claims a name." CaP
Risks of the Game, The. Adam Lindsay Gordon. *Fr.* Ye Wearie Wayfarer, Fytte II. OtMeF
Rispetto: "Eyes that without a tongue can speak to me." Angelo Poliziano, *tr. fr. Italian by* L. R. Lind. LyPI
Rispetto: "I ask no other vengeance, Love, from you." Angelo Poliziano, *tr. fr. Italian by* L. R. Lind. LyPI

Rispetto: "This little girl's so gay and fidgety." Angelo Poliziano, *tr. fr. Italian by* L. R. Lind. LyPI
Rispetto: "What good is there, ah me, what good is Love?" Agnes Mary Frances Robinson. Tuscan Cypress, II, XII, *and* XV. AV; HBMV
Rispetto: "When, these eyes closed in death, you look on me." Angelo Poliziano, *tr. fr. Italian by* L. R. Lind. LyPI
Risposta. *Unknown.* ElSeCe; HBV
Risus Dei. Thomas Edward Brown. PoVP
Rite and Fore-Time. David Jones. *Fr.* The Anathemata. AtBAP
Rite at a Brother's Grave. Catullus, *tr. fr. Latin by* George Lamb. OnPM
Rite of Spring. Leo Kennedy. CaP
Ritter Hugo. Charles Godfrey Leland. *See* Ballad of the Mermaid.
Ritual. Ibn Abd Rabbihi, *tr. fr. Arabic by* A. J. Arberry. MooP
Ritual Not Religion. *Unknown.* WGRP
Ritual of the Grape. Omar Khayyám. *See* Omar and Death.
Ritual to Read to Each Other, A. William Stafford. NePA
Rival, The. Gertrude Hall. BAP
Rival, The. James Whitcomb Riley. LBMV
Rival, The. Sylvia Townsend Warner. BLV; BoLiVe (1939 ed.); MBP; MoAB; MoBrPo
Rival Curates, The. W. S. Gilbert. CenHV; MBP
Rival Friends, The, *sels.* Peter Hausted.
Have Pity, Grief. EG; SeCL
("Have pity, grief, I cannot pay.") TuPP
(Song, The: "Have pity (Grief) I can not pay.") SeEP
"Have you a desire to see." TuPP
Of His Mistress. EG; SeCL
Rival Poets, The. Aristophanes, *tr. fr. Greek by* Marshall MacGregor. *Fr.* The Frogs. OxBG
(Rivals, The, *tr. by* Benjamin Bickley Rogers.) GrR
Rival Sisters, The, *sel.* Robert Gould.
Song: "Fair, and soft, and gay, and young," *fr.* III. CEP; SeCL
Rivalry in Love. William Walsh. *See* Rivals.
Rivals, The. Aristophanes. *See* Rival Poets, The.
Rivals, The. *sel.* Sir William Davenant.
Song: "My lodging it is on the cold ground." SeCL
Rivals, The. W. H. Davies. ChMo; CMP
Rivals, The. Paul Laurence Dunbar. IHA
Rivals, The. James Stephens. AlDL; BoTP; FaPON; GTBS-D; InvP; MoVE; OBEV (new ed.); OBMV; OTPC (1946 ed.); PoRh; RAR; SP; UTS
Rivals, The. *Unknown.* PIAE
Rivals. William Walsh. HBV; LoPo; OBEV
(Rivalry in Love.) LPS-1
(Rivals in Love.) EV-3
(Song: "Of all the torments, all the cares.") LiTL; OBEC; ViBoPo
Rivals, The. Robert Whitaker. OQP; QP-2
Rivals in Love. William Walsh. *See* Rivals.
River, The. Struthers Burt. NoCaPo (1941 ed.)
River, The. Hart Crane. *Fr.* The Bridge: Powhatan's Daughter. AmP; AmPP; AnFE; CoAnAm; CoBA; CoBMV; CoV; LiTA; MoAB; MoAmPo; NAMP; OxBA; TwAmPo; ViBoPo (1958 ed.)
Sels.
"Down, down—born pioneers in time's despite." TrGrPo
"You will not hear it as the sea." ViBoPo
River, The. Ibn Sa'id of Alcala la Real, *tr. fr. Arabic by* A. J. Arberry. MooP
River, The. Mary Sinton Leitch. HBMV
River, The, *sel.* Pare Lorentz.
"Black spruce and Norway pine." NAMP
River, The. Patrick MacDonogh. NeIP
River, The, *sel.* Coventry Patmore.
"It is a venerable place." EnSW
River, The. Alan Porter. MoP
River, The. Ellis M. Potter. VOD
River, The, *abr.* Sir Ronald Ross. BSV
River, The. Frederick George Scott. CPG
River, The. Thomas Tod Stoddart. EBSV
River boat had loitered down its way, The. Gamesters All. DuBose Heyward. HBMV; InP; LS
River Boats. *Unknown.* MW
River Bridge, The. James S. Tippett. GFA
River Duddon, The, *sels.* Wordsworth.
After-Thought, XXXIV. EnL; EnRP; EPN; FaBoEn; MeRV; SeCePo
(After-Thought Appended to "The River Duddon.") EM-2
(After-Thought—River Duddon.) ES
(After-Thought to "The River Duddon.") BPN; OAEP; OBRV; PIAE; TCEP
("I thought of thee, my partner and my guide.") EnLi-2; EPP
(Sonnet: "I thought of thee . . . .") CoEV
(Valedictory Sonnet to the River Duddon.) OBEV
"Old inventive poets, had they seen, The," XX. EnLi-2
(Plain of Donnerdale, The.) PeBoSo
"Return, Content! for fondly I pursued," XXVI. EnLi-2
"Sole listener, Duddon! to the breeze that played," V. EnLi-2
(Sonnet: "Sole listener, Duddon!") EnSW
River Fight, The. Henry Howard Brownell. PaA; PAH; PAP
"Would you hear of the river-fight," *sel.* AA; EtS; GA, *abr.;* MDAH
River flows to the East, The. The Red Cliff. Su T'ung-po. OnPC
River-Fog. Kiyowara Fukayabu, *tr. fr. Japanese by* Arthur Waley. *Fr.* Shui Shu. FaPON
("Because river-fog.") AWP; JAWP; LiTW; WBP
River Glideth in a Secret Tongue, The. Anthony Ostroff. NePoAm-2
River God, The ("I am this fountain's god"). John Fletcher. *Fr.* The Faithful Shepherdess, III, i. TrGrPo
River God, The. Sacheverell Sitwell. MBP; MoBrPo
River God, The. Stevie Smith. FaBoTw
River god cries far, The. Tao. Alfred Goldsworthy Bailey. CaP
River-God's Song, The. John Fletcher. *Fr.* The Faithful Shepherdess, III, i. FaPON; MoShBr; PCH
("Do not fear to put thy feet.") ElSeCe; TuPP
(Song: "Do not fear to put thy feet.") ElL; OBS; ThWaDe
(Song of the River God to Amoret, The.) EV-2
River has not any care, The. Francis Thompson. *Fr.* Contemplation. FaBoEn
River hemmed with leaning [*or* leafing] trees, The. A Mystery. Whittier. IAP; UnW
River in the Meadows, The. Léonie Adams. AnAmPo; LA; MAP; MoAB; MoAmPo; NP
River is a page, The. The River. Ibn Sa'id of Alcala la Real. MooP
River Izumi, The. Fujiwara no Go-Kanesuke, *tr. fr. Japanese by* Kenneth Rexroth. OnPJ
River laps the isle, The. Flow and Ebb. Ibn Safar. MooP
River Lea, The, with music. Sam Peck. SoAmSa
River-long Love, A. Li Chih-yi, *tr. fr. Chinese by* Ch'u Ta'kao. ChLP
River-Mates. Padraic Colum. AnIV; AWP; JAWP; LEAP; WBP
River meads of vanished Clonard hold, The. Clonard. Thomas S. Jones, Jr. HBMV; VOD
River Merchant's Wife, The; a Letter. Li Po, *tr. fr. Chinese by* Ezra Pound. AmP; AmPP; AnAmPo; AWP; CoAnAm; InPo; LA; LiTA; LiTL; LiTW; MoAB; MoAmPo (1950 ed.); MOAP; MoPo; NAMP; NP; OBMV; OxBA; PG (1945 ed.); TwAmPo; WBP
River murmurs, and the breathing gale, The. Evening at the Abbey. William Julius Mickle. *Fr.* Pollio; an Elegy. RO
River Nile, The. Leigh Hunt. *See* Nile, The.
River of billows, to whose mighty heart. The Shannon. Sir Aubrey De Vere. TIP
River of Commerce, The. "O.L." CAG
River of Grace, A. Molly Anderson Haley. ChIP
River of Heaven, The. *Unknown, tr. fr. Japanese by* Lafcadio Hearn. *Fr.* Manyo Shu. AWP; LiTW
River of Life, The. Thomas Campbell. BSV; FaFP; GTBS; GTBS-D; GTBS-W; GTSE; GTSL; HBV; LiTB; LiTG; LPS-3
(Thought Suggested by the New Year, A.) EBSV
River of Oblivion. Alfonso Reyes, *tr. fr. Spanish by* Samuel Beckett. AnMP
River of Seville. Al-Kutandi, *tr. fr. Arabic by* A. J. Arberry. MooP
River, on its way to sea, The. Still Voyager. *Unknown.* DDA
River Rhondda. Alun Lewis. MoWP
River Roses. D. H. Lawrence. ViBoPo
(All of Roses.) LEAP
River Sawdde. Keidrych Rhys. MoWP
River Skater. Winifred Welles. PoeMoYo
River Song. Elizabeth Brewster. CaP
River this November afternoon, The. The Double Vision. C. Day Lewis. AtBAP
River Traffic. Frederick Mortimer Clapp. VOD (1935 ed.)
River Walk, The. Padraic Fallon. OxBI
River widens to a pathless sea, The. On a Ferry Boat. Richard Burton. AA
Rivermouth Rocks are fair to see. The Wreck of Rivermouth. Whittier. IAP; MOAP
Rivers. J. C. Squire. PtOT
Rivers. Thomas Storer. ElL; FaBoCh
Rivers Arise; a Fragment. Milton. ChTr
Rivers I have seen which were beautiful. Rivers. J. C. Squire. PtOT
Rivers level granite mountains. Sulpicius Lupercus Servasius, Jr., *tr. fr. Latin by* Kenneth Rexroth. LaP
Rivers of France, The. "H. J. M." PTA-1
Rivers of the West. "Sunset Joe." PoOW
Rivers rush into the sea, The. The Song of the Bird. Longfellow. BoTP

Rivers seek each other through the world. Hydrographic Poem. Jorge Carrera Andrade. TwSpPo
Rivers Till and Tweed, The. *Unknown.* WhC
(Still Waters.) BLV
(Till and Tweed.) CBOV
(Two Rivers.) ChTr; OBEV; ShBV-1
"Rivers Unknown to Song." Alice Meynell. HBMV; NP
Riverton. Edmund Wilson. AnFE; CoAnAm; TwAmPo
Riverward they took him flying. My Old Hound Pack. Archibald Rutledge. AlBD
Rivery field spread out below, A. W. B. Yeats. *Fr.* Let All Things Pass Away. ChTr
Riveter, The. Joseph Auslander. PoeMoYo
Riveter, The. Margaret E. Sangster. PEDC
Rivets. N. S. Olds. EtS
Rivulet, The. Lucy Larcom. PRWS; TVSH
Rivulet crossing my ground. Tennyson. Maud, Pt. I, xxi. BPN
Rivulet with rush of sound, The. Midwinter Thaw. Lenore Pratt. CaP
Rizpah. Swinburne. EmBrPo
Rizpah. Tennyson. BEL; BMEP; BPN; DaM; EM-2; EmBrPo; EnLi-2; EPN; MotAn; PIAE; PoEL-5; PoVP; TCEP; TOP; VA; VLEP
Rizpah's Lullaby. *Unknown.* BOL
Road, The. Conrad Aiken. MAP; MoAmPo
Road, The. Patrick R. Chambers. HBV
Road, The. John Gould Fletcher. HBMV; TSW
Road, The. Helene Johnson. BANP; CDC; GoSl; PoNe
Road, The. Herbert Morris. NePoAm-2
Road, The. Edwin Muir. FaBoEn; FaBoMo; FaFP; LiTB; LiTG; LiTM; ViBoPo (1958 ed.)
Road, The. Nikolay Platonovich Ogarev, *tr. fr. Russian by* P. E. Matheson. AWP
Road, The. Hyam Plutzik. FiMAP
Road, The. Siegfried Sassoon. MCCG
Road, The. Zalman Schneour, *tr. fr. Yiddish by* Joseph Leftwich. TrJP
Road, The. Sir Philip Sidney. *See* Astrophel and Stella: Sonnets, LXXXIV.
Road, The. James Stephens. HBMV; PoeMoYo; VOD
Road, The. Humbert Wolfe. QS
Road and a Memory, A. Jim Thompson. CAG
Road and the End, The. Carl Sandburg. NP
Road at My Door, The. W. B. Yeats. Meditations in Time of Civil War, V. LiTB; SoV
Road at the top of the rise, The. The Middleness of the Road. Robert Frost. CrMA; LiTA
Road Fellows. Barbara Young. BrR
Road from Election to Christmas, The. Oscar Williams. NAMP
Road-Hymn for the Start. William Vaughn Moody. MAP; MoAmPo (1942 ed.)
Road in the Weald, A. Richard Church. HaMV
Road is burnt to dust, like more dust meadow rue, The. Harvest Dust. Winifred Welles. MAP
Road is left that once was trod, The. The Old Road. Jones Very. AA
Road is thronged with women, The: soldiers pass. The Road. Siegfried Sassoon. MCCG
Road is wide and the stars are out, The. Roofs. Joyce Kilmer. VOD
Road like brown ribbon, A. September. Edwina Fallis. SUS; TiPo; YeAr
Road Makers. *Unknown.* *See* Pioneers ("We shall not travel . . .").
Road Menders, The. Laurence Binyon. PoeT
Road Might Lead to Anywhere, A. Rachel Field. *See* Roads.
Road Not Taken, The. Robert Frost. AmPP; AnFE; AnNE; APA; BAP; BrBE; ChMo; ChTr; CMP; CoAnAm; CoBA; CoBMV; CV; FaBoCh; FaFP; GTBS-D; GTBS-W; InP; LEAP; LiTA; LiTG; LiTM; LoGBV; MAP; MAPA; MM; MoAB; MoAmPo; MOAP; NePA; OBAV; OxBA; PG; PoE; PreP; ReMP; SBMV; SeCeV; TwAmPo; TwP
Road of Ireland, A. Charles L. O'Donnell. HBMV
Road of Life, The. Yevgeny Abramovich Boratynsky, *tr. fr. Russian by* Babette Deutsch. TrRV
Road of Midnight Pageants, The. Hilton Ross Greer. HiLiAm
Road of Remembrance, The. Lizette Woodworth Reese. HBV
Road of Suffering, The. Chaim Grade, *tr. fr. Yiddish by* Sarah Zweig Betsky. OnCuPl
Road, route, footpath, alley of solitude with its myrmidons. Elegy for All Ages. "Pablo de Rokha." TwSpPo
Road Song. James Stuart Montgomery. NLK
Road Song. Margaret E. Sangster. PoMa
Road Song, A. Duncan Campbell Scott. PC
Road Song. W. G. Tinckom-Fernandez. NLK
Road Song, A. *Unknown.* PSO
Road Song. Louis Untermeyer. StaSt
Road-Song of the Bandar-Log. Kipling. *Fr.* The Jungle Book. NV; OAEP (2d ed.); VLEP
Road that I came by mounts eight thousand feet, The. The Waters of Lung-t'ou. Hsü Ling. TrCh
Road That Leads to Home, The. Ethel E. Mannin. NLK
Road, the hedge, the trees, The. The Caravan. J. Redwood Anderson. TCPD
Road to Anywhere, The. Bert Leston Taylor. HBMV; MPB; TSW; TSWC
Road to Babylon, The. Margaret Adelaide Wilson. HBMV
Road to Bethlehem, The. Watson Kirkconnell. MaRV
Road to Castaly, The, *sel.* Alice Brown.
Revelation. WGRP
Road to China, The. Olive Beaupré Miller. MPB
Road to Cook's Peak, The. *Unknown.* CoSo; CSF
Road to Dieppe, The. John Huston Finley. MCCG
Road to Emmaus, The. Vyacheslav Ivanov, *tr. fr. Russian by* C. M. Bowra. BoR
Road to Emmaus, The. Ida Norton Munson. ChIP
Road to Firenze, A. Agnes Kendrick Gray. TBM
Road to France, The. Daniel Henderson. HBV; MC; PaA; PAH
Road to Nijmegen, The Earle Birney. BoCaPo (1948 ed.)
Road to Raffydiddle, The. Mildred Plew Meigs. GoBP; TiPo (1952 ed.)
"Road to Ruin, The." *Unknown.* SCC
Road to Slumberland, The. Mary Dow Brine. BOL
Road to Tartary, The. Bernard Freeman Trotter. CPG
Road to the Bow, The. James David Corrothers. BANP
Road to the Pool, The. Grace Hazard Conkling. HBMV; VOD
Road to Town, The. H. M. Sarson. BoTP
Road to Vagabondia, The. Dana Burnet. AlBD; DDA; NLK; POT; PoTo
Road winds up the hill to meet the height, The. Faith. Emma Carleton. MaRV
Roads. Ruth Dallas. AnNZ
Roads. Rachel Field. BrR; FaPON; StVeCh; TiPo; WaKn
(Road Might Lead to Anywhere, A.) DDA
Roads. Katharine Knight. TVSH
Roads. Lizette Woodworth Reese. DaM
Road's End, The. Theodosia Garrison. HBMV
Roads Go Ever On and On. J. R. R. Tolkien. FaPON
(Roads Go Ever Ever On.) TiPo (1959 ed.)
Roads in the Dew, The. *Unknown, tr. fr. Chinese.* WhP
Roads lead southward, blue, The. To Argos. Lawrence Durrell. MoPo
Roads of spring wind gallantly, The. Weary Peddlers. Elias Lieberman. BAP
Roadside Fire, The. Robert Louis Stevenson. *See* Romance.
Roadside Flowers. Bliss Carman. CPG; CV; HBMV
Roadside forests here and there were touched with tawny gold, The. Mistress Hale of Beverly. Lucy Larcom. PAH
Roadside inn this summer Saturday, A. Sonnet. Thomas Caulfield Irwin. IrPN
Roadside near Moscow. R. A. D. Ford. PeCV; TwCaPo
Roadside nut-tree planted, here I stand, A. The Mournful Nut-Tree. Antipater. OnPM
Roadside Song, A. Lu Yu, *tr. fr. Chinese by* Pai Chwen-yu. WhP
Roadside thistle, eager, The. Matsuo Basho, *tr. fr. Japanese by* Curtis Hidden Page. AWP; LiTW
Roadway has a flinten face, The. The Old Inn-Sign. Wilfrid Thorley. BrR
Roadways. John Masefield. BEL; BoTP; GTSL; MCCG
Roamer, The, *sel.* George Edward Woodberry.
"Love is the bread that feeds the multitudes." MaRV
Roaming the lonely garden, he and I. From a Chinese Vase. Winifred Welles. MAP
Roan, The. Ibn Khafaja, *tr. fr. Arabic by* A. J. Arberry. MooP
Roan Stallion. Robinson Jeffers. AmPP (4th ed.); BeLS; CoV; NAMP
Roar of Niagara dies away, The. H. W. L. John Nichol. VA
Roar of the lion is the fearless man speaking, The. The Song of Experiencing the Tao. *Unknown.* WhP
Roar of the world is in my ears, The. Thanksgiving. Joyce Kilmer. MaRV
Roaring Days, The. Henry Lawson. BoAV; NeLNL
Roaring Frost, The. Alice Meynell. AlDL; NLK (1947 ed.)
Roaring Lad and the Ranting Lass, The; or, A Merry Couple Madly Met. *Unknown.* CoMu
Roaring of the wheels has filled my ears, The. A Cry from the Ghetto. Morris Rosenfeld. TrJP
Roaring Wind, soaring Wind. The Wind's Song. Eduard Mörike. AnGP
Roast Beef of Old England The. Henry Fielding. *Fr.* Don Quixote in England, I. CEP; LPS-2 (*with* 4 *add. sts. by* Richard Leveridge); OBEC
Roast Beef of Old England, The. Richard Leveridge. BHV; LPS-2
(Song in Praise of Old English Roast Beef.) OBEC
Roast Swan Song. *Unknown, tr. fr. Latin by* George F. Whicher. LiTW
Rob Rool and Rattlin Willie. Allan Cunningham. EBSV
Rob Roy. Eleanor *and* Herbert Farjeon. OnPP
Rob Roy, *sel.* Sir Walter Scott.
Black Prince, The, *fr. ch.* 2. CBPC

Rob Roy. *Unknown.* BaBo; ESPB (A *and* B *vers.*)
Rob Roy Macgregor. Rob Roy. Eleanor *and* Herbert Farjeon. OnPP
Robber, The. Ivy O. Eastwick. SiSoSe
Robber, The. W. J. Turner. MBP; MoBrPo
Robber in England, The. Marguerite Wilkinson. OBAV
Robber Kitten, The. *At. to* George M. Baker. CIV; FTB
Robe of Grass, The. John Le Gay Brereton. BoAu; MM
Robene and Makyne. Robert Henryson. BSV; EBSV; GoTS
(Robin and Makin.) OAEP; PoEL-1
(Robin and Makyne.) OBEV
Robert Barnes, fellow fine. Mother Goose. OxNR; RIS
Robert Bridges. Humbert Wolfe. PtP
Robert Bruce's Address to His Army, before the Battle of Bannockburn. Burns. *See* Scots Wha Hae.
Robert Burns. William Alexander. HBV
Robert Burns. Longfellow. PtP
Robert E. Lee. Julia Ward Howe. BlG; DD; GA; HiLiAm; MC; PAH; PoRL
Robert Frost. Louis Untermeyer. BOHV
Robert Gould Shaw. William Vaughn Moody. *Fr.* An Ode in Time of Hesitation. AA; MDAH
Robert Louis Stevenson. Lizette Woodworth Reese. HBV
Robert of Lincoln. Bryant. AnNE; APW; BLA; BoChLi; DD; EV-4; FaBoBe; FaPON; GFA; HBV; HBVY; HH; IAP; LPS-2; MPB; MW; OTPC (1946 ed.); PCH; PECK; PIR; PRWS; PTA-1; TCAP; WBLP, *abr.;* WhBS
Robert of Sicily, brother of Pope Urbane. King Robert of Sicily [*or* The Sicilian's Tale]. Longfellow. *Fr.* Tales of a Wayside Inn. AnNE; BeLS; CoV; MW; OHIP; OnSP; PCD; PCN; PFE; PTA-1; TCAP; YT
Robert Rowley rolled a round roll 'round. Mother Goose. OxNR; StVeCh
Robert, Second Duke of Normandy, *sel.* Thomas Lodge.
Pluck the Fruit and Taste the Pleasure. ElL; EV-1
(Carpe Diem.) OBSC
Robert Whitmore. Frank Marshall Davis. PoNe
Robes loosely flowing, and aspect as free. Seeing Her Dancing. Sir Robert Heath. OBS; SeEP
Robin, The. Laurence Alma-Tadema. BoTP; GFA; OTPC (1946 ed.)
Robin, The. O. M. Bent. BoTP
Robin, A. Robert Bridges. CMP
Robin. Robert Burns. *See* There Was a Lad.
Robin, The George Daniel. OBS; UnPo (1st ed.)
Robin, A. Walter de la Mare. ChMo; ChTr; CMP
Robin, The. Emily Dickinson. BLA; HBVY; NLK; WhBS
Robin. Anne Blackwell Payne. GFA
Robin, The. Jones Very. AnNE; APW
Robin-a-bobbin. *Unknown.* OxNR
Robin-a-Thrush. *Unknown.* PreP
Robin Adair. Lady Caroline Keppel. BCEP; FaBoBe; HBV; LPS-1; OIF
Robin and a robin's son, A. *Unknown.* OxNR
Robin and Gandelyn. *Unknown.* *See* Robyn and Gandeleyn.
Robin and Makin [*or* Makyne]. Robert Henryson. *See* Robene and Makyne.
Robin and Richard [*or* Richard and Robin] were two pretty [*or* little] men. Mother Goose. BoTP; OTPC (1946 ed.); OxBoLi; OxNR; RIS; SAS
Robin and the Cows, The. William Dean Howells. GoTP
Robin and the red-breast, The. A Rule for Birds' Nesters. *Unknown.* DD; HBV; HBVY; OTPC; OxNR
Robin and the Wren, The. *Unknown.* OxNR; PIAE
(Four Birds.) ChTr
Robin chants when the thrush is dumb, The. To-Morrow. Florence Earle Coates. AA
Robin dwelt in greenë wood. The Death of Robin Hood. *Unknown.* EnSB
Robin Friend has gone to bed. Bed-Time. Laurence Alma-Tadema. BoTP
Robin Goodfellow ("From Oberon, in fairy land"). *Unknown, wr. at. to* Ben Jonson. EV-2; FaBoCh; HOAH, *abr.;* ViBoPo
(Mad Merry Pranks of Robin Good-Fellow, The.) SeCL, *abr.;* SeEP
Robin Goodfellow, His Mad Prankes and Merry Jestes, *sels.* *Unknown.*
And Can the Physician Make Sick Men Well, *fr.* Pt. II. AtBAP
(Lily, Germander, and Sops-in-Wine.) AnFE
(Song: "And can the physician make sick men well?") ElL; LoBV; ThWaDe
Robin Good-Fellow's Song: "Round about, little ones," *fr.* Pt. II. ElL
Robin has flown away up in a tree, A. A May Basket. Lilian Bayne West. GFA
Robin he's gane to the wast. The Wife Wrapt in Wether's Skin (B *vers.*). *Unknown.* ESPB
Robin Hood. Keats. AWP; BEL; BPN; EM-2; EmBrPo; EnLi-2; EnLit; EnRP; EPN; EV-4; GEPC; InPo; OTPC (1946 ed.); PCD; PCN
Robin Hood. W. J. Linton. BHV
Robin Hood. Rachel MacAndrew. BoTP
Robin Hood, *wr. title.* John O'Keeffe. *See* Merry Sherwood.
Robin Hood. Patience Adrian Ross. PCH
Robin Hood/ Has gone to the wood. *Unknown.* OxNR
Robin Hood and Allen [*or* Allan *or* Alan *or* Allin]-a-Dale. *Unknown.* BaBo; BoChLi; CG; EnLit; ESPB; EV-2; FaBoBe; GoTP; HBV; LoEn; LPS-2; MCCG; MoShBr; OBB; OnSP; PYM; StVeCh (1940 ed.); TyEnPo
Robin Hood and Guy of Gisborne. *Unknown.* ATP (1935 ed.); BaBo; BEL; CoBE; EM-1; EPP; ESPB; OAEP; OBB, *sl. diff., abr.;* PFE; TOP
Robin Hood and Little John. *Unknown.* BaBo (A *and* B *vers.*); BHV; OTPC (1946 ed.); StaSt; StVeCh; ViBoFo
Robin Hood and Maid Marian. *Unknown.* BaBo; ESPB
Robin Hood and Queen Katherine. *Unknown.* BaBo; ESPB (A *and* B *vers.*)
Robin Hood and the Beggar, I ("Come light and listen, you gentlemen all"). *Unknown.* BaBo; ESPB
Robin Hood and the Beggar, II ("Lyth and listen, gentlemen"). *Unknown.* BaBo; ESPB
Robin Hood and the Bishop of Hereford. *Unknown.* BaBo; CG; ESPB; OBB
(Robin Hood and the Bishop, *sl. diff.*) BaBo; ESPB
Robin Hood and the Butcher. *Unknown.* ESPB (A *and* B *vers.*); OBB; REAL; RG
Robin Hood and the Curtal Friar. *Unknown.* BaBo; EM-1; ESPB (A *and* B *vers.*); EV-2; OBB
Robin Hood and the Golden Arrow. *Unknown.* ESPB
Robin Hood and the Grey Friars. Thomas Love Peacock. *Fr.* Maid Marian. EV-4
Robin Hood and the Monk. *Unknown.* BaBo; ESPB; MeEV, *tr. fr. Middle English;* OBB; TCEP; ViBoFo
"In somer [*or* summer], when the shawes be sheyne," *first* 5 *sts.* ViBoPo
(In Summer.) CH
(In the Fair Forest, *first* 2 *sts., mod.*) BoTP
(May in the Green-Wood.) OBEV
(Morning of May, A, *mod.*) PoLi
(Whitsuntide.) CBOV
Robin Hood and the Pedlars. *Unknown.* ESPB
Robin Hood and the Pinder of Wakefield. *Unknown.* *See* Jolly Pinder of Wakefield, The.
Robin Hood and the Potter. *Unknown.* BaBo; ESPB
Robin Hood and the Prince of Aragon. *Unknown.* ESPB
Robin Hood and the Ranger. *Unknown.* ESPB; StVeCh
Robin Hood and the Scotchman (A *and* B *vers.*) *Unknown.* ESPB
Robin Hood and the Shepherd. *Unknown.* ESPB
Robin Hood and the Tanner. *Unknown.* BaBo; ESPB; MaC
Robin Hood and the Three Squires. *Unknown.* *See* Robin Hood and the Widow's Three Sons.
Robin Hood and the Tinker. *Unknown.* BaBo; ESPB
Robin Hood and the Valiant Knight. *Unknown.* ESPB
Robin Hood and the Widow's Three Sons. *Unknown.* EV-2; OBB
(How Robin Hood Rescued the Widow's Sons.) StPo
(Robin Hood and the Three Squires.) EnSB
(Robin Hood and the Widow's Sons.) GoTP
(Robin Hood Rescuing the Widow's Three Sons.) EnLi-1; TiPo (1952 ed.)
(Robin Hood Rescuing Three Squires.) ESPB (A *and* B *vers.*); ViBoFo
Robin Hood hee was and a tall young man. Robin Hood's Progress to Nottingham *Unknown.* BaBo; ESPB
Robin Hood Newly Revived. *Unknown.* BaBo; ESPB
Robin Hood Rescuing Three Squires [*or* the Widow's Three Sons]. *Unknown.* *See* Robin Hood and the Widow's Three Sons.
Robin Hood Rescuing Will Stutly. *Unknown.* BaBo; ESPB
Robin Hood, Robin Hood,/ In the mickle wood! Mother Goose. BoTP; OTPC; OxNR
"Robin Hood, Robin Hood,"/ Said Little John. Robin Hood and Little John. Mother Goose. PCH
Robin Hood's Birth, Breeding, Valor, and Marriage. *Unknown.* ESPB
Robin Hood's Chase. *Unknown.* BaBo; ESPB
Robin Hood's Death. *Unknown.* BaBo; EM-1; ESPB (A *and* B *vers.*); TrGrPo; ViBoFo
(Death of Robin Hood, The.) EnSB; OBB; OnSP
Death of Robin Hood: "I never hurt maid," *last* 3 *sts.* ViBoPo
Robin Hood's Delight. *Unknown.* ESPB
Robin Hood's End. *Unknown.* A Gest of Robyn Hode, Fytte VIII. GoTL
Robin Hood's Golden Prize. *Unknown.* BaBo; ESPB; OBB
Robin Hood's Progress to Nottingham. *Unknown.* BaBo; ESPB
Robin in the Rain, The. Charles Coke Woods. POT
Robin in Winter, The. William Cowper. *Fr.* The Task, VI. RO
Robin is a lovely lad. The Dance. *Unknown, at. to* Thomas Campion. ElL; ElSeCe; FaBoCh; LiTL; LoBV; LoGBV
Robin is a mendicant, The. Lauds. Leonard Mahoney. SaFP

Robin is the one, The. The Robin. Emily Dickinson. BLA; HBVY; NLK; WhBS
Robin Knows Great A. *Unknown. See* Come Hither, Little Puppy-Dog.
Robin laughed in the orange tree, The. Tampa Robins. Sidney Lanier. PoRL
Robin of the Red Breast, The. *Unknown.* PoMS
Robin on da Fence. Edith Himstedt. CAG
Robin on my lawn, The. February. Francis Brett Young. HBMV; HBVY; LBBV; PoTo
Robin Redbreast. William Allingham. BoChLi; CBPC; CG; DD; EV-5; FaBoBe; HBV; HBVY; MoShBr; MPB; OTPC; PEDC; PRWS; TVC; TVSH
(Child's Song, A.) UTS
Robin Redbreast, A, *much abr.* Blake. *Fr.* Auguries of Innocence. SiSoSe; UTS
(Auguries, *much abr.*) MuP
(Our Lesser Kindred, *abr.*) BCEP
("Robin redbreast in a cage, A," *sl. abr.*) OxBoLi
(Things to Remember, *br. sel.*) RIS
(Three Things to Remember, *br. sel.*) BLA; CBPC; FaPON; MoShBr; OTPC (1946 ed.); PCD
Robin Redbreast. George Washington Doane. AA; DD; HBV; HBVY
Robin Redbreast. John Banister Tabb. StJW
Robin Red Breast. Lula Lowe Weeden. CDC
Robin redbreast in a cage, A. A Robin Redbreast [*or* Auguries *or* Three Things to Remember *or* Our Lesser Kindred]. Blake. *Fr.* Auguries of Innocence. BCEP; BLA; CBPC; FaPON; MoShBr; MuP; OTPC (1946 ed.); OxBoLi; PCD; RIS; SiSoSe; UTS
Robin Redbreasts, The. Ann Hawkshaw. OTPC (1923 ed.); SAS
(I'll Try.) PPL
Robin rents a tree-top house. Honest Mr. Robin. Eleanor Hammond. GFA
Robin sang sweetly/ In the Autumn days. *Unknown.* BoTP
Robin [*or* Robene] sat on gude green hill. Robene [*or* Robin] and Makyne [*or* Makin]. Robert Henryson. BSV; EBSV; GoTS; OAEP; OBEV; PoEL-1
Robin, sing to the rainbow! Sing-Time. Rose Waldo. GFA
Robin sings in the elm, The. The Robin and the Cows. William Dean Howells. GoTP
Robin sings of willow-buds, The. Bird Song. Laura E. Richards. HBV
Robin skimmed into the room, A. The Bird in the Room. Rudolph Chambers Lehmann. HBMV; HBVY
Robin Song. Elisabeth Scollard. BLA
Robin the Bobbin. *Unknown.* BoN; OxNR
Robin to His Mate, The. Ann A. G. Carter. OTPC (1923 ed.); PPL; SAS
Robin was a rovin boy. There Was a Lad. Burns. EBSV
Robinets and Jenny Wrens. *Unknown.* OxNR
Robin's Come. William W. Caldwell. DD, *abr.;* HBVY; SN
Robin's Cross. George Darley. OnYI
Robin's Egg, The. Annie Charlotte Dalton. CaP; CPG; OCL
Robin's egg blue and mother of pearl. The Confluence. "John Crichton." CPG
Robin's Grave, The. Samuel Rogers. *See* Epitaph on a Robin Redbreast, An.
Robins in the treetop. Marjorie's Almanac. Thomas Bailey Aldrich. FaPON; GFA; MPB; PRWS; RAR
Robin's on the wing again, The; I hear the call o' spring. The Wander Lure. Kendall Banning. NLK
Robins sang in England. Robin's Song. Rodney Bennett. BoTP
Robin's Secret. Katharine Lee Bates. AA
Robin's Song. Rodney Bennett. BoTP
Robin's Song, The. *Unknown, at. to* C. Lovat Fraser. BoTP; MoShBr
Robin's Song. E. L. M. King. TiPo
Robinson, *sel.* Maria Louise Weissmann, *tr. fr. German by* Elizabeth Selden.
Robinson Finds Friday. BoFr
Robinson Crusoe Returns to Amsterdam. Francis Jammes, *tr. fr. French by* Jethro Bithell. *Fr.* Amsterdam. FaPON
Robinson Crusoe's Story. Charles Edward Carryl. *Fr.* Davy and the Goblin, *ch.* 11. BeLS; BoChLi; BOHV; FiBHP; InMe; LEAP; MCCG; OnPP; OTPC (1946 ed.); PCD; PCN; PoRA; PoRh; TSW; TSWC
(Robinson Crusoe.) AA; HBV; HBVY; LHV; MPB
Robinson Finds Friday. Maria Louise Weissmann, *tr. fr. German by* Elizabeth Selden. *Fr.* Robinson. BoFr
Robyn and Gandeleyn. *Unknown.* BaBo; ESPB; OBB
(Robin and Gandelyn.) EnSB
Rock, The, *sels.* T. S. Eliot.
"And now you live dispersed on ribbon roads." TiPo
Eagle Soars in the Summit of Heaven, The, *fr.* Chorus I. NAMP; OBMV; OnHM; QS; TwCV
(Knowledge without Wisdom.) MaRV
"I have known two worlds." OxBoCh
"If humility and purity be not in the heart." TiPo
"In the beginning God created the world," *fr.* Chorus VII. OxBoCh
"It is hard for those who have never known persecution," Chorus VI. LiTM; QS
Men Who Turn from God, *fr.* Chorus III. MaRV
"O Light Invisible, we praise Thee!" *fr.* Chorus X. OxBoCh; TrPWD; TwCV
There Shall Always Be the Church. MaRV
When the Church Is No Longer Regarded, *fr.* Chorus VII. MaRV
"Word of the Lord came unto me, The," *fr.* Chorus III. LiTB
"World turns and the world changes, The." TiPo
"You have seen the house built, you have seen it adorned," Chorus X. QS
Rock, The. Hovhannes Hovhannessian, *tr. fr. Armenian by* Zabelle C. Boyajian. ArmLP
Rock, *sel.* Kathleen Raine.
"There is stone in me that knows stone." ImOP
Rock, The. *Unknown, tr. fr. Welsh.* ChTr
Rock and Hawk. Robinson Jeffers. MoVE; OxBA
Rock away, passenger, in the Third Class. *Unknown.* CenHV
Rock, Ball, Fiddle. *Unknown.* CH; OxBoLi
("He that lies at the stock.") OxNR; SiTL
Rock, Be My Dream. MacKnight Black. NP
Rock Carving. Douglas Stewart. NeLNL; SeCePo
Rock Constancy. Aurelian Townsend. *See* Though Regions far Divided.
Rock Crumbles, The. Else Lasker-Schüler, *tr. fr. German by* Ralph Manheim. TrJP
Rock-like mud unfroze a little and rills, The. The Manor Farm. Edward Thomas. EV-5; ExPo; HaMV; NP; SeCeV
Rock-like the souls of men. Men Fade like Rocks. W. J. Turner. OBMV; POTE
Rock-Lily's Pale Spray, The. Roland Robinson. BoAV
Rock Me to Sleep. Elizabeth Akers Allen. AA; BLPA; DD, *abr.;* FaBoBe; FaFP; LPS-1; MOAH; MotAn; NeHB; OBAV; PTA-1; TreF; WBLP
Rock of Ages. Augustus Montague Toplady. BLRP; FaFP; HBV; MaRV; NeHB; OIF; OTPC; OxBoCh; TOP; TreF; WGRP
(Prayer, Living and Dying, A.) CEP; OBEC
"Rock of Ages." *Unknown, at. to* E. Maud Moore *and to* Edward H. Rice. LPS-2; PEOR
Rock of Cashel, The. Sir Aubrey De Vere. IrPN; TIP
Rock of My Salvation. Mordecai ben Isaac, *tr. fr. Hebrew by* Solomon Solis-Cohen. TrJP
Rock of Rubies, The. Robert Herrick. InMe
(Julia.) OTPC (1923 ed.)
(Rubies and Pearls.) HBV
Rock there is whose homely front, A. The Primrose of the Rock. Wordsworth. BPN
Rock well my cradle. Rewards and Punishments—English. *Unknown.* BOL
Rock-a-by, baby up in a tree. The Tree Buds. Kate L. Brown. BOL; TVC; TVSH
"Rock-a-by, baby, up in the tree-top!" In the Tree-Top. Lucy Larcom. BOL
Rock-a-by, hush-a-by, little papoose. Indian Lullaby. Charles A. Myall. BOL; MPB; RAR
Rock-a-by Lady, The. Eugene Field. BoChLi; BOL; BoTP; HBVY; MPB; PCH; RIS; TiPo
Rockaby, Lullaby. Josiah Gilbert Holland. *See* Lullaby: "Rockaby, lullaby, bees in the clover."
Rockaby, rockaby. Sleepy-Time. Ellen V. Talbot. BOL
Rock-a-by, rock-a-by, little brown baby. An Indian Lullaby. *Unknown.* BOL; RAR
"Rock-a-bye, baby, in the tree-top." American Cradle Song. Robert J. Burdette. BOL
Rock-a-bye, baby, on the tree top! *See* Hush-a-bye, baby, on the tree top.
Rock-a-bye [*or* Hush-a-bye], baby, thy cradle is green. Mother Goose. BOL; BoTP; FaFP; HBVY; OTPC; OxNR; PCH; PPL; RIS; SAS
Rock-a-bye Song, A. Helen Wing. GFA
Rocked in the Cradle of the Deep. Emma Hart Willard. AA; BAV; BPP; FaBoBe; FaFP; HBV; LEAP; OBAV; OIF; TreF; WBLP; WGRP
(Cradle of the Deep, The.) MaRV
Rocket Show. James K. Baxter. AnNZ
Rocket was as sleek as any ship, The. Extraordinary Visit. Vincent Starrett. DaM
Rockets bubble upward and explode, The. 14 July 1956. L. D. Lerner. BoSA
Rockferns. Norman Nicholson. MoBrPo (1950 ed.); NeMA
Rocking. *Unknown, tr. fr. Czech carol.* ChrBoLe
Rocking Chair, The. A. M. Klein. CaP; PeCV
Rocking Hymn, A. George Wither. *Fr.* Hallelujah. AnEC; BOL
(Hymn L: Rocking Hymn, A.) SeCV-1
(Lullaby, A: "Sweet baby, sleep; what ails my dear.") EV-1, *abr.;* OxBoCh, *abr.* [*wr. at. to* William Austin]
Rocks flow and the mountain shapes flow, The. The Songs of the Birds. Edward Carpenter. WGRP

Rocks in de Mountens. *Unknown. See* My Old Hammah.
Rocks of my country! let the cloud. The Cliffs of Dover. Felicia Dorothea Hemans. DiM
Rocky Acres. Robert Graves. LiTB; UnPo (3d ed.)
Rocky Landscape. Mary Chandler. *Fr.* The Description of Bath. BeR
Rocky Mountain Sheep, The. Mary Austin. MPB
Rocky nook with [*or* and] hilltops three, The. Boston. Emerson. BoHiPo, 4 *ll.*; MC; PAP
Rococo. John Payne. OBVV
Rococo. Swinburne. HBV; PIR; ViBoPo
Rod, The. Robert Herrick. LiTB
Rod of Jesse, The. Isaiah XI: 1–10, Bible, *O.T.* AWP; OuHeWo, XI: 1–9, LIII: 10–12
(And There Shall Come Forth, XI: 1–9.) TrJP
Rodeo Days. S. Omar Barker. PoOW
Rodeo Parade. Berta Hart Nance. *Fr.* Arizona Nights. HiLiAm
Roderick Dhu [and Fitz-James]. Sir Walter Scott. *See* Fitz-James and Roderick Dhu.
Rodney's Glory. Owen Roe O'Sullivan. OnYI
Rodney's Ride. Elbridge Streeter Brooks. GA; MC; OTPC; PAH
Roe (and my joy to name) th'art now, to go. To William Roe. Ben Jonson. OBS
Roger and Dolly. Henry Carey. CoMu
("Young Roger came tapping at Dolly's window," *st.* 1, *sl. diff.*) OxNR
Roger Francis. Wilfrid Thorley. BrR
Roger Williams. Hezekiah Butterworth. PAH
Rogero heard the call in joyous vein. Ariosto. *Fr.* Orlando Furioso, XXXVI. PrPoCR
Rogue, The. Aristophanes, *tr. fr. Greek by* Arthur S. Way. *Fr.* The Frogs. LiA
Roisin Dubh. Aubrey Thomas De Vere. AnIV
Roisin Dubh. *Unknown. See* Dark Rosaleen.
Roistering gypsy went away, The. Ballad of Federico García Lorca. Luis Cardoza y Aragón. AnCL
Rokeby, *sels.* Sir Walter Scott.
Allen-a-Dale, *fr.* III. BCEP; BPN; EmBrPo; EnRP; ERP; OTPC (1946 ed.); TOP; TVSH
Ballad: "And whither would you lead me then?" *fr.* V. ERP
Brignal[l] Banks, *fr.* III. BCEP; BEL; BPN; EBSV; EmBrPo; EnRP; EPN; ERP; OBEV; PCN; TOP; TyEnPo
(Edmund's Song.) EnLi-2
(Outlaw, The.) GTBS; GTBS-D; GTBS-W; GTSE; GTSL; LH; OtMeF
(Song: Brignall Banks.) EV-4
(Song: "O Brignall banks are wild and fair.") HBV; OAEP; OBRV
Cypress Wreath, The, *fr.* V. ERP
Man the Enemy of Man, *fr.* III. WBLP
Song: Cavalier, The, *fr.* V. EV-4
(Cavalier, The.) TVSH
Song: Harp, The, *fr.* V. EV-4
Song: "Weary lot is thine, fair maid, A." EV-4; OBRV; ViBoPo
(Rover, The.) GTSE; GTSL
(Rover's Adieu, The.) EBSV; HBV; OBEV
(Rover's Farewell, The.) PoE
(Weary Lot Is Thine, A.) BSV; CH; EG; EmBrPo
Roland. Napoléon Peyrat, *pr. tr. fr. French by* A. W. Evans. LiA
Roll a river wide and strong. The Flag. "M. W. S." FOAH
Roll a Rock Down. Henry Herbert Knibbs. AnAmPo; PFY
Roll and Go. *Unknown.* SG
Roll-Call. Nathaniel Graham Shepherd. AA; BBV (1923 ed.); DD; HBV; MDAH; OHIP; PaA; PTA-2
Roll de Ol' Chariot Along, *with music. Unknown.* BoAN-1
Roll forth, my song, like the rushing river. The Nameless One. James Clarence Mangan. ACP; BCEP; CBOV; EnRP; EPN; EV-4; GoBC; GTBS; GTIV; GTSE; HBV; IrPN; OBEV; OnYI; OxBI; TIP
Roll, Jordan, Roll. *Unknown.* AA; BoAN-1, *with music;* OIF
Roll, *Julia,* Roll, *with music. Unknown.* ShS
(Row, Bullies, Row, *diff. vers., with music.*) SoAmSa
Roll of a chariot, The. *Unknown. Fr.* The Combat of Ferdiad and Cuchulain. OnYI
Roll on, and with thy rolling crust. One in the Infinite. George Francis Savage-Armstrong. PC; VA
Roll on, roll on, you restless waves. The Waves on the Sea-Shore. Ann Hawkshaw. OTPC (1923 ed.)
Roll On, Sad World! Frederick Goddard Tuckerman. AnNE; TreFS
Roll on, thick haze, roll on! Ode to a London Fog. *Unknown.* PA
Roll on, thou ball, roll on! To the Terrestrial Globe. W. S. Gilbert. BMEP; BOHV; HBV; LEAP; LiTG; LPS-3; MBP; PoeMoYo; SiTL; TrGrPo; WhC
Roll on, thou deep and dark blue ocean—roll! The Ocean [*or* Address to the Ocean]. Byron. *Fr.* Childe Harold's Pilgrimage, IV. AtBAP; BCEP; BLV; BoLiVe; CoEV; EtS; FaPON; GDAH; GN; PIAE; PYM; TreFS; TrGrPo; UnPo (1st ed.); WBLP; WGRP
Roll on, ye stars! exult in youthful prime. Immortal Nature. Erasmus Darwin. *Fr.* The Botanic Garden: The Economy of Vegetation. OBEC
Roll Out, O Song. Frank Sewall. AA
Roll out ye drums, peal organs' loudest thunder. Elegy on Albert Edward the Peacemaker. *Unknown.* CoMu
"Roll out!" yell cookee. The Lumberyak. William F. Kirk. IHA
Roll the Chariot. *Unknown. See* We'll Roll the Golden Chariot Along.
Roll the Cotton Down. *Unknown.* SG; ShS, 3 *vers., with music;* SoAmSa, *with music*
Rolled Over on Europe. Stephen Spender. ChMo
Roller Skates. John Farrar. FaPON; GFA
Rollicking Bill the Sailor. *Unknown.* AmSS
Rollicking Mastodon, The. Arthur Macy. BOHV; NA
Rollicking Robin is here again. Sir Robin. Lucy Larcom. BoChLi; MeMeAg; MPB; OTPC (1946 ed.); TiPo (1952 ed.)
Rollin and Me. Charles Ballard. DDA
Rolling clouds of greasy smoke. The Forest Fire. Arthur W. Monroe. PoOW
Rolling Down to Old Maui. *Unknown.* SoAmSa
Rolling English Road, The. G. K. Chesterton. FaBoCh; HBMV; LoGBV; OBEV (new ed.); OBMV; OtMeF; SeCeV; ShBV-2; TCPD
(Before the Roman Came to Rye.) GTBS
Rolling Home, *with music. Unknown.* AmSS; ShS, 2 *vers.*
Rolling King, *with music. Unknown.* SoAmSa
(South Australia, *with music.*) ShS
Rolling wave is on thy shore, Jerseyland, The. Ode to New Jersey. Elias F. Carr. PoRL
Rolling wheel that runneth often round, The. Amoretti, XVIII. Spenser. PeBoSo; TwHP
Roly! poly! pudding and pie! The Tale of a Tart. Frederic E. Weatherly. SUS
Rom. Cap. 8. Ver. 19. Henry Vaughan. *See* And Do They So?
Roma Mater Sempaeterna. Shaemas O'Sheel. JKCP
Roman, The, *sel.* Sydney Dobell.
Monk's Song. BMEP
Roman and Jew upon one level lie. In Galilee. Mary Frances Butts. AA
Roman, A, had an/ artist, a freedman. The Jerboa. Marianne Moore. AtBAP; MoPo
Roman de la Rose. Guillaume de Lorris *and* Jean de Meun. *See* Romance of the Rose, The.
Roman Elegy. Hildebert of Lavardin, *pr. tr. fr. Latin.* LiA
Roman Father's Sacrifice, The. Macaulay. *Fr.* Lays of Ancient Rome: Virginia. LPS-3
Roman Fountain. Rainer Maria Rilke, *tr. fr. German by* David Luke. AnGP
Roman host descended from the height, A. Mater Amabilis. Aubrey Thomas De Vere. ISi
Roman Lady, The. *Unknown. See* Romish Lady, The.
Roman Legions, The. John Mitford. VA
Roman Lullaby. *Unknown, ad. by* Louis Untermeyer. RIS
Roman Matron to Her Husband, A. Propertius, *tr. fr. Latin by* James Cranstoun. Elegies, IV, 11. RoL
Roman Mirror, A. Sir Rennell Rodd. OBVV; VA
Roman Nose Rides. John G. Neihardt. *Fr.* The Song of the Indian Wars. TCPD
Roman Officer Writes Home, A. C. M. Doughty. *Fr.* The Dawn in Britain. FaBoTw
Roman Road, The. Thomas Hardy. AWP; InPo; MBP; MoBrPo
Roman Road, The. Rachel Annand Taylor. EBSV
Roman Road runs straight and bare, The. The Roman Road. Thomas Hardy. AWP; MBP; MoBrPo
Roman soldiers come ridin' at full speed. The Man of Calvary. "Sin Killer" Griffin. OuSiCo
Roman Virgil [*or* Vergil], thou that singest Ilion's lofty temples robed in fire. To Virgil [*or* Vergil]. Tennyson. BPN; ChTr; EM-1; EmBrPo; EPN; GEPC; GTML; InP; InPo; PoEL-5; PoFS; PoVP; PtP; TCEP; ViPo; ViPP; VLEP; WHA
Romance. Mavis Clare Barnett. BAP
Romance. Samuel Taylor Coleridge. *See* Kubla Khan.
Romance. Anton Delvieg, *tr. fr. Russian by* C. M. Bowra. BoRS
Romance. W. E. Henley. In Hospital, XXI. EnLit; MC; PAH; POTT
Romance. Karen Hildebrandt, *tr. fr. Danish by* Charles W. Stork. BoDS
Romance. Mildred Howells. AA
Romance. Jules Laforgue, *tr. fr. French by* William Jay Smith. AnFP
Romance. Andrew Lang. BSV; HBV; PCD; VA
Romance. Scudder Middleton. SBMV
Romance. Poe. AmPP; AnAmPo; AnFE; APA; APW; AtBAP; ATP; BLV; BoLiVe; CoAnAm; CoV; FaBoEn; IAP; LA; MOAP; NePA; OxBA; PoE; RO; SPP

Romance. "Gabriel Setoun." BoTP; OTPC; PRWS
Romance. Robert Louis Stevenson. EBSV; EV-5; GoTS; GTSL; HBV; LBBV; LEAP; LiTL; LoPo; LoPS; MBP; MoBrPo; NeMA; OBEV; OBVV; OtMeF; PoeMoYo; PoFS; PoRA; RG; TrGrPo
(I Will Make You Brooches.) CP; PoE; PoeT; POTT; PoVP; WP
(My Valentine, *st.* 1.) FaPON; MPB; PoRL; SiSoSe
(Roadside Fire, The.) GTSE
(Song of a Traveller, The.) BoTP
Romance. Walter James Turner. AlDL; BMEP; CH; HBMV; HBVY; LBBV; LiTM; MBP; MoBrPo; OBMV; PoMS; PoRA; POTE; PtOT; ShBV-1; TCPD; ThWaDe; TrGrPo; TwCV; VOD (1935 ed.); WHA; WP
Romance. *Unknown.* DDA
Romance beside his unstrung lute. Realism. Thomas Bailey Aldrich. AnNE
Romance VIII. St. John of the Cross, *tr. fr. Spanish by* E. Allison Peers. ISi
Romance of a Christmas Card, The. Kate Douglas Wiggin. MaRV
(Christmas Eve.) OQP; QP-2
Romance of Nick Van Stann, The. John Godfrey Saxe. PTA-2
Romance of the Carpet, The. Robert J. Burdette. BOHV
Romance of the Living Corpse. Enrique González Martínez, *tr. fr. Spanish by* Samuel Beckett. AnMP
Romance of the Range. Robert V. Carr. PoOW
Romance of the Rose, The, *sels.* Guillaume de Lorris *and* Jean de Meun, *tr. fr. French.*
"Briddes that han left their song, The," *tr. by* Chaucer. EG
Dream of the Romaunt of the Rose, The. Guillaume de Lorris, *tr. by* Chaucer. LoBV
Garden of Amour, The. Guillaume de Lorris, *tr. by* Chaucer. PoEL-1
Love vs. Marriage, *fr.* LII. Jean de Meun, *tr. by* Bernard D. N. Grebanier. EnLi-1
"Right many times with hand assured," *fr.* III. Guillaume de Lorris, *tr. by* Bernard D. N. Grebanier. EnLi-1
Table Manners for the Hostess, *fr.* LXXIII. Jean de Meun, *tr. by* Bernard D. N. Grebanier. EnLi-1
"Well I looked upon each face," *fr.* II. Guillaume de Lorris, *tr. by* Bernard D. N. Grebanier. EnLi-1
"Zeuxis, the painter, strove in vain." Jean de Meun, *tr. by* F. S. Ellis. WoL
Romance of the Swan's Nest, The. Elizabeth Barrett Browning. BPN; CG, *abr.*; GN; LPS-1; OTPC, *abr.*
Romance, who loves to nod and sing. Romance. Poe. AmPP; AnAmPo; AnFE; APA; APW; AtBAP; ATP; BLV; BoLiVe; CoAnAm; CoV; FaBoEn; IAP; LA; MOAP; NePA; OxBA; PoE; RO; SPP
Romancer, far more coy than that coy sex! Hawthorne. Amos Bronson Alcott. AA
Romans, *sels.* Bible, *N.T.*
Duties of Man, The, XII: 3-21. TreF
Living Sacrifice, A, XII. *Tr. by* Edgar J. Goodspeed. GrCo-1
Romans first with Julius Caesar came, The. The English Race. Daniel Defoe. *Fr.* The True-born Englishman, I. OBEC
Romans, rheumatic, gouty, came. La Condition Botanique. Anthony Hecht. NePoEA
Romantic, The. Louise Bogan. NP
Romantic, The. "Sagittarius" (Olga Katzin). DiM
Romantic Fool. Harold Monro. TCPD
Romantic subject of the Great White Queen. The Explorer. William Plomer. BoSA
Romantic to Burlesque. Byron. *See* Author's Purpose, The.
Romany Girl, The. Emerson. BAV; CoBA; TCAP
Romany Gold. Amelia Josephine Burr. HBMV
Romany Lullaby, A. Edith De Charms. BOL
Romanza of the Guitarrist. Raúl Otero Reiche, *tr. fr. Spanish by* Rolfe Humphries. AnCL
Romanzo to Sylvia. George Darley. *See* Song: "I've taught thee love's sweet lesson o'er."
Romaunt of Humpty Dumpty, The. Henry S. Leigh. BOHV
Romaunt of the Rose. Austin Dobson. LPS-1
Romaunt of the Rose, The. Guillaume de Lorris *and* Jean de Meun. *See* Romance of the Rose, The.
Rome. Byron. *Fr.* Childe Harold's Pilgrimage, IV. BEL; EPP, *abr.*; MaPo; ShBV-3; TCEP, *abr.*
("Oh Rome! my country! City of the soul!") InP
(On Rome.) ERP
(Rome and Freedom.) EPN
(Ruins of Rome, The, *abr.*) CBOV
Rome. Arthur Hugh Clough. Amours de Voyage, Canto I, ii. BPN
("Rome disappoints me still.") EPN
Rome. Joachim du Bellay, *tr. fr. French by* Ezra Pound. Ruins of Rome, I. AWP; JAWP; WBP; LiTW, *tr. by* Spenser
Rome. Thomas Hardy. EmBrPo; EnLi-2; MoAB
Rome. Marcelino Menéndez y Pelayo, *tr. fr. Spanish by* Roderick Gill. CAW
Rome. Milton. *Fr.* Paradise Regained, IV. OBS
Rome. Ianus Vitalis Panormitanus, *tr. fr. Latin by* J. V. Cunningham. LaP
Rome. Samuel Rogers. *Fr.* Italy. LPS-2
Rome. *Unknown, tr. fr. Greek by* R. A. Knox. OxBG
Rome a Greek City. Juvenal, *tr. fr. Latin by* William Gifford. *Fr.* Satires, III. RoL
Rome and Freedom. Byron. *See* Rome.
Rome did its worst; thorns platted for his brow. Praetorium Scene; Good Friday. Elinor Lennen. PGD
Rome disappoints me still; but I shrink and adapt myself to it. Rome. Arthur Hugh Clough. *Fr.* Amours de Voyage, I. BPN; EPN
Rome, from thy queenly walls lest glory die. Rome. *Unknown.* OxBG
Rome had her Roscius and her theater. In Ed. Allen. John Weever. ReIE
Rome had its Caesar, great and brave; but stain was on his wreath. Washington. Eliza Cook. WOAH
Rome in Her Ruins. Francisco de Quevedo y Villegas, *tr. fr. Spanish by* Felicia Dorothea Hemans. AnSpL-1; TeCS
Rome Is Fallen, I Hear. Arthur Hugh Clough. Amours de Voyage, Canto V, vi. BEL
(Sceptic Moods.) BPN
Rome Remember. Sidney Keyes. MoAB; PoN
Rome still holds her rod of power. Nazareth. Thomas Curtis Clark. ChIP
Rome Unvisited, *sel.* Oscar Wilde.
"And yet what joy it were for me." VLEP
Romeo and Juliet, *parody.* Fred Newton Scott. InMe
Romeo and Juliet, *sels.* Shakespeare.
Come Night, Come Romeo, *fr.* III, ii. LiTL
Everlasting Rest, *fr.* V, iii. WHA
"O here/ Will I set up my everlasting rest," 7 *ll.* EtPaEn
Romeo's Last Words. FiP
("How oft when men are at the point of death.") AtBAP; NBE
Thus with a Kiss I Die. TrGrPo
(Here Lies Juliet.) FaFP; TreFS
With a Kiss I Die. LiTL
Friar Laurence's Cell, II, vi. GoBC
He Jests at Scars [That Never Felt a Wound], *fr.* II, ii. LiTB; LiTG; LiTL
(Balcony Scene, The.) TreF
(Living Juliet, The.) TrGrPo
Juliet's Yearning, *fr.* III, ii. TreFS
Music's Silver Sound, *fr.* IV, v. GN; HH
"O Romeo, Romeo, wherefore art thou Romeo!" *fr.* II, ii. WHA
Queen Mab, *fr.* I, iv. BCEP, *abr.*; CG, *abr.*; EV-1; FaPON; FiP; GoTP; HOAH, *abr.*; LPS-3; MPB; OTPC, *abr.*; PC, *abr.*; PoFS
(From "Romeo and Juliet.") LEAP
(Mercutio Describes Queen Mab.) TrGrPo
(Mercutio's Queen Mab Speech.) LiTB; TreF
(Queene Mab.) BoW
(Shakespeare Gallery, A: Queen Mab.) MaC
"Soft, what light through yonder window breaks," *fr.* II, ii.
(Shakespeare Gallery, A: Juliet.) MaC
"Wilt thou be gone? It is not yet near day," *fr.* III, v. LoPS
Romeo's Last Words. Shakespeare. *Fr.* Romeo and Juliet, V, iii. FiP
("How oft when men are at the point of death.") AtBAP; NBE
Rome's guns are spiked; and they'll stay so. Of Rome. Herman Melville. *Fr.* Clarel. OxBA
Romira, stay. The Call. John Hall. AEV; FaBoEn; LO; MeLP; MePo; OBS; SeCL; ViBoPo
Romish Lady, The, *with music. Unknown.* OuSiCo
(Death of a Romish Lady, The.) ABS
Romney, The. Harriet Monroe. HBMV
Romney and Aurora. Elizabeth Barrett Browning. *Fr.* Aurora Leigh, IX. VA
Romney, expert infallibly to trace. Sonnet to George Romney. William Cowper. BoFr
Rondeau: "By Jove, 'tis done with me, for Isabeau." Vincent Voiture, *tr. fr. French by* Henry Carrington. LiA
Rondeau: "Help me to seek, for I lost it there." Sir Thomas Wyatt. *See* Help Me to Seek.
Rondeau: "Homage to change that scatters the poppy seed." Ronald Bottrall. MoVE
Rondeau: "Jenny kissed me when we met." Leigh Hunt. *See* Jenny Kissed Me.
Rondeau: "Land-locked I lie, in idleness." Theodora Bates. CAG
Rondeau: "Lord, I'm done for: now Margot." William Jay Smith, *after* Vincent Voiture. FiBHP
Rondeau: "Thou fool! if madness be so rife." Charles Cotton. SeCL
Rondeau: Well, The. Charles d'Orléans, *tr. fr. French by* Barbara Howes. LyMA
Rondeau: "What? No, perdie [*or* perdy]! ye may be sure." Sir Thomas Wyatt. ElSeCe; LoBV; OBSC

Rondeau: "White as a lily, redder than a rose." Guillaume de Machault, *tr. fr. French by* Ralph N. Currey. FoS
Rondeau: "Year his winter cloak lets fall, The." Charles d'Orléans. *See* Spring.
Rondeau, The: "You bid me try, Blue-Eyes, to write." Austin Dobson, *after* Vincent Voiture. BOHV; HBV
(You Bid Me Try.) BPN; PoVP
Rondeau, The: "Your rondeau's tale must still be light." Don Marquis. PFE
Rondeau Humbly Inscribed to the Right Hon. William Eden, Minister Plenipotentiary of Commercial Affairs at the Court of Versailles. *At. to* George Ellis. OBEC
Rondeau in Wartime. James Bertram. AnNZ
Rondeau of Remorse, A. Burges Johnson. HBMV
Rondeau of Spring. Charles d'Orléans, *tr. fr. French by* W. E. Henley. LyMA
Rondeau Redoublé. John Payne. *See* My Day and Night.
Rondeau to Ethel, A. Austin Dobson. VA
(In Teacup Times.) PFE
Rondel: "As we look at these gay flowers." Charles d'Orléans, *tr. fr. French by* Ralph N. Currey. FoS
Rondel: "Death, I denounce thy cruelty." Villon, *tr. fr. French by* Alan Conder. TrFP
Rondel: "First day of the month of May, The." Charles d'Orléans, *tr. fr. French by* Ralph N. Currey. FoS
Rondel: "Good-by, the tears are in my eyes." Villon, *tr. fr. French by* Andrew Lang. AWP; JAWP; WBP
Rondel: "Grant him eternal rest, poor wight!" Villon, *tr. fr. French by* Alan Conder. TrFP
Rondel: "Greet all the company for me." Charles d'Orléans, *tr. fr. French by* Ralph N. Currey. FoS
Rondel: "Heart, thou must learn to do without." George Macdonald. BSV
Rondel: "If I'm at church these days." Christine de Pisan, *tr. fr. French by* Ralph N. Currey. FoS
Rondel: "It's dark, child, snatcher of sparks!" Tristan Corbière, *tr. fr. French by* Kate Flores. AnFP
Rondel: "Johnny of the Avenue." Villon, *tr. fr. French by* Alan Conder. TrFP
Rondel: "Kissing her hair, I sat against her feet." Swinburne. BMEP; BPN; FaBoBe; HBV; MBP; Po; PoVP; ViBoPo; ViPP
(Kissing Her Hair.) LPS-1; PIR
Rondel: "Now welcome, somer, with thy sunne softe." Chaucer. *See* Roundel, A: "Now welcom, somer . . ."
Rondel: "Stephen Le Gout, in the nominative." Charles d'Orléans, *tr. fr. French by* Ralph N. Currey. FoS
Rondel: "Strengthen, my Love, this castle of my heart." Charles d'Orléans. *See* Rondel to His Mistress.
Rondel: "Summer has sent his stewards on." Charles d'Orléans, *tr. fr. French by* Ralph N. Currey. FoS
Rondel: "These many years since we began to be." Swinburne. HBV; PIR
Rondel: To His Mistress, to Succor His Heart. Jean Froissart, *tr. fr. French by* Longfellow. AWP
Rondel: "Winter, you're nothing but a lout." Charles d'Orléans, *tr. fr. French by* Ralph N. Currey. FoS
Rondel: "Year has put his cloak away, The." Charles d'Orléans. *See* Spring.
Rondel for Middle Age. Louise Townsend Nicholl. NePoAm
Rondel for September. Karle Wilson Baker. HBMV; PoTo; VOD
Rondel of Love, A. Alexander Scott. BSV; EBSV; OBEV
Rondel of Merciles Beautè, A. Chaucer. *See* Merciles Beaute.
Rondel; the Wanderer. Austin Dobson. *See* Wanderer, The.
Rondel to His Mistress. Charles d'Orléans, *tr. fr. French by* Andrew Lang. LyMA
(Rondel: "Strengthen, my Love, this castle of my heart.") AWP
Rondelay: "Chloe found Amyntas lying." Dryden. ElSeCe; MaPo; SeCL; ViBoPo
(Roundelay.) ALV; SeEP
Rondelay, A: "Man is for woman made." Peter Anthony Motteux. BOHV
Rondo: "Did I love thee? I only did desire." George Moore. LoPS
Ronsard. Miriam Allen deFord. HBMV
Ronsard. Andrew Lang. PtP
Ronsard and Hélène. Humbert Wolfe. PtP
Ronsard to His Mistress. Thackeray. HBV
Rood is my name. Once long ago I bore. Brussels Cross Inscription. *Unknown.* InP
Roof is high and arched and blue, The. The Green Inn. Theodosia Garrison. HBMV; NLK
Roof it has a lazy time, The. The Lazy Roof. Gelett Burgess. BOHV; NA; RIS
Roof of midnight, hushed and high, The. Nocturnal. Os Marron. NeBP
Roof-Tops. Charles Hanson Towne. *See* City Roofs.
Roof Whirled Away by Winds, The. Tu Fu, *tr. fr. Chinese.* WhP
Roofed o'er by the blue of the near-bending sky. Dr. John Goodfellow—Office Upstairs. James Ball Naylor. DDA
Roofs. Witter Bynner. TCAP
Roofs. Joyce Kilmer. VOD
Roofs are shining from the rain, The. April. Sara Teasdale. FaPON; GFA; OTPC (1946 ed.); PCH; StVeCh; TiPo; TSW; YeAr
Rook Sits High, The. Eliza Cook. BLA
Rookery, The. Charles Tennyson Turner. VA
Rookhope Ryde. *Unknown.* ESPB
Rookie's Lament, A, *with music. Unknown.* ABF
Rooks. Charles Hamilton Sorley. BLA; HBMV; MBP; MoBrPo
Rooks are alive, The. What the Weather Does. Hamish Hendry. BoTP
Rooks are cawing up and down the trees, The. Nests in Elms. "Michael Field." BLA
Rooks' nests do rock on the tree-top, The. Lullaby. William Barnes. BOL
Rooks; New College Gardens. Louise Imogen Guiney. BLA
Room, The. Conrad Aiken. LiTG; LiTM (rev. ed.); MAP; MAPA; MoAmPo; MOAP; NePA
Room, The. Louis Ginsberg. UnW
Room, The. Francis Jammes, *tr. fr. French by* Alan Conder. TrFP
Room above the Square, The. Stephen Spender. ChMo; ChMP
Room after room. Love in a Life. Robert Browning. BMEP; BPN; EM-2; EmBrPo; EPN; GEPC; HBV; InvP; LiTL; OAEP; OBVV; PoVP; TOP; VLEP
Room after room, table after table. Public Library. Candace T. Stevenson. GoYe
Room and the Windows, The. Feng Chih, *tr. fr. Chinese by* Chu K'an. LiTW
Room dark and tight, The. Vestiges. Denis Devlin. OnHM
Room for a Jovial Tinker; Old Brass to Mend. *Unknown.* CoMu
Room for a soldier! lay him in the clover. Dirge: For One Who Fell in Battle. Thomas William Parsons. AA; APW; GN; HBV; LBAP; OBAV; PaA; PAH
Room for all else but love. Nor House nor Heart. Elinor Lennen. PGD
Room for Him! Room! Mary Artemisia Lathbury. *See* Song of Hope.
"Room for the leper! Room!" and as he came. The Leper. Nathaniel Parker Willis. LPS-2; StJW; WGRP
Room I Once Knew, A. Henry Birnbaum. GoYe
Room is open to the turquoise sky, The. Young Couple. Arthur Rimbaud. AnFP
Room is prepared, the incense burned, The. The Southern Room over the River. Su T'ung-po. OnPC
Room of peering shadows holds her fast, The. Sonnet of Departure. J. R. Hervey. AnNZ
Room, room for a Blade of the Town. The Bully [*or* Song]. *At. to* the Earl of Rochester *and to* Thomas D'Urfey. BeR; InvP; SeCePo; SeCL
Room! room! [*or* Roome, roome,] make room for the bouncing belly. Hymn to Comus [*or* Hymn to the Belly]. Ben Jonson. *Fr.* Pleasure Reconciled to Virtue. ElL; OAEP; SeCePo; SeEP; SiTL
Room! room to turn round in, to breathe and be free. Kit Carson's Ride. Joaquin Miller. AmPP (3d ed.); HiLiAm; IAP; TreFS
Room under Bombardment. Phyllis Allfrey. NeTW
Room was low and small and kind, The. Bible Stories. Lizette Woodworth Reese. BrR; MoSiPe; MPB; StJW; TSW; TSWC
Room was suddenly rich and the great bay-window was, The. Snow. Louis MacNeice. ExPo; GTBS-W; LiTM; ReMP
Roome make roome you that are fled. *Unknown.* SeCSL
Roome, roome, make roome for the bouncing bellie. *See* Room! room! . . .
Rooming-House Melancholy. Eric Kästner, *tr. fr. German by* Howard Hugo. LiTW
Room's Width, The. Elizabeth Stuart Phelps Ward. AA
Roosevelt. Samuel Valentine Cole. *See* Theodore Roosevelt.
Roosevelt. Robert H. Davis. GA; HH; PEDC
Roosevelt. Peter Fandel. PEDC
Roosevelt. T. E. Thomas. PEDC
Roosevelt and the *Antinoe*, The. E. J. Pratt. HeT
Burial at Sea, *sel.* CaP; TwCV
Roosevelt—Pilot and Prophet! Charles Hanson Towne. *See* Pilot and Prophet!
Roosevelt's in the White House, doing his best. The White House Blues. *Unknown.* OuSiCo
Rooster her sign. At the Sign of the Cock. Sir Owen Seaman. BOHV; PA
Roosters. Elizabeth Bishop. CrMA; FiMAP; LiTM; NePA; OnHM
Roosters. Boris Pasternak, *tr. fr. Russian by* Babette Deutsch. TrRV
Rooster's crowed, de big bell's rung, De. The Crown of Power. John Charles McNeill. NoCaPo
Root, The. Francis Maguire. JKCP (1926 ed.)
Root Cellar. Theodore Roethke. FiMAP

Root Hog or Die, *parody.* Floyd B. Small. PoOW
Root Hog or Die ("When I was a young man I lived on the square"). *Unknown. See* Bad Boy, The.
Rooting in packing case of/ dirty straw. Digdog. Ruth Pitter. AnFE
Roots. Louis Ginsberg. TrJP
Roots. Harold Telemaque. PoNe
Roots and Leaves Themselves Alone. Walt Whitman. NePA
Roots Go Down. Lloyd Frankenberg. AnEnPo
Ropero, El ("Ropero, so sad and so forlorn"). Antonio de Montoro, *tr. fr. Spanish.* TrJP
Ropin' of yearlin's and tyin' 'em down. Rodeo Days. S. Omar Barker. PoOW
Rorate Coeli Desuper. William Dunbar. BSV; CBOV; EBSV
(On the Nativity of Christ.) OBEV; OxBoCh
Rory of the Hill. Charles Joseph Kickham. OnYI; TIP
Rory O'More; or, Good Omens. Samuel Lover. BOHV; HBV; LPS-1; TIP; VA
Rosa, *with music. Unknown, tr. fr. Dutch.* TrAS
Rosa Mystica. Gerard Manley Hopkins. ACP; GoBC
Rosa Mystica. Denis A. McCarthy. JKCP
Rosa Mystica. *Unknown.* CAW; GoBC; ISi; PoLi
("There is no rose of such virtu[e].") AnEC; EG
(Two Carols to Our Lady, 2.) ACP
Rosa Nascosa. Maurice Hewlett. OBVV
Rosa Rosarum. Agnes Mary Frances Robinson. HBMV; VA
Rosabelle. Sir Walter Scott. *Fr.* The Lay of the Last Minstrel, VI. BeLS; BSV; CG; EBSV; GTBS; GTBS-D; GTBS-W; GTSE; GTSL; HBV; OTPC
(Dirge of Lovely Rosabelle, The.) EV-4
(Harold's Song [to Rosabelle].) EmBrPo; EnLi-2; ERP
(Harold's Song: Rosabelle.) EnRP
(Lay of Rosabelle, The.) EPP
Rosader's Sonnet ("In sorrow's cell"). Thomas Lodge. *Fr.* Rosalynde; or, Euphues' Golden Legacy. EPP; ReIE
Rosader's Sonnet ("Turn I my looks"). Thomas Lodge. *Fr.* Rosalynde; or, Euphues' Golden Legacy. OBSC
(Rosader's Second Sonetto.) EPP
Rosaders Sonnet, Sent to Rosalynde ("Two sunnes at once"). Thomas Lodge. *Fr.* Rosalynde; or, Euphues' Golden Legacy. BrBE
Rosalie. Washington Allston. AA; LPS-1
Rosalind. Hubert Church. BoAu
Rosalind. Thomas Lodge. *See* Rosalynde: Rosaline.
Rosalind has come to town! Rosalind. Hubert Church. BoAu
Rosalind; or, Euphues' Golden Legacy. Thomas Lodge. *See* Rosalynde; or, Euphues' Golden Legacy.
Rosalind's Scroll. Elizabeth Barrett Browning. *Fr.* The Poet's Vow. HBV; OBEV (1st ed.)
Rosalynde; or, Euphues' Golden Legacy, *sels.* Thomas Lodge.
Blith and Bonny Country Lass, A. ALV
(Corydon's Song.) ReIE
Contents of the Scedule Which Sir John of Bordeaux Gave to His Sons, The. ReIE; SiCE
Fancy, A. ElL; LoBV; OBSC
("First shall the heavens want starry light.") SiCE
(Lover's Protestation, A.) GoBC
(Love's Protestation.) ACP
"Phoebe sat,/ Sweet she sat." SiCE
(Montanus' Sonnet.) AtBAP; PoEL-2; TuPP
Rosader's Sonnet ("In sorrow's cell"). EPP; ReIE
Rosader's Sonnet, Sent to Rosalynde ("Two sunnes at once"). BrBE
Rosalind's Madrigal. ALV; BEL; BLV; CoBE; ElL; ElSeCe; EM-1; EnLit; EPP; GoBC; HBV; InvP; LEAP; LoBV; OBEV; OBSC; SeCePo; SiCE; TCEP; TOP; TuPP; ViBoPo
(Love in My Bosom like a Bee.) EG; LiTG; LiTL
(Rosalindes Madrigall.) FaBoEn
(Rosalind's Complaint.) LPS-1
(Rosalynde.) PoEL-2
(Rosalynde's Madrigall.) AtBAP; BrBE; EV-1; PoEL-2; ReIE; TrGrPo
(Rosalynd's Madrigal.) GTSL
Rosaline. BLV; GoBC; GTSE; GTSL; LiTB; LiTG; LO; LPS-1; OBEV
(Rosalind.) ElL
(Rosalind's Description.) ElSeCe; OBSC
(Rosalynde.) GTBS; GTBS-D; GTBS-W; TrGrPo
(Rosalynde's Description.) EV-1
Sonetto: "Of all chaste birds the phoenix doth excel." ReIE; SiCE
(Of Rosalind.) GoBC
(Of Rosalynd.) PoLi
"Turn I my looks unto the skies." SiCE
(Rosader's Sonnet.) OBSC
(Rosader's Second Sonetto.) EPP; TuPP
Rosamond, *sel.* Swinburne.
Rosamond at Woodstock. VA
Rosamond's Appeal. Samuel Daniel. *Fr.* The Complaint of Rosamond. OBSC
Rosamunde. Guillaume Apollinaire, *tr. fr. French by* Alan Conder. TrFP
Rosarie, The. Robert Herrick. *See* Rosary, The.
Rosario d'Arabeschi; Poems and Rose Portraits. Sacheverell Sitwell. POTE (1959 ed.)
Belle Isis; Ballad of a Rose, I.
O Rose with Two Hearts, II.
Rosary, The. Robert Herrick. EPS (1942 ed.)
(Rosarie, The.) InMe
Rosary, The, *abr.* Sister Maura. ISi
Rosary, The. Robert Cameron Rogers. AA; BPP; FaBoBe; HBV; LBMV; LEAP; TreF; WBLP
Rosary of My Tears, The. Abram J. Ryan. HBV; LPS-3
Rosary Songs, *sels.* Georg Trakl, *tr. fr. German by* Kate Flores. AnGP
Amen.
Nearness of Death.
To Sister.
Rosciad, The, *sel.* Charles Churchill.
Critical Fribble, A. OBEC
(Criticaster, A.) FaBoEn
Rose, The. "Angelus Silesius," *tr. fr. German by* Thomas Walsh. CAW
Rose, The. Ariosto, *tr. fr. Italian by* John Hoole. *Fr.* Orlando Furioso, I. LiA
Rose, A. Arlo Bates. HBV; PR
Rose, The. William Browne. Visions, V. CH; ES; EV-2; HBV; OBEV; OTPC (1923 ed.)
("Rose, as fair as ever saw the north, A.") CenL; ViBoPo
(Vision, A.) SeCL; SeEP
Rose, The. William Cowper. LPS-2
Rose, The. Isabella Valancy Crawford. BMEP; CPG
Rose, A. Sir Richard Fanshawe, *after* Luis de Góngora. *Fr.* Il Pastor Fido (*after* Guarini). ES; HBV; OBEV; OBS; PoEL-2; SeCePo; SeCL; SeEP; TeCS
(Rose of Life, The.) AWP
Rose, The. Goethe, *tr. fr. German by* Andrew Lang. AWP; JAWP; WBP
Rose, The. Gudmundur Gudmundsson, *tr. fr. Icelandic by* Jakobina Johnson. IcP
Rose, The. William Hammond. OBS
Rose, The. George Herbert. AtBAP; LiTB; PoEL-2
Rose, The. Thomas Howell. ElL; OBSC; PrWP; ReIE; TuPP
(Red Rose, The.) ElSeCe
Rose, The. Thomas Lodge. *Fr.* The Life and Death of William Longbeard. OBSC
(Fancy, A.) ElL
Rose, The. Richard Lovelace. EG; EPS (1942 ed.); EV-2; HBV; SeCL; ViBoPo
(To Lucasta: The Rose.) SeCV-1
Rose, The. Sigbjörn Obstfelder, *tr. fr. Norwegian by* Charles W. Stork. AnNoLy
Rose, The. Kathleen Raine. DiM
Rose, The. Pierre de Ronsard, *tr. fr. French by* Andrew Lang. AWP; JAWP; WBP
(Ode: "See, Mignonne, hath not the rose.") LiA
Rose, The. G. A. Studdert-Kennedy. MaRV
Rose. Swinburne. YT
Rose, The. Bayard Taylor. *Fr.* Hassan Ben Khaled. LPS-2
Rose. Lewis Thompson. AtBAP
Rose, The. Humbert Wolfe. MBP; MoBrPo; NP
Rose, The,/ 'Tis the rose I love. The Rose. Sigbjörn Obstfelder. AnNoLy
Rose Adair. Malachy Ryan. TIP
Rose aloft in sunny air, The. Rose and Root. John James Piatt. AA
Rose and amber was the sunset on the river. The Syrian Lover in Exile Remembers Thee, Light of My Land. Ajan Syrian. LiTL; NP
Rose and God, The. Charles Wharton Stork. HBMV
Rose and Root. John James Piatt. AA
Rose and the Gardener, The. Austin Dobson. *See* Fancy from Fontenelle, A.
Rose and the Gauntlet, The. "Christopher North." BeLS; LPS-3
Rose and the lily, the moon and the dove, The. Die Rose, die Lilie, die Taube, die Sonne. Heine. AWP; JAWP; WBP
Rose and the Ring, The, *sel.* Thackeray.
Betsinda's Bun. BoN
Rose and the Thorn, The. Paul Hamilton Hayne. AA; TCAP
(Rose and Thorn, The.) FaBoBe; HBV
Rose and the Wind, The. Philip Bourke Marston. OBVV; VA
Rose, as fair as ever saw the north, A. The Rose [*or* A Vision]. William Browne. *Fr.* Visions. CenL; CH; ES; EV-2; HBV; OBEV; OTPC (1923 ed.); SeCL; SeEP; ViBoPo
Rose Aylmer. Walter Savage Landor. AEV; AnFE; AWP; BCEP; BEL; BLV; BoLiVe; BPN; CBOV; CH; EmBrPo; EnLi-2; EnRP; EPN; EPP; ERP; EtPaEn; EV-4; ExPo; FaBoEn; FaFP; GTBS; GTBS-D;

Rose Aylmer (*continued*) GTBS-W; GTML; GTSL; HBV; HoPM; InP; InPo; JAWP; LEAP; LiTB; LiTG; LiTL; LO; LoBV; LoPo; LoPS; OAEP; OBEV; OBRV; OBVV; OTPC (1923 ed.); PIAE; PoE; PoEL-4; PreP; RiBV; SeCeV; TCEP; TOP; TreFS; TrGrPo; TyEnPo; UnPo; VA; WBP; WHA; WoL; WP
(Ah! What Avails the Sceptred Race.) CaAE; EG; EnLoPo; ViBoPo
Rose Aylmer's Hair, Given by Her Sister. Walter Savage Landor. BPN; TriL; VA
Rose Bloom. Hafiz, *tr. fr. Persian by* Gertrude Bell. PeP
Rose-bosom'd and rose-limb'd. The Evening Sky. John Freeman. MM; TwCV
Rose-Bud. *See* Rosebud.
Rose-Bush. *See* Rosebush.
Rose, A, but one, none other rose had I. Worm within a Rose. Tennyson. *Fr.* Idylls of the King: Pelleas and Ettarre. PoEL-5; VLEP
Rose-cheeked [*or* cheek'd *or* cheekt] Laura [Come]. Thomas Campion. AtBAP; BLV; EnL; EnLoPo; ExPo; InPo; InvP; LoBV; OAEP; PoE; PoEL-2; ReaPo; ReEn; RiBV; SeCeV; SiCE; TrGrPo; TuPP; TyEnPo; ViBoPo
(Laura.) AnFE; EIL; EV-2; GTSE; OBEV; OBSC; SeCePo; UnS
(Song: "Rose-cheekt Laura, come.") BrBE
Rose, die Lilie, die Taube, die Sonne, Die. Heine, *tr. fr. German by* Richard Garnett. AWP; JAWP; WBP
(Rose, the Fair Lily, the Dove, and the Sunlight, The, *tr. by* Howard E. Gugo.) AnGP
Rose Family, The. Robert Frost. PR
Rose for a young head, A. The Watcher. James Stephens. HBV; MBP; MoBrPo; OBEV (new ed.); OBVV
Rose Found in a Greek Dictionary, A. Edmund Wilson. CAG
Rose-Fragrance. Kostes Palamas, *tr. fr. Modern Greek by* Rae Dalven. *Fr.* City and Solitude. MoGP
Rose. Fresh and Fair. *Unknown, tr. fr. Spanish by* George Ticknor. AnSpL-1
Rose-Girl, The. Dionysius the Sophist, *tr. fr. Greek by* F. L. Lucas. GrPE
Rose had been washed, just washed in a shower, The. The Rose. William Cowper. LPS-2
Rose, harsh rose. Sea Rose. Hilda Doolittle ("H. D."). ChMo; CMP; FaBoMo
Rose has flushed red, the bud has burst, The. Rose Bloom. Hafiz. PeP
Rose in Jericho, A. Christina Rossetti. MeRV
Rose in October, The. Mary Townley. SN
Rose in the breast. On Waking. Alida Carey Gulick. GoYe
Rose in the garden slipped her bud, The. A Fancy from Fontenelle [*or* The Rose and the Gardener]. Austin Dobson. BLP; BMEP; HBV; MPB; OBVV; POTT
"Rose is a mystery, The"—where is it found? Rosa Mystica. Gerard Manley Hopkins. ACP; GoBC
Rose is a rose, The. The Rose Family. Robert Frost. PR
Rose Is a Royal Lady, The. Charles G. Blanden. HBMV
Rose is fairest when 'tis budding new, The. Sir Walter Scott. *Fr.* The Lady of the Lake. ViBoPo
Rose is made of little frills, The. Somebody's Garden. Margaret Steele Anderson. DD
Rose Is Not the Rose, The. Hafiz, *tr. fr. Persian by* Richard Le Gallienne. *Fr.* Odes. LiTW
("Rose is not the rose, unless thou see, The.") AWP
Rose is red, The. *See* Roses are red.
Rose is red, the grass is green, The. *Unknown.* OxNR
Rose is red, the rose is white, The. *Unknown.* OxNR
Rose is red, the violet blue, The/ The gillyflower sweet, and so are you. Easter Gloves. *Unknown.* PCH; SiTL
Rose is red, the violet's blue, The/ The honey's sweet, and so are you. *Unknown.* OxNR
Rose is sleeping beside the marjoram, The. *Unknown, tr. fr. Greek by* Sir James Rennell Rodd. BOL
Rose is the fairest flower of all, The. The Rose of Ryse. *Unknown.* AnEC
Rose is weeping for her love, The. Helen's Song. Philip James Bailey. *Fr.* Festus. VA
"Rose, it is a royal flower, The." The Peace of the Roses. Thomas Philipps. ACP
Rose kissed me to-day. A Kiss. Austin Dobson. *Fr.* Rose-Leaves. ALV; BPN; CBOV; CenHV; EnLit; HBV; InP; MBP; MoBrPo (1942 ed.); PoVP
Rose-Leaves. Austin Dobson. CenHV; PoVP; VLEP
Sels.
Circe. BPN
(To Rose.) PFE
Greek Gift, A. BPN; MBP; MoBrPo (1942 ed.)
Kiss, A. ALV; BPN; CBOV; EnLit; HBV; InP; MBP; MoBrPo (1942 ed.)
Tear, A. BPN
"Urceus Exit." ATP (1935 ed.); BPN; GTSL; HBV; MBP; MoBrPo (1942 ed.); PreP; TCEP; TOP
(I Intended an Ode.) OBEV; PIAE
(Triolet.) BMEP; LEAP
Rose, like dim battlements, the hills and reared. Macbeth. Walter de la Mare. TCEP
Rose Looks Fair, The. Shakespeare. *See* Sonnets, LIV.
Rose looks out in the valley, The. The Nightingale. Gil Vicente. LPS-2
Rose of Eden, The. Susan K. Phillips. BeLS
Rose of England, The. *Unknown.* ESPB
Rose of Flame, The. "Fiona Macleod." PoVP
Rose of Life, The. Sir Richard Fanshawe. *See* Rose, A.
Rose of Love, The. Nossis, *tr. fr. Greek by* F. L. Lucas. GrPE
Rose of May, The. Mary Howitt. HBV
Rose of Peace, The. W. B. Yeats. OBVV
Rose of Roses, The. Adam Oehlenschläger, *tr. fr. Danish by* Charles W. Stork. BoDS
Rose of Ryse, The. *Unknown.* AnEC
Rose of Stars, The. George Edward Woodberry. Wild Eden, IX. AA; HBV
Rose of that Garland! fairest and sweetest. To the Most Beautiful Lady, the Lady Bridget Manners. Barnabe Barnes. EnLoPo
Rose of the World, The. John Masefield. PoRA
Rose of the World, The. Coventry Patmore. The Angel in the House, I, iv, 1. HBV; LPS-1
Rose of the World, The. W. B. Yeats. BoLiVe; CBOV; ChMo; CMP; EnLi-2 (1949 ed.); EnLit; FaBoEn; HBV; MBP; MoAB; MoBrPo; OBVV; PoLFOT; PoVP; TIP; TwCV; VA; VLEP
Rose of the World, she came to my bed. The Dark Man. Nora Hopper. HBV; TIP
Rose of Tralee, The. William Pembroke Mulchinock. OnYI
Rose-Petals. Ibn al-Zaqqaq, *tr. fr. Arabic by* A. J. Arberry. MooP
Rose-red, russet-brown. A Letter to Elsa. Grace Hazard Conkling. HBMV; HBVY
Rose, round whose bed. Rose. Swinburne. YT
Rose Song, The. Gil Vicente. *See* I Come from the Rose Garden, Mother.
Rose Still Grows beyond the Wall. A. L. Frink. BLPA
Rose that here our mortal eyes behold, The. The Rose. "Angelus Silesius." CAW
Rose that leans its chin, The. Sleep. J. P. McAuley. NeLNL
Rose, the Fair Lily, the Dove, and the Sunlight, The. Heine. *See* Rose, die Lilie, die Taube, die Sonne, Die.
Rose the Red and White Lily. *Unknown.* ESPB; OBB, *abr., sl. diff.*
Rose Thou Gav'st, The. Charles Swain. VA
Rose to the Living, A. Nixon Waterman. HBV; MaRV; PoToHe
Rose to the roseburst break of day. The Cliff Rose. Ernest Fewster. CaP; OCL
Rose Tree, The. W. B. Yeats. EnLP; GTBS-D; OBMV; PoFr
Rose was given to man for this, The. The Rose. Isabella Valancy Crawford. BMEP; CPG
Rose was gone, The. When to the empty tent. Concerning the Rose and the Nightingale. Grigoris of Aghtamar. ArmLP
Rose was sick and smiling died, The. The Funeral Rites of the Rose. Robert Herrick. EV-2; OBEV
Rose, when I remember you. To Rose. Sara Teasdale. HBV
Rose when shaken fragrance shed around, The. Inscription on an Ancient Bell. *Unknown.* ISi
Rose White, Yellow, Silver. Ezra Pound. *Fr.* Phanopoeia. CoV
Rose Will Fade, A. Dora Sigerson Shorter. HBV; TIP
Rosebud, The. Hans Christian Andersen, *tr. fr. Danish by* Charles W. Stork. BoDS
Rose-Bud. The. William Broome. CEP; LoBV; OBEC; OBEV, *abr.*
Rosebud, A. Burns. OTPC
Rosebud firm and round and rare. The Rosebud. Hans Christian Andersen. BoDS
Rosebud that grew by the settle, The. The Gossips. Nathalia Crane. MAP
Rosebush. Hermann Claudius, *tr. fr. German by* Herman Salinger. TwGV
Rose-Bush, The. *Unknown, tr. fr. German by* William W. Caldwell. LPS-3
Rosebush and the Trinity, The. Alfred Barrett. GoBC
Rose bushes lean against the wall. The Convent Garden. Marie Kirkwood. PraNu
Rose-Marie. Zakarias Topelius, *tr. fr. Swedish by* Charles W. Stork. AnSL
Rose-Marie of the Angels. Adelaide Crapsey. HBV
Rosemary nods upon the grave, The. Poe. *Fr.* The Sleeper. PoD
Rosemary, Rosemary. A Sad Song. Stephen Vincent Benét. NV
Rosemary Spray, The. Luis de Góngora, *tr. fr. Spanish by* Edward Churton. AnSpL-1; AWP; LiTW
Rosen the Bow. *Unknown.* *See* Rosin the Bow.
Roses. Al-Ghassani, *tr. fr. Arabic by* A. J. Arberry. MooP

Roses. Thomas Campion. *Fr.* Lord Hay's Mask. OBSC
(Now Hath Flora Robbed Her Bowers.) EV-2
Roses. "George Eliot." BoTP
Roses. Dorothy Choate Herriman. CPG
Roses. John Masefield. *See* Roses Are Beauty.
Roses. J. Corson Miller. CAW
Roses. Pierre de Ronsard, *tr. fr. French by* Andrew Lang. AWP; JAWP; WBP; FoS, *abr., tr. by* Ralph N. Currey; LiTW, *tr. by* Vernon Watkins; TrFP, *tr. by* Alan Conder
("I send to you a nosegay that but now," *tr. by* Curtis Hidden Page.) PrPoCR
Roses. Thomas Stanley, *after the Greek of* Anacreon. AWP
Roses. *Unknown.* PEOR
Roses and butterflies snared on a fan. A Painted Fan. Louise Chandler Moulton. AA
Roses and gold. Places. Carl Sandburg. NP
Roses and Lilies. William Diaper. *Fr.* Nereides; or, Sea-Eclogues. BeR
Roses and lilies grow above the place. Life Hidden. Christina Rossetti. VLEP
Roses and lilies have wilted away. Regret. Benedikt Gröndal. IcP
Roses and pinks will be strewn where you go. Song. Sir William Davenant. *Fr.* The Unfortunate Lovers. ViBoPo
Roses and Rain. Archibald T. Strong. BoAu
Roses Are Beauty. John Masefield. *Fr.* Sonnets ("Long, long ago"). TOP
(Roses.) ES
("Roses are beauty, but I never see.") EnLi-2 (1949 ed.); HBV; TCPD
Roses are blossoming. Joy and Sorrow. Sadi. PeP
Roses are dead, The. Les Roses Mortes. Rosamund Marriott Watson. PFE
Roses are red [*or* The rose is red]. Mother Goose. OxNR; RIS; StVeCh
Roses are red,/ Violets are blue,/ What you need. *Unknown.* SiTL
Roses at first were white. How Roses Came Red. Robert Herrick. BEL; EnL; EPS (1942 ed.); TCEP; TyEnPo
Rose's bloom is short; and when it goes, The. When the Rose Is Dead. *Unknown.* OxBG
Rose's crimson stain, A. Roses of Memory. A. C. Gordon. AA
Rose's Cup, The. Frank Dempster Sherman. AA
Roses for My King. Sister Mary Madeleva. SaFP
Roses for the Flush of Youth. Christina Rossetti. *See* Song: "Oh roses for the flush of youth."
Roses from Paestan rosaries! Glories. Lionel Johnson. TriL
Roses have been his bed so long that he. Jeremiah. Witter Bynner. CrMA
Roses in December. G. A. Studdert-Kennedy. BLPA
Roses in my garden, The. Ballad. Maurice Baring. HBV
Roses in the Subway. Dana Burnet. BAP; NV; POT; PoTo
Roses (Love's delight) let's join. Roses. Thomas Stanley. AWP
Roses of Memory. A. C. Gordon. AA
Roses of Saadi [*or* Sa'adi], The. Marceline Desbordes-Valmore, *tr. fr. French.* LiTW, *tr. by* Barbara Howes; TrFP, *tr. by* Alan Conder
Roses of Saint Francis, The. Thomas S. Jones, Jr. SaFP
Roses of Thy Cheeks, The. Rafi of Merv, *tr. fr. Persian by* R. A. Nicholson. LiTW
Roses of yesteryear, The. At Twilight. Peyton Van Rensselaer. AA
Roses Only. Marianne Moore. AnFE; CoAnAm; LiTM
Roses over against your window. George Ivanov, *tr. fr. Russian by* Maud F. Jerrold. BoRS
Roses Red. Arno Holz, *tr. fr. German by* Jethro Bithell. AWP
Roses Red. *Unknown.* PCD; PCH
Roses red upon my neighbor's vine, The. My Neighbor's Roses. Abraham L. Gruber. BLPA; NeHB; OQP; PoToHe; OP-2
Rose's red, vi'let's blue. Roses Red. *Unknown.* PCD; PCH
Roses red wind themselves. Roses Red. Arno Holz. AWP
Roses, roses fresh and fair. Roses. Al-Ghassani. MooP
Roses' Song. Philip Bourke Marston. *Fr.* Garden Fairies. VA
Roses sweeter than red dates and grapes. The Beautiful Boy. *Unknown. Fr.* The Thousand and One Nights. LiTW
Roses, their sharp spines being gone. Bridal Song. Fletcher *and* Shakespeare. *Fr.* The Two Noble Kinsmen. BrBE; CBOV; CenL; EG; ElL; ElSeCe; EV-1; MyFE; OBEV; OBSC; SiCE; ViBoPo
Rosette, in this brief absence see. Villanelle. Philippe Desportes. TrFP
Rosie, *with music. Unknown.* ABF
Rosie-fingerd morne, no sooner shone, The. The Sacrifice. Homer. *Fr.* The Odyssey, III. OBS
Rosie Nell, *with music. Unknown.* AS
Rosies. Agnes I. Hanrahan. HBV
Rosin the Bow. *Unknown.* CSF
(Old Rosin, the Beau.) CoSo
(Rosen the Bow, *sl. abr.*) ABS
Rosleen. Sir Gilbert Parker. CPG
Roslin and Hawthornden. Henry van Dyke. AA
Rosny. Robert Browning. BPN
Rosses, The. "Seumas O'Sullivan." *See* Starling Lake, The.
Rostov. G. S. Fraser. LiTM (rev. ed.); WaP
Rosy Apple, Lemon or Pear. *Unknown.* CH; HH
(Wedding, A.) PCH
Rosy Bosom'd Hours, The. Coventry Patmore. EnLoPo
Rosy cloud of the dawn I see, A. Almond Blossoms. Charles Dalmon. *Fr.* Three Pictures. TSW; TSWC
Rosy clouds float overhead, The. The Sandman. "Margaret Vandegrift." BOL; HBV; HBVY; PRWS; PTA-2; TVC; TVSH
Rosy Days Are Numbered, The. Moses ibn Ezra, *tr. fr. Hebrew by* Solomon Solis-Cohen. *Fr.* Wine-Songs. TrJP
Rosy egret, sunset, The. The Old Bayou. Madison Cawein. PFY; PoeMoYo
Rosy lamp, the leaping flame, The. The Shadowed Star. Ada Foster Murray. LEAP
Rosy mouth and rosy toe, The. A Bunch of Roses. John Banister Tabb. HBVV; PRWS; SP
Rosy Musk-Mallow, The. Alice E. Gillington. VA
Rosy plum-tree, think of me. A Little Girl's Song. Hilda Conkling. NP
Rosy-Posy. Ann Augusta Carter. BOL
Rosy shield upon its back, A. The Dead Crab. Andrew Young. FaBoTw; LoBV
Rosy the water. Evening Sigh. Emil Aarestrup. BoDS
Rosy Wreath, The. Rufinus, *tr. fr. Greek by* Maurice Baring. OxBG
Rotten, heart-rotten, that is the word for you. Euripides. *Fr.* Medea. GrPo
Rotten Lake Elegy. Muriel Rukeyser. MoPo; NePA
Rotten Row. Frederick Locker-Lampson. ALV
Rou-cou spoke the dove. Song of Fixed Accord. Wallace Stevens. NePoAm
Rouge Bouquet. Joyce Kilmer. CV; DD; DDA; HBV; MC; NV; OBAV; PaA; PAH; PFY; SBMV; TreFS
Rough green wealth of wheaten fields that sway, The. Sonnet. Thomas Caulfield Irwin. IrPN
Rough old nut, A. Skipper. Cicely Fox Smith. AlDL
Rough pasture where the blackberries grow! A Pasture. Frederic Lawrence Knowles. AA
Rough Rhyme on a Rough Matter, A. Charles Kingsley. *Fr.* Yeast, *ch.* 11. BMEP; LPS-1; PIR
(Bad Squire, The.) EV-5
Rough Sea. Archilochus, *tr. fr. Greek by* C. M. Bowra. OxBG
Rough, shaggy furze. Our Dog. Janet Vaughn. PCD
Rough wind, that moanest loud. A Dirge. Shelley. BCEP; BEL; BoLiVe; BPN; CaAE; ChTr; EmBrPo; EnLi-2; EnLit; EnRP; EPN; ERP; GEPC; GTSL; MCCG; OAEP; PoFS; PoRA; PreP; RO; TCEP; TOP; TrGrPo; WHA
Roughchin, the Pirate. Arthur Boswell. EtS
Rougher than death the road I choose. The Dark Way. Joseph Mary Plunkett. LBBV
Roughly, so to say, you know. John William Mackail. *Fr.* The Masque of Balliol. CenHV
Round, A: "Hey nonny no!" *Unknown. See* Hey Nonny No!
Round, A: "Now that the spring hath filled our veins." William Browne. ElSeCe; ViBoPo
Round: "Wind takes the moon riding, The." Vicente Huidobro, *tr. fr. Spanish by* Donald Devenish Walsh. AnCL
Round: "Worlds, you must tell me." Louis Untermeyer. WhC
Round, a round, a round, boys, a round, A. Richard Brome. *Fr.* A Jovial Crew; or, The Merry Beggars. TuPP
Round about in a fair ring-a. *Unknown.* BoTP
Round about, little ones, quick, quick and nimble. Robin Good-Fellow's Song. *Unknown.* ElL
Round about Me. Sappho, *tr. fr. Greek by* William Ellery Leonard. AWP; JAWP; WBP
Round about, round about. The Elves' Dance [*or* Fairy Dances]. *Unknown, at. to* John Lyly *and to* Thomas Ravenscroft. *Fr.* The Mayde's Metamorphosis. CH; ElL; FaPON; HH; MPB; PoRh
Round about, round about, catch a wee mouse. *Unknown.* OxNR
Round about, round about, here sits the hare. *Unknown.* OxNR
Round about, round about, maggotty pie. *Unknown.* OxNR
Round about the cauldron go. Witches' Song [*or* Charm]. Shakespeare. *Fr.* Macbeth, IV, i. OnHT; SiTL
Round about the rosebush. *Unknown.* OxNR
Round about there / Sat a little hare. *Unknown.* OxNR
Round Achilles rose/ The boiling wave tremendous. Achilles and the Scamander. Homer. *Fr.* The Iliad, XXI. OxBG
Round among the quiet graves. Love's Resurrection Day. Louise Chandler Moulton. AA; HBV; LEAP

Round and Round. Dorothy Brown Thompson. ChBR
Round and round the garden. *Unknown.* OxNR
Round and round the rugged rock. *Unknown.* OxNR
Round as a biscuit. *Unknown.* RIS
Round Barrow, The. Andrew Young. SeCePo
"Round Cape Horn." *Unknown.* EtS
Round de meadows am a-ringing. Massa's in de Cold [Cold] Ground. Stephen Collins Foster. AA; APW; IHA; LEAP; OBAV; OlF; TreF
Round eye-socket holds all space, pulling, The. Star Gazer. Coleman Rosenberger. DaM
'Round Father's Grip. Strickland W. Gillilan. FAOV
Round her red garland and her golden hair. Of His Last Sight of Fiammetta [*or* Fiammetta]. Boccaccio. *Fr.* Sonnets. AWP; GoBC; JAWP; OnPM; WBP
Round-hoof'd, short-jointed, fetlocks shag and long. A Horse. Shakespeare. *Fr.* Venus and Adonis. ExPo
Round is the spacious pile; and in its heart. Tasso. *Fr.* Jerusalem Delivered, XVI. PrPoCR
Round moon hangs above the rim, The. Moment Musicale. Bliss Carman. HBMV; TCAP
Round moon hangs like a yellow lantern in the trees, The. The Ancient Thought. Watson Kerr. WGRP
'Round my Indiana homestead wave the cornfields. On the Banks of the Wabash, Far Away. Paul Dresser. PoRL
Round Number, A. Keith Douglas. NeBP
Round Our Restlessness. Elizabeth Barrett Browning. *Fr.* Rhyme of the Duchess May. MaRV
Round Quebec's embattled walls. Montgomery at Quebec. Clinton Scollard. GA; PAH
Round Robin. Bhartrihari, *tr. fr. Sanskrit by* Paul Elmer More. LiTW
Round Table, The. Layamon, *tr. fr. Middle English. Fr.* The Brut. EnLi-1, *pr. tr. by* Stith Thompson; MeEV
Round Table, The. Robert Mannyng. ACP
Round the Bay of Mexico, *with music. Unknown.* OuSiCo
Round the cape of a sudden came the sea. Parting at Morning. Robert Browning. AWP; BEL; BMEP; BPN; CaAE; EM-2; EmBrPo; EnL; EnLi-2; EnLit; EPN; EtPaEn; FaBoEn; FiP; GBV (1952 ed.); GEPC; GTML; GTSL; HBV; JAWP; LEAP; MCCG; OAEP; OBEV; OBVV; PCD; PIR; PoVP; PreP; ShBV-3; TOP; TwP; UnPo (3d ed.); VA; ViPo; ViPP; VLEP; WBP
Round the Corner, *with music. Unknown.* SoAmSa
Round the 'dobe rank sands are thickly blowing. The Deserted Adobe. *Unknown.* CSF
Round the foot of Amiata, like a bride. Dictator's Holiday. F. L. Lucas. NeTW
Round the island of Zipangu. The Mimshi Maiden. Hugh McCrae. MoAuPo; NeLNL
Round the Year. Coventry Patmore. *See* Year, The.
Round Trip, The. McLandburgh Wilson. BLP
Round Us the Wild Creatures. Robert Browning. *Fr.* Ferishtah's Fancies, I. BPN; VLEP
Roundabout Turn, A. Robert E. Charles. MoShBr
Roundabouts and Swings. Patrick R. Chalmers. PCN; PoeT; ShGoBo
Rounded Up in Glory. *Unknown.* CoSo, *with music;* CSF
Rounded world is fair to see, The. Nature. Emerson. IAP; MOAP
Roundel, A: "Now welcom, somer, with thy sonne softe." Chaucer. *Fr.* The Parlement of Foules. ATP; CBOV; EPP
(Foules Rondel, *orig., with mod. vers.* [The Birds' Rondel] *by* Louis Untermeyer.) TrGrPo
(Now Welcom[e] Somer.) SeCePo; TyEnPo
(Now Welcome Summer.) PoLi
(Qui Bien Aime à Tard Oublie.) AEV; EnLoPo
(Rondel: "Now welcome, somer . . .") LyMA
(St. Valentine Rondel, A, *mod. by* Edwin Markham.) BCEP
Roundel, The: "Roundel is wrought as a ring or a star-bright sphere, A." Swinburne. ATP (1935 ed.); BPN; EmBrPo; EPN; PIAE; PoVP; TOP; VA; VLEP
Roundel: "Your eyën two will slay me suddenly." Chaucer. *See* Merciles Beaute.
Roundel in the Rain. *Unknown.* FiBHP
Roundel of Passion-Tide. *Unknown.* CAW
Roundel of Rest, A. Arthur Symons. HBV
Roundelay: "Chloe found Amyntas lying." Dryden. *See* Rondelay: "Chloe found . . ."
Roundelay, The: "Gorbo, as thou cam'st this way." Michael Drayton. *See* Gorbo and Batte.
Roundelay, A: "It fell upon a holy eve." Spenser. *See* Perigot and Willie's Roundelay.
Roundelay: "O sing unto my roundelay." Thomas Chatterton. *See* Minstrel's Song.
Roundelay: "O Sorrow,/ Why dost borrow." Keats. *See* Song of the Indian Maid.
Roundelay, A: "Tell me, thou skilful shepherd's swain." Michael Drayton. *See* Sylvia.
Roundelay: "They are not only nightingales." Luis de Góngora. *See* Not All Sweet Nightingales.
Roundhouse, The. William Rose Benét. PoMa
Roundhouse in Cheyenne is filled every night, The. The Dreary Black Hills. *Unknown.* AS; CoSo
Rounding the Cape. Roy Campbell. BoSA
Rounding the Horn. John Masefield. *Fr.* Dauber, VI. EtS; MBP; MoAB; MoBrPo; NeMA; WHA
(Dauber Rounds Cape Horn, The.) BBV
Round-up, The. Sarah Elizabeth Howard. PoOW
Roundup Cook, The. Robert V. Carr. PoOW
Rous'd by the light from soft repose. The Poet. Christopher Smart. *Fr.* The Blockhead and Beehive. BeR
Rouse, Britons! at length. A New Ballad. *Unknown.* PAH
Rouse every generous, thoughtful mind. The Blasted Herb. Meshech Weare. PAH
Rousing Canoe Song, The. Hermia Harris Fraser, *ad. fr. Haida Indian song.* BoCaPo; CaP
Rousing to rein his pad's head back. Song. Geoffrey Taylor. NeIP; OxBI
Rousseau. Schiller, *tr. fr. German by* Sir Edward Bulwer-Lytton. PoFr
Rousseau—Voltaire—our Gibbon—and De Staël. Sonnet to Lake Leman. Byron. BPN
Roustabout Holler, *with music. Unknown.* OuSiCo
Roustabout Moon, The. Dorothy Marie Davis. DDA
Rout of Belgravia, The. "Jon Duan." PA
Rout of San Romano, The. Jon Manchip White. NePoEA
Route March. Charles Hamilton Sorley. *See* All the Hills and Vales Along.
Route of evanescence, A. Emily Dickinson. AmP; AmPP; PoE; PoEL-5
(Humming Bird, The.) AmPo; CoBA; GoTP; NeMA
Routine trickery of the examination, The. Examiner. F. R. Scott. TwCaPo
Rover, The. Sir Walter Scott. *See* Weary Lot Is Thine, A.
Rovers, The, *sel.* George Canning, George Ellis, *and* John Hookham Frere.
Song: "Whene'er with haggard eyes I view," *fr.* I. ALV; OBEC
(Song by Rogero the Captive.) CEP; TOP
(Song of One Eleven Years in Prison.) BOHV; FiBHP
Rover's Adieu, The. Sir Walter Scott. *See* Weary Lot Is Thine, A.
Rover's Apology, The. W. S. Gilbert. *Fr.* Trial by Jury. ALV
Rover's Farewell, The. Sir Walter Scott. *See* Weary Lot Is Thine, A.
Roving Alley-Cat, A. Mary Cockburn Bomke. CIV
Roving breezes come and go, The. On Kiley's Run. Andrew Barton Paterson. BoAu
Roving Gambler, The. *Unknown.* ABF; AS; TrAS, *with music*
(Gamboling Man, The, *diff. vers.*) AS
(Yonder Comes My Pretty Little Girl, *diff. vers.*) AS
Roving god, whose playfellows. To Dionysus. Anacreon. GrL; LiTW; OxBG
Roving Rebel, The. D. F. Lemarr. BlG
Roving Worker, The. *Unknown, tr. fr. Modern Irish by* George Sigerson. OnYI
Row after row with strict impunity. Ode to the Confederate Dead. Allen Tate. AnFE; ATP (1953 ed.); CoAnAm; FaBoMo; InPo; LiTA; LiTM; MAP; MoAB; MoAmPo; MOAP; MoPo; MoVE; NP; OxBA; ReMP; SeCeV; SPP; TwAmPo; UnPo; ViBoPo (1958 ed.)
Row, Bullies, Row. *Unknown. See* Roll, *Julia,* Roll.
Row-diddy, dow de, my little sis. Grampy Sings a Song. Holman F. Day. BOHV
Row Gently Here. Thomas Moore. HBV
"Row me o'er the strait, Douglas Gordon." Douglas Gordon. Frederic Edward Weatherly. VA
Row, row, Manoli. Swing Song. *Unknown.* PCH
Row till the land dip 'neath. Rower's Chant. T. Sturge Moore. PoeT; PtOT; SG
Row us out from Desenzano, to your Sirmione row! "Frater Ave atque Vale." Tennyson. BPN; ChTr; EM-2; EmBrPo; EPN; GEPC; GTML; PoVP; PtP; TCEP; ViPo; VLEP
Row Weel, My Boatie. *Unknown.* EBSV
Rowan County Crew, The, *with music. Unknown.* OuSiCo
Rowan Tree, The. Lady Nairne. HBV
Rowdy Soul, *with music. Unknown.* StDa
Rowers, The. Laura Benét. GoYe
Rower's Chant. T. Sturge Moore. PoeT; PtOT; SG
Rowers now are rowing. Song of the Three Angels. Gil Vicente. *Fr.* The Auto of the Bark of Purgatory. CAW
Rowing at Night on the West Lake. Su T'ung-po, *tr. fr. Chinese.* WhP
Rowing, I reach'd a rock—the sea was low. Gerard Manley Hopkins. *Fr.* A Vision of the Mermaids. ChTr
Rowland's Rhyme. Michael Drayton. *Fr.* The Shepherd's Garland, Eclogue II. OBSC
Rowley Powley. *Unknown.* OTPC
Rows of cells are unroofed, The. The Old Prison. Judith Wright. NeLNL

Roxbury Garden, A, *abr.* Amy Lowell. LaNeLa
Roxie, Roxie, if you were mine. O Lawd, I Went up on the Mountain. *Unknown.* OuSiCo
Roy Bean. *Unknown, at. to* Charles J. Finger. ABF; BeLS; CoSo, *with music*
Roy Kloof. Sydney Clouts. BoSA
Roy Kloof Went Riding. Sydney Clouts. BoSA
Royal Adventurer, The. Philip Freneau. PAH
Royal and saintly Cashel! I would gaze. The Rock of Cashel. Sir Aubrey De Vere. IrPN; TIP
Royal Angler, The, *sel.* Earl of Rochester.
"Methinks, I see our mighty Monarch stand." BeR
Royal banners forward go, The. Vexilla Regis [*or* Hymn to the Holy Cross]. Venantius Fortunatus. CAW; LiA; LiTW; LyMA; WHL
Royal Barge, A. Shakespeare. *See* Cleopatra.
Royal Bounty. Ibn Hani, *tr. fr. Arabic by* A. J. Arberry. MooP
Royal Bounty. Ibn Sa'id of Alcala la Real, *tr. fr. Arabic by* A. J. Arberry. MooP
Royal Charlie's now awa. Will He No Come Back Again? *Unknown.* OBEC; OBEV (new ed.)
Royal Crown, The, *abr.* Solomon ibn Gabirol, *tr. fr. Hebrew by* Israel Zangwill. AWP
My God, *sel., tr. by* Alice Lucas. TrJP
Royal feast was done; the King, The. The Fool's Prayer. Edward Rowland Sill. AA; AnNE; BAP; BeLS; FaBoBe; HBV; IAP; LBAP; LEAP; LHV; MAP; MaRV; MoAmPo (1942 ed.); NeHB; OBAV; OHFP; PFY; PG; TCAP; TreF; WBLP; WGRP
Royal Fisherman, The. *Unknown.* ChTr
Royal George, The. William Cowper. *See* On the Loss of the *Royal George.*
Royal Guest, The. Julia Ward Howe. BoFr; LPS-1
Royal Guest, A. *Unknown.* *See* Yet If His Majesty, Our Sovereign Lord.
Royal hand is this, A. The King's Hand. Mu'tamid, King of Seville. MooP
Royal Mummy to Bohemia, The. Charles Warren Stoddard. AA; OBAV
Royal Palace of the Highest Heaven, The. *At. to* Alexander Montgomerie. GoTS
Royal Palm. Hart Crane. ChMo; MAP; MoAB; MoAmPo; TrGrPo
Royal Pickle, A. Carlton Talbott. ALV
Royal Presents. Nathaniel Wanley. MaRV; OxBoCh
(Royall Presents.) OBS
"Instead of incense (Blessed Lord) if wee," *sel.* TrPWD
Royal Pride. Al-Nasir, *tr. fr. Arabic by* A. J. Arberry. MooP
Royal Slave, The, *sel.* William Cartwright.
Drinking Song. SeCL
Royal spouse, the season is now at hand. Sonnet. Tasso. LyPI
Royal Tour, The. "Peter Pindar." OxBoLi
Royal Victory, The. *Unknown.* SG
Royall Lady. John Ford. *Fr.* The Broken Heart, V, ii. LiA
Royall Presents. Nathaniel Wanley. *See* Royal Presents.
Royalty. Stéphane Mallarmé, *tr. fr. French by* Alan Conder. TrFP
Royalty. Stuart Merrill, *tr. fr. French by* Alan Conder. TrFP
Royalty. Arthur Rimbaud, *tr. fr. French by* Angel Flores. AnFP
Roy's Wife of Aldivalloch. Mrs. Grant. EBSV
Rub-a-dub-dub,/ Three men in a tub. Mother Goose. BoN; HBV; HBVY; OTPC; OxNR; RIS
Rub and scrape of a city's feet, The. The Pavement Artist. James Kirkup. HaMV
Rub thou thy battered lamp; nor claim nor beg. The State of Age. George Meredith. VLEP
Rubaiyat, The. Edwin Meade Robinson. Limericised Classics, III. HBMV
Rubáiyát of Omar Khayyám of Naishápúr. Omar Khayyám, *tr. fr. Persian by* Edward Fitzgerald. AtBAP, *abr.;* AWP; BCEP; BEL; BPN; CaAE, *abr.;* EmBrPo; EnL, *abr.;* EnLi-2; EPN; EPP, *abr.;* EV-5; FaBoBe; FaFP; GTBS; GTSL, *abr.;* HBV; JAWP, *abr.;* LEAP, *abr.;* LiA; LiTB; LiTG; LoBV, *abr.;* NeHB, *abr.;* OtMeF; OuHeWo; PeP (2 *vers.*); PIAE, *abr.;* PIR, *abr.;* PoEL-5; PoVP; PreP, *much abr.;* PYM, *much abr.;* REAL, *sl. abr.;* ReaPo; ShBV-4, *abr.;* TCEP; TOP; TrGrPo; UnPo (1st ed.), *much abr.;* VA, *abr.;* ViBoPo; ViP; ViPo; ViPP; VLEP; WBP, *abr.;* WHA, *abr.;* WoL, *abr.*
Sels.
"Ah, with the grape my fading life provide." GTBS-W; OBEV; OBVV
(Omar and Death, *abr.*) GTSE
(Ritual of the Grape.) OnPM
"And those who husbanded the golden grain." PoFr
"Awake! for Morning in the bowl of Night." GTBS-D; OxBI; PoFS
Ball, The. OnPM
"Book of verses underneath the bough, A." AnFE; EG; GTBS-W; HoPM; LiTL; LoPo; OBEV; OBVV; OQP; PC; QP-2; SeCeV; SiTL; YT
(Paradise.) OnPM
(Quatrains.) SeCePo
"But leave the Wise to wrangle, and with me." RiBV
Careless Delight. OnPM
"Come, fill the cup, and in the fire of spring." CBOV; InP; TreF; WGRP
(Bird of Time, The.) OnPM
(Fifteen Rubaiyat.) LiTW
Equity with God. OnPM
("O Thou, who man of baser earth didst make.") SeCeV
Fatalism. MaRV
("We are no other than a moving row.") PC
Heaven and Hell ("I sent my Soul through the Invisible"). MaRV
I Myself Am Heaven and Hell. GrCo-1
"I sometimes think that never blows so red." EG; InP; LO
(So Red the Rose.) OnPM
Iram Indeed Is Gone. OnPM
Long While, The. OnPM
Master-Knot, The. OnPM
Minister of Wine, The. OnPM
"Moment's halt, A—a momentary taste." PoFr
"Moving finger writes, The." EG; GTBS-W
(Moving Finger, The.) OnPM
New Year, The. OnPM
Omar's Lament ("Alas, that spring should vanish . . ."). GTML
Predestination. OnPM
Prefer the Cash. OnPM
Soul Is All, The. OnPM
There Is No Sin. OnPM
"They say the lion and the lizard keep." GTML
(Sleep Unbroken.) OnPM
"Think, in this batter'd Caravanserai." ChTr; OBVV
This Life Flies. OnPM
"Wake! For the Sun, who scattered into flight." SeCeV
(Wake!) FaPON
Waste Not Your Hour. OnPM
Wish, A. OnPM
Worldly Hope, The. MaRV
(Like Snow.) OnPM
Worldly Wisdom. MaRV
(Great Argument.) OnPM
("Myself when young did eagerly frequent.") EG; WGRP
"Yet Ah, that Spring should vanish with the Rose." SeCeV
Rubber Boots. Rowena Bastin Bennett. GFA
Rubbish, IV *and* VII. Luis Carlos López, *tr. fr. Spanish by* H. R. Hays. TwSpPo
Rubicon, The. William Winter. HBV; LBAP
Rubies. Emerson. BoFr
Rubies and Pearls. Robert Herrick. *See* Rock of Rubies, The.
Rubinstein Staccato Etude, The. R. Nathaniel Dett. BANP
Rubric. Josephine Preston Peabody. AA
Ruby wine is drunk by knaves. Heroism. Emerson. AtBAP; OnAP; ViBoPo
Ruddigore, *sels.* W. S. Gilbert.
Darned Mounseer, The. TSW; TSWC
Mad Margaret's Song. RIS
Sir Roderic's Song ("When the night wind howls in the chimney cowls"). GBV (1952 ed.); PoMS; WhC
Ruddy drop of manly blood, A. Friendship. Emerson. AmPP (3d ed.); IAP; LPS-1; MOAP
Ruddy poppies bend and bow, The. To Diane. Helen Hay Whitney. AA; HBV
Ruddy sunset lies, The. In November. Duncan Campbell Scott. VA
Rude architect, rich instinct's natural taste. The Mole. John Clare. SeCeV
Rude Militia, The. Dryden. *Fr.* Cymon and Iphigenia. CoEV
Rude rebuffs of bay-besieging winds, The. Patrick Moloney. Sonnets—Ad Innuptam, II. BoAu
Rudel to the Lady of Tripoli. Robert Browning. BPN; EmBrPo; LoBV; NBE; OtMeF; PoVP
Rudely blows the winter blast. Flora. *Unknown.* LyMA
Rudely forced to drink tea, Massachusetts, in anger. Epigram. *Unknown.* PAH
Rudely thou wrongest my dear heart's desire. Sonnet. Spenser. Amoretti, V. ElL; PeBoSo; ReIE; SiCE
Rudeness. Elizabeth Turner. OTPC (1923 ed.)
Rudiments of War. Christopher Marlowe. *Fr.* Tamburlaine the Great, Pt. II, Act III, sc. ii. KN
Rudolph Is Tired of the City. Gwendolyn Brooks. TiPo (1959 ed.)
Rue, *sel.* Laurence Housman.
Resurrection, *fr* III. MaRV
Rue Bonaparte. Joseph Warren Beach. NP
Rue des Vents, *sel.* Arthur Davison Ficke.
"It was an old house; and there seemed to live." UnW

Rueful Lamentation on the Death of Queen Elizabeth, A. Sir Thomas More. LiTB; LiTG; OBSC
(Ruful Lamentacion of the Deth of Quene Elisabeth, Mother to King Henry the Eighth, A.) NBE
Rufflecumtuffle. Annette Bishop. FTB
Rufty and Tufty. Isabell Hempseed. BoTP
Rufus, I trusted you. How vain that trust. Two Poems against His Rival, 2. Catullus. LiTW
Rufus is wondrous rich, but what of that? Henry Parrot. SiCE
Rufus Prays. L. A. G. Strong. MBP; MoBrPo; PC
Rufus the courtier, at the theater. In Rufum. Sir John Davies. ReIE
Rufus's Mare, *with music.* George Calhoun. ShS
Rug, The. Michael McClure. NeAP
Rugby Chapel [November, 1857]. Matthew Arnold. ATP (1935 ed.); BEL; BPN; EM-2; EmBrPo; EnL; EnLi-2; EnLit; EPN; EV-5; GEPC; GTBS; OAEP; OxBoCh; PIAE; PoE; PoEL-5; PoVP; TOP; TyEnPo; ViPo; ViPP; VLEP; WGRP
Sels.
Contagion of Courage. MaRV
Leaders and Friends of Mankind. GrCo-1
"What is the course of the life." MaRV
Rugged forehead that with grave foresight, The. Love. Spenser. *Fr.* The Faerie Queene, IV. OBSC
Ruin, The. Olaf Bull, *tr. fr. Norwegian by* Charles W. Stork. AnNoLy
Ruin, The. Richard Hughes. OBMV; POTE
Ruin, The. *Unknown, tr. fr. Anglo-Saxon.* AnOE, *tr. by* Charles W. Kennedy; EnLit, *tr. by* Harold S. Stine
(Ruined City, *tr. by* Chauncey B. Tinker.) EPP
Ruin and death held sway. In Apia Bay. Sir Charles G. D. Roberts. PAH
Ruin of Bobtail Bend, The. James Barton Adams. PoOW
"Ruin seize thee, ruthless King!" The Bard. Thomas Gray. BEL; BHV; CEP; EiPP; EM-1; EnL; EnLi-2; EnRP; EV-3; GTBS; GTBS-D; GTBS-W; GTSE; GTSL; LH; OAEP; OBEC; Po; PoFr; ShBV-4; TOP
Ruined and ill—a man of two score. Remembering Golden Bells. Po Chü-i. AtBAP; AWP; JAWP; TrCh; WBP
Ruined Cabin, The. Alfred Castner King. PoOW
Ruined Chapel, The. William Allingham. IrPN; TIP
Ruined Chapel, The. Andrew Young. POTE
Ruined City, The. *Unknown. See* Ruin, The.
Ruined Farm, The. William Plomer. BoSA
Ruined Glories. Joachim du Bellay, *tr. fr. French by* Alan Conder. Antiquities of Rome. XXVII. TrFP
Ruined Harbour, A. Johannes Barbucallus, *tr. fr. Greek by* Sir William Marris. OxBG
(Desolation of Berytus, The, *tr. by* F. L. Lucas.) GrPE
Ruined Maid, The. Thomas Hardy. FiBHP; LiTB; MaPo; SeCeV; SiTL; ViP
Ruined Nest, The. *Unknown. See* Deserted Home, The.
Ruinous Abbey, The. Walter de la Mare. MeRV
Ruins at Sunset. William Allingham. IrPN
Ruins of Athens, The. Byron. *Fr.* Childe Harold's Pilgrimage, II. CBOV
Ruins of Corinth, The. Antipater of Sidon. *tr. fr. Greek.* LiA, *tr. by* Goldwin Smith; OxBG, *tr. by* Walter Leaf
(Lament for Corinth, *tr. by* Robert Allason Furness.) GrR
(On Corinth Fallen, *tr. by* the Earl of Cromer.) GrPo
Ruins of Itálica, The. Rodrigo Caro, *tr. fr. Spanish by* Bryant. AnSpL-1
Ruins of Lo-yang, The. Ts'ao Chih, *tr. fr. Chinese by* Arthur Waley. TrCh
Ruins of Rome. Joachim du Bellay, *tr. fr. French by* Spenser. OnPM
"All that which Egypt whilom did devise," VIII.
"Such as the Berecynthian Goddess bright," III.
"Thou stranger, which for Rome in Rome here seekest," I. (Rome, *tr. by* Ezra Pound.) AWP; JAWP; WBP; LiTW, *tr. by* Spenser
"Thou that at Rome astonished dost behold." VII.
"When that brave honor of the Latin name," V.
"Who list the Roman greatness forth to figure," VI.
"Who lists to see whatever nature, art," II.
"Ye sacred ruins and ye tragic sights," IV.
Ruins of Rome. Byron. *See* Rome.
Ruins of Rome, The. *sel.* John Dyer.
"Fall'n, fall'n, a silent heap." BeR; OBEC
Rule, A. John Wesley. *See* John Wesley's Rule.
Rule a Wife and Have a Wife, *sel.* John Fletcher.
"I cast my cloud off, and appear myself." MyFE
Rule, Britannia! James Thomson. *Fr.* Alfred, a Masque, II, v (*by* Thomson *and* David Mallet). AEV; BEL; BHV; CEP; EiPP; EnLi-2 (1949 ed.); EnLit; EPP; EV-3; GTBS; GTBS-D; GTBS-W; GTSE; GTSL; HBV; LEAP; LPS-2; OAEP; OBEC; PoFr; TCEP; TreF; WBLP
(Ode, An: "When Britain first, at heaven's command.") CaAE
Rule for Birds' Nesters, A. *Unknown.* DD; HBV; HBVY; OTPC
("Robin and the redbreast, The.") OxNR
Rule of Fair Play. Solon, *tr. fr. Greek by* Henry Nelson Coleridge. GrR; PoFr
(Lawgiver's Boast, The, *tr. by* Gilbert Highet.) OxBG
Rule of Life, A. Lucian, *tr. fr. Greek by* Walter Leaf. OxBG
Rule of Money, The. *Unknown.* PoFr
Rule to Play, A. Sir John Harington. SiCE
Ruler of the Queen's Navee, The. W. S. Gilbert. *See* When I Was a Lad.
Rulers. Fenton Johnson. PoNe
(Rulers; Philadelphia.) GoSL
Rulers. *Unknown, tr. fr. Spanish by* Havelock Ellis. OnPM
Rules for the Road. Edwin Markham. OQP; OTPC (1946 ed.); PoRL; QP-2; RIS; StaSt
Rules of Behavior. *Unknown. See* Hearts, like Doors.
Rules of Life. Samuel Butler. *See* Saintship versus Conscience.
Rules of the Road. *Unknown. See* Sailor's Grace, The.
Ruling Passion, The. Pope. *Fr.* Moral Essays, Epistle I. BOHV, *br. sel.*; LPS-3, *abr.*
("Search then the ruling passion: there, alone.") ViBoPo
Rum Tum Tugger, The. T. S. Eliot. FaPON; TiPo
Rumba of the Three Lost Souls. Charles Madge. NeBP
Rumble along, over the water. A Street Car Symphony. Roy Helton. PC
Rumble of distant thunder, The. The Christ. Edgar William Whan. ChIP
Rumble of guns, A—not earthly ones. Electric Storm. Michael C. Martin. WaP
Rumble, rumble, rumble, goes the gloomy "L." Roller Skates. John Farrar. FaPON; GFA
Rumbling and rattly good green Bus. Good Green Bus. Rachel Field. BrR
Rumbling and rolling, and rocking, the battle swept up from the valley. Chickamauga. *Unknown.* MDAH
Rumbling under blackened girders, Midland, bound for Cricklewood. Parliament Hill Fields. John Betjeman. FaBoTw; HaMV
Rumination. Richard Eberhart. FiMAP; LiTA; LiTM (rev. ed.)
Rumour. Harold Monro. PtOT
Rumor came to Frei Egidio, The. Egidio of Coimbra (A.D. 1597). Thomas Walsh. JKCP
Rumor Laetalis [*or* Letalis]. *At. to* Peter Abelard, *tr. fr. Latin by* Kenneth Rexroth. LaP; LiTW; LyMA
"Rumoresque Senum Severiorum." Marcus Argentarius, *tr. fr. Greek by* Dudley Fitts. LiTW
Rumors from an Aeolian Harp. Henry David Thoreau. MOAP
Rumpled sheet, A/ of brown paper. The Term. William Carlos Williams. InvP; LiTA; ThWaDe
Rumpty-iddity. row, row, row. *Unknown.* OxNR
Run along, Bobby. Bobby [*or* Ego Sum]. Gelett Burgess. InMe; LauV
Run Along, You Little Dogies. *Unknown. See* Whoopee, Ti Yi Yo.
"Run faster, love," you say and I. Of Love and Time. John Henderson. BoAV
Run from Manassas Junction, The. *Unknown.* PAH
Run, little rivulet, run! The Rivulet. Lucy Larcom. PRWS; TVSH
Run, Mary, Run. *Unknown.* BoAN-2, *with music;* OIF
Run mighty hard for office. Consolation. James Larkin Pearson. NoCaPo
Run, Nigger, Run, *with music. Unknown.* ABF; SoAF
Run on, run on, in a way causing shaking motion on the sidewalk. Autolycus' Song (in Basic English). Richard L. Greene. WhC
Run out—run out from the insane gold world. Escape at Moonrise. Josephine Pinckney. LS
Run? Run? See this flank, sir, and I do love him so! Kit Carson's Ride. Joaquin Miller. IAP
Run, shepherds, run where Bethlehem blest appears. The Angels. William Drummond of Hawthornden. AnEC; COAH; GN; HBV; OBS; OxBoCh
Run with the Bullgine, *with music. Unknown.* SoAmSa
Runagate Runagate. Robert E. Hayden. PoNe
Runaway. Rhoda Coghill. NeIP; OxBI
Runaway, The. Robert Frost. AlDL; AnNE; AWP; BBV (1951 ed.); BoChLi; CH; DDA; FaBoCh; FaPON; GoTP; GTBS-D; HaMV; InPo; JAWP; LoGBV; MAP; MCCG; MoAB; MoAmPo; MOAP; MPB; NeMA; NLK; NV; PIAE; PoRL; PoTo; ShBV-3; StVeCh; TiPo; TSW; TSWC; TwP; WBP
Runaway, The. Daniel Whitehead Hicky. BrR
Runaway, The. Kim Kurt. NePoAm-2
Runaway, The. Cale Young Rice. VOD
Runaway. *sel.* James Whaler.
Pond, The. MAP; MoAmPo (1942 ed.)
Runaway Boy, The. James Whitcomb Riley. MPB
Runaway Brook. Eliza Lee Follen. GFA

Runaway Chorus, A. *Unknown. See* Drunken Sailor, The.
Runaway Cupid. Meleager, *tr. fr. Greek by* Walter Leaf. GrR
(Child Eros, The, *tr. by* John Herman Merivale.) OnPM
("Lost a boy! A runaway!" *tr. by* Walter Leaf.) GrPo
(Love the Rascal, *tr. by* Sir William Marris.) OxBG
(Love, the Vagrant, *tr. by* John Herman Merivale.) WoL
Runaway Slave, The. Walt Whitman. *Fr.* Song of Myself, X. PoNe
("Runaway slave came to my house and stopt outside.") PoFr
Runaway Slave at Pilgrim's Point, The. Elizabeth Barrett Browning. PoNe
Runaway slave came to my house and stopt outside, The. The Runaway Slave. Walt Whitman. *Fr.* Song of Myself, X. PoFr; PoNe
Runaways, The. Mark Van Doren. PoRA
Rune of Hospitality, The. *Unknown, tr. fr. Irish by* Thomas Walsh. CAW; WHL
(Gaelic Rune of Hospitality.) BoFr
Rune of Praise, A. *Unknown, tr. fr. Irish.* WHL
Rune of Riches, A. Florence Converse. BoTP; NLK; SUS
Rune of St. Patrick, The. *Unknown, tr. fr. Irish.* MeRV
Runes on Weland's Sword, The. Kipling. AtBAP; PoEL-5
Runic Ode, A. Thomas Warton, the Elder. CEP
Runilda's Chant. George Darley. *See* O'er the Wild Gannet's Bath.
Runnable Stag, A. John Davidson. AnFE; EBSV; EV-5; GoTS; GTML; GTSL; HBV; LiTG; OBEV (new ed.); OBVV; OnSP; PoVP; ShBV-2; VLEP
Runner, The. Walt Whitman. APW; MOAP; PCH; TSW; TSWC
Runner in the Skies, The. James Oppenheim. AnEnPo; BAP; CP; LEAP; MAP; MoAmPo (1942 ed.); NP; NV; PFY; SBMV; TrJP
Runner with the Lots, The. Léonie Adams. MoPo; NePA
Running along a bank, a parapet. The Path. Edward Thomas. MoVE
Running barefoot all the day. Lullaby in Undertones. "Feodor Sologub." BoR
Running in single drops. Sexual Water. "Pablo Neruda." TwSpPo
Running the Batteries. Herman Melville. PaA; PAH
Running the Blockade. Nora Perry. PAH
Running to Paradise. W. B. Yeats. BLV; BoLiVe; OxBoLi
Running Vines [in a Field]. H. L. Davis. AnAmPo; LA; NP
Runs all day and never walks. Mother Goose. TiPo
Runs the wind along the waste. Were-Wolf. Julian Hawthorne. AA
Rupert Brooke. James B. Dollard. CPG
Rupert Brooke ("He's gone"). W. W. Gibson. *See* Going, The.
Rupert Brooke ("Your face was lifted to the golden sky"). W. W. Gibson. HBMV; POTT; PtOT; PtP
"Once in my garret—you being far away," *sel.* ChMo; CMP; LBBV; PoeMoYo; TwCV; VOD
Rupture. Boris Pasternak, *tr. fr. Russian by* Babette Deutsch. TrRV
Rural Bliss. Anthony C. Deane. InMe
Rural Content. Andrew Scott. EBSV
Rural Dance about the Maypole, The. *Unknown.* OxBoLi; SeCL
Rural Evening. Lord De Tabley. EnSW
Rural Legend. Mary Elizabeth Osborn. NePoAm
Rural Poesy. Sir Philip Sidney. *Fr.* Arcadia. ElL; ElSeCe
(O Words Which Fall like Summer Dew on Me.) MaPo
Rural Postman, The, *sel.* Edward Capern.
"O, the postman's is as pleasant a life." AlDL
Rural Raptures. *Unknown.* BOHV
Rural Scenery—Eclogue I, *sel.* John Scott of Amwell.
"Then soon gay summer brings his gaudy train." EnSW
Rural Walk, The. William Cowper. *Fr.* The Task, I. TOP
("For I have lov'd the rural walk through lanes.") EnRP
Ruris Opes Saturi, Gnavoque Agitanda Colono. Politian, *tr. fr. Latin by* D. C. Allen. LaP
Rus in Urbe. Clement Scott. HBV; VA
Rush Hour, The. Fuyuhiko Kitagawa, *tr. fr. Japanese by* Takamichi Ninomiya *and* D. J. Enright. PoLJ
Rush Hour. Joachim Smet. QS
Rush Leaves, The. *Unknown, tr. fr. Chinese.* WhP
Rush of the *Oregon,* The. Arthur Guiterman. PAH
Rushes in a Watery Place. Christina Rossetti. ChTr
Rushing along on a narrow reach. The Main-Sheet Song. Thomas Fleming Day. EtS
Rushing thence, in one diffusive band. The Sheep Shearing. James Thomson. *Fr.* The Seasons: Summer. CoBE
Russet and white and gray is the oak wood. The Winter Scene. Bliss Carman. VOD
Russet leaves of the sycamore, The. The Last Days. George Sterling. AnAmPo; CP; HBMV; LA; NP; NV; OBAV; TCAP
Russia. "Andrei Bely," *tr. fr. Russian by* C. M. Bowra. BoRS
Russia. Aleksandr Blok, *tr. fr. Russian by* Babette Deutsch *and* Avrahm Yarmolinsky. AWP; JAWP; WBP; WoL
Russia. Nathan Haskell Dole. AA
Russia. Elliott Napier. BoAu
Russia,/ My country. "Andrei Bely." *Fr.* Christ Is Risen. TrRV
Russia, my life! are we tied to one fate for us? Aleksandr Blok, *tr. fr. Russian by* C. M. Bowra. BoR
Russian and Turk. Robert J. Burdette. *See* "Soldier, Rest!"
Russian Cathedral. Claude McKay. CDC; PoNe
Russian Cradle Song, A. David Nomberg, *tr. fr. Yiddish by* Alter Brody. TrJP
Russian Fantasy, A. Nathan Haskell Dole. AA
Russian sailed over the blue Black Sea, A. "Soldier, Rest!" Robert J. Burdette. BOHV
Russian Song: "Ah, you night, you." Anton Delvieg, *tr. fr. Russian by* C. M. Bowra. BoRS
Russian Song, A: "On the forest laces morning's pink is shed." "Igor Severyanin," *tr. fr. Russian by* Babette Deutsch. TrRV
Russian Song: "Sang a little bird, and sang." Anton Delvieg, *tr. fr. Russian by* C. M. Bowra. BoRS
Russian Spring. Ivan Alekseyevich Bunin, *tr. fr. Russian by* Babette Deutsch. TrRV
Russian Spring Song with Minaiev, A. Thomas Walsh. GoBC
Rust. Mary Caroline Davies. BAP; HBMV
Rust. Virginia Moore. BAP
Rust on the Latch. Marion Lee. MuM
Rust-red apricot and golden pear, The. A Fruit Piece. Eden Phillpotts. PtOT
Rustem and Akwan Dev. Firdausi, *tr. fr. Persian by* E. H. Palmer. *Fr.* Shah Namah. PeP
Rustem Slays Sohráb. Firdausi, *tr. fr. Persian by* James Atkinson. *Fr.* Shah Namah. PeP
Rustic at the Play, The. George Santayana. HBV; MAP; MoAmPo; OBVV; ReaPo
Rustic Courtship. *Unknown.* PTA-2
Rustic Lad's Lament in the Town, The. David Macbeth Moir. LPS-1
Rustic Serenade. Theocritus, *tr. fr. Greek by* R. C. Trevelyan. *Fr.* Idylls, III. GrR
(Serenade: "O beautiful Amaryllis.") OxBG
Rustic Song, A. Anthony C. Deane. FiBHP; InMe
Rustle and stir, 'mid the tall meadow grasses, A. The Mayonette River. *Unknown.* CAG
Rustle of each falling leaf, The. Love. Samuele Romanelli. TrJP
Rustler, The. *Unknown.* CoSo
Rustling leaves of the willow-tree. Alone in April. James Branch Cabell. HBMV
Ruth. Bible, *O.T.* EM-1, *ad.*; WoL, I: 1–IV: 17
(Ruth, Naomi, and Boaz, I: 1–IV: 13, *abr.*) BoFr
(Story of Ruth, The.) EnLi-1 (I: 1–IV: 13); OuHeWo (I: 1–IV: 10)
Sels.
Intreat Me Not to Leave Thee, I: 16–17. InP; TreF
(Address of Ruth to Naomi.) GBV (1952 ed.)
("And Ruth said, Intreat me not to leave thee.") LO
(Ruth to Naomi.) MaRV; TrGrPo
Naomi and Ruth, I: 8–17. TrJP
Ruth. Thomas Hood. EnLoPo; EnRP; EPN; EPP; ERP; EV-4; GN; GTBS-W; HBV; InP; LiTG; LiTL; LoBV; LPS-1; OBEV; OBRV; OnPP; OTPC; TOP; TreFS; VA; WP
Ruth. Wordsworth. ChER; EnRP; ERP; GEPC; GTBS; GTBS-D; GTBS-W; GTSE; GTSL; PoEL-4; REAL
"And many an endless, endless lake," *br. sel.* MyFE
Ruth Goes By. Edna Tucker Muth. PEDC
Ruth, Naomi, and Boaz. Ruth, Bible, *O.T. See* Ruth.
Ruth; or, The Influences of Nature. Wordsworth. *See* Ruth.
Ruth to Naomi. Ruth, Bible, *O.T. See* Intreat Me Not to Leave Thee.
Rutherford McDowell. Edgar Lee Masters. *Fr.* Spoon River Anthology. LiTA; NP; OxBA; SBMV; TOP
Ruthless unrest has urged slow feet. Rescue. Olive Tilford Dargan. GoYe
Ruthlessly 'twixt palm and thumb. For a Girl in Love. Florence Hynes Willette. GoBC
Rutted roads are all like iron, The; the skies. The Winter Scene. Bliss Carman. VOD
Rutterkin. W. Cornish. PoMS
Ruy Blas, *sel.* Victor Hugo, *tr. fr. French by* Mrs. Newton Crosland.
Love, *fr.* III, iv. LiA
Ruyter the while, that had our Ocean curb'd. The Dutch in the Medway. Andrew Marvell. *Fr.* Last Instructions to a Painter. OBS
Rwose in the Dark, The. William Barnes. AtBAP
Rye Bread. William Stanley Braithwaite. CDC
Rye Field, The. Jeppe Aakjaer, *tr. fr. Danish by* Charles W. Stork. BoDS

Rye Unharvested, The. Yulia Drunina, *tr. fr. Russian by* Jack Lindsay. RuPo
Rye Whisky [*or* Whiskey]. *Unknown.* ABF, *with music;* CoSo (A *and* B *vers.*), *with music;* OxBoLi; SiTL; TrAS, *with music*
(Way Up on Clinch Mountain, A *and* B *vers., with music.*) AS
Ryght as the stern of day begouth to schyne. *See* Right as the stern of day . . .
Ryogoku. Mokutaro Kinoshita, *tr. fr. Japanese by* Takamichi Ninomiya *and* D. J. Enright. PoLJ
Ryton Firs. Lascelles Abercrombie. TCPD

S

S. M. S. (Sister Mary Stanislaus, O.P.). Patrick Augustine Sheehan. PraNu
SOS. Kenneth Fearing. AmP
S.P.C.A. Sermon. Stuart Hemsley. FiBHP
S.S. *City of Benares.* G. S. Fraser. NeBP; OnHM
"S.S.R., Lost at Sea."—The *Times.* Ralph Gustafson. PeCV
S. T. Coleridge Dismisses a Caller from Porlock. Gerard Previn Meyer. GoYe
S. V. B. William Rose Benét. PtP
Saadabad. James Elroy Flecker. SeCePo
Saadi. Emerson. AmP; IAP; OxBA
"Trees in groves," *sel.* LEAP
Saagin. Sidney Goodsir Smith. AtBAP; PoN
Sabbath, The, *sel.* James Grahame.
"How still the morning of the hallow'd day!" EnSW; LPS-2
(Sunday Morning.) OBRV
Sabbath-Day Chace. Philip Freneau. WoL
Sabbath day was ending in a village by the sea, The. The Last Hymn. "Marianne Farningham." BLPA; PTA-1
Sabbath Eve. August Strindberg, *tr. fr. Swedish by* Charles W. Stork. AnSL
Sabbath Morn. Nicolai Grundtvig. EOAH
Sabbath Morning, The. John Leyden. LPS-2
Sabbath Morning Worship. Dwight Edwards Marvin. PraP
Sabbath, My Love. Judah Halevi, *tr. fr. Hebrew by* Solomon Solis-Cohen. TrJP
Sabbath of Rest, A. Isaac Luria, *tr. fr. Hebrew by* Nina Davis Salaman. TrJP
Sabbath of the Soul, The. Anna Letitia Barbauld. LPS-2
Sabbath Reflection. Denis Wrafter. NeIP
Sabbath Sonnet. Felicia Dorothea Hemans. EnSW
Sabidi, I love thee not, nor why I wot. Translat. ex Martial. Martial, *tr. by* John Weever. TuPP
Sabina has a thousand charms. A Love-Song. *Unknown.* ElSeCe; SeCL; SeEP
Sabine Farmer's Serenade, The. Francis Sylvester Mahony. BOHV; HBV
Sable is my throat. Negro Spiritual. Perient Trott. PoNe
Sable garb of darkness clothes the land, The. Night on the Prairie. Rufus B. Sage. PoOW
Sable mantle of the silent night, The. Night. William Browne. EV-2
Sabrina ("There is a gentle nymph"). Milton. *See* Nymph of the Severn, The.
Sabrina Fair. Milton. *Fr.* Comus. AtBAP; ATP (1935 ed.); EG; ElSeCe; FaBoCh; InPo; LoGBV; OBEV; PoEL-3; SeCL; TOP; ViBoPo
(Sabrina.) CH; HOAH; UnPo (1st ed.)
(Song: "Sabrina fair.") LoBV; SeCeV
Sa-Ca-Ga-We-A. Edna Dean Proctor. BoHiPo; PAH
Sachem voices cloven out of the hills, The. Miramichi Lightning. Alfred G. Bailey. TwCaPo
Sack of Baltimore, The. Thomas Osborne Davis. IrPN; LPS-3; TIP; VA
Sack of Deerfield, The. Thomas Dunn English. PAH
Sack of Old Panama, The, *abr.* Dana Burnet. PFY; PoeMoYo
Sack of straw suspended from a tree, A. The Barrack Yard. Nettie Palmer. NeLNL
Sacrament, The. Charles L. Ford. OQP; QP-1
Sacrament. Una W. Harsen. ChIP
Sacrament of Fire, The. John Oxenham. BMEP; POT; PoTo; VOD (1935 ed.)
Sacrament of Work, The. J. S. Hoyland. PraP
Sacrament of Work, The. John Oxenham. MaRV
(Gratitude for Work.) PGD
Sacramental Meditations, *sels.* Edward Taylor.
Am I Thy Gold? First Series, VI. AmPP (4th ed.)
("Am I thy gold? Or Purse, Lord, for thy Wealth.") NePA; OxBA
(Meditation Six.) AtBAP; LiTA
Experience, The, First Series, III. AmPP (4th ed.); CoV
"I kenning through Astronomy Divine," First Series, VIII. AmPP (4th ed.); OxBA; PoEL-3
(Meditation Eight.) AmP; AmPP; AtBAP; LiTA
Like to the Marigold, Second Series, III. AnNE
"My Lord, my Life, can Envy ever bee," First Series, XXXIII. PoEL-3
(Meditation Thirty-three.) AtBAP
"Oh! What a thing is Man? Lord, Who am I?" First Series, XXXVIII. OxBA
(Oh! What a Thing Is Man.) AnNE
(Meditation Thirty-eight.) CoV
"Prest down with sorrow, Lord, not for my Sin," Second Series, XXX.
(Meditation Thirty.) CoV
"Should I with silver tooles delve through the hill," Second Series, LVI. OxBA
(Meditation Fifty-six.) CoV
"Still I complain; I am complaining still," First Series, XL. OxBA; PoEL-3
"Stupendious Love! All Saints Astonishment!" First Series, X. OxBA
(Meditation Ten.) CoV
"Thy human frame, my glorious Lord, I spy," First Series, VII.
(Meditation Seven.) LiTA
"What Love is this of thine, that cannot bee," First Series, I. PoEL-3
(What Love Is This.) AmPP (4th ed.); AnNE
"Ye Angells bright, pluck from your wings a quill," Second Series, LX. PoEL-3
Sacramento, *with music.* *Unknown.* ShS (3 *vers.*); SoAmSa; TrAS
Sacraments of Nature, The. Aubrey Thomas De Vere. ACP; CAW
Sacramentum Supremum. Sir Henry Newbolt. CBE; GTML; GTSL
Sacred ape, now, children, see, The. The Ape. Roland Young. WhC
Sacred armies and the godly Knight, The. Tasso. *Fr.* Jerusalem Delivered, I. CAW
Sacred Book, The. *At. to* Zoroaster. *See* Zoroaster Devoutly Questions Ormazd.
Sacred day is this, A. Lincoln's Birthday. John Kendrick Bangs. DD; HH; MeMeAg; PGD
Sacred Elegy V: "These errors loved no less than the saint loves arrows." George Barker. *See* Elegy V: Separation of Man from God.
Sacred Emily, *sel.* Gertrude Stein.
"Noisy pearls noisy pearl coat." AtBAP
Sacred Flora crowne this feild. *Unknown.* SeCSL
Sacred Formula to Attract Affection. *Unknown, tr. fr. Cherokee by* James Mooney. LiTA
Sacred Formula to Destroy Life. *Unknown, tr. fr. Cherokee by* James Mooney. LiTA
Sacred Grove, A. Edward Cracroft Lefroy. *Fr.* Echoes from Theocritus. AWP
Sacred Heart, The. Adelaide Anne Procter. JKCP
Sacred Hearth, The. David Gascoyne. FaBoTw
Sacred keep of Ilion is rent, The. Homeric Unity. Andrew Lang. HBV
Sacred lake of Fundisi is an eye of moonstone, The. Fundisi. Ruth Miller. BoSA
Sacred muse that first made love divine, The. Gulling Sonnets, VI. Sir John Davies. TuPP
Sacred Night. Michelangelo, *tr. fr. Italian by* John Addington Symonds. OnPM
Sacred Ode. Juan Meléndez Valdés, *tr. fr. Spanish.* AnSpL-2
Sacred Order, The. May Sarton. ImOP
Sacred Poetry. "Christopher North." WBLP
Sacred Songs, *sels.* "Novalis," *tr. fr. German.* AnGP
I See Thee in a Thousand Pictures, XV, *tr. by* Herman Salinger.
There Come Such Troubled Hours, II, *tr. by* Eileen Hutchins.
Though All Are Faithless Growing, I, *tr. by* Eileen Hutchins.
When in Sad and Weary Hour, III, *tr. by* Eileen Hutchins.
Sacred, sonorous, is heard the long-muted speech of the Hellenes. On the Translation of the Iliad. Pushkin. TrRV
Sacred to Helen. Pierre de Ronsard, *tr. fr. French by* Alan Conder. TrFP
Sacred Trinity, The. *Unknown.* *See* Rann of the Three.
Sacred watcher, wave thy bells! To a Bluebell. Emily Brontë. VLEP
Sacred Way, The. Angelos Sikelianos, *tr. fr. Modern Greek by* Rae Dalven. MoGP
Sacrifice. "Æ." ChMo; CMP; TIP
Sacrifice. Al-Tutili, *tr. fr. Arabic by* A. J. Arberry. MooP
Sacrifice, The. Chu Yuan, *tr. fr. Chinese by* Shen Yu-ting. *Fr.* The Nine Songs. WhP
Sacrifice. Emerson. *Fr.* Quatrains. HBV; HBVY; MaRV
(Faith.) OtMeF
(Quatrain: "Though love repine.") OQP; QP-2

Sacrifice, The. George Herbert. AtBAP; PoEL-2; ReEn
Sacrifice. Hans Egon Holthusen, *tr. fr. German by* Herman Salinger. TwGV
Sacrifice, The. Homer, *tr. fr. Greek by* George Chapman. *Fr.* The Odyssey, III. OBS
Sacrifice. Walter Savage Landor. *See* Iphigenia and Agamemnon.
Sacrifice. Frederick Manning. NP
Sacrifice. Ada Foster Murray. NV
Sacrifice of Iphigenia, The. Aeschylus, *tr. fr. Greek. Fr.* Agamemnon. GrR, *tr. by* G. M. Cookson; LiA, *shorter sel., tr. by* George Thomson; OxBG, *tr. by* Jack Lindsay
Sacrifice of Polyxena, The. Euripides, *tr. fr. Greek by* Hugh Owen Meredith. *Fr.* Hecuba. GrR
Sacrifice of the Bacchantes in Honor of Bacchus. Angelo Poliziano, *tr. fr. Italian by* Hubert Creekmore. *Fr.* Orfeo. LyPI
Sacrifice of the Will, The. *Unknown. See* Laid on Thine Altar.
Sacrifice of Youth. Simonides, *tr. fr. Greek by* Robert Guthrie MacGregor. OnPM
Sacrifice to Apollo, The. Michael Drayton. OBS; SeEP
Sacrifice to Pan, The. Keats. *Fr.* Endymion, I. BCEP
Sacrilege, The. Thomas Hardy. VLEP
Sacrilege of Tiresias, The. Callimachus. *See* Blinding of Tiresias, The.
Sad Air. Carmen Alicia Cadilla, *tr. fr. Spanish by* Dudley Fitts. AnCL
Sad, all alone, not long I musing sat. Licia, I. Giles Fletcher. ReIE; SiCE; TuPP
Sad and dismal is the tale/ I now relate to you. Invasion Song. *Unknown.* PoOW
Sad and dismal is the tale I will relate to you. The *Persia's* Crew. *Unknown.* SoAmSa
Sad and solemn night, The. Hymn to the North Star. Bryant. OTPC
Sad at night were thoughts of the dear things vanished. Consolation. John Frederick Nims. UnW
Sad bells sound, The. Strangers. Walter de la Mare. POTE
Sad Complaint of Poor People, The. *Unknown. See* All Things Be Dear but Poor Mens Labour.
Sad Day, The. Thomas Flatman. OBEV
(Death.) SeCL
Sad Dido. Virgil, *tr. fr. Latin by* Sidney Godolphin. *Fr.* The Aeneid, IV. LiA
Sad eyes, that were patient and tender. The Eyes of Lincoln. Walt Mason. OQP; QP-1
Sad-faced little fellow sits alone in deep disgrace, A. The Boy Who Didn't Pass. *Unknown.* PTA-2
Sad Goat, The. *Unknown.* WaKn
Sad Green. Sylvia Townsend Warner. MBP; MoBrPo
Sad Hesper o'er the buried sun. In Memoriam A. H. H., CXXI. Tennyson. EmBrPo; EPN; GEPC; OAEP; ViPo; VLEP
Sad in the glooming dark. A Fatalist. John W. Garvin. CPG
Sad is my lot; among the shining spheres. Earth. William Caldwell Roscoe. VA
Sad Is Our Youth. Aubrey Thomas De Vere. *See* Human Life.
Sad is the fate of those. The Worst. *Unknown.* OnPM
Sad is yonder blackbird's song. The Ruined Nest [*or* The Blackbird's Nest]. *Unknown, tr. by* George Sigerson. SiB; TIP
Sad, lost in thought, and mute I go. Medieval Norman Songs, IX. *Unknown, tr. by* John Addington Symonds. AWP; JAWP; WBP
Sad Love. Tavallali, *tr. fr. Persian by* A. J. Arberry. PeP
Sad Love and Sad Song. Homei Iwano, *tr. fr. Japanese by* Yone Noguchi. LiTW
Sad Memories. Charles Stuart Calverley. CIV
Cat, The, *sel.* ChTr
Sad Mother, The. Katharine Tynan. MOAH; VA
Sad nymph, Gaho, followed to the shadie woods, The. *Unknown.* SeCSL
Sad One, The, *sel.* Sir John Suckling.
Song to a Lute, A. EPS; ReEn; TrGrPo
(Hast Thou Seen the Down in the Air, *abr.*) PIAE
Sad painter of the green midnight, A. The New Dummy. Geoffrey Grigson. LiTM (rev. ed.)
Sad! Sad! Thomas Edward Brown. VLEP
Sad, sad—lean with long illness. Illness. Po Chü-i. MoPW; TrCh
Sad, Sad Story, A. *Unknown, at. to* John Gay. *See* Three Children.
Sad searching eyes with benediction in their gaze. Galilean. Margielea Stonestreet. ChIP
Sad September Sentiments. Edwin Meade Robinson. YT
Sad Shepherd, The, *sels.* Ben Jonson.
Here She Was Wont to Go. ElSeCe; EPS; TuPP
(Aeglamour Seeks His Shepherdess.) CoEV
(Aeglamour's Lament.) CH
Karolin's Song. AtBAP; LiTL; LoBV; PoEL-2
(Love and Death.) SeCL
(Though I Am Young.) OAEP; TuPP
("Though I am young and cannot tell.") ElSeCe
Mother Maudlin the Witch. ChTr
"Spring, A, now she is dead! of what? of thorns." GoBC
Sad Shepherd, The. W. B. Yeats. BrBE
Sad Song, A. William Allingham. GTIV
Sad Song, The. Beaumont *and* Fletcher. *See* Away, Delights!
Sad Song, A. Stephen Vincent Benét. NV
Sad Song, A. Philip Massinger. *See* Song: "Why art thou slow, thou rest of trouble, Death."
Sad Song of Finian, The. "Ethna Carbery." DiM
Sad Stories of the Death of Kings. Shakespeare. King Richard II, *fr.* III, ii. BCEP
("Of comfort no man speak.") PIR
Sad Story. Clarence Day. InMe
Sad Strains of a Gay Waltz. Wallace Stevens. OxBA
Sad Sunsets. Zacharias Papondoniou, *tr. fr. Modern Greek by* Rae Dalven. MoGP
Sad Tale of Mr. Mears, The. *Unknown.* HBV; StPo; TreFS; YaD
Sad Thyrsis weeps till his blue eyes are dim. Thyrsis. Edward Cracroft Lefroy. *Fr.* Echoes from Theocritus. AWP
Sad to fare from the hills of Fál. A Farewell to Fál. Gerald Nugent. OnYI
"Sad Years, The." Eva Gore-Booth. HBMV
Sadder. *Unknown, tr. fr. Spanish by* Havelock Ellis. OnPM
Saddest fish that swims the briny ocean, The. The Catfish. Oliver Herford. BOHV
Saddest place that e'er I saw, The. Screaming Tarn. Robert Bridges. CMP; ExPo; VLEP
Saddest Words, The. Whittier. *Fr.* Maud Muller. NePA; SiTL
Saddle! saddle! saddle! After the Comanches. *Unknown.* PAH
Saddle smells of sweat, The. In patches. The Rider. Mikhail Svetlov. RuPo
Saddled and briddled. Bonnie James Campbell (B *vers.*). *Unknown.* ESPB
Sadie. *Unknown. See* Frankie and Johnny.
Sadly as some old mediaeval knight. My Books. Longfellow. AA
Sadly I walk't within the field. The Olive Branch. Robert Herrick. OnPM
Sadly talks the blackbird here. The Deserted Home [*or* The Ruined Nest]. *Unknown.* OnYI; OxBI
Sadly the dead leaves rustle in the whistling wind. The Church of a Dream. Lionel Johnson. GTIV; OBMV; PoVP; TIP
Sadly through the factory doors. The Little Children. Irwin Granich. MaRV
Sadness. F. S. Flint. MBP; MoBrPo (1942 ed.)
Sadness and Joy. W. H. Davies. PC
Sadness and stillness. What a bright transparency! Vyacheslav Ivanovich Ivanov. *Fr.* Fallow Land and Stubble Fields, III. TrRV
Sadness, Glass, Theory. Roy Fuller. WaP
Sadness of Olympio, The. Victor Hugo, *tr. fr. French by* Sir George Young. *Fr.* Les Rayons et les ombres. LiA
Sadness of the Moon. Baudelaire, *tr. fr. French by* Alan Conder. TrFP
Sae rantingly, sae wantonly. M'Pherson's Farewell. Burns. BSV; EBSV; LH; MCCG
Saecla Ferarum. William Ellery Leonard. ADAH
Saeter Girl's Sunday, The. Jörgen Moe, *tr. fr. Norwegian by* Charles W. Stork. AnNoLy
"Safe for Democracy." L. A. G. Strong. HBMV
Safe home, safe home in port. The Finished Course. St. Joseph of the Studium. WGRP
Safe in Bed. *Unknown. See* Matthew, Mark, Luke, and John.
Safe in his fortress. The Tortoise. Herbert Asquith. RIS
Safe in His Keeping. Edgar Cooper Mason. BLRP
Safe in our chariot. *Unknown, tr. fr. Chinese by* Yu Minchuan. The Stone Drums, IV. WhP
Safe in the arms of Jesus. Fanny Crosby. OIF
Safe in the earth they lie, serenely waiting. Bulbs. Louise Driscoll. MW
Safe in their alabaster chambers. Emily Dickinson. AnFE; APA; CoAnAm; EG; MAPA; MoPo; OxBA; TwAmPo
Safe sleeping on its mother's breast. The Baby. Ann Taylor. DD; MOAH; OHIP
Safe tethered by his master's loving hand. To a Dog, Grown Blind. Mazie V. Caruthers. AlBD
Safe upon the solid rock the ugly houses stand. Second Fig. Edna St. Vincent Millay. AmP
Safe where I cannot die yet. Is It Well with the Child? Christina Rossetti. OBEV (1st ed.)
Safely through another week. John Newton. OIF
Safety. Rupert Brooke. 1914, II. EnLoPo; LoPo; PoFr; VOD
(1914.) HBV; NP
Safety-Valve, The. Ruth Pitter. PoC
Saffron-elbow'd Morning up the slope, The. William Tennant. *Fr.* Anster Fair. EnSW

Saffron Flower. Babette Deutsch. BAP
Sag' mir wer einst die Uhren erfund. Heine, *tr. fr. German by* Richard Garnett. AWP; JAWP; WBP
(Who Was It, Tell Me.) TrJP
Sag', wo ist dein schönes Liebchen. Heine, *tr. fr. German by* James Thomson. AWP; OuHeWo
(Ashes, *tr. by* Asa Hughes.) LiTW
(Love Dead, *tr. by* James Thomson.) OnPM
Saga of King Olaf, The. Longfellow. Tales of a Wayside Inn: The Musician's Tale, Pt. I, i–iv. APW
Sels.
Building of the *Long Serpent,* xiii. EtS
Challenge of Thor, The, i. AmPP (4th ed.)
Einar Tamberskelver, xx. AmPP (4th ed.); YT
King Olaf's Death-Drink, xxi. AmPP (4th ed.)
King Olaf's Return, ii. AmPP (4th ed.)
King Olaf's War-Horns, xix. AmPP (4th ed.); PFY
Nun of Nidaros, xxii. PraNu
Saga of Leif the Lucky, *sel.* Hervey Allen.
"Leif was a man's name." EtS
Sagacity. William Rose Benét. MAP; MoAmPo; NeMA
Sagamore. Corinne Roosevelt Robinson. BAP; HBMV; PoRL
Sage, The. *Unknown, tr. fr. Greek by* F. L. Lucas. GrPE
Sage Counsel. Sir Arthur Quiller-Couch. HBV; HBVY; LBN; LiL; NA
("Lion is a beast to fight, The.") CenHV
Sage his satire ended, The; and the Shah. The Birth of Salámán. Jami. *Fr.* Salámán and Absál. PeP
Sage is not ostentatious, The, and therefore he shines. The Way of the Sage. Lao-tse. GrCo-2
Sage lectured brilliantly, The. The Black Riders, LVIII. Stephen Crane. AnAmPo; LA; YaD
Sage once to a maiden sung, A. The Green Leaves All Turn Yellow. James Kenney. IrPN
Sagebrusher's Wife. Howard McKinley Corning. MuM
Sages, The. Adam Mickiewicz. *tr. fr. Polish by* Dorothy Todd *and* George R. Noyes. CAW
Sagesse, *sels.* Paul Verlaine, *tr. fr. French.*
"Fairer is the sea," *tr. by* Arthur Symons.
(From "Sagesse.") AWP; JAWP; WBP
Sky Is Up above the Roof, The, *tr. by* Ernest Dowson. AWP; JAWP; WBP
(Sagesse.) EnLi-2
"Slumber dark and deep," *tr. by* Arthur Symons.
(From "Sagesse.") AWP; JAWP; WBP
Sagittarius or the Archer. Joseph Gordon Macleod. NP
Said a bad little youngster named Beauchamp. Limerick. *At. to* Carolyn Wells. PIAE; TSW; TSWC
Said a Blade of Grass. Kahlil Gibran. NV
Said a frog on a log. *Unknown.* BoTP
Said a girl from beyond Pompton Lakes. Limerick. Morris Bishop. LiBL
Said a great Congregational preacher. Limerick. *At. to* Oliver Wendell Holmes. GoTP; LiBL; SiTL; WhC
Said a lady whose surname was Beaulieu. Limerick. Franklin P. Adams. PIAE
Said a people to a poet—"Go out from among us straightway!" The Poet and the Bird. Elizabeth Barrett Browning. VLEP
Said a poet to a woodlouse, "Thou art certainly my brother." The Poet and the Woodlouse. Swinburne. PA
Said a pumpkin to me. A Pumpkin Speaks. Amanda Barris. PCH
Said a Snake to a Frog with a wrinkled skin. Hospitality. John Banister Tabb. PPL
Said Abner, "At last thou art come! Ere I tell, ere thou speak." Saul. Robert Browning. BEL; BHV; BoFr; BPN; EM-2; EmBrPo; EnLi-2; EPN; GBV (1922 ed.); GEPC; MaRV; OAEP; OxBoCh; PoVP; TCEP; TOP; TwCrTr; ViPo; VLEP; WHA
Said an ancient hermit, bending. The Olive Tree. Sabine Baring-Gould. GN; OTPC (1946 ed.)
Said Aristotle unto Plato. Owen Wister. WhC
Said Brier-Rose's mother to the naughty Brier-Rose. Brier-Rose. Hjalmar Hjorth Boyeson. PTA-1
Said Burgoyne to his men, as they passed in review. The Progress of Sir Jack Brag. *Unknown.* PAH
Said Christ our Lord, "I will go and see." A Parable. James Russell Lowell. ChIP; MaRV
Said Death to Passion. Emily Dickinson. MoVE
Said Descartes, "I extoll." Theological. Clifton Fadiman. FiBHP
Said Fading-leaf to Fallen-Leaf. Fading-Leaf and Fallen-Leaf. Richard Garnett. OBVV; TOP
Said Folly to Wisdom. On the Road. Tudor Jenks. NA
Said God, "You sisters, ere ye go." Hope and Despair. Lascelles Abercrombie. HBV; OBMV
Said I Not So? George Herbert. LPS-2
Said I to Lord & Taylor. A Father Does His Best. E. B. White. ALV; WhC
Said I to Myself, Said I. W. S. Gilbert. *Fr.* Iolanthe. PoVP
Said Jove one day: "Let every creature meet." The Wallet. La Fontaine. TrFP
Said lady once to lover. The Three Bushes. W. B. Yeats. LiTG; LiTL
Said Life to Death: "Methinks, if I were you." Recrimination. Ella Wheeler Wilcox. AA
Said Lizzie the big blonde barmaid, "There." In the Township. Denis Glover. AnNZ
Said Mr. Smith, "I really cannot." Bones. Walter de la Mare. FiBHP
Said my landlord, white-headed Gil Gomez. Battle of the King's Mill. Thomas Dunn English. MC; PAH
Said Nero to one of his train. Limerick. *Unknown.* LiBL
Said of the Earth and the Moon. Léonie Adams. TCPD
Said Old Gentleman Gay, "On a Thanksgiving Day." A Good Thanksgiving. "Marian Douglas." TVC
Said old Peeping Tom of Fort Lee. Limerick. Morris Bishop. LiBL; WhC
Said Opie Read. Julian Street *and* James Montgomery Flagg. BOHV; HBV
(To Be Continued.) FiBHP; InMe
Said Orville Wright to Wilbur Wright. Wilbur Wright and Orville Wright. Rosemary *and* Stephen Vincent Benét. PoMa
Said, Pull her up a bit will you, Mac, I want to unload there. Reason. Josephine Miles. FiMAP
Said Robin to his pretty mate. The Robin to His Mate. Ann A. G. Carter. OTPC (1923 ed.); PPL; SAS
Said Simple Sam: "Does Christmas come." Simple Sam. Leroy F. Jackson. ChBR; GaP
Said Sir Christopher Wren. *Unknown.* RIS
Said the Archangels, moving in their glory. Voice. Harriet Prescott Spofford. AA
Said the bird in search of a cage. A Bird in Search of a Cage. Robert Pack. NePoEA
Said the Captain. Alan Pryce Jones. MoWP
Said the Captain: "There was wire." Our Modest Doughboys. Charlton Andrews. PAH
Said the child to the youthful year. The Child and the Year. Celia Thaxter. DD; HH; PEOR
Said the crab unto the serpent. The Crab and the Snake. *Unknown.* OxBG
Said the Daisy. Isabella Valancy Crawford. CPG
Said the Duck to the Kangaroo. The Duck and the Kangaroo. Edward Lear. BoChLi; GFA; OTPC (1946 ed.); PoRh; TiPo (1952 ed.)
Said the expert: "All right, let's call it a day." Rhapsody of the Deaf Man. Tristan Corbière. LiTW; OnHM
Said the first little chicken. Five Little Chickens [*or* The Chickens *or* Wishes]. *Unknown.* BoTP; FaPON; GFA; GoBP; GoTP; MeMeAg; MoShBr; OTPC (1946 ed.); RAR; SAS; UTS
Said the grave Dean of Westminster. A Refusal. Thomas Hardy. LiTB
Said the Lion to the Lioness—"When you are amber dust." Heart and Mind. Edith Sitwell. AtBAP; ChMP; CoEV; FaBoTw; GTBS-D; MoPo; OAEP (2d ed.); Po
Said the Lord God, "Build a house." The Kingdom of Heaven. G. K. Chesterton. OQP; QP-1
Said the lord to his lady as he went away from home. False Linfinn. *Unknown.* BaBo
Said the monkey to the donkey. *Unknown.* FaFP; SiTL
Said the Old Young Man to the Young Old Man. A Catch for Singing. W. W. Gibson. AnFE
Said the Raggedy Man on a hot afternoon. The Man in the Moon. James Whitcomb Riley. BOHV; HBV; HBVY; InMe; NA; OTPC; YT
Said the Reverend Jabez McCotton. Limerick. James Montgomery Flagg. LiBL
Said the Robin to the Sparrow. Overheard in an Orchard. Elizabeth Cheney. BLRP; MaRV
Said the Rose. George H. Miles. BLPA
Said the Sword to the Axe, 'twixt the whacks and the hacks. Ned Braddock. John Williamson Palmer. MC; PAH
Said the Table to the Chair. The Table and the Chair. Edward Lear. BoChLi; GoTP; HBVY; MPB; OTPC (1946 ed.); PCH; PPL; RAR; SAS; StVeCh
Said the tooler to the driller, "Will you dance me a jig?" Turkey in the Straw (C *vers.*). *Unknown.* AS
Said the voice of Evil to the ear of Good. Epilogue. Isabella Valancy Crawford. *Fr.* Gisli, the Chieftain. BoCaPo
Said the Watcher by the Way. The Town down the River. E. A. Robinson. ChMo; CMP; CoBA; CV; IAP
Said the Wind to the Moon, "I will blow you out." The Wind and the Moon. George Macdonald. GoTP; HBV; HBVY; MoShBr; OnHT; OTPC; PECK; PTA-1; StVeCh (1940 ed.); SUS; TreFS; TVC; TVSH
Said this little fairy. The Five Little Fairies. Maud Burnham. HBVY; OTPC (1946 ed.); PCH; PPL
Said Venus, "Cupid, you're no more." Love and Reason. George Hill. APW
Saies, "Come here, cuzen Gawaine so gay." King Arthur and King Cornwall. *Unknown.* ESPB; OBB

Sail, A. Mikhail Yurevich Lermontov, *tr. fr. Russian by* Babette Deutsch. LiTW; OnPM; TrRV; WoL
—— *Tr. by* C. M. Bowra. BoR
—— *Tr. by* Max Eastman. AWP; JAWP; WBP
—— *Tr. by* Sir Cecil Kisch. WaL
"Sail, A! a sail! Oh, whence away." Heart's Content. *Unknown.* HBV; OTPC (1923 ed.)
Sail fast, sail fast. A Song of the Future. Sidney Lanier. TCAP
Sail of Claustra, Aelis, Azalais. The Alchemist. Ezra Pound. LiTA; NePA
Sail On, O Ship of State! Longfellow. *See* Ship of State, The.
Sail on, sail on, fair cousin cloud. Individuality. Sidney Lanier. SPP
Sail on, sail on, O Ship of State! The Ship of State [*or* Sail On, O Ship of State]. Longfellow. *Fr.* The Building of the Ship. BTP; HBVY; OHIP; OQP; PAP; PECK; PoFr; PSO; QP-1; TreF
Sail Peacefully Home. Simeon Frug, *tr. fr. Yiddish.* TrJP
Sail, sail thy best, ship of Democracy. The Voyage of Democracy. Walt Whitman. GrCo-1
Sail with the Wind. Palladas, *tr. fr. Greek by* J. A. Pott. OxBG
("Stream that carries you doth carry all, The.") GrPo
Sailing. Godfrey Marks. OlF; TreFS
Sailing after Lunch. Wallace Stevens. MoPo
Sailing at Dawn. Sir Henry Newbolt. CP; EtS
Sailing beyond Seas. Jean Ingelow. UnW; VA
Sailing Homeward. Chan Fang-sheng, *tr. fr. Chinese by* Arthur Waley. AWP; FaBoCh; JAWP; LoGBV; TrCh; WBP
Sailing of Odysseus from Ogygia, The. Homer, *tr. fr. Greek by* F. L. Lucas. *Fr.* The Odyssey, V. GrPE
Sailing of the Argo, The. Apollonius Rhodius, *tr. fr. Greek. Fr.* Argonautica, I. GrR, *tr. by* Arthur S. Way; OxBG, *tr. by* George Allen
(Sailing of Argo, The, *tr. by* F. L. Lucas.) GrPE
Sailing of the Fleet, The. *Unknown.* PAH
Sailing of the Pilgrims from Sandwich towards St. James of Compostella, The. *Unknown.* SG
(Pilgrims at Sea, *in mod. Eng.*) TMEV
Sailing of the *Sword*, The. William Morris. BPN; CoBE; EmBrPo; OAEP; OBVV; PoVP; TCEP; VLEP
Sailing on the Lake to the Ching River. Lu Yu, *tr. fr. Chinese by* Kenneth Rexroth. OnPC
Sailing Pine, The; the Cedar, proud and tall. Kinds of Trees to Plant. Spenser. *Fr.* The Faerie Queene, I, i. OHIP
Sailing ships with joy at length do touch the long-desired port, The. Wanting His Desire, He Complaineth. Richard Edwards. ReIE
Sailing to Byzantium. W. B. Yeats. AnFE; AnIL; AtBAP; ATP (1953 ed.); CaAE; ChMo; ChMP; CMP; CoBMV; CoEV; EnL; EnLi-2 (1949 ed.); EnLit; EnLP; ExPo; FaBoEn; FaFP; GTBS-W; HoPM; InPo; InvP; LiTB; LiTG; LiTM; MaPo; MBP; MoAB; MoBrPo; MoP; MoPo; MoPW; MoVE; NAMP; OAEP (2d ed.); OBMV; OxBI; PoFS; PoLFOT; POTE; PoVP; ReaPo; ReMP; RiBV; SeCePo; SeCeV; ShBV-4; TriL; TwHP; TwP; UnPo (3d ed.); ViBoPo
Sailing Weather. Hesiod, *pr. tr. fr. Greek by* Samuel Butler. *Fr.* Works and Days. OxBG
Sailor, The. William Allingham. CG; HBV; VA
Sailor. Eleanor Farjeon. BrR; PoRh
Sailor. Langston Hughes. GoSl
Sailor, The. Goodridge MacDonald. CaP
Sailor, A. *Unknown.* SG
Sailor, The. Sylvia Townsend Warner. NV; OBMV
Sailor and Inland Flower. Hamish Maclaren. EtS
Sailor and the Shark, The. Paul Fort, *tr. fr. French by* Frederick York Powell. OBMV
Sailor Ben had just been wed, The. Ballad of the Sailor Ben. Jack Mitchell. PCD
Sailor Boy, The. Tennyson. BHV; BLP; BPN
Sailor Boy, The. *Unknown.* BaBo; ShS, *with music*
Sailor boy who leant over the side, The. The Mermaid. Allen Upward. *Fr.* Scented Leaves from a Chinese Jar. NP
Sailor from Dover, The. *Unknown. See* Brown Girl, The.
Sailor Girl, The. Alfred Perceval Graves. RIS
"Sailor Home from the Sea, The." Palladas. *See* Life a Voyage.
Sailor is blythe and bonny O, A. A Sailor. *Unknown.* SG
Sailor Laddie, The ("My love has been in London City"). *Unknown.* SG
Sailor Man. H. Sewall Bailey. EtS
Sailor tells the children, The. Kingdoms. Oliver St. John Gogarty. AlDL
Sailor to His Parrot, The. W. H. Davies. EtS; ViBoPo
Sailor Uncle, A. *Unknown.* OnHT
Sailor, What of the Isles? Edith Sitwell. ChMP
"Sailorman, I'll give to you." The Silver Penny. Walter de la Mare. ExPo; OBMV
Sailors. Patric Dickinson. NeTW
Sailors. Théophile Gautier, *tr. fr. French by* Alan Conder. TrFP
Sailors. *Unknown. See* Wrap Me Up in My Tarpaulin Jacket.
Sailors. *Unknown, tr. fr. Spanish by* Havelock Ellis. OnPM
(Folk Songs, 2.) LiTW
(Spanish Folk Song.) AWP
Sailors, The. Karel van de Woestijne, *tr. fr. Dutch by* Adriaan J. Barnouw. OnPM
Sailor's Apology for Bow-Legs, A. Thomas Hood. EtS
Sailor's Carol. Charles Causley. AtBAP
Sailors come/ To the drum. Hornpipe. Edith Sitwell. MoVE; SeCePo
Sailors' "Come-All-Ye." *Unknown.* SoAmSa
Sailor's Consolation, The. William Pitt, *wr. at. to* Charles Dibdin. BBV; BeLS; CBOV; EtS; HBV; LBN; LPS-2; OTPC (1946 ed.); PYM; StVeCh (1955 ed.); TreFS; TVSH
Sailor's Dedication, The. Macedonius, *tr. fr. Greek by* T. F. Higham. OxBG
Sailor's Delight. Cicely Fox Smith. AlDL
Sailor's Delight. *Unknown.* SG
Sailors for My Money. Martin Parker. SeCL; TuPP
(Saylors for My Money.) CoMu
Sailor's Grace, The. *Unknown.* ShS
(Blow the Man Down, *vers.* V.) ShS
(Rules of the Road.) SoAmSa
Sailor's Grave, The. Eliza Cook. BLPA
Sailor's Grave, The, *with music. Unknown, diff. vers. of song by* Eliza Cook. ShS; SoAmSa
Sailor's Harbor. Henry Reed. MoAB
Sailor's Mother, The, *sl. abr.* Wordsworth. CG
Sailor's Onely Delight, The. *Unknown. See* George Aloe and the *Sweepstake,* The, *and* High Barbaree, The.
Sailor's Prayer, A. George Hornell Morris. TrPWD
Sailor's Return, The. *Unknown.* OxBoLi
("As I walked out one night.") LO
Sailor's Return, The ("Madame, I come straight from sea battles"), *with music. Unknown, tr. fr. French by* Janet E. Tobitt. SaSa
Sailors' Song. Thomas Lovell Beddoes. *See* To Sea, to Sea!
Sailor's Song, A. Hazel Harper Harris. EtS
Sailor's Sweetheart, The. Duncan Campbell Scott. PeCV
Sailor's Way, The. *Unknown.* ShS
Sailors' Weather Proverbs. *Unknown.* PCH
Sailor's Wife, A. Clara Bernhardt. CaP
Sailor's Wife, The. William Julius Mickle, *also at. to* Jean Adam. BeLS; BSV; GTBS; GTBS-D; GTBS-W; GTSL; HBV
("And are ye sure the news is true?") LO
(Mariner's Wife, The.) ViBoPo
(There's Nae Luck about the House.) CBOV; EPP; EV-3; GN; GTSE; LPS-1; OBEC
Sailor's Woman. Annette Patton Cornell. GoYe
Sailor's Yarn, A. James Jeffrey Roche. BOHV; NA
Sails. Ibn Billita, *tr. fr. Arabic by* A. J. Arberry. MooP
Sails. George Sterling. EtS
Sainclaire's Defeat. *Unknown.* PAH
Saint. Stéphane Mallarmé, *tr. fr. French.* AnFP, *tr. by* Hubert Creekmore; TrFP, *tr. by* Alan Conder
Saint. Kersti Merilaas, *tr. fr. Estonian by* W. K. Matthews. LiTW
Saint, The, *sels.* Humbert Wolfe. *Fr.* Requiem.
"Do you remember, Joan." CAW; TwCV; VOD (1935 ed.)
"Saint Francis of Assisi, do you remember." SaFP
St. Agnes; a Responsory. Thomas Merton. MeRV
St. Agnes' Eve. Tennyson. BPN; CoBE; EM-2; EmBrPo; EnL; EnLit; EPP; EV-5; GEPC; GoBC; GTBS-W; GTSL; HBV; LiTB; LiTG; OAEP; OBEV; OBVV; OTPC; OxBoCh; PoVP; REAL; StJW; TCEP; TriL; ViPo; VLEP
(St. Agnes.) CAW
St. Agnes' Eve—ah, bitter chill it was! The Eve of St. Agnes. Keats. AEV; AtBAP; ATP; BCEP; BEL; BeLS; BLV; BoLiVe; BPN; CBOV; ChER; CoBE; EmBrPo; EnL; EnLi-2; EnLit; EnLP; EnRP; EPN; EPP; ERP; EV-4; ExPo; FiP; GEPC; GoTL; HiLiEn; HoPM; LEAP; LiA; LiTL; LPS-1; MyFE; OAEP; OBRV; OnSP; PIAE; PIR; PoE; PoEL-4; PreP; REAL; ReaPo; RiBV; SeCeV; ShBV-4; TCEP; TOP; TreF; TrGrPo; TwCrTr; TwHP; TwP; TyEnPo; UnPo (1st ed.); WHA
St. Andrews by the Northern Sea. Almae Matres. Andrew Lang. BSV; OBVV; POT; TOP
St. Andrew's Voyage to Mermedonia. *Unknown, tr. fr. Anglo-Saxon by* Charles W. Kennedy. *Fr.* Andreas. AnOE
Saint Anthony at church. St. Anthony's Sermon to the Fishes. "Abraham à Sancta-Clara." BOHV
Saint Anthony of Padua, whom I bear. A Prayer to Saint Anthony of Padua. Arthur Symons. VLEP
St. Anthony's Sermon to the Fishes. "Abraham à Sancta-Clara." BOHV

St. Anthony's Township. Gilbert Sheldon. CH
Saint Apollinare in Classe. R. N. D. Wilson. CAW
Saint Augustine! well hast thou said. The Ladder of St. Augustine. Longfellow. IAP; PTA-2; REAL; TCAP
Saint Balshemtov. Itzik Manger, *tr. fr. Yiddish by* Sarah Zweig Betsky. OnCuPl
St. Bartholomew's on the Hill. Bliss Carman. NLK
St. Bee's Head. Thomas Edward Brown. VLEP
Saint Bernard's Prayer to Our Lady. Dante, *tr. fr. Italian by* Louis How. *Fr.* Divina Commedia; Paradiso, XXXIII. ISi
(St. Bernard's Prayer to the Virgin Mary, *tr. by* Laurence Binyon.) MeRV
("Thou Virgin Mother, daughter of thy Son," *tr. by* Longfellow.) CAW
(Vision of the Divine Mystery, *longer sel., tr. by* Laurence Binyon.) LiTW
Saint Bernard's Verses. *At. to* St. Bernard of Clairvaux, *tr. fr. Latin by* Thomas Tusser. SiCE
Saint Brandan. Matthew Arnold. PoVP; VLEP
Saint Brendan's Prophecy. *Unknown, tr. fr. Late Middle Irish by* Thomas Crofton Croker. OnYI
Saint Bride's Lullaby. "Fiona Macleod." BOL; PraNu
Saint Bridget was/ A problem child. The Giveaway. Phyllis McGinley. PoRA
St. Bridget's Lullaby. Dorothy Una Ratcliffe. CAW
Saint Brigid. Denis A. McCarthy. JKCP
Saint Brigid. Rosa Mulholland. PraNu; TIP
St. Catherine, St. Catherine. The Milton Abbas Rhyme. *Unknown.* SiTL
St. Christopher of the Gael. "Fiona Macleod." CLS
St. Clare Hears St. Francis. Sarah Norcliffe Cleghorn. AV; NV
St. Columcille the Scribe. *At. to* St. Columcille, *tr. fr. Middle Irish by* Kuno Meyer. AnIL
(Columcille the Scribe.) OnYI
St. Columcille's Island Hermitage. *Unknown, tr. fr. Middle Irish by* Kenneth Jackson. AnIL
St. Dunstan, as the story goes. *Unknown.* OxNR
St. Elizabeth of Hungary. Whittier. MeRV
Saint Erkenwald. *Unknown, tr. fr. Middle English.* MeEV
Saint Francis. Dorothy Bennett. SaFP
Saint Francis. Amanda Benjamin Hall. SaFP
St. Francis. Vachel Lindsay. OQP; QP-1
(Franciscan Aspiration.) CAW
Saint Francis. Gertrude Huntington McGiffert. SaFP
Saint Francis. Brother Rudolph. SaFP
Saint Francis. Horace Shipp. SaFP
Saint Francis. Eliot Kays Stone. SaFP
Saint Francis. Tennyson. *Fr.* Locksley Hall Sixty Years After. SaFP
Saint Francis and Saint Benedight. A House Blessing. William Cartwright. ChTr
Saint Francis and the Birds. Robert Hugh Benson. SaFP
Saint Francis and the Birds. Roy McFadden. OxBI
Saint Francis and the Cloud. Marie de L. Welch. SaFP
St. Francis and the Wolf. Katharine Tynan. TIP
Saint Francis Borgia; or, A Refutation for Heredity. Phyllis McGinley. NePoAm-2
St. Francis, Buddha, Tolstoi, and Saint John. Above the Battle's Front. Vachel Lindsay. StJW
Saint Francis called to the birds. Saint Francis. Eliot Kays Stone. SaFP
Saint Francis came to preach. With smiles he met. Sermon without Words. Elizabeth Patton Moss. MaRV
St. Francis Einstein of the Daffodils. William Carlos Williams. AtBAP; MoPo
Saint Francis Endeth His Sermon. Louise Imogen Guiney. SaFP
Saint Francis' Lesson to His Brothers, *sel.* *Unknown.*
"My Brothers, when the north wind bites us sharply." SaFP
Saint Francis loved the Lady Poverty. Paradox. Sister Maryanna. SaFP
Saint Francis, lover of laughter. Saint Francis Sings a New Song. Imogen Clark. SaFP
Saint Francis? No indeed, although at that. Old Man in the Park. Mary Elizabeth Osborn. NePoAm-2
Saint Francis of Assisi, *sel.* Jane C. Crowell.
"He went to meet death singing." SaFP
Saint Francis of Assisi. Harry F. Leary. SaFP
Saint Francis of Assisi. Shane Leslie. SaFP
Saint Francis of Assisi. "Joan Ramsay." MaRV
Saint Francis of Assisi. Pierson Ricks. SaFP
Saint Francis of Assisi. Tom Sweeney. SaFP
Saint Francis of Assisi, do you remember. The Saint. Humbert Wolfe. *Fr.* Requiem. SaFP
Saint Francis of Assisi Talks with a Priest. Jay G. Sigmund. SaFP
St. Francis of the mountain cave and wattle hut. A Little Litany to St. Francis. Philip Murray. NePoAm
Saint Francis prayed in a double darkness chill. Music. Daniel Sargent. SaFP
St. Francis' Prayer. St. Francis of Assisi. *See* Lord, Make Me an Instrument of Your Peace.
Saint Francis' Salute to Our Lady. St. Francis of Assisi, *tr. fr. Latin by* Marion A. Habig. SaFP
Saint Francis' Sermon to the Birds. Longfellow. OTPC, *abr.*; SaFP
Saint Francis Sings a New Song. Imogen Clark. SaFP
Saint Francis to the Birds. Clement Cook. SaFP
Saint Francis to the Birds. Katharine Tynan. SaFP
St. Francis walked in Umbria. The Singing Saint. J. B. Morton. SaFP
Saint Francis Weds the Three Maidens. Helene Mullins, *after* Sassetta. SaFP
St. Francis, who were ever friend. To Saint Francis. A. Babington Smith. SaFP
Saint Francis' Wood. Alexander J. Cody. SaFP
Saint Frideswida, *br. sel.* Aubrey Thomas De Vere. PraNu
St. George he was for England. The Englishman. G. K. Chesterton. WhC
Saint George of England. Cicely Fox Smith. BBV
St. George's Day, *sel.* John Davidson.
"I cannot see the stars." BMEP
St. George's Day—Ypres 1915. Sir Henry Newbolt. GTML; GTSL
Saint-Germain-des-Prés. Léon Paul Fargue, *tr. fr. French by* Wallace Fowlie. MiCF
St. Gervais. Michael Roberts. FaBoCh; LoGBV
St. Gregory's Day. *Unknown, tr. fr. Czech.* PCH
St. Helena Lullaby, A. Kipling. AtBAP; FaBoCh; MoVE; OAEP (2d ed.); OBMV; OtMeF; PoEL-5; POTE; ShBV-2; ViPP
Saint Hugh. Thomas Dekker. *See* Cold's the Wind.
Saint I heard of saw the world, A. The Plastic Glass. Josephine Miles. FiMAP
Saint Ita's Fosterling. *At. to* Saint Ita. See Jesukin.
Saint Ite. Robin Flower. MM; PraNu
St. James Hospital. *Unknown. See* Bad Girl's Lament, The.
St. James, hover near him. In Extremis. Angelico Chavez. JKCP (1955 ed.)
St. James Infirmary Blues. *Unknown. See* Gambler's Blues.
St. James's Street. Frederick Locker-Lampson. HBV
St Jean B'ptiste. S. Frances Harrison. *Fr.* Down the River. CPG
Saint Jeanne. Theodosia Garrison. PEDC
(Sainte Jeanne.) HH
Saint Jo, Buchanan County. Lover's Lane, Saint Jo. Eugene Field. PR
St. John, *sels.* Bible, *N.T.*
Be of Good Cheer; I Have Overcome the World, XVI. TreFS (19–33); WoL (1–33)
Children of the Light, XII: 23–36. WoL
Good Shepherd, The, X. TreFS (7–18); WoL (1–30)
Gospel According to Saint John, The ("For God so loved the world"), III: 16–17. LO
Gospel According to Saint John, The ("On the first day of the week cometh Mary Magdalene"), XX: 1–17. LO
I Am the Bread of Life, VI: 35–40. TreFS
In the Beginning Was the Word, I: 1–17. TreF
(Word, The, I: 1–5.) MaRV; TrGrPo
Jesus and Lazarus, XI: 1–44, *abr.* BoFr
Jesus Answers the Pharisees, VIII: 12–32. TreFS
Last Supper, The, XIII: 1–XVI: 16. OuHeWo
Light of the World, The, XII: 44–50. WoL
My Peace I Give unto You, XIV: 1–31. WoL
(Peace of Christ, The, XIV: 1–27.) TreFS
Neither Do I Condemn Thee, VIII: 1–11. GrCo-1
New Commandment, The ("He riseth from supper"), XIII: 4–38, *abr.* BoFr
New Commandment, The ("This is my commandment, That ye love one another"), XV: 12–13, 15. BoFr
"Then said Jesus to those Jews which believed on him," VIII: 31–36. PoFr
True Vine, The, XV: 1–27. WoL
Way, the Truth, and the Life, The—Love One Another, XIV: 1–19, XV: 12–17. EM-1
Saint John, The. George Frederick Clarke. CaP
St. John. Whittier. PAH
Saint John Baptist. William Drummond of Hawthornden. *See* For the Baptist.
St. John Baptist. Arthur O'Shaughnessy. HBV
Saint John Damascene. The Rosebush and the Trinity. Alfred Barrett. GoBC
St. John's, Cambridge. Longfellow. OBEV
St. John's Eve. Charles J. Kickham. TIP
St. Joseph to the Carpenters said on a Christmas Day. A Christmas Song for Three Guilds. G. K. Chesterton. TCPD
St. Joseph, when the day was done. To St. Joseph. Charles L. O'Donnell. JKCP
St. Kevin. Samuel Lover. OnYI
St. Kilda. William Collins. *Fr.* Ode on the Popular Superstitions of the Highlands. FaBoEn
St. Kilda. Barrie Reid. BoAV

St. Kilda Maid's Song, The. *Unknown, tr. fr. Gaelic by* Alexander Stewart. EBSV
St. Lawrence and the Saguenay, The, *sels.* Charles Sangster.
"On, through the lovely Archipelago." PeCV
Thousand Islands, The. BoCaPo
Saint Leger. Clinton Scollard. PAH
St. Louis Blues. W. C. Handy.
(Group of Negro Songs, A, 10.) NAMP
St. Luke, *sels.* Bible, *N.T.*
Adoration of the Shepherds, The. ChrBoLe (II: 1–16); CLS (II: 1–20)
(Birth of Jesus, The, II: 1–20.) EM-1
(Christmas Eve, II: 8–14.) ChBR; GaP; PCH; SiSoSe
(Christmas Story, The, II: 8–14.) MaRV
(First Christmas, The.) OTPC (1946 ed.) (II: 8–16); PoRL (II: 8–16); TreFS (II: 1–19)
(Tidings of Great Joy, II: 8–14.) FaPON
Benedictus, I: 68–79. MaRV
Child of Nazareth, The, II: 40–52. ChrBoLe
Death of Jesus, The, XXIII: 1–46. TreF
(Gospel According to Saint Luke, The: "And there followed him a great company," XXIII: 27–44.) LO
First Easter, The, XXIII: 54–56, XXIV. EOAH
Good Samaritan, The, X: 25–37. TreF
(On Compassion: "He, willing to justify himself," X: 29–37.) BoFr
(Who Is My Neighbor? X: 25–37.) GrCo-1
Good Tidings, IV: 18–19. MaRV
Gospel According to Saint Luke, The ("One of the Pharisees desired [Jesus] that he would eat with him"), VII: 36–50. LO
Jesus, Judas, and Peter, XXII: 31–62, *abr.* BoFr
Lost Sheep, The, XV: 4–7. TreF
Magnificat, The, I: 46–55. ISi (*Douay vers.*); MaRV; WGRP; WHL
(Hymn of the Blessed Virgin.) CAW
Mary and Elizabeth, I: 39–45, *Douay vers.* ISi
Mary and Gabriel, I: 26–38, *Douay vers.* ISi
Mary and Simeon, II: 34–35, *Douay vers.* ISi
Nunc Dimittis, II: 29–32. WGRP; WHL
On Compassion ("And as ye would that men should do to you"), VI: 31–32, 36. BoFr
On the Road to Emmaus, XXIV: 13–36. TreFS
Parable of the Pharisee and the Publican, XVIII: 10–14. GrCo-1
Poems by the Roadside ("Fear not, little flock"), XII: 32–37. CAW
Prelude of the New Testament ("Hail Mary full of grace!"), I: 28, 38, 42, II: 10–11, 14, *Douay vers.* CAW
Prodigal Son, The, XV: 11–32. EM-1; TreF
(Gospel According to Saint Luke, The: "And Jesus said . . .") LO
To His Disciples, XII: 24–25, 27–28. CAW
Widow's Mites, The, XXI: 2–4. GrCo-1
St. Luke the Painter. Dante Gabriel Rossetti. The House of Life, LXXIV. BPN; GoBC; PoVP; ViPo
St. Maixent. Allen Crafton. POT
St. Margaret's bells. London Voluntaries. W. E. Henley. Po; PoVP
St. Mark, *sel.* Bible, *N.T.*
Parables from Nature, IV: 3–9, 26–29. GrCo-1
St. Martin and the Beggar. Thom Gunn. ShBV-3
Saint Mary Magdalene. Richard Crashaw. *See* Weeper, The.
Saint Mary, mother mild. Mater Salutaris. *Unknown.* AnEC
St. Matthew, *sels.* Bible, *N.T.*
Come Unto Me, XI: 28–30. MaRV
(My Yoke Is Easy.) TreFS
Easter Morning, XXVIII: 1–10. TreF
Forgiveness, XVIII: 15, 21–22. BoFr
Greatest Commandments, The, XXII: 35–40. GrCo-2
("Then one of them, which was a lawyer.") PoFr
Jesus and the Children, XVIII: 1–6, XIX: 13–14. GrCo-1
Parable of the Talents, The, XXV: 14–30. EnLi-1
Poems by the Roadside, V: 14–16, XVI: 17–19. CAW
Rich Man and the Kingdom of Heaven, The, XIX: 13–30. TreF
Sermon on the Mount, The, V: 1–VII: 29. EM-1; GoTP (V: 3–10); OuHeWo; TreF; WoL
"And seeing the multitudes, he went up into a mountain," V: 1–48. ReIE
Beatitudes, The, V: 3–12. GrCo-1; MaRV; TrGrPo (V: 3–10)
(Blessed Are the Poor in Spirit.) ExPo
Fairness, VII: 1–5, 12. BoFr
God Provides, VI: 26–34, *abr.* BLRP
Lord's Prayer, The, VI: 9–13. MaRV; TrGrPo
(Poem of the Our Father, The.) CAW
Love Your Enemies, V: 38–48. GrCo-1
Pure Light, The, V: 14–16, VI: 22–23, VII: 3–5. GrCo-1
Treasures [in Heaven], VI: 19–21. GoTP; TrGrPo
Things That Are Caesar's, The, XXII: 15–22. TreF
Transfiguration, The, XVII: 1–8. GrCo-2
Unto the Least, XXV: 32–40. GrCo-1
Visit of the Wise Men, The, II: 1–12. ChrBoLe; CLS
When the Son of Man Shall Come in His Glory, XXV: 31–46. TreF
Wise and Foolish Virgins, The, XXV: 1–13. TreF
Saint Michael of the Flaming Sword. Ballade of the Harrowing of Hell. D. B. Wyndham Lewis. CoBE; JKCP (1955 ed.)
St. Michael the Weigher. James Russell Lowell. AnFE; AnNE; APA; CAW; CoAnAm; OBAV
St. Michael's Mount. John Davidson. HBV
St. Michan's Churchyard. Rose Kavanagh. TIP
St. Monica. Francis Thompson. MeRV
Saint Olaf and the Trolls. *Unknown, tr. fr. Danish by* E. M. Smith-Dampier. BoDaBa
Saint on the pillar stands, The. Stylite. Louis MacNeice. MoPo
Saint Patrick. Henry Bennett. *See* St. Patrick Was a Gentleman.
Saint Patrick. Edwin Markham. HH
Saint Patrick for Ireland, *sel.* James Shirley.
Bard's Chant. ACP
St. Patrick of Ireland, My Dear! William Meginn. BOHV; InMe
Saint Patrick, slave to Milcho of the herds. The Proclamation. Whittier. GA; LBAH; PAH
St. Patrick Was a Gentleman. Henry Bennett. DD, *abr.;* LPS-3; PoRL, *abr.;* SiSoSe, *abr.*
(Saint Patrick.) HBV
St. Patrick's Breastplate. *At. to* St. Patrick. *See* Deer's Cry, The.
St. Patrick's Day. Eleanor Hammond. GFA
Saint Patrick's day in 'sixty-five. Bound Down to Newfoundland. *Unknown.* ShS
St. Patrick's Day is with us. I'll Wear a Shamrock. Mary Carolyn Davies. BrR; SiSoSe; TiPo (1952 ed.); YeAr
St. Patrick's Day it is—it is. Dawn Song—St. Patrick's Day. Violet Alleyn Storey. YeAr
St. Patrick's dean, your country's pride. To Dr. Swift on His Birthday. Esther Johnson ("Stella"). EnLoPo; TriL
St. Patrick's Hymn before Tara[h]. James Clarence Mangan, *after the Irish.* EnRP; GoBC
"Christ, as a light," *sel.* TriL
St. Patrick's Treasure. Patrick J. Carroll. JKCP
Saint Paul, *abr.* F. W. H. Myers. PGD
Sels.
Alpha and Omega. OQP; QP-1
"Christ, I am Christ's and let the name suffice you." ChIP
(Christ, All-sufficient.) MaRV
Experience ("Oh could I tell ye surely would believe it!"). MaRV
"God, who, whatever frenzy of our fretting." PC
Knowledge. OQP; QP-1
Lo, as some bard on isles of the Aegean. VA
(Inner Light, The.) MaRV
"Lo! as some venturer, from his stars receiving." ChIP
(Advent.) MaRV
Not in Solitude. OQP; QP-2
St. Paul on Charity. First Corinthians, Bible, *N.T. See* Charity.
St. Paul's Church, Her Bill for the Parliament, *sel.* Henry Farley.
To See a Quaint Outlandish Fowl. ViBoPo
(Bounty of Our Age, The.) FaBoCh; SeCePo; SeCL
("To see a strange outlandish fowl.") CenL
Saint Peray. Thomas William Parsons. HBV
St. Peter. Eileen Duggan. WHL
St. Peter at the Gate. Joseph Bert Smiley. BLPA
Saint Peter sat by the celestial gate. The Vision of Judgment. Byron. BPN; CoEV; EM-2; EmBrPo; EnRP; ERP; GEPC; NBE; OxBoLi; ReaPo; TOP
St. Peter stood guard at the golden gate. St. Peter at the Gate. Joseph Bert Smiley. BLPA
Saint Peter's Complaint, *sel.* Robert Southwell.
"Weep balm and myrrh."
(Stanzas from Saint Peter's Complaint.) ACP; CAW
St. Peter's Shadow. Richard Crashaw. ACP
St. Philip and St. James, *sels.* Christopher Smart.
"Beeches, without order seemly." RO
Spring. OBEC
("Now the winds are all composure.") LoBV
St. Philip in Himself. Cardinal Newman. GoBC
Saint R. L. S. Sarah Norcliffe Cleghorn. HBMV
Saint, Revolutionist. Delmore Schwartz. FiMAP
St. Romuald. Robert Southey. CG
St. Saviour's, Aberdeen Park, Highbury, London, N. John Betjeman. MoVE
St. Sebastian. Valery Yakovlevich Bryusov, *tr. fr. Russian by* Babette Deutsch. TrRV
St. Simon and St. Jude's Day. Cecil Frances Alexander. IrPN
St. Stephen and [King] Herod. *Unknown.* BaBo, *Middle English vers.;* BLV, *mod. vers.;* BoLiVe, *Middle English vers.;* CBOV; EPP; ESPB, *Middle English vers.;*

St. Stephen and [King] Herod (*continued*)
MeEV, *mod. vers.*; OBB, *mod. vers.*; OxBoCh, *Middle English vers.*; OxBoLi, *Middle English vers.*; TrGrPo, *mod. vers.*
(Carol for St. Stephen's Day, A, *Middle English vers.*) CH
(St. Stephen, *mod. vers.*) TMEV
(Saint Stephen Was a Clerk, *mod. vers.*) AnEC; SDH; StJW
St. Stephen's cloistered hall was proud. Columbus. Lydia Huntley Sigourney. AA; DD; HBV; HH; MC; OTPC; PAH
St. Stephen's Day. John Keble. CoBE
St. Stephen's Word. Rayner Heppenstall. ChMP
St. Swithin. Daniel Henderson. HBMV
St. Swithin's Chair. Sir Walter Scott. *Fr.* Waverley. HOAH
St. Swithin's Day. *Unknown.* OTPC (1946 ed.)
("St. Swithin's Day, if thou dost rain.") GoTP; RIS
(Signs and Charms.) StaSt
Saint Teresa. Richard Crashaw. *See* Flaming Heart, The.
Saint Teresa. Thomas S. Jones, Jr. PraNu
Saint Teresa of Avila. Sister Mary Saint Virginia. PraNu
Saint Teresa's Book-Mark. St. Theresa of Avila, *tr. by* Longfellow. *See* Santa Teresa's Book-Mark.
Saint Thomas Aquinas. Thomas S. Jones, Jr. CAW
St. Thomas Aquinas. J. Corson Miller. JKCP (1955 ed.)
St. Thomas's Day is past and gone. *Unknown.* OxNR
St. Uncumber and St. Trunnion. The Palmer. John Heywood. *Fr.* The Four P's. ACP; CAW
St. Ursanne. Michael Roberts. LiTM
St. Valentine Rondel, A. Chaucer. *See* Roundel, A: "Now welcom, somer, with thy sonne softe."
St. Valentine, though wide your fame. To St. Valentine. Jennie Betts Hartswick. DD
St. Valentine's Day. Wilfrid Scawen Blunt. The Love Sonnets of Proteus, LV. EnLoPo; ES; EtPaEn; OBEV (1st ed.); OBVV; PoeT; ViBoPo
St. Valentine's Day. Theophilus Hunter Hill. NoCaPo
Saint Valentine's Day. Thomas William Parsons. PR
Saint Valentine's Day. Coventry Patmore. *Fr.* The Unknown Eros, XLIII. EV-5; FaBoEn; GoBC; GTML; PoLi
Saint Valentine's Day. Shakespeare. *See* Tomorrow Is [*or* Good Morrow, 'Tis] Saint Valentine's Day.
Saint Wears a Halo, The. "Peter." BoTP
St. Winefred's Well, *sel.* Gerard Manley Hopkins.
"My heart, where have we been?" NBE
Saint Winefride. C. W. Barraud. PraNu
Sainte Anne de Beaupre. Richard Eberhart. NePoAm
Sainte Jeanne. Theodosia Garrison. *See* Saint Jeanne.
Sainte Margérie. *Unknown.* BOHV
Saint's Delight, The, *with music. Unknown.* TrAS
Saints have adored the lofty soul of you. Two Sonnets [on Death], I. Charles Hamilton Sorley. HBMV; MBP; MoBrPo; NeMA; TrGrPo (1942 ed.)
Saint's Hours. Sarah Norcliffe Cleghorn. POT; SBMV
Saints, I give myself up to thee. Chorus. Jack Kerouac. *Fr.* Mexico City Blues. NeAP
Saints in Glory, The. Dante, *tr. fr. Italian by* Henry F. Cary. *Fr.* Divina Commedia: Paradiso, XXXI. WGRP
Saint's Parade. Robert Layzer. NePoEA
Saint's Tragedy, The, *sels.* Charles Kingsley.
Crusader Chorus, *abr.* VA
Guta's Song. ReTS
Song: "Oh! that we two were Maying." HBV; VA
When I Was a Greenhorn and Young. PoVP
Saints who love the Crucified, The. A Proud Song. Marguerite Wilkinson. BAP; HBMV
Saintship versus Conscience. Samuel Butler. *Fr.* Hudibras, III, 1. BCEP
(Rules of Life.) BeR
Saith man to man, We've heard and known. No Master. William Morris. BPN; EmBrPo; PoFr; PoVP
Saith the Spirit. Holy Song. *Tr. by* Natalie Curtis. APW
Saki. Al-Taliq, *tr. fr. Arabic by* A. J. Arberry. MooP
Saki, for God's love, come and fill my glass. Odes. Hafiz. AWP
Saki Refusing to Drink Wine, A. Ibn al-Tarawa, *tr. fr. Arabic by* A. J. Arberry. MooP
Salad. Mortimer Collins. ALV; BOHV
Salad, A. Sydney Smith. BOHV; HBV
(Recipe for a Salad, A.) LPS-3
Salad—after Tennyson. Mortimer Collins. CenHV
Salad of greens! Salad of greens! The Universal Favorite. Carolyn Wells. InMe
Salámán and Absál. *sels.* Jami, *tr. fr. Persian by* Edward Fitzgerald. PeP
Absál Tempts Salámán.
Birth of Salámán, The.
Burning of Absál, The.
Lovers Flee, The.
Preliminary Invocation.
Simple Arab, The.
(Bewildered Arab, The.) WoL
Salámán bow'd his forehead to the dust. The Burning of Absál. Jami. *Fr.* Salámán and Absál. PeP
Salamanca. Miguel de Unamuno, *tr. fr. Spanish by* Eleanor L. Turnbull. TeCS
Salamis. Aeschylus, *tr. fr. Greek by* G. M. Cookson. *Fr.* Persians. OxBG; WaaP, *shorter sel.*
(Battle of Salamis, The, *tr. by* Gilbert Murray.) PoFr
(Victory at Salamis, *tr. by* Gilbert Murray.) GrR
Salangadou, *with music. Unknown, tr. fr. French.* ABF; TrAS
Salary. Billy B. Cooper. DDA
Salcombe Hill and three hills more. A Sidmouth Soul. Cale Young Rice. TBM
Salcombe Seaman's Flaunt to the Proud Pirate, The. *Unknown.* CBPC; ChTr; SG
(Pirate of High Barbary, The.) EtS
Sale. Josephine Miles. FiMAP
Sale began—young girls were there, The. The Slave Auction. Frances E. W. Harper. PoNe
Sale of Saint Thomas, The, *abr.* Lascelles Abercrombie. LBBV
Tormented by the World, *sel.* POTE
Sale of the Pet Lamb, The. Mary Howitt. CH
Salem Robert Lowell. AnNE; NePoEA
Salem. Edmund Clarence Stedman. AA; PAH
Salem Witch, A. Ednah Proctor Clarke. PAH
Salerne Schoole, The, *sel. Unknown, tr. fr. Latin.*
"Salerne Schoole doth by these lines impart, The." PoP
Salesman, The. Robert Mezey. NePoEA
Salesman Is an It That Stinks Excuse, A. E. E. Cummings. AmP; OxBA
Salley Gardens, The. W. B. Yeats. *See* Down by the Salley Gardens.
Sallow dawn is in the sky, A. Lola Ridge. *Fr.* The Ghetto. MAP; MoAmPo (1942 ed.); TCPD
Sallow faces. Tokyo Imperial University Students. Shigeharu Nakano. PoLJ
Sallow waiter brings me six huge oysters, A. Storm on Fifth Avenue. Siegfried Sassoon. MoVE
Sallows like heads in Polynesia. Into the Salient. Edmund Blunden. ViBoPo
Sally and Manda. Alice B. Campbell. GoBP; PoMa
Sally Birkett's Ale. *Unknown.* ChTr
Sally Brown. *Unknown.* AmSS, *with music*; SG; ShS, 2 *vers., with music*; SoAmSa, *with music*
Sally Centipede. Helen Cowles LeCron. GFA
Sally from Coventry, The. George Walter Thornbury. HBV
Sally Go Round the Sunshine, *with music. Unknown.* OuSiCo
("Sally go round the sun," *sl. diff.*) OxNR
Sally, having swallowed cheese. Cruel Clever Cat. Geoffrey Taylor. ChTr; LiTM; SiTL
Sally in Our Alley. Henry Carey. AWP; BOHV; BTP; CBOV; CoMu; EV-3; FaBoBe; FaFP; GTBS; GTBS-D; GTBS-W; GTSE; GTSL; HBV; InMe; JAWP; KN; LEAP; LiTG; LiTL; LPS-1; NeHB; OBEV; OIF; PG (1945 ed.); RIS; SiTL; TOP; TreF; ViBoPo; WBP
(Ballad of Sally in Our Alley, The.) CEP; EiPP; OBEC; PoE
("Of all the girls that are so smart.") LO; TiPo (1952 ed.)
Sally is gone that was so kindly. Ha'nacker Mill. Hilaire Belloc. HBMV; MBP; MM; MoBrPo
Sally Monroe, *with music. Unknown.* ShS
Sally Ring, The. Patrick Kelly. GTIV
Sally, Sally Waters. *Unknown.* OxNR
Sally Salter, she was a young teacher who taught. The Lovers [*or* Love's Moods and Tenses]. Phoebe Cary. BOHV; HBV; LPS-3
Sally Simpkin's Lament. Thomas Hood. BOHV; EnRP; ERP
Sally Sweetbread. Henry Carey. CoMu
Salmon Drowns Eagle. Malcolm Lowry. BoCaPo (1948 ed.); TwCaPo
Salmon-fishing. Robinson Jeffers. AnEnPo; PC
Salome. Guillaume Apollinaire, *tr. fr. French by* Dudley Fitts. AnFP
Salonikan Grave. Kipling. *Fr.* Epitaphs of the War, 1914–18. LiA; OAEP (2d ed.)
Saloon is gone up the creek, The. Hemmed-in Males. William Carlos Williams. *Fr.* A Folded Skyscraper. AnAmPo; LA; MoVE
Saloon is sometimes called a Bar, The. The Bar. *Unknown.* PoToHe (new ed.)
Salopia Inhospitalis. Douglas Brooke Wheelton Sladen. VA
Sal's Gap. Olive Tilford Dargan. LS
Salt. Monk Gibbon. OxBI
Salt and Pepper Dance. Jimmy Garthwaite. GFA
Salt creek mouths unflushed by the sea. The South Coast. Brother Antoninus. NeAP
Salt Flats, The. Sir Charles G. D. Roberts. CaP; OCL
Salt Garden, The. Howard Nemerov. FiMAP; NePoEA

Salt of the Earth, The. Swinburne. BPN; EmBrPo; EPP; PoVP
Salt, Salt Sea, The. *Unknown. See* Daemon Lover, The.
Salt Sea Wind. W. B. Yeats. *Fr.* At the Hawk's Well. LiA
Salt Song, The. Nikolai Alekseyevich Nekrasov, *tr. fr. Russian by* Babette Deutsch. *Fr.* Who Lives Happily in Russia? TrRV
Salt Tides. Lucia Trent. MuM
Salts were formed by acids combined with bases. Scientia Vincit Omnia? Merrill Moore. AnAmPo; LA
Saltus goes booted to the dancing school. Videantur Quae Non Sunt. Henry Parrot. SiCE
Salty Dogs. *Unknown.* CoSo
Salut au Monde, *abr.* Walt Whitman. BoFr
"My spirit has pass'd in compassion and determination around the whole earth," *sel.* AtBAP
Salutamus. Sterling A. Brown. CDC
Salutation. "Æ." OnYI
Salutation. T. S. Eliot. *Fr.* Ash Wednesday. AnAmPo; LA; TCPD
("Lady, three white leopards sat under a juniper-tree.") LO; LoBV
Salutation. Zerea Jacob. *See* Hymn to Mary.
Salutation. Ezra Pound. LoGBV; MoAB; MoAmPo (1950 ed.); MoPW; OxBA
Salutation, The. Thomas Traherne. AtBAP; BrBE; EPS; InvP; OBS; SeCL; SeCV-2; SeEP
Sels.
"From dust I rise." FaBoEn
"These little limbs." ElSeCe; OxBoCh
"When silent I." AlDL
Salutation. George Sylvester Viereck. LPS-1
Salutation of the Blessed Virgin, The. John Byrom. ISi
Salutation of [*or* to] the Dawn, The. *Unknown, at. to* Kalidasa, *ad. fr. Sanskrit.* MaRV; PoToHe (new ed.)
(Look to This Day.) OQP; QP-1
Salutation the Second. Ezra Pound. OxBA
Salutation to Cardinal Wolsey. John Skelton. *Fr.* Speak, Parrot. CoEV
Salutation to Jesus Christ. John Calvin. MaRV; WGRP
Salutation to the Kelts. Thomas D'Arcy McGee. TIP
Salutations: To Mary, Virgin. *Unknown, tr. fr. Latin by* Raymond F. Roseliep. ISi
Salute. Archibald MacLeish. ChMo; CMP
Salute. James Schuyler. NeAP
Salute, Czechoslovakia! William Rose Benét. NeTW
Salute the Flag. H. C. Bunner. *See* Old Flag, The.
Salute the last and everlasting day. Ascention. John Donne. OBS
Salute to Greece. "Clemence Dane." NeTW; PoFr
Salute to Recife. Manuel Bandeira, *tr. fr. Portuguese by* Dudley Poore. AnCL
Salute to the Modern Language Association, A, Convening in the Hotel Pennsylvania, December 28th–30th. Morris Bishop. WhC
Salute to Trees, A. Henry van Dyke. StVeCh
(Trees.) NLK
Salvage. Beatrice Ravenel. LS
Salvation. Aaron Zeitlin, *tr. fr. Yiddish by* Sarah Zweig Betsky. OnCuPl
Salvation comes by Christ alone. An Evening Thought. Jupiter Hammon. PoNe
Salvation Prospect. LeRoy Smith, Jr. NePoAm
Salvation to all that will is nigh. Annunciation. John Donne. ISi; OBS
Salvator mundi, Domine,/ Father of heaven, blessed Thou be,/ And Thy Son that cometh of Thee. Alleluia, Alleluia,/ De Virgine Maria. *Unknown.* AnEC
Salvator mundi, Domine,/ Father of heaven, blessed Thou be,/ Thou greetest a maid with an avé. Alleluia, Alleluia, Alleluia. *Unknown.* AnEC
Salve! Thomas Edward Brown. HBV; OBEV; OBVV; POTT; TOP
Salve. "H. T. R." CAG
Salve Regina ("Mary, we hail thee"). *At. to* Hermanus Contractus, *tr. fr. Latin by* Winfred Douglas. ISi
Salve Regina! *in mod. Eng.* ("Blessed be thou, Lady"). *Unknown.* TMEV
Salve Regina ("Hail, holy Queen"). *Unknown.* WHL
Salve Regina, Mater Misericordie ("O blessedful bird."). *Unknown.* AnEC
Salve, Virgo Florens. *Unknown.* WHL
Salvos for Randolph Bourne. Horace Gregory. ChMo; NAMP
Sam. Arthur St. John Adcock. WhC
Sam. Walter de la Mare. MBP; MoAB; MoBrPo; NeMA; PoMS; TiPo; TwCV
Sam Bass. *Unknown.* ABF, *with music;* ABS; AS; BeLS; CoSo, *with music;* CSF, *with music;* ViBoFo
Sam Brown was a fellow from way down East. In the Catacombs. Harlan Hoge Ballard. BOHV; YaD
Sam Davis. John Trotwood Moore. SPP
Sam had spirits naught could check. Impetuous Samuel. Harry Graham. NA
Sam Hall, *with music. Unknown.* ABF; CoSo; ViBoFo
(Samuel Hall, *sl. diff. vers.*) ChTr
Sam, Sam, the butcher man. *Unknown.* FaFP; SiTL
Samadhi. Conrad Aiken. MAPA
Samarian Nights. Yaakov Fichman, *tr. fr. Hebrew by* Dov Vardi. LiTW
Samaritan Woman. Mother Francis d'Assisi. JKCP (1955 ed.)
Sambo's Right to be Kilt. Charles Graham Halpine. AA
Same, The ("Milton! thou shouldst be living at this hour"). Wordsworth. *See* London, 1802.
Same, The ("What awful perspective! while from our sight"). Wordsworth. *Fr.* Ecclesiastical Sonnets. EnLP
(Same, The [King's College Chapel].) Wordsworth. *Fr.* Ecclesiastical Sonnets. GEPC
Same blue sky, the same wide waste of sea, The. Immutabilis. Mahlon Leonard Fisher. MuM
Same Complaint, The. Norman Gale. PIAE
Same Forever, The. Horatius Bonar. BePJ
Same great angel who had once, The. On the Death of Mary. Rainer Maria Rilke. ISi
Same old charitable lie, The. The Lie of the Land. Margaret Fishback. SiTL
Same old fable, The. On Being Told That One's Ideas Are Victorian. Sara Henderson Hay. InMe
Same Old Jazz, The. Philip Whalen. NeAP
Same Old Story, The. James J. Montague. HBMV
Same Old Story. Harry B. Smith. BOHV
Same Train. *Unknown.* APW; BoAN-2, *with music*
Samela. Robert Greene. *See* Doron's Description of Samela.
Samis Idyll. Dachine Rainer. NePoAm
Samoan Revel. Nicaenetus, *tr. fr. Greek by* Walter Leaf. GrR
Samor, *sel.* Henry Hart Milman.
Beacons, The. OBRV
Sampler, The. Theognis, *tr. fr. Greek by* J. M. Edmonds. GrR
Sampling the books the moderns bring. Deep Stuff. Keith Preston. WhC
Sam's Three Wishes; or, Life's Little Whirligig. Walter de la Mare. ChMo; CMP; PCN
Samson. Frederick George Scott. CPG; VA
Samson, *with music. Unknown.* OuSiCo
Samson Agonistes. Milton. EnLi-1; EPS; PoEL-3; TwCrTr
Sels.
All Is Best. SeCePo
("All is best, though we oft doubt.") MyFE; OBEV; OBS; SeCeV
(Epilogue.) FaBoEn
(Final Chorus.) ExPo
(Last Chorus.) ShBV-4
Blindness of Samson, The. LiTB; UnPo
(Samson on His Blindness.) LPS-1
"I, dark in light, exposed," 5 *ll.* TrGrPo
"But who is this, what thing on sea or land?"
(Delilah.) SeCePo
(Milady's Face.) BoHiPo
"Come, come, no time for lamentation now." FiP
(Brave Epitaph, A.) BHV
(Death of Samson.) ChTr
Eyeless at Gaza. LH
("Can this be he," *shorter sel.*) InP
(Hero in Prison, A.) BHV
(Samson Fallen, *longer sel.*) OBS
Hero in Despair, A. BHV
"It is not vertue, wisdom, valour, wit."
(Woman.) OBS
"Little onward lend thy guiding hand, A." AtBAP; BrBE; NBE; ViBoPo
"Many are the sayings of the wise." SeCeV
(Ways of God to Men, The.) OBS
"O dearly-bought revenge, yet glorious!" TwHP
(Heroic Vengeance.) OBS
"Oh, how comely it is and how reviving." OBEV; SeCeV
(Deliverer, The.) OBS
(Out of Adversity.) LH
"O that torment should not be confin'd." BrBE
"O wherefore was my birth from heaven foretold." AnFE
(O Dark, Dark, Dark, *abr.*) WHA
"Why was my breeding order'd and prescrib'd," 12 *ll.* PoFr
"Occasions drew me early to this city." BHV; ShGoBo
(Samson at Gaza; His Last Trial of Strength.) EV-2
Samson Hath Quit Himself. LoBV
Transcendence of God, The. OBS
With Them That Rest, 5 *ll.* LiA
Samson to His Delilah. Richard Crashaw. TrGrPo
Samuel. Alan Paton. BoSA
Samuel, Book I. Bible, *O.T. See* First Samuel.
Samuel, Book II. Bible, *O.T. See* Second Samuel.
Samuel Brown. Phoebe Cary. PA
Samuel Hall. *Unknown. See* Sam Hall.
Samuel Hoar. Franklin Benjamin Sanborn. AA
Samuel Pepys. Allan M. Laing. FiBHP

Samuel Sewall. Anthony Hecht. NePoEA
Samuel Taylor Coleridge. Dante Gabriel Rossetti. Five English Poets, 3. BPN; EmBrPo; PoVP; PtP
San Francesco d'Assisi. Catherine Parmenter. SaFP
San Francisco. John Vance Cheney. PAH
San Francisco. Joaquin Miller. PAH
San Francisco. Walter Adolphe Roberts. PoNe
San Gloria. "Tom Redcam." PoNe
San Juan Capistrano. Alice Cecilia Cooper. GoBC
San Lorenzo Giustiniani's Mother. Alice Meynell. HBV
(San Lorenzo's Mother.) POTT; TriL
San Marco Museum, Florence. Sister Maris Stella. GoBC
San Martino del Carso. Giuseppe Ungaretti, *tr. fr. Italian by* Glauco Cambon. OnPM
San Miguel de la Tumba. Gonzalo de Berceo, *tr. fr. Spanish by* Longfellow. *Fr.* The Miracles of Our Lady. CAW; TeCS
San Sabas. Luis Palés Matos, *tr. fr. Spanish by* Muna Lee. CAW
San Terenzo. Andrew Lang. VA
Sanary. Katherine Mansfield. AnNZ
Sancho. William Edwin Collin. CaP
Sancta Maria Dolorum, or the Mother of Sorrows. Richard Crashaw. LiA
Sancte Confessor. Rhabanus Maurus, *tr. fr. Latin by* Alan G. McDougall. CAW
Sanctity. Patrick Kavanagh. FaBoTw
Sanctuary. Kendall Banning. MuM
Sanctuary. J. B. Boothroyd. FiBHP
Sanctuary. Bruce Boyd. NeAP
Sanctuary. Louise Imogen Guiney. AA
Sanctuary. Thomas S. Jones, Jr. Four Sonnets, I. SBMV
Sanctuary. Aline Kilmer. LEAP
Sanctuary. Elinor MacArthur. BLA
Sanctuary, The. Howard Nemerov. NePoEA
Sanctuary. Clinton Scollard. MaRV; OQP; QP-1
Sanctuary. Mildred Wojtalewicz. WHL
Sanctuary. Elinor Wylie. MAP; MoAB; MoAmPo; PoMa
Sanctuary in a maze, A, XII. Frances Crawford. PtPa
Sanctuary in Po-shan Temple. Chang Ch'ien, *tr. fr. Chinese.* WhP
Sanctum, The. T. A. Daly. TrPWD
Sanctus. David Gascoyne. *Fr.* Miserere. NeBP
Sand. Jorge Guillén, *tr. fr. Spanish by* Eleanor L. Turnbull. CoSP
Sand. Ibn al-Arabi, *tr. fr. Arabic by* A. J. Arberry. MooP
Sand and Spray; a Sea Symphony, *sel.* John Gould Fletcher. Gale, The. PIAE
Sand and the Waves, The. Po Chü-i, *tr. fr. Chinese by* Ching Ti. WhP
Sand below the border-mountain lies like snow, The. On Hearing a Flute at Night from the Wall of Shou-hsiang. Li Yi. UnS
Sand-between-the-Toes. A. A. Milne. TiPo (1959 ed.)
Sand Castles. W. Graham Robertson. CBPC; MPB
Sand Cooking. *Unknown.* PCH
Sand Dunes. Robert Frost. MAP; MoAB; MoAmPo
Sand Dunes and Sea. John Richard Moreland. HBMV; LS
Sand Paintings. Alice Corbin. AnAmPo; LA; NP
Sand, sand, hills of sand. The Hidden Mermaids. Walter de la Mare. OTPC
Sandalled with morning and with evening star. To Pain. George Sterling. JKCP (1926 ed.)
Sandalphon. Longfellow. AmPP (3d ed.); AnNE; APW; IAP; OBAV; TCAP
Sande ("Sande's crucifix, that criss-cross star"). Glyn Jones. MoWP
Sandgate Girl's Lamentation, The. *Unknown.* CoMu
Sandhill Crane, The. Mary Austin. TiPo
Sandhill People. Carl Sandburg. ChMo; CMP
Sand-Man, The. Elmer Ruán Coates. BOL
Sand-Man, The. George Cooper. BOL
Sandman, The. Mary White Slater. BOL
Sandman, The ("The flowers have gone to bed"). *Unknown, tr. fr. German.* BOL
Sandman, The ("I have a pair of boots so rare"). *Unknown, tr. fr. German by* Louis Untermeyer. RIS
Sand-Man ("What has this man got?"). *Unknown.* BOL
Sandman, The. "Margaret Vandegrift." BOL; HBV; HBVY; PRWS; PTA-2; TVC; TVSH
Sandpiper, The. Witter Bynner. BLA; HBMV; WhBS
Sandpiper, The. Ivan Swift. BLA
Sandpiper, The. Celia Thaxter. AA; BAP; BBV (1923 ed.); BLA; BoChLi; BTP; DD; DDA; FaBoBe; FaPON; GN; HBV; HBVY; LBAP; LEAP; LPS-2; MPB; MW; PECK; SN; UTS; WBLP
Sandpipers. Helen Merrill Egerton. CaP; CPG; OCL
Sands Are Alive with Sunshine, The. W. E. Henley. PoVP
Sands of [*or* o'] Dee, The. Charles Kingsley. *Fr.* Alton Locke. BBV (1923 ed.); BeLS; BLP; BMEP; BoChLi; CBE; CBOV; CBPC; CG; CH; DaM; EV-5; FaPON; GBV (1952 ed.); GN; GTBS; GTBS-D; GTML; GTSE; GTSL; HBV; LEAP; LPS-2; MCCG; MPB; MuP; MW; NeHB; OBEV (1st ed.); OnSP; OTPC; PECK; PFE; PoMS; PoVP; RG; ShBV-2; TreF; TSW; TSWC; TVSH; UnW; VA; WBLP; WP
(O Mary, Go and Call the Cattle Home!) PIR
Sandstone. Anne Marriott. CaP; TwCV
Sandwich Man, The. Louis Johnson. AnNZ
Sandy—A Small Dog. Alan Anderson. PCD
Sandy cat by the Farmer's chair, The. Summer Evening. Walter de la Mare. MBP; MoAB; MoBrPo; MoShBr; NeMA; TiPo (1959 ed.); TSW
Sandy Dan he had red hair. The Erie Canal. *Unknown.* ABF
Sandy he belongs to the mill. *Unknown.* OxNR
Sandy Hook. George Houghton. AA
Sandy Kildandy. *Unknown.* OxNR
Sandy Lan', *with music.* *Unknown.* ABF
Sandy spits, the shore-lock'd lakes, The. A Southern Night. Matthew Arnold. GEPC
Sandy Star and Willie Gee (*Complete,* I–V). William Stanley Braithwaite. BANP
Sandy Star, *sel.,* V. BAP; HBMV
Sang: "My Peggy is a young thing." Allan Ramsay. *See* My Peggy.
Sang: Recoll o Skaith. Sidney Goodsir Smith. NeBP
Sang a little bird, and sang. Russian Song. Anton Delvieg. BoRS
Sang old Tom the lunatic. Tom the Lunatic. W. B. Yeats. OnYI
Sang Solomon to Sheba. Solomon to Sheba. W. B. Yeats. GTBS-D
Sang the sunrise on an amber morn. An April Adoration. Sir Charles G. D. Roberts. HBV
Sangar. John Reed. NP
Sanna. Alan Paton. BoSA
Sans Souci. Lisel Mueller. NePoAm-2
Sanskrit Stanza, A. S. Helen Wijesinhe. MM
Santa Anna [*or* Ana] came storming, as a storm might come. The Defense [*or* Defence] of the Alamo. Joaquin Miller. BeLS; DD; FaBoBe; HBV; LEAP; MC; PaA; PAH
Santa Anna; or, The Plains of Mexico, *with music.* *Unknown.* AmSS
(Santy Anna, *with music.*) ShS, *2 vers.;* SoAmSa
(Santy Anno, *longer vers., with music.*) OuSiCo
Santa Barbara. Francis Fisher Browne. AA
Santa Barbara Beach. Ridgely Torrence. HBMV; NV; TBM
Santa Claus ("He comes in the night!") *Unknown.* BoTP; ChBR; COAH; HBVY; HH; MeMeAg; PEDC; PRWS; TVC
Santa Claus ("Little fairy snowflakes"). *Unknown.* MeMeAg; OTPC (1946 ed.)
Santa Claus ("Old Santa Claus puts on his cap"). *Unknown.* GFA
Santa Claus and the Mouse. Emilie Poulsson. ChBR; GFA; UTS
Santa Claus, I hang for you. A Real Santa Claus. Frank Dempster Sherman. ChBR; GaP
Santa Claus' Petition. Julie Mathilde Lippmann. SDH
Santa Fé Trail. Barbara Guest. NeAP
Santa Fé Trail, The, *with music.* *Unknown.* CoSo
Santa-Fé Trail, The (A Humoresque). Vachel Lindsay. CoBA; CP; CV; IAP; MOAP; NV; PFE; PoeMoYo; PYM
"I am a tramp by the long trail's border," *sel.* LaNeLa
Santa Filomena. Longfellow. PEDC; PoRL; PTA-2
Santa Maria! cover the child. *Unknown, tr. fr. Greek by* C. B. Sheridan. BOL
Santa Maria del Fiore. George Herbert Clarke. CaP; OCL
Santa Maria, well thou tremblest down the wave. The Triumph. Sidney Lanier. *Fr.* The Psalm of the West. PAH
Santa Teresa's Book-Mark. St. Theresa of Avila, *tr. fr. Spanish by* Longfellow. PoEL-5; TriL
(Alone God Sufficeth.) OQP; QP-1
(Let Nothing Disturb Thee.) AnSpL-1
(Lines Written in Her Breviary.) AWP; CAW; MaRV; OnPM
(Saint Teresa's Book-Mark.) MeRV; MW; WHL
(Who God Possesseth.) GrCo-1
Santiago. Thomas A. Janvier. MC; PAH
Santorin. James Elroy Flecker. FaBoTw; OBMV
Santos; New Mexico. May Sarton. NeTW; QS
Santy Anna [*or* Anno]. *Unknown.* *See* Santa Anna.
Sanyassi, The. Philip Gilbert Hamerton. VA
Saon of Acanthus. Callimachus, *tr. fr. Greek by* John Addington Symonds. AWP
(Good Live for Ever, The, *tr. by* Hugh Macnaghten.) OxBG
(In Memory of Saon of Acantus, *tr. by* F. A. Wright.) GrR
(Saon, *tr. by* Gerard Mackworth Young.) BoFr
Sap dripped from a broken twig. Youth of the Mountain. Walter Hard. AnNE
Sap is bubbling in the tree, The. For Old Lovers. T. A. Daly. OBAV
Sapho and Phao, *sels.* John Lyly.

"My shag-hair Cyclops, come, let's ply," *fr.* IV, iv. ElSeCe
(Song in Making of the Arrows, The.) LoBV; OBSC; TuPP
(Vulcan's Song.) ElL
Sapho's Song: "O cruel Love!" OBSC
Sapientia Lunae. Ernest Dowson. EnLi-2; HBV; POTT
Sapphic Stanzas. Aleksandr Radishchev, *tr. fr. Russian by* V. de S. Pinto. BoRS; LiTW
Sapphics. George Canning *and* John Hookham Frere. *See* Friend of Humanity and the Knife-Grinder, The.
Sapphics. Sir Philip Sidney. *Fr.* Arcadia. SiPS
Sapphics. Swinburne. AnEnPo; BPN; EmBrPo; Po; PoEL-5; POTT, *sts.* 1–6; PoVP; PtP; TOP; ViP; ViPo; VLEP
(Sappho.) GTML
Sapphics upon the Passion of Christ. *Unknown.* ReIE
Sapphire, nor diamond, nor emerald. No Jewel so Worthy. Jacopo da Lentino. OnPM
Sappho, *sel.* Bliss Carman.
"When in the spring the swallows all return," XCIII. PeCV
Sappho. Catullus, *tr. fr. Latin by* William Ellery Leonard. AWP; JAWP; WBP
(Catullus' Translation of the Ode to Anactoria, *tr. by* Sir William Marris.) LiA
Sappho. Poseidippus, *tr. fr. Greek by* F. L. Lucas. GrPE
Sappho ("All the night sleep came not"). Swinburne. *See* Sapphics.
Sappho ("Love's priestess"). Swinburne. *Fr.* On the Cliffs. GTML; VA
Sappho. Sara Teasdale. LBMV
Sappho and Phao. John Lyly. *See* Sapho and Phao.
Sappho, Be Comforted. William Carlos Williams. NePoAm-2
Sappho in Levkas. William Alexander Percy. LS
Sappho Rehung ("Sappho saw three stars"). LeRoy Smith, Jr. NePoAm
Sappho thou coverest, Aeolian land! To Sappho. Antipater of Sidon. GrPo
Sappho to Hesperus. Walter Savage Landor, *after the Greek of* Sappho. *Fr.* Pericles and Aspasia, CL. BPN
Sappho's Tomb. Arthur Stringer. CaP; OCL
Sapporo City. Kenji Miyazawa, *tr. fr. Japanese by* Takamichi Ninomiya *and* D. J. Enright. PoLJ
Sarah. "Robin Hyde." AnNZ
Sarah and William Adams! here we stood. Walkley. Ebenezer Elliott. EnSW
Sarah Byng. Hilaire Belloc. CenHV
Sarah kissed me when we met. Osculation. Henry Sydnor Harrison. InMe
Sarah Lorton. Mary Finnin. BoAV
Sarah Threeneedles. Katharine Lee Bates. BAP; HBMV
Sarah's Halls. "Judy." PA
Saratoga Song. *Unknown.* PAH
Sarcophagi. Bernard Spencer. FaBoMo
Sardanapalus. Earl of Surrey. SiPS
(Portrait of Henry VIII, The.) ACP (1952 ed.)
Sardine was lurking behind in the tin, The. The Fisherman on Toast. Edward Abbott Parry. BoN
Sardinia from a Liner. Leonora Speyer. PoeMoYo
Sardinian Lullaby. *Unknown.* RIS
("Oh! ninna and anninia!") BOL
(Sleep, Baby Boy.) FaPON
Sardonic master, you that dare betray. Zuloaga. Charles Wharton Stork. TBM
Sargent's Portrait of Edwin Booth at "The Players." Thomas Bailey Aldrich. AA
Sargon is dust, Semiramis a clod! The Dust Dethroned. George Sterling. *Fr.* Three Sonnets on Oblivion. BAP; HBV; LBMV
Saris go by me from the embassies, The. The Woman at the Washington Zoo. Randall Jarrell. UnPo (3d ed.)
Sarmèd, whom they intoxicated from the cup of love. Quatrain. Sarmèd the Yahud. TrJP
Sarolla's women in their picture hats. Lawrence Ferlinghetti. Pictures of the Gone World, Sec. 8. NeAP
Sarpedon and Glaucus. Homer, *tr. fr. Greek by* Maurice Hewlett. *Fr.* The Iliad, XII. OxBG
("Nor had great Hector and his friends the rampire overrun." *tr. by* George Chapman.) AtBAP
(Sarpedon and Glaucus; the Equation of Duty and Privilege, *tr. by* William Cowper.) GrR
(Sarpedon to Glaukos, *shorter sel., tr. by* Richmond Lattimore.) WaaP
(Sarpedon's Speech, *shorter sel., tr. by* George Chapman.) OBS
("Whence is it, Glaucus, that in Lycian land," *shorter sel., tr. by* the Earl of Derby.) GrPo
Sarpedon's words bit deep in Hector's heart. The Rally. Homer *tr. by* Sir William Marris. *Fr.* The Iliad, V. OxBG
Sarrazine's Song [to Her Dead Lover]. Marie de France. *See* Song from "Chartivel."
Sarsen-stone, The,/ Door-post of temple. In Course of Time. W. W. Gibson. ChMo; CMP
Sarsfield went out the Dutch to rout. A Ballad of Sarsfield. Aubrey Thomas De Vere. GoBC; HBV
Sartorial Solecism. R. E. C. Stringer. FiBHP
Sarum Primer, 1558, *sel. Unknown.*
God Be in My Head. MaRV; OxBoCh; PoLi
(Hymnus.) ChTr
(Knight's Prayer, The.) BoTP
(Mihi Adhaerere Deo Bonum Est.) PG (1955 ed.)
Sarvant, Marster! Yes, sah, dat's me. Uncle Gabe's White Folks. Thomas Nelson Page. AA; OBAV
Sary "Fixes Up" Things. Albert Bigelow Paine. BOHV
Sassafras. Samuel Minturn Peck. AA
Sassafras Tea. Mary Effie Lee Newsome. CDC; GoSl
Sat on a telephone pole talking to his girl. Lineman Calling. Josephine Miles. FiMAP
Sat Will & Kate. Those Troublesome Disguises. Jonathan Williams. NeAP
Satan. Milton. *Fr.* Paradise Lost, I. BLV, *ll.* 36–543, *abr.;* CBOV, *ll.* 34–75; LiA, *ll.* 589–599; SeCePo, *Bk.* I, *ll.* 283–313, *Bk.* II, *ll.* 1010–1055; TrGrPo, *ll.* 36–75, 221–237, 522–543
Satan and His Host. Milton. *Fr.* Paradise Lost, I. OBS
Satan and Pilate's Wife. *Unknown.* ACP (1952 ed.)
Satan and the Fallen Angels. Milton. *Fr.* Paradise Lost, I. CoEV; LiTB; OBS
(Satan.) SeCePo
(Satan Rallies the Fallen Angels, *abr.*) BCEP
(Superior Fiend, The.) MaPo
Satan Beholds Eve. Milton. *See* Eve and the Serpent.
Satan Defiant. Milton. *Fr.* Paradise Lost, I. WHA
(Fallen Angels, The.) FaBoEn
(". . . Him the Almighty Power/ Hurl'd headlong flaming.") AnFE; MyFE
Satan Discovers Eden. Milton. *See* Garden of Eden, The.
Satan from hence now on the lower stair. The Panorama. Milton. *Fr.* Paradise Lost, III. BrBE; WHA
Satan Greets Hell. Milton. *Fr.* Paradise Lost, I. LiA
Satan in Sight of Eden. Milton. *Fr.* Paradise Lost, IV. TCEP
Satan in Profile. Harold Vinal. MuM
Satan Is on Your Tongue. George Barker. MoAB; MoBrPo (1950 ed.)
Satan Journeys to the Garden of Eden. Milton. *Fr.* Paradise Lost, IV. ChTr
Satan Looks upon Adam and Eve in Paradise. Milton. *See* Adam and Eve in the Garden.
Satan on War. Milton. *Fr.* Paradise Lost, II. MaRV
Satan Ponders His Fallen State. Milton. *See* Fall of the Angels, The.
Satan Rallies the Fallen Angels. Milton. *See* Satan and the Fallen Angels.
Satan Reflects. Milton. *Fr.* Paradise Lost, IV. CoEV
("O thou that with surpassing glory crown'd.") NBE
(Satan Speaks, *abr.*) PIAE
(Satan's Address to the Sun.) EV-2
(Satan's Soliloquy.) LiTB; OBS
Satan Views the World. Milton. *Fr.* Paradise Lost, II. WHA
Satan's a Liar [*or* Liah]. *Unknown.* AS, *with music;* IHA; SoAF, *with music*
Satan's Address to the Sun. Milton. *See* Satan Reflects.
Satan's Adjuration. Milton. *Fr.* Paradise Lost, I. FaBoEn
Satan's First Meeting with Death. Milton. *Fr.* Paradise Lost, II. CBE
Satan's Guile. Milton. *Fr.* Paradise Regained, I. LiTB; OBS
Satan's Kingdom. Milton. *See* Fall of the Angels, The.
Satan's Presumption and Fall. Cædmon(?). *See* Fall of Satan, The.
Satan's Pride. Milton. *Fr.* Paradise Lost, IV. MaRV
Satan's Soliloquy. Milton. *See* Satan Reflects.
Satan's Survey of Greece. Milton. *See* Athens.
Sate the heavy burghers. The Brave Women of Tann. William James Linton. BHV
"Sated Guest, The." Mimnermus, *tr. fr. Greek by* F. L. Lucas. GrPE
Sather Gate Illumination. Allen Ginsberg. NeAP
Satin Shoes, The. Thomas Hardy. CoBMV
Satira Prima. Everard Guilpin. *Fr.* Skialetheia. ReIE
Satire, *sel.* John Marston. *Fr.* Certaine Satyres, V.
"Ambitious Gorgons, wide-mouthed Lamians." ViBoPo
Satire, A, *sel.* John Oldham.
"But, grant thy poetry should find success." ViBoPo
Satire, The, *sel.* Sulpicia II, *tr. fr. Latin by* Jack Lindsay.
"Look back. Two powers have raised Rome's lofty head." LaP
Satire I: "Alas, man's care, and O the vacuity." Persius, *tr. fr. Latin by* Robert A. Brooks. *Fr.* Satires. LaP
Satire VI: "Another scorns the homespun thread of rhymes." Joseph Hall. *Fr.* Virgidemiarum. SiCE; TuPP
Satire: "Ask you what provocation I have had?" Pope. *Fr.* Epilogue to the Satires, Dialogue II. OBEC
(In Defence of Satire.) CoBE
(Provocation to Satire.) BeR

Satire: "Away, thou fondling motley humorist." John Donne. Satires, I. OAEP
Satire VIII: "Curio, ay me! Thy mistress' monkey's dead!" John Marston. *Fr.* The Scourge of Villainy. ReEn; ReIE
Satire I: Garnet's Ghost Addressing to the Jesuits. John Oldham. *Fr.* Satires upon the Jesuits. SeEP
Satire: "Gentle squire would gladly entertain, A." Joseph Hall. *See* Trencher-Chaplain, The.
Satire: "Great is the folly of a feeble brain." Joseph Hall. *See* Love-sicke Poet, The.
Satire: "Great Osmond knows not how he shall be known." Joseph Hall. *Fr.* Virgidemiarum. ReIE
Satire VI: "Has winter brought you to the Sabine fire." Persius, *tr. fr. Latin by* Robert A. Brooks. *Fr.* Satires. LaP
Satire X: Humors, *sel.* John Marston. *Fr.* The Scourge of Villainy.
"Sleep, grim reproof, my jocund muse doth sing." SiCE, *longer sel.;* TuPP
Satire II: "I cannot hold, I cannot, I, indure." John Marston. *Fr.* The Scourge of Villainy. ReIE
Satire: "I wot not how the world's degenerate." Joseph Hall. *Fr.* Virgidemiarum. ReIE
Satire III: "Kind pity [*or* Kinde pitty] chokes my spleen; brave scorn forbids." John Donne. *Fr.* Satires. MaPo; MeLP; OBS; PoEL-2; ReIE; SeEP; TuPP
(Religion.) ReEn
(Satire III: On Religion.) EPS (1942 ed.)
(Satyre III: "Kinde pitty chokes my spleene; brave scorn forbids.") EnLP; SeCV-1
(Satyre: Of Religion.) MePo
(Truth.) SeCePo
"But unmoved thou," *fr.* III. NBE
Satire VII: "'Man, a man, a kingdom for a man, A!'" John Marston. *Fr.* The Scourge of Villainy. ReIE
Satire: "Mine own John Poynz." Sir Thomas Wyatt. *See* Of the Courtier's Life.
Satire I: "Nor lady's wanton love, nor wand'ring knight." Joseph Hall. *Fr.* Virgidemiarum. TuPP
("Nor ladies' wanton love, nor wandering knight.") SiCE
Satire: "Satire, my friend ('twixt me and you)." Alexander Geddes. ACP
Satire: "Sir: though (I thank God for it) I do hate." John Donne. Satires, II. PoFS; ViBoPo
Satire III: "Still at it? Morning stares between the shutters." Persius, *tr. fr. Latin by* Robert A. Brooks. *Fr.* Satires. LaP
Satire IV: "Vice, from privation of that sacred grace." John Marston. *Fr.* The Scourge of Villainy. ReIE
Satire IV: "Well; I may now receive, and die; my sinne." John Donne. *Fr.* Satires. SeEP
Satire II: "Yes; thank my stars! as early as I knew." Pope. *Fr.* The Satires of Dr. John Donne, Versified. PoFS
Satire against Mankind, A. Earl of Rochester. EiPP; SiTL
(Satyr against Mankind, A.) CEP; NBE; OBS, *abr.;* PoEL-3; SeCV-2
Sels.
"Were I, who to my cost already am." CoEV; FaBoEn; LiTB; LiTG
Wretched Man. SeCePo
Satire, be kind, and draw a silent veil. Daniel Defoe. *Fr.* The True-born Englishman, I. TOP
Satire Dissuading from Poetry, A, *sel.* John Oldham.
"'Tis so, 'twas ever so, since heretofore," (*abr.*). EPP
Satire, my friend ('twixt me and you). Satire. Alexander Geddes. ACP
Satire of Circumstance, A ("I stood at the back of the shop . . ."). Thomas Hardy. *Fr.* Satires of Circumstance. NeMA
Satire of the Three Estates, The, *sels.* Sir David Lindsay.
"Have I nocht made ane honest shift." GoTS
Prologue: "Father and founder of faith and felicity," *in mod. Eng.* TMEV
Satire on London, A. Earl of Surrey. SiPS
(London, Hast Thou Accusèd Me.) OAEP; ReEn; TuPP
Satire on Mahmúd. Firdausi, *tr. fr. Persian by* Joseph Champion. *Fr.* Shah Namah. PeP
Satire on Paying Calls [in August]. Ch'eng Hsiao, *tr. fr. Chinese by* Arthur Waley. TrCh; WoL
Satire on Riches. Pope. *See* Timon's Villa.
Satire on the People of Kildare, A. *Unknown, at. to* Friar Michael of Kildare, *mod. vers. by* St. John Seymour. OnYI
Satire on the Royal Society, A. Samuel Butler. BeR
Satire on the Toun Ladies. Sir Richard Maitland. EBSV
Satire should be like the porcupine, The. Joseph Hall. *Fr.* Virgidemiarum. ReEn
Satires, *sels.* John Donne.
"Away, thou fondling motley humorist," I. OAEP
"Kind pity [*or* Kinde pitty] chokes my spleen; brave scorn forbids," III. MaPo; MeLP; OBS; PoEL-2; ReIE; SeEP; TuPP
(Religion.) ReEn
(Satire III: On Religion.) EPS (1942 ed.)
(Satyre III: "Kinde pitty chokes my spleen; brave scorn forbids.") EnLP; SeCV-1
(Satyre: Of Religion.) MePo
(Truth.) SeCePo
"But unmoved thou," *fr.* III. NBE
"Sir, though (I thank God for it) I do hate," II. PoFS; ViBoPo
"Well; I may now receive, and die; my sinne," IV. SeEP
Satires, *sels.* Horace, *tr. fr. Latin.*
Bore, The, I, 9. ATP, *tr. by* John Conington; EnLi-1, *tr. by* Sir Theodore Martin; OuHeWo, *tr. by* Sir Theodore Martin; RoL, *tr. by* B. L. Ullman
"Fig-tree log I used to be, A," I, 8, *tr. by* George F. Whicher. LaP
"I left great Rome. Aricia offered me," I, 5, *tr. by* Jack Lindsay. LaP
Satires, The, *sels.* Juvenal, *tr. fr. Latin.*
Against Women, Satire VI, *abr., tr. by* Dryden. LiTW
"But you should know what Everywoman does, *fr.* VI, *tr. by* Gilbert Highet. LaP
Celestial Wisdom, X, *tr. by* Samuel Johnson. AWP; JAWP; WBP
Fair Field for Satire, A, *fr.* I, *tr. by* William Gifford. RoL
"Grieved though I am to see the man depart," III, *tr. by* William Gifford. EnLi-1
In Saturn's Reign, *fr.* VI, *tr. by* Dryden. BeR
Life at Rome, III, *tr. by* Miriam Allen deFord. LaP
Mood and Figure Bride, A, *fr.* VI, *tr. by* Dryden. BeR
New Woman, The, *fr.* VI, *tr. by* William Gifford. RoL
On Poets Who Recite in Public—and Other Sinners, I, *tr. by* L. R. Lind. LaP
Rome a Greek City, *fr.* III, *tr. by* William Gifford. RoL
Tenth Satire of Juvenal, The, *tr. by* Dryden. WoL
Vanity of Human Wishes, The, X. LaP, *tr. by* L. R. Lind; RoL, *tr. by* William Gifford
Satires, *sels.* Persius, *tr. fr. Latin.*
"Alas, man's care, and O the vacuity," I, *tr. by* Robert A. Brooks. LaP
"Has winter brought you to the Sabine fire," VI, *tr. by* Robert A. Brooks. LaP
Prologue to the First Satire, *tr. by* Dryden. AWP
"Still at it? Morning stares between the shutters," III, *tr. by* Robert A. Brooks. LaP
Satires, *sels.* Sir Thomas Wyatt.
"Mine [*or* Myne] own John Poynz," I. PoEL-1; ReEn; SiPS
(Of the Courtier's Life.) CoBE; GoTL; OBSC; ReIE; SiCE; TuPP
"My mother's maids, when they did sew and spin," II. SiPS
(Of the Mean and Sure Estate.) BEL; EPP; ReIE; SiCE; TuPP
"Spending hand, A," III.
(To Sir Francis Brian.) SiPS
Satires: In the Service of the Duke. Ariosto, *tr. fr. Italian by* L. R. Lind. LyPI
Satires of Circumstance, *sels.* Thomas Hardy.
At Tea, I. EPP; PoVP; TyEnPo
At the Altar-Rail, IX. MBP; MoAB; MoBrPo; PoVP
At the Draper's, XII. EnLi-2 (1949 ed.); MBP; MoAB; MoBrPo; NeMA
By Her Aunt's Grave, III. MBP; MoAB; MoBrPo; PoVP
"I stood at the back of the shop, my dear."
(Satire of Circumstance, A.) NeMA
In Church, II. MBP; MoAB; MoBrPo
In the Restaurant, XI. MBP; MoAB; MoBrPo
Satires of Dr. John Donne, Versified, The, *sel.* Pope.
Satire II: "Yes; thank my stars! as early as I knew." PoFS
Satires [*or* Satyrs] upon the Jesuits, *sels.* John Oldham.
Garnet's Ghost Addressing to the Jesuits, I. SeEP
Prologue: "For who can longer hold?" CEP; SeCV-2
"When shaven crown, and hallow'd girdle's power," III. SeCV-2
Words from a Wooden Image. BeR
Satirical Elegy on the Death of a Late Famous General, A (the Duke of Marlborough). Swift. BeR; HoPM; PoEL-3
(Satyrical Elegy on the Death of a Late Famous General, A, 1722.) ExPo; SeCeV
Satirical Letrilla III: "Such is, dear girl, my tenderness." Manuel Bretón de los Herreros, *tr. fr. Spanish by* James Kennedy. AnSpL-2
Satirical Letrilla: "That much a widowed wife will moan." José de Cadalso Vazquez, *tr. fr. Spanish.* AnSpL-2
Satirical Letrilla IV: "Whene'er Don Juan has a feast at home." Manuel Bretón de los Herreros, *tr. fr. Spanish by* James Kennedy. AnSpL-2
Satirical Poems on Daimyos. Issa, *tr. fr. Japanese by* Max Bickerton. PoFr
Satirist, The. Harry Lyman Koopman. AA
Satirist, The. Swift. *Fr.* Epistle to a Lady. BeR
Satisfied. Samuel Valentine Cole. BLRP
Satisfied. Edgar Cooper Mason. BLRP
Satisfying Portion, The. *Unknown.* BLRP

Satrapy. C. P. Cavafy, *tr. fr. Modern Greek by* Rae Dalven. MoGP
Saturday Afternoon. Lilian Bowes-Lyon. AlDL
Saturday. Dove calls to running wave. Beach Queen. David Campbell. BoAV
Saturday Market, *sel.* Charlotte Mew.
"In Saturday Market, there's eggs a-plenty." FaPON; HBMV; NV
Saturday Night. Langston Hughes. MAP; MoAmPo
Saturday Night. James Oppenheim. HBV; TSW
Saturday Night. *Unknown.* SAS
"Saturday night, A/ a Sunday morning!" Battarias. Miltiades Malakassis. MoGP
Saturday; or, The Flights. John Gay. *Fr.* The Shepherd's Week. EiPP
Saturday Sundae. Francis Reginald Scott. BoCaPo (1948 ed.); CaP
Saturday Towels. Lysbeth Boyd Borie. UTS
Saturday's Child. Countee Cullen. PoNe
Saturday's Party in Fairyland, The. Mary Carolyn Davies. TVC; TVSH
Saturn. Keats. *Fr.* Hyperion, I. LoBV; TrGrPo
(Saturn Fallen.) AnEnPo
Saturn. Sir Arthur Quiller-Couch. BMEP; LBBV
Saturn Fallen. Keats. *See* Saturn.
Saturnian mother! why dost thou devour. Russia. Nathan Haskell Dole. AA
Saturninus. Katherine Eleanor Conway. AA; JKCP
Satyr, The. André Chénier, *tr. fr. French by* Alan Conder. TrFP
Satyr, The. John Fletcher. *Fr.* The Faithful Shepherdess, I, i.
("Here be grapes, whose lusty blood.") EV-2
Satyr, The, *sel.* Ben Jonson.
Queen Mab. HBV; OTPC (1923 ed.)
(Mab the Mistress-Fairy.) ElL
("This is Mab, the mistress fairy.") ElSeCe; SiCE
Satyr, The. James Stephens. OnYI
Satyr III: "When shaven Crown, and hallow'd Girdle's Power." John Oldham. *Fr.* Satyrs upon the Jesuits. SeCV-2
Satyr Address'd to a Friend That Is About to Leave the University, and Come Abroad in the World, A, *sel.* John Oldham.
"If you for Orders." OBS
Satyr against Mankind, A. Earl of Rochester. *See* Satire against Mankind, A.
Satyr in the Periwig, The. Edith Sitwell. *Fr.* Façade. AnEnPo
Satyr, The; or, The Song of Nudity. Kostes Palamas, *tr. fr. Modern Greek by* Rae Dalven. MoGP
Satyr Scarabombardon, The. The Satyr in the Periwig. Edith Sitwell. *Fr.* Façade. AnEnPo
Satyra Quinta. Everard Guilpin. *Fr.* Skialetheia. TuPP
("Let me alone, I prithee, in this cell.") SiCE
Satyre III: "Kinde pitty chokes my spleene; brave scorn forbids." John Donne. *See* Satire III: "Kind pity chokes my spleen . . ."
Satyre: Of Religion. John Donne. *See* Satire III: "Kind pity chokes my spleen . . ."
Satyre Entituled the Witch, A. *Unknown.* CoMu
Satyre, Heracleia, Euphro, three. A Dedication to Athene. Archias. OxBG
Satyrical Elegy on the Death of a Late Famous General, A, 1722. Swift. *See* Satirical Elegy . . .
Satyricon, *sel.* Petronius, *tr. fr. Latin by* John Peale Bishop.
"Can it indeed be, Jove, you have grown old?" LaP
Satyrs and the Moon, The. Herbert S. Gorman. HBV; PFY; TSW; TSWC
Satyr's Farewell, The. John Fletcher. *Fr.* The Faithful Shepherdess, V, v. OBS
(Satyr's Leave-taking, The.) LoBV (2d ed.)
("Thou divinest, fairest, brightest.") LO
Satyr's Song ("See, the day begins to break"). John Fletcher. *Fr.* The Faithful Shepherdess, IV, iv. OBS
Satyrs upon the Jesuits. John Oldham. *See* Satires upon the Jesuits.
Saucy Sailor, The, *with music.* *Unknown.* SaSa
Saul. Nathan Alterman, *tr. fr. Hebrew by* Dov Vardi. TrJP
Saul. Robert Browning. BEL; BHV, *much abr.*; BoFr, *much abr.*; BPN; EM-2; EmBrPo; EnLi-2; EPN; GBV (1922 ed.); GEPC; MaRV; OAEP; OxBoCh; PoVP; TCEP; TOP; TwCrTr; ViPo; VLEP; WHA
Sels.
God with Us, 6 *ll. fr.* XVII. GrCo-2
"I believe it! 'Tis thou, God, that givest, 'tis I who receive," XVIII. ChIP; StJW
"I have gone the whole round of creation," XVII-XVIII. EPP
"I know not too well how I found my way home in the night," XIX. LoBV
"Then I tuned my harp, took off the lilies we twine round its chords," V. BBV (1951 ed.); FiP (V-IX); PreP (V-XVIII, *abr.*)
"Then the truth came upon me," XVI-XIX. PIAE
Wild Joys of Living, The, *fr.* IX. BLV; MuP
(David Sings to Saul.) GTML
(David's Song: "Oh, our manhood's prime vigor!") BoLiVe
(Joy of Living, The.) ShBV-2
(Saul: "Oh, our manhood's prime vigor!") OtMeF
(Saul: "Oh, the wild joys of living.") PC
(Youth.) BoTP
"Yea, my King," XIII-XIX, *sl. abr.* WGRP
Saul, *sels.* Charles Heavysege.
David Exorcising Malzah, the Evil Spirit from the Lord. VA
Flight of Malzah, The. VA
Hell's Road. BMEP
"Lo! I Am Saul." BoCaPo
Malzah and the Angel Zelehtha. VA
Malzah Speaks. BoCaPo
Malzah's Song. BoCaPo
Saul's Faithfulness. BMEP
"To hunt and to be hunted make existence." CaP
"What now? Thou look'st surprised." PeCV
Zaph Describes the Haunts of Malzah. BoCaPo
Saul. George Sterling. HBMV; TBM
Saul, David, and Jonathan. First Samuel XVI: 15-XXIV: 20; Second Samuel I: 2-27, Bible, *O.T.* BoFr
"Saul Kane," she said, "when next you drink." Another Cross. John Masefield. *Fr.* The Everlasting Mercy. MaRV
Saul, King of Israel, *sels.* Victor Starbuck.
David's Song to the Troubled King. NoCaPo
Gilboa. MuM
Jabesh Gilead. MuM
Saul's Faithfulness. Charles Heavysege. *Fr.* Saul. BMEP
Sauntering hither on listless wings. To a Sea-Bird. Bret Harte. BLA; EtS; LBAP; SN
Sauntering the pavement or riding the country by-road. Faces. Walt Whitman. Po; PoEL-5
Sauntering through Chao Village at Apricot-blossoming Time. Po Chü-i, *tr. fr. Chinese by* Ching Ti. WhP
Sausage-Seller's Triumph, The. Aristophanes, *tr. fr. Greek by* Benjamin Bickley Rogers. *Fr.* The Knights. GrR
Savage, A. John Boyle O'Reilly. AA; OBAV
Savage Grandeur. Sir Walter Scott. The Lord of the Isles, IV. EV-4
Savage I was sitting in my house, late, lone. Epilogue [*or* The Householder]. Robert Browning. *Fr.* Fifine at the Fair. BPN; LO; NBE
Savage loves his native shore, The. The Irishman. James Orr. DD
Savage Nomad Hordes. Anatoly Borisovich Marienhof, *tr. fr. Russian by* Babette Deutsch. TrRV
Savage Portraits. Don Marquis. HBMV
Savages, The. Josephine Miles. FiMAP
Savannah. Alethea S. Burroughs. PAH
Savannah River. Roselle Mercier Montgomery. LS
Save love of thee a soul in me I cannot see, I cannot see. I Cannot See. Iraqi. PeP
Save me, Lord! thou King Eternal! Oratio ad Dominum. Hildebert of Lavardin. LaP
Save the Tiger! A. P. Herbert. OnSP
Save up. Your very death won't dim an eye. Put Money in Thy Purse. Theognis. GrL; OxBG
Saved by Grace. Fanny Crosby. BPP
Saving God, The. Fulke Greville. *See* Caelica: "Down in the depth of mine iniquity."
Saviour, The. Piotr Vasilievich Oreshin, *tr. fr. Russian by* George Z. Patrick. BoFr
Saviour, The. Samuel Wesley. BePJ
Saviour, bowed beneath His cross, climbed up the dreary hill, The. Why the Robin's Breast Was Red. James Ryder Randall. AA; CAW; JKCP
Saviour, Breathe an Evening Blessing. James Edmeston. MaRV
(Evening Blessing, An.) BePJ
Saviour came, The. With trembling lips. The Second Coming. Norman Gale. BLP; HBV; MaRV; PC
Saviour Can Solve Every Problem, The. Oswald J. Smith. BePJ
Savior Eternal, night and day before Thee my sighs ascend. Psalm Eighty-eight. Théodore Agrippa d'Aubigné. LiA
Saviour [*or* Savior], I've no one else to tell. Emily Dickinson. CoBA; TrPWD
(Dost Thou Remember Me?) MaRV
Saviour looked on Peter, The. Aye, no word. The Look [*or* "The Lord Turned, and Looked upon Peter"]. Elizabeth Barrett Browning. ChIP; MaRV
Saviour of mankind, Man! Emmanuel! Lines Written at the Temple of the Holy Sepulchre. George Sandys. BePJ
Saviour, on Thy birthday dear. Christmas. Nancy Byrd Turner. PraP
Saviour Teach Me. Jane Eliza Leeson. MaRV
Saviour, the world's and mine. Draw Me, Saviour, after Thee Charles Wesley. BePJ

Saviour! Thy dying love. Something for Jesus. S. D. Phelps. BLRP
Saviour, when in dust to thee. Litany. Robert Grant. LPS-2
Saviour, Who Died for Me. Mary J. Mason. BePJ
Saviour, Whose Love Is like the Sun. Howard Chandler Robbins. TrPWD
Saviors, The. *Unknown, tr. fr. Greek by* Lord Neaves. OnPM
Savonarola. E. C. Bentley. OxBoLi
Savor. "Pablo Neruda," *tr. fr. Spanish by* H. R. Hays. TwSpPo
Saw God Dead but Laughing. José Garcia Villa. AnFE; CoAnAm; TwAmPo
Saw Ye Bonie Lesley. Burns. *See* Bonnie Lesley.
Saw Ye Johnnie Comin'? Joanna Baillie. EBSV
Saw ye Neece O'Hagan. Neece the Rapparee. "Ethna Carbery." BOL
Saw Ye Never in the Meadows, *abr.* Cecil Frances Alexander. OTPC (1923 ed.)
Saw you never in the twilight. The Adoration of the Wise Men. Cecil Frances Alexander. COAH; HBVY; PRWS
Sawney Was Tall. Thomas D'Urfey. *Fr.* The Virtuous Wife. OAEP
Saws Were Shrieking, The. W. W. E. Ross. CaP; PeCV
Saxon Grit. Robert Collyer. HBV; OTPC (1923 ed.)
Saxon Song, A. V. Sackville-West. MBP; MoBrPo (1942 ed.)
Saxons of Flint, The. Lewys Glyn Cothi, *tr. fr. Welsh by* Mrs. M. C. Llewelyn. PrWP
Say, are you she that came to me last. The Second Vision. Tadhg Dall O'Huiginn. AnIL
Say, birdies, when your bed-time comes. The Bye-low Song. *Unknown.* BOL
"Say, bold but blessed thief." The Thief. *Unknown.* CenL; LO; MeRV; OBS; OxBoCh; SeCL
Say, bud, ya got a cigarette? Refugee. Naomi Long Witherspoon. PoNe
Say, but did you love so long? An Answer. Sir Tobie Matthew. SeCL; SeCV-1
Say, crimson rose and dainty daffodil. A Nosegay [*or* The Garden's Queen]. John Reynolds. OBEV; SeCL
Say, darkeys [*or* darkies] hab you seen de massa. Year of Jubilo [*or* Jubilee]. Henry Clay Work. PAH; TrAS
Say, did his sisters wonder what could Joseph see. Regina Coeli. Coventry Patmore. ISi; JKCP; MOAH; POTT; PoVP; VA; VLEP
Say, earth, why hast thou got thee new attire. Easter Morn. Giles Fletcher, the Younger. *Fr.* Christ's Victory and Triumph. EIL
Say, fair maids maying. Of Life. Andrew Lang. VA
"Say, fellers, that ornery thief must be nigh us." Denver Jim. Sherman D. Richardson. SCC
Say first . . . which is it men call Pylades? Tidings of Home [*or* Agamemnon's Children]. Euripides. *Fr.* Iphigenia in Tauris. GrR; OxBG
Say, from what golden quivers of the sky. Abraham Cowley. *Fr.* Hymn: To Light. LPS-2
Say goodnight to him and shut the door. Exquisite Lady. Mary Elizabeth Osborn. NePoAm-2
Say, guiltless pair. The Winged Worshippers. Charles Sprague. AA; HBV; LPS-2; SN
Say he was sad, for there was none to love him. Epitaph. Robert Nathan. MuM
Say—if men ask for him—he has gone home. Lincoln. Wendell Phillips Stafford. HH
Say, in a hut of mean estate. The Soul of Man. Dora Reed Goodale. AA
Say, is it day, is it dusk in thy bower. The Song of the Bower. Dante Gabriel Rossetti. EmBrPo; HBV; PoVP; TCEP
Say it is life that matters. Say the bone. Address to the Doomed, I. George Dillon. NP
Say It Now. *Unknown.* BLPA; WBLP
(If You Have a Friend.) FaFP
(Seeds of Kindness.) PoToHe
(Sermon in Rhyme, A.) PTA-2
Say it were true that thou outliv'st us all. To My Tortoise Ἀνάγκη (Ananke). Eugene Lee-Hamilton. OBVV
Say, Lad, Have You Things to Do? A. E. Housman. A Shropshire Lad, XXIV. BPN; NeMA; PoVP
Say, Little Maiden. Arthur Upson. BOL
Say, lovelorn heart, that art condemned upon despair to feed. Lament of a Despised Lover. Juan Ruiz, Archpriest of Hita. TeCS
Say, Lovely Dream. Edmund Waller. OAEP
Say, lovely nymph, where dost thou dwell? To the Echo; in a Clear Night upon Astrop Walks. Countess of Winchilsea. EiPP
Say, lovely Tory, why the jest. To Miss Eleanor Ambrose on the Occasion of Her Wearing an Orange Lily at a Ball in Dublin Castle on July the 12th. Earl of Chesterfield. EnLoPo
Say Me Wiit in the Brom. *Unknown.* OAEP
Say, Mr. McGregor, do still you go hoeing. Paging Mr. McGregor. Edgar A. Guest. OnHT
Say, Moll, now don't you 'llow to quit. Cowboy's Valentine. Charles Fletcher Lummis. SCC
Say, Muse, who first, who last, on foot or steed. On the Road to Anster Fair. William Tennant. *Fr.* Anster Fair. OBRV
Say my love is easy had. Fighting Words. Dorothy Parker. InMe; LauV; NAMP
Say Nay. Sir Thomas Wyatt. *See* Earnest Suit to His Unkind Mistress Not to Forsake Him, An.
Say not, "I live!" A Song of Life. Angela Morgan. BLP
Say not I write to a metre's measure. The Cry of the Song Children. Wilson MacDonald. CPG
Say not, "It matters not to me." Where Is Thy Brother? *Unknown.* MaRV
Say not of Beauty she is good. Beauty. Elinor Wylie. NP; OxBA
Say not our hands are cruel. The Angler's Vindication. Thomas Todd Stoddart. EBSV
Say not so briefly that the stars to-night. Vide Astra. Julia Cooley. LEAP
Say Not that Beauty. Robin Flower. HBMV; HBVY; PtOT
Say not that death is king, that night is lord. Easter. Thomas Curtis Clark. OQP; QP-1
Say not that, its treasure exhausted. Rima IV. Gustavo Adolfo Bécquer. *Fr.* Rimas. AnSpL-2
Say Not That the Past Is Dead. W. E. H. Lecky. EPN (Unconscious Cerebration.) InP
Say not the good are dead. In Memory of Saon of Acantus. Callimachus. GrR
Say Not the Struggle [Nought Availeth]. Arthur Hugh Clough. AEV; AnFE; ATP; AWP; BEL; BLP; BMEP; BPN; CaAE; CBOV; CoEV; EmBrPo; EnLi-2; EnLit; EPN; EPP; EV-5; FaBoEn; FaFP; GTBS; GTBS-D; GTBS-W; GTML; GTSL; HBV; HBVY; JAWP; LEAP; LiTB; LiTG; LoBV; MaRV; OAEP; OBEV; OBVV; OtMeF; PC; PCD; PIAE; PoeMoYo; PoFr; PoVP; PreP; PTA-1; ReaPo; ShBV-3; ShGoBo; StaSt; TCEP; TOP; TreF; TrGrPo; TVSH; ViBoPo; ViP; ViPo; ViPP; VLEP; WaaP; WBP; WGRP
(Hope.) BHV
(Keeping On.) CBPC; MoShBr
Say Not 'Tis Dark. Caroline Norton. UnW
Say not you *love* a roasted fowl. Loving and Liking. Dorothy Wordsworth. OTPC (1923 ed.)
"Say, O Fool, hast thou riches?" The Lover and the Belovèd. Ramon Lull. CAW
Say of them/ They knew no Spanish. To the Veterans of the Abraham Lincoln Brigade. Genevieve Taggard. PoFr
Say over again, and yet once over again. Sonnets from the Portuguese, XXI. Elizabeth Barrett Browning. BPN; EmBrPo; EPP; HBV; PIR; ViPo
Say, pard, have you sighted a schooner. The Santa Fe Trail. *Unknown.* CoSo
Say puritan ist come to passe. *Unknown.* SeCSL
Say sheaphards boy who makes thee greeve soe sore. *Unknown.* SeCSL
Say, sweet, my grief and I, we may not brook. Je ne veux de personne auprès de ma tristesse. Henri de Régnier. AWP; JAWP; WBP
Say That He Loved Old Ships. Daniel Whitehead Hicky. EtS; PoMa; PoTo
Say That I Should Say [I Love Ye]. Nicholas Breton. EIL; OBSC; ReEn; TuPP
Say that the men of the old black tower. The Black Tower. W. B. Yeats. ChMo
Say that thou didst forsake me for some fault. Sonnets, LXXXIX. Shakespeare. OAEP; PeBoSo; SiCE
Say there! P'r'aps. "Jim." Bret Harte. AA; BOHV; IAP; LEAP; LPS-3; MAP; MoAmPo (1942 ed.); NeMA; TCAP; WhC
Say this city has ten million souls. Refugee Blues. W. H. Auden. InPo; LiTA; LiTM; SoV
Say This of Horses. Minnie Hite Moody. DDA; PoeMoYo
Say this when you return. The Wrong Road. Richard Church. POTE
Say thou who liest here beneath. For a Gravestone in Spain. Walter Savage Landor. TriL
Say well and do well. *Unknown.* OxNR
Say, what blinds us, that we claim the glory. Self-Deception. Matthew Arnold. BPN; EmBrPo; PoVP; VLEP
Say! what is life? 'Tis to be born. The Story of Life. John Godfrey Saxe. PoToHe (new ed.)
Say, what is the spell, when her fledgings are cheeping. A Song of Love. "Lewis Carroll." GN
Say what you like. Nature's Friend. W. H. Davies. BMEP; CP; LBBV; PoRL; POT; PoTo; RG; TSW; TSWC
Say What You Will. Edna St. Vincent Millay. BLV; BoLiVe
(Sonnet: "Say what you will.") HBMV

Say what you will, there is not in the world. Chanclebury Ring. Wilfrid Scawen Blunt. MM; PoeT
"Say, where did you get that spear there?" I asked of the hunter old. Smoke of the Camp Fire. Brian Brooke. BoSA
"Say, where have you been, Frank—say, where have you been?" The Old Man in the Moon. *Unknown.* PCH
"Say, where is the maiden sweet." Sag', wo ist dein schönes Liebchen [*or* Love Dead]. Heine, *tr. by* James Thomson. AWP; OnPM; OuHeWo
Say, where is your Love so lovely. Ashes. Heine, *tr. by* Asa Hughes. LiTW
Say, whose is the watch? The Watch before Dawn [*or* Night Watch]. Euripides. *Fr.* Rhesus. GrR; OxBG
Say, wilt thou go with me, sweet maid. Invitation to Eternity. John Clare. PoEL-4; TriL; UnW
Say with a friend we contemplate some scene. Caroline Anne Bowles. *Fr.* The Birthday. EnSW
Say, would'st thou be. The Last Hour. Henry Augustus Rawes. CAW
Say, wouldst thou guard thy son. Of Caution. Francesco da Barberino. AWP; JAWP; LyPI; OnPM; WBP
Say, ye that know, ye who have felt and seen. Lambs at Play. Robert Bloomfield. LPS-2
Say you, my life, that we shall ever love? Lesbia's Vow. Catullus. OnPM
Saye, must wee part. *Unknown.* SeCSL
Sayes "Christ thee save, good Child of Ell!" Earl Brand (F *vers.*) ESPB
Saying a Prayer. Rowena Bennett. MPB (1956 ed.)
Saying Farewell to a Friend. Li Po, *tr. fr. Chinese.* WhP
Saying Not Meaning. William Basil Wake. BOHV
Saying "There is no hope," he stepped. A Generous Creed. Elizabeth Stuart Phelps Ward. WGRP
Sayings of the High One, The. *Unknown, tr. fr. Icelandic by* Henry Adams Bellows. *Fr.* The Elder Edda. PaOS
Hava-Mal, The ("Happy is he/ Who for himself winneth"), *sel.* BoFr
Saylors for My Money. Martin Parker. *See* Sailors for My Money.
Saylor's Onely Delight, The. *Unknown. See George Aloe* and the *Sweepstake,* The, *and* High Barbaree, The.
Saylor's Song, The. *Unknown.* SG
Says Aucassin [*wr.* Auccasain] to Nicolette. Ballade Morale. Neil Tracy. BoCaPo
Says Hyam to Moses. A Practical Answer. Shirley Brooks. SiTL
Says I to Myself. Edward Lear. FiBHP; WhC
Says my uncle, I pray you discover. Molly Mog; or, The Fair Maid of the Inn. John Gay. CEP; CoMu
Says Phoebe Snow. The D. L. and W's Phoebe Snow. *Unknown.* TreF
Says She. Winifred M. Letts. MW
Says Stonewall Jackson to "Little Phil": "Phil, have you heard the news?" Joined the Blues. John Jerome Rooney. AA
Says the Colonel to the sergeant, "I was kept awake all night." Raggles. Robert C. V. Meyers. AlBD
Says the master to me, is it true? I am told. My Master and I. *Unknown.* CoMu
Says this gravestone sorrow-laden: "Death has taken to his keeping." "Man Is Born to Sorrow." Philitas. GrPE
Says Tweed to Till. The Rivers Till and Tweed [*or* Still Waters *or* The Two Rivers]. *Unknown.* BLV; CBOV; ChTr; OBEV; ShBV-1; WhC
Scabby walls of tenements, The. John Henry in Harlem. M. B. Toleson. GoSl
Scale of Being, The. Pope. *Fr.* An Essay on Man, Epistle I. BeR
("For as creation's ample range extends.") ImOP
(Great Chain of Being, The.) ExPo
Scales, The. William Empson. LiTM (rev. ed.)
Scales of Love, The. Hartmann von Aue, *tr. fr. German by* Jethro Bithell. LiTW; LyMA
Scales of War, The. Homer, *tr. fr. Greek by* F. L. Lucas. *Fr.* The Iliad, VIII. GrPE
(Scales of Zeus, The, *shorter sel.*) GrR, *tr. by* George Chapman; OxBG, *tr. by* William Cowper.
Scalp, The. George Francis Savage-Armstrong. TIP
Scamander the River God. Homer, *tr. fr. Greek by* the Earl of Derby. *Fr.* The Iliad, XXI. GrR
(Achilles and the Scamander, *shorter sel., tr. by* Sir William Marris.) OxBG
("Now bursting on his head with thundering sound," *shorter sel., tr. by* Pope.) GrPo
Scandal. Pope. *Fr.* Epistle to Dr. Arbuthnot. LPS-3
Scandal among the Flowers, A. Charles S. Taylor. BLPA
Scandalous Tale of Percival and Genevieve, The. Newman Levy. WhC
Scanderbeg. Longfellow. *Fr.* Tales of a Wayside Inn: The Spanish Jew's Second Tale, Pt. III. PFY
Scanty the hour and few the steps beyond the bourn of care. The World outside the World. Keats. *Fr.* Lines Written in the Highlands after a Visit to Burns's Country. RO
'Scaped. Stephen Crane. The Black Riders, LXV. AA
Scapegoats. Eleanor D. Breed. MaRV; PGD
Scar, The. W. W. Gibson. CMP
Scar not earth's breast that I may have. The Last Camp-Fire. Sharlot Mabridth Hall. HBV
Scarabic creeping deep in the white bath. The Murder. Bertram Warr. BoCaPo (1948 ed.)
Scarabs for the Living. R. P. Blackmur. AnFE; CoAnAm; TwAmPo
Sels.
In the Wind's Eye, II. CrMA
On Common Ground, III. CrMA
Too Much for One: Not Enough to Go Around, I. CrMA
Scaramouche waves a threatening hand. Fantoche. Paul Verlaine. AWP; OBMV
Scarborough Fair. *Unknown.* OxBoLi
("Where are you going? To Scarborough Fair.") LO
Scarce a broadside was ended, till another began again. How the British Fleet Bombarded New York. Philip Freneau. LauV
Scarce had Aurora ris'n with grateful ray. Tasso. Jerusalem Delivered, XV. PrPoCR
Scarce had I learned that all was dross. Beckett and the Rest. Eugene P. Adamov. KiPP
Scarce had they brought the bodies down. Ballad of Dead Girls. Dana Burnet. OBAV
Scarce lay the blossoms of her golden hair. Mary on Her Way to the Temple. Ruth Schaumann. ISi
Scarce sixteen years old was bold Robin Hood. Robin Hood and Little John (B *vers.*). *Unknown.* BaBo
Scarcely . . . Alfonso Reyes, *tr. fr. Spanish by* Samuel Beckett. AnMP
Scarcely a street, too few houses. The Village. R. S. Thomas. HaMV
Scarcely had the ancient mountain tops. Man. Friedrich Hölderlin. AnGP
Scarcely Spring. Louis Untermeyer. GoTP; MAP; MoAmPo (1942 ed.)
Scarcity. Lizette Woodworth Reese. GBOV; NP
Scarecrow, The. Walter de la Mare. MBP; MoBrPo; PoeT; ShBV-1
Scarecrow, The. H. L. Doak. OnYI
Scarecrow, The. Michael Franklin. BoTP; SUS
Scarecrow, The. Andrew Young. FaBoTw
Scarf, The. Ivy O. Eastwick. BoTP
Scaring Crows. *Unknown.* BoTP
("O all you little blackey tops.") OxNR
Scarlet spaces of sand and ocean. The Shrimp-Gatherers. Bayard Taylor. PA
Scarlet Tanager, The. Joel Benton. AA; BLA
Scarlet Tanager, The. Mary Augusta Mason. AA
Scarlet Thread, The. Daniel Henderson. HBMV
Scarlet tide of summer's life, The. To an Autumn Leaf. Albert Mathews. AA
Scarlet Woman, The. Fenton Johnson. BANP; PoNe
Scarred on a hundred fields before. The Last Charge at Appomattox. Henry Jerome Stockard. BIG
Scars. David Morton. TBM
Scatheless. Marguerite Wilkinson. BAP; HBMV; TBM
Scatter by this jar of wine. Roses. Pierre de Ronsard. FoS
Scatter grey ash to the darkness, break. Shining Dark. Michael Roberts. FaBoMo
Scatter Seeds of Kindness. May Riley Smith. BLPA; WBLP
Scattered. Walter C. Smith. TVSH
Scattered Moluccas. Mauberley, IV. Ezra Pound. *Fr.* Hugh Selwyn Mauberley. CoBMV; CoV; LiTA; LiTM (rev. ed.); MoPo
Scattered to East and West and North. Scattered. Walter C. Smith. TVSH
Scattering Flowers. St. Thérèse of Lisieux. WHL
Scaurus hates Greek, and is become. Epigram. *Unknown.* SPP
Scel lem duib. *Tr. fr. Irish by* Brian O'Nolan. OxBI
Scenario. D. S. Savage. NeBP
Scene à Faire. Morton Dauwan Zabel. NP
Scene, The: a public square in Ruritania. The Belle of the Balkans. Newman Levy. ALV; FiBHP
Scene in a Garden. Robert Browning. *Fr.* Paracelsus, I. PCH
Scene in a Madhouse. Aubrey Thomas De Vere. OnYI
Scene in front two sloping mountain sides, The. Richard Henry Horne. *Fr.* Orion. BCEP
Scene in Paradise, A. Milton. *Fr.* Paradise Lost, IV. GN
Scene is different, The, and the place, the air. Dipsychus. Arthur Hugh Clough. EmBrPo
Scene of War, The; Fear. Sir Herbert Read. TwCV
Scene of War, The; the Happy Warrior. Sir Herbert Read. TwCV
Scene on the Banks of the Hudson, A. Bryant. APW
Scene-Shifter Death. Mary Devenport O'Neill. NeIP
Scene with Figure. Babette Deutsch. TrJP

Scenes, *sel.* Gertrude Stein.
"Pale rose is a smell that has no fountain, A." AtBAP
Scenes from the Life of the Peppertrees. Denise Levertov. NeAP
Scenes of Infancy, *sel.* John Leyden.
"Again, beside this silver rivulet's shore." EnSW
Scenes of Youth, *sel.* William Holloway.
"Remember'd long, adown the far-stretch'd vale." EnSW
Scent of esparto grass—and again I recall, A. By the Weir. W. W. Gibson. MoVE; POTE
Scent of jasmines in the sultry air, The. Tropic Storm. Walter Adolphe Roberts. *Fr.* Boyhood Etchings. PoNe
Scent of guava-blossoms and the smell, A. At Set of Sun. Mary Ashley Townsend. AA
Scent of hyacinths, like a pale mist, lies between me and my book, The. Vernal Equinox. Amy Lowell. MAPA
Scent of rotted apples, The. Late October. Sara King Carleton. GoYe
Scented Leaves from a Chinese Jar. Allen Upward. NP
Sceptic Moods. Arthur Hugh Clough. *See* Rome Is Fallen, I Hear.
Schelynlaw Tower is fair on the brae. The Laird of Schelynlaw. John Veitch. VA
Scheme of Redemption, The. Milton. *Fr.* Paradise Lost, III. StJW
Schemer, A. Edgar L. Warren. PEOR
Schenectady, Schenectady. A Trip on the Erie. *Unknown.* ABF
Scherzando. W. E. Henley. London Voluntaries, III. POTT
("Down through the ancient Strand.") BPN
(From "London Voluntaries," III-IV, *abr.*) LEAP
(London Voluntary, A.) AlDL
(Wind-Fiend, The, *fr.* III-IV, *abr.*) BMEP
Schiller! that hour I would have wish'd to die. To the Author of "The Robbers." Samuel Taylor Coleridge. PtP
Schipman was ther, wonyng fer by weste, A. The Shipman. Chaucer. *Fr.* The Canterbury Tales: Prologue. EtS; SG
Schir, though your grace has put great order. Ane Supplication in Contemptioun of Syde Taillis. Sir David Lindsay. GoTS
Schir William Wallace. Henry the Minstrel. *See* Wallace, The.
Schism, A/ Nurtured by foppery and barbarism. Keats. *Fr.* Sleep and Poetry. InP
Schlof, Bobbeli, *with music. Unknown, tr. fr. German.* TrAS
Schmaltztenor. M. W. Branch. FiBHP
Scholar, The. Ch'en Sheng Chi, *tr. fr. Chinese by* Henry H. Hart. PoHN
Scholar, The. Robert Southey. *See* My Days among the Dead Are Past.
Scholar, The. Sir Henry Taylor. *Fr.* Edwin the Fair. LPS-3
Scholar and the Cat, The. *Unknown. See* Monk and His Pet Cat, The.
Scholar and the Dog, The. John Marston. AlBD
Scholar-Gipsy, The. Matthew Arnold. AEV; AnFE; BEL; BPN; CaAE; ChTr; CoEV; EM-2; EmBrPo; EnL; EnLi-2; EnLit; EnSW; EPN; EPP; EV-5; FaBoEn; FiP; GEPC; GoTL; GTBS; GTML; HBV; LEAP; LoBV; MaPo; OAEP; OBEV; OBVV; Po; PoE; PoEL-5; PoFS; PoVP; REAL; ReaPo; SeCeV; ShBV-4; TOP; TyEnPo; UnPo (1st ed.); ViBoPo; ViPo; ViPP; VLEP; WP
Flee fro' the Press, *sel.* LH
Scholar in the Narrow Street, The. Tso Ssu, *tr. fr. Chinese by* Arthur Waley. AWP; JAWP; TrCh; WBP
Scholar newly entered marriage life, A. Samuel Rowlands. TuPP
Scholar Recruit, The. Pao Chao, *tr. fr. Chinese by* Arthur Waley. SoV; TrCh
Scholarly person named Finck, A. Poets at a House-Party. Carolyn Wells. PA
Scholars. *Unknown, tr. fr. Irish by* Frank O'Connor. KiLC
Scholars, The. W. B. Yeats. TwP
Scholar's Life, The. Samuel Johnson. *Fr.* The Vanity of Human Wishes. FaBoEn; OBEC; SeCePo
Scholar's Sweetheart, The. Edgar Fawcett. PR
Scholfield Huxley. Edgar Lee Masters. *Fr.* Spoon River Anthology. ChMo; CMP; LiTA; MoPo; TrPWD
Schöne Rothraut. John Arthur Goodchild. VA
School. James Kenneth Stephen. BOHV
School. Winifred Welles. BAP; PoeMoYo; VOD
School after Christmas. Wymond Garthwaite. ChBR
School and Schoolfellows. Winthrop Mackworth Praed. EV-4; OBRV
School Begins. Nell Goodale Price. BrR
School-Bell. Eleanor Farjeon. BrR; FaPON; SiSoSe
School Boy. *See* Schoolboy.
School Days. Maltbie D. Babcock. MaRV
School Days in New Amsterdam. Arthur Guiterman. FaPON
School Fencibles. William Cory. LH
School for Scandal, The, *sels.* Sheridan.
Let the Toast Pass, *fr.* III, iii. HBV; LPS-1; OnYI; OxBI; PreP
(Famous Toast, A.) TreF
(Here's to the Maiden.) ALV; EV-3; LiTL; SiTL
(Song: "Here's to the maiden [*or* maid] of bashful fifteen.") CEP; NeHB; OBEC; OxBoLi; PoRA; ViBoPo
School Girl, The. William Henry Venable. AA
School Greeting. G. Scott. MeMeAg
School Is Out. Frances Frost. SiSoSe
School is over. Kate Greenaway. TiPo
School of Sorrow, The. Harold Hamilton. BLRP
School was out. The boys were quelling Mars. A Time of Light, a Time of Shadow. Samuel Yellen. NePoAm-2
School Boy, The. Blake. *Fr.* Songs of Experience. CH; EM-1; EV-3; FaBoCh; GTBS-D
Schoolboy [*or* School Boy] Reads His Iliad, The. David Morton. BAP; MCCG; PFE; PoMa; POT; PoTo; TBM
Schoolboys in Winter. John Clare. InvP; PoEL-4
Schoolgirls Hastening. John Shaw Neilson. BoAV
Schoolmaster, The. Charles Stuart Calverley. BOHV
Schoolmaster, The. Goldsmith. *See* Village Schoolmaster, The.
Schoolmaster, The. Whittier. *Fr.* Snow-bound. GoTP
Schoolmaster's Guests, The. Will M. Carleton. IHA; PTA-2
Schoolmistress, The. William Shenstone. CEP; EiPP; EPP, *much abr.*; GoTL; LaA
Sels.
"Ah, me! full sorely is my heart forlorn." EV-3
Village Schoolmistress, The. LPS-2
Schoolroom on a Wet Afternoon. Vernon Scannell. HaMV
Schoolroom: 158. James E. Warren, Jr. GoYe
School's Out. W. H. Davies. MuP; OBMV; POTE
School-Time. Wordsworth. The Prelude, II. BEL; EM-2; GEPC
Schooner, The. Thomas Edward Brown. MBP
Schooner *Blizzard*, The, *with music.* Henry Burke. ShS
Schooner *Kandahar*, The, *with music. At. to* Sepley Collin. ShS
Schooners. Ibn Lubbal, *tr. fr. Arabic by* A. J. Arberry. MooP
Science. Robinson Jeffers. AmPP; CoBA; OxBA
Science. Pope. *See* Epitaph Intended for Sir Isaac Newton.
Science and Prayer. William Cowper. *Fr.* The Task, III. RO
Science drove his plow. Pasts. Alfred Kreymborg. NP
Science in God. Robert Herrick. ImOP
Science is what the world is, earth and water. The Laboratory Midnight. Reuel Denney. ImOP; NePA
Science long watched the realms of space. A World Beyond. Nathaniel Ingersoll Bowditch. AA
Science—so the savants say, A. With a Daisy. Emily Dickinson. ImOP
Science! thou fair effusive ray. Hymn to Science. Mark Akenside. CEP; PoEL-3
Science! true daughter of Old Time thou art! Sonnet to Science. Poe. Al Aaraaf: Prologue. AmP; AmPo; AmPP; AnAmPo; AnFE; APA; CoAnAm; CoBA; CoV; IAP; LA; MOAP; NePA; OnAP; OxBA; PeBoSo; SPP
Scientia Vincit Omnia? Merrill Moore. AnAmPo; LA
Scientific Attack, The. Frederick Bertolet. CAG
Scientific Proof. J. W. Foley. BOHV
Scientist, The. Ptolemy, *tr. fr. Greek by* F. L. Lucas. GrPE
Scientist living at Staines, A. Genius. R. J. P. Hewison. FaFP; SiTL
Scientists have not made known. Those Who Soar. Margaret Lathrop Law. PoMa
Scillaes [*or* Scilla's *or* Scylla's] Metamorphosis, *sels.* Thomas Lodge.
Earth Late Choked with Showers, The. ElL; ElSeCe; SiCE; ViBoPo
(Sonnet: "Earth, late choked with showers, The.") TuPP
Melancholy. OBSC
Most Pithy and Pleasant History of Glaucus and Scylla, The. ReIE
Scintilla. William Stanley Braithwaite. BANP; CDC
Scintillate, scintillate, globule orific. The Little Star. *Unknown.* BOHV; InMe
Scissor-Man, The. Madeleine Nightingale. BoTP; GaP; MPB; RAR; TiPo
Scissors and string, scissors and string. *Unknown.* OxNR
Scissors-Grinder, The. Vachel Lindsay. *Fr.* Poems about the Moon. MAPA; TwAmPo
Scoffers, The. Blake. *See* Mock On, Mock On, Voltaire, Rousseau.
Scolding Wives Vindication, The; or, An Answer to the Cuckold's Complaint. *Unknown.* CoMu
Score of years had come and gone, A. John Underhill. Whittier. PAH, TCAP
Scorn me as reason, who am always there. To a Friend. Charles Gullans. NePoEA
Scorn Not the Least. Robert Southwell. ElSeCe; SiCE
Scorn Not the Sonnet. Wordsworth. ATP; BoLiVe; BPN; EM-2; EmBrPo; EnL; EnLit; EnRP; EPN; EPP; ERP;

HBV; InP; LEAP; OAEP; OBRV; PeBoSo; PFE; PoeMoYo; PreP; TOP; TyEnPo
(Sonnet, The: "Scorn not the Sonnet; critic, you have frowned.") BCEP; BLV; LPS-3; OBEV; TrGrPo
(Sonnet on the Sonnet.) PIAE
"Scorn not the sonnet," though its strength be sapped. On a Magazine Sonnet. Russell Hilliard Loines. AA; BOHV; InP; PC; SiTL
Scorna Boy [*or* Scorney Bwee] the Barretts' bailiff, lewd and lame. The Welshmen of Tirawley. Sir Samuel Ferguson. OBVV; OnYI; PoVP
Scorne then their censure, who gave out thy wit. Jasper Mayne. *Fr.* To the Memory of Ben Johnson. OBS
Scorned. Alexander Smith. OBVV
Scorney Bwee. the Barretts' bailiff, lewd and lame. *See* Scorna Boy, the Barretts' bailiff . . .
Scornfu' Nancy. *Unknown.* EBSV
Scorpion, The William Plomer. AtBAP; BoSA; OBMV; POTE
Scorpion under Every Stone, A. *Unknown, tr. fr. Greek by* T. F. Higham. OxBG
Scot to Jeanne d'Arc, A. Andrew Lang. VA
Scotch Air. Thomas Moore. *See* Oft in the Stilly Night.
Scotch Song. Thomas D'Urfey. *Fr.* The Campaigners; or, The Pleasant Adventures at Brussels, III, i. CEP
Scotch Te Deum. William Kethe. *See* Hundredth Psalm, The.
Scotland. Charles Churchill. *Fr.* The Prophecy of Famine. BeR
Scotland. Alexander Gray. GoTS
Scotland. Sir Walter Scott. *Fr.* The Lay of the Last Minstrel, VI. BSV; LPS-2
Scotland, when it is given to me. With a Lifting of the Head. "Hugh MacDiarmid." MoBrPo
Scotland Yet. Henry Scott Riddell. EBSV; HBV
Scotland Yet *Unknown, at. to* John Galt. *Br. sel. fr.* The Canadian Boat Song. OtMeF
Scotland's Tribute to Wallace. James MacFarlan. PoFr
Scot's Farewell to His Golf Ball, A. James J. Montague. LHV; PoMa
Scots Wha Hae [wi' Wallace Bled]. Burns. ATP; BEL; BHV; CEP; CoBE; EBSV; EiPP; EM-1; EnLi-2; EnRP; EPP; HiLiEn; OAEP; OBEC; OuHeWo; PIAE; SeCeV; TOP; TrGrPo; TVSH; TyEnPo; WHA
(Bannockburn.) Burns. BBV (1923 ed.); BCEP; GN; LPS-2; PECK; PYM; RG; TCEP; TreF; WBLP
(Before Bannockburn.) FaBoCh; LoGBV
(Bruce to His Army.) OTPC
(Bruce to His Men at Bannockburn.) BLP; EnLit; HBV; LEAP
(Bruce's Address to His Army at Bannockburn.) InP; MW
(Bruce's March to Bannockburn.) BLV; BoLiVe; TrGrPo
(Robert Bruce's Address to his Army before the Battle of Bannockburn.) PoFr
(Robert Bruce's March to Bannockburn.) EV-3; PIR
"Scots Wha' Hae!" Reversed. *Unknown.* TMEV
Scott and the Veteran. Bayard Taylor. PaA; PAP
Scott, your last fragments I arrange tonight. On Editing Scott Fitzgerald's Papers. Edmund Wilson. CrMA
Scottish Hinds too poor to house, The. A Receipt to Restore Stella's Youth. Swift. Po
Scottish Widow's Lament, The. Thomas Smibert. EBSV
Scourge, The. Stanley Kunitz. CrMA
Scourge of Villainy [*or* Villanie *or* Villany], The, *sels.* John Marston.
Proemium in Librum Primum. ReIE
Satire VIII: "Curio, aye me! thy mistress' monkey's dead." ReEn; ReIE
Satire X: Humors. TuPP
("Sleep grim Reproof; my jocund Muse doth sing," *longer sel.*) SiCE
Satire II: "I cannot hold, I cannot, I, indure." ReIE
Satire VII: "Man, a man, a kingdom for a man, A!" ReIE
Satire IV: "Vice, from privation of that sacred grace." ReIE
To Detraction [I Present My Poesie]. LoBV; OBSC; ReIE; SiCE; TuPP
To Everlasting Oblivion. LoBV (1949 ed.); OBSC; ReIE; SiCE; TuPP
(Oblivion.) BLV
Scow on Cowden Shore, The, 3 *vers., with music.* Larry Gorman. ShS
Scrape no more your harmless chins. Advice to the Old Beaux. Sir Charles Sedley. BeR; CEP; SeCV-2
Scraping sound, A: The grasshopper. The Grasshopper's Song. H. N. Bialik. FaPON; YeAr
Scratch a Jew and you'll find a Wailing Wall. The Wall. Eve Merriam. TrJP
Screaming Tarn. Robert Bridges. CMP; ExPo; VLEP
Screamlight streams of gleaming waterbreasts smiling. Poem II. David Evans. MoWP
Screech Owl, The. *Unknown.* GFA
Screech-Owl, The. Ethelwyn Wetherald. CPG; OCL
Screech owl lives in a hole in a tree, The. The Screech Owl. *Unknown.* GFA
Screech-owl sings, The; death follows at her cries. Demophilus. Henry Wellesley. ALV
Screech owls moan in the yellowing. Travelling Northward. Tu Fu. OnPC
Screw-Guns. Kipling. ViBoPo
Scribe, The. Walter de la Mare. AnFE; AtBAP; ChMo; CMP; FaBoCh; LoGBV; OBMV; QS; TCPD; TrPWD
Scribe, The. F. R. Higgins. JKCP (1926 ed.)
Scribe, The. *Unknown, tr. fr. Old Irish.* AnIL, *tr. by* Kuno Meyer; OnYI, *tr. by* Whitley Stokes *and* John Strachan, *arr. by* Kathleen Hoagland
Scribe's Prayer, The. Arthur Guiterman. TrPWD
Scribe's Prayer, The. Robert Service. TrPWD
Script of trees before the hill, A. Winter Spring. Richard Wilbur. FiMAP
Scriptures, The. Dryden. *Fr.* Religio Laici. OBS
Scroggam. Burns. RO
Scroll-Section. Robert Finch. BoCaPo; PeCV
Scrub Oak. E. Merrill Root. MAP
Scrubber. W. E. Henley. *Fr.* In Hospital. PoVP
Scruple. Sophocles, *tr. fr. Greek by* Lewis Campbell. *Fr.* Philoctetes. GrR
Scrutiny [*or* Scrutinie], The. Richard Lovelace. EG; ElSeCe; EnLit; EnLoPo; EPS; LO; MeLP; MePo; OBS; SeEP; TrGrPo
(Song: "Why should you swear I am forsworn.") BOHV; InMe
Sculptor, The. *Unknown. See* Piece of Clay, A.
Sculptor first in breath and blood, A. With Metaphor. Sarah Wingate Taylor. GoYe
Sculptor of the Soul. Toyohiko Kagawa. MaRV
Sculptor, wouldst thou glad my soul. Odes of Anacreon. *Tr. by* Thomas Moore. OuHeWo
Sculptor's Country, The? Sicyon. His name? A Statue by Lysippus. Poseidippus. OxBG
Sculptors of Life. George Washington Doane. *See* Life Sculpture.
Sculpture. *Unknown. See* Piece of Clay, A.
Sculpture and Song. Sir William Watson. *See* Epigram: "Statue. The—Buonarroti said—doth wait."
Sculptured Worship. William Stanley Braithwaite. Sandy Star and Willie Gee, I. BANP
"Scum o' [*or* of] the Earth." Robert Haven Schauffler. CP; GDAH; HBV; IDAH; LBMV; NV; OBAV; PaA; PC; PoFr; POT; PoTo; TCAP
Scum of churchmen! clergy's dregs! On the Gift of a Cloak. Hugo Primas of Orléans. LaP
Scunner. "Hugh MacDiarmid." FaBoTw
Scurrilous Scribe, The. Philip Freneau. AA
Scurvy Entertainment. Abu Abd Allah, *tr. fr. Arabic by* A. J. Arberry. MooP
Scurvy-grass creeps down the strand, The. January. Daniel James O'Sullivan. NeIP
Scuttle, scuttle, little roach. Nursery Rhymes for the Tender-hearted, I. Christopher Morley. FaFP; HBMV; SiTL; TCAP; YaD
Scylla and Charybdis. Homer, *tr. fr. Greek by* George Chapman. *Fr.* The Odyssey, XII. OBS
Scylla Toothless. *Unknown.* SiTL
Scylla's Lament. Thomas Hood. *Fr.* Hero and Leander. EnRP
Scylla's Metamorphosis. Thomas Lodge. *See* Scillaes Metamorphosis.
Scyros. Karl Shapiro. HoPM; LiTA; LiTM; MoVE; NePA; SeCeV; WaP
Scythe, The. Stanley Snaith. POTE
Scythe Song. Andrew Lang. BLP; GN; HBV; PCD; PoeMoYo; POTT; PoVP; SN; VA
Scythians, The. Aleksandr Blok, *tr. fr. Russian by* Babette Deutsch *and* Avrahm Yarmolinsky. AWP; WaaP; RuPo, *tr. by* Jack Lindsay; TrRV, *rev. tr. by* Babette Deutsch
Sea, The. E. M. Adams. BoTP
Sea, The. Rafael Alberti. *See* Sea, the Sea, The.
Sea, The. Bernard Barton. LPS-2
Sea, The. Thomas Lovell Beddoes. *See* To Sea, to Sea!
Sea, The. Björnstjerne Björnson, *tr. fr. Norwegian by* Charles W. Stork. AnNoLy
Sea, The. Byron. *See* Ocean, The.
Sea, The "Barry Cornwall." BHV; GN; HBV; HBVY; LPS-2; NLK; OTPC; SN; TreFS; TVSH; VA
(Sea, The! The Sea!) BTP
(Song of the Sea.) LH; PTA-1
Sea, The. Hart Crane. Voyages, I. CrMA
("Above the fresh ruffles of the surf.") ChMo; OxBA; Po; ReaPo
Sea, The. George Darley. *Fr.* Nepenthe. BLV
(Lines: "Hurry me Nymphs! O, hurry me.") HoPM
Sea, The ("An everywhere of silver"). Emily Dickinson. TCAP
Sea, The. Emerson. *Fr.* Sea-Shore. LPS-2
Sea, The. Lloyd Frankenberg. AnFE; CoAnAm; TwAmPo

Sea. Don Gordon. EtS
Sea, The. Herman Gorter, *tr. fr. Dutch by* A. J. Barnouw. LiTW
Sea, The. Nora Hopper. NLK
Sea, The. Richard Hovey. *Fr.* Seaward. NLK
Sea, The. Ignace M. Ingianni. MuM
Sea, The. Keats. *See* On the Sea.
Sea, The. D. H. Lawrence. NAMP; POTE
Sea, The. Richard Henry Stoddard. AA; HBV; TCEP
Sea, The Swinburne. *Fr.* The Triumph of Time. BLV; BoLiVe; PIAE; TrGrPo; TSW
(Disappointed Lover, The.) LPS-2
(From the "Triumph of Time.") LEAP
(Return, The.) EtS; NLK
(Stanzas: "I will go back to the great sweet mother.") HBV
(Triumph of Time.) BMEP, *longer sel.*; GTSL; MBP; OAEP; POTT
Sea, The ("Behold the wonders of the mighty deep"). *Unknown.* NA
Sea, The ("Look, wild and wide"). *Unknown, tr. fr. Irish by* Frank O'Connor. KiLC
Sea, The. Vasili Zhukovsky, *tr. fr. Russian by* C. M. Bowra. BoRS
Sea and Land Victories. *Unknown.* PAH
Sea and Shore. Harry Lyman Koopman. AA
Sea and strand, and a lordlier land than sea-tides rolling. England; an Ode. Swinburne. ViPo
Sea and the Eagle, The. Sydney Clouts. BoSA
Sea and the Hills, The. Kipling. OtMeF
Sea and the Mirror, The, *sels.* W. H. Auden.
Alonso to Ferdinand. MoPo
"At Dirty Dick's and Sloppy Joe's." FaBoTw
Gonzalo's Song. MeRV
Miranda's Song. FaBoMo
Pretace. LiTA; SeCeV
Sing, Ariel, Sing. TwHP
Sea and the Skylark, The. Gerard Manley Hopkins. LiTB; OBMV; POTT; PoVP
Sea at evening moves across the sand, The. Soldiers Bathing. F. T. Prince. ChMP; LiTB; LiTM; MoVE; PoN; WaP
Sea awoke at midnight from its sleep, The. The Sound of the Sea. Longfellow AnFE; APA; CoAnAm; CoV; EtS; IAP; OBAV; Po; UnW
Sea Ballad. Sydney Dobell. *Fr.* Balder. VA
Sea Battle, The. Dryden. *Fr.* Annus Mirabilis. FiP
Sea beyond sea, sand after sweep of sand. A Solitude. Swinburne. BPN
Sea Bird, The. Keith Douglas. ChMP
Sea Bird to the Wave, The. Padraic Colum. BMEP; EtS; LEAP; SUS
Sea-Birds. Elizabeth Akers Allen. AA; BLA; FaBoBe; HBV; LBAP
Sea-Birds. Fray Angelico Chavez. ISi
Sea-Birds. Elinor MacArthur. BLA
Sea-Birds. James Thomson. EtS
Sea-birds are asleep. Sea Slumber-Song. Roden Noel. BOL; MOAH; VA
Sea-Bird's Cry, The. Edith F. Parsons. CAG
Sea-Birds Crying above the Ruins of Corinth, The. Antipater of Sidon, *tr. fr. Greek by* F. L. Lucas. GrPE
Sea-Blown. Joaquin Miller. LBAP
Sea bluely gleaming. Dalmatian Nocturne. Aleksa Santic. LiTW
Sea Born. Harold Vinal. HBMV; TBM
Sea-bound landsman looking back to shore, The. John Brown. Harry Lyman Koopman. AA
Sea Breeze Stéphane Mallarmé. *See* Sea-Wind.
Sea Burial. Robina Monkman. EtS
Sea by the Wood, The. Duncan Campbell Scott. CPG
Sea Call. Margaret Widdemer. NLK; TSW
Sea-Captain, The. Gerald Gould. EtS
Sea Captain, The ("It was of a sea captain that followed the sea"). *Unknown.* ViBoFo
Sea-Captain, The ("There was a sea captain lately come to shore"). *Unknown.* BaBo
Sea Cathedral, The. E. J. Pratt. CaP; OCL
Sea-Change. W. W. Gibson. ChMo; CMP
Sea-Change. John Masefield. AtBAP; FaBoTw; OBMV
Sea Change, A. Dorothy Peace. NLK
Sea-Change. Genevieve Taggard. EtS; NP
Sea Child, A. Bliss Carman. HBV; VA
Sea-Child, The. Eliza Cook. VA
Sea-Chill. Arthur Guiterman. NLK (1947 ed.)
Sea-Chronicles. Rex Ingamells. BoAV
Sea-coast of Bohemia, The. Perdita. James Hebblethwaite. BoAu
Sea contains a destiny, The. The Sea and the Eagle. Sydney Clouts. BoSA
Sea crashed over the grim gray rocks, The. Flotsam and Jetsam. *Unknown.* LPS-2
Sea cries to the land, The, "You have taken from me." Seaweed. Monk Gibbon. BMEP
Sea Danceth, The. Sir John Davies. *See* Dancing Sea, The.
Sea Dawn. Francis Hackett. AnIV
Sea-Deeps, The. Thomas Miller. EtS
Sea Dialogue, A. Oliver Wendell Holmes. EtS
Sea Dike, The. M. Vasalis, *tr. fr. Dutch by* A. J. Barnouw. LiTW
Sea Dirge. Archias of Byzantium, *tr. fr. Greek by* Andrew Lang. AWP
Sea Dirge, A. "Lewis Carroll." CenHV; StaSt
Sea Dirge, A. Shakespeare. *See* Ariel's Song: "Full fathom five thy father lies."
Sea drained off, my poverty's uncovered, The. All Gone. C. Day Lewis. FaBoMo
Sea Dream, A. Whittier. IAP; TCAP
Sea Dreams, *sel.* Tennyson.
What Does Little Birdie Say? GFA; HBV; HBVY; HH; LPS-1; MeMeAg; MPB; OTPC
(Baby-Song.) BOL
(Cradle Song: "What does little birdie say.") BoTP; PPL; TVC; TVSH
(Little Birdie.) PTA-1; SAS
Sea-drinking Cities. Josephine Pinckney. LS; SPP
Sea Eclogue: "Otys, begin." William Diaper. Nereides; or, Sea-Eclogues, X. LoBV
Sea-Elephant, The. William Carlos Williams. LiTA
Sea Fairies. Eileen Mathias. BoTP
Sea-Fairies, The. Tennyson. ViPP
Sea, False Philosophy. Laura Riding. TCPD
Sea Fever. John Masefield. BEL; BLV; BMEP; BoChLi; BoLiVe; CaAE; CBOV; ChMo; CMP; CV; EnLi-2 (1949 ed.); EnLit; EtS; FaBoBe; FaPON; GBV; GTBS; GTSL; HBV; HBVY; HiLiEn; LBBV; LEAP; MBP; MCCG; MoAB; MoBrPo; MPB; NeHB; NeMA; NLK; OBVV; OHFP; OtMeF; OTPC (1946 ed.); PCD; PFE; PoeMoYo; PoMa; POT; PoTo; POTT; PreP; PYM; RG; ShBV-1; SP; StVeCh; TCEP; TiPo; TOP; TreF; TrGrPo; TwCV; VOD; WHA; YT
Sea-Fight, A. Timotheus, *tr. fr. Greek by* Gilbert Highet. *Fr.* The Persae. OxBG
Sea Fight, The. *Unknown.* LPS-2
Sea-Fight, A. Walt Whitman. Song of Myself, XXXV. LH
(Battle of the *Bonhomme Richard* and the *Serapis.*) UnPo (3d ed.)
(Old-Time Sea-Fight, An.) MaC
("Would you hear of an old-time sea-fight?") CoBA; SeCeV; TrGrPo
Sea-Fight at Sluys, The. Laurence Minot. SG
Sea-Flowers. Dorothy Livesay. OCL
Sea folk have speech that is not quite their own. Of Mariners. Harold Vinal. BAP
Sea Fowler, The. Mary Howitt. VA
Sea-fowls build in wrinkles on my face, The. Inscription. Sir William Watson. BLP
Sea-Garden. Cecilia MacKinnon. CPG
Sea Gipsy, The. Richard Hovey. *See* Sea Gypsy, The.
Sea gives her shells to the shingle, The. Dedication to Poems and Ballads. Swinburne. BPN; PIR; PoVP; ViPo; VLEP
Sea go dark, go dark with wind. Wild Iron. Allen Curnow. AnNZ
Sea-Goddess, The. Margaret Cavendish, Duchess of Newcastle. *Fr.* The Convent of Pleasure. SeCL
Sea Gods. Hilda Doolittle ("H. D."). AtBAP; ChMo; CMP; CP; LiTA; MOAP; NV; PFE
Sea-God's Address to Bran, The. *Unknown, tr. fr. Middle Irish by* Kuno Meyer. OnYI
(Sea-God's Song to Bran, The, *tr. by* Howard Mumford Jones.) LiTW
Sea-Grief. Dowell O'Reilly. BoAu
Sea guards warily its treasures, The. The Heart. Jacob Steinberg. TrJP
Seagull, The. Dafydd ap Gwilym, *tr. fr. Welsh by* David Bell. LyMA
Sea-Gull. Mary Carolyn Davies. BLA
Sea-Gull, The. Mary Howitt. BoTP
Sea Gull, The. Leroy F. Jackson. GFA; UTS
Sea-Gull, The. Ogden Nash. FaFP; LiTM; NePA; SiTL
Sea Gull, The. *Unknown, tr. fr. Gaelic.* GFA; RAR
Sea gull curves his wings, The. Elizabeth J. Coatsworth. TiPo
Seagull flying from the sea. A Feather for My Cap. Ivy O. Eastwick. BoTP
Sea-gull poises, The. Things Not Seen. Mark Turbyfill. NP
Seagull, spreadeagled, splayed on the wind, The. Memorial (For Two Young Seamen Lost Overboard in a Storm in Mid-Pacific, January, 1940). George Barker. LiTG; LiTM; ReMP; WaP
Sea-gull swooping. Sea-Gull. Mary Carolyn Davies. BLA
Sea-Gulls. Norah M. Holland. MCCG
Seagulls, The. Sir John Morris-Jones, *tr. fr. Welsh by* Gwyn Williams. PrWP
Sea-Gulls. Tatsuji Miyoshi, *tr. fr. Japanese by* Takamichi Ninomiya *and* D. J. Enright. PoLJ
Sea Gulls. R. W. Page. CAG
Sea Gulls. E. J. Pratt. EtS; TwCaPo

Seagull's narrow sails of feather lift, The. Winged Mariner. Grace Clementine Howes. EtS
Seagulls on the Serpentine. Alfred Noyes. EtS
Seagulls whiten and dip, The. In the Bay. Arthur Symons. PoVP
Sea Gypsy, The. Richard Hovey. BBV; BTP; CBPC; FaPON; GBV; GoTP; HBVY; LBMV; OBAV; OQP; PIAE; POT; PoTo; QP-2; StaSt; TCAP; TreFS; TSW; TSWC; YT
(Sea Gipsy, The.) AlDL; BAP; HBV; LEAP; MCCG; PYM
Sea has a laugh, The. The Frowning Cliff. Herbert Asquith. BrR
Sea Hath Its Pearls, The. Heine, *tr. fr. German by* Longfellow. AWP; JAWP; OnPM; OuHeWo; WBP
Sea Hath Many Thousand Sands, The. *Unknown.* CenL; ElL; ElSeCe; LiTB; OBSC; TuPP; ViBoPo
(Advice to a Lover.) GTSL; HBV
Sea hath tempered, The; the mighty sun. The Fountain. Mu'tamid, King of Seville. AWP; JAWP; WPB
Sea Holly. Conrad Aiken. LiTM; MAPA; NePA; TCPD
Sea Hunger. John Hanlon Mitchell. EtS
Sea, The—in Calm. "Barry Cornwall." EtS
Sea Irony. John Langdon Heaton. AA
Sea is a lonely thing, The. In Exile. B. E. Baughan. AnNZ
Sea is an acre of dull glass, the land is a table, The. Lusty Juventus. Charles Madge. FaBoMo
Sea, The, is an innumerable sword, an abundance of poverty. A Day's Run. Jorge Luis Borges. TwSpPo
Sea is at ebb, and the sound of her utmost word, The. The Seaboard. Swinburne. BPN
Sea is awake, and the sound of the song of the joy of her waking is rolled, The. In the Water. Swinburne. *Fr.* A Midsummer Holiday. BPN; PoVP; VLEP
Sea is calm tonight, The. Dover Beach. Matthew Arnold. AEV; AnEnPo; ATP; AWP; BEL; BoLiVe; BLV; BMEP; BPN; CBOV; CoBE; CoEV; EM-2; EmBrPo; EnL; EnLi-2; EnLit; EPN; EtS; ExPo; FaBoBe; FaBoEn; FaFP; FiP; GBV; GEPC; GTBS-D; GTBS-W; GTSL; HBV; HoPM; InP; InPo; InvP; JAWP; KN; LEAP; LiTB; LiTG; LiTL; LoBV; LoPo; LoPS; LPS-2; MaPo; MaRV; MCCG; NBE; NeHB; OAEP; OBVV; OTPC (1946 ed.); OuHeWo; PFE; PG; PIAE; Po; PoF; PoEL-5; PoFS; PoLFOT; PoRA; PoVP; PreP; PYM; REAL; ReaPo; RiBV; SeCePo; SeCeV; SN; TCEP; TOP; TreFS; TrGrPo; TwCrTr; TwHP; TyEnPo; UnPo; VA; ViBoPo; ViPo; ViPP; VLEP; WBP; WHA
Ah, Love, Let Us Be True, *sel.* OQP; QP-2
Sea is flecked with bars of gray, The. Les Silhouettes. Oscar Wilde. *Fr.* Impressions. Po; PoVP; VLEP
Sea Is Full of Loveliness and Tears, The. John Richard Moreland. MuM
Sea is green, the sea is grey, The. In Arcadie. Helen Merril Egerton. CPG
Sea Is His, The. Edward Sanford Martin. EtS
Sea is never still, The. Young Sea. Carl Sandburg. NLK (1947 ed.)
Sea Is Wild, The. John Hall Wheelock. POT
Sea is wild marble waiting a stonecutter's hand. Sea. Don Gordon. EtS
Sea Island Miscellany, *sels.* R. P. Blackmur.
Mirage, IX. GTBS-W; LiTM; MoVE
"One grey and foaming day." V. MoVE
"Where shall I go then," XIV. MoVE
Sea-island winds sweep through Palmetto Town. Palmetto Town. Hervey Allen. LS
Sea-King, The. L. Frank Tooker. EtS
Sea-King's Burial, The. Charles Mackay. PCN
Sea-kings' daughter from over the sea. A Welcome to Alexandra. Tennyson. PoVP
Sea-Lands, The. Orrick Johns. HBV; LBMV
Sea Lavender. Louise Morey Bowman. BoCaPo (1943 ed.); CaP; CPG; OCL
Sea Life. James Montgomery. *Fr.* The Pelican Island. LPS-2
Sea like a vast quicksilvered glass, The. Symphony in Gray Major. Rubén Darío. LiTW
Sea-Limits, The. Dante Gabriel Rossetti. AnEnPo; BMEP; BPN; EmBrPo; EPN; EtS; GrCo-2; PoVP; TOP; VA; VLEP
Sea Longing. Harold Vinal. NLK; PoMa
Sea Longings. Thomas Bailey Aldrich. SN
Sea Love. Charlotte Mew. AV; BLV; LBBV; MBP; MoAB; MoBrPo; NeMA; TrGrPo; ViBoPo
Sea Lullaby. Elinor Wylie. NeMA
Sea Lyric. William Stanley Braithwaite. GoSl
Sea Lyric, A. William Hamilton Hayne. EtS
Sea-Maiden, The. J. W. De Forest. EtS
Sea-maids, hitherward winging. Hymn to the Sirens. Euripides, *tr. by* Arthur S. Way. *Fr.* Helen. GrR
Sea-Maids' Music, The. Ernest Myers. VA
Sea-Marge. Alexander Smith. *Fr.* A Life-Drama. VA
(Autumn.) GTSE
Sea Mark. *See* Seamark.
Sea Marsh. George Crabbe. *Fr.* The Borough, Letter XXII. RO
Sea Memories. Longfellow. *Fr.* My Lost Youth. CBPC; FaPON; MPB
Sea-Mew, The. Elizabeth Barrett Browning. HBV; OTPC
Sea Monsters. Spenser. *Fr.* The Faerie Queene, II, 12. ChTr; FaBoEn
("Waves come rolling, and the billowes rore, The.") AtBAP
Sea-mosses hide the massive architrave. The Birds of Whitby. Thomas S. Jones, Jr. BLA
Sea Music. Theodore Harding Rand. CPG
Sea-nurtured. Jean Ingelow. EtS
Sea-Nymph's Parting, The. Walter Savage Landor. *Fr.* Gebir. FaBoEn
Sea of Death, The. Thomas Hood. FaBoEn; LiTB; LoBV; PoEL-4; RO; UnW
Sea of Death, The. *Unknown.* CH
Sea of Faith, The. Walt Whitman. *Fr.* Passage to India, XIII. OQP; QP-1
("Passage to more than India.") PC
Sea of Night. Ibn Sa'id of Alcala la Real, *tr. fr. Arabic by* A. J. Arberry. MooP
Sea of Peace, The. Ruth McEnery Stuart. MaRV
Sea of the years that endure not, The. Dedication. Swinburne. EmBrPo
Sea-Prayer, A. William Stanley Braithwaite. OBAV; PraP
Sea Princess, The. Katharine Pyle. PCH; TVC; TVSH
Sea—quick pugilist, The. Training. Demetrio Herrera S. AnCL
Sea retains such images, The. Louis Dudek. *Fr.* Europe. PeCV
Sea Ritual, The. George Darley. *Fr.* Syren Songs. OBRV; OnYI; OxBI; TriJ.
(Deadman's Dirge.) CH
Sea Road, The. Martha Haskell Clark. NLK
Sea Rose. Hilda Doolittle ("H. D."). ChMo; CMP; FaBoMo
Sea-Sand and Sorrow. Christina Rossetti. ChTr
Sea sang sweetly to the shore, The. Hymn Written for the Two Hundredth Anniversary of the Old South Church, Beverly, Massachusetts. Lucy Larcom. OHIP
Sea Serpant, The. Wallace Irwin. FiBHP
Sea-Serpent, The. James Robinson Planché. NA
Sea Shell. Elizabeth Stanton Hardy. MaRV; MuM
Sea Shell. Amy Lowell. BoTP; BrR; CBPC; FaPON; GFA; GoBP; MPB; PCH; RAR; StVeCh; TSW; TSWC
Sea shell is a castle, A. Shell Castles. Rowena Bastin Bennett. GFA; UTS
Sea shell is a palace, A. Palace. Dorothy Vena Johnson. GoSl
Sea-Shell Murmurs. Eugene Lee-Hamilton. VA
Sea Shell, Sea Shell,/ Sing me a song, O please! Sea Shell. Amy Lowell. BoTP; BrR; CBPC; FaPON; GFA; GoBP; MPB; PCH; RAR; StVeCh; TSW; TSWC
Sea Shells. Clinton Scollard. BrR
Sea Side. *See* Seaside.
Sea-Sleep. Thomas Lake Harris. AA
Sea Slumber-Song. Roden Noel. BOL; MOAH; VA
Sea-smooth stones imprison a moon. Forgotten Objects on a Beach. Patricia Excell. BoAV
Sea Snatches. *Unknown, tr. fr. Old Irish by* Seán O'Faoláin. SiB
Sea Song. Thomas Lovell Beddoes. *See* To Sea, to Sea!
Sea-Song. Martha Haskell Clark. NLK
Sea Song, A. Allan Cunningham. *See* Wet Sheet and a Flowing Sea, A.
Sea Song [*or* Seasong]. Stefan George, *tr. fr. German by* Kenneth Gee. AnGP; LiTW
Sea Song. Norah Holland. CaP; OCL
Sea Song. "Laurence Hope." AV; BMEP; LBBV
Sea-Song. Irene Rutherford McLeod. YT
Sea Song, A. John Richard Moreland. DDA; LS
Sea Song from the Shore, A. James Whitcomb Riley. BoTP; GaP; PRWS; TiPo; TVC; TVSH
Sea Sonnet. Norma Lay. GoYe
Sea Sorrow. Rose Mills Powers. TBM
Sea Spell, A. Fannie Stearns Davis. VOD
Sea still plunges where as naked boys, The. The Grotto. Francis Scarfe. NeBP
Sea Story, A. Emily Henrietta Hickey. JKCP; VA
Sea Story. Vincent Starrett. DaM
Sea-Stretch. Rena Cary Sheffield. BLA
Sea Surface Full of Clouds. Wallace Stevens. AnAmPo; AnFE; CoAnAm; CoBA; CoBMV; LA; MAP; MoAB; MoAmPo; TwAmPo
Sea tells something but it tells not all, The. Reserve. Mary Ashley Townsend. AA
Sea, the earth, the sky, fire and wind, The. Light. Vicente Aleixandre. CoSP
Sea, The! The Sea! "Barry Cornwall." *See* Sea, The.
Sea, the Sea, The. Rafael Alberti, *tr. fr. Spanish by* Eleanor L. Turnbull. CoSP; OnPM
(Sea, The.) AnSpL-2

Sea through a brief streamlet seeks to pass, The. A Streamlet Flows into the Sea. Luis de Góngora. *Fr.* The Solitudes. TeCS
Sea Town. Frances Frost. EtS
Sea Trade. Isidorus, *tr. fr. Greek by* Sir William Marris. OxBG
(Farmer Lost at Sea, The, *tr. by* F. L. Lucas.) GrPE
Sea Urge. *Unknown.* NLK; PoMa
Sea Variations. E. J. Pratt. CPG
Sea-Voyage. John Hall Wheelock. EtS; MuM
Sea Wall, The. W. Wesley Trimpi. PtPa
Sea was bright, and the bark rode well, The. The White Squall. "Barry Cornwall." LPS-2
Sea-Wash. Carl Sandburg. BrR
Sea-Watcher, The. Aubrey Thomas De Vere. IrPN
Sea waves are green and wet. Sand Dunes. Robert Frost. MAP; MoAB; MoAmPo
Sea-Way. Ellen Mackay Hutchinson Cortissoz. AA
Sea Weed. *See* Seaweed.
Sea-Wind, The. Arthur Ketchum. NLK
Sea-Wind. Stéphane Mallarmé, *tr. fr. French by* Arthur Symonds. AWP; JAWP; VLEP; WBP
(Sea Breeze.) AnFP, *tr. by* Kate Flores; ReMP, *tr. by* Warren Carrier
(Sea Winds, *tr. by* Patricia Terry.) OnPM
Sea, with waters unspeaking, with waters of azure. The Sea. Vasili Zhukovsky. BoRS
Sea Wolf, The. Violet McDougal. FaPON; MPB
Sea Words. Mary Sinton Leitch. EtS
Sea would flow no longer, The. The Frozen Ocean. Viola Meynell. CH
Sea Wrack. "Moira O'Neill." OnYI
Seaboard, The. Swinburne. BPN
Seace o seace this hum of greiveing. *Unknown.* SeCSL
Seafarer. Archibald MacLeish. CoV; TwHP
Seafarer, The. Earl of Surrey. *See* Complaint of the Absence of Her Lover . . .
Seafarer, The ("May I for my own self song's truth reckon"). *Unknown, tr. fr. Anglo-Saxon by* Ezra Pound. AmP; AnAmPo; EnL, Pt. I; ExPo; FaBoTw; KN; LA; LiTA; LiTW; LyMA; OxBA; PoE; AnOE, Pt. I, *tr. by* Charles W. Kennedy; EnLi-1 (1949 ed.), Pt. I, *tr. by* Stith Thompson; EtS, Pt. I, *tr. by* Charles W. Kennedy; REAL, Pt. I, *mod. vers.*
Sels.
Afar on the Floodways, Pt. I, *mod vers. by* Mother Margaret Williams. PoLi
Hour of Death, The, Pt. II, *abr., mod. vers. by* Mother Margaret Williams. PoLi
Seafarer, The ("Shall I thus ever long . . ."). *Unknown. See* Lady Prayeth the Return of Her Lover . . . , The.
Seafarers say there is an eastern land, The. Dreaming of Wandering through the Tien-mu Mountain. Li Po. WhP
Seafaring Towns. "Pablo de Rokha," *tr. fr. Spanish by* H. R. Hays. TwSpPo
Seagreen, admiral of the greens. Election Handbill of Green. Jorge Carrera Andrade. TwSpPo
Seal, A. Oliver Herford. *Fr.* Child's Natural History. HBV; HBVY
Seal. William Jay Smith. GoTP
Seal Lullaby. Kipling. *See* White Seal, The.
Seal thou the window! Yea, shut out the light. Cloistered. Alice Brown. AA; BAP; LEAP; MaRV
Seal Up Her Eyes, O Sleep. William Cartwright. *Fr.* The Siege. EG; SeCL
Sealed Bags of Ducats. Martial, *tr. fr. Latin by* Paul Nixon. LiTW
Sealed in Vain. Shakespeare. *See* Take, O Take Those Lips Away.
Sealed Orders. Richard Burton. HBV; OQP; QP-2
Sealed with the seal of Life, thy soul and mine. The Inscription. Elsa Barker. *Fr.* The Spirit and the Bride. HBMV
Sealights reflected on the rocks. The Mothers. John Peale Bishop. SPP
Seals, The. Dorothy Aldis. *Fr.* At the Circus. TiPo (1952 ed.); UTS
Seals, The. L. A G. Strong. LO; POTE
Seals all flap, The. The Seals. Dorothy Aldis. *Fr.* At the Circus. TiPo (1952 ed.); UTS
Seals at play off Western Isle, The. Seals, Terns, Time. Richard Eberhart. FiMAP; MoAB
Seals of Love. Shakespeare. *See* Take, O Take Those Lips Away.
Seals, Terns, Time. Richard Eberhart. FiMAP; MoAB
Seaman's Compass, The. *Unknown.* SG
Seaman's Confession of Faith, A. Harry Kemp. TrPWD
Seaman's Happy Return, The. *Unknown.* ChTr; SG
Sea-Man's Renown, The. John Playford. *See* Jovial Marriner, The.
Seaman's Reply, The. *Unknown.* SG
Seaman's Tomb, A. Plato, *tr. fr. Greek by* Lord Neaves. OnPM
Seamark, A. Bliss Carman. PeCV
Sea Mark, The. John Smith. SPP
Seamarks, *sel.* "St.-J. Perse," *tr. fr. French by* Wallace Fowlie.
And You, Seas. MiCF
Seamen shout once and together, The. A Leave-Taking. Sir Frederick Napier Broome. AnNZ
Seamen Three. Thomas Love Peacock. *See* Three Men of Gotham.
Seamy Side of Motley, The. Sir Owen Seaman. InMe
Search. T. Moore Atkinson. ChIP
Search, The. Thomas Curtis Clark. MaRV; WGRP
Search, The. Ernest Crosby. AA; BAP; OQP; QP-1
Search, The. Sara Henderson Hay. MaRV
Search, The. James Russell Lowell. MaRV; StJW
Search. Anne Marriott. MaRV
Search, The. Psalms, XLII *and* XLIII, Bible, *O.T.* (*Moulton, Modern Reader's Bible*). WGRP
Search. Raymond Souster. BoCaPo (1948 ed.)
Search, The. Henry Vaughan. ElSeCe
Search. Margaret Widdemer. TrPWD
Search after Happiness, The, *sel.* Hannah More.
Solitude. WBLP
Search for God, The. Thomas Heywood. *Fr.* Hierarchie of the Blessed Angels, I. MaRV, *abr.*; OxBoCh, *abr.*; QS, 1 *st.*
("I sought Thee round about, O Thou my God.") WGRP
Search for Pearls, The. Christopher Smart. *Fr.* Jubilate Agno. RO
Search for Perfection. W. Wesley Trimpi. PtPa
Search for St. Truth, The. William Langland, *tr. fr. Middle English. Fr.* The Vision of Piers Plowman. MeEV
Search for Truth, The. Boethius, *tr. fr. Latin by* Jack Lindsay. LyMA
Search then [*or* thou] the ruling passion: there, alone. The Ruling Passion. Pope. *Fr.* Moral Essays. LPS-3; ViBoPo
Searcher of Hearts, The. Psalms, CXXXIX, 1-12, 23-24, Bible, *O.T.* GrCo-1
(Searcher of Hearts Is Thy Maker, The, 1-24, *Moulton, Modern Reader's Bible.*) CBOV; WGRP
Searchers of majesty shall all be slain by glory, The. Presumption. Eileen Duggan. CAW; SaFP
Searching for the Hermit in Vain. Chia Tao, *tr. fr. Chinese.* WhP
Searching my heart for its true sorrow. Exiled. Edna St. Vincent Millay. EtS; OBAV; PoRA
Searchlights. Edward Shanks. NV
Seas, The. Stella Gibbons. AlDL
Seas. Juan Ramón Jiménez, *tr. fr. Spanish by* Eleanor L. Turnbull. TeCS
Seas are quiet when the winds give o'er, The. Old Age [*or* Last Verses]. Edmund Waller. *Fr.* Of the Last Verses in the Book. BCEP; CBOV; EV-2; LEAP; LPS-3; MaRV; OBEV; OxBoCh
Seas netted with ambushes, The. Two Christmas-Cards. Robinson Jeffers. NeTW
Seas' sound and the seas' drifting, The. The Shores of Night. August Derleth. DaM
Sea's Spell, The. Susan Marr Spalding. AA; EtS
Sea's Voice, The. William Prescott Foster. EtS
Seascape. Elizabeth Bishop. MoAB
Seascape. Langston Hughes. BrR
Seascape. Stephen Spender. AtBAP; ChMP; CoBMV; GTBS-D
Seascape. Francis Brett Young. PtOT
Seashore [*or* Sea-Shore]. Emerson. AmPP (4th ed.); AnAmPo; EtS; IAP; LA; LiTA; MOAP; OBAV; OxBA
Sea, The, *sel.* LPS-2
Sea Side. Robert Graves. MoPo
Seaside Grave, A. Archias of Byzantium, *tr. fr. Greek by* F. L. Lucas. GrPE
Seaside Nursery Song. "M. La T." BOL
Seaside Well, The. *Unknown.* LPS-3
Season comes, a day comes, A. Aleksandr Blok, *tr. fr. Russian by* C. M. Bowra. BoRS
Season in Hell, A, *sel.* Arthur Rimbaud, *tr. fr. French by* William M. Davis.
"Once, long ago—if I remember rightly—my life was a sumptuous feast." AnFP
Season of love, The. Elegies, IV. Philippe Thoby-Marcelin. PoNe
"Season of Mellow Fruitfulness." Theocritus. *See* Late Summer in the Country.
Season of mists and mellow fruitfulness. To Autumn [*or* Ode to Autumn]. Keats. AEV; AnEnPo; AnFE; AtBAP; ATP; AWP; BCEP; BEL; BLV; BoLiVe; BoTP; BPN; CaAE; CBE; CBOV; CBPC; CH; ChER; CoBE; CoEV; DD; EG; EM-2; EmBrPo; EnL; EnLi-2; EnLit; EnLP; EnRP; EPN; EPP; ERP; EV-4; ExPo; FaBoEn; FiP; GEPC; GoTP; GTBS; GTBS-D; GTBS-W; GTSE; GTSL; HBV; HBVY; InPo; InvP; JAWP; LEAP; LiTB; LiTG; LoBV; MaPo; MCCG; MyFE; OAEP; OBEV; OBRV; OuHeWo; PIAE; Po;

PoE; PoEL-4; PoeMoYo; PoFS; ReaPo; SeCeV; ShBV-3; SN; TCEP; TOAH; TOP; TreFS; TrGrPo; TVSH; TwHP; TwP; TyEnPo; UnPo; ViBoPo; WBP; WHA
Season 'Tis, My Lovely Lambs, The. E. E. Cummings. UnPo (3d ed.)
Seasonal Moraine. L. F. Gerlach. PtPa
Seasons, The. John Vance Cheney. DD
Seasons, The, *sels.* Kalidasa, *tr. fr. Sanskrit by* Arthur W. Ryder.
  Autumn. AWP; JAWP; WBP
  Early Spring. AWP
  Rains, The. AWP
  Spring. AWP
  Summer. AWP
  Winter. AWP
Seasons, The. William Julius Mickle. *Fr.* Ode on Vicissitude. RO
Seasons, The. William Morris. BPN
Seasons, The. Lynette Roberts. MoPW; MoWP
Seasons. Christina Rossetti. YeAr
Seasons. Spenser. *See* Pageant of the Seasons and the Months, The.
Seasons, The, *sels.* James Thomson.
  Autumn ("Crowned with the sickle"). CEP
    Autumn ("But see the fading many-coloured woods"), *sel.* EnRP; EnSW; LoBV
    "Fled in the blasted verdure." OAEP
    Lavinia. OBEC
    Love of Nature. OBEC
    Moonlight, 6 *ll.* BeR
    Moonlight in Autumn, *abr.* OBEC
    Stag Hunt, The. LPS-2
    Storm in Harvest. EPP
  Hymn on the Seasons, A. EnRP; EV-3; OxBoCh; PoE
    (Hymn, A: "These, as they change, Almighty Father, these.") CEP; EiPP; LPS-2
  Spring ("Come, gentle Spring"), *abr.* TCEP
    Angling. LPS-2
    Birds in Spring. OBEC
    Coming of the Rain, The. EPP
    Connubial Life. LPS-1
    Domestic Birds. BCEP; LPS-2
    Nightingale Bereaved, The. BCEP
    Plea for the Animals. LPS-3
    Prelude: "North-east spends his rage, The." CoEV
    Songsters, The. LPS-2
    Spring ("As rising from the vegetable world"), *sel.* PoEL-3
    Spring ("As yet the trembling year"), *sel.* EnSW
    Spring ("At length the finished garden"), *sel.* ViBoPo
    Spring ("Now, when the first foul torrent"), *sel.* EV-3
    Spring Flowers. AtBAP; OBEC
    Swan, Turkey, Dove, and the Bull in the Broom. BeR
    Woodland Choir, The. CoBE
  Summer.
    Bathing. LPS-2
    Britannia. BeR
    Happy Britannia. OBEC; SeCePo
    Sheep-washing, The EnLi-2; EPP
      (Sheep Shearing, The.) CoBE
    Storm, The. LoBV
    Summer ("Still let me pierce into the midnight depth"), *sel.* EnRP
    Summer Evening and Night. OBEC
    Summer Morning. OBEC
    Venus Shines Out. BeR
  Winter ("See, Winter comes, to rule the varied year"). BEL, *sl. abr.*; CEP; EiPP; EM-1, *shorter sel.*; EnL, *shorter sel.*, EnLi-2, *shorter sel.*; EnLit, *shorter sel.*; OAEP, *abr.*; PlAE, *abr.*; Po, *abr.*; TyEnPo, *shorter sel.*
    Approach of Winter. OBEC
    "Clear frost succeeds, and thro' the blew serene." FaBoEn
    Frost at Night. CoEV; OBEC
    "Late, in the louring sky, red, fiery, streaks." FaBoEn
    Lo! from the Livid East. AtBAP
      ("Lo! from the livid East, or piercing North.") FaBoEn
    Lost Shepherd, The. CoBE
    "Now, solitary, and in pensive guise." FaBoEn
    "Now when the cheerless empire of the sky." BSV
    Storm, The. CoBE
    Winter ("As thus the snows arise, and, foul and fierce"), *sel.* SeCePo
    Winter ("The keener tempests come"), *sel.* EnRP; ViBoPo
      (Snow Scene, A.) EPP
      (Storm in Winter, A.) EV-3
      (Winter Scenes.) LPS-2
      (Winter Storm, A.) TOP
    Winter Scene, A ("Through the hushed air"). OBEC
    Winter Winds ("Nature, great parent"). UnPo (1st ed.)
Seasons Alter, The. Shakespeare. *Fr.* A Midsummer Night's Dream, II, i. BoW
Season's anguish, crashing whirlwind, ice, The. Winter Garden. David Gascoyne. ChMP; GTBS-D
Seasons came, The. Wordsworth. *Fr.* The Prelude, II. NBE
Seasons' Fool, The. Goronwy Rees. MoWP
Seasons of the Gods, The. Albert E. S. Smythe. CPG
Seasons of the Soul. Allen Tate. CrMA; MoPo; NePA; OxBA
  Autumn, II. MoVE
Seasons pass, The. Glorying. Miyauchi. SoLD
Seat for Three, A; Written on a Settle. Walter Crane. OBVV; VA
Seat on the Cassiopeian stars, A. Listen. Albert Durrant Watson. CPG
Seated at breakfast, in the indigent country. A Summer Shower. A. Fleming MacLiesh. OnAP
Seated at church in the winter. The Lost Voice. "A. H. S." PA
Seated I see the two again. The Household Sovereign. Longfellow. *Fr.* The Hanging of the Crane. LPS-1
Seated in the swing. The Angelus. Gerardo Diego. CoSP
Seated once by a brook, watching a child. The Brook. Edward Thomas. MoVE; SeCeV
Seated one day at the organ. D. B. Wyndham Lewis. WhC
Seated one day at the organ. A [*or* The] Lost Chord. Adelaide Anne Procter. BPP; CAW; FaFP; HBV; LPS-3; MaRV; OlF; PTA-1; TreF; WBLP; WGRP
Seated one day at the typewriter. The Lost Word. Charles Henry Webb. PA
Seated one day on an organ. The Lost Ape. "J. W. G. W." PA
Seated, the harpist waits. Marble Statuette Harpist. Sara Van Alstyne Allen. GoYe
Seaward. Jeannette Bliss Gillespy. CAG
Seaward, *sel.* Richard Hovey.
  Sea, The. NLK
Seaward. Celia Thaxter. AA
Seaward. George Edward Woodberry. Wild Eden, XLI. AA
Seaward, at morn, my doves flew free. Three Doves. James Jeffrey Roche. JKCP
Seaward Bound. Alice Brown. TrPWD
Seaward goes the sun, and homeward by the down. The Cliffside Path. Swinburne. EmBrPo
Seaward the gentle Cyprian loves to gaze. Anyte, *tr. fr. Greek by* the Earl of Cromer. GrPo
Seaweed [*or* Sea Weed]. Longfellow. APW; CoBA; CoV; HBV; IAP; LPS-2; MOAP; OxBA; PCD
  Equinox, The, *sel.* EtS
Sea-Weed, The. Elisabeth Cavazza Pullen. AA
Sea-Weeds. Annie Chambers Ketchum. BlG
Sebastian in Dream. Georg Trakl, *tr. fr. German by* Kate Flores. AnGP
Sebastopol. *Unknown.* SG
2nd afternoon I come, The. A Poem for the Insane. John Wieners. NeAP
Second Air Force. Randall Jarrell. CoBMV; FiMAP; WaP
Second Anniversary, The. John Donne. *See* Of the Progress of the Soul.
Second Asgard, The. Matthew Arnold. *Fr.* Balder Dead. FiP
Second Avenue. Orrick Johns. BAP
Second Best, The. Matthew Arnold. BPN; EM-2; EmBrPo; EPN; GEPC
Second Best. Rupert Brooke. MBP; MoBrPo; OBVV
Second-Best. Robinson Jeffers. CoV
Second Brother, The, *sels.* Thomas Lovell Beddoes.
  Daisy and the Flood, The. RO
  "I should not say." AtBAP
  Strew Not Earth with Empty Stars. ERP
Second Canzone. Nikolai Stepanovich Gumilev, *tr. fr. Russian by* Harold Furth. TrRV
Second Chap. of the Cant. from the 10. Verse to the 13. John Norris. *See* Canticle.
Second Coming, The. Stanton A. Coblentz. ChIP
Second Coming, The. Norman Gale. BLP; HBV; MaRV; PC
Second Coming, The. W. B. Yeats. AtBAP; CoBMV; CoEV; EnL; EnLP; ExPo; FaBoEn; FaBoMo; GTBS-W; HoPM; InPo; LiTB; LiTG; LiTM; LoBV; MaPo; MoAB; MoVE; OAEP (2d ed.); OxBI; Po; PoE; PoFS; PoLFOT; ReaPo; ReMP; RiBV; SeCePo; SeCeV; TwHP; TwP; UnPo (3d ed.); WaP
Second Coming 1942. Henry Treece. MoWP
Second Coming of Christ, The. Harrington Green. CAG
Second Concession of Deer, The. William Wye Smith. BoCaPo (1943 ed.)
Second Corinthians, *sel.* Bible, *N.T.*
  Glory of God Revealed in Jesus, The, IV: 6. MaRV
Second Crucifixion, The. Richard Le Gallienne. HBV; MaRV; OBEV (1st ed.); OBVV; WGRP
Second Cycle of Love Poems, *sels.* George Barker.
  O Tender under Her Right Breast. MoAB; MoBrPo (1950 ed.); NeMA
    (Love Poem: "O tender under her right breast.") NeBP
  Verses for a First Birthday. MoAB; MoBrPo (1950 ed.)
Second Dirge. Thomas Lovell Beddoes. *See* Sibylla's Dirge.

Second Dream. Bernardo Ortiz de Montellano, *tr. fr. Spanish by* Thelma Lamb, Donald Devenish Walsh, *and* Dudley Fitts. AnCL
Second Duke of Buckingham, The. Pope. *See* Death of Buckingham, The.
Second Egloge Entituled Fortunatus, The. Mantuan, *tr. fr. Latin by* George Turberville. *Fr.* The Eglogs of the Poet B. Mantuan Carmelitan. ReIE
Second Epistle of the Essay on Man, The. Pope. GoTL
Second Epistle of the Second Book of Horace, The, *sel.* Pope.
 Has Life No Sourness? BeR
Second Fig. Edna St. Vincent Millay. AmP
Second Growth. Winifred Welles. BAP
Second Hyperion, The. Keats. *See* Fall of Hyperion, The.
Second Idyll, The. Theocritus. *See* Incantation, The.
Second Iron Age (1939–1945), The. Michael Harrington. CaP
Second Jungle Book, The, *sels.* Kipling.
 Bagheera's Song. PoFr
 Fear. PtOT
 Law of the Jungle, The. BoChLi; LiTB; PoEL-5; PoVP; ShBV-1; VA
 Song of the Little Hunter, The. ShBV-1
Second Life of My Mother. Jorge Carrera Andrade, *tr. fr. Spanish by* Muna Lee. AnCL
Second Maccabees [*or* Machabees]. *sel.* Bible, Apocrypha.
 Mother and Her Seven Sons, A, VII: 1–14. BHV
Second Man, The. Julian Symons. WaP
Second Mask, Which Was of Beauty, The, *sel.* Ben Jonson.
 Had Those That Dwell in Error Foul. TuPP
Second Mate, The. Fitz-James O'Brien. *See* Lost Steamship, The.
Second News Item. *Unknown.* SiTL
Second Night, The. Thomas Hardy. VLEP
Second Nimphall, The, *sel.* Michael Drayton. *Fr.* The Muses' Elysium.
 "With full-leav'd lillies I will stick." AtBAP
Second Nun's Tale, The, *sel.* Chaucer. *Fr.* The Canterbury Tales.
 Invocatio ad Mariam, *mod. vers. by* Frank Ernest Hill, *fr. Prologue.* ISi
 ("Thou maid and mother, daughter of thy Son," *mod. vers.*) GoBC
 (Two Invocations of the Virgin, I.) ACP
Second of November, The. *Unknown.* SG
Second of November Tolls, The. César Vallejo, *tr. fr. Spanish by* Donald Devenish Walsh. AnCL
Second Part of Absalom and Achitophel, The. Dryden. *See* Absalom and Achitophel, Pt. II.
Second Poem: "Morning again, nothing has to be done." Peter Orlovsky. NeAP
Second Quest, The. Joseph Rodman Drake. *Fr.* The Culprit Fay. AA
Second Review of the Grand Army, A. Bret Harte. BlG; HBV; MC; MDAH; PAH
Second Samuel, *sels.* Bible, *O.T.*
 David and Bathsheba, XI: 2–XII: 18. OuHeWo
 (David and Uriah, the Hittite.) EM-1
 David's Lament, I: 19–27. ChTr (17–27); TrGrPo; TrJP
 ("Beauty of Israel is slain upon thy high places, The," I: 19–26.) LO
 (David's Lament for Saul and Jonathan.) AWP
 (David's Lament over Saul and Jonathan.) ShBV-3
 (How Are the Mighty Fallen.) LiTW; WaaP
 (Lament over Saul.) BHV
 (Saul, David, and Jonathan, I: 2–27, *abr.*) BoFr
 "It came to pass after this, that Absalom the son of David had a fair sister." XIII: 1–19. LO
 Leader, The, XXIII: 3–4. PCD; PCH
Second Seeing. Louis Golding. WGRP
Second Settler's Story, The. Will Carleton. IHA
Second Shepherds' Play, The. *Unknown.* EM-1, *mod. Eng.*; EnLit, *mod. Eng.*; MeEV, *mod. Eng.*; PoEL-1
 Haylle, Comly and Clene, *sel.* OBEV (new ed.); OxBoLi
 (Hail, Comely and Clean.) AnEC
 (Hayll, Comly and Clene.) AtBAP; BoW
 (Shepherds at Bethlehem, The.) ChTr; CoEV
Second Song from Cyprus. Hilda Doolittle ("H. D."). *See* Song: "Where is the nightingale."
Second Song of Chang-kan, A. Li Po, *tr. fr. Chinese.* WhP
Second Sonnet on "Tetrachordon." Milton. *See* On the Detraction Which Followed . . . ("I did but prompt the age").
Second Stanza for Dr. Johnson, A. Donald Hall. FiBHP
Second Table, The. Nixon Waterman. PTA-1
Second Thanksgiving, The; or, The Reprisal. George Herbert. OAEP
Second Three-Man's [*or* Men's] Song, The. Thomas Dekker. *See* Cold's the Wind.
Second Timothy. *sel.* Bible, *N.T.*
 "For God hath not given us the spirit of fear," I: 7. TiPo (1952 ed.)
Second Vision, The. Tadhg Dall O'Huiginn, *tr. fr. Late Middle Irish by* the Earl of Longford. AnIL
Second Volume, The. Robert Mowry Bell. AA
Second Walk in the Garden, The. John Gould Fletcher. MAPA
Second Wisdom. Henry Morton Robinson. GoYe
Second Woman's Lament. Brenda Chamberlain. NeIP
 (Fisherman Husband.) PrWP
Secrecy. Samuel Daniel. *See* Eyes, Hide My Love.
Secrecy Protested. Thomas Carew. LoPS; OAEP
 (Fear Not, Dear Love.) LiTL
Secret, The. "Æ." MBP; MoBrPo
 (Unity.) PoVP
Secret. Gwendolyn B. Bennett. CDC
Secret, The. José Joaquin Casas, *tr. fr. Spanish by* Thomas Walsh. CAW
Secret, The. Marchette Chute. GoBP
Secret, The. Ralph Spaulding Cushman. MaRV; PraP
 (His Presence Came like Sunrise.) BLRP
Secret, The. Henri de Régnier, *tr. fr. French by* Alan Conder. TrFP
Secret, The ("A fuzzy fellow without feet"). Emily Dickinson. RIS
Secret, The ("I have not told my garden yet"). Emily Dickinson. *See* I have not told my garden yet.
Secret, A ("A secret told"). Emily Dickinson. CoBA
Secret, The ("Some things that fly there be"). Emily Dickinson. *See* Some things that fly there be.
Secret. Esther Hull Doolittle. YeAr
Secret, The. Elizabeth Fleming. BoTP
Secret, A. Mrs. G. M. Howard. PEOR
Secret. Catherine Haydon Jacobs. GoYe
Secret, The. Mary Sinton Leitch. LS
Secret, The. James Russell Lowell. IAP
Secret, The. Cosmo Monkhouse. VA
Secret, The. John Richard Moreland. NLK; OQP; QP-2
Secret, The. Arthur Wallace Peach. HBMV
Secret, The. Jessie B. Rittenhouse. PC
Secret, The ("Hark, Celia, hark!"). *Unknown.* SeCL
Secret, The ("I loved, I kissed, I was happy"). *Unknown, tr. fr. Greek by* F. L. Lucas. GrPE
Secret, A ("If I had wit for to indite"). *Unknown.* OBSC
Secret, The ("We have a secret"). *Unknown.* BoChLi; MPB (1956 ed.); OTPC (1946 ed.); RAR; StVeCh (1940 ed.); TiPo; UTS
Secret, The ("The weary one had rest"). *Unknown.* PraP
Secret, The. George Edward Woodberry. Wild Eden, VI. AA; BAP; HBV; LBMV
Secret Cavern, The. Margaret Widdemer. FaPON; MPB
Secret Combination, The. Ellis Parker Butler. BOHV
Secret draught of wine and love repressed, The. Comfort. Hafiz. PeP
Secret Garden, The. Robert Nichols. WGRP
Secret Gate, The. "Fiona Macleod." ReTS
Secret Heart The. Robert P. Tristram Coffin. PoRL; TwCV
Secret in bed the lustful with soft cries. Sonnet against the Too-facile Mystic. Elizabeth B. Harrod. NePoEA
Secret Joy, The. Mary Webb. BoTP
Secret Laughter. Christopher Morley. FAOV; TreFS
Secret Love, The. "Æ." HBV
Secret Love. John Clare. LiTL; PoEL-4; TrGrPo
 (I Hid My Love.) AtBAP
 "And even silence found a tongue," *br. sel.* LO
Secret Love; or, The Maiden Queen, *sels.* Dryden.
 "I feed a flame within, which so torments me." InPo; LO; LoPS; MaPo; SeCL
 (Hidden Flame, The.) OBEV
 (Song.) AWP; CoEV; JAWP; LiTL; WBP
 (Song of Secret Love, The.) BeR
 One Long Nuptial Day. BeR
Secret mystery lights up my spirit, A. Who Is She? Félix Arvers. TrFP
Secret Ode. Paul Valéry, *tr. fr. French by* Alan Conder. TrFP
Secret of Death, The ("She is dead"). Sir Edwin Arnold. *See* He and She.
Secret of the Cross, The. M. J. Clarkson. BePJ
Secret of the Deeps, The. Sidney Royse Lysaght. EtS
Secret of the King possesses me, The. As One Finding Peace. Sister Mary Madeleva. JKCP
Secret of the Machines, The. Kipling. PoMa; PoTo; StVeCh
Secret of the Nightingale, The. Roden Noel. VA
Secret of the Sea, The. Longfellow. AnNE; CBPC; EtS; GoTP; IAP; RIS; TCAP
 (Galley of Count Arnaldos, The.) OBEV (new ed.); OBVV
Secret of these hills was stone, The. The Pylons. Stephen Spender. AWP; ChMo; EnLi-2 (1949 ed.); EnLit
Secret Parting. Dante Gabriel Rossetti. The House of Life, XLV. EtPaEn; PoVP; ViPo
Secret People, The. G. K. Chesterton. OtMeF; PoFr
Secret Place, The. Henry Francis Lyte. VA
Secret Places. Irene Thompson. BoTP
Secret Rose, The. W. B. Yeats. GTIV
Secret Saint, The, *sel.* Moyshe Kulbak, *tr. fr. Yiddish by* Sarah Zweig Betsky.

Jew, The. OnCuPl
Secret Service. Richard Church. MoP
Secret Service. Gertrude Robinson Dugan. PraP
Secret Temple, The. Marjorie Allen Seiffert. BAP
Secret told, A. A Secret. Emily Dickinson. CoBA
Secret Town, The, *sel.* Abraham Sutzkever, *tr. fr. Yiddish by* Jacob Sonntag.
"Remember the sun in the autumn, its rays." TrJP
Secret Voices, The. Ethel Mannin. NLK
Secret was the garden. The Mistress of Vision. Francis Thompson. CH; OBVV
Secret Weapon. Ammonides, *tr. fr. Greek by* Dudley Fitts. LiTW
Secret Wood, The. Andrew Young. POTE
Secretary, The. Matthew Prior. CEP; PoE; PoFS
Secrets. Emily Dickinson. TCAP
Secrets. E. Kathryn Fowler. ChBR
Secrets. Luisa Hewitt. PCH
Secrets of Angling, The, *sel.* John Dennys.
"Let me live harmlessly, and near the brink," 4 *sts.* MyFE
(Angler's Song, The, 6 *sts.*) EIL
Secrets of Our Garden, The. Rupert Sargent Holland. OTPC
Section and brick and grass. The Houses, VI. "Robin Hyde." AnNZ
Section men a-workin' there all side by side. Mike. *Unknown.* ABF
Secular Litany. M. K. Joseph. AnNZ
Secular Masque, The. Dryden. ExPo; MaPo; PoEL-3; SeCeV; SeCV-2; SeEP; TCEP
Sels.
"All, all of a piece throughout." BeR; ChTr; GTBS-W
(Chorus.) ViBoPo
(Chorus from "The Secular Masque.") OnPM
Songs from "The Secular Masque": Momus. InPo
"With horns and with hounds I waken the day." ElSeCe
(Diana's Hunting-Song.) SeCePo; SeCL
(Songs from "The Secular Masque": Diana.) InPo
Secular Power. Pushkin, *tr. fr. Russian by* Babette Deutsch. TrRV
(Crucifix, The, *tr. by* Frances Cornford *and* E. P. Salaman.) LiTW
("When the last great and solemn act was played," *tr. by* Frances Cornford.) BoRS
Secure it falls upon its feet, not upon its back. Aeschylus. *Fr.* Suppliants. GrPo
Security. Denis Glover. AnNZ
Security. Charles L. O'Donnell. TrPWD
Security. Margaret E. Sangster. BLRP
Sed Non Satiata. Baudelaire, *tr. fr. French by* Arthur Symons. OnPM
Seder-Night. Israel Zangwill. TrJP
Sedge Songs. Nikolaus Lenau, *tr. fr. German by* Dwight Durling. AnGP
"On the motionless pond waters," III.
"Sunlight leaves the west," II.
"Yonder sinks the sun; the wearied," I.
Sedge Warblers. Edward Thomas. LO
Sedges, The. "Seumas O'Sullivan." AnIV; LBBV
See a pin and pick it up. Old Superstitions [*or* Some Proverbs in Verse]. *Unknown.* FaBoBe; GoTP; HBV; HBVY; RIS; TreF
See, above this mortal cloudland. Gwel uwchlaw cymylau amser. Islwyn. PrWP
See, already over the earth. Dawn. Euripides. *Fr.* Ion. OxBG
See an old unhappy bull. The Bull. Ralph Hodgson. AnFE; BMEP; ChMo; CMP; EnLi-2 (1949 ed.); EnLit; LiTG; LiTM (rev. ed.); MBP; MoAB; MoBrPo; MoVE; NV; OBMV; ShBV-2; TOP; YT
See, as the Carver Carves a Rose. Conrad Aiken. Priapus and the Pool, XVI [XIX]. MM; PFY
(Carver, The.) HBMV
("See, as the carver carves a rose.") AnAmPo; LA
See, as the prettiest graves will do in time. Fame. Robert Browning. *Fr.* Earth's Immortalities. BPN; PoVP; VLEP
See! cherubs drop their feathers from their wings. On a Snow Storm. Edward Capern. AlDL
See, chil-dren, the fur-bear-ing seal. A Seal. Oliver Herford. *Fr.* Child's Natural History. HBV; HBVY
See, cold island, we stand. Clare Coast. Emily Lawless. GTIV; OxBI
See colic, gout, and stone, a cruel train. Sir Richard Blackmore. *Fr.* Creation. PoP
"See, Corydon, see, here's the stall." Corydon and Tityrus. *Unknown.* CAW
See! down the red road by the brown tree. The End of Exploring. David Campbell. SeCePo
See, Fairest! virgins gather dew. To Eliza, upon May Day Morning, 1649. Robert Baron. SeCL
See, far above the starry height. The Eagle Swift. Adam of St. Victor. BePJ
See, from his head, his hands, his feet. Crucifixion to the World, by the Cross of Christ. Isaac Watts. *Fr.* When I Survey the Wond'rous Cross. BeR
See! from the brake the whirring pheasant springs. The Pheasant [*or* The Flames of Death]. Pope. *Fr.* Windsor Forest. BeR; FaBoEn; GoTP; PoEL-3
See, from this counterfeit of him. On a Bust of Dante. Thomas William Parsons. AA; AnAmPo; APW; BAP; CBOV; HBV; LBAP; LEAP; LPS-3; OBAV
See from yon looming summit the beacon, Cyrnus, beckon. The Soldier. Solon. GrPE
See, gallants, see this gallery of delights. Anthony Munday unto All Young Gentlemen in Commendation of this Gallery and Workmen Thereof. Anthony Munday. ReIE
See! He trails his toes. Haunted. Amy Lowell. DaM
See, here's the grand approach. On Blenheim [*or* Verses on Blenheim]. Swift, *after the Latin of* Martial. AWP; OnPM
See him, prone on his belly behind the mesquite. The Apache in Ambush. Bailey Millard. BAP
See him, the gentle Bible beast. The Toy Horse. Edwin Muir. FaBoMo
See, his beard is sprouting yet. The Youth. Ibn Sara. MooP
See, his slender fingers shine. Golden Glow. Abul Hasan of Seville. MooP
See how a king can slumber on his throne. Winter-Song for Pan. John Erskine. CAG
See how Flora smiles to see. On Clarastella Walking in Her Garden. Robert Heath. OBS; SeCL
See how from far upon the eastern road. The Magi. Milton. *Fr.* On the Morning of Christ's Nativity. ChTr
See how he dives. Seal. William Jay Smith. GoTP
See How He Gallops. Mikhail Yurevich Lermontov, *tr. fr. Russian by* Babette Deutsch. TrRV
See how it is teed up on the nest, enabling. A Flamingo's Egg. Terence Heywood. BoSA
See how it rains on the river! Straying. Jorge Guillén. CoSP
See, how like twilight slumber falls. Song. Charles Cotton. CaAE; OBS; SeCL
See how the dying west puts forth her song. Nocturne. Richard Church. ChMP
See how the flowers, as at parade. A Garden. Andrew Marvell. *Fr.* Upon Appleton House. CEP; EPS (1942 ed.); HBV; OBEV; ShGoBo; TrGrPo
See how the gently falling rain. Poems Translated from the Chinese. *Unknown, tr. by* John Francis Davis. RO
See how the goat in purple chains. The Billy Goat. Anyte. GrR
See how the mightiest gods, and best-beloved. Demetrius Enters Athens [*or* Processional for Demetrius Poliorcetes]. Hermocles. GrPo; OxBG
See, how the orient dew. On a Drop of Dew [*or* A Drop of Dew]. Andrew Marvell. EnLi-1; EV-2; GoBC; GTBS-W; LiTB; LiTG; LPS-2; MeLP; MePo; OBS; OuHeWo; OxBoCh; PoFS; ReEn; SeCV-1; SeEP; UnPo (1st ed.); WoL
See how the poppies nod. A Lullaby. Agnes H. Begbie. BOL
See how the sky. The Moon. Louise Ayres Garnett. SiSoSe
See! how the stubborn damsel doth deprave. Amoretti, XXIX. Spenser. PeBoSo
See how the sun has somewhat not of light. El Greco. E. L. Mayo. HoPM; MiAP
See how the Yellow River's waters move from heaven. Bringing in the Wine. Li Po. OuHeWo
See how this violet which before. On a Violet in Her Breast. Thomas Stanley. OBS
See! I give myself to you, Beloved! A Gift. Amy Lowell. BAP; ChMo; CMP; LEAP; NP
See, I have bent thee by thy saffron hair. The Sunflower. Peter Quennell. AtBAP; POTE
See, in the circle how we stand. In a Convex Mirror. Rosemary Dobson. MoAuPo
See, in the garden there, it hops and lurches about. On a Child with a Wooden Leg. Bertram Warr. BoCaPo (1948 ed.)
See in the Midst of Fair Leaves. Marianne Moore. MoAB
See, in yonder field. Corn in the Wind. Iyad. MooP
See love, whose kingdom as the world is ample. Pierre de Ronsard. *Fr.* Sonnets pour Hélène. PrPoCR
See me with all the terrors on my roads. The Face. Edwin Muir. ChMP; FaBoMo
See, Mignonne, hath not the rose. The Rose [*or* Ode]. Pierre de Ronsard. AWP; JAWP; LiA; WBP
See, my belovèd, how the sun. Nightfall. Kalidasa. LiTW
See my lov'd Britons, see your Shakespeare rise. Prologue. Dryden. *Fr.* Troilus and Cressida. CEP; SeCV-2
See my mast, a pen! The Voyage. Vachel Lindsay. MAP
See my pretty little nest. Oriole. Marion Mitchell Walker. GFA
See now, dead friend. Duty to Death, LD. Dick Roberts. WaP
See, O see!/ How every tree." Song. George Digby, Earl of Bristol. *Fr.* Elvira. SeCL

See on the mountain's southern side. John Dyer. *Fr.* Grongar Hill. CoEV
See on what mighty draughts of life. O Spring, Come Prettily In. Adolf Strodtmann. CAW
See, one physician, like a sculler, plies. Two Heads Are Better than One. Joseph Jekyll. WhC
See Phoebus breaking from the willing skies. The Consolation. Countess of Winchilsea. TriL
See represented here, in light and shade. The Salutation of the Blessed Virgin. John Byrom. ISi
See saw. *See also* Seesaw.
See-saw, down in my lap. *Unknown.* OxNR
See saw, Margery Daw. Mother Goose. BoChLi; OTPC; OxNR; RIS
See-saw, Margery Daw,/ The old hen flew over the malt house. *Unknown.* OxNR
See-saw, Margery Daw,/ Sold her bed and lay upon straw. *Unknown.* OxNR
See-saw! Margery Daw!/ Sold her bed. Margery Daw. Daniel Henry Holmes. BAP
See-saw, Margery Daw,/ This is the tale of Saint Margery Daw. Margery Daw. Ruth Manning-Sanders. OS
See-saw, sacradown. Mother Goose. OTPC; OxNR; PCH; PPL
See, see, mine own sweet jewel. Canzonet. *Unknown.* EG; EIL; LO
See, see, she wakes! Sabina wakes! Song. Congreve. HBV
See! see the bright light shines. *Unknown.* SeCSL
See! see! the swallow is here! Rhodian Swallow Song. *Unknown.* GrR
See, see, what shall I see? *Unknown.* OxNR
See, see where royal Snowdon rears. Liberty. John Ceiriog Hughes. PoFr
See, Sir, here's the grand approach. On Blenheim House. Abel Evans. OBEC
See! some strange comfort every state attend. Life's Poor Play. Pope. *Fr.* An Essay on Man. OBEC; SeCePo
See, stretching yonder o'er that low divide. The Old Mackenzie Trail. John A. Lomax. SCC
See that building, which, when my mistress living. A Well-wishing to a Place of Pleasure. *Unknown.* SeCL
See that satan pollarding a tree. Progression. Francis Scarfe. NeBP
See that upon my shield the sheen is brighter. Plautus. *Fr.* Miles Gloriosus. LaP
See the bunnies sitting there. Timid Bunnies. Jeannie Kirby. BoTP
See the chariot at hand here of Love. The Triumph of Charis [*or* Her Triumph]. Ben Jonson. *Fr.* A Celebration of Charis. AEV; AnFE; AtBAP; BEL; CoEV; EIL; ElSeCe; EPP; EPS; EV-2; ExPo; FaBoEn; GoBC; HBV; InPo; InvP; LiTB; LiTL; LoBV; MaPo; OAEP; OBEV; Po; PoEL-2; SeCeV; SeCV-1; SeEP; SiCE; TCEP; TOP; TuPP; TwHP; TyEnPo; ViBoPo; WHA
See the Crocus' Golden Cup. Joseph Mary Plunkett. OnYI
See the day begins to break. Satyr's Song. John Fletcher. *Fr.* The Faithful Shepherdess, IV, iv. OBS
See the dazzled stripling stand. Apocryphal Soliloquies [*or* Goliath and David]. Louis Untermeyer. TCPD; TrJP
See the fur coats go by! Poems. Hilda Conkling. ExPo; NP
See the happy moron. The Moron. *Unknown.* CenHV; DDA; YaD
See the ink bottle on the desk. The Poets at a House-Party. Carolyn Wells. PA
See the kinder shepherds round him. Isaac Watts. *Fr.* A Cradle Hymn. BeR
See the kitten on the wall. The Kitten at Play. Wordsworth. *Fr.* The Kitten and Falling Leaves. BoTP; CG; FaPON; GoTP; MPB (1956 ed.); OTPC; PRWS
See the land, her Easter keeping. Easter Week. Charles Kingsley. DD; EOAH; OHIP
See the little maunderer. A Love for Patsy. John Thompson, Jr. GTBS-W; LiTA; LiTL; LiTM; NePA; WaP
See the madly blowing dust. A Colorado Sand Storm. Eugene Field. PoOW
See! The Mother Corn comes hither, making all hearts glad! An Indian Hymn of Thanks to Mother Corn. *Unknown.* PCH
See, the pretty planet! Blowing Bubbles [*or* The Bubble]. William Allingham. GN; OnYI
See the pretty snowflakes. Falling Snow. *Unknown.* BoChLi; GFA; TiPo (1952 ed.)
See, the ruthless victor comes. Song for Peace. W. R. Rodgers. NeBP
See, the see, the Bishop's see, The. The Bishop's See. *Unknown.* CoMu
See the Smoking Bowl before Us. Burns. *Fr.* The Jolly Beggars. ALV, *abr.*; ATP (1935 ed.); BSV; GoTS (Jolly Mortals, Fill Your Glasses.) EnLi-2 (1949 ed.)
See, the spring herself discloses. Spring. Thomas Stanley. AWP; JAWP; SeCL; WBP
See, the sun! His chariot-light. Dawn. Euripides. *Fr.* Ion. GrR
See the sword: on either shank. The Bloody Sword. Ibn al-Zaqqaq. MooP
See the white stillness of the unicorn. Sonnet. Roy Daniells. PeCV
See the yellow catkins cover. A Spring Song. Mary Howitt. BoTP; EV-4
See them joined by strings to history. Puppets. Patricia K. Page. BoCaPo (1948 ed.)
See there! God's signpost, standing at the ways. The Cross at the Crossways. John Oxenham. MaRV
See! There he stands; not brave, but with an air. Brothers. James Weldon Johnson. BANP; PreP
See! There stands the temple. Hu Chiu Shan. Hsüeh Lan Ying. PoHN
See, they are clearing the sawdust course. A Circus Garland. Rachel Field. StVeCh
See, they return; ah, see the tentative/ Movements. The Return. Ezra Pound. AnEnPo; CoAnAm; CoBMV; FaBoEn; MoAB; MoAmPo; MoP; MoPo; NePA; OxBA; TwAmPo; TwCV; ViBoPo
"See this my garden." The Philosopher's Garden. John Oxenham. PoMa
See thou character. Give thy thoughts no tongue. *See* Look thou character . . .
See, though the oil be low, more purely still and higher. Terence MacSwiney [*or* A Prisoner]. "Æ." AnIL; AnIV; PoFr
See, through this air, this ocean, and this earth. The Unity of Nature. Pope. *Fr.* An Essay on Man. CBOV
See to thyself: but, sirrah, thou to me. A Chariot-Race. Sophocles. *Fr.* Electra. GrR
See twilight standing on the brink. At the Edge of the Day. Clarence Urmy. HBMV
See what a lovely shell. The Shell. Tennyson. *Fr.* Maud. BoTP; BPN; GN; PoEL-5; SN; VA
See what a mass of gems the city wears. Impression de Nuit; London. Lord Alfred Douglas. ES; OBEV (new ed.); OBVV; PoVP
See, what a wonderful smile! Does it mean. Slumber-Songs of the Madonna, III. Alfred Noyes. BOL
See, when a fireship in mid ocean blazes. Surrender to Christ. Frederic William Henry Myers. OxBoCh
See where Calisto wheels about. Serenade, to Two Ladies. Thomas Porter. *Fr.* The Villain. SeCL
See Where Capella with Her Golden Kids. Edna St. Vincent Millay. Epitaph for the Race of Man, VI. MAP; MoAB; MoAmPo
See where enamoured Thyrsis lies. The Amorist. Nahum Tate. SeCL
See Where My Love a-Maying Goes. *Unknown.* EIL
See where she sits upon the grassy green [*or* grassie greene]. A Ditty. Spenser. *Fr.* The Shepheardes Calender: April. FaBoCh; OBEV; ViBoPo
See where the farmer, with a master's eye. Robert Dodsley. *Fr.* Agriculture; a Poem. EnSW
See, whilst thou weep'st, fair Cloe, see. To Cloe Weeping. Matthew Prior. CaAE; CEP; EiPP
See, Will, 'Ere's a Go. *Unknown.* ChTr ("Civile, si ergo," *sl. diff.*) WhC
See, Winter comes, to rule the varied year. Winter [*or* The Storm]. James Thomson. *Fr.* The Seasons. BEL; CEP; CoBE; EiPP; EM-1; EnL; EnLi-2; EnLit; OAEP; OBEC; PIAE; Po; TyEnPo
See with what constant motion. Gratiana Dancing [*or* Dauncing] and Singing. Richard Lovelace. ElSeCe; EPS; EV-2; LiTL; LoBV; MeLP; MePo; OAEP; OBS; ReEn; SeCL; SeCV-1; SeEP
See with what simplicity. The Picture of Little T. C. in a Prospect of Flowers. Andrew Marvell. CaAE; EPS; EV-2; ExPo; GTSL; HBV; LiTB; MeLP; MePo; OBEV; OBS; PoE; SeCeV; SeCV-1
See yon blithe child that dances in our sight. The Child. Sara Coleridge. MotAn; OBEV (1st ed.)
See yon robin on the spray. The English Robin. Harrison Weir. LPS-2
See yonder cliff—how ghastly bare. The Cliff. John Henry Boner. NoCaPo
See yonder goes old Mendax, telling lies. Mendax. Gotthold Ephraim Lessing. BOHV
See yonder hallow'd fane! the pious work. Church and Church-yard at Night. Robert Blair. *Fr.* The Grave. EnSW; OBEC; ViBoPo
See yonder melancholy gentleman. Meditations of a Gull. Sir John Davies. SiCE
See, yonder, the belfry tower. At Midnight. Frank Dempster Sherman. AA; MAP
See yonder, where a gem of night. Es fällt ein Stern herunter. Heine. AWP; JAWP
See you him yonder who sits o'er the stage. Of Cornelius. Everard Guilpin. *Fr.* Skialetheia. SiCE; TuPP
See you not Heng Mountain towering over Hunan hills. Song of the Vermeil Phoenix. Tu Fu. WhP
See you the ferny ride that steals. Puck's Song. Kipling. *Fr.* Puck of Pook's Hill. FaBoCh; LoGBV; POTT

Seed. H. C. Bosman. BoSA
Seed-Eaters, The. Robert Francis. NePoAm-2
Seed Growing Secretly, The. Henry Vaughan. OxBoCh; SeCV-1
Seed is dug under, A. Shekhinah. Karl Wolfskehl. TrJP
Seed, Lord, falls on stony ground, The. Process. Charles L. O'Donnell. TrPWD
Seed Pods. John Wheelwright. MeRV
Seed Shop, The. Muriel Stuart. DiM; GoTP; GoTS; MBP; MW; NP; POTE
Seed Time. *See* Seedtime.
Seeds. Walter de la Mare. StVeCh; TiPo (1959 ed.)
Seeds. John Oxenham. WGRP
Seeds. Augusta Webster. OBVV
('Tween Earth and Sky.) VA
Seeds clutched in my hand. Hunting. "Yehoash." TrJP
Seeds I sowed, The. Seeds. Walter de la Mare. StVeCh; TiPo (1959 ed.)
Seeds in a dry pod, tick, tick, tick. Petit the Poet. Edgar Lee Masters. *Fr.* Spoon River Anthology. AnFE; APA; ChMo; CMP; CoAnAm; InPo; LaNeLa; LoGBV; MAP; MoAmPo; MoVE; NeMA; OxBA
Seeds of Kindness. *Unknown. See* Say It Now.
Seeds of Love, The. *At. to* Mrs. Fleetwood Habergham. FaBoCh; LoGBV; OxBoLi
Seeds with wings, between earth and sky. Seeds [*or* 'Tween Earth and Sky]. Augusta Webster. OBVV; VA
Seedsmen of Old Saturn's Land. Herman Melville. *Fr.* Clarel. AmPP (3d ed.)
Seed-Time. Patrick James Coleman. TIP
Seed-Time. George Meredith. BrBE
Seedtime and Harvest. Sir Henry Head. PoP
Seed Time Hymn. John Keble. VA
Seein' Things. Eugene Field. BoChLi; DDA; HBV; HBVY; HOAH; MAP; MoAmPo (1942 ed.); MPB; NeMA; OTPC; PoMa; PTA-1; RIS; TCAP; TreF
Seeing. John Lyle Donaghy. NeIP
Seeing a Lady. John Tatham. *Fr.* Ostella. SeCL
("Oh, she is fair: fair as the eastern morn.") LO
Seeing her Cnidian self Cypris cried "Hey!" On Praxiteles' Statue of Aphrodite at Cnidus. Plato. GrR
Seeing Her Dancing. Sir Robert Heath. OBS; SeEP
Seeing how I love you utterly. Song for a Lute, I. Edna St. Vincent Millay. BoFr
Seeing how the world suffered and bled. Angela Morgan. *Fr.* The Humanitarian. OQP; QP-2
Seeing Hsia Chan Off by River. Po Chü-i, *tr. fr. Chinese by* Ching Ti. WhP
Seeing Li Po in a Dream. Tu Fu, *tr. fr. Chinese by* Witter Bynner. BoFr
Seeing myself thus cleansed by solitude. The Stranger. Georges Duhamel. BoFr
Seeing the great moon rising. Moonrise. Abbie Huston Evans. NP
Seeing the martyred corpse of Sparta's king. Philip of Thessalonica, *tr. fr. Greek by* John Addington Symonds. GrPo
"Seeing the plum tree I thought of the Western Island." Ballad of the Western Island in the North Country. *Unknown.* TrCh
Seeing those mountains, distant and obscure. Mellin de Saint-Gelais. *See* Sonnet of the Mountain, The.
Seek a convenient time to take heed to thyself. Of Love of Silence and of Solitude. Thomas à Kempis. *Fr.* Imitation of Christ. TreF
Seek a Haven ("O navis referent"). Horace, *tr. fr. Latin by* Charles Stuart Calverley. Odes, I, 14. OnPM
Seek Flowers of Heaven. Robert Southwell. ReIE
Seek it by pole or equator. Atlantis Regained. Edwin Björkman. NoCaPo (1941 ed.)
Seek music in the wolf's fierce howl. The Irish Wolf. James McCarroll. TIP
Seek not afar for beauty. Lo! it glows. Earth's Common Things. Minot J. Savage. MaRV; OQP; QP-1
Seek not for me within a tomb. L'Envoi. John G. Neihardt. MaRV. *See also* Oh, seek me not within a tomb.
Seek not, for thou shalt not find it, what my end, what thine shall be. To Leuconöe [*or* Mistrust To-Morrow]. Horace, *tr. by* Charles Stuart Calverley. Odes, I, 11. LoBV; OnPM
Seek not in borrowed hues your cheeks to dress. To a Lady Who Used Cosmetics. Johannes Secundus. LaP
Seek not, Leuconöe, to know how long you're going to live yet. To Leuconöe. Horace, *tr. by* Eugene Field. AA; ALV
Seek not the tree of silkiest bark. Song. Aubrey Thomas De Vere. JKCP; OBVV; PoVP; VA
Seek not to know (the ghost replied with tears). Marcellus. Virgil, *tr. by* Dryden. *Fr.* The Aeneid, VI. OBS
Seek otherwhere for happiness? Answer. Harriet Hoock. WHL
Seek the Lord. Thomas Campion. OxBoCh
Seek the Lord in Prayer. *Unknown.* PraP
Seek Those Things Which Are Above. William Newell. EOAH
Seek true religion. Oh, where? Mirreus. Truth. John Donne. *Fr.* Satires, III. SeCePo
Seek up and down, both fair and brown. Kate o' Belashanny. William Allingham. IrPN
Seeker, The. Lascelles Abercrombie. *Fr.* The Fool's Adventure. WGRP
Seeker after God, The. Harry Kemp. OQP; QP-2
Seeker in the Marshes, The. Daniel Lewis Dawson. AA
Seeker in the Night, A. Florence Earle Coates. TrPWD
Seeker of far millenniums, stop here. Man Plowing. Edith Mirick. MuM
Seekers, The. Lucia Trevitt Auryansen. OQP; QP-2
Seekers, The. John Masefield. HBV; MaRV; OQP; QP-1; QS; TVSH; WGRP
Seekers, The. Charles Hamilton Sorley. WGRP
Seekers, The. Victor Starbuck. BPP; MaRV; WGRP
Seekers, The. Arthur Stringer. CPG
Seeking. Mary Carolyn Davies. OQP; QP-1
(Feet.) WGRP
Seeking and Finding God. John C. Earle. MaRV
Seeking, Finding. Pedro Salinas, *tr. fr. Spanish by* Eleanor L. Turnbull. CoSP
Seeking God. Edward Dowden. GrCo-1; MaRV; WGRP
Seeking Narcissus in my weariness. The Divine Narcissus. Sister Juana Inéz de la Cruz. CAW
Seeking of Self, The. Vyacheslav Ivanovich Ivanov, *tr. fr. Russian by* Babette Deutsch. TrRV
Seeking Spring beyond the City. Su T'ung-po, *tr. fr. Chinese by* Yu Min-chuan. WhP
Seeking the Mayflower. Edmund Clarence Stedman. ADAH
Seeking the Pastures of Christ the Shepherd. Isaac Watts. BeR
Seeking the prow of thought piercing the black. February Night. Wyn Griffith. MoWP
Seek'st thou the Highest—the Greatest? The Plant. Schiller. RO
Seele im Raum. Randall Jarrell. CoBMV; FiMAP
Seeming Dead, The. Paul Valéry, *tr. fr. French by* Alan Conder. TrFP
Seemingly as other men, yet always. Momist. Amy Groesbeck. GoYe
Seems lak [*or* like] to me de stars don't shine so bright. Sence You Went Away. James Weldon Johnson. BANP; PoNe
Seems not our breathing light? Renunciants. Edward Dowden. GTIV; OBVV; VA
Seen from these cliffs the sea circles slowly. Zennor. Anne Ridler. MoVE
Seen in a Glass. Kathleen Raine. ChMP
Seen in moonlight's silver ray. Oriental. José Zorrilla. AnSpL-2
Seen my lady home las' night. A Negro Love Song. Paul Laurence Dunbar. BANP; PoNe
Seen on the sea, no sign; no sign, no sign. The Dead Wingman. Randall Jarrell. MiAP
Seen you down at chu'ch las' night. Discovered. Paul Laurence Dunbar. LEAP; MAP; MoAmPo (1942 ed.)
Seer of the triple realm invisible. Paola and Francesca. Frances Anne Kemble. DiM
Seer saw on, The. Ebenezer Jones. *Fr.* Ways of Regard. NBE
Seesaw. *See also* See saw.
Seesaw. Gerardo Diego, *tr. fr. Spanish by* Eleanor L. Turnbull. CoSP; LiTW
Seesaw, The. Oscar Williams. LiTA; LiTG
See'st Not My Love. William Bosworth. *Fr.* The Chaste and Lost Lovers. SeCL
Seest thou how gayly my young master goes. Joseph Hall. *Fr.* Virgidemiarum. SiCE
Seest thou, my friend, with envious eye. Martial Rage. Horace. OnPM
See'st [*or* Seest] thou not in clearest dayes. Philarete Praises Poetry. George Wither. *Fr.* The Shepherd's Hunting. EPS; OBS
Seest thou not nann to day my pretty nanny. *Unknown.* SeCSL
"See'st thou o'er my shoulders falling." Love Song. Judah Halevi. TrJP
Seest thou those dyamonds which she weares. *Unknown.* SeCSL
Seest thou yon woodland child. Gardening. John Keble. OTPC (1923 ed.)
Segovia and Madrid. Rose Terry Cooke. AA; OBAV
Seguidilla. José de Valdivielso, *tr. fr. Spanish by* Thomas Walsh. CAW
Sehnsucht. Arthur Hugh Clough. EPN; VLEP
Sehnsucht. Anna Wickham. BMEP; MBP; MoBrPo; TwCV
Sehnsucht; or, What You Will. "Corinna." FiBHP; InMe
Seicheprey. *Unknown.* PAH
Seine. Rhys Davies. MoWP
Seine flows out of the mist, The. September Day. Sara Teasdale. ChMo; CMP

Seismograph. A. M. Sullivan. JKCP (1955 ed.)
Seize, O seize the sounding lyre. The Hero of Bridgewater. Charles L. S. Jones. PAH
Seized with a sudden fancy for fresh meat. *Unknown. Fr.* Homeric Hymns. GrPo
Seldom "can't." Christina Rossetti. *Fr.* Sing-Song. SAS
(Good Advice.) PPL
(Rules of Behavior.) HBV; HBVY
Select Passages from a Coming Poet. "F. Anstey." BOHV
Selection, A, *sel.* Juan Díaz Covarrubias, *tr. fr. Spanish by* Edna Worthley Underwood.
"Woe is he who sees vanish and then melt away." PoP
Selector's Wife, The. Mary Fullerton. MoAuPo
Selestial apoley which didest inspire. Odd to a Krokis. *Unknown.* NA
Self, The. *Unknown, tr. fr. Sanskrit by* Joseph Nadin Rawson. *Fr.* The Upanishads. OnPM
Self-Abandonment. Li Po, *tr. fr. Chinese by* Arthur Waley. TrCh
Self-Analysis. Anna Wickham. BLV; MBP; MoBrPo; TrGrPo (1942 ed.)
Self and the Otherself. Elizabeth, Queen of England. DiM
("I grieve, and dare not show my discontent.") LO
Self Banished, The. Edmund Waller. EPS; SeEP
(Selfe Banished, The.) FaBoEn; MePo; OBS
Self-composed Epitaph on a Doctor by the Name of I. Letsome. *Unknown. See* On Dr. Isaac Letsome.
Self-Control. Polly Chase Boyden. GoBP
Self-Criticism in February. Robinson Jeffers. AmPP; CoV
Self-Deception. Matthew Arnold. BPN; EmBrPo; GEPC; PoVP; VLEP
Self-Defense. Santob de Carrion, *tr. fr. Spanish by* George Ticknor. TrJP
Self-Dependence. Matthew Arnold. BBV; BEL; BLP; BPN; CRP; EM-2; EmBrPo; EnLi-2; EnLit; EPN; GEPC; HBV; MCCG; OAEP; OQP; Po; PoVP; QP-1; ReTS; TCEP; TreFS; ViPP; VLEP; WGRP
Self-Discipline. "Æ." MoBrPo; VA
Self-Esteem. Edward Coote Pinkney. SPP
Self-Esteem. Anna Wickham. PIAE
Self-evident. James Robinson Planché. PA
Self-exiled, The. Walter C. Smith. VA
Self-Guidance. Dante, *tr. fr. Italian by* Jefferson Butler Fletcher. *Fr.* Divina Commedia: Purgatorio, XXVII. GrCo-2
Self-Interrogation. Emily Brontë. EmBrPo
Self-Knowledge. Samuel Taylor Coleridge. SeCePo
Self-Love. Shams Tabrez, *tr. fr. Persian by* Puran Singh. OnPM
Self-love (which never rightly understood). Tyrannic Love: Prologue. Dryden. OAEP; ViBoPo
Self-made hero, marked by virtue man, The. Conversation in Clichés. James Edward Tobin. JKCP (1955 ed.)
Self-Mastery. Bayard Taylor. MaRV
Self-pleasing souls that play with beauty's bait. Robert Southwell. LO
Self-Portrait. William Cowper. *See* Stricken Deer, The.
Self Portrait. Edward Lear. *See* How Pleasant to Know Mr. Lear.
Self-Portrait. Moses Mendelssohn, *tr. fr. German.* TrJP
Self-Portrait of the Laureate of Nonsense. Edward Lear. *See* How Pleasant to Know Mr. Lear.
Self-praise is a wonderful thing! The Unawkward Singers. David Ferry. NePoAm-2
Self-Reliance. Emily Dickinson. *See* We never know how high we are.
Self-reverence, self-knowledge, self-control. The Way to Power. Tennyson. *Fr.* Oenone. MaRV; OQP; QP-2
Self-Righteousness. John Byrom. MaRV
Self-Server, A. Cale Young Rice. LS
Self Unsatisfied Runs Everywhere, The. Delmore Schwartz. FiMAP
Self-unseeing, The. Thomas Hardy. FaBoEn; GTBS-D; MoBrPo; MoPW; ViPP
Selfe-banished, The. Edmund Waller. *See* Self-banished, The.
Selfe-pitties teares, wherein my hope lyes drown'd. Caelica, VIII. Fulke Greville. AtBAP
Selfishness. Margaret E. Bruner. MaRV; PoToHe
Selfsame Song, The. Thomas Hardy. ChMo; CMP; TOP
Selfsame toothless voice for death or bridal, The. Bell Speech. Richard Wilbur. MoAB; MoVE
Selindra, *sel.* Sir William Killigrew.
Beauty Paramount. SeCL
Selkirk Grace, The. Burns. *See* Child's Grace, A.
"Sell all thou hast and give it to the poor." A Certain Rich Man. Theodore Maynard. OQP; QP-2
Sell him!—just as he lies there in his mother's arms a-sleeping! Love for Sale. Meleager, *tr. by* F. L. Lucas. GrPE
Sell him! though snuggled at his mother's breast. A Child for Sale. Meleager, *tr. by* Humbert Wolfe. OxBG
Selling a Dog. Irwin Russell. AIBD
Selma. Herman Wildenvey, *tr. fr. Norwegian by* Charles W. Stork. AnNoLy
Selves of myself, these waning days. Out of November; Speaking for One. David McCord. MAP
Semandra's Death. Nathaniel Lee. *Fr.* Mithridates, King of Pontus. BeR
Semi-Revolution, A. Robert Frost. LiTM; SiTL
Seminary. Constance Carrier. NePoAm
Seminary. Meurig Walters. MoWP
Sempronius,/ Sends greeting, warden of this Roman shore. A Roman Officer Writes Home. C. M. Doughty. *Fr.* The Dawn in Britain. FaBoTw
Sempronius, why, why wilt thou urge the fate. Addison. *Fr.* Cato, III, v. PoFr
Sempronius's Speech for War. Addison. *Fr.* Cato, II, i. LPS-2
("My voice is still for war.") PoFr
Sen throw virtue increases dignitie. Good Counsel. James I, King of Scotland. ACP; EBSV
Sence You Went Away. James Weldon Johnson. BANP; PoNe
Senchi Ferry; Gold Coast. L. D. Lerner. BoSA
Send Antipatra naked to meet the Parthian cavalry. Secret Weapon. Ammonides. LiTW
Send but a song oversea for us. To Walt Whitman in America. Swinburne. BEL; BPN; EmBrPo; EnLi-2; EnLit; EPN; InP; PoVP; ViP; ViPo; ViPP; VLEP
Send down thy truth, O God! For the Gifts of the Spirit. Edward Rowland Sill. TrPWD
"Send down your shining men!" we cried. The Ambuscade. Florence Cecilia Roberts. UnW
Send Forth, O God, Thy Light and Truth. John Quincy Adams. MaRV
Send Forth the High Falcon. Léonie Adams. InPo; MOAP; NP
Send Her a Valentine. Edgar A. Guest. ATP (1935 ed.)
Send Her On Along. *Unknown.* IHA
Send home my long-strayed [*or* stray'd] eyes to me. The Message. John Donne. ATP (1935 ed.); ElL; EnLit; EPS; GTBS-W; HBV; LiTG; MeLP; OBS; TuPP; ViBoPo; WHA
Send Me. Christina Rossetti. MaRV
Send Me. *Unknown.* MaRV
Send me no messages, for they are lies. Popular Sicilian Love Songs, 1. *Unknown.* LyPI
Send me some token that my hope may live. Sonnet [*or* The Token]. John Donne. LoPo; LoPS
Send-off, The. Wilfred Owen. CoEV; LiTB; MoAB; MoBrPo (1950 ed.); MoVE
Sending of the Magi, The. Bliss Carman. ChrBoLe
Sending Taro to sleep—it slowly blankets Taro's roof. Snow. Tatsuji Miyoshi. PoLJ
Senec. Traged. ex Thyeste Chor. 2. Seneca, *tr. by* Andrew Marvell. *See* Chorus: "Climb at Court for me that will."
Seneca Lake. James Gates Percival. *See* To Seneca Lake.
Seneca's Epitaph. Hildebert of Lavardin, *tr. fr. Latin by* L. R. Lind. LaP
Senex to Matt. Prior. James Kenneth Stephen. *Fr.* Two Epigrams. BOHV; CenHV; FiBHP; WhC
Senior Arbiter of Fate, The. Chu Yuan, *tr. fr. Chinese by* Shen Yu-ting. *Fr.* The Nine Songs. WhP
Senlin, a Biography, *sels.* Conrad Aiken.
Evening Song of Senlin ("It is evening"), II, ix. HBMV; MOAP
Evening Song of Senlin ("It is moonlight"), II, x. SBMV
Morning Song [of Senlin], II, ii. AmP; CBOV; ChMo; CMP; HBMV; InP; LiTA; LiTM; MAP; MoAB; MoAmPo; MOAP; NeMA; NP; NV; OxBA; PIAE; PoMa; PoTo; ReMP; SBMV; TrGrPo; WoL
(Senlin, a Biography.) PoMa
Sennacherib. Byron. *See* Destruction of Sennacherib, The.
Señora, it is true the Greeks are dead. Invocation to the Social Muse. Archibald MacLeish. CoV; LiTM; NAMP; OnAP
Sensation. Arthur Rimbaud, *tr. fr. French by* Jethro Bithell. AWP; JAWP; WBP
Sensation of the birth beat, softer. Strange within the Dividing. Ormond Thomas. MoWP
Sense and Spirit. George Meredith. EmBrPo; EPN; PoVP; WGRP
Sense, if You Can Find It. Hartley Coleridge. UnW
Sense of an earnest will, A. Small Things. Richard Monckton Milnes. NeHB
Sense of Death, The. Helen Hoyt. HBMV; TBM
(Since I Have Felt the Sense of Death.) LiTM (1946 ed.); NP
Sense of Humor, A. Vachel Lindsay. *Fr.* Poems about the Moon. MAPA; TwAmPo
Sense of the Sleight-of-Hand Man, The. Wallace Stevens. CoBMV; LiTM (rev. ed.); MoAB; MoAmPo (1950 ed.); MoPo
Sense of the world is short, The. Eros. Emerson. AnNE; FaBoBe; HBV; IAP; TCAP

Sense with keenest edge unused. Pater Filio. Robert Bridges. ChMo; CMP; OBEV; OBVV; POTT; PoVP; ViBoPo; ViP; VLEP
Sensemaya; Chant for Killing a Snake. Nicolás Guillén, *tr. fr. Spanish by* H. R Hays. TwSpPo
Senses loving Earth, or well or ill, The. Sense and Spirit. George Meredith. EmBrPo; EPN; PoVP; WGRP
Sensitive Plant, The. Shelley. BPN; EmBrPo; EnRP; ERP; EV-4; GoTL
(Garden, A, *abr.*) OTPC
Sels.
"In this life/ Of error, ignorance, and strife," *fr.* Conclusion. LO
Plants Decay, The. RO
Sensitive Sydney. Wallace Irwin. FiBHP
Sensitiveness. Cardinal Newman. PoVP
Sensual and the Dark rebel in vain, The. Rebellion. Samuel Taylor Coleridge. *Fr.* France; an Ode. RO
Sensualists, The. Theodore Roethke. NePoAm-2
Sensuality. Coventry Patmore. *Fr.* The Angel in the House, I, xi, 2. OBVV
Sensuality. Kenneth Slessor. NeLNL
Sent Ahead. John Hay. NePoAm
Sent as a present from Annam. The Red Cockatoo. Po Chü-i. ChTr; LiTW; MoPW; OuHeWo; TrCh
Sent from Egypt with a Fair Robe of Tissue to a Sicilian Vinedresser. T. Sturge Moore. GTML; OBEV (new ed.); OBVV
Sent to Home. Li Shang-Yin, *tr. fr. Chinese.* ChLP
(Letter Home, A, *diff. tr.*) WhP
Sent with a Rose to a Young Lady. Margaret Deland. AA
Sentence. Witter Bynner. HBV; LBMV
Sentence of Death. Palladas, *tr. fr. Greek by* T. F. Higham. OxBG
Sentences of Wisdom, *sel.* Thomas Lake Harris.
"When love cools down, ice forms upon the heart." BAP
Sentencing goes blithely on its way, The. In a Poem. Robert Frost. CoV
Sentimental blockade! Deliveries from the Sun held up! Winter Is Coming. Jules Laforgue. TrFP
Sentimental Colloquy. Paul Verlaine. *See* Colloque sentimentale.
Sentimental Dialogue. Paul Verlaine. *See* Colloque sentimentale.
Sentimental Journey. "Elspeth." WhC
Sentimental Lines to a Young Man Who Favors Pink Wallpaper, While I Personally Lean to the Blue. Margaret Fishback. FiBHP
Sentimentalist sends his mauve balloon, The. The Celebration in the Plaza. Adrienne Cecile Rich. NePoEA
Sentinel, The. Annie Johnson Flint. PraP
Sentinel, The. *Unknown.* BLRP; MaRV; OQP; QP-2
Sentinel angel, A. sitting high in glory. A Woman's Love. John Hay. HBV; LPS-1
Sentinel Songs. Abram J. Ryan. DD, *abr.;* GA, *abr.;* HBV; LPS-2
Sentry, The. Fu Chih Tao, *tr. fr. Chinese by* Henry H. Hart. PoHN
Sentry, The. W. W. Gibson. NeTW
Sentry, The. Alun Lewis. MoWP
Sentry, The. Wilfred Owen. AnEnPo; SoV
Separate Peace. Harrison S. Morris. MC
Separate place between the thought and felt, A. The Corridor. Thom Gunn. NePoEA
Separated from you, I lament in Yeh-lang beyond the clouds. To My Wife from Yeh-lang, the Place of Exile. Li Po. WhP
Separation. Matthew Arnold. HBV
Separation. Martha Dickinson Bianchi. AA
Separation. Alice Learned Bunner. Vingtaine, I. AA
Separation, The. Abraham Cowley. EPS (1942 ed.)
Separation. Charles Dalmon. TCPD
Separation. Laurence Housman. BMEP
Separation. Empress Kogyoku, *tr. fr. Japanese by* Ishii *and* Obata. OnPM
Separation. Walter Savage Landor. EtPaEn; LoPo; OBEV (1st ed.); TOP
Separation. Po Chü-i, *tr. fr. Chinese by* Arthur Waley. TrCh
Separation. D. S. Savage. NeBP
Separation. Tu Mu, *tr. fr. Chinese.* WhP
Separation. Wu Tsung Ai, *tr. fr. Chinese by* Henry H. Hart. PoHN
Separation Deed, A. Sir Lewis Morris. OBVV
Sephestia's Song to Her Child [or Childe]. Robert Greene. *Fr.* Menaphon. AtBAP; BOL; CoBE; ElSeCe; EnLi-1 (1949 ed.); EnLit; EPP; EV 1; GTSL; LoBV; PoEL-2; ReEn; ReIE; SiCE; TrG-Po; TuPP
(Sephestia's Lullaby.) HBV; LEAP; OBEV
(Sephestia's Song.) OBSC
(Weep Not, My Wanton.) ElL; SeCePo; ViBoPo
Sept ans sur mer, *with music. Unknown.* OuSiCo
Septem contra Thebas. Aeschylus. *See* Seven against Thebes.
September. George Arnold. DD; HBV; LPS-2; PTA-2
September. Sara Hamilton Birchall. NLK
September. Gabriele D'Annunzio, *tr. fr. Italian by* Glauco Cambon. OnPM
September. Edwina Fallis. SUS; TiPo; YeAr
September. S. Frances Harrison. VA
September. Mary Howitt. BoTP; OTPC (1923 ed.)
September. Helen Hunt Jackson. BoChLi; FaPON; GoTP; MPB; OnHT; OTPC (1946 ed.); PEDC; PoRL; PRWS; RAR; TiPo (1959 ed.)
(September Days Are Here.) YeAr
September. Archibald Lampman. PeCV
September. Dorothy Frances McCrae. BoAu
September. Katharine Pyle. PCH
September. Edward Bliss Reed. DD; HBMV; HBVY; MPB
(September Is Here.) YeAr
September. Thomas Tusser. ReIE
September Afternoon. Margaret Haley Carpenter. GoYe
September brings the golden sheaves. Sign of Fall in the Carolinas. Helen Bevington. NoCaPo (rev. ed.)
September Day. Sara Teasdale. ChMo; CMP
September Days. Helen L. Smith. PTA-2
September Days Are Here. Helen Hunt Jackson. *See* September.
September, 1815 ("While not a leaf seems faded"). Wordsworth. PEOR
(Sonnet: September, 1815.) ChER
September, 1819. Wordsworth. BPN
September, 1802. Near Dover. Wordsworth. *See* Near Dover, September, 1802.
September, 1802 (Upon the Same Occasion) ("Departing summer hath assumed"). Wordsworth. BPN
September Evening, 1938. William Plomer. SeCePo
September evenings such as these. Watching the Moon. David McCord. YeAr
September Fires. Sir Herbert Read. TwCV
September 1, 1802 ("We had a female Passenger who came"). Wordsworth. BPN; EmBrPo
(Sonnet: September 1, 1802: "Driven from the soil of France, a female came.") ChER
September 1, 1939. W. H. Auden. CoBMV; ExPo; InPo; LiTA; LiTM; MaPo; MoAB; MoBrPo (1950 ed.); MoVE; NePA; OAEP (2d ed.); OxBA; PoFS; ReMP; SeCeV; TwHP; WaP
(1st September 1939.) FaBoEn
September Gale, The. Oliver Wendell Holmes. PTA-2
"It chanced to be our washing day," *sel.* FiBHP
September in Australia. Henry C. Kendall. BoAu; OBVV; VA
September Is Here. Edward Bliss Reed. *See* September.
September! Let us go, it's time to wander. September. Gabriele D'Annunzio. OnPM
September Morning. Eduard Mörike, *tr. fr. German by* James Edward Tobin. AnGP
September 1913. W. B. Yeats. ChMo; CMP; CoBMV; MoPW; PoRA; TCPD
September 17. Sister M. Margaret Patricia. SaFP
September sky expands, The. Death of a Hornet. D. G. Jones. PeCV
September Sun: 1947. David Gascoyne. AtBAP; FaBoMo; POTE (1959 ed.)
September twenty-second, Sir: today. After the Surprising Conversions. Robert Lowell. CoBMV; FiMAP; NePoEA; SeCeV
September Violet, A. *Unknown.* PEOR
Septimius held his Acme close. Catullus, *tr. fr. Latin by* Gilbert Highet. LaP
Septimius with his arms entwined round his Acme. Catullus, *tr. fr. Latin by* Horace Gregory. RoL
Sepulcher in the Garden, The. John Finley. ChIP
Sepulchral Imprecation. Crinagoras, *tr. fr. Greek by* Dudley Fitts. LiTW
Sepulchral Inscription. Jorge Luis Borges, *tr. fr. Spanish by* Robert Stuart Fitzgerald. AnCL
Sequel to Finality. Patrick F. Kirby. GoBC; MaRV
Sequel to the Chariot Race. Homer. See After the Chariot-Race.
Sequence. Jami, *tr. fr. Persian by* A. J. Arberry. PeP
Sequence. Edgar Daniel Kramer. BLRP
Sequence. Elinor Wylie. AV
Sequence of Sonnets on the Death of Robert Browning, A, *sels.* Swinburne.
"Among the wondrous ways of men and time," V. BPN
"But he—to him who knows what gift is thine," IV. BPN
"Clearest eyes in all the world they read, The," I. BPN
"Death, what hast thou to do with one for whom," II. BPN
"He held no dream worth waking: so he said," VII. BPN
(On the Death of Robert Browning.) EmBrPo; EnLit; EPN; PoVP; VLEP
Sequence, with Strophes in Paraphrase Thereof, A. Francis Burke. CAW
Seraglio of the Sultan Bee! A Hollyhock. Frank Dempster Sherman. AA; ADAH; BAP

Seraph Abdiel, faithful found, The. The Faithful Angel, Milton. *Fr.* Paradise Lost, V. LPS-2
Seraph and the Snob, The. May Kendall. CenHV
Seraph of Heaven. Shelley. *Fr.* Epipsychidion. ISi
Seraphion. James K. Baxter. AnNZ
Seraphita. Ernest Dowson. VLEP
Seraphs in Heaven, The. Elizabeth Rowe. *Fr.* On Heaven. BeR
Sere and Yellow Leaf, The. Homer, *tr. fr. Greek by* F. L. Lucas. *Fr.* The Iliad, VI. GrPE
Serenade, A: "Ah! County Guy, the hour is nigh." Sir Walter Scott. *See* County Guy.
Serenade: "Ah, sweet, thou little knowest how." Thomas Hood. HBV
Serenade: "Awake thee, my Lady-love." George Darley. *See* Morning-Song.
Serenade: "Blue waves are sleeping, The." Jeremiah Joseph Callanan. IrPN, *abr.;* OnYI
Serenade: "By day my timid passions stand." Richard Middleton. HBV
Serenade: "Come now, let us wake them; time." *Unknown, tr. fr. German by* Jethro Bithell. AWP; JAWP; WBP
Serenade: "Come on, don't be afraid you'll spoil me." Emanuel Carnevali. AnAmPo; LA
Serenade: "Dogs on a summer night." Burges Johnson. AlBD
Serenade: "Harken how the flute complains." Clemens Brentano, *tr. fr. German by* Herman Salinger. AnGP
Serenade: "Heart of my heart, awake! awake!" H. W. Bell. CAG
Serenade: "Hide, happy damask, from the stars." Henry Timrod. HBV; PR
Serenade: "High in the dark the moon rides white." Paul Fearon. CIV
Serenade: "I'm a gay tra, la, la." Bret Harte. LBN (Swiss Air.) NA
Serenade, A: "Look out upon the stars, my love." Edward Coote Pinkney. AA; AnFE; APA; APW; BAP; BAV; BLV; CoAnAm; HBV; MOAP; OBAV; PIAE; PR; SPP
Serenade, A: "Lullaby, O, lullaby." Thomas Hood. BOL
Serenade: "O beautiful Amaryllis." Theocritus. *See* Rustic Serenade.
Serenade: "On a mandolin with slender/ Strings." Vilhelm Krag, *tr. fr. Norwegian by* Charles W. Stork. AnNoLy
Serenade: "Softly, O midnight hours!" Aubrey Thomas De Vere. HBV; OBEV
(Song: "Softly . . .") IrPN
Serenade: "Sometimes you seem a star." John Bunker. JKCP (1955 ed.)
Serenade: "Stars of the summer night!" Longfellow. *Fr.* The Spanish Student, I, iii. AA; AmPP (3d ed.); FaBoBe; HBV; IAP; LEAP; LoBV; MOAP; NeHB; OnPM; OuHeWo; PFY; REAL; ViBoPo
(Stars of the Summer Night.) BTP; LoPo; OlF
Serenade, The: "This age-old church." Sister Mary Madeleva. Christmas in Provence, I. WHL
Serenade: "Venus and the young new moon." Leon W. Kellogg. CAG
Serenade: "Wake, Isias, lips of fragrance, lips ten times sweeter, tasted." Marcus Argentarius, *tr. fr. Greek by* F. L. Lucas. GrPE
Serenade: "Western wind is blowing fair, The." Oscar Wilde. HBV
Serenade: "When maidens are young, and in their spring." Aphra Behn. *Fr.* The Emperor of the Moon. SeCL
Serenade: "While my lady sleepeth." John Gibson Lockhart. OBRV
Serenade at the Villa, A. Robert Browning. NBE; VLEP
Serenade at the Window of the Wise Man. Zacharias Papondoniou, *tr. fr. Modern Greek by* Rae Dalven. MoGP
Serenade of a Loyal Martyr. George Darley. *See* Song: "Sweet in her green dell . . ."
Serenade of Laughing Life. Vicente Huidobro, *tr. fr. Spanish by* H. R. Hays. TwSpPo
Serenade, to Two Ladies. Thomas Porter. *Fr.* The Villain. SeCL
Serenader. George Dillon. NP
Serendipity of Love, A. Richard Aldridge. NePoAm-2
Serene, and fitted to embrace. Dion. Wordsworth. GEPC
Serene, cool and composed, and easygoing. "One in a Thousand of Years of the Nights." Delmore Schwartz. FiMAP
Serene descent, as a red leaf's descending. Epitaph. Sara Teasdale. MM
Serene, I fold my hands and wait. Waiting [*or* My Own Shall Come to Me]. John Burroughs. AA; AnAmPo; AnFE; APA; BAP; BLPA; BTP; CoAnAm; DD; DDA; FaBoBe; HBV; LA; LBAP; LEAP; MaRV; NeHB; OBAV; OHFP; OQP; PC; PECK; QP-1; TreF; WGRP
Serene Immediate Silliest and Whose. E. E. Cummings. MoVE
Serene the silver fishes glide. At the Aquarium. Max Eastman. AnAmPo; FaPON; HBMV; LA; LEAP; OTPC (1946 ed.); PoMa; StaSt; WGRP
Serene, vast head, with silver cloud of hair. A Tribute of Grasses. Hamlin Garland. AnAmPo; LA
Serenity of Faith, The. Psalms, XXVII, Bible, *O.T. See* My Light and My Salvation.
Serf, The. Roy Campbell. BoSA; LiTB; LiTM; MoBrPo; NAMP; OBMV; ReMP; TrGrPo (1942 ed.)
Serfs. Cale Young Rice. BLA
Serf's Secret, The. William Vaughn Moody. HBV
Sergeant Champe. *Unknown.* PAH
Sergeant, He Is the Worst of All, The, *with music. Unknown.* AS
Sgt. stands so fluently in leather, The. On a Photo of Sgt. Ciardi a Year Later. John Ciardi. MiAP
Sergeant, the sergeant he is the worst of all, The. The Sergeant, He Is the Worst of All. *Unknown.* AS
Sergeant's Prayer, A. Hugh R. Brodie. *See* Airman's Prayer, An.
Serious Omission. John Farrar. GoBP; RIS; UTS
Serious over my cereals I broke one breakfast my fast. Breakfast with Gerard Manley Hopkins. Anthony Brode. FiBHP
Serious Question, A. Carolyn Wells. CIV
Serious Sonnets: Sleep, Ariosto! Pietro Aretino, *tr. fr. Italian by* Samuel Putnam. LyPI
Seriously, when I am dead, my mate. Wild Past. Paul Verlaine. TrFP
Sermon. Emanuel Carnevali. NP
Sermon, The. Richard Hughes. OBMV
Sermon, A. Lady Margaret Sackville. HBMV
Sermon in a Churchyard. Macaulay. OBRV
Sermon in a Stocking. Ellen A. Jewett. BLPA
Sermon in Rhyme, A. *Unknown. See* Say It Now.
Sermon of Saint Francis, A. Edward F. Garesché. SaFP
Sermon on the Mount, The. St. Matthew, V: 1–VII: 29, Bible, *N.T.* EM-1; OuHeWo; TreF; WoL
Sels.
"And seeing the multitudes, he went up into a mountain," V: 1–48. ReIE
Beatitudes, The, V. GrCo-1 (3–12); TrGrPo (3–10)
Blessed Are the Poor in Spirit, V. ExPo (3–12); GoTP (3–10)
Lord's Prayer, The, VI: 9–13. TrGrPo
Love Your Enemies, V: 38–48. GrCo-1
Pure Light, The, V: 14–16, VI: 22–23, VII: 3–5. GrCo-1
Treasures, VI: 19–21. TrGrPo
Sermon to the Birds. St. Francis of Assisi, *tr. fr. Italian by* Thomas W. Arnold. TreF
Sermon to the Fishes. Joaquin Antonio Peñalosa, *tr. fr. Spanish by* Arthur Train, Jr. SaFP
Sermon to the Rebels at Blackheath. John Ball. PoFr
Sermon without Words. Elizabeth Patton Moss. MaRV
Sermons in Stones. Shakespeare. *See* Uses of Adversity, The.
Sermons We See. Edgar A. Guest. MaRV
Serpent, The, *sel.* Paul Valéry, *tr. fr. French by* Mark Wardle.
"Eve, as once I came upon her." MiFP
Serpent Bride, The. *Unknown, tr. fr. Danish by* E. M. Smith-Dampier. BoDaBa
Serpent Curls. Ibn Jakha, *tr. fr. Arabic by* A. J. Arberry. MooP
Serpents. Isaac Watts. *Fr.* Flying Fowl and Creeping Things, Praise Ye the Lord. BeR
Serpent's Nature, The. *Unknown, tr. fr. Middle English. Fr.* The Bestiary. MeEV
Serpents, who o'er the meadows slide. Serpents. Isaac Watts. *Fr.* Flying Fowl and Creeping Things, Praise Ye the Lord. BeR
Serranilla VIII: "Early once in Robledillo." Marqués de Santillana, *tr. fr. Spanish by* Ida Farnell. AnSpL-1
Serranilla VI: "I ne'er on the border." Marqués de Santillana, *tr. fr. Spanish by* Jeremiah Holmes Wiffen. AnSpL-1
(Serranilla: "From Calatrava as I took my way," *tr. by* John Pierrepont Rice.) TeCS
Serried hosts stood man to man, The. The Oranges. Abu Dharr. MooP
Servant, A. Kipling. *Fr.* Epitaphs of the War. PoVP
Servant Girl and Grocer's Boy. Joyce Kilmer. LHV; YaD
Servant of God, The. Isaiah, LII: 13–LIII: 11, *Eng. Rev. Vers.,* Bible, *O.T.* GrCo-1
(Behold, My Servant, LII: 13–LIII: 9.) OuHeWo
Servant of God, well done! Well Done. James Montgomery. MaRV
Servant of the eternal Must. Pagan Epitaph. Richard Middleton. BMEP; OBVV; TOP
Servant of the Nymphs, who loves the showers, The. The Bronze Frog. *Unknown.* OnPM
Servant of the Prophet, The. Abbie Huston Evans. QS
Servant to Servants, A. Robert Frost. AmPo
Servants, The. Richard Wightman. WGRP
Servants of God! or sons. Leaders and Friends of Mankind. Matthew Arnold. *Fr.* Rugby Chapel. GrCo-1
Servants of the Great Adventure. Percy Dearmer. MaRV

Servants then (commanded) soone obaid, The. Nausicaa. Homer. *tr. by* George Chapman. *Fr.* The Odyssey, VI. OBS
Serve God truly. Colophon. *Unknown.* TMEV
Serve in Thy Post. Arthur Hugh Clough. *Fr.* Last Words. Napoleon and Wellington. PGD
Servian Lullaby, A. Nora Hopper. BOL
Service. Eduardo Anguita, *tr. fr. Spanish by* Lloyd Mallan. AnCL
Service. Anna Hempstead Branch. AV
Service. Robert Browning. *See* All Service Ranks the Same with God.
Service. Washington Gladden. *See* O Master, Let Me Walk with Thee.
Service. Hermann Hagedorn. OQP; QP-1
Service, The. Burges Johnson. HBMV; PreP; StaSt; VOD
Service. Georgia Douglas Johnson. CDC
Service Flag, The. William Herschell. PEDC; PTA-2
Service is joy, to see or swing. Tennis. Margaret Avison. PeCV
Service of Al' the Dead. D. H. Lawrence. NP; TCEP
Service of Song, A. Emily Dickinson. *See* Some keep the Sabbath going to church.
Service of the Lutherans, The. Feodor Tyutchev, *tr. fr. Russian by* Babette Deutsch. OnPM; TrRV
Serviceable thing, A. Herbs. Lizette Woodworth Reese. TBM
Serving Girl, The. Gladys May Casley Hayford (Aquah Laluah). CDC; GoSl; PoNe
Serving Men's Song, A. John Lyly. *Fr.* Alexander and Campaspe, I, iii. *Also in* A Mad World, My Masters (*by* Thomas Middleton). ALV; OBSC
(O for a Bowl of Fat Canary. Middleton.) OnPM; ViBoPo
Serving No Haughty Muse. Wordsworth. ERP
Servitor of learning, A. The Inkstand. Ibn Lubbal. MooP
Sery. Richard Watson Gilder. *See* Christmas Tree in the Nursery, The.
Sesostris. Lloyd Mifflin. AA; BAP; HBV
Session of the Poets, A. Sir John Suckling. PtP; SeCV-1
Session with Uncle Sidney, A, *sel.* James Whitcomb Riley. It. MeMeAg
Sessions of Sweet Silent Thought. Shakespeare. *See* Sonnets, XXX.
Sestina. James K. Baxter. Cressida, XV. AnNZ
Sestina. Richard Eberhart. FiMAP
Sestina. Sir Edmund Gosse. InP
Sestina. Donald Hall. NePoEA
Sestina. Donald Justice. NePoEA
Sestina. Sir Philip Sidney. *See* Double Sestine.
Sestina; Altaforte. Ezra Pound. AmP; CoBMV; FaBoTw; LiTA; LiTG; LiTM (1946 ed.); MoAB; MoAmPo (1950 ed.); ReaPo
Sestina; of the Lady Pietra degli Scrovigni. Dante, *tr. fr. Italian by* Dante Gabriel Rossetti. AWP; JAWP; LyPI; ViP; WBP
Sestina 2; to the Lady Pietra of Siena. Dante. *See* Canzone: To the Lady Pietra, of Sienna.
Sestina for Cynthia, A. David Lougée. NePA
Sestina of the Tramp-Royal. Kipling. LiTB; MBP; MoBrPo; OtMeF; PoVP; SiTL
Sestina of Youth and Age. Gelett Burgess. PIAE
Sestina on Her Portrait. Howard Nemerov. WaP
Set Down, Servant, *with music.* *Unknown.* ABF
Set every stitch of canvas to woo the fresh'ning wind. The Slave Chase. *Unknown.* CoMu
Set forty thousand on a row. Constant Affection. *Unknown.* SeCL
'Set he that hat on his head?" Cardinal Fisher. John Heywood. ACP
Set high your head above the nameless flood. To a Survivor of the Flood. John Gould Fletcher. AnAmPo; LA
Set in this stormy northern sea. Ave Imperatrix! Oscar Wilde. HBV; VA
Set Love in order, thou that lovest me. Cantica: Our Lord Christ [*or* Of Order in Our Lord Christ]. *At. to* St. Francis of Assisi *and to* Jacopone da Todi. AWP; CAW; GoBC; JAWP; LyPI; OnPM; SaFP; WBP
Set Me as a Seal. Song of Solomon, Bible, *O.T.* *See* Love.
Set me over the main again. More Life . . . More! Lee Wilson Dodd. PC
Set Me Where Phoebus' Heat. Petrarch, *tr. fr. Italian.* Sonnets to Laura: To Laura in Life, CXIII. TuPP
(Last Trial, The.) OBSC
Set Me Whereas the Sun Doth Parch the Green. Petrarch, *tr by* the Earl of Surrey. *See* Vow to Love Faithfully.
Set not thy foot on graves. To J. W. Emerson. IAP
Set of Phrases learn't by Rote, A. The Furniture of a Woman's Mind. Swift. CEP
Set silver cone to tulip flame! Inscription for a Mirror in a Deserted Dwelling. William Rose Benét. LoPS; MAP; MoAmPo; TriL
Set the great orb of Hector's shield to lie. Child-Burial; Sequel to Battles. Euripides. *Fr.* Trojan Women. GrR
Set where the upper streams of Simoïs flow. Palladium. Matthew Arnold. BPN; EPN; FaBoEn; OAEP; PoVP; TwCrTr; ViPP; VLEP
Set your face to the sea, fond lover. Refuge. William Winter. HBV; LBAP
Set your heart at rest. Shakespeare. *Fr.* A Midsummer Night's Dream, II, i. MotAn
Seth Compton. Edgar Lee Masters. *Fr.* Spoon River Anthology. ChMo; CMP; LiTA; NP
Sett to the sun, a diall that doth passe. *Unknown.* SeCSL
Settin'—and sewin'—and fixin' supper—and settin'. Old. John V. A. Weaver. DDA
Settin' on de Fence. *Unknown.* WBLP
Settin' [*or* Sittin'] round the stove, last night. A Liz-Town Humorist. James Whitcomb Riley. IHA
Setting my bulbs a-row. Planting Bulbs. Katharine Tynan. JKCP
Setting Sun, The. Ibn Sa'id of Alcala la Real, *tr. fr. Arabic by* A. J. Arberry. MooP
Setting Sun, The. Stesichorus. *See* Voyage of the Sun.
Setting sun, The. Farewell. Han Hung. PoHN
Setting sun leaves the poet to the dreary night, The. Early Summer Night. Wen Yi-tuo. LiTW; WhP
Setting the Table. Dorothy Aldis. FaPON; MPB; TiPo
Settled Men, The. George M. Brady. NeIP
Settler, The. Roy Macnab. BoSA
Settler, The. Alfred Billings Street. AA; BAP; FaBoBe; LPS-2; MC; PAH
Settlers, The. Laurence Housman. HBV; OBVV
Seumas Beg. James Stephens. FaPON; GaP; PCN; TSW; TSWC
Seurat. James Schevill. FiMAP
Seurat looked well to see these people. La Grande Jatte; Sunday Afternoon. Thomas Cole. NePoAm
Seven against Thebes, *sels.* Aeschylus, *tr. fr. Greek.*
Amphiaraus, *tr. by* Gilbert Murray. GrR
Gathering War Clouds, *tr. by* Gilbert Murray. GrR
(News of War, *tr. by* E. R. Bevan.) OxBG
Hour of National Emergency, *tr. by* Lewis Campbell. GrR
Lament for the Two Brothers Slain by Each Other's Hand, *tr. by* A. E. Housman. AWP; JAWP; WBP
"O wailing and sorrow, O wailing and woe!", *tr. by* J. S. Blackie. GrPo
Seven Ages of Man, The. Shakespeare. *See* All the World's a Stage.
Seven are the lights that wander in the skies. Licia, XXV. Giles Fletcher. ReEn; ReIE; SiCE; TuPP
Seven centuries are counted. Ecco il Santo. Katharine Lee Bates. QS
Seven Cities of America, The. Edgar Lee Masters. ChMo; CMP
Seven daughters had Lord Archibald. The Seven Sisters; or, The Solitude of Binnorie. Wordsworth. CG; OTPC
Seven days he travelled. The Crowning of Dreaming John. John Drinkwater. HBMV
Seven Days of the Sun, The, *sel.* W. J. Turner.
"I had watched the ascension and decline of the moon." OBMV
Seven Deadly Sins, The. Stephen Hawes. *Fr.* The Pastime of Pleasure. PoEL-1
Seven dog-days we let pass. Queens. J. M. Synge. ChTr; MoBrPo; OBMV; OnYI; TIP
Seven Evils Proverbs, VI: 16–19, Bible, *O.T.* TrGrPo
(Sower of Discord, A, *Moulton, Modern Reader's Bible.*) MaRV
Seven Fiddlers, The. Sebastian Evans. PoMS; RIS
Seven-fold star of the Pleiades hangs low in the sky, The. Mount Rhodope. Yiannis Griparis. MoGP
Seven Grecian cities vied for Homer dead. The Poet in Life and Death. *Unknown.* OnPM
Seven hundred and a half of years. The Old Woman Remembers. Lady Gregory. OnYI
Seven invasions, seven dynasties. Morocco. R. N. Currey. BoSA
Seven lang years I hae served the king. The Whummil Bore. *Unknown.* CH; ESPB
Seven Little Pigs. *Unknown.* BoTP
Seven Long Years in State Prison, *with music.* *Unknown.* AS
Seven lovely poplars. Poplars. Helen Leuty. BoTP
Seven men from all the world back to docks again. The Ballad of the *Bolivar.* Kipling. CaAE; EPP; TCEP
Seven Metal Mountains, The. Book of Enoch, LII: 6–9, Bible, Pseudepigrapha. TrJP
Seven notes of grief. Motif for Mary's Dolors. Sister Mary Madeleva. ISi
Seven of My Sweet Loves. Blake. *See* My Spectre around Me Night and Day.
Seven Old Men, The. Baudelaire, *tr. fr. French by* Barbara Gibbs. AnFP
Seven Penitential Psalms, *sel.* Petrarch, *tr. fr. Italian by* George Chapman.
To Young Imaginaries in Knowledge. ReEn

Seven Pilgrims. Chaucer. *See* Canterbury Tales, The: Prologue.
Seven Sad Sonnets. Mary Aldis. HBMV
Seven Seals, The. Nietzsche, *tr. fr. German by* Thomas Common. *Fr.* Also sprach Zarathustra. LiA
Seven Sisters, The; or, The Solitude of Binnorie. Wordsworth. CG; OTPC
Seven Sleepers, The. Sir Herbert Read. FaBoMo; SeCePo
Seven Sonnets, *sel.* Arthur Hugh Clough.
"But whether in the uncoloured light of truth," IV. ViPP
Seven Sonnets. Christopher Logue. PoN
Seven South African Poems. David Wright. BoSA
Seven Spiritual Ages of Mrs. Marmaduke Moore, The. Ogden Nash. MoAmPo (1950 ed.)
Seven stars in the still water. The Dole of the King's Daughter. *Unknown.* AWP
Seven sweet singing birds up in a tree. The Dream of a Girl [*or* Little Girl] Who Lived at Seven-Oaks. William Brighty Rands. GaP; OTPC; PPL; RIS
Seven Times, The. Thomas Hardy. VLEP
Seven Times Five. Jean Ingelow. *Fr.* Songs of Seven. GBV (1922 ed.); HBV
Seven Times Four. Jean Ingelow. *Fr.* Songs of Seven. GBV (1922 ed.); HBV; LPS-1; MOAH; PTA-1
(Heigh Ho!) BoTP
(Maternity.) OHIP
Seven times hath Janus ta'en new year by hand. A Sonnet upon the Author's First Seven Years' Service. Thomas Tusser. ElL; SiCE; TuPP
Seven Times One. Jean Ingelow. *Fr.* Songs of Seven. BLPA; EV-5; FaPON; GBV (1922 ed.); GoTP; HBV; LPS-1; MeMeAg; MPB; OTPC; PCH; PRWS; PTA-1; RAR; TreF; TVC; TVSH
Seven Times Seven. Jean Ingelow. *Fr.* Songs of Seven. GBV (1922 ed.); HBV; MOAH
(Longing for Home.) WGRP
Seven times seven/ the beads I toll. To the Queen of Dolors. Sister Mary Maura. ISi
Seven Times Six. Jean Ingelow. *Fr.* Songs of Seven. GBV (1922 ed.); HBV; LPS-1; MOAH
Seven times the centuple wheels of life have whirled. The Blessing of St. Francis. Sister Maura. CaP; SaFP
Seven Times the Moon Came. Jessie B. Rittenhouse. HBMV
Seven Times Three. Jean Ingelow. *Fr.* Songs of Seven. GBV (1922 ed.); HBV; LPS-1; PTA-1
(I Leaned out My Window.) AV
Seven Times Two. Jean Ingelow. *Fr.* Songs of Seven. GBV (1922 ed.); GN; HBV; LPS-1; OTPC (1923 ed.); PTA-1
Seven Virgins, The. *Unknown.* CH, *sl. abr.;* ChTr; OBB; OBEV; OxBoCh
(All under the Leaves, and the Leaves of Life.) AnEC
Seven we were, and two are gone. Two Long Vacations: Grasmere. Arthur Gray Butler. OBVV
Seven wealthy towns contend for Homer dead. A Cure for Poetry. *Unknown.* SiTL
Seven weeks of sea, and twice seven days of storm. Gibraltar. Wilfrid Scawen Blunt. ACP; ES; GTML; GTSL; HBV; OBEV; OBVV; OTPC (1923 ed.); SoV; VA
Seven Whistlers, The. Alice E. Gillington. VA
Seven white roses on one tree. Seven Years Old. Swinburne. HBV
Seven Wise Men. Alfred Noyes. *See* Thomas Dekker's Song.
Seven-year-old Poet. Arthur Rimbaud, *tr. fr. French by* Norman Cameron. OnHM
(Poets Seven Years Old, *tr. by* Kenneth Koch *and* George Guy.) AnFP
Seven Years. Marquess of Crewe. OBVV
Seven years are now elapsed, dear rambling volume. To My Book. Philip Freneau. IAP
Seven Years at Sea. *Unknown. See* Sept ans sur mer.
Seven Years Old. Swinburne. HBV
Seven years ye shall be a stone. The Maid and the Palmer. *Unknown.* ACP; ESPB; OBS
1750. Archibald MacLeish. *Fr.* The Farm. CMP
Seventeen hundred and thirty-nine. The Ballad of "Beau Brocade." Austin Dobson. EV-5
Seventeen Old Poems. *Unknown, tr. fr. Chinese by* Arthur Waley. *See* Nineteen Han Poems, The.
Seventeen rosebuds in a ring. Lucy's Birthday. Thackeray. OTPC (1923 ed.)
1777, *sels.* Amy Lowell.
City of Falling Leaves, The, II. MAPA; SUS; TCPD; TiPo; TwAmPo
Trumpet-Vine Arbour, The, I. MAPA; NP
Seventeen years ago, the sun so glaring. Cypress. John Peter. BoSA
Seventeen years ago you said. A Quoi Bon Dire. Charlotte Mew. HBMV
Seventeenth Kiss, The; Neaera's Lips. Johannes Secundus, *tr. fr. Latin by* F. A. Wright. LaP
Seventh City of Cibola, The. Harry Noyes Pratt. MuM
Seventh Day. Kathleen Raine. ChMP
VII Properte, The. Sir Thomas More. *Fr.* The XII Properties or Condicyons of a Lover. CoBE
Seventh Station. Paul Claudel, *tr. fr. French by* Henry M. Robinson. CAW
Seventy-five percent of his debt did the wine-bleared Hylas. Martial, *tr. fr. Latin by* Robert R. Schnorr. Epigrams, VIII, 9. LaP
Seventy-four and Twenty. Thomas Hardy. WhC
Seventy-six. Bryant. DD; HBV; MC; PAH
Several Voices Out of a Cloud. Louise Bogan. ExPo; MoVE
Severed Selves. Dante Gabriel Rossetti. The House of Life, XL. BPN; EmBrPo; PoVP; ViPo
Severed wasp yet drank the juice, A. The Wasp. Eden Phillpotts. BMEP
Severely now will we dance. Apollo Alone Approves. Mark Turbyfill. NP
Severn, The. Michael Drayton. *Fr.* The Baron's War, I. ChTr
Severus is extreme in eloquence. Samuel Rowlands. TuPP
Seville. Al-Tutili, *tr. fr. Arabic by* A. J. Arberry. MooP
Seville. L. D'O. Walters. HBMV
Sev'n skunks lumbering in a row. Black and White Shuffle. Harry Elmore Hurd. WhC
Sew the Flags Together. Vachel Lindsay. AOAH
Sewanee Hills of dear delight. The Hills of Sewanee. George Marion McClellan. BANP
Sewing. William H. Hayne. *Fr.* Pine Needles. GFA; MeMeAg; OTPC (1946 ed.)
(Pine Needles.) ADAH; PCH
Sex among Lions. Virgil, *tr. fr. Latin by* Dryden. *Fr.* Georgics, III. BeR
Sexsmith the Dentist. Edgar Lee Masters. *Fr.* Spoon River Anthology. NePA
Sextain. William Drummond of Hawthornden. TriL
Sextains, *sels.* William Baylebridge.
Master-Foe, The. BoAV
Troubled Unquickening, The. BoAV
Sextant, The. A. M. Sullivan. GoBC
Sextant of the meetinouse, which sweeps, The. A Appeal for Are to the Sextant of the Old Brick Meetinouse [*or* To the "Sextant"]. Arabella M. Willson. BOHV; LPS-3
Sextus the Usurer. Martial, *tr. fr. Latin by* Kirby Flower Smith. AWP
Sexual Water. "Pablo Neruda," *tr. fr. Spanish by* H. R. Hays. TwSpPo
Seynt Stevyn [*or* Stevene] Was a Clerk. *Unknown. See* Saint Stephen and Herod.
Sez Alderman Grady. Officer Brady. Robert W. Chambers. BOHV; DDA; InMe
Sez Corporal Madden to Private McFadden. The Recruit. Robert W. Chambers. AA; BOHV; HBV; LEAP; PFY
"Sh." James S. Tippett. SUS; TiPo
Shabby fellow chanced one day to meet, A. An Actor. "Peter Pindar." BOHV
Shabby Old Dad. Anne Campbell. PoToHe (new ed.)
Shack, The. Nellie Burget Miller. PoOW
Shack Bully Holler, *with music. Unknown.* ABF
Shadbush. Christina Rainsford. GoYe
Shade. Theodosia Garrison. MaRV; OHIP; PoeMoYo
Shade-Catchers, The. Charlotte Mew. AlDL
Shade of Cornelia Consoles Her Husband, The. Propertius, *pr. tr. fr. Latin by* H. E. Butler. Elegies, IV, 11. LiA
("Cease, Paullus, to oppress my tomb with tears," *tr. by* Frances Fletcher.) LaP
Shade of His hand shall cover us, The. His Hand Shall Cover Us. Isaac ben Samuel of Dampière. TrJP
Shade of our greatest, O look down to-day! To the Spirit of Abraham Lincoln. Richard Watson Gilder. LBAH
Shade of Patroclus, The. Homer. *See* Ghost of Patroclus, The.
Shade of the Trees, The. Margaret Junkin Preston. *See* Under the Shade of the Trees.
Shade, the light, the figures, the horizon as, The. October, 1942. Roy Fuller. WaP
Shade within shade! for deeper in the glass. Francis Thompson. *Fr.* From the Night of Forebeing. VLEP
Shaded lamp and a waving blind, A. An August Midnight. Thomas Hardy. EmBrPo; PoMa
Shaded Pool, The. Norman Gale. HBV; OBVV
Shaded Water, The. William Gilmore Simms. LPS-2
Shades are half-drawn on classroom and hall, The. Discourse on the Real. Samuel Yellen. NePoAm
Shades are real, The. Death is not the end. Propertius. Elegies, IV, 7. LaP
Shades of Agamemnon and Iphigeneia, The. Walter Savage Landor. BPN
Shades of Callimachus, and holy rites of Philetas. Propertius, *tr. by* Frances Fletcher. Elegies, III, 1. LaP
Shades of Callimachus, Coan Ghosts of Philetas. Ezra Pound. *Fr.* Homage to Sextus Propertius. MoAB; MoVE; OxBA
Shades of eve had crossed the glen, The. The Pretty Girl of Loch Dan. Sir Samuel Ferguson. HBV; LPS-1
Shades of Night, The. A. E. Housman. ChTr; FiBHP
Shades of night were falling fast, The. Excelsior. Long-

fellow. FaPON; HBV; HBVY; IAP; LPS-3; NeHB; OTPC; PoFS; PTA-2; TCAP; TreF; WBLP
Shadow. Guillaume Apollinaire, *tr. fr. French by* Jessie Degen *and* Richard Eberhart. WaaP
Shadow. Richard Bruce. CDC
Shadow. Mary Elizabeth Coleridge. PoVP
Shadow, The. Walter de la Mare. BoChLi (1950 ed.); ChMo; CMP; MeRV
Shadow. William Griffith. BAP
Shadow, The. Ben Jonson. *See* Song: That Women Are but Men's Shadows.
Shadow, The. Amy Lowell. ChMo; CMP
Shadow. Ann Mars. GoYe
Shadow. Louise Owen. PFE
Shadow, The. Richard Henry Stoddard. AA
Shadow, The. Arthur Symons. OBVV
Shadow, A. *Unknown. See* I Heard a Noise.
Shadow, The. William Carlos Williams. NP
Shadow and Shade. Allen Tate. InPo; LiTA; SPP; ViBoPo
Shadow and the Light, The, *sel.* Whittier.
"All souls that struggle and aspire." TrPWD
Shadow Boat, A. Arlo Bates. HBV
Shadow by my finger cast, The. 1904's Sundial at Wells College. Henry van Dyke. DDA
Shadow Child, The. Harriet Monroe. BAP; HBV; LBAP
Shadow Dance. Ivy O. Eastwick. TiPo
Shadow Dance, The. Louise Chandler Moulton. AA; HBV
Shadow-Evidence. Mary Mapes Dodge. AA
Shadow falls, the path I cannot trace, The. Satisfied. Samuel Valentine Cole. BLRP
Shadow House of Lugh, The. "Ethna Carbery." AnIV
Shadow like a creeping creature puts his nose out from the wood. Shadow. Louise Owen. PFE
Shadow Line, The. George S. Greene. CAG
Shadow-Love. Heine, *tr. fr. German by* Emma Lazarus. *Fr.* Songs to Seraphine. TrJP
Shadow March. Robert Louis Stevenson. *Fr.* North-West Passage. HOAH
Shadow of Cain, The. Edith Sitwell. CoBMV
Shadow of Flowers, The. Su T'ung-po, *tr. fr. Chinese by* Kenneth Rexroth. OnPC
Shadow of Night, The, *sels.* George Chapman.
Hymnus in Noctem. PoEL-2; ReIE, *abr.*
"All you possessed with indepressed spirits." TuPP
"Great goddesse to whose throne in Cynthian fives." AtBAP
Night ("Kneel then with me"). OBSC
Shadow of Night, The. Coventry Patmore. CH
Shadow of Smoke. Andrew Hewitt. NoCaPo (1941 ed.)
Shadow of the Night, A. Thomas Bailey Aldrich. AA
Shadow of the Rock, The. Frederick W. Faber. GoBC
Shadow of twilight. Barcarole. Sigbjörn Obstfelder. AnNoLy
Shadow on the Loom, The. Nellie Burget Miller. OQP; QP-2
Shadow People, The. Francis Ledwidge. GaP; HOAH; MCCG; MPB; PCH; POT; PoTo; RAR; SP; TSW; TSWC; VOD
Shadow Remains, The. Lynette Roberts. NeBP
Shadow River. E. Pauline Johnson. BoCaPo; CaP; OCL
Shadow Rose, The. Robert Cameron Rogers. AA
Shadow streamed into the wall, The. Shadow and Shade. Allen Tate. InPo; LiTA; SPP; ViBoPo
Shadow to Shadow. Hervey Allen. HBMV
Shadowed in midnight green. The Pond. James Whaler. *Fr.* Runaway. MAP; MoAmPo (1942 ed.)
Shadowed Star, The. Ada Foster Murray. LEAP
Shadows. Paul Claudel, *tr. fr. French by* Joseph T. Shipley. CAW
Shadows. Samuel Daniel. *See* Are They Shadows?
Shadows, The. Mary Lundie Duncan. OTPC (1923 ed.)
Shadows. Sebastian Evans. PrWP
Shadows, The. Robert Finch. TwCaPo
Shadows. William Sloane Kennedy. SN
Shadows. D. H. Lawrence. BrBE; OAEP (2d ed.)
Shadows. Richard Monckton Milnes. HBV; OBEV (1st ed.)
Shadows. Arthur J. Peel. MoSiPe
Shadows, The. Frank Dempster Sherman. AA
Shadows. Clark Ashton Smith. DaM
Shadows. "Yehoash," *tr. fr. Yiddish by* Elias Lieberman. TrJP
Shadows and Lights. "Æ." PoeT
Shadows Are Black. A. M. Sullivan. PFE
Shadows are descending, The. Outgoing Sabbath. *Unknown.* TrJP
Shadows cover the village lanes. The Village of Love. "Petros Vlastos." MoGP
Shadows do every where for substance passe. The Church-Windows. *Unknown. Fr.* A Poem, in Defence of the Decent Ornaments of Christ-Church, Oxon . . . OBS
Shadows gather round me, while you are in the sun, The. Next of Kin. Christina Rossetti. HBV
Shadows I alone can see. Ballad of the Two Grandfathers. Nicolás Guillén. TwSpPo
Shadows in the Water. Thomas Traherne. AtBAP; EnLi-1; EPS (1942 ed.); LiTB; MePo; OBS; PoEL-2; SeCL; UnPo (1st ed.)
Shadows lay along Broadway, The. Unseen Spirits [*or* Two Women]. Nathaniel Parker Willis. AA; AnAmPo; APW; BAP; BAV; BeLS; HBV; IAP; LA; LBAP; LEAP; LPS-1; OBAV; OBVV; TCAP
Shadows miss you, as they gather round your chair, The. Gone! Ethel Runyon Knott. BPP
Shadows of Chrysanthemums. E. J. Scovell. MoVE
Shadows of clouds. Clouds across the Canyon. John Gould Fletcher. *Fr.* The Grand Canyon of the Colorado. TCPD
Shadows of His Lady. Jacques Tahureau, *tr. fr. French by* Andrew Lang. AWP
Shadows of night were a-comin' down swift, The. Higher. *Unknown.* FiBHP; PA
Shadows of Sails. John Anderson. EtS
Shadows of the Evening Hours, The. Adelaide A. Procter. MaRV; TreFS
Shadows of the mountains stretch cool on the valley, The. August Evening. Olive Tilford Dargan. NoCaPo
Shadows of the ships, The. Sketch. Carl Sandburg. HBMV; NP
Shadows on the Wall. Aleksandr Blok, *tr. fr. Russian by* C. M. Bowra. BoR
Shadows on the Wall. Tsun Tsao, *tr. fr. Chinese by* Henry H. Hart. PoHN
Shadows There Are. A. J. M. Smith. BoCaPo
Shadows there are, mixed in the other shadows. The Shadows. Robert Finch. TwCaPo
Shadows To-Day. Christina Rossetti. OxBoCh
Shadows Worship, The. *Unknown, tr. fr. Arabic by* Sir Edwin Arnold. OnPM
Shadowy Swallows. Gustavo Adolfo Bécquer, *tr. fr. Spanish by* L. R. Lind. LiTW
Shadrach, Meshach, Abednego. Warm Babies. Keith Preston. FiBHP; HBMV; WhC
Shadwell. Dryden. *Fr.* MacFlecknoe. AnFE; EV-3; NBE ("All human things are subject to decay.") CoBE; TrGrPo; ViBoPo
(Laureate of Dulness, The.) CoEV
(Poet Shadwell, The.) FiP
(Primacy of Dullness, The.) OBS
Shadwell Stair. Wilfred Owen. FaBoTw; PoD
Shady arbor, The. The South Arbor. Chao Chia. PoHN
Shady friend for torrid days, A. Emily Dickinson. NePA
Shady, Shady. Tao Yuan-ming, *tr. fr. Chinese by* Arthur Waley. AWP; JAWP; WBP; WoL
(Twelve Poems, 1.) TrCh
Shady Woods. E. M. Adams. BoTP
Shaemus. Conrad Aiken. OxBA
Shaft of fire that falls like dew, A. The Burning-Glass. "Æ." LEAP
Shaftesbury. Dryden. *See* Achitophel.
Shag Rookery William Hart-Smith. AnNZ
Shaggy, and lean, and shrewd, with pointed ears. The Woodman's Dog. William Cowper. *Fr.* The Task. AlDL; BoTP; OTPC (1946 ed.); PCD; PCH
Shaggy camels kneel upon the sand, The. Caravans. Emily Patterson. ChIP
Shags or, they say, occasional a white. Incident at Matauri. Kendrick Smithyman. AnNZ
Shah Namal [Book of Kings], *sels.* Firdausi, *tr. fr. Persian.* PeP
Birth of Rustem, The, *tr. by* Joseph Champion.
Kiumers, *tr. by* Joseph Champion.
Rustem and Akwan Dev, *tr. by* E. H. Palmer.
Rustem Slays Sohráb, *tr. by* James Atkinson.
Satire on Mahmúd, *tr. by* Joseph Champion.
Sohráb Is Born, *tr. by* James Atkinson.
Shake back your hair, O red-headed girl. Red-headed Restaurant Cashier. Carl Sandburg. ChMo; CMP
Shake Hands, We Shall Never Be Friends, All's Over. A. E. Housman. More Poems, XXX. BoFr
Shake, Mulleary, and Go-ethe. H. C. Bunner. ALV; AnAmPo; BOHV; FiBHP; InMe; LA; PFE
Shake off thy sloth, my drowsy soul, awake. Thomas Traherne. *Fr.* On Christmas Day. OxBoCh
Shake Off Your Heavy Trance. Francis Beaumont. *Fr.* Masque of the Inner Temple and Gray's Inne. ElSeCe; EV-2; OBS; OnPM; ViBoPo
(Dance, A.) BLV
(Fit Only for Apollo.) ChTr
(Song for a Dance.) ElL; FaBoCh; LoGBV
(Songs from a Masque.) TrGrPo
(Superlative Dance and Song.) UnS
(Three Songs. I.) GoBC
Shake off your sadness and your will regain. Sow Your Self! Miguel de Unamuno. TeCS
Shakespeare. Matthew Arnold. AEV; AnFE; ATP; BEL; BLV; BMEP; BoLiVe; BPN; CaAE; CoBE; EM-2; EmBrPo; EnLi-2; EnLit; EPN; EPP; ES; EV-5; FiP; GEPC; GTBS; GTSE; GTSL; HBV; InP; InvP; LEAP; OAEP; OBEV; OBVV; OnPP; OTPC (1923 ed.); OuHeWo; PFE; PIAE; PoeMoYo; PoRL; PoVP;

Shakespeare (*continued*)
REAL; ReTS; TCEP; TOP; TrGrPo; TyEnPo; ViBoPo; ViPo; ViPP; VLEP; WHA
(Shakspeare.) PtP
Shakespeare. Henry Ames Blood. AA
Shakespeare. Hartley Coleridge. *See* To Shakespeare.
Shakespeare. Emerson. AnNE
Shakespeare. Agnes MacCarthy Hickey. PFE
Shakespeare. Thomas Hood. *Fr.* The Plea of the Midsummer Fairies. OBRV
Shakespeare. Samuel Johnson. *See* Prologue Spoken by Mr. Garrick at the Opening of the Theatre-Royal, 1747.
Shakespeare. Agnes Lee. NP
Shakespeare. Longfellow. AWP; IAP; InPo; MOAP; TOP
Shakespeare. John Sterling. PtP; VA
Shakespeare. Henry Jerome Stockard. NoCaPo
Shakespeare. Sir William Watson. HBV
Shakespeare; an Epistle to Mr. Garrick, *sel.* Robert Lloyd. Critic's Rules, The. OBEC
Shakespeare and Jonson. Samuel Johnson. *See* Prologue Spoken by Mr. Garrick at the Opening of the Theatre-Royal, 1747.
Shakespeare and Later. Harry Kemp. MoP
Shakespeare and Milton. Walter Savage Landor. BPN; MeRV; PtP; VA
Shakespeare and Milton—what third blazoned name. Tennyson. Thomas Bailey Aldrich. AA
Shakespeare Dead. Hugh Holland. ACP (1952 ed.)
(Sonnet to Shakespeare.) PrWP
Shakespeare is dust, and will not come. To and Fro about the City. John Drinkwater. MaRV; StJW
Shakespeare Might Have Boiled Othello. Edwin Meade Robinson. Limericised Classics, II. HBMV
Shakespeare Milton Keats are dead. Song of Allegiance. R. A. K. Mason. AnNZ
Shakespeare, Possibly, in California. Reed Whittemore. MoVE
Shakespeare Reads the King James Version. Richard Burton. PoeMoYo
Shakespeare, that nimble Mercury thy brain. To Master W. Shakespeare. Thomas Freeman. SiCE
Shakespeare, thy legacy of peerless song. At Stratford-on-Avon. Mackenzie Bell. VA
Shakespeare! to such name's sounding, what succeeds. The Names. Robert Browning. PtP
Shakespeare was king of seasons. Shakespeare and Later. Harry Kemp. MoP
Shakespearean Bear, The. Arthur Guiterman. BOHV; CenHV
Shakespeare's Fairies. Shakespeare. *Fr.* A Midsummer Night's Dream *and* The Tempest. CBPC
Shakespeare's Grave. Robinson Jeffers. TriL
Shakespeare's Mourners. John Banister Tabb. AmP
Shaking gold and silver bells. Translations from Modern Japanese Poetry. Takeko Kujo. PFE
Shako, The. Robert Lowell, *after the German of* Rainer Maria Rilke. OnHM
Shakspeare. Matthew Arnold. *See* Shakespeare.
Shall a Frown or Angry Eye. *Unknown.* ElL
Shall clammy clay shroud such a gallant gloze. A Mirror of Mortality. Thomas Proctor. ReIE
Shall dumpish melancholy spoil my joys. On Christmas-Day. Thomas Traherne. OBS; PoEL-2
Shall Earth No More Inspire Thee? Emily Brontë. EmBrPo; GTBS-D
(Lines: "Shall earth no more inspire thee.") LoBV
Shall hearts that beat no base retreat. The Enthusiast. Herman Melville. APW
Shall I be fearful thus to speak my mind. Irene Rutherford McLeod. *Fr.* Sonnets. HBMV
"Shall I be your first love, lady, shall I be your first?" Love-in-Idleness. Thomas Lovell Beddoes. LiTL; ViBoPo
Shall I call it fortune or my froward folly. How Jacke Cade Traiterously Rebelling agaynst His Kyng, Was for His Treasons and Cruell Doinges Wurthely Punished. *At. to* William Baldwin. *Fr.* A Mirror for Magistrates. SiCE
Shall I come, if I swim? wide are the waves, you see. Thomas Campion. EnLoPo
Shall I Come, Sweet Love, to Thee. Thomas Campion. CaAE; EG; ElL; FaBoEn; LoBV; OAEP; OBSC; OxBoLi; PoEL-2; ViBoPo
Shall I compare thee to a summers day? Sonnets, XVIII. Shakespeare. AnFE; AtBAP; ATP; AWP; BEL; BLV; BoLiVe; CaAE; CoBE; CoEV; EG; ElL; ElSeCe; EM-1; EnL; EnLi-1; EnLit; EnLoPo; ES; EtPaEn; EV-1; ExPo; FaBoBe; FaBoEn; FaFP; FiP; GTBS; GTBS-D; GTBS-W; GTSE; GTSL; HBV; InP; InvP; LiTB; LiTL; LoBV; LoPo; MaPo; MCCG; NeHB; OAEP; OBEV; OBSC; OuHeWo; PeBoSo; PIAE; PIR; PoEL-2; PoFS; PoMa; PoRA; REAL; ReaPo; ReEn; ReIE; RiBV; SeCePo; SeCeV; ShBV-4; SiCE; TOP; TrGrPo; TwHP; TwP; TyEnPo; ViBoPo; WHA
Shall I Complain? Louise Chandler Moulton. PoToHe
Shall I complain or keep silence, nor set down a charge. Ovid. *Fr.* Epistle from Pontus. BoFr
Shall I despaire of my resolv'd intent. *Unknown.* SeCSL
Shall I die wasting in despair. *See* Shall I, Wasting in Despair.
Shall I dip, shall I dip it, Dolores? The Poets at a House-Party. Carolyn Wells. PA
Shall I Do This? Purohit. OBMV
Shall I get drunk or cut myself a piece of cake. Cairo Jag. Keith Douglas. NePoEA
Shall I Go Bound and You Go Free? Padraic Colum. AnFE; PoFr
Shall I, I wonder, ever find. Peace. Irwin Edman. TrJP
Shall I kill myself? Remorse. Tennyson. *Fr.* Idylls of the King: Guinevere. MaRV
Shall I let myself be caught. Pygmalion. Hilda Doolittle ("H. D."). AnAmPo; LA
Shall I (like a hermit) dwell. His Further Resolution. *Unknown.* HBV
Shall I live always. A Hawk's Thoughts. Aleksey Koltsov. BoR
Shall I look on when states step on the stage. How Thomas Wolsey Did Arise unto Great Authority and Government . . . Thomas Churchyard. *Fr.* A Mirror for Magistrates. SiCE
Shall I look to ease my grief? What Remains but Only Dying? *Unknown.* ElL
Shall I Love Again. William Browne. ViBoPo
Shall I, mine affections slack. Answer to Master Wither's Song, "Shall I, Wasting in Despair?" Ben Jonson. BOHV; InMe; PA
Shall I, Mother, Shall I, Shall I Do So? *Unknown.* AnEC
Shall I no way win you to grant my desire? Being Importunate, at the Length He Obtaineth. Richard Edwards. TuPP
Shall I Pray On? Edith L. Mapes. PraP
Shall I say that I love you. Of Disdainful Daphne. M. H. Nowell. ElL
Shall I say that what heaven gave. Sentence. Witter Bynner. HBV; LBMV
Shall I sing the song you made of Philocles. The Song of Secret Love. Dryden. *Fr.* Secret Love. BeR
Shall I sonnet-sing you about myself? House. Robert Browning. BPN; OAEP; PoVP; PreP; ViPo; VLEP
Shall I still miche in silence and give aim. Satira Prima. Everard Guilpin. *Fr.* Skialetheia. ReIE
Shall I stray/ In the middle air. *Fr.* The Faithful Shepherdess, V, v. John Fletcher. ViBoPo
Shall I strew on thee rose or rue or laurel. Ave atque Vale. Swinburne. BMEP; CaAE; EnLi-2; LEAP; LiA; OAEP; OBEV; POTT; PoVP; PtP; ViBoPo; ViP; ViPP; VLEP
Shall I tell you who will come. Words from an Old Spanish Carol [*or* On Christmas Morn]. *Unknown, tr. by* Ruth Sawyer. BrR; ChBR; ChrBoLe; FaPON
Shall I Tell You Whom I Love? William Browne. *Fr.* Britannia's Pastorals, II, Song 2. ElL; EV-2; SeEP
(My Choice.) BCEP; LPS-1
(Song: "Shall I tell you whom I love?") HBV
(What Wight He Loved.) ElSeCe
"Shall I, then, covet riches? The lot that the Blest have made." Content at Home. Pindar. GrPE
Shall I then silent be or shall I speak? Amoretti, XLIII. Spenser. PeBoSo
Shall I then weep or shall I sing. *Unknown.* SeCSL
Shall I thus ever long, and be no whit the near? The Lady Prayeth the Return of Her Lover Abiding on the Seas [*or* The Seafarer *or* To Her Sea-faring Lover]. *Unknown.* ElL; OBEV; OBSC
Shall I to the Byre Go Down? Eleanor Farjeon. SDH
Shall I, Wasting in Despair. George Wither. *Fr.* Fair Virtue, the Mistress of Philarete, *and also* Fidelia. ALV; AnFE; BEL; EG; ElL; EM-1; EnLi-1; EV-2; LiTB; LiTG; LoPo, *abr.*; OBS; OuHeWo; PreP; ReEn; WHA
(Author's Resolution [in a Sonnet], The.) BCEP; CaAE; EPS; ViBoPo
(Lover's Resolution, The.) AWP; EnLit; HBV; InMe; JAWP; LEAP; LiTL; OBEV; PG; TOP; TreFS; WBP
(Manly Heart.) GTBS; GTBS-D; GTBS-W; GTSE; GTSL; MCCG; TVSH
(Resolution, The.) ElSeCe
(Shepherd's Resolution.) LPS-1
(Sonnet: "Shall I, wasting in despair.") EPP; SeCV-1; SeEP
(What Care I?) BLV; CoEV; TrGrPo
Shall I write pretty poetry. The Egoist. Anna Wickham. FaBoTw
Shall I your beauties with the moon compare? Pierre de Ronsard. *Fr.* Sonnets pour Hélène. PrPoCR
Shall it be given us to have the luck. Sleep. Kostas Kariotakis. MoGP
Shall mine eyes behold thy glory, oh, my country? After Death [*or* Post Mortem]. Fanny Parnell. AnIV; GTIV; OBVV; OnYI; OxBI; PoFr; TIP; VA
Shall misery make mirth. Christmas after War. Katharine Lee Bates. SDH

Shall reason rule where reason hath no right. To His Love. George Turberville. TuPP
Shall She Never Out of My Mind. *Unknown.* ReIE
Shall Simon Suckegg, simple Simkins' son. Henry Parrot. SiCE
Shall summer wood where we have laughed our fill. Apocalypse. Theodore Maynard. JKCP
Shall the great soul of Newton quit this earth. A Poem Sacred to the Memory of Sir Isaac Newton. James Thomson. CEP; EiPP
Shall the mole, in his dark underground, call the beasts from the day-glare to flee? Spiritual Vision. Solomon Solis-Cohen. MaRV
Shall these early fragrant hours. Henry Vaughan. LO
Shall they bury me in the deep. My Grave. Thomas Osborne Davis. OnYI
Shall this double anniversary, today, tonight. November 7th. "Pablo Neruda." PoFr
Shall Thor with his hammer. March. Isabella Valancy Crawford. OCL
Shall we but turn from braggart pride. England. Laurence Binyon. PoeT
Shall we die, both thou and I. One and His Mistress a-Dying. *Unknown.* LO; SeCL
Shall we for ever stealing looks of fire. Love or Death. Paulus Silentiarius. OxBG
Shall We Forget. William Mitchell. BePJ
Shall we forget, when Nations meet. Forget-Me-Not Day. Nan Terrell Reed. HH
Shall we go dance the hay, the hay? Country Song [*or* A Report Song]. Nicholas Breton. OBSC; SeCePo; TrGrPo
Shall we make love. A Bright Night. *Unknown.* *Fr.* Manyo Shu. AWP; LiTW; WoL
Shall we meet no more, my love, at the binding of the sheaves. Adonais. Will Wallace Harney. AA; HBV
Shall we not open the human heart. Give Way! Charlotte Perkins Gilman. WGRP
Shall we not weary in the windless days. Hereafter. Rosamund Marriott Watson. VA
Shall we renounce our ancient friends. Sonnets to Orpheus, Pt. I, XXIV. Rainer Maria Rilke. AnGP
Shall we say heaven is not heaven. One Kind of Humility. Jean Starr Untermeyer. MAP; MoAmPo (1942 ed.); NLK (1947 ed.)
Shall we send back the Johnnies their bunting. Those Rebel Flags. John H. Jewett. FOAH
Shall we win at love or shall we lose. Hotel Transylvanie. Frank O'Hara. NeAP
Shallo Brown, *with music.* *Unknown.* ShS; SoAmSa
Shallow dark but mocks the eyes. Night's Ancient Cloud. Thomas Keohler. AnIV
Shallows of the Ford, The. Henry Herbert Knibbs. SCC
Shalom Aleichem. *Unknown, tr. fr. Hebrew.* TrJP
Shamash of the glade, The. The Venerable Bee. A. M. Klein. TrJP
Shambles come ready-made these years/ are found. On Common Ground. R. P. Blackmur. Scarabs for the Living, III. CrMA
Shame. Hesiod, *tr. fr. Greek by* Sir William Marris. *Fr.* Works and Days. OxBG
Shame. Coventry Patmore. *Fr.* The Angel in the House, I, xi, 2. OBVV
Shame. Arthur Rimbaud, *tr. fr. French by* Louise Varèse. AnFP
Shame. James Stephens. ChMo; CMP
Shame checks our first attempts, but then 'tis proved. Sins Loathed, and Yet Loved. Robert Herrick. LiTB
"Shame!" Cypris cries her statue when she sees. The Aphrodite of Praxiteles. *Unknown.* OxBG
Shame Hitherto. Al Mutanabbi, *tr. fr. Arabic by* R. A. Nicholson. LiTW
Shame of Losing Salamis, The. Solon, *tr. fr. Greek by* F. L. Lucas. GrPE
Shame to my thoughts, how they stray from me! On the Flightiness of Thought. *Unknown.* OnYI
Shame upon thee, savage monarch-man, proud monopolist of reason. Of Cruelty to Animals. Martin Farquhar Tupper. *Fr.* Proverbial Philosophy. LPS-3
Shame upon you, Robin. Milkmaid's Song [*or* The Song of the Milkmaid]. Tennyson. *Fr.* Queen Mary. BPN; EPN; HBV; LPS-1
Shameful Death. William Morris. BPN; CBOV; ChTr; EmBrPo; GoTP; GTBS; HBV; MaC; MBP; MuP; OAEP; OBVV; POTT; PoVP; ShBV-2; VA; ViP; ViPo; ViPP; VLEP
Shamrock, The. Andrew Cherry. *See* Green Little Shamrock of Ireland, The.
Shamrock, The. Maurice Francis Egan. AA; DD; HBV; HH
Shamrock, The. *Unknown.* HH
Shamus is an Irish dog. To an Irish Setter Pup. "Campaspe." AlBD
Shan Van Vocht, The. *Unknown.* AnIL; AnIV, *2 sts.;* OnYI; OxBoLi, *diff. vers.;* PoFr; TIP
Shanadore, I love your daughter. Shenandoah. *Unknown.* ShS
Shancoduff. Patrick Kavanagh. OxBI
Shandon Bells, The. Francis Sylvester Mahony. *See* Bells of Shandon, The.
Shane O'Neill. Seumas MacManus. OnYI
Shaneen and Maurya Prendergast. Patch-Shaneen. J. M. Synge. LoBV
Shane's Head. John Savage. TIP
Shang Ya!/ I want to be your friend. Oath of Friendship. *Unknown.* BoFr
Shankill. Eileen Shanahan. NeIP
Shannon, The. Sir Aubrey De Vere. TIP
Shannon and the *Chesapeake,* The. Thomas Tracy Bouvé. GA; MC; PAH
Shannon and the *Chesapeake,* The. *Unknown.* AmSS (*Chesapeake* and *Shannon.*) PAH
Shanty Boy, The. *Unknown.* *See* Bung Yer Eye.
Shanty-Boy and the Farmer's Son, The, *with music.* *Unknown.* ABF; APW; IHA
Shantyboys' Song, The. Kenneth Zwicker. ShS
Shantyman's Life, The, *with music.* *Unknown.* AS; ShS, *2 vers.;* TrAS, *diff. vers.*
Shapcot! to thee the Fairy State. Oberon's Feast. Robert Herrick. BLV; BoLiVe; EPS; OAEP; OTPC (1923 ed.); SeCV-1; TrGrPo
Shape alone let others prize, The. Song. Mark Akenside. HBV; LPS-1
Shape-Changer. Ella Young. BoChLi (1950 ed.)
Shape God Wears, The. Sara Henderson Hay. GoTP; QS
Shape, like folded light, embodied air, A. Aishah Schechinah. Robert Stephen Hawker. ACP (1926 ed.); EV-4; GoBC; ISi; NBE; OxBoCh
Shape of a Bird, The. Laurence Whistler. MoVE
Shape of Autumn, The. Virginia Russ. GoYe
Shape of the Fire, The. Theodore Roethke. AmP; LiTA; MiAP; MoAB; OnAP
Shape of the Heart, The. Louise Townsend Nicholl. ImOP
Shaped and vacated. The Event. T. Sturge Moore. OBMV
Shaped long and arrowy. Express Trains. MacKnight Black. PoMa
Shapes. Mark Turbyfill. NP
Shapes and Signs. James Clarence Mangan. ERP; OnYI; TIP
Shapes of Death [Haunt Life]. Stephen Spender. MoPW; OBMV
Shapes that frowned before the eyes, The. The Eclipse of Faith. Theodore Dwight Woolsey. AA
Shards. Aline Kilmer. PFY
Sharecropper. Stewart Atkins. NoCaPo
Shared, *abr.* Lucy Larcom. NLK
Sharing Eve's Apple. Keats. ChER (Eve's Sweet Pippin.) RO
Sharing His Cross. Gracia L. Fero. BePJ
Sharks, The. Denise Levertov. NeAP
Shark's Fin. Eithne Wilkins. NeBP
Sharks' jaws are glittering through the eternal ocean. Ebenezer Jones. *Fr.* Ways of Regard. NBE
Sharks tooth is perfect for biting, The. Canticle. Michael McClure. NeAP
Sharp is the night, but stars with frost alive. Winter Heavens. George Meredith. BLV; BoLiVe; Po; ViP
Sharp Shares, The. *Unknown, tr. fr. Chinese.* WhP
Sharp triangles of red rubber and white. Consuelo at the Country Club. Selden Rodman. NAMP
Sharp wind stirs, The. The Mountain Courtyard. Ch'üan Shen. PoHN
Shatter'd rocks and strata seem to say, The. Rocky Landscape. Mary Chandler. *Fr.* The Description of Bath. BeR
Shattered, O Lord, is each enclosing wall. Heart's Poverty. Gloria T. Stein. JKCP (1955 ed.)
Shattered water made a misty din, The. Once by the Pacific. Robert Frost. AmPP; AnFE; CoAnAm; CoBMV; GTBS-W; InPo; LiTA; LiTM; MAP; MoAB; MoAmPo; MOAP; NePA; NP; PoFS; PreP; TwP
Shaven Beauty, The. Al-Ramadi, *tr. fr. Arabic by* A. J. Arberry. MooP
Shawls, The. Monk Gibbon. NeIP; OxBI
She. Vicente Huidobro, *tr. fr. Spanish by* Dudley Fitts. AnCL
She. Ben Jonson. *See* Have You Seen a Bright Lily Grow.
She, a Tung-yang girl, stands barefoot on the bank. The Women of Yueh. Li Po. ChLP
She always leaned to watch for us. The Watcher-Mother. Margaret Widdemer. CV; DD; HBMV; MaRV; OHIP; OOP; OP-1; TCAP; TSW; TSWC
"She always seems so tied," is what friends say. Just to Be Needed. Mary Eversley. PoToHe
She and He. Sir Edwin Arnold. *See* He and She.
She answered by return of post. The Perfect Guest. *Unknown.* DDA
She answered, standing dark against the west in the window. Robinson Jeffers. *Fr.* Tamar. PC

She, as a veil down to the slender waist. Milton. *Fr.* Paradise Lost, IV. LoPS

She Asks for New Earth. Katharine Tynan. HBMV

She bade us listen to the singing lark. On a Lady Singing. Isaac Rosenberg. FaBoTw

She bared her spirit to her sorrow. Escape. Lionel Johnson. VLEP

She beat the happy pavement. Gratiana Dancing [*or* Dauncing] and Singing. Richard Lovelace. EPS; EV-2; OAEP; OBS

She Being Brand. E. E. Cummings. OxBA

She, being woman, had two wines to pour. Circe Remembers. Sherman Conrad. CAG

She Bewitched Me. Thomas Burbidge. EnLoPo

She brings Him, smiling, in her arms to me. Stella Matutina. Lillian Doherty. WHL

She brings such gay and shining things to pass. Mary Sets the Table. David Morton. POT; PoTo

She brought a drinking-cup to him. Two. Hugo von Hofmannsthal. TrJP

She by the river sate, and sitting there. Upon Julia Weeping. Robert Herrick. ExPo

She called from her cell. Madness. Harry Lee. MaRV

She Called Him Mr. *Unknown. See* Limerick: "She frowned and called him Mr."

She called the famous smith Hephaestus, saying. Thetis and Hephaestus. Homer. *Fr.* The Iliad, XVIII. OxBG

She came. Dirge. Alfred Kreymborg. NP

She came alone from far away. The Stranger. Stefan George. AnGP

She came among the gathering crowd. Common Sense. James Thomas Fields. AA

She came and stood in the Old South Church. In the "Old South." Whittier. AA; APW

She Came and Went. James Russell Lowell. AA; BAP, *sts.* 1-3; CoBA; HBV; IAP; LBAP; LEAP; TCAP; ViBoPo

She came and went as comes and goes. Under the Red Cross. Chauncey Hickox. AA

She came in beauty beaming. Moon of Beauty. Ibn al-Faras. MooP

She came in from the snowing air. Ice. Stephen Spender. AtBAP; FaBoMo; SeCePo

She came like music: when she went. Ann Rutledge. Edwin Markham. MW: TBM

She came on Earth soon after the creation. The Fairy Maimounè. John Moultrie. OBRV

She Came Out of the Frost. Aleksandr Aleksandrovich Blok, *tr. fr. Russian by* Babette Deutsch. TrRV

She came to him in dreams—her ears. The Tame Hare. Norman Nicholson. FaBoMo

She came to him without eyes, yet her face held a smile. Ghost. Joseph Corson Miller. UnW

She came to me in hidden guise. Mater Incognita. Sister Mary Benvenuta. ISi

She came to us recommended. For Louise, Age 17. Irving Layton. PeCV

She can be as wise as we. Marian. George Meredith. EV-5; GTML; HBV

She cannot tell my name. Prayer. Edward Bliss Reed. HBMV

She carried her water pitcher. The Burden. Märta af Sillén. AnSL

She casts a spell, oh, casts a spell! My Love, Oh, She Is My Love. *Tr. by* Douglas Hyde. AnIV; GTIV; TIP

She chops the meat with a golden knife. The Richest Woman. Elizabeth Madox Roberts. GaP

She comes, an exile fair. The Stork. Al-Hajjam. MooP

She comes, and straight [*or* streight] therewith her shining twins do move. Astrophel and Stella, LXXVI. Sir Philip Sidney. ReIE; SiPS

She Comes as Comes the Summer Night. Frank S. Williamson BoAu

She comes like the hush and beauty of the night. Poetry. Edwin Markham. AA

She comes majestic with her swelling sails. Homeward Bound Robert Southey. EtS

She comes not: in the summer night. O Ubi? Nusquam. R. W. Dixon. LO

She Comes Not When Noon Is on the Roses. Herbert Trench. EtPaEn; GTIV; GTML; HBMV; LBBV; OBEV (new ed.); OBVV
(Song: "She comes not when noon is on the roses.") MBP

She comes! she comes! the sable throne behold. Chaos on Her Throne, or the Triumph of Dullness. Pope. *Fr.* The Dunciad. BeR; NBE

She comes She's here. Dryden. *Fr.* All for Love, III. MyFE

She comes! the spirit of the dance! A Dancing Girl [*or* Celeste Dancing]. Frances Sargent Osgood. AA; BAP

She cometh no more. At the Last. "Fiona Macleod." VLEP

She could die laughing. Minnie and Mrs. Hoyne. Kenneth Fearing. AnEnPo; PoRA

She could not sleep all night for happiness. Convent Morning. Sister Mary Eugene. PraNu

She cried aloud "Father!" yet they heard not. The Sacrifice of Iphigenia. Aeschylus. *Fr.* Agamemnon. LiA

She Crosses Her Knees. *Unknown.* SiTL

She crouched outside my door at break of dawn. Cruelty. Margaret E. Bruner. CIV

She danced, near nude, to tom-tom beat. Zalka Peetruza. Ray Garfield Dandridge. BANP

She dances, and I seem to be. Perdita. Florence Earle Coates. AA

She dared not wait my coming, and shall look. Canute the Great. "Michael Field." VA

She dealt her pretty words like blades. Emily Dickinson. MOAP

She-Devil. Douglas Goldring. HBMV

She Died in Beauty. Charles Doyne Sillery. HBV

She died in meekness, like the noiseless lamb. Thomas Holly Chivers. *Fr.* The Dying Beauty. PoP

She died last night (How deep the snows of May). Annie Ferguson. Mary W. Findlater. DiM

She died—this was the way she died. Emily Dickinson. OBAV
(Vanished.) AA; BAP

She died when earth was fair beyond all price. On the Death of a Favorite Cat. *Unknown.* CIV

She does not know. No Images. Waring Cuney. BANP; CDC; GoSl; PoNe

She doth not leave me comfortless, nor e'er. Ideal Passion, IV. George Edward Woodberry. MOAP

She dreams of Love upon the temple stair. A Sleeping Priestess of Aphrodite. Robert Cameron Rogers. AA

She dresses aye so clean and neat. From His First Song. Burns. *Fr.* O, Once I Lov'd a Bonie Lass. BLP

She drew back; he was calm. The Subverted Flower. Robert Frost. CoV; OxBA

She droops like a dew-dropping lily. The Widow's Lullaby. Sydney Dobell. BOL

She dropped the bar, she shot the bolt, she fed the fire anew. The Only Son. Kipling. *Fr.* All the Mowgli Stories. VLEP

She dwelleth in Elysium. Elysium. Edward Coote Pinkney. MOAP

She dwells, pale midnight sun, beyond the river. Une Idole du Nord. Francis Stuart. NeIP

She Dwelt among the Untrodden Ways. Wordsworth. ATP; AWP; BEL; BoLiVe; BTP; CBOV; CoBE; EG; EM-2; EnL; EnLit; EnLoPo; EnRP; EPN; ERP; EtPaEn; GTSL; HBVY; InP; InPo; JAWP; LEAP; LiTB; LiTG; LiTL; MaPo; MCCG; OAEP; OBRV; OTPC; OuHeWo; PG; PoE; PoFS; REAL; ReaPo; ShBV-4; TCEP; TOP; TVSH; TwHP; TwP; TyEnPo; ViBoPo; WBP; WHA; WP
(Lost Love, The.) GTBS; GTBS-D; GTBS-W; GTSE; PIR
(Lucy.) AnFE; BCEP; BLPA; BLV; CBE; EmBrPo; EnLi-2; EPP; EV-3; FaBoEn; FiP; HBV; LEAP; LoBV; LoPo; LPS-1; MaC; NeHB; OBEV; PECK; TreF; TrGrPo
Violet, The, *sel.* PCH

She even thinks that up in heaven. *See* She thinks that even up in heaven.

She fears him, and will always ask. Eros Turannos. E. A. Robinson. AnAmPo; AnFE; AnNE; APA; CoAnAm; CoBA; CoBMV; CrMA; LA; LiTA; LiTM (rev. ed.); MAP; MAPA; MoAB; MoAmPo; MOAP; MoPo; MoVE; NePA; NP; OnAP; OxBA; PoE; PoFS; RiBV; TwAmPo; TwP

She feeds the starving love, with hands. Love in Hunger. Philip Oakes. PoN

She fell asleep on Christmas Eve. My Sister's Sleep. Dante Gabriel Rossetti. BPN; EmBrPo; EnL; EPN; ExPo; LoBV; MyFE; OAEP; POTT; PoVP; SeCeV; ViP; ViPo; ViPP; VLEP

She fell away in her first ages spring. Spenser. *Fr.* Daphnaida OBEV

She felt, I think, but as a wild-flower can. An Irish Wild-Flower. Sarah Morgan Bryan Piatt. AA

She fled in anguish; he pursued desire. First Love. Charles Gullans. NePoEA

She flourished in the 'Twenties, "hectic" days of Peace. Mews Flat Mona. William Plomer. FaBoTw

She flung the parlour window wide. Quite by Chance. Frederick Langbridge. BOHV

She follows me about my house of life. The Child in Me. May Riley Smith. BAP; SBMV

She frowned and called him Mr. Limerick [*or* She Called Him Mr.]. *Unknown.* FaPON; GoTP; TSWC

She gamboll'd on the greens. Olivia. Tennyson. *Fr.* The Talking Oak. GN

She gathers white asters. The White Asters. *Unknown.* WhP

She gave her life to love. She never knew. The Old Maid. George Barlow. VA

She gave me all that woman can. Monna Lisa. James Russell Lowell. MOAP
She gave up beauty in her tender youth. A Portrait. Christina Rossetti. POTT; VLEP
She gaz'd into the fresh-thrown mould, as though. The Kernel of the Grave. Keats. *Fr.* Isabella. LiA
She gazed upon the burnished brace. The Tender Heart. Helen Gray Cone. PR
She gives most dangerous sight. For a Marriage. Louise Bogan. MOAP
She goes all so softly. Song. Edward J. O'Brien. SBMV
She goes but softly, but she goeth sure. Upon the Snail. Bunyan. ChTr
She goes by many names; Diana of the sacred wood. The Goddess. Kathleen Raine. FaBoTw
She had a cock hight Chaunteclere. The Poor Widow's Cock. Chaucer. *Fr.* The Canterbury Tales: The Nun's Priest's Tale. MyFE
She had a name among the children. A Cat. Edward Thomas. PoC
She had [*or* has] an understanding with the years. A Woman. Scudder Middleton. BAP; NV; PC
She had been ill for years and years. The Sick Wife. *Unknown.* TrCh
She had cornflowers in her ear. Gipsy Jane. William Brighty Rands. BoTP; FaPON; TiPo
She had green eyes, that excellent seer. Bast. William Rose Benét. HBMV; PoC
She had no business doin' it, but she come out o' the East. The Peeler's Lament. *Unknown.* CoSo
She had no saying dark enough. The Oft-repeated Dream. Robert Frost. *Fr.* The Hill Wife. ChMo; CMP; IAP; MOAP; NP; PG (1945 ed.); SBMV
She had thought the studio would keep itself. Living in Sin. Adrienne Cecile Rich. NePoEA
She hangs the garland in her hair. The Spirit Watches. Ruth Pitter. TriL
She has a beauty of her own. An Australian Girl. Ethel Castilla. VA
She has a bright and clever mind. A Disagreeable Feature. Edwin Meade Robinson. BAP; HBMV; PYM
She has a primrose at her breast. A Primrose Dame. Gleeson White. HBV; VA
She has an understanding with the years. *See* She had an understanding . . .
"She has beauty, but [still] you must keep your heart cool." Dear Fanny. Thomas Moore. HBV; InMe
She has been teaching now for thirty years. Old Teacher. Gerald Raftery. BPP
She has calld to her her bower-maidens. Young Hunting (G *vers.*) *Unknown.* ESPB
She has dancing eyes and ruby lips. My Mistress's Boots. Frederick Locker-Lampson. BOHV; HBV; PIAE; TOP
She has finished and sealed the letter. Parting, without a Sequel. John Crowe Ransom. BLV; LiTL; MAP; MoAB; MoAmPo; MoVE; NP; OxBA
She has gone—she has left us in passion and pride. Brother Jonathan's Lament for Sister Caroline. Oliver Wendell Holmes. APW; CoBA; HBV; IAP; MDAH; PaA; PAH
"She has gone to be with the angels." The Vision of the Snow. Margaret Junkin Preston. AA
She has gone to the bottom! the wrath of the tide. The *Alabama.* Maurice Bell. PAH
She has laughed as softly as if she sighed. A Woman's Shortcomings. Elizabeth Barrett Browning. BLPA; NeHB; HBV
She has left me, my pretty. Song. Sylvia Townsend Warner. MBP; MoAB; MoBrPo
She has new leaves. New Love. Richard Aldington. *Fr.* Epigrams. PFE
She has no need to fear the fall. Portrait. Louise Bogan. HBMV
She has not grown uncivil. Her Race. W. B. Yeats. Upon a Dying Lady, V. LiTB
She has opened an immense hole in the soft ground. The Goddess. Théodore de Banville. OnPM
She has returned from Paris, I am told. Fable of a Forgotten Woman. Louis Johnson. AnNZ
She has rolled up the beaded screen. Resentment. Li Po. WhP
She has that quality of innocence. Virgin Country. Roy McFadden. NeIP
She has the strange sweet grace of violets. Elizabeth. George Brandon Saul. HBMV
She has tightened her cinch by another inch. Over the Hills with Nancy. Gelett Burgess. WhC
She hastens through the dingy street. The Sister of Charity. Alexander J. Cody. PraNu
She hath the apple in her hand for thee. Venus Verticordia. Dante Gabriel Rossetti. EmBrPo
She heard the children playing in the sun. Pain. Harriet Monroe. NP
She heard with patience all unto the end. Prince Arthur. Spenser. *Fr.* The Faerie Queene, I. OBSC
She Hears the Storm. Thomas Hardy. ATP; BMEP; NP; TOP
She hears, upon that water without sound. Sunday Morning, II [VIII]. Wallace Stevens. AnFE; AnNE; APA; CoAnAm; MAP; MAPA; MoAmPo; TriL
She held my stirrup. *Unknown, tr. fr. Italian by* L. R. Lind. LyPI
She hid herself in the soirée kettle. A Ballade of the Nurserie. John Twig. NA
She hung a pendant in between her breasts. Redemption of the Ridiculous. Donald F. Drummond. PtPa
She hung the cage at the window. Caprice. William Dean Howells. ALV; PR
She I love (alas in vain!). Walter Savage Landor. GTSE
She I love leaves me and I leave my friends. False Bay. F. T. Prince. BoSA
She in whose lipservice. The Goddess. Denise Levertov. NeAF
She is a nun, withdrawing behind her veil. The Desert. Charles E. S. Wood. *Fr.* The Poet in the Desert. AnAmPo; LA; MAP
She is a person here in her own right. Memling's Virgin with Apple. Adèle Naudé. BoSA
She is a queen, seated on a throne of gold. The Desert. Charles E. S. Wood. *Fr.* The Poet in the Desert. BAP
She is a reed,/ straight and simple. The Reed. Caryll Houselander. ISi
She is a rich and rare land. My Land [*or* This Native Land]. Thomas Davis. BoTP; DD; HBV; MPB (1956 ed.); OTPC
She is a winsome wee thing. My Wife's a Winsome Wee Thing. Burns. HBV; LiTL; LPS-1
She is all so slight. After Two Years. Richard Aldington. BLV; CP; GTML; GTSL; HBV; LBBV; LEAP; MBP; MoBrPo; NV; PG; WHA
She is as in a field a silken tent. The Silken Tent. Robert Frost. CoV; ExPo; InPo; MoPo; NePA
She is bravest and best of a cursed race. Chipeta. Eugene Field. PoOW
She is coming, coming. The Red Gown. Ibn al-Sabuni. MooP
She is content to live in heaviness. The Cloister. George Allen. MotAn
She is dead, nor did she ever live! On a Dead Lady. Alfred de Musset. EnL1-2 (1949 ed.)
"She is dead!" they said to him; "come away." He and She [*or* The Secret of Death *or* She and He]. Sir Edwin Arnold. BLPA; BMEP; HBV; LPS-1; UnW
She is fair and debonair. Debonair. *Unknown.* WhP
She is false. O Death, she is fair! Betrayed. Lizette Woodworth Reese. TBM
She Is Far from the Land. Thomas Moore. AnIL; EnRP; ERP; EV-4; HBV
She is foremost of those that I would hear praised. Her Praise. W. B. Yeats. Po
She is free of the trap and the paddle. The Half-Breed Girl. Duncan Campbell Scott. CaP; CPG; OCL
She is gamesome and good. Nature. Emerson. MOAP
She is gathering lotos seed in the river of Yueh. The Girl of Yueh. Li Po. WhP
She Is Gentle and Also Wise. *Unknown.* KN; LO
("She is gentil and al so wise.") EG
(That Ever I Saw.) TrGrPo
She is gone, she is lost, she is found, she is ever fair. My Woe Must Ever Last. Sir Walter Ralegh. EIL
She is gone whom I loved so long, my girl that I loved so dear. Propertius. *Fr.* Elegies. LaP
She is gray but beautiful; lovely as the beggar-maid of King Cophetua. Dedication to My Gray Lady. Fra Jerome. SaFP
She is here, she is here, the swallow! Swallow Song. *Unknown.* GrPo
She is like pearls, of course, and rubies, and other. Valentine. Hollis Summers. GoYe
She is like the great rains. A Woman in Winter Costume. John Gould Fletcher. ChMo; CMP
She is more sparkling beautiful. A Bridal Song. Hugh McCrea. BoAu
She Is More to Be Pitied than Censured. William B. Gray. BeLS; BLPA; TreF
She is most fair. The Unknown. Edward Thomas. BMEP; LEAP
She Is My Dear. *Unknown, tr. fr. Irish by* Frank O'Connor. KiLC
She is not a pale visionary thing. Ideal Passion, XVI. George Edward Woodberry. MOAP
She is not cold, as mortal maidens are. Ideal Passion, II. George Edward Woodberry. MOAP
She Is Not Fair to Outward View. Hartley Coleridge. *See* Song: "She is not fair to outward view."
She is not holy like the Virgin One. Ideal Passion, III. George Edward Woodberry. MOAP

She is not mistress here, the arrows shake themselves. Lady with Arrows. Margaret Marks. MAP
She is not old, she is not young. The Woman with the Serpent's Tongue. Sir William Watson. BMEP; HBV
She is not yet; but he whose ear. Dominion of Australia, The (a Forecast, 1877). Brunton Stephens. BoAu; VA
She is older than the rocks among which she sits. Mona Lisa. Walter Pater. OBMV
She Is Overheard Singing. Edna St. Vincent Millay. InMe
She is playing like a child. The End of Day. W. B. Yeats. Upon a Dying Lady, IV. LiTB
She is risen from the dead! America Resurgent. Wendell Phillips Stafford. MC
She is slender and elegant and not yet fourteen. Bestowed in Farewell. Tu Mu. ChLP
She is so beautiful, so pure, dear God. Prayer for a Bride. Helen Welshimer. PraP
She is so proper and so pure. My Sweet Sweeting. *Unknown.* CH; LPS-1
She is so winsome and so wise. She Just Keeps House for Me. Jean Blewett. CPG
She is so young, dear Lord, so very young. Prayer for a Bride's House. Christie Lund. PraP
She is so young for this grave sacrifice! Young Nun. Grace Noll Crowell. PraNu
She is standing at the gate. Mid-Forest Fear. Roderic Quinn. BoAu
She is still, she is cold. Shelley. *Fr.* Ginevra. ChER
She is submarine, she is an octopus, she is/ A biological process. Ezra Pound. *Fr.* Canto XXIX. MoPo
She is the clernesse and the verray light. Chaucer. *Fr.* The Legend of Good Women. LO
She is the fairies' midwife, and she comes. Queen Mab [*or* Mercutio Describes Queen Mab]. Shakespeare. *Fr.* Romeo and Juliet, I, iv. GoTP; MaC; PoFS; TrGrPo
She is the Rose, the glorie of the day. Lament for Daphnaida. Spenser. FiP
She is too cruell, alas too cruell. *Unknown.* SeCSL
She is too old to work—too young to die. Fifth Wheel. Dorothy Brown Thompson. DDA
She is touching the cycle—her tender tread. Tennessee. Virginia Fraser Boyle. PAH
She is up in the dark and out in the cowyard. The Milker. Eileen Duggan. CoBE
She Is Wise, Our Ancient Mother. Karle Wilson Baker. OQP; QP-2
She issues radiant from her dressing-room. Modern Love, VII. George Meredith. ViPo
She it is where they lie down. Young Love. Lloyd Frankenberg. TwAmPo
She Just Keeps House for Me. Jean Blewett. CPG
She keeps her clavichord. The Clavichord. May Sarton. UnS
She keeps her nook, sitting with folded hands. The Old Woman. John Bunker. CAW
She kept her secret well, oh, yes. My Angeline. Harry B. Smith. *Fr.* The Wizard of the Nile. BOHV; InMe
She kissed me on the forehead. Windle-Straws. Edward Dowden. HBV
She kneeled before me begging. Confession. Donald Jeffrey Hayes. CDC
She kneeled before the dead lamb weeping. Synekdechestai. C. M. Schmid. GoYe
She knelt upon her brother's grave. Dora. Thomas Edward Brown. MBP; MotAn; OBEV (1st ed.); POTT; PoVP; ReaPo
She knew it not:—most perfect pain. The Mirror. Dante Gabriel Rossetti. EmBrPo
She knew that she was growing blind. Blind Louise. George Washington Dewey. AA
She knows a cheap release. The Movies. Florence Kiper Frank. MW; NP; POT; PoTo
She laid it where the sunbeams fall. Motherhood. Charles Stuart Calverley. LPS-3
She lay, and serving-men her lithe arms took. Abishag. Rainer Maria Rilke. AWP
She lay as if at play. Emily Dickinson. LiTA
She lay there in the stone folds of his life. Private Worship. Mark Van Doren. LiTL; MoVE
She lay unconscious there through all the day. Feodor Tyutchev, *tr. fr. Russian by* C. M. Bowra. BoRS
She leads me on through storm and calm. My Guide. George Francis Savage-Armstrong. VA
She leaned [*or* lean'd] her back unto [*or* upon] a thorn. The Cruel Mother [*or* Fine Flowers in the Valley]. *Unknown.* ESPB (C *vers.*); OBB; PIAE; ViBoFo
She leaned her cheek upon her hand. The Ballad of Oriskany. Obadiah Cyrus Auringer. AA
She Leaves Memphis, *with music.* *Unknown.* StDa
She leaves the puddle where she drinks. A Cow at Sullington. Charles Dalmon. TSW; TSWC
She left her love. Parting and Meeting. Kao Shih. ChLP
She left the keys and dropped. Silent Piano. W. Wesley Trimpi. PtPa
She lies far inland. Inland City. John Crowe Ransom. ChMo
She lies in her little bed. Little Spring. *Unknown.* GFA
She lies in silence. She Walks. Joseph Joel Keith. ISi
She lies on her left side her flank golden. Landscape as a Nude. Archibald MacLeish. Frescoes for Mr. Rockefeller's City, I. AmPP (4th ed.); ReaPo; UnPo
She lies there, her full firm teats not denied. Force. "Nikolai Maksimovich Minski." LiTW; TrRV
She lifted up her head. Loreine, a Horse. Arthur Davison Ficke. TCPD
She lifts her face. Chayah. Thomas Moult. NV
She like the Moon Arises. James McAuley. MoAuPo
She, like the morning, is still fresh and fair. Her Praises. Anthony Scoloker. ElL
She limps with halting painful pace. Portrait of an Old Woman. Arthur Davison Ficke. BAP; MAP; NP; PC
She listen'd like a cushat dove. Christina Rossetti. EG
She listen'd to the music of the spheres. Λειριόεσσα Κάλυξ (Leirioessa Kalyx). Maurice Baring. OBVV
She lived beside the Anner. The Irish Peasant Girl. Charles Joseph Kickham. AnIV; JKCP (1926 ed.); TIP
She lived in storm and strife. That the Night Come. W. B. Yeats. CoBMV; NP; PoEL-5
She lived shut in by flowers and trees. Sister Saint Luke. John Hay. PraNu
She lived, we knew not how. They Called Her Sunshine. Mary Gilmore. NeLNL
She lived where the mountains go down to the sea. Golden Rowan. Bliss Carman. VA
She lives a prisoner within. The Shut-in. Nellie De Hearn. PoToHe (new ed.)
She lives in light, not shadow. Of One Who Neither Sees nor Hears. Richard Watson Gilder. AA
She lives in the porter's room; the plush is nicotined. Bitter Sanctuary. Harold Monro. ChMo; CMP; FaBoMo; LiTB; OBMV
She Lives with the Furies of Hope and Despair. Delmore Schwartz. FiMAP
"She looked alluring that day, I confess." In the Public Ward. Florence Randal Livesay. CPG
She looked at [*or* on] me with sadder eyes than Death. Never Again. Hugh McCrae. BoAu; UnW
She looked over his shoulder. The Shield of Achilles. W. H. Auden. NePA; OAEP (2d ed.)
She looked over the hills for many a day. The Golden Ball. *Unknown.* BaBo
She looked to east, she looked to west. Mater Dei. Katharine Tynan. GTIV; ISi
She loved not the walk to and fro before the loom. Cyrene. Pindar. *Fr.* Pythian Odes. OxBG
She loved the Autumn, I the Spring. Spirit of Sadness. Richard Le Gallienne. HBV
She loves him; for her infinite soul is Love. True Woman, 2. Dante Gabriel Rossetti. The House of Life, LVII. BPN; EmBrPo; EPN; PoVP; ViPo
She loves me and she loves me not. The Coquette. Witter Bynner. PR
She loves me! From her own bliss-breathing lips. Sonnet. Charles Harpur. BoAu
She luminously wavered and I tentatively understood. The Poets at a House-Party. Carolyn Wells. PA
She made a little shadow-hidden grave. The Dead Faith. Fanny Heaslip Lea. HBV; WGRP
She made a nunnery of her life. A Sister of Charity. Frederick G. Scott. PraNu
She Made Home Happy. Henry Coyle. DD; MOAH
She makes thee seek, yet fear to find. Love's Servile Lot. Robert Southwell. ACP
She May Be Called a Sovereign Lady. *Unknown.* AnEC
She met me, Stranger, upon life's rough way. True Love. Shelley. *Fr.* Epipsychidion. LoBV
She might have borne them had they come. Breaking Point. Sylvia Auxier. GoYe
She might have known it in the earlier spring. Feminine. H. C. Bunner. AA; PR
She mixes blue and mauve and green. The Patchwork Quilt. Elizabeth Fleming. BoTP
She Moved through the Fair. Padraic Colum. GTBS-D; InvP; TwCV
She moved through the garden in glory because. Marigold. Richard Garnett. CIV
She moves as other women move. To One with Hands of Sleep. Harold Vinal. PC
She moves in tumult; round her lies. The Teresian Contemplative. Robert Hugh Benson. ACP; CAW; JKCP; PraNu
She must go back, she said. The Housewife. W. W. Gibson. *Fr.* The Battle. NP
She never climbed a mountain. Farm Wife. John Hanlon Mitchell. CaP; OCL
She never could sleep in the earth, in the cold dark grave. Fire Burial. Edgar McInnis. CaP; OCL
She never met a fairy. Mrs. C. (Or Any Other Too Practical Person). Rowena Bastin Bennett. GaP
She never puts her toys away. Patty-Poem. Nick Kenny. PoToHe

She Never Told Her Love. Shakespeare. *Fr.* Twelfth Night, II, iv. BCEP
(Love Concealed.) TreFS
(Patience on a Monument.) TrGrPo
(Unrequited Love, *longer sel.*) LPS-1
She No Longer Loves Him. Charles Dalmon. TCPD
She of the Garden. Emile Verhaeren, *tr. fr. French by* Alma Strettell. CAW
She of the Impudent Face. Proverbs, VII: 6–27, Bible, *O.T.* TrJP
She of whose soul, if we may say 'twas gold. John Donne. *Fr.* Of the Progress of the Soul. TuPP
She once was a lady of honor and wealth. The Sister of Charity. Gerald Griffin. PraNu
She only knew the birth and death. At Dawn. Arthur Symons. VLEP
She oped the portal of the palace. In the Sultan's Garden. Clinton Scollard. InP
She paced the silent hall. Sleep. Robert Eyres Landor. *Fr.* The Impious Feast, VII. OBRV
She passed away, like morning dew. Early Death. Hartley Coleridge. HBV; MaRV; OBEV; TreFS
She passed like a running flame. On the Mountain. Olive Tilford Dargan. NoCaPo
She passes in her beauty bright. The Secret. Cosmo Monkhouse. VA
She Plans Her Funeral. Louise Morey Bowman. CaP; CPG; OCL
She play'd me false, but that's not why. Our Photographs. Frederick Locker-Lampson. ALV
She played upon her music-box a fancy air by chance. Her Polka Dots. Peter Newell. NA
She plays her harp by hidden rills. The Muses of Australia. Victor Daley. BoAu
She Promised She'd Meet Me, *with music. Unknown.* AS
She Reports No Progress. Patience Eden. DDA
She rested by the Broken Brook. The Unforgotten, II. Robert Louis Stevenson. VLEP
She rose amid the Nations, tall and fair. Australia. John Laurence Rentoul. PoFr
She rose among us where we lay. The Vampire. Conrad Aiken. HBMV
She rose from her untroubled sleep. Chamber Scene. Nathaniel Parker Willis. HBV
She rose to his requirement, dropped. Emily Dickinson. FaBoEn; MOAP
She rose up from her resemblances. To the Infinite. Paul Eluard. MiCF
She roves through shadowy solitudes. Tacita. James Benjamin Kenyon. AA
She Said . . . Jonathan Henderson Brooks. PoNe
She said, 'I was not born to mope at home in loneliness." The Ride round the Parapet. Friedrich Rückert. AWP; JAWP; WBP
She said, in her profound manner. Pierrots (One Has Principles). Jules Laforgue. AnFP
She said, "Not only music; brave men marching." She Said . . . Jonathan Henderson Brooks. PoNe
She said she would come. The Monk Sosei, *tr. fr. Japanese by* Kenneth Rexroth. OnPJ
She said she'd been to Camden Town. She Reports No Progress. Patience Eden. DDA
She Said the Same to Me, *with music. Unknown.* AS
She said: The world is empty that we loved. Eternal. Agnes Foley Macdonald. CaP
She said: then, raging to Sir Plume repairs. Pope. *Fr.* The Rape of the Lock. MyFE
She said, "They gave me of their best." After Aughrim. Emily Lawless. GTIV; OBEV (new ed.); OxBI
She sang beyond the genius of the sea. The Idea of Order in Key West. Wallace Stevens. AmP; AmPP; CoBMV; MAP; MoAB; MoAmPo; MoPo; OxBA; Po
She sang her little bedtime air. Evening Prayer. Hermann Hagedorn. GoBC
She sang of lovers met to play. A Casual Song. Roden Noel. HBV
She sat and sewed that hath done me the wrong. Of His Love That Pricked Her Finger with a Needle. Sir Thomas Wyatt. ReIE; TCEP
She sat and wept beside His feet; the weight. "Multum Dilexit." Hartley Coleridge. EnRP; ERP; EV-4; HBV; VA
She sat beside her window through. O Plaguy Spring. Pierre Jean de Béranger. TrFP
She sat beside the mountain springs. The Forsaken. Hamilton Aidé. VA
She sat down below a thorn. The Cruel Mother [*or* Fine Flowers in the Valley]. *Unknown.* BaBo (A *vers.*); CBOV; ESPB (B *vers.*)
She sat her down upon his back and smiled. Europa and the Bull. Moschus. GrR
She sat just like the other ones at tea. Going Blind. Rainer Maria Rilke. TwGV
She sat on the sliding cushion. A Laugh in Church. *Unknown.* PTA-2
She sat upon the ground; there lay. Feodor Tyutchev, *tr. fr. Russian by* Maud F. Jerrold. BoR
She sate upon her Dobie. The Cummerbund. Edward Lear. CenHV
She saw the bayonets flashing in the sun. Memorial Day [*or* Decoration Day]. Richard Watson Gilder. MDAH; OHIP
She Says, Being Forbidden. Leonora Speyer. AV
She says, "But in contentment I still feel." Sunday Morning, IV [V]. Wallace Stevens. AnFE; AnNE; APA; CoAnAm; MAP; MAPA; MoAmPo; TriL
She says: "I am content when wakened birds." Sunday Morning, III [IV]. Wallace Stevens. AnFE; AnNE; APA; CoAnAm; MAP; MAPA; MoAmPo; TriL
She says, "The cock crows—hark!" The Parting Lovers. *Unknown.* LPS-1
She scarce had entered in the gate. Club Woman. Phyllis McGinley. QS
She Scorns Her Husband the Caliph. Lady Maisun, *tr. fr. Arabic by* R. A. Nicholson. LiTW
She seemed an angel to our infant eyes! A Mother's Picture. Edmund Clarence Stedman. MOAH; OHIP
She seemed so bored. The Great Offence. Abu Nuwas. LiTW
She sees her image in the glass. The Shadow Dance. Louise Chandler Moulton. AA; HBV
She sent eight sons against the foe. To a Spartan Mother. Dioscorides. GrR
She served love well. Elegy, Montreal Morgue. Goodridge MacDonald. CaP
She Sews Fine Linen. Julia Johnson Davis. HBMV
She shall attend the gods and be. The Daughters of Asopus. Corinna. OxBG
She sharpened her knife both sharp and keen. Young Hunting. *Unknown.* OxBoLi
She, she is dead; she's dead: when thou knowst this. John Donne. *Fr.* An Anatomy of the World. MyFE
She shook the flowering almond tree. The Almond Tree. Georgios Drossinis. MoGP
She Should Have Died Hereafter. Shakespeare. *See* Tomorrow and Tomorrow and Tomorrow.
"She should have had. . . ," I said, and there I stopped. After Speaking of One Dead a Long Time. Padraic Colum. GoYe
She should have had the state. Requiescat. Katherine Anne Porter HBMV
She should never have looked at me. Cristina. Robert Browning. BPN; EM-2; EmBrPo; EPN; GEPC; OAEP; PoVP; ViPo; VLEP
She shrank from all, and her silent mood. The Female Convict. Letitia Elizabeth Landon. LPS-1
She sighed, toward me turning. Frankincense. Ibn al-Zaqqaq. MooP
She Sighs on Her Jade Lute. Wen T'ing-yun, *tr. fr. Chinese by* Witter Bynner. ChLP
She sings a pious ballad wearily. The Street-Singer. Arthur Symons. POTT
She sings her wild dirges, and smiles 'mid the strain. Scene in a Madhouse. Aubrey Thomas De Vere. OnYI
She sits a queen whom none shall dare despoil. Australia, 1894. William Gay. BoAu
She sits all day plaiting a wild-rose wreath. June. *Unknown.* FEOR
She sits beneath the elder-tree. The Death-Child. "Fiona Macleod." VA
She sits in Sarras, delicate and strange. Our Lady with Two Angels. Wilfred Rowland Childe. ISi
She sits in the gathering shadows. At Fourscore. Eben E. Rexford. MotAn
She sits upon her pallet bed. A French Nun. Dinah Maria Mulock Craik. PraNu
She sits upon the tumulus [*or* on tumulus Savoor] and stares. Flax. Ivan Bunin. AWP; JAWP; TrRV; WBP
She sits with a son on her nursery knee. Mother. Keith Sinclair. AnNZ
She sits within a subway car. Girl in the Subway. Sydney King Russell. StaSt
She sits within the white oak hall. Helen. Edward A. U. Valentine. AA
She sitteth still who used to dance. Today for Me. Christina Rossetti. PoVP; VLEP
She sleeps;—Amaryllis. Amaryllis. *Unknown.* TeCS
She sleeps in bronze, the Helen of his dream. Noel Dark. W. W. Gibson. *Fr.* Casualties. VOD
She sleeps: peace crown thine eyes, sweet dreams in deep. Sickness, Not Sleep. *Unknown.* LO; SeCL
She smil'd, and more of pleasure than disdain. The Sea-Nymph's Parting. Walter Savage Landor. *Fr.* Gebir. FaBoEn
She Smiled like a Holiday. *Unknown.* OxBoLi
She smiles and smiles, and will not sigh. Urania. Matthew Arnold. HBV
She softly droops her maiden eyes. A Russian Spring Song with Minaiev. Thomas Walsh. GoBC
She sought him east, she sought him west. Rare Willy Drowned in Yarrow (B *vers.*). *Unknown.* ESPB

She sought the Studios, beckoning to her side. Heiress and Architect. Thomas Hardy. PoVP; ViP
She spake, and as she turned away, her roseate neck flashed bright. Venus the Goddess. Virgil. *Fr.* The Aeneid, I. LiA
She spends her life, far from the noisy mart. In the Cloister. William J. Fischer. PraNu
She spent her time recalling. Play-acting. Frances Barber. GoYe
She spoke and laughed, his back she sat upon. Europa and the Bull. Moschus. OxBG
She spoke, and rose, and opened the room-door. Medea's Hesitation. Apollonius Rhodius. *Fr.* Argonautica. OxBG
She spoke, and sadly from Oenone's eyes. Paris Is Dead. Quintus Smyrnaeus. *Fr.* Posthomerica. OxBG
She spoke to me gently with words of sweet meaning. Song. Patrick MacDonogh. NeIP
She sprawled on the border. Stolen Pleasure. Ibn Shuhaid. MooP
She stands as pale as Parian statues stand. A Soul. Christina Rossetti. BPN; EmBrPo
She stands full-throated and with careless pose. The Onondaga Madonna. Duncan Campbell Scott. PeCV
She stands in rusty black upon the curb. A Beggar for God. John Stigall. PraNu
She stands within the shadow, at the foot. Mater Dolorosa. John Fitzpatrick. JKCP
She stares from out the wagon as/ It trails the dimming road. The Woman in the Wagon. Clyde Robertson. PoOW
She stepped two paces forward. She. Vicente Huidobro. AnCL
She stole his eyes because they shone. Kleptomaniac. Leonora Speyer AnAmPo; HBMV; LA
She stood alone amidst the April fields. The Late Spring [*or* The Spring Is Late]. Louise Chandler Moulton. HBV; LPS-1
She stood at the bar of justice. "Guilty or Not Guilty?" *Unknown.* BeLS; BLPA; PTA-1
She stood beneath the mistletoe. Under the Mistletoe. George Francis Shults. BOHV
She stood breast high amid the corn. Ruth. Thomas Hood. EnLoPo; EnRP; EPN; EPP; ERP; EV-4; GN; GTBS-W; HBV; InP; LiTG; LiTL; LoBV; LPS-1; OBEV; OBRV; OnPP; OTPC; TOP; TreFS; VA; WP
She stood in all her slender grace. Moon of Loveliness. Mu'tamid, King of Seville. MooP
She Stoops to Conquer, *sel.* Goldsmith.
Song: "Let schoolmasters puzzle their brain[s]," *fr.* I, ii. OAEP; ViBoPo
("Let schoolmasters puzzle their brain.") EnLi-1 (1949 ed.)
(Three Jolly Pigeons, The.) PoRA
She surrendered without complaining. Konstantin Dmitreyevich Balmont, *tr. fr. Russian by* C. M. Bowra. BoR
She sweeps with many-coloured brooms. Evening. Emily Dickinson. BoTP
She Swims Back in the Crowning Hour. Bilhana, *formerly at. to* Chauras, *tr. fr. Sanskrit by* E. Powys Mathers. *Fr.* Black Marigolds. OnPM
She swings the lantern. Night around her. The Lantern. Richard Church. MBP; MoBrPo (1942 ed.)
She Tells Her Love While Half Asleep. Robert Graves. FaBoTw
She Tells Him How to Win the Fleece. Apollonius Rhodius, *tr. fr. Greek by* F. L. Lucas. *Fr.* Argonautica, III. GrPE
She that but little patience knew. On a Political Prisoner. W. B. Yeats. OBMV; PoE
She that denies me, I would have. Valerius on Women. Thomas Heywood. *Fr.* The Rape of Lucrece. HBV; LO
She that has that is clad in cómplete steel. Milton. *Fr.* Comus; a Masque. InP
She that I pursue, still flies me. Les Amours. Charles Cotton. ElSeCe; HBV
She That with Love Is Not Possessed. Elkanah Settle. *Fr.* Cambyses. SeCL
She, the one who should put me on to Woman! Another Lament of Lord Pierrot. Jules Laforgue. AnFP
She, then, like snow in a dark night. Like Snow. Robert Graves. AtBAP
She thinks that even up in heaven [*or* She even thinks that up in heaven]. A Lady I Know [*or* For a Lady I Know]. Countee Cullen. CDC; GoSl; MAP; MaRV; MoAmPo; PoNe
She, to Him. Thomas Hardy. BEL; ES; OBEV (new ed.); OBVV; TOP
She told the story, and the whole world wept. Harriet Beecher Stowe. Paul Laurence Dunbar. AA; DD
She, too, the voyaging in doors and Keys. This Alice. Herbert Morris. PoRA
She, too, whom men call "Iris" is but a mist in the skies. Rainbow. Xenophanes. GrPE
She took her then aside, and bade her heed. Lucius Apuleius, *tr. by* Robert Bridges. *Fr.* Eros and Psyche. BrBE
She took the last egg out of the basket. Evvie's Mother. Olive Tilford Dargan. LS; NoCaPo
She took the veil—how light a thing. Taking the Veil. *Unknown.* CAG
She tripped and fell against a star. Innocence. Anne Spencer. CDC
She turned in the high pew, until her sight. A Church Romance. Thomas Hardy. FaBoTw
She turned [*or* turn'd] the fair page with her fairer hand. Home, in War-Time. Sydney Dobell. VA
She turned the page of wounds and death. The Heart-Cry. Francis W. Bourdillon. POT
She Turns the Dolls' Faces to the Wall. W. B. Yeats. Upon a Dying Lady, III. LiTB
She used to let her golden hair fly free. Sonnet. Petrarch. Sonnets to Laura: To Laura in Life, LXIX. LyPI
She used to rock the cradle. They would leave her. Stepan Shchipachev, *tr. fr. Russian by* C. M. Bowra. BoRS
She wadna bake, she wadna brew. The Wife Wrapt in Wether's Skin. *Unknown.* BaBo (A *vers.*); ESPB
She walked along the crowded street. Revelation. Blanche Taylor Dickinson. CDC
She walked among the lilies. Mary. Margaret E. Sangster. DD; EOAH
She Walked Unaware. Patrick MacDonogh. FaBoTw; NeIP; OnYI; OxBI
She walked with God upon a golden morn. Vocation. Sister Mary David. PraNu
She Walks. Joseph Joel Keith. ISi
She walks among the loveliness she made. The Island. V. Sackville-West. *Fr.* The Land. MM
She walks as lightly as the fly. Charms. W. H. Davies. CaAE
She Walks in Beauty. Byron. AEV; AnFE; AtBAP; ATP; AWP; BEL; BLPA; BLV; BoLiVe; BPN; BTP; CaAE; CBOV; ChER; CoBE; EG; EM-2; EmBrPo; EnL; EnLi-2; EnLit; EnRP; EPN; EPP; ERP; EV-4; ExPo; FaBoBe; FaBoEn; FaFP; FiP; GBV (1952 ed.); GEPC; GTSE; GTSL; HBV; HBVY; HoPM; InP; InPo; JAWP; LEAP; LiTB; LiTG; LiTL; LO; LoBV; LoPo; LPS-1; MaPo; MCCG; NeHB; OAEP; OBEV; OBRV; OlF; OnPP; OTPC; OuHeWo; PFE; PG; PIR; PoEL-4; PoFS; PTA-1; REAL; ReaPo; SeCeV; ShBV-4; TreF; TrGrPo; TyEnPo; UnPo (1st ed.); WoL ("She walks in beauty, like the night.") GTBS-D; GTBS-W
She walks—the lady of my delight. The Shepherdess. Alice Meynell. ACP; AEV; AWP; CP; DD; EnLit; EPP; GBV; GoBC; GTSE; HBV; HBVY; JAWP; JKCP; MBP; MoBrPo; OBVV; OnPP; PoeT; PoVP; TCEP; TCPD; TreFS; TSW; TSWC; TVSH; VOD; WBP
"She Wandered after Strange Gods." Laura Benét. HBMV
She wanders in the April woods. Agatha. Alfred Austin. HBV; VA
She wanders like a shuttlecock, from side to side she flutters. The Girl from Tarentum. Naevius. LaP
She wanders up and down the main. Derelict. Elisabeth Cavazza Pullen. AA
She Warns Him. Frances Cornford. Two Poems, I. EnLoPo
She Was a Beauty. H. C. Bunner. AA; HBV
She Was a Child of February. Percy MacKaye. PR
She was a creature framed by love divine. A Wife. Sir Henry Taylor. *Fr.* Philip van Artevelde. LPS-1
She was a high-class bitch and a dandy. Epitaph. Theodore Spencer. LiTA
She was a little girl who smelled/ of nice cologne. Two Weeks. Nicolás Guillén. PoNe
She Was a Phantom of Delight. Wordsworth. AnFE; ATP (1935 ed.); BEL; BPN; BTP; EM-2; EmBrPo; EnLi-2; EnLit; EnRP; EPN; EPP; ERP; EV-3; FaBoBe; FaFP; GEPC; GTBS; GTBS-D; GTBS-W; GTSE; GTSL; HiLiEn; LiTB; LiTL; LoBV; LPS-1; MCCG; NeHB; OAEP; OBRV; OHFP; OnPP; OTPC; OuHeWo; PECK; PIAE; PIR; PoEL-4; PTA-2; TCEP; TOP; TrGrPo; TVSH; TwP; ViBoPo (Perfect Woman.) BCEP; HBV; LEAP; OBEV; TreF
She Was a Pretty Little Girl. Ramón Pérez de Ayala, *tr. fr. Spanish by* Alida Malkus. FaPON
She Was a Queen. Hartley Coleridge. *See* Solitary-hearted, The.
She was a quiet little body. Silence. Winifred Welles. HBMV
She was a stately lady. Changeling. Barbara Young. MoSiPe
She was a "sunbeam." Portrait. Hal Chadwick. DDA
She was a sweet country lassie. Blackpool Breezes. *Unknown.* CoMu
She was a Texas maiden, she came of low degree. The Transformation of a Texas Girl. James Barton Adams. SCC
She Was a Treasure. William Canton. TVC; TVSH
She was a Virgin of austere regard. Christ's Victory in Heaven. Giles Fletcher. *Fr.* Christ's Victory and Triumph. ViBoPo
She was a wild, wild song, and she is gone. Along the Wind. Chard Powers Smith. TBM

She was a woman now, with the heart and hopes of a woman. Longfellow. *Fr.* Evangeline. MotAn
She was a woman peerless in her station. Sonnet on Mistress Nicely [*or* On Mistress Nicely, a Pattern for Housekeepers]. Thomas Hood. NBE; OBRV
She Was All That You Loved. Halldór Laxness, *tr. fr. Icelandic by* Magnús Á. Árnason. LiTW
She was as lovely as a flower. Dream Tryst. Richard Le Gallienne. HBMV
She was born inland in the open country. Flood Tide. Marjorie Alice Miller. NLK (1947 ed.)
She Was Carrying the Lamp. Rafael Méndez Dorich, *tr. fr. Spanish by* Donald Devenish Walsh. AnCL; OnPM
She was in a village by a forest side. "Feodor Sologub," *tr. fr. Russian by* V. de S. Pinto. BoR
She was lufly of lere and of lore wise. Medea. *Unknown. Fr.* Gest Hystoriale of the Destruction of Troy. NBE
She was never a dog that had much sense. Of an Ancient Spaniel in Her Fifteenth Year. Christopher Morley. WaKn
She was not as pretty as women I know. My Kate. Elizabeth Barrett Browning. OBVV; OHFP; WBLP
She was only a woman, famished for loving. A Tragedy. Théophile Marzials. BMEP; HBV; LEAP
She Was Poor but She Was Honest. *Unknown. See* Poor but Honest.
She was skilled in music and the dance. Alas! Poor Queen. Marion Angus. GoTS
She was so aesthetic and culchud. The Cultured Girl Again. Ben King. FiBHP
She was so beautiful, she could not see. Dirge for Beauty. Marion Eells. CAG
She was so little—little in her grave. The Mother Who Died Too. Edith M. Thomas. AA
She was the daughter of Glubstein the Glover. Villanelle of a Villaness. Edwin Meade Robinson. HBMV
She Was the Girl within the Picture Frame. Delmore Schwartz. FiMAP
She was the human chalice. Venite Adoremus. Margery Cannon. GoBC
She was wearing the coral taffeta trousers. Full Moon. V. Sackville-West. AlDL; DiM; MBP; MoBrPo (1942 ed.); MoShBr; PtOT; TwCV
She Was Young and Blithe and Fair. Harold Monro. HBV
She wears a rose in her hair. Under the Rose. Richard Henry Stoddard. PR
She wears, my beloved, a rose upon her head. Requiem. John Frederick Matheus. CDC
She weaves away at the bower. To-and-Fro of Saint Theresa. Alfonso Reyes. AnMP
She Weeps over Rahoon. James Joyce. NP; TIP; ViBoPo
She welcomes him with pretty impatience. The Visit. Ogden Nash. FiBHP
She went about accustomed tasks. Loss. Julia Johnson Davis. HBMV
She went into the wood where serpents are. Legend. Vincent Starrett. DaM
She went round and asked subscriptions. A Cosmopolitan Woman. Sam Walter Foss. BOHV
She went to buy a brand new hat. Red. Countee Cullen. GoSl
She went to plain-work and to purling brooks. Away from London. Pope. *Fr.* An Epistle to Martha Blount on Her Leaving Town after the Coronation. BeR
She went up the mountain to gather sweet orchids. Old Song. *Unknown.* WhP
She went up the mountain to pluck wild herbs. Old and New. *Unknown, tr. by* Arthur Waley. AWP; LiTW; TrCh
She wept, sweet lady. La Bella Donna. Dante Gabriel Rossetti. TCEP
She, who could neither rest nor sleep. Alas! Sadi. *Fr.* The Gulistan. AWP; WoL
She who had lured them. Lilith. Calvin Holmes. CAG
She who hath felt a real pain. John Gay. EnLoPo
She who refuses to her young ones lip. Infancy. Hugh Downman. PoP
She, who so long has lain. New Love, New Life. Amy Levy. OBVV
She who to Heaven more Heaven doth annex. On a Virtuous Young Gentlewoman That Died Suddenly. William Cartwright. OBEV
She who was easy for any chance lover. Effie. Sterling A. Brown. BANP
She who with innocent and tender hands. The Monstrous Marriage. William Carlos Williams. MoPo
She who yielded once. On a Bereaved Girl. Alun Lewis. SoV
She whom I love will sit apart. Song. Gerald Gould. MBP; MoBrPo (1942 ed.)
She whose matchless beauty staineth. *Unknown.* OBSC
She, wild with wantonness, to her two suitors. The Wanton's Death. Norman Cameron. FaBoTw
She will come yet I think, although she said. Pleasure and Guilt. Arthur Hugh Clough. *Fr.* Dipsychus Continued. VLEP
She Will Go Softly. Mildred Anne Cook. CAG
She, with heavy heart. Demeter at Eleusis. Hesiod. *Fr.* Homeric Hymns. OxBG
She with his sight made breathless haste to meet him. Homer, *tr. by* George Chapman. *Fr.* The Iliad, VI. ViBoPo
She with Young Limbs. Bilhana, *formerly at. to* Chauras, *tr. fr. Sanskrit by* E. Powys Mathers. *Fr.* Black Marigolds. OnPM
She woke at length, but not as sleepers wake. The Death of Haidée. Byron. *Fr.* Don Juan, IV. FiP
She wore a new "terra-cotta" dress. A Thunderstorm in Town. Thomas Hardy. EnLoPo
She Wore a Wreath of Roses. Thomas Haynes Bayly. BeLS; VA
She wore her halo rakishly. Haloes. Idella Purnell. DDA
She Would. Dixie Willson. GFA
She would have liked the smallest things. Exile. Kathryn White Ryan. TBM
She Would if She Could, *sel.* Sir George Etherege.
To Little or No Purpose I Spent Many Days. SeCL; SeEP
She wrapped her flesh in raiment which the Hours. Flowery Garments. Cypria. OxBG
She yields: my Lady in her noblest mood. Modern Love, XXXIX. George Meredith. ViPo
Sheaf, The. Andrew Young. ChTr
Sheaf, a sheaf, send, send a great sheaf, A. Songs of Work. *Unknown.* OxBG
Shear sheep that have them, cry we still. A Round. William Browne. ElSeCe
Shearer's Wife, The. Louis Esson. BoAu
Shearing. David McKee Wright. AnNZ
Shears and paper. The Kite. Fang Che Chai. OnPM; PoHN
Sheath and Knife. *Unknown.* CH; ESPB (A *and* E *vers.*); ViBoFo
("One king's daughter said to anither.") LO
Sheaves, The. E. A. Robinson. AWP; CoBMV; InPo; JAWP; MAP; MaPo; MoAB; MoAmPo; MOAP; NePA; OxBA; ReaPo; ReMP; RiBV; TBM; TOP; TwP; WBP; WHA; YT
Sheba, now let down your hair. The Puppet Dreams. Conrad Aiken. *Fr.* Punch, the Immortal Liar. MAP; MoAmPo
Shebear, The. William Douw Lighthall. CPG
Shed, The. Charles L. O'Donnell. ISi
Shed no tear! oh shed no tear! Faery Song [*or* Fairy Song]. Keats. CH; EV-4; FaPON; HBV; HOAH; LPS-3; OTPC; PECK
Shed not a tear upon this burial place. Epitaph for Elizabeth Ranquet. Corneille. CAW
Shed Not Too Many Tears. *Unknown.* MaRV
Shed o'er our choir, Olympian dominations. To Athens. Pindar. OxBG
Shee brought her to her joyous paradize. The Garden of Adonis. Spenser. *Fr.* The Faerie Queene, III. PoEL-1
Shee is dead; and all which die. The Dissolution. John Donne. OAEP; SeCV-1
Shee said: Lullabye, mine owne deere child! *Unknown.* BOL
Shee with whom troopes of Bustuary slaves. A Satyre Entituled the Witch. *Unknown.* CoMu
Sheep. W. H. Davies. BMEP; ChMo; CMP; LiTM; MBP; MoBrPo; PoTo; PrWP; StPo
Sheep. Samuel Hoffenstein. AnAmPo; LA; TrJP
Sheep, The "Seumas O'Sullivan." GTIV; OxBI
Sheep, The. Hal Porter. NeLNL
Sheep. Keidrych Rhys. MoWP
Sheep, The. Ann Taylor. BoChLi; BoTP; MPB; OTPC; RAR; UTS
(Boy and the Sheep, The.) PRWS
Sheep!/ Unhappy connotation. Bleat of Protest. Mildred Weston. FiBHP
Sheep and Lambs. Katharine Tynan. AnIV; BoTP; GTIV; HBV; JKCP; MBP; OBEV; OBVV; OnYI; OTPC (1946 ed.); OxBI; PoRL, *abr.*; PRWS; StJW; VA; WHL
Sheep are coming home in Greece, The. The Homecoming of the Sheep. Francis Ledwidge. EnLit; HBMV; LBBV; TIP; VOD; YT
Sheep are yarded, an' I sit, The. The Old Black Billy an' Me. Louis Esson. BoAu; NeLNL
Sheep Beezness, The. S. Omar Barker. IHA
Sheep-bell tolleth curfew-time, The. An Evening Scene. Coventry Patmore. BLV
Sheep Fair, The. Thomas Hardy. NV
Sheep Herd. *See* Sheepherd.
Sheep in the Ruins, The. Archibald MacLeish. CoV
Sheep in the Shade. William Barnes. EnSW
Sheep-washing, The. James Thomson. *Fr.* The Seasons: Summer. EnLi-2; EPP
(Sheep Shearing, The.) CoBE
Sheepfol', De ("Po' lil' brack sheep"). *At. to* Paul Laurence Dunbar, *also to* Sarah Pratt McLean Greene. MaRV
(Little Black Sheep, The.) WBLP

Sheepfol', De ("De Massa . . ."). Sarah Pratt McLean Greene. AA; CBOV; HBV
(Massa ob de Sheepfol, De.) BAP; LBMV; OQP; POT; QP-2
Sheepheard, what's Love, I pray thee tell? The Shepherd's Description of Love. Sir Walter Ralegh *and* Edward de Vere. EPP; EV-1
Sheepheards Daffadill, The. Michael Drayton. *See* Gorbo and Batte.
Sheep Herd, The. Sister Mariella. ChrBoLe; WHL
Sheep-Herder, The. Badger Clark. IHA; SCC
Sheepherder, The. Lew Sarett. FaPON; GaP
Sheep Herders. Maurice Lesemann. NP
Sheepstor. L. A. G. Strong. HBMV
Sheer over to the other side,—for see. The Idiot. Hart Crane. PoFS
Sheer through his neck's soft skin the point of the weapon sprang. The Fallen Olive-Tree. Homer. *Fr.* The Iliad, XVII. GrPE
Sheer whistles, noon's rejoinder to the wheel's spin. Whistles and Wheels. Alfred G. Bailey. PeCV
Sheet Lightning. Edmund Blunden. HaMV
Sheet of water which reflects the house, The. Ornamental Water. Louise Townsend Nicholl. NePoAm
Sheets of night mist travel a long valley, The. Mist Forms. Carl Sandburg. ChMo; CMP
Sheets were frozen hard, and they cut the naked hand, The. Christmas at Sea. Robert Louis Stevenson. BBV (1951 ed.); CH; EtS; FaBoBe; HBV; MCCG; OBVV; OTPC (1946 ed.); PCN; PoVP; SG; ShBV-2; StaSt; StPo
Sheffield Dawn. D. G. Bridson. MuP
Shekel in the Fish's Mouth, The. Francis Quarles. StJW
Shekhinah. Karl Wolfskehl, *tr. fr. German by* Carol North Valhope *and* Ernst Morwitz. TrJP
Sheldonian Soliloquy. Siegfried Sassoon. UnS
Shell, The. James Stephens. AlDL; BLV; BoTP; CH; ChMo; CMP; EPP; MBP; MM; MoAB; MoBrPo; MoShBr; MoVE; NeMA; PoeMoYo; POT; POTE; PoTo; YT
Shell, The. Tennyson. *Fr.* Maud, Pt. II, ii. BoTP; GN; SN; VA
("See what a lovely shell.") BPN; PoEL-5
Shell, The. Mary Webb. AlDL
She'll Be Comin' round the Mountain (A *and* B *vers.*), *with music.* *Unknown.* AS
Shell Castles. Rowena Bastin Bennett. GFA; UTS
She'll come at dusky first of day. August. Francis Ledwidge. OxBI
Shell Secrets. *Unknown.* BoTP
Shellbrook. William Barnes. EnSW
Shelley. Robert Browning. *Fr.* Pauline. OBRV
Shelley. Paul Hamilton Hayne. SPP; TCAP
Shelley. Alexander Hay Japp. VA
Shelley. Henry van Dyke. VOD
Shelley and Harriet Westbrook. Sir William Watson. BMEP
(From "Epigrams.") LEAP
Shelley, madman, made his rhymes. Wiser than the Children of Light. Monk Gibbon. NeIP
Shelley! whose song so sweet was sweetest here. To Shelley. Walter Savage Landor. ViBoPo
Shelley's Centenary. Sir William Watson. BMEP; PoVP; TCPD
Shelley's loves/ On fancies ripened. For a Little Lady. Fred Saidy. InMe; LauV
Shelley's Skylark. Thomas Hardy. CoBMV; PoVP; PtP; VLEP
Shellfish and octopus, and all the insane. Crab. John Blight. BoAV
Shelling Peas. Elizabeth Fleming. DDA
Shells, The. Walter Savage Landor. *Fr.* Gebir. BCEP
Shells. T. Sturge Moore. SeCePo
Shells. Kathleen Raine. ImOP
Shells in Rock. Elizabeth Madox Roberts. AnAmPo; LA
Shell's Song, The. Keats. EtS
Shelly. James McIntyre. FiBHP
Shelter. Charles Stuart Calverley. PCD
Shelter. Gene Derwood. NePA
Shelter, Food, and Company. Roger Williams. *See* God Makes a Path.
Sheltered beneath white hawthorn boughs. Anonymous Alba. *Unknown.* OuHeWo
Sheltered from the Spring wind by. The Old Anguish. Chu Shu Chen. OnPC
Sheltered Garden. Hilda Doolittle ("H. D."). PG
Sheltered garden in a sheltered land, A. Homer in a Garden. James Larkin Pearson. NoCaPo
Shema Yisrael. *Unknown.* TrJP
Shemuel. Edward Ernest Bowen. HBV
Shemus O'Brien. Joseph Sheridan Le Fanu. TIP
Shenandoah. Carl Sandburg. PaA
Shenandoah, *sel.* Delmore Schwartz.
Let Us Consider Where the Great Men Are. MoAB; MoAmPo
Shenandoah, The ("It's of a famous American ship"). *Unknown.* SoAmSa
Shenandoah ("Oh, Shenandoah, I love your daughter [*or* long to hear you]"), *with music.* *Unknown.* ABF, *diff. vers.*; AmSS; ShS; SoAmSa; TrAS
(Wide Mizzoura, The, *with music.*) AS
(Wild Miz-zou-rye, The, *longer vers.. with music.*) ABF
Shepard upon a hill he sat, The. *Unknown.* *See* Can I Not Sing.
Shepeheards boye, A (no better doe him call). January [Eclogue]. Spenser. *Fr.* The Shepheardes Calender. FiP; ReIE
Sheperd upon a hill he satt, The. *Unknown.* *See* Can I Not Sing.
Shepheard and the Milkmaid, The. *Unknown.* CoMu
Shepheard, What's Loue? *At. to* Sir Walter Ralegh. *See* Shepherd's Description of Love, The.
Shepheardes [*or* Shepheards *or* Shepherd's] Calender, The, *sels.* Spenser.
April [*or* Aprill]. EnLi-1; PoEL-1; ReEn; ReIE; SiCE
Ditty, A: "See where she sits upon the grassy green," 6 *sts.* FaBoCh; OBEV
("See where she sits upon the grassy green," 2 *sts.*) ViBoPo
Elisa. CoEV; OBSC
(Hobbinal's Lay of Fair Elisa.) ElSeCe
("Ye dayntye nymphs, that in this blessed brooke.") AtBAP
August. OAEP; ReEn
Perigot and Willie's [*or* Willye's] Roundelay. ElSeCe; EV-1
(It Fell upon a Holy Eve.) PoE
(Perigot and Willye.) LoBV
(Roundelay, A: "It fell upon a holy eve.") EIL
December. BrBE
Februarie. EPP
Oak and the Brere, The. OBSC
January Eclogue. FiP
(January.) ReIE
July. ReIE
June. EnLit
November. MaPo; PoEL-1
Dido My Dear, Alas, Is Dead. ChTr
"Up then Melpomene thou mournefulst muse of nyne." AtBAP
October. NBE; ReEn; ReIE; SiCE
(Contempt of Poetry, The.) OBSC
"But, ah! Maecenas is yclad in clay," *br. sel.* MyFE; PoD
To His Book[e], *dedicatory sonnet.* CaAE; ReIE; SiCE
Shepheards boy (best knowen by that name), The. Spenser. *Fr.* Colin Clout's Come Home Again. ReIE
Shepheard's Hunting, The. George Wither. See Shepherd's Hunting, The.
Shepheards Sirena, The. Michael Drayton. *See* Shepherd's Sirena.
Shepheards that wont on pipes of oaten reed. Astrophel [*or* Death of Astrophel]. Spenser. EV-1; LiA
Shepherd, The. Blake. *Fr.* Songs of Innocence. BoTP; BrBE; EiPP; EnRP; ExPo; GaP; GoTP; HBV; KN; LoBV; OBEC; OTPC; PoRh; ThWaDe; TiPo (1959 ed.); TOP; TVC; TVSH
Shepherd. Edmund Blunden. HBMV
Shepherd. Leonidas of Tarentum. *See* Dead Shepherd, The.
Shepherd, The. Sir Walter Scott. *Fr.* Marmion, *introd. to* IV. ERP
(Shepherd in Winter, The.) OTPC (1923 ed.)
Shepherd and a shepherdess, A. Carol. Clément Marot. FoS
Shepherd and His Dog, The. William Lisle Bowles. EnSW
Shepherd and Shepherdess. Nicholas Breton. *See* Merry Country Lad, The.
Shepherd and Shepherdess. Thomas Hennell. FaBoTw
Shepherd and the Hawk, The. William Hart-Smith. AnNZ
Shepherd and the King, The. Eleanor Farjeon. TiPo (1952 ed.)
Shepherd and the King, The. Robert Greene. *See* Shepherd's Wife's Song, The.
Shepherd and the Philosopher, The. John Gay. CEP
Shepherd Boy, The. Heine, *tr. fr. German.* BoTP
Shepherd Boy, The. Edward Joseph O'Brien. HBMV
Shepherd Boy, The. Marjorie Pickthall. CPG
Shepherd boy a kingdom rules, The. The Shepherd Boy. Heine. BoTP
Shepherd-Boy and the Wolf, The. Aesop, *rhymed tr. fr. Greek by* William Ellery Leonard. AWP; JAWP; MPB; WBP
Shepherd boy lies on the hill, The. Noontide. John Keble. OTPC (1923 ed.)
Shepherd Boy Sings [in the Valley of Humiliation], The. Bunyan. *See* Shepherd Boy's Song, The.
Shepherd-boy, that hastens now and then, The. John Clare. *Fr.* The Shepherd's Calendar. GTBS-D
Shepherd Boys, The. Nicolas Saboly, *tr. fr. Provencal.* OHIP
Shepherd Boy's Day, The. Stefan George, *tr. fr. German by* David Luke. AnGP

Shepherd boys have met in their assembly, The. The Shepherd Boys. Nicolas Saboly. OHIP
Shepherd Boy's Song, The. Bunyan. *Fr.* The Pilgrim's Progress. BOL; BoTP; LEAP, *abr.*; MaRV; OTPC (1923 ed.); PCH, *st.* 1; TVSH
(Enough.) BLRP
("He that is down, needs fear no fall.") SeEP
(Shepherd Boy Sings [in the Valley of Humiliation], The.) EG; GBV; GN; GoTP; HBV; HBVY; OBEV; OQP; QP-2; WGRP
(Shepherd Boy's Song in the Valley of Humiliation, The.) CaAE
(Shepherd's Song, The.) OxBoCh
(Song [of the Shepherd] in the Valley of Humiliation.) BCEP; EV-2; OBS
Shepherd Dog and the Wolf, The. John Gay. AlBD
Shepherd Dog of the Pyrenees, The. Ellen Murray. PoRL
Shepherd: Echo, I ween, will in the wood reply. *See* Echo, I ween . . .
Shepherd Folk Go to Bethlehem, The. Nicolas Saboly, *tr. fr. Provençal by* Anne Macdonnell. CAW
Shepherd in Winter, The. Sir Walter Scott. *See* Shepherd, The.
Shepherd Jesus, in Thy arms. A Child's Evening Hymn. George Herbert Clarke. BOL
Shepherd Kept Sheep on a Hill so High, A. Thomas D'Urfey. CoMu
Shepherd Left Behind, The. Mildred Plew Meigs. ChBR
Shepherd Maiden, A. Edward Cracroft Lefroy. *Fr.* Echoes from Theocritus. VA
Shepherd of Eager Youth. Clement of Alexandria, *tr. fr. Greek by* Henry M. Dexter. MaRV, 3 *sts.*
(Earliest Christian Hymn, The.) BePJ
Shepherd of King Admetus, The. James Russell Lowell. HBVY; IAP; MOAP; OBAV; OnHT; PECK; TOP
Shepherd of Meriador, The. Wilfred Rowland Childe. HBMV
Shepherd of souls, refresh and bless. James Montgomery. OIF
Shepherd of tender youth. The Earliest Christian Hymn. Clement of Alexandria. BePJ
Shepherd saw thou not my fair lovely Philis. *Unknown.* SeCSL
Shepherd set him under a thorn, A. The Merry Bagpipes. *Unknown.* CoMu
Shepherd, Shepherd, Hark. St. Theresa of Avila, *tr. fr. Spanish by* Arthur Symons. AWP; CAW; LiTW
Shepherd, show me how to go. Mary Baker Eddy. OIF
Shepherd Song. Sir Philip Sidney. *Fr.* Arcadia. SiPS
Shepherd Speaks, The. John Erskine. ChIP; MaRV; OQP; QP-1
Shepherd! that [*or* who] with thine amorous, sylvan song. The Good Shepherd. Lope de Vega, *tr. by* Longfellow. BePJ; CAW; TeCS
Shepherd to His Love, The. Christopher Marlowe. *See* Passionate Shepherd to His Love, The.
Shepherd to the Poet, The. Agnes Kendrick Gray. BAP; POT; PoTo
Shepherd, to yon tall poplars tune your flute. Song of Poplars. Aldous Huxley. MBP; MoBrPo (1942 ed.); TwCV
Shepherd upon a [*or* the] Hill, The. *Unknown.* *See* Can I Not Sing.
Shepherd, what's love, I pray thee tell? The Shepherd's Description of Love [*or* Shepheard, What's Loue?]. *At. to* Sir Walter Ralegh. EPP; EV-1; NBE; ViBoPo
Shepherd, who can pass such wrong. The Nymph Selvagia [*or* Song]. Jorge de Montemayor, *tr. by* Bartholomew Young. *Fr.* Diana. ElL; ElSeCe; SiCE; TuPP
Shepherd Who Stayed, The. Theodosia Garrison. ChrBoLe; MW; OHIP; SDH
Shepherd! who with thine amorous, sylvan song. *See* Shepherd! that with . . .
Shepherd, wilt thou take counsel of the bird. Philomel to Corydon. William Young. AA
Shepherd Wind, The. Virna Sheard. CPG
Shepherd, wouldst thou here obtain. Inscription: On the Back of a Gothic Seat. William Shenstone. EiPP
Shepherdes Calender, The. Spenser. *See* Shepheardes Calender, The.
Shepherdess. Norman Cameron. Three Love Poems, III. FaBoTw
Shepherdess, The. Alice Meynell. ACP; AEV; AWP; CP; DD; EnLit; EPP; GBV; GoBC; GTSE; HBV; HBVY; JAWP; JKCP; MBP; MoBrPo; OBVV; OnPP; PoeT; PoVP; TCEP; TCPD; TreFS; TSW; TSWC; TVSH; VOD; WBP
(Lady of the Lambs, The.) GTSL; LEAP; OBEV
Shepherdess of porcelain, facing a snowy flock. Porcelain of the North. Rafael Méndez Dorich. AnCL
Shepherdess of the Shell, The. Stanley Pillsbury. CAG
Shepherdess' Song. Sir Philip Sidney. *See* My True Love Hath My Heart.
Shepherds, The. Samuel Taylor Coleridge. *See* Christmas Carol, A: "Shepherds went their hasty way, The."
Shepherds, The. William Drummond of Hawthornden. COAH
(For the Nativity of Our Lord—Shepherds.) StJW
Shepherds, The. Sophie Jewett. ChrBoLe
Shepherds, The. Laura Spencer Portor. PEDC
Shepherds, The. Beren Van Slyke. GoYe
Shepherds, The. Henry Vaughan. AnEC
Shepherds all, and maidens fair. Evening Song [*or* Folding the Flocks]. John Fletcher. *Fr.* The Faithful Shepherdess, II, i. CaAE; CenL; CG; CH; ElL; EV-2; GN; LPS-2; OBS; OTPC (1923 ed.); WP
Shepherds all, that wander this ridge of the mountains, feeding. The Shepherd's Last Sleep. Leonidas of Tarentum. GrPE
Shepherds almost wonder where they dwell, The. November. John Clare. GoTP
Shepherds and stars are quiet with the hills. V. Sackville-West. *Fr.* The Land. ShBV-4
Shepherd's Anthem, The. Michael Drayton. ReIE
Shepherds at Bethlehem, The. *Unknown.* *See* Haylle, Comly and Clene.
Shepherd's boy, A (he seeks no better name). Summer. Pope. *Fr.* Pastorals. CaAE; CEP; EiPP; ReaPo
Shepherds buried the sun in a naked forest. Rest and Silence. Georg Trakl, *tr. by* Werner Heider. LiTW
Shepherds buried the sun in the bare wood. Peace and Silence. Georg Trakl, *tr. by* Glauco Cambon. OnPM
Shepherd's Calendar, The, *sels.* John Clare.
"Loud is the summer's busy song," *fr.* July. GoTP; OBRV
"Milkmaid singing, The," *fr.* February. OBRV
"Shepherd-boy, that hastens now and then, The," *fr.* March. GTBS-D
Shepherd's Calendar, The. Spenser. *See* Shepheardes Calender, The.
Shepherd's Coat, A. Lilian Bowes-Lyon. ChMP; GTBS-D
Shepherd's Complaint, A. Richard Barnfield. *See* Unknown Shepherd's Complaint, The.
Shepherd's Complaint, The, *sel.* John Dickenson.
Tityrus to His Fair Phyllis. ElL
Shepherd's Conceit of Prometheus, The. Sir Edward Dyer. *See* Prometheus When First from Heaven.
Shepherd's Daffodil, The. Michael Drayton. *See* Gorbo and Batte.
Shepherd's daughter watching sheep, A. The Knight and Shepherd's Daughter (B *vers.*). *Unknown.* BaBo
Shepherd's Description of Love, The. *At. to* Sir Walter Ralegh. EPP; EV-1; ViBoPo
(Shepheard, What's Loue?) NBE
Shepherd's Despair, The. Thomas Dermody. OnYI
Shepherd's Dirge, The. George Peele. *See* Dirge: "Welladay, welladay, poor Colin."
Shepherd's Dream, A. Nicholas Breton. ReIE
Shepherd's Garland, The, *sels.* Michael Drayton.
Batte's Song: "Love is the heaven's fair [*or* fayre] aspect," *fr.* Eclogue VII (1593 ed.). LO; NBE
Batte's Song: "What is love but the desire," *fr.* Eclogue VII (1606 ed.). LoBV
Cassamen and Dowsabell, *fr.* Eclogue VIII (1593 ed.). OBSC
(Ballad of Dowsabell, The.) LoBV
(Eighth Eclogue, The.) ReEn; TuPP
Eclogue IX: "Late 'twas in June" (1606 ed.). OBSC
Gorbo and Batte, *fr.* Eclogue IX (1606 ed.). LoBV
(Daffodil.) EV-1; WP
("Gorbo, as thou cam'st [*or* camest] this way.") CenL; ViBoPo
(Ninth Eclogue, The.) OAEP; TuPP
(Roundelay, The.) ElSeCe
(Shepherd's Daffodil, The.) ElL
Ninth Eglog, The: "What time the weatherbeaten flocks" (1593 ed.). ReIE
Rowland's Rhyme, *fr.* Eclogue II (1606 ed.). OBSC
Song to Beta: "O thou fair silver Thames," *fr.* Eclogue III (1593 ed.). OBSC
("Stay, Thames, to heare my song," *fr.* Eclogue III, 1606 ed.) PoEL-2
Sylvia, *fr.* Eclogue IX (1606 ed.). LoBV (1949 ed.)
(Roundelay, A: "Tell me, thou skilful shepherd's swain.") ElL
Shepherd's Gift, A. Anyte. *See* On a Fountain.
Shepherd's Gratitude, The. Virgil, *tr. fr. Latin.* Eclogues, I. AWP, *tr. by* Charles Stuart Calverley; RoL, *pr. tr. by* Minnie Jameson Smith
Shepherds Had an Angel, The. Christina Rossetti. MaRV; OHIP; SDH
(Christmas Carol, A: "Shepherds had an angel, The.") BoChLi
Shepherds him with praise attended. Queen Pastores Laudaverunt. *Unknown.* LaP
Shepherd's Holiday, The, *sel.* Joseph Rutter.
Hymen. SeCL
Shepherd's Holiday. Elinor Wylie. CrMA; HBMV; PoTo
Shepherd's Home, The. William Shenstone. *See* Hope.
Shepherd's Hour, The. Paul Verlaine, *tr. fr. French by* Muriel Kittel. AnFP

Shepherd's Hunting, The, *sels.* George Wither.
Fourth Eglogue, The, *abr.* SeCV-1
"None ere drunke the Thespian spring," *fr.* Eclogue IV. NBE
On the Muse of Poetry, *fr.* Eclogue IV. EV-2
Philarete Praises Poetry, *fr.* Eclogue IV. OBS
("Seest thou not in clearest days," *longer sel.*) EPS
Shepherd's Hut, The. Andrew Young. ThWaDe
Shepherds Hymn Their Saviour. Richard Crashaw. *See* Hymn Sung as by the Shepherds, A.
Shepherds, I have lost my love. The Banks of Banna. George Ogle. IrPN
Shepherds in Judea, The. Mary Austin. ChrBoLe; COAH; DD; SDH
Shepherd's Lament, The. Goethe, *tr. fr. German by* Bayard Taylor. AWP; JAWP; WBP
Shepherd's Last Sleep, The. Leonidas of Tarentum. *See* Dead Shepherd, The.
Shepherd's Life, A. Shakespeare. *See* King Henry VI Yearns for the Simple Life.
Shepherd's Madrigal, The. Geraldine Farrar. StJW
Shepherd's Moan, A. William Browne. *See* Glide Soft, Ye Silver Floods.
Shepherd's Ode, The. Robert Greene. *Fr.* Tullie's Love. OBSC
Shepherd's Oracles, The, *sel.* Francis Quarles.
Christmas Carol, A: "Glory to God on high, and jolly mirth." AnEC
Shepherd's Pipe, The, *sels.* William Browne.
Dawn of Day, *fr.* Eclogue III. EIL
Fourth Eclogue. EPS
Shepherd's Plea, The. Christopher Marlowe. *See* Passionate Shepherd to His Love, The.
Shepherd's Praise of Diana, The. Sir Walter Ralegh. *See* Praised Be Diana's Fair and Harmless Light.
Shepherd's Psalm, The. Psalms, XXIII, Bible, *O.T. See* Lord Is My Shepherd, The.
Shepherds Rejoice. Isaac Watts. SDH
Shepherd's Resolution, The. George Wither. *See* Shall I, Wasting in Despair.
Shepherds, rise, and shake off sleep! Morning Song. John Fletcher. *Fr.* The Faithful Shepherdess, V. EV-2
Shepherd's [*or* Shepheards] Sirena, The, *sel.* Michael Drayton.
Sirena ("Near to the silver Trent"). EV-1; OBEV, *abr.*; SeCL
(Jovial Shepheard's Song, The.) PoEL-2
("Near to the silver Trent.") SeEP; TuPP
(Song to Sirena.) AtBAP
Shepherd's Song, The. Joanna Baillie. EBSV; EV-3
Shepherd's Song, The. Edmund Bolton. AnEC; COAH; EV-1
(Carol, A: "Sweet music, sweeter far.") OxBoCh
Shepherd's Song, The. Bunyan. *See* Shepherd Boy's Song, The.
Shepherd's Song. Norah M. Holland. ChrBoLe
Shepherd's Song. Tennyson. *See* Come Down, O Maid.
Shepherd's Song of Venus and Adonis, The. Henry Constable. TuPP
Shepherd's Star, The. Juan Ramón Jiménez, *tr. fr. Spanish by* Anna Pursche. LiTW
Shepherd's star with trembling glint, The. En bateau. Paul Verlaine. AWP
Shepherd's Tale, A. Sir Philip Sidney. *Fr.* Arcadia. SiPS
Shepherds that on this mountain ridge abide. Cleitagoras. Leonidas of Tarentum. AWP
Shepherds there were who in the fields by night. Peace on Earth. Helen Wieand Cole. ChIP; OQP; QP-1
Shepherd's Tree, The. John Clare. GTML
Shepherd's Week, The, *sels.* John Gay.
Ballad Monger, The, *abr.* EV-3
Ditty, The. LoBV
Friday; or, The Dirge. CEP; EiPP
Blouzelinda's Death. BeR
Blouzelinda's Funeral. OBEC
Saturday; or, The Flights. EiPP
Thursday; or, The Spell. CEP; EiPP; PoEL-3
Shepherds went their hasty way, The. A Christmas Carol [*or* The Shepherds]. Samuel Taylor Coleridge. ISi; OxBoCh; StJW
Shepherds Who Pastures Seek. Herbert Trench. MM; NLK (1947 ed.)
(Song of the Larks at Dawn.) TVSH
Shepherd's Wife's Song, The. Robert Greene. *Fr.* Greene's Mourning Garment. CoEV; EIL; ElSeCe; EnLit; EPP; EV-1; HBV; LoBV; OBSC; PG; ReEn; SiCE; TOP; TuPP; ViBoPo
("Ah what is love? It is a pretty thing.") EG
(Shepherd and the King, The.) LPS-1
Shepherd's Wooing Dulcina, The. *At. to* Sir Walter Ralegh. *See* Dulcina.
Shepherds, ye that haunt these rocks. The Dead Shepherd. Leonidas of Tarentum, *tr. by* Walter Leaf. GrPo; GrR
Shepherds, ye who wander with your white flocks feeding. Shepherd. Leonidas of Tarentum, *tr. by* E. R. Bevan. OxBG
Sheppard in faith tell me. *Unknown.* SeCSL
Sheridan at Cedar Creek. Herman Melville. APW; BBV (1923 ed.); GA; LiTA; PAH; PreP
Sheridan's Ride. Thomas Buchanan Read. BBV; BeLS; BlG; BoHiPo; CBPC; CoBA; DD; FaBoBe; FaFP; GA; GN; HBV; HBVY; IAP; LPS-2; MC; MDAH; OBAV; OHFP; OHIP; OnHT; OnSP; OTPC; PaA; PAH; PAP; PECK; PTA-1; PYM; TCAP; TreF; TVSH; WBLP; YaD
Sheriff, The. Madison Cawein. *Fr.* The Mountain Still. SPP
Sheriff, The. William Morris. *Fr.* A Dream of John Ball. PoVP
Sheriff followed hard and fast, a muy hombre he. Dodge City, the End of the Trail. *Unknown.* CoSo
Sheriff is made a mighty lord, The. The Sheriff. William Morris. *Fr.* A Dream of John Ball. PoVP
Sherman. Richard Watson Gilder. AA; GA; MDAH; OBAV
Sherman's in Savannah. Oliver Wendell Holmes. GA; MC; PAH
Sherman's March to the Sea. Samuel H. M. Byers. DD; GA; PAH; PAP
(Song of Sherman's March to the Sea.) HBV; MC; OTPC
Sherpa gasped out as they mounted the slope, The. Poem, neither Hilláryous Norgay. Gardner E. Lewis. FiBHP
Sherry. Mokutaro Kinoshita, *tr. fr. Japanese by* Takamichi Ninomiya *and* D. J. Enright. PoLJ
Sherwood. Alfred Noyes. *See* Song of Sherwood, A.
She's a saucy fast packet and a packet of fame. The *Dreadnought, vers.* II. *Unknown.* ShS
She's All My Fancy Painted Him. "Lewis Carroll." ALV; BoN; CenHV; LiTL; NA; StaSt
She's an enchanting little Israelite. Orientale. W. E. Henley. BPN
She's bin out here a-teachin' fer this winter now a-past. Romance of the Range. Robert V. Carr. PoOW
She's But a Lassie Yet. James Hogg. *See* My Love She's But a Lassie Yet.
She's coming down the meadow from the hall of Sjugareby. The Virgin Mary. Erik Axel Karlfeldt. *Fr.* Poems on Dalecarlian Paintings. AnSL
She's Hoy'd Me Out o' Lauderdale. *Unknown.* CoMu
She's loveliest of the festal throng. The Rose and the Thorn. Paul Hamilton Hayne. AA; FaBoBe; TCAP
She's Pretty to Walk With. Sir John Suckling. *Fr.* The Discontented Colonel. ALV; SeCL
She's running up for Callao in the blue Pacific weather. Callao. Crosbie Garstin. PoeMoYo
She's somewhere in the sunlight strong. Song. Richard Le Gallienne. HBV; LBMV; OBEV; OBVV
She's tall and gaunt, and in her hard, sad face. Scrubber. W. E. Henley. *Fr.* In Hospital. PoVP
She's taught me that I mustn't bark. Remarks from the Pup. Burges Johnson. AIBD
She's the darlin' of the parish, she's the pride of Inniskillen. Rosleen. Sir Gilbert Parker. CPG
She's up there—Old Glory—where lightnings are sped. The Old Flag Forever [*or* Our Flag Forever]. Frank L. Stanton. DD; FOAH; HH; PGD; PSO; PTA-2
Sheskinbeg. Elizabeth Shane. HBMV
Shet yo' eyes, ma little pickaninny, go to sleep. You's Sweet to Yo' Mammy Jes' de Same. James Weldon Johnson. BOL
Shi King [*or* Shih Ching *or* Book of Odes *or* Book of Songs], *sels. Unknown, tr. fr. Chinese.*
Alienation of an Old Friend, *tr. by* William Jennings. BoFr
Book of Songs, The, *sels.* WhP
Elms of the Eastern Gate, *tr. by* Arthur Waley. LiTW
Fallen Leaves, *tr. by* Arthur Waley. LiTW
Farming, *tr. by* Arthur Waley. LiTW
Forsworn, *tr. by* Bernhard Karlgren. ChLP
Friendship Veers with Fortune, *tr. by* William Jennings. BoFr
Girl in the Carriage, The, *tr. by* Arthur Waley. LiTW
Glimpse of a Plain Cap, The, *tr. by* Arthur Waley. LiTW
How Goes the Night, *tr. by* Helen Waddell. AWP; JAWP; WBP
I Wait My Lord, *tr. by* Helen Waddell. AWP; JAWP; WBP
If Along the Highroad, *tr. by* Arthur Waley. LiTW
In Our Lane, *tr. by* Arthur Waley. LiTW
Maytime, *tr. by* L. Cranmer-Byng. AWP
Morning Glory, The, *tr. by* Helen Waddell. AWP; JAWP; WBP
Mulberry Trees, The, *tr. by* Bernhard Karlgren. ChLP
Ode I/XI/8: "How shall it be said that you have no clothes?" *tr. by* James Legge. BoFr
Ode I/X/7: "Lamb's wool and leopard's cuffs," *tr. by* James Legge. BoFr
Ode II/I/5: "On the trees go the blows," *st.* 1, *tr. by* James Legge. BoFr

Ode I/VI/10: "There is a solitary russet pear tree/ But its leaves," *tr. by* James Legge. BoFr
Ode I/X/10: "There is a solitary russet pear tree/ Growing," *tr. by* James Legge. BoFr
Ode I/X/12: "Would you gather the liquorice," *tr. by* James Legge. BoFr
Old Love Should Not Be Ruptured, *tr. by* William Jennings. BoFr
Pear-Tree, The, *tr. by* Allen Upward. AWP; JAWP; WBP
Philanderer, The, *tr. by* Henry H. Hart. PoHN
Soldier Thought Dead Returns Home, The, *tr. by* Arthur Waley. LiTW
Stirred Waters, The, *tr. by* Bernhard Karlgren. ChLP
Sun in the East, *tr. by* Arthur Waley. LiTW
Ten Acres, The, *tr. by* Bernhard Karlgren. ChLP
That Crafty Youth, *tr. by* Bernhard Karlgren. ChLP
"There grows an elm tree," *tr. by* Arthur Waley.
(Book of Odes.) MBP; MoBrPo (1942 ed.)
Trust Thy Last Friend against the World, *tr. by* William Jennings. BoFr
Under the Pondweed, *tr. by* Helen Waddell. AWP
We Achieve Our Joy, *tr. by* Bernhard Karlgren. ChLP
Wedding Song, *tr. by* Arthur Waley. LiTW
Wife, The, *tr. by* Henry H. Hart. OnPM; PoHN; WoL
Wind and Violent Weather, *tr. by* Bernhard Karlgren. ChLP
Woman, *tr. by* H. A. Giles. AWP; LiTW
You Will Die, *tr. by* H. A. Giles. AWP; JAWP; WBP
Shield, The. Hafsa, *tr. fr. Arabic by* A. J. Arberry. MooP
Shield. *Unknown, tr. fr. Anglo-Saxon by* Charles W. Kennedy. *Fr.* Riddles. AnOE
Shield from every dart, The. What Christ Is to Us. *Unknown.* BLRP
Shield of Achilles, The. W. H. Auden. NePA; OAEP (2d ed.)
Shield of Achilles, The. Homer, *tr. fr. Greek. Fr.* The Iliad, XVIII. GrPE, *tr. by* F. L. Lucas; GrR, *tr. by* Pope; OxBG, *abr., tr. by* Pope
(Achilles' Shield, *tr. by* George Chapman.) ReEn
("This said, he left her there, and forth did to his bellows go," *tr. by* George Chapman.) TuPP
(Vulcan Forges the Shield of Achilles, *tr. by* George Chapman.) KN
Shield of Heracles, *sels.* Hesiod, *tr. fr. Greek.*
Battle-Piece, *tr. by* Arthur S. Way. GrR
("These were men that in harness of battle fought.") PoFr
Combat of Heracles and Cycnus, *tr. by* Sir William Marris. OxBG
Shields of myriad vanquished crowd my walls, The. Theseus. Price Day. CAG
Shifting Fortune. Euripides. *See* Dawn of Woman's Day, The.
Shiftless and shy, gentle and kind and frail. An Epitaph. J. C. Squire. BMEP; HBMV
Shifty limpet on his rocky shore, The. Every Earthly Creature. John Malcolm Brinnin. LiTA
Shih Ching. *Unknown. See* Shi King.
Shillin' a Day. Kipling. OAEP (2d ed.); ViBoPo
Shilling life will give you all the facts, A. Who's Who. W. H. Auden. CaAE; ChMo; CoBMV; MoAB; MoBrPo (1950 ed.); MoPW; NeMA; ReMP
Shiloh; a Requiem. Herman Melville. APW; LiTA; OxBA; PaA; PoFS; SoV; ViBoPo
"Shimmer of Evil, The." Theodore Roethke. NePoAm-2
Shimmering world, A. The Wave. Nordahl Grieg. AnNoLy
Shine and shock, A. Sight. Anne Welsh. BoSA
Shine forth into the night, O Flame. Give Our Conscience Light. Aline Badger Carter. ChIP; TrPWD
Shine in, O sun, on this dull place! For Martha's Kitchen. Fay Inchfawn. OQP; QP-2
Shine On, *with music.* Luke Schoolcraft. TrAS
Shine on me, oh, you gold, gold sun. Vacation Song. Edna St. Vincent Millay. YeAr
Shine on Me, Secret Splendor. Edwin Markham. TrPWD
Shine Out, Fair Sun, with All Your Heat. *Unknown, at. to* George Chapman. *Fr.* The Masque of the Twelve Months. ChTr
(Song: "Shine out, fair Sun, with all your heat.") EIL
Shine out, O hornèd Moon, O festal night's befriender. Moonlight. Philodemus of Gadara. OxBG
Shine, Perishing Republic. Robinson Jeffers. AmP; AmPP; AnAmPo; ChMo; CMP; InP; LA; LiTA; LiTM; MAP; MoAB; MoAmPo; MoVE; NAMP; NePA; NP; OxBA; PoLFOT; PreP; ReaPo; UnPo (3d ed.); ViBoPo
Shine, twy-horned Lady of the Night, shine on! Philodemus of Gadara, *tr. fr. Greek by* the Earl of Cromer. GrPo
Shingle, sand, sea, shells, the tracks. For Sheila. Margaret Allonby. BoSA
Shining and ponderous goblet, The. Bright Death. "Andrei Bely." TrRV
Shining black in the shining light. To a Black Greyhound. Julian Grenfell. AlDL; MM; OtMeF
Shining daggers of the harbor lights, The. Evening on the Harbor. Virginia Lyne Tunstall. HBMV
Shining Dark. Michael Roberts. FaBoMo
Shining Eye of Horus cometh, The. He Kindleth a Fire. *Unknown. Fr.* Book of the Dead. AWP
Shining Fool, The. Jacob Glatstein, *tr. fr. Yiddish by* Sarah Zweig Betsky. OnCuPl
Shining Hope, A. Julia H. Thayer. OQP; QP-1
Shining line of motors, The. May Day. Sara Teasdale. *Fr.* The Dark Cup. CP; MM
Shining marguerite. Marguerite. Ibn Billita. MooP
Shining moon burns the blue water, The. Song of the Blue Water. Li Po. WhP
Shining neutral summer has no voice, The. In Memory of Ernst Toller. W. H. Auden. AtBAP
Shining Night, A; or, Dick Daring, the Poacher. *Unknown.* CoMu
Shining of your golden eyes I bless, The. Benediction. Valery Yakovlevich Bryusov, *tr. by* Babette Deutsch. TrRV
Shining Spaces of the South, The. Joseph Campbell. JKCP
Shining splendour, The, of your eyes I bless! Benediction. Valery Yakovlevich Bryusov, *tr. by* C. M. Bowra. BoR
Shining Streets of London, The. Alfred Noyes. AlDL
Shining Things. Elizabeth Gould. BoTP
Shining waters of Seville. River of Seville. Al-Kutandi. MooP
Shining waters rise and swell, The. The Drowning of Conaing. *Unknown.* AnIL; SiB
Shiny Little House, The. Nancy M. Hayes. BoTP; SUS
Ship, The. Richard Church. AlDL
Ship, The. Louise A. Doran. EtS
Ship, The. J. F. Hendry. NeBP
Ship, The. Ibn Safar, *tr. fr. Arabic by* A. J. Arberry. MooP
Ship, The. Charles Mackay. BLPA
Ship, The. Lloyd Mifflin. AA; LEAP
Ship, The. J. C. Squire. CH; PtOT; TCPD; WP
Ship, an Isle, a Sickle Moon, A. James Elroy Flecker. PoeT
Ship and Her Makers, The. John Masefield. CoBE
Ship and the Sea, The. B. E. Baughan. AnNZ
Ship Bottom. Richmond Lattimore. NePoAm-2
Ship-broken Men Whom Stormy Seas Sore Toss. William Fowler. GoTS
Ship-Builders, The. Whittier. AnNE; EtS
Ship Canal from the Atlantic to the Pacific, The. Francis Lieber. PAH
Ship Comes In, A. Oliver Jenkins. DDA; EtS; PCH
Ship for Singapore, A. Daniel Whitehead Hicky. MoSiPe; PoTo
Ship from Thames. Rex Ingamells. MoAuPo
Ship I have got [*or* have] in the North Country, A. The *Golden Vanity. Unknown.* FaBoCh; OBB; SG; ShBV-1
Ship in Storm. Ibn Darraj, *tr. fr. Arabic by* A. J. Arberry. MooP
Ship in the Midst of the Sea, The. Christopher Wordsworth. BePJ
Ship is floating in the harbour now, A. Shelley. *Fr.* Epipsychidion. OBRV
Ship is sailing for Singapore, A. A Ship for Singapore. Daniel Whitehead Hicky. MoSiPe; PoTo
Ship-Love. Ethel E. Mannin. NLK
Ship, *Mayblossom,* left Magellan Straits, The. The *Mayblossom.* John Masefield. AlDL
Ship near Shoals. Anna Wickham. HBMV
Ship o' Bed, The. Robert P. Tristram Coffin. TSW; TSWC
Ship of Death, The. D. H. Lawrence. FaBoTw; KN; LiTB; LoBV; MoAB; OAEP (2d ed.); ViBoPo
"I sing of autumn and the falling fruit," *sel.* NAMP
Ship of Fools, The, *sels.* Sebastian Brant, *tr. fr. German by* Alexander Barclay.
Ballade to Our Lady. ISi
Geographers. ACP
Preachment for Preachers. ACP; CAW
Star of the Sea. ACP; CAW
Tudor Rose, The. ACP
Ship of Rio, The. Walter de la Mare. CenHV; EtS; LiL; TiPo; UTS
Ship of State, The. Alcaeus, *tr. fr. Greek by* James S. Easby-Smith. GrR
("I cannot understand how the winds are set," *tr. by* Richmond Lattimore.) GrPo
Ship of State, The ("O Navis, referent"). Horace, *tr. fr. Latin by* William Ewart Gladstone. Odes, I, 14. AWP; JAWP; RoL; WBP; OuHeWo, *tr. by* Sir Stephen E. De Vere
Ship of State, The. Longfellow. *Fr.* The Building of the Ship. BTP; FaBoBe; GrCo-1; HBVY; MaRV; NeHB; OHIP; OOP; PAP; PECK; PSO; QP-1
(O Ship of State.) FaFP
(Republic, The.) AA; DD; HH; IDAH; LEAP; MC; PAH; WGRP
(Sail On, O Ship of State!) FaPON; PoFr; TreF

Ship of State, The (*continued*)
("Thou, too, sail on, O Ship of State!") GDAH; HiLiAm; PaA; PGD; PTA-1; YaD
Ship of State, beware! The Ship of State. Horace, *tr. by* Sir Stephen E. De Vere. OuHeWo
Ship *Rambolee*, The, *with music*. *Unknown*. ShS
Ship Sails Up to Bideford, A. Herbert Asquith. BoTP; BrR
Ship Starting, The. Walt Whitman. MOAP
Ship That Never Returned, The, *with music*. *Unknown, diff. vers. of song by* Henry Clay Work. AS
Ship That Never Returned, The. Henry Clay Work. BLPA
Ship That Sails, The. *Unknown*. PoToHe (new ed.)
Ship to the roadstead rolled. O Navis. Austin Dobson. VA
Ship was built in Glasgow, and oh, she looked a daisy, A. In Prize. Cicely Fox Smith. WhC
"Ship was cheered, the harbour cleared, The." Samuel Taylor Coleridge. *Fr*. The Rime of the Ancient Mariner. MyFE
Ship with shields before the sun, The [*or* A]. Near Avalon. William Morris. BPN; PoVP
Shiperd-boy, what is yer trade? The Beggar-Laddie. *Unknown*. ESPB
Shipman, The. Chaucer. *Fr*. The Canterbury Tales: Prologue. ACP, *mod.*; EtS; SG
Shipmates, if you'll listen to me. Can't They Dance the Polka! *Unknown*. ShS
Shipmen, The. William Hunnis. *See* No Pains Comparable to His Attempt.
Shipment to Maidenek. Ephim G. Fogel. TrJP
Ships. Margaret Barrington. MW
Ships, The. John Joy Bell. BoTP; TVSH
Ships. John Masefield. CP; LEAP; NP; NV
Ships, The. Theodore Maynard. EtS
Ships. Nancy Byrd Turner. SUS
Ships are fitted, and the convoy sails, The. Convoy. William Jay Smith. WaP
Ships are lying in the bay, The. The Wanderer. Zoë Akins. BAP; HBMV; LEAP; NLK; NP; SBMV
Ships at Sea. Robert Barry Coffin. EtS; LPS-1
Ship's Cook, a Captive Sings, The. Hugo von Hofmannsthal, *tr. fr. German by* Charles Wharton Stork. TrJP
Ships glide in at the harbor's mouth, The. Our Father's World. Margaret E. Sangster. MaRV
Ships in Harbor [*or* Harbour]. David Morton. EtS; OBAV; VOD
Ships of Arcady, The. Francis Ledwidge. EtS
Ships of Saint John, The. Bliss Carman. EtS
Ships of Yule. The. Bliss Carman. CaP; CPG; HBVY; OCL
Ships That Pass in the Night. Paul Laurence Dunbar. BANP; CDC
Ships That Pass in the Night. Longfellow. *Fr*. Tales of a Wayside Inn: The Theologian's Tale. EtS; PoToHe (new ed.)
Ships with Your Silver Nets. Wade Oliver. EtS
Shipwreck, The. Byron. *Fr*. Don Juan, II. BPN; LiA; MCCG, *much abr.*; OBRV; PoD, *much abr.*; TCEP, *longer sel.*; WHA
Shipwreck, The, *sels*. William Falconer.
All Hands Unmoor! *fr*. I. EtS
"But now Athenian mountains they descry," *fr*. III. GoTL
"In vain the cords and axes were prepared," *fr*. III. LPS-2; OBEC
"It comes! the dire catastrophe draws near." EV-3
Shortening Sail, *fr*. II. EtS; SG
Shipwreck, The. E. Harriet Palmer. BOHV; NA
Shipwreck. Viktor Rydberg, *tr. fr. Swedish by* Charles W. Stork. AnSL
Shipwreck of the Trojans; Landing at Carthage. Virgil, *tr. fr. Latin by* Theodore C. Williams. The Aeneid, I. RoL
Shipwrecked Heart. *Unknown, tr. fr. Greek by* Lord Neaves. OnPM
Shipwrecked I, a farmer he. Farmer and Sailor. Plato. LiTW; OxBG
Shipwrecked Youth Reaches Land, A. Luis de Góngora, *tr. fr. Spanish by* Edward Meryon Wilson. *Fr*. The Solitudes. TeCS
Shiraz. Sadi, *tr. fr. Persian by* E. G. Browne. PeP
Shiv and the Grasshopper. Kipling. *Fr*. The Jungle Book. VLEP
Shiver, The. Thomas Hardy. InPo
Shivering cicada wailed heart-rendingly, The. A Farewell to My Love. Liu Yung. ChLP
Shivering in fever, weak and parched to sand. Dream of Dying. Thomas Lovell Beddoes. *Fr*. Fragments Intended for the Dramas. ERP
Sho-sho-ne Sa-ca-ga-we-a—captive and wife was she. Sa-Ca-Ga-We-A. Edna Dean Proctor. BoHiPo; PAH
Shoal of idlers, A, from a merchant craft. Pelters of Pyramids. Richard Henry Horne. VA
Shoal of Slime-Fish, The. Oppian, *tr. fr. Greek by* William Diaper. *Fr*. Halieuticks. BeR
Shock, The. Francis Reginald Scott. *Fr*. Armageddon. BoCaPo (1948 ed.)
Shock-headed Peter. Heinrich Hoffman, *tr. fr. German at. to* J. R. Planché. BoN
Shocking Rape and Murder of Two Lovers. *Unknown*. CoMu
Shock's fate I mourn; poor Shock is now no more. An Elegy on a Lap Dog. John Gay. HBV; PoE
Shoe a little horse. *Unknown*. OxNR
Shoe Factory, The. Ruth Harwood. HBMV
Shoe or Stocking. Edith M. Thomas. SDH
Shoe the colt, shoe the colt. Mother Goose. OxNR; RIS
Shoe the [old] horse, and shoe the mare. *Unknown*. PPL; SAS
Shoe the steed with silver. Sheridan at Cedar Creek. Herman Melville. APW; BBV (1923 ed.); GA; LiTA; PAH; PreP
Shoemaker, The ("As I was a-walking the other day"). *Unknown*. FaPON; GFA
Shoemaker, The ("I am a shoemaker by my trade"), *with music*. *Unknown*. TrAS
Shoemaker makes shoes without leather, A. *Unknown*. OxNR
Shoemakers, The. Whittier. AmPP (4th ed.); AnNE; CoBA; IAP; MOAP
Shoemaker's Holiday, The, *sels*. Thomas Dekker.
"Cold's the wind, and wet's the rain," *fr*. V, iv. ElSeCe; ReEn; TuPP
(Catch, A.) CBOV
(Cold's the Wind.) ViBoPo
(Drinking Song.) TrGrPo
(Hey Derry Derry.) SeCePo
(Saint Hugh.) OBSC
(Second Three-Man's Song, The.) EV-2
(Second Three Men's Song, The.) EPP
(Troll the Bowl!) ElL
Oh, the Month of May! *fr*. III, v. ElL; ViBoPo
(First Three-Man's Song, The.) EV-2
(May.) OBSC
(Maytime.) TrGrPo
Shoes. Tom Robinson. TiPo
Shoes. Louis Untermeyer. StaSt
Shoes have tongues. Ilo Orleans. RIS
Shoheen sho! There's a new moon setting. Slumber Song. Alice Furlong. BOL
Sholom Aleichem. Elias Lieberman. TrJP
Shoo, Shoo, Shoo-Lye, *with music*. *Unknown*. ABF
Shoogy-Shoo, The. Winthrop Packard. HBV
Shoon-a-shoon/ I sing no psalm/ Little Man. The Virgin's Slumber Song. Francis Carlin. BOL; ISi; NV; YeAr
Shoot down the "rebels"—men who dare. Rebels. Ernest Crosby. MC; PAH
Shoot, false Love, I care not. Song. *Unknown*. OBSC
Shoot the Buffalo, *with music*. *Unknown*. ABF; TrAS, *incl*. Hunt the Buffalo
Shoot your dice and have your fun, sugar babe. Sugar Babe. *Unknown*. ABF
Shooting of Dan McGrew, The. Robert W. Service. BAP; BeLS; BoCaPo; FaBoBe; FaFP; MaC; NeHB; PoRA; TreF
Shooting of His Dear. *Unknown*. *See* Molly Bawn.
Shooting of the Cup, The. John G. Neihardt. *Fr*. The Song of Three Friends. PoOW
Shooting of Werfel, The. Vernon Watkins. WaP
Shooting Song, A. William Brighty Rands. OTPC (1923 ed.)
Shooting Stars. Grace Noll Crowell. BoChLi
Shooting Stars. Otto C. Fønss, *tr. fr. Danish by* Charles W. Stork. BoDS
Shooting the Sun. Amy Lowell. MoAmPo (1950 ed.)
Shop. Robert Browning. AEV; PoVP; ViPo; VLEP
Shop, The. W. W. Gibson. BEL
Shop and Freedom. *Unknown*. PAH
Shop of Dreams. Mary Jane Carr. BrR
Shop Windows. Rose Fyleman. TiPo; UTS
Shopman, The. Eleanor Farjeon. HBVY; PCH
Shopper, The. Martial, *tr. fr. Latin by* Paul Nixon. RoL
(Unchanged.) WoL
Shopping Day. Orrick Johns. InMe
Shopping for Meat in Winter. Oscar Williams. GTBS-W; LiTA; LiTM; NePA
Shops. John Farrar. PCH
Shops. Winifred M. Letts. MoSiPe; MW
Shore. Mary Britton Miller. SUS; TiPo (1952 ed.)
Shore, The. Pedro Salinas, *tr. fr. Spanish by* Eleanor L. Turnbull. CoSP
Shore Birds. Vi Gale. GoYe
Shore-lark soars to his topmost flight, The. Ecstasy. Duncan Campbell Scott. CaP; OCL
Shore Roads of April. Bill Adams. EtS
Shoreham. Samuel Palmer. RO
Shoreless Sea, The. Li Hung-chang, *tr. into English by* James Whitall *fr. the Chinese-to-French translation of* Judith Gautier. ChLP
Shores of my native land. Farewell. Isaac Toussaint-L'Ouverture. PoNe

Shores of Night, The. August Derleth. DaM
Shores of Styx are lone forevermore, The. Idle Charon. Eugene Lee-Hamilton BMEP; ES; LEAP; OBVV
Shorn of his strength by time, these wornout nets. An Old Fishing Net. Julianus. OxBG
Short and sweet, and we've come to the end of it. Da Capo. H. C. Bunner. HBV; PR
Short Beach. Richard Hovey. NLK
Short is my say, O stranger. Stay and read. *Unknown. Fr.* Carmina Epigraphica. LaP
Short Lay of Sigurd, The. *Unknown, tr. fr. Icelandic by* William Morris *and* Eirikur Magnússon. *Fr.* The Elder Edda. EnLi-1
(Lay Called the Short Lay of Sigurd, The.) OuHeWo
(Lay of Sigurd, The.) AWP
Short Measures. Ben Jonson. *See* It Is Not Growing like a Tree.
Short seemed the space 'twixt sunset and the night. Nineveh. Robert Eyres Landor. *Fr.* The Impious Feast, V. OBRV
Short Sermon. *Unknown, ad. fr. German by* Louis Untermeyer. RIS; TiPo
Short Short Story. Josephine Jacobsen. NePoAm-2
Short Song of Congratulation, A. Samuel Johnson. *See* One-and-twenty.
Short Story, A. Euripides, *tr. fr. Greek by* Gilbert Murray. *Fr.* Electra. GrR
Short Story in Sonnet Form. Maxwell Bodenheim. MOAP
Short Visit, A. *Unknown.* SeCL
Shorten Sail. George Bubb Dodington. *See* Ode: "Love thy country . . ."
Shortenin' Bread, *with music. Unknown.* ABF
Shortening Sail. William Falconer. *Fr.* The Shipwreck, II. EtS; SG
Shortest Poem in the World, The. Eli Siegel. SiTL
(Lines [2] on the Questionable Importance of the Individual.) PIAE
Shortly After. Louis Smirnow. PoP
Shortly unto the wasteful woods she came. Venus in Search of Cupid, Coming to Diana. Spenser. *Fr.* The Faerie Queene, III, 6. BCEP
Shortness of Life, and the Goodness of God, The. Isaac Watts. BeR
Shorty George, *with music. Unknown.* ABF
Shot at Random, A. D. B. Wyndham Lewis. FaFP; FiBHP; SiTL
Shot gold, maroon and violet, dazzling silver, emerald, fawn. A Prairie Sunset. Walt Whitman. CaAE; CoBA
Shot in the back, in the courthouse square. Will Warner. William Aspenwall Bradley. BAP
Shot My Pisto' in de Heart of Town, *with music. Unknown.* ABF
Shot? so quick, so clean an ending? A. E. Housman. A Shropshire Lad, XLIV. PoVP
Shot Who? Jim Lane! Merrill Moore. MAP; MoAmPo; MOAP; SPP
Should a monkey wear a crown. Swift. *Fr.* To a Lady Who Desired I Would Write Some Verses in the Heroic Style. PoFr
Should a painter join a human head. The Art of Poetry. Horace. LaP
Should a plan we suggest, just that minute. Limerick. "R. K. B." LiBL
Should all the world so wide to atoms fall. Our Insufficiency to Praise God Suitably for His Mercy. Edward Taylor. *Fr.* God's Determinations. LiTA
Should any ask me on His form to dwell. He Hath No Parallel. Sadi. *Fr.* The Gulistan. AWP; LiTW
Should any one there in Rome remember Ovid the exile. Ovid. *Fr.* Tristia. LaP
Should auld acquaintance be forgot. Auld Lang Syne. Burns. AWP; BCEP; BEL; BSV; CaAE; CBE; CBOV; CEP; CoBE; EBSV; EiPP; EM-1; EnLi-2; EnLit; EnRP; EV-3; FaFP; GoTS; GTBS-W; HBV; HiLiEn; InP; InPo; JAWP; LEAP; LH; LiTB; LiTG; LiTL; LPS-1; MCCG; NeHB; OAEP; OBEC; OBEV; OlF; OuHeWo; PC; PoE; PreP; PYM; SiTL; TCEP; TOP; TreF; WBP
Should chance strike out of me some human heat. Gentleman of Fifty Soliloquizes. Don Marquis. HBMV; LEAP
Should D——s print, how once you robb'd your brother. Epigram. Pope. CEP
Should Ellen from the rectory come. A Windy Night. Lizette Woodworth Reese. DaM
Should Gaelic speech be e'er forgot. Gaelic Speech; or, "Auld Lang Syne" Done Up in Tartan. *Unknown.* PA
Should he but offer thee in part. Late Love. Dorothy Wellesley. DiM
Should he upon an evening ramble fare. Keats. *Fr.* Epistle to George Keats. ChER
Should I Be a Rabbi? Hayyim Nahman Bialik, *tr. fr. Hebrew by* Grace Goldin. TrJP
Should I get married? Should I be good? Marriage. Gregory Corso. NeAP
Should I long that dark were fair? The Dark. "George Eliot." *Fr.* The Spanish Gypsy. VA
Should I tread with ease the path He trod with sorrow? Sharing His Cross. Gracia L. Fero. BePJ
Should I with silver tooles delve through the hill. Meditation Fifty-six. Edward Taylor. *Fr.* Sacramental Meditations. CoV; OxBA
Should Lanterns Shine. Dylan Thomas. FaBoMo; GTBS-W
Should man oppose a rash rigidity. Meditation on a March Wind. Sister Mary Gilbert. JKCP (1955 ed.)
Should not the glowing lilies of the field. In His Steps. Katharine Lee Bates. PGD
Should old acquaintance be forgot. Auld Lang Syne. Burns. *See* Should auld acquaintance . . .
Should old acquaintance be forgot. Old-long-syne. *Unknown.* OBS
"Should one of us remember." He and She. Christina Rossetti. VLEP
Should the building totter, run for an archway! The Fallen Tower of Siloam. Robert Graves. WaP
Should thy love die. George Meredith. GTBS-D
Should you ask me, whence these stories? The Song of Hiawatha: Introduction. Longfellow. AnNE; IAP; LEAP; OBAV; PG (1945 ed.); TCAP
Should You Go First. Albert Rowswell. PoToHe (new ed.)
Should you meet a little saint. Identity. Sister Mary Helen. GoBC
Should you, of mirth and hope bereft. Song. Alfred de Musset. OnPM; TrFP
Shoulder up your [*or* yuh] gun and call your [*or* an' call up yuh] dog. Ground Hog. *Unknown.* SoAF; TrAS
Shouldering shapes of the skies of Broceliande. Taliessin's Song of the Unicorn. Charles Williams. FaBoTw
Shout All over God's Heaven. *Unknown.* IHA
Shout for the mighty men. Leonidas. George Croly. HBV
Shout from a clump of bathing boys. Bridge. S. Foster Damon. AnAmPo; LA
Shovel-gnats gnaw at the open wound, The. On the Edge of the Copper Pit. Pauline Henson. GoYe
Shovellin' Iron Ore, *with music. Unknown.* AS
Show, The. Emily Dickinson. *See* Show is not the show, The.
Show, The. Wilfred Owen. LiTB; LiTG; LiTM (rev. ed.); MoAB; MoBrPo (1950 ed.); NAMP; WaaP; WaP
Show is not the show, The. Emily Dickinson. CoBA
(Show, The.) TCAP
Show me a sight. The Irish Spinning-Wheel. Alfred Perceval Graves. TIP
Show me dear[e] Christ, thy spouse, so bright and clear. John Donne. Holy Sonnets, XVIII. EnLP; EPS; ExPo; MeLP; OAEP; OBS; SeEP; TuPP
Show Me More Love. *Unknown.* OxBoCh
Show me the face, cold mirror, that the world. Her Decision. James K. Baxter. Cressida, XI. AnNZ
Show Me Thyself. Margaret E. Sangster. TrPWD
"Show me your cloister," asks the Lady Poverty of the friars. Cloister. Charles L. O'Donnell. CAW; SaFP
"Show me your God!" the doubter cries. Blind. John Kendrick Bangs. MaRV; OQP; POT; PoToHe; QP-1
Show not to the poor thy pride. The Poor. *Unknown. Quoted by* George Crabbe *in* The Borough, *at head of* Letter XVIII. AEV
Show pity, Lord; O Lord, forgive. Psalm Fifty-one. R. A. Lapsley. PraP
Show-window manikins. Three Links of Light Armour. Richard Armour. SiTL
Shower, A. Izembo, *arr. by* Olive Beaupré Miller. SUS; TiPo
Shower, The. Henry Vaughan. AtBAP; ChTr; LiTB; OBS; ViBoPo
(Showre, The.) MePo
Shower and Sunshine. Maud Morin. BoTP
Shower came. A Shower. Izembo. SUS; TiPo
Shower hath past, ere it hath well begun, The. After the Shower. Archibald Lampman. CaP; OCL
Shower in spring, A. Chums. Buson. GaP
Shower is over, The. Let us play. Jesus at Play with His School-Mates. Longfellow. *Fr.* Christus; a Mystery. APW
Shower of green gems on my apple-tree, A. May Garden. John Drinkwater. HBMV
Shower, shower! Rain, Rain! *Unknown.* OnPM
Showers fall as softly, The. High and Low. Dora Read Goodale. PRWS
Showing How the Cavern Followed the Hut's Advice. John Hookham Frere. OTPC (1923 ed.)
Showing Off. *Unknown, tr. fr. Irish by* Frank O'Connor. KiLC
Showmen, The. Leconte de Lisle, *tr. fr. French by* Alan Conder TrFP
Show'r upon us. Attic Flagon. For an Epicurean Club Dinner. Poseidippus. GrR
Showre, The. Henry Vaughan. *See* Shower, The.
Shrew, The. Ogden Nash. CenHV

Shrill, a joyous scream. December Daybreak. W. W. Gibson. NeTW
Shrill the fife, kettle the drum. Baldy Bane. W. S. Graham. NePoEA
Shrilling locust slowly sheathes, The. The Beetle. James Whitcomb Riley. FaPON; PCD
Shrimp-Gatherers, The. Bayard Taylor. PA
Shrine, The. Digby Mackworth Dolben. DD; GoBC; GTML; HBV
Shrine, The. Hilda Doolittle ("H. D."). AnAmPo; LA; MAPA; NP
Shrine, The. Ethna MacCarthy. PoC
Shrine in Nazareth. Sister Mary St. Virginia. ISi
Shrines fill with festival and with sacrificing. Croesus. Bacchylides. OxBG
Shropshire Lad, A. John Betjeman. ShBV-4
Shropshire Lad, A. A. E. Housman. *Poems indexed separately by titles and first lines.*
Shropshire Lad, A. *Unknown.* ChTr
Shroud, The. Edna St. Vincent Millay. NP
Shroud My Body Down, *sel.* Paul Green.
Plants in the Earth. NoCaPo
Shrouded Stranger, The. Allen Ginsberg. NeAP
Shrouding of the Duchess of Malfi, The. John Webster. *See* Hark, Now Everything Is Still.
Shrouds and Away. Alfred G. Bailey. PeCV
Shrubbery, The. William Cowper. CEP; EiPP; FaBoEn; GTSL; NBE; OBEC; TwHP
Sh-ta-ra-dah-dey, *with music. Unknown.* AS
Shu Has Gone Hunting. *Unknown, tr. fr. Chinese.* WhP
Shu is away in the hunting-fields. In Our Lane. *Unknown. Fr.* Shi King. LiTW
Shudd'ring sheet of rain athwart the trees, The! Jack and Jill: As Swinburne Might Have Written It. Charles Battell Loomis. PA
Shub's Hunting. Ching, *tr. fr. Chinese. Fr.* Odes of Ching. RAR
Shui Shu, *sels. Tr. fr. Japanese by* Arthur Waley.
"Because river-fog." Kiyowara Fukuyabu. AWP; JAWP; LiTW; WBP
(River-Fog.) FaPON
"Deer which lives, The." Onakatomi Yoshinobu. AWP
("Deer on pine mountain, The," *tr. by* Kenneth Rexroth.) LiTW; OnPJ
"If it were not for the voice." Nakatsukasa. AWP
"Since I am convinced." Saigyo Hoshi. AWP; PFE
"Time I went to see my Sister, The." Tsurayuki. AWP
"When halting in front of it." Hitomaro. AWP; JAWP; PFE; WBP
"Winter has at last come." Minamoto no Shigeyuki. AWP
Shule, Agrah! "Fiona Macleod." OBVV
(Shule, Shule, Shule, Agrah!) PoVP
Shule Aroon. *Unknown.* GTIV; TIP
Shule, Shule, Shule, Agrah! "Fiona Macleod." *See* Shule, Agrah!
Shu-lin was a parrot who sat on the shoulder. Deprecating Parrots. Beulah May. EtS
Shun delays, they breed remorse. Loss in Delay. Robert Southwell. OBSC; SiCE
Shun Passion. Emerson. AmPP (3d ed.)
Shun when you be gray and old. "Crabbed Age and Youth." Theognis. GrR
Shunting. Basil Dowling. AnNZ
Shut Door, The. *Unknown.* PraP
Shut Doors along the Hall like Sleeping Eyes. Pauline Avery Crawford. MuM
Shut-Eye Train, The. Eugene Field. PFE
Shut fast again in beauty's sheath. Monochrome. Louise Imogen Guiney. AnAmPo; LA
Shut-in, The. Nellie De Hearn. PoToHe (new ed.)
Shut in from all the world without. Firelight. Whittier. *Fr.* Snow-bound. AA; LaNeLa
Shut not so soon; the dull-eyed [*or* dull-ey'd] night. To Daisies, Not to Shut So Soon. Robert Herrick. AtBAP; BLV; BoLiVe; CH; EG; EV-2; HBV; OBEV; OBS; SeCV-1; SeEP; TrGrPo
Shut Not Your Doors. Walt Whitman. APW; IAP; OxBA
Shut Out That Moon. Thomas Hardy. ChMo; CMP; MoVE; ViBoPo
"Close up the casement, draw the blind," *sel.* PoD
Shut, shut the door, good John! Epistle to Dr. Arbuthnot. [*or* Prologue to the Satires *or* The Author's Miseries]. Pope. BCEP; BEL; CEP; CoBE; EiPP; EM-1; EnLi-1; EnLit; EPP; EV-3; GEPC; HoPM; LEAP; LoBV; NBE; OAEP; OxBoLi; PoE; PoEL-3; ReaPo; TOP; TyEnPo; WHA; WoL
Shut the Seven Seas against Us. George Barker. *Fr.* Third Cycle of Love Poems. MoAB; MoBrPo (1950 ed.); NeMA
Shutter of time darkening ceaselessly, The. August. Louis MacNeice. ChMo; FaBoEn; LiTM
Shutters unhinge the bat, and brazen sun. Praise to Light. Thomas Cole. NePoAm-2
Shuttle of the sunburnt grass. The Grasshopper. Edith M. Thomas. SN
Shuttles of trains going north, going south, drawing threads of blue. Morning Sun. Louis MacNeice. MBP; MoAB; MoBrPo; NeMA
Shuttling spindles spun swiftly under the blue-electric. Love in a Cotton Mill. Stewart Atkins. NoCaPo
Shy, amorous. Apple Blossoms. Arthur L. Phelps. CPG
Shy and timid, Gloom to me. The Outcast. James Stephens. MBP; MoBrPo
Shy as the April weather. Armor the Bud. Frances Frieseke. JKCP (1955 ed.)
Shy as the squirrel and wayward as the swallow. George Meredith. *Fr.* Love in the Valley. PoeT
Shy Geordie. Helen B. Cruickshank. GoTS
Shy in their herding dwell the fallow deer. Deer. John Drinkwater. CH
Shy little garden! Ode to a Garden. Annie Charlotte Dalton. OCL
Shy one, I said, you can take me away in a breath. I Spoke to the Violet. John Shaw Neilson. BoAV
Shy one, shy one. To an Isle in the Water. W. B. Yeats. AWP; JAWP; WBP
Shy, woodland creatures perched upon your shoulders. Francis of Assisi. Bertha Gerneaux Woods. SaFP
Shylock's Defense. Shakespeare. *Fr.* The Merchant of Venice, III, i. TreFS
Shyly the silver-hatted mushrooms make. May. John Shaw Neilson. NeLNL
Si Descendero in Infernum, Ades. James Russell Lowell. BAV
Si Filius Dei Es, Dejice Te. Richard Crashaw, *tr. fr. Latin by* D. C. Allen. Epigrammata Sacra, I, 72. LaP
Si Hubbard. *Unknown.* AS, *with music;* IHA
Si Jeunesse Savait! Edmund Clarence Stedman. AA
(Why?) BLP
Si talked with Dauber, standing by the side. John Masefield. *Fr.* Dauber. InP
Si Vis Celsi Iura Tonantis. Boethius, *tr. fr. Latin by* Helen Waddell. TriL
Siasconset Song. Philip Booth. NePoAm
Siberia. James Clarence Mangan. CBOV; ERP; GTIV; IrPN; TIP
Sibrandus Schafnaburgensis. Robert Browning. Garden Fancies, II EnLi-2 (1949 ed.); VLEP
Sibyl, The. Thomas Gordon Hake. VA
Sibyl, The. Joan LaBombard. GoYe
Sibyl. John Payne. VA
Sibylla Palmifera. Dante Gabriel Rossetti. *See* Soul's Beauty.
Sibylla's Dirge. Thomas Lovell Beddoes. *Fr.* Death's Jest Book, V, iv. GTBS-D; NBE; PoD; TriL
(Second Dirge.) VA
(We Do Lie beneath the Grass.) ERP
Sibylline Prophecy, The. Virgil, *tr. fr. Latin by* Roderick Gill. *Fr.* Eclogues, IV. CAW; ISi, *tr. wr. at. to* Thomas Walsh
Sic a Wife as Willie Had. Burns. GoTS
Sic Ars Diluditur Arte. Henry Parrot. SiCE
Sic et Non. Sir Herbert Read. FaBoTw
Sic Semper Tyrannis. Aldis Dunbar. DDA
Sic Transit. Thomas Campion. *See* Come, Cheerful Day!
Sic Transit. Joseph Mary Plunkett. ACP
Sic Transit. Simonides. *See* Monuments Perish.
Sic Transit. *Unknown. See* Proper Sonnet, A, How Time Consumeth . . .
Sic Transit Gloria Mundi. James Wreford Watson. CaP
Sic Vita. William Stanley Braithwaite. BANP; CP; LBMV; NLK; OQP; QP-2
Sic Vita. Henry King, *wr. at. to* Francis Beaumont. BrBE; ElSeCe; HBV (8th ed.); LPS-1, *composite vers. by* Henry King, William Browne, Simon Wastell, *and* William Strode; MePo; OBS; PoFS; UnPo (1st ed.)
(Even Such Is Man.) BEL
(Like to the Falling of a Star.) EG; GTBS-W; LiTG; SeCePo
(Of Human Life.) BLV; PoD; TrGrPo
(On the Life of Man.) CBOV; GoBC; HBV (6th ed.); TOP; WHA
Sic Vita. Henry David Thoreau. *See* I Am a Parcel of Vain Strivings Tied.
Siccine separat amara mors? Knowledge after Death. Henry Charles Beeching. OBVV; VA
Sicelides, *sel.* Phineas Fletcher.
Woman's Inconstancy, *fr.* II, ii. ElL
("Who sows the seas, or ploughs the easy shore?") ElSeCe
Sich a li'l feller, en he settin' up so wise! A Lullaby. Frank L. Stanton. BOL
Sicilian Cyclamens. D. H. Lawrence. ChMP; MoVE
Sicilian Muse, begin a loftier strain! The Messiah. Virgil, *tr. by* Dryden. Eclogues, IV. AWP; JAWP; OuHeWo; WBP

Sicilian Night, A. Edward Cracroft Lefroy. Echoes from Theocritus, IV. VA
Siciliana; the Landings at Gela. G. Stanley Koehler. NePoAm-2
Sicilian's Tale, The. Longfellow. *See* King Robert of Sicily.
Sicily and Naples, *sel.* Samuel Harding.
Of Death. SeCL
Sick and used Cambridge in the suck-/ Ing sound. The Morning Light for One with Too Much Luck. Delmore Schwartz. FiMAP
Sick Autumn. Guillaume Apollinaire, *tr. fr. French by* Alan Conder. TrFP
Sick Child, A. Randall Jarrell. InvP
Sick Child, The. Robert Louis Stevenson. CH
Sick, Cornificius, is thy friend. The Complaint. Catullus. OnPM
Sick Face below the Surface of the Earth, A. Sakutaro Hagiwara, *tr. fr. Japanese by* Takamichi Ninomiya *and* D. J. Enright. PoLJ
Sick fretful upper berths—below, long rows. Hospital Train. John Allan Wyeth. PoP
Sick King in Bokhara, The. Matthew Arnold. EmBrPo; PoVP; VLEP
Sick Leave. Po Chü-i, *tr. fr. Chinese by* Arthur Waley. TrCh
Sick Leave. Siegfried Sassoon. LBBV; MM; NP
Sick Lion and the Fox, The. La Fontaine, *tr. fr. French by* Elizur Wright. OnPM
Sick Love. Robert Graves. CoEV; POTE
(O Love in Me.) FaBoMo
Sick Man, The. Jules Supervielle, *tr. fr. French by* Wallace Fowlie. MiCF
Sick Man and the Angel, The. John Gay. CEP
Sick man, though, had wit who thought you up, The. For Two Girls Setting Out in Life. Peter Viereck. MiAP
Sick Nought, The. Randall Jarrell. OxBA
Sick of thy northern glooms, come, shepherd, seek. Philip Freneau. *Fr.* The Beauties of Santa Cruz. CoBA
Sick one, see the day dies radiant. Sweet Death. Lorenzo Mavilis. MoGP
Sick Room. Francis D. Clare. JKCP (1955 ed.)
Sick Rose, The. Blake. *Fr.* Songs of Experience. AtBAP; AWP; BEL; BLV; BoLiVe; BoW; BrBE; ChER; ChTr; EiPP; EnL; EnLoPo; EPP; ExPo; FaBoEn; GTBS-D; InPo; JAWP; LoBV; MaPo; OAEP; OnPM; PoEL-4; PoFS; SeCeV; ShBV-4; TOP; TrGrPo; TwHP; ViBoPo; WBP
("O Rose, thou art sick.") EG
Sick Stockrider, The. Adam Lindsay Gordon. BoAu; OBVV; VA
"I've had my share of pastime," *sel.* OtMeF
Sick Wife, The. *Unknown, tr. fr. Chinese by* Arthur Waley. TrCh
Sick-Bed. Edmund Blunden. PtOT
Sickles sound. Harvest Song. Ludwig Hölty. AWP; JAWP; WBP; WoL
Sickness, intending my love to betray. Sir John Davies. *Fr.* Sonnets to Philomel. SiPS
Sickness, Not Sleep. *Unknown.* SeCL
("She sleeps: peace crown thine eyes, sweet dreams in deep.") LO
Sickness of Adam, The. Karl Shapiro. *Fr.* Adam and Eve. CoBMV; MoAB
Sickness of desire, that in dark days, The. Melancholia. Robert Bridges. ChMo
Sickness, 'tis true. Samuel Taylor Coleridge. *Fr.* A Tombless Epitaph. OBRV
Sickness Which Is Love, The. Lucretius, *tr. fr. Latin by* Gilbert Highet. *Fr.* De Rerum Natura, IV. LaP
Side by side in the crowded streets. The Cantelope. Bayard Taylor. BOHV; PA
Side by side let elder sheep roll over on spring earth. During Lambing Season. Keidrych Rhys. MoWP
Side by side the two lovers shy. *Unknown, tr. fr. Spanish by* Eleanor L. Turnbull. TeCS
Side Street, A. Louis Untermeyer. CBOV
Sidewalks of New York, The. James W. Blake. BLPA; BoHiPo; FaBoBe; LPS-1; TreFS; YaD
Sidmouth Soul, A. Cale Rice. TBM
Sidney, according to report, was kindly hearted. Various Ends. Ruthven Todd. NeBP; SeCePo
Sidney Godolphin. Clinton Scollard. AA; OBAV
Sidney, in whom the heydey of romance. Sonnet to Sidney. Alan Seeger. BTP
Sidrophel, the Rosicrucian Conjurer. Samuel Butler. *Fr.* Hudibras. OxBoLi
Siege, The, *sel.* William Cartwright.
Seal Up Her Eyes, O Sleep. SeCL
Siege. Edna St. Vincent Millay. BAP
Siege, The. Sir John Suckling. ElSeCe; EPS; OxBoLi; ReEn; ViBoPo
(Besieged Heart, The.) TrGrPo
('Tis Now, Since I Sat[e] Down [Before].) EnL; PoEL-3; SeCV-1; SeEP
Siege Conditions. Robert Herring. MoWP
Siege of Belgrade, The. *Unknown, at. to* Alaric Alexander Watts. BLPA; BOHV; HBV; LPS-3; TreF
(Alliteration; or, The Siege of Belgrade.) ChTr
(Austrian Army, An.) FiBHP; SiTL
Siege of Chapultepec, The. William Haines Lytle. MC; PAH
Siege of Corinth, The. Byron. GoTL
Sels.
Assault, The. EV-4
Storming of Corinth, The. LH
Siege of Derry, The. Cecil Frances Alexander. TIP
Siege of Ismail, The. Byron. *Fr.* Don Juan, VII *and* VIII. WoL
Siege of Numancia, The, *sel.* Cervantes, *tr. fr. Spanish by* Elizabeth Selden.
"I am bringing you, my sweet beloved." BoFr
Siege of Plattsburg, *with music. Unknown.* ABF
Siege of Rhodes, The, *sel.* Sir William Davenant.
"This cursèd jealousy, what is't?" LO
Siege of Valencia, The, *sel.* Felicia Dorothea Hemans.
Dirge: "Calm on the bosom of thy God." BCEP; EV-4; HBV, *longer sel.* OBEV
(Death-Hymn, A.) OBRV
Siegfried. Randall Jarrell. MiAP; ReMP
Siena. Swinburne. ViPo
Laud of Saint Catherine, The, *sel.* CAW
"Siene Mi Fe'; Disfecemi Maremma." Ezra Pound. *Fr* Hugh Selwyn Mauberley. CoBMV; CoV; LiTA; LiTM (rev. ed.): MoPo
Sierra. Jorge Carrera Andrade, *tr. fr. Spanish by* Muna Lee. AnCL
Sierra Nevada. Théophile Gautier, *tr. fr. French by* Alan Conder. TrFP
Sierran Vigil. Ewart Milne. NeIP
Siesta, The ("Airs! that wander and murmur round"). *Unknown, tr. fr. Spanish by* Bryant. AnSpL-1; AWP; JAWP; WBP
Siesta ("Fling yourself here, O traveller"). *Unknown, tr. fr. Greek by* F. L. Lucas. GrPE
Siesta in Andalusia! Villafranca de Córdoba. Pedro Garfias. PoFr
Sieve, The. Sadi, *tr. fr. Persian by* Edward B. Eastwick. LiTW
Sifting. Victor E. Beck. GoYe
Sigar riding did Helgi send. Helgi Thrice Born. *Unknown. Fr.* The Elder Edda. PaOS
Sigh, The. Thomas Hardy. VLEP
Sigh. Stéphane Mallarmé, *tr. fr. French by* Arthur Symons. AWP; JAWP; WBP
—— *Tr. by* Alan Conder. OnPM; TrFP
—— *Tr. by* Frederick Morgan. AnFP
Sigh, A. Harriet Prescott Spofford. AA; HBV; PR
Sigh, The. Nathaniel Wanley. OBS; OxBoCh
Sigh, A. Countess of Winchilsea. CEP
Sigh for Knockmany, A. William Carleton. TIP
Sigh from a Staircase of Jade, A. Li Po, *tr. fr. Chinese by* Witter Bynner. ChLP
Sigh, heart, and break not; rest, lark, and wake not! Nuptial Song. Lord De Tabley. OBVV
Sigh his name into the night. Love's Secret Name. John Arthur Blaikie. VA
Sigh in Winter, A. August, Graf von Platen, *tr. fr. German by* Edwin Morgan. AnGP
Sigh, my lute, sigh. Justin Huntly M'Carthy. *Fr.* If I Were King. ReTS
Sigh No More [Ladies, Sigh No More]. Shakespeare. *Fr.* Much Ado about Nothing, II, iii. AnFE; AWP; CenL; EG; ElL; EM-1; EnLi-1 (1949 ed.); EnLit; EPP; EV-1; ExPo; HBV; InMe; InPo; JAWP; LiTB; LiTG; LiTL; LoPo; MCCG; OAEP; PoEL-2; SeCeV; SiCE; SiTL; TOP; TreFS; TrGrPo; TwP; TyEnPo; ViBoPo; WBP
(Balthasar's Song.) ALV; BoLiVe; OBSC
(Fraud of Men, The.) BLV
(Song: "Sigh no more, ladies, sigh no more.") FiP
(Song from "Much Ado about Nothing.") LEAP
Sigh Not for Love. Helen Hay Whitney. AA
Sigh of Silence, The. Keats. *See* I Stood Tiptoe . . .
Sigh of the Forest, The. Bernhard Elis Malmström, *tr. fr. Swedish by* Charles S. Stork. AnSL
Sigh sent wrong, A. Finale. W. E. Henley. VOD
Sigh, Sigh, Rushes! Gustaf Fröding, *tr. fr. Swedish by* Charles W. Stork. AnSL
Sigh That Heaves the Grasses, The. A. E. Housman. Last Poems, XXVII. MoVE; POTT
Sigh, wind in the pine. Lament. Douglas Stewart. MoAuPo
Sighs. *Unknown.* SeCL
("All night I muse, all day I cry.") LO
Sighs and Grones. George Herbert. AtBAP; PoEL-2
Sighs are air, and are lost in air. Three Rimas, 2. Gustavo Adolfo Bécquer, *tr. by* Harold Morland. *Fr.* Rimas. LiTW
Sighs are air, and go to the air. Rima XXXVIII. Gustavo Adolfo Becquer, *tr by* Young Allison. *Fr.* Rimas. AnSpL-2

Sighs are my food, [my] drink are my tears. Wyatt Being in Prison, to Bryan [*or* Epigram]. Sir Thomas Wyatt. SiCE; SiPS; TuPP
Sight. Sir John Davies. LoBV (2d ed.)
Sight. W. W. Gibson. BMEP; ChMo; CMP; MBP; MoBrPo; NeMA; PoMa
Sight. Cora Ball Moton. GoSl
Sight. Ida Norton Munson. ChIP
Sight. Anne Welsh. BoSA
Sight and Insight. Eleanor Slater. TrPWD
Sight in Camp [in the Daybreak Gray and Dim], A. Walt Whitman. AA; AmPo; AmPP (4th ed.); BoFr; ExPo; GTBS-W; IAP; LO; MOAP; OxBA; PoEL-5; SoV; TCAP
Sighted Sub. *Unknown.* WhC
Sightless, I breathe and touch; this night of pines. The Cicadas. Aldous Huxley. POTE; TwCV
Sights and Sounds of the Night. Carlos Wilcox. AnAmPo; LA
(Northern Lights.) APW
Sights o'er yonder snowy range, The. Lines. Aubrey Thomas De Vere. BMEP
Sight-Seer's Dream, A. Baudelaire, *tr. fr. French by* Alan Conder. TrFP
Sightseers in a Courtyard. Nicolás Guillén, *tr. fr. Spanish by* Langston Hughes. PoNe
Sigismonda and Guiscardo, *sel.* Dryden.
Ave atque Vale. OBS
Sign, The. Bhartrihari, *tr. fr. Sanskrit by* Paul Elmer More. LiTW
Sign, The. Frederic Manning. LBBV; NP
Sign of Fall in the Carolinas. Helen Bevington. NoCaPo (rev. ed.)
Sign of Spring, A. Eben Eugene Rexford. PCH
(Bluebird, The.) PEDC
Sign of the Cross, The. Cardinal Newman. GoBC; JKCP; PoVP; VA
Sign of the Love Divine. The Red Cross. Henry van Dyke. PEDC
Sign of the Pleiades [*or* Pleiads], The. Hesiod, *tr. fr. Greek. Fr.* Works and Days. GrR, *tr. by* Arthur S. Way; OxBG, *tr. by* T. F. Higham
Sign-Post. *See* Signpost.
Sign says HOSPITAL—a blue haze wraps it now, The. Spring, the Vet, and I. "Eduard Bagritsky." TrRV
Signal, The. Eugenio Florit, *tr. fr. Spanish by* H. R. Hays. OnPM; TwSpPo
Signal Fires. Edward Everett Hale. From Potomac to Merrimac, II. PAH
Signals spelled summer but for me it was spring, The. Evergreen. Ewart Milne. OxBI
Signature, A. Robert H. Davis. GA
Signature for Tempo. Archibald MacLeish. MoVE
Signature of Pain, The. Alan Porter. POTE
Significance of John Brown, The. Stephen Vincent Benét. *Fr.* John Brown's Body. PaA
("Out of his body grows revolving steel," *shorter sel.*) VOD (1935 ed.)
Signpost. Robinson Jeffers. GoYe; ViBoPo
Sign-Post, The. Edward Thomas. ViBoPo
Signs. Beatrice M. Murphy. GoSl
Signs and Charms. *Unknown.* StaSt
Signs and Seasons. *Unknown.* RIS
Signs Everywhere of Birds Nesting, While. William Carlos Williams. *Fr.* Paterson. MoVE
Signs of Christmas. Edwin Lees. OHIP; SDH
Signs of Love. Petrarch. *See* If Amorous Faith.
Signs of Rain. Aratus, *tr. fr. Greek by* F. L. Lucas. *Fr.* Phaenomena. GrPE
Signs of Rain Edward Jenner. BLPA; CG; LPS-2; OTPC; PoP; PRWS; RIS, *abr.*
Signs of Rain. Alex Rogers, *after* Edward Jenner. StaSt
Signs of the Season in the Kitchen. *Unknown.* SDH
Signs of the times are full of promise, The. Words of Cheer. Thomas H. Barker. PEOR
Signs of Winter. John Clare. PoE; WaKn
Signum Cui Contradicetur. Sister Mary Angelita. GoBC; JKCP (1926 ed.)
Sigurd of yore. The Short Lay of Sigurd [*or* The Lay of Sigurd]. *Unknown, tr. by* William Morris *and* Eirikur Magnusson. *Fr.* The Elder Edda. AWP; EnLi-1; OuHeWo
Sigurd Rideth to the Glittering Heath. William Morris. *Fr.* The Story of Sigurd the Volsung, II. PoEL-5
Sigurd the Volsung. William Morris. *See* Story of Sigurd the Volsung, The.
Sigurth and I. *Unknown, tr. fr. Icelandic by* Henry Adams Bellows. *Fr.* The Elder Edda. LiA
Sigurth in Faeroëse. *Unknown, tr. fr. Icelandic by* E. M. Smith-Dampier. PaOS
Silence. Mavis Clare Barnett. BLP; OQP; QP-2
Silence. Walter de la Mare. BrBE
Silence, The. John Gould Fletcher. Down the Mississippi, VII. ChMo; CMP; LiTA; MOAP; NP; SPP; TCAP
Silence, The. Federico García Lorca, *tr. fr. Spanish by* Eleanor L. Turnbull. CoSP
Silence. Thomas Hood. BCEP; CH; CoBE; EnLi-2 (1949 ed.); EnRP; ERP; ES; FaBoEn; GTML; GTSL; LEAP; OBEV; OBRV; PeBoSo; PoEL-4; ShBV-4; ViBoPo
Silence. Toyohiko Kagawa, *tr. fr. Japanese by* Lois J. Erickson. SoLD
Silence. Inez Barclay Kirby. MuM
Silence, The. Archibald MacLeish. HBMV
Silence. Edgar Lee Masters. LaNeLa; MAP; MoAmPo; NP; PoMa; PoToHe (new ed.); SBMV
Silence. Marianne Moore. FaBoEn; FaBoMo; LiTA; MoP; PG (1955 ed.); ViBoPo
Silence. James Herbert Morse. AA
Silence. John Lancaster Spalding. AA
Silence. Charles Hanson Towne. BPP; MaRV; OQP; QP-1; WGRP
Silence. W. J. Turner. MoBrPo
Silence. Alfred de Vigny, *tr. fr. French by* Alan Conder. TrFP
Silence. Winifred Welles. HBMV
Silence. John Hall Wheelock. LiTM
Silence, The. Anna Wickham. NP
Silence. Humbert Wolfe. ReTS
Silence. A while ago. A Sea Story. Emily H. Hickey. JKCP; VA
Silence—and a muted bell rings. Consecration. Patrick F. Kirby. GoBC
Silence and Solitude may hint. An Uninscribed Monument on One of the Battle-Fields of the Wilderness. Herman Melville. AA
Silence and Speech. Richard Garnett. *See* Epigram: "I hardly ever ope my lips."
Silence and Stealth of Day[e]s! Henry Vaughan. SeCV-1; WHA
("Silence, and stealth of day[e]s! 'tis now.") MePo; SeEP
(Since Thou Art Gone.) SeCL
Silence augmenteth grief, writing increaseth rage. An Epitaph on [the Right Honorable] Sir Philip Sidney [*or* Another of the Same]. *At. to* Fulke Greville *and to* Sir Edward Dyer. AnFE; LiTB; LiTG; LoBV; OBSC; PtP; ReIE; SiCE; TuPP
Silence before/ Sound. Zacchaeus in the Leaves. Vernon Watkins. FaBoTw
Silence crumbles before the cavalcade. Andean Crossing. Alejandro Peralta. AnCL
Silence, Dryads' leafy keep. Country Gods. Plato. OxBG
Silence here bears gunfire in its breath. Cozzo Grillo. H. B. Mallalieu. WaP
Silence holds for it, taut and true, The. Click o' the Latch. Nancy Byrd Turner. HBMV
Silence instead of thy sweet song, my bird. Lament of a Mocking-Bird. Frances Anne Kemble. AA; HBV
Silence Invoked. Richard Flecknoe. *See* Invocation of Silence.
Silence is strange when the voices eddy and fade, The. Wills Dies in Solitude. Colin Thiele. *Fr.* Burke and Wills. NeLNL
Silence. . . . Listen to/ The sad list. Complaint of Fantomas. Robert Desnos. MiCF
Silence: now he has shriven me. Confession. "Anna Akhmatova." TrRV
Silence of a city, how awful at midnight, The! Fragments on a Theme. Samuel Taylor Coleridge. AIDL
Silence of Ajax, The. Homer, *pr. tr. fr. Greek by* T. E. Lawrence. *Fr.* The Odyssey, XI. LiA
(Of the Shade of Ajax, *tr. by* T. F. Higham.) OxBG
Silence of God, The. Sir Osbert Sitwell. WaKn
Silence of Love, The. "Æ." ChMo; CMP
Silence Sings. T. Sturge Moore. GTML; MBP
Silence sleeping on a waste of ocean. Rest. Percy Somers Payne. TIP
Silence slipping around like death, A. A Winter Twilight. Angelina W. Grimké. CDC; PoNe
Silence Spoke with Your Voice. Ryah Tumarkin Goodman. GoYe
Silence still and no sun burns above, The. Alone. Hubert Witheford. AnNZ
Silence was envious of the only voice. Robert Underwood Johnson. *Fr.* The Voice of Webster. AA
Silence, with its ragged edge of lost communication, The. Barbed Wire. Eithne Wilkins. NeBP
Silenced Singer, The. William James Linton. VA
Silences. Arthur O'Shaughnessy. VA
Silences. E. J Pratt. BoCaPo (1943 ed.); TwCV
Silent. Iwan Goll, *tr. fr. French by* Claire Goll. OnPM
Silent,/ Above the chaste bushes. Ulysses S. Grant. Paul Southworth Bliss. StaSt
Silent amidst unbroken silence deep. India. Florence Earle Coates. AA
Silent and alone I climb the west tower. To the Tune of "Crows Crying by Night." Li Yu. WhP
Silent, and in face/ Confounded, long they sat, as stricken mute. Milton. *Fr.* Paradise Lost, IX. EnL

Silent as thou, whose inner life is gone. To a Skull. Thomas Caulfield Irwin. TIP
Silent at Joseph's side he stood. The Carpenter. Phyllis Hartnoll. ChIP; QS
Silent Baby. Ellen Bartlett Currier. LPS-1
Silent bird is hid in the boughs, The. Song. Rosa Mulholland. TIP
Silent bivouac of the dead, we say, A. Decorating the Soldiers' Graves. Minot J. Savage. OHIP
Silent Christmas stars shine cool and clear, The. Stars of Cheer. Caroline D. Swan. JKCP
Silent Cockatoo, The. H. P. Stoddard. MuM
Silent Day, The. Luis G. Urbina, *tr. fr. Spanish by* Samuel Beckett. AnMP
Silent Folk, The. Charles Wharton Stork. SBMV
Silent Generation, The. Louis Simpson. NePoAm-2
Silent and tearful. A Song of Mo Shang Sang. Wang T'ai Ch'ing PoHN
Silent are the singers in the purple halls of Emain. Death of Cuchulain. Eleanor Rogers Cox. JKCP
Silent are the woods, and the dim green boughs are. On Eastnor Knoll. John Masefield. CH; MCCG; ShBV-3; VOD
Silent Grand Army, The. "E. M. H. C." PEOR
Silent he watched them—the soldiers and dog. With Little Boy Blue. Sarah Beaumont Kennedy. PTA-2
Silent Hour. Rainer Maria Rilke, *tr. fr. German by* Jessie Lemont. AWP; OnPM; WoL
Silent House it standeth wide, The. The House of the Silent Years. Lizette Woodworth Reese. MOAP
Silent I gaze at the cataract. By the Waterfall. Friedrich Adler. TrJP
Silent I sit by the prison's high window. Captive Knight. Mikhail Yurevich Lermontov. TrRV
Silent is Ida, with great Jove asleep. Reveille. Ada Foster Murray. VOD
Silent is Orpheus now, and silent now. Elegy VIII. William Bell. FaBoTw
Silent is the dark. Hope's Song. Francis Carlin. HBMV
Silent Is the House. Emily Brontë *and* Charlotte Brontë. *See* Visionary, The.
Silent light penetrates the panes, The. Death in the Sun. Eugenio Florit. TwSpPo
Silent Love. John Clare. EnRP
Silent Love. *Unknown, tr. fr. German by* Longfellow. LiTW
Silent Lover, The. Sir Walter Ralegh. BCEP, *abr.;* ElL; EPP; LiTB; OBEV, *abr.;* PG, *abr.;* ViBoPo
(Merit of True Passion, The.) LiTB
(Sir Walter Raleigh to the Queen.) OAEP
(To His Mistress.) SiPS
(To Queen Elizabeth.) TuPP
(To the Queen.) CaAE; ElSeCe; OBSC
Wrong Not, Sweet Empress of My Heart, *sel.* HBV, *abr.;* LoPS, *abr.;* OBS, *sl. diff., at. to* Sir Robert Ayton
Silent moment comes at last, The. Scène à Faire. Morton Dauwen Zabel. NP
Silent my robe, when I rest on earth. The Swan. *Unknown, tr. fr. Anglo-Saxon. Fr.* Riddles. CoBE
Silent Night [Holy Night]. Joseph Mohr, *tr. fr. German.* ChrBoLe; FaFP; MaRV; OIF; TreF; YaCaBo, *with music*
(Stille Nacht, *tr. by* Thomas Walsh.) CAW
(Stille Nacht, Heilige Nacht.) SDH
Silent Noon. Dante Gabriel Rossetti. The House of Life, XIX. BEL; BLV; BoLiVe; BPN; EmBrPo; EnLi-2; EnLit; EPN; GTBS-D; HBV; LiTL; LO; LoPo; LoPS; OAEP; PIAE; PoEL-5; POTT; PoVP; RiBV; TCEP; TrGrPo; TwHP; TyEnPo; ViP; ViPo; ViPP; VLEP; WHA
Silent nymph, with curious eye! Grongar Hill. John Dyer. CEP; ChTr; EiPP; EnRP; EPP; EV-3; GoTL; LoBV; LPS-2; OBEC; PIAE; PoE; PoEL-3; TOP
Silent, O Moyle, be the roar of thy water. The Song of Fionnuala. Thomas Moore. AnIL; ERP; OnYI; TIP
Silent Piano. W. Wesley Trimpi. PtPa
Silent Places, The. Harold M. Hildreth. OQP; QP-2
Silent Pool, The. Harold Monro. ChMo; CMP
Silent Ranges, The. Stephen Moylan Bird. HBMV
Silent, Silent Night. Blake. LiA
Silent Slain, The. Archibald MacLeish. *See* Too-late Born, The.
Silent Snake, The. *Unknown.* BoTP; FaPON; TiPo (1959 ed.)
Silent Songs. Richard Henry Stoddard. TCAP
Silent Stars, The. Eric H. Daniell. MaRV
Silent Stars Go By, The. Harriet Hartridge Tompkins. MaRV
Silent Sufferer. John Gilland Brunini. JKCP (1926 ed.)
Silent tepees stand like shocked corn, The. Always the Melting Moon Comes. Margot Osborn. CaP
Silent Testimony. Catherine Parmenter. PGD
Silent the Forests. Tasso, *tr. fr. Italian by* Edwin Morgan. LyPI
Silent Tongue, *sel.* Thomas Lake Harris.
"Exterior speech is oft a curse." BAP
Silent Tower of Bottreau[x], The. Robert Stephen Hawker. GoBC; OBRV; TCEP; VA
Silent Town, The. Richard Dehmel, *tr. fr. German by* Jethro Bithell. AWP; JAWP; WBP
"Silent upon a peak in Darien." Darien. Sir Edwin Arnold. MC; PAH
Silent Voices, The. Tennyson. BMEP; EPP; LEAP; MaRV; OQP; QP-2; VA
Silent Wail. Kenji Miyazawa, *tr. fr. Japanese by* Takamichi Ninomiya *and* D. J. Enright. PoLJ
Silent Woman, The. Ben Jonson. *See* Epicoene; or, The Silent Woman.
Silent Wooded Place, The. Rachael E. Miller. CAG
Silent words ripen of themselves. *Unknown, tr. fr. Chinese.* Tao Teh Ching, XIII. WhP
Silentium. Feodor Tyutchev, *tr. fr. Russian by* Babette Deutsch. LiTW; OnPM; TrRV; BoR, *tr. by* R. M. Hewitt; WoL, *tr. by* Babette Deutsch *and* Avrahm Yarmolinsky
Silentium Altum. Blanche Mary Kelly. CAW
Silently, every hour, a pair would rise. Turkey-Buzzards. Mark Van Doren. BLA
Silently fell/ The snow on the waters. Snow at Sea. John Gould Fletcher. ChMo; CMP
Silently gazing from the tower, apart. Cleopatra. Albert Samain. MiFP
Silently, slowly falls the snow from an ashen sky. Snowfall. Giosuè Carducci. AWP; JAWP; WBP
Silenus in Proteus. Thomas Lovell Beddoes. EnRP; ERP
Silet. Ezra Pound. MAP; MoAB; MoAmPo
Silex Scintillans. Henry Vaughan. *See* They Are All Gone.
Silhouette. Kathleen Hewitt. DiM
Silhouette. Violet Alleyn Storey. CIV
Silhouette and Oil. Rebecca Cushman. NoCaPo
Silhouette in Sepia. Robert V. Carr. PoOW
Silhouette on the face of the moon. Shadow. Richard Bruce. CDC
Silk,/ Satin. *Unknown.* OxNR
Silk Curtain, The. Tu Mu, *tr. fr. Chinese.* WhP
Silk I have for you, Madonna—you shook your small dear head. Needs. Elizabeth Rendall. HBMV
Silk Merchant's Daughter, The, *2 vers., with music. Unknown.* ShS
Silken curtain veils the skies, A. Indian Summer. Henry van Dyke. VOD
Silken-sheathed Angelica, The. Daily Paradox. Sara Henderson Hay. InMe
Silken Shoe upon Golden Last. Jens Peter Jacobsen, *tr. fr. Danish by* Charles W. Stork. BoDS
Silken Tent, The. Robert Frost. CoV; ExPo; InPo; MoPo; NePA
Silkie o' Sule Skerrie, The. *Unknown. See* Great Silkie of Sule Skerry, The.
Silkweed. Philip Henry Savage. AA; OBAV
Silkworm, The. Marco Girolamo Vida, *tr. fr. Latin by* Francis Sylvester Mahony. *Fr.* De Bombycibus. CAW
Silkworms. Mary Elliott. OTPC (1923 ed.)
Siller Croun [*or* Crown], The. Susanna Blamire. AV; DiM; HBV; LPS-1
Silly Boy, there is no cause. Song. Thomas Pestel. ElL
Silly boy, 'tis full moon yet, thy night as day shines clearly. First Love. Thomas Campion. LO; OxBoLi; SiCE
Silly Fair. Congreve. *See* Lesbia.
Silly Fool, The. W. H. Auden. *See* Happy Ending.
Silly girl! Yet morning lies. To a Pretty Girl. Israel Zangwill. TrJP
Silly heart forbeare. *Unknown.* SeCSL
Silly little fireflies, The. Demaru, *tr. fr. Japanese by* Lois J. Erickson. SoLD
Silly Old Man, The. *Unknown.* CoMu
Silly shepherd lately sate, A. A Shepherd's Dream. Nicholas Breton. ReIE
Silly Song, A. Louis How. PR
Silly swain whose love breeds discontent, The. Tityrus to His Fair Phyllis. John Dickenson. *Fr.* The Shepherd's Complaint. ElL
Silly Sweetheart. *Unknown.* CH
Silly young cricket, accustomed to sing, A. The Ant and the Cricket. GoTP; HBV; HBVY; OnHT; OTPC (1923 ed.); PRWS; TVSH
Silly young fellow named Hyde, A. Limerick. *Unknown.* LiBL; WhC
Silus hath sold his crimson satin suit. Henry Parrot. SiCE
Silva Gadelica, *sel. Unknown, tr. fr. Irish by* George Sigerson. Solace in Winter. TIP
Silvae, *sel.* Statius, *tr. fr. Latin by* J. V. Cunningham.
"What was my crime, youthful most gentle god," V, 4. LaP
Silver. Walter de la Mare. AnEnPo; BoChLi; BoTP; BrR; CaAE; ChMo; CMP; CP; CV; FaPON; GFA; GoTP; GTSL; MBP; MoAB; MoBrPo; MW; NeMA; NV; PCD; PoeMoYo; PoMa; PoMS; PoTo; PtOT; RAR; ShBV-1; SiSoSe; StVeCh; SUS; TCEP; TiPo; TreF; WaKn

Silver Age, The, *sel.* Thomas Heywood.
Praise of Ceres. ElL
Silver bark of beech, and sallow. Counting-out Rhyme. Edna St. Vincent Millay. MoShBr
Silver Bells. Hamish Hendry. BoTP
Silver birch is a dainty lady, The. Child's Song in Spring [*or* Bird's Song in Spring]. Edith Nesbit. BoTP; DD; HBV; HH; MeMeAg; MW; OHIP; OTPC; PRWS; RAR
Silver birch-tree like a sacred maid, A. Recollection. Amelia Walstien Carpenter. AA
Silver Bird of Herndyke Mill, The. Edmund Blunden. GoTL (1949 ed.)
Silver Bird's Nest, The. *Unknown.* PEOR
Silver Bowl, The, *sel.* Joseph Ezobi, *tr. fr. Hebrew by* D. I. Friedmann.
Barren Soul, A. TrJP
Silver Canoe, The. Arthur Guiterman. TBM
Silver carolling of Matins woke, The. On the Annunciation of Fra Angelico. Manuel Machado. CAW
Silver clouds are lightly sailing. Midsummer Lullaby. *Unknown.* BOL
Silver Crook, The. Alfred Noyes. ChMo; CMP
Silver Dagger, The. *Unknown.* ABS (A *and* B *vers.*); BaBo
Silver dust/ lifted from the earth. Pear Tree. Hilda Doolittle ("H. D."). HBMV; MAP; MoAmPo; NeMA; UnPo
Silver herring throbbed thick in my seine, The. Sonnet. Kenneth Leslie. *Fr.* By Stubborn Stars. BoCaPo; PeCV; TwCaPo
Silver House, The. John Lea. BoTP
Silver Jack. *Unknown.* CoSo; CSF
Silver Jubilee. Wyn Griffith. MoWP
Silver key of the fountain of tears. A Fragment: To Music [*or* Music]. Shelley. BoLiVe; ERP; TrGrPo
Silver Lamps. W. C. Dix. BePJ
Silver Lantern, A. Karle Wilson Baker. HBMV
Silver Leaf, The. John Hay. NePoAm
Silver Moon, The. Sappho, *tr. fr. Greek by* John Addington Symonds. EnLi-1
Silver moon's enamoured beam, The. Kate of Aberdeen. John Cunningham. HBV
Silver Penny, The. Walter de la Mare. ExPo; OBMV
Silver Poplars. Grace Noll Crowell. LS
Silver Question, The. Oliver Herford. NA
Silver rain, the shining sun, The. The Harvest. Alice Corbin. BoTP
Silver Road, The. Hamish Hendry. BoTP
Silver sand, silver sand. Sea-Garden. Cecilia MacKinnon. CPG
Silver Sheep. Anne Blackwell Payne. GFA; SiSoSe; UTS
Silver Ships. Mildred Plew Meigs. FaPON; TiPo
Silver sky is faintly etched, A. January. Michael Lewis. GoTP
Silver Spoon, The. Po Chü-i, *tr. fr. Chinese by* Arthur Waley. TrCh
Silver Stag, The. Kathleen Raine. FaBoMo
Silver Sty, The. *Unknown. See* Lady Who Loved a Swine, The.
Silver Swan, The. *Unknown.* ChTr; ElL; ElSeCe; ExPo; FaBoCh; LoGBV; OAEP; PoD; TuPP
(Silver Swan [*or* Swanne], Who Living Had No Note, The.) AtBAP; PoEL-2; ReEn; SiCE
Silver Tassie, The. Burns. *See* My Bonnie Mary.
Silver that shies off the silver-leaf maple, The. The Silver Leaf. John Hay. NePoAm
Silver Threads among the Gold. Eben E. Rexford. FaFP; OlF; TreF
Silver Tree, The. Francis Keppel. BLA
Silver trumpets rang across the dome, The. Easter Day in Rome. Oscar Wilde. EOAH
Silver-vested monkey trips, A. Cortège. Paul Verlaine. AWP; OnPM; WoL
Silver Wedding. Ralph Hodgson. HBMV; TrGrPo
Silvered hills. Fields of Soria, VII. Antonio Machado. TeCS
Silvery dewdrops that in autumn light, The. Jewels. Asayasu. OnPM
Silvery the olives on Ravello's steeps. Above Salerno. Ada Foster Murray. HBV
Silvia. Sir George Etherege. SeCL
Silvia. Shakespeare. *See* Who Is Sylvia?
Silvia, let us from the crowd retire. To Silvia. Countess of Winchilsea. *Fr.* The Cautious Lovers. HBV
Silvy. *Unknown. See* On a Time.
Sim Ines. Jane Stubbs. FiBHP
Simaetha. Hilda Doolittle ("H. D."). MAPA
Simaetha. Theocritus. *See* Incantation, The.
Simchas Torah. Morris Rosenfeld, *tr. fr. Yiddish.* TrJP
Simeon's Light Remembered. John W. Simons. JKCP (1955 ed.)
Simhat Torah. Judah Leib Gordon, *tr. fr. Hebrew by* Alice Lucas *and* Helena Frank. TrJP
Similar Cases. Charlotte Perkins Stetson Gilman. BAP; BBV; DDA; HBV; OBAV
Simile. Sir Samuel Ferguson. *Fr.* Congal. IrPN
Simile, A. Mrs. J. Hunter. DiM
Simile, A. Matthew Prior. BOHV; CEP; CoBE; EiPP; FaBoEn; TCEP
Simile for Her Smile, A. Richard Wilbur. FiMAP; HoPM; MiAP
Similes. Edward Moxon. OBRV
Similes. *Unknown.* BOHV; HBVY
(Comparisons.) GoTP
Similitude, A. Charles Harpur. BoAu
Simmer's a Pleasant Time. Burns. PoEL-4
Simon and Judas. Kenneth W. Porter. ChIP; OQP; QP-2
Simon and Susan. *Unknown.* OxBoLi
"Simon Bar-Jona, lovest thou Me?" Upon This Rock. James L. Duff. JKCP
Simon, called Peter, and Andrew his brother. Fishers. Edwin Meade Robinson. LHV
Simon Danz. Longfellow. *See* Dutch Picture, A.
Simon Lee. Wordsworth. BEL; BPN; EM-2; EmBrPo; EnRP; EPN; ERP; GEPC; GTBS; GTSE; GTSL; REAL
(Simon Lee the Old Huntsman.) GTBS-D; GTBS-W
Simon Legree—a Negro Sermon. Vachel Lindsay. The Booker Washington Trilogy, I. CoBA; HBMV; InMe; LiTA; LoGBV; MoVE; NAMP; NePA; PCN; PFY; ShBV-2
("Legree's big house was white and green.") LA
(Negro Sermon, A: Simon Legree.) AnAmPo; ATP (1935 ed.); MAP; MoAmPo; PFY
Simon of Cyrene. Georgia Harkness. ChIP
Simon, Son of Onias. Ecclesiasticus, L: 5–14, Bible, Apocrypha. BHV
Simon Surnamed Peter. Edgar Lee Masters. QS
Simon the Cyrenean. Lucy Lyttelton. HBV
Simon the Cyrenian Speaks. Glen Baker. ChIP
Simon the Cyrenian Speaks. Countee Cullen. BBV (1951 ed.); MAP; MaRV; MoAmPo; NeMA; OQP; PoNe; QP-1; QS; StJW
Simonetta ("Candid the Lady was"). Angelo Poliziano, *tr. fr. Italian by* Iain Fletcher. *Fr.* La Giostra. LyPI
Simonetta ("When la bella Simonetta was borne forth"). Angelo Poliziano, *pr. tr. fr. Latin by* Richard Aldington. LaP
Simple and fresh and fair from winter's close emerging. The First Dandelion. Walt Whitman. ADAH; APW; CBOV; NePA; TSW; TSWC
Simple Arab, The. Jami, *tr. fr. Persian by* Edward Fitzgerald. *Fr.* Salámán and Absál. PeP
(Bewildered Arab, The.) WoL
Simple Autumnal. Louise Bogan. MAP; MoAB; MoAmPo; MOAP
Simple bee that do's no harme, The. *Unknown.* SeCSL
Simple child, A/ That lightly draws its breath. We Are Seven. Wordsworth. BLPA; BPN; EM-2; EmBrPo; EnLi-2; EnRP; EPN; EPP; ERP; GEPC; GN; HBV; HiLiEn; LPS-1; NeHB; OnPP; PIR; PoE; PTA-1; TCEP; TreF; WBLP
Simple Duty, A. Poe. *See* To Frances S. Osgood.
Simple, erect, severe, austere, sublime. The Pantheon. Byron. *Fr.* Childe Harold's Pilgrimage. LPS-2
Simple Faith. William Cowper. *Fr.* Truth. OBEC
Simple Field That I Shall Buy, The. Mildred I. McNeal Sweeney. PFY
Simple-hearted Child was He, A. The Little Child. Albert Bigelow Paine. AA; ChIP; MaRV
Simple Horizontal, The. Margaret Avison. BoCaPo (1948 ed.)
(Old Adam.) BoCaPo (1943 ed.)
Simple Life, The. Toyohiko Kagawa, *tr. fr. Japanese by* Lois J. Erickson. SoLD
Simple light from all contagion free, A. An Infant's Eye. Thomas Traherne. CoBE
Simple Maid, A. Lord De Tabley. VA
Simple Nature. George John Romanes. HBV
Simple Pleasures. Antiphilus of Byzantium, *tr. fr. Greek by* F. L. Lucas. GrPE
Simple Ploughboy, The. *Unknown.* FaBoCh; LoGBV; OBB
Simple ring with a single stone, A. A Pearl, a Girl. Robert Browning. BPN; PoVP; VLEP
Simple Sam. Leroy F. Jackson. ChBR; GaP
Simple Simon. Harriet S. Morgridge. *Fr.* Mother Goose Sonnets. AA
Simple Simon met a pieman. Mother Goose. BoChLi; BoTP; FaBoBe; GaP; GoTP; HBV; HBVY; OTPC; OxNR; PPL; RIS; SiTL; StVeCh; WP
Simple Song. Paul Verlaine, *tr. fr. French by* Alan Conder. TrFP
Simple Tastes. Archilochus, *tr. fr. Greek by* C. M. Bowra. OxBG
Simple Things. Paul Jean Toulet, *tr. fr. French by* Joseph T. Shipley. CAW
Simple Verses, *sel.* José Martí, *tr. fr. Spanish by* Elizabeth Selden.

"I cultivate a white rose." BoFr
Simple was I and was young. After Reading Psalms XXXIX, XL, etc. Thomas Hardy. NBE
Simple Way, The. *Unknown, at. to* Lao-tze. *See* Tao Teh King.
Simpler Thing, a Chair, A. Robert Mezey. NePoEA
Simples. James Joyce. CaAE; HBMV; NP
Simpleton looks in love for rest, A. Three Love Poems, III. Stepan Petrovich Shchipachev. RuPo
Simplex Munditiis. Ben Jonson, *tr. fr. the Latin of* Jean Bonnefons. *Fr.* Epicoene; or, The Silent Woman, I, i. AWP; BCEP; CBOV; CoBE; EnLi-1; EnLit; EPS; GoBC; HBV; HoPM; InPo; JAWP; LEAP; OBEV; TOP; WBP
(Clerimont's Song.) BoLiVe; CaAE; LoBV; PreP; SeCV-1; SiCE; TrGrPo
(Freedom in Dress.) LPS-2
(Simplicity and Sweet Neglect.) EV-2
(Song: "Still to be neat, still to be dressed.") AnEnPo; CoEV; ElSeCe; LiTL; NeHB; OBS; ViBoPo
(Still to Be Neat [Still to Be Dressed].) ALV; ElL; EM-1; EnL; GTBS-W; MaPo; OAEP; OuHeWo; PoE; PoFS; ReEn; SeCePo; TuPP; TyEnPo; WHA
("Still to be neat, still to be drest.") EG; LO; ReaPo; ReEn
(Sweet Neglect.) BLV
Simplicity Franklin P. Adams, *after* Horace. *See* Persian Fopperies.
Simplicity. Emily Dickinson. *See* How happy is the little stone.
Simplicity. Horace, *tr. fr. Latin by* T. R. Clark. Odes, III, 1. RoL
Simplicity. Semyon Kirsanov, *tr. fr. Russian by* Jack Lindsay. RuPo
Simplicity and Sweet Neglect. Ben Jonson. *See* Simplex Munditiis.
Simplicity's Song. Robert Wilson. *Fr.* Three Ladies of London. OBSC
Simplify Me When I'm Dead. Keith Douglas. *See* Remember Me.
Simplon Pass, The. Wordsworth. *Fr.* The Prelude, VI. BPN; EM-2; ERP; InPo; PoFS
(Alpine Descent: "Downwards we hurried.") WHA
("Brook and road, The.") EV-2; OBRV
(Down the Simplon Pass: "Downwards we hurried.") EPN
("Melancholy slackening that ensued, The.") PoEL-4
Simply being drunk makes it. Drunk; on Crutches. Raymond Souster. PeCV
Simply by sailing in a new direction. Landfall in Unknown Seas. Allen Curnow. AnNZ
Simply I would sing for the time being. Interlude. Keidrych Rhys. MoWP
Simply she stands, by the cathedral portal. Eva. Rainer Maria Rilke. TwGV
Simpson's Rest. George S. Simpson. PoOW
Simson settled in the timber when his arm was strong and true. Peter Simson's Farm. Edward Dyson. BoAu
Simultaneously, as soundlessly. Prime. W. H. Auden. PoLFOT
Sin. George Herbert. BCEP; EPS; ES; EV-2; PeBoSo; ViBoPo
Sin, The; a Definition. Francis Maguire. JKCP (1955 ed.)
Sin and Satiety. Aeschylus, *tr. fr. Greek by* E. D. A. Morshead. *Fr.* Agamemnon. GrR
Sin, Despair, and Lucifer. Phineas Fletcher. *Fr.* The Locusts, or Apollyonists. OBS
Sin I fro Love escaped am so fat. Escape. Chaucer. *Fr.* Merciles Beaute. CaAE; LEAP; LoPS; OBEV (1st ed.)
Sin Is Sin. *Unknown.* BLP
Sin of Omission, The. Margaret E. Sangster. BLPA; HBV; MaRV; PoToHe; PTA-2; TreFS
Sin of self-love [*or* Sinne of selfe-love] possesseth all mine eye [*or* al mine eie]. Sonnets, LXII. Shakespeare. PeBoSo; PoEL-2
Sin of the Coppenter Man. Edmund Vance Cooke. PTA-2
Sin-satiate. and haggard with despair. Tannhäuser. William Morton Payne. AA
Since after all we were born to marry strangers. To Marry Strangers. Winfield Townley Scott. FiMAP
Since all my life out of my death derives. Ballata: Of Love's Power. Guido Cavalcanti. LiTW; LyMA; LyPI
Since all that I can ever do for thee. The Last Wish. "Owen Meredith." LoPS; OBEV (1st ed.); OBVV
Since all the riches of all this world. Two Kinds of Riches. Blake. EPP
Since All the World's Thus Gay and Free. Earl of Rochester. BeR
Since ancient Time began. Washington at Trenton. Richard Watson Gilder. WOAH
Since as in night's deck-watch ye show. Herman Melville. *Fr.* John Marr. ViBoPo
Since beauty is honored all over the empire. The Beautiful Hsi-shih. Wang Wei. OuHeWo
Since Bonny-Boots Was Dead. *Unknown.* OxBoLi; PoEL-2
(Madrigal: "Since Bonny-boots was dead, that so divinely.") SiTL
Since brass[e], nor stone, nor earth, nor boundless[e] sea. Sonnets, LXV. Shakespeare. AEV; AtBAP; AWP; BEL; BoFr; BoLiVe; BrBE; CBOV; CoEV; EM-1; EnLi-1 (1949 ed.); EPP; ES; EV-1; FaFP; FiP; GTBS; GTBS-D; GTBS-W; GTSE; GTSL; JAWP; LiTB; LiTL; MaPo; MCCG; OuHeWo; PeBoSo; PIAE; PoD; PoFS; PoRA; ReaPo; SeCeV; SiCE; TCEP; TOP; TwP; UnPo (1st ed.); WBP
Since Celia's my foe. Celia. Thomas Duffett. SeCL
Since Christ was born in Bethlehem. The Heavenly Runaway. John Daniel Logan. CPG
Since Christmas. Frederick R. McCreary. MAP
Since Cleopatra Died. Thomas Wentworth Higginson. AA; OBAV
Since counterfeit plots have affected this age. A Ballad upon the Popish Plot. John Gadbury. CoMu
Since, dearest Harry, you will needs request. Addison. *Fr.* An Account of the Greatest English Poets. PtP
Since earth has put you away, O sons of Barmak. Abu Nowas for the Barmacides. *Unknown. Fr.* The Thousand and One Nights. AWP
Since earth in winter yields. New Hampshire Sexton. James A. Notopoulos. CAG
Since Feeling Is First. E. E. Cummings. LoPo; MoAB; MoAmPo; PoLFOT
Since First I Saw Your Face. *Unknown.* EV-1; LiTB; OBEV
("Since first I saw your face I resolved to honour and renown ye.") EG; LO; OBSC
Since first the beams of summer lit. The Baby of Saint Brigid. Francis Carlin. PraNu
Since first the stone was rolled away. This Easter Day. Martha Snell Nicholson. BePJ
Since first to exhibit his plays he began. The Poet and the People [*or* The Poet and His Public]. Aristophanes. *Fr.* The Acharnians. GrR; OxBG
Since for kissing thee, Minguillo,/ Mother's ever scolding me. The Kiss, *tr. by* Sir John Bowring. AnSpL-1
Since for kissing thee, Minguillo, my mother scolds me all the day. Minguillo's Kiss, *tr. fr. Spanish.* BOHV
Since fortune's wrath envieth the wealth. Earl of Surrey. SiPS
Since God Is There. Mme Guyon, *tr. fr. French by* William Cowper. MaRV
Since gratious Lord if thou withhold thy hand. *Unknown.* SeCSL
Since he will call some night to sup. Most Honored Guest. Walter Shea. ChIP
Since honour from the honourer proceeds. Concerning the Honour of Books [*or* Of Books]. John Florio. ElL; ES
Since hopeless of thy love I go. Hopeless Love. *Unknown.* IrPN
Since I am coming [*or* comming] to that holy room. Hymn [*or* Hymne] to God, My God, in My Sickness. John Donne. AtBAP; CaAE; ChTr; CoEV; ElSeCe; EnL; EnLP; FaBoEn; GoBC; LoBV; MaPo; MeLP; MePo; NBE; OAEP; OBS; OxBoCh; PoEL-2; ReEn; SeCL; SeCV-1; SeEP; TrPWD; TuPP; UnS
Since I am convinced. Saigyo Hoshi, *tr. fr. Japanese by* Arthur Waley. AWP; LiTW; PFE
Since I am free,/ Offending no just law, let no law make. George Chapman. *Fr.* Bussy d'Ambois, II, i. MyFE
Since I believe in God the Father Almighty. Johannes Milton, Senex. Robert Bridges. EPP; LiTB; NAMP; PoEL-5
Since I did leave the presence of my love. Amoretti, LXXXVI. Spenser. EG; PeBoSo; ReEn
Since I do not hope to return ever. Ballata 11: Last Song; from Exile. Guido Cavalcanti. LyPI
Since I for Love. *Unknown.* TMEV
Since I have been so quickly done for. On an Infant Eight Months Old. *Unknown.* SiTL; WhC
Since I Have Felt the Sense of Death. Helen Hoyt. *See* Sense of Death, The.
Since I have lacked the comfort of that light. Amoretti, LXXXVII. Spenser. PeBoSo
Since I have learned Love's shining alphabet. Ignorance. John Masefield. BEL
Since I have seen a bird one day. The Truth. W. H. Davies. FaBoTw
Since I Have Seen Death's Face. Fania Kruger. UnW
Since I have set my lips to your full cup, my sweet. More Strong than Time. Victor Hugo. AWP; JAWP; WBP
Since I heard/ Faintly the voice. Mitsune. *Fr.* Kokin Shu. AWP
Since I heard them speak of her great shame. One Woman. Zoë Akins. BLP; LEAP
Since I keep only what I give away. Sonnet. George Hetherington. NeIP
Since I Lay Ill. Po Chü-i, *tr. fr. Chinese by* Arthur Waley. TrCh

Since I left her. Mibu no Tadamine, *tr. fr. Japanese by* Kenneth Rexroth. OnPJ
Since I left my home to seek official state. Po Chü-i to Yüan Chen. Po Chü-i. BoFr
Since I left you mine eye is in my mind. Sonnets, CXIII. Shakespeare. PeBoSo
Since I lived a stranger in the City of Hsün-yang. Rain. Po Chü-i. TrCh
Since I noo mwore do zee your feäce. The Wife a-Lost. William Barnes. EnLoPo; EV-4; GTBS; GTBS-D; OBEV; OBVV
Since I renounced the rose. Renunciation. Mary Brent Whiteside. LS
Since I returned from garrison in the west, my hairs have turned gray. Dying Spring. Lu Yu. WhP
Since I took quiet to my breast. Quiet. Léonie Adams. MOAP
Since I was a child. Rebel. Irene Rutherford McLeod. BMEP; HBMV
Since I was in Syracuse is a month ago. Quarries in Syracuse. Louis Golding. TrJP
Since, if you stood by my side to-day. Alas! Phoebe Cary. LBAP
Since in a land not barren still. Love and Discipline. Henry Vaughan. EPS; TrPWD
Since just disdain began to rise. Being Scorned, and Disdained, He Inveighs against His Lady. *Unknown.* SiCE
Since, Lord, to thee/ A narrow way and little gate. Holy [*or* H.] Baptism[e]. George Herbert. HBV; PoEL-2; SeCV-1
Since love is such that as ye wot. Sir Thomas Wyatt. SiPS
Since Love will needs that I shall love. Sir Thomas Wyatt. SiPS
Since lovers' joys then leave so sick a taste. Henry King. *Fr.* Paradox: That Fruition Destroys Love. LO
Since man has been articulate. Every Thing. Harold Monro. AnEnPo; ChMo; CMP; EPP; MBP; MoBrPo; NeMA; NV
Since men grow diffident at last. Youth Sings a Song of Rosebuds. Countee Cullen. BANP; CaAE; PoNe
Since more than half my hopes came true. Contented at Forty. Sarah N. Cleghorn. HBMV
Since My Birth. Iwan Goll, *tr. fr. French by* Claire Goll. OnPM
Since Nature's works be good, and death doth serve. Why Fear to Die? Sir Philip Sidney. *Fr.* Arcadia. SiPS
Since neither Bach nor Paganini speak. Morning Concert—Nantucket. Isabel Harriss Barr. JKCP (1955 ed.)
Since Nine o'Clock. C. P. Cavafy, *tr. fr. Modern Greek by* Rae Dalven. MoGP
Since nought avails, let me arise and leave. Love's Last Resource. Sadi. *Fr.* The Gulistan. AWP; LiTW
Since ocean rolled and ocean winds were strong. Sonnets on the Sea's Voice. George Sterling. EtS
Since o'er thy footstool here below. Heaven's Magnificence. William Augustus Muhlenberg. AA
Since of earth, air and water. Gratias Age. Geoffrey Howard. NLK
Since one anthologist put in his book. Anthologistics. Arthur Guiterman. InMe; WhC
Since our country, our God—Oh, my Sire. Jephtha's Daughter. Byron. EmBrPo
Since our hair was plaited and we became man and wife. To His Wife. Su Wu. LO; TrCh
Since Pa put in the radio we have a lot of fun. The Radio. Edgar A. Guest. PEDC
Since perfect happiness, by princes sought. To the Highborn Prince of Men, Henry. George Chapman. *Fr.* The Epistle Dedicatory. ReEn; ReIE
Since Reverend Doctors now declare. The Respectable Burgher. Thomas Hardy. ViP
Since She Is Gone. William Browne. *See* Memory ("So shuts the marigold . . .").
Since she must go, and I must mourn, come night. His Parting from Her. John Donne. Elegies, XII. OBS
Since she whom I lov'd [*or* loved] hath payd [*or* paid] her last debt. Holy Sonnets, XVII. John Donne. EnLP; MePo; NBE; OAEP; PeBoSo; PoD; SeEP; TwP
Since, Sir, you have made it your study to vex. The Lady's Receipt for a Beau's Dress. *Unknown.* CoMu
Since So Mine Eyes. Sir Philip Sidney. *Fr.* Arcadia. SiPS
Since so ye please to hear me plain. Sir Thomas Wyatt. SiPS
Since succour to the feeblest of the wise. Remembered Grace. Coventry Patmore. CoEV; OxBoCh
Since that the dewdrop holds the star. My Star. John Banister Tabb. BPN; VLEP
Since that this thing we call the world. An Epicurean Ode. John Hall. EG; MeLP; MePo; SeEP
Since the Conquest none of us. The Conquest. Oliver St. John Gogarty. OBMV
Since the day. Loneliness. Hsiao Wu Ti. PoHN
Since the external disorder, and extravagant lies. Dedication. W. H. Auden. *Fr.* Look, Stranger! CaAE
Since the first day of creation. The Fates. Alfred de Vigny. LiA
Since the lily's white is not so white as you. Song. Pierre de Ronsard. TrFP
Since the meadow hides its face in satin shot with greens and blues. The Branding. Farrukhi. PeP
Since the wise men have not spoken, I speak that am only a fool. The Fool. Padraic Pearse. OnYI
Since, then, my planet has looked on. My Fortune. Francisco de Quevedo y Villegas. AnSpL-1
Since then, there has been always, suspended on my brow and hurting me. Léon Paul Fargue. *Fr.* Aeternae Memoriae Patris. MiFP
Since there are saints in the islands still. To Ultima Thule. George Dangerfield. CAW
Since There Is No Escape. Sara Teasdale. AnAmPo; LA
Since there's no help, come let us kiss and part. Idea, LXI [*or* The Parting *or* Sonnet *or* Love's Farewell]. Michael Drayton. AEV; AnEnPo; AtBAP; ATP; AWP; BCEP; BEL; BLV; BrBE; CaAE; CBOV; CoEV; EG; EiL; ElSeCe; EM-1; EnL; EnLi-1; EnLit; EnLoPo; EPP; ES; EtPaEn; EV-1; ExPo; FaBoEn; GTBS; GTBS-D; GTBS-W; GTSE; GTSL; HBV; HoPM; InP; JAWP; LEAP; LiTB; LiTG; LiTL; LO; LoBV; LoPo; LoPS; LPS-1; OAEP; OBEV; OBSC; OtMeF; OuHeWo; PeBoSo; PIAE; PoE; PoEL-2; ReEn; ReIE; RiBV; SeCePo; SeCeV; ShBV-4; SiCE; TCEP; TOP; TreFS; TrGrPo; TuPP; TwHP; TyEnPo; ViBoPo; WBP; WHA
Since this ingenious earth began. In Praise of Diversity. Phyllis McGinley. SiTL
Since Those We Love and Those We Hate. W. E. Henley. OBMV
Since Thou Art Gone Henry Vaughan. *See* Silence, and Stealth of Days!
Since thou art gone, my friend, I seek in vain for peace. On Parting with Moses ibn Ezra. Judah Halevi. TrJP
Since thou desirest, I will then unveil. The Demon Speaks. Calderón de la Barca. *Fr.* El Magico prodigioso. CAW
Since Thou Hast Given Me This Good Hope, O God. Robert Louis Stevenson. TrPWD
Since thou hast view'd some Gorgon, and art grown. The Double Rock. Henry King. AtBAP; BoW; NBE
Since thou, O fondest and truest. Song. Robert Bridges. LoPS
Since thou wilt goe fond hart and I, must lye. *Unknown.* SeCSL
Since through vertue encreaseth dignity. Good Counsel. James I, King of Scotland. ACP; EBSV
Since Thursday he'd been working overtime. The Machine. W. W. Gibson. PCN; PoTo; PtOT
Since 'tis resolvd that I must dy. *Unknown.* SeCSL
Since to be loved endures. Robert Bridges. GTML; GTSL
Since to thy brimming cup my lips I oft have set. The Vase. Victor Hugo. TrFP
Since Tomorrow Is Sunday. Jacinto Fombona Pachano, *tr. fr. Spanish by* H. R. Hays. TwSpPo
Since tonight the wind is high. The Viking Terror. *Unknown.* KiLC
Since we are born in blood to be convinced. La Ci Darem la Mano. John Frederick Nims. MiAP
Since we had changed. Message. Allen Ginsberg. NeAP
Since We Parted. "Owen Meredith." HBV
Since we parted, spring is half over. To the Tune of "A Clear Calm Music." Li Yu. WhP
Since We Said Good-Bye. Arthur Upson. PR
Since we were first married. On the Death of His Wife. Mei Yao Ch'en. OnPC
Since who'd begin must make an end. "I Die Daily." Phil. J. Fisher. MaRV
Since without Thee we do no good. Hymn. Elizabeth Barrett Browning. TrPWD
Since ye delight to know. Sir Thomas Wyatt. SiPS
Since you all will have singing, and won't be said nay. The King's Own Regulars. *Unknown.* PAH
Since you and I. To a Husband. Su Wu. PoHN
Since You Are Gone. Wang Jung, *tr. fr. Chinese by* Henry H. Hart. PoHN
Since you are gone. Devotion. Pao Chao. PoHN
Since you are what my days have brought. To Failure. Marguerite Wilkinson. TriL
Since you have come thus far. Chorus. C. Day Lewis. *Fr.* Noah and the Waters. OAEP (2d ed.)
Since you have left my side. Gathering Bamboo. Ku Jo P'u. PoHN
Since you have turned unkind. To a Lady Friend. W. H. Davies. MBP; MoBrPo
Since you left, I know not whether you are far or near. Waiting for News. Ou-yang Hsiu. ChLP
Since you lie buried in the hill. To Senna Hoy. Else Lasker-Schüler. OnPM
Since you must go, and I must bid farewell. An Elegy. Ben Jonson. LoBV; TriL
Since you remember Nimmo, and arrive. Nimmo. E. A. Robinson. HBMV

Since you will have it so, I sing the rose. Paul Claudel. *Fr.* Canticle for Three Voices. MiFP

Since You Will Needs. Sir Thomas Wyatt. ReIE; TuPP ("Since you will needs [*or* Sins you will nedes] that I shall sing.") NBE; SiCE; SiPS

Since your limbs were laid out. Anthony O'Daly. James Stephens. BoFr

Since your voice like a soft vapour laps me. I Honour You in Dread. Ramón López Velarde. AnMP

Since Youth has all too brief a stay. What Is Worth the Singing? Cecil French. GTIV

Since Youth Is All for Gladness. Glenn Ward Dresbach. BAP; HBMV

Sincere Flattery. James Kenneth Stephen. *See* Imitation of Walt Whitman.

Sincere Man, The. Alfred Grant Walton. PoToHe (new ed.)

Sincere Praise. Isaac Watts. CEP
"Almighty Maker God!" *sel.* TrPWD

Sincerest Critic of my Prose, or Rhyme. Letter to Viscount Cobham. Congreve. LoBV

Sindbad, *with music. Unknown.* SoAmSa

Sine Amore Nil Est Jucundum. Mimnermus, *tr. fr. Greek by* G. Lowes Dickinson. GrL; OxBG

Sinfonia Domestica. Jean Starr Untermeyer. HBMV; LEAP; MAP; MoAmPo; NP

Sinfonia Eroica. Alice Archer James. AA

Sinful father, The/ Seem'd not to strike. Shakespeare. *Fr.* Pericles. I, ii. PoFr

Sing a little as the feet unwearied. Voyageur. R. E. Rashley. CaP

Sing a Song of Books. Nancy Byrd Turner. MOB

Sing a song of cobbler! Jeremy Hobbler. *Unknown.* BoTP

Sing a song of hollow logs. Song of Summer Days. J. W. Foley. BoTP

Sing a Song of Joy, *sel.* Thomas Campion.
"Sing a song of joy!" UnS

Sing a song of mincemeat. Mincemeat. Elizabeth Gould. BoTP

Sing a song of monkeys. The Monkeys. Edith Osborne Thompson. TiPo; UTS

Sing a Song of Moonlight. Ivy O. Eastwick. SiSoSe

Sing a song of picnics. Picnic Day. Rachel Field. SiSoSe; TiPo

Sing a song of pop corn. A Pop Corn Song. Nancy Byrd Turner. FaPON; GFA; MPB

Sing a song of rockets. Fourth of July Song. Lois Lenski. SiSoSe

Sing a song of scissor-men. The Scissor-Man. Madeleine Nightingale. BoTP; GaP; MPB; RAR; TiPo

Sing a Song of Seasons! Robert Louis Stevenson. OTPC (1946 ed.)

Sing a song of sixpence. Mother Goose. BoChLi; BoN; FaBoBe; FTB; HBV; HBVY; LiTG; OlF; OnHT; OTPC; OxBoLi; OxNR; PCH; PPL; RIS; SAS; SiTL; StVeCh; TiPo

Sing a Song of Sixpence, *parody.* Frank Sidgwick. WhC

Sing a song of Spring-time. The Song of the Seasons. Cosmo Monkhouse. DD; HBV

Sing a Song of Sunshine. Ivy O. Eastwick. SiSoSe

Sing a Song of the Cities. Morris Bishop. WhC

Sing a song of washing-up. The Washing-up Song. Elizabeth Gould. BoTP

Sing a song of winter. A Sledding Song. Norman C. Schlichter. FaPON

Sing Again. Marie van Vorst. AA

Sing again the song you sung. Egyptian Serenade. George William Curtis. HBV

Sing all the earth, ye hills break forth with singing! Rejoice! He Liveth! Kathryn Blackburn Peck. BePJ

Sing All Ye Joyful. J. R. R. Tolkien. PoRh

Sing aloud, harmonious spheares. William Strode. SeCSL

Sing aloud, his praise rehearse. The Philosopher's Devotion. Henry More. SeCL

Sing and be glad, O nations, in these hours. Edwin Markham. *Fr.* A Song of Victory. AOAH

Sing and heave, and heave and sing. The Banks of the Sacramento. *Unknown.* AmSS

Sing, Ariel, Sing. W H. Auden. *Fr.* The Sea and the Mirror. TwHP

Sing, Ballad-singer, raise a hearty tune. The Ballad Singer. Thomas Hardy. At Casterbridge Fair, I. BEL; ChMo; EmBrPo; EnLi-2 (1949 ed.); EnLit; LO; PoVP

Sing bird, on green Missouri's plain. The Death of Lyon. Henry Peterson. BIG; GA; PAH

Sing, Brothers, Sing! W. R. Rodgers. MoAB; MoBrPo (1950 ed.)

Sing care away with sport and play. A Song to the Tune of Heart's Ease. *Unknown. Fr.* Misogonus. ReEn; TuPP

Sing, children, sing! A Song of Easter. Celia Thaxter. EOAH; HH

Sing clear, O! throstle. To a Thrush. T. A. Daly. CAW; JKCP; SaFP

Sing Cuccu. *Unknown* *See* Sumer Is Icumen In.

Sing for the Garish Eye. W. S. Gilbert. BOHV; NA

Sing for the sun your lyric, lark. Raptures. W. H. Davies. CMP; EPP; WP

Sing forth a hymn sublime and solemn, grateful to glorious Varuna, imperial ruler. Hymn to Varuna, God of Fire and Light. *Unknown. Fr.* The Rigveda. LiTW

"Sing from the chamber to the grave!" The Dirge. Robert Stephen Hawker. AEV

Sing, Goddess, of Achilles, Peleus' son. The Quarrel. Homer, *tr. by* Sir William Marris. *Fr.* The Iliad, I. WoL

Sing, goddess, the anger of Peleus' son Achilleus. Homer, *tr. by* Richmond Lattimore. *Fr.* The Iliad, I. GrPo

Sing, goddess, the wrath of Achilles Peleus' son. Homer, *pr. tr. by* Lang, Leaf, *and* Myers. *Fr.* The Iliad, I. GrL

Sing Heigh-ho! Charles Kingsley. ALV; HBV (There Sits a Bird.) GBV (1952 ed.)

Sing hey, and sing ho, and sing down-a-down-derry. The Ballad of the Merry Ferry. Emma Rounds. MPB; RIS

Sing hey diddle diddle, the cat and the fiddle. *See* Hey, diddle, diddle . . .

Sing hey! for bold George Washington. George Washington. Rosemary Benét *and* Stephen Vincent Benét. FaPON; MaC

Sing hey! Sing hey!/ For Christmas Day. Christmas Greeting [*or* An Old Christmas Greeting]. *Unknown.* BrR; ChBR; FaPON; MeMeAg; MPB; SiSoSe; TiPo

Sing His Praises. John Fletcher. *See* Hymn to Pan.

Sing ho! for a brave and a gallant ship. Ten Thousand Miles Away. *Unknown.* SoAmSa

Sing Ho for the Herring. Grace Blackburn. CPG

Sing; how 'a would sing! Julie-Jane. Thomas Hardy. MoVE

Sing how the uncreated Light. Carmen Genesis. Francis Thompson. CoBE; PoLi

Sing I for a brave and gallant barque, and a stiff and a rattling breeze. Ten Thousand Miles Away. *Unknown.* AS

Sing, I must sing to my dear dolly, sing. Dolly's Lullaby. Mariana Griswold Van Rensselaer. BOL

Sing, I pray, a little song. Golden-tressed Adelaide. "Barry Cornwall." VA

Sing it, Mother; sing it low. A Cradle-Song. John Banister Tabb. BOL

Sing Ivy. *Unknown.* *See* Mad Farmer's Song.

Sing jigmijole, the pudding bowl. *Unknown.* OxNR

Sing, Klio, thou giver of guerdons of sweetness. For Hiero of Syracuse. Bacchylides. GrL

Sing low, my heart, lest we be overheard. The Heart Has Its Reasons. *Unknown.* GoBC

Sing Lullaby, as Women Do. George Gascoigne. *See* Lullaby of a Lover, The.

Sing, magnarello, merrily. The Leaf-Picking. Frédéric Mistral. AWP; JAWP; WBP

Sing me a hero! Quench my thirst. Tray. Robert Browning. BPN

Sing Me a Song. Christina Rossetti. *Fr.* Sing-Song. BoChLi

Sing Me a Song [of a Lad That Is Gone]. Robert Louis Stevenson. AlDL; InP; PFE; POTT; PoVP; VOD (Lad That Is Gone, A.) HBV (Over the Sea to Skye.) EBSV; EtS; ShBV-1

Sing me a sweet, low song of night. A Song. Hildegarde Hawthorne. AA; FaBoBe; HBV

Sing me at morn but only with your laugh. Song of Songs. Wilfred Owen. NAMP

Sing me of Hermes' beloved son, O Lady of Song. To Pan. *Unknown. Fr.* Homeric Hymns. GrR

Sing me the men ere this. He Would Have His Lady Sing. Digby Mackworth Dolben. CAW; GoBC; GTML

Sing Muse, of the anger of Haroun the Caliph. The Vizier's Apology. Arthur Guiterman. PoeMoYo

Sing, Muse, the beacon gleaming bright above. Musaeus. *Fr.* Hero and Leander. GrPo

Sing, Muse! the force and all-informing fire. *Unknown. Fr.* Homeric Hymns. GrPo

Sing, Muse, the son of Maia and of Jove. *Unknown. Fr.* Homeric Hymns. GrPo

Sing, my tongue, the Saviour's glory. Hymn [*or* Pange Lingua Gloriosa]. St. Thomas Aquinas. CAW; WGRP; WHL

Sing, nigger in the distance, coming up the hill. Night Song. Wallace Gould. AnAmPo; LA

Sing No Sad Songs for Me. *Unknown.* TriL, 8 *ll.* ("When from the world I shall be ta'en.") LO

Sing not, nightingale. Song. Aleksey Koltsov. BoR

Sing, O goddess, the wrath, the ontamable dander of Keitt. The Fight over the Body of Keitt. *Unknown.* PAH

Sing, O Muse. Homer. *See* Wrath of Achilles, The.

Sing, O Muse, of the man so wary and wise, who in far lands. Homer, *tr. by* H. B. Cotterill. *Fr.* The Odyssey, I. GrPo

Sing of romantic palaces. Idle Thoughts. V. Sackville-West. AlDL

Sing On, Blithe Bird! William Motherwell. DD; GN; HBV; HBVY; OTPC (1923 ed.) (I've Plucked the Berry.) EV-4

"Sing on," he said, "but let me dream of bliss." William Morris. *Fr.* The Life and Death of Jason. EV-5
Sing out, my soul, thy songs of joy. Songs of Joy. W. H. Davies. MBP; MoBrPo; OBVV; PC; YT
Sing out pent Soules, sing cheerefully! The Vintage to the Dungeon. Richard Lovelace. SeCV-1
Sing, Poet, 'tis a merry world. Glasgow. Alexander Smith. BSV; EBSV
Sing Sally O! *with music.* *Unknown.* SoAmSa
Sing, Sing for Christmas. J. H. Egar. OHIP
Sing sing Syren though thy notes bring death. *Unknown.* SeCSL
Sing, sing! what shall I sing? Mother Goose. OTPC; OxNR
Sing, sing, what shall we sing? A Musical Evening. Joseph G. Francis. CIV
Sing, Singsingetjie, sing, sing, sing. Singsingetjie. Arthur Vine Hall. MM
Sing soft, ye pretty birds, while Caelia sleeps. Sonnet to Caelia. William Browne. CaAE
Sing-Song. *See* Singsong.
Sing, soul of mine, this day of days. Easter. *Unknown.* OQP; QP-1
"Sing sweet, my bird; oh! sing, I pray." Lucy's Canary. Adelaide O'Keeffe. OTPC (1923 ed.)
Sing, sweet thrushes, forth and sing. The Angler's Trysting Tree. Thomas Tod Stoddard. LPS-2
Sing the old song, amid the sounds dispersing. Song. Aubrey Thomas De Vere. HBV
Sing the song of wave-worn Coogee, Coogee in the distance white. Coogee. Henry Clarence Kendall. VA
Sing Thou, My Soul. Theodosia Garrison. CAW
Sing-Time. Rose Waldo. GFA
Sing to Apollo, god of day. Song to Apollo. John Lyly. *Fr* Midas. AtBAP; ElSeCe; OBSC
Sing to Ashtaroth and Bel. To Ashtaroth and Bel. Saul Tchernichowsky. TrJP
Sing unto Jehovah [*or* the Lord]. Psalms, XCVIII, Bible, *O.T.* *See* Floods Clap Their Hands, The.
Sing unto the Lord with thanksgiving. Psalm CXLVII, Bible, *O.T.* OHIP; PoRL
Sing We All, for Time It Is. *Unknown.* *See* Christ, the Fleur-de-Lis.
Sing we all merrily. A Catch by the Hearth [*or* Christmas Hearth Rhyme]. *Unknown.* ChBR; MeMeAg; OHIP; PCH; RAR
Sing we and chant it. To Live in Pleasure [*or* Song]. *Unknown.* ElSeCe; OBSC; TrGrPo
Sing we for love and idleness. An Immorality. Ezra Pound. ChMo; CMP; HBV; LiTL; LiTM; MAP; MoAB; MoAmPo; NeMA; NePA; OBAV; SiTL
Sing we seamen now and then. A Ballad of Dansekar the Dutchman. *Unknown.* SG
Sing we the two lieutenants, Parer and M'Intosh. The Flight [to Australia]. *Fr.* A Time to Dance. C. Day Lewis. MoVE; ShBV-3
Sing we to the Trinity. The Way of Daily Living. *Unknown.* TMEV
Sing We to This Merry Company. *Unknown.* AnEC
Sing We with Mirth, Joy and Solace. *Unknown.* AnEC
Sing while you may, O bird upon the tree! Dark Wings. James Stephens. NP
"Sing while you work" and be full of cheer. To a Young Woman on the *World* Staff. Franklin P. Adams. ALV
Sing! Why should I sing. Wayfaring. Francisco A. de Icaza. AnMP
Sing with me, you little amorous birds. Madrigal. Matteo Maria Boiardo. LyPI
Singē We, Singē We. *Unknown.* AnEC
Singee a songee sick a pence. Nursery Song in Pidgin English. *Unknown.* BOHV; PA; WhC
Singer, The. Al-Buqaira, *tr. fr. Arabic by* A. J. Arberry. MooI
Singer, The. Edward Dowden. IrPN
Singer, The. Kadie Molodowsky, *tr. fr. Yiddish by* Sarah Zweig Betsky. OnCuPl
Singer, The. Edmund Clarence Stedman. PRWS
Singer, The. Anna Wickham. BMEP; HBMV; MBP; MoBrPo; NeMA; NP; TSW; TSWC
Singer and conqueror of battles vast. On an Icelandic Skald. Henry Adams Bellows. PaOS
Singer Asleep, A. Thomas Hardy. OAEP; POTE; POTT; PtP
Singer in the Mist, The. Robert Ervin Howard. DaM
Singer in the Prison, The. Walt Whitman. BeLS
Singer of High State, The. Louis Golding. MBP
Singer of hymns, by Sinai who adored. Israel. William Ellery Leonard. QS
Singer of One Song, The. Henry Augustin Beers. AA
Singer Saith of His Song, The. Francis Thompson. VLEP
Singer within the little streets. Song. Monk Gibbon. NeIP
Singers are gone from the cornmarket-place, The. After the Fair. Thomas Hardy. At Casterbridge Fair, VII. BEL; ChMo; CMP; EmBrPo; EnLi-2 (1949 ed.); EnLit; PoVP
Singers have hushed their notes of clear song, The. The Harper of Chao. Po Chü-i. MoPW; TrCh; UnS
Singers in a Cloud, The. Ridgely Torrence. AnAmPo; CP; HBMV; LA; LEAP; UnS
Singers in the Snow, The. *Unknown.* OHIP; SDH
Singers of Israel, O ye singers sweet. An Ode to Eight Cats Belonging to Israel Mendez, a Jew. "Peter Pindar." PoC
Singers of serenades, The. Mandoline. Paul Verlaine. AWP; JAWP; OBMV; WBP
Singer's Prayer, A. Johan Sebastian Cammermeyer Welhaven, *tr. fr. Norwegian by* Charles W. Stork. AnNoLy
Singer's Prelude, The. William Morris. *See* Apology, An: "Of Heaven or Hell. . ."
Singer's Quest, The. Odell Shepard. NLK
Singers, sing! The hoary world. The Servants. Richard Wightman. WGRP
Singin' wid a Sword in Ma Han'. *Unknown.* APW; BoAN-1, *with music*
Singing. Dorothy Aldis. GFA
Singing. Robert Louis Stevenson. GaP; GFA; MeMeAg; OnHT; PCH; SUS
Singing as she dips. The Broken Water-Wheel. Al-Hajjam. MooP
Singing Fairy, The. Rose Fyleman. BoChLi
Singing firework, A; the sun's darling. Lark Descending. Edmund Blunden. MoP
Singing Furies, The. Richard Hughes. PtOT
Singing Girl, The. Joyce Kilmer. JKCP
Singing Huntsman, The. Witter Bynner. MAP; MoAmPo (1942 ed.)
Singing in the Dark. Irma Wassall. PoNe
Singing is sweet; but be sure of this. Art, III. James Thomson. EnLi-2
Singing Leaves, The. James Russell Lowell. GN; LoEn; MPB; OnSP; OTPC; PTA-2; StVeCh
Singing Lesson, The. Jean Ingelow. DD; HBV; OTPC (1946 ed.)
Singing Lesson, A. Swinburne. BPN; HBV; VLEP
Singing Man, The. Josephine Preston Peabody. HBV; LEAP, *first 3 sts.*; PoFr, *abr.*
Singing my days. Passage to India. Walt Whitman. AmPo; AmPP (4th ed.); CoBA; CoV; IAP; Po; PoEL-5
Singing My Doubts Away. *Unknown.* BePJ
Singing Nigger. Carl Sandburg. OnAP
Singing of birds is as certain as the long, The. Bird Music. James Rorty. BLA
Singing of your words is to be heard on a bended knee, The. Your Mouth. Jenab Shehabuddin. LiTW
Singing on the Moselle. Ausonius, *tr. fr. Latin by* Howard Mumford Jones. LaP
Singing places surge in me, sorrow-stirred. Biography. Jacob Glatstein. OnCuPl
Singing Saint, The. J. B. Morton. SaFP
Singing Saviors, The. Clement Wood. BAP; MaRV; OQP; QP-1
Singing Stars. Katharine Tynan. VA
Singing the Reapers Homeward Come. *Unknown.* OHIP; PoRL
Singing through the forests. Rhyme of the Rail [*or* Railroad Rhyme *or* Riding on the Rail]. John G. Saxe. APW; BOHV; InMe; LPS-3; MoShBr; PTA-1
Singing-Time. Rose Fyleman. SiSoSe; TiPo
Singing Tortoise, The. *Unknown.* *See* Tortoise-Shell, The.
Singing Water. Rudolph Chambers Lehmann. HBMV
Singing white-throat poured my gladness out, The. The White-Throat. *Unknown.* BLA
Singing-Woman from the Wood's Edge, The. Edna St. Vincent Millay. HBMV
Singing World, The. Emerson. *See* Music.
Singing you go, and laughing through the water. Fortunate Being. Juan Ramón Jiménez. TeCS
Single cause why you invite, The. Dinner with Ligurinus. Martial. OnPM
Single clenched fist lifted and ready, The. Choose. Carl Sandburg. NP
Single Famished Kiss, A. Shakespeare. *Fr.* Troilus and Cressida, IV, iv. LiA
Single flow'r he sent me, since we met. A. One Perfect Rose. Dorothy Parker. ALV; FiBHP; PFE
Single Girl, The. *Unknown.* *See* When I Was Single.
Single-handed, and surrounded by Lecompton's black brigade. Lecompton's Black Brigade. Charles Graham Halpine. PAH
Single Sonnet. Louise Bogan. AnEnPo
Single star has Freya, A. Freya's Star. Christian K. F. Molbech. BoDS
Single step, that freed me from the skirts, A. Sky after Storm. Wordsworth. *Fr.* The Excursion. BLV; BoLiVe
Single tree there was, A. Wordsworth. *Fr.* The Prelude, VI. OBRV
Singsingetjie. Arthur Vine Hall. MM
Sing-Song; a Nursery Rime Book, *sels.* Christina Rossetti. Sing-Song, *first 15 rhymes.* EmBrPo

Other sels.
"All the bells were ringing." TiPo
(Broken Doll, The.) MPB
"And timid, funny, brisk little bunny." TiPo
Baby, Sleep. OTPC (1946 ed.)
("Lie a-bed,/ Sleepy head.") BOL
Boats Sail on the Rivers. BoChLi; BoTP; BrR; CoBE; OTPC (1946 ed.); PCH; PoVP; RAR; RIS; StVeCh; TiPo; TSW
(Rainbow, The.) GFA
"Bread and milk for breakfast." EmBrPo; SAS
(Winter.) PCH
Brownie, Brownie, Let Down Your Milk. RIS
"But give me holly, bold and jolly." BrR; ChBR; TiPo
Caterpillar, The. BoChLi (1950 ed.); BoTP; FaPON; GFA; GoTP; MPB; OTPC (1946 ed.); RIS; StVeCh
(Brown and Furry.) SUS; UTS
City Mouse and the Garden Mouse, The. BoChLi; BoTP; FaBoBe; FaPON; GoTP; HBV; HBVY; MeMeAg; MPB; OTPC; PPL; SeVeCh; UTS
(City Mouse and the Country Mouse, The.) PCH
("City mouse lives in a house, The.") SUS; TiPo
Daisies. RIS
(Sing-Song.) MBP
"Days are clear, The." RIS; TiPo
(Stay, June, Stay!) YeAr
"Dead in the cold, a song-singing thrush." EmBrPo; MBP
"Eight o'clock/ The postman's knock." EmBrPo; RIS; SAS; TiPo
(Postman, The.) GaP; GFA; PCH
"Emerald is as green as grass, An." AlDL; TiPo
(Precious Stones.) GoTP
Ferry Me across the Water. ChTr; GaP; PoRh; SUS
(Boatman, The.) PCH
(Ferryman, The.) BoTP
"Fly away, fly away over the sea." CoBE; PoVP; SUS
(Swallow, The.) GoTP; OTPC (1946 ed.); StVeCh
Frisky Lamb, A. BoTP
Growing in the Vale. BrR; GFA; RAR; RIS; TiPo
(Sweet Daffodowndilly.) BoChLi
"Hope is like a harebell trembling from its birth." MBP
Horses of the Sea, The. FaPON; GFA; PCD; PoRh; RAR; SUS; UTS
House of Cards, A. PCH
Hurt No Living Thing. FaPON; PCH; PoRL; RIS; SiSoSe
"I planted a hand." MBP
If a Pig Wore a Wig. BoChLi
"If hope grew on a bush." MBP
If I Were a Queen. CoBE; GaP; PoVP; SiSoSe
"If stars dropped out of heaven." RIS
Is The Moon Tired? BoTP; StVeCh
"Kookoorookoo! Kookoorookoo." EmBrPo; RIS
"Lily has a smooth stalk, The." MBP; OuHeWo
Love Me—I Love You. BoTP; EmBrPo
(Mother's Song, A.) BOL; OTPC (1946 ed.)
Lullaby: "Lullaby, oh lullaby." BoChLi; BOL; OTPC (1946 ed.); RIS
Minnie and Mattie. BoTP; GaP; InvP; SUS; TiPo
(Minnie, Mattie and May.) RAR; TSW
Mix a Pancake. GFA; MeMeAg; OTPC (1946 ed.); PoRh; RAR; SUS; TiPo (1952 ed.)
(Pancake, The.) BoTP; HBVY; PCH
Months, The ("January cold"). FaPON; RIS
"Mother shake the cherry-tree." PoVP; TiPo
(Let's Be Merry.) FaPON
Motherless Soft Lambkin, A. RIS
Neighboring. GaP; PCH
"No dandelions tell the time."
(Sing-Song Verses.) BoN
Oh, Fair to See. DD; FaPON; MPB; OHIP; OTPC (1946 ed.); RAR; TiPo; YeAr
O Lady Moon. PRWS
(Lady Moon.) PCH
O Sailor, Come Ashore. BoTP; BrR; GaP
(Coral.) GFA
O Wind, Where Have You Been? BoTP
"O wind, why do you never rest." TiPo
On the Grassy Banks. RAR; UTS
(Lambs at Play.) BoTP
(Woolly Lambkins.) StVeCh
"Peacock has a score of eyes, The."
(Sing-Song Verses.) BoN
Pin Has a Head, A. RIS
(Paradoxes.) OTPC (1946 ed.)
Pocket Handkerchief to Hem, A. RIS; SAS
(Stitching.) OTPC (1946 ed.); PPL
"Pussy has a whiskered face." TiPo
(Four Pets.) PPL
"Seldom 'can't.'" SAS
(Good Advice.) PPL
(Rules of Behavior.) HBV; HBVY
Sing Me a Song. BoChLi
Skylark and Nightingale. RIS
(Heaven Is Heaven.) YeAr
(Sing-Song.) MBP
Stars, The. MeMeAg; OTPC (1946 ed.)
"There is but one May in the year." TiPo
(May-Time.) BoTP
"There is one that has a head without an eye." OTPC (1946 ed.); PPL
There's Snow on the Fields. BoTP; EmBrPo
Three Plum Buns. BoTP
(Snack, A.) PCH
"Toadstool comes up in a night, A."
(Lesson, A.) RIS
"Twist me a crown of wind-flowers." MBP; VA
Watching Angels. PPL
("Angels at the foot.") EmBrPo
What Does the Bee Do? BoTP; RIS; SUS; TiPo
"What is pink? a rose is pink." SUS; TiPo
(Color.) GoBP; RAR
"When fishes set umbrellas up."
(Sing-Song Verses.) BoN
When the Cows Come Home. OTPC (1946 ed.); RAR; UTS
(Do You Know?) StVeCh
(Milking Time.) GFA; MPB; PRWS
Who Has Seen the Wind? BoTP; BPN; BrR; CoBE; FaPON; GoBP; HBV; HBVY; MPB; NLK; OnHT; OTPC; OuHeWo; PCH; PoRh; PoVP; PPL; PTA-1; RAR; StVeCh; SUS; TiPo; TSW; TSWC
(Sing-Song.) MBP
(Wind, The.) BoChLi; FaBoBe; GFA; MaRV; NeHB; RIS
"Wind has such a rainy sound, The." BrR; PoVP; TiPo
(Sing-Song.) MBP
(Sound of the Wind, The.) BoTP
"Wrens and robins in the hedge." GFA; SUS; TiPo
Sing-Song of Old Man Kangaroo, The. Kipling. FaPON; TiPo (1952 ed.)
Sing-Song Rhyme ("One! two! three!/ Outside the school"). *Unknown.* BoTP; SiSoSe
Singular Sangfroid of Baby Bunting, The. Guy Wetmore Carryl. NA
Sinister Dialogue. Callimachus, *tr. fr. Greek by* Robert Guthrie MacGregor. OnPM
("Rests Charidas beneath this tomb?") GrPo
Sinister presence changed life in a twelvemonth, A. Mountain Convent. Laura Benét. GoYe
Sinister voice of life, thou wilt be stilled! Solvet Saeclum. Leconte de Lisle. TrFP
Sink the world! Can that dismay us? A Pair. Karl Gjellerup. BoDS; OnPM
Sinking of the *Merrimac[k]*. Lucy Larcom. MC; PAH
Sinks the sun below the desert. Cleopatra Dying. Thomas Stephens Collier. BLPA; FaBoBe; NeHB
Sinless Child, The, *sel.* Elizabeth Oakes Smith.
"Her ways were gentle." AA
Sinless saint I was, mine eyes on honour fixed, The! Menander. *Fr.* Arbitrants. GrPo
Sinne of selfe-love possesseth al mine eie. *See* Sin of self-love possesseth all mine eye.
Sinner, The. Alcman, *tr. fr. Greek by* A. C. Benson. GrR
Sinner, The. Margaret E. Bruner. PoToHe
Sinner. Galatea Kazantzakis, *tr. fr. Modern Greek by* Rae Dalven. MoGP
Sinner Contemplates, A. Frances Boal Mehlek. DDA
Sinner, Please Don't Let Dis Harves' Pass, *with music. Unknown.* BoAN-2
Sinner-Saint, The. Wilfrid Scawen Blunt. ACP; CAW
Sinners. D. H. Lawrence. ViBoPo
Sins Loathed, and Yet Loved. Robert Herrick. LiTB
Sins of Kalamazoo, The. Carl Sandburg. CoV
Sins of Youth, The. Thomas, Lord Vaux. ACP (1952 ed.)
Sins' Round. George Herbert. ExPo; LoBV; ReEn
Sins you will nedes that I shall sing. *See* Since you will needs . .
Sion lies [*or* Syon lyes] waste, and Thy Jerusalem. Caelica, CIX [CX]. Fulke Greville. OxBoCh; PoEL-1; ReIE; SiCE; TriL; TuPP
Sion the son of Evan sang. Microcosmos, XLVI. Nigel Heseltine. NeBP
Sion, thy bridal-bower prepare. The Purification. St. Cosmas. *Fr.* Menaion. ISi
Sioux, The. Eugene Field. FiBHP
Sioux Indians. *Unknown.* CoSo, *with music;* CSF
Sippets of Gruel. Dryden. *Fr* Prologue to Nahum Tate's "The Loyal General." BeR
Sipping judiciously, he saw come near. Narcissus in a Cocktail Glass. Frances Minturn Howard. GoYe
Sir Aldingar. *Unknown.* BaBo (A *vers.*); ESPB (A, B, *and* C *vers.*); OBB
(Ravngard and Memering, B *vers.*) BaBo
Sir Andrew Barton. *Unknown.* BaBo; EnSB; ESPB; EV-2; OBB; SG, *diff. vers.;* ViBoFo
Sir Antony Love, *sel.* Thomas Southerne.

Sir Antony Love (*continued*)
Song: "Pursuing beauty, men descry." SeCL
(Song in the Second Act, A.) SeEP
Sir 'Arry, though lately created a knight. Catullus, *tr. fr. Latin.* LaP
Sir Bailey Barre. W. S. Gilbert. *Fr.* Utopia, Limited. PCD
Sir Balaam. Pope. *Fr.* Moral Essays. MaPo
Sir Beelzebub. Edith Sitwell. *Fr.* Façade. CoBMV; HoPM; MBP; MoAB; MoBrPo
(When Sir Beelzebub.) FaBoMo
Sir Björn rode up by land and lea. The Mother under the Mould. *Unknown.* BoDaBa
Sir Bosmer in Elfland. *Unknown, tr. fr. Danish by* E. M. Smith-Dampier. BoDaBa
Sir, can you tell where my young master lives. Henry Parrot. SiCE
Sir Cawline. *Unknown.* ESPB; OBB
Sir Christopher Wren. E. C. Bentley. *Fr.* Biography for Beginners. BOHV; CenHV; FiBHP; InMe; LauV; LiTG; MoShBr; ShBV-3; SiTL; WhC
(Important People, 8.) StaSt
("Said Sir Christopher Wren.") RIS
Sir Cock, to you the first place I award. Fortitude. Reinmar von Zweter. LiTW; LyMA
Sir David and His Stepsons. *Unknown, tr. fr. Danish by* E. M. Smith-Dampier. BoDaBa
Sir Drake, whom well the world's end knew. Epigram: On Sir Francis Drake [*or* On Francis Drake]. *Unknown.* CenL; OBS; TriL
Sir Eggnogg. Bayard Taylor. PA
Sir Eglamore. *Unknown.* OnSP
Sir Eglamour, *parody.* Samuel Rowlands. *Fr.* The Melancholy Knight. EIL; FaBoCh; InvP; LoGBV; WaKn
(Sir Eglamore.) MuP
Sir Egrabell had sonnes three. Sir Lionel. *Unknown.* BaBo (A *vers.*); ESPB
Sir Eustace Grey. George Crabbe. MyFE
Sels.
Demons of Opium, The. RO
"Peace, peace, my friend; these subjects fly." PoEL-4
"There was I fix'd." NBE
Sir Francis Drake, *sels.* Charles Fitzgeffrey.
Bee, The ("Look how the industrious bee"). EIL
English Captains. The. SG
"Heart-stealing Homer, marrow of the Muses," *br. sel.* PtP
Last Voyage of Sir Francis Drake, and Sir John Hawkins. SG
On Sir Francis Drake ("You, whose exploits the world itself admired"). SG
Sir Francis Drake Reviv'd. Sir William Davenant. *Fr.* The History of Sir Francis Drake. SG
Sir Francis, Sir Francis, Sir Francis is come. Upon Sir Francis Drake's Return from His Voyage about the World, and the Queen's Meeting Him. *Unknown.* CoMu; EIL; FaBoCh
Sir Franklin must to the Landsting go. Dame Gundelil's Harping. *Unknown.* BoDaBa
Sir Galahad. Tennyson. BEL; BHV; BMEP; BPN; EM-2; EmBrPo; EPN; EPP; GTBS; HBV; LiTG; OBVV; OnPP; OTPC; PECK; PoVP; TCEP; TVSH; VA; ViPo; ViPP; VLEP
Pure Heart, The ("My good blade carves the casques of men"), *br. sel.* MaRV; TreF
Sir Gawain and the Green Knight. *Unknown, tr. fr. Middle English.* BEL, *tr. by* Jessie L. Weston; EM-1, *tr. by* Jessie L. Weston; EnL, *tr. by* George B. Pace; EnLi-1, *tr. by* Theodore Howard Banks; EnLit, *tr. by* Jessie L. Weston; MeEV, *tr. by* Theodore Howard Banks; OuHeWo, *tr. by* Theodore Howard Banks
Sels.
"He dowelles ther al that day," *fr.* II. NBE
Passage of a Year, The, *fr.* II. PoEL-1
Temptation of Sir Gawain, The. ACP
"Ther wacz lokyng on lenthe," *fr.* I. EPP
Sir Gawain Encounters Sir Priamus. *Unknown. Fr.* Morte Arthure. PoEL-1
Sir Gawaine and the Green Knight. Yvor Winters. AnFE; CoAnAm; MoVE; TwAmPo
Sir Geoffrey Chaucer. Robert Greene. *See* Description of Sir Geoffrey Chaucer, The.
Sir George Prevost, with all his host. The Battle of Plattsburg. *Unknown.* PAH
Sir Giles' War-Song. William Morris. BPN; EmBrPo; PoVP; ViPo
Sir Guy the Crusader. W. S. Gilbert. BOHV
Sir have you ever heard of Paris-sur-Seine. Paris-am-Seine. Jean Malaquais. MiFP
Sir Helmer Blaa and His Bride's Brothers. *Unknown.* BaBo
Sir Henry Clinton's Invitation to the Refugees. Philip Freneau. PAH
Sir Hjelm. *Unknown, tr. fr. Danish by* E. M. Smith-Dampier. BoDaBa
Sir Hudibras. Samuel Butler. *Fr.* Hudibras. UnPo (1st ed.)
Sir Hudibras's Religion. Samuel Butler. *See* Religion of Hudibras, The.
Sir Hugh; or, The Jew's Daughter. *Unknown.* BaBo (A, B, *and* D *vers.*); CH; EM-1; ESPB (A, B, C, *and* N *vers.*); ViBoFo (A, B, *and* C *vers.*)
(Hugh of Lincoln.) ACP; EnSB; OBB
(Jew Lady, The, B *vers.*) ABS
(Jewish Lady, The.) ABS (A *vers.*); BaBo (C *vers.*)
Sir Humphrey Gilbert. Longfellow. BHV; EtS; HBV; HBVY; MC; OnSP; OTPC; PAH; TCAP; TOP; TVSH
Sir Humphry Davy. E. C. Bentley. *Fr.* Biography for Beginners. CenHV; ImOP; LauV; ShBV-3
Sir, I Admit Your General Rule. Pope. *See* Epigram: "Sir, I admit your general rule."
Sir, I pray you, be you not master god? John Heywood. *Fr.* The Play of the Weather. CoBE
Sir, I shall tell you news, except you know it. Of Don Pedro and His Poetry. Sir John Harington. SiCE
Sir, if there be within this hall an individual man. The Temperance Pledge. Thomas Francis Marshall. PEOR
Sir Inigo doth fear it, as I hear. An Epigram of Inigo Jones. Ben Jonson. EPS (1942 ed.)
Sir J. S. Sir John Suckling. *See* Constant Lover, The.
Sir James the Rose. *Unknown.* ESPB
Sir Jens he sat with cup in hand. Two Brides and One Groom. *Unknown.* BoDaBa
Sir John Butler. *Unknown.* ESPB
Sir John Franklin; On the Cenotaph in Westminster Abbey. Tennyson. EPP; InP; LiA
Sir John got him an ambling nag. Sir John Suckling's Campaign. *Unknown.* CG
Sir John Graeme and Barbara Allen. *Unknown. See* Barbara Allen.
Sir John Suckling's Campaign. *Unknown.* CG
Sir John the Outlaw. *Unknown, tr. fr. Danish by* E. M. Smith-Dampier. BoDaBa
Sir Joseph's Song. W. S. Gilbert. *See* When I Was a Lad.
Sir Joshua Reynolds. Blake. FiBHP; LiTG; OxBoLi
(Epigram.) SiTL
Sir Joshua Reynolds. Goldsmith. *Fr.* Retaliation. OBEC; SeCePo
Sir Karel's Lykewake. *Unknown, tr. fr. Danish by* E. M. Smith-Dampier. BoDaBa
Sir Lancelot, *sel.* Frederick William Faber.
"Fishy pool, The/ With willow-herb was edged." EnSW
Sir Lancelot beside the mere. Lancelot and Guinevere. Gerald Gould. HBV
Sir Lancelot du Lake. *Unknown.* CG
Sir Lark and King Sun. George Macdonald. *Fr.* Adela Cathcart, *ch.* 16. HBV; HBVY; OTPC
Sir Launcelot and Queen Guinevere. Tennyson. PIR; VA
Sir Launfal. Thomas Chester, *tr. fr. Middle English by* Jessie L. Weston. ATP
Sir Launfal, *sel.* John Moultrie.
"But here at starting." OBRV
Sir Launfal and the Leper. James Russell Lowell. *Fr.* The Vision of Sir Launfal, I. GN; OTPC
Sir Laurens Steals a Bride. *Unknown, tr. fr. Danish by* E. M. Smith-Dampier. BoDaBa
Sir Lionel. *Unknown.* BaBo (A *vers.*); ESPB (A, B, *and* C *vers.*)
(Old Bangham, *with music.*) OuSiCo
(Old Bangum, B *vers.*) BaBo
Sir Luno and the Mermaid. *Unknown, tr. fr. Danish by* E. M. Smith-Dampier. BoDaBa
Sir Magnus and the Elf-Maid. *Unknown.* BaBo
Sir Marmaduke. George Colman. GoTP; LPS-3; MW
Sir Marmaduke's Musings. Theodore Tilton. AA
Sir Martyn. William Julius Mickle. *See* Concubine, The.
Sir, more than kisses, letters mingle souls. To Sir Henry Wotton. John Donne. ReEn
Sir Moses, Sir Aaron, Sir Jamramajee. A New Order of Chivalry. Thomas Love Peacock. CenHV
Sir Nicketty Nox. Hugh Chesterman. BoTP
Sir, No Man's Enemy [Forgiving All]. W. H. Auden. CoEV; FaBoMo; NAMP; ReaPo
(Petition.) CoBMV; GTBS-W; LiTB; LiTM; MoPo; OAEP (2d ed.); ReMP; TwHP
(Poems, XXX.) CaAE
Sir Ogey and Lady Elsey. *Unknown.* See Sweet William's Ghost.
Sir Olaf. Johann Gottfried von Herder, *tr. fr. German by* Elizabeth Craigmyle. AWP; JAWP; PoMS; WBP
Sir Oluf and His Gilded Horn. *Unknown, tr. fr. Danish by* E. M. Smith-Dampier. BoDaBa
Sir Oluf he rideth over the plain. The Elected Knight. *Unknown.* AWP; JAWP; LyMA; WBP
Sir Oluf lay smitten with sickness sore. The Lover's Death. *Unknown.* BoDaBa
Sir Oluf rode by East and West. The Elfin Shaft. *Unknown.* BoDaBa
Sir Orfeo. *Unknown, ad. fr. Middle English by* Edward Eyre Hunt. MeEV
"His harp, whereon was al his gle," *orig. vers.* AtBAP

Sir Palle's Bridal. *Unknown, tr. fr. Danish by* E. M. Smith-Dampier. BoDaBa
Sir Patrick Spens [*or* Spence]. *Unknown.* AnFE; AtBAP; ATP; AWP; BaBo (A, B, *and* C *vers.*); BBV (1923 ed.); BCEP; BEL; BLV; BoChLi; BoLiVe; BSV; CaAE; CBOV; CH; CoBE; CoEV; EBSV; EM-1; EnL; EnLi-1; EnLit; EnRP; EnSB; EPP; ESPB (A, B, *and* G *vers.*); EV-1; ExPo; FaBoCh; GN; GoTS; HBV; HoPM; InP; InPo; InvP; JAWP; LH; LiTB; LoBV; LoGBV; MCCG; OAEP; OBB; OBEV; OnSP; OtMeF; OTPC (1946 ed.); OuHeWo; PCN; PFE; PIAE; PoEL-1; PoMa; PoRA; PYM; REAL; ReaPo; RG; RiBV; SeCeV; SG; ShBV-1; TCEP; TiPo (1952 ed.); TOP; TreF; TrGrPo; UnPo; ViBoFo (A *vers., with music;* B *vers.*); ViBoPo; WBP; WHA
(Ballad of Sir Patrick Spens, The.) EtS
Sir Peter and Kirsteen sat over the board. Sir Peter's Leman. *Unknown.* BoDaBa
Sir Peter rode to the castle door. The Avenging Sword. *Unknown.* BoDaBa
Sir Peter went forth all in the garth. Proud Ellensborg. *Unknown.* BoDaBa
Sir Peter's Harp. *Unknown, tr. fr. Danish by* E. M. Smith-Dampier. BoDaBa
Sir Peter's Leman. *Unknown. See* Lord Thomas and Fair Annet.
Sir Philip Sidney. Eleanor *and* Herbert Farjeon. OnPP
Sir Philip Sidney. Matthew Royden. *See* On Sir Philip Sidney.
Sir Richard Grenville's Farewell, on His Sailing for Foreign Parts in the Year 1585. *Unknown.* SG
Sir Richard's Song. Kipling. OtMeF
Sir Robert Bolton had three sons. Sir Lionel (C *vers.*). *Unknown.* ESPB
Sir Robin. Lucy Larcom. BoChLi; MeMeAg, *st.* 1; MPB; OTPC (1946 ed.); TiPo (1952 ed.)
Sir Roderic's Song. W. S. Gilbert. *Fr.* Ruddigore. GBV (1952 ed.); PoMS; WhC
Sir, say no more. Dramatic Fragment. Trumbull Stickney. OxBA
Sir Sidney Smith. Thomas Dibdin. CG
Sir Sidrophel, the Conjuror. Samuel Butler. *See* Portrait of Sidrophel.
Sir Stig and His Runes. *Unknown, tr. fr. Danish by* E. M. Smith-Dampier. BoDaBa
Sir T. J.'s Speech to His Wife and Children. *Unknown.* CoMu
Sir, the night is darker now. A Nightly Deed. Charles Madge. NeBP
Sir Thomas, stark green until he crept acurl. A Contempt for Dylan Thomas. Wilfred Watson. PeCV
Sir Thomas was a merry man, he laughed deep in his throat. A Ballad of St. Thomas. Charles A. Brady. JKCP (1955 ed.)
Sir Thopas. Chaucer. *Fr.* The Canterbury Tales. BEL; EM-1, *abr.*
Sir, though (I thank God for it) I do hate. Satires, II. John Donne. PoFS; ViBoPo
Sir Tristram was a Bear, in listed field. Tristram and Isolt. Don Marquis. HBMV
Sir Turlough; or, The Churchyard Bride. William Carleton. IrPN; TIP
Sir Verner's Escape. *Unknown, tr. fr. Danish by* E. M. Smith-Dampier. BoDaBa
Sir Walter Ralegh the Night before His Death. Sir Walter Ralegh. *See* Conclusion, The.
Sir Walter Raleigh. E. C. Bentley. *Fr.* Biography for Beginners. CenHV
Sir Walter Raleigh. Henry Jerome Stockard. NoCaPo
Sir Walter Raleigh. William Carlos Williams. *Fr.* In the American Grain. OnHM
Sir Walter Raleigh has built a ship. The Sweet Trinity; or, The Golden Vanity (A *vers.*). *Unknown.* BaBo
Sir Walter Raleigh Sailing in the Low-lands. *Unknown. See* Golden Vanity, The.
Sir Walter Raleigh to a Caged Linnet. Eugene Lee-Hamilton. VA
Sir Walter Raleigh to His Son. Sir Walter Ralegh. *See* Wood, the Weed, the Wag, The.
Sir Walter Raleigh to the Queen. Sir Walter Ralegh. *See* Silent Lover, The.
Sir Walter Raleigh's Verses, Found in His Bible in the Gatehouse at Westminster. Sir Walter Ralegh. *See* Conclusion, The.
Sir Walter Rauleigh His Lamentation. *Unknown.* CoMu
Sir Walter Scott's Tribute. Sir Walter Scott. *See* Book of Books, The.
Sir, welcome. Shakespeare. *Fr.* The Winter's Tale, IV, iii. AtBAP
Sir, whatsoever you are pleas'd to do. Dedications [*of* Orchestra], II: To the Prince. Sir John Davies. SiPS
Sir; when I flew to seize the bird. Beau's Reply. William Cowper. FaBoCh; OTPC (1923 ed.); PRWS
Sir, when you say. 15th Raga: For Bela Lugosi. David Melter. NeAP
Sir, while at the helm of state you ride. A Letter to Sir Robert Walpole. Henry Fielding. CEP
Sir William and his plighted maid. The Mighty Harp. *Unknown.* BoDaBa
Sir Wind, why blow so rough? The Squirrel and the Wind. *Unknown.* PCH
Sir, you should [shall, *wr.*] notice me: I am the Man. Epitaph. Lascelles Abercrombie. MoBrPo; POTE; ViBoPo
"Sire," announced the servant to the King. Rabindranath Tagore. *Fr.* Fruit-gathering. NV
Sire of the rising day. An Ode. Lord De Tabley. OBVV; PoVP
Sired by Zeus in a barren tower, unseen. The Growth of Perseus. W. Wesley Trimpi. PtPa
Siren, The. Meleager, *tr. fr. Greek by* F. L. Lucas. GrPE
Siren Chorus. George Darley. *See* Mermaidens' Vesper-Hymn.
Siren cries that ran like mad and naked screaming women, The. Eine Kleine Nachtmusik. Robert E. Hayden. PoNe
Siren sang, and Europe turned away, A. To the Western World. Louis Simpson. NePoAm-2
Siren Song. William Browne. *See* Siren's Song, The.
Siren-Spirits. Euripides. *See* Hymn to the Sirens.
Sirena. Michael Drayton. *Fr.* The Shepherd's Sirena. EV-1; OBEV, *abr.*; SeCL
(Jovial Shepheard's Song, The.) PoEL-2
("Near to the Silver Trent.") SeEP; TuPP
(Song to Sirena.) AtBAP
Sirens, The. Laurence Binyon. TwCV
Sels.
"Hymn the Finders! Hymn the Bold." TCPD
"Mystery of Dawn, ere yet the glory streams." GoTL (1949 ed.)
"Whither is she gone, wing'd by the enemy airs." MM
"World-besieging storm, from horizon heaped and menacing." GoTL (1949 ed.)
Sirens, The. Donald Finkel. NePoEA
Sirens, The. John Manifold. LiTB; LiTM; WaP
Sirens, The; Scylla and Charybdis. Homer, *tr. fr. Greek.* *Fr.* The Odyssey, XII. GrPE, *tr. by* F. L. Lucas; LiTW, *tr. by* Pope
Sirens' Song, The. William Browne. *Fr.* The Inner Temple Masque. BCEP; EtS; EV-2; LPS-3, *sl. abr.*; OBEV
(Siren Song.) EG
(Song of the Sirens.) CoEV; ElL
(Song of the Syrens.) ChTr; OBS, *sl. abr.*
("Steer hither, steer your wingèd pines.") ElSeCe; ViBoPo
Sirens' Song, The. Homer. *Fr.* The Odyssey, XII. EV-1
Sirens wailed and moaned, The. Two Silences. Robert Haven Schauffler. AOAH
Sirmio. Catullus, *tr. fr. Latin by* Charles Stuart Calverley. AWP; JAWP; WBP
Sirocco at Deyá. Robert Graves. MoVE
Sirs—though we fail you—let us live. To Men. Anna Wickham. MBP; MoBrPo
Sirventes: "I have made a sirventes against the city of Toulouse." Paul Blackburn. NeAP
Sirventes: "Paramours, to those who would accuse, The." Peire Cardenal, *tr. fr. Provençal by* Hubert Creekmore. LyMA
Sis Joe, *with music.* *Unknown.* OuSiCo
Sisiphus is he, whom noise and strife, The. The Fear of Death. Lucretius, *tr. by* Dryden. *Fr.* De Rerum Natura. LoBV
Sissinghurst. V. Sackville-West. DiM; POTE
Sister. Marian Osborne. CPG
Sister, A. "A. Page." PraNu
Sister. Whittier. *Fr.* Snow-bound; a Winter Idyl. AA
Sister, A. Wordsworth. *See* Sparrow's Nest, The.
Sister Agatha. Mary A. McMullen. PraNu
Sister and I. *Unknown.* PTA-1
Sister and mother and diviner love. To the One of Fictive Music. Wallace Stevens. AnAmPo; AnFE; APA; BLV; CoAnAm; CoBMV; CoV; LA; MAP; MoAB; MoAmPo; MoVE; TwAmPo
Sister and Nun. "A. Page." PraNu
Sister Ann Raphael, S.N.D. E. Mary. PraNu
Sister Anne, Sister Anne. Perspectives Are Precipices. John Peale Bishop. LiTA; LiTM; MoVE; NePA
Sister Anne, Sister Anne. The Ballad of Sister Anne. Sir Osbert Sitwell. AtBAP
Sister, Awake! *Unknown.* CH; DD; ElL; ElSeCe; HBV; OBEV; RG
(Madrigal: "Sister, awake, close not your eyes.") BoTP
("Sister awake, close not your eyes.") CenL
Sister Fidèle stands at the convent gate. Sœur Fidèle. Frances Gill. PraNu
Sister Helen. Dante Gabriel Rossetti. BEL; BeLS; BMEP; BPN; CBOV; DaM; EmBrPo; EnL; EnLi-2; EnLit; EPN; EPP; OAEP; PIAE; PoE; POTT; PoVP; REAL; ShBV-2; TCEP; TOP; TyEnPo; ViPo; ViPP; VLEP

Sister Lights the Candles, A. Sister Mary Jeremy. PraNu
Sister Lou. Sterling Brown. GoSl; PoNe
Sister Margaret Bourgeoys. Thomas D'Arcy McGee. PraNu
Sister Mary Alphonsa. Eleanor C. Donnelly. PraNu
Sister Mary Conceptia. Helene Mullins. PraNu
Sister Mary of the Love of God. Rosa Mulholland. VA
Sister Mary Philomena. James M. Hayes. PraNu
Sister Mary Veronica. Nancy Byrd Turner. PraNu
Sister Nell. *Unknown.* FaPON
Sister of Charity, The. Alexander J. Cody. PraNu
Sister of Charity, The. Gerald Griffin. PraNu
Sister of Charity, A. Frederick G. Scott. PraNu
Sister of Charity Comforts a Wounded Soldier, A. "Owen Meredith." *Fr.* Lucile. PraNu
Sister Saint Luke. John Hay. PraNu
Sister Simplicitie. Fragment of a Sleep-Song [*or* Sleepy Song]. Sydney Dobell. BOL; RAR; VA
"Sister, sister, go to bed!" Brother and Sister. "Lewis Carroll." ChTr
Sister Songs, *sels.* Francis Thompson.
"Ah, help, my daemon." VLEP
"But lo! at length the day." OBMV; VLEP
"Kiss? for a child's kiss, A." BMEP
"Thou canst foreshape thy word." VLEP
Sister Sun. Ibn Malik of Granada, *tr. fr. Arabic by* A. J. Arberry. MooP
Sister, the bride-bed waits: sister for thee. Epithalamium. Arthur Symons. FaBoTw
Sister! these woods have seen ten summers fade. In Memoriam. Sir William Stirling-Maxwell. EBSV
Sister to sister said. The Avenging Daughters. *Unknown.* BoDaBa; LiTW; LyMA
Sister Veronica. Margaret Holmes. PraNu
Sister, what talk is this, you come and cry. Light and Shadow. Sophocles. *Fr.* Electra. GrR
Sisterhood of God, The. Patrick F. Durkan. PraNu
Sistern and Brethren, *with music.* *Unknown.* TrAS
Sisters. Olga Berggolts, *tr. fr. Russian by* Jack Lindsay. Songs of the Spanish Children, I. RuPo
Sisters, The. Roy Campbell. ChMP; FaBoTw; MoVE; OBMV
Sisters. Eleanor Farjeon. FaPON
Sisters, The. Robert Finch. BoCaPo
Sisters. "Robin Hyde." AnNZ
Sisters, The. Amy Lowell. AnNE; MAP; MoAmPo
Sisters. Dorothy Roberts. CaP
Sisters, The, *sels.* Swinburne.
Love and Sorrow, I. POTT
There's Nae Lark, II. POTT
(Lyric, A.) HBV
Sisters, The. John Banister Tabb. AA; BAP; LEAP; MaRV
Sisters, The ("They have left the doors ajar"), *sel.* Tennyson.
Song: "O diviner air." BPN
Sisters, The ("We were two daughters of one race"). Tennyson. InvP; ReTS
Sisters, The. Whittier. AWP; InPo; MOAP
Sister's Best Feller. Joseph C. Lincoln. PTA-1
Sisters Kastemaloff, The. Carlton Talbott. ALV
Sisters, stay; we want our dame. Witches' Charms. Ben Jonson. *Fr.* The Masque of Queens. TwHP
Sit all beneath fair leaves of spreading bay. Under a Laurel. Anyte. OxBG
Sit Down, Sad Soul. "Barry Cornwall." CAW; LPS-2; VA
Sit on the bed. I'm blind, and three parts shell. A Terre. Wilfred Owen. LiTM (rev. ed.); WaP
Sit quiet in my lap while solemnly. Evensong. Carleton Drewry. GoYe
Sit tight, little hills, little valleys. Dame Liberty Reports from Travel. Dorothy Cowles Pinkney. GoYe
Sitalkas. Hilda Doolittle ("H. D."). ViBoPo
Sith earth is stage whereon we play our parts. Man's Life Likened to a Stage Play. Thomas Howell. SiCE
Sith gone is my delight and only pleasure. Sextain. William Drummond of Hawthornden. TriL
Sith, in dark, speech, Carvilios hymn unfolds. Druids' Hymn to the Sun. C. M. Doughty. *Fr.* The Dawn in Britain. FaBoTw
Sith my desire is prest to please. Reward Doth Not Always Answer Desert. Thomas Howell. SiCE
Sith my life from life is parted. Marie Magdalens Complaint at Christs Death. Robert Southwell. MePo
Sith of our language he was the lode-star. John Lydgate. *Fr.* The Fall of Princes. PtP
Sith sickles and the shearing scythe. Madrigals: Hawking for the Partridge. Thomas Ravenscroft. OxBoLi
Sith that you both are like in life. To a Married Couple That Could Not Agree. Martial, *tr. by* Timothe Kendall. TuPP
Sitteth alle stille and herkneth to me! The Song of Lewes [*or* On Richard, Duke of Cornwall, Brother to Henry III]. *Unknown.* NBE; OxBoLi
Sittin' around the stove last night. A Liz-Town Humorist. James Whitcomb Riley. IHA
Sittin' on the Porch. Edgar A. Guest. TreFS
Sitting, The. C. Day Lewis. FaBoMo
Sitting,/ Reflecting,/ On what has been passing. Shortly After. Louis Smirnow. PoP
Sitting all day in a silver mist. In the Mist. "Susan Coolidge." LPS-3
Sitting at evening in the warm grass. For My Wife. Julian Symons. NeBP; WaP
Sitting at her [*or* a] window in her cloak and hat. Mother Tabbyskins [*or* Old Mother Tabbyskins]. *Unknown, at. to* Elizabeth Anna Hart. CenHV; CIV; FTB
Sitting at Night. Po Chü-i, *tr. fr. Chinese by* Ching Ti. WhP
Sitting at Night with My Nephew Who Has Just Come from Afar. Su T'ung-po, *tr. fr. Chinese by* Yu Min-chuan. WhP
Sitting at times over a hearth that burns. Minora Sidera. Sir Henry Newbolt. PoeT; TCPD
Sitting by a river [*or* river's] side. Philomela's Ode [That She Sung] in Her Arbor. Robert Greene. *Fr.* Philomela, the Lady Fitzwater's Nightingale. ElSeCe; EPP; LO; OBSC; ReIE; SiCE; TuPP
Sitting cross-legged in a wooden chair. The Gulf of Tartary and a Butterfly. Fuyue Anzai. PoLJ
Sitting, He travels afar. Tranquility. *Unknown. Fr.* The Upanishads. OnPM
Sitting Here. Elizabeth J. Coatsworth. UTS
Sitting here behind bars in a dank cell am I. The Prisoner. Pushkin. BoRS
Sitting here in our usual chairs. Sitting Here. Elizabeth J. Coatsworth. UTS
Sitting here in the glow of my study-lamp. The Debt. Jesse Edgar Middleton. NeTW
Sitting in his rocker waiting for your tea. The View at Gunderson's. Joseph Warren Beach. NP
Sitting in this [*or* our] garden you cannot escape symbols. Of the Unscathing Fire [*or* The Phoenix Answered]. Anne Ridler. ChMP; LiTL; POTE
Sitting on a bench one evening in spring. Spring Evening on the Boulevards. Jules Laforgue. AnFP
Sitting on the flower-bed beneath the hollyhocks. The Fairy Tailor. Rose Fyleman. PoRh; TVC; TVSH
Sitting silent by the window while the evening's fading beam. The Old Thanksgiving Days. Ernest W. Shurtleff. PEOR
Sittinge downe to her repast. *Unknown.* SeCSL
Situation, The. Sydney Clouts. BoSA
Situation is blue and white, The. The Crucifixion of Noel. Marsden Hartley. AnAmPo; LA
Situation Normal. Hank Chernick. WhC
Siva, Destroyer. George Perry. OBAV
Six!/ Such different minds and faces! Mistresses. *Unknown.* KiLC
Six Carpenters' Case, The. Sir Frederick Pollock. VA
Six days Salámán on the Camel rode. The Lovers Flee. Jami. *Fr.* Salámán and Absál. PeP
Six Epigrams, *sel.* Gerard Manley Hopkins.
"No, they are come; their horn is lifted up." SeCePo
Six Feet of Earth. *Unknown.* BLPA
Six Green Singers. Eleanor Farjeon. SDH
Six Jolly Wee Miners. *Unknown.* CoMu
Six Letters. Euripides, *tr. fr. Greek by* C. M. Bowra. OxBG
Six [*or* Some *or* Ten] little mice sat down [*or* in a barn] to spin. Mother Goose. BoN; BoTP; HBV; OTPC; OxNR; PoC; PPL; RIS; SAS
Six month child, The. Slippery. Carl Sandburg. FaPON; TiPo
Six o'Clock. Owen Dodson. PoNe
Six o'Clock. Trumbull Stickney. MOAP; OxBA
Six Poets Gazed upon the Moon. Morris Abel Beer. PFE
Six Poets in Search of a Lawyer. Donald Hall. SiTL
Six Questions. *Unknown. See* Captain Wedderburn's Courtship.
Six Rubaiyat. Abu Said ibn Abi-l-Khair, *tr. fr. Persian by* E. G. Browne. LiTW
Six Significant Landscapes. Wallace Stevens. CoV
Six skeins and three, six skeins and three! A Spinster's Stint. Alice Cary. LPS-1
Six street-ends come together here. Blue Island Intersection. Carl Sandburg. MAP; MoAmPo; PIAE
Six Strings. Federico García Lorca, *tr. fr. Spanish by* Eleanor L. Turnbull. AnSpL-2; CoSP
Six thankful weeks—and let it be. Written in a Volume of Goethe. Emerson. IAP
Six thousand years in these dull regions pass'd. Discovery. Philip Freneau. WoL
Six Winters. Ruthven Todd. NeBP
Six years had passed, and forty ere the six. "Age, with Stealing Steps . . ." [*or* The Approach of Age]. George Crabbe. *Fr.* Tales of the Hall. BCEP; LEAP; LPS-1
Six Yoke. Edwin Ford Piper. NV
"Sixpence a week," says the girl to her lover. By Her Aunt's Grave. Thomas Hardy. *Fr.* Satires of Circumstance. MBP; MoAB; MoBrPo; PoVP
Sixt Nimphall, The. Michael Drayton. *See* Fine Day, A.

Sixteen Dead Men. Dora Sigerson Shorter. ACP; OnYI
Sixteen years ago I built this house. A World within a War. Sir Herbert Read. MoPo
Sixth Book of the Aeneis, The, *sel.* Virgil, *tr. fr. Latin by* Dryden. *Fr.* The Aeneid.
"Let others better mold the running mass." SeCV-2
Sixth Nymphal, The. Michael Drayton. *See* Fine Day, A.
Sixth Pastoral, The ("How still the sea!"). Ambrose Philips. *Fr.* Pastorals. CEP
(Pastoral Landscape, *abr.*) OBEC
Sixth was August, being rich arrayed, The. August. Spenser. *Fr.* The Faerie Queene, VII, 7. GN
Sixty-eighth Birthday. James Russell Lowell. PoEL-5
Sixty seconds make a minute. *Unknown.* RIS
Siyalila, siyalila, inkomo yetu ifile! Lament for a Dead Cow. F. C. Slater. BoSA
Skaian Gate, The, *sel.* Geoffrey Scott.
"Hector, the captain bronzed." OBMV
Skammel he dwells up North in Ty. Ebbe Skammelson. *Unknown.* BoDaBa
Skater of Ghost Lake, The. William Rose Benét. TBM
Skaters, The. John Gould Fletcher. MAP; MoAmPo; NeMA; PFY; PoMa
Skaters, The. John Williams. NePoAm-2
Skater's Valentine, A. Arthur Guiterman. SiSoSe
Skating. Herbert Asquith. BoChLi; BrR; FaPON; StVeCh; SUS; TiPo
Skating. Wordsworth. *See* On the Frozen Lake.
Skating Song. Christopher Morley. PCH
'Skeeters am a-hummin' on de honeysuckle vine. Kentucky Babe. Richard Henry Buck. AA; BOL; HBV
Skeleton, The. G. K. Chesterton. FaBoTw
Skeleton at the Feast, The. James Jeffrey Roche. AA; LEAP
Skeleton in Armor, The. Longfellow. AA; AmPP; AnNE; AFW; AWP; BeLS; CoBA; FaBoBe; GBV (1922 ed.); GoTP; HBV; HBVY; IAP; LEAP; LoEn; MaC; MCCG; MOAP; OnSP; PAH; PECK; PFE; REAL; RG; TCAP; TOP; TreF
Skeleton in the Cupboard, The. Frederick Locker-Lampson. HBV; VA
Skeleton of the Future, The. "Hugh MacDiarmid." GoTS; MoBrPo; OBMV; ShBV-4
Skeleton of the moa on iron crutches, The. Attitudes for a New Zealand Poet, III. Allen Curnow. AnNZ
Skelton Laureate, upon a Dead Man's Head. John Skelton. *See* Upon a Dead Man's Head.
Skeltoniad, A Michael Drayton. PoEL-2
Skeptic, The. Witter Bynner. PR
Skeptic Christmas. Jules Laforgue, *tr. fr. French by* Kate Flores. AnFP
Skerryvore ("For love of lovely words"). Robert Louis Stevenson. VLEP
Skerryvore; the Parallel ("Here all is sunny"). Robert Louis Stevenson. VLEP
Sketch, A. Byron. NBE; OBRV
Sketch. Donald Jeffrey Hayes. DDA
Sketch. "Seumas O'Sullivan." AnIV
Sketch. Carl Sandburg. HBMV; NP
Sketch from Bowden Hill after Sickness, *sel.* William Lisle Bowles.
"Upon the point/ Of the descending steep I stand." EnSW
Sketch from the Life, A. Arthur Guiterman. BOHV
Sketch of His Own Character. Thomas Gray. BEL; CEP; EnLit; TOP
Sketch of Lord Byron's Life, *sel.* Julia A. Moore.
"'Lord Byron' was an Englishman." FiBHP
Sketch of the Frontier Woman. "Claudia Lars," *tr. fr. Spanish by* Donald Devenish Walsh. AnCL
Skew-Ball Black, The. *Unknown.* CoSo; CSF
Ski Train. Patrick Anderson. TwCaPo
Skialetheia, *sels.* Everard Guilpin.
"As in the greatest of societies." SiCE
(Proemium I.) ReIE
De Ignoto. ReIE
"Fie on these Lydian tunes which blunt our sprights." SiCE
"Let me alone, I prithee, in this cell." SiCE
(Satyra Quinta.) TuPP
Of Cornelius. SiCE; TuPP
Of Pansa. ReIE
Of Titus. ReIE; SiCE; TuPP
Of Zeno. SiCE
Satira Prima: "Shall I still miche in silence and give aim." ReIE
To Clodius. ReIE
To Deloney. ReIE
To Licus SiCE
To the Reader. ReIE; SiCE
Skiers, The. Anthony Frisch. TwCaPo
Skies again are deep and bare. Afanasi Fet, *tr. fr. Russian by* Oliver Elton. BoRS
Skies are low, the winds are slow, The. Under the Blue. Francis Fisher Browne. AA
Skies can't keep their secret, The. Secrets. Emily Dickinson. TCAP
Skies contain still groves of silver clouds, The. Spring 1943. Roy Fuller. LiTB; LiTM; WaP
Skies gan scowl, o'ercast with misty clouds, The. Gascoigne's De Profundis. George Gascoigne. TuPP
Skies have sunk, and hid the upper snow, The. Ite Domum Saturae, Venit Hesperus [*or* Home, Rose . . . *or* Les Vaches]. Arthur Hugh Clough. BEL; BPN; EmBrPo; EnLit; EV-5; NBE; OAEP; PoVP; TCEP; VA; ViP; VLEP
Skies is different than they was, The. A Spring Lay. Oliver Opdyke. InMe
Skies they were ashen and sober, The. Ulalume. Poe. AA; AmP; AmPo; AmPP; AnAmPo; AnEnPo; AnFE; APA; APW; ATP; AWP; BAP; BAV; CoAnAm; CoBA; CoV; DaM; IAP; JAWP; LA; LEAP; LiTA; LiTG; LO; MOAP; NePA; OBAV; OuHeWo; OxBA; PoFS; REAL; SPP; TCAP; TOP; TreF; UnPo; ViBoPo; WBP; WHA
Skies they were ashen and sober, The, *parody.* The Willows. Bret Harte. BOHV; InMe
Skies to the West are stained with madder. Gloaming. Robert Adger Bowen. HBV
Skies were dim and vast and deep, The. Comfort. "Æ." ChMo
Skiff, The. Al-Munsafi, *tr. fr. Arabic by* A. J. Arberry. MooP
Skiff I spied, A. Sails. Ibn Billita. MooP
Skilful Listener, The. John Vance Cheney. AA
Skimbleshanks; the Railway Cat. T. S. Eliot. FaBoCh; LoGBV
Skimming lightly, wheeling still. Shiloh; a Requiem. Herman Melville. APW; LiTA; OxBA; PaA; PoFS; SoV; ViBoPo
Skin creamy as the furled magnolia bud. The Dancer. Ednah Proctor Clarke. AA
Skin-flakes, repetitions, erosions. Ezra Pound. *Fr.* Canto XV. MoPo
Skin more pure than Ida's snow. My Mistress. Richard Brathwaite. *Fr.* The English Gentlewoman. SeCL
Skinner, Skinner, You Know the Rule, *with music.* *Unknown.* StDa
Skinny Mrs. Snipkin. Mrs. Snipkin and Mrs. Wobblechin. Laura E. Richards. PoRh; StVeCh (1955 ed.); TiPo
Skip-Scoop-Anellie. Tom Prideaux. FiBHP
Skip, skip, skipping toward the fountain. The Flowers of Nazareth. Kaj Munk. BoDS
Skip to My Lou, *with music. Unknown.* ABF; TrAS
Skipper. C. Fox Smith. AlDL
Skipper-Hermit, The. Hiram Rich. EtS
Skipper Ireson's Ride. Whittier. AmP; AmPP; AnNE; APW; BeLS; BOHV; CoBA; DDA; GA, *abr.*; GBV; HBV; HiLiAm; IAP; InMe; InP; MOAP; OBAV; OnHT; OnSP; OTPC; OxBA; PAH; PFE; PFY; PIAE; StPo; StVeCh (1940 ed.); TCAP; TreFS; YaD; YT
Skippery Boo, The. Earl L. Newton. GoTP
Skippets, the Bad One. Christine E. Bradley. BoTP
Skipping Along Alone. Winifred Welles. TiPo
Skipping Ropes. Dorothy Aldis. StVeCh
Skirting the river road, (my forenoon walk, my rest). The Dalliance of the Eagles. Walt Whitman. AA; APW; FaBoEn; MOAP
Skoal! Charles Lindbergh, Skoal! *Unknown.* GA
Skottes out of Berwik and of Aberdene. A Song of Lawrence Minot. Lawrence Minot. BEL
Skreak and skritter of evening gone, The. Autumn Refrain. Wallace Stevens. LiTA
Skull, The. Charles Edward Eaton. NoCaPo (rev. ed.)
Skull, The. Mary E. Fullerton. BoAu
Skull of Haydn returned to his bones, The. The Turtle. James Schevill. FiMAP
Skull of Shakespeare, The. George Sterling. *See* On the Skull of Shakespeare.
Skunk, The. Robert P. Tristram Coffin. FaPON; TiPo
Sky, The. Elizabeth Madox Roberts. GFA; MAP; MoAmPo; VOD
Sky. Betty Shippe. DDA
Sky, The. Richard Henry Stoddard. AA; OBAV; TCAP
Sky, The/ is that beautiful old parchment. Old Manuscript. Alfred Kreymborg. BAP; CP; LEAP; MAP; NeMA; NP; NV; PFE; SBMV
Sky above London, The. London Night. Kathleen Raine. NeBP
Sky above the roof, The. Paul Verlaine. *See* Sky Is Up above the Roof, The.
Sky above us here is open again, The. Traveling Storm. Mark Van Doren. MoSiPe
Sky a-Clearèn, The, *abr.* William Barnes. RO
Sky after Storm. Wordsworth. *Fr.* The Excursion, II. BLV; BoLiVe
Sky, be blue, and more than blue. Denouement. Kenneth Fearing. OnHM
Sky bent down his piercing gaze one day, The. Earth and Sky. Hovhannes Toumanian. ArmLP
Sky came tripping, The. Ilo Orleans. RIS
Sky-Goer, The. Zona Gale. LEAP

Sky grew darker with each minute, The. Before the Storm. Richard Dehmel. AWP; JAWP; WBP
Sky hangs heavy tonight, The. Negro Woman. Lewis Alexander. CDC
Sky immense, bejewelled with rain of stars, The. Night of Stars. John Gould Fletcher. BAP
Sky in its lucent splendor lifted. A Tropical Morning at Sea. Edward Rowland Sill. EtS; PIAE
Sky is a drinking-cup, The. The Sky. Richard Henry Stoddard. AA; OBAV; TCAP
Sky is an immortal tent built by the sons of Los. Immortal Tent. Blake. *Fr.* Milton. PoF
Sky is black, the earth is white, The. Nowel. Théophile Gautier. TrFP
Sky is blue, is blue, today, The. In Absence. Robert Cameron Rogers. PR
Sky is changed, The! and such a change! Oh night. Sky, Mountains, River! Byron. *Fr.* Childe Harold's Pilgrimage, III. WHA
"Sky is clouded, the rocks are bare, The." Fate. Bret Harte. BAP
Sky is cold as pearl, The. Ancient. "Æ." SeCePo
Sky is dark, and the hills are white, The. Norse Lullaby. Eugene Field. BOL; BoTP; MPB; SUS
Sky is dotted like th' unleavened bread, The. Haggadah. A. M. Klein. TrJP
Sky is full of clouds to-day, The. Clouds. Frank Dempster Sherman. OnHT; PRWS; RAR; TVSH
Sky is glad that stars above, The. A Morisco [*or* Song]. Jasper Fisher. *Fr.* Fuimus Troes. SeCL; SeEP; TuPP
Sky is gray as gray may be, The. No Songs in Winter. Thomas Bailey Aldrich. OBAV
Sky is gray with rain that will not fall, The. At the Zoo. Israel Zangwill. TrJP
Sky is grayer [*or* greyer] than doves, The. Drought. Katharine Tynan. DiM; GTIV
Sky is hid in a snowy shroud, The. The Snowstorm. Frederick George Scott. PeCV
Sky is his ceiling, grass is his bed. Speaking of Cowboy's Home. *Unknown.* CoSo
Sky is just the top of day, The. The Top of Day. Anne Blackwell Payne. GFA
Sky is laced with fitful red, The. Impression: Le Réveillon. Oscar Wilde. PoVP
Sky is low, the clouds are mean, The. Emily Dickinson. AmPo; AmPP; CoBA; CoV; FaBoEn; MAP; MoAmPo; MoPW; OBAV; OnPM; OxBA; PoEL-5
(Beclouded.) AA; NeMA
Sky is overcast, The. A Night-Piece. Wordsworth. BPN; EmBrPo; EnRP; GEPC; SN
Sky is perfectly clear, The. Maximian Elegy V. Kenneth Rexroth. CrMA
Sky is ruddy in the East, The. The Ship-Builders. Whittier. AnNE; EtS
Sky Is Up above the Roof, The. Paul Verlaine, *tr. fr. French by* Ernest Dowson. AWP; FaPON; JAWP; WBP
(Sagesse.) EnLi-2
(Sky above the Roof, The, *tr. by* Muriel Kittel.) AnFP
Sky, lazily disdaining to pursue, The. Georgia Dusk. Jean Toomer. AnAmPo; CDC; LA; MAP; PoNe
Sky-like limpid eyes, The. Brennbaum. Ezra Pound. *Fr.* Hugh Selwyn Mauberley. CoBMV; CoV; LiTA; LiTM (rev. ed.); MoPo
Sky-making. Mortimer Collins. BOHV
Sky, Mountains, River ("The sky is changed"), *abr.* Byron. *Fr.* Childe Harold's Pilgrimage, III. WHA
Sky, mountains, river, winds, lake, lightnings! ye! The Poet's Impulse. Byron. *Fr.* Childe Harold's Pilgrimage, III. LPS-3
Sky of deepening bronze, A. Moon Rider. William Rose Benét. YT
Sky Pair, A. Robert Frost. MAP; MoAB; MoAmPo
Sels.
Canis Major. AlBD; AlDL
Peaceful Shepherd, The. QS
Sky Pictures. Mary Effie Lee Newsome. CDC; GoSl
Sky-riding on a Beetle. Aristophanes, *tr. fr. Greek by* Benjamin Bickley Rogers. *Fr.* The Peace. GrR
Sky seemed so small that winter day, The. Two Illustrations That the World Is What You Make of It. Wallace Stevens. NePoAm
Sky-Signs. Frederick Mortimer Clapp. PoeMoYo; VOD
Sky so bright. A Song in Praise of the Lord of Heaven and Earth. *Unknown.* GBV
Sky so pale, and the trees, such frail things, The. A la promenade. Paul Verlaine. AWP
Sky spreads out its poor array, The. Evening Sky. John Gould Fletcher. ChMo; CMP
Sky that has never known sun, moon, or stars, A. Rear Porches of an Apartment Building. Maxwell Bodenheim. AnAmPo; LA; NP
Sky unfolding its blankets to free, The. Morning Workout. Babette Deutsch. NePoAm-2
Sky was blue, so blue, that day, The. For the Candle Light. Angelina W. Grimké. CDC; PoNe
Sky was cold December blue, The. Steelhead. Robinson Jeffers. WoL
Sky was like a waterdrop, The. Remembrance. Walter de la Mare. ChMo; CMP
Sky was on the hill, The. When You Reach the Hilltop the Sky Is on Top of You. Etta Blum. GoYe
Sky was violet hued, The. The Shepherd's Star. Juan Ramón Jiménez. LiTW
Sky where the white clouds stand in prayer. Easter. Mary Carolyn Davies. OHIP
Sky-wide an Estuary. C. Day Lewis. POTE
Sky! Why are you so very gay. In a Garden. Theda Kenyon. NLK
Sky with clouds was overcast, The. Washing Day. *Unknown.* CoMu
Sky Writers. *See* Skywriters.
Skye. Alexander Nicolson. EBSV
Skylark, The. Richard Watson Dixon. *Fr.* Mano; a Poetical History. VA
Skylark, The. James Hogg. ATP; BLA; BSV; CBPC; DD; EBSV; EV-3; GN; HBV; HBVY; LPS-2; OTPC; PECK; PIR; TVSH
(Lark, The.) SN
Skylark, The. Christina Rossetti. *See* Green Cornfield, A.
Skylark, The. Frederick Tennyson. GN, *abr.*; HBV; SN
Skylark and Nightingale. Christina Rossetti. *Fr.* Sing-Song. RIS
(Heaven Is Heaven.) YeAr
(Sing-Song.) MBP
Skylark, how I envy you. Gayetez. Pierre de Ronsard. PrPoCR
Skylark's Nest, The. R. H. Long. BoAu
Skylark's nest among the grass, The. Birds' Nests. *Unknown.* BoTP; MPB; RAR; TVSH
Sky-Lark's Song, The. John Bennett. *Fr.* Master Sky-Lark. AA
Sky's a faded blue and taut-stretched flag, The. Jardin du Palais Royal. David Gascoyne. MoPo
Sky's the very blue Madonna wears, The. The Monk in the Garden. Adelaide Crapsey. VOD (1935 ed.)
Sky's unresting cloudland, that with varying play, The. Robert Bridges. *Fr.* The Testament of Beauty. MoVE
Skyscraper. Carl Sandburg. HiLiAm; PoMa; VOD (1935 ed.)
Skyscraper. Byron Vazakas. OnHM
Skyscraper Is a City's House. Clara Lambert. MPB
Skyscrapers. Rachel Field. FaPON; GFA; StVeCh
Skyscrapers. John Gould Fletcher. ChMo; CMP; VOD (1935 ed.)
Sky Writers. William Rose Benét. PoF
Skywriting. Mary Maxtone. BrR
Slabs of the Sunburnt West. Carl Sandburg. CoV
Finale, *sel.* NeMA
"Slack your rope, hangs-a-man [*or* hangsaman]." The Maid Freed from the Gallows [*or* Hangsaman]. *Unknown.* AS; ExPo; TOP; TrAS
Slacker Apologizes, The. Peter Viereck. MiAP
Slain by the arrows of Apollo, lo. Rupert Brooke. James B. Dollard. CPG
Slain Eagle, The. William Gilmore Sims. APW
Slain eye has not died, The. Cries Out of Blindness. Tristan Corbière. LiTW
Slainthe! Patrick MacGill. AnIV; LBBV
(Dedication: "I speak with a proud tongue.") OnYI
Slander! Aristophanes, *tr. fr. Greek by* Benjamin Bickley Rogers. *Fr.* The Thesmophoriazusae. GrR
Slander. Ibn Hazm, *tr. fr. Arabic by* A. J. Arberry. MooP
Slanderer, A. *Unknown, tr. fr. Greek by* Lord Neaves. OnPM
Slant of Sun, A. Stephen Crane. *See* Hymn: "Slant of sun on dull brown walls, A."
Slant sun falls at shut of day, The. Our Comrades. *Unknown.* PEOR
Slant-windowed belt-footed enormously long-boomed, A. Bucyrus. John Holmes. CrMA; NePoAm
Slanted faces of men. Study; for Ezra Pound. Peter Hellings. MoWP
Slanting the ragged peaks of the mind, Eagles. Calling Eagles. Leo Kennedy. TwCaPo
Slapandergosheka. *Unknown. See* Snapoo.
Slatey skies and a whistling wind. Marsh Marigolds. Godfrey Fox Bradby. ReTS; TVSH
Slaughter-House, The. Alfred Hayes. LiTA; LiTM
Slaughter-House, The. Palladas, *tr. fr. Greek by* F. L. Lucas. GrPE
Slaughter of Grendel by Beowulf, The. *Unknown. See* Slaying of Grendel, The.
Slaughter of the Innocents by Order of King Herod, The. Caelius Sedulius, *tr. fr. Latin by* George Sigerson. *Fr.* Carmen Paschale. OnYI
Slaughter of the Laird of Mellerstain, The. *Unknown.* ESPB
Slav Ho! *with music. Unknown.* SoAmSa

Slave. Hafiz, *tr. fr. Persian by* J. H. Hindley. PeP
Slave, The. Richard Henry Horne. VA
Slave, The. James Oppenheim. BAP; CP; MAP; MaRV; MoAmPo (1942 ed.); NP; PFE; PFY; PoeMoYo; PoFr; PoMa; PoTo; PYM; TrJP; VOD
Slave, The. Wu Shang Yeh, *tr. fr. Chinese by* Henry H. Hart. PoHN
Slave Auction, The. Frances E. W. Harper. PoNe
Slave Chase, The. *Unknown.* CoMu
Slave Girl, A. Damascius, *tr. fr. Greek by* J. A. Pott. OxBG
Slave I Languish, A. Joachim du Bellay, *tr. fr. French by* Alan Conder. Regrets, XXXIX. TrFP
Slave of my madness and bereft of wit. The Hunt. Pierre de Ronsard. TrFP
Slave Quarter. Carl Carmer. MoSiPe
Slave Ship, The. Heine, *tr. fr. German by* Ernst Feise. AnGP
Slave-Ships, The. Whittier. APW
Slave with long eyes charged with soft chains changes, A. Interior. Paul Valéry. TrFP
Slaver, The. Stephen Vincent Benét. *Fr.* John Brown's Body. AmPP; TwCV
Slavery. William Cowper. *Fr.* The Task. CoBE; LPS-2
("Oh for a lodge in some vast wilderness.") EnRP; EPP; OAEP
Slavery. Shelley. BCEP
Slaves. James Russell Lowell. *Fr.* Stanzas on Freedom. NeHB; OQP; PCD; QP-2; WBLP
(Freedom.) ShGoBo
(Stanza on Freedom, A.) AA; HiLiAm; WaKn
Slaves. George Sylvester Viereck. LPS-1
Slaves Cannot Breathe in England. William Cowper. *Fr.* The Task. OBEC
Slave's Complaint, The. George Moses Horton. NoCaPo
Slave's Dream, The. Longfellow. AnNE; CoBA; GTBS; IAP; MOAP; OBVV; PoNe; PYM; TSW; TSWC
Slave's Epitaph, A. Dioscorides. *See* Faithful Servant, A.
Slaves of Thy Shining Eyes. Hafiz, *tr. fr. Persian by* Gertrude L. Bell. LiTW
Slaves to London. Peter Anthony Motteux. *Fr.* Love's a Jest. OAEP
(London.) SeCL
(Song, A: "Slaves to London, I'll deceive you.") SeEP
Slav'ry Chain, *with music.* *Unknown.* TrAS
Slay fowl and beast; pluck clean the vine. Cavalier. Richard Bruce. CDC
Slayer of the winter, art thou here again? March. William Morris. *Fr.* The Earthly Paradise. HBV; LPS-2; OtMeF; POTT; VLEP
Slayer standeth where his stroke is sure, The. Ajax's Death [*or* Ajax before His Suicide]. Sophocles. *Fr.* Ajax. LiA; LiTW
Slaying, The. Homer, *tr. fr. Greek by* William Morris. *Fr.* The Odyssey, XXI *and* XXII. OxBG
Slaying of Grendel, The. *Unknown, tr. fr. Anglo-Saxon by* Chauncey B. Tinker. *Fr.* Beowulf. EPP
(Slaughter of Grendel by Beowulf, The, *tr. by* Charles W. Kennedy.) LiTW
Slaying of Hector, The. Homer. *See* Last Fight, The.
Slaying of Patroclus, The. Homer, *tr. fr. Greek by* F. L. Lucas. *Fr.* The Iliad, XVI. GrPE
Slaying of the Earth-born, The. Apollonius Rhodius, *tr. fr. Greek by* Arthur S. Way. *Fr.* Argonautica, III. GrR
Slaying of the Niblungs, The. William Morris. *Fr.* Sigurd the Volsung. LH
Slaying of the Suitors, The. Homer, *tr. fr. Greek. Fr.* The Odyssey, XXI *and* XXII. GrPE, *tr. by* F. L. Lucas; GrR, *fr.* XXII, *tr. by* William Morris
Slaying of the Witch, The. George Sterling. MOAP
Slaying of Thord Iverson, The. *Unknown, tr. fr. Danish by* E. M. Smith-Dampier. BoDaBa
Sledburn Fair. *Unknown.* CH
Sledding Song, A. Norman C. Schlichter. FaPON
Sleek and lax as a slug in the grass. The Sun-Bather. Kim Kurt. NePoAm-2
Sleek iron-gray horses, The. The Iron-gray Horses. *Unknown.* WhP
Sleep. Baltasar del Alcázar, *tr. fr. Spanish by* Sir John Bowring. AnSpL-1
Sleep. Thomas Bailey Aldrich. AA; IAP
Sleep ("Come, Sleep, and with thy sweet deceiving"). Beaumont *and* Fletcher. *Fr.* The Woman-Hater. *See* Come, Sleep.
Sleep. Alice Brown. AA
Sleep, The. Elizabeth Barrett Browning. EV-4; HBV; LPS-3; MaRV; VA; WGRP
(To Sleep.) BPP
"Of all the thoughts of God that are," *sel.* AlDL
Sleep, *sel.* Abraham Cowley.
"Sleep is a god too proud to wait in palaces." ChTr
Sleep. Samuel Daniel. *See* Care-Charmer Sleep.
Sleep ("Sleep is supposed to be"). Emily Dickinson. OnPM
Sleep ("Care-charming Sleep"). John Fletcher. *Fr.* The Tragedy of Valentinian. *See* Care-charming Sleep.
Sleep. Bartholomew Griffin. Fidessa, More Chaste than Kind, XV. OBSC
("Care-charmer sleep, sweet ease in restless misery.") ReEn; ReIE; SiCE; TuPP
Sleep. Sophie Jewett. PC
Sleep. Kostas Kariotakis, *tr. fr. Modern Greek by* Rae Dalven. MoGP
Sleep. Keats. *Fr.* Endymion, I. BCEP
(Life Again.) SeCePo
Sleep. Robert Eyres Landor. *Fr.* The Impious Feast, VII. OBRV
Sleep. J. P. McAuley. NeLNL
Sleep. John Bruce MacCallum. PoP
Sleep. "Fiona Macleod." GBV; TSW
Sleep. Ada Louise Martin. HBV
Sleep, *sel.* Christopher Morley.
"Yet, in the end." PC
Sleep. "Peter Pindar." LPS-3
Sleep. Thomas Sackville. *Fr.* The Induction to "The Mirror for Magistrates." CBOV; WHA
Sleep ("How many thousand"). Shakespeare. *See* Henry IV's Soliloquy on Sleep.
Sleep ("Methought I heard a voice"). Shakespeare. *See* Sleep—Innocent Sleep.
Sleep ("Come, sleep! O Sleep"). Sir Philip Sidney. *See* Astrophel and Stella: Sonnets, XXXIX.
Sleep ("Lock up, fair lids"). Sir Philip Sidney. *Fr.* Arcadia. OBSC; SiPS
"Lock up, fair lids, the treasure of my heart.") SiCE
(Sonnet: "Lock up, fair lids.") EG; ElL
Sleep. Kenneth Slessor. BoAV; MoAuPo
Sleep! Sophocles, *tr. fr. Greek by* Robert Whitelaw. *Fr.* Philoctetes. GrR
Sleep. Publius Papinius Statius, *tr. fr. Latin by* W. H. Fyfe. AWP
Sleep. John Banister Tabb. PC
Sleep. A. S. J. Tessimond. POTE
Sleep. Lewis Frank Tooker. AA
Sleep. *Unknown, tr. fr. Arabic by* A. J. Arberry. MooP
Sleep. *Unknown. See* Weep You No More, Sad Fountains.
Sleep. Théophile de Viau, *tr. fr. French by* Sir Edmund Gosse. AWP
Sleep. Wordsworth. *See* To Sleep.
Sleep a little, a little little. The Sleep Song of Diarmaid and Grainne [*or* The Sleep-Song of Grainne over Dermuid]. *Unknown.* AnIV; OnYI; SiB
Sleep, a ni-na-na, a nice long sleep. *Unknown.* BOL
Sleep after Toil. Spenser. *Fr.* The Faerie Queene, I, 9. ChTr
("He there does now enjoy eternal[l] rest.") MyFE; PoD
Sleep: and between the Closed Eyelids of Sleep. Conrad Aiken. Preludes to Attitude, II. LiTA; LiTG; TwAmPo
Sleep and death, the darkling eagles. Lament. Georg Trakl. AnGP
"Sleep and His Brother Death." William Hamilton Hayne. AA
Sleep; and my song shall build about your bed. Slumber Song. Siegfried Sassoon. MCCG
Sleep and Poetry. Keats. ATP, *abr.*; BNP; EmBrPo; EnRP; GEPC
Sels.
"Could all this be forgotten? Yes, a schism." ChER
"Schism, A/ Nurtured by foppery and barbarism." InP
"Is there so small a range." BEL
"O Poesy! For thee I grasp my pen." ERP
"Stop and consider! life is but a day." OBRV; SeCePo
(From "Sleep and Poetry.") EV-4
(What Is Life?) CBE
"What is more gentle than a wind in summer?" AtBAP; ATP
(From "Sleep and Poetry.") EV-4
Sleep, Angry Beauty. Thomas Campion. CaAE; ElL; GTSE; HBV; LoPo; LoPS; TrGrPo
("Sleep, angry beauty, sleep, and fear not me.") CoEV; EG; GTSL; LO
Sleep, Ariosto! in a fine marble pure. Serious Sonnets: Sleep, Ariosto! Pietro Aretino. LyPI
Sleep at Sea. Christina Rossetti. PoEL-5
Sleep, Baby Boy. *Unknown. See* Sardinian Lullaby.
Sleep, Baby Dear. *Unknown.* BOL
Sleep, Baby Jesukin. Mary Sings. Norah M. Holland. ChrBoLe
Sleep, baby mine, enkerchieft on my bosom. The Lullaby of a Female Convict to Her Child, the Night Previous to Execution. Henry Kirke White. BOL
Sleep, Baby, Sleep. Tristan Corbière, *tr. fr. French by* Kate Flores. AnFP
Sleep, Baby, Sleep. Ione L. Jones. BOL
Sleep, Baby, Sleep ("Sleep, baby, sleep!/ Thy father watches [*or* father's watching] the sheep"), *2 sts. Unknown, tr. fr. German at. to* Elizabeth Prentiss. BoChLi; FaPON;

Sleep, Baby, Sleep (*continued*)
GFA; MOAH; MPB; OTPC; PPL; PTA-1; RAR; SAS
(Cradle Song, A.) BoTP, 5 *sts.*; PCH, 3 *sts.*
(Slumber Song, A, 5 *sts.*) BOL
Sleep, Baby, Sleep. George Wither. HBV; OTPC (1923 ed.)
Sleep, baby, sleep!/ Our cottage vale is deep. Cradle Song. *Unknown.* BOL; CBPC
Sleep, baby, sleep!/ Once more upon. The Death Lullaby. *Unknown.* BOL
Sleep, baby, sleep./ Thy father guards the sheep. Holy Lullaby. *Unknown.* GoTP
Sleep, baby, sleep./ Waiting near with outstretched hands. Lullaby. Virginia Bioren Harrison. BOL
Sleep, baby, sleep,/ The wind is driving the red, red leaves. A Lullaby. Robert Ellice Mack. BOL
Sleep, baby, sleep!/ Dad is not nigh. Lullaby. *Unknown.* BOL
Sleep, baby, sleep,/ I can see two little sheep. Lullaby. *Unknown.* BOL
Sleep, baby, sleep!/ Your father herds his sheep. Nurse's Song. *Unknown.* ThWaDe
Sleep, baby, sleep,/ Thy father herds the sheep. Old German Lullabies, 1. *Unknown, ad. by* Louis Untermeyer. RIS
Sleep, baby, sleep!/ Fondly I keep. Sleep, Baby, Sleep. Ione L. Jones. BOL
Sleep, baby, sleep! The Christmas stars are shining. A Mother-Song. Julia C. R. Dorr. BOL
Sleep, baby, sleep! The Mother sings. A Christmas Lullaby. John Addington Symonds. AnEC; COAH; PRWS
Sleep, baby, sleep! what ails my dear. Sleep, Baby, Sleep. George Wither. HBV; OTPC (1923 ed.)
Sleep, Beloved, Sleep. *Unknown.* BOL
Sleep breathes at last from out thee. To a Child during Sickness. Leigh Hunt. LPS-1
Sleep Brings No Joy. Emily Brontë. ViBoPo
Sleep, child, lie quiet, let be. A Lullaby. James Agee. OnHM
Sleep, Child—Thy mother's first-born, Thou. Lullaby of the Virgin. *Unknown.* BOL
Sleep, Comrades, Sleep. Longfellow. *See* Decoration Day.
Sleep, Darling, Sleep. Mary B. C. Slade. BOL
Sleep, darling, stayed. Sleep. *Unknown.* MooP
Sleep, dear child, as mother bids. Lullaby for a Sick Child. *Unknown.* BOL
Sleep, Dolly, sleep. Doll's Cradle-Song. *Unknown.* BOL
Sleep enfold thee./ Jesukin. Cradle Song. James L. Duff. ISi
Sleep Fairy. Annie E. Tynan. BOL
Sleep falls, with limpid drops of rain. Bells in the Rain. Elinor Wylie. PC; YT
Sleep, gray brother of death. On Waking. Joseph Campbell. AnIV; NP
Sleep, grim Reproof, my jocond muse doth sing. Satire X: Humors. John Marston. *Fr.* The Scourge of Villainy. SiCe; TuPP
Sleep, happy Pamphilus. Lay down your head. Nightfall before Syracuse. Walter Hauk. CAG
Sleep, Holy Babe. Edward Caswall. BePJ; BOL
Sleep in love, naughty tuner of cicadas! Kazoo. Tristan Corbière. AnFP
Sleep in your silent glory. The Cliff Dwelling. Arthur W. Monroe. PoOW
Sleep—Innocent Sleep. Shakespeare. *Fr.* Macbeth, II, ii. EV 1
(Conscience.) MaRV
(Sleep.) TreFS
Sleep is a god too proud to wait in palaces. Abraham Cowley. *Fr* Sleep. ChTr
Sleep is a merciful Medusa, bending. Merciful Medusa. Winifred Welles. PIAE
Sleep Is a Reconciling. *Unknown.* *See* Weep You No More, Sad Fountains.
Sleep Is a Suspension. Carl Sandburg. *Fr.* The People, Yes. NAMP
Sleep is no servant of the will. Sleep. Baltasar del Alcázar. AnSpL-1
Sleep is supposed to be. Sleep. Emily Dickinson. OnPM
Sleep, kinsman thou to death and trance. In Memoriam A. H. H., LXXI. Tennyson. EmBrPo; EPN; GEPC; ViPo; VLEP
Sleep late with your dream. Poems for My Brother Kenneth. Owen Dodson. PoNe
Sleep, let me sleep, for I am sick of care. Looking Forward [*or* Let Me Sleep]. Christina Rossetti. EmBrPo; PC
Sleep, li'l boy an' I rock-a you low. A Song of Sleep-Time. *Unknown.* BOL
Sleep, li'l chillun, daddy gone ter fight. The Little Dreamers. Frank L. Stanton. BOL
Sleep, little baby, I love thee. Slumber-Songs of the Madonna, I. Alfred Noyes. BOL
Sleep, little baby of mine. Cradle Song. *Unknown.* BOL; MOAH; LPS-1
Sleep, little baby, sleep and rest. Lullaby. Elinor Chipp. HBMV
Sleep, little baby, sleep, sleep, sleep. Harvest Slumber Song. Wilfred Campbell. BOL
Sleep, little Baby, sleep; the holy angels love thee. Holy Innocents. Christina Rossetti. BOL; BPN; HBV; HBVY
Sleep, little brother, you must not awaken. The Little Sister Left in Charge. Cecil Frances Alexander. OTPC (1923 ed.)
Sleep, Little Dove. *Unknown, tr. fr. Alsatian.* BOL
Sleep, little moon of my delight. Syrian Lullaby. Alice Hathaway Cunningham. BOL
Sleep, little one, and be good. Lullaby. *Unknown.* BOL
Sleep, little one, in thy tiny bed. My Baby Dear. Samuel Abbott. BOL
Sleep, little one, sleep. Schlof, Bobbeli. *Unknown.* TrAS
Sleep, little pigeon, and fold your wings. Little Blue Pigeon [*or* Japanese Lullaby]. Eugene Field. BOL; GBV (1922 ed.); MOAH; TVSH
Sleep, love, sleep! Watching. "Fanny Forester." AA; LPS-3
Sleep, Madame, Sleep. Annemarie Ewing. NePoAm
Sleep, Mr. Speaker; it's surely fair. Stanzas on Seeing the Speaker Asleep in His Chair. Winthrop Mackworth Praed. EnRP
Sleep, mouseling, sleep. Lullaby. Elizabeth J. Coatsworth. SiSoSe
Sleep, my babe, lie still and slumber. All through the Night [*or* Lullaby *or* Welsh Lullaby]. *Unknown.* BOL; FaPON; GoTP
Sleep, my babe, your road of dreams. Cradle-Song. Laurence Housman. BOL
Sleep, my baby, all the night! Lullaby. Wendell Phillips Stafford. BOL
Sleep, my baby; sleep, my boy;/ Rest your little weary head. Lullaby [*or* Sweetly Sleep]. *At. to* Eliza Lee Follen, *also to* Jane Taylor. BOL; MOAH
Sleep, my baby, sleep, my darling. Cradle-Song. *Unknown.* BOL
Sleep, my baby, while I sing. Bed-Time Song. Emilie Poulsson. BOL; HBV; HBVY
Sleep, my boy, the night is treading. A Ghetto Cradle-Song. Philip M. Raskin. BOL
Sleep, My Child. Sholom Aleichem, *tr. fr. Yiddish by* Alter Brody. TrJP
Sleep, my child. Lullaby for a Baby Toad. Stella Gibbons. AlDL
Sleep, my child; because of you. Night. "Gabriela Mistral." LiTW
Sleep, my child, my darling child, my lovely child, sleep! *Unknown.* BOL
Sleep, my child, my joy, my treasure. Sleep, My Child. Sholom Aleichem. TrJP
Sleep, my child, my little daughter. Cradle Song. *Unknown.* TrJP
Sleep, my child, no care can cumber. Greek Mother's Lullaby. Zitella Cocke. *Fr.* A Doric Reed. BOL
Sleep, my child, sleep, my child. *Unknown, tr. fr. Japanese by* Mrs. M C Ayrton. BOL
Sleep, my childie, sleep. Cradle Song for Summer. Roden Noel. BOL
Sleep, my darling, calm and fearless. *Unknown.* BOL
Sleep, my darling, sleep. Cradle Song. Louis MacNeice. OxBI
Sleep, my darling, sleep! A Lullaby. Celia Thaxter. BOL
Sleep, my daughter, sleep an hour. *Unknown.* BOL
Sleep, my dear one, sleep. A Lullaby. George Edgar Montgomery. BOL
Sleep, my dear one, sleep my laddie. *Unknown, tr. fr. Russian by* L. Edna Walter. BOL
Sleep, my eye, sleep, sleep a slumber hale. Cradle Song. *Unknown.* BOL
Sleep, My Infant Saviour. George T. Rider. BOL
Sleep, my little baby, sleep. Lullaby. Samuel Hoffenstein. TrJP
Sleep, my little flax-haired fairy. Cossack Cradle-Song. Mikhail Yurevitch Lermontov. BOL
Sleep, my little Jesus. Mary's Manger-Song. William Channing Gannett. BOL
Sleep, my little one, sleep. Lullaby. Sarah Jane S. Harrington. RAR
Sleep, my little papoose, sleep on. An Indian Lullaby. Claude Bryan. BOL
Sleep, My Little 'Simmin-colored Coon. William H. Plass. BOL
Sleep, my love, and peace attend thee. All through the Night. Harold Boulton. OlF; TreFS
Sleep, my own baby, my darling thou art. Cradle Song. *Unknown.* BOL
Sleep, my own darling. Home and Mother. Mary Mapes Dodge. BOHV
Sleep, My Soul, Sleep. Miguel de Unamuno, *tr. fr. Spanish by* Eleanor L. Turnbull. TeCS
Sleep, My Treasure. Edith Nesbit. BOL; PRWS
Sleep Not, Dream Not, *sel.* Emily Brontë. LoBV, 2 *sts.*

Sleep. Now that the charge is won. Taps. Lizette Woodworth Reese. DD, HH; OHIP
Sleep, O my babe, not thine a manger. Lullaby. James B. Kenyon. BOL
Sleep, O my darling, sleep. Song. C. Kathleen Carman. BOL
Sleep, O my little Babe, my Son, my King! Mary to Her Babe. "L. L. O'K." BOL
Sleep, O Sleep! Thomas Hastings. BOL
Sleep, O sleep. Song. John Gay. Polly, Air XXIII. EG; FaBoEn; ViBoPo
Sleep, oh sleep, dear Baby mine. The Virgin's Lullaby. *Unknown.* BOL
Sleep, O sleep! While breezes so softly are blowing. Sleep, O Sleep! Thomas Hastings. BOL
Sleep of Bronze, A. Homer, *pr. tr. fr. Greek by* A. T. Murray. *Fr.* The Iliad, XI. LiA
Sleep of the Brave, The. William Collins. *See* How Sleep the Brave.
Sleep of the Just. *Unknown, tr. fr. Greek by* Lord Neaves. OnPM
Sleep on, and dream of Heaven awhile. The Sleeping Beauty. Samuel Rogers. EV-3; GTBS; GTBS-D; GTBS-W; GTSE; GTSL; HBV; LPS-1
Sleep on, baby, on the floor. Sleeping and Watching. Elizabeth Barrett Browning. BOL
Sleep on, beloved, sleep, and take thy rest. The Christian's "Good-Night." Sarah Doudney. BLPA
Sleep on, brave heart, thy broken sword beside thee! Requiem for a Dead Warrior. Edgar McInnis. PEDC
Sleep on, I lie at heaven's high oriels. Nirvana. John Hall Wheelock. HBMV; MAP; MoAmPo; NP; NV; SBMV; TSW
Sleep on my Love, in thy cold bed. Henry King. *Fr.* The Exequy. BCEP; CH; LoPS; PoFS; TrGrPo
Sleep, our lord, and for thy peace. Night Song for a Child [*or* Night Song]. Charles Williams. AlDL; OBEV (new ed.)
Sleep, Robin, Sleep. James Gowdy Clark. BOL
Sleep Serene, Avoid the Backward. Louis MacNeice. *Fr.* Autumn Journal. ChMo
Sleep, Silence' Child. William Drummond of Hawthornden. *See* Sonnet: "Sleep, Silence' child . . ."
Sleep, Sleep, Beauty Bright. Blake. *See* Cradle Song, A: "Sleep! sleep! beauty bright."
Sleep, Sleep, come to me, Sleep. A Charm to Call Sleep. Henry Johnston. PRWS
Sleep, sleep, little Cain! Eve's Cradle-Song. Walter Satterlee. BOL
Sleep, sleep, little mouse! Lullabies of Various Lands—Danish. *Unknown.* BOL
Sleep, sleep, lovely white soul. Lullaby. Walter de la Mare. BOL; GBV
Sleep, sleep mine Holy One! The Virgin Mary to the Child Jesus. Elizabeth Barrett Browning. BOL; ISi
Sleep, Sleep, My Babe. James B. Kenyon. BOL
Sleep, sleep, my darling. Lullaby. *Unknown.* BOL
Sleep, Sleep, My Soul. *Unknown.* SeCL
Sleep, sleep, my treasure. Sleep, My Treasure. Edith Nesbit. BOL; PRWS
Sleep, sleep old Sun, thou canst not have repast. Resurrection. John Donne. StJW
"Sleep, sleep on! forget thy pain." The Magnetic Lady to Her Patient. Shelley. EmBrPo
Sleep, sleep, sleep! All nature now is steeping. A Welsh Lullaby. John Ceiriog Hughes. BOL
Sleep, sleep, sleep, in thy folded waves, O Sea! Sea-Sleep. Thomas Lake Harris. AA
Sleep, sleep softe, you colde clay cindars that late clad. *Unknown.* SeCSL
Sleep, sleep, sweetly sleep. Lady Day in Harvest. Sheila Kaye-Smith. ISi
Sleep, sleep that comest from the mountains. *Unknown.* BOL
Sleep, sleep, that hover'st round. *Unknown.* BOL
Sleep, sleep, the south wind blows. Rizpah's Lullaby. *Unknown.* BOL
Sleep, sleep to-day, tormenting cares. The Sabbath of the Soul. Anna Letitia Barbauld. LPS-2
Sleep soft and long, no morn is worth the waking. Lullaby. Alice Herbert. BLP
Sleep soft, baby mine! A Lullaby. Monica Peveril Turnbull. BOL
Sleep softly . . . eagle forgotten . . . under the stone. The Eagle That Is Forgotten. Vachel Lindsay. AmP; AnFE; APA; ATP; AWP; BAP; ChMo; CMP; CoAnAm; CP; HBV; IAP; InP; JAWP; LBMV; LEAP; LiTA; MAP; MoAB; MoAmPo; MOAP; NeMA; NePA; NP; OxBA; PFY; Po; PoeMoYo; PoFr; TCPD; TOP; TwAmPo; ViBoPo (1958 ed.); WBP; WHA
Sleep Song, A. *Unknown, tr. fr. Irish by* Padraic Pearse. BOL
Sleep Song of Diarmaid and Grainne, The. *Unknown, tr. fr. Late Middle Irish by* Eoin MacNeill. OnYI
(Sleep-Song for Diarmuid, The, *tr. by* Seán O'Faoláin.) SiB
(Sleep-Song of Grainne over Dermuid, The, *tr. by* Eleanor Hull.) AnIV
Sleep sound, O soldier, through the night. Pillow Cases. Richard Armour. WhC
Sleep Sweet. Ellen M. Huntington Gates. BLPA; BLRP; FaBoBe; MaRV; NeHB; PC
Sleep, sweet babe! my cares beguiling. The Virgin's Cradle-Hymn. *Tr. by* Samuel Taylor Coleridge. AnEC; BOL
Sleep sweet within this [*or* thy] quiet room. Sleep Sweet [*or* Good-Night]. Ellen M. Huntington Gates. BLPA; BLRP; MaRV; NeHB; PC
Sleep sweetly, gentle one. Our Treasure in Heaven. Francis Orray Ticknor. PoP
Sleep sweetly in your humble graves. At Magnolia Cemetery [*or* Ode]. Henry Timrod. AA; AmP; AmPP; AnAmPo; BAP; BAV; BIG; BoHiPo; DD; HBV; IAP; LA; LBAP; LPS-2; MC; MDAH; MOAP; OBAV; OxBA; PaA; PoeMoYo; SPP; TCAP
Sleep sweetly, little child; lie quiet and still. *Unknown.* BOL
Sleep That like the Couchèd Dove. Gerald Griffin. *See* Nocturne: "Sleep that like the couched dove."
Sleep the Mother. Florence Kiper. NP
Sleep, this is the time for sleep. Old German Lullabies, 2. *Unknown, ad. by* Louis Untermeyer. RIS
Sleep, Thou little Child of Mary. The Song of a Shepherd-Boy at Bethlehem. Josephine Preston Peabody. ChrBoLe; CLS; OHIP; SDH; StJW
Sleep-Time in Darktown. *Unknown.* BOL
Sleep Unbroken. Omar Khayyám, *tr. fr. Persian by* Edward Fitzgerald. *Fr.* The Rubáiyát. OnPM
("They say the Lion and the Lizard keep.") GTML
Sleep upon the World. Alcman. *See* Fragment: "Mountain summits sleep, The."
Sleep walks over the hill. Lady Sleep. Rowena Bastin Bennett. GaP
Sleep, wayward thoughts, and rest you with my love. So Sleeps My Love. *Unknown.* EG; ReEn; TrGrPo
Sleep well, my dear, sleep safe and free. A Mother's Evening Hymn. Martin Luther. BOL; MOAH
Sleep, white little angel of God. *Unknown.* BOL
Sleep Will Come Singly. W. H. Oliver. AnNZ
Sleepe, babie mine, Desire's nurse, Beautie, singeth. Child-Song. Sir Philip Sidney. BOL
Sleepe, close not up mine eyes, and if thou doe. *Unknown.* SeCSL
Sleepe in your lidds thou loved shades. *Unknown.* SeCSL
Sleepe O sleepe thou sacred dust. *Unknown.* SeCSL
Sleepe, sleepe faire virgin, sleepe in peace. *Unknown.* SeCSL
Sleeper, The. Sydney Clouts. BoSA
Sleeper, The. Walter de la Mare. MBP; MoAB; MoBrPo; SeCeV; YT
Sleeper, The. "Isobel Hume." HBMV
Sleeper, The. Poe. AA; AmPo; AmPP; AnFE; APA; APW; BAP; CoAnAm; CoBA; IAP; InP; LiTA; NePA; OBAV; OBVV; OxBA; PoEL-4; PoFS; ReaPo; TCAP; TrGrPo; UnPo (1st ed.)
"Rosemary nods upon the grave, The," *sel.* PoD
Sleeper, The. Clinton Scollard. HBV; MuM; OBAV
Sleeper, The. Duncan Campbell Scott. BoCaPo (1948 ed.)
Sleeper, The. *Unknown, tr. fr. Arabic by* E. Powys Mathers. *Fr.* The Thousand and One Nights. AWP; LiTW
Sleeper from the Amazon, A. *Unknown.* *See* Limerick: "Sleeper from the Amazon, A."
Sleeper of the Valley, The. Arthur Rimbaud, *tr. fr. French by* Ludwig Lewisohn. AWP; JAWP; WBP
(Sleeper in the Valley, The.) TrFP, *tr. by* Alan Conder; WaaP, *tr. by* Selden Rodman
Sleeper, the palm-trees drink the breathless noon. The Sleeper. *Unknown.* *Fr.* The Thousand and One Nights. AWP; LiTW
Sleepers, The. W. H. Davies. AnFE; BMEP; ChMo; CMP; LBBV; PoeMoYo; POTT; PYM; TwCV; WoL
Sleepers. J. Corson Miller. TBM
Sleepers, The. Walt Whitman. AmP
Indian Woman, The, *sel.* PCD; PCH
Sleepers, Wake! *sel.* Johann Sebastian Bach, *tr. fr. German.* "Now let every tongue adore Thee!" OlF
Sleepers, Wake, *with music.* Philip Nicolai, *tr. by* Catherine Winkworth. YaCaBo
Sleepest or wakest thou, jolly shepherd? The Jolly Shepherd. Shakespeare. *Fr.* King Lear, III, vi. PCH
Sleepin' at the Foot of the Bed. Luther Patrick. BLPA; BoHiPo
Sleeping Alone at the Hsien-yu Temple. Po Chü-i, *tr. fr. Chinese by* Ching Ti. WhP
(Going Alone to Spend a Night at the Hsien-yu Temple, *tr. by* Arthur Waley.) TrCh
Sleeping and Watching. Elizabeth Barrett Browning. BOL
Sleeping at Last. Christina Rossetti. EmBrPo; PoVP; TrGrPo; VLEP
Sleeping-Bag, The. Herbert George Ponting. CenHV
Sleeping Beauty. William Drummond of Hawthornden. LiTL

Sleeping Beauty, The. Robert Layzer. NePoEA
Sleeping Beauty, The. Samuel Rogers. EV-3; GTBS; GTBS-D; GTBS-W; GTSE; GTSL; HBV; LPS-1
Sleeping Beauty, The, *sel.* Edith Sitwell.
"When we come to that dark house." MoVE; OBMV
Sleeping Beauty, The. Tennyson. *Fr.* The Day-Dream. CG; LPS-1
Sleeping Beauty. Elinor Wylie. MuM
Sleeping Beauty, The; Variation of the Prince. Randall Jarrell. FiMAP
Sleeping Child, A. Arthur Hugh Clough. PRWS
(To a Sleeping Child.) BOL
Sleeping earth, with thick white veil, The. Flower Dreams. *Unknown.* PEOR
Sleeping Fury, The. Louise Bogan. LiTM
Sleeping Giant, The. Donald Hall. NePoEA
Sleeping Giant, The. Pauline Johnson. OCL
Sleeping, he is not blind. The Blind Man's Morning. Viola Meynell. MoBrPo (1942 ed.)
Sleeping Heroes. Edward Shanks. OBMV
Sleeping House, The. Tennyson. *Fr.* Maud. FaBoEn
Sleeping in a cabin is as jolly as can be. The Boat. Rose Fyleman. BrR
Sleeping Now in Coventry. Arthur Stanley Bourinot. NeTW
Sleeping on a Summer Day. Yang W'an-li, *tr. fr. Chinese.* WhP
Sleeping on Her Couch. Richard Leigh. FaBoEn; MePo
Sleeping on Horseback Po Chü-i, *tr. fr. Chinese by* Arthur Waley. LiTW; TrCh
Sleeping on the Ceiling. Elizabeth Bishop. MiAP
"Sleeping or waking, thou sweet face." Popular Songs of Tuscany. *Unknown.* AWP; JAWP; WBP
Sleeping Priestess of Aphrodite, A. Robert Cameron Rogers. AA
Sleeping They Bear Me. Alfred Mombert, *tr. fr. German by* Jethro Bithell. AWP; JAWP; WBP
Sleeping Together. Katherine Mansfield. *Fr.* Two Nocturnes. HBMV
Sleeping waters. Beauty. Miguel de Unamuno. TeCS
Sleeping Youth, A. Keats. *See* Adonis in Slumber.
Sleepless. Meng Hao-jan, *tr. fr. Chinese by* Henry H. Hart. PoHN
Sleepless Dreams. Dante Gabriel Rossetti. The House of Life, XXXIX. OAEP; PoVP; ViPo
Sleepless hours who watch me as I lie, The. Hymn of Apollo. Shelley. EmBrPo; EnL; EnLit; EnRP; HBV; OAEP; OBRV
Sleepless in the dark I lie. Verses Written during a Sleepless Night. Pushkin. OnPM; TrRV
Sleepless Night. Annette von Droste-Hülshoff, *tr. fr. German by* Herman Salinger. AnGP
Sleepless Night, A. Egan O'Rahilly, *tr. fr. Modern Irish by* Frank O'Connor. AnIL; KiLC
Sleepless Palinurus. Silvina Ocampo, *tr. fr. Spanish by* Dudley Fitts. AnCL
Sleeplessness. Dwight Edwards Marvin. PraP
Sleeplessness. Wordsworth. *See* To Sleep.
"Sleeps Charidas beneath you?" "If you would ask concerning." "Pulvis et Umbra." Callimachus. GrPE
Sleep's mantle sifted dust from far-off skies. Poppies. Laura Livingston Speyer. CAG
Sleeps tranquilly the lake—a slender throat. Bohernabreena. Leslie Daiken. OnYI
Sleepward. Edith M. Thomas. TBM
Sleepy Harry. Ann *or* Jane Taylor. SAS
Sleepy Harry. *Unknown.* OTPC (1923 ed.)
Sleepy little, creepy little goblins in the gloaming. Lullaby. James W. Foley. BOL; PTA-2
Sleepy Man. Sir Charles G. D. Roberts. *See* When the Sleepy Man Comes.
Sleepy Maple Trees, The. Eleanor Hammond. GFA
Sleepy Song. Thomas Bailey Aldrich. *See* Cradle Song: "Ere the moon begins to rise."
Sleepy Song, The. Josephine Dodge Daskam Bacon. BOL; OTPC (1946 ed.); PCH; PPL; RAR; StVeCh; SUS; UTS
Sleepy Song, A. Carrie Jacobs Bond. BOL
Sleepy Song, A. Charles Buxton Going. BOL; RAR; SP; VOD
Sleepy-Time. Ellen V. Talbot. BOL
Sleepy Tulips, The. Marion Mitchell Walker. GFA
Sleepy vines on the chalk-white houses. Sancho. William Edwin Collin. CaP
Sleepyhead. Walter de la Mare. TiPo
Sleepyland. Laura E. Richards. SAS
Sleepytown Express, The. James J. Montague. HBMV
Sleet Storm. James S. Tippett BrR; SiSoSe
Sleigh Bells at Night. Elizabeth J. Coatsworth. SiSoSe
Sleighride. Patrick Anderson. CaP
Sleigh-Ride, A. Laura E. Richards. GFA
Sleigh Song. G. W. Pettee. LPS-2
Sleighing Song. John Shaw. AA
Sleighride. *See* Sleigh Ride.
Slender bough a-swing. Saki. Al-Taliq. MooP
Slender he was, and fair. In the Mosque. Ibn Malik of Murcia. MooP
Slender her flank. The Ant. Al-Tulaitili. MooP
Slender I saw her stand, stooped a little, her arms akimbo. The White Sand. Edmund Wilson. NePoAm
Slender moon and one pale star, The. The Voice and the Dusk. Duncan Campbell Scott. CPG; OCL
Slender one, white one. Alcibiades to a Jealous Girl. Arthur Davison Ficke. HBMV
Slender Spring. Jorge Guillén, *tr. fr. Spanish.* AnSpL-2, *tr by* Anne Sawyer Durand; CoSP, *tr. by* Eleanor L. Turnbull
Slender young blackbird built in a thorn-tree, A. The Blackbird. Dinah Maria Mulock Craik. BoTP; GoTP
Slender young peach tree, The. The Young Peach Trees. *Unknown.* WhP
Slender's Ghost. William Shenstone. *See* O Sweet Anne Page.
Sliced with shade and scarred with snow. Inverberg. J. F. Hendry. NeBP
Slide at the Empire Mine, The. Harriet L. Wason. PoOW
Slide, Kelly Slide. J. W. Kelly. FaFP; TreFS
Sliding. Marchette Chute. TiPo (1959 ed.)
Sliding. Myra Cohn. SiSoSe
Sliding down the banisters. On the Banisters. Margaret E. Gibbs. BoTP
Slieve Gua. *Unknown, tr. fr. Old Irish.* ChTr
Slievenamon. *Unknown, tr. fr. Irish by* Frank O'Connor. KiLC
Slight, The. Thomas Flatman. LO; SeCL
Slight as thou art, thou art enough to hide. To a Daisy. Alice Meynell. BMEP; JKCP; MBP; MoBrPo; PoeT; WGRP
Slim Cunning Hands. Walter de la Mare. SeCePo
Slim feet than lilies tenderer. Sainte Margérie. *Unknown.* BOHV
Slim Greer. Sterling A. Brown. BANP
Sling, The. Roy Campbell. BoSA
Slings. Rubén Darío, *ad. fr. Spanish by* William Rose Benét. PoFr
Slinky and black. Our Cat. Janet Vaughn. PCD
Slip into sleep as easy as a gown. Kind Sleep. Isabel Fiske Conant. PC
Slip of loveliness, slim, seemly. In Praise of a Girl. Huw Morus. PrWP
Slip-Shoe Lovey. Edgar Lee Masters. NP
Slippery. Carl Sandburg. FaPON; TiPo
Sliprails and the Spur, The. Henry Lawson. BoAu
Slog brute streets [*or* the squares] with rebel tramping! Our March. Vladimir Mayakovsky. AWP; PoFr; TrRV
Sloth, The. Theodore Roethke. FiBHP; NePA; NePoAm; SiTL; WaKn
Slow and reluctant, I have waited. Taking Leave of Wang Wei. Meng Hao-jan. BoFr
Slow and reluctant was the long descent. Sonnets, II. George Santayana. MOAP
Slow are the years of light. Lachrymae. David Gascoyne. *Fr.* Miserere. AtBAP; BoW; NeBP; POTE
Slow bells at dawn. Bells. Duncan Campbell Scott. CaP; OCL
Slow bleak awakening from the morning dream. Living. Harold Monro. ChMo; CMP; FaBoMo; LiTB; LiTM; SeCePo
Slow blush yon breaking clouds—the sun's uproll'd. A Wintry Sunrise. Richard Savage. *Fr.* The Wanderer. BeR
Slow breaks the hushed June dawn. The Voices. *Unknown.* BoHiPo; MCCG; PoMa
Slow but steady, the twilight and the incessant. Evening Sea. Shizuo Ito. PoLJ
Slow Death. Hazel Hall. MAP; MoAmPo (1942 ed.)
Slow dripping of a fountain, The. Impression of a Fountain. Hakushu Kitahara. LiTW
Slow, groping giant, whose unsteady limbs. Doubt. Robert Cameron Rogers. AA
Slow, horses, slow. Night of Spring. Thomas Westwood. AlDL; BoTP; OBVV; PIAE; TOP
Slow Movement. Louis MacNeice. FaBoMo
Slow Movement. William Carlos Williams. NP
Slow Pergamus, you always were a dunce. On Scribe Pergamus, a Slave Who Vainly Fled. Ausonius. LaP
Slow resistless flow of life goes on, The. Sonnet. Richard House. CAG
Slow sail'd the weary mariners and saw. The Sea-Fairies. Tennyson. ViPP
Slow sinks, more lovely ere his race be run. Summer. Byron. *Fr.* The Corsair, III. OBRV
Slow, Slow, Fresh Fount. Ben Jonson. *Fr.* Cynthia's Revels, I. ii. AtBAP; ChTr; EIL; EnLi-1 (1949 ed.); ExPo; RiBV; SeCeV; TuPP; TyEnPo; UnPo; WHA
(Dirge for Narcissus.) BLV
(Echo's Dirge for Narcissus.) CBOV
(Echo's Lament of Narcissus.) AnEnPo; EV-2
(Echo's [*or* Eccho's] Song.) BoLiVe; LoBV; SeCV-1; TrGrPo
("Slow, slow, fresh fount; keep time with my salt tears.")

AEV; CenL; CH; EG; ElSeCe; NBE; OAEP; OBS; ReEn; SiCE
(Song: "Slow, slow, fresh fount, keep[e] time with my salt tear[e]s.") FaBoEn; PoEL-2; ViBoPo
(Song of Echo.) GoBC
Slow Spring. Katharine Tynan. BLV; BoTP; MBP
Slow spring between two wheat-fields, A. High on the hill. The Old Are Sleepy. H. L. Davis. NP
Slow strings are vibrant in the first deep note. Valse Triste. Ruth Guthrie Harding. MuM
Slow the Kansas sun was setting o'er the wheat fields far away. Towser Shall Be Tied Tonight. *Unknown.* AlBD; BLPA; PTA-2
Slow the moon rises, wraith of a moon long drowned. Fog-Horn. George Herbert Clarke. CaP; OCL
Slow to resolve, but in performance quick. King James II. Dryden. *Fr.* The Hind and the Panther, III. ACP
Slow turns the water by the green marshes. Virginiana. Mary Johnston. HBMV
Slowly,/ Over the mountains, piercing the haze. Which? Hsi P'ei Lan. PoHN
Slowly by God's hand unfurled. Evening Hymn [*or* The Light of Stars]. William Henry Furness. AA; FaBoBe; HBV; TCAP; TrPWD
Slowly comes a hungry people, as a lion creeping nigher. Tennyson. *Fr.* Locksley Hall. PoFr
Slowly England's sun was setting o'er the hilltops far away. Curfew Must Not Ring Tonight. Rose Hartwick Thorpe. BeLS; BLPA; FaBoBe; FaPON; HBV; LPS-1; NeHB; PTA-1; WBLP
Slowly forth from the village church. Little Christel. William Brighty Rands. PRWS
Slowly he rode home at the end of day. The Captain. Jon Manchip White. NePoEA
Slowly I followed on. The Lame Shepherd. Katharine Lee Bates. SDH
Slowly I mount the stairs to have/ my picture taken. The Progress of Photography. Byron Vazakas. MoPo
Slowly I smoke and hug my knee. Ballade by the Fire. E. A. Robinson. InP; PFE; POT; PoTo
Slowly, my lords, go slowly. The Case of Thomas More. Sister Mary St. Virginia. GoBC
Slowly Nan the widow goes. Planter's Charm. Fay M. Yauger. HiLiAm; InP
Slowly, O so slowly, longing rose up. Christ Walking on the Water. W. R. Rodgers. AnIL; MoAB; OxBI
Slowly, one by one. Autumn. Forrest Reid. GTIV
Slowly! Patience! I remind the rings. The Goldsmith. Rainer Maria Rilke. TwGV
Slowly, silently, now the moon. Silver. Walter de la Mare. AnEnPo; BoChLi; BoTP; BrR; CaAE; ChMo; CMP; CP; CV; FaPON; GFA; GoTP; GTSL; MBP; MoAB; MoBrPo; MW; NeMA; NV; PCD; PoeMoYo; PoMa; PoMS; PoTo; PtOT; RAR; ShBV-1; SiSoSe; StVeCh; SUS; TCEP; TiPo; TreF; WaKn
Slowly, Slowly. Ovid, *tr. fr. Latin by* Kirby Flower Smith. Elegies, I, 14. WoL
(Lente, Lente.) AWP; LiTW
Slowly, slowly, slowly we oxidize! Isaac N. Himes. *Fr.* The Doctor's Life. PoP
Slowly, slowly, swinging low. Swinging. Irene Thompson. BoTP
Slowly the Bible of the race is writ. The Bible of the Race. James Russell Lowell. OQP; QP-1
Slowly the black earth gains upon the yellow. Odes. IV. George Santayana. AnFE; APA; CoAnAm; TwAmPo
Slowly the daylight left our listening faces. Early Chronology. Siegfried Sassoon. FaBoTw; PtOT
Slowly the flakes came down through the ash-gray skies and the shouting. First Snowfall. Giosuè Carducci. LiTW
Slowly the fog. The Fog. F. R. McCreary. BAP
Slowly the great head turned. Elephant. N. H. Brettell. BoSA
Slowly the mist fades! Ah! the cypress tree. The Home-coming of Ulysses. Stephen Phillips. *Fr.* Ulysses. MW; ReTS
Slowly the mist o'er the meadow was creeping. Lexington. Oliver Wendell Holmes. DD; MC; PAH
Slowly the moon is rising out of the ruddy haze. Aware. D H. Lawrence. MBP; MoBrPo
Slowly the night blooms, unfurling. Flowers of Darkness. Frank Marshall Davis. PoNe
Slowly the poison the whole blood stream fills. Missing Dates. William Empson. ChMP; CoBMV; FaBoEn; FaBoMo; LiTB; LiTM; MoAB; MoPo; ViBoPo (1958 ed.)
Slowly the roses bleed into the water. The Vase. Terence Tiller. ChMP
Slowly the sun descends at fall of night. Twilight. Joaquín A. Pagaza. CAW
Slowly the thing comes. Panic. Archibald MacLeish. MAP; MoAmPo
Slowly they pass. The Sheep. "Seumas O'Sullivan." GTIV; OxBI; TIP
Slowly through the tomb-still streets I go. The Lover's Farewell. James Clarence Mangan. IrPN
Slowly ticks the big clock. The Big Clock. *Unknown.* TiPo
Slowly two charring logs grew white and cold. Embers. J. E. Cadden. CAG
Slowly we learn; the oft repeated line. On National Vanity. J. E. Clare McFarlane. PoNe
Slowly, without force, the rain drops into the city. The Bombardment. Amy Lowell. NV; YT
Slug in Woods. Earle Birney. BoCaPo; CaP; PeCV
Sluggard, The. A. E. Coppard. MBP; MoBrPo (1942 ed.)
Sluggard, The. W. H. Davies. OBMV
Sluggard, The. Isaac Watts. CEP; CH; HBV; HBVY; MoShBr; OBEC; OnPP; OTPC; OxBoLi; PoEL-3; TreFS
Sluggard, The—a Sonnet. Proverbs, Bible, *O.T. See* Reproof, A.
Sluggish morn[e] as yet undrest [*or* undressed], The. Upon Phyllis [*or* Phillis] Walking in a Morning before Sun-rising. John Cleveland. EG; EPS; LiTL; MeLP
Sluggish smoke curls up from some deep dell, The. Smoke in Winter. Henry David Thoreau. AnNE
Sluice gates of sleep are open wide, The. Viaticum. Ethna MacCarthy. NeIP
Slumber and dream of the fast coming years. Slumber Song. *Unknown.* BOL
Slumber Angel, The. Virna Sheard. CPG
Slumber dark and deep. Paul Verlaine. *Fr.* Sagesse. AWP; JAWP; WBP
Slumber Did My Spirit Seal, A. Wordsworth. AnEnPo; AWP; BEL; BoLiVe; BPN; CBOV; EG; EM-2; EnL; EnLit; EnLoPo; EnRP; EPN; EPP; ERP; EtPaEn; ExPo; FaBoCh; FaBoEn; GEPC; GTBS; GTBS-D; GTBS-W; GTSE; GTSL; InPo; InvP; JAWP; LEAP; LiTB; LiTG; LoGBV; MaPo; OAEP; OBRV; OnPM; OuHeWo; Po; PoE; PoEL-4; PoFS; PoRA; REAL; ReaPo; RiBV; SeCeV; ShBV-4; TCEP; TOP; TreFS; TrGrPo; TriL; TwHP; TwP; TyEnPo; UnPo (3d ed.); ViBoPo; WBP; WP
(Lines.) LoBV
(Lucy.) AnFE; BLV; CoEV; EmBrPo; EnLi-2; FiP; HBV; LEAP; LiTL; OBEV
Slumber Fairies. Katharine Lee Bates. BOL
Slumber in Spring. Elizabeth Gould. BoTP
Slumber, Jesu, lightly [*or* o'er Thy] dreaming. Lullaby [*or* Latin Lullaby]. *Unknown.* CAW; ISi
Slumber, my darling, no danger is near. The Mother to Her Infant. Thomas Miller. BOL; OTPC (1923 ed.)
Slumber, Sleep—they were two brothers, servants to the gods above. The Brothers. Goethe. LPS-3
Slumber, slumber, darling, the old mocking-bird is singing. *Unknown.* BOL
Slumber, slumber, dearest, sweetest treasure. Cradle Song. *Unknown.* BOL
Slumber, slumber, little one, now. Lullaby. Frank Dempster Sherman. BOL
Slumber, Small One. Though She Slumbers. Joseph Joel Keith. ISi
Slumber Song: "All is still in sweetest rest." *Unknown.* BOL
Slumber Song, A: "Beautiful bird at the casement sings, A." A. Holcombe Aiken. BOL
Slumber Song: "Drowsily come the sheep." Louis V. Ledoux. FaPON; HBMV; MPB; SBMV; UTS; VOD
Slumber Song: "Lo, in the west." John Banister Tabb. BOL
Slumber Song: "Now the golden day is ending." Mary H. Poynter. BOL
Slumber Song: "Shoheen sho! There's a new moon setting." Alice Furlong. BOL
Slumber Song: "Sleep; and my song shall build about your bed." Siegfried Sassoon. MCCG
Slumber Song, A: "Sleep, baby, sleep, thy father watches the sheep." *Unknown. See* Sleep, Baby Sleep.
Slumber Song: "Slumber and dream of the fast coming years." *Unknown.* BOL
Slumber Song: "Thou little child, with tender clinging arms." Celia Thaxter. BOL
Slumber Song: "When the low flying wind, awake." Marie van Vorst. BOL
Slumber-Song of the Blessed Mother. *Unknown, tr. fr. Tuscan folk song by* Grace Warrack. ChrBoLe
Slumber-Songs of the Madonna. Alfred Noyes. BOL
Slumber, sweet slumber. *Unknown.* BOL
Slumbering darkly yesterday. A Day After. Bedros Tourian. ArmLP
Slump in Sybaris, The. Franklin P. Adams, *after* Horace. *See* Questioning Lydia.
Slums. James Oppenheim. BAP
Slung between the homely poplars at the end. Ursa Major. James Kirkup. ImOP
Slurred and drawled and crooning sounds, The. A Toast. Louis MacNeice. ChMo; GTBS-D
Slushy snow splashes and sploshes, The. Mary Ann Hoberman. TiPo (1959 ed.)

Sly Beelzebub took all occasions. Job [*or* Epigram]. Samuel Taylor Coleridge. BOHV; LPS-3
Sly-Boots. Arthur Rimbaud, *tr. fr. French by* Alan Conder. TrFP
Sly merchants plotted newer, greater gains. Renaissance. Robert Avrett. GoYe
Sly Santa Claus. Mrs. C. S. Stone. COAH
Sly Thoughts. Coventry Patmore. *See* Kiss, The.
Smack in School, The. William P. Palmer. BOHV; HBV; LPS-1; PTA-1
Smack of Lord Cromer, A, Jeff Davis a touch of him. Theodore Roosevelt. *Unknown.* BoHiPo
Small activity of mice, The. Mad Boy's Song. Leo Kennedy. BoCaPo; TwCaPo
Small and Early. Tudor Jenks. AA; PCD
Small April sobbed. April Fool. Eleanor Hammond. GFA
Small astonished angels, The, said: Who can that be? Mozart in Heaven. Manuel Bandeira. AnCL
Small Beginnings. Charles Mackay. LPS-3; PTA-2
(Little and Great.) HBV; HBVY
(Little but Great.) TVSH
(Song of Life.) PECK
Small Birds. Peter Quennell. MoVE
Small Boy, The. *Unknown, tr. fr. Chinese.* ChLP
Small boy has thrown a stone at a statue, A. The Statue. Robert Finch. BoCaPo (1948 ed.); PeCV
Small Boy Points a Moral, The. Wilbur D. Nesbit. OnHT
Small boy went away, and so, A. A Dog—Lost. Helen Brosi McLeod. AlBD
Small Boy's Loquitur, The. *Unknown.* CH
Small Boy's Prayer, A. Helen Gleaves Nunn. DDA
Small, busy flames play through the fresh laid coals. To My Brothers. Keats. EmBrPo; EnLi-2; PeBoSo
Small Celandine, The. Wordsworth. *See* Lesson, A.
Small City on a Rock, A. Phocylides, *tr. fr. Greek by* C. M. Bowra. OxBG; WoL
Small Cleodemus. Antistius, *tr. fr. Greek by* Robert Guthrie MacGregor. OnPM
Small Death to Laugh. Tristan Corbière, *tr. fr. French by* Kate Flores. AnFP
Small Fountains. Lascelles Abercrombie. *Fr.* Emblems of Love: Epilogue. CH
Small Girl, A. *Unknown, tr. fr. Chinese.* ChLP
Small gnats that fly. Song: One Hard Look. Robert Graves. LoPo; MBP; MoAB; MoBrPo
Small Hours, The. Mary Ursula Bethell. OnPM
Small house with a pointed roof, A. Epiphany. Eileen Shanahan. NeIP
Small is Eumenes' Cleodemus, yet. Small Cleodemus. Antistius. OnPM
Small men make love on stilts, and hold their poise. A Forked Radish. Jonathan Price. PoN
Small offender, small innocent child. To a Small Boy Who Died at Diepkloof Reformatory. Alan Paton. BoSA
Small on the skylit plain. Birds in the Flax. Stanley Snaith. HaMV
Small Perfect Manhattan. Peter Viereck. MiAP
Small piteous thing in the sun's yellow blaze. The Mole. Frederick William Harvey. MM
Small poets sing of little, foolish things. Which Will Scarcely Be Understood. Robert Ervin Howard. DaM
Small Rain. Alice Lawry Gould. MoSiPe
Small service is true service while it lasts. To a Child [*or* In a Child's Album]. Wordsworth. HBV; HBVY; LPS-1; PCH; OBRV
Small shining drop, no lady's ring. For a Dewdrop. Eleanor Farjeon. HBVY; YT
Small Silver-coloured Bookworm, The. Thomas Parnell. OnYI
Small skill is gained by those who cling to ease. *Unknown.* GoTP
Small Soldiers with Drum in Large Landscape. Robert Penn Warren. Mexico Is a Foreign Country, IV. FiMAP
Small Song. Daniel Whitehead Hicky. MaRV
Small Stars, The. *Unknown, tr. fr. Chinese.* WhP
Small Talk. Don Marquis. *Fr.* Archy Does His Part. StPo
Small tendrils of a morning glory to the well ropes cling. Chiyo Ni, *tr. fr. Japanese by* Lois J. Erickson. SoLD
Small Things. Richard Monckton Milnes. NeHB
Small Things. Lizette Woodworth Reese. MuM
Small town bears the mark of Cain, A. Estevan, Saskatchewan. E. W. Mandel. PeCV
Small traveler from an unseen shore. To a New-born Child. Cosmo Monkhouse. HBV
Small wasp lies in state. The. Dead Wasp. Kenneth Slade Alling. NePoAm
Small wind whispers through the leafless hedge, The. Winter. John Clare. ATP
Smallest Angel, The. Elsie Binns. ChBR
Smallest of the Drums, The. James Buckham. MDAH
Smart Lady, The. Edward Young. *Fr.* The Love of Fame, Satire V. BeR
Smart Yankee packet lay out in the bay, A. A Long Time Ago (B *vers.*). *Unknown.* SoAmSa
Smatterers. Samuel Butler. BOHV
Smell. William Carlos Williams. MoAB; MoAmPo
Smell of arnica is strong, The. When Father Played Baseball. Edgar A. Guest. PEDC
Smell of burning weeds, The. The Good Earth. Sir Charles G. D. Roberts. CPG
Smell of cigar smoke, Sunday, after dinner. Cigar Smoke, Sunday, after Dinner. Louise Townsend Nicholl. NePoAm
Smell of death was in the air, The. Farewell. John Press. PoRA
Smell of hay is on the field, The. The Hay Harvest. Apollon Nikolayevich Maikov. TrRV
Smell of ruin in the autumn air, The. Scars. David Morton. TBM
Smell of the heat is boxwood, The. To Daphne and Virginia. William Carlos Williams. CrMA
Smell of woodyards in the rain is strong, The. Woodyards in the Rain. Anne Marriott. CaP; TwCaPo; TwCV
Smelling the End of Green July. "Peter Yates." ChMP
Smells. Christopher Morley. PoeMoYo; PoMa; POT; PoTo; ShBV-1; YT
Smells. Kathryn Worth. BrR
Smells are surer than sounds or sights. Lichtenberg. Kipling. EnLit
Smells (Junior). Christopher Morley. BoChLi; GFA; MPB; TiPo
Smelting Furnace, The. Hugo Tigerschiöld, *tr. fr. Swedish by* Charles W. Stork. AnSL
Smile, The. Blake. CaAE; OBRV
(Smile and Frown.) BoFr
Smile, The. Anthony Euwer. *See* Limerick: "No matter how grouchy you're feeling."
Smile, The. Robert Frost. *Fr.* The Hill Wife. ChMo; CMP; IAP; MOAP; NP
Smile, The. Sophus Michaëlis, *tr. fr. Danish by* Charles W. Stork. BoDS
Smile, A ("Let others cheer"). *Unknown.* BLPA; WBLP
Smile ("Like a bread"). *Unknown.* BLPA; WBLP
Smile, A ("A smile costs nothing but gives much"). *Unknown.* PoToHe
Smile and Frown. Blake. *See* Smile, The.
Smile and Never Heed Me. Charles Swain. HBV; LPS-1
Smile, and the world smiles with you. Hustle and Grin. *Unknown.* WBLP
Smile at us, pay us, pass us; but do not quite forget. The Secret People. G. K. Chesterton. OtMeF; PoFr
Smile costs nothing but gives much, A. A Smile. *Unknown.* PoToHe
Smile, Massachusetts, smile. A Song. *Unknown.* PAH
Smile not, nor think the legend vain. Contentment. Sadi. LiTW
Smile of one face is like a fierce mermaid, The. Soldiers. Maxwell Bodenheim. MAPA
Smile of Reims, The. Florence Earle Coates. VOD
Smile of the Goat, The. Oliver Herford. FiBHP
Smile of the Walrus, The. Oliver Herford. FiBHP
Smile then, children, hand in hand. Epithalamion. James Elroy Flecker. POTT
"Smile, The," they called her,—"La Sourire" and fair. The Smile of Reims. Florence Earle Coates. VOD
Smiles on my lips, while quick tears blind my eyes. Chiyo Ni, *tr. fr. Japanese by* Lois J. Erickson. SoLD
Smiling. Dixie Willson. GFA
Smiling Demon of Notre Dame, A. Sophie Jewett. AA
Smiling girls, rosy boys. Mother Goose. GaP; OxNR
Smiling Morn, the Breathing Spring, The. The Birks of Invermay [*or* Endermay]. David Mallet. EBSV; OBEC
Smiling Phyllis has an air. Phyllis. *Unknown.* SeCL
Smith, The. Juana de Ibarbourou, *tr. fr. Spanish by* Beatrice Gilman Proske. OnPM
Smith/ a refugee from the Black Country. One Race, One Flag. A. R. D. Fairburn. AnNZ
Smith makes me, A. The Runes on Weland's Sword. Kipling. AtBAP; PoEL-5
Smith, of the Third Oregon, Dies. Mary Carolyn Davies. SBMV
Smiths of the heavens are mending the weather, The. Thunderstorm. Arthur Guiterman. PoMa
Smith's seventh wife has joined the batch. Martial, *tr. fr. Latin by* "T. W. M." Epigrams, X, 43. LaP
Smith's Song. George Sigerson, *ad. fr. the Irish.* OnYI
Smoke. Henry David Thoreau. *Fr.* Walden, *ch.* 13. AA; AmPP; AnAmPo; AnFE; AnNE; APA; AWP; BAV; CoAnAm; CoBA; IAP; InPo; JAWP; LA; LBAP; LPS-2; MOAP; OxBA; PIR; SN; TOP; WBP
(Light-winged Smoke.) ViBoPo
(Light-winged Smoke, Icarian Bird.) CoV; OnPM
Smoke, *sels.* Bernard Freeman Trotter. CPG
"Beyond a sky-swept crest of hills," III.
"I built for myself a lodge in a fringe of the forest." II.
Smoke and Steel. Carl Sandburg. CV; HeT; PIAE
Sels.
"Bar of steel, A—it is only." PoeMoYo; VOD (1935 ed.)

"Smoke of the fields in spring is one." MAP; MoAmPo; NeMA; PoMa
Smoke-blue Plains, The. Badger Clark. YaD
Smoke from the train-gulf hid by hoardings blunders upward. Birmingham. Louis MacNeice. ChMo; MBP; MoAB; MoBrPo
Smoke in Winter. Henry David Thoreau. AnNE
Smoke of the Camp Fire. Brian Brooke. BoSA
Smoke of the fields in spring is one. Smoke and Steel. Carl Sandburg. CV; HeT; MAP; MoAmPo; NeMA; PIAE; PoMa
Smoke Rings. *Unknown.* CAG
Smoke Rose Gold. Carl Sandburg. NeMA; VOD; YT
Smoke Stack. A. M. Sullivan. WaKn
Smoke-veiled chill waters, moon veiling the sands. Morning at Chien-wei River. Tu Mu. WhP
Smoked Herring, The. Charles Cros, *tr. fr. French by* A. L. Lloyd. MiFP
Smokin' my pipe on the mountings. Screw-Guns. Kipling. ViBoPo
Smoking Flax. Mary Josephine Benson. CaP
Smoky blue of evening wreathes from fields, The. Living. D. S. Savage. NeBP
Smooth between Sea and Land. A. E. Housman. MaPo; MoPo
Smooth-browed they stand, these marble forms of old. To Rodin. Charles Wharton Stork. TBM
Smooth Divine, The. Timothy Dwight. *Fr.* The Triumph of Infidelity. AA; AnAmPo; IAP; LA; TCAP; WGRP (Minister, New Style, A.) AmPP
Smooth hill is bare, and the cannons are planted, The. At Fredericksburg. John Boyle O'Reilly. MC; PAH
Smooth, unobtrusive walls say "Hush!" in a voice of honey and meal, The. Mortuary Parlors. Stephen Vincent Benét. NV
Smooth was the water, calm the air. Song. Sir Charles Sedley. CEP; SeCV-2
Smooth-worn coin and threadbare classic phrase, The. Andromeda. Thomas Bailey Aldrich. AA
Smoothing a cypress beam. The Builder. Willard Wattles. AnAmPo; BAP; HBMV; LA; OQP; PoeMoYo; PYM; QP-1; TBM
Smoothly riding. The Carpenter's Plane. Vasily Kazin. OnPM; TrRV
Smothered streams of love, which flow, The. The Atlantides. Henry David Thoreau. MOAP; ViBoPo
Smothering dark engulfs relentlessly, The. A Child's Winter Evening. Gwen John. CH
Smuggler, The. *Unknown.* CBPC; SG; WhC
Smuggler's Song, A. Kipling. *Fr.* Puck of Pook's Hill. ShBV-1
Snack, A. Christina Rossetti. *See* Three Plum Buns.
Snagtooth Sal. Lowell O. Reese. ABF, *with music;* SCC, *abr.*
Snail, The ("The frugal snail with forecast of repose"). Vincent Bourne, *tr. fr. Latin by* Charles Lamb. *See* Housekeeper, The.
Snail, The ("To grass, or leaf, or fruit, or wall"). Vincent Bourne, *tr. fr. Latin by* William Cowper. BoTP; CG; GFA; GoTP; HBV; HBVY; OTPC (1923 ed.); PoRh; WaKn
Snail, The. Grace Hazard Conkling. SUS; UTS
Snail. John Drinkwater. AlDL
Snail. Langston Hughes. FaPON; GoSl; TiPo
Snail. C. Lindsay McCoy. GFA
Snail, The ("Little snail"). *Unknown, tr. fr. Chinese by* Isaac Taylor Headland. PCH
Snail, The ("The snail he lives in his hard round house"). *Unknown.* OTPC (1946 ed.); PPL
Snail is very odd and slow, The. The Snail. Grace Hazard Conkling. SUS; UTS
Snail, The, says, "Alas!" The Poor Snail. J. M. Westrup. BoTP
Snail, snail, put out your horns. *Unknown.* OxNR
Snail upon the wall. Snail. John Drinkwater. AlDL
Snail who had a way, it seems, A. The Snail's Dream. Oliver Herford. PCH; UTS
Snail's a lucky fellow, he can go, The. The Lucky Snail. Winifred Welles. StVeCh (1940 ed.)
Snail's Dream, The. Oliver Herford. PCH; UTS
Snail's Moving Day, The. Hesiod. *See* When the Snail Climbs.
Snake, The. Roy Campbell. AtBAP
Snake, A [*or* The]. Emily Dickinson. *See* Narrow fellow in the grass, A, *and* Sweet is the swamp . . .
Snake, The. Francis Flagg. DaM
Snake. D. H. Lawrence. AtBAP; BBV (1951 ed.); BMEP; BrBE; CoBMV; CoEV; FaBoMo; GoTL (1949 ed.); HoPM; LBBV; LiTB; LiTM; LoBV; MM; MoAB; MoPo; MoPW; MoVE; OAEP (2d ed.); ReMP; SeCeV; ShBV-3; TwCV
Snake. John Russell McCarthy. BAP
Snake, The. Kenneth Mackenzie. BoAV
Snake, The. Thomas Moore. HBV
Snake, The. Virgil, *tr. fr. Latin by* Dryden. *Fr.* Georgics, III. LiA
Snake and the Mouse, The. Bhartrihari, *tr. fr. Sanskrit by* Paul Elmer More. OnPM
Snake came to my water-trough, A. Snake. D. H. Lawrence. AtBAP; BBV (1951 ed.); BMEP; BrBE; CoBMV; CoEV; FaBoMo; GoTL (1949 ed.); HoPM; LBBV; LiTB; LiTM; LoBV; MM; MoAB; MoPo; MoPW; MoVE; OAEP (2d ed.); ReMP; SeCeV; ShBV-3; TwCV
Snake Charmer, The. Muriel Earley Sheppard. IHA
Snake in Paradise, The. Tove Ditlevsen, *tr. fr. Danish by* Charles W. Stork. BoDS
Snake It Was That Died, The. Demodocus, *tr. fr. Greek by* J. H. Merivale. OxBG
Snake of a Man, A. *Unknown.* AlBD
Snake Story. Henry Johnstone. PPL
Snakes, Mongooses, Snake-Charmers and the Like. Marianne Moore. ExPo
Snakeskin and Stone. Keith Douglas. NePoEA
Snap back the canopy. Parachute Descent. David Bourne. WaP
Snapdragon. Cardinal Newman. GoBC
Snapoo (Slapandergosheka: "Oh, a little Dutch soldier from over the Rhine") (*orig. vers. of* Mademoiselle from Armentières). *Unknown.* SoAmSa
Snapshot: Ambassadress. George Garrett. NePoAm-2
Snapshot of a Pedant. George Garrett. NePoAm-2
Snapshot: Politician. George Garrett. NePoAm-2
Snare, The. Edward Davison. BMEP; PG (1955 ed.); ViBoPo (1941 ed.)
Snare, The. Patrick MacDonogh. NeIP
Snare, The. James Stephens. BMEP; BoTP; CBE; CH; ChMo; CMP; HBMV; LEAP; MM; MoSiPe; OxBI; PCN; PoRL; ReaPo; ShBV-1; TCPD; TiPo; UTS; YT
Snare me the soul of a dragon-fly. Miyoko San. Mary McNeil Fenollosa. AA
Snare of sleep held fast his struggling will, The. Epitaph on a Sentry. L. A. G. Strong. NeMA
Snares, The. Nahab Koutchak, *tr. fr. Armenian by* Thomas Walsh. CAW
Snark, The. "Lewis Carroll." *See* How to Recognize a Snark.
Snarlers, The. Arthur Guiterman. PaA
Snarleyyow; or, The Dog Fiend, *sel.* Frederick Marryat.
Captain Stood on the Carronade, The. BBV (1923 ed.); EtS; HBV; OTPC; SG
(Old Navy, The.) CBE; CBOV; EV-4; LH; TVSH
Snatch the departing mood. To a Town Poet. Lizette Woodworth Reese. AA
Snayl, The. Richard Lovelace. AtBAP; NBE; PoEL-3
Sneel, Snaul. *Unknown.* OTPC
Sneeze on a Monday, you sneeze for danger. *See* If you sneeze on Monday . . .
Sneezing. Leigh Hunt. HBV; LPS-3
Sniff. Frances Frost. BrR; SiSoSe; TiPo (1959 ed.)
Snore in the foam; the night is vast and blind. Tristan da Cunha. Roy Campbell. CoEV; MBP; MM; MoBrPo; MoVE; OnHM; TwCV
Snow. Dorothy Aldis. TiPo
Snow. Elizabeth Akers Allen. HBV; SN
Snow. Margaret Avison. PeCV
Snow, The. Joseph Beaumont. StJW
Snow. Madison Cawein. MAP; PFY; SPP
Snow. Elizabeth J. Coatsworth. SiSoSe
Snow, The ("It sifts from leaden sieves"). Emily Dickinson. GoTP; RG
Snow, The. Clifford Dyment. MoVE; POTE
Snow, The. F. Ann Elliott. BoTP
Snow. Robert Frost. IAP
Snow, The. W. W. Gibson. BEL
Snow. Jorge Guillén, *tr. fr. Spanish by* Eleanor L. Turnbull. CoSP
Snow, The. Sidney Keyes. NeBP
Snow. Archibald Lampman. PeCV
Snow. Longfellow. *See* Snow-Flakes.
Snow. Louis MacNeice. ExPo; GTBS-W; LiTM; ReMP
Snow, The. Mao Tse-tung, *tr. fr. Chinese.* WhP
Snow, The. Nellie Burget Miller. GFA
Snow. Tatsuji Miyoshi, *tr. fr. Japanese by* Takamichi Ninomiya *and* D. J. Enright. PoLJ
Snow. Munetake, *tr. fr. Japanese by* Asataro Miyamori. OnPM
Snow. Alfred Noyes. AlDL
Snow. W. R. Rodgers. LiTG; LiTM (rev. ed.)
"Out of the grey air grew snow and more snow," *sel.* AlDL
Snow. Jane Taylor. OTPC (1923 ed.); PCH; PPL
Snow. Edward Thomas. FaBoTw; MoVE
Snow. *Unknown.* *See* Riddle: "White bird featherless."
Snow, The. Emile Verhaeren, *tr. fr. French by* Alma Strettell. MiFP
Snow. Alfred de Vigny, *tr. fr. French by* Alan Conder. TrFP
Snow, The. Whittier. *See* Winter Day.
Snow. Alice Wilkins. GFA; TiPo
Snow. Humbert Wolfe. TwCV

Snow/ is an anthology. Snow Anthology. Arthur S. Bourinot. GoYe; TwCaPo
Snow—a Winter Sketch. Ralph Hoyt. LPS-2
Snow Advent. Joseph Auslander. DDA; MoSiPe
Snow, The, Ah, yes; ah, yes, indeed. Vista. Alfred Kreymborg. MAPA
Snow and hail and flash and gloom. Asclepiades, *tr. fr. Greek by* William Wallace *and* Mary Wallace. GrPo
Snow and sleet came to armor the earth, The. Pigeons and Snow. Andrew Hewitt. NoCaPo
Snow and stars, the same as ever. Age. William Winter. HBV
Snow and the silence came down together, The. Out in the Snow. Louise Chandler Moulton. PTA-2
Snow Anthology. Arthur S. Bourinot. GoYe; TwCaPo
Snow at Christmas. Stan Granlund, *tr. fr. Swedish by* Charles W. Stork. AnSL
Snow at Midnight; the Elevated. Frederick Mortimer Clapp. VOD (1935 ed.)
Snow at Sea. John Gould Fletcher. ChMo; CMP
Snow Ball, The. Petronius Arbiter, *tr. fr. Latin by* Soame Jenyns. LiTW
Snow-beaten, winter-bound, all that I see. First Words before Spring. Louis Untermeyer. MAP
Snow breaks the hushed June dawn. The Voices. *Unknown.* MCCG
Snow-Bunting, The. Thorsteinn Erlingsson, *tr. fr. Icelandic by* Runólfur Fjeldsted. IcP
Snow-Buntings. Frank Prewett. MBP
Snow came down like stars tonight, The. Fall of Stars. George Dillon. NP
Snow can come as quietly, A. Snow. Elizabeth J. Coatsworth. SiSoSe
Snow cannot melt too soon for the birds left behind, The. Rag Doll and Summer Birds. Owen Dodson. PoNe
Snow-Dance for the Dead. Lola Ridge. AnAmPo; LA
Snow dissolv'd no more is seen, The. Spring's Return. Horace, *tr. by* Samuel Johnson. Odes, IV, 7. LiA; TriL
Snow Dust. Robert Frost. *See* Dust of Snow.
Snow-dust driven over the snow. Winter Noon. Sara Teasdale. YeAr
Snow falling and night falling fast, oh, fast. Desert Places. Robert Frost. AmPP (4th ed.); AnFE; AtBAP; ChMo; CoAnAm; CoBMV; MAP; MoAB; MoAmPo; MoVE; OxBA; ReMP; RiBV; TwAmPo; TwP; UnPo
Snow falls/ flake on flake. Winter in the Wood. Ivy O. Eastwick. YeAr
Snow falls deep; the forest lies alone, The. Gipsies [*or* The Gipsy Camp]. John Clare. CH; ChTr; PoEL-4; ShBV-2
Snow Falls on China. Ai Ching, *tr. fr. Chinese.* WhP
Snow falls silently through the unnatural forest. The Campaign. Frederic Prokosch. NeTW; SoV
Snow fell slowly over the long sweep, The. Landscape. Alfred W Purdy. CaP
Snow fell softly all the night, The. Snow. Alice Wilkins. GFA; TiPo
Snow Fell with a Will. Richard Gillman. NePoAm-2
Snow-filled Nest, The. Rose Terry Cooke. SN
Snow Forest. Frank Ernest Hill. PoTo
Snow-Gardens, The. Zoë Akins. AV
Snow Globe, The. Howard Nemerov. FiMAP
Snow had begun in the gloaming, The. The First Snow-Fall. James Russell Lowell. AA; AnNE; BLPA; BTP; FaBoBe; FaPON; GFA; HBV; IAP; LPS-1; MCCG; NeHB; PCD; PEOR; PIR; PTA-1; REAL; TCAP; TreF; WBLP
Snow had fallen many nights and days, The. The End of the World. Gordon Bottomley. CH; MBP; MoBrPo; MoVE; NV
Snow, hail, make darkness, lighten, thunder, shake out on the earth. The Power of Love. Asclepiades. GrL
Snow has been falling. After midnight, drunk with purple. Winter Night. Georg Trakl. AnGP
Snow has fallen lightly on the earth, The. Prose Poem: Sadness of the Husbandman. Judith Gautier. OnPM
Snow has gone from Chung-nan; spring is almost come, The. Passing T'ien-men Street in Ch'ang-an and Seeing a Distant View of Chung-nan Mountain. Po Chü-i. TrCh
Snow in April. Leonora Speyer. PG (1955 ed.)
Snow, in bitter cold, The. The Snow. F. Ann Elliott. BoTP
Snow in Europe. David Gascoyne. MoPW
Snow in October. Alice Dunbar Nelson. CDC
Snow in the City. Rachel Field. TiPo
Snow in the Suburbs. Thomas Hardy. AlDL; ChMo; CMP; MBP; MoAB; MoBrPo; OBMV; PoVP; ShBV-3; ThWaDe; ViPP; VLEP
Snow in Town. Rickman Mark. BoTP; TVC; TVSH
Snow is a strange white word. On Receiving News of the War. Isaac Rosenberg. MoBrPo
"Snow is deep, The," the Justice said. The Green Mountain Justice. Henry Reeves. PTA-1
Snow is lying very deep, The. Convention. Agnes Lee. BAP; HBMV; PoMa; SBMV
Snow is out of fashion. Snow in the City. Rachel Field. TiPo
Snow, The, is soft, and how it squashes! Thaw. Eunice Tietjens. BrR
Snow is still on the ground. Winter's Turning. Amy Lowell. CV
Snow is white, the wind is cold, The. Night. Mary Frances Butts. BOL; OTPC (1946 ed.); PRWS
Snow Lay on the Ground, The, *with music. Unknown.* YaCaBo
Snow-Leopard, The. Randall Jarrell. MoPo
Snow, less intransigeant than their marble, The. At the Grave of Henry James. W. H. Auden. LiTA; MoPo
Snow lies crisp beneath the stars, The. Christmas Pastoral. Robert Hillyer. MaRV
Snow lies deep, The: nor sun nor melting shower. Winter at Tomi. Ovid. AWP; JAWP; WBP
Snow Lies Light, The. W. W. Christman. BLA
Snow Lies Sprinkled on the Beach, The. Robert Bridges. PoVP
Snowlight. Nancy Byrd Turner. MW
Snow makes whiteness where it falls. First Snow. Marie Louise Allen. TiPo
Snowman, The. E. M. Adams. BoTP
Snow Man, The. Wallace Stevens. AnEnPo; CoBMV; CoV; CrMA; NP; Po; PoFS; ReMP
Snowman. *Unknown.* GFA
Snow-masked and bell-bewitched the village. Christmas on Three Continents. John Peter. BoSA
Snow may come as quietly, A. January. Elizabeth J. Coatsworth. BoChLi (1950 ed.)
Snow Meditation. Francis Beauchesne Thornton. JKCP (1955 ed.)
Snow-Messengers, The. Paul Hamilton Hayne. SPP
Snow of Stones, The. Homer, *tr. fr. Greek by* Michael Balkwill. *Fr.* The Iliad, XII. OxBG
Snow of the Crane. Nikolai Tikhonov, *tr. fr. Russian by* Jack Lindsay. RuPo
Snow on! hail on! cast darkness all around me! The Power of Love. Asclepiades. GrR
Snow on the East Wind. Lord Dunsany. MBP; MoBrPo (1942 ed.)
Snow on the level, three feet deep. The Mulligan Stew. *Unknown.* DDA
Snow Queen comes on dazzling feet, The. The North Wind. Dorothy Gradon. BoTP
Snow Scene, A. James Thomson. *See* Winter.
Snow-Shower, The. Bryant. AnNE; APW; HBV; LEAP; LPS-2
Snow, snow faster. *Unknown.* OxNR
Snow-Sparrow, The. Elias Sehlstedt, *tr. fr. Swedish by* Charles W. Stork. AnSL
Snow Storm. *See* Snowstorm.
Snow Story. L. A. MacKay. TwCaPo
Snow swirls its wavering noiseless fringes against my window. The Bay; December. Frederick Mortimer Clapp. VOD (1935 ed.)
Snow toward Evening. Melville Cane. MAP; MoAmPo; SUS; TiPo
Snow upon my lifeless mountains, The. The Day of Love. Shelley. *Fr.* Prometheus Unbound. EPN; NBE
Snow Water. Frank Ernest Hill. TBM
Snow whispers about me, The. Chinoiseries: Falling Snow. Amy Lowell. AnAmPo; LA; NP
Snow-white gull, oh, would to you 'twere given. To a Sea-Gull in the Steamer's Wake. Daniel Fallström. AnSL
Snow white shawls. Daisies. Hilda Conkling. NV
Snow wind-whipt to ice. Winter. Richard Hughes. AlDL; OBMV; ThWaDe
Snow-Bird, The. Hezekiah Butterworth. PCH; PRWS
Snow-Bird, The. Frank Dempster Sherman. SiSoSe; TiPo; UTS
Snowbird, The. John Banister Tabb. SPP
Snow-Bird's Song, The. Francis C. Woodworth. PPL; SAS
Snow-bound. Edward Sandford Martin. PR
Snow-bound; a Winter Idyl. Whittier. AmPP; AnNE; APW, *sl. abr.;* CoBA; GN, *sels.;* HiLiAm; IAP; MCCG, *abr.;* MOAP; OxBA; PIAE, *much abr.;* SN; TCAP; TOP
Sels.
"Alas for him who never sees." InP
"And yet, dear heart! remembering thee." MaRV
"As night drew on, and, from the crest." YT
(Fireside, The.) MW
(Winter Night.) TrGrPo
Faith in Time of Darkness ("What matter how the night behaved"). GrCo-2
Life and Love. BLRP
New England in Winter. LPS-2
"O Time and Change—with hair as gray." BPP
"Our mother, while she turned her wheel." MotAn
(Mother.) AA; MW; OHIP; PFY

Prophetess ("Another guest that winter night"). AA
Schoolmaster, The ("Brisk wielder of the birch and rule"). GoTP
"Shut in from all the world without." LaNeLa
(Firelight.) AA
Sister ("As one who held herself apart"). AA
"Sun that brief December day, The." AtBAP; OnAP
(Lines.) BBV (1951 ed.)
(Snow, The.) StVeCh
(Winter Day.) TrGrPo
Uncle, The ("Our uncle, innocent of books"). GoTP
"Unwarmed by any sunset light." BBV (1923 ed.); GBV
(Snow-Storm, The.) MW
(World Transformed, The.) AA
Yet Love Will Dream. MaRV
Snow-bound in woodland, a mournful word. Postponement. Thomas Hardy. PoVP
Snow-bound mountains, snow-bound valleys. Carol of the Russian Children. *Unknown.* OHIP; SDH
Snow-Drift. Hugo T. Saglio. CAG
Snow-Drop, The. Samuel Taylor Coleridge. TriL
Snowdrop. Anna Bunston de Bary. BoTP; HBMV; MaRV
Snowdrop, A, *abr.* Harriet Prescott Spofford. GN
Snowdrop. William Wetmore Story. HBV; PR
Snowdrop. Tennyson. OTPC (1946 ed.); PCH; PoRL
Snowdrops. Laurence Alma-Tadema. BoTP; PRWS
Snowdrops. W. Graham Robertson. OTPC; PPL
Snowdrops. Mary Vivian. BoTP
Snowfall. Giosuè Carducci, *tr. fr. Italian by* Romilda Rendel. AWP; JAWP; WBP
Snowfall. Marjorie Meeker. TBM
Snowfall. "I. V. S. W." InMe
Snowfall on Plum Trees After They Had Bloomed, A. Charles Dalmon. *Fr.* Three Pictures. TSW; TSWC
Snowflake, The. W. H. Davies. ChMo; CMP
Snowflake, The. Walter de la Mare. AlDL
Snowflake, The. Mary Mapes Dodge. *See* Snowflakes ("Whenever a snowflake")
Snowflake. Stepan Shchipachev, *tr. fr. Russian by* C. M. Bowra. BoRS
Snowflake on Asphodel. Conrad Aiken. ChMo
Snow-flake Song. Hilda Conkling. NP
Snowflakes. Ruth M. Arthur. BoTP
Snowflakes. Alice Behrend. GoYe
Snowflakes ("Little white feathers"). Mary Mapes Dodge. MPB
Snowflakes ("Whenever a snowflake"). Mary Mapes Dodge. HBVY; OTPC (1946 ed.); PRWS
(Snowflake, The.) AA
(Winter, *st.* 1.) GFA
Snow-Flakes. Longfellow. AnNE; BBV (1951 ed.); ChTr; LPS-2; PCH, *st.* 1; PoEL-5
(Snow, *st.* 1.) BoTP
Snow-flakes come in fleets. Snow-flake Song. Hilda Conkling. NP
Snowfrid. Viktor Rydberg, *tr. fr. Swedish by* Charles W. Stork. AnSL
Snowing of the Pines, The. Thomas Wentworth Higginson. AA; ADAH; GN; LBAP
Snowless hang the clouds to-night. Charm Verses. *Unknown.* ArmLP
Snows, The. Charles Sangster. LPS-2
Snow's a snuggly blanket, The. The Snow. Nellie Burget Miller. GFA
Snows are fled away, leaves on the shaws, The. Horace, *tr. by* A. E. Housman. Odes, IV, 7. LaP
Snows are gone, the grass returns again, The. To Manlius Torquatus. Horace, *tr. by* Thomas Creech. Odes, IV, 7 BeR
Snows cloaked/ Mountain cliffs. Lament. Gudmundur Gudmundsson. IcP; LiTW
Snows have fled, the hail, the lashing rain, The. Diffugere Nives, 1917. Maurice Baring. AlDL; HBMV; POTE
Snows have joined the little streams and slid into the sea, The. One Morning When the Rain-Birds Call. Lloyd Roberts. CaP; OCL
Snowshoeing Song. Arthur Weir. POT; PoTo; VA
Snowshoers, The. A. M. Klein. BoCaPo (1948 ed.)
Snowstorm, The. Pearl Riggs Crouch. PoOW
Snow-Storm, A Charles Gamage Eastman. LPS-2
Snow-Storm, The. Emerson. AA; AmP; AmPo; AmPP; AnNE; APW; BAP; BAV; BLV; BoLiVe; CoBA; FaBoBe; GN; GTBS-D, GTBS-W; IAP; InP; LaNeLa; LEAP; LiTA; LiTG; LPS-2; MOAP; NePA; OBAV; OHFP; OnAP; OTPC; OuHeWo; OxBA; PG (1945 ed.); PIAE; PoE; PoEL-4; PoeMoYo; PoFS; TCAP; TrGrPo; YT
"Announced by all the trumpets of the sky," *sel.* PCH; PYM; TiPo
Snow Storm. Sister Mary Madeleva. GoBC
Snowstorm, The Frederick George Scott. PeCV
Snow Storm, The. Seba Smith.
(Mother's Sacrifice, The.) LPS-1
"Cold winds swept the mountain-height, The," *sel.* MotAn
Snow Storm. Tu Fu, *tr. fr. Chinese by* Kenneth Rexroth. OnPC
Snow Storm, The. Ethelwyn Wetherald. VA
Snow-Storm, The. Whittier. *See* World Transformed, The.
Snowstorms Sleep, The. Ludmila Tatyanicheva, *tr. fr. Russian by* Babette Deutsch. TrRV
Snowy Day, A. Dafydd ap Gwilym, *tr. fr. Welsh by* H. Idris Bell. LyMA
Snowy lamb I've bred, so full of play, A. Bright Offerings from Shepherds. Elizabeth Rowe. *Fr.* A Pastoral in Imitation of Drayton's Second Nymphal. BeR
Snowy-smooth beneath the pen. White Paper. Sydney Jephcott. BoAu
Snub nose, the guts of twenty mules are in your cylinders and transmission. New Farm Tractor. Carl Sandburg. FaPON
Snuff Boxes. Hortense Flexner. PFE; VOD
Snuff-Boxes, The. *Unknown.* StPo
Snug in My Easy Chair. W. W Gibson. EPN; TCEP
(Proem: "Snug in my easy chair.") HBMV
So,/ After all these long, long years. The Years Between. Chiang Yün. PoHN
So/ Went this little pig from the mainland to the market. Mother Goose Up-to-Date. Louis Untermeyer. MoAmPo
So Abram rose, and clave the wood, and went. The Parable of the Old Men and the Young. Wilfred Owen. TwCV
So active they seem passive, little sheep. Grace. Richard Wilbur. LiTA
So, after bath, the slave-girls brought. Dressing the Bride. Thomas Bailey Aldrich. BAV
So after the wedding, the husband. Newlyweds. Nikolai Alekseyevich Nekrasov. TrRV
So Ajax spake and the others lifted the dead on high. The Struggle for Patroclus. Homer. *Fr.* The Iliad, XVII *and* XVIII. GrPE
So all day long I followed through the fields. Gentian. Elizabeth Green Crane. AA
So all day long the noise of battle roll'd. Morte [*or* Mort] d'Arthur. Tennyson. AnEnPo; ATP; BBV; BEL; BMEP; BoLiVe; BPN; CBOV; EmBrPo; EnL; EnLi-2; EPP; EV-5; FaBoBe; FiP; GEPC; HBV; LPS-2; OAEP; OnSP; PIR; PoE; PoEL-5; PoVP; SeCeV; ShBV-3; TCEP; TOP; TwCrTr; UnPo (1st ed.); ViPo; ViPP; VLEP; WHA
So all men come at last to their Explorers' Tree. Burke and Wills. Ken Barratt. BoAV
So am I as the rich, whose blessed key. Sonnets, LII. Shakespeare. OBSC; PeBoSo
So-and-So Reclining on Her Couch. Wallace Stevens. LiTM; SiTI
So, April, here thou art again. Lady April. Richard Le Gallienne. YeAr
So are you to my thoughts as food to life. Sonnets, LXXV. Shakespeare. PeBoSo; PoEL-2
So as they traveild, lo they gan espy. The Cave of Despair. Spenser. *Fr.* The Faerie Queene, I, 9. LoBV
So, as we lay there resting, thick rustled overhead. The Festival. Theocritus. *Fr.* Idylls, VII. GrPE
So, at the last, I think that we must follow. Envoy. Du Bose Heyward. NV
So, back again? To a Dog. Josephine Preston Peabody. BLPA; CV; WGRP
So be it; you must bring the body inside. Electra and Orestes. Euripides. *Fr.* Electra. OxBG
So Be My Passing. W. E. Henley. *See* Margaritae Sorori.
So Beautiful You Are, Indeed. Irene Rutherford McLeod. AV; BMEP; HBMV; LBBV; NV
So begins the day. Dawn. Frances Cornford. AV; LoPS
So blessed a sight it was to see. Lullay, Jesu, Lullay, Lullay! *Unknown.* AnEC
So blest are they who round a family board. The Family. Donna R. Lydston. PoToHe (new ed.)
So! Breakers of broncos! with miles of jagged wire. Breakers of Broncos. Lew Sarett. HiLiAm
So, British Public, who may like me yet. Robert Browning. *Fr.* The Ring and the Book, XII. NBE
So by your edict Christ once more lies slain. Word to a Dictator. Adelaide Love. MaRV
So careful is Isa, and anxious to last. On a Valetudinarian. Ibn al-Rumi. LiTW
"So careful of the type?" but no. In Memoriam A. H. H., LVI. Tennyson. AnFE; BPN; CoBE; EM-2; EmBrPo; EnL; EPN; GEPC; HBV; InP; LoBV; MaPo; OAEP; OBEV (1st ed.); OuHeWo; PIAE; ReaPo; SeCeV; TCEP; TOP; ViPo; VLEP
So Castlereagh has cut his throat! The worst. Epigrams on Castlereagh, I. Byron. ExPo
So, Christ, I bought Thee with a Roman throne. Julian the Apostate. Ernest Denny. QS
So Cold. Tamiko Yamamuro, *tr. fr. Japanese by* Lois J. Erickson. SoLD
So cold the first Thanksgiving came. The First Thanksgiving. Nancy Byrd Turner. YeAr

So, contrary to Nature's normal ways. Petronius, *tr. fr. Latin by* Jack Lindsay. LaP
So cried she: but for him far less she mourned. Quintus Smyrnaeus. *Fr.* Posthomerica, X. GrPo
So crowded was the little town. Christmas Carol. James S. Park. COAH
So cruel prison how could betide, alas. Prisoned in Windsor, He Recounteth His Pleasure There Passed. Earl of Surrey. BEL; CoBE; FaBoEn; OAEP; OBSC; PoE; ReEn; ReIE; SeCePo; SiCE; SiPS; TuPP
So dainty in plumage and hue. The English Sparrow. Mary Isabella Forsyth. SN
So dark this night, with neither moon nor stars. Strange Night. Mary Willis Shelburne. UnW
So dear, so dainty, so demure. To a Persian Cat. F. C. W. Hiley. PoC
So dear, so dear she is to me. Prayer for a College Girl. Ella Broadus Robertson. PraP
So death-still are the hours, when you are gone. Palpable Silence. Leonora Clawson Stryker. MuM
So Deep Is Death. Frank Kendon. MBP; MoBrPo (1942 ed.)
So deep your eyes that as I lean to drink. Elsa's Eyes. Louis Aragon. MiFP
So delicate, so airy,/ The almond on the tree. Pink Almond. Katharine Tynan. BoTP
So detached and cool she is. The Mask. Clarissa Scott Delany. CDC; PoNe
So did he chide with the band; was none dared meet his eye. Apollonius Rhodius. *Fr.* Argonautica, I. GrPo
So did the son of Priam, the princely, speak his word. Achilles and Lycaon. Homer. *Fr.* The Iliad, XXI. OxBG
So did the world from the first hour decay. John Donne. *Fr.* An Anatomy of the World. TuPP
So die, thou child of stormy dawn. On the Death of a Certain Journal. Charles Kingsley. BMEP
So difficult the meeting, so difficult the parting. Li Shang-yin. WhP
So does the sun withdraw his beames. On His Mistress Going from Home. *Unknown.* OBS
So down the silver streams of Eridan. Giles Fletcher. *Fr.* Christ's Victory and Triumph: Christ's Triumph over Death. LoBV
So dream thy sails, O phantom bark. The Phantom Bark. Hart Crane. ChMo
So dress me down and douse me as you will. Refined Gold. Theognis. GrL; OxBG
So eager and so clamorous a throng. Cordial Soul. Sara Henderson Hay. BAP
So early lost, I cannot tell the lift. A. L. G. William Channing Gannett. GrCo-2
So earnest with thy God, can no new care. Of His Majesties Receiving the News of the Duke of Buckingham's Death. Edmund Waller. SeCV-1
So endlessly the gray-lipped sea. The Dead Aviator. Francis Hackett. JKCP (1926 ed.); LEAP
So ends the winning of the Golden Fleece. Invocation to Chaucer [*or* To Chaucer]. William Morris. *Fr.* The Life and Death of Jason. BPN; EmBrPo
So Ends the Wrath of Achilles. Homer. *See* Achilles' Remorse.
So every spirit, as it is most pure. Beauty. Spenser. *Fr.* An Hymne in Honour of Beautie. LPS-3
So faint, no ear is sure it hears. Silence Sings. T. Sturge Moore. GTML; MBP
So fair and fine her skin, so blue her eye. Reporter. Ethel Louise Knox. DDA
So fair, so dear, so warm upon my bosom. The Firstborn. John Arthur Goodchild. HBV
So Fair, So Sweet, Withal So Sensitive. Wordsworth. BPN; EmBrPo; EnRP
Daisy, The, *br. sel.* RO
So fair, so young, so innocent, so sweet. Epitaph on Mrs. Margaret Paston of Barningham, in Norfolk. Dryden. CaAE
So faire a church as this, had Venus none. Love at First Sight. Christopher Marlowe. *Fr.* Hero and Leander, First Sestiad. FaBoEn
So faith is strong. The Tide of Faith. "George Eliot." *Fr.* A Minor Prophet. MaRV; OQP; QP-2; WGRP
So fallen! so lost! the light withdrawn. Ichabod. Whittier. AA; AmP; AmPP; AnAmPo; AnFE; AnNE; APA; APW; BAP; CoAnAm; CoBA; CoV; DD; GA; HBV; IAP; LA; LBAP; LiTA; LPS-3; MOAP; OxBA; PAH; PG; PIAE; Po; PoEL-4; REAL; TCAP; TOP
So far as I can see. Meditations of a Tortoise Dozing under a Rosetree near a Beehive at Noon While a Dog Scampers About and a Cuckoo Calls from a Distant Wood. E. V. Rieu. FiBHP
So far as our story approaches the end. A Light Woman. Robert Browning. AEV; BPN; HBV; PoVP; VLEP
So far I set the scope extreme. Aspiration. Ibn Hani. MooP
So Far, So Near. Christopher Pearse Cranch. MaRV; TrPWD
So fare ye well, my darlin', so fare ye well, my dear. Fare Ye Well, My Darlin'. *Unknown.* OuSiCo
"So Farewell." Wang Wei, *tr. fr. Chinese by* W. J. B. Fletcher. OnPM
So Fast Entangled. *Unknown. See* Her Hair the Net.
So fell our statesman—for he stood sublime. Everett. Thomas William Parsons. DD; GA
So flashing-eyed Athene spoke, and went her way. Nausicaä. Homer. *Fr.* The Odyssey, VI. GrPE
"So fleet the works of men, back to the earth again." The Curtain (Old Tabor Grand Opera House). Jean Milne Gower. PoOW
So flies love's meteor to her shroud of winds. The Dead Words. Vernon Watkins. LiTM (rev. ed.); MoWP
So Fly by Night. Charles Osborne. BoAV
So, forth issew'd [*or* issued] the Seasons of the year[e]. The Pageant of the Seasons and the Months [*or* The Mask of Mutability *or* The Procession of Times and Seasons]. Spenser. *Fr.* The Faerie Queene, VII, 7. EV-1; GN; NBE; OBSC
So frail our life, perchance to-morrow's sun. An Elegy. Tsurayuki. OnPM
So, Freedom, thy great quarrel may we serve. Our Cause. William James Linton. VA
So, friend, your shop was all your house! Shop. Robert Browning. AEV; PoVP; ViPo; VLEP
So frisky and fit. Simchas Torah. Morris Rosenfeld. TrJP
So from the east unto the farthest west. The Vaunts of Tamburlaine. Christopher Marlowe. *Fr.* Tamburlaine, Pt. I. BCEP
So from the ground we felt that virtue branch. The Transfiguration. Edwin Muir. FaBoMo
So from the years the gifts were showered. In Time of War. W. H. Auden. ChMo
So gentle Ellen now no more. Samuel Taylor Coleridge. *Fr.* The Three Graves. ChER
So Ghostly Then the Girl Came In. Robert Hillyer. TriL; UnW
So glad I done done. I Done Done What Ya' Tol' Me to Do. *Unknown.* BoAN-1
So go forth to the world, to the good report and the evil. Envoi. Arthur Hugh Clough. *Fr.* Amours de Voyage. BPN
So—good-by! The dreamy splendor of the mornings. Pards. Hugh J. Hughes. POT; PoTo
So good-luck came, and on my roofe did light. The Comming of Good Luck. Robert Herrick. AtBAP
So Great a Sweetness. W. B. Yeats. *Fr.* Friends. LiA
So green are the cypresses on the hills. *Unknown, tr. fr. Chinese.* The Nineteen Han Poems, III. WhP
So Handy, *with music. Unknown.* ShS; SoAmSa
So happy the song he sings. Bluebird. Hilda Conkling. GFA
So happy were Columbia's eight. A Crew Poem. Edward Augustus Blount, Jr. AA; PC
So hath he fallen, the Endymion of the air. Chavez. Mildred I. McNeal Sweeney. HBV; LBMV; VOD (1935 ed.)
So have I seen a silver swan. Song. *At. to* John Webster. LO; SeCL
So having said, Aglaura him bespake. Colin Clout at Court. Spenser. *Fr.* Colin Clout's Come Home. OBSC
So he died for his faith. That is fine. How Did He Live [*or* Life and Death]. Ernest H. Crosby. MaRV; OQP; QP 1
So he droned on, of parish work and claims. City Priest. Anne Higginson Spicer. OQP; QP-1
So He has cut his throat at last! He? Who? Epigrams on Castlereagh, II. Byron. ExPo
So He made woman last—a melody. The Masterpiece. Kathleen Millay. BAP
So he sat down and slowly, slowly. Foreclosure. Mark Van Doren. CrMA
So he spake, and all the Wooers laughed on him pleasantly. The Slaying. Homer. *Fr.* The Odyssey, XXI–XXII. OxBG
So he spake, and all those people they sat in silence there. Farewell to Kind Hosts and a Godspeed. Homer. *Fr.* The Odyssey, XIII. GrR
So he spake, and fell to cleaving the logs with the ruthless brass. Homer. *Fr.* The Odyssey, XIV. GrPo
So he spake; but the Grey-eyed, the Goddess Athene, smiled and now. Homer. *Fr.* The Odyssey, XIII. GrPo
So he spoke in her honour. Downward she cast her gaze. She Tells Him How to Win the Fleece. Apollonius Rhodius. *Fr.* Argonautica, III. GrPE
So he trassed away dreamin' of Nora na Mo. The Girl with the Cows. Alfred Perceval Graves. TIP
So heavy and so fraught with pain. The Cross. Shirley Dillon Waite. ChIP; OQP; QP-2
So Hector; and loud the Trojans acclaimed the words he spoke. The Trojans Encamp before the Achaean Wall. Homer. *Fr.* The Iliad, VIII *and* IX. GrPE

So Hector spake; the Trojans roared applause. Homer. *Fr.* The Iliad, VIII. GrPo
So here confin'd, and but to female clay. Fragment. Countess of Winchilsea. TriL
So here hath been dawning. To-Day. Thomas Carlyle. BCEP; EBSV; HBV; HBVY; MaRV; MW; NeHB; OQP; OTPC (1946 ed.); PTA-1; QP-2; TVSH; WGRP
So here is my desert and here am I. In Paris. Thomas MacDonagh. OnYI
So, here, tied in that crooked line. "Chart Showing Rain, Winds, Isothermal Lines and Ocean Currents." Louise Owen. PFE
So here, twisted in steel, and spoiled with red. Trapped Dingo. Judith Wright. NeLNL
So here we are in April, in showy, blowy April. April. Ted Robinson. GoTP
So, here we meet—after long seeking. Linota Rufescens. Lyle Donaghy. OnYI
So High. John Russell McCarthy. UnW
So high reached my sorrow. Manuel Altolaguirre, *tr. fr. Spanish by* Eleanor L. Turnbull. CoSP
So hot shines the sun on the Nile's fertile shore. Birds of Passage. Esaias Tegnér. AnSL
So I am your "darling girl"! Remonstrance. Philodemos the Epicurean. LiTW
So I arm thee for the final night. The Page of Lancelot. May Kendall. VA
So I came down the steps to Lenin. Dorothy Wellesley. *Fr.* Lenin. OBMV
So I from that black pool whereinto Hell. William Ellery Leonard. *Fr* Two Lives, Pt. III. MOAP
So I go on, not knowing. Faith and Sight. Mary Gardiner Brainard. *Fr.* Not Knowing. MaRV
So I have known this life. Lollingdon Downs. John Masefield. LiTB
So I live in my nook, turning my face from the world. The Poet in His Poverty. Nizami. LiTW
So I lived in a thatched cottage on a narrow lane. A Fire Burns Down My Cottage. Tao Yuan-ming. WhP
So I May Feel the Hands of God. Anna Hempstead Branch. PC
So I may gain thy death, my life I'll give. Qui Perdiderit Animam Suam. Richard Crashaw. ACP
So I possess a perfect thing. A Bed of Campanula. "John Crichton." CaP; OCL
So I proposed, without an overture. E. A. Robinson. *Fr.* Isaac and Archibald. BoFr
So I said underneath the dusky trees. Two Thoughts of Death. Christina Rossetti. DiM
So, I shall see her in three days. In Three Days. Robert Browning. BPN; EmBrPo; EPN; EtPaEn; PoVP
So I spake, and he took it and drank, and became exceeding fain. Of Noman and Cyclops. Homer. *Fr.* The Odyssey, IX. OxBG
So I went wrong, grievously wrong, but folly crushed itself. Revival. Arthur Hugh Clough. VLEP
So I: when swift Achilles' long-limbed ghost. Of the Shade of Ajax. Homer. *Fr.* The Odyssey, XI. OxBG
So in a one man Europe I sit here. George Barker. NeBP
So, in the Evening, to the Simple Cloister. Conrad Aiken. *See* Cloister.
So in the sinful streets, abstracted and alone. Easter Day, II. Arthur Hugh Clough. BMEP; BPN; EPN; EPP; OAEP; PoVP; ViP; ViPP; VLEP
So infinitely vast. The Old Battlefield. Li Hua. WhP
So innocent, so quiet—yet. The Pond. W. H. Davies. ChMP
So is it not with me as with that Muse. Sonnets, XXI. Shakespeare. InvP; OBSC; PeBoSo; ReEn; SiCE
So, is this then the spot, Jens Baggesen's birthplace? Korsør. Adam Oehlenschläger. *Fr.* Langelands Rejsen. BoDS
So It Begins. James Agee. Sonnets, I. ATP (1953 ed.) ("So it begins. Adam is in his earth.") MAP; MoAmPo
So it happened, exactly as I tell you. Being. Jacob Glatstein. *Fr.* The Bratzlav Rabbi to His Scribe. LiTW
So it is, my dear. Even So. Dante Gabriel Rossetti. EmBrPo
So it is, they say, that the men in the bay. Merrimac Side, and Agiochook. Edward Everett Hale. From Potomac to Merrimac, III. PAH
So it was when Jesus came in his gentleness. Jesus. Robert Bridges. *Fr.* The Testament of Beauty. MaRV; MeRV
So Kings and Chiefs and Bards, in Eman of the Kings. The Fate of the Sons of Usna. John Todhunter. *Fr.* The First Duan: The Coming of Deirdre. TIP
So large a morning, so itself, to lean. Song. W. H. Auden. NePoAm-2
So Late Removed from Him She Swore. Walter Savage Landor. OBRV
So late, so late, so haunting. On the Threshold. Karl Kraus. TrJP
So laughing in lap laid. Christmas Carol [*or* Mater Dulcissima]. *Unknown.* CBOV; EPP
So leave her and cast care from thy heart. His Camel. Alqamah. *Fr.* The Mufaddiliyat. AWP; JAWP; WBP
So Let Me Hence. W. E. Henley. EnLit
So let them laugh, exulting in his fall. Tecmessa. Sophocles. *Fr.* Ajax. GrR
So, let us laugh—lest vain rememberings. Retractions, XIV. James Branch Cabell. HBMV
So Let Us Love. Spenser. *See* Amoretti, LXVIII.
So like a god I sit here. The Sitting. C. Day Lewis. FaBoMo
So like a queen she moves/ among the rabble. Our Lady on Calvary. Sister Michael Marie. ISi
So like a Quiet Rain. Lew Sarett. BAP
So like the corn, moon-ripened last. George Macdonald. Songs [*or* Song] of the Autumn Night, II. BSV; EBSV
So Little and So Much. John Oxenham. BLRP
So little time, time's guest. In the Year's Morning. David Ross. PG (1955 ed.)
So Live. Bryant. *Fr.* Thanatopsis. BLP; PoToHe (Be Ye Also Ready.) MaRV ("So live, that when thy summons comes.") DD; OQP; QP-2
So lively, so gay, my dear Mother, I'm grown. Taste and Spirit. Christopher Anstey. *Fr.* The New Bath Guide. CEP
So Long! Walt Whitman. AmP; AmPo; PreP; TCAP
From "So Long," *sel.* LEAP
So long,/ So far away. Afro-American Fragment. Langston Hughes. PoNe
So Long Ago. Morris Rosenfeld, *tr. fr. Yiddish by* Elbert Aidline. TrJP
So long ago, and not forgotten yet! To All People. Clement Wood. SDH
So long as light shall shine upon a world. E. J. Pratt. *Fr.* Dunkirk. NeTW
So long as tears can still fall from mine eyes. Memories. Louise Labé. TrFP
So Long As There Are Homes. Grace Noll Crowell. MaRV
So long as you live and move. Teach Us to Mark This, God. Franz Werfel. TrJP
So Long Folks, Off to the War. Anthony Ostroff. NePoAm-2
So Long Had I Travelled. W. W. Gibson. ChMo; CMP (Home.) HBMV
So long he rode he drew anigh. The King's Visit. William Morris. *Fr.* The Earthly Paradise. VA
So long I sat and conned. The Elm Beetle. Andrew Young. LoBV
So long you wandered on the dusky plain. To His Friend in Elysium. Joachim du Bellay. AWP; JAWP; WBP
So loud the deer cries, calling to his mate. Deer and Echo. Otomo Yakamochi. OnPM
So Love is dead that has been quick so long! Hic Jacet. Louise Chandler Moulton. AA; AnAmPo; AnFE; APA; CoAnAm; LA; LBAP; LEAP; OBAV
So madly noisy are men's battle ways. The Soldier and the Nun. Sister Eleanore. PraNu
So make your impassive passage to the act. Poem in Time of War. William Abrahams. WaP
So, Man? Gene Derwood. NePA
So Many! Frank L. Stanton. BPP; MaRV
So many cares to vex the day. Summer Magic. Leslie Pinckney Hill. BANP
So many dwell in Denmark. The King-slaying in Finderup. *Unknown.* BoDaBa
So many evenings, on the red-tiled terrace. Lost Garden. "Katherine Hale." CaP; OCL
So many folk are happy folk. A Song of Happiness. Muna Lee. NP
So many gods, so many creeds. The World's Need. Ella Wheeler Wilcox. BLP; LBAP; PC
So many laws, so many creeds. The One Need. Ella Wheeler Wilcox. BAP
So many little flowers. Cycle. Langston Hughes. FaPON; GoSl
So many monarchs with their mighty state. Death. Lucretius, *tr. by* Dryden. *Fr.* De Rerum Natura. BeR
So Many Monkeys. Marion Edey. TiPo
So many moral matters, and so little used. John Skelton. *Fr.* Speak, Parrot. CoBE; ViBoPo
So many pussy cats have multiplied. Sonnet: The Cats of Santa Anna. Tasso. LyPI
So many songs he had to sing. Vachel Lindsay. Sydney King Russell. MuM
So many stars in the infinite space. So Many! Frank L. Stanton. BPP; MaRV
"So many unlived lives," she said; and idle. An Idyl in Idleness. Robert Pack. NePoEA
So many worlds, so much to do. In Memoriam A. H. H., LXXIII. Tennyson. EM-2; EmBrPo; EPN; GEPC; HBV; LPS-1; ViPo; VLEP
So Many Years Have Gone! Léon Paul Fargue, *tr. fr. French by* Wallace Fowlie. MiCF
So may the auspicious Queen of Love. To the Ship in Which Virgil Sailed to Athens. Horace. Odes, I, 3. AWP

So merrily singeth the nightingale! John Skelton. *Fr.* Magnificence. PoFr
So merry the knights sat drinking. Tit for Tat. *Unknown.* BoDaBa
So Might is Right, you say; I fight in vain. "Might Is Right." Israel Zangwill. TrJP
So Miss Myrtle is going to marry? The Charming Woman. Helen Selina Sheridan. ALV; OBRV
So, Mistress Anne, faire neighbor myne. *See* Soe, Mistress Anne . . .
So much depends. The Red Wheelbarrow. William Carlos Williams. HoPM; LiTA; MoAB; MoAmPo; ThWaDe; UnPo (3d ed.)
So much have I forgotten in ten years. Flame-Heart. Claude McKay. BANP; CDC; PoNe
So much have I received at Dido's hands. Christopher Marlowe *and* Thomas Nashe. *Fr.* The Tragedy of Dido. SG
So much he mourns the queen beyond the seas. Aeschylus. *Fr.* Agamemnon. GrPo
So much I know, for I was there and heard. Calchas the Seer. Sophocles. *Fr.* Ajax. GrR
So much loving, so much loving. Mozarabic Songs, 5. *Unknown.* TeCS
So much to do: so little done! Three Days. James Robert Gilmore. LPS-3
"So much to do," said Turgot, "and so little/ Time to do it." Georgian Dublin. Maurice James Craig. PoN
So much to tell you. 2 Variations: All About Love. Philip Whalen. NeAP
So much true resolution wrought in those. The Death of Talbot. Samuel Daniel. *Fr.* The Civil Wars. EV-1
So must he be, who in the crowded street. "Is Thy Servant a Dog?" John Banister Tabb. JKCP
So, my Kathleen, you're going to leave me. Terence's Farewell. Helen Selina Sheridan. TIP
So Nigh Is Grandeur. Emerson. *See* Duty.
So nigh is grandeur to man. —— Cook. YaD
So nigh is grandeur to our dust. Duty [*or* Heroism]. Emerson. *Fr.* Voluntaries, III. BAP; CBOV; FaFP; GN; HBV; OQP; QP-2; TreF; YaD
So now I have confessed that he is thine. Sonnets, CXXXIV. Shakespeare. InvP; PeBoSo
So, Now Is Come Our Joyful'st Feast. *See* Christmas Carol, A: "So, now is come our joyfullest feast."
So now let them do with me just what they will. Aristophanes. *Fr.* The Clouds. GrPo
So now my summer task is ended, Mary. To Mary; Dedication. Shelley. *Fr.* The Revolt of Islam. BPN; EmBrPo; EnRP; EPN; ERP
So now the very bones of you are gone. Doricha. E. A. Robinson. AWP; JAWP; MOAP; WBP
So now, this poet, who forsakes the stage. Prologue to "Love Triumphant." Dryden. OxBoLi; SiTL
So oft as homeward I from her depart. Amoretti, LII. Spenser. PeBoSo
So oft as I her beauty do behold. Amoretti, LV. Spenser. BLV; BoLiVe; ElSeCe; HBV; PeBoSo; SiCE; TrGrPo
So oft as I with state of present time. Prologue. Spenser. *Fr.* The Faerie Queene, V. PoFS
So oft have I invoked thee for my Muse. Sonnets, LXXVIII. Shakespeare. EM-1; PeBoSo
So oft our hearts, belovèd lute. Dream and the Song. James David Corrothers. BANP
So often is the proud deed done. The Captain of the Northfleet. Gerald Massey. BMEP
So often, Lord, I come to Thee. Thanksgiving for Benefits Received. Lois Givens Vaughan. PraP
So on both sides they battled and an iron clangour there. The Horses of Achilles. Homer. *Fr.* The Iliad, XVII. GrPE
So on he fares, and to the border comes. The Garden of Eden. Milton. *Fr.* Paradise Lost, IV. EV-2; ExPo; PreP
So on he pricked, and loe, he gan espy. Variation I. Edmund Spenser. Barry Pain. *Fr.* Theme with Variations. PA
So on his Nightmare through the evening fog. Fuseli's "Nightmare." Erasmus Darwin. *Fr.* The Botanic Garden: The Loves of the Plants. RO
So, on the bloody sand, Sohrab lay dead. The Oxus. Matthew Arnold. *Fr.* Sohrab and Rustum. NBE; VA
So once again the trouble's o'er. The Matron Cat's Song. Ruth Pitter. PoC
So parc has a gate! Epithalamion. Nigel Heseltine. MoWP
So pass my Days. But when Nocturnal Shades. The Thirsty Poet. John Philips. *Fr.* The Splendid Shilling. OBEC
So passed the morning away. The Church Scene. Longfellow. *Fr.* Evangeline. TreF
So passed they naked on, nor shunned the sight. Adam and Eve. Milton. *Fr.* Paradise Lost, IV. SeCePo
So passeth, in the passing of a day. The Song. Spenser. *Fr.* The Faerie Queene, II, 12. MyFE
So Pleasant It Is to Have Money. Arthur Hugh Clough. *Fr.* Dipsychus. SeCePo
So poor old Prunes has cashed in.—Too bad. Me and Prunes. Rupe Sherwood. PoOW
So questioning, I was bold to dare. The Shape God Wears. Sara Henderson Hay. GoTP; QS
So Quicke, So Hot, So Mad Is Thy Fond Sute. Thomas Campion. PoEL-2
So quickly to have lost the summertime. Mint by Night. Alfred Barrett. JKCP (1955 ed.)
So Quietly. Leslie Pinckney Hill. BANP
So Ranolf felt when over wood and wild. Alfred Domett. *Fr.* Ranolf and Amohia. AnNZ
So rare, so mere. Presence of Snow. Melville Cane. GoYe
So Red the Rose. Omar Khayyám, *tr. fr. Persian by* Edward Fitzgerald. *Fr.* The Rubáiyát. OnPM
("I sometimes think that never blows so red.") InP; LO
So rest, forever rest, O princely pair! The Tomb. Matthew Arnold. *Fr.* The Church of Brou. PoVP; TriL
So restless Cromwell could not cease. Andrew Marvell. *Fr.* A Horatian Ode upon Cromwell. ViBoPo
So rich a treasure in yourself you bring. Waste. Edward Shanks. LBBV
So rich and proud a damsel. King Erik and the Scornful Maid. *Unknown.* BoDaBa
So round that sturdy ship the battle raged. Achilles and Patroclus. Homer. *Fr.* The Iliad, XVI. OxBG
So Runs Our Song. Mary Eva Kitchel. ChIP; PGD
"So Runs the World Away," *in mod. Eng. Unknown.* TMEV
So said he, and the crone went down the hall. Penelope Dreams. Homer. *Fr.* The Odyssey, XIX. OxBG
So said, he rusht at him, and by the crest. Paris Rescued by Aphrodite. Homer. *Fr.* The Iliad, III. GrR
So said the valiant master of the lance. Bacchylides. *Fr.* Theseus. OxBG
So sang he: and as meeting rose and rose. Willowwood, 4. Dante Gabriel Rossetti. The House of Life, LII. BPN; EmBrPo; OAEP; POTT; PoVP; ReaPo; TCEP; ViP; ViPo; VLEP
So sang I in the springtime of my years. Morton Luce. Thysia, XXXVI. HBV
So sang the hierarchies: meanwhile the Son. The First Day of Creation. Milton. *Fr.* Paradise Lost, VII. OxBoCh
So Satan spake, and him Beelzebub. The Council of Satan. Milton. *Fr.* Paradise Lost, I. PoEL-3
"So say the foolish! Say the foolish so, Love?" Poetics. Robert Browning. BPN; PoVP
So saying back to the dark house the ghost. Of His Mother's Shade. Homer. *Fr.* The Odyssey, XI. OxBG
So saying he passed from Thetis to where his bellows lay. The Shield of Achilles. Homer. *Fr.* The Iliad, XVIII. GrPE
So saying, light-foot Iris pass'd away. Achilles on the Rampart [*or* Achilles' Shout]. Homer. *Fr.* The Iliad, XVIII. GrPo; LiA; OxBG
So saying she came from her cavern; and with her, tearfully. Achilles' Remorse. Homer. *Fr.* The Iliad, XVIII. GrPE
So saying she left the cave, whom all her nymphs. So Ends the Wrath of Achilles. Homer. *Fr.* The Iliad, XVIII. GrR
So saying, the Goddess into Helen's soul. Helen. Homer. *Fr.* The Iliad, III. OxBG
So saying, to Olympus with its long ridge stretched afar. The Meeting of Priam and Achilles. Homer. *Fr.* The Iliad, XXIV. GrPE
So shall I live, supposing thou art true. Sonnets, XCIII. Shakespeare. InvP; PeBoSo
So shall it ever be. As Thy Days. Grant Colfax Tullar. BLRP
So shalt thou come to a court as clear as the sun. The Palace of Truth. *At. to* William Langland. *Fr.* The Vision of Piers Plowman. ACP
So she became a bird and bird-like danced. Procne. Peter Quennell. ChMP; FaBoMo; GTBS-W; LiTB; LiTM; MBP; MoBrPo
So she spoke in tears but the wife of Hektor had not yet/ heard. Homer. *Fr.* The Iliad, XXII. GrPo
So she went into the garden. The Great Panjandrum [Himself]. Samuel Foote. FaBoCh; LiL; LoGBV; MoShBr; RIS; WhC
So shoots a star as doth my mistress glide. Sonnet. John Davies of Hereford. ElL
So short the road from Bethlehem. "The Way." Leslie Savage Clark. PGD
So Shuts the Marigold Her Leaves ("Marina's gone . . ."). William Browne. *See* Memory ("Marina's gone . . .").
So shuts the marigold her leaves. Memory [*or* Since She Is Gone]. William Browne. *Fr.* Britannia's Pastorals. CBOV; EG; EV-2; LiTL; OBEV; ViBoPo
So, sick at heart, we watched the piccanins. Outside Kimberley. N. H. Brettell. BoSA
So sleep undoes itself and I arrive. For My Twenty-fifth Birthday in Nineteen Forty-one. John Ciardi. WaP

So Sleeps My Love. *Unknown.* TrGrPo
("Sleep, wayward thoughts, and rest you with my love.") EG; ReEn
So Slow to Die. George Edward Woodberry. Wild Eden, XXXVIII. AA
So slowly you walk, and so quickly you eat. To a Slow Walker and Quick Eater. Gotthold Ephraim Lessing. BOHV
So smell those odours that do rise. To the Most Fair and Lovely Mistress, Anne Soame, Now Lady Abdie. Robert Herrick. AtBAP; ViBoPo
So smile the heavens upon this holy act. Friar Laurence's Cell. Shakespeare. Romeo and Juliet, II, vi. GoBC
So smooth a field. Deduction. Mark Van Doren. BAP
So smooth and clear the Fountain was. To a Lady Sitting before Her Glass. Elijah Fenton. OBEC
So smooth, so sweet, so silvery [*or* silv'ry] is thy voice. Upon Julia's Voice. Robert Herrick. AtBAP; BoW; ExPo; MyFE; SeCePo; SeCL
So, so,/ Lo, lilies fade, before the roses show. Song. William Clerke. SeCL
So, so, break[e] off this last lamenting kiss[e]. The Expiration. John Donne. AtBAP; ATP; EG; ElL; ElSeCe; EV-2; MeLP; MePo
So, so; I feel the signal. Malzah and the Angel Zalehtha. Charles Heavysege. *Fr.* Saul. VA
So soft and gentle falls the rain. Rain in the Spring. "Gabriel Setoun." PPL
So soft in the hemlock wood. Pastoral. Robert Hillyer. MAP; MoAmPo
So soft streams meet, so springs with gladder smiles. The Welcome to Sack. Robert Herrick. SeCV-1
So, some tempestuous morn in early June. The Cuckoo's Parting Cry [*or* The Departure of the Cuckoo]. Matthew Arnold. *Fr.* Thyrsis. CBOV; SN
So soon as day forth dawn from the East. Artegall and Radigund. Spenser. *Fr.* The Faerie Queene, V, 5. OBSC
So soon grown old! hast thou been six years dead? The Anniverse. Henry King. NBE
So soon my body will have gone. Immortal. Sara Teasdale. WGRP
So Soon Tired. Richard Le Gallienne. BMEP
So spake he, and the clouds at his command. Odysseus Puts to Sea. Homer. *Fr.* The Odyssey, V. OxBG
So spake I, and straightway the fair goddess. At Sparta; Menelaus and Proteus. Homer. *Fr.* The Odyssey, IV. OxBG
So spake our Mother Eve, and Adam heard. The Banishment. Milton. *Fr.* Paradise Lost, XII. OBS
So spake the archangel Michael; then paused. Milton. *Fr.* Paradise Lost, XII. EnL
So spake the prudent governess; whose words. Hector and Andromache; the Parting. Homer. *Fr.* The Iliad, VI. GrR
So spake the Son, and into terrour changed. The Victor. Milton. *Fr.* Paradise Lost, VI. BCEP; NBE
So spoke London, immortal guardian. I heard in Lambeth's shades. Blake. *Fr.* Jerusalem. NBE
So spoke Priam's noble son, with many and many a word. Homer. *Fr.* The Iliad, XXI. GrPE
So spoke the noble Achilles; they followed where he led. Achilles Rejects the Embassy. Homer. *Fr.* The Iliad, IX. GrPE
So stands my cut-throat fitliest for its work. Before Death [*or* O Welcome! Gentle Death]. Sophocles. *Fr.* Ajax. GrR; OxBG
So still the pond in morning's gray. The Pond. Annette von Droste-Hülshoff. AnGP
So Still the World. Gerald Bullett. *Fr.* Winter Solstice. POTE
So stood of old the holy Christ. Whittier. *Fr.* The Healer. MaRV; PGD
So straight, so slender, and so tall. The Heaven's Mould. William Cavendish, Duke of Newcastle. LO; SeCL
So Sweet a Kiss. Shakespeare. *Fr.* Love's Labour's Lost, IV, iii. ElL; InvP
So Sweet Is She. Ben Jonson. *See* Have You Seen a Bright Lily Grow.
So sweet is thy discourse to me. Thomas Campion. SiCE
So Sweet Love Seemed [That April Morn]. Robert Bridges. EG; EnLit; EPN; EtPaEn; GTML; GTSL; HBV; LiTL; LoPS; PoVP; TCPD; TyEnPo; VA; VLEP
So sweet my love, her face so fair. Fortunio's Song. Alfred de Musset. *Fr.* Le Chandelier. LiA
So sweet, so sweet the roses in their blowing. In June. Nora Perry. SN; YeAr
So sweet the plum trees smell! Plum Trees [*or* Plum Blossoms]. Ranko. FaPON; MPB; SUS
So swift to bloom, so soon to pass, Love's flower! Ulysses Returns, II. Roselle Mercier Montgomery. BAP; HBMV; LPS-1; LS; TBM
So take a happy view. A Happy View. C. Day Lewis. ChMo
So talked the spirited sly snake; and Eve. Milton. *Fr.* Paradise Lost, IX. EnL
So tall she is, and slender, and so fair. The Poet Describes His Love. Robert Nathan. HBMV
So tame, so languid looks this drowsing sea. Calm. Stanton A. Coblentz. EtS
So Telemachus spoke. But Pallas Athene sent. The Vision of Theoclymenus. Homer. *Fr.* The Odyssey, XX. GrPE
So Telemachus spoke; then laughter loud and gay. The Slaying of the Suitors. Homer. *Fr.* The Odyssey, XXI *and* XXII. GrPE
So, thank God, my own beloved. My Wife's Return. Henrik Wergeland. AnNoLy
So that soldierly legend is still on its journey. Kearney at Seven Pines. Edmund Clarence Stedman. AA; DD; DDA; GA; HBV; HBVY; MC; MDAH; OTPC (1923 ed.); PaA; PAH; PAP
So that the vines burst from my fingers. Canto XVII. Ezra Pound. ExPo; LoBV; NAMP; OBMV; Po; ReMP
So that's Cleopathera's Needle, bedad. Reflections on Cleopathera's Needle. Cormac O'Leary. BOHV
So that's your Diary—that's your private mind. On Reading the War Diary of a Defunct Ambassador. Siegfried Sassoon. ChMo; CMP; PoeMoYo; TwCV
So, the All-great were the All-loving too. The All-loving. Robert Browning. *Fr.* An Epistle Containing the Strange . . . ChIP; MaRV; OQP; QP-1
So the distances are Galatea. The Distances. Charles Olson. NeAP
So the eyes accost and sunder. Emily Dickinson. CoBA
So the fisherman goes to his drink. The Fisherman. Su T'ung-po. WhP
"So the foemen have fired the gate, men of mine." The Knight's Leap. Charles Kingsley. BHV; PCD; StPo; TVSH
So the fugitives of the Trojans, that had fled as fawns in the brake. The Slaying of Hector. Homer. *Fr.* The Iliad, XXII. GrPE
So the last day's come at last, the close of my fifteen year. The Old Place (New Zealand). Blanche Edith Baughan. AnNZ; BoAu
So the long absent winter sun. A Short Visit. *Unknown.* SeCL
So the noble Odysseus wakened, once more on his native ground. Odysseus' Return to Ithaca. Homer. *Fr.* The Odyssey, XIII. GrPE
So the old nurse took a basin of brass bright-glittering. Odysseus and Eurycleia. Homer. *Fr.* The Odyssey, XIX. GrPE
So, the powder's low, and the larder's clean. The Last Cup of Canary. Helen Gray Cone. AA; PFY
So the red Indian, by Ontario's side. Lords of the Wilderness. John Leyden. OBRV
So the silver-feathered swan. Song to a Viol. Jasper Fisher. *Fr.* Fuimus Troes. LO; LoPS; SeCL; SeEP; TuPP
So the soldier replied to the poet. The Volunteer's Reply to the Poet. Roy Campbell. *Fr.* Talking Bronco. ViBoPo (1958 ed.)
So, the truth's out. I'll grasp it like a snake. Only a Woman. Dinah Maria Mulock Craik. LPS-1
So the wind blew all that night. A Bucket of Bees. David McCord. MAP; MoAmPo (1942 ed.)
So the wood finches too. Wood Finches. Boethius. WhBS
So the Wooers spake; but Odysseus, that many a rede did know. The Test of the Bow. Homer. *Fr.* The Odyssey, XXI. GrR
So, the year's done with! Love. Robert Browning. *Fr.* Earth's Immortalities. BPN; EnLoPo; PIR; PoVP; VLEP
So then, at last, let me awake this sleep. Purpose. Langdon Elwyn Mitchell. *Fr.* To a Writer of the Day. AA
So Then, I Feel Not Deeply! Walter Savage Landor. BPN; EmBrPo; EnRP; EPN; ERP
So then the lover, wounded by Venus' darts. The Sickness Which Is Love. Lucretius. *Fr.* De Rerum Natura, IV. LaP
So then the noble Odysseus with a fair wind off shore. The Sailing of Odysseus from Ogygia. Homer. *Fr.* The Odyssey, V. GrPE
So then to bed and bid the world goodnight. Ebb Tide. Robert Nathan. MuM
So then, to tell you plainly. The Crime of Orestes. Aeschylus. *Fr.* Choephoroe. LiA
So, then, we were no new device at all. America. Donald C. Babcock. NePoAm
"So thence with heavy hearts we sailed the seas again." Circe. Homer. *Fr.* The Odyssey, X. GrPE
So there he lay asleep, the steadfast goodly Odysseus. Homer. The Odyssey, VI. GrL
So, there, when sunset made the downs look new. Charles Hamilton Sorley. *Fr.* Marlborough. WGRP
So there you lie. In a Museum. Anne Elizabeth Wilson. CIV

So they begin. With two years gone. Poem. Boris Pasternak. BoRS; TrJP
So they carried the dead man out of the fighting. Patroclus' Body Saved. Homer. *Fr.* The Iliad, XVII. OxBG; WaaP
So they in Heav'n their Odes and Vigils tun'd. The Messiah. Milton. *Fr.* Paradise Regained, I. OBS
"So . . ." they said. The Dinner-Party. Amy Lowell. ChMo; CMP; TCPD
"So they went deeper into the forest," said Jacob Grimm. Deeper into the Forest. Roy Daniells. TwCaPo
So they were married, and lived/ Happily for ever? Marriage of Two. C. Day Lewis. ChMP
So they *will* have it! Sumter. Henry Howard Brownell. MC; PaA; PAH
So they would leave him there to die alone. The Death of a Friar. Lascelles Abercrombie. MM
So this is life. the ranger said. Optimism. Blanaid Salkeld. NeIP
So this is life! Towns, deserts, ocean. Reincarnation. Nikolai Gumilev. BoRS
So This Is Middle Age! Francis Whiting Hatch. WhC
So this is the red? Tanka, V. Lewis Alexander. CDC
So this, my good Sabinus, is the one. On a Stone at Corinth. *Unknown.* OxBG
So thou art come again, old black-winged Night. To Night. Thomas Lovell Beddoes. LoBV
So thou hast left us and our meadows. Ascension Day. Sheila Kaye-Smith. CAW
So threaten'd hee, but Satan to no threats. Milton. *Fr.* Paradise Lost, IV. BrBE
So through the darkness and the cold we flew. Skating. Wordsworth. *Fr.* The Prelude. CH
So through the sun-laced woods they went. The Sphere of Glass. John Lehmann. ChMP
So thus you love me now—you come to me. Bacaote to Alexis. Gillespie Evans. CAG
So thy rare virtues fixed in mine eyes. In Caium. Thomas Bastard. SiCE
So Tir'd Are All My Thoughts. Thomas Campion. LoBV
So to his perch appropriate with owls. Alexander Pope at Stanton Harcourt. Sidney Keyes. *Fr.* Sour Land. FaBoTw
So to Sion's hill there come up together. The Human Race Comes to Be Judged. Cynewulf. *Fr.* Christ. PoLi
So to the Gate of the three Queens we came. The Quest of the Grail. Tennyson. *Fr.* Idylls of the King: The Holy Grail. BHV
So to the sacred wood those two drew nigh. Apollonius Rhodius. *Fr.* Argonautica, IV. GrPo
So to the sea we came; the sea, that is. Her Heards Be Thousand Fishes. Spenser. *Fr.* Colin Clout's Come Home Again. ChTr
So unwarely was never no man caught. Sir Thomas Wyatt. SiPS
So up the road I wander slow. John Masefield. *Fr.* The Everlasting Mercy. MM
So vainly through the night prayed Morreus, sick for love. Chalcomede Prays to Be Saved from Love. Nonnus. *Fr.* Dionysiaca. OxBG
So very like a painter drew. The Painter Who Pleased Nobody and Everybody. John Gay. CEP
So Wags the World. Ellen Mackay Hutchinson Cortissoz. AA
So was He framed; and such his course of life. Margaret; or, The Ruined Cottage. Wordsworth. *Fr.* The Excursion. EnRP
So was it even then. So soundlessly. A Trysting. Richard Dehmel. AWP
So was Menoetius' gallant [*or* valiant] son employ'd. The Wall [of the Greeks]. Homer. *Fr.* The Iliad, XII. GrR; OxBG
So was the dread fray of Trojans and Achaians. Homer. *Fr.* The Iliad, VI. GrL
So wayward is the wind tonight. Wind in the Dusk [*or* The Wind]. Harold Monro. NeMA; OBVV; VOD
So we made our way. The Henchman's Speech. Euripides. *Fr.* Hippolytus. ReTS
So we, no distance from the sea-wet shore. The Doom of Hippolytus. Euripides. *Fr.* Hippolytus. OxBG
So we ride, and ride through milked heaven. Rides. Gene Derwood. LiTM; NePA
So we some antique hero's strength. On the Head of a Stag. Edmund Waller. Po
So we, who've supped the self-same cup. After the Quarrel. Paul Laurence Dunbar. CDC
So, We'll Go No More a-Roving. Byron. AlDL; AnFE; AtBAP; AWP; BEL; BoW; CaAE; EG; EM-2; EmBrPo; EnL; EnLi-2; EnRP; EPN; EPP; ERP; EV-4; ExPo; FaBoEn; FaFP; FiP; GEPC; HoPM; InPo; JAWP; LEAP; LiTB; LO; LoBV; MaPo; MyFE; OAEP; OBRV; PG (1955 ed.); PIR; Po; PoEL-4; PoRA; PreP; REAL; ReaPo; SeCeV; ShBV-3; TCEP; TOP; TreFS; TyEnPo; ViBoPo; WBP; WHA
(Impromptus.) BPN
(Song: "So, we'll go no more a-roving.") CBE; CoEV; EnLoPo
(We'll Go No More a-Roving.) ATP; BLV; CH; HBV; LoPS; OBEV; OnPM; OtMeF; PoFS; TrGrPo
So well that I can live without. Emily Dickinson. CoBA
So were we at destruction's very edge. Robert Browning. *Fr.* Balaustion's Adventure. PtP
So What? Vladimir Mayakovsky, *tr. fr. Russian by* Babette Deutsch. TrRV
So what said the others and the sun went down. Mrs. Alfred Uruguay. Wallace Stevens. MoPo; NePA
So what the lame four-poster gathered here. Obituary: In Mem. S. B. V. 1834–1909. Allen Tate. MOAP
So when the Queen of Love rose from the seas. To a Very Young Gentleman at a Dancing-School. Elizabeth Rowe. SeCL; SeEP
So when the old delight is born anew. Immortality. Frederic William Henry Myers. VA
So when the shadows laid asleep. The Kingfisher. Andrew Marvell. *Fr.* Upon Appleton House. AtBAP; FaBoEn
So where have you been, my good old man? Where Have You Been, My Good Old Man? *Unknown.* OuSiCo
So White, So Soft, So Sweet. Ben Jonson. *See* Have You Seen a Bright Lily Grow.
So, with the wan waste grasses on my spear. G. K. Chesterton. *Fr.* The Wild Knight. MaRV
So, without overt breach, we fall apart. Estrangement. Sir William Watson. ES; LBBV; MBP; MoBrPo (1942 ed.); PoeT
So without voice, without murmur, they stood there face to face. Accordingly Medea Met Jason in the Temple of Hecate. Apollonius Rhodius. *Fr.* Argonautica, III. GrPE
So Work the Honey-Bees. Shakespeare. *See* Commonwealth of the Bees, The.
So worn with passing through the bars. The Panther. Rainer Maria Rilke. AnGP
So, you are back. The Scar. W. W. Gibson. CMP
So you are gone, and are proved bad change, as we had always known. Address Not Known. John Heath-Stubbs. ChMP
So you are gone, dear Chalse! Chalse a Killey. Thomas Edward Brown. POTT; PoVP
So you are married, girl. It makes me sad. Epithalamium. Roy McFadden. NeIP
So you beg for a story, my darling, my brown-eyed Leopold. How He Saved St. Michael's. Mary A. P. Stansbury. BLPA; PTA-1, *sl. abr.*
So you bid me to Thanksgivin'! Thank you, neighbor, it is kind. Thanksgivin' Pumpkin Pies. Margaret Elizabeth Sangster. TOAH
So you came/ with a hyacinth, a poem and a thousand kisses. Meeting. Sam Harrison. NeIP
So you go back—because they bid you come. Sonnets of a Portrait Painter, XXXVI. Arthur Davison Ficke. AnAmPo; LA
So you have wondered at me,—guessed in vain. Her Explanation. Edward Rowland Sill. OBAV
So you think it is all a matter of love? Venus' Speech. Louis MacNeice. ChMo
So you will not believe he is God's son. Si Filius Dei Es, Dejice Te. Richard Crashaw. Epigrammata Sacra, I, 72. LaP
So you would like to become Mrs. Prisca?—Well, I understand that. Martial, *tr. fr. Latin by* Robert R. Schnorr. Epigrams, IX, 10. LaP
So Young ane King. Sir David Lindsay. SeCePo
So young, the little Callaeschrus—ah, Death, why must thou take him. The Dead Child. *Unknown.* GrPE
So you're back from your travels, old fellow. The Return of Belisarius; Mud Flat, 1860. Bret Harte. IHA
So you're leaving now. To Chu Ta. Meng Hao-jan. B Fr; PoHN
So, you're stretched on the planks, you schemer. The Nails. Charles Wharton Stork. StJW
So, you've come to the tropics, heard all you had to do. Down and Out. Clarence Leonard Hay. BeLS; BLPA
So zestfully canst thou sing? The Blinded Bird. Thomas Hardy. AnFE; BMEP; ChMo; CMP; LiTM (rev. ed.); MeRV; VLEP
So Zeus in Crete throve mightily, unespied. The Childhood of Zeus. Moero. OxBG
Soak your lungs with wine, for now. Two Drinking Songs. Alcaeus. LiTW
Soap is green. Ilo Orleans. RIS
Soap, the Oppressor. Burges Johnson. DDA
Soar for us, Ace of flame and joy! for us, who have no wings. Hail to Thee, Blithe Spirit. Laurie Simmons. BAP
Soar up, my soul, unto thy rest. Seek Flowers of Heaven. Robert Southwell. ReIE
Sob, fiery element. Native Land. "Andrei Bely." RuPo
Sob of fall, and song of forest, come you here on haunting

quest. The Trail to Lillooet. E. Pauline Johnson. CaP; OCL
Sober Advice from Horace to the Young Gentlemen about Town, *sel.* Pope.
Fufidia (Lady Mary Wortley Montagu). BeR
Sober and gray the afternoon. Afternoon in the Tropics. Rubén Darío. LiTW
Social Future, The. John Kells Ingram. OnYI
Social Heredity. John Kells Ingram. TIP
Social Hymn for Children. Jeanette E. Perkins. PraP
Social Note. Dorothy Parker. BOHV
(Some Beautiful Letters: Social Note.) InMe
Social Religion. Ebenezer Elliott. *See* When Wilt Thou Save the People?
Society. George Meredith. EPN
Society upon the Stanislaus [*or* Stanislow], The. Bret Harte. AA; BAP; BeLS; BOHV; HBV; InMe; LEAP; LPS-3; MaC; SiTL
Society Woman. Lucia Trent. PR
Sockeye Salmon. Ronald Hambleton. BoCaPo; CaP; PeCV
Socrates' Experiments. Aristophanes, *tr. fr. Greek by* Thomas Mitchell. *Fr.* The Clouds. OxBG
(Lampoon; in the School of Socrates, *longer sel., tr. by* Benjamin Bickley Rogers.) GrR
Socrates' Ghost Must Haunt Me Now. Delmore Schwartz. AnFE; CoAnAm; LiTM; TwAmPo
Socrates' House ("Socrates, the philosopher wise"). Yasimi, *tr. fr. Persian by* A. J. Arberry. PeP
Socrates Prays a Day and a Night. George O'Neil. AnAmPo; LA
Socrates Snooks. Fitz Hugh Ludlow. BLPA
Socratic. Hilda Doolittle ("H. D."). AnEnPo; HoPM
Sod-Breaker, The. Arthur Stringer. CaP; OCL
Sodden color of the clouds had run, The. The Idealist. James Coale Sappington, Jr. CAG
Sodenly Afraide. *Unknown. See* "Who Cannot Weep Come Learn of Me."
Sodom. Chaim Grade, *tr. fr. Yiddish by* Joseph Leftwich. TrJP
Sodoma's Christ Scourged. George Edward Woodberry. StJW
Soe, Mistress Anne, faire neighbour myne. Salem. Edmund Clarence Stedman. AA; PAH
Soe Phebus rose as if hee had last night. *Unknown.* SeCSL
Soe Well I Love Thee. Michael Drayton. AtBAP
(Last Verses.) FaBoEn
Sœur Fidèle. Frances Gill. PraNu
"Sœur Monique." Alice Meynell. PraNu
Sofa, The, *sel* William Cowper. *Fr.* The Task, I.
"For I have lov'd the rural walk through lanes." EnRP
Soffermati sull' arida sponda, *sel.* Alessandro Manzoni, *tr. fr. Italian by* Lorna de' Lucchi.
"With humble and discouraged mien." PoFr
Soft and low a voice breathed o'er me. The Dream. Smpad Shahaziz. ArmLP
Soft and pale is the moony beam. Joseph Rodman Drake. *Fr.* The Culprit Fay. PFY
Soft and pure fell the snow. Infant Spring. Fredegond Shove. HBMV
Soft answer turneth away wrath, A. The Lips of the Wise [*or* A Merry Heart]. Proverbs, Bible, *O.T.* StVeCh; TiPo (1952 ed.); TrGrPo
Soft are the clouds, and the moon is weak. Leaving Ching-k'ou. Su T'ung-po. WhP
Soft as the bed in the earth. The Shadow. William Carlos Williams. NP
Soft as the voice, as the voice of a/ Zephyr. Hope. *Unknown.* MaRV
Soft as the wind your hair. Love Song. "Adam Drinan." NeBP; OnHM
Soft breezes blowing, and low in the west. Hushabye Sea. Harry Noyes Pratt. BOL
Soft child of love, thou balmy bliss. To a Kiss. "Peter Pindar." HBV
Soft Day, A. Winifred M. Letts. AnIV; OnYI; VOD
Soft-eyed, a girl's, your face is. To Cleobulus. Anacreon. GrL; OxBG
Soft fall the February snows, and soft. Bereavement of the Fields. Wilfred Campbell. CaP; OCL
Soft falls the night. Evening Song. Edith King. BoTP
Soft from the linden's bough. A Legend of the Dove. George Sterling. NP
Soft, gray buds on the willow. The Turn of the Road. Alice Rollit Coe. HBV
Soft gray hands of sleep, The. Forgotten Dreams. Edward Silvera. PoNe
Soft hangs the opiate in the brain. An Opium Fantasy. Maria White Lowell. AnFE; APA; CoAnAm
Soft light from a stable door, The. Never Night Again. Lilian Cox. ChIP; MaRV
Soft-littered is the new-year's lambing-fold. Spring. Dante Gabriel Rossetti. EmBrPo
Soft little hands that stray and clutch. Little Hands. Laurence Binyon. HBV; MaRV
Soft, lovely, rose-like lips, conjoined with mine. Barnabe Barnes. *Fr.* Parthenophil and Parthenophe. EnLoPo
Soft malice of the silence. Per Amica Silentia Lunae. Ronald de Carvalho. LiTW
Soft midland cottage with the little brook. William Ellery Leonard. *Fr.* Two Lives, Pt. III. MOAP
Soft Musick. Robert Herrick. SeEP
Soft new grass is creeping o'er the graves, The. By the Potomac. Thomas Bailey Aldrich. PAH
Soft on the sunset sky. Ashes of Roses. Elaine Goodale Eastman. AA; HBV; OBAV
Soft-sandalled twilight, handmaid of the night. Winter Twilight. George Tracy Elliot. AA
Soft-shod nuns have laid the last fold straight, The. Sister Mary Veronica. Nancy Byrd Turner. PraNu
Soft Sleep, profoundly pleasing power. Ode to Sleep. Tobias George Smollett. PoP
Soft sleeps the earth in moonlight blest. A Mother-Song. Harriet Prescott Spofford. BOL
Soft slow song. Preface. Michizo Tachihara. PoLJ
Soft Snow. Blake. AtBAP; BoW
Soft sound of bells floats over the river, The. Returning at Night. Lu Yu. WhP
Soft sounds and odours brim up through the night. Guided Missiles Experimental Range. Robert Conquest. PoLFOT; PoN
Soft, sweet, and sad in its pathetic glory. In November. Susan Kelly Phillips. TOAH
Soft the angelus at even. A Rhapsody. T. H. Gould. CAG
Soft the barges glide with banners flying. King Erik. Carl Snoilsky. AnSL
Soft Venus do I serve, and round the bed. Paulus Silentiarius, *tr. fr. Greek by* F. A. Wright. GrPo
Soft! what light through yonder window breaks? A Shakespeare Gallery: Juliet. Shakespeare. *Fr.* Romeo and Juliet, II, ii. MaC
Soft you; a word or two before you go. Othello's Death [*or* Death of Othello *or* Othello's Farewell]. Shakespeare. *Fr.* Othello, V, ii. FiP; LiA; TreFS
Soft-throated South, breathing of summer's ease. South-Wind. George Parsons Lathrop. AA
Softer than silence, stiller than still air. The Snowing of the Pines. Thomas Wentworth Higginson. AA; ADAH; GN; LBAP
Softest whisperings of the scented South, The. An Old Battle-Field. Frank L. Stanton. OQP; QP-2
Softly along the road at evening. Nod. Walter de la Mare. AtBAP; BLV; BoLiVe; BoTP; CaAE; CV; EnLit; GoTP; HBMV; MBP; MM; MoAB; MoBrPo; PoeMoYo; PoeT; TCEP; ThWaDe; TSW; TSWC; TwCV; VOD
Softly and gently, drearly-ransom'd soul. Angel. Cardinal Newman. *Fr.* The Dream of Gerontius. OxBoCh
Softly and humbly to the Gulf of Arabs. Beach Burial. Kenneth Slessor. BoAV; MoAuPo
Softly and quietly across the waiting mountains. Francis Carey Slater. *Fr.* Drought. MM
Softly and unhampered an empty boat glides on. The Empty Boat. Tao Yuan-ming. WhP
Softly at dawn a whisper stole. Spring Song. William Griffith. BAP; BLA; MPB; SBMV
Softly blow lightly. Nocturne. Donald Jeffrey Hayes. CDC
Softly, by night, the deer come down to drink. The Deer Come Down, I. Edward Weismiller. MuM
Softly, drowsily,/ Out of sleep. A Child's Day Begins. Walter de la Mare. StVeCh; SUS; TiPo (1952 ed.)
Softly I closed the book as in a dream. The Book. Winfred Ernest Garrison. OQP; QP-1
Softly, in the dusk, a woman is singing to me. Piano. D. H. Lawrence. CoEV; InvP; LiTB; MBP; MoAB; MoBrPo; NeMA; OAEP (2d ed.); PoE; UnPo (3d ed.)
Softly, let the measure break. Harp Music. Rolfe Humphries. UnS
Softly Let Us All Vanish. Zisha Landau, *tr. fr. Yiddish by* Sarah Zweig Betsky. OnCuPl
Softly, My Heart! Bernhard Elis Malmström, *tr. fr. Swedish by* Charles W. Stork. AnSL
Softly now the burn is rushing. Lullaby. Seumas MacManus. AnIV; BOL
Softly Now the Light of Day. George Washington Doane. OlF; TreFS
(Evening.) AA; HBV
(Evening Contemplation.) BLPA; FaBoBe; NeHB
(Evening Hymn.) BPP
Softly, O midnight hours! Serenade [*or* Song]. Aubrey Thomas De Vere. IrPN; HBV; OBEV
Softly, on little feet that make no sound. Revenants des Enfants. Frederic Manning. UnW
Softly out of the dove-grey sky. Ralph Straker. W. W. Gibson. *Fr.* Casualties. VOD
Softly, pretty baby, sleeping. Cossack Cradle-Song. Mikhail Lermontov. BoR
Softly rustled the oaks, whispered low in my ear. The Graveyard. Hayyim Nahman Bialik. TrJP

Softly! She is lying. Dirge. Charles Gamage Eastman. AA
Softly sighs the April air. Bel m'es quan lo vens m'alena [*or* Canso]. Arnaut Daniel. AWP; JAWP; LiTW; LyMA; WBP
Softly sink in slumbers golden. Lullaby. Gerald Massey. BOL
Softly sinking through the snow. Roses' Song. Philip Bourke Marston. *Fr.* Garden Fairies. VA
Softly, softly, softly croon. Cradlesong. Clemens Brentano. AnGP
Softly, softly, through the darkness. Christmas Night. B. E. Milner. BoTP
Softly the car goes with the music in it. Mollesse. Josephine Jacobsen. NePoAm-2
Softly the darkness folds the sun away. The Last Tavern. Francis Beatrice Taylor. CPG
Softly the day dies out behind the pines. Evening Landscape. Pol de Mont. LiTW
Softly the dews upon my forehead light. Stars as Spray. *Unknown.* OnPM
Softly the waters ripple. Ares. Albert Ehrenstein. TrJP
Softly the west wind blows. A Maiden's Complaint in Spring-Time. *Unknown.* LiA
Softly through the Mellow Starlight. *Unknown.* OHIP; PoRL
Softly Woo Away Her Breath. "Barry Cornwall." HBV; LPS-1
Soggarth Aroon. John Banim. GoBC; TIP; VA
Sohrab and Rustum. Matthew Arnold. BEL; BPN; EmBrPo; EPN; EPP; EV-5; GEPC; HeT; PoVP; REAL; ShBV-2, *abr.*; TCEP; TOP; TyEnPo; ViPo; ViPP; VLEP
Sels.
Combat, The. VA
Death of Sohrab, The ("He spoke, and Sohrab kindled at his taunts"). LH
(Sohrab's Death.) WHA
Death of Sohrab, The ("He spoke; and Sohrab smiled on him, and took/ The spear"). FiP
Oxus ("But the majestic river floated on"). VA
Oxus ("So, on the bloody sand, Sohrab lay dead"). NBE
Sohráb Is Born. Firdausi, *tr. fr. Persian by* James Atkinson. *Fr.* Shah Namah. PeP
Soil. Pedro Salinas, *tr. fr. Spanish by* Eleanor L. Turnbull. AnSpL-2
("Soil. Nothing more.") CoSP
Soil intended for Pierian seeds, The. More Advice. Earl of Roscommon. *Fr.* An Essay on Translated Verse. BeR
Soil is quick with dust of men, The. What Far Kingdom. Arthur S. Bourinot. CaP
Soil luxuriant, and the fruit divine, The. Paradise. Dryden. *Fr.* The State of Innocence and the Fall of Man. BeR
Soil. Nothing more. Soil. Pedro Salinas. AnSpL-2; CoSP
Soil now gets a rumpling soft and damp, The. The Strong Are Saying Nothing. Robert Frost. ChMo; PoE
Soil ysowpit into water wak, The. Winter. Gawin Douglas. *Fr.* Prologues to the Aeneid. SeCePo
Sois sage, o ma douleur. Baudelaire, *tr. fr. French by* Lord Alfred Douglas. AWP; JAWP; WBP
Sojourner, The. Sara Hamilton Birchall. NLK
Solace. Clarissa Scott Delany. CDC; PoNe
Solace in Winter. *Unknown, tr. fr. Irish by* George Sigerson. *Fr.* Silva Gadelica. TIP
Solace of Art, The. Amphis, *tr. fr. Greek by* T. F. Higham. OxBG
Solace of Books, The. *Unknown.* MOB
Solar Creation. Charles Madge. FaBoMo; OBMV
Solar Myth. Genevieve Taggard. MAP; MoAmPo
Solar Road, The. Francis Carlin. JKCP
Soldier, The, *sels.* Conrad Aiken.
I. The Wars. WaaP
II. The Unknown Soldier. WaaP; WaP
Soldier, The. Rupert Brooke. 1914, V. AEV; AnFE; AOAH; BBV; BEL; BLV; BMEP; BoLiVe; BTP; CaAE; CBOV; CP; EnLit; EPN; EPP; ES; EV-5; ExPo; FaBoEn; FaFP; GTBS; GTBS-W; GTML; GTSL; HiLiEn; InP; LBBV; LEAP; LiTB; LiTM; MaC; MaRV; MBP; MCCG; MoBrPo; MoVE; NeHB; NeMA; OBEV (new ed.); OTPC (1946 ed.); PIAE; PoeT; PoMa; PoRA; POT; POTE; PoTo; POTT; PreP; PYM; ShBV-3; TCEP; TCPD; TOP; TreF; TrGrPo; TVSH; TwCV; ViBoPo; VOD; WaP; WHA; WP; YT
(1914.) HBV; NP
Soldier, The. John Clare. SoV
Soldier, A. Robert Frost. MoPo; NePA; SeCeV; SoV; TriL; TwP; WaaP; WaP
Soldier, A. A. G. Herbertson. NeTW
Soldier, The. Gerard Manley Hopkins. WaaP
Soldier, The. Sophie Jewett. PC
Soldier, The. Alun Lewis. MoWP
Soldier, A. Sir John Suckling. SeCV-1
Soldier, The. Theognis, *tr. fr. Greek by* F. L. Lucas. GrPE
Soldier, The ("I once knew a soldier just from the war"). *Unknown. See* Erlinton.
Soldier, A ("In obedience to the imperial command"). *Unknown, tr. fr. Japanese by* Ishii *and* Obata. OnPM
Soldier, The. Jones Very. IAP; TCAP
Soldier, The. George Wither. BHV
Soldier, The ("Down some cold field"). Humbert Wolfe. *Fr.* Requiem. TCPD
Soldier, The ("I do not ask God's purpose"). Humbert Wolfe. *Fr.* Requiem. TCPD
Soldier and a Sailor, A. Congreve. *Fr.* Love for Love. CoMu
(Buxom Joan.) BOHV; InMe
(Song: "Soldier [*or* Souldier] and a Sailor, A.") EV-3; OAEP
Soldier and a Scholar, A, *sel.* Swift.
"Thus spoke to my Lady the Knight full of care." OBEC
Soldier and Girl Sleeping. Sheila Shannon. SoV
Soldier and Sailor. Thomas Campbell. *See* Napoleon and the British Sailor.
Soldier and singer of Erin. In Memoriam; Francis Ledwidge. Norreys Jephson O'Conor. HBMV
Soldier and statesman, rarest unison. Washington [*or* George Washington *or* Ours, and All Men's]. James Russell Lowell. *Fr.* Under the Old Elm. DD; GN; GrCo-2; HH; MC; MW; OHIP; OQP; OTPC; PEDC; PGD; PSO; QP-1
Soldier and the Nun, The. Sister Mary Eleanore. PraNu
Soldier and the Sailor, The, *with music.* *Unknown.* ShS
Soldier-Boy, The. William Maginn. *See* I Give My Soldier Boy a Blade.
Soldier Boy, The. Johan Ludvig Runeberg, *tr. fr. Swedish by* Charles W. Stork. AnSL; WoL
Soldier-boy, soldier-boy. Return. Josephine Preston Peabody. CV
Soldier boy, soldier boy,/ Gallantly you go. Widow-Mother. Ada Jackson. NeTW
Soldier brave, sailor true. *Unknown.* OxNR
Soldier-Dead. Gilbert Emery. PEDC
Soldier fought his battle silently, The. Soldier. Sophie Jewett. PC
Soldier from the Wars Returning. A. E. Housman. Last Poems, VIII. LiTB; OBMV; PoLFOT; SoV
Soldier, full of battles and renown, The. The Returned Soldier. John Clare. SoV
Soldier Going to the Field, The. Sir William Davenant. EV-2
(Souldier Going to the Field, The.) MePo
Soldier, A—His Prayer. Gerald Kersh. QS; TreFS
Soldier, I Can't Figure Why. Nicolás Guillén, *tr. fr. Spanish by* H. R. Hays. AnCL
Soldier I watch so proudly pass. In a London Terminus. John Lehmann. AtBAP
Soldier in the Rain, The. Julia L. Keyes. BlG
Soldier loves his rifle, The. Foxtrot from a Play. W. H. Auden. LiTM
Soldier of Neither Camp. Aleksey Konstantinovich, Count Tolstoy, *tr. fr. Russian by* Babette Deutsch. TrRV
Soldier of the Cromwell stamp, A. Heredity. Thomas Bailey Aldrich. AA; AnAmPo; LA; LEAP; MAP; PFY
Soldier of the Legion lay dying in Algiers, A. Bingen on the Rhine. Caroline Norton. BeLS; BLPA; HBV; LPS-2; NeHB; PTA-1; TreF; WBLP
Soldier of the Russians, A. A New Version. William James Lampton. BOHV; PA
Soldier of the Silences, The. William Herschell. PEDC
"Soldier of the Union mustered out, A." A Nameless Grave. Longfellow. IAP
Soldier of Weight, A. John Kendall. WhC
Soldier Overseas. Leonard Mann. BoAu
Soldier passed me in the freshly-fallen snow, A. To a Conscript of 1940. Sir Herbert Read. ChMP; ExPo; LiTB; LiTM; WaP
Soldier Poet, A. Rossiter Johnson. AA; MDAH
Soldier Relieved, The. Robert Browning. CBPC
"Soldier, Rest!" Robert J. Burdette. BOHV
(Russian and Turk.) NA
Soldier, Rest! [Thy Warfare O'er]. Sir Walter Scott. *Fr.* The Lady of the Lake, I. AOAH; ATP (1935 ed.); AWP; BCEP; BEL; BPN; BTP; CBPC; CoBE; DD; EmBrPo; EnLi-2; EnLit; EPN; EPP; ERP; GN; HBV; HBVY; HH; JAWP; LPS-2; MoShBr; OTPC (1946 ed.); PIAE; PoRA; PYM; TCEP; TOP; TreFS; TrGrPo; WaKn; WBP
(Ellen's Song, *abr.*) CBE
(Song: "Soldier rest! thy warfare o'er.") BHV; OAEP; OBRV
Soldier-Statesman Returns, The. Tu Fu, *tr. fr. Chinese by* Arthur Christy. OnPM
Soldier (T. P.). Randall Jarrell. WaP
Soldier, There Is a War [between the Mind]. Wallace Stevens. *Fr.* Notes toward a Supreme Fiction. LiTM (rev. ed.); NePA
Soldier Thought Dead Returns Home, The. *Unknown, tr. fr. Chinese by* Arthur Waley. *Fr.* Shi King. LiTW

Soldier to His Wife, A. Liu Chi, *tr. fr. Chinese by* Henry H. Hart. OnPM; PoHN
Soldier; Twentieth Century. Isaac Rosenberg. ChMP
Soldier Walks under the Trees of the University, The. Randall Jarrell. OxBA; WaP
Soldier, What Did You See? Don Blanding. BBV (1951 ed.); MaRV
Soldier, Won't You Marry Me? *Unknown.* OxBoLi
Soldiers. Maxwell Bodenheim. MAPA
Soldiers, The. Giuseppe Ungaretti, *tr. fr. Italian by* Glauco Cambon. OnPM
Soldier's Amen, The. *Unknown.* BlG
Soldiers are citizens of death's gray land. Dreamers. Siegfried Sassoon. CaAE; ChMo; CMP; HBMV; MBP; MCCG; MoBrPo; NeMA; PoeMoYo; PtOT; SoV; VOD
Soldiers are weapons of evil. Weapons of Evil. *Tr. by* Lin Yutang. *Fr.* Tao Teh King. MaRV
Soldiers, as we come to lay. More than Flowers We Have Brought. Nancy Byrd Turner. SiSoSe
Soldiers Bathing. F. T. Prince. ChMP; LiTB; LiTM; MoVE; PoN; WaP
Soldiers beat the hour, The. The Sentry. Fu Chih Tao. PoHN
Soldier's Burial, The. Caroline Elizabeth Sarah Norton. PEOR
Soldier's Death, A. Cyril Tourneur. *Fr.* The Atheist's Tragedy. SeCePo
Soldier's Death, The. Countess of Winchilsea. BLV; OtMeF
(All Is Vanity.) PoD
(Trail All Your Pikes.) ExPo
Soldier's Dirge, A. Elizabeth Harman. DD; HH
Soldier's Dog. Ethel Barnett de Vito. AlBD
Soldier's Dove. James Forsyth. WaP
Soldier's Dream, The. Thomas Campbell. BeLS; BHV; BTP; CBE; CG; EnRP; EV-4; GTBS; GTBS-D; GTBS-W; GTSE; GTSL; HBV; LPS-2; MCCG; TreFS
Soldier's Farewell to Manchester, The. *Unknown.* CoMu
Soldiers fight by land and air. Ilo Orleans. RIS
Soldier's Friend, The. George Canning. OBEC
Soldier's Grave, A. John Albee. AA
Soldier's Grave, A. Anacreon, *tr. fr. Greek by* A. C. Benson. GrR
Soldier's Grave, The. Henry D. Muir. OHIP
Soldiers have to fight and swear. Unequal Distribution. Samuel Hoffenstein. TrJP
Soldiers of Christ, arise. Charles Wesley. OlF
Soldiers of the cross, arise! William Walsham How. OlF
Soldiers of the Plough, The. Charles Sangster. *Fr.* The Happy Harvesters. BoCaPo (1943 ed.); CPG
Soldiers's Prayer, A. Robert Freeman. *See* Prayer: "White Captain of my soul, lead on."
Soldier's Return, The. Robert Bloomfield. LPS-2
Soldier's Return, The. Samuel Taylor Coleridge. BHV
Soldier's Riches, A. Hybrias, *tr. fr. Greek by* Thomas Campbell. OxBG
("My wealth's a burly spear and brand.") GrPo
(Song of a Legionnaire, *tr. at. to* H. Rushton Fairclough.) GrR
Soldier's Song. David Campbell. BoAV; NeLNL
Soldier's Song. Goethe, *tr. fr. German by* Bayard Taylor. *Fr.* Faust. AWP
Soldier's Song, The. Peadar Kearney. OnYI
Soldier's Song ("Our vicar still preaches that Peter and Poule"). Sir Walter Scott. *Fr.* The Lady of the Lake, VI. ViBoPo
Soldier's Song ("I joined the army when I was fifteen"). *Unknown, tr. fr. Chinese by* Ho Yung. WhP
Soldier's Song, The ("I sing the praise of honored wars"). *Unknown.* ElSeCe; ReEn; TuPP
Soldiers suddenly struck by love, The. In Postures That Call. Oscar Williams. WaP
Soldier's Tale. Aleksey Nedogonov, *tr. fr. Russian by* Jack Lindsay. RuPo
Soldier's Tear, The. Alexander Lee. BHV
Soldiers! who freely for our country's glory. Decoration Hymn. William H. Randall. PEOR
Soldier's Wife, A. Li Po, *tr. fr. Chinese by* Henry H. Hart. OnPM
Soldier's Wife, A. Gerald Massey. UnW
Soldier's Wife, The. Robert Southey. OBEC
Soldier's Wite to Her Husband, A. Liu Chi, *tr. fr. Chinese by* Henry H. Hart. ChLP; OnPM; PoHN
Soldier's Wooing, The. *Unknown. See* Erlinton.
Soldier's Wound, The. Wallace Stevens. *See* How Red the Rose That Is the Soldier's Wound.
Sole listener, Duddon! to the breeze that played. The River Duddon, V. Wordsworth. EnLi-2; EnSW
Sole Lord of Lords and very King of Kings. Sesostris. Lloyd Mifflin. AA; BAP; HBV
Sole Positive of Night! Ne Plus Ultra. Samuel Taylor Coleridge. NBE
Sole thing I hate is Hate, The. Love and Hate. Longfellow. *Fr.* Christus; a Mystery. MaRV
Soledad. Federico García Lorca, *tr. fr. Spanish by* Eleanor L. Turnbull. CoSP
Solemn and slow they move. The Sod-Breaker. Arthur Stringer. CaP; OCL
Solemn Conceit, A. Nicholas Breton. SiCE
Solemn fields breathe out to me, The. English Easter, 7 A.M. Evelyn Underhill. MM
Solemn he paced upon that schooner's deck. The Captain. John G. C. Brainard. EtS
Solemn Hour. Rainer Maria Rilke, *tr. fr. German by* C. F. MacIntyre. TrJP
Solemn Meditation, A. Ruth Pitter. OxBoCh
Solemn Noon of Night, The. Thomas Warton, the Younger. *Fr.* The Pleasures of Melancholy. OBEC; SeCePo
Solemn Rondeau. Charles Dent Bell. OBVV
Solemn, solemn the coachman gets ready to go. Ch'in Chia's Farewell [*or* To His Wife]. Ch'in Chia. ChLP; LiTW; TrCh
Solemnly, mournfully,/ Dealing its dole. Curfew. Longfellow. AA; MCCG; MOAP; OxBA; PCD
Soles Occidere et Redire Possunt, *sel.* Aldous Huxley.
"'Misery,' he said, 'to have no chin,'" VIII. ViBoPo (1941 ed.)
Soliloquy, A. Walter Harte. LPS-2
Soliloquy. Frederick E. Laight. BoCaPo (1943 ed.); CaP
Soliloquy. Francis Ledwidge. EnLit
Soliloquy. Moschus, *tr. fr. Greek by* Henry Harmon Chamberlain. GrR
Soliloquy by the Shore. Martin Scholten. GoYe
Soliloquy from "Hamlet." Shakespeare. *See* To Be or Not to Be.
Soliloquy in an Air-Raid. Roy Fuller. LiTM
Soliloquy of a Tortoise on Revisiting the Lettuce Beds after an Interval of One Hour While Supposed to Be Sleeping in a Clump of Blue Hollyhocks. E. V. Rieu. FiBHP
Soliloquy of a Water-Wagtail. James Montgomery. OTPC (1923 ed.)
Soliloquy of Cicero. Colgate Dorr. PtPa
Soliloquy of Lincoln before Manassas. Stephen Vincent Benét. *Fr.* John Brown's Body. PaA
Soliloquy of the Returned Gold Adventurer. *Unknown.* PoOW
Soliloquy of the Spanish Cloister. Robert Browning. ATP; BEL; BLV; BMEP; BoLiVe; CBOV; EM-2; EmBrPo; EnL; EnLi-2; EnLit; EPN; ExPo; LiTB; OAEP; OtMeF; PIAE; PoE; PoVP; PreP; RiBV; SeCeV; ShBV-4; TOP; TrGrPo; TwCrTr; TwP; UnPo (1st ed.); ViPo; ViPP; VLEP
Soliloquy on Death. Shakespeare. *See* To Be or Not to Be.
Soliloquy on Immortality. Addison. *See* Cato.
Soliloquy on Sleep. Shakespeare. *See* Henry IV's Soliloquy on Sleep.
Soliloquy to Imogen, *sels.* Christopher Hassall.
"I heard a voice say 'Look into your heart.'" LO
"We danced/ Shyly, not speaking, more as partial friends." LO
Solipsism. George Santayana. AnFE; APA; CoAnAm; TwAmPo
Solitaire. John Zollie Howard. CAG
Solitaire. Amy Lowell. LaNeLa; MAP; MAPA; MoAmPo; NeMA; NP
Solitariness. Sir Philip Sidney. *See* O Sweet Woods.
Solitary, The. Nietzsche, *tr. fr. German by* Ludwig Lewisohn. AWP
Solitary, The. Rainer Maria Rilke, *tr. fr. German by* C. F. MacIntyre. TrJP
Solitary, The. Sara Teasdale. MAP; MoAmPo; NeMA; WHA
Solitary, The. Wordsworth. *Fr.* The Excursion, II. EnRP; ERP
Solitary, before daybreak, in a garden. An Old Man Sees Himself. Conrad Aiken. NV
Solitary bird of night, The. Ode to Wisdom. Elizabeth Carter. OBEC
Solitary-hearted, The. Hartley Coleridge. HBV; OBEV (1st ed.); OnPP
(She Was a Queen.) EV-4
Solitary invalid in a fuchsia garden, A. The Philosopher and the Birds. Richard Murphy. PoN
Solitary Life, A. William Drummond of Hawthornden. *See* Thrice Happy He.
Solitary Lyre, The. George Darley. GTBS-W; LiTB; LiTG; OBEV (new ed.)
(Lyre, The, I.) OBVV
(Wherefore, Unlaurelled Boy.) NBE; OBRV; TriL
Solitary Mourner, The. Euripides, *tr. fr. Greek by* Gilbert Murray. *Fr.* Rhesus. GrR
Solitary Pine. Prince Ichihara, *tr. fr. Japanese by* Ishii *and* Obata. OnPM
Solitary Reaper, The. Wordsworth. AEV; AnEnPo; AnFE; AtBAP; ATP; AWP; BCEP; BEL; BLV; BoLiVe; BPN; BrBE; CBE; CBOV; CH; ChER; CoBE; CoEV; EM-2; EmBrPo; EnL; EnLi-2; EnLit; EnLP; EnRP; EPN; EPP; ERP; EV-3; ExPo; FaBoCh; FaBoEn;

Solitary Reaper, The (*continued*)
FiP; GBV; GEPC; GN; HBV; HiLiEn; HoPM; InP; InPo; JAWP; KN; LEAP; LiA; LiTB; LiTG; LiTL; LoBV; MaPo; MCCG; OAEP; OBEV; OBRV; OnPP; OTPC; OuHeWo; PCD; PIAE; PoE; PoEL-4; PoeMoYo; PoFS; PoRA; PYM; REAL; ReaPo; RG; RiBV; SeCeV; ShBV-3; TCEP; ThWaDe; TOP; TreF; TrGrPo; TwHP; TwP; TyEnPo; UnPo; UnS; WBP; WHA
("Behold her, single in the field.") EG
(Reaper, The.) GTBS; GTBS-D; GTBS-W; GTSE; GTSL; WP
Solitary sail that rises, A. A Sail. Mikhail Lermontov. BoR
Solitary Shepherd's Song, The. Thomas Lodge. *See* Sonnet: "O shady vales . . ."
Solitary wayfarer! George Darley. *Fr.* Nepenthe. OBRV
Solitary Woodsman, The. Sir Charles G. D. Roberts. BoCaPo; CaP; OCL; TwCV
Solitude. William Allingham. BLP; PC
Solitude. James Beattie. *Fr.* Retirement. OBEC
Solitude. Byron. *See* Ocean, The.
Solitude, *sel.* "Lewis Carroll."
"I love the stillness of the wood." AlDL
Solitude. John Clare. EnRP; ERP
Solitude. Walter de la Mare. ChMo; FaBoEn
Solitude. Babette Deutsch. BAP; HBMV
Solitude. James Grainger. CEP; OBEC, *abr.*
Sels.
Ode to Solitude ("O solitude, romantic maid"). ViBoPo
"What is fame? an empty bubble." PoP
Solitude. Jami, *tr. fr. Persian by* Stephen Weston. PeP
Solitude. Keats. *See* To Solitude.
Solitude. Archibald Lampman. BoCaPo; ExPo; PeCV
Solitude. Harold Monro. CMP; MBP; MoBrPo; StaSt; TrGrPo; TSW
Solitude. Hannah More. *Fr.* Search after Happiness. WBLP
Solitude. Frederick Peterson. AA
Solitude. Pope. *See* Ode on Solitude.
Solitude. Rainer Maria Rilke, *tr. fr. German.* OnPM, *tr. by* Jessie Lemont; TrJP, *tr. by* C. F. MacIntyre
(Loneliness, *tr. by* Kate Flores.) AnGP
Solitude, *sel.* V. Sackville-West.
I Find My God. QS
Solitude. Philip Henry Savage. AA
Solitude. Edward Rowland Sill. AnNE
Solitude, A. Swinburne. BPN
Solitude. James Thomson. *Fr.* Hymn on Solitude. BeR
Solitude. Thomas Traherne. OBS; SeEP
"I do believ," *sel.* FaBoEn
Solitude. Ella Wheeler Wilcox. FaFP; HBV; LEAP; OHFP; PTA-2; YaD
(Laugh, and the World Laughs with You.) BAP; PYM
(Way of the World, The.) TreF; WBLP
Solitude. Wordsworth. *Fr.* The Prelude, III. LiA
Solitude and the Lily. Richard Henry Horne. OBVV; VA
Solitude is like rain. Solitude. Rainer Maria Rilke. TrJP
Solitude is very sad. Solitude. William Allingham. BLP; PC
Solitude of Alexander Selkirk, The. William Cowper. *See* Verses Supposed to Be Written by Alexander Selkirk . . .
Solitude that unmakes me one of men. Compensation. Robinson Jeffers. MAP; MoAB; MoAmPo; NeMA
Solitudes, The, *sels.* Luis de Góngora, *tr. fr. Spanish by* Edward Meryon Wilson.
Dedication to the Duke of Bejar. TeCS
Shipwrecked Youth Reaches Land, A. TeCS
Streamlet Flows into the Sea, A. TeCS
"'Twas now the blooming season of the year," *tr. by* Thomas Stanley. AnSpL-1
Wedding Hymn, A. TeCS
Solo. Bocho Yamamura, *tr. fr. Japanese by* Takamichi Ninomiya *and* D. J. Enright. PoLJ
Solo for Ear-Trumpet. Edith Sitwell. MBP; MoAB; MoBrPo; NeMA
Solo (Teterboro Airport). A. Fleming MacLiesh. Exploration by Air, I. PoF
Solomon. Hermann Hagedorn. GoBC
Solomon. Heine, *tr. fr. German by* Emma Lazarus. TrJP
Solomon. Matthew Prior. *See* Solomon on the Vanity of the World.
Solomon, *sels. Unknown.*
Inspiration, VI. WGRP
To Truth, XXXVIII. WGRP
Solomon and the Bees. John Godfrey Saxe. GN; GoTP; OTPC
Solomon, Clown, put by your crown. Conrad Aiken. *Fr.* Punch; the Immortal Liar. NP
Solomon Grundy/ Born on a Monday. Mother Goose. BoN; HBV; HBVY; OTPC; OxBoLi; OxNR; PPL; RIS; SiTL
Solomon Kane's Home-coming. Robert Ervin Howard. DaM
Solomon on the Vanity of the World, *sels.* Matthew Prior.
Knowledge; Solomon Discourses. BeR
Love and Reason, *fr.* Bk. II. OBEC
Man and the Universe. BeR
"Pass we the ills, which each man feels or dreads," *fr.* Bk. III. PoEL-3
(Power.) LoBV
Solomon Pease. *Unknown.* WhC
Solomon to Sheba. W. B. Yeats. GTBS-D
Solomon! where is thy throne? It is gone in the wind. Gone in the Wind. James Clarence Mangan. ACP; BCEP; CAW; GoBC; GTIV; IrPN; MaRV; OBVV; OnYI; OxBI; PoLi; SeCePo; TIP
Solomon's Hymn to the Moon. Oscar Levertin, *tr. fr. Swedish by* Charles W. Stork. AnSL
Solon's Song. Thomas D'Urfey. *See* Hunting Song.
Solsequium, The. Alexander Montgomerie. GoTS
Solstice. Charles Weekes. GTIV; OnYI
Solstices. Richard Church. POTE
Solstitium Saeculare. Robert Fitzgerald. MoVE
Solution. Jack Luzzatto. UnW
Solutions. Edmund Blunden. FaBoTw
Solvet Saeclum. Leconte de Lisle, *tr. fr. French by* Alan Conder. TrFP
Solvitur Acris Hiems. Francis Sylvester Mahony. IrPN
Solway Ford. W. W. Gibson. TCPD
Solway Sands. Elizabeth Craigmyle. VA
Solyman and Almena, *sel.* John Langhorne.
Farewell Hymn to the Valley of Irwan, A. CEP
Som tyme [*or* Sometime] this world was so stedfast and stable. Lak [*or* Lack] of Stedfastnesse. Chaucer. AWP; CoEV; PoLi
Sombre [*or* Somber] and rich, the skies. By the Statue of King Charles at Charing Cross. Lionel Johnson. BMEP; CaAE; CoBE; GTIV; GTML; HBV; JKCP; LEAP; MBP; MoBrPo; OBEV (new ed.); OBMV; OBVV; PoEL-5; PoeT; POTT; PoVP; ShBV-4; ViP; ViPP; VLEP
Sombre the night is. Returning, We Hear the Larks. Isaac Rosenberg. FaBoMo; WaaP
Some act of love's bound to rehearse. Why I Write Not of Love. Ben Jonson. ElSeCe; EnLit; OAEP; TuPP
Some ages hence, for it must not decay. Under a Lady's Picture. Edmund Waller. EnLoPo
Some are laughing, some are weeping. Sound Sleep. Christina Rossetti. BPN
Some are sick for spring and warm winds blowing. The Hound. Babette Deutsch. HBMV; NLK
Some are stout. Professors. Harold A. Larrabee. InMe
Some are teethed on a silver spoon. Saturday's Child. Countee Cullen. PoNe
Some are too much at home in the role of wanderer. Poem. Denise Levertov. NeBP
Some asked [*or* ask'd] me where the rubies grew? The Rock of Rubies [*or* Rubies and Pearls *or* Julia]. Robert Herrick. HBV; InMe; OTPC (1923 ed.)
Some awful Powers have been placed. Desert Dangers. Jakob Thorarensen. IcP
Some Beautiful Letters. Dorothy Parker. InMe
Comment. ALV
News Item. TreF; YaD
Observation. FiBHP
Résumé. ALV; PoeMoYo; TCPD; TrS; WhC
Social Note. BoHV
Some Blesseds. John Oxenham. WGRP
Some bloodied sea-bird's hovering decay. The Lie. Howard Moss. AtBAP; MoAB; NePoAm
Some *bon vivant* of the heart might have come for her. "There'll Be Others but Non So for Me." Delmore Schwartz. FiMAP
Some books are lies frae end to end. Death and Doctor Hornbook. Burns. DaM; EBSV; PIR
Some boys are mad when comp'ny comes to stay for meals. The Second Table. Nixon Waterman. PTA-1
Some, by their monarch's fatal mercy grown. Lord Shaftesbury. Dryden. *Fr.* Absalom and Achitophel, Pt. I. LoBV
Some candle clear burns somewhere I come by. The Candle Indoors. Gerard Manley Hopkins. CoEV; EmBrPo; FaBoMo; GTBS-W; LiTB; LiTM; MeRV; OxBoCh; PeBoSo; PoEL-5; ReMP; ViPP
Some Cannibal. *At. to* Samuel Wilberforce. BoN
("If I were a Cassowary.") CenHV
Some children like gay weather. A Preference. John Farrar. GFA
Some children live in palaces. Other Children. Helen Wing. GFA; OTPC (1946 ed.)
Some clerks aver that as the free doth fall. The Utmost. "Owen Meredith." VA
Some coasting vessels can be seen on the ocean. Victor Hugo. *Fr.* Choses du soir. LiA
Some cool medieval calm hath settled here. Cwm Farm near Capel Curig. Huw Menai. MoWP
Some crumpled-rose-leaf mountains, from forty miles away. A Song of Wandering. Lord Dunsany. BMEP
Some cry up Haydn, some Mozart. Free Thoughts on Several Eminent Composers. Charles Lamb. OBRV; OxBoLi

Some Day. *See also* Someday.
Some Day of Days. Nora Perry. HBV; LBAP
Some days are fairy days. The minute that you wake. Sometimes. Rose Fyleman. SiSoSe
Some days my thoughts are just like cocoons. Days. Karle Wilson Baker. GFA; OQP; QP-2; SBMV; SP; TiPo
Some days, you say, are good days. Warp and Woof. Harry Halbisch. BLRP
Some die too late and some too soon. The Lost Occasion. Whittier. CoBA; GA; IAP; PTA-2; TCAP
Some dogs are brats. For a Good Dog. Arthur Guiterman. AlBD
Some doleful thing there is at hand. Egloga Quinta. Barnabe Googe. ReIE
Some dreams we have are nothing else but dreams. The Haunted House. Thomas Hood. AnEnPo; BCEP; DaM; LiA; UnW
Some ears are tuned to catch. Wafu, *tr. fr. Japanese by* Lois J. Erickson. SoLD
Some eat the countries; these are kings. *Unknown. Fr.* The Panchatantra. LiTW
Some Europeans. *Unknown.* SiTL
Some evening, when the forest is a mist. Song to Say a Farewell. Howard McKinley Corning. NP
Some evening when you are sitting alone. The White Dress. Humbert Wolfe. LoPS; NP
Some Faith at Any Cost. Harriet Du Autermont. MaRV
Some faults, though small, no husband yet can bear. The The New Woman. Juvenal. *Fr.* Satires, VI. RoL
Some few yards from the hut the standing beeches. Poem in the Matukituki Valley. James K. Baxter. AnNZ
Some find love late, some find him soon. When Will Love Come? Pakenham Beatty. HBV
Some Fishy Nonsense. Laura E. Richards. TiPo
Some Flowers o' the Spring. Shakespeare. *Fr.* The Winter's Tale, IV, iii. ChTr
("Now (my fairst Friend).") NBE
Some fly through the storm and the night. Not One Thing Alone. Marius Bohun-Greene. PoP
Some folk like the chaffinch. The Robin. O. M. Bent. BoTP
Some folks are drunk, yet do not know it. An English Ballad, on the Taking of Namur by the King of Great Britain, 1695. Matthew Prior. PoEL-3
Some folks as can afford. Under a Wiltshire Apple Tree. Anna Bunston De Bary. CH
Some Folks I Know. Samuel Hoffenstein. ALV
Some folks in looks take so much pride. *Unknown.* PoToHe (new ed.)
Some folks say dat de Dummy don' run. The Dummy Line. *Unknown.* SoAF
Some folks say dat de worry blues ain' bad. Dink's Blues. *Unknown.* ABF
Some fools keep ringing the dumb waiter bell. Chant Royal of the Dejected Dipsomaniac. Don Marquis. HBMV
Some for the glories of this world; and some. Prefer the Cash. Omar Khayyám, *tr. by* Edward Fitzgerald. *Fr.* The Rubáiyát. OnPM
Some Future Day When What Is Now Is Not. Arthur Hugh Clough. Songs in Absence, VI. BPN; EmBrPo; EPN
(Meeting, The.) EV-5
Some Geese. Oliver Herford. *See* Geese.
Some glory in their birth, some in their skill. Sonnets, XCI. Shakespeare. PeBoSo
Some grave is known to God. Weary. George A. Chadwick. GTIV
Some gypsies are like her. The Ballad of Adam's First. Leland Davis. HBMV
Some had in courts been great, and thrown from thence. The Earl of Shaftesbury. Dryden. *Fr.* Absalom and Achitophel. FaBoEn
Some hae meat and [*or* that] canna eat. A Child's Grace. Burns. BrR; FaBoCh; FaPON; LoGBV; MeMeAg; MoShBr; MPB; PCH; PRWS; StVeCh
Some hae mickle, and to thaim. Hoo the Warld Wags. Heine, *tr. by* Edwin Morgan. AnGP
Some Hallucinations. "Lewis Carroll." *See* Gardener's Song, The.
Some hang above the tombs. On Such a Day. Mary Elizabeth Coleridge. GTBS-D; LO; MoVE
Some have at first for wits, then poets past. Insects from the Nile. Pope. *Fr.* An Essay on Criticism. BeR
Some hearts go hungering thro' the world. Hungering Hearts. *Unknown.* PoToHe
Some hot, some cold. Thomas Campion. LO
Some in the town go betimes to the Downs. The Hunt. *Unknown.* CoMu
Some innocent girlish kisses by a charm. Wild Rose. William Allingham. GN; OTPC
Some keep the Sabbath [*or* Sunday] going to church. Emily Dickinson. MoAB; MoAmPo (1950 ed.); WGRP
(Keeping the Sabbath.) CoBA
(Service of Song, A.) TCAP
Some Ladies. Frederick Locker-Lampson. BOHV; InP
Some ladies love the jewels in Love's zone. Love's Lovers. Dante Gabriel Rossetti. The House of Life, VIII. BPN; EmBrPo; PoVP; ViPo
Some ladies now make pretty songs. Some Ladies. Frederick Locker-Lampson. BOHV; InP
Some lasses are nice and strange. The Innocent Country-Maid's Delight; or, A Description of the Lives of the Lasses of London. *Unknown.* CoMu
Some laws there are too sacred for the hand. Liberty of the Press. Sir Aubrey De Vere. PoFr; TIP
Some leaders lead too far ahead. Leaders. *Unknown.* WBLP
Some like drink. Not I. Robert Louis Stevenson. BoN; NA
"Some likes picturs o' women," said Bill, "an' some likes 'orses best." Pictures. Cicely Fox Smith. EtS
Some Lines in Three Parts. Peter Viereck. MiAP; MoAmPo 1950 ed.)
I. "One tawny paw is all it takes to squash."
II. "But 'I' being less than soul."
III. "What hubbub rocks the nest?"
Some little boys get shushed all day. Mokie's Madrigal. Ronald McCuaig. NeLNL
Some Little Bug. Roy Atwell. BOHV
Some little mice sat in a barn to spin. *See* Six little mice . . .
Some love Marce and some love Venus. *Unknown.* SeCSL
Some Lovers Make Comparison in Love. Gerald Gould. TCPD
Some lovers speak, when they their muses entertain. Astrophel and Stella, VI. Sir Philip Sidney. PeBoSo; ReEn; ReIE; SiPS; TuPP
Some lucky day each November great waves awake and are drawn. November Surf. Robinson Jeffers. CrMA; MoPo; OxBA
Some man unworthy to be possessor. Confined Love. John Donne. AnEnPo; EnLP; TuPP
Some may have blamed you that you took away. Reconciliation. W. B. Yeats. TwP
Some may wish for city streets, jewels or silken gown. Wishes. A. C. Child. PoToHe
Some men are born, while others seem to grow. Great Oak. Bennet Chapple. HH
Some men are troubled by the sea. The River. Struthers Burt. NoCaPo (1941 ed.)
Some men break your heart in two. Experience. Dorothy Parker. InMe; WhC
Some men deem. Ideals. Robert Greene. PoToHe (new ed.)
Some men for sudden joy do weep. *Unknown.* SiCE
Some men marriage do commend. De Se. John Weever. TuPP
Some men there be which like my method well. Idea, XLII. Michael Drayton. SiCE; TuPP
Some misbelieving and profane in love. To Miracle. Michael Drayton. Idea, XXXV. SiCE; TuPP
Some modest windfalls from the tree. Vacation Trip. Donald C. Babcock. NePoAm
Some moons the world can nevermore forget. Moons. David Morton. MuM
Some morning I shall rise from sleep. The Last Voyage. Katharine Tynan. HBMV
Some Mother's Child. Francis L. Keeler. MotAn
Some Murmur When Their Sky Is Clear. Richard Chenevix Trench. HBVY
(Different Minds.) LPS-2
Some must delve when the dawn is nigh. The King of Dreams. Clinton Scollard. HBV
Some names there are of telling sound. The *Cumberland.* Herman Melville. PAH
Some night, John Carter, you will dream of hands. No Envy, John Carter. Merrill Moore. NeMA
Some observations touching speech and grief. William Ellery Leonard. *Fr.* Two Lives, Pt. III. MOAP
Some of our dead are famous, but they would not care. W. H. Auden. *Fr.* Commentary. MoPo
Some of the boys in our school. A Boy's Speech. *Unknown.* MeMeAg
Some of the hurts you have cured. *See* Some of your hurts you have cured.
Some of the roofs are plum-color. Not Three—but One. Esther Lillian Duff. HBMV
Some of their chiefs were princes of the land. Zimri. Dryden. *Fr.* Absalom and Achitophel, Pt. I. AnFE; AWP; EV-3; InPo; JAWP; LPS-3; WBP
Some of these poems are good, some are medium, many are poor stuff. Martial, *tr. fr. Latin by* Robert R. Schnorr. Epigrams, I, 16. LaP
Some of Wordsworth. Walter Savage Landor. ChTr
Some of you will be glad I did what I did. Not Quite Social. Robert Frost. CoV
Some of your [*or* the] hurts you have cured. Borrowing [*or* Anxiety]. Emerson. MaRV; WhC
Some officers take them away: good guard. Lear and Cordelia. Shakespeare. *Fr.* King Lear, V, iii. FiP
Some Old School-Books. *Unknown.* PEOR
Some one. *See* Someone.
Some opulent force of genius, soul, and race. Abraham Lincoln. Joel Benton. DD; LBAH

Some painters paint the sapphire sea. The Clean Platter. Ogden Nash. BOHV
Some part of life becomes oblivion. The Covered Bridge. Anderson M. Scruggs. DDA
Some passionate hour before my own deep stripe. To an Enemy. E. J. Pratt. MaRV; QS
Some People. Rachel Field. FaPON
Some people hang portraits up. A Likeness. Robert Browning. NBE; PoVP
Some people, now, like mountains, where the shafts. Horizontal World. Thomas Saunders. CaP
Some people say the world's all a stage. The Gate at the End of Things. *Unknown.* BLPA
Some people seem to go around. Fun. Douglas Malloch. OnHT
Some people shave before bathing. And Three Hundred and Sixty-six in Leap Year. Ogden Nash. NePA
Some people think I think I'm good. Oh, if They Only Knew! Edith L. Mapes. BLRP; WBLP
Some people understand all about machinery. Up from the Wheelbarrow. Ogden Nash. FaBoBe
Some poets, Lady, still of Jove do crave. Il Filostrato. Boccaccio. PrPoCR
Some poets sing of sweethearts dead. Ballade of Forgotten Loves. Arthur Grissom. BOHV
Some primal termite knocked on wood. The Termite. Ogden Nash. CenHV; WhC
Some prisoned moon in steep cloud-fastnesses. The Soul's Sphere. Dante Gabriel Rossetti. The House of Life, LXII. PoVP; ViPo
Some Prodigies. Charles Fisher. MoWP
Some Questions to Be Asked of a Rajah, Perhaps by the Associated Press. Preston Newman. FiBHP
Some rainbow shreds of hope and joy. Patchwork. Clinton Scollard. OQP; QP-2
Some reckon their age by years. The Rosary of My Tears. Abram J. Ryan. HBV; LPS-3
Some say, compar'd to Bononcini. Epigram on [*or* on the Feuds between] Handel and Bononcini. John Byrom. CEP; OBEC; UnS
Some say, good Will (which I in sport do sing). To Our English Terence, Mr. Will. [*or* Master William] Shakespeare. John Davies of Hereford. PtP; SiCE
Some say he's from Georgia. John Henry. *Unknown.* GoSl
Some say kissin's ae [*or* that kissing's a] sin. Kissin' [*or* Kissing's No Sin]. *Unknown.* FiBHP; HBV; LiTG; LiTL; LPS-1; SiTL; TreF
Some say Love. Menaphon's Song. Robert Greene. *Fr.* Menaphon. ElSeCe; LoBV; OBSC; ReIE
Some say my satires over-loosely flow. Joseph Hall. *Fr.* Virgidemiarum. SiCE
Some say no evil thing that walks by night. Milton. *Fr.* Comus. LO
Some say Noah was a foolish man. Noah's Ark. *Unknown.* APW
Some say that ever 'gainst that season comes. The Gracious Time [*or* Christmas]. Shakespeare. *Fr.* Hamlet, I, i. ChIP; ChrBoLe; ChTr; EV-1; GN; MaRV; TiPo (1952 ed.)
Some say that kissing's a sin. *See* Some say kissin's ae sin.
Some say the dead are lonely where they lie. Sonnets to My Mother. Arthur S. Bourinot. CaP
Some say the deil's deid. *Unknown.* FaBoCh; LoGBV
Some say the Phoenix dwells in Aethiopia. The Phoenix. Siegfried Sassoon. ChTr
Some say the world will end by fire. Frostbite. Conrad Aiken. SiTL
Some say the world will end in fire. Fire and Ice. Robert Frost. AmPP; AnFE; AnNE; APA; CaAE; ChMo; CMP; CoAnAm; CoBMV; CoV; FaFP; GTBS-W; HBMV; IAP; LiTA; LiTM; MAP; MoAB; MoAmPo; MoVE; NePA; OnPM; OxBA; PoLFOT; SiTL; TreFS; TrGrPo; TwAmPo; TwP; ViBoPo (1958 ed.); WHA; WoL
Some say thy fault is youth, some wantonness. Sonnets, XCVI. Shakespeare. PeBoSo
Some say we're bound for Liverpool. Heave Away. *Unknown.* SoAmSa
Some say, when nights are dry and clear. The Fatal Vision. Shelley. *Fr.* The Two Spirits. LO; RO
Some sayes that ever 'gainst that season comes. *See* Some say that ever . . .
Some seek a heaven for rest. Heaven. Edwin Hatch. MaRV
Some seek for ecstasies of joy. The One Thing Needful. Max Isaac Reich. BLRP
Some she binds 'prentice to the spade. Nature and the Poet. Swift. *Fr.* Ode to Sir William Temple. BeR
Some shining April I shall be asleep. The Last Sleep. Charles Hanson Towne. TBM
Some space beyond the garden close. The Hollyhocks. Craven Langstroth Betts. AA
Some speakis of lords, some speakis of lairds. *See* Sum speiks of lords, sum speiks of lairds.
Some Star within Orion. Jessie B. Rittenhouse. MuM
Some starlit garden gray with dew. W. E. Henley. Rhymes and Rhythms, XII. POTT
Some Stories of the Beauty Wapiti. Ebbe Borregaard. NeAP
Some take to liquor, some turn to prayer. A la carte. Kenneth Fearing. ChMo
Some talk of Alexander, and some of Hercules. The British Grenadiers. *Unknown.* ABV; OBEC; OxBoLi
Some Talk of Peace. Edmund Blunden. SoV
Some tell us 'tis a burnin' shame. Sambo's Right to be Kilt. Charles Graham Halpine. AA
Some ten or twelve old friends of yours and mine. A Gentleman of Fifty Soliloquizes. Don Marquis. HBMV; LEAP
Some ten or twenty times a day. Ballade of a Friar. Clément Marot. HBV
Some that have deeper digged [*or* digg'd] love's mine [*or* myne] than I. Love's Alchemy [*or* Alchymie]. John Donne. EnLP; LiTL; MePo; OAEP; ReEn; TuPP; ViBoPo
Some That Report. Thomas Watson. *Fr.* Hecatompathia; or, Passionate Century of Love. TuPP
Some, the great Adepts, found it. The Adepts. Lawrence Durrell. *Fr.* Eight Aspects of Melissa. NeBP
Some there are as fair to see to. Her Commendation [*or* Madrigal]. Francis Davison. EIL; OBSC; TuPP
Some there are who say that the fairest thing seen. Sappho, *tr. fr. Greek by* Richmond Lattimore. GrPo
Some there be that sow the seed and reap the golden grain. The Mother. Sarah Louise Arnold. PEDC
Some they will talk of bold Robin Hood. Robin Hood and the Bishop of Hereford. *Unknown.* BaBo; CG; ESPB; OBB
Some things a man must surely know. Recipe for Living. Alfred Grant Walton. PoToHe (new ed.)
Some things a man should tell his wife. *Unknown. Fr.* The Panchatantra. LiTW
Some things are very dear to me. Sonnets, II. Gwendolyn B. Bennett. BANP; CDC; PoNe
Some things go to sleep in such a funny way. How They Sleep. *Unknown.* PPL
Some things persist by suffering change, others. Homage to the Philosopher. Babette Deutsch. ImOP; TrJP
Some things take issue with the loveliest hours. Mood. Raymond Peckham Holden. CAG
Some Things That Easter Brings. Elsie Parrish. MeMeAg; PCH
Some things that fly there be. Emily Dickinson. AmP; AmPP (4th ed.); CoV; MaPo; OxBA
(Secret, The.) OnPM
Some Things There Are. Margaret Yale. PreP
Some Thracian now goes strutting with the shield I left behind me. The Better Part of Valour. Archilochus, *tr. by* F. L. Lucas. GrPE
Some Thracian strutteth with my shield. The Poet's Shield. Archilochus, *tr. by* Paul Shorey. GrL; GrPo
Some time. *See also* Sometime.
Some Time. Eugene Field. MOAH
Some time ago—two weeks or more. The Cowboy at Church. *Unknown.* CoSo; CSF
Some Time at Eve. Elizabeth Clark Hardy. HBV
(When I Sail Away.) MaRV
Some time now past in the autumnal tide. Contemplations. Anne Bradstreet. AmPP; AnFE; AnNE; APA; APW; CoAnAm; IAP; MOAP; Po; PoEL-3
Some Time We'll Understand. Maxwell N. Cornelius. BLRP; WBLP
Some Towns of Texas. Karle Wilson Baker. HiLiAm
Some twenty cats repose. A Philosophical Poem on Cats. Fillmore Hyde. CIV
Some two score years ago when I was young. The Doctor. E. O. Laughlin. PoP
Some vast amount of years ago. Gemini and Virgo. Charles Stuart Calverley. WhC
Some Verses to Snaix. *Unknown.* NA
Some vex their souls with jealous pain. On One Who Died Discovering Her Kindness. John Sheffield, Duke of Buckingham and Normanby. LO; OBEV
Some water—about a half a cup. Mud Cakes. Mildred D. Shacklett. GFA
Some we see no more, tenements of wonder. Emily Dickinson. MoVE
Some weep because they part. The Difference. Thomas Bailey Aldrich. TOP
Some were unlucky. Blown a mile to shoreward. Moonlight Night on the Port. Sidney Keyes. PoD
Some who are uncertain compel me. At This Moment of Time. Delmore Schwartz. TwAmPo
Some Who Do Not Go to Church. *Unknown.* WBLP
Some wifis of the burrows-toun. Satire on the Toun Ladies. Sir Richard Maitland. EBSV
Some will talk of bold Robin Hood. *See* Some they will talk of bold Robin Hood.
Some winter night, shut snugly in. Ronsard to His Mistress. Thackeray. HBV

Some wit of old—such wits of old there were. Paper. Benjamin Franklin. LHV; LPS-3; MOB
Some with molasses grace the luscious treat. The Eating of the Pudding. Joel Barlow. *Fr.* The Hasty Pudding, III. APW
Some Women. Semonides, *tr. fr. Greek by* Gilbert Highet. OxBG
("In the beginning God made various kinds of women," *tr. by* Richmond Lattimore.) GrPo
(On Women. *pr. tr. by* J. M. Edmonds.) GrL
(Women, *tr. by* F. L. Lucas.) GrPE
Some women herd such little things. Women. Lizette Woodworth Reese. MAP; MoAmPo; MOAP; NP
Some words are tall white candles to honor Mary's name. Ad Mariam. Sister M. Edwardine. WHL
Some would know. His Answer to a Question. Robert Herrick. EPS; ReEn
Some wretched creature, savior take. Emily Dickinson. MoVE
Some write for pleasure. *Unknown.* SiTL
Some years ago, ere time and taste. The Vicar. Winthrop Mackworth Praed. *Fr.* Every-Day Characters. BCEP; EnRP; EPN; ERP; EV-4; InMe; OBEV (new ed.); OBRV; OBVV; PoEL-4; VA
Some years ago you heard me sing. Sarah Byng. Hilaire Belloc. CenHV
Some Years in Washington's Life. M. Lizzie Stanley. WOAH
Some years of late, in eighty-eight. The Defeat of the [Spanish] Armada [*or* The Spanish Armado]. *Unknown, at. to* William Warner. CoBE; EV-2; FaBoCh; LiTG; LoGBV; SG; ShGoBo
Some young and saucy dandelions. The Dandelions. *Unknown.* BoTP
Some Youngster's Dad. Douglas Malloch. FAOV
Somebody. Burns. *See* For the Sake of Somebody.
Somebody ("Och hon for somebody"). *Unknown.* CBOV
Somebody ("Somebody did a golden deed"). *Unknown.* FaFP
Somebody ("Somebody's courting somebody"). *Unknown.* LPS-1
Somebody ("Somebody's tall and handsome"), *with music. Unknown.* AS
Somebody,/ Cut his hair. Young Poet. Myron O'Higgins. PoNe
Somebody called Walt Whitman. Witter Bynner. *Fr.* The New World. InP
Somebody did a golden deed. Somebody. *Unknown.* FaFP
Somebody has got to tell me something real. Runaway. Rhoda Coghill. NeIP
Somebody is whispering on the stair. Rumour. Harold Monro. PtOT
Somebody knew Lincoln Somebody Xerxes. Portrait X. E. E. Cummings. TCPD
Somebody left a mirror. Twenty Foolish Fairies. Nancy Byrd Turner. SUS
Somebody poisoned my dog today. A Snake of a Man. *Unknown.* AlBD
Somebody said that it couldn't be done. It Couldn't Be Done. Edgar A. Guest. BLPA; FaBoBe; FaFP; NeHB; TreFS; WBLP; YaD
Somebody up in the rocky pasture. The Ant Village. Marion Edey. FaPON; TiPo
Somebody's Boy. Katharine Lee Bates. PEDC
Somebody's Child. Louise Chandler Moulton. HBV
Somebody's courting somebody. Somebody. *Unknown.* LPS-1
Somebody's Darling. Marie La Coste [*or* La Conte]. BIG; BLPA; DD; HBV; LPS-2; PTA-2; TreF; WBLP
Somebody's Garden. Margaret Steele Anderson. DD
Somebody's knockin' at th' door. The Collier's Wife. D. H. Lawrence. HaMV
Somebody's Knockin' at Yo' Do', *with music. Unknown.* BoAN-1
Somebody's Mother. Mary Dow Brine. BeLS; BLPA; FaFP; OTPC (1946 ed.); PTA-1; TreF; WBLP
Somebody's Song. Dorothy Parker. *Fr.* Songs of a Markedly Personal Nature. TCPD
Somebody's tall and handsome. Somebody. *Unknown.* AS
Some Day. Medora Addison. HBMV
Some Day. F. P. Doveton. PA
Someday/ Jane shall/ Have. Skipping Ropes. Dorothy Aldis. StVeCh
Some day, all unawares, alone in the deep forest. My Death. Carl Zuckmayer. TrJP
"Some day," I said. "before Life is over." The Ballad of the Quest. Virna Sheard. CPG
Someday I'd like to climb the Puig. Balearic Idyll. Frederick Packard. FiBHP
Someday I'm going to have a store. General Store. Rachel Field. BoChLi; GaP; GoBP; MPB (1956 ed.); StVeCh (1955 ed.); SUS
Some day my spirit will grow up tall and wise. My Spirit Will Grow Up. Ruth Evelyn Henderson. OQP; QP-2
Some day perhaps I too may speak your name. Some Day. Medora Addison. HBMV
Some Day, Some Day (Alguna Vez). Cristóbal de Castillejo, *tr. fr. Spanish by* Longfellow. AnSpL-1; AWP; JAWP; ViBoPo; WBP
Some day, some day of days, threading the street. Some Day of Days. Nora Perry. HBV; LBAP
Some day, some happy day. The Reign of Peace. Mary Starck. WBLP
Some day the silver cord will break. Saved by Grace. Fanny Crosby. BPP
Some day there would be an escape, she knew. Escape. Daniel Whitehead Hicky. JKCP (1955 ed.)
Some day we shall be going home to find. Sonnets from Camp, II. Jesse Stuart. MuM
Someday when I'm braver. Courage. Dorothy Dezouche. DDA
Some day, when the stern seeker in my brain. Prodigal. Du Bose Heyward. SPP; TCAP
Some day, when trees have shed their leaves. After the Winter. Claude McKay. BANP; GoSL; PoNe
Somehow a solitude/ With neither swan nor quay. Little Air, I. Stéphane Mallarmé. AnFP
Somehow, but God knows how, we'll meet again. Somehow, Somewhere, Sometime. Winifred M. Letts. BMEP; HBMV
Somehow come to the calm of this present, a Sunday in summer. To Lighten My House. Alastair Reid. NePoEA
Somehow her very delicacy was strength. The Strong Woman. Roscoe Gilmore Stott. NV
Somehow, not only for Christmas. The Joy of Giving. Whittier. ChBR
Somehow, Somewhere, Sometime. Winifred M. Letts. BMEP; HBMV
Somehow this world is wonderful at times. The East in Gold. W. H. Davies. CBPC
Someone [*or* Some One]. Walter de la Mare. BoChLi; BoTP; FaPON; GaP; GoBP; MBP; MeMeAg; MoBrPo; MoShBr; MPB; RAR; SP; StVeCh; SUS; TiPo
Some One Attains to a Glimpse of Paradise. Jorge Guillén, *tr. fr. Spanish by* Eleanor L. Turnbull. CoSP
Someone came knocking. Someone [*or* Some One]. Walter de la Mare. BoChLi; BoTP; FaPON; GaP; GoBP; MBP; MeMeAg; MoBrPo; MoShBr; MPB; RAR; SP; StVeCh; SUS; TiPo
Some one complained to the Master. The Estuary. Allen Upward. *Fr.* Scented Leaves from a Chinese Jar. NP
Someone Could Certainly Be Found. Anne Hébert, *tr. fr. French by* F. R. Scott. CaP
Someone had been walking in and out. The Origin of Baseball. Kenneth Patchen. Po
Someone Had Prayed. Grace Noll Crowell. PraP
Some one has been in the garden. Jack Frost. *Unknown.* PEOR
Someone has got to tell me something real. Runaway. Rhoda Coghill. OxBI
Someone has left a stack. The Stack. Stanley Snaith. ChMP
Someone has lived here where twin chimneys. The Grapevine. Zoe Kincaid Brockman. GoYe
Someone has opened and undone. Beyond the Tapestries. Norma Farber. GoYe
Someone has shut the shining eyes, straightened and folded. Beside the Bed. Charlotte Mew. AnEnPo; BLV; MBP; MoAB; MoBrPo; NeMA; NP; TrGrPo
Someone is always sitting there. The Little Green Orchard. Walter de la Mare. DaM; MBP; MW; POTT; TiPo (1952 ed.)
Some one [*or* Someone] is coming to call. Afternoon. Fannie Stearns Davis. POT; PoTo
Someone is knocking at the door. The Rice Seller. *Unknown, tr. by* Isaac Taylor Headland. PCH
Someone painted pictures on my. Jack Frost. Helen Bailey Davis. GFA; MBP
Someone passes. Lady Murasaki Shikibu, *tr. fr. Japanese by* Kenneth Rexroth. OnPJ
Some one started the whole day wrong—was it you? Was It You? Stewart I. Long. WBLP
Somerset Farmer, The. Marguerite Wilkinson. CP
Something. Beth Lacy. CAG
Something befell. At the Bottom of the Well. Louis Untermeyer. MAP
Something Better. Clara J. Denton. WOAH
Something Beyond. Mary Clemmer. OQP; QP-1
Something calls and whispers, along the city street. Song. Georgiana Goddard King. *Fr.* The Way of Perfect Love. HBV; NLK
"Something characteristic," eh? The Babes in the Woods. Bret Harte. BAV
Something Childish, but Very Natural. Samuel Taylor Coleridge. *See* If I Had but Two Little Wings.
Something for Jesus. S. D. Phelps. BLRP
Something goes wrong with my synthetic brain. The Case for the Miners. Siegfried Sassoon. PoFr
Something happened the other day, that never happened before. Shovellin' Iron Ore. *Unknown.* AS

Something has ceased to come along with me. Death of a Son. Jon Silkin. NePoEA; PoN; POTE (1959 ed.)
Something Has Spoken to Me in the Night. Thomas Wolfe. OnAP
(Toward Which.) QS
Something I saw or thought I saw. On the Heart's Beginning to Cloud the Mind. Robert Frost. ChMo
Something inspires the only cow of late. The Cow in Apple-Time. Robert Frost. CV; MAP; MoAB; MoAmPo; NV; TwP
Something Is Bound to Happen. W. H. Auden. *See* Doom Is Dark.
Something is dead. Prologue to "Rhymes and Rhythms." W. E. Henley. BPN; PoVP
Something is happening—that he seems to sense. The Summer Cat. Ella Augusta Fanning. CIV
Something more than the lilt of the strain. Poetry. Lucius Harwood Foote. AA
Something of chivalry he lacks. Revelation. *Unknown.* LauV
Something of glass about her, of dead water. Circe. Louis MacNeice. LO; OBMV
Something Private. Richard Church. NeTW
Something so noble in that lifted brow. Clio. Ernest Rhys. POTE
Something Sorto' Healing. Margaret E. Bruner. AlBD
Something Starting Over. Thomas Hornsby Ferril. AnAmPo
Something startles me where I thought I was safest. This Compost. Walt Whitman. AWP; LiTA; MoAmPo (1950 ed.); MOAP; SN
Something surrounds him when he walks alone. Henry Vaughan. Thomas S. Jones, Jr. PtP
Something tapped at my window pane. April. Theodosia Garrison. DD; HBMV; MPB; NLK; TCAP; VOD
Something there is that doesn't love a wall. Mending Wall. Robert Frost. AmP; AmPP; AnNE; BAP; BoFr; CBOV; ChMo; CMP; CoBA; CoBMV; CP; ExPo; FaFP; GTBS-W; HBV; IAP; InP; InPo; LaNeLa; LiTA; LiTM; MAP; MaRV; MCCG; MoAB; MoAmPo; MOAP; MoPW; MoVE; NeMA; NePA; NP; OHFP; OtMeF; OxBA; PFE; PFY; PoE; PoeMoYo; PoLFOT; PoMa; POT; PoTo; PreP; PYM; ReaPo; SeCeV; TCAP; TCPD; TOP; TwP; ViBoPo; WHA
Something to Be Thankful For. Clara J. Denton. HH; TOAH
Something to do with territory makes them sing. Birds All Singing. Norman MacCaig. ChMP
Something to live for came to the place. Only. Harriet Prescott Spofford. HBV
Something to Remember. Robert Browning. *See* Memorabilia.
Something Told the Wild Geese. Rachel Field. BrR; SiSoSe; StVeCh (1955 ed.); TiPo; WaKn; WhBS; YeAr
Something wakes and stirs within me. On Hearing Jazz. Alice Phelps-Rider. PoMa
Sometime. *See also* Some Time.
Sometime. Jean McCrum. CAG
Sometime. May Riley Smith. BLPA; HBV; MaRV
Sometime [*or* Some time] at eve when the tide is low. Some Time at Eve [*or* When I Sail Away]. Elizabeth Clark Hardy. HBV; MaRV
Sometime I sigh, sometime I sing. Sir Thomas Wyatt. SiPS
Sometime It May Be. Arthur Willis Colton. HBV
(To Faustine.) AA; LEAP; OBAV
Sometime it may be pleasing to remember. Olim Meminisse Juvabit. Aline Kilmer. JKCP
Sometime, it may be, you and I. To Faustine [*or* Sometime It May Be]. Arthur Willis Colton. AA; HBV; LEAP; OBAV
Sometime, should I no longer flee forever. To His Dead Brother. Ugo Foscolo. OnPM
Sometime, Somewhere. Ophelia Guyon Browning. BLRP; PraP
(Pray without Ceasing.) BLPA; NeHB
Sometime [*or* Some time] there ben a lyttel boy. The Lyttel Boy. Eugene Field. AA; LEAP
Sometime this world was so steadfast and stable. *See* Som tyme this world . . .
Sometime we shall remember them, the little camping places. Black Ashes. Martha Haskell Clark. NLK
Sometime, when all life's lessons have been learned. Sometime. May Riley Smith. BLPA; HBV; MaRV
Sometime—when lilacs are in blossom. Sometime. Jean McCrum. CAG
Sometimes. Rose Fyleman. SiSoSe
Sometimes. Thomas S. Jones, Jr. BAP; BLP; HBV; InP; LBMV; LEAP; MaRV; OQP; PoMa; POT; PoTo; QP-2
Sometimes. *Unknown.* DDA
Sometimes/ I help my dad. Automobile Mechanics. Dorothy Baruch. FaPON; TiPo
Sometimes,/ Reading late in my bookroom. Gooseflesh. Vincent Starrett. DaM
Sometimes,/ I wish I knew the magic word. A Sometimes Wish. Mildred D. Shacklett. GFA
Sometimes a lantern moves along the night. The Lantern Out of Doors. Gerard Manley Hopkins. ChMo; EmBrPo; LiTB; OxBoCh
Sometimes a light surprises. In Him Confiding. William Cowper. MaRV; OlF
Sometimes a Little House Will Please. Elizabeth J. Coatsworth. BrR
Sometimes a right white mountain. Sky Pictures. Mary Effie Lee Newsome. CDC; GoSl
Sometimes a still small voice of music steals. The Harp. Jakob Jóhannesson Smári. IcP
Sometimes a waking dream my life will be. The Guardian Angel. Thomas S. Jones, Jr. UnW
Sometimes an effluence rises. Scarcely . . . Alfonso Reyes. AnMP
Sometimes, apart in sleep, by chance. The Trance. Stephen Spender. ChMP; CoBMV
Sometimes, as if forewarned, before we die. Views of Boston Common and Nearby. R. P. Blackmur. MoVE
Sometimes at evening travellers have heard. Delusions IV. Charles Madge. FaBoMo
Sometimes at night when human-kind. Sorrow Turned into Joy. John Alexander Bouquet. MaRV
Sometimes at night when the heart stumbles and stops. Caesura. Kenneth Mackenzie. BoAV
Sometimes, beneath the trees' green murmurous height. Sonnets on the Death of Laura, II. Petrarch. *Fr.* Sonnets to Laura. UnW
Sometimes deeply immured in white-washed tower. The Tingling Back. Karl Shapiro. FiMAP
Sometimes, for sport, the men of the crew. The Albatross. Baudelaire. ReMP
Sometimes God seems so far away. The Fault Is Mine. Edith M. Lee. PraP
Sometimes goldfinches one by one will drop. Goldfinches. Keats. GN
Sometimes he roars among the leafy trees. The Wind. W. H. Davies. SeCePo
Sometimes I am a tapster new. The Jolly Trades-Men. *Unknown.* CoMu
Sometimes I dare believe that time and space. I Dare Believe. Rose Mills Powers. BAP
Sometimes I fain would find in thee some fault. The Lamp's Shrine. Dante Gabriel Rossetti. The House of Life, XXXV. PoVP; ViPo
Sometimes I Feel like a Motherless Child. *Unknown.* BoAN-2, *with music;* OlF
Sometimes I Feel Like an Eagle in de Air. *Unknown.* NAMP; OnAP
Sometimes I have to cross the road. Bobby Blue. John Drinkwater. FaPON; GaP
Sometimes I hear fine ladies sing. Strong Moments. W. H. Davies. CMP
"Sometimes I hear my name." A Boy of Twenty. Horace Gregory. NV
Sometimes, I know not why, nor how, nor whence. Inspirations. William James Dawson. MaRV; WGRP
Sometimes I know the way. Absence. Charlotte Mew. ChMP; MoAB; MoBrPo
Sometimes I pause and sadly think. It Might Have Been Worse. G. J. Russell. PoToHe (new ed.)
Sometimes I say an extra prayer. The Extra Prayer. Annie Willis McCullough. PraP
Sometimes I see, against a storm-whipped sky. In the Storm. Stanton A. Coblentz. ChIP
Sometimes I seem to see gliding the green. Nilotic Elegy. G. S. Fraser. WaP
Sometimes I sit in the old arm chair. Sometimes. *Unknown.* DDA
Sometimes I think God grew tired of making. The Soul of a Mother. Margaret Sangster. PEDC
Sometimes I think my woman, she too sweet to die. Cornfield Holler. *Unknown.* ABF
Sometimes I think the hills. The Hills. Rachel Field. GFA
Sometimes, I think, the things we see. Phoebe Cary. *Fr.* Dreams and Realities. MaRV
Sometimes I walk in the shadow. Walking with God. *Unknown.* BLRP
Sometimes I wish that I his pillow were. Sonnet. Richard Barnfield. ReIE
Sometimes I wish that I might do. Patience. G. A. Studdert-Kennedy. OQP; QP-2; TrPWD
Sometimes I wonder what dead soldiers dream. Forgotten Wars. Grantland Rice. DDA
Sometimes I write with the stub of a pencil. The Poet Confides. Herbert T. J. Coleman. CaP
Sometimes, in a woman's brow. In a Woman's Face. Richard Church. LO; LoPS
Sometimes, in bitter fancy, I bewail. George Henry Boker. *Fr.* Sonnets. MOAP
Sometimes in bonnet that she. Heart-summoned. Jesse Stuart. GoYe
Sometimes, in morning sunlights by the river. Resurrection. Sidney Lanier. PoEL-5

Sometimes in summer months, the matrix [*or* gestate] earth. Summer Idyll. George Barker. FaBoMo; MoPo
Sometimes in the hills. Burma Hills. Bernard Gutteridge. WaP
Sometimes in the summer. Sprinkling. Dorothy Mason Pierce. SUS; TiPo
Sometimes it seems as if a dog can sense. Understanding. Margaret E. Bruner. AlBD
Sometimes it seems as though some puppet player. The Puppet Player. Angelina Weld Grimké. CDC
Sometimes I've seen. A Little Bird's Song. Margaret Rose. BoTP
Sometimes my brother lets me look. Neighbors. Helen Wing. GFA
Sometimes my thoughts in fervor teeming. Spanish Moonlight. Birger Sjöberg. AnSL
Sometimes, old pal, in the morning. Is It Really Worth the While? *Unknown.* BLPA
Sometimes passing late at night. Weldon House. August Derleth. DaM
Sometimes she is a child within mine arms. Heart's Haven. Dante Gabriel Rossetti. The House of Life, XXII. EmBrPo; EPN; OAEP; PoVP; ViPo; VLEP
Sometimes that promised glory haunts my sleep. Two Married, II. Helen Frazee-Bower. HBMV
Sometimes the girl on boyhood's silver screen. She Was the Girl within the Picture Frame. Delmore Schwartz. FiMAP
Sometimes the Man of Nazareth. When Spring Came to Nazareth. Mary Sinton Leitch. ChIP
Sometimes the pencil, in cool airy halls. James Thomson. *Fr.* The Castle of Indolence. PoEL-3
Sometimes the road was a twisted riddle. The Road's End. Theodosia Garrison. HBMV
Sometimes the sun turns hostile to men. The Hostile Sun. D. H. Lawrence. CaAE
Sometimes the weather is a man. The Weather. Nancy Byrd Turner. POT; PoTo
Sometimes thou seem'st not as thyself alone. Heart's Compass. Dante Gabriel Rossetti. The House of Life, XXVII. BPN; EmBrPo; EPN; Po; PoVP; ViPo; VLEP
Sometimes, tired, I imagine your death. To L. B. S. Winfield Townley Scott. FiMAP
Sometimes, to entertain themselves, the men of the crew. The Albatross. Baudelaire. WoL
Sometimes toward Eden, which now in his view. Satan in Sight of Eden. Milton. *Fr.* Paradise Lost, IV. TCEP
Sometimes, upon the coldest winter day. Snow-Drift. Hugo T. Saglio. CAG
Sometimes we go our way carefree. Rebirth. Margaret E. Bruner. PoToHe
Sometimes (we know not how, nor why, nor whence). Richard Realf. *Fr.* Symbolisms. UnW
Sometimes we peep beneath the blinds. The Tide. Marjorie Wilson. OTPC (1946 ed.); PCH
Sometimes w'en I am playin' with some fellers 'at I knows. Little Willie's Hearing. *Unknown.* FAOV; PTA-2
Sometimes we're bound to New York town and others we're bound to France. Heave Away, *vers.* II. *Unknown.* ShS
Sometimes, When after Spirited Debate. William Dean Howells. *See* Change.
Sometimes when all the world seems gray and dun. While Loveliness Goes By. Anna Hempstead Branch. MAP; MoAmPo (1942 ed.)
Sometimes when alone. The Outcast. "Æ." GTIV; LO; OxBI; POTE
Sometimes when fragrant summer dusk comes in with scent of rose and musk. Night for Adventures. Victor Starbuck. HBV
Sometimes when I am at tea with you. Things. Aline Kilmer. MCCG
Sometimes when I am very sick. His Promises. Martha Snell Nicholson. BePJ
Sometimes when I am walking in a wood. A Thought about Saint Francis. Denis A. McCarthy. SaFP
Sometimes when I come in at night. The Way He Used to Do. James W. Foley. FAOV
Sometimes when I feel hurried or dismayed. For One Who Is Serene. Margaret E. Bruner. PoToHe (new ed.)
Sometimes when I lie all alone. A Child-Thought. Wilfrid Thorley. PCH
Sometimes When I Sit Musing All Alone. Agnes Mary Frances Robinson. WHA
Sometimes when I think of things. Evidence. Arthur Kober. InMe
Sometimes when I wake up I lie. Roughchin, the Pirate. Arthur Boswell. EtS
Sometimes when it is bedtime. The Critic. John Farrar. GaP
Sometimes when life has gone wrong with you. A Friend. Esther Birdsall Darling. AlBD
Sometimes when morning lights the sky. God Is Near. Elizabeth McE. Shields. PraP
Sometimes, when Nature falls asleep. Night Mists. William Hamilton Hayne. AA
Sometimes When Night. V. Sackville-West. DiM
Sometimes when on night-herd I'm ridin', and the stars are a-gleam in the sky. The Range Rider's Soliloquy. Earle Alonzo Brininstool. PoOW
Sometimes, when the grind of the city beats on my heart. Memories. Charles Hanson Towne. OQP; QP-2
Sometimes, When Winding Slow. Frederick Goddard Tuckerman. AnNE
Sometimes wind and sometimes rain. Children's Song. Ford Madox Ford. HBV
Sometimes Wish, A. Mildred D. Shacklett. GFA
Sometimes with One I Love. Walt Whitman. BoFr; LoPo; LoPS
Sometimes, with Secure Delight. Milton. *Fr.* L'Allegro. MPB
Sometimes you hear, fifth-hand. Poetry of Departures. Philip Larkin. NePoEA
Sometimes you seem a star. Serenade. John Bunker. JKCP (1955 ed.)
Somewhar down thar round Hodgensville, Kaintucky. The Boy from Hodgensville. Robertus Love. GA
Somewhat apart from the village, and nearer the Basin of Minas. Evangeline in Acadie. Longfellow. *Fr.* Evangeline. AA
Somewhat back from the village street. Desolation. Tom Masson. PA
Somewhat back from the village street. The Old Clock on the Stairs. Longfellow. BLP; CoBA; HBV; IAP; OTPC; PTA-1; TCAP; WBLP
Somewhere. Sir Edwin Arnold. *See* Destiny.
Somewhere. John Vance Cheney. LBMV
Somewhere. J. C. Cochrane. OQP; QP-2
Somewhere. Walter de la Mare. BrR; FaPON
Somewhere a hungry muzzle rooted. Design for Mediaeval Tapestry. A. M. Klein. CaP
Somewhere a sapling is growing. Ponder It, O Soul! Eduard Mörike. AnGP
Somewhere afield here something lies. Shelley's Skylark. Thomas Hardy. CoBMV; PoVP; PtP; VLEP
Somewhere Beauty dwells, all undefiled. Prophecy. Nellie Burget Miller. BAP
Somewhere beneath the sun. Amaturus. William Johnson Cory. EV-5; GTBS; GTML; HBV
Somewhere—but where I cannot guess. Arthur Hugh Clough. *Fr.* Songs in Absence. EPN
Somewhere he failed me, somewhere he slipped [*or* slipt] away. The Lost Shipmate. Theodore Goodridge Roberts. BoCaPo; CaP; CPG; OCL
"Somewhere," he mused, "its dear enchantments wait." The Land of Heart's Desire. Emily Huntington Miller. HBV
Somewhere I Chanced to Read. Gustav Davidson. HBMV; TBM
Somewhere I Have Never Travelled [Gladly Beyond]. E. E. Cummings. AmPP; AnNE; AtBAP; BoLiVe (1939 ed.); CoBMV; FaBoEn; GTBS-W; LiTA; LiTL; LiTM; LoPS; MoAB; MoAmPo; MOAP; MoPo; OnAP; TrGrPo; TwAmPo
Somewhere I read a strange old rusty tale. Sangar. John Reed. NP
Somewhere I read, in an old book whose name. With the Tide. Edith Wharton. PEDC
Somewhere, in deeps. Sport. Hamlin Garland. BAP
Somewhere—in desolate wind-swept space. Identity. Thomas Bailey Aldrich. AA; AnNE; BAP; BPP; MAP; PFY; PoeMoYo; UnW
Somewhere-in-Europe-Wocky. F. G. Hartswick. BOHV
"Somewhere in France," upon a brown hillside. The First Three. Clinton Scollard. MC; PAH
Somewhere in India, upon a time. An Oriental Apologue. James Russell Lowell. PoEL-5
Somewhere in the division between aspiration. Exploration by Air: Solo (Teterboro Airport). A. Fleming MacLiesh. PoF
Somewhere inside of me. Altar Smoke. Rosalie Grayer. GoTP
Somewhere is music from the linnets' bills. The Lost Ones. Frances E. Ledwidge. TCEP
Somewhere Is Such a Kingdom. John Crowe Ransom. ChMo; LiTA
Somewhere it is always light. The Sun. Thomas Miller. OTPC (1923 ed.)
Somewhere Jack-in-the-Pulpit stands. Where the Wood-Thrush Calls. Jessie Wallace Hughan. TSW
Somewhere lost in the haze. Lord Dunsany. Songs from an Evil Wood, II. BMEP; MBP; MoBrPo (1942 ed.)
Somewhere, O sun, some corner there must be. Battle Sleep. Edith Wharton. VOD
Somewhere or Other. Christina Rossetti. AV; ViPo; VLEP
Somewhere, out on the blue seas sailing. When My Ship Comes In Robert Jones Burdette. FaFP; PTA-2

Somewhere people are peeling onions. Stanzas in the Infrared. Ethel Jacobson. DDA
Somewhere, somewhen I've seen. The Parrots. W. W. Gibson. CH
Somewhere there lies the dust. Somewhere. J. C. Cochrane. OQP; QP-2
Somewhere there waiteth in this world of ours. Destiny [*or* Somewhere]. Sir Edwin Arnold. MaRV; PoToHe (new ed.)
Somewhere they lie and are quiet. Who Hold the Steps Tonight. James Cresse, Jr. CAG
Somme Valley, The, 1917. Frank Prewett. MM
Somnambulant [*or* Somnambule *or* Somnambulistic] Ballad. Federico García Lorca. *See* Ballad Walking in Sleep.
Somnus, the Humble God. Sir John Denham. *Fr.* The Sophy. EPS (1942 ed.)
(Somnus.) SeCL
Son, A. Kipling. *Fr.* Epitaphs of the War. ChMP; PoVP
Son. Josephine Miles. FiMAP
Son, The. Ridgely Torrence. BAP; HBMV; InP; InvP; MAP; MoAmPo (1942 ed.); MotAn; NP; PFY; PoeMoYo; SBMV; TCPD; WaKn
Son am I of the rolling plain, A. The Departure of Martin Fierro. José Hernández. PoFr
Son and Mother. Cale Young Rice. LS
Son and Surf. Julia Hurd Strong. GoYe
Son Cotton! these light idle brooks. Izaac Walton, Cotton, and William Oldways. Walter Savage Landor. PoEL-4
Son-Dayes. Henry Vaughan. AtBAP
"Son, fit the grooves and join them well." The Carpenter's Son. Kathryn Blackburn Peck. BePJ
Son in December, A. Frank Kendon. POTE
Son just born, A. Mary Britton Miller. TiPo (1959 ed.)
Son, my son! Lament of a Man for His Son. *Tr. fr. Paiute Indian.* AWP; FAOV; JAWP; WBP
Son of a Gambolier, The, *with music. Unknown.* AS
Son of a Gun. *Unknown.* CoSo
Son of a mystic race, he came. Heinrich Heine. Ludwig Lewisohn. TrJP
"Son of Anchises, born of godly lineage." The Lower World (the Sibyl Speaks). Virgil. *Fr.* The Aeneid, VI. LaP
Son of Cronos spake, and bowed his dark brow in assent, The. Zeus on Olympus. Homer. *Fr.* The Iliad, I. LiA
Son of Erebus and Night. William Browne. *Fr.* The Inner Temple Masque. ElSeCe; ViBoPo
Son of God, The. Charles L. O'Donnell. JKCP
"Son of God am I, The," he humbly said. Good Friday. Alice B. Jurica. ChIP
Son of God goes forth for Peace, The. A Hymn of Peace. Ernest Bourner Allen. MaRV
Son of God Goes Forth to War, The. Reginald Heber. HBV; MaRV; OTPC; TreFS
(Who Follows in His Train?) WGRP
Son of God in the Wilderness, The; His Dream. Milton. *Fr.* Paradise Regained, II. EV-2
"Son of heaven and earth." Free to Serve. Milton. *Fr.* Paradise Lost, V. GrCo-2
Son of Man. Leslie Savage Clark. ChIP
Son of Man, The. Dorothy J. Langford. BePJ
Son of man shall come, The. Unto the Least. St. Matthew, Bible, *N.T.* GrCo-1
Son of the Father of heavenly bliss, The. Verbum Patris Hodie Processit ex Virgine. *Unknown.* AnEC
Son of the King of Moy, The. *Unknown, tr. fr. Old Irish by* Myles Dillon. AnIL
Son of the King of the River Muad, The. Love Epigram. *Unknown.* SiB
Son of the lightning and the light that glows. For the Feast of Giordano Bruno. Swinburne. PoFr; ViPo
Son of the Mountain. Eifion Wyn, *tr. fr. Welsh by* Gwyn Williams. PrWP
Son of the ocean isle! England's Dead. Felicia Dorothea Hemans. HBV
Son of the old moon-mountains African! To the Nile. Keats. HBV
Son of the Sea, A. Bliss Carman. EtS; NLK
Son of the Supreme Lord descends the northern stairway, The. The Lady of Hsiang. Chu Yuan. *Fr.* The Nine Songs. WhP
"Son," said my mother. The Ballad of the Harp-Weaver. Edna St. Vincent Millay. MaC; StPo; YT
Sona Dialect. David Evans. MoWP
Sonata and Destructions. "Pablo Neruda," *tr. fr. Spanish by* Angel Flores. AnCL
Sonatina. Rubén Darío, *tr. fr. Spanish by* G. W. Umphrey *and* Laura Forsberg. WoL
Sonet: "Fra bank to bank, fra wood to wood I rin." Mark Alexander Boyd. *See* Sonnet: "Fra bank to bank . . ."
Sonet, A: "Her face, her tongue, her wit." *At. to* Sir Walter Ralegh. *See* Her Face, Her Tongue, Her Wit.
Sonet, A: "His golden lockes, Time hath to silver turn'd." George Peele. *See* His Golden Locks . . .
Sonet to the Tune of A Hone a Hone, A. Nicholas Breton. SiCE
Sonetto: "Of all chaste birds the phoenix doth excel." Thomas Lodge. *See* Of Rosalind.
Song: "A ho! A ho!/ Love's horn doth blow." Thomas Lovell Beddoes. *See* Love Goes a-Hawking.
Song, A: "Absent from thee, I languish still." Earl of Rochester. CoEV; EnLoPo; EPS; FaBoEn; LoBV; MePo; OBS; PoFS; SeCePo; SeCV-2; SeEP; ViBoPo
(Absent from Thee [I Languish Still].) AEV; SeCL
("Absent from thee, I languish still!") LO
(Return.) OBEV
Song: "Across the Sea." William Allingham. IrPN
(Song: "I walk'd in the lonesome evening.") EnLoPo
Song: "Adieu, farewell, earth's bliss." Thomas Nashe. *See* Adieu, Farewell, Earth's Bliss!
Song: "After the pangs of a desperate lover." Dryden. *See* After the Pangs of a Desperate Lover.
Song: "Again rejoicing Nature sees." Burns. *See* Again Rejoicing Nature Sees.
Song: "Ah Cloris! that I now could sit." Sir Charles Sedley. *See* Child and Maiden.
Song: "Ah! County Guy, the hour is nigh." Sir Walter Scott. *See* County Guy.
Song: "Ah, fading joy! how quickly art thou past!" Dryden. *See* Ah, Fading Joy.
Song: "Ah, how sweet it is to love." Dryden. *See* Ah, How Sweet It Is to Love.
Song: "Ah, me! when shall I marry me?" Oliver Goldsmith. GTIV
Song: "Ah stay! ah turn! ah whither would you fly." Congreve. *Fr.* The Fair Penitent (*by* Nicholas Rowe). AtBAP; LoBV; OBEC
Song: "Ah, vale of woe, of gloom and darkness moulded." Rachel Morpurgo, *tr. fr. Hebrew by* Nina Davis Salaman. TrJP
Song: A-Hunting We Will Go. Henry Fielding. *See* A-Hunting We Will Go.
Song: "All in green went my love riding." E. E. Cummings. *See* All in Green . . .
Song: "All my love for my sweet." John Hall Wheelock. NP
Song: "All my past life is mine no more." Earl of Rochester. *See* Love and Life.
Song: "All service ranks the same with God." Robert Browning. *See* All Service Ranks the Same with God.
Song: "All the flowers of the spring." John Webster. *See* All the Flowers of the Spring.
Song: "Always before your voice my soul." E. E. Cummings. *See* Always before Your Voice.
Song: "Among the level valley lands." Aleksey Merzlyakov, *tr. fr. Russian by* C. M. Bowra. BoRS
Song: "And can the physician make sick men well?" *Unknown. See* And Can the Physician Make Sick Men Well.
Song: "And did those feet in ancient time." Blake. *See* And Did Those Feet in Ancient Time.
Song: "And ye maun braid your yellow hair." Swinburne. *Fr.* Mary Stuart. BPN
Song: "Apple, beach and cedar fair." *Unknown.* ADAH
Song: "April, April,/ Laugh thy girlish laughter." Sir William Watson. BLV; BMEP; CaAE; DD; HBV; HBVY; LEAP; MBP; MoBrPo (1942 ed.); OBVV; PoRL; PYM; TreF; TrGrPo; TSW; TSWC; YT
(April.) BoTP; GoTP; LBBV
(April, April.) NLK
(Song to April.) GN
Song: "Are they shadowes that we see?" Samuel Daniel. *See* Are They Shadows?
Song: "Art thou poor, yet hast thou golden slumbers?" Thomas Dekker. *See* Happy Heart, The.
Song: "As I lay in the early sun." Edward Shanks. BMEP
Song: As I Walked Out One Evening. W. H. Auden. *See* As I Walked Out One Evening.
Song: "Ask me no more: the moon may draw the sea." Tennyson. *See* Ask me no more: the moon may draw the sea.
Song, A: "Ask me no more where Jove bestows." Thomas Carew. *See* Ask Me No More Where Jove Bestows.
Song: "At setting day and rising morn." Allan Ramsay. HBV; LPS-1
Song: "Awake thee, my Bessy, the morning is fair." Jeremiah Joseph Callanan. IrPN; OnYI
Song: "Back and side go bare, go bare." *At. to* William Stevenson. *See* Back and Side Go Bare.
Song: "Balkis was in her marble town." Lascelles Abercrombie. *See* Balkis
Song, A: "Be not too quick to carve our rhyme." Herbert P. Horne. LEAP
Song: Beautiful Mistress, A. Thomas Carew. *See* Beautifull Mistress, A.
Song: "Beauty clear and fair." John Fletcher. *See* Beauty Clear and Fair.
Song: "Beauty no more the subject be." Thomas Nabbes. *Fr.* Hannibal and Scipio. SeCL; TuPP
Song: "Because I love, I weep." Mary Carolyn Davies. TBM
Song: "Because the rose must fade." Richard Watson Gilder. HBV
Song: "Bee to the heather, The." Sir Henry Taylor. OBVV

Song: "Before the barn-door crowing." John Gay. *See* Before the Barn-Door Crowing.
Song: "Before we shall again behold." Sir William Davenant. MeLP; SeEP
(Endimion Porter and Olivia.) MePo
(Song: Endymion and Olivia.) TriL
(Song: Endymion [*or* Endimion] Porter and Olivia.) MeRV; OBS
Song: "Bells of Sunday rang us down, The." John Ciardi. WaP
Song: "Belovèd, it is morn!" Emily Henrietta Hickey. *See* Belovèd, It Is Morn.
Song: "Beneath the poplar's shadow lay me." Nathaniel Lee. *Fr.* Sophonisba; or, Hannibal's Overthrow. BeR, 4 *ll.*
Song: "Bird in my bower, A." Francis Howard Williams. AA
Song: "Birds of the air, they sing it, The." John Vance Cheney. NLK
Song: Black-eyed Susan. John Gay. *See* Black-eyed Susan.
Song: "Blow, blow, thou winter wind." Shakespeare. *See* Blow, Blow, Thou Winter Wind.
Song: "Blow there, sweet Zephyrus!" *Unknown.* SeCL
Song: "Blushing rose and purple flower, The." Philip Massinger. *Fr.* The Picture, III, v. LiTL; ViBoPo
(Song of Pleasure, A.) SeCL
Song: "Boat is chafing at our long delay, The." John Davidson. BMEP; EBSV; OBEV; OBVV
Song: "Bone-aged is my white horse." Brenda Chamberlain. NeIP
(Song-Talysarn.) MoWP; NeBP
Song: "Bride, she wears a white, white rose—the plucking it was mine, The." Margaret Steele Anderson. SBMV
Song: Brignall Banks. Sir Walter Scott. *See* Brignall Banks.
Song: "Bring from the craggy haunts of birch and pine." John Todhunter. OBVV; PoVP; TIP
(O Mighty, Melancholy Wind.) OnYI
Song: Bunthorne. W. S. Gilbert. *See* Bunthorne's Song.
Song: "Call for the robin redbreast and the wren." John Webster. *See* Call for the Robin Redbreast.
Song: "Calm was the even, and cleer was the sky." Dryden. *See* Calm Was the Even, and Clear Was the Sky.
Song: "Can life be a blessing." Dryden. *See* Can Life Be a Blessing.
Song: "Can love be controll'd by advice?" John Gay. *Fr.* The Beggar's Opera. LoBV
Song: "Can you paint a thought? or number?" John Ford. *See* Can You Paint a Thought?
Song: "Care charming Sleep, thou easer of all woes." John Fletcher. *See* Care-charming Sleep.
Song: Cavalier, The. Sir Walter Scott. *See* Cavalier, The.
Song: Celia Singing. Thomas Carew. *See* Celia Singing ("You that think Love can convey").
Song "Child, is thy father dead?" Ebenezer Elliott. BCEP
Song: "Chloris farewell: I now must go." *At. to* Edmund Waller *See* Chloris Farewell.
Song, A: "Chloris, when I to thee present." *Unknown.* OBS
("Cloris when I to thee present.") SeCSL
Song: "Christ keep the Hollow Land." William Morris. *Fr.* The Hollow Land. PoD; PoEL-5; ThWaDe
(Hollow Land, The.) AtBAP; ChTr
Song: "Cloris, it is not thy disdaine." Sidney Godolphin. BrBE; MeLP
("Cloris, it is not thy disdaine.") EG
(To Chloris.) SeCL
(To the Tune of, In Fayth I Cannot Keepe My Fathers Sheepe.) OBS
Song: "Closes and courts and lanes." John Davidson. HBV; PoVP
Song: "Cold's the wind, and wet's the rain." Thomas Dekker. *See* Cold's the Wind.
Song: Colonel. W. S. Gilbert. *Fr.* Patience. PoVP
Song: "Come away, come away death." Shakespeare. *See* Come Away, Come Away, Death.
Song: 'Come away! come, sweet love!" *Unknown.* BrBE
Song: "Come. Celia, let's agree at last." John Sheffield. HBV
Song, A: "Come, cheer up, my lads, like a true British band." *Unknown.* PAH
Song: "Come down, O maid, from yonder mountain height." Tennyson. *See* Come Down, O Maid.
Song: "Come into the garden, Maud." Tennyson. *See* Come into the Garden, Maud.
Song: "Come, rest in this bosom, my own stricken deer." Thomas Moore. *See* Come, Rest in This Bosom.
Song "Come unto these yellow sands." Shakespeare. *See* Ariel's Song.
Song: "Cupid and my Campaspe played." John Lyly. *See* Apelles' Song.
Song: "Daughter of Egypt, veil thine eyes!" Bayard Taylor. AA; LBAP; LEAP
Song: "Day departs this upper air." Edward Coote Pinkney. MOAP; SFP
Song: "Dear, do not your fair beauty wrong." Thomas May. *See* Love's Prime.
Song: "Delicious beauty, that doth lie." *At. to* John Marston. EIL
Song: "Do I venture away too far." Keith Douglas. NePoEA
Song: "Do not fear to put thy feet." John Fletcher. *See* River God's Song, The.
Song: "Don't Tell Me What You Dreamt Last Night." Franklin P. Adams. FiBHP
Song: "Dorinda's sparkling wit, and eyes." Charles Sackville. CEP; OBS; SeCV-2; SeEP
(Dorinda.) CEP; OBEV (new ed.); SeCePo; SeCL
(On a Lady Who Fancied Herself a Beauty.) ElSeCe
Song: "Down lay in a nook my lady's brach." Sir Henry Taylor. *Fr.* Philip van Artevelde. VA
Song: "Down the dimpled green-sward dancing." George Darley. *See* Gambols of Children.
Song: "Draw near, and see." *Unknown.* SeCL
Song: "Dressed up in my melancholy." M. Carl Holman. PoNe
Song [*or* Songe], The: "Drink [*or* Drinke] and be merry, merry, merry boys [*or* boyes]." Thomas Morton. *Fr.* New English Canaan. AmPP; IAP
Song: "Drink and sing, and eat and laugh." Thomas Love Peacock. PoD
Song: "Drink today, and drown all sorrow." John Fletcher, *and others. See* Drink To-Day.
Song: "Earl March looked on his dying child." Thomas Campbell. *See* Maid of Neidpath, The.
Song: "Echo, tell me, while I wander." Addison. BOHV
Song: Endymion and Olivia. Sir William Davenant. *See* Song: "Before we shall again behold."
Song: Eternity of Love Protested. Thomas Carew. *See* Eternity of Love Protested.
Song: "Fain would I change that note." *Unknown. See* Fain Would I Change That Note.
Song: "Fair and fair, and twice so fair." George Peele. *See* Fair and Fair.
Song: "Fair, and soft, and gay, and young." Robert Gould. *Fr.* The Rival Sisters. CEP; SeCL
Song: "Fair Iris I love, and hourly I die." Dryden. *Fr.* Amphitryon, IV, i. AWP; JAWP; LiTL; WBP; WoL
(Fair Iris I Love.) InPo; OnPM
(Mercury's Song to Phaedra.) CEP; EPS (1942 ed.); LoPS; PoEL-3; SeCV-2
Song: "Fair is the night, and fair the day." William Morris. *See* Song from "The Story of Acontius and Cydippe."
Song: "Fair, sweet and young, receive a prize." Dryden. BrBE; LiTL; OBS; SeEP
(Fair, Sweet, and Young.) SeCL
Song: "Fairy band are we, A." Alfred Noyes. GBV (1922 ed.)
Song: "False though she be to me and love." Congreve. CaAE; EnLoPo; FaBoEn; LiTL; OBEC; ViBoPo
(False Though She Be.) EV-3; HBV; OBEV
Song: "Farewell, adieu, that courtly [*or* court-like] life!" John Pickering. *See* Haltersick's Song.
Song: "Farewell, ungrateful traitor!" Dryden. *See* Farewell, Ungrateful Traitor.
Song: "Fear no more the heat o' the sun." Shakespeare. *See* Fear No More the Heat o' the Sun.
Song: "Fearless follow, thou sad soul." *Unknown.* SeCL
Song: "Feathers of the willow, The." Richard Watson Dixon. CBE; CH; FaBoCh; GTBS-D; GTML; LoBV; LoGBV; OBVV; ThWaDe; ViP; YeAr
(Feathers of the Willow, The.) ShBV-4
(November.) GTSL
(Willow.) OBEV (new ed.)
Song: "Few more windy days, A." Helen Dudley. NP
Song: "Find me a lonely cave." *Unknown.* SeCL
Song: "Fine young folly, though you were." William Habington. *See* Fine Young Folly.
Song: "First month[s] of his absence, The." Alun Lewis. ChMP; LiTM; WaaP
Song: Fish in the Unruffled Lakes. W. H. Auden. *See* Fish in the Unruffled Lakes.
Song: "Flame at the core of the world." Arthur Upson. HBV
Song "Fleeing I go from death." Emilio Prados, *tr. fr. Spanish by* Eleanor L. Turnbull. CoSP
Song: "Flower-born Blodueda, The." Richard Hovey. *Fr.* The Marriage of Guenevere. OBAV
Song: "Flowers that in thy garden rise, The." Sir Henry Newbolt. FaBoTw
Song: "Fly, fly, you happy shepherds, fly." Sir John Vanbrugh. *See* Philira.
Song: "Fly hence, shadows, that do keep." John Ford. *See* Fly Hence Shadows.
Song: "Follow thy faire sunne, unhappy shadowe!" Thomas Campion. *See* Follow Thy Fair Sun.
Song: "Fond affection, hence, and leave me!" *At. to* Robert Parry. *Fr.* The Mirror of Knighthood. EIL
Song: "Fond men! whose wretched care the life soon ending." Phineas Fletcher. *Fr.* Brittain's Ida. EIL
Song: "Fool, take up thy shaft again." Thomas Stanley. EnLoPo

Song: "For her gait, if she be walking." William Browne. *See* Complete Lover, The.
Song: "For me the jasmine buds unfold." Florence Earle Coates. HBV; LBMV; NV; PoMa; VOD
(World Is Mine, The.) AA
Song, A: "For Mercy, Courage, Kindness, Mirth." Laurence Binyon. BMEP; BoTP; CP; HBMV; MBP; MoBrPo; WP
(For Mercy, Courage, Kindness, Mirth.) CBE; PC
Song: "For the tender beech and the sapling oak." Thomas Love Peacock. *Fr.* Maid Marian. ADAH; OHIP; PRWS
(For the Slender Beech and the Sapling Oak.) EnRP; ERP
(Greenwood Tree, The.) GTSE
(Oak and the Beech, The.) OTPC
Song: "Fortunate are the feet of the swallow." Walter James Turner. LO
Song: "Fortune smiles: cry holiday." Thomas Dekker. *See* Fortune and Virtue.
Song: "Four arms, two necks, one wreathing." *Unknown.* ElL
Song: "Fresh from the dewy hill, the merry year." Blake. CoBE; EiPP; EnLit; EnRP
Song: "Friend and lover mine." Dinis, King of Portugal, *tr. fr. Portuguese by* Aubrey F. G. Bell. CAW
Song: "Fringéd vallance of your eyes advance, The." Thomas Shadwell. *Fr.* Timon of Athens. ViBoPo
(Good-Morrow, A.) SeCL
Song: "From White's and Will's." Ambrose Philips. CEP
Song: "Full fathom [*or* fadom] five thy father lies." Shakespeare. *See* Ariel's Song: "Full fathom five . . ."
Song: "Gather Kittens while you may." Oliver Herford. PA
Song: "Girls, when I am gone away." Edward Dowden. GTIV
Song: "Give her but a least excuse to love me." Robert Browning. *Fr.* Pippa Passes, sc. ii. EPN; GTBS; GTSL; ViBoPo
Song, A: "Give me leave to rail at you." Earl of Rochester. EG; EPS
Song: "Give me more love or more disdain." Thomas Carew. *See* Mediocrity in Love Rejected.
Song: "Glories of our blood and state, The." James Shirley. *See* Death the Leveller.
Song: "Glories, pleasures, pomps, delights, and ease." John Ford. *See* Glories, Pleasures.
Song: "Go and catch a falling star." John Donne. ATP; AWP; BCEP; BOHV; BoLiVe; ElL; ElSeCe; EM-1; EnL; EnLi-1; EPS; EV-2; FaFP; HBV; InMe; InPo; JAWP; LEAP; LoBV; LoPo; MaPo; OAEP; OBEV; OuHeWo; PG (1945 ed.); PIAE; PreP; ReEn; ReIE; SeCeV; SeEP; SiTL; TOP; TrGrPo; TuPP; TwHP; ViBoPo; WBP; WHA
(Go and Catch a Falling Star.) BEL; EG; EnLit; GTBS-W; LiTB; LiTG; LiTL; PoRA; ReaPo; TwP; TyEnPo
(Goe, and Catche a Falling Starre.) AtBAP
(Song: "Goe, and catche a falling starre.") AnFE; EnLP; HoPM; MeLP; MePo; PoEL-2; SeCV-1
Song: "Go lovely Rose." Edmund Waller. *See* Go, Lovely Rose.
Song: "Go not, happy day." Tennyson. *See* Go Not, Happy Day.
Song: "Go with your tauntings, go." John Clare. OBRV
Song: "God Lyaeus, ever young." John Fletcher. *See* God Lyaeus.
Song: "Goe, and catche a falling starre." John Donne. *See* Song: "Go and catch a falling star."
Song: "Going down the old way." Margaret Widdemer. HBMV
Song: "Gold wings across the sea!" William Morris. *See* Gold Wings across the Sea.
Song: "Good day my heart, my sweetest life good day." Pierre de Ronsard, *tr. fr. French by* Alan Conder. TrFP
Song. "Good morrow, 'tis Saint Valentine's day." Shakespeare. *See* Tomorrow Is Saint Valentine's Day.
Song: "Grace and beauty has the maid." Gil Vicente. *See* Grace and Beauty Has the Maid.
Song: "Great is the rose." Nathalia Crane. *Fr.* Tadmor. MAP; MoAmPo (1942 ed.)
Song: Green Grow the Rashes. Burns. *See* Green Grow the Rashes.
Song: "Had I a heart for falsehood framed." Sheridan. *Fr.* The Duenna, I, v. CEP; HBV; OBEV; TIP
(Had I a Heart for Falsehood Framed.) EV-3
Song: "Hang sorrow, cast away care." *Unknown.* OBS
Song: "Happiest mortals once were we, The." George Granville. *See* Happiest Mortals Once Were We, The.
Song: "Hark, hark, the lark at heaven's gate sings." Shakespeare. *See* Hark! Hark! the Lark.
Song, A: "Hark! 'tis Freedom that calls, come, patriots, awake!" *Unknown.* PAH
Song: Harp, The. Sir Walter Scott. *Fr.* Rokeby, V. EV-4
Song: "Has summer come without the rose?" Arthur O'Shaughnessy. HBV; LEAP; VLEP
(Has Summer Come without the Rose?) VA
Song: "Hast thou seen." Heinrich von Morungen, *tr. fr. German by* Edgar Taylor. LyMA
Song, A: "Hast thou seen the down in the air." Sir John Suckling. *See* Song to a Lute, A.
Song, The: "Have pity (Grief) I can not pay." Peter Hausted. *See* Have Pity, Grief.
Song: "Haymakers, rakers, reapers, and mowers." Thomas Dekker *and* John Ford. *See* Country Glee.
Song: "He came unlook'd for, undesir'd." Sara Coleridge. *See* He Came Unlook'd For.
Song: "He found me sitting among flowers." Aubrey Thomas De Vere. IrPN
Song: "He or she that hopes to gain." *Unknown.* SeCL
Song: "Heap cassia, sandal-buds and stripes." Robert Browning. *See* Heap Cassia, Sandal-Buds and Stripes.
Song: "Hear, sweet spirit." Samuel Taylor Coleridge. *See* Invocation, An: "Hear, sweet spirit."
Song: "Hear, ye sullen Pow'rs below." Dryden. *Fr.* Oedipus. PoD
Song: "Heare ye Ladies that despise." John Fletcher. *See* Hear, Ye Ladies.
Song: "Hears not my Phyllis how the birds." Sir Charles Sedley. *See* Hears Not My Phyllis.
Song: "Heath this night must be my bed, The." Sir Walter Scott. *See* Heath This Night Must Be My Bed, The.
Song: "Hence, all you vain delights." John Fletcher *and* (*at.*) Thomas Middleton. *See* Melancholy.
Song: "Here she was wont to go, and here, and here!" Ben Jonson. Aeglamour's Lament.
Song: "Here the sudden iron sound." Arthur C. Coe. CAG
Song: "Here's a health unto His Majesty!" *Unknown, at. to* Jeremy Savile. EV-2
(Health unto His Majesty, A.) ChTr
(His Majesty's Health.) SeCL
Song: "Here's to the maiden of bashful fifteen." Sheridan. *See* Let the Toast Pass.
Song: "Heron is harsh with despair." Brenda Chamberlain. NeBP; NeIP
Song: "His golden locks time hath to silver turned." George Peele. *See* His Golden Locks.
Song: "Hither haste, and gently strew." Thomas Lovell Beddoes. EG
Song: "Hold back thy hours, dark Night, till we have done." Beaumont *and* Fletcher. *See* Bridal Song ("Hold back thy hours").
Song: "Home they brought her warrior dead." Tennyson. *See* Home They Brought Her Warrior Dead.
Song: "Honest lover whosoever [*or* whatsoever]." Sir John Suckling. ElSeCe; EPS
(Art of Love, The.) LO
Song: Hopeless Comfort, The. Robert Gould. CEP
Song: "Hot sun, cool fire, tempered with sweet air." George Peele. *See* Bethsabe's Song.
Song: "Hound was cuffed, The." Sidney Lanier. *See* Hound, The.
Song: "How blest are lovers in disguise!" George Farquhar. *Fr.* Love and a Bottle. SeCL
Song: "How blest he appears." Thomas Otway. *Fr.* Friendship in Fashion. SeCL
Song: "How can that tree but withered be." *Unknown.* ElL
Song: "How delicious is the winning." Thomas Campbell. *See* Freedom and Love.
Song: "How do I love you?" Irene Rutherford McLeod. HBV; VOD
Song: "How happy the lover." Dryden. *See* How Happy the Lover.
Song: "How happy were my days." Isaac Bickerstaffe. *Fr.* Love in a Village. OBEC
Song: "How many times do I love thee, dear?" Thomas Lovell Beddoes. *Fr.* Torrismond. AnFE; CaAE; LiTB; LiTG; LiTL; LoPo; OBEV (1st ed.); OBRV; PCD; PoEL-4; TrGrPo; VA; ViBoPo
(How Many Times.) TSW; TSWC
(How Many Times Do I Love Thee, Dear?) EnRP; ERP; GTBS-D; NeHB
Song: "How near to good is what is fair." Ben Jonson. *Fr.* Love Freed from Ignorance and Folly. LPS-2
Song: "How pleasant it is that always." Florence Smith. BLPA
Song: "How should I your true love know." Shakespeare. *See* How Should I Your True Love Know.
Song: "How strongly does my passion flow." Aphra Behn. EV-3
Song: "How sweet I roamed [*or* roam'd] from field to field." Blake. AtBAP; BCEP; BLV; BoLiVe; BrBE; CaAE; CH; ChER; ChTr; EiPP; EM-1; EnL; EnLi-2; EnLoPo; EnRP; EV-3; FaBoEn; GTBS-D; KN; LiTB; LiTG; LiTL; LoPS; OAEP; OBEC; PoE; PoEL-4; SeCeV; TCEP; TrGrPo; TVSH; ViBoPo; WHA; WP
(How Sweet I Roamed.) OTPC (1923 ed.); TyEnPo
(How Sweet I Roam'd from Field to Field.) EG; GTBS-W; MaPo; SeCePo

(Prisoner of Love.) PIAE
Song: "I am a passion; I am a flame." Gustavo Adolfo Bécquer, *tr. fr. Spanish by* Muna Lee. Rimas, XI. OnPM
("I am a passion; I am a flame.") TeCS
Song: "I came to the door of the House of Love." Alfred Noyes. HBV
Song: "I cannot change as others do." Earl of Rochester. *See* Constancy.
Song: "I can't be talkin' of love, dear." Esther Mathews. FaFP; LiTL; LiTM; LyMo; NePA; SiTL
Song: "I could make you songs." Dorothy Dow. HBMV
Song: "I dream'd that I woke from a dream." George Macdonald. VA
Song: "I feel a flame within, which so torments me." Dryden. *Fr.* Secret Love; or, The Maiden Queen. AWP; CoEV; JAWP; LiTL; LO; LoPS; WBP
(Hidden Flame, The.) OBEV
(I Feed a Flame Within [Which So Torments Me].) InPo; MaPo; SeCL
(Song of Secret Love, The.) BeR
Song: "I had a dove and the sweet dove died." Keats. *See* I Had a Dove.
Song: "I have halted my horse by the tree of the doves." "St.-J. Perse," *tr. fr. French by* T. S. Eliot. *Fr.* Anabasis. LiTW
Song: "I have twelve oxen that be fair and brown." *Unknown. See* I Have Twelve Oxen.
Song: "I kept neat my virginity." Glyn Jones. NeBP
Song: "I know a little garden close." William Morris. *See* I Know a Little Garden Close.
Song: "I know a room where tulips tall." V. Sackville-West. *Fr.* Mirage. AlDL
Song: "I know, I know." Arthur Cleveland Coxe. SDH
Song: "I know that any weed can tell." Louis Ginsberg. *See* I Know That Any Weed Can Tell.
Song: "I love the jocund dance." Blake. EiPP
("I love the jocund dance.") EG
Song: "I made another garden, yea." Arthur O'Shaughnessy. BMEP; CaAE; GTIV; HBV; LEAP; LoPo; OBEV; OBVV; PoVP; TCEP; VLEP
(New Love and the Old, The.) BLV; GTML; GTSL; MBP; MoBrPo (1942 ed.)
Song: "I make my shroud, but no one knows." Adelaide Crapsey. AnAmPo; HBV; LA; MAP; MoAmPo (1942 ed.); NP; SBMV; TOP
Song, The: "I met a ragged man." Theodore Roethke. CrMA; FiMAP
Song: "I pass all my hours in a shady old grove." *At. to* Charles II, King of England. SeCL
Song: "I prithee let my heart alone." Thomas Stanley. ElSeCe; ViBoPo
Song: "I prithee send me back my heart." Sir John Suckling. *See* I Prithee Send Me Back My Heart.
Song: "I promised Sylvia to be true." Earl of Rochester. SeCePo
Song: "I saw the day's white rapture." Charles Hanson Towne. HBV; OBAV
Song, A: I Thought No More Was Needed. W. B. Yeats. AtBAP
Song: "I try to knead and spin, but my life is low the while." Louise Imogen Guiney. *See* In Leinster.
Song: "I walk'd in the lonesome evening." William Allingham. *See* Song: "Across the Sea."
Song: "I wander'd by the brook-side." Richard Monckton Milnes. *See* Brookside, The.
Song: "I was brought up under the Stone Castle." Tsang Chih, *tr. fr. Chinese by* Arthur Waley. TrCh
Song: "I was so chill and overworn, and sad." Anna Wickham. BLV; CBOV; LoPS; MBP; MoBrPo; NeMA
Song: "I who love you bring." Theodore Spencer. AnFE; CoAnAm; TwAmPo
Song: "If a daughter you have, she's the plague of your life." Sheridan. *Fr.* The Duenna, I, iii. CEP; NeHB
Song: "If any wench Venus's girdle wear." John Gay. *Fr.* The Beggar's Opera, I, i. PoEL-3
Song: "If everywhere in the street." Denis Glover. Songs, II. AnNZ
Song, A: "If for a woman I would die." Countess of Winchilsea. ViBoPo
Song: "If I freely may discover." Ben Jonson. *See* If I Freely May Discover.
Song: "If I only had loved your flesh." V. Sackville-West. HBMV
Song: "If love were but a little thing." Florence Earle Coates. HBMV; LBMV; NV
Song: "If once I could gather in song." W. W. Gibson. OBVV; TOP
Song: "If she be not as kind as fair." Sir George Etherge. *See* If She Be Not as Kind as Fair.
Song: "If the heart of a man is deprest with cares." John Gay. *See* If the Heart of a Man.
Song: "If thou art sleeping, maiden." Gil Vicente, *tr. fr. Spanish by* Longfellow. AWP; JAWP; LiTW; WBP
Song: "If to be absent were to be." Richard Lovelace. *See* To Lucasta, [on] Going beyond the Seas.
Song, A: "If wine and music have the power." Matthew Prior. ATP (1935 ed.); CEP; LoBV
Song: "If ye would drink delight." Clément Marot, *tr. fr. French by* Alan Conder. TrFP
Song: "If you love God, take your mirror between your hands and look." Mahmud Djellaladin Pasha, *tr. fr. Turkish by* E. Powys Mathers. LiTW
Song: "If you refuse me once, and think again." Sir John Suckling. BrBE
Song: "I'll tell her the next time, said I." George Granville. *See* I'll Tell Her.
Song, A: "I'm a plain girl whose hands are stained with earth." Ivan Bunin, *tr. fr. Russian by* Babette Deutsch. TrRV
Song: "In a drear-nighted December." Keats. *See* Stanzas: "In a drear-nighted December."
Song: "In crystal towers and turrets richly set." Geffrey Whitney. *See* In Crystal Towers.
Song: "In his last bin Sir Peter lies." Thomas Love Peacock. *Fr.* Headlong Hall. OBRV; ViBoPo
(In His Last Binn Sir Peter Lies.) EnRP
Song: "In summer when the rose-bushes." Edith Sitwell. NP
Song, A: "In the air there are no coral-/ Reefs." Duncan Campbell Scott. PeCV; TwCV
Song, A: In the Name of a Lover, to His Mistress; Who Said, She Hated Him for His Grey Hairs, Which He Had at Thirty. William Wycherley. *See* To His Mistress, Who Said She Hated Him for His Grey Hairs.
Song: "In thy white bosom Love is laid." John Arthur Blaikie. VA
Song, A: "In vain you tell your parting lover." Matthew Prior. HBV
Song: "Indeed, my Caelia, 'tis in vain." Sir John Henry Moore. LO; OBEC
Song: Inviting the Influence of a Young Lady upon the Opening Year. Hilaire Belloc. *See* Song: "You wear the morning like your dress."
Song, A: "Is it only to-day." Tzu Yeh, *tr. fr. Chinese by* Henry H. Hart. PoHN
Song: "It autumne was, and on our hemispheare." William Drummond of Hawthornden. OBS
Song: "It is all one in Venus' wanton school." John Lyly. SeCePo
Song: "It is not Beauty I demand." George Darley. *See* Loveliness of Love, The.
Song: "It is the miller's daughter." Tennyson. *See* Miller's Daughter, The.
Song: "It was a friar of orders free." Thomas Love Peacock. *Fr.* Maid Marian. ViBoPo
Song: "It was a lover and his lass." Shakespeare. *See* It Was a Lover and His Lass.
Song: "I've taught thee love's sweet lesson o'er." George Darley. *Fr.* Sylvia; or, The May Queen. OBRV
(Romanzo to Sylvia.) VA
Song: "Jack and Joan they think no ill." Thomas Campion. *See* Jack and Joan.
Song: "Johnnie Crack and Flossie Snail." Dylan Thomas. *See* Johnnie Crack and Flossie Snail.
Song: "Join once again, my Celia." Charles Cotton. ViBoPo
Song: "Keep the dream alive and growing always." Edwin Rolfe. TrJP
Song: "Kind lovers, love on." John Crowne. *Fr.* Calisto. ALV; SeCL
(Kind Lovers, Love On.) InvP
Song: Kiss, The. Ben Jonson. *See* Song: "O, that joy so soon should waste."
Song: "Kiss me, sweet; the wary lover." Ben Jonson. *See* To Celia ("Kiss me, sweet . . .").
Song: "Ladies, though to your conquering eyes." Sir George Etherege. *Fr.* The Comical Revenge, V, iii. HBV; LO; OBEV (1st ed.); OBS
Song: "Lady, you are with beauties so enriched." Francis Davison. EIL
Song: "Lake and a fairy boat, A." Thomas Hood. HBV; OTPC (1946 ed.); PCH
(Lake and a Fairy Boat, A. MPB (1956 ed.)
Song: Landskip, The. William Shenstone. CEP; OBEC
(Landscape, The.) SeCePo
Song: "Lark now leaves his wat'ry nest, The." Sir William Davenant. *See* Lark Now Leaves . . . , The.
Song. "Lawn as white as driven snow." Shakespeare. *See* Lawn as White as Driven Snow.
Song: "Lay a garland on my hearse." Beaumont *and* Fletcher. *See* Aspatia's Song.
Song: "Lay your sleeping head, my love." W. H. Auden. *See* Lay Your Sleeping Head.
Song: "Lean out of the window." James Joyce. *See* Goldenhair.
Song: "Let it be forgotten, as a flower is forgotten." Sara Teasdale. *See* Let It Be Forgotten.

Song: "Let my voice ring out and over the earth." James Thomson. Sunday up the River, XVII. EmBrPo; HBV; MaRV; OBVV; POTT; VLEP
Song, A: "Let not the sluggish sleep." *Unknown. See* Let Not the Sluggish Sleep.
Song: "Let schoolmasters puzzle their brains." Goldsmith. *Fr.* She Stoops to Conquer, I, ii. OAEP; ViBoPo
("Let schoolmasters puzzle their brain.") EnLi-1 (1949 ed.)
(Three Jolly Pigeons, The.) PoRA
Song: "Let the bells ring, and let the boys sing." John Fletcher. *Fr.* The Spanish Curate, III, ii. OBS; TuPP
Song: "Let's sing a song together once." Louis Simpson. NePoAm
Song: "Life, in one semester." Charles G. Blanden. OQP; QP-2
Song: "Light of spring, The." Alice Duer Miller. AA
Song: "Like violets pale i' the spring o' the year." James Thomson. Sunday up the River, IX. OBVV
Song: "Linnet in the rocky dells, The." Emily Brontë. EmBrPo; EnLit; HBV; OAEP; PoVP; VA
(Linnet in the Rocky Dells, The.) OTPC
(My Lady's Grave.) EV-5; OBEV (1st ed.); OBVV; TOP
Song: "Little Black Rose shall be red at last, The!" Aubrey Thomas De Vere. *See* Little Black Rose, The.
Song: "Lo! here we come a-reaping, a-reaping." George Peele. *Fr.* The Old Wives' Tale. OBSC
Song: "Long betwixt love and fear Phillis tormented." Dryden. *See* Long betwixt Love and Fear.
Song, A: "Lord, when the sense of Thy sweet grace." Richard Crashaw. EPS (1942 ed.); MeRV; PoE; SeCeV; TriL; TrPWD; TwHP; ViBoPo
(Divine Love.) MaRV
(Ecstacy, An.) EV-2
(Song of Divine Love, A.) ElSeCe; GoBC
Song: "Lost is my quiet for ever." *Unknown. See* Lost Is My Quiet.
Song: "Lost, lost! yet come." Robert Browning. *See* Lost, Lost! Yet Come.
Song: "Love a thousand sweets distilling." James Shirley. *See* Love, a Thousand Sweets Distilling.
Song, A: "Love a woman! you're an ass." Earl of Rochester. BeR
Song: "Love and harmony combine." Blake. EnRP; LiTL
Song: Love Arm'd [*or* Armed]. Aphra Behn. *See* Song: "Love in fantastic triumph sate."
Song: "Love, by that loosened hair." Bliss Carman. BAP; HBV; VA
Song: "Love for such a cherry lip." Thomas Middleton. *Fr.* Blurt, Master Constable. EG; ElL; ElSeCe; ViBoPo
(Lips and Eyes.) HBV
Song: "Love in fantastic [*or* fantastique] triumph sate [*or* satt]." Aphra Behn. *Fr.* Abdelazer. AtBAP; EV-3; HBV; OBEV; TrGrPo; ViBoPo
(Love Armed.) ElSeCe; SeCL
(Love in Fantastic[k] Triumph [Sate].) DiM; OAEP; OnPM
(Song: Love Arm'd [*or* Armed].) CaAE; CoEV; OBS
Song: "Love in her eyes sits playing." John Gay. *See* Love in Her Eyes Sits Playing.
Song: "Love in my heart: oh, heart of me, heart of me." "Fiona Macleod." AA
Song: "Love is a sickness full of woes." Samuel Daniel. *See* Love Is a Sickness.
Song: "Love is cruel, Love is sweet." Thomas MacDonagh. ACP
Song: Love Is like a Lamb. Thomas Middleton. *Fr.* Blurt, Master Constable. AtBAP
Song: "Love is the blossom where there blows." Giles Fletcher. *See* Wooing Song.
Song: "Love laid his sleepless head." Swinburne. BLV; BoLiVe; PIAE; TrGrPo
Song: "Love lives beyond the tomb." John Clare. OBVV; TOP
(Love.) ChTr
("Love lives beyond.") GTBS-D
(Love Lives beyond the Tomb.) FaBoEn; RO
Song: "Love, love me only." Robert Crawford. BoAu
Song: "Love, love today, my dear." Charlotte Mew. MBP; MoBrPo
Song: "Love me because I am lost." Louise Bogan. AV; MOAP; NP; PG (1955 ed.)
Song: "Love still has something of the sea." Sir Charles Sedley. CEP; CoEV; ElSeCe; EPP; EPS (1942 ed.); EV-3; FaBoEn; HBV; NBE; OBS; SeCV-2; SeEP; ViBoPo
(Love Still Has Something of the Sea.) AEV; EtS; LoBV; SeCL
Song: "Love that is hoarded, moulds at last." Louis Ginsberg, *wr. at. to* Harold C. Sandall. MaRV; PoToHe (new ed.)
Song: "Love, that looks still on your eyes." William Browne. EG
Song, A: "Love, thou art best of human joys." Countess of Winchilsea. *See* On Love.
Song: "Love took my life and thrill'd it." Lewis Morris. OBVV; VA
(Surface and the Depths, The.) HBV
Song: "Love was true to me." John Boyle O'Reilly. *See* Love Was True to Me.
Song: "Lovely hill-torrents are." W. J. Turner. MBP; MoBrPo
Song: "Lovely kind and kindly loving." Nicholas Breton. *See* Odd Conceit, An.
Song: "Lovers, avoid the shafts that fly." Charles d'Orléans, *tr. fr. French by* Ralph N. Currey. FoS
Song: "Love's but the frailty of the mind." Congreve. *See* Love's but the Frailty of the Mind.
Song: "Love's on the highroad." Dana Burnet. HBV; PFE; PoMa; POT; PoTo; PR; PrPoTo; VOD
Song: "Low whispers the wind from Malaya." Jayadeva, *tr. fr. Sanskrit by* Sir Edwin Arnold. *Fr.* The Gita Govinda. LiTW
Song: "Maid of Athens, ere we part." Byron. *See* Maid of Athens, Ere We Part.
Song: "Maidens came, The." *Unknown. See* Maidens Came, The.
Song: "Man's a poor deluded bubble." Robert Dodsley. CEP
Song: "Mars in a fury 'gainst love's brightest queen." Robert Greene. *See* Mars and Venus.
Song: Mary Morison. Burns. *See* Mary Morison.
Song: "Mary, the mother, sits on the hill." Langdon Elwyn Mitchell. *See* Carol: "Mary, the mother . . ."
Song: May Morning, A. Milton. *See* Song on May Morning.
Song: "Maydens came, The." *Unknown. See* Maidens Came, The.
Song: "Me Cupid made a happy slave." Sir Richard Steele. OBEC
Song: "Memory, hither come." Blake. BCEP; EG; EiPP; EnLit; EV-3; LiA; PoEL-4
Song: "Men of thought! be up and stirring." Charles Mackay. PoFr
Song: "Merchant, to secure his treasure, The." Matthew Prior. *See* Ode, An: "Merchant to secure his treasure, The."
Song: "Merry waves dance up and down, and play, The." Abraham Cowley. *See* Sport.
Song: "Methinks the poor town has been troubled too long." Charles Sackville. *See* Bonny Black Bess.
Song: Miller's Daughter, The. Tennyson. *See* Miller's Daughter, The.
Song: "Moth's kiss, first! The." Robert Browning. *See* Moth's Kiss, First, The.
Song: "My days have been so wondrous free." Thomas Parnell. *See* My Days Have Been So Wondrous Free.
Song: "My dear mistress has a heart." Earl of Rochester. HBV; LiTL; LoBV; SeCV-2
(Jealousy.) LoPo
(My Dear Mistress.) SeCL
Song: "My dreams were doleful and drear." Thomas Caulfield Irwin. IrPN
Song: "My Fair, no beauty of thine will last." Alice Meynell. VA
Song: "My gen'rous heart disdains." Francis Hopkinson. PreP
Song: "My limbs I will fling." William Strode. *Fr.* The Floating Island. CenL; SeCL
Song: "My lodging it is on the cold ground." Sir William Davenant. *Fr.* The Rivals. SeCL
Song: "My love bound me with a kiss." *At. to* Thomas Campion. *See* Kisses.
Song: "My love is the flaming sword." James Thomson. Sunday up the River, XVI. EmBrPo; OBVV
Song: "My luve is like a red, red rose." Burns. *See* Red, Red Rose, A.
Song: My Nanie, O. Burns. *See* My Nanie, O.
Song: "My shag-hair Cyclops, come, let's ply." John Lyly. *See* Song in Making of the Arrows, The.
Song: "My silks and fine array." Blake. BEL; CBE; CBOV; CEP; CoBE; EG; EiPP; EM-1; EnLi-2; EnLit; EnRP; EV-3; FaBoEn; GTBS-D; HBV; LoBV; OAEP; OBEC; OBEV (1st ed.); PoD; PoE; TOP; TrGrPo
(My Silks and Fine Array.) BLV; BoLiVe; ChTr; LEAP; TyEnPo
Song: "My spirit like a shepherd boy." V. Sackville-West. HBMV
Song: "My true love hath my heart, and I have his." Sir Philip Sidney. *See* My True Love Hath My Heart.
Song: "My windows open to the autumn night." Lionel Johnson. *See* Cadgwith.
Song: "Nay, but you, who do not love her." Robert Browning. AnFE; BLV; BoLiVe; BPN; EmBrPo; EPN; EPP; GTBS-W; HBV; LiTL; LoPS; MaPo; OBEV (1st ed.); PIAE; PoVP; TrGrPo; ViBoPo; VLEP
Song: "Neath blue-bell or streamer." Poe. *Fr.* Al Aaraaf. AmPP; AnFE; APA; CoAnAm; IAP; NePA; OxBA

Song: "Neither sighs, nor tears, nor mourning." *Unknown.* SeCL

Song: "Never seek to tell thy love." Blake. *See* Love's Secret.

Song: "Night has a thousand eyes, The." Francis William Bourdillon. *See* Night Has a Thousand Eyes, The.

Song: "Night is an ancient sorceress, The." Simeon S. Frug, *tr. fr. Yiddish by* Isaac Goldberg. LiTW

Song: "Nightingale, as soon as April bringeth, The." Sir Philip Sidney. *See* Nightingale, The.

Song: "No, no, fair heretic[k], it needs must be." Sir John Suckling. *Fr.* Aglaura, IV, i. AtBAP; LiTL; LoBV; OBS; ReEn; RiBV; SeEP

Song: "No, no, no, no, I cannot hate my foe." Sir Philip Sidney. SiPS

Song: "No, no, no, no, resistance is but vain." Anthony Henly. SeCL

Song: "No, no, poor suff'ring heart no change endeavour." Dryden. *See* No, No, Poor Suffering Heart.

Song: "No, no, the falling blossom is no sign." George Meredith. EnLit

Song: Noble Name of Spark, The. *At. to* the Earl of Rochester *and to* Thomas D'Urfey. *See* Bully, The.

Song: "Noe more unto my thoughts appeare." Sidney Godolphin. MePo; MeLP
(Quatrains.) OBS

Song: "Not, Celia, that I juster am." Sir Charles Sedley. *See* To Celia.

Song: "Not faster yonder rowers' might." Sir Walter Scott. *Fr.* The Lady of the Lake, II. EV-4

Song: "Not from the whole wide world I chose thee." Richard Watson Gilder. The New Day, Pt. IV, Song IV. AA; LBAP

Song, A: "Not he, that knows how to acquire." Thomas May. *See* Not He That Knows.

Song: "Not to sigh and to be tender." Aphra Behn. *Fr.* Lycidus. CaAE

Song: "Nothing I have is worth a tear." E. N. da Costa Andrade. POTE

Song: "Now are the Tritons heard, to Loving-land to call." Michael Drayton. *Fr.* Polyolbion. AtBAP

Song: "Now do the birds in their warbling words." Patrick Hannay. SeCL

Song: "Now go I quietly." Garcilaso de la Vega, *tr. fr. Spanish by* Beatrice Gilman Proske. TeCS

Song: "Now I see thy looks were feigned." Thomas Lodge. *See* Ode, An: "Now I find thy looks were feigned."

Song: "Now is the month of maying." *Unknown.* EG; OBSC

Song: "Now sleeps the crimson petal." Tennyson. *See* Now Sleeps the Crimson Petal.

Song: "Now that Fate is dead and gone." Edith Sitwell. MoAB; MoBrPo (1950 ed.); NeMA

Song: "Now the lusty spring is seen." John Fletcher. *See* Love's Emblems.

Song: "Now the purple night is past." Alfred Noyes. *Fr.* Drake, I. ChMo; CMP

Song: "Now winter nights enlarge." Thomas Campion. *See* Now Winter Nights Enlarge.

Song: "Nymphs and shepherds, dance no more." Milton. *Fr.* Arcades. AtBAP; ElSeCe; FiP; SeCL; ViBoPo

Song: "O bird, thou dartest to the sun." Maria White Lowell. AA; LBAP

Song: "O Brignall banks are wild and fair." Sir Walter Scott. *See* Brignall Banks.

Song: "O come, soft rest of cares! come, Night!" George Chapman. *See* Bridal Song ("O come . . .")

Song: "O Death, that maketh life so sweet." William Morris. *See* O Death, That Maketh Life So Sweet.

Song: "O diviner air." Tennyson. *Fr.* The Sisters. BPN

Song: "O, do not wanton with those eyes." Ben Jonson. *See* O, Do Not Wanton.

Song: "O fair! O sweet! when I do look on thee." Sir Philip Sidney. SiPS
(O Faire! O Sweete!) AtBAP

Song: "O fair[e] sweet face, O eyes celestial[l] bright." John Fletcher. *Fr.* Women Pleas'd. OBS; PoEL-2

Song: "O fly not, Pleasure, pleasant-hearted Pleasure." Wilfrid Scawen Blunt. *Fr.* The Love Lyrics of Proteus: A Rhapsody. JKCP; OBEV (1st ed.); OBVV; ViBoPo

Song: "O harmless feast." Barten Holyday. *Fr.* Technogamia. ElL

Song: "O heart that gave its first sweet love!" Joseph William Holden. NoCaPo (rev. ed.)

Song: "O, I have been in the land where you were born." Olga Berggolts, *tr. fr. Russian by* Jack Lindsay. *Fr.* Parting. RuPo

Song: "O, inexpressible as sweet." George E. Woodberry. *See* O, Inexpressible as Sweet.

Song: "O, it was out by Donnycarney." James Joyce. Chamber Music, XXXI. MBP; MoBrPo; OBVV

Song: "O lady, leave thy silken thread." Thomas Hood. HoPM

Song: "O, let the solid ground." Tennyson. Maud, I, xi. BPN; GEPC; HBV

Song: "O, like a queen's her happy tread." Sir William Watson. HBV

Song: "O Love, how strangely sweet." John Marston. *See* O Love, How Strangely Sweet.

Song: "Oh Love! that stronger art than wine." *At. to* Aphra Behn, *also to* —— Ousley. *Fr.* The Lucky Chance (*by* Aphra Behn). BrBE; LO
(Of Love.) SeCL

Song: "'Oh! Love,' they said, 'is King of Kings.'" Rupert Brooke. HBV; TSW; TSWC

Song: "O lovely April, rich and bright." Gustave Kahn, *tr. fr. French by* Ludwig Lewisohn. TrJP

Song: "O lovers, this song I give to you." A. R. D. Fairburn. *Fr.* To Daphnis and Chloe in the Park. AnNZ

Song: "O memory, thou fond deceiver." Goldsmith. *See* Memory.

Song: "Oh mistress mine, where are you roaming?" Shakespeare. *See* O Mistress Mine.

Song: "Oh, my love was more hot." Aleksey Koltsov, *tr. fr. Russian by* C. M. Bowra. BoRS

Song: "O my luve's like a red, red rose." Burns. *See* Red, Red Rose, A.

Song: "O Nancy, wilt thou go with me?" Thomas Percy. *See* O Nancy, Wilt Thou Go with Me?

Song: "Oh, no more, no more, too late." John Ford. *Fr.* The Broken Heart, IV, iii. BrBE; KN; LO; LoBV; OBS; PoEL-2; SeCePo; SeEP; ViBoPo
(Now Love Dies.) SeCL
(Oh No More, No More, Too Late.) AtBAP; TuPP

Song: "Oh roses for the flush of youth." Christina Rossetti. BPN; EmBrPo; GTBS; LoBV; ViBoPo; ViPo
(Roses for the Flush of Youth.) BMEP

Song: "O ruddier than the cherry." John Gay. *See* O Ruddier than the Cherry.

Song: "O say not that my heart is cold." Charles Wolfe. EV-4

Song: "Oh! say not woman's love [*or* heart] is bought." Isaac Pocock, *wr. at. to* Thomas Love Peacock. *Fr.* The Heir of Vironi. HBV

Song: "O shadie vales, O faire inriched meades." Thomas Lodge. *See* Sonnet: "O shady vales . . ."

Song: "O sing unto my roundelay." Thomas Chatterton. *See* Minstrel's Song.

Song: "O Sorrow,/ Why dost borrow." Keats. *See* Song of the Indian Maid.

Song: "Oh! Sorrow, Sorrow, scarce I knew." Charlotte Mew. BrBE; MM

Song: "O spirit of the Summertime!" William Allingham. IrPN

Song: "O stay, Madonna! stay." Macaulay. EtPaEn

Song: "O, strew the way with rosy flowers." James Clarence Mangan. IrPN

Song: "O Swallow, Swallow, flying, flying South." Tennyson. *See* O Swallow, Swallow . . .

Song: "O sweet delight, O more than human bliss." Thomas Campion. *See* O Sweet Delight.

Song: "O, that joy so soon should waste." Ben Jonson. *Fr.* Cynthia's Revels, IV, iii. LiTL; ViBoPo
(Kiss, The.) HBV
(Oh, That Joy So Soon Should Waste.) TuPP
(Song: Kiss, The.) EV-2

Song: "Oh! that we two were Maying." Charles Kingsley. *Fr.* The Saint's Tragedy. HBV; VA

Song: "Oh, the fickle state of lovers!" Francis Quarles. *See* O, the Fickle State of Lovers.

Song: "O thou that sleep'st like pig in straw." Sir William Davenant. *Fr.* News from Plymouth. CenL; EG; ElSeCe; SeCL; SeEP
(O Thou That Sleep'st like Pig in Straw.) InvP

Song: "Oh welcome, bat and owlet gray." Joanna Baillie. EV-3

Song: "'O where are you going?' said reader to rider." W H. Auden. *See* O Where Are You Going.

Song: "Oh, why did e'er my thoughts aspire." Charles Sackville. SeCL

Song: "Oh, you hear sweet music." John McClure. LS

Song: "O'er desert plains, and rushy meers." William Shenstone. *See* O'er Desert Plains and Rushy Meers.

Song: "O'er the hills far away, at the birth of the morn." Francis Hopkinson. IAP

Song: "O'er [*or* O're] the smooth enamel[l]ed green." Milton. *Fr.* Arcades. BLV; BoLiVe; ElSeCe; LEAP; LoBV; OBEV; SeCL; ThWaDe; TrGrPo; ViBoPo
(O'er [*or* O're] the Smooth Enamelled Green.) AtBAP; InPo

Song: "Of all the torments, all the cares." William Walsh. *See* Rivals.

Song: "Of Pan we sing, the best of singers, Pan." Ben Jonson. *Fr.* Pan's Anniversary. ElSeCe

Song: "Of thee (kind boy) I ask no red and white." Sir John Suckling. *See* Sonnet: "Of thee (kind boy) . . ."

Song: "Often I have heard it said." Walter Savage Landor. *See* Her Lips.
Song: "Old Adam, the carrion crow." Thomas Lovell Beddoes. *Fr.* Death's Jest Book, V, iv. ChER; EPP; LiTB; OBRV; PoD; PoEL-4; TOP
(Carrion Crow, The.) TrGrPo
(Old Adam, the Carrion Crow.) EnRP; ERP; PoMS
(Song That Wolfram Heard in Hell, The.) NBE
(Wolfram's Song.) BCEP; EV-4; GTBS-D; OBEV; OBVV; SiTL
Song: "Old England is eaten by knaves." Alexander McLachlan. *Fr.* The Emigrant. BoCaPo
Song: "Old Farmer Oats and his son Ned." John Jay Chapman. PoEL-5
Song: "On a day—alack the day." Shakespeare. *See* On a Day—Alack the Day!
Song: On Captain Barney's Victory over the Ship *General Monk.* Philip Freneau. PAH
Song: "On the Eastern Way at the city of Lo-yang." Sung Tzu-hou, *tr. fr. Chinese by* Arthur Waley. TrCh
Song: "On thy waters, thy sweet valley waters." Thomas Holley Chivers. *See* Georgia Waters.
Song: "Once my heart was a summer rose." Edith Sitwell. ChMP; GTBS-D
Song: "One day the god of fond desire." James Thomson. EnLoPo
Song: "One gloomy eve I roam'd about." John Clare. EG
Song: One Hard Look. Robert Graves. *See* One Hard Look.
Song: "Only a little while since first we met." Brian Hooker. HBMV
Song: "Only joy, now here you are." Sir Philip Sidney. *See* Only Joy, Now Here You Are.
Song: "Only tell her that I love." Lord Cutts. BCEP; HBV; OBEV (1st ed.)
(Only Tell Her That I Love.) SeCL
Song: "Or love me less [*or* mee lesse], or love me more." Sidney Godolphin. ElSeCe; MePo; OBS; SeCL; SeEP
Song: "O're the smooth enamel'd green." Milton. *See* Song: "O'er the smooth enameled green."
Song: "Orpheus with his lute made trees." *At. to* Fletcher, *also to* Shakespeare. *See* Orpheus with His Lute.
Song: "Out upon it, I have loved." Sir John Suckling. *See* Constant Lover, The.
Song: "Over hill, over dale." Shakespeare. *See* Over Hill, over Dale.
Song: "Over the sea our galleys went." Robert Browning. *Fr.* Paracelsus, Pt. IV. BPN; OBRV; VA
(Over the Sea Our Galleys Went.) EmBrPo; EV-5; PoVP
(Song from "Paracelsus.") SG
(Wanderers, The.) OBEV; OBVV
Song: Owl, The. Tennyson. *See* Owl, The.
Song: "Pack, clouds, away, and welcome day." Thomas Heywood. *See* Pack, Clouds, Away.
Song: "Peace, wayward barne! O cease thy moan!" Richard Brome. *Fr.* The Northern Lass. SeCL
Song: "Peasant sun went crushing grapes, The." Laurence Dakin. *Fr.* Tancred, I, i. CaP
Song: Perswasions to Enjoy. Thomas Carew. *See* Persuasions to Joy.
Song: "Phillis, for shame let us improve." Charles Sackville. *See* Song: "Phyllis, for shame . . ."
Song: "Phillis is my only joy." Sir Charles Sedley. *See* Phyllis Is My Only Joy.
Song: "Phillis, let's shun the common Fate." Sir Charles Sedley. SeCV-2
("Phillis, let's shun the common fate.") LO
Song: "Phoebus, arise." William Drummond of Hawthornden. *See* Phoebus, Arise!
Song: "Phyllis [*or* Phillis], for shame, let us improve." Charles Sackville. BrBE; CEP; ElSeCe; SeCV-2
(Advice, The.) EPS (1942 ed.); SeCL
(Phillis for Shame Let Us Improve.) OBS
Song: "Phyllis [*or* Phillis] is my only joy." Sir Charles Sedley. *See* Phyllis Is My Only Joy.
Song: "Pious Selinda goes to prayers." Congreve. *See* Pious Selinda.
Song: "Place in thy memory, dearest, A." Gerald Griffin. *See* Place in Thy Memory, A.
Song: "Pleasures of love, and the joys of good wine, The." Sir George Etherege. *Fr.* The Man of Mode, IV, i. CEP
Song: "Poor old pilgrim Misery." Thomas Lovell Beddoes. *See* Hesperus Sings.
Song: "Poppies paramour the girls." Haniel Long. HBMV; LEAP
Song, A: "Pouring music, soft and strong, The." Frederic William Henry Myers. VA
Song: "Pride and ambition, and peevishness too." *Unknown.* SeCL
Song: "Primrose in the green forest, The." Thomas Deloney. *Fr.* The Gentle Craft. AIDL; TiPo (1959 ed.); ViBoPo
Song: "Proverb reporteth, no man can deny, The." *Unknown.* *Fr.* Tom Tyler and His Wife, sc. i. ElSeCe
Song: "Pursuing beauty, men descry." Thomas Southerne. *Fr.* Sir Antony Love. SeCL
(Song in the Second Act, A.) SeEP
Song: "Queen and huntress, chaste and fair." Ben Jonson. *See* Hymn to Diana.
Song: "Quoth tongue of neither maid nor wife." Sir Henry Taylor. *See* Elena's Song.
Song: "Rarely, rarely, comest thou." Shelley. BPN; CBE; CBOV; EM-2; EmBrPo; EnRP; EPN; ERP; EV-4; HBV; OAEP; OBRV; TrGrPo
(Invocation: "Rarely, rarely, comest thou.") GTBS; GTBS-D; GTBS-W; GTSE
(Invocation: To the Spirit of Delight.) BLV
(Rarely, Rarely, Comest Thou.) CH
(Spirit of Delight.) BoLiVe
"I love snow and all the forms," 3 *ll.* TiPo (1959 ed.)
Song: "Ribs and terrors in the whale, The." Herman Melville. *See* Father Mapple's Hymn.
Song: "Rise Lady Mistresse, rise." Nathaniel Field. *See* Rise, Lady Mistress, Rise!
Song: "Room, room for a blade of the town." *At. to* the Earl of Rochester *and to* Thomas D'Urfey. *See* Bully, The.
Song: "Rose-cheekt Laura, come." Thomas Campion. *See* Rose-cheeked Laura.
Song: "Roses and pinks will be strewn where you go." Sir William Davenant. *Fr.* The Unfortunate Lovers. ViBoPo
Song: "Roses, their sharp spines being gone." Fletcher *and* Shakespeare. *See* Bridal Song.
Song: "Rousing to rein his pad's head back." Geoffrey Taylor. NeIP; OxBI
Song: "Sabrina fair." Milton. *See* Sabrina Fair.
Song: Scrutiny, The. Richard Lovelace. ReEn
Song: "See, how like twilight slumber falls." Charles Cotton. CaAE; SeCL
(Song; Set by Mr. Coleman.) OBS
Song: "See, O See!/ How every tree." George Digby, Earl of Bristol. *Fr.* Elvira. SeCL
Song: "See, see, she wakes! Sabina wakes!" Congreve. HBV
Song: "Seek not the tree of silkiest bark." Aubrey Thomas De Vere. JKCP; OBVV; PoVP; VA
Song: "Shake off your heavy trance." Francis Beaumont. *See* Shake Off Your Heavy Trance.
Song: "Shall I tell you whom I love?" William Browne. *See* Shall I Tell You Whom I Love?
Song: "Shape alone let others prize, The." Mark Akenside. HBV; LPS-1
Song: "She comes not when noon is on the roses." Herbert Trench. *See* She Comes Not When Noon Is on the Roses.
Song: "She goes all so softly." Edward J. O'Brien. SBMV
Song: "She has left me, my pretty." Sylvia Townsend Warner. MBP; MoAB; MoBrPo
Song: "She is not fair to outward view." Hartley Coleridge. BBV (1951 ed.); CaAE; EG; EnRP; ERP; EV-4; GTBS; GTBS-D; GTBS-W; GTSE; GTSL; HBV; LEAP; MCCG; OBEV; OBRV; OBVV; TreFS; VA; ViBoPo
(She Is Not Fair to Outward View.) LiTL; LPS-1; PIAE; TOP
Song: "She spoke to me gently with words of sweet meaning." Patrick MacDonogh. NeIP
Song: "She whom I love will sit apart." Gerald Gould. MBP; MoBrPo (1942 ed.)
Song: "Shepherd, who can pass such wrong." Jorge de Montemayor, *tr. by* Bartholomew Young. *See* Nymph Selvagia, The, Her Song.
Song: "She's somewhere in the sunlight strong." Richard Le Gallienne. HBV; LBMV; OBEV; OBVV
Song: "Shine out, fair Sun, with all your heat." *Unknown.* *See* Shine Out, Fair Sun . . .
Song: "Shoot, false Love, I care not." *Unknown.* OBSC
Song: "Should you, of mirth and hope bereft." Alfred de Musset, *tr. fr. French by* Alan Conder. OnPM; TrFP
Song: "Sigh no more, ladies, sigh no more." Shakespeare. *See* Sigh No More.
Song: "Silent bird is hid in the boughs, The." Rosa Mulholland. TIP
Song: "Silly boy, there is no cause." Thomas Pestel. ElL
Song: "Since the lily's white is not so white as you." Pierre de Ronsard, *tr. fr. French by* Alan Conder. TrFP
Song: "Since thou, O fondest and truest." Robert Bridges. LoPS
Song: "Sing his praises that doth keep." John Fletcher. *See* Hymn to Pan.
Song, A: "Sing me a sweet, low song of night." Hildegarde Hawthorne. AA; FaBoBe; HBV
Song: "Sing not, nightingale." Aleksey Koltsov, *tr. fr. Russian by* C. M. Bowra. BoR
Song: "Sing the old song, amid the sounds dispersing." Aubrey Thomas De Vere. HBV
Song: "Sing to Apollo, god of day." John Lyly. *See* Song to Apollo.
Song: "Sing we and chant it." *Unknown.* *See* To Live in Pleasure.
Song: "Singer within the little streets." Monk Gibbon. NeIP

Song, A: "Slaves to London, I'll deceive you." Peter Motteux. *See* Slaves to London.
Song: "Sleep, O my darling, sleep." C. Kathleen Carman. BOL
Song: "Sleep, O sleep." John Gay. Polly, Air XXIII. FaBoEn
("Sleep, O sleep.") EG; ViBoPo
Song: "Slow, slow, fresh fount, keep[e] time with my salt tear[e]s." Ben Jonson. *See* Slow, Slow, Fresh Fount.
Song, A: "Smile, Massachusetts, smile." *Unknown.* PAH
Song: "Smooth was the water, calm the air." Sir Charles Sedley. CEP; SeCV-2
Song: "So have I seen a silver swan." *Unknown.* SeCL
Song: "So large a morning, so itself, to lean." W. H. Auden. NePoAm-2
Song, The: "So passeth, in the passing of a day." Spenser. *Fr.* The Faerie Queene, II, 12. MyFE
Song: "So, so,/ Lo, lilies fade, before the roses show." William Clerke. SeCL
Song: "So, we'll go no more a-roving." Byron. *See* So We'll Go No More a-Roving.
Song: "Softly, O midnight hours!" Aubrey Thomas De Vere. *See* Serenade: "Softly, O midnight hours."
Song: "Soldier and a sailor, A." Congreve. *See* Soldier and a Sailor, A.
Song: "Soldier, rest! thy warfare o'er." Sir Walter Scott. *See* Soldier, Rest!
Song: "Something calls and whispers, along the city street." Georgiana Goddard King. *Fr.* The Way of Perfect Love. HBV; NLK
Song: "Song is so old." Hermann Hagedorn. *See* Song Is So Old.
Song, The: "Song lay silent in my pen, A." John Erskine. AA
Song, A: "Song of grass. A,/ A Song of earth." "Yehoash," *tr. fr. Yiddish by* Isidore Goldstick. TrJP
Song: "Soules joy, now I am gone." *Unknown, at. to* the Earl of Pembroke. OBS
Song: "Spirit haunts the year's last hours, A." Tennyson. AtBAP; CBE; EmBrPo; GEPC; GTML; GTSL; KN; LEAP; NBE; OAEP; PoEL-5; PoVP; TOP; ViPP; VLEP
(Spirit Haunts the Years Last Hours, A.) InvP
Song: "Spirit! that dwellest where." Poe. *Fr.* Al Aaraaf. CoBA
(Song of Nesace.) APW
Song: "Splendour falls on castle walls, The." Tennyson. *See* Bugle Song.
Song: Spring and Winter. Shakespeare. *See* When Daisies Pied and Violets Blue.
Song: "Spring lights her candles everywhere." Fredegond Shove. HBMV
Song: "Spring, the sweet spring, is the year's pleasant king." Thomas Nashe. *See* Spring, the Sweet Spring.
Song: "Spring will come when the year turns, The." Margaret Widdemer. SBMV
Song: "Star that bids the Shepherd fold, The." Milton. *See* Star That Bids the Shepherd Fold, The.
Song: "Stars are with the voyager, The." Thomas Hood. ERP
Song: "Stay, Phoebus, stay!" Edmund Waller. ElSeCe
(Stay, Phoebus!) TriL
Song: "Stay, stay at home, my heart, and rest." Longfellow. *See* Home Song.
Song, A: "Steal from the meadows, rob the tall green hills." Lord Alfred Douglas. JKCP (1926 ed.); PoVP
Song: "Steer hither, steer your wingèd pines." William Browne. *See* Sirens' Song, The.
Song: "Still to be neat, still to be dressed." Ben Jonson. *See* Simplex Munditiis.
Song: "Stop all the clocks." W. H. Auden. *See* Stop All the Clocks.
Song: "Stranger, you who hide my love." Stephen Spender. FaBoTw
Song: "Strew not earth with empty stars." Thomas Lovell Beddoes. *See* Strew Not Earth with Empty Stars.
Song: "Sun a-beatin' on the deck." A. Gregg. CAG
Song: "Sunlight on the garden, The." Louis MacNeice. *See* Sunlight on the Garden, The.
Song: "Sunny shaft did I behold, A." Samuel Taylor Coleridge. *See* Glycine's Song.
Song: "Sweet and low, sweet and low." Tennyson. *See* Sweet and Low.
Song: "Sweet are the charms of her I Love." Barton Booth. OBEC
Song: "Sweet are the thoughts that savor of content." Robert Greene. *See* Sweet Are the Thoughts . . .
Song: "Sweet Cupid, ripen her desire." *Unknown.* LoBV; OBSC; ViBoPo
Song: "Sweet Echo, sweetest nymph, that liv'st unseen." Milton. *See* Sweet Echo.
Song: "Sweet in her green dell the flower of beauty slumbers." George Darley. EV-4; GTBS-D; LO; OBEV; OBVV
(Flower of Beauty.) HBV; VA
(Serenade of a Loyal Martyr.) OBRV; OnYI
Song: "Sweet, yet cruel unkind is she." *Unknown.* SeCL
Song: "Sweetest love, I do not go[e]." John Donne. ATP; AWP; BLV; BoLiVe; CBOV; CoEV; EG; ElL; ElSeCe; EnL; EnLit; EPS; EV-2; FaBoEn; InvP; KN; LiTL; LoPS; MaPo; MeLP; MePo; OAEP; OBS; PoE; PoEL-2; ReaPo; ReEn; ReIE; SeCV-1; SeEP; TOP; ViBoPo; ViV
(Sweetest Love [I Do Not Go].) BEL; EnLi-1; TrGrPo; TwP
"O how feeble is man's power," *br. sel.* LO
Song: "Sylvia the fair, in the bloom of fifteen." Dryden. LiTG; LiTL; ViBoPo
(Sylvia the Fair.) SiTL
Song: "Take it love!" Richard Le Gallienne. HBV
Song: "Take, O take those lips away." Shakespeare. *See* Take, O Take Those Lips Away.
Song: "Tears, idle tears." Tennyson. *See* Tears, Idle Tears.
Song: "Tell me, dearest, what is love?" Beaumont *and* Fletcher. *See* Tell Me, Dearest, What Is Love?
Song: "Tell me no more I am deceived." Congreve. ALV
Song: "Tell me not I my time misspend." *At. to* Sir John Eaton *and to* Phillip King. SeCL
Song: "Tell me where is fancy bred." Shakespeare. *See* Tell Me Where Is Fancy Bred.
Song, The: "That day, in the slipping of torsos and straining flanks." Lola Ridge. NP
Song: That Women Are but Men's Shadows [*or* Shaddowes]. Ben Jonson. CaAE; ElSeCe; EnLit; FaBoEn; HBV; LiTL; OBS; ReIE
(Follow a Shadow.) ALV
(Shadow, The.) OBEV
(That Women Are but Men's Shadows [*or* Shaddowes].) AtBAP; ElL; ViBoPo
(Women Men's Shadows.) WBLP
Song: "That zephyr every year." William Drummond of Hawthornden. EBSV
(Spring Bereaved, 1.) OBEV
Song: "There is many a love in the land, my love." Joaquin Miller. HBV
Song: "There is no joy in water apart from the sun." R. N. Currey. BoSA
Song: "There is no land like England." Tennyson. *Fr.* The Foresters, II, i. VA
Song: "There stands a lonely pine-tree." Heine, *tr. fr. German by* Emma Lazarus. TrJP
Song: "There was a jolly miller once." Isaac Bickerstaffe. *See* There Was a Jolly Miller.
Song: "There was a Knight of Bethlehem." Henry Neville Maugham. *See* Knight of Bethlehem, A.
Song: "There's one great bunch of stars in heaven." Théophile Marzials. OBVV
Song: "These songs will not stand." Denis Glover. Songs, I. AnNZ
Song: "Think of dress in ev'ry light." John Gay. *See* Think of Dress in Every Light.
Song: "This is Mab, the mistress-fairy." Ben Jonson. *See* Queen Mab.
Song: "This peach is pink with such a pink." Norman Gale. HBV; VA
Song: "Thou the golden fruit dost bear." Blake. LiA
Song: "Though I am young and cannot tell." Ben Jonson. *See* Though I Am Young.
Song: "Though regions farr devided." Aurelian Townshend. *See* Though Regions Far Divided.
Song: "Though richer swains thy love pursue." Joanna Baillie. *Fr.* The Country Inn. OBRV
Song: "Though veiled in spires of myrtle-wreath." Samuel Taylor Coleridge. ERP; RO
Song: "Though your little word is light." Louis Ginsberg. TBM
Song: "Three little maidens they have slain." Maurice Maeterlinck, *tr. fr. French by* Jethro Bithell. AWP; JAWP; WBP
Song: "Three Moorish girls I loved." *Unknown.* *See* Axa, Fátima, and Marién.
Song: "Three score and ten by common calculation." James Robinson Planché. BOHV
Song: "Thrice the brinded cat hath mewed." Shakespeare. *See* Witches' Song.
Song: "Thus the Mayne glideth." Robert Browning. *See* Thus the Mayne Glideth.
Song: "Thus, thus begin the yearly rites." Ben Jonson. *See* Thus, Thus Begin.
Song: "Thus when the swallow, seeking prey." John Gay. *Fr.* The Beggar's Opera, II, ii. PoEL-3
Song: "Thy face I have seen as one seeth." Sophie Jewett. AA
Song: "Thy fingers make early flowers of all things." E. E. Cummings. *See* Thy Fingers Make Early Flowers.
Song: "Thy voice is heard thro' rolling drums." Tennyson. *See* Thy Voice is Heard . . .
Song: "Thyrsis, when we parted, swore." Thomas Gray. OAEP

Song: "'Tis said that absence conquers love!" Frederick William Thomas. AA; HBV
Song, A: "'Tis strange, this heart within my breast." Countess of Winchilsea. BLV
Song: "'Tis sweet to hear the merry lark." Hartley Coleridge. *See* Lark and the Nightingale, The.
Song: "'Tis true our life is but a long disease." Katherine Philips. ElSeCe
Song: To a Lady with Many Names. John Wickham. JKCP (1955 ed.)
Song: "To all you ladies now at land." Charles Sackville. BEL; EPS (1942 ed.); EV-3; HBV; SeCV-2; TOP
(Song: Written at Sea, in the First Dutch War, 1665, the Night before an Engagement.) CEP; EnLoPo; LiTG; OBEV; OBS
(Song Written at Sea.) CoMu; EnLi-1 (1949 ed.); SiTL
(To All You Ladies.) SG
(Written at Sea, in the First Dutch War.) LEAP; SeCL; SeEP
Song: To Althea, from Prison. Richard Lovelace. *See* To Althea from Prison.
Song: To Celia ("Come, my Celia, let us prove"). Ben Jonson. *See* Come, My Celia, Let Us Prove.
Song: To Celia ("Drink to me only with thine eyes"). Ben Jonson. *See* To Celia ("Drink to me . . .").
Song: To Celia ("Kiss me, sweet; the wary lover"). Ben Jonson. *See* To Celia ("Kiss me, sweet . . .").
Song: To Chloris. Sir Charles Sedley. *See* Child and Maiden.
Song: To Comus. Ben Jonson. *See* Hymn to Comus.
Song: To Cynthia. Ben Jonson. *See* Hymn to Diana.
Song: To Lucasta, Going beyond the Seas. Richard Lovelace. *See* To Lucasta, Going beyond the Seas.
Song: To Lucasta, Going to the Warres. Richard Lovelace. *See* To Lucasta, Going to the Wars.
Song: To Mary. Charles Wolfe. *See* To Mary.
Song: To My Inconstant Mistress. Thomas Carew. *See* To My Inconstant Mistress.
Song: To Myra. George Granville. *See* Happiest Mortals Once Were We, The.
Song: To Psyche. William Morris. *See* Song from "The Story of Cupid and Psyche."
Song: To the Masquers Representing Stars. Thomas Campion. *Fr.* The Lords' Mask. LoBV
(Stars Dance, The.) OBSC
Song: "To the ocean now I fly." Milton. *See* To the Ocean Now I Fly.
Song: "To what bliss could my spirit aspire." Victor Hugo, *tr. fr. French by* Alan Conder. TrFP
Song: "Toils are pitched, The." Sir Walter Scott. *Fr.* The Lady of the Lake, IV. EmBrPo
(Toils Are Pitched, The.) EnRP; ERP
Song. "Tomorrow is [*or* Good morrow, 'tis] Saint Valentine's day." Shakespeare. *See* Tomorrow Is Saint Valentine's Day.
Song: "Too late, alas! I must confess." Earl of Rochester. HBV; LPS-1
Song: "Trip it gipsies, trip it fine." Thomas Middleton *and* William Rowley. *See* Trip It Gipsies.
Song: "Trust the form of airy things." Henry Harington. *See* Trust the Form of Airy Things.
Song: "Turn, turn thy beauteous face away." Beaumont *and* Fletcher. *See* Turn, Turn Thy Beauteous Face Away.
Song: "'Twas in this shade." Pope. CaAE
Song: "Under a southern wind." Theodore Roethke. CrMA
Song: "Under the bronze leaves a colt was foaled." "St. J. Perse," *tr. fr. French by* T. S. Eliot. *Fr.* Anabasis. AtBAP; LiTW
Song: "Under the greenwood tree." Shakespeare. *See* Under the Greenwood Tree.
Song: "Under the lime-tree, on the daisied ground." Walther von der Vogelweide. *See* Tandaradei.
Song: "Under the winter, dear." Eugene Lee-Hamilton. OBVV
Song, A: "Upon a time I had a heart." Oliver Herford. *See* Song of a Heart.
Song: "Urnes and odours bring away!" Fletcher *and* Shakespeare. *See* Funeral Song.
Song: "Victor was a little baby." W. H. Auden. AnFE
Song: "Victorious men of earth, no more." James Shirley. *See* Victorious Men of Earth.
Song: "Violet in her lovely hair, A." Charles Swain. *See* Violet in Her Hair, A.
Song: "Virtue's branches wither, virtue pines." Thomas Dekker. *See* Priest's Song, A.
Song: "Wait but a little while." Norman Gale. HBV; VA
Song: "Wake all the dead! What hoa! What hoa!" Sir William Davenant. *See* Wake All the Dead . . .
Song: "Wake not, but hear me, love!" Lew Wallace. *Fr.* Ben-Hur. AA
Song: "Warm are the still and lucky miles." W. H. Auden. FaBoMo; GTBS-D; POTE
Song: "Was it a form, a gait, a grace." Henry Reynolds. LO; SeCL
(Was It a Form?) ElSeCe; TuPP
("Was it a forme, a gate, a grace.") SeCSL
Song: "We break the glass, whose sacred wine." Edward Coote Pinkney. APW; HBV; LBAP; MOAP; SPP
Song: "We came to Tamichi in 1880." Scott Judy *and* "Doc" Hammond. PoOW
Song: "We cannot die, for loveliness." Mary Carolyn Davies. TBM
Song: "We cobblers lead a merry life." *At. to* George Peele. *See* Cobblers' Song, The.
Song: "We have bathed, where none have seen us." Thomas Lovell Beddoes. *See* Bridal Song to Amala.
Song: "We only ask for sunshine." Helen Hay Whitney. HBV
Song: "We sail toward evening's lonely star." Celia Thaxter. AA; PR
Song: "Weary lot is thine, fair maid, A." Sir Walter Scott. *See* Weary Lot Is Thine, A.
Song: "Weep, weep, ye woodmen, wail." Anthony Munday *and* Henry Chettle. *See* Weep, Weep, Ye Woodmen.
Song: "Were I laid on Greenland's coast." John Gay. *Fr.* The Beggar's Opera, I, i. BeR; CaAE; CEP; OBEC; OxBoLi; PoEL-3; SeCeV
(Macheath and Polly.) LoBV
(Over the Hills and Far Away.) ATP (1935 ed.); EnLi-1 (1949 ed.)
(Were I Laid on Greenland's Coast.) AtBAP; EnLoPo
Song: "Westron wynde [*or* Western wind] when wyll thou blow." *Unknown.* *See* Western Wind, When Wilt Thou Blow?
Song: "What a dainty life the milkmaid leads!" Thomas Nabbes. *Fr.* Tottenham Court. EG; SeCL
Song: "What have the years left us?" Charles G. Blanden. OQP; QP-1
Song: "What is there hid in the heart of a rose." Alfred Noyes. CH
Song: "What trees were in Gethsemane." Charles G. Blanden. ChIP; OQP; QP-1
Song: "What will be left when my life is over?" Audrey Alexandra Brown. TwCV
Song: "Whaur yon broken brig hings owre." William Soutar. GoTS
Song: "When as the rye [*or* rie] reach to the chin." George Peele. *See* Whenas the Rye Reach to the Chin.
Song: "When Britain really ruled the waves." W. S. Gilbert. *See* House of Peers, The.
Song: "When daffodils begin to peer." Shakespeare. *See* When Daffodils Begin to Peer.
Song: "When daisies pied and violets blue." Shakespeare. *See* When Daisies Pied . . .
Song: "When, dearest, I but think of thee." *At. to* Sir John Suckling *and to* Owen Felltham. *See* When, Dearest, I but Think of Thee.
Song: "When Delia on the plain appears." George Lyttelton. CEP; LoPS; OBEC
(Tell Me, My Heart, if This Be Love.) HBV; LPS-1; OBEV (1st ed.)
Song: When Friends Are Met o'er Merry Cheer. Sir Walter Scott. *Fr.* The Doom of Devorgoil, II, ii. EmBrPo
Song: "When I am dead, my dearest." Christina Rossetti. ATP; AWP; BMEP; BPN; BTP; CaAE; CH; DiM; EmBrPo; EnLi-2; EPP; EtPaEn; FaFP; GTBS; GTSL; HBV; JAWP; LBAP; LiTG; LiTL; OAEP; OBEV; OBVV; OuHeWo; PCD; PIR; PoE; PoFS; PoRA; POTT; PoVP; PreP; TOP; TreFS; ViBoPo; ViP; ViPo; VLEP; WBP; WHA
(Requiem.) OtMeF
(When I am Dead [My Dearest].) AV; BLV; BoLiVe; GTBS-D; GTBS-W; LiTB; MBP; MCCG; NeHB; PFE; PG (1955 ed.); PIAE; TrGrPo; TyEnPo
Song: "When I behold my mistress' face." *Unknown.* *See* When I Behold.
Song: "When I lie burning in thine eye." Thomas Stanley. ViBoPo
Song: "When I was young, I said to Sorrow." Aubrey Thomas De Vere. GTBS-D; TIP
(When I Was Young.) GTIV
Song: "When icicles hang by the wall." Shakespeare. *See* When Icicles Hang by the Wall.
Song: "When in Celia's heav'nly eye." Thomas Godfrey. NoCaPo
Song: "When love at first did move." Ben Jonson. *Fr.* The Masque of Beauty. GoBC
Song: "When love on time and measure makes his ground." *At. to* John Lilliat. ElL; LO
(False Love.) OBSC
(Love, Time and Measure.) BLV
Song: "When lovely woman stoops to folly." Goldsmith. *Fr.* The Vicar of Wakefield, *ch.* 24. AWP; BEL; CEP; EiPP; EV-3; GTBS; GTSE; GTSL; JAWP; LiTL; OBEC; PoFS; SeCePo; TOP; TrGrPo; TyEnPo; ViBoPo; WBP
(On Woman.) CaAE; LPS-1
(Stanzas on Woman.) EnLit; ExPo; OnYI; OxBI

(When Lovely Woman [Stoops to Folly].) EnLi-1; GTBS-D; GTBS-W; HBV; InP; SeCeV; TreF
(Woman.) LEAP; LiTB; LiTG; OBEV; PIR; PoP
Song: "When our banner went down." *Unknown.* FOAH
Song: "When that I was and a little tiny boy." Shakespeare. *See* When That I Was and a Little Tiny Boy.
Song: "When the rose came I loved the rose." Arthur O'Shaughnessy. PoVP
Song: "When thy beauty appears." Thomas Parnell. EiPP; EV-3; LO; LoPS; OBEC; OBEV
(Angel or Woman.) CBOV
(When Your Beauty Appears.) LPS-1
Song: "When Time, who steals our years away." Thomas Moore. TreFS
Song: "Whenas the rye reach to the chin." George Peele. *See* Whenas the Rye Reach to the Chin.
Song: "Whene'er with haggard eyes I view." George Canning, George Ellis, *and* John Hookham Frere. *Fr.* The Rovers, I. ALV; OBEC
(Song by Rogero the Captive.) CEP; TOP
(Song of One Eleven Years in Prison.) BOHV; FiBHP
Song: "Where is the Nightingale." Hilda Doolittle ("H. D."). *Fr* Songs from Cyprus. CBOV
(Second Song from Cyprus.) TCPD
(Song from Cyprus, A.) NeMA; TriL
(Songs from Cyprus.) MAP; MoAmPo; TwCV
Song: "Where is the nymph, whose azure eye." Thomas Moore. EnLoPo
Song: "Where, my days, are you." Aleksey Koltsov. BoRS
Song: "Where shall Celia fly for shelter." Christopher Smart. EnLoPo
Song: "Where shall the lover rest." Sir Walter Scott. *See* Where Shall the Lover Rest.
Song: "Where the bee sucks, there suck I." Shakespeare. *See* Ariel's Song: "Where the bee sucks."
Song: "Wherever I am, and whatever I do." Dryden. *See* Wherever I Am, and Whatever I Do.
Song: "While Morpheus thus doth gently lay." Henry Killigrew. CH
Song: "Who calls me bold because I won my love." Cosmo Monkhouse. VA
Song: "Who can say." Tennyson. FaBoCh; LoGBV
Song: Who Finds a Woman Good and Wise. George Wither. AEV
Song: "Who has robbed the ocean cave." John Shaw. AA; HBV; PR; SPP
Song: "Who hath his fancy pleasèd." Sir Philip Sidney. *See* Who Hath His Fancy Pleasèd.
Song: "Who is it that, this dark night." Sir Philip Sidney. *See* Astrophel and Stella: Eleventh Song.
Song: "Who is lord of lordly fate." Charles Heavysege. *Fr.* Count Filippo. PeCV
Song: "Who is Silvia? what is she." Shakespeare. *See* Who Is Silvia?
Song: "Who sows the seas, or ploughs the easy shore?" Phineas Fletcher. *See* Woman's Inconstancy.
Song: "Who tames the lion now?" Thomas Lovell Beddoes. PoE; ViBoPo
Song: "Why art thou slow, thou rest of trouble, Death." Philip Massinger. *Fr.* The Emperor of the East, V, iii. ElSeCe; EV-2; ViBoPo
(Death Invoked.) ACP (1952 ed.)
(Sad Song, A.) OBS; SeCL
("Why art thou slow, thou rest of trouble, Death.") SeEP; TuPP
Song: "Why canst thou not, as others do." *Unknown.* *See* Why Canst Thou Not.
Song: "Why do the bells of [*or* do bells for] Christmas ring?" Eugene Field. *See* Christmas Song.
Song: "Why do the houses stand." George Macdonald. OBVV
Song, A: "Why doth the world study vain glory to attain." Thomas Ingelend. *Fr.* The Disobedient Child. CaAE
Song: "Why fadest thou in death." Richard Watson Dixon. ChTr
("Why fadest thou in death.") CBE
Song: "Why, lovely charmer, tell me why." Sir Richard Steele. *Fr.* The Tender Husband. LiTL; ViBoPo
(Why, Lovely Charmer.) HBV; LPS-1
Song: "Why should a foolish marriage vow." Dryden. *See* Why Should a Foolish Marriage Vow.
Song: "Why should you swear I am forsworn." Richard Lovelace. *See* Scrutiny, The.
Song: "Why so pale and wan, fond lover?" Sir John Suckling. *See* Why So Pale and Wan?
Song: "Widow bird sate mourning for her love, A." Shelley. *See* Widow Bird, A.
Song: "Wind blows out of the gates of the day, The." W. B. Yeats. *See* Fairy Song.
Song, A: "With Love among the haycocks." Ralph Hodgson. AlDL
Song: "With whomsoever I share the spring." Jan Burroway. NePoAm-2
Song: "Woman's face is full of wiles, A." Humphrey Gifford. *Fr.* A Delectable Dream. ElL; ElSeCe; SiCE; TuPP
Song: "World is full of loss, The; bring, wind, my love." Muriel Rukeyser. MiAP
Song: "World is young to-day, The." Digby Mackworth Dolben. LoBV
Song: "Would you know what's soft? I dare." Thomas Carew. BEL; EG; EnLi-1; EPP; TOP
Song: "Would you wish me to sing to you." *Unknown, tr. fr. French by* Claude C. Abbott. LyMA
Song: Written at Sea, in the First Dutch War. Charles Sackville. *See* Song: "To all you ladies now at land."
Song: "Ye happy swains, whose hearts are free." Sir George Etherege. ElSeCe; HBV; LiTL; ViBoPo
(Ye Happy Swains, Whose Hearts Are Free.) EV-3
Song: "Ye little birds that sit and sing." *At. to* Thomas Heywood. *See* Ye Little Birds
Song: "Year's at the spring, The." Robert Browning. *See* Year's at the Spring, The.
Song, A: "Years have flown since I knew thee first." Richard Watson Gilder. The New Day, Pt. IV, Song VII. AA; BAP; LBAP
Song: "You are as gold." Hilda Doolittle ("H. D."). AnFE; APA; CoAnAm; CoBA; LiTA; LiTM; MAP; MAPA; MoAmPo; TwAmPo
Song: "You are my sky; beneath your circling kindness." J. C. Squire. LBBV
Song: "You charm'd me not with that fair face." Dryden. *Fr.* An Evening's Love, II, i. BrBE; CEP; ElSeCe; SeCV-2
(You Charm'd Me Not.) ATP (1935 ed.)
Song: "You spotted snakes with double tongue." Shakespeare. *See* You Spotted Snakes.
Song: "You virgins that did late despair." James Shirley. *See* Piping Peace.
Song: "You wear the morning like your dress." Hilaire Belloc. OBEV (new ed.)
(Song: Inviting the Influence of a Young Lady upon the Opening Year.) OBVV
Song: "You wrong me, Strephon, when you say." "Ephelia." DiM; LiTL
Song: "You'll love me yet! and I can tarry." Robert Browning. *See* You'll Love Me Yet.
Song, A: "Young Thyrsis with sighs often tells me his tale." Thomas Godfrey. IAP
Song: "Your hay it is mow'd and your corn is reap'd." Dryden. *See* Harvest Song.
Song: "Your heart is a music-box, dearest!" Frances Sargent Osgood. AA
Song: "Youth's the season made for joys." John Gay. *Fr.* The Beggar's Opera, II, i. CEP; EV-3; OBEC
Song; a Morisko. Jasper Fisher. *See* Morisco, A.
Song, a poem of itself—the word itself a dirge, A. Yonnondio. Walt Whitman. MCCG
Song about a Bitch. Sergei Yesenin, *tr. fr. Russian by* C. M. Bowra. BoRS
Song about Charleston, A. *Unknown.* PAH
Song about Great Men, A. Michael Hamburger. NePoEA
Song about Myself, A. Keats. BoTP, *sts.* 1–2; CoBE; InvP; PoEL-4; ReTS
(Naughty Boy, The.) GaP; GoBP; OTPC (1946 ed.); RIS
(There Was a Naughty Boy.) AlDL, *st.* 4; FaBoCh, *sts.* 1 *and* 4; LiTB; LiTG; LoGBV; MoShBr; SiTL, *sts.* 1 *and* 4
Song about Singing, A. Anne Reeve Aldrich. AA
Song about Whiskers. P. G. Wodehouse. FiBHP
Song above Death. James Edward Tobin. JKCP (1955 ed.)
Song after Harvest. Erik Axel Karlfeldt, *tr. fr. Swedish by* Charles W. Stork. AnSL
Song after Rain. *Tr. fr. Hopi Indian by* Natalie Curtis. APW
Song against Children. Aline Kilmer. CP; FAOV; SP; TSW; TSWC
Song against Grocers, The. G. K. Chesterton. CenHV
Song against Servants. Gertrude Jane Codd. JKCP (1926 ed.)
Song against Songs, The. G. K. Chesterton. ALV
Song against the Evil Days, A. Edgar McInnis. MM
Song against Women. Willard Huntington Wright. HBV
Song and Music. Dante Gabriel Rossetti. EmBrPo
Song and Science. Milicent Washburn Shinn. AA
Song and Wine. Bacchylides. *See* Fecundi Calices.
Song as Yet Unsung, A. "Yehoash," *tr. fr. Yiddish by* Isidore Goldstick. TrJP
Song at Amala's Wedding. Thomas Lovell Beddoes. *See* Bridal Song to Amala.
Song at Capri. Sara Teasdale. ChMo; CMP
Song at Easter, A. Charles Hanson Towne. BLRP; ChIP; MaRV
Song at Night. Norman Nicholson. FaBoTw
Song at Santa Cruz. Francis Brett Young. HBMV; PtOT
Song at Summer's End. A. R. D. Fairburn. AnNZ
Song at the Beginning of Autumn. Elizabeth Jennings. PoN

Song at the Feast of Brougham Castle. Wordsworth. EmBrPo; EnRP; ERP; GEPC
Two Victories, *sel.* LH
Song at the Frontier. Hsu Hun, *tr. fr. Chinese.* WhP
Song at the Moated Grange, A. Shakespeare. *See* Take, O Take Those Lips Away.
Song at the Ruin'd Inn. Tennyson. *Fr.* The Vision of Sin. PoEL-5
Song at the Well, The. George Peele. *Fr.* The Old Wives' Tale. AtBAP; ExPo; SeCeV
(Celanta at the Well of Life.) LoBV; ThWaDe
(Fair Maiden.) PoEL-2
(Voice from the Well [of Life Speaks to the Maiden], The.) ChTr; FaBoEn
Song Be Delicate. John Shaw Neilson. BoAV
Song before Action, *sel.* Kipling.
O Mary Pierced with Sorrow. ISi
Song before Grief, A. Rose Hawthorne Lathrop. AA; CAW; JKCP
Song before Night. Richard Dehmel, *tr. fr. German by* Babette Deutsch *and* Avrahm Yarmolinsky. OnPM
Song before Offering Wine. Li Po, *tr. fr. Chinese.* WhP
Song between the Queen's Majesty and England, A. William Birche. TuPP
(Songe betwene the Quenes Majestie and Englande, A.) CoMu
Song between two silences Life sings, A. The Silence. Archibald MacLeish. HBMV
Song-Bird. Brian Vrepont. NeLNL
Song-birds, The? are they flown away? Flight. Madison Cawein. AA
Song-Books. *See* Songbooks.
Song by a Person of Quality. *At. to* Pope *and to* Swift. *See* Lines by a Person of Quality.
Song by Apelles. John Lyly. *See* Apelles' Song.
Song by Fairies. John Lyly. *Fr.* Endymion. OAEP; ReEn; TuPP
(Fairy Revels.) EPP
(Fairy Song, A.) OBSC
Song, by Mr. Cypress. Thomas Love Peacock. *See* There Is a Fever of the Spirit.
Song, *ex improviso.* Samuel Taylor Coleridge. ERP
Song-Flower and Poppy, *sels.* William Vaughn Moody.
At Assisi. LEAP; SaFP
In New York. LEAP
Song for a Babe. Jean Ingelow. BOL
Song for a Ball-Game. Wilfrid Thorley. BoTP
Song for a Blue Roadster. Rachel Field. FaPON; TiPo (1950 ed.)
Song for a Camper. John Farrar. YeAr
Song for a Cracked Voice. Wallace Irwin. InMe
Song for a Dance. Francis Beaumont. *See* Shake Off Your Heavy Trance.
Song for a Dark Girl. Langston Hughes. CDC; PoNe
Song for a Fishing Party near Burlington, on the Delaware, in 1776. Jonathan Odell. BoCaPo (1948 ed.)
Song for a Forgotten Shrine to Pan. John Farrar. BAP
Song for a 'Fraid Cat. Patience Eden. DDA
Song for a Hot Day. Elizabeth J. Coatsworth. StVeCh (1955 ed.)
Song for a Jewess. Iwan Goll *tr. fr. French by* Joseph T. Shipley. TrJP
Song for a Listener, *sel.* Leonard Feeney.
Because of Her Who Flowered So Fair. ISi
Song for a Little Cuckoo Clock. Elizabeth J. Coatsworth. SiSoSe
Song for a Little House. Christopher Morley. BoTP; FaPON; MPB; StVeCh; TreF; TSW; TSWC
Song for a Lute ("For you there is no song"), II. Edna St. Vincent Millay. BoFr
Song for a Lute ("Seeing how I love you utterly"), I. Edna St. Vincent Millay. BoFr
Song for a Lyre. Louise Bogan. LiTA
Song for a May Morning. Herbert Trevelyan. AlDL
Song for a Proud Relation. Patrick MacDonogh. OnYI
Song for a Slight Voice. Louise Bogan. NP
Song for a Venison Dinner at Mr. Bunyan's, New York, 1781. Joseph Stansbury. BoCaPo (1948 ed.)
Song for Afterwards. Francisco López Merino, *tr. fr. Spanish by* Richard O'Connell. AnCL
Song for All Seas, All Ships. Walt Whitman. CH; FaBoBe; HBV; HBVY; MCCG; NePA; SG
Song for Apollo. Matthew Arnold. *See* Callicles' Song.
Song for Colin, The. Sara Teasdale. ChMo; CMP; MOAP
Song for Dark Days. Anderson M. Scruggs. MuM
Song for December Thirty-first. Frances Frost. YeAr
Song for Decoration Day. Helen C. Bacon. HH
Song for Fine Weather. *Tr. fr. Haida Indian by* Constance Lindsay Skinner. AWP; JAWP; WBP
Song for Flag Day, A. Lydia Avery Coonley Ward. *See* Flag Song.
Song for Government. Raymond Holden. PoFr
Song for Heroes, A. Edwin Markham. PEDC
Song for July 12th, 1843. John de Jean Frazer. TIP
Song for Lexington, A. Robert Kelley Weeks. AA; IDAH; OBAV
Song for Lovers. T. I. Moore. MoAuPo
Song for Love's Coming of Age. J. Corson Miller. JKCP (1955 ed.)
Song for Mariana. Shakespeare. *See* Take, O Take Those Lips Away.
Song for May Day, A. Frederick Herbert Adler. DD
Song for Memorial Day. Clinton Scollard. OHIP
Song for Midsummer Night. Elizabeth J. Coatsworth. YeAr
Song for Music. G. S. Fraser. ChMP
Song for Music. Sir Edmund Gosse. VA
Song for Music. William Morris. *See* Love Is Enough.
Song for Music, A. *Unknown. See* Weep You No More, Sad Fountains.
Song for My Lady. A. Godwhen. *See* Now Would I Fain.
Song for My Mate, A. Marguerite Wilkinson. AV
Song for My Mother, A: Her Hands. Anna Hempstead Branch. *See* Her Hands.
Song for My Mother, A: Her Stories. Anna Hempstead Branch. *Fr.* Songs for My Mother. MotAn; OHIP
Song for My Mother, A: Her Words. Anna Hempstead Branch. *See* Her Words.
Song for New Year's Eve, A. Bryant. DD; MPB; PoRL
Song for Old Apis, A. James Schevill. FiMAP
Song for our banner, the watch-word recall, A. The Flag of Our Union Forever. George Pope Morris. FOAH
Song for Our Flag, A. Margaret E. Sangster. FaFP
Song for Peace. W. R. Rodgers. NeBP
Song for Saint Cecelia, A. Marya Zaturenska. TriL
Song for St. Cecilia's Day. W. H. Auden. FaBoTw
Song for St. Cecilia's Day, A, 1687. Dryden. AtBAP; ATP; AWP; BCEP; BEL; BoLiVe; CBOV; CEP; CoEV; EiPP; ElSeCe; EnL; EnLi-1 (1949 ed.); EnLit; EV-3; ExPo; FaBoEn; GEPC; GoBC; GTBS; GTBS-D; GTBS-W; GTSE; GTSL; HBV; InPo; JAWP; LiTB; LiTG; LPS-3; MaPo; OAEP; OBEV; Po; PoEL-3; PoLi, *much abr.;* PreP; RiBV; SeCV-2; SeEP; TCEP; TOP; TrGrPo; TriL; TwCrTr; UnS, *abr.;* WBP
Instruments, The, *sel.* BLV
(Fife and Drum, 8 *ll.*) GN
Song for Simeon, A. T. S. Eliot. BLV; BoLiVe; CoBE; LiTB; MAP; MaRV; MM; MoAmPo (1942 ed.); OxBoCh; POTE; TwCV
Song for Souls under Fire, A. Mark Turbyfill. NP
Song for the Asking, A. Francis Orrery Ticknor. AA
Song for the baby, A, sweet little Bopeep. Lullaby. Shirley Dare. BOL
Song for the beautiful trees, A. Forest Song. William Henry Venable. PEDC
Song for the Bronze God. Li Ho, *tr. fr. Chinese by* Ho Chih-yuan. WhP
Song for the Centennial Celebration of Harvard College, A. 1836. Oliver Wendell Holmes. TCAP
Song for the Clatter-Bones. F. R. Higgins. LiTB; LiTM; OBMV; OnYI; OxBI; SiTL
Song for the Flag, A. Denis A. McCarthy. PEDC
Song for the Greenwood Fawn. I. L. Salomon. GoYe
Song for the Heroes. Alex Comfort. MoBrPo (1950 ed.); NeBP
Song for the heroes who saw the sign, A. A Song for Heroes. Edwin Markham. PEDC
Song for "The Jacquerie" ("The hound was cuffed"). Sidney Lanier. *See* Hound, The.
Song for the Last Act. Louise Bogan. NePoAm
Song for the Least of All Saints, A. Christina Rossetti. BePJ
Song for the Luddites. Byron. PoFr
Song for the Moon on Mount Omei. Li Po, *tr. fr. Chinese.* ChLP; WhP
Song for the New Year. W. H. Auden. EnLi-2 (1949 ed.)
Song for the Old, A. The New Year. George Cooper. DD; PEDC; PEOR
Song for the Passing of a Beautiful Woman. *Unknown, tr. fr. Paiute Indian by* Mary Austin. LiTA
Song for the Pike's Peaker. *Unknown.* PoOW
Song for the plant of my own native West, A. The Maize. William Fosdick. LPS-2
Song for the Season, A. Katharine Tynan. SDH
Song for the Seasons, A. "Barry Cornwall." HBV
Song for the Sick Emperor. John Fletcher. *See* Care-charming Sleep.
Song for the Spanish Anarchists, A. Sir Herbert Read. ChMP
Song for the Spinning Wheel. Wordsworth. OBRV
Song for the Squeeze-Box. Theodore Roethke. NePoAm
Song for the States, A. Walt Whitman. PoRL
Song for the unsung heroes who rose in the country's need, A. The Unsung Heroes. Paul Laurence Dunbar. PoFr
Song for the Virgin Mother, A. Lope de Vega, *tr. fr. Spanish by* Ezra Pound. LiTW
Song for These Days. Patrick F. Kirby. GoBC
Song for Thrift Week. Mildred Weston. WhC
Song for Tomorrow. Lucia Trent. PGD

Song for Two Voices, A. *Unknown. See* What Can We Poor Females Do.
Song for Unbound Hair. Genevieve Taggard. AV; PG; PoRA; TBM
Song for War. W. R. Rodgers. NeBP
Song for Wei City, A. Wang Wei, *tr. fr. Chinese.* WhP
Song for Youth. Dana Burnet. MBP
Song from a Booke of Ayres, A. Thomas Campion. *See* Follow Thy Fair Sun, Unhappy Shadow.
Song from a Drama. Edmund Clarence Stedman. AA
Song from a Masque. Margaret Widdemer. TBM
Song from a Play. W. B. Yeats. *See* Two Songs from a Play.
Song from "Aella." Thomas Chatterton. *See* Minstrel's Song.
Song from "Al Aaraaf." Poe. *See* Song: "Neath blue-bell or streamer."
Song from an Evil Wood. Lord Dunsany. *See* Songs from an Evil Wood.
Song from "April." Irene Rutherford McLeod. CP; SUS; VOD
Song from "Chartivel." Marie de France, *tr. fr. French by* Arthur O'Shaughnessy. *Fr.* Chartivel. AWP; JAWP; LEAP, *abr.*; LiTW; LyMA; WBP
("Hath any loved you well, down there.") EnLoPo; PoVP
(Sarrazine's Song [to Her Dead Lover].) GTIV; HBV
Song from "Cymbeline." Shakespeare. *See* Hark! Hark! the Lark.
Song from Cyprus, A. Hilda Doolittle ("H. D."). *See* Songs from Cyprus.
Song from Fragment of an Eccentric Drama. Henry Kirke White. OBRV
Song from "Hamlet." Shakespeare. *See* How Should I Your True Love Know.
Song from "In a Gondola." Robert Browning. *See* Moth's Kiss, First, The.
Song from "Maud" ("Come into the garden, Maud"). Tennyson. *See* Come into the Garden, Maud.
Song from "Maud" ("Go not, happy day"). Tennyson. Maud, Pt. I, xvii. ATP
Song from "Much Ado about Nothing." Shakespeare. *See* Sigh No More.
Song from "Ogier the Dane." William Morris. *Fr.* The Earthly Paradise. BPN; OAEP; POTT; PoVP; VLEP
(Antiphony.) VA
("In the white-flowered hawthorn brake.") EG; ViBoPo
Song from Old Spain, A. Alice Corbin. NP
Song from "Osorio." Samuel Taylor Coleridge. *See* Invocation, An: "Hear, sweet spirit."
Song from "Paracelsus." Robert Browning. *See* Song: "Over the sea our galleys went."
Song from "Pippa Passes." Robert Browning. *See* Year's at the Spring, The.
Song from Portugal, 1940. Frederic Prokosch. Three Songs from Portugal, II. LoPo
Song from Shakespeare's "Cymbeline," A ("To fair Fidele's grassy tomb"). William Collins. BEL; CaRE; CEP; EiPP; EM-1; EnRP; EPP; OAEP; RiBV; TCEP; TOP; TriL; TyEnPo
(Dirge: "To fair Fidele's grassy tomb.") BrBE; TVSH
(Dirge for Fidele.) EV-3
(Dirge in "Cymbeline.") ATP; CBOV; EnLi-2 (1949 ed.); HBV; OBEC; PoFS; SeCePo; ViBoPo
(Fidele.) OBEV
(Fidele's Dirge.) BCEP; LEAP
Song from "Sylvan," A. *Unknown. See* Out in the Fields with God.
Song from the Bride of Smithfield. Sylvia Townsend Warner. MBP; MoBrPo
Song from "The Hill of Venus." William Morris. *Fr.* The Earthly Paradise. POTT; PoVP; VLEP
Song from the Italian, A. Dryden. *Fr.* Limberham; or, The Kind Keeper, III, i. CEP; SeCV-2
Song from "The Land East of the Sun and West of the Moon." William Morris. *See* Outlanders, Whence Come Ye Last?
Song from "The Only Jealousy of Emer." W. B. Yeats. *Fr.* The Only Jealousy of Emer. MoAB
Song from the Persian. Thomas Bailey Aldrich. OBAV; LBAP
Song from the Ship. Thomas Lovell Beddoes. *See* To Sea, to Sea!
Song from "The Story of Acontius and Cydippe." William Morris. *Fr.* The Earthly Paradise. BPN; POTT; VLEP
(Song: "Fair is the night and fair the day.") HBV
Song from "The Story of Cupid and Psyche." William Morris. *Fr.* The Earthly Paradise. BPN; POTT; VLEP
(Song: To Psyche.) VA
Song from the Traffic. Margaret Bell Houston. LS
Song from "The Two Gentlemen of Verona." Shakespeare. *See* Who Is Silvia?
Song from "The Winter's Tale." Shakespeare. *See* When Daffodils Begin to Peer.
Song from "Twelfth Night." Shakespeare. *See* O Mistress Mine.
Song from "Zapolya." Samuel Taylor Coleridge. *See* Glycine's Song.
Song I sing of my sea-adventure, A. The Seafarer. *Unknown.* AnOE; EtS
Song I sing of sorrow unceasing, A. The Wife's Lament. *Unknown.* AnOE; LiTW; LyMA
Song in a Siege. Robert Heath. OBS
Song in a suffocating night, A. The Toad. Tristan Corbière [*wr.* Jules Laforgue], *tr. by* Patricia Terry. OnPM
Song in a windless night, A. The Toad. Tristan Corbière, *tr. by* Vernon Watkins. AnFP; MiFP
Song in Absence. Arthur Hugh Clough. *See* Green Fields of England.
Song in Autumn, A. Theodosia Garrison. NLK
Song in Camp, The. Bayard Taylor. *See* Song of the Camp, The.
Song in Imitation of the Elizabethans. Sir William Watson. VA
Song in Leinster. Louise Imogen Guiney. *See* In Leinster.
Song in Making of the Arrows, A. John Lyly. *Fr.* Sapho and Phao LoBV; OBSC; TuPP
("My shag-hair Cyclops, come, let's ply.") ElSeCe
(Vulcan's Song.) EIL
Song in March. Clinton Scollard. NLK
Song in March. William Gilmore Simms. AA; BPP; DD; HBV
Song, in Praise of a Beggers Life, A. "A. W." *See* In Praise of a Beggar's Life.
Song in Praise of Old English Roast Beef, A. Richard Leveridge. *See* Roast Beef of Old England, The.
Song in Praise of Paella. C. W. V. Wordsworth. FiBHP
Song in Praise of the Lord of Heaven and Earth, A. *Unknown.* GBV
Song in Season, A. Swinburne. EmBrPo
Song in Spring. Louis Ginsberg. YeAr
Song in Spring, A. Thomas S. Jones, Jr. LBMV; POT; PoTo
(Two Songs in Spring, 1.) VOD
Song in the Dell, The. Charles Edward Carryl. AA
Song in the Second Act, A. Thomas Southerne. *See* Song: "Pursuing beauty, men descry."
Song in the Songless. George Meredith. BMEP; EmBrPo; GTML; GTSL; OTPC (1946 ed.); PCD; POTT; PoVP; VLEP
Song in the Valley of Humiliation. Bunyan. *See* Shepherd Boy's Song, The.
Song in the valley of Nemea, A. Nemea. Lawrence Durrell. ChMP; FaBoTw
Song in the Wood. John Fletcher. *Fr.* The Little French Lawyer. EIL; ThWaDe
Song in Time of Order, A. Swinburne. BPN; POTT; PoVP; VLEP
Song in Time of Plague. Pushkin, *tr. fr. Russian by* V. de S. Pinto. *Fr.* The City of the Plague. BoRS
Song is but a little thing, A. The Poet and His Song. Paul Laurence Dunbar. PoRL
"Song is ended and the singer fled, The." After. Theodora Bates. CAG
Song is gone, The; the dance. Bora Ring. Judith Wright. NeLNL
Song Is So Old. Hermann Hagedorn. LBMV
(Song: "Song is so old.") HBV
Song is such a curious thing, A. Written in a Song Book. Lizette Woodworth Reese. NP; VOD
Song lay silent in my pen, A. The Song. John Erskine. AA
Song Made by F. B. P., A. *Unknown. See* New Jerusalem, The.
Song Maker, The. Kingsley Fairbridge. BoSA
Song-Maker, The. Anna Wickham. MBP; MoBrPo
Song Making. Sara Teasdale. WGRP
Song My Paddle Sings, The. E. Pauline Johnson. CaP; CPG; FaPON; HBV; OCL; OTPC; PoRL; POT; PoTo; VA
Song of a boat, A. Songs of Seven: Seven Times Seven [*or* Longing for Home]. Jean Ingelow. GBV (1922 ed.); HBV; MOAH; WGRP
Song of a Factory Girl. Marya Zaturenska. HBMV; NP
Song of a Happy Rising, The. John Thewlis. ACP
Song of a Heart, A. Oliver Herford. PA
(Song, A: "Upon a time I had a heart.") PR
Song of a Heathen, The. Richard Watson Gilder. AA; BAP; BePJ; ChIP; LEAP; MaRV; OQP; QP-1; StJW; WGRP
Song of a Jewish Boy. "M. J.," *tr. fr. Polish by* A. Glanz-Leyeless. TrJP
Song of a Legionnaire. Hybrias. *See* Soldier's Riches, A.
Song of a Man Who Has Come Through. D. H. Lawrence. ChMP; CoBMV; FaBoMo; LiTM; MoPo; SeCeV; ViBoPo

Song of a man who was dead, The. Felo-de-Se. James Elroy Flecker. LBBV
Song of a Modest Woman. Chang Chi, *tr. fr. Chinese*. WhP
Song of a Pure-hearted Girl, A. Meng Chiao, *tr. fr. Chinese by* Witter Bynner. ChLP
Song of a Second April. Edna St. Vincent Millay. ChMo; CMP; LoPo; OxBA
Song of a Shepherd-Boy at Bethlehem, The. Josephine Preston Peabody. ChrBoLe; CLS; OHIP; SDH; StJW
Song of a Soldier. "Monk of Eight Fingers," *tr. fr. Chinese by* Wang Sheng-chih. WhP
Song of a Thousand Years, *sel.* Don Marquis.
"Methuselah!" BAP
Song of a Traveller, The. Robert Louis Stevenson. *See* Romance.
Song of a Young Lady to Her Ancient Lover, A. Earl of Rochester. BeR; MePo
Song of Accius and Silena. John Lyly. *See* O Cupid! Monarch over Kings.
Song of Adoration to God. Thomas Holley Chivers. SPP
Song of Aerial Spirits. Sir Robert Howard *and* John Dryden. *Fr.* The Indian Queen. AtBAP
Song of Albert Graeme. Sir Walter Scott. *See* It Was an English Ladye Bright.
Song of Ale, A. *At. to* William Stevenson. *See* Back and Side Go Bare, Go Bare.
Song of Allegiance. R. A. K. Mason. AnNZ
Song of Always, A. Efraim Rosenzweig. TiPo (1952 ed.)
Song of American Freedom, A. John Dickinson. *See* Liberty Song, The.
Song of an Australian. Flexmore Hudson. BoAu
Song of Angiola in Heaven, A. Austin Dobson. HBV
Song of Apelles. John Lyly. *See* Apelles' Song.
Song of Apple Gathering, A. Gordon Bottomley. ReTS
Song of April, A. Francis Ledwidge. VOD
Song of Arbor Day. Sarah J. Pettinos. PEOR
Song of Ariel. Shakespeare. *See* Ariel's Song: "Come unto these yellow sands."
Song of Arno, A. Grace Ellery Channing. AA
Song of Autumn, A. Arthur Hugh Clough. *See* My Wind Is Turned to Bitter North.
Song of Autumn, A. Adam Lindsay Gordon. BoAu
Song of Autumn, A. Sir Rennell Rodd. HBV
Song of Autumn. Tu Fu, *tr. fr. Chinese by* Pu Hsiang-hsing. WhP
Song of Autumn. Paul Verlaine. *See* Chansons d'automne.
Song of Babek. Ilya Selvinsky, *tr. fr. Russian by* Jack Lindsay. *Fr.* The Man with an Eagle on His Shoulder. RuPo
Song of Ballyshannon. Jeanne Robert Foster. NLK
Song of Basket-weaving. Constance Lindsay Skinner. AnAmPo; LA
Song of Battle. Bertrand de Born. *See* Well Pleaseth Me the Sweet Time of Easter.
Song of birds which leaps from leaf to leaf, The. Sonnet. Matteo Maria Boiardo. LyPI
Song of Braddock's Men, The. *Unknown.* MC; PAH
Song of Bread and Honey, A. Richard Le Gallienne. PCH
Song of Breath, A. Stephen Vincent Benét. *See* Song of the Breath, The.
Song of Breath. Peire Vidal, *tr. fr. French by* Ezra Pound. AWP; JAWP; WBP
Song of Callicles, The ("Far, far from here"). Matthew Arnold. *See* Cadmus and Harmonia.
Song of Callicles, The ("Through the black, rushing smoke-bursts"). Matthew Arnold. *See* Callicles' Song.
Song of canaries, The. The Canary. Ogden Nash. FiBHP
Song of Carroll's Sword, The. *At. to* Dallan MacMore, *tr. fr. Middle Irish by* Kuno Meyer. OnYI
(Carroll's Sword, *tr. by* Frank O'Connor.) KiLC
Song of Cash, A. *Unknown, tr. fr. Latin by* Jack Lindsay. LyMA
Song of Chang-kan, A. Li Po, *tr. fr. Chinese.* WhP
Song of Ch'ang-kan, A. Ts'uei Hao, *tr. fr. Chinese by* Witter Bynner. BoFr
Song of Cherry-Time, A. Tzu Yeh, *tr. fr. Chinese by* Henry H. Hart. ChLP; PoHN
Song of Chess, The. *At. to* Abraham ibn Ezra, *tr. fr. Hebrew by* Nina Davis Salaman. TrJP
Song of Ching-ping, A. Li Po, *tr. fr. Chinese.* WhP
Song of Christian Workingmen. Thomas Curtis Clark. OQP; PSO; QP-1
Song of Chun-k'u. Li Ho, *tr. fr. Chinese by* Ho Chih-yuan. WhP
Song of Clan-Alpine. Sir Walter Scott. *See* Boat Song.
Song of Clover, A. Helen Hunt Jackson. GN; OTPC
Song of Colours, A. Theodore Maynard. JKCP
Song of Content, A. Frederic Lawrence Knowles. PR
Song of Coridon and Melampus. George Peele. *Fr.* The Hunting of Cupid. OBSC
(Coridon and Melampus' Song.) TuPP
Song of Cradle-making. Constance Lindsay Skinner. CaP; CPG; OCL
Song of Crede, The. *Unknown, tr. fr. Middle Irish by* Howard Mumford Jones. LiTW
(Song of Crede, Daughter of Gooary, The, *tr. by* Kuno Meyer.) OnYI
Song of Dagger-Dancing, A, *sel.* Tu Fu, *tr. fr. Chinese by* Witter Bynner.
"There lived years ago the beautiful Kung-sun." UnS
Song of Daily Life, A. Utako Hayashi, *tr. fr. Japanese by* Lois J. Erickson. SoLD
Song of Dalliance, A. William Cartwright. ALV; NBE
Song of Daphne to the Lute, A. John Lyly. *See* Daphne.
Song of Dark Waters, The. Roy Helton. IHA; PC
Song of David, The. Christopher Smart. *See* Catholic Amen, The.
Song of Deborah, A. Deborah. William Weaver Christman. DDA
Song of Deborah [and Barak], The. Judges, V: 2-31, Bible, *O.T.* AWP; LiTW
(Then Sang Deborah and Barak, 1-31.) TrJP
(War Song of Kishon, 1-23.) BHV
Song of Denmark, *sel.* Soeren Haller, *tr. fr. Danish by* Joy Davidman.
"This is the ironhard winter foretold." PoFr
Song of Departing May. Rofu Miki, *tr. fr. Japanese by* Takamichi Ninomiya *and* D. J. Enright. PoLJ
Song of Derivations, A. Alice Meynell. GTML; MaRV; PoVP; TCPD; WGRP
(Modern Poet, The.) VA
Song of Desire, A. Frederic Lawrence Knowles. HBV; NLK
Song of Diana's Nymphs, A. John Lyly. *See* Cupid's Indictment.
Song of Diego Valdez, The. Kipling. OtMeF
Song of Diligence, A. Helen Frazee-Bower. HBMV
Song of Divine Love, A. Richard Crashaw. *See* Song, A: "Lord, when the sense of Thy sweet grace."
Song of Doubt, A. Josiah Gilbert Holland. WGRP
Song of Dreams, A. "Fiona Macleod." VLEP
Song of Dust, A. Lord De Tabley. EnLoPo
Song of Early Autumn, A. Richard Watson Gilder. DD; HBV; NLK (1947 ed.); SN
Song of Easter. Celia Thaxter. EOAH; HH
Song of Echo. Ben Jonson. *See* Slow, Slow, Fresh Fount.
Song of Egla. Maria Gowen Brooks. AA; AnAmPo; BAV; LA; LEAP
(Day, in Melting Purple Dying.) LPS-1
Song of Enchantment, A. Walter de la Mare. GTML; GTSL; PG (1955 ed.)
Song of Eros. George Edward Woodberry. *Fr.* Agathon. AA; HBV
Song of Eve to Cain, The. John Sterling. BOL
Song of Exile, A. Psalms, CXXXVII, Bible, *O.T.* TrGrPo
(Lament in Exile, A.) CBOV
(Psalm CXXXVII.) AWP; ExPo; JAWP; LiTW; OnPM; StaSt (1-6, *ad.*)
Song of Experiencing the Tao, The. *Unknown, tr. fr. Chinese.* WhP
Song of Fairies Robbing an Orchard. Thomas Randolph. *See* Fairies' Song.
Song of Fairly Utter Despair. Samuel Hoffenstein. CIV
Song of Faith, A. Josiah Gilbert Holland. *Fr.* Bitter-sweet. WGRP
Song of Faith Forsworn, A. Lord De Tabley. VA
Song of Farewell, A. Dora Greenwell. VA
Song of Fate. Friedrich Hölderlin, *tr. fr. German by* Emery Neff. WoL
(Hyperion's Song, *tr. by* Lola Gruenthal.) AnGP
Song of Finis, The. Walter de la Mare. MoBrPo
Song of Finn, The. *Unknown. See* May Day ("May day").
Song of Fionnuala, The. Thomas Moore. ERP; OnYI; TIP
Song of Fixed Accord. Wallace Stevens. NePoAm
Song of Fleet Street, A. Alice Werner. HBV
Song of Flight, A. Christina Rossetti. CAW; GTML
Song of Four Priests Who Suffered Death at Lancaster, A. *Unknown.* ACP
Song of Freedom, A. Alice Milligan. AnIV; OnYI; PoFr
Song of Freedom and the Sea, The. Yiannis Sphakianakis, *tr. fr. Modern Greek by* Rae Dalven. MoGP
Song of Glenann, A. "Moira O'Neill." HBV; LBBV
Song of grass, A,/ A song of earth. A Song. "Yehoash." TrJP
Song of Greatness, A. *Unknown, tr. fr. Chippewa Indian by* Mary Austin. BoChLi; FaPON; TiPo
Song of Green, A. Phyllis Reid. DiM
Song of Grief, A. Pan Chieh-yu, *tr. fr. Chinese by* Florence Ayscough *and* Amy Lowell. ChLP
Song of Gwythno. Thomas Love Peacock. *Fr.* The Misfortunes of Elphin. OBRV
Song of Handicrafts, A. Annie Matheson. OBVV
Song of Hannah, The. First Samuel, II: 1-10, Bible, *O.T.* LiTW
(Hannah's Song of Thanksgiving.) AWP
Song of Hannibal; Rome. Marcus B. Christian. GoSl
Song of Happiness, A. Muna Lee. NP
Song of Happiness, A. Ernest Rhys. NP

Song of Hate. Jacob ben David Frances, *tr. fr. Hebrew by* A. B. Rhine. TrJP
Song of hate is a song of Hell, A. A Chant of Love for England. Helen Gray Cone. LBAP; LEAP; VOD
Song of Heaven, A. Li Ho, *tr. fr. Chinese by* Ho Chih-yuan. WhP
Song of Hiawatha, The, *sels.* Longfellow.
Death of Minnehaha, The, *fr.* XX. AA
Famine, The, XX. BAV; IAP
Firefly Song, *fr.* III. PCD
Four Winds, The, II. AnNE
Ghosts, The, XIX. DaM; HOAH, *abr.*; LoBV
Hiawatha and Mudjekeewis, IV. AnNE; EV-1; IAP; TCAP
Hiawatha's Brothers, *fr.* III. BoTP; PCH, *br. sel.*
(Hiawatha's Chickens, *br. sel.*) PCH
Hiawatha's Childhood, III. AnNE; BoChLi, *sel.*; BoTP, *sel.*; FaPON, *sel.*; GFA, *sel.*; IAP; MPB, *sel.*; OHFP, *sel.*; PECK, *sel.*; PoRh, *sel.*; RAR, *sel.*; RIS, *abr.*; ShBV-1, *sel.*; StVeCh, *sel.*; TiPo, *sel.*; TreF, *sel.*; TVSH, *sel.*; WBLP, *sel.*
Hiawatha's Departure, XXII. IAP
Hiawatha's Sailing, VII. BBV; IAP; PCH, *sel.*; TVSH
(Hiawatha's Canoe.) OHIP, *sel.*; StVeCh, *abr.*
Hiawatha's Wedding-Feast, *fr.* XI. PEOR
Hiawatha's Wooing, X. BeLS; IAP; TreFS
Hunting of Pau-Puk-Keewis, The, XVII. CoBA
Introduction. AnNE; IAP; LEAP; OBAV; PG (1945 ed.); TCAP
Legend of the Cornstalk, *abr., fr.* V. GrCo-1
Lullaby of Nokomis, *abr., fr.* III. PCH
Pau-Puk-Keewis, XVI. CoBA
Peace-Pipe, The, I. AnNE; IAP
Song of Honour [*or* Honor], The. Ralph Hodgson. AtBAP; CAW, *abr.*; CBE; ChMo; CMP; CP; GTML; GTSL; LiTB; MBP; MCCG; MM; MoBrPo; OtMeF; TSW; TSWC, *abr.*
(Hymn of Being, The, *abr.*) GrCo-2
Sels.
"I heard it all, each, every note." TwCV
"I heard the hymn of being sound." LO
Song of Hope. Mary A. Lathbury. BLPA; MaRV
(Room for Him! Room!) ChIP
Song of Impossibilities, A. Winthrop Mackworth Praed. BOHV; InMe; NA
Song of Industrial America. Sherwood Anderson. NP
Song of Iowa, The. S. H. M. Byers. PoRL
Song of Ithamore, The. Christopher Marlowe. *Fr.* The Jew of Malta, IV. WHA
Song of Jehane du Castel Beau, The. William Morris. *See* Gold Wings across the Sea.
Song of Jeppe, The. Alfred Noyes. *Fr.* Watchers of the Sky. EPP
Song of Jonah in the Whale's Belly, The. Michael Drayton. *Fr.* The Harmony of the Church. ReIE
Song of Joys, A. Walt Whitman. *Fr.* A Poem of Joys. LEAP
Song of Labor, The. Ninette M. Lowater. PEDC
Song of Laughter, A. Theodore Maynard. JKCP
Song of Laurence Minot. Laurence Minot. BEL
Song of Lazarus, The, *sel.* Alex Comfort.
Notes for My Son, VI. MoBrPo (1950 ed.); NeBP; SeCePo
Song of Lewes, The. *Unknown.* OxBoLi
(On Richard, Duke of Cornwall, Brother to Henry III.) NBE
Song of Liang Chou. Ou-yang Hsiu, *tr. fr. Chinese by* Kenneth Rexroth. OnPC
Song of Liangchow, The. Wang Han, *tr. fr. Chinese.* WhP
Song of Liberty, A. Blake. EiPP; EnLi-2; EnRP
Song of Liberty, *sel.* Louise Ayres Garnett.
"Lead on, lead on, America." PGD
Song of Life. Florence Earle Coates. BAP; POT; PoTo
Song of Life. Hugo von Hofmannsthal, *tr. fr. German by* Dwight Durling. AnGP
Song of Life. Charles Mackay. *See* Small Beginnings.
Song of Life, A. Angela Morgan. BLP
Song of Life, A. Franz Werfel, *tr. fr. German by* Edith Abercrombie Snow. TrJP
Song of Light, A. Marguerite Wilkinson. MeRV
Song of Living, A. William Stanley Braithwaite. BPP
Song of Living, A. Amelia Josephine Burr. HBV; OBAV; POT; PoTo
Song of Lo-fu, The. *Unknown, tr. fr. Chinese.* AWP, *tr. by* Arthur Waley; WhP
Song of Loneliness. Judah Halevi, *tr. fr. Hebrew by* Nina Davis Salaman. TrJP
Song of Louisiana. Vashti R. Stopher. PoRL
Song of Love, A. "Lewis Carroll." GN
Song of Love, The. Rainer Maria Rilke, *tr. fr. German by* Ludwig Lewisohn. AWP
Song of Maelduin. Thomas William Rolleston. HBMV; TIP
Song of Maldoror, The, *sel.* "Comte de Lautréamont," *tr. fr French by* John Rodker.
"Leech's brother walked slowly in the forest, The." MiFP
Song of Marion's Men. Bryant. AnNE; APW; BoHiPo; CoBA; DD; DDA; GA, *abr.*; HBV; HBVY; HiLiAm; IAP; IDAH; LPS-2; MC; MOAP; PAH; PAP; PTA-2; TCAP; TreF
Song of Mary, A. Agnes H. Begbie. BOL
Song of Mary-of-the-Angels, The. Jean Richepin, *tr. fr. French by* Alan Conder. TrFP
Song of Mary the Mother of Christ, The. *At. to* Henry Walpole. ISi
Song of Mehitabel, The. Don Marquis. *Fr.* Archy and Mehitabel. FiBHP; TreFS
Song of Men. Edgar Lee Masters. *Fr.* Canticle of the Race. ChMo; CMP
Song of Milkanwatha, The, *parody, sel.* George A. Strong.
Modern Hiawatha, The. BBV (1951 ed.); BOHV; FaFP; FaPON; FiBHP; HBV; InMe; LiTG; MoShBr; NA; PA; PIAE; SiTL; TreFS; WhC; YaD
(Hiawatha's Mittens.) ShBV-1
Song of Mr. Toad, The. Kenneth Grahame. *See* World Has Held Great Heroes, The.
Song of Mo Shang Sang, A. Wang T'ai Ch'ing, *tr. fr. Chinese by* Henry H. Hart. PoHN
Song of Moses, The. Exodus Bible, *O.T. See* Triumphal Chant.
Song of Myself. Walt Whitman. AmP; AmPo; AmPP; AnFE; APA; APW, *abr.*; ATP (1935 ed.), *much abr.*; BAP, *much abr.*; BLV, *much abr.*; BoLiVe, *much abr.*; CoAnAm; CoBA, *abr.*; CoV, *abr.*; IAP; LEAP, *abr.*; LiTA; MAP, *abr.*; MoAmPo, *abr.*; NeMA, *abr.*; OxBA; PECK, *much abr.*; REAL, *abr.*; TrGrPo, *abr.*; ViBoPo, *much abr.*
(I Celebrate Myself, *much abr.*) OnAP
(Walt Whitman, *much abr.*) WHA
Sels.
"All truths wait in all things," *fr.* XXX–XXXI. PFY; PoLFOT (XXX)
"Alone far in the wilds and mountains I hunt," X. SeCeV
Animals, *fr.* XXXII. EV-5; FaFP; GTBS-W; LiTG; MCCG; NePA; SiTL
(Beasts, The.) HBV; OBVV; PC
("I think I could turn and live with animals.") AnEnPo; LoBV (1949 ed.); PG (1955 ed.); PoMa; TrGrPo; WGRP
Battle of the *Bonhomme Richard* and the *Serapis*, XXXV–XXXVI. UnPo (3d ed.)
(Old-Time Sea-Fight, An, XXXV.) MaC
(Sea-Fight, A, XXXV.) LH
("Would you hear of an old-time sea-fight?") SeCeV
Beholding God, *fr.* XLVIII. GrCo-1
Dazzling and Tremendous How Quick the Sun-Rise Would Kill Me, *fr.* XXV. AtBAP
Drayman, The, *fr.* XIII. PoNe
Dying Heroes, *fr.* XXXIII. BHV
(Dying Fireman, The, *shorter sel.*) EV-5; LH
Earth at Night, *fr.* XXI. PIAE
(Bare-bosom'd Night.) SN
Grass, The, VI. GTBS-W; LiTG; NePA; NLK, *sel.*; PIAE
("Child said, *What is the Grass?*, A.") AtBAP; BLV; BoLiVe; InP; MaPo; PG (1955 ed.); TrGrPo
(From "Walt Whitman.") PFY
(Leaves of Grass, *fr.* VI *and* XX.) AA; ADAH
(Lines from "Song of Myself.") BBV (1951 ed.)
(What Is the Grass?) PCD, *abr.*; PCH; TSW, *sel.*; TSWC, *sel.*
I Am an Acme of Things Accomplished, *fr.* XLIV. SN
I Am He That Walks with the Tender and Growing Night, *fr.* XXI. AtBAP; ChTr; ExPo; MCCG; TSW
"I am the poet of the body," XXI. BAV, 11 *ll.*; CoBA; RiBV; SeCeV; TrGrPo
"I am the teacher of athletes," XLVII. CoBA; PreP, *abr.*
"I celebrate myself, and sing myself," I. OBAV (I *and* VI); PoFS (I–XLVIII, *much abr.*); PoLFOT; TCAP
(I Celebrate Myself.) NePA
(Myself.) AA; FaBoBe
I Dote upon Myself, *fr.* XXIV. AnEnPo
"I have heard what the talkers were talking, the talk of the beginning and the end," III. PoLFOT
"I have said that the soul is not more than the body," XLVIII. BAV; CoBA; CoV; TrGrPo
(Hub for the Universe, A.) FaFP
(Letters from God.) CBOV
"I hear and behold God in every object," *fr.* XLVIII. WGRP
I Know I Am Deathless, *fr.* XX. MaRV
"I open my scuttle at night and see the far-sprinkled systems," *fr.* XLV. PFY
I Tramp a Perpetual Journey, *fr.* XLVI. OQP; QP-2
(Perpetual Journey, The.) GrCo-2
"I understand the large hearts of heroes," *fr.* XXXIII. PoFr
(Heroes, *fr.* XXXIII *and* XXXV.) AA

Song of Myself (*continued*)
Infinity ("My feet strike an apex"), *fr.* XLIV–XLV. AA
"It is time to explain myself," *fr.* XLIV. MaRV
"Little one sleeps in its cradle, The," VIII. MaPo
Miracles, *fr.* XXXI. CBOV; MaRV; PoeMoYo
("I believe a leaf of grass is no less than the journey-work of the stars.") PG (1955 ed.); SeCeV; TiPo
(Leaf of Grass, A.) OQP; QP-2
(Leaves of Grass.) YT
(Microcosm, The.) SN
My Barbaric Yawp, LII. NePA
("Spotted hawk swoops by and accuses me, The.") PoLFOT
"Now I will do nothing but listen," XXVI. HoPM; MaPo
Oxen That Rattle the Yoke and Chain, *fr.* XIII. SN
"Pure contralto sings in the organ loft, The," XV. MaPo
Runaway Slave, The, *fr.* X. PoNe
("Runaway slave came to my house, The.") PoFr
Twenty-eight Young Men Bathe by the Shore, XI. ExPo; MaPo
"Walt Whitman, a kosmos, of Manhattan the son," XXIV. BAV, XXIV–XXXIII, *abr.*; PoFr, 11 *ll.*
With Music Strong I Come, *fr.* XVIII–XIX. AtBAP
Wounded Person, The, *fr.* XXXIII. PoNe
You Sea, *fr.* XXII. SN
Song of Mystic Unity, The. Jami, *tr. fr. Persian by* R. A. Nicholson. LiTW
Song of Nature. Emerson. AnNE; HBV; SN
Song of Nature. Elizabeth Selden. BoFr
Song of Nesace. Poe. *See* Song: "Spirit! that dwellest where."
Song of Nidderdale, The. Dorothy Una Ratcliffe. HBMV
Song of Nuns, A. James Shirley. *See* O Fly My Soul.
Song of Oenone and Paris. George Peele. *See* Fair and Fair.
Song of One Eleven Years in Prison. George Canning, George Ellis, *and* John Hookham Frere. *See* Song: "Whene'er with haggard eyes I view."
Song of Orpheus ("O surely now the fisherman"). William Morris. *Fr.* The Life and Death of Jason, IX. LEAP
Song of O'Ruark, Prince of Breffni, The. Thomas Moore. OnYI
Song of Our Flag, A. Wilbur D. Nesbit. *See* Your Flag and My Flag.
Song of Our Glorious Southland. Mary Ware. BIG
Song of Panama, A. Damon Runyon. PAH
Song of Paris and Oenone. George Peele. *See* Fair and Fair.
Song of Parting, A. Chang Yung, *tr. fr. Chinese by* Henry H. Hart. PoHN
Song of Parting, A. Compton Mackenzie. HBV; OBVV
Song of Past Feelings. Po Chü-i, *tr. fr. Chinese by* Arthur Waley. TrCh
Song of Perfect Propriety. Dorothy Parker. InMe
Song of Phillida and Coridon. Nicholas Breton. TuPP
Song of Pierrot, A. Maurice A. Hanline. LEAP
Song of Pleasure, A. Philip Massinger. *See* Song: "Blushing rose and purple flower, The."
Song of Ploughing. *Unknown.* LyMA
Song of Poplars. Aldous Huxley. MBP; MoBrPo (1942 ed); TwCV
Song of Power, A. Berton Braley. PoMa
Song of Praise, A. Psalms, VIII, Bible, *O.T.* *See* What Is Man?
Song of Praise, A. Psalms, CXLVIII, Bible, *O.T.* TrGrPo
(Psalm CXLVIII: "Praise ye the Lord.") TriL; TrJP
Song of Praise, A. Countee Cullen. LoPS; NP
Song of Praise to Mary. "Angelus Silesius," *tr. fr. German by* Mary E. Mannix. CAW
Song of Quetzalcoatl, *sels.* *Unknown, tr. fr. Aztec by* John Hubert Cornyn. LiTW
Hymn to the Wind God.
White Kite, The.
Song of Quoodle, The. G. K. Chesterton. SiTL
Song of Renaud. *Unknown, pr. tr. fr. French.* LiA
Song of Renunciation, A. Sir Owen Seaman. CenHV; PA
Song of Returning to Kwei-chi. Li Ho, *tr. fr. Chinese by* Ho Chih-yuan. WhP
Song of Riches, A. Katharine Lee Bates. AA
Song of Right and Wrong, The. G. K. Chesterton. *See* Feast on Wine or Fast on Water.
Song of Robin Goodfellow, A. Shakespeare. *See* Now the Hungry Lion Roars.
Song of Roland, The, *sels.* *Unknown, tr. fr. Old French.*
Last Battle, The, *tr. by* C. K. Scott Moncrieff. LiTW
Ready They Make Hauberks Sarrazinese, *tr. by* C. K. Scott Moncrieff. WaaP
"When Roland saw that life had fled," *tr. by* John O'Hagan. EnLi-1; OuHeWo
Death of Roland, The, *shorter sel., tr. by* Henry Adams. LiA; MeRV
Song of Sack, A. *Unknown.* OBS
Song of Safety, A. Psalms, CXXI, Bible, *O.T.* *See* I Will Lift Up Mine Eyes unto the Hills.
Song of Satisfaction on Completing an Overhauling of Fishing Tackle, A. Leslie P. Thompson. WhC
Song of Saul before His Last Battle. Byron. BPN; Po
Song of Secret Love, The. Dryden. *See* Song: "I feed a flame within . . ."
Song of Self-Pity, A. Geoffrey Vivien. TwCaPo
Song of Shadows, The. Walter de la Mare. BLV; BoLiVe; ChMo; CMP; CoBE; MBP; MoBrPo; MoP; ShBV-3; TrGrPo
("Sweep thy faint strings, Musician.") CBE
Song of Sherman's Army, The. Charles Graham Halpine. GA; MC; PAH; PAP
Song of Sherman's March to the Sea. Samuel H. M. Byers. *See* Sherman's March to the Sea.
Song of Sherwood, A. Alfred Noyes. BBV; FaPON; HBV; HBVY; MCCG; MPB; OTPC (1946 ed.); PCD; POT; PoTo; PYM; RG; SP; TiPo (1959 ed.); VOD
(Sherwood.) BMEP; BoTP; MBP; MoBrPo; PCN; ShBV-1
Song of Sighing, A. James Thomson. EnLit
Song of Slaves in the Desert. Whittier. AmPP; AnAmPo; LA; OBVV; OxBA
(Song of the Slaves in the Desert.) PFY
Song of Sleep-Time, A. *Unknown.* BOL
Song of Snow-white Heads. Cho Wen-chün, *tr. fr. Chinese by* Arthur Waley. ChLP; TrCh
Song of Soldiers, The. Walter de la Mare. SoV
Song of Solomon, The. Bible, *O.T.*
(Song of Songs, The.) AWP; TrGrPo
Sels.
"Awake! Oh, north wind," IV: 16. SUS
"Behold, thou art fair, my love," IV: 1–16. LoPS
(Behold, Thou Art Fair, 1–7.) TrJP
(Song of Songs, 1–16.) WoL
"For, lo, the winter is past," II: 11–12. SUS; TiPo
(For, Lo, the Winter Is Past, 10–13.) TreF
(Hark! My Beloved! 8–13.) TrJP
(Lo, the Winter Is Past.) FaPON (11–12); ShBV-3 (11–13)
(Spring, 11–12.) PCD; PCH
"How beautiful are thy feet with shoes, O prince's daughter!" VII: 1–13. LoPS
(Return, Return, O Shulammite, 1–10.) TrJP
"I adjure you, O daughters of Jerusalem," V: 8–16 (*King James Version, Revised*). LiTW
"I am come into my garden, my sister, my spouse," V: 1–16. LoPS
I Am My Beloved's, VII: 11–14. TrJP
"I am the flower of the field," II: 1, 2, 14, *Douay vers.*
(Canticle of Canticles.) ISi
I Sleep, but My Heart Waketh, V: 2–VI: 3. TrJP
Love Idyll, A ("I am the rose of Sharon"), II: 1–14, 16–17, III: 1–5. CBOV
(I Am the Rose of Sharon, II: 1–17.) ChTr
(Song of Songs, II: 1–17.) GBV, *abr.*; PG
"My beloved spake, and said unto me," II: 10–III: 4. LO
On My Bed I Sought Him, III: 1–5. TrJP
"Set me as a seal upon thine heart," VIII: 6–7. LiTW (*King James Version, Revised*); LoPo
(As a Seal upon Thy Heart.) TrJP
(Love.) CBOV; LiA; MaRV
"Thou art beautiful, O my love," VI: 3, 8, 9, *Douay vers.*
(Canticle of Canticles.) ISi
"Voice of my beloved, The," II: 8–14. EnLi-1; LiTW (*King James Version, Revised*)
(Arise, My Love, My Fair One.) LoPo
(Love Lyrics.) OuHeWo
Song of Solomon, A. Josephine Preston Peabody. NP; OBAV
Song of Songs, The. Bible, *O.T.* *See* Song of Solomon, The.
Song of Songs. Wilfred Owen. NAMP
Song of Songs. Tzu Yeh, *tr. fr. Chinese by* Henry H. Hart. ChLP; PoHN
Song of Sorrow, A. Charles Battell Loomis. BOHV
Song of Sprats, A. Jørgen Vibe, *tr. fr. Danish by* Charles W. Stork. BoDS
Song of Spring. Keats. *Fr.* At Teignmouth. BoTP
Song of Steam, The. George W. Cutter. LPS-2
Song of Sten Sture, A. Edvard Bäckström, *tr. fr. Swedish by* Charles W. Stork. AnSL
Song of Street Labor, A. Caroline A. Lord. DD
Song of Summer. Paul Laurence Dunbar. MCCG; OTPC (1946 ed.); TSW; TSWC; VOD
Song of Summer Days. J. W. Foley. BoTP
Song of Summer Days, A. Virna Sheard. OCL
Song of sunshine through the rain, A. Calvary and Easter [*or* Easter Song]. "Susan Coolidge." BLRP; EOAH; OQP; PGD; PSO; QP-1; WBLP
Song of Supplication, A. Psalms, CXXX, Bible, *O.T.* *See* De Profundis.
Song of Switzerland. Stoddard King. WhC
Song of Texas. William Henry Cuyler Hosmer. PAH
Song of Thamesis. Dryden. *Fr.* Albion and Albanius. TCEP
(Song of the River Thames, A.) FaBoEn

Song of Thanatos, The. Thomas Lovell Beddoes. *See* Mighty Thoughts of an Old World, The.
Song of Thanks, A. Edward Smyth Jones. BANP
Song of Thanksgiving. John Richard Moreland. PGD
Song of the All-Wool Shirt. Eugene Field. StPo
Song of the Ancient People, The, *sel.* Edna Dean Proctor.
"We are the Ancient People." AA
Song of the Angels. Nahum Tate. *See* While Shepherds Watched Their Flocks by Night.
Song of the Argonauts. William Morris. *See* O Bitter Sea.
Song of the Arrow, The. Isabella Valancy Crawford. *Fr.* Gisli, the Chieftain. BoCaPo
Song of the Arrowhead. Li Ho, *tr. fr. Chinese by* Ho Chih-yuan. WhP
Song of the Ascension. William Drummond of Hawthornden. *See* Hymn of the Ascension, An.
Song of the Athenians. Viktor Rydberg, *tr. fr. Swedish by* Charles W. Stork. *Fr.* Dexippos. AnSL
Song of the Autumn Nights. George Macdonald. BSV
(Songs of the Autumn Night: "So, like the corn, moon-ripened last.") EBSV
Song of the Bacchanals. Euripides, *tr. fr. Greek by* Gilbert Murray. *Fr.* Bacchae. GrR
(Bacchanal, *shorter sel., tr. by* T. F. Higham.) OxBG
(Home of Aphrodite, The, *shorter sel., tr. by* Gilbert Murray.) AWP
Song of the Ballet. J. B. Morton. FiBHP
Song of the Banishment of the Two Dukes, A. Thomas Deloney. SiCE
Song of the Banjo, The. Kipling. BPN; FaBoCh; OtMeF; PoVP; VLEP
Song of the Bath, The. Margaret Gibbs. BoTP
Song of the Battle-Skald. Bengt Lidner, *tr. fr. Swedish by* Charles W. Stork. *Fr.* Medea. AnSL
Song of the Bees. Hannah Flagg Gould. OTPC
Song of the Beggars. Richard Brome. *Fr.* A Jovial Crew, I, i. CenL; SeCL
Song of the Bell. Schiller, *tr. fr. German by* Longfellow. LiA
Epilogue of Schiller's "Song of the Bell": "He was our own!" *abr.* Goethe, *tr. by* Edgar A. Bowring. BoFr
Song of the Billows, The. Nils Collett Vogt, *tr. fr. Norwegian by* Charles W. Stork. AnNoLy
Song of the Bird, The. Wilhelm Müller, *tr. fr. German by* Longfellow. BoTP
Song of the Blue Water. Li Po, *tr. fr. Chinese.* WhP
Song of the Borderguard, The. Robert Duncan. NeAP
Song of the Bow, The. Sir Arthur Conan Doyle. *Fr.* The White Company. BHV; HBV; MCCG; MuP
Song of the Bower, The. Dante Gabriel Rossetti. EmBrPo; HBV; PoVP; TCEP
Song of the Breath, The. Stephen Vincent Benét. *Fr.* John Brown's Body. AmP
(Song of Breath, A.) MoVE
Song of the Broad-Axe. Walt Whitman. WoL
Sels.
Broad-Axe, The, *fr.* I. APW; MAP; MoAmPo
Great City, The, V. BAP; GrCo-1 (*fr.* IV *and* V)
What Endures, *fr.* IV. BHV
Song of the Brook. Tennyson. *See* Brook, The; an Idyl.
Song of the Camels. Elizabeth J. Coatsworth. FaPON; RIS
(Twelfth Night.) ChBR
Song of the Camp, The. Bayard Taylor. AA; BeLS; BTP; GN; HBV; HBVY; LPS-1; OBAV; OTPC; PTA-1; TCAP; WBLP
(Song in Camp, The.) BBV (1923 ed.); PECK
Song of the Candle, The. Li Shih-ming, *tr. fr. Chinese by* Henry H. Hart. PoHN
Song of the Cannon, The. Sam Walter Foss. IDAH
Song of the Cattle Trail. John Milton Hagen. *See* Cowboy and His Love, The.
Song of the Centennial, The, *sel.* Joaquin Miller.
People's Song of Peace, The. LPS-2
Song of the Chattahoochee. Sidney Lanier. AA; AmP; AmPP; AnAmPo; AnEnPo; BBV (1923 ed.); CoBA; FaBoBe; HBV; IAP; InP; LA; LaNeLa; LEAP; LiTA; MAP; MCCG; MoAmPo (1942 ed.); MOAP; NePA; OBAV; OHFP; OTPC (1946 ed.); PCD; PFE; PoeMoYo; PTA-2; PYM; RG; SPP; TCAP; TreF; YaD; YT
Song of the Chickadee. *Unknown.* OTPC (1946 ed.); PCH
Song of the Child, The. Anna Wickham. QS
Song of the Children, The. G. K. Chesterton. AlDL
Song of the Children in Paladore. Sir Henry Newbolt. MM
Song of the Christmas Trees. Blanche Elizabeth Wade. OHIP; SDH
Song of the Cid, The. *Unknown. See* Cid, The.
Song of the Clouds. Aristophanes, *tr. fr. Greek. Fr.* The Clouds. AWP, *tr. by* Oscar Wilde; GrL, *tr. by* T. F. Higham; OxBG, *tr. by* T. F. Higham
(Chorus of Clouds, *tr. by* Benjamin Bickley Rogers.) GrR
(Chorus of the Clouds, *tr. by* T. F. Higham.) LiTW
(Cloud-maidens that float on forever, *tr. by* Oscar Wilde.) GrPo
Song of the Colorado, The. Sharlot Mabridth Hall. HBV
Song of the Columns. Paul Valéry, *tr. fr. French by* Vernon Watkins. AnFP; MiFP; TrFP, *tr. by* Alan Conder
Song of the Cornpopper, The. Laura E. Richards. BoChLi
Song of the Corsairs. Byron. *Fr.* The Corsair, I. EtS
(Corsair's Life, The.) EV-4
(Song of the Rover.) LPS-2
Song of the Cossack Girl. Ilya Selvinsky, *tr. fr. Russian by* Jack Lindsay. RuPo
Song of the Courtesans. Ting Liu Niang, *tr. fr. Chinese by* Florence Ayscough *and* Amy Lowell. ChLP
Song of the Creatures, The. St. Francis of Assisi. *See* Canticle of the Sun.
Song of the Crusaders. *Unknown. See* Fairest Lord Jesus.
Song of the Cyclops, The. Thomas Dekker. *Fr.* London's Tempe. NBE; ShBV-1
("Brave iron! brave hammer! from your sound.") TuPP
Song of the Dawn, *sel.* John Ruskin.
"Awake! awake! the stars are pale, the east is russet gray." HBV; PoFr
Song of the Death of Daphnis, The. Theocritus. *See* Death of Daphnis, The.
Song of the Demented Priest, The. John Berryman. MoPo
Song of the Derelict, The. John McCrae. EtS
Song of the Dew. *Unknown, tr. fr. Hebrew by* Solomon Solis-Cohen. TrJP
Song of the Dial, The. Peter Airey. OQP; QP-2
Song of the Dove. Fredrika Bremer, *tr. fr. Swedish by* Mary Howitt. *Fr.* The Home. BOL
(Swedish Mother's Lullaby.) MOAH
Song of the Drift Weed. Jessie Mackay. BoAu
Song of the drowsy sky, The. Lied V. José María Eguren. AnCL
Song of the Dumb Waiter, The. James Reeves. AlDL
Song of the Earth. *Tr. fr. Navaho Indian by* Natalie Curtis. APW
Song of the Elfin Miller. Allan Cunningham. OTPC (1946 ed.); TVSH
Song of the Elfin Steersman. George Hill. AA; APW
Song of the Emigrants in Bermuda. Andrew Marvell. *See* Bermudas.
Song of the Emperor Yu on the Making of the Nine Tripods. *Unknown, tr. fr. Chinese. Fr.* The Fountain of Old Poems. WhP
Song of the Engine, The. H. Worsley-Benison. BoTP
Song of the English, A. Kipling. BPN
Song of the Exposition, *sels.* Walt Whitman.
"Ah little recks the laborer," I–IV, *abr.* IAP
"And thou America," VIII, *abr.* GA
Muse in the New World, The, II, III, *abr.* APW; MAP; MoAmPo
(Come Muse Migrate from Greece and Ionia, *longer sel.*) OnAP
Song of the Faeries, The. W. B. Yeats. *See* Fairy Song.
Song of the Fairies. Shakespeare. *See* You Spotted Snakes.
Song of the Fairies. *Unknown, tr. fr. Middle Irish by* A. H. Leahy. OnYI
Song of the Fairies, The. W. B. Yeats. *See* Fairy Song.
Song of the Fairy ("Over hill, over dale"). Shakespeare. *See* Over Hill, over Dale.
Song of the Falcon. *Unknown, tr. fr. Danish by* E. M. Smith-Dampier. BoDaBa
Song of the fields and a song of the woods, A. Lord De Tabley. *Fr.* A Song of the Rolling Wind. GTBS-D
Song of the Figurehead. Kai Friis-Møller, *tr. fr. Danish by* Charles W. Stork. BoDS
Song of the Fire. Edward Fitzgerald. OTPC (1923 ed.)
Song of the Fire. Sister M. Maura. SaFP
Song of the Fishes, *with music.* *Unknown.* AmSS
Song of the Five Joys, A. *Unknown.* TMEV
Song of the Flags, The. S. Weir Mitchell. PAH
Song of the Flea. Judah Al-Harizi, *tr. fr. Hebrew.* TrJP
Song of the Foot-Track. Elsie Cole. BoAu
Song of the Forerunners. Karle Wilson Baker. HiLiAm
Song of the Forest Ranger, The. Herbert Bashford. HBV; OHIP
Song of the Forest Trees. *Unknown, tr. fr. Middle Irish by* Standish Hayes O'Grady. OnYI
(Wood to Burn and Not to Burn.) SiB
Song of the Forsaken. William Thom. EBSV
Song of the Four Colors. Wang Jung, *tr. fr. Chinese by* Henry H. Hart. PoHN
Song of the Four Seasons, A. Austin Dobson. BMEP; HBV; POTT; VLEP
Song of the Four Seasons, The. Li Po, *tr. fr. Chinese.* WhP
Song of the Four Winds, The. Thomas Love Peacock. *Fr.* The Misfortunes of Elphin. OBRV
Song of the Full Catch. Constance Lindsay Skinner. *Fr.* Songs of the Coast Dwellers. BoCaPo; CaP; NV; OCL; TBM
Song of the Future, A. Sidney Lanier. TCAP

Song of the Galley, The. *Unknown, tr. fr. Spanish by* John Gibson Lockhart. AWP; PoFr
Song of the Galley-Slaves. Kipling. *Fr.* Many Inventions. ChTr; PoEL-5; PoFr
Song of the General Strike. Mario Bravo, *tr. fr. Spanish by* Alice Stone Blackwell. PoFr
Song of the Ghost, The. Alfred Perceval Graves. AnIV; DaM
Song of the Golden Pavilion for Liang Fen. Nalan Hsinteh, *tr. fr. Chinese by* Hsiung Ting. WhP
Song of the Good Samaritan, The. Vernon Watkins. LiTM (rev. ed.)
Song of the Grail Seekers. Hermann Hagedorn. VOD
Song of the Grass, The. Sarah Roberts Boyle. *See* Voice of the Grass, The.
Song of the Graves, The. *Unknown, tr. fr. Welsh by* Ernest Rhys. OBMV
Song of the Greek Poet [*or* Bard]. Byron. *See* Isles of Greece, The.
Song of the Gulf Stream. Francis Alan Ford. EtS
Song of the Happy Shepherd, The. W. B. Yeats. PoFS
Song of the Harlot. Isaiah, XXIII: 16, Bible, *O.T.* TrJP
Song of the Harper. *Unknown, tr. fr. Egyptian by* T. Eric Peet. LiTW
Song of the Harvest. Henry Stevenson Washburn. OHIP
Song of the Hatteras Whale, A. *Unknown.* EtS
Song of the Hawk. Maxim Gorki, *tr. fr. Russian by* C. M. Bowra. BoRS
Song of the Heads, The. *Unknown, tr. fr. Irish by* Frank O'Connor. KiLC
Song of the Hermit Thrush, The. James B. Thomas. BLA
Song of the Highest Tower. Arthur Rimbaud, *tr. fr. French by* Edgell Rickword. AWP; JAWP; WBP; AnFP, *tr. by* Kate Flores
Song of the Hill. Edith Lodge. GoYe
Song of the Holly. Shakespeare. *See* Blow, Blow, Thou Winter Wind.
Song of the Horse. *Tr. fr. Navajo Indian by* Natalie Curtis. APW; AWP; JAWP; WBP
Song of the House. *Unknown, tr. fr. Navajo Indian.* GrCo-1
Song of the Human Spirit. Edgar Lee Masters. *Fr.* Canticle of the Race. ChMo; CMP
Song of the Hunt, The. John Bennett. *Fr.* Master Sky-Lark. AA
Song of the Ill-Beloved, The. Guillaume Apollinaire, *tr. fr. French by* Dudley Fitts. AnFP
Song of the Indian Maid. Keats. *Fr.* Endymion. EV-4; OAEP; OBEV
(O Sorrow! *abr.*) CH
(Roundelay: "O Sorrow.") ATP (1935 ed.); BPN
(Song: "O Sorrow," *shorter sel.*) LoBV
Song of the Indian Mother. James Gowdy Clark. BOL
Song of the Indian Wars, The, *sels.* John G. Neihardt.
At Beecher's Island. TCPD
Roman Nose Rides. TCPD
Sowing of the Dragon, The. TCAP
Song of the Initiated. Euripides, *tr. fr. Greek by* Sir Gilbert Murray. OxBG
Song of the Jellicles, The. T. S. Eliot. FaBoCh; LiL; LoGBV
Song of the King's Minstrel, The. Richard Middleton. HBV
Song of the Kings of Gold. Ebenezer Jones. VA
Song of the Lark, The. George Macdonald. BMEP
Song of the Larks at Dawn. Herbert Trench. *See* Shepherds Who Pastures Seek.
Song of the Leadville Mine Boss. Don Cameron. PoOW
Song of the Lightning. George W. Cutter. LPS-3
Song of the Lilies, The. Lucy Wheelock. OHIP
Song of the Little Hunter, The. Kipling. *Fr.* The Second Jungle Book. ShBV-1
(Fear.) PtOT
Song of the Little Hypertrophic Child. Jules Laforgue, *tr. fr. French by* Vernon Watkins. AnFP
Song of the Little Villages. James B. Dollard. CAW; JKCP
Song of the Little Winds. Laura E. Richards. BOL
Song of the Long River. Constance Lindsay Skinner. AV; CPG; TBM
Song of the Lotos-Eaters. Tennyson. *See* Choric Song.
Song of the Love of Jesus, A. Richard Rolle of Hampole. PoEL-1
Song of the Lower Classes, The. Ernest Charles Jones. CoMu; OBVV
Song of the Lute in the Praise of God and Dispraise of Idolatry, A. John Hall. ReIE
Song of the Mad Prince, The. Walter de la Mare. AtBAP; FaBoCh; LBBV; LoGBV; MoVE; OAEP (2d ed.); POTT; ShBV-4
Song of the Maple. R. M. Streeter. PEOR
Song of the Mariner's Needle. C. R. Clarke. EtS
Song of the Mayers: "Remember us poor Mayers all." *Unknown.* CH; PoD, *sl. abr.*
(Hitchen May-Day Song, The.) CG
Song of the Men of Chin-ling. Hsieh T'iao, *tr. fr. Chinese by* Arthur Waley. TrCh
Song of the Mermaids. George Darley. *See* Mermaidens' Vesper-Hymn.
Song of the "Metis" Trapper, The. *Unknown.* CSF
Song of the Micmac, The. Joseph Howe. BoCaPo; CaP
Song of the Milkmaid. Tennyson. *See* Milkmaid's Song.
Song of the Mischievous Dog, The. Dylan Thomas. FaFP; SiTL
Song of the Moderns. John Gould Fletcher. AWP; InPo; MOAP
Song of the Moon, A. Claude McKay. PoNe
(Moon Song.) TSW
Song of the Moon-Spirit. Mary Josephine Benson. CPG
Song of the Mound. Wincenty Pol, *tr. fr. Polish by* Paul Soboleski. PoFr
Song of the Mountain Girl, The. Juan Ruiz, Archpriest of Hita, *tr. fr. Spanish by* Elisha K. Kane. *Fr.* The Book of Good Love. AnSpL-1
Song of the Mountebank. Jules Supervielle, *tr. fr. French by* Alan Conder. TrFP
Song of the Movie Mexican, A. Edwin Meade Robinson. LHV
Song of the Musicians. Shakespeare. *Fr.* Cymbeline. *See* Hark! Hark! the Lark.
Song of the Musicians. Shakespeare. *Fr.* Two Gentlemen of Verona. *See* Who Is Silvia.
Song of the Mystic. Abram J. Ryan. JKCP; SPP
Song of the Narcissus, The. *Unknown, tr. fr. Arabic by* E. Powys Mathers. *Fr.* The Thousand and One Nights. AWP
Song of the Navajo. Albert Pike. PoOW
Song of the Negro Boatman. Whittier. *Fr.* At Port Royal. GN
Song of the New World. Angela Morgan. BAP; CP; CV; HBMV; HBVY; OQP; QP-2
Song of the Nibelungs, The, *sels.* *Unknown, pr. tr. fr. Middle High German by* Margaret Armour.
Fall of Siegfried, The, *abr.* WoL
Fall of the Nibelungs, The. LiA
Song of the Night at Daybreak. Alice Meynell. CH; PoVP; VA
Song of the Norns, The. *Unknown.* *See* Song of the Valkyries, The.
Song of the Old Days, A. Patrick MacGill. MaRV
Song of the Old Love. Jean Ingelow. *Fr.* Supper at the Mill. HBV
Song of the Old Man. John Gould Fletcher. MOAP
Song of the Old Man in Chains. Anatoli Vasilyevich Lunacharsky, *tr. fr. Russian by* L. A. Magnus *and* K. Walter. *Fr.* Faust and the City. PoFr
Song of the Old Mother, The. W. B. Yeats. AnIV; BEL; CV; GTSL; MBP; MCCG; MOAH; MoBrPo; MotAn; NeMA; VA
Song of the Open. Sara Hamilton Birchall. NLK
Song of the Open Country. Dorothy Parker. PC
Song of the Open Road, A. Louis J. McQuilland. NLK
Song of the Open Road. Ogden Nash. LiTM; NAMP; NLK (1947 ed.); SiTL; TreFS; WhC
Song of the Open Road, A. *Unknown, tr. fr. Latin by* John Addington Symonds. AWP; JAWP; WBP; WHA
Song of the Open Road. Walt Whitman. APW, *cond.;* FaFP; IAP; LEAP, *abr.;* MAP, *abr.;* MoAmPo, *abr.;* NePA; PC, *much abr.;* PoMa; ViBoPo, *abr.;* WHA, *sl. abr.*
(Open Road, The, *much abr.*) StaSt
Sels.
"Afoot and light-hearted I take to the open road," *7 ll.* AtBAP, *longer sel.;* HBVY; NeMA; NLK, *6 ll.;* OQP; QP-2; TiPo
(Open Road, The.) GTSE
Be Not Afraid. MaRV
Human Progress. GrCo-1
"Listen! I will be honest with you." PoFr
Song of the Outlaws. Joanna Baillie. *See* Outlaw's Song, The.
Song of the Pacifist, The. Robert W. Service. ReTS
Song of the Palm. Tracy Robinson. AA
Song of the Parrot. Elizabeth J. Coatsworth. StVeCh
Song of the Partridge, The. *Unknown, tr. fr. Armenian by* Zabelle C. Boyajian. ArmLP
Song of the Passion, A. Richard Rolle of Hampole. OxBoCh
(My Trewest Tresowre.) AtBAP
("My trewest tresowre so trayturly was taken.") NBE
(My Truest Treasure, *mod.*) TMEV
Song of the Passion, A. *Unknown.* TMEV
Song of the Peasants. *Unknown, tr. fr. Chinese.* *Fr.* The Fountain of Old Poems. WhP
Song of the Pen, The. Judah Al-Harizi, *tr. fr. Hebrew by* Joseph Chotzner. TrJP
Song of the Phoenix, A. George Darley. *See* Phoenix, The.
Song of the Pilgrims, The. Rupert Brooke. QS
"O Thou/ God of all long desirous roaming," *sel.* TrPWD
Song of the Pilgrims. Thomas Cogswell Upham. MC; PAH
Song of the Pine, The. James Buckham. PEOR

Song of the Pines. Po Chü-i, *tr. fr. Chinese by* Ching Ti. WhP
Song of the Pirates. *Unknown. Fr.* Common Conditions. MuP
("Lustily, lustily, let us sail forth.") ReEn; SiCe; TuPP
Song of the Plow, The, *sels.* Maurice Hewlett.
"He loathed his bond, but could not stir," *fr.* V. PoFr
Hodge in the Strife, *fr.* VIII. PoFr
London, *abr., fr.* V. PoFr
Man on the Hill, The. POTE
1914 Autumn and Winter, *fr.* Envoy. PoFr
Old Thought, An, *abr., fr.* Envoy. PoFr
Poll Tax (1378), *fr.* V. PoFr
Song of the Pop-Bottlers. Morris Bishop. FaPON; FiBHP
Song of the Press, The. William Hurd Hillyer. PoeMoYo
Song of the Rabbits outside the [*or* a] Tavern. Elizabeth J. Coatsworth. AnNE; RIS
(Rabbits' Song outside the Tavern, The.) PoMa; SUS; TiPo
Song of the Rain. Hugh McCrae. BoAV; MoAuPo
Song of the Rain Chant. *Tr. fr. Navajo Indian by* Natalie Curtis. AWP; JAWP; WBP
Song of the Reed, The. Jalal ed-Din Rumi, *tr. fr. Persian by* Sir William Jones. PeP
Song of the Reim-Kennar, The. Sir Walter Scott. *Fr.* The Pirate, *ch.* 6. OAEP
Song of the Riders. Stephen Vincent Benét. *Fr.* John Brown's Body. MAP; MoAmPo
Song of the River. Charles Kingsley. *See* Clear and Cool.
Song of the River. Li Po, *tr. into English by* James Whitall *fr. the Chinese-to-French translation of* Judith Gautier. ChLP
Song of the River God to Amoret, The. John Fletcher. *See* River God's Song, The.
Song of the River Thames, A. Dryden. *See* Song of Thamesis.
Song of the Road, A. Fred G. Bowles. MaRV; NLK; OQP; QP-2
Song of the Road, A. Robert Louis Stevenson. OTPC (1946 ed.); POTT; PoVP; YT
Song of the Robin, The. Beatrice Bergquist. SUS
Song of the Rolling Earth, A, *sel.* Walt Whitman.
Great Mother, The. GrCo-2
Song of the Rolling Wind, A, *sel.* Lord De Tabley.
"Song of the fields and a song of the woods, A." GTBS-D
Song of the Rover. Byron. *See* Song of the Corsairs.
Song of the Samma. Haruo Sato, *tr. fr. Japanese by* Takamichi Ninomiya *and* D. J. Enright. PoLJ
Song of the saw, The. Busy Carpenters. James S. Tippett. StVeCh
Song of the Scarlet Banners over John Reed. Marya Zaturenska. *Fr.* Elegies over John Reed. BAP
Song of the Screw. *Unknown.* NA
Song of the Sea. Richard E. Burton. EtS; NLK
Song of the Sea, A. "Barry Cornwall." *See* Sea, The.
Song of the Sea. *Unknown, at. to* Rumann MacColmain, *tr. fr. Middle Irish.* OnYI, *tr. by* Kuno Meyer; SiB, *diff. tr by* Kuno Meyer
Song of the sea-adventurers, that never were known to fame, The. The Pageant of Seamen. May Byron. HBV
Song of the sea was an ancient song, The. Song of the Sea. Richard E. Burton. EtS; NLK
Song of the Search. Constance Lindsay Skinner. *Fr.* Songs of the Coast-Dwellers. CPG
Song of the Seasons. Blanche De Good Lofton. YeAr
Song of the Seasons, A. Cosmo Monkhouse. DD; HBV
Song of the Seaweed, *sel.* Eliza Cook.
"Many a lip is gaping for drink." FiBHP
Song of the Settlers. Jessamyn West. FaPON
Song of the Shepherd in the Valley of Humiliation, The. Bunyan. *See* Shepherd Boy's Song, The.
Song of the Shepherds, The. Edwin Markham. SDH
Song of the Shirt, The. Thomas Hood. BCEP; BEL; BTP; CoBE; EnLi-2; EnLit; EnRP; EPN; EPP; ERP; EV-4; HBV; LEAP; LPS-1; MaC; MCCG; OBVV; OHFP; OnHT; OTPC (1946 ed.); PCD; PoFr; PreP; PTA-1; PYM; StaSt; TCEP; TreF; VA; WBLP
Sweated Labor, *sel.* MaRV
Song of the Siberian Exiles, The, *abr.* Nikolai Alekseyevich Nekrasov, *tr. fr. Russian by* Martha Dickinson Bianchi. PoFr
Song of the Silent Land. Johann Gaudenz von Salis-Seewis, *tr. fr. German by* Longfellow. AWP; HBV; JAWP; LEAP; OQP; WBP
Song of the Sirens. William Browne. *See* Sirens' Song, The.
Song of the Ski, The. Wilson MacDonald. CaP; PCN
Song of the Slaves in the Desert. Whittier. *See* Song of Slaves in the Desert.
Song of the Snowflakes. Annette Wynne. GFA
Song of the Soldier. Charles G. Halpine. *See* Comrades Known in Marches Many.
Song of the Soldier-born, The. Robert W. Service. LEAP
Song of the Son. Jean Toomer. CDC; MAP; PoNe
Song of the Songless. George Meredith. EPP
Song of the Sons of Esau, The. Bertha Runkle. AA
Song of the sorrow of Melisande is a weary song and a dreary song, The. The Song against Songs. G. K. Chesterton. ALV
Song of the Soul and the Bridegroom. St. John of the Cross, *tr. fr. Spanish by* David Lewis. LiA
(Spiritual Canticle between the Soul and Christ, *tr. by* Jessie Read Wendell.) TeCS
Song of the South Wind. *Unknown, tr. fr. Chinese. Fr.* The Fountain of Old Poems. WhP
Song of the Spanish Main, The. John Bennett. HBV
Song of the Spirits, The. Joseph Sheridan Le Fanu. *Fr.* The Legend of the Glaive. OnYI
Song of the Splendid Clouds. *Unknown, tr. fr. Chinese. Fr.* The Fountain of Old Poems. WhP
Song of the Spring Days. George Macdonald. BSV
Song of the Springtide. *Unknown.* BOHV
Song of the Squatter. Robert Lowe. VA
Song of the Standard, The. Swinburne. PoVP; VLEP
Song of the Steamer Engine. Caroline B. Le Row. PEOR
Song of the Stork, The. *Unknown, tr. fr. Armenian by* Zabelle C. Boyajian. ArmLP
Song of the Storm. Albert Durrant Watson. CPG
Song of the Storm-Finch, The. Maxim Gorki, *tr. fr. Russian by* Alice Stone Blackwell. PoFr
Song of the Strange Ascetic, The. G. K. Chesterton. HBMV
Song of the Stygian Naiades. Thomas Lovell Beddoes. EnRP; ERP; NBE
Song of the Summer Days. George Macdonald. BSV
Song of the Summer Winds. George Darley. *See* Summer Winds.
Song of the Sword, The. W. E. Henley. BPN
Song of the Syrens. William Browne. *See* Sirens' Song, The.
Song of the Texas Rangers. *Unknown.* BIG
Song of the Thames, A. Ernest Myers. TVSH
Song of the Three Angels. Gil Vicente, *tr. fr. Spanish by* Aubrey F. G. Bell. *Fr.* The Auto of the Bark of Purgatory. CAW
Song of the Three Minstrels. Thomas Chatterton. *Fr.* Aella. TrGrPo
("Budding floweret blushes at the light, The.") ViBoPo
(Mynstrelles Songe.) EnRP
(There Lacketh Somethynge Stylle, *abr.*) EV-3
Song of the Three Seeds in the Macaw's Beak. Elizabeth J. Coatsworth. TCPD
Song of the Thrush, The. T. A. Daly. BAP; MAP; NeMA
Song of the Times. Jacob Adler, *tr. fr. Yiddish by* Sarah Zweig Betsky. OnCuPl
Song of the Toad, The. John Burroughs. DDA; FaPON
Song of the Train. David McCord. FaPON
Song of the Trees. Mary Colborne-Veel. BoAu
Song of the Trip-Hammer. C. H. Collester. CAG
Song of the Turnkey, The. Harry Bache Smith. AA
Song of the Turtle and Flamingo. James Thomas Fields. *See* Turtle and Flamingo, The.
Song of the Two Brothers. Shakespeare. *See* Fear No More the Heat o' the Sun
Song of the Two Pages. Shakespeare. *See* It Was a Lover and His Lass.
Song of the Ungirt Runners, The. Charles Hamilton Sorley. EnLit; HBMV; MBP; MoBrPo; MuP; NeMA; OBEV (new ed.); PIAE; PreP; ShBV-2; TrGrPo (1942 ed.); TSW; TSWC; TVSH
Song of the Universal, *sels.* Walt Whitman.
"All, all for immortality," *fr.* IV. MaRV
"And thou, America," *fr.* IV. PGD
Song of the Unsuccessful, The. Richard Burton. LBMV; OQP; QP-2; WGRP
Song of the Valkyries, The. *Unknown, tr. fr. Norse by* Lee M. Hollander. LiTW; WaaP
(Song of the Norns, The.) PaOS
Song of the Vanquished, The. Nicholas Karvounis, *tr. fr. Modern Greek by* Rae Dalven. MoGP
Song of the Vermeil Phoenix. Tu Fu, *tr. fr. Chinese by* Hsieh Wen Tung. WhP
Song of the Vineyard Knife. Clément Marot, *tr. fr. French by* Ralph N. Currey. FoS
Song of the Virgin Mother, A. Lope de Vega, *tr. fr. Spanish by* Ezra Pound. AWP; JAWP; WBP
Song of the Vulture, The. Elia Demirjibashian, *tr. fr. Armenian by* Zabelle C. Boyajian. ArmLP
Song of the Wage-Slave, The. Ernest Charles Jones. PoFr
Song of the Water-Nymph. Roden Noel. *See* I Flung Me round Him.
Song of the Wave, A. George Cabot Lodge. AA; EtS
Song of the Well. Numbers, XXI: 17-18, Bible, *O.T.* TrJP
Song of the Western Men, The. Robert Stephen Hawker. AEV; CBE; EnRP; ERP; GoBC; HBV; LH; OBRV; OBVV; PoFr; TCEP; TVSH; VA
(And Shall Trelawn[e]y Die?) BCEP; EV-4; GTBS; GTSL; OtMeF; ShBV-1; WP
(Trelawny.) ACP (1926 ed.)
Song of the Wheat in Flower. *Unknown, tr. fr. Chinese. Fr.* The Fountain of Old Poems. WhP

Song of the White Clouds. *Unknown, tr. fr. Chinese. Fr.* The Fountain of Old Poems. WhP
(Ditty of the White Clouds, The, *tr. by* James Legge.) BoFr
Song of the Wild Storm-Waves, The. Percy F. Sinnett. VA
Song of the Wind and the Rain. Solomon ibn Gabirol, *tr. fr. Hebrew by* Solomon Solis-Cohen. TrJP
Song of the Wise Men. Edith Lovejoy Pierce. PGD
Song of the Witless Boy. Hugh McCrae. MM
Song of the Wood, The. Frederic Edward Weatherly. OTPC (1946 ed.)
Song of the Wulfshaw Larches. Ernest Rhys. VA
Song of the Young Girls. *Unknown, tr. fr. Sanskrit by* Puran Singh. OnPM
Song of the Zambra Dance. Dryden. *Fr.* The Conquest of Granada, Pt. I. AtBAP; OAEP; PoEL-3
(Zambra Dance, The.) CEP; SeCV-2
Song of the Zincali. "George Eliot." *Fr.* The Spanish Gypsy. VA
Song of Theodolinda, The. George Meredith. EmBrPo; NBE
"In their heaven the sainted hosts," *sel.* MeRV
Song of Thirst. Alcaeus, *tr. fr. Greek by* J. M. Edmonds. GrR
Song of Thomas, Departed. "Winétt de Rokha," *tr. fr. Spanish by* H. R. Hays. AnCL
Song of Three Friends, The, *sels.* John G. Neihardt.
Prairie Fire, The. TCPD
Shooting of the Cup, The. PoOW
Song of Thyrsis. Philip Freneau. *Fr.* Female Frailty. AA; AnFE; APA; APW; CoAnAm; HBV; LBAP; LEAP; LiTA; OnPM; PR; ViBoPo
Song of Troilus. Chaucer, *after* Petrarch. *Fr.* Troilus and Criseyde. AWP; LoPS
(Canticus Troili.) AtBAP
("If no love is, O God, what fele I so?") LO
(Troilus Soliloquizes.) EG
Song of Troy. Euripides. *See* Troy ("In Salamis, filled with the foaming").
Song of Trust, A. Psalms, CXXI, Bible, *O.T. See* I Will Lift Up Mine Eyes unto the Hills.
Song of Twilight, A. *Unknown.* HBV
Song of Two Angels, A. Laura E. Richards. AA
Song of Two Wanderers, A. Marguerite Wilkinson. BAP; HBMV; PoTo; SBMV
Song of Venus. Dryden. *Fr.* King Arthur, V, i. LoBV; OxBoLi; PoEL-3; SeCeV
(Song Sung by Venus in Honor of Britannia.) EPS (1942 ed.)
Song of Victory, A, *sel.* Edwin Markham.
"Sing and be glad," III *and* IV. AOAH
Song of Waking, A. Katharine Lee Bates. DD; OHIP; PEOR
Song of Wandering, A. Lord Dunsany. BMEP
Song of Wandering Ængus, The. W. B. Yeats. AEV; BLV; BMEP; BoLiVe; CBOV; CH; ChMo; CMP; CP; EnLi-2 (1949 ed.); EnLit; FaBoCh; GoTP; GTIV; InP; KN; LoGBV; MaPo; MBP; MoAB; MoBrPo; NV; OnSP; PG; PoEL-5; PoMS; PoRA; POTT; RG; SP; TCPD; ThWaDe; TiPo; TwCV; TyEnPo; VLEP; WaKn
Song of War, A. Li Po, *tr. fr. Chinese.* WhP
Song of Welcome. Hermia Harris Fraser, *ad. fr. Haida Indian song.* BoCaPo; CaP
Song of Whip-plaiting. Constance Lindsay Skinner. *Fr.* Songs of the Coast Dwellers. BoCaPo; NP
Song of White and Red, A. Sister Mary Benvenuta. JKCP (1926 ed.)
Song of White Snow, A. Ts'en Ts'an. *See* Farewell: "North wind sweeps over the land, The."
Song of Winter, A. Emily Davis Pfeiffer. PrWP; VA
Song of Winter, A. *Unknown, tr. fr. Middle Irish by* Kuno Meyer. AnIL; CH; OnYI
Song of Women. Edgar Lee Masters. *Fr.* Canticle of the Race. ChMo; CMP
Song of Women, A. Anna Wickham. OS
Song of Wood-Nymphs. "Barry Cornwall." LPS-3
Song of Work, A. Mary Blake. HH
Song of Youth, The. Orrick Johns. *Fr.* Songs of Deliverance. BAP
Song of Youth. Austin Melvin Works. CAG
Song of Zephyrus and the Spring. Ben Jonson. *Fr.* Chloridia. EPS (1942 ed.)
Song-Offering, A. Rabindranath Tagore, *tr. fr. Bengali by* Rabindranath Tagore. LiTW
Song on a May Morning. Milton. *See* Song on May Morning.
Song on Beholding an Enlightment. Matías de Bocanegra, *tr. fr. Spanish by* Samuel Beckett. AnMP
Song on King William. *Unknown. See* As I Walked by Myself.
Song on May Morning. Milton. BLV; BoLiVe; CBE; CH; DD; ElSeCe; EPS; GN; HBV; HBVY; OTPC; PIAE; TrGrPo
(May Morning.) LPS-2; YeAr
(On a May Morning.) ExPo
(On May Morning.) BCEP; CBOV; CG; RG; WP
(Song: May Morning, A.) ADAH
(Song on a May Morning.) PoRL; TyEnPo
Song (on Seeing Dead Bodies Floating off the Cape). Alun Lewis. *See* Song: "First month of his absence, The."
Song on the Ivy and the Holly, A. *Unknown. See* Nay, Ivy, Nay.
Song on the Water. Thomas Lovell Beddoes. EG; ERP; FaBoCh; LoGBV; PoE
Song on the Way, The *Unknown.* BrR; MPB
Song, Set by H. Purcell, and Sung by Mrs. Hodgson, A. Thomas Southerne. *See* Though You Make No Return.
Song; Set by Mr. Coleman. Charles Cotton. *See* Song: "See, how like twilight slumber falls."
Song; Set by Mr. John Eccles. Congreve. *See* Nymph and a Swain, A.
Song soars from a sordid city street, A. A Street Melody. Belle Cooper. GoBC
Song Sparrow, The. Archibald Lampman. BoCaPo
Song-Sparrow, The. George Parsons Lathrop. SN
Song-Sparrow, The. Percy MacKaye. BLA
Song Sparrow, The. Henry van Dyke. MPB; SN
Song Sparrow's Nest, The. Ethelwyn Wetherald. CPG
Song sprang to their lips, A. A Good Year. Alejandro Carrión. AnCL
Song Sung by Venus in Honor of Britannia. Dryden. *See* Song of Venus.
Song-Talysarn. Brenda Chamberlain. *See* Song: "Bone-aged is my white horse."
Song that I'm going to sing, The. The Crafty Farmer. *Unknown.* BaBo; ESPB; TiPo (1952 ed.)
Song That Lovers Sing, The. Victor Hugo, *tr. fr. French by* Alan Conder. TrFP
Song That Wolfram Heard in Hell, The. Thomas Lovell Beddoes. *See* Song: "Old Adam, the Carrion crow."
Song, the chariot of delight. Thrasybulus. Pindar. OxBG
Song the Eighth: "That Jenny's my friend." Edward Moore. CEP
Song the Grass Sings, A. Charles G. Blanden. HBV; NLK
Song the Ninth: "You tell me I'm handsome." Edward Moore. CEP
Song the Oriole Sings, The. William Dean Howells. HBV; SN
Song—the Owl. Tennyson. *See* Owl, The.
Song-Throe, The. Dante Gabriel Rossetti. The House of Life, LXI. BPN; PoVP; ViPo
Song, 'tis my will that thou do seek out Love. Dante. *Fr.* La Vita Nuova. AWP
Song to a Dead Girl. Vicente Aleixandre, *tr. fr. Spanish by* Eleanor L. Turnbull. CoSP
Song to a Fair Young Lady Going Out of [the] Town in the Spring. Dryden. AEV; EV-3; HBV; LiTL; MaPo; OBEV; OBS; SeEP
(To a Fair Young Lady Going Out of [the] Town in the Spring.) ElSeCe; SeCL
Song to a Lute, A. Sir John Suckling. *Fr.* The Sad One. EPS; ReEn; TrGrPo
(Hast Thou Seen the Down in the Air, *abr.*) PIAE
(Song, A: "Hast thou seen the down in the air.") EnLoPo; SeEP
Song to a Minuet. Dryden. *See* How Happy the Lover.
Song to a Negro Wash-Woman. Langston Hughes. GoSl
Song to a Tree. Edwin Markham. FaPON; MPB
Song to a Viol. Jasper Fisher. *Fr.* Fuimus Troes. LO; LoPS; SeCL
("So the silver-feathered swan.") SeEP; TuPP
Song to Amoret, A. Henry Vaughan. AEV; HBV; LiTL; NBE; ViBoPo
Song to Apollo. John Lyly. *Fr.* Midas. AtBAP; OBSC
("Sing to Apollo, god of day.") ElSeCe
Song to April. Sir William Watson. *See* Song: "April, April."
Song to Bacchus. John Fletcher. *See* God Lyaeus.
Song to Be Sung by the Father of Infant Female Children. Ogden Nash. MoAmPo
Song to Belinda, A. Theodosia Garrison. VOD
Song to Beta ("O thou fair silver Thames"). Michael Drayton. *Fr.* The Shepherd's Garland, Eclogue III (1953 ed.). OBSC
(Third Eclogue, The: "Stay, Thames to heare my song" [1606 ed.].) AtBAP; PoEL-2
Song to Celia ("Come, my Celia, let us prove"). Ben Jonson. *See* Come, My Celia, Let Us Prove.
Song to Celia ("Drink to me only with thine eyes"). Ben Jonson. *See* To Celia ("Drink to me . . .").
Song to Celia ("Kiss me, sweet; the wary lover"). Ben Jonson. *See* To Celia ("Kiss me, sweet . . .").
Song to Celia. Sir Charles Sedley. *See* To Celia.
Song to David, A. Christopher Smart. AtBAP; CEP; ChTr; EiPP; EV-3, *abr.*; GoTL; LaA; LiA; LoBV, *abr.*; OBEC; PoEL-3; TrGrPo, *abr.*; TriL; WoL, *abr.*
Sels.
"For adoration all the ranks," 28 *sts.* CoEV
"For adoration, David's psalms," 23 *sts.* AnFE

"For adoration seasons change."
(Adoration, 12 *sts.*) FaBoEn
(Mermaid's Pap, The, 3 *sts.*) BeR
Glorious the Sun in Mid Career, *last* 3 *sts.* FaBoCh; LiTG; LoGBV
"He sang of God—the mighty source." BLV, 18 *sts.*; GBV, 3 *sts.*; GTSL, 3 *sts.*; LiTG, 3 *sts.*
(Catholic Amen, The, 15 *sts.*) GoBC
(Song of David, The, 3 *sts.*) GTBS-W
"O David, highest in the list," 38 *sts.* OxBoCh
"O servant of God's holiest charge," 45 *sts.* ViBoPo
"O thou, that sit'st upon a throne." PtP, 17 *sts.*; UnS, 2 *sts.*
"Strong is the horse upon his speed." AlDL, 8 *sts.*; BeR, 6 *sts.*; MyFE, 3 *sts.*
(Man of Prayer, The, 3 *sts.*) BBV (1951 ed.); LiTB; LiTG
(Strength, 3 *sts.*) OtMeF
"Sublime—invention ever young," 18 *sts.* HBV; OBEV
"Sweet is the dew that falls betimes." BrBE, 8 *sts.*; CaAE, 15 *sts.*; LEAP, 5 *sts.*; Po, 15 *sts.*
"Tell them, I am, Jehovah said." BCEP, 8 *sts.*; WGRP, 14 *sts.*
Song to Death. Juan Escrivá. *See* Welcome Death.
Song to Five Toes. *Unknown.* OTPC (1946 ed.); PCH
Song to His Cynthia. Fulke Greville. *See* Of His Cynthia.
Song to Imogen. Shakespeare. *See* Hark! Hark! the Lark.
Song to Imogen (in Basic English). Richard L. Greene. WhC
Song to Isa Singing. Thomas Holley Chivers. APW; MOAP
(Song to Isa.) SPP
Song to Mary. —— Thomson. SG
Song to My Love. Laurence McKinney. InMe
Song to Night. Elizabeth J. Coatsworth. WaKn
Song to One, A. T. A. Daly. PIAE; YT
Song to Our Lady. *Unknown.* *See* Hymn to the Virgin, A.
Song to Pan. John Fletcher. *See* God of Sheep, The.
Song to Say a Farewell. Howard McKinley Corning. NP
Song to Silvia. Shakespeare. *See* Who Is Silvia?
Song to Sirena. Michael Drayton. *See* Sirena.
Song to Sleep. John Fletcher. *See* Care-charming Sleep.
Song to the Evening Star ("Gem of the crimson-colour'd even"). Thomas Campbell. *See* To the Evening Star.
Song to the Evening Star ("Star that bringest . . ."). Thomas Campbell. ERP; GTBS; GTSE; GTSL; HBV; LoPo
(Evening Star, The.) LPS-2
(Star That Bringest Home the Bee.) EBSV
(To the Evening Star.) EV-4; GTBS-D; GTBS-W
Song to the Glory of the Sky of America. Emilio Oribe, *tr. fr. Spanish by* Muna Lee. AnCL
(Ode to the Sky of the New Atlantis.) PoFr
"Song, to the Gods, Is Sweetest Sacrifice." Annie Fields. AA
Song to the Men of England. Shelley. AnFE; EmBrPo; EnL; EnLi-2 (1949 ed.); EnRP; ERP; ExPo; FiP; PoFr; SeCeV; TrGrPo; ViBoPo; WoL
(Men of England.) BCEP
Song to the Most Holy Name of Jesus. Fernando de Córdova y Bocanegra, *tr. fr. Spanish by* Samuel Beckett. AnMP
Song to the Mountains. *Tr. fr. Pawnee Indian by* Alice C. Fletcher. AWP; JAWP; WBP
Song to the oak, the brave old oak, A. The Brave Old Oak. Henry Fothergill Chorley. FaBoBe; HBV; LPS-2; PIR
Song to the Soviet Union. Manuel Crespo, *tr. fr. Spanish by* Muna Lee. PoFr
Song to the Sun. Esaias Tegnér, *tr. fr. Swedish by* Charles W. Stork. AnSL
Song to the Tune of Heart's Ease, A. *Unknown. Fr.* Misogonus. TuPP
("Sing care away with sport and play.") ReEn
Song to the Virgin, A. *Unknown.* *See* Hymn to the Virgin, A.
Song to the Virgin Mary. Pero López de Ayala, *tr. fr. Spanish by* Thomas Walsh. CAW
Song to the Wanderer. Hermia Harris Fraser, *ad. fr. Haida Indian song.* BoCaPo
Song to the Wind, A. Taliesin, *tr. fr. Welsh by* A. P. Graves. FaBoCh
Song Tournement: New Style. Louis Untermeyer. CrMA
Song unto Liberty's brave buccaneer, A. Paul Jones. *Unknown.* GA; PAH
Song, A, upon, "Now Must I Sing." *Unknown.* AnEC
Song, A? What goes to make a poet's song? Plea. Eileen Duggan. JKCP (1955 ed.)
Song, A! What songs have died. A Song for the Asking. Francis Orrery Ticknor. AA
Sang with a Discord, A. Arthur Colton. AA
Song with Words. James Agee. MAP; MoAmPo
Song without a Sound. Sir Edwin Arnold. *Fr.* With Sa'di in the Garden. VA
Song, Written at Sea, in the First Dutch War. Charles Sackville. *See* Song: "To all you ladies now at land."
Song You Love, The. William Alexander Percy. *Fr.* In New York. SPP
Song, Youth, and Sorrow. William Cranston Lawton. AA
Songbooks of the War. Siegfried Sassoon. InP; PtOT
Songe, The: "Drinke and be merry, merry, merry boyes." *See* Song, The: "Drink and be merry . . ."
Songe betwene the Quenes Majestie and Englande, A. William Birche. *See* Song between the Queen's Majesty and England, A.
Songs ("If I were told that I must go tonight"). Grace Noll Crowell. LS
Songs ("I would make songs for you"). Babette Deutsch. HBMV
Songs. Denis Glover. AnNZ
"If everywhere in the street," II.
"These songs will not stand," I.
Songs ("How are songs begot and bred?"). Richard Henry Stoddard. AA; OBAV
Songs: Spring and Winter. Shakespeare. *See* When Daisies Pied *and* When Icicles Hang by the Wall.
Songs above the Dust. Grantland Rice. DDA; PaA
Songs and Chorus of the Flowers. Leigh Hunt. ADAH
Songs and Lyrics. Sir Thomas Wyatt. *Poems indexed separately by titles and first lines.*
Song's Apostasy. Sir William Watson. EPN
Songs Ascending. Witter Bynner. *Fr.* To Celia. HBV; LoPS; NP
Songs at Amala's Wedding. Thomas Lovell Beddoes. *See* Bridal Song to Amala.
Songs before Sunrise, *sel.* Swinburne.
Prelude: "Between the green bud and the red." ViP
Songs' End. John Payne. VA
Song's Eternity. John Clare. BLV; FaBoCh; LoGBV; PG; WaKn
Songs for a Colored Singer. Elizabeth Bishop. MiAP; PoNe
Songs for Fragoletta. Richard Le Gallienne. HBV
"Blue eyes, against the whiteness pressed," IV.
"Blue eyes, looking up at me," II.
"Fragoletta, blessed one!" I.
"That, Fragoletta, is the rain," III.
Songs for My Mother, *sels.* Anna Hempstead Branch.
Her Hands. MPB; PoTo
(My Mother's Hands.) DD; MW, *abr.*
(Song for My Mother, A: Her Hands.) OHIP; RG
(Songs for My Mother: Her Hands.) HH; LBMV; MOAH; OBAV; OnPP; PoRL; POT; YT
Her Words. FaPON; NV; PoTo
(My Mother's Words.) CV
(Song for My Mother, A: Her Words.) BoChLi; OHIP; SiSoSe; TiPo (1959 ed.); YeAr
(Songs for My Mother: Her Words.) HH; LBMV; MOAH; OBAV; OnPP; POT; YT
Song for My Mother, A: Her Stories. MotAn; OHIP
Songs from a Masque. Francis Beaumont. *See* Masque of the Inner Temple and Gray's Inne, The.
Songs from an Evil Wood. Lord Dunsany. MBP; MoBrPo (1942 ed.)
Sels.
"I met with Death in his country," III.
(Song from an Evil Wood.) LBBV
"Somewhere lost in the haze," II. BMEP
"There is no wrath in the stars," I. BMEP
Songs from Cyprus, *sels.* Hilda Doolittle ("H. D.").
"Bring myrrh and myrtle bud." TwCV
"Gather for festival." MAP; MoAmPo; TwCV
"Where is the nightingale." MAP; MoAmPo; TwCV
(Second Song from Cyprus.) TCPD
(Song: "Where is the nightingale.") CBOV
(Song from Cyprus, A.) NeMA; TriL
Songs from "The Princess." Tennyson. *See* Princess, The.
Songs from the Rockies, *sel.* Hermann Hagedorn.
Day's End. VOD
Songs from "The Secular Masque." Dryden. *See* Secular Masque, The.
Songs I Sing, The. Charles G. Blanden. HBV
Songs in Absence. Arthur Hugh Clough. EmBrPo
Sels.
O Ship, Ship, Ship, XIV. PoVP
Some Future Day When What Is Now Is Not, VI. BPN; EmBrPo; EPN
(Meeting, The.) EV-5
Where Lies the Land [to Which the Ship Would Go], VII. AlDL; AWP; BEL; BMEP; BoTP; ChTr; EmBrPo; EtS; EV-5; FaBoBe; FaBoCh; GN; HBV; JAWP; LoGBV; MCCG; NLK (1947 ed.); OBVV; OTPC (1946 ed.); TOP; TVSH; VA; ViPo; ViPP; VLEP; WBP; WGRP
(Songs in Absence.) OQP; QP-2
(Two Ships, 2.) ES
("Where lies the land to which the ship would go?") BPN; EPN; GTBS; GTBS-D; GTSL
Ye Flags of Piccadilly, II. PoVP
Song's Indenture. Humbert Wolfe. MM
Songs, lords of the lyre! what God shall we hymn? For Theron, Tyrant of Akragas. Pindar. *Fr.* Olympian Odes. GrL

Songs of adolescence, The. Lyric. John Thompson. BoAu
Songs of an Empty House, *sels.* Marguerite Wilkinson.
End, The. HBMV; SBMV
Vista. SBMV
Songs of Autolycus. Shakespeare. *See* Jog On, Jog On *and* Lawn as White as Driven Snow *and* When Daffodils Begin to Peer *and* Will You Buy Any Tape.
Songs of Conn the Fool, The, *sel.* Fannie Stearns Davis.
Moon Folly. CP; NV; RG; SP
Songs of Deliverance, *sel.* Orrick Johns.
Song of Youth, The. BAP
Songs of Education, *sel.* G. K. Chesterton.
Geography. HBMV
Songs of Experience, *sels.* Blake.
Ah! Sunflower. AtBAP; AWP; EiPP; EnLi-2; EnLit; EnRP; EV-3; ExPo; GTBS-D; GTBS-W; InPo; JAWP; LEAP; MaPo; NBE; OAEP; OBEC; OuHeWo; PoE; PoEL-4; RiBV; SeCeV; ShBV-4; TCEP; TOP; UnPo; ViBoPo; WBP
(Ah! Sunflower, Weary of Time.) BLV; EG; ReaPo
(Sunflower, The.) BEL; BoLiVe; ChTr; PoFS; TrGrPo
Angel, The. CH; EiPP; EnRP
Chimney Sweeper, The. AtBAP; BoW; CBOV; EiPP; EnL; EnLi-2 (1949 ed.); EnLit; EV-3
Clod and the Pebble, The. AWP; BEL; BoLiVe; CoEV; EiPP; EM-1; EnL; EnLi-2; EnLit; EnLoPo; EnRP; EPP; FaBoEn; JAWP; LoBV; NBE; OAEP; OBEC; OnPM; OtMeF; TOP; TrGrPo; ViBoPo; WBP
("Love seeketh not itself to please.") LO
Earth's Answer. EiPP; EnRP
Fly, The. BLV; BoLiVe; EiPP; EM-1; EnL; GoTP; MaPo; OTPC (1923 ed.); TrGrPo
Garden of Love, The. AWP; EM-1; EnLi-2 (1949 ed.); EnLoPo; EnRP; ExPo; InPo; JAWP; LEAP; LiTB; LiTG; LiTL; LO; LoBV; OAEP; PoE; PoFS; SeCeV; TOP; TyEnPo; ViBoPo; WBP
Holy Thursday ("Is this a holy thing to see"). CEP; CoBE; EiPP; EM-1; EnL; EnLi-2 (1949 ed.); EnRP; OAEP; PoE; ReaPo
Human Abstract, The. EiPP; EnRP; MaPo; PoEL-4
Infant Sorrow. BLV; BoLiVe; EiPP; EnL; FaBoEn; PoEL-4; PoFS
Introduction: "Hear the voice of the bard!" EiPP; EnRP; LoBV; OAEP; PoEL-4
(Ancient Trees, The.) LiA
(Bard, The.) WGRP
(Hear the Voice [of the Bard].) GTBS-D; OBEC; OBEV
(Introduction to "Songs of Experience.") ExPo
(Voice of the Bard, The.) LEAP
Little Boy Lost, A. CEP; EM-1; EnLi-2; EnLit; EnRP; OAEP; ViBoPo
London. AtBAP; AWP; CEP; ChER; ChTr; CoEV; EiPP; EM-1; EnL; EnLi-2 (1949 ed.); EnRP; ExPo; FaBoEn; InPo; LiTB; MaPo; NBE; OnPM; PoE; PoEL-4; PoFS; RiBV; SeCePo; SeCeV; TwHP; TyEnPo; UnPo; ViBoPo; WoL
("I wander thro' each chartered street.") LO
Nurse's Song. CEP; EiPP; EnLi-2 (1949 ed.); EnRP; PoFS; TOP
Poison Tree, A. AnFE; AWP; BoLiVe; CaAE; EM-1; EnL; EnLi-2; EnLit; EnRP; EPP; FaFP; HoPM; InPo; JAWP; LEAP; LiTB; LiTG; MaPo; OAEP; OtMeF; PoEL-4; PoFS; PoMS; PreP; TOP; TreFS; TrGrPo; TyEnPo; WBP
("I was angry with my friend.") EG; GTBS-W
Schoolboy, The. CH; EM-1; EV-3; FaBoCh; GTBS-D
Sick Rose, The. AtBAP; AWP; BEL; BLV; BoLiVe; BoW; BrBE; ChER; ChTr; EiPP; EnL; EnLoPo; EPP; ExPo; FaBoEn; GTBS-D; InPo; JAWP; LoBV; MaPo; OAEP; OnPM; PoEL-4; PoFS; SeCeV; ShBV-4; TOP; TrGrPo; TwHP; ViBoPo; WBP
("O Rose, thou art sick.") EG
Tiger, The. AEV; ATP; AWP; BBV; BCEP; BEL; BoLiVe; CaAE; CBE; CG, *abr.*; ChTr; CoEV; EiPP; EM-1; EnL; EnLi-2; EnLit; EPP; EV-3; FaBoBe; FaFP; FaPON; GN; GoTP; GTBS-W; HBV; JAWP; LEAP; LiTB; LiTG; LPS-2; MaPo; MaRV; MCCG; MPB; MuP; MW; MyFE; NeHB; OAEP; OBEC; OBEV; OnPM; OtMeF; OTPC; OuHeWo; PC; PFE; PG; PIAE; PIR; Po; PoeMoYo; PoFS; PoRA; PreP; PYM; ReaPo; RG; ShBV-2; SN; StaSt; TCEP; TOP; TreF; TVSH; TwCrTr; TwHP; TyEnPo; ViBoPo; WBP; WGRP; WHA; WoL; WP
(Beauty of Terror, The.) LH
(Tyger, The.) AnFE; AtBAP; BLV; BoTP; CEP; CH; EnRP; ExPo; FaBoCh; FaBoEn; GTBS-D; HoPM; InPo; KN; LoBV; LoGBV; PoE; PoEL-4; RiBV; SeCePo; SeCeV; TrGrPo; WaKn
("Tyger, Tyger, burning bright.") EG
To Tirzah. EiPP; EnRP; LO; MeRV; OxBoCh
Songs of Guthrum and Alfred, The. G. K. Chesterton. *Fr.* The Ballad of the White Horse. HBV

Songs of Home, *sel.* Ola Hansson, *tr. fr. Swedish by* Charles W. Stork.
"Dull and muffled now the tumult of the city comes to me." AnSL
Songs of Innocence, *sels.* Blake.
Chimney Sweeper, The. AtBAP; BCEP; BoW; CEP; CH; EiPP; EnRP; KN
Cradle Song, A: "Sweet dreams, form a shade." AnFE; BEL; BOL; EiPP; EM-1; EnLi-2; EnLit; EnRP; OAEP; RIS; ViBoPo
(Sweet Dreams Form a Shade.) OTPC
Divine Image, The. BoTP; CEP; CoEV; EiPP; EM-1; EnL; EnLit; EnRP; FaBoEn; GrCo-2; LiTG; MaPo; MaRV; OAEP; OBEC; OnPM; OxBoCh; PoEL-4; ReaPo; TwCrTr; ViBoPo; WGRP
("To Mercy Pity Peace and Love.") LO
Dream, A. CH; EnRP; EV-3; MPB; NBE; PECK; PoRh; RAR; TVC; TVSH
Echoing Green, The. BoTP; CBE; CEP; CH; EiPP; EV-3; GBV (1952 ed.); KN; OBEC; OTPC; PCH; PoRh
Holy Thursday ("'Twas on a Holy Thursday"). AnFE; CEP; CH; CoBE; EiPP; EnL; EnRP; EV-3; HBV; OAEP; OBEC; OTPC; PoE; PoFS
Infant Joy. BCEP; EiPP; EM-1; EnLi-2; EnLit; FaPON; GoTP; GTSL; HBV; HBVY; KN; LEAP; LoBV; NeHB; OTPC; PRWS; SiSoSe; ThWaDe; TiPo; ViBoPo
Lamb, The. AnFE; BCEP; BEL; BLV; BoChLi; BoLiVe; BoTP; BTP; CAW; CBPC; CEP; CH; CoBE; EiPP; EM-1; EnL; EnLi-2; EnLit; EnRP; EV-3; ExPo; FaBoBe; FaBoCh; FaPON; GoTP; HBV; LiTB; LiTG; LoBV; LoGBV; MaPo; MaRV; MeMeAg; MPB; NeHB; OAEP; OBEC; OTPC; OuHeWo; OxBoCh; PG (1945 ed.); PoFS; PoRh; PRWS; PTA-2; RAR; RIS; SeCeV; StaSt; StVeCh; SUS; TOP; TreF; TrGrPo; TVC; TVSH; TwCrTr; TwHP; UTS; WaKn; WGRP; WHA
Laughing Song. BoTP; BrR; CBOV; EiPP; EnLi-2; EnRP; GoTP; KN; OTPC; PCH; PoRh; SUS; TiPo; ThWaDe; WaKn; WP
(When the Green Woods Laugh.) CH
Little Black Boy, The. AnFE; AtBAP; AWP; BCEP; BEL; CEP; CH; CoEV; EiPP; EM-1; EnL; EnLi-2; EnLit; EnRP; EV-3; HBV; InPo; LoGBV; MotAn; MyFE; OAEP; OBEC; OBEV; OxBoCh; PoEL-4; PoFr; PoNe; RiBV; SeCeV; TOP; TreFS; TrGrPo
Little Boy Found, The. EnRP; TiPo (1952 ed.)
Little Boy Lost, The. EnRP; FAOV; TiPo (1952 ed.)
Night. AIDL, *st.* 1; AnFE; AtBAP; BCEP; BoTP; BrBE; CaAE; CBE; CBOV; CEP; CH; CoBE; EnRP; EV-3; FaBoBe; FaPON; GoTP; GTBS-D; HBV; HBVY; MaPo; MyFE; OBEC; OBEV; OTPC (1923 ed.); OxBoCh; PoE; RAR, *st.* 1; RIS; SAS; ShBV-3; StaSt, *abr.*; WP
Nurse's Song. AWP; BoChLi; BOL; CBE; CEP; CH; EiPP; EnRP; EV-3; FaBoBe; GaP; GoTP; HBV; HBVY; InPo; KN; MPB; OBEC; OnPM; OTPC (1923 ed.); RG; ThWaDe; TiPo; WoL; WP
On Another's Sorrow. AWP; CEP; EnRP; EV-3; LiTG; MaRV; OTPC (1923 ed.); PoEL-4; ViBoPo
Piping down the Valleys Wild. BTP; FaBoCh; GBV; HiLiEn; InvP; LoGBV; OBEC; PoRh; PRWS; TreFS; TVSH; TyEnPo; UnS
(Child and the Piper, The.) CG
(Happy Piper, The.) CBPC
(Happy Songs.) GoTP; MeMeAg; RIS
(Introduction: "Piping down the valleys wild.") AnFE; BEL; BrBE; CEP; EiPP; EnLit; EnRP; EV-3; OAEP; PoE; PoEL-4; SeCeV; ThWaDe; TrGrPo
(Introduction to "Songs of Innocence.") CaAE; CoBE; EM-1; EnLi-2; ExPo; FaBoBe; KN; NeHB; OuHeWo; PG (1945 ed.); Po; TCEP; TiPo; TrGrPo; ViBoPo; WHA
(Piper, The.) AWP; BoChLi; BoTP; GaP; InPo; JAWP; LPS-1; MPB; OTPC; PIR; TOP; WBP
(Reeds of Innocence.) BCEP; GTBS-W; HBV; HBVY; LEAP; LiTB; LiTG; OBEV
(Songs of Innocence.) WP
(Songs of Innocence: Introduction.) EiPP; EPP; LoBV
"Piper, sit thee down and write," *last 2 sts.* YT
Shepherd, The. BoTP; BrBE; EiPP; EnRP; ExPo; GaP; GoTP; HBV; KN; LoBV; OBEC; OTPC; PoRh; ThWaDe; TiPo (1959 ed.); TOP; TVC; TVSH
Spring. BoChLi; BoTP; FaBoCh; FaPON; GoTP; KN; LoGBV; MoShBr; OTPC; RIS; SUS; TiPo (1952 ed.); YeAr
Songs of Jesus. Louis F. Benson. MaRV
Songs of Joy. W. H. Davies. MBP; MoBrPo; OBVV; PC; YT
Songs of Kabir. Kabir, *tr. fr. Hindi by* Rabindranath Tagore.
"How could the love between Thee and me sever?"
(Two Songs, 2.) LiTW
"Moon shines in my body, but my blind eyes cannot see it, The." WGRP
(Two Songs, 1.) LiTW

"Tell me, O Swan, your ancient tale." WGRP
Songs of La Mouche. Sir Henry Head. PoP
Songs of Labor: Dedication. Whittier. *See* Dedication: "I would the gift I offer here."
Songs of Maximus, The. Charles Olson. NeAP
Songs of Nature and Love, *sel.* Erik Axel Karlfeldt, *tr. fr. Swedish by* Charles W. Stork.
My Forefathers, *introd.* AnSL
Songs of Orpheus and the Sirens. William Morris. *Fr.* The Life and Death of Jason, XIV. BPN
("O happy seafarers are ye.") ViBoPo
Songs of Play. *Unknown, tr. fr. Greek by* J. M. Edmonds. OxBG
Songs of Selma, The. James MacPherson.
Alpin. CEP
Argument. CEP
Colma. CEP
(From "Songs of Selma," *abr.*) BEL
Ryno. CEP
Songs of Seven. Jean Ingelow. GBV (1922 ed.); HBV
Seven Times Five. GBV (1922 ed.); HBV
Seven Times Four. GBV (1922 ed.); HBV; LPS-1; MOAH; PTA-1
(Heigh Ho!) BoTP
(Maternity.) OHIP
Seven Times One. BLPA; EV-5; FaPON; GBV (1922 ed.); GoTP; HBV; LPS-1; MeMeAg; MPB; OTPC; PCH; PRWS; PTA-1; RAR; TreF; TVC; TVSH
Seven Times Seven. GBV (1922 ed.); HBV; MOAH
(Longing for Home.) WGRP
Seven Times Six. GBV (1922 ed.); HBV; LPS-1; MOAH
Seven Times Three. GBV (1922 ed.); HBV; LPS-1; PTA-1
(I Leaned out My Window.) AV
Seven Times Two. GBV (1922 ed.); GN; HBV; LPS-1; OTPC (1923 ed.); PTA-1
Songs of Several Lands. Antonio Machado, *tr. fr. Spanish by* Florence Lewis May. AnSpL-2
Songs of shepherds and rustical roundelays. The Hunting of the Gods. Walter Wasse. OxBoLi; SeCL
Songs of the Autumn Night. George Macdonald.
"O Night, send up the harvest moon," I. EBSV
"So, like the corn, moon-ripened last," II. EBSV
(Song of the Autumn Nights.) BSV
Songs of the Birds, The. Edward Carpenter. WGRP
Songs of the Coast Dwellers, *sels.* Constance Lindsay Skinner.
Chief's Prayer after the Salmon Catch, The. BoCaPo; NP
Song of the Full Catch. BoCaPo; CaP; NV; OCL; TBM
Song of the Search. CPG
Song of Whip-plaiting. BoCaPo; NP
Songs of the Common Day, *sels.* Sir Charles G. D. Roberts.
Flight of the Geese, The. BLA; PeCV; SN; VA
Herring Weir, The. PeCV
Pea-fields, The. PeCV
Songs of the Greenwood. Shakespeare. *See* Blow, Blow, Thou Winter Wind *and* Under the Greenwood Tree.
Songs of the Night Watches, *sel.* Jean Ingelow.
"Come out and hear the waters shoot, the owlet hoot, the owlet hoot." AlDL
(Apprenticed.) LiTL; OBVV
Songs of the People, *sels.* Hayyim Nahman Bialik, *tr. fr. Hebrew by* Maurice Samuel.
"On a hill there blooms a palm," 2. AWP; JAWP; WBP
"Two steps from my garden rail," 1. AWP; JAWP; WBP
Songs of the Pixies. Samuel Taylor Coleridge. OBEC
Songs of the Plains, I–IV. Glenn Ward Dresbach. NP
Songs of the Seasons. Meta E. B. Thorne. PEOR
Songs of the Slave, *sel.* Svatopluk Cech, *tr. fr. Czech by* Otto Koutouc.
"Here and there, Freedom is an empty name." PoFr
Songs of the Soul. St. John of the Cross. *See* Obscure Night of the Soul, The.
Songs of the Spanish Children. Olga Berggolts, *tr. fr. Russian by* Jack Lindsay. RuPo
Meeting, II.
Sisters, I.
Songs of Work. *Unknown, tr. fr. Greek.* OxBG
Songs, so old and bitter, The. The Coffin. Heine. AWP; JAWP; WBP
Songs to a Woman. Maxwell Bodenheim. NP
Songs to Seraphine, *sel.* Heine, *tr. fr. German by* Emma Lazarus. TrJP
Shadow-Love.
Waves Gleam in the Sunshine, The.
Songs to the Peonies. Li Po, *tr. fr. Chinese by* Florence Ayscough *and* Amy Lowell. ChLP
Songs We Need, The. Bernard Freeman Trotter. MaRV
"Songs without Words." Robert J. Burdette. BOHV; PA
Song's Worth, A. Susan Marr Spalding. AA
Songster, The. E. Pauline Johnson. CPG
Songsters, The. James Thomson. *Fr.* The Seasons: Spring. LPS-2
Songstress, in all times ended and begun. To Christina Rossetti. Sir William Watson. InP
Sonnet, The ("A sonnet is a moment's monument"). Dante Gabriel Rossetti. The House of Life, *introd.* BEL; BMEP; BPN; CoBE; EmBrPo; EnL; EnLi-2; EnLit; EPN; EPP; ES; GTBS-W; HBV; InP; LEAP; OAEP; PFE; PoVP; TCEP; TOP; ViBoPo; ViP; ViPo; ViPP; VLEP
(Introductory.) VA
Sonnet: "Accuse me not, beseech thee, that I wear." Elizabeth Barrett Browning. Sonnets from the Portuguese, XV. DiM; PoVP; VLEP
Sonnet: "Accuse me thus: that I have scanted all." Shakespeare. Sonnets, CXVII. PeBoSo
Sonnet: "Across the heath, the monolith's pubic arch." Alfred Jarry, *tr fr. French by* Francis Scarfe. MiFP
Sonnet: "Across the shaken bastions of the year." Arthur Davison Ficke. Sonnets of a Portrait Painter, XLVII. AnAmPo; LA
Sonnet: Addressed by a Father Mourning His Recently Deceased Married Daughter to the Father Whose Daughter Had Entered a Convent. Jacopo Vitorelli. *See* On a Nun.
Sonnet: Addressed to Haydon Keats. *See* Addressed to Haydon.
Sonnet: "Afar from you and very near to care." Marqués de Santillana, *tr. fr. Spanish by* Beatrice Gilman Proske. AnSpL-1
Sonnet: After Dark Vapors. Keats. *See* After Dark Vapours Have Oppressed Our Plains.
Sonnet: "After long storms and tempests' sad assay." Spenser. *See* Amoretti, LXIII.
Sonnet: "Against my love shall be as I am now." Shakespeare. Sonnets, LXIII. OBSC; PeBoSo; ReEn; SiCE
Sonnet: "Against that time (if ever that time come)." Shakespeare. Sonnets, XLIX. PeBoSo
Sonnet: Age. Richard Garnett. *See* Age.
Sonnet: "Ah, had I ever thought the world would care." Petrarch, *tr. fr. Italian by* Joseph Auslander. Sonnets to Laura: To Laura in Death, XXV. LyPI
Sonnet: "Ah, sweet Content, where is thy mild abode?" Barnabe Barnes. Parthenophil and Parthenophe, LXVI. ElL; ElSeCe; PeBoSo; ReEn; TuPP
(Content.) ES; OBSC
Sonnet: "Ah, we are neither heaven nor earth, but men." John Masefield. *Fr.* Sonnets ("Long long ago"). EPN; PoeMoYo
Sonnet: "Ah wherefore with infection should he live." Shakespeare. Sonnets, LXVII. PeBoSo; SiCE
Sonnet: "Alack, what poverty my Muse brings forth." Shakespeare. Sonnets, CIII. PeBoSo
Sonnet: "Alas, 'tis true I have gone here and there." Shakespeare. *See* Sonnets, CX.
Sonnet: "Alexis, here she stayed; among these pines." William Drummond of Hawthornden. EBSV; ElL; ElSeCe; OBS
(Alexis, Here She Stay'd.) HBV
(Primitiae.) ES
(Spring Bereaved.) LO; OBEV
Sonnet: "All beautiful things bring sadness, nor alone." Richard Chenevix Trench. VA
Sonnet: "All other joys of life he strove to warm." George Meredith. Modern Love, IV. EmBrPo; GTBS-D; OAEP; VA; ViPo
Sonnet: "Almighty God, whose justice like a sun." Hilaire Belloc. *See* Almighty God, Whose Justice Like a Sun.
Sonnet: "Alone and ever weary with dark care." Petrarch, *tr. fr. Italian by* T. G. Bergin. Sonnets to Laura: To Laura in Life, XXVIII. LyPI
Sonnet: "Along the garden terrace." George Meredith. Modern Love, XXXVII. ViPo
Sonnet: "Already I grow weary thinking how." Petrarch, *tr. fr. Italian by* Joseph Auslander. Sonnets to Laura: To Laura in Life, LIV. LyPI
Sonnet: "Altarwise by owl-light in the halfway-house." Dylan Thomas. *See* Altarwise by Owl-Light.
Sonnet: "Am I failing? For no longer can I cast." George Meredith. Modern Love, XXIX. EmBrPo; ViPo
Sonnet: "Ambition—following down this far-famed slope." Wordsworth. SoV
Sonnet: "Ancient greybeard shoulders on his load, The." Petrarch, *tr. fr. Italian by* Morris Bishop. Sonnets to Laura: To Laura in Life, XIV. LyPI
Sonnet: "And from the windy West came two-gunned Gabriel." Dylan Thomas. Sonnets, V. LiTM
Sonnet: "And I have seen again the marvellous child." Paul Verlaine. *See* And I Have Seen Again the Marvelous Child.
Sonnet: "And then I sat me down, and gave the rein." Gustav Rosenhane. *tr. fr. Swedish by* Sir Edmund Gosse. *Fr.* Sonnets. AWP; JAWP; WBP
Sonnet: "And what is beauty? It is a going-home." Arthur Davison Ficke. MuM
Sonnet: "And what were roses." E. E. Cummings. NP

Sonnet: "And wilt thou have me fashion into speech." Elizabeth Barrett Browning. Sonnets from the Portuguese, XIII. BPN; DiM; PoVP; VLEP
Sonnet: "And yet, because thou overcomest so." Elizabeth Barrett Browning. Sonnets from the Portuguese, XVI. BPN; OAEP; PoVP; ViPo; VLEP
Sonnet: "And yet I cannot reprehend the flight." Samuel Daniel. *See* To Delia: "And yet I cannot . . ."
Sonnet: "And you as well must die, beloved dust." Edna St. Vincent Millay. Unnamed Sonnets, VIII. BAP; NP
Sonnet: Anniversary, February 23, 1795. William Mason. OBEC
Sonnet: "Apples ripen under yellowing leaves, The." Thomas Caulfield Irwin. IrPN
Sonnet: "Arms and the leader I sang whose piety." Tasso, *tr. fr. Italian by* L. R. Lind. LyPI
Sonnet: "As a decrepit father takes delight." Shakespeare. Sonnets, XXXVII. PeBoSo
Sonnet: "As a seed deeply sheathed within a cone." Phyllis Reid. DiM
Sonnet: "As an unperfect actor on the stage." Shakespeare. *See* Sonnets, XXIII.
Sonnet: "As due by many titles I resign." John Donne. Holy Sonnets, II. EPS; MePo; NBE; OBS; SeEP
(Resignation to God.) EV-2
Sonnet: "As fast as thou shalt wane, so fast thou grow'st." Shakespeare. Sonnets, XI. PeBoSo
Sonnet: "As in a duskie and tempestuous night." William Drummond of Hawthornden. *See* As in a Dusky and Tempestuous Night.
Sonnet: "As in the midst of battle there is room." George Santayana. Sonnets, XXV. AnFE; APA; AWP; BAP; CoAnAm; JAWP; LBMV; LEAP; LiTM; MAP; MoAmPo; MOAP; ReaPo; WBP
Sonnet: "As on a branch, in May, we see the rose." Pierre de Ronsard, *tr. fr. French by* Ralph N. Currey. FoS
Sonnet: "As one who late hath lost a friend adored." Mary Tighe. DiM
Sonnet: "As one who lingers over some old store." Phyllis Reid. DiM
Sonnet: "As over the fresh grass her golden feet." Petrarch, *tr. fr. Italian by* Joseph Auslander. Sonnets to Laura: To Laura in Life, CXXXII. LyPI
Sonnet: "As soon as I begin to overtake." Louise Labé. *See* Dreams.
Sonnet: "As when the scepter dangles from the hand." George Santayana. Sonnets, XLII. ATP
Sonnet: "Ashamed at times that I am silent." Petrarch. *See* Praises of Laura Transcend His Poetic Power, The.
Sonnet: At Dover Cliffs, July 20, 1787. William Lisle Bowles. *See* Dover Cliffs.
Sonnet: At Last, Beloved Nature. Henry Timrod. SPP
(Elusive Nature.) SN
Sonnet: At Ostend, July 22, 1787. William Lisle Bowles. OBEC
(Bells of Ostend, The.) EnRP; PTA-2
(Ostend on Hearing the Bells at Sea.) ES
Sonnet: "At the round earth's imagin'd [*or* imagined] corners, blow." John Donne. Holy Sonnets, VII. AnEnPo; AtBAP; ATP (1953 ed.); CoBE; CoEV; ElSeCe; EnLP; EPS; ExPo; FaBoEn; InPo; LiTB; LiTG; LoBV; MaPo; MeLP; MePo; MyFE; NBE; OAEP; OBS; OxBoCh; PeBoSo; Po; PoD; PoEL-2; PoFS; ReaPo; ReEn; SeCeV; SeCV-1; SeEP; ShBV-4; TuPP; TwCrTr; TwHP; TwP; ViBoPo
(Blow Your Trumpets, Angels.) ChTr
(Death.) EV-2
(Divine Sonnet.) TriL
Sonnet: Avenge O Lord Thy Slaughter'd Saints. Milton. *See* On the Late Massacre in Piedmont.
Sonnet: "Awakened, I behold through dewy leaves." Thomas Caulfield Irwin. IrPN
Sonnet: "Away with these self-loving lads." Fulke Greville. *See* Of His Cynthia.
Sonnet: "Azured vault, the crystal circles bright, The." James I, King of England. *See* Heaven and Earth.
Sonnet: "Batter my heart, three-person'd God." John Donne. Holy Sonnets, XIV. AnEnPo; AnFE; BoLiVe; CaAE; CoEV; EnL; EnLP; EPS; ExPo; GoBC; GTBS-W; LiTB; LiTG; MaPo; MaRV; MeLP; NBE; OAEP; OBS; OxBoCh; PeBoSo; Po; PoE; PoEL-2; PoFS; RiBV; SeCeV; SeCV-1; SeEP; TrGrPo; TrPWD; TuPP; TwCrTr
(Prayer for Violence.) BLV
Sonnet: "Be secret, heart; and if your dreams have come." Anna Virginia Mitchell. OQP; QP-2
Sonnet: "Be wise as thou art cruel." Shakespeare. Sonnets. CXL. PeBoSo
Sonnet: "Beatrice is gone up into high Heaven." Dante, *tr fr. Italian by* D. G. Rossetti. *Fr.* La Vita Nuova. GoBC
Sonnet: "Beauty of ladies of compassionate heart." Guido Cavalcanti, *tr. fr. Italian by* G. S. Fraser. LyPI
Sonnet: "Beauty, sweet love, is like the morning dew." Samuel Daniel. To Delia, XLII [XLVII]. ElL; ElSeCe; FaBoEn; HBV; OBSC; TuPP; ViBoPo
(Beauty, Time, and Love, 5.) OBEV
(Beauty's Lease.) ES
Sonnet: "Because I breathe not love to every one." Sir Philip Sidney. *See* Astrophel and Stella, LIV.
Sonnet: "Because mine eyes can never have their fill." Dante. *See* Ballata: He Will Gaze upon Beatrice.
Sonnet: "Because my faltering feet may fail to dare." Hilaire Belloc. *See* Because My Faltering Feet.
Sonnet: "Because my grief seems quiet and apart." Robert Nathan. *See* Because My Grief Seems Quiet and Apart.
Sonnet: "Because the misery of some great men." Owen Barfield. PtOT
Sonnet: "Because thou hast the power and own'st the grace." Elizabeth Barrett Browning. Sonnets from the Portuguese. XXXIX. BPN; PoVP; VA; VLEP
Sonnet: "Being myeself [*or* my selfe] captyved here in care." Spenser. *See* Amoretti, LXXIII.
Sonnet: "Being your slave, what should I do but tend." Shakespeare. *See* Sonnets, LVII.
Sonnet: "Belovèd, my Belovèd, when I think." Elizabeth Barrett Browning. *See* Sonnets from the Portuguese: "Belovèd, my Belovèd . . ."
Sonnet: "Belovèd, thou hast brought me many flowers." Elizabeth Barrett Browning. Sonnets from the Portuguese, XLIV. BPN; OAEP; PoVP; ViP; ViPo; VLEP
Sonnet: "Beshrew that heart that makes my heart to groan." Shakespeare. Sonnets, CXXXIII. InvP; PeBoSo; ReIE
Sonnet: "Between my love and me there runs a thread." Irene Rutherford McLeod. *Fr.* Sonnets. HBMV
Sonnet: "Betwixt mine eye and heart a league is took." Shakespeare. Sonnets, XLVII. PeBoSo
Sonnet: "Beyond the sphere which spreads to widest space." Dante, *tr. fr. Italian by* Dante Gabriel Rossetti. *Fr.* La Vita Nuova. AWP; JAWP; LyPI; OuHeWo; WBP
(Beyond the Sphere.) OnPM
Sonnet: "Bird that discoursest from yon poplar bough." James Clarence Mangan. IrPN
Sonnet: "Black pitchy night, companion of my woe." Michael Drayton. Idea's Mirrour, LXX [XLV]. LoBV; OBSC; ReIE; SiCE; TuPP
Sonnet: "Blast of wind, A, a momentary breath." Barnabe Barnes. *Fr.* A Divine Century of Spiritual Sonnets. SiCE; TuPP
Sonnet: "Bow down, my song, before her presence high." Morton Luce. *Fr.* Thysia. HBV
Sonnet: "Bright star of beauty, on whose eyelids sit." Michael Drayton. Idea, IV. ElSeCe; EPP; HBV; SiCE
Sonnet: "Bright star, would I were steadfast as thou art." Keats. *See* Bright Star, Would I Were . . .
Sonnet: "But be contented: when that fell arrest." Shakespeare. Sonnets, LXXIV. BoFr; OBSC; PeBoSo; TCEP
Sonnet: "But do thy worst to steal thyself away." Shakespeare. Sonnets, XCII. PeBoSo
Sonnet: "But love whilst that thou may'st [*or* maist] be loved again." Samuel Daniel. *Fr.* To Delia, XXXVII. AtBAP; ElL; OBSC; SiCE; TuPP
Sonnet: "But now my muse, toil'd with continual care." Richard Barnfield. ReIE
Sonnet: "But only three in all God's universe." Elizabeth Barrett Browning. Sonnets from the Portuguese, II. BPN; ES; PoVP; VLEP
Sonnet: "But wherefore do not you a mightier way." Shakespeare. Sonnets, XVI. FaBoEn; PeBoSo
Sonnet: "But whether in the uncoloured light of truth." Arthur Hugh Clough. Seven Sonnets, IV. ViPP
Sonnet: "By this he knew she wept with waking eyes." George Meredith. Modern Love, I. AnEnPo; BEL; BMEP; EmBrPo; EnLi-2; EnLit; EnLoPo; HBV; HoPM; LEAP; OAEP; Po; PoEL-5; POTT; PoVP; TyEnPo; ViP; ViPo; ViPP; VLEP
Sonnet: "Cambridge ladies who live in furnished souls, The." E. E. Cummings. *See* Cambridge Ladies, The.
Sonnet: "Can it be right to give what I can give?" Elizabeth Barrett Browning. Sonnets from the Portuguese, IX. BPN; HBV; PoVP; VA; VLEP
Sonnet: "Canst thou, O cruel, say I love thee not." Shakespeare. Sonnets, CXLIX. PeBoSo
Sonnet: "Captain or Colonel, or Knight in Arms." Milton. *See* When the Assault Was Intended to the City.
Sonnet: "Care-charmer Sleep, son of the sable Night." Samuel Daniel. *See* Care-Charmer Sleep.
Sonnet: "Cartoons of slashes on the tide-traced crater." Dylan Thomas. Sonnets, VI. LiTM
Sonnet: Cats of Santa Anna, The. Tasso, *tr. fr. Italian by* L. R. Lind. LyPI
Sonnet: "Cherish you then the hope I shall forget." Edna St. Vincent Millay. Unnamed Sonnets, XII. NP; TCPD
(Cherish You Then the Hope I Shall Forget.) AV
Sonnet, A: "Chloris, whil'st thou and I were free." Charles Cotton. BrBE; ViBoPo

Sonnet: "Circean cup, and Epicurus' sty." Luis de Góngora, *tr. fr. Spanish by* Thomas Roscoe. AnSpL-1
Sonnet: "Cleere Ankor, on whose silver-sanded shore." Michael Drayton. Idea's Mirrour, XIII. BrBE
Sonnet, A: "Cold are the crabs that crawl on yonder hills." Edward Lear. CenHV
Sonnet: "Come back to me, who wait and watch for you." Christina Rossetti. Monna Innominata, I. AV; EmBrPo; MBP; TCEP; ViPo
Sonnet: "Come, sleep, O sleep, the certain knot of peace." Sir Philip Sidney. *See* Astrophel and Stella, XXXIX.
Sonnet: "Comes the New Year; wailing the north winds blow." Morton Luce. Thysia, XVI. HBV
Sonnet: "Comming to kisse her lyps (such grace I found)." Spenser. *See* Amoretti, LXIV.
Sonnet: Composed after a Journey across the Hamilton Hills, Yorkshire. Wordsworth. ChER
Sonnet: Composed by the Side of Grasmere Lake. Wordsworth. *See* Composed by the Side of Grasmere Lake.
Sonnet: Composed upon Westminster Bridge, Sept. 3, 1802. Wordsworth. *See* Composed upon Westminster Bridge.
Sonnet: Composed While the Author Was Engaged in Writing a Tract Occasioned by the Convention of Cintra. Wordsworth. ChER
Sonnet: "Could then the babes from yon unshelter'd cot." Thomas Russell. OBEC
Sonnet: "Cupid laid by his brand and fell asleep." Shakespeare. Sonnets, CLIII. PeBoSo
Sonnet: "Cynthia, because your horns look divers ways." Fulke Greville. Caelica, LV. ElSeCe; SiCE
Sonnet: "Cynthia, whose glories are at full forever." Fulke Greville. Caelica, XVII. ElSeCe
Sonnet: "Cyriack, this three years' day." Milton. *See* To Cyriack Skinner ("Cyriack, this three years' day").
Sonnet: "Cyriack, whose grandsire on the royal bench." Milton. *See* To Cyriak Skinner ("Cyriak, whose grandsire . . .").
Sonnet: Dante. Michelangelo. *See* Dante.
Sonnet: "Dante was naif although he had an inkling." Leonard Bacon. Sonnets, II. TBM
Sonnet: "Daughter of her whose face, and lofty name." Sir William Watson. Sonnets to Miranda, I. HBV
Sonnet: "Daughter to that good Earl, once President." Milton. *See* To the Lady Margaret Ley.
Sonnet: "Day slipped out of the web of her fog-wet gown." Kenneth Leslie. *Fr.* By Stubborn Stars. BoCaPo
Sonnet: "Dead men of 'ninety-two, also of 'ninety-three." Arthur Rimbaud, *tr. fr. French by* Norman Cameron. WaaP
Sonnet, A: "Dear, if you love me, hold me most your friend." Alice Duer Miller. AA
Sonnet: "Dear quirister, who from those shadows sends." William Drummond of Hawthornden. ElSeCe; ViBoPo (To the Nightingale.) EV-2; HBV; LO
Sonnet: "Dear to my soul! then leave me not forsaken!" Henry Constable. *Fr.* Diana. ElL; OBSC; ReEn; ReIE; SiCE; TuPP
Sonnet: "Dear [*or* Deare], why should you command me to my rest." Michael Drayton. *See* Idea: "Dear, why should you . . ."
Sonnet: Death. William Walsh. *See* Sonnet on Death.
Sonnet: "Death, be not proud, though some have called thee." John Donne. *See* Death, Be Not Proud.
Sonnet: "Death is all metaphors, shape in one history." Dylan Thomas. *Fr.* Two Sonnets. LiTM; MoAB; MoBrPo (1950 ed.)
Sonnet: Death Is Not without but within Him. Cino da Pistoia, *tr. fr. Italian by* Dante Gabriel Rossetti. AWP
Sonnet: Death of Virgil, The. Angelo di Costanzo, *tr. fr. Italian by* David Wright. LyPI
Sonnet: Death Warnings. Francisco de Quevedo y Villegas, *tr. fr. Spanish by* John Masefield. AWP; JAWP; TeCS; WBP; WoL
(Death Warnings.) AnSpL-1, *tr. by* John Masefield; CAW, *tr. by* Thomas Walsh
Sonnet I: Dedication of These Rimes to His First Love. Francis Davison. ReIE
Sonnet: "Deep in a vale where rocks on every side." Gustav Rosenhane, *tr. fr. Swedish by* Sir Edmund Gosse. *Fr.* Sonnets. AWP; JAWP; WBP
Sonnet: "Determined with one sally to erase." Petrarch, *tr. fr. Italian by* T. G. Bergin. Sonnets to Laura: To Laura in Life, II. LyPI
Sonnet: "Devouring Time, blunt thou the lion's paws." Shakespeare. *See* Sonnets, XIX.
Sonnet: "Did not the heavenly rhetoric of thine eye." Shakespeare. *See* Did Not the Heavenly Rhetoric . . .
Sonnet: "Distraction is the panacea, Sir!" George Meredith. Modern Love, XXVII. ViPo
Sonnet: "Divers doth use (as I have heard and know)." Sir Thomas Wyatt. *See* Divers Doth Use . . .
Sonnet: "Do not be angry with me for the word." Phyllis Reid. DiM
Sonnet: "Dost see how unregarded now." Sir John Suckling. ElSeCe; NBE
Sonnet: "Down in a valley, by a forest's side." William Browne. *See* Down in a Valley . . .
Sonnet: "Down [*or* Downe] in the depth of mine iniquity." Fulke Greville. *See* Caelica: "Down in the depth . . ."
Sonnet: "Down to the Puritan marrow of my bones." Elinor Wylie. *See* Puritan Sonnet.
Sonnet: "Drawn with th' attractive virtue of her eyes." Samuel Daniel. To Delia, XLVIII. ReIE
Sonnet: Dream, The. Gaspara Stampa, *tr. fr. Italian by* Richard Aldington. LyPI
Sonnet: "Each man me telleth I change most my devise." Sir Thomas Wyatt. Sonnets, II. SiPS
Sonnet: "Earth has not anything to show more fair." Wordsworth. *See* Composed upon Westminster Bridge.
Sonnet: "Earth, late choked [*or* chok'd] with showers, The." Thomas Lodge. *See* Earth, Late Choked with Showers, The.
Sonnet: "Earth with thunder torn, with fire blasted, The." Fulke Greville. Caelica, LXXXVII. ElSeCe; PeBoSo; SiCE; TuPP
Sonnet: Effigy, The. Guido Cavalcanti. *See* Effigy, The.
Sonnet: 1811. Wordsworth. SoV
Sonnet: England in 1819. Shelley. *See* England in 1819.
Sonnet: "England! the time is come." Wordsworth. ViBoPo
Sonnet: "Eternal [*or* Eternall] Truth, almighty, infinite." Fulke Greville. Caelica, XCVII [XCVIII]. OBS; OxBoCh; SiCE
Sonnet: "Euclid alone has looked on beauty bare." Edna St. Vincent Millay. *See* Euclid Alone Has Looked on Beauty Bare.
Sonnet: "Even as love grows more, I write the less." Robert Hillyer. Sonnets, XVI. HBMV
Sonnet: "Evening, as slow thy placid shades descend." William Lisle Bowles. CEP
Sonnet: "Evening bends upon a stubborn day, The." Pearce Young. PtPa
Sonnet: "Evil spirit, your beauty haunts me still, An." Michael Drayton. Idea, XX. CoBE; ElL; ElSeCe; EPP; LoBV; OAEP; OBSC; SiCE; TuPP
Sonnet: "Expense of Spirit in a waste of shame, The." Shakespeare. *See* Sonnets, CXXIX.
Sonnet: "Face of all the world is changed, I think, The." Elizabeth Barrett Browning. *See* Sonnets from the Portuguese: "Face of all the world . . ."
Sonnet: "Fair and lovely maid, look from the shore." Samuel Daniel. To Delia, XLII. ReIE
Sonnet: "Fair is my Love, and cruel as she's fair." Samuel Daniel. *See* To Delia: "Fair is my Love . . ."
Sonnet: "Fair is my love, for April in her face." Robert Greene. *See* Fair Is My Love, for April in Her Face.
Sonnet: "Fair [*or* Faire] is my Love that feeds among the lilies." Bartholomew Griffin. Fidessa, More Chaste than Kind, XXXVII. BCEP; EG; ElL; LO; NBE; PeBoSo; PoEL-2; TuPP; ViBoPo
(My Love.) TrGrPo
Sonnet: "Fair is my love, when her fair golden hairs [*or* heares]." Spenser. *See* Amoretti, LXXXI.
Sonnet: "Fair Naiads of the river, that reside." Garcilaso de la Vega, *tr. fr. Spanish by* Jeremiah H. Wiffen. TeCS
Sonnet: "Fair room, the presence of sweet beauty's pride." Thomas Nashe. CaAE
Sonnet: "Fair star of evening, splendor of the west." Words worth. *See* Composed by the Sea-Side, near Calais, August, 1802.
Sonnet: "Fairest, when by the rules of palmistry." William Browne. Caelia, III. ElSeCe
Sonnet: "Farewell, Love, and all thy laws forever." Sir Thomas Wyatt. *See* Renouncing of Love, A.
Sonnet: "Farewell! thou art too dear for my possessing." Shakespeare. *See* Sonnets, LXXXVII.
Sonnet: "Farewell, you children that I might have borne." Eleanor Farjeon. DiM
Sonnet: "Father in heaven! after the days misspent." Petrarch, *tr. fr. Italian by* Lady Dacre. Sonnets to Laura: To Laura in Life. CAW
Sonnet: "Fie, foolish earth, think you the heaven wants glory." Fulke Greville. *See* Caelica: "Fie, foolish Earth . . ."
Sonnet: "First there was the lamb on knocking knees." Dylan Thomas. Sonnets, III. LiTM
Sonnet: "First time he kissed me, he but only kissed." Elizabeth Barrett Browning. *See* Sonnets from the Portuguese: "First time he kissed . . ."
Sonnet: "First time that the sun rose on thine oath, The." Elizabeth Barrett Browning. *See* Sonnets from the Portuguese: "First time that the sun . . ."
Sonnet: "Flesh, I have knocked at many a dusty door." John Masefield. *Fr.* Sonnets ("Long long ago"). GTSL; LEAP; LiTM; MBP; MoBrPo; SeCePo
Sonnet: "Flower of the dust am I: for dust will flower." Clement Wood. Eagle Sonnets, VII. HBMV
Sonnet: "For her gait if she be walking." William Browne. *See* Complete Lover, The.

Sonnet: "For I have dreamed a dream where Fate and God." Arthur Davison Ficke. MuM

Sonnet: "For I have seen this Light. I did not dream." Leonora Speyer. Fr. Sonnets for the Beloved. UnW

Sonnet: "For shame deny that thou bear'st love to any." Shakespeare. Sonnets, X. PeBoSo

Sonnet: "For this true nobleness I seek in vain." James Russell Lowell. See For This True Nobleness.

Sonnet: "Forward violet thus did I chide, The." Shakespeare. See Sonnets, XCIX.

Sonnet: "Fountain of sorrow, inn of cursed ire." Petrarch, tr. fr. Italian by Joseph Auslander. Sonnets to Laura: To Laura in Life, CVII. PoFr

Sonnet [or Sonet]: "Fra bank to bank, fra wood to wood I rin." Mark Alexander Boyd. AnFE; BSV; EBSV; ES; LO; LoBV (2d ed.); OBEV; SeCeV (Cupid and Venus.) GoTS (Fra Bank to Bank.) ExPo

Sonnet: French and the Spanish Guerrillas, The. Wordsworth. See French and Spanish Guerrillas, The.

Sonnet: "Fresh spring, the herald of love's mighty king." Spenser. See Amoretti, LXX.

Sonnet: "From afar so lov'd and near, so cloudless fair." Stéphane Mallarmé, tr. fr. French by Arthur Ellis. LiA

Sonnet: "From fairest creatures we desire increase." Shakespeare. See Sonnets, I.

Sonnet: "From low to high doth dissolution climb." Wordsworth. See Mutability.

Sonnet: "From the oracular archives and the parchment." Dylan Thomas. Sonnets, IX. LiM

Sonnet LIV: "From thy fair face I learn, O my loved lord." Michelangelo, tr. fr. Italian by John Addington Symonds. BoFr

Sonnet: "From you have I [or I have] been absent in the spring." Shakespeare. See Sonnets, XCVIII.

Sonnet: "Full faith I have she holds that rarest gift." George Meredith. Modern Love, XXXII. ViPo

Sonnet: "Full many a glorious morning have I seen." Shakespeare. See Sonnets, XXXIII.

Sonnet: "Give me, full-handed, lilies, give me the rose." Matteo Maria Boiardo, tr. fr. Italian by L. R. Lind. LyPI

Sonnet: "Give me the darkest corner of a cloud." R. W. Dixon. LO

Sonnet: "Give to imagination some pure light." George Meredith. Modern Love, XXXVIII. ViPo

Sonnet: "Go from me. Yet I feel that I shall stand." Elizabeth Barrett Browning. See Sonnets from the Portuguese: "Go from me . . ."

Sonnet: "Go, spend your penny, Beauty, when you will." John Masefield. Fr. Sonnets ("Long long ago"). AEV; TCPD

Sonnet: "Go, Valentine, and tell that lovely Maid." Robert Southey. ERP

Sonnet: "Go you, O winds that blow from north to south." Alexander Craig. See To Pandora.

Sonnet XIII: "God of pity and love, return to this earth." Robert Nathan. QS

Sonnet: "Gods are dead, The. The earth has covered them." Frank Belknap Long. DaM

Sonnet: "Golden spring redeems the withered year, The." Robert Hillyer. Sonnets, II. HBMV

Sonnet: Good Friday 1327. Petrarch, tr. fr. Italian by T. G. Bergin. Sonnets to Laura: To Laura in Life, III. LyPI

Sonnet: Grief. Thomas Holley Chivers. SPP

Sonnet: "Happy as Ulysses, his voyage done." Joachim du Bellay, tr. by Ralph N. Currey. See Heureux qui, comme Ulysse . . .

Sonnet: "Happy ye leaves when as those lilly hands." Spenser. See Amoretti, I.

Sonnet: "Hard is yon rock, around whose head." Fernando de Herrera, tr. fr. Spanish by Sir John Bowring. AnSpL-1

Sonnet: "Hardness of her heart and truth of mine, The." Sir John Davies. Gulling Sonnets, IV. ElSeCe

Sonnet: "Have patience; it is fit that in this wise." George Santayana. Sonnets, IX. MOAP; WGRP

Sonnet: "Having this day my horse, my hand, my lance." Sir Philip Sidney. See Astrophel and Stella, XLI.

Sonnet: He Argues His Case with Death. Cecco Angiolieri da Siena, tr. fr. Italian by Dante Gabriel Rossetti. AWP

Sonnet: "He came in silvern armour, trimmed with black." Gwendolyn B. Bennett. CDC; PoNe

Sonnet: He Compares All Things with His Lady. Guido Cavalcanti, tr. fr. Italian by Dante Gabriel Rossetti. AWP

Sonnet: He Craves Interpreting of a Dream of His. Dante da Maiano, tr. fr. Italian by Dante Gabriel Rossetti. AWP; LiTW

Sonnet I: He Demands Pardon for Looking, Loving, and Writing. Walter Davison. ReIE

Sonnet: "He felt the wild beast in him between whiles." George Meredith. Modern Love, IX. EmBrPo; POTT; ViPo

Sonnet: "He found her by the ocean's moaning verge." George

Meredith. Modern Love, XLIX. BEL; BMEP; EmBrPo; EnLi-2; HBV; OAEP; PoE; POTT; ViP; ViPo

Sonnet: He Is Out of Heart with His Time. Guerzo di Montecanti, tr. fr. Italian by Dante Gabriel Rossetti. AWP

Sonnet: He Is Past All Help. Cecco Angiolieri da Siena. See Past Help.

Sonnet: He Jests Concerning His Poverty. Bartolomeo di Sant' Angelo, tr. fr. Italian by Dante Gabriel Rossetti. AWP

Sonnet: He Rails against Dante. Cecco Angiolieri da Siena, tr. fr. Italian by Dante Gabriel Rossetti. AWP; JAWP; WBP

Sonnet: He Speaks of a Third Love. Guido Cavalcanti, tr. fr. Italian by Dante Gabriel Rossetti. AWP

Sonnet: "He who created time, and out of nothing." Michelangelo, tr. fr. Italian by Creighton Gilbert. LyPI

Sonnet: "He who in spring's rebirth." Robert Hillyer. MuM

Sonnet: "He who loves life, and has the winging thought." Arthur Davison Ficke. MuM

Sonnet: "He who would like to see what art and nature." Joachim du Bellay, tr. fr. French by Ralph N. Currey. FoS

Sonnet: He Will Not Be Too Deeply in Love. Cecco Angiolieri da Siena, tr. fr. Italian by Dante Gabriel Rossetti. AWP (Not Too Deeply in Love.) OnPM

Sonnet: He Will Praise His Lady. Guido Guinicelli, tr. fr. Italian by Dante Gabriel Rossetti. AWP (Praise.) OnPM

Sonnet: "Hear, O Self-Giver, infinite as good." Morton Luce. Thysia, XXXVII. HBV

Sonnet VI: "Heart in wonder, like a lonely wren, The." Robert Nathan. See Heart in Wonder, The.

Sonnet: "Hence away, you sirens, leave me." George Wither. See Hence, Away, You Sirens!

Sonnet: "Here in the self is all that man can know." John Masefield. Fr. Sonnets ("Long long ago"). AWP; JAWP; WBP

Sonnet XVIII: "Here lies, and none to mourn him but the sea." Edna St. Vincent Millay. See Epitaph for the Race of Man.

Sonnet: "High walls and huge the body may confine." William Lloyd Garrison. See Sonnet Written While in Prison for Denouncing the Domestic Slave Trade.

Sonnet: "Highway, since you my chief Parnassus be." Sir Philip Sidney. See Astrophel and Stella, LXXXIV.

Sonnet XIV: "Him not the golden fang of furious heaven." Edna St. Vincent Millay. AtBAP

Sonnet: "His golden locks time hath to silver turn'd." George Peele. See His Golden Locks.

Sonnet: "How all men wrongly death to dignify." A. J. M. Smith. PeCV

Sonnet: "How can I then return in happy plight." Shakespeare. Sonnets, XXVIII. OBSC; PeBoSo

Sonnet: "How can my Muse want subject to invent." Shakespeare. Sonnets, XXXVIII. EnLit; PeBoSo; ReEn

Sonnet: "How careful was I, when I took my way." Shakespeare. Sonnets, XLVIII. PeBoSo

Sonnet: "How do I love thee? Let me count the ways." Elizabeth Barrett Browning. See Sonnets from the Portuguese: "How do I love thee . . ."

Sonnet: "How fruitless is each human hope, how vain." Lorenzo de' Medici, tr. fr. Italian by L. R. Lind. LyPI

Sonnet: "How healthily their feet upon the floor." Edna St. Vincent Millay. Sonnets, XXI. CP

Sonnet: "How heavy do I journey on the way." Shakespeare. Sonnets, L. EtPaEn; PeBoSo; ReEn; ReIE; SiCE

Sonnet: "How like a winter hath my absence been." Shakespeare. See Sonnets, XCVII.

Sonnet: "How little do they know of sorrow." William Ellery Leonard. Fr. Two Lives, Pt. III. MOAP; MuM

Sonnet: "How many bards gild the lapses of time!" Keats. See How Many Bards Gild the Lapses of Time.

Sonnet: "How many paltry, foolish, painted things." Michael Drayton. See Idea: "How many paltry, foolish, painted things."

Sonnet: "How oft, when thou, my music, music play'st." Shakespeare. See Sonnets, CXXVIII.

Sonnet: "How shall I tell the measure of my love?" Morton Luce. Thysia, XLV. HBV

Sonnet: "How soon hath Time, the subtle thief of youth." Milton. See On His Having Arrived at the Age of Twenty-three.

Sonnet: "How sweet and lovely dost thou make the shame." Shakespeare. Sonnets, XCV. PeBoSo; ReEn; TrGrPo

Sonnet: "How sweet it is, when mother Fancy rocks." Wordsworth. EnSW

Sonnet: "How sweet only to delight in lambs." Rex Warner. LO

Sonnet: "How that vast heaven intitled First is rolled." William Drummond of Hawthornden. EIL

Sonnet: "I abide and abide and better abide." Sir Thomas Wyatt. Sonnets, VI. EnLoPo; SiPS

Sonnet: "I am a little world made cunningly." John Donne. Holy Sonnets, V. EnL; EPS; MyFE; OBS; OxBoCh; PeBoSo; ReEn; SeEP; TwP
Sonnet: "I am a tongue for beauty. Not a day." Clement Wood. Eagle Sonnets, XIX. HBMV
Sonnet: "I am for ever bathed in tears, I rend." Garcilaso de la Vega, *tr. fr. Spanish by* Jeremiah H. Wiffen. TeCS
Sonnet: "I cannot think that thou shouldst pass away." James Russell Lowell. LPS-1
Sonnet: "I cast these lyrics offerings at your feet." Sir William Watson. Sonnets to Miranda, V. HBV
Sonnet: "I could not sleep for thinking of the sky." John Masefield. *See* I Could Not Sleep for Thinking of the Sky.
Sonnet: "I dare but sing of you in such a strain." Sir William Watson. Sonnets to Miranda, III. HBV
Sonnet: I Die with Too Transporting Joy. *Unknown, tr. fr. French by* John Hughes. AEV
Sonnet: "I dreamed I moved among the Elysian fields." Edna St. Vincent Millay. *See* I Dreamed I Moved among the Elysian Fields.
Sonnet: "I dreamed last night I stood with God on high." Snow Longley. *See* I Dreamed Last Night.
Sonnet: "I dreamed that I was thrown from a crag." Francisco de Terrazas, *tr. fr. Spanish by* Samuel Beckett. AnMP
Sonnet: "I envy not Endymion now no more." Earl of Stirling. Aurora, XXIX. EIL
Sonnet: "I feele my selfe endaungered beyond reason." Thomas Lodge. PoP
Sonnet: "I find no peace, and all my war is done." Petrarch, *tr. by* Sir Thomas Wyatt. *See* Description of the Contrarious Passions in a Lover.
Sonnet: "I find no peace and bear no arms for war." Petrarch, *tr. by* T. G. Bergin. Sonnets to Laura: To Laura in Life, CIV. LyPI
Sonnet: "I fly the crowded roads where thousands hurry." Pierre de Ronsard, *tr. fr. French by* Humbert Wolfe. LiA
Sonnet: "I grant thou wert not married to my Muse." Shakespeare. Sonnets, LXXXII. PeBoSo
Sonnet: "I had no thought of violets of late." Alice Dunbar Nelson. BANP; CDC; PoNe
Sonnet: "I hate the money-lending avarice." Joachim du Bellay. *See* I Hate.
Sonnet: "I have been sure of three things all my life." Clement Wood. Eagle Sonnets, III. HBMV
Sonnet: "I have not spent the April of my time." Bartholomew Griffin. *Fr.* Fidessa, More Chaste than Kind, XXXV. EIL; ElSeCe; ReEn; SiCE; TuPP
(Youth.) OBSC
Sonnet: "I have seen beauty where light stabs the hills." Arthur Davison Ficke. Sonnets of a Portrait Painter, XVI. AnAmPo; LA
Sonnet: "I heard beneath the quiet stars last night." Florence Wilson Roper. *Fr.* Return of Proserpine. UnW
Sonnet: "I hereby swear that to uphold your house." Elinor Wylie. *See* I Hereby Swear . . .
Sonnet: "I know I am but summer to your heart." Edna St. Vincent Millay. *See* I Know I Am But Summer to Your Heart.
Sonnet: I Know Not Why. Henry Timrod. *See* I Know Not Why, but All This Weary Day.
Sonnet: "I know that all beneath the moon decays." William Drummond of Hawthornden. *See* I Know That All . . .
Sonnet: "I lift my heavy heart up solemnly." Elizabeth Barrett Browning. *See* Sonnets from the Portuguese: "I lift my heavy heart . . ."
Sonnet: "I lived with visions for my company." Elizabeth Barrett Browning. *See* Sonnets from the Portuguese: "I lived with visions . . ."
Sonnet: "I might—unhappy word!—oh me, I might." Sir Philip Sidney. *See* Astrophel and Stella, XXXIII.
Sonnet: "I move amid your throng, I watch you hold." Sir William Watson. Sonnets to Miranda, VI. HBV
Sonnet: "I must be ill: my mind is dumb and bored." Nikolai Gumilev, *tr. fr. Russian by* Y. Hornstein. BoRS
Sonnet: "I must not grieve my Love, whose eyes would read." Samuel Daniel. To Delia, XLVIII. EIL; HBV
(Beauty, Time and Love, VI.) OBEV
Sonnet: "I never gave a lock of hair away." Elizabeth Barrett Browning. *See* Sonnets from the Portuguese: "I never gave . . ."
Sonnet: "I never saw that you did painting need." Shakespeare. Sonnets, LXXXIII. PeBoSo
Sonnet: "I never see the red rose crown the year." John Masefield. *See* I Never See the Red Rose.
Sonnet: "I never swung a staff and deep, oh deep." Roy Daniells. PeCV
Sonnet: "I never used to think myself so fine." Michelangelo, *tr. fr. Italian by* Creighton Gilbert. LyPI
Sonnet: "I once may see when years shall wreck my wrong." Samuel Daniel. To Delia, XXXIV. ReIE
Sonnet: "I said I splendidly, loved you; it's not true." Rupert Brooke. POTT
Sonnet: "I sat within the temple of her heart." Charles Sangster. CPG
Sonnet: "I saw my lady by a cool, fresh stream." Lorenzo de' Medici, *tr. fr. Italian by* L. R. Lind. LyPI
Sonnet: "I saw the eyes, where Amor took his place." Guido Cavalcanti, *tr. fr. Italian by* Ezra Pound. LyPI
Sonnet: "I saw the fiure of a lovely maid." Wordsworth. *See* I Saw the Figure of a Lovely Maid.
Sonnet: "I saw the object of my pining thought." Thomas Watson. *Fr.* The Tears of Fancy. EIL; TuPP
Sonnet: "I stood beside a pool, from whence ascended!" Richard Chenevix Trench IrPN
Sonnet: "I thank all who have loved me in their hearts." Elizabeth Barrett Browning. Sonnets from the Portuguese, XLI. BPN; CoBE; PoVP; VA; ViPo; VLEP
Sonnet: "I thought of thee, my partner and my guide." Wordsworth. *See* After-Thought.
Sonnet: "I thought once how Theocritus had sung." Elizabeth Barrett Browning. *See* Sonnets from the Portuguese: "I thought once . . ."
Sonnet: "I thought our love at full, but I did err." James Russell Lowell. LPS-1
Sonnet: "I tossed my golden anchor to the sea." Idris Davies. MoWP
Sonnet: "I wake and feel the fell of dark, not day." Gerard Manley Hopkins. *See* I Wake and Feel the Fell of Dark.
Sonnet: "I walk of grey noons by the old canal." Thomas Caulfield Irwin. EnSW; IrPN
Sonnet: "I walked, in meditation that was pain." Arthur Davison Ficke. MuM
Sonnet: "I wandered out a while agone." George Wither. *See* I Wandered Out.
Sonnet: "I watch beside you in your silent room." Morton Luce. Thysia, VII. HBV
Sonnet: "I watched the sea for hours blind with sun." Winfield Townley Scott. MiAP
Sonnet: "I will fling wide the windows of my soul." Robert Hillyer. Sonnets, XII. HBMV
Sonnet: "I, with whose colors Myra dressed her head." Fulke Greville. *See* Myra.
Sonnet: "I would not have this perfect love of ours." James Russell Lowell. *See* I Would Not Have This Perfect Love of Ours.
Sonnet: "I write to soothe that inward grief alone." Vittoria Colonna, *tr. fr. Italian by* L. R. Lind. LyPI
Sonnet, A: "Icarus is fallen here, the marvelous boy." Philippe Desportes. *See* Icarus.
Sonnet: "Idiots will prate and prate of suicide." Leonard Bacon. Sonnets, III. TBM
Sonnet: "If dreaming of thee be a waste of time." George Henry Boker. Sonnets; a Sequence of Profane Love, XXXV. LoP
(Sonnets, XVI.) MOAP
Sonnet: "If ever Sorrow spoke from soul that loves." Henry Constable. *Fr.* Diana. EIL; SiCE
Sonnet: "If faithful souls be alike glorified." John Donne. Holy Sonnets, VIII. OBS; SeEP
Sonnet XXIX: "If I could come again to that dear place." John Masefield. *See* If I Could Come Again to That Dear Place.
Sonnet: "If I could get within this changing I." John Masefield. *Fr.* Sonnets ("Long, long ago"). EPP; WGRP
Sonnet: "If I had never known your face at all." Sir William Watson. Sonnets to Miranda, VIII. FaBoBe; HBV
Sonnet: "If I leave all for thee, wilt thou exchange." Elizabeth Barrett Browning. *See* Sonnets from the Portuguese: "If I leave all . . ."
Sonnet: "If I might choose where my tired limbs shall lie." John Anster. *See* If I Might Choose.
Sonnet: "If I should pray this lady pitiless." Guido Cavalcanti, *tr. fr. Italian by* Ezra Pound. LyPI
Sonnet: "If I were fire, I'd burn the world away." Cecco Angiolieri da Siena. *See* Sonnet: Of All He Would Do.
Sonnet: "If it must be; if it must be, O God!" David Gray. EBSV
Sonnet: "If life on earth be less than is a day." Joachim du Bellay. *See* Sonnet to Heavenly Beauty, A.
Sonnet: "If my dear love were but the child of state." Shakespeare. Sonnets, CXXIV. PeBoSo
Sonnet: "If, of a wretched state and all forlorn." Leonard Digges. LO; SeCL; SeEP
Sonnet: "If of our life the span be not a day." Joachim du Bellay. *See* Sonnet to Heavenly Beauty, A.
Sonnet XXXI: "If one pure love, if one supreme devotion." Michelangelo, *tr. fr. Italian by* S. Elizabeth Hall. BoFr
Sonnet: "If poisonour minerals, and if that tree." John Donne. *See* If Poisonous Minerals . . .
Sonnet: "If the dull substance of my flesh were thought." Shakespeare. Sonnets, XLIV. PeBoSo
Sonnet: "If there be nothing new, but that which is." Shakespeare. Sonnets, LIX. FaBoEn; PeBoSo; ReEn
Sonnet: "If thou must love me, let it be for nought." Elizabeth Barrett Browning. *See* Sonnets from the Portuguese: "If thou must love me . . "

Sonnet: "If thou survive my well-contented day." Shakespeare. *See* Sonnets, XXXII.
Sonnet: "If thy soul check thee that I come so near." Shakespeare. Sonnets, CXXXVI. PeBoSo
Sonnet: "If you had lived in that more stately time." Sir William Watson. Sonnets to Miranda, II. HBV
Sonnet: In Absence. Gaspara Stampa, *tr. fr. Italian by* Richard Aldington. LyPI
Sonnet: In Absence from Becchina. Cecco Angiolieri da Siena, *tr. fr. Italian by* Dante Gabriel Rossetti. AWP; JAWP; WBP
Sonnet: "In faith, I do [*or* doe] not love thee with mine eyes." Shakespeare. Sonnets, CXLI. EtPaEn; MaPo; PeBoSo; PoEL-2; TrGrPo
Sonnet: "In heaven there is a star I call my own." Irene Rutherford McLeod. *Fr.* Sonnets. HBMV
Sonnet: "In love his kingdom great two fools there be." Robert Tofte. Laura, VIII. ElSeCe
Sonnet: "In loving thee thou know'st I am forsworn." Shakespeare. Sonnets, CLII. PeBoSo; ReIE
Sonnet: "In minds pure glasse when I my selfe behold." William Drummond of Hawthornden. OBS
Sonnet: "In so much as the lily and the rose." Garcilaso de la Vega, *tr. fr. Spanish by* James Cleugh. TeCS
Sonnet: "In the old age black was not counted as fair." Shakespeare. Sonnets, CXXVII. PeBoSo; ReIE; TwP
Sonnet: "In this deep hush and quiet of my soul." George Henry Boker. *Fr.* Sonnets. MOAP
Sonnet: "In thousands toward the south the swallows fly." Arthur Davison Ficke. MuM
Sonnet: "In truth, O Love, with what a boyish kind." Sir Philip Sidney. *See* Astrophel and Stella, XI.
Sonnet: "In what divine ideal, what lofty sphere." Petrarch, *tr. fr. Italian by* T. G. Bergin. Sonnets to Laura: To Laura in Life, CXXVI. LyPI
Sonnet: "Indeed this very love which is my boast." Elizabeth Barrett Browning. Sonnets from the Portuguese, XII. BPN; HBV; LPS-1; PoVP; VLEP
Sonnet: "Innumerable Beauties, thou white haire." Lord Herbert of Cherbury. BoW; PoEL-2
(Innumerable Beauties.) AtBAP
Sonnet: "Into the golden vessel of great song." Edna St. Vincent Millay. *Fr.* Unnamed Sonnets. NP
Sonnet: "Into the wood at close of rainy day." Thomas Caulfield Irwin. IrPN
Sonnet: "Into these loves, who but for passion looks." Michael Drayton. Idea, *introd. sonnet.* BEL; HBV; ViBoPo
Sonnet XI: "Is God invisible? This very room." Adele Greeff. GoYe
Sonnet: "Is it for fear to wet a widow's eye." Shakespeare. Sonnets, IX. PeBoSo
Sonnet: "Is it indeed so? If I lay here dead." Elizabeth Barrett Browning. Sonnets from the Portuguese, XXIII. BPN; PoVP; VA; VLEP
Sonnet: "Is it thy will thy image should keep open." Shakespeare. Sonnets, LXI. LO; LoPo; PeBoSo; PoEL-2
Sonnet: "Is there a great green commonwealth of Thought." John Masefield. *Fr.* Sonnets ("Long, long ago"). LiTM; MBP; MoBrPo
Sonnet: "Isle of trees full foliaged in a meadow, An." Thomas Caulfield Irwin. IrPN
Sonnet: "It is a beauteous evening, calm and free." Wordsworth. *See* It Is a Beauteous Evening . . .
Sonnet: "It is as true as strange, else trial feigns." John Davies of Hereford. ElL
Sonnet: "It is not death." Thomas Hood. *See* Death.
Sonnet: "It is not to be thought of that the flood." Wordsworth. *See* It Is Not to Be Thought Of.
Sonnet: "It shall be said I died for Coelia!" William Percy. Coelia, XIX. ElL; ReEn; ReIE
Sonnet: "It was the time, when rest, soft sliding downe." Joachim du Bellay, *tr. fr. French by* Spenser. *Fr.* Visions. AWP; OnPM
Sonnet: "Italia, O Italia, upon whom." Vincenzo da Filicaja. *See* Italy.
Sonnet: "Joy of my life! full oft for loving you." Spenser. *See* Amoretti, LXXXII.
Sonnet: "Keen, fitful gusts are whisp'ring here and there." Keats. *See* Keen, Fitful Gusts Are Whisp'ring Here and There.
Sonnet: "Lacking my love, I go from place to place." Spenser. *See* Amoretti, LXXVIII.
Sonnet: "Lady, if grace to me so long be lent." Petrarch. *See* He Hopes That Time Will Render Her More Merciful.
Sonnet: Lady Laments, A. *Unknown, tr. fr. Italian by* Dante Gabriel Rossetti. AWP
Sonnet: "Lame, impotent conclusion to youth's dreams." Wilfrid Scawen Blunt. The Love Sonnets of Proteus, LII. ViBoPo
Sonnet: "Languid, and sad, and slow, from day to day." William Lisle Bowles. CEP
Sonnet: "Last All Saints' holy-day, even now gone by." Dante. *See* Sonnet: Of Beatrice de Portinari on All Saints' Day.
Sonnet: "Last night I kissed you with a brutal might." Arthur Davison Ficke. Sonnets of a Portrait Painter, XXXVII. AnAmPo; LA
Sonnet: "Late tired with woe, even ready for to pine." Sir Philip Sidney. Astrophel and Stella, LXII. EnLit; HBV; ReEn; SiPS
Sonnet XVII: "Lawrence of vertuous father vertuous son." *See* To Mr. Lawrence.
Sonnet: "Leave me, all sweet refrains my lip hath made." Luís de Camões, *tr. fr. Portuguese by* Richard Garnett. AWP; CAW; JAWP; WBP
Sonnet: "Leave me, O Love, which reachest but to dust." Sir Philip Sidney. *See* Leave Me, O Love.
Sonnet: "Let all men see the ruins of the shrine." Robert Hillyer. Sonnets, XIV. HBMV
Sonnet: "Let him who wishes seek pomp and honor, follow." Lorenzo de' Medici, *tr. fr. Italian by* L. R. Lind. LyPI
Sonnet: "Let me confess that we two must be twain." Shakespeare. Sonnets, XXXVI. OAEP; PeBoSo
Sonnet: "Let me not to the marriage of true minds." Shakespeare. *See* Sonnets, CXVI.
Sonnet: "Let not my love be called [*or* call'd] idolatry." Shakespeare. Sonnets, CV. BoFr; PeBoSo
Sonnet: "Let others of the world's decaying tell." Earl of Stirling. Aurora, XCVIII. ElL
Sonnet: "Let others sing of knights and paladins." Samuel Daniel. *See* To Delia: "Let others sing . . ."
Sonnet: "Let the tale's sailor from a Christian voyage." Dylan Thomas. Sonnets, X. LiTM
Sonnet: "Let the world's sharpness, like a clasping knife." Elizabeth Barrett Browning. Sonnets from the Portuguese, XXIV. PoVP; VLEP
Sonnet: "Let those who are in favor with their stars." Shakespeare. *See* Sonnets, XXV.
Sonnet: "Let us leave talking of angelic hosts." Elinor Wylie. *Fr.* One Person. OxBA
Sonnet: "Life hurries on, a frantic refugee." Petrarch, *tr. fr. Italian by* Morris Bishop. Sonnets to Laura: To Laura in Death, IV. LyPI
Sonnet: "Lift not the painted veil." Shelley. EmBrPo; EnRP; ERP; FaBoEn
(Lift Not the Painted Veil.) EPN
Sonnet: "Lift up your hearts in Gumber, laugh the Weald." Hilaire Belloc. AlDL
Sonnet: "Like as a huntsman after weary chase." Spenser. *See* Amoretti, LXVII.
Sonnet: "Like as the waves make towards the pebbled shore." Shakespeare. *See* Sonnets, LX.
Sonnet: "Like as to make our appetites more keen." Shakespeare. Sonnets, CXVIII. PeBoSo; UnPo
Sonnet: "Like Memnon's rock, touched [*or* touch'd] with the rising sun." Giles Fletcher. Licia, XLVII. ElL; ReEn; ReIE; SiCE; TuPP
Sonnet: "Like some lone miser, dear, behold me stand." Morton Luce. Thysia, XXIII. HBV
Sonnet: "Like some small hungry bird that sees and hears." Vittoria Colonna, *tr. fr. Italian by* L. R. Lind. LyPI
Sonnet: "Like to an hermit poor, in place obscure." *At. to* Sir Walter Ralegh. *See* Like to a Hermit.
Sonnet: "Little Love-god lying once asleep, The." Shakespeare. Sonnets, CLIV. EM-1; PeBoSo; ReIE
Sonnet: "Lo, as a careful housewife runs to catch." Shakespeare. Sonnets, CXLIII. OAEP; PeBoSo; ReEn
Sonnet: "Lo, in the orient when the gracious light." Shakespeare. Sonnets, VII. PeBoSo; ReIE; SiCE
Sonnet: "Lock up, fair lids, the treasure of my heart." Sir Philip Sidney. *See* Sleep.
Sonnet: London 1802. Wordsworth. *See* London, 1802.
Sonnet: Long Time a Child. Hartley Coleridge. *See* Long Time a Child.
Sonnet: "Look, Delia, how we esteem the half-blown rose." Samuel Daniel. *Fr.* To Delia. ElL; ElSeCe; EnLit; HBV; SiCE; TuPP; WHA
Sonnet: "Look how the flower which lingeringly doth fade." William Drummond of Hawthornden. *See* No Trust in Time.
Sonnet: "Look in thy glass, and tell the face thou viewest." Shakespeare. Sonnets, III. EG; GTBS-W; LiTB; OBSC; PeBoSo; SiCE; TwP
Sonnet: "Looking into the windows that doom has broken." George Woodcock. NeBP
Sonnet: "Lord of my love, to whom in vassalage." Shakespeare. Sonnets, XXVI. PeBoSo; PoFS; ReEn
Sonnet: "Lord, what a change within us one short hour." Richard Chenevix Trench. *See* Prayer: "Lord, what a change . . ."
Sonnet: "Love guards the roses of thy lips." Thomas Lodge. *See* Love Guards the Roses . . .
Sonnet: "Love, how ignobly hast thou met thy doom!" Wilfrid Scawen Blunt. The Love Sonnets of Proteus, XIV. ViBoPo
Sonnet: "Love is my sin and thy dear virtue hate." Shakespeare. Sonnets, CXLII. PeBoSo
Sonnet: "Love is that orbit of the restless soul." George Henry Boker. *Fr.* Sonnets. MOAP

Sonnet: "Love is too young to know what conscience is." Shakespeare. Sonnets, CLI. PeBoSo; PoEL-2; ReEn
Sonnet: "Love still a boy, and oft a wanton is." Sir Philip Sidney. *See* Astrophel and Stella, LXXIII.
Sonnet: Love's Assize. Guido Cavalcanti. *See* Love's Assize.
Sonnet: "Loving in truth, and fain in verse my love to show." Sir Philip Sidney. *See* Astrophel and Stella, I.
Sonnet: "Low full sweep of instrumental string, A." *Unknown.* CAG
Sonnet: "Luxuriant, fragrant, fresh the new-blown rose." José de Espronceda, *tr. fr. Spanish by* Eleanor L. Turnbull. TeCS
Sonnet: "Lyke as a huntsman after weary chace." Spenser. *See* Amoretti, LXVII.
Sonnet: "Lyke as a ship, that through the ocean wyde." Spenser. *See* Amoretti, XXXIV.
Sonnet: "Man, dreame no more of curious mysteries." Fulke Greville. Caelica, LXXXVIII. MePo; OBS
Sonnet: "Man has his unseen friend, his unseen twin." John Masefield. *Fr.* Sonnets ("Long long ago"). PoeMoYo
Sonnet: "Mark when she smiles with amiable cheer." Spenser. *See* Amoretti, XL.
Sonnet: "Men call you fair, and you do credit it." Spenser. *See* Amoretti, LXXIX.
Sonnet XCIV: "Men, that delight to multiply desire." Fulke Greville. Caelica, XCIV [XCV]. OBS; SiCE
Sonnet: "Merry cuckoo, messenger of spring, The." Spenser. *See* Amoretti, XIX.
Sonnet: "Methinks ofttimes my heart is like some bee." Ella Wheeler Wilcox. LBAP
Sonnet: "Methought I saw my late espousèd saint." Milton. *See* On His Deceased Wife.
Sonnet: "Milton, thou shouldst be living at this hour." Wordsworth. *See* London, 1802.
Sonnet: "Mine eye and heart are at a mortal war." Shakespeare. Sonnets, XLVI. PeBoSo
Sonnet: "Mine eye hath played the painter and hath steeled." Shakespeare. Sonnets, XXIV. PeBoSo
Sonnet: "Mine eyes beheld the blessed pity spring." Dante. *See* Mine Eyes Beheld the Blessed Pity.
Sonnet: "Mists on the mountain, mists far down the vale." Arthur Davison Ficke. MuM
Sonnet: "Mole, which sleeps beneath the woven peat, The." W. Wesley Trimpi. PtPa
Sonnet: "More my own poor wishes would commend me, The." Petrarch, *tr. fr. Italian by* Joseph Auslander. Sonnets to Laura: To Laura in Life, CVIII. PoFr
Sonnet: "Most glorious Lord of life [*or* lyfe]! that on this day." Spenser. *See* Amoretti, LXVIII.
Sonnet: Most Men Know Love. Henry Timrod. *See* Quatorzain.
Sonnet: "Muses that sing love's sensual empery." George Chapman. A Coronet for His Mistress Philosophy, I. BrBE; CoBE; ElL; ElSeCe; LoBV; LPS-1; PoE; RiBV; TuPP
(Love and Philosophy.) OBSC; SeCePo
Sonnet: "Music [*or* Musick] to hear, why hear'st thou music sadly?" Shakespeare. Sonnets, VIII. PeBoSo; PoEL-2; ViBoPo
Sonnet: "My future will not copy fair my past." Elizabeth Barrett Browning. Sonnets from the Portuguese, XLII. BPN; PoVP; VLEP
Sonnet: "My galley chargèd with forgetfulness." Sir Thomas Wyatt. *See* Lover Compareth His State to a Ship . . . , The.
Sonnet: "My glass shall not persuade me I am old." Shakespeare. Sonnets, XXII. EG; EM-1; OBSC; PeBoSo
Sonnet: "My heart is like a ship on Neptune's back." "E. C." Emaricdulfe, XXIX. ElSeCe
Sonnet: "My heart the anvil where my thoughts do beat." Michael Drayton. Idea, XL. HBV
Sonnet: "My honoured lord, forgive the unruly tongue." Elinor Wylie. *Fr.* One Person. NP
Sonnet: "My lady carries love within her eyes." Dante. *See* My Lady Carries Love.
Sonnet: "My lady looks so gentle and so pure." Dante, *tr. fr. Italian by* Dante Gabriel Rossetti. *Fr.* La Vita Nuova. AWP; JAWP; LyPI; WBP
Sonnet: "My Lady's face it is they worship there." Guido Cavalcanti, *tr. fr. Italian by* Ezra Pound. LyPI
Sonnet: "My lady's presence makes the roses red." Henry Constable. *Fr.* Diana. CoBE; ElL; HBV; LEAP; OBSC; ReIE; SiCE
Sonnet: "My letters all dead paper, mute and white!" Elizabeth Barrett Browning. *See* Sonnets from the Portuguese: "My Petters . . ."
Sonnet: "My Love, I cannot thy rare beauties place." William Smith. *See* My Love, I Cannot . . .
Sonnet: "My Love, I have no fear that thou shouldst die." James Russell Lowell. LPS-1
(My Love, I Have No Fear That Thou Shouldst Die.) IAP
Sonnet: "My love is as a fever, longing still." Shakespeare. *See* Sonnets, CXLVII.
Sonnet: "My love is like to ice, and I to fire." Spenser. *See* Amoretti, XXX.
Sonnet: "My love is sleeping; but her body seems." Kenneth Leslie. *Fr.* By Stubborn Stars. BoCaPo
Sonnet: "My love is strengthened, though more weak in seeming." Shakespeare. *See* Sonnets, CII.
Sonnet: "My love took scorn my service to retain." Sir Thomas Wyatt. Sonnets, VIII. SiPS
Sonnet: "My lute, be as thou wast when thou didst grow." William Drummond of Hawthornden. BSV; EG; ElL; ElSeCe; EPS; LoBV; OBS; ViBoPo
(To His Lute.) EBSV; EV-2; GTBS; GTBS-D; GTBS-W; GTSE; GTSL; UnS
Sonnet: "My mistress' eyes are nothing like the sun." Shakespeare. *See* Sonnets, CXXX.
Sonnet: "My own Belovèd, who has lifted me." Elizabeth Barrett Browning. Sonnets from the Portuguese, XXVII. BPN; PoVP; VLEP
Sonnet: "My Phyllis [*or* Phillis] hath the morning sun." Thomas Lodge. *See* To Phyllis, the Fair Shepherdess.
Sonnet: "My poet, thou canst touch on all the notes." Elizabeth Barrett Browning. *See* Sonnets from the Portuguese: "My poet . . ."
Sonnet: "My simple heart, bred in provincial tenderness." G. S. Fraser. NeBP
Sonnet: "My soul surcharged with grief now loud complains." Rachel Morpurgo, *tr. fr. Hebrew by* Nina Davis Salaman. TrJP
Sonnet: "My spotless love hovers, with purest wings." Samuel Daniel. *See* To Delia: "My spotless love . . ."
Sonnet: "My tameless will doth recklessly pursue." Petrarch. *See* Of His Foolish Passion for Laura.
Sonnet: "My tongue-tied Muse in manners holds her still." Shakespeare. Sonnets, LXXXV. EM-1; PeBoSo
Sonnet: "My true love hath my heart, and I have his." Sir Philip Sidney. *See* My True Love Hath My Heart.
Sonnet: Netley Abbey. William Lisle Bowles. CEP
Sonnet: "Never until our souls are strong enough." E. A. Robinson. PoLFOT
Sonnet: "Newcomer, you who look in Rome for Rome." Joachim du Bellay, *tr. fr. French by* Ralph N. Currey. FoS
Sonnet: "Night is my sister, and how deep in love." Edna St. Vincent Millay. LoPS
Sonnet: "No longer mourn for me when I am dead." Shakespeare. *See* Sonnets, LXXI.
Sonnet: "No more be grieved at that which thou hast done." Shakespeare. Sonnets, XXXV. PeBoSo; UnPo
Sonnet: "No more, my dear, no more these counsels try." Sir Philip Sidney. *See* Astrophel and Stella, LXIV.
Sonnet LII: "No mortal object did these eyes behold." Michelangelo. *See* Celestial Love.
Sonnet: "No, Time, thou shalt not boast that I do change." Shakespeare. *See* Sonnets, CXXIII.
Sonnet: "No worst, there is none. Pitched past pitch of grief." Gerard Manley Hopkins. *See* No Worst, There Is None.
Sonnet: "Nor happiness, nor majesty, nor fame." Shelley. *See* Political Greatness.
Sonnet: "Nor mine own fears, nor the prophetic soul." Shakespeare. *See* Sonnets, CVII.
Sonnet: "Not at first sight, nor yet with a dribbed shot." Sir Philip Sidney. *See* Astrophel and Stella, II.
Sonnet: "Not from the stars do I my judgment pluck." Shakespeare. Sonnets, XIV. PeBoSo; SiCE
Sonnet: "Not, I'll not, carrion comfort, Despair, not feast on thee." Gerard Manley Hopkins. *See* Carrion Comfort.
Sonnet: "Not marble, nor the gilded monuments." Shakespeare. *See* Sonnets, LV.
Sonnet: "Not mine own fears, nor the prophetic soul." Shakespeare. *See* Sonnets, CVII.
Sonnet: "Not with libations but with shouts and laughter." Edna St. Vincent Millay. Unnamed Sonnets, III. HBMV; NP
(Not with Libations.) WHA
Sonnet: "Not with vain tears, when we're beyond the sun." Rupert Brooke. BrBE
Sonnet: "Not wrongly moved by this dismaying scene." William Empson. PreP; WaP
(Not Wrongly Moved.) LiTM (rev. ed.)
Sonnet VI: "Now from the world the light of God is gone." Robert Nathan. *See* Now from the World the Light of God Is Gone.
Sonnet: "Now I go grieving for the days on earth." Petrarch, *tr. fr. Italian by* Morris Bishop. Sonnets to Laura: To Laura in Death, LXXXVI. LyPI
Sonnet: "Now keep that long revolver at your side." George Hetherington. NeIP
Sonnet: "Now perish, Baïa, root and stock and name." Boccaccio, *tr. fr. Italian by* T. G. Bergin. LyMA; LyPI
Sonnet: "Now stamp the Lord's Prayer on a grain of rice." Dylan Thomas. GTBS-W; LiTM
Sonnet: "Now stands our love on that still verge of day." James Agee. Sonnets, XX. MoAmPo

Sonnet: "Now they are gone with all their songs and sins." John Masefield. *Fr.* Sonnets ("Like bones the ruins of the cities stand"). InP
Sonnet: "Now while the wind and earth and heavens rest." Petrarch, *tr. fr. Italian by* T. G. Bergin. Sonnets to Laura: To Laura in Life, CXXXI. LyPI
Sonnet: "Now, winter's dolorous days are o'er, and through." Thomas Caulfield Irwin. IrPN
Sonnet: "Nuns fret not at their convent's narrow room." Wordsworth. *See* Nuns Fret Not.
Sonnet: "O bitter moon, O cold and bitter moon." Clement Wood. Eagle Sonnets, IX. HBMV; NV
Sonnet: "Oh, breath is sweet, here in this mountain land!" Eunice Tietjens. BAP
Sonnet: "O call not me to justify the wrong." Shakespeare. Sonnets, CXXXIX. PeBoSo; ReIE
Sonnet: "Oh dear love tokens that did work me harm." Garcilaso de la Vega, *tr. fr. Spanish by* Eleanor L. Turnbull. TeCS
Sonnet: "Oh! Death will find me, long before I tire." Rupert Brooke. MBP; MoBrPo; NeMA
(Oh! Death Will Find Me.) HBV; PoRA
Sonnet: "O false and treacherous Probability." Fulke Greville. Caelica, CIII [CIV]. OBS; OxBoCh; RiBV
Sonnet: "O Fate, implacable in my pursuit." Garcilaso de la Vega, *tr. fr. Spanish by* Caroline B. Bourland. TeCS
Sonnet: "O for my sake do you with Fortune chide." Shakespeare. *See* Sonnets, CXI.
Sonnet: "Oh, for some honest lover's ghost." Sir John Suckling. *See* Doubt of Martyrdom, A.
Sonnet: "O Friend! I know not which way I must look." Wordsworth. *See* Written in London, September, 1802.
Sonnet: "O from what power [*or* powre] hast thou this powerful might." Shakespeare. Sonnets, CL. NBE; PeBoSo
Sonnet: "O had she not been fair and thus unkind." Samuel Daniel. To Delia, VII. ReIE
Sonnet: "O happy Thames that didst my Stella bear!" Sir Philip Sidney. *See* Astrophel and Stella, CIII.
Sonnet: "O how I faint when I of you do write." Shakespeare. Sonnets, LXXX. PeBoSo; ReEn; SiCE
Sonnet: "Oh, how much more doth beauty beauteous seem." Shakespeare. *See* Sonnets, LIV.
Sonnet: "O how thy worth with manners may I sing." Shakespeare. Sonnets, XXXIX. PeBoSo
Sonnet: "O, I could wish, most richly yellowing." Pierre de Ronsard, *tr. fr. French by* Ralph N. Currey. FoS
Sonnet: "Oh, if thou knew'st how thou thyself dost harm." Earl of Stirling. *See* To Aurora.
Sonnet: "Oh! leave the Past to bury its own dead." Wilfrid Scawen Blunt. The Love Sonnets of Proteus, LXII. ViBoPo
Sonnet: "O lest the world should task you to recite." Shakespeare. Sonnets, LXXII. PeBoSo
"O, lest your true love may seem false in this," 4 *ll.* LO
Sonnet: "O little room, my harbor from the sea." Petrarch, *tr. fr. Italian by* Morris Bishop. Sonnets to Laura: To Laura in Life, CXCVIII. LyPI
Sonnet: "O little self, within whose smallness lies." John Masefield. *Fr.* Sonnets ("Long long ago"). GTML; HBV; PoeMoYo; POTE; WGRP
Sonnet: "Oh, love of woman, you are known to be," VIII. Alan Seeger. BAP
Sonnet: "O lovely little bird, I watch you fly." Petrarch, *tr. fr. Italian by* Morris Bishop. Sonnets to Laura: To Laura in Death, XC. LyPI
Sonnet: "Oh, make me see thy face in every place!" Michelangelo, *tr. fr. Italian by* Edwin Morgan. LyPI
Sonnet: "O me, what eyes hath Love put in my head." Shakespeare. *See* Sonnets, CXLVIII.
Sonnet: "O might those sighs and tears return again." John Donne. Holy Sonnets, III. AnEnPo; OBS; PeBoSo; SeEP
Sonnet: "Oh, my beloved, have you thought of this." Edna St. Vincent Millay. Unnamed Sonnets, X. HBMV
Sonnet: "O my black Soul! now thou art summonèd." John Donne. Holy Sonnets, IV. MePo; MyFE; OBS
Sonnet "O never say that I was false of heart." Shakespeare. *See* Sonnets, CIX.
Sonnet: "O Nightingale, that on yon bloomy spray." Milton. *See* To the Nightingale.
Sonnet: "O patience, that dost wait eternally!" Pedro Malon de Chaide, *tr. fr. Spanish by* E. Allison Peers. CAW
Sonnet X: "O precious locket, found by luckless me." Garcilaso de la Vega, *tr. fr. Spanish by* Seymour Resnick. AnSpL-1
Sonnet: "O shady vales, O fair enriched meads." Thomas Lodge. *Fr.* A Margarite of America. EIL; OBSC
(All Things Revive save the Lover.) ES
(O Shady Vales! O Fair Enrichèd Meads.) PeBoSo
(Solitary Shepherd's Song, The.) ReIE
(Song: "O shadie vales, O faire inriched meades.") BrBe
Sonnet: "O Solitude! if I must with thee dwell." Keats. *See* To Solitude.
Sonnet: "O sweetest sleep, come now at last to stay." Lorenzo de' Medici, *tr. fr. Italian by* L. R. Lind. LyPI
Sonnet: "O that you were yourself! but, love, you are." Shakespeare. Sonnets, XIII. OAEP; PeBoSo; SiCE
Sonnet: "Oh, think not I am faithful to a vow!" Edna St. Vincent Millay. *See* Oh, Think Not I Am Faithful to a Vow!
Sonnet: "O thou, my lovely boy, who in thy power." Shakespeare. *See* Sonnets, CXXVI.
Sonnet: "O Thou to whom the musical white springs." E. E. Cummings. *See* O Thou to Whom the Musical White Springs.
Sonnet: "O Time! who know'st a lenient hand to lay." William Lisle Bowles. *See* Time and Grief.
Sonnet: "Oh, to vex me, contraries [*or* contraryes] meet in one." John Donne. Holy Sonnets, XIX. EPS (1942 ed.); NBE; PeBoSo; PoEL-2
(Devout Fits.) SeCePo
(Inconstancy.) MaRV
Sonnet: "O truant Muse, what shall be thy amends." Shakespeare. Sonnets, CI. PeBoSo
Sonnet: "O unforgiving thoughts, I pray you: Peace!" Petrarch. *tr. fr. Italian by* T. G. Bergin. Sonnets to Laura: To Laura in Death, VI. LyPI
Sonnet: "O World, thou choosest not the better part!" George Santayana. *See* O World.
Sonnet: "October's gold is dim—the forests rot." David Gray. EV-5
Sonnet: Of All He Would Do. Cecco Angiolieri da Siena, *tr. fr. Italian by* Dante Gabriel Rossetti. AWP; JAWP; WBP
(Of All He Would Do.) OnPM
(Sonnet: "If I were fire I'd burn the world away.") LyMA; LyPI
Sonnet: Of an Ill-favoured Lady. Guido Cavalcanti, *tr. fr. Italian by* Dante Gabriel Rossetti. AWP; JAWP; WBP
Sonnet: Of Beatrice de Portinari on All Saints' Day. Dante, *tr. fr. Italian by* Dante Gabriel Rossetti. AWP; JAWP; WBP
(Sonnet: "Last All Saints' holy-day, even now gone by.") GoBC
(To Beatrice on All Saints' Day.) OnPM
Sonnet: Of Beauty and Duty. Dante. *See* Beauty and Duty.
Sonnet: Of Becchina in a Rage. Cecco Angiolieri da Siena, *tr. fr. Italian by* Dante Gabriel Rossetti. AWP; JAWP; WBP
Sonnet: Of Becchina, the Shoemaker's Daughter. Cecco Angiolieri da Siena, *tr. fr. Italian by* Dante Gabriel Rossetti. AWP
Sonnet: Of His Lady in Heaven. Jacopo da Lentino, *tr. fr. Italian by* Dante Gabriel Rossetti. AWP; JAWP; LyPI; WBP
Sonnet: Of His Lady's Face. Jacopo da Lentino. *See* Of His Lady's Face.
Sonnet VII: Of His Lady's Weeping. Walter Davison. ReIE
Sonnet: Of His Pain from a New Love. Guido Cavalcanti, *tr. fr. Italian by* Dante Gabriel Rossetti. AWP
Sonnet: Of Love, in Honor of His Mistress Beechina. Cecco Angiolieri da Siena, *tr. fr. Italian by* Dante Gabriel Rossetti. AWP
(In Honor of His Mistress.) OnPM
Sonnet: Of Love in Men and Devils. Cecco Angiolieri da Siena, *tr. fr. Italian by* Dante Gabriel Rossetti. AWP
(Love in Men and Devils.) OnPM
Sonnet: Of Moderation and Tolerance. Guido Guinicelli, *tr. fr. Italian by* Dante Gabriel Rossetti. AWP; JAWP; WBP
Sonnet: Of the Eyes of a Certain Mandetta. Guido Cavalcanti, *tr. fr. Italian by* Dante Gabriel Rossetti. AWP
Sonnet: Of the Grave of Selvaggia. Cino da Pistoia, *tr. fr. Italian by* Dante Gabriel Rossetti. AWP; JAWP; WBP
(At the Grave of Selvaggia.) OnPM
Sonnet: Of the Making of Master Messerin. Rustico di Filippo, *tr. fr. Italian by* Dante Gabriel Rossetti. AWP; JAWP; LiTW; WBP
(Making of Master Messerin, The.) OnPM
(Sonnet: "When God had finish'd Master Messerin.") LyMA
Sonnet: Of the 20th June 1291. Cecco Angiolieri da Siena, *tr. fr. Italian by* Dante Gabriel Rossetti. AWP
Sonnet: "Of thee (kind boy) I ask no red and white." Sir John Suckling. LO; MeLP; MePo; OBS; OxBoLi; ReEn; SeCV-1; SeEP
(Of Thee, Kind Boy.) SeCL
(Song.) CoEV; LoBV
Sonnet, "Of this fair volume which we World do name." William Drummond of Hawthornden. *See* Book of the World, The.
Sonnet: Of Virtue. Folgore da San Geminiano, *tr. fr. Italian by* Dante Gabriel Rossetti. AWP; JAWP; WBP
Sonnet: Of Why He Is Unhanged. Cecco Angiolieri da Siena, *tr. fr. Italian by* Dante Gabriel Rossetti. AWP
Sonnet: Of Why He Would Be a Scullion. Cecco Angiolieri da Siena, *tr. fr. Italian by* Dante Gabriel Rossetti. AWP

Sonnet: Oft o'er My Brain. Samuel Taylor Coleridge. ChER
Sonnet: "Oft when my spirit doth spread her bolder wings." Spenser. *See* Amoretti, LXXII
Sonnet: On a Distant View of England. William Lisle Bowles. CEP
Sonnet: On a Picture of Leander. Keats. *See* On a Picture of Leander.
Sonnet: On First Looking into Chapman's Homer. Keats. *See* On First Looking into Chapman's Homer.
Sonnet: On His Being Arrived at the Age of Twenty-three. Milton. *See* On His Having Arrived at the Age of Twenty-three.
Sonnet: On King Arthur's Round Table at Winchester. Thomas Warton, the Younger. Sonnets, VIII. EiPP
Sonnet: On Seeing the Elgin Marbles. Keats. *See* On Seeing the Elgin Marbles.
Sonnet: On Sleep. Sir Philip Sidney. *See* Astrophel and Stella, XXXIX.
Sonnet: On the Death of Cino da Pistoia. Petrarch, *tr. fr. Italian by* T. G. Bergin. Sonnets to Laura: To Laura in Life, LXXI. LyPI
Sonnet: On the Death of Richard West. Thomas Gray. *See* Sonnet on the Death of Richard West.
Sonnet: On the Detection of a False Friend. Guido Cavalcanti, *tr. fr. Italian by* Dante Gabriel Rossetti. AWP
Sonnet: On the Grasshopper and Cricket. Keats. *See* On the Grasshopper and Cricket.
Sonnet: On the Late Massacre in Piedmont. Milton. *See* On the Late Massacre in Piedmont.
Sonnet: On the 9th of June 1290. Dante, *tr. fr. Italian by* Dante Gabriel Rossetti. AWP
Sonnet XIV: On the Religious Memorie of Mrs. Catherine Thomason My Christian Friend Deceased Dec. 16, 1646. Milton. *See* On the Religious Memory of Mrs. Catherine Thomson.
Sonnet: "Once in good hour there came in company." Matteo Maria Boiardo, *tr. fr. Italian by* L. R. Rind. LyPI
Sonnet: "One day I wrote her name upon the strand." Spenser. *See* Amoretti, LXXV.
Sonnet: "Open wound which has been healed anew," An. Richard Chenevix Trench. TrPWD
Sonnet: "Or I shall live your epitaph to make." Shakespeare. Sonnets, LXXXI. OAEP; OBSC; PeBoSo
Sonnet: "Or whether doth my mind, being crowned with you." Shakespeare. Sonnets, CXIV. PeBoSo
Sonnet: "Other two, The, slight air and purging fire." Shakespeare. Sonnets, XLV. PeBoSo
Sonent: Our Dead. Robert Nichols. QS
Sonnet: "Our doom is in our being." James Agee. Sonnets, II. MAP; MoAmPo
Sonnet: "Our love is not a fading, earthly flower." James Russell Lowell. *See* Our Love Is Not a Fading Earthly Flower.
Sonnet: "Out of the dusk into whose gloom you went." Arthur Davison Ficke. Sonnets of a Portrait Painter, L. AnAmPo; LA
Sonnet: "Out of this world's imperial terror." Peter Johnson. PoN
Sonnet: "Over the waters but a single bough." Robert Hillyer. Sonnets, XXIII. HBMV
Sonnet: "Passing glance, a lightning long the skies, A." William Drummond of Hawthornden. EPP; ViBoPo
Sonnet XXVI: "Pasture is a forest where we lie, The." Olive Tilford Dargan. NoCaPo
Sonnet: "Patience, hard thing! the hard thing but to pray." Gerard Manley Hopkins. FaBoEn
(Patience, Hard Thing!) CoBMV
Sonnet: "Penelope, for her Ulysses' sake." Spenser. *See* Amoretti, XXIII.
Sonnet: Philosophic Flight, The. Giordano Bruno, *tr. fr. Italian by* John Addington Symonds. LyPI
(Philosophic Flight, The.) AWP; PoFr
(Spurning the Earth.) OnPM
Sonnet: Pity Me Not. Edna St. Vincent Millay. *See* Pity Me Not.
Sonnet: "Point where beauty and intelligence meet, The." Gavin Ewart. WaP
Sonnet: Political Greatness. Shelley. *See* Political Greatness.
Sonnet: "Ponder thy cares, and sum them all in one." Sir David Murray. *Fr.* Caelia. EIL
Sonnet: "Poor drooping flowers and pallid violets." Matteo Maria Boiardo, *tr. fr. Italian by* Peter Russell. LyPI
Sonnet: "Poor soul, the centre of my sinful earth." Shakespeare. *See* Sonnets, CXLVI.
Sonnet: "Quickly and pleasantly the seasons blow." Robert Hillyer. Sonnets, I. HBMV
(From a Sonnet Sequence.) OBAV
Sonnet: Quiet Work. Matthew Arnold. *See* Quiet Work.
Sonnet: "Rain fire from Heaven down upon thy head." Petrarch, *tr. fr. Italian by* Joseph Auslander. Sonnets to Laura: To Laura in Life, CV. LyPI
Sonnet: "Rainbow o'er the sea of afternoon, The." Thomas Caulfield Irwin. IrPN
Sonnet: Rapture concerning His Lady, A. Guido Cavalcanti. *tr. fr. Italian by* Dante Gabriel Rossetti. AWP
Sonnet: "Red sun, that with thy taper shining bright." Fernando de Herrera, *tr. fr. Spanish by* Eleanor L. Turnbull. TeCS
Sonnet: "Regions of soft clear air, of cold green leaves." Thomas Caulfield Irwin. IrPN
Sonnet: "Reign in my thoughts, fair hand, sweet eye, rare voice!" Samuel Daniel. To Delia, XXV. ReIE
Sonnet: "Remember me when I am gone away." Christina Rossetti. *See* Remember.
Sonnet: "Remote from smoky cities, aged and grey." Thomas Caulfield Irwin. IrPN
Sonnet: "Restore thy tresses [*or* treasure] to the golden ore." Samuel Daniel. To Delia, XVIII. ElSeCe; EPP [XIX]
Sonnet: "'Rise,' said the Master, 'come unto the feast.'" Henry Alford. *See* Bride, The.
Sonnet: "Rise up and do begin the day's adorning." Hilaire Belloc. AlDL
Sonnet: "Roadside inn this summer Saturday, A." Thomas Caulfield Irwin. IrPN
Sonnet: "Rolling wheele that runneth often round, The." Spenser. *See* Amoretti, XVIII.
Sonnet: "Rough green wealth of wheaten fields that sway, The." Thomas Caulfield Irwin. IrPN
Sonnet: "Royal spouse, the season is now at hand." Tasso, *tr. fr. Italian by* L. R. Lind. LyPI
Sonnet: "Rudely thou wrongest my dear heart's desire." Spenser. Amoretti, V. EIL; PeBoSo; ReIE; SiCE
Sonnet: "Saints have adored the lofty soul of you." Charles Hamilton Sorley. Two Sonnets, I. HBMV; MBP; MoBrPo; NeMA; TrGrPo
Sonnet: "Say over again, and yet once over again." Elizabeth Barrett Browning. Sonnets from the Portuguese, XXI. BPN; EmBrPo; EPP; HBV; PIR; PoVP; ViPo; VLEP
Sonnet: "Say that thou didst forsake me for some fault." Shakespeare. Sonnets, LXXXIX. OAEP; PeBoSo; SiCE
Sonnet: "Say what you will, and scratch my heart to find." Edna St. Vincent Millay. *See* Say What You Will.
Sonnet, The: "Scorn not the Sonnet." Wordsworth. *See* Scorn Not the Sonnet.
Sonnet: "See the white stillness of the unicorn." Roy Daniells. PeCV
Sonnet: "Send me some token, that my hope may live." John Donne. LoPS
(Token, The.) LoPo
Sonnet: September, 1815. Wordsworth. *See* September, 1815.
Sonnet: September, 1802. Wordsworth. *See* Near Dover, September, 1802.
Sonnet: September 1, 1802. Wordsworth. *See* September 1, 1802.
Sonnet: "Set me whereas the sun doth parch the green." Petrarch. *See* Vow to Love Faithfully, Howsoever He Be Rewarded, A.
Sonnet: "Shall I be fearful thus to speak my mind." Irene Rutherford McLeod. *Fr.* Sonnets. HBMV
Sonnet: "Shall I compare thee to a summer's day?" Shakespeare. *See* Sonnets, XVIII.
Sonnet: "Shall I, wasting in despair." George Wither. *See* Shall I, Wasting in Despair.
Sonnet: "She loves me! From her own bliss-breathing lips." Charles Harpur. BoAu
Sonnet: "She used to let her golden hair fly free." Petrarch, *tr. fr. Italian by* Morris Bishop. Sonnets to Laura: To Laura in Life, LXIX. LyPI
Sonnet: "Show me deare Christ, thy spouse, so bright and cleare." John Donne. Holy Sonnets, XVIII. EnLP; EPS; ExPo; MeLP; OAEP; OBS; SeEP; TuPP
Sonnet: "Sidney, in whom the heyday of romance." Alan Seeger. LPS-1
Sonnet: Silence. Poe. APW; CoV; IAP
Sonnet: Silkworm, The. Michelangelo, *tr. fr. Italian by* John Addington Symonds. LyPI
Sonnet: "Silver herring throbbed thick in my seine, The." Kenneth Leslie. *Fr.* By Stubborn Stars. BoCaPo; PeCV; TwCaPo
Sonnet: "Sin of self-love possesseth all mine eye." Shakespeare. Sonnets, LXII. PeBoSo
(Sonnet: "Sinne of selfe-love possesseth al mine eie.") PoEL-2
Sonnet: "Since brass, nor stone, nor earth, nor boundless sea." Shakespeare. *See* Sonnets, LXV.
Sonnet: "Since I keep only what I give away." George Hetherington. NeIP
Sonnet: "Since I left you mine eye is in my mind." Shakespeare. Sonnets, CXIII. PeBoSo
Sonnet: "Since she whom I lov'd [*or* loved] hath payd [*or* paid] her last debt." John Donne. Holy Sonnets, XVII. EnLP; MePo; NBE; OAEP; PeBoSo; PoD; SeEP; TwP
Sonnet: "Since there's no help, come let us kiss and part." Michael Drayton. *See* Idea: "Since there's no help . . ."

Sonnet: "Sion lies [*or* Syon lyes] waste, and thy Jerusalem." Fulke Greville. Caelica, CIX [CX]. OxBoCh; PoEL-1; ReIE; SiCE; TriL; TuPP
Sonnet: "Sleep, Silence' child, sweet father of soft rest." William Drummond of Hawthornden. EBSV; ElL; EPS; OBS
(Sleep, Silence' Child [Sweet Father of Soft Rest].) BSV; HBV
(To Sleep.) ES
Sonnet: "Slow resistless flow of life goes on, The." Richard House. CAG
Sonnet: "So am I as the rich, whose blessed key." Shakespeare. Sonnets, LII. OBSC; PeBoSo
Sonnet: "So are you to my thoughts as food to life." Shakespeare. Sonnets, LXXV. PeBoSo; PoEL-2
Sonnet: "So is it not with me as with that Muse." Shakespeare. Sonnets, XXI. InvP; OBSC; PeBoSo; ReEn; SiCE
Sonnet: "So it begins. Adam is in his earth." James Agee. Sonnets, I. ATP (1953 ed.); MAP; MoAmPo
Sonnet: "So, now I have confessed that he is thine." Shakespeare. Sonnets, CXXXIV. InvP; PeBoSo
Sonnet: "So oft as I her beauty do behold." Spenser. *See* Amoretti, LV.
Sonnet: "So oft have I invoked thee for my Muse." Shakespeare. Sonnets, LXXVIII. EM-1; PeBoSo
Sonnet: "So sang I in the springtime of my years." Morton Luce. Thysia, XXXVI. HBV
Sonnet: "So shall I live, supposing thou art true." Shakespeare. Sonnets, XCIII. InvP; PeBoSo
Sonnet: "So shoots a star as doth my mistress glide." John Davies of Hereford. ElL
Sonnet: "So you go back—becouse they bid you come." Arthur Davison Ficke. Sonnets of a Portrait Painter, XXXVI. AnAmPo; LA
Sonnet: "Sole listener, Duddon! to the breeze that played." Wordsworth. The River Duddon, V. EnLi-2; EnSW
Sonnet: "Some glory in their birth, some in their skill." Shakespeare. Sonnets, XCI. PeBoSo
Sonnet: "Some say thy fault is youth, some wantonness." Shakespeare. Sonnets, XCVI. PeBoSo
Sonnet: "Some things are very dear to me." Gwendolyn Bennet. Sonnets, II. BANP; CDC; PoNe
Sonnet: "Sometimes I wish that I his pillow were." Richard Barnfield. ReIE
Sonnet: "Song of birds which leaps from leaf to leaf, The." Matteo Maria Boiardo, *tr. fr. Italian by* Peter Russell. LyPI
Sonnet, The: "Sonnet is a fruit which long hath slept, The." John Addington Symonds. HBV; VA
Sonnet: "Sonnet is a moment's monument, A." Dante Gabriel Rossetti. *See* Sonnet, The ("A sonnet is a moment's monument").
Sonnet: "Soul's Rialto hath its merchandise, The." Elizabeth Barrett Browning. Sonnets from the Portuguese, XIX. BPN; PoVP; VLEP
Sonnet: "Spit in my face you Jews, and pierce my side." John Donne. Holy Sonnets, XI. EPS; OBS; OxBoCh; SeEP
Sonnet, A: "Spring has departed; early days' sweet scent." Jóhann Sigurjónsson, *tr. fr. Icelandic by* Skuli Johnson. IcP
Sonnet: "Star of my mishap impos'd this paining, The." Samuel Daniel. To Delia, XXXI. OBSC; ReIE
Sonnet: "Stella! since thou so right a Princess art." Sir Philip Sidney. *See* Astrophel and Stella, CVII.
Sonnet: "Stella, think not that I by verse seek fame." Sir Philip Sidney. *See* Astrophel and Stella, XC.
Sonnet: "Stoics think, The (and they come near the truth)." Richard Barnfield. ReIE
Sonnet: "Striving to sing glad songs, I but attain." James Thomson. Two Sonnets, II. EmBrPo
Sonnet: "Such, such is Death: no triumph: no defeat." Charles Hamilton Sorley. Two Sonnets, II. BLV; HBMV; MBP; MoBrPo; NeMA; TrGrPo
Sonnet: Suppos'd to Be Written at Lemnos. Thomas Russell. CEP; OBEC
(Philoctetes.) LoBV
(Supposed to Be Written at Lemnos.) ES
Sonnet: "Surprised by joy—impatient as the wind." Wordsworth." *See* Surprised by Joy—Impatient as the Wind.
Sonnet: Swallow, The. Tasso, *tr. fr. Italian by* L. R. Lind. LyPI
Sonnet: "Sweet is the rose, but grows upon a brere." Spenser. *See* Amoretti, XXVI.
Sonnet: "Sweet love, renew thy force; be it not said." Shakespeare. Sonnets, LVI. LO; PeBoSo; UnPo (1st ed.)
Sonnet: "Sweet poets of the gentle antique line." John Hamilton Reynolds. OBRV
Sonnet: "Sweet semi-circled Cynthia played at maw." John Taylor. *Fr.* Odcomb's Complaint. ElL
Sonnet: "Sweet soul, which in the April of thy years." William Drummond of Hawthornden. TriL
Sonnet: "Sweet Spring, thou turn'st with all thy goodly train." William Drummond of Hawthornden. EBSV; ElL; FaBoEn
(Spring Bereaved, 2.) OBEV
(Spring, Wanting Her.) ES
(Sweet Spring, Thou Turn'st.) EV-2
Sonnet: "Sweet, when I think how summer's smallest bird." Irene Rutherford McLeod. *Fr.* Sonnets. HBMV
Sonnet: "Take all my loves, my love." Shakespeare. Sonnets, XL. InvP; OBSC; PeBoSo
Sonnet, A: "Take all of me—I am thine own, heart, soul." Amélie Rives. AA; BAP
Sonnet: "Tell me no more how fair she is." Henry King. *See* Tell Me No More.
Sonnet: "That learned Grecian (who did so excel)." William Drummond of Hawthornden. EPS; OBS; SeEP
Sonnet: "That thou art blamed shall not be thy defect." Shakespeare. Sonnets, LXX. PeBoSo
Sonnet: "That thou hast her, it is not all my grief." Shakespeare. Sonnets, XLII. EM-1; InvP; PeBoSo
Sonnet: "That time of year thou mayst in me behold." Shakespeare. *See* Sonnets, LXXIII.
Sonnet: "That window where the sun at midday shows." Petrarch, *tr. fr. Italian by* Morris Bishop. Sonnets to Laura: To Laura in Life, LXXIX. LyPI
Sonnet: "That you were once unkind befriends me now." Shakespeare. Sonnets, CXX. InvP; PeBoSo
Sonnet: "Then hate me when thou wilt; if ever, now." Shakespeare. *See* Sonnets, XC.
Sonnet: "Then judge me as thou wilt I cannot flee." Robert Hillyer. Sonnets, III. HBMV
Sonnet: "Then let not winter's ragged hand deface." Shakespeare. Sonnets, VI. PeBoSo; SiCE
Sonnet: "Then whilst that Latmos did contain her bliss." Earl of Stirling. Aurora, XXVIII. ViBoPo
Sonnet: "There are strange shadows fostered of the moon." Arthur Davison Ficke. *See* November Dusk.
Sonnet: "There have been many cats I loved and lost." Margaret E. Bruner. CIV
Sonnet: There Is a Bondage Worse. Wordsworth. ChER
Sonnet: "There is a dream that comes to me by night." Florence Wilson Roper. *Fr.* Dusty Answer. UnW
Sonnet: "There is a little unpretending rill." Wordsworth. *See* There Is a Little Unpretending Rill.
Sonnet: "There was an Indian, who had known no change." J. C. Squire. *See* There Was an Indian.
Sonnet XI: "These are the chosen people. He has set." Robert Nathan. *See* These Are the Chosen People.
Sonnet: "These flowers that were resplendent, a delight." Pedro Calderón de la Barca, *tr. fr. Spanish by* Eleanor L. Turnbull. TeCS
Sonnet: "They say that shadows [*or* shadowes] of deceased ghosts." Joshua Sylvester. *See* They Say That Shadows . . .
Sonnet: "They that have power to hurt and will do none." Shakespeare. *See* Sonnets, XCIV
Sonnet: "Thine eyes I love, and they, as pitying me." Shakespeare. Sonnets, CXXXII. OAEP; OBSC; PeBoSo; SiCE
Sonnet, A: "Think, when a starry night of bitter frost." Conrad Aiken. AnEnPo
Sonnet: "Thirty-eight years. Yes, neither less nor more." Leonard Bacon. Sonnets, I. TBM
Sonnet: "This infant world has taken long to make." George Macdonald. *See* This Infant World.
Sonnet: "This is my play's last scene, here heavens appoint." John Donne. Holy Sonnets, VI. AnEnPo; EPS; LoBV; MeLP; MePo; MyFE; OAEP; OBS; OxBoCh; PeBoSo; PoFS; SeEP; TuPP
Sonnet: "This is the garden: colours come and go." E. E. Cummings. *See* This Is the Garden.
Sonnet: "This was the crucifixion on the mountain." Dylan Thomas. Sonnets, VIII. LiTM
Sonnet, A: "Those eyes that hold the hand of every heart." Nicholas Breton. ReIE
Sonnet: "Those flakes of fire, brilliant sparks of light." Pedro Calderón de la Barca, *tr. fr. Spanish by* Eleanor Turnbull. TeCS
Sonnet: "Those former loves wherein our lives have run." James Agee. Sonnets, XIX. MAP; MoAmPo
Sonnet: "Those hours that with gentle work did frame." Shakespeare. Sonnets, V. PeBoSo; ReEn; SiCE
Sonnet: "Those lines that I before have writ do lie." Shakespeare. Sonnets, CXV. PeBoSo; SiCE
Sonnet: "Those lips that Love's own hand did make." Shakespeare. Sonnets, CXLV. PeBoSo
Sonnet: "Those parts of thee that the world's eye doth view." Shakespeare. Sonnets, LXIX. PeBoSo
Sonnet: "Those pretty wrongs that liberty commits." Shakespeare. Sonnets, XLI. InvP; PeBoSo; ReEn
Sonnet: "Thou art as tyrannous, so as thou art." Shakespeare. Sonnets, CXXXI. PeBoSo
Sonnet: "Thou art indeed just, Lord." Gerard Manley Hopkins. *See* Thou Art Indeed Just, Lord.

Sonnet: "Thou blind fool, Love." Shakespeare. Sonnets, CXXXVII. PeBoSo

Sonnet: "Thou blind man's mark, thou fool's self-chosen snare." Sir Philip Sidney. *See* Thou Blind Man's Mark.

Sonnet: "Thou comest! all is said without a word." Elizabeth Barrett Browning. Sonnets from the Portuguese, XXXI. BPN; PoVP; VLEP

Sonnet: "Thou hast made me, and shall Thy work decay?" John Donne. Holy Sonnets, I. AnEnPo; EG; EPS; FaBoEn; MaPo; MeLP; NBE; OAEP; OBS; OxBoCh; PeBoSo; Po; PoEL-2; PoFS; SeEP; TwCrTr

Sonnet: "Thou hast thy calling to some palace floor." Elizabeth Barrett Browning. Sonnets from the Portuguese, IV. EmBrPo; EnLi-2; EV-4; PoVP; PtP; TCEP; VA; VLEP

Sonnet LV: "Thou knowest, love, I know that thou dost know." Michelangelo. *See* Love's Entreaty.

Sonnet XLIX: "Though not a hill be holy, and no spring." Arthur Davison Ficke. QS

Sonnet: Thought of a Briton on the Subjugation of Switzerland. Wordsworth. *See* Thought of a Briton on the Subjugation of Switzerland.

Sonnet CV: "Three things there be in man's opinion deare." Fulke Greville. *See* Three Things There Be.

Sonnet: "Thrice happy he, who by some shady grove." William Drummond of Hawthornden. *See* Thrice Happy He.

Sonnet: "Through savage woods I walk without demur." Petrarch, *tr. fr. Italian by* T. G. Bergin. Sonnets to Laura: To Laura in Life, CXLIII. LyPI

Sonnet: "Through twenty-one long years love held me burning." Petrarch, *tr. fr. Italian by* T. G. Bergin. Sonnets to Laura: To Laura in Death, LXXXV. LyPI

Sonnet: "Thus can my love excuse the slow offence." Shakespeare. Sonnets, LI. PeBoSo; PoFS

Sonnet: "Thus ends my love, but this doth grieve me most." Lord Herbert of Cherbury. LiTL; ViBoPo

Sonnet: "Thus is his cheek the map of days outworn." Shakespeare. Sonnets, LXVIII. OBSC; PeBoSo; ReIE; UnPo (1st ed.)

Sonnet: "Thy bosom is endearèd with all hearts." Shakespeare. Sonnets, XXXI. ES; OBEV; OBSC; PeBoSo
(Sonnet: "Thy bosome is indeared with all hearts.") PoEL-2

Sonnet: "Thy gift, thy tables, are within my brain." Shakespeare. Sonnets, CXXII. PeBoSo

Sonnet: "Thy glass will show thee how thy beauties wear." Shakespeare. Sonnets, LXXVII. PeBoSo; RiBV

Sonnet: "Thy head with flames, thy mantle bright with flowers." William Drummond of Hawthornden. ElSeCe

Sonnet: "Time and the mortal will stand never fast." Luís de Camões, *tr. fr. Portuguese by* Richard Garnett. AWP

Sonnet: "Tired with all these, for restful death I cry." Shakespeare. *See* Sonnets, LXVI.

Sonnet: "'Tis better to be vile than vile esteemed." Shakespeare. *See* Sonnets, CXXI.

Sonnet: "'Tis love that moveth the celestial spheres." George Santayana. Sonnets, XXII. MOAP

Sonnet: To ——. Wordsworth. ChER

Sonnet: To a Balcony. Matteo Maria Boiardo, *tr. fr. Italian by* Richard Aldington. LyPI

Sonnet: To a Friend. Hartley Coleridge. *See* Friendship.

Sonnet: To a Friend Who Does Not Pity His Love. Guido Cavalcanti, *tr. fr. Italian by* Dante Gabriel Rossetti. AWP

Sonnet: To a Friend Who Sent Me Some Roses. Keats. GEPC

Sonnet: To Brunetto Latini. Dante, *tr. fr. Italian by* Dante Gabriel Rossetti. AWP

Sonnet: To Certain Ladies. Dante, *tr. fr. Italian by* Dante Gabriel Rossetti. AWP

Sonnet: To Dante Alighieri (He Commends the Work of Dante's Life). Giovanni Quirino, *tr. fr. Italian by* Dante Gabriel Rossetti. AWP
(To Dante Alighieri.) OnPM

Sonnet: To Dante Alighieri (He Conceives of Some Compensation in Death). Cino da Pistoia, *tr. fr. Italian by* Dante Gabriel Rossetti. AWP

Sonnet: To Dante Alighieri (He Interprets Dante Alighieri's Dream). Dante da Maiano, *tr. fr. Italian by* Dante Gabriel Rossetti. AWP

Sonnet: To Dante Alighieri (He Interprets Dante's Dream). Guido Cavalcanti, *tr. fr. Italian by* Dante Gabriel Rossetti. AWP

Sonnet: To Dante Alighieri (He Interprets Dante's Dream. Cino da Pistoia, *tr. fr. Italian by* Dante Gabriel Rossetti. AWP

Sonnet: To Dante Alighieri (He Mistrusts the Love of Lapo Gianni). Guido Cavalcanti, *tr. fr. Italian by* Dante Gabriel Rossetti. AWP

Sonnet: To Dante Alighieri (He Reports the Successful Issue of Lapo Gianni's Love.) Guido Cavalcanti, *tr. fr. Italian by* Dante Gabriel Rossetti. AWP

Sonnet: To Dante Alighieri (He Writes to Dante, Defying Him). Cecco Angiolieri da Siena, *tr. fr. Italian by* Dante Gabriel Rossetti. AWP

Sonnet: To Dante Alighieri (On the Last Sonnet of the "Vita Nuova"). Cecco Angiolieri da Siena, *tr. fr. Italian by* Dante Gabriel Rossetti. AWP

Sonnet: "To every heart which the sweet pain doth move." Dante. *See* To Every Heart.

Sonnet: To Guido Cavalcanti. Dante, *tr. fr. Italian by* Shelley. AWP; JAWP; LyPI; WBP
(To Guido Cavalcanti.) LyMA

Sonnet: To His Lady Joan, of Florence. Guido Cavalcanti, *tr. fr. Italian by* Dante Gabriel Rossetti. AWP; JAWP; WBP

Sonnet: To His Mistress. Alexander Montgomerie. EBSV

Sonnet: To Homer. Keats. *See* To Homer.

Sonnet: To Love, in Great Bitterness. Cino da Pistoia, *tr. fr. Italian by* Dante Gabriel Rossetti. AWP
(In Great Bitterness.) OnPM

Sonnet: "To me, fair friend, you never can be old." Shakespeare. *See* Sonnets, CIV.

Sonnet: To Mr. H. Lawes, on His Aires. Milton. *See* To Mr. H. Lawes on His Airs.

Sonnet: "To nothing fitter can I thee compare." Michael Drayton. Idea, X. BEL; EIL; HBV; OBSC; SiCE; TrGrPo; TuPP; ViBoPo

Sonnet: "To one who has been long in city pent." Keats. *See* To One Who Has Been Long in City Pent.

Sonnet: To Oxford. Thomas Russell. ATP; CEP; OBEC; PeBoSo

Sonnet: "To rail or jest, ye know I use it not." Sir Thomas Wyatt. Sonnets, IX. SiPS

Sonnet: To Science. Poe. *See* Sonnet to Science.

Sonnet: To Sleep. Keats. *See* To Sleep.

Sonnet: "To that fair kingdom, o my gentle lord." Boccaccio, *tr. fr. Italian by* T. G. Bergin. Sonnets, CXXVI. LyPI

Sonnet: To the Critic. *See* Idea: "Methinks I see . . ."

Sonnet: To the Emperor Charles V and to King Francis I of France. Veronica Gambara, *tr. fr. Italian by* T. G. Bergin. LyPI

Sonnet: To the Hudson. George S. Hellman. CAG

Sonnet: To the Lady Beaumont. Wordsworth. ChER

Sonnet: To the Lady Pietra degli Scrovigni. Dante, *tr. fr. Italian by* Dante Gabriel Rossetti. AWP
(Sonnet to the Lady Pietra.) LyMA

Sonnet: To the Nightingale. Milton. *See* To the Nightingale.

Sonnet: To the River Lodon [*or* Loddon]. Thomas Warton, the Younger. Sonnets, IX. CEP; OBEC; ViBoPo
(To the River Lodon.) CoBE

Sonnet: To the River Otter. Samuel Taylor Coleridge. ChER; EnSW

Sonnet: To the River Seine. Luigi Alamanni, *tr. fr. Italian by* T. G. Bergin. LyPI

Sonnet: To the Same Ladies. Dante, *tr. fr. Italian by* Dante Gabriel Rossetti. AWP

Sonnet: "To travel like a bird, lightly to view." C. Day Lewis. *Fr.* O Dreams O Destinations. ChMP

Sonnet: To Valclusa. Thomas Russell. CEP; OBEC

Sonnet: To Vittoria Colonna. Michelangelo, *tr. fr. Italian by* John Addington Symonds. LyPI

Sonnet: "To-day, all day, I rode upon the Down." Wilfrid Scawen Blunt. *See* St. Valentine's Day.

Sonnet XXXVI: "Today I went among the mountain folk." Olive Tilford Dargan. AV; NoCaPo

Sonnet: "Too soon the winter cold and heavy frost." Fernando de Herrera, *tr. fr. Spanish by* Jean Willard Burnham. TeCS

Sonnet: Trance of Love, A. Cino da Pistoia, *tr. fr. Italian by* Dante Gabriel Rossetti. AWP

Sonnet: True Ambition. Benjamin Stillingfleet. OBEC

Sonnet: "Twin songs there are, of joyance, or of pain." Morton Luce. Thysia, II. HBV

Sonnet: "Two flowers I love, the March-flower and the rose." Pierre de Ronsard, *tr. fr. French by* Henry Francis Cary. RO

Sonnet: "Two loves I have of comfort and despair." Shakespeare. *See* Sonnets, CXLIV.

Sonnet, A: "Two voices are there: one is of the deep." James Kenneth Stephen. FiBHP; PC; VA; WhC
(Sonnet on Wordsworth, A.) CenHV
(Two Voices Are There.) EnLi-2 (1949 ed.)
(Wordsworth.) HBV

Sonnet: "Tyr'd with all these for restful death I cry." Shakespeare. *See* Sonnets, LXVI.

Sonnet: "Under a throne I saw a virgin sit." Fulke Greville. Caelica, LXXXI [LXXXII]. ReIE; SiCE; TuPP

Sonnet: "Under the bark remembers now my heart." Roy Daniells. PeCV

Sonnet: "Understanding of a medical man, The." Rex Warner. ChMP

Sonnet: "Unlike are we, unlike, O princely Heart." Elizabeth Barrett Browning. *See* Sonnets from the Portuguese: "Unlike are we . . ."

Sonnet: "Unthrifty loveliness, why dost thou spend." Shakespeare. Sonnets, IV. PeBoSo

Sonnet: "Unto the boundless ocean of thy beauty." Samuel Daniel. To Delia, I. LiTL; LoBV; OAEP; OBSC; ReIE; SiCE

Sonnet: "Upon an upland orchard's sunny side." Thomas Caulfield Irwin. IrPN

Sonnet III: Upon His Absence from Her. Francis Davison. ReIE

Sonnet: "Upon our fullness shines the dawning day." Francis Lyman Windolph. MaRV

Sonnet: "Very names of things beloved are dear, The." Robert Bridges. *See* Very Names of Things Beloved Are Dear, The.

Sonnet: "Voice that resounds from pole to pole, The." Jean Ogier de Gombauld, *pr. tr. fr. French.* LiA

Sonnet: "Warm rain whispers, A, but the earth knows best." Kenneth Leslie. *Fr.* By Stubborn Stars. BoCaPo; PeCV; TwCaPo

Sonnet: "Was it the proud full sail of his great verse." Shakespeare. *See* Sonnets, LXXXVI.

Sonnet: "Was it the work of Nature or of Art." Spenser. *See* Amoretti, XXI.

Sonnet: "We are a part of all things that we see." William Gilmore Simms. SPP

Sonnet: "We are the singing shadows beauty casts." Clement Wood. Eagle Sonnets, XX. HBMV

Sonnet: "We saw the swallows gathering in the sky." George Meredith. *See* Modern Love: "We saw the swallows . . ."

Sonnet: "We two, O true-heart, who have learned so well." Odell Shepard. CAG

Sonnet: "We will not whisper, we have found the place." Hilaire Belloc. Sonnets, XIX. MBP; MoBrPo

Sonnet: "Weary with toil, I haste me to my bed." Shakespeare. *See* Sonnets, XXVII.

Sonnet: "Weary yeare his race now having run, The." Spenser. Amoretti, LXII. OBSC; PeBoSo; ReaPo; ReIE; SiCE

Sonnet LIX: "Well may sure hope at times, on wings elate." Michelangelo, *tr. fr. Italian by* S. Elizabeth Hall. BoFr

Sonnet: "Were I as base as is the lowly plain." *At. to* Joshua Sylvester. *See* Were I as Base . . .

Sonnet: "Were 't aught to me I bore the canopy." Shakespeare. Sonnets, CXXV. PeBoSo

Sonnet: "What am I, Life? A thing of watery salt." John Masefield. *See* What Am I, Life?

Sonnet: "What can I give thee back." Elizabeth Barrett Browning. *See* Sonnets from the Portuguese: "What can I give thee back . . ."

Sonnet: "What doth it serve to see sun's burning face." William Drummond of Hawthornden. EIL; ElSeCe

Sonnet: "What god forbid, that made me first your slave." Shakespeare. Sonnets, LVIII. PeBoSo

Sonnet: "What guile is this, that those her golden tresses." Spenser. *See* Amoretti, XXXVII.

Sonnet: "What have I thus betrayed my libertie?" Sir Philip Sidney. *See* Astrophel and Stella, XLVII.

Sonnet: "What if this present were the world's last night?" John Donne. Holy Sonnets. XIII. ElSeCe; ExPo; GTBS-W; LiTB; MeLP; MeRV; OAEP; OBS; SeCeV; SeEP; TuPP

Sonnet, The: "What is a sonnet? 'Tis the pearly shell." Richard Watson Gilder. AA; HBV

Sonnet: "What is the metre of the dictionary?" Dylan Thomas. Sonnets, IV. LiTM

Sonnet: "What is your substance, whereof are you made." Shakespeare. *See* Sonnets, LIII.

Sonnet: "What lips my lips have kissed, and where, and why." Edna St. Vincent Millay. *See* What Lips My Lips Have Kissed.

Sonnet. "What needs my Shakespeare for his honour'd bones." Milton. *See* On Shakespeare.

Sonnet: "What potions have I drunk of Siren tears." Shakespeare. *See* Sonnets, CXIX.

Sonnet: "What riches have you that you deem me poor. George Santayana. *See* What Riches Have You?

Sonnet: "What sugared terms, what all-persuading art." Richard Lynche. Diella, IV. ElSeCe

Sonnet: "What's in the brain, that ink may character." Shakespeare. Sonnets, CVIII. PeBoSo

Sonnet: "When as mans life, the light of human lust." Fulke Greville. *See* Sonnet: "Whenas man's life . . ."

Sonnet: "When down the windy vistas of the years." Clement Wood. Eagle Sonnets, XI. HBMV

Sonnet: "When forty winters shall besiege thy brow." Shakespeare. *See* Sonnets, II.

Sonnet: "When, from the tower whence I derive love's heaven." *Unknown. Fr.* Zepheria. EIL

Sonnet: "When God had finish'd Master Messerin." Rustico di Filippo. *See* Sonnet: Of the Making of Master Messerin.

Sonnet: "When I consider every thing that grows." Shakespeare. *See* Sonnets, XV.

Sonnet: "When I consider how my light is spent." Milton. *See* On His Blindness.

Sonnet: "When I do count the clock that tells the time." Shakespeare. *See* Sonnets, XII.

Sonnet: "When I had turned Catullus into rhyme." Thomas Caulfield Irwin. IrPN

Sonnet: "When I have fears that I may cease to be." Keats. *See* When I Have Fears . . .

Sonnet: "When I have seen by Time's fell hand defaced." Shakespeare. *See* Sonnets, LXIV.

Sonnet: "When I perceive the sable of your hair." Elinor Wylie. *See* When I Perceive . . .

Sonnet: "When I was marked for suffering, Love forswore." Cervantes, *tr. fr. Spanish by* Sir Edmund Gosse. AWP; PoFr

Sonnet: "When, in disgrace with Fortune and men's eyes." Shakespeare. *See* Sonnets, XXIX.

Sonnet: "When in the chronicle of wasted time." Shakespeare. *See* Sonnets, CVI.

Sonnet: "When men shall find thy flower, thy glory, pass." Samuel Daniel. *See* To Delia: "When men shall find . . ."

Sonnet: "When most I wink, then do mine eyes best see." Shakespeare. Sonnets, XLIII. PeBoSo

Sonnet: "When my love swears that she is made of truth." Shakespeare. *See* Sonnets, CXXXVIII.

Sonnet: "When nature made her chief work, Stella's eyes." Sir Philip Sidney. Astrophel and Stella, VII. ElSeCe; ReEn; ReIE; SiCE; SiPS; TuPP

Sonnet: "When our two souls stand up erect and strong." Elizabeth Barrett Browning. *See* Sonnets from the Portuguese: "When our two souls . ."

Sonnet: "When Phoebe form'd a wanton smile." William Collins. EnLoPo

Sonnet: "When sane men gather in to talk of love." Irene Rutherford McLeod. *Fr.* Sonnets. HBMV

Sonnet: "When she was born she came with smiling eye." Robert Tofte. Laura, VII. ElSeCe

Sonnet: "When thou hast taken thy last applause." E. E. Cummings. NP

Sonnet: "When thou shalt be disposed to set me light." Shakespeare. Sonnets, LXXXVIII. BoFr; PeBoSo

Sonnet: "When to the sessions of sweet silent thought." Shakespeare. *See* Sonnets, XXX.

Sonnet: "When we met first and loved, I did not build." Elizabeth Barrett Browning. Sonnets from the Portuguese, XXXVI. BPN; PoVP; VLEP

Sonnet: "When winter snows upon thy sable hairs [*or* golden hears]." Samuel Daniel. To Delia, XXXVIII [XXXIX]. OBS; ReIE; TuPP

Sonnet: "When you to Acheron's ugly water come." Hilaire Belloc. Sonnets, XVIII. TCPD

Sonnet: "Whenas [*or* When as] man's life, the light of human lust." Fulke Greville. Caelica, LXXXVII [LXXXVIII]. ElSeCe; GTBS-W; LiTB; MePo; OxBoCh; PoD ("When as mans life, the light of human lust.") OBS; PoEL-1

Sonnet: "Where are we to go when this is done?" Alfred A. Duckett. PoNe

Sonnet: "Where art thou, Muse, that thou forget'st so long." Shakespeare. Sonnets, C. OBSC; PeBoSo

Sonnet: Where Lies the Land. Wordsworth. *See* Where Lies the Land to Which Yon Ship Must Go?

Sonnet: "Whilst I alone did call upon thy aid." Shakespeare. Sonnets, LXXIX. EM-1; PeBoSo

Sonnet: "Who is it that says most, which can say more." Shakespeare. Sonnets, LXXXIV. PeBoSo

Sonnet: "Who is she that comes, makyng turn every man's eye." Guido Cavalcanti, *tr. fr. Italian by* Ezra Pound. LyMA
(Chi è questa, *tr. by* Ezra Pound.) ReMP
(Sonnet: "Who's this that comes, as each man looks at her," *tr. by* G. S. Fraser.) LyPI

Sonnet: "Who will believe my verse in time to come." Shakespeare. *See* Sonnets, XVII.

Sonnet: "Whoever hath her wish, thou hast thy 'Will.'" Shakespeare. Sonnets, CXXXV. PeBoSo; ReEn

Sonnet: "Who's this that comes, as each man looks at her." Guido Cavalcanti. *See* Sonnet: "Who is she that comes, makyng turn every man's eye."

Sonnet: "Whoso list to hunt, I know where is an hind." Sir Thomas Wyatt. *See* Hind, The.

Sonnet: "Why are we by all creatures waited on?" John Donne. Holy Sonnets, XII. MaPo; OBS; PeBoSo; PoEL-2; TuPP

Sonnet: "Why are your songs all wild and bitter sad." James Thomson. Two Sonnets, I. EmBrPo; PeBoSo

Sonnet: "Why did I laugh to-night?" Keats. *See* Why Did I Laugh To-Night?

Sonnet: "Why didst thou promise such a beauteous day." Shakespeare. Sonnets, XXXIV. OBSC; PeBoSo; PoE

Sonnet: "Why is my verse so barren of new pride." Shakespeare. *See* Sonnets, LXXVI.

Sonnet: "Why practise, love, this small economy?" Wilfrid Scawen Blunt. The Love Sonnets of Proteus, LVIII. ViBoPo
Sonnet: "Why should I hate you, love, or why despise." Wilfrid Scawen Blunt. The Love Sonnets of Proteus, XXVIII. ViBoPo
Sonnet: "Why should I think that heaven hears my prayer." Ariosto, *tr. fr. Italian by* L. R. Lind. LyPI
Sonnet: Wild Duck's Nest, The. Wordsworth. *See* Wild Duck's Nest, The.
Sonnet: "Wind has blown the rain away and blown, A." E. E. Cummings. AmPP; AnNE; MAP; MoAB; MoAmPo
Sonnet: "With heart and breast of brimstone, flesh of flax." Michelangelo, *tr. fr. Italian by* Edwin Morgan. LyPI
Sonnet: "With how sad steps, O Moon, thou climb'st the skies." Sir Philip Sidney. *See* Astrophel and Stella, XXXI.
Sonnet: "With sighs my bosom always laboureth." Dante, *tr. fr. Italian by* D. G. Rossetti. *Fr.* La Vita Nuova. GoBC. *sl. abr.*
Sonnet: "Within her hair Venus and Cupid sport them." "E. C." Emaricdulfe, VI. ElL
Sonnet: "Witless gallant, a young wench that wooed, A." Michael Drayton. Idea, XXI. PeBoSo; SiCE; TuPP
Sonnet: "Woman's face with Nature's own hand painted, A." Shakespeare. Sonnets, XX. InvP; PeBoSo; ReEn
Sonnet: "Wonderfully out of the beautiful form." Dante, *tr. fr. Italian by* D. G. Rossetti. *Fr.* La Vita Nuova. GoBC
Sonnet, A: "World is too much with us, The; late and soon." Wordsworth. *See* World Is Too Much with Us, The.
Sonnet: "World, that all contains, is ever moving, The." Fulke Greville. *See* Change.
Sonnet: "World's bright comforter, whose beamsome light, The." Barnabe Barnes. *See* World's Bright Comforter, The.
Sonnet: "Wretched thing it were, to have our heart, A." Richard Chenevix Trench. *See* Retirement.
Sonnet: Written after Seeing Wilton-House. Thomas Warton, the Younger. Sonnets, V. OBEC
Sonnet: Written at Stonehenge. Thomas Warton, the Younger. Sonnets, IV. CEP; EiPP; EPP
Sonnet: Written at the End of "The Floure and the Lefe." Keats. EmBrPo; EnRP
(Written on the Blank Space at the End of Chaucer's Tale of "The Floure and the Lefe.") PtP
Sonnet: Written in a Blank Leaf of Dugdale's "Monasticon." Thomas Warton, the Younger. Sonnets, III. EiPP; OBEC; SeCePo
(Written in a Blank Leaf of Dugdale's "Monasticon.") EV-3
Sonnet: Written in January, 1818. Keats. *See* When I Have Fears.
Sonnet: Written in London, September 1802. Wordsworth. *See* Written in London, September, 1802.
Sonnet: Written on a Blank Page in Shakespeare's Poems, Facing "A Lover's Complaint." Keats. *See* Bright Star, Would I Were . . .
Sonnet: Written on the Day That Mr. Leigh Hunt Left Prison. Keats. ChER; GEPC
(Written on the Day That Mr. Leigh Hunt Left Prison.) EM-2; PoFr
Sonnet: "Ye pilgrim-folk, advancing pensively." Dante, *tr. fr. Italian by* Dante Gabriel Rossetti. *Fr.* La Vita Nuova. LyPI
("Ye pilgrim-folk . . .") AWP; JAWP; WBP
Sonnet: "Ye tradeful merchants that, with weary toil." Spenser. *See* Amoretti, XV.
Sonnet: "Ye two fair trees that I so long have known." Thomas Caulfield Irwin. IrPN
Sonnet: "Yea, Love is strong as life; he casts out fear." Lady Blanche Elizabeth Lindsay. VA
Sonnet: "Yes! hope may with my strong desire keep pace." Michelangelo, *tr. fr. Italian by* Wordsworth. LyPI
Sonnet: "Yes! mourn the soul, of high and pure intent." John Kells Ingram. TIP
Sonnet: "Yet love, mere love, is beautiful indeed." Elizabeth Barrett Browning. *See* Sonnets from the Portuguese: "Yet love, mere love . . ."
Sonnet: "You are the faintest freckles on the hide." Elinor Wylie. MuM
Sonnet: "You ask my love. What shall my love then be?" Wilfrid Scawen Blunt. The Love Sonnets of Proteus, XXII. ViBoPo
Sonnet: "You have in you the flowers and the green grass." Guido Cavalcanti, *tr. fr. Italian by* G. S. Fraser. LyPI
Sonnet: "You little stars that live in skies." Fulke Greville. *See* You Little Stars That Live in Skies.
Sonnet: "You that in love find luck and abundaunce." Sir Thomas Wyatt. Sonnets, X. SiPS
(May Time.) OBSC
(You That in Love Find Luck and Abundance.) MaPo
Sonnet: "You waken slowly. In your dream you're straying." William Bell. NePoEA
Sonnet: "You were born; must die." Stephen Spender. EnLit; MoAB; MoBrPo (1950 ed.)
Sonnet: "You whispered, 'still the stars shine cold above me.'" William Bell. FaBoTw
Sonnet: "You, who do breach mine eyes and touch the heart." Guido Cavalcanti, *tr. fr. Italian by* Ezra Pound. LyPI
Sonnet: "You who give ear to sorrow, as you scan." Petrarch, *tr. fr. Italian by* Morris Bishop. Sonnets to Laura: To Laura in Life, I. LyPI
Sonnet: "Your love and pity doth the impression fill." Shakespeare. Sonnets, CXII. PeBoSo
Sonnet: "Your words, my friend (right healthful caustics), blame." Sir Philip Sidney. *See* Astrophel and Stella, XXI.
Sonnet: "You're [*or* You] not alone when you are still alone." Michael Drayton. *See* Idea: "You're not alone . . ."
Sonnet: "Zephyr returns, and scatters everywhere." Petrarch, *tr. fr. Italian by* Morris Bishop. Sonnets to Laura: To Laura in Death, XLII. LyPI
Sonnet against the Too-facile Mystic. Elizabeth B. Harrod. NePoEA
Sonnet and Limerick. Morris Bishop. FiBHP
Sonnet at Christmas. Allen Tate. *See* Sonnets at Christmas.
Sonnet at Easter. Howard Nemerov. FiMAP
Sonnet Claims More Freedom, The. Keats. *See* On the Sonnet.
Sonnet Composed upon Westminster Bridge, September 3, 1802. Wordsworth. *See* Composed upon Westminster Bridge.
Sonnet Entitled How to Run the World. E. E. Cummings. NePA
Sonnet for a Marriage. Ann Louise Hayes. PtPa
Sonnet for a Picture. Swinburne. *Fr.* The Heptalogia. OAEP
Sonnet for Christmas. Vincent G. Burns. MaRV
Sonnet for My Dog. Thomas Curtis Clark. AlBD
Sonnet for My Son. Melanie Gordon Barber. GoYe
Sonnet for Myself. Mildred Plew Meigs. DDA
Sonnet for Selvaggia. Cino da Pistoia, *tr. fr. Italian by* L. R. Lind. LyPI
Sonnet for the Madonna of the Cherries. A. P. Wavell. OtMeF
Sonnet Found in a Deserted Madhouse. *Unknown.* BoHV; InvP; NA; SiTL
Sonnet from an Oilfield. Dorothy McFarlane. DDA
Sonnet from "Idea." Michael Drayton. *See* Idea: "Since there's no help . . ."
Sonnet from "One Person." Elinor Wylie. *See* I Hereby Swear That to Uphold Your House.
Sonnet in a Garden. Josephine Preston Peabody. AA
Sonnet in a Pass of Bavaria. Richard Chenevix Trench. OBRV
Sonnet in Dialogue, A. Austin Dobson. YT
Sonnet in 1862. John James Piatt. *See* To Abraham Lincoln.
Sonnet in Sorrow. B. Y. Williams. MuM
Sonnet is a fruit which long hath slept, The. The Sonnet. John Addington Symonds. HBV; VA
Sonnet is a moment's monument, A. The Sonnet. Dante Gabriel Rossetti. The House of Life, *introd.* BEL; BMEP; BPN; CoBE; EmBrPo; EnL; EnLi-2; EnLit; EPN; EPP; ES; GTBS-W; HBV; InP; LEAP; OAEP; PFE; PoVP; TCEP; TOP; VA; ViBoPo; ViP; ViPo; ViPP; VLEP
Sonnet is an opal, The. In its white. The White Opal. "R. K. K." CAG
Sonnet, July 18th, 1787. William Lisle Bowles. *See* Time and Grief.
Sonnet Made on Isabella Markham, A. John Harington. ElL; ElSeCe; OBSC; TuPP
(Lines on Isabella Markham.) LPS-1
Sonnet of a Little Girl. Ernest Dowson. CaAE
Sonnet of Black Beauty. Lord Herbert of Cherbury. AtBAP; BoW; MePo; SeCL; SeEP
(Of Black Beauty.) ElSeCe
Sonnet of Brotherhood. R. A. K. Mason. AnNZ
Sonnet of Departure. J. R. Hervey. AnNZ
Sonnet of Fishes. George Barker. FaBoMo
Sonnet of the Moon, A. Charles Best. CH; ElSeCe; HBV; TuPP
(Looke How the Pale Queene.) EtS
(Moon, The.) ES; OBSC
(Of the Moon.) ElL
Sonnet of the Mountain, The. Mellin de Saint-Gelais, *tr. fr. French by* Austin Dobson. AWP
(Flame and Snow, *tr. by* Alan Conder.) TrFP
("Seeing those mountains, distant and obscure," *tr. by* Alan Conder.) LO
Sonnet of the Sea. Florence La Bau. CAG
Sonnet of the Unsleeping Dead. "Anthony Boucher." DaM
Sonnet on a Family Picture. Thomas Edwards. CEP; OBEC
Sonnet on a Monkey, A. Marjory Fleming. FaFP; FiBHP; LiTG; SiTL
(Sonnet to a Monkey, A.) ALV
(To a Monkey.) GoTP
Sonnet on a Picture of Leander. Keats. *See* On a Picture of Leander.

Sonnet on a Somewhat Inferior Radio Outfit. Cary Ross. AnAmPo; LA
Sonnet on a Sonnet. Lope de Vega, *tr. fr. Spanish by* James Young Gibson. AnSpL-1; TeCS
Sonnet on Catherine Wordsworth. Wordsworth. *See* Surprised by Joy—Impatient as the Wind.
Sonnet on Chillon. Byron. *Fr.* The Prisoner of Chillon. AnEnPo; ATP; BEL; BLP; BoLiVe; BPN; EM-2; EmBrPo; EnLi-2; EnLit; EnRP; EPN; EPP; ExPo; FiP; GEPC; HiLiEn; InP; LEAP; LiTB; LoBV; OAEP; OBRV; PoFr; PoFS; REAL; SeCeV; TCEP; TOP; TreFS; TrGrPo
(Chillon.) BCEP; PFE
(Freedom's Hero.) MaRV
(On Chillon.) ES
(On the Castle of Chillon.) GTBS; GTBS-D; GTBS-W; GTSE; GTSL; PYM
(Prisoner of Chillon, The, *introd. sonnet.*) LPS-2; MCCG
Sonnet on Death. William Walsh. ViBoPo
(Death; a Sonnet.) SeCL
(Sonnet: Death.) SeEP
Sonnet on First Looking into Chapman's Homer. Keats. *See* On First Looking . . .
Sonnet on Hearing the *Dies Irae* Sung in the Sistine Chapel. Oscar Wilde. TrPWD
Sonnet on His Blindness. Milton. *See* On His Blindness.
Sonnet on His Deceased Wife. Milton. *See* On His Deceased Wife.
Sonnet on Holy Week. Oscar Wilde. JKCP (1926 ed.)
Sonnet on Life. Sir Brooke Boothby. ViBoPo
Sonnet on Mistress Nicely, a Pattern for Housekeepers. Thomas Hood. *See* On Mistress Nicely, a Pattern for Housekeepers.
Sonnet on Seeing the Elgin Marbles. Keats. *See* On Seeing the Elgin Marbles.
Sonnet on Stewed Prunes. William F. Kirk. WhC
Sonnet on the Death of Paul Ehrlich, Discoverer of Salvarsan. Jerome Meyers. PoP
Sonnet on the Death of Richard West [*or* Mr. Richard West]. Thomas Gray. CEP; EiPP; EM-1; EnLit; EnRP; ES; OAEP; OBEC; PoE; PoEL-3; SeCePo; ViBoPo
(On the Death of Mr. Richard West.) TrGrPo
(On the Death of Richard West.) PeBoSo
Sonnet on the Sea. Keats. *See* On the Sea.
Sonnet on the Sonnet. Lord Alfred Douglas. MBP; MoBrPo (1942 ed.)
Sonnet on the Sonnet. Wordsworth. *See* Scorn Not the Sonnet.
Sonnet on Turning a Radio Dial. Anderson M. Scruggs. PoMa
Sonnet on Wordsworth, A. James Kenneth Stephen. *See* Sonnet: "Two voices are there . . ."
Sonnet or Dittie: "Mars in a fury gainst love's brightest queen." Robert Greene. *See* Mars and Venus.
Sonnet-Prison, The. Wordsworth. *See* Nuns Fret Not at Their Convent's Narrow Room.
Sonnet Sequence. Kimball Flaccus. CAG
"Long after the last wall."
"Noble gods will not be long alone, The."
"Once more as in the days."
Sonnet Series of French Canada, A, *sels.* Frank Oliver Call.
Blue Homespun. CaP; CPG; OCL
La Terre. CPG
Old Habitant, An. CaP; CPG; OCL
Sonnet Suppos'd to be Written at Lemnos. Thomas Russell. FaBoEn
Sonnet to ——. John Hamilton Reynolds. OBRV
Sonnet to a Cat. Heine, *tr. fr. German.* CIV
Sonnet to a Clam. John Godfrey Saxe. AnNE; APW; BOHV
Sonnet to a Friend Who Asked How I Felt When the Nurse First Presented My Infant to Me. Samuel Taylor Coleridge. EnRP; MotAn
Sonnet to a Monkey. Marjorie Fleming. *See* Sonnet on a Monkey, A.
Sonnet to a Negro in Harlem. Helene Johnson. BANP; CDC
Sonnet to a Plow-Woman of Norway. Margaret Tod Ritter. TBM
Sonnet to a Young Lady Who Sent Me a Laurel Crown. Keats. EmBrPo; EnRP
Sonnet to an Octogenarian. Wordsworth. BPN; EmBrPo
Sonnet to Britain. W. E. Aytoun. SoV
Sonnet to Byron. Shelley. PtP
Sonnet to Caelia. William Browne. CaAE
Sonnet to Edgar Allan Poe ("On our lone pathway"). Sarah Helen Whitman. *Fr.* Sonnets from the Series Relating to Edgar Allan Poe. AnAmPo; LA
(Sonnets.) AA; BAP; LEAP
Sonnet to Gath. Edna St. Vincent Millay. CoBA; MAP; MoAB; MoAmPo
Sonnet to George Romney. William Cowper. BoFr
Sonnet to Heavenly Beauty, A. Joachim du Bellay, *tr. fr. French by* Andrew Lang. Olive, CXIII. AWP; JAWP; WBP
(Home, *tr. by* Alan Conder.) TrFP
(Sonnet: "If life on earth be less than is a day," *tr. by* Armel O'Conner.) CAW
(Sonnet: "If of our life the span be not a day," *tr. by* Eleanor L. Turnbull.) WoL
Sonnet to Lake Leman. Byron. BPN
Sonnet to Liberty. Oscar Wilde. BMEP; LBBV; LEAP; PoFr
Sonnet to Mrs. Reynolds' Cat. Keats. *See* To a Cat.
Sonnet to Mrs. Unwin. William Cowper. *See* To Mary Unwin.
Sonnet to My Mother. George Barker. FaFP; GTBS-W; LiTB; LiTM; MoAB; PeBoSo; PG (1955 ed.); SeCePo; ViBoPo (1958 ed.); WaP
(To My Mother.) FaBoMo; GTBS-D; MoPW
Sonnet to My Mother, A. Heine. *See* To My Mother.
Sonnet to My Mother. Poe. *See* To My Mother.
Sonnet to Night, A. Joseph Blanco White. *See* To Night.
Sonnet to Orpheus, A ("O not till the time when flight"). Rainer Maria Rilke, *tr. fr. German by* M. D. Herter Norton. Sonnets to Orpheus, Pt. I, XXIII. PoF
Sonnet to Science. Poe. Al Aaraaf: Prologue. AmP; AmPo; AmPP; AnAmPo; AnFE; CoBA; CoV; NePA; OnAP; OxBA
(Sonnet: To Science.) APA; CoAnAm; IAP; LA; MOAP
(To Science.) PeBoSo; SPP
Sonnets to Shakespeare. Hugh Holland. *See* Shakespeare Dead.
Sonnet to Sidney. Alan Seeger. BTP
Sonnet to Sleep. Keats. *See* To Sleep.
Sonnet to Solitude. Keats. *See* To Solitude.
Sonnet to That Great Mother Schumann-Heink, A. Marian Leland. MotAn
Sonnet to the Lady Pietra. Dante. *See* Sonnet: To the Lady Pietra degli Scrovigni.
Sonnet to the Moon. Yvor Winters. TwAmPo
Sonnet to the River Lodon. Thomas Warton, the Younger. *See* Sonnet: To the River Lodon.
Sonnet to the River Otter. Samuel Taylor Coleridge. *See* Sonnet: To the River Otter.
Sonnet to the Sea Serpent. John G. C. Brainard. EtS
Sonnet to the Virgin. Wordsworth. *See* Virgin, The.
Sonnet to Vauxhall. Thomas Hood. PoEL-4
Sonnet to William Hayley. William Cowper. BoFr
Sonnet to William Wilberforce, Esq. William Cowper. CEP; OAEP
(To William Wilberforce.) CoBE
Sonnet to Zante. Poe. IAP
Sonnet upon a Stolen Kiss. George Wither. *See* Stolen Kiss, A.
Sonnet upon the Author's First Seven Years' Service, A. Thomas Tusser. SiCE; TuPP
(Upon the Author's First Seven Years' Service.) EIL
Sonnet upon the Pitiful Burning of the Globe Playhouse in London, A. *Unknown.* TuPP
Sonnet with her Mona Lisa smile, The. Sonnet and Limerick. Morris Bishop. FiBHP
Sonnet Written at the Close of Spring. Charlotte Smith. OBEC
(Elegiac Sonnet.) FaBoEn
Sonnet Written during His Residence in College. Charles Wolfe. TIP
Sonnet; Written on a Blank Page in Shakespeare's Poems, Facing "A Lover's Complaint." Keats. *See* Bright Star, Would I Were Steadfast as Thou Art.
Sonnet Written While in Prison for Denouncing the Domestic Slave-Trade. William Lloyd Garrison. *See* Freedom for the Mind.
Sonnets, *sels.* James Agee. MAP; MoAmPo
"Now stands our love on that still verge of day," XX.
"Our doom is in our being," II.
"So it begins," I.
"Those former loves wherein our lives have run," XIX.
Sonnets. Leonard Bacon. TBM
"Dante was naïf, although he had an inkling," II.
"Idiots will prate and prate of suicide," III.
"Thirty-eight years. Yes, neither less nor more," I.
Sonnets, *sels.* Hilaire Belloc.
"Almighty God, whose justice like a sun," XXI. QS; TrPWD
"Because my faltering feet may fail to dare," XVII. OxBoCh; POTE
(Her Faith.) GoBC
"We will not whisper, we have found the place," XIX. MBP; MoBrPo
"When you to Acheron's ugly water come," XVIII. TCPD
Sonnets. Gwendolyn B. Bennett.
"He came in silvern armour," I. CDC; PoNe
"Some things are very dear to me," II. BANP; CDC; PoNe
Sonnets, *sels.* Boccaccio, *tr. fr. Italian by* Dante Gabriel Rossetti.
Inscription for a Portrait of Dante. AWP; JAWP; WBP
(Inscription for Portrait of Dante.) OnPM
(Tribute to Dante, A.) GoBC

"Now perish, Baia, root and stock and name," *tr. by* T. G. Bergin. LyMA; LyPI
Of Fiammetta Singing. AWP
(Fiammetta.) GoBC
Of His Last Sight of Fiammetta. AWP; JAWP; OnPM; WBP
(Fiammetta.) GoBC
Of Three Girls and [of] Their Talk. AWP; JAWP; OnPM; WBP
To Dante in Paradise, after Fiammetta's Death. AWP
(Fiammetta.) GoBC
To One Who Had Censured His Public Exposition of Dante. AWP
(Tribute to Dante, A.) GoBC
"To that fair kingdom, o my gentle lord," *tr. by* T. G. Bergin. LyPI
Sonnets, *sels.* George Henry Boker. MOAP
"Either the sum of this sweet mutiny."
"Here part we, love, beneath the world's broad eye."
"I have been mounted on life's topmost wave."
"I'll call thy frown a headsman passing grim."
(To My Lady.) AA
"In this deep hush and quiet of my soul."
"Love is that orbit of the restless soul."
"My lady sighs, and I am far away."
"Not when the buxom form which nature wears."
"Sometimes, in bitter fancy, I bewail."
"Thou who dost smile upon me, yet unknown."
"What fancy, or what flight of wingèd thought."
"Your love to me appears in doubtful signs."
Sonnets. Samuel Daniel. *See* To Delia.
Sonnets. Michael Drayton. *See* Idea *and* Idea's Mirrour.
Sonnets (I–VIII.) Feng Chih, *tr. fr. Chinese by* Chu K'an. *Fr.* Twenty-seven Sonnets. WhP
Sonnets, *sels.* Robert Hillyer.
"Even as love grows more, I write the less," XVI. HBMV
"Golden spring redeems the withered year, The," II. HBMV
"I will fling wide the windows of my soul," XII. HBMV
"Let all men see the ruins of the shrine," XIV. HBMV
"Long after both of us are scattered dust," XXXIV.
(From a Sonnet Sequence.) OBAV
"Over the waters but a single bough," XXIII. HBMV
"Quickly and pleasantly the seasons blow," I. HBMV
(From a Sonnet Sequence.) OBAV
"Then judge me as thou wilt, I cannot flee," III. HBMV
Sonnets (I–XIV.) Thomas Caulfield Irwin. IrPN
Sonnets, *sels.* Muna Lee.
"Along my ways of life you never came," XII. HBMV; NP
"I have a thousand pictures of the sea," IV. HBMV
"I make no question of your right to go," III. HBMV
"It were easiest to say: the moon and lake." NP
"It will be easy to love you when I am dead," XI. BAP; HBMV
"Life of itself will be cruel and hard enough," V. HBMV
"What other form were worthy of your praise," Foreword. HBMV
Sonnets, *sels.* Irene Rutherford McLeod. HBMV
"Between my love and me there runs a thread."
"In heaven there is a star I call my own."
"Shall I be fearful thus to speak my mind."
"Sweet, when I think how summer's smallest bird."
"When sane men gather in to talk of love."
Sonnets, *sels.* Mary Queen of Scots. DiM
"For him what countless tears I must have shed," IX.
"I seek but one thing," X.
"Into his hands, utterly into his power," VI.
"O you High Gods, have pity," V.
"That you trust her, alas, is plain enough," VIII.
"When you so wildly loved her, she was cold," VII.
Sonnets ("Like bones the ruins of the cities stand"), *sel.* John Masefield.
"Now they are gone with all their songs and sins," II. InP
Sonnets ("Long long ago"), *sels.* John Masefield.
"Ah we are neither heaven nor earth, but men." EPN; PoeMoYo
"Flesh, I have knocked at many a dusty door." GTSL; LEAP; LiTM; MBP; MoBrPo; SeCePo
"Go, spend your penny, beauty, when you will." AEV; TCPD
"Here in the self is all that man can know." AWP; JAWP; WBP
"How many ways, how many times." WGRP
(How many Ways.) LiTB
"I never see the red rose crown the year." ChMo; CMP; EnLi-2 (1949 ed.); EPP; GoYe; InP; PeBoSo
"If I could come again to that dear place." CMP; EPP; HBV; TwCV
(Revelation.) ChMo
(Sonnet, *wr. at. to* Herbert P. Horne.) LEAP
"If I could get within this changing I." EPP; WGRP
"Is there a great green commonwealth of Thought." LiTM; MBP; MoBrPo
"It may be so with us that in the dark." ATP; TOP
(Life Is a Miracle.) GrCo-2
"Let that which is to come be as it may." HBV
"Long long ago, when all the glittering earth." EPP; HBV
"Man has his unseen friend, his unseen twin." PoeMoYo
"Men are made human by the mighty fall." EPN
"O little self, within whose smallness lies." GTML; HBV; PoeMoYo; POTE; WGRP
"Roses are beauty, but I never see." HBV; TCPD
(Roses.) ES
(Roses Are Beauty.) TOP
"There is no God, as I was taught in youth." ChMo; CMP; HBV; WGRP
"There, on the darkened deathbed, dies the brain." CMP
(End, The.) ChMo
"What am I, Life? A thing of watery salt." PoeMoYo
(What Am I, Life?) ImOP; NP
"What is this atom which contains the whole." GTML
Sonnets. Gustav Rosenhane, *tr. fr. Swedish by* Sir Edmund Gosse. AWP; JAWP; WBP
"And then I sat me down and gave the rein," II.
"Deep in a vale where rocks on every side," I.
Sonnets, *sels.* George Santayana.
"After gray vigils, sunshine in the heart," XLIX. MAP; MoAmPo; MOAP; WHA
"As in the midst of battle there is room," XXV. AnFE; APA; AWP; BAP; CoAnAm; JAWP; LBMV; LEAP; LiTM; MAP; MoAmPo; MOAP; NePA; ReaPo; WBP
"As when the sceptre dangles from the hand," XLII. ATP; MOAP
"Deem not, because you see me in the press," XI. TrGrPo
(Deem Not.) AnEnPo
"Have patience; it is fit that in this wise," IX. MOAP; WGRP
"I sought on earth a garden of delight," I. AnEnPo
(Sorrow.) WGRP
"I would I might forget that I am I," IV. AWP; JAWP; LBMV; MOAP; TOP; WBP
"O world, thou choosest not the better part," III. ATP; InP; MAP; MoAmPo; PFE; TreFS
(Faith.) OQP; PoeMoYo; QP-1; WGRP
(Light of Faith, The.) GrCo-1
(O World.) HBMV; MaRV; TrGrPo
"Slow and reluctant was the long descent," II. MOAP
"Sweet are the days we wander with no hope," XIII. MOAP
"These strewn thoughts by the mountain pathway," XX. OBAV
"Tis love that moveth the celestial spheres," XXII. MOAP
"We needs must be divided in the tomb," XXXV. LBMV; OBAV; ViBoPo
"What riches have you that you deem me poor," XXIX.
(What Riches Have You?) BAP; HBV; LEAP; POT; PoTo; TrGrPo
Sonnets (*Complete,* I–CLIV). *Shakespeare.* PeBoSo
Sels.
I. "From fairest creatures we desire increase." AtBAP; EG; FaBoEn; LiTB; LiTL; OAEP; OBSC; SiCE; TrGrPo
II. "When forty winters shall besiege thy brow." EG; EM-1; LiTB; OBSC; ReEn; ReIE; SiCE; TwP
III. "Look in thy glass, and tell the face thou viewest." EG; GTBS-W; LiTB; OBSC; SiCE; TwP
V. "Those hours that with gentle work did frame." ReEn; SiCE
VI. "Then let not winter's ragged hand deface." SiCE
VII. "Lo, in the orient when the gracious light." ReIE; SiCE
VIII. "Music to hear, why hear'st thou music sadly." PoEL-2; ViBoPo
XII. "When I do count the clock that tells the time." AWP; BEL; EG; ElL; ElSeCe; EM-1; EnLi-1; EPP; ES; EV-1; FaFP; InPo; JAWP; OBSC; OuHeWo; Po; REAL; ReEn; ReIE; SiCE; TOP; TwP; ViBoPo; WBP
(Approach of Age, The.) LPS-3
XIII. "O! that you were yourself; but, love, you are." OAEP; SiCE
XIV. "Not from the stars do I my judgment pluck." SiCE
XV. "When I consider every thing that grows." AWP; BEL; CoBE; EM-1; EnLi-1; EPP; EtPaEn; OAEP; OBSC; OuHeWo; PoFS; ReEn; ReIE; SiCE; TrGrPo; TwP; TyEnPo
XVI. "But wherefore do not you a mightier waie." FaBoEn
XVII. "Who will believe my verse in time to come." AEV; EM-1; EnLi-1; EPP; OBSC; SiCE
XVIII. "Shall I compare thee to a summer's day?" AnFE; AtBAP; ATP; AWP; BEL; BoLiVe; CaAE; CoBE; CoEV; EG; ElL; ElSeCe; EM-1; EnL; EnLi-1; EnLit; EnLoPo; ES; EtPaEn; EV-1; ExPo; FaBoBe; FaBoEn; FaFP; FiP; HBV; InP; InvP; LiTB; LiTG; LiTL; LoBV; LoPo; MaPo; MCCG; NeHB; OAEP; OBEV; OBSC; OuHeWo; PIAE; PIR; PoE; PoEL-2; PoFS; PoRA; REAL; ReaPo; ReEn; ReIE; RiBV; SeCePo; SeCeV; ShBV-4; SiCE; TOP; TrGrPo; TwHP; TwP; TyEnPo; ViBoPo; WHA
(Eternal Summer.) BLV

Sonnets. Shakespeare (*continued*)
(To His Love.) GTBS; GTBS-D; GTBS-W; GTSE; GTSL; PoMa
XIX. "Devouring time, blunt thou the lion's paws." AtBAP; AWP; ChTr; CoEV; EG; GTBS-W; InPo; LiA; OBSC; PoEL-2; ReIE; RiBV; SiCE; TrGrPo; TwP; WHA
XX. "Woman's face, with nature's own hand painted, A." InvP; ReEn
XXI. "So is it not with me as with that Muse." InvP; OBSC; ReEn; SiCE
XXII. "My glass shall not persuade me I am old." EG; Em-1; OBSC
XXIII. "As an unperfect actor on the stage." BEL; EM-1; EnL; EtPaEn; HBV; InvP; OAEP; REAL; ReEn; SiCE
XXV. "Let those who are in favor with their stars." EM-1; EnL; EnLi-1; OBSC; ReIE; SiCE; WoL
XXVI. "Lord of my love, to whom in vassalage." PoFS; ReEn
XXVII. "Weary with toil, I haste me to my bed." OBSC; PoFS; ReEn; SiCE
XXVIII. "How can I then return in happy plight." OBSC
XXIX. "When, in disgrace with fortune and men's eyes." AEV; AnFE; AtBAP; ATP; AWP; BCEP; BEL; BoLiVe; BrBE; CaAE; CBE; CoBE; CoEV; ElL; ElSeCe; EM-1; EnL; EnLi-1; EnLit; EPP; ES; EtPaEn; EV-1; ExPo; FaBoEn; GrCo-2; HBV; HiLiEn; InP; InPo; InvP; JAWP; LEAP; LiTB; LiTG; LiTL; LoBV; LoPo; LoPS; MaPo; OAEP; OBEV; OBSC; OuHeWo; PFE; PG; PIR; Po; PoE; PoEL-2; PoFS; PoRA; REAL; ReaPo; ReEn; ReIE; SeCeV; SiCE; TCEP; TOP; TreF; TrGrPo; TwHP; TwP; TyEnPo; ViBoPo; WBP; WHA
(Consolation, A.) GTBS; GTBS-D; GTBS-W; GTSE; GTSL; PoMa
(For Thy Sweet Love.) MaRV
(Fortune and Men's Eyes.) BLV
XXX. "When to the sessions of sweet silent thought." AEV; AnFE; ATP; BCEP; BEL; BoFr; CBE; CoBE; EG; ElL; ElSeCe; EM-1; EnL; EnLi-1; EnLit; EPP; ES; EtPaEn; EV-1; ExPo; FaBoEn; GTBS-W; HBV; InPo; JAWP; KN; LEAP; LiTB; LiTG; LoBV; LPS-1; MaPo; NeHB; OAEP; OBEV; OBSC; OuHeWo; PFE; PIAE; PIR; PoE; PoEL-2; PoeMoYo; PoFS; PoRA; REAL; ReaPo; ReEn; ReIE; SeCeV; ShBV-4; SiCE; TCEP; TOP; TreFS; TrGrPo; TwHP; TwP; TyEnPo; ViBoPo; WBP; WHA; WoL; WP
(Memory.) GTSL
(Remembrance [of Things Past].) BLV; FaFP; GTBS; GTBS-D; GTSE
(Sessions of Sweet Silent Thought.) BoLiVe
XXXI. "Thy bosom is endeared with all hearts." ES; OBEV; OBSC; PoEL-2
XXXII. "If thou survive my well-contented day." BEL; BoLiVe; ElL; EM-1; EnL; EnLit; EPP; ES; EtPaEn; EV-1; HBV; LiTL; OBSC; SiCE; TOP
(Post Mortem.) GTBS; GTBS-D; GTBS-W; GTSE; GTSL
(These Lines.) BLV
XXXIII. "Full many a glorious morning have I seen." AEV; ATP; AWP; BCEP; BEL; BoLiVE; CoBE; CoEV; EG; ElL; ElSeCe; EM-1; EnL; EnLi-1; ES; EV-1; FaBoEn; FaFP; HBV; InPo; JAWP; KN; LEAP; LiTB; LiTG; LoBV; OAEP; OBSC; OtMeF; OuHeWo; PIAE; PoRA; ReaPo; ReEn; ReIE; RiBV; SeCePo; SeCeV; SiCE; SN; TOP; TreFS; TrGrPo; TwHP; TwP; TyEnPo; UnPo (1st ed.); ViBoPo; WBP
(Suns and Clouds.) BLV
XXXIV. "Why didst thou promise such a beauteous day." OBSC; PoE
XXXV. "No more be grieved at that which thou hast done." UnPo
XXXVI. "Let me confess that we two must be twain." OAEP
XXXVIII. "How can my Muse want subject to invent." EnLit; ReEn
XL. "Take all my loves, my love, yea, take them all." InvP; OBSC
XLI. "Those pretty wrongs that liberty commits." InvP; ReEn
XLII. "That thou hast her, it is not all my grief." EM-1; InvP
L. "How heavy; do I journey on the way." EtPaEn; ReEn; ReIE; SiCE
LI. "Thus can my love excuse the slow offense." PoFS
LII. "So am I as the rich, whose blessed key." OBSC
LIII. "What is your substance, whereof are you made." AtBAP; ElL; EtPaEn; EV-1; FaFP; GTBS-W; LiTB; LiTG; LiTL; OAEP; OBEV; OBSC; RiBV; ViBoPo
LIV "O, how much more doth beauty beauteous seem." AWP; ElL; EnLi-1 (1949 ed.); EV-1; JAWP; OBEV; OBSC; ReEn; ReIE; SiCE; TOP; ViBoPo; WBP
(Rose Looks Fair, The.) LiTG
LV. "Not marble, nor the gilded monuments." AEV; AnEnPo; AnFE; ATP; AWP; BEL; CoBE; CoEV; EG; EM-1; EnL; EnLi-1; EnLit; EPP; ExPo; FaBoEn; FaFP; GTBS-W; InPo; JAWP; LEAP; LiTB; LiTG; LiTL; LoBV; OAEP; OBSC; OuHeWo; PoE; PoEL-2; PoRA; REAL; ReEn; ReIE; SeCeV; SiCE; TOP; TrGrPo; TwHP; TwP; TyEnPo; ViBoPo; WBP
LVI. "Sweet love, renew thy force; be it not said." LO; UnPo (1st ed.)
LVII. "Being your slave, what should I do but tend." EG; ES; EtPaEn; EV-1; LiA; LiTL; LoPo; LoPS; OBEV; PoEL-2; ViBoPo; WoL
(Absence.) GTBS; GTBS-D; GTBS-W; GTSE; GTSL
LIX. "If there be nothing new, but that which is." FaBoEn; ReEn
LX. "Like as the waves make towards the pebbled shore." AnFE; ATP; BEL; BoFr; BoLiVe; ChTr; CoBE; CoEV; ElL; ElSeCe; EM-1; EnL; EnLi-1; EnLit; ES; EtPaEn; EV-1; ExPo; FaBoEn; FaFP; HBV; LEAP; LiTB; LiTL; LoBV; NBE; OBSC; Po; PoRA; ReaPo; ReEn; ReIE; SeCeV; ShBV-4; SiCE; TwHP; UnPo; ViBoPo
(Revolutions.) GTBS; GTBS-D; GTBS-W; GTSE; GTSL
(Time.) BLV
LXI. "Is it thy will thy image should keep open." LO; LoPo; PoEL-2
LXII. "Sinne of selfe-love possesseth al mine eie." PoEL-2
LXIII. "Against my love shall be, as I am now." OBSC; ReEn; SiCE
LXIV. "When I have seen by Time's fell hand defaced." AWP; BEL; CoEV; ElL; ElSeCe; EM-1; EnL; EnLi-1 (1949 ed.); EnLit; EnLoPo; ES; EV-1; FaFP; InP; InPo; JAWP; LiTB; LiTL; LO; MCCG; OBSC; OuHeWo; PFE; PoFS; PoRA; ReaPo; ReEn; ReIE; SeCeV; SiCE; TCEP; TOP; TwHP; TwP; ViBoPo; WBP
(Time and Love, 1.) GTBS; GTBS-D; GTBS-W; GTSE; GTSL
LXV. "Since brass, nor stone, nor earth, nor boundless sea." AEV; AtBAP; AWP; BEL; BoFr; BoLiVe; BrBE; CBOV; CoEV; EM-1; EnLi-1 (1949 ed.); EPP; ES; EV-1; FaFP; FiP; JAWP; LiTB; LiTL; MaPo; MCCG; OuHeWo; PIAE; PoD; PoFS; PoRA; ReaPo; SeCeV; SiCE; TCEP; TOP; TwP; UnPo (1st ed.); WBP
(Time and Love, 2.) GTBS; GTBS-D; GTBS-W; GTSE; GTSL
LXVI. "Tired with all these, for restful death I cry." AnFE; AWP; BEL; BLV; BoLiVe; EnL; EnLi-1; EPP; EtPaEn; EV-1; ExPo; FaFP; InPo; JAWP; LiTB; LiTG; MyFE; OBSC; PFE; PIAE; ReEn; SeCeV; SiCE; TOP; TrGrPo; ViBoPo; WBP; WHA
("Tyr'd with all these for restfull death I cry.") PoEL-2
(World's Way, The.) GTBS; GTBS-D; GTBS-W; GTSE; GTSL
LXVII. "Ah, wherefore with infection should he live." SiCE
LXVIII. "Thus is his cheek the map of days outworn." OBSC; ReIE; UnPo (1st ed.)
LXXI. "No longer mourn for me when I am dead." AWP; BEL; BoLiVe; CoBE; ElL; ElSeCe; EM-1; EnL; EnLi-1; EnLit; EPP; ES; EV-1; HBV; InPo JAWP; LiTB; LO; OAEP; OBSC; OuHeWo; PIAE; PoE; PoRA; ReaPo; ReEn; ReIE; SeCeV; SiCE; TOP; TrGrPo; ViBoPo; WBP; WHA
(Triumph of Death, The.) GTBS; GTBS-D; GTBS-W; GTSE; GTSL
LXXII. "O! lest the world should task you to recite."
"O, lest your true love may seem false in this," *sel.* LO
LXXIII. "That time of year thou may'st in me behold." AnFE; ATP (1935 ed.); AWP; BCEP; BEL; BoLiVe; BPF; BrBE; CaAE; ChTr; CoBE; CoEV; EG; ElL; ElSeCe; EM-1; EnL; EnLi-1; EnLit; EnLoPo; EPP; ES; EtPaEn; EV-1; ExPo; FaBoEn; FiP; GTBS; GTBS-D; GTBS-W; GTSE; GTSL; HBV; HoPM; InPo; InvP; JAWP; KN; LEAP; LiTB; LoBV; MaPo; NLK (1947 ed.); OAEP; OBEV; OBSC; OHFP (1958 ed.); OuHeWo; PFE; PG (1955 ed.); PIAE; PoE; PoEL-2; PoFS; PoMa; PoRA; PreP; REAL; ReaPo; ReEn; ReIE; RiBV; SeCeV; SiCE; TCEP; TOP; TrGrPo; TwHP; TwP; TyEnPo; ViBoPo; WBP
(Twilight of Love, A.) BLV
(Where Late the Sweet Birds Sang.) LiTG
LXXIV. "But be contented: when that fell arrest." BoFr; OBSC; TCEP
LXXV. "So are you to my thoughts as food to life." PoEL-2
LXXVI. "Why is my verse so barren of new pride." AEV; EnLi-1 (1949 ed.); InvP; NBE; ReEn; ReIE; SiCE
LXXVII. "Thy glass will show thee how thy beauties wear." RiBV
LXXVIII. "So oft have I invoked thee for my Muse." EM-1
LXXIX. "Whilst I alone did call upon thy aid." EM-1

LXXX. "Oh how I faint when I of you do write." ReEn; SiCE
LXXXI. "Or I shall live your epitaph to make." OAEP; OBSC
LXXXV. "My tongue-tied Muse in manners holds her still." EM-1
LXXXVI. "Was it the proud full sail of his great verse?" EM-1; InvP; NBE; OAEP; PtP; ReEn; ReIE; SiCE; TwP
LXXXVII. "Farewell! thou art too dear for my possessing." AnFE; BLV; BoLiVe; CaAE; CoBE; ElL; EM-1; ES; EtPaEn; EV-1; GTBS; GTBS-D; GTBS-W; GTSE; GTSL; InvP; LiTB; LiTG; LPS-1; OAEP; OBEV; OBSC; PG (1955 ed.); PIAE; PoEL-2; PoFS; ReIE; SiCE; TOP; TrGrPo; TwP; ViBoPo
LXXXVIII. "When thou shalt be dispos'd to set me light." BoFr
LXXXIX. "Say that thou didst forsake me for some fault." OAEP; SiCE
XC. "Then hate me when thou wilt; if ever, now." ATP; AWP; BoFr; CoEV; ElL; ES; EtPaEn; EV-1; JAWP; LO; MaPo; OBEV; OBSC; PG; PoEL-2; ReIE; TOP; WBP; WHA; WoL
(Spight of Fortune, The.) LiA
XCIII. "So shall I live, supposing thou art true." InvP
XCIV. "They that have power to hurt and will do none." AnFE; BoLiVe; CaAE; CoEV; ElL; ES; ExPo; FaBoEn; LiTB; LiTG; MaPo; OBEV; PG (1955 ed.); PoEL-2; ReEn; TrGrPo; ViBoPo
(Life without Passion, The.) GTBS; GTBS-D; GTBS-W; GTSE; GTSL
(Lilies That Fester.) BLV
XCV. "How sweet and lovely dost thou make the shame." ReEn; TrGrPo
XCVII. "How like a winter hath my absence been." ATP; AWP; BEL; CaAE; ElL; EM-1; EnLi-1; EnLoPo; EPP; ES; EV-1; FaBoEn; GTBS; GTBS-D; GTBS-W; GTSE; GTSL; JAWP; LiTG; LoPo; LoPS; OBEV; OBSC; PIAE; PoFS; PoRA; REAL; ReaPo; ReIE; TOP; TrGrPo; WBP
XCVIII. "From you have I [*or* I have] been absent in the spring." AWP; BEL; ChTr; EG; ElL; EM-1; EnLi-1; EPP; ES; InPo; JAWP; LiTB; LiTG; LoPo; OBEV; OBSC; ReEn; ReIE; SiCE; TOP; TwP; ViBoPo; WBP
XCIX. "Forward violet thus did I chide, The." EG; EnLi-1; EPP; ES; LPS-1; OAEP; OBSC; PIAE
C. "Where art thou, Muse, that thou forget'st so long." OBSC
CII. "My love is strengthen'd, though more weak in seeming." AWP; CaAE; CoEV; ElL; ES; LiTG; LiTL; LoPS; OAEP; OBEV; OBSC; SiCE; TOP; ViBoPo
CIV. "To me, fair friend, you never can be old." BEL; CaAE; EG; ElL; ElSeCe; EM-1; EnLi-1 (1949 ed.); EnLit; ES; EtPaEn; EV-1; FaBoEn; GTBS; GTBS-D; GTBS-W; GTSE; GTSL; HBV; InP; LEAP; OAEP; OBEV; OBSC; ReEn; ReIE; SiCE; TOP; ViBoPo
(You Never Can Be Old.) LiTL
CV. "Let not my love be call'd idolatry." BoFr
CVI. "When in the chronicle of wasted time." AnFE; AWP; BCEP; BEL; BoLiVe; CaAE; CoBE; EG; ElL; ElSeCe; EM-1; EnL; EnLi-1; EnLit; EnLoPo; EPP; ES; EtPaEn; EV-1; ExPo; FaBoCh; FaBoEn; FiP; HBV; InPo; JAWP; LEAP; LiTB; LiTG; LiTL; LoBV; LoGBV; LPS-1; MaPo; MCCG; OAEP; OBEV; OBSC; OuHeWo; PIAE; Po; PoE; PoFS; PoRA; REAL; ReaPo; ReEn; ReIE; SeCeV; ShBV-3; SiCE; TOP; TrGrPo; TwCrTr; TwHP; TwP; TyEnPo; ViBoPo; WBP; WHA
(Chronicle of Wasted Time.) BLV
(Her Beauty.) GTSL
(To His Love.) GTBS; GTBS-D; GTBS-W; GTSE; WP
CVII. "Not mine own fears, nor the prophetic soul." AWP; EG; EM-1; EnLi-1; EPP; ES; EV-1; FiP; InPo; JAWP; LiTB; LoBV; MaPo; OAEP; OBSC; OuHeWo; PoFr; ReaPo; ReEn; ReIE; SeCeV; SiCE; TOP; WBP
(I'll Live in This Poor Rime.) LiTG
CIX. "Oh, never say that I was false of heart." BEL; ElL; EM-1; EPP; ES; EtPaEn; EV-1; HBV; LiTG; LiTL; LO; LoPo; OBEV; OBSC; ReaPo; SiCE; TwP; WoL
(Unchangeable, The.) GTBS; GTBS-D; GTBS-W; GTSE; GTSL
CX. "Alas, 'tis true I have gone here and there." EM-1; EnLi-1 (1949 ed.); EPP; EtPaEn; EV-1; MaPo; NBE; OAEP; OBSC; PoE; ReEn; ReIE; SiCE; ViBoPo
CXI. "O, for my sake do you with fortune chide." EM-1; EPP; EV-1; SiCE; TOP
CXV. "Those lines that I before have writ do lie." SiCE
CXVI. "Let me not to the marriage of true minds." AnFE; ATP; AWP; BCEP; BEL; BoFr; CaAE; CoBE; CoEV; EG; ElL; ElSeCe; EM-1; EnL; EnLi-1; EnLit; EnLoPo; EPP; ES; EtPaEn; EV-1; ExPo; FaBoEn; FaFP; GrCo-2; HBV; InPo; InvP; JAWP; KN; LEAP; LiTB; LiTG; LO; LoBV; LoPo; LPS-1; MaPo; MCCG; OAEP; OBEV; OBSC; OuHeWo; PFE; PG; PIR; Po; PoE; PoEL-2; PoeMoYo; PoRA; PreP; REAL; ReaPo; ReEn; ReIE; RiBV; SeCePo; SeCeV; ShBV-4; SiCE; TOP; TrGrPo; TwP; TyEnPo; UnPo; ViBoPo; WBP; WHA
(Love Is Not Love Which Alters.) BLV
(Love's Eternity.) PIAE
(Love's Not Time's Fool.) LiTL; TreF
(Marriage of True Minds, The.) AnEnPo; BoLiVe; LiA
(True Love.) BBV; GBV; GoBC; GTBS; GTBS-D; GTBS-W; GTSE; GTSL; MaRV
CXVIII. "Like as, to make our appetites more keen." UnPo (1st ed.)
CXIX. "What potions have I drunk of Siren tears." EtPaEn; EV-1; NBE; ReIE; WHA
CXX. "That you were once unkind befriends me now." InvP
CXXI. "'Tis better to be vile than vile esteemed." InvP; MaPo; PoEL-2
CXXIII. "No, Time, thou shalt not boast that I do change." BoLiVe; OAEP; OBSC; SiCE; TrGrPo
(Despite Time.) BLV
CXXVI. "O thou, my lovely boy, who in thy power." MyFE; ReIE
CXXVII. "In the old age black was not counted fair." ReIE; TwP
CXXVIII. "How oft, when thou, my music, music play'st." ElL; EM-1; EnLit; EnLi-1 (1949 ed.); ReEn; ReIE
CXXIX. "Expense [*or* Expence] of spirit in a waste of shame, The." AWP; BrBE; CaAE; CBE; CoBE; CoEV; EnL; ElSeCe; ES; ExPo; FaBoEn; GTBS-W; InPo; JAWP; KN; LiTB; LiTG; LiTL; LO; LoBV; MaPo; OBEV; OBSC; OtMeF; PoE; PoEL-2; PoFS; ReaPo; ReEn; ReIE; RiBV; SeCePo; SeCeV; ShBV-4; TOP; TrGrPo; UnPo (3d ed.); ViBoPo; WBP
(Lust.) AnEnPo
(Past Reason [Hunted].) BLV; LiA
CXXX. "My mistress' eyes are nothing like the sun." ATP; AWP; BEL; CoBE; ElSeCe; EM-1; EnL; EnLi-1 (1949 ed.); EnLit; ExPo; HBV; HoPM; InvP; JAWP; LiTB; LiTL; OAEP; OtMeF; PoE; ReEn; ReIE; SeCeV; SiCE; TOP; TwP; TyEnPo; WBP
(Love's Concession.) PIAE
CXXXII. "Thine eyes I love, and they, as pitying me." OAEP; OBSC; SiCE
CXXXIII. "Beshrew that heart that makes my heart to groan." InvP; ReIE
CXXXIV. "So now I have confessed that he is thine." InvP
CXXXV. "Whoever hath her wish, thou hast thy Will." ReEn
CXXXVIII. "When my love swears that she is made of truth." AWP; InPo; JAWP; OAEP; PoEL-2; ReEn; TrGrPo; TwP; ViBoPo; WBP
CXXXIX. "O, call not me to justify the wrong." ReIE
CXLI. "In faith, I do not love thee with mine eyes." EtPaEn; MaPo; PoEL-2; TrGrPo
CXLIII. "Lo, as a careful housewife runs to catch." OAEP; ReEn
CXLIV. "Two loves I have of comfort and despair." EM-1; InvP; LoBV; OAEP; PoEL-2; ReEn; ReIE
CXLVI. "Poor soul, the centre [*or* center] of my sinful earth." AtBAP; ATP; AWP; BEL; BoLiVe; CAW; CoBE; ElL; EM-1; EnL; EnLi-1; EPP; ES; EV-1; ExPo; FaBoEn; HBV; InPo; JAWP; LEAP; LiTB; LiTG; LO; MaPo; MyFE; OBEV; OBSC; OxBoCh; PIAE; PoEL-2; ReaPo; ReEn; ReIE; RiBV; SeCeV; SiCE; TOP; TrGrPo; TwP; UnPo (1st ed.); ViBoPo; WBP; WHA
(Body and Soul.) BLV
(Death of Death, The.) TreFS
(Outer and the Inner Man, The.) MaRV
(Soul and Body.) GoBC; GTBS; GTBS-D; GTBS-W; GTSE; GTSL
CXLVII. "My love is as a fever, longing still." HoPM; LO; PoEL-2; ReEn; ReIE; TwP
CXLVIII. O me! what eyes hath Love put in my head." EV-1
(Blind Love.) GTBS; GTBS-D; GTBS-W; GTSE; GTSL
CL. "Oh, from what powre hast thou this powerful might." NBE
CLI. "Love is too young to know what conscience is." PoEL-2; ReEn
CLII. "In loving thee thou know'st I am forsworn." ReIE
CLIV. "Little Love-god lying once asleep, The." EM-1; ReIE
Sonnets. Spenser. *See* Amoretti.
Sonnets, *sels.* Dylan Thomas.

Sonnets. Dylan Thomas (*continued*)
"Altarwise by owl-light in the halfway-house," I. LiTM
  (Two Sonnets.) MoAB; MoBrPo (1950 ed.)
"And from the windy West came two-gunned Gabriel," V.
  LiTM
"Cartoons of slashes on the tide-traced crater," VI. LiTM
"Death is all metaphors, shape in one history," II. LiTM
  (Two Sonnets.) MoAB; MoBrPo (1950 ed.)
"First there was the lamb on knocking knees," III. LiTM
"From the oracular archives and the parchment," IX. LiTM
"Let the tale's sailor from a Christian voyage," X. LiTM
"Now stamp the Lord's Prayer on a grain of rice," VII.
  GTBS-W; LiTM
"This was the crucifixion on the mountain," VIII. LiTM
"What is the metre of the dictionary?" IV. LiTM
Sonnets, *sels.* Thomas Warton, the Younger.
  Sonnet: On King Arthur's Round Table at Winchester,
    VIII. EiPP
  Sonnet: To the River Lodon [*or* Loddon], IX. CEP;
    OBEC; ViBoPo
    (To the River Lodon.) CoBE
  Sonnet: Written after Seeing Wilton-House, V. OBEC
  Sonnet: Written at Stonehenge, IV. CEP; EiPP; EPP
  Sonnet: Written in a Blank Leaf of Dugdale's "Monasticon,"
    III. EiPP; OBEC; SeCePo
    (Written in a Blank Leaf of Dugdale's "Monasticon.")
    EV-3
Sonnets; a Sequence of Profane Love, *sels.* George Henry
  Boker. MOAP
  "All the world's malice, all the spite of fate," XVI.
  "As some new ghost, that wanders to and fro," XXXIII.
  "Death on his mission sought my lady's side," XCV.
  "I strive to live my life in whitest truth," LV.
  "If dreaming of thee be a waste of time," XXXV.
  "Love sat at ease upon Time's bony knee," CCCVIII.
  "Perhaps in mercy is the future masked," XIII.
  "Thus in her absence is my fancy cool," LXXVII.
  "Today her majesty was wroth and cold," LXXXIX.
  "When I look back upon my early days," XLV.
Sonnets—Actualities, *sel.* E. E. Cummings.
  "Notice the convulsed orange inch of moon." AnAmPo; LA
Sonnets—Ad Innuptam (I–VII). Patrick Moloney. BoAu
Sonnets after the Italian. Richard Watson Gilder. HBV
  "I know not if I love her overmuch."
  "I like her gentle hand that sometimes strays."
Sonnets are full of love, and this my tome. To My First Love,
  My Mother [*or* Dedicatory Sonnet]. Christina Rossetti.
  MOAH; MotAn; OHIP; VLEP
Sonnets at Christmas. Allen Tate. AmP; GTBS-W; LiTA;
  LiTM; NePA; OxBA
  (Sonnet at Christmas.) ReMP
Sonnets by the Night Sea, *sel.* George Sterling.
  Wind of Night, The. UnW
Sonnets for the Beloved, *sel.* Leonora Speyer.
  Sonnet: "For I have seen this Light. I did not dream."
  UnW
Sonnets from a Hospital, *sel.* David Morton.
  Spring. TBM
Sonnets from a Sequence, *sels.* Shirley Barker. AnAmPo
  "Down the black highway where no whisper stirs," XXIV.
  "Thin rain seeps along the apple boughs, A," XXI.
Sonnets from Camp. Jesse Stuart. MuM
Sonnets from Greece, *sels.* Trumbull Stickney.
  Mt. Lykaion. AnAmPo; AnFE; APA; CoAnAm; LA;
    MOAP; MoVE; NePA; OxBA; TrGrPo
    (Alone on Lykaion.) MAP; MoAmPo (1942 ed.)
  Near Helikon. AnFE; CoAnAm; LiTA; MOAP; TwAmPo
Sonnets from Moabite Prison, *sels.* Albrecht Haushofer, *tr.*
  fr. German by Herman Salinger. TwGV
  In Chains.
  Rats, The.
Sonnets from "One Person." Elinor Wylie. *See* One Person.
Sonnets from the Portuguese (*Complete*, I–XLIV). Elizabeth
  Barrett Browning. PoVP; VLEP
  Sels.
  "Accuse me not, beseech thee, that I wear," XV. DiM;
    PoVP; VLEP
  "And wilt thou have me fashion into speech," XIII. BPN;
    DiM; PoVP; VLEP
  "And yet, because thou overcomest so," XVI. BPN;
    OAEP; PoVP; ViPo; VLEP
  "Because thou hast the power and own'st the grace,"
    XXXIX. BPN; PoVP; VA; VLEP
  "Belovèd, my Belovèd, when I think," XX. AV; BPN;
    CoBE; EmBrPo; EPP; MaRV; OAEP; PoVP; TOP;
    VA; ViP; VLEP
  "Belovèd, thou hast brought me many flowers," XLIV.
    BPN; OAEP; PoVP; ViP; ViPo; VLEP
  "But only three in all God's universe," II. BPN; ES;
    PoVP; VLEP
  "Can it be right to give what I can give," IX. BPN;
    HBV; PoVP; VA; VLEP
  "Face of all the world is changed, I think, The," VII.
    ATP; BEL; BPN; CoBE; EmBrPo; EnLi-2; EnLit;

EPN; EPP; HBV; OAEP; OuHeWo; PFE; PoVP;
    TOP; ViPo; VLEP
  "First time he kissed me, he but only kiss'd," XXXVIII.
    BLPA; BPN; DiM; FaBoBe; HBV; LPS-1; NeHB;
    PoVP; RiBV; VA; ViBoPo; ViPo; VLEP
  "First time that the sun rose on thine oath, The," XXXII.
    BPN; LPS-1; PoVP; ViBoPo; ViPo; VLEP
  "Go from me. Yet I feel that I shall stand," VI. AV;
    BCEP; BPN; CaAE; EmBrPo; EPN; ES; EV-4; GBV;
    GTSL; HBV; LEAP; LoPo; LoPS; LPS-1; OBEV;
    OBVV; PG (1955 ed.); PIAE; PIR; PoVP; TreFS;
    TrGrPo; VA; ViBoPo; ViPo; VLEP
    (Nevermore Alone.) MaRV
  "Heavy heart, belovèd, have I borne, A," XXV. PoVP;
    VLEP
  "How do I love thee? Let me count the ways," XLIII.
    AnFE; ATP; AV; BBV (1951 ed.); BCEP; BEL;
    BPN; CoBE; DiM; EmBrPo; EnLi-2; EnLit; EPN;
    EPP; EV-4; FaBoBe; FaFP; GTBS; GTBS-W; GTML;
    GTSL; HBV; HiLiEn; HoPM; InP; LEAP; LiTB;
    LiTG; LiTL; LO; LoPo; LPS-1; MaRV; OAEP; OQP;
    OuHeWo; PFE; PG; PIR; Po; PoeMoYo; PoFS; PoMa;
    PoRA; PoRL; PoToHe (new ed.); PoVP; PreP; PYM;
    QP-2; ReaPo; ShBV-4; TCEP; TreF; TrGrPo; TyEnPo;
    UnFo; VA; ViBoPo; ViP; ViPo; VLEP; WHA; YT
    (Love.) BLV
    (Ways of Love.) PIAE
  "I lift my heavy heart up solemnly," V. BPN; EmBrPo;
    PoVP; TOP; VA; ViPo; VLEP
  "I lived with visions for my company," XXVI. BEL;
    BPN; CoBE; EmBrPo; EnLi-2; EnLit; OAEP; PoVP;
    TOP; VA; ViPo; VLEP
  "I never gave a lock of hair away," XVIII. BPN; HBV;
    LEAP; LPS-1; PoVP; VA; VLEP
  "I thank all who have loved me in their hearts," XLI.
    BFN; CoBE; PoVP; VA; ViPo; VLEP
  "I think of thee!—my thoughts to twine and bud," XXIX.
    BPN; EPN; PoVP; VLEP
  "I thought once how Theocritus had sung," I. AnFE;
    BCEP; BEL; BoHiPo; BPN; CaAE; CoBE; EmBrPo;
    EnLi-2; EnLit; EPN; EPP; EtPaEn; EV-4; GTBS;
    GTBS-D; GTSL; HBV; HiLiEn; LEAP; OAEP; OBEV;
    OuHeWo; PeBoSo; PFE; PoE; PoVP; TCEP; TOP;
    VA; ViBoPo; ViP; ViPo; VLEP
  "If I leave all for thee, wilt thou exchange," XXXV.
    BEL; BPN; EmBrPo; EnLi-2; EnLit; PoVP; TOP;
    VA; ViBoPo; ViPo; VLEP
  "If thou must love me, let it be for naught," XIV. AnFE;
    ATF (1935 ed.); AV; BCEP; BEL; BoFr; BPN; CaAE;
    CBOV; CoBE; DiM; EmBrPo; EnLi-2; EnLit; EPN;
    EPP; ES; EV-4; FaFP; GTBS; GTBS-W; GTSE;
    GTSL; HBV; LEAP; LiTB; LiTG; LiTL; LoPS;
    LPS-1; MaRV; OBEV; OBVV; PG; PoVP; TCEP;
    TOP; TreFS; TrGrPo; TyEnPo; ViBoPo; ViPo; VLEP;
    WHA
    (For Love's Sake Only.) PoToHe (new ed.)
    (Love.) BLV
    (Ways of Love.) PIAE
  "Indeed this very love which is my boast," XII. BPN;
    HBV; LPS-1; PoVP; VLEP
  "Is it indeed so? If I lay here dead," XXIII. BPN;
    PoVP; VA; VLEP
  "Let the world's sharpness, like a clasping knife," XXIV.
    PoVP; VLEP
  "My future will not copy fair my past," XLII. BPN;
    PoVP; VLEP
  "My letters! all dead paper, mute and white!" XXVIII.
    BPN; CoBE; EmBrPo; EnLi-2; EnLit; EPP; EV-4;
    HBV; LPS-1; PoVP; ViBoPo; ViPo; VLEP
  "My own belovèd, who hast lifted me," XXVII. BPN;
    PoVP; VLEP
  "My poet, thou canst touch on all the notes," XVII.
    BPN; EmBrPo; EPP; HBV; PoVP; PtP; VLEP;
    WHA
  "Say over again, and yet once over again," XXI. BPN;
    EmBrPo; EPP; HBV; PIR; PoVP; ViPo; VLEP
  "Soul's Rialto hath its merchandise, The," XIX. BPN;
    PoVP; VLEP
  "Thou comest! all is said without a word," XXXI. BPN;
    PoVP; VLEP
  "Thou hast thy calling to some palace floor," IV. EmBrPo;
    EnLi-2; EV-4; PoVP; PtP; TCEP; VA; VLEP
  "Unlike are we, unlike, O princely Heart," III. AnFE;
    BPN; EmBrPo; EnLi-2; ES; EV-4; GTSL; HBV;
    LEAP; OAEP; OBEV; OBVV; PIAE; PoVP; TCEP;
    TrGrPo; ViPo; VLEP
  "What can I give thee back, O liberal," VIII. BPN;
    EV-4; GTBS; GTSL; HBV; OBVV; PoVP; ViPo;
    VLEP
    (Gift, The.) BrBE
  "When our two souls stand up erect and strong," XXII.
    AnFE; BEL; BPN; CBOV; EmBrPo; EnLi-2; EnLit;
    EPN; EPP; ES; EtPaEn; GTML; GTSE; GTSL; HBV;
    LiTL; LoPo; LoPS; OAEP; OBEV; PIAE; PoVP;

ReaPo; TCEP; TrGrPo; ViBoPo; ViP; ViPo; VLEP; WHA
"When we met first and loved, I did not build," XXXVI. BPN; PoVP; VLEP
"Yet, love, mere love, is beautiful indeed." X. BPN; EV-4; GTBS; GTML; HBV; PoVP; VLEP
Sonnets from the Series Relating to Edgar Allan Poe, *sels.* Sarah Helen Whitman.
"If thy sad heart, pining for human love," VI. AA; LEAP
(Sonnets.) BAP
(To Edgar Allan Poe.) LBAP
"Oft since thine earthly eyes have closed on mine," III. AA
"On our lone pathway bloomed no earthly hope," V. AA; LEAP
(Sonnet to Edgar Allan Poe.) AnAmPo; LA
(Sonnets.) BAP
"When first I looked into thy glorious eyes," II. AA
(To Edgar A[llan] Poe.) DD; GA
Sonnets in Quaker Language. Hildegarde Flanner. NP
Sonnets in Wartime. Cullen Jones. MuM
I Gained a Greater Strength.
While Life Sits Idly.
Sonnet's like a measured minuet, A. The Minuet. Dorothy Leonard. VOD
Sonnets of a Portrait Painter, *sels.* Arthur Davison Ficke.
"Across the shaken bastions of the year," XLVII. AnAmPo; LA
Come Forth! for Spring Is Singing in the Boughs, XI. PFE; TBM
(April Moment.) HBMV
Her Pedigree, IX. HBMV
I Am in Love with High Far-seeing Places, XIII. LEAP; LoPo; NP; NV; OQP; QP-2
(View from Heights.) HBMV
"I have seen beauty where light stabs the hills," XVI. AnAmPo; LA
"Last night I kissed you with a brutal might," XXXVII. AnAmPo; LA
"Out of the dusk into whose gloom you went," L. AnAmPo; LA
"So you go back—because they bid you come," XXXVI. AnAmPo; LA
Sonnet: "There are strange shadows fostered of the moon," XLV. MAP
(November Dusk.) UnW
Spring Landscape, XII. HBMV
Summons, XIV. HBMV
There Stretch between Us Wonder-woven Bonds, XXI. TBM
"They brought me tidings; and I did not hear," XLIX. PFE
Troubadours, X. HBMV
What If Some Lover in a Far-off Spring, XLIII. TBM
Sonnets of an Old Town. Virginia Lyne Tunstall.
Old April, II. LS
Spring Dusk in Williamsburg, I. LS
They Sleep So Quietly, III. BLP; LS; TBM
Sonnets of Christian Passions, *sels.* Henry Lok.
(Sundry Christian Passions.)
"It is not, Lord, the sound of many words." SiCE; TuPP
"Words may well want, both ink and paper fail." ReEn; SiCE; TuPP
Sonnets of the Empire, *sels.* Archibald T. Strong.
Australia, 1905. BoAu
Australia, 1914. BoAu
Australia to England. BoAu; PoFr
Dawn at Liverpool. BoAu
Gloriana's England. BoAu
Hawke. BoAu
Nelson. BoAu
Oxford. BoAu
Sonnets of the Midnight Hours. Donald Wandrei. DaM
Sonnets of the Months. Folgore da San Gemignano, *tr. fr. Italian by* Dante Gabriel Rossetti.
(Of the Months.) AWP
Sels.
"And now take thought, my sonnet, who is he," *Conclusion.* LyPI
"For August, be your dwelling thirty towers." LyPI
"For January I give you vests of skins." LyPI
"I give you horses for your games in May." LyPI
(May.) LyMA
"I give you meadow-lands in April, fair." LyPI
"Last, for December, houses on the plain." LyPI
March. LyMA
"Next, for October, to some sheltered coign." LyPI
"Unto the blithe and lordly Fellowship," *Dedication.* LyPI
Sonnets of the Saints. Thomas S. Jones, Jr. TBM
Blessing of Columcille, The, I.
Brindled Hare, The, II.
Sonnets on English Dramatic Poets (1590–1650), *sels.* Swinburne.
Beaumont and Fletcher, IV. PoVP
Ben Jonson, III. BEL; EmBrPo; PeBoSo; PoVP; PtP; VLEP
Christopher Marlowe, I. BEL; PoVP; PtP; TOP; TrGrPo; VLEP
John Webster, VII. InvP; PtP; VLEP
Philip Massinger, V. EmBrPo; PtP; VLEP
Many, The, XIX. PoVP
Thomas Decker, VIII. PtP; VLEP
William Shakespeare, II. BMEP; BPN; PIAE; PoVP; TrGrPo; VLEP
Sonnets on the Death of Laura. Petrarch, *tr. fr. Italian by* Brooks Vaughan. *See* Sonnets to Laura: To Laura in Death.
Sonnets on the Sea's Voice. George Sterling. EtS
Sonnets on the Seasons, *sel.* Hartley Coleridge.
November, XII. LoBV; OBRV; PEOR; PoRL
Sonnets pour Hélène, *sels.* Pierre de Ronsard, *tr. fr. French by* Humbert Wolfe.
"Count me the stairs I climbed to your retreat." PrPoCR
"Cruel, farewell, since I do but annoy thee." PrPoCR
(No Other Slave, *tr. by* Alan Conder.) TrFP
"Dance, lovely lady, dance and mask your face." PrPoCR
"Hate me, or love, my Helen, as you list."
(Four Sonnets to Helen, 2.) LiTW
"Helen, this age, by your exceeding worth." PrPoCR
"I consecrate this fountain Helen's, praying." PrPoCR
"In these long winter nights when moon doth steer." PrPoCR
(Four Sonnets to Helen, 3.) LiTW
"Madam, when we two walked, the rest unheeding." PrPoCR
"No other torch save what my dreams discover." PrPoCR
"Only your arm, and nothing more, I found." PrPoCR
"Out of her lattice gazing on the leas." PrPoCR
"See love, whose kingdom as the world is ample." PrPoCR
(Beauty's Paradigm, *tr. by* Alan Conder.) TrFP
"Shall I your beauties with the moon compare?" PrPoCR
"That century to century may tell," *tr. by* Curtis Hidden Page. PrPoCR
"That evening when love bad you take the floor." PrPoCR
"Tossed by the seas of love how have I striven."
(Four Sonnets to Helen, 1.) LiTW
"What though the spirit of man, by Plato taught." PrPoCR
"When you are old and sit by candlelight," *tr. by* Alan Conder. TrFP
"When you are old, at evening candle-lit."
(Four Sonnets to Helen, 4.) LiTW
"When you are very old, by the hearth's glare," *tr. by* Curtis Hidden Page. PrPoCR
" 'Who,' cried the elders on the Trojan wall." PrPoCR
Sonnets—Realities, *sel.* E. E. Cummings.
"Cambridge ladies who live in furnished souls, The." AnAmPo; CoBA; LA; MoPW; MoVE; OxBA; TCPD; ViBoPo (1958 ed.)
Sonnets Relating to Edgar Allan Poe. Sarah Helen Whitman. *See* Sonnets from the Series Relating to Edgar Allan Poe.
Sonnets to Aurelia, *sels.* Robert Nichols. OBMV
"But piteous things we are—when I am gone," III.
"Come, let us sigh a requiem over love," IV
"Though to your life apparent stain attach," II.
"When the proud World does most my world despise," I.
Sonnet to Delia. Samuel Daniel. *See* To Delia.
Sonnets to George Sand, *sels.* Elizabeth Barrett Browning.
Desire, A. LPS-3
To George Sand; a Recognition. EmBrPo
(Recognition, A.) LPS-3
Sonnets to "Idea." Michael Drayton. *See* Idea.
Sonnets to Laura, *sels.* Petrarch, *tr. fr. Italian.*
To Laura in Death.
"Ah, had I ever thought the world would care," XXV, *tr. by* Joseph Auslander.
(Sonnet.) LyPI
"Alas! that liquid look, that lovely face!" I, *tr. by* Joseph Auslander. PrPoCR
"All my green years and golden prime of man," XLVII, *tr. by* Lady Dacre. PrPoCR
"Ecstasy of thought upraised me where, An," XXXIV, *tr. by* Joseph Auslander. PrPoCR
"Eyes, the face, the limbs of heavenly mould, The," XXIV, *tr. by* Lady Dacre. PrPoCR
"First day she passed up and down through the Heavens, The," LXXV, *pr. tr. by* J. M. Synge.
(Laura Waits for Him in Heaven.) OBMV; TwCV
"If the lone bird lament or the green leaves," XI, *tr. by* Joseph Auslander. PrPoCR
"In the years of her age the most beautiful," X, *pr. tr. by* J. M. Synge
(He Wishes He Might Die and Follow Laura.) OBMV; TwCV
"In thought I traveled to the high abode," XXXIV, *tr. by* Brooks Vaughan.
(Sonnets on the Death of Laura, I.) UnW
"Life ever flies with course that nought may stay," IV, *tr. by* Lady Dacre. PrPoCR

Sonnets to Laura (*continued*)
"Life hurries on, a frantic refugee," IV, *tr. by* Morris Bishop.
(Sonnet.) LyPI
"Lofty Column and the Laurel fall, The," II, *tr. by* Joseph Auslander. PrPoCR
"Love kept me one and twenty years a slave," LXXXV, *tr. by* Joseph Auslander. PrPoCR
"My flowery and green age was passing away," XLVII, *pr. tr. by* J. M. Synge.
(He Understands the Great Cruelty of Death.) OBMV; TwCV
"My mind! prophetic of my coming fate," XLVI, *tr. by* Lady Dacre. PrPoCR
"Never a mother spoke advice so wise," XVII, *tr. by* Brooks Vaughan.
(Sonnets on the Death of Laura, III.) UnW
"Ne'er to the son, in whom her age is blest," XVII, *tr. by* Lady Dacre. PrPoCR
"Not skies serene, with glittering stars inlaid," XLIV, *tr. by* Lady Dacre. PrPoCR
"Now I go grieving for the days on earth," LXXXVI, *tr. by* Morris Bishop.
(Sonnet.) LyPI
"Now of my life each gay and greener year," XLVII, *tr. by* Thomas LeMesurier.
(Jealous Enemy, The.) LiTW
"O lovely little bird, I watch you fly," XC, *tr. by* Morris Bishop.
(Sonnet.) LyPI
"O sweet severity, repulses mild," LXXXVII, *tr. by* Lady Dacre. PrPoCR
"O unforgiving thoughts, I pray you: Peace!" VI, *tr. by* T. G. Bergin.
(Sonnet.) LyPI
"Poor solitary bird, that pour'st thy lay," XC, *tr. by* Lady Dacre. PrPoCR
"Sometimes, beneath the trees' green murmurous height," XI, *tr. by* Brooks Vaughan.
(Sonnets on the Death of Laura, II.) UnW
"Sorrow and love did thrust me in the way," LXXIV, *tr. by* Agnes Tobin.
(Flying Lesson, The.) CAW
"Soul of my soul, how often you return," XIV, *tr. by* Joseph Auslander. PrPoCR
"Spring returns, the spring wind softly blowing, The," XLII, *tr. by* Joseph Auslander. PrPoCR
"That nightingale, who weeps so sweetly, grieves," XLIII, *tr. by* Joseph Auslander. PrPoCR
"That nightingale, whose strain so sweetly flows," XLIII, *tr. by* Thomas LeMesurier.
(Nightingale, The.) LiTW; LyMA
"Through twenty-one long years love held me burning," LXXXV, *tr. by* T. G. Bergin.
(Sonnet.) LyPI
"To that pure look which honours Paradise," LXXII, *tr. by* Joseph Auslander. PrPoCR
"Valley familiar with my desperate din," XXXIII, *tr. by* Joseph Auslander. PrPoCR
"Weeping, I still regret the years that went," LXXXVI, *tr. by* Joseph Auslander. PrPoCR
"What a grudge I am bearing the earth," XXXII, *pr. tr. by* J. M. Synge.
(He Is Jealous of the Heavens and Earth.) TwCV
(Translation from Petrarch, A.) MBP; MoBrPo; NeMA
"What pity-driven angel proved his speed," LXX, *tr. by* Joseph Auslander. PrPoCR
"When my heart was the amorous worms' meat," XXXVI, *tr. by* Anna Maria Armi.
(Amorous Worms' Meat, The.) LiTW
"Zephyr returns, and scatters everywhere," XLII, *tr. by* Morris Bishop.
(Sonnet.) LyPI
To Laura in Life.
"Ah Liberty, so lovely, so denied!" LXXVI, *tr. by* Joseph Auslander. PrPoCR
"Alone and ever weary with dark care," XXVIII, *tr. by* T. G. Bergin.
(Sonnet.) LyPI
"Alone, thought-sick, I pace where none has been," XXVIII, *tr. by* Joseph Auslander. PrPoCR
"Already I grow weary thinking how," LIV, *tr. by* Joseph Auslander.
(Sonnet.) LyPI
"Already in the east the amorous star," XXVI, *tr. by* Joseph Auslander. PrPoCR
"Although from falsehood I with all my will," XLI, *tr. by* Joseph Auslander. PrPoCR
"Ancient graybeard shoulders on his load, The," XIV, *tr. by* Morris Bishop.
(Sonnet.) LyPI
"As over the fresh grass her golden feet," CXXXII, *tr. by* Joseph Auslander.
(Sonnet.) LyPI
"Ashamed at times that I am silent," XVIII, *tr. by* Robert Guthrie MacGregor.
(Praises of Laura Transcend His Poetic Power, The.) EnLi-1; OuHeWo
"Determined with one sally to erase," II, *tr. by* T. G. Bergin.
(Sonnet.) LyPI
"Fair ladies, weep, the while Love's own tears fall," LXXI, *tr. by* T. G. Bergin.
(Sonnet: On the Death of Cino da Pistoia.) LyPI
"Father in heaven! after the days misspent," XLVIII, *tr. by* Barbarina Lady Dacre.
(Sonnet.) CAW
"Father of heaven! after the days all lost," XLVIII, *tr. by* Joseph Auslander. PrPoCR
"Fountain of sorrow, inn of cursèd ire," CVII, *tr. by* Joseph Auslander.
(Sonnet.) PoFr
"Golden upon the wind her loose hair streaming," LXIX, *tr. by* Joseph Auslander. PrPoCR
"I find no peace, and all my war is done," CIV, *tr. by* Sir Thomas Wyatt. ReEn
(Contrarious Passions in a Lover, The.) LiTL
(Description of the Contrarious Passions [in a Lover].) BLV; EnLi-1 (1949 ed.); ElSeCe; OAEP; PeBoSo; PoFS; ReIE; TrGrPo; TuPP
(I Find No Peace.) LiTB
(Love's Inconsistency.) AWP; JAWP; OuHeWo; PreP; WBP
(Sonnet: "I find no peace . . .") SiPS
"I find no peace and bear no arms for war," CIV, *tr. by* T. G. Bergin.
(Sonnet.) LyPI
"I find no peace, yet from all wars abstain me," CIV, *tr. by* Joseph Auslander. PrPoCR
"If amorous faith, a heart of guileless ways," CLXXXVIII, *tr. by* C. B. Cayley.
(Signs of Love.) AWP; JAWP; WBP
"If faith most true, a heart that cannot feign," CLXXXVIII, *tr. by* Lady Dacre. PrPoCR
"If it be destined that my life, from thine," XI, *tr. by* Edward Fitzgerald. AWP; JAWP; OnPM; WBP
"If this should not be Love, O God, what shakes me?" CII, *tr. by* Joseph Auslander. PrPoCR
"In what bright realm, what sphere of radiant thought," CXXVI, *tr. by* Joseph Auslander. PrPoCR
"In what divine ideal, what lofty sphere," CXXVI, *tr. by* T. G. Bergin.
(Sonnet.) LyPI
"It was the day the sun had overcast," III, *tr. by* T. G. Bergin.
(Sonnet: Good Friday 1327.) LyPI
"It was the morning of that blessed day," III, *tr. by* Joseph Auslander. PrPoCR
"Lady, if grace to me so long be lent," XI, *tr. by* Robert Guthrie MacGregor.
(He Hopes That Time Will Render Her More Merciful.) EnLi-1; OuHeWo
"Long love that in my thought doth harbor, The," CIX, *tr. by* Sir Thomas Wyatt. ReEn; SiCE
(Lover for Shamefastness Hideth His Desire within His Faithful Heart, The.) CoBE; ReIE; TuPP
"Long Love that is sovereign to my mind, The," CIX, *tr. by* Joseph Auslander. PrPoCR
"Love that liveth and reigneth in my thought," CIX, *tr. by* the Earl of Surrey. ReEn; SiPS
(Complaint of a Lover Rebuked.) AWP; BEL; CoBE; ElSeCe; EnLi-1 (1949 ed.); EnLit; EPP; LiTW; LyMA; OAEP; OnPM; ReIE; SiCE; TrGrPo; TuPP; TyEnPo
"More my own poor wishes would commend me, The," CVIII, *tr. by* Joseph Auslander.
(Sonnet.) PoFr
"My galley charged with forgetfulness," CLVI, *tr. by* Sir Thomas Wyatt. EnL; LiTB; MaPo; NBE; ReEn; SiCE; SiPS; TwHP
(Galley, The.) OBSC
(Lover Compareth His State to a Ship [in Perilous Storm Tossed on the Sea], The.) BEL; CoBE; ElL; ElSeCe, EnLi-1; EnLit; PoE; PoEL-1; PoFS; ReIE; TuPP
(Lover like to a Ship Tossed on the Sea.) EtS
"My tameless will doth recklessly pursue," VI, *tr. by* Susan Wollaston.
(Of His Foolish Passion for Laura.) EnLi-1; OuHeWo
"My vessel, cargoed with oblivion, cleaves," CLVI, *tr. by* Joseph Auslander. PrPoCR
"Nearer I approach that final day, The," XXV, *tr. by* Joseph Auslander. PrPoCR
"Now while the wind and earth and heavens rest," CXXXI, *tr. by* T. G. Bergin.
(Sonnet.) LyPI

"O little room, my harbor from the sea," CXCVIII, *tr. by* Morris Bishop.
(Sonnet.) LyPI
"O rich and happy flowers forever apart," CXXIX, *tr. by* Joseph Auslander. PrPoCR
"Palmer bent. with locks of silver gray, The," XIV, *tr. by* Lady Dacre. PrPoCR
"Place me where herb and flower the sun has dried," CXIII, *tr. by* Lady Dacre. PrPoCR
"Rain fire from Heaven down upon thy head," CV, *tr. by* Joseph Auslander
(Sonnet.) LyPI
"Set me where phoebus's heat the flowers slayeth," CXIII, *tr. unknown.* TuPP
(Last Trial, The.) OBSC
"Set me whereas the sun doth parch the green," CXIII, *tr. by* the Earl of Surrey. OnPM; PeBoSo; ReEn; SiPS
(Love's Fidelity.) AWP; JAWP; WBP
(To His Lady.) OBSC; RiBV
(Vow to Love Faithfully.) BLV; PIAE
(Vow to Love Faithfully, Howsoever He Be Rewarded, A.) ElL; ElSeCe; EnLi-1 (1949 ed.); EnLit; ES; LiTL; PoFS; SiCE; TrGrPo; TuPP; ViBoPo
"She used to let her golden hair fly free," LXIX, *tr. by* Morris Bishop.
(Sonnet.) LyPI
"That touching pallor which, like a soft cloud," XCVIII, *tr by* Joseph Auslander. PrPoCR
"That window where the sun at midday shows," LXXIX, *tr. by* Morris Bishop.
(Sonnet.) LyPI
"Thou green and blooming, cool and shaded hill," CCV, *tr. by* C. B. Cayley.
(Heart on the Hill, The.) AWP
"Thousand times, O my sweet warrior, A," XIX, *tr. by* Joseph Auslander. PrPoCR
"Through savage woods I walk without demur," CXLIII, *tr. by* T. G. Bergin.
(Sonnet.) LyPI
"Two glowing roses, fresh from Paradise," CCVII, *tr. by* Joseph Auslander. PrPoCR
"Vengeaunce must fall on thee, thou filthie whore," CVII, *tr. by* Sir Thomas Wyatt.
(Against the Court of Rome.) LiTW; LyMA
"When Love his flaming image on her brow," XII, *tr. by* Joseph Auslander. PrPoCR
"Ye, who may listen to each idle strain," I, *tr. by* Lady Dacre. PrPoCR
"You who give ear to sorrow, as you scan," I, *tr. by* Morris Bishop.
(Sonnet.) LyPI
Songs.
Canzone 126: "Clear, fresh, and dulcet streams." To Laura in Life, Canzone XIV, *tr. by* Leigh Hunt. LyPI
Canzone: "Clear, fresh, sweet waters. To Laura in Life, Canzone XIV, *tr. by* William D. Foulke. LiTW
Canzone 129: "From thought to thought, from mountain-peak to mountain." To Laura in Life, Canzone XVII, *tr. by* Morris Bishop. LyPI
"Clear, cool, and lovely brook." To Laura in Life, Canzone XIV, *tr. by* Anna Maria Armi.
(Here Rules Love.) LiA
"Fair Virgin,/ Vestured with the sun!" To Laura in Death, Canzone VIII, *tr. by* Helen Lee Peabody. PrPoCR
(Ode to the Virgin, *tr. by* Helen Lee Peabody.) ISi
(To the Virgin, *tr. by* Anna Maria Armi.) LiA
(To the Virgin Mary, *abr., tr. by* Robert Guthrie MacGregor.) CAW
"From hill to hill I roam, from thought to thought." To Laura in Life, Canzone XVII, *tr. by* Barbarina Lady Dacre.
(Distance and Solitude.) LiA
Visions, The. To Laura in Death, Canzone III, *tr. by* Spenser. AWP; EnLi-1; JAWP, *abr.;* WBP, *abr.*
I Saw a Phoenix in the Wood Alone, *sel.* ChTr
Sonnets to Miranda, *sels.* Sir William Watson.
"Daughter of her whose face, and lofty name," I. HBV
"I cast these lyric offerings at your feet," V. HBV
"I dare but sing of you in such a strain," III. HBV
"I move amid your throng, I watch you hold," VI. HBV
"If I had never known your face at all," VIII. FaBoBe; HBV
"If you had lived in that more stately time, II. HBV
Sonnets to My Mother. Arthur S. Bourinot. CaP
Sonnets to Orpheus, *sels.* Rainer Maria Rilke, *tr. fr. German.*
"All we have achieved, the machine threatens to rule," Pt. II, X, *tr. by* Jessie Lemont. OnPM
"All we have gained the machine threatens," Pt. II, X, *tr. by* M. D. Herter Norton. PoFr
"Almost a girl it was and issued forth," Pt. I, II, *tr. by* M. D. Herter Norton.
(Four Sonnets to Orpheus.) LiTW
"Almost a girl it was, then, issuing," Pt. I, II, *tr. by* W. D. Snodgrass. ReMP
"Call me at the one among your hours," Pt. II, XXIII, *tr. by* Ruth Speirs. AnGP
"Dancer: O you translation," Pt. II, XVIII, *tr. by* Jessie Lemont. OnPM
"Hark, already you can hear the working song," Pt. II, XXV, *tr. by* Jessie Lemont. OnPM
"Mirrors; never yet has anyone described," Pt. II, III, *tr. by* M. D Herter Norton.
(Four Sonnets to Orpheus.) LiTW
"Oh, come and go, you almost child, entrancing," Pt. II, XXVIII, *tr. by* J. B. Leishman. UnS
"O fountain-mouth, O giving, O mouth that speaks," Pt. II, XX, *tr. by* M. D. Herter Norton.
(Four Sonnets to Orpheus.) LiTW
"O no: till the time when flight," Pt. I, XXIII, *tr. by* M. D. Herter Norton.
(Sonnet to Orpheus, A.) PoF
"O this is the beast that does not have being!" Pt. II, IV, *tr. by* W. D. Snodgrass. ReMP
"Only one who has lifted the lyre," Pt. I, IX, *tr. by* M. D. Herter Norton.
(Four Sonnets to Orpheus.) LiTW
"Our kinship is with flower, vine leaf, fruit," Pt. I, XIV, *tr. by* R. F. C. Hull. AnGP
"Ours is the storm and stress," Pt. I, XXII, *tr. by* R. F. C. Hull. AnGP
Poet, The, Pt. I, III, *tr. by* Selden Rodman. OnHM
"Praise is the thing! Like one destined for singing," Pt. I, VII, *tr. by* R. F. C. Hull. AnGP
"Ripe apple, the banana and the pear," Pt. I, XIII, *tr. by* Jessie Lemont. OnPM
"Shall we renounce our ancient friends," Pt. I, XXIV, *tr. by* Ruth Speirs. AnGP
"Though the world is changing fast," Pt. I, XIX, *tr. by* Jessie Lemont. OnPM
"Tree ascending there, A, O pure transcension!" Pt. I, I, *tr. by* J. B. Leishman. UnS
"Tree rose up, A. O clear transcendency!" Pt. I, I, *tr. by* W. D. Snodgrass. ReMP
"Where, in whichever blissfully watered gardens, on which," Pt. II, XVII, *tr. by* Ruth Speirs. AnGP
Sonnets to Philomel, *sels.* Sir John Davies.
"If you would know the love which I you bear." SiPS
"Oft did I hear our eyes the passage were." SiPS
"Once did my Philomel reflect on me." SiPS
"Sickness, intending my love to betray." SiPS
Sonnets to the Fairest Coelia. William Percy. *See* Coelia.
Sonnets—Unrealities, *sel.* E. E. Cummings.
It May Not Always Be So; and I Say. AnAmPo; LA; MOAP
Sonnet's Voice, The. Theodore Watts-Dunton. EtS; HBV; InP; PIAE; TOP; VA
Sonnets Written in the Fall of 1914. George Edward Wood berry. HBV; MC; PAH
Sonnets Written in the Orillia Woods, *sel.* Charles Sangster.
"Blest Spirit of Calm that dwellest in these woods!" PeCV
Sons. Grace Noll Crowell. DDA
Sons of Aeacus, The. Pindar, *tr. fr. Greek by* C. J. Billson. *Fr.* Isthmian Odes, V. OxBG
Sons of Belial. Lola Ridge. BAP; PFY; TCPD
Sons of Erechtheus, the olden, The. Interlude. Euripides. *Fr.* Medea. GrR
Sons of Failure. Edith Lovejoy Pierce. MaRV
Sons of Indolence. James Thomson. *Fr.* The Castle of Indolence, I. OBEC
Sons of landsmen, sons of seamen, hear the tale of grief and me. The Land of Biscay. A. E. Housman. ReaPo
Sons of Martha, The. Kipling. EPN; HBV; WGRP
Sons of Mughira! I love well. The Tailor's Apprentice. Ibn Kharuf. MooP
Sons of New England, in the fray. Treason's Last Device. Edmund Clarence Stedman. PAH
Sons of Our Sons, The. Ilya Ehrenburg, *tr. fr. Russian by* Babette Deutsch. TrJP; TrRV; RuPo *tr. by* Jack Lindsay
Sons of Patrick, The. James B. Dollard. JKCP
Sons of pleasure, listen to me. James Bird. *Unknown.* ABS
Sons of Promise. Thomas Curtis Clarke. PoToHe
Sons of the Empire, bond and free. The Hands-across-the-Sea Poem. J. C. Squire. HBMV
Sons of the Greeks, arise! Greek War-Song. *Unknown, tr. by* Byron. PoFr
Sons of the Island race, wherever ye dwell. The Guides at Cabul, 1879. Sir Henry Newbolt. MBP
Sons of the King. Joan Agnew. BoTP
Sons of the Prophet are brave men [*or* valiant] and bold, The. Abdul A-Bul-Bul A-Mir [*or* Abdul, the Bulbul Ameer *or* Ye Ballade of Ivan Petrofsky Skevar]. *Unknown.* ABF; AS; BLPA; StPo; TreF
Sons of the youth and the truth of a nation. The Name of Washington. George Parsons Lathrop. DD; HH

Sons of valor, taste the glories. Off from Boston. *Unknown.* MC; PAH
"Sooeep!" Walter de la Mare. BoTP
Soon, ah, soon the April weather. April Weather. Bliss Carman. NLK
Soon as she sees the Ilian ranks and Turnus' troops. Jupiter Sends a Fury to Baffle Turnus in Battle. Virgil. *Fr.* The Aeneid, XII. LiA
Soon as the azure-colored gates of th' east. Diella, II. Richard Lynche. TuPP
Soon as the day begins to waste. The Constant Swain and Virtuous Maid. *Unknown.* HBV
Soon as the sound had ceased whose thunder filled Shelley. *Fr.* Prometheus Unbound, III, iv. ChER
Soon as the sun forsook the eastern main. An Hymn to the Evening. Phillis Wheatley. BAV
Soon at Last My Sighs and Moans. Louis Ginsberg. TrJP
Soon may the edict lapse, that on you lays. To a Friend. Sir William Watson. PC
Soon now Sir Mullet, when the scent reacheth him. Temptation. Oppian. *Fr.* Halieutica. OxBG
Soon of the shock of battle men surfeit and grow sick. The Barren Battlefield. Homer. *Fr.* The Iliad, XIX. GrPE
Soon One Mornin' Death Come Creepin', *with music. Unknown.* OuSiCo
Soon one mornin', was mistin' rain. The Wreck on the Somerset Road. *Unknown.* OuSiCo
Soon Shall the Winter's Foil Be Here. Walt Whitman. CaAE
Soon shall thy arm, Unconquered Steam! afar. Steam Power. Erasmus Darwin. *Fr.* The Botanic Garden: The Economy of Vegetation. BoHiPo; OBEC
"Soon—soon—soon" the prophet stars foretell. Strong Arms. Frances O'Connell Corridan. JKCP (1926 ed.)
Soon the night in mantle dark. The Ploughboy. John Clare. PoEL-4
Soon we entered in the woods. In the Forest. Alexander McLachlan. *Fr.* The Emigrant. BoCaPo
Soon wilt thou pass to earth; waste not thy breath. The Rest Is Silence. Palladas. OxBG
Soon with the Lilac Fades Another Spring. Patrick MacDonogh. OxBI
Soote [*or* Sweet] season, that bud and bloom forth brings, The. Description of Spring, Wherein Each Thing Renews Save Only the Lover [*or* Sonnet *or* Summer Comes]. Earl of Surrey. AnEnPo; AtBAP; AWP; BCEP; BEL; BrBE; CaAE; CoBE; EG; ElL; ElSeCe; EnLi-1; EnLit; EPP; ES; JAWP; LEAP; LiTB; LoBV; OAEP; OBEV; OBSC; OnPM; OuHeWo; PeBoSo; PoE; ReEn; ReIE; SeCePo; SeCeV; SiCE; SiPS; TCEP; TOP; TuPP; TyEnPo; WBP
Soothd by the murmurs of a plaintive streame. A Wild [*or* Wyld] Romantic Dell. William Julius Mickle. *Fr.* The Concubine. OBEC; RO
Soothing it is, when over mighty seas. From the Shore of Life. Lucretius. *Fr.* De Rerum Natura, II. LaP
Soothsay. Dante Gabriel Rossetti. BPN; EmBrPo
Sooth-Sayer, The. Sadi, *tr. fr. Persian by* Sir Edwin Arnold. *Fr.* The Gulistan. AWP
Sop, The. *Unknown.* StJW
Sophia, her age between. Wisdom of the Gazelle. George P. Solomos. GoYe
Sophie, my bold gallows' gal. Gallows' Brother's Song. Christian Morgenstern. AnGP
Sophisticate. Barbara Young. SiSoSe
Sophisticated, worldly-wise. I Found God. Mary Afton Thacker. MaRV
Sophocles. Phrynichus, *tr. fr. Greek by* T. F. Higham. OxBG
Sophocles' Tomb. Simmias. *tr. fr. Greek by* Walter Leaf. OxBG (On Sophocles.) GrR
Sophonisba; or, Hannibal's Overthrow, *sel.* Nathaniel Lee.
Song: "Beneath the poplar's shadow lay me," 4 *ll.* BeR
Sophy, The, *sel.* Sir John Denham.
Somnus [the Humble God]. EPS (1942 ed.); SeCL
Sopolis. Callimachus, *tr. fr. Greek by* William M. Hardinge. AWP
("Now would to God swift ships had ne'er been made!") GrPo
Sops of Light. Fredegond Shove. ChMP
Sorcerer, The, *sel.* W. S. Gilbert.
My Name Is John Wellington Wells. PoMS
("Oh! my name is John Wellington Wells.") PIAE
Sorceress, The. Theocritus. *See* Incantation, The.
Sorceress and sorcerer. Resurrection. Clark Ashton Smith. DaM
Sorceress of the Moon, The. William Rose Benét. DaM
Sordello, *sels.* Robert Browning.
And What Sordello Would See There. MyFE
At Ecelin. MyFE
How a Poet's Soul Comes into Play. MyFE
Sordello's Birth-Place. MyFE
Vault inside the Castle at Goito, A. MyFE
Sore wounded by love, the heron. *Unknown, tr. fr. Spanish by* Eleanor L. Turnbull. TeCS
Sores. Douglas Malloch. OnHT
Sorrento. Carl Snoilsky, *tr. fr. Swedish by* Charles W. Stork. AnSL
Sorrow. Samuel Daniel. *See* Had Sorrow Ever Fitter Place.
Sorrow. Aubrey Thomas De Vere. BLPA; EPN; GoBC; HBV; JKCP; MaRV; NeHB; OBEV (1st ed.); OQP; QP-1; TIP; VA; WGRP
Sorrow ("They say that 'Time assuages'"). Emily Dickinson. WGRP
Sorrow. Helen Parry Eden. JKCP
Sorrow. Reginald C. Eva. OQP; QP-2
Sorrow. Goethe, *tr. fr. German by* Gretchen Warren. *Fr.* Wilhelm Meister's Apprenticeship, *Bk.* II, *ch.* 13. MaRV (Who Never Ate with Tears His Bread, *tr. by* Farnsworth Wright.) WGRP
Sorrow. D. H. Lawrence. OBMV
Sorrow. Mei Yao Ch'en, *tr. fr. Chinese by* Kenneth Rexroth. OnPC
Sorrow. Marie Tello Phillips. GoYe
Sorrow. George Santayana. *See* I Sought on Earth.
Sorrow. Jóhann Sigurjónsson, *tr. fr. Icelandic by* Magnús A. Árnason. IcP
Sorrow. Katrina Trask. AA
Sorrow ("I will not gather the vervain sweet"). *Unknown, tr. fr. Spanish by* Sir John Bowring. OnPM
Sorrow ("Whither shall I, the fair maiden, flee from sorrow?"). *Unknown, tr. fr. Russian by* W. R. S. Ralston. AWP
Sorrow and love did thrust me in the way. The Fying Lesson. Petrarch. Sonnets to Laura: To Laura in Death, LXXIV. CAW
Sorrow can wait. Folded Power. Gladys Cromwell. HBMV; NP
Sorrow has a harp of seven strings. The Harp of Sorrow. Ethel Clifford. HBV; WGRP
Sorrow has a thousand joys. A Little Love Song. Helen Cecilia Willis. CAG
Sorrow heaped on sorrow, ruin on disaster. On My Sorrowful Life. Moses ibn Ezra. TrJP
Sorrow in a Garden. May Riley Smith. NLK
Sorrow in my own yard. *See* Sorrow is my own yard.
Sorrow, in vain why dost thou seek to tempt. To Sorrow. *Unknown.* SeCL
Sorrow is [*or* in] my own yard. The Widow's Lament in Springtime. William Carlos Williams. CoBMV; NP
Sorrow is over the fields. The Land War. "Seumas O'Sullivan." GTIV; OxBI
Sorrow lay upon my breast more heavily than winter clay. Desolation Is a Delicate Thing. Elinor Wylie. MAP; MoAmPo
Sorrow, lie still and wear. Dirge. Thomas Lovell Beddoes. TriL
Sorrow, my friend. A Song before Grief. Rose Hawthorne Lathrop. AA; BMC; CAW; JKCP
Sorrow of Love, The. W. B. Yeats. LBBV; MBP; MoAB; MoBrPo; PoEL-5
Sorrow of Mydath. John Masefield. MBP; MoBrPo
Sorrow of the Knights at Bruce's Death. John Barbour. *Fr.* The Bruce, XX. EBSV
Sorrow of the Sea, The. *Unknown.* PEOR
Sorrow of Troilus, The. Chaucer. *Fr.* Troilus and Criseyde, V. PoEL-1
Sorrow on the acres. Winter Field. A. E. Coppard. MBP; MoBrPo (1942 ed.)
Sorrow of Unicume, The. Sir Herbert Read. ChMP
Sorrow seldom killeth any. Francis Davison. EG
Sorrow shared divides the trouble, A. Rhymes to Remember. *Unknown.* StaSt
Sorrow Shatters My Heart. Moses ibn Ezra, *tr. fr. Hebrew by* Solomon Solis-Cohen. LiTW
Sorrow Stays. Sir Walter Ralegh. *See* Farewell to the Court.
Sorrow That Cries. Samuel Hoffenstein. TCPD
Sorrow Turned into Joy. John Alexander Bouquet. MaRV
Sorrow, who to this house scarce knew the way. Elegy on the L. C. John Donne. ATP (1953 ed.)
Sorrowful grew the eagle's spirit and heart. The Eagle. Khanlari. PeP
Sorrowful Lamentation of Callaghan, Greally and Mullen, The. *Unknown.* TIP
Sorrowful Verses Made on the Death of Our Most Sovereign Lady Queen Elizabeth My Gracious Mistress. Thomas Churchyard. ReIE
Sorrows Humanize Our Race. Jean Ingelow. MaRV; WGRP
Sorrow's Ladder. Gertrude Callaghan. CAW
Sorrows of Armenia, The. *Unknown.* ArmLP
Sorrows of Werther, The. Thackeray. ALV; BLPA; BMEP; BOHV; CenHV; EnLi-2; FiBHP; HBV; InMe; InP; LEAP; LiTL; NA; NeHB; OnSP; PoVP; SiTL; TOP; TreF; VA
Sorry Hamlets. Feodor Ivanovich Tyutchev, *tr. fr. Russian by* Babette Deutsch. TrRV
("These poor hamlets, humbly faring," *tr. by* C. M. Bowra.) BoRS
Sorry I am, my God, sorry I am. Sins' Round. George Herbert. ExPo; LoBV; ReEn

Sorry prophet this, a witless seer, A. Apollonius Rhodius. *Fr.* Argonautica, III. GrPo
Sorry world is sighing now, The. Fin de Siècle. Newton Mackintosh. NA
Sort of a Song, A. William Carlos Williams. HoPM; SeCeV
Sort of Girl He Prefers, The. Ausonius, *tr. fr. Latin by* Jack Lindsay. LaP
Sortin' the Mail. W. Scott Stranahan. DDA
Sory beuerech it is and sore it is abouth, A. Christ's Prayer in Gethsemane. *Unknown.* SeCePo
Sospetto d'Herode, *sels.* Richard Crashaw, *after the Italian of* Giambattista Marini.
"Casting the times with their strong signs." EPS (1942 ed.)
"Mongst all the palaces in Hells command." SeCV-1
Sospiri di Roma, *sels.* "Fiona Macleod."
Red Poppies. VA
Susurro. BMEP; VA
Vision, The. BMEP; VLEP
White Peacock, The. PoVP; VA
Sotus hates wise men, for himself is none. Impar Impares Odit. Henry Parrot. SiCE; TuPP
Sou'-sou'east of the Woods of Penn. The Blue Hen's Chickens. Arthur Guiterman. PaA
Sought by the greatest and the least as friend. "H. H." John H. Finley. BAP
Sought by the World. *Unknown.* TuPP
(Love's Ending.) OBSC
Soul, The. George Barlow. OBVV
Soul, The. Madison Cawein. AA
Soul, The. Richard Henry Dana. LPS-2
Soul, The. Pindar, *tr. fr. Greek by* Lionel W. Lyde. GrR
Soul, A. Christina Rossetti. BPN; EmBrPo; EPN
Soul Alone, The. Emily Dickinson. *See* Departed to the judgment.
Soul alone, like a neglected harp, The. Harriet Beecher Stowe. *Fr.* Abide in Me. ChIP
Soul and Body. Shakespeare. *See* Sonnets, CXLVI.
Soul and Body. Samuel Waddington. OBVV; VA
Soul and Body of John Brown, The. Muriel Rukeyser. MoAmPo
Soul and Country. James Clarence Mangan. VA
Soul and Sense. Hannah Parker Kimball. AA
Soul and the Body, The. Sir John Davies. *Fr.* Nosce Teipsum. OBSC
(In what Manner the Soul[e] Is United to the Body.) LiTB; PoEL-2
Soul, art thou sad again. Triumphalis. Bliss Carman. HBMV; PG
Soul as full of Worth, A, as void of Pride. To James Craggs, Esq.; Secretary of State. Pope. CEP
Soul, be your own. The Outcast. John Davidson. MBP; MoBrPo (1942 ed.)
Soul before God, The. Cardinal Newman. *Fr.* The Dream of Gerontius. OxBoCh
Soul came to him of his hapless friend, The. The Ghost of Patroclus. Homer. *Fr.* The Iliad, XXIII. OxBG
"Soul-cheering Light, most bountiful of things." The Churchyard among the Mountains. Wordsworth. *Fr.* The Excursion, VII. ERP
Soul, do you hear the trumpets down in the valley. Reveillé. Audrey Alexandra Brown. CaP
Soul Eternal, The. Sir John Bowring. MaRV
Soul-feeding Hyacinths. Corinne Farley. ChIP
Soul Growth. Annerika Fries. OQP; QP-2
Soul, he said, is composed, The. Anecdote of Men by the Thousand. Wallace Stevens. Po
Soul, heart, and body, we thus singly name. Love's Trinity. Alfred Austin. OBVV
Soul in the Body, The. Edith M. Thomas. AA
Soul in the Kiss, The. *Unknown, tr. fr. Latin by* Sir Stephen Gaselee. *Fr.* Attic Nights (*by* Aulus Gellius). LaP
Soul Is All, The. Omar Khayyám, *tr. fr. Persian by* Edward Fitzgerald. *Fr.* The Rubáiyát. OnPM
(Heaven and Hell.) MaRV
Soul Is Form. Spenser. *See* Beauty ("What time this world's great workmaster did cast").
Soul is like to iron, The. The Soul like Iron. *Unknown.* SoLD
Soul lies haunted in unfathomed deeps, The. Solution. Jack Luzzatto. UnW
Soul Lifted. Albert Durrant Watson. CaP; OCL
Soul-Light. Dante Gabriel Rossetti. The House of Life, XXVIII. CoBE; EPP; PoVP; ViPo; VLEP
Soul like Iron, The. *Unknown, tr. fr. Japanese by* Lois J. Erickson. SoLD
Soul Longs to Return Whence It Came, The. Richard Eberhart. AmP; ExPo; LiTM; TriL
Soul, Mind, and Body. Lillah A. Ashley. MuM
Soul must have, for its great need, The. Neoplatonic Soliloquy. Donald C. Babcock. NePoAm
Soul of a Mother, The. Margaret E. Sangster. PEDC
Soul of a tree ungrown, new life out of God's life proceeding. Yosemite. Milicent Washburn Shinn. *Fr.* The Washington Sequoia. AA
Soul of Christ, be my sanctification. Anima Christi. St. Ignatius Loyola. WHL
Soul of Dante, The. Michelangelo, *tr. fr. Italian by* John Addington Symonds. GoBC
(On Dante Alighieri.) OnPM
Soul of him who is self-conquered, The. Union with the Eternal. *Unknown.* *Fr.* Bhagavad-Gita. GrCo-1
Soul of Jesus Is Restless, The. Cyprus R. Mitchell. ChIP; OQP; QP-1
Soul of Karnaghan Buidhe, The. James B. Dollard. JKCP
Soul of Lincoln, The. Chauncey R. Piety. PGD
Soul of Man, The. Dora Reed Goodale. AA
Soul of Man is larger than the sky, The. To Shakespeare [*or* Shakespeare]. Hartley Coleridge. LPS-3; PtP; VA
Soul of Man Must Quicken, The. T. S. Eliot. *Fr.* The Rock. MoP
Soul of Man Seeketh, The. John W. Garvin. CPG
Soul of mine, may my soul. Held Fast. Sadi. PeP
Soul of my soul, how often you return. Petrarch. Sonnets to Laura: To Laura in Death, XIV. PrPoCR
Soul of my soul! it cannot be. The Sympathy. Owen Feltham. LO; SeCL
Soul of Poetry, The. Johan Sebastian Cammermeyer Welhaven, *tr. fr. Norwegian by* Charles W. Stork. AnNoLy
. . . Soul of the Age! Ben Jonson. *Fr.* To the Memory of My Beloved Master William Shakespeare, and What He Hath Left Us. PIR
Soul of the deceased, although it live, The. Euripides. *Fr.* Helen. MaRV
Soul of the sunny South! thy voice is heard. To Idealon. Thomas Holley Chivers. SPP
Soul of the World, The. Ernest Crosby. AA
Soul of Time, The. Trumbull Stickney. LiTA; NePA
Soul Remembers, The. Richard Burdick Eldridge. GoYe
Soul, secure in her existence, smiles, The. Lines. Addison. *Fr.* Cato: Cato's Soliloquy. UnW
Soul selects her own society, The. Emily Dickinson. AmP; AnFE; AnNE; CoAnAm; CoBA; CoV; GTBS-W; InPo; MaPo; MOAP; NePA; OnPM; OxBA; PoEL-5; TwP; WHA
(Exclusion.) AWP; BAP; JAWP; WBP
(Soul Selects, The.) AmPP; APA; CBOV; MAP; MoAB; MoAmPo; PoLFOT; TrGrPo; UnPo
Soul shall burn her fetters, The. The Soul. George Barlow. OBVV
Soul Speaks, The. Edward H. Pfeiffer. HBMV; LPS-1
Soul Stithy, The. James Chapman Woods. VA
Soul, The, to love created prone and free. Freedom of the Will. Dante. *Fr.* Divina Commedia: Purgatorio. GrCo-1
Soul to the Body, The. *Unknown.* PoLi
Soul unto Soul Glooms Darkling. Charles Leonard Moore. AA
Soul, Wherefore Fret Thee? "Stuart Sterne." AA
Soul Wherein God dwells, The. "Angelus Silesius," *tr. fr. German.* CAW
Souldier and a Sailor, A. *See* Soldier and a Sailor, A.
Souldier Going to the Field, The. Sir William Davenant. *See* Soldier Going to the Field, The.
Souldiers Farewell to His Love, The. *Unknown.* CoMu
Soules Ignorance in This Life and Knowledge in the Next, The. John Donne. *Fr.* Of the Progresse of the Soule. OBS
Soules joy, now I am gone. Song. *Unknown, at. to* the Earl of Pembroke. OBS
Soulless, colorless strain, thy words are the words of wisdom. The Didactic Poem. Richard Garnett. VA
Souls. Fannie Stearns Davis. HBMV; LBMV; SP
Souls. Paul Wertheimer, *tr. fr. German by* Jethro Bithell. TrJP
Soul's Adventure. Stanley J. Kunitz. NP
Soul's Beauty. Dante Gabriel Rossetti. The House of Life, LXXVII. BMEP; BPN; CoBE; EmBrPo; EnLit; OAEP; OBEV (new ed.); OBVV; POTT; PoVP; ViP; ViPo; ViPP; VLEP
(Sibylla Palmifera.) EV-5; GTML
Soul's Bitter Cry, The. *Unknown.* WGRP
Soul's Calm Sunshine, The. Pope. *Fr.* An Essay on Man, Epistle IV. BeR
Soul's Cry, The. Ray Palmer. LPS-2
Soul's Dark Cottage, The. Edmund Waller. *Fr.* Of the Last Verses in the Book. ChTr
Soul's Defiance, The. Lavinia Stoddard. AA
Soul's Departure, The. James Smetham. RO
Soul's Desire, The. *Tr. fr. Irish by* Eleanor Hull. OxBI
Soul's Errand, The. Sir Walter Ralegh. *See* Lie, The.
Soul's Garment, The. Margaret Cavendish, Duchess of Newcastle. MeRV; OxBoCh; SeCePo; SeCL
Souls Groan to Christ for Succour, The. Edward Taylor. *Fr.* God's Determinations. PoEL-3
Soul's Harmony, The, *sels.* Nicholas Breton. SiCE
"What is the gold of all this world but dross."
"Worldly prince doth in his scepter hold, The."

Souls in the east, awake. An Easter Reveille. John R. Slater. MaRV
Soul's joy, bend not those morning stars from me. Astrophel and Stella, XLVIII. Sir Philip Sidney. MaPo; SiPS
Soul's joy, when thou are gone. A Parodie. George Herbert. OBS
Soul's Kiss. Samuel Greenberg. LiTA
Souls Lake. Robert Fitzgerald. MoPo
Soul's Liberty. Anna Wickham. MBP; MoBrPo
Souls of Black and White, The. Gladys May Casely Hayford (Aquah Laluah). PoNe
Souls of men! why will ye scatter. God Our Father. Frederick W. Faber. WGRP
Souls of Poets dead and gone. Lines on the Mermaid Tavern [*or* The Mermaid Tavern]. Keats. ATP; AWP; BCEP; BEL; BPN; CoBE; EM-2; EmBrPo; EnLi-2; EnLit; EnRP; EPN; EPP; ERP; EV-4; FaBoBe; GEPC; GTBS; GTBS-D; GTBS-W; GTSE; GTSL; HBV; InMe; InPo; InvP; LoBV; OAEP; OBRV; OTPC (1923 ed.); PoFS; PoRA; PreP; ReTS; SeCeV; TCEP; TOP; TreFS; TwP; ViBoPo
Souls of the patriot dead. The Kidnapping of Sims. John Pierpont. PAH
Souls of the Slain, The. Thomas Hardy. LiTB; PoEL-5; PoVP
Soul's Pilgrimage, The. Sir Walter Ralegh. *See* Passionate Man's Pilgrimage, The.
Soul's Prayer, The. Sarojini Naidu. MaRV
Soul's Rialto hath its merchandise, The. Sonnets from the Portuguese, XIX. Elizabeth Barrett Browning. BPN
Soul's Soliloquy, A. Wenonah Stevens Abbott. BLPA; NeHB
Soul's Sphere, The. Dante Gabriel Rossetti. The House of Life, LXII. PoVP; ViPo
Soul's Springtime, The. Georg Trakl, *tr. fr. German by* David Luke. AnGP
Soul's Tendency towards Its True Centre, The. John Byrom. CEP
Sound, A, a sigh; a whip of rushing air. As It Began to Dawn. George Edward Hoffman. ChIP
Sound all to arms! Catiline to the Roman Army. George Croly. *Fr.* Catiline, V, ii. LPS-2
Sound and Sense ("True ease in writing . . ."). Pope. *Fr.* An Essay on Criticism, Pt. II. UnPo, 14 *ll.*
(Craft of Verse, The, 12 *ll.*) BLV; BoLiVe
(Ease in Writing, 12 *ll.*) CBOV
(Sound and the Sense, The: "'Tis not enough . . . ," 10 *ll.*) LiA
("True ease in writing comes from art, not chance.") ExPo, 12 *ll.*; TrGrPo, 22 *ll.*
Sound but from an Echo made, A. The Cuckoo. Francis Carlin. NV
Sound came booming through the air, A. The Philosopher and Her Father. Shirley Brooks. CenHV
Sound Country Lass, The. *Unknown.* CoMu
Sound me brass trumpets of the sun! Song for Love's Coming of Age. J. Corson Miller. JKCP (1955 ed.)
Sound of Breaking. Conrad Aiken. AnAmPo; AWP; InPo; LA; MAPA; MOAP
Sound of Footsteps, The. Homer, *pr. tr. fr. Greek by* A. T. Murray. *Fr.* The Odyssey, XVI. LiA
"Sound of Going in the Tops of the Mulberry Trees, A." Henry Bellamann. TBM
Sound of her silk skirt has stopped, The. Li Fu-jen. Wu Ti. AtBAP; BoW; LO; TrCh
Sound of many waters, A!—now I know. Sonnet in a Pass of Bavaria. Richard Chenevix Trench. OBRV
Sound of Rain, The. Cale Young Rice. MuM
Sound of the closing outside door was all, The. The Valley's Singing Day. Robert Frost. UnS
Sound of the Heart, The. Ramón López Velarde, *tr. fr. Spanish by* H. R. Hays. TwSpPo
Sound of the Horn, The. Alfred de Vigny, *tr. fr. French by* Wilfrid Thorley. AWP; JAWP; WBP
(Horn, The, *tr. by* Alan Conder.) TrFP
Sound of the Sea, The. Longfellow. AnFE; APA; CoAnAm; CoV; EtS; IAP; OBAV; Po; UnW
Sound of the Sea, The. John Hall Wheelock. EtS
Sound of the Trees [*or* of Trees], The. Robert Frost. AnFE; APA; AtBAP; BrBE; ChMo; CMP; CoAnAm; MAPA; NV; OxBA; PG; PoeMoYo; TwAmPo; TwCV; VOD
Sound of the Wind, The. Christina Rossetti. *See* Wind Has Such a Rainy Sound, The.
Sound of Thy Sweet Name, The. Francis Davison. TuPP
(Madrigal: "Sound of thy sweet name, my dearest treasure, The.") EIL
Sound of Trees. Robert Frost. *See* Sound of the Trees.
Sound out, proud trumpets. Sir Osbert Sitwell. *Fr.* England Reclaimed. ViBoPo
Sound over all waters, reach out from all lands. A Christmas Carmen. Whittier. COAH; SDH
Sound Sleep. Christina Rossetti. BPN
Sound smashes through the dark. It is a wall. Joseph Schull. *Fr.* I. Jones. Soldier. TwCaPo
Sound, sound forever, clarions of thought! The Trumpets of the Mind. Victor Hugo. WoL
Sound, Sound the Clarion. Thomas Osbert Mordaunt, *formerly at. to* Sir Walter Scott. *Fr.* Old Mortality (*by* Scott), *ch.* 34. AnFE; BCEP; BHV; EBSV; EV-4; OQP; QP-2; TOP
(Answer.) OBEV (1st ed.)
(Call, The.) GTBS-W; OBEV (new ed.)
(Clarion.) BEL; BPN; EmBrPo; EnLit
(Motto from "Old Mortality.") CaAE
(One Crowded Hour.) CBOV; MaRV; TrGrPo
("Sound, sound the clarion, fill the fife!") InP; OAEP
(Sound the Clarion.) ERP; TreFS
Sound that the whippoorwill sobbed adown the mountain. Lost Corner. John Gould Fletcher. ChMo; CMP
Sound the Clarion. Thomas O. Mordaunt. *See* Sound, Sound the Clarion.
Sound the deep waters. Sleep at Sea. Christina Rossetti. PoEL-5
Sound the flute! Spring. Blake. *Fr.* Songs of Innocence. BoChLi; BoTP; FaBoCh; FaPON; GoTP; KN; LoGBV; MoShBr; OTPC; RIS; SUS; TiPo (1952 ed.); YeAr
Sound the Loud Timbrel. Thomas Moore. GoBC; MaRV; PIR
Sound Thy Trumpet, God of Action. Arthur B. Dale. PraP
Sound Trumpets, ho!—weigh anchor—loosen sail. The Voyager's Song. Edward Coote Pinkney. APW; SPP
Sound ye no trumpets. Martyrs of Nazareth. Sister Margaret Maria. PraNu
Soundest of all literary legal tenders. Old Bill's Memory Book. William Rose Benét. InMe
Sounding, The. Conrad Aiken. CrMA
Sounding. Doris Ferne. CaP
Sounding battles leave him nodding still, The. The School Boy Reads His Iliad. David Morton. BAP; MCCG; PFE; PoMa; POT; PoTo; TBM
Sounding brass and tinkling cymbal. Music. G. K. Chesterton. JKCP (1955 ed.)
Sounding cataract, The. Wordsworth. *Fr.* Lines Composed a Few Miles above Tintern Abbey. FaBoEn; WGRP
Sounding of the Last Trump. Michael Wigglesworth. *Fr.* The Day of Doom. TCAP
(Summons, The.) APW
Sounding Portage, The. Annie Charlotte Dalton. CaP
Soundings at Memphis, *with music. Unknown.* StDa
Soundings from Tee Collins, *with music. Unknown.* StDa
Soundings from Uncle Mac, *with music. Unknown.* StDa
Soundless and almost weightless. In Woods near the Frontline. Mikhail Isakovsky. RuPo
Soundless the moth-flit, crisp the death-watch tick. Maerchen. Walter de la Mare. CoBMV
Sounds. Mary Austin. NP
Sounds in the Morning, The. Eleanor Farjeon. BoChLi; SUS
Sounds of Dawn, The. Efraín Huerta, *tr. fr. Spanish by* Dudley Fitts. AnCL; LiTW
Sounds Out of Sorrow. Edgar Lee Masters. ChMo; CMP
Soupy, soupy, soupy, without a single bean. Words for Army Bugle Calls: Mess Call. *Unknown.* TreF
Sour fiend, go home and tell the Pit. Ghoul Care. Ralph Hodgson. AnEnPo; MoBrPo
Sour Land, *sel.* Sidney Keyes.
Alexander Pope at Stanton Harcourt. FaBoTw
Sour taste of strawberries lingers in my mouth and teeth, The. Sleeping on a Summer Day. Yang W'an-li. WhP
Sour Wine. Arthur Stringer. BoCaPo (1943 ed.)
Source. Leigh Mitchell Hodges. LPS-1
Source immaterial of material naught. The Rejected "National Hymns," IV. "Orpheus C. Kerr." ALV; BOHV; InMe; PA
Source of News. *Unknown.* TreF
Source of the Danube, The. Friedrich Hölderlin, *tr. fr. German by* R. F. C. Hull. AnGP
Sources of the Past, The. Kingsley Amis. PoLFOT
Sourdough Mountain Lookout. Philip Whalen. NeAP
Sourwood Mountain (*diff. versions*). *Unknown.* ABF, *with music*; APW; AS, *with music*; IHA; TrAS, *with music*
(I Got a Gal at the Head of the Holler, *with music.*) AS
South, The. Wang Chien, *tr. fr. Chinese by* Arthur Waley. AWP; TrCh
South and west winds joined, and, as they blew, The. John Donne. *Fr.* The Storm. EtS
South Arbor, The. Chao Chia, *tr. fr. Chinese by* Henry H. Hart. PoHN
South Australia. *Unknown. See* Rolling King.
South Carolina, The. *Unknown.* PAH
South Carolina to the States of the North. Paul Hamilton Hayne. PAH
South Coast, The. Brother Antoninus. NeAP
South Coast Idyll, A. Rosamund Marriott Watson. OBVV
South Country, The. Hilaire Belloc. ACP (1952 ed.); EPP; GoBC; HBV; JKCP; LBBV;; MBP; MoBrPo; OBVV; PoeT; POTE; ShBV-3; TCPD; TwCV
South End. Conrad Aiken. MoVE; OxBA
South-Folk in Cold Country. Ezra Pound. CrMA

South is green with coming spring, The. The Trial. Muriel Rukeyser. NAMP; PoNe
South Mountain towered upon [*or* towering on] our right. The Pride of Battery B. Frank H. Gassaway. BlG; PTA-2
South of Guardafui with a dark tide flowing. The Dhows. Francis Brett Young. EtS
South of My Days. Judith Wright. NeLNL
South of the City We Fight. *Unknown, tr. fr. Chinese.* WhP
South of the Great Sea. *Unknown, tr. fr. Chinese by* Arthur Waley. ChLP; TrCh
South of the Line, inland from far Durban. A Christmas Ghost-Story. Thomas Hardy. EmBrPo; EnLi-2
South of the river, north of the river, lies my native land. Native Land. Li Yu. WhP
South of the River We Gather Lotos. *Unknown, tr. fr. Chinese.* WhP
South of the Thames by Chelsea Reach. Power Station. T. W. Ramsey. HaMV
South Street. Francis E. Falkenbury. EtS; PFY; PoeMoYo; VOD (1935 ed.)
South Street. Edward S. Silvera. CDC
South Wind, The. Charles Kingsley. EV-5
South-Wind. George Parsons Lathrop. AA
South Wind. George O'Neil. PFE
South Wind. Siegfried Sassoon. BoTP; NLK (1947 ed.)
South Wind. Georg Trakl, *tr. fr. German by* David Luke. AnGP
South Wind. Tu Fu, *tr. fr. Chinese by* Kenneth Rexroth. OnPC
South wind, The, blows the mountains; the mountains become plains. A Great Song. Li Ho. WhP
South-wind brings, The/ Life, sunshine. Threnody. Emerson. AA; AnNE; EOAH; IAP; MOAP; TCAP; TOP
South wind brings wet weather, The. Weather Wisdom [*or* Country Proverbs *or* Winds and Weathers]. *Unknown.* HBV; HBVY; RIS; StaSt; TreF
South Wind laid his moccasins aside, The. Isabella Valancy Crawford. *Fr.* Malcolm's Katie. BoCaPo
South-wind strengthens to a gale, The. Low Barometer. Robert Bridges. CoBMV; LiTB; LoBV (2d ed.); MeRV; RiBV; UnPo (3d ed.)
Southeast the Peacock Flies. *Unknown, tr. fr. Chinese.* WhP
Southerly. E. J. Brady. NeLNL
Southerly Wind, *with music. Unknown.* ShS
Southern Cross. Hart Crane. *Fr.* The Bridge: Three Songs. LiTA
Southern Cross, The. Robert Stephen Hawker. *See* Mystic Magi, The.
Southern Cross. Herman Melville. AnFE; CoAnAm; LiTA
Southern Cross, The. St. George Tucker. FOAH
Southern Dead, The. Morton Bryan Wharton. BlG
Southern Girl, A. Samuel Minturn Peck. AA
Southern Lullaby, A. Virna Sheard. CPG
Southern Mansion. Arna Bontemps. BANP; PoNe
Southern Mansion. John Crowe Ransom. *See* Old Mansion.
Southern Night, A. Matthew Arnold. GEPC
Southern Republic, The. Olivia Thomas. BlG
Southern Road. Sterling A. Brown. BANP
Southern Room over the River, The. Su T'ung-po, *tr. fr. Chinese by* Kenneth Rexroth. OnPC
Southern Snow-Bird, The. William Hamilton Hayne. AA
Southern Soldier Boy, The. Abram Joseph Ryan. BlG
Southern Summer. Francis Stuart. NeIP
Southern Whip-Poor-Will, A. Clinton Scollard. BLA
Southerndown Beach. George Woodcock. MoWP
Southerner, The. Karl Shapiro. FiMAP; PoNe
Southey and Wordsworth. Byron. *See* Dedication: "Bob Southey! You're a poet—Poet-laureate."
Southrons, hear your country call you! Dixie. Albert Pike. AA; APW; HBV; MC; MDAH; PaA; PAH; SPP; TCAP
Southward and eastward had our seamen steered. The Dutch Seamen and New Holland. William Pember Reeves. AnNZ
Southward Returning. Donald Davidson. SPP
Southward Sidonian Hanno. Hervey Allen. EtS
Southward the birds go, every wing. Prague Students' Song Joseph von Eichendorff. AnGP
Southward through Eden went a river large. Milton. *Fr.* Paradise Lost, IV. GEPC; ViBoPo
Southward with fleet of ice. Sir Humphrey Gilbert. Longfellow. BHV; EtS; HBV; HBVY; MC; OnSP; OTPC; PAH; TCAP; TOP; TVSH
Southwest wind blows in from the sea unceasing, The. Return to Life. Abbie Huston Evans. NePoAm
South-west wind is blowing, The. Autumn Morning. Adeline White. BoTP
Southwestern Night. Angelico Chavez. JKCP (1955 ed.)
South-westward, where th' autumnal sun went down. Ruins at Sunset. William Allingham. IrPN
Souvenir. Alfred de Musset, *tr. fr. French by* George Santayana. AWP; WoL
Souvenir. E. A. Robinson. InP
Souvenirs. Margaret E. Bruner. CIV
Sovereign [*or* Soverayne] beauty which I do[o] admire [*or* admyre], The. Amoretti, III. Spenser. ATP; HBV; OAEP; PeBoSo; PoEL-1; SiCE; TwHP
Sovereign Emblem, The. James Russell Lowell. *Fr.* The Cathedral. MaRV
("Whatsoe'er/ The form of building or the creed professed.)" ChIP
Sovereign Goddess, thou who lovest Golgoi, and Idalion. The Adonis Song. Theocritus. *Fr.* Idylls. GrR
Sovereign Poet, The. Sir William Watson. BMEP; LBBV; PoVP; WGRP
Sovereigns, The. Lloyd Mifflin. AA; AnAmPo; HBV; LA (Sovereign Poets.) WGRP
Sovereignty. Leslie Savage Clark. ChIP
Soviet Union, immense resplendence of blood. Song to the Soviet Union. Manuel Crespo. PoFr
Sow came in with the saddle, The. *Unknown.* OxNR
Sow it with salt where men went to and fro. Carthage. Miriam Allen deFord. MuM
Sow one acorn has, The. Wayward Desire. *Unknown.* OxBG
Sow Your Self! Miguel de Unamuno, *tr. fr. Spanish by* Eleanor L. Turnbull. TeCS
Sow your wheat in muddy weather. Country Lore. *Unknown.* OxBG
Sower, The. R. Olivares Figueroa, *tr. fr. Spanish by* Dudley Fitts. AnCL; FaPON; OnPM
Sower, The. Sir Charles G. D. Roberts. CaP; OCL
Sower and His Seed, The. W. E. H. Lecky. TIP
Sower of Discord, A. Proverbs, Bible, *O.T. See* Seven Evils.
Sower trudged and swung, leaning, The. Dust. Stanley Snaith. POTE
Sower's Song, The. Thomas Carlyle. DDA; OBVV; VA
Sowing. Miguel Otero Silva, *tr. fr. Spanish by* Donald Devenish Walsh. AnCL
Sowing. Edward Thomas. AlDL; BMEP; CBOV; HBMV; NP; POTE
Sowing of the Dragon, The. John G. Neihardt. *Fr.* The Song of the Indian Wars. TCAP
Sowing Season. Victor Hugo, *tr. fr. French by* Alan Conder. TrFP
Sowing Seed. Laurence Binyon. POTE
Sowing Seeds. Ursula Cornwall. BoTP
Sown fields./ Herds. Constantino Suasnavar. *Fr.* Numbers. AnCL
Space. William Hart-Smith. *See* Columbus Goes West.
Space and Dread and the Dark. W. E. Henley. PoVP; VLEP; WHA
Space, and the twelve clean winds of heaven. The Most-sacred Mountain. Eunice Tietjens. BAP; CP; HBMV; NLK (1947 ed.); NV; PoTo; QS; SBMV
Space and Time! now I see it is true, what I guess'd at. Song of Myself, XXXIII. Walt Whitman. CoBA; CoV
Space Being Curved. E. E. Cummings. PoLFOT
Space in the Air, A. Jon Silkin. NePoEA; TrJP
Space is ample, east and west. Unity. Emerson. APW
Space is azure and the mountains bathe. Ignacio Rodríguez Galván. *Fr.* Prophecy of Cuauhtémoc. AnMP
Space long was ours, factories to frame our guns. Warsaw, 27 September, 1939. Leo Minster. NeTW
Space-time, our scientists tell us, is impervious. Archibald MacLeish. *Fr.* Reply to Mr. Wordsworth. ImOP
Spacialesque trumpets corrode. Ideogram. Alfred G. Bailey. BoCaPo
'Spacially Jim. Bessie Morgan. BOHV; HBV
('Specially Jim.) PTA-2
Spacious Firmament on High, The. Addison. FaBoBe; GN; HBV; HBVY; LEAP; MCCG; OIF; OTPC; Po; PoEL-3; PoeMoYo; PreP; ShBV-2
(Hymn: Confirmation of Faith, The.) EV-3
(Hymn: "Spacious firmament on high, The.") AWP; EPP; JAWP; LiTG; OBEV; PIAE; TOP; TyEnPo; WBP
(Hymn to the Creation.) DD; OHIP
(Ode: "Spacious firmament on high, The.") BLPA; BPP; CEP; CoBE; LPS-2; MaRV; NeHB; OBEC; OxBoCh
(Ode to Creation.) TVSH
(Psalm XIX.) WGRP
(Spacious Firmament, The.) BCEP; GrCo-1; GTBS-W; TriL
Spacious hall in brazen splendour gleams, The. The Armory. Alcaeus. GrR
Spacious hive well stocked with bees, A. The Grumbling Hive; or, Knaves Turned Honest. Bernard Mandeville. CEP; EiPP
Spade, A! a rake! hoe! The Lay of the Laborer. Thomas Hood. DD; ERP; HH; VA
Spades. Cale Young Rice. PR
Spaewife, The. Robert Louis Stevenson. POTT; PoVP; VA
Spain. W. H. Auden. *See* Spain, 1937.
Spain. Emily Lawless. *See* In Spain.
Spain drew us proudly from the womb of night. Full Cycle. John White Chadwick. PAH

Spain, 1809. F. L. Lucas. HaMV
Spain, 1937. W. H. Auden. EnLit; LiTB
(Spain.) LiTG; WaP
Spain, Take from Me This Cup. César Vallejo, *tr. fr. Spanish by* Donald Devenish Walsh. AnCL
Spain's Last Armada. Wallace Rice. PAH
Spake full well, in language quaint and olden. Flowers. Longfellow. ADAH; DD; HBV
Spake the Lord Christ—"I will arise." An Easter Hymn. Richard Le Gallienne. OHIP
Span of Life, The. Robert Frost. HoPM; LiTM; SiTL
(Old Dog, The.) RIS
Span of Man, The. Psalms, XC, Bible, *O.T.* *See* God, Our Dwelling Place.
Spangled Pandemonium, The. Palmer Brown. LiL; TiPo (1959 ed.)
Spaniard's long time care and cost, invincible surnam'd, The. William Warner. *Fr.* Albion's England, *Bk.* IX, *ch.* 49. SG
Spaniel, Beau, that fares like you, A. On a Spaniel Called Beau Killing a Young Bird. William Cowper. AlBD; FaBoCh; PRWS
Spanish Alleluja. James J. Galvin. JKCP (1955 ed.)
Spanish Armada, The. Macaulay. *See* Armada, The.
Spanish Armado, The. *Unknown, at. to* William Warner. *See* Defeat of the Spanish Armada, The.
Spanish Bawd, The. James Mabbe, *after the Spanish of* Fernando de Rojas. *See* Celestina.
Spanish Cabineer, The. *Unknown.* ABS
Spanish Cavalier, The. William D. Hendrickson. OlF
Spanish Curate, The, *sels.* John Fletcher.
Dearest, Do Not You Delay Me, *at. to* Fletcher, *fr.* II, iv. SeCL; ViBoPo
Song: "Let the bells ring, and let the boys sing," *fr.* III, ii. OBS
("Let the bells ring, and let the boys sing.") TuPP
Spanish Elegy. Luis Cernuda, *tr. fr. Spanish by* Eleanor L. Turnbull. CoSP
Spanish Folk Songs. *Unknown, tr. fr. Spanish by* Havelock Ellis.
"Let the rich man fill his belly." AWP; JAWP; WBP
"My father was a sailor." AWP
(Folk Songs, 2.) LiTW
(Sailors.) OnPM
Spanish Friar, The, *sel.* Dryden.
Farewell, Ungrateful Traitor! *fr.* V, i. ElSeCe; InPo; LiTB; LiTG; SeCL; ViBoPo
("Farewell ungratfull traytor.") EnLoPo
(Love's Despair.) ACP
(Song: "Farewell ungrateful[l] traitor.") BCEP; EiPP; FaBoEn; FiP; LEAP; OBS; SeCV-2; SeEP
Spanish Gipsy, The, *sel.* Thomas Middleton *and* William Rowley.
Trip It, Gipsies [Trip It Fine], *fr.* III, i. OAEP; SeCL
(Song: "Trip it gipsies, trip it fine.") OBS
Spanish Gypsy, The, *sels.* "George Eliot."
Dark, The. VA
Day Is Dying. LPS-2
I Am Lonely. GN; HBV
"It was in the prime." DiM
Spring Song. PRWS
Song of the Zincali. VA
Spanish is the lovin' tongue. Border Affair. Badger Clark. SCC
Spanish Johnny. Willa Cather. ABF, *with music;* BAP; FaPON; HBMV; MPB; MW; NP; PFY; WaKn
Spanish Ladies. *Unknown.* AmSS, *with music;* FaBoCh; LoGBV; SG
Spanish Lady's Love, The. *Unknown.* CG; OBB
Spanish Ledges. Crosbie Garstin. ReTS
Spanish Lullaby. *Unknown, ad. by* Louis Untermeyer. RIS
Spanish Man, The. F. R. Higgins. JKCP (1926 ed.)
Spanish Moonlight. Birger Sjöberg, *tr. fr. Swedish by* Charles W. Stork. AnSL
Spanish Needle, The. Claude McKay. GoSl
Spanish Point. Sir Aubrey De Vere. TIP
Spanish Ships Reach Mexico, The. Dryden. *Fr.* The Indian Emperor, I, ii. BeR
Spanish Song. Charles Divine. HBMV
Spanish Student, The, *sel.* Longfellow.
Serenade: "Stars of the summer night," *fr.* I, iii. AA; AmPP (3d ed.); FaBoBe; HBV; IAP; LEAP; LoBV; MOAP; NeHB; OnPM; OuHeWo; PFY; REAL; ViBoPo
(Stars of the Summer Night.) BTP; LoPo; OlF
Spanish Trilogy, The. Rainer Maria Rilke, *tr. fr. German by* "Hugh MacDiarmid." AnGP
Spanish Waters. John Masefield. BeLS; ChMo; CMP; FaBoBe; FaPON; MCCG; MW; PCD; PFE; PoMa; ShBV-3; WaKn
Spanking is something that must go. Character Building. Edward Anthony. GoTP
Spare. Ibn Ammar, *tr. fr. Arabic by* A. J. Arberry. MooP
Spare!/ There is one, yes I have one. The Golden Echo. Gerard Manley Hopkins. *Fr.* The Leaden Echo and the Golden Echo. ChMo; LiA; LiTM; LoBV; MBP; MoAB; MoBrPo; OBMV; PreP; ReaPo; TwCV; ViPo; VLEP
Spare all who yield; alas, that we must pierce. The Death of Hampden. Pakenham Beatty. VA
Spare, Gen'rous Victor, spare the Slave. To a Lady; She Refusing to Continue a Dispute with Me, and Leaving Me in the Argument. Matthew Prior. BrBE; CEP; EiPP; LiTL; SeCL; WHA
Spare my sweetheart, boar, whether in grass-sweet meadow. Cerinthus Forgiven; Once More Tibullus Speaks for the Girl [*or* Sulpicia's Rival]. Tibullus. LaP; LiTW
Spare then the person, and expose the vice. Name No Names. Pope. *Fr.* Epilogue to the Satires. BeR
Spare to this humble hillock, this stone that stands so lowly. The Farmer's Rest. Leonidas of Tarentum. GrPE
Spare us this silence after the guns. Map Reference T994724. John Pudney. WaP
Sparhawk proud did hold in Wicked jail, A. A Sparrow-Hawk. *Unknown.* CH
Spark, The. Helen Gray Cone. PC
Spark, The. Joseph Mary Plunkett. AnIV; AWP; JAWP; TIP; WBP
Spark o' Nature's Fire, A. Burns. *Fr.* Epistle to John Lapraik. BLP
Sparkle up, little tired flower. Tired. Hilda Conkling. NP
Sparkles from the Wheel. Walt Whitman. FaBoEn
Sparkling and Bright. Charles Fenno Hoffman. AA; BAV; HBV; LHV
Sparkling and warm the breezes drift. The Bridal Voyage. Andreas Munch. AnNoLy
Sparkling Bowl, The. John Pierpont. AnAmPo; LA
Sparkling sunset, oranged to gold, A. First Frost. Edwin Curran. HBMV; TSW; TSWC
Sparrow. Stephen Vincent Benét. DDA
Sparrow, The. Psalms, LXXXIV: 3, Bible, *O.T.*, *and* St. Matthew, X: 29, Bible, *N.T.* FaPON
Sparrow dips in his wheel-rut bath, The. The Five Students. Thomas Hardy. ExPo; PoEL-5
Sparrow has gone home into the tree, The. 1914. Frank Wilmot. BoAu; MoAuPo
Sparrow hath found an house, The. The Sparrow. Psalm LXXXIV, Bible, *O.T.* FaPON
Sparrow-Hawk, A. *Unknown.* CH
Sparrow Hills. Boris Pasternak. *See* Vorobyev Hills.
Sparrow, my mistress' pet. Catullus, *tr. fr. Latin by* W. K. Newton. LaP
Sparrow, O, sweet sparrow. Catullus, *tr. fr. Latin by* Horace Gregory. RoL
Sparrow told it to the robin, The. Early News. Anna Maria Pratt. AA
Sparrows. Adeline D. T. Whitney. PEOR
Sparrows at the Airport, The. Anthony Ostroff. NePoAm-2
Sparrow's Dirge, The ("Pla ce bo"). John Skelton. *Fr.* Phyllyp Sparowe. OBSC
("Pla ce bo/ Who is there, who?") AtBAP; CoBE, *abr.*; NBE; OxBoLi, *abr.*; ReEn; TuPP
Sparrow's Dirge, The ("When I remember again"). John Skelton. *Fr.* Phyllyp Sparowe. FaBoCh; LoGBV
("When I remember again.") SeCePo
Sparrows in gossip outside the bedroom eaves. Come Not Near. Mary Elizabeth Osborn. NePoAm-2
Sparrow's Nest, The. Wordsworth. BPN; EmBrPo; EnRP; ERP
(Sister, A.) WP
Sparta. Terpander, *tr. fr. Greek by* C. M. Bowra. OxBG; WoL
Sparta, the proud inviolate city, sees. Lacedaemon. *Unknown.* OxBG
Spartan Monument, The. Simonides, *tr. fr. Greek by* Hugh Macnaghten. GrL; OxBG
(Dead of Sparta at Plataea, The, *tr. by* F. L. Lucas.) GrPE
(On the Lacedaemonian Dead at Plataea, *tr. by* Richard Eberhart.) WaaP
Spartan Three-Choir Festival. *Unknown, tr. fr. Greek by* T. F. Higham. OxBG
Spasskoye. Boris Pasternak, *tr. fr. Russian by* C. M. Bowra. BoRS
Spastara's Death, *sel.* Bengt Lidner, *tr. fr. Swedish by* Charles W. Stork.
"On Nova Zembla's peaks, in vales of parched Ceylon." (Introduction to "Spastara's Death.") AnSL
Spattering of the rain upon pale terraces, The. Irradiations, I. John Gould Fletcher. AnFE; APA; CoAnAm; MAPA; TwAmPo
Spawn of fantasies. Love Songs. Mina Loy. AnAmPo; LA
Speak! Wordsworth. *See* Why Art Thou Silent?
Speak and tell us, our Ximena, looking northward far away. The Angels of Buena Vista. Whittier. BeLS; PAH; TCAP
Speak fair to him that hates thee, till he falls in thy hand at last. Vendetta. Theognis. GrPE

Speak from the Distance! Clemens Brentano, *tr. fr. German by* Mabel Cotterell. AnGP
Speak, gentle heart, where is thy dwelling place? Thomas Watson. LO
Speak Gently. David Bates, *wr. at. to* G. W. Langford. PoToHe
"Speak gently, kindly, to the poor," *sel.* BPP
Speak gently, Spring, and make no sudden sound. Four Little Foxes. Lew Sarett. BAP; FaPON; GoTP; NP; NV; PCD; PoeMoYo; PoMa; PoTo; PYM; TBM; TCPD; WaKn; YeAr
Speak gently to the herring and kindly to the calf. Kindness to Animals. Joseph Ashby-Sterry. BOHV; InMe; NA
Speak, God of Visions. Emily Brontë. *See* Plead for Me.
Speak, Goddess! since 'tis thou that best canst tell. Sir Samuel Garth. *Fr.* The Dispensary. PoP
Speak, gracious Lord, oh speak; Thy servant hears. A Paraphrase on Thomas à Kempis. Pope. GoBC; OBEC; TrPWD
Speak, History! Who are life's victors? William Wetmore Story. *Fr.* Io Victis. ChIP
Speak holy words—too many blasphemies. To Pulpit and Tribune. Amos N. Wilder. MaRV
Speak low to me, my Saviour, low and sweet. Comfort. Elizabeth Barrett Browning. HBV
Speak No Evil. *Unknown.* GoTP
Speak no more of life. The Dying Enthusiast. James Clarence Mangan. IrPN
Speak not ill of womankind. Against Blame of Women. Gerald, Earl of Desmond. AnIL
Speak not too much lest speech make thee speechless. Of the Senses. John Heywood. ReIE
Speak not—whisper not. The Sunken Garden. Walter de la Mare. HBMV; TCEP
"Speak, O man, less recent! Fragmentary fossil!" To the Pliocene Skull. Bret Harte. BOHV; LPS-3
Speak [*or* Speke], Parrot, *sels.* John Skelton.
"My name is Parrot, a byrd of paradyse." OxBoLi
(Parrot, The.) ACP
(Parrot's Soliloquy.) PoEL-1
Salutation to Cardinal Wolsey. CoEV
"So many moral matters, and so little used." CoBE; ViBoPo
Speak, quiet lips, and utter forth my fate. An English Girl. F. Wyville Home. VA
Speak Roughly to Your Little Boy. "Lewis Carroll." *Fr.* Alice's Adventures in Wonderland. FaBoCh; LoGBV
Speak! said my soul, be stern and adequate. Exordium. George Cabot Lodge. LBMV
Speak, Satire; for there's none can tell like thee. The Introduction. Daniel Defoe. *Fr.* The True-born Englishman. BEL
"Speak! speak! thou fearful guest!" The Skeleton in Armor. Longfellow. AA; AmPP; AnNE; APW; AWP; BeLS; CoBA; FaBoBe; GBV (1922 ed.); GoTP; HBV; HBVY; IAF; LEAP; LoEn; MaC; MCCG; MOAP; OnSP; PAH; PECK; PFE; REAL; RG; TCAP; TOP; TreF
"Speak! speak! thou fearless boy!" Skoal! Charles Lindbergh, Skoal! *Unknown.* GA
Speak the speech, I pray you, as I pronounced it to you. Hamlet's Instruction to the Players. Shakespeare. *Fr.* Hamlet, III, ii. TreFS
Speak the Word. Charles Wesley. BePJ
Speak This Kindly to Her. Robert Bagg. NePoAm-2
Speak thou and speed, where will or power aught help'th. That Speaking or Proffering Brings Alway Speeding. Sir Thomas Wyatt. TuPP
Speak: thy strong words may never pass away. Epilogue of Prometheus. Shelley. *Fr.* Prometheus Unbound, IV. CBE
Speak to me, oh, speak to me. Incantation for Healing. Constance Lindsay Skinner. NV
Speak to me. Take my hand. What are you now? Effort at Speech between Two People. Muriel Rukeyser. MoAB; MoAmPo; TrGrPo (rev. ed.); TrJP
Speak to the Sun. Dedie Huffman Wilson. GoYe
Speak to us only with the killer's tongue. Sursum Corda. Conrad Aiken. ReMP
Speak to us who/ are also split. Tiresias. George Garrett. NePoAm-2
Speak when you're spoken to,/ Come for one call. *Unknown.* OxNR
Speak when you're spoken to,/ Do as you're bid. *Unknown.* CenHV
Speak with contempt of none, from slave to king. Speak No Evil. *Unknown.* GoTP
Speak with the Sun. David Campbell. NeLNL; SeCePo
Speake, speake, at last replye. *Unknown.* SeCSL
Speake you that heare, now Cloris sings. *Unknown.* SeCSL
Speakers, Columbus Circle. Raymond Souster. CaP
Speakin' in general, I'ave tried 'em all. Sestina of the Tramp-Royal. Kipling. LiTB; MBP; MoBrPo; OtMeF; PoVP; SiTL
Speakin' of dorgs, my bench-legged fyce. The Bench-legged Fyce. Eugene Field. AlBD
Speaking My Mind. Yüan Chi, *tr. fr. Chinese.* WhP
Speaking of Cowboy's Home. *Unknown.* CoSo
Speaking of Joe, I should have said. Fred. David McCord. TiPo (1959 ed.)
Speaking of Poetry. John Peale Bishop. LiTA; LiTM (rev. ed.); OxBA
Speaking of wine. The Grapes of Wrath. Christopher Morley. WhC
Spear, The. Abu Zakariya, *tr. fr. Arabic by* A. J. Arberry. MooP
Spear-points of young men blossom there. Sparta. Terpander. OxBG; WoL
Speargrass crackles under the billy and overhead is the winter sun, The. While the Billy Boils. David McKee Wright. AnNZ
Spearmen heard the bugle sound, The. Beth Gêlert. William Robert Spencer. BeLS; BLPA; GoTP; LPS-2; OnSP; OTPC; TreFS
Spear's my bread, the spear's my wine, The. Staff of Life. Archilochus. GrR
Special Delivery. Elizabeth Winton. PCH
Special Place, A. Dorothy Quick. MuM; QS
Specialist told him, The: "Fine, let's leave it at that." Rhapsody of the Deaf Man. Tristan Corbière. AnFP
'Specially Jim. Bessie Morgan. *See* 'Spacially Jim.
Specimen of an Induction to a Poem. Keats. EmBrPo; ERP
Speck that would have been beneath my sight, A. A Considerable Speck. Robert Frost. AmP; AmPP; MoAB; MoAmPo; WhC
Speck went blowing up against the sky, A. A Visit from Abroad. James Stephens. PoMS
Speckeldy hen, speckeldy hen. *Unknown, tr. fr. German.* SAS
Speckled bird sings in the tree, The. The Nightingale. Katharine Tynan. BoTP
Speckled cat and a tame hare, A. Responsibilities. J. C. Hall. HaMV
Speckled cat and a tame hare, A. W. B. Yeats. *Fr.* Two Songs of a Fool. AlDL
Speckled sky is dim with snow, The. Midwinter. John Townsend Trowbridge. AA; AnAmPo; AnFE; APA; CoAnAm; GN; HBV; LA; LBAP; LEAP; OBAV; OTPC
Speckled with glints of star and moonshine. Mr. Walter de la Mare Makes the Little Ones Dizzy. Samuel Hoffenstein. SiTL
Spectator ab Extra. Arthur Hugh Clough. OxBoLi; SiTL
"As I sat at the cafe I said to myself," *also in* Dipsychus. ALV; FiBHP; LiTG
Specter, The. Ernst Hardt, *tr. fr. German by* Jethro Bithell. AWP
Specter's Tale, The. Yetza Gillespie. DaM
Spectra, *sel.* Witter Bynner.
"If I were only dafter," *st.* 1 *fr.* Opus 6. LiTM
Spectral Lovers. John Crowe Ransom. SPP; TCPD; TriL
Spectre, The. Walter de la Mare. WhC
Spectre Boat, The. Thomas Campbell. UnW
Spectre Ship, The. Thomas Stephens Collier. EtS
Spectres. Samuel Minturn Peck. BAP
Spectrum, The. Cosmo Monkhouse. VA
Specula. Thomas Edward Brown. OQP; QP-1
Speculative. Robert Browning. EPN; PoVP
Speculative Evening. Marguerite Young. LiTA
Speech, A. Thaddeus Mason Harris. MeMeAg
Speech after long silence; it is right. After Long Silence. W. B. Yeats. CaAE; EnLoPo; GTBS-W; HoPM; LiTL; LiTM; OBMV; POTE; TwP; UnPo
Speech, both pithy and concise, A. "Exactly So." Lady T. Hastings. BOHV
Speech for the Repeal of the McCarran Act. Richard Wilbur. NePoAm
Speech of Abbot Stephen. Petar Petrovic Njegos, *tr. fr. Serbian by* James William Wiles. *Fr.* The Mountain Wreath. PoFr
Speech of Emer, The. William Larminie. *Fr.* Fand. TIP
Speech of Night, The. Michelangelo, *tr. fr. Italian by* John Addington Symonds. OnPM
Speech of the Dead, The. Anne Ridler. ChMP
Speech to a Crowd. Archibald MacLeish. MoAB; MoAmPo; NePA
Speech to Those Who Say Comrade. Archibald MacLeish. AmPP; BoFr; OxBA; PoLFOT; PreP; ReaPo
Speechless Sorrow sat with me. The Guest. Harriet McEwen Kimball. AA; LEAP
Speechless tree and animal and bird. A Lesson from Van Gogh. Howard Moss. MoAB
"Speed not afar, thou wandering Wraith." Heaven and Hell. Sir William Watson. QS
Speed on, speed on, good Master! The Walker of the Snow. Charles Dawson Shanly. BoCaPo (1943 ed.); OnYI; UnW; VA
Speed Track, The. "Peter." BoTP
Speke, Parrot. John Skelton. *See* Speak, Parrot.

Spell, The. Medora Addison. HBMV
Spell, The. John Gay. DD; HOAH
Spell, The. Henry Martyn Hoyt. HBMV
Spell, A. George Peele. *Fr.* The Old Wives' Tale. ChTr
Spell Eva back and Ave shall you find. Our Lady's Salutation. Robert Southwell. ISi
Spell is past, the dream is o'er, The. We Never Speak as We Pass By. *Unknown.* TreFS
Spell of Creation. Kathleen Raine. FaBoCh; LoGBV; WaKn
Spell of France, The. Edmund Blunden. POTE
Spell of Invisibility, A. *At. to* Christopher Marlowe. ChTr
Spell of Sleep. Kathleen Raine. HaMV
Spell of the Pool, The. L. Burton Crane, Jr. NLK
Spell of the Yukon, The. Robert W. Service. BLPA; FaBoBe; FaFP; NeHB; TreF
Spelling Bee at Angels, The. Bret Harte. StPo
Spelling with love the Word among the flowers. Holy Thursday. Leonard McCarthy. JKCP (1955 ed.)
Spells. Thomas Campion. *See* Thrice Toss These Oaken Ashes in the Air.
Spells. James Reeves. AlDL; PoMS
Spelt from Sibyl's Leaves. Gerard Manley Hopkins. ChMo; CoBMV; CoEV; FaBoMo; LiTM; MaPo; MoPo; ViPP; VLEP
Spend and God will send, but wot ye what follows. John Davies of Hereford. SiCE
Spending and Sparing. Hesiod, *tr. fr. Greek by* Sir William Marris. *Fr.* Works and Days. OxBG
(Golden Mean of Thrift, *tr. by* Arthur S. Way.) GrR
Spending hand that alway poureth out, A. To Sir Francis Brian. Sir Thomas Wyatt. Satires, III. SiPS
Spendthrift. Vega Curl. CAG
Spendthrift. Sister M. Genoveva. SaFP
Spenser! a jealous honorer of thine. To Spenser. Keats. CoBE
Spenserian Stanzas on Charles Armitage Brown. Keats. InMe
(Portrait, A.) BOHV; PA
Spenser's Ireland. Marianne Moore. GTBS-W; LiTA; LiTG; LiTM (rev. ed.); NePA; OxBA
Spent purpose of a perfectly marvellous, The. In Favor of One's Time. Frank O'Hara. NeAP
Spent Wave. John Hall Wheelock. LiTM (1946 ed.)
Sphere of Glass, The. John Lehmann. ChMP
Sphere, which is as many thousand spheres, A. Shelley. *Fr.* Prometheus Unbound. ImOP
Sphinx, The. Henry Howard Brownell. AA
Sphinx, The. Lord Alfred Douglas. PtOT
Sphinx, The. Emerson. AmPP (3d ed.); IAP; MOAP; OxBA; REAL
Sphinx. D. H. Lawrence. MoP
Sphinx, The. Agnes Repplier. *See* Le Repos en Egypte.
Sphinx, The. James Thomson. The City of Dreadful Night, XX. EPN
("I sat me weary on a pillar's base.") OAEP; POTT
Sphinx, The. Oscar Wilde. PoVP; ViPP; VLEP
"How subtle-secret is your smile," *sel.* MBP; MoBrPo
Sphinx is drowsy, The. The Sphinx. Emerson. AmPP (3d ed.); IAP; MOAP; OxBA; REAL
Sphinx Speaks, The. Francis Saltus Saltus. AA; BAP; LEAP; OBAV
Sphinx with lion's feet, The. The Phoenix. Theodore Spencer. CrMA
Spice-Tree, The. John Sterling. LPS-2
Spicewood. Lizette Woodworth Reese. BLV; MAP; MoAmPo; MOAP; NeMA; SPP
Spider, The. Robert P. Tristram Coffin. ImOP; OTPC (1946 ed.); PoeMoYo
Spider, The. A. P. Herbert. RIS
Spider, The. David McCord. MAP
Spider, The. César Vallejo, *tr. fr. Spanish.* AnCL, *tr. by* Donald Devenish Walsh; TwSpPo, *tr. by* H. R. Hays
Spider and His Wife, The. Jane Taylor. OTPC (1923 ed.)
Spider and the Fly, The, *abr.* John Heywood. ReIE
Spider and the Fly, The. Mary Howitt. BeLS; FaFP; FaPON; GFA; HBV; HBVY; OHFP; OnHT; OnSP; OTPC; RIS; TreFS; TVC; TVSH; WBLP
Spider, from his flaming sleep. Little City. Robert Horan. CrMA; LiTM (rev. ed.); NePA
Spider in the bath, A. The image noted. The Image. Roy Fuller. ChMP; PoN
Spider Silverlegs. Carolyn Sherwin Bailey. PCH
Spider! Spider! The Spider's Web. Charlotte Druitt Cole. GFA
Spider spreads her webs, whether she be, The. Letter to Maria Gisborne. Shelley. GEPC
Spider weaves his silver wire, The. Of a Spider. Wilfrid Thorley. BrR; FaPON
Spider Web, The. Mattie Lee Hausgen. GFA
Spider Webs. James S. Tippett. UTS
Spiders are spinning their webs. Mid-August. Louise Driscoll. MW; YeAr
Spider's Web, The. Charlotte Druitt Cole. GFA
Spiel of the Three Mountebanks. John Crowe Ransom. MAP; MoAB; MoAmPo
Spight of Fortune, The. Shakespeare. *See* Sonnets, XC
Spike of Green, A. Barbara Baker. AlDL
Spikenard. Laurence Houseman. TrPWD
Spiky children pour through resined schools, The. Childhood and Age. Diana Witherby. PoN
Spilled Flame. Joseph Auslander. BAP
Spilled into the cup. Bubbling Wine. Abu Zakariya. MooP
Spin cheerfully. Leave the Thread with God. *Unknown.* BLRP
Spin, Dame, spin. *Unknown.* OxNR
Spin, daughter Mary, spin. The Making of Viola. Francis Thompson. POTT; PoVP
Spin Love from Out Your Heart. Adam Mickiewicz, *tr. fr. Polish by* Dorothea Prall Radin. BoFr
Spindle-wood, spindle-wood, will you lend me, pray. Alms in Autumn. Rose Fyleman. NLK; PCH
Spinks, The. Don Marquis. LEAP
Spinner, The. "Madeline Bridges." AA
Spinner, The. Charles L. O'Donnell. GoBC; ISi
Spinners at Willowsleigh. Marya Zaturenska. HBMV; TBM
Spinner's Song, The. Clemens Brentano, *tr. fr. German by* Wyatt A. Surrey. AnGP
Spinner's Song, The. Kathleen Millay. BAP
Spinning. Helen Hunt Jackson. BLP; CV; HBV; LBAP; OQP; QP-1; TCAP
Spinning Heart, The. John Berryman. LiTM (1946 ed.)
Spinning in April. Josephine Preston Peabody. HBV
Spinning Song, A. John Francis O'Donnell. IrPN; TIP
Spinning Song. Edith Sitwell. MBP; MoAB; MoBrPo
Spinning Top, The. Sister Mary Angelita. WHL
Spinning Top. Frank Dempster Sherman. GFA
Spinning-Wheel. Hakushu Kitahara, *tr. fr. Japanese by* Takamichi Ninomiya *and* D. J. Enright. PoLJ
Spinning Wheel, The. A. M. Klein. CaP
Spinning-Wheel, The. John Francis Waller. AnIV; ChTr; StPo; TIP
(Spinning-Wheel Song, The.) LPS-1; VA
Spinning-wheel, spinning-wheel—quiet and deep hums the hand-spinning. Spinning-Wheel. Hakushu Kitahara. PoLJ
Spinning Woman, The. Leonidas of Tarentum, *tr. fr. Greek by* Andrew Lang. AWP; JAWP; WBP
Spinoza. Thomas S. Jones, Jr. MuM
Spinozaism, A. John Swanwick Drennan. IrPN
Spinster Song. Virginia Lyne Tunstall. HBMV
Spinsterish/ silver/ Before the shuttered window. Men Walked To and Fro. Blanaid Salkeld. NeIP
Spinster's Stint, A. Alice Cary. LPS-1
Spiral, The. John Holmes. MiAP
Spire cranes, The. Its statue is an aviary. Poem. Dylan Thomas. MoWP
Spires of Oxford, The. Winifred M. Letts. BEL; BLP; BMEP; CV; EnLit; FaFP; HBV; HiLiEn; InP; LBBV; LEAP; MaRV; MCCG; NeHB; OHFP; OnYI; PoMa; PoRA; POT; PoTo; PYM; TCEP; TOP; TreF; VOD (1931 ed.); WGRP
Spirit, The. Harold Lenoir Davis. NP
Spirit and the Bride, The, *sels.* Elsa Barker. HBMV
Caresses.
Confession.
Consummation.
Fulfilment.
Inscription, The: "Sealed with the seal of Life, thy soul and mine."
Love's Immortality.
Spirit breathes upon the Word, The. The Spirit's Light. William Cowper. BLRP
Spirit from Whom Our Lives Proceed. Howard Chandler Robbins. TrPWD
Spirit going with me here. Time and Spirit. Léonie Adams. MOAP; NLK (1947 ed.)
Spirit has its passion as the sense, The. Monasticism. Aubrey Thomas De Vere. PraNu
Spirit haunts the year's last hours, A. Song. Tennyson. AtBAP; CBE; EmBrPo; GEPC; GTML; GTSL; InvP; KN; LEAP; NBE; OAEP; PoEL-5; PoVP; TOP; ViPP; VLEP
Spirit in me/ why are you so sad? Sadness. F. S. Flint. MBP; MoBrPo (1942 ed.)
Spirit, in Our Hearts, The. H. U. Onderdonk. BePJ
Spirit is caged, they said, its prison flesh. The Master-Welder. Sarah Wingate Taylor. JKCP (1955 ed.)
Spirit-Land, The. Jones Very. AnAmPo; LA; LPS-2
(Present Heaven, The.) IAP
Spirit long shaping for sublime endeavor. Woodrow Wilson. Katharine Lee Bates. GA
Spirit Muses, A. Franklin B. Williams. CAG
Spirit of beauty walks the hills, A. The Return of Spring. Bayard Taylor. ADAH
Spirit of Britannia, The. Ode to the Germans. Thomas Campbell. PoFr
Spirit of Christ my sanctification. Prayer. *Unknown.* CAW

Spirit of death, so soft, so sweet. Epitaph. John Bruce MacCallum. PoP
Spirit of Delight. Shelley. *See* Song: "Rarely, rarely comest thou."
Spirit of Earth, with still, restoring hands, The. The Last Furrow. Edwin Markham. AA
Spirit of "fire and dew." To O. S. C. Annie Eliot Trumbull. AA
Spirit of Freedom, The, *abr.* *Unknown.* PoFr
Spirit of Freedom, Thou Dost Love the Sea. Henry Nehemiah Dodge. EtS
Spirit of God [Descend upon My Heart]. George Croly. MaRV; PraP
Spirit of man shall triumph and reign o'er all the earth, The. A Psalm of Confidence. Horace Westwood, *at. also to* Stanton Coit. MaRV
Spirit of Night, The. Thomas Rogers. ElL
Spirit of old summers long departed, The. Going Upstairs. Arnold Wall. MM
Spirit of Plato. *Unknown, tr. fr. Greek by* Shelley. AWP; JAWP; LiA; UnW; WBP
(Epigram: "Eagle! why soarest thou above that tomb?") EnLi-1
(Plato's Tomb.) FaBoCh; LoGBV; OxBG
Spirit of Poetry, The. Longfellow. CoBA; IAP; MOAP
Spirit of Sadness. Richard Le Gallienne. HBV
Spirit of self-sacrifice, The. Christ's Giving. Anna E. Hamilton. ChIP; OQP; QP-1
Spirit of shades and shadows, The. Vale. *Unknown.* CAG
Spirit of Shakespeare, The. George Meredith. BMEP; EmBrPo; EPN; PoVP; PtP; VA; ViPo
Spirit of song, whose shining wings have borne. Song and Science. Milicent Washburn Shinn. AA
Spirit of Spring, thy coverlet of snow. The Waking of Spring. Olive Custance. VA
Spirit of the Birch, The. Arthur Ketchum. *Fr.* Legends for Trees. MPB; MW; OHIP; SP
Spirit of the *Bluenose,* The. Claire Harris MacIntosh. CaP
Spirit of the Fall, The. Danske Dandridge. AA; LBAP
Spirit of the Fountain never dies, The. *Unknown, tr. fr. Chinese.* Tao Teh Ching, III. WhP
Spirit of the Lord is upon me, The. Good Tidings. St. Luke, Bible, *N.T.* MaRV
Spirit of the *Maine,* The. Tudor Jenks. AA; MC; PAH
Spirit of the Mountain, The. Chu Yuan, *tr. fr. Chinese by* Shen Yu-ting. *Fr.* The Nine Songs. WhP
Spirit of the Saints, The. Jalal ed-Din Rumi, *tr. fr. Persian by* R. A. Nicholson. PeP
Spirit of the Time-to-be, The. Resurgence. Laura Bell Everett. PGD
Spirit of the Wheat, The. Edward A. U. Valentine. AA
Spirit of the world, The. Heine. Matthew Arnold. *Fr.* Heine's Grave. BPN
Spirit of Twilight, through your folded wings. Twilight. Olive Custance. CAW; HBV; JKCP; VA
Spirit of Wine, The. W. E. Henley. Echoes, XLI. HBV
Spirit of Wisdom and of Love. Sir William Rowan Hamilton. ES
(O Brooding Spirit.) GTIV
(Prayer, A: "O brooding Spirit of Wisdom and of Love.") IrPN
Spirit of wordless love! that in the lone. Love. James Clarence Mangan. IrPN
Spirit seems to pass, A. Lausanne. Thomas Hardy. EmBrPo; FaBoTw; TriL; ViPo
Spirit, Silken Thread. Margot Ruddock. OBMV
Spirit speeding down on All Soul's Eve, A. The One Forgotten. Dora Sigerson Shorter. PoRL; TIP
Spirit that breathest through my lattice. The Evening Wind. Bryant. AA; AnNE; APW; BAP; BAV; CoBA; IAP; LaNeLa; LPS-2; MCCG; MOAP; PIR; REAL; TCAP
Spirit! that dwellest where. Song [*or* Song of Nesace]. Poe. *Fr.* Al Aaraaf. APW; CoBA
Spirit That Form'd This Scene. Walt Whitman. IAP
Spirit that moves the sap in spring. A Prelude. Maurice Thompson. HBV; LBAP
Spirit Tower, The. *Unknown, tr. fr. Chinese.* WhP
Spirit Watches, The. Ruth Pitter. TriL
Spirit, who lov'st Britannia's Isle. Fragment. Blake. RO
Spirit who sweepest the wild Harp of Time. Ode to the Departing Year. Samuel Taylor Coleridge. EmBrPo; EnRP
Spirit Whose Work Is Done. Walt Whitman. CoV
Spiritism. Robert Hillyer. WHL
Spirits. Robert Bridges. *See* Angel Spirits of Sleep.
Spirits and illusions have died. Life from the Lifeless. Robinson Jeffers. ChMo
Spirits and Men, *sels.* Ebenezer Elliott.
"Again a child, where childhood rov'd, I run." EnSW
I sing of men and angels." OBRV
Spirit's Epochs, The. Coventry Patmore. The Angel in the House, I, viii, 3. EPP; GoBC
("Not in the crisis of events.") EG
Spirits Everywhere. Ludwig Uhland, *tr. fr. German by* James Clarence Mangan. AWP
Spirit's Grace, The. Janie Screven Heyward. HBMV
Spirit's House. Sara Teasdale. Interlude: Songs Out of Sorrow, I. OQP; QP-1; QS
Spirit's Light, The. William Cowper. BLRP
Spirits of patriots, hail in heaven again. The Flag. George Henry Boker. FOAH; HH
Spirits of the Dead. Poe. APW; TriL
Spirits of the dead are with us still, The. The Unseen World. Craven Langstroth Betts. OQP; QP-1
Spirits of well-shot woodcock, partridge, snipe. "New King Arrives in His Capital by Air . . ."—Daily Newspaper. John Betjeman. OxBoLi; WhC
Spirit's Song, The. Arthur Hugh Clough. *See* "There Is No God," the Wicked Saith.
Spirit's Song in "Prometheus." Shelley. *See* Poet's Dream, The.
Spirit's Warfare, The. Blake. *See* Morning.
Spiritual Canticle between the Soul and Christ. St. John of the Cross. *See* Song of the Soul and the Bridegroom.
Spiritual Explorations, *sel.* Stephen Spender.
"I am that witness through whom the whole," VI. PoLFOT
Spiritual Gifts. First Corinthians, XII: 1–XIII: 13, Bible, *N.T.* WoL
Spiritual Isolation. Isaac Rosenberg. TrJP
Spiritual Love. William Caldwell Roscoe. OBVV
Spiritual Passion. George Barlow. OBVV
Spiritual Song, A. Franz Werfel, *tr. fr. German by* Elizabeth Selden. BoFr
Spiritual, the carnal, are one, The. Dorothy Wellesley. *Fr.* Matrix. OBMV
Spiritual Vision. Solomon Solis-Cohen. MaRV
Spirituality. Samuel Greenberg. LiTA
Spiritus Intactus. Robert Germain Cole. CAG
Spiritus Sanctus. Sara Jackson. DiM
Spirk Troll-Derisive. James Whitcomb Riley. BOHV; LBN; NA
Spit-Bug, The. William H. Matchett. WaKn
Spit in my face you Jews, and pierce my side. Holy Sonnets, XI. John Donne. EPS; OBS; OxBoCh; SeEP
Spite hath no power to make me sad. Sir Thomas Wyatt. SiPS
Spite o' the tempests a-blowin'. "Tollable Well!" Frank L. Stanton. FaFP
Spiteful will slander, the timid will clamor, The. A Man. Arthur Guiterman. LPS-1
Spitz, dear Spitz, for a moment come here. Pug-Dog and Spitz. F. Hey. SAS
Splash of darkness on the face of day, A. The Crow. Albert Durrant Watson. CPG; OCL
Splashing along the boggy woods all day. Together. Siegfried Sassoon. AlDL
Spleen ("The bored rain-god spills his irritation over"). Baudelaire, *tr. fr. French by* David Paul. MiFP
(Spleen LXXV: "January, angry at the whole damned town," *tr. by* Warren Carrier.) ReMP
Spleen ("When the oppressive sky weighs like a cover"). Baudelaire, *tr. fr. French by* Barbara Gibbs. AnFP
Spleen ("Let us go hence"). Ernest Dowson. MBP; MoBrPo
Spleen, The. Matthew Green. EiPP
Sels.
"And may my humble dwelling stand." LoBV
"But now more serious let me grow." PoEL-3
Cure for the Spleen, A. OBEC
Idyll. BeR
On Even Keel [with Gentle Gale]. BeR; CoEV; OBEC
(Voyage of Life, The.) LPS-3
"This motley piece," *abr.* CEP
Spleen. Paul Verlaine, *tr. fr. French by* Ernest Dowson. AWP; EnLi-2; JAWP; OnPM; WBP
Spleen, The, *sel.* Countess of Winchilsea.
"O'er me alas. thou dost too much prevail." BeR
Spleen LXXV. Baudelaire. *See* Spleen ("The bored rain-god").
Splendid and Terrible [Your Love]. "Seumas O'Sullivan." HBMV; NP
Splendid burns the huge house with bronze. An Armoury. Alcaeus. OxBG; WaaP
Splendid Fellow, A. H. C. Dodge. BOHV
Splendid Flower, The. Etta May Van Tassel. JKCP (1955 ed.)
Splendid glories of the past, The. The Garden of the Gold Valley. Tu Mu. WhP
Splendid Isolation. Katharine Lee Bates. LHV
Splendid Lover, The. John Richard Moreland. ChIP; PGD
Splendid moon shines on the fiery night, The. *Unknown, tr. fr. Chinese.* The Nineteen Han Poems, VII. WhP
Splendid Shilling, The. John Philips. BOHV; CEP; EiPP; EV-3; LPS-3
Thirsty Poet, The, *sel.* OBEC
Splendid Spur, The. Sir Arthur Quiller-Couch. BMEP; HBV; HBVY; LBBV; LEAP; VA
Splendid Village, The, *sel.* Ebenezer Elliott.
"Path of the quiet fields! that oft of yore." EnSW

Splendidis Longum Valedico Nugis. Sir Philip Sidney. *See* Leave Me, O Love . . . .
Splendor [*or* Splendour] Falls [on Castle Walls], The. Tennyson. *See* Bugle Song.
Splendour is mine and power and loneliness! Sun-Song. Mary Josephine Benson. CPG
Splendour of my Spring I destroy here, The. Abishag. Jacob Fichman. TrJP
Splendor of the kindling day, The. Fluttered Wings. Christina Rossetti. VA
Splendor of Thine Eyes, The. Moses ibn Ezra, *tr. fr. Hebrew by* Solomon Solis-Cohen. TrJP
Splendor-throned Queen, immortal Aphrodite. Ode to Aphrodite. Sappho. EnLi-1; OuHeWo
Splendours of this passing world, The. "Peace Is the Tranquillity of Order." Robert Wilberforce. GoBC; JKCP (1955 ed.)
Spliced between Milan and Carthage this strip of days. Moment in Ostia. Sister Mary Thérèse. JKCP (1955 ed.)
Splinter. Carl Sandburg. FaPON; SUS; TiPo; UTS
Splinter, The. James Kenneth Stephen. CenHV
Splitting of his cheek, The. The Portent. Ibn al-Zaqqaq. MooP
Spoil. William E. Brooks. QS
Spoil not her rest by singing threnodies. In Memory of Mother Seraphine Ireland. Sister Maris Stella. PraNu
Spoils of War, The. Vernon Watkins. WaP
Spoke my heart in the dearth of the night. John Francis O'Donnell. *Fr.* Ossian. IrPN
Spoken at a Castle Gate. Donald Davidson. MAP; MoAmPo (1942 ed.)
Spoken by the God Pan. *Unknown, tr. fr. Greek by* Lord Neaves. OnPM
Spoken Extempore. Earl of Rochester. SeCePo
Spoken Is But the Surface Foam, The. *Unknown.* DDA
Spoken through Glass. Eithne Wilkins. NeBP
"Spoken Word, The." Christopher Morley. PoFr
Spontaneous Me. Walt Whitman. OxBA
Spontaneous Us! Presto Furioso. Sir Owen Seaman. BOHV
Spooks. Nathalia Crane. StaSt
Spool of Thread, A. Sophie E. Eastman. PAH
Spoon River Anthology, *sels.* Edgar Lee Masters.
Aaron Hatfield. LiTA; NP
Alexander Throckmorton. BAP; SBMV
Anne [*or* Ann] Rutledge. AmP; BAP; ChMo; CMP; CP; FaFP; InPo; LiTA; LiTM (rev. ed.); LoPo; MAP; MoAmPo; MoVE; NeHB; NeMA; NePA; NP; NV; OHFP; OxBA; PaA; PG (1945 ed.); PYM; SBMV; TCAP; TrGrPo; VOD
Archibald Higbie. InP; NP
Arlo Will. ChMo; CMP; LiTA; NP
Benjamin Pantier. AlBD
Bert Kessler. AnFE; APA; CoAnAm
"Butch" Weldy. NePA
Carl Hamblin. AmP; ChMo; CMP; LiTA; LiTM (rev. ed.)
Cassius Hueffer. OxBA
Daisy Fraser. MoVE; NP
Davis Matlock. ChMo; CMP; LiTA; LiTM (rev. ed.)
Doc Hill. BAP; NP
Doctor Meyers. ChMo; CMP
Editor Whedon. CrMA; NP; OxBA
Edmund Pollard. AnFE; APA; CoAnAm
Elliott Hawkins. OxBA
Elsa Wertman. OxBA
Emily Sparks. BoFr
English Thornton. OxBA
Father Malloy. NP; OxBA
Fiddler Jones. AmP; LiTA; LoGBV; NP; OxBA; TrGrPo; UnS
George Gray. TOP
Hamilton Greene. OxBA
Hare Drummer. TOP
Harmon Whitney. SBMV
Henry C. Calhoun. AmP; LiTA; LiTM (rev. ed.); NP
Herman Altman. OxBA
Hill, The. AmP; ExPo; LiTA; LiTM; NePA; NP; OxBA; ReMP; SeCeV; ViBoPo
Isaiah Beethoven. NV
J. Milton Miles. CrMA
Jacob Godbey. ChMo; CMP; LiTA
James Garber. ChMo; CMP
John Hancock Otis. PoFr; TOP
John Horace Burleson. CrMA
John Wasson. LaNeLa
Jonathan Houghton. OxBA
Julia Miller. MoVE
Knowlt Hoheimer. OxBA
Lucinda Matlock. BAP; BAV; ChMo; CMP; CP; InP; LaNeLa; LiTA; LiTL; LiTM; MAP; MCCG; MoAmPo; MotAn; MoVE; NeMA; NP; NV; OnPP; OxBA; ReMP
Mrs. Meyers. ChMo; CMP
Mrs. Williams. NAMP
Mollie [*or* Ollie] McGee. BAP; NP
Perry Zoll. CrMA; NP
Petit, the Poet. AnFE; APA; ChMo; CMP; CoAnAm; InPo; LaNeLa; LoGBV; MAP; MoAmPo; MoVE; NeMA; OxBA
Reuben Pantier. BoFr
Rutherford McDowell. LiTA; NP; OxBA; SBMV; TOP
Scholfield Huxley. ChMo; CMP; LiTA; MoPo; TrPWD
Seth Compton. ChMo; CMP; LiTA; NP
Sexsmith the Dentist. NePA
Thomas Rhodes. NP
Thomas Trevelyan. AnFE; APA; CoAnAm; MoPo; SBMV
Village Atheist, The. AmP; ChMo; CMP; LiTA; MaRV
Washington McNeeley. SBMV
Webster Ford. NP
William H. Herndon. NP; SBMV; TOP
William Jones. ImOP
Spoon River Anthology. Edwin Meade Robinson. Limericised Classics, V. HBMV
Sport. Abraham Cowley. *Fr.* Love's Riddle. EPS (1942 ed.); SeCL
(Song: "Merry waves dance up and down, and play, The.") AlDL
Sport. Hamlin Garland. BAP
Sport, an adventitious sprout, A. Perspective. Margaret Avison. BoCaPo (1948 ed.); PeCV
Sport-Fellows, The. Li Po, *tr. fr. Chinese by* Shigeyoshi Obata. BoFr
Sport for Gods. Jewell Bothwell Tull. CIV
Sporting Cowboy, The, *with music. Unknown.* OuSiCo
Sporting through the forest wide. Little Children. Mary Howitt. PRWS
Sporting white-throat on some twig's end borne, The. Thrush and Blackthorn. Robert Bloomfield. *Fr.* The Farmer's Boy. RO
Sportive Love-god in this worldly sea, The. The Angler. Bhartrihari. LiTW
Sports and gallantries, the stage, the arts, the antics of dancers. Boats in a Fog. Robinson Jeffers. AmPP; OxBA; TCPD
Sportsman's Prayer, A. *Unknown.* MaRV
Sportsmen in Paradise. T. P. Cameron Wilson. BMEP; PoMa
Sporus. Pope. *Fr.* Epistle to Dr. Arbuthnot. AWP; ChTr; JAWP; LPS-3; MaPo; WBP
(Characters from the Satires: Sporus.) InPo
("Let Sporus tremble—What? that thing of silk.") ViBoPo
(Lord Hervey.) CoEV
Spotless Maid, The. Vincent McNabb. ISi
Spotted cow that's light and freckled. The Woman of Llyn y Fan's Call to Her Cattle. *Unknown.* PrWP
Spotted hawk swoops by and accuses me, The. My Barbaric Yawp. Walt Whitman. *Fr.* Song of Myself. CoBA; CoV; NePA; PoLFOT; TrGrPo
Spouse. Witter Bynner. AnFE; CoAnAm
Spouse I Do Hate. William Wycherley. *Fr.* Love in a Wood. OAEP
Spouse of Christ, The. D. A. Casey. JKCP; PraNu
Spouse! Sister! Angel! Pilot of the Fate. Shelley. *Fr.* Epipsychidion. BCEP; ChER; LoPS
Spouse to the Beloved, The. William Baldwin. *See* Christ, My Beloved.
Spratt vs. Spratt. Louis Untermeyer. *See* Owen Seaman.
Sprawled on the bags and crates in the rear of the truck. El Aghir. Norman Cameron. FaBoTw
Spray of Honeysuckle, A. Mary Emily Bradley. AA
Spray of song that springs in April, light of love that laughs through May. The Sunbows. Swinburne. BPN; EmBrPo; EPN
Spraying the Potatoes. Patrick Kavanagh. OxBI
Spread the board with linen snow. Invitation to the Dance. Sidonius Apollinarius. AWP
Spread the feast, and let there be. The Wedding Morning. Francis Ledwidge. TCPD
Spread the Light. John Oxenham. PraP
Spread thy close curtain, love-performing night. Juliet's Yearning. Shakespeare. *Fr.* Romeo and Juliet, III, ii. TreFS
Spread We Our Nets. Bilhana, *formerly at. to* Chauras, *tr. fr. Sanskrit by* E. Powys Mathers. *Fr.* Black Marigolds. OnPM
Spreeng ees com', Da; but oh, da joy. Da Leetla Boy. T. A. Daly. CP; CV; HBV; NV; PoTo; YT
'Spress! Jimmy Garthwaite. GFA
Sprig Fever. Margaret Fishback. BOHV
Sprig of Lime, The. Robert Nichols. MM; POTE; TwCV
Sprightly youth, The. Bathing. James Thomson. *Fr.* The Seasons: Summer. LPS-2
Sprin' Fevah. Ray Garfield Dandridge. BANP
Spring. William Allingham. IrPN
Spring, The. William Barnes. HBV
Spring. Harry Behn. TiPo

Spring. Muggurdich Beshigtashlian, *tr. fr. Armenian by* Zabelle C. Boyajian. ArmLP
Spring. Song of Solomon, Bible, *O.T. See* For, Lo, the Winter Is Past.
Spring. Blake. *Fr.* Songs of Innocence. BoChLi; BoTP; FaBoCh; FaPON; GoTP; KN; LoGBV; MoShBr; OTPC; RIS; SUS; TiPo (1952 ed.); YeAr
Spring. Anne Bradstreet. *Fr.* The Four Seasons of the Year. AnNE; TCAP
Spring. The. Thomas Carew. *See* Now That the Winter's Gone.
Spring. John Alden Carpenter. RIS
Spring, The. Chang Chung-sur, *tr. fr. Chinese by* W. J. B. Fletcher. OnPM
Spring. Chu Shu Chen. *tr. fr. Chinese by* Kenneth Rexroth. OnPC
Spring. Marchette Chute. TiPo (1959 ed.)
Spring. William Cornish. *See* Pleasure It Is.
Spring, The. Abraham Cowley. *Fr.* The Mistress. ElSeCe; EPS (1942 ed.); EV-2; LO; MeLP; OBS; ReEn; SeEP (Love's Absence in the Spring.) LiTL
Spring. E. E. Cummings. *See* Spring Is like a Perhaps Hand.
Spring Aubrey Thomas De Vere. *Fr.* The Year of Sorrow: Ireland—1849. IrPN; TIP
Spring. Gerardo Diego, *tr. fr. Spanish by* Eleanor L. Turnbull. CoSP
Spring. Ebenezer Elliott. EV-4; LPS-2
Spring. John Gould Fletcher. NV; PFY; SBMV
Spring. Jean Föyen, *tr. fr. Norwegian by* Charles W. Stork. AnNoLy
Spring, The. Rose Fyleman. BrR; FaPON
Spring. Norman Gale. NLK
Spring, The. Théophile Gautier, *tr. fr. French by* Alan Conder. TrFP
Spring. Caroline Giltinan. HBMV
Spring. Thorsteinn Gíslason, *tr. fr. Icelandic by* Skuli Johnson. IcP
Spring. Thomas Gray. *See* Ode on the Spring.
Spring. Giovanni Battista Guarini, *tr. fr. Italian by* Leigh Hunt. AWP; JAWP; OnPM; WBP
Spring. Hannes Hafstein, *tr. fr. Icelandic by* Jakobina Johnson. IcP
Spring. Gerard Manley Hopkins. AlDL; BLV; BoLiVe; FaBoEn; InvP; JKCP; LiTM; MaPo; MBP; MoAB; MoBrPo; MoVE; OAEP (2d ed.); OBMV; OnHM; OxBoCh; PoLi; TwCV; ViP; ViPP; VLEP
("Nothing is so beautiful as spring.") EG; LO
Spring. Horace, *tr. fr. Latin by* J. O. Sargent. Odes, I, 4. RoL
Spring. Richard Hovey. ADAH, *abr.*; NLK, *abr.*
Sels.
"I said in my heart, 'I am sick of four walls and a ceiling.'" BBV (1951 ed.); PoMa
Stein Song, A. CP; HBV; LA; MAP; MoAmPo (1942 ed); NeMA; PFY
("Give a rouse, then, in the Maytime.") AnAmPo
Spring. Hovhannes Hovhannessian, *tr. fr. Armenian by* Zabelle C. Boyajian. ArmLP
Spring. Mary Howitt. PEOR
Spring. Thomas Caulfield Irwin. IrPN
Spring. Orrick Johns. InMe
Spring. Toyohiko Kagawa, *tr. fr. Japanese by* Lois J. Erickson. SoLD
Spring. Kalidasa, *tr. fr. Sanskrit by* Arthur W. Ryder. *Fr.* The Seasons. AWP
Spring. Robert Loveman. AA
Spring ("O little city-gals, don't never go it"). James Russell Lowell. *Fr.* The Biglow Papers, 2nd Series, No. VI. MCCG
Spring, The. John Lyly. *See* Trico's Song.
Spring. John Charles McNeill. NoCaPo
Spring. Anne Elizabeth Maddock. OQP; QP-2
Spring ("Now the bright crocus flames"). Meleager. *See* In the Spring.
Spring ("Now Winter's winds are banished from the sky"). Meleager, *tr. fr. Greek by* William M. Hardinge. AWP; JAWP; WBP
Spring. Charlotte Mew. *See* In the Fields.
Spring. Edna St. Vincent Millay. MAP; MoAB; MoAmPo; NePA; NP
Spring, *sel.* William Miller.
"Spring comes linking and jinking through the woods, The." AlDL
Spring. Thomas Moore, *after the Greek of* Anacreon. LPS-2
Spring. David Morton. *Fr.* Sonnets from a Hospital. TBM
Spring. Thomas Nashe. *See* Spring, the Sweet Spring.
Spring, The. John Francis O'Donnell. IrPN
Spring ("The year has changed his mantle cold"). Charles d'Orléans, *tr. fr. French by* Andrew Lang. AWP; JAWP; LiA; WBP
(Return of Spring: "Now Time throws off his cloak again," *tr. by* Longfellow.) ADAH
(Rondeau: "Year his winter cloak lets fall, The," *tr. by* J. G. Legge.) LiTW
(Rondel: "Year has put his cloak away, The," *tr. by* R. N. Currey.) FoS
(Spring: "Time hath laid his mantle by, The," *tr. unknown.*) DD; LPS-2
(Year Hath Doffed His Cloak To-Day, The, *tr. by* Alan Conder.) TrFP
Spring ("How many buds"). Boris Pasternak, *tr. fr. Russian by* Babette Deutsch. LiTW; TrRV
Spring ("It's spring, I leave a street"). Boris Pasternak, *tr. fr. Russian by* C. M. Bowra. BoRS
(Spring: "I've come from the street," *tr. by* Babette Deutsch.) TrRV
Spring. Pindar, *tr. fr. Greek by* F. L. Lucas. GrPE
Spring, The. Ezra Pound. MOAP; Po; TBM
Spring. W. R. Rogers. AnIL; OnYI
Spring. Pierre de Ronsard, *tr. fr. French by* Alan Conder. Odes, I, 17. TrFP
("Sweet-heart, come see if the rose," *tr. by* Curtis Hidden Page.) PrPoCR
Spring. Isaac Rosenberg. TrJP
Spring. Christina Rossetti. BPN
Spring. Dante Gabriel Rossetti. EmBrPo
Spring. V. Sackville-West. *Fr.* The Land. MoP
Spring. Shakespeare. *See* When Daisies Pied and Violets Blue.
Spring. Shelley. *Fr.* The Revolt of Islam. EV-4
Spring. Edith Sitwell. OAEP (2d ed.)
Spring. Christopher Smart. *Fr.* St. Philip and St. James. OBEC
("Now the winds are all composure.") LoBV
Spring. André Spire, *tr. fr. French by* Jethro Bithell. AWP
Spring. Thomas Stanley, *after the Greek of* Anacreon. AWP; JAWP; SeCL; WBP
Spring. Earl of Surrey. *See* Description of Spring.
Spring. Su T'ung-po, *tr. fr. Chinese by* Kenneth Rexroth. OnPC
Spring ("Dip down upon the northern shore"). Tennyson. *See* In Memoriam A. H. H.: "Dip down upon . . ."
Spring ("Now fades the last long streak of snow"). Tennyson. *See* In Memoriam, A. H. H.: "Now fades . . ."
Spring. Celia Thaxter. BoChLi; DD; HH; OTPC (1946 ed.); PRWS; RAR
Spring ("Come, gentle Spring"), *abr.* James Thomson. *Fr.* The Seasons. TCEP
Sels.
Angling. LPS-2
"As rising from the vegetable world." PoEL-3
"As yet the trembling year." EnSW
"At length the finished garden to the view." ViBoPo
Birds in Spring. OBEC
Coming of the Rain, The. EPP
Connubial Life. LPS-1
Domestic Birds. BCEP; LPS-2
Nightingale Bereaved, The. BCEP
"Now, when the first foul torrent of the brooks." EV-3
Plea for the Animals. LPS-3
Prelude: "North-east spends his rage, The." CoEV
Songsters, The. LPS-2
Spring Flowers. AtBAP; OBEC
Swan, Turkey, Dove, and the Bull in the Broom. BeR
Woodland Choir, The. CoBE
Spring. Meta E. B. Thorne. *Fr.* Songs of the Seasons. PEOR
Spring. Henry Timrod. HBV; HiLiAm; IAP; LBAP; NLK; SPP; TCAP
(Spring in Carolina.) LPS-2
Spring. Tu Fu, *tr. fr. Chinese.* WhP
Spring. Feodor Tyutchev, *tr. fr. Russian by* C. M. Bowra. BoRS
Spring ("Lenten ys come with love to toune"). *Unknown. See* Lenten Is Come.
Spring ("When from her winter-prison"). *Unknown, tr. fr. Japanese.* SUS
Spring ("When the nightingale singeth the woods waxen green"), *mod. Unknown.* TMEV
("When the nyhtegale singes, the wodes waxen grene.") NBE
Spring ("Ye spring is here, beyond all doubt"). *Unknown.* CAG
Spring. Louis Untermeyer. VOD
Spring. Yiannis Vilaras, *tr. fr. Modern Greek by* Rae Dalven. MoGP
Spring. Prince Vyazemsky, *tr. fr. Russian by* Babette Deutsch. TrRV
Spring. Oscar Williams. LiTA
Spring, The. Luis Fabio Xammar, *tr. fr. Spanish by* Muna Lee. AnCL
Spring Air. Gene Derwood. FaFP; GTBS-W; LiTL
Spring all the Graces of the age. Chorus. Ben Jonson. *Fr.* Neptune's Triumph. OBS; SeCL
Spring am I, too soft of heart. The Seasons. William Morris. BPN

Spring and All. William Carlos Williams. *See* By the Road to the Contagious Hospital.
Spring! And all our valleys turning into green. In Excelsis. Thomas S. Jones, Jr. SBMV
Spring and Autumn. William James Linton. VA
Spring & Co. Jorge Carrera Andrade, *tr. fr. Spanish by* Richard O'Connell. AnCL
Spring and Fall. Gerard Manley Hopkins. AnFE; ChTr; CoEV; EmBrPo; EnL; ExPo; GTBS-W; KN; LiTB; LiTM; MoAB; MoPo; MoVE; OAEP; PoE; PoEL-5; PoFS; PoRA; POTT; ReaPo; ReMP; SeCeV; ThWaDe; TwHP; ViP; ViPP
Spring! And her hidden bugles up the street. The Laughers. Louis Untermeyer. GDAH
Spring and Summer. "A." PRWS
Spring and summer. Tennyson. *Fr.* Vastness. OQP; QP-2
Spring! and the buds against the sky. Spring. Caroline Giltinan. HBMV
Spring, and the sharpness of the golden dawn. On Newblown Roses. Ausonius. LaP
Spring and Winter ("When daisies pied . . ."). Shakespeare. *See* When Daisies Pied and Violets Blue.
Spring and Winter ("When icicles hang . . ."). Shakespeare. *See* When Icicles Hang by the Wall.
Spring Apple Tree. "Igor Severyanin," *tr. fr. Russian by* Babette Deutsch. TrRV
Spring Arithmetic. *Unknown.* FiBHP
Spring at her height on a morn at prime. Ballade of Youth and Age. W. E. Henley. PoVP
Spring at the Capital. Elizabeth Akers Allen. *See* In April.
Spring Beauties, The. Helen Gray Cone. AA
Spring, beautiful spring! Spring Song. *Unknown, tr. fr. Russian.* PCH
Spring Bereaved ("Alexis, here she stayed"). William Drummond of Hawthornden. *See* Sonnet: "Alexis, here she stayed . . ."
Spring Bereaved ("Sweet Spring, thou turn'st with all thy goodly train"). William Drummond of Hawthornden. *See* Sonnet: "Sweet Spring, thou turn'st . . ."
Spring Bereaved ("That zephyr every year"). William Drummond of Hawthornden. *See* Song: "That zephyr every year."
Spring blew trumpets of color, The. Blind. Harry Kemp. BAP; HBMV; NLK; PFY; PoMa; POT; PoTo; SBMV
Spring Blossoms. Li Yu, *tr. fr. Chinese by* Hsiung Ting. WhP
Spring bursts to-day. An Easter Carol. Christina Rossetti. DD; EOAH; HH; MaRV; MPB; OHIP; PoRL; TriL
Spring Called Parthenius, The. Hesiod, *tr. fr. Greek by* Sir William Marris. OxBG
Spring came earlier on, The. A Song for Lexington. Robert Kelley Weeks. AA; IDAH; OBAV
Spring came with tiny lances thrusting. Blossom Time. Wilbur Larremore. AA
Spring Cellar. Gladys McKee. GoYe
Spring Cleaning. Sam Walter Foss. ADAH
Spring comes early to the gardens. Green Jade Plum Trees in Spring. Ou-yang Hsiu. OnPC
Spring comes hither. Spring Song. "George Eliot." *Fr.* The Spanish Gypsy. OTPC (1946 ed.); PRWS
Spring comes hurrying. Hello! Louise Ayres Garnett. SiSoSe
Spring comes in with all her hues and smells, The. A Spring Morning. John Clare. RO
Spring comes laughing down the valley. New Life. Amelia Josephine Burr. HBV
Spring comes linking and jinking through the woods, The. William Miller. *Fr.* Spring. AlDL
Spring Comes to Murray Hill. Ogden Nash. FiBHP
Spring Comes to Our Garden. Sister Mary Immaculata. JKCP (1955 ed.)
Spring comes to town like some mad girl who runs. Spring in Town. Charles Hanson Towne. *Fr.* Manhattan. TBM
Spring comes with silent rush of leaf. Resurrection. Laurence Housman. *Fr.* Rue. MaRV
Spring Cricket. Frances Rodman. FaPON; SiSoSe
Spring-Dance. W. R. Rodgers. PoN
Spring Dawn. Li Po, *tr. fr. Chinese.* WhP
Spring Day. Hermann Hesse, *tr. fr. German by* Herman Salinger. TwGV
Spring day is clad in brightest green, The. Green Spring. Chang Shou. PoHN
Spring Day on West Lake. Ou-yang Hsiu, *tr. fr. Chinese by* Kenneth Rexroth. OnPC
Spring Days. Basho, *tr. fr. Japanese by* H. G. Henderson. OnPM
Spring Doggerel. Rhoda Coghill. NeIP
Spring Dreams. Ts'en Ts'an, *tr. fr. Chinese by* Henry H. Hart. PoHN
Spring Dusk in Williamsburg. Virginia Lyne Tunstall. Sonnets of an Old Town, I. LS
Spring Ecstasy. Lizette Woodworth Reese. MAP; MoAmPo
Spring Equinox, The. Anne Ridler. NeBP
Spring, etc. Reed Whittemore. WaKn
Spring Evening on the Boulevards. Jules Laforgue, *tr. fr. French by* William Jay Smith. AnFP
Spring Flowers. Shakespeare. See Flowers ("O Proserpina!").
Spring Flowers. James Thomson. *Fr.* The Seasons: Spring. AtBAP; OBEC
Spring flowers, Autumn moons. Plaint. Chu Shu Chen. OnPC
Spring Flowers from Ireland. Denis Florence MacCarthy. ACP; GoBC; TIP
Spring, for Julian, was amber in the hand. In the Henry James Country. William Abrahams. WaP
Spring for Travelers. *Unknown, tr. fr. Greek by* Lord Neaves. OnPM
Spring Fragment. Ken Etheridge. MoWP
Spring Garland, A. Meleager. *See* Heliodora's Wreath.
Spring Garland, A. James Rorty. MOAP
Spring Goeth All in White. Robert Bridges. BoTP; ChTr; HBMV; PoeT; TCEP; TwCV
Spring Grass. Carl Sandburg. FaPON
Spring-Grass. Oscar Stjerne, *tr. fr. Swedish by* Charles W. Stork. AnSL
Spring grass, there is a dance to be danced for you. Spring Grass. Carl Sandburg. FaPON
Spring Grief and Resentment. Li Po, *tr. fr. Chinese by* Florence Ayscough *and* Amy Lowell. ChLP
Spring has caught up the eager earth. Spring in the Valley. Duncan Campbell Scott. TwCV
Spring Has Come ("Hark! the tiny cowslip bell"). *Unknown.* BoTP
Spring Has Come ("Lenten is come with love to town"). *Unknown. See* Lenten Is Come.
Spring has come and the snow has gone. Captive. Peretz Hirshbein. TrJP
Spring has come back again. Spring. Toyohiko Kagawa. SoLD
Spring has come. I try to forget. Spring. Chu Shu Chen. OnPC
Spring has come to St. Marie. White Thorn. Rose Darrough. PoTo
Spring has come to the Pass. Two Springs. Li Ch'ing-chao. OnPC
Spring has come up from the South again. The Immortal. Cale Young Rice. NLK; VOD
Spring has departed; early days' sweet scent. A Sonnet. Jóhann Sigurjónsson. IcP
Spring has stolen all poetry from my heart, The. Springtime Theft. Marie Emilie Gilchrist. VOD
Spring Heart-break. Liu Fang-p'ing, *tr. fr. Chinese by* Witter Bynner. ChLP
Spring in Carmel. George Sterling. SBMV
Spring in Carolina. Henry Timrod. *See* Spring.
Spring in England. Charles Buxton Going. HBMV; VOD
Spring in Florida. C. B. Roth. LPS-1
Spring in Hiding. Frances Frost. YeAr
Spring Holidays. Catullus, *tr. fr. Latin by* George Lamb. OnPM
Spring in his death abounds among the lily islands. Elegy on My Father. Allen Curnow. AnNZ
Spring in Kentucky hills will soon awaken. Kentucky Mountaineer. Jesse Stuart. *Fr.* Man with a Bull-Tongue Plow. PoeMoYo
Spring in My Hut. Sodo, *tr. fr. Japanese by* H. G. Henderson. OnPM
Spring in New England, *sel.* Thomas Bailey Aldrich. Bluebird, The. BLA; SN
Spring in New England. Carlos Wilcox. APW
Spring in New Hampshire. Claude McKay. BANP; GoSl; PoNe
Spring in New Zealand. Hubert Church. BoAu
Spring in Oxford Street. "John Presland." VOD
Spring in the Convent. Sergei Gorodetsky, *tr. fr. Russian by* C. M. Bowra. BoRS
Spring in the South. Henry van Dyke. ADAH
Spring in the Students' Quarter. Henry Murger, *tr. fr. French by* Andrew Lang. AWP
Spring in the Valley. Duncan Campbell Scott. TwCV
Spring in the world! The New-born Year. Richard Hovey. GrCo-2
Spring in Town. Bryant. APW
Spring in Town. Charles Hanson Towne. *Fr.* Manhattan, V. TBM
Spring in War Time. Sara Teasdale. OHIP
Spring is a requiem rehearsed. Spring Song. LeRoy Smith, Jr. NePoAm
Spring Is at Work with Beginnings of Things. Greta Leora Rose. CaP
Spring is come to town with love. Spring Song. *Unknown.* EnLi-1
Spring Is Coming. Mary Howitt. *See* Coming of Spring, The.
Spring is coming by a many signs, The. Young Lambs. John Clare. EG; GoTP; TrGrPo

Spring is coming, spring is coming. May Song [or Oxfordshire Children's May Song]. *Unknown.* BoTP; HH; MeMeAg; OTPC
Spring is growing up. Spring and Summer. "A." PRWS
Spring is here again. Caring for Silkworms. Sung Shih. PoHN
Spring is here, beyond all doubt, Ye. Spring. *Unknown.* CAG
Spring is in her eyes. A Little Girl. Charles Angoff. GoYe
Spring Is in the Making. Nona Keen Duffy. YeAr
Spring Is Late, The. Louise Chandler Moulton. *See* Late Spring, The.
Spring Is like a Perhaps Hand. E. E. Cummings. GTBS-W; NePA
(Spring.) AnEnPo
Spring is showery, flowery, bowery. Mother Goose. TiPo
Spring is the morning of the year. The Golden Rod. Frank Dempster Sherman. BoChLi; FaPON
Spring It Is! Eduard Mörike, *tr. fr. German by* Charles E. Passage. AnGP
Spring it is cheery. What Can an Old Man Do but Die? [or Ballad]. Thomas Hood. ERP; LPS-1; VA
Spring Journey, A. Alice Freeman Palmer. HBV
Spring Landscape. Arthur Davison Ficke. Sonnets of a Portrait Painter, XII. HBMV
Spring Lay, A. Oliver Opdyke. InMe
Spring lights her candles everywhere. Song. Fredegond Shove. HBMV
Spring Lilt, A. *Unknown.* HBV; MPB; OTPC
"June! June! June!" *sel.* PCH
Spring made little promise. Portrait of an Indian. R. E. Rashley. CaP
Spring Market. Louise Driscoll. HBMV; HBVY; NLK
Spring Morning. William Browne. WP
Spring Morning, A. John Clare. RO
Spring Morning. Frances Cornford. BoTP
Spring Morning. D. H. Lawrence. MBP; MoAB; MoBrPo
Spring Morning. Coley B. Taylor. *Fr.* Chinoiseries. PFE
Spring Morning—Santa Fé. Lynn Riggs. TBM
Spring Mountain Climb. Richard Eberhart. GoYe
Spring, my dear, The. Out of Tune. W. E. Henley. BPN; MBP; MoBrPo
Spring Night. Richard Aldridge. NePoAm
Spring Night. Sidney Keyes. POTE
Spring Night. Su T'ung-po, *tr. fr. Chinese by* Kenneth Rexroth. OnPC
Spring Night. Coley B. Taylor. *Fr.* Chinoiseries. PFE
Spring Night. Sara Teasdale. ChMo; CMP; FaBoBe; HBMV; LiTA; LiTL; LiTM (1946 ed.); MAP; MoAmPo; NeMA; PG (1945 ed.)
Spring night, the owls crying. Spring Night. Sidney Keyes. POTE
Spring Nights, *sel.* Gerasimos Markoras, *tr. fr. Modern Greek by* Rae Dalven.
"Ocean laughs, The." MoGP
Spring 1940. W. H. Auden. OAEP (2d ed.)
Spring MCMXL. David Gascoyne. MoVE
Spring 1944. Boris Pasternak, *tr. fr. Russian by* C. M. Bowra. BoRS
Spring 1943. Roy Fuller. LiTB; LiTM; WaP
Spring 1942. Roy Fuller. LiTM; NeBP; WaaP
Spring Nocturne. Abraham Liessin, *tr. fr. Yiddish.* TrJP
Spring, A, now she is dead! of what? of thorns. Ben Jonson. *Fr.* The Sad Shepherd. GoBC
Spring Oak. Galway Kinnell. NePoAm
Spring Ode. Don Marquis. PC
Spring of God, The. William Alexander Percy. *Fr.* In April Once. OQP; QP-2
Spring of Hermes, The. Anyte, *tr. fr. Greek by* F. L. Lucas. GrPE; GrR
Spring of Joy Is Dry, The. *Unknown.* EIL
Spring of the Year, The. Allan Cunningham. BCEP; BSV; EV-4; HBV; OBEV (1st ed.)
(Gane Were But the Winter-Cauld.) EBSV
(Gone Were But the Winter Cold.) CH
Spring Offensive. Wilfred Owen. LiTB; MoVE
Spring Omnipotent Goddess. E. E. Cummings. OxBA
Spring on a wind-swept hill! On a Hill. Irene Rutherford McLeod. NLK; VOD
Spring on the Ochils. J. Logie Robertson. EBSV; OBVV
Spring once said to the nightingale. The Birds' Ball. William Bardeen. BLPA
Spring Passion. Joel Elias Spingarn. HBV
Spring Pastoral. Elinor Wylie. AnEnPo
Spring Ploughing. Hesiod, *tr. fr. Greek by* F. L. Lucas. *Fr.* Works and Days. GrPE
Spring Poem. Julian Symons. NeBP
Spring Poem. Colleen Thibaudeau. TwCaPo
Spring Poem. Nikolai Ushakov, *tr. fr. Russian by* Jack Lindsay. RuPo
Spring Pools. Robert Frost. MoAB; MOAP; OxBA
Spring Prayer. *Unknown, at. to* Emerson. *See* We Thank Thee.
Spring Questions. Clara Doty Bates. PPL
Spring Quiet. Christina Rossetti. BoTP; CH; LoBV; PoEL-5; ThWaDe
("Gone were but the winter.") EG
Spring Rain. Harry Behn. TiPo
Spring Rain. Marchette Chute. TiPo
Spring Rain. Ko I, *tr. fr. Chinese by* Henry H. Hart. PoHN
Spring Rain. Li Shang-yin, *tr. fr. Chinese by* Witter Bynner. ChLP
Spring rain! And as yet. Taniguchi Buson, *tr. fr. Japanese by* Harold Gould Henderson. LiTW
Spring rain is soft rain, The. Rainy Day Song. Violet Alleyn Storey. YeAr
Spring Returns. Li Ch'ing-chao, *tr. fr. Chinese by* Sophia H. Chen. WhP
Spring Returns, The. Charles Leonard Moore. HBV
Spring returns, and blended meet. Spring Holidays. Catullus. OnPM
Spring returns, the long awaited. Ver Redit Optatum. *Unknown. Fr.* Carmina Burana. LaP
Spring returns, the spring wind softly blowing, The. Petrarch. Sonnets to Laura: To Laura in Death, XLII. PrPoCR
Spring returns, The! What matters then that war. The Spring Returns. Charles Leonard Moore. HBV
Spring rides down, The; from Judith and the Larb. A Missouri Traveller Writes Home, 1830. Robert Bly. NePoEA
Spring Ring-Jingle. Michael Lewis. RIS
Spring River, The. Po Chü-i, *tr. fr. Chinese by* Arthur Waley. TrCh
Spring Sailing. Agathias Scholasticus, *tr. fr. Greek by* F. L. Lucas. GrPE
Spring Sailing. Leonidas, *tr. fr. Greek by* Robert Guthrie MacGregor. OnPM
Spring, St. Stephen's Green. Leslie Daiken. OnYI
Spring scattered the seed with a lavish hand. Summer. Meta E. B. Thorne. *Fr.* Songs of the Seasons. PEOR
Spring Scene. Su T'ung-po, *tr. fr. Chinese by* Yu Min-chuan. WhP
Spring Scene at River Town. *Unknown, tr. fr. Korean by* Grace W. Mitchell. OnPM
Spring Serpent, A. Yvor Winters. ExPo
Spring shall rouse my buried Lord, The. Easter Poem. Kathleen Raine. LiTB
Spring, The—she is a blessed thing. The Spring. Mary Howitt. PEOR
Spring Sigh, A. Chin Ch'ang-hsü, *tr. fr. Chinese by* Witter Bynner. ChLP
Spring Signs. Mildred Bowers Armstrong. GoBP
Spring Signs. Rachel Field. InMe
Spring Snow and Tui. Mary Ursula Bethell. AnNZ
Spring Song. Jean Antoine de Baïf, *tr. fr. French by* Alan Conder. TrFP
Spring Song. Robert Browning. *See* Year's at the Spring, The.
Spring Song. Bliss Carman. BAP, *much abr.*; CPG; HBV; LEAP, *abr.*; NLK; OCL; VA; YT
Make Me Over, Mother April, *sel.* HBVY
Spring Song. Hilda Conkling. GBV (1922 ed.); HH; MPB; PoTo; TSW; TSWC
Spring Song. John Davidson. BMEP
Spring Song. Aubrey Thomas De Vere. IrPN
Spring Song. "George Eliot." *Fr.* The Spanish Gypsy. OTPC (1946 ed.); PRWS
Spring Song. William Griffith. BAP; BLA; MPB; SBMV
Spring Song. Rayner Heppenstall. NeBP
Spring Song. Hermann Hesse, *tr. fr. German by* Ludwig Lewisohn. AWP; JAWP; WBP
Spring Song, A. Mary Howitt. BoTP; EV-4
Spring Song. Nahum, *tr. fr. Hebrew by* Emma Lazarus. TrJP
Spring Song. Katharine O'Brien. GoYe
Spring Song. Dollie Radford. DiM
Spring Song. Pierre de Ronsard, *tr. fr. French by* Alan Conder. Odes, IV, 21. TrFP
("God guard you, and greet you well," *tr. by* Curtis Hidden Page.) PrPoCR
Spring Song. George Brandon Saul. GoYe
Spring Song. LeRoy Smith, Jr. NePoAm
Spring Song. Theodore Spencer. AnFE; CoAnAm; TwAmPo
Spring Song. Swinburne. PCD
Spring Song ("Lenten is come with love to towne"). *Unknown. See* Lenten Is Come.
Spring Song, A ("Old Mother Earth"). *Unknown.* ADAH
Spring Song ("Spring, beautiful spring!"). *Unknown, tr. fr. Russian.* PCH
Spring Song ("Spring is come to town with love"), *mod. vers. of* Lenten Is Come. *Unknown.* EnLi-1
Spring Song ("Storks fly over the fields"). *Unknown, tr. fr. Czech.* PCH
Spring Song in the City. Robert Buchanan. HBV; OTPC (1923 ed.); SN; VA
Spring Song in Winter. Michael Hamburger. PoN
Spring-Song, 1939. F. L. Lucas. NeTW

Spring Song of a Super-Blake. Louis Untermeyer. HBMV
Spring Song of Aspens. Lilian White Spencer. PoOW
Spring Song of the Birds. James I, King of Scotland. *Fr.* The Kingis Quair. OBEV
("Worship, ye that lovers been, this May.") TrGrPo
Spring Sorrow. Wei Chuang, *tr. fr. Chinese.* ChLP
Spring Sows Her Seeds. Mary Carolyn Davies. NV
Spring still makes spring in the mind. We Are Never Old. Emerson. *Fr.* The World-Soul. OQP; PoRL; QP-2
Spring Stops Me Suddenly. Valentin Iremonger. OnYI
Spring Storm. Miltiades Malakassis, *tr. fr. Modern Greek by* Rae Dalven. MoGP
Spring, summer, autumn, winter. The Builders. Ebenezer Elliott. VA
Spring Sun. Chu Hsi, *tr. fr. Chinese by* Kenneth Rexroth. OnPC
Spring Symphony, *sel.* Yiannis Ritsos, *tr. fr. Modern Greek by* Rae Dalven.
"You pace/ through my dusty rooms." MoGP
Spring, the Sweet Spring. Thomas Nashe. *Fr.* Summer's Last Will and Testament. CG; CH; EnLi-1 (1949 ed.); EV-2; GTBS; GTSE; GTSL; HBV; KN; LiTB; LPS-2; OBEV; PoRA; TOP; ViBoPo
(Birds in Spring.) PRWS
(Spring.) AtBAP; BLV; CBE; CBOV; CoEV; ElL; GTBS-D; GTBS-W; LiTG; MCCG; OBSC; OTPC; PCH; RG; RIS; ShBV-2; TrGrPo
("Spring, the sweet spring, is the year's pleasant king.") CenL; EG; ElSeCe; MyFE; ReEn; SiCE; TuPP
Spring, the Travelling Man. Winifred M. Letts. BoTP; VOD
Spring, the Vet, and I. "Eduard Bagritsky," *tr. fr. Russian by* Babette Deutsch. TrRV
Spring Thoughts. Li Po, *tr. fr. Chinese by* Arthur Christy. ChLP
Spring Thunder. Feodor Tyutchev, *tr. fr. Russian by* V. de S. Pinto. BoR
Spring to Winter. George Crabbe. *Fr.* The Ancient Mansion. ChTr
Spring Trip of the Schooner *Ambition,* The, *with music. Unknown.* ShS
Spring up, O well—sing ye unto it. Song of the Well. Numbers, Bible, *O.T.* TrJP
Spring wakens the birds' voices, but for me. For St. Felix' Day. Paulinus of Nola. LaP
Spring Walk, The. Thomas Miller. OTPC (1923 ed.)
Spring Walk to the Pavilion of Good Crops and Peace. Ou-yang Hsiu, *tr. fr. Chinese by* Kenneth Rexroth. OnPC
Spring, Wanting Her. William Drummond of Hawthornden. *See* Sonnet: "Sweet Spring, thou turn'st . . ."
Spring Was Late That Year, The. V. Sackville-West. *Fr.* The Land. AtBAP
Spring Waters. Feodor Tyutchev, *tr. fr. Russian by* C. M. Bowra. BoRS
Spring which has its appeal in ghosts. The Seasons. Lynette Roberts. MoPW; MoWP
Spring will come again, dear friends, The. A Song of Farewell. Dora Greenwell. VA
Spring will come when the year turns, The. Song. Margaret Widdemer. SBMV
Spring Wind, The. Ho Hung, *tr. fr. Chinese by* Henry H. Hart. PoHN
Spring Wind. Nancy Byrd Turner. SiSoSe
Spring wind raises fine dust from the road, The. A Walk in the Country. Su T'ung-po. OnPC
Spring wind will never reach, The. An Answer to Ting Yuan Ch'en. Ou-yang Hsiu. OnPC
Spring winds that blow. Allegro Maëstoso. W. E. Henley. *Fr.* London Voluntaries. ViP
Spring Wish. John Farrar. GFA
Spring, with that nameless pathos in the air. Spring [in Carolina]. Henry Timrod. HBV; HiLiAm; IAP; LBAP; LPS-2; NLK; SPP; TCAP
Spring Work at the Farm. Thirza Wakley. BoTP
Spring Workman. Alan Creighton. CaP; TwCaPo
Springboard, The. Louis MacNeice. ChMP
Springfield Calibre Fifty, The. Joseph Mills Hanson. PoOW
Springfield Mountain (*diff. versions*). *Unknown.* ABS; BaBo; Po; SoAF, *with music;* TrAS, *with music;* ViBoPo (A, B, *and* C *vers.;* D *vers., with music*)
(In Springfield Mountain.) ABS; APW; IHA
(O Johnny Dear, Why Did You Go?) ABS
(Woodville Mound, *sl. abr.*) ABS
Springful of larks in a rolling, A. October. Dylan Thomas. *Fr.* Poem in October. YeAr
Spring's Answer. Edwin Osgood Grover. NLK
Spring's Arrival. *Unknown.* FaPON
Spring's Delights. Joseph Ashby-Sterry. CenHV
Spring's Glory, The, *sel.* Thomas Nabbes.
On a Mistress of Whose Affections He Was Doubtful. SeCL
Spring's glow and glamour over Baltimore. At the Grave of Poe. Clinton Scollard. GA
Spring's Immortality. Mackenzie Bell. VA
Spring's on the Curb. Hildegarde Flanner. AnAmPo
Spring's Procession. Sydney Dobell. *See* Chanted Calendar, A.
Spring's Return ("Diffugere nives"). Horace, *tr. fr. Latin by* Samuel Johnson. Odes, IV, 7. LiA
("Snows are fled away, leaves on the shaws, The," *tr. by* A. E. Housman.) LaP
(To Manlius Torquatus, *tr. by* Thomas Creech.) BeR
(Translation of Horace, *tr. by* Samuel Johnson.) TriL
Spring's Saraband. Bliss Carman. TwCV
Spring's silver poplars stand apart. For Any Lady's Birthday. Lawrence Lee. TBM
Spring's Torch-Bearer. Maurice Thompson. BLA
Spring's Welcome. John Lyly. *See* Trico's Song.
Spring-Tide. *Unknown. See* Lenten Is Come.
Springtide of spirits, at the Altar rail. Nam Semen Est Verbum Dei. Louise Imogen Guiney. CAW; QS
Springtime. Alfred Kreymborg. MAPA
Springtime. *Unknown. See* Lenten Is Come.
Springtime—a Humble Cry from the Depths. Clemens Brentano, *tr. fr. German by* Mabel Cotterell. AnGP
Springtime in Cookham Dean. Cecil Roberts. HBMV; VOD
Springtime in Donegal. Mabel Rose Stevenson. StVeCh
Springtime is a green time. Four Seasons. Rowena Bennett. SiSoSe; TiPo (1959 d.)
Springtime of the dead! I was uneasy with its mildness. Good Friday Rhapsody. Pierre Emmanuel. MiCF
Spring-Time Sweetheart, A (If I Had Had One). Gustaf Fröding, *tr. fr. Swedish by* Charles W. Stork. AnSL
Springtime Theft. Marie Emilie Gilchrist. VOD
Springtime with One Love. Wordsworth. *Fr.* The Excursion, VI. LiA
Springtime's bright blue ribbon flies. Spring It Is! Eduard Mörike. AnGP
Springy motion in her gait, A. Charles Lamb. *Fr.* Hester. LO
Springy red bow, The. The Red Bow. *Unknown.* WhP
Sprinkling. Dorothy Mason Pierce. SUS; TiPo
Spritely Dead, The. Oscar Williams. *Fr.* Variations on a Theme. LiTA; NePA
Sprouting Beard, The. Al-Isra'ili, *tr. fr. Arabic by* A. J. Arberry. MooP
Sprouting flowers and leaves and the May time, The. Fealty. Wolfram von Eschenbach. LiTW
Sprouts the Bitter Grain. Phyllis Webb. PeCV
Spruce Macaronis, and pretty to see. The Maryland Battalion. John Williamson Palmer. AA; HBV; IDAH; MC; PaA; PAH
Spruce Tree, The. Dorothy Choate Herriman. CPG
Sprung from a race that had long till'd the soil. The Adventures of Simon Swaugum, a Village Merchant. Philip Freneau. PoEL-4
Spun by the weir. The Wheel. Ibn al-Abbar. MooP
Spur is red upon the briar, The. An Outdoor Litany. Louise Imogen Guiney. TrPWD
Spurning the Earth. Giordano Bruno. *See* Sonnet: Philosophic Flight, The.
Sputter, city! Bead with fire. To Chicago at Night. Mildred Plew Meigs. HBMV
Squabble of the Sea Nymphs, The, or the Sacrifice of the Tuscararoes. Mercy Warren. BAV
Squalid village set in wintry mud, A. Born without a Chance. Edmund Vance Cooke. BLPA
Squall, The. Leonora Speyer. POT; PoTo; VOD
Square of Saint-Germain-des-Prés, The. Saint-Germain-des-Prés. Léon Paul Fargue. MiCF
Square sheets—they saw the marble into. Island Quarry. Hart Crane. CrMA
Square, squat room, A (a cellar on promotion). Waiting. W. E. Henley. In Hospital, II. BPN; PoVP; VLEP
Square-stanced hind-legs; body rectangular. Mantis. Terence Heywood. BoSA
Squat in swamp shadows. Burning. Gary Snyder. Myths & Texts, III. NeAP
Squats on a Toad-Stool under a Tree. Thomas Lovell Beddoes. *See* Isbrand's Song.
Squatted on their hunkers at the corner of the street. The White Whippet. W. W. Gibson. MM
Squatter's Children. Elizabeth Bishop. NePoAm-2
Squawking they rise from reeds into the sun. Mallard. Rex Warner. PoF
Squeak the fife, and beat the drum. Independence Day. Royall Tyler. HS, *abr.;* PAH
Squeak's heard in the orchestra, A. Quatrain. George T. Lanigan. WhC
Squeal. Louis Simpson. FiBHP
Squealing under city stone. Rapid Transit. James Agee. AnAmPo; MoAmPo; NAMP
Squealshrilling mosquitoes, fraternity lost to shame. Against Mosquitoes. Meleager. LiTW
Squire, A. Chaucer, *mod. by* Louis Untermeyer. *Fr.* The Canterbury Tales: Prologue. GoTP
Squire Adam had two wives, they say. Ballade of My Lady's Beauty. Joyce Kilmer. HBV; LBMV; LEAP; PR

Squire and Milkmaid; or, Blackberry Fold. *Unknown.* CoMu
Squire her hent in arms two, The. Medieval Mirth. *Unknown. Fr.* The Squire of Low Degree. ACP
Squire of Alsatia, The, *sels.* Thomas Shadwell.
  Expostulation, The. OAEP
  Victory in Hungary, The. SeCL
Squire of Low Degree, The, *sel. Unknown.*
  Medieval Mirth. ACP
Squirrel, The. Bernard Barton. OTPC (1923 ed.)
Squirrel, The. William Cowper. GoTP
Squirrel. Frances Frost. BoChLi
Squirrel, The. Mary Howitt. BoTP
Squirrel, The. Ogden Nash. CenHV
Squirrel, The. Ian Serraillier. AlDL
Squirrel, The ("Whisky Frisky"). *Unknown.* BoChLi; FaPON; RIS; StVeCh; SUS; TiPo; UTS
  (Whisky Frisky.) GFA; MeMeAg; OTPC (1946 ed.)
Squirrel, The ("The winds they did blow"). *Unknown.* BoTP; OxNR
Squirrel and the Wind, The. *Unknown.* PCH
Squirrel, dear Squirrel, up there on the tree. The Boy and the Squirrel. F. Hey. SAS
Squirrel, flippant, pert, and full of play, The. The Squirrel. William Cowper. GoTP
Squirrel is happy, the squirrel is gay, The. The Squirrel. Bernard Barton. OTPC (1923 ed.)
Squirrel is the curliest thing, The. The Curliest Thing. *Unknown.* BoTP
Squirrel to some is a squirrel, A. The Squirrel. Ogden Nash. CenHV
Squirrels' Christmas, The. Winifred Howard. ChBR
Ssu-ming had a man of madness. In Memoriam; Ho Chi-chang. Li Po. BoFr
Stab, The. Will Wallace Harney. AA; BTP
Stabat Mater. Jozef Wittlin, *tr. fr. Polish by* Joy Davidman. PoFr
Stabat Mater Dolorosa [*or* Stabat Mater]. *At. to* Jacopone da Todi, *tr. fr. Latin.*
  "At the cross her station keeping." *Tr. by* Richard Mant *and* Edward Caswall. OlF; TreFS; WGRP; WHL
  "By the cross of expiation/ The Mother stood, and kept her station." *Tr. by* Aubrey Thomas De Vere. ISi
  "Near the cross her vigil keeping." *Comp. by* Louis F. Benson. MaRV
  "Stood the afflicted mother weeping." *Tr. by* Abraham Coles. HBV; LPS-2
  "Stood the Mother in her anguish." *Tr. by* Thomas Walsh. CAW
Stabat Mater Speciosa. *At. to* Jacopone da Todi, *tr. fr. Latin by* Thomas Walsh. CAW
Stable-Talk. Raymond Knister. BoCaPo; CaP
Staccato! Staccato! The Rubinstein Staccato Etude. R. Nathaniel Dett. BANP
Staccato to O Le Lupe, A, *parody.* Bliss Carman. PA
Stack, The. Stanley Snaith. ChMP
"Stack Arms!" Joseph Blynth Alston. BlG; PAH; SPP
Stacker Lee. *Unknown. See* Stagolee.
Stacking the Needles. Theda Kenyon. AOAH
Staff and Scrip, The. Dante Gabriel Rossetti. OAEP; POTT; PoVP; VLEP
Staff-Nurse: New Style. W. E. Henley. In Hospital, X. PoVP
Staff-Nurse: Old Style. W. E. Henley. In Hospital, VIII. BPN; InP; PIAE; PoVP
Staff of Aesculapius, The. Marianne Moore. ImOP
Staff of Life. Archilochus, *tr. fr. Greek by* J. M. Edmonds. GrR
Staff Officer, The. Shakespeare. *See* My Liege, I Did Deny No Prisoners.
Stafford's Cabin. E. A. Robinson. CV; DDA; TCAP
Stag, The. Padraic Colum. *See* Deer of Ireland, The.
Stag, The. Harold Lewis Cook. MM
Stag and Jackals. Homer, *tr. fr. Greek by* F. L. Lucas. *Fr.* The Iliad, XI. GrPE
Stag does not lay his side to sleep. Grania. *Unknown.* KiLC
Stag Hunt, The. Sir Walter Scott. *See* Chase, The.
Stag Hunt, The ("The stag too, singled from the herd where long"). James Thomson. *Fr.* The Seasons: Autumn. LPS-2
Stag of the Ogura Mountain, The. Cry of the Stag. Emperor Jomei. OnPM
Stage Directions. William Rose Benét. ShBV-2
Stage Driver's Story, The. *Unknown.* IHA
Stage is about to be swept of corpses, The. Horatian Epode to the Duchess of Malfi. Allen Tate. FaBoMo
Stage is lighted, the first act half over, The. Third Row, Centre. William Rose Benét. WhC
Stage Love. Swinburne. PoEL-5; ViPP
Stage Poets. Dryden. *Fr.* The Conquest of Granada: Prologue. BeR
Staggering down the road at midnite. The Encounter. Paul Blackburn. NeAP
Staggering homeward between the stream and the trees the unhappy drunkard. New Year's Eve. Robinson Jeffers. CoV
Stagirius. Matthew Arnold. *See* Desire.
Stagnant tower foretold the doom, The. The Kind Look. Willard Maas. LiTM (1946 ed.)
Stagolee. *Unknown.* ABF (2 *vers.*), *with music;* BaBo (A *and* B *vers.*); OxBoLi; ViBoFo (A *and* B *vers.*)
  (Stacker Lee, 1, 2, *and* 3; *br. vers., with music.*) StDa
Stained-Glass Window, A. John Henry Boner. NoCaPo
Stainless Fair Appearance, The. Bilhana, *formerly at. to* Chauras, *tr. fr. Sanskrit by* E. Powys Mathers. *Fr.* Black Marigolds. OnPM
Stainless soldier on the walls. Emerson. *Fr.* Voluntaries. WGRP
Stains. Theodosia Garrison. BAP; BPP; HBV; LBMV; LEAP; MaRV; TCAP; WGRP
Stair-carpet is Turkey red, The. On the Staircase. Eleanor Farjeon. SiSoSe
Staircase narrow as the way, The. The Haunted Stairs. Yetza Gillespie. DaM
Stairs. Oliver Herford. FiBHP; InMe; WhC
Stairway to the stars, The. William Ludlum. PraP
Stalingrad. Huw Menai. MoWP
Stalker of Dreams. Lilith Lorraine. UnW
Stalker of Geese, A. *Unknown, tr. fr. Greek by* Sir William Marris. OxBG
Stalky Jack. William Brighty Rands. BoTP; RIS
Stalled on the sidelines we must hope and wait. We Who Build Visions. Stanton A. Coblentz. PGD
Stallions I must have, The, good wife! the red one and the brown. At Welbedacht. A. M. Buckton. BoSA
Stalwart soldier comes, the spring, A. The Seasons: Spring. Kalidasa. AWP
Stamp Battalion. E. V. Lucas. StVeCh (1955 ed.)
Stamp not your little foot! A Plea. Arthur Guiterman. PR
Stampede, The. Earl Alonzo Brininstool. PoOW
Stampede, The. Wallace D. Coburn. PoOW
Stampede, The. *Unknown.* CoSo
Stamp's a tiny, flimsy thing, A. Stamp Battalion. E. V. Lucas. StVeCh (1955 ed.)
Stan' Still Jordan, *with music. Unknown.* BoAN-1
Stances, *sel.* Jean Moréas, *tr. fr. French by* James Elroy Flecker.
  "Garden rose I paid no honour to, The." MiFP
Stand by the Flag. John Nichols Wilder. FOAH, *abr.;* GN, *abr.;* HH; PGD, *abr.*
  "Stand by the flag," *sel.,* 2 *sts.* PEDC
Stand close around, ye Stygian set. Dirce. Walter Savage Landor. *Fr.* Pericles and Aspasia. AEV; AnFE; AWP; BCEP; BLV; BoLiVe; BPN; CBOV; ChTr; CoEV; EG; EnRP; EV-4; ExPo; FaBoEn; GTBS-D; InPo; JAWP; LEAP; LiA; LiTB; LoBV; OAEP; OBEV; OBRV; PoEL-4; PoRA; SeCeV; TOP; TrGrPo; VA; ViBoPo; WBP; WHA; WhC
Stand Fast, O My Heart. *Unknown, tr. fr. Egyptian by* Alan H. Gardiner. LiTW
Stand Forth! Angela Morgan. MaRV
Stand forth, Seithenyn: winds are high. Song of Gwyntho. Thomas Love Peacock. *Fr.* The Misfortunes of Elphin. OBRV
Stand gentle in my words. Wilfred Watson. *Fr.* Canticle of Darkness. MeRV
Stand here by my side and turn, I pray. The Snow-Shower. Bryant. AnNE; APW; HBV; LEAP; LPS-2
Stand like an anvil, when 'tis beaten. Abraham Lincoln. Frank Moore. LBAH
Stand Not Uttering Sedately. Victor Plarr. *See* Epitaphium Citharistriae.
Stand on the highest pavement of the stair. La Figlia Che Piange. T. S. Eliot. APA; BLV; BoLiVe; CaAE; ChMo; CMP; CoAnAm; FaBoTw; LiTA; LoPo; LoPS; MAP; MoAmPo (1942 ed.); NP; NV; PG (1945 ed.); POTE; PreP; ReMP; TCPD; TwP; ViBoPo
Stand stately Tavie out of the codpis rise. *Unknown.* SeCSL
Stand still, and I will read to thee. A Lecture upon the Shadow. John Donne. AnEnPo; AtBAP; AWP; ElSeSe; EPS (1942 ed.); EV-2; InPo; OBS; Po; ReEn; SeEP; TuPP
Stand still, true poet that you are! Popularity. Robert Browning. BPN; PoVP; PtP; TCEP
Stand still you floods doe not deface. On Sight of a Gentlewomans Face in the Water. Thomas Carew. SeCV-1
Stand straight:/ Step firmly, throw your weight. Rules for the Road. Edwin Markham. OQP; OTPC (1946 ed.); PoRL; QP-2; RIS; StaSt
Stand! the ground's your own, my braves! Warren's Address to the American Soldiers [*or* at Bunker Hill]. John Pierpont. AA; AnNE; APW; BoHiPo; DD; FaBoBe; GA; GN; HBV; HBVY; IDAH; LEAP; LPS-2; MC; PaA; PAH; PAP; PECK; PEDC; PoFr; PTA-2; TreF; WBLP
Stand there, magnificent, with free, unbowed head. The Old World to the New. Florence Ellenwood Allen. CAG
Stand-to, The. C. Day Lewis. SoV

Stand-to; Good Friday Morning. Siegfried Sassoon. FaBoTw
Stand to Your Glasses. Bartholomew Dowling. *See* Revel, The.
"Stand to your guns, men!" Morris cried. On Board the *Cumberland.* George Henry Boker. IAP; PAH
Stand up—erect! Thou hast the form. The Laborer. William Davis Gallagher. APW
Stand Up for Jesus. George Duffield, Jr. TreFS
("Stand up, stand up, for Jesus.") OlF
Stand, Whoso List, upon the Slipper Top. Sir Thomas Wyatt. *See* Stond Who So List . . .
Stand ye calm and resolute. Shelley. *Fr.* The Masque of Anarchy. LoBV
Standard Forgings Plant. William Stephens. NAMP
Standard on the Braes o' Mar, The. Alexander Laing. EBSV
Standardization. A. D. Hope. BoAV
Standards. Nathalia Crane. *See* Colors, The.
Standards. Charles Wharton Stork. BLP; NV; TBM
Standin' on the Walls of Zion, *with music. Unknown.* AS
Standing against the snow, a tall Being of beauty. Being Beauteous. Arthur Rimbaud. AnFP
Standing aloof in giant ignorance. To Homer [*or* Sonnet: To Homer]. Keats. BPN; BrBE; ChER; EM-2; EmBrPo; ES; EV-4; OBRV; PtP; TriL
Standing at the portal. At the Portal. Frances Ridley Havergal. BLRP
Standing between the sun and moon preserves. Einstein. Archibald MacLeish. AnFE; APA; ChMo; CoAnAm; CMP; MoPo; TwAmPo
Standing by the shore of the great bitter water. The Indian. Arthur S. Bourinot. BoCaPo
Standing erect in the mire. Sketch of the Frontier Woman. "Claudia Lars." AnCL
Standing on Earth. Milton. *Fr.* Paradise Lost, VII. ChTr
Standing on high Olympus' topmost peak. Homer. *Fr.* The Iliad, XIV. GrPo
Standing on the fire-step. Front Line. William Rose Benét. AOAH
Standing on Tiptoe. George Frederick Cameron. BoCaPo; CaP; CPG; OCL; VA
Standing there. Just Sixteen. Hsü Chien. ChLP; OnPM
Standing together side by side on high mountains. Sonnets, II. Feng Chih. *Fr.* Twenty-seven Sonnets. WhP
Standing upon the margent of the Main. The Tempest. Charles Cotton. SeCePo
Standing with folded wings of mystery. The New Year. Lillian Gilchrist Gard. OQP; PSO; QP-1
Stands a lady/ on a mountain. David Jones. *Fr.* The Anathemata. PrWP
Stane wi Its Runes Rises frae the Sea, The. Heine, *tr. fr. German into Scottish by* Edwin Morgan. AnGP
Stans Puer ad Mensam. Sir Walter Raleigh. WhC
Stanza: "Often rebuked, yet always back returning." *At. to* Emily Brontë. *See* Stanzas: "Often rebuked . . ."
Stanza: "When a man hath no freedom to fight for at home." Byron. *See* When a Man Hath No Freedom.
Stanza of Anglo-Saxon Poetry. "Lewis Carroll." *See* Jabberwocky.
Stanza on Freedom, A. James Russell Lowell. *See* Stanzas on Freedom.
Stanzas: "Away! the moor is dark beneath the moon." Shelley. *See* Stanzas—April, 1814.
Stanzas: "Black absence hides upon the past." John Clare. EnLoPo
Stanzas: "Brightly lit from above, I am sitting." Vladislav Khodasevich, *tr. fr. Russian by* Vladimir Nabokov. BoRS
Stanzas: "Could love for ever." Byron. HBV; ViBoPo, *abr.*
Stanzas: "Dead leaves strew the forest walk, The." John G. C. Brainard. AnAmPo; BAV; LA
Stanzas: "Farewell, Life! my senses swim." Thomas Hood. *See* Farewell, Life!
Stanzas: "I will go back to the great sweet mother." Swinburne. *See* Sea, The.
Stanzas: "If, Marchioness, you can descry." Corneille, *tr. fr. French by* Henry Carrington. LiTW
(Stanzas: "Lady fair, if on the page," *tr. by* John Payne.) LiA
(Stanzas to the Marquise, *tr. by* Alan Conder.) TrFP
Stanzas: "I'll not weep that thou art going to leave me." Emily Brontë. LoBV
Stanzas: "In a drear-nighted December." Keats. ChER; EmBrPo; ERP; HBV; OBEV; OBRV; TVSH
(December.) GN; OTPC
(Happy Insensibility.) GTBS; GTBS-D; GTBS-W; GTSE; GTSL
(In a Drear-nighted December.) BCEP; BPN; CBOV; CH; EG; EnRP; EPN; PoE; TCEP; TOP
(Song: "In a drear-nighted December.") EM-2; EV-4
Stanzas: "Lady fair, if on the page." Corneille. *See* Stanzas: "If, Marchioness, you can descry."
Stanzas: Little While, a Little While, A. Emily Brontë. *See* Little While, a Little While, A.
Stanzas: "Mighty thought of an old world, The." Thomas Lovell Beddoes. *See* Mighty Thoughts of an Old World, The.
Stanzas: "My life is like the summer rose." Richard Henry Wilde. *See* My Life Is like the Summer Rose.
Stanzas: "Nature doth have her dawn each day." Henry David Thoreau. MOAP
Stanzas: "No tongue can tell, no pen describe." Philip Freneau. CoBA
Stanzas: "Often rebuked, yet always back returning." *At. to* Emily Brontë. ChER; CoEV; EmBrPo; FaBoEn; HBV; KN; LiTB; LoBV; OAEP; OBVV; VA
(Often Rebuked, Yet Always Back Returning.) EnLit; GTML; PoVP
(Stanza: "Often rebuked . . .") OBEV (new ed.)
Stanzas: "We have forgot what we have been." Thomas William Parsons. UnW
Stanzas: "When a man hath no freedom to fight for at home." Byron. *See* When a Man Hath No Freedom.
Stanzas: "When down the loud streets I go straying." Pushkin. *See* Along the Noisy Streets.
Stanzas: "When these assaults proove vain, the Enemy." Edward Taylor. *Fr.* God's Determinations: Difficulties Arising from Uncharitable Cariages of Christians. OnAP
Stanzas: "Where forlorn sunsets flare and fade." W. E. Henley. *See* Over the Hills and Far Away.
Stanzas: "With tears thy grief thou dost bemoan." Solomon ibn Gabirol, *tr. fr. Hebrew by* Emma Lazarus. TrJP
Stanzas—April, 1814. Shelley. BPN; CaAE; ChER; EM-2; EmBrPo; EnRP; ERP; FiP; MyFE; OAEP
("Away! the moor is dark beneath the moon.") CBE
(Remorse.) OBEV
(Stanzas: "Away! the moor is dark beneath the moon.") BrBE; LoBV
Stanzas Cancelled from the Elegy. Thomas Gray. ViBoPo
Stanzas concerning Love. Stefan George, *tr. fr. German by* Ludwig Lewisohn. AWP; JAWP; WBP
Stanzas for Lent. James Howell. PrWP
Stanzas for Music ("Bright be the place"). Byron. *See* Bright Be the Place of Thy Soul.
Stanzas for Music ("There be none of beauty's daughters"). Byron. AWP; BEL; BPN; CaAE; ChER; EmBrPo; EnL; EnLi-2 (1949 ed.); EnLit; EnRP; EPN; ERP; EV-4; FiP; HBV; MCCG; NeHB; OAEP; OBRV; OuHeWo; PoE; PoFS; PoRA; REAL; RiBV; TOP; TrGrPo; TyEnPo
(For Music.) OBEV (1st ed.)
(There Be None of Beauty's Daughters.) CBE; GTBS; GTBS-D; GTBS-W; GTSE; GTSL; LiTB; LoBV; LiTG; LiTL; ReaPo
Stanzas for Music ("There's not a joy"). Byron. BEL; BPN; CoBE; EM-2; EmBrPo; EnLi-2; EnLit; EnRP; EPN; EV-4; HBV; MaPo; OAEP; OuHeWo; PoFS; RiBV; TOP
(Youth and Age.) GTBS; GTBS-D; GTBS-W; GTSE; GTSL
Stanzas for Music ("They say that Hope"). Byron. BPN; EmBrPo
Stanzas for My Daughter. Horace Gregory. *See* Poems for My Daughter.
Stanzas for the Harp. *Unknown, tr. fr. Welsh by* Gwyn Williams. PrWP
Stanzas from "Elegy for Edward Thomas." Charles Dalmon. POTE
Stanzas from "Epithalamion" ("Now cease, ye damsels, your delights forepast"). Spenser. *Fr.* Epithalamion. CoEV
Stanzas from "Milton." Blake. *See* And Did Those Feet in Ancient Time.
Stanzas from "Saint Peter's Complaint." Robert Southwell. *Fr.* Saint Peter's Complaint. ACP
Stanzas from "The Church Porch." George Herbert. TVSH
Stanzas from the Grande Chartreuse. Matthew Arnold. BPN; CoBE; EM-2; EmBrPo; EPN; GEPC; OAEP; PoEL-5; PoVP; TyEnPo; ViPo; ViPP; VLEP
Sels.
"Approach, for what we seek is here." BMEP
"For rigorous teachers seized my youth." ViBoPo
"What helps it now, that Byron bore." PtP
Stanzas from "The Ivory Gate." Thomas Lovell Beddoes. *See* Mighty Thoughts of an Old World, The.
Stanzas in Meditation VI (1940). Gertrude Stein. OnAP
Stanzas in Memory of the Author of "Obermann." Matthew Arnold. BPN; EM-2; EPN; GEPC; PoVP; ViPo; ViPP; VLEP
"By England's lakes, in grey old age," *sel.* PtP
Stanzas in the Infrared. Ethel Jacobson. DDA
Stanzas Occasioned by the Ruins of a Country Inn, Unroofed and Blown Down in a [*or* by the] Storm. Philip Freneau. APW; DDA; IAP; MOAP; OxBA; TCAP
(On the Ruins of a Country Inn.) AA
Stanzas on Freedom. James Russell Lowell. AOAH; CoBA; GN, *2 sts.;* IAP; MaRV, *abr.;* MC; OHIP; PGD, *abr.;* PoFr; PoNe
(Freedom.) PEOR, *abr.*

Slaves, *last st.* NeHB; OQP; PCD; QP-2; WBLP
(Freedom.) ShGoBo
(Stanza on Freedom, A.) AA; HiLiAm; WaKn
Stanzas on Mutability. Hugo von Hofmannsthal, *tr. fr. German by* Jethro Bithell. AWP; TrJP
Stanzas on Oliver Cromwell. Dryden. *Fr.* Heroic Stanzas. EPP
Stanzas on Seeing the Speaker Asleep in His Chair. Winthrop Mackworth Praed. EnRP
Stanzas on Woman. Goldsmith. *See* Song: "When lovely woman stoops to folly."
Stanzas to —— ("Well, some may hate"). Emily Brontë. EmBrPo; LoBV
Stanzas to an Alien. Philip Freneau. CoV
Stanzas to Augusta ("Though the day of my destiny"). Byron. BCEP; BPN; EM-2; EmBrPo; EnRP; ERP
Stanzas to Augusta ("When all around grew drear and dark"). Byron. ERP
Stanzas to Mr. Bentley. Thomas Gray. EiPP; EV-3
Stanzas to Pale Ale. *Unknown.* BOHV
Stanzas to the Marquise. Corneille. *See* Stanzas: "If, Marchioness, you can descry."
Stanzas to the Memory of Thomas Hood. Bartholomew Simmons. *See* To the Memory of Thomas Hood.
Stanzas Written in Dejection near Naples. Shelley. BEL; BPN, CBE, *abr.;* ChER; CoBE; EM-2; EmBrPo; EnL; EnLi-2; EnLit; EnRP; EPN; ERP; EV-4; FiP; GEPC; GTBS; GTBS-D; GTBS-W; GTSE; GTSL; MCCG; OAEP; OBRV; PoRA; ViBoPo; WHA
(Sun Is Warm, the Sky Is Clear, The, *abr.*) LPS-1
Stanzas Written in My Pocket Copy of Thomson's "Castle of Indolence." Wordsworth. EnRP
Stanzas Written in Sickness. Thomas Hood. *See* Farewell, Life!
Stanzas Written on Battersea Bridge during a Southwesterly Gale. Hilaire Belloc. GoBC
Stanzas Written on the Road between Florence and Pisa. Byron. BPN; EmBrPo; EnLi-2 (1949 ed.); EnRP; ERP; EV-4; HBV; MCCG; OBRV; PoFS; TCEP
(All for Love.) GTBS; GTBS-D; GTBS-W; GTSE; GTSL; LiTL; LoPo
(O Talk Not to Me.) InP
("Oh talk not to me of a name.") CBE
Star. Guillaume Apollinaire, *tr. fr. French by* W. S. Merwin. AnFP
Star, The. Grace Hazard Conkling. HBMV
Star. Gene Derwood. NePA
Star [*or* Starre], The. George Herbert. AtBAP; MeRV
Star. "The Knight of Kürenberg," *tr. fr. German by* Margaret R. Richey. LyMA
Star. The. Bertha Palmer Lane. ChrBoLe
Star. Vladimir Lugovskoi, *tr. fr. Russian by* Jack Lindsay. RuPo
Star, The. Ida Norton Munson. ChIP
Star. Plato. *See* Morning and Evening Star.
Star, The. Beatrice Redpath. CaP; CPG; OCL
Star, The. William Soutar. NeBP
Star, The. Jane Taylor. *See* Twinkle, Twinkle, Little Star.
Star, A ("A star has stopped"). *Unknown.* BPP
Star, The ("This other night so cold"). *Unknown.* ChrBoLe
Star, The. Willoughby Weaving. HBMV; HBVY
Star,/ If you are. A Christmas Tree. William Burford. NePA
Star, A—a star in the west! Hymn of the New World. Percy MacKaye. PEDC; PoRL
Star and Face. *Unknown, tr. fr. Spanish by* Havelock Ellis. OnPM
Star Bearer, The. Edmund Clarence Stedman. CLS
Star bright, starlight. *See* Star light, star bright.
Star-crowned cliffs seem hinged upon the sky, The. Glencoe. G. K. Chesterton. LEAP
Star darkly gleaming hides its dim light, The. Star. "The Knight of Kürenberg." LyMA
Star, The; Dedicated to Theodore Roosevelt, Following His Death, January 6, 1919. Marion Couthouy Smith. DD: PAH
Star-dust and vaporous light. Noel. Richard Watson Gilder. AA
Star-Fear. Leonora Speyer. AnEnPo
Star-filled seas are smooth tonight, The. The Isle of Portland. A. E. Housman. A Shropshire Lad, LIX. MoBrPo; PoVP
Star Flowers. Ibn al-Zaqqaq, *tr. fr. Arabic by* A. J. Arberry. MooP
Star from out the heavens, A. Star and Face. *Unknown.* OnPM
Star Gazer. Coleman Rosenberger. DaM
Star-gazing, O my Star, would I could be. My Star. Plato. *tr. by* Alexander Lothian. EnLi-1; OuHeWo
Star has stopped above my heart, A. A Star. *Unknown.* BPP
Star in the West, The. Hezekiah Butterworth. PEOR
Star in the West, The. Eliza Cook. PEDC
Star, A, is gone! a star is gone! The Fallen Star. George Darley. AnFE; BCEP; HBV; OBEV; TIP
Star is not extinguished when it sets, The. Reappearing. Horatius Bonar. EOAH
Star Light. *See also* Starlight.
"Star Light, Star Bright." Dorothy Parker. LoPo
Star light, star bright [*or* Star bright, starlight]. Star Wish [*or* Signs and Charms]. *Unknown.* HBVY; OxNR; PCH; RIS; SiTL; StaSt; StVeCh (1955 ed.); TiPo
Star looked down on Bethlehem, A. Holier Night. Leslie Savage Clark. ChIP
Star looks down at me, A. Waiting Both. Thomas Hardy. ChMo; CMP; MBP; MoAB; MoBrPo; NeMA; OxBoLi; WaKn; WHA
Star Map, A. Sara Teasdale. TCAP
Star Morals. Friedrich Wilhelm Nietzsche, *tr. fr. German by* Ludwig Lewisohn. AWP
Star must cease to burn with its own light, The. Et Mori Lucrum. John Lancaster Spalding. *Fr.* God and the Soul. AA
Star of Bethlehem. Florence Van Cleve. OQP; QP-2
Star of Bethlehem, The; a Nativity Play for Children. Alice Corbin Henderson. ChrBoLe
Star of Calvary, The. Nathaniel Hawthorne. AA
Star of Columbia, *with music.* Timothy Dwight. *See* Columbia.
Star of descending night! fair is thy light in the west! The Songs of Selma. James MacPherson. CEP
Star of Eternal Possibles and Joy. "Peter Yates." ChMP
Star of Ethiopia. Lucian B. Watkins. BANP
Star of My Heart. Vachel Lindsay. OQP; QP-1; SDH; VOD
Star of my mishap imposed [*or* impos'd] this pain [*or* paining], The. To Delia, XXXI. Samuel Daniel. OBSC; ReIE
Star of ocean fairest. Ave Maris Stella. *Unknown.* ISi
Star of Sangamon, The. Lyman Whitney Allen. PGD
Great American, The, *sel.* PSO
Star of the Covenant, The, *sel.* Stefan George, *tr. fr. German by* Herman Salinger.
"In purple fire spoke the heavenly wrath." TwGV
Star of the East. Eugene Field. HH; OQP; PGD; PoRL; QP-1
Star of the mead! sweet daughter of the day. The Daisy. John Leyden. LPS-2
Star of the Morning. D. V. Johnstone. BePJ
Star of the North! though night winds drift. The Fugitive Slave's Apostrophe to the North Star. John Pierpont. AA
Star of the Sea. Sebastian Brant, *tr. fr. German by* Alexander Barclay. *Fr.* The Ship of Fools. ACP; CAW
Star of the Sea. Richard Webb Sullivan. ISi
Star of the Sea, to whom, age after age. To Ask Our Lady's Patronage for a Book on Columbus. Thomas D'Arcy McGee. JKCP
Star proves never traitor, and a weed, A. Thrift. Lizette Woodworth Reese. NP
Star-Pudding. Robert P. Tristram Coffin. DDA
Star Sirius and the Pole Star dwell afar. Christina Rossetti. *Fr.* Later Life. VA
Star-Song. Hans Carossa, *tr. fr. German by* Herman Salinger. TwGV
Star Song. Robert Underwood Johnson. HBV
Star Song, The; a Carol to the King. Robert Herrick. OxBoCh
(Star Song, The, *abr.*) GN
Star-spangled Banner, The. Francis Scott Key. AA; APW; BAV; BBV; BIG; BLPA; BoHiPo, 3 *sts.;* DD; FaBoBe; FaFP; FaPON; FOAH; HBV; HBVY; HH; InP; LEAP; LPS-2; MaRV; MC; NeHB; NePA; OIF; OnHT; OTPC; PaA; PAH; PAP; PECK; PEDC; PoFr; PoRL; PSO; SPP; TCAP; TreF; TVSH; WBLP; YaD
Star-Splitter, The. Robert Frost. ChMo; CMP; ImOP; PoLFOT
Star, star, shining bright. Star. Gene Derwood. NePA
"Star stood over where the young child was, The." A Christmas Prayer. Molly Anderson Haley. PGD; PSO
Star-Talk. Robert Graves. AIDL; HBMV; MBP; MoBrPo; PtOT; RG; TCPD; TwCV; WP
Star That Bids the Shepherd Fold, The. Milton. *Fr.* Comus. EG; FaBoCh; LoGBV; OBEV, *abr.;* TOP; ViBoPo; WHA
(Comus' Invocation to His Revelers.) BoLiVe; TrGrPo
(From "Comus.") LEAP
(Invocation of Comus, The.) OBS
(Mask, A.) FiP
(Night Mysteries.) BCEP
(Song: "Star that bids the shepherd fold, The.") SeCeV
(Songs.) BLV
Star That Bringest Home the Bee. Thomas Campbell. *See* Song to the Evening Star.
Star, that gives a gracious dole. "Star Light, Star Bright." Dorothy Parker. LoPo

Star that watched above your sleep has just put out his light, The. The Child's Star. John Banister Tabb. PPL
Star There Fell, A. Zalman Schneour, *tr. fr. Hebrew by* Harry H. Fein. TrJP
Star Thought. Frances Shaw. NP
Star-throned, incorruptible Aphrodite. Ode to Aphrodite. Sappho. AWP
Star upon the south hangs low, The. Legend of Noël. Frances Frost. PoTo
Star Wagon, The, *sel.* Maxwell Anderson.
Holy City, A. QS
Star Wish. *Unknown.* HBVY; PCH
(Signs and Charms.) StaSt
("Star-light, star-bright.") OxNR; RIS; SiTL; TiPo
Stare deeply inside. Waterdrop. Sergei Smirnov. RuPo
Stare's Nest by My Window, The. W. B. Yeats. Meditations in Time of Civil War, VI. LiTB
Starfish, The. Robert P. Tristram Coffin. ImOP
Starfish. Winifred Welles. FaPON; SiSoSe
Staring into the deep darkness. The Raven. Shinkichi Takahashi. PoLJ
Stark by the Eastern gate. Two Men in Armour. John Heath-Stubbs. NeBP
Stark in the pasture on the skull-shaped hill. Pieta. David Gascoyne. *Fr.* Miserere. NeBP; POTE
Stark the row of corpses lies. Death Feast. Viktor Khlebnikov. BoRS
Starkness of Earth, The. Frank O'Connor, *fr. the Irish.* TriL
Starless and chill is the night. A Night by the Sea. Heine, *tr. by* Howard Mumford Jones. *Fr.* The North Sea. AWP
Starless and cold is the night. Night on the Shore. Heine, *tr. by* Emma Lazarus. *Fr.* The North Sea. LiTW
Starlight. John White Chadwick. AA
Starlight. Harold Lewis Cook. NP
Starlight. William Meredith. NePoEA
Starlight. J. C. Squire. PtOT
Starlight like Intuition Pierced the Twelve. Delmore Schwartz. AmP; LiTM (1946 ed.); MiAP
(Starlight's Intuitions Pierced the Twelve, The.) MoPo; NePA
Starlight Night, The. Gerard Manley Hopkins. ACP; AlDL; CaAE; CAW; EmBrPo; EV-5; GoBC; GTBS; GTBS-W; JKCP; LiTM; MBP; MeRV; MoAB; MoBrPo; MoPW; MoVE; OBVV; OxBoCh; PoVP; SeCePo; ShBV-4; ThWaDe; ViBoPo; ViP; WoL
Starlight through the curve of space. Starlight. Harold Lewis Cook. NP
Starlight! with deep and quiet breathing slept. Palinurus. George Cronyn. BAP
Starlighter, The. Arthur Guiterman. GaP; MoSiPe; SiSoSe
Starlight's Intuitions Pierced the Twelve, The. Delmore Schwartz. *See* Starlight like Intuition Pierced the Twelve.
Starling, The. Aleksandr Trifonovich Tvardovsky, *tr. fr. Russian by* Babette Deutsch. TrRV
Starling Lake, The. "Seumas O'Sullivan." AnIV; AWP; JAWP; WBP
(My Sorrow.) HBV; NP
(Rosses, The.) LBBV
Starling's Spring Rondel, A. James Cousins. HBV; HBVY
Starre, The. George Herbert. *See* Star, The.
Starre, The. Henry Vaughan. MePo
Starred Mother, The. Robert Whitaker. PGD
Starry amorist, starward gone. A Dead Astronomer. Francis Thompson. VLEP
Starry Classroom. E. Merrill Root. DDA
Starry Heavens Without. Ptolemy. *See* Immortality.
Starry Host, The. John Lancaster Spalding. *Fr.* God and the Soul. AA; HBV
Starry light and the lady bright, The. Children's Song. *Unknown.* ABS
Starry Night. Hermann Hagedorn. MaRV
Starry Sky. *Unknown, tr. fr. Old Irish by* Seán O'Faoláin. AnIL; SiB
Stars. Rhoda W. Bacmeister. BrR
Stars, The. "Barry Cornwall." CG; OTPC
Stars, The. Mary Carolyn Davies. DD; HH
Stars, The. Mary Mapes Dodge. AA
Stars. Florence S. Edsall. MoSiPe
Stars. Carolyn Hancock. RIS
Stars. Dowell O'Reilly. BoAu
Stars, The. Christina Rossetti. *Fr.* Sing-Song. MeMeAg; OTPC (1946 ed.)
Stars. Kenneth Slessor. BoAV
Stars, The. Christopher Smart. RO
"Stars of the superior class," *sel.* ChTr
Stars. Sara Teasdale. BoChLi; CP; FaPON; HBMV; NP; SP; TiPo; YT
Stars ("I'm glad the stars"). *Unknown.* GFA
Stars ("A little boy"). *Unknown.* GFA
Stars and atoms have no size. Measurement. A. M. Sullivan. WaKn
Stars and Moon on the River. Tu Fu, *tr. fr. Chinese by* Kenneth Rexroth. OnPC
Stars and Silence. *Unknown, tr. fr. Spanish by* Havelock Ellis. OnPM
Stars and Stripes, The. James T. Fields. FOAH; HH
Stars and Stripes, The. Lucretia Gray Noble. FOAH
Stars and Stripes, The. Henry van Dyke. PSO
Stars are foam-flecks, white, The. Sea of Night. Ibn Sa'id of Alcala la Real. MooP
Stars are forth, the moon above the tops, The. The Coliseum [by Moonlight]. Byron. *Fr.* Manfred, III, iv. BCEP; LPS-2; MCCG
Stars Are Glittering in the Frosty Sky, The. Charles Heavysege. *See* Winter Galaxy, The.
Stars are gone out spark by spark, The. At Cockcrow. Lizette Woodworth Reese. TrPWD
Stars are heard, The. Lament of This Good Moon. Jules Laforgue. AnFP
Stars are hidden, The. A Group of Verse. Charles Reznikoff. NP
Stars are lighted candles, The. The Stars. Mary Carolyn Davies. DD; HH
Stars Are Lit, The. Hayyim Nahman Bialik, *tr. fr. Hebrew by* Florence L. Friedman. TrJP
Stars are pale, The. The Break of Day. Shaw Neilson. BoAu; BoAV
Stars are shining cheerily, cheerily, The. Turn Ye to Me. "Christopher North." EBSV
Stars Are True, The. *Unknown.* MaRV
Stars Are with the Voyager, The. Thomas Hood. EnRP; ERP
Stars as Spray. *Unknown, tr. fr. Japanese by* Basil Hall Chamberlain. OnPM
Stars at Tallapoosa. Wallace Stevens. MOAP
Stars began to peep, The. The Little Ghost. Katharine Tynan. HBV
Stars Begin to Fall. *Unknown.* AA
Stars burnt out in the pale blue air, The. Shelley. *Fr.* The Boat on the Serchio. MyFE
Stars catch my eyes, The. A Thought for My Love. Bruce Williamson. NeIP
Stars Dance, The. Thomas Campion. *See* Song: To the Masquers Representing Stars.
Stars Fade. Peretz Hirshbein, *tr. fr. Yiddish by* Joseph Leftwich. TrJP
Stars flicker and there is little left of night, The. Reveille for the Dead. Yiannis Griparis. MoGP
Stars Go By, The. Lilian Bowes-Lyon. ChMP
Stars Go over the Lonely Ocean, The. Robinson Jeffers. GTBS-W; LiTA; LiTM (rev. ed.); NePA; WaP
Stars Have Not Dealt Me, The. A. E. Housman. EnLi-2 (1949 ed.); OxBoLi; SeCeV
Stars have their glory and, or near or far. The Sun Men Call It. John Hall Wheelock. NePoAm-2
Stars have ways I do not know. I Look into the Stars. Jane Draper. HBMV
"Stars," he said, "are very low, The." A Knight of La Mancha. Frank Belknap Long. DaM
Stars, I Have Seen Them Fall. A. E. Housman. More Poems, VII. ChTr; EnLi-2 (1949 ed.); MaPo
Stars in My Country's Sky—Are Ye All There? Lydia Huntley Sigourney. FOAH
Stars in the heaven turn. The Turning Dervish. Arthur Symons. MBP; MoBrPo
Stars know a secret, The. Force. Edward Rowland Sill. AA
Stars Lean Close, The. Lucille Evans. MuM
Stars lie broken on a lake. Reflections. Edna Becker. MaRV; OQP; QP-2
Stars Look at Love, The. Heine. *See* When Young Hearts Break.
Stars Look Down, The. Huw Menai. MoWP
Stars must make an awful noise, The. One Blackbird. Harold Monro. *Fr.* Strange Meetings. NLK; RIS; StaSt; WP
Stars never had any mystery for me, The. Sailor and Inland Flower. Hamish Maclaren. EtS
Stars of Cheer. Caroline D. Swan. JKCP
Stars of midnight shall be dear, The/ To her. Nature's Gifts to Lucy. Wordsworth. *Fr.* Three Years She Grew in Sun and Shower. LiA
Stars of Night contain the glittering Day, The. The Dying Words of Stonewall Jackson. Sidney Lanier. PAH
Stars of the early dawning, set in a field of blue. Ode to the Flag. Charles C. Crellin. PEDC
Stars of the morn, The/ On our banner borne. The Flag of the *Constellation.* Thomas Buchanan Read. EtS; FOAH; PaA
Stars of the Summer Night. Longfellow. *See* Serenade: "Stars of the summer night."
Stars of the superior class. The Stars. Christopher Smart. ChTr; RO
Stars on a winter night. Winter Starset. Elliott Coleman. NoCaPo (1941 ed.)

Stars over snow. Night [*or* It Is Not Far]. Sara Teasdale. BrR; FaPON; MeMeAg; MoSiPe; StVeCh; SUS; TiPo
Stars raced headlong. Seaward headlands lathered. Boris Pasternak, *tr. fr. Russian by* C. M. Bowra. BoRS
Stars Sang in God's Garden, The. Joseph Mary Plunkett. JKCP
Stars scribble on our eyes the frosty sagas. The Aeroplane. Hart Crane. *Fr.* The Bridge: Cape Hatteras. VOD (1935 ed.)
Stars shine forth from the blue sky, The. Even-Song. *Unknown.* BOL
Stars sleep upon the calm black stream; there, pale. Ophelia. Arthur Rimbaud. TrFP
Stars' Song, The. Greville MacDonald. BOL
Stars, Songs, Faces. Carl Sandburg. ChMo; CMP
Stars Stand Up in the Air, The. *Tr. fr. Irish by* Thomas MacDonagh. AnIV; GTIV
Stars that swing from twilight to far dawn, The. Sanctuary. Mildred Wojtalewicz. WHL
Stars trembling o'er us and sunset before us. In Our Boat. Dinah Maria Mulock Craik. HBV
Stars wheel in purple, yours is not so rare. Let Zeus Record. Hilda Doolittle ("H. D."). MAP; MoAmPo
Stars wheel past the windows, The. For the New Year. Norman Nicholson. NeBP
Stars with their laughter are shaken, The. A Song of Laughter. Theodore Maynard. JKCP
Starscape, A. John Bellenden. ACP
Starshine on the Arch is silver white, The. Villanelle of Washington Square. Walter Adolphe Roberts. PFE; PoNe
Start, A. Transfigured Swan. Louis Untermeyer. MAP
Start not—nor deem my spirit fled. Lines Inscribed upon a Cup Formed from a Skull. Byron. RO
Start Where You Stand. Berton Braley. PoToHe
Starting Early from the Ch'u-ch'eng Inn. Po Chü-i, *tr. fr. Chinese by* Arthur Waley. TrCh
Starting from Paumanok. Walt Whitman. AtBAP
Sels.
Necessity of Religion, The. MaRV
(For Religion's Sake.) GrCo-1
"Starting from fish-shape Paumanok." ViBoPo
Starting on the Journey. Verner von Heidenstam, *tr. fr. Swedish by* Charles W. Stork. AnSL
Startled/ By a single scream. Saigyo Hoshi, *tr. fr. Japanese by* Arthur Waley. AWP; PFE, *tr. wr. at. to* Curtis Hidden Page
Startling all spirits, dreams, and secrets. To Our Catchment Board. Edmund Blunden. MoPW
Starvation Peak Evening. David O'Neil. AnAmPo; LA
Starved Rock. Edgar Lee Masters. ChMo; CMP
Starving, savage, I aspire. The Tiger of Desire. Tom MacInnes. BoCaPo
Starving to Death on a Government Claim. *Unknown. See* Lane County Bachelor, The.
Starving wolves along the main sea prowl, The. The Ocean of Ice. Ambrose Philips. *Fr.* A Winter Piece. BeR
State, The. Randall Jarrell. MiAP
State, The. Sir William Jones. *See* What Constitutes a State?
State of Age, The. George Meredith. VLEP
State of Arkansas [*or* Arkansaw], The. *Unknown.* CoSo, *with music;* CSF; TrAS, *abr., with music*
(Arkansaw Traveler, The, *diff. vers.*) ViBoFo
State of Innocence and the Fall of Man, The, *br. sel.* Dryden. Paradise. BeR
State of Maine Song. Roger Vinton Snow. PoRL
State Street is lonely today. Aunt Jane Allen. Fenton Johnson. GoSl; PoNe
State versus Conscience, The. Sophocles, *tr. fr. Greek by* Gilbert Murray. *Fr.* Antigone. GrR
(Higher Command, The, *tr. unknown.*) MaRV
(Undying Law, The, *tr. by* C. M. Bowra.) OxBG
State We Honor, The. Fanny J. Crosby. PoRL
State with the prettiest name, The. Florida. Elizabeth Bishop. AmP
Stateliest Measure, The. Virgil, *pr. tr. fr. Latin by* H. R. Fairclough. *Fr.* Georgics, III. LiA
Stately dames of Rome their pearls did wear, The. Ferdinando Ieronimi's Sonnet. George Gascoigne. ElSeCe
Stately homes of England, The. The Homes of England. Felicia Dorothea Hemans. CG; DiM; LPS-1; PECK; WhC
Stately Homes of England, The, *parody.* E. V. Knox. WhC
Stately, kindly, lordly friend. To a Cat. Swinburne. CIV; PoC
Stately Lady, The. Flora Sandstrom. BoTP
. . . Stately-sailing swan, The. Swan, Turkey, Dove, and the Bull in the Broom. James Thomson. *Fr.* The Seasons: Spring. BeR
Stately Southerner, The. *Unknown. See* Yankee Man-of-War, The.
Stately the feast, and high the cheer. The Grave of King Arthur. Thomas Warton, the Younger. CEP; EnRP; GoTL
Stately Verse. *Unknown.* FaPON; TiPo (1959 ed.)
States are not great except as men may make them. John Brown. Eugene F. Ware. GA
States Crowning Washington, The. Kate Bowles Sherwood. WOAH
Statesman and priest alike must yield her place. Jane Addams. Marguerite Wilkinson. CAG
Statesman, I thank thee! and, if yet dissent. To William H. Seward. Whittier. GA
Statesman in Retirement. William Cowper. *Fr.* Retirement. OBEC
Statesman who in speaking all surpassed, A. Eupolis, *tr. fr. Greek by* F. A. Paley. GrPo
Statesman's Holiday, The. W. B. Yeats. AtBAP
Static. Rolfe Humphries. UnS
Static. Gertrude Van Winkle. GFA
Station, The. Kitty Parsons. PCH
Station-Master's Story, The. George R. Sims. PTA-2
Stationary blasts of waterfalls, The. Wordsworth. *Fr.* The Prelude. MeRV
Stationary Journey, The. Edwin Muir. POTE
Stationed Scout, The. Lyman H. Sproull. PoOW
Stations of the Cross, The. Padraic Colum. GoBC
Stations of the Cross, The, *sels.* William A. Donaghy.
He Falls. JKCP (1955 ed.)
He Is Buried. JKCP (1955 ed.)
He Is Condemned. QS
He Meets His Mother. QS
(Fourth Station.) ISi
Thirteenth Station. ISi
Statistician, The. Charles Wharton Stork. PoMa
Statistics. Stephen Spender. MBP; MoBrPo
Statue, The. Hilaire Belloc. ACP (1952 ed.); MoVE
Statue, The. John Berryman. LiTM (1946 ed.)
Statue, The. Robert Finch. BoCaPo (1948 ed.); PeCV
Statue, A. R. Pier. CAG
Statue and Birds. Louise Bogan. MAP; MoAB; MoAmPo
Statue and the Bust, The. Robert Browning. BEL; BMEP; BPN; EM-2; EmBrPo; EnLi-2 (1939 ed.); EPN; GEPC; OAEP; PIAE; PoVP; TOP; ViPP; VLEP
Statue and the Perturbed Burghers, The. Denis Devlin. OnYI
Statue, The—Buonarroti said—doth wait. Epigram [*or* Sculpture and Song]. Sir William Watson. MBP; MoBrPo (1942 ed.); PIAE
Statue by Lysippus, A. Poseidippus, *tr. fr. Greek by* John Addington Symonds. OxBG
Statue in a Garden, A. Agnes Lee. HBMV; NP
Statue Inscribed "Lee," Richmond. Mary Sinton Leitch. LS
("Lee.") BoHiPo
Statue of a Dog. Macedonius, *tr. fr. Greek by* T. F. Higham. OxBG
Statue of Berenice, A. Callimachus, *tr. fr. Greek by* G. M. Young. GrL
Statue of Cypris, A. Anyte, *tr. fr. Greek by* Sir William Marris. OxBG
Statue of Liberty, The. Sheila Jane Crooke. DDA; YaD
Statue of Liberty, The. Thomas Hardy. EPN; LiTB
Statue of Liberty, The. Edgar Lee Masters. HiLiAm
Statue of Lorenzo de' Medici, The. J. E. Nesmith. AA
Statue of Love, A. *At.* to Zenodotus, *tr. fr. Greek by* H. Wellesley. OxBG
Statue of Pan, A. *Unknown, tr. fr. Greek by* R. A. Furness. OxBG
Statue of Shadow, The. John Peale Bishop. LiTA
Statue, The, stood/ Of Newton. Newton. Wordsworth. *Fr.* The Prelude, III. ImOP
Statue, tolerant through years of weather, The. The Statue. John Berryman. LiTM (1946 ed.)
Statues, The. Laurence Binyon. OBEV (new ed.); OBVV
Statues, The. W. B. Yeats. AnIL
Statuette; Late Minoan. C. Day Lewis. EnLit; OxBI
Status. Alberta Robison. MuM
Status Quo. Binga Dismond. PoNe
Statute. Josephine Miles. FiMAP
Stave of Roving Tim, A. George Meredith. EmBrPo
Stavin' Chain, *with music. Unknown.* OuSiCo; StDa, *diff. song, with same opening stanza*
Stay as the tree—go as the wind. Motto for a Tree-planting. Richard Watson Gilder. PoRL
Stay at Home, The. Martha Haskell Clark. VOD
Stay-at-Home, The. Marjorie Charles Driscoll. DDA
Stay-at-Home, The. Josephine Preston Peabody. CV
Stay, Christmas! Ivy O. Eastwick. SiSoSe
Stay, fellow-traveler, let us stop and think. The Poets at a House-Party. Carolyn Wells. PA
Stay, Fortunatus, once more hear me speak. Thomas Dekker. *Fr.* Old Fortunatus. ViBoPo
Stay here, above the portal set. The Desolate Wreath. Asclepiades. GrR
Stay here fond youth and ask no more, be wise. Against Fruition. Sir John Suckling. NBE

Stay, jailer, stay, and hear my woe! The Maniac. Matthew Gregory Lewis. LPS-1
Stay, June, Stay! Christina Rossetti. *Fr.* Sing-Song. YeAr
("Days are clear, The.") RIS; TiPo
Stay Little Always. Jessie Corrigan Pegis. JKCP (1955 ed.)
Stay near me—do not take thy flight! To a Butterfly. Wordsworth. BPN; EmBrPo; EnRP; ERP; GEPC
Stay near me. Speak my name. Oh, do not wander. Mid-century Love Letter. Phyllis McGinley. ViBoPo (1958 ed.)
Stay not for me, O sailor, your vessel's swift careering. The Desolation of Berytus. Johannes Barbucallus, *tr. by* F. L. Lucas. GrPE
Stay not your course, nor, shipman, drop your sail. A Ruined Harbour. Johannes Barbucallus, *tr. by* Sir William Marris. OxBG
Stay now with me, and list to my sighs. Dante. *Fr.* La Vita Nuova. AWP
Stay, O Stay. A. E. Coppard. MBP; MoBrPo (1942 ed.)
Stay O stay why dost thou fly me. *Unknown.* SeCSL
Stay! O Stay! Ye Winged Howers. Matthew Stevenson. *See* At the Florists' Feast in Norwich.
Stay, O sweet, and do not rise! Break of Day [*or* Day-break]. John Donne. EG; ElL; LoPS; OBEV; TOP; TrGrPo
Stay, Phoebus! Edmund Waller. *See* Song: "Stay, Phoebus, stay!"
"Stay!" she said. "Keep at least one soul unspecked." Robert Browning. *Fr.* A Forgiveness. ReTS
Stay, ship from Thames, with fettered sails. Ship from Thames. Rex Ingamells. MoAuPo
Stay, speedy Time, behold, before thou pass. To Time. Michael Drayton. Idea, XVII. OBSC; SiCE
Stay, Spring. Andrew Young. FaBoTw
Stay, Stay at Home, My Heart, and Rest. Longfellow. *See* Home Song.
Stay, Stay, Old Time. *Unknown.* SeCL
Stay, stay, sweet Time! Behold, or ere thou pass. Michael Drayton. Idea's Mirrour, VII. ReIE
Stay, stay, thou lovely, fearful snake. An American Love-Ode. Thomas Warton, the Elder. CEP
Stay, stay, ye greedy merchants, stay. Chloris a Constant Comfort. Henry Hughes. SeCL
Stay, Thames, to heare my song, thou great and famous flood. Michael Drayton. *Fr.* The Third Eclogue. AtBAP; PoEL-2
Stay, Time. James Wreford Watson. CaP
Stay we here/ With the wild hawks? Robert Browning. *Fr.* Pauline. MyFE
Stay weary traveler, stay! The Fountain at the Tomb. Nicias. AWP; JAWP; WBP
Stay with me, God. The night is dark. A Soldier—His Prayer. Gerald Kersh. QS; TreFS
Stay, woodsman, stay thy hand awhile, and hark. Pierre de Ronsard. *Fr.* Elegies. PrPoCR
Stay yet, my friends, a moment stay. A Song for New Year's Eve. Bryant DD; MPB; PoRL
Staye, staye Aeneas, for thyne owne sake staye. *Unknown.* SeCSL
Staying at the Official Residence on a Spring Night. Tu Fu, *tr. fr. Chinese.* WhP
(Night Vigil in the Left Court of the Palace, A, *tr. by* Witter Bynner.) LiTW
Staying in bed and being sick. Being Sick. Jimmy Garthwaite. BrR
Steadfast. Arthur Hugh Clough. *See* "With Whom Is No Variableness, neither Shadow of Turning."
Steadfast Cross! *Unknown.* *See* Holy Cross.
Steadfast Mind, The. Thomas Carew. *See* Disdain Returned.
Steadfast they stood, as mists that upon windless days. Clouds upon Windless Peaks. Homer. *Fr.* The Iliad, V. GrPE
Steadfastness. Sir Thomas Wyatt. *See* Forget Not Yet.
Steady, boys, steady! Wounded to Death. John W. Watson. LPS-2
Steady heart, which in its steadiness, The. Angina Pectoris. W. R. Moses. LiTA
Steal Away to Jesus. *Unknown.* BoAN-1, *with music;* OlF
(Steal Away.) *Unknown.* APW; SPP; TrGrPo
Steal from the meadows, rob the tall green hills. A Song. Lord Alfred Douglas. JKCP (1926 ed.); PoVP
Steal up, young ladies. Mah Mammy Stoled a Cow. *Unknown.* SoAF
Stealing. James Russell Lowell. MaRV; TreF
Stealthy the silent hours advance, and still. On a Sundial. Hilaire Belloc. MoVE
Steam. Frederick Mortimer Clapp. VOD
Steam Power. Erasmus Darwin. *Fr.* The Botanic Garden: The Economy of Vegetation, I. BoHiPo; OBEC
Steam Shovel. Charles Malam. PoMa
Steam Shovel, The. Eunice Tietjens. NP; PoeMoYo
Steam-shovels had sunk their teeth, The. The Riveter. Joseph Auslander. PoeMoYo
Steam Threshing-Machine, The. Charles Tennyson Turner. CBOV; PoVP
Steamboat is a slow poke, The. Boats. Rowena Bastin Bennett. GFA; TiPo
Steamboat's a dange'ous thing. Down the Rivuh, Down, Boys. *Unknown.* StDa
Steamboat's coming 'round the bend. *Unknown.* LaNeLa
Steamfitter had no notion of buying an opal, The. Opal. Josephine Miles. FiMAP
Steed, a steed of matchless speed, A. The Cavalier's Song. William Motherwell. EBSV; GN; HBV; OTPC
Steed bit his master, The. On a Clergyman's Horse Biting Him. *Unknown.* GoTP; LiTG; OxBoLi; SiTL; WhC
Steeds of Heaven, The. Homer, *tr. fr. Greek by* F. L. Lucas. *Fr.* The Iliad, V. GrPE
Steel. Joseph Auslander. TBM; TCPD
Steel. Henri DeWitt Saylor. PoMa
Steel fibrous slant & ribboned glint, The. The Turncoat. LeRoi Jones. NeAP
Steel Glass, The, *sels.* George Gascoigne.
"Behold him, priests, and though he stink of sweat." ReEn
"But that my lord may plainly understand." ReEn
"For whiles I mark this weak and wretched world." ReIE; SiCE; TuPP
Steel, hard to dent, once dented. If Scars Are Worth the Keeping. Glenn Ward Dresbach. TBM
Steel Laying Holler, *with music.* *Unknown.* ABF
Steel Mill. Louis Untermeyer. TCPD
(Munitions Plant.) PIAE
Steel Mills after Midnight. Louise Crenshaw Ray. JKCP (1955 ed.)
Steel the Flint abused, The. The Flint and the Steel. Tomás de Iriarte. BoChLi
Steel Valley, 1938. George Woodcock. MoWP
Steelhead. Robinson Jeffers. WoL
Steelyards, The. Charles Bruce. BoCaPo (1948 ed.)
Steep Slopes of Morning, The. Mary Weeden. MuM
Steep, Stone Steps. Norman Cameron. MoPW
Steeped in ecstasies of perfume. Spring Nocturne. Abraham Liessin. TrJP
Steeple-Jack, The. Marianne Moore. *Fr.* Part of a Novel, Part of a Poem, Part of a Play. AmPP; CoBMV; CrMA; ExPo; FaBoMo; MoPo; OnHM; OxBA
Steer, Bold Mariner, On! Schiller, *tr. fr. German.* MC
Steer hither, steer, your wingèd pines. The Siren's Song [*or* Song of the Sirens]. William Browne. *Fr.* The Inner Temple Masque. BCEP; ChTr; CoEV; EG; ElL; ElSeCe; EtS; EV-2; LPS-3; OBEV; OBS; ViBoPo
Steering Home. Timothy Daniel Sullivan. TIP
Stein Family, The. *Unknown.* BOHV
Stein Song, A. Richard Hovey. *Fr.* Spring. CP; HBV; LA; MAP; MoAmPo (1942 ed.); NeMA; PFY
("Give a rouse, then, in the Maytime.") AnAmPo
Stella. Charles Henry Crandall. AA
Stella Flammarum. Wilfred Campbell. CPG; WoL
Stella is sick, and in that sick-bed lies. Astrophel and Stella, CI. Sir Philip Sidney. SiPS
Stella Looked On. Sir Philip Sidney. *See* Astrophel and Stella, XLI.
Stella Maris. Katherine Drayton Mayrant Simons. LS
Stella Maris, *sels.* John Addington Symonds.
"Give me thyself! It were as well to cry." PoVP
(Thyself.) VA
"How often have I now outwatched the night." PoVP
"Venice, thou Siren of sea-cities, wrought." HBV; PIAE; PoVP; VA
Stella Maris, I remember. Stella Maris. Katherine Drayton Mayrant Simons. LS
Stella Matutina. Lilian Doherty. WHL
Stella oft sees the very face of woe. Astrophel and Stella, XLV. Sir Philip Sidney. PoE; ReEn; SiCE; SiPS; TuPP
Stella, since thou so right a princess [*or* princesse] art. Astrophel and Stella, CVII. Sir Philip Sidney. EV-1; HBV; MaPo; ReEn; SiPS
Stella Sleeping. Sir Philip Sidney. Astrophel and Stella: Second Song. SiPS
Stella, the fullness of my thoughts of thee. Astrophel and Stella, L. Sir Philip Sidney. ReEn; SiPS
Stella, the only planet of my light. Astrophel and Stella, LXVIII. Sir Philip Sidney. OBSC; ReEn; SiPS
Stella, think not that I by verse seek fame. Astrophel and Stella, XC. Sir Philip Sidney. ElSeCe; EnLit; OBSC; ReEn; SiCE; SiPS; TuPP
Stella this day is thirty-four. Stella's Birth-Day, Written in the Year 1718. Swift. CEP; EiPP; EnLoPo
Stella, whence doth these new assaults arise. Astrophel and Stella, XXXVI. Sir Philip Sidney. SiPS
Stella, while now by Honour's cruel might. Astrophel and Stella, XCI. Sir Philip Sidney. SiPS
Stella's Birthday ("This day, whate'er the Fates decree"). Swift. EiPP; LoBV
(Stella's Birthday; March 13, 1726-27.) CEP; GTIV; OBEC; PoEL-3
Stella's Birthday, 1720 ("All travellers at first incline"). Swift. CBOV; EV-3; OxBI

(Stella's Birth-Day; Written A.D. 1720-21.) PoEL-3
Stella's Birth-Day, Written in the Year 1718 ("Stella this day is thirty-four"). Swift. CEP
(On Stella's Birthday.) EiPP
(Stella's Birth-day.) EnLoPo
Stenographers, The. P. K. Page. BoCaPo; CaP; PeCV; TwCaPo
. . . Step, A/ A single step, that freed me. Mist Opening in the Hills. Wordsworth. *Fr.* The Excursion. UnW
Step by step, step by step. Evening Walk. David Einhorn. OnCuPl
Step lightly across the floor. The Passer-by. Edith M. Thomas. AV
Step lightly on this narrow spot! Emily Dickinson. NePA
Step out from your curtain of silvered shadow. Hymn to the Harvest Moon. Erik Axel Karlfeldt. AnSL
Step silently if you would hear. Woodland Magic. S. Omar Barker. HiLiAm
Step-stream pavement bears. Victoria Dancing. Anne Welsh. BoSA
Step to silence taken, The. Wild Philomela. William Rose Benét. NP
Stephano's Song. Shakespeare. *See* Master, the Swabber, The.
Stephen and Time. Lines for the Tombstone of a Singing-Master. *Unknown.* LauV
Stephen Le Gout, in the nominative. Rondel. Charles d'Orléans. FoS
Stephen ostler now doth drive. An Old New-Year's Song. Oscar Levertin. AnSL
Stepney Green. John Singer. WaP
Steppe in the Nazas Country, A. Manuel José Othón, *tr. fr. Spanish by* Samuel Beckett. AnMP
Stepping Stones, The. Conrad Aiken. CrMA
Stepping Westward. Wordsworth. BEL; BPN; CH; EmBrPo; EnLi-2; EnRP; ERP; ExPo; GEPC; HBV; OBRV; PoEL-4; SeCeV; ShBV-4
Steps, The. Paul Valéry, *tr. fr. French by* Donald Petersen. ReMP
Steps of the Commander, The. Aleksandr Blok, *tr. fr. Russian by* C. M. Bowra. BoR
Stern be the pilot in the dreadful hour. To Abraham Lincoln [*or* Sonnet in 1862]. John James Piatt. AA; BlG; LBAH
Stern Daughter of the Voice of God! Ode to Duty. Wordsworth. AWP; BCEP; BEL; EM-2; EmBrPo; EnLit; EnLP; EnRP; EPN; EPP; ERP; EV-3; GEPC; GrCo-1; GTBS; GTBS-D; GTBS-W; GTSE; GTSL; HBV; HBVY; InPo; JAWP; LH; MaRV; OBEV; OBRV; PIAE; PoFS; REAL; TCEP; TOP; TreFS; TyEnPo; WBP; WGRP
Stern destroyer struck out my life, A. A Bible. *Unknown. Fr.* Riddles. EnLi-1; OuHeWo
Stern eagle of the far north-west. The Song of the Reim-Kennar. Sir Walter Scott. *Fr.* The Pirate. OAEP
Stern granite Gate of Wicklow, with what awe. The Scalp. George Francis Savage-Armstrong. TIP
Stern gray glory of old days is still, The. St. Maixent. Allen Crafton. POT
Stern lover in your helm of steel. The Only Pretty Ringtime. A. V Bowen. POTE
Stern Parent, The. Harry Graham. ChTr
(Some Ruthless Rhymes, I.) CenHV
Stethoscope tells what everyone fears, The. Academic. Theodore Roethke. CrMA; MiAP
Stevedores, The. John Gould Fletcher. Down the Mississippi, V. ChMo; CMP; HiLiAm; LiTA; MOAP; NP; PoTo; TCAP
Stevenson's Birthday. Katherine Miller. AA; PECK
Stewball, *with music. Unknown.* ABF
Sthreets of Home. Denis A. McCarthy. PoTo
Stick, The. May O'Rourke. HBMV
Stick to It. Edgar A. Guest. FaFP
Stick your patent name on a signboard. The River. Hart Crane. *Fr.* The Bridge: Powhatan's Daughter. AmP; AmPP; AnFE; CoAnAm; CoBA; CoBMV; CoV; LiTA; MoAB; MoAmPo; NAMP; OxBA; TwAmPo; ViBoPo (1958 ed.)
Stiff are the warrior's muscles. Lines Written after a Battle. *Unknown.* BOHV; InMe
Stifling day was harsh and hot, The. "Feodor Sologub," *tr. fr. Russian by* C. M. Bowra. BoRS
Stigmata. Edwin McNeill Poteat. MaRV
Stigmata. Charles Warren Stoddard. JKCP; TrPWD
Stigmata. A. M. Sullivan. SaFP
Still a bare, silent, solitary glen. Thalaba and the Banquet. Robert Southey. *Fr.* Thalaba the Destroyer. SeCePo
Still am I haunting. Come Down. George Macdonald. TrPWD
Still Amathea thou art fayre. *Unknown.* SeCSL
Still and calm. The Blue Ridge. Harriet Monroe. HBMV
Still and dark along the sea. Twilight on Sumter. Richard Henry Stoddard. PAH; PAP
Still are the meadowlands, and still. In September. Francis Ledwidge. POTE; TCPD
Still are the ships that in haven ride. Outwards and Homewards. Francis William Bourdillon. BTP
Still as/ On windless nights. Moon Shadows. Adelaide Crapsey. AnAmPo; LA; NeMA; PFE
Still, as each night dwindles, new-born each dawn we find us. "To-Morrow Is a New Day." Palladas. GrPE
Still as I move thou movest. Her Shadow. Elisabeth Cavazza Pullen. AA
Still as of Old. Hester H. Cholmondeley. *See* Betrayal.
Still as the holy of holies breathes the vast. Dawn. "Æ." BEL
Still at it? Morning stares between the shutters. Persius. Satires, III. LaP
Still bathed in its moonlight slumber, the little white house by the cedar. Reveille. W. W. Gibson. ChMo; CMP
Still by meadow and stream. The Whisperer. Arthur Bullen. HBMV (2d ed.)
Still by the Cloud Stricken. Stéphane Mallarmé, *tr. fr. French by* Kate Flores. AnFP
Still chirp the crickets/ Cheerfully. Basho, *tr. fr. Japanese by* Lois J. Erickson. SoLD
Still, Citizen Sparrow. Richard Wilbur. MiAP; MoAB; MoPo; NePA; ReMP
Still Day in Autumn, A. Sarah Helen Whitman. LPS-2
Still do the stars impart their light. Falsehood. William Cartwright. OBEV
Still Falls the Rain. Edith Sitwell. ChMP; CoBMV; FaBoEn; FaBoMo; LiTM; MoAB; MoBrPo (1950 ed.); MoPo; POTE; SeCePo; TrGrPo; TriL; WaaP
Still farther would I fly, my child. An Aboriginal Mother's Lament. Charles Harpur. MOAH; VA
Still fields and silent ways. To Font-Georges. Théodore de Banville. TrFP
Still, for all slips of hers. Rhymes. Thomas Hood. *Fr.* The Bridge of Sighs. LiA
Still glowing from the red-lipped kiss of noon. Twilight. Virginia McCormick. HBMV
Still half in dream, upon the stair I hear. We Meet at Morn. Hardwicke Drummond Rawnsley. POT; PoTo
Still-Heart. Frank Pearce Sturm. OBMV
Still heavy with may, and the sky ready to fall. Before Invasion, 1940. John Betjeman. MoVE
Still herald of the morn, whose ray. The Morning Star. John Hall. SeCL
Still I am patient, tho' you're merciless. The Patriarchal Home. Charles Jeremiah Wells. *Fr.* Joseph and His Brethren. VA
Still I complain; I am complaining still. Edward Taylor. *Fr.* Sacramental Meditations. OxBA; PoEL-3
Still in her native glory, unsubdued. Babylon. Robert Eyres Landor. *Fr.* The Impious Feast. OBRV
Still, in some hidden towns of our Dispersion. The Talmud Student. Hayyim Nahman Bialik. TrJP
Still, it is dear defiance now to carry. Love Note II: Flags. Gwendolyn Brooks. PoNe
Still let me pierce into the midnight depth. Summer. James Thomson. *Fr.* The Seasons. EnRP
Still let my tyrants know, I am not doom'd to wear. Emily Brontë. *Fr.* The Prisoner. BrBE; ChER; EG; GTML; LEAP; OBEV; OBVV; UnW
Still let us go the way of beauty. A Prayer for the Old Courage. Charles Hanson Towne. PC; TrPWD
Still Life. Kathleen Raine. NeBP
Still more, still more: I feel the demon move. David Exorcising Malzah, the Evil Spirit from the Lord. Charles Heavysege. *Fr.* Saul. VA
Still must I hear?—shall hoarse Fitzgerald bawl. Byron. *Fr.* English Bards and Scotch Reviewers. AtBAP; BCEP
Still, O Lord, for Thee I Tarry. Charles Wesley. OxBoCh
Still of Andromache the wail we hear. Life through Verse. Alpheus of Mitylene. OnPM
Still on my cheeks I feel their fondling breath. Stanzas on Mutability. Hugo von Hofmannsthal. AWP; TrJP
Still on the tower stood the vane. The Letters. Tennyson. HBV
Still onward winds the dreary way. In Memoriam A. H. H., XXVI. Tennyson. EmBrPo; EnLi-2; EPN; GEPC; ViPo; VLEP
Still Poem 9. Philip Lamantia. NeAP
Still Pool, The. Kathleen Raine. MoAB
Still round thy towers descend the fertile rain! Cordova. Ibn Zaydun. AWP; LiTW
Still Search, The. Genevieve Taggard. NV
Still, serene, soft day, A; enough of sun. To a Bride. Walter Savage Landor. BPN; EmBrPo
Still shall the tyrant scourge of Gaul. Ode to the Inhabitants of Pennsylvania. *Unknown.* PAH
Still sing the morning stars remote. Matins. John Banister Tabb. SPP
Still sits the school-house by the road. In School-Days. Whit-

Still sits the school-house by the road (*continued*)
tier. AA; AnNE; BLPA; BTP; CoBA; FaBoBe; FaPON; IAP; MPB (1956 ed.); MW; NeHB; OTPC (1946 ed.); PCD; PTA-1; PYM; StVeCh (1940 ed.); TCAP; TreF
Still sleeps the unknown soldier. Memorial. Mae Winkler Goodman. PGD
Still Small Voice, The. A. M. Klein. PeCV
Still Small Voice, The. Alexander Smart. PRWS
Still small voice spake unto me, A. The Two Voices. Tennyson. EmBrPo; PoVP
Still sometimes in my secret heart of hearts. Cor Mio. Christina Rossetti. BPN
Still south I went and west and south again. Prelude. J. M. Synge. AWP; ChTr; HBMV; JAWP; MBP; MoBrPo; NeMA; OBMV; PoFr; TSW; WBP
Still stands the forest primeval; but far away from its shadow. Longfellow. *Fr.* Evangeline: Conclusion. IAP
Still, Still with Thee. Harriet Beecher Stowe. BLRP; BPP; MaRV
(When I Awake I Am Still with Thee.) OQP; QP-1; PraP; TrPWD
Still the Cross. E. Merrill Root. MaRV; StJW
Still the Emasculated. Heine, *tr. fr. German by* Lola Gruenthal. AnGP
Still the faint harps & silver voices calm the weary couch. Night. Blake. *Fr.* The Four Zoas. BoW
Still the ghost of Joseph Alston. Theodosia Burr. Myra Burnham Terrell. GoYe
Still the heat of mid-July. July 14, at Night. Feodor Ivanovich Tyutchev. OnPM; TrRV
Still the mighty mountains stand. Epilogue to Alun Mabon. John Ceiriog Hughes. PrWP
Still the Mind Smiles. Robinson Jeffers. ChMo; CMP
Still the same function, still the same habit come. Preludes to Definition, III. Conrad Aiken. TwAmPo
Still the Wonder Grew. Goldsmith. *Br. sel. fr.* The Deserted Village. TreF
Still the world is wondrous large, seven seas from marge to marge. The Wide, Wide World. Kipling. OtMeF
Still thirteen years: 'tis autumn now. Palinode. James Russell Lowell. AA; IAP
Still Thou Art Question. *Unknown.* ChIP; PGD; StJW
Still Though the One I Sing. Walt Whitman. AA; IAP
Still through Egypt's desert places. Hermes Trismegistus. Longfellow. OBAV
Still through the dusk of dead, blank-legended. Octaves, XI. E. A. Robinson. CoV
Still Thy Sorrow, Magdalena! *Tr. by* E. A. Washburn. BePJ
Still to Be Neat, Still to Be Dressed [*or* Drest]. Ben Jonson. *See* Simplex Munditiis.
Still tow'rd new shores we wend our unreturning way. The Lake. Alphonse de Lamartine. LiA
Still Undaunted. George B. Ryan. CIV
Still under the leaves green. The Murning Maiden. *Unknown.* EBSV
Still Voyager. *Unknown.* DDA
Still was the night, serene & bright. Sounding of the Last Trump [*or* The Summons]. Michael Wigglesworth. *Fr.* The Day of Doom. AWP; TCAP
Still Waters. *Unknown. See* Rivers Till and Tweed, The.
Still we behold Troy city from her foundations shaken. Homer. Alpheus. GrPE
Still we think of it. It is as if. A Young Girl's Tomb. Rainer Maria Rilke. AnGP
Still we who follow Christ in deed. Eucharist. E. Merrill Root. ChIP; OQP; QP-2
Still wilt thou sigh, and still in vain. The Expostulation. Thomas Shadwell. *Fr.* The Squire of Alsatia. OAEP
Stillborn Love. Dante Gabriel Rossetti. The House of Life, LV. BPN; EmBrPo; EnLi-2; EPN; PoVP; ViPo
Stillborn Silence, thou that art. Invocation of Silence [*or* Silence Invoked]. Richard Flecknoe. GoBC; SeCL
Stille Nacht. Joseph Mohr. *See* Silent Night.
Stilled the meek glory of thy music. The Ruinous Abbey. Walter de la Mare. MeRV
Stillness. James Elroy Flecker. BLV; CH; GTBS-D; MBP; MoBrPo; POTT
Stillness and Sound. Simonides, *tr. fr. Greek by* C. M. Bowra. GrL; OxBG
Stillness of the Poem, The. Ron Loewinsohn. NeAP
Stimulus of Friendship, The. *Unknown.* OQP; QP-1
Sting of Death, The. Frederick George Scott. BoCaPo; PeCV
Stinger and Gonoph and Peterman. Another Villon-ous Variation. Don Marquis. HBMV
Stinging/ gold swarms. Sunset [*or* Impression]. E. E. Cummings. MAP; MoAB; MoAmPo
Stinging Nettle, The. A. E. Housman. More Poems, XXXII. POTE
(With Seed the Sowers Scatter.) EnLi-2 (1949 ed.)
Stir not, whisper not. The River. Patrick MacDonogh. NeIP
Stir—shake off sleep. Love Lyric. Max Michelson. NP
Stir the pot and mix the brew. Devil's Cauldron. Monk Gibbon. HaMV
Stirred Waters, The. *Unknown, tr. fr. Chinese by* Bernhard Karlgren. *Fr.* Shi King. ChLP
Stirring suddenly from long hibernation. Mid-Winter Waking. Robert Graves. CoEV; MoAB
Stirrup Cup, The. Douglas Ainslie. EBSV; GoTS
Stirrup-Cup, The. John Hay. AA; HBV; LBAP
Stirrup Cup, The. Aline Kilmer. CAW
Stirrup-Cup, The. Sidney Lanier. AA; AmP; BAP; CoBA; IAP; LBAP; MOAP; OBAV; OQP; PFY; QP-2; SPP; TCAP; TOP
Stirrup Cup, The. William Alexander Percy. WHA
Stitches over and over. Lesbia Sewing. Harold Vinal. HBMV
Stitching. Christina Rossetti. *See* Pocket Handkerchief to Hem, A.
Stock whom Cromwell planted here, The. Lines Written in a Country Parson's Orchard. Leslie Daiken. OnYI
Stockdove, The. Ruth Pitter. HaMV; SeCePo
Stockdoves, The. Andrew Young. POTE
Stockholm in White. Daniel Fallström, *tr. fr. Swedish by* Charles W. Stork. AnSL
Stocking Fairy. Winifred Welles. BoChLi; FaPON; TiPo
Stocking Song on Christmas Eve. Mary Mapes Dodge. ChBR; OHIP
Stockings are a trouble; so many times my toes. Troubles. Dorothy Aldis. StVeCh
Stockman, The. David Campbell. MoAuPo
Stoic, The. Theognis, *tr. fr. Greek by* F. L. Lucas. GrPE
Stoic, The; for Laura von Courten. Edgar Bowers. NePoEA; PtPa
Stoics, The. E. J. Pratt. NeTW
Stoic's Resignation, The. Cleanthes. *See* God Leads the Way.
Stoics think, The (and they come near the truth). Sonnet. Richard Barnfield. ReIE
Stoic's Wedding, The. Lucan, *tr. fr. Latin by* Gilbert Highet. *Fr.* Pharsalia, II. LaP
Stolen Boat, The. Wordsworth. *See* Prelude, The: "One summer evening . . ."
Stolen Bow, The. Sophocles, *tr. fr. Greek by* C. M. Bowra. *Fr.* Philoctetes. OxBG
(Philoctetes Robbed of His Bow, *tr. by* Sir George Young.) GrR
Stolen Bride, The. *Unknown, tr. fr. Danish by* E. M. Smith-Dampier. BoDaBa
Stolen Child, The. W. B. Yeats. BEL; EnLi-2 (1949 ed.); GTIV; GTML; MPB; OnYI; OxBI; PoMS; POTE; PoVP; TVSH
Stolen Fifer, The. Padraic Fiacc. NeIP
Stolen Heart, The. Arthur Rimbaud, *tr. fr. French by* Norman Cameron. MiFP
Stolen Kiss, A. George Wither. *Fr.* Fair Virtue, the Mistress of Philarete. HBV; LiTL; PeBoSo; SeCL
(Sonnet upon a Stolen Kiss.) LPS-1
Stolen Penknife, The. Ibn Sa'id of Alcala la Real, *tr. fr. Arabic by* A. J. Arberry. MooP
Stolen Pleasure. William Drummond of Hawthornden. EnLoPo
Stolen Pleasure. Ibn Shuhaid, *tr. fr. Arabic by* A. J. Arberry. MooP
Stol'n to this paradise, and so entranced. Keats. *Fr.* The Eve of St. Agnes. LO
Stond [*or* Stand] Who So List upon the Slipper Toppe [*or* Top]. Seneca, *tr. fr. Latin by* Sir Thomas Wyatt. *Fr.* Thyestes. PoEL-1; SiPS
(Of the Mean and Sure Estate.) SiCE
Stone, The. Emily Dickinson. *See* How happy is the little stone.
Stone, A. Richard Eberhart. NePoAm-2
Stone, The. W. W. Gibson. CV; LBBV; MBP; MoBrPo; NeMA
Stone, The. Anne Morrow Lindbergh. SaFP
Stone, The. Peter McArthur. PCN
Stone, The. Kenneth W. Porter. ChIP; PSO
Stone, The. Thomas Vaughan. OBS; PrWP
Stone, The/ would like to be. Evolution. May Swenson. TrGrPo (rev. ed.)
Stone-Age Sea, The. Helen Hoyt. NP
Stone, bronze, stone, steel, stone, oakleaves, horses' heels. Triumphal March. T. S. Eliot. *Fr.* Coriolan. KN; PoLFOT; ShBV-4; SoV; WaaP
Stone cries from the wall, The. Epitaph. *Unknown.* TrJP
Stone Crop, The. Robert P. Tristram Coffin. PaA
Stone Drums, The. *Unknown, formerly at. to* Hsuan, *tr. fr. Chinese by* Yu Min-chuan. WhP
Stone Fleet, The. Herman Melville. BAV; EtS
Stone from the Gods. Irma Wassall. GoYe
Stone goes straight, The. Washington Monument by Night. Carl Sandburg. ChMo; CMP; FaPON; OHIP

Stone-gray roses by the desert's rim, The. The Princess. W. J. Turner. HBMV
Stone Horse Shoals. Malcolm Cowley. TwAmPo
Stone jug and a pewter mug, A. The Kavanagh. Richard Hovey. HBV; LBAP
Stone Mountain. Mary Brent Whiteside. HiLiAm; LS
Stone of the Sepulcher, The. "Susan Coolidge." EOAH
Stone-Pit. John Clare. RO
Stone Staircase Overlooking the Sea. Fuyuji Tanaka, *tr. fr. Japanese by* Takamichi Ninomiya *and* D. J. Enright. PoLJ
Stone the size of man was my stone, A. A Stone. Richard Eberhart. NePoAm-2
Stone Trees. John Freeman. LBBV; MBP; TCPD
Stone Venus fixed and still. The Venus of Bolsover Castle. Sacheverell Sitwell. HBMV
Stone Walls. Julie Mathilde Lippmann. AA
Stone walls do not a prison make. Richard Lovelace. *Fr.* To Althea from Prison. CBE; MaRV; OQP; QP-2
Stone Well, The. Chien Hsu, *tr. fr. Chinese.* WhP
Stonebreaker, The. Jeppe Aakjaer, *tr. fr. Danish by* Charles W. Stork. BoDS
Stonecutter, The. Valery Yakovlevich Bryusov, *tr. fr. Russian by* C. M. Bowra. BoR
Stone-cutters fighting time with marble, you foredefeated. To the Stone-Cutters. Robinson Jeffers. AmP; AmPP; InP; MAP; MoAB; MoAmPo; MoVE; NeMA; OxBA; PC; PoLFOT; TBM; TrGrPo
Stonefish and Starfish. John Blight. BoAV; NeLNL
Stone Fish Lake. Yüan Chieh, *tr. fr. Chinese by* Arthur Waley. TrCh
Stones and Blossoms. *Unknown, tr. fr. Spanish by* Havelock Ellis. OnPM
Stones of Greece. Stephen Gwynn. NeTW
Stones towards the earth descend. The Soul's Tendency towards Its True Centre. John Byrom. CEP
Stonewall Jackson. Henry Lynden Flash. AA; DD; GA; PAH
Stonewall Jackson's Way. John Williamson Palmer. AA; BlG; DD; GA; HBV; MC; OTPC (1946 ed.); PaA; PAH; SPP
Stonewall's Requiem. M. Deeves. BlG
Stony fields and lonely roads. Northern Graveyards. "Katherine Hale." BoCaPo (1943 ed.); CPG
Stony Town. John Shaw Neilson. BoAV; NeLNL
Stood, at the closed door, and remembered. Prelude LII [*or* One-eyed Calendar]. Conrad Aiken. Preludes for Memnon, LII. BLV; LiTM
Stood the afflicted mother weeping. Stabat Mater Dolorosa. *At. to* Jacopone da Todi, *tr. by* Abraham Coles. HBV; LPS-2
Stood the lovely Mother smiling. Stabat Mater Speciosa. *At. to* Jacopone da Todi, *tr. by* Thomas Walsh. CAW
Stood the Mother in her anguish. Stabat Mater Dolorosa. *At. to* Jacopone da Todi, *tr. by* Thomas Walsh. CAW
Stood the tall Archangel weighing. St. Michael the Weigher. James Russell Lowell. AnFE; AnNE; APA; CAW; CoAnAm; OBAV
Stool Ball. *Unknown.* CH
Stoope, stoope, proud heart, and mounting hopes downe, downe descend. *Unknown.* NBE
Stop All the Clocks. W. H. Auden. NeMA
(Song: "Stop all the clocks.") MoBrPo (1950 ed.)
Stop and consider! life is but a day. What Is Life? Keats. *Fr.* Sleep and Poetry. CBE; EV-4; OBRV; SeCePo
Stop, Christian passer-by!—Stop, child of God. Epitaph [on Himself]. Samuel Taylor Coleridge. BCEP; CH; EmBrPo; EnRP; EPN; ERP; EV-4; FiP; LEAP; MaRV; OAEP; OBRV; OxBoCh; TriL
"Stop, Cuckoo," said the Bee. The Bee and the Cuckoo. Tomás de Iriarte. BoChLi
Stop—Go. Dorothy W. Baruch. FaPON; SUS; TiPo
Stop, let me have the truth of that! Dis Aliter Visum; or, Le Byron de Nos Jours. Robert Browning. ViPP
Stop look &/ listen Venezia. Memorabilia. E. E. Cummings. OnHM
Stop, mortal! Here thy brother lies. A Poet's Epitaph [*or* Burns]. Ebenezer Elliott. BCEP; LPS-3; VA
Stop!—not to me, at this bitter departing. Separation. Matthew Arnold. HBV
Stop on the Appian Way. On the Campagna. Elizabeth Stoddard. AA
Stop playing, poet! May a brother speak? Transcendentalism; a Poem in Twelve Books. Robert Browning. PoVP; VLEP
Stop Pondering on Things Imponderable. Stefan George, *tr. fr. German by* Peter Viereck. AnGP
Stop, Science—Stop! A. P. Herbert. FiBHP
Stop still on the stair. Sops of Light. Fredegond Shove. ChMP
"Stop, stop!" The Maid Freed from the Gallows (B *vers.*). *Unknown.* ViBoFo
Stop, stop and listen for the bough top. The Blackbird of Derrycairn. Austin Clarke. NeIP
"Stop, stop, pretty water!" Runaway Brook. Eliza Lee Follen. GFA
Stop Thief. Herman Knickerbocker Vielé. PR
Stopping at a Friend's Farm-House. Meng Hao-jan, *tr. fr. Chinese by* Witter Bynner. BoFr
Stopping by Woods on a Snowy Evening. Robert Frost. AmP; AmPo; AmPP; AnFE; AnNE; APA; BLV; BoLiVe; CaAE; CBOV; ChMo; CMP; CoAnAm; CoBA; CoBMV; CoV; DDA; ExPo; FaBoCh; FaFP; FaPON; GBV (1952 ed.); GTBS-W; HBMV; HoPM; IAP; InP; InPo; LiTA; LiTG; LiTM; LoGBV; MAP; MaPo; MoAB; MoAmPo; MOAP; MoShBr; MoVE; MW; NeMA; NePA; NP; OTPC (1946 ed.); OxBA; PCD; PG (1955 ed.); PoE; PoeMoYo; PoFS; PoLFOT; PoRA; PoTo; PreP; ReMP; RiBV; ShBV-1; SiSoSe; StaSt; StVeCh; SUS; TBM; ThWaDe; TiPo; TreFS; TrGrPo; TSW; TSWC; TwCV; TwAmPo; TwP; UnPo (3d ed.); UTS; ViBoPo (1958 ed.); WaKn; WHA
Stopping the Night at Jung-yang. Po Chü-i, *tr. fr. Chinese by* Arthur Waley. TrCh
Stopwatch and an Ordnance Map, A. Stephen Spender. BoFr
Store cattle from Nelanjie! The mob goes feeding past. From the Gulf. Will H. Ogilvie. BoAu
Store-House, A. Louis Dudek. CaP
Stories of many slants, gods of sea and sky. Ephemerae for Bruska. Keidrych Rhys. MoWP
Stories of passion make sweet dust. The Garden of the Golden Valley. Tu Mu. ChLP
Stories of Snow. Patricia K. Page. BoCaPo (1948 ed.)
Stork, The. Al-Hajjam, *tr. fr. Arabic by* A. J. Arberry. MooP
Stork, I welcome thy return. The Song of the Stork. *Unknown.* ArmLP
Storks fly over the fields. Spring Song. *Unknown.* PCH
Storm, The. Alcaeus, *tr. fr. Greek by* John Herman Merivale. AWP; JAWP; OnPM; WBP
Storm, The. "Robin Christopher." RIS
Storm, The. Emily Dickinson. *See* There came a wind like a bugle.
Storm, The. John Donne. ReIE; SeEP
Sels.
"England, to whom we owe what we be and have." SG
"South and west winds joined, and, as they blew, The." EtS
Storm. Hilda Doolittle ("H. D."). TiPo; TSW; TSWC
Storm, The. Heine, *tr. fr. German by* Louis Untermeyer. AWP; JAWP; WBP
Storm. Ibn al-Bain, *tr. fr. Arabic by* A. J. Arberry. MooP
Storm, The. Imr el Kais, *tr. fr. Arabic by* Sir Charles Lyall. LiTW
Storm, The, *sel.* Islwyn, *tr. fr. Welsh by* Gwyn Williams.
"For everything is sacred, poetry." PrWP
Storm, The, *sel.* Egan O'Rahilly, *tr. fr. Modern Irish by* P. S. Dinneen *and* T. O'Donoghue.
"Pitiful the playing of the flood with dire destruction!" OnYI
Storm, The. Coventry Patmore. EnLoPo
Storm, The. Pushkin, *tr. fr. Russian by* Sir Cecil Kisch. WaL
Storm, The. Frederick George Scott. CPG
Storm, The. Edward Shanks. AlDL; PtOT
Storm, The. George Alexander Stevens. LPS-2
Storm, The ("Behold, slow-settling . . ."). James Thomson. *Fr.* The Seasons: Summer. LoBV
Storm, The ("See, winter comes . . ."). James Thomson. *Fr.* The Seasons: Winter. CoBE
Storm, A, I, II, *and* III. *Unknown, tr. fr. Anglo-Saxon by* Stith Thompson. *Fr.* Riddles. OuHeWo
Storm, A. Riddles, I. EnLi-1
Storm, The. Richard Untermeyer *and* Louis Untermeyer. *See* Concerning a Storm.
Storm Along. *Unknown. See* Stormalong.
Storm and peril overpast, The. Garrison. Whittier. GA
Storm at Nightfall, The. Morton Dauwen Zabel. NP
Storm at Sea. Alcaeus, *tr. fr. Greek by* C. M. Bowra. GrL; OxBG
Storm at Sea, A. *Unknown, tr. fr. Middle Irish by* Robin Flower. AnIL; LyMA; KiLC, *tr. by* Frank O'Connor
Storm-beaten old watch-tower, A. Symbols. W. B. Yeats. OBMV
Storm came up so very quick, The. Spring Rain. Marchette Chute. TiPo
Storm-Child, The. May Byron. HBV
Storm clouds dim the sky; the tempest. Winter Evening. Pushkin. TrRV
Storm-clouds whirl and storm-clouds scurry. Devils. Pushkin. BoR
Storm Cone, The. Kipling. ChMP; POTE; PoVP
Storm cries every night, The. Spring Song. Hermann Hesse. AWP; JAWP; WBP
Storm-dances of gulls, the barking game of seals, The. Divinely Superfluous Beauty. Robinson Jeffers. LiTL; MAP; MoAmPo

Storm Fear. Robert Frost. DDA; HBV; NP; OBAV; OxBA; TCAP; ViBoPo
Storm had strong intention in its flow, The. Cleavage. Louise Townsend Nicholl. NePoAm
Storm in Harvest. James Thomson. *Fr.* The Seasons: Autumn. EPP
Storm in the Distance, A. Paul Hamilton Hayne. AA; HiLiAm; OBAV
Storm in the skies in the evening. Afanasi Fet, *tr. fr. Russian by* Oliver Elton. BoR
Storm in the sky of an even. Afanasi Fet, *tr. fr. Russian by* Sir Cecil Kisch. WaL
Storm in Winter, A. James Thomson. *See* Winter.
Storm is a bandit, The. The Bandit. Rowena Porter Baker. CAG
Storm is out, The; the land is roused. Men and Boys. Karl Theodor Körner. LPS-2
Storm Is Over, The. Robert Bridges. LiTB; LiTM (rev. ed.); MoPo; OBMV
Storm is riding on the tide, A. The Tragedienne. Zoë Akins. NP
Storm Lines. Bayard Taylor. BAV
Storm on Fifth Avenue. Siegfried Sassoon. MoVE
Storm over Rockefeller Center. Raymond Holden. AnAmPo
Storm Snapped Its Fingers, The. Elizabeth J. Coatsworth. BrR
Storm Song. Bayard Taylor. BBV (1923 ed.); EtS; HBV
Storm-sudden summer filled the dongas with thunder. Estrangement. John Peter. BoSA
Storm upon the mountain. The Lost Lamb. Thomas Westwood. OTPC (1923 ed.); PCH
Stormalong, *with music. Unknown.* AmSS; ShS; SoAmSa
(Storm Along.) SG
Storming of Corinth, The. Byron. *Fr.* The Siege of Corinth. LH
Storming of Stony Point, The. Arthur Guiterman. MC; PAH
Storming of the Achaean Wall, The. Homer, *tr. fr. Greek by* F. L. Lucas. *Fr.* The Iliad, XII *and* XIII. GrPE
Storms are past, the clouds are overblown, The. Bonum Est Mihi Quod Humiliasti Me. Earl of Surrey. SiPS
Storms come and sorrows come. Security. Margaret E. Sangster. BLRP
Storms have beaten on this point of land. Cumulatives. Carl Sandburg. MOAP
Storms once hurled my howls about. The Lighthouse Keeper's Offspring. James Broughton. CrMA
Stormy Day. W. R. Rodgers. AIDL, *abr.*; LiTB
Stormy March is come at last, The. March. Bryant. DD; GN; OTPC
Stormy Night. W. R. Rodgers. OxBI
Stormy Night in Autumn. Chu Shu Chen, *tr. fr. Chinese by* Kenneth Rexroth. OnPC
Stormy Petrel, The. "Barry Cornwall." BLA; EtS; HBV; LPS-2; OTPC; SN; VA
Stormy Petrel, The. Ibsen, *tr. fr. Norwegian by* Charles W. Stork. AnNoLy
Stormy Petrel, The. James Harold Manning. CPG
Stormy Sea. Janet Vaughn. PCD
Stormy sea, A! Waves dashing high! He Shall Speak Peace unto the Nations. Lila V. Walters. BePJ; WBLP
Story. Dorothy Parker. InMe; MaC
Story, a story to you I will tell, A. The Cunning Cobbler Done Over. *Unknown.* CoMu
Story Books. E. V. Lucas. MOB
Story for a Child, A. Bayard Taylor. HBV; HBVY; OTPC (1923 ed.); PCD
(Night with a Wolf, A.) GN; GoTP; PTA-2; TVC; TVSH
Story in the Snow, A. Pearl Riggs Crouch. MPB; TiPo
Story of a Dream, The. Jun Yamamura, *tr. fr. Japanese by* Takamichi Ninomiya *and* D. J. Enright. PoLJ
Story of a fisher lad, The. An Incident of French History. James I. Whitman. PCD
Story of a Summer Day, The. Alexander Hume. *See* Summer Day.
Story of Acontius and Cydippe, *sel.* William Morris. *Fr.* The Earthly Paradise.
Song: "Fair is the night and fair the day." BPN; HBV; POTT; VLEP
Story of Augustus Who Would Not Have Any Soup, The. Heinrich Hoffmann, *tr. fr. German at. to* J. R. Planché. BoN; HBV; HBVY; MoShBr; OnHT; OTPC; TiPo
Story of Baby's Blanket, The. Emilie Poulsson. PPL
Story of Baby's Pillow, The. Emilie Poulsson. PPL
Story of Bellerophon, The. Homer. *See* Glaukos and Diomedes
Story of Cruel Frederick, The. Heinrich Hoffmann, *tr. fr. German at. to* J. R. Planché. BoN
Story of Cruel Psamtek. *Unknown.* NA
Story of Eleusis, The, *sel.* Louis V. Ledoux.
Hymn to Demeter. LEAP
Story of Fidgety Philip, The. Heinrich Hoffmann, *tr. fr. German at. to* J. R. Planché. BoN
Story of Flying Robert, The. Heinrich Hoffmann, *tr. fr. German at. to* J. R. Planché. BoN; RIS
Story of Frederick Gowler, The. The King of Canoodle-Dum. W. S. Gilbert. CenHV
Story of Johnny Head-in-Air, The. Heinrich Hoffmann, *tr. fr. German at. to* J. R. Planché. BoN; TiPo
Story of Jonah, The. Jonah, I: 3-17, Bible, *O.T.* SG
Story of Life, The. John Godfrey Saxe. PoToHe (new ed.)
Story of Little Suck-a-Thumb, The. Heinrich Hoffmann, *tr. fr. German at. to* J. R. Planché. BoN; HBV; HBVY
Story of Macha, The. *Unknown, tr. fr. Middle Irish by* Sir Samuel Ferguson. *Fr.* Dinnshenchas. OnYI
Story of passion's conflict that the laughter-lover told, A. Chalcomede Wards Off Her Lover. Nonnus. *Fr.* Dionysiaca. OxBG
Story of Phaeton, The. Ovid, *tr. fr. Latin by* Zechariah Chafee, Jr. *Fr.* Metamorphoses, II. LaP
Story of Phoebus and Daphne Applied, The. Edmund Waller. EPP; InvP; OBS; SeEP
Story of Ponce de Leon, A. The Fountain of Youth. Hezekiah Butterworth. PAH
Story of Prince Agib, The. W. S. Gilbert. BOHV; InMe; LBN; NA
Story of Pyramid Thothmes, The. *Unknown.* NA
Story of Rimini, The, *sels.* Leigh Hunt.
"One day—'twas on a gentle autumn noon." ERP
Places of Nestling Green. OBRV
("Noble range it was, of many a rood, A.") EnRP
Story of Ruth, The. Bible, *O.T.* *See* Ruth.
Story of Samuel Jackson, The. Charles Godfrey Leland. StPo
Story of Self-Sacrifice, A. James W. Foley. FAOV
Story of Sigurd the Volsung, The, *sels.* William Morris.
Brooding of Sigurd, The. SeCePo
Gunnar in the Pit of Adders, *fr.* IV. PoVP; ViPo
Of the Passing Away of Brynhild, *fr.* III. PoVP; TCEP; VA; VLEP
Sigurd Rideth to the Glittering Heath, *fr.* II. PoEL-5
Slaying of the Niblungs, The, *fr.* IV. LH
Story of Svetaketu, The. *Unknown, tr. fr. Sanskrit by* F. Max Müller. *Fr.* The Upanishads. WoL
Story of the Alchemist, The. Eugene Williams. PCD
Story of the Baby Squirrel, The. Dorothy Aldis. TiPo
Story of the Corn. K. Fisher. BoTP
Story of the Flowery Kingdom. James Branch Cabell. HBMV; PCD
Story of the Inky Boys, The. Heinrich Hoffmann, *tr. fr. German at. to* J. R. Planché. BoN
Story of the Little Rid Hin, The. F. W. Sweetser. SAS
Story of the Man That Went Out Shooting, The. Heinrich Hoffmann, *tr. fr. German at. to* J. R. Planché. BoN
(Story of the Wild Huntsman, The, *sl. diff.*) NA
Story of the Red Cross Knight, or of Holiness, The. Spenser. *See* Legend of the Knight of the Red Cross.
Story of the Shepherd, The. *Unknown, tr. fr. Spanish.* OHIP; SDH
Story of the Wild Huntsman, The. Heinrich Hoffmann. *See* Story of the Man That Went Out Shooting, The.
Story of Thebes, The, *sel.* John Lydgate.
"At a posterne forth they gan to ryde." EPP
Story of Thisbe of Babylon, Martyr, The. Chaucer. *Fr.* The Legend of Good Women. TCEP
Story of Ug, The. Edwin Meade Robinson. HBMV; LHV; YaD
Story of Ulysses, The, *mod.* John Gower. *Fr.* Confessio Amantis, I. SG
Story of Uriah, The. Kipling. LEAP; PIR
Story of Vinland, The. Sidney Lanier. *Fr.* Psalm of the West. PAH
Stoush o' Day, The. C. J. Dennis. NeLNL
Stout. Rue Carpenter. RIS
Stout Didrik dwells in Berneland. Holger Danske and Stout Didrik. *Unknown.* BoDaBa
Stove is orphaned now, The; the old housewife has died. A Cottage Song. Nikolai Alekseyevich Kluyev. TrRV
Stove Pipe Hole, De. William Henry Drummond. IHA
Stowaway. Bill Adams. EtS
Stowed away in a Montreal lumber room. O God! O Montreal! Samuel Butler OxBoLi
Stradivarius. "George Eliot."
(God Needs Antonio, *abr.*) GrCo-2
Working with God, *sel.* MaRV
Strahan, Tonson, Lintot of the times. Impromptus. Byron. BPN
Straight and swift the swallows fly. Rococo. John Payne. OBVV
Straight from a mighty bow this truth is driven. The Arrow. Clarence Urmy. HBMV
Straight from the feast, Akhti, you went to Hell. Epitaph for a Tyrannous Governor Who Choked on Wine. Adib-i Sabir. LiTW
Straight is the downward journey, tho' it be. The Way to Hades. *Unknown.* OxBG
Straight Road, The. Ellen Hooper. HBV

Straight strength pitched into the surliness of the ditch. To a Discarded Steel Rail. Maxwell Bodenheim. NP; PFY
Straight to his heart the bullet crushed. Apocalypse. Richard Realf. PaA; PAP
Straight to Syr Martins hall the Hunters bend. Sunset. William Julius Mickle. *Fr.* The Concubine. OBEC
Straightway Virginius led the maid. The Roman Father's Sacrifice. Macaulay. *Fr.* Lays of Ancient Rome: Virginia. LPS-3
Strain, strain thine eyes, this parting is for aye! Lohengrin. William Morton Payne. AA
Strains upraise of joy and praise, The. Cantemus Cuncti Melodum. Notker Balbulus. CAW
Straiten'd am I, O Lord, upon a pillar. Liberty. Leopold Staff. PoFr
Strampin' the bent, like the Angel o' Daith. Molecatcher. Albert D. Mackie. GoTS
Strand, The. Louis MacNeice. AnIV
Strand-Thistle. Gustav Falke, *tr. fr. German by* Jethro Bithell. AWP
Stranded soldier's epaulet, A. The Silver Bird's Nest. *Unknown.* PEOR
Strange. Stanley Burnshaw. TrJP
Strange. Kirby Doyle. NeAP
Strange. Dorothy Quick. DaM
Strange. Arthur Upson. BAP
Strange, All-absorbing Love. Digby Mackworth Dolben. GoBC; TrPWD
Strange and unnatural! lets stay and see. Destinie. Abraham Cowley. MeLP
Strange are the feelings arising within me. The Love of Hell. Abraham Burstein. TrJP
Strange—as I sat brooding here. Lucy. Walter de la Mare. ChMo; CMP
Strange as it seems, the smallest mammal. The Shrew. Ogden Nash. CenHV
Strange beauty, eight-limbed and eight-handed. Octopus. Arthur Clement Hilton. CenHV
Strange bed, whose recurrent dream we are, The. Hotel de l'Univers et Portugal. James Merrill. MoAB; NePoAm
Strange Bird. Yüan Chi, *tr. fr. Chinese by* Yang Chi-sing. WhP
Strange, bright dancers, The. Poppies. P. A. Ropes. BoTP
Strange Companion, The. Harold Monro. NP
Strange Description of a Rare Garden-Plot, A. Nicholas Breton. ReIE
Strange Experience, A. Josephine Pollard. PEOR
Strange fabled face! From sterile shore to shore. Mirage. Walter de la Mare. MM
Strange Fits of Passion Have I Known. Wordsworth. BPN; CoBE; EG; EM-2; EnL; EnLit; EnRP; EPN; ERP; EV-3; GEPC; LiTB; LiTG; LiTL; OAEP; OBRV; Po; PoE; PoFS; REAL; TCEP; TwP; ViBoPo (Lucy.) EmBrPo; EnLi-2; FiP; HBV; LEAP; LO; OBEV; TrGrPo
Strange foreboding is o'er me, A. The Lorelei. Heine. PoMS
Strange Fortunes of Two Excellent Princes, The, *sel.* Nicholas Breton.
His Wisdom. ALV; OBSC
(I Would Thou Wert Not Fair [*or* I Were Wise].) ElL; InvP
Strange friend, past, present and to be. Tennyson. *Fr.* In Memoriam A. H. H., CXXIX. LO
Strange Girl. Clark Ashton Smith. MuM
Strange grows the river on the sunless evenings! Vesperal. Ernest Dowson. OBMV
Strange Guest. Gertrude Jane Codd. JKCP (1955 ed.)
Strange Guest, The. Alfred Noyes. LBBV
Strange harp! with eerie murmurings. The Wind and the Wires. Benjamin Sledd. NoCaPo
Strange Holiness. Robert P. Tristram Coffin. TwCV
Strange how much sentiment. A Bundle of Letters. Frank Dempster Sherman. PR
Strange, how the moon will come. Moon Magic. Leigh Hanes. StaSt
Strange, how this smooth and supple joint can be. Hands. Louis Untermeyer. AnAmPo; LA
Strange how you go along all day. Strange. Kirby Doyle. NeAP
Strange, in a room closed to the wintry air. Was It the Wind That Stirred? Florence Wilson Roper. UnW
Strange Interlude, A. Margaret Fishback. BOHV
Strange, Is It Not. Edward D. Kennedy. HBMV
Strange is it not if scholars yell. Scholars. *Unknown.* KiLC
Strange, is it not, that youth will always sing. Strange, Is It Not. Edward D. Kennedy. HBMV
Strange is my story, passing prodigy. The Mock Caliph. *Unknown.* EnLi-1
Strange is this thing! My horse I cannot make. Robert Tofte. *Fr.* Laura. ReIE; TuPP
Strange justice walks abroad tonight. Woodrow Wilson. Donald Gillies. DD; GA
Strange land holds thy bones, A. Lost at Sea. Simonides. GrL; OxBG; WoL
Strange Lands. Laurence Alma-Tadema. DD; HBVY; OTPC; PRWS
Strange lesson taught by war. Lessons. Helen Weber. PGD
Strange little spring, by channels past our telling. To a Mountain Spring. Richard Le Gallienne. CV
Strange little tune, so thin and rare. To a Scarlatti Passepied. Robert Hillyer. HBMV; OBAV; VOD
Strange Love. Moses ibn Ezra, *tr. fr. Hebrew by* Solomon Solis-Cohen. TrJP
Strange Man, The. *Unknown.* FaPON; MPB; OTPC (1946 ed.); StVeCh (1940 ed.)
Strange Meeting. Leslie Nelson Jennings. MuM
Strange Meeting. Wilfred Owen. AnFE; AtBAP; BMEP; CaAE; ChMP; CoBE; CoBMV; CoEV; EnLi-2 (1949 ed.); ExPo; FaBoEn; FaBoMo; GTBS-W; KN; LBBV; LiTB; LiTM; LoBV; MBP; MM; MoAB; MoBrPo; MoP; MoPo; MoVE; NAMP; NP; NV; OAEP (2d ed.); PIAE, *abr.*; PoE; POTE; SeCeV; ShBV-4; TrGrPo; TwCV; WaaP; WaP
Strange Meeting. Harper Poulson. UnW
Strange Meetings, *sels.* Harold Monro.
Flower Is Looking through the Ground, A. LBBV; MBP; MoBrPo; TCPD
If Suddenly a Clod of Earth. EPP; LBBV; MBP; MoBrPo
One Blackbird. NLK; RIS; StaSt
("Stars must make an awful noise, The.") WP
Strange misapprehension 'tis—and yet, A. Galileo. Albert Durrant Watson. CPG
Strange Music, The. G. K. Chesterton. OtMeF
Strange Night. Mary Willis Shelburne. UnW
Strange now to think of you, gone without corsets and eyes, while I walk on the sunny pavement of Greenwich Village. Allen Ginsberg. *Fr.* Kaddish. NeAP
Strange old man, A/ Stops me. Kakinomoto no Hitomaro, *tr. fr. Japanese by* Kenneth Rexroth. OnPJ
Strange Pangs of a Poor Passionate Lover, The. *Unknown.* TuPP
Strange Passion of a Lover, A. George Gascoigne. ElSeCe; EnLit; ReIE; SiCE; TuPP
("Amid my bale I bathe in bliss.") ReEn
Strange pie that is almost a passion. A Melton Mowbray Pork-Pie. Richard Le Gallienne. BOHV; PA
Strange Power, I know not what thou art. To Memory. Mary Elizabeth Coleridge. GTML
Strange Promise. Inez Barclay Kirby. UnW
Strange rumours gripped Olympus. Apollo's hand. Home Thoughts. Guy Butler. BoSA
Strange sickness fell upon this perfect creature. On Maou Dying at the Age of Six Months. Frances Cornford. PoC
Strange, since they had made him free. The Convict. Beatrice Redpath. CPG
Strange spirit with inky hair. The Lion. W. J. Turner. MBP; MoBrPo; TrGrPo (1942 ed.)
Strange Talk. L. E. Yates. BoTP
Strange Teeth, The. Nancy Birckhead. RIS
Strange that a sod for just a thrill or two. Strange. Arthur Upson. BAP
Strange that I did not know him then. An Old Story. E. A. Robinson. AnNE; HBMV; MAP; MaRV; MoAmPo; NeMA; TreFS
Strange, that in this nigger place. Esthete in Harlem. Langston Hughes. BANP
Strange that such horror and such grace. To a Fair Lady Playing with a Snake. Edmund Waller. HoPM; PoEL-3
Strange that the spring has come. Only a Flower. Toyohiko Kagawa. MaRV
Strange the formation of the eely race. Eels, Tortoises, Soles, Lampreys. Oppian, *tr. by* William Diaper. *Fr.* Halieuticks. BeR
Strange the world about me lies. World-Strangeness. Sir William Watson. BMEP; MBP; MoBrPo (1942 ed.); PoVP; TCPD; UnW
Strange thing, that a lark and robin sky, A. The Wild Duck. Leroy McLeod. BLA
Strange things happen at night. Rainy Night. James Rorty. MOAP
Strange to be torn away from your embrace. Strange. Stanley Burnshaw. TrJP
Strange Tree. Elizabeth Madox Roberts. BoChLi; FaPON; MPB; NP; SP
Strange violin! Dost thou follow me? The Neighbor. Rainer Maria Rilke. OnPM
Strange Visitor, The. *Unknown.* ChTr; FaBoCh
Strange wanderer out of the deeps. Stella Flammarum. Wilfred Campbell. CPG; WoL
Strange wares are handled on the wharves of sleep. The Wharf of Dreams. Edwin Markham. HBV
Strange was the wooing! Lullaby of the Catfish and the Crab. William Rose Benét. WhC
Strange Wild Song, A. "Lewis Carroll." *See* Gardener's Song, The.

Strange within the Dividing. Ormond Thomas. MoWP
Strangely assorted, the shape of song and the bloody man. The Military Harpist. Ruth Pitter. FaBoTw; MoVE
Strangeness of Heart. Siegfried Sassoon. PtOT; TrJP
Stranger, The. Aleksandr Blok, *tr. fr. Russian by* Babette Deutsch. TrRV
Stranger, The. Jorge Carrera Andrade, *tr. fr. Spanish by* H. R. Hays. BoFr; TwSpPo
Stranger, The. John Clare. OxBoCh
Stranger, The. Walter de la Mare. MoVE; OAEP (2d ed.)
Stranger, The. Georges Duhamel, *tr. fr. French by* Elizabeth Selden. BoFr
Stranger, The. Jean Garrigue. LiTA; LiTM
Stranger, The. Stefan George, *tr. fr. German by* Kenneth Gee. AnGP
Stranger, The. Amanda Benjamin Hall. MuM
Stranger, The. Daniel Henderson. HBMV; TBM
Stranger, The. James Montgomery. BCEP
Stranger, The. John Richard Moreland. ChIP; OQP; QP-1
Stranger. Elizabeth Madox Roberts. MAP; MoAmPo
Stranger, The. Richard Sullivan. JKCP (1955 ed.)
Stranger and countryman to me. Greet All Equally. Macedonius. OnPM
Stranger, approach this spot with gravity. Epitaph on a Dentist [*or* A Dentist *or* On a Dentist]. *Unknown.* GoTP; LiTG; OxBoLi; TreFS; WhC
Stranger at the Peace Table. Esther Baldwin York. MaRV
Stranger! awhile upon this mossy bank. Inscription for a Tablet on the Banks of a Stream. Robert Southey. OBEC
Stranger came one night to Yussouf's tent, A. Yussouf. James Russell Lowell. BBV (1951 ed.); BeLS; BHV; BLPA; BoTP; FaBoBe; LPS-3; MPB; NeHB; OTPC (1946 ed.); PYM; TVSH
Stranger Here, A ("A stranger here, as all my fathers were"). *Unknown.* ElSeCe
(Motect, A.) SeEP
Stranger, I threaded sunken-hearted, A. The Woman I Met. Thomas Hardy. AtBAP
Stranger! if e'er thine ardent step hath traced. Savage Grandeur. Sir Walter Scott. *Fr.* The Lord of the Isles, IV. EV-4
Stranger, if passing by you seek to learn. The Author Writes His Own Epitaph. Edward Thompson. MM
Stranger, if thou hast learned a truth which needs. Inscription for the Entrance to a Wood. Bryant. ADAH; AmP; AmPP; AnNE; APW; BAV; CoBA; CoV; IAP; MCCG; MOAP; OxBA
Stranger, if you passing meet me. To You. Walt Whitman. BoFr; LEAP
Stranger in my gates, The—lo! that am I. Omnia [*or* Omnium] Exeunt in Mysterium. George Sterling. AnAmPo; BAP; LA; LEAP; NP; SBMV; TBM; WGRP
Stranger in Scythopolis, A. Katharine Lee Bates. StJW
Stranger in the Night. August Derleth. DaM
Stranger, in this land of goodly steeds. The Glories of Athens. Sophocles. *Fr.* Oedipus at Colonus. LiA
Stranger might say if he see heem drink till he almos' fall, A. William Henry Drummond. *Fr.* Doctor Hilaire. PoP
Stranger on the Sill, The. Thomas Buchanan Read. PTA-2
Stranger pass by and waste no time. Suffolk Epitaph. *Unknown.* SiTL
Stranger stood without the gates, A. Homeless. Ts'ao Chih. PoHN
Stranger, the bark you see before you says. The Yacht. Catullus. AWP; JAWP; WBP
Stranger, the world expected You for long days. Messias. Thomas Merton. JKCP (1955 ed.)
Stranger to Europe. Guy Butler. BoSA
Stranger, to His own, A. Christ the Mendicant. John Banister Tabb. MOAH
Stranger, where thy feet now rest. The Grove of Colonus. Sophocles. *Fr.* Oedipus at Colonus. OxBG; WoL
Stranger, whoe'er thou art, that stoop'st to taste. The Fountain. Sir Edward Sherburne. ElSeCe
Stranger! whoe'er thou art, whose restless mind. Verses Copied from the Window of an Obscure Lodging-House. *Unknown.* LiTL; ViBoPo
Stranger, you freeze to this: there ain't no kinder gin-palace. Home, Sweet Home, with Variations, II. H. C. Bunner. CenHV
Stranger, you who hide my love. Song. Stephen Spender. FaBoTw
Strangers. Walter de la Mare. POTE
Strangers. Leviticus, XIX: 33-34, Bible, *O.T.* BoFr
Strangers. Mark Turbyfill. NP
Strangers, The. Jones Very. APW; OxBA
Strangers Are We All upon the Earth. Franz Werfel, *tr. fr. German by* Edith Abercrombie Snow. TrJP
Stranger's Grave, The. Emily Lawless. OnYI
Strangers! your eyes are on that valley fixed. The Field of the Grounded Arms. Fitz-Greene Halleck. PoEL-4
Strangest of adventures, The. Lord Arnaldos. James Elroy Flecker. StPo
Strappado for the Devil, A, *sels.* Richard Brathwaite.
Of Maids' Inconstancy. ElL
(Wooer's Song, The.) ElSeCe
To the Precision. SiCE
Strapped at the center of the blazing wheel. A Pilot from the Carrier. Randall Jarrell. MoPo
Strapped to an iron frame and racked. On a Dead Cripple. Ronald Allison Kells Mason. MM
Strapping young stockman lay dying, A. The Dying Stockman. *Unknown.* ViBoFo
Stratagem. Allen Curnow. AnNZ
Stratagem. Euripides, *tr. fr. Greek by* Witter Bynner. *Fr.* Iphigenia in Tauris. GrR
Strategy. Ibn Sa'id of Alcala la Real, *tr. fr. Arabic by* A. J. Arberry. MooP
Stratford upon Avon. Ivor Brown. NeTW
Stratton Water. Dante Gabriel Rossetti. EmBrPo
Stravaigin galliard laudie, gang your gate! Tuscan Folk Songs, 2. *Unknown, tr. into Scottish by* Edwin Morgan. LyPI
Straw, The. Robert Graves. MoVE
Straw ("Straw on the silent London street"). Mary Ellis Peltz. DDA
Strawberries that in gardens grow. Wild Strawberries. Robert Graves. FaBoCh; LoGBV
Strawberry Jam. May Justus. FaPON
Strawberry Plant, The. Ruth Pitter. DiM; POTE
Strawberry Roan, The, *with music. Unknown.* ABF
Strawberry shortcake, blueberry pie. *Unknown.* LoGBV
Stray Memories of Natal and Zululand, *sels.* Charles Barter. BoSA
Changes.
Dingaan and Retief.
Strayed Reveller, The. Matthew Arnold. BPN; GEPC; LoBV; MyFE, *abr.*; ViPo; ViPP
Sels.
"Old Silenus, The." VLEP
Strayed Reveller to Ulysses, The. OBEV (new ed.)
("Gods are happy, The.") BrBE
Straying. Jorge Guillén, *tr. fr. Spanish by* Eleanor L. Turnbull. CoSP
Straying Sheep, The. *Unknown, tr. by* Eleanor Hull. JKCP (1926 ed.)
Straying Student, The. Austin Clarke. AnIL; MoAB; NeIP; OxBI
Streak of Blood, A. Stefan George, *tr. fr. German by* Elizabeth Closs. AnGP
Streaks of green and yellow iridescence. An Aquarium. Amy Lowell. PFY
Stream, The. Al-Rusafi, *tr. fr. Arabic by* A. J. Arberry. MooP
Stream, The. William Cowper. *See* To a Young Lady.
Stream, The. Lula Lowe Weeden. CDC
Stream and Sun at Glendalough. W. B. Yeats. MaPo; MoPW
Stream descends on Meru mountain, A. Robert Southey. *Fr.* The Curse of Kehama. OBRV
Stream is frozen hard, The. Going by. Antenora. "Hugh MacDiarmid." SeCePo
Stream of arms and backs, A. Las Sierpes Street. Oliverio Girondo. AnCL
Stream of Faith, The. William Channing Gannett. OQP; QP-1; WGRP
Stream of Life, The. Bryant. AnNE
Stream of Life, The. Arthur Hugh Clough. BPN
Stream of Life, The. W. W. E. Ross. BoCaPo
Stream of silver [*or* tender] gladness, A. Shadow River. E. Pauline Johnson. BoCaPo; CaP; OCL
Stream of the living world. New York. Richard Watson Gilder. BoHiPo
Stream swirls, The. The wind moans in. Jade Flower Palace. Tu Fu. OnPC
Stream that carries you doth carry all, The. Sail with the Wind. Palladas. GrPo; OxBG
Stream was smooth as glass, we said, The. The Ballad of the Boat. Richard Garnett. CG; HBV; VA
Streaming beneath the eaves, the sunset light. The Old Bed. W. W. Gibson. NV
Streamlet Flows into the Sea, A. Luis de Góngora, *tr. fr. Spanish by* Edward Meryon Wilson. *Fr.* The Solitudes. TeCS
Streamlined Stream-Knowledge. Arthur W. Bell. WhC
Streams. Clinton Scollard. NLK; PoMa
Streams of Lovely Nancy, The. *Unknown.* LO; OxBoLi
Streams of the spring a-singing. In Media Vita. Willa Cather. OBAV
Stream's Secret, The. Dante Gabriel Rossetti. EmBrPo
Stream's Song, The. Lascelles Abercrombie. OBMV; POTE
Streams would wander, bridges stay. The Bridge. Willibald Köhler. CAW
Street. Alan Brown. TwCaPo
Street, The. James Russell Lowell. BAP; OQP; QP-2
Street Beggar. Anderson M. Scruggs. PoMa

Street below is dull and cold, The. I Must to Prayer. Frank Buchanan. QS
Street Car Miracle, A. Minnie Leona Upton. POT
Street Car Symphony, A. Roy Helton. PC
Street Corner College. Kenneth Patchen. MoAmPo
Street Cries. Josephine Pinckney. LS; SPP
Street Cry. Rafael Alberti, *tr. fr. Spanish by* Eleanor L. Turnbull. AnSpL-2; CoSP
Street Cry under Sea. Rafael Alberti, *tr. fr. Spanish by* Eleanor L. Turnbull. AnSpL-2; CoSP
Street Fight. Harold Monro. FaBoTw
Street Hawker. Allen Dow. CAG
Street in April, A. Louis Dudek. BoCaPo (1948 ed.)
Street in our town, A. The Watchmaker's Shop. *Unknown.* BoTP
Street Lanterns. Mary Elizabeth Coleridge. BoTP; PoeT
Street lies folded in pale composure, The. After Snow. Anne Blackwell Payne. NoCaPo
Street light, The. Late Corner. Langston Hughes. NePoAm-2
Street Melody, A. Belle Cooper. GoBC
Street Music. "John Presland." VOD
Street Musician. *Unknown.* TSW; TSWC
Street of Cats. William Rose Benét. PoC
Street of Doctors, The. Thomas Walsh. PoMa
Street Scene. W. E. Henley. BoTP
Street Scene, A. Lizette Woodworth Reese. PCH; TSW; VOD
Street Scene—1946. Kenneth Porter. PoNe
Street-Singer, The. Arthur Symons. POTT
Street Song. Juan Ruiz, Archpriest of Hita, *tr. fr. Spanish by* Hubert Creekmore. LyMA
Street Song. Edith Sitwell. CoBMV; MoPo; MoVE; OnHM; POTE
Street Sounds to the Soldiers' Tread, The. A. E. Housman. A Shropshire Lad, XXII. PoVP; SoV
Street, the store, the station especially the bar, The. The Pioneers; or, Twenty Years After. William Plomer. BoSA
Street there is in Paris famous, A. The Ballad of Bouillabaisse. Thackeray. ALV; BOHV; EV-5; HBV; InMe; OBEV (new ed.); OBVV; PoVP; VA; ViBoPo
Street-Walker in March. Samuel L. Albert. NePoAm-2
Streets. Douglas Goldring. HBMV
Streets of Baltimore. *Unknown.* BLPA; BoHiPo
Streets of Laredo, The. Louis MacNeice. ChTr
Streets of Laredo, The. *Unknown. See* Cowboy's Lament, The.
Streets of the roaring town. On a Soldier Fallen in the Philippines. William Vaughn Moody. AmPP (3d ed.); HBV; LBAP; MAP; MC; MoAmPo (1942 ed.); PaA; PAH
Streets that slept all afternoon in sun, The. Camptown. John Ciardi. WaP
Strength. Jessie Wilmore Murton. ChIP; MaRV; OQP; QP-2
Strength. Christopher Smart. *See* Strong Is the Horse upon His Speed.
Strength and dignity are her clothing. The Mother of the House. Proverbs, Bible, *O.T.* GoTP; OQP; PGD; PSO; QP-1
Strength in Weakness. Richard Burton. MaRV
Strength in Weakness. Philip E. Howard. PraP
Strength, Love, Light. Robert II, King of France. WGRP
Strength of Fate, The. Euripides, *tr. fr. Greek by* A. E. Housman. *Fr.* Alcestis. AWP; JAWP; WBP
Strength to War. Stephen Stepanchev. WaP
Strengthen, my Love, this castle of my heart. Rondel to His Mistress. Charles d'Orléans. AWP; LyMA
Strengthened to live, strengthened to die. In Distrust of Merits. Marianne Moore. AmPP; CoBMV; LiTA; LiTM; MoAB; MoAmPo (1950 ed.); NePA; OxBA; PoRL; SeCeV; TrGrPo (rev. ed.); UnPo (3d ed.); ViBoPo (1958 ed.); WaaP; WaP
Strephon. John Smith. SeCL
Strephon and Klaius. Sir Philip Sidney. *See* Double Sestine.
Strephon kissed me in the spring. The Look. Sara Teasdale. ALV; HBV; LiTL; LiTM; MOAP; PR
Strephon the brisk and gay. Strephon. John Smith. SeCL
Strepsiades of Thebes. Pindar, *tr. fr. Greek by* C. J. Billson. *Fr.* Isthmian Odes, VII. OxBG
(To a Nation's Hero, *longer sel.*) GrR
Stretch'd and still lies the midnight. Song of Myself, XXXVI. Walt Whitman. CoBA
Stretched in full cry. The Weathercock. H. H. Abbott. TVSH
Stretched in the shadow of the broad beech. The Shepherd's Gratitude. Virgil. Eclogues, I. AWP
Stretched out full length, his eighty years too ripe. The Old Peasant in the Billiard Saloon. Huw Menai. MoWP
Stretching his hands out of the bed. A Peaceful Man. Henri Michaux. MiCF
Strew lightly o'er the soldier's grave. The Soldier's Grave. Henry D. Muir. OHIP
Strew me with blossoms when I die. Popular Songs of Tuscany. *Unknown.* AWP; JAWP; WBP
Strew Not Earth with Empty Stars. Thomas Lovell Beddoes. *Fr.* The Second Brother. ERP
(Song: "Strew not earth with empty stars.") ViBoPo
Strew on her bloaters, bloaters—for her God. Poem for D. Robert Griffiths. Davis Aberpennar. MoWP
Strew on her roses, roses. Requiescat. Matthew Arnold. AWP; BEL; BLV; BMEP; BoLiVe; BPN; CaAE; CBOV; DD; EM-2; EmBrPo; EnLi-2; EnLit; EPN; EV-5; FiP; GEPC; GTBS; GTBS-D; GTBS-W; GTML; GTSL; HBV; InP; InPo; InvP; JAWP; LEAP; LiTB; LiTG; LiTL; OAEP; OBEV; OBVV; OHIP; OuHeWo; PG; PoFS; PoRA; PoVP; PYM; ReaPo; RiBV; TCEP; TOP; TreFS; TrGrPo; TyEnPo; ViBoPo; ViPo; ViPP; VLEP; WBP; WHA
Strew the fair garlands where slumber the dead. Memorial Day. Samuel F. Smith. *Fr.* Our Honored Heroes. OQP; QP-2
Stricken. *Unknown.* BPP
Stricken Deer, The. William Cowper. *Fr.* The Task, III. FiP; LoBV; RO
(Dreams, Empty Dreams.) BHV
("I was a stricken deer.") BrBE; EnRP; LEAP; MaRV; OAEP; OxBoCh
(Self-Portrait.) CoBE
(Sum of Life, The.) LPS-3
Stricken Deer, The. Thomas Moore. *See* Come, Rest in This Bosom.
Stricken South to the North, The. Paul Hamilton Hayne. PAH
Stricken to earth, the sword snapped in his hand. I Am the Last [*or* One Love]. Edward Shillito. MaRV; OQP; QP-1
Strict hairshirt of circumstance wears the flesh. The Veterans. Donagh MacDonagh. JKCP (1955 ed.); OnYI
Strict I walk my ordered way. The Mummer. Anna Wickham. TwCV
Strictly at noon the mist was there. The Orchard Ghost. Mark Van Doren. DaM
Strictly Germ-proof. Arthur Guiterman. BAP; BLPA; BOHV; HBV; PC; PFE; PoeMoYo; TCAP; TreF; TrJP; YaD
Stride the hill, sower. The Furrow and the Hearth. Padraic Colum. NV; TwCV
Strife. Hafiz, *tr. fr. Persian by* R. A. Nicholson. PeP
Strife in Metellus' year first stirred. Horace. Odes, II, 1. LaP
Strife is grown between Virtue and Love, A. Astrophel and Stella, LII. Sir Philip Sidney. ReEn; SiPS
Strife Is O'er [the Battle Done], The. *Unknown, tr. fr. Latin by* Francis Pott. EOAH; OlF; OQP; QP-1
(Victory.) MaRV
Strife on Ilium's windy plain is still, The. To Helen, Middle-aged. Roselle Mercier Montgomery. LS
Strife, War's Sister Urges On the Host. Homer. *See* Two Hosts, The.
Strike again, O Sorrow, if you find the place! Hymn to Sorrow. Alphonse de Lamartine. LiA
Strike among the Poets, A. *Unknown.* BOHV; FiBHP; SiTL
Strike, churl; hurl, cheerless wind, then; heltering hail. Fragment. Gerard Manley Hopkins. NAMP
Strike down into my breast, O sun, and cleanse my soul. Hymn to the Sun. William Alexander Percy. TrPWD
Strike home, strong-hearted man! Down to the root. To Ronge. Whittier. AnEnPo
"Strike me blind!" we swore. The Blind Sailor. Theodore Goodridge Roberts. CPG
Strike the Blow. "F. McK." PAH
Strike the concertina's melancholy string! The Story of Prince Agib. W. S. Gilbert. BOHV; InMe; LBN; NA
"Strike the sails!" King Olaf said. King Olaf's War-Horns. Longfellow. *Fr.* Tales of a Wayside Inn, Pt. I. AmPP (4th ed.); PFY
Strike up, you lusty gallants, with musick and sound of drum. Captain Ward and the *Rainbow. Unknown.* BaBo; ESPB; SG
Striking. Charles Stuart Calverley. CenHV; PA
Striking of the Tent, The. Ibn al-Khabbaza, *tr. fr. Arabic by* A. J. Arberry. MooP
String Quartet. Babette Deutsch. UnS
String Stars for Pearls. J. U. Nicolson. HBMV
Strings' Excitement, The. W. H. Auden. MoAB; MBP; MoBrPo
(Family Ghosts.) ReMP
Strings in the Earth [and Air]. James Joyce. Chamber Music, I. CBOV; GTIV; HBMV; MoBrPo; OnYI; ReMP
Strings of camels come in single file, The. He Cometh Late. *Unknown.* OQP; QP-1
Strip of Blue, A. Lucy Larcom. AA; HBV; LBAP; MaRV, *abr.;* NLK; OBAV; OQP; OTPC; QP-2; SN; WGRP

Striped blouse in a clearing by Bazille, A. Ceremony. Richard Wilbur. FiMAP; MiAP; Po; ReMP
Stripes and the Stars, The. Edna Dean Proctor. FOAH
Stripped country, shrunken as a beggar's heart. The Golden Corpse. Stephen Vincent Benét. TCPD
Stripping an almond tree in flower. Little Joke. Elinor Wylie. LHV
Strive No More. Thomas Lodge. CoBE; TuPP
Strive not, Leuconoe, to know what end. Carpe Diem. Horace. Odes, I, 11. RoL
Strive Not, Vain Lover, to Be Fine. Richard Lovelace. OAEP
Strive though it may, no power in earth or sky. Prayer Reaches Him. Nagata. SoLD
Strive, Wait and Pray. Adelaide Anne Procter. PraP
Striving is past. Ah, I must sink and drown. Fidessa, More Chaste than Kind, XXIV. Bartholomew Griffin. ReIE
Striving to sing glad songs, I but attain. Two Sonnets, II. James Thomson. EmBrPo; PoVP
Stroke of One. Jorge Carrera Andrade, *tr. fr. Spanish by* Muna Lee. AnCL; OnPM
Stroke of time within my breast, The. Requiem. Douglas V. Kane. UnW
Strolling fox, famished and underfed, A. The Greedy Fox and the Elusive Grapes. Aesop. MaC
Strolling in a Village. Liu Teh-jen, *tr. fr. Chinese.* WhP
Strolling on the green grass. *Unknown.* RIS
Strolling one afternoon along a street. Monody on the Demolition of Devonshire House. Siegfried Sassoon. FaBoTw
Strolling under the Moon. Lu Yu, *tr. fr. Chinese by* Pai Chwen-yu. WhP
Strong, The. John Vance Cheney. AA; OBAV
Strong, The. John Curtis Underwood. BAP; MaRV
Strong and slippery, built for the midnight grass-party confronted by four cats. Peter. Marianne Moore. AnAmPo; LA; OxBA
Strong Are Saying Nothing, The. Robert Frost. ChMo; PoF
Strong Arms. Frances O'Connell Corridan. JKCP (1926 ed.)
Strong as Death. H. C. Bunner. HBV; LBAP; OBAV
Strong City, The. Alfred Noyes. *Fr.* The Last Voyage. GoBC
Strong God which made the topmost stars. The Prophet Lost in the Hills at Evening. Hilaire Belloc. JKCP; OxBoCh
Strong grow stronger in their faith, The. To My Father. Donald F. Drummond. PtPa
Strong Grow the Young Reed Shoots. *Unknown, tr. fr. Chinese.* WhP
Strong Hand, A. Aaron Hill. HBV
Strong Hera's daughter. Eileithyia, hear! Hearken! O Eileithyia. Pindar. *Fr.* Nemean Odes, VII. GrR
Strong Heroic Line, The. Oliver Wendell Holmes. AA
Strong imagination from my youth has been combined, A. The Caulker. M. A. Lewis. StPo
Strong in a dream of perfect bloom. To the Brave Soul. Wilbur Underwood. WGRP
Strong in thy steadfast purpose, be. Purpose. John James Piatt. AA
Strong Is the Horse upon His Speed. Christopher Smart. *Fr.* A Song to David. AlDL; BeR; MyFE
(Man of Prayer, The.) BBV (1951 ed.); GTBS-W; LiTB; LiTG
(Strength.) OtMeF
Strong Love. A. E. Housman. Additional Poems, IV. OtMeF
Strong man awhile in his kingdom is lord, The. The Eternal. Esaias Tegnér. AnSL; LiTW
Strong Men. Sterling A. Brown. BANP
Strong men have trembled at thy name O Death. Death. John Bruce MacCallum. PoP
Strong men keep coming on, The. Upstream. Carl Sandburg. HBMV; MAP; MoAB; MoAmPo; NeMA; PoFr; TBM
Strong Moments. W. H. Davies. CMP
Strong prophetick dream, A. William Chamberlayne. *Fr.* Pharonnida. NBE
Strong, simple, silent are the [steadfast] laws. On a Bust of General Grant. James Russell Lowell. GA
Strong sob of the chafing stream, The. Orara. Henry C. Kendall. BoAu
Strong Son of God, immortal Love. In Memoriam A. H. H., Proem. Tennyson. BBV; BEL; BoLiVe; BPN; ChIP; CoBE; EmBrPo; EnL; EnLit; EPN; EPP; GEPC; GTBS-W; HBV; LEAP; LiTB; LPS-2; MaRV; NeHB; OAEP; OQP; OuHeWo; OxBoCh; PIAE; PIR; PoFS; PoVP; QP-1; REAL; RiBV; SeCeV; StJW; TOP; TreF; TrGrPo; TriL; TrPWD; TyEnPo; UnPo (1st ed.); ViPo; ViPP; VLEP; WGRP; WHA
Strong, still light upon the verge of Being. To the Angel. Rainer Maria Rilke. LiTW
Strong sun across the sod can make. Song for the Passing of a Beautiful Woman. *Unknown.* LiTA
Strong Swimmer, The. William Rose Benét. PoNe
Strong wind is gathering the storm-clouds together, The. The Song of the Storm-Finch. Maxim Gorki. PoFr
Strong Woman, The. Roscoe Gilmore Stott. NV
Stronger Faith, A. Tennyson. *Fr.* In Memoriam A. H. H., XCVI. MaRV
Stronger Lessons. Walt Whitman.
(Have You Learned Lessons Only of Those Who Admired You?) GrCo-1
Stronger than Death. Paulus Silentiarius, *tr. fr. Greek by* F. L. Lucas. GrPE
Strongest, The. "Yehoash," *tr. fr. Yiddish by* Marie Syrkin. TrJP
Strongest and the noblest argument, The. Dedication II. Sir John Davies. *Fr.* Nosce Teipsum. SiPS
Strophes: "There is one who takes all men within his hand." Rainer Maria Rilke, *tr. fr. German by* Jessie Lemont. OnPM
Strophes to a Statue. Eugenio Florit, *tr. fr. Spanish by* Donald Devenish Walsh. AnCL
Stropshire Lad, A. David McCord. PIAE
Struck into a mountain one black cross. Saint. Kersti Merilaas. LiTW
Struck was I, nor yet by lightning. Emily Dickinson. AnNE
Structural Iron Workers. MacKnight Black. NP
Structure of the Plane, The. Muriel Rukeyser. PoF
Struggle. Sidney Lanier. LiTA; OxBA
Struggle, The. Sully-Prudhomme, *tr. fr. French by* Arthur O'Shaughnessy. AWP
Struggle, The. Miriam Teichner. BLP
Struggle for Patroclus, The. Homer, *tr. fr. Greek by* F. L. Lucas. *Fr.* The Iliad, XVII *and* XVIII. GrPE
Struggle is over, the boys are defeated, The. Bold Robert Emmet. Tom Maguire. OnYI
Struggle is strong and splendid, The. Sounding. Doris Ferne. CaP
Struggling Fancies. Bhartrihari, *tr. fr. Sanskrit by* Arthur W. Ryder. OnPM
Strumbo, Dorothy, Trumpart, Cobbling Shoes. *At. to* George Peele. *See* Cobblers' Song, The.
Strut and wiggle. To Midnight Nan at LeRoy's. Langston Hughes. AnAmPo; LA
Strutting cock, with swelling chest. The Cock [*or* For a Cock]. Eleanor Farjeon. PoRh; RIS
Stuart Mill on Mind and Matter. Charles Neaves. EBSV
Stubborn Fool, The. Bhartrihari, *tr. fr. Sanskrit by* Arthur W. Ryder. OnPM
Stuck in a bottle on the window-sill. Geraniums. W. W. Gibson. AEV; POTT; TCPD
Student, The. *Unknown, tr. fr. Early Modern Irish by* Frank O'Connor. AnIL; KiLC; OBMV
Student, at his book so placed, A. Of a New-married Student. *Unknown.* SiCE; TuPP
Student came from Oxford town also, A. Seven Pilgrims. Chaucer. *Fr.* The Canterbury Tales. TrGrPo
Students. Florence Wilkinson Evans. HBV; SBMV
Students, *much abr.* Haniel Long. AnAmPo; LA
Student's Kiss, A. *Unknown, tr. fr. Spanish by* Havelock Ellis. OnPM
Student's life is pleasant, The. The Student. *Unknown.* AnIL; KiLC; OBMV
Studies at Delhi. Sir Alfred Comyn Lyall. OBVV
Badminton.
Hindu Ascetic, The.
Studios Photographic, The, *sel.* Paul Shivell.
In God's Eternal Studios. HBV
Study; for Ezra Pound. Peter Hellings. MoWP
Study in a Late Subway. Muriel Rukeyser. OnHM
Study in aesthetics, The. Ezra Pound. ChMo; CMP; NP
Study of a People. H. I. Phillips. LauV
Study of a Spider, The. Lord De Tabley. BMEP
Study of an Elevation, in Indian Ink. Kipling. BOHV; InMe
Study of Images, I. Wallace Stevens. ReMP
Study of Two Pears. Wallace Stevens. AmPP (4th ed.); OxBA
Study was once my dearest joy, but jealous Poverty. Dulce Mihi Quondam Studium Fuit. Politian. LaP
Stuff God uses to make folks [*or* men], The. Lincoln. James Larkin Pearson. BAP; NoCaPo
Stuff of the moon. Nocturne in a Deserted Brickyard. Carl Sandburg. AmPP; CoBA; MAP; MoAmPo; NP; PFE; TCPD
Stumbling over fallen logs. Lost in a Blizzard. Arthur W. Monroe. PoOW
Stumbling, we see the future as a cup. Dedication. Lilian Shuman Dreyfus. *Fr.* In Praise of Leaves. MOAH
Stung. *Unknown, tr. fr. Greek by* Thomas Stanley. OuHeWo
Stung by a spiteful wasp. Forgiveness. W. H. Davies. ChMo; CMP
Stung by the tail of a scorpion. Jet Plane. A. M. Sullivan. JKCP (1955 ed.)
Stunned in the stone light, laid among the lilies. Ophelia. Vernon Watkins. MoVE
Stupendious Love! All Saints Astonishment. Meditation Ten. Edward Taylor. *Fr.* Sacramental Meditations. CoV; OxBA

Stupid horse and cow, they say, A. Noel. Leonard Feeney. QS
Stupid Kite, The. Allen Upward. *Fr.* Scented Leaves from a Chinese Jar. NP
Stupid men, forever prone. Redondillas. Sister Juana Inés de la Cruz. CAW
Stupid Old Body, The. Edward Carpenter. WGRP
Stupidity Street. Ralph Hodgson. AtBAP; BLA; BMEP; CaAE; CBOV; CH; ChMo; CMP; EnLit; HBV; LiTM (rev. ed.); MBP; MoAB; MoBrPo; NeMA; NP; PoeMoYo; PoFr; PtOT; PYM; SiSoSe; SP; TCEP; TOP; TreFS; TwCV; UTS; WP
Sturdiest of forest trees, The. The Holly. Walter de la Mare. ChMo; CMP
Sturdy rock, for all his strength, The. Man's Flitting Life Finds Surest Stay, Where Sacred Virtue Beareth Sway. John Thorn. SiCE
Stygian Oath, The. Angelos Sikelianos, *tr. fr. Modern Greek by* Rae Dalven. MoGP
"Styles that at present are regnant, The." Limerick. *Unknown.* LiBL
Stylite. Louis MacNeice. MoPo
Styx River Anthology. Carolyn Wells. BOHV
Suave body of the Queen, she gave me you. Body of the Queen. Donald Evans. AnAmPo; LA
Suave Mari Magno. Lucretius, *tr. fr. Latin by* W. H. Mallock. *Fr.* De Rerum Natura. AWP
Suave Mari Magno. Sophocles, *tr. fr. Greek by* Walter Headlam. OxBG
Sub-average *Time* Reader, The. Ernest Wittenberg. FiBHP
Sub Pondere Crescit. James Russell Lowell. MaRV
Sub Terra. William Carlos Williams. NP
Subalterns, The. Thomas Hardy. ChMo; MaPo; MBP; MoAB; MoBrPo
Subaltern's Love Song, A. John Betjeman. ChMP; ShBV-4
Subject for Prophecy. Gemma D'Auria. JKCP (1955 ed.)
Subject of Heroic Song, The. Milton. *Fr.* Paradise Lost, IX. OBS
("No more of talk where God or Angel guest.") SeEP
Subject of the Bishop's Miracle, The. John Philip. BoAV
Subject today, my friends, is stinted praise, The. "The Art of Our Necessities Is Strange." Forrest Izard. WhC
Subjectivity. Helen Pinkerton. PtPa
Subjects' Joy, The. *Unknown. See* England's Triumph.
Sublime, The. Wilfrid Scawen Blunt. BMEP
Sublime—invention ever young. Christopher Smart. *Fr.* A Song to David. HBV; OBEV
Sublimer strains, O rustic Muse, prepare. Saturday; or, The Flights. John Gay. *Fr.* The Shepherd's Week. EiPP
Sublimity! Sublimity! I lay thee down. Wilfred Campbell. *Fr.* Lines on a Re-reading of Parts of the Old Testament. InP
Submarine Bed, The. John Peale Bishop. LiTA
Submarine Landscape. William Diaper. *Fr.* Nereides; or, Sea-Eclogues. BeR
Submarine Mountains. Cale Young Rice. EtS
Submergence. Hazel Hall. NP
Submission. Jessie E. Williams. OQP; QP-1
Submission and Rest. Anna Temple Whitney. *See* Kneeling Camel, The.
Submite submitted to her heavenly king. *Unknown.* WhC
Subsiding from those heavenly wings the air. Hymn for the Feast of the Annunciation. Aubrey Thomas De Vere. ISi
Substance and Shadow. Cardinal Newman. GoBC
Substance, Shadow, and Spirit. Tao Yuan-ming, *tr. fr. Chinese.* TrCh, *tr. by* Arthur Waley; WhP, *tr. by* Yang Yeh-tzu
Substitution. Elizabeth Barrett Browning. MaRV; WGRP
Substitution. Anne Spencer. CDC
Subterranean City, A. Thomas Lovell Beddoes. ERP; HoPM
Subterranean Days and Nights. "Pablo de Rokha," *tr. fr. Spanish by* H. R. Hays. TwSpPo
Subtle almost beyond thought are these dim colours. Dun-Colour. Ruth Pitter. MoVE
Subtle chain of countless rings, A. Emerson. *Fr.* Nature (essay). AmPP; AWP; IAP; InPo; MOAP
Subtle evil that the mind engenders, The. I. Frances Crawford. PtPa
Subtle tracery of the leafless bough, The. Ad Matrem in Coelis. Linda Lyon Van Voorhis. GoBC
Suburb. Harold Monro. ChMo; CMP; HBV
Suburban Lullaby. J. S. Manifold. BoAV
Suburbs, The. Enid Derham. BoAu
Suburbs Is a Fine Place, The. *Unknown.* CoMu
Suburbs on a Hazy Day. D. H. Lawrence. OBMV
Subverted Flower, The. Robert Frost. CoV; OxBA
Subway, The. Morris Abel Beer. VOD (1935 ed.)
Subway Builders. Lawrence Lee. PoMa
Subway Engineer. C. R. Holmes. PtPa
Success ("It's doing your job . . ."). Berton Braley. WBLP
(That's Success!) PoToHe
Success. C. C. Cameron. PoToHe (new ed.)
Success. Emily Dickinson. *See* Success is counted sweetest.
Success. Edgar A. Guest. TreF
Success. *Unknown.* FaFP; PoToHe (new ed.)
Success. Wang Chi, *tr. fr. Chinese by* Henry H. Hart. PoHN; WoL
Success is counted sweetest. Emily Dickinson. AmP; AmPo; AmPP (4th ed.); GTBS-W; InPo; LiTA; LiTM; MoAB; MoAmPo (1950 ed.); MOAP; NeMA; OxBA; PG; PoLFOT; PoRA; TwP; WaaP
(Success.) AWP; CoBA; JAWP; MCCG; WBP
Success is speaking words of praise. Success. *Unknown.* FaFP; PoToHe (new ed.)
Succession, The. Frances Laughton Mace. AA
Succession of the Four Sweet Months, The. Robert Herrick. OTPC (1946 ed.); PCH; YeAr
(Four Sweet Months, The.) BoTP; CBPC
(July; the Succession of the Four Sweet Months.) FaPON
Such a Blustery Day! Elizabeth Gould. BoTP
Such a fine pullet ought to go. A Blue Ribbon at Amesbury. Robert Frost. NePA
"Such a little king's eye," said my mother. Roy Kloof. Sydney Clouts. BoSA
Such a morning it is when love. Day of These Days. Laurie Lee. AtBAP; FaBoMo; MoVE
Such a Starved Bank of Moss. Robert Browning. The Two Poets of Croisic: Prologue. EPN; LoPo; VLEP
(Apparitions.) EPP; TSW; TSWC
(Prologue: "Such a starved bank of moss.") BMEP; BPN
(Prologue to "The Two Poets of Croisic.") HiLiEn
Such a wide, still landscape, all cold and white! A Greenland Winter. Lucy Diamond. BoTP
Such a Woman, the Principle of Life, the Ideal Questioner. Paul Eluard, *tr. fr. French by* Ruthven Todd. MiFP
Such are the stillness and peace that prevail through the Sultan's dominions. A Triplet on the Reign of the Great Sultan. James Clarence Mangan. IrPN
Such as into himself at last Eternity changes him. The Tomb of Edgar Poe. Stéphane Mallarmé. AnFP
Such as it is. Such as two men. The Clothing's New Emperor. Donald Finkel. NePoEA
Such as, retired from sight of men, like thee. To St. Mary Magdalen. Henry Constable. CoBE; TriL; TuPP
Such as the Berecynthian Goddess bright. Ruins of Rome, III. Joachim du Bellay. OnPM
Such beautiful, beautiful hands. Beautiful Hands [*or* My Mother's Hands]. *Unknown, at. to* Ellen M. H. Gates. TreF; TreFS
Such, British Public, ye who like me not. Dedication. Robert Browning. *Fr.* The Ring and the Book. BPN
Such captivating quantities of dirt. A Dog's Life. Lew Sarett. AlBD
Such churlish brutes his guardians be. The Guardians. Ibn Sa'id of Alcala la Real. MooP
Such darkness as when Jesus died! San Francisco. Joaquin Miller. PAH
Such dubious nomenclatures crowding in. Basic Communication. Thomas Hornsby Ferril. NePoAm-2
Such glorious faith as fills your limpid eyes. Verse for a Certain Dog. Dorothy Parker. AlBD
Such great complaints brake forth out of her breast. Departure of Aeneas from Dido. Virgil. *Fr.* The Aeneid, IV. TCEP
Such hap as I am happèd in. Sir Thomas Wyatt. SiPS
Such hints as untaught Nature yields! Nature, the Artist. Frederic Lawrence Knowles. AA
Such is, dear girl, my tenderness. Satirical Letrilla III. Manuel Bretón de los Herreros. AnSpL-2
Such Is Love. Rodrigo Cota de Maguaque, *tr. fr. Spanish by* Thomas Walsh. OnPM
(Love.) AnSpL-1
Such Is the Death the Soldier Dies. Robert Burns Wilson. AA; HBV
Such is the endless exile of dead men. Last Words of Byron. George Chapman. *Fr.* Byron's Tragedy. CoEV
Such is the mode of these censorious days. On Mr. Hobbs, and His Writings. John Sheffield, Duke of Buckingham and Normanby. PoEL-3
Such is the mystery of man's freedom, says God. Charles Péguy. *Fr.* Freedom. PoFr
Such Is the Way of the World. "St.-J. Perse," *tr. fr. French by* T. S. Eliot. Anabasis, Pt. IV. AtBAP; MiFP
(Thus Was the City Founded.) OnHM
Such light is in sea-caves. Musica No. 3. Richard Duerden. NeAP
Such little, puny things are words in rhyme. Quickening. Christopher Morley. HBMV
Such love is like a smoky fire. George Chapman. LO
Such lovers as shall haunt this grove. *Unknown.* SeCSL
Such majestic rhythms, such tiny disturbances. A Grain of Rice. F. R. Scott. PeCV
Such maner time there was (what time I n'ot). Sir Philip Sidney. *Fr.* Arcadia. NBE
Such marvellous ways to kill a man! The Bofors A.A. Gun. Gavin Ewart. WaP

Such moving sounds from such a careless touch. Of My Lady Isabella Playing on the Lute. Edmund Waller. MePo
Such natural depths of love our Oxford knows. Martyr's Memorial. Louise Imogen Guiney. AA
Such offer did the Libyan also make. The Prize. Pindar. *Fr.* Odes. LiA
Such old, illustrious tidings you proclaim. To a Young Priest. Anne Blackwell Payne. MaRV
Such our love of liberty, our country and our laws. In the Garb of Old Gaul. Sir Henry Erskine. EBSV
Such perfect Bliss, fair Cloris, we. To a Lady; in a Letter. Earl of Rochester. SeEP
Such pictures of the heavens were never seen. The Invisible. Richard Watson Gilder. WGRP
Such quiet gray and green! Such peaceful farms. Flood Tide. Hermann Hagedorn. PC
Such special sweetness was about. That Day You Came. Lizette Woodworth Reese. AV; HBV; LBMV
"Such Stuff as Dreams." Franklin P. Adams. FiBHP; PC
"Such Stuff as Dreams Are Made Of." Thomas Wentworth Higginson. AA
Such Stuff as Dreams Are Made On. Shakespeare. *See* Our Revels Now Are Ended.
Such, such is Death: no triumph: no defeat. Two Sonnets [on Death], II. Charles Hamilton Sorley. BLV; HBMV; MBP; MoBrPo; NeMA; TrGrPo (1942 ed.)
Such the arraignment, and I answer not. William Ellery Leonard. *Fr.* Two Lives, Pt. III. MOAP
Such the fair garden of untrammeled ease. Childhood's Immunity from Inward Sorrows. Sophocles. *Fr.* Trachiniae. GrR
Such times as windy moods do stir. The Spirit of the Wheat. Edward A. U. Valentine. AA
Such was he, our Martyr-Chief. Abraham Lincoln [*or* Our Martyr-Chief *or* Lincoln]. James Russell Lowell. *Fr.* Ode Recited at the Harvard Commemoration, July 21, 1865. AnNE; GDAH; InP; OHIP; PAP; PEDC
Such was his greed of life and dread of the voidness of the tomb. A Self-Server. Cale Young Rice. LS
Such was old Chaucer. Such the placid mien. For a Statue of Chaucer at Woodstock. Mark Akenside. SeCePo
Such was the boy—but for the growing youth. Communion. Wordsworth. *Fr.* The Excursion, I. MaRV; OBRV
Such was the rise of this prodigious fire. The Fire of London. Dryden. *Fr.* Annus Mirabilis. EV-3
Such wayward ways hath Love, that most part in discord. Earl of Surrey. SiPS
Such were those epigrams of elder times. Henry Parrot. SiCE
Such Wisdom. *Unknown.* GFA
Suck the bare sob out of the heart. Microcosmos, X. Nigel Heseltine. NeBP
Sucking Cider through a Straw, *with music. Unknown.* AS
Sudas, the gardener, plucked from his tank. Rabindranath Tagore. *Fr.* Fruit-gathering. NV
Sudbury Fight, The. Wallace Rice. PAH
Sudden along the city street. To a Thorn Tree Blooming on a City Street. Virginia McCormick. LS
Sudden amid the slush and rain. In the City. Israel Zangwill. WGRP
Sudden blow, A: the great wings beating still. Leda and the Swan. W. B. Yeats. AnIL; AtBAP; ChMP; CoBMV; CoEV; EnL; EnLi-2 (1949 ed.); EnLP; ExPo; FaBoEn; InPo; LiTM; MaPo; MBP; MoAB; MoBrPo; MoVE; OAEP (2d ed.); PeBoSo; PoE; PoFS; PoLFOT; SeCeV; TrGrPo; TwHP
Sudden Call, The. Narihira, *tr. fr. Japanese by* Mabel Lorenz Ives. PFE
Sudden cry in sleep, A; wind rushes through dark streets. The Soul's Springtime. Georg Trakl. AnGP
Sudden hush of silence, A. My Belief. Albert Teodor Gellerstedt. AnSL
Sudden Light. Dante Gabriel Rossetti. BrBE; BMEP; EmBrPo; FaBoEn; GTBS-D; InP; LO; LoBV; LoPS; NBE; OAEP, *sl. diff.;* Po; POTT, *sl. diff.;* PoVP; TrGrPo; TwHP; UnW; VA; VLEP
Sudden night is here at once, The. Poppies. Charles Weekes. OnYI
Sudden refreshment came upon the school. Physical Geography. Louise Townsend Nicholl. ImOP
Sudden Shower. John Clare. EV-4; OBRV
Sudden Shower, A. James Whitcomb Riley. PRWS
Sudden Spring. Margaret Coulby. TwCaPo
Sudden Squall, A. David Gascoyne. AIDL
Sudden storms that heave me to and fro. The Noble Voyage. Earl of Surrey. PoLi
Sudden sun, and the white spring rain, The. Picnic. Ray Mathew. BoAV
Sudden swallows swiftly skimming. Susan Simpson. *Unknown.* BOHV
Sudden the desert changes. Bridge-Guard in the Karroo. Kipling. BoSA
Sudden thrust of speech is no mean test, The. The Fire i' the Flint. Lucy Catlin Robinson. AA
Sudden transport seiz'd the melting maid, A. Apollonius Rhodius. *Fr.* Argonautica, III. GrPo
Sudden wakin', a sudden weepin', A. Man's Days [*or* The Gaffer's Song]. Eden Phillpotts. HBV; MBP; OBEV (new ed.); OBVV
Sudden waking when a saffron glare, A. A Transvaal Morning. William Plomer. BoSA
Suddenly. Leonora Speyer. PG (1945 ed.)
Suddenly/ as the darkness fell. Anguish. José Moreno Villa. CoSP
Suddenly,/ out of the faint gray smother. White Fox. Elizabeth Alsop Shepard. GoYe
Suddenly./ Suddenly and certainly, as I watched elsewhere, locked. The First Morning of the Second World. Delmore Schwartz. FiMAP
Suddenly afraid [*or* Sodenly afraide], half waking, half sleeping. "Who Cannot Weep Come Learn of Me" [*or* Sodenly Afraide]. *Unknown.* EnLit; TMEV
Suddenly, after the quarrel, while we waited. The Quarrel. Conrad Aiken. LiTL; MAP; MoAB; MoAmPo
Suddenly all the fountains in the park. The Fountains. W. R. Rodgers. MoVE
Suddenly—all the sky is hid. James Russell Lowell. *Fr.* Summer Storm. PEOR
Suddenly as I came. Ducks. Roy Daniells. TwCaPo
Suddenly, as I crouched low on a ledge. The Swooping Wings. W. W. Gibson. ChMo
Suddenly, as you are clinging to my hands. My Son Stands Alone. John V. A. Weaver. FAOV
Suddenly bells and flags! Peace. Agnes Lee. BAP; SBMV
Suddenly discovering in the eyes of the very beautiful. Pagani's, November 8. Ezra Pound. ReaPo
Suddenly flickered a flame. Suddenly. Leonora Speyer. PG (1945 ed.)
Suddenly from a wayside station. In the Train. Clifford Bax. InP; TCPD
Suddenly I saw the cold and rock-delighting Heaven. The Cold Heaven. W. B. Yeats. AWP; InPo; JAWP; MoVE; NAMP; NP; OAEP (2d ed.); WBP
Suddenly in the midnight on mortal men. The Last Judgment. Cynewulf. *Fr.* Christ. AnOE
Suddenly into my dream why should they come. Lament for the Great Yachts. Patric Dickinson. HaMV
Suddenly, jeweled eyes. A Fawn's First Snow. Glenn Ward Dresbach. PoTo
Suddenly lifting and rising heavily from the reeds. Image of Silenus. Douglas Le Pan. BoCaPo (1948 ed.)
Suddenly light shone out from the dark window. Snow Story. L. A. Mackay. TwCaPo
Suddenly night crushed out the day and hurled. The Unreturning. Wilfred Owen. MBP; MoBrPo
Suddenly night flung wide the sapphire gate. Charles Erskine Scott Wood. *Fr.* The Poet in the Desert. PoFr
Suddenly, out of dark and leafy ways. Tenants. W. W. Gibson. ChMo; CMP; HBV; NP
Suddenly out of its stale and drowsy lair, the lair of slaves. Europe. Walt Whitman. IAP
Suddenly, out of my darkness, shines Thy beauty, O Brother. A Psalm to the Son. Marguerite Wilkinson. TrPWD
Suddenly the last boundary broke. The Shock. Francis Reginald Scott. *Fr.* Armageddon. BoCaPo (1948 ed.)
Suddenly the sky turned gray. Snow toward Evening. Melville Cane. MAP; MoAmPo; SUS; TiPo
Suddenly to become John Benbow, walking down William Street. Metempsychosis. Kenneth Slessor. ViBoPo (1958 ed.)
Suffenus, whom so well you know. To Varus. Catullus. AWP
Sufferance of her race is shown, The. "Formerly a Slave." Herman Melville. PoNe
Suffering. Nathalia Crane. TSWC
Suffering. Albert Ehrenstein, *tr. fr. German by* Babette Deutsch. TrJP
Suffering God, The. Raymond Kresensky. ChIP
Suffering God, The. G. A. Studdert-Kennedy. MaRV
Peace and Joy, *sel.* MaRV
Suffering has settled like a sly disguise. A Korean Woman Seated by a Wall. William Meredith. NePoEA
Sufferings of the Poor, The. William Langland, *mod. by* Henry W. Wells. *Fr.* The Vision of Piers Plowman. PoLi
("Needy are our neighbors, The," *mod. by* Henry W. Wells.) PoFr
(Poor, The, *shorter sel., Middle English vers.*) PoEL-1
Sufficèd not, madame, that you did tear. Sir Thomas Wyatt. SiPS
Sufficeth it to you, my joys interred. The Ocean's Love [*or* The Ocean] to Cynthia. Sir Walter Ralegh. OBSC; ReIE; SiPS
Sufficiency. Gleeson White. VA
Suffolk Epitaph. *Unknown.* SiTL
Suffolk Miracle, The. *Unknown.* BaBo (A *and* B *vers.*); CG; ESPB; OBB

Suffolk Shore, The. George Crabbe. *Fr.* The Borough, Letter XXIII. RO
Sugar Babe, *with music. Unknown.* ABF
Sugar Loaf is a philosophic fisherman, The. Bay of Guanabara. Menotti del Picchia. AnCL
Sugar-Maker, The. Frank Oliver Call. CPG
Sugar-Plum Tree, The. Eugene Field. FaFP; GoBP; HBV; HBVY; MPB; OTPC (1946 ed.); PCH; TreF
Sugar Weather. Peter McArthur. CaP; CPG; OCL
Suggested Device of a New Western State. John James Piatt. AnAmPo; LA
(Farther.) AA
Suibne Geilt. *Unknown. See* Sweeney the Mad.
Suicidal Cat, The. *Unknown.* CIV
Suicide? Elias Nandino, *tr. fr. Spanish by* Margaret Allison. PoP
Suicide, The. Hugh Wilgus Ramsaur. UnW
Suicides, The. Vera Bax. DiM
Suicide's Grave, The. W. S. Gilbert. *Fr.* The Mikado. ALV; LiTG; LiTL; TreF; WhC
(Ko-Ko's Song.) FaFP
(Ko-Ko's Winning Song.) LiTB
(Tit-Willow.) OlF; SiTL
(Willow, Titwillow.) PoVP
Suicide's Note. Langston Hughes. CDC
Suicide's Stone. Robinson Jeffers. MM; PC; TwCV
Suilven and the Eagle, *sel.* Gordon Bottomley.
Eagle Song. MBP; MoBrPo
Suire, The. Thomas Caulfield Irwin. IrPN
Suit of sheep's clothing, A. Policy. Carolyn Wells. WhC
Suits hang half a year in. Tyburn and Westminster. John Heywood. ACP
Sukey, you shall be my wife. *Unknown.* OxNR
Sulk when you're spoken to. *Unknown.* CenHV
Sullen and dark [*or* dull], in the September day. The Last Reservation. Walter Learned. AA; PaA; PAH
Sullen carre why dost thou keepe. *Unknown.* SeCSL
Sullen Moods. Robert Graves. LBBV
Sullen skies today. Joy and Sorrow. Aubrey Thomas De Vere. OQP; QP-2
Sullen, sullen, my brows are ever knit. To His Brother Hsing-chien, Who Was Serving in Tung-ch'uan. Po Chü-i. TrCh
Sullen, the stream gives no clear image back. Henley on Taieri. Charles Brasch. AnNZ
Sulpicia's Rival. Tibullus. *See* Cerinthus Forgiven; Once More Tibullus Speaks for the Girl.
Sultan was vexed by a dream, The. Fact. Arthur Guiterman. PFE
Sultry air, the smoke of shavings. A Night in a Village. Ivan Savvich Nikitin. AWP; JAWP; WBP
Sultry and brazen was the August day. Saint R. L. S. Sarah N. Cleghorn. HBMV
Sultry noon, not in the summer's prime, A. A Summer Noon. Carlos Wilcox. APW
Sultry Sunday, noon. Tropic Siesta. Luis Carlos López. AnCL; WoL
Sum, A. "Lewis Carroll." BoN
Sum, Es, Est ("Sum—I am a gentleman"). *Unknown.* ChTr
Sum of him is not here, The. Book Review. David Ross. PG (1945 ed.)
Sum of Kisses, A. Juan Meléndez Valdés, *tr. fr. Spanish by* Thomas Walsh. OnPM
(Nisé.) AnSpL-2
Sum of Life, The. William Cowper. *See* Stricken Deer, The.
Sum of Things, The. Arthur W. Jose. BoAu
Sum of Wisdom, The. Milton. *Fr.* Paradise Lost, XII. MaPo
Sum [*or* Some] speiks of lords, sum speiks of lairds. Johnie Armstrong. *Unknown.* EBSV; ESPB (C *vers.*); OBB; ViBoPo (B *vers.*)
Sumach and Birds. Carl Sandburg. YT
Sumacs burn beside the country lane, The. October Prelude. "Joseph Upper." MuM
Sumer Is Icumen In. *Unknown.* AWP; BEL; InPo; InvP; JAWP; ReaPo; SeCePo; SeCeV; SiTL; TOP; TyEnPo; WBP
(Cuckoo.) ShBV-1
(Cuckoo [*or* Cuccu] Song.) BCEP; BLA; BLV, *Middle English and mod. vers.;* CaAE; CBOV; ChTr; CoEV; EnL; EnLi-1; EnLit; EV-1; LiTG; OBEV; PreP, *with music;* PYM; TCEP; TrGrPo
(Sing Cuccu.) ViBoPo
(Summer.) LyMA
(Summer Has Come.) PoLi
(Summer Is a-Coming In, *st.* 1.) PCH
(Summer Is I-Comen In.) LEAP
Summa is i-cumen in. Baccalaureate, *parody.* David McCord. WhC
Summah night and sighin' breeze. Lover's Lane. Paul Laurence Dunbar. BANP
Summary of the Distance between the Bomber and the Objective. Walter Benton. WaP
Summer. Johannes Carl Andersen. BoAu
Summer. Richard Burton. *Fr.* Dumb in June. NLK
Summer. Byron. *Fr.* The Corsair. OBRV
Summer. John Davidson. VLEP
Summer. Aubrey Thomas De Vere. *Fr.* The Year of Sorrow: Ireland, 1849. TIP
Summer. Hesiod, *tr. fr. Greek by* F. L. Lucas. *Fr.* Works and Days. GrPE
Summer. Kalidasa. *Fr.* The Seasons. AWP
Summer. Thøger Larsen, *tr. fr. Danish by* Charles W. Stork. BoDS
Summer. Lloyd Mifflin. *Fr.* The Fields of Dawn. SN
Summer. P. K. Page. PeCV
Summer. Boris Pasternak, *tr. fr. Russian by* C. M. Bowra. BoRS
Summer. Pope. *Fr.* Pastorals. CaAE; CEP; ReaPo
(Summer; the Second Pastoral, or Alexis.) EiPP
Summer. Christina Rossetti. *See* Summer Days.
Summer. Spenser. *Fr.* The Faerie Queene, VII, 7. GN
Summer, *sels.* James Thomson. *Fr.* The Seasons.
Bathing. LPS-2
Britannia. BeR
Happy Britannia. OBEC
Sheep-washing, The. EnLi-2; EPP
(Sheep Shearing, The.) CoBE
"Still let me pierce into the midnight depth." EnRP
Storm, The. LoBV
Summer Evening and Night. OBEC
Summer Morning. OBEC
Venus Shines Out. BeR
Summer. Meta E. B. Thorne. *Fr.* Songs of the Seasons. PEOR
Summer ("The cock's on the housetop"). *Unknown. See* All Busy.
Summer ("Sumer is icumen in"). *Unknown. See* Sumer Is Icumen In.
Summer,/ the plain's vehement season. Cicada. Libero de Libero. LiTW
Summer Acres. Anne Wilkinson. CaP
Summer Afternoon. Basil Dowling. AnNZ
Summer Afternoon. Elizabeth B. Harrod. NePoEA
Summer and autumn had been so wet, The. God's Judgment on a Wicked Bishop [*or* Bishop Hatto]. Robert Southey. CG; ChTr; EnRP; EV-4; HBV; HBVY; LPS-3; OBRV; OTPC (1923 ed.); PCN; PECK; PTA-1; StPo; TVSH
Summer, and noon, and a splendour of silence, felt. A Nympholept. Swinburne. VLEP
Summer and spring the lovely rose. Not Quite Fair. H. S. Leigh. InMe
Summer and Winter. G. S. Fraser. FaBoMo
Summer and Winter. Shelley. EV-4; UnPo (3d ed.)
Summer as it passes owes to night, The. Incense. Louise Townsend Nicholl. NePoAm-2
Summer, autumn, winter, spring. The Changing Year. Lloyd Roberts. DD
Summer Ball. Viktor Viktorovich Hofman, *tr. fr. Russian by* Babette Deutsch. TrRV
Summer Bayou. John T. Westbrook. MuM
Summer Beach. Frances Cornford. ChMP
Summer Breeze. *Unknown.* BoTP
(Breeze, The.) PCH
Summer by the Lakeside. Whittier. IAP
Summer Cat, The. Ella Augusta Fanning. CIV
Summer Comes. Edith Agnew. SiSoSe
Summer comes. Magalu. Helene Johnson. CDC; PoNe
Summer Comes. Earl of Surrey. *See* Description of Spring.
Summer Commentary, A. Yvor Winters. LiTM; UnPo (3d ed.)
Summer Dawn. William Morris. AtBAP; BPN; EV-5; FaBoEn; GTBS; GTBS-D; GTSL; LoBV; OBEV; OBVV; PeBoSo; ViBoPo; ViPo; VLEP
Summer dawn's reflected hue, The. Dawn on Lake Katrine. Sir Walter Scott. *Fr.* The Lady of the Lake, III. EV-4
Summer Day, A. Henry Charles Beeching. VA
Summer Day, A. Florence Harrison. BoTP
Summer Day. Alexander Hume. EV-1, *abr.;* LoBV; OBEV (1st ed.), *much abr.*
(Of the Day Estivall.) BSV; EBSV, *abr.*
(Story of a Summer Day, The, *abr.*) LPS-2
Summer's Day, A, *br. sel.* CH
Summer Day, A. Li Po, *tr. fr. Chinese by* Shigeyoshi Obata. OnPM
Summer Day. Boris Pasternak, *tr. fr. Russian by* C. M. Bowra. BoRS
Summer Day, A. *Unknown.* PEOR
Summer Day in Old Sicily, A. Edward Cracroft Lefroy. *Fr.* Echoes from Theocritus. OBVV
Summer day is closed, The—the sun is set. An Evening Revery. Bryant. AA; OBAV
Summer Days. Wathen Marks Wilks Call. LPS-1; VA
Summer Days. Roy Daniells. CaP
Summer Days. Christina Rossetti. MCCG; OTPC; PRWS
(Summer.) AlDL; BPN

Summer days moved with the pace of a caged lion, The. July in the Jardin des Plantes. Claire McAllister. NePA
Summer dieth: o'er his bier. A Dirge for Summer. Sebastian Evans. VA
Summer Drought. J. P. Irvine. SN
Summer ends now; now, barbarous in beauty, the stooks arise. Hurrahing in Harvest. Gerard Manley Hopkins. ChTr; InvP; LO; MBP; MoAB; MoBrPo; MoP; MoPo; MoVE; PoVP
Summer Evening. John Clare. BoTP; GTML
Summer Evening. Charles Cotton. *See* Evening Quatrains.
Summer Evening. Walter de la Mare. MBP; MoAB; MoBrPo; MoShBr; NeMA; TiPo (1959 ed.); TSW
Summer Evening. Sara Henderson Hay. PoMa
Summer Evening, A. Archibald Lampman. PeCV; TwCV
Summer Evening, A. Isaac Watts. LPS-2
Summer Evening and Night. James Thomson. *Fr.* The Seasons: Summer. OBEC
Summer Evening Churchyard, A. Shelley. EmBrPo; EnSW
Summer Evening's Meditation, A, *sel.* Anna Letitia Barbauld.
"'Tis past! the sultry tyrant." BCEP; LPS-2
Summer flows in golden waves, The. The Invasion Weather. Douglas Newton. NeBP
Summer Gone, A. Howard Moss. NePoEA
Summer gone. A Frost Fancy. Richard Le Gallienne. OTPC (1946 ed.)
Summer grass. Haiku. Basho, *tr. by* Kenneth Rexroth. OnPJ
Summer grasses grow, The. The Afterglow. Basho, *tr. by* Harold Gould Henderson. WoL
Summer harvest day begun, The. July. *At. to* Whittier. YeAr
Summer Has Come ("Summer has come"). *Unknown, tr. fr. Middle Irish by* Kuno Meyer. LiTW; OnYI; SiB
Summer Has Come ("Summer is i-cumen in"). *Unknown. See* Sumer Is Icumen In.
Summer has doft his latest green. Winter. W. D. Landor. BoTP
Summer has gone. Life in the Autumn Woods. Philip Pendleton Cooke. LPS-2; SPP
Summer has sent his stewards on. Rondel. Charles d'Orléans. FoS
Summer has sunk us and we lie. Blackbirds in the Rain. Joyce Horner. WhBS
Summer has two beginnings. Emily Dickinson. InPo
Summer Holiday. Robinson Jeffers. CrMA; MAP; MoAmPo; MoVE; OxBA
Summer Holidays. W. R. Rodgers. LiTB
Summer Idyll. George Barker. FaBoMo; MoPo
Summer Images, *sels.* John Clare.
"Green lane now I traverse, where it goes, The." OBRV
"I love at early morn, from new-mown swath." ChTr; EG, *abr.*; ERP
"I see the wild flowers, in their summer morn." CoEV
Summer in England 1914. Alice Meynell. SoV
Summer Interlude. Lionel Stevenson. CaP
Summer Invocation. William Cox Bennett. *See* Invocation to Rain in Summer.
Summer Is a-Coming In. *Unknown. See* Sumer Is Icumen In.
Summer is all a green air. Summer Music. May Sarton. NePoAm
Summer Is Come. Earl of Surrey. *See* Description of Spring.
Summer is come and winter gone. A Song of the Passion. *Unknown.* TMEV
Summer is come. The beetle's wings. Plenitude. A. M. Sullivan. JKCP (1926 ed.)
Summer Is Coming, The. Bryan Guinness. OxBI
"Summer is coming, summer is coming." The Throstle. Tennyson. BMEP; BoChLi; BPN; DD; EmBrPo; EPN; FaPON; HBV; HBVY; MCCG; NLK; OTPC; PFE; PoRL; PoVP; ShBV-1; SN; VLEP; WaKn
Summer is dying, is dying. I Sail in the Fall. David Stefánsson. IcP
Summer Is Ended, The. Christina Rossetti. HBV
Summer is fading; the broad leaves that grew. Farewell to Summer. George Arnold. AA; DD
Summer is full of things that are good. Belonging to Summer. Mildred Shacklett. GFA
Summer Is Gone. *Unknown, tr. fr. Old Irish by* Seán O'Faoláin. AnIL; LyMA; SiB
——*Tr. by* Kuno Meyer. FaBoCh; LoGBV; OnYI
Summer Is I-Comen [*or* I-cumen] In. *Unknown. See* Sumer Is Icumen In.
Summer Is Nigh. *Unknown.* BoTP
Summer is over, The. October. Rose Fyleman. SiSoSe; TiPo (1959 ed.)
Summer is over, the old cow said. Moo! Robert Hillyer. WhC
Summer is sadness and its vivid light. Old Montague. *Fr.* The Lovers and the City. M. K. Joseph. AnNZ
Summer Joys. Theocritus, *tr. fr. Greek by* J. M. Edmonds. *Fr.* Idylls, VII. LiA
Summer joys are o'er. Winter Song. Ludwig Hölty. LPS-2
Summer Landscape. Jules Laforgue, *tr. fr. French by* William Jay Smith. AnFP
Summer Lightning. Emil Lange-Müller, *tr. fr. Danish by* Charles W. Stork. BoDS
Summer Longings. Denis Florence MacCarthy. HBV; LPS-2
Summer Lullaby, A. Eudora S. Bumstead. BoTP; MOAH
Summer Magic. Leslie Pinckney Hill. BANP
Summer Malison, The. Gerard Manley Hopkins. PoEL-5
Summer Matures. Helene Johnson. CDC; PoNe
Summer Moods. John Clare. LPS-2
Summer Morning, A. Rachel Field. BoChLi; StVeCh (1955 ed.); SUS; TiPo
Summer Morning. James Thomson. *Fr.* The Seasons: Summer. OBEC
Summer Music. May Sarton. NePoAm
Summer Night, A. "Æ." TCEP; TCPD
Summer Night, A. Matthew Arnold. BMEP; BPN; EmBrPo; EM-2; EnLi-2; EPN; EV-5; ExPo; GEPC; GTBS; GTSE; GTSL; MCCG; OAEP; PoVP; SeCePo; SeCeV; TyEnPo; ViPo; ViPP; VLEP
"Plainness and clearness," *sel.* PC
Summer Night, A. Elizabeth Stoddard. AA
Summer Night. Tennyson. *See* Now Sleeps the Crimson Petal.
Summer Night. Tu Fu, *tr. fr. Chinese by* Nee Wen-yei. WhP
Summer night, A/ With breezes sweet. Buson, *tr. fr. Japanese by* Lois J. Erickson. SoLD
Summer Night, Riverside. Sara Teasdale. TCPD
Summer—Noon. Thomas Gisborne. *Fr.* Walks in a Forest. EnSW
Summer Noon, A. William Howitt. LPS-2
Summer Noon, A. Carlos Wilcox. APW
Summer Noon at Sea, A. Epes Sargent. EtS
Summer Noon, 1941. Yvor Winters. CrMA
Summer of 'sixty-three, sir, and Conrad was gone away. Kentucky Belle. Constance Fenimore Woolson. BeLS; BlG; BLPA; FaBoBe; GoTP; MaC; PAH; PTA-1; StPo
Summer on the Great American Desert. Rufus B. Sage. PoOW
Summer Palace burnt, the Winter Palace, wherever it was, The. Forty-five Years Since the Fall of the Ch'ing Dynasty. Philip Whalen. NeAP
Summer Pool, The. Robert Buchanan. VA
Summer Rain. Laurie Lee. MoVE
Summer Rain. Apollon Nikolayevich Maikov, *tr. fr. Russian by* Babette Deutsch. TrRV
Summer Rain. Sir Herbert Read. LiTM; POTE
Summer Rain, The. Henry David Thoreau. AmP; AnNE; OnAP
(My Books I'd Fain Cast Off, I Cannot Read.) CoV
Summer Resort. P. K. Page. CaP
Summer Sabbath. Jessie E. Sampter. TrJP
Summer Sanctuary, A. John Hall Ingham. AA
Summer season at Tyne Dock, The. Tyne Dock. Francis Scarfe. NeBP
Summer set lip to earth's bosom bare. The Poppy. Francis Thompson. EmBrPo; MBP; MoBrPo; OBEV (1st ed.); PoP; POTT; PoVP; VLEP
Summer Shower, A. A. Fleming MacLiesh. OnAP
Summer Shower, The. Thomas Buchanan Read. CG
Summer Shower. Selma Robinson. MoSiPe
Summer Shower, A ("'Hurry!' said the leaves"). *Unknown.* BoTP
Summer sits wilting like a lilac woman. The Garden. Marvin Solomon. NePoAm
Summer Sky. Ruth McKee Gordon. TiPo (1959 ed.)
Summer Song. Edith Nesbit. AlDL
Summer Song. George Barker. ChMP; FaBoTw; GTBS-D
Summer Song. Percy MacKaye. VOD
Summer Song, A. George Peele. *See* Whenas the Rye Reach to the Chin.
Summer Song. W. W. Watt. FiBHP
Summer Song. Wu Ti, *tr. fr. Chinese by* Arthur Waley. AlDL
Summer Stars. Carl Sandburg. YeAr
Summer Storm, A. Lord Alfred Douglas. JKCP (1926 ed.)
Summer Storm. James Russell Lowell. LPS-2
"Suddenly—all the sky is hid," *sel.* PEOR
Summer Storm, A. Charles Whitehead. OBRV
Summer, stream and stillness. A Level of Abstraction. Robert Conquest. PoLFOT
Summer Sun. Robert Louis Stevenson. MBP; MoBrPo
Summer sun is falling soft on Carbery's hundred isles, The. The Sack of Baltimore. Thomas Osborne Davis. IrPN; LPS-3; TIP; VA
Summer sun is sinking low, The. Sunset. Longfellow. BoTP
Summer sun was sinking, The. The Fairy Child. John Anster. LPS-3
Summer Sunday morning, A. A Battle Ballad. Francis Orrery Ticknor. BlG; PAH
Summer Sunshine. Mary A. Lathbury. YeAr
Summer-sweet. Katharine Tynan. TIP

Summer that I was ten, The. The Centaur. May Swenson. NePoAm-2
Summer; the Second Pastoral, or Alexis. Pope. *See* Summer.
Summer, this is our flesh. Seasons of the Soul. Allen Tate. CrMA; MoPo; NePA; OxBA
Summer Time on Bredon. A. E. Housman. *See* Bredon Hill.
Summer Twilight, A. Charles Tennyson Turner. OBRV
Summer twilight gently yields, The. The Flower of Battle. Ralph Hale Mottram. MM
Summer Vacation. Wordsworth. *See* Prelude, The.
Summer vapours, soft and white. A May Sunday. Thomas Caulfield Irwin. IrPN
Summer Walk, A. Elizabeth Winton. PCH
Summer Wind. Bryant. AA; APW; BAV; PoEL-4; TCAP
Summer Winds. George Darley. VA
(Song of the Summer Winds.) LPS-2
Summer Wish. Louise Bogan. AnFE; CoAnAm; TwAmPo
Summer Wish. John Farrar. GFA
Summer Wish, A. Christina Rossetti. BPN
Summer Wooing, A. Louise Chandler Moulton. HBV
Summerhouse. Melvin Walker La Follette. NePoEA
Summers and summers have come, and gone with the flight of the swallow. Tantramar Revisited. Sir Charles G. D. Roberts. BoCaPo; CaP; OCL; TwCV
Summer's Day, A. Alexander Hume. *See* Summer Day.
Summer's End. Ethel Kirk Grayson. TwCaPo
Summer's Farewell. Thomas Nashe. *Fr.* Summer's Last Will and Testament. PoEL-2
Summer's Harbingers Are Here, The. Charles d'Orléans, *tr. fr. French by* Alan Conder. TrFP
Summer's Joe. Patrick Anderson. BoCaPo
Summer's Last Will and Testament, *sels.* Thomas Nashe.
Adieu, Farewell, Earth's Bliss [*or* Blisse]! AtBAP; CH; ElL; ElSeCe; InvP; LoBV; OAEP; PoD; PoE; ReaPo; SiCE; TuPP; ViBoPo
(Death's Summons.) HBV
(Dust Hath Closed Helen's Eye.) SeCePo
(In a Time of Pestilence [1593].) CoEV; HoPM; LiTG; MeRV; OBEV; OtMeF; PIAE; PoFS; TrGrPo
(In Plague Time.) FaBoCh; LoGBV; OBSC; RiBV
(Lament in Time of Pestilence, A.) EV-2
(Litany in Time of Plague, A.) BEL; EnLi-1 (1949 ed.); PoRA; ReEn
(Lord, Have Mercy on Us.) ChTr
(Song: "Adieu, farewell earth's blisse.") FaBoEn; MyFE; PoEL-2
A-Maying, a-Playing. ElL
(Clownish Song, A.) OBSC
Autumn. ElL; LoBV; OBSC; RiBV; TrGrPo
("Autumn hath all the summer's fruitful treasure.") CenL; TuPP
(Winter, Plague and Pestilence.) BLV
Death's Summons ("Beauty is but a flower"). CBOV
("Beauty is but a flower.") LO
Fair Summer Droops. ElL; LoBV; TuPP
(Waning Summer.) OBSC
Harvest. OBSC
Spring, the Sweet Spring. CG; CH; EnLi-1 (1949 ed.); EV-2; GTBS; GTSE; GTSL; HBV; KN; LiTB; LPS-2; OBEV; PoRA; TOP; ViBoPo
(Birds in Spring.) PRWS
(Spring.) AtBAP; BLV; CBE; CBOV; CoEV; ElL; GTBS-D; GTBS-W; LiTG; MCCG; OBSC; OTPC; PCH; RG; RIS; ShBV-2; TrGrPo
("Spring, the sweet spring, is the year's pleasant king.") CenL; EG; ElSeCe; MyFE; ReEn; SiCE; TuPP
Summer's Farewell. PoEL-2
Summer's Revel, The. Pierre de Ronsard. Odes, II, 18. WoL
Summery Windermere, sweet lake! From Four Lakes' Days. Richard Eberhart. MiAP
Summit gained, behold the proud alcove, The. Landscape. William Cowper. *Fr.* The Task. CoBE
Summit Redwood, The. Robinson Jeffers. AmPP (3d ed.); MOAP
Summit Temple, The. Li Po, *tr. fr. Chinese.* OnPM, *tr. by* Shigeyoshi Obata; WhP
Summits and vales, slim cypresses and pines. Santa Maria del Fiore. George Herbert Clarke. CaP; OCL
Summon the Workers. Clara Lambert. MPB
Summoned by love and heat and God knows what. News from the Court. David Wagoner. NePoAm-2
Summoning sun, the sun that looks on London, The. The Hours of the Planets. Charles Madge. FaBoMo
Summons. Arthur Davison Ficke. Sonnets of a Portrait Painter, XIV. HBMV
Summons, The. James Laughlin. ExPo; LiTA
Summons, The. Elizabeth Roberts MacDonald. CaP; OCL
Summons, The. Milton. *Fr.* Paradise Lost, I. WHA
Summons, The. Sir Charles G. D. Roberts. CPG
Summons, The. W. W. E. Ross. CaP
Summons, *sel.* Louis Untermeyer.
With Energy Renewed, *abr.* GrCo-2
Summons, The. Michael Wigglesworth. *See* Sounding of the Last Trump.
Summons to Execution. John Webster. *See* Hark, Now Everything Is Still.
Summons to Love. William Drummond of Hawthornden. *See* Phoebus, Arise!
Summons was urgent; and forth I went, The. Her Death and After. Thomas Hardy. PoVP
Summum Bonum. Abu-l-Ala al-Maarri, *tr. fr. Arabic by* R. A. Nicholson. LiTW
Summum Bonum. Robert Browning. BPN; EmBrPo; EnLi-2 (1949 ed.); EPN; GEPC; GTML; GTSL; HBV; LEAP; LiTL; LoPo; NeHB; OHFP; PG (1955 ed.); PoVP; VLEP
Sumner, *abr.* Whittier. GA
Sumter. Henry Howard Brownell. MC; PaA; PAH
Sumter. Edmund Clarence Stedman. MC; PAH
Sumter—a Ballad of 1861. *Unknown.* PAH
Sumter's Band. James Wright Simmons. GA; PAH
Sun, The. Baudelaire, *tr. fr. French by* David Paul. MiFP
Sun, The. John Davis. NA
Sun, The. Emily Dickinson. *See* I'll tell you how the sun rose.
Sun, The. John Drinkwater. FaPON; TiPo
Sun. Iwan Goll, *tr. fr. German by* Charles Guenther. OnPM
Sun. Langston Hughes. *Fr.* A House in Taos. CDC
Sun, The. Thomas Miller. OTPC (1923 ed.)
Sun! Marianne Moore. MeRV; NP
Sun. Henry Rowe. OBEV
Sun, The. Francis Thompson. *Fr.* Ode to the Setting Sun. MBP; MoAB; MoBrPo
Sun, The. Georg Trakl, *tr. fr. German by* Christopher Middleton. AnGP
Sun, The. W. J. Turner. MoBrPo
Sun,/ inventory of colour. Zoo. Gonzalo Escudero. AnCL
Sun a-beatin' on the deck. Song. A. Gregg. CAG
Sun, about to part, The. The Setting Sun. Ibn Sa'id of Alcala la Real. MooP
Sun am des a golden ball. Sleep-Time in Darktown. *Unknown.* BOL
Sun and Cloud. Abus Salt, *tr. fr. Arabic by* A. J. Arberry. MooP
Sun and Moon. Charlotte Druitt Cole. BoTP
Sun and moon, that ceaselessly obey, The. Immortal Israel. Judah Halevi. TrJP
Sun and Rain. Christina Rossetti. PPL
Sun and rain at work together. Orange Tree by Day. Sacheverell Sitwell. *Fr.* The Red-gold Rain. AtBAP; MBP; MoBrPo
Sun and skies and clouds of June. October's Bright Blue Weather. Helen Hunt Jackson. BBV; BLPA; CV; DD; GN; HBVY; PTA-1
Sun and the Moon, The. *Unknown, tr. fr. Chinese.* WhP
Sun and the serenest Moon sprang forth, The. Shelley. *Fr.* Ode to Liberty. NBE
Sun and Wind. Eleanor Farjeon. OTPC (1946 ed.)
Sun and wind and beat of sea. Adventure. Adelaide Crapsey. NP
Sun appeared so smug and bright, The. The Silver Question. Oliver Herford. NA
Sun, as hot as he was bright, The. In Search of the Picturesque. William Combe. *Fr.* Dr. Syntax in Search of the Picturesque. OBRV
Sun at noon to higher air, The. March. A. E. Housman. A Shropshire Lad, X. FaBoCh; LoGBV; PoVP; ViP
Sun, autumnly thin and timid. Whispered to the Afternoon. Georg Trakl. OnPM
Sun-Bather, The. Kim Kurt. NePoAm-2
Sunbather, The. Vernon Watkins. MoPo; MoVE; MoWP
Sun blazed while the thunder yet, The. The Mill-Pond. Edward Thomas. POTE
Sun bombed the happy fields, The. Airborn. Louis Grudin. PG (1955 ed.)
Sun brings out a satin day, The. In Autumn. Francis Kiely. CAG
Sun burns on its sultry wick, The. Elegy Written on a Frontporch. Karl Shapiro. MoPo
Sun comes up and the sun goes down, The;/ The night mist shroudeth the sleeping town. The Fallow Field. Julia C. R. Dorr. AA
Sun comes up and the sun goes down, The,/ And day and night are the same as one. Vanity. Harriet Prescott Spofford. LPS-3
Sun, departing, kissed the summer Sky, The. A Sunset. Robert Loveman. AA
Sun descending in the west, The. Night. Blake. *Fr.* Songs of Innocence. AlDL, *st.* 1; AnFE; AtBAP; BCEP; BoTP; BrBE; CaAE; CBE; CBOV; CEP; CH; CoBE; EnRP; EV-3; FaBoBe; FaPON; GoTP; GTBS-D; HBV; HBVY; MaPo; MyFE; OBEC; OBEV; OTPC (1923 ed.); OxBoCh; PoE; RAR, *st.* 1; RIS; SAS; ShBV-3; StaSt; WP
Sun-Dial, The. Austin Dobson. LPS-1

Sun-Dial, The. Thomas Love Peacock. *Fr.* Melincourt. OBRV
Sun does [*or* doth] arise, The. The Echoing Green. Blake. *Fr.* Songs of Innocence. BoTP; CBE; CEP; CH; EiPP; EV-3; GBV (1952 ed.); KN; OBEC; OTPC; PCH; PoRh
Sun drew off at last his piercing fires, The. Witchcraft; New Style. Lascelles Abercrombie. MBP; MoBrPo
Sun Drops Red, The. Nellie Burget Miller. PoOW
Sun falls warm, The: the southern winds awake. In March. Archibald Lampman. CPG
Sun fell in love and married the moon, The. The Wedding Song. *Unknown.* MoGP
Sun five times the earth had compassed, The. Episode of Adamastor off the Cape of Good Hope [*or* The Cape of Tempests]. Luís de Camões. *Fr.* The Lusiads. LiA; LiTW
Sun from the east tips the mountains with gold, The. Hunting Song. Paul Whitehead. *Fr.* Apollo and Daphne. OBEC; OxBoLi
Sun gas coughed, A. A million miles of flame. In the Year of Many Conversions and the Private Soul. John Ciardi. MiAP
Sun-glad day is a wondrous dream, The. The Trip. "Lambros Porphyras." MoGP
Sun God, The. Aubrey Thomas De Vere. ACP; BMEP; ES; OBVV; PoVP; TIP
Sun goes down, The. Midsummer Night. Elizabeth Gould. BoTP
Sun goes down and over all, The. Low Tide on Grand-Pré. Bliss Carman. BoCaPo; CaP; CPG; OCL; PeCV; TwCV
Sun goes down, and with him takes, The. The Romany Girl. Emerson. BAV; CoBA; TCAP
Sun Gonna Shine in My Door Some Day, *with music. Unknown.* OuSiCo
Sun had clos'd the winter day, The. Burns. *Fr.* The Vision. BSV
Sun had gone down, The. Her White Bosom Bare. *Unknown.* CSF
Sun had set behind the hill across the dreary moor, The. The Farmer's Boy. *Unknown.* ABS
Sun had set, The; the leaves with dew. Keenan's Charge. George Parsons Lathrop. AA; BBV (1923 ed.); HBV; MC; MDAH; OBAV; PAH; PAP; PFY
Sun had sunk beneath the west, The. The Ocean-Fight. *Unknown.* PAH
Sun has come, I know, The. The Sun. W. J. Turner. MoBrPo
Sun has gane down o'er the lofty Benlomond, The. Jessie, the Flower o' Dunblane [*or* The Flower o' Dumblane]. Robert Tannahill. EBSV; EV-4; HBV; LPS-1
Sun has gone from the shining skies, The. A Summer Lullaby. Eudora S. Bumstead. BoTP; MOAH
Sun has kissed the violet sea, The. Betrayal. Sidney Lanier. *Fr.* The Jacquerie. AA
Sun Has Long Been Set, The. Wordsworth. YeAr
Night in June, A, *sel.* BoTP
Sun has returned to the west mountains, The. Journey among Ruins. Li Ho. WhP
Sun has risen on the eastern brim of the world, The. The Song of Lo-fu. *Unknown.* AWP
Sun Has Set, The. Emily Brontë. ViBoPo
Sun has set, the stars are still, The. The Fair-haired Girl. *Unknown.* OnYI
Sun has sunk behind the hills, The. Good-Night. George Hill. BOL
Sun has touched the mountain's crest, The. The Song of the Partridge. *Unknown.* ArmLP
Sun has turned the dusky hill, The. The Voice. Richard Mansfield. POTE
Sun hath twice brought forth his [*or* the] tender green, The. The Restless State of a Lover. Earl of Surrey. GoTL; SiPS
Sun, his journey ending in the west, The. Henry Constable. *Fr* Diana. OBSC
Sun in the East. *Unknown, tr. fr. Chinese. Fr.* Shi King. LiTW, *tr. by* Arthur Waley; WhP
Sun in the heavens, The. The Young Reaper. Aleksey Koltsov. WoL
Sun in the mist this morning. November 11th, 1942. Lawrence Toynbee. NeTW
Sun, in wanton pride, The. In the Barn. Josephine Pinckney. NP
Sun is a fire, The. A Minor Poet. John Richard Moreland. LS
Sun is a glorious thing, The. Common Things. Ann Hawkshaw. OTPC (1923 ed.)
Sun is a huntress young, The. An Indian Summer Day on the Prairie. Vachel Lindsay. StVeCh; WaKn; YT
Sun is always in the sky, The. Breakfast Time. James Stephens. SUS
Sun is ashining to welcome the day, The. Come to the Fair. Helen Taylor. OlF
Sun is blue and scarlet on my page, The. Falling Asleep over the Aeneid. Robert Lowell. CoBMV; CrMA; FiMAP; OxBA
Sun is careering in glory and might, The. Joy of Life. Mary Russell Mitford. OTPC
Sun is clear of bird and cloud, The. Alulvan. Walter de la Mare. GBV (1952 ed.); MoVE
Sun is down, and time gone by, The. Good-Night. Joanna Baillie. OTPC (1923 ed.)
Sun Is First to Rise, The. Elizabeth J. Coatsworth. StVeCh (1955 ed.)
Sun is gone: those glorious chariot-wheels, The. Evening. Edward Rowland Sill. AnAmPo; LA
Sun is hidden from our sight, The. The Little Boy's Good-Night. Eliza Lee Follen. OTPC (1923 ed.)
Sun, The, is in the sky, mother, the flowers are springing fair. The Biter Bit. William E. Aytoun. BOHV; InMe; PA
Sun is lord and god, sublime, serene, The. The Lake of Gaube. Swinburne. PoVP; VLEP
Sun is low, to say the least, The. The Sunset [*or* Nonsense Rhymes]. Gelett Burgess. HBVY; PIAE; TSW; TSWC
Sun is melting the last rosy snow, The. Snow of the Crane. Nikolai Tikhonov. RuPo
Sun is nigh the verge, The. Soon we must part. A Walk. Hedwig Lachmann. TrJP
Sun, The, is not a-bed, when I. The Sun's Travels. Robert Louis Stevenson. FaPON; GFA; MPB; StVeCh (1940 ed.)
Sun, The, is set; the swallows are asleep. Evening; Ponte al Mare, Pisa. Shelley. KN
Sun is setting, and the toiler halts, The. The Dignity of Labor. *Unknown.* PEOR
Sun is sinking over hill and sea, The. At Night. George Edward Montgomery. AA
Sun is sleeping in the skies, The. Good-Night. Elizabeth Hays Wilkinson. BOL
Sun Is Warm, the Sky Is Clear, The. Shelley. *See* Stanzas Written in Dejection near Naples.
Sun is weary, for he ran, The. A Child's Evensong. Richard Le Gallienne. BOL
Sun itself was cheering, so they said, The. Independence. Roy McFadden. OxBI
Sun lay warm on tawny fields, The. Remembrance. Leslie Savage Clark. ChIP
Sun lies light on a jade-green hill, The. Spring. Anne Elizabeth Maddock. OQP; QP-2
Sun looked from his everlasting skies, The. My Old Counselor. Gertrude Hall. AA; OBAV
Sun, Lord and Master, and sacred flame. Hecate. Sophocles. OxBG
Sun makes music as of old, The. Prologue in Heaven. Goethe. *Fr.* Faust. AWP; JAWP; WBP
Sun may set and rise, The. Lines from Catullus. Sir Walter Ralegh. SiPS
Sun Men Call It, The. John Hall Wheelock. NePoAm-2
Sun, Moon and Thunder. *Unknown, tr. fr. Russian by* W. R. S. Ralston. OnPM
Sun o'er the steppeland is sinking, The. The Convicts. Aleksey Konstantinovich Tolstoy. WaL
Sun of all suns, seed of dandelion seeds. Llewelyn's Chariot. Vernon Watkins. MoWP
Sun of Austerlitz had dawned and shone and set in blood, The. The Vengeance of the Duchess. John Davidson. VLEP
Sun of grace Him shineth in, The. All the Merrier Is That Place. *Unknown.* AnEC
Sun of Ivera, The. *See* Sun on Ivera, The.
Sun of life has crossed the line, The. Equinoctial. Adeline D. H. Whitney. HBV
Sun of my soul, Thou Saviour dear. Evening Hymn. John Keble. BePJ; MaRV; OlF
Sun of Righteousness. William Austin. *See* Chanticleer.
Sun of the moral world; effulgent source. To Freedom. Joel Barlow. AnAmPo; AnNE; LA; PoFr
Sun of the Sleepless! Byron. AtBAP
Sun of the stately day. The National Ode. Bayard Taylor. PAH
Sun, of whose terrain we creatures are, The. Solar Creation. Charles Madge. FaBoMo; OBMV
Sun on [*or* upon *or* of] Ivera, The/ No longer shines brightly. The Lament for [*or* of *or* Dirge of] O'Sullivan Bear[e]. *Tr. by* Jeremiah Joseph Callanan. AnIV; GTIV; IrPN; TIP
Sun on the dewy grasslands where late the frost hath shone. In the Mushroom Meadows. Thomas Walsh. SBMV
Sun on the steppes is sinking, The. The Convicts. Aleksey Konstantinovich Tolstoy. BoR
Sun on the tree-tops no longer is seen, The. Queen Sabbath. Hayyim Nahman Bialik. TrJP
Sun Orchids. Douglas Stewart. NeLNL
Sun over all and air over all and clover. Merrill's Brook. Winfield Townley Scott. FiMAP
Sun overwhelms the city with his terrible and direct light, The. The Fair Dorothy. Baudelaire. MiFP

Sun-Parasol, The. Fredrik August Dahlgren, *tr. fr. Swedish by* Charles W. Stork. AnSL
Sun Rises Bright in France, The. Allan Cunningham. BSV; EBSV; HBV; OBEV (1st ed.); OBRV
Sun rises in the east, The. The Song of Lo-fu. *Unknown.* WhP
Sun [*or* Sunne] Rising, The. John Donne. AnFE; AtBAP; BLV; BoLiVe; EnLP; ExPo; GTSE; InvP; LiTB; LiTG; LiTL; LoBV; MeLP; MePo; OAEP; PoE; PoEL-2; PoFr; PoFS; ReEn; ReIE; SeCePo; SeCeV; SeCV-1; SeEP; TrGrPo; TuPP; TwHP; TwP
("Busie old foole, unruly sun.") EG
Sun, The, rushed up the sky; the taxi flew. Parting as Descent. John Berryman. LiTA; MoAmPo (1950 ed.)
Sun saw on that widening shore, The. Sainte Anne de Beaupre. Richard Eberhart. NePoAm
Sun set, and up rose the yellow moon, The. 'Tis Sweet to Hear. Byron. *Fr.* Don Juan, I. MCCG
Sun set, but set not his hope, The. Character. Emerson. AnFE; AnNE; CoAnAm; LiTA
Sun shines bright in the [*or* in our *or* on my] old Kentucky home, The. My Old Kentucky Home [Good-Night]. Stephen Collins Foster. AA; AnAmPo; AnFE; APA; APW; CoAnAm; FaBoBe; FaFP; HBV; IAP; LA; LEAP; LPS-1; OBAV; OIF; OTPC; PECK; PoeMoYo; PoRL; PYM; StaSt; TrAS; TreF; TrGrPo
Sun shines bright on Arlington, the drowsy sheep creep by, The. Arlington. David McKee Wright. AnNZ
Sun shines high on yonder hill, The. The False Lover Won Back (B *vers.*). *Unknown.* ESPB
Sun shines on the chamber wall, The. The Death of Marlborough. George Walter Thornbury. VA
Sun shines, The. The coltsfoot flowers. Tommies in the Train. D. H. Lawrence. NP
Sun sinks down, the tremulous daylight dies, The. Plainte Eternelle. Lord Alfred Douglas. PoVP
Sun sinks softly to his Ev'ning Post, The. The Rejected "National Hymns," V. "Orpheus C. Kerr." BOHV; InMe; LPS-3; PA
Sun sinks towards the horizon, The. Clear Evening after Rain. Tu Fu. OnPC
Sun-Song. Mary Josephine Benson. CPG
Sun strikes gold the dirty street, The. Brest Left Behind. John Farrar. AOAH; PAH
Sun strikes those windows blind. The Library. Mary Mills. NePoAm
Sun strikes, through the windows, up the floor, The. Sursum Corda. Elizabeth Barrett Browning. *Fr.* Casa Guidi Windows. VA
Sun-swept beaches with a light wind blowing. The Unchanging. Sara Teasdale. ChMo; CMP
Sun that brief December day, The. Snow-bound. Whittier. AmPP; AnNE; APW; AtBAP; BBV; CoBA; GN; HiLiAm; IAP; MCCG; MOAP; OnAP; OxBA; PIAE; SN; StVeCh; TCAP; TOP; TrGrPo
Sun, that bright swan, stoops, The. Sunlight on the Sea. Ibn Sa'id of Alcala la Real. MooP
Sun that shines all day so bright, The. Night. *Unknown.* BoTP
Sun, The, the moon, the stars, the seas, the hills, and the plains. The Higher Pantheism. Tennyson. BEL; BMEP; BPN; EM-2; EmBrPo; EnLi-2; EPP; GrCo-1; MaRV; PoVP; ViPo; ViPP; VLEP; WGRP
Sun, the Rose, the Lily, the Dove, The. Love's Résumé. Heine. TrJP
Sun-treader—life and light be thine for ever. Shelley. Robert Browning. *Fr.* Pauline. OBRV
Sun-up in March. Abbie Huston Evans. NePoAm
Sun upon Ivera, The. *See* Sun on Ivera, The.
Sun upon the Lake Is Low, The. Sir Walter Scott. *Fr.* The Doom of Devorgoil, I. EBSV
(Datur Hora Quieti.) GTBS; GTBS-D; GTBS-W; GTSE; GTSL
(Leonard: "Sun upon the lake is low, The.") EmBrPo
Sun upon the snow shows up, The. The Warm Front and the Cold. James Wreford Watson. BoCaPo (1948 ed.)
Sun upon the Weirdlaw Hill, The. Sir Walter Scott. BPN; BSV; EmBrPo; EPN
Sun Used to Shine, The. Edward Thomas. FaBoTw
Sun was bright when we went in, The. At the Theater. Rachel Field. FaPON
Sun was down, and twilight grey, The. In the Room. James Thomson. OBVV
Sun was drowned in the western tide, The. An Easter-Tide Deliverance, A.D. 430. Maria H. Bulfinch. EOAH
Sun was drowning in the ocean's brim, The. Khustina—The Kerchief. Fedkovich. CPG
Sun was gold over the water and the voices golden, The. The Flower. John Holmes. LiTL
Sun was gone, and the moon was coming, The. August Moonrise. Sara Teasdale. TCAP
Sun was in the summer grass, The. The Stockman. David Campbell. MoAuPo
Sun was now withdrawn, The. Damon and Cupid. John Gay. EnLoPo; SeCeV
Sun was setting, and its golden glow, The. The Throne of the King. Francis Clement Kelley. JKCP
Sun was setting, and vespers done, The. Thursday. Frederick E. Weatherly. BOHV
Sun was shining on the sea, The. The Walrus and the Carpenter. "Lewis Carroll." *Fr.* Through the Looking-Glass. BeLS; BMEP; BoChLi; BOHV; BoN; FaBoBe; FaFP; FaPON; FiBHP; GN; GoBP; HBV; HBVY; InMe; LBN; LiTB; LiTG; MaC; MBP; MCCG; NA; NeHB; OnSP; OTPC; PFE; PIR; PoRA; PoRh; PoVP; PTA-1; PYM; SAS; ShBV-1; StVeCh; TreF; TVC; TVSH; YT
Sun was sinking in the west, The. The Dying Ranger [*or* Soldier]. *Unknown.* CoSo; CSF; ShS
Sun Was Slumbering in the West, The. Thomas Hood. FiBHP
Sun was warm but the wind was chill, The. Early April. Robert Frost. YeAr
Sun Went Down, The. Avetis Isahakian, *tr. fr. Armenian by* Zabelle C. Boyajian. ArmLP
Sun went down, and the work of the Achaians was accomplished, The. Homer. *Fr.* The Iliad, VII. GrPo
Sun went down in flame and smoke, The. Under One Blanket. James Barton Hope. TCAP
Sun went down—'twas summer time—from evening skies outwelling, The. The Girl of the Cottage. Johan Ludvig Runeberg. AnSL
Sun, when it shines on traffic, has a look. Noon on Alameda Street. Hildegarde Flanner. LiTM
Sun, which doth the greatest comfort bring, The. Master [*or* Mr.] Francis Beaumont's Letter to Ben Jonson [*or* A Letter to Ben Jonson]. Francis Beaumont. BEL; ElSeCe; EPP; LoBV; OBS; PtP; SeEP; ViBoPo
Sun, who never stops to dine, The. The Town-Meeting, P.M. John Trumbull. *Fr.* M'Fingal. TCAP
Sun, with his great eye, The. The Daisy's Song. Keats. ADAH; OTPC; PRWS
Sun, yon glorious orb of day, The. The Sun. John Davis. NA
Sunbather. *See* Sun Bather.
Sunbeam, The ("I dined with a friend"). *Unknown.* NA
Sun-beames in the East are spread, The. Epithalamion Made at Lincolnes Inne. John Donne. LEAP; OBS
Sunbeams drip, drip, incessantly, The. Lonely Spring. Saisei Muro. PoLJ
Sunbeams streamed without, The. In the Morgue. Israel Zangwill. TrJP
Sunbows, The. Swinburne. BPN; EmBrPo; EPN
Sunburn. Abu Hafs, *tr. fr. Arabic by* A. J. Arberry. MooP
Sunburnt Boys. John Charles McNeill. NoCaPo
Sunburnt mowers are in the swath, The. The Mowers. Myron B. Benton. LPS-2
Sunday. Jorge Carrera Andrade, *tr. fr. Spanish by* Muna Lee. AnCL
Sunday. Elizabeth J. Coatsworth. WaKn
Sunday, A. Walter de la Mare. POTE
Sunday. George Herbert. EPS; OBS; SeCV-1; SeEP
Sunday. Carlos Pellicer, *tr. fr. Spanish by* Dudley Fitts. AnCL
Sunday Afternoon Service in St. Enodoc Church, Cornwall. John Betjeman. MoVE
Sunday and sunlight ashen on the Square. The Self Unsatisfied Runs Everywhere. Delmore Schwartz. FiMAP
Sunday at Hampstead, *sels.* James Thomson.
"As we rush, as we rush in the train," X. EBSV; EmBrPo; EV-4; GTBS; GTBS-W; LiTG; POTT; PoVP; ViBoPo
(In the Train.) BoTP; LoPo; OBEV; PCD
"Day after day of this azure May," XI. EmBrPo
"How your eyes dazzle down into my soul!" II. EmBrPo
"O mellow moonlight warm," XII. EmBrPo
"This is the Heath of Hampstead," I. EmBrPo; POTT
"Was it hundreds of years ago, my Love," III. EmBrPo
Sunday Bells. William Allingham. IrPN
Sunday Evening. Barbara Guest. NeAP
Sunday Evening in the Common. John Hall Wheelock. HBV; MAP; MoAmPo; NP; PFY
Sunday evening. The thick-lipped men binoculared. Merthymawr. George Woodcock. MoWP; NeBP
Sun-Day Hymn, A. Oliver Wendell Holmes. *Fr.* The Professor at the Breakfast Table, *ch.* 12. AnNE; APW; IAP; InP; MaRV; TrPWD; WGRP
(Lord of All Being.) GrCo-1
("Lord of all being, throned afar.") OIF
Sunday in Old England. *Kearsarge.* S. Weir Mitchell. PAH
Sunday in the Country. May Swenson. NePoAm-2
Sunday in the Park. William Carlos Williams. *Fr.* Paterson. CrMA
Sunday, July 14th; a Fine Day at the Baths. Julian Symons. WaP
Sunday Morning. James Grahame. *Fr.* The Sabbath. OBRV
(Sabbath, The.) EnSW; LPS-2

Sunday Morning. Louis MacNeice. CoBMV; FaBoMo; LiTB; MBP; MoAB; MoBrPo; MoVE; NeMA; PoE
Sunday Morning. James Rorty. MOAP
Sunday Morning. Isidor Schneider. AnAmPo; LA
Sunday Morning (*Complete,* I-VIII). Wallace Stevens. AmP; AmPP (4th ed.); CoBA; CoBMV; CoV; CrMA; FaBoEn; InPo; LiTA; LiTG; LiTM; MoAB; MOAP; MoVE; OxBA; NePA; ReMP; RiBV; SeCeV; TwAmPo
Sels.
"Complacencies of the peignoir, and late," I. AnFE; AnNE; APA; CoAnAm; MAP; MAPA; MoAmPo; TriL
"She hears, upon that water without sound," II [VIII]. AnFE; AnNE; APA; CoAnAm; MAP; MAPA; MoAmPo; TriL
"She says, 'But in contentment I still feel,'" IV [V]. AnFE; AnNE; APA; CoAnAm; MAP; MAPA; MoAmPo; TriL
"She says: 'I am content when wakened birds,'" III [IV]. AnFE; AnNE; APA; CoAnAm; MAP; MAPA; MoAmPo; TriL
"Supple and turbulent, a ring of men," V [VII]. AnFE; AnNE; APA; CoAnAm; GTBS-W; MAP; MAPA; MoAmPo; TriL
Sunday Morning. L. A. G. Strong. WhC
Sunday Morning Apples. Hart Crane. NAMP
Sunday morning just at nine. Down Went McGinty. Joseph Flynn. TreF; YaD
Sunday night and the park policemen. The Picnic Boat. Carl Sandburg. WoL
Sunday Night Walk. Raymond Souster. CaP
Sunday on Hampstead Heath. George Woodcock. NeBP
Sunday shuts down on a twentieth-century evening. Boy with His Hair Cut Short. Muriel Rukeyser. ExPo; FiMAP; MoAB; NAMP; TwAmPo
Sunday the sea made morning worship, sang. Half-Tide Ledge. R. P. Blackmur. AnFE; CoAnAm; TwAmPo
Sunday, the shout of hosannas. His Last Week. Elinor Lennen. PGD
Sunday up the River, *sels.* James Thomson.
"Church bells are ringing, The," IV. EmBrPo; OAEP
"Could we float thus ever," XX. EmBrPo
"Drink! drink! open your mouth!" XIX. EmBrPo
"Give a man a horse he can ride," XV. CaAE; EBSV; EmBrPo; EnLi-2; EPP; GTSL; LEAP; POTT; PoVP; VLEP
(Gifts.) BBV; HBV; OBEV; OBVV; TOP; TreF
"I looked out into the morning," I. EmBrPo; OAEP; PoVP; ViBoPo; VLEP
"I love all hardy exercise," V. EmBrPo
"In the vast vague gray," III. EmBrPo
"Let my voice ring out and over the earth," XVII. EmBrPo; POTT; PoVP; VLEP
(Song.) HBV; MaRV; OBVV
"Like violets pale i' the spring o' the year," IX
(Song.) OBVV
"My love is the flaming sword," XVI. EmBrPo
(Song.) OBVV
"My Love o'er the water bends dreaming," XII. EBSV; OBEV (1st ed.)
(Reflection.) EnLit
"'Oh, what are you waiting for here, young man?'" II. EmBrPo; PoVP; VLEP
(Bridge, The.) OBVV; TOP
"Were I a real poet, I would sing," X. OAEP
"Wine of Love is music, The," XVIII. EmBrPo; POTT; PoVP; ViBoPo; VLEP
(Vine, The.) HBV; LEAP; LoPS; MBP; OBEV; OBVV
Sunday; Wherein a Man Laments like a Man. Eduardo Carranza, *tr. fr. Spanish by* Donald Devenish Walsh. AnCL
Sunder me from my bones, O sword of God. The Sword of Surprise. G. K. Chesterton. LBBV; MBP; MoBrPo
Sundered. Sidney Henry Morse. LBAP
Sundered. Israel Zangwill. TrJP
Sundered from this beauty is its fond lover. Elegy in the Orongorongo Valley. Hubert Witheford. AnNZ
Sundew, The. Swinburne. CoEV; ViP
Sundown. Léonie Adams. MAP; MoAB; MoAmPo; TrGrPo; TwAmPo
Sundown. Chu Shu Chen, *tr. fr. Chinese by* Henry H. Hart. PoHN
Sundown. John Charles McNeill. NoCaPo
Sundown. Bert Leston Taylor. OQP; QP-1
Sundown is but the mortal eye's confusion. Illusion. Nevah Trebor. PC
Sundry Christian Passions. Henry Lok. *See* Sonnets of Christian Passions.
Sunflower, The. Blake. *See* Ah! Sunflower.
Sunflower. André Breton, *tr. fr. French by* Edouard Roditi. LiTW
Sunflower, The. Gilles Durant, *tr. fr. French by* Alan Conder. TrFP
Sunflower, The. Eugenio Montale, *tr. fr. Italian by* Glauco Cambon. OnPM
Sunflower, The. Peter Quennell. AtBAP; POTE
Sunflower. Stepan Petrovich Shchipachev, *tr. fr. Russian by* Babette Deutsch. TrRV
Sunflower ain't de daisy, De. Doan't You Be What You Ain't. Edwin Milton Royle. BLPA
Sunflower has nowhere, The. Sunflower. Stepan Petrovich Shchipachev. TrRV
Sunflower Sutra. Allen Ginsberg. NeAP
Sunflower to the Sun, The. Mary Elizabeth Hewitt Stebbins. AA
Sunflowers. Clinton Scollard. HBMV; MPB; NLK; VOD
Sunflowers, The. Douglas Stewart. BoAV
Sung by the nightingale to birth. Pomegranates. Roy Campbell. AtBAP
Sung in Spring. Oliver St. John Gogarty. AlDL
Sung on a By-Way. "Æ." TOP
Sung on a Sunny Morning. Jean Starr Untermeyer. TrPWD
Sunium. Trumbull Stickney. MOAP
Sunk in sleep a song is ringing. The Divining Rod. Joseph von Eichendorff. AnGP
Sunk in the vale, whose concave depth receives. Winter—Frost. Thomas Gisborne. *Fr.* Walks in a Forest. EnSW
Sunk Lyonesse. Walter de la Mare. CoBMV; FaBoCh
Sunken City. Wilhelm Müller, *tr. fr. German by* James Clarence Mangan. LPS-3
Sunken Evening. Laurie Lee. PoN
Sunken Garden, The. Walter de la Mare. HBMV; TCEP
Sunken Gold. Eugene Lee-Hamilton. EtS; VA
Sunless your caverns are; the fever damps. Baudelaire, *tr. by* Aldous Huxley. *Fr.* Femmes Damnées. MeRV
Sunlight and summer wind are never sure. The Attic. Charles Bruce. *Fr.* The Flowing Summer. CaP
Sunlight drawing from shadow, up and down the street. Passages. Larry Eigner. NeAP
Sunlight falls happily upon this sea. Tranquil Sea. Claire Aven Thomson. EtS
Sunlight fills the trembling air, The. Betrothed Anew. Edmund Clarence Stedman. LPS-2
Sunlight from the sky's own heart. A Song of Handicraft. Annie Matheson. OBVV
Sunlight glitters keen and bright, The. Hampton Beach. Whittier. LPS-2; MOAP
Sunlight is beautiful, mother, The. Katie's Secret. *Unknown.* ABS
Sunlight laughs along the serried stone, The. Dawn at Liverpool. Archibald T. Strong. *Fr.* Sonnets of the Empire. BoAu
Sunlight leaves the west. Sedge Songs, II. Nikolaus Lenau. AnGP
Sunlight, moonlight. Dream-Song. Walter de la Mare. BOL
Sunlight on the Garden, The. Louis MacNeice. CaAE; ChMo; CoBMV; LiTB; MoPo; OAEP (2d ed.); OxBI; ReaPo; TwHP
(Song: "Sunlight on the garden, The.") MoP
Sunlight on the Sea. Ibn Sa'id of Alcala la Real, *tr. fr. Arabic by* A. J. Arberry. MooP
Sun-light recedes on the mountains, in long gold shafts. Interlude. Maxwell Bodenheim. MAPA
Sunlight shone on walls of stone, The. The King and the Child. Eugene J. Hall. PTA-2
Sunlight speaks, and its voice is a bird, The. The Humming Bird. Harry Hibbard Kemp. FaPON; HBMV; MPB
Sunlight the tall women may never have seen. Children, the Sandbar, That Summer. Muriel Rukeyser. FiMAP
Sunlit Vale, The. Edmund Blunden. ChMP; GTBS-D; MoVE
Sunne Rising, The. John Donne. *See* Sun Rising, The.
Sunning. James S. Tippett. AlBD; SiSoSe; SUS; TiPo
Sunny hair and eyes of wonder. A Little Person. Brian Hooker. HBMV
Sunny rounds of earth contain, The. Proletaria. Bernard O'Dowd. BoAu
Sunny shaft did I behold, A. Glycine's Song. Samuel Taylor Coleridge. *Fr.* Zapolya. BoTP; BPN; CEP; EmBrPo; ERP; LO; OBEV; OTPC (1946 ed.); TCEP; TwHP
Sunrise. Rowena Bennett. TiPo (1959 ed.)
Sunrise. Robert Browning. *Fr.* Pippa Passes. NLK; OQP; QP-2
("Day!/ Faster and more fast.") AlDL; EmBrPo; GTSL; PoVP; SN; ViPP
Sunrise. Edgar A. Guest. NLK
Sunrise. Sidney Lanier. Hymns of the Marshes, I. AA; ADAH; HiLiAm; PoEL-5; SPP; TCAP
"Tide's at full, The: the marsh with flooded streams," *sel.* FaBoEn
Sunrise. Lizette Woodworth Reese. TSW; TSWC
Sunrise. Charles Erskine Scott Wood. *Fr.* The Poet in the Desert, III. GoTP; MAP; PFY
Sunrise along Shore. L. M. Montgomery. CPG
Sunrise and Sunset. Emily Dickinson. *See* I'll tell you how the sun rose.
Sunrise at Sea. Edwin Atherstone. EtS

Sunrise at Sea. Epes Sargent. EtS
Sunrise at Sea. Swinburne. *Fr.* Tristram of Lyonesse: The Sailing of the Swallow. EtS
Sunrise in the Hills of Satsuma. Mary McNeil Fenollosa. AA
Sunrise; Maine Coast. Robert P. Tristram Coffin. CAG
Sunrise Never Failed Us Yet, The. Celia Thaxter. PEOR
Sunrise of the Poor, The. Robert Burns Wilson. AA
Sunrise on Mansfield Mountain. Alice Brown. HBV
Sunrise on Rydal Water. John Drinkwater. GBV; HBV; LiTM; NP; NV; TCEP
Sunrise on the Sea. Shakespeare. *Fr.* A Midsummer Night's Dream, III, ii. ChTr
Sunrise over the Pyramids. Lorentz Dietrichson, *tr. fr. Norwegian by* Charles W. Stork. AnNoLy
Sunrise tints the dew, The. Crocuses. Josa. MBP; TiPo
Sunrise Trumpets. Joseph Auslander. AnAmPo; LA; TrJP
Sunrise wakes the lark to sing, The. Bird Raptures. Christina Rossetti. ViPo; VLEP
Sun's a bright-haired shepherd boy, The. Silver Sheep. Anne Blackwell Payne. GFA; SiSoSe
Suns and Clouds. Shakespeare. *See* Sonnets, XXXIII.
Sun's Darling, The, *sels.* Thomas Dekker *and* John Ford.
"Cast away care, he that loves sorrow." ReEn; TuPP
"Haymakers, rakers, reapers, and mowers," *fr.* III, i. CenL; ElSeCe; ViBoPo
(Country Glee.) CoEV
(Song: "Haymakers, rakers . . .") EV-2
Live with Me Still. EV-2; SeCL
Sun's Golden Bowl, The. Mimnermus, *tr. fr. Greek by* Kirby Flower Smith. GrL; LiTW
Sun's gone dim, The. Two-Volume Novel. Dorothy Parker. InMe
Sun's over the Foreyard, The. Christopher Morley. EtS
Sun's Perpendicular Rays, The. W. L. Mansel. ChTr
Sun's relentless hand, The. Sunburn. Abu Hafs. MooP
Sun's Shame, The. Dante Gabriel Rossetti. The House of Life, XCII–XCIII. PoVP; ViPo
Sun's snow, conversing, lowly slides from limbs. To a Young Lady Swinging Upside Down on a Birch Limb over a Winter-swollen Creek. James H. Koch. GoYe
Sun's Travels, The. Robert Louis Stevenson. FaPON; GFA; MPB; StVeCh (1940 ed.)
Sunset. Laurence Alma-Tadema. *See* Blessing for the Blessed, A.
Sunset. Herbert Bashford. AA
Sunset. Hayyim Nahman Bialik, *tr. fr. Hebrew by* Helena Frank. TrJP
Sunset, The. Gelett Burgess. HBVY; PIAE
(Nonsense Rhymes.) TSW; TSWC
Sunset. E. E. Cummings. MAP; MoAmPo
(Impression.) MoAB
Sunset. George Darley. *Fr.* Harvest Home. RO
Sunset. Friedrich Hölderlin, *tr. fr. German by* Lola Gruenthal. AnGP
Sunset, A. Victor Hugo, *tr. fr. French by* Francis Thompson. AWP; JAWP; WBP; TrFP, *tr. by* Alan Conder
Sunset, A. Aldous Huxley. MBP; MoBrPo (1942 ed.)
Sunset. Longfellow. BoTP
Sunset, A. Robert Loveman. AA
Sunset. William Julius Mickle. *Fr.* The Concubine. OBEC
Sunset. Shelley. *Fr.* Queen Mab. LPS-2
Sunset. Tu Fu, *tr. fr. Chinese by* Kenneth Rexroth. OnPC
Sunset. *Unknown, tr. fr. Japanese by* Lois J. Erickson. SoLD
Sunset and evening star. Crossing the Bar. Tennyson. BEL; BLV; BLRP; BMEP; BoLiVe; BPN; BTP; DD; EM-2; EmBrPo; EnL; EnLi-2; EnLit; EOAH; EPN; EPP; EtS; FaBoEn; FaFP; FiP; GEPC; GTBS-W; GTSL; HBV; HBVY; HiLiEn; InP; LEAP; LiTB; LiTG, MaRV; MCCG; NeHB; OAEP; OBEV (new ed.); OBVV; OHFP; OlF; OQP; OTPC (1946 ed.); OuHeWo; PECK; PFE; PG (1945 ed.); PIAE; PIR; PoE; PoeMoYo; PoRA; PoVP; PTA-1; PYM; QP-1; REAL; ReaPo; ShBV-3; StJW; TCEP; TOP; TreF; TrGrPo; TSW; TSWC; TwHP; TyEnPo; UnPo (1st ed.); VA; ViBoPo; ViPo; ViPP; VLEP; WBLP; WGRP; WHA; YT
Sunset and Landscape. Richard Savage. *Fr.* The Wanderer, V. BeR
Sunset and Sea. Wordsworth. *See* It Is a Beauteous Evening, Calm and Free.
Sunset and silence! A man: around him earth savage, earth broken. The Plougher [*or* Plower]. Padraic Colum. AnFE; EPP; GoBC; GTIV; GTML; GTSL; HBMV; MBP; MoBrPo; NeMA; OHIP; OnYI; TwCV
Sunset and Sunrise. Emily Dickinson. *See* I'll tell you how the sun rose.
Sunset; and the mountain tops are afire. Mountain Evenings. Jamie Sexton Holme. PoOW
Sunset at Les Eboulements, A. Archibald Lampman. BoCaPo
Sunset City, The. Henry Sylvester Cornwell. HBV; LPS-3
Sunset City, The. Isabel Ambler Gilman. PTA-2
Sunset Clouds. Henrik Wergeland, *tr. fr. Norwegian by* Charles W. Stork. AnNoLy
Sunset deepens in the West, The. A Prairie Mother's Lullaby. E. A. Brininstool. BOL
Sunset flamed: a hundred suns, The. A Most Extraordinary Adventure. Vladimir Mayakovsky. TrRV
Sunset Garden, The. Marion St. John Webb. TVC; TVSH
Sunset glitters on the beads. Sunset. Tu Fu. OnPC
Sunset—God's face from which grief radiates. Sodom. Chaim Grade. TrJP
Sunset has faded, there's but a tinge, The. Barley Fields. Jean Blewett. OCL
Sunset Horn. Myron O'Higgins. PoNe
Sunset in the Lake Country. Wordsworth. *Fr.* An Evening Walk. EPN
Sunset in the rosy west, The. A Little Song. Duncan Campbell Scott. VA
Sunset is golden on the steep. The Flock at Evening. Odell Shepard. HBMV; OBAV
Sunset Joy. Arne Garborg, *tr. fr. Norwegian by* Charles W. Stork. AnNoLy
Sunset on an English Hill. Marion Acton-Bond. ReTS
Sunset on Calvary. *Unknown.* AtBAP
Sunset on Sixth Avenue. J. E. Cadden. CAG
Sunset on the Bearcamp. Whittier. TCAP
Sunset on the Cunimbla Valley, Blue Mountains. Douglas Brooke Wheelton Sladen. VA
Sunset on the Spire. Elinor Wylie. CoBA
Sunset; St. Louis. Sara Teasdale. PoMa; VOD
Sunset swept, The. Valley Song. Carl Sandburg. SBMV
Sunset was a crown of spiked flame, The. Montezuma. Witter Bynner. *Fr.* Chapala Poems. NP
Sunset, when the eyes suddenly closed. Death of an Elephant. Bertram J. Warr. TwCaPo
Sunset Wings. Dante Gabriel Rossetti. EmBrPo; HBV; RO
Sunsets. Richard Aldington. PFE
Sunsets. Florence Boyce Davis. OQP; QP-2
Sunsets. Carl Sandburg. MAP; MoAmPo
Sunset's kiss, with lingering desire, The. The Wind in the Elms. J. Corson Miller. HBMV
Sunset's mounded cloud, A. An Evening. William Allingham. EnLoPo; IrPN
Sunshine. Fujita, *tr. fr. Japanese by* Lois J. Erickson. SoLD
Sunshine. Ibn Abi Bishr, *tr. fr. Arabic by* A. J. Arberry. MooP
Sunshine after a Shower. Thomas Warton, the Younger. *Fr.* On the Approach of Summer. OTPC
Sun-shine and hoe-shine! Love Pagan. Arthur Shearly Cripps. MM
Sunshine and Music. Ripley Dunlap Saunders. PoToHe (new ed.)
Sunshine, come softly here. Prayer for a Play House. Elinor Lennen. TrPWD
Sunshine let it be or frost. After St. Augustine. Mary Elizabeth Coleridge. MaRV; MeRV; TriL; TrPWD
Sunshine melts away in twilight golden-red, The. Angelus. "Yehoash." LiTW
Sunshine of the Gods, The, *sel.* Bayard Taylor.
"Ah, moment not to be purchased." AA
Sunshine of Thine Eyes, The. George Parsons Lathrop. AA; LBAP; PR
Sunshine set to music! The First Song-Sparrow. *Unknown.* PCH
Sunshiny shower, A. Weather Signs [*or* Signs and Charms *or* Rhymes about the Weather]. *Unknown.* FaBoBe; GoTP; HBV; HBVY; OTPC; OxNR; PCH; PPL; RIS; StaSt; TreF
Sunstruck spray sifts back breakwater waves, A. The Pavilion on the Pier. Byron Vazakas. NePA
Sunt Lacrimae Rerum. Virgil, *tr. fr. Latin by* James Rhoades. *Fr.* The Aeneid, I. LiA
Sunthin' in the Pastoral Line. James Russell Lowell. The Biglow Papers, 2d Series, No. VI. AmPP (3d ed.); APW, *abr.*; CoBA; IAP; PFY, *abr.*
(Biglow Papers, The, *abr.*) SN
Bobolink, The, *very br. sel.* BLA
Spring, *sel.* MCCG
Supai Hill Patrol. Jack O'Brien. HiLiAm
Super Flumina Babylonis. Swinburne. AnFE; LiA; OBVV; PoEL-5; PoFr, *abr.*; PoVP; ViPo; VLEP
Unto Each [Man] His Handiwork, *sel.* OQP, *2 sts.*; QP-2, *2 sts.*
("Whoso Loseth His Life," *4 sts.*) MaRV
Super-Lark, The. R. H. Long. BoAu
Superannuation. Sister M. Eleanore. GrCo-2
Superb and sole, upon a plumèd spray. The Mocking Bird. Sidney Lanier. AA; AmPP (3d ed.); BLA; HiLiAm; IAP; TCAP
Superb creator,/ All being that wrought. Hymn to Satan. Giosuè Carducci. PoFr
Superbus sold a gallant manor place. In Superbum. Thomas Freeman. SiCE
Supercargo Mynheer van Koek, The. The Slave Ship. Heine. AnGP

Supercilious nabob of the East, A. A Modest Wit. Selleck Osborne. BLPA; BOHV; HBV; PECK
Superfluous Bite. Heine. *See* Mir träumte wieder der alte Traum.
Superintindint wuz Flannigan. Finnigin to Flannigan. Strickland Gillilan. BOHV; FaBoBe; HBV; StPo; TreF; YaD
Superior Fiend, The. Milton. *See* Satan and the Fallen Angels.
Superior Nonsense Verses. *Unknown.* NA
Superiority to fate. Emily Dickinson. BAV; TwP
Superlative Dance and Song. Francis Beaumont. *See* Shake Off Your Heavy Trance.
Superman, The. Albert Bigelow Paine. MaRV
Supermarket in California, A. Allen Ginsberg. NeAP
Supernal Dialogue. Harriet Monroe. NP
Superscription, A. Dante Gabriel Rossetti. The House of Life, XCVII. BEL; BMEP; BPN; EmBrPo; EnL; EnLi-2; EnLit; EPP; FaBoEn; HBV; LEAP; LO; NBE; PG (1955 ed.); PoEL-5; PoVP; SeCePo; TOP; VA; ViPo; ViPP; VLEP; WHA
(Nevermore, The.) LPS-3
Superseded, The. Thomas Hardy. TOP
Supersensual. Evelyn Underhill. WGRP
Superstitious Ghost, The. Arthur Guiterman. DaM
Supine the wanderer lay. The Wanderer. Wordsworth. *Fr.* The Excursion. GEPC
Supper at the Mill, *sel.* Jean Ingelow.
Song of the Old Love. HBV
Supper is o'er, the hearth is swept, The. Sermon in a Stocking. Ellen A. Jewett. BLPA
Supple and turbulent, a ring of men. Sunday Morning, V [VII]. Wallace Stevens. AnFE; AnNE; APA; CoAnAm; GTBS-W; MAP; MAPA; MoAmPo; TriL
Supple body bends to will, The, VI. Frances Crawford. PtPa
Supplement of an Imperfect Copy of Verses of Mr. Wil. Shakespeare, A. Sir John Suckling. SeEP
Suppliant. Florence Earle Coates. TrPWD
Suppliant, The. Sir Edmund Gosse. TCPD
Suppliant, The. Georgia Douglas Johnson. CDC; PoNe
Suppliant. Alan Sullivan. CaP; CPG; OCL
Suppliant Maidens, The. Aeschylus. *See* Suppliants.
Suppliants, *sels.* Aeschylus, *tr. fr. Greek.*
Io, *tr. by* Walter Headlam. OxBG
Litany for Argos, *tr. by* Lewis Campbell. GrR
Prayer for Deliverance, *tr. by* Gilbert Murray. OxBG
(O Zeus, Our Spirit Fails.) GrR
"Secure it falls upon its feet, not upon its back," *tr. by* Moses Hadas. GrPo
"To whom of the gods could I more fitly appeal?" *tr. by* Moses Hadas. GrPo
World's Harmonious Plan, The, *tr. by* Walter Headlam. LiA
Suppliants, *sels.* Euripides, *tr. fr. Greek.*
Aethra's Intercession, *tr. by* Arthur S. Way. GrR
(Chivalry, *tr. by* C. M. Bowra.) OxBG
Democratic Way, The; Pro and Con, *tr. by* Arthur S. Way. GrR
Dirge: "I bring from funeral," *tr. by* George Allen. OxBG
"Eloquent herald this, a speech-crammed babbler, An," *tr. by* Arthur S. Way. PoFr
Evadne, *tr. by* Arthur S. Way. GrR
Three Classes of Citizens, *tr. by* M. Wodhull. GrR
Voice of Enlightenment, The, *tr. by* Arthur S. Way. GrR
Supplication, A. Nicholas Breton. *See* Corydon's Supplication to Phyllis.
Supplication. Joseph Seamon Cotter, Jr. BANP; CDC; PoNe
Supplication, A. Abraham Cowley. *Fr.* The Davideis. GTBS; GTBS-D; GTBS-W; GTSE; GTSL
(Awake, Awake, My Lyre!) SeCL
(Invocation: "Awake, awake, my lyre!") LPS-3
(Music.) EV-2
Supplication. Josephine Johnson. QS; TrPWD
Supplication. Dorothy A. Linney. HiLiAm
Supplication. Edgar Lee Masters. ChMo; CMP; TrPWD
"Dost Thou not see about our feet," *sel.* MaRV
Supplication, A. Michelangelo. *See* For Inspiration.
Supplication. Edith Lovejoy Pierce. TrPWD
Supplication, A. Clinton Scollard. QS
Supplication. Louis Untermeyer. HBMV
Supplication, A. Sir Thomas Wyatt. *See* Forget Not Yet.
Supplication of the Black Aberdeen. Kipling. BLPA
Supplices. Aeschylus. *See* Suppliants.
Supplices. Euripides. *See* Suppliants.
Suppose. Anne Reeve Aldrich. HBV
Suppose. Phoebe Cary. BLPA; PTA-1
Suppose. Walter de la Mare. PtOT; TSW; TSWC
Suppose. Epes Sargent, *sometimes at. to* Fanny Crosby. *See* Deeds of Kindness.
Suppose a painter to a human head. The Art of Poetry. Horace. RoL
Suppose . . . and suppose that a wild little horse of magic. Suppose. Walter de la Mare. PtOT; TSW; TSWC
Suppose I put my babe to sleep. A Lullaby. Kate Wisner McClusky. BOL
Suppose in Perfect Reason. Howard Griffin. CrMA
Suppose it, for the last time, in that moment. The Coming of the White Man. Patrick Anderson. *Fr.* Poem on Canada. BoCaPo (1948 ed.)
Suppose it is nothing but the hive. Davis Matlock. Edgar Lee Masters. *Fr.* Spoon River Anthology. ChMo; CMP; LiTA; LiTM (rev. ed.)
Suppose, my little lady. Suppose. Phoebe Cary. BLPA; PTA-1
Suppose that Christ Had Not Been Born. Martha Snell Nicholson. BePJ
Suppose that we part (work done, comes play). Pambo. Robert Browning. VLEP
Suppose that We, To-Morrow or the Next Day. C. Day Lewis. *Fr.* From Feathers to Iron. CoEV; TwCV
Suppose the little cowslip. Deeds of Kindness [*or* Suppose]. Epes Sargent, *sometimes at. to* Fanny Crosby. HBV; HBVY; OTPC; PPL; TVC; TVSH
Suppose you screeve? or go cheap-jack? Villon's Straight Tip to All Cross Coves. W. E. Henley, *after* Villon. AWP; BOHV; CenHV; HBV; InMe; InvP; NA; SeCePo
Supposed Confessions of a Second-rate Sensitive Mind. Tennyson. ViPP
Supposed of Pamphylax the Antiochene. A Death in the Desert. Robert Browning. GoTL; OxBoCh; PoVP; StJW
Supposed to be Written at Lemnos. Thomas Russell. *See* Sonnet: Suppos'd to Be Written at Lemnos.
Supposing I Dreamed This. E. E. Cummings. MOAP
Supreme Dominion. Thomas Gray. *Fr.* The Progress of Poesy. LiA
Supreme Sacrifice, The. John Stanhope Arkwright. POT; WGRP
Supreme Surrender. Dante Gabriel Rossetti. The House of Life, VII. EtPaEn; POTT; PoVP; ViPo
Supreme, the Best Being of all, the Source of Light, The. Divine Songs to Ahura Mazda. Zoroaster. LiTW
Supremest fictions grow with fungus speed. Poem. Arthur Boyars. PoN
Surcloying the Stomach. J. Sylvester. *Fr.* Tetrasticha. MOB
Sure. Ted Robinson. MaRV
Sure, afther all the winther. The Green o' the Spring. Denis A. McCarthy. POT; PoTo
Sure and exact, the master's quiet touch. The Dead Player. Robert Burns Wilson. AA
Sure he's five months old, an' he's two foot long. Johneen. "Moira O'Neill." TIP
Sure, I am a wild young Irish boy and from Dubalin town I came. I Am a Wild Young Irish Boy. *Unknown.* ShS
Sure, if we were all Sirens, we should sing pitifully. John Ford. *Fr.* The Broken Heart. PoD
Sure, I'm sitting here this evening, while the firelight flickers low. Kitty's Feet. Norah M. Holland. CPG
Sure, it was so. Man in those early days. Corruption. Henry Vaughan. CAW; EPS; FaBoEn; MeRV; OBS; OxBoCh; SeCV-1
Sure maybe ye've heard the storm-thrush. Birds. "Moira O'Neill." BLA; HBV
Sure Sign, A. Nancy Byrd Turner. PCH; TiPo
Sure the last end. Peace the End of the Good Man. Robert Blair. *Fr.* The Grave. EV-3
Sure there are poets which did never dream. Cooper's Hill. Sir John Denham. CEP; EPS; SeCV-1; SeEP
Sure, this world is full of trouble. It's Fine Today [*or* "Ain't It Fine Today!"]. Douglas Malloch. BLPA; WBLP
Sure thou didst flourish once! and many springs. The Timber. Henry Vaughan. EM-1; EPP; EV-2; OBEV; SeCV-1
Sure 'twas by Providence design'd. On a Beautiful Youth Struck Blind with Lightning. Goldsmith. OAEP
Sure, 'twas like the angels' footsteps when your baby feet went racin'. Relinquishing. Theda Kenyon. AOAH
"Sure, we can," said the man. Heartbeat of Democracy. Virginia Brasier. StVeCh (1955 ed.)
Surely a voice hath called her to the deep. Lines. George Arthur Greene. TIP
Surely among a rich man's flowering lawns. Ancestral Houses. W. B. Yeats. *Fr.* Meditations in Time of Civil War. ChMP; LiTB; MoVE
Surely enough of rain and rattling showers. Horace. Odes, I, 2. LaP
Surely I dreamt to-day, or did I see. Keats. *Fr.* Ode to Psyche. LO
Surely I think the wild beasts fear your white bones. Epitaph of a Thessalian Hound. Simonides. LiTW
Surely in no benignant mood. Chorus. William Alexander Percy. SPP
Surely it is not you! Sit, nevertheless. Conversation Galante. Humbert Wolfe. HBMV; MAP
Surely My Soul. Jacob Cohen, *tr. fr. Hebrew by* I. M. Lask. TrJP
Surely that is not a man. A Circus Garland: Acrobat. Rachel Field. StVeCh

Surely that town's the scansion of my life. Revenant. Ernest Rhys. UnW
Surely the Author. Donald Parson. MuM
Surely the finger of God that governs the stars. Yeats' Tower. Vernon Watkins. NeBP
Surely the hand of God has spread this peace. Country Sabbath. Minnie Hite Moody. MuM
Surely the saints you loved visibly came. Joyce Kilmer. Amelia Josephine Burr. DD; HBMV
Surely the sun has labour all his days. The Never-Resting Sun. Mimnermus. OxBG
Surely the toothpaste magnate who controls. The Broadcast. John W. Simons. JKCP (1955 ed.)
Surely there is a vein for the silver. The Price of Wisdom. Job, Bible, *O.T.* TrGrPo
Surely upon his shoulders, gaunt and worn. Lincoln. Laura Simmons. LPS-1; PSO
Surety. Lizette Woodworth Reese. MAP; MoAmPo
Surface and the Depths, The. Lewis Morris. *See* Song: "Love took my life and thrill'd it."
Surface of the flowing stream, The. Flowing Stream. Ibn Hamdis. MooP
Surge mea sponsa, swete [*or* sweet] in sight. Veni, Coronaberis. *Unknown.* AtBAP; BoW; TMEV
Surgeon, The. George W. Caldwell. PoP
Surgeon, The. W. J. Funk. PoMa
Surgeon's Hands, The. Ida Norton Munson. OQP; QP-1
Surgeons must be very careful. Emily Dickinson. ImOP; TCAP; TwP
Surgery of the Liver. Merrill Moore. PoP
Surgical Art Versus Beauty. Rodulfo Figueroa, *tr. fr. Spanish by* Margaret Allison. PoP
Surging sea of human life forever onward rolls, The. A Hundred Years from Now. Mary A. Ford. BLPA
Surnames. James Smith. BOHV
Surprise, The. William Barnes. PoVP
Surprise. Harry Behn. TiPo (1959 ed.)
Surprise, A. Malcolm Douglas. MeMeAg
Surprise. Federico García Lorca, *tr. fr. Spanish by* Eleanor L. Turnbull. CoSP
Surprise. *Unknown, tr. fr. Japanese by* Lois J. Erickson. SoLD
Surprise, A. Elizabeth Winton. PCH
Surprise at Ticonderoga, The. Mary A. P. Stansbury. GA; MC; PAH
Surprised by Joy—Impatient as the Wind. Wordsworth. BPN; EmBrPo; EnRP; ERP; ExPo; GEPC; LO; SeCeV
(Desideria.) GTBS; GTBS-D; GTBS-W; GTSE; GTSL; OBEV
(Of His Daughter Catherine Dead Long Since.) ES
(Sonnet: Surprised by Joy.) ChER
(Sonnet: "Surprised by joy—impatient as the wind.") CoEV; ViBoPo
(Sonnet on Catherine Wordsworth.) PoD
(Surprised by Joy.) EPN; HBV; LiTB; OBRV
(To Catherine Wordsworth 1808–1812.) FaBoEn
Surrealist Poem of the Elephant and the Song. Carlos Oquendo de Amat, *tr. fr. Spanish by* H. R. Hays. AnCL
Surrender. Amelia Josephine Burr. HBV
Surrender, The. Thomas Flatman. EV-3
Surrender. Angelina W. Grimké. CDC
Surrender. Ruth Guthrie Harding. HBMV
Surrender, The. Henry King. BLV; CoEV; ElSeCe; LO; MePo; TrGrPo
Surrender. "S. M. M." JKCP
Surrender at Appomattox, The. Herman Melville. MC; PAH
Surrender of Burgoyne, The. James Watts de Peyster. IDAH
Surrender of Cornwallis, The. *Unknown.* PAH
Surrender of New Orleans, The. Marion Manville. PAH
Surrender of Spain, The. John Hay. AA
Surrender to Christ. Frederic William Henry Myers. OxBoCh
Surrexit Dominus de sepulchro. On the Resurrection of Christ. *At. to* William Dunbar. TMEV
Surrounded by beakers, by strange coils. The Naked World. Sully-Prudhomme. ImOP
Surrounded by unnumbered foes. His Banner over Me. Gerald Massey. HBV; VA; WGRP
Surrounding woods are burning with subdued fire, The. Treason. Lora Dunetz. NePoAm
Sursum. Guillermo Valencia, *tr. fr. Spanish by* Thomas Walsh. CAW
Sursum Corda. Conrad Aiken. ReMP
Sursum Corda. Archilochus. *See* Be Still, My Soul.
Sursum Corda. Elizabeth Barrett Browning. *Fr.* Casa Guidi Windows. VA
Sursum Corda, *sel.* Edith M. Thomas.
"Up and rejoice." PC
Sursum Corda. Annie Lake Townsend. OQP; QP-1
Survey, my fair! that lucid stream. Ode to a Young Lady, Somewhat too Sollicitous about Her Manner of Expression. William Shenstone. CEP
Survey of Literature. John Crowe Ransom. FaBoCh; LiTA; LoGBV; LS; SiTL
Survey our progress from our birth. John Webster. LO
Surview. Thomas Hardy. ChMP; EmBrPo
(Surview; Cogitavi Vias Meas.) LO
Survival, The. Edmund Blunden. OBEV (new ed.); OBMV
Survival. Florence Earle Coates. AA
Survival. Margaret Moore Meuttman. MaRV
Survival of the Fittest, The. Sarah N. Cleghorn. BAP; HBMV
Survivor, The. Robert Graves. MoVE
Survivor, The. Frederic L. Knowles. OQP; QP-2
Survivor sole, and hardly such, of all. Yardley-Oak. William Cowper. LaA
Susaki Waterfront. Saisei Muro, *tr. fr. Japanese by* Takamichi Ninomiya *and* D. J. Enright. PoLJ
Susan. Frederick Locker-Lampson. BOHV
Susan. *Unknown.* NA
Susan; a Poem of Degrees, *sel.* Arthur Joseph Munby.
Sweet Nature's Voice. VA
Susan Blue. Kate Greenaway. MPB; OTPC (1946 ed.); RAR
("Oh, Susan Blue.") TiPo
Susan poisoned her grandmother's tea. Susan. *Unknown.* NA
Susan Simpson. *Unknown.* BOHV
Susan to Diana. Frances Cornford. MoVE
Susan Van Dusan. *Unknown.* ABF
Susanna and the Elders. Adelaide Crapsey. AnAmPo; LA; MAP; MoAmPo (1942 ed.); NP
Susanna Fair, Sometime of Love Requested. *Unknown.* ReIE
Susannah and the Elders ("Susannah the fair with her Beauties all bare"). *Unknown.* ALV
Susceptible Chancellor, The. W. S. Gilbert. *Fr.* Iolanthe. ALV; PoVP
Suscipe Flos Florem. *Unknown, tr. fr. Latin by* L. R. Lind. *Fr.* Carmina Burana. LaP
Susiana, *with music.* *Unknown.* ShS
Susie's galoshes. Galoshes. Rhoda W. Bacmeister. BrR; TiPo
Suspended in a moving night. Corner Seat. Louis MacNeice. MoVE
Suspended Moment. Mariana B. Davenport. GoYe
Suspense. Emily Dickinson. *See* Elysium is as far as to.
Suspense. William J. Grace. JKCP (1955 ed.)
Suspense. D. H. Lawrence. MBP; MoBrPo
Suspicious Truth, The, *sel.* Juan Ruiz de Alarcón, *tr. fr. Spanish by* Samuel Beckett.
Feast by the Manzanares. AnMP
Suspiria. Longfellow. ViBoPo
Suspiria. *Unknown.* OBEV (new ed.)
Sussex. Kipling. GTML; PoeT; POTT; TCPD; ViPP; VLEP
Sussex Legend, A. Charles Dalmon. BoTP
Susurro. "Fiona Macleod." *Fr.* Sospiri di Roma. BMEP; VA
Susy Miller. Elizabeth Prentiss. SAS
Suum Cuique Pulchrum. Henry Parrot. TuPP
Sven Duva. Johan Ludvig Runeberg, *tr. fr. Swedish by* Charles W. Stork. AnSL
Svend of Vollerslov. *Unknown, tr. fr. Danish by* E. M. Smith-Dampier. BoDaBa
Svetasvatara Upanishad. *Unknown.* *See* Upanishads, The.
Swaggering Damsel, The, *sel.* Robert Chamberlain.
"Farewell this company." TuPP
Swallows, The. Thomas Aird. VA
Swallow, The. John Burroughs. BLA
Swallow, The. John Clare. ERP
Swallow, The. Abraham Cowley. BCEP; BEL; CoBE; EV-2; OBEV; SeCL; TOP
Swallow, A. Euenus, *tr. fr. Greek by* William Cowper. OxBG; WoL
Swallow, The. Ralph Hodgson. CMP; LBBV
Swallow, The. Pamphilus, *tr. fr. Greek by* Humbert Wolfe. OxBG
Swallow, The. Christina Rossetti. *Fr.* Sing-Song. GoTP; OTPC (1946 ed.); StVeCh
("Fly away, fly away over the sea.") CoBE; PoVP; SUS
Swallow, The. Charlotte Smith. *See* First Swallow, The.
Swallow, The. Thomas Stanley, *after the Greek of* Anacreon. AWP
Swallow, The. *Unknown, tr. fr. Greek by* Thomas Girdlestone. GrR
Swallow, bonny birdie, comes sharp twittering o'er the sea, The. The Swallow. Thomas Aird. VA
Swallow, The, comes! She comes, she brings. Folk Song. *Unknown, tr. fr. Greek.* PCH
Swallow comes winging, The. Swallow Song. *Unknown, tr. fr. Greek.* GrL; OxBG
Swallow flew like lightning over the green, The. Solutions. Edmund Blunden. FaBoTw
Swallow Flight. Sara Teasdale. NP
Swallow has come again, The. The Children's Song [*or* Greek Children's Song]. *Unknown.* FaPON; OTPC (1946 ed.)

Swallow in the spring, A. Perseverance. R. S. S. Andros. LPS-2
Swallow is a mason, The. Bird Trades. *Unknown.* DD; HH
Swallow is flying over, The. Tears in Spring. William Ellery Channing. AA; LBAP
Swallow Leaves Her Nest, The. Thomas Lovell Beddoes. *See* Dirge: "Swallow leaves her nest, The."
Swallow, my sister, O sister swallow. Itylus. Swinburne. BLA; ChTr; EmBrPo; EnLi-2; EPP; EV-5; GTBS; GTSL; HBV; MBP; OBEV (1st ed.); PIR; POTT; PoVP; ReaPo; ViPo; ViPP; VLEP; WHA
Swallow Song. Marjorie Pickthall. CaP; OCL
Swallow Song. *Unknown. tr. fr. Greek.* GrL; OxBG; GrPo, *tr. by* John Addington Symonds
(Children's Song, The.) FaPON
(Folk Song.) PCH
(Greek Children's Song.) OTPC (1946 ed.)
Swallow Tails. Tom Robinson. FaPON
Swallowed thud of cattle shouldering through, The. Enigma. Joseph Auslander. NP
Swallows, The. Agathias Scholasticus, *tr. fr. Greek.* GrPE, *tr. by* F. L. Lucas; LiTW, *tr. by* Dudley Fitts; OxBG, *tr. by* Sir William Marris
Swallows, The. Sir Edwin Arnold. DD; PoRL; WhBS
Swallows, The. Patric Dickinson. ChMP
Swallows. Afanasi Afanasievich Fet, *tr. fr. Russian.* BoR; OnPM, *tr. by* Babette Deutsch; TrRV, *tr. by* Babette Deutsch
Swallows. Apollon Nikolayevich Maikov, *tr. fr. Russian by* Sir Cecil Kisch. WaL
Swallows. Cale Young Rice. VOD
Swallows,/ Swallows,/ Come back. I Call the Swallows. Toyohiko Kagawa. SoLD
Swallows, The; an Elegy. Richard Jago. CEP
Swallow's Flight, The. Louis Levy, *tr. fr. Danish by* Martin S. Alwood *and* Sanford Kaufman. TrJP
Swallows in their torpid state, The. To the Rev. Mr. Newton. William Cowper. LoBV
Swallow's Nest, The. Sir Edwin Arnold. OTPC (1946 ed.); PRWS
Swamp, The. Beatrice Ravenel. TBM
Swamp Fox, The. William Gilmore Simms. AA; BeLS; DD; FaBoBe; GA, *abr.;* MC; PaA; PAH; SPP; TCAP
Swampstrife and spatterdock. The Marsh. W. D. Snodgrass. NePoEA
Swampy State of Illinois, The. Excelsior. *Unknown.* PA
Swan, The. Baudelaire, *tr. fr. French by* Joseph Bennett. AnFP
Swan, The. Elizabeth J. Coatsworth. BLA; WhBS
Swan, The. John Gould Fletcher. MM; OTPC (1946 ed.); PoeMoYo; SPP; TwCV
Swan, The. F. S. Flint. NP
Swan, The. Jorge Guillén, *tr. fr. Spanish by* Eleanor L. Turnbull. CoSP
Swan, A. Henrik Ibsen, *tr. fr. Norwegian by* Charles W. Stork. AnNoLy
Swan, The. Jay Macpherson. PeCV
Swan, The. Stéphane Mallarmé, *tr. fr. French by* Alan Conder. TrFP
Swan, The. Yakov Polonsky, *tr. fr. Russian by* J. S. Phillimore. BoR
Swan, The. W. R. Rodgers. NeBP
Swan, The. Johan Ludvig Runeberg, *tr. fr. Swedish by* Charles W. Stork. AnSL
Swan, The. Stephen Spender. UnS
Swan, The. *Unknown.* ChTr; FaPON
("Swan swam over the sea.") BoChLi; OxNR
Swan, The. *Unknown, tr. fr. Anglo-Saxon. Fr.* Riddles. BEL, *tr. by* F. B. Snyder; CoBE; EPP, *tr. by* Herbert B. Brougham; OuHeWo, *tr. by* Stith Thompson
Swan and the Cook, The. La Fontaine, *tr. fr. French.* BoChLi
Swan and the Goose, The. Aesop, *rhymed tr. fr. Greek by* William Ellery Leonard. AWP; FaPON; JAWP; LiTW; UnS; WBP
Swan Bathing, The. Ruth Pitter. MoBrPo
Swan bears on its neck the initial of sleep, The. Entreaty to the Cloud. Amado Nervo. AnMP
Swan Boat, A. Robert Palfrey Utter. PCH
Swan existing, The. Voyage à l'Infini. Walter Conrad Arensberg. AnAmPo; LA; SBMV
Swan-Neck, The. Charles Kingsley. EV-5
Swan Song. Samuel Taylor Coleridge. *See* On a Bad Singer.
Swan Song. Swinburne. *Fr.* The Garden of Proserpine. OtMeF
Swan Song of Parson Avery, The. Whittier. *See* Parson Avery.
Swansong on the Moorlands. Steingrimur Thorsteinsson, *tr. fr. Icelandic by* Jakobina Johnson. IcP; LiTW
Swan swam over the sea. The Swan. *Unknown.* BoChLi; ChTr; FaPON; OxNR
Swan, the Pike, and the Crab, The. Ivan Andreyevich Krylov, *tr. fr. Russian by* I. Henry Harrison. BoChLi
Swan, Turkey, Dove, and the Bull in the Broom. James Thomson. *Fr.* The Seasons: Spring. BeR
Swanee River. Stephen Collins Foster. *See* Old Folks at Home.
Swannanoa. *Unknown.* NoCaPo
Swannanoa Town. *Unknown. See* My Old Hammah.
Swans. Lawrence Durrell. FaBoMo; SeCePo
Swans, The. Clifford Dyment. MoVE
Swans, The. John Irvine. UnW
Swans, The. Catulle Mendès, *tr. fr. French by* Stuart Merrill. OnPM
Swans, The. Edith Sitwell. FaBoMo; GTBS-D; MoVE
Swans. Leonora Speyer. BLA
Swans, The. Randall Swingler. POTE
Swans. Wordsworth. *Fr.* An Evening Walk. OBEC
Swans, The. Andrew Young. MoBrPo (1942 ed.); POTE
Swans at Night, *sel.* Mary Gilmore.
"Within the night, above the dark." MoAuPo
Swan's Feet, The. E. J. Scovell. FaBoMo
Swans from the North, The. Hans Hartvig Seedorff Pedersen, *tr. fr. Danish by* Charles W. Stork. BoDS
Swans, Lilies and Doves. Christopher Smart. RO
Swans rise up with their wings in day, The. The Boy and the Geese. Padraic Fiacc. NeIP
Swans sing before they die—'twere no bad thing. On a Bad Singer [*or* The Desired Swan-Song]. Samuel Taylor Coleridge. BOHV; GoTP; TreF; UnS; WhC
Swan's Singing, The. *Unknown, tr. fr. Spanish by* Havelock Ellis. OnPM
"Swans, whose pens as white as ivory, The." Robert Greene. *Fr.* A Madrigal. ViBoPo
Swansea Bay. John Prichard. MoWP
Swansea Market. Peter Hellings. MoWP
Swansea Town, *with music. Unknown.* ShS
Swansong. *See* Swan Song.
Swapping Song, The. *Unknown.* RIS
("My father he died, but I can't tell you how.") OxNR
Swapping yarns, two Mountain Men. Mountain Liars. Ann Woodbury Hafen. PoOW
Swarm of bees in May, A. Weather Signs [*or* Proverbs *or* Rhymes about Months and Days]. *Unknown.* FaBoBe; HBV; OTPC; OxNR; PPL; RIS; SiTL; StaSt
Swarms of minnows show their little heads. Minnows. Keats. *Fr.* I Stood Tiptoe upon a Little Hill. FaPON; GN; GoTP; RIS
Swart, sweaty smiths, smutched with smoke. The Blacksmiths. *Unknown.* EnL
Swarthy bee is a buccaneer, The. A More Ancient Mariner. Bliss Carman. NLK; SN; VA
Swashbuckler's Song, The. James Stuart Montgomery. HBMV
Swathe Uncut, The. John Hewitt. NeIP
Swaying greenery. Garden in Liberty Square. Carlos Drummond de Andrade. AnCL
Swear by what the sages spoke. Under Ben Bulben. W. B. Yeats. AnIV; CoBMV; LiTM (rev. ed.); LoBV; OxBI
Swear, "Rather death than tyrants in the land." Manuel José Quintana. *Fr.* Ode to Spain—after the Revolution of March. PoFr
Swearing. Henry Fitzsimon. ACP (1952 ed.)
Sweat-Shop Slaves. Charles Erskine Scott Wood. BAP
Sweat, thought, and prayer—engage. The Ages of Man. Hesiod. OxBG
Sweated Labor. Thomas Hood. *Fr.* The Song of the Shirt. MaRV
Sweden. Verner von Heidenstam, *tr. fr. Swedish by* Charles W. Stork. AnSL
Swedes. Edward Thomas. MoVE
Swedish Angel. Winfield Townley Scott. LiTM
Swedish Folk Song: "Three ships I saw come sailing." *Unknown, tr. fr. Swedish by* Florence Christine Svenson. PCH
Swedish Mother's Lullaby. Fredrika Bremer. *See* Song of the Dove.
Swedish National Hymn. Karl Vilhelm August Strandberg, *tr. fr. Swedish by* Charles W. Stork. AnSL; PoFr
Swedish Poem, A. *Unknown.* PEOR
Swee-swee go the sharp shares. The Sharp Shares. *Unknown.* WhP
Sweeney among the Nightingales. T. S. Eliot. AnEnPo; AnFE; APA; BLV; BoLiVe; ChMo; ChMP; CMP; CoAnAm; CoBMV; CoEV; EnL; EnLit; FaBoMo; InPo; InvP; LiTA; LiTM; MAP; MAPA; MaPo; MoAmPo (1942 ed.); MOAP; MoVE; NePA; NP; OAEP (2d ed.); OBMV; OxBA; ReaPo; ReMP; SeCeV; TwAmPo; TwHP
Sweeney Erect. T. S. Eliot. TwP
Sweeney the Mad. *Unknown, tr. fr. Old Irish by* J. G. O'Keeffe.
(Mad Sweeney.) AnIL
Sels.
"Cold is the snow tonight." SiB
"He came to me in his swift course." OnYI
"O little stag, thou little bleating one." SiB
(Crazy Sweeney's Song of the Woods, *tr. by* Owen Masters.) LyMA

"O Suibhne from lofty Sliabh na nEach." SiB
Sweep the house clean. Love Song. William Carlos Williams. MoAB; MoAmPo (1950 ed.)
Sweep thy faint strings, Musician. The Song of Shadows. Walter de la Mare. BLV; BoLiVe; CBE; ChMo; CMP; CoBE; MBP; MoBrPo; MoP; ShBV-3; TrGrPo
Sweeper, The. Agnes Lee. BAP; HBMV; NP
Sweeper of the Floor, The. George Macdonald. BMEP; MaRV
Sweeping the Skies. Elizabeth Anna Hart. CenHV
Sweet. *Unknown, tr. fr. Spanish by* Havelock Ellis. OnPM
Sweet, acidulous, down-reaching thrill, A. Ode on a Jar of Pickles. Bayard Taylor. PA
Sweet Adon', dar'st not glance thine eye? Infida's Song. Robert Greene. *Fr.* Never Too Late. AtBAP; LO; OBSC
Sweet after showers, ambrosial air. In Memoriam A. H. H., LXXXVI. Tennyson. BEL; BPN; EM-2; EmBrPo; EPN; GEPC; OAEP; TOP; ViPo; VLEP
Sweet Afton. Burns. *See* Flow Gently, Sweet Afton.
Sweet Amarillis, by a spring's. Upon Mrs. Eliz. Wheeler, under the Name of Amarillis. Robert Herrick. EV-2
Sweet and Bitter. Bhartrihari, *tr. fr. Sanskrit by* Arthur W. Ryder. OnPM
Sweet and clean and dainty. A Franciscan Dream. Enid Dinnis. SaFP
Sweet and ghostly laughter of the owl, The. The Owl. Hildegarde Flanner. BLA
Sweet and goodly fellowship. There's No Lust like to Poetry. *Unknown.* AWP
Sweet and humble and gladly poor. To Two Little Sisters of the Poor. Aline Kilmer. PraNu
Sweet and Low [Sweet and Low]. Tennyson. *Fr.* The Princess, Pt. II. BEL; BMEP; BoChLi; BoTP; BPN; BTP; CBPC; CoBE; EnLi-2; EnLit; EPN; EtS; EV-5; FaBoBe; FaPON; GEPC; GFA; GoTP; InP; MCCG; MPB; NeHB; OlF; OTPC; PC; PECK; PG (1945 ed.); PIR; PoE; PoVP; PRWS; PTA-1; REAL; ShBV-1; StVeCh; TCEP; TreF; TrGrPo; TSW; TSWC; VA; ViPP; WP
(Cradle Song.) CBE
(Lullaby.) GBV (1922 ed.); HBV; HBVY; LPS-1; MOAH; OnHT; PoRh; TVC
(Lyrics from "The Princess.") OuHeWo
(Song: Sweet and Low.) BOL; RAR; ThWaDe
(Songs from "The Princess.") EmBrPo; MotAn; ViPo; VLEP
Sweet and Sour. Spenser. *See* Amoretti, XXVI.
Sweet-and-twenty. Shakespeare. *See* O Mistress Mine.
Sweet Apple. James Stephens. ChMo; CMP
Sweet are iced bowls in drought. Glory to Cypris. Asclepiades. GrR
Sweet are the charms of her I love. Song. Barton Booth. OBEC
Sweet are the days we wander with no hope. George Santayana. Sonnets, XIII. MOAP
Sweet are the moonbeams, sweet the grass-grown wood. Sweet and Bitter. Bhartrihari. OnPM
Sweet are the omens of approaching Spring. Approach of Spring. John Clare. ERP
Sweet are the pleasures that to verse belong. Epistle to George Felton Mathew. Keats. EmBrPo; GEPC
Sweet are the rosy memories of the lips. "Owen Meredith." *Fr.* A Night in Italy. BMEP; OBEV (1st ed.)
Sweet Are the Thoughts That Savor of Content. Robert Greene. *Fr.* Farewell to Folly. BEL; CoBE; EG; EM-1; PoToHe; ReIE; SiCE; TuPP; TyEnPo
(Content.) EnLit; LPS-3; OnPM; WoL
(Maesia's Song.) ElSeCe; EV-1; HBV; OBSC; ReEn; WP
(Mind Content, A.) ElL; ViBoPo
(Poor Estate, The.) TrGrPo
(Song: "Sweet are the thoughts that savor of content.") CaAE; EnLi-1; EPP; OuHeWo; PoEL-2
Sweet Are the Uses of Adversity. Shakespeare. *See* Uses of Adversity, The.
Sweet are the ways of death to weary feet. Lord De Tabley. Chorus from "Medea." OBEV (new ed.); OBVV
Sweet are the whispers of yon pine that makes. The Death of Daphnis. Theocritus. Idylls, I. AWP; JAWP; WBP
Sweet as Eden is the air. Woodland Peace. George Meredith. POTT; TwCV
Sweet as violets to a weary heart. The Pleiades. Elizabeth J. Coatsworth. ImOP
Sweet, as this morn I chanced. Buen Matina. Sir John Salusbury. ElL
Sweet Athens! I dream once more. O Sweet Athens. Sotiris Skipis. MoGP
Sweet Auburn! loveliest village of the plain. The Deserted Village. Goldsmith. BEL; BeLS; CEP; CoBE; EiPP; EnL; EnLi-1; EnLit; EnRP; EPP; EV-3; FaFP; GoTL; HBV; HiLiEn; LaA; LEAP; LiTB; LoBV; LPS-2; MCCG; OAEP; OBEC; OnYI; OTPC; OuHeWo; OxBI; Po; PoE; PoEL-3; PYM; REAL; SeCePo; TCEP; TOP; TreFS; TrGrPo; TyEnPo; ViBoPo; WP
Sweet Auburn! parent of the blissful hour. Blest Retirement. Goldsmith. *Fr.* The Deserted Village. OBEC
Sweet babe, a golden cradle holds thee. *Unknown.* BOL
Sweet babe! a golden cradle holds thee. The Fairy Nurse. Edward Walsh. BOL; OnYI
Sweet baby, sleep; what ails my dear? A Rocking Hymn [*or* A Lullaby]. George Wither. *Fr.* Hallelujah. AnEC; BOL; EV-1; OxBoCh [*wr. at. to* William Austin]; SeCV-1
Sweet, Be No Longer Sad. Charles Webbe. SeCL
Sweet, be not proud of those two eyes. To Dianeme. Robert Herrick. BCEP; BrBE; CaAE; EG; EV-2; FaBoEn; GTBS; GTBS-D; GTBS-W; GTSE; GTSL; HBV; LiTL; LoBV; LPS-1; OBEV; OBS; OnPM; RiBV; SeCV-1; SeEP; TOP; TrGrPo; ViBoPo; WoL
Sweet bell of Stratford, tolling slow. The Passing Bell at Stratford. William Winter. AA
Sweet Benjamin, since thou art young. John Hoskins to His Little Child Benjamin, from the Tower. John Hoskins. TuPP
Sweet Betsy from Pike, *with music. Unknown.* ABF; AmPP (4th ed.); AS; CoSo; CSF; SoAF; TrAS; ViBoFo
(Betsy from Pike.) BaBo
(Sweet Betsy from Pike.) OxBoLi
Sweet bird that shunn'st the noise of folly. Milton. *Fr.* Il Penseroso. CH; SN
Sweet bird, that sing'st away the early hours. To the Nightingale. William Drummond of Hawthornden. EV-2
Sweet birds! that sit and sing amid the shady valleys. A Pastoral [*or* Phyllis]. Nicholas Breton. CBOV; EG; ElL; OBSC; ReIE; SiCE; TrGrPo
Sweet blackbird is silenced with chaffinch and thrush. Winter. Christina Rossetti. BoTP
Sweet-breathed and young. A Woman's Execution. Edward King. AA; LEAP
Sweet brother, if I do not sleep. For My Brother. Thomas Merton. InPo; TreFS
Sweet, can I sing you the song of your kisses. Kisses. Arthur Symons. VLEP
Sweet Castle Hyde. Edward Kenealy. RO
(Castle Hyde.) IrPN
(Castlehyde, *sl. diff.*) OnYI
Sweet Chance, that led my steps abroad. A Great Time. W. H. Davies. AlDL; AnFE; BLV; BMEP; ExPo; LBBV; LiTB; MBP; MoBrPo; MoVE; POTE; WHA; YT
Sweet child of April, I have found thy place. The Pyxidanthera. Augusta Cooper Bristol. AA
"Sweet child of woe! who pour'st thy love-lorn lays." Royall Tyler. PIAE
Sweet chimes! that in the loneliness of night. Chimes. Longfellow. OBAV
Sweet Clover. Wallace Rice. HBV
Sweet columns, with. Song of the Columns. Paul Valéry. AnFP; MiFP
Sweet Content. Thomas Dekker. *See* Happy Heart, The.
Sweet country life, to such unknown. The Country Life. Robert Herrick. EPS; EV-2
Sweet Cupid, ripen her desire. Song. *Unknown.* LoBV; OBSC; ViBoPo
Sweet cyder is a great thing. Great Things. Thomas Hardy. GTML; GTSL; MoVE
Sweet Cynthia, take the book away. To Cynthia, Not to Let Him Read the Ladies' Magazines. P. M. Hubbard. FiBHP
Sweet Daffadowndilly. Christina Rossetti. *See* Growing in the Vale.
Sweet daughter of a rough and stormy sire. Ode to Spring. Anna Letitia Barbauld. EV-3
Sweet day, so cool, so calm, so bright. Virtue [*or* Vertue]. George Herbert. AtBAP; ATP; AWP; BCEP; BEL; BLV; BoLiVe; CaAE; CBOV; CenL; CH; CoBE; CoEV; EG; ElSeCe; EM-1; EnLi-1; EnLit; EOAH; EPP; EPS; EV-2; ExPo; FaBoEn; HBV; InPo; InvP; JAWP; LEAP; LH; LoBV; LPS-1; MeLP; MePo; OBEV; OBS; OnPM; PG (1955 ed.); PIAE; Po; PoE; PoFS; PoRA; SeCeV; SeCL; SeCV-1; SeEP; ShBV-4; TCEP; TOP; TrGrPo; TVSH; TwCrTr; TwHP; TyEnPo; UnPo (1st ed.); ViBoPo; WBP; WGRP; WHA
Sweet Death. Lorenzo Mavilis, *tr. fr. Modern Greek by* Rae Dalven. MoGP
Sweet death com vissit my sicke hart. *Unknown.* SeCSL
Sweet dimness of her loosened hair's downfall. Love-Sweetness. Dante Gabriel Rossetti. The House of Life, XXI. BEL; BPN; EmBrPo; EnLit; EPN; EPP; EtPaEn; EV-5; OAEP; POTT; PoVP; TOP; ViPo; VLEP
Sweet Disorder. Robert Herrick. *See* Delight in Disorder.
Sweet, doe not frowne on me though I must goe. *Unknown.* SeCSL
Sweet Dreams Form a Shade. Blake. *See* Cradle Song: "Sweet dreams form a shade."
Sweet Echo [Sweetest Nymph, That Liv'st Unseen]. Milton. *Fr.* Comus. AtBAP; ExPo; KN; SeCL

Sweet Echo (*continued*)
(Echo.) CoEV; OBEV; OBS
(Lady's Song.) BoLiVe; TrGrPo
(Song: "Sweet Echo, sweetest Nymph, that liv'st unseen.") BrBE; LoBV
(Songs: "Sweet Echo, sweetest nymph, that liv'st unseen.") BLV
(Songs from Comus.) SeCeV
("Sweet Echo, sweetest nymph, that liv'st unseen.") EG; ElSeCe; TOP; ViBoPo
Sweet Eden was the arbor of delight. In Gethsemane. Giles Fletcher. MaRV; StJW
Sweet Emma Moreland of yonder town. Edward Gray. Tennyson. OBVV
Sweet England, call for grace! The Four Wonders. *Unknown.* TuPP
Sweet eyes by sorrow still unwet. Wonderland. Harry Thurston Peck. AA
Sweet fellow, whom I sware such sure, affected love. The Preamble to N[icholas] B[reton] His Garden-Plot. Nicholas Breton. ReIE
Sweet Fields of Violo. *Unknown.* ABS
Sweet flower, that art so fair and gay. Medieval Norman Songs, XI. *Unknown, tr. fr. French by* John Addington Symonds. AWP
Sweet for a little even to fear, and sweet. Erotion. Swinburne. EtPaEn; PoEL-5
Sweet friend, when you and I are gone. Patience with the Living. Margaret Elizabeth Sangster. PoToHe
Sweet Genevieve. George Cooper. OlF; TreFS
Sweet girl graduate, lean as a fawn, A. Nancy Hanks, Mother of Abraham Lincoln. Vachel Lindsay. ATP (1935 ed.); ChMo; CMP; MAP
Sweet Grass Range. Edwin Ford Piper. *See* Sweetgrass Range.
Sweet hand! the sweet yet cruel bow thou art. Love's Franciscan. Henry Constable. ACP; GoBC; SaFP
Sweet, hard and wise, your choice so early made. To a Friend. Lionel Johnson. POTT
Sweet, harmless livers! on whose holy leisure. The Shepherds. Henry Vaughan. AnEC
Sweet have I known the blossoms of the morning. Because of You. Sophia Almon Hensley. HBV
Sweet Highland Girl, a very shower. To a Highland Girl [of Inversneyde]. Wordsworth. BPN; EmBrPo; EnRP; EPN; ERP; GEPC; GTBS-D; GTBS-W; LoBV; LPS-1
Sweet Hour of Prayer. William W. Walford. BLRP; PraP; WBLP
Sweet I am not come too soone. *Unknown.* SeCSL
Sweet if thou wilt be. Come Turn to Mee, Thou Pretty Little One. *Unknown.* CoMu
Sweet, If You Like and Love Me Still. Francis Davison. *See* His Farewell to His Unkind and Unconstant Mistress.
Sweet in goodly fellowship. There's No Lust like to Poetry. *Unknown.* AWP
Sweet in her green dell [*or* cell] the Flower of Beauty slumbers. Song [*or* Flower of Beauty]. George Darley. EV-4; GTBS-D; HBV; LO; OBEV; OBRV; OBVV; OnYI; VA
Sweet Infancy!/ O heavenly fire! The Rapture. Thomas Traherne. OBS
Sweet Innisfallen. Thomas Moore. HBV
Sweet is a voice in the land of gold. Things Delightful. Oisin. TIP
Sweet Is Childhood. Jean Ingelow. TreFS
Sweet is my Lais' smile, and sweet the tide. The Tears of Fear. Paulus Silentiarius. GrL; OxBG
Sweet is my sleep, but more to be mere stone. The Speech of Night. Michelangelo. OnPM
Sweet Is the Breath of Morn. Milton. *Fr.* Paradise Lost, IV. TyEnPo
(World Beautiful, The, *shorter sel.*) GN
Sweet is the dew that falls betimes. Christopher Smart. *Fr.* A Song to David. BrBE; CaAE; LEAP; Po
Sweet is the hermit's evening bell. The Mourning Dove. W. W. Christman. BLA
Sweet is the highroad when the skylarks call. Wanderers. George Sylvester Viereck. LBMV
Sweet is the image of the brooding dove! Caroline Elizabeth Sarah Norton. *Fr.* The Dream. MOAH
Sweet is the music of yon whispering pine. The Song of the Death of Daphnis. Theocritus. EnLi-1
Sweet is the pleasure. True Rest. Goethe. LPS-2
Sweet is the rose, but grows upon a brere [*or* brier]. Amoretti, XXVI. Spenser. ElL; HBV; PeBoSo; ReEn
Sweet is the snow to drink in summer heat. Love Is Best. Asclepiades. GrL
Sweet is the swamp with its secrets. A Snake. Emily Dickinson. MAPA; TwAmPo
Sweet is the time for joyous folk. Hora Christi. Alice Brown. HBV; LBMV; MaRV; QS; SDH; TrPWD; WGRP
Sweet is the voice that calls. September. George Arnold. DD; HBV; LPS-2; PTA-2
Sweet is the whisper, goatherd, of yonder pine that sings. Daphnis. Theocritus. Idylls, I. GrPE
Sweet is true love tho' given in vain, in vain. Elaine's Song. Tennyson. *Fr.* Idylls of the King: Lancelot and Elaine. BPN; FaBoEn
Sweet it is to see the sun. Every Day Thanksgiving Day. Harriet Prescott Spofford. DD; OHIP; PEDC
Sweet Jesus. Friar Michael of Kildare, *mod. vers. by* Russell K. Alspach. OnYI
Sweet Jesus with Thy Mother mild. England's Prayer. William Blundell of Crosby. GoBC
Sweet kiss, thy sweets I fain would sweetly indite. Astrophel and Stella, LXXIX. Sir Philip Sidney. ReEn; SiPS
Sweet Kitty Wells. *Unknown. See* Kitty Wells.
Sweet lady & sole mistres of my love. *Unknown.* SeCSL
Sweet lament of two Castilian swains, The. Eclogue I. Garcilaso de la Vega. AnSpL-1; TeCS
Sweet Land. Francis Maguire. JKCP (1955 ed.)
"Sweet land"/ at last! St. Francis Einstein of the Daffodils. William Carlos Williams. AtBAP; MoPo
Sweet land of song, thy harp doth hang. The War Ship of Peace. Samuel Lover. PAH
Sweet, Let Me Go! *Unknown.* ElL; ElSeCe; InvP; LO; LoPS; OnPM; TrGrPo; ViBoPo
Sweet life, if life were stronger. Before Dawn. Swinburne. PIR; VLEP
Sweet little bell. The Bell of the Hermitage. *Unknown.* CAW
Sweet little bell, struck on a windy night. The Church Bell at Night. *Unknown.* AnIL; OnYI
Sweet little bird in russet coat. The Autumn Robin. John Clare. BoTP
Sweet little maid with winsome eyes. The Other One. Harry Thurston Peck. AA
Sweet Lotus blossoms white and red. A Sanskrit Stanza. S. Helen Wijesinhe. MM
Sweet Love,—but oh! most dread Desire of Love. Love's Fatality. Dante Gabriel Rossetti. The House of Life, LIV. PoVP; ViPo
Sweet love has twined his fingers in my hair. Love's Prisoner. Mariana Griswold Van Rensselaer. HBV
Sweet Love, If Thou Wilt Gain a Monarch's Glory. *Unknown.* EG; RiBV
(Picture, A.) BTP; GTSL
Sweet Love, Mine Only Treasure. "A. W." ElSeCe
(Where His Lady Keeps His Heart.) ElL; OBSC
Sweet love, renew thy force; be it not said. Sonnets, LVI. Shakespeare. LO; PeBoSo; UnPo (1st ed.)
Sweet, Low Speech of the Rain, The. Ella Higginson. NLK
Sweet Lullaby, A. Nicholas Breton. BOL; ElL; GTSL; OBSC; SiCE; TOP; TuPP; ViBoPo
(Cradle Song, A: "Come little babe, come silly soul.") EV-1; HBV; LEAP; MotAn; OBEV
Sweet maid, if thou wouldst charm my sight. A Persian Song [of Hafiz]. Hafiz. AWP; OBEC; OuHeWo; PeP; PrWP
Sweet maiden of Passamaquoddy. Lines to Miss Florence Huntington [*or* The Maiden of Passamaquoddy]. *Unknown, at. to* James De Mille. BOHV; NA; WhC
Sweet Marie. Cy Warman. TreFS
Sweet Mary Lulled Her Blessed Child. H. E. Nichol. BOL
Sweet Mary was a servant girl. Young Edwin in the Lowlands Low (B *vers.*). *Unknown.* BaBo
Sweet Meeting of Desires. Coventry Patmore. LPS-1
Sweet, meseems, is the whispering sound of yonder pine tree. The Daphnis Song. Theocritus. *Fr.* Idylls. GrL
Sweet Month of April, The. Remy Belleau. *See* April.
Sweet mother, let the weaving be. Mother, I Cannot Mind My Wheel. Sappho. GrL; OxBG
Sweet mouth, that send'st a musky-rosed breath. Joshua Sylvester. EnLoPo
Sweet Muse. Isaac Watts. OxBoCh
(Meditation in a Grove.) CEP
Sweet Music. *At. to* John Fletcher, *also to* Shakespeare. *See* Orpheus with His Lute.
Sweet music [*or* musicke], sweeter far [*or* farre]. The Shepherd's Song [*or* A Carol]. Edmund Bolton. AnEC; COAH; EV-1; OxBoCh
Sweet, my child, in slumber lie. The Widow. *Unknown.* BOL
Sweet my musings used to be. Mot eran dous miei cossir. Arnaut Daniel. AWP
Sweet names, the rosary of my evening prayer. Love's Rosary. George Edward Woodberry. AA
Sweet Nature's Voice. Arthur Joseph Munby. *Fr.* Susan; a Poem of Degrees. VA
Sweet "Nay" with an equally sweet smile, A. Of "Yea" and "Nay." Clément Marot. TrFP
Sweet Nea!—for your lovely sake. Because. Edward Fitzgerald. HBV
Sweet Neglect. Ben Jonson. *See* Simplex Munditiis.
Sweet night of joyous merriment. Night by the River. Mu'tamid, King of Seville. MooP
Sweet "No, no," A—with a sweet smile beneath. Yes and

No [*or* A Love Lesson]. Clément Marot. AWP; JAWP; OnPM; WBP
Sweet nymphs, if, as ye stray. Love Vagabonding [*or* Madrigal: Love Vagabonding]. William Drummond of Hawthornden. EG; ElSeCe; LoBV
Sweet on Anders Anna was, but Anna she was shy. The Rye Field. Jeppe Aakjaer. BoDS
Sweet Pastoral, A. Nicholas Breton. LO; SiCE
(To His Muse.) OBSC
Sweet Peace. Henry Vaughan. *See* Peace.
Sweet Peace, where dost thou dwell? I humbly crave. Peace. George Herbert. AWP; ChTr; EPS; ExPo; InPo; JAWP; OxBoCh; ReEn; SeCeV; SeEP; WBP
Sweet Peas. Keats. *Fr.* I Stood Tiptoe upon a Little Hill. ADAH; GN; MPB (1956 ed.); PCH
Sweet Peas. *Unknown.* PEOR
Sweet peas and roses, strawberries on the vine. Way Over in the Blooming Garden. *Unknown.* ABF
Sweet Peridarchus was a Prince. The Prince. Walter de la Mare. LiL
Sweet Peril. George Macdonald. BLPA; FaBoBe; NeHB; TreFS
Sweet Phosphor, Bring the Day. Francis Quarles. EPS (1942 ed.)
Sweet Phyllis [*or* Phillis], if a silly swain. Corydon's Supplication to Phyllis [*or* A Supplication]. Nicholas Breton. ElSeCe; OBSC; SiCE
Sweet Pity, Wake. *Unknown.* ElL
Sweet poets of the gentle antique line. Sonnet. John Hamilton Reynolds. OBRV
Sweet pretty fledglings, perched on the rail arow. Flycatchers. Robert Bridges. MoVE; POTE
Sweet rain falls, The. *Unknown, tr. fr. Chinese by* Yu Minchuan. The Stone Drums, V. WhP
Sweet reader, whom I've never seen. Apostrophic Notes from the New-World Physics. E. B. White. ImOP
Sweet Riley. *Unknown.* *See* Willy Reilly.
Sweet Risen Christ! They shall not gag our song. Spanish Alleluja. James J. Galvin. JKCP (1955 ed.)
Sweet Robin, I have heard them say. Robin Redbreast. George Washington Doane. AA; DD; HBV; HBVY
Sweet Robinette. *Unknown.* CoMu
Sweet Rose, Fair Flower. *At. to* Shakespeare. The Passionate Pilgrim, X. ElL
Sweet rose [*or* Sweit roiss] of virtue [*or* vertew] and of gentleness [*or* gentilnes]. To a Lady. William Dunbar. BSV; EBSV; EG; GoBC; OAEP; OBEV
Sweet rose, whence is this hue. Madrigal. William Drummond of Hawthornden. ElSeCe
Sweet, sacred hill! on whose fair brow. Mount of Olives. Henry Vaughan. Po; ReaPo
Sweet Saint, thou better canst declare to me. To Saint Mary Magdalen. Henry Constable. ACP
Sweet saint! whose rising dawned upon the sight. Ariana. Franklin Benjamin Sanborn. AA
Sweet-scented flowers on beauty's grave. On the Death of Decatur. William Crafts. GA
Sweet season, that bud and bloom forth brings, The. *See* Soote season, that bud . . .
Sweet secrecy, what tongue can tell thy worth? Idea's Mirrour, XLVI. Michael Drayton. SiCE; ViBoPo
Sweet semi-circled Cynthia played at maw. Sonnet. John Taylor. *Fr.* Odcomb's Complaint. ElL
Sweet September. George Arnold. GN
Sweet, serene, sky-like flower. The Rose [*or* To Lucasta: The Rose]. Richard Lovelace. EG; EPS (1942 ed.); EV-2; HBV; SeCL; SeCV-1; ViBoPo
Sweet she was, as kind a love. She Smiled like a Holiday. *Unknown.* OxBoLi
Sweet Silence after Bells. Christopher Brennan. BoAV
Sweet Simplicity. Timothy Dwight. *Fr.* Greenfield Hill. AmPP
Sweet singer of the Spring, when the new world. On a Thrush Singing in Autumn. Sir Lewis Morris. OBVV; VA
Sweet sixteen is shy and cold. Growing Old. Walter Learned. HBV
Sweet! sleep, lie still, my dear! A Cavalier's Lullaby for His Mistress. Thomas Jordan. *Fr.* An Alarm in 1645. SeCL
Sweet Sleep, with dewy poppies crowned. Ode to Sleep. Fernando de Herrera. TeCS
Sweet slumber now creeps o'er thee slow. Cradle Song. Raphael Patkanian. ArmLP
Sweet smile! the daughter of the Queen of Love. Amoretti, XXXIX. Spenser. PeBoSo
Sweet smiling village, loveliest of the lawn. Goldsmith. *Fr.* The Deserted Village. AnFE; PoFr; PreP
Sweet Soldier of the Silences! The Soldier of the Silences. William Herschell. PEDC
Sweet Solitude, thou placid queen. Solitude. Hannah More. *Fr.* The Search after Happiness. WBLP
Sweet Song Sung Not Yet to Any Man, A. William Morris. *See* I Know a Little Garden Close.
Sweet soul, do with me as thou wilt. In Memoriam A. H. H., LXV. Tennyson. EmBrPo; EPN; GEPC; ViPo; VLEP
Sweet soul, which in the April of thy years. Sonnet. William Drummond of Hawthornden. TriL
Sweet sounds, oh, beautiful music, do not cease! On Hearing a Symphony of Beethoven. Edna St. Vincent Millay. GTBS-W; InP; LiTA; LiTM; MAP; MoAB; MoAmPo; NeMA; NePA; NP; TrGrPo; TwAmPo; UnS
Sweet Spirit! Sister of that orphan one. Epipsychidion. Shelley. BPN; EmBrPo; EPN; ERP
Sweet Spring Is Your. E. E. Cummings. OnAP
Sweet spring, like man in his minority. Spring. Anne Bradstreet. *Fr.* The Four Seasons of the Year. AnNE
Sweet Spring, Thou Turn'st. William Drummond of Hawthornden. *See* Sonnet: "Sweet Spring, thou turn'st . . ."
Sweet Stay-at-Home. W. H. Davies. *Fr.* Foliage. AtBAP; CH; GTBS; HBMV; POTE; POTT; PtOT; TCPD; TwCV
Sweet stream-fed glen, why say "farewell" to thee. Farewell to the Glen. Dante Gabriel Rossetti. The House of Life, LXXXIV. BPN; PoVP; ViPo
Sweet stream, that dost with equal pace. On His Mistress Drowned. Thomas Sprat. ATP; EnLoPo; SeCL
Sweet stream that winds through [*or* thro'] yonder glade. To a Young Lady [*or* The Stream]. William Cowper. EiPP; EnRP; EV-3; GTBS; GTBS-D; GTBS-W; GTSE; GTSL; HBV; LEAP; LiTL; LO; LPS-1
Sweet Suffolk Owl. *Unknown.* CBOV; CH; ChTr; ElL; ElSeCe; HBV
("Sweet Suffolk owl, so trimly dight.") CenL
Sweet Sunday Bells! your measured sound. Sunday Bells. William Allingham. IrPN
Sweet Surprises. S. Doudney. BoTP
Sweet Swan of Avon! what a sight it were. Ben Jonson. *Fr.* To the Memory of My Beloved; the Author Mr. William Shakespeare. ChTr
Sweet sweet Robinette all the shepherds do declare. Sweet Robinette. *Unknown.* CoMu
Sweet, sweet, sweet is the wind's song. Harvest. Ellen Mackay Hutchinson Cortissoz. AA; HBV
Sweet, sweet, sweet, sweet! My Canary's Rhapsody. Zöe Ackerman. VOD
Sweet-swelling lip, well mayst thou swell in pride. Astrophel and Stella, LXXX. Sir Philip Sidney. SiPS
Sweet Teviot, fare thee well! Less gentle themes. The Emigrants: Introductory Stanzas. Thomas Pringle. BoSA
Sweet Teviot! on Thy Silver Tide. Sir Walter Scott. *Fr.* The Lay of the Last Minstrel, IV. BSV; ERP; OBRV
Sweet Thing, *with music.* *Unknown.* OuSiCo
(Crawdad Song, The, *diff. vers.*) OuSiCo; SoAF, *diff.*
"Sweet, thou art pale." The Three Enemies. Christina Rossetti. CoBE; EV-5; MeRV; NBE; POTT; PoVP; TCEP; ViPo; VLEP
Sweet, thou hast trod on a heart. A False Step. Elizabeth Barrett Browning. BoFr; VLEP
Sweet thought—sweet model—that gloweth for all. The Opponent Charm Sustained. Samuel Greenberg. MoPo
Sweet timber land. Homing. Arna Bontemps. CDC
Sweet to the morning traveller. The Traveller's Return. Robert Southey. BoTP; OTPC
Sweet Trinity, The. *Unknown.* *See* Golden Vanity, The.
Sweet twining hedgeflowers wind-stirred in no wise. The Lovers' Walk. Dante Gabriel Rossetti. The House of Life, XII. BPN; OAEP; PoVP; TOP; ViPo
Sweet Unsure. Sir Walter Ralegh. SiPS
Sweet upland, to whose walks, with fond repair. To Hampstead. Leigh Hunt. EnRP
Sweet upland! where, like hermit old, in peace sojourn'd. In Mortem Venerabilis Andreae Prout Carmen. Francis Sylvester Mahony. IrPN
Sweet, use your time, abuse your time. Kingston Church. Thomas D'Urfey. SeCL
Sweet Violets, Love's Paradise. *Unknown.* ElL
(Violets and Roses.) OBSC
Sweet-voiced Hope, thy fine discourse. All's Well. David A. Wasson. BAP
Sweet-voiced Myrtis too I blame. Pindarum Quisquis. Corinna. OxBG
Sweet wantton wagg whose chaire of state. *Unknown.* SeCSL
Sweet warrior! when shall I have peace with you? Amoretti, LVII. Spenser. PeBoSo
Sweet Was the Song. Walter Savage Landor. ViBoPo
Sweet was the song the Virgin sung. *Unknown.* CenL
Sweet was the sound, when oft at evening's close. The Village [*or* Evening]. Goldsmith. *Fr.* The Deserted Village. BrBE; EnSW; FaBoEn; GTIV; ShBV-2
Sweet Weather. Lizette Woodworth Reese. LS
Sweet were the days when Thou didst lodge with Lot. Decay. George Herbert. EPS (1942 ed.); NBE; SeCV-1
Sweet were the joys that both might like and last. Sweet Unsure. Sir Walter Ralegh. SiPS
Sweet were the sauce would please each kind of taste. In Commendation of George Gascoigne's Steel Glass. Sir Walter Ralegh. SiPS

Sweet west wind, the prairie school a break in the yellow wheat, The. The Prairie School. Isabel Ecclestone Mackay. CPG
Sweet Western Wind, whose luck it is. To the Western Wind. Robert Herrick. HBV; OBEV; SeCV-1; SeEP
Sweet, when I think how summer's smallest bird. *Fr.* Sonnets. Irene Rutherford McLeod. HBMV
Sweet Wild April. William Force Stead. HBV; HBVY
Sweet William ("Sweet William arose on last May morning"). *Unknown. See* Douglas Tragedy, The.
Sweet William and May Margaret. *Unknown. See* Sweet William's Ghost.
Sweet William arose on last May morning. Sweet William. *Unknown.* ABS; BaBo
Sweet William he married a wife. The Wife Wrapped in Wether's Skin. *Unknown.* ABS; ESPB (F *vers.*); ViBoFo (B *vers.*)
Sweet William would a-wooing ride. Fair Margaret and Sweet William. *Unknown.* BaBo (A *vers.*); OBB; ViBoFo
Sweet William's Farewell to Black-eyed Susan. John Gay. *See* Black-eyed Susan.
Sweet William's Ghost. *Unknown.* BaBo (A *vers.*); CG; EBSV; ESPB (A, B, F, *and* G *vers.*); HOAH; InPo; ViBoFo (A *and* B *vers.*)
(Sir Ogey and Lady Elsey, B *vers.*) BaBo
(Sweet William and May Margaret.) CH; HBV, *abr.*
(William and Marjorie.) DaM
Sweet William's gone over seas. Lord William; or, Lord Lundy. *Unknown.* BaBo; ESPB
Sweet Willie was a widow's son. Willie and Maisry. *Unknown.* ESPB
Sweet Willy's ta'en him o'er the faem. *See* Willy's [*or* Willie's] Lady. *Unknown.* ESPB; OBB
Sweet wise death of old men honorable, The. The Fortunate Dead. Swinburne. *Fr.* Atalanta in Calydon. EmBrPo
Sweet, wooded way in life, forgetful Sleep! To Sleep. Maybury Fleming. AA
Sweet World, if you will hear me now. Envoy. Sarah Morgan Bryan Piatt. AA
Sweet Yak, I do adore you for your hair. The Yak. Nathalia Crane. StaSt
Sweet, yet cruel unkind is she. Song. *Unknown.* SeCL
Sweet Youth no more will tarry. Old Age. Anacreon. GrL; OxBG
Sweeter and sweeter. Thread and Song. John Williamson Palmer. LPS-1
Sweeter Far than the Harp, More Gold than Gold. "Michael Field." OBMV
Sweeter Saint I Serve, A. Sir Philip Sidney. *Fr.* Arcadia. SiPS
Sweeter than honey and the honeycomb. The Shed. Charles L. O'Donnell. ISi
Sweeter than water or cream or ice. The Watch on the Rhine. Gertrude Stein. *Fr.* Accents in Alsace. AtBAP
Sweetes' Li'l' Feller. Frank L. Stanton. *See* Mighty Lak' a Rose.
Sweetest Bud of Beauty! may. To a Very Young Lady. Sir George Etherege. BrBE; CEP; SeCL; ViBoPo
Sweetest Cloris lend a kisse. *Unknown.* SeCSL
Sweetest! if thy fairy hand. To a Little Girl Gathering Flowers. Mary Tighe. OTPC (1923 ed.)
Sweetest in Measure, Each Pleasure. Euripides, *tr. fr. Greek by* R. C. Trevelyan. *Fr.* Medea. GrR
Sweetest is the time of waiting. Time of Waiting. Erik Axel Karlfeldt. AnSL
Sweetest Jesus, gracious, free. Sweet Jesus. Friar Michael of Kildare. OnYI
Sweetest [*or* Sweetes'] li'l' feller. Mighty Lak' a Rose [*or* Sweetes' Li'l' Feller]. Frank L. Stanton. FaFP; OlF; TreFS
Sweetest Lives, The ("The sweetest lives are those to duty wed"). *At. to* Elizabeth Barrett Browning. *See* Reward of Service.
Sweetest Love, I Do Not Go. John Donne. *See* Song: "Sweetest love, I do not go."
Sweetest Melancholy. John Fletcher. *See* Melancholy.
Sweetest melody, The. Two Songs, 1. Abraham Reisen. LiTW
Sweetest Name, The. *At. to* St. Bernard of Clairvaux. *See* Jesus, the Very Thought of Thee.
Sweetest of all childlike dreams. The Vanishers. Whittier. AA; IAP
Sweetest of all delight is. Joy, Sorrow and Happiness. Axel Juel. BoDS
Sweetest of sweets, I thank you. Church-Music. George Herbert. EPS; SeCV-1; UnS
Sweetest Place, The. Mary Frances Butts. PPL
Sweetest Saviour, if my soul. Dialogue. George Herbert. EV-2; MePo; OBEV; OBS; SeCV-1
Sweetest sound our whole year round, The. Seeking the Mayflower. Edmund Clarence Stedman. ADAH
Sweetest spring/ adorned in flowers. Spring. Yiannis Vilaras. MoGP
Sweetest Story Ever Told, The. R. M. Stults. TreFS
Sweetest sweets that time hath rifled. Song in Imitation of the Elizabethans. Sir William Watson. VA
Sweetgrass Range. Edwin Ford Piper. LEAP; MAP; PFY; TBM
(Sweet Grass Range.) CBOV
Sweetgum Creek's got the bighead. Fall Freshet. Thad Stem, Jr. NoCaPo (rev. ed.)
Sweet-heart, come see if the rose. Odes, I, 17. Pierre de Ronsard. PrPoCR
Sweetheart Gate, Th'. Edwin Waugh. VA
Sweetheart in the Army, A (A *and* B *vers.*). *Unknown.* BaBo
(Pretty Fair Maid, A, *with music.*) AS
Sweetheart, Rejoice in Mind. Alexander Montgomerie. BSV
Sweetheart, young mistress mine. For One of Low Degree. Walther von der Vogelweide. LyMA
Sweethearts. Mary Gilmore. BoAu
Sweetly Breathing, Vernal Air. Thomas Carew. LPS-2
Sweetly-favored face, The. Canzonetta: Of His Lady in Absence. Giacomino Pugliese. AWP; LyPI
Sweetly Sleep. *At. to* Eliza Lee Follen, *also to* Jane Taylor. *See* Lullaby: "Sleep, my baby, sleep my boy."
Sweetly Sleep. *Unknown.* BOL
Sweetly sung, O blackbird of Derrycairn. The Blackbird of Derrycairn. *Unknown.* SiB
Sweetmeat, The. Sir Edward Sherburne. ElSeCe; SeCL
Sweetness of England, The. Elizabeth Barrett Browning. *See* England.
Sweetness of Nature, The. *Unknown, tr. fr. Irish by* Frank O'Connor. KiLC
Sweetness of Spring, The. *Unknown, tr. fr. Latin by* John Addington Symonds. LyMA
Sweetness of Spring memories bring. When It's Iris Time in Tennessee. Willa Mae Waid. PoRL
Sweetnesse in Sacrifice. Robert Herrick. NBE
Sweets, that bending o'er their banks, The. Moonrise. John Cunningham. *Fr.* Contemplation; a Night Piece. RO
Sweets That Die. Langdon Elwyn Mitchell. AA
Sweit roiss of vertew and of gentilnes. *See* Sweet rose of virtue . . .
Swell, The. Apollon Nikolayevich Maikov, *tr. fr. Russian by* Babette Deutsch. TrRV
Swell Me a Bowl. Ben Jonson. *Fr.* The Poetaster. TuPP
Swell within her billowed skirts, A. The Madwoman of Punnet's Town. L. A. G. Strong. MBP
Swell's Soliloquy. *Unknown.* FiBHP; LPS-3
Swept by the hot wind, stark, untrackable. Mohammed and Seid. Harrison Smith Morris. AA
Swept clean of leaves, with stripped boughs, the garden. Sestina. James K. Baxter. Cressida, XV. AnNZ
"Swerve to the left, son Roger," he said. The Judgment of God. William Morris. OBVV; POTT; SoV; ViPP; VLEP
Swete Ihesu King of Blisse. *Unknown.* OxBoCh
Swetnam, the Woman-Hater, *sel.* *Unknown.*
Ding Dong. ElL
Swevens came up round Harold the Earl, The. The Weird Lady. Charles Kingsley. DaM
Swift, *sel.* Thomas Caulfield Irwin.
"Two women loved him, shapes of Heaven." IrPN
Swift across the palace floor. Little Guinever. Annie Fields. AA
Swift as a spirit hastening to his task. The Triumph of Life. Shelley. ChER; ERP; PoEL-4
Swift as an arrow in the wind he goes. Polo Player. Daniel Whitehead Hicky. MoSiPe
Swift goes the sooty swallow o'er the heath. The Swallow. John Clare. ERP
Swift had pains in his head. January 1940. Roy Fuller. HoPM; LiTM; OnHM; SeCePo; WaP
Swift has sailed into his rest. Swift's Epitaph. W. B. Yeats. NAMP; PtP
Swift in his step and careless of his speech. Native Son. Gertrude Callaghan. JKCP (1955 ed.)
Swift kindnesses are best: a long delay. Be Kind Promptly. *Unknown.* OnPM
Swift o'er the sunny grass. Shadow-Evidence. Mary Mapes Dodge. AA
Swift red flesh, a winter king, The. The Dance. Hart Crane. *Fr.* The Bridge: Powhatan's Daughter. AnAmPo; AnFE; CoAnAm; LA; LiTA; LiTM; MoAB; MoAmPo; OxBA; SeCeV; TwAmPo
Swift spirit of Truth, unfaltering I pursue. Clues. Mary Sinton Leitch. LS
Swift summer into the Autumn flowed. The Plants Decay. Shelley. *Fr.* The Sensitive Plant. RO
Swift swallows sailing from the Spanish main. Homing Swallows. Claude McKay. TSW
Swift Things Are Beautiful. Elizabeth J. Coatsworth. StVeCh; TiPo (1952 ed.)
Swift thro' the Phrygian towns the rumour flies. Niobe. Ovid. *Fr.* Metamorphoses, VI. RoL
Swift through some trap mine eyes have never found. The Harlequin of Dreams. Sidney Lanier. AA; CoV; TCAP

Swift through the eyes unto the heart within. Carnal and Spiritual Love. Michelangelo. OnPM
Swift through the yielding air I glide. The Lark. *Unknown.* OBS; SeCL
Swift was sweet on Stella. Us Potes. Franklin P. Adams. WhC
Swift years slip and slide adown the steep, The. The End of Aodh-of-the-Songs. "Fiona Macleod." LBBV
Swifter and swifter the White Ship sped. The White Ship. Dante Gabriel Rossetti. POTT
Swifter far than summer's flight. Remembrance. Shelley. EmBrPo; EV-4
Swiftly as dart the thoughts of a man long used to fare. The Old Traveller. Homer. *Fr.* The Iliad, XV. GrPE
Swiftly ending their stories, feeling. Preoccupation with Death. Charles Fisher. MoWP
Swiftly Relight the Flame. Hilda Doolittle ("H. D."). *Fr.* A Tribute to the Angels. FaBoTw
Swiftly song of mine depart. Simple Song. Paul Verlaine. TrFP
Swiftly the dews of the gloaming are falling. The Bugles of Dreamland. "Fiona Macleod." OTPC (1946 ed.)
Swiftly the world retreats. Departure. L. A. G. Strong. HaMV
Swiftly the years, beyond recall. New Corn. T'ao Ch'ien. Twelve Poems, 9. TrCh
Swiftly through the forest brake. A Mountain Glen. *Unknown.* OxBG
Swiftly turn the murmuring wheel! Song for the Spinning Wheel. Wordsworth. OBRV
Swiftly walk o'er [*or* over] the western wave. To Night [*or* To the Night]. Shelley. AnFE; AtBAP; ATP; AWP; BCEP; BEL; BLV; BoLiVe; BPN; CaAE; CBE; CH; ChER; CoBE; EG; EM-2; EmBrPo; EnL; EnLi-2; EnLit; EnRP; EPN; EPP; ERP; EV-4; ExPo; GEPC; GTBS; GTBS-D; GTBS-W; GTSE; GTSL; HBV; HBVY; InP; InPo; JAWP; KN; LEAP; LoBV; LPS-2; MaPo; MCCG; MyFE; OAEP; OBRV; PCD; PIAE; PIR; PoE; PoFS; PoRA; REAL; ReaPo; SeCeV; ShBV-4; TOP; TreFS; TrGrPo; TVSH; TyEnPo; UnPo (1st ed.); ViBoPo; WBP; WHA
Swift's Epitaph. W. B. Yeats. NAMP; PtP
Swifts in the Chimney. Rose Mills Powers. BLA
Swimmer. Robert Francis. CrMA; NePoAm
Swimmer, The. Ibn Khafaja, *tr. fr. Arabic by* A. J. Arberry. MooP
Swimmer, The. Irving Layton. PeCV
Swimmer, The. Roden Noel. OBVV
Swimmer, The. John Crowe Ransom. PFY
Swimmer, A. Shakespeare. *Fr.* Julius Caesar, I, ii. BHV
Swimmer of Night. Pedro Salinas, *tr. fr. Spanish by* Eleanor L. Turnbull. AnSpL-2
("Swimmer of night, swimmer between.") CoSP
Swimmers, The. Edward Shanks. PtOT
Swimmers, The. Allen Tate. MoVE
Swimmers. Louis Untermeyer. PFY; PoeMoYo; TCPD
"O the swift plunge into the cool, green dark." *sel.* TSW
Swimming. Byron. *Fr.* The Two Foscari. GN; LPS-2
Swimming. Hafiz, *tr. fr. Persian by* Walter Leaf. PeP
Swimming. Clinton Scollard. FaPON; GFA; MPB; UTS
Swimming. Swinburne. *Fr.* Tristram of Lyonesse. GN
Swimming by Night. Alice Blaine Damrosch. LEAP
Swineherd, let us make for the moorland. The Wry Rowan. *Unknown.* OnYI
Swing, The. Mary I. Osborn. BoTP
Swing, The. Robert Louis Stevenson. BoChLi; FaBoBe; FaFP; GFA; GoBP; MBP; MeMeAg; NeHB; OTPC; PCH; StVeCh; SUS; TiPo; TreF; VLEP
Swing back the gate till it stumbles over the furrows. Chance Met. Rosemary Dobson. NeLNL
Swing, Cradle, Swing. George Cooper. BOL
Swing dat hammer—hunh. Southern Road. Sterling A. Brown. BANP
Swing Low, Sweet Chariot ("Oh, de good ole chariot swing so low"). *Unknown.* AA
Swing Low, Sweet Chariot ("Swing low, sweet chariot"). *Unknown.* ABF, *with music;* AmPP; BlG; BoAN-1, *with music;* FaPON; GoSl; InP; LoGBV; MaRV; OlF
Swing Low, Swing Low. *Unknown.* BOL
Swing on the Corner, *with music. Unknown.* TrAS
Swing on the cripple and hit the dying quail. An Astonished Listener Hears the Radio Announcer Bat Out the Long Balls of Verbs, Nouns and Adjectives. James Schevill. FiMAP
Swing out, oh bells. The Bells of Peace. Aileen Fisher. SiSoSe
Swing out thy doors, high gate that dreadst not night. The Gate of the Armies. Henri de Regnier. MiFP
Swing Ship, The. Mildred D. Shacklett. GFA
Swing Song, A. William Allingham. BrR; FaPON; MoShBr; MPB; OTPC (1946 ed.); PCD; PoRh; RAR; SUS
Swing Song. *Unknown, tr. fr. Turkish.* PCH
Swing! Swing! Swing! Skating Song. Christopher Morley. PCH
Swing thee low in thy cradle soft. Indian Cradle Song. *Unknown.* BoChLi; BOL
Swinging. Irene Thompson. BoTP
Swinging across the belfry tower. The Christmas Peal. Harriet Prescott Spofford. PEOR
Swinging Song, A. Mary Howitt. OTPC (1923 ed.)
Swinging Stair, The. Nathalia Crane. YT
Swinging toward the Light. Georgia Harkness. MaRV
Swirl of light follows me through the square, The. Rose White, Yellow, Silver. Ezra Pound. *Fr.* Phanopoeia. CoV
Swiss Air. Bret Harte. *See* Serenade: "I'm a gay tra, la, la."
Swiss Peasant, The. Wordsworth. OBEC
(On the Swiss.) PoFr
Swiss they are a hardy race, The. Song of Switzerland. Stoddard King. WhC
Switch Blade, The; or, John's Other Wife. Jonathan Williams. NeAP
Switch Cut in April, A. Clifford Dyment. MoP; MoVE
Switzerland. Matthew Arnold. OAEP; ViPP
Sels.
Absence, VI. PoVP
Isolation; to Marguerite, IV. BPN; GEPC; PoVP; VLEP
"Forgive me! forgive me!" *br. sel.* VLEP
To Marguerite (Continued), V. BMEP; BPN; CoEV; EnL; EnLi-2; EPN; EPP; FaBoEn; FiP; GEPC; GTBS-D; GTML; HBV; MaPo; OBEV; PoEL-5; PoVP; RiBV; SeCeV; TOP; ViPo; VLEP
(Isolation.) OBVV
("Yes! in the sea of life enisled.") ReaPo
Switzerland. James Sheridan Knowles. *Fr.* William Tell. LPS-2; PoFr
Swoon of noon, a trance of tide, A. In a Bye-Canal. Herman Melville. PoFS
Swooping Wings, The. W. W. Gibson. ChMo
Sword, The. Abu Bakr, *tr. fr. Arabic by* A. J. Arberry. MooP
Sword, The. Michael Joseph Barry. TIP
Sword, a sword, and a sword, A. Which Sword? Jason Noble Pierce. PGD; PSO
Sword and Lance. Ibn Shuhaid, *tr. fr. Arabic by* A. J. Arberry. MooP
Sword and the Sickle, The. Blake. BLV; BoLiVe; ChTr
(Gnomic Verses.) TrGrPo
Sword and the Skewer, The. Tomás de Iriarte, *tr. fr. Spanish by* Alice Jane McVan. AnSpL-2
Sword fell down, The: I heard a knell. The Leader. Hilaire Belloc. ACP (1952 ed.)
Sword-fish whose weariness is imputed above all, The. Without Light. Vicente Aleixandre. CoSP
Sword in the Spring Office, A. Li Ho, *tr. fr. Chinese by* Ho Chih-yuan. WhP
Sword is a sheathed rivulet, to whose brink, The. Sword and Lance. Ibn Shuhaid. MooP
Sword of Bunker Hill, The. William Ross Wallace. PEDC
Sword of Robert Lee, The. Abram Joseph Ryan. BlG; GA; JKCP; PaA; PoRL; SPP
Sword of silver cuts the fields asunder, A. Vigil of the Immaculate Conception. Maurice Francis Egan. CAW; JKCP
Sword of Surprise, The. G. K. Chesterton. LBBV; MBP; MoBrPo
Sword of Tethra, The. William Larminie. *Fr.* Moytura. OnYI; TIP
Sword, on my left side gleaming. Sword Song. Karl Theodor Körner. LPS-2
Sword sang [*or* sung] on the barren heath, The. The Sword and the Sickle [*or* Gnomic Verses]. Blake. BLV; BoLiVe; ChTr; TrGrPo
Sword Singing, The. The Song of the Sword. W. E. Henley. BPN
Sword Song. Karl Theodor Körner, *tr. fr. German by* Charles T. Brooks. LPS-2
Sword sung on the barren heath, The. *See* Sword sang on the barren heath, The.
Sword was sheathed, The: in April's sun. The Vow of Washington. Whittier. DD; GA; MC; PAH
Swords and Plowshares. Isaiah II: 2-4. Bible, *O.T.* GrCo-1
Swords crossed, but not in strife! The Crossed Swords. Nathaniel Langdon Frothingham. AA
Swordy Well. John Clare. WHA
Swung down from the fragrant branches. Boris Pasternak, *tr. fr. Russian by* C. M. Bowra. BoRS
Swung in the hollows of the deep. Cradle-Song of the Fisherman's Wife. Ella Higginson. BOL; MOAH
Sycamore. Vernon Watkins. MoWP
Sycophantic Fox and the Gullible Raven. Guy Wetmore Carryl. AA; AnAmPo; BLPA; CenHV; FaFP; FiBHP; HBV; InMe; LA; LEAP; LHV; MAP; MoAmPo (1942 ed.); PoeMoYo; ShBV-3
Syllables of grief are small, The. Text for Today. Phyllis McGinley. WhC
Sylly boy wert thou but wise. *Unknown.* SeCSL

Sylph, The. Paul Valéry, *tr. fr. French by* Alan Conder. TrFP
Sylvan Catch. Ben Jonson. *See* Buz, Quoth the Blue Fly.
Sylvan meant savage in those primal woods. Woods. W. H. Auden. NePA; NePoAm
Sylvan Morfydd. Lionel Johnson. VLEP
Sylvan Muses, can ye sing. Aglaia. Nicholas Breton. *Fr.* The Passionate Shepherd. OBSC
Sylvan Ode. José Santos Chocano, *tr. fr. Spanish by* John Pierrepont Rice. WoL
Sylvan Revel, A. Edward Cracroft Lefroy. Echoes from Theocritus, XXV. AWP; JAWP; WBP
Sylvan slopes with corn-clad fields, The. September, 1819. Wordsworth. BPN
Sylvester Vermicelli was a conscientious clerk. Ballad of the Faithful Clerk. Albert Stillman. InMe
Sylvia. Michael Drayton. *Fr.* The Shepherd's Garland, Eclogue IX. LoBV (1949 ed.)
(Roundelay, A: "Tell me, thou skilful shepherd's swain.") EIL
Sylvia. Shakespeare. *See* Who Is Silvia?
"Sylvia, hush!" I said, "come here." Dove's Nest. Joseph Russell Taylor. HBV
Sylvia; or, The May Queen, *sels.* George Darley.
Chorus of Spirits, I. OnYI; VA
Dirge: "Wail! wail ye o'er the dead!" OBRV
Morning-Song, II. VA
(Serenade.) HBV
Nephon's Song, III. VA
(Elfin Pedlar, The.) BoTP
(From "Sylvia.") LEAP
Song: "I've taught thee Love's sweet lesson o'er." OBRV
(Romanzo to Sylvia, IV.) VA
Sylvia, thanks in verses take. To Sylvia, Who Sent Me Music of Her Own Composing. Schuyler B. Jackson. CAG
Sylvia the fair, in the bloom of fifteen. Song. Dryden. LiTG; LiTL; SiTL; ViBoPo
Sylvie and Bruno, *sels.* "Lewis Carroll."
Gardener's Song, The, 8 *sts.* HBV; OTPC
(He Thought He Saw.) GBV (1952 ed.), 7 *sts.;* HBVY, 6 *sts.*
(He Thought He Saw a Banker's Clerk.) LBN; NA
("He thought he saw an Elephant," 5 *sts.*) EnLi-2
(Mad Gardener's Song, The, 9 *sts.*) BoN; FiBHP, 7 *sts.;* PoRh; SiTL; TreFS, 6 *sts.*
(Metamorphoses, 7 *sts.*) MBP
(Some Hallucinations, 7 *sts.*) BOHV
(Strange Wild Song, A, 7 *sts.*) StVeCh
Melancholy Pig, The. FaPON; OTPC (1946 ed.); PPL; RAR
Outland Fare. BoN
Sylvie and Bruno Concluded, *sels.* "Lewis Carroll."
King-Fisher Song, The. BoN; RIS
Little Birds. BoN; WhC
Little Birds Are Playing, *shorter sel.* KN; OxBoLi
Pig-Tale, The. BoN
Symbol, The. James Hebblethwaite. BoAu
Symbol. David Morton. HBMV; MaRV; OQP; POT; PoTo; QP-1; SBMV; StJW; VOD
Symbol from the first, of mastery, A. The Staff of Aesculapius. Marianne Moore. ImOP
Symbol of Hope. Carl S. Weist. *See* Cross on a Hill, A.
Symbol of star or lily of the snows. The Cloud of Carmel. Jessica Powers. ISi
Symbolism. "Æ." TIP
Symbolisms, *sels.* Richard Realf.
"O Earth! thou hast not any wind that blows." UnW
(Ever-present Spirit, The.) GrCo-1
(O Earth!) AnEnPo
(Word, The.) AA; WGRP
(World, The.) MaRV; OBAV
"Sometimes (we know not how)." UnW
Symbols. John Drinkwater. BMEP; NV; TCEP
Symbols. John Richard Moreland. ChIP; PGD
Symbols. Vance Thompson. AA
Symbols. W. B. Yeats. OBMV
Sympathetic. Burges Johnson. AIBD
Sympathizers, The. Josephine Miles. CrMA; FiMAP
Sympathy. Emily Brontë. OAEP
Sympathy. Paul Laurence Dunbar. CDC; PoNe
Sympathy, The. Owen Felltham. LO; SeCL
Sympathy. Althea Gyles. HBV; TIP
Sympathy. Anna E. Hamilton. OQP; QP-1
Sympathy. Reginald Heber. BeLS; BOHV
Sympathy. James B. Kenyon. UnW
Sympathy. Sir Thomas Noon Talfourd. *Fr.* Ion, I, ii. LPS-3
(Friend, A.) PoToHe
Sympathy. Henry David Thoreau. MOAP
Sympathy, The. *Unknown.* SeCL
Sympathy Explained. Emyr Humphreys. MoWP
Symphonie Symbolique, *sel.* Edmund John.
"And what I seek." BMEP
Symphony, The. Sidney Lanier. AmPP; ATP (1935 ed.); CoBA; CoV; LiTA; SPP
Sels.
"For the outside leagues of liberty." PoFr
"I speak for each no-tonguéd tree." ViBoPo
Symphony, The. Herman W. Stillman. PEDC
Symphony; First Movement. John Hall Wheelock. UnS
Symphony in Blue. Raymond F. Roseliep. ISi
Symphony in Gray Major. Rubén Darío, *tr. fr. Spanish by* Alice Jane McVan. LiTW
Symphony in Yellow. Oscar Wilde. MBP; MoBrPo; OTPC (1946 ed.); PCH; ViP
Symphony Pathétique. Ruth Comfort Mitchell. PoeMoYo; VOD
Symptoms of an Ailing Democracy. Aristophanes, *tr. fr. Greek by* Benjamin Bickley Rogers. *Fr.* The Frogs. GrR
Synce my joyes thoroughe Phillis frownes. *Unknown.* SeCSL
Synekdechestai. C. M. Schmid. GoYe
Synge's Grave. Winifred M. Letts. AnIV; LBBV
Synnöve's Song. Björnstjerne Björnson, *tr. fr. Norwegian by* Charles W. Stork. AnNoLy; LiTW
Synods are whelps of th' Inquisition. Presbyterian Church Government. Samuel Butler. *Fr.* Hudibras, I, 3. OBS
Synonym for God, A. John Fandel. JKCP (1955 ed.)
Synthesis. David Evans. MoWP
Synthesis, above Swansea. Peter Hellings. MoWP
Syon lyes waste, and thy Jerusalem. *See* Sion lies waste . . .
Syr Gawayn and the Grene Knight. *Unknown. See* Sir Gawain and the Green Knight.
Syracusan Women, The. Theocritus, *pr. tr. fr. Greek by* Andrew Lang. Idylls, XV. GrL
("Praxinoa in?/ Yes, Gorgo dear!" *tr. by* Leigh Hunt.) GrPo
Sels.
Adonis Song, The, *tr. by* R. C. Trevelyan. GrR
Syracusan Women, The, *tr. by* J. M. Chapman. WoL
(Gorgo and Proxinoa, *tr. by* Jack Lindsay.) OxBG
(Syracusan Women at the Adonis Festival, The, *tr. by* R. C. Trevelyan. GrR
Syracuse. Elizabeth J. Coatsworth. TBM
Syren Songs, *sels.* George Darley.
Mermaiden's Vesper Hymn, The, VI. KN; LoBV; OBRV; PoEL-4; RO
(Mermaids' Vesper-Hymn, The.) BLV
(Siren Chorus: "Troop home to silent grots and caves.") GTIV; OxBI; ViBoPo
(Song of the Mermaids.) ChTr
Sea-Ritual, The, V. OBRV; OnYI; OxBI; TriL
(Deadman's Dirge.) CH
Syren's Song. Dryden. *Fr.* King Arthur, IV, i. BeR
Syria. Thomas Moore. *Fr.* Lalla Rookh. LPS-2
Syrian Lover in Exile Remembers Thee, Light of My Land, The. Ajan Syrian. LiTL; NP
Syrian Lullaby. Alice Hathaway Cunningham. BOL
Syrian's Tale, The. Leslie Savage Clark. ChIP
Syrinx. John Lyly. *See* Pan's Song.
Syro-Phoenician Woman, The. *Unknown.* StJW
System. Robert Louis Stevenson. PoVP; RIS; VLEP
Systole and Diastole. Conrad Aiken. CrMA
Systolic city noise denies the thrush. Rural Legend. Mary Elizabeth Osborn. NePoAm

T

T. A. H. Ambrose Bierce. AA; AnAmPo; BAP; LA; LEAP; YaD
T.B.'s Progress, The. Norman Bethune. PoP
T.F.C. Mortimer Collins. HBV
T is for turkey so crispy and brown. The Feast Day. Amy McDonall. PCH
T.V.A., The, *with music. Unknown.* TrAS
Tabernacle Thought, A. Israel Zangwill. TrJP
Tabitha Soliloquizes. Minnie Leona Upton. CIV
Tabitha, sweet Tabitha, I never can forget. Concerning Tabitha's Dancing of the Minuet. Arthur Colton. PR
Tablada I was near. The Song of the Mountain Girl. Juan Ruiz, Archpriest of Hita. *Fr.* The Book of Good Love. AnSpL-1
Table and the Chair, The. Edward Lear. BoChLi; GoTP; HBVY; MPB; OTPC (1946 ed.); PCH; PPL; RAR; SAS; StVeCh
Table Blessing. Julia Budd Shafer. MeMeAg
Table Blessing. Bernice Ussery. MeMeAg
Table Blessing. Lew Wallace. MeMeAg
Table for One. John Holmes. WhC
Table is imposing, The. Sunday. Carlos Pellicer. AnCL
Table is spread, the lamp glitters and sighs, The. The Expected Guest. Sidney Keyes. PoN
Table Manners for the Hostess. Jean de Meun, *tr. fr. French by* Bernard D. N. Grebanier. *Fr.* The Romance of the Rose, *ch.* 73. EnLi-1

Table Richly Spread, A. Milton. *Fr.* Paradise Regained, II. FaBoCh; LoGBV
Table Talk, *sels.* William Cowper.
Fragment. WGRP
"Freedom has a thousand charms to show." PoFr
"In front of these came Addison." PtP
Table Talk. Donald Mattam. FiBHP
Tableau. Countee Cullen. BANP; TCPB
Tableau at Twilight. Ogden Nash. FiBHP
Table's long and gleaming, The. The Board Meets. John Gloag. FiBHP
Tables Turned, The. Wordsworth. BEL; BPN; EM-2; EmBrPo; EnL; EnLi-2; EnLit; EnRP; EPN; EPP; ERP; GEPC; HBV; OAEP; OBRV; TwP
(Up! Up! My Friend, and Quit Your Books.) NLK; PC; PoMa; SN
Let Nature Be Your Teacher, *sel.* MaRV
Taboo to Boot. Ogden Nash. FiBHP
Tabor was her dying bed, A. Sister Mary Philomena. James M. Hayes. PraNu
Tacita. James Benjamin Kenyon. AA
Taciturn Sea Captain. Kotaro Takamura, *tr. fr. Japanese by* Takamichi Ninomiya *and* D. J. Enright. PoLJ
Tacking Ship off Shore. Walter Mitchell. AA; EtS; FaBoBe; GN; HBV; LPS-2; OBAV; PFY; PoeMoYo
Tact. Harry Graham. ALV
Tact. Arthur Guiterman. PFE
Tactic. Margaret Marks. MAP
Taddeo Gaddi built me. I am old. The Old Bridge at Florence. Longfellow. BAV
Tadmor, *sel.* Nathalia Crane.
Song: "Great is the rose." MAP; MoAmPo (1942 ed.)
Tadoussac. Charles Bancroft. BLPA
Tadpole, The. Elizabeth Gould. BoTP
Tae titly. *Unknown.* OxNR
Taffy, the topaz-colored cat. In Honor [*or* Honour] of Taffy Topaz. Christopher Morley. CIV; PoMa; TiPo
Taffy was a Welshman, Taffy was a thief. Mother Goose. OTPC; OxNR; RIS; SiTL
Taffy was born. *Unknown.* OxNR
Tag him, forward him gently home. Message Received. Sonia Raiziss. PoF
Tagus, farewell [*or* farewel], that westward with thy streams [*or* stremes]. Of His Return from Spain [*or* In Spain]. Sir Thomas Wyatt. FaBoEn; OBSC; ReEn; ReIE; SeCePo; SiCE; TuPP
Tahiti, Tahiti. Vor a Gauguin Picture zu Singen. Kurt M. Stein. FiBHP
Tail behind, a trunk in front, A. The Elephant, or the Force of Habit. A. E. Housman. WhC
Tail for the Horse, A. *Unknown.* SiTL
Tail Piece. *Unknown. See* From the Chuck Wagon.
Taill of the Uponlandis Mous and the Burges Mous, The. Robert Henryson. BSV; EV-1
Tailor, The. "S. Ansky," *tr. fr. Yiddish by* Joseph Leftwich. TrJP
Tailor, The. Walter de la Mare. VOD
Tailor, The. Joseph Leftwich. TrJP
Tailor, The. Piotr Vasilyevich Oreshin, *tr. fr. Russian by* Babette Deutsch. TrRV
Tailor, A, a man of an upright dealing. Of a Precise Tailor. Sir John Harington. BOHV
Tailor Bills. Martial, *tr. fr. Latin by* Paul Nixon. RoL
Tailor of Bicester, The. *Unknown.* OxNR
Tailor That Came from Mayo, The. Denis A. McCarthy. OnYI
Tailor's Apprentice, The. Ibn Kharuf, *tr. fr. Arabic by* A. J. Arberry. MooP
Tailspinning from the shelves of sky. Jubilo. Allen Tate. WaP
'Tain't. *Unknown.* BPP
'Taint Gwine Rain No Mo', *with music. Unknown.* SoAF
'Tain't what we have. 'Tain't. *Unknown.* BPP
Tak Your Auld Cloak about Ye. *Unknown.* See Old Cloak, The.
Take a blessing from my heart to the land of my birth. The Fair Hills of Eirè, O! Donogh Mac-Con-Mara (Macnamara), *tr. by* James Clarence Mangan. IrPN; OBVV
Take a common little bronco. The Cowboy up to Date. Charles S. Thomas, Jr. CoSo
Take a dainty paradox. Finale. A. P. Herbert. *Fr.* Perseverance; or, Half a Coronet. InMe
Take a father's admonition, from a heart disturbed. A Father's Testament. Judah ibn Tibbon. TrJP
Take a harp. Song of the Harlot. Isaiah, Bible, *O.T.* TrJP
Take a Letter to Dmitri Shostakovitch. Carl Sandburg. NeTW
Take a robin's leg. Homœopathic Soup. *Unknown.* BOHV
Take all my loves, my love, yea, take them all. Sonnets, XL. Shakespeare. InvP; OBSC
Take all of me—I am thine own, heart, soul. A Sonnet. Amélie Rives. AA; BAP
Take all; take all; take everything. Saint Francis of Assisi. Harry F. Leary. SaFP
Take as gold this old tradition. Schöne Rothraut. John Arthur Goodchild. VA
Take Away. Margot Ruddock. OBMV
Take away from me my eyes. Cantiga. Gil Vicente. LyMA
Take away your soft hair and your softer lips. Supplication. Louis Untermeyer. HBMV
Take back into thy bosom earth. Stanzas to the Memory of Thomas Hood [*or* To the Memory of Thomas Hood]. Bartholomew Simmons. LPS-3; VA
Take back the lute! I make no claim. Voltaire, Cobbett, and Gastronomy. Winthrop Mackworth Praed. *Fr.* A Preface. RO
Take Back the Virgin Page. Thomas Moore. HBV
Take Back Your Gold. Louis W. Pritzkow. TreF
Take back your suit. A Song of Faith Forsworn. Lord De Tabley. VA
Take Care. Rose Waldo. GFA
Take care, O wisp of a moon. To the Afternoon Moon, at Sea. Cale Young Rice. ETS
Take courage, lady: many fearful things. Night Fears. Sophocles. OxBG
Take down thy stars, O God! We look not up. These Latter Days. Olive Tilford Dargan. NoCaPo
Take earth, throw it up with thy right hand. Charm for Swarming Bees. *Unknown.* EPP
Take Frankincense, O God. Charles Fitzgeffrey. *Fr.* Holy Transportations. ChTr
Take from me something. Chance Meeting. Hilda Doolittle ("H. D."). MoP
Take from the earth its tragic hunger, Lord. Prayer. Hazel J. Fowler. TrPWD
Take from your head the garland too, Menechtenus. After the Festival. Stefan George. LiTW
Take hand and part with laughter. Rococo. Swinburne. HBV; PIR; ViBoPo
Take Heart. Edna Dean Proctor. BLP; HBV; LBAP
Take heart, for now the battle is half over. Truce. Sara Teasdale. ChMo; CMP
Take heed betime, lest ye be spied. Sir Thomas Wyatt. SiPS
Take heed; do not profane. James Shirley. *Fr.* The Maid's Revenge. BoFr
Take heed, my love. H. G. Andrews. LO
Take Heed of Gazing Overmuch. Thomas Richardson. *Fr.* A Proper New Song Made by a Student in Cambridge. EIL
Take heed of hating mee. John Donne. *Fr.* The Prohibition. BoFr
Take heed of loving me[e]. The Prohibition. John Donne. EG; ElL; MeLP; OBS; TuPP
Take heed of this small child of earth. The Poor Children [*or* The Children of the Poor]. Victor Hugo. AWP; JAWP; LiA; LiTW; WBP
Take heed, what time thou hearest, high in the clouds, the crane. Autumn Ploughing. Hesiod. *Fr.* Works and Days. GrPE
Take Her, Break Her. Anacreon, *tr. fr. Greek by* Walter Headlam. GrL; OxBG
Take him, earth, for cherishing. The Burial of the Dead. Prudentius, *tr. by* Helen Waddell. LiTW; TriL
Take him, O Braddan, for he loved thee well. In Memoriam. Thomas Edward Brown. VLEP
Take him this charm. The Orange. Frank Kendon. PtOT
Take him up tendahly. Parody on Thomas Hood's "The Bridge of Sighs." *Unknown.* FiBHP
Take Home This Heart. John Holmes. LiTL
Take home Thy prodigal child, O Lord of Hosts! Birthday Sonnet. Elinor Wylie. BLV; BoLiVe; MAP; MoAB; MoAmPo; OnPM; TriL
Take in good part these trifling toys. To the Reader [*or* Quip to the Reader]. Timothe Kendall, *after* Martial. OnPM; TuPP
Take it from me kiddo. Poem, or Beauty Hurts Mr. Vinal. E. E. Cummings. AmP; MoAB; MoAmPo; MoVE; OnAP; OxBA
Take it, love. Song. Richard Le Gallienne. HBV
Take it, my dear. Keep it beneath your pillow. Gift of a Mirror to a Lady. David Wagoner. NePoAm-2
Take Life as It Comes. Euripides, *tr. fr. Greek by* Walter Headlam. OxBG
Take me away, and in the lowest deep. The Dream of Gerontius: The Soul before God. Cardinal Newman. OxBoCh
Take me back to old Montana. *Unknown.* CoSo
Take me back to the days when the old red cradle rocked. The Old Red Cradle. Annie J. Granniss. PTA-1
Take me home to Ballyshannon, for there's music in the word. Song of Ballyshannon. Jeanne Robert Foster. NLK
Take Me in Your Arms, Miss Moneypenny-Wilson. Patrick Barrington. WhC
Take Me, Mother Earth. Anna Jameson. VA
Take me to some still abode. Learning. William Barnes. MOB
Take me upon thy breast. O Sleep. Grace Fallow Norton. HBV; LEAP

Take my hand and let us run. With the Winds. Matilda Hutchinson Turner. RAR
Take My Hand, O Blessed Master. Connie Calenberg. BePJ
Take my heart! for I cannot give it Thee. St. Augustine. PraP
Take My Life. Frances Ridley Havergal. MaRV; PraP
(Take My Life and Let It Be.) BLRP
Take my overcoat and hold it—I'll hit Bupalus in the eye. Pugilist. Hipponax. GrPE
Take my wish and all its meaning. From My Father. Michael Earls. FAOV
Take not away my wits, O God! Pushkin, *tr. fr. Russian by* C. M. Bowra. BoR
Take Nothing for Granite. Nate Salsbury. InMe
Take, O Take Those Lips Away. Shakespeare. *Fr.* Measure for Measure, IV, i; *also given, with add. st., in* The Bloody Brother (*by* John Fletcher, *and others*), V, ii. AnFE; AtBAP, *2 sts.;* BCEP; BEL; BrBE; ElL; ElSeCe; EM-1; EnLi-1; EnLit; EnLoPo, *2 sts.;* EPP; EtPaEn; EV-1; ExPo; HBV, *2 sts.;* InPo; LEAP, *2 sts.;* LiTB; LiTG; LiTL; LO; LPS-1, *2 sts.;* OAEP; OBEV; OnPM; OuHeWo; ReaPo; SeCeV; SiCE; TCEP; TOP; TuPP, *2 sts.;* TwP; ViBoPo; WHA
(Boy's Song to Mariana.) BoLiVe
(Frustra.) GTSL
(Love Forsworn.) MCCG
(Love Song.) FaBoEn. *2 sts.*
(Madrigal.) GTBS; GTBS-D; GTBS-W; GTSE
(Sealed in Vain.) WoL
(Seals of Love.) BLV; TrGrPo
(Song: "Take, O take those lips away.") FiP; LoPS; PoEL-2, *2 sts.;* REAL
(Song at the Moated Grange, A.) OBSC
(Song for Mariana.) EG
(Songs from the Plays.) AWP; JAWP; WBP
(Three Songs, 2.) UnPo (1st ed.)
Take of English earth as much. A Charm. Kipling. GTML; OtMeF
Take of letters the first. *Unknown. Fr.* Riddles. CoBE
Take of me what is not my own. Envoi. Kathleen Raine. NeBP
Take old Amyntor to thy heart, dear soil. The Good Farmer. *Unknown.* OnPM
Take one bowl, one valley. Florence; Design for a City. Elizabeth Jennings. HaMV
Take one example—to our purpose quite. Byron. Robert Pollok. *Fr.* The Course of Time. LPS-3
Take I, 4: II: 58. Philip Whalen. NeAP
Take Physic, Pomp. Shakespeare. *Fr.* King Lear, III, iv. TrGrPo
(Discovery of Pity.) UnPo (1st ed.)
Take pity, signors, ye who pass me by. For a Blind Beggar's Sign. Clemente Biondi. CAW
Take, proud ambition, take thy fill. A Sigh for Knockmany. William Carleton. TIP
Take strands of speech, faded and broken. Maker of Songs. Hazel Hall. HBMV
Take temperance to thy breast. A Talisman. Louise Imogen Guiney. CP
Take the cloak from his face, and at first. After [*or* The Avenger Speaks]. Robert Browning. BLV; BMEP; BoLiVe; EG; TrGrPo
Take the cloak of all my love. Song for a Jewess. Iwan Goll. TrJP
Take the Crust. Sadi, *tr. fr. Persian by* L. Cranmer-Byng. *Fr.* The Gulistan. AWP
Take the Glass Away. *Unknown.* SiTL
Take the good and cast the evil. Crusaders' Song. *Unknown.* CAW
Take the World as It Is. Charles Swain. VA
"Take the world as it is!—with its smiles and its sorrow," *sel.* PoToHe (new ed.)
Take them, O Death! and bear away. Suspiria. Longfellow. ViBoPo
Take then the music; plunge in the thickest of it. Samadhi. Conrad Aiken. MAPA
Take, then, your paltry Christ. To the Christians. Francis P. Adams. WGRP
Take these flowers which, purple waving. To a Lady [with Flowers from the Roman Wall]. Sir Walter Scott. BPN; BSV; OAEP
Take these stripes from, stripes from around my shoulder, huh! Lord It's All, Almost Done. *Unknown.* OuSiCo
Take these who will as may be. Permit Me Voyage. James Agee. MAP; MoAMPo; TriL
Take this counsel of me, who your safety am seeking. Advice to a Clansman. *Tr. by* Thomas Pattison. EBSV
Take This Hammer, *with music. Unknown.* OuSiCo
Take this kiss upon the [*or* thy] brow! A Dream within a Dream. Poe. AmP; AmPP; AnFE; APA; APW; BLV; BoLiVe; CoAnAm; CoBA; IAP; LO; OxBA; TrGrPo; UnW
Take Thou the burden, Lord. The Burden. Toyohiko Kagawa. MaRV
Take Thou This Rose. Pierre de Ronsard, *tr. fr. French by* Alan Conder. *Fr.* Armours de Cassandre. TrFP
("Take thou this rose, sweet even as thou art," *tr. by* Curtis Hidden Page.) PrPoCR
Take Thought. Plato, *tr. fr. Greek by* T. F. Higham. OxBG
Take Thy Bliss, O Man. Blake. *Fr.* Visions of the Daughters of Albion. EnRP
Take Thy Old Cloak about Thee. *Unknown. See* Old Cloak, The.
Take thy silent entity apart. Poem. Ann Louise Hayes. PtPa
Take time, my dear, ere time takes wing. Fading Beauty. *Unknown.* SeCL; SeEP
Take Time to Be Holy. W. D. Longstaff. BLRP
Take Time to Live. Thomas Curtis Clark. PoToHe
Take time unto Thyself, O Father. *Unknown.* OBSC; SiCE
Take unto Thyself, O Father. Prayer at the Close of a Marred Day. Elizabeth Stuart Phelps Ward. PraP
Take Up the Fish. *Unknown, tr. fr. Chinese.* WhP
Take up the oxen, boys, and harness up the mules. The Gold Seeker's Song. *Unknown.* PoOW
Take up the White Man's burden. The White Man's Burden. Kipling. BPN; EnLi-2 (1949 ed.); InP; PoVP; ViP
Take Up the Wings. Lawrence Lee. NeTW
Take Up Thy Cross. Francis Turner Palgrave. MaRV
Take us on the quest of beauty. The Prayer of the Quest. Eleanor B. Stock. MaRV
Take us size for size and he. A Fledgling Robin. Leonard Feeney. JKCP (1926 ed.)
Take weapon away, of what force is a man? The Preface to the Book of Housewifery. Thomas Tusser. SiCE
Take what God gives, O heart of mine. Your House of Happiness. Thomas Campion. MaRV
Take wings of fancy, and ascend. In Memoriam A. H. H., LXXVI. Tennyson. EmBrPo; EPN; GEPC; ViPo; VLEP
Take word to Lacedaemon, passer-by. The Dead of Sparta at Thermopylae. Simonides. GrPE
Take yesterday's worries and sort them all out. Worries. *Unknown.* PoToHe (new ed.)
Take Yo' Time, *with music. Unknown.* StDa
Take Yo' Time, Miss Lucy. *Unknown.* GoSl
Take you my brushes, child of light, and lay. Spring Landscape. Arthur Davison Ficke. *Fr.* Sonnets of a Portrait Painter, XII. HBMV
Take your bucket, and take your spade. The Sea. E. M. Adams. BoTP
Take Your Gun. Jacob Bronowski. POTE
Take your meals, my little man. The Little Gentleman. *Unknown. Fr.* Little Derwent's Breakfast. HBV; HBVY
Take your pleasure, dance and play. Invitation to Youth. *Unknown.* OnPM
Taking a charity. Confession in Holy Week. Christopher Morley. HBMV
Taking his trick, the crew being at their meal. The Boy. W. W. Gibson. NeTW
Taking Leave of a Friend. Li Po, *tr. fr. Chinese by* Ezra Pound. CoAnAm; PoFS; TwAmPo
Taking Leave of Wang Wei. Meng Hao-jan, *tr. fr. Chinese by* Witter Bynner. BoFr
Taking Long Views. May Kendall. CenHV
Taking my walk the other day. Commination. Walter Savage Landor. ALV
Taking of Cartagena, The. Thomas Greepe. *Fr.* The True and Perfecte Newes of the Worthy Enterprises of Sir Francis Drake, 1586. SG
Taking of the Name. *Unknown, tr. fr. Omaha Indian.* PCH
Taking of the Salmon, The. Thomas Tod Stoddart. EBSV
Taking of Troy, The, *sel.* Tryphiodorus, *tr. fr. Greek by* James Merrick.
"Meanwhile the Steed's deep caverns, op'ning wide." GrPo
Taking Off. Mary McB. Green. TiPo
Taking Off. Elizabeth Harrison. NeTW
Taking pity on this scrag-end of the city. One Kingfisher and One Yellow Rose. Eileen Brennan. NeIP
Taking the Veil. *Unknown.* CAG
Taking Turns. Emilie Blackmore Stapp. GFA
Taking us by and large, we're a queer lot. The Sisters. Amy Lowell. AnNe; MAP; MoAmPo
Taking your life as one long Eucharist. Imitation of Christ. Wilma C. Ludlow. ChIP
Takings. Tom Hood. BOHV
(What He Took.) CoMu
Takis Plumis. Miltiades Malakassis, *tr. fr. Modern Greek by* Rae Dalven. MoGP
Talcumed to a ghost, she slowly sways. Dancer. Vincent Starrett. LEAP
Tale, A. Louise Bogan. MOAP
Tale, A. Edward Thomas. ChTr
Tale for Husbands, A. Sir Philip Sidney. *Fr.* Arcadia. SiPS
Tale from the Garden, A. Margaret Wynne Jones. GFA
Tale half told and hardly understood, A. Exodus for Oregon. Joaquin Miller. AmPP (3d ed.); BAP; IAP; TCAP

Tale is every time the same, The. Fable. Maurice James Craig. NeIP
Tale of a Dog and a Bee, The. *Unknown.* BoTP
Tale of a Little Pig. *Unknown.* ABF
Tale of a Tart, The. Frederic E. Weatherly. SUS
Tale of Battle, The. Ibn Sa'id of Alcala la Real, *tr. fr. Arabic by* A. J. Arberry. MooP
Tale of Custard the Dragon, The. Ogden Nash. FaPON; GoBP; GoTP; PoRA; ShBV-1; TiPo (1959 ed.)
Tale of Drury Lane, A. Horace Smith. LPS-3
Tale of Eternity, *sel.* George Massey.
"Both heaven and hell." BMEP
Tale of Eumaeus, The. Homer. *See* Eumaeus the Swineherd.
Tale of How Fadey Learned of the Law Protecting Working-men, The, *sel.* Vladimir Mayakovsky, *and others, tr. fr. Russian by* Babette Deutsch.
"Fadey had fought on every front." TrRV
Tale of Hugelin, Count of Pisa, The. Chaucer. *Fr.* The Canterbury Tales: The Monk's Tale. MyFE
Tale of Lord Lovell, The. *Unknown.* PA
Tale of One Hill. Franklin D. Elmer, Jr. ChIP
Tale of Rosiphelee, The. John Gower. *Fr.* Confessio Amantis. ArmLP
Tale of Sigemund, The. *Unknown, tr. fr. Anglo-Saxon by* Charles W. Kennedy. *Fr.* Beowulf. AnOE
Tale of the Dixie-Belle, The. Frank Chase. InMe
Tale of the Golden Cockerel, The. Pushkin, *tr. fr. Russian by* Babette Deutsch. TrRV
Tale of the Golden Fleece, The. Pindar. *See* Quest of the Golden Fleece, The.
Tale of the Little Cossack, The. The Little Cossack. Laura E. Richards. PoRh
Tale of the times of old, A!/ Why, thou wanderer unseen! James Macpherson. *Fr.* Cath-Loda. BEL
Tale of the times of old, A! The deeds of days of other years! Carthon, a Poem. James Macpherson. EiPP; EnRP
Tale of the Wyf of Bathe, The. Chaucer. *See* Wife of Bath's Tale, The.
Tale was this, The. The Wind in the Pines. Henry Taylor. *Fr.* Edwin the Fair. VA
Talented Man, The. Winthrop Mackworth Praed. ALV; CoBE; EnRP; ERP; FiBHP; HBV
"Talents Differ." Laura E. Richards. TiPo
Tales, *sels.* George Crabbe.
Frank Courtship, The, *fr.* VI. OBRV
Jonas Kindred's Household, *fr.* VI. FaBoEn
Lover's Journey, The, *fr.* X. EnSW; EPP, *abr.*
Patron, The, *fr.* V. EnSW
Tales and talismans I have chronicled. The Task. Robert Bhain Campbell. MoPo
Tales of a Wayside Inn, *sels.* Longfellow.
Azrael (The Spanish Jew's Tale), *fr.* Pt. III. AnAmPo; LA
Bell of Atri, The (The Sicilian's Tale), *fr.* Pt. II. MW
Birds of Killingworth, The (The Poet's Tale), *fr.* Pt. I. APW; IAP; OxBA; PCN
"Do you ne'er think what wondrous beings these," 2 *sts.* WBLP
Charlemagne (The Poet's Tale), *fr.* Pt. III. AnAmPo; FaFP; LA
King Robert of Sicily (The Sicilian's Tale), *fr.* Pt. I. AnNe; BeLS; MW; OHIP; OnSP; PCD; PCN; PFE; PTA-1; TCAP; YT
(Sicilian's Tale, The.) CoV
Legend Beautiful, The (The Theologian's Tale), *fr.* Pt. II. CBPC; PTA-2
Legend of Rabbi Ben Levi, The (The Spanish Jew's Tale), *fr.* Pt. I. AnNe; BAV; DaM; EV-5; GBV (1952 ed.)
Manichaean's Prayer, The, *abr., fr.* Prelude to Pt. III. APW
Monk of Casal-Maggiore, The (The Sicilian's Tale), *fr.* Pt. III. AmPP (4th ed.); OxBA
Paul Revere's Ride (The Landlord's Tale), *fr.* Pt. I. AmPP (4th ed.); AnNE; APW; BAP; BAV; BBV; BeLS; BLPA; BoHiPo; CoBA; DD; EV-5; FaBoBe; FaFP; FaPON; GA; GoTP; HBV; HBVY; IAP; IDAH; LoGBV; LPS-2; MC; NeHB; OBAV; OHFP; OnHT; OnSP; PaA; PAH; PAP; PEDC; PIR; PoFr; PoRL; PTA-1; PYM; REAL; RIS; StPo; StVeCh; TCAP; TiPo (1952 ed.); TreF; TrGrPo; WBLP; YaD
Saga of King Olaf (The Musician's Tale), *fr.* Pt. I. APW (i–iv)
Building of the *Long Serpent*, xiii. EtS
Challenge of Thor, The, i. AmPP (4th ed.)
Einar Tamberskelvar, xx. AmPP (4th ed.); YT
King Olaf's Death-Drink, xxi. AmPP (4th ed.)
King Olaf's Return, ii. AmPP (4th ed.)
King Olaf's War-Horns, xix. AmPP (4th ed.); PFY
Nun of Nidaros, The, xxii. PraNu
Scanderbeg (The Spanish Jew's Second Tale), *fr.* Pt. III. PFY
Ships That Pass in the Night (The Theologian's Tale, iv), 4 *ll. fr.* Pt. III. EtS; PoToHe (new ed.)
Wayside Inn, The. Prelude to Pt. I. CoBA; TCAP
"Youth was there, of quiet ways, A," *fr.* Prelude to Pt. I. LEAP
Tales of the Hall, *sels.* George Crabbe.
"Age, with Stealing Steps," *fr.* X. BCEP; LEAP
(Approach of Age, The.) LPS-1
Cathedral-Walk, The, *fr.* XX. EnSW
Dejected Lover, The. FaBoEn
Delay Has Danger, *fr.* XIII. EnSW
"George loved the cause of freedom, but reproved," *fr.* I. PoFr
Tales of the Mermaid Tavern, *sels.* Alfred Noyes.
Black Bill's Honey-Moon, *abr., fr.* Pt. III. PCN
Thomas Dekker's Song, *fr.* Pt. II. ChMo; CMP
(Seven Wise Men.) InP
"Will Shakespeare's out like Robin Hood," *fr.* Pt. II. POTT
Tales the Barbers Tell, The. Morris Bishop. ALV
Taliesin, *sels.* Richard Hovey.
Death Song in Taliesin. PC
"Here falls no light." AA; OBAV
Taliessin's Song of Lancelot's Mass. Charles Williams. ReTS
Taliessin's Song of the Unicorn. Charles Williams. FaBoTw
Talisman, A. Louise Imogen Guiney. CP
Talisman, A. Marianne Moore. AnFE; APA; CoAnAm; MAP; MoAB; MoAmPo; NP; TCPD; ViBoPo
Talk. Philip A. Stalker. FiBHP
Talk about de lates', de lates' of this song. The Ballet of the Boll Weevil (B *vers.*). *Unknown.* ViBoFo
Talk Faith. Ella Wheeler Wilcox. OQP; QP-2
Talk Happiness. Ella Wheeler Wilcox. PoToHe
(Optimism.) BLPA; FaBoBe
Talk, if you will, of hero deed. Christianity and War. Ernest Crosby. PSO
Talk Is a Candle. Pierson Underwood. LoPS
Talk not of justice and her scales of woe. The Cross. Eva Gore-Booth. ChIP; MaRV
Talk not of strength, till your heart has known. Ella Wheeler Wilcox. PoToHe
Talk not of wasted affection! affection never was wasted. Longfellow. *Fr.* Evangeline. PoToHe (new ed.)
Talk not to me of all the frowns of fate. Woman's Jealousy. Baltasar del Alcázar. OnPM
Talk of Chocolate! Bacchus on Beverages. Francesco Redi. *Fr.* Bacchus in Tuscany. LiTW
"Talk of pluck!" pursued the sailor. Romance. W. E. Henley. In Hospital, XXI. EnLit; MC; PAH; POTT
Talk of the Greeks at Thermopylae! A Ballad of Redhead's Day. Richard Butler Glaenzer. MC; PAH
Talk of the Town, The. Ed Fisher. FiBHP
Talk to Me Tenderly. Vivian Yeiser Laramore. HBMV
Talk to the Boy, A. Strickland W. Gillilan. FAOV
Talker, The. Benjamin Appel. TrJP
Talking about men who are richer than they are. Old Men. Merrill Moore. MOAP
Talking Bronco, *sel.* Roy Campbell.
Volunteer's Reply to the Poet, The. ViBoPo (1958 ed.)
Talking in Their Sleep. Edith M. Thomas. ADAH; DD; OHIP; PEDC; PEOR
Talking Oak, The, *sel.* Tennyson.
Olivia. GN
Talking Oak, The/ To the ancients spoke. Be Different [*or* Deferent] to Trees. Mary Carolyn Davies. DD; FaPON; HBMV; MPB; OHIP
Talking of sects till [*or* quite] late one eve. No Sect [*or* Sects] in Heaven. Elizabeth H. Jocelyn Cleaveland. BLPA; PTA-2; TreFS
Talking to her, he knew it was the end. Hector. Valentin Iremonger. NeIP; OxBI
Talking with Soldiers. W. J. Turner. ChMP; FaBoTw; GTBS-D; MBP; MoBrPo; SoV
Tall Ambrosia. Henry David Thoreau. PoEL-4
Tall and clothed in samite. White Iris. Pauline B. Barrington. NV
Tall Axe-Man, The. Robert P. Tristram Coffin. PoFr
Tall, black,/ alone on the hill-top. Telegraph Pole. Enrique Bustamante y Ballivián. AnCL
Tall Braunighrindas left her bed. A Legend of Camelot. George du Maurier. CenHV
Tall camels of the spirit, The. A World without Objects Is a Sensible Emptiness. Richard Wilbur. FiMAP; Po
Tall clock is striking twelve, The. A Roxbury Garden. Amy Lowell. LaNeLa
Tall, cool and gentle, you are here. The Guest. Harold Monro. NeMA
Tall dancer dances, The. The Dancer. Joseph Campbell. GTIV; OBMV; OxBI; POTE
Tall deer upon snowy hills. Love. Itzik Manger. OnCuPl
Tall ears. What Is It? Marie Louise Allen. TiPo
Tall fir whispered in the wood, A. A Secret. Mrs. G. M. Howard. PEOR
Tall Fruit Trees, The. Ruth Pitter. DiM
Tall Girl, The. John Crowe Ransom. PeBoSo
Tall grove of towers that as he goes down. Salamanca. Miguel de Unamuno. TeCS

Tall knight met me in a haunted spot, A. Who Are the Dead? Lilith Lorraine. UnW
Tall, majestic monarch of the wood, The. The Mountain to the Pine. Clarence Hawkes. AA
Tall Men, The, *sels.* Donald Davidson.
  Andrew Jackson. SPP
  David Crockett. SPP
  Fire on Belmont Street, *Epilogue.* MAP; MoAmPo (1942 ed.); SPP
  "It was a hunter's tale." SPP
  John Sevier. SPP
Tall Nettles. Edward Thomas. BoTP; BrBE; ChTr; EPP; FaBoTw; HBMV; MBP; MoAB; MoBrPo; NeMA; POTE
Tall oak, who spread on high your shady boughs. Noontide Rest. Antiphilus of Byzantium. OxBG
Tall Oaks from Little Acorns Grow. David Everett. FaFP; TreF
  (Boy Reciter, The.) BLPA
Tall on the village hill the church stood lonely/ against the dark. New England Steeple. Frances Frost. QS
Tall people, short people. People. Lois Lenski. FaPON
Tall raking clipper ships driving hell-for-leather. Sailor's Delight. Cicely Fox Smith. AlDL
Tall She Was. *Unknown, tr. fr. Chinese.* WhP
Tall ships were wrecked here, and exotic cargoes. The Beachcomber. W. H. Oliver. AnNZ
Tall, somber [*or* sombre], grim. against the morning sky. Aspects of the Pines. Paul Hamilton Hayne. AA; AmPP (3d ed.); AnAmPo; HBV; HiLiAm; IAP; LA; SPP; TCAP
Tall Stately Plants with Spikes and Forks of Gold. Frederick Goddard Tuckerman. AnNE
Tall Tale God. Mark Van Doren. CrMA
Tall Toms, The. Edwin Honig. NePA
Tall Trees. Edgar Daniel Kramer. PEDC
Tall Trees. Eileen Mathias. BoTP
Tall unpopular men. Dedication. Oliver St. John Gogarty. OBMV
Tall, with tow-hair, the texture of hide. Aubade: Dick, the Donkey-Boy. Sir Osbert Sitwell. HaMV
Tall yellow hollyhocks stand, The. The Precinct—Rochester. Amy Lowell. OBAV; VOD
Tallahassee, *sel.* Andrew Merkel.
  "Ann stood and watched the combers race to shore." CaP
Taller Today, We Remember. W. H. Auden. ChMo; FaBoMo
Talmud, The, *sels. Tr. fr. Hebrew.* TrJP
  God to Man.
  Good Man, The.
  Why?
Talmud, The. Simeon Frug, *tr. fr. Yiddish by* Alice Stone Blackwell. TrJP
Talmud Student, The. Hayyim Nahman Bialik, *tr. fr. Hebrew by* Helena Frank. TrJP
Tam Glen. Burns. ALV; AWP; BEL; BSV; CEP; EBSV; EM-1; EnLi-2; EV-3; InPo; JAWP; OAEP; OBEC; TOP; WBP
Tam i' the Kirk. Violet Jacob. GoTS; HBMV; MM; POTE
Tam Lin. *Unknown.* BaBo; BSV, *longer vers.*; EBSV; ESPB; OBB, *longer vers.*; OBEV (new ed.), *longer vers.*; ViBoFo
Tam o' Shanter. Burns. AEV; BCEP; BEL; BeLS; BLV; BOHV; BoLiVe, *sl. abr.*; BSV; CBOV; CEP; DaM; EBSV; EiPP; EM-1; EnL; EnLi-2; EnLit; EnRP; EPP, *abr.*; EV-3; GoTL; GoTS; HBV; HOAH; LPS-3; OAEP; OBEC; OnSP; OuHeWo; PIAE; PoE; RiBV; SeCePo; ShBV-3; TCEP; TOP; TrGrPo, *sl. abr.*; TyEnPo; UnPo (1st ed.), *sl. abr.*; ViBoPo; WHA
Tam o' the linn cam up the gait. *Unknown.* FaBoCh
Tam Samson's Elegy. Burns. PoEL-4
Tamalpais, *sel.* Charles Warren Stoddard.
  "Hollow moon, The." BAP
Tamar, *sels.* Robinson Jeffers.
  California Vignette, A. PC
  "O swiftness of the swallow." TCPD
  "She answered, standing dark against the west in the window." PC
  "They two had unbridled the horses." AnAmPo; LA
Tamar and the Nymph. Walter Savage Landor. *See* Nymph, The.
Tamar's Wrestling. Walter Savage Landor. *Fr.* Gebir. EnRP
Tamburlaine the Great, *sels.* Christopher Marlowe.
  "Ah faire Zenocrate, divine Zenocrate," *fr.* Pt. I, Act V, sc. ii. AtBAP; NBE; PoEL-2; ViBoPo
  "And ride in triumph through Persepolis!" *fr.* Pt. I, Act II, sc. v. MyFE; TrGrPo; WHA
  "Black[e] is the beauty of the brightest day," *fr.* Pt. II, Act II, sc. iv. AtBAP; BoW; ViBoPo
  (Death of Zenocrate, The.) PoD
  (Divine Zenocrate.) WHA
  (To Entertain Divine Zenocrate.) ChTr
  "Disdains Zenocrate to live with me," *fr.* Pt. I, Act. I, sc. ii. ViBoPo
  (Tamburlaine to Zenocrate, *shorter sel.*) WHA
  Emperor of the Threefold World, *fr.* Pt. II, Act IV, sc. iii. TrGrPo
  (Bloody Conquests of Mighty Tamburlaine, The.) ChTr
  ("Forward, then, ye jades," *longer sel.*) ViBoPo
  Fair Is Too Foul an Epithet, *fr.* Pt. I, Act V, sc. ii. LiTB
  "I will with Engines never exercisde," *fr.* Pt. II, Act IV, sc. I. BrBE
  "Nature that framed us of four elements," *fr.* Pt. I, Act II, sc. vii. MyFE; PoEL-2; TrGrPo
  (Climbing after Knowledge.) EV-1
  (Perfect Bliss and Sole Felicity.) SeCePo
  Now Clear the Triple Region of the Air, *fr.* Pt. I, Act IV, sc. ii. TrGrPo
  Rudiments of War, *fr.* Pt. II, Act III, sc. ii. KN
  Tamburlaine's Dying Speech to His Sons, *fr.* Pt. II, Act V, sc. iii. PoD
  Tamburlaine's Love. ShBV-4
  "Thirst of reign [*or* raigne] and sweetness of a crown, The," *fr.* Pt. I, Act II, sc. vii. NBE; ViBoPo
  (Ambition.) CoEV
  "Those wallèd garrisons will I subdue," *fr.* Pt. I, Act III, sc. iii. ViBoPo
  Vaunts of Tamburlaine, The, *sels. fr.* Pt. I *and* Pt. II. BCEP
  "Virgins, in vain you labour to prevent," *fr.* Pt. I, Act V, sc. i. MyFE
  "What is beauty, saith my sufferings, then?" *fr.* Pt. I, Act V, sc. ii. MyFE; ReaPo
  (Beauty.) TrGrPo
  (If All the Pens That Ever Poets Held.) ChTr
  (Immortal Flowers of Poesy.) LiA
  (Poet's Pen, The.) EV-1
  (Tamburlaine on Poetry.) CoEV
Tame Animals I Have Known. Nixon Waterman. BoN
Tame Duck. Kenneth Kaufman. PoeMoYo
Tame Hare, The. Norman Nicholson. FaBoMo
Tamed Deer, The. Spenser. *See* Amoretti, LXVII.
Tameless in his stately pride, along the lake of islands. The Loon. Alfred Billings Street. AA; BLA
Tamer and Hawk. Thom Gunn. NePoEA
Tamerlane. Poe. AmP; IAP
  "I have no words—alas!—to tell," *sel.* LO
Tamerton Church Tower, *sel.* Coventry Patmore.
  "Gaps of blue shrank fast in span, The," *fr.* I, 6. EnSW
Taming of Pegasus, The. Pindar, *tr. fr. Greek by* C. J. Billson. *Fr.* Olympian Odes, XIII. GrR
  (Bellerophon.) OxBG
Taming of the Shrew, The, *sel.* Shakespeare.
  "Why, then thou canst not break her to the lute?" *fr.* II, i. UnS
Tammuz. Rayner Heppenstall. WaP
Tampa Robins. Sidney Lanier. PoRL
Tampico. Grace Hazard Conkling. HBMV; NV; SBMV
"Tan Ta Ra, Cries Mars . . ." David Wagoner. NePoAm-2
Tanagra! think not I forget. Corinna [from Athens] to Tanagra. Walter Savage Landor. *Fr.* Pericles and Aspasia. BPN; OBEV (new ed.); OBRV; OBVV; TOP; ViBoPo
Tancred, *sels.* Laurence Dakin. CaP
  "All night I raced the moon," *fr.* II, i.
  "How gently sings my soul and whets its wings," *fr.* III, i.
  Song: "Peasant sun went crushing grapes, The," *fr.* I, i.
Tandaradei ("Under der Linden"). Walther von der Vogelweide, *tr. fr. German* by Ford Madox Ford. AWP; LiA; LiTW
  (Song: "Under the lime-tree," *tr. by* Thomas Lovell Beddoes.) ERP
  (Under the Lime Tree, *tr. by* Thomas Lovell Beddoes.) RO
  (Under the Linden, *tr. by* O. L. Oliver.) LyMA
Tang! tang! went the gong's wild roar. Night Quarters. Henry Howard Brownell. GN
Tanger-orange, squeeshit sherp. Tuscan Folk Songs, 12. *Unknown, tr. into Scottish by* Edwin Morgan. LyPI
Tangled briars intertwisting. Henrik Wergeland. *Fr.* The Jewess. AnNoLy
Tangled in nets. Fishers. Albert Reginald Gold. ChIP; OQP; QP-1
Tangled was I [*or* I was] in love's snare. The Lover Rejoiceth [*or* Love's Snare]. Sir Thomas Wyatt. BLV; LiTL; LoPS; OBSC; SiPS; TrGrPo; TuPP
Tanglewood. Francis Sweeney. JKCP (1955 ed.)
Tanist. James Stephens. OnYI
Tanka (I–VIII). Lewis Alexander. CDC
Tanka: "Blossoms of the plum." *Unknown, tr. fr. Japanese by* Eunice Tietjens. InP
Tanka: Cry of the Crane, The. Tsurayuki, *tr. fr. Japanese by* Arthur Waley. InP
Tanka: "In the evening/ Quiet of the country town." Noin Hoshi, *tr. fr. Japanese by* Nobuyuki Yuasa. Po
Tanka: "Men of valor, The." Akahito, *tr. fr. Japanese by* Arthur Waley. *Fr.* Manyo Shu. InP
  ("Men of valor, The.") AWP; PFE, *tr. wr. at. to* Curtis Hidden Page

Tanka: Reflection, A. Saigyo Hoshi, *tr. fr. Japanese by* Arthur Waley. InP
("Those ships which left.") AWP; LiTW
Tanned blonde, The. The Once-over. Paul Blackburn. NeAP
Tannhäuser, *sel.* Heine, *tr. fr. German by* Emma Lazarus.
Best Religion, The. TrJP
Tannhäuser. William Morton Payne. AA
Tantalus. Paulus Silentiarius, *tr. fr. Greek by* Dudley Fitts. LiTW
(Tantalos.) LyMA
Tantalus; Texas. *Unknown, at. to* Joaquin Miller. HBV
(Llano Estacado, The.) CoSo
Tantivy [*or* Tantivee]! tivy! tivy! tivy! high and low. Hunting Song [*or* Solon's Song]. Thomas D'Urfey. *Fr.* The Marriage-Hater Match'd. CEP; SeCL; SeEP
Tantramar Revisited. Sir Charles G. D. Roberts. BoCaPo; CaP; OCL; TwCV
Tantum Ergo Sacramentum. *Unknown, tr. fr. Latin.* WHL
Tao. Alfred Goldsworthy Bailey. CaP
Tao. *Unknown, at. to* Lao-tzu, *tr. fr. Chinese by* Walter Gorn Old. *Fr.* Tao Teh King. GrGo-2
Tao Teh King [*or* Tao Teh Ching], *sels. Unknown, at. to* Lao-tzu, *tr. fr. Chinese.*
Endless Self, *tr. by* Witter Bynner. OnPM
Gentle Touch, A, *tr. by* Witter Bynner. OnPM
He Who Feels Punctured, *tr. by* Witter Bynner. OnPM
"How can a man's life keep its course," *tr. by* Witter Bynner. WaKn
In a Land, *tr. by* Witter Bynner. OnPM
Knowledge Studies Others, *tr. by* Witter Bynner. OnPM
Lesson of Water, *tr. by* Witter Bynner. OnPM
Life, *tr. by* Witter Bynner. OnPM
Simple Way, The, *tr. by* Walter Gorn Old. Paradoxes. GrCo-2
Tao. GrCo-2
Way of the Sage, The. GrCo-2
Tao Teh Ching, *sels.* WhP
Those Who Know Do Not Tell, *tr. by* Witter Bynner. OnPM
To Be, *tr. by* Witter Bynner. OnPM
True Freedom, *tr. by* Witter Bynner. OnPM
Weapons of Evil, *tr. by* Lin Yutang. MaRV
Taoism and Buddhism. Po Chü-i, *tr. fr. Chinese by* Arthur Waley. TrCh
Taoist Monk, The. Tu Hsün Hao, *tr. fr. Chinese by* Henry H. Hart. OnPM
Taoist Song. Chi K'ang, *tr. fr. Chinese by* Arthur Waley. TrCh
Taoping. James Elroy Flecker. SoV
Tap-tap! Who is it? It is the Devil. Who Is It? José Gorostiza. TwSpPo
Tapering stars glint cool. Challengers. Alfred Dorn. GoYe
Tapers in the great God's hall, The. By Night. Philip Jerome Cleveland. BPP; MaRV
Tapestry, The. Stefan George, *tr. fr. German by* Carol North Valhope *and* Ernst Morwitz. LiTW
Tapestry Trees. William Morris. FaPON; MPB; OHIP
Tapestry Weavers, The. Anson G. Chester. BLPA; BLRP; PTA-1; WBLP
Tapping the rails as he went by. The Platelayer. W. W. Gibson. POTT
Taps. Lizette Woodworth Reese. DD; HH; OHIP
Taps at Twilight. Arthur Stringer. NeTW
Tapster, fille another ale! Drinking Song. *Unknown.* EnLit
Tar for All Weathers, The. Charles Dibdin. CG; OTPC (1923 ed.)
Tar Heel. Helen Bevington. NoCaPo (rev. ed.)
Tara. Thomas Moore. *See* Harp That Once through Tara's Halls, The.
Tara. *Unknown, tr. fr. Middle Irish by* Edward Gwynn. *Fr.* Dinnshenchas. OnYI
Tara Is Grass. *Unknown, tr. fr. Modern Irish by* Padraic Pearse. AnIL; AnIV
Tara today in this fateful hour. The Rune of St. Patrick. *Unknown.* MeRV
Tarahumara Herbs. Alfonso Reyes, *tr. fr. Spanish by* Samuel Beckett. AnMP
Tarantella. Hilaire Belloc. CH; FaBoCh; GoBC; LoGBV; MoBrPo; MoShBr; MoSiPe; MuP; NeMa; OBMV; OtMeF; PtOT; ShBV-2
Tarantula rattling at the lily's foot, The. O Carib Isle! Hart Crane. MoPo; NePA; OnHM
Tardy George. *Unknown.* GA, *abr.;* PAH
Tardy Spring. George Meredith. EV-5; OBEV (1st ed.)
Tarpauling Jacket. *Unknown.* OxBoLi
Tarpeia's grove; Tarpeia's traitor-tomb; capture of. Propertius. Elegies, IV, 4. LaP
Tarras Moon. James K. Baxter. AnNZ
Tarry a moment, happy feet. The Statues. Laurence Binyon. OBEV (new ed.); OBVV
Tarry Buccaneer, The. John Masefield. MCCG; TCPD
Tarry, shadow of my scornful treasure. Sister Juana Inés de la Cruz, *tr. fr. Spanish by* Samuel Beckett. AnMP
Tarry sweete love. *Unknown.* SeCSL
Tartar captive, A. The Captive. Chang Yu Shu. PoHN
Tartar Horse, A. Herbert S. Gorman. TBM
Tartars led in chains. The Prisoner. Po Chü-i, *tr. by* Arthur Waley. PoFr; SoV; TrCh
Tartary. Walter de la Mare. BMEP; CP; EPP; GaP; GoTP; HBMV; MW; PC; PoRh; PtOT; PYM; SP
(Lord of Tartary.) ShBV-1
Tartuffe, *sel.* Molière, *tr. fr. French by* Curtis Hidden Page. Men of Religion, *fr.* I, vi. GrCo-2
Tarye [*or* Tary] no lenger [*or* longer]; toward thyn herytage [*or* heritage]. Vox Ultima Crucis. John Lydgate. OBEV; OxBoCh; StJW
Task, The. Robert Bhain Campbell. MoPo
Task, The, *sels.* William Cowper.
Bastille, The, *abr., fr.* V. RO
City and Country Life, *fr.* I. CoBE
Discipline in Education, *fr.* II. CoBE
England, *fr.* II. BHV; CoEV; EV-3; FiP, *shorter sel.;* LPS-2, *abr.;* OBEC; TOP
("England, with all thy faults, I love thee still," 9 *ll.*) BrBE
(Love of England.) LoBV
Flowering Shrubs, *fr.* VI. RO
"For I have lov'd the rural walk through lanes, *fr.* I. EnRP
(Rural Walk, The.) TOP
Freeman, The, *fr.* V. LPS-2
Garden, The, III. CEP; EiPP
God Made the Country, *fr.* I. FiP; NBE; PoEL-3
("God made the country, and man made the town.") AnFE
(Town and Country.) FaBoEn
"He is the happy man, whose life ev'n now," *fr.* VI. BrBE
(Happy Man, The.) LPS-3
Heedless Cruelty, *fr.* VI. BCEP
(Humanity.) LPS-3
"I was a striken deer, that left the herd," *fr.* III. BrBE; EnRP; LEAP; MaRV; OAEP; OxBoCh
(Dreams, Empty Dreams.) BHV
(Self-Portrait.) CoBE
(Stricken Deer, The.) FiP; LoBV, *longer sel.;* RO, *longer sel., abr.*
(Sum of Life, The.) LPS-3
Landscape, *fr.* I. CoBE
Nature and God, *fr.* I. CoBE
"Nor rural sights alone, but rural sounds," *fr.* I. BrBE
"Now roves the eye," *fr.* I. EnSW
"Now stir the fire, and close the shutters fast," *fr.* IV. LEAP
"Oh for a lodge in some vast wilderness," *fr.* II. EnRP; EPP; OAEP, *longer sel.*
(Slavery.) CoBE; LPS-2
Poetic Pains, *fr.* II. FiP
(Poetry; Satire and Pulpit.) CoBE
Postman, The, *fr.* IV. CoBE; CoEV
(Post-Boy, The.) FiP
Preachers; the True vs. the Insincere, *fr.* II. MaRV
Robin in Winter, The, *fr.* VI. RO
Science and Prayer, *fr.* III. RO
"Shaggy, and lean, and shrewd, with pointed ears," *fr.* V. AlDL
(Woodman's Dog, The.) BoTP; OTPC (1946 ed.); PCD; PCH
Slaves Cannot Breathe in England, 7 *ll. fr.* II. OBEC
(Time-Piece, The.) SDH
Sofa, The, I. CEP; OAEP, *abr.*
"There is in souls a sympathy with sounds," *fr.* VI. BrBE
"There often wanders one, whom better days," *fr.* I. EPP
Time-Piece, The, II. BEL
True Preacher, The, *fr.* II. MaRV
"Whose freedom is by suff'rance, and at will," *fr.* V. EnRP; PoFr
Winter, *fr.* IV. OBEC
("Oh Winter, ruler of th' inverted year," *longer sel.*) TyEnPo
Winter Evening ("Come, Evening"), *fr.* IV. CoBE
(Evening.) OBEC
Winter Evening, The ("Hark! 'tis the twanging horn"), IV. EiPP; EnLi-2; EnLit; EV-3, *sel.;* OAEP; SeCePo, *sel.;* TOP, *sel.*
Winter Morning Walk, The, *fr.* V. PoEL-3
("'Tis morning; and the sun, with ruddy orb.") EnSW; EPP
(Winter Morning, *abr.*) LPS-2
Winter Walk at Noon, The, *fr.* VI. EV-3
("Night was winter in his roughest mood, The.") BrBE; EnRP; EnSW; NBE
(Winter Noon, *abr.*) LPS-2
(Winter Scene.) OBEC
Wisdom ("Knowledge and wisdom, far from being one"), *fr.* VI. MaRV
Task, The. Ruth Pitter. MoBrPo; TrGrPo (1942 ed.)
Task That Is Given to You, The. Edwin Markham. WBLP
Tasker Norcross. E. A. Robinson. ChMo; CMP

Tasks in Hours of Insight Willed. Matthew Arnold. *Fr.* Morality. GrCo-1
(Morality, *st.* 1.) BLP; MaRV, *sts.* 1-2
(We Cannot Kindle.) OQP; QP-2
Taste. Thomas Campbell. *Fr.* Valedictory Stanza to Kemble. BCEP
Taste and Spirit. Christopher Anstey. *Fr.* The New Bath Guide. CEP
Taste, like the silent dial's power. Taste. Thomas Campbell. *Fr.* Valedictory Stanza to Kemble. BCEP
Taste of Prayer, The. Ralph W. Seager. TrPWD
Tasting the Earth. James Oppenheim. BAP; MAP; MoAmPo (1942 ed.); PFY; TBM; TCPD
Tattered Flag, The. James Buckham. FOAH
Tattered outlaw of the earth, The. The Donkey. G. K. Chesterton. BLV; BMEP; CBOV; HBVY; MBP; MM; PIAE; POT; TCEP; TCPD; TOP; WGRP; WP
Tattoo. Wallace Stevens. AnFE; APA; CoAnAm; LiTA; NP
Tattoo beats, the lights are gone, The. My Wife and Child. Henry R. Jackson. LPS-2
Tattooed. William Plomer. ChMP
Tattooed Man, The. Harry B. Smith. *Fr.* The Idol's Eye. InMe; LauV
Tatyana's Letter to Onegin. Pushkin, *tr. fr. Russian by* Babette Deutsch. *Fr.* Eugene Onegin, III. TrRV
(Tatyana's Letter, *tr. by* Oliver Elton.) BoR
Taught by no priest, but by our beating hearts. Faith to Each Other. *Unknown.* OQP; QP-1
Taught from your artfull straines my faire. *Unknown.* SeCSL
Tavern. Edna St. Vincent Millay. GaP; OTPC (1946 ed.)
Tavern, The ("What the divel hast thou brought there?"). Shakespeare. King Henry the Fourth, Pt. II, Act II, sc. iv. LiA
Tawny are the leaves turned, but they still hold. Antique Harvesters. John Crowe Ransom. AnFE; APA; CoAnAm; CoBMV; CrMA; FaBoEn; InPo; MAP; MM; MoAB; MoAmPo; MOAP; OxBA; WoL
Tawny gleam in the sunlight, A. The First Robin. Lilian Leveridge. CaP; OCL
Tawny in a pasture by the true sea. The Forgotten Rock. Richard Eberhart. NePA
Tax-Gatherer, The. John Banister Tabb. GN; UTS
Tax not the royal saint with vain expense. Inside of [*or* Within] King's College Chapel, Cambridge. Wordsworth. *Fr.* Ecclesiastical Sonnets. BPN; CBE; EM-2; EmBrPo; EnLi-2; EnLP; EnRP; EPN; ES; GEPC; GoBC; GTBS; GTBS-D; GTBS-W; GTSE; GTSL; MaRV; OAEP; OBRV; OxBoCh
Taxes. Tu Hsün Hao, *tr. fr. Chinese by* Henry H. Hart. OnPM
Taxi, The. Amy Lowell. AV; MAP; MoAmPo
Taxis. Rachel Field. FaPON; GFA; GoBP; MPB; PoRh; StVeCh (1940 ed.); TiPo
Tay Toy Babilarde Arondelle. Pierre de Ronsard, *tr. fr. French by* Jonathan Price. PoN
Taylor's Song. Björnstjerne Björnson, *tr. fr. Norwegian by* Charles W. Stork. *Fr.* Marie Stuart. AnNoLy
Tcheliabtraktrostroi Waltz, *sel.* Louis Aragon, *tr. fr. French by* Nancy Cunard.
"This is an ancient waltz." MiFP
Tchirek Song. Altun, *tr. fr. Chinese by* Arthur Waley. TrCh
Te Deum. Charles Reznikoff. TrJP
Te Deum Laudamus. *Unknown, tr. fr. Latin.* MaRV; WGRP; WHL, *sl. diff. tr.*
(Te Deum, The, *tr. by* Dryden.) AWP; JAWP; OuHeWo; WBP
Te Deum of the Commonplace, A. John Oxenham. *See* Little Te Deum of the Commonplace, A.
"Te Judice." Frederick George Scott. PeCV
Te Laudamus, Te Dominum. *Unknown.* AnEC
Te Martyrum Candidatus. Lionel Johnson. ACP; CAW; GTIV; HBV; JKCP; MuP; OBMV; OxBoCh; PoLi; TIP
Te-whit! te-whit! [*or* To-whit! to-whit!] te-whee!/ Will you listen to me? Who Stole the Bird's Nest? Lydia Maria Child. OTPC; PRWS; PTA-2; SAS
Tea. Jacqueline Embry. HBMV; YaD
Tea, The. Tom Hood. PA
Tea. Dorothy E. Reid. PFE
Tea at the Palaz of Hoon. Wallace Stevens. FaBoMo; NP
Tea Flowers. Rito, *tr. fr. Japanese by* William N. Porter. MPB
Tea of the dead/ Eyelid that shuts life away from us. Service. Eduardo Anguita. AnCL
Tea Party. Aileen Fisher. GoBP
Tea-Party, A [*or* The]. Kate Greenaway. MPB; OTPC; PPL
("In the pleasant green garden.") TiPo (1952 ed.)
Tea-rose tea-gown, etc., The. Hugh Selwyn Mauberley, III. Ezra Pound. CoBMV; CoV; LiTA; LiTM (rev. ed.); MoPo; OnAP
Tea, The! The tea! The beef, beef-tea! The Tea. Tom Hood. PA
Tea Trader, The. Daniel Henderson. PFE
Tea-Tree and the Lyrebird, The. Roland Robinson. NeLNL
Teach Me! Christian Richardt, *tr. fr. Danish by* Charles W. Stork. BoDS
Teach me, Father, how to go. A Prayer. Edwin Markham. BOL; BoTP; BPP; DD; HBMV; HBVY; MaRV; MW; NLK; OTPC (1946 ed.); PGD; PoRL; POT; PoTo; PraP; QS; RG; StVeCh; TrPWD; TSW; TSWC; WGRP
Teach me, life. Only the Heart. Marjorie Freeman Campbell. CaP
Teach me, my God and King. The Elixir. George Herbert. AEV; BCEP; BLV; BoLiVe; BoTP; FaBoCh; GN; GrCo-1; LoGBV; MaRV; OHIP; PCH; SeCV-1; TrGrPo; WGRP; WP
Teach me, stars, in beauty. Teach Me! Christian Richardt. BoDS
Teach me the ritual that runs beyond. Worship. Robert Whitaker. TrPWD
Teach me the secret of thy loveliness. To a Wind Flower. Madison Cawein. AA; ADAH; HBV; OBAV
Teach Me to Live. *Unknown.* PraP
(Harder Task, The.) BLRP; MaRV
Teach me to love? Go teach thy self more wit. The Prophet. Abraham Cowley. BLV; TrGrPo
Teach me your mood, O patient stars! Quatrains, 1. Emerson. *Fr.* Fragments on the Poet. CBOV
Teach not thy parent's mother to extract. *Unknown.* WhC
Teach the child to pray to the blue waves. The Child's Prayer. Robert de Montesquiou-Fezensac. CAW
Teach the Rover. *At. to* Benjamin Franklin. *See* Downfall of Piracy, The.
Teach Us to Die. Arthur Penrhyn Stanley. VA
Teach Us to Mark This, God. Franz Werfel, *tr. fr. German by* Jacob Sloan. TrJP
Teach you French? I will, my dear! French with a Master. Theodore Tilton. PR
Teacher, The. Leslie Pinckney Hill. BANP; GrCo-1; MaRV; PoNe; PraP; TrPWD
Teacher, The. Sister Monica. PraNu
Teacher, The. Hildegarde Hoyt Swift. ChIP; MaRV; OQP; QP-1
Teacher, The. Annette Wynne. GaP
Teacher, The. Virginia Brady Young. GoYe
Teacher should impart what's true, A. Flower for a Professor's Garden of Verses. Irwin Edman. InMe
Teachers, The. C. V. Pilcher. OQP; QP-2
Teacher's Dream, The. William Henry Venable. BeLS; PTA-1
Teacher's "If," The. R. J. Gale. PTA-2
Teacher's Prayer, The. "Gabriela Mistral," *tr. fr. Spanish by* James H. McLean. MaRV
Teacher's Prayer, The. Norman E. Richardson. PraP
Teacher's Prayer, The. Nancy Byrd Turner. PraP
Teaching of Mohammed, The. Mohammed, *tr. fr. Arabic by* J. M. Rodwell. *Fr.* The Koran. WoL
Teak Forest, The, *br. sel.* "Laurence Hope."
Wisdom? OtMeF
Teams, The. Henry Lawson. BoAu; NeLNL
Teamster's Farewell, A. Carl Sandburg. CoBA
Teamster's Song, *with music. Unknown.* TrAS
Teapot Dragon, The. Rupert Sargent Holland. OTPC; UTS
Tear, The. Richard Crashaw. EnLi-1; GTBS-W; LiTB; OAEP; UnPo
Tear, A. Austin Dobson. *Fr.* Rose-Leaves. BPN
Tear, The. Kristján Jónsson, *tr. fr. Icelandic by* Jakobina Johnson. IcP
Tear, The. Ramón López Velarde, *tr. fr. Spanish by* Samuel Beckett. AnMP
Tear. Arthur Rimbaud, *tr. fr. French by* Joseph Bennett. AnFP
Tear, A. Samuel Rogers. *See* On a Tear.
Tear bedews my Delia's eye, A. The Kid. William Shenstone. OTPC (1923 ed.)
Tear down the Ivory Tower! Bring Torches. A. M. Stephen. CaP
Tear Down the Walls! Edgar Cooper Mason. OQP; QP-2
Tear Is an Intellectual Thing, A. Blake. *Fr.* The Grey Monk. BCEP
("But vain the sword and vain the bow.") LEAP
Tear out my tongue: I shall still have hands. The Forest. Paul Zech. OnPM
Tear was in her eye, A. Three Rimas, 3. Gustavo Adolfo Bécquer. *Fr.* Rimas. LiTW
Teares does not spare. *Unknown.* SeCSL
Tearin' Out-a Wilderness, *with music. Unknown.* ABF
Tears. Elizabeth Barrett Browning. OQP; PC; PFE; QP-2; TCAP
Tears. George Rostrevor Hamilton. POTE
Tears. Huang Pien, *tr. fr. Chinese by* Henry H. Hart. PoHN
Tears. Jami, *tr. fr. Persian by* Stephen Weston PeP
Tears. Khansa, *tr. fr. Arabic by* R. A. Nicholson. AWP; JAWP; WBP
Tears. Lizette Woodworth Reese. AA; BAP; BLP; BLV; CBOV; CP; HBV; HBVY; InP; LBMV; LEAP; LS;

MAP; MaRV; MCCG; MM; MoAmPo; NeMA; OBAV; OQP; PC; PFY; PYM; QP-2; SPP; TCPD; TreFS; VOD; WGRP; WHA
Tears. Johan Ludvig Runeberg, *tr. fr. Swedish by* Charles W. Stork. AnSL
Tears. Edith Sitwell. MoPo
Tears. Edward Thomas. LiTB; MoPW; PoE
Tears. Feodor Ivanovich Tyutchev, *tr. fr. Russian by* Babette Deutsch. OnPM; TrRV
Tears. *Unknown. See* Weep You No More, Sad Fountains.
Tears. Paul Verlaine. *See* Il pleut doucement sur la ville.
Tears. Walt Whitman. AnAmPo; IAP; LA; MOAP; NePA
Tears against the Moon. Thomas Walsh. CAW
Tears and Rain. Paul Verlaine. *See* Il pleut doucement sur la ville.
Tears and Song. *Unknown, tr. fr. Spanish by* Havelock Ellis. OnPM
Tears Cost Her Nothing Anyway. Konstantin Simonov, *tr. fr. Russian by* Frances Cornford. BoRS
Tears, ere thy death, for many a one I shed. Tears. Khansa. AWP; JAWP; WBP
Tears fall in my heart, The. Tears. Paul Verlaine, *tr. by* Alan Conder. TrFP
Tears Fall within Mine Heart. Paul Verlaine. *See* Il pleut doucement sur la ville.
Tears Flow in My Heart. Paul Verlaine. *See* Il pleut doucement sur la ville.
Tears, Flow No More. Lord Herbert of Cherbury. AtBAP; ElL; OBS
Tears for my lady dead. Heliodora [*or* Heliodore Dead]. Meleager. OxBG; VA
Tears for Sale. Leonora Speyer. HBMV
Tears, human tears, that pour forth beyond telling. Tears. Feodor Ivanovich Tyutchev. OnPM; TrRV
Tears, Idle Tears [I Know Not What They Mean]. Tennyson. *Fr.* The Princess, Pt. IV. AnFE; AtBAP; BEL; BLV; BMEP; BoLiVe; BPN; EG; EM-2; EnL; EnLi-2; EnLit; EPN; EV-5; FaFP; FiP; GEPC; GTBS; GTBS-W; GTML; GTSL; HBV; InvP; LEAP; LiTB; LiTG; MaPo; MCCG; NeHB; OBVV; PC; PG (1945 ed.); PIR; PoE; PoEL-5; PoeMoYo; PoFS; PoVP; PYM; REAL; ShBV-4; TCEP; TreF; TrGrPo; TwHP; TyEnPo; UnPo; VA; ViBoPo; ViPP; WHA
(Days That Are No More, The.) LiA
(Lyrics from "The Princess.") OuHeWo
(Retrospection.) LPS-1
(Song: "Tears, Idle tears, I know not what they mean.") CoEV; FaBoEn; TOP
(Songs from "The Princess.") AWP; EmBrPo; InPo; JAWP; MotAn; OAEP; SeCeV; ViPo; VLEP; WBP
Tears, idle tears! Ah, who shall bid us weep. Alfred Tennyson. Wilfrid Scawen Blunt. PtP; VLEP
Tears in Spring. William Ellery Channing. AA; LBAP
Tears in the eyes of the surgeon. To My Friends. Peter De Vries. FiBHP
Tears, long-stayed, that well. Rain at Night. Helen Walker Homan. JKCP (1955 ed.)
Tears of a Muse in America, The. F. T. Prince. FaBoMo
Tears of Amynta, The, for the Death of Damon. Dryden. MaPo
Tears of Araxes, The. Raphael Patkanian, *tr. fr. Armenian by* Alice Stone Blackwell. ArmLP
Tears of Fancy, The, *sels.* Thomas Watson.
"Each tree did boast the wished spring-time's pride." TuPP
"I saw the object of my pining thought." TuPP
(Sonnet.) ElL
"In clouds she shines, and so obscurely shineth." TuPP
Tears of Fear, The. Paulus Silentiarius, *tr. fr. Greek by* Sir William Marris. GrL; OxBG
Tears of Harlequin, The. Theodosia Garrison. LBMV
Tears of Khorassan, The. Anvari, *tr. fr. Persian by* E. H. Palmer. PeP
Tears of Mary, The. Theodosia Garrison. BPP
Tears of Peace, The. George Chapman. *See* Euthymiae Raptus; or, The Teares of Peace.
Tears of Scotland, The. Tobias Smollett. CEP; EBSV; OBEC
Tears of the Poplars, The. Edith M. Thomas. AA; AnAmPo; LA; LEAP
Tears of the widower, when he sees. In Memoriam A. H. H., XIII. Tennyson. BPN; EmBrPo; EnLi-2; EPN; GEPC; ViPo; VLEP
Tears of the World. Mu'tamid, King of Seville, *tr. fr. Arabic by* Dulcie L. Smith. AWP
Tears on my pillow—who has wept. Tears against the Moon. Thomas Walsh. CAW
Tears on the Death of Meliades, *sel.* William Drummond of Hawthornden.
Lament: "Chaste maids which haunt fair Aganippe's well." LoBV
Tears pouring from the [*or* this] face of stone. The Vase of Tears. Stephen Spender. AtBAP; LO; POTE
Tears! tears! tears! Tears. Walt Whitman. AnAmPo; IAP; LA; MOAP; NePA
Tears that never quite touch earth. White Violets. Benjamin R. C. Low. HBMV
Tears that you spill, clown David, crouched by rock. To Dafydd Coed Mourning His Mountain-broken dog. Brenda Chamberlain. MoWP
Tears through the earth I send you, Heliodora. To Heliodora, Dead. Meleager, *tr. fr. Greek by* L. R. Lind. LiTW
Tears to thee even beneath the earth, my Heliodora. Meleager, *tr. fr. Greek by* H. N. Couch. GrPo
Tears will betray all pride, but when ye mourn him. Parnell [*or* Parnell's Memory]. Thomas Kettle. ACP; AnIV; JKCP (1926 ed.)
Teased and titillated by the need. Beyond Biology. Robert Francis. NePoAm
Technique. Burnham Eaton. GoYe
Technique. Langdon Elwyn Mitchell. *Fr.* To a Writer of the Day. AA
Technogamia, *sels.* Barten Holyday.
Song: "O harmless feast." ElL
"Tobacco's a musician." TuPP
Tecmessa. Sophocles, *tr. fr. Greek by* Robert Whitelaw. *Fr.* Ajax. GrR
Tecmessa's Fruitless Plea. Sophocles, *tr. fr. Greek by* Robert Whitelaw. *Fr.* Ajax. GrR
Tecumseh, *sels.* Charles Mair.
Enter General Brock and Lefroy, *fr.* IV, vi. CPG
Buffalo Herds. VA
"Tell me more of those unrivaled wastes." CaP; OCL
"He comes! Yohewah! the Great Spirit, comes," *fr.* V, ii. PeCV
("Once we were strong.") PeCV
(Tecumseh to General Harrison.) CPG
Iena's Song. VA
"Once all this mighty continent was ours," *fr.* II, iv. BoCaPo
"There was a time on this fair continent," *fr.* I, ii. BoCaPo
"This region is as lavish," *fr.* II, i. CPG
(Lefroy in the Forest, *abr.*) VA
"We left the silent forest," *fr.* IV, vi. BoCaPo
Tecumseh and the Eagles. Bliss Carman. PoFr
Tecumseh to General Harrison. Charles Mair. *Fr.* Tecumseh, II, iv. CPG
("Once all this mighty continent was ours.") BoCaPo
("Once we were strong.") PeCV
Ted Birkett. August Derleth. DaM
Teddy unt Me unt Gott. *Unknown.* BLPA
Tee Roo, *with music. Unknown. See* Farmer's Curst Wife, The.
Teeming city, full of dreams, where in broad. The Seven Old Men. Baudelaire. AnFP
Teeming the host, the ash-tree budding. Tercets. Llywarch Hen. LiTW
Teemothy Hatch. Wilson MacDonald. WhC
Teeney and Weeney together are going. Green Grass and White Milk. Winifred Welles. TiPo
Teeny Cow, The. *Unknown. See* Father Grumble.
Teeth Called Straight, The. Fairfax Downey. LauV
Teeth you see up here, The. Oisin. *Unknown.* KiLC
Teetotal? Theognis, *tr. fr. Greek by* J. M. Edmonds. GrR
Tegea. Simonides, *tr. fr. Greek by* T. F. Higham. GrL; OxBG
Tegnér's Drapa. Esaias Tegnér, *tr. fr. Swedish by* Longfellow. TCAP
Telegram. William Wise. TiPo (1959 ed.)
Telegraph, The. Annette Wynne. GFA
Telegraph Pole. Enrique Bustamante y Ballivián, *tr. fr. Spanish by* Muna Lee. AnCL
Telemachus Finds His Father. Homer. *See* Reunion of Ulysses and Telemachus.
Telephone, The. Hilaire Belloc. MoVE
Telephone, The. Robert Frost. AnFE; APA; CoAnAm; HBV; OBAV
Telephone Girl's Prayer, The. Oliver Herford. LauV
Telephone Message, A. *Unknown.* PEOR
Telephone Pole, The. Karel van den Oever, *tr. fr. Dutch by* Adriaan J. Barnouw. OnPM
Telescope, The. J. C. Hall. HaMV
Tell all the truth but tell it slant. Emily Dickinson. LiTA; LiTM; MaPo; NePA
Tell All the World. Harry Kemp. HBMV; NLK
Tell Forth His Fame. *Unknown.* BePJ
Tell her I love/ she will remember me. Poems [*or* Stanzas] for My Daughter. Horace Gregory. MAP; MoAmPo; MoVE; TriL
Tell Her So. *Unknown.* PoToHe (new ed.)
Tell him it's all [*or* the tale is] a lie. A Learned Mistress. *Unknown.* KiLC; OBMV
Tell Him, O Night. *Unknown, tr. fr. Arabic by* E. Powys Mathers. *Fr.* The Thousand and One Nights. AWP; LiTW
Tell Him So. James Arthur Edgerton. MaRV
Tell Him So. *Unknown.* BLPA; WBLP
Tell him the tale is a lie! *See* Tell him it's all a lie.
Tell hir he that sent hir this. *Unknown.* SeCSL

Tell it again in strong tones. Nature Cure. Jean Starr Untermeyer. PC
Tell It to God. Dorothy Dix Porges. PraP
Tell Jesus. *Unknown.* BePJ
Tell Me. Edith M. Thomas. *Fr.* The Inverted Torch. AA
(Cure-all.) TBM
(Lyric: "Tell me, is there sovereign cure.") OBAV
Tell me a story, Father, please do. Request Number. G. N. Sprod. FiBHP
Tell Me a Word. D. H. Lawrence. SiTL
Tell me about that harvest field. Real Property. Harold Monro. AlDL; ChMo; CMP; MoP; ReTS; TCEP; TCPD; WP
Tell me, and wouldst thou span the ends of earth. Palladas, *tr. fr. Greek by* F. A. Wright. GrPo
"Tell me, Belinda, prithee do." Celia and Belinda. Colley Cibber. *Fr.* Woman's Wit. SeCL
Tell me, daughter, my lovely daughter. Cossante. Pero Meogo. LyMA
Tell me, dear Garcilaso—thou. On the Death of Garcilaso. Juan Boscán Almogáver. BoFr
Tell me, dear, in terms laconic. The Conservative Shepherd to His Love. Jack D'Arcy. InMe
Tell Me, Dearest, What Is Love? 3 *sts.* Beaumont *and* Fletcher. *Fr.* The Captain, II, ii. ElL; SeEP; ViBoPo
(What Is Love?) HBV
Tell me, dearest, what is love? 2 *sts.* Beaumont *and* Fletcher. *Fr.* The Knight of the Burning Pestle, III, i. ElSeCe
Tell me, do you remember. Pedro Salinas, *tr. fr. Spanish by* Eleanor L. Turnbull. CoSP
Tell me, Echo fair! Lover and Echo. Carrol O'Daly. OnYI
Tell me, Fancy, sweetest child. Fancy's Home. W. H. Davies. AtBAP; ChMo; CMP; POTT
"Tell me, good dog, whose tomb you guard so well." The Tomb of Diogenes. *Unknown.* AWP; JAWP; OnPM; WBP
Tell me, good Hobbinoll, what garres thee greete? April[l]. Spenser. *Fr.* The Shepheardes Calender. EnLi-1; PoEL-1; ReEn; ReIE; SiCE
Tell me, hair of her head, where I should lie. The Hair's Breadth. Nicholas Moore. NeBP
"Tell me his name and you are free." Sam Davis. John Trotwood Moore. SPP
"Tell me honestly, Marcus, tell me, please do." Martial, *tr. fr. Latin by* Robert R. Schnorr. Epigrams, VIII, 76. LaP
Tell me in what far country is. Ballade of Fair Ladies of Olden Time. Villon. TrFP
Tell me is there anything lovelier. Greenness. Angelina Weld Grimké. CDC
Tell me, is there sovereign cure. Tell Me [*or* Cure-all *or* Lyric]. Edith M. Thomas. *Fr.* The Inverted Torch. AA; OBAV; TBM
Tell Me, Lydia ("Cum tu, Lydia"). Horace, *tr. fr. Latin by* William Boscawen. Odes, I, 13. OnPM
Tell me, maiden, dost thou use. Lines to Ellen. Emerson. IAP
Tell me more of those unrivalled wastes. Charles Mair. *Fr.* Tecumseh, IV, vi. CaP; OCL
Tell me, Muse, of that man, so ready at need, who wandered far and wide. Homer. *Fr.* The Odyssey, I. GrL
Tell Me, My Heart, if This Be Love. George Lyttelton. *See* Song: "When Delia on the plain appears."
Tell me, my patient friends—awaiters of messages. Speech to a Crowd. Archibald MacLeish. MoAB; MoAmPo; NePA
Tell Me No More. William Drummond of Hawthornden. TrGrPo
Tell Me No More. Henry King. SeCL
(Sonnet: "Tell me no more how fair she is.") AEV; ElSeCe; EnLoPo; EPS (1942 ed.); MeLP; MePo; NBE; OBS; SeEP; ViBoPo
("Tell me no more how fair she is.") EG
(That Distant Bliss.) TrGrPo
Tell me no more I am deceived. Song. Congreve. ALV
Tell me no more of gives of brasse. *Unknown.* SeCSL
Tell me no more of minds embracing minds. No Platonic [*or* Platonique] Love. William Cartwright. ElSeCe; InvP; LiTB; PoEL-2; SiTL
Tell me no more that I am one. Gifts. Viola Gerard Garvin. AlDL
Tell me noe more tis love. *Unknown.* SeCSL
Tell Me Not Here [It Needs Not Saying]. A. E. Housman. Last Poems, XL. BMEP; ChMP; CoBMV; FaBoEn; GTBS-D; LiTM; MaPo; MM; MoPo; MoPW; MoVE; TwCV
Tell me not I my time misspend. Song. *At. to* Sir John Eaton *and to* Phillip King. SeCL
Tell me not, in idle jingle, *parody.* A Psalm of Life. Phoebe Cary. PA
Tell me not, in mournful numbers. A Psalm of Life. Longfellow. AA; AnNE; BAP; BAV; BHV; CoBA; FaBoBe; HBV; HBVY; IAP; LEAP; LPS-3; MaRV; NeHB; OHFP; PECK; PIR; PreP; PTA-1; PYM; TCAP; TreF; TSWC; TVSH; UnPo; WBLP; YaD
Tell me not, O Soul that slumbers, *parody.* A Psalm of Life. Andrew Lang. CenHV
Tell me not of a face that's fair. The Resolve. Alexander Brome. EG; ElSeCe; LiTL; LO; OBEV; SeCL
Tell me not of joy: there's none. The Dead Sparrow. William Cartwright. CH; LO
Tell Me Not of Morrows, Sweet. Augusta Davies Webster. VA
Tell me not, sweet, I am unkind[e]. To Lucasta, [on] Going to the Wars [*or* Warres]. Richard Lovelace. AEV; ALV; AnFE; AtBAP; AWP; BBV (1923 ed.); BCEP; BEL; BLV; BTP; CaAE; CBE; CBOV; CBPC; CenL; CoBE; CoEV; ElSeCe; EM-1; EnL; EnLi-1; EnLit; EnLoPo; EPP; EPS; ExPo; FaBoEn; FaFP; GTBS; GTBS-D; GTBS-W; GTSE; GTSL; HBV; HoPM; InPo; JAWP; KN; LEAP; LH; LiA; LiTB; LiTG; LiTL; LoBV; LoPo; LoPS; LPS-1; MCCG; MeLP; MePo; NeHB; OAEP; OBEV; OBS; OuHeWo; PG (1945 ed.); PIAE; PIR; Po; PoEL-3; PoRA; ReEn; SeCePo; SeCeV; SeCL; SeCV-1; SeEP; ShBV-3; TCEP; TOP; TreF; TrGrPo; TVSH; TwHP; UnPo (1st ed.); ViBoPo; WBP; WHA; WP
Tell me not the good and wise. And There Will I Be Buried. Thomas Davidson. BSV; EBSV
Tell me not what too well I know. On Catullus. Walter Savage Landor. EV-4; OBEV; PtP; TOP; ViBoPo
Tell Me Now. Wang Chi, *tr. fr. Chinese by* Arthur Waley. FaBoCh; LoGBV; TrCh
(What Should a Man Want?) OuHeWo
Tell me now in what hidden way is. The Ballad of Dead Ladies. Villon, *tr. by* Dante Gabriel Rossetti. ALV; ATP (1935 ed.); AWP; BEL; EnLi-2; EPP; ExPo; FaFP; GoBC; HBV; InP; JAWP; LiA; LO; OuHeWo; PIR; PoFS; PoRA; POTT; PoVP; PreP; TOP; VA; ViBoPo; ViP; ViPP; VLEP; WBP
"Tell me now, what should a man want." Tell Me Now [*or* What Should a Man Want?]. Wang Chi. FaBoCh; LoGBV; OuHeWo; TrCh
Tell me O great All-knowing God! Paucitatem Dierum Meorum Nuncia Mihi. David. William Habington. MeRV
Tell me, O Love, why Celia, smooth. The Cruel Mistress. William Hammond. SeCL
Tell me, Oh Muse (for thou, or none canst tell). The Power of Numbers. Abraham Cowley. *Fr.* Davideis. OBS
Tell me, O Muses, of the man of many devices. The Man of Many Devices. Homer. *Fr.* The Odyssey, I. LiA
Tell me, O Octopus, I begs. The Octopus. Ogden Nash. NePA; TiPo
Tell me, O Swan, your ancient tale. Songs of Kabir. Kabir. WGRP
Tell me, O tell, what kind of thing is wit. Ode: Of Wit [*or* Of Wit]. Abraham Cowley. CEP; MeLP; MePo; OAEP; OBS; ReEn; SeCV-1; SeEP
Tell me of love, sweet Love, who is thy sire? Fidessa, More Chaste than Kind, XLIII. Bartholomew Griffin. TuPP
Tell me of progress if you will. Mountain Air. John Galsworthy. OQP; QP-2
Tell me of that Treasure State. Montana. Charles C. Cohan. PoRL
Tell me one thing; why do you follow Jesus? Conversion. Andrew Young. *Fr.* Nicodemus. MaRV
Tell me Perigot, what shalbe the game. August. Spenser. *Fr.* The Shepheardes Calender. OAEP; ReEn
Tell me, Praise, and tell me, Love. Praise and Love. William Brighty Rands. OBVV
Tell me quickly the secret of your existence. I Would Know. Vicente Aleixandre. CoSP
Tell me, sages, what shadowy street. Reminder. Sherry Kane. BoHiPo
Tell me, shepherd, tell me, pray. Country Gods. Cometas. FaBoCh; LoGBV; OxBG
Tell Me, Smiling Child. Emily Brontë. *See* Tell Me, Tell Me, Smiling Child.
Tell me, some pitying angel, quickly say. The Blessed Virgin's Expostulation. Nahum Tate. ISi
Tell Me Some Way. Lizette Woodworth Reese. PG
Tell me, speak to me. Spanish Elegy. Luis Cernuda. CoSP
Tell me, sweetest one, where I may find you. The Fair Unknown. Poul Martin Møller. BoDS
"Tell me, tell me." The Galliass. Walter de la Mare. FaBoTw
Tell me, tell me, gentle Robin. The Cat and the Bird. George Canning. ChTr
Tell Me, Tell Me, Smiling Child. Emily Brontë. AlDL; OAEP
(Tell Me, Smiling Child.) EmBrPo
(Tell Me, Tell Me.) LoBV (1949 ed.); ViBoPo
Tell me, tell me the secret of your virgin heart. Song to a Dead Girl. Vicente Aleixandre. CoSP
Tell me that the snow is red. Belief. Ruth Fitch Bartlett. InMe
Tell me the old, old story. Katherine Hankey. OlF
Tell Me the Stories of Jesus. William Henry Parker. MaRV; OlF

Tell me the tales that to me were so dear. Long, Long Ago. Thomas Haynes Bayly. OlF; TreF
Tell me, Thou common Father,—tell me why. Not of This World. Bartolomé Leonardo de Argensola. OnPM
Tell me, thou skilful shepherd's swain. Sylvia [*or* A Roundelay]. Michael Drayton. *Fr.* The Shepherd's Garland, Eclogue IX. ElL; LoBV (1949 ed.)
Tell Me, Thou Soul of Her I Love. James Thomson. EBSV (Ode: "Tell me, thou soul of her I love.") OBEC
Tell me, thou Star whose wings of light. The World's Wanderers. Shelley. BEL; BPN; EmBrPo; EnLit; EPN; ERP; ViBoPo
Tell me today, when all my tides are gone. Sea Sonnet. Norma Lay. GoYe
Tell me, was Venus more beautiful. Venus Transiens. Amy Lowell. MM; NP; OBAV; SBMV
Tell me, what is a poet's thought? A Poet's Thought. "Barry Cornwall." VA
Tell Me, What Is Poetry. Jeanne Robert Foster. POT; PoTo
Tell me what is that only thing. Women's Longing. John Fletcher. *Fr.* Women Pleased. HBV
Tell me what is this innumerable throng. A Christmas Hymn. Richard Watson Gilder. CLS; MaRV; StJW
Tell me what sail the seas. Under the Stars. Wallace Rice. AA; MDAH; OBAV; OHIP
"Tell me what you're doing over here, John Gorham." John Gorham. E. A. Robinson. ChMo; CMP; MAP; MAPA; MoAB; MoAmPo; NP
Tell me, when shall these weary [*or* wearie] woes have [*or* haue] end? Amoretti, XXXVI. Spenser. AEV; PeBoSo
Tell me, where do you live? A Song of Ch'ang-kan. Ts'uei Hao. BoFr
Tell me, where doth whiteness grow. Whiteness, or Chastity. Joseph Beaumont. LiTL; LoBV
Tell Me Where Is Fancy Bred. Shakespeare. *Fr.* The Merchant of Venice, III, ii. AnFE; AtBAP; BEL; CBE; CH; EG; ElL; ElSeCe; EM-1; EnLi-1; EnLit; EPP; EV-1; FaPON; InPo; LiTB; LiTG; LO; OAEP; PIR; ReaPo; RiBV; SeCeV; SiCE; TOP; TwP; TyEnPo; ViBoPo; WHA
(Casket Song, A.) OBSC
(Fancy.) BLV; CBPC; TreFS; TrGrPo
(Love.) LPS-1; OBEV
(Madrigal: "Tell me where is fancy bred.") GTBS; GTBS-D; GTBS-W; GTSE
(Song: "Tell me where is fancy [*or* fancie] bred.") BoLiVe; BrBE; PoEL-2
(Where Is Fancy Bred.) PC
(Young Love.) GTSL
Tell me where thy lovely love is. Heine. *Fr.* Die Heimkehr. AWP
Tell me, whither do they go. The Vanished Fay. Bert Leston Taylor. FAOV
Tell me whither, maiden June. The Reaper. John Banister Tabb. ACP
Tell Me Why. Anacreon. *See* Coy Mistress, The.
Tell me, wide wandering soul, in all thy quest. But Once. Theodore Winthrop. AA
Tell me widow up there on the terrace. Woman from Samos. Alexandros Pallis. MoGP
Tell Me, Wight in the Broom. *Unknown, tr. fr. Middle English by* Mabel Van Duzee. MeEV
Tell me, ye nymphs, and tell me right. Pan and Daphnis. Glaucus. OxBG
Tell Me, Ye Wingèd Winds. Charles Mackay. LPS-2; VA (Inquiry, The.) PEOR
Tell me you/ That sing in the black-thorn. You That Sing in the Blackthorn [*or* Bird Song *or* The Unconscious]. Alfred Noyes. *Fr.* The Last Voyage. BLA; GoBC; MM; POTT
Tell Me, You Wandering Spirits [of the Air]. *Unknown.* OBS; SeCL; SeEP
"Tell me your name," I challenged Christ. The Bargain. Anna Bunston de Bary. MaRV
Tell me your secrets, pretty shell. Shell Secrets. *Unknown.* BoTP
Tell mee shepherd dost thou love? *Unknown.* SeCSL
Tell my priests, when I am gone. *Unknown.* WhC
Tell now, good kit, of three months' age, or less. The Kitten's Eclogue. Ruth Pitter. PoC
Tell, O Tell. Thomas Campion. *See* When Thou Must Home.
Tell of the lamp that witnessed Love's secret, Goddess, tell. Hero and Leander. Musaeus. GrPE
Tell old Bill, when [*or* before] he leaves home dis mornin'. Dis Mornin', Dis Evenin', So Soon [*or* Old Bill]. *Unknown.* ABF; AS
Tell Tale. *See* Telltale.
Tell, tell our fortune, Mirabel. Fortune for Mirabel. Horace Gregory. TwAmPo
Tell the Disciples. *Unknown* PSO
Tell the story to your sons. The Fight of the *Armstrong* Privateer. James Jeffrey Roche. PAH
Tell the tune his feet beat. A Refrain. Arthur Shearly Cripps. PoeT; TVSH
Tell them, I am, Jehovah said. Christopher Smart. *Fr.* A Song to David. BCEP; WGRP
Tell them in Lakedaimon, passer-by. At Thermopylae [*or* The Three Hundred]. Simonides. ChTr; GrL; LiA; OnPM; OxBG; WaaP; WoL
Tell them, O Sky-born, when I die. Farewell. Harry Kemp. HBMV; NLK
Tell them, though 'tis an awful thing to die. Epitaph on Mrs. William Mason. Thomas Gray. MeRV
Tell them to go away. Insomnia. Ethna MacCarthy. NeIP
Tell them, when you are home again. Love's Caution. W. H. Davies. ChMP
Tell this to ladies: how a hero man. Man without Sense of Direction. John Crowe Ransom. LiTM (rev. ed.); OxBA
Tell thou the world, when my bones lie whitening. The Nameless One. James Clarence Mangan. ACP; BCEP; CBOV; EPN; EV-4; GTBS; GTIV; GTSE; HBV; OBEV; TIP
"Tell us a story, old Robin Gray!" Prelude. Robert Southey. ERP
Tell us, tell us, holy shepherds. Flowers for the Altar. Digby Mackworth Dolben. GoBC
Tell us that love/ returns. Chorus for Survival. Horace Gregory. ChMo
Tell us, thou clear and heavenly tongue. The Star Song; a Carol to the King. Robert Herrick. GN; OxBoCh
"Tell Ye the Faint of Heart." Francis J. Rock. JKCP (1955 ed.)
Tell ye the king: the carven hall is fallen in decay. The Fallen Shrine. Delphic Oracle. OxBG
Tell you I chyll. John Skelton. *Fr.* The Tunning [*or* Tunnynge] of Elinour Rumming [*or* Elynour Rummynge]. PoFS; ReIE; SiTL; TrGrPo; TwHP
Tell you what I like the best. Knee-deep in June. James Whitcomb Riley. OHFP
Tell youth to play with wine and Love and never bear away the scars! Compensation. Ridgely Torrence. *Fr.* The House of a Hundred Lights. AA
Tell-a me who dat had a rod? Mone, Member, Mone. *Unknown.* ABF
Telling Fortunes. W. H. Davies. ChMo; CMP
Telling the Bees. Andrew Lang, *after the Greek.* VA
Telling the Bees. Lizette Woodworth Reese. AA; LEAP
Telling the Bees. Whittier. AmPP (3d ed.); AnNE; APW; AWP; BAV; CoBA; GBV (1952 ed.); HBV; HiLiAm; IAP; InP; InPo; LaNeLa; MOAP; PFY; PTA-1; TCAP; TOP
Telltale, The. *Unknown.* LPS-2
Tell-Tale Tag, The. Aristophanes, *tr. fr. Greek by* Benjamin Bickley Rogers. *Fr.* The Frogs. GrR
Tellus. William Reed Huntington. AA
Temair noblest of hills. Tara. *Unknown.* Fr. Dinnshenchas. OnYI
Temeraire, The. Herman Melville. APW; WaaP
Temora, *sel.* James Macpherson.
"Waves crowd away, The." BCEP
Temper, The. George Herbert. AtBAP; EPS (1942 ed.); MePo; OBS; OxBoCh; PoEL-2; PoFS; SeCL; WHA
Temper. *Unknown.* PoToHe (new ed.)
Temper, blood and speech divide. Tears. George Rostrevor Hamilton. POTE
Temper my spirit, O Lord. The Passionate Sword. Jean Starr Untermeyer. BAP; GrCo-2; HBMV; MaRV; QS; TrJP; TrPWD
Temperament. Martial, *tr. fr. Latin by* Addison. AWP; JAWP; WPB
(In All the Humors.) OnPM
(To a Capricious Friend.) BOHV
Temperance ("Wine taken with excess"). *Unknown.* ACP; CAW
Temperance and Virginity. Milton. *Fr.* Comus. OBS
Temperance, exercise, and air. To His Son. John Dyer. PrWP
Temperance Note; and Weather Prophecy. James Agee. *Fr.* Two Songs on the Economy of Abundance. MAP; MoAmPo
Temperance, or the Cheap Physician [*or* Physitian]. Richard Crashaw. LPS-2; SeCV-1
Temperate Drinking. Anacreon, *tr. fr.* Greek by Thomas Moore. OnPM
Tempest, The. Charles Cotton. SeCePo
Tempest, A. Emily Dickinson. MCCG
Tempest, The. James Thomas Fields. *See* Ballad of the Tempest.
Tempest, The. Mabuchi, *tr. fr. Japanese by* Asataro Miyamori. OnPM
Tempest, A. Sir Walter Scott. *Fr.* The Lord of the Isles, III. EV-4
Tempest, The, *sels.* Shakespeare.
Ariel's Song: "Come unto these yellow sands," *fr.* I, ii.

Tempest, The (*continued*)
CBE; EG; EV-1; FaBoCh; GN; LoBV; LoGBV; MCCG; MPB (1956 ed.); PCH; RAR; ThWaDe
("Come unto these yellow sands.") AEV; AnFE; AtBAP; BEL; BoTP; CH; ElL; EM-1; InPo; KN; OBSC; OTPC (1923 ed.); PoEL-2; SiCE; TOP; TwHP; ViBoPo
(Fairy Land.) BCEP; OBEV
(Fairy Life, The, 2.) GTSL
(Fairy Songs.) HBV
(Shakespeare's Fairies; They Dance and Play.) CBPC
(Song of Ariel.) CG
(Songs from "The Tempest." LEAP
Ariel's Song: "Full fathom five thy father lies," *fr.* I, ii. BoLiVe; CoEV; EG; EV-1; FaBoEn; GN; LoBV; PFE; SeCePo
(Ariel's Dirge.) ThWaDe
(Ditty: "Full fadom five thy father lies.") LiA
(Fairy Land.) BCEP; OBEV
("Full fathom five thy father lies.") AnFE; AtBAP; ATP; BEL; CaAE; CenL; ChTr; ElL; ElSeCe; EM-1; EnLi-1; ExPo; FaBoCh; GTSL; HoPM; InPo; KN; LiTB; LiTG; LoGBV; MaPo; OAEP; OBSC; OTPC; OuHeWo; PIR; PoEL-2; PoRA; ReaPo; SeCeV; ShBV-1; SiCE; TOP; TwHP; TyEnPo; ViBoPo; WHA
(Sea Dirge, A.) AnEnPo; BLV; CBOV; CBPC; CG; EPP; EtS; GTBS; GTBS-D; GTBS-W; GTSE; HBV; MCCG; TrGrPo
(Song: "Full fathom five thy father lies.") BrBE; NeHB
(Songs from the Plays.) AWP; JAWP; WBP
(Songs from "The Tempest.") LEAP; SG
Ariel's Song: "Where the bee sucks," *fr.* V, i. AnEnPo; CaAE; EG; EV-1; GN; HOAH; MCCG; PCD; PFE; RAR
(Ariel's Last Song.) CBE
(Fairy Land.) BCEP; OBEV
(Fairy Life, The, 1.) GTSL
(Fairy Songs.) HBV; HBVY; RIS
(Fairy's Life, A.) PCH
(Shakespeare's Fairies; Ariel Sings.) CBPC
(Songs from the Plays.) AWP; JAWP; WBP
(Songs from "The Tempest.") LEAP
("Where the bee sucks, there suck I.") AnFE; BEL; BoTP; CH; ElL; EM-1; EnLi-1; EnLit; EPP; InPo; KN; MPB; OBSC; OTPC; PIR; PoRh; ReaPo; SeCeV; SiCE; ThWaDe; TiPo; TOP; TyEnPo; UTS; ViBoPo; WHA
"Be not afeard; the isle is full of noises," *fr.* III, ii. AtBAP; UnS
(Caliban.) FiP
(Caliban on the Island.) CoEV
(To Dream Again.) TrGrPo
"Boatswain," I, i.
(From "The Tempest." SG
Brave New World, *fr.* V, i. TrGrPo
"Ceres, most bounteous lady, thy rich leas," *fr.* IV, i. AtBAP
"Had I plantation of this isle, my lord," *fr.* II, i. PoFr
"Hast thou which art but aire a touch, a feeling," *fr.* V, i. NBE
No More Dams I'll Make, *fr.* II, ii. ViBoPo
"Now I want/ Spirits to enforce, art to enchant," *fr.* Epilogue. MyFE
Our Revels Now Are Ended, *fr.* IV, i. GTBS-W; LEAP; LiTB; LiTG; MaRV; PG; PIR; ShBV-3; WHA
(Airy Nothings.) LPS-3
(Finale.) BCEP
(Grand Style, The.) LiA
(Our Little Life.) OQP; QP-1
(Prospero.) FiP
(Prospero Ends the Revels.) TreF
(Such Stuff as Dreams Are Made On.) EV-1, *sl. abr.*; PC; TrGrPo
Prospero's Epilogue. KN
(Epilogue: "Now my charmes are all ore-throwne.") NBE
Stephano's Song, *fr.* II, ii. SG; WhC
("Master, the swabber, the boatswain, and I, The.") InPo; ViBoPo
(None of Us Cared for Kate.) OnPM
"Where should this music be? I' the air, or the earth?" *fr.* I, ii. UnS
"Ye elves of hills, brooks, standing lakes, and groves," *fr.* V, i.
(Magic, *after* Ovid.) AWP; JAWP; WBP
(Shakespeare's Fairies; Some of Them.) CBPC
You Nymphs, Call'd Naiads. *fr.* IV, i. ViBoPo
Tempest, The. Marya Zaturenska. MoAmPo; TrGrPo (1942 ed.)
Tempest cracked on the theatre, A. Repetitions of a Young Captain. Wallace Stevens. WaP
Tempest on the great seaborders! A Storm at Sea. *Unknown.* AnIL; LyMA
Tempest on the plain of Lir. Storm at Sea. *Unknown.* KiLC
Tempest over and gone, the calm begun, The. Easter Even. Christina Rossetti. EOAH
Tempest without: within the mellow glow. Hands. W. W. Gibson. PFE; PoMa; VOD
Tempio di Venere. T. Sturge Moore. GTML
Temple, The. Congreve. *See* Among the Dead.
Temple, The. Lee Wilson Dodd. BAP
Temple. John Donne. OBS
(Jesus in the Temple.) StJW
Temple, The. Clifford Dyment. ChMP
Temple, A. Mnasalcas, *tr. fr. Greek by* W. H. D. Rouse. OxBG
Temple, The. Po Chü-i, *tr. fr. Chinese by* Arthur Waley. OBMV
Temple, The. Tennyson. OQP; QP-2
Temple, The. Tu Fu, *tr. fr. Chinese by* Chi Hwang Chu *and* Edna Worthley Underwood. OnPM
Temple Bar. Rose Fyleman. UTS
Temple Bells of Yün Sui, The. Yang Wan Li, *tr. fr. Chinese by* Henry H. Hart. PoHN
Temple Garlands. Agnes Mary Frances Robinson. HBV
Temple is clean, The. A Song of Always. Efraim Rosensweig. TiPo (1952 ed.)
Temple of Fame, The, *sels.* Pope.
Honest Fame. OBEC
Thick as the Bees. BeR
Temple of the Trees, The. J. D. C. Pellow. PGD
Temple of Venus, The. Spenser. *Fr.* The Faerie Queene, IV, 10. WHA
Temple Offering. Leslie Savage Clark. ChIP
Temple That Charged Admission, The. Issa, *tr. fr. Japanese by* Max Bickerton. PoFr
Temple to Friendship, A. Thomas Moore. BeLS; HBV; LPS-1; NeHB
Templeogue. Blanaid Salkeld. NeIP
Temples Built with Hands. Su T'ung-po, *tr. fr. Chinese by* Henry H. Hart. PoHN
Tempora Acta. "Owen Meredith." *Fr.* Babylonia. OBVV; VA
Tempt Me No More. C. Day Lewis. *Fr.* The Magnetic Mountain, XXIV. AnFE; MBP; MoAB; MoBrPo; OAEP (2d ed.); OBMV; PoFr; POTE
("Tempt me no more: for I.") CaAE; EnLit; NAMP
Tempt me not now; it is not wanted. Dissuasion. Evgeni Baratynsky. BoRS
Temptation. Winfred Ernest Garrison. ChIP
Temptation. Robert Herrick. LiTB
Temptation. Cathleen Keegan. Three Sonnets, I, II. MuM
Temptation. Vladislav Khodasevich, *tr. fr. Russian by* C. M. Bowra. BoR
Temptation. Oppian, *tr. fr. Greek by* Gilbert Highet. *Fr.* Halieutica. OxBG
Temptation. Dionysios Solomos, *tr. fr. Modern Greek by* Rae Dalven. *Fr.* The Free Besieged. MoGP
Temptation and Fall of Man, The. *Unknown, tr. fr. Anglo-Saxon by* Charles W. Kennedy. *Fr.* Genesis. AnOE
Temptation of St. Anthony, The. R. L. Gales, *ad. fr. Old French.* WP
Temptation of Sir Gawain, The. *Unknown. Fr.* Sir Gawain and the Green Knight. ACP
Tempted. Katharine Lee Bates. ChIP; StJW
Tempted. Edward Rowland Sill. AA
Tempus Edax Rerum. Henry Parrot. SiCE
Tempus Instat Floridum. *Unknown. See* Flowering Time.
Ten Acres, The. *Unknown, tr. fr. Chinese by* Bernhard Karlgren. *Fr.* Shi King. ChLP
Ten Brothers. *Unknown, ad. fr. Yiddish by* Louis Untermeyer. MaC
"Ten bucks, he's yours. That dog," said he. The Dog Salesman. J. Harvey Haggard. AlBD
Ten Commandments, The. Exodus, Bible, *O.T.* GrCo-1 (XIX: 1–XX: 21, *abr.*); OHFP (XX: 2–26); TreF (XX: 1–17); WBLP (XX: 2–26)
Ten Commandments, Seven Deadly Sins, and Five Wits. *Unknown.* ChTr
Ten Days Leave. W. D. Snodgrass. UnPo (3d ed.)
Ten Definitions of Poetry. Carl Sandburg. MAP; MoAmPo
Ten Lepers, The. Katharine Tynan. MaRV; StJW
Ten little children/ Dancing on the shore. Dancing on the Shore. M. M. Hutchinson. BoTP
Ten Little Christmas Trees. Rodney Bennett. BoTP
Ten Little Dicky-Birds. A. W. I. Baldwin. BoTP
Ten Little Indian Boys. M. M. Hutchinson. BoTP
Ten Little Injuns. *Unknown.* OTPC (1946 ed.); RIS
Ten little mice sat down to spin. *See* Six little mice . . .
Ten little nigger boys went out to dine. *Unknown.* OxNR
Ten met the Master in a field. The Living Tithe. Mabel Munns Charles. ChIP
Ten-odd years I have journeyed since leaving school. Distant View of School. Kaoru Maruyama. PoLJ
Ten Per Cent; Then as Now. Pope. *Fr.* The First Epistle of the First Book of Horace Imitated. BeR
Ten pound hammer kill John Henry. John Henry (F *vers.*). *Unknown.* ViBoFo

Ten snowy white pigeons are standing in line. The Pigeons. Maud Burnham. PCH
Ten South Sea Island boys. Fun with Fishing. Eunice Tietjens. FaPON; GaP
Ten Thousand, The. James Thomson. BHV
Ten Thousand Cattle (A *vers.*), *with music*. *Unknown*. CoSo
Ten Thousand God-damn Cattle (B *vers. of* Ten Thousand Cattle), *with music*. *Unknown*. CoSo
Ten Thousand Miles Away, *with music*. *Unknown*. AS; SoAmSa
Ten Thousand Miles Away from Home, *with music*. *Unknown*. AS
Ten thousand times ten thousand. Henry Alford. OlF
Ten thousand tomes with pendant discs of jade. In an Old Library. Yuan Mei. LiTW
Ten Years After, *sel.* Lucia Trent *and* Ralph Cheyney.
  True Peace, A. PSO
  (Toward a True Peace.) PGD
Ten years ago, when I left home. The Fleeting Years. Wu Mou Ch'ien. PoHN
Ten years!—and to my waking eye. The Terrace at Berne. Matthew Arnold. Switzerland, VII. OAEP; ViPP
Ten Years Old. Louis Untermeyer. TSW; TSWC
Ten years together without yet a cloud. Firelight. E. A. Robinson. ChMo; CMP; InP; NP; PeBoSo
Tenancy, The. Mary Gilmore. BoAV
Tenancy. *Unknown, tr. fr. Greek by* Hugh Macnaghten. OxBG
Tenants, The. Leah Bodine Drake. DaM
Tenants. W. W. Gibson. ChMo; CMP; HBV; NP
Tend me my birds, and bring again. A Prayer. Norman Gale. TrPWD
Tendency, The. Heine, *tr. fr. German by* Louis Untermeyer. PoFr
Tender Adonis stricken is lying. Adonis. Sappho. GrR
Tender Babes. Thomas Hood. *Fr.* The Plea of the Midsummer Fairies. OBRV
Tender bud within herself [*or* itselfe] doth close, The. On a Rosebud Sent to Her Lover. *Unknown*. AtBAP; LO; SeCL
Tender child of summers three, A. The Light That Is Felt. Whittier. PEOR
Tender-handed stroke a nettle. A Strong Hand. Aaron Hill. HBV
Tender he was, perplexed and jealous; yet. The White Bird. "Anna Akhmatova." LiTW
Tender Heart, The. Helen Gray Cone. PR
Tender Husband, The, *sel.* Sir Richard Steele.
  Song: "Why, lovely charmer, tell me why." LiTL; ViBoPo
  (Why, Lovely Charmer.) HBV; LPS-1
Tender is the night and clear, and without wind. The Evening of the Feast-Day. Giacomo Leopardi. LiTW
Tender one, A, not ready yet to climb. To a Child. Gerda Dalliba. BAP
Tender Shepherd, The. Mary Lundie Duncan. *See* Child's Evening Prayer, A.
Tender song that sweeps across the hills, A. Echo. E. G. Bishop. CAG
Tender the flowers are. Requiem. Archibald Rutledge. LS
Tender willow. Haiku of a Day. José Juan Tablada. AnMP
Tenderfoot, The. D. J. O'Malley. *See* Horse Wrangler, The.
Tenderheartedness. Harry Graham. ALV; FaFP; NA; SiTL; WhC
  (Billy.) LiTM
  (Four Ruthless Rhymes.) MaC
  (Some Ruthless Rhymes, II.) CenHV
Tenderly, day that I have loved, I close your eyes. Day That I Have Loved. Rupert Brooke. BEL; GTSL
Tenderly, humbly, upon the charming tomb. The Buried Lady. Paul Valéry. AnFP
Tenderness of dignity of souls, The. Crass Times Redeemed by Dignity of Souls, II. Peter Viereck. HoPM
Tenebrae. Austin Clarke. AnIL; NeIP
Tenebrae. David Gascoyne. *Fr.* Miserere. NeBP
Tenebris. Angelina W. Grimké. CDC; PoNe
Tenebris Interlucentem. James Elroy Flecker. BMEP; MBP; MoBrPo; POTT
Tenement Room; Chicago. Frank Marshall Davis. GoSl
Teneriffe, *sel.* Frederic William Henry Myers.
  "Atlantid islands, phantom-fair." OBVV
Tennessee. Virginia Frazer Boyle. PAH
Tennessee. Francis Brooks. *Fr.* Intaglios. AA
Tennis. Margaret Avison. PeCV
Tennyson. Thomas Bailey Aldrich. AA
Tennyson. Florence Earle Coates. AA
Tennyson. Thomas Henry Huxley. HBV; VA
Tennyson. Henry van Dyke. AA; InP
  (In Lucem Transitus, October, 1892.) BTP
Tenour which my life, holds, The. Wordsworth. *Fr.* The Excursion, III. OBRV
Tense and whittled thundershaft he pulls, A. Herakles Archer. Morton Dauwen Zabel. NP
Tension in the tendons of her wing, The. Soldier's Dove. James Forsyth. WaP
Tent-lights glimmer on the land, The. At Port Royal. Whittier. PAH; PAP
Tent on the Beach, The, *sel.* Whittier.
  To Her Absent Sailor. LPS-1
Tent with rustling breezes cool, A. She Scorns Her Husband the Caliph. Lady Maisun. LiTW
Tenth Duino Elegy, The. Rainer Maria Rilke, *tr. fr. German by* Ruth Speirs. *Fr.* The Duino Elegies. AnGP
Tenth Elegy: Elegy in Joy. Muriel Rukeyser. MiAP
X Properte, The. Sir Thomas More. *Fr.* The XII Properties or Condicyons of a Lover. CoBE
Tenth Reunion. Edward Steese. GoYe
Tenth Satire of Juvenal, The, *abr.* Juvenal, *tr. fr. Latin by* Dryden. WoL
Tenting on the Old Camp Ground. Walter Kittredge. OlF; TreFS
  (Tenting To-Night, *with music*.) TrAS
  (We're Tenting To-Night.) BlG; PaA
Tenure of Kings and Magistrates, The, *sel.* Milton.
  "There can be slain/ No sacrifice," *3 ll., tr. fr. the Latin of* Seneca. PoFr
Tenzone. Ezra Pound. CoV
Tercets. Llywarch Hen, *tr. fr. Welsh by* Owen Masters. LiTW
Terence McDiddler. *Unknown*. OxNR
Terence MacSwiney. "Æ." AnIV; PoFr
  (Prisoner, A.) AnIL
Terence, This Is Stupid Stuff. A. E. Housman. A Shropshire Lad, LXII. ChMo; CMP; CoBMV; EmBrPo; EnL; EnLit; LiTB; LiTM (rev. ed.); MaPo; NAMP; OAEP; PoLFOT; PoVP; SeCeV; TwP; ViP; ViPo; VLEP; WHA
  (Epilogue: "Terence, this is stupid stuff.") MBP; MOAB; MoBrPo; OuHeWo; ReMP; TrGrPo
  Power of Malt, The, *sel.* HBV; LEAP
Terence's Farewell. Helen Selina Sheridan. TIP
Terenure. Blanaid Salkeld. NeIP
Teresian Contemplative, The. Robert Hugh Benson. ACP; CAW; JKCP; PraNu
Teresina's Face. Margaret Widdemer. HBMV; NP
Terly Terlow. *Unknown*. AtBAP
Term, The. William Carlos Williams. InvP; LiTA; ThWaDe
Term of Death, The. Sarah Morgan Bryan Piatt. AA
Terminus. Emerson. AA; AmPo; AmPP; AnNE; APW; AWP; CoBA; CoV; EOAH; HBV; IAP; InPo; LBAP; MOAP; OnAP; OuHeWo; OxBA; PoEL-4
Termite, The. Ogden Nash. CenHV; WhC
Termites. Charles G. Bell. NePoAm-2
Terms, The. Thorsteinn Erlingsson, *tr. fr. Icelandic by* Jakobina Johnson. IcP
Ternarie [*or* Ternary] of Littles, upon a Pipkin of Jellie [*or* Jelly] Sent to a Lady, A. Robert Herrick. ALV; BOHV; EPS; EV-2; FaBoCh; HBV; HBVY; LoGBV; MaPo; MyFE, *2 sts.*; OTPC (1923 ed.); PG (1955 ed.); PoEL-3; PoRA; WhC
  (Littles, *sl. abr.*) BoTP
Ternissa! You Are Fled! Walter Savage Landor. *Fr.* The Hellenics. ExPo; GTSE; LoBV; PoEL-4; SeCeV
  (Ternissa.) FaBoEn; TriL
Terra Australis. Douglas Stewart. BoAV; MoAuPo
Terrace, The. Richard Wilbur. MiAP
Terrace at Berne, The. Matthew Arnold. Switzerland, VII. OAEP; ViPP
Terrace in the Snow, The. Su T'ung-po, *tr. fr. Chinese by* Kenneth Rexroth. OnPC
Terrae Illuminatae. Robert P. Tristram Coffin. CAG
Terrapin War. *Unknown*. PAH
Terrible/ is the soft sound of a hardboiled egg. Late Rising. Jacques Prévert. OnHM
Terrible and splendid trust, A. Ways of War. Lionel Johnson. AnIV; GTIV; TIP
Terrible Dead, The. Mary Carolyn Davies. HBMV
Terrible Door, The. Harold Monro. EnLoPo; FaBoTw
Terrible Infant, A. Frederick Locker-Lampson. ALV; BOHV; FiBHP; HBV; InMe; LauV; TreFS; WhC
Terrible is the price. The Price. John Davidson. CaAE
Terrible Man, A. Alcaeus, *tr. fr. Greek by* John Addington Symonds. GrR
Terrible Meek, The, *sel.* Charles Rann Kennedy.
  "Already our kingdoms are beginning to totter." ChIP
Terrible People, The. Ogden Nash. NePA; SiTL
Terrible Robber Men, The. Padraic Colum. HBMV; RG
Terrible Sonnets, The. Gerard Manley Hopkins. *See* Carrion Comfort; I Wake and Feel the Fell of Dark; *and* No Worst, There Is None.
Terrible Sons, The. Eleazar ben Kalir, *tr. fr. Hebrew by* Israel Zangwill. TrJP
Terrible Thought, A. Eliezer Steinberg, *tr. fr. Yiddish by* Joseph Leftwich. TrJP
Terrifying are the attent sleek thrushes on the lawn. Thrushes. Ted Hughes. GoYe
Terrifying Tell-Tale, The. Antipater, *tr. fr. Greek by* Lord Neaves. OnPM
Terror. Thomas O'Brien. NeIP

Terror. Maximilian Aleksandrovich Voloshin, *tr. fr. Russian by* Babette Deutsch. TrRV
Terror. Robert Penn Warren. MoPo; NePA; WaP
Terror. "Yehoash," *tr. fr. Yiddish by* Isidore Goldstick. TrJP
Terror!/ O moving with the quickness of wings. The Furies. Euripides. *Fr.* Orestes. OxBG
Terror by Night. Leah Bodine Drake. UnW
Terror Conduction. Philip Lamantia. NeAP
Terror does not belong to open day. Counterpoint. Owen Dodson. PoNe
Terror in Beauty. M. Eugenie Perry. TwCaPo
Terror of Death. Keats. *See* When I Have Fears That I May Cease To Be.
Terse-tongued and sparely worded was the singing of Erinna. The Poetess Erinna. Antipater of Sidon. GrPE
Tess's Lament. Thomas Hardy. FaBoTw
Test, The. Emily Dickinson. TCAP
Test, The. Emerson. AA; BAP; IAP
Test, The. Walter Savage Landor. *See* I Held Her Hand.
Test. Helen Pursell Roads. OQP; QP-1
Test, The. John Banister Tabb. AnAmPo; LA
Test of Faith, The. Sidney Royse Lysaght. GrCo-2
Test of Manhood, The, *sel.* George Meredith.
"In fellowship religion has its founts." WGRP
Test of Men, The. Ecclesiasticus, XXVI: 5-8, Bible, Apocrypha. TrJP
Test of the Bow, The. Homer, *tr. fr. Greek by* William Morris. *Fr.* The Odyssey, XXI. GrR
Testament. Langston Hughes. NePoAm-2
Testament. F. Tennyson Jesse. DiM
Testament, The. Mikhail Yurevich Lermontov, *tr. fr. Russian.* BoR, *tr. by* Maurice Baring; TrRV, *tr. by* Babette Deutsch
Testament, A. *Unknown.* OBSC
Testament, The, *sels.* Villon, *tr. fr. French by* Alan Conder. TrFP
"In God's own name, as I have said."
"In Saint-Avoye, and not elsewhere."
"No angel's son am I, I own."
Testament of a Man Forbid, The, *sels.* John Davidson.
I Haunt the Hills That Overlook the Sea. BSV
"Mankind has cast me out." BrBE
Testament of a Prime Minister, The, *sels.* John Davidson.
"For whether earth already to its doom," I. BSV
"Like savage wood-nymphs with their hair on end," II. BSV
Testament of Beauty, The, *sels.* Robert Bridges.
"But love's true passion is of immortal happiness," *fr.* III. LO
Friendship, *fr.* IV. MaRV
"How was November's melancholy endear'd to me," *fr.* III. MoVE
"In higher natures, poetic or mystical," *fr.* III. LO; PtP, *longer sel.*
Introduction: "'Twas late in my long journey, when I had clomb to where," *fr.* I. MoVE
Jesus, *fr.* I. MaRV
("So it was when Jesus came in his gentleness.") MeRV
"Our happiest earthly comradeships hold a foretaste," *fr.* IV. MaRV
"Sky's unresting cloudland, that with varying play, The," *fr.* I. MoVE
"'Twas at thatt hour of beauty when the setting sun," *fr.* IV. MoVE; OxBoCh
Testament of Cathaeir Mor, The. *Unknown, tr. fr. Middle Irish by* James Clarence Mangan. *Fr.* Book of Rights. OnYI
Testament of Cresseid, The. Robert Henryson. GoTS; MeEV, *sl. abr., tr. fr. Middle English by* Marshall W. Stearns
Sels.
Assembly of the Gods, The. PoEL-1
Cresseid's Lament. CoEV
Cressida's Leprosy. SeCePo
Prologue: "Ane doolie season to ane careful dyte." BSV
"This duleful sentence Saturn took on hand." BSV
"When they togidder murnit had full lang." NBE
Testament of John Davidson, The, *sels.* John Davidson.
Last Journey, The. BSV; GoTS
"None should outlive his power." LEAP
Testamentum Domini, *in mod. Eng.* *Unknown.* TMEV
Testimony, A. Christina Rossetti. EmBrPo
Testimony. Eva Moad Turner. OQP; QP-1
Testimony to an Inquisitor. William Stafford. NePoAm-2
Testing, The. Edwin Markham. LPS-1; MaRV; OQP; QP-1
Tetélestai. Conrad Aiken. ChMo; CMP; LiTA; LiTM (rev. ed.); MAP; MAPA; MoAB; MoAmPo; MOAP
Tethys' Festival, *sel.* Samuel Daniel.
Are They Shadow[e]s [That We See]? AtBAP; ATP; ElL; ExPo; InP; LoBV; SeCeV; TuPP
("Are they shadows that we see?") CH; ElSeCe; SiCE
(Eidola.) LO
(Shadows.) EV-1; OBSC; RiBV
(Song: "Are they shadowes that we see?") PoEL-2
Tetrasticha, *sel.* Joshua Sylvester.
Surcloying the Stomach. MOB
Teufelsdröckh Minor. Morton Dauwen Zabel. NP
Teuton sang the "Wacht am Rhein," The. "Il Est Cocu—le Chef de Gare!" H. S. Mackintosh. WhC
Tewkesbury Road. John Masefield. BoTP; CV; EPN; EPP; GBV; MCCG; PoeT; POT; PoTo; StaSt; TCEP; TSW; TSWC; VOD
Texas. James Daugherty. TiPo (1959 ed.)
Texas. Amy Lowell. InP; PoMa; PoTo
Texas. Henry van Dyke. GDAH
Texas. Whittier. PAH
Texas Cowboy, The ("Oh, I am a Texas cowboy"), *with music. Unknown.* CoSo; CSF
Texas Cowboy and the Mexican Greaser, The. *Unknown.* SCC
Texas cowboy [lay down] on a barroom floor, A. The Hell bound Train. *Unknown.* BeLS; BLPA; CoSo
Texas Cowboys, The ("It's of those Texas cowboys . ."). *Unknown. See* Lone Buffalo Hunter, The.
Texas, Our Texas. Gladys Yoakum Wright. PoRL
Texas Rangers, The. *Unknown.* ABS; CoSo, *with music;* CSF; OuSiCo, *with music*
Texas Song, The: "I'm going to leave old Texas now." *Unknown.* CoSo
Texas Trains and Trails. Mary Austin. TiPo
Texas Types—"The Bad Man." William Lawrence Chittenden. PoOW
Texian Boys. *Unknown. See* Kansas Boys.
Text. Sara Henderson Hay. QS
Text. Aaron Zeitlin, *tr. fr. Yiddish by* Sarah Zweig Betsky. OnCuPl
Text for Today. Phyllis McGinley. WhC
Thaddeus Stevens. Phoebe Cary. GA; MOAH; PAH
Thaddeus Stevens was a burning scandal. Old Thad Stevens. Kenneth Porter. NePoAm-2
Thais. Newman Levy. BOHV; FiBHP; InMe
Thaisa's Dirge ("Thaisa fair, under the cold sea lying"). Herman Charles Merivale. VA
Thalaba the Destroyer, *sels.* Robert Southey.
Night [in the Desert], *fr.* I. GN; OTPC
Thalaba and the Banquet, *fr.* VI. SeCePo
Thalaba and the Magic Thread, *fr.* VIII. EV-4; SeCePo
Thalassius. Swinburne. PoVP; VLEP
Thalatta. Willis Boyd Allen. EtS
Thalatta! Thalatta! Joseph Brownlee Brown. AA; BAP; BTP; HBV; LBAP
Thalia. Thomas Bailey Aldrich. AA; HBV; InMe; LHV; OBAV
Thames, The. Sir John Denham. *Fr.* Cooper's Hill. BCEP; FaBoEn, *longer sel.*
Thames, The. M. M. Hutchinson. BoTP
Thames from Cooper's Hill, The. Sir John Denham. *Fr.* Cooper's Hill. CoEV; OBS; SeCePo
("My eye descending from the hill, surveys.") EPP; ReEn; ViBoPo
(Praise of the Thames.) EV-2
Thames nocturne of blue and gold, The. Impression du Matin. Oscar Wilde. MBP; MoBrPo; PoVP; ViP
Thames, the most lov'd of all the Ocean's sons. The Thames. Sir John Denham. *Fr.* Cooper's Hill. BCEP; FaBoEn
Thames will take us to London town, The. The Thames. M. M. Hutchinson. BoTP
Thammuz. William Vaughn Moody. MOAP
Than Deiphobus made this answer plain. The Entrance to Tartarus. Virgil, *tr. by* Gawin Douglas. *Fr.* The Aeneid, VI. BSV
Than forth I went into a meadow green. Stephen Hawes. *Fr.* The Pastime of Pleasure. ReIE
Than Longen Folk to Goon on Pilgrimages. Chaucer. *See* Canterbury Tales, The: Prologue.
Than love there's nothing sweeter. No joys are worth the weighing. The Rose of Love. Nossis. GrPE
Than Perseverance, in all goodly haste. Of the Great Marriage between Grand Amour and La Belle Pucelle. Stephen Hawes. *Fr.* The Pastime of Pleasure. ReIE
Than this great universe no less. Rowland's Rhyme. Michael Drayton. *Fr.* The Shepherd's Garland. Eclogue II. OBSC
Thanatopsis. Bryant. AA; AmP; AmPP; AnAmPo; AnFE; AnNE; APA; APW; AWP; BAP; BAV; BLV; BoLiVe; CoAnAm; CoBA; CoV; FaBoBe; FaFP; GTBS-W; HBV; HBVY; IAP; LA; LaNeLa; LBAP; LEAP; LiTA; LiTG; LPS-1; MCCG; MOAP; NeHB; NePA; OBAV; OBEV (new ed.); OBRV; OBVV; OHFP; OTPC (1946 ed.); OxBA; PFY; PG (1945 ed.); PIR; PoFS; PTA-1; REAL; TreF; TrGrPo; UnPo (1st ed.); ViBoPo; WBLP; WGRP; WHA
Sels.
"Earth that nourished thee." YT
"So live, that when thy summons comes." DD; OQP; QP-2
(Be Ye Also Ready.) MaRV
(So Live.) BLP; PoToHe
Thank God. Joseph Rolnik, *tr. fr. Yiddish by* Joseph Leftwich. TrJP
Thank God! *Unknown.* MaRV; OQP; PoToHe; PSO; QP-1

Thank God,/ No one knows. Thank God. Joseph Rolnik. TrJP
Thank God, a man can grow! Per Aspera. Florence Earle Coates. BLP; HBMV; VOD
Thank God, bless God, all ye who suffer not. Tears. Elizabeth Barrett Browning. OQP; PC; PFE; QP-2; TCAP
Thank God for Fools! *Unknown.* OQP; PoToHe (1941 ed.); QP-2
Thank God for home. Prayer at Thanksgiving Time. Nancy Byrd Turner. PraP
Thank God for Life. *Unknown.* PGD
Thank God for life!/ E'en though it bring much bitterness and strife. Thank God. *Unknown.* MaRV; OQP; PoToHe; PSO; QP-1
Thank God for Life!/ There! A meadowlark sings! The Things of the Spirit. Douglas Malloch. MaRV
Thank God for life; life is not sweet always. Thank God for Life. *Unknown.* PGD
Thank God for life, with all its endless store. Thomas Durley Landels. *Fr.* At Eighty-three. MaRV
Thank God for sleep in the long quiet night. Morning Thanksgiving. John Drinkwater. BoTP
Thank God! for that lovely spirit. Wondrous Motherhood. *Unknown.* PGD; PSO
Thank God for the Country! Mrs. Major Arnold. WBLP
Thank God my brain is not inclined to cut. The Menagerie. William Vaughn Moody. AmPP (3d ed.); OnAP; PFY; TCAP; TCPD; TOP; YaD
Thank God our liberating lance. The Road to France. Daniel Henderson. HBV; MC; PaA; PAH
Thank God that God shall judge my soul, not man! The Eternal Justice. Anne Reeve Aldrich. AA
Thank God we can see, in the glory of morn. The Stars and Stripes. Henry van Dyke. PSO
Thank God we do not live by bread alone. Twice Fed. A. A. Bassett. HBV
Thank God who seasons thus the year. The Fall of the Leaf. Henry David Thoreau. AmP
Thank Heaven! the crisis. For Annie. Poe. AmP; AmPP; AnFE; APA; APW; BAV; CoAnAm; EV-5; HBV; IAP; LiTA; LO; LPS-1; MOAP; NePA; OBEV; OBVV; OxBA; TreFS
Thank him who isled us here, and roughly set. Tennyson. *Fr.* Ode on the Death of the Duke of Wellington. PoFr
Thank Thee. Egi, *tr. fr. Japanese by* Lois J. Erickson. SoLD
Thank Thee, O Giver of life, O God! Thanksgiving. Angela Morgan. TrPWD
Thank You. Kenneth Koch. NeAP
Thank You for Friends, A. Rodney Bennett. BoTP
Thank You, God. Nina Stiles. PoToHe (new ed.)
Thank You, Pretty Cow. Ann *or* Jane Taylor. *See* Cow, The.
Thank you very much indeed. Thanks. Norman Gale. GoTP; NLK (1947 ed.); OQP; OTPC (1946 ed.); QP-2; YT
"Thank you, whatever comes." And then she turned. Erat Hora. Ezra Pound. CoV; MOAP
Thankful Country Lass, The; or, The Jolly Batchelor Kindly Entertained. *Unknown.* CoMu
Thankful Heart, A. Robert Herrick. *See* Thanksgiving to God for His House, A.
Thankful Heart, A. *Unknown.* PraP
Thankfulness. Adelaide Anne Procter. MaRV; PraP; TrPWD
Thanks. Norman Gale. GoTP; NLK (1947 ed.); OQP; OTPC (1946 ed.); QP-2; YT
Thanks. Marty Hale. AlBD
Thanks Be to God. Janie Alford. MaRV; PGD; PoToHe
Thanks be to God for the light and the darkness. The Irish Te Deum. *Unknown.* WHL
Thanks be to God! to whom earth owes. Thanksgiving. Frances Ridley Havergal. TOAH
Thanks, fair Urania; to your scorn. The Indifference. Sir Charles Sedley. CEP; SeCV-2
Thanks for Everything. Helen Isabella Tupper. *See* Give Thanks.
Thanks for Laughter. *Unknown.* OQP; QP-2
Thanks for New Opportunities. *Unknown.* PSO
Thanks for the lovely time. Concert. Ibn Sharaf. MooP
Thanks from Earth to Heaven. John Hall Wheelock. HBMV
"Holy Poet, I have heard," *sel.* TrPWD
Thanks in Old Age. Walt Whitman. MCCG
Thanks, Just the Same. *Unknown.* DDA
Thanks, my Lord, for your venison, for finer or fatter. The Haunch of Venison. Goldsmith. CEP; EV-3; TCEP
Thanks: not for thoughts that give the mind more mirth. To Thomas Hardy. Laurence Housman. MaRV
Thanks, thanks! With the Muse is always love and light. The Poet. Philip James Bailey. *Fr.* Festus. VA
Thanks to My World for the Loan of a Fair Day. Stella Benson. AV
Thanks to Saint Matthew, who had been. Comrade Jesus. Sarah N. Cleghorn. AnAmPo; BAP; BoFr; HBMV; LA; MaRV; NAMP; NV; OQP; PoFr; QP-1; StJW; WGRP
Thanks to Spring. Mary Anderson. BoTP
Thanks to the morning light. The World-Soul. Emerson. IAP
Thanksgivin' Pumpkin Pies. Margaret E. Sangster. TOAH
Thanksgiving. David Abenatar Melo, *tr. fr. Spanish by* Henry Hart Milman. TrJP
Thanksgiving, A. John Kendrick Bangs. MaRV
Thanksgiving. Amelia E. Barr. PEDC
(Poetic Responses.) TOAH
Thanksgiving. Susie M. Best. QS; TrPWD
Thanksgiving. Alice Williams Brotherton. PGD
Thanksgiving. Phoebe Cary. TOAH
Thanksgiving. Florence Earle Coates. PEDC; TrPWD
Thanksgiving. Louise Driscoll. YeAr
Thanksgiving. Emerson. MeMeAg; PCH
Thanksgiving. Hannah E. Garey. TOAH
Thanksgiving. Frances Ridley Havergal. TOAH
Thanksgiving. Robert Herrick. LiTB
Thanksgiving. William Dean Howells. *See* Undiscovered Country, The.
Thanksgiving. Emily Read Jones. TOAH
Thanksgiving. Joyce Kilmer. MaRV
Thanksgiving, A. Lucy Larcom. OHIP
"For the rosebud's break of beauty," *sel.* TrPWD
Thanksgiving. William Ludlum. PraP
Thanksgiving. Whitney Montgomery. PraP
Thanksgiving. Angela Morgan. TrPWD
Thanksgiving. Margarete Münsterberg. GFA
Thanksgiving, A. Cardinal Newman. TrPWD
Thanksgiving. Gene H. Osborne. PGD; PSO
Thanksgiving. John Oxenham. BLRP; OQP; QP-2; WBLP
Thanksgiving. Psalms, XCV: 1–7, C: 1–5, CXXXVI: 1–9, 26, Bible, *O.T.* BoChLi (1950 ed.)
Thanksgiving. Psalms, C, Bible, *O.T.* StVeCh
(Be Thankful unto Him.) FaPON
(Psalm of Praise.) SiSoSe; SUS
(Psalm C.) MPB; OHIP; OnPM; PG (1955 ed.); TiPo (1952 ed.); UnS
Thanksgiving ("For the days when nothing happens"). Margaret E. Sangster. BLRP
Thanksgiving ("I think God loves simplicity"). Margaret E. Sangster. PEDC
Thanksgiving. Odell Shepard. PEDC
Thanksgiving. Jeanie Rogers Sherman. TOAH
Thanksgiving. Charles Hanson Towne. PoMa
Thanksgiving. *Unknown.* PeOR
Thanksgiving, A. Carolyn Wells. PEDC
Thanksgiving. Amos Niven Wilder. MaRV
Thanksgiving. "Yehoash," *tr. fr Yiddish by* Isidore Goldstick. TrJP
Thanksgiving after Travel. Addison. *See* How Are Thy Servants Blest.
Thanksgiving Day. Thomas Bailey Aldrich. TOAH
Thanksgiving Day. Henry Alford. *See* Harvest Home.
Thanksgiving Day. John Kendrick Bangs. TrPWD
Thanksgiving Day. Marie Barton. PraP
Thanksgiving Day. Robert Bridges. MaRV; OHIP
Thanksgiving Day. Lydia Maria Child. DD; DDA; FaPON; GFA; GoTP; HH; MeMeAg, *sl. abr.*; MPB; OHIP; OTPC; PCH, *sl. abr.*; PEDC; PRWS; PTA-1, *sl. abr.*; SAS; SiSoSe; StVeCh; TOAH; TreFS
Thanksgiving Day. James J. Montague. HH; PEDC
Thanksgiving Day. *Unknown.* TOAH
Thanksgiving Day. Annette Wynne. OHIP
Thanksgiving Day came chill and bare. Farmer John's Thanksgiving. Isaac F. Eaton. TOAH
Thanksgiving Day Grace. Luther B. Cross. PraP
Thanksgiving Day I like to see. Thanksgiving Magic. Rowena Bastin Bennett. BrR; SiSoSe; TiPo
Thanksgiving Day will soon be here. Turkey Time. *Unknown.* PCH
Thanksgiving Exercise. Lizzie M. Hadley. TOAH
Thanksgiving Fable, A. Oliver Herford. HH; OnHT; PRWS; TOAH; UTS
Thanksgiving for a former, doth invite. Thanksgiving. Robert Herrick. LiTB
Thanksgiving for America, The. Hezekiah Butterworth. PAH
Thanksgiving for Benefits Received. Lois Givens Vaughan. PraP
Thanksgiving for His House, A. Robert Herrick. *See* Thanksgiving to God for His House, A.
Thanksgiving for Thanksgiving. Amos R. Wells. PEDC
Thanksgiving for the Body. Thomas Traherne. ImOP
Thanksgiving for the Earth. Elizabeth Goudge. YeAr
Thanksgiving for the ranks of corn. Thanksgiving Song. Clinton Scollard. PEDC
Thanksgiving Hymn ("The Lord above, in tender love"). *Unknown.* PAH
Thanksgiving Hymn ("O thou, whose eyes of love"). *Unknown.* PEOR; TOAH
Thanksgiving in Boston Harbor, The. Hezekiah Butterworth. AA; DD, *abr.*; MC; OHIP; PAH; TOAH
(First Boston Thanksgiving, The, July, 1630.) PEOR

Thanksgiving Magic. Rowena Bastin Bennett. BrR; SiSoSe; TiPo
Thanksgiving Night. Wilbur D. Nesbit. DD; HH; PEDC
Thanksgiving Ode. Whittier. *See* Harvest Hymn.
Thanksgiving Philosophy. Charlotte W. Thurston. TOAH
Thanksgiving Prayer, A. *Unknown.* PEOR
Thanksgiving Prayer, A. Ruth G. Winant. PSO
Thanksgiving Rosary, A. Edwin Markham. PEDC
(Rhyme for Thanksgiving Day, A). BLP
Thanksgiving Song. Clinton Scollard. PEDC
Thanksgiving stirs her ruddy fire. Two Festivals. Lucy Larcom. DD; TOAH
Thanksgiving Time. *Unknown.* MeMeAg; OTPC (1946 ed.); PCH
Thanksgiving to God for His House, A. Robert Herrick. AEV; BEL; CenL; ChTr; ElSeCe; EM-1; EnLi-1; EnLit; EPS; EV-2; FaBoBe; HBV; InPo; LEAP; MaRV, *much abr.*; NeHB; OBS; OHIP; OTPC; PGD, *much abr.*; Po; PoE; PoRA; ReEn; SeCeV; SeCV-1; SeEP; TiPo (1952 ed.); TOP; TrPWD; UnPo (1st ed.); ViBoPo; WGRP; WoL; WP
(Thankful Heart, A, *much abr.*) OQP: PoToHe; QP-1
(Thanksgiving for His House, A.) BCEP; PEOR
Thanksgiving to the gods! The Seeker in the Marshes. Daniel Lewis Dawson. AA
Thanksgivings for the Beauty of His Providence. Thomas Traherne. FaBoCh; LoGBV
Thanksgivings of Old. E. A. Smuller. PEOR
Thanksliving. Chauncey R. Piety. OQP; PGD; QP-1
Thar she goes a-lopin', stranger. Our Little Cowgirl. *Unknown.* SCC
Thar was an ol' man who lived in de West. De Ol' Man. Alonzo W. Combs. IHA
Thar's lots o' music in 'em—the hymns o' long ago. The Old Hymns. Frank L. Stanton. BLRP
Thar's More in the Man than Thar Is in the Land. Sidney Lanier. CoBA
Thar's the bread, thar's the meat. Cowboy Grace. *Unknown.* CoSo
Tha'rt welcome, little bonny brid. Welcome, Bonny Brid! Samuel Laycock. VA
Thasos. Archilochus, *tr. fr. Greek by* C. M. Bowra. OxBG
That. Charles Weekes. GTIV
That after horror that was Us. Emily Dickinson. MoPo
That aged woman with the bass voice. The Great-Grandmother. Robert Graves. MoPW
That all should change to ghost and glance and gleam. The Transmutation. Edwin Muir. FaBoEn
That all things should be mine. Amendment. Thomas Traherne. SeCV-2
That amazing holiday. The Unscarred Fighter Remembers France. Kenneth Slade Alling. HBMV
That American Poet's future. The Line of an American Poet. Reed Whittemore. MoVE
That angel so adored. The Lost Angel. Al-Kasad. MooP
That angel whose charge was Eiré sang thus. The Three Woes. Aubrey Thomas De Vere. AnIV
That any thing should be. Axle Song. Mark Van Doren. MoPo; TwAmPo
That autumn when the partridges called in the stubble. Microcosmos, XLI. Nigel Heseltine. NeBP
That balmy eve, within a trellised bower. The Marriage of Pocahontas. Mrs. M. M. Webster. GA; MC; PAH
That best portion of a good man's life. Wordsworth. *Fr.* Lines Composed a Few Miles above Tintern Abbey. PoToHe
That blazing galleon the sun. Mutiny. "Æ." ChMo; CMP; SoV
That blessèd mood. Wordsworth. *Fr.* Lines Composed a Few Miles above Tintern Abbey. LEAP
That Bright Chimeric Beast. Countee Cullen. PoNe
That brown girl's swagger gives a twitch. To a Brown Boy. Countee Cullen. TBM
That cactus recalled the despairing gestures of marble. The Cactus. Manuel Bandeira. AnCL
That Cat. Ben King. FiBHP
That celestial power, to whom the care. Spenser. *Fr.* The Faerie Queene, II. MyFE
That century to century may tell. Pierre de Ronsard. *Fr.* Sonnets pour Hélène. PrPoCR
That childish thoughts such joys inspire. The Approach. Thomas Traherne. OxBoCh
"That Christ may dwell." Christ Liveth in Me. Toyohiko Kagawa. SoLD
That civilisation may not sink. Long-legged Fly. W. B. Yeats. FaBoEn; FaBoTw; LiTM; PoE
That cloud now! Just below that strip of blue! We Visit My Estate. Richard R. Kirk. BPP; LS
That Consciousness that wonders at its spright. Mind. Paul C. Boomer. PoP
That Corner. Blanaid Salkeld. OnYI; OxBI
That Crafty Youth. *Unknown, tr. fr. Chinese by* Bernhard Karlgren. *Fr.* Shi King. ChLP
That "Craning of the Neck." Isabella Gardner. NePA
That Day. Poul la Cour, *tr. fr. Danish by* Charles W. Stork. BoDS
That Day. Mark Van Doren. WaP
That day—/ Day was more beautiful than a bitter gem. Hawk Shadow. Florence Wilkinson Evans. TBM
That day church bells chimed gaily overhead. Country Wedding. Francis Jammes. TrFP
That day her eyes were deep as night. Once. Trumbull Stickney. LBMV
That day, in the slipping of torsos and straining flanks. The Song. Lola Ridge. NP
That day of wrath, that dreadful day,/ Shall the whole world. Dies Irae. Thomas of Celano, *tr. by* the Earl of Roscommon. *See* Day of wrath . . .
That day of wrath, that dreadful day/ When heaven and earth. Dies Irae. Thomas of Celano, *par. by* Sir Walter Scott. *Fr.* The Lay of the Last Minstrel, VI. EmBrPo; GoBC; MaRV
That day of wrath, that dreadful day,/ When heaven and earth. Dies Irae. Thomas of Celano, *tr. by* Father Wingfield *and* Father Alward. WHL
That day the doves with burnished breasts. Told in the Market-Place. Edwina Stanton Babcock. StJW
That day the eggshell of appearance split. Transfigured Bird. James Merrill. MoAB
That day the guns fell silent at a word. Armistice Day, 1918–1928. Nancy Byrd Turner. AOAH
That day the small Christ hurt His hand. Mary. Sara Henderson Hay. BAP
That Day You Came. Lizette Woodworth Reese. AV; HBV; LBMV
That day you wrought for me. Thanks to My World for the Loan of a Fair Day. Stella Benson. AV
That Death Is Not So Much to Be Feared as Daily Diseases Are. George Turberville. ReIE
That Delightful Time. Mark Akenside. *Fr.* The Pleasures of Imagination. SeCePo
"That Did in Luve So Lively Write." Georgine M. Adams. InMe
That Distant Bliss. Henry King. *See* Tell Me No More.
That dolphin-torn, that gong-tormented face. The Death of Yeats. George Barker. LiTB
That Dreary Lake. Emily Brontë. VLEP
That dusky child upon your knee. Guardianship. Georgia Douglas Johnson. GoSl
That Each Thing Is Hurt of Itself. *Unknown.* ElL
That each, who seems a separate whole. In Memoriam A. H. H., XLVII. Tennyson. EmBrPo; EnLi-2; EPN; GEPC; PIAE; ViPo; VLEP
That England lost, that learning lov'd, that every mouth commended. An Epitaph upon the Death of Sir Philip Sidney, Knight, Lord-Governor of Vlissing. Richard Barnfield. ReIE
That epigram that last you did rehearse. To Sextus, an Ill Reader. Sir John Harington. TuPP
That evening all in fond discourse was spent. The Dejected Lover. George Crabbe. *Fr.* Tales of the Hall. FaBoEn
That evening the stranger was carried to the chamber of death. On the Way. Georg Trakl. LiTW
That evening when love bad you take the floor. Pierre de Ronsard. *Fr.* Sonnets pour Hélène. PrPoCR
That evening, when the fire was lit. The Dream. Helen Spalding. ChMP; DiM
That Ever I Saw. *Unknown.* *See* She Is Gentle and Also Wise.
That face which no man ever saw. Sargent's Portrait of Edwin Booth at "The Players." Thomas Bailey Aldrich. AA
That famous Nico swore. To a Faithless Mistress. Asclepiades. GrR
That Far Lone Mountain. Sister Mary Stephanie. JKCP (1955 ed.)
That fearful day, that day of speechless dread. The Canon for Apocreos. St. Theodore of Studium. CAW
That fellow Singer, it is said. Martial, *tr. fr. Latin by* "T. W. M." Epigrams, III, 9. LaP
That firewood pale with salt and burning green. Gigha. W. S. Graham. FaBoMo; NeBP
That first Christmas night of all. First Christmas Night of All. Nancy Byrd Turner. PEDC; SDH
That flame is borne of earthly fire. *Unknown.* SeCSL
That flying angel's torrent cry. Eastern Tempest. Edmund Blunden. PtOT
That for seven Lusters I did never come. To the Reverend Shade of His Religious Father. Robert Herrick. OBS; SeCV-1; SeEP
That, Fragoletta, is the rain. Songs for Fragoletta, III. Richard Le Gallienne. HBV
That Garden of sedate Philosophy. The Garden of Epicurus. George Meredith. ATP (1953 ed.); EPN
That Gentle Man from Boston Town. Joaquin Miller. BOHV

That girl who always wore the Harris tweeds. The English Rider. "Robin Hyde." AnNZ

That gloomy trip is lifted off your sweetheart's mind. Later, to Cerinthus. Sulpicia. LaP

That God Made. Will Herford. QS

That God, which ever lives and loves. The Truths That Never Can Be Proved. Tennyson. *Fr.* In Memoriam A. H. H., Epilogue. MaRV

That grave small face, but twelve hours here. The Chart. Walter de la Mare. CoBMV

That gusty spring, each afternoon. Love's Calendar. William Bell Scott. HBV

That Harp You Play so Well. Marianne Moore. HBMV; MAP; MoAB; MoAmPo; NV; TBM; TCPD
(Harp You Play So Well, The.) NP

That haughty tyranny of thine. Love Song. Luis de León. TrJP

That He Findeth [or Finds] Others as Fair, but Not So Faithful as His Friend. George Turberville. EIL; SiCE; TuPP
(Others as Fair, but Not So Faithful.) ElSeCe

That he to his unmeasur'd mightie acts. Praise of Homer. George Chapman. OBS

That He Who lay on Mary's knee. Rabboni! Master! Mother Loyola. WHL

That he would never have any rest this side of his death. Hagiograph. Rayner Heppenstall. NeBP

That heart which stands aloof from pain and woe. Thy Love. Sana'i. PeP

That Heathen Chinee. Bret Harte. *See* Plain Language from Truthful James.

That heavens are void, and that no gods there are. Against an Atheist. Sir John Harington. SiCE

That her serene influence should spread. Two Loves. Richard Eberhart. FiMAP

That Hill. Blanche Taylor Dickinson. CDC

That Hollow space, where now in living rowes. Fairies. Thomas Tickell. *Fr.* Kensington Garden. OBEC

That Holy Thing. George Macdonald. *Fr.* Paul Faber, Surgeon, *ch.* 49. ChIP; HBV; MaRV; OBEV; OBVV; OQP; QP-1; SDH; StJW; TrPWD; WGRP

That horse whose rider fears to jump will fall. Masters. Kingsley Amis. NePoEA; PoLFOT

That house, a stone's throw from the shell-strewn shore. Boat-Haven, Co. Mayo. Geoffrey Taylor. NeIP

That houses forme within was rude and strong. The Cave of Mammon [or The House of Richesse]. Spenser. *Fr.* The Faerie Queene, II. BCEP; CH; LiA

"That humble, simple duty of the day." Serve in Thy Post. Arthur Hugh Clough. *Fr.* Last Words: Napoleon and Wellington. PGD

That I am writing you this letter. Tatyana's Letter. Pushkin. *Fr.* Eugene Onegin. BoR

That I have felt the rushing wind of Thee. A [or The] Poet's Prayer. Stephen Phillips. CP; WGRP

That I have lived I know; that I. Tragic Books. Lizette Woodworth Reese. TBM

That I love thee, charming maid, I a thousand times have said. Waiting for the Grapes. William Maginn. LPS-1

That I may not in blindness grope. A Little Prayer. Samuel Ellsworth Kiser. BLP; MaRV; PraP

That I now call you by your name. Martial, *tr. fr. Latin* by J. V. Cunningham. Epigrams, II, 68. LaP

That I Shall Die ("That I shall die before the winter snow"). John W. Thompson. PoP

That I to God, unfettered, may aspire. A Nun. J. O. Austin. PraNu

That I went to warm my self in Lady Betty's chamber, because I was cold. To Their Excellencies the Lords Justices of Ireland, the Humble Petition of Frances Harris [or Mrs. Frances Harris's Petition]. Swift. BeR; CEP; EV-3; GTIV; KN; LiA; PoEL-3

That in Jesus' heart should be. In the Heart of Jesus. Murdoch O'Daly. CAW

That innocence is not a shield. The Wolf and the Lamb. La Fontaine. OuHeWo

That Is All I heard. "Yehoash," *tr. fr. Yiddish* by Isidore Goldstick. TrJP

"That is important. I do not watch the birds." He Said the Facts. Merrill Moore. CrMA

That is no country for old men. Sailing to Byzantium. W. B. Yeats. AnFE; AnIL; AtBAP; ATP (1953 ed.); CaAE; ChMo; ChMP; CMP; CoBMV; CoEV; EnL; EnLi-2 (1949 ed.); EnLit; EnLP; ExPo; FaBoEn; FaFP; GTBS-W; HoPM; InPo; InvP; LiTB; LiTG; LiTM; MaPo; MBP; MoAB; MoBrPo; MoP; MoPo; MoPW; MoVE; NAMP; OAEP (2d ed.); OBMV; OxBI; PoFS; PoLFOT; PoTE; PoVP; ReaPo; ReMP; RiBV; SeCePo; SeCeV; ShBV-4; TriL; TwHP; TwP; UnPo (3d ed.); ViBoPo

That is what they say, who were broken off from love. Children's Elegy. Muriel Rukeyser. *Fr.* Eighth Elegy. FiMAP

That Jenny's my friend, my delight, and my pride. Song the Eighth. Edward Moore. CEP

That lady of all gentle memories. Dante. *Fr.* La Vita Nuova. AWP

That lamp thou fill'st in Eros' name tonight. Hero's Lamp. Dante Gabriel Rossetti. The House of Life, LXXXVIII. PoVP; ViPo

That last best effort of thy skill. Hymn to Science. Mark Akenside. PoP

That Learned Graecian (who did so excel). Sonnet. William Drummond of Hawthornden. EPS; OBS; SeEP

That light, that sight, that thought. Fullness. Thomas Traherne. CaAE

That Little Dog. James Whitcomb Riley. AlBD

That little grey-haired lady. The Little Old Lady. Rodney Bennett. BoTP

That Love—whose power and sovranty we own. The Creation of My Lady. Francesco Redi. AWP

That lover of a night. Crazy Jane on God. W. B. Yeats. AtBAP; MeRV; MoAB

That man,/ this man, never. Night Song for Two Mystics. Paul Blackburn. NeAP

That man is great, and he alone. True Greatness. "Owen Meredith." MaRV

That man must lead a happy life. Panegyric on the Ladies. *Unknown.* BOHV

That man or woman which will look. To the Reader. *Unknown.* SeCL

That man seems to me peer of gods. Ode to Anactoria. Sappho. LiA

That man's a fool who tries by art and skill. Woman's Will. *Unknown.* HBV

That matter of the murder is hushed up. The Cenci. Shelley. EnRP

That Men Should Fear. Shakespeare. *See* Cowards ("Cowards die many times before their deaths").

That mighty slave, whom the proud victor's rage. The Mortal Cage. John Oldham. *Fr.* To the Memory of Mr. Charles Morwent. BeR

That mighty smith, the wind. Coat of Mail. 'Asa the Blind. MooP

That moment all the world respired. First Communion. José Asunción Silva. CAW

That moment, fainting as he touch'd the shore. Homer. *Fr.* The Odyssey, V. PreP

That morn which saw me made a bride. Upon a Maid That Died the Day She Was Married. Meleager. AWP; GrPo

That morning, after the storm After the Storm. Elizabeth Bartlett. GoYe

That much a widowed wife will moan. Satirical Letrilla. José de Cadalso Vasquez. AnSpL-2

That my dead bones should lie in royal state. The Dead Feel Not. Theognis. GrL; OxBG

That my old bitter heart was pierced in this black doom. A Grey Eye Weeping. Egan O'Rahilly. AnIL; KiLC; OBMV; OxBI

That Nantucket Limerick, and What Followed. *Unknown.* TreF
(Limerick: "There was [or once was] an old man of [or a man from] Nantucket.") Dayton Voorhees. HBV (8th ed.); LiBL; LiTG

That Nature being sicke of mans unkindness. Shakespeare. *Fr.* Timon of Athens, IV, iii. NBE

That Nature Is a Heraclitean Fire and of the Comfort of the Resurrection. Gerard Manley Hopkins. AtBAP; CoBMV; FaBoMo; LiTB; MaPo; MoAB; MoPo; MoVE; OAEP (2d ed.); PoEL-5; ViP; ViPP
Of a Death in Winter, sel. BoW

That night I think that no one slept. The Last Fight. Lewis Frank Tooker. AA; FaBoBe; MDAH

That night, letting lie the copper kettle, she was saying. The Invasion of Greece. Jeremy Ingalls. PoFr

That night my angel stooped and strained. My Angel. Jonathan Henderson Brooks. PoNe

That night when all the clamor of the sea. Sonnet of the Unsleeping Dead. "Anthony Boucher." DaM

That night, when I woke suddenly, was sweet. Conversation with Rain. Louise D. Gunn. GoYe

That night when in Judean skies. The Miracle Dreams. Susie M. Best. QS

That night, when through the mooring-chains. The Ballad of Fisher's Boardinghouse. Kipling. PoRA

That night will long delight us, Nealce. Three Lyrics. Petronius Arbiter, *tr. fr. Latin* by Kenneth Rexroth. LaP; LiTW

That night your great guns, unawares. Channel Firing. Thomas Hardy. CoBMV; EnL; ExPo; LiTB; MaPo; MoPo; OAEP (2d ed.); PoEL-5; PoFS; PoRA; RiBV; SeCeV; UnPo; ViP; ViPP; WaaP

That nightee teem he come chop-chop. Topside Galah! *Unknown.* PA

That nightingale, who weeps so sweetly, grieves. Petrarch.

That nightingale, who weeps so sweetly, grieves (continued) tr. by Joseph Auslander. Sonnets to Laura: To Laura in Death, XLIII. PrPoCR

That nightingale, whost strain so sweetly flows. The Nightingale. Petrarch, tr. by Thomas LeMesurier. Sonnets to Laura: To Laura in Death, XLIII. LiTW; LyMA

That no fair woman will, wonder not why. Catullus, tr. fr. Latin by Richard Lovelace. LaP

That noise that Time makes in passing by. The Noise That Time Makes. Merrill Moore. TrGrPo (rev. ed.)

That None Beguiled Be. Sir John Suckling. PoEL-3; SeCL

That nose is out of drawing. With a gasp. Sonnet for a Picture. Swinburne. Fr. The Heptalogia. OAEP

That Nova was a moderate star. Nova. Robinson Jeffers. ChMo

That old monk confined in his cell. Monasteries. Charles David Webb. NePoAm-2

That on her lap she casts her humble eye. On the Blessed Virgin's Bashfulness. Richard Crashaw. EnLi-1; ISi; OAEP

That once the gentle mind of my dead wife. William Ellery Leonard. Fr. Two Lives, Pt. III. AnAmPo; LA; MOAP

That once this life was really mine. A Song of Life. Franz Werfel. TrJP

That One Face. Robert Browning. Fr. Dramatis Personae: Epilogue. ChIP; MaRV

That Out of Sight Is Out of Mind. Arthur Hugh Clough. Songs in Absence, IX. EmBrPo

That overnight a rose could come. Overnight, a Rose. Caroline Giltinan. HBMV; SBMV

That Path. Unknown, tr. fr. Japanese by Ishii and Obata. OnPM

That Pretty Little Gal. Unknown. ABF

That prudent Prince who ends Shakespearian plays. Elizabethan Tragedy; a Footnote. Howard Moss. NePoEA

That Radio Religion. William Ludlum. WBLP

"That rake up near the rafters, why leave it there so long?" Rory of the Hill. Charles Joseph Kickham. OnYI; TIP

That Rama whom the Indian sung. Of Rama. Herman Melville. AnFE; CoAnAm; LiTA

That Reminds Me. Ogden Nash. FiBHP

That sacred, solemn night, the last on earth. Intercession. L. M. Hollingsworth. PraP

That sea was greater than we knew. The Voyage. Edwin Muir. GTBS-W; LiTM (rev. ed.)

That season when the leaf deserts the bole. October 1. Karl Shapiro. FiMAP; MoAB; MoAmPo (1950 ed.)

That seat of science, Athens. Free America. At. to Joseph Warren. PAP; PoFr

That second time they hunted me. The Italian in England. Robert Browning. BPN; EmBrPo; GEPC; OAEP; PCN; PoVP; ViPo; VLEP

That shield some Saian decks, which 'gainst my grain. On the Loss of His Shield. Archilochus. GrR

That shining moon—watched by that one faint star. Night. Walter de la Mare. AlDL

That so many of the poor should suffer from cold. The Big Rug. Po Chü-i. TrCh

That soft autumnal time. The Indian Summer. John H. Bryant. TOAH

That son of Italy who tried to blow. Austerity of Poetry [or Jacopone da Todi]. Matthew Arnold. BEL; BMEP; BPN; CAW; EM-2; EmBrPo; EnLi-2; EPN; GoBC; OAEP; OBVV; PoFS; PoVP; PtP; TCEP; TOP; VLEP

That sovereign thought obscured? That vision clear. On a Great Man Whose Mind Is Clouding. Edmund Clarence Stedman. AA

That sovereign tyrant, Time, who can. On the Gout. Guillaume de Chaulieu. TrFP

That Speaking or Proffering Brings Alway Speeding. Sir Thomas Wyatt. TuPP

That spring in Palestine when airs went forth. The Annunciation. Margaret D. Conway. JKCP (1955 ed.)

That spring night I spent. Lady Suo, tr. fr. Japanese by Kenneth Rexroth. LiTW; OnPJ

That story which the bold Sir Bedivere. The Passing of Arthur. Tennyson. Fr. Idylls of the King. CoBE; EM-2; EPN; HeT; PCN; REAL

That Strain Again. Ronald Hambleton. CaP

That strange companion came on shuffling feet. The Strange Companion. Harold Monro. NP

That stream ran through the sunny grass so clear. The Ancestors. Judith Wright. BoAV

That stubborn crew. See He was of that stubborn crew.

That such have died enables us. Emily Dickinson. AA; AmPP

That summer we saw the Blue Horse. The Blue Horse. Melvin Walker La Follette. NePoEA

That Sunday, on my oath, the rain was a heavy overcoat. Mary Hynes. Padraic Fallon, after Anthony Raftery. AnIV; OxBI

That swollen paunch you are doomed to bear. Heredity. William Dean Howells. BAP

That ten-years-travelled Greek returned from sea. Elegy of His Lady's Not Coming to London. Michael Drayton. TriL

That Texan Cattle Man. Joaquin Miller. BOHV

That! That! There I was told. The Bible. Thomas Traherne. LoBV (1949 ed.)

That the glass would melt in heat. The Glass of Water. Wallace Stevens. AtBAP; CoBMV; MoAB; MoAmPo (1950 ed.); MoPo; OxBA

That the mere glimpse of a plain cap. The Glimpse of a Plain Cap. Unknown. Fr. Shi King. LiTW

That the Night Come. W. B. Yeats. CoBMV; NP; PoEL-5

That the Soul Is Immortal, and Cannot Die. Sir John Davies. Fr. Nosce Teipsum. TuPP

That There Are Powers above Us I Admit. Arthur Hugh Clough. ViPP

That there is falsehood in his looks. The Parson's Looks. Burns. OxBoLi

That there should be a barren garden. A House in Taos: Sun. Langston Hughes. CDC

"That They All May Be One." Roden Noel. VA

That Things Are No Worse, Sire. Helen Hunt Jackson. OHIP; PEOR

That this is not the best that did allow. "O Dark, Dark, Dark amid the Blaze of Noon." Sophocles. Fr. Oedipus Rex. GrR

That thou art blamed shall not be thy defect. Sonnets, LXX. Shakespeare. PeBoSo

That thou hast her it is not all my grief. Sonnets, XLII. Shakespeare. EM-1; InvP; PeBoSo

That thou so often held Him in thine arms. Mother Most Powerful. Giovanni Dominici. CAW

That Time and Absence Proves Rather Helps than Hurts to Loves. John Hoskins. See Absence.

That time great Hector stayed and comforted. Three Thousand Years After. Edith M. Tuttle. NeTW

That time of revolution being come. Reflections in Bed. Julian Symons. LiTM; WaP

That time of year thou may'st in me behold. Sonnets, LXXIII [or A Twilight of Love]. Shakespeare. AnFE; ATP (1935 ed.); AWP; BCEP; BEL; BLV; BoLiVe; BPP; BrBE; CaAE; ChTr; CoBE; CoEV; EG; EIL; ElSeCe; EM-1; EnL; EnLi-1; EnLit; EnLoPo; EPP; ES; EtPaEn; EV-1; ExPo; FaBoEn; FiP; GTBS-D; GTBS-W; GTSE; GTSL; HBV; HoPM; InPo; InvP; JAWP; KN; LEAP; LiTB; LiTG; LoBV; MaPo; NLK (1947 ed.); OAEP; OBEV; OBSC; OHFP (1958 ed.); OuHeWo; PeBoSo; PFE; PG (1955 ed.); PIAE; PoE; PoEL-2; PoFS; PoMa; PoRA; PreP; REAL; ReaPo; ReEn; ReIE; RiBV; SeCeV; SiCE; TCEP; TOP; TrGrPo; TwHP; TwP; TyEnPo; ViBoPo; WBP

That time that mirth did steer my ship. Sir Thomas Wyatt. SiPS

That time we went to Suffolk Downs to see. The Beautiful Horses. Donald Hall. NePoAm-2

That time when Bob got throwed. When Bob Got Throwed. Unknown. SCC

That 'tis well to be off with the old love. Dictum Sapienti. Charles Henry Webb. ALV; PR

That to this mountain-daisy's self were known. The Daisy. Wordsworth. Fr. So Fair, So Sweet, Withal So Sensitive. RO

That touching pallor which, like a soft cloud. Petrarch. Sonnets to Laura: To Laura in Life, XCVIII. PrPoCR

That twilight, dearest, as I spoke with thee. In the Face of Grief. Sister Juana Inéz de la Cruz. CAW

That vengeance [or vengeaunce] I ask and cry. O Cat of Carlish Kind. John Skelton. Fr. Phyllyp Sparowe. ChTr; SiCE

That very time I saw, but thou couldst not. Love-in-Idleness. Shakespeare. Fr. A Midsummer Night's Dream, II, i. TrGrPo

That very time I saw (but thou couldst not). Reuben. Phoebe Cary. BoHV

That voice makes lovely the land. Before Rain. Tr. by Mary Austin. APW

That voice, that presence, or that face. To His Mistress. T. Beaumont. SeCL

That was a brave old epoch. The Battle of La Prairie. William Douw Lighthall. MC; PAH; VA

That was a kindly storm, I know. Anniversary. Leonora Speyer. LoPS

That was a shocking day. Paul Engle. Fr. Beasts. ReMP

That was her beginning, an apparition. First Love. Laurie Lee. ChMP

That was his sort. The Father. W. W. Gibson. NV

That was I, you heard last night. A Serenade at the Villa. Robert Browning. NBE; VLEP

That Was My Woe. Robert Fairfax. TuPP

That was the chirp of Ariel. George Meredith. EG

That was the day they killed the Son of God. The Killing. Edwin Muir. ChMP

"That was the thrush's last good-night," I thought. The Singer. Edward Dowden. IrPN

That was the top of the walk, when he said. The Gypsy. Ezra Pound. ThWaDe
That was the year. A Poem to Delight My Friends Who Laugh at Science-Fiction. Edwin Rolfe. NePa; NePoAM
That way look, my infant, lo! The Kitten and Falling Leaves. Wordsworth. CIV; HBVY; PoC
That we are mortals and on earth must dwell. A Garden Prayer. Thomas Walsh. OQP; QP-2
That we may never lack two Sundays in a week. Secular Litany. M. K. Joseph. AnNZ
That which hath made them drunk, hath made me bold. The Murder. Shakespeare. *Fr.* Macbeth, II, ii. AtBAP; CBOV; LPS-3; MyFE; WHA
"That Which Hath Wings Shall Tell." Linda Lyon Van Voorhis. GoBC
That which her slender waist confined. On a Girdle. Edmund Waller. ALV; AWP; BEL; BLV; CEP; EG; ElSeCe; EM-1; EnLi-1; EnLit; EPP; EPS; EV-2; GTBS; GTBS-D; GTBS-W; GTSE; GTSL; HBV; InMe; InPo; JAWP; LEAP; LiTB; LiTG; LiTL; LoBV; LPS-1; OAEP; OBEV; OBS; PG (1945 ed.); PoFS; PoRA; SeCePo; SeCL; SeCV-1; SeEP; TCEP; TOP; TreFS; TrGrPo; ViBoPo; WBP; WHA
"That which I have myself seen and the fighting." Bernál Díaz's Preface to His Book. Archibald MacLeish. *Fr.* Conquistador. AmPP (3d ed.)
That which is marred at birth time shall not mend. Gertrude's Prayer. Kipling. FaBoEn
That Which Made Us. Tennyson. *Fr.* Locksley Hall Sixty Years After. OQP; QP-2
That which no one knows is the Highest. *Unknown, tr. fr. Chinese.* Tao Teh Ching, XXII. WhP
That which shall last for aye can have no birth. Or Ever the Earth Was. Charles Leonard Moore. AA
That which the long scythe whispered to the grass. Ruth Gilbert. *Fr.* And There Shall Be No More Death. AnNZ
That which we dare invoke to bless. In Memoriam A. H. H., CXXIV. Tennyson. BPN; EmBrPo; EnL; EPN; GEPC; GTSL; MaRV; OAEP; ViPo; VLEP; WGRP
That wife is best (as prudent men have found). Marriage. *Unknown.* OxBG
That Wind, I Used to Hear. Emily Brontë. EmBrPo
(That Wind.) CH
That Wind Is Best. Caroline Atherton Briggs Mason. *See* En Voyage.
That window where the sun at midday shows. Sonnet. Petrarch. Sonnets to Laura: To Laura in Life, LXXIX. LyPI
That winter love spoke and we raised no objection. Jig. C. Day Lewis. OxBI
That with this bright believing band. The Impercipient. Thomas Hardy. ChMo; CMP; MaPo; MaRV; OAEP; PoLFOT; POTT; TrGrPo; ViBoPo; ViPo; WGRP
That wolf, shivering by the palisade. Colonial Set. Alfred G. Bailey. BoCaPo
That woman with the somber eyes. Symphony Pathétique. Ruth Comfort Mitchell. PoeMoYo; VOD
That Women Are but Men's Shadows. Ben Jonson. *See* Song: That Women Are but Men's Shadows.
That wooded face of cliffs and shadows. Remembering Lincoln. Frank Mundorf. GoYe
That Wooden Cross. Austin Dobson. BPN
That word which never appears. Prelude. José Gorostiza. TwSpPo
That year! How often "Out you fall!" January, 1919. Boris Pasternak. BoRS
That year no wondering shepherds came. Christmas, the Year One, A.D. Sara Henderson Hay. PoRA
That year they fought in the snow. Rostov. G. S. Fraser. LiTM (rev. ed.); WaP
That year? Yes, doubtless I remember still. The World Well Lost. Edmund Clarence Stedman. AA; OBRV; PR
That you are fair or wise is vain. Destiny. Emerson. IAP
That you, enamoured so of life and art. To Virginia Woolf. Nathaniel Thornton. MuM
That you have wronged me, doth appear in this. Brutus and Cassius. Shakespeare. *Fr.* Julius Caesar, IV, iii. CBE
That you like me not. Referring to Flowers. *Unknown. Fr.* Manyo Shu. OnPM
That you, struck down by fortune's angry hand. Letter to Manlius Torquatus. Catullus. LiTW
That you trust her, alas, is plain enough. Sonnets, VIII. Mary Queen of Scots. DiM
That you were once unkind befriends me now. Sonnets, CXX. Shakespeare. InvP; PeBoSo
That your trees may be bold. Man's Inhumanity to Man. Martial. RoL
That zephyr every year. Song [*or* Spring Bereaved]. William Drummond of Hawthornden. EBSV; OBEV
Thatcher of Thatchwood went to Thatchet a-thatching, A. *Unknown.* OxNR
"That's a detestable thing you did!" A Deep Discussion. Richard Moore. HoPM
That's a Lie! Luis de Góngora, *tr. fr. Spanish by* Sir John Bowring. AnSpL-1
That's a rather bold speech, my Lord Bacon. Franciscus de Verulamio Sic Cogitavit. James Russell Lowell. TCAP
That's Ethan Allen on the monument. Green Mountain Boy. Florida Watts Smyth. GoYe
That's Jesus! Grace B. Renfrow. BePJ
That's July. Mary F. Butts. YeAr
That's June. Mary F. Butts. YeAr
That's my last Dutchess painted on the wall. My Last Duchess. Robert Browning. ATP; AWP; BEL; BeLS; BLV; BMEP; BoLiVe; BPN; CaAE; CBOV; CoBE; CoEV; EM-2; EmBrPo; EnL; EnLi-2; EnLit; EPN; EPP; EV-5; ExPo; FaBoEn; FaFP; FiP; GEPC; HBV; HiLiEn; HoPM; InP; InPo; JAWP; LiTB; MCCG; OAEP; OnPP; OtMeF; OuHeWo; PFE; PIAE; PIR; PoE; PoEL-5; PoVP; PYM; REAL; ReaPo; RiBV; SeCeV; ShBV-4; TCEP; TOP; TreFS; TrGrPo; TwHP; TwP; TyEnPo; UnPo (1st ed.); VA; ViPo; ViPP; VLEP; WBP; WHA
That's not a broom you're using, soldier. The Bayonet. Shawn O'Leary. MoAuPo
That's Success! Berton Braley. *See* Success.
That's the man who made the treaty. Dicaeopolis and the Case for the Enemy. Aristophanes. *Fr.* The Acharnians. GrR
That's the strange regalia of souls. Orpheus, Eurydice, and Hermes. Rainer Maria Rilke. AnGP
That's what misery is. Poetry Is a Destructive Force. Wallace Stevens. CoV; OxBA
Thaw. Walker Gibson. NePoAm
Thaw. Edward Thomas. FaBoTw; HaMV; MBP; MoAB; MoBrPo; NeMA
Thaw, The. Henry David Thoreau. CoV
Thaw. Eunice Tietjens. BrR
Thaw. Jean Starr Untermeyer. AtBAP
Thay walkit furth so derk oneith they wist. The Entrance to Hell. Virgil, *tr. by* Gawin Douglas. *Fr.* The Aeneid, VI. GoTS
Thealma and Clearchus, *sel.* John Chalkhill.
Rhotus on Arcardia. OBS
Theatre, The, *sel.* Horace Smith *and* James Smith.
"John Richard William Alexander Dwyer." OBRV
Thebes of the golden shield, my mother, I will put. Pindar. *Fr.* Isthmian Odes. GrPo
Thebes of the Seven Gates. Sophocles. *See* Victory over Aggressors.
Thee, dear friend, a brother soothes. To Rhea. Emerson. TCAP
Thee finds me in the garden, Hannah—come in! The Quaker Widow. Bayard Taylor. AA; IAP
Thee for my recitative. To a Locomotive in Winter. Walt Whitman. AmPP; InP; MCCG; MoAmPo (1950 ed.); PoE; PoEL-5; PoFS
Thee, holiest minister of Heaven—thee, envoy, usherer, guide at last of all. Peaceful Death. Walt Whitman. OQP; QP-1
Thee I Adore. Baudelaire, *tr. fr. French by* Arthur Symons. OnPM
"Thee, Mary, with this ring I wed." To His Wife on the Fourteenth [*or* Sixteenth] Anniversary of Her Wedding-Day [*or* To Mary]. Samuel Bishop. CBOV; HBV; LO; ViBoPo
Thee, May and Mother, I entreat. Author's Entreaty for His Lay. Eysteinn Asgrímsson. *Fr.* Lilya. ISi
Thee, O Mary, will I praise. Song of Praise to Mary. "Angelus Silesius." CAW
Thee sets a bell to swinging in my soul. Sonnets in Quaker Language. Hildegarde Flanner. NP
Thee, Sovereign God, our grateful accents praise. Te Deum. *Unknown, tr. by* Dryden. AWP; JAWP; OuHeWo; WBP
Thee too, modest tressèd maid. Moon. Henry Rowe. OBEV
Thee too the years shall cover. Anactoria. Swinburne. ViBoPo
Thefts of the Morning. Edith M. Thomas. AA
Their Banishment. Milton. *Fr.* Paradise Lost, XII. SeCePo
("... For now too nigh/ Th' Archangel stood.") BrBE
Their brown, harmless flack. The Sparrows at the Airport. Anthony Ostroff. NePoAm-2
Their cheeks are blotched for shame, their running verse. The Bards [*or* Lust in Song]. Robert Graves. FaBoMo; GTBS-W; LiTM (rev. ed.); OxBI; SeCePo. *See also* Bards falter in shame, their running verse, The
Their Conscience as Their King. Tennyson. *Fr.* Idylls of the King: Guinevere. MaRV
Their country's need is more to them than personal demands. The Medical Corps. Beatrice Barry. PEDC
Their dufflebags sprawl like a murder. Words without Music. Irving Layton. CaP
Their eyelids are drooping, no tears lie beneath. Weavers. Heine. TrJP
Their eyes had known the quiet color blue. Prisoner of War. Gertrude May Lutz. GoYe

Their hearts are filled with Pity's mead. A Gaelic Christmas. Liam P. Clancy. ISi
Their heels slapped their bumping mules. Merchants from Cathay. William Rose Benét. CV; HBMV; MAP; MoAMoP; NeMA; NV
Their height in heaven comforts not. Emily Dickinson. NePA
Their horses are black, the shoes of their horses are black. Ballad of the Spanish Civil Guard. Federico García Lorca. LiTW
Their Last Will and Testament. Louis MacNeice. NAMP
Their little room grew light with cries. Proper Clay. Mark Van Doren. LoPS; PoRA; TrGrPo; UnW
Their masses whiten the shore. Crimea Red. John Lehmann. MBP
Their memories behind them. Salvation Prospect. LeRoy Smith, Jr. NePoAm
Their mouths have drunken the eternal wine. The Night of Gods. George Sterling. MAP; MoAmPo (1942 ed.); PFY; WHA
Their noonday never knows. Fame. John Banister Tabb. AA; BAP
Their opaque, restless eyes. Notes by a Foreigner. Bernard Spencer. PoN
Their pail they must fill. Jack and Jill: As Austin Dobson Might Have Written It. Charles Battell Loomis. PA
Their poet, a sad trimmer, but no less. The Isles of Greece; Ways of Poets. Byron. *Fr.* Don Juan, III. EPN
Their quick feet pattered on the grass. Night Dancers. Thomas Kennedy. MoSiPe
Their scythes upon the adverse bank. The Mowers. Christopher Smart. *Fr.* A Noon Piece; or, The Mowers at Dinner. RO
Their sense is with their senses all mixed in. Modern Love, XLVIII. George Meredith. EmBrPo; EnLi-2; ViP; ViPo
Their several ends pursuing, one will roam. Diversity of Gifts. Solon. OxBG
Their shoulders you shook. The Preacher. Al-Mahdi. MooP
Their Silent Ministry. Frederick Lucian Hosmer. *See* My Dead.
Their slender shadows fill the enclosure. Poems Translated from the Chinese. *Unknown, tr. by* John Francis Davis. RO
Their souls escaped from Earth and fled. The Suicides. Vera Bax. DiM
Their steel-carved loveliness from tier to tier. A Letter from the Metropolis. Mildred D. Ingalls. CAG
Their Thanksgiving Day. Louise Driscoll. PCH
Their time past, pulled down. Burning the Christmas Greens. William Carlos Williams. CoBMV; MoPo; NePA
Their verdure dare not show. Valediction. Louis MacNeice. AnIL; MoVE
Their Victory Won. Florence Earle Coates. PEDC
Their Wedded Love. Milton. *See* Wedded Love.
Their world stands all on end; no place at all. An Alpine Village. Anne Goodwin Winslow. LS
Theirs is a white a green life, a smooth. Red Cross Nurses. Gervase Stewart. WaP
Theirs is the courage of flesh and bone. Of Things Not Seen. Leslie Savage Clark. ChIP
Theirs is the gentle finger on the pulse. For the Quakers. Bianca Bradbury. BoFr; NeTW
Theirs is the house whose windows—every pane. On the Asylum Road. Charlotte Mew. MoBrPo (1950 ed.)
Theirs is yon house that holds the village poor. The Parish Workhouse. George Crabbe. *Fr.* The Village. BCEP; LEAP
Thekla's Song. Schiller, *tr. fr. German by* Samuel Taylor Coleridge. *Fr.* The Piccolomini. AWP; JAWP; WBP
Thel's Motto. Blake. *Fr.* The Book of Thel. ChTr
("Does the eagle know what is in the pit?") LO
Them ez wants, must choose. A Baker's Duzzen uv Wize Sawz. Edward Rowland Sill. FaBoBe; FaFP; HBV; HBVY; InMe; SiTL; TreFS
Them Yankee Blankits. Samuel W. Small. MDAH
Theme. James Stephens. POTE
Theme in Yellow. Carl Sandburg. MPB; PCD; StVeCh (1955 ed.); TiPo; YeAr
Theme of morning was the sound of rain, The. Rain. Sam Harrison. NeIP
Theme Song for a Songwriters' Union. Al Graham. WhC
Theme with Variations, A. Barry Pain. PA
Theme with Variations, *sel.* James Stephens.
"No pride hath he who sings of escape from love." POTE
Themes. Denis Glover. AnNZ
Themistocles. Timocreon, *tr fr. Greek by* C. M. Bowra. OxBG
Then. Rose Terry Cooke. HBV
Then. Walter de la Mare. GaP; TVC; TVSH
Then a ploughman said, Speak to us of Work. Of [*or* On] Work. Kahlil Gibran. *Fr.* The Prophet. GrCo-2; PoToHe (new ed.)
Then a thousand men thronged together. The Search for St. Truth. William Langland. *Fr.* The Vision of Piers Plowman. MeEV
Then after show'rs, 'tis easy to descry. After the Rain. Virgil, *tr. by* Dryden. *Fr.* Georgics. BeR
Then Agamemnon said, the King of Men. Agamemnon; Peace Offerings to Achilles. Homer. *Fr.* The Iliad, IX. GrR
Then Ag'in. Sam Walter Foss. BAP; BOHV; HBV
Then all the minutes of my life to come. Thomas Lovell Beddoes. *Fr.* Death's Jest Book, II. LO
Then Almighty God, High Lord of heaven, was filled with wrath. The Fall of the Angels. Cædmon(?). *Fr.* Genesis. EPP
Then among them the father of gods and men began to speak. Blame Not the Gods! Homer. *Fr.* The Odyssey, I. GrR
Then and Now. Samuel Daniel. *See* To Delia: "When men shall find thy flower . . ."
Then and Now. A. E. Housman. *See* Oh, When I Was in Love With You.
Then and Now. Charles Frederick Johnson. AA
Then and Now. Sir Rennell Rodd. VA
Then and Now. George Sterling. PoMa
Then answer thus Antenor sage return'd. Menelaus and Odysseus. Homer. *Fr.* The Iliad, III. OxBG
Then answered him Antinoüs and said: "What god has brought to us this pest." Homer. *Fr.* The Odyssey, XVII. GrPo
Then Aphrodite, the lover of laughter, was clad. Aphrodite on Ida. *Unknown. Fr.* Homeric Hymns. OxBG
Then as Now. Walter de la Mare. WaKn
Then As to Feasting. Oliver Wendell Holmes. WhC
Then backed the griffin-horse, and soared a flight. Ariosto. *Fr.* Orlando Furioso, XXXIV. PrPoCR
Then before All they stand—the holy vow. Marriage. Samuel Rogers. *Fr.* Human Life. LPS-1
Then beheld our Creator. The Garden of Eden. Cædmon(?). *Fr.* Genesis. TCEP
Then bold Dankwart strode in through the door. The Fall of the Nibelungs. *Unknown. Fr.* The Song of the Nibelungs. LiA
Then bold Robin Hood to the north he would go. Robin Hood and the Scotchman. *Unknown.* ESPB
Then by Athena the goddess, the daughter of Zeus the Almighty. Nausicaa; the Ingenue. Homer. *Fr.* The Odyssey, VI. GrR
Then Byrhtnoth drew up his battle in order. The Battle of Maldon. *Unknown.* EPP
Then came a man, some years awhile. Dedicated to Dr. Harvey Cushing. Temple Fay. PoP
Then came Dunkirk to mitigate the news. Martyn Skinner. *Fr.* Letters to Malaya, IV. AlDL
Then came fair May, the fairest maid on the ground. May. Spenser. *Fr.* The Faerie Queene, VII. GN; PoRL
Then Came I to the Shoreless Shore of Silence. Conrad Aiken. Preludes for Memnon, XXXIII. LiTA; NePA; OxBA (Preludes to Attitude, VII.) TwAmPo
Then came old January, wrapped well. Old January. Spenser. *Fr.* The Faerie Queene, VII, 7. YeAr
Then came the Autumn all in yellow clad. Autumn. Spenser. *Fr.* The Faerie Queene, VII. GN; HOAH
Then came the cry of "Call all hands on deck!" Rounding the Horn [*or* Dauber Rounds Cape Horn]. John Masefield. *Fr.* Dauber. BBV; EtS; MBP; MoAB; MoBrPo; NeMA; WHA
Then came the Nightingale, from such a draught. The Nightingale. Ferid ed-Din Attar. *Fr.* The Bird-Parliament. PeP
Then came the subtle Parrot in a coat. The Parrot. Ferid ed-Din Attar. *Fr.* The Bird-Parliament. PeP
Then Christ, the Gardener, said, "These many years." Transplanted. Helen Hunt Jackson. EOAH
Then close at hand came Athene. Odysseus and His Son. Homer. *Fr.* The Odyssey, XVI. GrPE
Then come his sister and his village-friend. The Suffolk Shore. George Crabbe. *Fr.* The Borough. RO
Then Constantine, mindful of the Holy Cross. Helena Embarks for Palestine. Cynewulf. *Fr.* Elene. AnOE
Then, couched at night in hunter's wattled shieling. Thomas Pringle. *Fr.* The Desolate Valley. BoSA
Then dar'd I words to him, and did present. Noman and the Cyclops. Homer. *Fr.* The Odyssey, IX. GrR
Then, day by day, her broidered gown. The Earth in Spring. Judah Halevi. TrJP
Then did Guthrun think to die. "Home They Brought Her Warrior Dead." *Unknown. Fr.* The Elder Edda. PaOS
Then did Siddartha raise his eyes, and see. The End Which Comes. Sir Edwin Arnold. *Fr.* The Light of Asia. LoBV
Then did the sage old Medon, the herald, address her in answers. Penelope; New Woes on Old. Homer. *Fr.* The Odyssey, IV. GrR
Then did Ulysses cast his rags aside. Homer. *Fr.* The Odyssey, XXII. GrPo
Then die! Outside the prison gawk. For St. Bartholomew's Eve. Malcolm Cowley. NAMP
Then die, thou Year—thy work is done. Autumn. Aubrey

Thomas De Vere. *Fr.* The Year of Sorrow: Ireland, 1849. TIP
Then dread no more the Argive foeman's spear. Macaria and Iolaus. Euripides. *Fr.* Children of Heracles. GrR
Then Eurycleia, the dear nurse, rejoined. Homer. *Fr.* The Odyssey, XXIII. GrPo
Then farewell, Horace; whom I hated so. Byron. *Fr.* Childe Harold's Pilgrimage, IV. PtP
Then first he form'd the immense and solid shield. The Shield of Achilles. Homer. *Fr.* The Iliad, XVIII. GrR; OxBG
Then forth issewed (great goddesse) great Dame Nature. Dame Nature. Spenser. *Fr.* The Faerie Queene, VII. PoEL-1
Then from a Wood was heard unseen to coo. The Ring-Dove. Ferid ed-Din Attar. *Fr.* The Bird-Parliament. PeP
Then from His throne the Godhead bowed. A Christmas Song. Laurence Housman. SDH
Then from the seas [*or* sea] the dawning 'gan arise. Dido's Hunting [*or* The Fourth Book of Virgil]. Virgil, *tr. by* the Earl of Surrey. *Fr.* The Aeneid, IV. OBSC; ReEn
Then, from the skeletons of trams. Kenneth Slessor. *Fr.* Last Trams. MoAuPo
Then from the well-laced cars leapt down the twain to earth apace. Combat of Heracles and Cycnus. Hesiod. *Fr.* Shield of Heracles. OxBG
Then from their poverty they rose. The Ordinary Women. Wallace Stevens. OxBA
Then gently scan your brother man. Burns. *Fr.* Address to the Unco Guid, or the Rigidly Righteous. MaRV
Then Glutton got ready to go to confession. Glutton and Bat the Brewer. William Langland. *Fr.* The Vision of Piers Plowman, Passus V. CoBE
Then haste ye, Prescott and Revere! The Battle of Lexington. Sidney Lanier. *Fr.* The Psalm of the West. PaP
Then hate me when thou wilt: if ever, now. Sonnets, XC. Shakespeare. ATP; AWP; BoFr; CoEV; ElL; ES; EtPaEn; EV-1; JAWP; LiA; LO; MaPo; OBEV; OBSC; PeBoSo; PG; PoEL-2; ReIE; TOP; WBP; WHA; WoL
Then have mercy upon me. Mercury. Josephine Miles. FiMAP
Then he made of the stars, in my mind. Baiamai's Never-failing Stream. William Hart-Smith. BoAV
Then He summoned an archangel. Romance VIII. St. John of the Cross. ISi
Then hear me bounteous Heaven. Jaffier Parting with Belvidera. Thomas Otway. *Fr.* Venice Preserved. LPS-1
Then hearkened the Argus-slayer, Hermes the Heavenly Guide. The Message of Hermes to Calypso. Homer. *Fr.* The Odyssey, V. GrPE
Then heavenly branches did I see arise. The Visions of Petrarch. *Tr. by* Spenser. EnLi-1
Then here's an end of me: fare-well day-light. John Webster. *Fr.* The White Devil, V, vi. AtBAP
Then here's to the city of Boston. Boston. Franklin P. Adams. BoHiPo
Then hey for the whisky, and hey for the meal. A Cogie o' Yill. Andrew Shirrefs. EBSV
Then Hippolochos' glorious son made answer to him. Glaukos and Diomedes. Homer. *Fr.* The Iliad, VI. GrR
Then his might no longer did Zeus refrain. The Doom of the Titans. Hesiod. *Fr.* Theogony. GrR
Then Hrothgar's minstrel rehearsed the lay. The Lay of Finn. *Unknown. Fr.* Beowulf. AnOE
Then I Saw What the Calling Was. Muriel Rukeyser. FiMAP
Then I tuned my harp—took off the lilies we twine round its chords. Robert Browning. *Fr.* Saul. BBV (1951 ed.); FiP; PreP
Then I was dead. Dream of Dying. Thomas Lovell Beddoes. *Fr.* Fragments Intended for the Dramas. RO
Then I was sealed, and like the wintering tree. Alas, Kind Element. Léonie Adams. MoVE
Then I'll say this—life is so still. Endymion. Humbert Wolfe. NP
Then in the corb Aegisthus set his hand. Euripides. *Fr.* Electra. ReTS
Then in the field the Trojans supped; but the Argives kept. Homer. *Fr.* The Iliad, XVIII. GrPE
Then in two several bands I did portion and number my comrades. Homer. *Fr.* The Odyssey, X. GrPo
Then, indeed, did I yearn to die. The Parting. Sappho. LiTW
Then indeed had the sons of Achaea, led by Patroclus' might. The Slaying of Patroclus. Homer. *Fr.* The Iliad, XVI. GrPE
Then it came to pass that a pestilence fell on the city. The Finding of Gabriel. Longfellow. *Fr.* Evangeline, II. AA
Then it was dusk in Illinois, the small boy. First Song. Galway Kinnell. NePoAm
Then it was faith and fairness. The Age of Herbert & Vaughan. Edmund Blunden. PtP
Then it was hound. Its force compelled the jaw. Famine. Georg Heym. LiTW
Then it's a hooraw, and a hooraw. Standin' on the Walls of Zion. *Unknown.* AS
Then Job answered and said. Not Flesh of Brass. Job, Bible, *O.T.* TrJP
Then Job arose, and rent his mantle. The Lord Gave. Job, Bible, *O.T.* TreF
Then Jove's daughter Helen. At Sparta; Helen and Menelaus. Homer. *Fr.* The Odyssey, IV. OxBG
Then judge me as thou wilt, I cannot flee. Sonnets, III. Robert Hillyer. HBMV
Then, lady, at last thou art sick of my sighing. A West-Country Lover. Alice Brown. HBV; LBMV; LEAP; PR
Then Laugh. Bertha Adams Backus. BLPA; NeHB; PoToHe (new ed.); WBLP; YaD
Then leave complaints: Fools only strive. The Moral to "The Grumbling Hive." Bernard Mandeville. *Fr.* The Grumbling Hive; or, Knaves Turn'd Honest. BeR
Then left the sons of Urizen the plow & harrow, the loom. The Arts of Death. Blake. *Fr.* The Four Zoas. CoEV
Then Lelex rose, an old experienced man. Baucis and Philemon. Ovid. *Fr.* Metamorphoses. AWP; JAWP; WBP
Then let not winter's ragged hand deface. Sonnets, VI. Shakespeare. PeBoSo; SiCE
Then let the chill Sirocco blow. The Winter Glass. Charles Cotton. HBV
Then let the village bells, as often wont. James Hurdis. *Fr.* The Village Curate. EnSW
Then life is—to wake not sleep. Life. Robert Browning. *Fr.* Christmas-Eve and Easter-Day. OP-2
Then lift up the head with a song! Praise. *Unknown.* PCH
Then, like a miracle, the violets came out. Bay Violets. Sister Maris Stella. GoBC
Then like the ship at rest in the bay. Love Poem. George Barker. First Cycle of Love Poems, IV. FaBoMo; MoPo
Then listen, as I listened unto you. Thomas Lovell Beddoes. *Fr.* Death's Jest Book, III. PoFr
Then Mahoney, standing in the surf. Mahoney. Seán Jennett. NeIP
Then mass was sung, and prayers were said. Dies Irae [*or* Hymn for the Dead]. *Par. fr. Latin by* Sir Walter Scott. *Fr.* The Lay of the Last Minstrel, VI. EmBrPo; GoBC
Then Menelaus, shaking his own long-shadowed spear. Paris Is Worsted by Menelaus and Returns to Helen. Homer. *Fr.* The Iliad, III. GrPE
Then Mercury 'gan bend him to obey. Virgil, *tr. by* the Earl of Surrey. *Fr.* The Aeneid, IV. ViBoPo
Then muster thy folk, play the captain thyself. July. Thomas Tusser. ReIE
Then my well-greaved fellows I numbered into two companies. Of Circe. Homer. *Fr.* The Odyssey, X. OxBG
Then night drew darkness over the earth; on the lonely sea. Vigil and Remorse. Apollonius Rhodius. *Fr.* Argonautica. GrR
Then night throbs on; O, let me pray, dear Lord! Motherhood. Josephine Dodge Daskam Bacon. HBV
Then no one hears me. O! the world's too loud. Thomas Lovell Beddoes. *Fr.* Death's Jest Book, IV. ERP
Then Oberon spake the word of might. The Flitting of the Fairies. Jane Barlow. *Fr.* The End of Elfintown. TIP
Then Odysseus of many counsels stripped him of his rags. Homer. *Fr.* The Odyssey, XXII. GrL
Then on his arm he settled the massy weight of his shield. Achilles' Arms. Homer. *Fr.* The Iliad, XIX. GrPE
Then once more men's ears were full of "Yankee Doodle." Harry Brown. *Fr.* The Poem of Bunker Hill. PoFr
Then one of them, which was a lawyer. St. Matthew, Bible, *N.T.* PoFr
Then our music is in prime. A Good Eating Song. William Cartwright. *Fr.* The Ordinary. SeCL
Then out spake brave Horatius. Horatius at the Bridge. Macaulay. *Fr.* Lays of Ancient Rome. LEAP; PoFr
Then out-streamed a Light. Death of Saint Guthlac. Cynewulf. *Fr.* Guthlac. ACP
Then Perceveraunce in all goodly haste. Of the Great Mariage betwene Graunde Amour and Labell Pucell. Stephen Hawes. *Fr.* The Pastime of Pleasure, *ch.* 39. EPP
Then piped a tiny voice hard by. Chickadee. Emerson. *Fr.* The Titmouse. PCH
Then Roland feels that death is taking him. The Death of Roland. *Unknown, tr. by* Henry Adams. *Fr.* The Song of Roland. LiA
Then Roland feels that his last hour has come. The Death of Roland. *Unknown, tr. by* Henry Adams. *Fr.* The Song of Roland. MeRV
Then rose from sea to sky the wild farewell. The Shipwreck. Byron. *Fr.* Don Juan, II. LiA
Then rose the King and moved his host by night. Tennyson. *Fr.* Idylls of the King: The Passing of Arthur. NBE
Then round the Bay of Mexico. Round the Bay of Mexico. *Unknown.* OuSiCo
Then sad he sung "The Children in the Wood." The Ballad Monger. John Gay. *Fr.* The Shepherd's Week. EV-3
Then said another, "Ah! so may that desire be fulfilled." Buonconte Relates His Fate. Dante. *Fr.* Divina Commedia: Purgatorio. LiA

Then said Jesus to those Jews which believed on him. St. John, Bible, *N.T.* PoFr
Then said Jesus unto them again, Verily, verily, I say unto you, I am the door of the sheep. The Good Shepherd. St. John, Bible, *N.T.* TreFS
Then said the Cid, who in good hour had girded on the steel. Pawning the Coffers of Sand. *Unknown. Fr.* The Cid. LiTW
Then saith another, "We are kindly things." Tender Babes. Thomas Hood. *Fr.* The Plea of the Midsummer Fairies. OBRV
Then Sang Deborah and Barak. Judges, Bible, *O.T. See* Song of Deborah, The.
Then Sang Moses. Exodus, Bible, *O.T. See* Triumphal Chant.
"Then saw I many broken hinted sights." On the Death of Beatrice: The Dream. Dante. *Fr.* La Vita Nuova. MeRV
Then saw I, with gray eyes fulfilled of rest. In Hades. Anna Callender Brackett. AA
Then saw they how there hove a dusky barge. Tennyson. *Fr.* Idylls of the King: The Passing of Arthur. VA
Then seeing him the noble Achilles, the swift of foot, was moved. Patroclus Intercedes for the Achaeans. Homer. *Fr.* The Iliad, XVI. GrPE
Then shall he lie in the earth. Death. *Unknown.* OxBG
Then shall the kingdom of heaven be likened unto ten virgins. The Wise and Foolish Virgins. St. Matthew, Bible, *N.T.* TreF
Then Shall We See. Charles Leonard Moore. AA
Then shame to manhood, and opprobrious more. The Bastille. William Cowper. *Fr.* The Task, V. RO
Then she came to the pillar of the bed. The Tyrant's Death. Judith, Bible, Apocrypha. BHV; PoFr
Then since from God those lesser lives began. From God to God. Virgil. MaRV
Then sing, ye birds, sing, sing a joyous song! The Gladness of the May. Wordsworth. YeAr
Then slanting off towards the left he took the road to Pyxa. "Season of Mellow Fruitfulness." Theocritus. *Fr.* Idylls, VII. GrR
"Then sleep, Thou little Child." Thus sweet and high. Choir-Boys on Christmas Eve. Louise Townsend Nicholl. TSW
Then, soon as night o'ershades my dying eyes. The Lover's Death. Propertius. *Fr.* Elegies. RoL
Then soon gay summer brings his gaudy train. John Scott of Amwell. *Fr.* Rural Scenery, Eclogue I. EnSW
Then spake Jesus unto them, saying, I am the light of the world. Jesus Answers the Pharisees. St. John, Bible, *N.T.* TreFS
Then spake the old dame cheerily: "Right well I wot, perdie." Endrina and Trota-Conventos. Juan Ruiz, Archpriest of Hita. TeCS
Then step by step walks Autumn. Autumn's Processional. Dinah Maria Mulock Craik. GN
Then swift Achilles answer'd him. Achilles' Reply to the Embassy. Homer. *Fr.* The Iliad, IX. OxBG
Then tell me how to woo thee, love, *refrain.* O Tell Me How to Woo Thee. Robert Graham. EBSV. *See also* If Doughty Deeds.
Then that dread angel near the awful throne. Fiat Lux. Lloyd Mifflin. AA; AnAmPo; LA; LBMV; PFY
Then the armies came out. Plautus. *Fr.* Amphitryon. LaP
Then the assembly was broken up. Homer. *Fr.* The Iliad, XXIV. GrL
Then the Courage-hearted quakes, when the King he hears. *Fr.* Christ. Cynewulf. TCEP
Then the Ermine. Marianne Moore. NePoAm
Then the fierce trumpet-flourish. The Battle. Macaulay. *Fr.* Lays of Ancient Rome. BHV
Then the golden hour. Length of Moon. Arna Bontemps. CDC; PoNe
Then the King in low deep tones. The King. Tennyson. *Fr.* Idylls of the King: The Coming of Arthur. BHV
Then the little Hiawatha. Hiawatha's Brothers [*or* Hiawatha's Chickens]. Longfellow. *Fr.* The Song of Hiawatha, III. BoTP; PCH
Then the Lord Answered. Job, Bible, *O.T. See* Voice Out of the Whirlwind Answers Job, The.
Then the Lord God spoke and said unto Noah. Noah's Flood. *Unknown. Fr.* Genesis. AnOE
Then the Master/ With a gesture. Longfellow. *Fr.* The Building of the Ship. OHFP
Then the old dame went up to the upper chamber. Odysseus and Penelope Meet. Homer. *Fr.* The Odyssey, XXIII. LiA
Then the pair followed Pa to Manhasset. Limerick [*or* That Nantucket Limerick and What Followed]. *Unknown.* LiBL; TreF
Then the son of Weohstan, stalwart in war. The Funeral Pyre. *Unknown. Fr.* Beowulf. AnOE
Then the truth came upon me. No harp more—no song more! Robert Browning. *Fr.* Saul. PIAE
Then the white-armed Goddess Hera heeded the words he said. The Steeds of Heaven. Homer. *Fr.* The Iliad, V. GrPE
Then there came at that time a valiant man riding. Arthur's Dream. Layamon. *Fr.* The Brut. MeEV
Then there is this civilizing love of death, by which. Ignorance of Death. William Empson. CoBMV; LiTM (rev. ed.); ReMP
Then there were the grapes turned purple in the sun. Grapes. Sister Maris Stella. GoBC
. . . Then they saw/ Forth and forward faring. The Approach [*or* Coming] of Pharaoh. Cædmon(?). *Fr.* Genesis. ACP; CAW; WaaP
Then thou, Achilles, reverence the Gods. Homer. *Fr.* The Iliad, XXIV. GrPo
Then thought within his mind the Lord of hosts. The Beginning of Creation. Cædmon(?). *Fr.* Genesis. BCEP
Then thus we have beheld. Chorus. Samuel Daniel. *Fr.* Cleopatra. OBSC
Then thus with gentle tones. Helen; the Penitent. Homer. *Fr.* The Iliad, VI. GrR
Then to Emmaus with him I, too, walked. Contemporary. Sara Bard Field. ChIP; QS
Then to keep covenant in Greece is well! Medea's Parting Words. Apollonius Rhodius. *Fr.* Argonautica. OxBG
Then to the bar all they drew near. The Infants' Petition [*or* Damnation of the Infants]. Michael Wigglesworth. *Fr.* The Day of Doom. AnNE; APW
Then to the bees one said. The Bees. Monk Gibbon. OnYI
Then took the generous host. The Rose. Bayard Taylor. *Fr.* Hassan Ben Khaled. LPS-2
Then touch then park; the leaves are stained to lure you. Counter-Serenade; She Invokes the Autumn Instant. Peter Viereck. CrMA
Then Twist the Neck of This Delusive Swan. Enrique González Martínez, *tr. fr. Spanish by* John Peale Bishop. AnCL; LiTW
Then unto Hrothgar was given success in battle. The Slaying of Grendel. *Unknown. Fr.* Beowulf. EPP
Then up aloft this yard must go. A Long Time Ago, *vers.* VI. *Unknown.* ShS
Then up shake Sigurd Sigmundarson. Sigurth in Faeroese. *Unknown.* PaOS
Then up sprang storm-foot Iris to bear the word He gave. Homer. *Fr.* The Iliad, XXIV. GrPE
Then was earth made anew where'er He went. The Law of Love. John Oxenham. OQP; QP-2
Then was Gunnar silent a little. Gunnar in the Pit of Adders. William Morris. *Fr.* The Story of Sigurd the Volsung. PoVP; ViPo
Then was I cast out from my state. The Demons of Opium. George Crabbe. *Fr.* Sir Eustace Grey. RO
Then was not non-existent nor existent. The Creation Hymn. *Unknown. Fr.* The Rig-Veda. OuHeWo
Then we came to the isle Aeolian. Homer. *Fr.* The Odyssey, X. GrL
Then we'll sing of Lydia Pinkham. Lydia Pinkham. *Unknown.* AS
Then went the ancient matron forth. Penelope's Dream. Homer. *Fr.* The Odyssey, XIX. GrR
Then went the Pharisees, and took counsel. The Things That Are Caesar's. St. Matthew, Bible, *N.T.* TreF
Then were brought near with trembling fear, a number numberless. The Heathen and the Infants. Michael Wigglesworth. *Fr.* The Day of Doom. AmPP (3d ed.)
Then were brought nigh a company. Men of Good Works. Michael Wigglesworth. *Fr.* The Day of Doom. AmPP
Then were there brought unto him little children. The Rich Man and the Kingdom of Heaven. St. Matthew, Bible, *N.T.* TreF
Then what does it avail me, that you once. What Does It Avail Me? Louise Labé. LiTW
Then what is the answer?—Not to be deluded by dreams. The Answer. Robinson Jeffers. ChMo; GoYe; PoLFOT
Then, When I Am Thy Captive, Talk of Chains. Milton. *Fr.* Paradise Lost, IV. WHA
Then When the Ample Season. Richard Wilbur. MiAP
Then whilst that Latmos did contain her bliss. Sonnet. Earl of Stirling. Aurora, XXVIII. ViBoPo
Then wide-ruling Agamemnon seized the spear in his hand. A Sleep of Bronze. Homer. *Fr.* The Iliad, XI. LiA
Then with the rich harp came Pontonous. Homer. *Fr.* The Odyssey, VIII. GrPo
Then woes, and wars, and wasting tides of blood. Lycophron. *Fr.* Alexandra. GrPo
Then You'll Remember Me. Alfred Bunn. *See* When Other Lips and Other Hearts.
Then you'll see our oars with feathered spray. In Measure Time We'll Row. *Unknown.* ShS
Then Zeus no longer held back his power. Zeus and the Titans. Hesiod. *Fr.* Theogony. OxBG
Thence, in his saffron robe, for distant Thrace. Orpheus and Eurydice. Ovid. *Fr.* Metamorphoses, X. RoL
Thence onward by the well-known road. Changes. Charles Barter. *Fr.* Stray Memories of Natal and Zululand. BoSA

Thence passing forth, they shortly do arrive. The Bower of Bliss. Spenser. *Fr.* The Faerie Queene, II. ATP; FiP
Thenot Protests. "C. N. S." InMe
Theobalds' Roads. Charles Williams. LO
Theocritus. Annie Fields. AA; LBAP
Theocritus. Sir Edmund Gosse. PtP; VA
Theocritus. Charles Hartley Langhorne. PtP; VA
Theocritus. Oscar Wilde. BMEP; EV-5; HBV; LBBV; OxBI; PIAE; ShBV-4; VLEP
Theocritus! Theocritus! ah, thou hadst pleasant dreams. Theocritus. Charles Hartley Langhorne. PtP; VA
Theodor Herzl. Israel Zangwill. TrJP
Theodore and Honoria. Dryden, *paraphrased fr. the Italian of* Boccaccio. GePC; SeEP
Theodore Roosevelt. Samuel Valentine Cole. PEDC
Theodore Roosevelt. Kipling. *See* Great-Heart.
Theodore Roosevelt. William W. Peavyhouse. HH
Theodore Roosevelt. Edna Dean Proctor. BoHiPo
Theodore Roosevelt. *Unknown.* BoHiPo
Theodore Roosevelt. McLandburgh Wilson. BoHiPo
Theodore Roosevelt—Pilot and Prophet! Charles Hanson Towne. *See* Pilot and Prophet.
Theodosia Burr. Myra Burnham Terrell. GoYe
Theodosia Burr; the Wrecker's Story. John Williamson Palmer. GA; PAH
Theodosius; or, The Force of Love, *sel.* Nathaniel Lee.
Dead Night. BeR
Theogony, *sels.* Hesiod, *tr. fr. Greek.*
"Amid the foremost, towering in the van," *tr. by* C. A. Elton. GrPo
Birth of the Muses, *tr. by* Arthur S. Way. GrR
Coming of Aphrodite, The, *tr. by* F. L. Lucas. GrPE
Mountains, *tr. by* F. L. Lucas. GrPE
Muses' Gift, The, *tr. by* Jack Lindsay. OxBG
(Gift of the Muses, *tr. by* Arthur S. Way.) GrR
Poetry, *tr. by* F. L. Lucas. GrPE
Religion, *tr. by* F. L. Lucas. GrPE
Zeus and the Titans, *tr. by* Jack Lindsay. OxBG
(Doom of the Titans, The, *tr. by* Arthur S. Way.) GrR
Theological. Clifton Fadiman. FiBHP
Theology. Joyce Kilmer. TSW; TSWC
Theology. William Langland, *mod. by* Henry W. Wells. *Fr.* The Vision of Piers Plowman. PoLi
(Grace for Theology.) GoBC
Theology in Extremis. Sir Alfred Comyn Lyall. LH
Theonichos and Mnesarete. Constantine Trypanis. PoN
Theophany. Evelyn Underhill. MaRV; WGRP
Theophila; or, Love's Sacrifice, *sels.* Edward Benlowes.
Evening Prayer. FaBoEn
Life and Death. FaBoEn
To His Muse. SeCL
Theophilus Thistledown. *Unknown.* LiL
("Theophilus Thistledown, the successful thistle sifter.") OxNR
Theory. Dorothy Parker. BOHV
Theory. Wallace Stevens. CoV
Theory if you hold it hard enough, A. Etherealizing. Robert Frost. CoV
Theoxenus. Pindar, *tr. fr. Greek by* C. M. Bowra. OxBG
Ther wacz lokyng on lenthe, the lude to beholde. *Unknown.* *Fr.* Sir Gawain and the Green Knight. EPP
Ther was a lady fair an rear. The Kitchie-Boy. *Unknown.* ESPB
Ther was also a Nonne, a Prioresse. *See* There also was a nun, a Prioress.
Ther was in Asie [*or* Asye], in a greet citee. The Prioress's Tale. Chaucer. *Fr.* The Canterbury Tales. BEL; EM-1; GEPC; LoBV; OAEP. *See also* There was in Asia . . .
Therania. William Allingham. TIP
There a king once went in dancing. Shadows on the Wall. Aleksandr Blok. BoR
There ain' no liars there in my Father's house. In My Father's House. *Unknown.* AS
There ain' no mo' cane on de Brazis. Ain' No Mo' Cane on de Brazis. *Unknown.* ABF
There aince was a very pawky duke. The Pawky Duke. David Rorie. GoTS
There all the golden codgers lay. News for the Delphic Oracle. W. B. Yeats. CoBMV; LiTB; LiTM; MoPo; OAEP (2d ed.)
There also was a nun [*or* Ther was also a Nonne], a Prioress. A Prioress [*or* Seven Pilgrims *or* Three Canterbury Pilgrims]. Chaucer. *Fr.* The Canterbury Tales: Prologue. CBOV; MaC; TrGrPo
There always is a noise when it is dark! In the Night. James Stephens. OBMV
There Ance Was a May. Lady Grizel Baillie. *See* Were Na My Heart Light I Wad Dee.
There—and Back. Rodney Bennett. BoTP
There are a few things I shall not forget. 1917–1919. Henry Martin Hoyt. HBMV
There are a number of us creep. Insignificant Existence [*or* Horace Paraphrased]. Isaac Watts. LoBV; LPS-3; UnPo (3d ed.)
There are abandoned corners of our exile. The Mathmid. Hayyim Nahman Bialik. AWP; PoFr
There are all kinds of men. A Thank You for Friends. Rodney Bennett. BoTP
There Are Big Waves. Eleanor Farjeon. BoTP
There are blind eyes. A Prayer in Time of Blindness. Clement Wood. TrPWD
There are canines old and mangy. The Dog That Howls at Night. Herbert J. Bryce. AlBD
There are certain things—as, a spider, a ghost. A Sea Dirge. "Lewis Carroll." CenHV; StaSt
There Are Children in the Dusk. Bertram Warr. PeCV
There are dealers in pictures named Agnew. Tom Agnew, Bill Agnew. Dante Gabriel Rossetti. ChTr
There are emerald herbs by the riverbank. The Nineteen Han Poems, II. *Unknown, tr. fr. Chinese.* WhP
There are fairies at the bottom of our garden! The Fairies. Rose Fyleman. FaPON; HBMV; HBVY; HOAH; MPB; OTPC (1946 ed.); StVeCh; TSW; TSWC; TVC; TVSH
There are ferns in the garden of the Soul, as well as flowers. God's Ferns. John Henry Jowett. CBOV
There are figures like the dark figures. Microcosmos, XXXII. Nigel Heseltine. NeBP
There are fish that go bathing in the sand. Open Letter. Rafael Alberti. CoSP
There Are Four Doors Which Open on the Skies. Robert Nathan. MaRV; MuM
There are four good legs to my father's chair. My Father's Chair. Kipling. FAOV
There are four men mowing down by the Isar. A Youth Mowing. D. H. Lawrence. MBP; MoAB; MoBrPo; TrGrPo
There are four vibrators, the world's exactest clocks. Four Quartz Crystal Clocks. Marianne Moore. ImOP
There are four wild steeds that the witches ride. The Witches' Steeds. Will H. Ogilvie. TVSH
There Are Gains for All Our Losses. Richard Henry Stoddard. *See* Flight of Youth, The.
"There are gains for all our losses." An Old Song Reversed. Richard Henry Stoddard. AA; LEAP
There are harps that complain to the presence of night. Music of the Night. John Neal. AA; APW
There are hermit souls that live withdrawn. The House by the Side of the Road. Sam Walter Foss. BAP; BLPA; BTP; CV; DDA; FaBoBe; FaFP; HBV; HBVY; MaRV; NeHB; OHFP; OQP; POT; PoTo; PTA-1; QP-1; FreF; WBLP; WGRP
There are hours I imagine. Romance of the Living Corpse. Enrique González Martínez. AnMP
There are human beings who seem to regard the place as craftily. Dock Rats. Marianne Moore. AnAmPo; LA
There are in our existence spots of time. Wordsworth. *Fr.* The Prelude, XII. LO; NBE; PoEL-4
There are in Paradise. The Shepherd Who Stayed. Theodosia Garrison. ChrBoLe; MW; OHIP; SDH
There are jasmine-petaled hands that droop. Hands. Margaret Lathrop Law. PoMa
There are lilies for her sisters. To the End. Christina Rossetti. POTT; VLEP
There are lions and roaring tigers, and enormous camels and things. At the Zoo. A. A. Milne. FaPON; TiPo (1959 ed.)
There are lonely cemeteries. Death Alone. "Pablo Neruda." AnCL; OnHM
There are lonely hearts to cherish. While the Days Are Going By. George Cooper. BLRP; WBLP
There are lots of queer things that discoverers do. Christopher Columbus. Rosemary Benét *and* Stephen Vincent Benét. PoRh
There are loved ones who are missing. The Blessings That Remain. Annie Johnson Flint. BLRP
There are loyal hearts, there are spirits brave. Life's Mirror. "Madeline Bridges." BLPA; FaBoBe; MaRV; NeHB; PoToHe; PTA-1; TreF; WBLP
There are many dead in the brutish desert. First Elegy. Hamish Henderson. ChMP
There are many flags in many lands. Our Flag. Mary H. Howliston. GFA
There are many like him there—unsymbolled heap. A Grave in Ukraine. Saul Tchernichowsky. TrJP
There are many ways to die. History among the Rocks. Robert Penn Warren. Kentucky Mountain Farm, III. MAP; MoVE; SPP
There are many who say that a dog has his day. The Song of the Mischievous Dog. Dylan Thomas. FaFP; SiTL
There are many who think of Quintia in terms of beauty. Catullus, *tr. fr. Latin by* Horace Gregory. RoL
There are men in the village of Erith. The Village of Erith. *Unknown.* ChTr
There are monsters who are very good. Monsters. Quillevic. OnPM

There are mushrooms in the paddock. The Wagon in the Barn. John Drinkwater. MoSiPe
There are no bells in all the world. Sleigh Bells at Night. Elizabeth J. Coatsworth. SiSoSe
There are no colors in the fairest sky. Walton's Book of Lives. Wordsworth. *Fr.* Ecclesiastical Sonnets. LPS-3
There are no frontiers in the air. "Nation Shall Speak Peace . . ." William Soutar. POTE
There are no gloomy days. Kyohaku, *tr. fr. Japanese by* Lois J. Erickson. SoLD
There Are No Gods. Euripides, *tr. fr. Greek by* John Addington Symonds. *Fr.* Bellerophon. OxBG
There are no handles upon a language. Languages. Carl Sandburg. CoV
There are no hills for climbing. Lucifer at Leisure. Sister Mary Maura. JKCP (1955 ed.)
There are no hollows any more. Ironic; LL.D. William Stanley Braithwaite. BANP
There are no instructions here for that dazzling man. Old Iron. Douglas Stewart. BoAV
There are no late-hour devotees. Those Who Read in Bed. Persis Greely Anderson. DDA
There are no stars tonight. My Grandmother's Love Letters. Hart Crane. ChMo; FaBoBe; MoAB; MOAP; PG (1945 ed.)
There are no trenches dug in the park, not yet. Nightmare at Noon. Stephen Vincent Benét. OxBA
There Are No Wolves in England Now. Rose Fyleman. HBMV; UTS
There are one or two things I should just like to hint. To His Countrymen. James Russell Lowell. *Fr.* A Fable for Critics. AA
There are pears against the wall. The Thorn of Somerset. Elliott Coleman. NoCaPo (1941 ed.)
"There are people so dumb," my father said. Plain Talk. William Jay Smith. FiBHP
There are people who perhaps would say. Never Again Will I Say. Moishe-Leib Halpern. OnCuPl
There are persons, mole-blind to the soul's make and style. Emerson. James Russell Lowell. *Fr.* A Fable for Critics. OnAP
There are potent perfumes to which nothing. The Vial. Baudelaire. AnFP
There are pumpkins in the field. Fall Days. Marion Conger. SiSoSe
There are questions that must be asked. Incidents in Playfair House. Nicholas Moore. NeBP
There Are Roughly Zones. Robert Frost. ChMo; PoLFOT
There are seven men in Moy Castle. Moy Castle. *Unknown.* GoTP; OnSP
"There are sixteen lang miles, I'm sure." The Bent Sae Brown. *Unknown.* ESPB
There are so many things I have forgot. The Word. Edward Thomas. NP
There are so many things to do to-day. Every Day. Mary I. Osborn. BoTP
There Are So Many Ways of Going Places. Leslie Thompson. FaPON
There are sobs when death is the cause of parting. Seeing Li Po in a Dream. Tu Fu. BoFr
There are solemn figures walking up the Tocaima roadway. The Feast of Padre Chala. Thomas Walsh. CAW
There Are Some Birds in These Valleys. W. H. Auden. ChMo
There are some days the happy ocean lies. Seascape. Stephen Spender. AtBAP; ChMP; CoBMV; GTBS-D
There are some hearts like wells, green-mossed and deep. Living Waters. Caroline S. Spencer. LPS-3
There are some heights in Wessex, shaped as if by a kindly hand. Wessex Heights. Thomas Hardy. FaBoEn; PoEL-5; UnPo
There are some men, of course, some men, I know. Harold Monro. *Fr.* Trees. PtOT; TwCV
There are some qualities—some incorporate things. Sonnet: Silence. Poe. AWP; CoV; IAP
There are some quiet ways. The Wayside. James Herbert Morse. AA
There are some scenes that we should not. Broken and Desolate. John Henry Boner. NoCaPo
There are sounds in the sky when the year grows old. Christmas Bells. *Unknown.* COAH
There are stepping-stones in the deepest waters. As Thy Day Thy Strength Shall Be. *Unknown.* PEOR
There Are Still Kingfishers. A. Y. Campbell. BLA; GTML
There are strange shadows fostered of the moon. November Dusk. Arthur Davison Ficke. Sonnets of a Portrait Painter, XLV. MAP; UnW
There are strange things done in the midnight sun. The Cremation of Sam McGee. Robert W. Service. FaFP; MaC; StPo; TreF; TwCaPo; YT
There are strange ways of serving God. Service. Hermann Hagedorn. OQP; QP-1
"There are stranger guests come hither, Menelaus God-bred king." Homer. *Fr.* The Odyssey, IV. GrPo
There are sunsets who whisper a good-by. Sunsets. Carl Sandburg. MAP; MoAmPo
There Are Sweet Flowers. Walter Savage Landor. EnRP
There are the fair-limbed nymphs o' the woods. Leigh Hunt. *Fr.* The Nymphs. OBRV
There are things/ Feet know. Feet. Dorothy Aldis. BoChLi; SUS
There are things/ Hands do. Hands. Dorothy Aldis. SUS
There are things you almost see. Almost. Rachel Field. SUS
There are thirteen months in all the year. *See* There are twelve months . . .
There are three central figures preoccupied by toplighting. Composition for a Nativity. John Ciardi. MiAP
There are three lessons I would write. Three Words of Strength [*or* Lessons]. Schiller. MaRV; OQP; QP-2
There are three tame ducks in our back yard. Tame Duck. Kenneth Kaufman. PoeMoYo
There are three things which are too wonderful for me. Too Wonderful. Proverbs, Bible, *O.T.* TrJP
There are three valleys where the warm sun lingers. The Long Harbour. Mary Ursula Bethell. AnNZ
There are three ways in which men take. The Music Grinders. Oliver Wendell Holmes. WhC
There Are Times. Hermann Hesse, *tr. fr. German by* Herman Salinger. TwGV
There are, to whom too poignant I appear. The Bold Satirist. Horace. WoL
There are too many heart-shaped words for one. Too Much for One; Not Enough to Go Around. R. P. Blackmur. Scarabs for the Living, I. CrMA
There are trails that a lad may follow. Silver Ships. Mildred Plew Meigs. FaPON; TiPo
There are twelve [*or* thirteen] months in all the year. Robin Hood and [*or* Rescuing] the Widow's Three Sons [*or* the Three Squires]. *Unknown.* EnLi-1; EnSB; ESPB (B *vers.*); EV-2; GoTP; OBB; StPo; TiPo (1952 ed.); ViBoFo
There are twelve months throughout the year. September. Mary Howitt. BoTP; OTPC (1923 ed.)
There are twenty dead who're sleeping near the slopes of Bud Dajo. The Fight at Dajo. Alfred E. Wood. PAH
There are two births; the one when light. William Cartwright. *Fr.* To Chloe, Who Wished Herself Young Enough for Me. BCEP; GTBS-W; LO; LoPS; OBEV; PoToHe (new ed.)
There are two kinds of people on earth today. Lifting and Leaning [*or* Leaners or Lifters *or* The Two Kinds of People]. Ella Wheeler Wilcox. BLPA; MaRV; PoToHe; PTA-2; WBLP
There are two sights that make my heart feel gay. Good Morning, America. Harry Kemp. PEDC; PoTo
There are two sisters, one is a rose. The Sisters. Robert Finch. BoCaPo
There are two sorts of rat. The Wandering Rats. Heine. AnGP
There are veils that lift, there are bars that fall. Song of Maelduin. Thomas William Rolleston. HBMV; TIP
There are veins in the hills where jewels hide. The Best Treasure. John J. Moment. MaRV
There are white clouds in the heaven. Song of the White Clouds. *Unknown.* *Fr.* The Fountain of Old Poems. WhP
There are white moon daisies in the mist of the meadow. Summer Song. Edith Nesbit. AlDL
There Are Who Say. Walter Savage Landor. EPN
There are who say the lover's heart. Love. Thomas Kibble Hervey. LPS-1
There are who say we are but dust. There Are Who Say. Walter Savage Landor. EPN
There are willow pussies. Pussy Willows. *Unknown.* GFA
There are wolves in the next room waiting. The Wolves. Allen Tate. LiTA; LiTG; LiTM; MOAP; OxBA
There are words like freedom. Refugee in America. Langston Hughes. WaKn
There are words that can only be said on paper. Words. Robert Finch. BoCaPo
There are words that wait. Words to Sleep Upon. Leonora Speyer. NP
There are wrongs done in the fair face of heaven. The Deeds That Might Have Been. Wilfred Scawen Blunt. *Fr.* In Vinculis. TrGrPo
There as she lay, a deep sleep brought relieving. Medea's Dream. Apollonius Rhodius. *Fr.* Argonautica. OxBG
There, as she sewed, came floating through her head. Past. Winifred Howells. AA
There at the factory I like to see. The Porcelain Factory. Carl Snoilsky. AnSL
There, at the window that doth hold. Saint. Stéphane Mallarmé. TrFP
There be five things to a man's desire. Hrolf's Thrall, His Song. Willard Wattles. SBMV
There be four things which are little upon the earth. Four Things. Proverbs, Bible, *O.T.* FaPON; GoTP

There be lovers who bring me roses. A Question of Lovers. Sister Mary Madeleva. PraNu
There be many kinds of parting—yes, I know. Separation. Martha Dickinson Bianchi. AA
There Be None of Beauty's Daughters. Byron. *See* Stanzas for Music.
There be six things which the Lord hateth. A Sower of Discord. Proverbs, Bible, *O.T.* (*Moulton, Modern Reader's Bible*). MaRV
There be the greyhounds! lo'k! an' there's the heäre. The Heäre. William Barnes. VA
There be those who are afraid to fear. The Courage of the Lost. Edith M. Thomas. BAP
There be three things seeking my death. Prayer for the Speedy End of Three Great Misfortunes. *Tr. by* Frank O'Connor. OBMV
There be two men of all mankind. Two Men. E. A. Robinson. BOHV; GoTP; LaNeLa; OBAV; WhC
There be who say, in these enlighten'd days. Byron. *Fr.* English Bards and Scotch Reviewers. PtP
There beams no light from thy hall to-night. The Dark Palace. Alice Milligan. AnIV; TIP
There Blooms No Bud in May. Walter de la Mare. MBP; MoAB; MoBrPo; NeMA
There breaks on me, burning upon me. Three Songs to Steingerd, 1. Cormac Ogmundarson. LyMA
There breaks upon my sight. Frank Wilmot. *Fr.* The Gully. BoAV; NeLNL
There breathes a sense of Spring in the boon air. Accidian. Henry Charles Beeching. OBVV
There by the window in the old house. William H. Herndon. Edgar Lee Masters. *Fr.* Spoon River Anthology. NP; SBMV; TOP
There calleth me ever a marvelous horn. Home-Sickness. Justinus Kerner. AWP; JAWP; UnW; WBP
There cam' seven Egyptians on a day. The Gypsy Countess. *Unknown.* OBB
There came a bird out o a bush. Lady Isabel and the Elf-Knight (B *vers.*). *Unknown.* ESPB
There came a day. Wayfaring Fools. Frances Beatrice Taylor. CPG
There came a day at summer's full. Renunciation. Emily Dickinson. MoAmPo (1950 ed.); TCAP
There came a ghost to Margaret's [*or* Margret's] door. Sweet William's Ghost [*or* Sweet William and May Margaret]. *Unknown.* BaBo; CG; CH; ESPB; HBV; InPo; ViBoFo (A *vers.*)
There came a little light-foot breeze a-dancing down the bay. The Isle of Apple-Trees. Fritz S. Burnell. BoAu
There came a man, making his hasty moan. Mahmoud. Leigh Hunt. CG; LPS-2
There came a satyr creeping through the wood. The Satyr. James Stephens. OnYI
There came a seaman up from the sea. The Drowned Seaman. Maude Goldring. HBMV
There came a soul to the gate of Heaven. The Self-exiled. Walter C. Smith. VA
There came a time when roses bloomed again. May. C. R. Saunders. CAG
There came a whisper from the night to me. God's Remembrance. Francis Ledwidge. GTIV
There came a wind like a bugle. Emily Dickinson. AmPP (4th ed.); AtBAP; FaBoEn; IAP; LoBV; MoAB; NePA; OxBA; PoE
(Storm, The.) MAPA; TSW; TSWC; TwAmPo
There came a youth upon the earth. The Shepherd of King Admetus. James Russell Lowell. HBVY; IAP; MOAP; OBAV; OnHT; PECK; TOP
There Came an Ancient Huron. *Unknown.* IHA
There came an ancient man and slow. The Call to a [*or* of the] Scot. Ruth Guthrie Harding. BoHiPo; HBV
There came an image in Life's retinue. Death-in-Love. Dante Gabriel Rossetti. The House of Life, XLVIII. BPN; EmBrPo; PoVP; ViP; ViPo
There came an officer knocking by night at my door. The Grain-Tribute. Po Chü-i. TrCh
There came an old soldier to my door. The Old Soldier. Walter de la Mare. SoV
There came by the post. Special Delivery. Elizabeth Winton. PCH
There came tidings to Arthur the king. The Battle of Bath. Layamon. *Fr.* The Brut. MeEV
There came to port last Sunday night. The New Arrival. George Washington Cable. AA; HBV; PA; PECK
There came to the beach a poor Exile of Erin. Exile of Erin. Thomas Campbell. HBV; LPS-2
There Came You Wishing Me. José Garcia Villa. LoPS; TwAmPo
There can be no tears. Farewell in Secret. Po Chü-i. ChLP
There can be slain/ No sacrifice. Milton, *tr. fr. the Latin of* Seneca. *Fr.* The Tenure of Kings and Magistrates. PoFr
There cannot yet remain a lengthened span. A Meditation. Samuel Walter Kelly. PoP
There chanced to be a pedlar bold. The Bold Pedlar and Robin Hood. *Unknown.* BaBo; ESPB
There Come Such Troubled Hours. "Novalis," *tr. fr. German by* Eileen Hutchins. Sacred Songs, II. AnGP
There comes a moment late in Summer. Prognostic. Samuel Yellen. NePoAm
There comes a moment when to believe is not enough. Action. James Oppenheim. TrJP
There comes a night when the once full-orbed moon. *Unknown.* LO
There comes a ship far sailing then. There Comes a Ship. *Unknown.* AnEC
There comes a wail of anguish. A Cry for Light. *Unknown.* BLRP
There comes an old man to our street. Street Music. "John Presland." VOD
There comes at times to take a seat near mine. Amid the Shadows. Antero de Quental. UnW
There comes Emerson first, whose rich words, every one. Emerson. James Russell Lowell. *Fr.* A Fable for Critics. AmPP (4th ed.); AnNe; APW; CoBA; OuHeWo; OxBA; PtP; TCAP
There comes Poe, with his raven, like Barnaby Rudge. Poe and Longfellow. James Russell Lowell. *Fr.* A Fable for Critics. AnNE; APW; CoBA; OxBA; PtP
There cometh sixth a man of wisdom high. Amphiaraus. Aeschylus. *Fr.* Seven against Thebes. GrR
There died a myriad. Hugh Selwyn Mauberley, V. Ezra Pound. CoBMV; CoV; LiTA; LiTM (rev. ed.); MoPo; OnAP
There dropped a leaf upon my hand. Balance. Melanie Hyman. PtPa
There dwells a lady in Denmark. Merman Rosmer. *Unknown.* SG
There dwelt a dame in Bredeby. Svend of Vollerslov. *Unknown.* BoDaBa
There dwelt a fair maid in the West. James Harris. *Unknown.* BaBo (A *vers.*); ESPB
There dwelt a man in faire Westmerland. Johnie Armstrong. *Unknown.* BaBo; BoLiVe; EnLi-1 (1949 ed.); ESPB; GDAH; HoPM; PC; ReaPo; TOP; TrGrPo; UnPo; ViBoFo (A *vers.*)
There dwelt a man in Ribe town. The Bride of Ribe. *Unknown.* BoDaBa
There dwelt a miller hale and bold. The Miller of the Dee. Charles Mackay. BTP; HBV; OTPC; PTA-1; TVSH
There dwelt the man, the flower of human kind. Mount Vernon, the Home of Washington. William Day. DD; GA; OHIP; PoRL; WOAH
There Falls with Every Wedding Chime. Walter Savage Landor. VA
(Last Fruit off an Old Tree, The.) SeCePo
There fared a mother driven forth. The House of Christmas. G. K. Chesterton. GoBC; HBV; HBVY; MaRV; MBP; MoBrPo; QS; TSW; TwCV
There fell an April shower, one night. April Showers. Mary E. Wilkins Freeman. PTA-2
There fell red rain of spears athwart the sky. Last Judgment. John Gould Fletcher. AWP; MOAP
There flames the first gay daffodil. Daffodils. Ruth Guthrie Harding. HBMV; VOD
There flew a bird at the close of day. Bird-Notes. Johan Sebastian Cammermeyer Welhaven. AnNoLy
There flourished once a potentate. The King of Yvetot. Pierre Jean de Béranger. AWP; JAWP; WBP; WoL
There, from its entrance, lost in matted vines. The Covered Bridge. Madison Cawein. YT
There, go to sleep, Dolly, in own mother's lap. The Little Girl to Her Dolly. Ann Taylor. SAS
There goes the clock; there goes the sun. Epitaph for John and Richard. Karl Shapiro. TwAmPo
There goes the dog of the mind. Soliloquy by the Shore. Martin Scholten. GoYe
There goes the roistering wind. The Adventurer. José Moreno Villa. CoSP
There goes the Wapiti. The Wapiti. Ogden Nash. MoShBr
There grew a goodly tree him faire beside. Balme. Spenser. *Fr.* The Faerie Queene, I, 11. CH
There grew a lowly flower by Eden-gate. Eden-Gate. Sydney Dobell. OBVV
There grew an aged tree on the green. The Oak and the Brere. Spenser. *Fr.* The Shepheardes Calender: February. OBSC
There grows an elm-tree on the hill. *Unknown, tr. by* Arthur Waley. *Fr.* The Book of Odes. MBP; MoBrPo (1942 ed.)
There had been years of passion—scorching, cold. "And There Was a Great Calm." Thomas Hardy. ChTr; LiTM
There hangs the long bow, the strong bow, once was bent. The Death of Robin Hood. William Rose Benét. OTPC (1946 ed.)
There, hard by the highway, anguished at heart, she sat her

There, hard by the highway (*continued*)
down. Demeter Welcomed at Eleusis. *Unknown. Fr.* Homeric Hymns. GrR
There hartes ware so roted in the popes lawes. Fragment of an Anti-Papist Ballad. *Unknown.* CoMu
There has something gone wrong. Keep a Stiff Upper Lip. Phoebe Cary. FaFP
There hath come an host to see Thee. Lullaby in Bethlehem. Henry Howarth Bashford. BOL; HBV; HBVY
There haunts in Time's bare house an active ghost. Polonius. Walter de la Mare. AtBAP
There have been many cats I loved and lost. Sonnet. Margaret E. Bruner. CIV
There have been three storms in my heart. Summerhouse. Melvin Walker La Follette. NePoEA
There have been times when I have looked at life. Vision. Elizabeth N. Hauer. PoToHe
There have been times when I well might have passed. In Tenebris, III. Thomas Hardy. ViPo
There have been times when on a city street. On City Streets. Margaret E. Bruner. PoToHe
There he arriuing, round about doth flie. The Butterfly. Spenser. *Fr.* Muiopotmos. EV-1
There he lay dead in the street. Surprise. Federico García Lorca. CoSP
There he lies—the saviour, the lord of the earth. The Iron Messiah. Vladimir Timofeevich Kirillov. PoFr
There he moved, cropping the grass at the purple canyon's lip. The Horse Thief. William Rose Benét. BBV (1951 ed.); CP; HBMV; MAP; MoAmPo; TCAP; TSW; TSWC
There headlong into the calm black night. Orestes Pursued. Charles David Webb. NePoAm-2
There hung about me others of the departed. The Silence of Ajax. Homer. *Fr.* The Odyssey, XI. LiA
There in a bare place, in among the rocks. The Little Lough. John Hewitt. NeIP
There in a woodland, to my thought more bright. Ballata 9. Guido Cavalcanti. LyPI
There in close covert by some brook. Milton. *Fr.* Il Penseroso. PC
There in his room, whene'er the moon looks in. Ode for a Master Mariner Ashore. Louise Imogen Guiney. AA; GoBC; JKCP
There in its old historic splendour stands. Sonnet: To the Hudson. George S. Hellman. CAG
There in the broom I killed her. *Unknown. Fr.* William Grismond's Downfall. SG
There in the crotch of a naked branch. A Bird's Nest in Winter. "John Crichton." CPG
There in the dusty alcove of the room. The Waiting Harp. Gustavo Adolfo Bécquer. CAW
There in the fane a beauteous creature stands. Woman. Kalidasa. HBV; LPS-3
There in the flower garden. *Unknown, tr. fr. Spanish by* Eleanor L. Turnbull. TeCS
There in the garden, a little fox. Crafty Fox. Toson Shimazaki. PoLJ
There in the half-dark of the winter wood. I Gained a Greater Strength. Cullen Jones. *Fr.* Sonnets in Wartime. MuM
There, in the night, where none can spy. Robert Louis Stevenson. *Fr.* The Land of Story-Books. YT
There in the northwest lies a lofty mansion. The Nineteen Han Poems, V. *Unknown, tr. fr. Chinese.* WhP
There is/ One great society alone on earth. The Noble. Wordsworth. *Fr.* The Prelude, IX. ChTr
There Is a Beauty. Archibald Lampman. *Fr.* The Largest Life. MaRV
There is a bird bath on our grass. The Bird Bath. Florence Hoatson. BoTP
There is a bird I know so well. The Song Sparrow. Henry van Dyke. MPB; SN
There is a bird in the poplars. Metric Figure. William Carlos Williams. MAP; MoAB; MoAmPo; MOAP; NeMA; NP
There is a bird that comes and sings. The Song the Oriole Sings. William Dean Howells. HBV; SN
There is a bird, who by his coat. The Jackdaw. Vincent Bourne. CBOV; HBV; HBVY; OTPC (1923 ed.); TCEP
There is a blossom sprung of a thorn. Alleluia! Alleluia!/ Deo Patri Sit Gloria. *Unknown.* AnEC
There is a blue star, Janet. Baby Toes. Carl Sandburg. FaPON; LaNeLa; SUS; TSW
There is a bondage worse, far worse, to bear. Sonnet: There Is a Bondage Worse. Wordsworth. ChER
There is a book, tho' not a book of rhymes. On a Hessian Debarkation. Philip Freneau. MOAP
There is a book, who runs may read. Who Runs May Read. John Keble. VA
There is a bridge, whereof the span. The Unseen Bridge. Gilbert Thomas. HBMV; MaRV; PraP
There is a brook I must hear. Morning. Hilda Conkling. NP
There is a budding morrow in midnight. "Found." Dante Gabriel Rossetti. EmBrPo; PoVP; VLEP
There is a castle on a hill. Gold. John Drinkwater. TCPD
There is a change—and I am poor. A Complaint. Wordsworth. ATP; OBRV; PoEL-4
There Is a Charming Land. Adam Oehlenschläger, *tr. fr. Danish by* Robert Hillyer. AWP; FaPON
There is a Child born of Mary. Conditor Alme Siderum. *Unknown.* AnEC
There is a Child born of our blessed Virgin. Gloria Tibi Domine. *Unknown.* BOL
There is a choice in spoons. A Choice in Spoons. Joel Barlow. *Fr.* The Hasty Pudding. OnAP
There Is a City. *At. to* "The Jewish Sibyl," *tr. fr. Greek by* Bohn. *Fr.* The Fourth Book of Sibylline Oracles. TrJP
There is a city, builded by no hand. Paradisi Gloria. Thomas William Parsons. AA; APW; OBAV; OQP; QP-1
There is a city, Chaldean Ur. There Is a City. *At. to* "The Jewish Sibyl." *Fr.* The Fourth Book of Sibylline Oracles. TrJP
There is a city where God's happy children. The Life to Come. Edward Shillito. OQP; QP-2
There is a clang of gongs within my ears. Nostalgia. Mary Elizabeth Counselman. DaM
There is a close companionship of pain. Sons of Failure. Edith Lovejoy Pierce. MaRV
There is a clouded city, gone to rest. The Aztec City. Eugene Fitch Ware. AA; HBV
There is a coarseness. Jungle Taste. Edward S. Silvera. CDC
There is a core of suffering that the mind. The Stone. Anne Morrow Lindbergh. SaFP
There is a country full of wine. Two Voices. Alice Corbin. HBMV; NP; NV
There is a creator named God. Limerick. James Abbott McNeill Whistler. BOHV; LiBL
There is a dale in Ida, lovelier. *See* There lies a vale in Ida, lovelier.
There is a day that comes in spring. Apple Blossoms. Ralph Bergengren. GFA
There is a destiny that makes us brothers. A Creed [*or* Inbrothered]. Edwin Markham. BLPA; FaBoBe; FaFP; GrCo-1; MaRV; NeHB; TreFS
There is a dish to hold the sea. Imagination. John Davidson. *Fr.* New Year's Eve. MBP; MoBrPo
There is a dream that comes to me by night. Sonnet. Florence Wilson Roper. *Fr.* Dusty Answer. UnW
There is a dungeon in whose dim drear light. Filial Love. Byron. *Fr.* Childe Harold's Pilgrimage, IV. LPS-1
There is a far country where there is a hall for dreams. The Far Country. Robert Greacen. NeIP
"There is a fashion in this land." The Knight's Ghost. *Unknown.* ESPB
There is a feast in your father's house. Leesome Brand. *Unknown.* ESPB (B *vers.*); OBB
There Is a Fever of the Spirit. Thomas Love Peacock. *Fr.* Nightmare Abbey, *ch.* 11. EPN; GTSE
(Mr. Cypress's Song.) LO
(Song, by Mr. Cypress.) OBRV
There is a field sown with mines in rows. The Plow. Max Barthel. TwGV
There is a fine stuffed chavender. A False Gallop of Analogies. Warham St. Leger. CenHV; FiBHP; WhC
There is a flash packet, flash packet [*or* 'n' a packet] of fame. The *Dreadnought. Unknown.* ShS (*vers.* I); SoAmSa
There Is a Flower, *in mod. Eng. At. to* John Awdlay. TMEV
(Flower of Jesse, The.) AnEC
(There Is a Floure Sprung of a Tree.) AtBAP
There is a flower, a little flower. The Daisy [*or* A Field Flower]. James Montgomery. BoTP; HBV; LPS-2; OTPC (1923 ed.); SN
There is a flower I wish to wear. Hearts-Ease. Walter Savage Landor. BPN; EnRP; VA
There is a flower [*or* floure] sprung of a tree. There Is a Flower [*or* The Flower of Jesse]. *At. to* John Awdlay. AnEC; AtBAP; TMEV
There is a flower that bees prefer. Purple Clover. Emily Dickinson. MoAmPo (1950 ed.)
There is a flower, the lesser Celandine. A Lesson [*or* The Small Celandine]. Wordsworth. CoEV; EM-2; GTBS; GTBS-D; GTBS-W; GTSE; GTSL; HBV; OBRV
There is a flower within my heart. Daisy Bell. Harry Dacre. TreF
There is a fountain filled with blood. Praise for the Fountain Opened. William Cowper. CEP; EiPP
There is a fountain in a wood. The Puppet Dreams. Conrad Aiken. *Fr.* Punch; the Immortal Liar. MAP; NeMA
There is a fountain in the forest called. The Fountain of the Fairies. Robert Southey. OTPC
There Is a Fox. *Unknown, tr. fr. Chinese.* WhP

There is a friendship that exists between. A Dog's Vigil. Margaret E. Bruner. AlBD; PoToHe
There is a funny little man. Mr. Nobody. *Unknown.* DDA; HBVY; OTPC; RAR
There is a gal in our town. Cl'ar de Kitchen. *Unknown.* SoAF
There Is a Garden. Thomas Campion. *See* Cherry-ripe.
There is a garden enclosed. Wild Eden, III. George Edward Woodberry. HBV
There Is a Garden in Her Face. Thomas Campion. *See* Cherry-ripe.
There is a garden where lilies. Eutopia. Francis Turner Palgrave. OBVV; TOP
There is a garden where the seeded stems of thin long grass are bowed. Merrill's Garden. John Freeman. MM
There is a garden, which I think He loves. The Garden. Digby Mackworth Dolben. GoBC
There is a gentle nymph not far from hence. The Nymph of the Severn. Milton. *Fr.* Comus. LPS-3; MyFE; OBS; SeEP
There Is a Girl in Our Coach. *Unknown, tr. fr. Chinese.* WhP
There is a glorious city in the sea. Venice. Samuel Rogers. *Fr.* Italy. LPS-2
There is a glory in the autumn wood. On Reading Arthur Machen. Frank Belknap Long. DaM
There is a glory past the heart's believing. Cotton Field. Minnie Hite Moody. MuM
There is a glory setting him apart. Night unto Night. Inez Barclay Kirby. MuM
There is a great amount of poetry in unconscious/ fastidiousness. Critics and Connoisseurs. Marianne Moore. AnAmPo; AnEnPo; LA; MoP; NePA; OxBA
There Is a Green Hill Far Away. Cecil Frances Alexander. BLRP; GTIV; HBV; MaRV; OlF; VA; WGRP
There is a green island in lone Gougaune Barra. Gougaune Barra. Jeremiah Joseph Callanan. LPS-2
There is a harp set above us. Harp in the Rigging. Hamish Maclaren. EtS
There is a hatred that endures. Hatred. Arthur C. Coe. CAG
There is a hill and on that hill is a stone. The Heart of the World. Nahman of Bratzlav. TrJP
There Is a Hill beside the Silver Thames. Robert Bridges. EV-5; OAEP; PoeT; POTT; PoVP; VLEP
There is a hill in England. Three Hills. Everard Owen. StJW
There is a hole. A Bar at Night. Sakutaro Hagiwara. LiTW
There is a honey none shall taste. The Bees of Christ. Clifford J. Laube. JKCP (1955 ed.)
There is a house in New Orleans, they call the Rising Sun. The Rising Sun Blues. *Unknown.* OuSiCo
There is a hunger in my heart tonight. Music. Charles Phillips. CAW; JKCP
There is a hush that comes on Christmas Eve. Christmas Eve Meditation. Margaret E. Bruner. MaRV
There is a hush this golden afternoon. Classroom in October. Elias Lieberman. GoYe
There is a jewel which no Indian mines. Risposta. *Unknown.* ElSeCe; HBV
There is a joy I have not known, a splendor. After Reading Saint Teresa, Luis de Leon and Ramon Lull. Muna Lee. CAW
There is a jungle, there is a jungle. Travelogue in a Shooting-Gallery. Kenneth Fearing. PoLFOT
There is a knack in doing many a thing. The Pilgrims and the Peas. "Peter Pindar." BOHV; LPS-3
There Is a Laddie. Albert Teodor Gellerstedt, *tr. fr. Swedish by* Charles W. Stork. AnSL
There Is a Lady Conquering with Glances. Walther von der Vogelweide, *tr. fr. German by* Jethro Bithell. AWP; OnPM; WoL
There Is a Lady Sweet and Kind. *Unknown.* BCEP, *abr.;* BLV, *abr.;* CBOV, *abr.;* CH, *abr.;* EG, *abr.;* ElL; ElSeCe; FaFP; GoBC; GTBS-W; LiTB; LiTL; LoPS; NeHB; OAEP; OBEV, *abr.;* OBS; SiTL; TreFS; TrGrPo (Passing By.) OTPC (1946 ed.); ShBV-4
There is a lake—but I forget its name. The Lake. Eleanour Norton. NLK
There Is a Land. James Montgomery. PEDC; PGD (My Country, *abr.*) LPS-2
There is a land of Dream. Dream Fantasy. "Fiona Macleod." WGRP
There is a land, of every land the pride. There Is a Land [*or* My Country]. James Montgomery. LPS-2; PEDC; PGD
There is a land of pure delight. Heaven [*or* A Prospect of Heaven]. Isaac Watts. EiPP; OBEC; OlF; WGRP
There is a law of stern necessity. The Blood-Guilty. Empedocles. OxBG
There is a legend that the love of God. The Birth. Don Marquis. NV
There is a little church in France to-day. Saint [*or* Sainte] Jeanne. Theodosia Garrison. HH; PEDC
There is a little garden path. A Garden Path. May Justus. PCH
There is a little gentleman. The Bee. *Unknown.* PCH
There is a little hill in Picardy. A Hill in Picardy. Clinton Scollard. VOD (1931 ed)
There is a little hint of spring. A Hill Song. Helen Merrill Egerton. CPG
There is a little man. The Merry Man of Paris. Stella Mead. SUS
There is a little mole. The Mole. Al-Munfatil. MooP
There Is a Little Unpretending Rill. Wordsworth. EPN (Sonnet: "There is a little unpretending rill.") EnSW
There is a locust. Dislike of a Governor. Issa. PoFr
There Is a Loneliness. Margaret E. Bruner. PoToHe
There is a lonely mountain-top. Jephthah's Daughter. "Yehoash." TrJP
There is a lonely stream in a lone dim land. The Washer of the Ford. "Fiona Macleod." LBBV; PoVP
There is a loud noise of Death. To Dear Daniel. Samuel Greenberg. LiTA; MoPo
There Is a Man on the Cross. Elizabeth Cheney. ChIP; MaRV; OQP; PGD; QP-1
There is a marble fragment from an old. A Statue. R. Pier. CAG
There is a memory stays upon old ships. Old Ships. David Morton. BAP; BBV; EtS; OBAV; PoTo; PYM; SBMV; StVeCh; TSW; TSWC
There is a mirror in my room. My Mirror. Aline Kilmer. AnAmPo; LA; NP; NV
There is a moment between day and night. Dusk from a Train Window. Cale Young Rice. LS; MuM
There is a moment blind with light, split by the hum. Icarus in November. Alec B. Stevenson. SPP
There is a moment country children know. Village before Sunset. Frances Cornford. LoGBV
There is a morn by men unseen. Emily Dickinson. OxBA
There is a mountain and a wood between us. Separation. Walter Savage Landor. EtPaEn; LoPo; OBEV (1st ed.); TOP
There is a mountain everyone must climb. The Mountain. Robert Finch. CaP
There Is a Mystery in Human Hearts. *Unknown.* PoToHe
There is a mystery too deep for words. Silence. John Hall Wheelock. LiTM
There Is a Mystic Borderland. Helen Field Fischer. *See* Mystic Borderland.
There Is a Mystic Splendor. Raymond Barrow. PoNe
There is a myth, a tale men tell. The Pearl. Hans Christian Andersen. BoDS; LiTW
There is a name all names above. The Name of Jesus. Annie Johnson Flint. BePJ
There Is a Name I Love to Hear. Frederick Whitfield. BePJ
There is a niland on a river lying. Collusion between a Alegaiter and a Water-Snaik. J. W. Morris. LPS-3; NA
There is a painted bus. The Bus. "Peter." BoTP
There is a panther caged within my breast. The Black Panther. John Hall Wheelock. BAP; HBMV; LiTG; LiTM; PFY
There is a path through a marsh. The Path through the Marsh. Leah Bodine Drake. DaM
There is a peace which cometh after sorrow. Peace after Sorrow. Jessie Rose Gates. MaRV
There is a peewee bird that cries. California Dissonance. James Rorty. MOAP
There is a people mighty in its youth. Tribute to America. Shelley. PaA
There is a pirate in my blood. Heredity. Theda Kenyon. DDA
There is a pity in forgotten things. The Triumph of Forgotten Things. Edith M. Thomas. HBV
There is a place that some men know. The Cross. Allen Tate. AWP; MAP; MoAmPo; MOAP; MoVE; OxBA; SPP
There is a place where love begins and a place where love ends. Explanations of Love. Carl Sandburg. ChMo; CMP; LiTL; LoPo
There is a place where, wisdom won, right recorded. Elegy for Our Dead. Edwin Rolfe. WaP
There is a plan far greater than the plan you know. There Is No Death. *Unknown.* BLPA; NeHB
There is a pleasure in poetic pains. Poetic Pains [*or* Poetry; Satire and Pulpit]. William Cowper. *Fr.* The Task. CoBE; FiP
There is a pleasure in the pathless woods. The Ocean [*or* Communion with Nature *or* Roll On, Thou Deep and Dark Blue Ocean]. Byron. *Fr.* Childe Harold's Pilgrimage, IV. CBE; ChTr; EPN; EV-4; FaBoBe; FiP; GrCo-1; HBV; InP; LEAP; LiTB; LiTG; LPS-2; MaPo; MaRV; MCCG; NLK; OBRV; OHFP; PC; PreP; SG; ShBV-3; SN; TCEP; TreF; ViBoPo; WHA
There Is a Poem Everywhere. Charles Davies. MoWP
There is a poem I have read, and which is quoted far. If We Could Only Be! Lee Shippey. PEDC
There Is a Pool on Garda. Clinton Scollard. HBV; OBAV
There is a pretty piece of work. The Naughty Lord & the Gay Young Lady. *Unknown.* CoMu

There is a poverty that trees may show. City Trees. Anderson M. Scruggs. PoMa
There is a quest that calls me. The Mystic. Cale Young Rice. BLP; LBMV; LS; MaRV; MuM; QS; WGRP
There is a quiet kingdom's strand. The Quiet Kingdom. Carl Busse. AWP; JAWP; WBP
There is a quiet spirit in these woods. The Spirit of Poetry. Longfellow. CoBA; IAP; MOAP
There is a race from eld descent. Hey Nonny No. Marguerite Merington. AA
There is a ragged piper walks the byways of the town. The Ragged Piper. Dana Burnet. OBAV
There is a rainbow in the east. The Rainbow. *Unknown.* WhP
There is a reaper whose name is Death. The Reaper and the Flowers. Longfellow. AnNE; HBV; IAP; LEAP; LPS-2; PIR; TCAP
There Is a River. Jane Addams. QS
There is a river clear and fair. Fragment in Imitation of Wordsworth [*or* An Imitation of Wordsworth]. Catherine Fanshawe. ALV; BOHV; HBV; NA; PA
"There is a river the streams whereof." There Is a River. Jane Addams. QS
There is a road that turning always. The Road. Edwin Muir. FaBoEn; FaBoMo; FaFP; LiTB; LiTG; LiTM; ViBoPo (1958 ed.)
There is a rumour hereabout of summer. The Overgrown Back Yard. John Holmes. CrMA; NePoAm
There is a sad carnival up the valley. Are They Dancing. Edward Dorn. NeAP
There is a safe secret place. The Secret Place. Henry Francis Lyte. VA
There is a secret laughter. Secret Laughter. Christopher Morley. FAOV; TreFS
There is a sense of journeying. A Sound of Going in the Tops of the Mulberry Trees. Henry Bellamann. TBM
There is a sentinel before the gate. The City Church. "E. H. K." WGRP
There is a serpent in perfection tarnished. True Vine. Elinor Wylie. AnFE; APA; CoAnAm; LiTA; MOAP; TwAmPo
There is a shame of nobleness. Emily Dickinson. NePA
There is a sheeling hidden in the wood. The Lay of Prince Marvan. *Tr. by* Eleanor Hull. AnIV
There is a ship we understand. Ho, for Lubberland [*or* An Invitation to Lubberland]. *Unknown.* CoBE; SG
There is a shrine whose golden gate. The Shrine. Digby Mackworth Dolben. DD; GoBC; GTML; HBV
There is a silence. Christmas. Catherine Parmenter. DD; SDH
There is a silence I carry about with me always. The Silence. John Gould Fletcher. Down the Mississippi, VII. ChMo; CMP; LiTA; MOAP; NP; SPP; TCAP
There is a silence where hath been no sound. Silence. Thomas Hood. BCEP; CH; CoBE; EnLi-2 (1949 ed.); EnRP; ERP; ES; FaBoEn; GTML; GTSL; LEAP; OBEV; OBRV; PeBoSo; PoEL-4; ShBV-4; ViBoPo
There is a silence which I carry about with me always. *See* There is a silence I carry about with me always.
There is a singer everyone has heard. The Oven Bird. Robert Frost. AmPP (4th ed.); AWP; BLA; CoBMV; CrMA; InPo; JAWP; MAPA; MaPo; MOAP; OxBA; Po; RiBV; TwAmPo; UnS
There is a singing in the summer air. The Summer Pool. Robert Buchanan. VA
There is a sleepy dusk, an odorous shade. Encounter with Sleep. Keats. *Fr.* Endymion. ERP
There is a small store-house of knowledge in which I sit sometimes on hard wooden cases. A Store-House. Louis Dudek. CaP
There is a smile of love. The Smile [*or* Smile and Frown]. Blake. BoFr; CaAE; OBRV
There is a solitary russet pear tree. Ode I/VI/10. *Unknown.* BoFr
There is a solitary russet pear tree. Ode I/X/10. *Unknown.* BoFr
There is a sorrow in the hills tonight. Benjamin F. Musser. *Fr.* Poverello. SaFP
There is a soul above the soul of each. Humanity. Richard Watson Dixon. EPN; OBVV; OQP; QP-2; VA
There is a Soul Gethsemane. Easter Sacraments. Henry Park Schauffler. EOAH; OQP; QP-1
There is a sound I would not hear. Fear. Langdon Elwyn Mitchell. AA
There is a sound of going. Sounds. Mary Austin. NP
There is a sound that's dear to me. The Lay of the Levite. William E. Aytoun. HBV
There is a spark dwells deep within my soul. Verner von Heidenstam. *Fr.* Thoughts in Loneliness. AnSL
There Is a Spell, for Instance. Hilda Doolittle ("H. D."). MoPo
There is a spot, 'mid barren hills. Emily Brontë. *Fr.* A Little While. EnSW
There is a spray the bird clung to. Misconceptions. Robert Browning. BPN; EPN; GEPC; GTBS; OBEV; OBVV; PIAE; TOP; VA; VLEP
There is a stane in yon water. Burd Isabel and Earl Patrick. *Unknown.* BaBo; ESPB
There is a star that runs very fast. Moon Song. Hilda Conkling. SP; TiPo
There is a stillness in October air. In His Will. Howard Mumford Jones. LS
There is a stillness in the heart of night. Nocturne. Minnie Markham Kerr. MuM
There is a stranger in the council hall. Stranger at the Peace Table. Esther Baldwin York. MaRV
There is a stream (I name not its name, lest inquisitive tourist). The Bathers. Arthur Hugh Clough. *Fr.* The Bothie of Tober-na-Vuolich. EV-5; VA
There is a stream that flowed before the first beginning. Kathleen Raine. *Fr.* Water. ImOP
There is a strength in knowing that it can be borne. Emily Dickinson. MaPo
There is a strong wall about me to protect me. Love Song. Mary Carolyn Davies. AV
There is a stubblefield, where a black rain falls. De Profundis. Georg Trakl. OnPM
There is a supreme God in the ethnological section. Homage to the British Museum. William Empson. FaBoMo; LiTM (rev. ed.); MoAB
There is a sweet air on the side of the hill. Mary Hynes. Lady Gregory, *after* Anthony Raftery. DiM; GTIV
There is a tale, beloved of old Japan. The Chrysanthemum Legend. Arthur Davison Ficke. PoMa
There Is a Tavern in the Town. *Unknown.* ABS; FaFP; OlF; TreF; YaD
There is a temple in my heart. Temple Garlands. Agnes Mary Frances Robinson. HBV
There is a thin line. Border. Isabel Fisk Conant. BAP
There is a thing that much is us'd. *Unknown.* SeCSL
There is a thing which in my brain. Mea Culpa. Edward Sandford Martin. PR
"There is a thorn—it looks so old." The Thorn. Wordsworth. BPN; EmBrPo; EnRP
There Is a Tide. Josephine Johnson. BPP
There Is a Tide [in the Affairs of Men]. Shakespeare. *Fr.* Julius Caesar, IV, iii. BCEP; BTP; MaRV (Time to Strike, The.) TreFS
There is a time for vine leaves in the hair. Morgan Oakley. Edgar Lee Masters. *Fr.* The New Spoon River. LEAP
There is a time to mount; to humble thee. On the Fitness of Seasons. Enzo, King of Sardinia. OnPM
There is a time, we know not when. The Hidden Line [*or* The Doomed Man]. Joseph Addison Alexander. BLPA; MaRV; NeHB
There is a time wherein eternity. The Last Communion. Leo Ward. CAW; GoBC
There is a tomb in Arqua; rear'd in air. Byron. *Fr.* Childe Harold's Pilgrimage, IV. PtP
There is a toy called the kaleidoscope. Kaleidoscope. Frances Angevine Gray. MuM
There is a tree, by day. Tenebris. Angelina W. Grimké. CDC; PoNe
There is a tree I love to pass. My Blue-eyed Boy. *Unknown.* ABS
There is a tree native in Turkestan. Note on Local Flora. William Empson. AtBAP; FaBoMo; MoVE
There is a tree of praise and dower. The Year. *Unknown.* MeMeAg; OTPC (1946 ed.)
There is a truck that rumbles by. The Grumbling Truck. Rowena Bennett. MPB (1956 ed.)
There is a vale which none hath seen. Rumors from an Aeolian Harp. Henry David Thoreau. MOAP
There Is a Wail in the Wind To-Night. Sir Joseph Noel Paton. EBSV
There is a wall of which the stones. The Rebel. Hilaire Belloc. BMEP; CoBE; PoFr
There is a Water that flows down from Heaven. The Spirit of the Saints. Jalal ed-Din Rumi. PeP
There Is a Way of Life. Merrill Moore. OnPM
There is a way that calls to me. In April. John Richard Moreland. LS
There is a way, that sages tell. The Advantage of the Outside. Richard Eberhart. NePA
There is a way which man hath trod. Gethsemane. Charles Russell Wakeley. OQP; QP-1
There is a well, a willow-shaded spot. The Cherwell Water Lily [*or* Waterlily]. Frederick W. Faber. CAW; GoBC
There is a white horse with a gold bridle to the East of the Liao Sea. Spring Grief and Resentment. Li Po. ChLP
There is a white mare that my love keeps. The Postures of Love, II. Alex Comfort. FaBoMo; NeBP
There is a wild boar in these woods. Old Bangum. *Unknown.* BaBo
There is a wild flower growing. Jean. Paul Potts. NeBP
There is a willow grows aslant a brook. Ophelia's Death. Shakespeare. *Fr.* Hamlet, V, i. ChTr

There is a willow grows beside a pool. A Bread and Butter Letter. Alice Duer Miller. VOD

There is a wind in Cornwall that I know. Cornish Wind. Arthur Symons. LBBV

There is a wind where the rose was. Autumn [*or* The Lost Playmate]. Walter de la Mare. GTBS-D; OTPC (1923 ed.); POTE

There is a wolf in me. Wilderness. Carl Sandburg. AnAmPo; LA

There is a woman like a seed. Another Generation. J. C. Squire. HBMV

There is a wonderful family called Stein. Limerick. *Unknown.* BOHV. *See also* Wonderful Family is Stein, A.

There is a word/ Which bears a sword. Emily Dickinson. BoFr

There is a word of Fate, an old decree. Empedocles, *tr. fr. Greek by* W. E. Leonard. GrPo

There is a world of tenderness, within. To a Nun Violinist. Sister Mary Louise. PraNu

There is a world of wonder in this rose. The Rose. G. A. Studdert-Kennedy. MaRV

There is a world that's floored with clouds. The World at the Bottom of the Lake. Karle Wilson Baker. LS

There is a worm in the world, well man knoweth him. The Serpent's Nature. *Unknown. Fr.* The Bestiary. MeEV

There is a worthy man in the east. The Hermit. Tao Yuan-ming. WhP

There is a yew-tree, pride of Lorton Vale. Yew-Trees. Wordsworth. BCEP; BEL; BPN; EmBrPo; EnLi-2; EnRP; ERP; UnPo (3d ed.)

There is a young artist called [*or* named] Whistler. Limerick. Dante Gabriel Rossetti. BOHV; LiBL

There is a young lady whose nose/ Continually prospers and grows. Limerick. Edward Lear. OTPC (1946 ed.). *See also* There was a young lady whose nose/ Was so long . . .

There is about old houses such a charm. Old Houses. Struthers Burt. NoCaPo (1941 ed.)

There Is Always a Place for You. Anne Campbell. PoToHe

There is always room for beauty; memory. The Poetry of Earth. Florence Earle Coates. BAP

There is always the sound of falling water here. Night Piece. Robert Hillyer. MAP; MoAmPo

There is an air for which I fain would give. Fantasia. Gérard de Nerval, *tr. by* Alan Conder. TrFP

There is an air for which I would disown. An Old Tune. Gérard de Nerval, *tr. by* Andrew Lang. AWP; HBV; JAWP; WBP

There is an air for which I'd gladly give. Fantasy. Gérard de Nerval, *tr. by* Anthony Bower. AnFP; LiTW

There is an ape in Paris. The Ape. La Fontaine. OnPM

There is an architecture grander far. The Builders. Henry van Dyke. OQP; QP-2

There is an eagle screaming from a roof. The Painted Desert. Elizabeth J. Coatsworth. PoeMoYo

There is an earthly glimmer in the tomb. Love after Death. Arthur O'Shaughnessy. GTIV

There is an eerie music, Tabary. Villon Strolls at Midnight. Vincent Starrett. BAP; LEAP

There Is an Eminence. Wordsworth. Poems on the Naming of Places, III. ERP

There is an enchanted orange orchard. The Enchanted Orchard. Henry Mackenzie Green. MM

There is an end of joy and sorrow. Ilicet. Swinburne. EmBrPo; PoD; PoVP; VLEP

There is an evening hour when light is laid. Saffron Flower. Babette Deutsch. BAP

There is an exquisite torture in living with dull people. Always Battling. Thomas O'Brien. NeIP

There is an eye that never sleeps. God the Omniscient [*or* The Power of Prayer]. *At. to* James Cowden Wallace, *also to* John Aikman Wallace. BLRP; PraP; WGRP

There is an hour of peaceful rest The Hour of Peaceful Rest. William Bingham Tappan. AA; HBV

There Is an Inn, a Merry Old Inn. J. R. R. Tolkien. LiL

There is an island in a far-off sea. Where the Single Men Go in Summer. Nina Bourne. FiBHP

There is an island in the warm Pacific. Easter Island. Richard Leon Spain. MuM

There is an isle beyond our ken. The Isle of Lost Dreams. "Fiona Macleod." VA

There is an octopus in my orchard. Beauty and the Beast. Edwin Björkman. NoCaPo (1941 ed.)

There is an ode in every swaying tree. Reflection. Kurt M. Stein. InMe

There is an old and very cruel god. Vicarious Atonement. Richard Aldington. MBP; WGRP

There Is an Old City. Karl Bulcke, *tr. fr. German by* Ludwig Lewisohn. AWP; JAWP; WBP

There is an old Cook in N. Y *Unknown.* SiTL

There is an old he-wolf named Gambart. Limerick. Dante Gabriel Rossetti. CenHV

There is an old low room I love. An Old Room. Gustaf Fröding. AnSL

There is an old pond in the hills. An Old Pond. Bocho Yamamura. PoLJ

There is an old woman/ Who ought to die. The Old Woman. Marjorie Allen Seiffert. AnAmPo; NP

There is an old woman/ Who lives in the town. The Old Woman Who Lives in the Town. Pringle Barret. PCH

There is an old woman who looks each night. A Man's Daughter. John Drinkwater. LEAP

There is an Order by a northern sea. Religio Novissima. Aubrey Thomas De Vere. IrPN

There is at least one thing I would less rather have in the neighborhood than a gangster. What's the Matter, Haven't You Got Any Sense of Humor? Ogden Nash. SiTL

There is beauty in the bellow of the blast. Ko-Ko's Song. W. S. Gilbert. *Fr.* The Mikado. PCD

There is beauty in the forest. When the Heart Is Full of Love. *Unknown.* MaRV

There is, besides the warmth, in this new love. Scarabs for the Living, V. R. P. Blackmur. TwAmPo

There is blood on thy desolate shore. Apostrophe to the Island of Cuba. James Gates Percival. PAH

There is bright light. Its Name Is Known. Daniel Lawrence Kelleher. NeIP

There is Bryant, as quiet, as cool, and as dignified. Bryant. James Russell Lowell. *Fr.* A Fable for Critics. AnNE; CoBA; PtP

There is but one great sorrow. The Shadow. Richard Henry Stoddard. AA

There is but one May in the year. May-Time. Christina Rossetti. *Fr.* Sing-Song. BoTP; TiPo

There is comfort in old houses. Old Houses. Homer D'Lettuso. PoToHe (new ed.)

There is darkness still, gross darkness, Lord. Spread the Light. John Oxenham. PraP

There is death enough in Europe without these. Dead Ponies. Brenda Chamberlain. NeBP

There is delight in singing, tho' none hear. To Robert Browning. Walter Savage Landor. BCEP; BEL; BPN; EmBrPo; EnLi-2; EnRP; EPN; EPP; ERP; EV-4; GTBS; GTSL; InP; LEAP; MCCG; MyFE; OAEP; PeBoSo; PoRL; PreP; PtP; ViBoPo

There is dogwood in my soul. Leonard Bacon. Animula Vagula, XXVII. NV

There is enchantment on you lips. To a "Friend." Emil Aarestrup. BoDS

There is fear in. Eskimo Song. *Unknown.* PeCV

There is fire in the lower hold, there's fire down below. Fire Down Below. *Unknown.* SoAmSa

There is great mystery, Simone. Hair. Remy de Gourmont. AWP

There Is Hallelujah Hannah. A. E. Housman. WhC

There is hardly a mouthful of air. Nelson Street. "Seumas O'Sullivan." GTIV; OxBI

There is Hawthorne, with genius so shrinking and rare. Hawthorne. James Russell Lowell. *Fr.* A Fable for Critics. AmPP (4th ed.); AnNE; CoBA; OxBA

There is health in thy gray win- To a Marsh Hawk in Spring. Henry David Thoreau. PoEL-4

There is heard a hymn when the panes are dim. The Feast of the Snow. G. K. Chesterton. HBV

There is here an ancient anchorite. San Sabas. Luis Palés Matos. CAW

There is immortal living now and here. Immortal Living. Harold T. Pulsifer. MaRV

There is in all the sons of men. God's Altar. Emerson. MaRV

There is in certain ancient things a trace. Continuity. H. P. Lovecraft. UnW

There is, in famous Yankee-land. A Yankee Lyric. Hugh Peters. LauV

There is in souls a sympathy with sounds. William Cowper. *Fr.* The Task, VI. BrBE

There is Lowell, who's striving Parnassus to climb. Lowell [*or* On Himself]. James Russell Lowell. *Fr.* A Fable for Critics. AA; AmPP (4th ed.); CoBA; OxBA

There is many a love in the land, my love. Song. Joaquin Miller. HBV

There is many a slipton. Lady Tree. WhC

There is many a wild Canadian boy who leaves his happy home. Harry Dunne, *vers.* II. *Unknown.* ShS

There is midsummer. Midsummer. Stephen Spender. AtBAP

There is much to be said. Mac Diarmod's Daughter. Francis Carlin. HBMV

There is much to be said for the portrait painted in winter. Portrait in Winter. Katherine Garrison Chapin. GoYe

There is music in me, the music of a peasant people. The Banjo Player. Fenton Johnson. AnAmPo; BANP; GoSl; LA; PoNe

There is naught for thee by thy haste to gain. The Created. Jones Very. AmP

There Is Never a Day So Dreary. Lilla M. Alexander. BLRP

There is never any trusting. Foam. *Unknown.* OnPM
There is no balm on earth. Invocation. Gilbert Thomas. TrPWD
There is no bargain basement. Early Willows. James Wreford Watson. BoCaPo
There is no bountie to be shew'd to such. Ben Jonson. *Fr.* The Poetaster. PoEL-2
There is no breeze upon the fern. Beal' an Dhuine. Sir Walter Scott. *Fr.* The Lady of the Lake. LPS-2
There is no chance, no destiny, no fate. Will. Ella Wheeler Wilcox. BLPA; NeHB; PoToHe
There is no change of time and place with Thee. The Ark. Jones Very. IAP
There is no chapel on the day. Oscar Wilde. *Fr.* The Ballad of Reading Gaol. GTIV; OxBI
There is no cock crowing in our bedroom. No Cock Crows at Morning. Horace Gregory. ChMo
There is no comfort in adversity. The Solace of Art. Amphis. OxBG
There is no comfort to be found for pain. Oh, Gentle Beauty [*or* Chanson]. Thibaut of Champagne. LiA; LyMA
There Is No Country. Juljan Tuwim, *tr. fr. Polish by* Watson Kirkconnell. TrJP
There is no creator but One. Do Mercy before Thy Judgement. *Unknown.* TMEV
There is no dearer lover of lost hours. Idleness. Silas Weir Mitchell. AA; OBAV
There Is No Death. John Luckey McCreery. BLPA; FaBoBe; HBV; NeHB; TreF; WBLP
"There is no death! The stars go down," *sel.* MaRV
There Is No Death. *Unknown.* BLPA; NeHB
There is no death, O child divine. The Great Victory. R. V. Gilbert. BLRP
There is no death! The stars go down. There Is No Death. John Luckey McCreery. BLPA; FaBoBe; HBV; MaRV; NeHB; TreF; WBLP
There is no death! What seems so is transition. Resignation. Longfellow. MaRV
There is no denying. At the Last. Witter Bynner. TwAmPo
There Is No Dream. Margaret E. Sangster. PEDC
There is no end to the/ Deception of quiet things. The Chinese Banyan. William Meredith. NePoEA
There is no escape by the river. At the End of the Day. Richard Hovey. HBVY; LBMV; PC; StaSt; YT
There is no fire of the crackling boughs. Glenaradale. Walter Chalmers Smith. EBSV; OBEV (new ed.); OBVV
There is no flock, however watched and tended. Resignation. Longfellow. CoBA; HBV; LPS-1; TCAP
There is no flower that hath no hue. The Heart's Flower. Karl Jonas Love Almquist. AnSL
There is no force however great. Physics. William Whewell. LPS-3
There is no frigate like a book. Emily Dickinson. BBV (1951 ed.); CoBA; MAP; MoAmPo; PoMa; SiSoSe; TrGrPo; YeAr
(Book, A.) ATP; CV; FaPON; HH; InP; MPB; NeMA; TreFS
There Is No God. Arthur Hugh Clough. *See* "There Is No God," the Wicked Saith.
There is no God, as I was taught in youth. John Masefield. *Fr.* Sonnets ("Long long ago"). ChMo; CMP; HBV; WGRP
"There is no God," the foolish saith. Convinced by Sorrow. Elizabeth Barrett Browning. *Fr.* The Cry of the Human. BLRP; MaRV; OQP; PoVP; QP-2; WBLP
"There Is No God," the Wicked Saith. Arthur Hugh Clough. *Fr.* Dipsychus, Pt. I, sc. v. TreFS; ViPP; VLEP
(Spirit's Song, The.) LoBV
("'There is no God!' the wicked saith.") BHV; BMEP; BPN; EPN; PoVP
There is no great and no small. The Informing Spirit [*or* No Great, No Small]. Emerson. *Fr.* History. AWP; BBV (1951 ed.); IAP; InPo; MaRV; MOAP; WGRP
There is no happy life. Love's Vision [*or* Love's Matrimony]. Duke of Newcastle. LO; LoPS; SeCePo; SeCL
There is no haven past the sky and sun. Lonely Trek. Joseph Joel Keith. MuM
There is no joy in water apart from the sun. Song. R. N. Currey. BoSA
There is no land has sorrow for me. Prison Songs. *Unknown.* TMEV
There is no land like England. Song. Tennyson. *Fr.* The Foresters. VA
There is no latch on books, to say: "Stand back!" The Negro Student. Marguerite Steffan. MuM
There is no laughter in the natural world. Laughter and Death. Wilfrid Scawen Blunt. The Love Sonnets of Proteus, XCI. BMEP; MBP; MoBrPo (1942 ed.); PoMa; VA
There is no light in any path of Heaven. The Dark Road. Ethel Clifford. HBV
There is no love like the love of Jesus. The Heart of God. W. E. Littlewood. BePJ
There Is No Loving after Death. Asclepiades, *tr. fr. Greek by* R. A. Furness. GrL; OxBG
(Carpe Diem.) GrR
There is no means to annul. Permanence. Francis Meynell. LoPo
There is no "mighty purpose" in this book. To Laurence Hutton. Austin Dobson. BPN
There is no music that man has heard. A Sea Lyric. William Hamilton Hayne. EtS
There is no name for thee! To Her. Vasili Zhukovsky. BoRS
There is no name in all our country's story. Abraham Lincoln. Robert Whitaker. GA; HH
There is no name so sweet on earth. The Blessed Name. George W. Bethune. BLRP
There Is No Nearer Nearness. Cha Liang-cheng, *tr. fr. Chinese by* Cha Liang-cheng. LiTW
There is no need to run outside. To Be. *Unknown, at. to* Lao-tzu. *Fr.* Tao Teh King. OnPM
There is no one among men who [*or* that] has not a special failing. Madly Singing in the Mountains. Po Chü-i. AlDL; MoPW; OuHeWo; TrCh
There is no one beside thee and no one above thee. Insufficiency. Elizabeth Barrett Browning. AV; BPN; EmBrPo
There Is No Opera like "Lohengrin." John Wheelwright. OnHM; WhC
There is no page or servaunt, most or least. The VII Properte. Sir Thomas More. *Fr.* The XII Properties or Condicyons of a Lover. CoBE
There is no path in this desert waste. My Guide. Robert Jones Burdette. MaRV
There is no peace on earth today save the peace in the heart. Anselmo Speaks. Edna St. Vincent Millay. *Fr.* Conversation at Midnight. TwCV
There is no peace with you. Enigma. Jessie Redmond Fauset. PoNe
"There is no permanence," you sagely said. Two Sonnets for a Lost Love, I. Samuel A. De Witt. GoYe
There is no person lonelier. Visit the Sick. James J. Metcalfe. PoToHe (new ed.)
"There is no place to turn," she said. The Sensualists. Theodore Roethke. NePoAm-2
There is no point in work. Work. D. H. Lawrence. MM; MoP; OBMV; ShBV-3; TwCV
There is no power to change. Permanence. Francis Meynell. HBMV; MBP; MoBrPo (1942 ed.)
There is no quiet in the earth. In Time of Peace. Michael Roberts. MoP
There is no Rachel any more. One Shall Be Taken and the Other Left. Aline Kilmer. LEAP; NP; TBM
There is no rest for the mind. Interior; the Suburbs. Horace Gregory. AnAmPo; LA; NP
There is no rest in falling, even so. Snow Meditation. Francis Beauchesne Thornton. JKCP (1955 ed.)
There is no rhyme that is half so sweet. Proem. Madison Cawein. AA
There Is No Rose of Such Virtue. *Unknown. See* Rosa Mystica.
There Is No Sanctuary for Brave Men. A. G. Herbertson. NeTW
There is no sense in asking those who fought. Anabasis. Eithne Wilkins. NeBP
There is no siding for the brain. Listening to a Broadcast. John Manifold. WaP
There is no silence lovelier than the one. To a Tree in Bloom. Hildegarde Flanner. VOD (1935 ed.)
There is no silence upon the earth or under the earth. Silences. E. J. Pratt. BoCaPo (1943 ed.); TwCV
There Is No Sin. Omar Khayyám, *tr. fr. Persian by* Edward Fitzgerald. *Fr.* The Rubáiyát. OnPM
There is no sky now for the slender song. Plover. Luella Boynton. MuM
There is no small work unto God. Anna Hempstead Branch. *Fr.* The Monk in the Kitchen. MaRV
There is no soft beatitude in Death. Death is but Death. Will Dyson. BoAV; MoAuPo
There is no sorrow. Away. Walter de la Mare. ChMo
There is no sorrow anywhere. Homeward Bound. L. Frank Tooker. EtS
There is no sound. Portent. Richard Church. MBP; MoBrPo (1942 ed.)
There Is No Sound save through the Sweltry Sheet. Pauline Avery Crawford. MuM
"There is no sun!" the blind man said. Unfaith. Ted Robinson. MaRV
There is no sweeter sight, I swear; in Heaven. The Crimson Cherry Tree. Henry Treece. LiTM (1946 ed.); MoWP; TriL; WaP
There is no thing in all the world but love. The Camel Rider. *Unknown.* AWP; FaBoTw
There is no town but London town. London. Irene Rutherford McLeod. VOD
There Is No Trumpet like the Tomb. Emily Dickinson. BLV; BoLiVe
There Is No Unbelief. Elizabeth York Case. HBV; NeHB; OQP; QP-1; TreFS; WBLP; WGRP
(Unbelief.) MaRV

There is no vacant chair. The loving meet. Afterward. Elizabeth Stuart Phelps Ward. HBV
There is no way here, shepherds, read the wooden sign. Eclogue by a Five-barred Gate. Louis MacNeice. MoP; ReaPo
There is no way in this starless night. Christ. Robert Jones Burdette. *Fr.* My Guide. BePJ
There is no whispering of any friend. No Friend like Music. Daniel Whitehead Hicky. PoToHe
There is no word of thanks to hear. Pioneers. Arthur W. Jose. BoAu
There is no worldly pleasure here below. On Love. Sir Robert Ayton. LPS-1
There is no wrath in the stars. Songs from an Evil Wood, I. Lord Dunsany. BMEP; MBP; MoBrPo (1942 ed.)
"There is none good save God," said Jesus Christ. Elizabeth Barrett Browning. *Fr.* Aurora Leigh, IV. VLEP
There Is None like Her. Tennyson. *Fr.* Maud. FaBoEn
There Is None, O None but You. Thomas Campion, *wr. at. to* Robert Devereux, Earl of Essex. AtBAP; EIL; HBV; OBSC
There is none other medicine, Nicias, against Love. The Cyclops in Love. Theocritus. *Fr.* Idylls. GrL
There is none under sun like to her. The Black Rose. Clement Wood. TBM
There is nor great nor small in Nature's plan. Great and Small. Charles Mackay. BSV
There is not a grand inspiring thought. Mother. Emily Taylor. PGD
There is not half so warm a fire. Against Fulfillment of Desire. *Unknown.* TrGrPo
There is not in the wide world a valley so sweet. The Meeting of the Waters [*or* The Vale of Avoca]. Thomas Moore. AnIL; ERP; LPS-1; OxBoLi; PoEL-4
There is not now that mankind, which was then. An Anatomy [*or* Anatomie] of the World. John Donne. EPS; NBE
There is nothing in the quince. The Quince. Ibn Sara. MooP
There is nothing moving there, in that desert of silence. Priapus and the Pool, IX [X]. Conrad Aiken. ChMo; CMP; MOAP
There is nothing new to be written of tears and man's shuddering breath. On a Fly-Leaf of Schopenhauer's "Immortality." Ruth Guthrie Harding. MaRV; MuM
There Is Nothing Strange. Archilochus, *tr. fr. Greek by* J. H. Merivale. GrL; OxBG
There is nothing to remember in me. On Deck. Robert Browning. James Lee's Wife, IX. EtPaEn
There is one/ race of men. Nemean Ode, VI. Pindar. *Fr.* Odes. LiTW
"There is one at the door, Wolfe O'Driscoll." The Fair Little Maiden. Dora Sigerson Shorter. DaM
There Is One Creed, and Only One. E. A. Robinson. MaRV
There is one form of life to which I unconditionally surrender. Oh, Please Don't Get Up! Ogden Nash. NePA; SiTL
There is one I love. Odi et Amo. Ibn al-Hajj. MooP
There is one Mind, one omnipresent Mind. Samuel Taylor Coleridge. *Fr.* Religious Musings. WGRP
There is one sin: to call a green leaf grey. Ecclesiastes. G. K. Chesterton. MoBrPo
There Is One Spot for Which My Soul Will Yearn. Myron B. Benton. SN
There is one story and one story only. To Juan at the Winter Solstice. Robert Graves. CoBMV; FaBoMo; LiTB; LiTM (rev. ed.); MoPo; OnHM; SeCeV; UnPo (3d ed.)
There is one that has a head without an eye. Christina Rossetti. *Fr.* Sing-Song. OTPC (1946 ed.); PPL
There is one who takes all men within his hand. Strophes. Rainer Maria Rilke. OnPM
There is only one love. Sappho, Be Comforted. William Carlos Williams. NePoAm-2
There Is Pleasure in the Pathless Woods. Byron. *See* Ocean, The.
There is rust on the latch of poetry's house. Rust on the Latch. Marion Lee. MuM
There Is Shrill Music in High Winds at Night. Jesse Stuart. Man with a Bull-Tongue Plow, *st.* 293. PoMa
There is so much bad in the best of us. A Thought to Remember. *Unknown.* BLP
There is so much good in the worst of us. Charity [*or* Good and Bad]. *Unknown, at. to* Edward Wallis Hoch. BLPA; NeHB; TreFS
There is so much of loneliness. *Unknown.* PoToHe
There is some soul of goodness in things evil. Goodness in Things Evil. Shakespeare. King Henry V, *fr.* IV, i. EV-1
There is some that like the city Ridin'. Badger Clark. IHA
There is some will talk of lords and knights. Robin Hood's Delight. *Unknown.* ESPB
There is something in the autumn that is native to my blood. A Vagabond Song [*or* Autumn Song]. Bliss Carman. BTP; FaPON; GBV; GN; GoTP; HBV; HBVY; HOAH; LBMV; MAP; MCCG; MM; MoAmPo (1942 ed.); MPB; NeMA; NLK; OTPC (1946 ed.); PoeMoYo; PoMa; POT; PoTo; StaSt; StVeCh (1940 ed.); TCAP; VOD; YT
There is something in the word home. Home. *Unknown.* HBV
There is somewhere a secret garden, which none hath seen. The Secret Garden. Robert Nichols. WGRP
There is sorrow enough in the natural way. The Power of the Dog. Kipling. AlBD; BLPA
There Is Still Splendour. Laurence Binyon. NeTW
There is stone in me that knows stone. Kathleen Raine. *Fr.* Rock. ImOP
There is strange holiness around. Strange Holiness. Robert P. Tristram Coffin. TwCV
There Is Strength in the Soil. Arthur Stringer. OHIP
There is sweet music here that softer falls. Choric Song [*or* Song of the Lotos-Eaters]. Tennyson. *Fr.* The Lotos-Eaters. BMEP; CBE; CBOV; CoEV; FaFP; GTBS-W; GTML; GTSL; LiTG; OBEV; OuHeWo; PC; ReTS; ViBoPo; WHA
There is that in the air, an imminence. Death Ray. Lola Ridge. TBM
There is that whispering gallery where. Letter to a Young Poet. George Barker. ChMP
There is the caw of a crow. Jonathan Houghton. Edgar Lee Masters. *Fr.* Spoon River Anthology. OxBA
There is the hat. Only the Clothes She Wore. Nathaniel Graham Shepherd. LPS-1
There is the loneliness of peopled places. Solitude. Babette Deutsch. BAP; HBMV
There is the quaintest little girl. A Little Girl in Bloom. Anne Blackwell Payne. GFA
There is the sea—shall any stanch it up? The Purple Carpet. Aeschylus. *Fr.* Agamemnon. OxBG
There is the star bloom of the moss. Forest. Jean Garrigue. LiTM
There is this distance between me and what I see. Still Poem 9. Philip Lamantia. NeAP
There is waiting a work where only his hands can avail. The Day and the Work. Edwin Markham. OQP; PEDC; PSO; QP-1
There is weeping on Cnoc-Aulin and on hoary Slieve-na-mon. The Passing of the Sidhe. James B. Dollard. CPG
There is Whittier, whose swelling and vehement heart. Whittier. James Russell Lowell. *Fr.* A Fable for Critics. AmPP (4th ed.); AnNE; APW; CoBA; OxBA; PtP
There is wind indeed and violent weather. Wind and Violent Weather. Unknown. *Fr.* Shi King. ChLP
There is wind where the rose was. The Lost Playmate. Walter de la Mare. OTPC (1923 ed.)
There is, within three leagues and less of Padua. Samuel Rogers. *Fr.* Italy. PtP
There Is Yet Time. Arvel Steece. PGD
There isn't a prettier sight, I think. Bare-Back Rider. Dorothy Aldis. *Fr.* At the Circus. UTS
There Isn't Time. Eleanor Farjeon. BoTP; FaPON
There it stands, the *flamboyant*, dead or alive we hardly know. The Phoenix' Throne. D. J. Enright. PoN
There it was I saw what I shall never forget. The Fawn. Edna St. Vincent Millay. LaNeLa
There Lackethe Somethynge Stylle. Thomas Chatterton. *See* Song of the Three Minstrels.
There lay upon the ocean's shore. The Finding of the Lyre. James Russell Lowell. PECK; PTA-2; TVSH
There leeft a may, an a weel-far'd may. Katharine Jaffray (C *vers.*). *Unknown.* ESPB
There leeved a wee man at the fit o' yon hill. Get Up and Bar the Door (B *vers.*). *Unknown.* ESPB
There Let Thy Bleeding Branch Atone. Emily Brontë. SeCePo
There lies a city inaccessible. The Unknown City. Sir Charles G. D. Roberts. CaP; CPG; OCL
There lies a cold corpse upon the sands. Death Song. Robert Stephen Hawker. OBRV; OBVV
There lies a little city in the hills. Home. Edward Rowland Sill. AnNE; HBV
There lies a little city leagues away. The Deserted City. Sir Charles G. D. Roberts. BMEP; VA
There lies a lone isle in the tropic seas. Easter Island. Frederick George Scott. BoCaPo
There lies a somnolent lake. In the Past. Trumbull Stickney. MAP; MoAmPo (1942 ed.); MOAP; OxBA
There lies a vale [*or* There is a dale] in Ida, lovelier. Oenone. Tennyson. BEL; BPN; BrBE; EM-2; EmBrPo; EnLi-2; EnLit; EPN; GEPC; OAEP; OBRV; PoVP; TCEP; TwCrTr; ViBoPo; ViPo; ViPP; VLEP
There lies afar behind a western hill. The Town without a Market. James Elroy Flecker. MBP; MoBrPo
There lies her fan, gold-flecked. The Fan. Fan Tseng Hsiang. PoHN
There lies no magic in this bit of bread. Sacrament. Una W. Harsen. ChIP
There lies the port; the vessel puffs her sail. Work May Yet Be Done. Tennyson. *Fr.* Ulysses. EtS; GrCo-1; MaRV; OQP; OTPC; PC; QP-2

There! little girl, don't cry! A Life-Lesson. James Whitcomb Riley. AA; BAP; HBV; LEAP; OBAV; TreFS
There liv'd a lady in Lauderdale. She's Hoy'd Me Out o' Lauderdale. *Unknown.* CoMu
There livd a laird down into Fife. The Wife Wrapt in Wether's Skin (D *vers.*). *Unknown.* ESPB
There livd a lass in yonder dale. *See* There lived . . .
There livd a lord on yon sea-side. Fair Annie (B *vers.*) *Unknown.* ESPB
There liv'd of late in Luteners Lane. A Westminster Wedding; or, Like unto Like, Quoth the Devil to the Collier. *Unknown.* CoMu
There lived a bold and valiant dinge who made the heathen Paynim cringe. Othello. Newman Levy. PIAE
There Lived a King. W. S. Gilbert. *Fr.* The Gondoliers. FiBHP; StPo; WhC
(King Goodheart.) ALV; InMe
There Lived a lady in Milan. William Rose Benét. HBMV; OnPP; TCPD
There lived [*or* livd] a lass in yonder dale. Katharine Jaffray. *Unknown.* BaBo; ESPB; InP; TCEP; ViBoFo (A *vers.*)
There Lived a Man. Thomas Curtis Clark. ChIP
There lived a man at the foot of a hill. Get Up and Bar the Door. *Unknown.* EnSB
There Lived a Romish lady. *See* There was a Romish lady.
There lived a sage in days of yore. A Tragic Story. Adelbert von Chamisso, *tr. by* Thackeray. BoChLi (1950 ed.); BOHV; BoTP; FaPON; GaP; GoTP; HBV; HBVY; MoShBr; MPB; OTPC; RIS; StVeCh (1940 ed.)
There lived a singer in France of old. A Farewell. Swinburne. *Fr.* The Triumph of Time. GTML; GTSL
There lived a wife at Usher's Well. The Wife of Usher's Well. *Unknown.* AnFE; AtBAP; AWP; BaBo (A *vers.*); BEL; BLV; BoLiVe; BrBE; BSV; CBE; CBOV; CH; ChTr; DaM; EBSV; EM-1; EnL; EnLi-1; EnRP; EnSB; ESPB; EV-2; ExPo; GoTS; HBV; InP; InPo; JAWP; LiTB; LoBV; OAEP; OBB; OBEV; OuHeWo; PoEL-1; REAL; ReaPo; RiBV; SeCeV; ShBV-2; TCEP; TiPo (1952 ed.); TOP; TreF; TrGrPo; TwHP; UnPo; UnW; ViBoFo (A *vers.*); WBP
There lived an honest man and true. The Cruel Sister. *Unknown.* BaBo
There lived an old lord by the Northern Sea. The Two Sisters. *Unknown.* PoMa
There lived an old man in a garret. D'Arcy Wentworth Thompson. *Fr.* Nursery Nonsense. BoN
There lived an old man in the Kingdom of Tess. The New Vestments. Edward Lear. BOHV; BoN; OnPP
There lived in a laburnum tree. The Yellow Fairy. Charlotte Druitt Cole. BoTP
There lived in Gothic days, as legends tell. Edwin, the Minstrel. James Beattie. *Fr.* The Minstrel. EV-3
There lived once Svetaketu Aruneya, the grandson of Aruna. The Story of Svetaketu. *Unknown.* *Fr.* The Upanishads. WoL
There lived years ago the beautiful Kung-sun. Tu Fu. *Fr.* A Song of Dagger-Dancing. UnS
There lives a cat across the way. A Parlor Cat. Louella C. Poole. CIV
There lives a lassie i' the braes. Lizzy Liberty. John Skinner. PoFr
There lives a man in Rynie's land. Lang Johnny More. *Unknown.* ESPB
There lives a pig in Georgia's far land. Pipes in the Sty. John Kendall. WhC
There lives beside me here an unknown woman. The Ascension and the Assumption. Ramón López Velarde. TwSpPo
There may be finer pleasures than just tramping with your boy. The Finest Fellowship. Edgar A. Guest. FAOV
There May, of Course, Be Mice. Richard R. Kirk. LS
There men micht see men freshly ficht. Bannockburn. John Barbour. *Fr.* The Bruce. EBSV
There mounts in squalls a sort of rusty mire. The Exile's Return. Robert Lowell. MiAP; NePA; OxBA
There mournful cypress grew in greatest store. The Garden of Proserpina. Spenser. *Fr.* The Faerie Queene, II, 7. ChTr
There must be fairy miners. Buttercups. Wilfrid Thorley. DD; FaPON; GaP; HBV; HBVY; NLK; OBVV; PC
There must be magic. Otherwise. Aileen Fisher. GoBP; SUS
There must be many Theobalds' Roads in the universe. Theobalds' Roads. Charles Williams. LO
There Must Be Silence. Anne Tansey. JKCP (1955 ed.)
There, my blessing with thee! Polonius' Advice to Laertes [*or* To Thine Own Self Be True]. Shakespeare. *Fr.* Hamlet, I, iii. EV-1; FaFP; LiTB; LiTG; MaRV; OHFP; OQP; PIR; PTA-1; QP-1; TVSH
There ne'er was blown out of the yellow east. Said the Daisy. Isabella Valancy Crawford. CPG
There never breathed a man, who, when his life. Gabriello Chiabrera. Epitaphs, IV. AWP; JAWP; WBP
"There never was a grandma half so good!" Flattering Grandma. *Unknown.* PEOR
There never was a man besmitten so. A Man Besmitten So. Alfred Kreymborg. TBM
There never was a mood of mine. I Remembered. Sara Teasdale. LoPo; LoPS; TCPD
There never were such radiant noons. Then and Now. Sir Rennell Rodd. VA
There never yet was honest man. Loving and Beloved. Sir John Suckling. FaBoEn; OBS; SeEP
There, obedient to her praying, did I read aloud the poems. The Poets. Elizabeth Barrett Browning. *Fr.* Lady Geraldine's Courtship. BCEP
There often wanders one, whom better days. William Cowper. *Fr.* The Task, I. EPP
There, on the Darkened Deathbed [Dies the Brain]. John Masefield. *Fr.* Sonnets ("Long, long ago"). CMP; LiTB
(End, The.) ChMo
There on the hill it's holiday. Alyona. Aleksandr Yashin. RuPo
"There, on the left!" said the colonel. Marthy Virginia's Hand. George Parsons Lathrop. BlG; MC; PAH
There on the top of the down. June Bracken and Heather. Tennyson. EnLoPo; GEPC; PoVP; VLEP
There once did live in days of old. Florent and the Loathly Hag. John Gower. *Fr.* Confessio Amantis. MeEV
There once the penitents took off their shoes. Our Lady of Walsingham. Robert Lowell. *Fr.* The Quaker Graveyard in Nantucket. MeRV
There once the walls. A Tale. Edward Thomas. ChTr
There once was a bird that lived up in a tree. Fiddle-Dee-Dee. Eugene Field. DDA
There once was a bonnie Scotch laddie. Limerick. *Unknown.* LiBL; WhC
There once was a boring young Rev. *Unknown.* SiTL
There once was a boy of Bagdad. Limerick [*or* New Limericks]. *Unknown.* RIS; StaSt
There once was a cobbler. The Kind Mousie. Natalie Joan. BoTP
There Once was a Cow with a Double Udder. The Cow. Theodore Roethke. FiBHP
There once was a Dormouse who lived in a bed. The Dormouse and the Doctor. A. A. Milne. WhC
There once was a frog. A Legend of Lake Okeefinokee [*or* A Legend of Okeefinokee]. Laura E. Richards. BoChLi; PoRh; RIS; StPo
There once was a girl of New York. Limerick. Cosmo Monkhouse. LiBL; NA
There once was a girl of Pitlochry. Limerick. *Unknown.* CenHV
There once was a guy named Othello. Shakespeare Might Have Boiled Othello. Edwin Meade Robinson. *Fr.* Limericised Classics. HBMV
There once was a happy hyena. The Happy Hyena. Carolyn Wells. PCH
There once was a maid with such graces. *Unknown.* SiTL
There once was a man from Nantucket. *See* There was an old man of Nantucket.
There once was a man of Bengal. Limerick. *Unknown.* CenHV
There once was a man of Calcutta. Limerick. *Unknown.* LiBL; LiL; TSWC; WhC
There once was a man [*or* was a young man] who said: "Damn!" Limerick. Maurice Evan Hare. CenHV; LiBL; OxBoLi
There once was a man [*or* was a young man] who said, "God." Limerick [*or* Rhyme]. Ronald Arbuthnott Knox. LiBL; OxBoLi
There once was a man who said, "How." Limerick. *Unknown.* LiBL; NA
There once was a monarch, a pompous old Persian. The King and the Clown. *Unknown.* MaC
There once was a noble ranger. Mustang Gray. *Unknown.* ABF; CoSo; CSF
There once was a painter named Scott. Limerick. Dante Gabriel Rossetti. CenHV
There once was a peach on a tree. The Peach. Abbie Farwell Brown. GFA
There once was a person of Benin. Limerick. Cosmo Monkhouse. LiBL; NA
There once was a pious young priest. Limerick. *Unknown.* TSWC
There once was a popular crooner. Limerick. M. B. Thornton. LiBL
There Once Was a Puffin. Florence Page Jaques. TiPo
(There Was Once a Puffin.) GoBP
There once was a sculptor called [*or* named] Phidias. Limerick. Oliver Herford. BOHV; LiBL
There once was a Shah had a second son. Noureddin, the Son of the Shah. Clinton Scollard. BOHV
There once was a Warden of Wadham. The Folkways of Sodom. "E. W." SiTL
There once was a Willow, and he was very old. The Willowman. Juliana Horatia Ewing. TVC; TVSH

There once was a witch of Willowby Wood. The Witch of Willowby Wood. Rowena Bennett. PoMS
There once was a wood, and a very thick wood. The First Tooth. William Brighty Rands. HBV; HBVY
There once was an arch armadillo. The Arch Armadillo. Carolyn Wells. PCH
There once was an Ichthyosaurus. The Ichthyosaurus. *Unknown.* MeMeAg; OTPC (1946 ed.)
There once was an old man of Lyme. *Unknown, at. to* Edward Lear, *also to* Cosmo Monkhouse. NA; PreP. *See also* There was an old party of Lyme.
There once were some learned M.D.'s. Limerick. Oliver Herford. BOHV; LiBL
There once were some people called Sioux. The American Indian [*or* The Indian]. *Unknown.* FiBHP; LiTG; SiTL
There once were two cats of Kilkenny. *See* There wanst was two cats of Kilkenny.
There our murdered brother lies. The Wake of William Orr. William Drennan. GTIV; OnYI; OxBI; TIP
There out of hell the Old One bellows. Lamentations of the Fallen Angels. Cædmon(?) *Fr.* Christ and Satan. AnOE
There overtook me and drew me in. The Gum-Gatherer. Robert Frost. NV
There pass the careless people. A. E. Housman. A Shropshire Lad, XIV. PoVP; ViPo
There passed the low door of the Nazareth home. The Open Door. Ida Norton Munson. ChIP
There passed with fitful flight. Nothing but Flight. José Moreno Villa. CoSP
There piped a piper in the wood. The Magic Piper. E. L. Marsh. BoTP; SiSoSe
There rests a shade above yon town. Letitia E. Landon. *Fr.* The Factory. BCEP
There roamed a Bear by Dalby lea. The Bear of Dalby. *Unknown.* BoDaBa
There rolls the deep where grew the tree. In Memoriam A. H. H., CXXIII. Tennyson. BPN; CaAE; CoBE; EmBrPo; EPN; GEPC; GTML; GTSL; MaPo; OAEP; OuHeWo; SeCePo; SeCeV; TOP; ViPo; VLEP
There rose a song out of Denmark's grief. Niels Ebbesen. Nikolai Frederik Severin Grundtvig. BoDS
There runs a rhythm thro' the woods and seas. The Woodland Singer. John Jerome Rooney. MaRV
"There!" Said a Stripling Pointing with Meet Pride. Wordsworth. BEL; BPN; EmBrPo; EPN; PeBoSo
There sat a happy fisherman. The Reed. Mikhail Yurevich Lermontov. AWP; JAWP; WBP
There sat an old man on a rock. Too Late. Fitzhugh Ludlow. BOHV; LPS-3
There sat two glasses, filled to the brim. The Two Glasses. Ella Wheeler Wilcox. BLPA; PEOR; PTA-1
There sat upon the linden tree. The Linden Tree. Dietmar von Aist. LyMA
There saugh I stonden, out of drede. Chaucer. *Fr.* The Hous of Fame. PtP
There see the clover, pea, and bean. Idyll. Matthew Green. *Fr.* The Spleen. BeR
There Seemed a Strangeness. Thomas Hardy. ChMo; CMP
There seems to be a spirit on the mountain. The Spirit of the Mountain. Chu Yuan. *Fr.* The Nine Songs. WhP
There, set in green. Ocean and Stars. Edward Young. *Fr.* Ocean, an Ode. BeR
There Shall Always Be the Church. T. S. Eliot. *Fr.* The Rock. MaRV
"There Shall Be More Joy." Ford Madox Ford. MBP; MoBrPo (1942 ed.)
There Shall Be New Songs. Clifford Gessler. PSO
There Shall Be No Night. Revelation, XXII: 1-5, Bible, *N.T.* TrGrPo
There shall be touching of hands. Pavane. Donald Davidson. BAP
There shall come from out this noise of strife and groaning. Sir Lewis Morris. *Fr.* Brotherhood. PGD
There She Blows! *Unknown.* EtS; SoAmSa, *with music*
There she goes up the street with her book in her hand. Martin's Puzzle. George Meredith. EmBrPo
There she sits in her Island-home. England. Gerald Massey. HBV
There should be no despair for you. Sympathy. Emily Brontë. OAEP
There should be two words, dearest, one made up. Alone. Carolyn Wells. PoToHe
There Sits a Bird. Charles Kingsley. *See* Sing Heigh-ho!
There sits a piper on the hill. The Piper on the Hill. Dora Sigerson Shorter. HBV; HBVY; OnYI; OTPC (1923 ed.)
There sitteth a dove, so white and fair. Song of the Dove [*or* Swedish Mother's Lullaby]. Fredrika Bremer. *Fr.* The Home. BOL; MOAH
There Sleeps in the Churchyard. Peter Hopegood. MoAuPo
There smiled the smooth Divine, unused to wound. The Smooth Divine [*or* A Minister, New Style]. Timothy Dwight. *Fr.* The Triumph of Infidelity. AA; AmPP (3d ed.); AnAmPo; IAP; LA; TCAP; WGRP
There souls of men are bought and sold. London. Blake. *Fr.* The Human Image. ChTr
There splashes an ocean of bell chimes. From a Church Tower. Eduard Mörike. AnGP
There stands a decree of Destiny, from the immemorial past. Karma. Empedocles. GrPE
There stands a fountain in a darksome wood. Narcissus. Ovid. *Fr.* Metamorphoses, III. RoL
There stands a knicht at the tap o' yon hill. The Elfin Knight. *Unknown.* EBSV
There stands a lady on a mountain. Kiss in the Ring. *Unknown.* OxBoLi
There stands a lonely pine-tree. Song. Heine. TrJP
There stands death, a bluish liquid. Death. Rainer Maria Rilke. AnGP
There stood a courteous damsel. The Serpent Bride. *Unknown.* BoDaBa
There stood an unsold captive in the mart. Parrhasius. Nathaniel Parker Willis. AA
There stood of old a temple. The Ruin. Olaf Bull. AnNoLy
There Stretch between Us Wonder-woven Bonds. Arthur Davison Ficke. Sonnets of a Portrait Painter, XXI. TBM
There sunk the greatest, nor the worst of men. Napoleon. Byron. *Fr.* Childe Harold's Pilgrimage. LPS-3; OBRV
There sways,/ up there, upon the neck. World of the Seven Wells. Alfonsina Storni. AnCL
There the brown barrow curves its sullen breast. Robert Stephen Hawker. *Fr.* The Quest of the Sangraal. EnSW
There the moon leans out and blesses. In a September Night. F. Wyville Home. VA
There the most daintie paradise on ground. The Bower of Bliss. Spenser. *Fr.* The Faerie Queene, II. BCEP; LPS-3
There the voluptuous nightingales. Shelley. *Fr.* Prometheus Unbound, II, ii. ViBoPo
There the wrinkled, old Nokomis. Hiawatha's Childhood. Longfellow. *Fr.* The Song of Hiawatha. RIS
"There, there, there." Magruder's Lullaby. *Unknown.* BOL
There they are, my fifty men and women. One Word More. Robert Browning. BMEP; BPN; EmBrPo; EPP; EtPaEn; FiP; GEPC; HBV; OtMeF; PoEL-5; PoVP; REAL; VA; ViBoPo; ViPP; VLEP
There they dismounting, drew their weapons bold. Britomart in the House of Busirane. Spenser. *Fr.* The Faerie Queene, III. FiP
There they dwelt in the wrennet's cot. The Poe Cottage. Nathalia Crane. TCAP
There they stand, on their ends, the fifty faggots. Fifty Faggots. Edward Thomas. EPP; MBP; MoAB; MoBrPo
There, 'tis the shepherd's task the winter long. Wordsworth. *Fr.* The Prelude. CoEV
There towered the hall. The Anglian Tradition. *Unknown.* *Fr.* Beowulf. PaOS
There used to be a custom then. The Open Gate. John Masefield. *Fr.* The Everlasting Mercy. GrCo-2
There Uther the king took Ygerne for queen. The Birth of Arthur. Layamon. *Fr.* The Brut. MeEV
There walked on Plover's shady banks. Driving Saw Logs on the Plover. *Unknown.* AS; IHA
There wanst was [*or* once were] two cats of Kilkenny. The Kilkenny Cats [*or* Limerick]. *Unknown.* BOHV; CenHV; CIV; FaFP; LiL; LiTG; TreF
There was a battle in the north. Geordie. *Unknown.* BaBo (A *vers.*); ESPB
There was a Being whom my spirit oft. Shelley. *Fr.* Epipsychidion. EnLi-2
There was a big bear. Honey Bear. Elizabeth Lang. BoTP
There was a bonny blade. The Dumb Wife Cured. *Unknown.* MaC
There Was a Boy. Wordsworth. *Fr.* The Prelude, V. BoLiVe; BPN; ChER; ERP; FaBoCh; FaBoEn; GEPC; LoGBV; MaPo; MCCG; MyFE; NBE; OBRV; PoEL-4; PTA-2; REAL; RO, *abr.*; SN; TwP
("There was a Boy: ye knew him well, ye cliffs.") CoEV; TCEP
(Winander Lake.) FiP
There was a Boy bedded in bracken. Carol. John Short. FaBoCh; FaBoTw; LoGBV
There was a boy of other days. Lincoln. Nancy Byrd Turner. FaPON; MOB; MPB; TiPo
There was a boy whose name was Jim. Jim. Hilaire Belloc. AlDL; CenHV; ChTr; HBMV; LiL; MaC; OnSP; ShBV-2; TSW; TSWC
There was a boy whose name was Phinn. A Fishing Song. William Brighty Rands. CenHV
There was a brave girl of Connecticut. Benjamin. Ogden Nash. NePA; SiTL
There was a bride (the Gospel goes). Nuptial. Mary Fabyan Windeatt. JKCP (1955 ed.)
There was a bright and happy tree. The Happy Tree. Gerald Gould. MBP; MoBrPo (1942 ed.); WGRP

There Was a Brisk Girle. *Unknown.* CoMu
There was a butcher cut his thumb. *Unknown.* PPL
There was a Cameronian cat. The Cameronian Cat. *Unknown.* BOHV; CIV
There was a captain-general who ruled in Vera Cruz. El Capitan-General. Charles Godfrey Leland. AA; HBV; YaD
There was a chalice in the ancient East. Two Chalices. Edwin McNeill Poteat. ChIP
There Was a Chandler. *Unknown.* OTPC (1923 ed.)
There was a chap—I forget his name. The Gemlike Flame. R. P. Lister. FiBHP
There was a child, as I have been told. The Comical Girl. M. Pelham. BOHV
There Was a Child Went Forth. Walt Whitman. AmPP; AWP; CoBA; CoV; GoTP; IAP; InPo; LaNeLa; MOAP; OnPP; OQP; OxBA; Po; QP-2, *much abr.*; SN; WoL
"Mother at home quietly placing the dishes on the supper-table, The," *sel.* MotAn
There was a Christmas Brownie. Christmas Brownie. Rowena Bennett. ChBR
There was a company of young folk living. The Pardoner's Tale. Chaucer. *Fr.* The Canterbury Tales. EnL
There Was a Cot. Hartley Coleridge. BoFr
There was a crooked man, and he went [*or* walked] a crooked mile. Mother Goose. BoChLi; BoN; BoTP; FaBoBe; FaFP; HBV; HBVY; OTPC; OxBoLi; OxNR; PPL; RIS; SiTL; StVeCh; WP
There was a cruel darkey boy. The Naughty Darkey Boy. *Unknown.* BOHV
There was a dark and awful wood. Wood. Thomas Hornsby Ferril. PoRA
There was a darkness in this man; an immense and hollow darkness. John Gould Fletcher. *Fr.* Lincoln. PoFr
There was a day I wasted long ago. Wasted Hours. Medora Addison. NLK
There was a day, so country legends tell. The Legend of the Tortoise. Pamela Tennant. GBV (1922 ed.)
There was a day when death to me meant tears. Afterwards. Mahlon Leonard Fisher. MuM; SBMV
There was a dear lady of Eden. Limerick. *Unknown.* LiBL; NA
There was a devil and his name was I. Malzah's Song. Charles Heavysege. *Fr.* Saul. BoCaPo
There was a dreamer once, whose spirit trod. The Seeker after God. Harry Kemp. OQP; QP-2
There was a duke's daughter lived in York. The Cruel Mother (P *vers.*). *Unknown.* ESPB
There was a fair lady far crossed in love. The Fair Maid by the Seashore. *Unknown.* BaBo
There was a fair maid from Decatur. Limerick. *Unknown.* LiBL
There was a fairy once. The Singing Fairy. Rose Fyleman. BoChLi
There was a faith-healer of Deal. Limerick [*or* Mind and Matter *or* Faith-Healer]. *Unknown.* CenHV; FaFP; GoTP; LiBL; LiTM; PIAE; PreP; SiTL; TSWC; WhC
There was a farmer had two sons. Bohunkus. *Unknown.* YaD
There was a farmer's daughter near Dublin town did dwell. The Constant Farmer's Son. *Unknown.* ABS
There was a fat canon of Durham. Limerick. *Unknown.* WhC
There was a fat man of Bombay. Limerick. *Unknown.* BoChLi; RIS
There Was a Frog. *Unknown.* NA
There Was a Frog Lived in a Well. *Unknown.* OTPC (1923 ed.)
There was a froge swum in the lake. *Unknown.* SeCSL
There was a funny little man. Fussy. Laura E. Richards. MPB
There was a gallant ship, and a gallant ship was she. The Golden Vanity [*or* The Sweet Trinity]. *Unknown.* AtBAP; CH; ESPB (B *vers.*); OnSP; SG; ViBoFo
There Was a Garden. Marie Barton. OQP; QP-1
There was a garden planned in Spring's young days. Vos Non Vobis. Edith M. Thomas. AV
There was a gather'd stillness in the room. My Mother. William Bell Scott. MOAH; VA
There was a gay damsel of Lynn. Limerick. *Unknown.* LiBL; NA
There was a gay maiden lived down by the mill. The Ferry. George Henry Boker. AA; OBAV
There was a gentle hostler. Gates and Doors. Joyce Kilmer. ChrBoLe; CV; GBV (1952 ed.); HBV; HBVY; QS; SDH
There was a gentle Maiden. God's Handmaid. Hugh F. Blunt. PraNu
There was a giant in times of old. The Dorchester Giant. Oliver Wendell Holmes. FaPON; MPB
There was a gifted Mexican who came up here to paint. Sad Story. Clarence Day. InMe
There was a girl in our town. Riddles. *Unknown.* HBV; HBVY; OTPC (1946 ed.); OxNR; PPL; RIS
There was a girl with us in our carriage. The Girl in the Carriage. *Unknown.* *Fr.* Shi King. LiTW
There was a good Canon of Durham. Limerick. William Ralph Inge. CenHV
There was a great white wall—bare, bare, bare. The Smoked Herring. Charles Cros. MiFP
There was a green branch hung with many a bell. The Dedication to a Book of Stories Selected from the Irish Novelists. W. B. Yeats. NAMP
There was a grove Pelasgian men had planted. Erysichthon. Callimachus. OxBG
There Was a Guinea-Pig. *Unknown.* OTPC (1946 ed.)
(Guinea-Pig, The.) GoTP; LiL; NA
("There was a little guinea-pig.") BoN; OxNR
There was a Hag who kept two chambermaids. The Hag and the Slavies. La Fontaine. AWP
There was a high majestic fooling. Laughing Corn. Carl Sandburg. MOAP; TCAP
There was a jolly beggar, and a begging he was born. The Jolly Beggar. *At. to* James V, King of Scotland. CoMu
There was a jolly blade that married a country maid. Dumb, Dumb, Dumb. *Unknown.* OnYI
There was a jolly harper-man. The Lochmaben Harper. *Unknown.* BaBo
There Was a Jolly Miller. Isaac Bickerstaffe. *Fr.* Love in a Village, I. HBV; GoTP; OnPP; OTPC (1946 ed.), *st.* 1; ViBoPo, *st.* 1; WP, *st.* 1
(Jolly Miller, The.) OlF, *st.* 1; RIS, *st.* 1
(Song: "There was a jolly miller once," *st.* 1.) OBEC; OnYI
("There was a jolly miller once," *st.* 1.) OxNR
There was a jovial beggar. The Jovial Beggar. *Unknown.* BoTP; CG
There was a jury sat at Perth. The Earl of Errol. *Unknown.* ESPB
There was a kind curate of Kew. Limerick. *Unknown.* CenHV
There Was a King. *Unknown.* OxBoLi
There was a king, and a very great king. Lady Diamond. *Unknown.* BaBo; ESPB
There was a king, and he had three daughters. *Unknown.* BoN; OxNR
There was a king in Brentford, of whom no legends tell. The King of Brentford. Thackeray, *after* Béranger. HBV; OtMeF
There was a king in Thule. The King of Thule. Goethe. *Fr.* Faust. LPS-3
There was a king met a king. *Unknown.* OxNR
There was a king of the north countree. The Twa Sisters (C *vers.*). *Unknown.* ViBoFo
There was a king of Yvetot. The King of Yvetot. Thackeray, *after* Béranger. OnPP; RIS
There was a kingdom known as the Mind. The Barbarous Chief. Ella Wheeler Wilcox. PEOR
There was a knicht riding frae the east. Riddles Wisely Expounded [*or* Jennifer Gentle and Rosemary *or* The Riddling Knight]. *Unknown.* AtBAP; BEL; CH; EM-1; ESPB (C *vers.*); HBV; OxBoLi; ViBoFo (A *vers.*)
There was a knight, an he had a daughter. Erlinton (B *vers.*). *Unknown.* ESPB
There was a knight and a lady bright. The Broomfield Hill. *Unknown.* BaBo; ESPB; OBB; ViBoFo
There Was a Knight and He Was Young. *Unknown.* *See* Baffled Knight, The.
There was a knight, in a summer's night. The Bonny Birdy. *Unknown.* ESPB
There was a Knight of Bethlehem. A Knight of Bethlehem [*or* Song]. Henry Neville Maugham. *Fr.* The Husband of Poverty. BoTP; CBPC; ChIP; MaRV; OQP; QP-2
There Was a Lad. Burns. EBSV
(Robin.) BSV
There was a lady fair and gay. The Wife of Usher's Well. *Unknown.* ESPB (D *vers.*); ViBoFo (C *vers.*)
There was a lady fine and gay. Willie o Winsbury (D *vers.*) *Unknown.* ESPB
There was a lady from the town. The Cruel Mother. *Unknown.* PIAE
There was a lady in this land. The Tinker. *Unknown.* CoMu
There was a lady liv'd at Leith. The Irishman and the Lady. William Maginn. BOHV; HBV; VA
There was a lady lived in a hall. Two Red Roses across the Moon. William Morris. BLV; BPN; EmBrPo; EnLit; PoRA; PoVP; ViP; VLEP
There was a lady lived in York. The Cruel Mother (C *vers.*). *Unknown.* BaBo
There was a lady loved a swine. The Lady Who Loved a Swine [*or* The Lady and the Swine *or* Hunc, Said He *or* The Silver Sty]. *Unknown.* ChTr; OuSiCo; OxNR; Po; RIS
There was a lady of Erskine. *Unknown.* SiTL
There was a lady of the North Country. Riddles Wisely Expounded. *Unknown.* BaBo (B *vers.*); ESPB

There was a lame soldier in time of the war. The Lame Soldier. *Unknown.* OuSiCo
There was a land where lived no violets. The Violets. Stephen Crane. War Is Kind, XXIII. AA; AnAmPo; LA
There was a Lass of Islington. The Lass of Islington. *Unknown.* CoMu
There was a lily and rose sea-maiden. The Sea-Maiden. J. W. De Forest. EtS
There was a little Baby once. A Child's Christmas Carol. Christine Chaundler. BoTP
There was a little boy. Sir Hugh; or, The Jew's Daughter (D *vers.*). *Unknown.* BaBo
There was a little boy and a little girl. Mother Goose. CG; OTPC (1923 ed.); OxNR; RIS. *See also* Little boy and a little girl, A.
There was a little boy, and he had a little dog. Tumbling Doggie. *Unknown.* SAS
There was a little boy, and he had a piece of bread. Walter and His Dog. Eliza Lee Follen. SAS
There was a little boy went into a barn. *Unknown.* OxNR
There was a little dog, and he had a little tail. *Unknown.* BoTP
There was a little, Elvish man. The Man Who Hid His Own Front Door. Elizabeth MacKinstry. FaPON; GaP; TiPo
There was a little family. The Little Family. *Unknown.* BaBo
There Was a Little Girl. *St.* 1, Mother Goose; *sts.* 2 *and* 3, *unknown, at. to* Longfellow. BoChLi; BOHV; BLPA, *st.* 1; FaFP; HBV; HBVY; LBN; LiTG, *st.* 1; NA; NeHB, *st.* 1; OnHT; OnPP; OTPC; RIS, *st.* 1; SAS, *st.* 1; TreF; YaD, *st.* 1
(Jemima, *diff. vers.*) FaBoCh; GoTP; LoGBV
("There was a little girl, and she had a little curl.") OxNR
There was a little goblin. Agnes Grozier Herbertson. GFA
There was a little guinea-pig. There Was a Guinea-Pig [*or* The Guinea Pig]. *Unknown.* BoN; GoTP; LiL; NA; OTPC (1946 ed.); OxNR
There was a little hobby-horse. A Little Hobby-Horse. Eliza Grove. OTPC
There was a little maid, and she was afraid. *Unknown.* OxNR; SiTL
There was a little maiden. The Singing Girl. Joyce Kilmer. JKCP
There was a little man and he had a little can. No More Booze [*or* Fireman Save My Child]. *Unknown.* AS; TrAS; TreF
There was a little man, and he had a little gun. Mother Goose. FaFP; HBV; HBVY; OTPC; OxNR; PPL
There was a little man and he had a little wife. The Crabfish. *Unknown.* SaSa
There was a little man, and he woo'd a little maid. Mother Goose. OTPC (1923 ed.); OxNR; SiTL
There Was a Little Nobby Colt. *Unknown.* OTPC (1923 ed.); PPL
There was a little one-eyed gunner. *Unknown.* OxNR
There Was a Little Rabbit Sprig. *Unknown.* BoTP; OTPC (1923 ed.)
(True Story, A.) RIS
There was a little serpent and he wouldn't go to school. Snake Story. Henry Johnstone. PPL
There was a little turtle. The Little Turtle. Vachel Lindsay. BoChLi; FaPON; GFA; GoBP; MeMeAg; PCH; RAR; SP; StVeCh; SUS; TiPo; UTS
There was a little woman, as I've heard tell. *See* There was an old woman, so I've heard tell.
There was a locked door. Don Marquis. *Fr.* I Have Looked Inward. PFY
There was a long, old road anear the town. The Ghost's Promenade. Thomas Caulfield Irwin. IrPN
There was a lovely lady Gnu. The Gnu Wooing. Burges Johnson. HBVY
There was a low, dull droning in my ears. Life. Edward H. Pfeiffer. UnW
There was a mad lad had an acre of ground. Mirth. *Unknown.* SeCL
There Was a Maid. *Unknown. See* Maid of Kent, A.
There was a maid, richly arrayd. Blancheflour and Jellyflorice. *Unknown.* ESPB
There Was a Man. Thomas Curtis Clark. ChIP
There Was a Man. Stephen Crane. *See* There Was a Man with a Tongue of Wood.
There Was a Man. *Unknown.* Po
("There was a man of double deed.") OxNR
There was a man,/ And his name was Dob. *Unknown.* OxNR
There was a man. The Painter on Silk. Amy Lowell. CV
There was a man/ Named Iky Small. The Sad Goat. *Unknown.* WaKn
There was a man/ Whose name was Peter. The Tragedy of Pete. Joseph Seamon Cotter, Sr. CDC; PoNe
There was a man and he had nought. *Unknown.* OxNR
There Was a Man and He Went Mad. *Unknown.* OTPC (1923 ed.)
("There was a man, he went mad.") OxNR; SiTL
"There was a man in Arkansaw." A Great Fight. Robert Henry Newell. BoHV
There was a man in Denver. The Man Who Thought He Was a Horse. Thomas Hornsby Ferril. NePoAm-2
There Was a Man in Our Toone. *Unknown.* OTPC (1923 ed.)
There was a man in [*or* of] our town [*or* of Newington],/ And he was wondrous wise. Mother Goose. FaFP; HBV; HBVY; OTPC; PPL; RIS; SAS; StVeCh (1940 ed.); WP; YT
There was a man in our town whose Christian name was Jim. It Happens, Often. Edwin Meade Robinson. BAP; HBMV
There was a man in Westmoreland. Johnny Armstrong. *Unknown.* MaC; StaSt
There was a man lived in the moon. Aiken Drum. *Unknown.* BoN; FaBoCh; LoGBV; OxNR
There was a man lived in the west. Dandoo. *Unknown.* TrAS
There was a man lived under the hill. The Devil and the Farmer's Wife. *Unknown.* TrAS
There was a man named Ferguson. The Suicidal Cat. *Unknown.* CIV
There was a man of double deed. There Was a Man. *Unknown* OxNR; Po
There was a man of Newington. *See* There was a man in our town.
There was a man of our town. *See* There was a man in our town.
There was a man of Thessaly. The Man of Thessaly. *Unknown.* BoN; LiTG; OxNR; SiTL
There was a man—or was he but a man? There Was a Man. Thomas Curtis Clark. ChIP
There was a man rode through our town. *Unknown.* OxNR
There was a man was son and lover. A Soldier. A. G. Herbertson. NeTW
There was a man well fastened to a nose. To a Nose. Francisco de Quevedo y Villegas. AnSpL-1
There was a man who had a clock. The Sad Tale of Mr. Mears. *Unknown.* HBV; StPo; TreFS; YaD
There was a man who had no eyes. *Unknown.* BoN; OxNR
There was a man who [*or* and he] lived in England. The Turkish Lady. *Unknown.* BaBo; MaC
There was a man who married a maid. She laughed as he led her home. I Love My Love. Helen Adam. NeAP
There was a man who saw God face to face. To Love, at Last the Victory. David Starr Jordan. OQP; QP-1
There was a man who watched the river flow. The Cranes of Ibycus. Emma Lazarus. AA; PFY
There was a man whom Sorrow named his friend. The Sad Shepherd. W. B. Yeats. BrBE
There Was a Man with a Tongue of Wood. Stephen Crane. War Is Kind, XVI. LiTA; NePA
(There Was a Man.) MoAmPo (1950 ed.)
There was a man within our tenement. The Spritely Dead. Oscar Williams. *Fr.* Variations on a Theme. LiTA; NePA
There was a mayde cam [*or* maid came] out of Kent. The Maid of Kent. *Unknown.* ElL; LO; OxBoLi
There was a mighty city. Two Towns. Ralph Linton. DDA
There Was a Monkey. *Unknown.* NA; OTPC (1923 ed.)
("There was a monkey climbed a tree.") OxNR
There was a multitude striving to build. Babel and Bethel. Frank Buchanan. QS
There was a murkier tinge in London's air. Lionel Johnson. Joyce Kilmer. PtP
There was a music throbbed athwart the street. Hubert Church. *Fr.* A Fugue. AnNZ
There was a naked greatness in those times. The Festival. Robert Eyres Landor. *Fr.* The Impious Feast. OBRV
There Was a Naughty Boy. Keats. *See* Song about Myself, A.
There was a negro preacher, I have heard. The Learned Negro. *Unknown.* BOHV
There was a noble ranger. Mustang Gray. *Unknown.* ABF; CSF
There was a Pig that sat alone. The Melancholy Pig [*or* The Pig-Tale]. "Lewis Carroll." *Fr.* Sylvie and Bruno. BoN; FaPON; OTPC (1946 ed.); PPL; RAR
There was a piper had [*or* he had] a cow. Mother Goose. OTPC (1946 ed.); OxNR; RIS
There was a poet whose untimely tomb. Shelley. *Fr.* Alastor. EPP
There was a poor chap called Rossetti. Limerick. Dante Gabriel Rossetti. CenHV
There was a Presbyterian cat. The Auld Seceder Cat. *Unknown.* FaBoCh; LoGBV; SiTL
There was a pretty dandelion. Dandelion. *Unknown.* GFA
There was a priest in the land; Layamon was he called. The Prolog. Layamon. *Fr.* The Brut. MeEV
There was a princess of Bengal. Limerick. Walter Parke. NA
There was a pussy in the stable. In the Stable. Elizabeth Goudge. ChBR

There was a queen that fell in love with a jolly sailor bold. The Sailor and the Shark. Paul Fort. OBMV
There was a queer fellow named Woodin. Limerick. "Cuthbert Bede." BoN; CenHV
There was a ragman and a madman. The Ragman. *Unknown.* FTB
There was a rat, for want of stairs. *Unknown.* OxNR; SiTL
There was a rich Dutchman. Villkins and His Dinah (B *vers.*). *Unknown.* BaBo
There was a rich lady, from England she came. The Brown Girl (B *vers.*). *Unknown.* BaBo
There was a rich lord, and he lived in Forfar. Bonnie Annie. *Unknown.* ESPB; OBB
There was a rich old rancher who lived in the country by. The Rambling Cowboy. *Unknown.* CoSo; CSF
There was a rich young farmer. The Rich Young Farmer. *Unknown.* ABS
There was a road ran past our house. The Unexplorer. Edna St. Vincent Millay. MoShBr; SUS
There was a roar of stormy gates, a cry. Babylon. Virgil Markham. BAP
There was a roaring in the wind all night. Resolution and Independence. Wordsworth. AEV; BEL; BPN; CBE; ChER; EM-2; EmBrPo; EnL; EnLi-2; EnLit; EnLP; EnRP; EPN; ERP; EV-3; GEPC; LiTB; NBE; OAEP; OBRV; PoE; PoEL-4; ShBV-4; TriL; TwP
There was [*or* lived] a Romish [*or* Roman] lady. The Romish Lady [*or* The Death of a Romish Lady]. *Unknown.* ABS; OuSiCo
There Was a Rose. Arthur L. Phelps. CPG
There was a rose-tree grew so high. White Roses. Cora Randall Fabbri. AA
There was a round pond, and a pretty pond too. The Pond. Jane Taylor. OTPC (1923 ed.)
There was a rover from a western shore. Mother England. Edith M. Thomas. AA; HBV
There was a Russian came over the sea. Russian and Turk. Robert J. Burdette. NA
There was a scent of heavy purple lilacs. Romance. Karen Hildebrandt. BoDS
There was a score of likely girls. Cerelle. Margaret Bell Houston. PoMa
There was a sea captain lately come to shore. The Sea-Captain. *Unknown.* BaBo
There was a shepherd's daughter/ Came tripping on the way. The Knight and Shepherd's Daughter (A *vers.*). *Unknown.* ESPB
There was a shepherd's dochter/ Kept sheep upon yon hill. The Knight and Shepherd's Daughter. *Unknown.* BaBo (A *vers.*); ESPB (B *vers.*); ViBoFo
There was a shepherd's son. Blow the Winds, I-ho! *Unknown.* OxBoLi
There was a ship, and a ship of fame. William Glen [*or* Captain Glen]. *Unknown.* BaBo; SG
There was a ship called *The Golden Vanitie.* The Golden Vanitie. *Unknown.* EnSB
There was a ship of Rio. The Ship of Rio. Walter de la Mare. CenHV; EtS; LiL; TiPo; UTS
There was a ship—she sailed to Spain. Roll and Go. *Unknown.* SG
There was a silk merchant. Jackaro. *Unknown.* IHA
There was a Slug who ate and ate. A Tale from the Garden. Margaret Wynne Jones. GFA
There was a small boy [*or* young man] of [*or* from *or* in] Quebec. Limerick [*or* In Quebec]. Kipling. HBV; HBVY; LiBL; NA; TSWC
There was a snake that dwelt in Skye. The Fastidious Serpent. Henry Johnstone. BoHV; HBV; HBVY; LiL; OTPC (1946 ed.); PPL
There was a soldier once. E. A. Robinson. *Fr.* Captain Craig. BoFr
There was a sound of revelry by night. Waterloo [*or* The Eve of Waterloo]. Byron. *Fr.* Childe Harold's Pilgrimage. AnFE; BBV; BCEP; BeLS; BHV; BLV; BoHiPo; CBPC; EPP; EV-4; FaBoBe; FaBoCh; FaBoEn; FaFP; FiP; GN; HBV; HiLiEn; LPS-2; MCCG; OBRV; OnSP; OtMeF; OTPC; PECK; PIR; PTA-2; PYM; ShBV-3; TCEP; TreF; TrGrPo; TVSH; ViBoPo; WaaP; WBLP; WHA
There was a squire lived in this town. The Suffolk Miracle (B *vers.*). *Unknown.* BaBo
There was a strangeness on your lips. Consummation. Witter Bynner. *Fr.* To Celia. NP
There was a student out of Oxford town. The Clerk of Oxenford. Chaucer. *Fr.* The Canterbury Tales: Prologue. OnPP
There was a stunted handpost just on the crest. Near Lanivet, 1872. Thomas Hardy. AWP; LoBV
There was a thick-headed marine. *Unknown.* GoTP
There was a thing a full month old. *Unknown.* OxNR
There Was a Time. Emily Brontë. EmBrPo
There was a time before our time. Clipper Ships and Captains. Rosemary Benét *and* Stephen Vincent Benét. StVeCh (1955 ed.)
There was a time for discoveries. Voyage West. Archibald MacLeish. CoV
There was a time I watched with fortitude. Love's Unveiling. Tessa Sweazy Webb. MuM
There was a time in boyhood, ere life ceased. Dedication. Alfred Gordon. CPG
There was a time in former years. She Hears the Storm. Thomas Hardy. ATP; BMEP; NP; TOP
There was a time, O Lesbia, when you said Catullus. Transformation. Catullus. LiTW; RoL
There was a time on this fair continent. Charles Mair. *Fr.* Tecumseh. BoCaPo
There was a time, so ancient records tell. Revolutions. Sir Henry Taylor. *Fr.* Philip Van Artevelde. PoFr; VA
There was a time when Death and I. Beyond Recall. Mary E. Bradley. AA
There was a time when I wanted to live in a south village. Moving House. Tao Yuan-ming. WhP
There was a time when I was very small. Childhood. Jens Baggesen. AWP; JAWP; WBP
There was a time when I would magnify. Elegy for an Unknown Soldier. James K. Baxter. AnNZ
There was a time when meadow, grove, and stream. Ode: Intimations of Immortality from Recollections of Early Childhood. Wordsworth. AnFE; AtBAP; ATP; AWP; BCEP; BEL; BLV; BoLiVe; BPN; BrBE; CaAE; CBOV; CBPC; ChER; CoBE; EM-2; EmBrPo; EnL; EnLi-2; EnLit; EnLP; EnRP; EPN; EPP; ERP; EV-3; ExPo; FaFP; FiP; GEPC; GTBS; GTBS-D; GTBS-W; GTSE; GTSL; HBV; HiLiEn; InP; InPo; InvP; JAWP; LEAP; LiA; LiTB; LiTG; LoBV; LPS-3; MaPo; MaRV; MCCG; OAEP; OBEV; OBRV; OHFP; OQP; OuHeWo; PIAE; PIR; Po; PoEL-4; PoFS; PreP; QP-2; REAL; ReaPo; RiBV; SeCeV; ShBV-4; TCEP; TOP; TreF; TrGrPo; TVSH; TwHP; TyEnPo; UnW; ViBoPo; WBP; WHA; WoL
There was a time when men for love did marry. Nuptiae post Nummos. Henry Parrot. SiCE; TuPP
There was a time when Mother Nature made. First Miracle [*or* Gladness]. Genevieve Taggard. HBMV; NV
There was a time when my cheek burned. There Was a Time. Emily Brontë. EmBrPo
There was a tinker liv'd of late. The Jovial Tinker; or, The Willing Couple. *Unknown.* CoMu
There was a tower/ In the land of Shinar. The Towers of New York. Joseph Auslander. MuM
There was a tree stood in the ground. The Green Grass Growing All Around. *Unknown.* HBVY; MoShBr; MPB
There was a trim maiden named Wood. Limerick. William A. Lockwood. LiBL
There was a troop of merry gentlemen. The Broom of Cowdenknows (A *vers.*). *Unknown.* ESPB
There was a tumult in the city. *See* There was tumult in the city.
There was a wealthy merchant. Lily Munro. *Unknown.* OuSiCo
There was a wealthy merchant. The Wars of Germany. *Unknown.* CSF
There was a weasel lived in the sun. The Gallows. Edward Thomas. BMEP; ChMP; GTBS-D; HaMV; LiTB; MBP; MoAB; MoBrPo; PoE; UnPo (3d ed.)
There Was a Wee Bit Mousikie. *Unknown.* MoShBr (Cheetie-Poussie-Cattie, O.) FaBoCh
There was a wee bit wifie. *Unknown.* OxNR
There was a wee cooper who lived in Fife. The Wife Wrapt [*or* Wrapped] in Wether's Skin. *Unknown.* BaBo (B *vers.*); ViBoFo (A *vers.*)
There was a whispering in my hearth. Miners. Wilfred Owen. GTBS-D; MBP; MoAB; MoBrPo
There was a widow-woman lived in far Scotland. The Wife of Usher's Well. *Unknown.* ESPB (C *vers.*); ViBoFo (B *vers.*)
There Was a Wife from Bath, a well-appearing. The Wife of Bath and the Parson [*or* Seven Pilgrims]. Chaucer. *Fr.* The Canterbury Tales: Prologue. NBE; TrGrPo
There was a wife wonn'd in Cockpen. Scroggam. Burns. RO
There was a wild colonial boy, Jack Dollin was his name. The Wild Colonial Boy. *Unknown.* OuSiCo
There was a wild Montana boy, Jack Nolan was his name. The Wild Montana Boy. *Unknown.* CoSo
There was a woman lived in Ardell. The Wife of Usher's Well (B *vers.*). *Unknown.* BaBo
There was a yellow pumpkin. Coach. Eleanor Farjeon. PoRh
There was a young bard of Japan. Limerick. *Unknown.* CenHV
There was a young belle of Old Natchez. Requiem [*or* Limerick]. Ogden Nash. LiBL; SiTL
There was a young chap not so nice. *Unknown.* SiTL
There was a young critic of King's. Limerick. Arthur Clement Hilton. CenHV
There was a young curate of Hants. Limerick. E. V. Knox. CenHV

There was [*or* was once] a young curate of Salisbury. Limerick. *Unknown, at. to* George Libaire. BoN; LiBL
There was a young farmer of Leeds. Limerick [*or* New Limericks]. *Unknown.* RIS; StaSt
There was a young fellow called Green. Limerick. *Unknown.* CenHV
There was a young fellow from Fife. Limerick. T. R. Ybarra. LiBL
There was a young fellow named Clyde. Limerick. *Unknown.* BOHV
There was a young fellow named Dice. Limerick. *Unknown.* LiBL
There was a young fellow named Hall. Limerick [*or* A Happy Time]. *Unknown.* LiTG; LiTM; SiTL; WhC
There was a young fellow named Hatch. Limerick. *Unknown.* LiBL
There was a young fellow named Sydney. Limerick [*or* A Young Fellow Named Sydney]. Don Marquis. LiBL; SiTL
There was a young fellow [*or* person] named Tate [*or* Tait]. *At. to* Carolyn Wells. GoTP; HBV; HBVY; LiBL; PIAE; PoeMoYo; PreP; TSW; TSWC; WhC
There was a young fellow of Ceuta. Limerick. *Unknown.* CenHV
There was a young fellow of Lyme. *See* There was an old party of Lyme.
There was a young fellow of Perth. Limerick [*or* New Limericks]. *Unknown.* RIS; StaSt; WhC
There was a young genius of Queens'. Limerick. Arthur Clement Hilton. CenHV
There was a young girl of Asturias. *Unknown.* GoTP
There was a young girl of Lahore. Limerick. Cosmo Monkhouse. HBV
There was a young girl of Majorca. Limerick. Edward Lear. LiBL
There was a young gourmand of John's. Limerick. Arthur Clement Hilton. CenHV
There was a young lady at Bingham. Limerick. *Unknown.* LiBL
There was a young lady called Starky. *See* There was a young woman called Starkie.
There was a young lady from Joppa. Limerick. *Unknown.* BoHV; LiBL
There was a young lady from Woosester. *See* There was a young lady of Woosester.
There was a young lady [*or* woman] named [*or* called] Bright. Limerick [*or* Relativity]. *Unknown, at. to* Arthur Buller. CenHV; FaFP; FaPON; ImOP; LiBL; LiTM; OxBoLi; SiTL; WhC
There was a young lady named Rood. *Unknown.* SiTL
There was a young lady named Wemyss. Limerick. *Unknown.* TSWC
There was a young lady of Bute. Limerick [*or* Nonsense Verses]. Edward Lear. OTPC (1946 ed.); StVeCh
There was a young lady of Byde. Limerick. *Unknown.* LiBL
There was a young lady of Corsica. Limerick. Edward Lear. BoN; CenHV; ChTr
There was a young lady of Ealing. Limerick. *Unknown.* CenHV
There was a young lady of Flint. Limerick. *Unknown.* CenHV
There was a young lady of Hull. Limerick. Edward Lear. MoShBr
There was a young lady of Kent. Limerick. *Unknown.* CenHV; LiBL; SiTL
There was a young lady of Limerick. Limerick. Andrew Lang. CenHV
There was a young lady of Lynn,/ Who was deep in original sin. Limerick. *Unknown.* BOHV; LiBL; TSWC
There was a young lady of Lynn/ Who was so exceedingly thin. Limerick [*or* The Young Lady of Lynn]. *Unknown.* CenHV; ChTr; InP; OnPP
There was a young lady of Milton. Limerick. *Unknown.* NA
There Was a Young Lady of Niger. *Unknown, at. to* Cosmo Monkhouse. *See* Limerick: "There was a young lady of Niger."
There was a young lady of Norway. Limerick [*or* A Young Lady of Norway]. Edward Lear. FaPON; OTPC (1946 ed.); StVeCh; TiPo; TSW; TSWC
There was a young lady of Oakham. Limerick. *Unknown.* BOHV
There was a young lady of Portugal. Limerick. Edward Lear. LiTG; OxBoLi
There was a young lady of Rheims. Moonshine. Walter de la Mare. FiBHP
There was a young lady of Riga. Limerick. *Unknown.* BoN; CenHV
There was a young lady of Russia. Limerick. Edward Lear. MoShBr
There was [*or* was once] a young lady of Ryde/ Who ate a green apple and died. Limerick. *Unknown.* BoN; CenHV
There was a young lady of Ryde/ Whose shoe-strings were seldom untied. Limerick. Edward Lear. OxBoLi; WhC
There was a young lady ot Spain. Limerick [*or* A Young Lady of Spain]. *Unknown.* LiTG; LiTM (rev. ed.)
There was a young lady of station. Limerick. "Lewis Carroll." BOHV; CenHV; GoTP
There was a young lady of Truro. Limerick. *Unknown.* BOHV
There was a young lady of Twickenham. Limerick. Oliver Herford. BOHV; LiBL; WhC
There was a young lady of Venice. Limerick. *Unknown.* BOHV; LiBL
There was a young lady of Wales. Limerick. *Unknown.* NA
There was a young lady of Wantage. Real Estate. *Unknown.* SiTL
There was a young lady of Warwick. Limerick. *Unknown.* PIAE
There was a young lady of Wilts. Limerick. *Unknown.* HBV
There was a young lady of [*or* from] Woosester. *Unknown.* GoTP; LiBL; WhC
There was a young lady whose bonnet. Limerick. Edward Lear. GFA; PCH; StVeCh
There was a young lady whose chin. Limerick. Edward Lear. BoChLi; BoN; RIS; StaSt; TiPo
There was a young lady whose eyes. Limerick. Edward Lear. RIS; StaSt; TSW; TSWC
There was a young lady whose nose/ Was so long . . . Limerick. Edward Lear. BoChLi; BoN; FaPON; SAS. *See also* There is a young lady whose nose/ Continually prospers . . .
There was a young maid from Madras. *Unknown.* SiTL
There was a young maid of Manila. Limerick. *Unknown.* OnPP
There was a young maid who said, "Why." Limerick [*or* New Limericks]. *Unknown.* LiBL; NA; RIS; StaSt
There was a young maiden. a Sioux. Limerick. *Unknown.* LiBL
There was a young man at St. Kitts. *See* There was a young man of St. Kitts.
There was a young man down in Ga. Limerick. *Unknown.* OnPP
There was a young man from Chapultepec. A Dublin Limerick. Ray Bradbury. SiTL
There was a young man from Cornell. Limerick. *Unknown.* BOHV
There was a young man from Japan. Limerick. *Unknown.* LiBL; LiTM; SiTL
There was a young man from Quebec. *See* There was a small boy of Quebec.
There Was a Young Man from Trinity. *Unknown.* ImOP
There was a young man named Achilles. How Homer Should Have Written the Iliad. Edwin Meade Robinson. HBMV
There was a young man named Willie the Weeper. Willie the Weeper. *Unknown.* ABF; APW; BLPA
There was a young man of Bengal. Limerick. *Unknown.* GoTP; OxBoLi; TSWC
There was a young man of Cohoes. Limerick. Robert J. Burdette. BoHV; NA
There was a young man of Devizes. Limerick. *Unknown, at. to* Archibald Marshall. CenHV; WhC
There was a young man of Fort Blain[e]y. Limerick. *Unknown.* BoHV; LiBL
There was a young man of Hong Kong. Limerick. *Unknown.* LiBL
There was a young man of Laconia. Limerick. *Unknown.* BoHV
There was a young man of Madrid. Limerick. *Unknown.* LiBL; WhC
There was a young man of Montrose. Limerick [*or* It Pays]. Arnold Bennett. CenHV; FaFP; LiTM; OxBoLi; SiTL
There was a young man of Ostend. Limerick. *Unknown.* BOHV; LiBL
There was a young [*or* an old] man of St. Bees. Limerick [*or* Old Man of St. Bees]. W. S. Gilbert. BOHV; InvP; LBN; LiBL; LiTG; SiTL; TSWC
There was a young man of [*or* at] St. Kitts. Limerick. *Unknown.* BOHV; LiBL; NA
There was a young man of Sid. Sussex. Limerick. Arthur C. Hilton. WhC
There was a young man of the Cape. *See* There was an old man of the Cape.
There was a young man of the Clyde. Just for the Ride. *Unknown.* FaFP; SiTL
There was a young man so benighted. Limerick. *Unknown.* HBV; OnPP
There was a young man who said, "Damn!" *See* There once was a man who said, "Damn!"
There was a young man who said, "God." *See* There once was a man who said, "God."
There was a young man who said, "Run." Limerick. *Unknown.* LiBL
There was a young man who was bitten. Limerick. *Unknown, at. to* Walter Parke. LiBL; NA; TSWC

There was a young person named Tate. *See* There was a young fellow named Tate.
There was a young person of Ayr. Limerick. Edward Lear. BoN
There was a young person of Crete. Limerick. Edward Lear. OTPC (1946 ed.)
There was a young person of Janina. Limerick. Edward Lear. BoN
There was a young person of Smyrna. Limerick. Edward Lear. OxBoLi
There was a young poet of Thusis. Limerick. *Unknown.* OxBoLi
There was a young poet of Trinity. Limerick. *Unknown.* HBMV; TSWC
There was a young servant at Drogheda. Limerick. *Unknown.* TSWC
There was a young woman, and what do you think? A Lost Illusion. George Du Maurier. CenHV
There was a young woman [*or* lady] called Starkie [*or* Starky]. Mendelian Theory [*or* Limerick]. *Unknown.* CenHV; LiTM; SiTL
There was a young woman named Bright. *See* There was a young lady named Bright.
There was a youth, and a well-belovèd [*or* well belovd] youth. The Bailiff's Daughter of Islington. *Unknown.* BaBo (A *vers.*); ESPB; EV-2; GN; GoTP; HBV; LoEn; OAEP; OBB; OnSP; OTPC; OxBoLi; ReaPo; SaSa; ViBoFo; WP
There was airy music and sport at the fair. The Fair at Windgap. Austin Clarke. OnYI; SeCePo
There was also a Nun, a Prioress. *See* There also was a nun, a Prioress.
There Was an Aged Monarch. Heine, *tr. fr. German by* Lola Gruenthal. AnGP
There was an ancient carver that carved of a saint. The Figure-Head. Crosbie Garstin. EtS; StPo
There was an ancient Grecian boy. A Tiger's Tale. John Bennett. TiPo (1959 ed.)
There was an ape in the days that were earlier. Darwin. Mortimer Collins. LPS-3
There was an Archbishop named Tait. Archbishop Tait. *Unknown.* ChTr
There was an Archdeacon who said. Limerick. *Unknown.* OxBoLi
There was an auld birkie ca'ed Milton. Limerick. Andrew Lang. CenHV
There was an ease of mind that was like being alone in a boat at sea. Prologues to What Is Possible. Wallace Stevens. NePoAm
There was an hour when I saw the shore. There Is a Tide. Josephine Johnson. BPP
There Was an Indian. J. C. Squire. InP; ReTS; ShBV-2 (Discovery, The.) PoMa; PtOT; TCPD; WaKn (Sonnet: "There was an Indian, who had known no change.") CH; FaPON; MBP
There was an island in the sea. Priapus and the Pool, XV [XVIII]. Conrad Aiken. ChMo; CMP
There was an old crow. *Unknown.* OxNR; SiTL
There was an old farmer in Sussex did dwell. The Farmer's Curst Wife. *Unknown.* BaBo (A *vers.*); ESPB; ViBoFo
There was an old fellow of Lynn. Limerick. *Unknown.* LiBL
There was an old Fellow of Trinity,/ A doctor well versed in Divinity. Limerick. *Unknown.* CenHV; LiBL
There was an old fellow of Trinity/ Who solved the square root of Infinity. Limerick. *Unknown.* LiBL; WhC
There was [*or* There was once] an old Fox. The Owl and the Fox [*or* The Tragic Tale of Hooty the Owl]. *Unknown.* BLPA; FTB
There was an old lady. Godmother. Phyllis B. Morden. BrR; MoSiPe
There was an old lady of Chertsey. Limerick. Edward Lear. BoN
There was an old lady of Wales. Limerick. *Unknown.* RIS
There was an old lady who lived in Dundee. A Long Time Ago, *vers.* V. *Unknown.* ShS
There was an old lady who said. Limerick [*or* New Limericks]. *Unknown.* RIS; StaSt
There was an old lady whose folly. Limerick. Edward Lear. RIS; StaSt
There was an old looney of Rhyme. An Old Looney of Rhyme. *Unknown.* SiTL
There Was an Old Man and He Had a Calf. *Unknown.* OTPC (Nursery Tales.) MeMeAg ("There was an old man.") OxNR; PPL; RIS; SiTL
There was an old-man and a jolly old-man. The Old Man and Young Wife. *Unknown.* CoMu
There was an old man and he lived in a wood. *See* There was an old man lived out in the wood.
There was an old man from Antigua. *Unknown.* SiTL
There was an old man from [*or* of] Peru/ Who dreamt he was eating his shoe. Limerick [*or* An Old Man from Peru]. *Unknown.* CenHV; FaFP; LiTG; LiTM (rev. ed.); SiTL
There was an old man from the Rhine. *See* There was an old man of the Rhine.
There was an old man in a barge. Limerick [*or* Nonsense Pictures in Rhyme]. Edward Lear. MPB; PoVP
There was an old man in a boat. Limerick [*or* Nonsense Verses]. Edward Lear. BoChLi (1950 ed.); HBV; OTPC; StVeCh
There was an old man in a pew. Limerick. Edward Lear. MoShBr
There was an old man in a pie. Limerick. *Unknown.* BOHV
There was an old man in a tree. Limerick. Edward Lear. BoChLi; BOHV; GoTP; HBV; InvP; LBN; LiBL; NA; OTPC; PoVP; SAS; TiPo (1952 ed.)
There was an old man in a trunk. Limerick. Ogden Nash. CenHV
There was an old man in a velvet coat. *Unknown.* OxNR
There was an old man in the North Countree [*or* Countrie]. The Old Man in the North Countree [*or* The Twa Sisters]. *Unknown.* ABS; ViBoFo
There was an old man lived out in the wood [*or* and he lived in a wood]. Green Broom [*or* Broom, Green Broom]. *Unknown.* ALV; CH; KN; LiTB; LiTG; LoEn; OnSP; OxBoLi; SiTL; StPo
There was an old man lived under the hill. Father Grumble. *Unknown.* ViBoFo
There was an old man named Michael Finnegan. *Unknown.* GoTP; TiPo
There was an old man of Ancona. Limerick. Edward Lear. BoN
There was an old man of Aosta. Limerick. Edward Lear. BoN
There was an old man of Bengal. Limerick. "F. Anstey." CenHV
There was an old man of Berlin. Limerick. Edward Lear. PoVP
There was an old man of Blackheath. Limerick. *Unknown.* CenHV; LiL; TSWC
There was an old man of Boulogne. Limerick [*or* An Old Man of Boulogne]. *Unknown.* CenHV; LiTM; OxBoLi; SiTL
There was an old man of Calcutta. Arthur. Ogden Nash. FiBHP
There was an old man of Cape Horn. Limerick. Edward Lear. TSW; TSWC
There was an old man of Cashmere. Limerick. Edward Lear. BoN
There was an old man of Coblenz. Limerick. Edward Lear. BoN
There was an old man of Dumbree. Edward Lear. GoTP
There was an old man of Hawaii. *Unknown.* SiTL
There was an old man of Kamschatka. Limerick. Edward Lear. NA
There was an old man of Khartoum. Limerick. *Unknown.* LiBL; OxBoLi
There was an old man of Leghorn. Limerick. Edward Lear. BoN; NA
There was an old man of Madras. Limerick. Edward Lear. BoN
There was an old man of Melrose. Limerick. Edward Lear. LBN
There was an old man of [*or* once was a man from] Nantucket. Limerick [*or* That Nantucket Limerick]. Dayton Voorhees. HBV; LiBL; LiTG; TreF
There was an old man of Nepaul. Limerick. Edward Lear. BoN
There was an old man of Peru/ Who dreamt he was eating his shoe. *See* There was an old man from Peru . . .
There was an old man of Peru/ Who never knew what he should do. Limerick. Edward Lear. BoN
There was an old man of Peru/ Who watched his wife making stew. Limerick. Edward Lear. BoN
There was an old man of Port Grigor. Limerick. Edward Lear. BoN
There was an old man of St. Bees. *See* There was a young man of St. Bees.
There was an old man of Spithead. Limerick. Edward Lear. BoN
There was an old man of Tarentum. Limerick. *Unknown.* HBV; LiBL; LiL; PoeMoYo; TSWC; WhC
There was an old [*or* a young] man of the Cape. Limerick [*or* Wear and Tear]. *At. to* Robert Louis Stevenson. BOHV; LiBL; PIAE; TSWC
There was an old man of the coast. Limerick. Edward Lear. BoN; CenHV; LiBL; MoShBr; PoVP; RIS; StaSt
There was an old man of the Dargle. Limerick. Edward Lear. BoN; ChTr
There was an old man of The Hague. Limerick. Edward Lear. BoN
There was an old man of the Isles. Limerick. Edward Lear. OTPC (1946 ed.); StVeCh
There was an old man of [*or* from] the Rhine. Limerick. *Unknown.* BOHV; GoTP
There was an old man of the South. Limerick. Edward Lear. BoN

There was an old man of the West. Limerick. Edward Lear. BoN; RIS; StaSt
There was an old man of Thermopylae. Limerick. Edward Lear. BoN; CenHV; LBN; LiBL; NA
There was an old man of Tobago. Limerick. *Unknown.* BOHV; LiBL; RIS
There was an old man of Toronto. Andrew Lang. BoN
There was an old man of Vesuvius. Limerick. Edward Lear. LiBL
There was an old man of West Dumpet. Limerick. Edward Lear. BoN
There was an old man on the Border. Limerick. Edward Lear. CenHV; PoVP
There was an old man on whose nose. Limerick. Edward Lear. BoChLi; BoN
There was an old man who lived in a wood. The Old Man Who Lived in a Wood. *Unknown.* MoShBr; MPB; StVeCh
There was an old man who lived in Middle Row. *Unknown.* OxNR
There was an old man who lived in the West. The Wife Wrapt in Wether's Skin (C *vers.*). *Unknown.* BaBo
There was an old man who lived on a common. The Wonderful Old Man. *Unknown.* NA
There was an old man who lived under the hill. The Old Man under the Hill. *Unknown.* CSF
There was an old man who owned a small farm. The Farmer's Curst Wife (B *vers.*). *Unknown.* BaBo
There was an old man who said, "Do." Limerick [*or* New Limericks]. *Unknown.* FaPON; ImOP; LiBL; MeMeAg; NA; RIS; StaSt
There was an old man who said, "Gee!" Limerick. *Unknown.* BOHV
There was an old man who said, "How." Limerick [*or* Nonsense Verses]. Edward Lear. BoChLi; BoN; GFA; PIAE; SAS; StVeCh; TSW; TSWC
There was an old man who said: "Hush!" Limerick [*or* Nonsense Verses]. Edward Lear. BoN; GoTP; HBV; LiTG; NA; OTPC; OxBoLi; PIAE; StVeCh
There was an old man who said, "Well!" Limerick. Edward Lear. OTPC (1946 ed.); RIS; StaSt
There was an old man who supposed. Limerick. Edward Lear. BoN; LBN; LiBL; NA; RIS; StaSt; WhC
There was an old man, who when little. Limerick. Edward Lear. BoN; GoTP
There was an old man with a beard,/ Who said, "It is just as I feared!" Limerick [*or* Old Man with a Beard]. Edward Lear. BoChLi; BoN; ChTr; FaPON; HBV; LBN; LiBL; NA; OTPC; PoVP; RAR; StVeCh; TiPo; TSW; TSWC
There was an old man with a beard,/ Who sat on a horse when he reared. Limerick. Edward Lear. LiBL
There was an old man with a nose. Limerick. Edward Lear. BoN
There was an old man with a poker. Limerick [*or* Nonsense Verses]. Edward Lear. HBV; OTPC
There was an old monk of great renown. The Monk of Great Renown. *Unknown.* CoMu
There was an old monk of Siberia. Limerick. *Unknown.* LiBL
There Was an Old Owl. *Unknown.* GFA
("There was an old owl [who] lived in an oak.") CenHV; GoTP
There was an old party called Pennycomequick. Mr. Pennycomequick. P. M. Stone. BoTP
Theer was an old party [*or* old person *or* a young fellow] of Lyme. Limerick. *Unknown.* CenHV; LiBL; LiTG; OxBoLi; PIAE; SiTL. *See also* There once was an old man of Lyme.
There was an old person of Anerly. Limerick. Edward Lear. LiBL
There was an old person of Blythe. Limerick. Edward Lear. BoN
There Was an Old Person of Bradley. Edward Lear. UnS
There was an old person of Bray. Limerick. Edward Lear. BoN
There was an old person of Burton. Limerick. Edward Lear. RIS; StaSt
There was an old person of Cassel. Limerick. Edward Lear. BoN
There was an old person of Dean. Limerick. Edward Lear. BoChLi; MoShBr; PCH
There was an old person of Diss. Edward Lear. BoN
There was an old person of Ewell. Limerick. Edward Lear. BoN
There was an old person of Grange. Limerick. Edward Lear. BoN
There was an old person of Gretna. Limerick. Edward Lear. BoN; ChTr
There was an old person of Ickley. Limerick. Edward Lear. BoN
There was an old person of Leeds. Limerick. *Unknown.* WhC
There was an old person of Lyme. *See* There was an old party of Lyme.
There was an old person of Pinner. Limerick. Edward Lear. BoN
There was an old person of Rheims. Limerick. Edward Lear. BoN
There was an old person of Rye. Limerick. Edward Lear. BoN
There was an old person of Skye. Edward Lear. ChTr
There was an old person of Slough. Limerick. Edward Lear. BoN
There was an old person of Spain. Limerick. Edward Lear. BoN
There was an old person of Sparta. Limerick. Edward Lear. BoChLi (1939 ed.)
There was an old person of Tring/ Who embellished his nose with a ring. Limerick. Edward Lear. BoN
There was an old person of Tring/ Who, when somebody asked her to sing. Limerick. *Unknown.* LiBL; WhC
There was an old person of Ware. Limerick [*or* The Moppsikon Floppsikon Bear]. Edward Lear. BoChLi; BoN; CenHV; GoTP; LiBL; NA; PCH; SAS
There was an old person of Wick. Limerick. Edward Lear. NA
There was an old person of Wilts. Limerick. Edward Lear. BoN
There was an old person of Woking. Limerick. Edward Lear. NA
There was an old person whose habits. Limericks. Edward Lear. BoChLi (1950 ed.); BoN; FaPON; LBN
There Was an Old Soldier, *with music.* *Unknown.* AS; TrAS, *with* Old Zip Coon
There was an old soldier of Bister. Limericks. *Unknown.* BOHV
There was an old stump of an old tree standing. The New View. John Holmes. MiAP
There was an old stupid who wrote. Limerick. Walter Parke. LiBL; NA
There was an old tailor of Bicester. Limerick. *Unknown.* CenHV
There was an old wife and she lived all alone. The Old Wife and the Ghost. James Reeves. PoMS
There was an old woman/ Lived under a hill. Mother Goose. HBV; HBVY; OTPC; RIS; SAS; StVeCh
There was an old woman/ Lived up on a hill. Mother Goose. RIS
There was an old woman,/ And nothing she had. *Unknown.* OxNR
There was an old woman/ Sold puddings and pies. *Unknown.* OxNR
There was an old woman/ Who lived in Dundee. *Unknown.* OxNR
There was an old woman/ Went blackberry picking. Berries. Walter de la Mare. AtBAP; BoChLi; MBP; MoBrPo; OnSP; RG; StaSt; TiPo
There was an old woman/ Went out one morning. Fairies. Louis Untermeyer. StaSt
There was an old woman all skin and bone. Old Woman All Skin and Bone. *Unknown.* TrAS
There was an old woman and she had a little pig. Tale of a Little Pig. *Unknown.* ABF
There was an old woman and she lived in a shoe. The Old Woman Who Lived in a Shoe. *Unknown.* LiTG; OxBoLi. *For* Mother Goose *vers., see* There was an old woman who lived in a shoe.
There was an old woman, and what do you think. Mother Goose. FaBoCh; HBV; LoGBV; OTPC; OxNR
There was an old woman, as I've heard tell. *See* There was an old woman, so I've heard tell.
There was an old woman called Nothing-at-all. Mother Goose. BoN; OxNR; RIS
There was an old woman had three cows. *Unknown.* OxNR
There was an old woman, her name [it] was Peg. *Unknown.* BoN; OxNR
There was an old woman in Ireland, in Ireland she did dwell. The Wife of Kelso. *Unknown.* ShS
There was an old woman in Surrey. Mother Goose. BoChLi
There was an old woman lived down in a dell. Was She a Witch? Laura E. Richards. MPB
There Was an Old Woman Lived in the West. *Unknown.* *See* Two Sisters, The.
There was an old woman lived on the sea shore. The Twa Sisters (B *vers.*). *Unknown.* BaBo
There was an old woman lived under a hill/ And if she's not gone. Mother Goose HBV; HBVY; OTPC; OxNR; RIS; SAS; StVeCh (1940 ed.)
There was an old woman lived under a hill/ She put a mouse in a bag. Mother Goose. OxNR
There was an old woman of Harrow. *Unknown.* BoN
There was an old woman of Leeds. Limerick. *Unknown.* RIS
There was an old woman sat spinning. *Unknown.* GoTP; OxNR
There was an old [*or* a little] woman, so [*or* as] I've heard tell. The Little Old Woman. Mother Goose. BoChLi;

There was an old woman, so I've heard tell *(continued)* BoN; CG; GoTP; InvP; MeMeAg; MoShBr; OTPC; OxNR; RIS; SAS; SiTL; StPo; TiPo
There was an old woman tossed [*or* went] up in a basket. Mother Goose. BoChLi; BoN; OTPC; OxNR; PCH; PPL; RIS; SAS; SiTL; StVeCh
There was an old woman who lived in a shoe. Mother Goose. BoChLi; BoN; FaBoBe; FaFP; HBV; HBVY; OnHT; OTPC; OxNR; PPL; RIS; SAS; SiTL; StVeCh; TiPo. *See also* There was an old woman and she lived in a shoe.
There was an old woman who lived on the strand. Johnny and Betsy. *Unknown.* ABS
There was an ould man down by Killyburn brae. Killyburn Brae. *Unknown.* OnYI
There was an owl lived in an oak. *Unknown.* GFA; OxNR; RIS
There was an ox, there was a flea. Partners. Jaime Castiello. WaKn
There was ance a may, and she lo'ed na men. Were Na My Heart Light I Wad Dee. Lady Grizel Baillie. EBSV
There was blood [*or* bullud] on the saddle. Blood on the Saddle [*or* Trail End]. *Unknown, at. to* Everett Chatham [*or* Cheetham]. CoSo; SoAF
There was crying in Granada when the sun was going down. Flight from Granada. *Unknown.* AnSpL-1
There was feasting in the hall. King Edwin's Feast. John White Chadwick. OTPC (1923 ed.)
There was glory on the windy street. Avalon. Donald Davidson. LS
There was Hep and Texas an' Bronco Jack. Campfire and Bunkhouse. *Unknown.* CoSo
There was I fix'd, I know not how. George Crabbe. *Fr.* Sir Eustace Grey. NBE
There was in Arll a little cove. The Piper of Arll. Duncan Campbell Scott. BoCaPo; CPG; PeCV; SG
There was in Asia, in a city great [*or* great city]. The Prioress's Tale (*mod. vers.*). Chaucer. *Fr.* The Canterbury Tales. ACP; ISi. *See also* Ther was in Asie . . .
There was in him a vital scorn of all. Byron. *Fr.* Lara. OBRV
There was king's daughter lived in the north. The Cruel Mother (B *vers.*). *Unknown.* BaBo
There was lifted up one voice of woe. A Lamentation for the Death of Sir Maurice Fitzgerald, Knight of Kerry. Pierce Ferriter. IrPN
There was monie a braw noble. Glenlogie. *Unknown.* GN
There was movement at the station, for the word had passed around. The Man from Snowy River. A. B. Paterson. NeLNL
There was never a leaf on bush or tree. A Winter Morning [*or* January]. James Russell Lowell. *Fr.* The Vision of Sir Launfal. GN; PoRL
There was never a queen like Balkis. True Royalty. Kipling. *Fr.* Just-so Stories. PECK
There was never a sound beside the wood but one. Mowing. Robert Frost. AmPo; AmPP; AnFE; AnNE; APA; CoAnAm; CoV; ExPo; HBMV; HoPM; LiTA; MM; MOAP; NeMA; NP; OxBA; PeBoSo; ShBV-3; TwAmPo; UnPo (3d ed.); YT
There was never nothing more me pained. Sir Thomas Wyatt. SiPS
There was no covert for the birds. Winter Birds. Elinor MacArthur. BLA; WhBS
There was no glory on the hills that day. Good Friday. Martha Provine Leach Turner. MaRV; OQP; QP-2
There was no hand to hold me back. The Ancient Track. H. P. Lovecraft. DaM
There was no hunted one. The Baying Hounds. Mary Gilmore. BoAV
There was no lady more refined. Mrs. Brown and the Famous Author. Stoddard King. ATP
There was no land, they used to tell. At the Grave of a Land-Shark. Ernest G. Moll. WhC
There Was No One. Juan Ramón Jiménez, *tr. fr. Spanish by* Eleanor L. Turnbull. TeCS
There was no one like 'im, 'Orse or Foot. "Follow Me 'Ome." Kipling. OAEP (2d ed.)
There Was No Place Found. Mary Elizabeth Coleridge. OxBoCh
There was no repose. Hero Song. Robert Duncan. CrMA
There was no road at all to that high place. The Grove. Edwin Muir. LiTM (rev. ed.); MoPo
There Was No Room on the Cross. *Unknown.* GoBC
There was no sight of man in the immense mountain. Desolation. Wang Wei. WhP
There was no song nor shout of joy. The Ship. J. C. Squire. CH; PtOT; TCPD; WP
There was no trace of Heaven. Bivouac. Alun Lewis. ChMP
There was no union in the land. Gettysburg. James Jeffrey Roche. BIG; MC; PaA; PAH
There was no west, there was no east. The Demon of the Gibbet. Fitz-James O'Brien. DaM; PoMS
There was (not certain[e] when) a certain[e] preacher. Of a Certain[e] Man. Sir John Harington. BOHV; LPS-3; SiCE
There was once a bird that lived up in a tree. Fiddle-dee-dee. Eugene Field. DDA
There was once a boat on a billow. Longing for Home. Jean Ingelow. *Fr.* Songs of Seven. WGRP
There was once a Filipino hombre. A Filipino Hombre. *Unknown.* AS
There was once a heron in a certain place on the edge of a pond. The Heron That Liked Crab-Meat. *Unknown.* *Fr.* The Panchatantra. OuHeWo
There was once a king of Guzzlemuchgate. The King of Guzzlemuchgate. Pierre Jean de Béranger. TrFP
There was once a little animal. Similar Cases. Charlotte Perkins Stetson Gilman. BAP; BBV; DDA; HBV; OBAV
There was once a little man, and his rod and line he took. The Usual Way. Frederic E. Weatherly. BOHV
There was once a maiden who loved a cheese. Quite the Cheese. H. C. Waring. PA
There was once a man who dreamt he went to Heaven. The Man Who Dreamed of Fairies. Po Chü-i. TrCh
There was once a man with a beard. *See* There was an old man with a beard.
There was once a pious young priest. *See* There once was a pious young priest.
There was once a pirate, greedy and bold. A Message of Peace. John Boyle O'Reilly. OnYI
There Was Once a Puffin. Florence Page Jaques. *See* There Once Was a Puffin.
There was once a small boy in Quebec. *See* There was a small boy of Quebec.
There was once a young curate of Salisbury. *See* There was a young curate of Salisbury.
There was once a young fir-tree of Bosnia. Dante Gabriel Rossetti. BoN
There was once a young lady of Riga. *See* There was a young lady of Riga.
There was once a young lady of Ryde. *See* There was a young lady of Ryde/ Who ate a green apple and died.
There was once a young man of Oporta. "Lewis Carroll." BoN
There was once an old fox. *See* There was an old fox.
There was once an old sailor my grandfather knew. The Old Sailor. A. A. Milne. CenHV
There was once two Irish labouring men; to England they came over. How Paddy Stole the Rope. *Unknown.* BLPA
There was once upon a time a man who lost the/ Dictionary. Doctor Bill Williams. Ernest Walsh. InvP
There was once't upon a time. The Story of the Little Rid Hin. F. W. Sweetser SAS
There was one little Jim. Dirty Jim. Jane Taylor. HBV; HBVY
There was revel of heroes and high carouse. The Slaughter of Grendel by Beowulf. *Unknown.* *Fr.* Beowulf. LiTW
There was silence in heaven, as if for half an hour. Mary's Assumption. Alfred J. Barrett. ISi
There was some jolly drivers on the Denver City Line. Root Hog or Die. Floyd B. Small. PoOW
There was such speed in her little body. Bells for John Whiteside's Daughter. John Crowe Ransom. AmP; AmPP; AnFE; ChMo; CoAnAm; CoBMV; CrMA; GTBS-D; InP; InPo; LiTA; LiTM (rev. ed.); LS; MAP; MoAB; MoAmPo; MOAP; MoVE; NePA; NP; OxBA; ReMP; TwAmPo; UnPo (3d ed.)
There was the battle stricken weill. The Battle of Bannockburn. John Barbour. *Fr.* The Bruce. BSV
There was the privy, there the porkers' pen. Inscription for an Old Well. John Fallon. PoP
There was the world that Jackson always found. Obituary. Louis Untermeyer. MAP
There was this road. The Legs. Robert Graves. FaBoMo; HaMV; LiTB; LiTM; MoP
There was three crows sat on a tree. Blow the Man Down, *vers.* IV. *Unknown.* ShS
There was [*or* were] three Kings into the east. John Barleycorn. Burns. BOHV; CG; CoEV; EV-3; FaBoCh; HBV; LoGBV; LPS-3; PECK; SeCeV; ShBV-1
There was three ladies played at the ba. *See* There were three ladies playd at the ba'.
There was, 'tis said, and I believe, a time. George Crabbe. *Fr.* The Parish Register: Burials. EiPP
There was too much swamp, too much blue in the sky. Nature Poem. Ruth Herschberger. OnHM
There was tumult [*or* a tumult] in the city. Independence Bell [*or* Liberty and Independence]. *Unknown.* BLPA; BoHiPo; DD; FaBoBe; IDAH; MC; PEDC; TreFS
There was twa sisters in a bowr. *See* There were twa sisters . . .
There was two little boys going to the school. The Twa Brothers (B *vers.*). *Unknown.* ESPB; ViBoFo
There was two lofty ships, from old England they set sail. High Barbaree. *Unknown.* SoAmSa

There went an incense through the land one night. Monk's Song. Sydney Dobell. *Fr.* The Roman. BMEP
There went out in the dawning light. A Pastoral [*or* Pastoral Dialogue]. *Unknown.* AWP; OnPM
There were blossoms all unblown. When You Came. Ada Foster Murray. LEAP
There were estrangements on the road of love. The Altar. Jean Starr Untermeyer. BAP; HBMV
There were faces to remember in the Valley of the Shadow. The Valley of the Shadow. E. A. Robinson. TCPD
There were four apples on the bough. August. Swinburne. AtBAP
There were four of us about that bed. Shameful Death. William Morris. BPN; CBOV; ChTr; EmBrPo; GoTP; GTBS; HBV; MaC; MBP; MuP; OAEP; OBVV; POTT; PoVP; ShBV-2; VA; ViP; ViPo; ViPP; VLEP
There were great steppes, and rocky table-lands. A Memory. H. P. Lovecraft. UnW
There were ladies, they lived in a bower. Mary Hamilton (B *vers.*). *Unknown.* ESPB
There Were Ninety and Nine. Elizabeth Cecilia Clephane. OlF; WGRP
(Lost Sheep, The.) HBV; OTPC; VA
(Ninety and Nine, The.) BPP; TreF, 4 *sts.*
There were ninety and nine of a flock, sleek and fine. The Good Shepherd. D. N. Howe. PTA-2
There were no footprints left upon the waters. Dies Irae. James L. Duff. ChIP; JKCP; MaRV
There were none of my blood in this battle. Wildwest. Archibald MacLeish. Frescoes for Mr. Rockefeller's City, II. ReaPo; ReMP; UnPo
There were not many at that lonely place. Lonely Burial. Stephen Vincent Benét. BAP; SBMV
There were once two cats of Kilkenny. The Cats of Kilkenny. *Unknown.* GoTP
There were only two or three of us. At Prayer Meeting. Margaret E. Sangster. PraP
There were saddened hearts in Mudville for a week or even more. Casey's Revenge. James Wilson. BLPA; PTA-1; TreFS
There were seven angels erst that spanned. The Star Bearer. Edmund Clarence Stedman. CLS
There were sights to be seen at the flaming end of summer. End of Summer. Jean Starr Untermeyer. YT
There were some kings, in number three. Jumbo Jee. Laura E. Richards. GaP; SUS
There were sparkles on the window-pane, and sparkles in the sky. The Waits. Madeline Nightingale. SDH; SUS
There were strange riders once, came gusting down. Earth-Visitors. Kenneth Slessor. BoAV
There were three brothers in merry Scotland. Henry Martyn. *Unknown.* SG; ViBoFo (B *vers.*)
There were three cherry trees once. The Three Cherry Trees. Walter de la Mare. ChMo; GBV
There were three cooks of Colebrook. *Unknown.* OxNR
There were three critics: Slip and Slop. Criticism. Sir William Watson. BMEP
There were three crows sat on a tree. The Three Ravens (The Twa Corbies) (C *vers.*) *Unknown.* BaBo; ViBoFo
There were three gipsies [*or* gypsies] a-come to my door. The Wraggle Taggle Gipsies [*or* The Raggle, Taggle Gypsies]. *Unknown.* BoTP; CH; FaPON; MPB; OnSP; OTPC (1946 ed.); PCD; StVeCh; ThWaDe; TiPo (1952 ed.)
There were three hills that stood alone. The Three Hills. J. C. Squire. BMEP; HBMV; InP; TCEP; TCPD
There were three in the meadow by the brook. The Code. Robert Frost. MaC; NP; YT
There were three jovial Welshmen [*or* huntsmen]. The Three Jovial Welshmen [*or* The Three Jovial Huntsmen]. *Unknown.* BoChLi; BOHV; CG; GaP; GoBP; HBVY; MoShBr; NA; OTPC; OxBoLi; OxNR; SiTL; StVeCh
There were three kings cam' frae the East. The Kings from the East. Heine, *tr. by* Alexander Gray. GoTS
There were three kings into the East. *See* There was three kings . . .
There were three ladies [*or* laides] lived in a bower. Babylon; or, The Bonnie Banks o' Fordie. *Unknown.* BaBo (A *vers.*); EnLi-1; ESPB; OBB; SeCePo; TOP
There were [*or* was] three ladies playd [*or* play'd] at the ba. The Cruel Brother. *Unknown.* BaBo (A *vers.*); EM-1; EnLit; ESPB; LoEn; OBB; PFE; TOP; ViBoFo
There were three lights that night. God with Us. Nancy Byrd Turner. ChIP; OQP; QP-1
There were three little birds in a wood. *Unknown.* GoTP
There were three maidens who loved a king. Three Loves. Lucy H. Hooper. BeLS; LPS 1
There were three maids lived in a barn. Babylon; or, The Bonnie Banks o Fordie (B *vers.*). Unknown. BaBo
There were three ravens sat on a tree. The Three Ravens. *Unknown.* AtBAP; BaBo (A *vers.*); BCEP; BEL; ChTr; EM-1; ESPB; EV-2; ExPo; HBV; OAEP; OBB; OBEV; OuHeWo; PoEL-1; SeCeV; TrGrPo; UnPo; ViBoFo (A *vers.*); ViBoPo
There were three sailors of Bristol City. Little Billee. Thackeray. BOHV; CBOV; CenHV; EtS; EV-5; FaBoCh; GaP; HBV; HBVY; LBN; LoGBV; LPS-3; MPB; NA; OnSP; OTPC; PECK; PoVP; TreFS; TSW; TSWC; TVSH
There were three sisters fair and bright. The Riddling Knight. *Unknown.* FaBoCh; LoGBV; OBB; PoEL-1
There were three sisters in a hall. *Unknown.* OxNR
There were three young maids of Lee. A Bird in the Hand. Frederic E. Weatherly. BOHV; VA
There were three young women of Birmingham. Limerick. *Unknown.* HBV
There were troths in the hedges. Naked Boughs. Harrison Smith Morris. PR
There were twa brethren in the north. The Twa Brothers. *Unknown.* ATP; BaBo (A *vers.*); CH; EM-1; ESPB; EV-2; OBB; PreP; ViBoFo (A *vers.*)
There were twa knights in fair Scotland. The Twa Knights. *Unknown.* ESPB
There were [*or* was] twa [*or* two] sisters in [*or* sat in] a bour [*or* bower *or* bowr]. The Twa [*or* Two] Sisters [*or* Binnorie]. *Unknown.* AnFE; BaBo; BEL; BLV; BoLiVe; BSV; CBOV; CH; CoBE; EBSV; EM-1; EnLit; EnSB; ESPB (B *vers.*); EV-2; GBV (1952 ed.); HBV; LEAP; OBB; OBEV; OnSP; OuHeWo; PCN; REAL; ShBV-1; StaSt; TOP; TrGrPo; ViBoFo (B *vers.*); WHA
There were two birds sat on a stone. Mother Goose. OxNR; PPL
There were two blackbirds sitting on a hill. Mother Goose. HBV; HBVY; OTPC
There were two little girls, neither handsome nor plain. Jane and Eliza. Ann Taylor. HBV; HBVY; OnPP
There were two little skeezucks who lived in the isle. The Two Little Skeezucks. Eugene Field. MPB
There were two lofty ships from old England came. The High Barbaree [*or* High Barbary]. *Unknown.* AmSS; BaBo; OuSiCo; ViBoFo
There were two of us left in the berry patch. Robert Frost Relates "The Death of the Tired Man." Louis Untermeyer. BOHV
There were two sisters sat in a bower. *See* There were twa sisters . . .
There were two sisters, they went playing. The Twa Sisters. *Unknown.* ESPB; ViBoFo (A *vers.*)
There were two wrens upon a tree. *Unknown.* OxNR
There were waving hands and banners, as the crowded car rolled by. The Color Guard. Charles F. Harwood. FOAH
There were years vague of measure. Her Apotheosis. Thomas Hardy. ViPP
There, where death's brief pang was quickest. Murat. Byron. *Fr.* Ode from the French. LPS-3
There where he sits, in the cold, in the gloom. The Hidden Weaver. Odell Shepard. WGRP
There where the rusty iron lies. Rooks. Charles Hamilton Sorley. BLA; HBMV; MBP; MoBrPo
There where the sea does not pulsate. Come, Come Thou. Vicente Aleixandre. CoSP
There, where the sun shines first. The Azalea. Coventry Patmore. GoBC; POTT; PoVP; ViP; VLEP
There where the woodcock his long bill among the alders. October—an Etching. Edna St. Vincent Millay. CaAE
There will always be songs. There Shall Be New Songs. Clifford Gessler. PSO
There will be a moon. Moonlit Night. Vladimir Mayakovsky. TrRV
There will be a rusty gun on the wall, sweetheart. A.E.F. Carl Sandburg. CoBA; HBMV; MAP; MoAB; MoAmPo; TCAP; WaaP
There will be butterflies. Butterflies. Haniel Long. HBMV
There will be news tomorrow. Tomorrow's News. "George Klingle." OQP; QP-1
There Will Be No Peace. W. H. Auden. NePoAm-2
There Will Be Peace. Margaret Miller Pettengill. PGD
There will be rose and rhododendron. Elegy before Death. Edna St. Vincent Millay. AnFE; APA; ChMo; CMP; CoAnAm; GTBS-W; LiTA; LiTM; MM; OBAV
There will be roses after you are gone. Eternity. Arthur M. Sampley. *Fr.* Fragments of Eternity. MuM
There Will Be Stars. Sara Teasdale. LoPS; TBM; TwCV
There will be those to-day who weep their own. Woodrow Wilson. S. Omar Barker. DD; GA
There will come a day. The Punching Clock. Milos Macourek. LiTW
There Will Come Soft Rains. Sara Teasdale. ChMo; CMP; LiTA; NP; SBMV
There will, of course, be other perfect days. Lux Aeterna. Irwin Edman. TBM
There, wrapped in his own roars, the lone airman. The Raider. W. R. Rodgers. AnIL; MoBrPo (1950 ed.)
There you are once more near me. Shadow. Guillaume Apollinaire. WaaP
There you flutter. Rejected. Wu Wen Ti. PoHN
Therefore, Achilles, rule thy high spirit. The Old Knight Phoenix. Homer. *Fr.* The Iliad, IX. GrR

Therefore all seasons shall be sweet to thee. All Seasons Shall Be Sweet. Samuel Taylor Coleridge. *Fr.* Frost at Midnight. BoTP; EnSW
Therefore come they the crowding maidens. The Virgin Martyrs. Sigebert of Gembloux. MeRV
Therefore death is nothing to us, it matters not one jot. Fear of Death. Lucretius. *Fr.* De Rerum Natura. RoL
Therefore doth heaven divide. Commonwealth of the Bees. Shakespeare. King Henry V, *fr.* I, ii. GN
Therefore I cannot think thee wholly gone. James Russell Lowell. *Fr.* Elegy on the Death of Dr. Channing. MaRV
Therefore I Must Tell the Truth. Torlino, *tr. fr. Navajo Indian by* Washington Matthews. ExPo
Therefore, my friends, I say. Bliss Carman. *Fr.* The Word at St. Kavin's. PC
Therefore Philippi saw once more the Roman battalions. We Have Paid Enough Long Since in Our Own Blood. Virgil. *Fr.* Georgics. WaaP
Therefore the Lord Himself/ shall give you a sign. Isaias, Bible, *O.T.* (*Douay vers*). ISi
Therefore thus saith the Lord; Ye have not hearkened unto me. Jeremiah, Bible, *O.T.* PoFr
Therefore to whom turn I but to thee, the ineffable Name? Robert Browning. *Fr.* Abt Vogler. MaRV; ReTS
Therefore We Preserve Life. Shen Ch'üan, *tr. fr. Chinese by* William C. White. TrJP
Therefore, We Thank Thee, God. Reuben Grossman, *tr. fr. Hebrew by* L. V. Snowman. TrJP
Therefore, when restless rage of wind and wave. Marcus Tullius Cicero's Death. Nicholas Grimald. ReIE
Therefore, when thou wouldst pray, or dost thine alms. The Right Use of Prayer. Sir Aubrey De Vere. OBVV; OQP; QP-2; WGRP
There'll be a glassy paradise. Eruption in Utopia. Genevieve Taggard. TCPD
"There'll be no roof to shelter you." The Fiddling Lad. Adelaide Crapsey. MW; NLK (1947 ed.)
"There'll Be Others but Non So for Me." Delmore Schwartz. FiMAP
There'll Never Be Peace till Jamie Comes Hame. Burns. CBE
There's a baby moon rocking far up in the sky. Cradle Song. Pauline Frances Camp. BOL
There's a barrel-organ carol[l]ing across a golden street. The Barrel-Organ. Alfred Noyes. BMEP; ChMo; CMP; EnLit; HBV; MBP; MCCG; MoBrPo; NeMA; PFE; PoeMoYo; PoRA; PYM; TCEP; TreF; TwCV; VOD
There's a bear in yon hill, and he is a brave fellow. The Bear in the Hill. *Unknown.* ABF
There's a beautiful island away in the West. The Land of the Evening Mirage. *Unknown.* WGRP
There's a big fat turkey. *Unknown.* GFA
There's a bit of sky across the street. My "Patch of Blue." Mary Newland Carson. BLPA; NeHB
There's a Black Bull barque coming down the river. Blow, Bullies, Blow. *Unknown.* SG
There's a black fog hiding London. Promise. Florence Lacey. BoTP
There's a blessing on the hearth. Robert Browning. *Br. sel. fr.* The Ring and the Book, VIII. PoToHe
There's a Bower of Bean-Vines. Phoebe Cary. BOHV; PA
There's a bower of roses by Bendemeer's stream. By Bendemeer's Stream [*or* Bendemeer]. Thomas Moore. *Fr.* Lalla Rookh. BLP; CBPC; OBRV; OTPC (1946 ed.); RG
There's a brand new wind a-blowin' down that Lincoln road. A New Wind a-Blowin'. Langston Hughes. TrAS
There's a breathless hush in the Close tonight. Vitai Lampada. Sir Henry Newbolt. BBV; BLPA; BTP; MaRV; NeHB; OQP; PCN; PoeT; POT; QP-2; TCEP; TCPD; TreF; TVSH; YT
There's a brief spring in all of us and when it finishes. To S.T.C. on His 179th Birthday, October 12th, 1951. Maurice Carpenter. FaBoTw
There's a brook on the side of Greylock that used to be full of trout. Dave Lilly. Joyce Kilmer. DaM; JKCP (1926 ed.); LEAP
There's a certain slant of light. Emily Dickinson. AmP; AmPo; AmPP; APA; AnFE; AtBAP; ATP (1953 ed.); CoAnAm; CoV; ExPo; LiTG; LoGBV; MAP; MoAB; MoAmPo; MoPo; NePA; OnPM; OxBA; PoEL-5; PoFS; PoLFOT; ReaPo; ReMP; RiBV (Certain Slant of Light, A.) GTBS-W; LiTA; LiTM (rev. ed.)
There's a certain young lady. A Certain Young Lady. Washington Irving. FaBoBe; HBV; OnPP; PT
There's a chirrupy cricket as guest in my room. The Chirrupy Cricket. Martha Banning Thomas. GFA; PCH
There's a church in the valley by the wildwood. The Little Brown Church in the Vale. William S. Pitts. OIF
There's a circus in the sky. Winter Circus. Aileen Fisher. YeAr
There's a city that lies in the Kingdom of Clouds. The Sunset City. Henry Sylvester Cornwell. HBV; LPS-3
There's a colleen fair as May. Pearl of the White Breast. *Unknown, tr. by* George Petrie. AnIV; OnYI
There's a combative artist named Whistler. Limerick. Dante Gabriel Rossetti. CenHV
There's a comforting thought at the close of the day. Touching Shoulders. *Unknown.* BLPA; MaRV
There's a Convent garden across the way. From My Window. Mother M. Columba. WHL
There's a crack in the city—down that sharp street. Brogan's Lane. Louis Esson. BoAu
There's a crackle of brown on the leaf's crisp edge. Romany Gold. Amelia Josephine Burr. HBMV
There's a craze among us mortals that is cruel hard to name. The Other Fellow's Job. Strickland W. Gillilan. WBLP
There's a crystal-arrowed riffle at the turning of the river. The Spell of the Pool. L. Burton Crane, Jr. NLK
There's a dandy little fellow. Dandelion. Nellie M. Garabrant. GFA; PTA-2
There's a dear little plant that grows in our isle. The Green Little Shamrock of Ireland [*or* The Shamrock]. Andrew Cherry. DD; HBV; HH; MPB; PoRL
There's a death-dealing custom/ Abroad in the land. Drilling Missed Holes. Don Cameron. PoOW
There's a desire. Simplicity. Semyon Kirsanov. RuPo
There's a door at the end of our garden. The Door at the End of Our Garden. Frederic E. Weatherly. OTPC (1946 ed.)
There's a dragon on our teapot. The Teapot Dragon. Rupert Sargent Holland. OTPC; UTS
There's a faerie at the bottom of my garden. My Garden. Janice Appleby Succorsa. HoPM
There's a family nobody likes to meet. The Grumble Family. *Unknown.* WBLP
There's a far high trail where the pines are. The Peak. Mary Carolyn Davies. POT; PoTo
There's a flag hangs over my threshold, whose folds are more dear to me. The Flag. Julia Ward Howe. FOAH
There's a flash packet, a flash packet of fame. The Dreadnought. *Unknown.* AmSS
There's a flower in the garden. *Unknown.* OTPC (1946 ed.)
"There's a footstep coming; look out and see." The Ghost's Petition. Christina Rossetti. DaM
There's a Friend for Little Children. Albert Midlane. OIF; OTPC (1923 ed.)
There's a funny tale of a stingy man. "The Penny Ye Meant to Gi'e." *Unknown.* PTA-1
There's a game much in fashion—I think it's called Euchre. The Game of Life. John Godfrey Saxe. BLPA; NeHB
There's a Garden. "John Crichton." CPG
There's a gathering in the village, that has never been outdone. The Country Doctor. Will M. Carleton. BLPA
There's a gift of elegance. The Mirror. Ibn al-Sabuni. MooP
There's a girl in these parts. No Names. *Unknown.* KiLC
There's a girl just come to town. Automedon, *tr. fr. Greek by* F. A. Wright. GrPo
There's a girl out in Ann Arbor, Mich. *Unknown.* GoTP
There's a glade in Aghadoe, Aghadoe, Aghadoe. Aghadoe. John Todhunter. AnIL; AnIV; GTIV; OBEV (1st ed.); OBVV; OxBI; PoVP
There's a good time coming, boys. The Good Time Coming. Charles Mackay. PEOR
There's a grass-grown road from the valley. Threnody. Ruth Guthrie Harding. BAP; HBV
There's a graveyard near the White House. The Unknown Soldier. Billy Rose. BLPA
There's a green hollow where a river sings. The Sleeper of the Valley. Arthur Rimbaud. AWP; JAWP; WBP
There's a grim one-horse hearse in a jolly round trot. The Pauper's Drive. Thomas Noel. LPS-1
There's a handsome steed. A White Horse with a Crimson Flash. Ibn Abdus. MooP
There's a hard wind yet and a sad road. The Walking Woman. Sidney Keyes. *Fr.* Against a Second Coming. AtBAP; POTE
There's a heap o' love in the human heart. The Human Heart. Frank Carleton Nelson. PoToHe (new ed.)
There's a hill above the harbor. In the Cove. Mary Fanny Youngs. HH
There's a hill somewhere, and a tree and birds. Town Child. Barbara Young. PoMa
There's a hole in the fence. Dorothy Dickinson. GFA
There's a humming in the sky. Aeroplane. Mary McB. Green. TiPo
There's a hush on the frosty furrow where the frozen loam lifts black. Chickadee. Martha Haskell Clark. BLA; WhBS
There's a joy without canker or cark. Ballade of Blue China [*or* Of Blue China]. Andrew Lang. BMEP; PoVP; TSW; TSWC; VA
There's a knowing little proverb. A Quarrel. *Unknown.* MeMeAg
There's a land that is fairer than day. Sanford Fillmore Bennett. OIF

"There's a leak in the sea-wall five miles out!" The Dragon Sees His Advantage. Lyon Sharman. CPG
There's a legend that's told of a gypsy who dwelt. The Flight into Egypt. Francis Sylvester Mahony. LPS-2
There's a lemondrop monkey that whistles and sings. The Land Where the Taffy Birds Grow. Margaret McBride Hoss. GFA
There's a light upon the mountains. A Light upon the Mountains. Henry Burton. MaRV
There's a little black train a-comin'. The Little Black Train. *Unknown.* OuSiCo
There's a little brown wren that has built in our tree. The Little Brown Wren. Clinton Scollard. WhBS
There's a little dog on the doorstep next. The Little French Dog. Tom Robinson. AlBD
There's a little grey friar in yonder green bush. The Grey Linnet. James McCarroll. CaP; OCL
There's a lone [*or* low] green valley by [*or* on] the old Kentucky shore. Darling Nelly Gray. B. R. Hanby. OlF; TrAS; TreFS
There's a lot of music in 'em—the hymns of long ago. The Old Hymns. Frank L. Stanton. BLRP
There's a low green valley on the old Kentucky shore. *See* There's a lone green valley by the old Kentucky shore.
There's a man goin' roun' takin' names. Man Goin' Round. *Unknown.* ABF; AS
There's a mellower light just over the hill. Morning Song. Karle Wilson Baker. BAP; HBMV; PCD
There's a merry brown thrush sitting up in the tree. The Brown Thrush. Lucy Larcom. BoChLi; BoTP; DD; FaPON; HBV; HBVY; MPB; OTPC; PEDC; PPL; PTA-1; RAR; RIS; TVC; UTS
There's a message, sweet and tender. Christmas Still Lives. William Hawkes. BePJ
There's a mockin' bird a-singin' in a tall pine tree. Spring in Florida. C. B. Roth. LPS-1
There's a Nation. Alfred Kreymborg. PG (1945 ed.)
There's a never dying chorus. Toil. *Unknown.* PEDC; PEOR
There's a noise of coming, going. Ballade of Spring. W. E. Henley. PIAE; TSW
There's a Notable Clan Yclept Stein. *Unknown.* SiTL
There's a one-eyed yellow idol to the north of Khatmandu. The Green Eye of the Yellow God. J. Milton Hayes. BLPA
There's a palace in Florence, the world knows well. The Statue and the Bust. Robert Browning. BEL; BMEP; BPN; EM-2; EmBrPo; EnLi-2 (1939 ed.); EPN; GEPC; OAEP; PIAE; PoVP; TOP; ViPP; VLEP
There's a part of the sun in the apple. Out of the Vast [*or* Each a Part of All]. Augustus Wright Bamberger. MaRV; OQP; QP-1; WBLP
There's a patch of old snow in a corner. A Patch of Old Snow. Robert Frost. ChMo; CMP; PoFS; TwP
There's a path that leads to Nowhere. The Path that Leads to Nowhere. Corinne Roosevelt Robinson. BLPA; HBMV; NeHB; NLK; SBMV
There's a pathos in the solemn desolation. The Ruined Cabin. Alfred Castner King. PoOW
There's a piping wind from a sunrise shore. Off to the Fishing Ground. L. M. Montgomery. CaP; CPG
There's a place called Far-away Meadow. The Last Mowing. Robert Frost. InP
There's a plump little chap in a speckled coat. Bob White. George Cooper. DD; GoTP; HBVY; MPB; OTPC (1946 ed.); StVeCh (1940 ed.)
"There's a pool in the ancient forest." The Picture. Frederick O. Sylvester. NLK
There's a Portuguese person named Howell. Limerick. Dante Gabriel Rossetti. CenHV
There's a pretty fuss and bother both in country and in town. A New Song on the Birth of the Prince of Wales. *Unknown.* CoMu
There's a quaint little place they call Lullaby Town. Lullaby Town. John Irving Diller. BLPA; NeHB
There's a race of men that don't fit in. The Men That Don't Fit In. Robert W. Service. BLPA
There's a ragged old man in the garden to-day. Mr. Scarecrow. Sheila Braine. BoTP
There's a red light on the track for Bolsum Brown. Bolsum Brown. *Unknown.* AS
There's a regret. W. E. Henley. AnEnPo
There's a regret that from my bosom aye. A Regret. Charles Harpur. BoAu
There's a road to heaven, a road to hell. My Road. Oliver Opdyke. HBV
There's a rosie-show in Derry. Rosies. Agnes I. Hanrahan. HBV
There's a sacred Shinto island. Torii. Dorothy Choate Herriman. CPG
There's a schooner out from Kingsport. Arnold, Master of the Scud. Bliss Carman. EtS
There's a season in life's spring. Theoxenus. Pindar. OxBG
"There's a seat, I see, still empty?" The Carrier. Thomas Hardy. BMEP
There's a silver house in the lovely sky. The Silver House. John Lea. BoTP
There's a softness, and a silence, and a whiteness by the Aisne. Christmas Day on the Aisne. Ernest E. Blau. CAG
There's a Song in the Air! Josiah Gilbert Holland. *See* Christmas Carol, A.
There's a song that rings in my ears to-night. The Voice of an Alumnus. S. N. Whitney. CAG
There's a sound on the hill. Monaltri. *Unknown.* EBSV
There's a stairway leading upward. The Stairway to the Stars. William Ludlum. PraP
There's a star in the west, that shall never go down. The Star in the West. Eliza Cook. PEDC
There's a stir among the trees. The Christmas Trees. Mary Frances Butts. OHIP; PRWS
There's a streak across the sky line. The Unfurling of the Flag. Clara Endicott Sears. PEDC
There's a sweet old story translated for man. The Gospel According to You. *Unknown.* BLRP
There's a tear in her eye. A Tear. Austin Dobson. *Fr.* Rose-Leaves. BPN
There's a Three-penny Lunch on Dover Street. Eat and Walk. James Norman Hall. BLPA
There's a thrush that sings in a shadowy wood. City Bird. Theda Kenyon. PoMa
There's a time each year that we always hold dear. In the Good Old Summer Time. Ren Shields. TreF
There's a Time to Be Jolly. Charles Godfrey Leland. PR
There's a town called Don't-You-Worry. The Town of Don't-You-Worry. I. J. Bartlett. BLPA; WBLP
There's a tramping of hoofs in the busy street. The Troop of the Guard. Hermann Hagedorn. HBV; OHIP
There's a tree out in our garden which is very nice to climb. The Tree in the Garden. Christine Chaundler. BoTP
There's a tree that is growing alone on the hill. The All Alone Tree. F. O'Neil Gallagher. PCH
There's a vaporish maiden in Harrison. Limerick. Morris Bishop. LiBL; WhC
There's a voice on the wind of the world. The Prophecy. Lon Woodrum. MaRV
There's a whisper down the field where the year has shot her yield. The Long Trail [*or* L'Envoi]. Kipling. HBV; LEAP; OBEV; OBVV; OtMeF; POTT; PoVP; ViBoPo; VLEP
There's a whisper down the line at 11:39. Skimbleshanks; the Railway Cat. T. S. Eliot. FaBoCh; LoGBV
There's a whisper in the orchard, there's a laughter in the breeze. Song of the Open. Sara Hamilton Birchall. NLK
There's a whisper of life in the grey dead trees. The White Canoe. Alan Sullivan. CaP; OCL
There's a Wideness in God's Mercy. Frederick William Faber. *Fr.* God Our Father. OlF; WBLP, *abr.*
(All-embracing, The.) BLRP
(God's Mercy.) MaRV
(Heart of the Eternal, The.) BPP; OQP; QP-1
There's a widow in sleepy Chester. The Grave of the Hundred Head. Kipling. PIR
There's a Woman like a Dewdrop. Robert Browning. *Fr.* A Blot in the 'Scutcheon. BPN
(Earl Mertoun's Song.) HBV; OBEV
There's a wonderful family, called Stein. The Stein Family. *Unknown.* BOHV
There's a wonderful weaver. The Wonderful Weaver. George Cooper. BoChLi; OTPC (1946 ed.); StVeCh (1940 ed.)
There's a wondrous peace lies on this earth. Christmas. Elizabeth Stanton Rice. StJW
There's About Two Million Fellows. Albert Jay Cook. PaA
There's an angel in our ward as keeps a-flittin' to and fro. V. A. D. *Unknown.* AOAH
There's an awful lot to fishin'. An Awful Lot to Fishin'. R. C. Calloway. DDA
There's an end to the duel long fought in the Dark. The End of the Duel. Rachel Annand Taylor. CAW
There's an [*or* the] Irishman, Arthur O'Shaughnessy. Limerick [*or* On the Poet O'Shaughnessy]. Dante Gabriel Rossetti. CenHV; ChTr
There's an odd fellow (I'll not tell his name). De Ignoto. Everard Guilpin. *Fr.* Skialetheia. ReIE
There's Asia on the avenue. Manhattan. Morris Abel Beer. BAP; BoHiPo; PoTo
There's beauty in the deep. The Deep. John Gardiner Calkins Brainard. AA; EtS
There's been a death in the opposite house. Emily Dickinson. BLV; BoLiVe
"There's been an accident!" they said. Mr. Jones [*or* Common Sense *or* Some Ruthless Rhymes]. Harry Graham. CenHV; FaFP; FiBHP; LiTG; MaC; OtMeF; SiTL
There's black grief on the plains, and a mist on the hills. Roisin Dubh. *Unknown.* OnYI
There's blood between us, love, my love. The Convent Threshold. Christina Rossetti. PoEL-5; PoVP

There's but one gift that all our dead desire. God's Gift. Alfred Noyes. POT; PoTo
There's But One Pair of Stockings to Mend To-Night. *Unknown.* PTA-1
There's but the twinkling of a star. The Astral Fates. Samuel Butler. *Fr.* Hudibras. BeR
There's cauld kail in Aberdeen. Cauld Kail in Aberdeen. Alexander, Duke of Gordon. EBSV
There's comfort in a horse's lean brown thighs. The Thoroughbred. Helen Magaret. StaSt
There's dew on the grass of the pastureland. Headin' Home. E. W. Patten. BTP
There's doubtless something in domestic doings. Love and the Poets. Byron. *Fr.* Don Juan, III. GEPC
There's folks that like the good dry land. When the Drive Goes Down. Douglas Malloch. StVeCh
There's good cooks and there's bad ones. The Roundup Cook. Robert V. Carr. PoOW
There's Gowd in the Breast. James Hogg. HBV
There's hardly a wheel rut left to show. The Old Coach Road. Rachel Field. GFA
There's heaven above, and night by night. Johannes Agricola in Meditation. Robert Browning. EmBrPo; OBVV; PoVP; TwP; ViPo; ViPP
There's her hair with which Love angles. Her Fairness. George Wither. *Fr.* Fair Virtue, the Mistress of Philarete. EV-2
There's Holmes, who is matchless among you for wit. Holmes. James Russell Lowell. *Fr.* A Fable for Critics. AnNE; CoBA
"There's just one Book!" cried the dying sage. Just One Book. *Unknown.* BLRP
There's light in the west, o'er the rims of the walnut. By the Turnstile. John Francis O'Donnell. IrPN
There's little in taking or giving. Coda. Dorothy Parker. BOHV; InMe; TreFS
There's little joy in life for me. On the Death of Anne Brontë. Charlotte Brontë. ViBoPo
There's little wildness in my city head. The Wind Blows. Donagh MacDonagh. NeIP
There's lots o' friendly fellers in this here fine ole town. Friendly People. John G. Herndon. MPB
There's lots of things I'd like to be. The Hurdy-Gurdy Man. Elizabeth Fleming. BoTP
There's Lowell, who's striving Parnassus to climb. On Himself. James Russell Lowell. *Fr.* A Fable for Critics. AA
There's Many a Man Killed on the Railroad, *with music. Unknown.* AS
There's many a pool that holds a cloud. In Spring-Time. W. H. Davies. MM; NLK (1947 ed.); TwCV
There's many a proud wizard in Araby and Egypt. Wizards. Alfred Noyes. POT
There's many a strong farmer. The Happy Townland. W. B. Yeats. ThWaDe
There's many a trick in Harvard yard. A Ballade of the Higher Learning. *Unknown.* CAG
There's many a young Canadian boy leaves home and friends so dear. Harry Dunne, *vers.* I. *Unknown.* ShS
There's moaning somewhere in the dark. Voice in Darkness. Richard Dehmel. AWP; JAWP; WBP
There's Money in Mother and Father. Morris Bishop. FiBHP
There's mony a man loves land and life. The Tyneside Widow. Swinburne. PoVP; ViP
There's much afoot in heaven and earth this year. The Rainy Summer. Alice Meynell. AlDL; MoVE
There's music in a hammer. *Unknown.* SiTL
There's Music in the Air. Fanny Crosby. OlF
There's Nae Lark. Swinburne. *Fr.* The Sisters. POTT (Lyric, A: "There's nae lark loves the lift, my dear.") HBV
There's Nae Luck about the House. William Julius Mickle, *also at. to* Jean Adam. *See* Sailor's Wife, The.
There's nae mair lands to tyne, my dear. A Jacobite's Farewell. Swinburne. POTT; PoVP; TOP
There's Nae Place like Otago Yet. John Barr of Craigielee. AnNZ
There's naught [*or* nought] but care on ev'ry han'. Green Grow the Rashes. Burns. HBV; LEAP. *See also* Green Grow the Rashes.
"There's no a bird in a' this foreste." Johnie Cock (K *vers.*). *Unknown.* ESPB
There's no a muir in my ain land but's fu' o' sang the day. The Comin' o' the Spring. Lady John Scott. EBSV
There's no defeat in life. *Unknown.* PoToHe (new ed.)
There's no dew left on the daisies and clover. Songs of Seven: Seven Times One. Jean Ingelow. BLPA; EV-5; FaPON; GBV (1922 ed.); GoTP; HBV; LPS-1; MeMeAg; MPB; OTPC; PCH; PRWS; PTA-1; RAR; TreF; TVC; TVSH
There's No Lust like to Poetry. *Unknown, tr. fr. Latin by* John Addington Symonds. AWP
"There's no one on the long white road." The Irish Mother's Lament. Cecil Frances Alexander. TIP
There's no respect for youth or age. The California Stage Company. *Unknown.* CoSo; CSF
"There's no sense of going further—it's the edge of cultivation." The Explorer [*or* Go]. Kipling. GrCo-2; PoTo; WHA
There's no smoke in the chimney. The Deserted House. Mary Elizabeth Coleridge. BoTP; CH; MoVE; PCD; ThWaDe
There's nobody left but God. The Salt Song. Nikolai Alekseyevich Nekrasov. *Fr.* Who Lives Happily in Russia? TrRV
There's not a breath the dewy leaves to stir. Moonlight in Italy. Elizabeth Clementine Kinney. AA
There's not a craving in the mind. He Satisfies. Frederick William Faber. BePJ
There's not a joy the world can give like that it takes away. Stanzas for Music [*or* There Be None of Beauty's Daughters *or* Youth and Age]. Byron. AWP; BEL; BPN; CBE; CoBE; EmBrPo; EnLi-2; EnLit; EnRP; EPN; ERP; EV-4; GTBS; GTBS-D GTBS-W; GTSE; GTSL; HBV; MaPo; MCCG; OAEP; OBEV; OBRV; OuHeWo; PoFS; RiBV; TOP
There's not a nook within this solemn pass. The Trosachs. Wordsworth. BPN; EM-2; EmBrPo; EnLi-2; EPN; ES; GTSL; HBV; OBEV; OBRV; SeCePo
There's not a person in the street. Empty Houses. Mary Colborne-Veel. BoAu
There's not a spider in the sky. A Love-Song by a Lunatic. *Unknown.* NA
There's not on earth a thing more vile and base. A Prayer for Faith. Michelangelo. OnPM
There's not the smallest orb which thou behold'st. Shakespeare. *Fr.* The Merchant of Venice, V, i. LO
There's nothing great. Nothing Small. Elizabeth Barrett Browning. BCEP
There's nothing grieves me but that age should haste. Idea, VIII. Michael Drayton. ReEn; ReIE; SiCE
There's nothing in the world like love. Plautus. *Fr.* Casina. LaP
There's Nothing like a Ship at Sea. Harry Kemp. MW
There's Nothing like the Rose. Christina Rossetti. PRWS
There's Nothing like the Sun. Edward Thomas. LBBV; NP; YT
There's nothing so good as a good bed. Mirelle of the Good Bed. Tom MacInnes. CPG
There's nothing very beautiful and nothing very gay. Little Things. Orrick Johns. AnAmPo; LA; MAP; NLK; NP; NV; PG (1945 ed.); PoToHe (new ed.); SBMV
There's nought but care on ev'ry han'. Green Grow the Rashes, O! Burns. SiTL. *See also* Green Grow the Rashes.
There's nought, no doubt, so much the spirit calms. The Shipwreck. Byron. *Fr.* Don Juan, II. PoD
There's one great bunch of stars in heaven. Song. Théophile Marzials. OBVV
There's one joins sweetly in the quavering hymn. Sunday Morning. L. A. G. Strong. WhC
There's one that I have loved so much. I Give Thanks. Grace Fallow Norton. NP
There's pain in parting, and a kind of hell. Robert Herrick. *Fr.* To His Dying Brother. LO
There's part of the sun in an apple. Out of the Vast [*or* Each a Part of All]. Augustus Wright Bornberger. OQP; QP-1; WBLP
There's recompense to balm your spirit's ire. Da Silva Gives the Cue. Walter Hart Blumenthal. TrJP
There's retribution in the Judgment Day. Occasion of Sin. Maurice James Craig. *Fr.* Three Cat Poems. PoC
There's room for most things: Tropic seas. A Sermon. Lady Margaret Sackville. HBMV
There's Rosemary. Olive Tilford Dargan. LBMV
There's scarce a point whereon mankind agree. On the Phrase, "To Kill Time." Voltaire. ALV
There's snakes on the mountain. Wanderin'. *Unknown.* AS
There's snow in every street. Winter. J. M. Synge. OBMV
There's Snow on the Fields. Christina Rossetti. *Fr.* Sing-Song. BoTP; EmBrPo
There's soap-suds on the waves. Morning at the Beach. John Farrar. RIS
There's some is born with their legs straight by natur. A Sailor's Apology for Bow-Legs. Thomas Hood. EtS
There's some o' the setter about him. My Old Dawg. Courtney Ryley Cooper. AlBD
"There's someone at the door," said gold candlestick. Green Candles. Humbert Wolfe. HBMV; MBP; MoBrPo; NeMA; NV; PoMS
There's something about the going down of the sun. Any Sunset. Louis Untermeyer. GoTP
There's something in a flying horse. The Crescent Boat [*or* Among the Stars]. Wordsworth. *Fr.* Peter Bell. GoTP; ThWaDe
There's something in a noble boy. The Torn Hat. Nathaniel Parker Willis. AA
There's something in a noble tree. The Trees. Samuel Valentine Cole. NLK; OHIP

There's something in the air. The Coming of [the] Spring. Nora Perry. DD; HBVY; HH; PRWS; YeAr
There's something very lovely. Snowlight. Nancy Byrd Turner. MW
There's somewhat on my breast, father. The Confession. "Thomas Ingoldsby." BOHV; FiBHP
There's such a tiny little mouse. The Mouse. Thirza Wakley. BoTP
There's ten of ye now, and twenty long years in between. Johneen. Patrick J. Carroll. WHL
There's that old hag [*or* thik wold hag] Moll Brown, look, see, just past! A Witch [*or* A Country Witch]. William Barnes. CG; GoTP; PoMS
There's the gals at the bar, there's the beer. The Homeward Bound. Bill Adams. EtS
There's the Irishman Arthur O'Shaughnessy. *See* There's an Irishman, Arthur O'Shaughnessy.
There's the last stick gone; well, one last look round. The Old Doctor. Habberton Lulham. PoP
There's the old, the waves that harvested. The Fisherman. Leonidas of Tarentum. AWP
There's thik wold hag, Moll Brown, look zee, jus' past! *See* There's that old hag Moll Brown, look, see, just past!
There's trampling of hoofs in the busy street. A Troop of the Guard. Hermann Hagedorn. HBV; OHIP
There's Wisdom in Women. Rupert Brooke. HBV
Therewith she left the cave, and with her went. Thetis and Achilles. Homer. *Fr.* The Iliad, XVIII. LiTW; OxBG
Therewith when he was ware, and gan behold. Chaucer. *Fr.* Troilus and Criseyde. LO
Thermometrical. Martial, *tr. fr. Latin by* Paul Nixon. RoL
Thermopylae. Robert Hillyer. AnAmPo; LA
(Thermopylae and Golgotha.) BAP; MaRV
Thermopylae. Simonides, *tr. fr. Greek by* William Lisle Bowles. AWP; JAWP; WBP
(At Thermopylae, *tr. unknown.*) GrL; OnPM; OxBG; WaaP; WoL
(Dead of Sparta at Thermopylae, The, *tr. by* F. L. Lucas.) GrPE
("Go tell the Spartans, thou that passest by," *tr. by* William Lisle Bowles.) GrPo
(Inscription to Spartans Dead at Thermopylae, *tr. by* William Lisle Bowles.) TreF
(On the Army of Spartans, Who Died at Thermopylae, *tr. unknown.*) ChTr
(On the Spartans Who Fell at Thermopylae, *tr. by* Walter Leaf.) GrR
(Three Hundred, The, *tr. unknown.*) LiA
Thermopylae and Golgotha. Robert Hillyer. *See* Thermopylae.
Thermopylae Ode, The. Simonides. *See* Greek Dead at Thermopylae, The.
Thersites. Homer, *tr. fr. Greek by* Maurice Hewlett. *Fr.* The Iliad, II. OxBG
("Rest now took their seats and kept to their own several places, The," *longer sel., pr. tr. by* Samuel Butler.) GrPo
(Thersites Out of Bounds, *tr. by* George Chapman.) GrR
Thesaurus Nightmare, A. J. Willard Ridings. WhC
These. William Carlos Williams. CoBMV; MoAB; MoAmPo; OxBA
These acres, always again lost. Lost Acres. Robert Graves. FaBoMo; LiTG; MoPW
These acres breathe my family. Summer Acres. Anne Wilkinson. CaP
These alternate nights and days, these seasons. Prologue. Archibald MacLeish. MAP; MoAmPo
These Apple Trees. Valentin Iremonger. NeIP
These are arrows that murder sleep. The Song of Crede, Daughter of Gooary. *Unknown.* LiTW; OnYI
These are but words, and I have more than these to give you. Gifts. Muna Lee. BAP
These are my murmur-laden shells that keep. On Some Shells Found Inland. Trumbull Stickney. AnFE; APA; CoAnAm; LiTA; LiTG; NePA; TwAmPo
These Are My People. Lucia Trent. PGD
These are my scales to weigh reality. Reality. Martha Dickinson Bianchi. AA
These are my tears that now you see. M. Kirwan. LO
These Are Not Lost. *At. to* Richard Metcalf *and to* Sarah Doudney. PoToHe
These are not words set down for the rejected. A Communication to Nancy Cunard. Kay Boyle. PoNe
These are our brave, these with their hands in on the work. Citation for Horace Gregory. Muriel Rukeyser. NAMP
These are really the thoughts of all men in all ages and lands. Song of Myself. XVII. Walt Whitman. CoV
These are stale tidings I foreknew. Prometheus in the Earthquake. Aeschylus. *Fr.* Prometheus Bound. LiTW; OxBG
These are the best of him. On a Flyleaf of Burns's Songs. Frederic Lawrence Knowles. HBV; LBMV; PoMa
These Are the Chosen People. Robert Nathan. TrJP
(Sonnet XI: "These are the chosen people. He has set.") QS
These are the days of falling leaves. Autumn Song. Elizabeth-Ellen Long. SiSoSe
These are the days of our youth, our days of glory and honor. The Days of Our Youth. *Unknown.* AWP; JAWP; WBP
These are the days when birds come back. Emily Dickinson. CoV
(Indian Summer.) AnNE; BoLiVe (1945 ed.); CoBA; DDA; GoTP; HBV; MAP; MoAmPo; NeMA; NLK; PFE
These are the desolate, dark weeks. These. William Carlos Williams. CoBMV; MoAB; MoAmPo; OxBA
These are the drab ones. They. Marjorie Meeker. BAP
These are the eggs that were put in a nest. The Story of Baby's Pillow. Emilie Poulsson. PPL
These are the fellows who smell of salt to the prairie. Words Are Never Enough. Charles Bruce. BoCaPo; CaP
These are the fields of light, and laughing air. The Pea-Fields. Sir Charles G. D. Roberts. *Fr.* Songs of the Common Day. PeCV
These are the first shapes: stonefish and starfish. Stonefish and Starfish. John Blight. BoAV; NeLNL
"These are the floating berries of the night." Stars. Kenneth Slessor. BoAV
These are the flowers for a mad bride. Indian Pipes. Winifred Welles. AnAmPo; LA
These are the forgeries of jealousie. Shakespeare. *Fr.* A Midsummer Night's Dream, II, i. NBE
These are the gardens of the Desert, these. The Prairies. Bryant. AmP; AmPP (3d ed.); AnAmPo; CoBA; CoV; IAP; InP; LA; MOAP; OxBA; Po; PoE; PoEL-4; TCAP
These are the generations of the heavens and of the earth. The Garden of Eden. Genesis, Bible, *O.T.* EnLi-1; OuHeWo
These Are the Gifts I Ask. Henry van Dyke. *Fr.* God of the Open Air. FaBoBe; NeHB; OQP; QP-1
These are the heroes, for their country's weal. Epitaph on Those Who Fell at the Battle of Chaeronea. Demosthenes. PoFr
These are the last men. For They Are England. Walter O'Hearn. NeTW
These are the letters which Endymion wrote. On the Recent Sale by Auction of Keats' Love Letters. Oscar Wilde. AnEnPo; BMEP; LBBV; LEAP
These are the live. Kenneth Fearing. NAMP
These are the patriot brave, who side by side. Epitaph for Chaeroneia. *Unknown.* GrPo
These are the saddest of possible words. Baseball's Sad Lexicon. Franklin P. Adams. FaFP; InMe; TreFS
These are the signs in which my days endure. Museum Piece. Lawrence P. Spingarn. GoYe
These are the strings of the Ægean lyre. Sunium. Trumbull Stickney. MOAP
These Are the Subtle Rhythms. Glenway Wescott. NP
These are the tales in all their valorous lore. The Morte d'Arthur. Wilfrid Scawen Blunt. VLEP
These are the things I hold divine. The Things Divine. Jean Brooks Burt. PTA-1
These are the things men seek at dusk. Dusk. Helen Welshimer. PoToHe
These are the things our Christmas Day should leave. Sonnet for Christmas. Vincent G. Burns. MaRV
These are the things that make me laugh. Villanelle of Things Amusing. Gelett Burgess. BOHV
These are the things which once possessed. True Happiness. Morris Talpalar. PoToHe (new ed.)
These are the three principles, friend. Constantino Suasnavar. *Fr.* Numbers. AnCL
These are the trees for hill folk—men that toil. Pines. Anderson M. Scruggs. PoMa
These are the Victoria Falls, whose noisy gushing. The Victoria Falls. William Plomer. BoSA
These are the wells of incredible wonder. Honey for the Heart. Louis J. Sanker. JKCP (1955 ed.)
These are the women whom no man has loved. The Unloved. Arthur Symons. PoVP; VLEP
These are the words. Stone from the Gods. Irma Wassall. GoYe
These are the words which Cato spoke—they well become a sage. The Disputation between the Greeks and the Romans. Juan Ruiz, Archpriest of Hita. *Fr.* The Book of Good Love. AnSpL-1
These Are the Young. Vachel Lindsay. ATP (1935 ed.); TCAP
These are things that pass too soon. Passage. Elliott Coleman. NoCaPo (1941 ed.)
These are thy glorious works, Parent of good. Adam's Morning Hymn [*or* Morning Hymn in Paradise]. Milton. *Fr.* Paradise Lost, V. BrBE; GrCo-1; LPS-2; MaRV; OxBoCh; TCEP; TrPWD; WGRP
These, as they change, Almighty Father! these. A Hymn on the Seasons [*or* A Hymn]. James Thomson. *Fr.* The Seasons. CEP; EiPP; EnRP; EV-3; LPS-2; OxBoCh; PoE
These barrows of the century-darkened dead. Prehistoric Burials. Siegfried Sassoon. MBP; MoBrPo

These be/ Three silent things. Triad. Adelaide Crapsey. BAP; BLV; CBOV; InP; MAP; MCCG; MoAmPo (1942 ed.); NeMA; NP; PFE; PFY; VOD (1935 ed.)
These be the little verses, rough and uncultured, which. By-the-Way. Patrick MacGill. BMEP
These be two men of all mankind. Two Men. E. A. Robinson. BOHV; OBAV
These being the haunts of those. The Death of Friends. Adele Levi. GoYe
These buildings are too close to me. Rudolph Is Tired of the City. Gwendolyn Brooks. TiPo (1959 ed.)
These burning fits but meteors be. A Fever. John Donne. MyFE
These by the streams of famed Eurymedon. On Those Who Fell. Simonides, the Younger. OnPM
These caverns yield. The Bats. Robert Hillyer. GoYe
These cherry flowers. Issa, *tr. fr. Japanese by* Lois J. Erickson. SoLD
These Children Singing. E. E. Cummings. PoLFOT
These courtesans are like the sea. Plautus. *Fr.* Truculentus. LaP
These days are long before I die. Yet a Little While. Christina Rossetti. BPN
These days are misty, insulated. Louis MacNeice. *Fr.* Autumn Journal. ChMo
These days, continually fuddled with drink. On Going to a Tavern. Wang Chi. OnPM; TrCh
These days of disinheritance, we feast. Cuisine Bourgeoise. Wallace Stevens. LiTA
These discords and these warring tongues are gales. A Solemn Meditation. Ruth Pitter. OxBoCh
These dreams abound. Prelude for Spring. Dorothy Livesay. BoCaPo; PeCV; TwCV
These dreary hours of hopeless gloom. The Face. Ebenezer Jones. VA
These errors loved no less than the saint loves arrows. Elegy V: Separation of Man from God [*or* Sacred Elegy V]. George Barker. FaBoTw; GTBS-W; LITB; MoPo
These evenings since the Child was born. Since Christmas. Frederick R. McCreary. MAP
These eyes, dear [*or* deare] Lord, once brandons of desire. For the Magdalene. William Drummond of Hawthornden. AtBAP; ElSeCe; LoBV; PoEL-2
These fallen boughs now never more will weave. The Fallen Tree. Patrick Maybin. NeIP
These Few Precepts. Shakespeare. *See* Polonius' Advice to Laertes.
These Fields at Evening. David Morton. *See* Fields at Evening.
These fields unsown the ploughman Stratonicus hallows. To Pan. Agathias Scholasticus. GrPE
These fishes take their own trip, scrape. Average. P. K. Page. TwCaPo
These flowers that were resplendent, a delight. Sonnet. Pedro Calderón de la Barca. TeCS
"These foreigners with strange and avid faces." Immigrants. Nancy Byrd Turner. PoeMoYo
These fought in any case Ezra Pound. *Fr.* Hugh Selwyn Mauberley. CoBMV; CoV; LiTA; LiTM (rev. ed.); MoPo; NP; OnAP; WaaP
These gay snuff-boxes will be whispering still. Snuff Boxes. Hortense Flexner. PFE; VOD
These gifts to Aphrodite. The Bacchante's Offering. Callimachus. GrL
These goblets of the son of Donnacha. *Unknown. Fr.* Eulogistic Snatches. SiB
These going home at dusk. French Peasants. Monk Gibbon. HaMV; NeIP; OxBI; POTE
These golden heads, these common suns. Dandelions. Howard Nemerov. NePA
These grand and fatal movements toward death. Rearmament. Robinson Jeffers. CoV; OxBA
These grasses, ancient enemies. Poem. Keith Douglas. NeBP
These had been together from the first. Leolin and Edith. Tennyson. *Fr.* Aylmer's Field. GN
These hands are shaped like God's, and so. Warning. Sara Henderson Hay. MaRV
These Hands of Ours. Temple Fay. PoP
These hands shall beate upon my pensive brest. *Unknown.* SeCSL
These have forsaken other lives and ways. The Monks at Ards. Patrick Maybin. NeIP
These have no Christ to spit and stoop. Black Magdalens. Countee Cullen. BANP; BAP; QS
These hearts were woven of human joys and cares. The Dead [*or* All This Is Ended]. Rupert Brooke. 1914, IV. AnFE; AOAH; ATP; CH; CP; EnLit; ES; GTBS-W; GTSL; HBV; HiLiEn; LiTB; LiTG; MCCG; NP; NV; OtMeF; PFE; PIAE; PoeMoYo; PoeT; PoRL; POTE; SeCeV; ShBV-4; TOP; TwCV; VOD; YT
These Helps Solicit. Wordsworth. *Fr.* The Excursion, IV. GrCo-2
These hemp-clothes which you take. Who Will Mend Them? *Unknown.* OnPM
These houres, and that which hovers o'er my end. The Recommendation. Richard Crashaw. PoLi
These hours are kin to the windy rain. Mount Holyoke. Phyllis Merrill. CAG
These I have loved. Rupert Brooke. *Fr.* The Great Lover. BMEP; NAMP; ShBV-2
These I have seen with my eyes. The Banished. Arturo Serrano Plaja. PoFr
These, in the day when heaven was falling. Epitaph on an Army of Mercenaries. A. E. Housman. BMEP; CoBMV; CoEV; GTBS; MM; MoAB; MoVE; OBEV (new ed.); OtMeF; PoFS; POTE; TwP; UnPo; ViBoPo; ViP; WaaP
These kingly piles the acres take. On Luxury. Horace. Odes, II, 15. RoL
These labouring wits, like paviours, mend our ways. The Black Militia of the Pen. Edward Young. *Fr.* Epistles to Mr. Pope Concerning the Authors of the Age. BeR
These lands are clothed in burning weather. The Arid Lands. Herbert Bashford. AA
These larger-than-life comic characters. Homage to Our Leaders. Julian Symons. NeBP
These Latter Days. Olive Tilford Dargan. NoCaPo
These Lines. Shakespeare. *See* Sonnets, XXXII.
These lines I send by waves of woe. Grief's Ship. *Unknown. Fr.* The Phoenix Nest. CoEV; NBE
These lions, each by a daisy queen. Dandelions. Sacheverell Sitwell. RIS
These little firs today are things. A Young Firwood. Dante Gabriel Rossetti. GN; PoRL
These little limbs [*or* limmes]. The Salutation. Thomas Traherne. AtBAP; BrBE; ElSeCe; EPS; InvP; OBS; OxBoCh; SeCL; SeCV-2; SeEP
These little songs. Day and Night Songs. William Allingham. LEAP; VA
These London wenches are so stout. The Sound Country Lass. *Unknown.* CoMu
These lost their bright youth by Eurymedon's side. To the Honoured Dead. Simonides. GrR
These lovely groves of fountain-trees that shake. Golden Bough. Elinor Wylie. MAP; MoAmPo
These many years since we began to be. Rondel. Swinburne. HBV; PIR
These market-dames, mid-aged, with lips thin-drawn. Former Beauties. Thomas Hardy. At Casterbridge Fair, II. BEL; EmBrPo; EnLi-2 (1949 ed.); EnLit; FaBoEn; OBMV; PoVP
These Men. Leon Gellert. BoAV; MoAuPo
These men lost heart and hope, let faith grow cold. Vichy. Dudley G. Davies. NeTW
These men, now both alert and watching. The Friends. *Unknown.* BoFr
These men, to set a crown of ever quenchless glory. The Dead of Sparta at Plataea. Simonides. GrPE
These mountains are too tall; these crags too starkly loom. Mountain Night. Ralph Cheyney. TBM
These mountains wake in me the self-same feeling. Recollections. Aasmund Olafsson Vinje. AnNoLy
These never knew or had a hint. Bones of a French Lady in a Museum. Richard Gillman. NePoAm
These next three days I'd read the Iliad through. To Corydon. Pierre de Ronsard. TrFP
These nights we fear the aspects of the moon. Full Moon; New Guinea. Karl Shapiro. MiAP
These nuts, that I keep in the back of the nest. My Treasures. Robert Louis Stevenson. SAS
These nymphs, I would make them endure. The Afternoon of a Faun. Stéphane Mallarmé, *tr. by* Frederick Morgan. AnFP
These nymphs I would perpetuate. The Afternoon of a Faun. Stéphane Mallarmé, *tr. by* Roger Fry. ReMP
These our actors. Shakespeare. *Fr.* The Tempest, IV, i. BCEP
These pains of mine, oh mother. *Unknown.* Fr. Four Songs. LyMA
These panting damsels, dancing for their lives. The Mother's Choice. *Unknown.* OxBoLi
These pearls of thought in Persian gulfs were bred. In a Copy of Omar Khayyám. James Russell Lowell. AA; TCAP
These People. Howard McKinley Corning. AnAmPo; LA
These people have not heard your name. In a Cathedral City. Thomas Hardy. EnLoPo
These places abound in the old. Limerick. George Libaire. LiBL
These plaintive verse, the posts of my desire. To Delia, IV. Samuel Daniel. OBSC; ReEn; SiCE
These Poems I Have So Loved. Leonora Speyer. PG (1955 ed.)
These pools that, though in forests, still reflect. Spring Pools. Robert Frost. MoAB; MOAP; OxBA
These poor hamlets, humbly faring. Feodor Ivanovich Tyutchev. *See* Sorry Hamlets.
These pretty little birds, see how. Human [*or* Humaine] Cares. Nathaniel Wanley. OBS; SeCL

These Puritans of Massachusetts Bay. Escape. Dorothy Brown Thompson. DDA
These quiet lazy mountains are my own. Coming Back to Mountains. Bianca Bradbury. MuM
These rioters, of whom I make my rime. Chaucer. *Fr.* The Canterbury Tales: The Pardoner's Tale. WHA
These roads that run from Redding Ridge to Kent. Connecticut Trilogy. Leila Jones. MuM
These royal kings that rear up to the sky. Thomas Sackville in Commendation of the Work to the Reader. Thomas Sackville. ReIE
These rugged, wintry days I scarce could bear. In Absence. James Russell Lowell. BAV
These sad last days, dear Claudia, which have brought. Letter to Claudia. Wrenne Jarman. DiM
These set a crown of glory on their land. On the Lacedaemonian Dead at Plataea. Simonides. WaaP
These six things doth the Lord Hate. Seven Evils. Proverbs, Bible, *O.T.* TrGrPo
These songs will not stand. Songs, I. Denis Glover. AnNZ
These Stoic Romans had a flair for dying. In the Annals of Tacitus. Philip Murray. NePoAm
These Stones. Menander, *tr. fr. Greek by* E. F. Watling. LiTW
These Strewn Thoughts by the Mountain Pathway Sprung. George Santayana. Sonnets, XX. OBAV
These summer birds did with thy master stay. To His Maid Prew. Robert Herrick. OBS
These Sunday mornings Londoners delight. In Regent's Park. Anne Ridler. DiM; POTE
These sweeter far than lilies are. Thanksgivings for the Beauty of His Providence. Thomas Traherne. FaBoCh; LoGBV
These take their leave and those remain. Quia Pulvis Es. Victor Hugo. TrFP
These Things Have I Loved. Codman Hislop. CAG
These things have I spoken unto you. Be of Good Cheer. St. John, Bible, *N.T.* WoL
These things I do engage to do. Matins. John Finley. PraP
These Things I Do Remember. Solomon Ephraim ben Aaron of Lenczicz, *tr. fr. Hebrew by* Nina Davis Salaman. TrJP
These things I wish you for our friendship's sake. Wishes for William. Winifred M. Letts. OnYI
These Things Shall Be. John Addington Symonds. *See* Loftier Race, A.
These thoughts, O Night! are thine. Night. Edward Young. *Fr.* Night Thoughts, IX. EV-3
These thoughts of mine. Thoughts. Duncan Campbell Scott. PeCV
These thoughts of you, the memories and pain. Mist. Georgie Starbuck Galbraith. MuM
These Times. Gertrude Ryder Bennett. MaRV; OQP; QP-2
These times strike monied worldings with dismay. October 1803. Wordsworth. EmBrPo
These to be thankful for: a friend. A Road Song. *Unknown.* PSO
These to His Memory—since he held them dear. Dedication [*or* To the Queen]. Tennyson. *Fr.* Idylls of the King. BHV; PoVP; ViPP
These to their country brought an endless name. Not to Die. Simonides. OnPM
These to you now, O, more than ever now. Epilogue to Rhymes and Rhythms [*or* Epilogue]. W. E. Henley. POTT; ViBoPo
"These Tourists, heaven preserve us! needs must live." The Brothers. Wordsworth. ERP
These trees that fling their leafy boughs aloft. London Trees. Beryl Netherclift. BoTP
These trucks and coaches, only yesterday. Shunting. Basil Dowling. AnNZ
These truly are the Brave. The Negro Soldiers. Roscoe Conkling Jamison. BANP
These tulips are, I think, Egyptian queens. Tulip Queens. Hilda Mary Hooke. CPG
These very pinnacles, and turrets small. The Ancient Mansion. George Crabbe. *Fr.* Posthumous Tales. EnSW
These walls will not forget, through later days. In a Girls' School. David Morton. PoRL
These were men that in harness of battle fought. Battle-Piece. Hesiod. *Fr.* The Shield of Heracles. GrR; PoFr
These were my end: a fierce down-squall from the east. Epitaph of a Sailor. Leonidas of Tarentum. LiTW
These were our brothers, the same kindly mother. On Looking at the School War Memorial. Joseph Manton. ShGoBo
These were our fields. Dust Bowl. Robert A. Davis. GoSl
. . These were poets true. Elizabeth Barrett Browning. *Fr.* A Vision of Poets. PtP
These were the distant fruits of a garden childhood. Fruit. Ruth Miller. BoSA
These were the ones who thanked their God. Psalm XII. A. M. Klein. *Fr.* The Psalter of Avram Haktani. PeCV
These were the seas that you knew, and these were the ways that you followed. To Columbus. John Gould Fletcher. AnAmPo; LA
These, who desired to live, went out to death. Epitaph [*or* Epitaph Written for the Liverpool University Roll of Honour]. Lascelles Abercrombie. AEV; TCPD
These Women all. —— Heath. TuPP
(Women.) OBSC
These Words I Write on Crinkled Tin. Lynette Roberts. ChMP
These words, Phocaea, were Theano's last. A Wife's Grave. Damagetus. OxBG
These words spake Don Henriquez. The Last Words of Don Henriquez. Zalman Schneour. TrJP
These words the poet heard in Paradise. President Garfield. Longfellow. PAH
These words were wingèd with his swift delight. The Power of Music. *Unknown. Fr.* Homeric Hymns. OxBG
Theseus. Bacchylides, *tr. fr. Greek by* Arthur S. Way. GrL
("Dark-prowed ship, The, through surges cleft her way.") GrPo
Sels.
"Lightning flashed, The," *tr. by* Arthur S. Way. GrR
"Lord of Athens' holy ground," *tr. by* C. M. Bowra. OxBG
"So said the valiant master of the lance," *tr. by* J. S. Phillimore. OxBG
Theseus. Price Day. CAG
Theseus. T. Sturge Moore. TCPD
Theseus and Ariadne. Lloyd Mifflin. AA
Theseus and Hippolyta. Walter Savage Landor. BPN
Theseus and Hippolyta. Shakespeare. *See* Music of Hounds, The.
Thesis and Antithesis. Arthur Hugh Clough. ViPP
Thesmophoriazusae, The, *sels.* Aristophanes, *tr. fr. Greek.* Euripides, *tr. by* Benjamin Bickley Rogers. GrR; OxBG
Male Inconsistency, *tr. by* Benjamin Bickley Rogers. GrR
(Chorus of Women, *tr. by* W. L. Collins.) BOHV
("They're always abusing the women," *tr. by* W. L. Collins.) GrPo
Slander! *tr. by* Benjamin Bickley Rogers. GrR
Thespians at Thermopylae, The. Norman Cameron. ChMP
Thetis. Aeschylus, *tr. fr. Greek by* C. M. Bowra. OxBG
Thetis and Achilles. Homer, *tr. fr. Greek by* Sir William Marris. *Fr.* The Iliad, XVIII. LiTW
Thetis and Hephaestus. Homer, *tr. fr. Greek by* Sir William Marris. *Fr.* The Iliad, XVIII. OxBG
(Visit of Thetis to Hephaistos, *longer sel., tr. by* George Chapman.) GrR
Thetis to Achilles. Homer, *pr. tr. fr. Greek by* Samuel Butler. *Fr.* The Iliad, I. LiA
Thevet waited in his workshop. Noël de Thevet. *Unknown.* ChrBoLe
They. Marjorie Meeker. BAP
"They." Siegfried Sassoon. BMEP; ChMo; CMP; HBMV; MaRV
They Accuse Me. Byron. SiTL
They, after the slow building of the house. Asmodai. Geoffrey Hill. NePoEA
They All Belong to Me. Eliza Cook. PGD
They All Love Jack, *with music. Unknown.* ShS
They All Want to Play Hamlet. Carl Sandburg. CoV; PFY
They all were looking for a king. That Holy Thing. George Macdonald. *Fr.* Paul Faber, Surgeon. ChIP; HBV; MaRV; OBEV; OBVV; OQP; QP-1; SDH; StJW; TrPWD; WGRP
They Also. Basho, *tr. fr. Japanese by* H. G. Henderson. OnPM
"They Also Serve . . ." Oliffe Richmond. NeTW
They Also Stand . . . Merrill Moore. CrMA
They always called her Love's detective. Love's Detective. Gamaliel Bradford. PR
They Answer Back; to His Ever-worshipped Will from W. H. "Francis." FiBHP
They are able, with science, to measure. C Stands for Civilization. Kenneth Fearing. TrJP
They Are All Gone [into the World of Light]. Henry Vaughan. ChTr, *abr.*; CoBE; EG; ElSeCe; EOAH; GTBS-W; LiTB; LiTG; LPS-1; MaPo; MePo; OAEP; OBS; OxBoCh; PoE; PoEL-2; ReEn; SeCePo; SeCL; SeEP; SeCV-1; TwHP; TyEnPo; ViBoPo; WHA
(Ascension-Hymn.) CaAE; MeLP; PrWP; SeCeV
(Beyond the Veil.) EV-2
(Departed Friends.) ATP (1935 ed.); AWP; EM-1; EnLi-1 (1949 ed.); EPS; InPo; MaRV; TreFS
(Friends Departed.) BCEP, *abr.*; CoEV; FaBoEn; HBV; LEAP; OBEV
(Friends in Paradise, *abr.*) GrCo-2; GTSL
(Silex Scintillans.) PoD
(World of Light, The.) CH; OHIP; WGRP
They are all gone away. The House on the Hill. E. A. Robinson. AA; AnNE; BAP; CoBA; CV; FaPON; HBMV; InP; LaNeLa; MAP; MoAmPo; MOAP; MPB; PCD; PFE; PG; PIAE; TCAP; TrGrPo; TSW; TSWC; TwP; WHA; YT
They Are All Gone into the World of Light. Henry Vaughan. *See* They Are All Gone.

They are asleep: the utmost crests and the cracks in the mountains. Asleep. Alcman. LiTW
They are at rest. Rest. Cardinal Newman. OBRV; OBVV
They are at rest, the heroes brave. Apotheosis. Joseph Bajza. PoFr
They are bearing him home through the old Virginia valley. Passing of the Unknown Soldier. Vilda Sauvage Owens. DD; MC
They are camped on Chickamauga! Chickamauga—1898. *Unknown.* ADAH
They are coy, these sisters, Autumn and Death. Autumn and Death. Amy Lowell. TBM
They are crying salt tears. Repetitions. Carl Sandburg. HBMV; NP
They are cutting down the great plane-trees at the end of the gardens. The Trees Are Down. Charlotte Mew. MBP; MoAB; MoBrPo; PoTo
They Are Dear Fish to Me. *Unknown.* LPS-1
They are dying! they are dying! where the golden corn is growing. Ireland. Denis Florence MacCarthy. LPS-2; PoFr
They are fluttering and fluttering, like birds upon the tree. Lullaby. Virginia Frazer Boyle. BOL
They Are Forewarned. Winifred Gray Stewart. MuM
They are gathered in the cloister, highest type of womankind. The Sisterhood of God. Patrick F. Durkan. PraNu
They are gathering round. A Concert Party. Siegfried Sassoon. EnLit
They are gone—all is still! Foolish heart, dost thou quiver? A Modern Sappho. Matthew Arnold. VLEP
They are gone who were the sum of summer. For a Parting. Keith Sinclair. AnNZ
They are immortal, voyagers like these. Flight. Harold Vinal. FaPON; GA; MPB; WaKn
They are left alone in the dear old home. They Two. Mrs. Frank A. Breck. WBLP
They are like tightrope walkers, unable to fall. The People at the Party. Lisel Mueller. NePoAm-2
They are living the poems we write. Hymn to Labor. Angela Morgan. MaRV
They are my laddie's hounds. My Laddie's Hounds. Marguerite Elizabeth Easter. AA
They are not all sweet nightingales. Not All Sweet Nightingales. Luis de Góngora, *tr. by* Sir John Bowring. CAW
They are not born secret, moon-eyed and still. Cats. Edith Richmond Blanchard. CIV
They are not dead, the soldiers fallen here. On a World War Battlefield. Thomas Curtis Clark. PGD
They are not gone who pass. They Softly Walk. Hugh Robert Orr. GrCo-1; OQP; MaRV; QP-2
They are not long, the weeping and the laughter. Vitae Summa Brevis Spem Nos Vetat Incohare Longam [*or* Envoy]. Ernest Dowson. AWP; BLV; CBOV; ChTr; EnLit; HBV; InPo; JAWP; LBBV; LoBV; MPB; MoBrPo; NeMA; OBEV (new ed.); OQP; PoRA; POTT; PoVP; QP-2; TOP; TrGrPo; ViBoPo; ViPP; VLEP; WBP; WGRP; WHA
They are not only nightingales. Roundelay. Luis de Góngora, *tr. by* Alice Jane McVan. TeCS
They are not those who used to feed us. The Puzzled Game-Birds. Thomas Hardy. VLEP
They are ordinary men like you and me. The Reporters. Newman Levy. InMe
They Are Ours. A. B. Magil. PoNe
They are rattling breakfast plates in basement kitchens. Morning at the Window. T. S. Eliot. AmPP; AnEnPo; AWP; ChMo; CMP; CoBA; InPo; JAWP; MAP; MoAmPo (1942 ed.); MOAP; NeMA; NePA; OnPM; WBP
They are remembering forests where they grew. Wooden Ships. David Morton. EtS; NV
They are rhymes rudely strung with intent less. A Dedication. Adam Lindsay Gordon. BoAu
They are slaves who fear to speak. Slaves. James Russell Lowell. *Fr.* Stanzas on Freedom. HiLiAm; NeHB; OQP; PCD; QP-2; ShGoBo; WaKn; WBLP
They are such dear familiar feet that go. Be Patient. "George Klingle." PoToHe
They are the arrows. Archery. Ibn Sa'id of Alcala la Real. MooP
They are the foes of silence and of time. Sonnet on Turning a Radio Dial. Anderson M. Scruggs. PoMa
They are the proudest who have met defeat. The Proud. Frances M. Frost. OQP; QP-2
They are unholy who are born. Wild Plum. Orrick Johns. DDA; HBMV; LEAP; MAP; NP; PG (1945 ed.); PoeMoYo; TBM
They are working, beneath the sun. A Song of Street Labor. Caroline A. Lord. DD
They are wrong. It is not the knowing of good from evil. Knowledge. "Jan Struther." QS
They ask me where I've been. Back [*or* Black]. W. W. Gibson. BMEP; ChMo; CMP; GTSL; LBBV; MaRV; PoeMoYo; PYM
They asked me: "Are you happy." Ugliness. Ibn Shakil. MooP
They bade me cast the thing away. Doubt. Helen Hunt Jackson. WGRP
They bade me to my spinning. The Warrior Maid. Anna Hempstead Branch. HBV; LoEn
They bear him through the channels of the crowd. Anno Santo. Stephen Spender. FaBoMo
They bear no laurels on their sunless brows. Failures. Arthur W. Upson. HBV; OQP; PoToHe (1941 ed.); QP-2; WGRP
They beat the tom-tom, they plucked the guitar. Fandango. "Stanley Vestal." IHA
They beat their drums with a loud noise. The Soldier Thought Dead Returns Home. *Unknown. Fr.* Shi King. LiTW
They bid us live each day afresh. On Looking Backward. Ernestine Mercer. MaRV
They bled a bullock, and stripped the hide. Res Publica. J. A. R. McKellar. MoAuPo
They borrow books they will not buy. Non-returnable. Carolyn Wells. DDA
They borrowed a bed to lay His head. The Cross Was His Own [*or* "Borrowed"]. *Unknown.* BePJ; BLPA; BLRP; MaRV
They bowed to him: "O man of God, we'll crown thy head." The Prophet. "Yehoash." TrJP
They bring me gifts, they honour me. If They Honoured Me, Giving Me Their Gifts. "Michael Field." OBMV; TCPD
They bring old ir'n and glass upon the stage. Stage Poets. Dryden. *Fr.* The Conquest of Granada: Prologue. BeR
They brought me ambrotypes. Rutherford McDowell. Edgar Lee Masters. *Fr.* Spoon River Anthology. LiTA; NP; OxBA; SBMV; TOP
They brought me rubies from the mine. Rubies. Emerson. BoFr
"They brought me tidings; and I did not hear." Arthur Davison Ficke. Sonnets of a Portrait Painter, XLIX. PFE
They brought us yesterday to Carcassonne. Carcassonne. Margaret Talbott Stevens. LPS-1
They burn!—nor shall you write them out anew. The Burning Letters. Nikolai Alekseyevich Nekrasov. WaL
They burned lime on the hill and dropped it down here in an iron car. Bixby's Landing. Robinson Jeffers. MOAP
They Bury Him. Marya Zaturenska. *Fr.* Elegies over John Reed. BAP
They call her fair. I do not know. Love's Blindness. William James Linton. VA
They call him Bill, the hired man. William Brown of Oregon. Joaquin Miller. BOHV
They call me and I go. Complaint. William Carlos Williams. PoP
They call me cruel. Do I know if mouse or songbird feels? The Cat. Charles Stuart Calverley. *Fr.* Sad Memories. ChTr
They call me Hanging Johnny. Hanging Johnny. *Unknown.* AmSS; SG
They call me now the Indian Priest. The Mandan Priest. Edward William Thomson. CPG
They call thee rich; I deem thee poor. Treasure. Lucilius. AWP; GrPo; LiTW
They call them pussy willows. The Willow Cats. Margaret Widdemer. BrR; OTPC (1946 ed.); RIS
They call us aliens, we are told. On Behalf of Some Irishmen Not Followers of Tradition. "Æ." AnIL; MM; PoFr
They Called Her Sunshine. Mary Gilmore. NeLNL
They called him a hermit, those who walked. Bart Hinch. August Derleth. DaM
They called him King; and I would have no King. Judas. Gamaliel Bradford. OQP; QP-1
"They called it Annandale—and I was there." How Annandale Went Out. E. A. Robinson. AmP; CoBMV; HBMV; MAP; MoAB; MoAmPo; TwP
They called me to the window, for. Emily Dickinson. MoVE
They called my love a poor blind maid. On a Blind Girl. Baha Ad-din Zuhayr. AWP
They came from only God knows where. Three Tarry Men. Edmund Leamy. MW; PoMa
They came from Persia to the Sacred Way. Peacocks. Walter Adolphe Roberts. PoNe
They came on to fish-hook Gettysburg in this way, after this fashion. The Battle of Gettysburg. Stephen Vincent Benét. *Fr.* John Brown's Body. BeLS
They came out of the sun undetected. The Raid. William Everson. OnHM
They came to tell your faults to me. Faults. Sara Teasdale. BoFr; ChMo; CMP
They Came to the Wedding. Babette Deutsch. NePoAm
They came, you know, and told me you were dead. News. Godfrey Elton. ReTS
They cannot change the hills; though they may hew. Changeless. Martha Haskell Clark. NLK
They cannot wholly pass away. The Departed. John Banister Tabb. AA; LEAP; SPP

They carried the corpse of a sailor drowned. From Dover. L. C. Nielsen. BoDS

They chained her fair young body to the cold and cruel stone. Andromeda. James Jeffrey Roche. AA; HBV; JKCP

They chose me from my brothers: "That's the." What Am I? Dorothy Aldis. OTPC (1946 ed.); RIS; StVeCh (1955 ed.)

They christened my brother of old. The Bell Buoy. Kipling. BLP; PIR; POTT

They claim no guard of heraldry. Aristocrats of Labor. W. Stewart. *Fr.* The True Aristocrat. OQP; PGD; PSO; QP-1

They clear away the grass, the trees. Farming. *Unknown. Fr.* Shi King. LiTW

They Closed Her Eyes. Gustavo Adolfo Bécquer, *tr. fr. Spanish by* John Masefield. Rimas, LXXIII. AnSpL-2; AWP; JAWP; WBP

They come again, those monsters of the sea. Icebergs. William Prescott Foster. EtS

They come, beset by riddling hail. Albuera. Thomas Hardy. *Fr.* The Dynasts. WaaP

They come fluttering helpless to the ground. Snow-Buntings. Frank Prewett. MBP

They come from beds of lichen green. The Assembling of the Fays. Joseph Rodman Drake. *Fr.* The Culprit Fay. GN

They Come! The Merry Summer Months. William Motherwell. LPS-2

They come!—they come!—the heroes come. Evacuation of New York by the British. *Unknown.* PAH

They come to me and talk about God's will. Soliloquy of Lincoln before Manassas. Stephen Vincent Benét. *Fr.* John Brown's Body. PaA

They come with, ah, fell footfall. Fêtes, Fates. John Malcolm Brinnin. LiTA

They could not shut you out of heaven. To ——. Katharine Duncan Morse. HBMV

They course the glass, and let it take no rest. The Vanity of the Beautiful. George Gascoigne. LPS-2

They covered her up with frozen sand. Aizmirstai Mihlai. Arthur Berthold. CAG

They cowered inert before the study fire. Certain American Poets. Odell Shepard. InP; NV

They cried: "Ha, you are hoary!" White Hair. Ibn Ghaiyath. MooP

They crossed her face with blood. A Hope for Those Separated by War. Sidney Keyes. LoPS

They crucified my Lord. Crucifixion. *Unknown.* APW; BoAN-1; TrGrPo

"They cut it in squares." Socratic. Hilda Doolittle ("H. D."). AnEnPo; HoPM

They danced all on the wold. The Wounded Maiden. *Unknown.* BoDaBa

They danced by the roadside on Saturday night. The Dance by the Roadside. Gustaf Fröding. AnSL; WoL

They did not crucify the Lord. Golgotha. Katherine Greenleaf Pedley. ChIP

They did not know that the moon had shone. Moon-Madness. Victor Starbuck. HBMV

They die—the dead return not—Misery. Death. Shelley. EmBrPo

They do but grope in learning's pedant round. Substance and Shadow. Cardinal Newman. GoBC

They do me wrong who say I come no more. Opportunity. Walter Malone. BLP; BLPA; DDA; FaBoBe; HBV; LBAP; MaRV; NeHB; OQP; PTA-1; QP-1; SPP; WBLP; YaD

They do neither plight nor wed. The City of the Dead [*or* City]. Richard Burton. HBV; LBAP; LEAP

They do not count the mountains that they climb. These People. Howard McKinley Corning. AnAmPo; LA

They do not live in the world. The Animals. Edwin Muir. MoPW

They do not speak but into their empty mood. Two Old Men Look at the Sea. J. R. Hervey. AnNZ

They do you wrong who paint you, wondrous Man. To the Master Poet. Thomas Curtis Clark. ChIP

They dogged him all one afternoon. On the Way to the Mission. Duncan Campbell Scott. CaP; OCL

They drafted Michael into the army. Michael. Kostas Kariotakis. MoGP

They dragged you from homeland. Strong Men. Sterling A. Brown. BANP

They Dreamt Not of a Perishable Home. Wordsworth. Ecclesiastical Sonnets, Pt. III, XLV. PeBoSo
(Continued [King's College Chapel].) GEPC

They dressed us up in black. The Funeral. Walter de la Mare. MoVE

They drift away. Ah, God! they drift for ever. Drifting Away. Charles Kingsley. OxBoCh

They drive home the cows from the pasture. Little Brown Hands. Mary Hannah Krout. PTA-1

They drop with periodic regularity. The Preacher Sought to Find Out Acceptable Words. Richard Eberhart. WaP

They dropped like flakes, they dropped like stars. Emily Dickinson. OBAV
(Battle-Field, The.) AA; OHIP

They drove the hammered nails into His hands. Sequel to Finality. Patrick F. Kirby. GoBC; MaRV

"They dug ten streets from that there hole," he said. Millom Old Quarry. Norman Nicholson. ChMP; HaMV

They dug us down and earthed us in, their hasty shovels plying. Old Soldiers. Crosbie Garstin. ReTS

They dwell in the odor of camphor. My Books. Austin Dobson. BPN; MOB

They err who count it glorious to subdue. Milton. *Fr.* Paradise Regained, III. PoFr

They err who say this long-withdrawing line. Paul Veronese: Three Sonnets, III. Sir Samuel Ferguson. IrPN

They fared bravely. The Gripsholm Stone. *Unknown.* PaOS

They find the way who linger where. The Way. Sidney Henry Morse. HBV

They Flee from Me. Sir Thomas Wyatt. *See* Lover, The, Showeth How He Is Forsaken . . .

They fling their flags upon the morn. Spain's Last Armada. Wallace Rice. PAH

They flutter out of white, and run. Bathers. Terence Tiller. ChMP; FaBoMo; NeBP

They follow each other like footsteps. The Air Raid. Archibald MacLeish. PoF

They followed the path all the way. The Last Fairy-Tale. "Lambros Porphyras." MoGP

They fought last year by the upper valley of Son-Kan. The Long War. Li Po. WaaP

They fought like demons of the night. Cats. John Banister Tabb. CIV

They fought south of the Castle. Fighting South of the Castle. *Unknown.* AWP; JAWP; PreP; SoV; TrCh; WaaP; WBP

They fought south of the ramparts. Fighting South of the Ramparts. *Unknown.* LiTW

They found/ Hard by a slab of rock a bubbling spring. Amycus. Theocritus. *Fr.* Idylls. OxBG

They Found Him Sitting in a Chair. Horace Gregory. MoAmPo

They found it in her hollow marble bed. A Roman Mirror Sir Rennell Rodd. OBVV; VA

They found Odysseus dear to Zeus, where hemmed him still. Stag and Jackals. Homer. *Fr.* The Iliad, XI. GrPE

They founded in the turbulent stream their bridge. The Bridge. Albert Verwey. LiTW

They gave him his orders at Monroe, Virginia. The Wreck of the Old 97. *Unknown.* ViBoFo

They gave his flesh the sting of knout. The Greater Guilt. John Richard Moreland. ChIP

They glare—those stony eyes! The Sphinx. Henry Howard Brownell. AA

They gleam, your gods, right fair to see. Dead Gods. Erik Blomberg. AnSL

They glide upon their endless way. The Stars. "Barry Cornwall." CG; OTPC

They grew in beauty, side by side. The Graves of a Household. Felicia Dorothea Hemans. CG; HBV; PTA-2; WBLP

They go along the graveled walks. Seminary. Constance Carrier. NePoAm

They had a picnic in the woods. The Picnic. Elizabeth Madox Roberts. GoBP; RIS

They had a pocketful of stories that they told. A High Place. Eithne Wilkins. NeBP

They had a tale on which to gloat. No Miracle. Daniel Corkery. AnIV

They had brought in such sheafs of hair. The Last Bowstrings. Edward Lucas White. AA

They had got used to him. But when they brought. Washing the Corpse. Rainer Maria Rilke. AnGP

They had known it all before, routine. New Wine, Old Bottles. Colin Newbury AnNZ

They Had No Poet. Don Marquis. DDA

They hailed him King as he passed by. He—They—We. John Oxenham. ChIP

They hailed him, trembling, to the Judgment Seat. Judgment. Kenneth W. Porter. ChIP

They hasten, still they hasten. The Were-Wolves. Wilfred Campbell. VA

They Have Blown the Trumpet. Florence Converse. QS

They have burned to Thee many tapers in many temples. Psalm. Jessie E. Sampter. NV; OQP; QP-1

They have chiseled on my stone the words. Cassius Hueffer. Edgar Lee Masters. *Fr.* Spoon River Anthology. OxBA

They have connived at those jewelled fascinations. Auspice of Jewels. Laura Riding. FaBoMo; LiTA

They have departed, there is no speech with them. *Unknown, tr. fr. Chinese.* The Nineteen Han Poems, XV. WhP

They have dreamed as young men dream. Old Black Men. Georgia Douglas Johnson. CDC; PoNe

They have dressed me up in a soldier's dress. The Jewish

They have dressed me up in a soldier's dress (*continued*)
Conscript. Florence Kiper Frank. BPP; OQP; QP-2; QS
They have dropped a bomb on St. Paul's. Trafalgar Day, 1940. "Clemence Dane." NeTW
They have gone home now, the labourers. Saturday Afternoon. Lilian Bowes-Lyon. AlDL
They have gone over, the god, the friend, the lover. The Purification. Richard Church. MBP; MoBrPo (1942 ed.); POTE
They have hanged Roger Casement to the tolling of a bell. On the Death of Roger Casement. Padraic Colum. PoFr
They have launched the little ship. The Ship. Richard Church. AlDL
They have left Thee naked, Lord; O that they had! Upon the Body of Our Blessed Lord, Naked and Bloody [*or* On Our Crucified Lord Naked, and Bloody]. Richard Crashaw. ACP; EnLi-1; InvP; OAEP; OBS; Po; RiBV; SeCV-1
They have made for Leonora this low dwelling in the ground. Leonora. E. A. Robinson. MaPo; NePA
They have met at last—as storm-clouds. Manassas. Catherine Anne Warfield. BlG; MC; MDAH; PAH
They have no pact to sign—our peaceful dead. The Pact. Alfred Noyes. MaRV
They have no song, the sedges dry. Song in the Songless. George Meredith. BMEP; EmBrPo; GTML; GTSL; OTPC (1946 ed.); PCD; POTT; PoVP; VLEP
They have not fought in vain, our dead. Carry On! Thomas Curtis Clark. OQP; QP-2
They have not gone from us. O no! they are. Sonnet: Our Dead [*or* Our Dead]. Robert Nichols. QS;WGRP
They have pictured Peace at the wheel and loom. Peace Must Come as a Troubadour. Marie Drennan. OQP; QP-1
They have planted them together—our gallant sires of old. The Palmetto and the Pine. Lucy Virginia Smith French. BlG
They have put my bed beside the unpainted screen. Last Poem. Po Chü-i. TrCh
They have said evil of my dear. Medieval Norman Songs, XIV. *Unknown, tr. by* John Addington Symonds. AWP; JAWP; WBP
They have sailed back into the endless night. Into the Endless Night. Lilith Lorraine. UnW
They have shaved his head. The Shaven Beauty. Al-Ramadi. MooP
They have slain you, Sean MacDermott. Lament for Sean MacDermott. "Seumas O'Sullivan." AnIV
They have taken his horse and plume. Eagle Youth. Karle Wilson Baker. AOAH
They Have Taken It from Me. Timothy Corsellis. WaP
They have taken the gable from the roof of clay. Swedes. Edward Thomas. MoVE
They have taken the tomb of our Comrade Christ. Crusaders. Elizabeth Waddell. ChIP; OQP; QP-1
They have triumphed who have died. The Victors. Charles Hanson Towne. OQP; QP-1
They have vanished, the immortal horses of Achilles. The Deathless Ones. Eleanor Glenn Wallis. NePoAm
They have watered the street. A London Thoroughfare Two A.M. Amy Lowell. PoeMoYo; VOD
They Have Yarns. Carl Sandburg. *Fr.* The People, Yes, Sec. 45. LiTA; MoAmPo; PreP
(American Yarns.) StVeCh (1955 ed.)
(Yarns.) GoTP
(Yarns of the People.) NeMA
They haven't got no noses. The Song of Quoodle. G. K. Chesterton. SiTL
They head the list. Horses. Richard Armour. WhC
They heard that she was dying, and they came. Harvest. Robert Haven Schauffler. PC
They heaved the stone; they heap'd the cairn. Sir Samuel Ferguson. *Fr.* Aideen's Grave. TIP
They held her south to Magellan's mouth. The Rush of the *Oregon*. Arthur Guiterman. PAH
They howled 'til Pilate. Crucifixion. Waring Cuney. BANP; GoSl
They hunt chameleon worlds with cameras. Adina. Harold Telemaque. PoNe
They hunt, the velvet tigers in the jungle. India. W. J. Turner. MoBrPo
They in the darkness gather and ask. Our Lady of Idleness. Florence Wilkinson Evans. BAP
They journeyed. Ode. Ibn al-Arabi. AWP; LiTW
They kill me for the death within them. Mihailovich. Roy McFadden. NeIP
They knelt in silent anguish by her bed. A Portrait, II. Christina Rossetti. POTT; VLEP
They knew him well, and could not err. God's Creatures. Christopher Smart. RO
They knew they were fighting our war. As the months grew to years. Pershing at the Tomb of Lafayette. Amelia Josephine Burr. PAH
They know not silence who have never heard. Silence. Inez Barclay Kirby. MuM
They know the lion's power. Killed in Action. Terence Tiller. NeBP
They know the time to go! Time to Go. "Susan Coolidge." GN; OTPC (1946 ed.)
They laid their hands upon my head. The False Friends. Dorothy Parker. PR
They leave the land of gems and gold. A Christmas Carol. Sir Aubrey De Vere. COAH
They leave their love-lorn haunts. Wedded. Isaac Rosenberg. FaBoEn; LO
They leave us nothing. Gray [*or* Grey] Matter. Ford Madox Ford. MBP; MoBrPo (1942 ed.); ReTS
They left behind the insistent strain. Retrospect. Roy Davis. WhC
They left the fury of the fight. Sportsmen in Paradise. T. P. Cameron Wilson. BMEP; PoMA
They left their Babylon bare. The Destruction of Jerusalem by the Babylonian Hordes. Isaac Rosenberg. MeRV
They left to me their house and lands. Inheritance. Anna Hempstead Branch. TBM
They lie on beaches and are proud to tan. Summer Resort. P. K. Page. CaP
They lie who say that love must be. No Sufferer for Her Love. *Unknown.* AnIL
"They lied, those lying traitors all." Medieval Norman Songs, XV. *Unknown, tr. fr. French by* John Addington Symonds. AWP
They lined the long perches like a living color spectrum. The Finches. Philip Murray. NePoAm
They list for me the things I can not know. Knowledge. Thomas Curtis Clark. OQP; QP-2
They Live. Randall Swingler. WaP
They live in their country. Restricted. Miriam Waddington. CaP
They live 'neath the curtain. Puk-Wudjies [*or* Pud-Wudjies]. Patrick R. Chalmers. BoTP; DD; HBVY; HOAH
They lived alone. The Romney. Harriet Monroe. HBMV
They locked his cage; and through the bars. The Ape and the Key. Mary W. Findlater. DiM
They look so solemn and fine. Who are they? The Unknown Soldier. Arthur B. Rhinow. OQP; QP-2
They look'd on each other and spake not; but Gunnar gat him gone. Of the Passing Away of Brynhild. William Morris. *Fr.* The Story of Sigurd the Volsung. TCEP; VA; VLEP
They looked up to the sky, whose floating glow. The Lovers. Byron. LiTL
They lost the Star one night. (Why do men lose.) The Three Magi. Roy Temple House. PSO
They made a feast in the banquet hall. The Prodigal. Sara Henderson Hay. StaSt
They made a myth of you, professor. Mr. Atilla. Carl Sandburg. ImOP
"They made her a grave, too cold and damp." The Lake of the Dismal Swamp. Thomas Moore. BLPA; DaM
They made her a grave where the tall grasses wave. Sister Mary Alphonsa. Eleanor C. Donnelly. PraNu
They made the chamber sweet with flowers and leaves. A Pause [*or* A Meeting]. Christina Rossetti. CBOV; GTBS-D; HBV; NBE; POTT
They made them idols in the elder days. Idols. Richard Burton. TrPWD
They made them ready and we saw them go. The Travellers. Mark A. De Wolfe Howe. AA
They make a scented white blur in the gloom. Flowers in a Library. Carrie Ward Lyon. MOB
They make it only more immortal still. The Cathedral of Rheims. Edmond Rostand. CAW
They marched,/ That sun-gold summer day. Via Dolorosa. Phoebe Smith. PGD
They Marched over the Field of Waterloo. John Masefield. NeTW
They May Rail at This Life. Thomas Moore. PoEL-4
They may talk of love in a cottage. Love in a Cottage. Nathaniel Parker Willis. BAV; HBV; LHV; PR
They meet with but unwholesome springs. Against Them Who Lay Unchastity to the Sex of Women. William Habington. *Fr.* Castara, II. ElSeCe; MePo; OBS; SeEP
They met and bowed and moved apart. The Whole Story. "Madeline Bridges." PR
They met in the red dust. A Meeting. Li Po. WhP
They met me in the day of successe. Shakespeare. *Fr.* Macbeth, I, v. AtBAP
They might have made an end of death. The Knights. Ibn Sa'id of Alcala la Real. MooP
They might not need me; but they might. Emily Dickinson. PoToHe (new ed.)
They mock'd the Sovereign of Ghaznin: one saith. Mahmoud and Ayaz; a Paraphrase of Sa'di. Sir Edwin Arnold. *Fr.* With Sa'di in the Garden. VA
They mouth love's language. A Memory of the Players in a Mirror at Midnight. James Joyce. InvP; TiP; ViBoPo

They move on tracks of never-ending light. The Master Singers. Rhys Carpenter. WGRP
They must to keep their certainty accuse. The Leaders of the Crowd. W. B. Yeats EnLit; MBP; MoAB; MoBrPo; TwP
They named it Aultgraat—Ugly Burn. The Black Rock of Kiltearn. Andrew Young. FaBoTw
They named your name and suddenly. Again for You. Sister Mary Catherine. JKCP (1955 ed.)
They nearly strike me dumb. My Mistress's Boots. Frederick Locker-Lampson. BOHV; HBV; InP; PIAE; TOP
They neither toil nor spin. Violets. Lucy Larcom. ADAH
They never fail who die/ In a great cause. Triumph of the Defeated. Byron. MaRV
They Never Quite Leave Us. Margaret Elizabeth Sangster. WBLP
They never seem to be far away. Within the Veil. Margaret Elizabeth Sangster. BLRP
They never sought; nay, they but woke and came. The Shepherds. Laura Spencer Portor. PEDC
They nod at me and I at stems. Open. Larry Eigner. NeAP
They noticed that virginity was needed. The Presumptuous. W. H. Auden. ChMo
They occupye them so. Worldly Prelates. John Skelton. *Fr.* Colyn Cloute. CoEV
They of the Mean Estate Are Happiest. *Unknown.* SiCE
They offered barter—love. Transaction on the Roman Exchange. Henrietta A. Burke. JKCP (1955 ed.)
They out-talked thee, hissed thee, tore thee. Matthew Arnold. *Fr.* The Last Word. GrCo-1
They paced the moor, 'twas cold and wild. The Heart. Elizabeth Fergusson. ReTS
They paper the walls of their world. The Recluses. Stuart Z. Perkoff. NeAP
They Part. Dorothy Parker. ALV
They parted, with clasps of hand. Comedy. Thomas Bailey Aldrich. PR
They pass me by like shadows, crowds on crowds. The Street. James Russell Lowell. BAP; OQP; QP-2
They pass so close, the people on the street. Footsteps. Hazel Hall. HBMV
They pass through the great iron gates. The Legion of Iron. Lola Ridge. NAMP
They pass upon their old, tremulous feet. The Old Women. Arthur Symons. PoVP
They pity me. Lonely. André Spire. AWP; JAWP; TrJP; WBP
They planned for Christ a cruel death. Revealment. John Richard Moreland. ChIP
They played him home to the House of Stones. The Burial of Sir John McKenzie. Jessie Mackay. AnNZ
They played till the dusk of summer in the wood. Coogan's Wood. Francis Stuart. NeIP
They pluck their palm branches and hail him as King. Palm Sunday and Monday. Edwin McNeill Poteat. ChIP; MaRV
They pushed him straight against the wall. At Sunrise. Rosa Zagnoni Marinoni. PoToHe
They put their finger on their lip. Eros. Emerson. HBV; IAP; TCAP
They put up big wooden gods. Manufactured Gods. Carl Sandburg. WGRP
They questioned my theology. Orthodox. Mark Guy Pearse. MaRV
They raised Him on the rood and pierced Him through. Christ on the Cross. *Unknown.* PSO
They ran through the streets of the seaport town. Greyport [*or* Grayport] Legend. Bret Harte. EtS; GN
They reached the low lying city of Lacedaemon. An At-Home in Sparta. Homer. *Fr.* The Odyssey, IV. GrR
They reached the Maryland bridge of Harper's Ferry. John Brown. Stephen Vincent Benét. *Fr.* John Brown's Body. WoL
They rear'd their lodges in the wilderness. The First Fathers. Robert Stephen Hawker. OBVV
They rise to mastery of wind and snow. Pioneers. Hamlin Garland. AA
They roamed between/ Delicious dells. Prose and Poesy; a Rural Misadventure. Thomas R. Ybarra. WhC
They rode from the camp at morn. Sidney Godolphin. Clinton Scollard. AA; OBAV
They rose in Freedom's rare sunrise. The Men of "Forty-eight." Gerald Massey. PoFr
They rose to where their sovran eagle sails. Montenegro. Tennyson. BPN; PoVP
They rose up in a twinkling cloud. The Stockdoves. Andrew Young. POTE
They roused him with muffins—they roused him with ice. The Baker's Tale. "Lewis Carroll." *Fr.* The Hunting of the Snark. BoChLi; MBP; PoVP
They said, It will be like snow falling. The Snow. Sidney Keyes. NeBP
They said, It will be like snow falling. Variations on a Theme by Sidney Keyes. Eithne Wilkins. NeBP
They said last night. Nusaib. *Unknown.* MOAH
They said: "Now here is gold." Pioneers. Frederick William Ophel. BoAu
They said, "The Master is coming." Unawares. Emma A. Lent. PTA-2
They said this mystery shall never cease. Blake. *Fr.* Gnomic Verses. TrGrPo
They said to him, "It is a very good thing." Homage. Kenneth Fearing. ChMo
They sailed from Argos, and brought down. An Epilogue to Polycrates. Ibycus. OxBG
They sat in a tavern in wicked Port Royal. Dana Burnet. *Fr.* The Sack of Old Panama. PFY; PoeMoYo
They Saw and Believed. Esther Lloyd Hagg. ChIP
They saw her standing in the field. Incarnation. "Maurine Halliburton." MuM; UnW
They saw the sun looke pale, and cast through aire. Presage of Storme. George Chapman. *Fr.* Eugenia. FaBoEn
They Say. Ella Wheeler Wilcox. WBLP
They say a snake the other day. On Jean Fréron. Voltaire. OnPM; TrFP
They say a tropic river threads the seas. The Gulf Stream. Henry Bellamann. EtS
They say a wife and husband, bit by bit. A Bridge Instead of a Wall. *Unknown.* PoToHe (new ed.)
They Say, and I Am Glad They Say. Hilaire Belloc. ALV
They say He was a serious child. The Gentlest Lady. Dorothy Parker. ISi
They say I do not love thee. The American Flag. Charles Constantine Pise. CAW
They say Ideal beauty cannot enter. Hiram Power's Greek Slave. Elizabeth Barrett Browning. BCEP
They say La Jac Brite Pink Skin Bleach avails not. Government Injunction [Restraining Harlem Cosmetic Co.]. Josephine Miles. FiMAP; PoNe
They Say My Verse Is Sad. A. E. Housman. More Poems, Introd. EmBrPo; EnLit
(Dedication.) EnLi-2 (1949 ed.)
They say old man your horse will die. The Dead Horse. *Unknown.* AmSS; AS
They say snow water is not good to drink. Snow Water. Frank Ernest Hill. TBM
They say that, afar in the land of the west. The Green Isle of Lovers. Robert Charles Sands. AA
They say that dead men tell no tales! Dead Men Tell No Tales. Haniel Long. HBMV; MCCG; NP; PC
They say that Edgar Allan Poe was buried in Baltimore. To the Least American, If Not the Greatest, of All American Poets. William Griffith. GA
They say that God lives very high! A Child's Thought of God. Elizabeth Barrett Browning. FaPON; MeMeAg; MPB; OTPC; PCH; PRWS; PTA-1
They say that Hope is happiness. Stanzas for Music. Byron. BPN; EmBrPo
They say that I was in my youth. Limerick. *Unknown.* CenHV
They say that Jockey'll speed weel o't. The Bridal o't. Alexander Ross. EBSV
They say that man is mighty. The Hand That Rules the World [*or* What Rules the World]. William Ross Wallace. DD; MotAn; OHIP; OTPC (1946 ed.); PoRL; PTA-1
They say that men whose veins with a mad dog's venom sicken. Love-Madness. Paulus Silentiarius. GrPE
They say that old age. Unbeliever. Dorothy Dow. HBMV
They say, that Pity in Love's service dwells. Modern Love, XLIV. George Meredith. VA; ViPo
They say that poison-sprinkled flowers. A Fragment. Adam Lindsay Gordon. CaAE
They Say That Shadows of Deceasèd Ghosts. Joshua Sylvester. PeBoSo
(Sonnet: "They say that shadows [*or* shadowes] of deceased ghosts.") EIL; OBS; SeEP
They say that the year is old and gray. New Year Song. Emily Huntington Miller. DD; LH; PoRL
They say that thou wert lovely on thy bier. Death's Alchemy. William Sidney Walker. VA
They say that "Time assuages." Sorrow. Emily Dickinson. WGRP
They Say That Time Is Swift. "Angelus Silesius," *tr. fr. German by* Paul Carus. OnPM
They say the blue king jays have flown. It Will Be a Hard Winter. Olive Tilford Dargan. TBM
They say the eyes of oxen and of sheep. Dead Waters. Georges Rodenbach. TrFP
They say the fate of the trumpeter is misery and sorrow. The Trumpeter. Ai Ching. WhP
They say the Lion and the Lizard keep. Sleep Unbroken. Omar Khayyám, *tr. by* Edward Fitzgerald. *Fr.* The Rubáiyát. GTML; OnPM
They say the Phoenix is dying, some say dead. News of the Phoenix. A. J. M. Smith. BoCaPo

They say the Spanish ships are out. The Dragon of the Seas. Thomas Nelson Page. PAH
They say the war is over. But water still. Redeployment. Howard Nemerov. NePA; TrJP
They say the world is round, and yet. Life's Scars. Ella Wheeler Wilcox. BLPA
They say the world's a sham, and life a lease. The Linnet. Ralph Hodgson. ChMo; CMP
They say there is/ A still pool. Whirlpool. *Unknown.* LiTW; WoL
They say there is a monk on the Tai-pei Mountains. Ode to a Monk on the Tai-pei Mountains. Ts'en Ts'an. WhP
They say there is a sweeter air. A Carriage from Sweden. Marianne Moore. LiTA; LiTM (rev. ed.); MoAB; NePA
They say there is no hope. Sea Gods. Hilda Doolittle. ("H. D."). AtBAP; ChMo; CMP; CP; LiTA; MOAP; NV; PFE
They say there's a high windless world and strange. Mutability. Rupert Brooke. POTT
They say this is His mother. Fourth Station. Ruth Schaumann. ISi
They say Thou art a Myth. Per Contra. Mahlon Leonard Fisher. BAP; ChIP; MaRV
They say, " 'Tis time, go, marry! go!" Cassandra's Song of Celibacy. Gil Vicente. AnSpL-1
They say, when first my mother bore me. Mother. Iraj. PeP
They say your lady friends have no long life. Epigram. Martial, *tr. by* J. A. Pott *and* F. A. Wright. ALV
They say you're in love with that keck-eyed lad. Braggart! Denis Wrafter. OnYI
They scold, that I engage. Bloom of Age. Abu Yahya. MooP
They scoured the hill with steel and living brooms. Mine No. 6. Malcolm Cowley. *Fr.* Blue Juniata. InP; MAP; MoAmPo (1942 ed.)
They see the rowan-trees above the fall. Visitors to the Waterfall. James Reeves. MoP
They seemed, to those who saw them meet. Shadows. Richard Monckton Milnes. HBV; OBEV (1st ed.)
They sell good beer at Haslemere. West Sussex Drinking Song. Hilaire Belloc. MoBrPo
They sent him back to her. The letter came. Not to Keep. Robert Frost. AmPP; AnAmPo; LA; OxBA; TCAP
They sent me to bed, dear, so dreadfully early. Cuddle Down, Dolly. Kate Douglas Wiggin. PPL
They set the fish upon the table. Pesci Misti. L. Aaronson. FaBoTw
They set the slave free, striking off his chains. The Slave. James Oppenheim. BAP; CP; MAP; MaRV; MoAmPo (1942 ed.); NP; PFE; PFY; PoeMoYo; PoFr; PoMa; PoTo; PYM; TrJP; VOD
They shall come in the black weathers. The Waiting Watchers. Henry Treece. NeBP
"They shall not die in vain," we said. Dedication. Ralph Gustafson. BoCaPo; CaP; TwCaPo; TwCV
They Shall Not Know. Wilfrid Scawen Blunt. VLEP
They shall not return to us, the resolute, the young. Mesopotamia 1917. Kipling. SoV
They shall sink under water. The Cities. "Æ." OBMV
They shot young Windebank just here. Young Windebank. Margaret L. Woods. HBV; HBVY; VA
They shut the road through the woods. The Way through the Woods. Kipling. CH; FaBoCh; FaPON; GTBS-D; LoGBV; MCCG; MM; MoVE; OBEV (new ed.); OBVV; Po; POTE; SeCeV; ShBV-2; ThWaDe; TwCV
They sin who tell us love can die. Immortality of Love. Robert Southey. *Fr.* The Curse of Kehama. EV-4; OBRV
They sing their dearest songs. During Wind and Rain. Thomas Hardy. ExPo; RiBV; SeCeV; ViPP
They sit at home and they dream and dally. The Adventurers. May Byron. GA; HBV
They sit at the green baize table. Congress, 1878. Victor Alexis de la Montagne. WoL
They sit in the roots. The Lost Tribe. Robert Finch. CaP
They sleep beneath no immemorial yews. We Shall Remember Them. James Terry White. PEDC
They sleep so calm and stately. Ode for Decoration Day. Theodore P. Cook. MDAH
They Sleep So Quietly. Virginia Lyne Tunstall. Sonnets of an Old Town, III. BLP; LS; TBM
They slept on the field which their valor had won. Beyond the Potomac. Paul Hamilton Hayne. BlG; PAH
They Softly Walk. Hugh Robert Orr. GrCo-1; MaRV; OQP; QP-1
They sold me candles by the pound. Candlemas. Hugh Francis Blunt. JKCP (1955 ed.)
They spake these words and straightway the tent upgathered then. The Cid's Prayer. *Unknown.* *Fr.* The Cid. TeCS
They spat in his face and hewed him a cross. Men Follow Simon. Raymond Kresensky. ChIP; OQP; QP-1
They Speak o' Wiles. William Thom. HBV
They speak of time, as if the hour were split. Madaket Beach. Isabel Harriss Barr. GoYe
They spoke of Progress spiring round. A Ballade of an Anti-Puritan. G. K. Chesterton. BoHV
They stand beside the pasture gate. Cows. Judy Van der Veer. MuM
They stand like penitential Augustines. Gothic Landscape. Irving Layton. TrJP
They stole her from the well beside the wood. Hazel Dorn. Bernard Sleigh. HOAH
They stood above the world. Yes. Richard Doddridge Blackmore. HBV
They stood on the bridge at midnight. How Often. Ben King. BoHV; HBV; PA
They stood rejoicing at his birth. Coming and Going. Grace Hyde Trine. BAP
They stretch across this earth-ball. Alone. Hermann Hesse. TwGV
They strew the lone and ghastly battleground. Our Dead. Victor Hugo. TrFP
They strolled down the lane together. A Farmer's Boy. *Unknown.* DDA
They sung how God spoke out the worlds vast ball. The Creation. Abraham Cowley. *Fr.* Davideis. OBS
They swear the dead come back at night. Waiting. Lizette Woodworth Reese. SPP
They talk of feavours that infect the brains. Sippets of Gruel. Dryden. *Fr.* Prologue to Nahum Tate's "The Loyal General." BeR
They talk of short-lived pleasure—be it so. Mutation. Bryant. AmPP (3d ed.); BAV
They teeter with an inane care among the skewbald stones. The Sheep. Hal Porter. NeLNL
They tell me (but I really can't). My Aunt's Spectre. Mortimer Collins. BoHV
They tell me I am beautiful: they praise my silken hair. Sad Memories. Charles Stuart Calverley. CIV
They tell me, I am shrewd with other men. The Royal Guest. Julia Ward Howe. BoFr; LPS-1
They tell me, Liberty, that in thy name. Liberty for All. William Lloyd Garrison. AA; GrCo-1; IDAH
They tell me she is beautiful, my City. Dusk. DuBose Heyward. HBMV; LS; SPP; TBM
They tell me that euphoria is the feeling of feeling wonderful. No Doctors Today, Thank You. Ogden Nash. ShBV-4
They tell me that I must not love. Love Unsought. Emma Catherine Embury. AA
They tell me that the earth is still the same. The Earth. "Æ." ChMo; CMP
They Tell Me Thou Art Rich. Henry van Dyke. *See* America's Prosperity.
They tell me 'tis decided; you depart. Julia's Letter. Byron. *Fr.* Don Juan. EV-4; ViBoPo
They tell themselves so many little lies, my beloved. Song of Industrial America. Sherwood Anderson. NP
They tell us of an Indian tree. To My Mother. Thomas Moore. MotAn; OHIP; PEDC; PoRL
They tell us there is no stability. Immortality. W. W. Gibson. ChMo; CMP
They tell you Lincoln was ungainly, plain? His Face. Florence Earle Coates. GA; OHIP
They tell you that Death's at the turn of the road. The Unillumined Verge. Robert Bridges. AA
They tell you the poet is useless and empty the sound of his lyre. The Poet. Bernard O'Dowd. BoAu
They That Go Down to the Sea in Ships. Psalms, CVII, Bible, *O.T.* BBV (1951 ed.) (23-31); ChTr (23-31); EtS (23-30); FaPON (23-24); GaP (23-24); MuP (23-31); WaKn (23-30)
(Ocean, The, *23-32, Moulton, Modern Reader's Bible.*) WGRP
They that have power to hurt and will do none. Sonnets, XCIV. Shakespeare. AnFE; BLV; BoLiVe; CaAE; CoEV; ElL; ES; ExPo; FaBoEn; GTBS; GTBS-D; GTBS-W; GTSE; GTSL; LiTB; LiTG; OBEV; MaPo; PeBoSo; PG (1955 ed.); PoEL-2; ReEn; TrGrPo; ViBoPo
They that in course of heavenly spheres are skilled. Amoretti, LX. Spenser. PeBoSo
They that never had the use. An Apologie [*or* Apology] for Having Loved Before. Edmund Waller. MePo; OAEP
They that wash on Monday. Mother Goose. FaBoBe; HBV; HBVY; OTPC (1946 ed.); PPL; TreF
They—the good people—heard her song. The Witch. Louise Morey Bowman. CPG
They thought him a magician, Tycho Brahe. The Torch Bearers: Tycho Brahe. Alfred Noyes. *Fr.* Watchers of the Sky. GrCo-1
They thought to kill old Socrates: instead. Bringers of the Hemlock. Stanton A. Coblentz. ChIP
They threw a stone, you threw a stone. After the Martyrdom. Scharmel Iris. ChIP; MaRV
They throw in Drummer Hodge, to rest. Drummer Hodge. Thomas Hardy. AWP; CoBMV; EnL; EPP; InPo; JAWP; PoE; POTE; PoVP; RiBV; SeCeV; ViP; ViPo; WBP

They tinkle laughter at the solemn hills. Spring Song of Aspens. Lilian White Spencer. PoOW
They to the flour-mill. Frothi's Meal. *Unknown.* *Fr.* The Younger [*or* Snorra *or* Prose] Edda. PaOS
They Toil Not neither Do They Spin. Christina Rossetti. *See* Prayer, A: "Clother of the lily . . ."
They told her she had hair the colour. Daphne. Hildegarde Flanner. HBMV; VOD (1935 ed.)
They told him gently he was made. Man's Place in Nature. *Unknown.* BoHV; PA
They told me Death had lost its sting, and yet. The Refugee. Helen Molyneaux Salisbury. PSO
They told me, Heraclitus, they told me you were dead. Heraclitus. William Johnson Cory, *after* Callimachus. AWP; EnLi-1; EV-5; GrL; GrPo;GrR; GTBS; GTBS-D; GTSE; GTSL; HBV; JAWP; LEAP; LiA; OBEV; OBVV; OuHeWo; OxBG; PCD; PIAE; PoRA; SeCePo; ShBV-4; TOP; TreF; TVSH; VA; ViBoPo; WBP; WoL; WP
They told me I had three months to live. Isaiah Beethoven. Edgar Lee Masters. *Fr.* Spoon River Anthology. NV
They told me I was heir: I turned in haste. My Legacy. Helen Hunt Jackson. HBV; LPS-3
They told me in their shadowy phrase. To Alfred Tennyson. Robert Stephen Hawker. VA
They told me that Life could be just what I made it. Life. Nan Terrell Reed. BLPA
They told me when I came. The Shoe Factory. Ruth Harwood. HBMV
They told me you had been to her. Evidence Read at the Trial of the Knave of Hearts [*or* Important Evidence]. "Lewis Carroll." *Fr.* Alice's Adventures in Wonderland. FaFP; LiTG; OxBoLi; SiTL; ViP
They told us that the King was coming up to see the base. The Inspection. Frederick B. Watt. CaP
They took him to a mountain top to see. Temptation. Winfred Ernest Garrison. ChIP
They took John Henry to the steep hillside. If I Die a Railroad Man. *Unknown.* AS
They took me from the forests and they put me in the town. Young Blood. Lloyd Roberts. CPG
They took the little London girl from out the city street. A Strange Experience. Josephine Pollard. PEOR
They took their stand where the appointed judges. Sophocles. *Fr.* Electra. GrPo
They tore down the toll-gate. The Toll-Gate Man. Wilson MacDonald. CaP; OCL
They tried to hold back Time. The Youth Seekers. Dorothy Brown Thompson. DDA
They trod the streets and squares where now I tread. London Poets. Amy Levy. DiM; OBVV
They Two. Mrs. Frank A. Breck. WBLP
They two had unbridled the horses. Robinson Jeffers. *Fr.* Tamar. AnAmPo; LA
They wait all day unseen by us, unfelt. The Stars. Mary Mapes Dodge. AA
They walk with surer step the paths of men. Motherhood. Karl M. Chworowsky. PGD
They walked by the frolicking sea. Amber. Holger Drachmann. BoDS; LiTW
They warned Our Lady for the Child. Our Lord and Our Lady. Hilaire Belloc. AIDL; GoBC; HBMV; ISi; JKCP; WHL
They was a lawyer from Fredericton came. Perigoo's Horse. *At. to* George Calhoun *and to* John Calhoun. ShS
They was twenty men on the Cabbage Rose. The Fate of the Cabbage Rose. Wallace Irwin. FiBHP
They wear their evening light as women wear. Fields at Evening [*or* These Fields at Evening]. David Morton. AnAmPo; BAP; HBMV; LA
They Went Forth to Battle, but They Always Fell. Shaemas O'Sheel. AnAmPo; AnFE; APA; BAP; CoAnAm; HBV; JKCP; LA; LEAP; LBMV; LiTM (1946 ed.); MaRV; OQP; QP-2; WaaP; WGRP
They went off on the buckboard in the rain. Ranchers. Maurice Lesemann. NP
They went to sea in a Sieve, they did. The Jumblies. Edward Lear. BOHV; BoN; ChTr; CoEV; EnLi-2 (1949 ed.); FaBoBe; FaFP; GFA; HBV; HBVY; KN; LBN; LiL; LiTB; NA; OtMeF; OTPC; OxBoLi; PC; PoE; PoRA; PoVP; RIS; SAS; SeCeV; SiTL; TiPo; VA; ViP
They went with axe and rifle, when the trail was still to blaze. Western Wagons. Stephen Vincent Benét. WaKn
They went with songs to the battle. Laurence Binyon. *Fr.* For the Fallen. ViBoPo
They wer' amid the shadows by night in loneliness obscure. Ibant Obscuri; Vision of Aeneas. Virgil. *Fr.* The Aeneid, VI. LaP
They were a couple well-content. For He Was Scotch and So Was She. Jean Blewett. CPG
They were a lovely pack for looks. John Masefield. *Fr.* Reynard the Fox. OtMeF
They were approaching the region where reigns perpetual summer. Longfellow *Fr.* Evangeline. FaBoEn
They were at play, she and her cat. Femme et chatte [*or* Cat and Lady *or* Woman and Cat]. Paul Verlaine. AWP; JAWP; OnPM; PoC; WBP; WoL
They were islanders, our fathers were. Knowledge. Frederick George Scott. VA
They were met in the Last Inn's tap-room, where the road strikes hands with the sea. Wayfarers. Dana Burnet. EtS
They Were Only Playing Leapfrog. *Unknown.* SiTL
They were passing the toy-shop, his Daddy and he. Dad's Birthday. Arthur Vine Hall. FAOV
They were the oaks and beeches of our species. The Stoics. E. J. Pratt. NeTW
They Were Welcome to Their Belief. Robert Frost. AtBAP
They wheeled me up the snow-cleared gardenway. Elfin Skates. Eugene Lee-Hamilton. OBVV
They which read Horace, Virgil, and the rest. Thomas Bastard. SiCE
They whispered when she passed—gave knowing looks. The Sinner. Margaret E. Bruner. PoToHe
They whisted all, with fixèd face attent. Certain Books of Virgil's Aeneis. Virgil, *tr. by* the Earl of Surrey. *Fr.* The Aeneid, II. EnLi-1; EPP; LiTB; SiCE; SiPS; TuPP
They who create rob death of half its stings. The Sovereigns [*or* Sovereign Poets]. Lloyd Mifflin. AA; AnAmPo; HBV; LA; WGRP
They who have best succeeded on the stage. Epilogue. Dryden. *Fr.* The Conquest of Granada, Pt. II. CEP; EiPP; FiP; GePC; SeCV-2; SeEP
They who once probed and doubted now believe. Beyond Electrons. Adelaide P. Love. OQP; QP-2
They Who Possess the Sea. Marguerite Janvrin Adams. EtS
They Who Wait. Charles Buxton Going. HBMV
They whose life is given utterly over to valor. Epitaph: Inscription from Anticyra. *Unknown.* WaaP
They will never die on that battlefield. Uccello. Gregory Corso. NeAP
They will not, then, with victory return. Poem. Ann Louise Hayes. PtPa
They Will Say. Carl Sandburg. PC
They will take us from the moorings, they will tow us down the Bay. Homeward Bound. D. H. Rogers. AnNZ; BoAu; EtS
They will tell—in a province of some simple folk. Corpus Christi. Margery Mansfield. NV
They wind a thousand soldiers round the king. A Ribbon Two Yards Wide. Alfred Kreymborg. HBMV
They with alternate change for one day keep. Castor and Polydeuces [*or* Twin Brothers]. Pindar. *Fr.* Nemean Odes, X. GrR; OxBG
They wondered why the fruit had been forbidden. W. H. Auden. *Fr.* In Time of War. ChMo
They worked at night, they went through. Terror. Maximilian Aleksandrovich Voloshin. TrRV
They would have fought again/ Had not the Major stepped between the men. The Shooting of the Cup. John G. Neihardt. *Fr.* The Song of Three Friends. PoOW
They wove for me a little cloak. Codes. Lois Seyster Montross. HBMV
They wrong with ignorance a royal choice. Magic. Lionel Johnson. POTT
They yell at the poet. The Worker Poet. Vladimir Mayakovsky. TrRV
They'll carve it in stone and the hand in the air. Duel. Stepan Shchipachev. RuPo
They'll come again to the apple tree. The Building of the Nest. Margaret Elizabeth Sangster. DD; HBV; HBVY
They'll None of 'em Be Missed. W. S. Gilbert. *See* Ko-Ko's Song ("As some day it may happen").
They'll talk of him for years to come. Popular Recollections of Bonaparte. Pierre Jean de Béranger, *tr. by* Francis Sylvester Mahony. LPS-3
They'll walk no longer to Mass on Sunday. The Shawls. Monk Gibbon. NeIP; OxBI
They're always abusing the women. Chorus of Women. Aristophanes. *Fr.* Thesmophoriazusae. BOHV; GrPo
They're big. Grownups. William Wise. TiPo (1959 ed.)
They're building a skyscraper. Building a Skyscraper. James S. Tippett. MPB
They're going to build a flathouse on the lot next door to me. The Vacant Lot. Nathalia Crane. LPS-1
They're hiding by the pebbles. Sea Fairies. Eileen Mathias. BoTP
They're holding a revival at New Hope Meeting house. The Mourner's Bench. Edgar Lee Masters. ChMo; CMP
They're nice—one would never dream of going over. A Healthy Spot. W. H. Auden. EnLit
They're Shifting Father's Grave. *Unknown.* CoMu
They're tunin' up the orchestray down at old Bill Haller's. Bill Haller's Dance. Robert V. Carr. PoOW
They've builded wooden timber tracks. Progress. Frank Wilmot. BoAu
They've Crucified Our Lord. Alice Mortenson. BePJ

They've got a brand-new organ, Sue. The New Church Organ. Will M. Carleton. BOHV; LPS-3
They've lost their way. Flower of Hemp. Louise Ayres Garnett. NV
They've marched them out of old Yorktown, the vanquished redcoat host. The Ride of Tench Tilghman. Clinton Scollard. GA; MC
They've named a cruiser *Dixie*—that's whut the papers say. The Warship *Dixie*. Frank L. Stanton. MDAH
They've paid the last respects in sad tobacco. Padraic O'Conaire—Gaelic Storyteller. F. R. Higgins. OBMV; OnYI; OxBI; PtP
They've putten her into prison strang. Sir Aldingar (C *vers.*). *Unknown.* ESPB
They've started a discussion. Being Danish. Kaj Munk. BoDS
They've taken the cosy bed away. Kit's Cradle. Juliana Horatia Ewing. CIV; SAS
They've turned at last! Good-by, King George. Haarlem Heights. Arthur Guiterman. PAH
Thick and stormy was the night. My Delight. Gamaliel Bradford. HBMV
Thick as the Bees. Pope. *Fr.* The Temple of Fame. BeR
Thick-fleeced lamb came trotting by, A. Tame Animals I Have Known. Nixon Waterman. BoN
Thick grow the green thistles. The Green Thistles. *Unknown.* WhP
Thick grow the plantains. The Plantains. *Unknown.* WhP
Thick in its glass. Poor Henry. Walter de la Mare. HBMV
Thick lids of Night closed upon me, The. The Souls of the Slain. Thomas Hardy. LiTB; PoEL-5; PoVP
Thick Lies the Dew. *Unknown, tr. fr. Chinese.* WhP
Thick rise the spear-shafts o'er the land. The Burghers' Battle. William Morris. BPN; PoVP; VA
Thick-sprinkled Bunting. Walt Whitman. IAP
Thick trees swallow a mountain trail. The Temple. Tu Fu. OnPM
Thick wool is muslin to-night and the wire. A Cold Night. Bernard Spencer. WaP
Thickly blossomed creeping vine tells, The. The Creeping Vine. Aristotelis Valaoritis. MoGP
Thickness of paint or flesh cannot deface. Sestina on Her Portrait. Howard Nemerov. WaP
Thief, The. Abraham Cowley. *Fr.* The Mistress. BEL; ElSeCe; EnLi-1; EnLit; OAEP; SeCL; WHA
Thief. Robert Graves. POTE
Thief, The. Irene F. Pawsey. BoTP
Thief, The. *Unknown.* LO; MeRV; OBS; OxBoCh; SeCL
Thief and the Cordelier, The. Matthew Prior. EV-3
Thief on the Cross, The. Harriet Monroe. OQP; QP-1
Thief that has leaped Heaven's star-spiked wall! Franciscus Christificatus. Francis Thompson. SaFP
Thiepval Wood. Edmund Blunden. AnFE
Thieves, The. Robert Graves. GTBS-W; LiTM (rev. ed.); OxBI
Thieves and the Ass, The. La Fontaine, *tr. fr. French by* Elizur Wright. OnPM
Thieving locksmith died of late, A. On a Thieving Locksmith. *Unknown.* GoTP
Thimble, The. Al-Liss, *tr. fr. Arabic by* A. J. Arberry. MooP
Thin air I breathe and birds use for flying. Air. Edwin Denby. CrMA
Thin are the night-skirts left behind. Insomnia. Dante Gabriel Rossetti. BPN; PoVP; VLEP
Thin birches stood on Stockholm's nesses. Visual Memory. Harry Martinson. LiTW
Thin Diocleia I would see, for though. Marcus Argentarius, *tr. fr. Greek by* Elsie Spoerl. GrPo
Thin, erect and silent. Alone. Elsie Laurence. CaP
Thin Façade for Edith Sitwell, A. John Malcolm Brinnin. FiBHP
Thin ghost of a man. Saint Francis. Brother Rudolph. SaFP
Thin gray shadow on the edge of thought, A. Apparitions. Alice Corbin. NP
Thin ice/ Free advice. David McCord. TiPo (1959 ed.)
Thin leaves wave on the *wu-t'ung* tree beside the well. Lonely Night in Early Autumn. Po Chü-i. ChLP; WhP
Thin-legged, thin-chested, slight unspeakably. Apparition. W. E. Henley. *Fr.* In Hospital. BEL; EnLi-2 (1949 ed.); POTT; PoVP; TCEP; TrGrPo
Thin lips can make a music. Redivivus. Donald Davidson. SPP
Thin mist, dense clouds sorrow over the whole day. The Mid-autumn Festival. Li Ch'ing-chao. WhP
Thin Potomac scarcely moves, The. The Potomac. Karl Shapiro. CoBMV
Thin rain seeps along the apple boughs, A. Sonnets from a Sequence, XXI. Shirley Barker. AnAmPo
Thin Rain, whom are you haunting. Wraith. Edna St. Vincent Millay. OBAV
Thin rank at regular intervals lines, A. The Proud Trees. Walter H. Kerr. NePoAm-2
Thin, scattered ranks of snow. The Lineman. William Hurd Hillyer. PoeMoYo
Thin shrill row of poplars, A. Pruned Trees. Gloria Goddard. BAP
Thin wind seemed uneasy, The. The Gallows Tree. F. R. Higgins. OnYI
Thine. Annie S. Hawks. PraP
Thine absence overflows the rose. Old Song. Hart Crane. ChMo
Thine arms, O Mother, be outspread. Inscription on a Shrine near Ischl. Elizabeth, Empress of Austria-Hungary. CAW
Thine Early Death. Theocritus, *tr. fr. Greek by* "D. M. P." LiA
Thine elder that I am, thou must not cling. Sweeter Far than the Harp, More Gold than Gold. "Michael Field." OBMV
Thine eyes, dear one, dot dot, are like, dash, what? Love-lilts. Marion Hill. BOHV
Thine eyes I love, and they, as pitying me. Sonnets, CXXXII. Shakespeare. OAEP; OBSC; PeBoSo; SiCE
Thine eyes shall see the light of distant skies. To Cole, the Painter, Departing for Europe. Bryant. AmPP (4th ed.); CoV
Thine Eyes Still Shined. Emerson. IAP; MOAP
Thine is the balmy breath of morn. Solitude. James Thomson. *Fr.* Hymn on Solitude. BeR
Thine is the mystic melody. Coleridge. George Sidney Hellman. AA
Thine, most gracious Lord. Thine. Annie S. Hawks. PraP
Thine old-world eyes—each one a violet. On a Miniature. Henry Augustin Beers. AA
Thine own wish wish I thee in every place. A Christmas Wish. Celia Thaxter. SDH
Thine was the corn and the wine. The Bells of San Gabriel. Charles Warren Stoddard. CAW; JKCP
Thing could barely stand, The. Yet taken. The Bull Calf. Irving Layton. PeCV
Thing, he said, would come that night at three, The. The Messenger. H. P. Lovecraft. DaM
"Thing is but a statue after all, The!" W. S. Gilbert. *Fr.* Pygmalion and Galatea. VA
Thing long sought, A. Prelude. Neil Tracy. BoCaPo
Thing Made Real, The. Ron Loewinsohn. NeAP
Thing of Beauty, A [Is a Joy Forever]. Keats. *Fr.* Endymion, I. ATP; BEL; BLV; BoLiVe; CoBE; EM-2; EnLit; EnRP; EV-3; FaFP; FiP; GrCo-2; LiTB; LiTG; LPS-2; MaRV; MCCG; OBRV; OTPC; PG; StVeCh, 5 *ll.*; TCEP; TOP; TreF; TrGrPo
(Beauty.) BCEP
(Credo.) ERP
(Endymion.) BBV (1951 ed.), 5 *ll.*; BPN; CBE; EmBrPo; EnLi-2; HiLiEn, 5 *ll.*; NeHB, 6 *ll.*; OAEP; PreP; TyEnPo; ViBoPo
(From "Endymion.") OuHeWo
Thing one learns too much, The. Learning. Mary Fullerton. NeLNL
Thing that goes the farthest towards making life worth while, The. Let Us Smile. Wilbur D. Nesbit. WBLP
Thing that numbs the heart is this, The. Firm Belief. *Unknown.* PoToHe (new ed.)
Thing that's rich in tears is sweet, A. Born of Tears. W. H. Davies. GTBS-D
Thing We Long For, The. James Russell Lowell. *Fr.* Longing. OQP; QP-2
Thing which fades, A. Ono no Komachi. *Fr.* Kokin Shu. AWP; JAWP
Things. Dorothy Dow. HBMV; TBM
Things. Aline Kilmer. MCCG
Things. William Jay Smith. TiPo (1959 ed.)
Things Dead. Marcel Schwob, *tr. fr. French by* William Brown Meloney. TrJP
Things Delightful. Oisin, *tr. fr. Irish by* George Sigerson. TIP
Things did not vibrate so when I was young. Lines Written in a Moment of Vibrant Ill-Health. Morris Bishop. WhC
Things Divine, The. Jean Brooks Burt. PTA-2
Things I Like. Marjorie H. Greenfield. BoTP
Things I Miss, The. Thomas Wentworth Higginson. PraP; TrPWD
Things I Used to Do, *with music. Unknown.* AS
Things Lovelier. Humbert Wolfe. LoPS; MBP; MoBrPo; TrJP
Things native sweetly grew. Thomas Traherne. *Fr.* Christendom. FaBoEn
Things never changed since the Time of the Gods. Four Folk-Songs in Hokku Form, I. *Unknown.* LiTW
Things Not Seen. Mark Turbyfill. NP
Things of every day are all so sweet, The. Life's Common Things. Alice E. Allen. WBLP
Things of the Spirit, The. Douglas Malloch. MaRV
Things owned by mortals needs must mortal be. Lucian, *tr. fr. Greek by* Lord Neaves. GrPo
Things she knew, let her forget again, The. Prayer for a New Mother. Dorothy Parker. QS

Things That Are Caesar's, The. St. Matthew, XXII: 15-22, Bible, *N.T.* TreF
Things that are good and great my land has given. The Great Land. William Rose Benét. NeTW
Things that are lovely. Things. Dorothy Dow. HBMV; TBM
"Things That Are More Excellent, The." Sir William Watson. OHFP
Things That Cause a Quiet Life, The. Martial. *See* Means to Attain Happy Life, The.
Things That Endure, The, *sel.* Florence Wilkinson Evans.
"What wish you, immortality?" OQP; QP-2
Things That Endure. Ted Olson. WBLP
Things that make a life to please, The. The Means to Attain Happy Life. Martial. WoL
Things that make a virgin please, The. The Virgin. Katherine Philips. LO
Things That Never Die. Charles Dickens. MaRV
Things, The, that one grows tired of—O be sure. Wonder and Joy. Robinson Jeffers. BAP; PoTo
Things to Be Loved. Sister Mary Madeleva. SaFP
Things to draw with compasses, The. Circles. Harry Behn. LiL
Things to Remember. Blake. *See* Robin Redbreast, A.
Things you heard that blessed be. Grenstone River. Witter Bynner. PFY; PoeMoYo
Thingumbob, The. *Unknown.* BOHV
Think. Charles Weekes. AnIV; OnYI
Think before You Act. Mary Elliott. HBVY
"Think, father, through all ages now." The Torch Bearers: Celeste and Galileo. Alfred Noyes. *Fr.* Watchers of the Sky. GrCo-1
Think, in this batter'd Caravanserai. Omar Khayyám, *tr. by* Edward Fitzgerald. *Fr.* The Rubáiyát. ChTr; OBVV
Think it not idolatry. In Gusts of Music. Sister Davida. JKCP (1955 ed.)
Think It Not Strange. Amy Carmichael. MaRV
Think, Marquise! what if my face. Stanzas to the Marquise. Corneille. TrFP
Think me not unkind and rude. The Apology. Emerson. AmPP (3d ed.); BAV; CoBA; IAP; OBAV; PG (1945 ed.)
Think naught a trifle. *Unknown.* PoToHe (new ed.)
Think No More, Lad [Laugh, Be Jolly]. A. E. Housman. A Shropshire Lad, XLIX. BPN; ChMo; CMP; EmBrPo; InP; InPo; PoLFOT; PoVP
Think No More of Me. Wilfrid Scawen Blunt. VLEP
Think not, because I wonder where you fled. Another Dark Lady. E. A. Robinson. LoPo; TwP
Think not, 'cause men flatt'ring say. To A. L.: Persuasions to Love. Thomas Carew. EPS; EV-2
Think not from pride, nor yet from bitterness. Prometheus' Gifts to Man. Aeschylus. *Fr.* Prometheus Bound. GrR
Think not I love him, though I ask for him. Love Dissembled. Shakespeare. *Fr.* As You Like It, III, v. LPS-1
Think not I may not know thee kneeling there. Dusk. Archibald MacLeish. HBMV
Think not, my dearest, though I love to speak. Gothic. Louis Untermeyer. AnAmPo; LA
Think not, my Phoebe [*or* Phebe], 'cause a cloud. To His Mistress [*or* Mistris] Confined. James Shirley. LO; OBS; SeCL
Think not, O King! thy sceptre or thy pow'r. Satire on Mahmúd. Firdausi. *Fr.* Shah Namah. PeP
Think not, O man that dwells herein. Upon the New-built House at Appleton. Thomas, Lord Fairfax. SeCL
Think not on me, as countless men have thought. Christ Speaks. Wade Oliver. MaRV
Think not that I for pride and stubbornness. Prometheus the Teacher of Men. Aeschylus. *Fr.* Prometheus Bound. LiTW; OxBG
Think not that mystery has place. Mystery. John Drinkwater. TCPD
Think not thy wisdom can illume away. Epigrams, XIX. Sir William Watson. LEAP
Think not to cozen me, my dear. To Philaenis. Poseidippus. GrR
Think of all the games you play. Trees Used in Games and Sports. Mary Isabel Curtis. GFA
"Think of Death!" the grave-stones say. Two Epitaphs. *Unknown.* PEOR
Think of Dress in Every Light. John Gay. *Fr.* Achilles. InvP
(Song.) OBEC
Think of each house you stay in as a tent. Campers. Robert Finch. TwCaPo
Think of me as your friend. The Heart's Anchor. William Winter. PoToHe
Think of the storm roaming the sky uneasily. Little Exercise. Elizabeth Bishop. CrMA; MoAB; MoAmPo (1950 ed.); UnPo (3d ed.)
Think of the things that make you happy. Thinking Happiness. Robert E. Farley. PoToHe
Think on him, Lord! we ask thy aid. In Extremity. Phoebe Cary. PraP
Think on St. Francis' feathered friends, dear heart. "That Which Hath Wings Shall Tell." Linda Lyon Van Voorhis. GoBC
Think on These Things. Philippians, IV: 8, Bible, *N.T.* GrCo-1
("Whatsoever things are true.") TiPo (1952 ed.)
Think that this world against the wind of time. Signature for Tempo. Archibald MacLeish. MoVE
Think, the ragged turf-boy urges. Think. Charles Weekes. AnIV; OnYI
Think [*or* Thinke] then, my soul, that death is but a groom. John Donne. *Fr.* Of the Progresse of the Soule; the Second Anniversary. CoEV; OBS; OxBoCh
Think thou and act; tomorrow thou shalt die. The Choice, 3. Dante Gabriel Rossetti. The House of Life, LXXIII. ATP; BEL; BPN; EmBrPo; EnL; EnLi-2; EPP; GTML; HBV; MyFE; OBEV (new ed.); OBVV; OHIP; PIAE; POTT; PoVP; PreP; TOP; ViBoPo; ViPo; VLEP; WHA
Think, when a starry night of bitter frost. A Sonnet. Conrad Aiken. AnEnPo
Think ye the desolate must live apart. Desolation. Henry T. Tuckerman. APW
Think ye the joys that fill our early day. Life. George Crabbe. OBEC
Think you I am not fiend and savage too? To the White Fiends. Claude McKay. BANP
Think you 'mid all this mighty sum. Communion with Nature. Wordsworth. *Fr.* Expostulation and Reply. MaRV
Think you the dead are lonely in that place? The Dead. David Morton. PAH
Think you to escape. Immunity. Thomas à Kempis. *Fr.* Imitation of Christ. ChIP; OQP; QP-1
Thinke then, my soule, that death is but a groome. *See* Think then, my soul, that death is but a groom.
Thinker, The. Berton Braley. BLPA; BTP; MW; NeHB; OQP; PEDC; PoMa; POT; PoTo; QP-1; StVeCh (1940 ed.); WBLP
Thinkers and airmen—all such. To Poets and Airmen. Stephen Spender. NeTW; PoF; WaP
Thinking. Walter D. Wintle. WBLP
Thinking, entangling shadows in deep solitude. Twenty Poems of Love, No. XVII. "Pablo Neruda." TwSpPo
Thinking Happiness. Robert E. Farley. PoToHe
Thinking of a Friend Lost in the Tibetan War. Chang Chi, *tr. fr. Chinese by* Witter Bynner. BoFr
Thinking of a Master. Richard Church. HaMV
Thinking of Her. Liu Yung, *tr. fr. Chinese.* ChLP
Thinking of Li Po. Tu Fu, *tr. fr. Chinese.* WhP
Thinking of My Brother. Su T'ung-po, *tr. fr. Chinese by* Yu Min-chuan. WhP
Thinking of My Brother in Shantung on the Ninth Day of the Ninth Moon. Wang Wei, *tr. fr. Chinese.* WhP
Thinking of My Brothers on a Moonlit Night. Tu Fu, *tr. fr. Chinese.* WhP
(Thinking of My Brothers, *tr. by* W. J. B. Fletcher.) OnPM
Thinking of My Love. Li Yu, *tr. fr. Chinese.* ChLP
Thinking of Shores. Laurence Binyon. LBBV; LoPo
Thinking of the Past. Po Chü-i, *tr. fr. Chinese by* Arthur Waley. TrCh
Thinking of you, and all that was, and all. Monna Innominata, IX. Christina Rossetti. EmBrPo; ViPo
Thinking of you, I think of the *coureurs de bois.* Coureurs de Bois. Douglas Le Pan. BoCaPo (1948 ed.); CaP
Thinking on thee, thy beauties then. Sir John Suckling. LO
Thinking to shrive me in the solitude. The Pagan. Mary Sinton Leitch. LS
Thinking tomorrow remains, thou heart's frail flower-of-cherry. Four Folk-Songs in Hokku Form, 2. *Unknown.* LiTW
Think'st Thou, Kate? *Unknown.* ElSeCe; TuPP
Think'st thou that this love can stand. Ametas and Thestylis Making Hay-Ropes. Andrew Marvell. ALV; InvP; SeCL
Think'st Thou to Seduce Me Then. Thomas Campion. ElL
Third and Fourth. Keidrych Rhys. NeBP
Third Cycle of Love Poems, *sels.* George Barker.
Shut the Seven Seas against Us. MoAB; MoBrPo (1950 ed.); NeMA
"This is that month, Elizabeth." NeBP
Third Dimension, The. Denise Levertov. NeAP
Third Duino Elegy, The. Rainer Maria Rilke, *tr. fr. German.* *Fr.* The Duino Elegies. AnGP, *tr. by* R. F. C. Hull; LiTW, *tr. by* Stephen Spender *and* J. B. Leishman
Third Eclogue, The. Michael Drayton. *See* Song to Beta.
Third in our Borough's list appears the sign. The Caroline. George Crabbe. *Fr.* The Borough. SeCePo
Third Kiss, The: Butterfly Kisses. Johannes Secundus, *tr. fr. Latin by* F. A. Wright. LaP
Third Limick. Ogden Nash. NePA
Third Madrigal. Gene Derwood. NePA
Third Mate. John Masefield
(Young Man's Fancy, A. *At. to* R. E. McGowan *by* Masefield.) SG

Third of February, The, 1852. Tennyson. PoFr
Third of November, The. Bryant. PEOR
Third Pastor's Song, The. Nicholas Breton. *See* Merry Country Lad, The.
Third Proposition, The. "Madeline Bridges." BOHV
Third Row, Centre. William Rose Benét. WhC
Third Sunday after Easter, The, and the first dominical day of the white month of Mary. Ave Maria. Henriette Charasson. CAW; ISi
Third Time. Carlos Pellicer, *tr. fr. Spanish by* Dudley Fitts. AnCL
Third Wonder, The. Edwin Markham. MAP
(Breathless Awe.) MaRV
Thirsis a youth of the inspired train. *See* Thyrsis, a youth . . .
Thirst. Ralph Bergengren. FAOV
Thirst. Emily Dickinson. WGRP
Thirst of reign [*or* raigne] and sweetness of a crown, The. Ambition. Christopher Marlowe. *Fr.* Tamburlaine the Great. CoEV; NBE; ViBoPo
Thirsting Amphora. Rafael Heliodoro Valle, *tr. fr. Spanish by* Muna Lee. AnCL
Thirsty earth soaks up the rain, The. Drinking [*or* Anacreontic on Drinking]. Abraham Cowley. ALV; CEP; EG; ElSeCe; EnLi-1 (1949 ed.); EPS; EV-2; HBV; LEAP; LoBV; MePo. OBEV; OtMeF; PG; PoFS; PoP; ReEn; SeCePo; SeCV-1; SeEP; ShBV-4; TrGrPo; WhC
Thirsty Flowers. Arthur A. Knipe. GFA
Thirsty Poet, The. John Philips. *Fr.* The Splendid Shilling. OBEC
Thirteen men by Ruan Shore. Dolor Oogo. Sir Arthur Quiller-Couch. SG
Thirteen o'Clock. Kenneth Fearing. ExPo
Thirteen Sisters, The. Stephen Vincent Benét. *Fr.* John Brown's Body, I. TreF
Thirteen Ways of Looking at a Blackbird. Wallace Stevens. CoBMV; CoV; LiTM; MAPA; OnAP; PoFS; TwAmPo
Thirteen's no age at all. Thirteen is nothing. Portrait of a Girl with Comic Book. Phyllis McGinley. CrMA
Thirteenth has come again, The . . . But is still the first. Artemis. Gérard de Nerval, *tr. by* Barbara Howes. AnFP
Thirteenth Kiss, The: Love, Life and Death. Johannes Secundus, *tr. fr. Latin by* F. A. Wright. LaP
Thirteenth one returns, The . . . Yet she's the first. Artemis. Gérard de Nerval, *tr. by* Hubert Creekmore. LiTW
Thirteenth Song, The, *abr.* Michael Drayton. *Fr.* Polyolbion. ReEn
Sels.
Forest of Arden ("My native country then, which so brave spirits hast bred"). SeEP
"Forest so much fallen from what she was before, The." SeCePo
"Of all the beasts." OBS
"Upon the midlands now th' industrious muse doth fall." ReIE; TuPP
"When Phoebus lifts his head." OBS
Thirteenth Station. William A. Donaghy. *Fr.* The Stations of the Cross. ISi
Thirteenth Station, The. Caroline Giltinan. LS
Thirty Bob a Week. John Davidson. FaBoTw; FaFP; LiTB; LiTG; LiTM (rev. ed.); PoFr, *abr.*; PoVP
Thirty days hath September. Mother Goose. FaBoBe; GoTP; HBV; HBVY; OTPC (1946 ed.); OxNR; PCH; PECK; PPL; RIS; SiTL; StVeCh
Thirty-eight years. Yes, neither less nor more. Sonnets, I. Leonard Bacon. TBM
Thirty elongated seconds. For Dinah, the Adeneys' Cat. Anne Wilkinson. PeCV
Thirty-first of May. Frederick Tennyson. VA
Thirty Pieces of Silver for Jesus. Helene Mullins. StJW
33 Days, *sel.* Nicephorus Vrettakos, *tr. fr. Modern Greek by* Rae Dalven.
"Thus it happened then in Greece." MoGP
Thirty [*or* Twenty] white horses upon a red hill. Mother Goose. HBV; HBVY; OTPC; OxNR; PPL; RIS; SiTL; StVeCh; TiPo
This a servant made me sworn. Her Virtue. George Wither. *Fr.* Fair Virtue, the Mistress of Philarete. EV-2
This Above All. Shakespeare. *See* Polonius' Advice to Laertes.
This Advent moon shines cold and clear. Advent. Christina Rossetti. PoVP; VLEP
This ae nighte, this ae nighte. A Lyke-Wake Dirge [*or* Cleveland Lyke-Wake Dirge *or* Final Dirge]. *Unknown.* ACP; AnFE; AtBAP; BCEP; BrBE; CBOV; CH; ChTr; DaM; EBSV; EnSB; FaBoCh; GoBC; HBV; HoPM; LoBV; MeRV; OBB; OBEV; OtMeF; OxBoCh; PoD; PoEL-1; PoLi; ReaPo; SeCeV; ShBV-2
This afternoon disturbs within the mind. Afternoon in Florence. Elizabeth Jennings. PoN
This afternoon I take the path alone. In Loco. Peter Jackson. BoSA
This afternoon in loud Jerusalem. Fourth Station [*or* He Meets His Mother]. William A. Donaghy. *Fr.* The Stations of the Cross. ISi; QS
This afternoon it is raining as never before, and I. Dregs. César Vallejo. AnCL
This afternoon on Willow-Walk alone. William Ellery Leonard. *Fr.* Two Lives, Pt. III. TBM
This age it is the same with less remembered. The Rape of Europa. R. P. Blackmur. CrMA
This age-old church, dream-stricken yesterday. The Serenade. Sister Mary Madeleva. Christmas in Provence, I. WHL
This Age, This Faust. George Reavey. SiTL
This Air That Blows In from the Sea. Elizabeth J. Coatsworth. BrR
This Alice. Herbert Morris. PoRA
This also said Phocylides. The Exception. Phocylides. OxBG
This also said Phocylides. A Small City on a Rock. Phocylides. OxBG; WoL
This Amber Sunstream. Mark Van Doren. GoYe; LiTA; LiTM (1946 ed.); MoPo; MoVE; TrGrPo (1942 ed.)
This ancient hag. Mexican Market Woman. Langston Hughes. GaP; TiPo (1952 ed.)
This ancient silver bowl of mine, it tells of good old times. On Lending a Punch-Bowl. Oliver Wendell Holmes. AA; CAP; CoBA; IAP; TCAP
This and That. Florence Boyce Davis. FaPON; GaP; TiPo (1952 ed.)
This Arrow. Dorothy Livesay. PeCV
This autumn, just before Thanksgiving hurries. Armistice. Margaret E. Sangster. PEDC
This autumn rainfall. November Rain. Maud E. Uschold. YeAr
This Babe to Us That Now Is Born. *Unknown.* AnEC
This baseness follows your profession. John Day. *Fr.* The Parliament of Bees. ViBoPo
This be my pilgrimage and goal. Vocation. John Drinkwater. BMEP
This Be Our Revenge. Saul Tchernichowsky, *tr. fr. Hebrew by* Shalom Spiegel. TrJP
This bears the seal of immortality. The Living Book. Charlotte Fiske Bates. AA
This beauty made me dream there was a time. Sedge Warblers. Edward Thomas. LO
This beauty where no hand, caressing, lingers. Antique Dresden Porcelain, Marked "Do Not Handle." Blanche D. Small. DDA
This bird is the keel-billed toucan. Limerick. Howard Ketcham. LiBL
This bit of foam, this nothing, a verse purely. Toast. Stéphane Mallarmé. AnFP
This blaze of leaves, your hand. October Garden. Pearce Young. PtPa
This Blind Rose. Humbert Wolfe. CaAE
This Blonde Girl. Kendrick Smithyman. AnNZ
This blue half circle of sea. Mersa. Keith Douglas. FaBoMo
This blue-washed, old, thatched summerhouse. The Old Summerhouse. Walter de la Mare. ChMo; MoPo
This body is my house—it is not I. My Faith. Frederic Lawrence Knowles. OQP; QP-1
This body of my mother, pierced by me. Epithalamium. Leo Kennedy. BoCaPo
This book is all that's left me now! My Mother's Bible. George Pope Morris. AA; BLRP; LPS-1; MOAH; MotAn; WBLP
This book may seem, as it sorteth in suit. An Epigram on This Book of Epigrams. John Heywood. ReIE
This bookplate, that thou here seest put. Book & Bookplate. John Masefield. WhC
This Bottle's the Sun of Our Table. Sheridan. *Fr.* The Duenna, III, v. EV-3
This Bread I Break Was Once the Oat. Dylan Thomas. FaBoTw
This brief common youth I was once in dread for it. Youth. Blanaid Salkeld. OxBI
This bronze doth keep the very form and mold. On the Life-Mask of Abraham Lincoln. Richard Watson Gilder. AA; HBV; LBAH; OBAV; PoRL
This bronze to liberty is loftier. The Statue of Liberty. Edgar Lee Masters. HiLiAm
This busy, vast, enquiring soul. The Enquiring Soul. Thomas Traherne. *Fr.* Insatiableness. ElSeCe; MaRV
This careful head, with divers thoughts distressed. Parthenophil and Parthenophe, XCIX. Barnabe Barnes. TuPP
This case befell at four of the clock. The Six Carpenters' Case. Sir Frederick Pollock. VA
This casual verdure, light and tremulous. Camouflage. Helen Frith Stickney. MuM
This celestial seascape, with white herons got up as angels. Seascape. Elizabeth Bishop. MoAB
This Chauntecleer stood hye up-on his toos. Chaucer. *Fr.* The Canterbury Tales: The Nun's Priest's Tale. FiP
This cheerful picture shows the fate. The Jungle Pest. Roland Young. BOHV
This Child. Norman Rosten. TrJP

This, children, is the famed Mon-goos. The Mon-goos. Oliver Herford. *Fr.* Child's Natural History. AA; HBV; LEAP
This Chinese emperor, loving beauty, longed for "the killer of Empires." The Everlasting Sorrow. Po Chü-i. WhP
This city and this country has brought forth many mayors. Good English Hospitality [*or* The Mayors.] Blake. *Fr.* An Island in the Moon. CH; CoMu
This city is the child of France and Spain. Vieux Carré. Walter Adolphe Roberts. PoNe
This claw remains alive. Painting of a Lobster by Picasso. Hy Sobiloff. NePA
This cloak of purple, Leonidas, Xerxes gives you. Imaginary Dialogue. Antiphilus of Byzantium, *tr. by* Dudley Fitts. TriL
This cluck of water in the tangles. The Voices of Nature. Thomas Edward Brown. PoVP
This cold, sad fear that holds me should not be. This Fear. Zoe Kincaid Brockman. NoCaPo (rev. ed.)
This coloured counterfeit that thou beholdest. Sister Juana Inés de la Cruz, *tr. fr. Spanish by* Samuel Beckett. AnMP
This Compost. Walt Whitman. AWP; LiTA; MoAmPo (1950 ed.); MoAP; SN
This cool night is strange. Nocturne. Gwendolyn Bennet. BANP
This Corruptible. Elinor Wylie. AnFE; CoAnAm; MAP; MoAB; MoAmPo; TwAmPo
This could I paint my inward sight. Lines for a Drawing of Our Lady of the Night. Francis Thompson. ISi; MeRV; POTT; VLEP
This country has literally gone to the dogs. Gone to the Dogs. William Hankins Chitwood. AlBD
This Cross-Tree Here. Robert Herrick. BEL; EM-1
This cruising caballero of the deep. Flying Fish. J. Corson Miller. EtS
This cursèd jealousy, what is't? Sir William Davenant. *Fr.* The Siege of Rhodes. LO
This curve I'm plotting? The Parabola. H. Reynolds Goodwin. PoMa
This damsel was brought up to read and to write. The Female Warrior. *Unknown.* ShS
This darksome burn, horseback brown. Inversnaid. Gerard Manley Hopkins. ACP; AlDL; ChMo; EmBrPo; FaBoMo; GTBS-W; GTML; LiTB; LiTG; LiTM (rev. ed.); LoBV; MoAB; MoBrPo; PoRA; POTT; PoVP; ShBV-3; UnPo (3d ed.)
This dawn when the mountain-cherry lifts. Easter in the Woods. Frances Frost. BrR; SiSoSe
This Day ("An heavenly song"). *Unknown.* AnEC
This day, Cerinthus, which gave you to the earth for me. He Speaks for the Girl, on Cerinthus' Birthday. Tibullus. LaP
This Day Christ Was Born. *Unknown.* AnEC
This day, I think, will be a common day. Help Me Today. Elsie Robinson. PoToHe
This day I'd have none by my sadness linger. The Voice. Henri de Régnier. TrFP
This day is for Israel light and rejoicing. A Sabbath of Rest. Isaac Luria. TrJP
This Day Is Thine. Verna Whinery. BLRP
This day, just fifteen years ago, was dated. Feodor Ivanovich Tyutchev, *tr. fr. Russian by* Sir Cecil Kisch. WaL
This day, O Father, give us daily bread. Francis Jammes. *Fr.* Géorgiques Chrétiennes. CAW
This day our Savior Christ was born. *Unknown.* SeCSL
This day relenting God. Lines Written after the Discovery by the Author of the Germ of Yellow Fever [*or* In Exile *or* Reply]. Sir Ronald Ross. ImOP; InP; MaRV; MM; PoeMoYo; PoP; TCPD
This Day, This Pure, Enduring, Beautiful Today. Stéphane Mallarmé, *tr. fr. French by* Joseph Bennett. AnFP
This day upon the bitter tree. Good Friday. A. J. M. Smith. CaP; MaRV; StJW; TwCV
This day was sacred once to Pan. Saint Valentine's Day. Thomas William Parsons. PR
This day, whate'er the Fates decree. Stella's Birthday; March 13, 1726–27. Swift. CEP; EiPP; GTIV; LoBV; OBEC; PoEL-3
This day winding down now. Prologue. Dylan Thomas. GTBS-W
This daylit doll, this dim divinity. Neo-classical Poem. William Jay Smith. WaP
This Dear English Land. Sydney Dobell. *Fr.* Balder. EV-5
This death-mask is my portrait by my son. For a Child's Drawing. Anton Vogt. AnNZ
This deep of night, with nature's law complying. Hazard. Nils Petersen. LiTW
This Defileth a Man. Menander, *tr. fr. Greek by* Gilbert Murray. OxBG
This delightful young man. Heine. *Fr.* Die Heimkehr. AWP
This Dim and Ptolemaic Man. John Peale Bishop. CrMA; ImOP; LiTA; LiTM (rev. ed.); NePA
This dirty little heart. Emily Dickinson. PoEL-5
This Discord in the Pact of Things. Boethius, *tr. fr. Latin by* Helen Waddell. LiTW
This Do in Remembrance of Me, *sel.* Horatius Bonar. "Here, O my Lord, I see Thee face to face." OlF; TrPWD
This door you might not open, and you did. Bluebeard. Edna St. Vincent Millay. BAV
This double anniversary, this day, this night. November 7; Ode to a Day of Victories. "Pablo Neruda." AnCL
This drop of ink chance leaves upon my pen. A Drop of Ink. Joseph Ernest Whitney. AA
This duleful sentence Saturn took on hand. Robert Henryson. *Fr.* The Testament of Cresseid. BSV
This Dust Was Once the Man. Walt Whitman. *Fr.* Memories of President Lincoln. PoRL (Epitaph for Lincoln.) WoL
This dust was Timas; and they say. The Dust of Timas [*or* Variations of Greek Themes]. E. A. Robinson, *after* Sappho. AWP; JAWP; MOAP; WBP
This dust was Timas'; ere her bridal hour. Sappho, *tr. fr. Greek by* C. A. Elton. GrPo
This earth is not the steadfast place. William Vaughn Moody. *Fr.* Gloucester Moors. PoFr; WGRP
This earth Pythonax and his brother hides. On Two Brothers. Simonides. AWP
This earth, this Asia, wide as east from west. Xerxes Defeated. Aeschylus. *Fr.* Persians. OxBG
This earthly tomb so low, and heaven so hie. Epitaph. *Unknown.* BSV
This Easter, Arthur Winslow, less than dead. Death from Cancer [*or* In Memory of Arthur Winslow]. Robert Lowell. FiMAP; MiAP
This Easter Day. Martha Snell Nicholson. BePJ
This egle, of whiche I have yow tolde. Chaucer. *Fr.* The Hous of Fame. NBE
This Endernight I Saw a Sight ("'Ah, my dear Son,' said Mary"). *Unknown.* AnEC (Ah My Dere.) AtBAP; BoW (Dream Carol, A.) BOL (This Endurs Night.) TwHP
This Endernight I Saw a Sight ("This endernight"). *Unknown.* AnEC (Child of Mary.) EV-2 (Christmas Carol, A: "Thys endernyght," *abr.*) TrGrPo (Madonna and Child, The.) BOL ("Thys ender nyght.") EPP ("Thys endris nygth.") OAEP
This endless gray-roofed city, and each heart. London Despair. Frances Cornford. OBMV
This endris night. Child of Mary [*or* The Madonna and Child]. *Unknown.* BOL; EV-2
This Endurs Night. *Unknown. See* This Endernight I Saw a Sight ("'Ah, my dear Son'").
This England ("This England never did"). Shakespeare. *Fr.* King John, V, vii. BoTP; EV-1 (England, 2.) OTPC (Words of Faulconbridge, The.) BHV
This England ("This royal throne of kings"). Shakespeare. King Richard II, *fr.* II, i. LiA; MuP; TreF; TrGrPo (England.) OTPC (Gaunt's Dying Speech.) CBE (John of Gaunt's Dying Speech, *longer sel.*) FiP (This Royal Throne of Kings.) BHV; EV-1, *longer sel.*; ShBV-2
This evening, our father. Prayer. *Unknown.* OuSiCo
This evening when I spake with thee, beloved. Sister Juana Inés de la Cruz, *tr. fr. Spanish by* Samuel Beckett. AnMP
This Excellent Machine. John Lehmann. MoP
This existence has, without the azure sphere, no reality. Quatrain. Sarmèd the Yahud. TrJP
This fable is a very short one. Showing How the Cavern Followed the Hut's Advice. John Hookham Frere. OTPC (1923 ed.)
This face you got. Phizzog. Carl Sandburg. TiPo (1952 ed.)
This fairest lady, who, as well I wot. Sonnet: Death Is Not without but within Him. Cino da Pistoia. AWP
This fairest one of all the stars, whose flame. Ballata: One Speaks of the Beginnings of His Love. *Unknown.* AWP
This faith in your beauty, woman, is false. Propertius. Elegies, III, 24. LaP
This fat woman in canvas knickers. Tourist Time. F. R. Scott. BoCaPo; WhC
This Fear. Zoe Kincaid Brockman. NoCaPo (rev. ed.)
This feast-day of the sun, his altar there. The Hill Summit. Dante Gabriel Rossetti The House of Life, LXX. BPN; CaAE; EmBrPo; PoVP; REAL; TCEP; ViPo
This Feast of the Law. *Unknown, tr. fr. Hebrew by* Israel Zangwill. TrJP
This Fevers Me. Richard Eberhart. FiMAP
This fighting grows more hideous hour by hour. The War in the Dark. Rolfe Humphries. NeTW

This figure, that thou here seest put. On the Portrait of Shakespeare Prefixed to the First Folio Edition, 1623. Ben Jonson. EV-2; HBV; LEAP; OTPC (1923 ed.)
This fine nature clear. The Fine Nature. Edmund Blunden. BoFr; NeTW
This first year/ Of the atom. There Is Yet Time. Arvel Steece. PGD
This flesh is but the symbol and the shrine. Hail Man! Angela Morgan. WGRP
This flimsy tent. Fourth Dimensional. "Katherine Hale." OCL
This flower that smells of honey and the sea. Relics. Swinburne. POTT; VLEP
This [or That] flying angel's torrent cry. Eastern Tempest. Edmund Blunden. MPB; MoBrPo; PtOT
This, for my soul's peace, have I heard from thee. The Transfiguration. *Unknown. Fr.* Bhagavad-Gita. OuHeWo
This fountain sheds her flowery spray. The Fountain. A. J. M. Smith. CaP
This fourteen six and fiftieth year. The Lesser Testament. Villon. WoL
This Fresshe Flour. Chaucer. *Fr.* The Legend of Good Women. SeCePo
This from that soul incorrupt whom Athens had doomed to the death. The Reply of Socrates. Edith M. Thomas. WGRP
This from the fluxing bagnio just dismist. City Magistrate. Daniel Defoe. *Fr.* Reformation of Manners. BeR
This fugitive between the earth and sky. Prelude. Tu Fu. WhP
This gapes for marriage, yet his fickle head. John Hall. *Fr.* On an Hour-Glass. LO
This Garden does not take my eyes. The Garden. James Shirley. OBS
This gentle and half melancholy breeze. An Autumn Breeze. William Hamilton Hayne. AA
This glorious title hath in it exprest. George Wither. *Fr.* The Protector. PoFr
This goblet is a little loving-cup. Fantasy for a Charming Friend. Arthur Davison Ficke. TCPD
This golden cockerel summer sun ruffles his feathers into sleep. Cockerel Sun. Rosemary Dobson. MoAuPo
This golden head has wit in it. Modern Love, XXXI. George Meredith. ViPo
This grave-yard with its umbrella pines. The Island Cemetery. W. H. Auden. NePoAm-2
This green wall to which I turn for sleep. Green Wall My Grave. Martin Seymour-Smith. MoPW
This grey-haired spinster, Catharine Plouffe. Catharine Plouffe. S. Frances Harrison. *Fr.* Down the River. CPG
This guest of summer,/ The temple-haunting Martlet. Fragments from the Old Masters. Shakespeare. *Fr.* Macbeth, I, vi. PoF
This Happy Day. Harry Behn. TiPo
This Heart That Flutters near My Heart. James Joyce. Chamber Music, XXIII. AnIV
This heaven is too clear and bright. Macrocosm. Philip Child. CaP
This helmet, I suppose. Arac's Song. W. S. Gilbert. *Fr.* Princess Ida. FiBHP; WhC
This Heritage to the Race of Kings. Joseph Mary Plunkett. AnIV; PoFr
(Our Heritage.) OnYI
This high-caught hooded Reason broods upon my wrist. The Falcon and the Dove. Sir Herbert Read. FaBoMo; POTE
This high-way beheld at break of day. March of the Three Kings. *Unknown.* OHIP
This Hill. Otomo Yakamochi, *tr. fr. Japanese by* Ishii *and* Obata. OnPM
This hinder year [or yeir] I heard [or hard] be tauld [or tald]. The Bludy Serk. Robert Henryson. CaAE; EBSV; OBEV (1st ed.); OxBoCh
This Holy Night. Eleanor Farjeon. ChBR
This Holy Night. Gertrude Hanson. ChIP
This holy season, fit to fast and pray. Amoretti, XXII. Spenser. ES; PeBoSo; ReEn; SiCE
This horn of full two cubits from his bull that turned a rover. The Trophy. Erycius. GrPE
This hound has had his day, and is content. Old Dog. Leonard Twynham. StaSt
This hound (no chase too stern for such a creature!). Statue of a Dog. Macedonius. OxBG
This hour by all rules of astrologie. George Chapman. *Fr.* The Conspiracy of Charles, Duke of Byron, III, i. NBE
This hour was set the time for heaven's descent. Twilit Revelation. Léonie Adams. AV; MAP; MoAB; MoAmPo
This Houre Her Vigill. Valentin Iremonger. *See* Recollection in Autumn.
This house is built within a sheltering. Back Road Farm. Charles Bruce. CaP
This house is haunted, this house is haunted. Calliope. *Unknown.* AS
This house of flesh was never loved of me! Protest in Passing. Leonora Speyer. BAP; HBMV; PC
This house that has been our home has been condemned. Packing a Photograph from Firenze. William H. Matchett. NePoEA
This House was built for Zeus, where he will find. *Unknown, tr. fr. Greek by* Humbert Wolfe. PIAE
This House Where Once a Lawyer dwelt. William Erskine. HBV; TreF; WhC
This household drudge, a slave whom all despise. Unseen Riches. Bianor. OxBG
This I admit, Death is terrible to me. Pure Death. Robert Graves. AWP; InPo
This I ask thee, O Ahura! tell me aright. O Great Creator. *At. to* Zoroaster, *tr. by* L. H. Mills. *Fr.* Gathas. GrCo-1
This I ask Thee—tell it to me truly, Lord! Zoroaster Devoutly Questions Ormazd [or The Sacred Book]. *At. to* Zoroaster, *tr. by* A. V. Williams Jackson. *Fr.* Gathas. AWP; WGRP
This I beheld, or dreamed it in a dream. Opportunity [or The Broken Sword]. Edward Rowland Sill. AnNE; BAP; BBV; BLPA; BLV; BTP; GN; GoTP; HBV; HBVY; IAP; LBAP; MAP; MaRV; MCCG; MoAmPo (1942 ed.); NeHB; NeMA; OBAV; OHFP; PCD; PoeMoYo; PoMa; PoToHe; PYM; TCAP; TreFS; TSW; TSWC; WGRP; YaD
This I do, being mad. Siege. Edna St. Vincent Millay. BaP
This I got on the day that Goring. The Three Scars. George Walter Thornbury. VA
This I have read in some old book and wise. To Elizabeth. Mary Dixon Thayer. JKCP (1955 ed.)
This I Know. Eliza M. Hickok. PraP
(Prayer: "I know not by what methods rare.") BLRP
This I know, though it be all my knowledge. Men of Religion. Molière. *Fr.* Tartuffe. GrCo-2
This I remember clearly: from stone to stepping-stone. Fragment. Clark Ashton Smith. UnW
This I say to you. To Youth. John V. A. Weaver. TBM
"This I shall write," he said. S. V. B. William Rose Benét. PtP
This I trow be truth—who can teach thee better. William Langland. *Fr.* The Vision of Piers Plowman. EG
This I will pray. Grief Must Go. Jane Barton. DiM
This I would like to be—braver and bolder. Lord, Make a Regular Man Out of Me. Edgar A. Guest. BLPA; NeHB
This Infant World. George Macdonald. *Fr.* A Memorial of Africa. EPN
(Sonnet: "This infant world has taken long to make.") OBVV
(World and Soul.) VA
This is a breath of summer wind. On Reading a Poet's First Book. H. C. Bunner. AA
This is a cat that sleeps at night. Cat. Sinclair Lewis. GoTP
This is a colder winter than last year. Ugga Byan. *Fr.* Her Absent Lord. LiTW
This is a fair in Magh Eala of the king. The Headless Phantoms. *Unknown.* AnIL
This is a fearful thing to bear. Horror. Peter Baum. AWP
This is a giant day. Wind. Phyllis Reid. DiM
This is a grove where the leaves of the trees. Altar of Liberty. Sophia Mavroidi Papadaky. MoGP
This is a land of forests, and of meres. The Land Within. Mary Webb. MM
This is a night to be out. Street-Walker in March. Samuel L. Albert. NePoAm-2
This is a night when ghosts come stalking. Now with the Moon. Louise Liebhardt. MuM
This is a piece too fair. Design. Dryden. *Fr.* To My Honor'd Friend Sir Robert Howard. MaRV
This is a pleasant place between the hills. Happiness. Katharine Beeman. BLP
This is a rocksaw seacoast. Memento. Winfield Townley Scott. FiMAP
This is a rune I ravelled in the still. The Cow. Bernard O'Dowd. BoAu
This is a sacred city built of marvellous earth. By a Bier-Side. John Masefield. PoeT
This is a salt steep-cobbled town. Sea Town. Frances Frost. EtS
This Is a Sin-tryin' World, *with music. Unknown.* TrAS
This is a song to celebrate banks. Bankers Are Just like Anybody Else, except Richer. Ogden Nash. ATP (1953 ed.); LiTA
This is a spray the bird clung to. Misconceptions. Robert Browning. AtBAP; BPN; EmBrPo; EnLi-2 (1949 ed.); EPN; EtPaEn; GEPC; GTBS; OBEV; OBVV; PIAE; PoVP; TOP; VA; VLEP
This is a surplus in a four-cornered. The Four-cornered Tower; Llanybri. Nigel Heseltine. MoWP
This is a tale to tell your sons. Wayne at Stony Point. Clinton Scollard. GA; MC; PAH

This is a theme for muted coronets. The Plot against Proteus. A. J. M. Smith. BoCaPo; PeCV
This is a wild land, country of my choice. Rocky Acres. Robert Graves. LiTB; UnPo (3d ed.)
This is a wrong that needs not my bespeaking. New Testament, Revised Edition. Sister Mary Catherine. ISi
This is all we ever say. Christopher Morley. WhC
"This Is Alone Life, Joy, Empire and Victory." Euripides. *See* Where Shall Wisdom Be Found?
This Is America. Thomas Curtis Clark. PGD
This Is America. Katharine Janeway Conger. PaA
This is an ancient pattern on these hills. American Vineyard. Mildred Cousens. GoYe
This is an ancient waltz. Louis Aragon. *Fr.* Tcheliabtraktrostroi Waltz. MiFP
This is an evening for a hallowed landfall. Pattern of Saint Brendan. Francis MacManus. AnIV; OxBI
"This is an evil night to go, my sister." The Fairy Thorn-Tree. Dora Sigerson Shorter. DaM
This is an old and very cruel god. Vicarious Atonement. Richard Aldington. MBP; MoBrPo; WGRP
This is Anacreon's tomb: the Teian swan. Man at Peace. Antipater of Sidon. OnPM
This is Charles Ives. Muriel Rukeyser. *Fr.* Ives. UnS
This is Don, the dog of all dogs. Don. James T. Fields. AlBD
This is enchanted country, lies under a spell. Bonac. John Hall Wheelock. MoVE
This Is England. Laurence Binyon. BoTP
This is Flag Day. Hang Out the Flags. James S. Tippett. SiSoSe
This is for poets . . . Reasoner and empiric. God Said: Let There Be Sky. James J. Donohue. JKCP (1955 ed.)
This is God's hive; the bees. Saint Apollinare in Classe. R. N. D. Wilson. CAW
This is God's house—the blue sky is the ceiling. In the Woods. Frederick George Scott. CaP; OCL
This Is Halloween. Dorothy Brown Thompson. BrR; TiPo; YeAr
This is he who, felled by foes. Worship. Emerson. IAP; MeRV; TCAP
This is her picture as she was. The Portrait. Dante Gabriel Rossetti. BMEP; BPN; EmBrPo; EV-5; GTML; GTSE; OAEP; POTT; PoVP; TriL; VA; ViPo; VLEP
This is her picture—Dolladine. Dolladine. William Brighty Rands. PRWS
This is high saintliness, I know. Earth-canonized. Henry Morton Robinson. CAW
This is how snowflakes play about. A Finger Play for a Snowy Day. *Unknown.* BoTP
This is how the flowers grow. How the Flowers Grow. "Gabriel Setoun." MPB
This is how to speed a night. Cock-Crow. Abbie Huston Evans. BAP
This Is Indeed the Blessed Mary's Land. Longfellow. *Fr.* The Golden Legend. ISi
This is just the weather, a wet May and blowing. A Memory. Katharine Tynan. OxBI
This Is Just to Say. William Carlos Williams. AmP; HoPM
This is like the nave of an unfinished cathedral. Broadway's Canyon. John Gould Fletcher. InP; VOD (1935 ed.)
This is Mab, the mistress-fairy. Queen Mab [*or* Mab the Mistress-Fairy]. Ben Jonson. *Fr.* The Satyr. EIL; ElSeCe; HBV; OTPC (1923 ed.); SiCE
This is Mister Beers. Mister Beers. Hugh Lofting. FaPON; GaP
This is Morgan's Country: now steady, Bill. Morgan's Country. Francis Webb. BoAV
This Is My Body. John Donne. ChIP; OQP; QP-1
"This is my body, which is given for you." The Sacrament. Charles L. Ford. OQP; QP-1
This is my commandment, that ye love one another. The New Commandment. St. John, Bible, *N.T.* BoFr
This is my country's flag. My Country's Flag. Juniata Stafford. HH
This is my creed: To do some good. My Creed. Samuel Ellsworth Kiser. PoToHe
This is my curse on thee. God send thou love. A Curse. Rabi'a, Daughter of Ka'b. LiTW
This Is My Father's World. Maltbie D. Babcock. MaRV (My Father's World.) BLRP
This Is My Hour. Zoë Akins. HBV; LEAP
This is my hour between the flight and the flight. Remember Me, Gulls! Joseph Auslander. YT
This is my letter to the world. Emily Dickinson. AmPo; AmPP (4th ed.); AnNE; OxBA; PoLFOT; TCAP (Letter to the World.) OnPM
This Is My Love for You. Grace Fallow Norton. HBV
This is my play's [*or* playes] last scene, here heavens appoint. Holy Sonnets, VI. John Donne. AnEnPo; EPS; LoBV; MeLP; MePo; MyFE; OAEP; OBS; OxBoCh; PeBoSo; PoFS; SeEP; TuPP
This is my prayer to Thee, my Lord. Prayer for Strength. Rabindranath Tagore. Gitanjali, XXXVI. MaRV
This Is My Rock. David McCord. FaPON; SiSoSe; StVeCh; TiPo (1959 ed.)
This is my secret, this is the chord most perfectly strung. The Beaches, V. "Robin Hyde." AnNZ
This Is My Song. Norma Davis. NeLNL
This is my world! within these narrow walls. My Study. Paul Hamilton Hayne. AmPP (3d ed.); SPP
This is my wrong to you, O man that I love. A Woman's Song. Muna Lee. NP
This Is New England. Margery Mansfield. DDA
This is no book. To a Poet. Sister Mary Angelita. GoBC
This Is No Case of Petty Right or Wrong. Edward Thomas. SoV
This is no common roadway. The Road of Midnight Pageants. Hilton Ross Greer. HiLiAm
This is no dreamworld, no nightmare country. Letter from the South. Robert E. Hayden. PoNe
This is no fallow field through which we travel. Golden Wedding. William W. Pratt. MaRV
This Is No My Ain House. *Unknown.* EBSV
"This is no place for a tree," said the sour black soil. The Mountain Tree. Hugh Connell. NeIP
This is no time for fear, for doubts of good. Challenge. Thomas Curtis Clark. MaRV; PGD
This is no wood for me to walk. Forest. Harriet Gray Blackwell. GoYe
This is nobleness, this is the one claim. Petronius, *tr. fr. Latin by* Jack Lindsay. LaP
This is not a struggle on marble threshing-floors. Resistance. Angelos Sikelianos. MoGP
This is not all I would have said. Arlington Cemetery Looking toward the Capitol. Winthrop Palmer. GoYe
This Is Not Death. Humbert Wolfe. MBP; MoBrPo
This Is Not Loneliness. Grace Hazard Conkling. TBM
This is not sorrow, this is work: I build. The Tomb of Lieutenant John Learmonth, A.I.F. John Manifold. BoAV; LiTM; NeLNL
This is not the classic torso. All the Farewells. Byron Vazakas. MoPo
This is not the moon. Ariwara no Narihira, *tr. fr. Japanese by* Kenneth Rexroth. OnPJ
This is not the sea, this is its image. Distant Sea. Pedro Salinas. CoSP
This is not you? These phrases are not you? Prelude VI. Conrad Aiken. *Fr.* Preludes for Memnon. MAP; MoAB; MoAmPo
This is of green—unclassic shade. The Final Green. Leah Bodine Drake. NePoAm
This is our love, these wheels and chains. The Night Loves Us. Louis Adeane. NeBP
This is our place of meeting; opposite. At the Saturday Club. Oliver Wendell Holmes. AmPP (3d ed.); CoBA; IAP
This is Palm Sunday; mindful of the day. To a Young Girl Dying. Thomas William Parsons. AA
This Is Pioneer Weather. William Carlos Williams. NePoAm-2
This is Popilia's tomb: my husband's care. Sleep of the Just. *Unknown.* OnPM
This is Proteus, a god. He comes from the ocean. Proteus; or, The Shapes of Conscience. Rolfe Humphries. LiTM (1946 ed.)
This Is She. Arthur Guiterman. LHV; PR
This is that bastioned rock where dwell the free. Canada Speaks of Britain. Sir Charles G. D. Roberts. NeTW
This is that [*or* the] blessed Mary, pre-elect. Mary's Girlhood. Dante Gabriel Rossetti. BPN; CAW; EmBrPo; GBV; GoBC; ISi; MeRV; PoVP; SDH; VLEP; WGRP
This is that month, Elizabeth. George Barker. *Fr.* Third Cycle of Love Poems. NeBP
This is the anniversary of the day. Wedding Anniversary. Margaret E. Bruner. PoToHe
This is the arsenal. From floor to ceiling. The Arsenal at Springfield. Longfellow. AmPP; AnNE; APW; CoBA; CoV; DD; GTBS; HBV; IAP; MCCG; TCAP; WaaP
This is the beautiful dress. Chu Yuan. *Fr.* The Nine Declarations. WhP
This is the best world that we live in. The World. *Unknown.* ALV
This is the birthday of our land. Prayer on Fourth of July. Nancy Byrd Turner. YeAr
This is the black sea-brute bulling through wave-wrack. Leviathan. W. S. Merwin. NePoEA
This is the blessed Mary, pre-elect. *See* This is that blessed Mary, pre-elect.
This is the blessing. A Child of Prayer. *Unknown.* SoLD
This is the breed that followed the tails. Nantucket Whalers. Daniel Henderson. EtS
This is the bricklayer; hear the thud. Sanctuary. Elinor Wylie. MAP; MoAB; MoAmPo; PoMa
This is the case of a high-school land. Canada: Case History. Earle Birney. TwCaPo
This is the cave of which I spoke. The Caves. Michael Roberts. ChMP
This is the chapel: here, my son. Clifton Chapel. Sir Henry Newbolt. OBEV (new ed.); OBVV; TwCV

This is the charge I keep as mine. My Charge. Leslie Pinckney Hill. MaRV
This is the children's playground, the home of the inner eye. The Children's Playground. Oscar Williams. SiTL
This Is the City Children Made. Frank Ernest Hill. PoMa
This is the convent where they tend the sick. Sister Mary of the Love of God. Rosa Mulholland. VA
This is the country of the Norman tower. A Warning to Conquerors. Donagh MacDonagh. OxBI
This is the Darkness that they told us of. In Tenebris. Sister Mary of the Visitation. JKCP (1955 ed.)
This is the day His hour of life draws near. Sonnets at Christmas, I. Allen Tate. AmP; GTBS-W; LiTA; LiTM; NePA; OxBA; ReMP
This is the day the Child was born. Christmas, 1943. James Boyd. NoCaPo (rev. ed.)
This is the day the circus comes. Parade. Rachel Field. *Fr.* A Circus Garland. StVeCh; UTS
This is the day the prophets have foretold. Without Regret. Lilith Lorraine. PGD
This is the day when all through the town. Sunday. Elizabeth J. Coatsworth. WaKn
This is the day when the fairy kind. Friday. Sir Walter Scott. BoTP
This is the day when we honor "Old Hickory." Old Hickory. Clinton Scollard. GA
This is the day, which down the void abysm. Demogorgon's Last Words [*or* Epilogue of "Prometheus" *or* The Ideal]. Shelley. *Fr.* Prometheus Unbound, IV. BHV; CBE; EnLit; KN; LoBV; OQP; QP-2; SeCeV; ShBV-3
This is the dead fiddle. Look where the wood. The Dead Fiddle. Humbert Wolfe. TrJP
This is the death by water. This is dying. Dead Marine. Louis O. Coxe. WaP
This is the debt I pay. The Debt. Paul Laurence Dunbar. BANP; CDC; GrCo-1; MaRV
This is the depth, the end of all despair. Street Beggar. Anderson M. Scruggs. PoMa
This is the dewy morning of the world. From the Cliffs at Puye, New Mexico. Katharine Shepard Hayden. MuM
This is the Doctor Johnson of the "Prayers." On a Portrait of Dr. Samuel Johnson, LL.D. Christopher Morley. PoeMoYo
This is the dream—this is the nightmare. Castle Howard. Lawrence Toynbee. NeTW
This is the dust of Timas, who, unwed/ Passed hence. Timas. Sappho, *tr. by* H. De Vere Stacpoole. GrR
This is the dust of Timas, whom unwed/ Persephone locked. Timas. Sappho, *tr. by* John Addington Symonds. LiTW
This is the earth he walked on. Holy Land. Richard Watson Gilder. StJW
This is the earth that God made. That God Made. Will Herford. QS
This is the end of him, here he lies. Epitaph. Amy Levy. LBBV; TrJP
"This is the end": the anguished word. The End. Walter de la Mare. OAEP (2d ed.)
This is the end of the book. Written at the End of a Book. Langdon Elwyn Mitchell. AA; OBAV
This is the feast time of the year. The Feast Time of the Year. Dora Read Goodale. OHIP; PEDC
This is the final man. The Final Man. Basil McFarlane. PoNe
This is the forest primeval. To What Base Uses! *parody.* Bert Leston Taylor. WhC
This is the forest primeval. The murmuring pines and the hemlocks. Evangeline. Longfellow. AmPP (3d ed.); AnNE; BeLS; CaAE; CoBA; HiLiAm; IAP; InP; LEAP; LPS-2; OBAV; PCD; PIAE; TCAP; TreF; WBLP
This is the freezing guilt I shall remember. Epigram on the Passing of Christmas. Edgar Bowers. PtPa
This is the fruit of that forbidden tree. On the Photograph of a Lynching. Wendell Phillips Stafford. PoFr
This Is the Garden. E. E. Cummings. BLV; BoLiVe; MoAmPo
(Sonnet: "This is the garden: colours come and go.") MoAB
This is the garden; its twenty paths. Geraldine's Garden. John Francis O'Donnell. IrPN
This is the gladness of our Easter morning. The Day of Joy. Lucy Larcom. HH
This is the glamour of the world antique. Sibyl. John Payne. VA
This is the gospel of labour, ring it, ye bells of the kirk! Henry van Dyke. *Fr.* The Gospel of Labour. OQP; PSO; QP-1; WBLP
This is the grave of famed Megistias. The Poet's Friend. Simonides. GrL; GrPo; OxBG
This is the grave of Hector: Troy lies in this small room. The Grave of Hector. Ausonius. LaP
This is the grave of Mike O'Day. Mike O'Day. *Unknown.* LiTG; LiTM (rev. ed.); SiTL; WhC
This is the greatest proof of power. Who Can Forget? Leslie Savage Clark. ChIP
This is the hand. At Cambridge. Audrey McGaffin. NePoAm
This is the hardest hour of all to bear. After Hour. Sydney King Russell. MuM
This is the hardest of my fate. The Rival. Gertrude Hall. BAP
This Is the Hay That No Man Planted. Elizabeth J. Coatsworth. BrR
This is the Heath of Hampstead. Sunday at Hampstead, I. James Thomson. EmBrPo; POTT
This is the height of our deserts. Deservings. *Unknown.* HBV
This is the hero; he is black or white. Fairy Tale. John Frederick Nims. MiAP
This is the hidden place that hiders know. Stephen Vincent Benét. *Fr.* John Brown's Body. ViBoPo
This is the hour of magic, when the Moon. The Hour of Magic. W. H. Davies. MBP; MoBrPo; NeMA
This is the hour that we must mourn. Tenebrae. Austin Clarke. AnIL; NeIP
This is the hour when the city. Sky-Signs. Frederick Mortimer Clapp. PoeMoYo; VOD
This is the house. On one side there is darkness. Portrait of One Dead. Conrad Aiken. *Fr.* The House of Dust. ChMo; CMP; HBMV; NP; WHA
This is the house that Jack built. Mother Goose. BoTP; FaBoBe; HBV; HBVY; OnHT; OxNR; Po; RIS; SiTL; StVeCh. *See also* This is the knife with a handle of horn.
This is the house we used to know so well. I. M. H. Maurice Baring. ACP (1952 ed.)
This is the house where Jesse White. Lowery Cot. L. A. G. Strong. MBP; MoBrPo
This is the huge dream of us that we are Heroes. The Flowers of Politics, I. Michael McClure. NeAP
This is the ironhard winter foretold. Soeren Haller. *Fr.* Song of Denmark. PoFr
This is the journey of this night. Journey, IV. Erik Lindegren. LiTW
This Is the Key. *Unknown.* CH; FaBoCh; FaFP; GBV (1952 ed.); LoGBV; MoShBr; OTPC (1946 ed.); OxBoLi; SiTL; ThWaDe; TreFS
(Key of the Kingdom, The.) OtMeF
("This is the key of the kingdom.") BoTP; OxNR; PPL
This is the key to the playhouse. The Playhouse Key. Rachel Field. BoTP; FaPON; MPB
This is the knife with a handle of horn. The House That Jack Built. *Unknown.* OxBoLi. *For* Mother Goose *vers., see* This is the house that Jack built.
This is the land our fathers came to find. New World. Brewster Ghiselin. MoVE
This is the land where hate should die. The Land Where Hate Should Die. Denis A. McCarthy. PGD; PSO; PTA-2
This Is the Last. Gilbert Waterhouse. PGD; PSO
This is the last full snowless moon. October Ending. Price Day. CAG
This is the last stroke my toungs clock must strike. Summer's Farewell. Thomas Nashe. *Fr.* Summer's Last Will and Testament. PoEL-2
This is the law of the Yukon, and ever she makes it plain. The Law of the Yukon Robert W. Service. CaP; CPG; HBV; OCL; TreFS
This is the lean year yet green year of my giving. Past Song. Joyce Rowe. DiM
This is the living thing that cannot stir. The Tree. John Masefield. GTML
This is the loggia Browning loved. Browning at Asolo. Robert Underwood Johnson. AA; BAP; LEAP
This is the magic month of all the year. The Magic Month. Gelett Burgess. SDH
This is the magic morning. Christmas Morning. Elsie Melchert Fowler. ChBR
This is *The Making of America in Five Panels.* Empire Builders. Archibald MacLeish. Frescoes for Mr. Rockefeller's City, V. AmP; OxBA; Po; ReaPo; UnPo
This Is the Making of Man. Priscilla Leonard. OQP; QP-2
(Making of Man, The.) MaRV
This is the man that shoots the hares. The Story of the Man That Went Out Shooting. Heinrich Hoffmann. BoN
This is the man they deemed of languid blood. The Leader. Robert Underwood Johnson. GA
This is the measured moment. More than the Moment. Sister Claude of Jesus. JKCP (1955 ed.)
This is the mew of God set high. Hawkesyard. Sister Mary Benvenuta. JKCP (1926 ed.)
This is the midnight—let no star. The Storm Cone. Kipling. ChMP; POTE; PoVP
This is the midnight of the century—hark! New Year's Eve, 1850. James Russell Lowell. MeRV
This is the month, and this the happy morn. On the Morning of Christ's Nativity [*or* Ode on the Morning of Christ's Nativity]. Milton. AnFE; AtBAP; BEL; CaAE; CoBE; EPP; ExPo; GBV; GEPC; GoTL; GTBS; GTBS-D; GTBS-W; GTSE; GTSL; HBV; LiTB; LiTG; MaRV;

MeLP; OBS; OxBoCh; PoE; PoEL-3; PoFS; ReaPo; SeCeV; SeEP; TCEP; TOP; TwCrTr; TwHP; UnPo (1st ed.); WGRP
This is the month of the Thunder Moon. The Month of the Thunder Moon. Marion Doyle. YeAr
This is the month of weeds. Weed Month. V. Sackville-West. *Fr.* The Land. MBP; MoBrPo (1942 ed.)
This is the month when hills turn white. The Long Night Moon; December. Frances Frost. YeAr
This is the mouth-filling song of the race that was run by a Boomer. The Sing-Song of Old Man Kangaroo. Kipling. FaPON; TiPo (1952 ed.)
This is the moving nakedness that swirls once and is night. Corliss Engine-Wheel. MacKnight Black. AnAmPo; LA
This is the muse of nonsense: see! The Muse of Nonsense. Gelett Burgess. PIAE
This is the naked unsurmountable truth. The True Lover. Abbie Huston Evans. NP
This is the nature we behold. Nature. Nikolai Gumilev. BoRS
This is the need/ Of every seed. What Every Gardener Knows. *Ad. by* Louis Untermeyer. StaSt
This is the night mail crossing the border. Night Mail. W. H. Auden. AlDL; ChTr; MuP; ShBV-3
This is the order of the music of the morning. The Santa-Fé Trail. Vachel Lindsay. CoBA; CP; CV; IAP; MOAP; NV; PFE; PoeMoYo; PYM
This is the pathway where she walked. Amy. James Matthew Legaré. AA
This is the pedigree of degradation. Charles Erskine Scott Wood. *Fr.* The Poet in the Desert. PoFr
This is the place. In a Meadow. John Swinnerton Phillimore. OBEV (new ed.)
This is the place, as wild as summer snow. The Track into the Swamp. Samuel French Morse. CrMA
This is the place. Even here the dauntless soul. William Blake. Dante Gabriel Rossetti. Five English Poets, 2. BMEP; BPN; EmBrPo; PoVP; PtP
This is the place I love. Here I belong. Mountain Creed. Medora Addison Nutter. GoYe
This Is the Place to Wait. Horace Gregory. The Passion of M'Phail, V. MoAmPo
This is the place where André met that death. André. Charlotte Fiske Bates. MC; PAH
This is the place where Dorothea smiled. The Elm. Hilaire Belloc. GTML
This is the place where far from the unholy populace. In a Meadow. J. S. Phillimore. OBVV
This is the poem of rustic love. Indian Girl. Emilio Vásquez. AnCL
This is the pool that Plato visited. The Pool. E. L. Mayo. MiAP
This is the road to Hades. We go down. Leonard Bacon. *Fr.* Animula Vagula. TCPD
This is the room to which she came that day. Her Pity. Philip Bourke Marston. VA
This is the season when I long for a pen as sadly eloquent as Verlaine's. Who Wants to Travel All Over Europe and See Nothing but a Lot of American Tourists? I Do. Ogden Nash. SiTL
This is the secret love. Joy. Sister Mary Irma. JKCP (1955 ed.)
This is the Seventh Day. Sunday Morning. James Rorty. MOAP
This is the shack where the old man died. Post Mortem. Verna Loveday Harden. CaP
This Is the Shape of the Leaf. Conrad Aiken. Priapus and the Pool, IV[V]. AnAmPo; AtBAP; ChMo; CMP; HBMV; MAPA; MOAP; NePA; OxBA; TBM; TrGrPo; WHA
(Portrait of a Girl.) MAP; MoAB; MoAmPo; TSW
("This is the shape of the leaf, and this of the flower.") LA
This is the ship of pearl, which, poets feign. The Chambered Nautilus. Oliver Wendell Holmes. *Fr.* The Autocrat of the Breakfast-Table. AA; AmP; AmPP; AnAmPo; AnNE; APW; BAP; BAV; BTP; DD; EOAH; EtS; EV-5; FaBoBe; FaFP; GN; GTBS; GTBS-W; HBV; HBVY; HoPM; IAP; IHA; LA; LBAP; LEAP; LiTA; LPS-2; MaRV; MCCG; NeHB; NePA; OBAV; OBVV; OHFP; OQP; OTPC; OuHeWo; PCD; PECK; PG (1955 ed.); PIR; PoEL-5; PoP; PTA-1; QP-1; TCAP; TreF; TVSH; UnPo (1st ed.); WGRP; YT
This is the sin against the Holy Ghost. The Unpardonable Sin. Vachel Lindsay. ChMo; CMP; LiTM (rev. ed.); MaRV; NePA; QS
This is the song I rested with. Mammy Hums. Carl Sandburg. PoNe
This is the song of Mehitabel. The Song of Mehitabel. Don Marquis. *Fr.* Archy and Mehitabel. FiBHP; TreFS
This is the song of the Empire Builder. The Empire Builder. John Jerome Rooney. JKCP
This is the song of the reed. The Reed. Audrey Alexandra Brown. BoCaPo
This is the song of the waters churning. A Song of Power. Berton Braley. PoMa
This is the song of the wave! The mighty one! A Song of the Wave. George Cabot Lodge. AA; EtS
This is the song of the wind as it came. The Avenue of the Allies. Alfred Noyes. PoFr
This is the song of youth. The Song of Youth. Orrick Johns. *Fr.* Songs of Deliverance. BAP
This is the sorrowful story. The Legends of Evil, I. Kipling. MoShBr
"This is the State above the Law." A Death-Bed, 1918. Kipling. ViP
This is the story of/ The brawny Brady riflemen. Brady's Bend. Martha Keller. StPo
This is the story of a coal miner's child. The Coal Miner's Child. *Unknown.* OuSiCo
This is the story told in Libyan tales. The Wounded Eagle. Aeschylus. *Fr.* Myrmidones. OxBG
This is the sum of things . . . that we. The Sum of Things. Arthur W. Jose. BoAu
This is the tale from first to last. Simon the Cyrenian. Lucy Lyttelton. HBV
This is the tale that Cassidy told. The Mornin's Mornin'. Gerald Brennan. BLPA
This is the tale that was told to me. A Sailor's Yarn. James Jeffrey Roche. BOHV; NA
This is the time lean woods shall spend. Sundown. Léonie Adams. MAP; MoAB; MoAmPo; TrGrPo; TwAmPo
This is the time man hath o'ercome. Easter. *Unknown.* TMEV
This is the time of wonder, it is written. It Rolls On. Morris Bishop. ImOP
This is the time to speak to those who will come after. From Men Who Died Deluded. May Sarton. NeTW
This is the time, the appointed place. The Impetuous Lover. A. R. D. Fairburn AnNZ
This is the time when bit by bit. Turn o' the Year. Katharine Tynan. HBV; NLK
This is the time when larks are singing loud. The End of April. Robert Fuller Murray. CenHV
This is the toll of the desert. The Toll of the Desert. Arthur W. Monroe. PoOW
This is the tomboy month of all the year. March. Madison Cawein. MW
This is the top. Here we can only go. Yet Nothing Less. Louis Untermeyer. TBM
This Is the Tragedy. Helen Frazee-Bower. MaRV; MuM
This Is the Trouble with Us All. Josephine Winslow Johnson. QS
This is the voice of high midsummer's heat. The Mowing. Sir Charles G. D. Roberts. BoCaPo; ExPo
This is the way a tree: from the rain down. From the Rain Down. Rhina P. Espaillat. GoYe
This is the way of a bird. Morning Bird. Louis Untermeyer. BLA
This is the way the baby slept. The Way the Baby Slept. James Whitcomb Riley. AA
This is the way the ladies ride,/ Nim, nim, nim, nim. *Unknown.* OxNR
This is the way the ladies ride. Rhymes about a Little Woman. William Canton. PPL
This is the way the ladies ride: Tri-tre-tre-tree! Mother Goose. PPL; TiPo
This is the way we dress the doll. Dressing the Doll. William Brighty Rands. PRWS; VA
This is the way we make our hay. Haymaking. A. P. Graves. BoTP
This is the way we wash our clothes. Wash-Day. Lilian McCrea. BoTP
This is the weather the cuckoo likes. Weathers. Thomas Hardy. AlDL; ALV; AnEnPo; BLV; BoLiVe; BoTP; CBE; CBOV; CBPC; CH; FaBoCh; GTSL; LoGBV; MBP; MoAB; MoBrPo; MuP; OBMV; OtMeF; POTE; ReMP; SeCePo; ShBV-1; TCEP; VOD; YT
This is the week when Christmas comes. In the Week When Christmas Comes. Eleanor Farjeon. ChBR; SiSoSe; TiPo (1952 ed.)
This is the wild huntsman that shoots the hares. The Story of the Wild Huntsman. Heinrich Hoffmann. NA
This is the wood my holy angel-child. Pierre de Ronsard. *Fr.* Amours de Cassandre. PrPoCR
This is the word whose breaking heart. Mathematics or the Gift of Tongues. Anna Hempstead Branch. ImOP
This is the Yak, so neg-li-gee. The Yak. Oliver Herford. *Fr.* Child's Natural History. HBV; HBVY
This is their moment, when the brimming skies. Evening in the Great Smokies. DuBose Heyward. LS
This Is Thy Gift, O Muse ("Quem tu, Melpomene, semel"). Horace, *tr. fr. Latin by* Christopher Smart. Odes, IV, 3. LiA
(Gift of Song, The.) LiTW
This is thy hour, O Soul, thy free flight into the wordless. A Clear Midnight. Walt Whitman. NeMA

This is true liberty, when free-born men. Milton, *tr. fr. the Greek of* Euripides. Fr. Areopagitica. PoFr
This is true love, by that true Cupid got. The Dance of Love. Sir John Davies. *Fr.* Orchestra. EIL; SeCePo
This Is War. Richard Le Gallienne. OQP; QP-1
(Illusion of War, The.) BMEP
(War.) MaRV
This is what I vow. Somebody's Story. Dorothy Parker. *Fr.* Songs of a Markedly Personal Nature. TCPD
This is what the fiddle said to the bow. The Fiddle and the Bow. Humbert Wolfe. NV
This Is What the Watchbird Sings, Who Perches in the Love-tree. Bruce Boyd. NeAP
This is what we really want. By Fiat of Adoration. Oscar Williams. GTBS-W; LiTL; LiTM; NePA
This is where the scarlet lords-and-ladies. Under the Cliff. Geoffrey Grigson. WaP
This is Willy Walker, and that's Tam Sim. *Unknown.* OxNR
This is your home to which you are returning. Return. Sister Mary Madeleva. JKCP (1955 ed.)
This Is Your Hour. Herbert Kaufman. PoToHe
This is your loveliest moment; now the song. On Her Twenty-fifth Birthday. Louis Hasley. JKCP (1955 ed.)
This is your month, the month of "perfect days." James Russell Lowell. Oliver Wendell Holmes. PEOR
This island is the world's end. The Island. Seán Jennett. JKCP (1955 ed.); NeIP; SeCePo
This Johnny Jones he thinks he's smart. Sores. Douglas Malloch. OnHT
This kind o' sogerin' aint a mite like our October trainin'. A Letter from Mr. Hosea Biglow to the Hon. J. T. Buckingham. James Russell Lowell. *Fr.* The Biglow Papers. OxBA
This kiss upon your fan I press. Two Triolets: What He Said. Harrison Robertson. HBV; PR
This labouring, vast, Tellurian galleon. To My Godchild. Francis Thompson. JKCP; PC; PoeT
This labyrinth of bridges and cramped streets. Venetian Sonnets, II. August, Graf von Platen. AnGP
This Land. Ian Mudie. BoAu
This last October working to a day of sun. Voyage. John Lyle Donaghy. OxBI
This Last Pain. William Empson. ChMP; CoBMV; FaBoMo; LiTM; MoAB; MoVE; SeCePo
This Latest Poet. *Unknown.* LiTM (rev. ed.); SiTL
This legend is told of me. Actaeon. Rayner Heppenstall. FaBoTw
This let who hate me know, and much admire. The Master-Foe. William Baylebridge. *Fr.* Sextains. BoAV
This Life. William Drummond of Hawthornden. *See* Madrigal: "This life which seems so fair."
This life a theatre we well may call. All the World's a Stage. Palladas. GrPo; OxBG
This life, and all that it contains, to him. The Scholar. Sir Henry Taylor. *Fr.* Edwin the Fair. LPS-3
This Life and the Next ("A truth it is few doubt but fewer trust"). Edward Young. *Fr.* Night Thoughts, Night III. GrCo-1
This Life Flies. Omar Khayyám, *tr. fr. Persian by* Edward Fitzgerald. *Fr.* The Rubáiyát. OnPM
This life is a hospital. Anywhere Out of the World. Baudelaire. AnFP
This life is but a game of cards. Life's a Game. *Unknown.* BLPA
This life is sweetest; in this wood. In the Country. W. H. Davies. BMEP; ChMo; CMP
This life were brutish did we not sometimes. Life's Purpose. James Russell Lowell. *Fr.* The Cathedral. MaRV
This Life Which Seems So Fair. William Drummond of Hawthornden. *See* Madrigal: "This life, which seems so fair."
This life's a hollow bubble. Fin de Siècle. Edmund Vance Cooke. BLPA
This light is loss backward; delight by hurt and by bias gained. March Twilight. Louise Bogan. NePoAm-2
This Lime-Tree Bower My Prison. Samuel Taylor Coleridge. BPN; EM-2; EmBrPo; EnRP; ERP; LoBV; PoEL-4; ShBV-4
This Little Bill, *in mod. Eng.* *Unknown.* TMEV
This little bunny said, "Let's play." Finger Play. *Unknown.* BoTP
This little child do not compare. On the Death of Mlle de Conty. François de Malherbe. LiA
This little child, so white, so calm. Challenge. Kenton Foster Murray. HBV
This Little Earth. Leslie Savage Clark. ChIP
This little fable heard. The Ass and the Flute. Tomás de Iriarte. AnSpL-2
This little fellow, we call him a thumb. To Be Said to Baby's Fingers. *Unknown.* SAS
This little flag to us so dear The Union Jack. Jeannie Kirby. BoTP
This little girl's so gay and fidgety. Rispetto. Angelo Poliziano. LyPI
This little house is sugar. Winter Sweetness. Langston Hughes. GoSl
This Little Moment. George Meredith. *See* Modern Love: "We saw the swallows . . ."
This little pig had a rub-a-dub. *Unknown.* OxNR
This little pig went to market. Mother Goose. BoChLi; HBV; HBVY; OTPC; OxNR; PCH; PPL; RIS; SAS; SiTL; StVeCh; TiPo
This little runt whom I outplay. Down the Field. Rolfe Humphries. AnAmPo; LA
This little talent goes to market. Rhyme from Grandma Goose. Annemarie Ewing. NePoAm
This little vault, this narrow room. An Epitaph [*or* Epitaph on a Young Girl *or* Epitaph on the Lady Villiers]. Thomas Carew. BEL; BLV; EnLi-1; EPS (1942 ed.); LiTL; OBEV; PIAE; SeCV-1; SeEP; UnPo (1st ed.)
This Little Vigil. Charles G. Bell. NePoAm
This living hand, now warm and capable. Lines. Keats. ChER
This Loneliness for You Is like the Wound. Dunstan Thompson. WaaP; WaP
This lonely hill has always/ Been dear to me. The Infinite. Giacomo Leopardi, *tr. by* Kenneth Rexroth. LiTW
This lonely hill was always dear to me/ And this hedge too. The Infinite. Giacomo Leopardi, *tr. by* Glauco Cambon. OnPM
This lonely hill was always dear to me,/ And this hedgerow. L'Infinito (The Infinite). Giacomo Leopardi, *tr. by* John Heath-Stubbs. Po
This long and lonely month. The Lonely Month. Ruthven Todd. NeBP
This lovely flower fell to seed For My Grandmother. Countee Cullen. CDC; GoSl; MAP; MoAmPo
This Lunar Beauty. W. H. Auden. MBP; MoAB; MoBrPo; OBMV
(Pur.) TwHP
This luxury they call the Flesh. Phineas Pratt. Gloria MacArthur. GoYe
This lyfe, I see, is but a cheyre feyre. A Cherry Fair. *Unknown.* ChTr
This Mad Carnival of Loving. Heine, *tr. fr. German by* Emma Lazarus. *Fr.* To Angélique. TrJP
This man escaped the dirty fates. Flyer's Fall. Wallace Stevens. MoAB
This man has written songs. Fellow-Passengers. Frank Wilmot. BoAu
This man is dead. Steel. Joseph Auslander. TBM; TCPD
This man is O so. Item. E. E. Cummings. MoAB; MoAmPo
This man that at the wheatstack side. A Yeoman. Edmund Blunden. NV
This man that is mean, that is nothing, this drudge—he too is known. "In Huts Where Poor Men Lie." Bianor. GrPE
This man, who his own fatherland forgets. He Is My Countryman. Antoni Slonimski. TrJP
This man whose homely face you look upon. Abraham Lincoln [*or* Lincoln's Birthday]. Richard Henry Stoddard. DD; GN; HH; LBAH; OHIP; OTPC (1946 ed.); PEDC; PGD; PoRL; PSO
This marquis hath hir spousèd with a ryng. Griselda. Chaucer. *Fr.* The Canterbury Tales: The Clerkes Tale. BHV
This mast, new-shaved, through whom I rive the ropes. Choosing a Mast. Roy Campbell. CaAE; FaBoTw; GTBS-D; TwCV
This master sprite has been too long maligned. The Mocking-Bird Misnamed. Percy MacKaye. BAP
This matter of baldness: we do it badly. Baldness and the Swan. Winfield Townley Scott. FiMAP
This may I prove withouten let. Now Be We Glad, and Not too Sad. *Unknown.* AnEC
This Measure. Léonie Adams. MAP; MoAB; MoAmPo; PIAE
This memory of my mother stays with me. Remembrance. Margaret E. Bruner. PoToHe
This merry pleasant springe. *Unknown.* SeCSL
This might have been a place for sleep. Thistledown. Harold Monro. GTBS-D; TCEP
This mild September mist recalls the soul. The Origin of Centaurs. Anthony Hecht. NePoEA
This mist has followed on an all-day rain. Spring Night. Richard Aldridge. NePoAm
This Moment. Annie Johnson Flint. BLRP
This Moment Yearning and Thoughtful. Walt Whitman. BoFr; MCCG; OTPC (1946 ed.); PoMa
This month of May, one pleasant eventide. Medieval Norman Songs, VI. *Unknown, tr. by* John Addington Symonds. AWP
This moonlight lies. Good Night. Mark Van Doren. BAP
This morn a young squire shall be made a knight. On Knighthood. Folgore da San Geminiano. AWP; JAWP; WBP
This morn I footed far. The Monk's Day. Arthur L. Phelps. CPG
This morn is merry June, I trow. Sir Walter Scott. LO

This morn it was she died, the little maid. To a Dead Infant. Philip Francis Little. GTIV
This Morning. Hildegarde Flanner. NP
This morning, as I walked to school. A Story in the Snow. Pearl Riggs Crouch. MPB; TiPo
This morning, as I wandered forth. Rags and Bones. W. H. Davies. ChMo; CMP
This morning as the scythe swung in my grasp. The Scythe. Stanley Snaith. POTE
This morning before breakfast time. The Dewdrops. Lydia Miller Mackay. GFA
This Morning I Wakened among Loud Cries of Seagulls. Patrick MacDonogh. NeIP
This morning I went out to look for roses. Moment Musicale. Wallace Gould. AnAmPo; LA
This morning I went to the tomb. To the Tomb. Raymond Kresensky. ChIP
This morning I will not/ Comb my hair. Kakinomoto no Hitomaro, *tr. fr. Japanese by* Kenneth Rexroth. OnPJ
This morning, in my garden. November Garden. Louise Driscoll. YeAr
This morning saw I, fled the shower. Contemplation. Francis Thompson. EmBrPo; LoBV
This morning take a holiday from unhappiness because. George Barker. First Cycle of Love Poems, I. MoPo
This morning, there flew up the lane. Lady Lost. John Crowe Ransom. AnFE; CoAnAm; MAP; MoAB; MoAmPo; NeMA; TrGrPo; TwAmPo
This morning, timely rapt [*or* wrapt] with holy fire. On Lucy, Countess[e] of Bedford. Ben Jonson. EPS; OAEP; OBS; SeCV-1; SeEP; TuPP
This morning we beheld with streaming eyes. Callimachus, *tr. fr. Greek by* H. W. Tytler. GrPo
This morning, when I heard the crows. The Crows. David McCord. MAP; MoAmPo
This morning with a blue flame burning. A Poem for Trapped Things. John Wieners. NeAP
This mossy bank they pressed. That aged oak. A Pastoral Dialogue. Thomas Carew. EV-2
This most afflicts me, that departing hence. Yonder Nether World. Milton. *Fr.* Paradise Lost, XI. LiA
This motion was of Love begot. Dances Inspired by Love. Ben Jonson. *Fr.* Love Restored. UnS
This motley piece to you I send. The Spleen. Matthew Green. CEP; EiPP
This mound the Achaeans reared—Achilles' tomb. Epitaph on Achilles. *Unknown.* AWP
This Much I Know. Florence Wilson Roper. MuM
This much, O heaven—if I should brood or rave. A Prayer in Darkness. G. K. Chesterton. BMEP; MBP; MoBrPo; TrGrPo
This much the gods vouchsafe today. To One Who Said Me Nay. Countee Cullen. PR
This music leads us far/ From all our creeds. Alfred Noyes. *Fr.* Watchers of the Sky. MaRV; OQP; QP-2
This Native Land. Thomas Davis. *See* My Land.
This Needle. Kurahashibe Otome, *tr. fr. Japanese by* Ishii *and* Obata. OnPM
This never-ended searching for the eyes. Egg-and-Dart. Robert Finch. BoCaPo
This new Diana makes weak men her prey. Diana. Ernest Rhys. OBVV; VA
This night is pure and clear as thrice refinèd silver. Fountains. Sacheverell Sitwell. LBBV; MBP; MoBrPo
This night oh hide thy crescent, kindly Moon. To the Moon. Pierre de Ronsard. TrFP
This night sees Eire desolate. The Flight of the Earls. *Unknown.* AnIL
This night there is a Child [y]born. All This Time This Song Is Best [*or* Three Christmas Carols, 3]. *Unknown.* ACP; AnEC
This night, while sleep begins with heavy wings. Astrophel and Stella, XXXVIII. Sir Philip Sidney. SiPS
This noiseless ball and top so round. Philocles. Leonidas of Tarentum. AWP
This now seemed to my mind to be counsel the best and the wisest. Homer. *Fr.* The Odyssey, IX. GrPo
This nycht befoir the dawing cleir. Followis How Dumbar Wes Desyrd to Be Ane Freir. William Dunbar. OAEP
This old crabbed man, with his wrinkled, fusty clothes. Old Crabbed Men. James Reeves. ChMP
This old hammer killed John Henry. John Henry (E *vers.*). *Unknown.* ViBoFo
This old tree in a/ blaze of Spring. Wild Willow. James Wreford Watson. TwCaPo
This Ole Worl' Ain't Goin' to Stan' Much Longer, *with music.* *Unknown.* StDa
This on thy posy-ring I've writ. The Posy Ring. Clément Marot. AWP; JAWP; WBP
This One Heart-shaken. Sister Maris Stella. GoBC
This one sits shivering in Fortune's smile. Pessimist and Optimist. Thomas Bailey Aldrich. AnNE; PIAE; TOP
This one was put in a jacket. Counting the Mad. Donald Justice. NePoEA; UnPo (3d ed.)
This onion-dome holds all intricacies. Greenwich Observatory. Sidney Keyes. MoAB
This Only Do I Know. *Unknown.* BePJ
This only grant me, that my means may lie. Of Myself [*or* A Wish]. Abraham Cowley. *Fr.* A Vote. ElSeCe; LPS-3; OAEP; OBS; ReTS; SeCL; SeEP; WP
This Other Night. *Unknown.* ISi
This other night so cold. The Star. *Unknown.* ChrBoLe
This our land—indeed we love it. National Song. Björnstjerne Björnson. AnNoLy
This Page My Pigeon. Earle Birney. PeCV
This palace standeth in the air. The Palace of the Fairies. Michael Drayton. OTPC (1923 ed.)
This paper flatness, yellow-isled, and neat. Chart of the Pacific. Clifford Gessler. MuM
This passeth yeer by yeer, and day by day. The Knight's Tale. Chaucer. *Fr.* The Canterbury Tales. BEL; GEPC; TOP
This passion, too, will end at last. This, Too. Helene Mullins. MuM
This pathway marked No Thoroughfare. Spiritism. Robert Hillyer. WHL
This peach is pink with such a pink. Song. Norman Gale. HBV; VA
This peasant cot of mine here. Castle and Cottage. Anna Maria Lenngren. AnSL
This piano travels within. Trilce, XLIV. César Vallejo. TwSpPo
This picture placed these busts between. On Beau Nash's Picture, Which Once Stood between the Busts of Newton and Pope. Jane Brereton. InP
This pig got in the barn. *Unknown.* OxNR
This Pine-Tree. Elizabeth Morrow. PEDC
This piston's infinite recurrence is. La Marche des Machines. A. S. J. Tessimond. MoP
This Place in the Ways. Muriel Rukeyser. MiAP
This place is wonderful; here old romance. In a Library. Richard Burton. MOB
This Place Rumord to Have Been Sodom. Robert Duncan. NeAP
This pleasant tale is like a little copse. Sonnet Written at the End of "The Floure and the Lefe." Keats. EmBrPo; EnRP; PtP
This plot, which failed for want of common sense. Dryden. *Fr.* Absalom and Achitophel, Pt. I. CoBE
This ploughman dead in battle slept out of doors. A Private. Edward Thomas. SoV
This poem is for my wife. Poem in Prose. Archibald MacLeish. LiTL; LoPS
This Poem Will Never Be Finished. Raymond Souster. CaP
This point then craves our cunning, to acquire. Scruple. Sophocles. *Fr.* Philoctetes. GrR
This Political Time-plotted Day. David Evans. MoWP
This pool, the quiet sky. March Evening. L. A. G. Strong. MBP; MoBrPo
This Prayer I Make. Wordsworth. *Fr.* Lines Composed a Few Miles above Tintern Abbey. PoToHe
This problem yet, this offspring of a guess. Man and the Universe. Matthew Prior. *Fr.* Solomon on the Vanity of the World. BeR
This prospect vast, what is it? At Home among the Stars. Edward Young. GrCo-1
This Pure Child. Jules Supervielle, *tr. fr. French by* Wallace Fowlie. MiCF
This Quiet Dust. Emily Dickinson. *See* This quiet dust was gentlemen and ladies.
This Quiet Dust. John Hall Wheelock. AnEnPo; MAP; MM; MoAmPo; QS; WHA
This quiet dust was gentlemen and ladies. Emily Dickinson. EG; IAP; InP; OxBA; PoeMoYo; TOP; ViBoPo (Cemetery, A.) CBOV; MAP; MoAB; MoAmPo; NeMA; RiBV
This quiet roof, where sail the doves, is bright. The Graveyard by the Sea. Paul Valéry. TrFP
This rain like silver corn, this northern rain. Count Orlo in England. Jon Manchip White. NePoEA
This realm is sacred to the silent past. In a Garret. Elizabeth Akers Allen. AA; LEAP
This red nun on my left hand leans away. Red Right Returning. Louis O. Coxe. MoVe; WaP
This red scabbard of rock. The Phoenix. W. H. Oliver. AnNZ
This region is as lavish of its flowers. Lefroy in the Forest. Charles Mair. *Fr.* Tecumseh. CPG; VA
This region, surely, is not of the earth. Naples. Samuel Rogers. *Fr.* Italy. LPS-2
This relative of mine. To My Grandmother. Frederick Locker-Lampson. ALV; EPP; HBV; InMe; OBVV; TOP; VA
This reverend shadow cast that setting sun. Upon Bishop Andrewes His Picture before His Sermons. Richard Crashaw. OBS
This rich marble doth inter. An Epitaph on the Marchioness of Winchester. Milton. OBS; TriL

This rite perform'd, all inly pleas'd and still. A Wondrous Show. James Thomson. *Fr.* The Castle of Indolence, I. OBEC
This river Crathis rolls us down. Metagenes, *tr. fr. Greek by* F. A. Paley. GrPo
"This river does not see the naked sky." The Coming of Dian. Keats. *Fr.* Endymion. BPN
This road isn't passable. Warning. Jesse Douglas. WhC
This room is very old and very wise. Poem. Sam Harrison. NeIP
This Rose Is Railed on a Ryse. *Unknown.* AnEC
This rose-tree is not made to bear. Envy. Charles *and* Mary Lamb. OTPC (1923 ed.)
This royal infant, heaven still move about her! England at Peace; a Vision. Shakespeare *and probably* John Fletcher. King Henry VIII, *fr.* V, v. EV-1
This Royal Throne of Kings. Shakespeare. *See* This England ("This royal throne of kings").
This rudely sculptured porter-pot. Undying Thirst. Antipater of Sidon. AWP; GrPo; OuHeWo
This said; he (begging) gather'd clouds from land. Ulysses in the Waves. Homer, *tr. by* George Chapman. *Fr.* The Odyssey, V. OBS
This said; he high Olympus reacht, the king then left his coach. Priam and Achilles. Homer, *tr. by* George Chapman. *Fr.* The Iliad, XXIV. OBS
This said, he left her there, and forth did to his bellows go. Vulcan Forges the Shield of Achilles [*or* Achilles' Shield]. Homer, *tr. by* George Chapman. *Fr.* The Iliad, XVIII. KN; ReEn; TuPP
This said, he turned about his steed. Sidrophel, the Rosicrucian Conjurer. Samuel Butler. *Fr.* Hudibras. NBE; OxBoLi
This said, he went to see. The Parting of Hector and Andromache. Homer, *tr. by* George Chapman. *Fr.* The Iliad, VI. SeEP
This said, our 'Squire, yet undismayed. John Trumbull. *Fr.* M'Fingal. IAP
This said Phocylides, also; where men live lawfully. "In Huts Where Poor Men Lie." Phocylides. GrPE
This said, the golden-throned Aurora rose. The Twelfth Book. Homer, *tr. by* George Chapman. *Fr.* The Odyssey, XII. EPP
This said unanimous, and other rites. Wedded Love. Milton. *Fr.* Paradise Lost, IV. PoFS
This sailor knows of wondrous lands afar. The Child and the Mariner. W. H. Davies. CH; POTT
This saith my Cloris bright. Madrigal. *Unknown.* LO
"This Same Flower That Smiles To-Day." Rufinus, *tr. fr. Greek by* F. L. Lucas. GrPE
This Satyr was not carved, but laid asleep. Peace to the Statue. *Unknown.* OnPM
This saying good-bye on the edge of the dark. Good-bye and Keep Cold. Robert Frost. ChMo; GoTP; NV; OBAV
This scheme of worlds, which vast we call. Turris Eburnea. Aubrey Thomas de Vere. *Fr.* May Carols. PoVP
This school: like larks, in the clod low down. The Teacher. Sister Monica. PraNu
This sely widwe, and eek hir doghtres two. Chasing the Fox. Chaucer. *Fr.* The Canterbury Tales: The Nonne Preestes Tale. CoEV
This Senseless Slug. Wade Oliver. PoP
This shade-bestowing pear-tree, thou. The Pear-Tree. *Unknown.* *Fr.* Shi King. AWP; JAWP; WBP
This shadow flesh of risen man. Night. Glyn Jones. NeBP
This Sharpening Tension. Sister Mary St. Virginia. JKCP (1955 ed.)
This she? no, this is Diomids Cressida. Shakespeare. *Fr.* Troilus and Cressida, V, ii. NBE
This shell, this slender spiral in the hand. The Enduring Music. Harold Vinal. EtS
This shepherdess/ serene of gaze. Christmas Hymn. Sister Juana Inés de la Cruz. AnMP
This short straight sword. Prelude. R. A. K. Mason. AnNZ
This Side and That Side. Mokutaro Kinoshita, *tr. fr. Japanese by* Takamichi Ninomiya *and* D. J. Enright. PoLJ
This Side of Calvin. Phyllis McGinley. QS
This side of madness, while the flames abate. Two Sonnets from a Sequence. Edgar Holt. BoAV
This Side of the Truth. Dylan Thomas. GTBS-W
This silken wreath, which circles thus mine arm. Upon a Ribbon Tied about His Arm by a Lady. Thomas Carew. EPS
This small, delightful book Erinna wrote. Asclepiades, *tr. fr. Greek by* William Wallace *and* Mary Wallace. GrPo
This Smoking World. Graham Lee Hemminger. InMe
This song is of no importance. Evensong. Conrad Aiken. HBMV; PG
This song of late autumn. Autumn. Itzig Manger. TrJP
This song of mine. Catawba Wine. Longfellow. LHV
This song of mine will wind its music around you, my child, like the fond arms of love. My Song. Rabindranath Tagore. MOAH; OHIP
This Speaking Were Enough. Ralph Gustafson. BoCaPo (1943 ed.); TwCV
This speech all Trojans did applaud; who from their traces loos'd. The Trojans outside the Walls. Homer, *tr. by* George Chapman. *Fr.* The Iliad, VIII. OBS
This spiritual love acts not nor can exist. Wordsworth. *Fr.* The Prelude, XIV. NBE
This spoke, a huge wave took him by the head. Homer, *tr. by* George Chapman. *Fr.* The Odyssey, V. PreP
This spot is the sweetest I've seen in my life. From a Churchyard in Wales. *Unknown.* FiBHP; WhC
This Spring of Love. Shakespeare. *Fr.* The Two Gentlemen of Verona, I, iii. ChTr
This spring there is a change in everything. Spring 1944. Boris Pasternak. BoRS
This starry world, and I in it. Death. James Oppenheim. WGRP
This statue of Liberty, busy man. The Statue of Liberty. Thomas Hardy. EPN; LiTB
This still roof where the doves walk slowly, waves. The Cemetery by the Sea. Paul Valéry. OnHM
This Stone. *Unknown, tr. fr. Greek by* Goldwin Smith. AWP
This street where I live, between two bends of the road. The Highway. Manuel Bandeira. AnCL
This sturdy squire, he had, as well. Samuel Butler. *Fr.* Hudibras, I. ViBoPo
This Suffenus, Varus, with whom you are acquainted. Catullus, *tr. fr. Latin by* Frances Fletcher. LaP
This summer is your perfect summer. Never will the skies. To a Child before Birth. Norman Nicholson. ChMP
This Summer's Love, *sel* Mikhail Alekseyevich Kuzmin, *tr. fr. Russian by* Babette Deutsch.
"Night was done; we rose and after." OnPM; TrRV
This sunlight shames November where he grieves. Autumn Idleness. Dante Gabriel Rossetti. The House of Life, LXIX. PoVP; ViPo; ViPP; VLEP
This Swan. Richard Ely Morse. CAG
This sweet and merry month of May. *Unknown.* SiCE
This sweet work is Erinna's: no great sum. Erinna's Poems [*or* Preface to Erinna's Poems]. Asclepiades. GrR; OxBG
This sweetness built our beauty. America Is Corn. Robert P. Tristram Coffin. WaKn
This sycamore, oft musical with bees. Inscription for a Fountain on a Heath. Samuel Taylor Coleridge. EV-4; MCCG; OAEP
This tale he utters I have known. Answer to Defiance; the Earthquake. Aeschylus. *Fr.* Prometheus Bound. GrR
This tempest sweeps the Atlantic! Night Storm. William Gilmore Simms. EtS
This that I give you now. Bread. Stanley Burnshaw. TrJP
This that is Neptune's own. Celebration for Neptune. Horace. *Fr.* Odes. LiA
This that is washed with weed and pebblestone. The Figurehead. Léonie Adams. NP
This the house of Circe, queen of charms. Circe. Lord De Tabley. VA
This the law of all war through all ages. The Waste of War. William L. Stidger. PGD
This the road I tread today. The Death of Moses. *Unknown.* TrJP
This the true sign of ruin to a race. The Decay of a People. William Gilmore Simms. AA; APW; SPP
This, then, is she. The Daguerreotype. William Vaughn Moody. AnAmPo; LA; LBMV; MOAH
This, then, is the covenant you shall keep. Covenant. Joseph Auslander. QS
This, then, the end of a dream of power. Basho, *tr. fr. Japanese by* Lois J. Erickson. SoLD
This thief the gallows mounting, there to die. Of Labienus. John Owen. *Fr.* Four Epigrams. PrWP
This thin elastic stick was plucked. A Switch Cut in April. Clifford Dyment. MoP; MoVE
This thing I pray, dearest Night, thou Mother of all the gods. A Lover's Curse. Meleager. LiTW
This thing you see, this brightly gay deceit. To Her Portrait Sister Juana Inés de la Cruz. LiTW
This, this is he; softly a while. Samson Fallen [*or* Eyeless at Gaza *or* A Hero in Prison]. Milton. *Fr.* Samson Agonistes. BHV; LH; OBS
This tiger is not Blake's tiger burning bright. The Wooden Tiger. Samuel Yellen. NePoAm
This time, I mean it. A Little Tumescence. Jonathan Williams. NeAP
This time is born a Child full good. Man, Be Merry as Bird on Berry. *Unknown.* AnEC
This time of year a twelvemonth past. A. E. Housman. A Shropshire Lad, XXV. BPN; EmBrPo; PoVP
This time the snow came fiercely down. Of Snow. Norman Brick. WaP
This to the crown, and blessing of my life. A Letter to Dafnis [*or* Daphnis]. Countess of Winchilsea. DiM; EnLoPo
This Tokyo. Gary Snyder. NeAP

This told, strange Teras touched her lute, and sung. The Wedding of Alcmane and Mya. George Chapman. *Fr.* Hero and Leander. OBSC
This tomb, by loving hands up-piled. At the Lincoln Tomb. John H. Bryant. PGD
This tomb inscribed to gentle Parnell's name. Epitaph on Dr. Parnell. Goldsmith. PtP
This, Too. Helene Mullins. MuM
This, too, be your glory great. Primroses. Alfred Austin. BMEP; OBVV
This too is an experience of the soul. Isis Wanderer. Kathleen Raine. FaBoMo
This, Too, Shall Pass Away. *Ad. fr. var. sources by* A. L. Alexander. PoToHe
This, Too, Shall Pass Away. Lanta Wilson Smith. BLPA; NeHB
This tooke; he stoopt Pierea. Calypso's Island. Homer. *Fr.* The Odyssey, V. GrR
This torment of love. Describes Rationally the Irrational Effects of Love. Sister Juana Inés de la Cruz. AnMP
This trade of mine, dear boy. Plautus. *Fr.* Asinaria. LaP
This tragical tale, which, they say, is a true one. Pyramus and Thisbe. John Godfrey Saxe. HBV
This Train. *Unknown.* ABF, *with music;* OxBoLi; SiTL
This tranquil roof whereon the white dove looms. The Marine Cemetery. Paul Valéry, *tr. by* Sidney Alexander. ReMP
This tranquil roof, with walking pigeons, looms. The Cemetery by the Sea. Paul Valéry, *tr. by* Barbara Gibbs. AnFP; LiTW
This tree, entrusted by the East. Gingo Biloba. Goethe. *Fr.* West-eastern Divan. BoFr
This troubled world is sighing now. *Unknown.* GoTP
This truth came borne with bier and pall. In Memoriam A. H. H., LXXXV. Tennyson. BPN; EmBrPo; EPN; GEPC; ViPo; VLEP
This tuft that thrives on saline nothingness. The Air Plant. Hart Crane. MAP; MoAB; MoAmPo
This twilight of two years, not past nor next. To the Countesse of Bedford on New-Yeares Day. John Donne. OBS; SeEP
This Unimportant Morning. Lawrence Durrell. NeBP
This valley sends another sound. Deserted Hollow. Mark Van Doren. MM
This valley wood is hedged. An English Wood. Robert Graves. YT
This vase you filled with roses, tender care displaying. The Broken Vase. Aleksey Nikolayevich Apukhtin. WaL
This vast web, of Nature's weaving. The Cosmic Fabric. Yakov Petrovich Polonsky. TrRV
This verse be thine, my friend, nor thou refuse. To Mr. Jervas, with Fresnoy's Art of Painting, Translated by Mr. Dryden. Pope. OBEC
This Very Hour. Lizette Woodworth Reese. AnAmPo; HBMV; LA
This very remarkable man. On Monsieur Coué. Charles Inge. FaFP; SiTL
This villa is raked of winds from fore and aft. Catullus, *tr. fr. Latin by* Ezra Pound. LaP
This village has no name. We wiped it out. Lidice. "Lucio." NeTW
This wall-paper has lines that rise. Missing My Daughter. Stephen Spender. AtBAP
This warning, Gallus, for thy love I send. Hylas. Propertius. *Fr.* Elegies. AWP
This war's dead heroes, who has seen them? Heroes. Kathleen Raine. DiM
This was a dog's day, when the land. Ice on the Round Pond. Paul Dehn. AlDL
This was a man of mighty mould. On a Bust of Lincoln. Clinton Scollard. PEDC
This was a mouse who played around. Tracks in the Snow. Marchette Chute. SiSoSe
This was a thing the saints never knew. Park Avenue Cat. Frances Frost. CIV
This was Briseis' way: she was a bridge. The Postures of Love, IV. Alex Comfort. NeBP
This was decreed by superior powers. Tower of Ivory. Leonard Bacon. WhC
This was her table, these her trim outspread. On the Toilet Table of Queen Marie-Antoinette. J. B. B. Nichols. PoeT
This was his life—overalls, cotton, sweat. Sharecropper. Stewart Atkins. NoCaPo
This Was My Brother. Mona Gould. CaP
This was no cargo of roses, nor charcoal, nor wood. Lament for a Dead Burro. Joaquin Antonio Peñalosa. SaFP
This was of old my wishes' utmost bound. The Town and the Country Mouse. Horace. *Fr.* Satires. WoL
This was our heritage. An Ode on the Despoilers of Learning in an American University (1947). Yvor Winters. ExPo
This was that mystery of clearest light. The Statue of Shadow. John Peale Bishop. LiTA
This was the color of coolness. Spring Cellar. Gladys McKee. GoYe
This was the crucifixion on the mountain. Sonnet. Dylan Thomas. Sonnets, VIII. LiTM
This was the end and yet, another start. Merlin in the Cave; He Speculates without a Book. Thom Gunn. NePoEA
This was the fire that ran in the wake of the promise. In a Class of Moral Theology. Francis Sweeney. JKCP (1955 ed.)
This was the first world, where the wild dove cries. Creation. Louise Townsend Nicholl. GoYe
This was the hand that knew to swing. The Hand of Lincoln. Edmund Clarence Stedman. PGD
This was the hawk's way. This way the hawk. Hawk's Way. Ted Olson. HoPM
This was the heavenly hiding place. Vale. "Æ." ChMo; CMP
This was the man God gave us when the hour. George Washington. John Hall Ingham. AA; HH; OHIP; PAH; WOAH
This was the noblest Roman of them all. Portrait of Brutus [*or* Brutus *or* A Man]. Shakespeare. *Fr.* Julius Caesar, V, v. BCEP; BHV; FaFP; GoTP; MaC; PECK; PIR; TreFS; TrGrPo
This was the song of the wakeupworld. The Wakeupworld. Countee Cullen. GoSl
This was the stroke that fired the stacks. Poll Tax (1378). Maurice Hewlett. *Fr.* The Song of the Plow. PoFr
This was the summer when the tired girls. Now Kindness. Peter Viereck. LiTA
This was the woman; what now of the man. Modern Love, III George Meredith. EmBrPo; ViPo
This was your butterfly, you see. After Wings. Sarah M. B Piatt. AA; HBV; LBAP
This watchful nurse and bundled boy at play. A Matter of Life and Death. Richard Aldridge. NePoAm
This water, like a sky that no one uses. Waters. Kenneth Slessor. NeLNL
This wax-mannequin nude, the florist rose. The Florist Rose. Robert Graves. AtBAP
This Way Out. Margaret Fishback. ALV
This way the noise was, if my ear be true. The Lady Lost in the Wood. Milton. *Fr.* Comus. LPS-3
This way, this way, come and hear. Song in the Wood. John Fletcher. *Fr.* The Little French Lawyer. EIL; ThWaDe
This way to salvation is swept. Museum Portico. H. L. R. Edwards. MoWP
This we had never known· the sea to build a town. London Elegies, II. Fred Marnau. BoFr
This Weariness and Grief. *Unknown, tr. fr Irish by* Douglas Hyde. GTIV
This Were to Pray. Richard Chenevix Trench. MaRV
This while does good duke Aymon's daughter mourn. Ariosto. *Fr.* Orlando Furioso, XXXII. PrPoCR
This while we are abroad. An Ode Written in the Peak[e]. Michael Drayton. OBS; ReIE
This whirlwind sounds a larger dissonance. Mid-Century. Mary Elizabeth Osborn. NePoAm
This Will Pass. Semyon Osipovich Kirsanov, *tr. fr. Russian by* Babette Deutsch. TrRV
This Will Remain. Semyon Osipovich Kirsanov, *tr. fr. Russian by* Babette Deutsch. TrRV
This wind brings all dead things to life. A Windy Day. Andrew Young. GoTP; MoPW; ThWaDe
This wind from Fife has cruel fingers, scooping. Double Life. Norman MacCaig. PoN
This wind upon my mouth, these stars I see. Epilogue. William Alexander Percy *Fr.* Enzio's Kingdom. LS; UnW
This winter air is keen and cold. Le Jardin des Tuileries. Oscar Wilde. JKCP (1926 ed.)
This winter austere and gaunt has closely hidden. Hungry Winter. Vladimir Mayakovsky. *Fr.* Good! RuPo
This winter day, we build our fire. The Fire. William Burford. NePA
This winter eve how soft! how mild! Elegy. Richard Chenevix French. IrPN
This Winter's Weather It Waxeth Cold. *Unknown. See* Old Cloak, The.
This wolf for many a day. St. Francis and the Wolf. Katharine Tynan. TIP
This World. Abu-l-Ala al-Maarri, *tr. fr. Arabic by* R. A. Nicholson. LiTW
This World. Abbie Huston Evans. NePoAm
This world a hunting is. The World a Game. William Drummond of Hawthornden. BSV; CenL; ElSeCe
This world and life are battered and shattered. Philosophy. Heine, *tr. by* James Thomson. OnPM
This world and this life are so scattered, they try me. Zu fragmentarisch ist Welt und Leben. Heine, *tr. by* Charles G. Leland. AWP
This world behind the faces that you see. A Little Distance Off. John Lehmann. MoP
This World Fares But as a Fantasy, *in mod. Eng. Unknown.* TMEV
This World Is All a Fleeting Show. Menander, *tr. fr. Greek by* Gilbert Murray. OxBG

This World Is All a Fleeting Show. Thomas Moore. HBV
This world is but illusion. The Buddhist to His Soul. Ch'en Sheng Chi. PoHN
This world is not conclusion Emily Dickinson. MaPo
This world is so full of a number of bugs. Happy Thought. Bert Leston Taylor. RIS
This world is unto God a work of art. Robert Bridges. *Fr.* The Growth of Love. PoVP
This world, O my friend, is like a carcase unsepulchred. This World. Abu-l-Ala al-Maarri. LiTW
This world of ours awakes the human will. Speech of Abbot Stephen. Petar Petrovic Njegos. *Fr.* The Mountain Wreath. PoFr
This world was not. The Golden Age. Ernest Francisco Fenollosa. AA
This world was once a fluid haze of light. Tennyson. *Fr.* The Princess. ImOP
This world we see, O Lord, is made so fair. Canto Espiritual. Juan Maragall. CAW
This world's a scene as dark as Styx. Lines Written in an Album. Willis Gaylord. LPS-3
This World's Joy. *Unknown. See* Wynter Wakeneth Al My Care.
This worthy limitour, this noble frere. Prologue. Chaucer. *Fr.* The Canterbury Tales: The Friar's Tale. EnLi-1 (1949 ed.)
This would be spring, if seasons could be found. Perhaps the Best Time. William Meredith. NePoEA
This wreath, O Rhodocleia, to thee I send. Rufinus, *tr. fr. Greek by* W. C. Lawton. GrPo
This year,/ Next year. *Unknown.* OxNR
This Year, before It Ends. Eve Langley. BoAV
This year, I said, when first along the lane. November. Richard Le Gallienne. LBBV
This year of fourteen fifty-six. The Little Testament. Villon. OuHeWo
This year the heavy winter hit me hard. Rose-Fragrance. Kostes Palamas. *Fr.* City and Solitude. MoGP
This year, till late in April, the snow fell thick and light. The Nineteenth of April. Lucy Larcom. MC; MDAH; PAH
This yellow velvet visitor. Caterpillar. R. E. Rashley. CaP
This youth too long has heard the break. A Tale. Louise Bogan. MOAP
This Yris, fro the high stage. The House of Sleep. John Gower. *Fr.* Confessio Amantis: Ceix and Alceone. AtBAP
Thisbe. Helen Gray Cone. AA; PR
Thise olde gentil Britons in hir dayes. The Franklin's Prologue. Chaucer. *Fr.* The Canterbury Tales. OAEP
Thise ryotoures three, of which I telle. Quest for Death. Chaucer. *Fr.* The Canterbury Tales: The Pardoner's Tale. CoEV; MyFE
Thistle and darnel and dock grew there. Nicholas Nye. Walter de la Mare. BoChLi; BoTP; HBMV; WP
Thistle and the Rose, The. William Dunbar. *See* Thrissil and the Rose, The.
Thistle, Yarrow, Clover. Kenneth Porter. NePoAm
Thistle-Down. Clara Doty Bates. AA
Thistledown. Denis Glover. AnNZ
Thistledown. Harold Monro. GTBS-D; TCEP
Thistledown. Lizette Woodworth Reese. YeAr
Thistledown's flying, The. Autumn. John Clare. PoEL-4
Thistles there are, and thwarted thyme. Unconcern. Virginia Moore. TBM
Thither when we came/ To the fair haven. Of the Laestrygones. Homer. *Fr.* The Odyssey, X. OxBG
Tho'. *See also* Though.
Tho' endowed with all the virtues of a Daniel. Tact. Harry Graham. ALV
Tho' grief and fondness in my breast rebel. London. Samuel Johnson. GoTL; PoEL-3
Tho' Grief had nipp'd her early bloom. The Maniac. Thomas Russell. OBEC
Tho' he inherit/ Nor the pride, nor ample pinion. Supreme Dominion. Thomas Gray. *Fr.* The Progress of Poesy. LiA
Tho' [*or* Though] He That Ever Kind and True. Robert Louis Stevenson. *See* Resurgence.
Tho' I am very old and wise. To Dick, on His Sixth Birthday. Sara Teasdale. TSW; TSWC
Tho' I can not your cruelty constrain. Sir Thomas Wyatt. SiPS
Tho' if an eye that's downward cast. In Memoriam A. H. H., LXII. Tennyson. EmBrPo; EPN; GEPC; ViPo; VLEP
Tho' I'm no Catholic. The Catholic Bells. William Carlos Williams. OxBA
Tho' my verse is exact. Hence These Rimes. Bert Leston Taylor. FiBHP
Tho' thou art worship'd by the names divine. In Weary Night. Blake. *Fr.* The Gates of Paradise. LiA
Tho' truths in manhood darkly join. In Memoriam A. H. H., XXXVI [*or* The Word *or* The Word Incarnate]. Tennyson. ChIP; EmBrPo; EPN; GEPC; GoBC; MaRV; ViPo; VLEP
Tho' world on world in myriad myriads roll. What Know We Greater than the Soul? Tennyson. *Fr.* Ode on the Death of the Duke of Wellington. MaRV
Tho' yer lamp o' life is burnin' with a clear and steady light. When the Light Goes Out. Harry S. Chester. PTA-2
Tho' you are conversant at Court. Mr. Diaper Wants Advancement. William Diaper. *Fr.* An Imitation of the Seventeenth Epistle of the First Book of Horace. BeR
Tho' you make no return to my passion. *See* Though You Make No Return.
Tho' You May Boast You're Fairer. *Unknown.* OBS
"Thoch raging stormes move us to shake." *See* Though raging stormes movis us to shake.
Thocht, The. William Soutar. NeBP
Thogorma in his imagination saw walls of iron arise. Charles Marie Leconte de Lisle. *Fr.* Qain. LiA
Thomas A. Edison/ Never took medicine. Important People. Louis Untermeyer, *and others.* StaSt
Thomas à Kempis. Richard Rogers Bowker. AA
Thomas à Kempis. Lizette Woodworth Reese. AA
Thomas a Tattamus took two T's. Riddles. *Unknown.* HBV; HBVY; OTPC; RIS
Thomas at Chickamauga. Kate Brownlee Sherwood. BIG; GA, *abr.*; PAH
Thomas Carlyle. *Unknown.* FiBHP
Thomas Chatterton. Dante Gabriel Rossetti. Five English Poets, 1. BPN; EmBrPo; PoVP; PtP (Two English Poets.) BMEP
Thomas Cromwell. *Unknown.* ESPB
Thomas Decker. Swinburne. *Fr.* Sonnets on English Dramatic Poets (1590–1650). PtP; VLEP
Thomas Dekker's Song. Alfred Noyes. *Fr.* Tales of the Mermaid Tavern, Pt. II. ChMo; CMP (Seven Wise Men.) InP
Thomas Hood. E. A. Robinson. HBMV; PtP
Thomas Hood. Sir William Watson. PoVP
Thomas Jefferson. Stephen Vincent Benét. FaPON; NAMP; TiPo
Thomas lay on the Huntlie bank. Thomas the Rimer [*or* Thomas Rymer]. *Unknown.* EnSB; ESPB (C *vers.*)
Thomas MacDonagh. Francis Ledwidge. GTIV; OnYI; OxBI; TCPD (Lament for Thomas MacDonagh.) AnIV
Thomas Moore at St. Anne's. Thomas D'Arcy McGee. BoCaPo (1943 ed.)
Thomas o Yonderdale. *Unknown.* ESPB
Thomas of Erceldoune. *Unknown, tr. fr. Middle English.* MeEV
Thomas Rhodes. Edgar Lee Masters. *Fr.* Spoon River Anthology. NP
Thomas Rymer. *Unknown. See* Thomas the Rhymer.
Thomas Sackville in Commendation of the Work to the Reader. Thomas Sackville. ReIE
Thomas Shadwell the Poet. Dryden. *Br. sel. fr.* Absalom and Achitophel, Pt. II. ChTr
Thomas Stuart was a lord. Lord Thomas Stuart. *Unknown.* BaBo; ESPB
Thomas the Rhymer. *Unknown.* AnFE; BSV; CBOV; EBSV; EV-2; FaBoCh; GoTS; HBV; LEAP; LiTB; LiTG; OBB; OBEV; SeCeV; ViBoPo (Ballad of True Thomas, The.) CBE (Queen of Elfland, The.) HOAH (Thomas Rymer.) ATP; BaBo (A *and* B *vers.*); BoChLi (1939 ed.); BoLiVe; CH; CoBE; EM-1; EnLi-1; ESPB (A *and* C *vers.*); InP; OAEP; PFE; TyEnPo; ViBoFo (Thomas Rymer and the Queen of Elfland.) ChTr (Thomas the Rimer.) EnSB (True Thomas.) BLV; CoEV; GBV (1952 ed.); GoTP; MaC; OtMeF; StPo; TrGrPo
"'Harp and carp, Thomas!' she said," *sel.* LO; LoPS
Thomas, the vagrant piper's son. Mother Goose Up-to-Date. Louis Untermeyer. MoAmPo
Thomas Trevelyan. Edgar Lee Masters. *Fr.* Spoon River Anthology. AnFE; APA; CoAnAm; MoPo; SBMV
Thomas Winterbottom Hance. W. S. Gilbert. InMe
Thompson Street. Samuel McCoy. HBMV
Thomson Green and Harriet Hale. W. S. Gilbert. TSWC
Thon bird, thon rossignel—ye hear its sang? Tuscan Folk Songs, 4. *Unknown, tr. into Scottish by* Edwin Morgan. LyPI
Thor Gets Back His Hammer. *Unknown. See* Lay of Thrym, The.
Thoralf and Synnöv. Hjalmar Hjroth Boyesen. AA
Thorberg Skafting, master-builder. The Building of the *Long Serpent.* Longfellow. *Fr.* Tales of a Wayside Inn. EtS
Thoreau. Amos Bronson Alcott. AA; GA; LBAP; OBAV
Thoreau. Genevieve Taggard PoTo
Thoreau,/ grabbing on, hard. The Distances to the Friend. Jonathan Williams. NeAP
Thoreau, you've come into your own. To Henry David Thoreau. Irwin Edman. WhC
Thoreau's Flute. Louisa May Alcott. AA; DD; GA; HBV; LBAP
Thorgerda. John Payne. VA

Thorn, The. *Unknown, tr. fr. Japanese by* Lois J. Erickson. SoLD
Thorn, The. Wordsworth. BPN; EmBrPo; EnRP
Thorn of Somerset, The. Elliott Coleman. NoCaPo (1941 ed.)
Thorn Piece. Amy Lowell. ChMo; CMP
Thoroughbred, The. Helene Magaret. StaSt
Thoroughgoing, The. Josephine Miles. FiMAP
Thorowe the halle the belle han sounde. The Accounte of W. Canynge's Feast. Thomas Chatterton. EnLi-2; EPP
Thorvaldur Thoroddsen. Thorsteinn Gislason, *tr. fr. Icelandic by* Jakobina Johnson. IcP
Those animals that follow us in dream. Lupus in Fabula. Malcolm Lowry. BoCaPo (1948 ed.); PeCV
Those arts which common beauties move. To Corinna. John Oldmixon. SeCL
Those Beauteous Maids. Moses ibn Ezra, *tr. fr. Hebrew by* Solomon Solis-Cohen. TrJP
Those Cambridge generations, Russell's, Keynes'. On Bertrand Russell's "Portraits from Memory." Donald Davie. PoN
Those charming eyes within whose starry sphere. On the Death of Catarina de Attayda. Luis de Camões. AWP; JAWP; WBP
Those Christmas bells as sweetly chime. Old Christmas. *Unknown.* PEOR
Those Dancing Days Are Gone. W. B. Yeats. AtBAP
Those days we spent on Lebanon. On Lebanon. David Gray. AA
Those delicate wanderers. Sacrifice. "Æ." ChMo; CMP; TIP
Those—dying, then. Emily Dickinson. MeRV
Those earlier men that owned our earth. The After-Comers. Robert Traill Spence Lowell. AA
Those envied places which do know her well. A Day of Love. Dante Gabriel Rossetti. The House of Life, XVI. PoVP; ViPo
Those Evening Bells. Thomas Moore. LPS-2
Those evening clouds, that setting ray. On the Setting Sun. Sir Walter Scott. MaRV
Those eyes that hold the hand of every heart. A Sonnet. Nicholas Breton. ReIE
Those Eyes Which Set My Fancy on Afire. Philippe Desportes, *tr. fr. French.* ReIE; SiCE
(Conquest.) AWP
(His Lady's Might.) OBSC
Those famous men of old, the Ogres. Ogres and Pygmies. Robert Graves. FaBoMo; LiTB; LiTM; SeCePo; SeCeV
Those fireflies sparkling in the willows. The Code. Christopher Morley. LHV
Those flakes of fire, brilliant sparks of light. Sonnet. Pedro Calderón de la Barca. TeCS
Those former loves wherein our lives have run. Sonnets, XIX. James Agee. MAP; MoAmPo
Those Gambler's Blues. *Unknown. See* Gambler's Blues.
Those golden seeds which thou on fertile earth. To Torquato Tasso. Don Angelo Grillo. BoFr
Those graves, with bending osier bound. A Night-Piece on Death. Thomas Parnell. SeCePo
Those guests from many climes had often heard. New Liberty Bell. "H. B. C." PEOR
Those hands, which you so clapped [*or* clapt], go now and wring. Shakespeare Dead [*or* Sonnet to Shakespeare]. Hugh Holland. ACP (1952 ed.); PrWP
Those heav'nly rayes of thyne. *Unknown.* SeCSL
Those hewers of the clouds, the Winds—that lair. The Winds. Madison Cawein. CP; MAP; NV; PIAE; SPP
Those horns, the envy of the moon. Death of the Bull. Roy Campbell. FaBoTw
Those hours that with gentle work did frame. Sonnets, V. Shakespeare. PeBoSo; ReEn; SiCE
Those hours were good to us. Hours Grey. Francis Vielé-Griffin. MiFP
Those Images. W. B. Yeats. POTE
Those in the vegetable rain retain. Stories of Snow. Patricia K. Page. BoCaPo (1948 ed.)
Those joys are very few. Lovely Things. *Unknown.* SoLD
Those lean and salty sires of ours. The Stone Crop. Robert P. Tristram Coffin. PaA
Those lines that I before have writ do lie. Sonnets, CXV. Shakespeare. PeBoSo; SiCE
Those lips that Love's own hand did make. Sonnets, CXLV. Shakespeare. PeBoSo
Those little woolly insect things. Preference. Berton Braley. AlBD
Those looks, whose beams be joy, whose motion is delight. Astrophel and Stella, LXXVII. Sir Philip Sidney. SiPS
Those lovers only hapye are. *Unknown.* SeCSL
Those lumbering horses in the steady plough. Horses. Edwin Muir. AlDL; FaBoCh; LoGBV; MoVE; SeCePo
Those moon-gilded dancers. The Gay. "Æ." OBMV; POTE
Those nights we said "Goodbye! goodbye!" and then. Decent Burial. Lois Seyster Montross. HBMV
Those nights with the glorious woes are over. Post-War Roll Call. Nicholas Pappas. MoGP
Those Not Elect. Léonie Adams. MOAP; MoVE
Those occasions involving the veering of axles. Munich Elegy No. 1. George Barker. LiTG; LiTM; SeCePo; WaP
Those on the top say they know you, Earth—they are liars. The Miner. Maxwell Bodenheim. NP
Those parts of thee that the world's eye doth view. Sonnets, LXIX. Shakespeare. PeBoSo
Those pretty wrongs that liberty commits. Sonnets, XLI. Shakespeare. InvP; PeBoSo; ReEn
Those ravens black that rested. Heavy-hearted. Judah Al-Harizi. TrJP
Those Rebel Flags. John H. Jewett. FOAH
Those reckless hosts rush to the wells. Elegy. Baruch of Worms. TrJP
Those rules of old discover'd, not devis'd. Pope. *Fr.* An Essay on Criticism. PoFS; PreP
Those saints, which God loves best. Temptation. Robert Herrick. LiTB
Those ships which left. Tanka: A Reflection [*or* Seven Poems, 5]. Saigyo Hoshi. AWP; InP; LiTW
Those stopped by the barrage. Dirge for the Barrel-Organ of the New Barbarism. Louis Aragon. OnHM; WaaP
Those That Come Back. Don Marquis. LEAP
Those trackless deeps, where many a weary sail. The Trackless Deeps. Shelley. *Fr.* The Daemon of the World. EtS
Those Troublesome Disguises. Jonathan Williams. NeAP
Those Two Boys. Franklin P. Adams. ALV; FiBHP; MAP; MoAmPo (1942 ed.); PFE; TrJP
Those Various Scalpels. Marianne Moore. LoBV
Those walléd garrisons will I subdue. Christopher Marlowe. *Fr.* Tamburlaine the Great, Pt. I. ViBoPo
Those we have loved the dearest. The Fallen. Duncan Campbell Scott. AOAH; TrPWD
Those We Love the Best. Ella Wheeler Wilcox. PoToHe
Those we love truly never die. Forever. John Boyle O'Reilly. BoFr; CAW; HBV; MaRV; OnYI; OQP; QP-2; WGRP
Those were good times, in olden days. Written on a Flyleaf of Theocritus. Maurice Thompson. AA; BAP; LEAP
Those were the conquered, still too proud to yield. The Battlefield. Lloyd Mifflin. PAH
Those which have travelled o'er the earth's round ball. John Heath. SiCE
Those who are not mine. The Feast. Nora B. Cunningham. OQP; QP-2
Those who are wise in heart and mind. Sic Transit. Simonides. GrR
Those who fling off, toss head. Meeting Together of Poles & Latitudes; in Prospect. Margaret Avison. PeCV
Those who have descended to the nethermost deeps. Bathymeter. William Hart-Smith. BoAV
Those who have laid the harp aside. To Wordsworth. Walter Savage Landor. BPN; EmBrPo
Those who have no agent paid to cry. Lucky Strike. Merrill Moore. MOAP
Those who have visited the North Pole. The World's End. Michael Roberts. FaBoMo
Those who in ancient days were the best commanders. *Unknown, tr. fr. Chinese.* Tao Teh Ching, XVI. WhP
Those who in quarrels interpose. The Mastiff. John Gay. AlBD
Those Who Know Do Not Tell. *Unknown, at. to* Lao-tzu, *tr. fr. Chinese by* Witter Bynner. *Fr.* Tao Teh King. OnPM
Those who live in country places. Epiphany. Eileen Duggan. ISi
Those who love cats which do not even purr. Cats. Francis Scarfe. NeBP
Those who love Thee may they find. A Prayer. George F. Chawner. BLRP
Those Who Read in Bed. Persis Greely Anderson. DDA
Those who said God is praised. For the New Railway Station in Rome. Richard Wilbur. NePoEA
Those Who Soar. Margaret Lathrop Law. PoMa
"Those who speak know nothing." Lao-tzu [The Philosopher]. Po Chü-i, *tr. by* Arthur Waley. LiTW; OnPM; TrCh; WhC; WoL
Those who were born in years of quiet. Aleksandr Blok, *tr. fr. Russian by* C. M. Bowra. BoR
Those who were born so beautifully. The Young Dead. Struthers Burt. AOAH
Thothmes, who loved a pyramid. The Story of Pyramid Thothmes. *Unknown.* NA
Thou alive on earth, sweet boy. Three Epitaphs upon the Death of a Rare Child of Six Years Old, 3. Francis Davison. OBSC; ReIE
Thou Alone Art Good. Michelangelo, *tr. fr. Italian by* John Addington Symonds. OnPM
(Prayer for Purification, A.) AWP
Thou Alone Canst Save. Amelia Wakeford. BePJ
Thou and I. Jalal ed-Din Rumi, *tr. fr. Persian by* R. A. Nicholson. BoFr
Thou and I and he are not gods made men for a span. Swinburne. *Fr.* The Hymn of Man. WGRP

Thou Art. Kawabuchi, *tr. fr. Japanese by* Lois J. Erickson. SoLD
"Thou art a fool," said my head to my heart. Retort. Paul Lawrence Dunbar. AA
Thou art all fair, O Mary. A Prayer of Praise to Mary. *Unknown.* WHL
Thou art as a lone watcher on a rock. England. Richard Edwin Day. AA
Thou art as tyrannous, so as thou art. Sonnets, CXXXI. Shakespeare. PeBoSo
Thou art beautiful, O my love. Canticle of Canticles (The Song of Solomon), Bible, *O.T.* (*Douay vers.*). ISi
Thou art come at length. Sitalkas. Hilda Doolittle ("H. D."). ViBoPo
Thou Art Coming! Frances Ridley Havergal. WGRP
Thou Art Even as a Flower Is. Heine. *See* Du bist wie eine Blume.
Thou Art God. Psalms, XC, Bible, *O.T. See* God, Our Dwelling Place.
Thou art God, and all things formed are Thy servants. The Royal Crown, VIII. Solomon ibn Gabirol. AWP
Thou art God's sky. Mary. Robert Farren. ISi
Thou art great, and compared with Thy greatness all greatness. The Royal Crown, V. Solomon ibn Gabirol. AWP
Thou art great, and Thou art good. *Unknown.* PraP
Thou art heav'n Olimpia. *Unknown.* SeCSL
Thou art in danger, Cincius, on my word. Epigram. Marcus Argentarius. ALV
Thou Art Indeed Just, Lord. Gerard Manley Hopkins. AWP; ChMo; CoBMV; EnLit; GTBS-W; InPo; LoBV; MeRV; MoAB; MoBrPo (1950 ed.); NeMA; OAEP (2d ed.); PG (1945 ed.); UnPo (3d ed.); ViP; ViPP
(Justus Quidem Tu Es, Domine.) CAW
(Sonnet: "Thou art indeed just, Lord.") CoEV; KN; LiA; MoVE
(Thou Art Indeed Just.) OxBoCh; VLEP
(Thou Art Indeed Just, Lord, If I Contend.) GTML; LiTM; TrPWD, 4 *ll.*
Thou art light and thou art free. The Immortal Muse. Richard Watson Dixon. CBE
Thou art Light celestial, and the eyes of the pure shall. The Royal Crown, VII. Solomon ibn Gabirol. AWP
Thou art like to [*or* unto] a flower. The Translated Way. Franklin P. Adams. BOHV; FiBHP
Thou art lost to me forever!—I have lost thee, Isadore! The Widowed Heart. Albert Pike. AA
Thou art mine, thou hast given thy word. Song from a Drama. Edmund Clarence Stedman. AA
Thou art my bright star in a world half-hidden. Peter Vyazemsky, *tr. fr. Russian by* C. M. Bowra. BoRS
Thou art my dream, but for my last delight. To A. C. M. Richard Middleton. LEAP
Thou art my God, sole object of my love. Prayer of St. Francis Xavier. Pope. TrPWD
Thou art my hiding place, O Lord! O Lord! My Hiding Place. Thomas Raffles. BePJ
Thou art my very own. The Unborn. Julia Neely Finch. AA
Thou art not, and thou never canst be mine. To Imperia. Thomas Burbidge. VA
Thou art not dead, although the spoiler's hand. Africa. Lewis Alexander. CDC
Thou art not dead, my Prote! thou art flown. To Prote. Simmias. AWP
Thou Art Not Fair. Thomas Campion. AtBAP; ElL; ElSeCe; InvP; ReIE; TuPP; ViBoPo
(Renunciation.) GTSL; OnPM
("Thou art not fair for all thy red and white.") EG; EnLoPo; OBSC; ReEn; RiBV
Thou Art Not False, but Thou Art Fickle. Byron. EmBrPo
Thou Art Not in a Place. "Angelus Silesius," *tr. fr. German by* Paul Carus. OnPM
Thou Art Not Lovelier than Lilacs. Edna St. Vincent Millay. Unnamed Sonnets (I–V), I. BLV; BoLiVe; ChMo; CMP
Thou art not, Penshurst, built to envious show. To Penshurst. Ben Jonson. APW; AtBAP; EPS; LoBV; OBS; PoEL-2; PoFS; ReEn; ReIE; SeCV-1; SeEP; TuPP
Thou art not so black, as my heart. A Jeat Ring Sent. John Donne. PoEL-2
Thou art, O God, the life and light. The Glory of God in Creation [*or* Thou Art, O God]. Thomas Moore. MaRV; OHIP; TrPWD
Thou Art of All Created Things. Pedro Calderón de la Barca, *tr. fr.* Spanish. WGRP
Thou art One, the first of every number and the foundation. The Royal Crown, II. Solomon ibn Gabirol. AWP
Thou art Orplid, my land. Weyla's Song. Eduard Mörike. AnGP
Thou art our Master! Thou of God the Son. The Master. S. D. Robbins. BePJ
Thou art present in my shadowiness. Venus Poised. Rafael López. AnMP
Thou art returned, great light, to that blest hour. Love's Anniversary to the Sun. William Habington. ES
Thou art so fair, and yong withall. Youth and Beauty. Aurelian Townshend. MePo
Thou Art So Sweet. Sayat Nova, *tr. fr. Armenian by* Zabelle C. Boyajian. ArmLP
Thou art the essence of all created things. Thou Art of All Created Things. Pedro Calderón de la Barca. WGRP
Thou art the flower of grief to me. The Woodruffe. Isa Craig Knox. VA
Thou art the joy of age. Light. George Macdonald. VA
Thou art the rock of empire, set mid-seas. At Gibraltar, II. George Edward Woodberry. AA; BAP; GN; LA; LBMV; LEAP
Thou art the sky and thou art the nest as well. Rabindranath Tagore. Gitanjali, LXVII. OBMV
Thou are the Star, blazing with beames bright. Star of the Sea. Sebastian Brant, *tr. by* Alexander Barclay. *Fr.* The Ship of Fools. ACP; CAW
Thou art the star for which all evening waits. Aldebaran at Dusk. George Sterling. PFY; TCPD
Thou art the Way. "I Am the Way." Alice Meynell. ACP; CAW; GoBC; JKCP; LBBV; MaRV; OBMV; OQP; POTT; PoVP; QP-1
Thou art the Way! The Way, the Truth, and the Life. *Unknown.* BePJ
Thou art the Way, to Thee alone. Christ, the Way [*or* The Way, the Truth, the Life]. George Washington Doane. BePJ; MaRV
Thou art to all lost love the best. To the Willow-Tree. Robert Herrick. HBV; OBEV
Thou art wise. And wisdom is the fount of life. The Royal Crown, IX. Solomon ibn Gabirol. AWP
Thou askest why such fury fills my heart. Anteros. Gérard de Nerval. TrFP
Thou barren waste; unprofitable strand. Winter in Lower Canada. Standish O'Grady. *Fr.* The Emigrant. BoCaPo
Thou beauteous off-spring of a syre as fair. On a Sunbeam. Thomas Heyrick. MePo
Thou Beautiful Sabbath. *Unknown, tr. fr. Yiddish by* Isidore Myers. TrJP
Thou bent and only motion of our lives. Lyttelton Harbour, XXXIII. D'Arcy Cresswell. AnNZ
Thou bid'st me change with every changing hour. The Branch. Jones Very. TriL
Thou bidst me come away. To Death. Robert Herrick. CoBE; EPS; EV-2; InPo
Thou Black, wherein all colours are composed. Another Sonnet to Black Itself. Lord Herbert of Cherbury. SeEP
Thou bleedest, my poor Heart! and thy distress. On a Discovery Made Too Late. Samuel Taylor Coleridge. EnRP
Thou blind fool, Love, what dost thou to mine eyes. Sonnets, CXXXVII. Shakespeare. PeBoSo
Thou Blind Man's Mark. Sir Philip Sidney. *Sometimes considered Sonnet CIX of* Astrophel and Stella; *also in* Certain Sonnets. TuPP; ViBoPo
(Desire.) LiTB; LiTG; PeBoSo; SiPS; TrGrPo
("Thou blind man's mark, thou fool's self-chosen snare.") ReEn; ReIE; SiCE
Thou blossom bright with autumn dew. To the Fringed Gentian. Bryant. AA; AmP; AmPP (3d ed.); AnAmPo; AnFE; AnNE; APA; APW; AWP; CBOV; CoAnAm; CoBA; DDA; FaBoBe; GN; HBV; IAP; LA; LPS-2; MOAP; MPB; NeHB; NePA; OBAV; OBRV; OTPC; PIR; PTA-1; TCAP; TOP; TriL; TSWC; YT
Thou bonnie wood o' Craigie-lea! Bonnie Wood o' Craigie-lea. Robert Tannahill. EBSV
Thou born to match the gale (thou art all wings). Walt Whitman. *Fr.* To the Man-of-War-Bird. InP
Thou, born to sip the lake or spring. On a Honey Bee [*or* To a Honey Bee *or* The Honey Bee]. Philip Freneau. AA; AmPP; BAP; CoBA; HiLiAm; IAP; LEAP; TCAP; YaD
Thou Bounteous Giver of the Light. St. Hilary of Arles, *tr. fr. Latin.* BePJ
Thou brown, bare-breasted, voiceless mystery. To the Colorado Desert. Madge Morris Wagner. BAP
Thou burden of all songs the earth hath sung. Autumn. Sir William Watson. LEAP; OBVV
Thou, burning Topaz. Invocation and Proposition. Carlos de Sigüenza y Góngora. *Fr.* Eastern Evangelic Planet. AnMP
Thou by the pleasant springe shalt lye. *Unknown.* SeCSL
Thou canst foreshape thy word. Francis Thompson. *Fr.* Sister Songs. VLEP
Thou canst hold my nose to the grindstone. Of Holding of a Nose. John Heywood. ReIE
Thou canst not die whilst any zeal abound. To Delia, XL. Samuel Daniel. EnLi-1 (1949 ed.); OAEP; OBSC; TuPP
Thou canst not prove that thou art body alone. Tennyson. *Fr.* The Ancient Sage. EPN; VLEP
Thou canst not prove the Nameless, O my Son. Faith. Tennyson. *Fr.* The Ancient Sage. MaRV
Thou canst not understand my words. A Mother to Her Sick Child. W. H. Davies. BOL

Thou canst not wave thy staff in air. Rhythm. Emerson. OQP; QP-2; TOP

Thou cheat'st us Ford, mak'st one seem two by Art. Upon Ford's Two Tragedies, "Love's Sacrifice" and "The Broken Heart." Richard Crashaw. OBS

Thou child of music and the Thracian flood. Rebuke. Euripides. *Fr.* Rhesus. GrR

Thou Christ, my soul is hurt and bruised. The Doubter [*or* Christ the Answer]. Richard Watson Gilder, *also at. to* George Macdonald. MaRV; TrPWD

Thou comest! all is said without a word. Sonnets from the Portuguese, XXXI. Elizabeth Barrett Browning. BPN

Thou comest, Autumn, heralded by the rain. Autumn. Longfellow. BAV; OBVV

Thou Comest Down to Die. "Michael Field." TCPD

Thou comest, much wept for; such a breeze. In Memoriam A. H. H., XVII. Tennyson. EmBrPo; EnLi-2; EPN; GEPC; OBEV (1st ed.); ViPo; VLEP

Thou comest to me, thou exultest, seeing my beauty. Hymn of Victory: Thutmose III. Amon-Re. WaaP

Thou cruel fair, I go. Virelay. Charles Cotton. LO; LoPS; SeCL

Thou cursed cock, with thy perpetual noise. On a Cock at Rochester. Sir Charles Sedley. BeR

Thou dancer of two thousand years. The Dancing Faun. Robert Cameron Rogers. AA

Thou dear and mystic semblance. Lines to the Blessed Sacrament. James Joseph Callanan. OnYI

Thou dearest disciple of Jesu Christ. Pray for Us to the Trinity. *Unknown.* AnEC

Thou didst deign to pluck us. The Soul as a Plucked Flower. Bhai Vir Singh. OnPM

Thou Didst Delight My Eyes. Robert Bridges. *Fr.* Indolence. GTBS-D; LoPS; MBP; MoAB; MoBrPo; VA; VLEP

Thou divinest, fairest, brightest. The Satyr's Farewell [*or* The Satyr's Leave-taking]. John Fletcher. *Fr.* The Faithful Shepherdess, V, v. LO; LoBV (2d ed.); OBS

Thou Dome, where Edward first enroll'd. An Ode Inscribed to the Earl of Sunderland at Windsor. Thomas Tickell. OBEC

Thou dost not fly, thou art not perched. The Hawk. W. H. Davies. BLA; GTML

Thou dreamer with the million moods. A Song of Desire. Frederic Lawrence Knowles. HBV; NLK

Thou dreges of Lethey O thou dull. *Unknown.* SeCSL

Thou, Earth, calm empire of a happy soul. To Suffer Woes Which Hope Thinks Infinite. Shelley. *Fr.* Prometheus Unbound, IV. EV-4; OBRV; RO

Thou ever young! Persephone but gazes. To Demeter. Maybury Fleming. AA

Thou existest, but hearing of ear cannot reach Thee. The Royal Crown, III. Solomon ibn Gabirol. AWP

Thou fair-haired [*or* -hair'd] angel of the evening. To the Evening Star. Blake. BCEP; CaAE; CEP; CH; ChER; ChTr; CoBE; EiPP; EM-1; EnLit; EnRP; EV-3; GBV (1952 ed.); KN; LoBV; MCCG; MW; OAEP; PeBoSo; PoFS; RO; StaSt; TrGrPo; TwHP

Thou fillest all of South America. To Bolivar. Rafael Pombo. PoFr

Thou fire, thou utter monster, thou hateful masterpiece of subtle villainy. Sophocles. *Fr.* Philoctetes. GrPo

Thou Flower of flowers! I'll follow thee. Hymn to the Virgin. Juan Ruiz, Archpriest of Hita. *Fr.* The Book of Good Love. AnSpL-1; TeCS

Thou Flower of Summer. John Clare. LoPS (Thou Flower of Spring.) LO

Thou fool! if madness be so rife. Rondeau. Charles Cotton. SeCL

Thou fool profane, be silent! Epigram II. *Unknown.* *Fr.* Duel with Verses over a Great Man. TrJP

Thou foolish blossom, all untimely blown! To a Wild Rose Found in October. Ednah Proctor Clarke. AA

Thou for whose birth the whole creation yearned. The Rise of Man. John White Chadwick. AA

Thou foul-mouthed wretch! Why dost thou choose. The Sailor to His Parrot. W. H. Davies. EtS; ViBoPo

Thou from th' enthroned martyrs blood-stain'd line. Henry King. *Fr.* An Elegy upon the Most Incomparable King Charles the First. OBS

Thou, from whom we never part. Evening Hymn. "R. W." BOL

Thou gallant chief whose glorious name. Washington. Denis O'Crowley. OHIP; PoRL

Thou gavest me birth, Eileithyia; Earth, thou wilt hide me sleeping. "Betwixt a Sleep and a Sleep." Macedonius. GrPE

Thou gavest me leave to kiss. *See* Thou gav'st me leave to kiss.

Thou gavest steel to us, Thou gavest brain. Frank Wilmot. *Fr.* To God, from the Warring Nations. BoAV

Thou gav'st me late to eat. The Sweetmeat. Sir Edward Sherburne. ElSeCe; SeCL

Tho gav'st [*or* gavest] me leave to kiss. Chop-Cherry. Robert Herrick. ALV; EnLoPo; MyFE; SeEP

Thou gav'st us learning, lit with many an hour. Oxford. Archibald T. Strong. *Fr.* Sonnets of the Empire. BoAu

Thou gazest on the stars. Aster. Plato. OxBG

"Thou Ghost," I said, "and is thy name Today?" The Morrow's Message. Dante Gabriel Rossetti. The House of Life, XXXVIII. GTSE; PoVP; ViPo; VLEP

Thou glorious mirror, where the Almighty's form. The Ocean. Byron. *Fr.* Childe Harold's Pilgrimage. MW

Thou glorious mocker of the world! I hear. To the Mocking-Bird. Albert Pike. AA

Thou God of all, whose presence dwells. Hymn. John Haynes Holmes. TrPWD

Thou God of all, whose spirit moves. Hymn of At-One-Ment. John Haynes Holmes. MaRV

Thou God, whose high, eternal love. Prayer at a Wedding [*or* Wedding-Hymn]. Sidney Lanier. PraP; TrPWD

Thou goest more and more. Ode on Advancing Age. Richard Watson Dixon. GTML

Thou goest then, and leavest none behind. Aeschylos and Sophocles. Walter Savage Landor. BPN; PtP

Thou goest; to what distant place. Farewell. John Addington Symonds. HBV

Thou golden sunshine in the peaceful day! Lament for King Ivor. Whitley Stokes. TIP

Thou Grace Divine, encircling all. The Love of God. Eliza Scudder. LPS-2

Thou great Supreme, whom angel choirs adore. Unseen. Fanny Crosby. TrPWD

Thou green and blooming, cool and shaded hill. The Heart on the Hill. Petrarch. Sonnets to Laura: To Laura in Life, CCV. AWP

Thou grim, unburied corpse of wind and sea! The Derelict. Robert Munger. LEAP

Thou Guide to doubt, be silent evermore. Epigram I. *Unknown.* *Fr.* Duel with Verses over a Great Man. TrJP

Thou half-unfolded flower. The Blossom of the Soul. Robert Underwood Johnson. AA

Thou happiest thing alive. To the Boy. Elizabeth Clementine Kinney. AA

Thou Happy Bridegroom. Sappho, *tr. fr. Greek by* Edwin Marion Cox. GrR

Thou happy, happy elf! A Parental Ode to My Son, Aged Three Years and Five Months [*or* To My Infant Son *or* To My Son]. Thomas Hood. BOHV; FAOV; FaPON; FiBHP; HBV; LauV; LPS-1; RIS

Thou happy vale of Tormes. Happy Vale of Tormes. *Unknown.* TeCS

Thou hast beauty bright and fair. Hermione. "Barry Cornwall." OBVV

Thou hast brought a vine out of Egypt: thou hast cast out the heathen, and planted it. A Vine Out of Egypt. Psalm LXXX, Bible, *O.T.* LiA

Thou hast burst from thy prison. The Butterfly's First Flight. *Unknown.* OTPC

Thou hast but foreign earth, O Cleisthenes, to hide thee. Lost at Sea. Simonides. GrPE

Thou hast clothed thy steepest hillsides/ With the fragrant fir and pine. To Pikes Peak. Elijah Clarence Hills. PoOW

Thou hast come from the old city. The Old City. Ruth Manning-Sanders. CH

Thou hast conquered, O pale Galilean; the world has grown gray from thy breath. Swinburne. *Fr.* Hymn to Proserpine. MBP; WHA

Thou Hast Diamonds. Heine, *tr. fr. German by* Emma Lazarus. *Fr.* Homeward Bound. TrJP

Thou hast done evil. The Judgment. Dora Read Goodale. AA; AnAmPo; LA; LEAP

Thou hast fill'd me a golden cup. To Christina Rossetti. Dora Greenwell. VA

Thou hast given so much to me. Our Prayer. George Herbert. MaRV

Thou hast gone forth, my darling one. My Warrior Boy. *Unknown.* BIG

Thou hast left behind/ Powers that will work for thee. Wordsworth. *Fr.* To Toussaint L'Ouverture. LiA

Thou hast lived in pain and woe. A Requiem. James Thomson. EnLit; HBV

Thou hast lost thy love, poor fool. A Simple Maid. Lord De Tabley. VA

Thou hast made me, and shall Thy work decay? Holy Sonnets, I. John Donne. AnEnPo; EG; EPS; FaBoEn; MaPo; MeLP; NBE; OAEP; OBS; OxBoCh; PeBoSo; Po; PoEL-2; PoFS; SeEP; TwCrTr

Thou hast made me known to friends whom I knew not. The Divine Companion [*or* When One Knows Thee]. Rabindranath Tagore. Gitanjali, LXIII. GrCo-2; NP; OQP; QP-2

Thou hast more music in thy voice. Lucifer's Song. Philip James Bailey. *Fr.* Festus. BMEP

Thou hast not drooped thy stately head. Savannah. Alethea S. Burroughs. PAH

Thou hast not toiled, sweet Rose. To a Rose. John Banister Tabb. CAW

Thou hast on earth a Trinity. To the Christ. John Banister Tabb. ChIP; TrPWD
Thou hast stirred! Song of Cradle-making. Constance Lindsay Skinner. CaP; CPG; OCL
Thou hast stolen again—I know it—on the path thy feet did follow. The Adder. Theognis. GrPE
Thou Hast Sworn by Thy God, My Jeanie. Allan Cunningham. LPS-1
Thou hast thine eyrie in the lifted lands. Colorado. John D. Dillenback. PoOW
Thou hast thy calling to some palace floor. Sonnets from the Portuguese, IV. Elizabeth Barrett Browning. EmBrPo; EnLi-2; EV-4; PtP; TCEP; VA
Thou hast thy ponds, that pay thee tribute fish. Ben Jonson. *Fr.* To Penshurst. FaBoEn
Thou Hast Wounded the Spirit That Loved Thee. Mrs. David Porter. BLPA
Thou hearest the nightingale begin the song of spring. Nightingale and Flowers [*or* Birdsong *or* The Choir of Day *or* Vision of Beulah]. Blake. *Fr.* Milton, II. EnRP; EV-3; FaBoEn; LoBV; NBE; OBRV
Thou hear'st me say that I do dote on thee. *Unknown. Fr.* Edward the Third. LO
Thou heavenly quivering beneath the deathlike above! To a Lark in War-Time. Franz Werfel. TrJP
Thou heaven-threat'ning rock, gentler then she! Echo to a Rock. Lord Herbert of Cherbury. AtBAP; PoEL-2
Thou, heedless Albion, what, alas, the while. England, Unprepared for War. Mark Akenside. *Fr.* An Ode to the Country Gentlemen of England. OBEC
Thou, Hesper, bringest homeward all. Evening. Sappho. GrL; OxBG; WoL
Thou hidden love of God, whose height. Hymn [*or* The Love of God Supreme]. John Wesley. CEP; LPS-2; OBEC
Thou holy daughter of Sion. Novus Sol de Virgine. *Unknown.* AnEC
Thou holy sky, ye swift and wingèd Winds. Prometheus Doomed. Aeschylus. *Fr.* Prometheus Bound. GrR
Thou honeysuckle of the hawthorn hedge. *Unknown.* LO
Thou hope of all the lowly! Thy Kingdom Come. St. Bernard of Clairvaux. CAW
Thou huntress swifter than the Moon! thou terror. Shelley. *Fr.* Ode to Liberty. PoFr
Thou idol of my constant heart. William Winter. *Fr.* Arthur. LEAP
Thou ill-form'd offspring of my feeble brain. The Author to Her Book. Anne Bradstreet. AmPP; IAP; NePA; OxBA
Thou in this wide cold church art laid. On the Dead. Walter Savage Landor. TriL
Thou inmost, ultimate. To the Body. Alice Meynell. ACP; GTML
"Thou jestedst when thou swor'st that thou betrothedst." Tudor Aspersions. R. A. Piddington. FiBHP
Thou Joy'st, Fond Boy. Thomas Campion. OAEP
Thou Knowest. Katharine Lee Bates. TrPWD
Thou knowest all; I seek in vain. The True Knowledge. Oscar Wilde. VLEP
Thou knowest, Lord! *Unknown.* MaRV
Thou knowest, Lord, with what flaming boldness. The Prayer. "Gabriela Mistral." AnCL
Thou knowest, love, I know that thou dost know. Love's Entreaty [*or* Sonnet LV]. Michelangelo. AWP; BoFr
Thou knowest my years entire, my life. Walt Whitman. *Fr.* Prayer of Columbus. TrPWD
Thou knowest, Thou who art the soul of all. Thou Knowest. Katharine Lee Bates. TrPWD
Thou knowest what is best. Trust and Obedience. *Unknown.* BLRP
Thou know'st, O man, how heavy is thy care. Thy Grief Is Thine. Viktor Rydberg. AnSL
Thou large-brained woman and large-hearted man. A Desire. Elizabeth Barrett Browning. *Fr.* Sonnets to George Sand. LPS-3
Thou laverock that springs frae the dews o' the lawn. My Nannie's Awa' [*or* My Nanie's Awa']. Burns. EBSV; GN; HBV; OTPC (1923 ed.)
Thou layest thy hand on the fluttering heart. Thy Presence [*or* Be Quiet: Fear Not]. Frances Ridley Havergal. MaRV; OQP; QP-1
Thou liest dead, and there will be no memory left behind. Sappho, *tr. fr. Greek by* Sir Edwin Arnold. GrPo
Thou Life within my Life. Eliza Scudder. MaRV
Thou Light of Ages. Rolland W. Schloerb. ChIP; MaRV; TrPWD
Thou Light of Life. *At. to* St. Bernard of Clairvaux. *See* Jesus, Thou Joy of Loving Hearts.
Thou lily-leaf, thou roseal-bud. To Mary. Gottfried von Strassburg. ISi
Thou Lingering Star. Burns. *See* To Mary in Heaven.
Thou little bird, thou dweller by the sea. The Little Beach-Bird. Richard Henry Dana. AA; AnAmPo; AnFE; AnNE; APA; APW; BLA; CoAnAm; EtS; HBV; LA; LBAP; LEAP; LPS-2; OTPC (1923 ed.); SN; TCAP
Thou little child, with tender, clinging arms. Slumber Song. Celia Thaxter. BOL
Thou livest, but not from any restricted season. The Royal Crown, IV. Solomon ibn Gabirol. AWP
Thou Livest, O Soul! Charles Leonard Moore. AA
Thou lookest not upon the prisoner. Sequence. Jami. PeP
Thou lookest up with meek, confiding eye. The Wind-Flower. Jones Very. AnNE; APW
Thou Lord of Life and glorious King of Heaven. The Holy Viaticum Comes to Me. Giovanni Prati. CAW
Thou lovely and belovèd, thou my love. Mid-Rapture. Dante Gabriel Rossetti. The House of Life, XXVI. BEL; BPN; EPP; FaBoBe; HBV; LEAP; OAEP; PoE; PoVP; TOP; TyEnPo; ViPo
Thou Lovely Fishermaiden. Heine, *tr. fr. German by* George Meredith. AnGP
(Du schönes Fischer-Mädchen, *tr. by* Sir Theodore Martin.) OuHeWo
(Fisher-Maiden, The, *tr. by* James Thomson.) OnPM
(Oh Lovely Fishermaiden, *tr. by* Louis Untermeyer.) AWP; JAWP; WBP
Thou Lovely One Far Distant. Ludvig Holstein, *tr. fr. Danish by* Charles W. Stork. BoDS
Thou lowly, meek and lovely flower. The Passion Flower. Charles G. Blanden. ChIP; OQP; QP-1
Thou maid and mother, daughter of thy Son. The Canterbury Tales: Prologue to the Second Nun's Tale. Chaucer. GoBC
Thou man, first-comer, whose wide arms entreat. Veneration of Images. Alice Meynell. GTBS
Thou mastering me. The Wreck of the *Deutschland.* Gerard Manley Hopkins. AtBAP; CoBMV; CoEV; FaBoMo; LiTB; LiTM (rev. ed.); MoVE; OAEP (2d ed.); OxBoCh; PoEL-5; PoVP; ReMP; SeCeV; TriL; ViP; ViPP
Thou mayst of double ignorance boast. On One Ignorant and Arrogant. John Owen, *tr. by* William Cowper. PC
Thou met'st, Euripides, a mournful fate! On Euripides. *Unknown.* OnPM
Thou mighty gulf, insatiate cormorant. To Everlasting Oblivion [*or* Oblivion]. John Marston. *Fr.* The Scourge of Villainy. BLV; LoBV (1949 ed.); OBSC; ReIE; SiCE; TuPP
Thou monarch of eight parts of speech. To a Schoolmaster. Martial. OnPM
Thou Moon, that aidest us with thy magic might. A Charm. Dryden. ChTr
Thou more than most sweet glove. The Glove. Ben Jonson. *Fr.* Cynthia's Revels. EIL
Thou Mother with Thy Equal Brood. Walt Whitman. CoBA; HiLiAm, *sl. abr.*
(Hymn to America, *abr.*) GrCo-1
"Beautiful world of new, superber birth," *sel.* PoFr
Thou Must Be True. Horatius Bonar. *See* Be True.
Thou Needst Not [Pitch upon My Hat]. Walter Savage Landor. EmBrPo; EPN
Thou need'st not flutter from thy half-built nest. The Robin. Jones Very. AnNE; APW
Thou needst not weave nor spin. The Power of Beauty. James Herbert Morse. LBAP
Thou ne're wilt [*or* wutt] riddle, neighbour John [*or* Jan]. A Devonshire Song. *Unknown, at. to* William Strode. OBS; PoEL-2
Thou noblest monument of Albion's isle! Sonnet: Written at Stonehenge. Thomas Warton, the Younger. Sonnets, IV. CEP; EiPP; EPP
Thou of the hill Heliconian. Bridal Hymn. Catullus. WoL
Thou old and faithful servant. In the Stillness of Dawn. Euripides. *Fr.* Iphigenia in Aulis. GrR
Thou only bird that singest as thou flyest. The Skylark. Richard Watson Dixon. *Fr.* Mano; a Poetical History. VA
Thou perceivest the flowers put forth their precious odours. Joy in the Flowers. Blake. *Fr.* Milton, II. RO
Thou priest that art behind the screen. Ipsissimus. Eugene Lee-Hamilton. BMEP
Thou, proud man, look upon yon starry vault. Man's Littleness in Presence of the Stars. Henry Kirke White. WBLP
Thou pure and glowing rose. To the Rose. Francisco de Rioja. AnSpL-1
Thou Remainest. Annie Johnson Flint. BLRP
Thou robb'st [*or* rob'st] my days of business [*or* bus'ness] and delights. The Thief. Abraham Cowley. *Fr.* The Mistress. BEL; ElSeCe; EnLi-1; EnLit; OAEP; SeCL; WHA
Thou say'st, "Take up thy cross." Take Up Thy Cross. Francis Turner Palgrave. MaRV
Thou Seemest like a Flower. Heine. *See* Du bist wie eine Blume.
Thou seest me here at midnight, now all rest. John Donne. *Fr.* Obsequies to the Lord Harrington. MeRV; MyFE
Thou seest the under side of every leaf. Omniscience. Blanche Mary Kelly. TrPWD
Thou seest this world is but a thoroughfare. Eternal Reward, Eternal Pain. Sir Thomas More. CoBE
Thou sent to me [*or* mee] a heart was crowned [*or* crown'd].

Upon a Diamond Cut in Form of a Heart . . . Sent in a New Year's Gift. Sir Robert Ayton. ElL; OBS
Thou settest splendors in my sight, O Lord! At the Grand Canyon. George Sterling. MuM
Thou shalt have no other gods before me. The Ten Commandments. Exodus, Bible, *O.T.* OHFP; WBLP
Thou shalt have one God only. The Latest Decalogue. Arthur Hugh Clough. BEL; BOHV; BPN; ChTr; CoEV; EmBrPo; EnLi-2 (1949 ed.); EnLit; EPN; ExPo; HoPM; InMe; LiTG; LoBV; OAEP; OBVV; OtMeF; PIAE; PoE; PoFS; PoVP; PreP; RiBV; SiTL; TOP; ViBoPo; ViP; ViPo; ViPP; VLEP; WGRP
Thou shalt know the nature of the Sky. Parmenides, *tr. fr. Greek by* Charles H. Kahn. GrPo
Thou Shalt Not Die. Euripides, *tr. fr. Greek by* C. M. Bowra. *Fr.* Heracles. OxBG
"Thou Shalt Purge Me with Hyssop and I Shall Be Clean." Anna Bunston de Bary. MaRV
"Thou shalt seek the beach of sand." The Fay's Sentence. Joseph Rodman Drake. *Fr.* The Culprit Fay. GN; LEAP
Thou shinest beautiful on the horizon of heaven. Hymn to the Sun. Ikhnaton (Amenhotep IV). LiTW
Thou should'st be living at this hour. Heathcote William Garrod. CenHV
"Thou Shouldst Be Living at This Hour!" Kenyon West. PGD
Thou shouldst have sung the swan song for the choir. James Russell Lowell. Oliver Wendell Holmes. DD; GA
Thou, Sibyl rapt! whose sympathetic soul. Margaret Fuller. Amos Bronson Alcott. AA
Thou simple bird what mak'st thou here to play? Upon the Lark and the Fowler. Bunyan. CH
Thou Sleepest Fast. *Unknown.* ElL; ElSeCe
Thou sleepest, Zenophila, tender flower. Zenophila. Meleager. GrL
Thou snatch of a man. *Unknown. Fr.* Abusive Snatches. SiB
Thou snowy farm with thy five tenements. Elinda's Glove [*or* The Glove]. Richard Lovelace. ALV; EG; OBS
Thou, so far, we grope to grasp thee. So Far, So Near. Christopher Pearse Cranch. MaRV; TrPWD
"Thou solitary!" the Blackbird cried. The Riddlers. Walter de la Mare. TCPD
Thou sorrow, venom elf[e]. Upon a Spider Catching a Fly. Edward Taylor. AmP; AmPP (4th ed.); CoV; GTBS-W; NePA; OxBA; PoEL-3
Thou spark of life that wavest wings of gold. Ode to a Butterfly. Thomas Wentworth Higginson. AA; FaBoBe; HBV
Thou sparkling bowl! thou sparkling bowl! The Sparkling Bowl. John Pierpont. AnAmPo; LA
Thou speaker of all wisdom in a word. A Prologue. Coventry Patmore. PoLi
Thou speakest always ill of me. To an Acquaintance. *Unknown.* FaFP; SiTL
Thou stately stream that with the swelling tide. The Lover to the Thames [of London to Favour His Lady Passing Thereon]. George Turberville. ChTr; ElL; ElSeCe; OBSC; ReIE
Thou still unravish'd bride of quietness. Ode on a Grecian Urn. Keats. AEV; AnEnPo; AnFE; AtBAP; ATP; AWP; BCEP; BEL; BLV; BoLiVe; BPN; CaAE; CBE; CBOV; ChER; CoBE; CoEV; EM-2; EmBrPo; EnL; EnLi-2; EnLit; EnLP; EnRP; EPN; EPP; ERP; EV-4; ExPo; FaBoBe; FaBoEn; FaFP; FiP; GEPC; GTBS-W; GTSL; HBV; HBVY; HiLiEn; HoPM; InP; InPo; JAWP; KN; LEAP; LiA; LiTB; LiTG; LoBV; LPS-2; MaPo; MCCG; OAEP; OBEV; OBRV; OHFP; OuHeWo; PC; PFE; PIAE; PIR; Po; PoE; PoEL-4; PoeMoYo; PoFS; PoMa; PreP; PYM; REAL; ReaPo; RiBV; SeCeV; ShBV-4; TCEP; TOP; TreF; TrGrPo; TVSH; TwCrTr; TwHP; TwP; TyEnPo; UnPo; ViBoPo; WBP; WHA
Thou stranger, which for Rome in Rome here seekest. Ruins of Rome, I [*or* Rome]. Joachim du Bellay. LiTW; OnPM
Thou swearst thou'lt drink no more: kind heaven, send. Epigram. *Unknown.* ALV
Thou sweetly-smelling fresh red rose. Dialogue; Lover and Lady. Ciullo d'Alcamo. AWP; LyPI
Thou talkest much, so soon to yield thy breath. Muse on Death. Palladas. OnPM
Thou that art wise, let wisdom minister. Sonnet: He Craves Interpreting of a Dream of His. Dante da Maiano. AWP; LiTW
Thou that at Rome astonished dost behold. Ruins of Rome, VII. Joachim du Bellay. OnPM
Thou that didst grant the wise King his request. The Sins of Youth. Thomas, Lord Vaux. ACP (1952 ed.)
Thou that didst leave the ninety and the nine. Missing. John Banister Tabb. QS; TrPWD
Thou that didst mark from Heircte's spacious hill. Hamilcar Barca. Roger Casement. JKCP (1926 ed.)
Thou that dost save through pain. Thanksgiving. Florence Earle Coates. PEDC
Thou that from the heavens art. Wanderer's Night-Songs. Goethe, *tr. by* Longfellow. AWP; InP; JAWP; OnPM; WBP; WoL
Thou that hast a daughter. The Sailor. William Allingham. CG; HBV; VA
Thou that hast given so much to me. Our Prayer. George Herbert. PGD; PraP; PSO
Thou that in fury with thy knotted tail. The Captive Lion. W. H. Davies. ChMo; CMP; PtOT
Thou that makest high heaven thy chariot course. Sophocles. *Fr.* Ajax. GrPo
Thou that mak'st gain thy end, and wisely well. To My Bookseller. Ben Jonson. TuPP
Thou that once, on mother's knee. A Little Child's Hymn. Francis Turner Palgrave. BOL; VA
Thou that spendst thy time to knowe. *Unknown.* SeCSL
Thou the golden fruit dost bear. Song. Blake. LiA
Thou thinkest that beard of thine brains can create. Ammianus, *tr. fr. Greek by* Norman Douglas. GrPo
Thou tiny solace of these prison days. Sir Walter Raleigh to a Caged Linnet. Eugene Lee-Hamilton. VA
Thou to wax fierce. The Zeal of Jehu. Cardinal Newman. OBRV
Thou, to whom my name bears witness. Be Not Silent. David ben Meshullam. TrJP
Thou, to whom the world unknown. Ode to Fear. William Collins. BrBE; CEP; EiPP; OAEP; PIAE; Po; TrGrPo
Thou too hast traveled, little fluttering thing. To a Swallow Building under Our Eaves. Jane Welsh Carlyle. HBV; OBRV; OTPC (1923 ed.); VA
"Thou, too, my Lancelot," ask'd the King, "my friend." Lancelot and the Grail. Tennyson. *Fr.* Idylls of the King. GoBC
Thou, too, O bronze-eyed darling of the feast. In an Autumn Wood. William Alexander Percy. HBMV
Thou, Too, Sail on! Longfellow. *See* Ship of State, The.
Thou unrelenting Past! The Past. Bryant. AA; BAP; BAV; IAP; MOAP; OBAV; TCAP; TOP
Thou vague dumb crawler with the groping head. To My Tortoise Chronos. Eugene Lee-Hamilton. VA
"Thou Virgin Mother, daughter of thy Son." Dante. *Fr.* Divina Commedia: Paradiso. CAW
Thou visitest the earth, and waterest it. *Fr.* Psalm LXV, Bible, *O.T.* OHIP
Thou wast all that [*or* that all] to me, love. To One in Paradise. Poe. *Fr.* The Assignation. AA; AmPo; AmPP; AnFE; APA; APW; BLV; BoLiVe; CoAnAm; CoBA; GTBS-D; HBV; IAP; LBAP; LEAP; LiTA; LiTL; LO; LoPS; MOAP; NePA; OBAV; OBEV (new ed.); OBRV; OBVV; OxBA; PG; PIR; SPP; TCAP; TrGrPo; TriL; UnW; ViBoPo; WHA; YT
Thou wast not born for death, immortal bird! The Nightingale. Keats. *Fr.* Ode to a Nightingale. DD
Thou water turn'st to wine (faire friend of life). To Our Lord, upon the Water Made Wine. Richard Crashaw. MePo
Thou we adore, eternal name. Worthington. *Unknown.* AS
Thou wert fair, Lady Mary. Lady Mary. Henry Alford. VA
Thou wert out betimes, thou busy, busy bee! To a Bee. Robert Southey. OTPC
Thou wert the morning-star among the living. Morning and Evening Star [*or* Aster *or* Star *or* To Stella]. Plato, *tr. by* Shelley. AWP; EnLoPo; GrL; GrPo; InPo; JAWP; LiA; LiTW; LO; OnPM; OxBG; ViBoPo; WBP; WoL
Thou which art I ('tis nothing to be so). The Storm. John Donne. ReIE; SeEP
Thou who art clothed in silk, who drawest on. Man Is a Weaver. Moses ibn Ezra. TrJP
Thou who art Lord of the wind and rain. A Hymn of Thanksgiving. Wilbur D. Nesbit. OHIP
Thou who at will canst fling. The Faithless and the Constant. Sir William Watson. CaAE
Thou, who didst lay all other bosoms bare. To Shakespeare. Richard Edwin Day. AA
Thou, who dost dwell alone. Desire [*or* Stagirius]. Matthew Arnold. GEPC; LPS-2; WGRP
Thou who didst multiply, by Galilee. Prayer. Frances Crosby Hamlet. ChIP
Thou, who dost all my worldly thoughts employ. Lines Written on Her Death-Bed. Mary Monk. DiM
Thou, who dost feel life's vessel strand. Edmund Clarence Stedman. *Fr.* The Ordeal by Fire. WGRP
Thou, who dost flow and flourish here below. The Garland. Henry Vaughan. AnEnPo; MeRV
Thou, who dost smile upon me, yet unknown. George Henry Boker. *Fr.* Sonnets. MOAP
Thou who hast fled from life's enchanted bowers. To a Cloistress. Juan de Tassis. CAW
Thou who hast made this world so wondrous fair. At High Mass. Robert Hugh Benson. CAW

Thou who hast [*or* has] slept all night upon the storm. To the Man-of-War Bird. Walt Whitman. AA; AmP; AmPP (4th ed.); BLA; CBOV; EtS; FaBoBe; HBV; IAP; MOAP; NePA; OBAV; PoF; TCAP
Thou who loved Juvenal, and filed. Indignation. Victor Hugo. WoL
Thou who lovest, like a crow. Jalal ed-Din Rumi, *tr. fr. Persian by* A. J. Arberry. PeP
Thou who on Sin's wages starvest. Barnfloor and Winepress. Gerard Manley Hopkins. ACP; CAW
Thou who ordainest, for the land's salvation. God Save the Nation! Theodore Tilton. AA
Thou who, when fears attack. Ode to Tobacco. Charles Stuart Calverley. ALV; BOHV; FiBHP; HBV; InMe; LPS-3; PIR; TOP; WhC
Thou who wouldst see the lovely and the wild. Monument Mountain. Bryant. BeLS; IAP; MOAP; PIAE; REAL
Thou who wouldst wear the name. The Poet. Bryant. AA; AmPP (3d ed.); CoBA; CoV; InP
Thou whom I lifted from her pallid lips. Crucifix. Alphonse de Lamartine. CAW
Thou whom my soul admires above. Seeking the Pastures of Christ the Shepherd. Isaac Watts. BeR
Thou, Whom rich and poor adore. An Offer. Arthur Guiterman. TrJP
Thou whom these eyes saw never, say friends true. Epitaph. Robert Browning. VA
Thou whose beauty. A Song in Season. Swinburne. EmBrPo
Thou whose birth on earth. Christmas Antiphon [*or* The Peace-Giver *or* A Christmas Antiphony]. Swinburne. CBE; CBPC; ChIP; MaRV; MeRV; OTPC (1946 ed.); PGD; TriL; TrPWD
Thou—whose endearing hand once laid in sooth. Invocation. Edmund Clarence Stedman. AA
Thou, whose exterior semblance doth belie. Trailing Clouds of Glory. Wordsworth. *Fr.* Ode: Intimations of Immortality from Recollections of Early Childhood. GrCo-2
Thou whose prayer doth vice destroy. Lux Advenit Veneranda. Adam of St. Victor. CAW
Thou whose sweet youth and early hopes enhance. George Herbert. *Fr.* The Church Porch. LPS-2
Thou whose thrilling hand in mine. George Darley. *Fr.* Nepenthe. OBRV
Thou, Whose Unmeasured Temple Stands. Bryant. *See* Dedication: "Thou whose unmeasured temple stands."
Thou wilt come with suddenness. Spring in New Zealand. Hubert Church. BoAu
"Thou wilt forget me." "Love has no such word." Spring and Autumn. William James Linton. VA
Thou wilt not cower in the dust. James Ryder Randall. *Fr.* Maryland, My Maryland. OlF; PoRL
Thou wilt not look on me? A Farewell. Alice Brown. HBV
Thou, with thy looks, on whom I look full oft. The Looks of a Lover Enamoured. George Gascoigne. ElL; SeCePo
Thou woman without peer. "Behold Thy Mother and Thy Brother." William Heribert. TMEV
Thou wonder of the Atlantic shore. To Aaron Burr, under Trial for High Treason. Sarah Wentworth Morton. GA; PAH
Thou wouldst be greate and to such height wouldst rise. Greatness. *Unknown.* OBS
Thou wouldst be loved?—then let thy heart. To Frances S. Osgood [*or* A Simple Duty]. Poe. APW; IAP; PoRL; TCAP
Thou youngest virgin-daughter of the skies. To the Pious Memory of the Accomplisht Young Lady Mrs. Anne Killigrew [*or* Ode to the Pious Memory . . .]. Dryden. AtBAP; BrBE; CEP; EiPP; EPS; HBV; LiA; LoBV; OBEV; PoEL-3; PoFS; PtP; SeCV-2; SeEP; TriL
Thou, Zion, old and suffering. David Levi. *Fr.* The Bible. TrJP
Though. *See also* Tho'.
Though All Are Faithless Growing. "Novalis," *tr. fr. German by* Eileen Hutchins. Sacred Songs, I. AnGP
Though all the Fates should prove unkind. Lines. Henry David Thoreau. MOAP
Though Amaryllis Dance in Green. *Unknown.* ElL; OAEP; ReEn; SiCE
Though an ill mind appear in simulation. Ariosto. *Fr.* Orlando Furioso, IV. EnLi-1; PrPoCR
Though art be on vacation. Leonard Feeney. WhC
Though aware of our rank and alert to obey orders. Which Side Am I Supposed to Be On? [*or* Ode: To My Pupils]. W. H. Auden. CoBMV; MBP; MoBrPo
Though beauty [*or* beautie] be the mark[e] of praise. An Elegy [*or* Elegie]. Ben Jonson. OBEV; SeCV-1
Though Bodies Are Apart C. Day Lewis. POTE
Though brave your beauty be. The Lover Exhorteth His Lady to Take Time While Time Is. George Turberville. ReIE
Though buds still speak in hints. Field-Glasses. Andrew Young. ChMP
Though by thy bounteous favor I be in. The Examination of His Mistress' Perfections. Francis Beaumont. GoBC
Though by wide seas and Time we sundered are. Pierre de Ronsard, *tr. fr. French by* Curtis Hidden Page. PrPoCR
Though Christ a thousand times. In Thine Own Heart. "Angelus Silesius." ChIP; MaRV
Though clasp'd and cradled in his nurse's arms. William Cowper. *Fr.* Hope. PoEL-3
Though clock/ To tell how night draws hence, I've none. His Grange, or Private Wealth. Robert Herrick. EG; EnLit; EPS; OAEP; OTPC (1923 ed.); SeCV-1; SeEP
Though Cupit be a god. *Unknown.* SeCSL
Though decked the tray, two things afar and near. Fragment. Jami. *Fr.* Baharistan. CIV
Though black the night, I know upon the sky. Prelude. John Drinkwater. TCPD
Though doubters doubt and scoffers scoff. Christmas, 1898. Edward Sandford Martin. DD
Though dusty wits dare scorn astrology. Astrophel and Stella, XXVI. Sir Philip Sidney. ReEn; SiPS
Though dusty wits of this ungrateful time. To Master Bastard, a Minister That Made a Pleasant Book of English Epigrams. Sir John Harington. SiCE
Though every way I try. Jalal ed-Din Rumi, *tr. fr. Persian by* A J Arberry. PeP
Though expedition bids, yet never stray. Of Narrow Streets. John Gay. *Fr.* Trivia; or, The Art of Walking the Streets of London. EnLi-1 (1949 ed.)
Though experts make to-day the dress. To Michal Meditating a New Costume. Charles Williams. TCPD
Though fast youth's glorious fable flies. Lone Founts. Herman Melville. AnFE; CoAnAm; LiTA; OnPM; ViBoPo
Though folks no more go Maying. The May Day Garland. Edmund Blunden. HBMV
Though frost, and snow, lock'd from mine eyes. To Saxham. Thomas Carew. OBS
Though gifts like thine the fates gave not to me. To Hafiz. Thomas Bailey Aldrich. AA
Though God, as one that is an householder. Old and New Art, 3: The Husbandman. Dante Gabriel Rossetti. The House of Life, LXXVI. BPN; PoVP;ViPo
Though he believe it, no man is strong. Chorus. W. H. Auden. *Fr.* Paid on Both Sides. CoEV
Though he hung dumb upon her wall. And One Shall Live in Two. Jonathan Henderson Brooks. PoNe
Though he lay on the ground. Little Boy Blue. Thomas Holley Chivers. MOAP
Though He That Ever Kind and True. Robert Louis Stevenson. *See* Resurgence.
Though heart grows faint and spirits sink. The Word of God. Annie Johnson Flint. BLRP
Though Heaven be high, the gate is low. Humility. Thomas Washbourne. *Fr.* God's Two Dwellings. MaRV
Though heaven's gate of light uncloses. Another Song. Victor Hugo. LiA
Though her mother told her. Leda and the Swan. Oliver St. John Gogarty. AnIL; OnYI
Though here and there a man is left. Heroics. Elinor Wylie. CoBA
Though Here in Flesh I Be. Philip Howard, Earl of Arundel. CoBE
(Through Thy Cross and Passion.) PoLi
Though here on earth men differ, in the grave. Of Death. Samuel Sheppard. SeCL
Though I am Chateaulaire who sings. Chanson de Chateaulaire. Herbert S. Gorman. AnAmPo; LA; TCPD
Though I am humble, slight me not. The Moss Supplicateth for the Poet. Richard Henry Dana. AA
Though I am little as all little things. Not Overlooked. James Oppenheim. NP
Though I am native to this frozen zone. Reminiscence. Thomas Bailey Aldrich. AA; AnAmPo; LA
Though I am seventy, I do not want to leave my books. The Wind and the Rain. Lu Yu. WhP
Though I am to-day against the breast of battle. Knightsbridge of Libya. Sorley Maclean. NeBP
Though I Am Young. Ben Jonson. *Fr.* The Sad Shepherd, I, v. OAEP; TuPP
(Karolin's Song.) AtBAP; LiTL; LoBV; PoEL-2
(Love and Death.) SeCL
("Though I am young and cannot tell.") ElSeCe
Though I Be Now a Gray, Gray Friar. Thomas Love Peacock. *Fr.* Maid Marian. ERP
(Friar's Hunting Song.) GoTP
Though I cannot see. The Spring Wind. Ho Hung. PoHN
Though I get home how late, how late! The Return. Emily Dickinson. MoAmPo (1950 ed.); NeMA
Though I go by with banners. Pageant. Margaret Widdemer. AV; TBM
Though I have given. Lines Written in a Mausoleum. Lillian Grant. GoYe
Though I have not seen the milk snake. Five Serpents. Charles Burgess. NePoAm-2
Though I have twice been [*or* beene] at the doors [*or* doores] of death. To Sir William Alexander [*or* From a Cypress Grove]. William Drummond of Hawthornden. OBS; PoEL-2; SeEP; TriL

Though I march until I drop. Soldier's Song. David Campbell. BoAV; NeLNL
Though I met her in the summer. The Ballad of Cassandra Brown. Helen Gray Cone. BOHV; InMe
Though I regarded not. Earl of Surrey. SiPS
Though I see the white azaleas on the shore. An Elegy. *Unknown. Fr.* Manyo Shu. OnPM
Though I should be maligned by those. Prayer for Strength. Margaret E. Bruner. MaRV; PoToHe
Though [*or* If] I speak with the tongues of men and of angels. Charity [*or* The Gospel of Love *or* St. Paul on Charity *or* The Greatest of These]. First Corinthians, Bible, *N.T.* BoFr; BPP; BrBE; EM-1; GrCo-1; LO; OuHeWo; PG (1955 ed.); PreP; ShBV-4; StVeCh; TreF; TrGrPo
Though I was born a Londoner. Oak and Olive. James Elroy Flecker. HBMV; POTT
Though I waste watches framing words to fetter. Revulsion. Thomas Hardy. EmBrPo
Though I with strange desire. Kisses Desired. William Drummond of Hawthornden. EnLoPo
Though I would take comfort against sorrow. The Cry of the Daughter of My People. Jeremiah, Bible, *O.T.* TrJP
Though I'm sad unto death. The Return of Spring. Sui Fu Jen. PoHN
Though it grieve you. Bequest to My Daughters. Lawrence Lee. FAOV
Though its heart was all aflame. The Incense Burner. Abus Salt. MooP
Though joy is better than sorrow, joy is not great. Joy. Robinson Jeffers. ChMo; CMP; NeMA; NP
Though leaves are many, the root is one. The Coming of Wisdom with Time. W. B. Yeats. TwP
Though little be the god of love. Love's Victories. James Shirley. *Fr.* Cupid and Death. GoBC
Though little be the tombstone, O passer-by, above me. The Cricket's Grave. Leonidas of Tarentum. GrPE
Though loath to grieve. Ode Inscribed to W. H. Channing. Emerson. AmP; AmPo; AmPP; AnNE; APW; CoBA; CoV; IAP; MOAP; OnAP; OxBA; PoLFOT; TOP; WoL
"Though logic choppers rule the town." Tom O'Roughley. W. B. Yeats. ChMo; CMP
Though love be deeper, friendship is more wide. Friendship. Corinne Roosevelt Robinson. BoFr
Though love repine, and reason chafe. Sacrifice [*or* Faith *or* Quatrain]. Emerson. HBV; HBVY; MaRV; OQP; OtMeF; QP-2
Though lovely are the tombs of the dead nymphs. Panope. Edith Sitwell. MBP; NP
Though many a year above his dust. His Living Monument. Minna Irving. PGD
Though many men had passed the ford, not one. Fight with a Water-Spirit. Norman Cameron. HaMV
Though men believe it not this thing I know. Parrhasius, *tr. fr. Greek by* Walter Leaf. GrPo
Though men may build their bridges high and plant their piers below the sea. John Curtis Underwood. *Fr.* Central. PoMa
Though mild clear weather. There Will Be No Peace. W. H. Auden. NePoAm-2
Though Mine Eye Sleep Not. *Unknown, tr. fr. Hebrew by* Theodor H. Gaster. *Fr.* The Dead Sea Scrolls. TrJP
Though moonlight dapples. Traditional Tune. Robert D. Fitzgerald. BoAV
Though my bodye be restraind. *Unknown.* SeCSL
Though My Carriage Be but Careless. *Unknown.* ElSeCe (Though My Carriage.) TuPP
Though my interest in viands is easy to whet up. Tirade on Tea. Phyllis McGinley. InMe
Though my soul may set in darkness, it will rise in perfect light. Sarah Williams. *Fr.* The Old Astronomer. MaRV
Though myriad voices ever fill thine ear. Prayer for Homecoming. Julius Polyaenus. OxBG
Though naked trees seem dead to sight. Hopeless Desire Soon Withers and Dies. "A. W." ReIE
Though Nature weigh our talents, and dispense. Conversation. William Cowper. BCEP
Though not a hill be holy, and no spring. Sonnet XLIX. Arthur Davison Ficke. QS
Though now no more the musing ear. Written on the First of December, 1793. Robert Southey. EV-4
Though now thou hast failed and art fallen despair not because of defeat. Hope in Failure. "Æ." PC
Though now 'tis neither May nor June. Love's Nightingale. Richard Crashaw. LoBV
Though now you are bereft and ways seem black. For One Lately Bereft. Margaret E. Bruner. PoToHe
Though nurtured like the sailing moon. First Love. W. B. Yeats. A Man Young and Old, I. TwP
Though of their glory all the earth is haven. In Memoriam. Alexander William Mair. MM
Though oft a heavy load it carries. The Wagon of Life. Pushkin, *tr. by* Sir Cecil Kisch. WaL
Though often somewhat heavy-freighted. The Coach of Life. Pushkin, *tr. by* Babette Deutsch. TrRV
Though old the thought and oft exprest. For an Autograph. James Russell Lowell. InP
Though one with all that sense or soul can see. Transcendence. Richard Hovey. OQP; QP-1; WGRP
Though other lands may boast of skies. No Land like Ours. J. R. Barrick. BlG
Though others may her brow adore. Love's Insight. *Unknown.* GTSL
Though our great love a little wrong his fame. Charles Lamb. Pakenham Beatty. VA
Though pain and care are everywhere. Reminder. *Unknown.* PIAE
Though parents think their children rude. In Defense of Children. Arthur Guiterman. FAOV
Though prejudice perhaps my mind befogs. I Think I Know No Finer Things than Dogs. Hally Carrington Brent. AlBD; BBV (1951 ed.); BLPA; NeHB
Though pride in damsels is a hateful vice. The Author to a Daughter of Nine Years Old. Sir John Harington, *after* Martial. SiCE
Though quaint indeed your riding habit. Quaint Rider. Francis Maguire. PraNu
Though [*or* Thoch] raging stormes movis [*or* move] us to shake. The Reeds in the Loch Sayis [*or* Say]. *Unknown.* EBSV; GoTS
Though Regions Far Divided. Aurelian Townsend. LoBV (Constant Lover, The.) OxBoLi (Rock Constancy.) CoEV (Song: "Though regions farr devided.") MePo (Though Regions Farr Devided.) PoEL-2
Though richer swains thy love pursue. Song. Joanna Baillie. *Fr.* The Country Inn. OBRV
Though Riders Be Thrown. *Unknown, tr. fr. Irish by* Douglas Hyde. GTIV
Though rulers spend a million men. Conquest. Leslie Savage Clark. ChIP
Though seated then on Afric's further coast. The Death of Chrysaor. Walter Savage Landor. *Fr.* The Hellenics. EmBrPo
Though Shakespeare's Mermaid, ocean's mightiest daughter. On a Prohibitionist Poem. G. K. Chesterton. ViBoPo
Though She Slumbers. Joseph Joel Keith. ISi
Though short her strain nor sung with mighty boast. Erinna [*or* Preface to Erinna's Poems]. Antipater of Sidon. AWP; OxBG
Though Sin too oft, when smitten by Thy rod. Doubt and Prayer. Tennyson. EPN
Though singing but the shy and sweet. Content. Norman Gale. HBV; VA
Though sitting beside the brazier. Buried Fire. Emperor Meiji. OnPM
Though sometimes narrowing as a wolf's might do. To a Dog. Stanton A. Coblentz. AlBD
Though Soporific Not a Little. Pushkin, *tr. fr. Russian by* Babette Deutsch. TrRV
Though Spring has come. Spring Rain. Ko I. PoHN
Though still the blue forget-me-nots. Hay-making. Karl Erik Forsslund. AnSL
Though surrender cut the heart. One. Marion Monks Chase. EOAH
Though the bee. In Him. James Vila Blake. WGRP
Though the bold wings of poesy affect. Ministration. Wordsworth. ES
Though the cover is worn. My Old Bible. *Unknown.* BLRP
Though the crocuses poke up their heads in the usual places. Vernal Sentiment. Theodore Roethke. MiAP
Though the day of my destiny's over. Stanzas to Augusta. Byron. BCEP; BPN; EM-2; EmBrPo; EnRP; ERP
Though the Earth Be Removed. Psalms, XLVI, Bible, *O.T. See* Our Refuge.
Though the evening comes with slow steps and has signalled for all songs to cease. The Bird. Rabindranath Tagore. LiTW
Though the fairies meet by night. At Dawn. Rose Fyleman. BoChLi
Though the goddess made you wonder, do believe the things she said. A Riddle. Sophocles. OxBG
Though the hands be raised to kill. A War-Time Prayer. Anna Bunston de Bary. MaRV
Though the hills are cold and snowy. A Day in the Pamfili Doria. Harriet Beecher Stowe. LPS-2
Though the long seasons seem to separate. Harvest. Eva Gore-Booth. CP; HBMV; OQP; QP-1; WGRP
Though the mills of God grind slowly, yet they grind exceeding small. Retribution. Friedrich von Logau, *tr. by* Longfellow. LPS 3; MaRV; PoToHc; TreF
Though the Muse be gone away. Persistency of Poetry. Matthew Arnold. PoVP
Though the privates may never return. Happy Thought for Some Struggling Nation. Morrie Ryskind. PIAE
Though the purity/ Of the moonlight. *Unknown, tr. fr. Japanese by* Kenneth Rexroth. OnPJ
Though the river still flows seaward. Separation. Wu Tsung Ai. PoHN

Though the rough, bitter-sweet haw of pioneering. American History. W. R. Moses. LiTA
Though the roving bee, as lightly. The Bridal Pair. William Young. *Fr.* Wishmakers' Town. AA
Though the sea-horse on the ocean. The Wandering Jew. *Unknown.* RO
Though the stars riot and the heavens fall. Arise! Arise! Louis Untermeyer. StaSt
Though the sun has set. Calm of Evening. Hsieh T'iao. PoHN
Though the world has slipped and gone. Lullaby. Edith Sitwell. AtBAP; ChMP; LiTM; POTE; WaP
Though the world is changing fast. Rainer Maria Rilke. *Fr.* Sonnets to Orpheus. OnPM
Though the world is torn with care. To a Woman. Denis Glover. AnNZ
Though they have loved me as the gentle roebuck. Deirdre and the Poets. Ewart Milne. NeIP
Though Thine ears be filled with voices—voices that pray Thee fearing. The Wanderer. Julius Polyaenus. GrPE
Though this the port, and I thy servant true. Sir Thomas Wyatt. SiPS
Though thou indeed hast quite forgotten ruth. Ballata: Of a Continual Death in Love. Guido Cavalcanti. AWP
Though thou, my ring, be small. To His Ring, Given to His Lady. George Turberville. EIL
Though thou well dost wish me ill. Na Audiart. Ezra Pound. ReaPo
Though three men dwell on Flannan Isle. Flannan Isle. W. W. Gibson. CH; GoTL (1949 ed.); GTML; MoVE; OBVV; PCN; PoRA; ShBV-2; ShGoBo; StPo; TOP
Though thy constant love I share. To M. T. Bayard Taylor. AA
Though time may prod against me and insist. Madrigal 95. Michelangelo. LyPI
Though Time's black mountain overhangs. Night Song. A. R. D. Fairburn. AnNZ
Though tiny things, ants must see very well. Such Wisdom. *Unknown.* GFA
Though to the root you eat me, goat, I swear. The Vine to the Goat. Euenus. LiTW
Though to the vilest things beneath the moon. Arthur Hugh Clough. "Blank Misgivings of a Creature Moving About in Worlds Not Realized," II. VLEP
Though to think. Love Song. Margot Ruddock. OBMV
Though to your life apparent stain attach. Sonnets to Aurelia, II. Robert Nichols. OBMV
Though tuneless, stringless, it lies there in dust. The Old Violin. Maurice Francis Egan. AA; JKCP
Though veiled in spires of myrtle-wreath. Song. Samuel Taylor Coleridge. ERP; RO
Though virtue be the same when low she stands. To the Lady Lucy, Countess of Bedford. Samuel Daniel. OBSC; ReIE; SiCE; TuPP
Though we are atoms and the self defined. Argument on Immortality. Lenore G. Marshall. BoFr
Though we love and suffer together. Meditation. Paul Géraldy, *tr. by* Joseph T. Shipley. ALV
Though we may waver, He remaineth steadfast. The Everlasting Love. Annie Johnson Flint. BLRP
Though when I cry. To Mistress Sarah Hickford. Chambers. SeCL
Though when I lov'd thee thou wert fair. A Deposition from Beauty [*or* When I Loved Thee]. Thomas Stanley. EG; EV-2; HBV; LiTL
Though, when other maids stand by. Smile and Never Heed Me. Charles Swain. HBV; LPS-1
Though wide earth's ranks of valor. Rank and File. Marion Lee. MuM
Though winter come with dripping skies. A Song with a Discord. Arthur Colton. AA
Though Winter's Barricade Delays. C. Day Lewis. *Fr.* The Magnetic Mountain. ChMo; EnLit
Though wisdom underfoot. The Fields. Witter Bynner. SBMV
Though with the North we sympathize. Shop and Freedom. *Unknown.* PAH
Though wolves against the silver moon do bark. To the Detracted. John Andrews. *Fr.* The Anatomy of Baseness. EIL; LO; SeEP
Though ye were hard-hearted. To Mistress Gertrude Statham. John Skelton. *Fr.* The Garlande of Laurell. OAEP
Though you are missing from the shelf. Hero of His Village. Nigel Heseltine. MoWP
Though you are young, and I am old. Young and Old. Thomas Campion. OBSC; PoP; SiCE
Though you be absent here, I needs must say. The Spring [*or* Love's Absence in the Spring]. Abraham Cowley. *Fr.* The Mistress. ElSeCe; EPS (1942 ed.); EV-2; LiTL; LO; MeLP; OBS; ReEn; SeEP
Though you be scholarly, beware. Bigot. Eleanor Slater. MaRV
Though you can tell me. Lady Sei Shonagon, *tr. fr. Japanese by* Kenneth Rexroth. OnPJ
Though you determine not to love. *Unknown.* SeCSL
Though You Make No Return. Thomas Southerne. *Fr.* The Maid's Last Prayer. SeCL
(Song, A, Set by H. Purcell, and Sung by Mrs. Hodgson.) SeEP
Though you never recite, you would like to pass for a poet. Martial, *tr. fr. Latin by* Robert R. Schnorr. Epigrams, II, 88. LaP
Though you on seas in stormes have bin. *Unknown.* SeCSL
Though you serve richest wines. A Total Abstainer. Martial. LiTW; RoL
Though you should whisper. Dirge. Muna Lee. NP
Though you think beautiful the valiant champions. Deirdre and Conchobar. *Unknown.* SiB
Though your eyes with tears were blind. A Leader. "Æ." HBMV
Though your little word is light. Song. Louis Ginsberg. TBM
Though Your Words Be Messengers of Hate. Sophie Himmell. MuM
Though Youth Be Gone. Sappho, *tr. fr. Greek by* H. De Vere Stacpoole. GrR
Thought. Christopher Pearse Cranch. *See* Gnosis.
Thought, A. W. H. Davies. GTML; GTSL; MoShBr; POTE
Thought. Emerson. AmPP (3d ed.); CoBA; IAP; MOAP
Thought, The. Lord Herbert of Cherbury. ElSeCe; InvP; LoBV (2d ed.); SeCL, SeEP
Thought, A. Walter Savage Landor. VA
Thought, A. Mikhail Yurevich Lermontov, *tr. fr. Russian by* Max Eastman. AWP; WoL
Thought, A. Juan Meléndez Valdés, *tr. fr. Spanish by* Eleanor L. Turnbull. TeCS
Thought, The. William Brighty Rands. BMEP; OBEV; OBVV; UnW
Thought. Johan Ludvig Runeberg, *tr. fr. Swedish by* Charles W. Stork. AnSL
Thought, A. James Kenneth Stephen. BOHV; FiBHP; VA
Thought, A. Robert Louis Stevenson. MeMeAg; OTPC; PCH; PPL
Thought. Walt Whitman. MaRV; MeRV
Thought about Saint Francis, A. Denis A. McCarthy. SaFP
Thought and the Poet. "Peter Yates." ChMP
Thought, behold yon bird there swinging. Thought. Johan Ludvig Runeberg. AnSL
Thought beneath so slight a film, The. Emily Dickinson. AmP; AmPP; CoV; OxBA
Thought Eternal, The. Goethe, *tr. fr. German by* Ludwig Lewisohn. AWP; JAWP; WBP
Thought for a Lonely Death-Bed, A. Elizabeth Barrett Browning. MaRV
Thought for a New Year. Gail Brook Burket. PGD
Thought for a Sunshiny Morning. Dorothy Parker. PoMa
Thought for Easter. Mary E. McCullough. MaRV
Thought for My Love, A. Bruce Williamson. NeIP
Thought for the Winter Season. Mary Elizabeth Osborn. NePoAm
Thought from Cardinal Newman, A. Matthew Russell. CAW; JKCP
Thought in Two Moods, A. Thomas Hardy. EPN
Thought is deeper than all speech. Gnosis [*or* Thought]. Christopher Pearse Cranch. AnAmPo; BAP; HBV; IAP; LA; LBAP; LPS-3; UnW; WGRP
Thought is false happiness: the idea. Crude Foyer. Wallace Stevens. LiTM (rev. ed.); NePA
Thought, Labor, Patience. Sydney Dobell. *Fr.* Balder. BMEP
Thought may, at times, be a very dangerous thing. A Tragedy of the Deep. Don Marquis. LHV
Thought may well be ever ranging. Love, Not Duty. Arthur Hugh Clough. VLEP
Thought of a Briton on the Subjugation of Switzerland. Wordsworth. BEL; BoLiVe; BPN; EM-2; EmBrPo; EnLi-2; EnRP; EPN; EPP; ES; GEPC; PeBoSo; PoFr; REAL; ReaPo; SeCeV; TOP; TwHP
(England and Switzerland, 1802.) GTBS; GTBS-D; GTBS-W; GTSE; GTSL; MCCG; PC
(On the Subjugation of Switzerland.) ShBV-3
(Sonnet: Thought of a Briton on the Subjugation of Switzerland.) ChER
(Thoughts of a Briton on the Subjugation of Switzerland.) EnL; HiLiEn; OBRV
(Two Voices Are There.) ERP
Thought of Death, A. Thomas Flatman. CEP; OBS
Thought of God, The. Frederick Lucian Hosmer. GrCo-1
Thought of God, The. Nagata, *tr. fr. Japanese by* Lois J. Erickson. SoLD
Thought of Her, The. Richard Hovey. LBMV
Thought of Marigolds, A. Janice Farrar. GoYe
Thought of old, dear things is in thine eyes, The. October. John Charles McNeill. NoCaPo
Thought on a News Item. Lucia Trent. ChIP
Thought Suggested by the New Year, A. Thomas Campbell. *See* River of Life, The.
Thought to Remember, A. *Unknown.* See Charity.

Thought went up my mind today, A. Emily Dickinson. AmP; AmPP; AnFE; APA; CoAnAm; CoBA
Thought, whose hard strife only midnight may see. Music. Erik Gustaf Geijer. AnSL
Thought, with good cause thou likest so well the night. Astrophel and Stella, XCVI. Sir Philip Sidney. ReEn; SiPS
Thoughtful men their praise withhold. Monuments Perish. Simonides. GrL; OxBG
Thoughtful nights, and restless waking. To Myra. George Granville. CEP
Thoughtful Quinctius, cease to ask. Horace. Odes, II, 11. LaP
Thoughtfulness. Yamaguchi, *tr. fr. Japanese by* Lois J. Erickson. SoLD
Thoughts. Roy Davis. WhC
Thoughts. Arthur L. Phelps. CPG
Thoughts. Duncan Campbell Scott. PeCV
Thoughts. Sara Teasdale. ChMo; CMP; PoTo
Thoughts are broken in my memory, The. Dante. *Fr.* La Vita Nuova. AWP; JAWP; WBP
Thoughts are strange that crowd into my brain, The. The Fall of Niagara. John Gardiner Calkins Brainard. LPS-2
Thoughts at the Museum. Eileen Brennan. OnYI
Thoughts at the Trysting Stile. Francis Ledwidge. TCEP
Thoughts during an Air Raid. Stephen Spender. MoBrPo (1950 ed.); NeMA; ViBoPo
Thought's End. Léonie Adams. MAP; MoAB; MoAmPo; PIAE
Thoughts for St. Stephen. Christopher Morley. WhC
Thoughts from Abroad. Patrick Maybin. NeIP
Thoughts in a Garden. Andrew Marvell. *See* Garden, The ("How vainly men themselves amaze").
Thoughts in Exile. Su T'ung-po, *tr. fr. Chinese by* Kenneth Rexroth. OnPC
Thoughts in Loneliness, *sel.* Verner von Heidenstam, *tr. fr. Swedish by* Charles W. Stork.
"There is a spark dwells deep within my soul." AnSL
Thoughts in School. Dorothy M. Young. DDA
Thoughts in Separation. Alice Meynell. ACP; GoBC; MeRV; POTT
Thoughts in the Cold. Li Shang-yin, *tr. fr. Chinese by* Witter Bynner. BoFr
Thoughts in the Gulf Stream. Christopher Morley. EtS
Thoughts like an empty cage. The Cage. Elizabeth Bartlett. NePoAm-2
Thoughts of a Briton in the Fourth Year of War. E. H. W. Meyerstein. *Fr.* Two War Sonnets. NeTW
Thoughts of a Briton on the Subjugation of Switzerland. Wordsworth. *See* Thought of a Briton on the Subjugation of Switzerland.
Thoughts of a Little Girl. Maria Enriqueta, *tr. fr. Spanish by* Emma Gutiérrez Suárez. FaPON
Thoughts of Death, The. Thomas à Kempis. *Fr.* Imitation of Christ. OuHeWo
Thoughts of Loved Ones. Margaret Fishback. FiBHP
Thoughts of men appear, The. Consummation. Thomas Traherne. SeCV-2
Thoughts of Phena at News of Her Death. Thomas Hardy. BrBE
Thoughts on Being Invited to Dinner. Christopher Morley. HBMV
Thoughts on Choosing. George MacBeth. PoN
Thoughts on Editors. Thomas Moore. WhC
Thoughts on One's Head. William Meredith. SiTL
Thoughts on Progress. David Daiches. SiTL
Thoughts on the Commandments. George Augustus Baker. AA; HBV; PR
Thoughts on the Cosmos. Franklin P. Adams. HBMV
Thoughts That Move the Heart of Man, The. Ebenezer S. Oakley. TrPWD
Thoughts that rain their steady glow, The. Despondency. Matthew Arnold. PoVP; VLEP
Thoughts Thought While Waiting for a Pronouncement from a Doctor, a Big Executive, the Department of Internal Revenue, or Any Other Momentous Pronouncer. Ogden Nash. SiTL
Thoughts upon a Walk with Natalie, My Niece, at Houghton Farm. Harold Trowbridge Pulsifer. HBMV
Thoughts while Reading. Chu Hsi, *tr. fr. Chinese by* Kenneth Rexroth. OnPC
Thou'rt my sleeping. The Island Boatman's Love-Croon. Robert Farren. CoBE
Thou's welcome, wean! mishanter fa' me. The Poet's Welcome to His Love-begotten Daughter. Burns. LiTB; OxBoLi; PoEL-4; SiTL; ViBoPo
Thousand, a thousand, a thousand, A. Triumphal Song of the Roman Army. *Unknown. Fr.* Aurelian (*by* Flavius Vopiscus). LaP
Thousand aeons, nailed in pain, A. Pandora's Song, V. William Vaughn Moody. *Fr.* The Fire-Bringer. MOAP
Thousand and One Nights, The, *sels. Unknown, tr. fr. Arabic by* E. Powys Mathers.
Abu Nowas for the Barmacides. AWP
Beautiful Boy, The. LiTW
Birds. AWP; LiTW
Book of a Thousand Nights and a Night, The, *tr. by* Sir Richard Francis Burton.
Mock Caliph, The. EnLi-1
Dates. AWP; FaPON; JAWP; LiTW; WBP
Death. AWP; JAWP; WBP
Drinking Song. LiTW
Haroun al-Rachid for Heart's-Life. AWP
Haroun's Favorite Song. AWP
Her Rival for Aziza. AWP
Inscriptions at the City of Brass. AWP; PG (1945 ed.); PoFr, *2 sts.;* WaaP, *3 sts.*
(Inscription at the City of Brass, *1 st.*) LiTW
Laments. AWP; JAWP; WBP
Love. AWP; LiTW
Pearls Seen though Amber. LiTW
Power of Love, The. LiTW
Psalm of Battle. AWP; JAWP; WBP
Sleeper, The. AWP; LiTW
Song of the Narcissus, The. AWP
Tell Him, O Night. AWP; LiTW
To Lighten My Darkness. AWP
Tumadir al-Khansa for Her Brother. AWP; JAWP; PG (1945 ed.); WBP
Wazir Dandan for Prince Sharkan, The. AWP; JAWP; WBP
Thousand burdened burros filled, A. The Rise and Fall of Creede. Cy Warman. PoOW
Thousand guileless sheep have bled, A. Song from the Bride of Smithfield. Sylvia Townsend Warner. MBP; MoBrPo
Thousand Islands, The. Charles Sangster. *Fr.* The St. Lawrence and the Saguenay. BoCaPo
Thousand knights have rein'd their steeds, A. Calais Sands. Matthew Arnold. OAEP
Thousand lights their glory shed, A. The Return from Egypt. Pope Leo XIII. CAW
Thousand martyrs I have made, A. The Libertine. Aphra Behn. OBEV (1st ed.)
Thousand miles from land are we, A. The Stormy Petrel. "Barry Cornwall." BLA; EtS; HBV; LPS-2; OTPC; SN; VA
Thousand minstrels woke within me. Emerson. *Fr.* Monadnoc. OBAV
Thousand Nights and One Night, The. *Unknown. See* Thousand and One Nights, The.
Thousand sea birds all pale gray, A. Romance. Jules Laforgue. AnFP
Thousand silent years ago, A. Praxiteles and Phryne. William Wetmore Story. AA; BeLS; LBAP; OBAV
Thousand sounds, A, and each a joyful sound. Omnipresence. Edward Everett Hale. WGRP
Thousand summers ere the time of Christ, A. The Ancient Sage. Tennyson. EPN; ViPP; VLEP
Thousand thoughts of tender vague regret, A. Autumn Moon. Chisato. OnPM
Thousand, thousand times I seek, A. If She Frown My Heart Would Break. Vicente Espinel. AnSpL-1
Thousand threads of rain and fine white wreathing of air-mist. Walking Home. *Unknown.* EPP
Thousand times, O my sweet warrior, A. Petrarch. Sonnets to Laura: To Laura in Life, XIX. PrPoCR
Thousand tymes have I herd men telle, A. The Prologue. Chaucer. *Fr.* The Legend of Good Women. NBE
Thousand years from this tonight, A. Survival. Margaret Moore Meuttman. MaRV
Thousand Years Have Come, A. Thomas T. Lynch. BLRP; OlF
Thousand years now had his breed, A. The Cachalot. E. J. Pratt. BoCaPo
Thousand Years of Peace, The. Tennyson. *Fr.* In Memoriam A. H. H., CVI. AOAH
Thousands and Again Thousands. Arthur Berthold. CAG
Thousands are building; in byways and backways. The Pioneers. Selden Rodman. PoF
Thousandth Man, The. Kipling. BoFr
Thou'st Had Thy Day. Anacreon, *tr. fr. Greek by* Thomas Moore. OnPM
Thouzandz of thornz there be. The Bees' Song. Walter de la Mare. LiL; OTPC (1946 ed.); WhC; YT
Thow thou be kyng of tour and town. A Warning. *Unknown.* EnLit
Thracian filly, tell me why. Tell Me Why. Anacreon, *tr. by* J. M. Edmonds. GrR
Thracian filly, why so heartless? Why, so shyly sidelong glancing. The Coy Mistress. Anacreon, *tr. by* F. L. Lucas. GrPE
Thracian Wonder, The, *sels. Unknown, at. to* John Webster *and* William Rowley.
Art Thou Gone in Haste? ElL; LO; OxBoLi; ThWaDe
("Art thou gon in haste Ile not forsake thee," *longer vers.*) SeCSL
(Chase, The.) CH
(Pursuit of Love.) ChTr
Love Is a Law. ElL

Thracian Wonder, The (*continued*)
(“Love is a law, a discord of such force.”) TuPP
Thraldome, The. Abraham Cowley. *Fr.* The Mistress. SeCV-1
Thrash away, you'll hev to rattle. A Letter from Mr. Ezekiel Biglow of Jaalam to the Hon. Joseph T. Buckingham. James Russell Lowell. *Fr.* The Biglow Papers, 1st Series, No. I. AmPP; AnNE; APW; CoBA; IAP; OxBA; PAH; TCAP
Thrasybulus. Pindar, *tr. fr. Greek by* T. F. Higham. OxBG
Thrasymedes and Eunoe. Walter Savage Landor. *Fr.* The Hellenics. BPN; EmBrPo
Overture, *sel.* VA
Thread and Song. John Williamson Palmer. LPS-1
Thread of Life, The, *sel.* Christina Rossetti.
Aloof, I. BLV; BoLiVe; ES; OBEV; OBVV; TrGrPo; TyEnPo; YT
(Irresponsive Silence of the Land, The.) MBP
(Thread of Life, The.) FaBoEn; VA
Thread the nerves through the right holes. Resurrection Song. Thomas Lovell Beddoes. PoE
Threading a darksome passage all alone. The Inverted Torch. Edith M. Thomas. LBMV
Threats. Menander, *tr fr. Greek by* C. M. Bowra. OxBG
Three accomplishments well regarded in Ireland: a clever/ verse. *Tr. by* Thomas Kinsella. *Fr.* The Triads of Ireland. OxBI
Three Acres of Land. *Unknown. See* Mad Farmer's Song.
Three American Women and a German Bayonet. Winfield Townley Scott. FiMAP; OnHM
Three ancient men in Bethlehem's cave. The Mystic Magi [*or* The Southern Cross]. Robert Stephen Hawker. ChTr; OxBoCh
Three Arrows, The. Edward Fitzgerald. OBVV
Three Arts, The. Minerva Florence Swigert. LPS-1
Three Babes, The. *Unknown. See* Babes in the Wood, The.
Three Ballate. Angelo Poliziano, *tr. fr. Italian by* John Addington Symonds.
“He who knows not what thing is Paradise,” II. AWP
(Ballata of Myrrha's Eyes.) LiTW
“I found myself one day all, all alone,” I. AWP
“I went a roaming, maidens, one bright day,” III. AWP
(Dance Song, *tr. by* John Heath-Stubbs.) LyPI
Three Barrows Down. Jocelyn Brooke. ChMP
Three Beggars, The. Walter de la Mare. RIS
Three Bells, The. Whittier. EtS
(*Three Bells* of Glasgow, The.) PECK
Three Best Things, The. Henry van Dyke. TCAP
Sels.
Life (“Let me but live my life from year to year”). BLP; MaRV; OQP; QP-1
Work. BTP; MaRV; OQP; PoeMoYo; PoMa; PoRL; POT; PoTo; PYM; QP-1; SP; YT
Three Black Crows, The. John Byrom. BOHV
Three Black Crows, The. *Unknown. See* Three Ravens, The.
Three Blessings. *Unknown.* ALV; PA
Three blind mice, see how they run! Mother Goose. BoN; OxNR; RIS; SiTL; StVeCh (1940 ed.)
Three blind mice, three blind mice,/ Dame Julian, Dame Julian. *Unknown.* OBS
Three bold brothers of merrie Scotland. Henry Martyn (E *vers.*). *Unknown.* ESPB
Three brightest blessings of this thirsty race. Three Blessings. *Unknown.* ALV; PA
Three brothers in old Scotland did dwell. Henry Martyn (A *vers.*). *Unknown.* ViBoFo
Three Bushes, The. W. B. Yeats. LiTG; LiTL
Lady's Third Song, The, *sel.* FaBoTw
Three Canterbury Pilgrims. Chaucer. *See* Canterbury Tales, The: Prologue.
Three Captains, The. *Unknown, tr. fr. French by* Andrew Lang. AWP
Three captains went to Indian wars. The Casterbridge Captains. Thomas Hardy. EV-5
Three Cat Poems. Maurice James Craig. PoC
Address of Welcome.
Book of Life, The.
Occasion of Sin.
Three Cherry Trees, The. Walter de la Mare. ChMo; GBV
Three Children. *Unknown, at. to* John Gay. BOHV; NA
(Sad, Sad Story, A.) RIS
(“Three children sliding on the ice.”) BoN; OxNR; PPL; StVeCh (1940 ed.)
Three children dash in the dim dooryard. Tree Tag. Mary E. Caragher. GoYe
Three Children near Clonmel. Eileen Shanahan. OnYI; OxBI
Three children sliding on the ice. Three Children [*or* A Sad, Sad Story]. *Unknown, at. to* John Gay. BOHV; BoN; NA; OxNR; PPL; RIS; StVeCh (1940 ed.)
Three Christmas Carols. *Unknown.* ACP
“Lake is born all of a May, A,” I.
“Man, be merry, I thee rede,” II.
“This night there is a child born,” III.
Three Cities. George Rostrevor Hamilton. POTE
Three City Cantos. Charles A. Wagner. GoYe
Three Classes of Citizens. Euripides, *tr. fr. Greek by* M. Wodhull. *Fr.* Suppliants. GrR
Three Colours, Black, and Red, and White. Swift. *Fr.* The Progress of Beauty. BrBE
Three Colts Exercising in a Six-Acre. Joseph Campbell. OnYI
Three Cottage Girls, The. Wordsworth. HBV
Three Counsellors, The. “Æ.” TIP
Three crests against the saffron sky. Twilight on Tweed. Andrew Lang. EBSV; OBVV; POTT; PoVP
Three crooked cripples went through Cripplegate. *Unknown.* OxNR
Three Crosses, The. Edmund Vance Cook. PEDC
Three Crosses. Leila Avery Rotherburger. ChIP; MaRV; StJW
Three crosses rose on Calvary against the iron sky. The Thief on the Cross. Harriet Monroe. OQP; QP-1
Three Crows, The. *Unknown. See* Three Ravens, The.
Three Cups of Cold Poison. *Unknown. See* Lord Randal.
Three Damsels in the Queen's Chamber. Swinburne. AnEC
(Christmas Carol, A.) StJW
Three Dangers. *Unknown, tr. fr. Spanish by* Havelock Ellis. OnPM
Three dark maids—I loved them when. Villancico. *Unknown.* AWP; JAWP; OnPM; WBP
Three Days. W. Boyd Carpenter. MaRV
Three Days. James Roberts Gilmore. LPS-3
Three days ago I found my love, and it's not so long. Je caresserai la belle par amitié. *Unknown.* OuSiCo
Three days from the Luapula still. The Explorer. Anthony Delius. BoSA
Three days I heard them grieve when I lay dead. Beyond the Stars. Charles Hanson Towne. UnW
Three days, I ween, make up our life. Three Days. W. Boyd Carpenter. MaRV
Three days through sapphire seas we sailed. The Bay Fight. Henry Howard Brownell. GA; PaA; PAH; PAP; PFY
Three Dead and the Three Living, The. George Barker. LiTB
Three Dogs. E. C. Brereton. BoTP
Three doors are in the temple. The Doors in the Temple. George Matheson. OQP; QP-1
Three Doves. James Jeffrey Roche. JKCP
Three dwarfs there were which lived in an isle. The Isle of Lone. Walter de la Mare. PtOT
Three Enemies, The. Christina Rossetti. CoBE; EV-5; MeRV; NBE; POTT; PoVP; TCEP; ViPo; VLEP
Three Epitaphs upon the Death of a Rare Child of Six Years Old. Francis Davison. OBSC; ReIE
“Lovely boy, thou art not dead,” II.
“Thou alive on earth, sweet boy,” III.
“Wit's perfection, Beauty's wonder,” I.
Three fellows were marching over the Rhine. The Hostess' Daughter. Ludwig Uhland. AWP; JAWP; WBP
Three Fields. Adolf Heyduk, *tr. fr. Czech by* Paul Selver. LiTW
Three fishermen/ fished in the old Round Pond. Fishes. Humbert Wolfe. RIS; StaSt
Three Fishers, The. Charles Kingsley. BBV; BeLS; BMEP; BTP; CaAE; CG; EtS; EV-5; HBV; LEAP; LPS-2; MCCG; NeHB; OTPC (1923 ed.); PoVP; ShBV-1; TreF; TVSH; VA; WBLP
(Three Fishers Went Sailing.) OtMeF
Three folds in my garment, yet only one garment I bear. The Rann of the Three. *Unknown, tr. by* Thomas Walsh. CAW; WHL
Three folds of the cloth, yet one only napkin is there. The Sacred Trinity [*or* Four Prayers]. *Unknown, tr. by* Eleanor Hull. JKCP (1926 ed.); OnYI
3 for 25. William Jay Smith. WaP
Three Foxes, The. A. A. Milne. MoShBr; StVeCh (1955 ed.)
Three Fragments. William Allingham. IrPN
“And from a northern coast the Lovers watch'd,” I.
“Black texture of the leafy trees,” III.
“Night a spongy dimness fill'd with moonshine, The,” II.
Three Friends of Mine. Longfellow. BAV; IAP
Three gables; clustered chimney stacks; a wall. The Vacant Farmhouse. Walter de la Mare. HaMV
Three Gannets, The. Fitz-James O'Brien. DaM
Three Gates. Beth Day, *after the Arabic.* BLP; BLPA; MaRV; NeHB; OQP; QP-1; TreFS
(Three Gates of Gold.) PoToHe
Three ghosts on the lonesome road, The. Stains. Theodosia Garrison. BAP; BPP; HBV; LBMV; LEAP; MaRV; TCAP; WGRP
Three Gifts. Edward Judson Hanna. ChIP; OQP; QP-1
Three gipsies [*or* gypsies] stood at the Castle gate. The Wraggle Taggle Gipsies. *Unknown.* BLV; CBOV; LiTL; OtMeF; SaSa; ShBV-1
Three Girls. Hazel Hall. BAP; PoTo
Three Graves, The, *sel.* Samuel Taylor Coleridge.
“So gentle Ellen now no more.” ChER

Three Green Trees. Angela Morgan. HBMV
Three grey geese in a green field grazing. *Unknown.* OxNR
Three Gypsies. Nikolaus Lenau, *tr. fr. German by* Dwight Durling. AnGP
Three gypsies stood at the Castle gate. *See* Three gipsies . . .
Three Haitian Creole Moods. Emile Roumer, *tr. fr. French by* Selden Rodman. OnHM
Three hand-spike raps on the forward hatch. Reefing Topsails. Walter Mitchell. EtS
Three Hermits, The. W. B. Yeats. AtBAP
Three Hills. Everard Owen. StJW
Three Hills, The. J. C. Squire. BMEP; HBMV; InP; TCEP; TCPD
Three horsemen dark 'gainst a daffodil sky. The Ballad of the Lady Lorraine. Padraic Gregory. ReTS
Three horsemen galloped the dusty way. On the Road to Chorrea. Arlo Bates. AA
Three Hours. Vachel Lindsay. ATP
Three hours ago he blundered up the trench. A Working Party. Siegfried Sassoon. ChMo; CMP; TCEP
Three Hundred, The. Simonides. *See* Thermopylae.
306. E. E. Cummings. AnEnPo
Three Hundred Thousand More. James Sloan Gibbons. MDAH; PaA; PAH; PoFr
Three hundred years ago or more, so runs the ancient tale. Jonathan Smith. Karl N. Llewellyn. SoAF
Three hundred years the world has looked at it. Raphael's San Sisto Madonna. George Henry Miles. CAW
Three Huntsmen, The. *Unknown. See* Three Jovial Welshmen, The.
Three jolly farmers. Off the Ground. Walter de la Mare. CBPC; MuP; RG; StaSt; StPo; YT
Three jolly gentlemen. The Huntsmen. Walter de la Mare. CenHV; HBMV; InP; PreP; SiSoSe; StVeCh; TiPo
Three Jolly Hunters, The. James Whitcomb Riley. WaKn
Three Jolly Huntsmen, The. *Unknown. See* Three Jovial Welshmen, The.
Three Jolly Pigeons, The. Goldsmith. *See* Song: "Let schoolmasters puzzle their brains."
Three Jovial Welshmen, The. *Unknown.* GaP; HBVY; SiTL
(Jovial Welshmen, The.) OTPC
("There were three jovial Welshmen.") BoChLi; CG; OxNR; StVeCh
(Three Huntsmen, The.) OxBoLi
(Three Jolly Huntsmen.) GoTP
(Three Jovial Huntsmen, The.) BOHV, *abr.;* GoBP, *diff. vers.;* NA, *abr.*
(Three Welshmen, The.) MoShBr
Three Khalandeers, The. James Clarence Mangan. OBVV
Three Kings, The. Eugene Field. *See* Three Kings of Cologne, The.
Three Kings, The. Longfellow. ChrBoLe; CLS; COAH; GBV (1952 ed.); GN; GoTP; HBV; HBVY; SDH
(Three Kings Came Riding.) StVeCh
Three Kings, The. *Unknown.* OBB
(Now Is Christmas Ycome.) AnEC
Three Kings Came Riding. Norah M. Holland. ChrBoLe
Three Kings came riding from far away. The Three Kings. Longfellow. ChrBoLe; CLS; COAH; GBV (1952 ed.); GN; GoTP; HBV; HBVY; SDH; StVeCh
Three kings from out the Orient. Carol. Thomas Edward Brown. VLEP
Three Kings of Cologne, The. Eugene Field. CLS; SDH; StJW
(Three Kings, The.) GN
Three Kings of Orient. *Unknown. See* We Three Kings of Orient Are.
Three Kings' Song. *Unknown, tr. fr. French by* Sabine Baring-Gould. BOL
Three Kings stepped out of my body. Poem for Epiphany. Norman Nicholson. StJW
Three kings there were from Orient who came. Gifts. Helen Wieand Cole. ChIP; OQP; QP-1
Three Knights from Spain. *Unknown.* AtBAP; CH
("We are three brethren out of Spain.") OxNR; RIS, *much abr.*
Three Ladies, The. Robert Creeley. NeAP
Three Ladies of London, The, *sels.* Robert Wilson.
New Brooms. ElL; EM-1
(Conscience's Song.) OBSC
Simplicity's Song. OBSC
Three ladies played at cup and ball. The Cruel Brother. *Unknown.* ABS; BaBo (B *vers.*)
Three Lessons. Schiller. *See* Three Words of Strength.
Three Links of Light Armour. Richard Armour. SiTL
Three Little Babes. *Unknown.* ABS
Three little chickens/ And one little worm. A Tug-of-War. M. M. Hutchinson. BoTP
Three little children sitting on the sand. All, All a-Lonely. *Unknown.* ChTr; ExPo; OxBoLi
Three Little Fishers. F. H. Stauffer. PA
Three little ghostesses. *Unknown.* OxNR
Three Little Kittens, The ("Three little kittens, they lost their mittens"). *Unknown, at. to* Eliza Lee Follen. BoTP; CIV; FaPON; GFA; OIF; OnHT; OTPC (1946 ed.); OxNR; PCH; SAS; StVeCh; TreFS; UTS
(Careless Kittens, The, *abr.*) RIS
("Three little kittens they lost their mittens.") PPL
Three little maidens they have slain. Song. Maurice Maeterlinck. AWP; JAWP; WBP
Three Little Maids from School. W. S. Gilbert. *Fr.* The Mikado. PoVP
Three Little Men in a Boat. Rodney Bennett. BoTP
Three little mice sat down to spin. Pussy and the Mice. *Unknown.* MoShBr
Three little mice walked into town. Three Mice. Charlotte Druitt Cole. BoTP
Three Little Pigs, The. Sir Alfred Scott-Gatty. BoTP
Three Little Puffins. Eleanor Farjeon. LiL; TiPo (1959 ed.)
Three little words you often see. Grammar in a Nutshell [*or* Grammar in Rhyme *or* The Parts of Speech]. *Unknown.* HBV; HBVY; MeMeAg; OTPC; PTA-2; TreFS
Three long breaths of the blessèd night. Night-Errantry. Maurice Hewlett. BMEP; GTML
Three long nights, an' three long days. Walk, Mary, down de Lane. *Unknown.* BoAN-2
Three long years a-sailing, three long years a-whaling. A Whaler's Confession. Harry Kemp. NV
Three Love Poems. Norman Cameron. FaBoTw
From a Woman to a Greedy Lover, I.
In the Queen's Room, II.
Shepherdess, III.
Three Love Poems. Stepan Petrovich Shchipachev, *tr. fr. Russian by* Jack Lindsay. RuPo
"Let men intently strip your grace," I.
"My memory fears," II.
"Simpleton looks in love for rest, A," III.
Three Lovely Holes. Winifred Welles. StVeCh
Three lovely notes he whistled, too soft to be heard. The Unknown Bird. Edward Thomas. FaBoEn; MoP
Three Loves. Lucy Hamilton Hooper. BeLS; LPS-1
Three Lullabies. Fred Emerson Brooks. BOL
Three Magi, The. Roy Temple House. PSO
Three maidens in their chamber. Sir Ogey and Lady Elsey. *Unknown.* BaBo
Three maidens sit in a bower. Aage and Else. *Unknown.* BoDaBa
Three Maids a-Milking Would Go. *Unknown.* CoMu
Three Memorial Sonnets. George Barker. *See* Memorial (for Two Young Seamen . . .).
Three Memories of Heaven. Rafael Alberti, *tr. fr. Spanish by* Eleanor L. Turnbull. CoSP
Three men came talking up the road. Nightpiece. John Manifold. LiTM; MoBrPo (1950 ed.); WaP
Three men coming down the winter hill, The. Winter Landscape. John Berryman. LiTA; LiTG; MoAmPo (1950 ed.)
Three men in a limousine travelling westward. The Three Dead and the Three Living. George Barker. LiTB
Three men lived yet when this dead man was young. After Looking into Carlyle's Reminiscences. Swinburne. ViPo
Three Men of Gotham. Thomas Love Peacock. *Fr.* Nightmare Abbey. CoEV; EV-4; FaBoCh; GTBS; GTBS-D; LiTG; MuP; MyFE, *st.* 1; OBEV; SiTL; TOP
(Catch, A: "Seamen three! What men be ye?") AlDL; ViBoPo
(Men of Gotham, The.) CH; OTPC (1946 ed.)
(Seamen Three.) CaAE; OBRV
("Seamen three, what men be ye?") EG
(Wise Men of Gotham, The.) LoBV
Three men shared death upon a hill. Upon a Hill. Miriam LeFevre Crouse. ChIP
Three Mice. Charlotte Druitt Cole. BoTP
Three Mice, The. Anthony C. Deane. PA
Three miles extended around the fields of the homestead. Frithiof's Homestead. Esaias Tegnér. *Fr.* Frithiof's Saga. AWP
Three months with clenched fists and thin bitten lips. William Ellery Leonard. *Fr.* Two Lives, Pt. III. MOAP
Three moons I trekked the woods without a trail. Trash. Robert Haven Schauffler. TCAP
Three Moorish girls I loved. Axa, Fátima, and Marién [*or* Song]. *Unknown.* AnSpL-1; LiTW; TeCS
Three Most Famous Tales, The. *Unknown, tr. fr. Old Irish by* Seán O'Faoláin. SiB
Three Musicians, The. Aubrey Beardsley. ACP (1926 ed.); JKCP (1926 ed.)
Three Nights Drunk (*diff. vers. of* Our Goodman), *with music. Unknown.* OuSiCo
Three Nocturns. Sir Osbert Sitwell. POTE
"Milky clouds, dispersing, The," III.
"Owl, horned wizard of the night, An," II.
"Valleys that we knew in sunlit hours, The," I.
Three o'Clock. Ridgely Torrence.
(Three o'Clock—Morning.) NP; TBM
Three o'Clock in the Morning. R. S. Palfrey. DD; MPB
Three of a Kind. Richard Hovey. PIAE

Three of us afloat in the meadow by the swing. Pirate Story. Robert Louis Stevenson. BeLS; FaPON; GFA; GoTP; OTPC (1946 ed.); PoVP; TiPo; VA
Three of us without a care. Three of a Kind. Richard Hovey. PIAE
Three Old Brothers. Frank O'Connor. OnYI
Three Old Cattlemen. Monica Shannon. GaP
Three old hermits took the air. The Three Hermits. W. B. Yeats. AtBAP
Three ounces are necessary, first of Patience. Recipe for a Happy Life. Margaret of Navarre. PoMa
Three Persons. Louise Townsend Nicholl. CAW
Three Peters, The. Molly Michaels. RIS
Three Pictures. Charles Dalmon. TSW; TSWC
Almond Blossoms.
Snowfall on Plum Trees after They Had Bloomed, A.
Wistaria Blossoms.
Three Pigs, *with music. Unknown.* ABF
Three Pipes, The. *Unknown, tr. fr. Russian by* W. R. S. Ralston. OnPM
Three Plum Buns. Christina Rossetti. *Fr.* Sing-Song. BoTP (Snack, A.) PCH
Three Poems about Mark Twain, *sel.* Vachel Lindsay.
When the Mississippi Flowed in Indiana, II. ChMo; CMP
Three Poems of the Atomic Bomb. *sel.* Edith Sitwell.
Dirge for the New Sunrise. AtBAP; MoAB; MoBrPo (1950 ed.); SeCePo
Three Poets, The. Lilian Whiting. PA
Three poets, in three distant ages born. Lines Printed under the Engraved Portrait of Milton [*or* Epigram on Milton]. Dryden. ACP; BCEP; BEL; BLV; BoLiVe; CEP; EiPP; EnLi-1 (1939 ed.); EnLit; EPP; EV-3; GEPC; HBV; InP; LEAP; LiA; LPS-3; PIR; PtP; SeCeV; SeCV-2; SeEP; TCEP; TOP; TrGrPo; WHA
Three poets went sailing down Boston Bay. The Three Poets. Lilian Whiting. PA
Three Poplars, The. Philip Francis Little. GTIV; OxBI
Three Portraits of Prince Charles. Andrew Lang. PoVP; VA
Three Princesses, The. Cecilia MacKinnon. CPG
Three Proverbs. James Clarence Mangan, *after the Ottoman (Turkish).* IrPN
"Hour of Good, a day of Ill, An," I.
"Nought, I hear thee say," III.
"Steed to the man who bestrides it newly, The," II.
Three Quatrains. E. A. Robinson. TwP
"As long as Fame's imperious music rings," I.
"Drink to the splendor of the unfulfilled," II.
"We cannot crown ourselves with everything," III.
Three quince trees dance, a windy row. Flower of Quince. Virginia Taylor McCormick. BAP
Three ranks there are of citizens. Three Classes of Citizens. Euripides. *Fr.* Suppliants. GrR
Three Ravens, The ("As I was walking all alane"). *Unknown. See* Twa Corbies, The.
Three Ravens, The ("There were three ravens sat on a tree"). *Unknown.* AtBAP; BCEP; BEL; ChTr; EM-1; ESPB; EV-2; HBV; OAEP; OBB; OBEV; OuHeWo; PoEL-1; SeCeV; TrGrPo; UnPo; ViBoFo (A, B, *and* C *vers.*); ViBoPo
Three Rimas. Gustavo Adolfo Bécquer. *See* Rimas.
Three roads led out to Calvary. The Blessed Road. Charles Buxton Going. ChIP
Three roads were shadowy and the sky over. Vanessa Vanessa. Ewart Milne. NeIP
Three Roses, The. Walter Savage Landor. BPN; EmBrPo
Three Roses. Dmitri Venevitinov, *tr. fr. Russian by* C. M. Bowra. BoRS
Three Sailor Boys. *Unknown.* ABS
Three Scars, The. George Walter Thornbury. VA
Three school-girls pass this way each day. Three Girls. Hazel Hall. BAP; PoTo
Three score and ten by common calculation. Song. James Robinson Planché. BOHV
Three score and ten! The tumult of the world. Life's Evening. William Dudley Foulke. OQP; QP-2; WGRP
Three Scotch Robbers, The. *Unknown. See* Henry Martin.
Three Seamstresses, The. Isaac Leibush Peretz, *tr. fr. Yiddish by* Joseph Leftwich. TrJP
Three Seasons. Christina Rossetti. HBV; POTT; VLEP
Three Sections from "Anabasis." "St.-J. Perse." *See* Anabasis.
Three Sermons to the Dead. Laura Riding.
Nor Is It Written, III. FaBoMo; LiTA
Not All Immaculate, II. LiTA
Way of the Air, The, I. LiTA
Three Shadows. Dante Gabriel Rossetti. BPN; EmBrPo; HBV; PoVP; ViBoPo; VLEP
Three ships I saw come sailing. Swedish Folk Song. *Unknown.* PCH
Three ships of war had Preble when he left the Naples shore. Reuben James. James Jeffrey Roche. GA; PAH
Three Silences of Molinos, The. Longfellow. AmPP; AnFE; APA; APW; CoAnAm; CoBA; IAP
Three Singing Birds, The. James Reeves. PoMS
Three Sisters, The. Arthur Davison Ficke. HBV; LEAP; MAP; SBMV
Three Sisters. *Unknown, tr. fr. French by* Richard Beaumont. LyMA
Three slender things that best support the world. *Unknown. Fr.* The Triads of Ireland. OnYI
Three Songs. Hart Crane. *Fr.* The Bridge. LiTA
National Winter Garden, *sel.* OxBA
Three Songs, The. Bayard Taylor. StPo
Three Songs from Portugal, *sel.* Frederic Prokosch.
Song from Portugal, 1940 ("Under the leafless arches"), II. LoPo
Three Songs to Steingerd. Cormac Ogmundarson, *tr. fr. Old Norse by* W. G. Collingwood *and* Jón Stefánsson. LyMA
"There breaks on me, burning upon me," I.
"Tree of my treasure and longing, The," III.
"Yea, black are the eyes that I bring ye," II.
Three Sonnets. Hartley Coleridge.
"Dark green summer, with its massive hues, The," III. RO
"Hast thou not seen an aged rifted tower," I. EnRP; RO
"How shall a man fore-doom'd to lone estate," II. RO
Three Sonnets. Cathleen Keegan. MuM
Renunciation.
Temptation, I, II.
Three Sonnets on Oblivion. George Sterling. HBV
Dust Dethroned, The, *sel.* BAP; LBMV
Three Sons, The. John Moultrie. LPS-1
Three Sorrowful Things. *Unknown, tr. fr. Middle English by* Mabel Van Duzee. MeEV
(Three Sorry Things, *mod. vers.*) TMEV
Three sorrows of story-telling fill me with pity. The Three Most Famous Tales. *Unknown.* SiB
Three Sorry Things. *Unknown. See* Three Sorrowful Things.
Three Spiritual Sonnets. W. W. E. Ross. BoCaPo
On Angels.
On the Supernatural.
Stream of Life, The.
Three Spring Notations on Bipeds. Carl Sandburg. AWP; InPo; JAWP; MOAP; WBP
Three Springs. Pushkin, *tr. fr. Russian.* BoR, *tr. by* Maud F. Jerrold; OnPM, *tr. by* Babette Deutsch; TrRV, *tr. by* Babette Deutsch
Three Stages. Christina Rossetti. EmBrPo
(Pause of Thought, A.) FaBoEn
Three Star Final. Conrad Aiken. OxBA
Three Stars of Prophecy, The. David Gascoyne. POTE
Three Steps. Katharine Lee Bates. OQP; QP-2
Three steps and I reach the door. Fate. Louis James Block. AA
Three steps there are our human life must climb. Three Steps. Katharine Lee Bates. OQP; QP-2
Three steps up from earthiness. Chapel in the Woods. Mary Newton Baldwin. UnW
Three stood listening to a fresh access, The. Snow. Robert Frost. IAP
Three strange men came to the inn. A Lady Comes to an Inn. Elizabeth J. Coatsworth. MAP; MoAmPo; NeMA; StPo
Three students once tarried over the Rhine. From the German of Uhland. *Tr. by* James Weldon Johnson. CDC
Three students were travelling over the Rhine. The Landlady's Daughter. Ludwig Uhland, *tr. by* John S. Dwight. LPS-1
Three summers since I chose a maid. The Farmer's Bride. Charlotte Mew. BMEP; HBMV; LBBV; MBP; MoAB; MoBrPo; NP; OnPP; PoRA; TCPD; TrGrPo
Three swart gypsies once I saw. Three Gypsies. Nikolaus Lenau. AnGP
Three Tarry Men. Edmund Leamy. MW; PoMa
Three then came forward out of darkness. The Road. Conrad Aiken. MAP; MoAmPo
Three Things. Joseph Auslander. BAP; HBMV; MPB; PoTo; TrJP
Three Things. Gertrude B. Gunderson. OQP; QP-2
Three Things. *Unknown, ad. fr. Persian by* Louis Untermeyer. GoTP
Three Things. W. B. Yeats. AtBAP; FaBoEn; OBMV
Three things are of the Evil One. Charm against Enemies. *Unknown.* JKCP (1926 ed.)
Three Things Come Not Back. *Unknown, tr. fr. Arabic.* MaRV; OQP; QP-2
Three things filled this day for me. Three Things. Joseph Auslander. BAP; HBMV; MPB; PoTo; TrJP
Three things I beg of Life to let me keep. Three Things. Gertrude B. Gunderson. OQP; QP-2
Three things in my house are my own. Salvage. Beatrice Ravenel. LS
Three things must a man possess if his soul would live. The New Trinity. Edwin Markham. BoFr; PGD
Three things seek my death. Inheritance. *Unknown.* KiLC
Three things the Master hath to do. Pray—Give—Go. Annie Johnson Flint. BLRP
Three things there are more beautiful. The Beautiful. W. H. Davies. POTE

"Three things there are," said one. "And I, if I Be Lifted Up, Shall Draw All Men." E. P. Dickie. ChIP; MaRV
Three things there are that will never come back. Three Things. *Unknown.* GoTP
Three things there are, worth living for. The Swashbuckler's Song. James Stuart Montgomery. HBMV
Three Things There Be. Fulke Greville. Caelica, CV [CVI]. LiTG
("Three things there be in man's opinion dear.") LiTB; OBS; PoEL-1; SiCE
Three things there be that prosper all [*or* up] apace. The Wood, the Weed, the Wag [*or* To His Son]. Sir Walter Ralegh. BLV; EnL; Po; PoD; PoE; PoEL-2; ReIE; SiPS; TrGrPo; TuPP
Three Things to Remember. Blake. *See* Robin Redbreast, A.
Three thousand dollars to repair the church! A Spirit Muses. Franklin B. Williams. CAG
Three thousand miles of border line! A Century of Peace. Guy Bilsford. BoHiPo
Three Thousand Years After. Edith M. Tuttle. NeTW
Three Threads of Gold. Leconte de Lisle, *tr. fr. French by* Alan Conder. TrFP
Three times a day my prayer is. *Unknown.* OBSC
Three times, all in the dead of night. Colin and Lucy [*or* Lucy and Colin]. Thomas Tickell. CEP; CG; EV-3; OBEC; OTPC (1923 ed.)
Three times he crossed our way. Old Man Pondered. John Crowe Ransom. MAP; MoAmPo
Three times in Bethany, that hallowed spot. At His Feet. Lois R. Carpenter. BePJ
Three times round the cuckoo waltz. Cuckoo Waltz. *Unknown.* AS
Three times we heard it calling with a low. The Ground-Swell. E. J. Pratt. CaP; CPG; OCL
Three Trees. Charles H. Crandall. OHIP; PEOR
Three Trees. Christopher Morley. NLK
Three Trees at Solstice. Mary Finnin. BoAV
Three Troopers, The. George Walter Thornbury. BeLS; BMEP; HBV; VA
Three turkeys fair their last have breathed. A Melancholy Lay. Marjory Fleming. FaBoCh; FiBHP; LoGBV; SiTL; ThWaDe
Three twangs of the horn, and they're all out of cover. The Glory of Motion. R. St. John Tyrwhitt. VA
Three Valkyries, The. Johannes Ewald, *tr. fr. Danish by* Charles W. Stork. BoDS
Three Variations. Boris Pasternak, *tr. fr. Russian by* Babette Deutsch. TrJP; TrRV
"Miles thick with torpor nauseate the gardens," II.
"Now tatters of denuded clouds," III.
"When consummate the day hangs before you," I.
Three viands in three different courses served. Oyster-Crabs. Carolyn Wells. PA
Three Warnings, The. Hester Thrale. BeLS; HBV; LPS-3
Three weeks gone and the combatants gone. Vergissmeinicht. Keith Douglass. ChMP; NePoEA; PoN
Three Welshmen, The. *Unknown. See* Three Jovial Welshmen, The.
Three White Birds of Angus. Eleanor Rogers Cox. HBMV
Three white things. New Triads. Constance Davies. MoWP
Three Winds, The. Laurie Lee. FaBoMo
Three Wise Couples, The. Mrs. E. T. Corbett. BLPA
Three Wise Kings. William E. Brooks. ChIP; PGD
Three Wise Men, The. John Finley. ChIP; OQP; QP-1
Three wise men of Gotham. Mother Goose. BoChLi; FaBoBe; FaFP; HBV; HBVY; OnHT; OTPC; OxNR; PPL; RIS; SiTL
Three Wise Monkeys, The. Florence Boyce Davis. WBLP
Three wise old couples were they, were they. The Three Wise Couples. Mrs. E. T. Corbett. BLPA
Three Wise Women, The. Mrs. E. T. Corbett. BLPA, *abr.*
Three Wishes ("I wish I had a yellow cat"). *Unknown.* DDA
Three Wishes, The ("You've saved my life"). *Unknown.* DDA
Three with the Moon and His Shadow. Li Po, *tr. fr. Chinese by* Shigeyoshi Obata. WoL
Three without slumber ride from afar. Five Carols for Christmastide, III. Louise Imogen Guiney. ISi
Three Witnesses, The. Coventry Patmore. MeRV
Three Woes, The. Aubrey Thomas De Vere. AnIV
Three words fall sweetly on my soul. Mother, Home, Heaven. William Goldsmith Brown. DD; FaBoBe; HBV
Three Words of Strength. Schiller, *tr. fr. German.* OQP; QP-2
(Three Lessons.) MaRV
Three workmen fashioning a cross. Cross Makers [*or* Free Enterprise]. Clyde McGee. ChIP; MaRV
Three Woulds, The. *Unknown.* DDA
Three years have passed of man's mortality. William Ellery Leonard. *Fr.* Two Lives, Pt. III. MOAP
Three years of night and nightmare, years of black. Daybreak. Louis Untermeyer. NV
Three Years She Grew [in Sun and Shower]. Wordsworth. AtBAP; AWP; BEL; BPN; CBOV; EM-2; EnL; EnLit; EnRP; EPN; EPP; ERP; EV-3; GBV (1922 ed.); GEPC; HBVY; LoBV; LPS-1; OAEP; OBRV; OnPP; OuHeWo; PoE; PoEL-4; PoFS; REAL; ReaPo; SeCeV; SN; TCEP; TOP; TreFS; TwP; TyEnPo
(Education of Nature, The.) GTBS; GTBS-D; GTBS-W; GTSE; GTSL
(Lucy.) EmBrPo; EnLi-2; EtPaEn; FiP; GN; HBV; LEAP; LiTL; OBEV; OTPC (1923 ed.); TrGrPo
Nature's Gifts to Lucy, *br. sel.* LiA
Three Young Rats ("Three young rats with black felt hats"). *Unknown.* AlDL; BoN; ChTr; InvP; LiL; LiTG; OxBoLi; OxNR; SiTL
Three youths went a-fishing. The Banished Duke of Grantham. *Unknown.* EnSB
Threefold terror of love; a fallen flare, The. The Mother of God. W. B. Yeats. EnLP; MeRV
Threefold the stride of Time, from first to last! Time. Schiller. OQP; QP-2
Threes. Carl Sandburg. OxBA
Threescore and Ten. Richard Henry Stoddard. HBV; LEAP
Threescore o' nobles rade to the king's ha! Glenlogie. *Unknown.* HBV
Threnodia Augustalis, *sel.* Dryden.
"O wondrous changes of a fatal scene." NBE
Threnody, A: Ahkoond of Swat, The. George Thomas Lanigan. *See* Threnody, A: "What, what, what."
Threnody: "Blow out the dying candles one by one." Richmond Lattimore. CAG
Threnody: "I have been a snob to-day." Alfred Kreymborg. MAPA
Threnody, A: In Memory of Albert Darasz, *sel.* William James Linton.
"O Blessed Dead! beyond all earthly pains." VA
Threnody: "In Plimmerton, in Plimmerton." Denis Glover. AnNZ
Threnody: "Lilacs blossom just as sweet." Dorothy Parker. InMe
Threnody: "No sunny ray, no silver night." Thomas Lovell Beddoes. EnRP; ERP; TriL
Threnody: "Only quiet death." Waring Cuney. BANP
Threnody: "Red leaves fall upon the lake, The." John Farrar. BoChLi; BrR; GFA; SUS
Threnody: "South-wind brings, The." Emerson. AA; AnNE; EOAH; IAP; MOAP; TCAP; TOP
Sels.
What Is Excellent Is Permanent. GrCo-1
"Wilt thou not ope thy heart to know." MaRV
Threnody: "There's a grass-grown road from the valley." Ruth Guthrie Harding. BAP; HBV
Threnody: "Truth is a golden sunset far away." I. O. Scherzo. HoPM
Threnody, A: "What, what, what." George Thomas Lanigan. AA; BoCaPo; FiBHP; HBV; InMe; LauV; LEAP; LHV; NA; PeCV
(Ahkoond of Swat, The.) BOHV; CaP; TreFS
(Threnody on the Ahkoond of Swat, A.) CenHV
Threnody for a Pet Cat. Mazie V. Caruthers. CIV
Threnody for a Poet. Bliss Carman. CaP; OCL
Threnody on the Ahkoond of Swat, A. George Thomas Lanigan. *See* Threnody: "What, what, what."
Threnos. J. R. Hervey. AnNZ
Threnos. Ezra Pound. MOAP
Threnos. Shelley. *See* Lament, A: "O world! O life! O time!"
Thresh seed and go fan, for the plow may not lie. September. Thomas Tusser. ReIE
Thresher's Labour, The, *sel.* Stephen Duck.
"Grass again is spread upon the ground, The." EnSW
Threshing Machine, The. Alice Meynell. SeCePo
Threshold. Edmund Blunden. HBMV
Threshold. Charles David Webb. NePoAm-2
Thrice, and above, blest (my soules halfe) art thou. A Country Life; to His Brother, M. Tho. Herrick. Robert Herrick. SeCV-1
Thrice Armed. Shakespeare. King Henry VI, Pt. II, *fr.* III, ii. BLP, 3 *ll.*; MaRV
(Justice.) BTP
Thrice at the huts of Fontenoy the English column failed. Fontenoy. Thomas Osborne Davis. HBV; OnYI
Thrice bless'd are they, who feel their loneliness. Melchizedek. Cardinal Newman. TriL
Thrice Blessed ("Thrice blessed are our friends"). Richard R. Kirk. LS
(Company.) BLP
Thrice Blessed Be the Giver. *Unknown.* ElSeCe
Thrice-cruel maid, may Heaven frown on thee. The Elusive Maid. Abraham ibn Chasdai. TrJP
Thrice hail, thou prince of jovial fellows. An Ode to Myself. Thomas Dermody. OnYI
Thrice happy day which sweetly dost combine. On the Coincidence of the Feasts of the Annunciation and the Resurrection in 1627. Sir John Beaumont. ACP (1926 ed.)

Thrice happy days! in rural business past. Blest Winter Nights. John Armstrong. *Fr.* The Art of Preserving Health, III. OBEC
Thrice Happy He. William Drummond of Hawthornden. ElSeCe; HBV
(Solitary Life, A.) EV-2; OBS
(Sonnet: "Thrice happy he, who by some shady grove.") EPS
Thrice happy he among the favoured few. *Unknown.* *Fr.* Homeric Hymns. GrPo
Thrice happy she that is so well assured. Amoretti, LIX. Spenser. PeBoSo
Thrice happy, who free from ambition and pride. The Fire Side; a Pastoral Soliloquy. Isaac Hawkins Browne. *Fr.* The Foundling Hospital for Wit, IV. OBEC
Thrice Holy. Reginald Heber. *See* Holy, Holy, Holy.
Thrice-holy thorns, encircling with thy fire. To the Most Holy Crown of Thorns. Sister Miriam Teresa. JKCP (1955 ed.)
Thrice is he armed that hath his quarrel just. Thrice Armed. Shakespeare. King Henry VI, Pt. II, *fr.* III, ii. BLP
Thrice summer and autumn passed into the west. William Ellery Leonard. *Fr.* Two Lives, Pt. III. MOAP; TBM
Thrice the brinded cat hath mewed. The Witches' Song [*or* The Charm]. Shakespeare. *Fr.* Macbeth, IV, i. ElL; ElSeCe; InvP; MyFE; PoMS
Thrice the crested cock has crowed. The Glory of Early Rising. Frank Sidgwick. WhC
Thrice Toss These Oaken Ashes [in the Air]. Thomas Campion. AnFE; AtBAP; CaAE; ElL; ElSeCe; EnLoPo; FaBoCh; LoBV; LoGBV; OBSC; PeBoSo; PoRA; TuPP; ViBoPo
(Spells.) ES
(Thrice Tosse These Oaken Ashes in the Ayre.) PoEL-2
Thrice Welcome Christmas. *Unknown.* *See* Now Thrice Welcome Christmas.
Thrice with her lips she touched my lips. Parting [*or* For Ever]. William Caldwell Roscoe. HBV; OBVV
Thrift. Lizette Woodworth Reese. NP
Thrissil and the Rose, The. William Dunbar. EBSV
Thro'. *See also* Through.
Thro' Grief and thro' Danger. Thomas Moore. *See* Irish Peasant to His Mistress, The.
Thro' Pope's soft song tho' all the Graces Breathe. Goodbye to Mr. Pope. Thomas Warton, the Younger. *Fr.* The Pleasures of Melancholy. BeR
Thro' the hushed air the whitening shower descends. A Winter Scene. James Thomson. *Fr.* The Seasons: Winter. OBEC
Thro' the night of doubt and sorrow. Pilgrim's Song. Bernhard S. Ingemann. WGRP
Thro' the night Thy angels kept. A Child's Prayer. William Canton. BoTP
Throat of thunder, a tameless heart, A. A Cyclone at Sea. William Hamilton Hayne. AA
Throats of the little trumpet-flowers are wide open, The. The Trumpet-Vine Arbor. Amy Lowell. *Fr.* 1777. MAPA; NP
Throb, throb, throb . . . the tall ship. Night Boat. Audrey Alexandra Brown. CaP
Throbs the Night with Mystic Silence. Hayyim Nahman Bialik, *tr. fr. Hebrew by* Bertha Beinkinstadt. TrJP
Thron'd in the sun's descending car. Benevolence. Mark Akenside. *Fr.* Against Suspicion. OBEC
Throne of the King, The. Francis Clement Kelley. JKCP
Throne of the Lily-King, The. Joseph Rodman Drake. *Fr.* The Culprit Fay. GN
Throned in splendor, deathless, O Aphrodite. Sappho, *tr. fr. Greek by* Richmond Lattimore. GrPo
Thrones, altars, judgment-seats and prisons. The Millennium. Shelley. *Fr.* Prometheus Unbound, III, iv. BHV; NBE
Thronged now the shrines with revel and sacrifice. Croesus. Bacchylides. GrPE
Throstle, The. Tennyson. BMEP; BoChLi; BPN; DD; EmBrPo; EPN; FaPON; HBV; HBVY; MCCG; NLK; OTPC; PFE; PoRL; PoVP; ShBV-1; SN; VLEP; WaKn
Through. *See also* Thro'.
Through a faire forrest as I went. The Wood-Man's Walk. Anthony Munday. EV-1
Through a Fog of Stars. John Nixon, Jr. MaRV
Through a Glass Darkly. Arthur Hugh Clough. BPN; PoVP; VLEP
(What We, When Face to Face We See.) ViPP
Through a green gorge the river like a fountain. The Sleeper in the Valley. Arthur Rimbaud. WaaP
Through a Porthole. Leon Gellert. BoAu
Through a Shop Window. Eleanor Farjeon. ChBr; GaP
Through a wild midnight all my mountainous past. The Monster. Henry Rago. SiTL
Through a window in the attic. Burglar Bill. "F. Anstey." CenHV; FiBHP
Through all the days of your secret, wishful planning. Letter from a Postulant. Sister Mary Irma. PraNu
Through all the early morning hours. The Workers. Mary Blake Woodson. PEDC
Through all the employments of life. John Gay. *Fr.* The Beggar's Opera, I, i. CEP
Through all the frozen winter. Smells. Kathryn Worth. BrR
Through all the long midsummer day. Midsummer. John Townsend Trowbridge. AA; DD; HBV; HBVY; OBAV
Through all the pleasant meadow-side. The Hayloft. Robert Louis Stevenson. GFA; OnHT; PCH; TSW
Through all the wind-blown aisles of May. A Benedictine Garden. Alice Brown. HBV
Through All the World, *with music.* *Unknown.* TrAS
Through all the years, dear, you would not reprove me. Aja's Lament over His Dead Wife. Kalidasa. LiTW
Through all this new-born day, O Lord. Hymn for the Day. "Gabriela Mistral." MaRV
Through Alpine meadows soft-suffused. Stanzas from the Grande Chartreuse. Matthew Arnold. BPN; CoBE; EM-2; EmBrPo; EPN; GEPC; OAEP; PoEL-5; PoVP; TyEnPo; ViPo; ViPP; VLEP
Through an Embrace. Paul Eluard, *tr. fr. French by* Stephen Spender *and* Frances Cornford. LiTW
Through an old field. Dakotsu, *tr. fr. Japanese by* Lois J. Erickson. SoLD
Through and through the inspired leaves. The Book-Worms. Burns. ChTr; FiBHP; RO
Through Arched Windows. Frank Oliver Call. CPG
Through Baltimore. Bayard Taylor. PAH
Through broken arches moonbeams softly shine. San Juan Capistrano. Alice Cecilia Cooper. GoBC
Through calm and storm the years have led. Centennial Hymn. Bryant. PAH
Through carnage, desolation, blood, and mire. The Army of the Red Cross. Katrina Trask. PEDC
Through centuries of cyclists' traffic-blocks. Robert Herring. Poem of Quietness, II. MoWP
Through Dangly Woods the aimless Doze. The Doze. James Reeves. GoTP
Through darkening pines the cavaliers marched on their sunset way. The Legend of Waukulla. Hezekiah Butterworth. PAH
Through Death to Love. Dante Gabriel Rossetti. The House of Life, XLI. BPN; PoVP; ViPo; VLEP
Through drowsy stillness drifts a sound of mowing. Summer Afternoon. Basil Dowling. AnNZ
Through every minute of this day. A Prayer. John Oxenham. BLRP; PraP
Through every sort of trouble Joe. Contrary Joe. L. A. G. Strong. PoMa
Through ev'ry age, eternal God. Highbridge. *Unknown.* AS
Through Fire in Mobile Bay. *Unknown, at. to* David Glascoe Farragut. BlG; PAH
Through glades and glooms! Oh, fair! Oh, sad! Collins. Lionel Johnson. EV-5
Through great Earl Norman's acres wide. Earl Norman and John Truman. Charles Mackay. VA
Through [*or* Thro'] grief and through danger thy smile hath cheer'd my way. The Irish Peasant to His Mistress. Thomas Moore. ACP; AnIV; EV-4; OBEV (1st ed.); PoFr; TIP
Through halls of vanished pleasure. Poppies in Ludlow Castle. Willa Cather. OBAV
Through harrowing hours now, O broken drake. Broken Drake. Lew Sarett. BAP
Through her forced abnormal quiet. Quakerdom. Charles G. Halpine. LPS-1
Through her lorgnette's disdainful glass. Lady in a Limousine. Lucia Trent. PR
Through his eye searching far. The Portrait. John Gould Fletcher. MOAP
Through his iron glades. Winter the Huntsman. Sir Osbert Sitwell. AlDL; AtBAP; BoW; POTE; ShBV-2
Through his might men work their wills. The Brute. William Vaughn Moody. PoeMoYo
Through his million veins are poured. William Bull Wright. *Fr.* The Brook. AA
Through his misshapen soul and brain. The Idiot. Frederick Peterson. PoP
Through intricate motions ran. Stream and Sun at Glendalough. W. B. Yeats. MaPo; MoPW
Through its sepulchral sewer mouth, oozing mud and rubies. The Tomb of Charles Baudelaire. Stéphane Mallarmé. AnFP
Through laughing leaves the sunlight comes. In the Wood. Herbert Edwin Clarke. VA
Through life's dull road, so dim and dirty. On My Thirty-third Birthday. Byron. OBRV
Through love to light! O, wonderful the way. After-Song. Richard Watson Gilder. AA; LBAP; TrPWD
"Through me is the way into the doleful city." Dante Enters the Gate of Hell. Dante. *Fr.* Divina Commedia: Inferno. LiA

Through meadow-ways as I did tread. A May Burden. Francis Thompson. HBV
Through miles of mist the lighthouse candle sweeps. Gentle Storm. Martha Banning Thomas. PoMa
Through mountain gorges so she won to where. Quintus Smyrnaeus. *Fr.* Posthomerica, X. GrPo
Through my north window in the wintry weather. My Aviary. Oliver Wendell Holmes. SN
Through my open window comes the sweet perfuming. Attainment. Algernon Tassin. AA
Through my small town I roamed, a taunting ghost. Rimbaud in Africa. Edgell Rickword. ChMP
Through night's middle darkness an angel did fly. The Angel. Mikhail Yurevich Lermontov. WaL
Through Nightmare. Robert Graves. Po
Through Nurseryland. *Unknown.* BoTP
Through or over the deathless feud. Pacific Door. Earle Birney. PeCV; TwCaPo
Through progress of the railroads our occupation's gone. The Camp Fire Has Gone Out. *Unknown.* CSF
Through reedy banks. The Nima. Jorge Isaacs. TrJP
Through restless waters of his mind. Poet. John Richard Moreland. BoHiPo
Through rifts of cloud the moon's soft silver slips. A Memory. Ina Donna Coolbrith. BAP
Through rocky arroyas so dark and so deep. Chopo. *Unknown.* CSF
Through rosy cloud and over thorny towers. Rooks; New College Gardens. Louise Imogen Guiney. BLA
Through savage woods I walk without demur. Sonnet. Petrarch. Sonnets to Laura: To Laura in Life, CXLIII. LyPI
Through seas of dreams and seas of phantasies. Nirvana. Sidney Lanier. BAV
Through sepia air the boarders come and go. Landlady. P. K. Page. CaP; TwCaPo
Through some strange sense of sight or touch. Death. Madison Cawein. AA
Through Sorrow to Service. *Unknown.* MaRV
Through storm and fire and gloom, I see it stand. The Celtic Cross. Thomas D'Arcy McGee. OnYI; VA
Through storm and wind. *Unknown.* OxNR
Through storms you reach them and from storms are free. The Enviable Isles. Herman Melville. AA; AnAmPo; APW; FaBoBe; LA; LEAP
Through street and square, through square and street. The Night Cat. W. E. Henley. *Fr.* London Voluntaries. BMEP
Through Streets Where Crooked Wicklow Flows. Horace Gregory. PoeMoYo
Through sun-bright lakes. The River. Thomas Tod Stoddart. EBSV
Through Tanglewood the thrushes trip. Thrushes. Karle Wilson Baker. BLA; MW
Through that pure virgin-shrine. The Night. Henry Vaughan. EPS; EV-2; LiTB; MeLP; MePo; MeRV; NBE; OBEV (new ed.); OBS; OxBoCh; PoEL-2; PoFS; ReaPo; ReEn; RiBV; SeCeV; SeCL; SeCV-1; SeEP; UnPo (1st ed.)
Through that window—all else being extinct. The Room. Conrad Aiken. LiTG; LiTM (rev. ed.); MAP; MAPA; MoAmPo; MOAP; NePA
Through the Ages. Margaret Hope. PGD
Through the ample open door of the peaceful country barn. A Farm Picture. Walt Whitman. IAP; MOAP; OnPM; WoL
Through the Appalachian valleys, with his kit a buckskin bag. A Ballad of Johnny Appleseed. Helmer O. Oleson. SiSoSe; TiPo (1959 ed.)
Through the Barber Shop Window. Violet Anderson. CaP
Through the black, rushing smoke-bursts. Callicles' Song [*or* Apollo]. Matthew Arnold. *Fr.* Empedocles on Etna, II. BMEP; BPN; ChTr; EmBrPo; FiP; GTBS; LH; LoBV; OBEV; OBVV; PoVP; ShBV-3; ViPo; VLEP
Through the blue and frosty heavens. The Angel's Story. Adelaide Anne Procter. DD
Through the blue shadowy valley I hastened in a dream. Recollection. "Æ." NV
Through the bound cable strands, the arching path. Atlantis. Hart Crane. *Fr.* The Bridge. AnFE; AtBAP; CoAnAm; CoV; LiTA; LiTM; MOAP; MoPo; NePA; TwAmPo
Through the brown shade of forests ivied o'er. Tasso. *Fr.* Jerusalem Delivered, VII. PrPoCR
Through the clangor of the cannon. Defeat and Victory. Wallace Rice. GA; MC; PAH
Through the dark aisles of the wood. Poem. Henry Treece. NeBP
Through the dark pine trunks. Images. Richard Aldington. BMEP; MBP; NP; PFE; PIAE; TOP
Through the deep monastic halls. The Abbey. José M. Eguren. CAW
Through the deep woods, at peep of day. The Canadian Herd-Boy. Susanna Moodie. BoCaPo
Through the dim pageant of the years. Lincoln. Julia Ward Howe. GA; PoRL
Through the dim window, I could see. In Passing. Roy Helton. HBMV
Through the eddying haze and shadows. Winter Road. Pushkin. BoRS
Through the eyes. Tanka. Lewis Alexander. CDC
Through the faintest filigree. The Ships of Arcady. Francis Ledwidge. EtS
Through the fierce fever I nursed him, and then he said. Little Wild Baby. "Margaret Vandegrift." AA; HBV
Through the forest the boy wends all day long. The Boy and the Flute. Björnstjerne Björnson. AWP; JAWP; WBP
Through the fresh fairness of the spring to ride. Ready for the Ride—1795. H. C. Bunner. PFE
Through the frosty air to the woods we go. Autumn Gloves. Mildred D. Shacklett. GFA
Through the gate. The Colt. Raymond Knister. TwCaPo
Through the great sinful streets of Naples as I passed. Easter Day. Arthur Hugh Clough. BMEP; BPN; EmBrPo; EPN; EPP; OAEP; PoVP; ViP; ViPP; VLEP
Through the green tassels of the weeper tree. Triumphal Ode MCMXXXIX. George Barker. LiTB; WaP
Through the high arches dusty sunbeams stream. Dunster Church. Margaret Willy. DiM
Through the house give glimmering light. Oberon and Titania to the Fairy Train Shakespeare. *Fr.* A Midsummer Night's Dream, V, ii. GN; SiCE
Through the house what busy joy. The First Tooth. Charles *and* Mary Lamb. OTPC (1923 ed.)
Through the leaves are statues gleaming. Villa Borghese. Sophus Michaëlis. BoDS
Through the long August day, mantled blue with a sky of Our Lady. Lady Day in Ireland. Patrick J. Carroll. JKCP
Through the long bending grass. The Heroes' Day. *Unknown.* PEOR
Through the long dark I watch and wake. The Vigil. Abbie Farwell Brown. CV
Through the Looking-Glass, *sels.* "Lewis Carroll."
Humpty Dumpty's Recitation, *fr. ch.* 6. BOHV; ChTr; FiBHP; GoTP; SiTL
(Humpty Dumpty's Song.) OxBoLi; SAS
Jabberwocky, *fr. ch.* 1. AlDL; ALV; BLV; BoChLi; BoN; EnLi-2 (1949 ed.); FaBoBe; FaFP; FaPON; FiBHP; GoTP; HBV; HoPM; InP; LBN; LEAP; LiTB; LiTG; MBP; NA; NAMP; OnSP; OTPC; PIAE; PoRA; PoVP; PreP; PYM; RAR; RIS; SeCeV; ShBV-2; SiTL; TiPo; TreF; TrGrPo; ViP; WhC
Stanza of Anglo-Saxon Poetry. BoN
Walrus and the Carpenter, The, *fr. ch.* 4. BeLS; BMEP; BoChLi; BOHV; BoN; FaBoBe; FaFP; FaPON; FiBHP; GN; GoBP; HBV; HBVY; InMe; LBN; LiTB; LiTG; MaC; MBP; MCCG; NA, NeHB; OnSP; OTPC; PFE; PIR; PoRA; PoRh; PoVP; PTA-1; PYM; SAS; ShBV-1; StVeCh; TreF; TVC; TVSH; YT
" 'Time has come, The,' the Walrus said," 1 *st.* TiPo
White Knight's Song, The, *fr. ch.* 8. EnLi-2; FaBoCh; GoTP; LoGBV; ViP
(Aged, Aged Man, The.) BoN; CoEV; OnPP
(A-Sitting on a Gate.) PoE
(I'll Tell Thee Everything I Can.) InvP
(Ways and Means.) BOHV; FiBHP; NA
(White Knight's Ballad, The.) PoRh
(White Knight's Tale, The.) RIS; ShBV-4
Through the low grey archway children's feet that pass. In a Rosary. Swinburne. VLEP
Through the Maze. *Unknown.* BLRP
Through the Metidja to Abd-el-Kadr. Robert Browning. BPN; EmBrPo; GEPC; PoVP
Through the new wound that fate opened in me. The Sacred Way. Angelos Sikelianos. MoGP
Through the night, through the night. The Sea. Richard Henry Stoddard. AA; HBV; TCEP
Through the Open Door. Patrick Kavanagh. AnIV
Through the Porthole. Marjorie Wilson. BoTP
Through the pregnant universe rumbles life's terrific thunder. Exhortation; Summer, 1919. Claude McKay. CDC
Through the purple dusk on this pathless heath. The Heath. Thomas Boyd. OnYI
Through the sea. Dance of the Lost Key. Jacinto Fombona Pachano. TwSpPo
Through the sea of money-changers he stormed. The Whip of Anger. Mary Ross. ChIP
Through the seedling grass. Red Poppies. "Fiona Macleod." *Fr.* Sospiri di Roma. VA
Through the shine, through the rain. Twilight Song. E. A. Robinson. HBV
Through the shrubs as I can crack[e]. Doron's Jig [*or* Jigge]. Robert Greene. *Fr.* Menaphon. AtBAP; ElL; ElSeCe; PoEL-2; TuPP
Through the silver mist. A Spring Lilt. *Unknown.* HBV; MPB; OTPC
Through the slush and the ruts of the highway. Aleksey Konstantinovich Tolstoy, *tr. fr. Russian by* Maurice Baring. BoR

Through the soft evening air enwinding all. Italian Music in Dakota. Walt Whitman. AmP; TCAP
Through the Solitudes. George Francis Savage-Armstrong. TIP
Through the still air of night. Night Coming Out of a Garden. Lord Alfred Douglas. MBP; MoBrPo (1942 ed.)
Through the street as I trot when the weather is hot. The Hottentot Tot. Newman Levy. RIS
Through the street of mist a grey man advances. Remorse in Garb of Night. Luis Cernuda. CoSP
Through the streets and bazaars. Old Books for New. Edwin Francis Edgett. POT; PoTo
Through the streets of the city. Where Mortals Dwell. Schiller. *Fr.* Die Braut von Messina. LiA
Through the sunny garden. Chillingham. Mary Elizabeth Coleridge. BoTP; PoeT
Through the thatched roof. Emperor Tenchi, *tr. fr. Japanese by* I. W. Furukami. LiTW
Through the vague morning, the heart preoccupied. Bombers. C. Day Lewis. ChMo; MoAB
Through the vales to my love! A Bride Song. Christina Rossetti. EtPaEn
Through the village a word. The Daybreak Call. Gwendolen Haste. PFE
Through the weary nights I strain. Fate's Malignity. Ibn Wahbun. MooP
Through the Windmills. Fairy Wings. Winifred Howard. SUS
Through the Year. Julian S. Cutler. BLPA
Through thee, Virginity, endure. Ad Castitatem. Francis Thompson. PoLi
Through These Pale Cold Days. Isaac Rosenberg. MeRV; TrJP
Through thick Arcadian woods a hunter went. Atalanta's Race [*or* Atalanta's Victory]. William Morris. *Fr.* The Earthly Paradise. BEL; BMEP; BPN; EV-5; LPS-1; VA; ViPo
Through thicke and thin, all night, all day, she driued. Erminia Wanders in the Fields and Dreams of Love. Tasso. *Fr.* Jerusalem Delivered. LiA
Through this our city of delight. Chiffons. William Samuel Johnson. HBV
Through this toilsome world, alas! I Shall Not Pass This Way Again. *Unknown.* BLPA; NeHB; TreFS
Through throats where many rivers meet, the curlews cry. In the White Giant's Thigh. Dylan Thomas. AtBAP; LiTB; PoLFOT; ReMP
Through Thy Cross and Passion. Philip Howard. *See* Though Here in Flesh I Be.
Through torrid entrances, past icy poles. To Shakespeare. Hart Crane. PeBoSo; PtP
Through tranquil years they watched the changes. Clearing for the Plough. E. G. Moll. MoAuPo
Through twenty-one long years love held me burning. Sonnet. Petrarch. Sonnets to Laura: To Laura in Death, LXXXV. LyPI
Through Unknown Paths. Frederick L. Hosmer. TrPWD
Through verdant banks where Thames's branches glide. The Assault on the Fortress. Timothy Dwight. PAH
Through villages of yelping tykes. Dreaming Spires. Roy Campbell. BoSA
Through weary days and sleepless nights. One Gift I Ask. Virginia Bioren Harrison. HBV
Through what long heaviness, assayed in what strange fire. Carthusians. Ernest Dowson. JKCP; PoVP; TriL
Through what rock-strewn tunnels, O companions. The D Minor. E. L. Mayo. MiAP
Through wild and tangled forests. On the Mississippi. Hamlin Garland. BAP
Through winter streets to steer your course aright. Trivia; or, The Art of Walking the Streets of London. John Gay. CEP
Through winter-time we call on spring. The Wheel. W. B. Yeats. MoVE; TwP
Through years our minds have wrestled—and how vain! Disillusioned. Thomas Curtis Clark. ChIP
Through your eyes' round and perfect pupils. Narrative. Louis Dudek. CaP
Through your grey eyes evasive heaven. Four Poems for April, III. Louis Adeane. NeBP
Through Your Window. Tzu Yeh, *tr. fr. Chinese by* Henry H. Hart. ChLP; PoHN
Throughe a forest as I can ryde. Crow and Pie. *Unknown.* ESPB
Throughout a garden greene and gay. The Rose of England. *Unknown.* ESPB
Throughout the day our sweet bells chime. Bluebells. P. A. Ropes. BoTP
Throughout the field I find no grain. Winter in Durnover Field. Thomas Hardy. MBP; MoBrPo
Throughout the soft and sunlit day. The Pines. Julie Mathilde Lippmann. AA
Throughout the vale again Narcissus cries. April. Thomas S. Jones, Jr. VOD
Throughout the world if it were sought. Honesty [*or* Of Dissembling Words]. Sir Thomas Wyatt. OBSC; SiCE
Throw away Thy rod. Discipline. George Herbert. BLV; BoLiVe; CaAE; CoBE; EG; EPS; EV-2; ExPo; HBV; LiTB; LoBV; MeLP; MePo; OBEV; OBS; OxBoCh; PG (1945 ed.); PIAE; PoFS; SeCePo; SeCeV; SeEP; TrGrPo; TwCrTr; TyEnPo; ViBoPo
Throw Him Down M'Closkey. John W. Kelly. TreF
Throw me, and yet I stand. The Celt Speaks. Arthur Stringer. PoFr
Throw of the Dice, A. Stéphane Mallarmé, *tr. fr. French by* Daisy Aldan. AnFP
Throw Out the Lifeline. Edward Smith Ufford. TreF
("Throw out the life-line across the dark wave.") OlF
Throw something to the gulls, any old scrap. Writing on the Wall. Padraic Fallon. NeIP
Throw your little dreams away. The Man of Science Speaks. Harriet Monroe. MaRV; PoeMoYo
Thrown. Ralph Hodgson. HBMV
Thrush, The. Laura Benét. BLA; HBMV
Thrush, The. Timothy Corsellis. LiTM; WaaP; WaP
Thrush, The. John Duffy. JKCP (1955 ed.)
Thrush and Blackthorn. Robert Bloomfield. *Fr.* The Farmer's Boy. RO
Thrush before Dawn, A. Alice Meynell. BLA; BMEP; HBMV; MBP; MoBrPo; POTT; TCEP
Thrush in February, The. George Meredith. EmBrPo
"Love born of knowledge, love that gains," *sel.* FaBoEn
Thrush is tapping a stone, A. Dawn. Gordon Bottomley. *Fr.* Night and Morning Songs. BoTP; MBP; MoBrPo; NP
Thrush, linnet, stare, and wren. In Glencullen. J. M. Synge. OBMV; OxBI; ThWaDe
Thrush Sings, A. W. E. Henley. YT
Thrush, the lark, and, chief, the nightingale, The. David ap Gwillam's Mass of the Birds. Padraic Colum. CAW
Thrushes. Karle Wilson Baker. BLA; MW
Thrushes. Ted Hughes. GoYe
Thrushes. Humbert Wolfe. MBP; MoBrPo; TwCV
Thrush's Nest, The. John Clare. AlDL; BCEP; BoTP; CG; GoTP; PoRL; ThWaDe; WP
Thrush's Song, The. *Unknown, tr. fr. Gaelic by* William MacGillivray. CH; GoTP
Thrust back by hands of air from the sanctuary door. Maria Aegyptiaca. John Heath-Stubbs. FaBoMo
Thrust up three hundred feet above the bleak. The Escorial. Théophile Gautier. TrFP
Thrustararorum. Henry Nehemiah Dodge. EtS
Thrusting glance grows dim, The. Portrait of a Very Old Man. Sara E. Carsley. CaP
Thrymskvitha. *Unknown. See* Lay of Thrym, The.
Thule, the period of cosmography. Wonders [*or* Madrigal]. *Unknown.* CenL; CoEV; ElL
Thumb bold. *Unknown.* OxNR
Thumb he. *Unknown.* OxNR
Thumbikin, Thumbikin, broke the barn. *Unknown.* OxNR
Thumkin says, I'll dance. *Unknown.* OxNR
Thumbprint. Celeste Turner Wright. MuM; PreP
"Thumbs in the thumb-place." The Mitten Song. Marie Louise Allen. BrR; SUS; TiPo
Thump—thud! Who is throwing. Nutting Time. Emilie Poulsson. BrR
Thumpin' sound o' hosses' hoofs, the clack o' runnin' cows, The. Hot Ir'n! S. Omar Barker. PoOW
Thunder and hail, and fire and storms. Isaac Watts. *Fr.* The Universal Hallelujah. BeR
Thunder and whirlwind pluck out the eyestone, A. Easter Poem. John Prichard. MoWP
Thunder-bird. Supplication. Dorothy A. Linney. HiLiAm
Thunder clouds are sweeping, shrouding. A Russian Cradle Song. David Nomberg TrJP
Thunder of riotous hoofs over the quaking sod. The Maid. Theodore Goodridge Roberts. CBPC; CPG; HBV; MoShBr
Thunder of the Rain God. A House in Taos: Rain. Langston Hughes. CDC
Thunder of Zeus, The. Homer, *tr. fr. Greek by* Sir William Marris. *Fr.* The Iliad, XX. LiA
Thunder our thanks to her—guns, hearts, and lips. *Mayflower.* John Boyle O'Reilly. AA; PAH
Thunder Shower. Hilda Conkling. NP
Thunder-Shower, The. John Hall Wheelock. NP
Thunder, the flesh quails, and the soul bows down. John Webster. Swinburne *Fr.* Sonnets on English Dramatic Poets. InvP; PtP; VLEP
Thunderbolt. Jules Laforgue, *tr. fr. French by* William Jay Smith. AnFP
Thunderchild's Lament. Edward William Thomson. CPG
Thunderdrums, I-VI. Lew Sarett. TCPD
Iron-Wind Dances, V. MAP
Thundering, shimmering, silvery gray. Summer Shower. Selma Robinson. MoSiPe
. . . Thundering sound, A/ He hears. All Hands Unmoor! William Falconer. *Fr.* The Shipwreck. EtS

Thunderstorm. Arthur Guiterman. PoMa
Thunderstorm, A. Archibald Lampman. CaP; OCL
Thunderstorm in Town, A. Thomas Hardy. EnLoPo
Thunderstorms. W. H. Davies. GTML; HBV; POTE; PtOT; TSW; TSWC
Thursday. Edna St. Vincent Millay. InMe; PR
Thursday. Frederic E. Weatherly. BOHV
Thursday; or, The Spell. John Gay. *Fr.* The Shepherd's Week. CEP; EiPP; PoEL-3
Thus all is here in motion, all is life. The Wool Trade. John Dyer. *Fr.* The Fleece, III. OBEC; SeCePo
Thus Answered. E. H. W. Meyerstein. *Fr.* Two War Sonnets. NeTW
Thus as he spake he collected the clouds and stirred up the ocean. Odysseus; the Shores of Scheria at Last. Homer. *Fr.* The Odyssey, V. GrR
Thus as he spoke, his sharp-edged sword he drew. Homer. *Fr.* The Iliad, XXII. GrPo
Thus briefly sketched the sacred Rights of Man. On Mr. Paine's "Rights of Man." Philip Freneau. PoFr
Thus by himself compell'd to live each day. The Foreshore [*or* Peter Grimes]. George Crabbe. *Fr.* The Borough. CoEV; FaBoEn; SeCePo
Thus, by the way, to human loves interring. George Chapman. *Fr.* Euthymiae Raptus; or, The Tears of Peace. LoBV
Thus can my love excuse the slow offence. Sonnets, LI. Shakespeare. PeBoSo; PoFS
Thus chydand with her drery desteny. Cressida's Leprosy. Robert Henryson. *Fr.* The Testament of Cresseid. SeCePo
Thus dark sett of my light, which like a ray. *Unknown.* SeCSL
Thus deaths hand clos'd his eyes. The Death of Hector. Homer, *tr. by* George Chapman. *Fr.* The Iliad, XXII. OBS
Thus doth the Great Foresightless mechanize. The Overworld. Thomas Hardy. *Fr.* The Dynasts, Pt. III. WoL
Thus drave they out that dear night with dances full noble. William Dunbar. *Fr.* The Tua Mariit Wemen and the Wedo. BSV
Thus ends my love, but this doth grieve me most. Sonnet. Lord Herbert of Cherbury. LiTL; ViBoPo
Thus ere another noon they emerged from the shades. The Lakes of the Atchafalaya. Longfellow. *Fr.* Evangeline. PoEL-5
Thus every creature, and of every kind. Sex among Lions. Virgil, *tr. by* Dryden. *Fr.* Georgics. BeR
Thus Far. Sophie Jewett. LBAP
Thus far, O Friend! Have we though leaving much. School-Time. Wordsworth. The Prelude, II. BEL; EM-2; GEPC
Thus far the Lord hath led us on—in darkness and in day. Light Shining Out of Darkness. Jane Borthwick. BLRP
Thus far the muse has traced in useful lays. Of Walking the Streets by Day. John Gay. *Fr.* Trivia; or, The Art of Walking the Streets of London, II. CEP; EiPP; EnLi-1 (1949 ed.)
Thus go the cries in Rome's fair town. Thomas Heywood. *Fr.* The Rape of Lucrece. NBE
Thus grief still treads upon the heels of pleasure. William Congreve. *Fr.* The Old Bachelor, V, iii. TreF
Thus groan the old, till, by disease oppress'd. George Crabbe. *Fr.* The Village. PoFS; PreP
Thus have I waded through a worthless task. Epilogus. Henry Parrot. SiCE
Thus having past all perill, I was come. The Happy Isle. Spenser. *Fr.* The Faerie Queene, IV. OBSC
Thus having said, brave Hector went to see. The Last Parting of Hector and Andromache. Homer. *Fr.* The Iliad, VI. SeEP
Thus hoping that Adonis is alive. Shakespeare. *Fr.* Venus and Adonis. EPP
Thus I/ Pass by. Upon His Departure Hence. Robert Herrick. PCD; PIAE; PreP
Thus I awaked and wrote what I had dreamed. The Vision of Jesus. William Langland. *Fr.* The Vision of Piers Plowman. ACP; CAW
Thus, I come underneath this chapel-side. To Oxford. Gerard Manley Hopkins. *Fr.* Low Sunday and Monday. NBE
"Thus I revealed to my comrades the warning Circe gave." The Sirens; Scylla and Charybdis. Homer. *Fr.* The Odyssey, XII. GrPE
Thus I sat one night by a blue-eyed girl. Categorical Courtship. *Unknown.* BOHV; CIV
Thus I woke, God wot, when I dwelt on Cornhill. Langland's Life. William Langland. *Fr.* The Vision of Piers Plowman. McEV
Thus I would walk abroad when gentle night. Walking at Night. Henry Treece. WaP
Thus in alternate uproar and sad peace. Keats. *Fr.* Hyperion, III. BrBE
Thus in her absence is my fancy cool. George Henry Boker. Sonnets; a Sequence of Profane Love, XIX [LXXVII]. MOAP
Thus is his cheek the map of days outworn. Sonnets, LXVIII. Shakespeare. OBSC; PeBoSo; ReIE; UnPo (1st ed.)
Thus it befell upon a nyht. Medea Goes to Gather Herbs for Her Incantations. John Gower. *Fr.* Confessio Amantis. LiA
Thus it happened then in Greece. Nicephorus Vrettakos. *Fr.* 33 Days. MoGP
Thus kept the Trojans watch. Homer. *Fr.* The Iliad, IX. GrL
Thus kiss I your fair hands, taking my leave. A Farewell. Henry King. LoPo
Thus Kitty, beautiful and young. The Female Phaeton. Matthew Prior. HBV; NBE
Thus lovely, sleep did first appear. Sleeping on Her Couch. Richard Leigh. FaBoEn; MePo
Thus man by his own strength to Heaven would soar. Dryden. *Fr.* Religio Laici. WGRP
Thus much the fates have allotted me. Turning Aside from Battles. Sextus Propertius. WaaP
Thus, near the gates conferring as they drew. Ulysses and His Dog. Homer, *tr. by* Pope. *Fr.* The Odyssey, XVII. FiP; OBEC
Thus pass the glories of the world! The Symbol. James Hebblethwaite. BoAu
Thus piteously Love closed what he begat. Modern Love, L. George Meredith. AnFE; BEL; BMEP; CaAE; EmBrPo; EnLi-2; EnLit; EnLoPo; EtPaEn; FaBoEn; GTBS-D; GTML; GTSL; HBV; InPo; LEAP; LoBV; LoPo; OAEP; PoE; PoEL-5; POTT; SeCePo; SeCeV; TrGrPo; UnPo (1st ed.); ViBoPo; ViP; ViPo; WHA
Thus pondering he stood; meantime approach'd. The Pursuit round the Walls. Homer. *Fr.* The Iliad, XXII. GrPo; OxBG
Thus, Prince, of all my goods bereft. Martial, *tr. fr. Latin by* "T. W. M." Epigrams, VII, 16. LaP
Thus quoth Alfred: "If thou hast sorrow." Proverbs of King Alfred. *At. to* Alfred, King of England. WaKn
Thus re-inforc'd, against the adverse fleet. The Fourth Day's Battle. Dryden. *Fr.* Annus Mirabilis. OBS
Thus round the well-mann'd ship they wag'd the war. Patroclus to Achilles. Homer. *Fr.* The Iliad, XVI. GrR
. . . Thus roving on. A Universe of Death. Milton. *Fr.* Paradise Lost, II. CoEV
Thus sadly I thought/ As that bird unsought. L'Envoy to W. L. H. Ainsworth, Esq. Francis S. Mahony. OnYI
Thus safely low, my friend, thou can'st not fall. To the Reverend Mr. Murdoch. James Thomson. OBEC
Thus said the Lord in the Vault above the Cherubim. The Last Chantey. Kipling. AnFE; BLV; BMEP; BoLiVe; ChMo; EPN; EtS; FaBoCh; GTBS; LoGBV; MoBrPo; MuP; OBVV; OtMeF; POTT; PoVP; SG; VA; VLEP
Thus said the Poet: "When Death comes to you." To Hafiz of Shiraz. Gertrude Lowthian Bell. PtP
Thus sailing, sailing on forevermore. The Lake. Alphonse Marie Louis de Lamartine. WoL
Thus saith the great god Thoth. He Is Declared True of Word. *Unknown.* *Fr.* Book of the Dead. AWP; JAWP; WBP
Thus saith the Lord:/ I return unto Zion. I Return unto Zion. Zechariah, Bible, *O.T.* TrJP
Thus saith the Lord,/ The Redeemer of Israel. Proclamation. Isaiah, Bible, *O.T.* StaSt
Thus sang Orpheus to his strings. *Unknown.* SeCSL
Thus sang she. The Wedding. *Unknown.* SAS
Thus Sang the Chian Singer. Simonides, *tr. fr. Greek by* J. M. Edmonds. GrR
Thus sang the sages of the Gael. Man Octipartite. *Tr. by* Whitley Stokes. TIP
Thus saying, from her husbands hand her hand. The Fall. Milton. *Fr.* Paradise Lost, IX. PoEL-3
Thus saying, from her side the fatal key. Milton. *Fr.* Paradise Lost, II. NBE
Thus saying he drew his sharp sword. The Slaying of Hector. Homer. *Fr.* The Iliad, XXII. GrR
Thus should have been our travels. Over 2000 Illustrations and a Complete Concordance. Elizabeth Bishop. FiMAP
Thus shouting onward these twain roused the Achaian battle. The Snow of Stones. Homer. *Fr.* The Iliad, XII. OxBG
Thus, some tall tree that long hath stood. On the Death of [Dr.] Benjamin Franklin. Philip Freneau. BAV; BoHiPo; DD; GA; MOAP; PAH
Thus spake she wailing. Andromache the Desolate. Homer. *Fr.* The Iliad, XXII. GrR
Thus spake the Lord. The Word of the Lord from Havana. Richard Hovey. HBV; PAH
Thus Spake Zarathustra. Nietzsche. *See* Also sprach Zarathustra.
Thus spake Zarathustra! Ah, my Persian, wait! Apotheosis. Alexander M. Stephen. OCL
Thus Speak the Slain. Carl Holliday. PGD
Thus Speaketh Christ Our Lord. *Unknown, tr. fr German.* ChIP; PGD
Thus Spoke My Love. Pieter Corneliszoon Hooft, *tr. fr. Dutch by* A. J. Barnouw. LiTW

Thus spoke Priam's shining son with words supplicating. Achilles to Lycaon. Homer. *Fr.* The Iliad, XXI. LiTW; WaaP

Thus spoke the heav'nly Guide, and on the car. Priam at the Feet of Achilles. Homer. *Fr.* The Iliad, XXIV. GrR

Thus spoke the lady underneath the tree[s]. Colonel Fantock. Edith Sitwell. AnFE; MBP; MM; MoAB; MoBrPo; MoVE; OBMV

Thus spoke to my Lady the Knight full of care. Swift. *Fr.* A Soldier and a Scholar. OBEC

Thus Steal the Silent Hours Away. Isaac Watts. *Fr.* Inscriptions on Dials. AEV

Thus sung, or could, or would, or should have sung. Byron. *Fr.* Don Juan, III. BPN

Thus systole addressed diastole. Systole and Diastole. Conrad Aiken. CrMA

Thus the heavens and the earth were finished. Genesis, Bible, *O.T.* LO

Thus the Mayne Glideth. Robert Browning. *Fr.* Paracelsus, Pt. V. OBEV; PoVP
(Song: "Thus the Mayne glideth.") OBRV

Thus the poor bird, by some disast'rous fate. Time's Balm. Cuthbert Shaw. *Fr.* Monody to the Memory of a Young Lady. OBEC

Thus then, one beautiful day, in the sweet, cool air of October. Beauty at the Plough. Arthur Joseph Munby. *Fr.* Dorothy; a Country Story. VA

Thus they throughout the city, scared like fawns. Homer. *Fr.* The Iliad, XXII. GrL

Thus, Thus Begin. Ben Jonson. *Fr.* Pan's Anniversary. TuPP
(Song: "Thus, thus begin the yearly rites.") EPS (1942 ed.)
("Thus, thus begin the yearly rites.") OBS

Thus, thus I steer my bark, and sail. On Even Keel [or The Voyage of Life]. Matthew Green. *Fr.* The Spleen. BeR; CoEV; LPS-3; OBEC

Thus to be lost and thus to sink and die. To Constantia, Singing. Shelley. EmBrPo; ERP

Thus Tophet look'd; so grinn'd the brawling fiend. Tophet; an Epigram. Thomas Gray. MyFE

Thus, usually, when he was asked to sing. Byron. *Fr.* Don Juan, III. EnLi-2

Thus Was the City Founded. "St.-J. Perse." *See* Such Is the Way of the World.

Thus was this place/ A happy rural seat of various view. Eden. Milton. *Fr.* Paradise Lost, IV. ATP; FaBoEn

Thus, weeping bitterly, the aged pair. Homer. *Fr.* The Iliad, XXII. GrPo

Thus, when soft love subdues the heart. Goldsmith, *after the French of* Paul Scarron. LO

Thus when the silent grave becomes. Belinda's Recovery from Sickness. William Broome. OBEV (1st ed.)

Thus when the swallow, seeking prey. Song. John Gay. *Fr.* The Beggar's Opera. PoEL-3

Thus while he spoke, each eye grew big with tears. The Pyre of Patroclus. Homer, *tr. by* Pope. *Fr.* The Iliad, XXIII. OBEC

Thus while he thinks, Antilochus appears. Dead Is Patroclus. Homer. *Fr.* The Iliad, XVIII. LiA

Thus while I ape the measure wild. To William Erskine, Esq. Sir Walter Scott. *Fr.* Marmion, *Introd. to* III. OBRV

Thus while the days flew by, and years passed on. Wordsworth. *Fr.* The Prelude, II, IV, *and* VI. UnW

Thus will I have the woman of my dream. Dawn of Womanhood. Harold Monro. HBV

Thus with a Kiss I Die. Shakespeare. *Fr.* Romeo and Juliet, V, iii. TrGrPo
(Here Lies Juliet.) FaFP; TreFS

Thus with imagin'd wing our swift scene flies. Shakespeare. King Henry V, Prologue to Act III. BHV; EV-1; LH

Thus with the year. Inner Light. Milton. *Fr.* Paradise Lost, III. MaRV

Thus would I have it. Exit. John Gould Fletcher. InP; MOAP; PFE

Thus writeth Meer Djafrit. To the Ingleezee Khafir, Calling Himself Djann Bool Djenkinzun. James Clarence Mangan. OnYI

Thy arms with bracelets I will deck. Homage. Gustave Kahn. TrJP

Thy beauty haunts me heart and soul. The Moon. W. H. Davies. AEV; MBP; MoBrPo; MoVE; NeMA; POTE; PtOT; StaSt; TCPD; WP

Thy beauty, O Israel, upon thy high places is slain! David's Lament. Second Samuel, Bible, *O.T.* TrJP

Thy black cylindric body, golden brass and silver steel. To a Locomotive in Winter. Walt Whitman. VOD (1935 ed.)

Thy Blessing, Lord, on All Vacation Days! Molly Anderson Haley. OQP; QP-1

Thy blessing on the boys—for time has come. Prayer. Haim Guri. TrJP

Thy blue waves, Patapsco, flowed soft and serene. Fort McHenry. *Unknown.* MC; PAH

Thy bosom is endearèd [or indeared] with all hearts. Sonnets,

XXXI. Shakespeare. ES; OBEV; OBSC; PeBoSo; PoEL-2

Thy Braes Were Bonny. John Logan. *See* Braes of Yarrow, The.

"Thy breath is far sweeter than honey." Far Sweeter than Honey. Abraham ibn Ezra. TrJP

Thy Brother. Theodore Chickering Williams. GrCo-1; MaRV

Thy Brother's Blood. Jones Very. OnAP; PoEL-4

Thy Cheek is o' the rose's hue. My Only Jo and Dearie, O. Richard Gall. EBSV

Thy Conquering Name. Charles Wesley. BePJ

Thy converse drew us with delight. In Memoriam A. H. H., CX. Tennyson. EmBrPo; EPN; GEPC; ViPo; VLEP

Thy coral-colored lips, how should I portray. *Unknown. Fr.* Zepheria. ReIE

Thy country, Wilberforce, with just disdain. Sonnet to [or To] William Wilberforce, Esq. William Cowper. CEP; CoBE; OAEP

Thy cruise is over now. Mr. Merry's Lament for "Long Tom." John Gardiner Calkins Brainard. AA

Thy dawn, O Master of the world, thy dawn. James Elroy Flecker. *Fr.* Hassan, II, ii. OtMeF

Thy dawn, O Ra, opens the new horizon. Adoration of the Disk by King Akhnaten and Princess Nefer Neferiu Aten. *Unknown. Fr.* Book of the Dead. AWP; JAWP; WBP

Thy dawning is beautiful in the horizon of the sky [or of heaven]. Hymn to the Sun. Ikhnaton (Amenhotep IV). GrCo-1; WoL

Thy Distaff Ply. Antipater of Thessalonica, *tr. fr. Greek by* Francis Wrangham. LiA

Thy epigrams are of no bastard race. Ad Tho. Bastardum Epigrammatistam. John Heath. TuPP

Thy error, Frémont, simply was to act. John Charles Frémont. Whittier. LPS-3

Thy face I have seen as one seeth. Song. Sophie Jewett. AA

Thy Faithful Sons. Eleazar, *tr. fr. Hebrew.* TrJP

Thy fan is a butterfly. The Fan. Serafín Alvarez Quintero *and* Joaquín Alvarez Quintero. OnPM

Thy father all from thee, by his last will. Disinherited. John Donne. PIAE

Thy Fingers Make Early Flowers. E. E. Cummings. MOAP
(Song: "Thy fingers make early flowers.") MAP; MoAmPo

Thy flattering picture, Phryne, is like thee. Phryne. John Donne. TuPP

Thy Form Is Lovely. Sappho, *tr. fr. Greek by* H. De Vere Stacpoole. GrR

Thy friendship oft has made my heart to ache. To [William] Hayley. Blake. PIAE; TrGrPo

Thy Garden. Mu'tamid, King of Seville, *tr. fr. Arabic by* Dulcie L. Smith. AWP

Thy gift, thy tables, are within my brain. Sonnets, CXXII. Shakespeare. PeBoSo

Thy gifts to us mortals fulfil all our needs. Rabindranath Tagore. Gitanjali, LXXV. InP

Thy gifts without Thy grace are lacking still. Grace for Grace. Mark Guy Pearse. OQP; QP-2

Thy glass will show thee how thy beauties wear. Sonnets, LXXVII. Shakespeare. PeBoSo; RiBV

Thy Glorious Face Above. Charles Wesley. BePJ

Thy glory alone, O God, be the end of all that I say. Ad Majorem Dei Gloriam. Frederick George Scott. MaRV; VA

Thy Glory dawns, Jerusalem, awake, thy bells to ring! Palm Sunday. John J. Moment. MaRV

Thy greatest knew thee, Mother Earth. The Spirit of Shakespeare. George Meredith. BMEP; EmBrPo; EPN; PoVP; PtP; VA; ViPo

Thy Grief Is Thine. Viktor Rydberg, *tr. fr. Swedish by* Charles W. Stork. AnSL

Thy hand, Harifa! bring it me. To Harifa, in an Orgy. José de Espronceda. AnSpL-2

Thy hands are like cool herbs that bring. The Candle and the Flame. George Sylvester Viereck. BAP; LBMV; LEAP

Thy hands are washt, but O the waters spilt. To Pontius Washing His Hands. Richard Crashaw. SeEP

Thy head with flames, thy mantle bright with flowers. Sonnet. William Drummond of Hawthornden. ElSeCe

Thy Heart. *Unknown.* NA

Thy heart and mine are one, my dear. Cradle Song. Florence Earle Coates. BOL

Thy heart is like some icy lake. Thy Heart. *Unknown.* NA

Thy hue, dear pledge, is pure and bright. To a Lock of Hair. Sir Walter Scott. GTBS; GTBS-D; GTBS-W; GTSE

Thy human frame, my glorious Lord, I spy. Meditation Seven. Edward Taylor. *Fr.* Sacramental Meditations. LiTA

Thy impious finger, would it, then, reborrow. Christ to Thomas. Richard Crashaw. StJW

Thy Joy in Sorrow. Chauncey Hare Townshend. VA

Thy Kingdom Come. St. Bernard of Clairvaux, *tr. fr. Latin.* CAW

Thy Kingdom Come! Thomas Curtis Clark. ChIP

Thy Kingdom Come. Frederick Lucian Hosmer. WGRP

Thy Kingdom Come. A. B. Simpson. BePJ

Thy Kingdom Come! Willard Wattles. OQP; QP-2
(Page from America's Psalter, A.) BPP
Thy Kingdom Come, O God! Lewis Hensley. TriL
"Thy Kingdom Come!" O Lord. Henry Warburton Hawkes. MaRV
Thy Kingdom Come, O Lord. Frederick Lucian Hosmer. MaRV; WGRP
(Prophecy Sublime, The.) TrPWD
Thy kingdom come—on bended knee. Thy Kingdom Come. Frederick Lucian Hosmer. WGRP
Thy Kingdom, Lord, We Long For. Vida D. Scudder. MaRV; WGRP
Thy knights, O Queen, ride forth by east and west. Regina Confessorum. *Unknown.* GoBC
Thy laugh's a song an oriole trilled. Kitty's Laugh. Arlo Bates. *Fr.* Conceits. AA
Thy lesson, Nature, let me learn from thee. *See* One lesson, Nature . . .
Thy life was given for me. Frances Ridley Havergal. OlF
Thy little footsteps on the sands. To William Shelley. Shelley. ChER
Thy Love. Sana'i, *tr. fr. Persian by* E. G. Browne. PeP
Thy love thou sentest oft to me. A Contrast. James Russell Lowell. IAP; TCAP
Thy lufe, thy lawtie, and thy gentilnes. Cresseid's Lament. Robert Henryson. *Fr.* The Testament of Cresseid. CoEV
Thy merits, Wolfe, transcend all human praise. The Death of Wolfe. *Unknown.* PAH
Thy Mother Was like a Vine. Ezekiel, XIX:10-14, Bible, *O.T.* TrJP
Thy name, O Washington renowned. Washington's Song. Edmond S. Meany. PoRL
Thy name of old was great. To My Totem. Henry Charles Beeching. VA
Thy Name We Bless and Magnify. John Power. BLRP
Thy Neighbor. *Unknown.* OQP; QP-1
Thy nights moan into my days. Psalms of Love. Peter Baum. AWP
Thy one white leaf is open to the sky. To a Cherokee Rose. William Hamilton Hayne. AA
Thy Peace, O God. *Unknown.* PraP
Thy peak transcends thy brother heights. Monastery on Kasbek [*or* Kazbek]. Pushkin. BoRS; WaL
Thy pendent diamonds let thy Fanny take. Advice to an Old Beauty. Thomas Parnell. *Fr.* An Elegy: To an Old Beauty. BeR
Thy praise, O Lord, will I proclaim. Palms and Myrtles. Eleazar ben Kalir. TrJP
Thy Presence. Frances Ridley Havergal. MaRV
(Be Quiet; Fear Not.) OQP; QP-1
Thy restless feet now cannot go. Christ Crucified. Richard Crashaw. BLV; GoBC; OBEV; PoRL
Thy Saints are comforted, I know. William Cowper. *Fr.* The Contrite Heart. MyFE
Thy Sea Is Great, Our Boats Are Small. Henry van Dyke. *See* Voyagers.
Thy Sea So Great. Winfred Ernest Garrison. MaRV; TrPWD
Thy shades, thy silence, now be mine. Solitude. James Beattie. *Fr.* Retirement. OBEC
Thy Shadow, Earth, from Pole to Central Sea. At a Lunar Eclipse. Thomas Hardy. MoPW; POTE; TOP
Thy shadow falls on the fount. Shadows. Clark Ashton Smith. DaM
Thy sorrow, and the sorrow of the sea. Ireland. Lionel Johnson. HBV
Thy soul is not enchanted by the moon. The Lilies of the Field. Compton Mackenzie. OBVV
Thy soul shall find itself alone. Spirits of the Dead. Poe. APW; TriL
Thy soul, unhearing and unspeaking. Complaint. Vyacheslav Ivanov. BoR
Thy soul within such silent pomp did keep. A Tranquil [*or* Quiet] Soul. John Oldham. *Fr.* To the Memory of Mr. Charles Morwent. EV-3; OBEV
Thy span of life was all too short. To a Withered Rose. John Kendrick Bangs. AA; ADAH
Thy spear rent Christ, when dead for me He lay. To My Patrons Lionel Johnson. JKCP
Thy spirit ere our fatal loss. In Memoriam A. H. H., XLI. Tennyson. EmBrPo; EPN; GEPC; ViPo; VLEP
Thy spirit, Independence, let me share! Independence [*or* Ode to Independence]. Tobias Smollett. OBEC; PoFr
Thy steps, the children of my hush. Footsteps. Paul Valéry. TrFP
Thy Strength and My Day. Annie Johnson Flint. PraP
Thy stricken daughter, now, O Lord, prepares. Hymn for the Eve of the New Year. Abraham Gerondi. TrJP
Thy summer voice, Musketaquit. Two Rivers. Emerson. AmPP; AnNE; APW; CoBA; DDA; IAP; MOAP; OBAV; OxBA: TrGrPo
Thy Sun Posts Westward. William Drummond of Hawthornden. *See* No Trust in Time.
Thy sword within the scabbard keep. Songs from "The Secular Masque": Momus. Dryden. InPo
Thy tale shall nothing scathe thee. The Revel. Euripides. *Fr.* Bacchae. GrR
Thy throne is ringed by amorous cavaliers. Patrick Moloney. Sonnets—Ad Innuptam, III. BoAu
Thy trivial harp will never please. Merlin [*or* The Poet]. Emerson. AA; AmP; AmPo; AmPP (4th ed.); AnNe; APW; BLV; BoLiVe; CoV; IAP; LEAP; MOAP; OxBA; TCAP
Thy various works, imperial queen, we see. On Imagination. Phillis Wheatley. APW; PoNe
Thy voice hath filled our forest shades. The Hope of the Resurrection. Frances Brown. EOAH
Thy Voice Is Heard [thro' Rolling Drums]. Tennyson. *Fr.* The Princess: Interlude. BHV; BPN; GEPC; OBVV; PoVP; TrGrPo
(Songs from "The Princess.") MotAn; ViPo; VLEP
Thy voice is hovering o'er my soul—it lingers. To Constantia Singing. Shelley. EnRP
Thy voice is on the rolling air. In Memoriam A. H. H., CXXX [*or* Truths That Never Can Be Proved]. Tennyson. BoFr; BPN; EM-2; EmBrPo; EnL; EnLi-2; EPN; EPP; GEPC; HBV; HiLiEn; MaPo; MaRV; OAEP; PIAE; PoFS; ReaPo; TOP; TyEnPo; UnPo; UnW; ViPo; VLEP
Thy Voice Is Sweet. Sayat Nova, *tr. fr. Armenian by* Zabelle C. Boyajian. ArmLP
Thy Way, Not Mine. Horatius Bonar. *See* God's Way.
"Thy Will Be Done." Charlotte Elliott. PraP
Thy Will Be Done. John Hay. *See* Not in Dumb Resignation.
Thy Will Be Done. Hugh Thomson Kerr. BLRP; MaRV
Thy Will Be Done. Lucy Larcom. PraP
Thy Will Be Done. Anna Norman Oates. PraP
Thy Will Be Done. Louise Peabody Sargent. OQP; QP-1
Thy Will Be Done. G. A. Studdert-Kennedy. MaRV
Thy Will Be Done. *Unknown.* BePJ
Thy Will Be Done. Whittier. LPS-2
Thy Will Be Done in Me. Fanny Crosby. MaRV
Thy Will be done. No greater words than these. Thy Will Be Done. G. A. Studdert-Kennedy. MaRV
Thy will be done, our Father. Thy Will Be Done. Anna Norman Oates. PraP
"Thy will be done." Why always bow the head. Thy Will Be Done. Louise Peabody Sargent. OQP; QP-1
Thy will, O God, is best. Thy Will Be Done. Hugh Thomson Kerr. BLRP; MaRV
Thy wisdom speaks in me, and bids me dare. Shelley. *Fr.* Epipsychidion. KN
Thy Word Is like a Garden, Lord. Edwin Hodder. PraP
Thy words are compounded of sweet-smelling myrrh. Words Wherein Stinging Bees Lurk. Judah Halevi. TrJP
Thyestes, *sels.* Seneca, *tr. fr. Latin.*
Chorus: "Climb at Court for me that will," *tr. by* Andrew Marvell. OnPM
("Climb at Court for me that will.") LaP
(Quiet Life, The.) LiTW
(Senec. Traged. ex Thyeste Chor. 2.) SeCV-1
Stond [*or* Stand] Who So List upon the Slipper Toppe [*or* Top], *tr. by* Sir Thomas Wyatt. PoEL-1; SiPS
(Of the Mean and Sure Estate.) SiCE
"Wealth can never produce a king," *tr. by* Asa M. Hughes. LaP
Thyroid Gland, The. "R. M." PA
Thyrsis. Matthew Arnold. BMEP; BPN; CP; EM-2; EmBrPo; EnLi-2; EnLit; EnSW; EV-5; FiP; GEPC; GTML; GTSL; LEAP; LiA; OAEP; OBEV (new ed.); OBVV; PoE; PoVP; ReaPo; TOP; TyEnPo; ViPo; ViPP; VLEP
Sels.
Cuckoo's Parting Cry, The. CBOV
(Departure of the Cuckoo, The.) SN
"How changed is here each spot." NBE
Thyrsis. Edward Cracroft Lefroy. Echos from Theocritus, XXVI. AWP
Thyrsis. Antonio Mario, *tr. tr. fr. Latin by* Richard Aldington. LaP
Thyrsis [*or* Thirsis], a youth of the inspired train. The Story of Phoebus and Daphne Applied. Edmund Waller. EPP; InvP; OBS; SeEP
Thyrsis and Milla, arm in arm together. The Never-certain Male. *Unknown.* EG
Thyrsis' Praise of His Mistress. William Browne. ReIE
"Thyrsis, Sleep'st Thou?" *Unknown.* InvP; OBSC
Thyrsis the village-shepherd, with the flocks of the Nymphs in his keeping. Love the Shepherd. Myrinus. GrPE
Thyrsis, when we parted, swore. Song. Thomas Gray. OAEP
Thys ender nyght [*or* endris nygth]. A Christmas Carol. *Unknown.* EPP; OAEP; TrGrPo
Thys Morneyngne Starre of Radcleves rysynge Raie. Epitaph of Robert Canynge. Thomas Chatterton. TCEP

Thyself. John Addington Symonds. *Fr.* Stella Maris. VA
("Give me thyself! It were as well to cry.") PoVP
Thyself and thy belongings. Not Thine Own. Shakespeare. *Fr.* Measure for Measure, I, i. MaRV
Thyself from love Thy heart didst not defend. To Jesus. Jacopone da Todi. MaRV
Thysia, *sels.* Morton Luce. HBV
"Bow down, my song, before her presence high," III.
"Comes the New Year; wailing the north winds blow," XVI.
"Hear, O Self-Giver, infinite as good," XXXVII.
"How shall I tell the measure of my love?" XLV.
"I watch beside you in your silent room," VII.
"Like some lone miser, dear, behold me stand," XXIII.
"So sang I in the springtime of my years," XXXVI.
"Twin songs there are, of joyance, or of pain," II.
Tiare Tahiti. Rupert Brooke. POTT; SeCeV
Tibbie Fowler. *Unknown.* EBSV
Tibetan Comforter, *sel.* Robert K. Ekvall.
Put Grief Away. MaRV
Tibur is beautiful, too, and the orchard slopes and the Anio. On Montorio's Height. Arthur Hugh Clough. *Fr.* Amours de Voyage, III. BPN
Tic-tic-tic!/ The sound of the sleet. Sleet Storm. James S. Tippett. BrR; SiSoSe
Tichborne's Elegy, Written [with His Own Hand] in the Tower before His Execution. Chidiock Tichborne. *See* Elegy: "My prime of youth . . ."
"Tick-tock," said the nursery clock. Christmas Eve. Florence Hoatson. GFA
Tick, tock, tick, tock/ Merrily sings the clock. The Clock. *Unknown.* MeMeAg; OTPC (1946 ed.); PCH
"Tick-Tock! Tick-Tock!"/ Sings the great time-clock. The Time-Clock. Charles Hanson Towne. CV; HBMV; NV
Ticket Agent, The. Edmund Leamy. HBMV; MW; PoMa; StVeCh
Ticking Clocks. Rachel Field. TiPo (1959 ed.)
Tickly, tickly, on your knee. *Unknown.* OxNR
Ticonderoga. V. B. Wilson. IDAH; OTPC; PaA; PAP
Tiddle liddle lightum. *Unknown.* OxNR
Tide, The. Joseph William Holden. NoCaPo
Tide, The. Harry Kemp. TBM
Tide, The. Marjorie Wilson. OTPC (1946 ed.); PCH
Tide be runnin' the great world over. Sea Love. Charlotte Mew. AV; BLV; LBBV; MBP; MoAB; MoBrPo; NeMA; TrGrPo; ViBoPo
Tide comes in, and out goes tide, The. In Robin Hood Cove. Marsden Hartley. AnFE; CoAnAm
Tide in the river, The. Eleanor Farjeon. TiPo
Tide of Faith, The. "George Eliot." *Fr.* A Minor Prophet. MaRV; OQP; QP-2; WGRP
(Tides of Faith, The, *longer sel.*) GrCo-1
Tide of Life, The, *sel.* Watson Kirkconnell.
"Ah, Flood of Life on which I am a wave." CaP
Tide Rises, the Tide Falls, The. Longfellow. AA; AmPP (4th ed.); AnNE; APW; ChTr; FaFP; IAP; NePA; OxBA; PG (1955 ed.); PoRA
Tide River, The. Charles Kingsley. *See* Clear and Cool.
Tide slips up the silver sand, The. Sea-Way. Ellen Mackay Hutchinson Cortissoz. AA
Tide Trapped. Floris Clark McLaren. TwCaPo
Tide Will Win, The. Priscilla Leonard. MaRV
Tides, The. Thomas Tapper. GFA
Tides. Josephine Williams. PCD
Tide's at full, The: the marsh with flooded streams. Sunrise. Sidney Lanier. *Fr.* Hymns of the Marshes. FaBoEn
Tides of Faith, The. "George Eliot." *See* Tide of Faith, The.
Tides of Love, The. T. A. Daly. InMe; LauV; WhC; YaD
Tides Run up the Wairau, The. Eileen Duggan. AnNZ
Tidewater, *sels.* Beatrice Ravenel.
Coasts, I. LS
Harbor Water, II. LS
Tidings I Bring You for to Tell. *Unknown.* AnEC
Tidings of Great Joy. St. Luke, Bible, *N.T.* *See* Adoration of the Shepherds, The.
Tidings of Home. Euripides, *tr. fr. Greek by* Gilbert Murray. *Fr.* Iphigenia in Tauris. GrR
(Agamemnon's Children.) OxBG
Tidings of Invisible Things. Wordsworth. *See* Faith.
Tidings of Union. Hafiz, *tr. fr. Persian by* Gertrude Bell. PeP
Tidings, Tidings That Be True. *Unknown.* AnEC
Tidings true, there be come new. Nowell, Nowell, Nowell, Nowell. *Unknown.* AnEC
Tie a bandage over his eyes. A Rebel. John Gould Fletcher. MAP; MoAmPo
Tie-shuffling Chant, *with music.* *Unknown.* ABF
Tie-tamping Chant, *with music.* *Unknown.* ABF
Tie the moccasin, bind the pack. Young Washington. Arthur Guiterman. FaPON; MPB; OHIP
Tien-ho Temple. Su T'ung-po, *tr. fr. Chinese by* Yu Min-chuan. WhP
Tien Shan snowed soon after the cold sea wind came, The. Following the Army to the North [*or* Northern Expedition]. Li I. OnPM; WhP
Tiger, The. Hilaire Belloc. MBP; MoBrPo
Tiger, The. Blake. *Fr.* Songs of Experience. AEV; ATP; AWP; BBV; BCEP; BEL; BoLiVe; CaAE; CBE; CBPC; CG, *abr.;* ChTr; CoEV; EiPP; EM-1; EnL; EnLi-2; EnLit; EPP; EV-3; FaBoBe; FaFP; FaPON; GN; GoTP; GTBS-W; HBV; JAWP; LEAP; LiTB; LiTG; LPS-2; MaPo; MaRV; MCCG; MPB; MuP; MW; MyFE; NeHB; OAEP; OBEC; OBEV; OnPM; OtMeF; OTPC; OuHeWo; PC; PFE; PG; PIAE; PIR; Po; PoeMoYo; PoFS; PoRA; PreP; PYM; ReaPo; RG; ShBV-2; SN; StaSt; TCEP; TOP; TreF; TVSH; TwCrTr; TwHP; TyEnPo; ViBoPo; WBP; WGRP; WHA; WoL; WP
(Beauty of Terror, The.) LH
(Tyger, The.) AnFE; AtBAP; BLV; BoTP; CEP; CH; EnRP; ExPo; FaBoCh; FaBoEn; GTBS-D; HoPM; InPo; KN; LoBV; LoGBV; PoE; PoEL-4; RiBV; SeCePo; SeCeV; TrGrPo; WaKn
("Tyger, Tyger, burning bright.") EG
Tiger, The. Laura Riding. FaBoMo
Tiger-Cat Tim. Edith H. Newlin. TiPo
Tiger Christ unsheathed his sword. For the One Who Would Take Man's Life in His Hands. Delmore Schwartz. FiMAP; LiTA; LiTM; MiAP; MoAB; MoAmPo; MoVE; NePA; WaP
Tiger in me I know late, not burning bright, The. The Tiger. Laura Riding. FaBoMo
Tiger in the tiger-pit, The. Lines for an Old Man. T. S. Eliot. FaBoTw; MoPW; OnAP
Tiger-Lilies. Thomas Bailey Aldrich. BAV; GN; GoTP; OBAV
Tiger of Desire, The. Tom MacInnes. BoCaPo
Tiger, on the other hand, is kittenish and mild, The. The Tiger. Hilaire Belloc. MBP; MoBrPo
"Tiger, strolling at my side." Triumph of Sensibility. Sylvia Townsend Warner. MBP; MoAB; MoBrPo
Tiger! Tiger [*or* Tyger! Tyger]! burning bright. The Tiger [*or* The Tyger *or* The Beauty of Terror]. Blake. *Fr.* Songs of Experience. AEV; AnFE; ATP; AtBAP; AWP; BBV; BCEP; BEL; BLV; BoLiVe; BoTP; CaAE; CBE; CBPC; CEP; CG; CH; ChTr; CoEV; EG; EiPP; EM-1; EnL; EnLi-2; EnLit; EnRP; EPP; EV-3; ExPo; FaBoBe; FaBoCh; FaBoEn; FaFP; FaPON; GN; GoTP; GTBS-D; GTBS-W; HBV; HoPM; InPo; JAWP; KN; LEAP; LH; LiTB; LiTG; LoBV; LoGBV; LPS-2; MaPo; MaRV; MCCG; MPB; MuP; MW; MyFE; NeHB; OAEP; OBEC; OBEV; OnPM; OtMeF; OTPC; OuHeWo; PC; PFE; PG; PIAE; PIR; Po; PoE; PoEL-4; PoeMoYo; PoFS; PoRA; PreP; PYM; ReaPo; RG; RiBV; SeCePo; SeCeV, ShBV-2; StaSt; TCEP; TOP; TreF; TrGrPo; TVSH; TwCrTr; TwHP; TyEnPo; ViBoPo; WaKn; WBP; WGRP; WHA; WoL; WP
Tiger, when a man goes by, The. The Dignity of Man—Lesson #1. Walter H. Kerr. NePoAm-2
Tiger's Tale, A. John Bennett. TiPo (1959 ed.)
Tiggady Rue. David McCord. RIS; TiPo (1959 ed.)
Tightly-folded bud. Born Yesterday. Philip Larkin. HaMV
Tigress, The. Ruth Pitter. FaBoTw; HaMV
Tiki. André Breton, *tr. fr. French by* Wallace Fowlie. MiCF
Till all sweet gums and juices flow. The Prince's Progress. Christina Rossetti. EmBrPo; EV-5
Till and Tweed. *Unknown.* *See* Rivers Till and Tweed, The.
Till dawn the winds' insuperable throng. In Extremis. George Sterling. HBV
"Till death" is narrow loving. Emily Dickinson. CoBA
Till Eve was brought to Adam, he. Nearest the Dearest. Coventry Patmore. *Fr.* The Angel in the House. HBV
Till Green Leaves Come Again. Thomas Haynes Bayly. *See* Oh! Where Do Fairies Hide Their Heads.
Till late our atheists turned aggressive eyes. Patronage. Thomas Thornely. QS
Till now the doubtful dusk reveal'd. Tennyson. *Fr.* In Memoriam A. H. H., XCV. AlDL
Till of the mighty host that fledged the dome. Attainment. Ferid ed-Din Attar. *Fr.* The Bird-Parliament. PeP
Till one dawn, above the green bloom of a gleaming lawn. The Death of Urgan. Swinburne. *Fr.* Tristram of Lyonesse. WHA
Till sacred morn had brighten'd into noon. The Scales of Zeus. Homer. *Fr.* The Iliad, VIII. OxBG
Till thinking had worn out my enterprise. Spring Mountain Climb. Richard Eberhart. GoYe
Till We Have Built Jerusalem. Blake. *See* And Did Those Feet in Ancient Time
Till yesterday we lived that moment of dreaming. Earth. Alfonso Gutiérrez Hermosillo. AnCL
Tillaquils, The. Laura Riding. FaBoMo
Tillers of the soil have few idle months. Watching the Reapers. Po Chü-i. TrCh
Tillie. Walter de la Mare. PoMS; TiPo
Tim, an Irish Terrier. Winifred M. Letts. TVSH

Tim and Tilly sauntered on. The Pussy-Cat Who Visited the Queen. Carolyn Wells. CIV
Tim Finnigan [or Finigan] lived in Walker Street. Finnigan's [or Finigan's or Finnegan's] Wake. *Unknown.* BLPA; OnAP; TrAS
Tim the Dragoon. Sir Arthur Quiller-Couch. WhC
Tim, the Fairy. Florence Randal Livesay. CaP; CPG; OCL
Tim Turpin. Thomas Hood. BOHV
Timarete, ere she wedded, gave the coif that tamed her tresses. The Young Bride. *Unknown, tr. by* F. L. Lucas. GrPE
Timareté, her wedding-day now near. A Girl's Treasures. *Unknown, tr. by* Lord Neaves. OnPM
Timas. Sappho, *tr. fr. Greek.* GrR, *tr. by* H. De Vere Stacpoole; LiTW, *tr. by* John Addington Symonds
("This dust was Timas'; ere her bridal hour," *tr. by* C. A. Elton.) GrPo
Timber, *with music. Unknown.* AS
Timber, The. Henry Vaughan. EPS; EV-2, *abr.;* SeCV-1
"Sure thou didst flourish once," *sel.* EM-1; EPP; OBEV
Timber Line Trees. Jamie Sexton Holme. PoOW
Timbers heaving to heaven we sailed at seven. Crabbing. Norman Levine. CaP
Timbuctoo. Thackeray. PA
Time. "Æ." ChMo; CMP
Time. Bhartrihari, *tr. fr. Sanksrit by* Paul Elmer More. AWP; JAWP; WBP
Time. Thomas Stephens Collier. AA
Time. Hilda Conkling. NV
Time. Allen Curnow. AnNZ
Time. Giles Fletcher. *See* In Time the Strong and Stately Turrets Fall.
Time, The. G. S. Fraser. WaP
Time. Robert Graves. AtBAP; CoEV; FaBoMo; LiTM (rev. ed.); MoP
Time. George Herbert. SeCL
Time. Robert Herrick. *See* To the Virgins, to Make Much of Time.
Time. Leonidas of Tarentum, *tr. fr. Greek by* Edwyn R. Bevan. GrL; OxBG
("Measureless time or ever thy years, O man, were reckon'd.") GrPo
Time. Jasper Mayne. *Fr.* The Amorous War. OBEV; SeCL
(First Song, Sung by Two Amazons, The.) SeEP
("Time is the feather'd thing.") EG
Time. Schiller, *tr. fr. German.* OQP; QP-2
Time. Clinton Scollard. VCU
Time. Frederick George Scott. VA
Time. Sir Walter Scott. *Fr.* The Antiquary, *ch.* 10. BPN; EmBrPo
(Aged Carle, The.) OAEP
(Omnipotent, The.) LH
(Why Sitt'st Thou by That Ruined Hall.) EnRP; EPN
Time ("Like as the waves"). Shakespeare. *See* Sonnets, LX.
Time ("Time hath, my lord, a wallet at his back"). Shakespeare. *Fr.* Troilus and Cressida, III, iii. CoEV
(Good Deeds Past.) LiA
(Ulysses Advises Achilles [Not to Let Slip Opportunity].) LiTB; LiTG
(Ulysses; the Instant Way.) EV-1
Time. Shelley. BEL; BPN; CBE; EM-2; EmBrPo; EnLi-2; EPN; EV-4
(Unfathomable Sea!) EtS
Time. Thomas Watson. *Fr.* Hecatompathia. OBSC
("Time wasteth years, and months, and hours.") SiCE
Time. Marguerite Wilkinson. HBMV
Time. Edward Young. *Fr.* Night Thoughts, I *and* II. LPS-3
(Lapse of Time, The, *longer sel.*) BCEP
Time and Account. Miguel de Guevara, *tr. fr. Spanish by* Samuel Beckett. AnMP
Time and Death. William Henry Whitworth. VA
Time and Eternity. Fulke Greville. Caelica, LXXXIII. OBSC
Time and Eternity. Stephen Hawes. *Fr.* The Pastime of Pleasure. PoEL-1
Time and Grief. William Lisle Bowles. BCEP; EV-3; HBV; OBEV; ReTS
(Healing.) ES
(Influence of Time on Grief.) ATP; EnRP
("O Time! who know'st a lenient hand to lay.") LO
(Sonnet: "O Time!") CEP; OBEC
(Sonnet, July 18th, 1787.) FaBoEn
Time and Love. Shakespeare. *See* Sonnets, LXIV *and* LXV.
Time and Motion Study. Iain Fletcher. PoLFOT; PoN
Time and Space, Torment. August, Graf von Platen, *tr. fr. German by* Edwin Morgan. AnGP
Time and Spirit. Léonie Adams. MOAP; NLK (1947 ed.)
Time and the mortal will stand never fast. Sonnet. Luís de Camões. AWP
Time approaches when I said good-bye, The. Some Star within Orion. Jessie B. Rittenhouse. MuM
Time as Variable. Lucian, *tr. fr. Greek by* Lord Neaves. OnPM
Time at my elbow plucks me sore. The Racers. James B. Kenyon. LBAP
Time at Timberline. Donald F. Drummond. PtPa
Time-Bomb. Earle Birney. TwCaPo
Time breaks our passion but the Virgin smiles. Our True Beginnings. Wrey Gardiner. NeBP
Time bringeth swift to end. Jalal ed-Din Rumi, *tr. fr. Persian by* A. J. Arberry. PeP
Time brings not death, it brings but changes. A Comrade Rides Ahead. Douglas Malloch. HBMV
Time brought me many another friend. Not Yet. Mary Elizabeth Coleridge. BoFr
Time can [or will] say nothing but I told you so. Villanelle [or Time Will Say Nothing]. W. H. Auden. LiTA; LoPo; MoAB; MoBrPo
Time cannot age thy sinews, nor the gale. Albatross. Charles Warren Stoddard. AA; BLA; EtS; SN
Time cannot break the bird's wing from the bird. To a Young Poet. Edna St. Vincent Millay. CrMA
Time-Clock, The. Charles Hanson Towne. CV; HBMV; NV
Time cost, time lost, time lusty I was. Englynion. *Unknown.* PrWP
Time, cruel Time, come and subdue that brow. To Delia, XXIII. Samuel Daniel. AtBAP; OBSC
Time demands a rolling eye, The. The Time. G. S. Fraser. WaP
Time—do you prefer night when lights are kindled? Lighted Night. Jorge Guillén. CoSP
Time Does Not Bring Relief. Edna St. Vincent Millay. Unnamed Sonnets (I–V), II. LoPo
Time draws near for flowers to spring, The. Flowering Time [or Tempus Instat Floridum]. *Unknown. Fr.* Carmina Burana. LaP; LyMA
Time draws near the birth of Christ, The. In Memoriam A. H. H., XXVIII [or Bells of Yule or The Birth of Christ]. Tennyson. BePJ; BPN; ChIP; COAH; EM-2; EmBrPo; EnLi-2; EnLit; EPN; GEPC; MaRV; OAEP; OQP; PEOR; PGD; QP-1; SDH; TOP; TVSH; ViPo; VLEP
Time draws near the birth of Christ, The. In Memoriam A. H. H., CIV. Tennyson. BPN; EM-2; EmBrPo; EnLi-2; EnLit; EPN; GEPC; OAEP; PoE; TCEP; ViPo; VLEP
Time draws nigh when I shall go forth, The. Prelude. Steen Steensen Blicher. *Fr.* Birds of Passage. BoDS
Time Eating. Keith Douglas. FaBoMo; NeBP; PoN
Time ends when vision sees its lapse in liberty. Beata l'Alma. Sir Herbert Read. LiTG
Time erodes the hills? Tale of One Hill. Franklin D. Elmer, Jr. ChIP
Time flies. Found on an English Sun Dial [or Love over All]. *Unknown.* OQP; PC; QP-2
Time Flies, Hope Flags. Christina Rossetti. Monna Innominata, X. EmBrPo; ViPo
Time flits away, time flits away, lady. Variation on Ronsard. T. Sturge Moore. OBMV
Time for Everything, A. Ecclesiastes, XII: 1–8, Bible, *O.T.* TrGrPo
Time for rain! for your long hot dry Autumn. The Englishman in Italy. Robert Browning. SeCePo
Time for toil is past, and night has come, The. Bringing Our Sheaves. Elizabeth Akers Allen. HBV
Time for Us to Leave Her. *Unknown. See* Leave Her Johnny.
Time, Gentlemen, Please! W. W. Gibson. ChMo
Time Goes by Turns. Joel Chandler Harris. *Fr.* Uncle Remus, His Songs and His Sayings. IHA
Time Goes by Turns. Robert Southwell. *See* Times Go by Turns.
Time goes, you say? Ah, no! The Paradox of Time. Austin Dobson. AWP; HBV: JAWP; PG (1945 ed.); VLEP; WBP
Time had come to kill himself, he said, The. Epitaph on a Madman's Grave. Morris Gilbert. YaD
Time has a magic wand! On an Old Muff. Frederick Locker-Lampson. CenHV; LPS-3; VA
Time has been that these wild solitudes, The. A Winter Piece. Bryant. AmPP (4th ed.); CoBA; MOAP; OxBA
Time Has Come, the Clock Says Time Has Come, The. Conrad Aiken. Preludes for Memnon, XXVIII. NePA; OxBA
"Time has come, The," the walrus said. "Lewis Carroll." *Fr.* The Walrus and the Carpenter. TiPo
Time has come to call a halt, The. Songs for a Colored Singer, II. Elizabeth Bishop. PoNe
Time has [or is] come to speak, I think, The. Mrs. Golightly. Gertrude Hall. AA; PR
Time has its ends and its beginnings. The Jungle. Louis Dudek. PeCV
Time has no flight—'tis we who speed along. Time. Thomas Stephen Collier. AA
Time has stored all, but keeps his chronicle. History. Laurence Binyon. POTE
Time has trailed lengthily since met. Postscript. Thomas Hardy. NV

Time hath laid his mantle by, The. Spring. Charles d'Orléans. DD; LPS-2
Time hath, my lord, a wallet at his back. Time [*or* Good Deeds Past *or* Ulysses; the Instant Way]. Shakespeare. *Fr.* Troilus and Cressida, III, iii. CoEV; EV-1; LiA; LiTB; LiTG
Time holds no purring hour-glass to your face. The Day. George M. Brady. NeIP
Time, I ever must complain. To Time. John Hagthorpe. SeCL
Time I went to see my sister, The. Tsurayuki. *Fr.* Shui Shu. AWP
Time in the Rock, *sels.* Conrad Aiken.
"And there I saw the seed upon the mountain," I. (Preludes to Definition, I.) TwAmPo
"And you who love, you who attach yourselves." ViBoPo
"But no, the familiar symbol, as that the," XCII *and* XCIII. FaBoMo
"On that wild verge in the late night he stood," XXXIX. (Preludes to Definition, II.) TwAmPo
"Or else, in an afternoon of minor reflection," XCIII. MoVE
"Still the same function, still the same habit come," XLV. (Preludes to Definition, III.) TwAmPo
"What without speech we knew and could not say," XLVI. (Preludes to Definition, IV.) TwAmPo
Time in the Sun. Louise Townsend Nicholl. NePoAm-2
Time is a [*or* the] feathered thing. Time [*or* The First Song, Sung by Two Amazons]. Jasper Mayne. *Fr.* The Amorous War. EG; OBEV; SeCL; SeEP
Time is a flat even plain. Manuel Altolaguirre, *tr. fr. Spanish by* Eleanor L. Turnbull. CoSP
Time is a fox on quick, velvet feet. Earthly Illusion. Louise Leighton. GoYe
Time is a harp. Time. Hilda Conkling. NV
Time is a heavy legend to be told. French Clock. Hortense Flexner. HBMV
Time is a thing. Epilogue. Stephen Spender. MBP; MoBrPo
Time is a treasure. New Time. *Unknown.* BLRP
Time is a withered monk whose pale hands write. Enigma. Hugh Wilgus Ramsaur. MuM
Time is as feather footed as the snow. Time. Clinton Scollard. VOD
Time is God's tenderness. Time. Marguerite Wilkinson. HBMV
Time is immovable; it is ourselves that pass. Life's Cloudy Quest. John Richard Moreland. MuM
Time is midsummer, The. In the Heat of the Day. Kyukin Susukida. PoLJ
Time is moving, people move up and down. The Parade. Ashton Greene. NePoAm
Time is never wasted, listening to the trees. The Trees. Lucy Larcom. NLK; OHIP
Time is no measure, there is only light. Villanelle of Light. A. M. Sullivan. JKCP (1955 ed.)
Time Is No Remedy. Ovid, *tr. fr. Latin by* Geoffrey Johnson. *Fr.* Tristia. LaP
Time is not remote, when I, The. Swift. *Fr.* Verses on the Death of Dr. Swift. BCEP; OBEC; OxBoLi; PoD; SiTL; ViBoPo; WoL
Time is of the essence. This is a highly skilled. Polo Grounds. Rolfe Humphries. HoPM; PreP
Time is the bound of things, where'er we go. Death Ends All Woe. Robert Herrick. EPS (1942 ed.)
Time is the feather'd thing. *See* Time is a feathered thing.
Time Is the Fire. Delmore Schwartz. The Repetitive Heart, IV. LiTA; LiTM
("Calmly we walk through this April's day.") MoVE
(For Rhoda.) MoAB; MoAmPo; OxBA
Time is the rest of all this earth. Time. Bhartrihari. AWP; JAWP; WBP
Time Is Today, The. John Farrar. GoYe
Time I've Lost in Wooing, The. Thomas Moore. ALV; BEL; EnLi-2; EnLit; EnRP; EPN; EPP; ERP; EV-4; HBV; HoPM; InP, *st.* 1; LiTL; OAEP; OnYI; PG (1945 ed.); PoFS; ReaPo; TreF
Light That Lies, The, *sel.* BTP
Time Lags Abed. D'Arcy Cresswell. AnNZ
Time like an Ever-rolling Stream. P. G. Wodehouse. FiBHP
Time like the repetitions of a child's piano. The Reconciliation. Archibald MacLeish. MoAmPo
Time Long Past. Shelley. BPN; EmBrPo; EPN; ERP; HBV
Time makes an ending of the Pyramids. Louise Labé. *Fr.* Elegy. FoS
Time never can produce men to o'ertake. William Browne. *Fr.* Britannia's Pastorals, II, Song 3. SG
Time nor place did I want, what held me tongue-tied. Phaleuciaks I. *Unknown.* SiCE
Time of gifts has come again, The. The Pressed Gentian. Whittier. AnAmPo; LA
Time of Light, a Time of Shadow, A. Samuel Yellen. NePoAm-2
Time of Roses. Thomas Hood. BLV; LoPS; OBEV; OBVV; PG (1945 ed.)
(Ballad: "It was not in the winter.") TOP, *abr.*; VA
(Ballad: Time of Roses.) EV-4
(It Was Not in the Winter.) LoPo
(It Was the Time of Roses.) CH; PFE
Time of school drags by with waiting, The. Childhood. Rainer Maria Rilke. AnGP
Time of the Barmecides, The. James Clarence Mangan. EnRP; TIP
Time of Waiting. Vicente Huidobro, *tr. fr. Spanish by* H. R. Hays. TwSpPo
Time of Waiting. Erik Axel Karlfeldt, *tr. fr. Swedish by* Charles W. Stork. AnSL
Time on her face has writ. A Woman. Thomas MacDonagh. TIP
Time Out. Frances Westgate Butterfield. GoYe
Time Out. Oliver Jenkins. GoYe
Time out of mind I have stood. The Old Grey Wall. Bliss Carman. CaP; OCL
Time passes, and the years. Come Up to Umbria. Charles Phillips. SaFP
Time-Piece, The. William Cowper. The Task, II. BEL
"Oh for a lodge in some vast wilderness," *sel.* EnRP
Time present and time past. Burnt Norton. T. S. Eliot. *Fr.* Four Quartets. AnFE; AtBAP; CoAnAm; LiTG; LiTM (rev. ed.); MoAB; MoAmPo (1950 ed.); MoPo; PoE; TwAmPo; TwHP
Time, Real and Imaginary. Samuel Taylor Coleridge. BPN; EmBrPo; EnRP; EV-4; OBEV; OBRV
Time Regained. Sir Herbert Read. FaBoMo
Time requires me to give account. Time and Account. Miguel de Guevara. AnMP
Time rolls his ceaseless course. Sir Walter Scott. *Fr.* The Lady of the Lake. ViBoPo
Time runs wild on the hilltops. Wild Thyme. Eleanor Farjeon. SiSoSe
Time seems not now beneath his years to stoop. Dryden. *Fr.* To His Sacred Majesty, a Panegyrick on His Coronation, 1661. OBS
Time-Servers. Judah Halevi, *tr. fr. Hebrew by* Solomon Solis-Cohen. TrJP
Time shall come, when, free as seas or wind, The. Pope. *Fr.* Windsor Forest. PoFr
Time shall come when wrong shall end, The. Chartist Song. Thomas Cooper. VA
Time sitting on the throne of memory. October XXIX, 1795. William Stanley Braithwaite. CDC
Time so tranquil is and still, The. A Summer Day. Alexander Hume. EV-1; OBEV
"Time stands still." The Unbeseechable. Frances Cornford. MBP; MoBrPo
Time stands still, with gazing on her face! *Unknown.* EnLoPo
Time taken by the forelock as he flies. Bluebell. Geoffrey Taylor. NeIP
Time takes the summer's loveliness. While Immortality Endures. Ernest Briggs. NeLNL
Time that brings children from the wizard den. Clock Symphony. John Frederick Nims. MiAP
Time, that has crumbled to impotent nothingness. The Voices of Hellas. Laurence Binyon. NeTW
Time that has lifted you over them all. Simon Surnamed Peter. Edgar Lee Masters. QS
Time that is fallen is flying, we are fooled by the passing hours. Venantius Fortunatus, *tr. by* Helen Waddell. TriL
Time that is moved by little fidget wheels. Five Bells. Kenneth Slessor. BoAV; MoAuPo; OnHM; PoRA; SeCePo
Time the Changer. Plato, *tr. fr. Greek by* T. F. Higham. OxBG
Time, the Faithless. Valentin Iremonger. *See* Evening in Summer.
Time time said old King Tut. Don Marquis. FiBHP
Time to Be Wise. Walter Savage Landor. *See* Yes; I Write Verses.
Time to Choose a Lover. Horace. *See* To Chloe.
Time to Dance, A, *sels.* C. Day Lewis.
Flight, The. FaBoMo; MoVE, *longer sel.*
(Flight to Australia.) ShBV-3
"For those who had the power." FaBoMo; MoP; POTE; TwCV
Time to Die. Ray Garfield Dandridge. BANP
Time to Go. "Susan Coolidge." GN; OTPC (1946 ed.)
Time to Leave Her. *Unknown.* *See* Leave Her Johnny.
Time to Rise. Robert Louis Stevenson. BoChLi; InP; MeMeAg; OTPC (1946 ed.); PCH; PoVP; RIS; SiSoSe; StVeCh; UTS
Time to Strike, The. Shakespeare. *See* There Is a Tide.
Time to Talk, A. Robert Frost. CoBA; LaNeLa
Time to Trust, The. *Unknown.* BLRP
Time was, and that was termed the time of gold. The Olden Days. Joseph Hall. *Fr.* Virgidemiarum. OBSC; SiCE
Time was away and somewhere else. Meeting Point. Louis MacNeice. ChMP; POTE
Time was come when he must choose, The. 1914 Autumn and Winter. Maurice Hewlett. *Fr.* The Song of the Plow. PoFr

Time was he sang the British Brute. Ballade of Expansion. Hilda Johnson. PAH
Time was, I shrank from what was right. Sensitiveness. Cardinal Newman. PoVP
Time was I was a plowman driving. Plowman. Sidney Keyes. MoAB; PoRA
Time was, in defence of his King and the Right. God Save the King. Joseph Stansbury. BoCaPo (1948 ed.)
Time was long and long ago, The. Ditty. Ted Robinson. MaRV
Time was long before I met her, but is longer since we parted. To One Unnamed. Li Shang-yin. ChLP
Time was night, when most the violent breathing winds, The. Leander's Death. Musaeus. *Fr.* Hero and Leander. OxBG
Time was, no archer with impunity. Archers of the King. Sister Mary Genoveva. GoBC
Time was, our hearts were young and stout. Spartan Three-Choir Festival. *Unknown.* OxBG
Time was that Strephon when he found. The Contemporary Suitor. Edward Sandford Martin. PR
Time was upon. Upon Time. Robert Herrick. EV-2; OBS
Time was when America hallow'd the morn. A Birthday Song. Jonathan Odell. BoCaPo (1948 ed.); IAP
Time was when his half million drew. Bewick Finzer. E. A. Robinson. AnNE; BoLiVe (1945 ed.); ChMo; CMP; CoBMV; MAP; MoAB; MoAmPo; NeMA; TwP
Time was when I was free as air. On a Goldfinch, Starved to Death in His Cage. William Cowper. CaAE
Time was when I was weapon and warrior. Horn. *Unknown.* *Fr.* Riddles. AnOE
Time was when we were closer, moon and earth. Moonlight. Lord Vansittart. NeTW
Time was when ye were powerless. The Young Priest to His Hands. Edward F. Garesché. CAW
Time wasted and time spent. The Times. Charles Madge. OBMV
Time wasteth years, and months, and hours. Time. Thomas Watson. *Fr.* Hecatompathia. OBSC; SiCE
Time went away, and left him lingering. The Last Romantic. Alexander Laing. AnAmPo; LA
Time! what an empty vapour 'tis! The Shortness of Life, and the Goodness of God. Isaac Watts. BeR
Time When First, The. *Unknown.* TuPP
Time When I Was Plowing, The. Maxwell Anderson. TBM
Time! Where Didst Thou Those Years Inter. William Habington. OxBoCh
(Recogitabo Tibi Omnes Annos Meos.) ACP (1926 ed.)
Time will come when, looking in a glass, The. The Frailty of Beauty. "J. C." *Fr.* Alcilia. ElL
Time Will Not Grant. Sidney Keyes. SeCePo
Time Will Say Nothing but I Told You So. W. H. Auden. *See* Villanelle.
Time winnows beauty with a fiery wind. The Harvest of Time. Harold Trowbridge Pulsifer. HBMV
Time-worn, the soldier lays aside the steel. Propertian. L. A. MacKay. *Fr.* Erotica Antiqua. PeCV
Time, wouldst thou hurt us? Never shall we grow old. The Double Fortress. Alfred Noyes. GoBC
Time, You Old Gipsy [*or* Gypsy] Man. Ralph Hodgson. BLV; BoLiVe; BoTP; CH; ChMo; CMP; EnLi-2 (1949 ed.); EnLit; EPP; FaPON; GaP; GBV (1952 ed.); HBV; InP; LBBV; LiTM (rev. ed.); MBP; MoAB; MoBrPo; MoShBr; NeMA; NP; PCD; PFE; PG; PoeMoYo; PoeT; RG; ShBV-1; SiSoSe; StaSt; TCPD; ThWaDe; TOP; TreF; TrGrPo; TwCV; ViBoPo; WaKn; WP
Time you won your town the race, The. To an Athlete Dying Young. A. E. Housman. A Shropshire Lad, XIX. ATP; BEL; BoLiVe; BPN; ChMo; CMP; CoBE; EmBrPo; EnL; EnLi-2; ExPo; GTBS-W; InP; LiTB; LiTG; LiTM (rev. ed.); MaC; MaPo; MBP; MoAB; MoBrPo; NeMA; OAEP (2d ed.); Po; PoEL-5; PoFS; PoMa; PoRA; POTT; PoVP; PreP; ReaPo; RiBV; SeCeV; TreF; TrGrPo; TriL; TwP; UnPo; ViP; ViPo; VLEP; WHA
Time Zones for Forty-four. Donald A. Stauffer. WaP
Timeless Island. Clifford Gessler. MuM
Timely blossom, infant fair. To Miss Charlotte Pulteney, in Her Mother's Arms [*or* To Charlotte Pulteney]. Ambrose Philips. CEP; EiPP; EV-3; FaBoEn; GTBS; GTBS-D; GTBS-W; GTSE; GTSL; HBV; OBEC
Timely Warning, A. *Unknown.* PoMa
Timers. Flora J. Arnstein. GoYe
Times, The, *sel.* Charles Churchill.
At Least. BeR
Times, The. Charles Madge. OBMV
Times, The. Marcus Manilius, *tr. fr. Latin by* Thomas Creech. LiTW
Times, The. *Unknown.* PAH
Time's a circumference. The Soul of Time. Trumbull Stickney. LiTA; NePA
Time's Alteration. *Unknown.* EV-2
"Time's an illusion," I heard the philosopher say. Realism. Ruth Samuels. CAG
Time's Balm, *abr.* Cuthbert Shaw. *Fr.* Monody to the Memory of a Young Lady. OBEC
Time's Bright Sand. Robert Finch. CaP
Time's Changes. James Bramston. *Fr.* The Art of Politicks. OBEC
Times come 'round again, The. To a Military Rifle, 1942. Yvor Winters. WaP
"Time's Conscience!" cried the allerion. Forever Morning. Laura Riding. LiTA
Time's Flying. *Unknown.* *See* Lauriger Horatius.
Time's Fool. Ruth Pitter. ChMP; MoBrPo; PoRA
Times Gettin' Hard, Boys, *with music.* *Unknown.* AS
Time's Glory. Shakespeare. *Fr.* The Rape of Lucrece. ChTr
Times Go [*or* Goe] by Turns. Robert Southwell. ACP; AEV; CoBE; ElL; ElSeCe; GoBC; GTBS-W; HBV; LiTB; LiTG; OBEV (1st ed.); OBSC; OxBoCh; PG; PoEL-2; SiCE
(Time Goes by Turns.) WP
(Tymes Goe by Turnes.) FaBoEn
Time's Hand Is Kind. Margaret E. Bruner. PoToHe
Times Have Altered, The. *Unknown.* CoMu
Times is mighty dull at Squawville, an' we've nothin' else to do. Patriotism at Squawville. *Unknown.* PAP
Time's Long Ago. Herman Melville. PoFS
Time's Long and Ever-flowing River. Gavril Derzhavin, *tr. fr. Russian by* Babette Deutsch. TrRV
Time's Revenge. Walter Learned. HBV
Time's Revenges. Robert Browning. BPN; GEPC; PoVP; PR; VLEP
Times she'll sit quiet by the hearth. The Woodcutter's Wife. William Rose Benét. AnAmPo; AWP; InPo; LA; MOAP
Time's Song. Winthrop Mackworth Praed. EnRP
Times wherein old Pompion was a saint, The. Benjamin Tompson. *Fr.* New England's Crisis. APW; IAP; TCAP
Times without Number Have I Pray'd. Charles Wesley. MaRV; OxBoCh
Timid Ash Tree, The. Kathleen Millay. PEDC
Timid Bunnies. Jeannie Kirby. BoTP
Timid child with heart oppressed, A. Buffalo Creek. John Le Gay Brereton. BoAu
Timid cringing little thing, A. My Dog. Marty Hale. AlBD
Timid fallow deer, his tender breast, The. The Useless Flight. Juan Meléndez Valdés. TeCS
Timid Gazelle, The. Kasmuneh, *tr. fr. Arabic.* TrJP
Timid Hortense. Peter Newell. NA
Timid little night moth, The. Moth Miller. Aileen Fisher. UTS
Timid Lover. Countee Cullen. BANP
Timidly, still half asleep, it has blossomed. The Purple Peach Tree. Su T'ung-po. OnPC
Timocreon. Simonides, *tr. fr. Greek by* C. M. Bowra. GrL; OxBG
(Mock Epitaph, A, *tr. by* Robert Allason Furness.) GrR
Timocritus fought well. This is his grave. War's Folly. Anacreon. GrPE
Timomachus. Simonides, *tr. fr. Greek by* T. F. Higham. GrL; OxBG
Timon ("'Timon, now dead'"). Callimachus, *tr. fr. Greek by* G. M. Young. GrL
Timon of Archimedes. Charles Battell Loomis. NA
Timon of Athens, *sel.* Thomas Shadwell.
Good-Morrow, A. SeCL
Timon of Athens, *sels.* Shakespeare.
"Ah, when the means are gone that buy this praise," *fr.* II, ii. MyFE
"Here lies a wretched corse," *fr.* V, iv. MyFE
"How came the noble Timon to this change?" *fr.* IV, iii. MyFE
"I am sicke of this false world, and will love nought," *fr.* IV, iii. NBE
"If Alcibiades kill my countrymen," *fr.* V, i. MyFE
"That Nature being sicke of mans unkindnesse," *fr.* IV, iii. NBE
Timon's Epitaph. Callimachus, *tr. fr. Greek by* Shakespeare. AWP; JAWP; WBP
("Here lie, I, Timon; who, alive, all living men did hate.") GrPo
Timon's Villa. Pope. *Fr.* Moral Essays, Epistle IV. CoEV; MaPo; OBEC
(At Timon's Villa.) ExPo
(Satire on Riches.) PoLi
Timor Mortis Conturbat Me. Sir Joseph Noel Paton. EBSV
Timothy. Rose Fyleman. UTS
Timothy. Wordsworth. *See* Childless Father, The.
Timothy Boon. Ivy O. Eastwick. TiPo
Timothy Tiggs and Tomothy Toggs. Some Fishy Nonsense. Laura E. Richards. TiPo
Timothy Tim was a very small cat. Tiger-Cat Tim. Edith H. Newlin. TiPo
Timothy Titus took two ties. *Unknown.* OxNR
Tin-bright and whistle-sharp the world occurs. The Body's Eye. Anne Welsh. BoSA
Tin Gee Gee, The. Fred Cape. PTA-2

Tin of corned beef, chained like a lorgnette, A. Fable. Alfred Jarry. MiFP
Tin-tinkle-tinkle-tinkle, went the bell. The Shop. W. W. Gibson. BEL
Tin-Whistle Player, The. Padraic Colum. UnS
Ting! ring! the sleigh bells jingle. A Sleigh-Ride. Laura E. Richards. GFA
Ting, ting goes the woodman's ax. The Woodman's Ax. *Unknown.* WhP
Tinged with my kisses go, go thou to her. Upon Returning a Silk Handkerchief. Herbert P. Horne. LEAP
Tinged with the blood of Aztec lands. El Vaquero. Lucius Harwood Foote. AA
Tingling Back, The. Karl Shapiro. FiMAP
Tingling, misty marvel, A. November Morning. Evaleen Stein. YeAr
Tink-a-tink, tink-a-tink. The Minaret Bells. Thackeray. RIS
Tinker, The. *Unknown.* CoMu
Tinker and the Monks, The. Nathaniel Whiting. *Fr.* Le Hore di Recreatione; or, The Pleasant Historie of Albino and Bellama. SeCL
Tinker out of Bedford, A. The Holy War. Kipling. TCPD
Tinker, Tailor. *Unknown.* OxNR
Tinkers, The. Joseph Campbell. OnYI
Tinker's Moon. Ewart Milne. OnYI
Tinkle, tinkle! The Waterfall. Frank Dempster Sherman. BoChLi; OTPC (1946 ed.); PRWS
"Tinkle, tinkle, tinkle": 'tis the muffin-man you see. The Muffin-Man's Bell. Ann Hawkshaw. BoTP; OTPC
Tint I cannot take is best, The. Emily Dickinson. CoBA; MAP; MoAmPo
Tintadgel bells ring o'er the tide. The Silent Tower of Bottreau [*or* Bottreaux]. Robert Stephen Hawker. GoBC; OBRV; TCEP; VA
Tintern Abbey. Wordsworth. *See* Lines Composed a Few Miles above Tintern Abbey.
Tiny bell the tree-toad has, A. The Tree-Toad. Orrick Johns. NP; PoeMoYo
Tiny cream-bricked lighthouse on the hill, The. Park. Glyn Jones. MoWP
Tiny fly fell down on my page, A. A Death to Us. Jon Silkin. NePoEA
Tiny moon as small and white as a single jasmine flower, A. A White Blossom. D. H. Lawrence. MBP; MoBrPo; NeMA
Tiny shoes so trim and neat. The Fairy Shoemaker. Phyllis Garlick. BoTP
Tiny slippers of gold and green. To a Pair of Egyptian Slippers. Sir Edwin Arnold. HBV; OBVV
Tiny stone, a jasper, here displays, A. A Carved Stone. *Unknown.* OnPM
Tip Sams of Kentucky. Cotton Noe. DDA
Tipperary. Mary Kelly. TIP; VA
Tipperary Recruiting Song. *Unknown.* OnYI
Tipperty-Toes, the smallest elf. Red in Autumn. Elizabeth Gould. BoTP
Tippler's Philosophy. *Unknown, tr. fr. Greek by* Thomas Girdlestone. GrR
Tipsiness. Clement Wood. VOD
Tiptoe Night. John Drinkwater. GaP; SiSoSe
Tip-Toe Tale. Dixie Willson. GFA
Tiptoeing twilight. Twilight. Hazel Hall. AnAmPo; HBMV; LA
Tir-Nan-Og. J. F. Hendry. NeBP
Tirade on Tea. Phyllis McGinley. InMe
Tir'd Nature's sweet restorer, balmy sleep! *See* Tired Nature's sweet restorer . . .
Tir'd with all these, for restful death I cry. *See* Tired with all these . . .
Tir'd with the noysom follies of the age. *See* Tired with the noisome follies of the age.
Tir'd with vain Toil, scar'd with each dreadful blast. Musaeus. *Fr.* Hero and Leander. GrPo
Tired. Hilda Conkling. NP
Tired. Fenton Johnson. BANP; PoNe
Tired, *sel.* William Wetmore Story.
I Have My Cruse of Oil. PSO
Tired air groans as the heavies swing over, The. Thiepval Wood. Edmund Blunden. AnFE
Tired and thirsty, weary of the way. After the Hunt. Detlev von Liliencron. AWP
Tired and Unhappy [You Think of Houses]. Delmore Schwartz. LiTM; MoAB; MoAmPo; NePA
Tired brain, there is a place of rest. Quiet. Ernest Radford. OBVV
Tired cars go grumbling by, The. When Dawn Comes to the City; New York. Claude McKay. GoSl
Tired Caterpillar, The. *Unknown.* UTS
Tired Doctor's Prayer, A. George David Stewart. PoP
Tired Man, The. Anna Wickham. BMEP; HBMV; LBBV; NP; ViBoPo (1941 ed.); YT
Tired Mothers. May Riley Smith. HBV; MOAH
Tired [*or* Tir'd] Nature's sweet restorer, balmy sleep! The Complaint [*or* Introduction]. Edward Young. *Fr.* Night Thoughts. CEP; EiPP; EnRP; EV-3; OBEC; SeCePo
Tired of being my dog, and with grave anger. A Dog Who Ate a Pond Lily. Winifred Welles. NP
Tired of embraces, yet happy and careless. Diminuendo. Tom Kristensen. BoDS
Tired of man's futile, petty cry. Wide Haven. Clement Wood. SBMV
Tired of play! Tired of play! On the Picture of a "Child Tired of Play." Nathaniel Parker Willis. HBV
Tired out with hours of study's task supreme. Smoke Rings. *Unknown.* CAG
Tired Petitioner, The, *sel.* George Wither.
"It may be 'tis observ'd, I want relations." SeCV-1
Tired summer sinks its head, The. Youth's Flight. Hermann Hesse. TwGV
Tired swimmer in the waves of time, A. Sissinghurst. V. Sackville-West. DiM; POTE
Tired Tim. Walter de la Mare. ALV; BMEP; BoTP; FaPON; GaP; MoShBr; MPB; OnPP; TiPo; TSW; TSWC
Tired, tired of soul she walked across the field. In the Pasture. Dora Hagemeyer. MuM
Tired vulture, A, nibbles at the bleak/ Flesh it thought ageless. Anatole France at Eighty. Gladys Oaks. AnAmPo; LA
Tired? Well, what of that? What of That? *Unknown.* PEOR
Tired [*or* Tir'd] with all these, for restful death I cry. Sonnets, LXVI. Shakespeare. AnFE; AWP; BEL; BLV; BoLiVe; EnL; EnLi-1; EPP; EtPaEn; EV-1; ExPo; FaFP; GTBS; GTBS-D; GTBS-W; GTSE; GTSL; InPo; JAWP; LiTB; LiTG; MyFE; OBSC; PeBoSo; PFE; PIAE; ReEn; SeCeV; SiCE; TOP; TrGrPo; ViBoPo; WBP; WHA
Tired [*or* Tir'd] with the noisome [*or* noysom] follies of the age. Farewell. Earl of Rochester. *Fr.* Farewell to the Court. BeR; TrGrPo
Tired Woman, The. Anna Wickham. AV; MBP; MoBrPo
Tired Worker, The. Claude McKay. BANP
Tireless budding and flowering of women. Image in a Lilac Tree. Terence Tiller. NeBP
Tireless flight of a pursuing gull, The. A Christmas Dawn at Sea. Evan Morgan. EtS
Tiresias. George Garrett. NePoAm-2
Tiresias' Lament. Ellen de Young Kay. NePoEA
Tiring of rest, of plain and fruitless toil. The Dreamer. Dorothy Gould. PGD
'Tis a cold, bleak night! with angry roar. The Red Jacket. George M. Baker. PTA-2
'Tis a dozen or so of years ago. Deborah Lee. William H. Burleigh. LPS-3
'Tis a dull sight. Old Song [*or* The Meadows in Spring]. Edward Fitzgerald. EV-5; GN; HBV; OBEV; OBVV
'Tis a fearful night in the winter time. A Snow-Storm. Charles Gamage Eastman. LPS-2
" 'Tis a hundred years," said the bosun bold. The Whale. *Unknown.* EtS
'Tis a last choice Havana. The Last Cigar. *Unknown.* PA
'Tis a lesson you should heed. Try Again [*or* Try, Try Again]. *Unknown, at. to* William Edward Hickson, *also to* T. H. Palmer. FaFP; FaPON; PTA-2; TreF; TVC
'Tis a Little Journey. *Unknown.* PoToHe
'Tis a little thing. Sympathy [*or* A Friend]. Sir Thomas Noon Talfourd. *Fr.* Ion. LPS-3; PoToHe
'Tis a new life; thoughts move not as they did. The New Birth. Jones Very. EOAH
'Tis a region calm of sunny groves. *Unknown. Fr.* The Phoenix. LiTW
'Tis a sad sight to see the year dying. Song of the Fire. Edward Fitzgerald. OTPC
'Tis a stern and startling thing to think. Her Death. Thomas Hood. *Fr.* Miss Kilmansegg and Her Precious Leg. VA
'Tis a strange place, this Limbo! not a place. Samuel Taylor Coleridge. *Fr.* Limbo. ERP; NBE
'Tis a substantial thing, and not a word. Fletcher *and* Massinger. *Fr.* The Double Marriage. PoFr
'Tis a wild spot, and even in summer hours. The Edge of the Swamp. William Gilmore Simms. APW; SPP
" 'Tis a wonderful story," I hear you say. The Boy Columbus. *Unknown.* HH; PEDC
'Tis a world of silences. I gave a cry. Silences. Arthur O'Shaughnessy. VA
'Tis advertised in Boston, New York and Buffalo. Blow, Ye Winds. *Unknown.* AmSS; IHA; SoAmSa
'Tis all a libel—Paxton (Sir) will say. One Thousand Seven Hundred and Thirty Eight, Dialogue II. Pope. CEP
'Tis all a myth that Autumn grieves. Autumn's Mirth. Samuel Minturn Peck. GN
'Tis all men's office to speak patience. Patience and Sorrow. Shakespeare. *Fr.* Much Ado about Nothing, V, i. EV-1
'Tis all the way to Toe-town. Foot Soldiers. John Banister Tabb. HBV; HBVY; PPL
'Tis always love in Arles the old. In Provence. Jean Aicard. CAW
'Tis an honorable thought. Emily Dickinson. *See* It is an honourable thought.

'Tis an old dial, dark with many a stain. The Sun-Dial. Austin Dobson. LPS-1
'Tis April, month of wondrous Helen's birth. Helen's Birthday. Pierre de Ronsard. TrFP
'Tis bad enough in man or woman. Epigram: On Inclosures. *Unknown.* OxBoLi
'Tis beauty truly blent, whose red and white. Olivia. Shakespeare. *Fr.* Twelfth Night, I, v. LPS-1
'Tis bedtime; say your hymn, and bid, "Good-night." Bedtime. Francis Robert St. Clair Erskine. HBV; HBVY; PRWS; VA
'Tis believed that this harp, which I wake now for thee. The Origin of the Harp. Thomas Moore. LPS-3
'Tis best sometimes your censure to restrain. The Treatment for Old Jades and Janes. Pope. *Fr.* An Essay on Criticism. BeR
'Tis better to be vile than vile esteemed. Sonnets, CXXI. Shakespeare. InvP; MaPo; PeBoSo; PoEL-2
'Tis Better to Have Loved and Lost. Tennyson. *See* In Memoriam A. H. H.: "I envy not in any moods."
'Tis bitter, yet 'tis sweet. Troubled with the Itch, and Rubbing with Sulphur. George Moses Horton. NoCaPo
'Tis bitter-sweet on winter nights to list. The Cracked Bell. Baudelaire. TrFP
'Tis busy in the grove here. The Forest Wedding. Christian Richardt. BoDS
'Tis but a foil at best, and that's the most. Emblem. Francis Quarles. Emblems, II, 14. LoBV
'Tis but a frowne, I prithee let me dye. *Unknown.* SeCSL
'Tis But a Little Faded Flower. Ellen Clementine Howarth. AA; HBV
'Tis But a Week. Gerald Gould. LBBV; PoeT; TVSH
'Tis but an ague that's reverst. Love. Samuel Butler. *Fr.* Hudibras. BeR
'Tis Christmas, and the North wind blows. A Christmas Letter from Australia. Douglas Brooke Wheelton Sladen. COAH; VA
'Tis Christmas morn. In other lands they sing. Ode on Christmas. J. E. Clinton. PEOR
'Tis Christmas night! The snow. The Light of Bethlehem. John Banister Tabb. CAW; ChIP; MaRV; PoRL
Tis Christmas now, 'tis Christmas now. *Unknown.* SeCSL
'Tis Christmas weather, and a country house. Modern Love, XXIII. George Meredith. EmBrPo; ViP; ViPo
'Tis dead night round about: norror doth creep. The Lamp. Henry Vaughan. SeCL
'Tis death! and peace, indeed, is here. Youth and Calm. Matthew Arnold. BPN; EmBrPo; PoVP; VLEP
'Tis done—but yesterday a King! Ode to Napoleon Bonaparte. Byron. BCEP; BPN; EV-4
'Tis done, the edict past, by Heaven decreed. Ode to the Fourth of July. Daniel George. TrAS
'Tis "Done"—the wondrous thoroughfare. The Pacific Railway. C. R. Ballard. PAH
'Tis dreadful! The Aisle of a Temple. Congreve. *Fr.* The Mourning Bride, II, i. EV-3
'Tis education forms the common mind. As the Twig Is Bent. Pope. *Fr.* Moral Essays. TreF
'Tis eight o'clock, a clear March night. The Idiot Boy. Wordsworth. ERP
'Tis Evanoe's. The House of Splendour. Ezra Pound. InPo; MOAP
'Tis evening now! Abide with Us. Horatius Bonar. BePJ; VA
'Tis fatal to tyrannic power, when they. Defoe. *Fr.* The Kentish Petition, 1701. PoFr
'Tis fine to play/ In the fragrant hay. A Boy's Summer Song. Paul Laurence Dunbar. SiSoSe
'Tis fine to see the Old World, and travel up and down. America for Me [*or* Home Thoughts from Europe]. Henry van Dyke. BAP; BLPA; BTP; CV; GA; FaFP; HBVY; MC; MPB; OHFP; OTPC (1946 ed.); PaA; PCD; POT; PoTo; PYM; SP; TreFS; WBLP
'Tis from high life high characters are drawn. The Gem and the Flower. Pope. *Fr.* Moral Essays, Epistle I. OBEC
'Tis God that girds our armor on. The American Soldier's Hymn. *Unknown.* PAH
'Tis gone at last, and I am glad; it stayed a fearful while. The Mortgage on the Farm. *Unknown.* PTA-2
'Tis gone, that bright and orbed blaze. John Keble. *Fr.* Evening. TrPWD
'Tis gone, the land of dreams! a grayer sky. Conclusion. Lord De Tabley. PoVP
'Tis Growing So Hushed around Me. Karl August Tavaststjerna, *tr. fr. Swedish by* Charles W. Stork. AnSL
'Tis Hard to Find God. Robert Herrick. LiTB
'Tis hard to find in life. True Friendship. *Unknown. Fr.* The Panchatantra. AWP; JAWP; LiTW; WBP
'Tis hard to say, if greater want of skill. An Essay on Criticism. Pope. ATP; BEL; CEP; CoBE; EiPP; EM-1; EnLi-1; EnLit; EPP; FaBoEn; FiP; GEPC; OAEP; OuHeWo; PIAE; PoEL-3; TCEP; TOP; TwP; TyEnPo; WHA
'Tis held that sorrow makes us wise. In Memoriam A. H. H., CXIII. Tennyson. BPN; EmBrPo; EPN; GEPC; ViPo; VLEP
'Tis highly rational, we can't dispute. Epigram. Richard Garnett. HBV
'Tis I go Fiddling, Fiddling. Nora Hopper. *See* Fairy Fiddler, The.
'Tis, in good truth, a most wonderful thing. Love. Sir William Davenant. *Fr.* The Unfortunate Lovers. SeCL
'Tis known, at least it should be, that throughout. Beppo. Byron. BEL
'Tis Late and Cold. John Fletcher. *See* Dead Host's Welcome, The.
'Tis late; the astronomer in his lonely height. The Appointment. Sully-Prudhomme. OxBI
'Tis Life Beyond. *Unknown.* MaRV (Horizon.) BPP
'Tis life in a half-breed shack. Life in a Half-Breed Shack. *Unknown.* CoSo; CSF
'Tis light makes colour visible: at night. Reality and Appearance. Jalal ed-Din Rumi. PeP
'Tis like a helmet, nicked. The Thimble. Al-Liss. MooP
'Tis like stirring living embers when, at eighty, one remembers. Grandmother's Story of Bunker Hill Battle. Oliver Wendell Holmes. GoTP; IAP; PAH; PAP
'Tis little I can give you, yet I can give you these. Oblation. A. Newberry Choyce. HBMV
'Tis little I could care for pearls. Emily Dickinson. AmPP
'Tis long since, long since, since I heard. The Tin-Whistle Player. Padraic Colum. UnS
'Tis love that moveth the celestial spheres. Sonnets, XXII. George Santayana. MOAP
'Tis March. Hope Nelson GFA
'Tis Merry in Greenwood. Sir Walter Scott. *Fr.* Harold the Dauntless. ADAH; FaPON; MPB; OHIP
'Tis Midnight. *Unknown.* BOHV; NA; RIS
'Tis midnight; and on Olive's brow. Jesus Prays Alone. William Bingham Tappan. BePJ
'Tis midnight, and the moonbeam sleeps. The Romaunt of Humpty Dumpty. Henry S. Leigh. BOHV
'Tis midnight, and the setting sun. 'Tis Midnight. *Unknown.* BOHV; NA; RIS
'Tis midnight hour, and the dead have power. "In the Dead Unhappy Midnight." Gerald Massey. UnW
'Tis midnight's holy hour, and silence now. The Closing Year. George Denison Prentice. LPS-3
'Tis mirth that fills the veins with blood. Mirth [*or* Laugh and Sing]. Beaumont *and* Fletcher. *Fr.* The Knight of the Burning Pestle. BLV; ElL; SiCE; TrGrPo
'Tis moonlight on the sea, boys. Dip, Boys, Dip the Oar. F. Sarona. OlF
'Tis morning; and the sun, with ruddy orb. The Winter Morning Walk. William Cowper. *Fr.* The Task, V. EnSW; EPP; LPS-2; PoEL-3
'Tis morning; well; I fain would yet sleep on. Abraham Cowley. *Fr.* Ode upon Liberty. PoFr
'Tis much immortal beauty to admire. Beauty. Edward Hovell Thurlow. LPS-3
'Tis mute, the word they went to hear on high Dodona mountain. The Oracles. A. E. Housman. AnFE; PoFr; POTT
'Tis my mother comes. "A Blot as Black as Death." Euripides. *Fr.* Electra. GrR
'Tis mystic union, man and wife. For the Right Honorable Lucy, Countess of Huntingdon, 1649. Thomas Pestel. ReEn
'Tis nearing the noonday on Massabielle. The Canticle of Bernadette. *Unknown.* WHL
'Tis nearly over; in this darkening hour. Thomas Dunn English. *Fr.* At Seventy-two. PoP
'Tis nigh two thousand years. Sir Lewis Morris. *Fr.* Christmas 1898. TrPWD
'Tis night, and tempests roar unceasingly. The Pilgrim before St. Just. August, Graf von Platen. LiA
'Tis night, dead night, and weary Nature lies. Dead Night. Nathaniel Lee. *Fr.* Theodosius; or, The Force of Love. BeR
'Tis night on the mountain. Cradle Song. Mary M. Bowen. BOL
'Tis night upon the lake. Our bed of boughs. The Voice of the Pine. Richard Watson Gilder. ADAH; SN
'Tis night, when meditation bids us feel. Night. Byron. *Fr.* Childe Harold's Pilgrimage, II. LPS-2; SN
" 'Tis no marvel," one to other said. The Elders of Troy Behold Helen. Homer. *Fr.* The Iliad, III. LiA
'Tis no matter to amaze. Bounty. Abus Salt. MooP
'Tis no wonder if my songs. Troubadour Song. Bernart of Ventadorn. EnLi-1
Tis noe shame to yeild. *Unknown.* SeCSL
'Tis noonday by the buttonwood, with slender-shadowed bud. The Minute-Men of North-Boro. Wallace Rice. PAH
'Tis not a freedom that, where all command. Andrew Marvell. *Fr.* The First Anniversary of the Government under His Royal Highness the Lord Protector. PoFr

'Tis not a game that plays at mates and mating. The Flame. Ezra Pound. CoAnA n
Tis not Boy thy amorous looke. *Unknown.* SeCSL
'Tis not by brooding on delight. Marcus Curtius. Oliver St. John Gogarty. OBMV
'Tis not by guilt the onward sweep. Edward Rowland Sill. *Fr.* The Fool's Prayer. TrPWD
'Tis not enough for one that is a wife. Chorus. Lady Elizabeth Carew. *Fr.* Mariam. LiTL
'Tis not enough no harshness gives offence. The Sound and the Sense. Pope. *Fr.* An Essay on Criticism. LiA
'Tis not enough that Christ was born. Day Dawn of the Heart. Mary T. Lathrop. ChIP; PGD
'Tis not every [*or* ev'ry] day, that I. Not Every Day Fit for Verse. Robert Herrick. PoRA; SeEP
'Tis not for man to trifle! Life is brief. Life. Horatius Bonar. OQP; QP-2
'Tis not from any feeling of ambition. Slander! Aristophanes. *Fr.* The Thesmophoriazusae. GrR
'Tis not great, what I solicit. Address to Plenty. John Clare. OBRV
'Tis not greatness they require. Sweetnesse in Sacrifice. Robert Herrick. NBE
'Tis not her birth, her friends, nor yet her treasure. Why I Love Her. Alexander Brome. HBV; LO
'Tis not how witty, nor how free. Upon Kind[e] and True Love. Aurelian Townsend. EG; MeLP; MePo; OBS; SeCL
'Tis not in blood that Liberty inscribes her civil laws. True Freedom. Charles Mackay. PGD
'Tis not my lady's [*or* ladies] face that makes me love her. Love's without Reason. Alexander Brome. OBS; SeEP
'Tis not so much, these men more forms survey. Charles Lloyd. *Fr.* An Essay on the Genius of Pope. OBRV
'Tis not that both my eyes are black. The Penalties of Baldness. Sir Owen Seaman. FiBHP
'Tis not that I am weary grown. Upon [His] Leaving His Mistress. Earl of Rochester. EnLoPo; TrGrPo; ViBoPo
'Tis not that I design to rob. An Epistle to Robert Lloyd, Esq. William Cowper. FiP
'Tis not the babbling of a busy world. Conscience. Charles Churchill. *Fr.* The Conference. OBEC
'Tis not the lily-brow I prize. Song, ex Improviso. Samuel Taylor Coleridge. ERP
'Tis not the President alone. McKinley. *Unknown.* GA; MC; PAH
'Tis not the stones that conquer now, nor the knotted flails. Seventh Station. Paul Claudel. CAW
Tis not the world not what can please. *Unknown.* SeCSL
'Tis not those paultry counterfeit/ French stones. The Lady's Answer. Samuel Butler. *Fr.* Hudibras. BeR
Tis not thy well-mixd red & whyte. *Unknown.* SeCSL
'Tis not to be told/ What servile villainies men will do for gold. Ben Jonson. *Fr.* The Case Is Altered. LO
'Tis not too late to build our young land right. To Reformers in Despair. Vachel Lindsay. InP
'Tis not what I am fain to hide. My Secret. John Banister Tabb. SPP; WaKn
'Tis not your beauty can engage. To Flavia. Edmund Waller. ElSeCe; HBV
'Tis now clear day: I see a rose. The Search. Henry Vaughan. ElSeCe
'Tis now since I began to die. To Mrs. M. A. upon Absence. Katherine Philips. NBE
Tis Now Since I Sate Down. Sir John Suckling. *See* Siege, The.
'Tis now the time in latter May. My Mother. Viggo Stuckenberg. BoDS
'Tis now we'd want to be wary, boys. Tipperary Recruiting Song. *Unknown.* OnYI
'Tis of a brisk young Farmer, in ——shire did dwel. The Frolicksome Farmer. *Unknown.* CoMu
'Tis of a fearless Irishman. Brennan on the Moor. *Unknown.* BaBo
'Tis of a gallant Yankee ship that flew the stripes and stars. The Yankee Man-of-War. *Unknown.* AA; AmSS; EtS; FaBoBe; GA; LaNeLa; LEAP; OBAV; PAH
'Tis of a little drummer. The Little Drummer. Richard Henry Stoddard. AA; PAH
'Tis of a silk merchant in London I write. The Silk Merchant's Daughter, *vers.* II. *Unknown.* ShS
'Tis of a stately Southerner who flew the Stripes and Stars. The Stately Southerner. *Unknown.* ShS
'Tis of a wild Colonial boy, Jack Doolan was his name. The Wild Colonial Boy. *Unknown.* NeLNL; ViBoFo
'Tis of Aucassin and Nicolete. Aucassin and Nicolete. *Unknown.* OuHeWo; WoL
'Tis of the Father Hilary. World's Worth. Dante Gabriel Rossetti. GoBC; PoVP
'Tis on Eilanowen. The Faery Reaper. Robert Buchanan. OBVV
'Tis only a half truth the poet has sung. Crowded Ways of Life [*or* Let Me Walk with the Men in the Road]. Walter J. Gresham. BLPA; PTA-2
'Tis only saints in youth. *Unknown.* *Fr.* The Panchatantra. LiTW
'Tis only with the Bible or with Walt Whitman's verse. To Roosevelt. Rubén Darío. WoL
'Tis past, the sultry tyrant of the South. Anna Letitia Barbauld. *Fr.* A Summer Evening's Meditation. BCEP; LPS-2
'Tis pity not to have a dog. A Dog. Edgar A. Guest. AlBD
'Tis Pity She's a Whore, *sel.* John Ford.
"Be not deceived, my brother." PoD
" 'Tis plain to see," said a farmer's wife. Mother's Fool. *Unknown.* PTA-1
'Tis pleasant on a fine spring morn. Merry Autumn Days. Charles Dickens. PCH
'Tis pleasant, stretched on grassy lawn. Thomas Caulfield Irwin. *Fr.* Elizabethan Days. IrPN
'Tis pleasing to be schooled in a strange tongue. Byron. *Fr.* Don Juan. ViBoPo
'Tis pretty to see the girl of Dunbwy. The Girl of Dunbwy. Thomas Osborne Davis. TIP
'Tis queer, it is, the ways o' men. The Ways o' Men. Angelina Weld Grimké. CDC
. . . 'Tis real love,/ Where nature triumphs over wretched art. Nat Lee's Images. Dryden. *Fr.* To Mr. Lee, on His Alexander. BeR
'Tis religion that can give. The Satisfying Portion. *Unknown.* BLRP
'Tis right for her to sleep between. In Memoriam. Richard Monckton Milnes. HBV
'Tis sad to see the sons of learning. He That Never Read a Line. *Unknown.* AnIL
'Tis said. A Legend about Color. Edwin McNeill Poteat. NoCaPo (rev. ed.)
'Tis said achievement dwells on a rock both steep and high. Per Ardua. Simonides. GrR
'Tis said, as Cupid danced among. How Roses Came Red. Robert Herrick. ChTr
'Tis said on earth that the felicity. Contemplation. Joachim du Bellay. Les Amours, XXV. TrFP
'Tis said that absence conquers love! Song. Frederick William Thomas. AA; HBV
'Tis Said That Some Have Died for Love. Wordsworth. BPN; EmBrPo; EnRP; LO
"Oh, move, thou cottage, from behind that oak," *sel.* EnSW
'Tis said that the gods on Olympus of old. The Mint Julep. Charles Fenno Hoffman. AA
'Tis said, the pipe and lute that charm our ears. Remembered Music. Jalal ed-Din Rumi. PeP
'Tis said the rose is Love's own flower. The Flower of Love. Thomas Love Peacock. *Fr.* Melincourt. EV-4
'Tis said the Turk, when passing down. A Turkish Tradition. *Unknown.* PEOR
'Tis said, when Schiller's death grew nigh. The Death of Schiller. Bryant. UnW
'Tis sailing time; the swallows come. "All Ashore!" Leonidas of Tarentum. GrR
'Tis Sair to Dream. Robert Gilfillan. VA
'Tis so, 'twas ever so, since heretofore. John Oldham. *Fr.* A Satire Dissuading from Poetry. EPP
'Tis solemn darkness; the sublime of shade. Night. Charles Heavysege. BoCaPo
'Tis something from that tangle to have won. Icarus. Harry Lyman Koopman. AA
'Tis Sorrow Builds the Shining Ladder Up. James Russell Lowell. *Fr.* On the Death of a Friend's Child. MaRV; WGRP
'Tis spent—this burning day of June! Wordsworth. *Fr.* The Waggoner. EnSW
'Tis splendid to live so grandly. Washington's Birthday. Margaret E. Sangster. GA; HH; PEDC; PEOR; WOAH
'Tis spring; come out to ramble. The Lent Lily. A. E. Housman. A Shropshire Lad, XXIX. AlDL; MPB; OHIP; PoRL; PoVP; ViP
'Tis still and cold, and nothing in the air. Thomas Lovell Beddoes. *Fr.* Death's Jest Book, III, iii. NBE
'Tis strange! I saw the skies. Dreams. Thomas Traherne. MeRV
'Tis strange how my head runs on! 'tis a puzzle to understand. The City Clerk. Thomas Ashe. OBVV
'Tis strange, my Theseus. Shakespeare. *Fr.* A Midsummer Night's Dream, V, i. NBE
'Tis strange that absence often does. At the Garden Rail. A. M. Buckton. BoSA
'Tis strange that I sit here in wakeful mood. Moonlight. Verner von Heidenstam. AnSL
'Tis strange, the miser should his cares employ. Of the Use of Riches. Pope. *Fr.* Moral Essays. EiPP; PoEL-3; TwP
'Tis strange, this heart within my breast. A Song. Countess of Winchilsea. BLV
'Tis strange to look across the street. The Old Collector. Beatrice Hanscom. PR
'Tis strange to me, who long have seen no face. From Country to Town. Hartley Coleridge. OBRV

'Tis Strange, You Think. George Frederick Cameron. BoCaPo

'Tis Sunday at home. Vespers. Louis Mercier. CAW

'Tis Sweet [to Hear]. Byron. *Fr.* Don Juan, I. MaPo; MCCG; PIR
(First Love.) LPS-1; OBRV
(Pleasant Things, *shorter sel.*) OTPC (1923 ed.)
("Tis sweet to hear.") ViBoPo

'Tis sweet at dewy eve to rove. Rural Raptures. *Unknown.* BOHV

'Tis sweet, O God, to steal away. Among the Spruces. Frederick George Scott. OCL

. . . 'Tis sweet to hear,/ At midnight on the blue and moonlit deep. 'Tis Sweet [*or* First Love]. Byron. *Fr.* Don Juan, I. LPS-1; MaPo; MCCG; OBRV; OTPC (1923 ed.); PIR; ViBoPo

'Tis sweet to hear of heroes dead. The Great Adventure. Henry David Thoreau. HBV; OBVV

'Tis sweet to hear the merry lark. The Lark and the Nightingale [*or* Song]. Hartley Coleridge. HBV; OTPC (1923 ed.)

'Tis Sweet to Roam. *Unknown.* BOHV; NA

'Tis sweet, when slanting light the field adorns. The Home Field; Evening. Charles Tennyson Turner. EnSW

'Tis the Arabian bird alone. The Chaste Arabian Bird. Earl of Rochester. SiTL

'Tis the blithest, bonniest weather for a bird to flirt a feather. Robin's Secret. Katharine Lee Bates. AA

'Tis the cause of my anguish and grief of heart. The Maiden's Complaint. Brian Merriman. *Fr.* The Midnight Court. LiTW

'Tis the day of the blessed St. Jean B'ptiste. St. Jean B'ptiste. S. Frances Harrison. *Fr.* Down the River. CPG

'Tis the fortress of St. Louis. The Star in the West. Hezekiah Butterworth. PEOR

'Tis the hour of fairy ban and spell. Fairy Dawn. Joseph Rodman Drake. *Fr.* The Culprit Fay. GN

'Tis the hour when white-horsed Day. Morning. Charles Stuart Calverley. FiBHP

'Tis the human touch in this world that counts. The Human Touch. Spencer Michael Free. FaBoBe; MaRV; NeHB; PoP; PoToHe

'Tis the Last Rose of Summer. Thomas Moore. ATP; BEL; BLPA; EnLi-2 (1949 ed.); EnLit; EPP; ERP; HBV; LEAP; LPS-2; NeHB; PG (1945 ed.); PIR; PoEL-4; TreF; WBLP; WHA
(Last Rose of Summer, The.) BCEP; FaBoBe; FaFP; OIF; OnYI; OxBoLi; PECK; PreP, *with music*

'Tis the laughter of pines that swing and sway. The Phantom Light of the Baie des Chaleurs. Arthur Wentworth Hamilton Eaton. CaP; CPG; OCL; PoMS

'Tis the merry nightingale. The Nightingale. Samuel Taylor Coleridge. ERP; EV-4; NBE; OBRV

'Tis the middle of night by the castle clock. Christabel. Samuel Taylor Coleridge. BCEP; BEL; BPN; BrBE; CH; CoBE; EM-2; EmBrPo; EnL; EnLi-2; EnLit; EnRP; EPN; EPP; ERP; EV-4; FiP; GoTL; LiA; NBE; OAEP; OBRV; REAL; SeCePo; ShBV-3; TCEP; TOP; WHA

'Tis the middle watch of a summer's night. The Culprit Fay. Joseph Rodman Drake. BAP; BAV; LPS-3; TCAP

'Tis the rose of the desert. Written to a Young Lady. Jeremiah Joseph Callanan. IrPN

'Tis the terror of tempest. The rags of the sail. A Vision of the Sea. Shelley. EmBrPo

'Tis the voice of a sluggard . . . *See* 'Tis the voice of the sluggard . . .

'Tis the voice of the Lobster; I heard him declare. The Voice of the Lobster [*or* The Lobster]. "Lewis Carroll." *Fr.* Alice's Adventures in Wonderland. BoN; SAS; SiTL

'Tis the voice of the [*or* a] sluggard; I heard him complain. The Sluggard. Isaac Watts. CEP; CH; HBV; HBVY; MoShBr; OBEC; OnPP; OTPC; OxBoLi; PoEL-3; TreFS

'Tis the voice of the Wanderer. The Ghost. Stevie Smith. DiM

'Tis the white anemone, fashioned so like the stars of the winter snow. "Owen Meredith." *Fr.* The White Anemone. GN; OTPC

'Tis the White Plum Tree. John Shaw Neilson. BoAV

'Tis the year's [*or* yeares] midnight, and it is the day's [*or* dayes]. A Nocturnal[l] upon St. Lucy's [*or* S. Lucies] Day, Being the Shortest Day. John Donne. AtBAP; BoW; CaAE; EnLP; FaBoEn; GTBS-W; LiTB; LiTG; MaPo; MeLP; MePo; OBS; PoE; PoEL-2; ReaPo; ReIE; SeCV-1; SeEP; TuPP; TwP

'Tis they, of a veritie. Deid Folks' Ferry. Rosamund Marriott Watson. VA

'Tis time, I think, by Wenlock town. Wenlock. A. E. Housman. A Shropshire Lad, XXXIX. BPN; LBBV; PoVP; SeCePo

'Tis Time, My Friend. Pushkin, *tr. fr. Russian.* BoR, *tr. by* C. M. Bowra; TrRV, *tr. by* Babette Deutsch

'Tis time this heart should be unmoved. On This Day I Complete My Thirty-sixth Year [*or* Byron's Latest Verses *or* Hail and Farewell]. Byron. AnFE; BEL; BPN; CoBE; EM-2; EmBrPo; EnL; EnLi-2; EnLit; EnRP; EPN; ERP; EV-4; FiP; GEPC; HBV; LEAP; LH; LPS-1; MaPo; MCCG; OAEP; OnPP; PIR; ViBoPo

'Tis to yourself I speak; you cannot know. Yourself. Jones Very. AA; LBAP; NePA; OxBA; PoEL-4

'Tis told by one whom stormy waters threw. Wordsworth. *Fr.* The Prelude, VI. ImOP

'Tis Too Late for a Coach. *Unknown.* SeCL

'Tis too much, the blind man's tread. October Myth. Innokenti Annensky. BoRS

Tis true (deare Ben:) thy just chastizing hand. To Ben. Jonson. Thomas Carew. MePo

'Tis true, fair Celia, that by thee I live. Against Platonick Love. *Unknown.* OBS

'Tis true. I am fettered. Chains. Patrick Carey. SeCL

'Tis true, I never was in love. A Mock Song. Alexander Brome. SeCL

'Tis true, no lover has that pow'r. The Art of Love. Samuel Butler. *Fr.* Hudibras. FaBoEn

'Tis true, one half of woman's life is hope. Her Horoscope. Mary Ashley Townsend. AA

'Tis true our life is but a long disease. Song. Katherine Philips. ElSeCe

'Tis True That Last Night I Adored Thee. William Gilmore Simms. SPP

'Tis true the beauteous star. A Paradox. Richard Lovelace. Po

'Tis true, the sun is beautiful. Light and Life. Victor Hugo. *Fr.* Les Burgraves. LiA

'Tis true, then why should I repine. In Sickness. Swift. CEP; OBEC

'Tis true, 'tis day; what though it be? Break of Day. John Donne. EG; EnLP; LiTB; LiTG; LiTL; TuPP; TwP

'Tis truth, too much wine's bad; don't blink it. Teetotal? Theognis. GrR

'Tis twelve o'clock! Within my prison dreary. New Year's Eve. F. A. Bartleson. PAP

'Tis Una has hair looped and twisty like horns of the kine. Una Bhan. Robert Farren. JKCP (1955 ed.)

"'Tis very sad," the onion said. The Onion. C. C. Ward. PCH

'Tis weak and worldly to conclude. The Retirement. *Unknown.* OBEC

'Tis well; 'tis something; we may stand. In Memoriam A. H. H., XVIII. Tennyson. BPN; EmBrPo; EnLi-2; EPN; GEPC; ViPo; VLEP

'Tis well, 'tis well with them, say I. All-over Love. Abraham Cowley. *Fr.* The Mistress. LiTL; SeCL

'Tis well you think me truly one of those. To John Keats. Leigh Hunt. PtP

'Tis what they say. The Red Man's Wife. *Unknown, tr. by* Douglas Hyde. GTIV; OnYI; OxBI; SeCePo

'Tis where the road-side rivulet expands. Girls Going to the Fair. William Allingham. IrPN

'Tis wine that inspires. The Excellency of Wine. Roger Boyle, Earl of Orrery. SeCL; SeEP

'Tis with our judgments as our watches. Pope. *Fr.* An Essay on Criticism. ViBoPo

'Tis years since last we met. Her Bright Smile. *Unknown.* SoAmSa

Tisket, a Tasket, A. *Unknown. See* Itiskit, Itaskit.

Tit for Tat. Esther Antin. RIS

Tit for Tat. Walter de la Mare. UTS

Tit for Tat. *Unknown, tr. fr. Danish by* E. M. Smith-Dampier. BoDaBa

Tit-tat-toe,/ My first go. A Baby Verse. *Unknown.* BoTP; OxNR

Tit-Willow. W. S. Gilbert. *See* Suicide's Grave, The.

Titan! to whose immortal eyes. Prometheus. Byron. BPN; EmBrPo; EnRP; EPN

Titania. Thomas Hood. *Fr.* The Plea of the Midsummer Fairies. OBRV

Titania's Bower. Shakespeare. *See* Violet Bank, A.

Titanic, The, *sels.* E. J. Pratt.
Iceberg, The. TwCaPo
Isador and Ida Strauss. TwCaPo
"Out on the water was the same display." PeCV

Titanic, The ("It was on one Monday morning"). *Unknown.* ViBoFo

Titanic, De ("De rich folks 'cided to take a trip"), *with music. Unknown.* AS

Tithonus. Tennyson. BPN; EmBrPo; EnL; EPN; FaBoEn; GEPC; GTBS-D; KN; LiTB; LoBV; NBE; OAEP; PoE; PoEL-5; PoFS; PoVP; ReaPo; TOP; TwCrTr; ViPo; ViPP; VLEP; WHA

Title divine is mine. Emily Dickinson. ViBoPo

Title to Fame. Horace, *tr. fr. Latin by* W. E. Gladstone. Odes, III, 30. RoL

Titles. Justin Richardson. ShBV-3
(What'll Be the Title?) FiBHP

Titmouse, The. Emerson. BLA; IAP; PRWS
Chickadee, *sel.* FaPON; GFA; OTPC (1946 ed.); PCH

Titty cum tawtay. *Unknown.* OxNR

Titus Andronicus, *sel.* Shakespeare.
"Victorius Titus, rue the tears I shed," *fr.* I, i. MotAn

Titus Oates. Dryden. *Fr.* Absalom and Achitophel. NBE
Titus oft vaunts his gentry everywhere. Of Titus. Everard Guilpin. *Fr.* Skialetheia. ReIE; SiCE; TuPP
Titus reads neither prose nor rhyme. The Writer. Hildebrand Jacob. SiTL
Titus, the brave and valorous young gallant. In Titum. Sir John Davies. ReIE; TuPP
Titwillow. W. S. Gilbert. *See* Suicide's Grave, The.
Tityrus to His Fair Phyllis. John Dickenson. *Fr.* The Shepherd's Complaint. ElL
To ——: "All good things have not kept aloof." Tennyson. OBRV
To ——: "Asleep within the deadest hour of night." Robert Nichols. HBMV; MBP
To ——: "Bound for your far-off native shore." Pushkin. *See* Abandoning an Alien Country.
To ——: "Bowers whereat, in dreams, I see, The." Poe. IAP; RO
To ——: "Broken moon lay, The." Alexander Smith. VA
To ——: "I fear thy kisses, gentle maiden." Shelley. *See* I Fear Thy Kisses . . .
To ——? "I have baptized thee Withy, because of thy slender limbs." Richard Dehmel, *tr. fr. German by* Jethro Bithell. AWP
To ——: "I heed not that my earthly lot." Poe. IAP
To ——: "I saw thee on thy bridal day." Poe. IAP
To ——: "I send you here a sort of allegory." Tennyson. The Palace of Art, *introd. poem.* ViPo
(To ——, with the Following Poem.) ViPP
To ——: "Lady—the lyre thou bid'st me take." Jeremiah Joseph Callanan. IrPN
To ——: Music, When Soft Voices Die. Shelley. *See* Music, When Soft Voices Die.
To ——: "O dearer far than light and life are dear." Wordsworth. ERP
To ——: "One word is too often profaned." Shelley. *See* One Word Is Too Often Profaned.
To ——: "Take this kiss upon thy brow!" Poe. *See* Dream within a Dream.
To ——: "They could not shut you out of heaven." Katharine Duncan Morse. HBMV
To ——: "We met but in one giddy dance." Winthrop Mackworth Praed. ERP; HBV
To ——: "When I grow old and my quick blood is chilled." Muriel Stuart. AV
To ——: "When I loved you, I can't but allow." Thomas Moore. *See* When I Loved You.
To ——: "When passion's trance is overpast." Shelley. *See* When Passion's Trance.
To ——: "When the fair one was here, the house was adorned with flowers." Li Po, *tr. fr. Chinese.* WhP
To ——, with the Following Poem. Tennyson. *See* To ——: "I send you here a sort of allegory."
To a Baffled Idealist. J. G. E. Hopkins. JKCP (1926 ed.); MaRV
To a Baked Fish. Carolyn Wells. FiBHP
To a Beautiful but Heartless Coquette. Francisco de Terrazas, *tr. fr. Spanish by* Peter H. Goldsmith. LiTW
To a Beautiful Lady Encountered on the Road. Li Po, *tr. fr. Chinese.* WhP
To a Bee. Robert Southey. OTPC
To a Believer. Marjorie Pickthall. PeCV
To a Bird. Edward Hovell-Thurlow. *See* Heron, The.
To a Bird at Dawn. Richard Le Gallienne. BLA; BMEP
To a Bird on a Downtown Wire. Hilton Ross Greer. BLA
To a Black Dog, Bereaved. Elizabeth J. Coatsworth. PCD
To a Black Greyhound. Julian Grenfell. AlDL; MM; OtMeF
To a Blind Bird. Hubbard Fulton Page. NoCaPo
To a Blockhead. Pope. BOHV
(Epigram: "You beat your pate, and fancy wit will come.") HBV; SiTL
To a Blue Flower. John Shaw Neilson. BoAV
To a Blue Hippopotamus. Ellen de Young Kay. NePoEA
To a Blue Tit. V. H. Friedlaender. BLA
To a Bluebell. Emily Brontë. VLEP
To a Bluebell. Helena Coleman. CPG
To a Book. Elinor Wylie. LiTA
To a Boon Companion. Oliver St. John Gogarty. OBMV
(Boon Companion, The.) OtMeF
To a Boy. *Unknown, tr. fr. Irish by* Frank O'Connor. KiLC
To a Boy-Poet of the Decadence. Sir Owen Seaman. CenHV; FiBHP; LEAP
To a Boy, with a Watch. Thomas Moore. FAOV
To a Bride. Walter Savage Landor. BPN; EmBrPo
To a Bride. Sappho, *tr. fr. Greek.* GrL, *tr. by* Walter Headlam; GrR, *tr. by* Edwin Marion Cox; OxBG, *tr. by* Sir William Marris; WoL, *tr. by* Walter Headlam
(Blest as the Immortal Gods, *tr. by* Ambrose Philips.) LPS-1
(Fragment from [*or* of] Sappho, *tr. by* Ambrose Philips.) EV-3; OBEC
(Ode: "Peer of gods he seemeth to me, the blissful," *tr. by* John Addington Symonds.) GrPo; LiTW
(Ode to Anactoria.) AWP, *tr. by* William Ellery Leonard; LiA, *pr. tr. by* Henry Thornton Wharton
(Peer of the Gods, *tr. by* John Addington Symonds.) EnLi-1
To a Brown Girl. Countee Cullen. TBM
To a Brownie. Pushkin, *tr. fr. Russian by* Oliver Elton. BoRS
To a Buddha Seated on a Lotus. Sarojini Naidu. MM
To a Bull-Dog. J. C. Squire. AlBD; ReTS
To a Butterfly. Lady Flora Hastings. OTPC (1923 ed.)
To a Butterfly ("I've watched you . . ."). Wordsworth. CG; GoTP; HBV; OTPC; PTA-1; SeCeV; SN
("I've watched you now a full half-hour.") EG
To a Butterfly ("Stay near me . . ."). Wordsworth. BPN; EmBrPo; EnRP; ERP; GEPC
To A. C. W. E. Henley.
(Rhymes and Rhythms, XXIII.) POTT
To A. C. M. Richard Middleton. LEAP
To a Cafeteria Rubber-Plant. Philip Wrenn. CAG
To a Caged Grasshopper. Meleager, *tr. fr. Greek by* Walter Leaf. GrR
To a Candle. Walter de la Mare. ChMP; GTBS-D
To a Capricious Friend. Martial. *See* Temperament.
To a Captive Crane. Hamlin Garland. BAP
To a Careful Young Man. John Holmes. CAG
To a Carmelite Postulant. Michael Earls. CAW; JKCP
To a Cat. Ibn Alalaf Alnaharwany, *tr. fr. Arabic by* J. D. Carlyle. PoC
To a Cat. Samuel Hoffenstein. CIV
To a Cat. Keats. FaBoCh; PoC
(Sonnet to Mrs. Reynolds' Cat.) CIV
To a Cat. Fanny Elizabeth Perkins. CIV
To a Cat. Swinburne. CIV; PoC
To a Cat Purring. Florence Small Edsall. CIV
To a Caty-did. Philip Freneau. AA; AmP; AmPP; APW; CoBA; IAP; LHV; SN; TCAP
To a Certain Civilian. Walt Whitman. CoBA; IAP; TCAP
To a Certain Lady, in Her Garden. Sterling A. Brown. CDC
To a Certain Little Boy. Charles Hanson Towne. FAOV
To a Certain Woman. Albert Rice. CDC
To a Chameleon. Marianne Moore. GoYe
To a Cherokee Rose. William Hamilton Hayne. AA
To a Child. Gerda Dalliba. BAP
To a Child. Babette Deutsch. FAOV
To a Child. Robert Herrick. *See* To His Saviour, a Child; a Present by a Child.
To a Child. Charles Kingsley. BoTP
To a Child, *sel.* Longfellow.
"By what astrology of fear or hope." FaBoEn
To a Child. David McCord. AnAmPo
To a Child. George Edgar Montgomery. AA
To a Child. Christopher Morley. BAP; HBMV
To a Child. Norreys Jephson O'Conor. HBMV
To a Child. John Sterling. VA
To a Child. Wordsworth. HBV; HBVY; LPS-1
(In a Child's Album.) GN; PCH
(Written in the Album of a Child, *diff.*) OBRV
To a Child. Judith Wright. BoAV
To a Child before Birth. Norman Nicholson. ChMP
To a Child Dancing in the Wind. W. B. Yeats. AlDL; GTIV
To a Child during Sickness. Leigh Hunt. LPS-1
To a Child Embracing His Mother. Thomas Hood. MOAH
To a Child in Death. Charlotte Mew. MBP; MoAB; MoBrPo; POTE; QS
To a Child of Fancy. Lewis Morris. HBV
To a Child of Noble Birth. Matthew Prior. *See* Letter to the Honourable Lady Miss Margaret Cavendish-Holles-Harley, A.
To a Child of Quality [Five Years Old]. Matthew Prior. AEV; CBOV; CoBE; EiPP EPP; EV-4; ExPo; GN; GTBS-W; HBV; InP; LiA; LiTB; OBEC; OBEV; PoEL-3; SeCeV; TCEP
To a Child Who Inquires. Olga Petrova. BLPA
To a Child with Eyes. Mark Van Doren. PCH
To a Cloistress. Juan de Tassis, *tr. fr. Spanish by* Felicia Dorothea Hemans. CAW
To a Cloud. Manuel Altolaguirre, *tr. fr. Spanish by* Harold Morland. LiTW
To a Common Prostitute. Walt Whitman. AnAmPo; APW; LA; LEAP; MAP; MoAmPo; ViBoPo
To a Comrade in Arms. Alun Lewis. FaBoTw
To a Conscript of 1940. Sir Herbert Read. ChMP; ExPo; LiTB; LiTM; WaP
To a Contemporary Bunkshooter. Carl Sandburg. CoBA; CoV; TCPD; WGRP
To a Coquet Beauty. John Sheffield, Duke of Buckingham and Normanby. CEP
To a Cricket. William Cox Bennett. BoTP; GN; HBV; OTPC
To a Critic of Tennyson. Ambrose Bierce. BAP
To a Crow. Robert Burns Wilson. AA
To a Crucifix. Anna Wickham. MBP; MoBrPo
To a Cyclamen. Walter Savage Landor. BPN; VA
To A. D. W. E. Henley. *See* Blackbird, The.

To a Daisy. John Hartley. VA
To a Daisy. Alice Meynell. BMEP; JKCP; MBP; MoBrPo; PoeT; WGRP
To a Dark Girl. Gwendolyn B. Bennett. BANP; CDC
To a Dead Actress. Luis de Sandoval y Zapata, *tr. fr. Spanish by* Samuel Beckett. AnMP
To a Dead Cockerel. Anyte. *tr. fr. Greek by* F. A. Wright. GrR
To a Dead Cricket. Mnasalcas, *ad. fr. Greek by* Louis Untermeyer. RIS
To a Dead Infant. Philip Francis Little. GTIV
To a Dead Poet (Armando Más Leite). Augusto Frederico Schmidt, *tr. fr. Portuguese by* Elizabeth Selden. BoFr
To a Dead Woman. H. C. Bunner. OBAV
To a Deaf and Dumb Little Girl. Hartley Coleridge. PoEL-4
To a Dear Friend Lately Given Over to Covetousness. Thomas Lodge. *Fr.* A Fig for Momus. SiCE
To a Defeated Saviour. James Wright. NePoEA
To a Dejected Friend. Morton Bryan Wharton. BlG
To a Depraved Lying Woman. Sorley Maclean. NeBP
To a Desolate Friend. William James Dawson. VA
To a Discarded Steel Rail. Maxwell Bodenheim. NP; PFY
To a Distant Friend. Wordsworth. *See* Why Art Thou Silent.
To a Dog. Anna Hempstead Branch. MAP; MoAmPo (1942 ed.)
To a Dog. Stanton A. Coblentz. AlBD
To a Dog. Luis Carlos López, *tr. fr. Spanish by* H. R. Hays. TwSpPo
To a Dog. Josephine Preston Peabody. BLPA; CV; WGRP
To a Dog Dreaming. Lord Dunsany. AlBD
To a Dog, Grown Blind. Mazie V. Caruthers. AlBD
To a Dog Injured in the Street. William Carlos Williams. MoAB; NePoAm; SeCeV
To a Dog's Memory. Louise Imogen Guiney. AnAmPo; LA; OBAV
To a Fair Gentlewoman, False to Her Friend. George Turberville. TuPP
To a Fair Lady Playing with a Snake. Edmund Waller. HoPM
(Of a Fair Lady Playing with a Snake.) PoEL-3
To a Fair Young Lady, Going Out of [the] Town in the Spring. Dryden. *See* Song to a Fair Young Lady . . .
To a Faithless Lover. Robert Greacen. OnYI
To a Faithless Mistress. Asclepiades, *tr. fr. Greek by* Walter Leaf. GrR
To a Famous Painter. John Dyer. *Fr.* Epistle to a Famous Painter. BeR
To a Fat Lady Seen from the Train. Frances Cornford. BLPA; LiTM; MBP; MoBrPo; NeMA; OBMV; OnPP; SiTL; TCPD; TwCV; YT
(To a Lady Seen from the Train.) LBBV; PoeMoYo; PoeT
To a Field-Mouse. Burns. *See* To a Mouse [on Turning Up Her Nest with the Plough, November, 1785.
To a Fish. Leigh Hunt. *See* To Fish.
To a Flirt. Horace. *See* To Pyrrha.
To a Fly. William Oldys. *See* On a Fly Drinking Out of His Cup.
To a Fly. "Peter Pindar." BOHV
To a Foil'd European Revolutionaire, *sel.* Walt Whitman. "Not songs of loyalty alone are these." PoFr
To a Foolish Wise Man. Sir William Watson. (From "Epigrams.") LEAP
To a Fossil Fern. John A. Foote. CAG
To a Fountain. Pierre de Ronsard, *tr. fr. French by* Ralph N. Currey. FoS
To a "Friend." Emil Aarestrup, *tr. fr. Danish by* Charles W. Stork. BoDS
To a Friend. Matthew Arnold. BPN; EM-2; EmBrPo; EnLi-2; EPN; GEPC; OAEP; PoVP; PtP; TCEP; TwCrTr; ViPo; ViPP; VLEP
To a Friend. Maxwell Bodenheim. LEAP
To a Friend. Hartley Coleridge. *See* Friendship.
To a Friend. Grace Strickler Dawson. BLPA; NeHB
To a Friend. Joseph Rodman Drake. IAP
To a Friend. David Gray. EnSW
To a Friend. Charles Gullans. NePoEA
To a Friend. Lionel Johnson. POTE
To a Friend. Boris Pasternak, *tr. fr. Russian by* Babette Deutsch. TrRV
To a Friend. Sir William Watson. PC
To a Friend before Taking a Journey. Katherine Philips. EV-2
To a Friend Bound North after the Rebellion. Ssu-k'ung Shu, *tr. fr. Chinese by* Witter Bynner. BoFr
To a Friend in the Country. Oliver St. John Gogarty. OnYI
To a Friend in the Wilderness, *sel.* A. R. D. Fairburn. "Old friend, dear friend." AnNZ
To a Friend on His Marriage. F. T. Prince. LiTM
To a Friend Parting. Robert Penn Warren. BoFr
To a Friend Recently Married. Struthers Burt. NoCaPo
To a Friend Whose Work Has Come to Nothing. W. B. Yeats. AnFE; AWP; CP; EnLP; GTBS-W; InPo; JAWP; LiTG; LiTM (rev. ed.); MoAB; MoBrPo; NP; OBMV; PC; TCPD; TwP; WBP
To a Gardener. Robert Louis Stevenson. AnEnPo
To a Gentlewoman Objecting to Him His Gray Hairs. Robert Herrick. MyFE
(Age Not to Be Rejected, *sl. diff.*) OBS
To a Giant Sequoia, Fallen and Enshrined in Calaveras County, California. Pearce Young. PtPa
To a Gipsy Child by the Sea-Shore. Matthew Arnold. ViPP
To a Golden-haired Girl in a Louisiana Town. Vachel Lindsay. MAP; MoAmPo; NeMA
To a Golden Heart, Worn round [*or* around] His Neck. Goethe, *tr. fr. German by* Margaret Fuller Ossoli. AWP; JAWP; LiTW; WBP
To a good man of most dear memory. Wordsworth. *Fr.* Written after the Death of Charles Lamb. CoBE
To a Good Physician. William Wycherley. ACP
To a Greek Girl. Austin Dobson. HBV; VA; VLEP
To a Greek Ship in the Port of Dublin. William Bedell Stanford. NeIP
To a Grosbeak in the Garden. Ivan Swift. BLA
To a Happy Warrior. Wilfrid Scawen Blunt. AnEnPo
To a Hedge-Sparrow. *Unknown.* OTPC (1923 ed.)
To a Highland Girl. Wordsworth. BPN; EmBrPo; EnRP; EPN; ERP; GEPC; LoBV; LPS-1
To a Honey Bee. Philip Freneau. *See* On a Honey Bee.
To a Human Skeleton. Richard Armour. WhC
To a Humble Bug. Linda Lyon Van Voorhis. GoYe
To a Humming Bird in a Garden. George Murray. SN; VA
To a Hurt Child. Grace Denio Litchfield. AA; BLP; LBAP; OBAV
To a Husband. Su Wu. *See* To His Wife.
To a Jack Rabbit. S. Omar Barker. IHA
To a Janitor. Ovid, *tr. fr. Latin by* George Howe. Amores, I, 6. RoL
To a Japanese Girl Grieved over the War on China. Belle Chapman Morrill. MaRV
To a Jazz Pianist, Dead. Stewart Atkins. NoCaPo
To a June Breeze. H. C. Bunner. AA
To a Junior Waiter. A. P. Herbert. FiBHP
To a Katydid. James J. Montague. LPS-1
To a King Snake. LeGarde S. Doughty. MuM
To a Kiss. "Peter Pindar." HBV
To a Kitten. Martha Haskell Clark. CIV
To a Kitten. Rena M. Manning. CIV
To A. L.: Persuasions to Love. Thomas Carew. EPS; EV-2
To a Lady. Franklin P. Adams. FiBHP
To a Lady. William Dunbar. BSV; GoBC, *mod. vers. by* Belle Cooper; OBEV
(Sweet Rose of Virtue.) EG
(To a Ladie.) EBSV
(To a Ladye.) OAEP
To a Lady. Sir George Etherege. *See* To a Lady Asking Him How Long He Would Love Her.
To a Lady. John Gay. OBEC; OBEV (new ed.)
To a Lady. John McClure. FR
To a Lady. Thomas William Parsons. AA
To a Lady. John James Piatt. AA
To a Lady. Pope. *See* Of the Characters of Women.
To a Lady. Sir Walter Scott. BPN; BSV
(To a Lady with Flowers from the Roman Wall.) OAEP
To a Lady across the Way. E. B. White. InMe
To a Lady Admiring Herself in a Looking-Glass. Thomas Randolph. EV-2; LPS-1
To a Lady Asking [Him] How Long He Would Love Her. Sir George Etherege. BrBE; CEP; ElSeCe; HBV; LiTL; LO; LoBV; LoPS; OBEV; OBS, *diff. vers.*; SeCL; SeEP; ViBoPo
(Lines to a Lady, Who Asked of Him How Long He Would Love Her.) EG
(To a Lady.) OnPM
To a Lady before Marriage. Thomas Tickell. LPS-1
"In some small hamlet on the lonely plain," *sel.* EnSW
To a Lady Friend. W. H. Davies. MBP; MoBrPo
To a Lady Going Veiled. Gómez Manrique, *tr. fr. Spanish by* Thomas Walsh. AnSpL-1
To a Lady Holding the Floor. Mildred Weston. FiBHP
To a Lady; in a Letter. Earl of Rochester. SeEP
To a Lady; of the Characters of Women. Pope. *Fr.* Moral Essays, Epistle II. OxBoLi
To a Lady on Her Marriage. William Bell. NePoEA
To a Lady on Her Passion for Old China. John Gay. EiPP; FaFP; LiTB; LoBV; PoE; SiTL
To a Lady Playing and Singing in the Morning. Thomas Hardy. TOP
To a Lady Resembling His Mistress. Thomas Carew. ElSeCe
To a Lady Seen from the Train. Frances Cornford. *See* To a Fat Lady Seen from the Train.
To a Lady; She Refusing to Continue a Dispute with Me, and Leaving Me in the Argument. Matthew Prior. BrBE; CEP; EiPP; LiTL; SeCL; WHA
To a Lady Singing a Song of His Own Composing. Edmund Waller. EV-2; ReEn; SeCL; SeEP
To a Lady Sitting before Her Glass. Elijah Fenton. OBEC

To a Lady That Desired I Would Love Her. Thomas Carew. CoEV; LiTL; LoBV; MeLP; MePo; OBS; SeCL; SeCV-1; SeEP
To a Lady to Answer Directly with Yea or Nay. Sir Thomas Wyatt. ElL; PoFS; ReIE; TuPP
("Madame, withouten many words.") EG; EnLoPo; LO; ReEn; SiPS
(To His Lady.) OBSC; SeCePo
To a Lady Troubled by Insomnia. Franklin P. Adams. InMe
To a Lady Who Desired I Would Write Some Verses in the Heroic Style, *sel.* Swift.
"Should a monkey wear a crown." PoFr
To a Lady Who Did Sing Excellently. Lord Herbert of Cherbury. OBS
To a Lady Who Used Cosmetics. Johannes Secundus, *tr. fr. Latin by* F. A. Wright. LaP
To a Lady with a Guitar. Shelley. *See* With a Guitar, to Jane.
To a Lady with Flowers from the Roman Wall. Sir Walter Scott. *See* To a Lady.
To a Lady, with Some Painted Flowers. Anna Letitia Barbauld. DiM; LPS-1
To a Ladye. William Dunbar. *See* To a Lady.
To a land rich in goodly horses. Sophocles. *Fr.* Oedipus at Colonus. GrPo
To a Lark in War-Time. Franz Werfel, *tr. fr. German by* Edith Abercrombie Snow. TrJP
To a Late Comer. Julia C. R. Dorr. AV; LBAP
To a Lily. James Matthew Legaré. AA; AnAmPo; LA; SPP
To a Linnet. Robert Allan. EBSV
To a Linnet in a Cage. Francis Ledwidge. OnYI; TIP
To a Little Girl. Helen Parry Eden. HBV; OTPC (1923 ed.)
To a Little Girl. Amory Hare. MuM
To a Little Girl. Gustav Kobbé. HBV
To a Little Girl Gathering Flowers. Mary Tighe. OTPC (1923 ed.)
To a Little Girl, One Year Old, in a Ruined Fortress. Robert Penn Warren. FiMAP
"It rained toward day. The morning came sad and white," *sel.* MoVE
To a Living Author. *Unknown.* SiTL
To a Lock of Hair. Sir Walter Scott. GTBS; GTBS-D; GTBS-W; GTSE
To a Locomotive in Winter. Walt Whitman. AmPP; InP; MCCG; MoAmPo (1950 ed.); PoE; PoEL-5; PoFS; VOD (1935 ed.)
To a Lofty Beauty, from Her Poor Kinsman. Hartley Coleridge. EV-4; OBVV
To a Lost Love. Stephen Phillips. GTML
To a Lost Spirit. Lord Dunsany. UnW
To a Lost Sweetheart, *sels.* Don Marquis.
"I oft stand in the snow at dawn." FiBHP
"When Whistler's Mother's Picture's frame." FiBHP
To a Louse [On Seeing One on a Lady's Bonnet at Church]. Burns. BLPA; CEP; CoBE; EM-1; EnL; EnLit; EnRP; FaFP; HiLiEn; InvP; LiTB; LiTG; LPS-2; OAEP; PIR; Po; PoE; SeCeV; SiTL; TCEP; TreF; ViBoPo; WoL
As Others See Us, *sel.* MaRV
To a Magnolia Flower in the Garden of the Armenian Convent at Venice. Silas Weir Mitchell. AA; OBAV
To a Maid Demure. Edward Rowland Sill. PR
To a Man on His Horse. F. T. Prince. MoPW
To a Maple Seed. Lloyd Mifflin. AA; ADAH
To a Married Couple That Could Not Agree. Martial, *tr. fr. Latin by* Timothe Kendall. TuPP
To a Marsh Hawk in Spring. Henry David Thoreau. PoEL-4
To a Mate. Roland Robinson. NeLNL
To a Mayflower. William E. Marshall. CaP
To a Medieval Workman, Winchester. Margaret Willy. DiM
To a Military Rifle, 1942. Yvor Winters. WaP
To a Missal of the Thirteenth Century. Austin Dobson. POTT
To a Mistress Dying. Sir William Davenant. GoBC; OBEV; PoD
(Lover and Philosopher.) ACP
(Philosopher and the Lover, The.) ElSeCe; FaBoEn; LO; MePo
To a Mocking Bird. Edwin Osgood Grover. BLA
To a Monkey. Marjory Fleming. *See* Sonnet on a Monkey, A.
To a Mosquito. Bryant. AnNE; LPS-2, *abr.*
To a Moth. Charles Edward Thomas. AA
To a Moth That Drinketh of the Ripe October. Emily Pfeiffer. VA
To a Mother. Sophia Mavroidi Papadaky, *tr. fr. Modern Greek by* Rae Dalven. MoGP
To a Mountain. Henry Clarence Kendall. NeLNL, *abr.*; VA
To a Mountain Daisy [On Turning One Down, with the Plow, in April, 1786]. Burns. ADAH; AnEnPo; ATP; BCEP; BEL; CEP; EBSV; EiPP; EM-1; EnLi-2; EnLit; EnRP; EPP; EV-3; GN, *abr.*; HBV; LiA; LPS-2; MPB; OAEP; OTPC (1923 ed.), *much abr.*; PECK; PIAE; PIR; REAL; SN; TCEP; UnPo (1st ed.); WBLP
To a Mountain Fen. Arne Garborg, *tr. fr. Norwegian by* Charles W. Stork. AnNoLy
To a Mountain Spring. Richard Le Gallienne. CV
To a Mouse [on Turning Her Up in Her Nest with the Plough, November, 1785]. Burns. AnEnPo; AnFE; ATP; BBV (1923 ed.); BCEP; BEL; BLV; BoLiVe; BSV; BTP; CaAE; CBE; CEP; CoBE; EBSV; EiPP; EM-1; EnL; EnLi-2; EnLit; EnRP; EPP; EV-3; FaFP; GoTS; GTBS; GTBS-D; GTBS-W; GTSL; HBV; HBVY; LiTG; LoBV; LPS-2; MCCG; MPB; OAEP; OBEC; OTPC; OuHeWo; PECK; PIR; PoeMoYo; PoFS; PoMa; PreP; PYM; RG; SeCeV; ShBV-2; SN; TCEP; TOP; TreFS; TrGrPo; TyEnPo; WaKn; WHA
(To a Field-Mouse.) GTSE
To a Musician. George Wither. *See* For a Musician.
To a Nation's Hero. Pindar. *See* Strepsiades of Thebes.
To a Neglectful Lover. Nancy Birckhead. PIAE
To a New-born Baby Girl. Grace Hazard Conkling. HBV
To a New-born Child. Cosmo Monkhouse. HBV
To a New Daughter-in-Law. *Unknown.* PoToHe (new ed.)
To a New York Shop-Girl Dressed for Sunday. Anna Hempstead Branch. CV; HBV; LBMV
To a Nightingale. William Drummond of Hawthornden. EBSV; LPS-2; OBS
(To the Nightingale.) EV-2
To a Nightingale. Keats. *See* Ode to a Nightingale.
To a Nose. Francisco de Quevedo y Villegas, *tr. fr. Spanish by* Jean Willard Burnham. AnSpL-1
To a Nun. Mary Terry Gill. PraNu
To a Nun Decorated with the Iron Cross. J. Corson Miller. PraNu
To a Nun of the Good Shepherd. Michael Earls. PraNu
To a Nun-Stigmatist. Sister Mary Thérèse. PraNu
To a Nun Violinist. Sister Mary Louise. PraNu
To A. P. Kern. Pushkin, *tr. fr. Russian.* BoR, *tr. by* C. M. Bowra; WaL, *tr. by* Sir Cecil Kisch
To a Painter. Walter Savage Landor. EmBrPo; RiBV
To a Painter. *Unknown, tr. fr. Greek by* J. M. Edmonds. GrL
To a Pair of Egyptian Slippers. Sir Edwin Arnold. HBV; OBVV
To a Passing Gypsy. Elizabeth Ruhnka. CAG
To a Persian Cat. F. C. W. Hiley. PoC
To a Persistent Phantom. Frank Horne. BANP; CDC
To a Person. Haruo Sato, *tr. fr. Japanese by* Takamichi Ninomiya *and* D. J. Enright. PoLJ
To a Pet Cobra. Roy Campbell. AtBAP
To a Petrel. Cale Young Rice. BLA
To a Phoebe Bird. Witter Bynner. BAP; BLA; CP; HBMV; PoeMoYo; VOD; WhBS; YT
To a Photograph. John Banister Tabb. AmP
To a Photograph. Parker Tyler. NePA
To a Photographer. Berton Braley. LEAP; PoeMoYo; POT; PoTo
To a place of ruined stone we brought you, and sea-reaches. To a Little Girl, One Year Old, in a Ruined Fortress. Robert Penn Warren. FiMAP
To a Plagiarist. Moses ibn Ezra, *tr. fr. Hebrew by* Solomon Solis-Cohen. TrJP
To a Plain Sweetheart. T. A. Daly. JKCP
To a Poet. Walter Conrad Arensberg. AnAmPo; LA
To a Poet. Sister Mary Angelita. GoBC
To a Poet. Carolyn Wells. PoMa
To a Poet a Thousand Years Hence. James Elroy Flecker. BMEP; CaAE; ChTr; HBV; InP; LEAP; MBP; MoBrPo; MoPW; PoRA; POT; PoTo; POTT; ReTS; ShBV-4; TCPD; TrGrPo (1942 ed.); TwCV
To a Poet Breaking Silence. Francis Thompson. EmBrPo; VA
To a Poet Who Has Never Travelled. Charles Causley. POTE (1959 ed.)
To a Poetic Lover. Martial, *tr. fr. Latin by* W. Hay. ALV
To a Polish Mother. Adam Mickiewicz, *tr. fr. Polish.* CAW, *tr. by* Jewell Parish *and* George R. Noyes; LiTW, *tr. by* Watson Kirkconnell
To a Pomeranian Puppy Valued at 2500 Dollars. Louis Untermeyer. AIBD
To a Poor Old Woman. William Carlos Williams. OnPM
To a Portrait. Arthur Symons. VA
To a Portrait of Whistler in the Brooklyn Art Museum. Eleanor Rogers Cox. HBMV; LEAP; SBMV
To a Portrait Painter Who Desired Him to Sit. Po Chü-i, *tr. fr. Chinese by* Arthur Waley. TrCh
To a Post-Office Inkwell. Christopher Morley. InP; LEAP; PoeMoYo
To a Pretty Girl. Israel Zangwill. TrJP
To a Pretty Woman. John Urban Nicholson. PR
To a Primrose. John Clare. GTSE; OTPC (1923 ed.)
(Primrose, The.) BCEP
To a Prince of the Church. Kenneth W. Porter. MaRV
To a Publisher . . . Cut-out. LeRoi Jones. NeAP
To a Recalcitrant Virgin. Asclepiades, *tr. fr. Greek by* L. R. Lind. LiTW

To a Recruiting Sergeant. James Russell Lowell. *See* Letter from Mr. Ezekiel Biglow of Jaalam to the Hon. Joseph T. Buckingham, A.
To a Republican Friend, 1848. Matthew Arnold. EmBrPo; EPN; PoFr; PoVP; ViPP; VLEP, *sl. diff.*
To a Republican Friend, 1848, Continued. Matthew Arnold. EmBrPo; EPN; ViPP; VLEP
(Continued.) PoVP
To a Revolutionist. Harold E. Fey. ChIP
To a Rich Uncultured Woman. Sappho, *tr. fr. Greek by* F. L. Lucas. GrPE
To a River in the South. Sir Henry Newbolt. CH; MM
To a Robin. T. A. Daly. JKCP
To a Roman. J. C. Squire. HBMV
To a Roman Doll. Mahlon Leonard Fisher. MuM
To a Romanticist. Allen Tate. MOAP
To a Rose. Frank Dempster Sherman. AA; LEAP; OBAV
To a Rose. John Banister Tabb. CAW
To a Run-away Pupil. Alcuin, *tr. fr. Latin by* Jack Lindsay. LyMA
To a Sacred Cow. *Unknown, tr. fr. Toda by* W. E. Mashiel. WGRP
To a Scarlatti Passepied. Robert Hillyer. HBMV; OBAV; VOD
To a Scarlet Tanager. Glenn Ward Dresbach. BAP; BLA
To a Schoolmaster. Martial, *tr. fr. Latin by* John Hay. OnPM
To a Sea-Bird. Bret Harte. BLA; EtS; LBAP; SN
To a Seabird. Sir William Watson. VA
To a Sea Eagle. "Hugh MacDiarmid." MoBrPo
To a Sea-Gull. Arthur Symons. BLA; PoVP
To a Sea-Gull in the Steamer's Wake. Daniel Fallström, *tr. fr. Swedish by* Charles W. Stork. AnSL
To a Seamew. Swinburne. BLA; EtS; MBP
To a Shade. W. B. Yeats. AnIL; LiTB; PoE; PoEL-5
To a Shining Falcon. Nikolai Aseyev, *tr. fr. Russian by* Jack Lindsay. RuPo
To a Siamese Cat. Michael Joseph. PoC
To a Silhouette. Hans Hartvig Seedorff Pedersen, *tr. fr. Danish by* Charles W. Stork. BoDS
To a Singer. Shelley. *See* Asia.
To a Sinister Potato. Peter Viereck. OnHM
To a Skeleton. *Unknown.* BLPA; BMEP; LPS-3
To a Skull. Thomas Caulfield Irwin. TIP
"Dumb are the heavens: sphere controlling sphere," *sel.* IrPN
To a Skull. Joshua Henry Jones. BANP
To a Skylark. George Meredith. EnLit
To a Skylark. Shelley. AnFE; AtBAP; ATP; BCEP; BEL; BLA; BLV; BoLiVe; BPN; BTP; CBOV; CBPC; CoBE; DD, *abr.*; EM-2; EmBrPo; EnL; EnLi-2; EnLit; EnRP; EPN; EPP; ERP; EV-4; FaBoBe; FaFP; FaPON, *abr.*; GBV; GePC; GN; GTBS; GTBS-D; GTBS-W; GTSE; GTSL; HBV; HH; HiLiEn; InP; InvP; LEAP; LiTB; LiTG; LoBV; MCCG; MPB; MyFE; NP; OAEP; OBEV; OBRV; OHFP; OTPC; OuHeWo; PFE; PIAE; PIR; PoFS; PTA-1; PYM; REAL; ReaPo; ShBV-4; TCEP; TOP; TreFS; TrGrPo; TVSH; TwHP; TyEnPo; WHA
(Ode to a Skylark.) PECK, *much abr.*
(To the Skylark.) LPS-2
Our Sweetest Songs ("We look before and after"), *sel.* MaRV
To a Skylark ("Ethereal minstrel!"). Wordsworth. BEL; BLA; BLV; BoLiVe; BPN; EM-2; EmBrPo; EnLi-2; EnLit; EnRP; EPN; EPP; ERP; EV-3; GEPC; HBV; HBVY; OAEP; PIAE; REAL; TCEP; TrGrPo
(To the Skylark.) FaFP; GTBS; GTBS-D; GTBS-W; GTSE; GTSL; LPS-2; PIR
To a Skylark ("Up with me!"). Wordsworth. BEL; BLA; BPN; DD; EM-2; EmBrPo; GEPC; HBV; MCCG; REAL; SN; TCEP; TOP
To a Skylark, Singing above Barnhill Poorhouse, Glasgow. Roger Quin. EBSV
To a Sleeping Child. Arthur Hugh Clough. *See* Sleeping Child, A.
To a Slow Walker and Quick Eater. Gotthold Ephraim Lessing. BOHV
To a Small Boy Standing on My Shoes While I Am Wearing Them. Ogden Nash. ALV; FiBHP
To a Small Boy Who Died at Diepkloof Reformatory. Alan Paton. BoSA
To a Snail. Marianne Moore. FaBoMo; OnPM
To a Snail in the Cemetery. Sara Henderson Hay. DDA
To a Snowdrop. Wordsworth. BPN; EmBrPo
To a Snowflake. Francis Thompson. AlDL; BLV; BMEP; BoLiVe; CP; GoTP; HBV; HiLiEn; ImOP; InP; LEAP; LoBV; MBP; MoAB; MoBrPo; NeMA; PIAE; PIR; PoeMoYo; PoeT; POTT; SeCePo; TCEP; ThWaDe; TrGrPo; TSW; TSWC; TVSH; VLEP; VOD (1935 ed.)
To a Solitary Sea-Gull. Cale Young Rice. BLA
To a Son and Daughter. Walter Savage Landor. (Lyrics and Epigrams.) ERP
To a Songster. John Banister Tabb. InP
To a Spanish Poet. Stephen Spender. ChMo; OAEP (2d ed.)
To a Sparrow. Francis Ledwidge. BLA; HBMV; TSW; VOD; WhBS
To a Sparrow. Sir Philip Sidney. Astrophel and Stella, LXXXIII. SiPS
To a Spartan Mother. Dioscorides, *tr. fr. Greek by* Robert Allason Furness. GrR
To a Spirit Seen in a Dream. Lord Dunsany. UnW
To a Squirrel at Kyle-na-no. W. B. Yeats. FaPON; ThWaDe
To a Staring Baby in a Perambulator. Nancy Byrd Turner. PC
To a Steam Roller. Marianne Moore. MAP; MoAB; MoAmPo; OxBA
To a Survivor of the Flood. John Gould Fletcher. AnAmPo; LA
To a Swallow Building under Our Eaves. Jane Welsh Carlyle. HBV; OBRV; OTPC (1923 ed.); VA
To a Talkative Guest. Po Chü-i, *tr. fr. Chinese by* Arthur Waley. TrCh
To a Tawny Thrush. Max Eastman. LEAP
To a Texas Primrose. Olive Tilford Dargan. LS
To a Thesaurus. Franklin P. Adams. BOHV; SiTL; WhC
To a Thinker. Robert Frost. PoLFOT; TwHP
To a Thorn Tree Blooming on a City Street. Virginia McCormick. LS
To a Thrush. T. A. Daly. CAW; JKCP; SaFP
To a Town Poet. Lizette Woodworth Reese. AA
To a Traveler. Lionel Johnson. AnEnPo; MBP; MoBrPo; TriL
To a Traveler. Su T'ung-po, *tr. fr. Chinese by* Kenneth Rexroth. HoPM; OnPC
To a Tree in Bloom. Hildegarde Flanner. VOD (1935 ed.)
To a Triumpher. José Maria de Heredia, *tr. fr. French by* Alan Conder. TrFP
To a Troublesome Fly. Thomas MacKellar. SN
To a Usurper. Eugene Field. FAOV
To a Vagabond. Constance Davies Woodrow. CaP; OCL
To a Very Beautiful Lady. Ruthven Todd. NeBP
To a Very Young Gentleman. Bliss Carman. FAOV
To a Very Young Gentleman. Christopher Morley. PoMa
To a Very Young Gentleman at a Dancing-School. Elizabeth Rowe. SeCL; SeEP
To a Very Young Lady. Sir George Etherege. BrBE; CEP; SeCL; ViBoPo
To a Very Young Lady. Sir Charles Sedley. *See* Child and Maiden
To a Very Young Lady. Edmund Waller. LO; OBS; PoFS; SeCL; TrGrPo; ViBoPo
(To My Young Lady, Lucy Sidney.) EV-2; MePo; OAEP; SeEP
("Why came I so untimely forth.") EG
To a Virtuous Young Lady. Milton. EM-1; ES; TOP
To a Waterfowl. Bryant. AA; AmP; AmPP; AnAmPo; AnFE; AnNE; APA; APW; AWP; BAP; BAV; BLA; BLV; BoLiVe; BTP; CG; CH; CoAnAm; CoBA; DD; DDA; EV-4; ExPo; FaBoBe; FaBoEn; FaFP; GN; GTBS; GTBS-D; HBV; HBVY; HiLiAm; HoPM; IAP; InP; LA; LBAP; LEAP; LiTA; LiTG; LPS-2; MaRV; MCCG; MOAP; NeHB; NePA; OBAV; OBRV; OHFP; OQP; OTPC; OxBA; PFE; PG (1945 ed.); PIAE; PIR; Po; PoE; PoEL-4; PoeMoYo; PTA-1; PYM; QP-1; REAL; RiBV; SeCeV; SN; TCAP; TOP; TreF; TrGrPo; TVSH; UnPo (1st ed.); WBLP; WGRP; YT
To a Wild Goose over Decoys. Lew Sarett. BLA; MAP; NP; PoeMoYo; PoTo
To a Wild Rose Found in October. Ednah Proctor Clarke. AA
To a Wind Flower. Madison Cawein. AA; ADAH; HBV; OBAV
To a Withered Rose. John Kendrick Bangs. AA; ADAH
To a Witty Man of Wealth and Quality; Who, after His Dismissal from Court, Said, He Might Justly Complain of It. William Wycherley. SeCV-2
To a Woman. Denis Glover. AnNZ
To a woman that I knew. Her Eyes. John Crowe Ransom. LiTM (rev. ed.); NePA
To a Wood-Violet. John Banister Tabb. HBV
To a Woodbine Tendril. August, Graf von Platen, *tr. fr. German by* Mabel Cotterell. AnGP
To a Writer of the Day. Langdon Elwyn Mitchell. AA
To a Young Artist. Robinson Jeffers. CoBA
To a Young Ass. Samuel Taylor Coleridge. EmBrPo; EnRP; OBEC
To a Young Beauty. W. B. Yeats. ChMo
To a Young Child. Eliza Scudder. AA
To a Young Friend, *br. sel.* Samuel Taylor Coleridge.
"And haply, bason'd in some unsunn'd cleft," *3 ll.* ChER
To a Young Friend. Robert Nathan. NeTW
To a Young Gentle-Woman. Councel Concerning Her Choice. Richard Crashaw. AtBAP; OBS
To a Young Girl. W. B. Yeats. TwP
To a Young Girl Dying. Thomas William Parsons. AA

To a Young Girl Leaving the Hill Country. Arna Bontemps. CDC
To a Young Heir. Samuel Johnson. *See* One-and-twenty.
To a Young Lady. William Cowper. EV-3; GTBS; GTBS-D; GTBS-W; GTSE; GTSL; HBV
(Addressed to a Young Lady.) EiPP; EnRP
(Comparison, A; Addressed to a Young Lady.) LEAP
(Stream, The.) LiTL; LO
(Sweet Stream, That Winds.) LPS-1
To a Young Lady. Pope. *See* Epistle to Martha Blount.
To a Young Lady. Richard Savage. OBEC
To a Young Lady. Wordsworth. BPN; EmBrPo; EnRP; ERP
("Dear Child of Nature, let them rail!") EG
To a Young Lady on Her Leaving the Town after the Coronation. Pope. *See* Epistle to Martha Blount.
To a Young Lady Swinging Upside Down on a Birch Limb over a Winter-swollen Creek. James H. Koch. GoYe
To a Young Leader of the First World War. Stefan George, *tr. fr. German by* E. B. Ashton. WaaP
To a Young Lover. Amur Mu'izzi, *tr. fr. Persian by* R. A. Nicholson. LiTW
To a Young Poet. Harry M. Meacham. GoYe
To a Young Poet. Edna St. Vincent Millay. CrMA
To a Young Poet Who Killed Himself. Joyce Kilmer. YT
To a Young Priest. Anne Blackwell Payne. MaRV
To a Young Woman on the *World* Staff. Franklin P. Adams. ALV
To a Young Wretch. Robert Frost. NeMA
To Aaron Burr, under Trial for High Treason. Sarah Wentworth Morton. GA; PAH
To Abraham Lincoln. John James Piatt. AA; BlG
(Sonnet in 1862.) LBAH
To Abraham Lincoln ("O Captain, My Captain"). Walt Whitman. *See* O Captain! My Captain!
To accompany the waistcoat. The Eastcoat. Christian Morgenstern. TwGV
To Aenone. Robert Herrick. HBV
(To Oenone.) OBEV
To Age. Walter Savage Landor. BEL; BPN; EmBrPo; EnRP; EPN; ERP; HBV; OQP, *abr.;* QP-1, *abr.;* TreFS; VA
To Ailsa Rock. Keats. BPN; EnRP; ES
To Aladore, to Aladore. Song of the Children in Paladore. Sir Henry Newbolt. MM
To Alcestis. Euripides, *tr. fr. Greek by* Richard Aldington. *Fr.* Alcestis. OxBG
(Praise of a Heroine, *tr. by* Gilbert Murray.) GrR
To Alexander Griboyedow, *sel.* Wilhelm Küchelbecker, *tr. fr. Russian.*
"Oh, when I reach the shores of misty Lethe." BoFr
To Alfred Tennyson. Robert Stephen Hawker. VA
To Alison Cunningham. Robert Louis Stevenson. PoVP
To All Angels and Saints. George Herbert. SeCV-1
To all men thou dost slander me. Epigram. Bernard de la Monnoye. TrFP
To All People. Clement Wood. SDH
To all the heart-wounds touched afresh this day. Memorial Day. Emerette H. Dunning. OQP; PSO; QP-1
To all the humble beasts there be. Prayer for Gentleness to All Creatures. John Galsworthy. BoTP
To all the spirits of Love that wander by. Supreme Surrender. Dante Gabriel Rossetti. The House of Life, VII. EtPaEn; POTT; PoVP; ViPo
To all those happy blessings which ye have. Amoretti, LXVI. Spenser. PeBoSo
To all to whom it now means nothing. Death of a Teacher. L. F. Gerlach. PtPa
To all who hope for Freedom's gleam. Our Country. Anna Louise Strong. MaRV; OQP; QP-2
To all you Ladies now at Bath. Farewell to Bath. Lady Mary Wortley Montagu. CEP
To all you ladies now at land. Song [*or* Written at Sea, in the First Dutch War]. Charles Sackville. BEL; CEP; CoMu; EnLi-1 (1949 ed.); EnLoPo; EPS (1942 ed.); EV-3; HBV; LEAP; LiTG; OBEV; OBS; SeCL; SeCV-2; SeEP; SG; SiTL; TOP
To all young men that love to wooe. To Chuse a Friend, but Never Marry. *At. to* the Earl of Rochester. CoMu
To Allegra Florence in Heaven. Thomas Holley Chivers. APW; SPP
To Althea from Prison. Richard Lovelace. AEV; AnEnPo; AnFE; ATP; AWP; BCEP; BEL; BLPA; BLV; BTP; CaAE; CBOV, *abr.;* CoBE; ElSeCe; EM-1; EnL; EnLi-1; EnLit; EPP; EPS; EV-2; FaBoBe; FaBoEn; GTBS; GTBS-D; GTBS-W; GTSE; GTSL; HBV; InPo; JAWP; LEAP; LiTB; LiTG; LiTL; LoBV; LPS-1; MCCG; MeLP; MePo; NeHB; OAEP; OBEV; OBS; OuHeWo; PC; PCD; PG (1945 ed.); PIAE; PIR; PoE; PoFS; PoRA; PreP; SeCeV; SeCL; SeCV-1; SeEP; TCEP; TOP; TreF; TrGrPo; TVSH; TwHP; TyEnPo; ViBoPo; WBP; WHA
(From Prison.) LH
(Song.) ReEn
"Stone walls do not a prison make," *1 st.* CBE; MaRV; OQP; QP-2
To Amanda. James Thomson. BSV
To Amanda Walking in the Garden. Nicholas Hookes. SeCL
To Amarantha, That She Would Dishevel Her Hair. Richard Lovelace. BLV; HBV; HoPM; LO; MePo; OBEV; PoFS; SeCV-1, *longer vers.;* TrGrPo
(To Amarantha.) LiTL; ViBoPo
(To Amarantha, to Dishevel Her Hair.) EG
To America. Alfred Austin. GN; HBV; PECK; POT; PoTo
(Britannia to Columbia.) PAH
(Voice from the West, A.) TVSH
To America. Richard Garnett. VA
To America, on Her First Sons Fallen in the Great War. E. M. Walker. PAH
To Amine. James Clarence Mangan. OBEV (new ed.); OBVV
To Amoret. Edmund Waller. ElSeCe; EnLoPo; SeCV-1
To Amoret Gone from Him. Henry Vaughan. MeLP; OBS
To an Acquaintance. *Unknown.* FaFP; SiTL
To an Alaskan Glacier. Charles Keeler. SN
To an Ambitious Friend ("Quid bellicosus"). Horace, *tr. fr. Latin by* Matthew Arnold. Odes, II, 11. AWP
To an Andalusian Fan. J. Rodríguez la Orden, *tr. fr. Spanish by* Thomas Walsh. OnPM
To an Anti-poetical Priest. Giolla Brighde MacNamee, *tr. fr. Middle Irish by* the Earl of Longford. AnIV
To an Araucaria. Salvador Díaz Mirón, *tr. fr. Spanish by* Samuel Beckett. AnMP
To an Artful Theatre Manager. Lorenzo da Ponte, *tr. fr. Italian by* John Mazzinghi. *Fr.* Il Capriccio Dramatico. TrJP
To an Athlete Dying Young. A. E. Housman. A Shropshire Lad, XIX. ATP; BEL; BoLiVe; BPN; ChMo; CMP; CoBE; EmBrPo; EnL; EnLi-2; ExPo; GTBS-W; InP; LiTB; LiTG; LiTM (rev. ed.); MaC; MaPo; MBP; MoAB; MoBrPo; NeMA; OAEP (2d ed.); Po; PoEL-5; PoFS; PoMa; PoRA; POTT; PoVP; PreP; ReaPo; RiBV; SeCeV; TreF; TrGrPo; TriL; TwP; UnPo; ViP; ViPo; VLEP; WHA
To an Attic Marble. Edna Worthley Underwood. VOD (1935 ed.)
To an Author. Philip Freneau. AmPP; CoBA; CoV; OxBA
To an Autumn Leaf. Albert Mathews. AA
To an Avenue Sport. Helen Johnson Collins. PoNe
To an Aviator. Daniel Whitehead Hicky. MoSiPe
To an Early Plum. Hsieh Hsieh, *tr. fr. Chinese by* Henry H. Hart. PoHN
To an Early Primrose. Henry Kirke White. HBV; OBRV; OTPC (1923 ed.)
(Early Primrose, The.) LPS-2
To an ebbing tide, all sail apeak. A Song of the Hatteras Whale. *Unknown.* EtS
To an Egyptian Boy. H. W. Berry. WhC
To an Egyptian Mummy. Donald Parson. MuM
To an Enchantress. Alice Brown. CIV
To an Enemy. Maxwell Bodenheim. NP; TrJP
To an Enemy. E. J. Pratt. MaRV; QS
To an English Setter. Thomas Walsh. PFY
To an Icicle. Blanche Taylor Dickinson. CDC
To an Imperilled Traveller. Nathan Haskell Dole. AA
To an Importunate Host. *Unknown.* BOHV; PA
To an Inconstant [Mistress *or* One]. Sir Robert Ayton. *See* I Loved Thee Once.
To an Independent Preacher. Matthew Arnold. *See* In Harmony with Nature.
To an Indian Skull, *sel.* Alexander McLachlan.
"And art thou come to this at last." CaP
To an Infant Newly Born. Sir William Jones. *See* Baby, The.
To an Infant Sleeping. Richard Chenevix Trench. BOL
To an Insect. Oliver Wendell Holmes. APW; DDA; HBV; HBVY; IAP; LPS-2; OTPC; SN; StaSt; TCAP; TreF
To an Irish Blackbird. James MacAlpine. BLA; HBMV; HBVY
To an Irish Setter Pup. "Campaspe." AlBD
To an Isle in the Water. W. B. Yeats. AWP; JAWP; WBP
To an Oak Tree. Sir Walter Scott. BHV
To an Obscure Poet Who Lives on My Hearth. Charles Lotin Hildreth. AA
To an Old Danish Song-Book. Longfellow. OBVV
To an Old Farmhouse. Edna Jaques. DDA
To an Old Fraud. Martial, *tr. fr. Latin by* L. R. Lind. LiTW
("On your bald, dirty head you wear.") LaP
To an Old Friend. Arthur Davison Ficke. LEAP
To an Old Lady. William Empson. AtBAP; CoBMV; CoEV; FaBoTw; MoAB; MoPW
To an Old Tenor. Oliver St. John Gogarty. WhC
To an Old Tune. William Alexander Percy. HBMV
To an Old Venetian Wine-Glass. Lloyd Mifflin. AA
To an open house in the evening. Home at Last. G. K. Chesterton. OQP; QP-1; WGRP

To an Oriole. Edgar Fawcett. BLA; HBV; LBAP; LEAP; OTPC; SN; WhBS
(Oriole.) GoTP
To an Unborn Pauper Child. Thomas Hardy. CoBMV; LiTB; PoLFOT; ReMP; ViBoPo
To an Uncultivated Woman. Sappho, tr. fr. Greek by C. T. Murphy. GrL
To an Ungentle Critic. Robert Graves. HBMV; InMe
To an Ungrateful Friend. Tasso, tr. fr. Italian. BoFr
To an Unknown Neighbor at the Circus. Rosemary Benét. InMe
To an Unknown Poet. Countee Cullen. BAP
To an Upland Plover. Percy MacKaye. BLA
To Anacreon. Antipater of Sidon, tr. fr. Greek by Thomas Moore. GrPo
To and Fro about the City. John Drinkwater. MaRV; StJW
To-and-Fro of Saint Theresa. Alfonso Reyes, tr. fr. Spanish by Samuel Beckett. AnMP
To Andrew Lang. Robert Louis Stevenson. POTT; PoVP
To Angélique, sel. Heine, tr. fr. German by Emma Lazarus. This Mad Carnival of Loving. TrJP
To Anne. Clément Marot, tr. fr. French by Louisa S. Costello. OnPM; WoL
To Anne. Sir William Stirling Maxwell. HBV
To Anthea ("Bid me to live"). Robert Herrick. See To Anthea Who May Command Him Anything.
To Anthea ("If dear Anthea"). Robert Herrick. OBS; SeEP
To Anthea ("Now is the Time"). Robert Herrick. NBE; OAEP; OBS; PoEL-3; SeEP
To Anthea Who May Command Him Anything. Robert Herrick. BLV; BoLiVe; CaAE; CoBE; ElSeCe; EM-1; EnLit; EPS; EV-2; GTBS-D; GTBS-W; HBV; LEAP; LH; LoBV; NeHB; PIAE; ReEn; SeCL; SeCV-1; SeEP; TOP; TrGrPo; TwHP; TyEnPo; ViBoPo
(To Anthea.) GTBS; GTSE; GTSL; OAEP; OBEV; OBS
To Anthea, Who May Command Him Anything (New Style). Alfred Cochrane. HBV
To Any Member of My Generation. George Barker. LiTM (rev. ed.); ViBoPo (1958 ed.); WaP
To Any Reader. Robert Louis Stevenson. MOB
To Anyone. Witter Bynner. SBMV
To Aphrodite. Sappho. See Ode to Aphrodite.
To Aphrodite; with a Mirror. Aline Kilmer. HBMV
To Apollo. Callimachus, tr. fr. Greek by Arthur S. Way. GrL
To Apollo. Unknown, tr. fr. Greek by Jack Lindsay. Fr. Homeric Hymns. OxBG
To Apollo and the Muses. Terpander, tr. fr. Greek by C. M. Bowra. OxBG
To Aratus. Callimachus, tr. fr. Greek by R. A. Furness. OxBG
To Arcady. Charles Buxton Going. HBV; LBAP; PR
To Archaeanassa, on whose furrow'd brow. On Archaeanassa. Plato. AWP
To Archbishop Stepinac. Sister Mary Eulalia. JKCP (1955 ed.)
To Archinus. Callimachus, tr. fr. Greek by F. A. Wright. AWP
To Argos. Lawrence Durrell. MoPo
To Aristius Fuscus. Horace. See Integer Vitae.
To Aristophanes. Plato, tr. fr. Greek by Humbert Wolfe. GrR
("Graces, seeking for a shrine, The," tr. by Charles Merivale.) GrPo
(On Aristophanes, tr. by Lord Neaves.) OnPM
To Arms. Park Benjamin. PAH
To arms, to arms! my jolly grenadiers! The Song of Braddock's Men. Unknown. MC; PAH
To Arolilia, sel. Herbert Trench.
"Ay, since beyond these walls no heavens there be." LO
To Artemis. Anacreon, tr. fr. Greek by T. F. Higham. GrL; OxBG
To Ashtaroth and Bel. Saul Tchernichowsky, tr. fr. Hebrew by L. V. Snowman. TrJP
To Ask for All Thy Love. Unknown. EIL
To Ask Our Lady's Patronage for a Book on Columbus. Thomas D'Arcy McGee. JKCP
To Ask the Hard Question Is Simple. W. H. Auden. ChMo
To Aster. Plato. See Morning and Evening Star.
To Astraea. Sir John Davies. Fr. Hymns of Astraea. SiCE
To Atalanta. Dorothy Dow. HBMV
To Athena. Alcaeus, tr. fr. Greek by T. F. Higham. OxBG
To Athena. Unknown, tr. fr. Greek by T. F. Higham. OxBG
To Athens. Pindar, tr. fr. Greek. GrR, tr. by Lionel W. Lyde; OxBG, tr. by Arthur S. Way
To Atthis. Sappho, tr. fr. Greek by C. M. Bowra. GrL; OxBG
To Augusta. Byron. See Epistle to Augusta.
To Augustus. Pope. See First Epistle of the Second Book of Horace, The.
To Aurora. Earl of Stirling. Aurora, Sonnet XXXIII. EBSV; FaFP; GTBS; GTBS-D; GTBS-W; GTSE; GTSL

("Oh, if thou knew'st how thou thyself dost harm.") EIL; EV-2
(Two in One.) ES
To Ausonius. Paulinus of Nola, tr. fr. Latin by Helen Waddell. LaP; LiA
To Austin Dobson. Sir Edmund Gosse. LEAP
To Autumn. Keats. AEV; AnEnPo; AnFE; AtBAP; ATP; AWP; BCEP; BEL; BoTP; BPN; CaAE; CBOV; CBPC; CH; ChER; CoBE; CoEV; DD; EmBrPo; EM-2; EnL; EnLi-2; EnLP; EnRP; EPN; EPP; ERP; FaBoEn; FiP; GePC; GoTP; HBV; HBVY; InPo; InvP; JAWP; LEAP; LiTB; LiTG; MaPo; MyFE; OAEP; OBEV; OBRV; OuHeWo; Po; PoE; PoEL-4; PoeMoYo; PoFS; ReaPo; SeCeV; ShBV-3; TCEP; TOP; TreFS; TVSH; TwHP; TwP; TyEnPo; UnPo; ViBoPo; WBP; WHA
(Ode to Autumn.) BLV; BoLiVe; CBE; EnLit; EV-4; ExPo; GTBS; GTBS-D; GTBS-W; GTSE; GTSL; LoBV; MCCG; PIAE; SN; TOAH; TrGrPo
("Season of mists and mellow fruitfulness.") EG
To Avisa. At. to Henry Willoby. Fr. Willobie His Avisa. EIL
To awake when dawn is breaking. "Anna Akhmatova," tr. fr. Russian by C. M. Bowra. BoRS
To B. R. Haydon. Wordsworth. BPN; EM-2; EmBrPo
To Baby. Kate Greenaway. MPB
To banish your shape from my mind. Exorcism. Oliver St. John Gogarty. AnIL
To Barbary I Have Not Sailed. Eleanor Rogers Cox. TBM
To Be. Manuel Gutiérrez Nájera, tr. fr. Spanish by Samuel Beckett. AnMP
To Be. Unknown, at. to Lao-tzu, tr. fr. Chinese by Witter Bynner. Fr. Tao Teh King. OnPM
To Be a Jew in the Twentieth Century. Muriel Rukeyser. Fr. Letter to the Front. TrJP
To be a Negro in a day like this. At the Closed Gate of Justice. James David Corrothers. BANP
To Be a Nurse. A. H. Lawrence. PoToHe (new ed.)
To be a poet and not know the trade. Sanctity. Patrick Kavanagh. FaBoTw
To be a poet is to be vanquished. Ars Poetica. Victor van Vriesland. TrJP
To be a stranger in a strange land. Thinking of My Brother in Shantung on the Ninth Day of the Ninth Moon. Wang Wei. WhP
To be a sweetness more desired than Spring. True Woman, 1. Dante Gabriel Rossetti. The House of Life, LVI. BPN; EmBrPo; EPN; POTT; PoVP; ViPo; ViPP
To be able to see every side of every question. Editor Whedon. Edgar Lee Masters. Fr. Spoon River Anthology. CrMA; NP; OxBA
To be alive in such an age! To-Day [or In Such an Age]. Angela Morgan. BLPA; MaRV; OQP; QP-1
To be an orphan. The Orphan. Unknown. TrCh
To Be and Not to Be. Unknown, tr. fr. Greek by Robert Guthrie MacGregor. OnPM
To Be Answered in Our Next Issue. Unknown. WaKn
To Be Black, to Be Lost. Hannah Kahn. GoYe
To be brave is not enough. The Hero. W. J. Turner. SoV
To Be Carved on a Stone. W. B. Yeats. MM
To Be Continued. Julian Street and James Montgomery Flagg. See Said Opie Read.
To Be Etched in Silver. Carolyn Wilson Link. MuM
To be forever young. Immortality. Frank Horne. BANP
To-be-forgotten, The. Thomas Hardy. PoVP
To be Himself a star most bright. Childhood. John Erskine. MaRV
To be honest, to be kind. My Task. Robert Louis Stevenson. BLP; MaRV
To be in any form, what is that? Song of Myself, XXVII. Walt Whitman. CoV
To Be or Not to Be. Shakespeare. Fr. Hamlet, III, i. EV-1; FaFP; FiP; GTBS-W; HoPM; LiA; LiTB; LiTG; PIR; TrGrPo; WHA
(From "Hamlet.") LEAP
(Hamlet Contemplates Death.) MaRV
(Hamlet Contemplates Suicide.) TreF
(Hamlet's Soliloquy.) BCEP; NeHB; PYM; WBLP
(Soliloquy from "Hamlet.") OHFP; OQP; QP-1
(Soliloquy on Death.) LPS-1
("To be, or not to be, that is the question.") AtBAP
To Be or Not to Be. Spenser. See Despair.
To Be or Not to Be. Unknown. AIDL; BOHV; FaFP; LiTM; MoShBr; SiTL
(I Sometimes Think.) GoTP
To Be Said at the Seder. Karl Wolfskehl, tr. fr. German by Carol North Valhope and Ernst Morwitz. TrJP
To Be Said to Baby's Fingers ("Peedy, Peedy; Pally, Ludy"). Unknown. SAS
To Be Said to Baby's Fingers ("This little fellow, we call him a thumb"). Unknown, tr. fr. German. SAS
To Be Sung on the Water. Louise Bogan. MoVE
To be unloved brings sweet relief. Lovers. Mary Fullerton. BoAV
To Beachey, 1912. Carl Sandburg. TiPo

To bear, to nurse, to rear. Seven Times Six. Jean Ingelow. *Fr.* Songs of Seven. GBV (1922 ed.); HBV; LPS-1; MOAH
To beast's cry in its forest lair. Echo. Pushkin. BoRS
To Beatrice on All Saints' Day. Dante. *See* Sonnet: Of Beatrice de Portinari on All Saints' Day.
To Beauty. Baudelaire, *tr. fr. French by* Frances Winwar. EnLi-2
To Becky in France. John Arey. LO
"To bed, to bed," says Sleepy-Head. *See* Come, let's to bed.
To Begin the Day. *Unknown. See* Moment in the Morning, A.
To begin with she wouldn't have fallen in. Our Silly Little Sister. Dorothy Aldis. FaPON
To Bellerie Spring. Pierre de Ronsard, *tr. fr. French by* Alan Conder. TrFP
To Ben Jonson. Thomas Carew. MePo
To Ben Jonson. Robert Herrick. *See* Ode for Ben Jonson, An.
To Benjamin West. Washington Allston. AnAmPo; LA
To Bethlehem town in the long ago. Three Wise Kings. William E. Brooks. ChIP; PGD
To Bethlehem's silly shed, methinks I see. The Bee. Henry Hawkins. ACP
"To Bethlem did they go, the shepherds three." Masters, in This Hall. William Morris. AnEC; ChTr; COAH
To Betsey-Jane, on Her Desiring to Go Incontinently to Heaven. Helen Parry Eden. HBMV
To Betty. "E. G. B." PCH
To Björnstjerne Björnson, on His Seventieth Birthday. Knut Hamsun, *tr. fr. Norwegian by* Charles W. Stork. AnNoLy
To Bliss God Brings Us, All and Some. *Unknown.* AnEC (2 vers.)
To Blossoms. Robert Herrick. CBOV; EG; EM-1; EV-2; GTBS; GTBS-D; GTBS-W; GTSE; GTSL; HBV; LoBV; LPS-2; OBEV; OBS; PYM; SeCL; SeCV-1; SeEP; UnPo (1st ed.)
To Bolívar. Rafael Pombo, *tr. fr. Spanish by* Alice Stone Blackwell. PoFr
To Borglum's Seated Statue of Abraham Lincoln. Charlotte B. Jordan. OHIP
To Boston. John Collins Bossidy. *See* Boston Toast, A.
To Bran around his coracle the billows crawl the crystal sea. The Sea-God's Song to Bran. *Unknown, tr. by* Howard Mumford Jones. LiTW
To Bran in his coracle it seems. The Sea-God's Address to Bran. *Unknown, tr. by* Kuno Meyer. OnYI
To Brander Matthews. Austin Dobson. *See* In Vain Today.
To brave and to know the unknown. The Unknown. John Davidson. MBP; MoBrPo
To break bolt and bar. Christmas Amnesty. Edith Lovejoy Pierce. PGD
To break the stillness of the hour. At Evening. Dora Wilcox. BoAu
To bring a smile once more to John Baptist's lips. Salome. Guillaume Apollinaire. AnFP
To Bring the Dead to Life. Robert Graves. FaBoMo
To bring yourself to be happy. Martial, *tr. fr. Latin by* Gilbert Highet. Epigrams, X, 47. LaP
To Britain—after War ("Well hast thou stood, my country"). Sir Walter Scott. *Fr.* The Field of Waterloo: Conclusion. ShGoBo
To Brooklyn Bridge. Hart Crane. *Fr.* The Bridge. AmPP; ChMo; CoBMV; CrMA; ExPo; FaBoEn; GTBS-W; LiTA; LiTM; MoAB; MoAmPo (1950 ed.); MoPo; NePA; OxBA; PoE; ReMP; SeCeV
(Proem: To Brooklyn Bridge.) AmP; CoV
To Browning, the Music Master. Robert Haven Schauffler. BAP
To build a life that's clean, upright, secure. Youth's Prayer. George W. Wiseman. PraP
To build the trout a crystal stair. The Whole Duty of Berkshire Brooks. Hilda Conkling. HBMV; HBVY; NLK; OBAV; PoTo
To Butterfly. William Alexander Percy. HBMV; LS
To buy, or not to buy; that is the question. Investor's Soliloquy. Kenneth Ward. FaFP; SiTL
To Byron. Keats. PtP
To Byron. Shelley. PtP
To C. L. M. John Masefield. POTE
To C. T. C. Joseph Bennett. LiTM (rev. ed.)
To Calista. Charles Cotton. Lo; NBE
To Campbell. Thomas Moore. LPS-3
To Cassandra. Pierre de Ronsard, *tr. fr. French.* FoS, *tr. by* Ralph N. Currey; TrFP, *tr. by* Alan Conder
To Castara: Of the Knowledge of Love. William Habington. *Fr.* Castara, II. EV-2
To Castara Praying. William Habington. *Fr.* Castara, I. MeRV
To Castara: The Reward of Innocent Love. William Habington. *Fr.* Castara, II. EV-2
(Reward of Innocent Love, The.) ACP
(To Castara.) LoBV
To Castara, upon Beauty. William Habington. *Fr.* Castara, II. CoBE
To Castor and Pollux. Alcaeus, *tr. fr. Greek by* Walter Petersen. GrR
To catch some fragment from her hands. Beauty. Kenneth Slade Alling. HBMV
To Catherine Wordsworth 1808–1812. Wordsworth. *See* Surprised by Joy—Impatient as the Wind.
To Cattraeth's vale in glittering row. Aneirin, *tr. fr. Welsh by* Thomas Gray. *Fr.* Gododdin. PrWP
To cause accord or to agree. Sir Thomas Wyatt. MaPo; SiPS
To Celia, *sels.* Witter Bynner.
Consummation. NP
During a Chorale by César Franck. AnAmPo; HBMV; LA; NP
Night. LoPo; LoPS; NP
Songs Ascending. HBV; LoPS; NP
To Celia. Charles Cotton. EV-2; HBV
(To Coelia.) OBEV
To Celia ("Come my Celia, let us prove"). Ben Jonson. *See* Come, My Celia, Let Us Prove.
To Celia ("Drink to me only with thine eyes"). Ben Jonson. AEV; ALV; AnFE; ATP; BCEP; BLV; BoLiVe; BTP; CaAE; CBOV; ElSeCe; EM-1; EnLi-1; EnLit; EnLoPo; EtPaEn; FaBoBe; FaBoEn; FaFP; GTBS; GTBS-D; GTBS-W; GTSE; GTSL; HBV; LiTB; LiTG; MCCG; NeHB; OBEV; OBS; OTPC (1946 ed.); OuHeWo; PFE; PG; PIR; PoeMoYo; PreP; ReEn; RiBV; SeCeV; ShBV-3; SiTL; TCEP; TrGrPo; ViBoPo; WHA
(Drink to Me Only with Thine Eyes.) EG; HiLiEn; LiTL; LPS-1; OlF; ReaPo
(From "The Forest.") LEAP
(Song to Celia.) AtBAP; AWP; BEL; CoBE; ElL; EnL; EPP; EPS; EV-2; InP; InPo; JAWP; LiA; LoPo; PIAE; PoE; PoEL-2; PoFS; ReIE; SeCV-1; SeEP; TOP; TreF; TuPP; TyEnPo; WBP
(To Celia: Song.) MaPo
(Two Songs to Celia.) TwHP
To Celia ("Kiss me, sweet; the wary lover"). Ben Jonson. AWP; JAWP; LoBV; LoPS, *sl. abr.;* WBP
("Kiss me, sweet; the wary lover.") LO
(Song: "Kiss me, sweet . . .") LiTL
(Song to Celia.) ElL; ElSeCe
(To the Same.) SeCV-1
To Celia ("I spend my sad life in sighs and in cries"). Daniel Kenrick. SeCL
To Celia. Sir Charles Sedley. AWP; CaAE; EPP; HBV; JAWP; LiTL; OBEV; SeCl; TOP; WBP
("Not, Celia, that I juster am.") EnLi-1 (1949 ed.); GTBS-D; GTBS-W; LO
(Song: "Not, Celia, that I juster am.") ElSeCe; EPS (1942 ed.); FaBoEn; GTBS; GTSE; GTSL; LoPS; SeEP; ViBoPo
(Song to Celia.) OBS; SeCePo
To Celia ("When, Celia, I intend to flatter you"). *Unknown. See* When, Celia, I Intend.
To Celia Pleading Want of Merit. Thomas Stanley. *See* To One That Pleaded Her Own Want of Merit.
To Celio. Sister Juana Inés de la Cruz, *tr. fr. Spanish by* Pauline Cook. LiTW
To Censorious Courtling. Ben Jonson. ReIE
To Ceres. Joachim du Bellay, *tr. fr. French by* Alan Conder. TrFP
To Cerinthus: "At last comes such a love that gossip that I conceal it." Sulpicia, *tr. fr. Latin by* Hubert Creekmore. LaP
To Cerinthus: "Have you no tender thoughts, Cerinthus, for your sweetheart." Sulpicia, *tr. fr. Latin by* Hubert Creekmore. LaP
To Cerinthus: "I thank you indeed that, sure of me, you assume such license." Sulpicia, *tr. fr. Latin by* Hubert Creekmore. LaP
To Cerinthus: "May I be, dear love, no more a caution so glowing." Sulpicia, *tr. fr. Latin by* Hubert Creekmore. LaP
To Cerinthus: "My hateful birthday is coming, and dismally I must spend it." Sulpicia, *tr. fr. Latin by* Hubert Creekmore. LaP
To Certain Men of Science. Kimball Flaccus. CAG
To Chaadayev. Pushkin, *tr. fr. Russian by* Babette Deutsch. TrRV
To Charles Cowden Clarke. Keats. *See* Epistle to Charles Cowden Clarke.
To Charlotte Corday. Sir Osbert Sitwell. ChMP
To Charlotte Pulteney. Ambrose Philips. GTBS; GTBS-D; GTBS-W; GTSE; GTSL; HBV
(To Miss Charlotte Pulteney in Her Mother's Arms.) CEP; EiPP; EV-3; FaBoEn; OBEC
To Chatterton. Keats. PtP
To Chaucer. Thomas Hoccleve. *Fr.* De Regimine Principum. ACP
To Chaucer. William Morris. *See* Invocation to Chaucer.

To Cheng on His Deposal. Tu Fu, *tr. fr. Chinese by* Chi Hwang Chu *and* Edna Worthley Underwood. OnPM
To Cherry-Blossomes. Robert Herrick. SeCV-1
To Chester Kallman. W. H. Auden. BoFr
To Chicago at Night. Mildred Plew Meigs. HBMV
(Chicago, *last 6 ll.*) BoHiPo
To Children of Girard, Pa. Whittier. PEOR
To Chile's coast we are bound away. Bangidero. *Unknown.* SoAmSa
To China. Leroy F. Jackson. StVeCh (1940 ed.)
To Chi Wu Ch'ien Bound Home after Failing in an Examination. Wang Wei, *tr. fr. Chinese by* Witter Bynner. BoFr
To Chloe. Thomas Burke. NoCaPo
To Chloe. William Cartwright. *See* To Chloe Who Wish'd Herself Young Enough for Me.
To Chloe. Thomas Cheek. SeCL
To Chloe ("Vitas hinnuleo"). Horace, *tr. fr. Latin by* Austin Dobson. Odes, I, 23. AWP; JAWP; WBP; LiTW, *tr. by* Patrick Branwell Brontë; OuHeWo, *tr. by* Goldwin Smith
(Time to Choose a Lover, *tr. by* Patrick Branwell Brontë.) OnPM
To Chloe. "Peter Pindar." LPS-1
To Chloe Jealous [a Better Answer]. Matthew Prior. *See* Answer to Chloe Jealous.
To Chloe, Who Wished Herself Young Enough for Me. William Cartwright. ElSeCe; EV-2; LiTL, *4 sts.*; MePo; OBS; SeCL; SeEP; ViBoPo
(To Chloe.) GTBS-W, *2 sts.*; LiTB, *4 sts.*; PoToHe (new ed.), *1 st.*
(To Chloe Who for His Sake Wished Herself Younger.) BCEP, *2 sts.*; CBOV, *abr.*; HBV; LO, *2 sts.*; LoPS, *2 sts.*; OBEV, *2 sts.*
To Chloris. John Cobbes. SeCL
To Chloris. Charles Cotton. EV-2
To Chloris. Sidney Godolphin. *See* Song: "Cloris, it is not thy disdaine."
To Chloris. Sir Charles Sedley. *See* Child and Maiden.
To Chloris. *At. to* —— Waldren. SeCL
To Christ. John Donne. *See* Hymn to God the Father, A.
To Christ Crucified. *Unknown, at. to* St. John of the Cross *and to* Miguel de Guevara, *tr. fr. Spanish.* AnSpL-1, *tr. by* James Young Gibson; CAW, *tr. by* Thomas Walsh; OnPM, *tr. by* Thomas Walsh; TeCS, *tr. by* Ida Farnell
("I am not moved to love thee, my Lord God," *tr. by* Samuel Beckett.) AnMP
To Christina at Nightfall. Ford Madox Ford. GTML
To Christina Rossetti. Dora Greenwell. VA
To Christina Rossetti. Sir William Watson. InP
To Christopher North. Tennyson. FiBHP
To Chromis. André Chénier, *tr. fr. French by* Alan Conder. TrFP
To Chuck—Concerning a Rendezvous in Siam. Jack Charles. WaKn
To church! I heard a sermon once in spring. God. Harold Monro. *Fr.* Dawn. WGRP
To Chuse a Friend, but Never Marry. *At. to* the Earl of Rochester. CoMu
To Chu Ta. Meng Hao-jan, *tr. fr. Chinese by* Henry H. Hart. BoFr; PoHN
To claim the Arctic came the sun. The Northern Lights. Benjamin Franklin Taylor. LPS-2
To Clair. Samuel Hoffenstein. LEAP
To Clarastella on St. Valentines Day Morning. Robert Heath. OBS
To Clarinda. *Unknown.* SeCL
To Claude McKay. Vivian L. Virtue. PoNe
To Claudia Homonoea. Elinor Wylie. TOP
To Clelia. Matthew Coppinger. SeCL
To Clelia, on the Pulling Down St. Martin's Church, *sel.* Aaron Hill.
Pulling Down St. Martin's Church. BeR
To Cleobulus. Anacreon, *tr. fr. Greek by* T. F. Higham. GrL; OxBG
To climb a hill that hungers for the sky. Fulfillment. Helene Johnson. CDC; PoNE
To Clodius. Everard Guilpin. *Fr.* Skialetheia. ReIE
To Cloe. Thomas Moore, *after the Latin of* Martial. AWP; OuHeWo
To Cloe Jealous [a Better Answer]. Matthew Prior. *See* Answer to Chloe Jealous.
To Cloe Weeping. Matthew Prior. CaAE; CEP; EiPP
To Cloris. Sir Charles Sedley. CEP
("Chloris, I cannot say your eyes.") LO
To clothe the fiery thought. Poet. Emerson. *Fr.* Quatrains. AnNe; APW; OnPM; OxBA
To Cocola Fernández del Castillo. José Martí, *tr. fr. Spanish by* Elizabeth Selden. BoFr
To Coelia. Charles Cotton. *See* To Celia.
To Cole, the Painter, Departing for Europe. Bryant. AmPP (4th ed.); CoV
To Coleridge. Shelley. *See* Oh! There Are Spirits.
To Colin Clout. Anthony Munday. *Fr.* Primaleon of Greece.
CenL; ElSeCe; OAEP; OBSC; TuPP; ViBoPo
(Beauty Bathing.) EV-1; OBEV; PG (1955 ed.)
(Beauty Sat Bathing by a Spring.) EIL
(Colin.) GTBS; GTBS-D; GTBS-W; GTSE; GTSL
To Columbus. John Gould Fletcher. AnAmPo; LA
To come back from the sweet South, to the North. Italia, Io Ti Saluto! Christina Rossetti. LO; OBVV; POTT; VLEP
To communicate with Mars, converse with spirits. The Dry Salvages, V. T. S. Eliot. *Fr.* Four Quartets. AmPP; ATP (1953 ed.)
To Comrade Intellectuals. Valery Bryusov, *tr. fr. Russian by* Jack Lindsay. RuPo
To conclude, I announce what comes after me. So Long! Walt Whitman. AmP; AmPo; PreP; TCAP
To Constantia, Singing. Shelley. EmBrPo; EnRP; ERP
To Cordelia. Joseph Stansbury. BoCaPo (1948 ed.); CaP
(To His Wife.) BAV
To Corinna. John Oldmixon. SeCL
To Corinth. Walter Savage Landor. ERP
To Corydon. Pierre de Ronsard, *tr. fr. French by* Alan Conder. TrFP
To Cotton Mather once there came. Ben Franklin's Head (1728). M. A. De Wolfe Howe. WaKn
To couple is a custom. *Unknown.* EG
To Craske's Statue at Gloucester. Russell Mayo Spear. CAG
To Crinog. *Unknown, tr. fr. Middle Irish by* Kuno Meyer. AnIL; OnYI
To Critics. Walter Learned. AA; AnAmPo; HBV; LA; LEAP
To Crucify the Son. Miguel de Guevara, *tr. fr. Spanish by* Samuel Beckett. AnMP
To Cupid. Francis Davison. OBSC; TuPP
("Love, if a god thou art.") EG
(Madrigal I: To Cupid.) ElSeCe; SiCE
To Cupid. Michael Drayton. EIL
To Cupid. Fulke Greville. Caelica, XII. ES
("Cupid, thou naughty boy, when thou wert loathed.") TuPP
To Cynara. Ernest Dowson. *See* Non Sum Qualis Eram Bonae sub Regno Cynarae.
To Cynthia. George Clifford. *See* My Thoughts Are Winged with Hopes.
To Cynthia. Congreve. NBE
To Cynthia. Sir Francis Kynaston. AEV
To Cynthia, Not to Let Him Read the Ladies' Magazines. P. M. Hubbard. FiBHP
To Cynthia on Concealment of Her Beauty. Sir Francis Kynaston. CaAE; HBV; LiTL; LO; MeLP; MePo; OBS; SeCL; SeEP; ViBoPo
("Do not conceal thy radiant eyes.") EG
To Cynthia, on Her Changing. Sir Francis Kynaston. MePo; SeCL
("Dear Cynthia, though thou bear'st the name.") EG
To Cynthia, on Her Embraces. Sir Francis Kynaston. LO
("If thou a reason dost desire to know.") EG
To Cynthia on His Love after Death. Sir Francis Kynaston. SeEP
To Cynthia Weeping and Not Speaking. Congreve. LiTL; Lo
To Cypros she passed and entered the fragrant temple. Hymn to Aphrodite. *Unknown. Fr.* Homeric Hymns. LiTW
To Cyriack Skinner ("Cyriack, this three years' day"). Milton. AnEnPo; ATP (1935 ed.); BEL; EnLi-1; EPP; EPS; GEPC; PeBoSo; RiBV; TCEP; TOP; TrGrPo
(On His Own Blindness.) LPS-3
(To Mr. Cyriack Skinner upon His Blindness.) OBS
(To the Same [upon His Blindness].) EM-1; ES
To Cyriack Skinner ("Cyriack, whose grandsire on the royal bench"). Milton. EM-1; ES; EV-2; GTBS; GTBS-D; GTBS-W; GTSE; GTSL; OBEV; PC
(Sonnet: "Cyriack, whose grandsire on the royal bench.") LoBV; SeEP
(Sonnet XVIII.) OBS
To Cyrnus. Theognis, *tr. fr. Greek by* John Addington Symonds. GrR
To Daffodils. Austin Dobson. InP
To Daffodils [*or* Daffadills]. Robert Herrick. AnEnPo; AtBAP; AWP; BCEP; BEL; BLV; BoLiVe; CaAE; CBOV; CBPC; CenL; CG; CoBE; CoEV; ElSeCe; EM-1; EnL; EnLi-1; EnLit; EPP; EPS; EV-2; ExPo; FaBoCh; FaBoEn; GBV; GN; GTBS; GTBS-D; GTBS-W; GTSL; HBV; HBVY; InPo; JAWP; LEAP; LiTB; LoBV; MaPo; OAEP; OBEV; OBS; OTPC; OuHeWo; PCN; PIAE; PoE; PoEL-3; PoFS; PoRA; ReaPo; ReEn; SeCeV; SeCL; SeCV-1; SeEP; ShBV-3; TOP; TrGrPo; TVSH; TwHP; TyEnPo; ViBoPo; WBP; WHA; WP
(Daffodils.) LPS-2; PEOR, *st. 2*
("Fair daffodils, we weep to see.") EG
To Dafydd Coed Mourning His Mountain-broken Dog. Brenda Chamberlain. MoWP
To Daisies. Francis Thompson. HBV
To Daisies, Not to Shut So Soon[e]. Robert Herrick. AtBAP; BLV; BoLiVe; CH; EG; EV-2; HBV; OBEV; OBS; SeCV-1; SeEP; TrGrPo

To D'Annunzio; Lines from the Sea. Robert Nichols. OBMV
To Dante. Vittorio Alfieri, *tr. fr. Italian by* Lorna de' Lucchi. AWP; JAWP; WBP
To Dante. Guido Cavalcanti, *tr. fr. Italian by* Shelley. AWP; JAWP; LyMA; WBP
To Dante. Tennyson. EPP; TCEP
To Dante Alighieri. Giovanni Quirino. *See* Sonnet: To Dante Alighieri.
To Dante in Paradise, after Fiammetta's Death. Boccaccio, *tr. fr. Italian by* Dante Gabriel Rossetti. *Fr.* Sonnets. AWP
(Fiametta.) GoBC
To Daphne. Sir Walter Besant. HBV; VA
To Daphne and Virginia. William Carlos Williams. CrMA
To Daphnis and Chloe in the Park, *sel.* A. R. D. Fairburn.
Song: "O lovers, this song I give to you." AnNZ
To Dear Daniel. Samuel Greenberg. LiTA; MoPo
To Death. Caroline Anne Bowles. DiM; OBEV (1st ed.)
To Death. Johann Christoph von Gluck, *tr. fr. German.* LPS-1
To Death. Oliver St. John Gogarty. MaRV; OBMV; OtMeF
To Death. Robert Herrick. CoBE; EPS; EV-2; InPo
To Death. Padraic Pearse, *tr. fr. Modern Irish by* Thomas MacDonagh. AnIV
To Death. Countess of Winchilsea. HBV
To Death of His Lady. Villon, *tr. fr. French by* Dante Gabriel Rossetti. AWP; OuHeWo
To deck with honours due the bridal bed. Apollonius Rhodius. *Fr.* Argonautica, IV. GrPo
To deities of gauds and gold. Ad Patriam [*or* Land of Our Fathers]. Clinton Scollard. MC; PaA; PAH; PEDC
To Delia, *sels.* Samuel Daniel.
"And yet I cannot reprehend the flight," XXX [XXXII]. HBV; OAEP
(Beauty, Time and Love, 3.) OBEV
(Moth, The, 2.) ES
"Beauty [*or* Beautie], sweet love, is like the morning dew," XLII *or* XLV [XLVII]. ElL; ElSeCe; FaBoEn; HBV; OBSC; TuPP; ViBoPo
(Beauty, Time and Love, 5.) OBEV
(Beauty's Lease.) ES
"But love whilst that thou may'st be loved again," XXXVII. AtBAP; ElL; OBSC; SiCE; TuPP
"Care-charmer Sleep, son of the sable Night," XXXV *or* XLIV *or* XLV *or* XLIX *or* LII *or* LIV [LI]. AtBAP; ATP; BCEP; BEL; CBOV; CoBE; EG; ElL; ElSeCe; EnLi-1; EnLit; EPP; EV-1; FaBoEn; GTBS; GTBS-D; GTBS-W; GTSE; GTSL; HBV; LEAP; LiTB; LiTG; LoBV; LPS-2; OAEP; OBSC; PeBoSo; PoEL-2; ReaPo; ReEn; ReIE; SiCE; TCEP; TOP; TreFS; TrGrPo; TuPP; ViBoPo
(Prayer to Sleep.) ES
(Sleep.) BLV
(Sonnet.) CoEV
"Drawn with th' attractive virtue of her eyes," XLVIII. ReIE
"Fair and lovely maid, look from the shore," XLII. ReIE
"Fair is my love, and cruel as she's fair," VI. CaAE; ElL; ES; GTBS-W; HBV; HoPM; LiTB; LiTG; LiTL; OAEP; OBSC; PoEL-2; ReEn; ReIE; SiCE; TrGrPo; TuPP; TwHP; ViBoPo
(Beauty, Time and Love, 1.) BCEP; OBEV
"I must not grieve my Love, whose eyes would read," XLVI [XLVIII]. ElL; HBV
(Beauty, Time and Love, 6.) OBEV
"I once may see when years shall wreck my wrong," XXXIV. ReIE
(Beauty's Glass, *sl. diff., after the French of* Philippe Desportes.) OnPM
"If it so hap this offspring of my care," III. ReEn
"If this be love, to draw a weary breath," IX. OBSC; ReEn; SiCE; TrGrPo
"Let others sing of knights and paladins," XLVI *or* L *or* LIII *or* LV [LII]. BEL; CoBE; ElL; ElSeCe; EnLi-1 (1949 ed.); EPP; FaBoEn; HBV; OAEP; OBSC; ReEn; ReIE; SiCE; TuPP; ViBoPo
(Beauty, Time and Love, 7.) BCEP; OBEV
(Trophies.) ES
"Like as the lute delights, or else dislikes," LIV. OAEP
"Lo, here the impost of a faith entire," LVII. TuPP
"Look, Delia, how we esteem [*or* 'steem] the half-blown rose," XXXI *or* XXXIX [XXXVI]. AtBAP; ElL; ElSeCe; EnLit; HBV; ReEn; SiCE; TuPP
(Half-blown Rose, The.) SeCePo
(Sonnet: "Look, Delia.") WHA
"Most fair and lovely maid, look from the shore," XLIII. TuPP
"My cares draw on mine everlasting night," XXX (1592 ed.). AtBAP; OBSC
"My spotless love hovers with purest [*or* white] wings," XII. HBV; OBSC; SiCE
(Beauty, Time and Love, 2.) OBEV
(Moth, The, 1.) ES
"None other fame mine unambitious muse," XLVIII [LV]. ReEn; SiCE; TuPP
"O had she not been fair and thus unkind," VII. ReIE
"Reign in my thoughts, fair hand, sweet eye, rare voice," XXV. ReIE
"Restore thy tresses [*or* treasure] to the golden ore," XVIII [XIX]. ElSeCe; EPP
"Star of my mishap imposed [*or* impos'd] this pain [*or* paining], The," XXXI. OBSC; ReIE
"These plaintive verse, the posts of my desire," IV. OBSC; ReEn; SiCE
"Thou canst not die whilst any zeal abound," XL. EnLi-1 (1949 ed.); OAEP; OBSC; TuPP
"Time, cruel Time, come and subdue that brow," XXIII. AtBAP; OBSC
To the Right Honorable, the Lady Mary, Countess of Pembroke. SiCE; TuPP
"Unto the boundless ocean of thy beauty," I. LiTL; LoBV; OAEP; OBSC; ReIE; SiCE
"When men shall find thy flow'r, thy glory pass," XXXVI [XXXVIII]. CaAE; EG; ElL; HBV; LiTL; OBSC; PIAE; PoE; ReEn; SiCE; TrGrPo; TuPP
(Beauty, Time and Love, 4.) LO; OBEV
(From "To Delia.") LEAP
(Quand Vous Serez Bien Vieille.) ES
(Then and Now.) BLV
"When winter snows upon thy sable hairs," XXXIX. OBSC; ReIE; TuPP
"Why should I sing in verse, why should I frame," XVII. TuPP
To Deloney. Everard Guilpin. *Fr.* Skialetheia. ReIE
To Delos. Callimachus, *tr. fr. Greek by* Robert Allason Furness. GrR
(Delos.) OxBG
To Delphi, to Apollo's festal games. A Chariot-Race. Sophocles. *Fr.* Electra. OxBG
To Demeter. Maybury Fleming. AA
To Demeter. Andrea Navagero, *pr. tr. fr. Latin by* Richard Aldington. LaP
To Detraction [I Present My Poesie]. John Marston. *Fr.* The Scourge of Villainy. LoBV; OBSC; ReIE; SiCE; TuPP
To Diana. Ben Jonson. *See* Hymn to Diana.
To Diane. Helen Hay Whitney. AA; HBV
To Dianeme. Robert Herrick. BCEP; BrBE; CaAE; EV-2; FaBoBe; FaBoEn; GTBS; GTBS-D; GTBS-W; GTSE; GTSL; HBV; LiTL; LoBV; NeHB; OBEV; OBS; OnPM; RiBV; SeCV-1; SeEP; TOP; TrGrPo; ViBoPo; WoL
(Sweet, Be Not Proud.) LPS-1
("Sweet, be not proud of those two eyes.") EG
To Dianeme, Again. Robert Herrick. LiTL
To Dick, on His Sixth Birthday. Sara Teasdale. TSW; TSWC
To Die. Paul Eluard, *tr. fr. French by* Glauco Cambon. OnPM
To die be given us, or attain! Resignation. Matthew Arnold. EmBrPo; OAEP; PoVP; ViPP; VLEP
To die in spring, to join one's fleeting breath. Taking Off. Elizabeth Harrison. NeTW
To die with a forlorn hope, but soon to be raised. The Survivor. Robert Graves. MoVE
To Dionysus. Anacreon, *tr. fr. Greek by* T. F. Higham. GrL; LiTW; OxBG
To Dionysus. *Unknown, tr. fr. Greek. See* Hymn to Dionysus.
To distant service my heart is well accustomed. The Silver Spoon. Po Chü-i. TrCh
To dive for the nimbus on the sea-floor. The Nimbus. Douglas Le Pan. PeCV
To Dives. Hilaire Belloc. CAW; HBMV
To do a thing alone is difficult. One with the Universe. Toyohiko Kagawa. SoLD
To Dr. Arbuthnot. Pope. *See* Epistle to Dr. Arbuthnot.
To Doctor Bale. Barnabe Googe. ReIE; TuPP
To Doctor Delany on the Libels Writ against Him, *sel.* Swift.
Critick Vermin, The. BeR
To Doctor Empiric. Ben Jonson. BOHV; TuPP
To Doctor Hake. Robert Louis Stevenson. VLEP
To Dr. Plot. John Norris. NBE
To Dr. Swift on His Birthday. Esther Johnson ("Stella"). EnLoPo; TriL
To Don Angelo Grillo. Tasso, *tr. fr. Italian* by Elizabeth Selden. BoFr
To Don Francisco Giner de los Rios. Antonio Machado, *tr. fr. Spanish by* Ida Farnell. AnSpL-2; TeCS
To Donnybrook steer, all you sons of Parnassus. The Humours of Donnybrook Fair. *Unknown.* OnYI
To Doris. Lee Wilson Dodd. FAOV
To draw no envy, Shakespeare, on thy name. To the Memory of My Beloved Master [*or* the Author, Mr.] William Shakespeare. Ben Jonson. BCEP; BEL; BoLiVe; CoBE; EM-1; EnL; EnLi-1; EnLit; EPP; EPS; EV-2; GoTL; HBV; LEAP; LiTB; LPS-3; MaPo; MyFE; OAEP;

OBS; PIAE; PoEL-2; PoFS; PtP; ReEn; SeCeV; SeCV-1; SeEP; TCEP; TOP; TreFS; TrGrPo; TriL; TuPP; TwHP; ViBoPo; WHA
To draw, or not to draw,—that is the question. Poker. *Unknown.* PA
To Dream Again. Shakespeare. *See* Caliban.
To dreamy languors and the violet mist. Dogwood Blossoms. George Marion McClellan. BANP
To drift with every passion till my soul. Hélas. Oscar Wilde. AnIV; BMEP; GTIV; GTSL; LBBV; LEAP; MBP; MoBrPo; PoVP; ViPP; VLEP
To drink a toast. The Man for Galway. Charles James Lever. OnYI
To drink in moderation, and to smoke. Party Knee. John Updike. FiBHP
To drive Paul out of any lumber camp. Paul's Wife. Robert Frost. AnAmPo; LA
To drive the kine one summer's morn. The Cow-Chace. John André. PAH
To drum-beat and heart-beat. Nathan Hale. Francis Miles Finch. DD; GA; MC; PAH; PAP; PoFr; PTA-1
To Duffy in Prison. Thomas D'Arcy McGee. TIP
To Duncan. Jessica Nelson North. NP
To Duty. Thomas Wentworth Higginson. AA; AnAmPo; LA; LEAP
To Duty. Wordsworth. *See* Ode to Duty.
To Dwell Together in Unity. Psalms, CXXXIII, Bible, *O.T.* TrJP
(Psalm CXXXIII.) AWP; JAWP; OnPM
To E. Sara Teasdale. ChMo; CMP
To E. A. R. Lola Ridge. NP; TBM
To E. FitzGerald. Tennyson. PoEL-5; PtP
(To Edward Fitzgerald.) LoBV
To E. L., on His Travels in Greece. Tennyson. SeCePo
To E. M. O. Thomas Edward Brown. WhC
To Each His Own. Margaret Root Garvin. HBV
To each his sufferings; all are men. Where Ignorance Is Bliss. Thomas Gray. *Fr.* On a Distant Prospect of Eton College. TreF
To each man is given a day and his work for the day. The Day and the Work. Edwin Markham. OQP; PEDC; PSO; QP-1
To each one is given a marble to carve for the wall. The Task That Is Given to You. Edwin Markham. WBLP
To Earth, the Mother of All. *Unknown. See* Hymn to Earth the Mother of All.
To Earthward. Robert Frost. AnFE; APA; BLV; BoLiVe; CoAnAm; CoBMV; GTBS-D; HBMV; InPo; LiTA; LO; MAP; MoAB; MoAmPo; MOAP; MoPo; MoVE; NePA; OnAP; OxBA; PoeMoYo; PreP; ReMP; TBM; TCPD; TwAmPo; TwP; WoL
To eastward ringing, to westward winging, o'er mapless miles of sea. When the Great Gray Ships Come In. Guy Wetmore Carryl. AA; EtS; FaBoBe; GDAH; HBV; LBAP; MC; PAH
To Edgar Allan Poe ("If thy sad heart, pining for human love"). Sarah Helen Whitman. LBAP
(Sonnets from the Series Relating to Edgar Allan Poe.) AA; BAP; LEAP
To Edgar Allan Poe ("When first I looked into thy glorious eyes"). Sarah Helen Whitman. DD; GA
(Sonnets from the Series Relating to Edgar Allan Poe.) AA
To Edom. Heine, *tr. fr. German.* TrJP
To Edward Allen (Alleyne). Ben Jonson. OAEP; OBS; ReIE
To Edward Fitzgerald. Tennyson. *See* To E. FitzGerald.
To Edward Thomas. Alun Lewis. MoWP; WaP
To Edwin Arlington Robinson. Winfield Townley Scott. CAG
To Electra. Robert Herrick. ALV; BEL; EM-1; EnLit; EV-2; ExPo; HBV; HoPM; LoBV; OBEV; OBS; PG (1945 ed.); RiBV; SeCV-1; TCEP
("I dare not ask a kiss.") EG
"No, no, the utmost share," *sel.* LO
To Eliza, Duchess of Dorset. Joseph Bennett. LiTA; NePA
To Eliza, upon May Day Morning, 1649. Robert Baron. SeCL
To Elizabeth. Mary Dixon Thayer. JKCP (1955 ed.)
To Elizabeth she came. The Visitation. Calvin Le Compte. ISi
To Ellen. Emerson. IAP; MOAP; TOP
To Ellen at the South. Emerson. LaNeLa
Wind in the Grass, The, *st.* 1. BoTP
To Elsie. William Carlos Williams. *See* Pure Products of America, The.
To Emily Dickinson. Hart Crane. ChMo; PtP
To Emma. Lady Burrell. DiM
To End Her Fear. John Freeman. OBMV
To Engineers. Roberta Teale Swartz. PoeMoYo
To England. George Henry Boker. AA; AnAmPo; HBV; LA; OTPC
To England. Byron. *Fr.* Childe Harold's Pilgrimage, IV. WHA
To England. Charles Leonard Moore. AA
To English Connoisseurs. Blake. OxBoLi
(Epigram: To English Connoisseurs.) SiTL
To engulf us, waters eddy. Travelers' Song. Hugo von Hofmannsthal. AnGP
To Enjoy the Time. Robert Herrick. EM-1
To Entertain Divine Zenocrate. Christopher Marlowe. *See* Divine Zenocrate.
To Envy. Sir John Davies. *Fr.* Hymns of Astraea. SiCE
To Eros. Anacreon, *tr. fr. Greek.* GrR, *tr. by* Judson France Davidson; LiTW, *tr. by* John Ounsted
"To Europe! Europe!"—"Hope!"—"Our hope is dead!" Columbus. Casimir Delavigne. TrFP
To Eva. Emerson. EV-4; GTBS
To Evening. William Collins. *See* Ode to Evening.
To Everlasting Oblivion. John Marston. *Fr.* The Scourge of Villainy. LoBV (1949 ed.); OBSC; ReIE; SiCE; TuPP
(Oblivion.) BLV
"To every form of being is assigned." Discourse of the Wanderer, and an Evening Visit to the Lake. Wordsworth. *Fr.* The Excursion. EnRP
To Every Heart. Dante, *tr. fr. Italian by* Dante Gabriel Rossetti. La Vita Nuova, 1. AWP; OnPM
(Sonnet: "To every heart which the sweet pain doth move.") LyPI
To every hearth a little fire. A Christmas Wish. Rose Fyleman. BoTP
To every man there openeth. The Ways [*or* A High Way and a Low]. John Oxenham. HBMV; MaRV; OQP; PoMa; QP-1
To every one on earth. The Burden. "Marianne Farningham." OQP; QP-2
To everything there is a season. A Time for Everything. Ecclesiastes, Bible, *O.T.* TrGrPo
To F——. Poe. IAP
To F. C. Mortimer Collins. HBV; TreFS
To F. C. in Memoriam Palestine. G. K. Chesterton. HBMV
To F. W. Edith Wyatt. NP
To face the arrows of the chance-drawn bow, VIII. Frances Crawford. PtPa
To failing strength a stick is given. The Stick. May O'Rourke. HBMV
To Failure. Marguerite Wilkinson. TriL
To fair Fidele's grassy tomb. A Song from Shakespeare's "Cymbeline" [*or* Dirge in "Cymbeline"]. William Collins. ATP; BrBE; CaAE; EiPP; EnLi-2 (1949 ed.); EnRP; PoFS; RiBV; SeCePo; TriL; TyEnPo; ViBoPo
To Fancy. Richard Watson Dixon. GTML
To Fancy. Keats. *See* Fancy.
To Fanny. Keats. EmBrPo; EnRP; ERP; LoPo; LoPS; TrGrPo; TwP
To Fanny. Thomas Moore. HBV
To far-off shores as merchant the false sea's promise drew me. The Farmer Lost at Sea. Isidorus Aegeates. GrPE
To farmstead nymphs and shaggy Pan. On a Fountain. Anyte. GrR
To Father Sun (from the Hako Ceremony). *Tr. fr. Pawnee Indian.* GrCo-1
To Faunus ("Faune, Nympharum"). Horace, *tr. fr. Latin by* Alfred Noyes. Odes, III, 18. LiTW
("Faunus, fleet-foot lover of flying wood-nymphs.") LaP
To Fausta. Matthew Arnold. *See* Question, A.
To Faustine. Arthur Colton. *See* Sometime It May Be.
To Favonius. Edmund Bolton. OBSC
To Fear. Clifford J. Laube. JKCP (1926 ed.)
To fear a violent good, abuseth goodness. George Chapman. *Fr.* The Conspiracy of Charles, Duke of Byron. MyFE
To February. Ethelwyn Wetherald. VA
To feel and speak the astonishing beauty of things—earth, stone and water. The Beauty of Things. Robinson Jeffers. CoV
To Felicity Who Calls Me Mary. Frances Chesterton. HBMV
To Fidele. Shakespeare. *See* Fear No More the Heat o' the Sun.
To Fidentinus. Martial, *tr. fr. Latin by* Timothe Kendall. TuPP
To fight aloud is very brave. Emily Dickinson. AmP; AmPo; AmPP; CoBA; LiTA, MOAP; PoLFOT
To fill my rising song with sacred fire. The Battle of the Frogs and Mice. *Unknown.* GrL; GrPo
To fill the gap, to bear the brunt. St. George's Day—Ypres, 1915. Sir Henry Newbolt. GTML; GTSL
To find a thousand cattle. A Marching Song. Kao Ang. PoHN
To Find [*or* Finde] God. Robert Herrick. EPS; WGRP
To find out Tom of Bedlam ten thousand years I'll travel. Mad Maudlin to Find Out Tom of Bedlam. *Unknown.* SiTL
To find the western path. Morning [*or* The Spirit's Warfare]. Blake. BLV; BoLiVe; CBE; EG; FaBoCh; LoBV; LoGBV; OBRV
To Fish. Leigh Hunt. *Fr.* The Fish, the Man and the Spirit. PIAE
(To a Fish.) FiBHP
To Flavia. Edmund Waller. ElSeCe; HBV

To Flaxman. Blake. OxBoLi
(Epigram: To Flaxman.) SiTL
To flee from memory. Emily Dickinson. Po
To Fletcher Reviv'd. Richard Lovelace. OBS; PtP
To fling my arms wide. Dream Variation. Langston Hughes. BAP; CDC; PoNe
To Flossie. William Carlos Williams. NePoAm-2
To Flush, My Dog. Elizabeth Barrett Browning. AlBD; BoFr, *abr.*
To fly off, a ripe pear in a storm. Definition of the Soul. Boris Pasternak. TrJP; TrRV
To fold my hands a little while in sleep. Death. Grace Noll Crowell. PraP
To Font-Georges. Théodore de Banville, *tr. fr. French by* Alan Conder. TrFP
To Foreign Lands. Walt Whitman. AmPP (3d ed.); IAP
To Fortune. Robert Herrick. SeCV-1
To Fortune. Sir Thomas More. ACP
To Fortune. James Thomson. *See* For Ever, Fortune.
To France. Ralph Chaplin. HBMV
To Frances S. Osgood. Poe. TCAP
(Simple Duty, A.) PoRL
(To F——s S. O——d.) APW; IAP
To Francesca Frazer. Dionysios Solomos, *tr. fr. Modern Greek by* Rae Dalven. MoGP
To Francis Beaumont. Ben Jonson. OAEP; OBS; PtP; SeEP; TuPP
To Frankfort I on *Schobbas* came. The Best Religion. Heine. *Fr.* Tannhäuser. TrJP
To Freedom. Joel Barlow. AnAmPo; LA; PoFr
(Freedom.) AnNE
To Freedom. James Russell Lowell. PSO
To Friend and Foe. *Unknown.* CoMu
To Friendship. Don Juan de Arguijo, *tr. fr. Spanish by* Elizabeth Selden. BoFr
To further this, Achitophel unites. The Malcontents. Dryden. *Fr.* Absalom and Achitophel, Pt. I. OBS
To Fuscus Aristus. Horace, *tr. fr. Latin by* Abraham Cowley. Epistles, I, 10. AWP; JAWP; WBP
To G. A. W. Keats. ERP; PIR
To G. K. Chesterton. Joseph Mary Plunkett. OnYI
To Gabriel of the Annunciation. Peter Abelard, *tr. fr. Latin by* H. T. Henry. CAW
To gallop off to town post-haste. Friar Lubin. Clément Marot. AWP; WoL
To Gather Flowers Sappha Went. Robert Herrick. KN
(Apron of Flowers, The.) SeCV-1
To General Hamley. Tennyson. SoV
To George Barker. Gene Derwood. NePA
To George Chapman. Thomas Freeman. SiCE
To George Sand; a Recognition. Elizabeth Barrett Browning. *Fr.* Sonnets to George Sand. EmBrPo
(Recognition, A.) LPS-3
To Germany. Charles Hamilton Sorley. LBBV; MBP; MoBrPo
To get and breed a man is easier done. The Truth of It. Theognis. GrR
To get off the ground has always been difficult. Dialectics of Flight. John Hall Wheelock. NePoAm-2
To Giacomo Leopardi. T. Sturge Moore. PtP
To Gild Refinèd Gold. Shakespeare. *Fr.* King John, IV, ii. BCEP; LiTB; LiTG
To Giotto. Wesley Trimpi. NePoEA
To Giovanni da Pistoia on the Painting of the Sistine Chapel, 1509. Michelangelo, *tr. fr. Italian by* John Addington Symonds. LyPI
To Giulia Grisi. Nathaniel Parker Willis. AA; IAP
To give a little from a shining store. Giving. William F. Kirk. MaRV
To give—and forgive. Short Sermon [*or* Proverbs]. *Unknown.* RIS; TiPo
To give me its bright plumes they shot a jay. A Flaw. "Michael Field." BLA
To Give One's Life. Mary Carolyn Davies. PoToHe
To gladden one poor heart of man is more. Six Rubaiyat. Abu Said ibn Abi-l-Khair. LiTW
To Glow-Worms. Andrew Marvell. *See* Mower to the Glow-worms, The.
To go, to leave the classics and the buildings. Poem. Gavin Ewart. NeBP
To go to Rome. The Pilgrim at Rome [*or* A Word of Warning]. *Unknown.* AnIL; KiLC
To God. Robert Herrick. TrPWD; WGRP
To God and Ireland True. Ellen O'Leary. TIP; VA
To God, from the Warring Nations. Frank Wilmot. BoAu
Sels.
"Thou gavest steel to us, Thou gavest brain," XV. BoAV
"We have been cruel in thought. Life's not so sweet," V. BoAV
"We pray for pity, Lord, not justice, we," II. BoAV; NeLNL
"We've smashed the tablets and the songs, forsworn," III. BoAV
To God on high be thanks and praise. Nicolaus Decius, *tr. fr. German by* Catherine Winkworth. OlE
To God, on His Sickness. Robert Herrick. OxBoCh
To God, the Architect. Harry Kemp. *See* God the Architect.
To God, the everlasting, who abides. An Invocation. John Addington Symonds. WGRP
To God the Father. Henry Constable. GoBC; PoLi
To God the Son. Henry Constable. OBSC
To God, Ye Choir Above. Philip Skelton. OxBoCh
To Goddess Luck. Pindar, *tr. fr. Greek by* C. J. Billson. *Fr.* Olympian Odes, XII. GrR
To Gottfried Benn. Else Lasker-Schüler, *tr. fr. German by* Glauco Cambon. OnPM
To grasp it; say that you have seized that hour. César Franck. Joseph Auslander. HBMV
To grasp, to grasp the evening, the pear and the statue. Grasp. Jules Supervielle. OnPM
To grass, or leaf, or fruit, or wall. The Snail. Vincent Bourne, *tr. by* William Cowper. BoTP; CG; GFA; GoTP; HBV; HBVY; OTPC (1923 ed.); PoRh; WaKn
To Grow Older. "Jan Struther." LO
To Guido Cavalcanti. Dante. *See* Sonnet: To Guido Cavalcanti.
To H. B. M. W. W. E. Henley. BPN
To H. C. Wordsworth. ChER; EmBrPo; EnRP; GEPC; LiA; NBE; OBRV; PoEL-4; RO
(To Hartley Coleridge.) BPN; HBV
To H. W. L. James Russell Lowell. *See* To Henry Wadsworth Longfellow.
To Hades' gate the road runs straight, with never a turning. All Roads Lead to Death. *Unknown.* GrPE
To Hafiz. Thomas Bailey Aldrich. AA
To Hafiz of Shiraz. Gertrude Lowthian Bell. PtP
To Hampstead. Leigh Hunt. EnRP; OBRV
To Harifa, in an Orgy. José de Espronceda, *tr. fr. Spanish by* James Kennedy. AnSpL-2
To Harold Jacoby. Irwin Edman. InMe
To Harriet ——. Shelley. Queen Mab: Dedication. EmBrPo; EPN
To Harriett. John Clare. AtBAP
To Hartley Coleridge. Wordsworth. *See* To H. C.
To Hasekawa. Walter Conrad Arensberg. HBV
To have it out or not. That is the question. Toothache. *Unknown.* PA
To have known him, to have loved him. Monody. Herman Melville. AnFE; CoAnAm; GTBS-W; LiTA; PoEL-5; TriL
To have lived [*or* liv'd] eminent, in degree. Upon the Death of My Ever-desired Friend, Doctor Donne, [Dean] of Paul's. Henry King. EPS (1942 ed.); NBE
To Hayley. Blake. *See* To William Hayley.
To hear an oriole sing. Emily Dickinson. AmPo; AmPP; AnFE; APA; CoAnAm; CoBA; PoEL-5; UnS
To Hear Him Tell It. *Unknown.* SCC
To hear the lark begin his flight. Milton. *Fr.* L'Allegro. SN
To hear then prepare of the discipline rare. Education vs. Fads. Aristophanes. *Fr.* The Clouds. GrR
To Heaven. Ben Jonson. ExPo; LiTB; LoBV; OBS; ReIE; RiBV; SeCeV; TrPWD; UnPo
(Good and Great God.) OxBoCh
To Heaven Approached a Sufi Saint. Jalal ed-Din Rumi, *tr. fr. Persian by* William R. Alger. LPS-2
To Heaven on a Beetle. Aristophanes, *tr. fr. Greek by* T. F. Higham. *Fr.* The Peace. OxBG
To Helen ("Helen, thy beauty is to me"). Poe. AA; AmP; AmPo; AmPP; AnAmPo; AnFE; APA; APW; AtBAP; ATP; AWP; BAP; BAV; BLV; BoLiVe; BTP; CaAE; CBE; CH; ChTr; CoAnAm; CoBA; CoV; DD; DDA; EtPaEn; EV-5; ExPo; FaBoBe; FaBoEn; FaFP; GA; GTBS-D; GTBS-W; GTSE; HBV; HBVY; HoPM; InP; InPo; InvP; JAWP; KN; LA; LaNeLa; LBAP; LEAP; LiA; LiTA; LiTG; LiTL; LoBV; LoPo; MCCG; MOAP; NeHB; NePA; OBAV; OBEV; OBRV; OtMeF; OTPC; OuHeWo; OxBA; PC; PFE; PFY; PG (1945 ed.); PIAE; PIR; Po; PoEL-4; PoFS; PoRA; REAL; ReaPo; RiBV; SeCeV; SPP; TCAP; TOP; TreF; TrGrPo; TSW; TSWC; TwCrTr; UnPo (1st ed.); ViBoPo; WBP; WHA; YT
("Helen, thy beauty is to me.") EG
To Helen ("I saw thee once—once only—years ago"). Poe. AmPo; CoV; IAP; UnW
To Helen. Winthrop Mackworth Praed. HBV; LoBV
To Helen. Pierre de Ronsard. *See* Of His Lady's Old Age.
To Helen in a Huff. Nathaniel Parker Willis. PR
To Helen, Middle-aged. Roselle Mercier Montgomery. LS
To Helene. George Darley. OBEV (1st ed.)
To Heliodora. Meleager. *See* Heliodore.
To Heliodora; a Fretful Monody. Meleager, *tr. fr. Greek by* Dudley Fitts. LiTW
To Heliodora, Dead. Meleager, *tr. fr. Greek by* L. R. Lind. LiTW
("Tears to thee even beneath the earth, my Heliodora," *tr. by* H. N. Couch.) GrPo

To Hell with It. Frank O'Hara. NeAP
To Hellas' bard all Hellas gives a tomb. *At. to* Thucydides, *tr. fr. Greek by* F. A. Paley. GrPo
To Hen Chu, Magistrate of Yangchow. Tu Mu, *tr. fr. Chinese by* Yuan K'o-chia. WhP
To Henry David Thoreau. Irwin Edman. WhC
To Henry Reynolds, of Poets and Poesy, *sel.* Michael Drayton.
Christopher Marlowe. ChTr
To Henry Wadsworth Longfellow. James Russell Lowell. LPS-3
(To H. W. L.) PtP
To Her. Vasili Zhukovsky, *tr. fr. Russian by* C. M. Bowra. BoRS
To Her Absent Sailor. Whittier. *Fr.* The Tent on the Beach. LPS-1
To her accustomed eyes. Nurse Edith Cavell. Alice Meynell. BoHiPo; CP
To her couch of evening rest. Dirge. Thomas Lovell Beddoes. ERP
To Her Eyes. Lord Herbert of Cherbury. OBS
To Her Hair. Lord Herbert of Cherbury. SeEP
To Her Husband, at the Wedding. Kaga no Chiyo, *tr. fr. Japanese by* Curtis Hidden Page. LiTW
To Her Portrait. Sister Juana Inés de la Cruz, *tr. fr. Spanish by* Pauline Cook. LiTW
To Her Sea-faring Lover. *Unknown. See* Lady Prayeth the Return of Her Lover . , The.
To Her—Unspoken. Amelia Josephine Burr. HBV
To Heracleitus. William Johnson Cory, *after* Callimachus. *See* Heraclitus.
To Hermes. *Unknown, pr. tr. fr. Greek by* Andrew Lang. *Fr.* Homeric Hymns. GrL
To Hermes, this fair ball of pleasant sound. Boy's Playthings. Leonidas. OnPM
To Hiero the Syracusan. Pindar. *See* For Hiero, Tyrant of Syracuse.
To Him All Life Was Beauty. "A. L. C." ChIP
To Him be praise who made. Deus Noster Ignis Consumens. Laurence Housman. HBMV
To Him I Love. Tzu Yeh, *tr. fr. Chinese by* Henry H. Hart. PoHN
To him she hasted; in her face excuse. Milton. *Fr.* Paradise Lost, IX. EnL
To him that overcometh. Victory. Marguerite Wilkinson. ChIP
To him that smote Egypt in their firstborn. Psalm CXXXVI, Bible, *O.T.* PoFr
To Him That Was Crucified. Walt Whitman. AnEnPo; BoFr; IAP; MaRV; StJW
To him the moon was a silver dollar, spun. Requiem for a Modern Croesus. Lew Sarett. MaRV
To him who felt a human sea. Ballad of the Common Man. Alfred Kreymborg. PoFr
To him who in the love of Nature holds. Thanatopsis. Bryant. AA; AmP; AmPP; AnAmPo; AnFE; AnNE; APA; APW; AWP; BAP; BAV; BLV; BoLiVe; CoAnAm; CoBA; CoV; FaBoBe; FaFP; GTBS-W; HBV; HBVY; IAP; LA; LaNeLa; LBAP; LEAP; LiTA; LiTG; LPS-1; MCCG; MOAP; NeHB; NePA; OBAV; OBEV (new ed.); OBRV; OBVV; OHFP; OTPC (1946 ed.); OxBA; PFY; PG (1945 ed.); PIR; PoFS; PTA-1; REAL; TreF; TrGrPo; UnPo (1st ed.); ViBoPo; WBLP; WGRP; WHA
To Him Who Is Feared. Eleazar ben Kalir, *tr. fr. Hebrew by* Lady Katie Magnus. TrJP
To Him Who Walks the Water. E. Merrill Root. ChIP
To him who wanders up and down. Town Lights. Clark Ashton Smith. MuM
To him whom reason cannot bless. A Dream. William Gaston. NoCaPo
To Himself. Richard Aldridge. NePoAm
To Himself. Anacreon, *tr. fr. Greek by* John Ounsted. LiTW
To Himself. Catullus, *tr. fr. Latin by* William Ellery Leonard. AWP; LiTW
To Himself. Ben Jonson. *See* Ode to Himself, An ("Where do'st thou careless lie").
To Himselfe and the Harpe, *abr.* Michael Drayton. OBS
To His Book. Martial, *tr. fr. Latin by* Robert Herrick. AWP; LiTW
To His Book ("Go little book: thyself present"). Spenser. The Shepheardes Calender, *Dedicatory sonnet.* CaAE; ReIE; SiCE
To His Book ("Happy ye leaves!"). Spenser. *See* Amoretti, I.
To His Book. William Walsh. CEP; EV-3
To His Books. Henry Vaughan. EPS (1942 ed.)
To His Book's End. Robert Herrick. EnLit
(End-Piece for His Book, An.) InP
("To his book's end this last line he'd have placed.") ReEn
To His Brother. Wei Ying-wu, *tr. fr. Chinese by* Henry H. Hart. PoHN
To His Brother Hsing-chien. Po Chü-i, *tr. fr. Chinese by* Arthur Waley. TrCh
To His Brother Hsing-chien, Who Was Serving in Tung-ch'uan. Po Chü-i, *tr. fr. Chinese by* Arthur Waley. TrCh
To His Brother in the Service of Nebuchadnezzar. Alcaeus, *tr. fr. Greek by* F. L. Lucas. GrPE
To His Conscience. Robert Herrick. MaPo; OxBoCh; PoEL-3
To His Countrymen. James Russell Lowell. *Fr.* A Fable for Critics. AA
To His Cousin. Martial, *tr. fr. Latin.* PoFr
To his cousin the Bat. An Inconvenience. John Banister Tabb. UTS
To His Coy Love. Michael Drayton. AEV; ElL; HBV; LiTL; LO; LoPS; OBEV; OBS; ReIE; SeEP; ViBoPo
(Call Home the Heart.) LoPo
(Canzonet, to His Coy Love.) ElSeCe
(I Pray Thee Leave, Love Me No More.) InvP
To His Coy Mistress. Andrew Marvell. AnFE; AtBAP; ATP; AWP; BCEP, *ll.* 1-24; BLV; BoLiVe; BrBE; CaAE; CBOV; CEP; CoBE; CoEV; ElSeCe; EnL; EnLi-1 (1949 ed.); EnLit; EnLoPo; EPP; EPS; EtPaEn; EV-2; ExPo; FaBoEn; FaFP; GTBS-W; HBV; HoPM; InPo; InvP; JAWP; KN; LiTB; LiTG; LiTL; LO; LoBV; LoPo; LoPS; MaPo; MeLP; MePo; NeHB; OAEP; OBEV; OBS; OtMeF; PoE; PoEL-2; PoFS; PoRA; ReaPo; ReEn; RiBV; SeCL; SeCePo; SeCeV; SeCV-1; SeEP; ShBV-4; SiTL; TrGrPo; TwHP; TyEnPo; UnPo; ViBoPo; WBP; WHA
("Had we but world enough.") EG
"Now therefore, while the youthful hue," *sel.* AlDL
To His Cup Bearer. Catullus, *tr. fr. Latin by* George Lamb. OnPM
To His Cup-Bearer. Horace. *See* Persian Fopperies.
To His Dead Brother. Ugo Foscolo, *tr. fr. Italian by* Glauco Cambon. OnPM
To His Dead Daughter. Victor Hugo, *tr. fr. French by* Alan Conder. TrFP
To His Dear God. Robert Herrick. WP
To His Disciples. St. Luke, XII: 24-25, 27-28, Bible, *N.T.* CAW
To His Dying Brother, Master William Herrick. Robert Herrick. EV-2; OAEP; PoD; SeCV-1
"There's pain in parting," *2 ll.* LO
To His Ever-loving God. Robert Herrick. TrPWD
To His Familiar Friend. Nicholas Grimald, *after the Latin of* Marc-Antoine Muret. TuPP
To His Forsaken Mistress. *At. to* Sir Robert Ayton. BCEP; ElL; HBV; LO; OBEV; OBS; SeCePo
(Inconstancy Reproved.) BSV; EBSV; LiTL
(Inconstant Mistress.) EV-2
To His Friend. George Turberville. *See* To His Friend, Promising . . .
To His Friend in Absence. Walafrid Strabo, *tr. fr. Latin by* Helen Waddell. LiTW; LyMA
To His Friend in Elysium. Joachim du Bellay, *tr. fr. French by* Andrew Lang. AWP; JAWP; WBP
To His Friend Master [*or* Maister] R. L., in Praise of Music and Poetry. Richard Barnfield. ElL; ES; ReEn; ReIE; SiCE; TuPP; UnS
(If Music and Sweet Poetry.) ViBoPo
(In Praise of Music and Poetry.) ElSeCe
To His Friend, Promising That Though Her Beauty Fade, Yet His Love Shall Last. George Turberville. OBSC; SiCE; TuPP
(I Wot Full Well That Beauty Cannot Last.) TriL
(To His Friend.) ElSeCe
To His Friend Riding to Londonward. George Turberville. ReIE
To His Godson Gerald C. A. Jackson. A. E. Housman. WhC
To His Good Friend, Sir Anthony Cooke. Sir John Davies. *Fr.* Gulling Sonnets. TuPP
To His Heart. Sir Thomas Wyatt. OBSC
("Ah my heart, ah, what aileth thee?") SiPS
To His Heart, Bidding It Have No Fear. W. B. Yeats. PC
To His Honoured Kinsman, Sir William Soame. Robert Herrick. AtBAP; BoW
To His Ideal. Padraic Pearse, *tr. fr. Irish by* Thomas MacDonagh. LEAP
To His Inconstant Mistress. Thomas Carew. *See* To My Inconstant Mistress.
To His Lady. Sir John Davies. SiPS
To His Lady. Robert Graham. *See* If Doughty Deeds.
To His Lady. Fulke Greville. *See* More than Most Fair.
To His Lady. Henry VIII, King of England. *See* Whereto Should I Express.
To His Lady. Petrarch. *See* Vow to Love Faithfully, Howsoever He Be Rewarded, A.
To His Lady. Sir Thomas Wyatt. *See* To a Lady to Answer Directly . . .
To His Lady, of Her Doubtful Answer. Thomas Howell. TuPP
To His Lady, Who Had Vowed Virginity. Walter Davison. OBSC

To His Late Majesty, Concerning the True Form of English Poetry. Sir John Beaumont. OBS, *abr.*; SeEP
To His Love. Shakespeare. *See* Sonnets, XVIII *and* CVI.
To His Love. George Turberville. TuPP
To His Love. *Unknown. See* Come Away, Come, Sweet Love.
To his loved daughter, on his dying bed. Thy Distaff Ply. Antipater of Thessalonica. LiA
To His Lovely Mistresses. Robert Herrick. OAEP; TriL
To His Lute. William Drummond of Hawthornden. *See* Sonnet: "My lute, be as thou wast . . ."
To His Lute. Sir Thomas Wyatt. *See* Lover Complaineth the Unkindness of His Love, The.
To His Lyre Franklin P. Adams. LHV
To His Maid Prew. Robert Herrick. OBS
To His Maiden Quire. Alcman. *See* Halcyons, The.
To His Mistress. Richard Barnfield. *Fr.* Cynthia. SiCE; TuPP
To His Mistress. Thomas Beaumont. SeCL
To His Mistress. *At. to* George Villiers, Duke of Buckingham. SeCL
To His Mistress. Samuel Butler. SeCL
To His Mistress. Henry Constable. *Fr.* Diana. TuPP
("Miracle of the world, I never will deny.") OBSC; ReEn
To His Mistress. Abraham Cowley. EV-2; SeCL
(Ode to His Mistress.) CaAE
("Tyrian dye why do you wear.") EG
To His Mistress. Gilles Durant, *tr. fr. French by* John Payne. LiA
To His Mistress. Robert Herrick. ViBoPo
To His Mistress. Sir Walter Ralegh. *See* Silent Lover, The.
To His Mistress. Earl of Rochester. EPP; LEAP; LO; OBEV
My Light Thou Art, *sel.* PG
(To His Mistress.) LiTL
To His Mistress. William Walsh. EV-3
To His Mistress Confined. James Shirley, *also at. to* Thomas Carew *and to* Samuel Pick. LO; SeCL
(To His Mistris Confined.) OBS
To His Mistress, Elizabeth of Bohemia. Sir Henry Wotton. *See* On His Mistress, the Queen of Bohemia.
To His Mistress Going to Bed. John Donne. *See* Going to Bed.
To His Mistress in Absence. Tasso, *tr. fr. Italian by* Thomas Stanley. AWP; JAWP; WBP
(Far from My Dearest Self.) OnPM
To His Mistress Objecting to Him Neither Toying or Talking. Robert Herrick. *See* You Say I Love Not.
To His Mistress; Sending Her the Arcadia. Thomas Beaumont. ElSeCe; SeCL
To His Mistress' Skull. Cyril Tourneur. *Fr.* The Revenger's Tragedy. CoEV
("And now methinks I could e'en chide myself.") PoD; ViBoPo
To His Mistress, Who Said She Hated Him for His Grey Hairs. William Wycherley. SeCL
(Song, A: In the Name of a Lover, to His Mistress . . .) SeCV-2
To His Mistris Confined. James Shirley. *See* To His Mistress Confined.
To His Mother. Heine. *See* To My Mother.
To His Mother. George Herbert. ElSeCe; PoFS
("My God, where is that ancient heat towards thee.") SeEP
(Resolve, The.) EPS
To His Mother. John Banister Tabb. The Child, III. AA
To His Mother, C. L. M. John Masefield. *See* C. L. M.
To His Muse. Edward Benlowes. *Fr.* Theophila; or, Love's Sacrifice. SeCL
To His Muse. Nicholas Breton. *See* Sweet Pastoral, A.
To His Muse. Robert Herrick. OAEP
To His Nose. Jean Le Houx, *formerly at. to* Olivier Basselin, *tr. fr. French by* Ralph N. Currey. FoS
To His Page. Pierre de Ronsard, *tr. fr. French by* Alan Conder. TrFP
To His Pandora, from England. Alexander Craig. TuPP
To His Pen. Sir Thomas Wyatt. OBSC
("My pen, take pain a little space.") SiPS
To His Posterity. Henry Parker, Baron Morley. TuPP
To His Reader. Samuel Daniel. OBSC
To His Retired Friend, *sel.* Henry Vaughan.
"Come! leave this sullen state, and let us wine." ViBoPo
To His Ring, Given to His Lady. George Turberville. ElL
To His Rival. Michael Drayton. ReEn
To His Sacred Majesty, a Panegyrick on His Coronation, 1661, *sel.* Dryden.
"Time seems not now beneath his years to stoop." OBS
To His Saviour, a Child; a Present by a Child. Robert Herrick. EV-2; OTPC (1923 ed.); OxBoCh; PRWS
(Child's Present to His Child-Saviour, A.) CBPC; OHIP
(Go, Pretty Child.) BoTP
(To a Child.) EG
To His Son. John Dyer. PrWP
To His Son. Sir Walter Ralegh. *See* Wood, the Weed, the Wag, The.
To His Son, Vincent [Corbet, on His Third Birthday]. Richard Corbet. ElSeCe; EV-2; FaBoCh; LoGBV; OBS; SeCL; SeEP; TrGrPo
(To Vincent Corbet, His Son.) FAOV
To His Sons. Lu Yu, *tr. fr. Chinese by* Pai Chwen-yu. WhP
To His Soul. Emperor Hadrian, *tr. fr. Latin by* Matthew Prior. EPP; InP; SeCL; LaP, *tr. by* Elinor Wylie
(Adriani Morientis ad Animam Suam, *tr. by* Matthew Prior.) CEP
(Animula Blandula Vagula, *tr. by* Charles Glenn Wallis.) LiTW
(On the Soul, *tr. by* Byron.) WoL
To his sweet lute Apollo sung the motions of the spheres. Thomas Campion. CenL
To His Three Friends. Li Po, *tr. fr. Chinese by* Shigeyoshi Obata. BoFr
To His Tomb-Maker. Robert Herrick. SeCV-1
To His Tutor. John Hall. EG
To His Valentine. Michael Drayton. AtBAP; PoEL-2
To His Verse. Walter Savage Landor. OBVV
(Lyrics, to Ianthe.) BPN
To His Very Friend, Master Richard Martin. Sir John Davies. Orchestra, Dedication I. SiPS
To His Watch. Gerard Manley Hopkins. MBP; MOAB; MoBrPo
To His Watch, When He Could Not Sleep. Lord Herbert of Cherbury. MePo; PoEL-2
To His Wife. Decimus Magnus Ausonius, *tr. fr. Latin by* Terrot Reaveley Glover. AWP; JAWP; WBP
——*Tr. by* Helen Waddell. LaP; LiTW
To His Wife. Ch'in Chia. *See* Ch'in Chia's Farewell.
To His Wife. Daniel Henry Deniehy. BoAV
To His Wife. Ovid, *tr. fr. Latin by* Geoffrey Johnson. *Fr.* Tristia, III, 3. LaP
To His Wife. Joseph Stansbury. *See* To Cordelia.
To His Wife. Su Wu, *tr. fr. Chinese by* Arthur Waley. TrCh
("Since our hair was plaited and we became man and wife.") LO
(To a Husband, *tr. by* Henry H. Hart.) PoHN
To His Wife on His Departure. Li Po, *tr. fr. Chinese by* Shigeyoshi Obata. ChLP
To His Wife, on the Fourteenth [*or* Sixteenth] Anniversary of Her Wedding-Day, with a Ring. Samuel Bishop. CBOV; LO; ViBoPo
(To Mary.) HBV
To His Young Mistress. Pierre de Ronsard, *tr. fr. French by* Andrew Lang. *Fr.* Amours de Marie. AWP; OuHeWo
("Fair flower of fifteen springs, that still.") PrPoCR
To his young Rose an old man said. To Rose. Walter Savage Landor. TriL
To Hölderlin. Rainer Maria Rilke, *tr. fr. German by* David Luke. AnGP
To Holy Jesus. Princess Philipa, *tr. fr. Portuguese by* Thomas Walsh. CAW
To Homer. John Malcolm Bulloch. ATP (1935 ed.)
To Homer. Keats. BPN; BrBE; EM-2; EmBrPo; ES; EV-4; OBRV; PtP
(Sonnet: To Homer.) ChER; TriL
"Aye, on the shores of darkness there is light," *sel.* PC
To Hope. Helen Maria Williams. *Fr.* Julia, a Novel. OBEC
To hope is good, but with such wild applause. Hope. Sir Richard Fanshawe. *Fr.* Il Pastor Fido. OBS
To horse! to horse, Sir Nicholas! The clarion's note is high. Marston Moor. Winthrop Mackworth Praed. BHV; ShGoBo
To Houston at Gonzales town, ride, ranger, for your life. The Men of the Alamo. James Jeffrey Roche. BoHiPo; PAH
To Hsü Ling. Yü Hsin, *tr. fr. Chinese by* Henry H. Hart. BoFr; PoHN
To Hunt. Blake. OxBoLi
(Epigram: To Hunt.) SiTL
To hunt and to be hunted make existence. Charles Heavysege. *Fr.* Saul. CaP
To hurt the Negro and avoid the Jew. University. Karl Shapiro. AmPP (4th ed.); CoBA; LiTA; OxBA
To Ianthe. Byron. *Fr.* Childe Harold's Pilgrimage. FaBoEn
To Ianthe. Walter Savage Landor. *See* You Smiled, You Spoke.
To Ianthe. Shelley. ATP
To Ianthe, Sleeping. Shelley. *Fr.* Queen Mab, Pt. I. LPS-2
To Idealon. Thomas Holley Chivers. SPP
To Idleness. T. Sturge Moore. *See* Idleness.
To Imagination. Emily Brontë. VLEP
To Imagination. Edith M. Thomas. AA
To Imperia. Thomas Burbidge. VA
To —— in Church. Alan Seeger. HBV
To intoxicate you with the wine of things. The Mangoes. Duraciné Vaval. AnCL; PoNe
To Ireland in the Coming Times. W. B. Yeats. OxBI

To Iron-Founders and Others. Gordon Bottomley. GTML; GTSL; OBEV (new ed.); OBMV; OBVV
To Italy. Giovanni Guidiccioni, *tr. fr. Italian by* Longfellow. PoFr
To Italy. Giacomo Leopardi, *tr. fr. Italian by* Romilda Rendel. AWP; WoL
To J. M. George Meredith. EPN
To J. M. K. Tennyson. PoVP; ViPo; VLEP
To J. S. Robert J. Misch. ALV
To J. S. Collis. Ruth Pitter. OxBoCh
To J. W. Emerson. IAP
To James. Frank Horne. GoSl
(More Letters Found near a Suicide.) BANP
To James Craggs, Esq., Secretary of State. Pope. CEP
To James McNeill Whistler. W E. Henley. PoVP
To James Smith. Burns. *See* Epistle to James Smith.
To James the VI, King of Scotland. Sir John Harington. SiCE
To James Warre. Ben Jonson. EV-2
(Truth.) PG
To James Whitcomb Riley. Bide Dudley. BLP
To James Whitcomb Riley. Kipling. YT
To Jane: The Invitation. Shelley. AlDL, *sl. abr.*; EmBrPo; ERP; HBV; OBRV; SeCeV
(Invitation, The.) GTBS; GTBS-D; GTBS-W; GTSE; GTSL; OBEV; OTPC; SN
(Invitation to Jane, The.) CH; PC
(To Jane.) EPN
Sels.
Away, Away! GoTP
"Radiant Sister of the Day." ThWaDe
To Jane: The Keen Stars Were Twinkling. Shelley. *See* Keen Stars Were Twinkling, The.
To Jane: The Recollection. Shelley. *See* Recollection, The.
To Jean. Duncan B. M. Emrich. CAG
To Jean Paul. August, Graf von Platen-Hallermund, *tr. fr. German by* Reginald B. Cooke. BoFr
To Jessie's Dancing Feet. William De Lancey Ellwanger. AA
To Jesus. Jacopone da Todi, *tr. fr. Italian.* MaRV
To Jesus. *Unknown. See* Rise, O My Soul!
To Jesus of Nazareth. Frederic Lawrence Knowles. TrPWD
To Jesus on His Birthday. Edna St. Vincent Millay. ChMo; CMP; LiTG; MaRV; ReaPo; StJW; TrGrPo
To Jesus on the Cross. Juan Manuel Garcia Tejada, *tr. fr. Spanish by* Thomas Walsh. CAW
To Joan of Arc on D-Day. Sister Mary Thérèse. MuM
To John C. Frémont. Whittier. GA; MC; PAH
To John Charles McNeill. Stewart Atkins. NoCaPo
To John Donne ("Donne, the delight of Phoebus, and each Muse"). Ben Jonson. MaPo; OAEP; OBS; PtP; ReEn; SeCV-1; SeEP
To John Donne ("Who shall doubt, Donne, where I a poet be"). Ben Jonson. MaPo; ReIE; SeCV-1; TuPP
To John Fiorini. C. R. Holmes. PtPa
To John G. Whittier. James Russell Lowell. PEOR
(To Whittier.) CoBA
To John Gorham Palfrey, *sel.* James Russell Lowell.
O Mother State. BHV
To John Greenleaf Whittier. William Hayes Ward. AA; GA
To John I ow'd [*or* owed] great obligation. Epigram [*or* More than Quit *or* Quits]. Matthew Prior, *after* Martial. ALV; AWP; CEP; FaFP; LiTG; OnPM; SiTL
To John Keats. Leigh Hunt. PtP
To John Keats. Amy Lowell. PtP
To John Keats, Poet. At Springtime. Countee Cullen. BANP; CDC
To John Taylor. Burns. WhC
To join the ages they have gone. Seven Years. Marquess of Crewe. OBVV
To José Maria Palacio. Antonio Machado, *tr. fr. Spanish by* Eleanor L. Turnbull. TeCS
To Joseph. Harriet Hoock. WHL
To Joseph Ablett. Walter Savage Landor. BPN; EmBrPo
To Joseph Joachim. Robert Bridges. TriL
To Juan at the Winter Solstice. Robert Graves. CoBMV; FaBoMo; LiTB; LiTM (rev. ed.); MoPo; OnHM; SeCeV; UnPo (3d ed.)
To Judith Asleep. John Ciardi. LiTL; MiAP
To Julia in Shooting Togs. Sir Owen Seaman. BOHV
To Julia under Lock and Key. Sir Owen Seaman. PA
To K. de M. W. E. Henley. POTT; PoVP
To K. H. Thomas Edward Brown. VLEP
Tò καλόν. Arthur Hugh Clough. BPN; PoVP; ViPo; VLEP
(I Have Seen Higher, Holier Things than These.) OAEP
To Kate, Skating Better than Her Date. David Daiches. FiBHP
To Keats. Lord Dunsany. BMEP
To Keep a True Lent. Robert Herrick. BEL; EM-1; EnLi-1; EPP; GrCo-1; HBV; MaRV; TOP
(True Lent, A.) DD; LPS-2; OHIP; PoRL
To keep, at noon, the windows open. Noon. Jaime Torres Bodet. AnCL
To keep my health! Resolve [*or* I Resolve]. Charlotte Perkins Gilman. BLP; OQP; PoToHe; QP-2; WGRP
To kinder skies, where gentler manners reign. France. Goldsmith. *Fr.* The Traveller. OBEC
To King James. Ben Jonson. OAEP
To kiss a fan! Two Triolets: What She Thought. Harrison Robertson. HBV; PR
To kiss my Celia's fairer breast. On Snowflakes Melting on His Lady's Breast. William Martin Johnson. AA; BAV
"To Know All Is to Forgive All." Nixon Waterman. BLPA; NeHB
(If I Knew You and You Knew Me.) PoToHe
(Understanding, *st.* 1.) MaRV
To know just how he suffered would be dear. Emily Dickinson. InvP
To know people is to be wise. *Unknown, tr. fr. Chinese.* Tao Teh Ching, XVIII. WhP
To know thy bent and then pursue. Ella Wheeler Wilcox. CenHV
To Kosciusko. Keats. PoFr
To L——. D'Arcy Cresswell. AnNZ
To L. B. C. L. M. Robert Bridges. *See* I Love All Beauteous Things.
To L. B. S. Winfield Townley Scott. FiMAP
To L. C. Lucy Hawkins. HBMV
To L. H. B. Katherine Mansfield. AnNZ; HBMV
To La Sanscœur. William Caldwell Roscoe. VA
To Labor Is to Pray. Frances Sargent Osgood. LPS-2
To Laddie. Anne Robinson. SUS
To Ladies' Eyes. Thomas Moore. OxBoLi; PoEL-4; SiTL
To Lady Anne Fitzpatrick, When about Five Years Old [with a Present of Shells]. Horace Walpole. CEP; OBEC
To Lady Jane Wharton, on Her Studying the Globe. Nicholas Rowe. LO
To Lake Aghmoogenegamook. The American Traveller. "Orpheus C. Kerr." BOHV; WhC
To Larr. Robert Herrick. BoW; SeCV-1
To Laura W——, Two Years Old. Nathaniel Parker Willis. HBV
To Laurels. Robert Herrick. ElSeCe; ExPo; SeCV-1
To Laurence Hutton. Austin Dobson. BPN
To leave behind a picture, fine to see. To One Who after Death Would Leave His Lively Picture. Thomas Howell. TuPP
To leave the old with a burst of song. A Way to a Happy New Year. Robert Brewster Beattie. OQP; PSO; QP-1
To Leigh Hunt, Esq. Keats. BPN; EmBrPo; EnRP; ERP
(Dedication: To Leigh Hunt.) ViBoPo
To Lesbia. Catullus. *See* Love Is All.
To Lesbia. John Godfrey Saxe. HBV
To Lesbia ("My sweetest Lesbia"). Thomas Campion, *after* Catullus. *See* My Sweetest Lesbia.
To Let. D. Newey-Johnson. BoTP
To Leuconöe ("Tu ne quaesieris"). Horace, *tr. fr. Latin.* Odes, I, 11. AA, *tr.* I *by* Roswell Martin Field, *tr.* II *by* Eugene Field; ALV, *tr. by* Eugene Field; LoBV, *tr. by* Charles Stuart Calverley
(Ad Leuconoen, *par. by* Franklin P. Adams.) AWP; JAWP; WBP
(Carpe Diem, *tr. by* Thomas Hawkins.) RoL
(Mistrust To-Morrow, *tr. by* Charles Stuart Calverley.) OnPM
To Leven Water. Tobias George Smollett. OBEV
To Liane-Neila. Iwan Goll, *tr. fr. German by* Claire Goll. OnPM
To Liberality. *Unknown, tr. fr. Vedic by* Ralph T. H. Griffith. *Fr.* Vedic Hymns: Rig-Veda, Bk. X, Hymn 117. PoFr
To Liberty. Casimir Sarbiewski, *tr. fr. Polish by* Sir John Bowring. PoFr
To Li Chien ("The province I govern is humble and remote"). Po Chü-i, *tr. fr. Chinese by* Arthur Waley. AWP; TrCh
To Li Chien ("Worldly matters again draw my steps"). Po Chü-i, *tr. fr. Chinese by* Arthur Waley. BoFr; LiTW; TrCh
To Licinius ("Rectius vives"). Horace, *tr. fr. Latin by* William Cowper. Odes, II, 10. AWP; JAWP; WBP
(Golden Mean, The.) HBV, *tr. by* William Cowper; RoL, *tr. by* Sir Philip Sidney
(To Licinius Murena, *tr. by* William Cowper.) EnLi-1; OuHeWo
(Translated out of Horace Which Begins Rectius Vives, *tr. by* Sir Philip Sidney.) ReIE
To Licus. Everard Guilpin *Fr.* Skialetheia. SiCE
To Life. Thomas Hardy. ChMo; CMP; EmBrPo; TOP
To Life I Said Yes. Chaim Grade, *tr. fr. Yiddish by* Joseph Leftwich. TrJP
To Lighten My Darkness. *Unknown, tr. fr. Arabic by* E. Powys Mathers. *Fr.* The Thousand and One Nights. AWP
To Lighten My House. Alastair Reid. NePoEA
To Lillian Russell. Bert Leston Taylor. WhC
To Li Po. Tu Fu, *tr. fr. Chinese.* WhP
To Li Po on a Spring Day Tu Fu, *tr. fr. Chinese.* WhP
To little Kirsteen spake Si Peter the knight. Sir Peter's Harp. *Unknown.* BoDaBa

To Little or No Purpose I Spent Many Days. Sir George Etherege. *Fr.* She Would if She Could. SeCL; SeEP

To Little Renée on First Seeing Her Lying in Her Cradle. William Aspenwall Bradley. HBV

To live as gently as I can. My Creed. Edgar A. Guest. MaRV

To live in hell, and heaven to behold. If This Be Love. Henry Constable. *Fr.* Diana. HBV; LiTL; OBSC; ReEn; ReIE; SiCE; TuPP

To Live in Pleasure. *Unknown.* TrGrPo
("Sing we and chant it.") ElSeCe
(Song: "Sing we . . .") OBSC

To Live Merrily and to Trust to Good Verses. Robert Herrick. AWP; BEL; EPS (1942 ed.); InPo; InvP; LoBV; MyFE, *st.* 1; OBS; ReEn; SeCV-1; SeEP
"Behold, Tibullus lies/ Here burnt," *sel.* PoD

To live within a cave—it is most good. Salve! Thomas Edward Brown. HBV; OBEV; OBVV; POTT; TOP

To live without you, seems to me. Little Mother. "M. P. D." PEDC

To Lizard Head. Clifford J. Laube. CAW

To Lizbie Browne. Thomas Hardy. EnLit; LO; ViP

To locate a person hidden in this room. Identity. Hyam Plutzik. FiMAP

To London once my steps I bent. London Lickpenny [*or* Lackpenny]. *Unknown.* EV-1; GoTL; MeEV; TMEV

To London the Train Gallops, Its Shrill Steel Hooves. Clifford Dyment. HaMV

To Longfellow. Paul Hamilton Hayne. SPP

To loosen with all ten fingers held wide and limber. Mossgathering. Theodore Roethke. CoBMV; FiMAP

To Lord Byron. Richard Henry Wilde. SPP

To Lorna. Eric Wilson Barker. MuM

To Losers. George Dillon. NP

To Louis Kossuth. Swinburne. BPN

To Love. Thomas Lodge. BCEP

To Love. Rolf Hjorth Schöyen, *tr. fr. Norwegian by* Charles W. Stork. AnNoLy

To Love. *Unknown. See* Fain Would I Change That Note.

To Love; a Sonnet. Philip Ayres. CEP

To Love and to Remember: That Is Good. Christina Rossetti. Later Life, VII. BoFr; LO, 4 *ll.*

To Love, at Last, the Victory. David Starr Jordan. OQP; QP-1

"To love is to give," said the crooked old man. Cupidon. William Jay Smith. NePoEA

To love our God with all our strength and will. The Whole Duty of Man. Henry Vaughan. OQP; QP-1

To love some one more dearly ev'ry day. My Task. Maude Louise Ray. MaRV

To love the girl you have conquered. To Love. Rolf Hjorth Schöyen. AnNoLy

To Love Unloved. Alexander Scott. *See* To Luve Unluvit.

To love with no return. Sadder. *Unknown.* OnPM

To loveliness of water, its faery ways. Ballade of the Things That Remain. Richard Le Gallienne. PFE

To Lovers. Amelia Josephine Burr. PR; TBM

To Lovers of Earth: Fair Warning. Countee Cullen. CDC

To Lucasta ("I laugh and I sing but cannot tell"). Richard Lovelace. OBS

To Lucasta ("Tell me not, sweet, I am unkind"). Richard Lovelace. *See* To Lucasta, Going to the Wars.

To Lucasta, from Prison. Richard Lovelace. PoFr

To Lucasta: Her Reserved Looks. Richard Lovelace. SeCV-1

To Lucasta, [on] going beyond the Seas. Richard Lovelace. AtBAP; CaAE; ElSeCe; EPS; EV-2; FaBoEn; GTBS-D; GTBS-W; GTSE; GTSL; HBV; LiTB; LiTG; LiTL; LO; LoBV; MeLP; OAEP; OBEV; OBS; SeCL; SeCV-1; SeEP; TriL; ViBoPo
("If to be absent were to be.") GTBS
(Song.) ReEn

To Lucasta, [on] Going to the Wars [*or* Warres]. Richard Lovelace. AEV; ALV; AtBAP; AWP; BBV (1923 ed.); BCEP; BEL; BLV; BTP; CaAE; CBE; CBOV; CBPC; CenL; CoBE; CoEV; ElSeCe; EM-1; EnL; EnLi-1; EnLit; EnLoPo; EPP; EPS; ExPo; FaBoEn; FaFP; GTBS; GTBS-D; GTBS-W; GTSE; GTSL; HBV; HoPM; InPo; JAWP; KN; LEAP; LiTB; LiTG; LiTL; LoBV; MCCG; MeLP; MePo; NeHB; OAEP; OBEV; OuHeWo; PG (1945 ed.); PIAE; PIR; Po; PoEL-3; PoRA; SeCePo; SeCeV; SeCL; SeCV-1; SeEP; ShBV-3; TCEP; TOP; TreF; TrGrPo; TVSH; TwHP; UnPo (1st ed.); ViBoPo; WBP; WHA; WP
(Going to the Warres [*or* Wars]. AnFE; LH; LoPS; OBS
(Song: To Lucasta, Going to the Warres [*or* Wars].) LiA; ReEn
(To Lucasta.) LoPo; LPS-1

"To Lucasta, on Going to the Wars." Edwin Meade Robinson. Limericised Classics, IV. HBMV

To Lucasta: The Rose. Richard Lovelace. *See* Rose, The.

To Lucia Playing on Her Lute. Samuel Pordage. SeCL

To Lucius Sestius ("Solvitur acris hiems"). Horace, *tr. fr. Latin by* Sir Theodore Martin. Odes, I, 4. OuHeWo

To Lucy, Countess[e] of Bedford, with Mr. Donne's Satires [*or* Satyres]. Ben Jonson. OBS; ReIE; SeCV-1; SeEP; TuPP

To Lupus. Martial, *tr. fr. Latin by* Paul Nixon. RoL

To Luve Unluvit. Alexander Scott. EBSV; GoTS
(To Love Unloved.) BSV
("To love unloved it is a pain.") LO

To "Lydia Languish." Austin Dobson. PoVP

To M. William Gay. BoAu

To M. E. W. G. K. Chesterton. HBV

To M. H. Wordsworth. Poems on the Naming of Places, V. ERP

To M. T. Bayard Taylor. AA

To Mackinnon of Strath. Iain Lom, *tr. fr. Gaelic.* GoTS

To Madame A. P. Kern. Pushkin, *tr. fr. Russian by* V. de S. Pinto. LiTW

To Madame de Sévigné. Mathieu de Montreuil. LPS-3

To Madame la Duchesse de Bauffremont. Louis Morpeau, *tr. fr. French by* Edna Worthley Underwood. PoNe

To Madame Lullin. Voltaire, *tr. fr. French by* Alan Conder. TrFP

To Madame N. Ménessier. Alfred de Musset, *tr. fr. French by* Alan Conder. TrFP

To Maecenas ("Tyrrhena regum progenies"). Horace, *paraphrased fr. Latin by* Dryden. Odes, III, 29. AWP; JAWP; PoFr, *sel.;* WBP
(Horat. Ode 29. Book 3.) CEP; SeCV-2
(Twenty-ninth Ode of the Third Book of Horace, The.) LiA
Sels.
Enjoy the Hour. BeR
Happy the Man, *br. sel.* MaRV
(Happiness, 4 *ll.*) TreF

To Maia. Keats. *See* Fragment of an Ode to Maia.

To Make a Bridge. Charles Madge. NeBP

To make a final conquest of all me. The Fair Singer. Andrew Marvell. EG; ElSeCe; EnLoPo; LiTL; LO; LoPo; MeLP; MePo; PoEL-2; ReEn; SeCL; UnPo (3d ed.)

To make a lover known by plain anatomy. The Anatomy of a Lover. George Gascoigne. ReIE

To make a prairie it takes a clover and one bee. Emily Dickinson. AmPP (4th ed.); AnNE; CoBA; CoV; HBVY; OxBA; Po; TCAP; VOD (1935 ed.); WoL; YT
(Revery.) BPP

To make a start. Paterson: Book One, Preface. William Carlos Williams. CoBMV

To make my lady's obsequies. The Fairest Thing in Mortal Eyes. Charles d'Orléans. LPS-1

To make quick way I'll leap o'er heavy blocks. Og and Doeg. Dryden. *Fr.* Absalom and Achitophel, Pt. II. BeR

To make this condiment, your poet begs. A Salad [*or* A Recipe for a Salad]. Sydney Smith. BOHV; HBV; LPS-3

To make your candles last for aye. *Unknown.* OxNR

To man that was i'th ev'ninge mad. *Unknown.* SeCSL

To Manlius Torquatus. Horace. *See* Spring's Return.

To Manon, as to His Choice of Her. Wilfrid Scawen Blunt. The Love Sonnets of Proteus, VIII. HBV
(As to His Choice of Her.) ViBoPo

To Manon, Comparing Her to a Falcon. Wilfrid Scawen Blunt. The Love Sonnets of Proteus, II. OBVV; VA
(Falcon, The.) ACP

To Manon, on Her Lightheartedness. Wilfrid Scawen Blunt. The Love Sonnets of Proteus, XI. VA

To Manon, on His Fortune in Loving Her. Wilfrid Scawen Blunt. The Love Sonnets of Proteus, III. CaAE; GTSL; LEAP; OBEV (1st ed.)

To Many Deaths Decreed. John Crowne. *Fr.* Regulus. SeCL

To Margot Heinemann. John Cornford. *See* Huesca.

To Marguerite. Matthew Arnold. Switzerland, V. BMEP; BPN; CoEV; EnL; EnLi-2; EPN; EPP; FaBoEn; FiP; GEPC; GTBS-D; GTML; HBV; MaPo; OAEP; OBEV; PoEL-5; PoVP; RiBV; SeCeV; TOP; ViPo; ViPP; VLEP
(Isolation.) OBVV
("Yes! in the sea of life enisled.") ReaPo

To Marie. John Bennett. BOHV; NA

To market, to market, to buy a fat pig. Mother Goose. BoTP; FaBoBe; FaFP; HBV; HBVY; OnHT; OTPC; OxNR; PCH; PPL; RIS; StVeCh; TiPo

To market, to market, to buy a plum bun. Mother Goose. OxNR; SAS

To Marry Strangers. Winfield Townley Scott. FiMAP

To Mars. *Unknown. See* Hymn to Ares.

To Mary. Samuel Bishop. *See* To His Wife on the Fourteenth Anniversary of Her Wedding-Day . . .

To Mary ("I sleep with thee and wake with thee"). John Clare. EnLoPo

To Mary. William Cowper. BEL; BoFr; EiPP; EM-1; EnLi-2 (1949 ed.); EnLoPo; EnRP; FiP; LO; OAEP; OBEC
(My Mary.) LiTL; OBEV; TreFS
(To the Same [1793].) EV-3; GTBS; GTBS-D; GTBS-W; GTSE; GTSL

To Mary. Gottfried von Strassburg, *tr. fr. German by* E. M. Sweetman. ISi
To Mary ("My dearest Mary, wherefore hast thou gone"). Shelley.
(To Mary Shelley.) MotAn
To Mary ("So now my summer task is ended, Mary"). Shelley. The Revolt of Islam: Dedication. BPN; EmBrPo; EnRP; EPN
(Dedication.) ERP
To Mary. Charles Wolfe. GTSL; HBV; LO; OBEV; OBRV; ViBoPo
(Lines Written to Music.) TIP
(Song: To Mary.) EV-4
To Mary at Christmas. John Gilland Brunini. ISi
To Mary; at the Thirteenth Station. Raymond F. Roseliep. ISi
To Mary in Heaven. Burns. ATP; BCEP; BEL; CoBE; EnLit; HBV; LEAP; LPS-1; OAEP; OuHeWo; TCEP
(Thou Lingering Star.) EBSV; EiPP; EnRP; OBEC
To Mary: It Is the Evening Hour. John Clare. *See* Mary.
To Mary Lady Wroth. Ben Jonson. OBS
To Mary Lamb. Walter Savage Landor. *See* To the Sister of Elia.
To Mary Magdalen. Bartolomé Leonardo de Argensola, *tr. fr. Spanish by* Bryant. CAW
To Mary, Mother of Christ. Una W. Harsen. ChIP
To Mary our Queen, that flower so sweet. The Marigold. William Forrest. ACP; CAW
To Mary Shelley. Shelley. *See* To Mary ("My dearest Mary").
To Mary Sinclair, with a Volume of His Poems. Thomas Campbell. ERP
To Mary Unwin ("Mary! I want a lyre with other strings"). William Cowper. CBOV; CoBE; EV-3; GTBS; GTBS-D; GTBS-W; GTSE; GTSL; HBV; LEAP; OBEV; PeBoSo; RiBV; TrGrPo
(Sonnet to Mrs. Unwin.) BEL; OAEP; OBEC
(To Mrs. Unwin.) BoFr; ES; TCEP
To Mary Unwin ("The twentieth year is well-nigh past"). William Cowper. *See* To Mary.
To Master Bastard, a Minister That Made a Pleasant Book of English Epigrams. Sir John Harington. SiCE
To Master Bastard, Taxing Him of Flattery. Sir John Harington. SiCE
To Master Everard Digby. Thomas Lodge. ReIE
To Master Henry Cobham of the Most Blessed State of Life. Barnabe Googe. SiCE
To Master John Davies. Sir John Harington. SiCE
To Master Michael Drayton. Thomas Lodge. ReIE
To Master W. Shakespeare. Thomas Freeman. SiCE
To Maystres Isabell Pennell. John Skelton. *See* To Mistress Isabel Pennell.
To Me. William Barnes. PoEL-4
To me/ The thought of God. The Thought of God. Nagata. SoLD
To Me and Not to Them. Alma Ellis Hoernecke. MuM
To me fair friend you never can be old. Sonnets, CIV. Shakespeare. BEL; CaAE; EG; EIL; ElSeCe; EnLi-1 (1949 ed.); EnLit; ES; EtPaEn; EV-1; FaBoEn; GTBS; GTBS-D; GTBS-W; GTSE; GTSL; HBV; InP; LEAP; LiTL; OAEP; OBEV; OBSC; PeBoSo; ReEn; ReIE; SiCE; TOP; ViBoPo
To me, one silly task is like another. Cassandra. Louise Bogan. AnAmPo; LA; MAP; MoAmPo; MOAP; MoVE; NP
To me reveal thy heavenly art. To a Famous Painter. John Dyer. *Fr.* Epistle to a Famous Painter. BeR
To me the earth once seemed to be. Then and Now. Charles Frederick Johnson. AA
To me the groaning of world-worshippers. E. A. Robinson. Octaves, III. CoV
To me 'twas giv'n to die. For My Own Tomb-Stone. Matthew Prior. LiA
To me way-ay-ay-yah!/ We'll pay Paddy Doyle for his Boots! Paddy Doyle. *Unknown.* SoAmSa
To me, whom in their lays the shepherds call. Inscription for a Grotto. Mark Akenside. CEP; OBEC; PoEL-3; RO; SeCePo
To Me Wide-eyed throughout the Alien Night. Pauline Avery Crawford. MuM
To Meadows. Robert Herrick. AEV; AWP; CBE; CBOV; CBPC; CenL; CH; EG; EPS; EV-2; HBV; InPo; KN; LEAP; LoBV; OBEV; OTPC (1923 ed.); SeCL; ViBoPo; WP
(To Meddowes.) AtBAP; FaBoEn; OBS; PoEL-3; SeCV-1
"Ye have been fresh and green," *sel.* MyFE
To Meath of the pastures. A Drover. Padraic Colum. AnIL; AnIV; AWP; HBV; JAWP; LBBV; MBP; MoBrPo; NP; OBMV; OxBI; ViBoPo; WBP
To Meddowes. Robert Herrick. *See* To Meadows.
To meditate upon the tiger, turn. Scarabs for the Living, II. R. P. Blackmur. CoAnAm; TwAmPo
"To meet and then to part," and that is all. The Close of Day. Wesley Curtwright. CDC
To meet the fountain of true life I run. Longing. Judah Halevi. TrJP
To Melanippus. Alcaeus, *tr. fr. Greek by* Walter Petersen. GrR
To Melissus of Thebes. Pindar, *tr. fr. Greek by* Abraham Moore. Isthmian Odes, III. PreP
To Melité. Rufinus Domesticus, *tr. fr. Greek by* Dudley Fitts. LiTW
To Melody. George Leonard Allen. CDC
To Melvin Gardner; Suicide. John Charles McNeill. NoCaPo
To Memory. Mary Elizabeth Coleridge. GTML
To Men. Anna Wickham. MBP; MoBrPo
To men of other minds my fancy flies. Goldsmith. *Fr.* The Traveller. BHV
To Men Unborn. David Osborne Hamilton. HH; PEDC
To Mercy, Pity, Peace and Love. The Divine Image. Blake. *Fr.* Songs of Innocence. BoTP; CEP; CoEV; EiPP; EM-1; EnL; EnLit; EnRP; FaBoEn; GrCo-2; LiTG; LO; MaPo; MaRV; OAEP; OBEC; OnPM; OxBoCh; PoEL-4; ReaPo; TwCrTr; ViBoPo; WGRP
To Michal Meditating a New Costume. Charles Williams. TCPD
To Midnight; an Epitaph. *Unknown.* CoSo
To Midnight Nan at LeRoy's. Langston Hughes. AnAmPo; LA
To Miguel de Cervantes Saavadra. Richard Kendall Munkittrick. AA
To Milton. Oscar Wilde. BMEP
To Milton. Wordsworth. *See* London, 1802.
To Milton—Blind. Stephen Phillips. MBP
To mine own self I am a wilderness. Stéphane Mallarmé. *Fr.* Herodiade. LiA
To Minerva. Thomas Hood. BCEP; BoHV; ChTr; FiBHP; HBV; InMe; OxBoLi; PIAE; SiTL; TOP; WhC
(Fewer Books, More Salad.) OnPM
To Miracle. Michael Drayton. *See* Idea: "Some misbelieving and profane in love."
To Miss Arundell. Walter Savage Landor. OBVV
To Miss Charlotte Pulteney, in Her Mother's Arms. Ambrose Philips. *See* To Charlotte Pulteney.
To Miss Eleanor Ambrose on the Occasion of Her Wearing an Orange Lily at a Ball in Dublin Castle on July the 12th. Earl of Chesterfield. EnLoPo
To Miss Margaret Pulteney. Ambrose Philips. CEP; EV-3
To Miss X, Buried in the West Wind. Rafael Alberti, *tr. fr. Spanish by* Eleanor L. Turnbull. CoSP
To Mr. Barbauld. Anna Letitia Barbauld. DiM
To Mr. Congreve, *sel.* Swift.
Animal Critics, The. BeR
To Mr. Cyriack Skinner upon his Blindness. Milton. *See* To Cyriack Skinner ("Cyriack, this three years' day").
To Mr. Gay, *sel.* Swift.
Politician and Mr. Gay, The. BeR
To Mr. Gray. David Garrick. OBEC
To Mr. Gray. Thomas Warton, the Younger. PtP
To Mr. H. Lawes on His Airs. Milton. AWP; EM-1; ES; InPo; JAWP; LoBV; WBP
(Sonnet XIII: To Mr. H. Lawes on His Aires.) OBS
To M. Henry Lawes, the Excellent Composer, of His Lyrics. Robert Herrick. OAEP
To Mr. Henry Lawes, Who Had Then Newly Set a Song of Mine, in the Year 1635. Edmund Waller. EPS; SeCV-1
To Mr. Hobbes [*or* Hobs]. Abraham Cowley. LoBV; ReEn; SeCV-1
To Mr. Izaak Walton. Charles Cotton. *See* Retirement, The.
To Mr. Jervas, with Fresnoy's "Art of Painting," Translated by Mr. Dryden. Pope. OBEC
To Mr. John Davies. Sir John Harington. TuPP
To Mr. Lawrence. Milton. AWP; EM-1; ES; EV-2; GTBS; GTBS-D; GTBS-W; GTSE; GTSL; InPo; JAWP; MyFE; OBEV; PC; PeBoSo; WBP
(Lawrence of Virtuous Father Virtuous Son.) MaPo; PoE
(Sonnet XVII: "Lawrence of vertuous father . ."). OBS; SeEP
(Two Sonnets.) LiA
To Mr. Lee, on His Alexander, *sel.* Dryden.
Nat Lee's Images. BeR
To Mr. Pope. Thomas Parnell. PtP
To Mr. R. W. ("Zealously my Muse doth salute all thee"). John Donne. BoFr
To Mr. Rowland Woodward ("Like one who'in her third widdowhood doth professe"). John Donne. MePo
To Mr. T. W. ("At once, from hence, my lines and I depart"). John Donne. BoFr
To Mr. T. W. ("Pregnant again with the old twins Hope, and Feare"). John Donne. BoFr
To Mr. Victor Hugo. Alfred de Musset, *tr. fr. French by* Elizabeth Selden. BoFr
To Mr. W. B. on the Birth of His First Child. William Cartwright. NBE
To Mrs. Ann Flaxman. Blake. OBRV

To Mistress Anne Cecil, upon Making Her a New Year's Gift, January 1, 1567–8. William Cecil, Lord Burghley. ElL; OBSC; PrWP
To Mistress Gertrude Statham. John Skelton. *Fr.* The Garlande of Laurell. OAEP
To Mistress [*or* Maystres] Isabel[l] Pennell. John Skelton. *Fr.* The Garlande of Laurell. AtBAP; KN; LiTG; LiTL; LO; OAEP; OBEV (new ed.); OBSC; OxBoLi; PoEL-1; PoFS; SeCeV; TrGrPo; TuPP; ViBoPo
("By Saint Mary, my lady.") EG
(In Praise of Isabel Pennell.) CH
To Mrs. Leigh upon Her Wedding-Day. George Canning. ALV
To Mrs. M. A. upon Absence. Katherine Philips. NBE
To Mrs. M. B. on Her Birthday [*or* Birth-Day]. Pope. CEP; EnLoPo; FaBoEn; MeRV; OBEC
To Mistress Margaret Hussey. John Skelton. *Fr.* The Garlande of Laurell. ACP; AnFE; AtBAP; CoEV; EnLoPo; EV-1; GN; GoBC; HBV; HoPM; InPo; KN; LiTL; LoBV; LPS-1; OAEP; OBEV; OBSC; OTPC (1923 ed.); PG (1955 ed.); PoEL-1; PoRA; ReEn; SeCeV; SiCE; ThWaDe; TrGrPo; TuPP; ViBoPo
(Merry Margaret.) GoTP; RIS
(Mistress Margaret Hussey.) FaBoCh; LoGBV
(To Mistress Margery Wentworth, *wr. title.*) LEAP
To Mistress Margery Wentworth. John Skelton. *Fr.* The Garlande of Laurell. CoEV; EnLoPo; EV-1; LoBV; OBEV; OBSC; TrGrPo; ViBoPo
("With marregain gentle.") EG
To Mistress Pyrrha. Horace. *See* To Pyrrha.
To Mistress Sarah Hickford. —— Chambers. SeCL
To Mrs. Unwin. William Cowper. *See* To Mary Unwin.
To Mnesidice. Sappho, *tr. fr. Greek by* H. De Vere Stacpoole. GrR
To Modigliani to Prove to Him That I Am a Poet. Max Jacob, *tr. fr. French by* Wallace Fowlie. MiCF; TrJP
To Mollidusta. James Robinson Planché. NA
To Monsieur de la Mothe le Vayer. Molière, *tr. fr. French by* Austin Dobson. AWP; JAWP; WBP
To Morfydd. Lionel Johnson. AnIV; GTIV; LBBV; MBP; MoBrPo; OBMV; POTT; PoVP; ThWaDe; ViPP; VLEP
To Morning. Blake. EnRP
To mortal men Peace giveth these goods things. Peace on Earth. Bacchylides. AWP; GrPo; JAWP; WBP
To Mother. Louisa May Alcott. MOAH
To Mother. Thomas W. Fessenden. MaRV
(Mother.) MotAn
To Mother Corn (from the Hako Ceremony). *Tr. fr. Pawnee Indian.* GrCo-1
To Mother Fairie. Alice Cary. OTPC (1946 ed.); PCH
To Mother—in Heaven. Bennett Weaver. OQP; QP-1
To Mother Nature. Frederic Lawrence Knowles. HBV
To Mount Aetna. Tristan Corbière, *tr. fr. French by* Dudley Fitts. AnFP
To murder one so young! Alfred Domett. *Fr.* A Christmas Hymn; New Style. VA
To Music. William Kean Seymour. HBMV
To Music. Shelley. *See* Fragment, A: To Music.
To Music Bent Is My Retired Mind. Thomas Campion. CoBE; OxBoCh; ReEn; SiCE; TriL; UnS
(To Music [*or* Musicke] Bent.) TrPWD; TuPP
To Music [*or* Musique], to Becalm[e] His Fever. Robert Herrick. ATP; CoEV; EG; ElSeCe; EPS; EV-2; HBV; OBEV; OBS; PIAE; ReEn; SeCL; SeCV-1; TyEnPo
"Charm me asleep, and melt me so," *sel.* UnS
To Musick ("Musick, thou Queen of Heaven, care-charming-spel"). Robert Herrick. UnS
To my,/ Ay[e]. Paddy Doyle. *Unknown.* AmSS; SG
To My Auld Dog Dash. John Barr of Craigielee. AnNZ
To My Blackthorn Stick. F. R. Higgins. POTE
To My Book. Philip Freneau. IAP
To My Book [*or* Booke]. Ben Jonson. MaPo; OAEP; Po; ReIE; SeCV-1; TuPP
To My Books. William Roscoe. MOB
To My Bookseller. Ben Jonson. TuPP
To My Brother George. Keats. *See* Epistle to My Brother George.
To My Brothers. Norman Gale. VA
To My Brothers. Keats. EmBrPo; EnLi-2; PeBoSo
To My Brothers and Sisters Adrift in Troubled Times This Poem of the Moon. Po Chü-i, *tr. fr. Chinese by* Witter Bynner. BoFr
To My Cat. Rosamund Marriott Watson. PoC; POT; PoTo; VA
To My Child Carlino. Walter Savage Landor. OBRV
To My Children. John J. Burchenal. FAOV
To My Children. Marion Strobel. NP
To My Country. "Rachel," *tr. fr. Hebrew by* Sholom J. Kahn. LiTW
To My Country. Marguerite Wilkinson. AOAH
To My Countrymen. Robert Underwood Johnson. OQP; QP-2
To My Daughter. H. C. Bunner. FAOV
To My Daughter. Victor Hugo, *tr. fr. French by* Nelson R. Tyerman. FAOV
To My Daughter. Archibald Lampman. CPG
To My Daughter Adèle. Victor Hugo, *tr. fr. French by* Alan Conder. TrFP
To My Daughter Betty [the Gift of God]. Thomas Michael Kettle. CAW; HBMV; JKCP (1955 ed.); OnYI
To My Dear and Loving Husband. Anne Bradstreet. AmP; AmPP; BAV; IAP; NePA; OxBA; PoEL-3
To My Dear and Most Worthy Friend, Mr. Isaac Walton. Charles Cotton. BoFr, *abr.;* FaBoEn
To My Dear Friend, Mr. Congreve [on His Comedy Called "The Double-Dealer"]. Dryden. CEP; EiPP; FiP; GEPC; NBE; OBS; PoE; PoEL-3; PtP; SeCV-2; SeEP
To my dear wife. Father Abbey's Will. John Seccomb. BHV
To My Dearest Son. Helen Selina Sheridan. *See* To My Son.
To My Distant Beloved. Alois Jeitteles, *tr. fr. German by* the Reverend Doctor Troutbeck. TrJP
To My Dog. John Galsworthy. AlBD
To My Dog Blanco. Josiah Gilbert Holland. AlBD
To My Egeria, *sl. abr.* George Darley. RO
To My Empty Purse. Chaucer. *See* Compleint of Chaucer to His Empty Purse, The.
To My Excellent Lucasia, on Our Friendship. Katherine Philips. ElSeCe; LO; MeLP; OBS; SeCL; SeEP
("I did not live until this time.") EG
To my fancy, idly roaming, comes a picture of the gloaming. The Echo of a Song. James W. Foley. PEDC
To My Father. James K. Baxter. AnNZ
To My Father. William Rose Benét. FAOV
To My Father. Donald F. Drummond. PtPa
To My Father. W. S. Graham. FaBoTw
To My Father. William Hamilton Hayne. SPP
To My Father. Grace Denio Litchfield. FAOV
To My Father. "Philardee." FAOV
To My Father. Iris Tree. FAOV; HBMV
To my father went and shyly asked consent. May I Woo the Lassie? *Unknown.* SaSa
To my father's garden will I with this crown. The Withered Crown. Marceline Desbordes-Valmore. TrFP
To My Fellow Writers. Aleksandr Yashin, *tr. fr. Russian by* Jack Lindsay. RuPO
To My First Love, My Mother. Christina Rossetti. MotAn; OHIP
(Dedications.) MOAH
(Dedicatory Sonnet.) VLEP
To My Firstborn. Bernard Isaac Durward. JKCP (1926 ed.)
To My Friend. Anne Campbell. PoToHe
To My Friend. Wilfred Owen. NaMP
To My Friend, behind Walls. Carolyn Kizer. NePoAm-2
To My Friend Butts I Write. Blake. EnRP
To My Friend, Dr. Charleton. Dryden. *See* To My Honor'd Friend, Dr. Charleton.
To My Friend, Grown Famous. Eunice Tietjens. HBMV
To My Friend, Master John Ford. James Shirley. PtP
To My Friend Mr. Jonson. Sir Thomas Roe. BoFr
To My Friends. Peter De Vries. FiBHP
To My Friends. Schiller, *tr. fr. German by* James Clarence Mangan. AWP; LiTW
To My Friends in São Paulo. Olavo Bilac, *tr. fr. Portuguese by* Elizabeth Selden. BoFr
To My Generation. Benyamin Galai, *tr. fr. Hebrew by* Jacob Sonntag. TrJP
To My Generation (1919–1933). Horace Gregory. *See* Valediction to My Contemporaries.
To My Gillyflower. Henrik Wergeland, *tr. fr. Norwegian by* Charles W. Stork. AnNoLy
(Wall-Flower, The, *tr. by* Sir Edmund Gosse.) AWP; JAWP; WBP
To My God. George Macdonald. TrPWD
To My Godchild. Francis Thompson. PC; PoeT
(To My Godchild—Francis M. W. M.) JKCP
To My Grandmother. Frederick Locker-Lampson. ALV; EPP; HBV; InMe; OBVV; TOP; VA
To My Hairdresser. Warham St. Leger. CenHV
To My Honor'd [*or* Honoured] Friend, Dr. Charleton. Dryden. CEP; EiPP; EnL; SeEP
(To My Friend, Dr. Charleton, on His Learned and Useful Works.) SeCV-2
To My Honor'd Friend Sir Robert Howard, on His Excellent Poems. Dryden. EiPP
Design, 4 *ll.* MaRV
To My Honour'd [*or* Honoured] Kinsman, John Dryden, of Chesterton [in the County of Huntingdon, Esq.]. Dryden. OBS, *abr.;* SeEP
To My Household Gods. Jean François Ducis, *tr. fr. French by* Alan Conder. TrFP
To My Inconstant Mistress [*or* Mistris]. Thomas Carew. ElSeCe; EnLit; EnLoPo; EPS; EV-2; HBV; LO; LoBV; MeLP; MePo; OBS; SeCePo; SeCL; SeCV-1; TrGrPo
(Song: To My Inconstant Mistress.) BrBE
(To His Inconstant Mistress.) OBEV
("When thou, poor excommunicate.") EG

To My Infant Son. Thomas Hood. *See* Parental Ode to My Son, Aged Three Years and Five Months, A.
To My Lady. George Henry Boker. *Fr.* Sonnets. AA
("I'll call thy frown a headsman passing grim.") MOAP
To My Lady Dear, *in mod. Eng. Unknown.* TMEV
To My Lady Mirriel Howard. John Skelton. *Fr.* The Garlande of Laurell. LoBV
To My Little Daughter. E. J. Francis Davies. FAOV
To My Little Son. Julia Johnson Davis. FAOV; HBMV
To My Lord Buckhurst, Very Young, Playing with a Cat. Matthew Prior. PoC
To My Love. John Godfrey Saxe. HBV
To My Love. Sir John Suckling. *See* I Prithee Send Me Back My Heart.
To My Lucasia, in Defence of Declared Friendship. Katherine Philips. MeLP
To My Mere English Censurer. Ben Jonson. TuPP
To My Mistress. Frederick Locker-Lampson. VA
To My Most Dearly-loved [Friend] Henry Reynolds, Esquire, of Poets and Poesy [*or* Poesie]. Michael Drayton. OAEP; OBS; PtP; ReEn; SeEP; TuPP
To My Most Gracious Dread Sovereign. Sir John Davies. *See* Dedication: "To that clear majesty which in the north."
To My Mother. George Barker. *See* Sonnet to My Mother.
To My Mother. Eugene Field. *Quoted in* The Mother of Eugene Field, *by* Ida Comstock Below. MOAH
To My Mother. Heine, *tr. fr. German by* Matilda Dickson. AWP; JAWP; WBP
(Sonnet to My Mother, A, *tr. by* Emma Lazarus.) TrJP
(To His Mother, *tr. by* Ralph Marcus.) OnPM
To My Mother. Felicia Dorothea Hemans. MOAH
To My Mother. W. E. Henley. PoVP
To My Mother. Hsing Ch'e, *tr. fr. Chinese by* Henry H. Hart. PoHN
To My Mother. Thomas Moore. MotAn; OHIP; PEDC; PoRL
To My Mother. Poe. AnAmPo; DD; IAP; LA; LaNeLa; MaRV; MCCG; MOAH; MotAn; NePA; OxBA
(Sonnet to My Mother.) APW
To My Mother. Robert Haven Schauffler. MOAH
To My Mother. "Petros Vlastos," *tr. fr. Modern Greek by* Rae Dalven. MoGP
To My Mother. Henry Kirke White. MOAH
To My Mouse-colored Mare. Tristan Corbière, *tr. fr. French by* Dudley Fitts. AnFP
To My Native City. Luis Carlos López, *tr. fr. Spanish by* H. R. Hays. TwSpPo
To My Native Land. James Clarence Mangan. AnIL
"Awake! arise! shake off thy dreams!"*sel.* IrPN
To My Ninth Decade. Walter Savage Landor. BEL; BPN; EmBrPo; EnRP
(Lyrics and Epigrams.) ERP
(On His Ninth Decade.) TrGrPo
To My Nose. Alfred A. Forrester. BLPA; BOHV; LPS-3
To my nose there came a whiff. Plautus. *Fr.* Curculio. LaP
To My Nun Sister. E. P. Tivnan. PraNu
To My Old, and Most Worthy Friend, Mr. Izaak Walton. Charles Cotton. SeEP
To My Patrons. Lionel Johnson. JKCP
To My People. Edwin Seaver. TrJP
To My Promised Wife. John Walsh. TIP
To my quick ear the leaves conferred. Emily Dickinson. AnFE; APA; CoAnAm; GTBS-D; MAPA; TwAmPo
To My Readers. Oliver Wendell Holmes. AmPP (3d ed.); IAP; TCAP
To My Retired Friend Wei. Tu Fu, *tr. fr. Chinese by* Witter Bynner. LiTW
To My Setter, Scout. Frank H. Seldon. BLPA
To my sick eyes. Loveliness. *Unknown.* SoLD
To My Sister. Hsi P'ei Lan, *tr. fr. Chinese by* Henry H. Hart. BoFr; PoHN
To My Sister, *sel.* Yiannis Ritsos, *tr. fr. Modern Greek by* Rae Dalven.
"My sister/ only you/ are left me." MoGP
To My Sister. Wordsworth. BPN; EmBrPo; EnRP; ERP; GEPC; OBRV; PoE; SN
Change in the Year, A, *sel.* BoTP
To My Soldier Brother. Sallie M. Ballard. BlG
To My Son. Babette Deutsch. NeTW
To My Son. John Drinkwater. PtOT
To My Son. Margaret Johnston Grafflin. *See* Like Mother, like Son.
To My Son. Thomas Hood. *See* Parental Ode to My Son, Aged Three Years and Five Months, A.
To My Son. Helen Selina Sheridan.
(To My Dearest Son.) DiM
Love Hath a Language, *sel.* HBV
To My Son. *Unknown.* PoMa
To My Son. John V. A. Weaver. FAOV
To My Son, Aged Three Years and Five Months. Thomas Hood. *See* Parental Ode to My Son, Aged Three Years and Five Months, A.
To My Son, Four Days Old. Leila Sprague Learned. MotAn
To My Soul. Phineas Fletcher. OxBoCh
(To My Soul in Its Blindness.) SeCL
To My Terrier Rex. Agnes Kendrick Gray. TBM
To My Tortoise 'Ἀνάγκη (Ananke). Eugene Lee-Hamilton. OBVV
To My Tortoise Chronos. Eugene Lee-Hamilton. VA
To My Totem. Henry Charles Beeching. VA
To my true king I offered free from stain. A Jacobite's Epitaph [*or* Epitaph on a Jacobite]. Macaulay. CBE; CBOV; EV-4; GTBS; InP; LH; OBEV; OBVV; VA; ViBoPo; WP
To My Truly Valiant, Learned Friend, Who in His Book Resolv'd the Art Gladiatory into the Mathematics. Richard Lovelace. PoEL-3
To My Unborn Son. Cyril Morton Horne. BLPA
To My Valentine. *Unknown.* PCH
To my village fair no lass can compare. The Lovely Village Fair; or, I Dont Mean to Tell You Her Name. *Unknown.* CoMu
To My Wife. John Bayliss. POTE
To My Wife. William Rose Benét. PoMa
To My Wife. James Forsyth. WaP
To My Wife. Robert Louis Stevenson. *See* My Wife.
To My Wife from Yeh-lang, the Place of Exile. LiPo, *tr. fr. Chinese.* WhP
To My Worthy and Honoured Friend, Mr. George Chapman, on His Translation of Hesiod's "Works and Days." Ben Jonson. PtP
To My Worthy Friend Master George Sands [*or* Sandys], on His Translation of the Psalms [*or* Psalmes]. Thomas Carew. EV-2; MePo; SeCV-1; SeEP
(To My Worthy Friend Mr. George Sandys.) MeLP; OBS
To My Worthy Friend Mr. George Chapman, and His Translated Hesiod. Michael Drayton. PtP
To My Worthy Friend Mr. George Sandys. Thomas Carew. *See* To My Worthy Friend Master George Sands . . .
To My Young Lady Lucy Sidney. Edmund Waller. *See* To a Very Young Lady.
To My Youngest Son. Tu Fu, *tr. fr. Chinese.* WhP
To Myra. George Granville. *See* Happiest Mortals Once Were We, The.
To Myra. Fulke Greville. *See* I, with Whose Colors Myra Dressed Her Head.
To N. Chapman, M.D., *sel.* John Kearsley Mitchell.
"I've aften wished for Burns's pen." PoP
To N. N. Pushkin, *tr. fr. Russian by* Babette Deutsch. TrRV
To N. V. de G. S. Robert Louis Stevenson. VA
To Naples. H. B. Mallalieu. WaP
To Napoleon in Exile. Walter Channing. PoP
To Natalie. Morrie Ryskind. HBMV
To Nature. Samuel Taylor Coleridge. ES; MaRV
To Nature. Mahlon Leonard Fisher. AnAmPo; LA
To Nature. Friedrich Hölderlin, *tr. fr. German by* Frederic Prokosch. LiTW
To Nature Seekers. Robert W. Chambers. MoShBr
To Ned. Herman Melville. PoEL-5; ViBoPo
To New Haven. Frederick Scheetz Jones. *See* On the Democracy of Yale.
To New Haven and Boston. Walter Foster Angell. TreFS
To Night. Thomas Lovell Beddoes. LoBV
To Night. Shelley. AnFE; AtBAP; ATP; AWP; BEL; BLV; BoLiVe; BPN; CaAE; CBE; ChER; CoBE; EM-2; EmBrPo; EnL; EnLi-2; EnLit; EnRP; EPN; EPP; ERP; EV-4; ExPo; GEPC; GTSL; HBV; HBVY; InP; InPo; JAWP; KN; LEAP; LoBV; LPS-2; MaPo; MCCG; MyFE; OAEP; OBRV; PCD; PIAE; PoE; PoFS; PoRA; PPD-1; REAL; ReaPo; SeCeV; TOP; TreFS; TrGrPo; TVSH; TyEnPo; UnPo (1st ed.); ViBoPo; WBP; WHA
(Night.) BCEP; OAEP
("Swiftly walk o'er the western wave.") EG
(To the Night.) CH; GTBS; GTBS-D; GTBS-W; GTSE; ShBV-4
To Night. Arthur Symons. POTT
To Night. *Unknown.* *See* O Night, O Jealous Night.
To Night. Joseph Blanco White. EV-4; GoBC; GTBS-W; HBV; LiA; MaRV; OBEV (new ed.); OBRV; PoeMoYo; TreFS; ViBoPo; WGRP
(Mysterious Night.) AnFE
("Mysterious night, when our first parent knew.") EG
(Night.) AnIV; BCEP; GTIV; JKCP (1926 ed.); LPS-1
(Night and Death.) EPN; ES; SN
(Sonnet to Night, A.) TVSH
"Hesperus with the Host of Heaven came," *sel.* MyFE
To nothing fitter can I thee compare. Idea, X. Michael Drayton. BEL; EIL; HBV; OBSC; SiCE; TrGrPo; TuPP; ViBoPo
To November. G. W. Adams. TOAH
To O. E. A. Claude McKay. BANP; PoNe
To O. S. C. Annie Eliot Trumbull. AA
To O. W. Holmes. Paul Hamilton Hayne. DD; GA
To Ocean Hazard; Gipsy. Lionel Johnson. VLEP
To Oenone. Robert Herrick. *See* To Aenone.

To Old Age. Walt Whitman. InP
To Old John Heywood the Epigrammatist, Wheresoever. John Davies of Hereford. SiCE
To Old Movitz, Ill with Consumption. Karl Mikael Bellman, *tr. fr. Swedish by* Charles W. Stork. AnSL
To Old Roscoff. Tristan Corbière, *tr. fr. French by* Alan Conder. TrFP
To Olive. Lord Alfred Douglas. OBEV (new ed.); OBVV
To Oliver Cromwell. Milton *See* To the Lord General Cromwell.
To Olivia. Francis Thompson. BMEP; MBP; MoBrPo
To Omar Khayyám. Maud Ludington Cain. MuM
To Omar Khayyám. Justin Huntly M'Carthy. LEAP
To One. Gustaf Munch-Petersen, *tr. fr. Danish by* Carl Nesjar *and* Martin S. Allwood. LiTW
To One Admiring Herself in a Looking Glass. Thomas Randolph. LiTL; ViBoPo
To One Afar. Chang Jung, *tr. fr. Chinese by* Henry H. Hart. PoHN
To One alone my thoughts arise. Longfellow. *Fr.* Coplas de Manrique. ChIP
To One Being Old. Langdon Elwyn Mitchell. AA; OBAV
To one fair Lady out of Court. The Challenge. Pope. PoEL-3
To one full sound and silently. The Man with Three Friends. Dora Greenwell. OBVV
To One in Bedlam. Ernest Dowson. ACP; BLV; EnLi-2; LBBV; MBP; MoBrPo; NeMA; OBMV; PoVP; ViPP; WHA
To One in Heaven. Nagata, *tr. fr. Japanese by* Lois J. Erickson. SoLD
To One in Paradise. Poe. *Fr.* The Assignation. AA; AmPo; AmPP; AnFE; APA; APW; BLV; BoLiVe; CoAnAm; CoBA; GTBS-D; HBV; IAP; LBAP; LEAP; LiTA; LiTL; LO; LoPS; MOAP, *abr.*; NePA; OBAV; OBEV (new ed.); OBRV; OBVV; OxBA; PG; PIR, *abr.*; SPP; TCAP, *abr.*; TrGrPo; TriL; UnW; ViBoPo; WHA; YT
To One of Little Faith. Hildegarde Flanner. HBMV
To One Older. Marion M. Boyd. HBMV
To One on Her Waste of Time. Wilfrid Scawen Blunt. The Love Sonnets of Proteus, LVIII. ViBoPo
To One Persuading a Lady to Marriage. Katherine Philips. EV-2; OBEV
To One Self-slain. Charles Hanson Towne. *See* Of One Self-slain.
To One Singing. Russell Mayo Spear. CAG
To One That Pleaded Her Own Want of Merit. Thomas Stanley. OBS
(To Celia Pleading Want of Merit.) MeLP
To One Unknown. Helen Dudley. AV; NP
To One Unnamed. Li Shang-yin, *tr. fr. Chinese by* Witter Bynner. ChLP
To One Who after Death Would Leave His Lively Picture. Thomas Howell. TuPP
To One Who Denies the Possibility of a Permanent Peace. Lady Margaret Sackville. HBMV; MaRV
To One Who Died in Autumn. Virginia McCormick. HBMV
To One Who Died Young. Georg Trakl, *tr. fr. German by* Christopher Middleton. AnGP
To One Who Had Censured His Public Exposition of Dante. Boccaccio, *tr. fr. Italian by* Dante Gabriel Rossetti. *Fr.* Sonnets. AWP
(Tribute to Dante, A.) GoBC
To One Who Has Been Long in City Pent. Keats. BEL; BLV; BoLiVe; BPN; CBE; CoBE; EM-2; EmBrPo; EnLi-2; EnLit; EnRP; ERP; EV-4; GTBS-W; GTSL; HBV; LiTB; LiTG; MCCG; PeBoSo; PoFS; SeCeV; TrGrPo; TwP; TyEnPo
(Sonnet: "To one who has been long in city pent.") BLPA; CaAE; FaBoBe; GEPC; LoBV; NeHB; PC; REAL
To One Who Has Passed. Wu Ti, *tr. fr. Chinese by* Henry H. Hart. PoHN
To One Who Said Me Nay. Countee Cullen. PR
To One Who Spoke of Eternal Things. John Cowper Powys. BAP
To One Who Wanted a Philosophy from Me. "Æ." ChMo
To One Who Worshipped Gods of Gold. John Richard Moreland. MaRV; MuM
To One Who Would Make a Confession. Wilfrid Scawen Blunt. The Love Sonnets of Proteus, LXII. HBV; LEAP; ViBoPo
To One with Hands of Sleep. Harold Vinal. PC
To onpreise womene it were a shame. *Unknown.* LO
To Orkney. David Vedder. EBSV
To others he was a presence—perhaps only. Matthew. Clive Sansom. HaMV
To Our Blessed Lady. Henry Constable. ACP; CAW; GoBC; ISi; OBSC
(To Our Lady.) CoBE
To Our Blessed Lord upon the Choice of His Sepulchre. Richard Crashaw. *See* Upon the Savior's Tomb.
To Our Catchment Board. Edmund Blunden. MoPW
To our country's soldiers. Tribute to Our Soldiers. Marion Kennedy. PEDC
To Our English Terence, Mr. Will. [*or* Master William] Shakespeare. John Davies of Hereford. PtP; SiCE
To Our Forefathers. Frances Crosby Hamlet. PSO
To Our Friends. Lucian B. Watkins. BANP
To Our House-Dog Captain. Walter Savage Landor. PoEL-4
To Our Ladies of Death. James Thomson. BSV; GoTS
To Our Lady. Henry Constable. *See* To Our Blessed Lady.
To Our Lady. Robert Henryson. ACP; CAW
To Our Lady. Mary Dixon Thayer. TreFS
To Our Lady, the Ark of the Covenants. Raymond E. F. Larsson. ISi
To Our Lord. Francisco Galvam, *tr. fr. Portuguese by* Thomas Walsh. CAW
To Our Lord in the Sacrament. St. Anselm, *tr. fr. Latin by* Romano Rios. CAW
To Our Lord, upon the Water Made Wine. Richard Crashaw. MePo
To Our Saviour. Agostinho da Cruz, *tr. fr. Portuguese by* Thomas Walsh. CAW
To outer senses there is peace. La Fuite de la Lune. Oscar Wilde. *Fr.* Impressions. Po; PoVP
To outer senses they are geese. More Impressions. "Oscuro Wildgoose." PA
To Oxford. Gerard Manley Hopkins. *Fr.* Low Sunday and Monday. NBE
To Oxford. Thomas Russell. *See* Sonnet: To Oxford.
To Pablo Picasso. Paul Eluard, *tr. fr. French by* Wallace Fowlie. MiCF
To Pain. George Sterling. JKCP (1926 ed.)
To Pan. Agathias Scholasticus, *tr. fr. Greek by* F. L. Lucas. GrPE
To Pan. John Fletcher. *See* God of Sheep, The.
To Pan ("Pan, who hast to thy command"). *Unknown, tr. fr. Greek by* T. F. Higham. OxBG
To Pan ("Sing me of Hermes' beloved son"). *Unknown, tr. fr. Greek by* Arthur S. Way. *Fr.* Homeric Hymns. GrR
(Hymn to Pan: "Of the dear son of Hermes, O Muse, sing now to me," *tr. by* F. L. Lucas.) GrPE
(To Pan: "Muse, tell of Pan," *tr. by* Jack Lindsay.) OxBG
To Pan ("Twy-horn Pan, the ridgy hills"). *Unknown, tr. fr. Greek by* Alexander Lothian. OxBG
To Pandora. Alexander Craig TuPP
(Sonnet: "Go you, O winds that blow from north to south.") EIL
To parents and friends: Mrs. June. Mrs. June's Prospectus. "Susan Coolidge." ADAH
To Paris, to Paris, to Paris. The Hobby Horse. *Unknown.* PCH
To part now, and, parting now. After Love. Arthur Symons. LEAP
To Pass the Place Where Pleasure Is. *Unknown.* CoMu
To Paths Unknown. Whittier. *See* At Last.
To Patricia, Eleven. Robert Underwood Johnson. PYM
To Peace. Katharine Lee Bates. AOAH
To Peace. Richard Watson Dixon. EV-5
To peace-white ashes sunk war's lurid flame. Appomattox. Ben D. House. BIG
To Peace, with Victory. Corinne Roosevelt Robinson. AOAH
To Penetrate That Room. John Lehmann. MBP
To Pensacola town we'll bid adieu. Homeward Bound. *Unknown.* AmSS
To Penshurst. Ben Jonson. AtBAP; AWP; EPS; LoBV; OBS; PoEL-2; PoFS; ReEn; ReIE; SeCV-1; SeEP; TuPP
"Thou hast thy ponds, that pay thee tribute fish," *sel.* FaBoEn
To Pentadius. Jacopo Sannazaro, *tr. fr. Latin by* Richard Lovelace. LaP
To people who allege that we. The Uses of Ocean. Sir Owen Seaman. ALV; FiBHP
To Perilla. Robert Herrick. AtBAP; ElSeCe; OBS; ReaPo; SeCV-1; SeEP; UnPo (1st ed.)
To Petronilla Who Has Put Up Her Hair. Henry Howarth Bashford. HBV
To Petronius Arbiter. Oliver St. John Gogarty. OBMV
To Phidyle ("Caelo supinas"). Horace, *tr. fr Latin by* Austin Dobson. Odes, III, 23. AWP
To Philaenis. Poseidippus, *tr. fr. Greek by* J. M. Edmonds. GrR
To Philippe Desportes. Jean Antoine de Baïf, *tr. fr. French by* Elizabeth Selden. BoFr
To Phillis. Robert Herrick. *See* To Phyllis, to Love and Live with Him.
To Phillis. Edmund Waller. *See* To Phyllis.
To Phillis, the Fair Shepherdess. Thomas Lodge. *See* To Phyllis, the Fair Shepherdess.
To Philomel. John Tatham. SeCL
To Phoebe. W. S. Gilbert. BOHV; InMe; InP; PFE
To Phoebus Seeing a Lady before Sunrise. Edmund Prestwich. SeCL

To Phyllis ("Est mihi"). Horace, *tr. fr. Latin by* Eugene Field. Odes, IV, 11. InMe
To Phyllis. Thomas Lodge. *See* Love Guards the Roses of Thy Lips.
To Phyllis. *Unknown.* SeCL
To Phyllis. Edmund Waller. ElSeCe; TrGrPo
(To Phillis.) CEP; OAEP
To Phyllis, the Fair Shepherdess. Thomas Lodge. Phyllis, XV. CBOV; ViBoPo
("My Phyllis [*or* Phillis] hath the morning sun.") CaAE; ElSeCe
(Phillis.) LoBV; OBEV, *12 ll.;* OBSC
(Phyllis.) ACP; ElL
To Phyllis [*or* Phillis], to Love and Live with Him. Robert Herrick. EPS (1942 ed.); LiTL; OAEP; ReaPo
(To Phillis.) AnEnPo
To Pikes Peak. Elijah Clarence Hills. PoOW
To Pillar's height reach up, and rest thee now. Dedication for a Spear. Simonides. OxBG
To Ping-ku, Asleep. Lawrence Durrell. ChMP; NeBP
To Piso from his pet friend. Philodemus, *tr. fr. Greek by* F. A. Wright. GrPo
To Pi Ssu Yao. Tu Fu, *tr. fr. Chinese by* Kenneth Rexroth. OnPC
To Pius X at Easter. John Hazard Wildman. JKCP (1955 ed.)
To place the precisely slippered toes. Portraits. Robert Fitzgerald. OnHM
To plant a seed and see it grow. Lesson. Harry Behn. TiPo (1959 ed.)
To plant a tree! How small the twig. Arbor Day. Dorothy Brown Thompson. SiSoSe
To Plead My Faith. Earl of Essex. TuPP
To Poets. George Darley. RO
To Poets. Walter Savage Landor. ViBoPo
To Poets. Charles Hamilton Sorley. GTML; LO
To Poets All Thomas Curtis Clark. MaRV
To Poets and Airmen. Stephen Spender. PoF; NeTW; WaP
To Polla. John Owen, *tr. fr. Latin by* Thomas Harvey. *Fr.* Four Epigrams. PrWP
To Pontius Washing His Hands. Richard Crashaw. SeEP
To popularize the mule, its neat exterior. The Labors of Hercules. Marianne Moore. AnAmPo; LA; OxBA
To Posterity. Bertolt Brecht, *tr. fr. German by* H. R. Hays. OnHM
To Postumus ("Etheu, fugaces"). Horace, *tr. fr. Latin by* Sir Stephen Edward De Vere. Odes, II, 14. LiTW; OuHeWo
(Death Inevitable, *tr. by* Thomas Creech.) RoL
("Postumus, Postumus, the years glide by us," *tr. by* Lord Lytton.) LaP
To Potapovitch. Hart Crane. UnS
To praise men as good, and to take them for such. Charity in Thought. Samuel Taylor Coleridge. WhC
To Praise thy life or wail thy worthy death. An Epitaph upon the Right Honorable Sir Philip Sidney, Knight, Lord Governor of Flushing [*or* Epitaph on Sir Philip Sidney]. *At. to* Sir Walter Ralegh. ReIE; SiCe; SiPS; TuPP
To praise, yet still with due respect to praise. To Mr. Pope. Thomas Parnell. PtP
To press my lips. Sons. Grace Noll Crowell. DDA
To Primal Matter. Luis de Sandoval y Zapata, *tr. fr. Spanish by* Samuel Beckett. AnMP
To Primroses Filled [*or* Fill'd] with Morning Dew. Robert Herrick. BCEP; EG; ElSeCe; EPS; EV-2; HBV; OBS; SeCL; SeCV-1; SeEP; ViBoPo
To print, or not to print—that is the question. Hamlet's Soliloquy Imitated. Richard Jago. SiTL
To print our poems, the propulsive cause. Fame Makes Us Forward. Robert Herrick. EPS (1942 ed.)
To Prote. Simmias, *tr. fr. Greek by* John Addington Symonds. AWP
To Psyche. Keats. *See* Ode to Psyche.
To Puck. Beatrice Llewellyn Thomas. HBMV
To Pulpit and Tribune. Amos N. Wilder. MaRV
To punish crime and spread dire terror. The Animals Ill with the Plague. La Fontaine. TrFP
To purge what I am pleased to call my mind. Ataraxia. Bert Leston Taylor. HBMV; InMe
To Purity and Truth. *Unknown, tr. fr. Chinese by* William C. White. TrJP
To put new shingles on old roofs. A Little Brother of the Rich. Edward Sandford Martin. AA; HBV
To Pyrrha ("Quis multa gracilis"). Horace, *tr. fr. Latin by* Milton. Odes, I, 5. AWP; JAWP; WBP; EnLi-1, *tr. by* Goldwin Smith; OuHeWo, *tr. by* Goldwin Smith
(Fifth Ode of Horace, The, *tr. by* Milton.) EnLoPo; LiA; PoEL-3
(For Whom, Pyrrha? *tr. by* Milton.) LiTW
(Horace to Pyrrha, *tr. by* Eugene Field.) LHV
(To a Flirt, *tr. by* Milton.) RoL
(To Mistress Pyrrha, *tr. by* Eugene Field.) PR
("What slim elegant youth, drenched in effusive scent," *tr. by* Gilbert Highet.) LaP
("What slim youth, moistened with liquid perfumes," *tr. by* Joseph Bennett.) LaP
To Q. H. F. Austin Dobson. PtP
To Queen Elizabeth. Sir John Davies. *See* Dedication: "To that clear majesty which in the north."
To Queen Elizabeth. Sir Walter Ralegh. *See* Silent Lover, The.
To Queen Radigunde with Herbs and Violets. Venantius Fortunatus, *tr. fr. Latin by* Jack Lindsay. LyMA
To Quintius. Catullus, *tr. fr. Latin by* George Lamb. OnPM
To Quintus. Martial, *tr. fr. Latin by* Paul Nixon. RoL
To Quintus Dellius ("Aequam memento"). Horace, *tr. fr. Latin by* John Herman Merivale. Odes, II, 3. OuHeWo
To R. B. Gerard Manley Hopkins. CoBMV; InvP; POTT; PoVP; ViP; ViPP
To R. K. James Kenneth Stephen. CenHV; EnLi-2 (1949 ed.); OtMeF; WhC
(Lapsus Calami.) VA
(Millennium, The.) BOHV
To R. L. S. W. E. Henley. Echoes, XXIX. BPN; POTT; VOD
(To Robert Louis Stevenson.) MBP; MoBrPo
To R. W. E. Ellen Hooper. AnAmPo; LA
To Rafael Cansinos Assens. Jorge Luis Borges, *tr. fr. Spanish by* Robert Stuart Fitzgerald. AnCL
To rail or jest, ye know I use it not. Sonnets, IX. Sir Thomas Wyatt. SiPS
To Rathlin's Isle I chanced to sail. The Enchanted Island. Luke Aylmer Conolly. OBRV; TIP
To read my book, the virgin shy. To His Book. Martial. AWP; LiTW
To rear a child is easy, but to teach. Theognis, *tr. fr. Greek by* J. H. Frere. GrPo
To recall and revision blue skies. Bertrand Hume. Edgar Lee Masters. *Fr.* The New Spoon River. LEAP
To reckon [*or* rekyn] of ever thing the circumstance. James I, King of Scotland. *Fr.* The Kingis Quair. BSV; NBE
To Reformers in Despair. Vachel Lindsay. InP
To remember . . . to forgive . . . to have loved. Manuel Gutiérrez Nájera. *Fr.* Pax Anima. AnMP
To Remi Belleau. Pierre de Ronsard, *tr. fr. French by* Ralph N. Currey. FoS
To Retirement. Luis de León, *tr. fr. Spanish by* Thomas Walsh. TrJP
To Rhea. Emerson. TCAP
To Rich Givers. Walt Whitman. AnAmPo; LA
To Richard. Vera Bax. DiM
To Richard Owen Cambridge. Thomas Edwards. ES
To Richard Watson Gilder. Austin Dobson. BoFr
To rise up and get away from all this. Escape. Leonard Mann. NeLNL
To Robert Browning. Witter Bynner. LPS-1
To Robert Browning. Walter Savage Landor. BCEP; BEL; BPN; EmBrPo; EnLi-2 (1949 ed.); EnRP; EPN; EPP; EV-4; GTBS; GTSL; InP; LEAP; MCCG; OAEP; PeBoSo; PoRL; PreP; PtP; ViBoPo
(Lyrics and Epigrams, XVIII.) ERP
"There is delight in singing, though none hear," *sel.* MyFE
To Robert Earl of Oxford and Earl Mortimer. Pope. CEP; OBEC
To Robert Louis Stevenson. W. E. Henley. *See* To R. L. S.
To Robin Redbreast. Robert Herrick. EPS; OBS; SeEP; TrGrPo
To Rodin. Charles Wharton Stork. TBM
To Ronge. Whittier. AnEnPo
To Roosevelt. Rubén Darío. *See* To Theodore Roosevelt.
To Rose. Austin Dobson. *See* Circe.
To Rose. Walter Savage Landor. TriL
To Rose. Sara Teasdale. HBV
To Rosemary. Stephen Vincent Benét. LaNeLa; LoPS
To Rosemounde [*or* Rosemound]; a Balade. Chaucer. InP; LoPS; PoLi
To Roses in the Bosom of Castara. William Habington. *Fr.* Castara, I. ElSeCe; EnLoPo; EV-2; GoBC; HBV; LoBV; MeLP; OBEV; SeCL; SeEP; ViBoPo
To Rosina Pico. William Wilberforce Lord. AA
To Ruin. Burns. CoBE
To Rupert Brooke. W. W. Gibson. *See* Going, The.
To Russia. Ilya Ehrenburg, *tr. fr. Russian by* Babette Deutsch. TrRV
To Russia. Joaquin Miller. AA; AnAmPo; LA
To S. R. Crockett. Robert Louis Stevenson. FaBoEn; GTBS-D; LO; PoeT; POTT; ShBV-4
(Blows the Wind To-Day.) BSV; CH; GTSE; LoBV
(Vailima.) CBE
(Whaups, The.) VA
To S.T.C. on His 179th Birthday, October 12th, 1951. Maurice Carpenter. FaBoTw
To Sabidius. Martial, *tr fr. Latin by* Timothe Kendall. TuPP
To Safeguard the Heart from Hardness. Sarah N. Cleghorn. PC
To Saint Catherine. Henry Constable. GoBC
To Saint Francis. Edwin Markham. SaFP

To Saint Francis. A. Babington Smith. SaFP
To St. Joseph. Charles L. O'Donnell. JKCP
To Saint Margaret. Henry Constable. ACP; GoBC
To St. Mary Magdalen. Henry Constable. ACP; CoBE; LoBV (2d ed.); PoEL-2; TriL; TuPP
To St. Mary Magdalen. Benjamin Dionysius Hill. AA
To St. Peter and St. Paul. Henry Constable. ReEn; TuPP
To St. Valentine. Jennie Betts Hartswick. DD
To Sally. John Quincy Adams, *after the Latin of* Horace. AA; ALV; AWP; JAWP; LHV; PR; WBP
To Samuel Daniel, Prince of English Poets. Francis Davison. ReIE
To San Francisco. S. J. Alexander. PAH
To Sappho. Alcaeus, *tr. fr. Greek by* Walter Petersen. GrR
To Sappho. Antipater of Sidon, *tr. fr. Greek by* Andrew Lang. GrPo
To Sappho, about Her Apple. Aline Kilmer. BAP; LEAP
To Satan. Luis Carlos López, *tr. fr. Spanish by* H. R. Hays. TwSpPo
To Saxham. Thomas Carew. OBS
To say, Change cometh, set the old scene straight. The Late Summer. John Malcolm Brinnin. TwAmPo
To Science. Poe. *See* Sonnet to Science.
To Sea, to Sea! Thomas Lovell Beddoes. *Fr.* Death's Jest Book, I, i. ETS; OTPC; PCD; VA
(Mariners' Song.) OBVV; YT
(Sailors' Song.) EV-4; HBV
(Sea, The.) CG
(Sea Song.) GoTP
(Song from the Ship.) GTBS-D; OBRV
(To Sea.) CH; LPS-2; SG
To search our souls. Lent. Jane McKay Lanning. MaRV
To See a Quaint Outlandish Fowl. Henry Farley. *Fr.* St. Paul's Church, Her Bill for the Parliament. ViBoPo
(Bounty of Our Age, The.) FaBoCh; SeCePo; SeCL
("To see a strange outlandish fowl.") CenL
To see a [*or* the] world in a grain of sand. Auguries of Innocence. Blake. AnFE; AtBAP; BEL; BLV; BoLiVe; BrBE; CoBE; EG; EiPP; EM-1; EnLi-2; EnLit; EnRP; EPP; FaBoCh; FaBoEn; FaFP; GoTP; GTBS-W; ImOP; InP; KN; LiTB; LiTG; LO; LoBV; LoGBV; MaRV; OAEP; OBRV; OnPM; OtMeF; PIAE; Po; PoEL-4; PoFr; PoFS; RiBV; SeCeV; TOP; TreFS; TrGrPo; TriL; TyEnPo; UnW; ViBoPo; WGRP; WHA; WoL
To See God's Bleedin' Lam', *with music.* *Unknown.* BoAN-2
To see my coat hanging there limp as a scarecrow's. On the Couch. Oscar Williams. WaP
To see the Kaiser's epitaph. The Laughing Willow. Oliver Herford. BOHV; HBV
To see the moment hold a madrigal. Sonnet on the Sonnet. Lord Alfred Douglas. MBP; MoBrPo (1942 ed.)
To see the world in a grain of sand. *See* To see a world in a grain of sand.
To see this flame of life, this flow. Mardi Gras. Joseph Auslander. MuM
To see us but receive, is such a sight. The Recovery. Thomas Traherne. EPS
To see you every hour. A Divided Thought. *Unknown.* OnPM
To seek each where where man doth live. Sir Thomas Wyatt. SiPS
To seeke new worlds, for golde, for prayse, for glory. Sir Walter Ralegh. *Fr.* The Last Booke of the Ocean to Scinthia. FaBoEn
To Seem the Stranger Lies My Lot. Gerard Manley Hopkins. CoBMV; ViPP
To Seneca Lake. James Gates Percival. BAV; BoTP; LPS-2; SN
(Seneca Lake.) AnNE
To Senna Hoy. Else Lasker-Schüler, *tr. fr. German by* Glauco Cambon. OnPM
To Septicianus. Martial, *tr. fr. Latin by* Paul Nixon. RoL
To Sextus. Martial, *tr. fr. Latin by* J. A. Pott *and* F. A. Wright. ALV
To Sextus, an Ill Reader. Sir John Harington. TuPP
To Shades of Underground. Thomas Campion. *See* When Thou Must Home.
To shaggy Pan, and all the wood-nymphs. A Shepherd's Gift. Anyte, *tr. by* John William Burgon. AWP
To shaggy Pan, and to the Fold-nymphs fair. By the Fountain. Anyte, *tr. by* Lord Neaves. OnPM
To Shakespeare. Hartley Coleridge. PtP; VA
(Shakespeare.) LPS-3
To Shakespeare. Hart Crane. PeBoSo; PtP
To Shakespeare. Richard Edwin Day. AA
To Shakespeare. Thomas Hardy. PtP; VLEP
To Sheila Playing Haydn. Sylvia Lynd. LO
To Shelley. Walter Savage Landor. ViBoPo
To Shelley. John Banister Tabb. AA; LBAP
To shoot, to shoot, would be my delight. A Shooting Song. William Brighty Rands. OTPC (1923 ed.)
To show that Africa is more than breadth. The Giraffe. Marvin Solomon. NePoAm-2
To show their love, the neighbours far and near. Blouzelinda's Funeral. John Gay. *Fr.* The Shepherd's Week: Friday. OBEC
To shred them: a narrow labor, and simply toss. Destruction of Letters. Babette Deutsch. HoPM
To Signora Cuzzoni. Ambrose Philips. CEP; LoBV; OBEC
To Sigurd. Katharine Lee Bates. CV
To "Silk." Marty Hale. AlBD
To Silver Birches. Charles G. Blanden. PoTo
To Silvia. Shakespeare. *See* Who Is Silvia?
To Silvia ("You I love, by all that's true"). *Unknown.* SeCL
To Silvia. Countess of Winchilsea. *Fr.* The Cautious Lovers. HBV
To Sin, Unshamed. Aleksandr Blok. *See* Russia.
To sing of wars, of captains, and of kings. [The] Prologue. Anne Bradstreet. AmPP (3d ed.); BAV; IAP; OxBA
To Sir Edward Herbert at Julyers. John Donne. SeCV-1
To Sir Francis Brian. Sir Thomas Wyatt. Satires, III. SiPS
To Sir Green-eyes Grimalkin de Tabby de Sly. The Dandy Cat. Laura E. Richards. CIV
To Sir H. W. at His Going Ambassador to Venice. John Donne. MeLP; SeEP
To Sir Henrie Savile [upon His Translation of Tacitus]. Ben Jonson. OBS; SeCV-1
To Sir Henry Goodyere. John Donne. SeEP
To Sir Henry Vane the Younger. Milton. ES; OBS
To Sir Henry Wotton ("Here's no more news than virtue"). John Donne. TuPP
To Sir Henry Wotton ("Sir, more than kisses, letters mingle souls"). John Donne. ReEn
To Sir Philip Sidney's Soul. Henry Constable. *See* On the Death of Sir Philip Sidney.
To Sir Robert Wroth. Ben Jonson. SeCV-1
To Sir Thomas Egerton. Samuel Daniel. OBSC
To Sir Toby. Philip Freneau. CoBA
To Sir William Alexander. William Drummond of Hawthornden. OBS; SeEP
(From a Cypress Grove, 1623.) TriL
(To Sir W. A.) PoEL-2
To Sir William Davenant upon His Two First Books of Gondibert. Abraham Cowley. CEP; SeCV-1
To Sister. Georg Trakl, *tr. fr. German by* Kate Flores. *Fr.* Rosary Songs. AnGP
To Sit in Solemn Silence. W. S. Gilbert. *Fr.* The Mikado. FiBHP; SiTL; WhC
To Sleep. Elizabeth Barrett Browning. *See* Sleep, The.
To Sleep. Giovanni della Casa, *tr. fr. Italian by* John Addington Symonds. AWP; JAWP; WBP
To Sleep. William Drummond of Hawthornden. *See* Sonnet: "Sleep, Silence' child, sweet father of soft rest."
To Sleep. Maybury Fleming. AA
To Sleep. John Fletcher. *See* Care-charming Sleep.
To Sleep, *sel.* Norman Gale.
"But thou, O Sleep, bend down and give." PC
To Sleep. Robert Graves. MoVE
To Sleep. Keats. BoLiVe; BPN; BrBE; ChTr; EM-2; EmBrPo; EnLi-2; EnRP; EPN; EPP; ES; EV-4; GTBS-W; LoBV; OAEP; OBEV; OBRV; PC; PeBoSo; PoE; PoEL-4; ReaPo; WHA
(Sonnet to Sleep.) AlDL; AtBAP; ViBoPo
To Sleep. Jan Kochanowski, *tr. fr. Polish by* Watson Kirkconnell. LiTW
To Sleep. Walter Savage Landor. VA
To Sleep. Percy MacKaye. HBMV
To Sleep. Frances Sargent Osgood. AA; LEAP
To Sleep. Sir Philip Sidney. *See* Astrophel and Stella, XXXIX.
To Sleep. Wordsworth. BoLiVe; BPN; EM-2; EnRP; EPN; EPP; ERP; GBV; GEPC; GTBS; GTBS-D; GTBS-W; GTSE; GTSL; HBV; InPo; MyFE; OBRV; PC; PeBoSo; PoFS; ShBV-4; TrGrPo; ViBoPo
(Sleep.) BLV; PIAE
(Sleeplessness.) LPS-3
To sleep easy all night. *Unknown.* OxNR
To Sleep I give my powers away. In Memoriam A. H. H., IV. Tennyson. EmBrPo; EnLi-2; EPN; GEPC; MaPo; OAEP; ViPo; VLEP
"To sleep: perchance to dream. . . ." He turned his head. Composition. George O'Neil. TBM
To sleep the corn is sinking. Cradle Song. Hoffmann von Fallersleben. BOL
To Sleep, to Sleep. Claire Goll, *tr. fr. French by* Claire Goll. OnPM
To Slumber Town. "M. E. W." BOL
To smash the simple atom. Atomic Courtesy. Ethel Jacobson. FaFP; LiTM (rev. ed.); SiTL
To So-kin of Rakuyo, ancient friend, Chancellor of Gen. Exile's Letter. Li Po, *tr. by* Ezra Pound. FaBoMo; NP; OxBA; PoE; SeCeV
To Solitude. Keats. BPN; EmBroPo
(O Solitude.) EPN
(O Solitude! If I Must with Thee Dwell.) ERP
(Solitude.) EnRP
(Sonnet: "O Solitude!") GEPC
(Sonnet to Solitude.) REAL

To Some Builders of Cities. Stanley Snaith. HaMV
To some folks he was just a dog. "Old Bob"—"Friend." Marty Hale. AlBD
To Some Philadelphia Sparrows. Jeannette Marks. MW
To Some Reviewers Who Have Wilfully Abused Certain True Poets. Herbert Palmer. FaBoTw
To some the fat gods give money. Humoresque. Alice Corbin. NP
To some, the pattering raindrops on the roof. Reprieve. Barbara Villy Cormack. CaP
To Someone in Berlin. Doris Peel. BoFr
To Song. Thomas S. Jones, Jr. HBV; VOD
To soothe a mad king's fevered brain. A Ballade of Playing Cards. Gleeson White. VA
To soothe and mild your lowland airs. Margaret's Song. Lascelles Abercrombie. *Fr.* The New God; a Miracle. GTBS; LBBV
To Sorrow. Steen Steensen Blicher, *tr. fr. Danish by* Charles W. Stork. BoDS
To Sorrow. *Unknown.* SeCL
To Sorrow, I bade good-morrow. Keats. *Fr.* Endymion. OBRV
To Southey, 1833. Walter Savage Landor. PtP
To Spain—a Last Word. Edith M. Thomas. MC
To speak of everyday things with ease. The Shadow Remains. Lynette Roberts. NeBP
To speak the rest, who better are forgot. Titus Oates. Dryden. *Fr.* Absalom and Achitophel. NBE
To speed my brother. Journeying Alone. Princess Oku. OnPM
To spend the long warm days. Rest. Margaret L. Woods. VA
To Spend Uncounted Years of Pain. Arthur Hugh Clough. *See* "Perchè Pensa? Pensando S'Invecchia."
To Spenser. Keats. CoBE
To spirits thrice ten thousand by God's will 'tis assigned. Daemones. Hesiod. *Fr.* Works and Days. GrPE
To Spring. Blake. ATP; BoTP; CEP; EnRP; EV-3; HBV; MuP; OBEC; OBEV; PoEL-4; UnPo
("O thou with dewy locks who lookest down.") EG
To Spring. Virginia Moore. AnEnPo
To Spring, *sel.* John Francis O'Donnell.
"From the grey wicket of the morn." IrPN
To Spring. William Stanley Roscoe. UnPo (1st ed.)
(To Spring; on the Banks of the Cam.) OBVV
To Spring. Henrik Wergeland, *tr. fr. Norwegian by* Charles W. Stork. AnNoLy
To spring belongs the violet, and the blown. A Petition. Thomas Bailey Aldrich. AA
To Spring; on the Banks of the Cam. William Stanley Roscoe. *See* To Spring.
To stand here in the wings of Europe. On a Return from Egypt. Keith Douglas. NeBP; NePoEA
To Stand Up Straight and Tread the Turning Mill. A. E. Housman. More Poems, XXVII. EmBrPo; EnLi-2 (1949 ed.); EnLit; TwP
To stand upon a windy pinnacle. The Sublime. Wilfrid Scawen Blunt. BMEP
To stand within a gently gliding boat. The Haunts of the Halcyon. Charles Henry Luders. AA
To Stars. Francis Thompson. EmBrPo
To Stella. Hester Chapone. OBEC
To Stella. Plato. *See* Morning and Evening Star.
To Stella. Sir Philip Sidney. *See* Astrophel and Stella: First Song.
To Stella; March 13, MDCCXXIII-IV. Swift. Po
To Stella, Who Collected and Transcribed His Poems, *sel.* Swift.
Poets and Poetasters. BeR
To Stephen Spender. Timothy Corsellis. WaP
To stone memorials of a bitter loss. November Eleventh. Katherine Burton. PoRL
To stones trust not your monument. To W. B. Yeats Who Says That His Castle of Ballylee Is His Monument. Oliver St. John Gogarty. AnIL
To streets (the people's region) early fame. Sir William Davenant. *Fr.* Gondibert, II, ii. SeEP
To Suffer Woes Which Hope Thinks Infinite ("Thou, Earth"). Shelley. *Fr.* Prometheus Unbound, IV. RO
("Thou, Earth, calm empire of a happy soul.") EV-4; OBRV
To suffer woes which Hope thinks infinite. The Promethean Ideal [*or* Peaks of Life *or* Victory]. Shelley. *Fr.* Prometheus Unbound, IV. BCEP; CBOV; GrCo-2; LEAP; PC
To Summer. Blake. CEP
To sup with thee thou didst me home invite. The Invitation. Robert Herrick. OAEP
To Suzette. Arthur S. Bourinot. CPG
To sweat a slave to a race of slaves. G. K. Chesterton. *Fr.* The Ballad of the White Horse. PoFr
To swoon, to dare, to anger yield. Varied Effects of Love. Lope de Vega. AnSpL-1
To Sydney. Louise Mack. BoAu
To Sylvia, Who Sent Me Music of Her Own Composing. Schuyler B. Jackson. CAG
To take things as they be. A Philosopher. John Kendrick Bangs. HBV; ShGoBo
To take thy calling thankfully. The Ladder to Thrift. Thomas Tusser. ReIE; SiCE
To talk with God. Wait On. Dnyanodaya. MaRV
To Tan Ch'iu. LiPo, *tr. fr. Chinese.* AWP, *tr. by* Arthur Waley; TrCh, *tr. by* Arthur Waley; WhP
To taste/ Wild wine of the mountain-spring. Five Prayers. Blanche Edith Baughan. BoAu
To Tell How I Love You. Thor Lange, *tr. fr. Danish by* Charles W. Stork. BoDS
To tell the truth about you, Robert Browning. To Robert Browning. Witter Bynner. LPS-1
To Teresa. José de Espronceda, *tr. fr. Spanish by* Ida Farnell. TeCS
To th' Minstrel Girl. T. A. Daly. BoHV
To Thaliarchus ("Vides ut alta"). Horace, *tr. fr. Latin by* Dryden. Odes, I, 9. AWP; JAWP; PreP; WBP
(Ode to Thaliarchus.) LiTW
(Winter.) RoL
To thank with a phrase. Old German Mottos [*or* Proverbs]. *Unknown.* RIS; StaSt
To that clear majesty which, in the north. Dedication I [*or* To Queen Elizabeth *or* To My Most Gracious Dread Sovereign]. Sir John Davies. *Fr.* Nosce Teipsum. OBSC; ReIE; SiCE; SiPS
To that fair kingdom, o my gentle lord. Sonnet. Boccaccio. *Fr.* Sonnets. LyPI
To that pure look which honours Paradise. Petrarch. *Fr.* Sonnets to Laura: To Laura in Death. PrPoCR
To the accordion he leaves the end of the world. Nature Vive. Vicente Huidobro. AnCL
To the Accuser Who Is the God of This World. Blake. The Gates of Paradise: Epilogue. TrGrPo; UnPo (1st ed.); ViBoPo
(Epilogue to the Accuser . . .) NBE
To the Admirable Transubstantiation of the Roses. Luis de Sandoval y Zapata, *tr. fr. Spanish by* Samuel Beckett. AnMP
To the Adventurous. Keats. *See* On First Looking into Chapman's Homer.
To the Afternoon Moon, at Sea. Cale Young Rice. EtS
To the Angel. Rainer Maria Rilke, *tr. fr. German by* J. B. Leishman. LiTW
To the Ashes of Claude Colet. Etienne Jodelle, *pr. tr. fr. French.* LiA
To the Atoyac. Ignacio Manuel Altamirano, *tr. fr. Spanish by* Samuel Beckett. AnMP
To the Author. George Peele. *Fr.* Hecatompathia (*by* Thomas Watson). ReIE
To the Author of "The Robbers." Samuel Taylor Coleridge. PtP
To the Balliol Men Still in Africa. Hilaire Belloc. JKCP
To the Bat. Edith King. BoTP
To the Bell-Ringer. Robert Farren. OnYI
To the Beloved. Alice Meynell. PoeT; TCPD
To the Birds. Peter McArthur. CPG
To the Blacksmith with a Spade. *Unknown, tr. fr. Irish by* Frank O'Connor. KiLC
To the Blessed Sacrament. Henry Constable. ACP; CAW
To the Blessed Virgin Mary. Gerald Griffin. *See* Nightingale, The.
To the Blest Evanthe. John Fletcher. *Fr.* A Wife for a Month. SeCL; SeEP
To the Body. Alice Meynell. ACP; GTML
To the Body. Coventry Patmore. The Unknown Eros, II, vii. GoBC; OxBoCh; PoEL-5; PoLi; POTT; ViP
To the bower went Riseli. The Maiden's Morning-Dream. *Unknown.* BoDaBa
To the Boy. Elizabeth Clementine Kinney. AA
To the Boy Elis. Georg Trakl, *tr. fr. German by* Kate Flores. AnGP
To the brave all homage render. Ashby. John Reuben Thompson. AA; BIG
To the Brave Soul. Wilbur Underwood. WGRP
To the Cambro-Britons [*or*-Britains] and Their Harp, His Ballad of Agincourt. Michael Drayton. *See* Agincourt.
To the Canadian Mothers. Duncan Campbell Scott. AOAH
To the Catbird. *Unknown.* BLA; SN
To the child, in love with maps and pictures. The Voyage. Baudelaire. AnFP
To the Child Jesus. Henry van Dyke. TrPWD
Nativity, The, *sel.* MaRV
To the Christ. John Banister Tabb. ChIP; TrPWD
To the Christian Reader. Robert Southwell. SiCE
To the Christians. Francis P. Adams. WGRP
To the Christians. Blake. *Fr.* Jerusalem, *prologue to ch.* 4. EnRP; WGRP
(I Give You the End of a Golden String.) OBRV; ShBV-4
(I Will Give You.) OTPC (1946 ed.)
To the City in the Snow. Agnes O'Gara Ruggeri. MoSiPe

To the City of London William Dunbar. *See* In Honour of the City of London
To the cold peak without their careful women. The Climbers. Elizabeth Jennings. NePoEA
To the Colorado Desert. Madge Morris Wagner. BAP
To the Commonplace. Gloria Goddard. BAP
To the Connecticut River. John G. C. Brainard. APW
To the Countess of Bedford ("Reason is our soul's left hand"). John Donne. ATP (1953 ed.)
To the Countesse of Bedford ("Honour is so sublime perfection"). John Donne. MeLP
To the Countesse of Bedford on New-Yeares Day ("This twilight of two years"). John Donne. OBS; SeEP
To the Countesse of Salisbury. Aurelian Townsend. MePo; OBS
(Loves Victory.) MeLP
To the Cowpens riding proudly, boasting loudly, rebels scorning. The Battle of the Cowpens. Thomas Dunn English. PAH; PAP
To the Critic. Michael Drayton. *See* Idea: "Methinks I see . . ."
To the Crocus—with My Love. Marion Sturges-Jones. BOHV
To the Cuckoo. Alcuin, *tr. fr. Latin by* Howard Mumford Jones. LaP
To the Cuckoo. Michael Bruce, *revised by* John Logan. BCEP; BSV; EV-3; HBV; LEAP; LPS-2; OBEV; SN; TVSH; ViBoPo
(Ode: To the Cuckoo.) CG; DD; EBSV; OBEC; OTPC
To the Cuckoo. F. H. Townsend. ChTr
To the Cuckoo. Wordsworth. BCEP; BEL; BLA; BLV; BoLiVe; BoTP; BPN; CoBE; EM-2; EmBrPo; EnLit; EnRP; EPN; EPP; ERP; EV-3; FaFP; FiP; GEPC; GoTP; GTBS; GTBS-D; GTBS-W; GTSE; GTSL; LEAP; LiTG; LoBV; LPS-2; MCCG; OBRV; OTPC; OuHeWo; PIR; ShBV-2; SN; TCEP; TOP; TrGrPo; TVSH; TwHP; WP
To the Daisy ("Bright flower! whose home is everywhere"). Wordsworth. BPN; CoBE; EmBrPo; EnRP; EPN; ERP
To the Daisy ("In youth from rock to rock I went"). Wordsworth. BPN; EmBrPo; EnRP; ERP; GEPC
To the Daisy ("With little here to do or see"). Wordsworth. EPN; GTBS; GTBS-D; GTBS-W; GTSE; GTSL; HBV; HBVY
(To the Same Flower.) BPN; EmBrPo; EnRP; ERP; GEPC
To the Dandelion. James Russell Lowell. CoBA; DD, *abr.*; GN; HBV; HBVY; IAP; MPB; NLK; OBAV; PEOR; SN; TCAP; TVSH
"Dear common flower," *sel.* ADAH; FaPON; YT
To the Dead. William Bell Scott. VA
To the Dead Butterfly. Eugenio Florit, *tr. fr. Spanish by* Richard O'Connell. AnCL
To the Dead Cardinal of Westminster. Francis Thompson. POTT; PoVP
To the Dead Doughboys. William Ellery Leonard. AOAH
To the Dead of '98. Lionel Johnson. HBV
To the Dead of the Revolution. Ernst Toller, *tr. fr. German by* R. Ellis Roberts. PoFr
To the Dear Child of the Muses and His Ever Kind Maecenas, Master Anthony Cooke, Esquire. Michael Drayton. *Fr.* Idea's Mirrour. ReIE; SiCE; TuPP
To the Dearest One, to the Beauty divine. Hymn. Baudelaire. TrFP
To the Defenders of New Orleans. Joseph Rodman Drake. DD; PAH
To the Detracted. John Andrews. *Fr.* The Anatomy of Baseness. ElL; LO; SeEP
To the dim light and the large circle of shade. Sestina; of the Lady Pietra degli Scrovigni. Dante. AWP; JAWP; LyPi; ViP; WBP
To the Distant One. Po Chü-i, *tr. fr. Chinese by* Ching Ti. WhP
To the Driving Cloud. Longfellow. ChTr; FaBoEn; Po; PoEL-5
To the Duke Alphonso. Tasso, *tr. fr.* Italian. BoFr
To the Earl of Dorset. Ambrose Philips. LoBV
To the Earl of Warwick on the Death of Mr. Addison. Thomas Tickell. CEP; EiPP; EV-3; HBV; LPS-3; OBEC; PtP
Addison's Funeral in the Abbey, *sel.* BeR
To the East and to the West. Walt Whitman. BoFr
To the Echo; in a Clear Night upon Astrop Walks. Countess of Winchilsea. EiPP
To the edge of the wood I am drawn, I am drawn. Sidney Lanier. *Fr.* The Marshes of Glynn. BBV (1951 ed.)
To the End. John E. Bode. BLRP
To the End. Christina Rossetti. POTT; VLEP
To the English Martyrs. Francis Thompson. JKCP; MeRV
To the Eretrian Dead. Plato, *tr. fr. Greek by* Robert Allason Furness. GrR
To the Evening Star. Mark Akenside. *See* Ode to the Evening Star.
To the Evening Star. Blake. BCEP; CaAE; CEP; CH; ChER; ChTR; CoBE; EiPP; EM-1; EnLit; EnRP; EV-3; GBV (1952 ed.); KN; LoBV; MCCG; MW; OAEP; PeBoSo; PoFS; RO; StaSt; TrGrPo; TwHP
To the Evening Star ("Gem of the crimson-colour'd even"). Thomas Campbell. GTBS; GTBS-D; GTBS-W; GTSE; GTSL
To the Evening Star ("Star that bringest home the bee"). Thomas Campbell. *See* Song to the Evening Star.
To the Evening Star. Edgar Fawcett. OBAV
To the Evening Wind. Bryant. *See* Evening Wind, The.
To the Excellent and Most Accomplish'd Lady, Lucy, Countess of Bedford. Michael Drayton. *Fr.* Mortimeriados. ReIE
To the Excellent Pattern of Beauty and Virtue, Lady Elizabeth, Countess of Ormond. James Shirley. GoBC
To the fair fields where loves eternal dwell. John Fletcher. *Fr.* The Mad Lover. MyFE
To the fairest! Winchester. Lionel Johnson. OBVV
To the Fates. Friedrich Hölderlin, *tr. fr. German by* Lola Gruenthal. AnGP
To the Federal Convention. Thomas Dwight. PAH
To the Fickle Gallery. Aristophanes. *See* Poet and His Rivals, The.
To the field I carried my milking pail. I Want to Be Married and Cannot Tell How. *Unknown.* OnYI
To the Fir-Tree. *Unknown, tr. fr. German.* COAH
To the Flag of Stars. Thomas Curtis Clark. PEDC
To the Forgotten Dead. Margaret L. Woods. BMEP; DiM; GTML; LBBV; PoeT; VA
To the Fountain of Bandusia ("O fons Bandusiae"). Horace, *tr. fr. Latin by* Eugene Field. Odes, III, 13. AA; AWP; JAWP; WBP
(Fountain of Bandusia, The.) OuHeWo, *tr. by* Austin Dobson; RoL, *tr. by* M. Jourdain
(O Fons Bandusiae, *tr. by* Austin Dobson.) VA
To the Four Courts, Please. James Stephens. BLV; BMEP; EPP; HBMV; MBP; MoAB; MoBrPo; NeMA; TCEP
To the fresh wet fields. April. Sir Herbert Read. *Fr.* Eclogues. BrBE
To the Fringed Gentian. Bryant. AA; AmP; AmPP (3d ed.); AnAmPo; AnFe; AnNe; APA; APW; AWP; CBOV; CoAnAm; CoBA; DDA; FaBoBe; GN; HBV; IAP; LA; LPS-2; MOAP; MPB; NeHB; NePA; OBAV; OBRV; OTPC; PIR; PTA-1; TCAP; TOP; TriL; TSWC; YT
To the Frivolous Muse. George Meason Whicher. InMe
To the front of yon old peaked hill, the sovereign of verdure returns. Poems Translated from the Chinese. *Unknown, tr. by* John Francis Davis. RO
To the galleys, thief, and sweat your soul out. Thief. Robert Graves. POTE
To the Garden God. Catullus, *tr. fr. Latin by* John Nott. OnPM
To the Ghost of a Kite. James Wright. NePoEA
To the Ghost of John Milton. Carl Sandburg. ReMP
To the Ghost of Martial. Ben Jonson. OAEP
To the Giver of all blessings. Thanksgiving Hymn. *Unknown.* PEOR
To the God of all sure mercies let my blessing rise to-day. Cassandra Southwick. Whittier. IAP; PAH
To the God of Love. Edmund G. V. Knox. ALV; HBMV
To the Goddess of Childbirth. Callimachus, *tr. fr. Greek by* F. A. Wright. GrR
To the Goddess of Liberty. George Sterling. PoFr
To the Gods intrust thou all things. God's Ways to Man. Archilochus. GrR
To the Gossamer-Light. Charles Tennyson Turner. VA
To the Grasshopper. Richard Lovelace. *See* Grasshopper, The.
To the Grasshopper and the Cricket. Leigh Hunt. EnLi-2; EnRP; EPN; ERP; ES; GBV (1922 ed.); GN; HBV; LEAP; LPS-2; OTPC (1946 ed.); PCD; TCEP
(Grasshopper and the Cricket, The.) BCEP; EV-4; TVSH
(On the Grasshopper and Cricket.) GoTP
To the Greatest City in the World. Rolfe Humphries. PoMa
To the green wood where I found my love. These Words I Write on Crinkled Tin. Lynette Roberts. ChMP
To the Guardian Angel. Mme Tastu, *tr. fr. French.* BOL
To the Guardian Angel. *Unknown.* WHL
To the Harp Player. Li Ho, *tr. fr. Chinese by* Ho Chih-yuan. WhP
To the Harpies. Arthur Davison Ficke. HBV; OBAV
To the Harvest Moon. Henry Kirke White. LPS-2
To the heart of youth the world is a highwayside. Youth and Love. Robert Louis Stevenson. PoeT
To the heavens above us. An Astrologer's Song. Kipling. MBP; MoBrPo; NeMA
To the Heirs of the Pilgrims. Benjamin Church. PoFr
To the Herald Honeysuckle. Emily Pfeiffer. VA
To the High-born Prince of Men, Henry. George Chapman. *Fr.* The Epistle Dedicatory to Chapman's Translation of the Iliad. ReIE
("Since perfect happiness, by princes sought.") ReEn

To the Highland Girl of Inversneyde. Wordsworth. GTBS; GTBS-D; GTBS-W; GTSE; GTSL
To the Holy Ghost. John Skelton. TriL
To the Holy Spirit. Yvor Winters. MoVE
To the Hon. Charles Montague. Matthew Prior. LPS-3
To the Honoured Dead. Simonides, *tr. fr. Greek by* Robert Allason Furness. GrR
To the Housatonic at Stockbridge. Robert Underwood Johnson. SN
To the Humblebee. Emerson. *See* Humble-Bee, The.
To the Immortal Memory and Friendship of That Noble Pair, Sir Lucius Cary and Sir H. Morison. Ben Jonson. *See* Pindaric Ode, A.
To the Immortal Memory of the Halibut, on Which I Dined This Day, Monday, April 26, 1784. William Cowper. CaAE; NBE; SeCePo
To the Imperial Eagle. Kostas Krystallis, *tr. fr. Modern Greek by* Rae Dalven. MoGP
To the Infant Martyrs. Richard Crawshaw. SeCV-1
To the Infinite. Paul Eluard, *tr. fr. French by* Wallace Fowlie. MiCF
To the Ingleezee Khafir, Calling Himself Djann Bool Djenkinzun. James Clarence Mangan. OnYI
To the International Brigade. Rafael Alberti, *tr. fr. Spanish by* Katherine Garrison Chapin. PoFr
To the judges of the prize, we wish to mention in a word. Aristophanes. *Fr.* The Birds. GrPo
To the kind, the tall Carpenter. Carpenter. Isabel Fiske Conant. StJW
To the King. Kaj Munk, *tr. fr. Danish by* Charles W. Stork. BoDS
. . . to the King./ Thou art the wall-stone the workers rejected. Advent Lyrics, I. *Unknown. Fr.* Christ 1. AnOE
To the King on His Navy Edmund Waller. CEP
To the Lady Lucy, Countess of Bedford. Samuel Daniel. OBSC; ReIE; SiCE; TuPP
To the Lady Margaret, Countess of Cumberland. Samuel Daniel. EV-1; LoBV; OBSC; ReIE; SiCE; TuPP
(Epistle to the Lady Margaret.) EPP
(High Mind, The.) AnEnPo
"Knowing the heart of man is set to be," *sel.* FaBoEn
To the Lady Margaret Ley. Milton. ES; EV-2; GTBS; GTBS-D; GTBS-W; GTSE; GTSL; OBEV
(Sonnet: "Daughter to that good Earl, once President.") OBS
(Two Sonnets.) LiA
To the Lady May. Aurelian Townsend. MePo; SeCL; SeEP
To the Lady Rogers, of Her Unprofitable Sparing. Sir John Harington. SiCE
To the Lady with a Book. *Unknown, tr. fr. Irish by* Frank O'Connor. KiLC
To the Ladybird. Caroline Anne Bowles. *See* Lady-Bird.
To the Laggards. Joseph Bovshover, *tr. fr. Yiddish by* Joseph Bovshover. TrJP
To the Lakes. Wilfred Campbell. VA
To the Lapland Longspur. John Burroughs. BLA; SN
To the Lark. Sir John Davies. *Fr.* Hymns of Astraea. SiCE
To the Lark. Robert Herrick. BLA; WP
To the last moment of his breath. Hope. Goldsmith. *Fr.* The Captivity. OBEC
To the Leanán Shee [*or* Sidhe]. Thomas Boyd. GTIV; OnYI; TIP
To the Learned and Accomplish'd Gentleman Maister Nicholas Blackleech of Gray's Inn. Richard Barnfield. ReIE
To the Learned Shepheard. Gabriel Harvey. PtP
To the Least American, If Not the Greatest, of All American Poets. William Griffith. GA
To the Liffey with the Swans. Oliver St. John Gogarty. AnIL; OxBI
To the Lighted Lady Window. Marguerite Wilkinson. CAW; ISi; WHL
To the Little House. Christopher Morley. BAP; HBMV; TCAP
To the Littlest of All. Arthur Guiterman. FAOV
To the Living. Ernst Toller, *tr. fr. German by* R. Ellis Roberts. PoFr
To the Lord Chancellor, *sel.* Shelley.
"Oh, let a father's curse be on thy soul." ViBoPo
To the Lord General Cromwell (May, 1652). Milton. AnEnPo; BEL; EM-1; EnLit; EPP; EPS; LH; LPS-3; OBS; OuHeWo; PeBoSo; PIR; TCEP; TrGrPo; TwCrTr; ViBoPo
(Cromwell, Our Chief of Men, Who through a Cloud.) MaPo
(To Oliver Cromwell.) SeCeV
(To the Lord General Cromwell, May 1652, on the Proposals of Certain Ministers at the Committee for Propagation of the Gospel.) ES
To the Lord General Fairfax. Milton. *See* Fairfax, Whose Name in Arms through Europe Rings.
To the Lord Love. "Michael Field." OBMV
To the Lords of Convention 'twas Claver'se who spoke. Bonny [*or* Bonnie] Dundee. Sir Walter Scott. *Fr.* The Doom of Devorgoil. BEL; BHV; BPN; EBSV; EmBrPo; EnRP; ERP; EV-4; FaBoCh; HBV; LH; LoGBV; OBRV; OTPC (1923 ed.); OxBoLi; SeCeV; TCEP; TOP
To the lucky now who have lovers or friends. Alexandria. Lawrence Durrell. MoVE; PoN
To the Maiden in the East. Henry David Thoreau. MOAP; OxBA
To the Maids Not to Walk in the Wind. Oliver St. John Gogarty. AnIL
To the man-in-the-street, who, I'm sorry to say. Note on Intellectuals. W. H. Auden. FiBHP; SiTL
To the Man-of-War-Bird. Walt Whitman. AA; AmP; AmPP (4th ed.); BLA; CBOV; EtS; FaBoBe; HBV; IAP; MOAP; NePA; OBAV; PoF; TCAP
"Thou born to match the gale (thou art all wings)," *sel.* InP
To the Marquesa Mancera. Sister Juana Inés de la Cruz, *tr. fr. Spanish by* Elizabeth Selden. BoFr
To the Master Poet. Thomas Curtis Clark. ChIP
To the Memory of a Lady, *abr.* George Lyttelton. OBEC
To the Memory of a Young Man. *Unknown.* WhC
To the Memory of Abraham Lincoln. Bryant. *See* Abraham Lincoln.
To the Memory of Ben Johnson, *sel.* Jasper Mayne.
"Scorne then their censure." OBS
To the Memory of Ben Jonson. John Cleveland. LPS-3
To the Memory of Fletcher Harper. Dinah Maria Mulock Craik. LPS-3
To the Memory of Hood. James Russell Lowell. PtP
To the Memory of John Burroughs. Catherine Parmenter. PEDC; PoRL
To the Memory of Mr. Charles Morwent, *sels.* John Oldham.
Infant Roses in Their Bloom. BeR
Mortal Cage, The. BeR
Tranquil Soul, A. EV-3
(Quiet Soul, A.) OBEV
To the Memory of Mr. Oldham. Dryden. ATP; AWP; CEP; CoEV; EiPP; EV-3; ExPo; FaBoEn; FiP; InPo; JAWP; LiA; LoBV; NBE; OBS; PoEL-3; PtP; RiBV; SeCeV; SeCV-2; SeEP; UnPo (1st ed.); ViBoPo; WBP
"Farewell, too little and too lately known," *br. sel.* PoD
To the Memory of My Beloved Master William Shakespeare. Ben Jonson. BEL; BoLiVe; EM-1; EnLi-1; EPP; GoTL; PIAE; PoFS; TOP; TreFS; TrGrPo; TriL; WHA
(To the Memory of My Beloved Master [*or* Mr.] William Shakespeare and What He Hath Left Us.) BCEP; EPS; HBV; LEAP; LPS-3, *abr.*; MyFE, *abr.*; TCEP, *sl. abr.*; TwHP
(To the Memory of My Beloved, the Author Mr. William Shakespeare [and What He Hath Left Us].) CoBE; EnL; EnLit; EV-2; LiTB; OAEP; OBS; PoEL-2; PtP; ReEn; SeCeV; SeCV-1; SeEP; TuPP; ViBoPo
(To the memory of . . . William Shakespeare.) MaPo
Sels.
". . . Soul of the Age!" PIR
"Sweet Swan of Avon! what a sight it were." ChTr
To the Memory of My Friend, Ben Jonson. Henry King. BoFr
To the Memory of Rupert Brooke. W. W. Gibson. *See* Going, The.
To the Memory of Sir Isaac Newton, *sel.* James Thomson.
"All-intellectual eye, our solar round." ImOP
To the Memory of the Brave Americans. Philip Freneau. AmP; AmPP; CoBA; IAP; MOAP; PaA; TCAP; TriL
(Eutaw Springs.) AA; BeLS; NeHB; PAH
(To the Memory of the Americans Who Fell at Eutaw.) PAP
To the Memory of the Incomparable Paire of Authors Beaumont and Fletcher. *Unknown.* BoFr
To the Memory of Thomas Hood. Bartholomew Simmons. LPS-3
(Stanzas to the Memory of Thomas Hood.) VA
To the Memory of Yale College. Phelps Putnam. AnAmPo; LA
To the Men of Kent. Wordsworth. BPN
To the Men Who Lose. George L. Scarborough. BLPA
To the Milkweed. Lloyd Mifflin. AA
To the Mocking-Bird. Albert Pike. AA
To the Mocking-Bird. Richard Henry Wilde. AA; AnAmPo; APW; BLA; HiLiAm; IAP; LA; LEAP; SN; SPP; TCAP
To the Modern Man. John Hall Wheelock. HBMV
To the Month of September. Sir John Davies. *Fr.* Hymns of Astraea. CaAE; CenL
To the Moon. Thomas Hardy. ChTR; CoBE
To the Moon. Pierre de Ronsard, *tr. fr. French. Fr.* Amours de Marie. AWP, *tr. by* Andrew Lang; TrFP, *tr. by* Alan Conder
("Hide this one night thy crescent, kindly Moon," *tr. by* Andrew Lang.) PrPoCR
To the Moon. Shelley. *See* Moon, The ("Art thou pale . . .").
To the Moon. Sir Philip Sidney. *See* Astrophel and Stella, XXXI.
To the Moon. Henry Longan Stuart. GTIV

To the Moon. *Unknown*. *See* Hymn to the Moon.
To the Moonflower. Craven Langstroth Betts. AA
To the Most Beautiful Lady, the Lady Bridget Manners. Barnabe Barnes. EnLoPo
To the Most Excellent and Learned Shepherd, Colin Clout. William Smith. *Fr.* Chloris. TuPP
("Colin, my dear and most entire beloved.") ReEn
To the Most Fair and Lovely Mistress [*or* Mistris], Anne Soame, Now Lady Abdie. Robert Herrick. AtBAP; ViBoPo
To the Most Holy Crown of Thorns. Sister Miriam Teresa. JKCP (1955 ed.)
To the Most Holy Mother of God. *Unknown, tr. fr. Greek by* Shane Leslie. ISi
To the Most Learned, Wise, and Arch-Antiquary, M. John Selden. Robert Herrick. SeCV-1
To the Mother of Christ, the Son of Man. Alice Meynell. ISi
To the Mothers. Ernst Toller, *tr. fr. German by* E. Ellis Roberts. TrJP
To the Mountains. Henry David Thoreau. PoEL-4
To the much-tossed Ulysses, never done. Ulysses. Robert Graves. ChMP; FaBoTw; OxBI
To the Muse. Robert Louis Stevenson. VLEP
To the Muse of Sirmio. Marc-Antonio Flaminio, *pr. tr. fr. Latin by* Richard Aldington. LaP
To the Muse of the North. William Morris. BPN; PoVP; ViP; VLEP
To the Muses. Blake. AnFE; BCEP; BLV; BoLiVe; CEP; ChER; ChTr; CoBE; EiPP; EM-1; EnLi-2; EnLit; EnRP; EV-3; GTBS-W; GTSL; HBV; LiTB; LiTG; LoBV; OAEP; OBEC; OBEV; OnPM; OuHeWo; PoFS; Ro; SeCeV; TCEP; TrGrPo; TwCrTr; TyEnPo; ViBoPo; WHA
To the Name above Every Name, the Name of Jesus, a Hymn. Richard Crashaw. *See* Hymn to the Name of Jesus.
To the Nativity. Fernán González de Eslava, *tr. fr. Spanish by* Samuel Beckett. AnMP
To the Nautilus. Hartley Coleridge. VA
To the New Men. John Davidson. EPN; PoVP; TOP
To the New Owner. Lucile Hargrove Reynolds. PoToHe
To the new wick/ Of freedom's torch. My Thread. David Hofstein. TrJP
To the New Women. John Davidson. PoVP
To the New Yeere. Michael Drayton. AtBAP; PoEL-2
To the Night. Shelley. *See* To Night.
To the Nightingale. Philip Ayres. CEP
To the Nightingale. Richard Barnfield. *See* Nightingale, The.
To the Nightingale. Sir John Davies. *Fr.* Hymns of Astraea. OBSC; SiCE; TrGrPo
To the Nightingale ("Dear quirister, who from those shadows sends"). William Drummond of Hawthornden. *See* Sonnet: "Dear quirister . . ."
To the Nightingale ("Sweet bird, that sing'st away the early hours"). William Drummond of Hawthornden. *See* To a Nightingale.
To the Nightingale. Milton. ATP (1953 ed.); BLA; ElSeCe; ES; HBV; LEAP; MyFE; PeBoSo
(O Nightingale.) SeCePo
(O Nightingale That on Yon Bloomy Spray.) EG; EV-2
(Sonnet: "O Nightingale, that on yon bloomy spray.") BrBE; OBS; SeCL; ViBoPo
To the Nightingale. Countess of Winchilsea. CEP; EiPP
To the Nile. Keats. OBRV
To the Nile. Shelley. OBRV
To the Nile. Bayard Taylor. TCAP
To the Noble and Patrician Iovinus, Governor of Provence. Venantius Fortunatus, *tr. fr. Latin by* L. R. Lind. LaP
To the Noble Sir Francis Drake. Thomas Beedome. SeEP
To the Noblest and Best of Ladies [*or* Ladyes], the Countess[e] of Denbigh. Richard Crashaw. EPS; MeLP; ReEn
(Against Irresolution, *diff. vers.*) OxBoCh
(Letter to the Countess of Denbigh against Irresolution and Delay in Matters of Religion, A.) MePo
To the Not Impossible Him. Edna St. Vincent Millay. PR
To the Nun. Dafydd ap Gwilym, *tr. fr. Welsh by* H. Idris Bell. LyMA
To the Nymphs Pursuing Hylas. Ausonius, *tr. fr. Latin by* Jack Lindsay. LaP
To the Oaks of Glencree. J. M. Synge. GTIV; MBP; MoBrPo; OxBI
To the Ocean. Byron. *See* Ocean, The.
To the Ocean Now I Fly. Milton. *Fr.* Comus. AtBAP; ElSeCe; OBEV; OBS; ViBoPo
(Farewell of the Attendant Spirit.) BoLiVe; TrGrPo
(From "Comus.") LEAP
(Songs.) BLV; SeCeV
To the old, long life and treasure. Gipsy Song. Ben Jonson. *Fr.* The Gypsies Metamorphosed. EPS (1942 ed.); SeCL
To the One of Fictive Music. Wallace Stevens. AnAmPo; AnFE; APA; BLV; CoAnAm; CoBMV; CoV; LA; MAP; MoAB; MoAmPo; MoVE; TwAmPo
To the Ottawa. Arthur S. Bourinot. CPG
To the Painted Columbine. Jones Very. IAP
To the Parotid Gland. —— Schlesinger. WhC
To the Parted One. Goethe, *tr. fr. German by* Christopher Pearse Cranch. AWP; JAWP; WBP
To the Pious Memory of the Accomplished [*or* Accomplisht] Young Lady, Mrs. Anne Killigrew. Dryden. CEP; EiPP; EPS; HBV; LiA; LoBV; PoEL-3; PoFS; PtP; SeEP
(Ode to the Pious Memory of the Accomplished [*or* Accomplisht] Young Lady, Mrs. Anne Killigrew, Excellent in the Two Sister Arts of Poesy and Painting.) AtBAP; BrBE; OBEV, *abr.*; SeCV-2; TriL
Poet's Resurrection, *sel.* WHA
(Last Day, The.) BeR
To the Pliocene Skull. Bret Harte. BoHV; LPS-3
To the Poet. Pushkin, *tr. fr.* Russian. TrRV, *tr. by* Babette Deutsch; WaL, *tr. by* Sir Cecil Kisch
To the Poet, John Dyer. Wordsworth. PtP
To the Poets. Keats. *See* Ode: "Bards of Passion and of Mirth."
To the Polyandrous Lydia. Franklin P. Adams, *after the Latin of Horace.* HBMV
To the Portrait of "A Gentleman." Oliver Wendell Holmes. BOHV; InMe
To the Portrait of Shakespeare. Ben Jonson. LPS-3
To the Preacher, *sel.* Charlotte Perkins Gilman.
"Preach about the old sins, Preacher!" MaRV
To the Precision. Richard Brathwaite. *Fr.* A Strappado for the Devil. SiCE
To the Priest of the Middles. Lynette Roberts. MoWP
To the Prince. Sir John Davies. Orchestra: Dedication II. SiPS
To the Princesses of Ferrara. Tasso, *tr. fr. Italian by* L. R. Lind. LyPI
To the Queen. Blake. *See* Door of Death, The.
To the Queen. Sir William Davenant. *See* To the Queen, Entertain'd at Night by the Countess of Anglesey.
To the Queen. Sir Walter Ralegh. *See* Silent Lover, The.
To the Queen ("O loyal to the royal in thy self"). Tennyson. *Fr.* Idylls of the King. PoVP
To the Queen ("Revered, beloved—O you that hold"). Tennyson. BPN
To the Queen ("These to his memory"). Tennyson. *See* Dedication: "These to his memory."
To the Queen, Entertain'd at Night by the Countess of Anglesey. Sir William Davenant. FaBoEn; MeLP; MePo; OBS; SeCL
(To the Queen.) SeEP
To the Queen of Dolors. Sister Mary Maura. ISi
To the quick brow Fame grudges her best wreath. The Guerdon. John James Piatt. AA
To the quick sense, how good feels rimy soil. Inviolable. Margaret Willy. DiM
To the Rainbow. Thomas Campbell. ERP; HBV; SN
(Rainbow, The.) PECK
To the Reader. Baudelaire, *tr. fr. French by* Stanley Kunitz. AnFP
To the Reader. Samuel Daniel. SiCE
To the Reader. Everard Guilpin. *Fr.* Skialetheia. ReIE; SiCE
To the Reader. Thomas Howell. SiCE
To the Reader. Ben Jonson. MaPo; OAEP; ReIE; SeCV-1; TuPP
To the Reader. Timothe Kendall, *after the Latin of* Martial. TuPP
(Quip to the Reader.) OnPM
To the Reader. *Unknown.* SeCL
To the Reader of These Sonnets. Michael Drayton. *See* Idea: "Into these loves . . ."
To the Returning Brave. Robert Underwood Johnson. PAH
To the Rev. F. D. Maurice. Tennyson. CBE
To the Rev. John M'Math. Burns. EiPP
To the Reverend Mr. Murdoch. James Thomson. OBEC
To the Rev. Mr. Newton. William Cowper. LoBV
To the Reverend Shade of His Religious Father. Robert Herrick. OBS; SeCV-1; SeEP
To the Reverend W. L. Bowles. Samuel Taylor Coleridge. EmBrPo; EnRP; ERP
To the Rt. Hon. John Hookham Frere in Malta. William Stewart Rose. EnSW
To the Right Honourable Robert Walpole, Esq. Ambrose Philips. CEP
To the Right Honorable, the Lady Mary, Countess of Pembroke. Samuel Daniel. *Fr.* Delia. SiCE; TuPP
To the Right Honorable William, Earl of Dartmouth. Phillis Wheatley. PoFr; TCAP
To the Right Noble and Valorous Knight, Sir Walter Raleigh. Spenser. PtP
To the Right Worshipful, My Singular Good Friend, M[aster] Gabriel Harvey, Doctor of the Laws. Spenser. ReIE
To the Right Worthy and Judicious Favorer of Virtue, Master [*or* Maister] Fulke Greville. Samuel Daniel. *Fr.* Musophilus. ReIE; SiCE
To the River Anker. Michael Drayton. *See* Idea: "Our floods' queen, Thames . . ."
To the River Duddon. Norman Nicholson. FaBoMo

To the River Lodon. Thomas Warton, the Younger. *See* Sonnet: To the River Lodon.
To the Rose. Sir John Davies. *Fr.* Hymns of Astraea. OBSC; SiCE; TuPP
To the Rose. Francisco de Rioja, *tr. fr. Spanish by* Ida Farnell. AnSpL-1
To the Rose; a Song. Robert Herrick. EPS; HBV; OBS
To the Rose upon the Rood of Time. W. B. Yeats. OAEP (2d ed.); Po
To the Rosella in the Poinsettia Tree. James Picot. BoAV
To the Royal Society. Abraham Cowley. CEP; EPS; EV-2
To the Ruins of Troy and Greece. George Chapman. ReIE
To the Rulers. John Frederick Nims. JKCP (1955 ed.)
To the Sacred Battalion Andreas Calvos, *tr. fr. Modern Greek by* Rae Dalven. MoGP
To the sages who spoke, to the heroes who bled. The Fourth of July. Charles Sprague. IDAH
To the Same [1793]. William Cowper. *See* To Mary.
To the Same. Ben Jonson. *See* To Celia ("Kiss me, sweet . . .").
To the Same [upon His Blindness]. Milton. *See* To Cyriack Skinner ("Cyriack, this three years' day").
To the Same Flower (Celandine). Wordsworth. BPN; EmBrPo; EnRP; GEPC
To the Same Flower (Daisy). Wordsworth. *See* To the Daisy ("With little here to do or see").
To the Same Purpos. Thomas Traherne. SeCV-2
To the scarlet plain and the holy place. The Red Sea. Aeschylus. *Fr.* Prometheus Unbound. OxBG
To the School at War. Cyril Argentine Alington. ShGoBo
To the Schooner *Casco.* Grace Hazard Conkling. PoeMoYo; VOD
To the Sea. Cally Monrad, *tr. fr. Norwegian by* Charles W. Stork. AnNoLy
To the Sea. William Morris. *See* O Bitter Sea.
To the Sea. Sara Teasdale ChMo; CMP
To the sea-shell's spiral round. Appreciation. Thomas Bailey Aldrich. AA
To the Seamen. John Masefield. NeTW
To the Senses. Michael Drayton. *See* Idea: "When conquering love . . ."
To the "Sextant." Arabella M. Willson. *See* Appeal for Are to the Sextant . . .
To the Shade of Washington. Richard Alsop. WOAH
To the Ship in Which Virgil Sailed to Athens ("Sic te diva potens Cypri"). Horace, *tr. fr. Latin by* Dryden. Odes, I, 3. AWP
To the Shore. May Swenson. NePoAm-2
To the Sister of Elia. Walter Savage Landor. EmBrPo; HBV; TriL
(To Mary Lamb.) BPN; TOP
To the Sistine Madonna. Cornelia Otis Skinner. ISi
To the Sky-Council on Star, Riga, Milky Way. Report on the Planet, Earth. James Oppenheim. PoMa
To the Skylark. Shelley. *See* To a Skylark.
To the Skylark. Wordsworth. *See* To a Skylark ("Ethereal minstrel!")
To the Small Celandine. Wordsworth. BPN; EmBrPo; EnRP; ERP; GEPC; HBV; OBRV; OTPC; SN
"Pansies, lilies, kingcups, daisies," *sel.* AlDL
To the Soul. John Collop. AEV; BCEP; TrGrPo
To the sound of the strange hooves on the midnight cobbles. The Ostler. Hyam Plutzik. Horatio, II. FiMAP
To the sound of timbrels sweet. Hebrew Wedding. Henry Hart Milman. *Fr.* The Fall of Jerusalem. LPS-1
To the Sour Reader. Robert Herrick. OAEP
To the South. Brewster Ghiselin. LiTA; LiTM (rev. ed.); NePA
To the south-east—three thousand leagues. Civilization. Yüan Chieh. LiTW
To the Spanish Main we are bound away. Slav Ho! *Unknown.* SoAmSa
To the Spirit Great and Good. Leigh Hunt. TrPWD
To the Spirit of Abraham Lincoln. Richard Watson Gilder. LBAH
To the Spirit of Keats. James Russell Lowell. BAV; IAP
To the Spirit of Poetry. Philip Bourke Marston. VA
To the Spring. Sir John Davies. *Fr.* Hymns of Astraea. ElL; SiCE; TuPP
To the Spring Sun. Freda Laughton. NeIP
To the Stall-Holders at a Fancy Fair. W. S. Gilbert. PA
To the Stars That Have Gone Out. Afanasi Fet, *tr. fr. Russian by* Oliver Elton. BoR
To the State of Love; or, The Senses Festival. John Cleveland. MePo
To the Stationer. Thomas Freeman. SiCE; TuPP
To the Stone-Cutters. Robinson Jeffers. AmP; AmPP; InP; MAP; MoAB; MoAmPo; MoVE; NeMA; OxBA; PC; PoLFOT; TBM; TrGrPo
To the Sultan. Sir William Watson. BMEP; LEAP
To the Sun. Roy Campbell. *Fr.* Mithraic Emblems. FaBoTw
("O let your shining orb grow dim.") MeRV
To the Sun. Guido Gezelle, *tr. fr. Flemish by* Jethro Bithell. LiTW
(To the Sun from a Flower.) FaPON
To the Sun. Patterické Jenkyn. SeCL
To the Sun. Last Song. James Guthrie. TiPo
To the Supreme Being. Michelangelo. *See* For Inspiration.
To the Swallow. *Unknown, tr. fr. Greek by* Thomas Stanley. GrL; OxBG
To the Terrestrial Globe. W. S. Gilbert. BMEP; BOHV; HBV; LEAP; LiTG; LPS-3; MBP; PoeMoYo; SiTL; TrGrPo; WhC
To the Thawing Wind. Robert Frost. AlDL; OxBA; RIS
To the Thirty-ninth Congress. Whittier. PAH
To the Tomb. Raymond Kresensky. ChIP
To the Translator of Lucan's Pharsalia (1614). Sir Walter Ralegh. SiPS
To the Trinity. Richard Stanyhurst. *See* Prayer to the Trinity, A.
To the Tune of "A Clear Calm Music." Li Yu, *tr. fr. Chinese by* Hsiung Ting. WhP
To the Tune of "A Sprig of Plum Blossom." Li Ch'ing-chao, *tr. fr. Chinese by* Sophia H. Chen. WhP
To the Tune of "Breaking through Battle." Li Yu, *tr. fr. Chinese by* Hsiung Ting. WhP
To the Tune of "Crows Crying by Night." Li Yu, *tr. fr. Chinese by* Hsiung Ting. WhP
To the Tune of "Gathering Mulberry Seeds." Nalan Hsinteh, *tr. fr. Chinese by* Hsiung Ting. WhP
To the Tune of "Horses Drinking by the Great Wall." Li Shih-ming, *tr. fr. Chinese by* Wang Sheng-chih. WhP
To the Tune of, In Fayth I Cannot Keepe My Fathers Sheepe. Sidney Godolphin. *See* Song: "Cloris, it is not thy disdaine."
To the Tune of "Like a Dream." Li Ch'ing-chao, *tr. fr. Chinese by* Sophia H. Chen. WhP
To the Tune of "Meeting Happiness." Li Yu, *tr. fr. Chinese by* Hsiung Ting. WhP
To the Tune of "Mountain Flowers." Li Yu, *tr. fr. Chinese by* Hsiung Ting. WhP
To the Tune of "Pusa Barbarian." Nalan Hsinteh, *tr. fr. Chinese by* Hsiung Ting. WhP
To the Tune of the Coventry Carol. Stevie Smith. FaBoTw
To the Tune of "The South River Song." Li Yu, *tr. fr. Chinese by* Hsiung Ting. WhP
To the Tune of "The Ugly Slave." Hsin Ch'i-chi, *tr. fr. Chinese by* Hsiung Ting. WhP
To the Tune, "Plum Blossoms Fall and Scatter." Li Ch'ing-chao, *tr. fr. Chinese by* Kenneth Rexroth. OnPC
To the Unco Guid. Burns. *See* Address to the Unco Guid, or the Rigidly Righteous.
To the Unconstant Cynthia. Sir Robert Howard. SeCL
To the Ungentilized Censurer. Henry Parrot. SiCE
To the Unimplored Beloved. Edward Shanks. TCPD
To the United States of America. Robert Bridges. HBV; HiLiEn; PaA; PAH; PoFr
To the University of Oxford, 1674. Dryden. *See* Epilogue Spoken at Oxford by Mrs. Marshall.
To the Unknown Eros. Coventry Patmore. The Unknown Eros, II, i. LO; NBE; OxBoCh; PoEL-5
To the Unknown God. *Unknown, tr. fr. Vedic by* Max Müller. The Rig-Veda, X, Hymn 121. GrCo-1, *sl. abr.;* OuHeWo
To the Unknown Light. Edward Shanks. NV; TrPWD
To the Ursulines. Caroline Gilman. PraNu
To the Veterans of the Abraham Lincoln Brigade. Genevieve Taggard. PoFr
To the Victor. William Ellery Leonard. MAP; MoAmPo (1942 ed.); PoFr
To the village of lace and stone. Lamentation. Lynette Roberts. MoWP
To the Virgin. John Lydgate. ACP; CAW; GoBC; PoLi
To the Virgin. Rodríguez del Padrón, *tr. fr. Spanish by* Roderick Gill. OnPM
To the Virgin Mary, *abr.* Petrarch, *tr. fr. Italian by* Robert Guthrie MacGregor. Sonnets to Laura: To Laura in Death, Canzone VIII. CAW
("Fair Virgin,/ Vestured with the sun," *tr. by* Helen Lee Peabody.) PrPoCR
(Ode to the Virgin, *tr. by* Helen Lee Peabody.) ISi
(To the Virgin, *tr. by* Anna Maria Armi.) LiA
To the Virginian Voyage. Michael Drayton. AtBAP; BHV; BrBE; CoBE; CoEV; ElSeCe; EV-1; HBV; MC, *sl. abr.;* OAEP; OBEV; OBS; PaA; PAH; PoEL-2; PoFr; ReEn; ReIE; RiBV; SeCePo; SeEP; SG; TuPP; ViBoPo, *sl. abr.*
(Ode to the Virginian Voyage.) EnLi-1 (1949 ed.)
(Virginian Voyage, The.) LoBV
To the Virgins, to Make Much of Time. Robert Herrick. ALV; AnFE; AWP; BEL; BLPA; BLV; BoLiVe; CaAE; ChTr; EG; ElSeCe; Em-1; EnL; EnLi-1; EnLit; EnLoPo; EPP; EPS; EV-2; ExPo; FaBoEn; FaFP; HBV; InMe; InP; InPo; JAWP; LEAP; LiTB; LiTG; LiTL; LoBV; LPS-3; MaPo; NeHB; OAEP; OBEV; OBS; OuHeWo; PG; PIAE; PoE; PoEL-3; PoFS; PreP; ReaPo; ReEn; SeCeV; SeCL; SeCV-1; SeEP; ShBV-2; TCEP; TOP; TreFS; TrGrPo; TwHP; TyEnPo; ViBoPo; WBP; WHA
(Counsel to Girls.) GTBS; GTBS-D; GTBS-W; GTSE; GTSL; PoMa

To the Virgins, to Make Much of Time *(continued)*
(Gather ye Rosebuds [While Ye May].) AnEnPo; LoPo; MCCG; PFE
(Time.) PIR
(To Virgins to Make Much of Time.) CBOV
To the wake of Tim O'Hara. The Wake of Tim O'Hara. Robert Buchanan. VA
To the wall of the old green garden. A Yellow Pansy. Helen Gray Cone. DD; GFA; HBMV; NLK; VOD
To the warm life that musically passes. Ants. López Velarde. TwSpPo
To the Water Nymphs, Drinking at the Fountain. Robert Herrick. EG; EPS; PoFS; ViBoPo
To the Wayfarer. *Unknown.* SiSoSe
To the wedding of Shon Maclean. Wedding of Shon Maclean. Robert Buchanan. EBSV
To the west of the towering mountain is a red cloud. The Soldier-Statesman Returns. Tu Fu. OnPM
To the West Wind. George Frederick Cameron. CPG
To the Western Wind. Judah Halevi, *tr. fr. Hebrew by* Solomon Solis-Cohen. TrJP
To the Western Wind. Robert Herrick. HBV; OBEV; SeCV-1; SeEP
To the Western World. Louis Simpson. NePoAm-2
To the White Fiends. Claude McKay. BANP
To the Willow-Tree. Robert Herrick. HBV; OBEV
To the Wind. Vicente Riva Palacio, *tr. fr. Spanish by* Samuel Beckett. AnMP
To the Winds. Philip Ayres. CEP
To the winds give our banner! St. John. Whittier. PAH
To the Winnowing Demeter, from his ploughland's scanty measure. Harvest-Home. Zonas. GrPE
To the Winter Wind. John Gould Fletcher. TSW; TSWC
To the Woman I Will Be Fifty Years Hence. Virginia Moore. BAP
To the Woman in Bond Street Station. Edward Weismiller. LiTA; NePA; WaP
To the World; the Perfection of Love. William Habington. ElSeCe
To the World's Edge. Donn Byrne. BPP
To the Young Man Jesus. Annie Charlotte Dalton. CaP
To the Younger Old-Americans, *sel.* Kenneth Porter.
Oration, An ("Too long we have cheated our bellies with crumbs of tradition"). PoFr
To Thee. *Unknown.* BePJ
To thee, fair freedom! I retire. Written at [*or* in] an Inn at Henley. William Shenstone. AWP; CEP; EPP; EiPP; EV-3; HBV; JAWP; LEAP; LoBV; OBEC; OBEV (new ed.); OTPC (1923 ed.); PoE; TOP; ViBoPo; WBP
To thee I dedicate this green retreat. To the Garden God. Catullus. OnPM
To thee I would bring. The Violet under the Snow. Rachel Capen Schauffler. ADAH
To thee, my love, for ever I have given wings to raise thee. The Beloved. Theognis. GrPE
To thee my way in epigrams seems new. To My Mere English Censurer. Ben Jonson. TuPP
To thee now, Christ's dear darling. Pray for Us to the Prince of Peace. *Unknown.* AnEC
To thee, O Father of the stately peaks. To a Mountain. Henry Kendall. NeLNL; VA
To thee, our peaceful ground invisibly defending. To a Brownie. Pushkin. BoRS
To thee that art the sommers nightingale. To the Right Noble and Valorous Knight, Sir Walter Raleigh. Spenser. PtP
To Their Excellencies the Lords Justices of Ireland, the Humble Petition of Frances Harris, Who Must Starve, and Die a Maid if It Miscarries. Swift. BeR; LiA; PoEL-3
(Humble Petition of Frances Harris, The.) CEP
(Mrs. Frances Harris's Petition.) EV-3; GTIV; OxBI
(Mrs. Harris's Petition to Their Excellencies the Lords Justices of Ireland.) KN
To Theocritus, in Winter. Andrew Lang. *See* Ballade to Theocritus, in Winter.
To Theodore Roosevelt. Rubén Darío, *tr. fr. Spanish by* Elijah Clarence Hills.
(To Roosevelt.) WoL
"United States are rich, they're powerful and great, The," *fr.* II. PoFr
To These I Turn, in These I Trust. Siegfried Sassoon. *See* Kiss, The.
To these, the gentle South, with kisses smooth and soft. Michael Drayton. *Fr.* Polyolbion. OBS
To these [*or* those] whom death again did wed. An Epitaph upon [*or* on] Husband and Wife [*or* a Young Married Couple] Who Died and Were Buried Together. Richard Crashaw. BLV; ElSeCe; EV-2; FaBoEn; LiTL; LO; MaRV; OAEP; OBEV; OBS; SeCePo; SeCL; SeEP; TreFS; TrGrPo; WHA
To Thine Own Self Be True. Shakespeare. *See* Polonius' Advice to Laertes.
To Think. Elizabeth J. Coatsworth. *See* Counters.
To think, Belleau, that such a man. To Remi Belleau. Pierre de Ronsard. FoS
To think I once saw grocery shops. Counters [*or* To Think]. Elizabeth J. Coatsworth. DDA; GaP; MPB; MW; PoRh; SUS
To think of it! He knows me. And Yet. Arthur B. Rhinow. BLRP
To Think of Time. Walt Whitman. AnFE; APA; CoAnAm; IAP; LiTA
To think of you to-night. Pedro Salinas, *tr. fr. Spanish by* Eleanor L. Turnbull. CoSP
To think one thought a hundred hundred ways. Pierre de Ronsard. *Fr.* Amours de Cassandre. PrPoCR
To think our cat was wandering. The Cat and Northern Lights. Elizabeth J. Coatsworth. CIV
To think that Keats once held this volume dear. Association Copy. Paula Kurth. JKCP (1955 ed.)
To Think That Two and Two Are Four. A. E. Housman. *Fr.* Last Poems, XXXV. ImOP
To think that where young Jesus lay. Thought on a News Item. Lucia Trent. ChIP
To think the face we love shall ever die. Etruscan Tombs. Agnes Mary Frances Robinson. WHA
To think to know the country and not know. A Hillside Thaw. Robert Frost. ExPo; IAP; NP; TSW; TSWC
To thirst and find no fill—to wail and wander. Fragment. Shelley. BLV
To this khan, and from this khan. The World; a Ghazel. James Clarence Mangan. OBVV
To this man, to his boned shoulders. The Sympathizers. Josephine Miles. CrMA; FiMAP
To this sad shrine, whoe'er thou art, draw near. On the Hon. Simon Harcourt. Pope. OnPM; WoL
To this the Panther, with a scornful[l] smile. Dryden. *Fr.* The Hind and the Panther. SeCV-2; SeEP
To this you answered, oh swineherd Eumaeus. Eumaeus Plays Host to His Master. Homer. *Fr.* The Odyssey, XIV. GrR
To Thomas Hardy. Laurence Housman. MaRV
To Thomas Lord Chancellor. Ben Jonson. OBS
To Thomas Moore ("My boat is on the shore"). Byron. ATP; BoFr; BPN; EM-2; EnLi-2 (1949 ed.); EnLit; EnRP; ERP; EV-4; InP; LPS-3; MCCG; OAEP; PtP; TCEP; TOP
(Friendship.) LH; OTPC (1946 ed.)
(My Boat Is on the Shore.) BCEP; BEL; EPN; LEAP
To Thomas Moore ("What are you doing now"). Byron. BoFr; EmBrPo; PtP
To those blest shades, and amarantine bow'rs. The Seraphs in Heaven. Elizabeth Rowe. *Fr.* On Heaven. BeR
To those dim alcoves, far withdrawn. The Monastic Scribe. Thomas Bailey Aldrich. MOB
To those who died for her on land and sea. Prepared for a Soldiers' and Sailors' Monument in Boston. James Russell Lowell. InP; TOP
To those who have tried and seemingly have failed. Courage to Live. Grace Noll Crowell. BPP; PoToHe
To those whom death again did wed. *See* To these whom death again did wed.
To those whose bosomes harbours woes. *Unknown.* SeCSL
To Those Who've Failed. Walt Whitman. TOP
To Throw Away the Key. W. H. Auden. *See* Chorus: "To throw away the key and walk away."
To Thy continual Presence, in me wrought. A Prayer. William Ellery Channing. TrPWD
To thy lover. Out of the Italian; a Song. Richard Crashaw. SeCV-1
To Time. Michael Drayton. Idea, XVII. SiCE
("Stay, speedy Time, behold, before thou pass.") OBSC
To Time. John Hagthorpe. SeCL
To Time. "A. W." ElL; TuPP
To Tirzah. Blake. *Fr.* Songs of Experience. EiPP; EnRP; LO; MeRV; OxBoCh
"To-to" pour down. Raindrops. *Unknown.* PCH
To Tomas [*or* Tomaus] Costello at the Wars. *At. to* Tomas O'Higgins, *tr. fr. Irish by* Frank O'Connor. AnIV; KiLC
To Torquato Tasso. Don Angelo Grillo, *tr. fr. Italian by* Elizabeth Selden. BoFr
To touch the cup with eager lips and taste, not drain it. Living. *Unknown.* BLPA; FaBoBe; NeHB; TreFS
To Toussaint L'Ouverture. Wordsworth. AnEnPo; BCEP; BEL; BPN; CBE; EM-2; EmBrPo; EnL; EnLi-2; EnLit; EnLP; EnRP; EPP; ERP; ES; ExPo; GEPC; LoBV; LPS-3; OAEP; OBRV; PeBoSo; PoNe; PoRA; TrGrPo
"Thou hast left behind," *sel.* LiA
To travel like a bird, lightly to view. Sonnet. C. Day Lewis. *Fr.* O Dreams O Destinations. ChMP
To tread the path of glory needs a braver soul than I. The Vagabond. Edgar A. Guest. NLK
To tremble, when I touch her hands. Divine Awe. George Edward Woodberry. Wild Eden, XVI. AA; LBAP
To trump, or not to trump, that is the question. The Whist-Player's Soliloquy. Carolyn Wells. PA
To Truth. *Unknown. Fr.* Solomon. WGRP
To Tu Fu. Li Po, *tr. fr. Chinese.* WhP

To Tu Fu from Sand Hill City. Li Po, *tr. fr. Chinese by* Shigeyoshi Obata. BoFr
To turn my volumes o'er nor find. How to Read Me. Walter Savage Landor. VA
To Two Bereaved. Thomas Ashe. OBEV (1st ed.)
To Two Little Sisters of the Poor. Aline Kilmer. PraNu
To Ulla at a Window in Fishertown, Noon of a Summer Day. Karl Mikael Bellman, *tr. fr. Swedish by* Charles W. Stork. AnSL
To Ultima Thule. George Dangerfield. CAW
To unfrequented worlds I soaring fly. Solitude. Jami. PeP
To Urn, or not to Urn? that is the question. Cremation. William Sawyer. BOHV
To us, goddess, who are in barbary. Charles Madge. *Fr.* Poem by Stages. BoSA
To Varus. Catullus, *tr. fr. Latin by* Walter Savage Landor. AWP
To Venus ("Intermissa, Venus"). Horace, *tr. fr. Latin by* Ben Jonson. Odes, IV, 1. AWP
To Venus garlands—braids of clustering hair. A Happy Woman. Agathias. OnPM
To Vergil. Tennyson. *See* To Virgil.
To Vernon Lee. Amy Levy. VA
To Verse Let Kings Give Place. Ovid, *tr. fr. Latin by* Christopher Marlowe. Elegies, XV. ChTr
To Victor Hugo. Swinburne. OBVV; PtP
To Victor Hugo. Tennyson. LPS-3; PtP
To Vida D. Scudder. Florence Converse. BoFr
To view these walls each night I come alone. Complains, Being Hindered the Sight of his Nymph. Philip Ayres. SeCL
To Vincent Corbet, His Son. Richard Corbet. *See* To His Son, Vincent.
To Vineyarders in cold Korea. Pinkletinks. Grace Elisabeth Allen. GoYe
To Violets. Robert Herrick. EG; EV-2; HBV; OBEV; OBS; RG; TrGrPo; ViBoPo
(Violets.) LPS-2; OTPC (1923 ed.)
"Welcome, Maids of Honour," *sel.* MyFE, *2 sts.*
To Virgil. Tennyson. BPN; ChTr; EM-2; EmBrPo; EPN; GEPC; GTML; InP; PoEL-5; PoFS; PoVP; PtP; TCEP; ViPo; ViPP; VLEP; WHA
(To Vergil.) AWP; InPo
To Virginia Woolf. Nathaniel Thornton. MuM
To Virgins ("Hear ye virgins . . ."). Robert Herrick. ViBoPo
To Virgins, to Make Much of Time. Robert Herrick. *See* To the Virgins, to Make Much of Time.
To Virtue. Aristotle, *tr. fr. Greek by* T. F. Higham. OxBG
To Vittoria Colonna. Michelangelo, *tr. fr. Italian by* Longfellow. AWP; JAWP; MeRV; WBP
To voyaging past Ind, sole care. Renouncement. Stéphane Mallarmé. TrFP
To W. A. W. E. Henley. Echoes, XXXVII. BPN; EnLi-2; OuHeWo; PoVP
(Echoes.) BLPA; TreF
(I Was a King in Babylon.) LoPo
("Or ever the knightly years were gone.") BMEP; HBV; VLEP
To W. B. Yeats Who Says That His Castle of Ballylee Is His Monument. Oliver St. John Gogarty. AnIL
To W. H. H. Paul Hamilton Hayne. SPP
To W. M. Alice Meynell. *See* At Night.
To W. M. Francis Thompson. VLEP
To W. P. (I–IV). George Santayana. OBAV
Sels.
"Calm was the sea," I. BoFr
"With you a part of me," II. BoFr; TrGrPo
"To wade the sea-mist, then to wade the sea." Stone Horse Shoals. Malcolm Cowley. TwAmPo
To wake at morn. Rebellion. Stephen Chalmers. NLK
To wake the soul by tender strokes of art. Prologue to Mr. Addison's Tragedy of Cato. Pope. CEP; EV-3
To Waken an Old Lady. William Carlos Williams. InPo
To walk abroad is, not with eyes. Walking. Thomas Traherne. BLV; ElSeCe; SeCL; TrGrPo
To Walk on Hills. Robert Graves. MoP
To Walt Whitman. Tom MacInnes. BoCaPo; CaP; OCL
To Walt Whitman in America. Swinburne. BEL; BPN; EmBrPo; EnLi-2; EnLit; EPN; PoVP; ViP; ViPo; ViPP; VLEP
"Send but a song oversea for us." *sel.* InP
To Wang Lun. Li Po, *tr. fr. Chinese by* Shigeyoshi Obata. BoFr
To warm life passing singing with the grace. Ants. Ramón López Velarde. AnMP
To wear out heart, and nerves, and brain. Life Is Struggle. Arthur Hugh Clough. BEL; BPN; EmBrPo; EnLi-2; PoVP; VLEP
To weary hearts, to mourning homes. The Angel of Patience. Whittier. LPS-1; WGRP
To wed, or not to wed? That is the question. The Bachelor's Soliloquy. *Unknown.* PA
To Weep Irish. Lionel Johnson. VLEP
To Wei Pa, a Retired Scholar. Tu Fu, *tr. fr. Chinese by* Kenneth Rexroth. OnPC
To Weland came woes and wearisome trial. Deor's Lament. *Unknown.* EnLi-1; OuHeWo
To Welcome in the Spring. John Lyly. *See* Trico's Song.
To western woods, and lonely plains. On the Emigration to America and Peopling the Western Country. Philip Freneau. AmPP (3d ed.); CoV; MOAP; PAH
To wet your eye withouten tear. Sir Thomas Wyatt. SiPS
To what a cumbersome unwieldiness. Love's Diet. John Donne. OAEP; PoFS
To What Base Uses! Bert Leston Taylor. WhC
To what bliss could my spirit aspire. Song. Victor Hugo. TrFP
To what dark purpose was the will employed. Sea-Voyage. John Hall Wheelock. EtS; MuM
To what new fates, my country, far. Unmanifest Destiny. Richard Hovey. AA; AnAmPo; CBOV; HBV; HBVY; LA; MAP; MaRV; MoAmPo (1942 ed.); NeMA; OBAV; PaA; PFY; PoFr; WGRP
To what purpose, April, do you return again? Spring. Edna St. Vincent Millay. MAP; MoAB; MoAmPo; NePA; NP
To What Serves Mortal Beauty. Gerard Manley Hopkins. NBE
To what shall a woman liken her beloved. A Woman's Beloved. Marguerite Wilkinson. NP
To what shall I liken this life? A Boat Lost. *Unknown.* OnPM
To while the long, long road away. The Shepherd Folk Go to Bethlehem. Nicolas Saboly. CAW
To-whit! to-whit! to-whee! *See* Te-whit! te-whit! te-whee!
To Whittier. James Russell Lowell. *See* To John G. Whittier.
To whom Achilles thus with scornful glance. Achilles and Agamemnon; the Fatal Feud. Homer. *Fr.* The Iliad, I. GrR
To Whom Else? Robert Graves. FaBoMo
To whom of the gods could I more fitly appeal? Aeschylus. *Fr.* Suppliants. GrPo
To whom our Saviour calmly thus replied. True and False Glory. Milton. *Fr.* Paradise Regained. LiTB; OBS
To whom Penelope, discrete, replied. Penelope's Constancy Rewarded. Homer. *Fr.* The Odyssey, XXIII. GrR
To whom shall I this dancing poem send. Dedications [*of* Orchestra], I: To His Very Friend, Master Richard Martin. Sir John Davies. SiPS
To Whom Shall the World Henceforth Belong? John Oxenham. OQP; QP-2; WBLP
To whom the Angel. Son of Heav'n and Earth. Milton. *Fr.* Paradise Lost, V. NBE
To whom the Tempter inly rackt reply'd. Milton. *Fr.* Paradise Regained. NBE
To whom thus also th' angel last replied. Milton. *Fr.* Paradise Lost, XII. FiP
To whome shall I complaine, to men or gods. *Unknown.* SeCSL
To Will. H. Low. Robert Louis Stevenson. PoeT
To William Allen White. Edna Ferber. InMe
To William Blake. Olive Tilford Dargan. HBMV
To William Camden. Ben Jonson. AWP; EPS; InPo; OBS; PoFS; ReEn; ReIE; SeCV-1; SeEP; TuPP
To William Carlos Williams. Galway Kinnell. NePoAm
To William Erskine, Esq. Sir Walter Scott. Marmion, *Introd. to* III. EBSV; OBRV, *abr.*
To William H. Seward. Whittier. GA
To William Hayley. Blake. PIAE
(To Hayley.) TrGrPo
To William Lloyd Garrison ("Champion of those"). Whittier. CoBA; GA; PAH
To William Morris. W. C. Greene. CAG
To William Roe. Ben Jonson. OBS; SeCV-1
To William Sharp. Clinton Scollard. HBV; LBMV
To William Shelley. Shelley. ChER
To William Simpson of Ochiltree. Burns. EBSV; MCCG
(Epistle to William Simpson, Ochiltree.) BSV
To William Stewart Rose, Esq. Sir Walter Scott. Marmion, *Introd. to* I. EBSV
(In Memoriam; Nelson, Pitt, Fox.) EV-4; LH
(Nelson, Pitt, [and] Fox.) BSV; OBEV
(November in Ettrick Forest.) BSV
("November's sky is chill and drear.") OBRV
(Pitt and Fox.) BCEP
To William Wilberforce. William Cowper. *See* Sonnet to William Wilberforce, Esq.
To William Wordsworth. Samuel Taylor Coleridge. BPN; EmBrPo; EnRP; ERP; PtP
To Win the World. John Oxenham. MaRV
To Winter. Blake. AnEnPo; EM-1; TyEnPo
To wish, and want, and not obtain. Sir Thomas Wyatt. SiPS
To Woman. Byron. HBV
"Woman! experience might have told me," *sel.*, 10 *ll.* ViBoPo
To Women. Laurence Binyon. CP

To wonder, Plato told, revealed the wise. The Astronomer. Kevin F. Doherty. JKCP (1955 ed.)
To Worcester Gardens next they strolled. Maggie's Visit to Oxford. "Lewis Carroll." CIV
To Wordsworth. Walter Savage Landor. BPN; EmBrPo
To Wordsworth. Shelley. EmBrPo; EnRP; EPN; ERP; FiP; MCCG; PoRL; PtP
To work a wonder, God would have her shown. The Virgin Mary. Robert Herrick. NBE
To write a sonnet doth Juana press me. Sonnet on a Sonnet. Lope de Vega. AnSpL-1; TeCS
To write a sonnet needs a quiet mind. At a Window Sill. Christopher Morley. OBAV
To write a verse or two is all the praise. Praise. George Herbert. LPS-2
To write as your sweet mother does. Advice. Walter Savage Landor. HBV; VA
To write down all I contain at this moment. The Moment. Kathleen Raine. MoPW
To write of war and wot not what it is. The Fruits of War. George Gascoigne. ReIE
To write poems,/ to be a poet with a passionate and romantic life. Poetry. Salvador Novo. AnCL
To ye,/ Winged squadron flights of awful mystery. Powers of Darkness. Euripides. *Fr.* Orestes. GrR
To yon fause stream that, by the sea. The Mermaid. *Unknown.* CH
To You ("Stranger, if you passing meet me"). Walt Whitman. BoFr; LEAP
To You ("Whoever you are, I fear"). Walt Whitman. APW; IAP
To you alone our shivering souls confess. A Toast to Poets. Laura Simmons. LPS-1
To you, bleak fenland, first of all. To a Mountain Fen. Arne Garborg. AnNoLy
To you, consummate drinkers. MS of Benedictbeuern. *Tr. by* Helen Waddell. DiM
To you, dear mother heart, whose hair is gray. Lines. John Charles McNeill. NoCaPo
To you he gave his laughter and his jest. The Tears of Harlequin. Theodosia Garrison. LBMV
To you, holding in spent hands all seasons' memories. To a Faithless Lover. Robert Greacen. OnYI
To you I hurrying come. O sacred arms. To Jesus on the Cross. Juan Manuel Tejada. CAW
To you, light throng. A Winnower of Wheat to the Winds. Joachim du Bellay. FoS
To you, my lordis, that standis by. So Young ane King. Sir David Lindsay. SeCePo
To you, my purse [*or* purs], and to non [*or* no *or* noon] other wight. The Compleint [*or* Complaint] of Chaucer to His [Empty] Purse. Chaucer. BEL; BOHV; CoBE; EM-1; EnL; EnLi-1; EnLit; EPP; GoBC; LEAP; LPS-3; SiTL; TCEP; TrGrPo; TyEnPo; ViBoPo; WHA
To you, that know the touch of true conceit. To the Learned and Accomplish'd Gentleman Maister Nicholas Blackleech of Gray's Inn. Richard Barnfield. ReIE
"To you the torch we fling." The Torch. Arthur B. Dale. OQP; QP-2
To You! To You! Sir Philip Sidney. *See* Astrophel and Stella: First Song.
To you, troop [*or* who troop] so fleet. Hymn to the Winds. Joachim du Bellay. AWP; WoL
To you, Virginia, Tennessee. Southward Returning. Donald Davidson. SPP
To you, who troop so fleet. *See* To you, troop so fleet.
To You Who Wait. John Pudney. WaP
To you, whose temperate pulses flow. On the Fly-Leaf of Manon Lescaut. Walter Learned. AA
To you who've lived your life elate. Dedication. William Aspenwall Bradley. *Fr.* The Garden Muse. MOAH
To Young Dreamers. Lucia Trent. OQP; QP-2
To Young Imaginaries in Knowledge. Petrarch, *tr. fr. Italian by* George Chapman. *Fr.* Seven Penitential Psalms. ReEn
To your hermitage here on the top of the mountain. After Missing the Recluse on the Western Mountain. Ch'iu Wei. BoFr
To Youth. Walter Savage Landor. BEL; BPN; EmBrPo; EnRP; EPN; HBV; VA
(Lyrics and Epigrams, XXIV.) ERP
To Youth. John V. A. Weaver. TBM
To youths, who hurry thus away. On a Painted Woman. Shelley. SiTL
To Zeus. Terpander, *tr. fr. Greek by* C. M. Bowra. OxBG
To Zion. Judah Halevi, *tr. fr. Hebrew by* Maurice Samuel. AWP; JAWP; WBP
Toad, The. Tristan Corbière, *tr. fr. French by* Vernon Watkins. AnFP; MiFP; OnPM [*wr. at. to* Jules Laforgue], *tr. by* Patricia Terry; TrFP, *tr. by* Alan Conder
Toad, A. Edgar Fawcett. SN
Toad, The. Louis Kent. WaKn
Toad and the Frog, The. *Unknown.* RIS
("Croak!" Said the Toad.) PCH
Toad-Eater, The. Burns. RO
Toad that lived on Albury Heath, A. A Roundabout Turn. Robert E. Charles. MoShBr
Toad the power mower caught, A. The Death of a Toad. Richard Wilbur. AmP; MiAP; MoVE
Toad the Tailor. N. E. Hussey. BoTP
Toads. Philip Larkin. NePoEA
Toad's Journal, The. Jane Taylor. LPS-3
Toadstool comes up in a night, A. A Lesson. Christina Rossetti. RIS
Toadstools. Elizabeth Fleming. BoTP
Toast, A. John Byrom. *See* Jacobite Toast.
Toast. Frank Horne. BANP; PoNe
Toast, A. Joseph Howe. BoCaPo (1948 ed.)
Toast, A. Louis MacNeice. ChMo; GTBS-D
Toast. Stéphane Mallarmé, *tr. fr. French by* Joseph Bennett. AnFP
Toast, A. June Provine. AlBD
Toast, The. Charles Warren Stoddard. CAW
Toast ("Here's to those who love us"). *Unknown.* SiTL
Toast, A ("Here's to ye absent lords"). *Unknown.* ALV; WhC
Toast ("Up to my lips and over my gums"). *Unknown.* CoSo
Toast, A. Marguerite Wilkinson. SDH
Toast to Heliodore, A. Meleager. *See* Heliodore.
Toast to Omar Khayyám. Theodore Watts-Dunton. VA
Toast to Our Native Land, A. Robert Bridges. HiLiAm; MC; PAH
Toast to Poets, A. Laura Simmons. LPS-1
Toast to the Flag, A. John Daly. BAP; POT
Tobacco. Graham Lee Hemminger. WhC
(This Smoking World.) InMe
Tobacco, Tobacco. *Unknown.* TuPP
("Tobacco, tobacco, sing sweetly for tobacco!") ReEn
Tobacconist of Eighth Street, The. Richard Eberhart. MiAP
Tobacco's a musician. Barten Holyday. *Fr.* Technogamia; or, The Marriage of the Arts. TuPP
Tobit, *sel.* Bible, Apocrypha.
Blessed Is God, XIII, *tr. fr. Greek by* D. C. Simpson. TrJP
Toby Tosspot. George Colman. LPS-3
Toccata of Galuppi's, A. Robert Browning. AnFE; ATP (1935 ed.); BPN; EmBrPo; EnLi-2 (1949 ed.); GEPC; HBV; LEAP; LiTB; LoBV; OAEP; OtMeF; PIAE; PoE; PoFS; PoVP; REAL; ReaPo; ViPo; ViPP; VLEP; WHA
Today. John Kendrick Bangs. PoToHe
To-Day. Mary Frances Butts. *See* Build a Fence of Trust.
To-Day [*or* Today]. Thomas Carlyle. BCEP; EBSV; HBV; HBVY; MaRV; MW; NeHB; OQP; OTPC (1946 ed.); PTA-1; QP-2; TVSH; WGRP
Today. Thomas Curtis Clark. ChIP
To-Day. Helen Gray Cone. LBMV
Today. Ozora Stearns Davis. OQP; QP-2
Today. Ethel Romig Fuller. PoToHe (new ed.)
To-Day. Kipling. CBE
To-Day. Benjamin R. C. Low. HBV
To-Day. Angela Morgan. BLPA; MaRV
(In Such an Age.) OQP; QP-1
To-Day. John Boyle O'Reilly. OnYI
To-Day. Sybil F. Partridge. *See* Just for Today.
To-Day. Sister Mary Philip. GoBC
To-Day. William James Price. LPS-1
Today. Lizette Woodworth Reese. SPP
Today ("And if tomorrow shall be sad"). *Unknown.* OQP; QP-2
To-Day. Lydia Avery Coonley Ward. HBV; MaRV
Today. Nixon Waterman. *See* What Have We Done Today?
Today. Celeste Turner Wright. MuM
To-day/ I sit in the halls of state. The Garment of Mortality. Shih Ling Yü. PoHN
Today,/ Hark! Heaven sings. On Christmas Day. Clement Paman. AlDL; MeRV; OBS; OxBoCh; SeCL
Today/ The sun shines brightly. Visiting the Chou Family Tombs. T'ao Yüan-ming. PoHN
To-day a rude brief recitative. Song for All Seas, All Ships. Walt Whitman. CH; FaBoBe; HBV; HBVY; MCCG; NePA; SG
To-Day a Shepherd. St. Theresa of Avila, *tr. fr. Spanish by* Arthur Symons. AWP
To-day, all day, I rode upon the down. St. Valentine's Day. Wilfrid Scawen Blunt. EnLoPo; ES; EtPaEn; OBEV (1st ed.); OBVV; PoeT; ViBoPo
To-Day and Thee. Walt Whitman. NePA
Today and Tomorrow. Martial. *See* Happy the Man.
To-Day and To-Morrow. Gerald Massey. BMEP
Today and Tomorrow. Edward N. Pomeroy. MaRV; OQP; QP-2
To-day as I went down the road. Turtle Town. Helen Wing. GFA
To-day as I went out to play. The Brown Frog. Mary K. Robinson. BoTP
Today at the time of falling leaves we meet only to part. Parting with Li Po on the Tung-ting Lake. Chia Chi. BoFr

Today carries me back. From Exile. Hsü Chu. ChLP; PoHN
To-day chance drove me to the wood. A Moment. Stopford Augustus Brooke. IrPN
Today dawned not upon the earth as other days have done. The Débutante. Guy Wetmore Carryl. POT; PoTo
Today, dear heart, but just today. Her Answer. John Bennett. AA; BLPA; NeHB
Today Death seems to me an infant child. Newborn Death, I. Dante Gabriel Rossetti. The House of Life, XCIX. BPN; EmBrPo; PoVP; ViPo
Today ees com' from Eetaly. Da Boy from Rome. T. A. Daly. FaPON; LBMV; MPB; POT
Today for Me. Christina Rossetti. PoVP; VLEP
Today from the Aurora's bosom. The Nativity of Christ. Luis de Góngora. CAW; TeCS
Today he sickens with his hurt. Valhalla for the Living. Léonie Adams. MOAP
Today her Majesty was wroth and cold. George Henry Boker. Sonnets; a Sequence of Profane Love, LXXXIX. MOAP
Today I found lean winter's. The Coming. Anthony Delius. BoSA
Today I have been thinking of very old men. Old Men. Nancy Keesing. BoAV
Today I have grown taller from walking with the trees. Good Company. Karle Wilson Baker. FaPON; HBV; HiLiAm; NLK; NV; OQP; POT; PoTo; QP-1; SBMV; VOD; WGRP
Today I Have Touched the Earth. William Jay Smith. WaP
Today I have wine. I Am Content with Life and at Peace with the World. Lo Yin. PoHN
Today I met a stranger. Translations from Modern Japanese Poetry. Akiko Yanagiwara. PFE
Today I pray for one thing. Give Us This Day. Josephine Royle. BAP
To-day I saw a butterfly. Teresa Hooley. TiPo (1959 ed.)
Today I saw a group of children running. Green Branches. "Joan Ramsay." MaRV
Today I saw a picture of the cancer cells. The Cancer Cells. Richard Eberhart. HoPM; MiAP
Today I saw a thing of arresting poignant beauty. Snow in October. Alice Dunbar Nelson. CDC
Today I saw a woman wrapped in rags. At the Slackening of the Tide. James Wright. UnPo (3d ed.)
To-Day I Saw Bright Ships. Eloise Robinson. HBMV
To-day, I saw the catkins blow. February. Dorothy Una Ratcliffe. BoTP
Today I saw the dragon-fly. The Dragon-Fly. Tennyson. *Fr.* Two Voices. SN
To-day I saw the shop-girl go. To a New York Shop-Girl Dressed for Sunday. Anna Hempstead Branch. CV; HBV; LBMV
Today I saw the sun come up, like Neptune from the sea. Sunrise. Edgar A. Guest. NLK
Today I sing/ A song to Atlantis in the glory of the sky. Song to the Glory of the Sky of America [*or* Ode to the Sky of the New Atlantis]. Emilio Oribe. AnCL; PoFr
Today I think. Digging. Edward Thomas. MBP; MoAB; MoBrPo
Today I went among the mountain folk. Sonnet XXXVI. Olive Tilford Dargan. AV; NoCaPo
Today in Bethlehem Hear I. St. John of Damascus, *tr. fr. Greek.* BePJ; MaRV
To-day, in the hall. Confession. Yüan Ti. PoHN
Today is a holiday in the Western heart. Today Is Armistice, a Holiday. Delmore Schwartz. TrJP
Today is a thought, a fear is tomorrow. Dirge Written for a Drama. Thomas Lovell Beddoes. EnRP
Today Is Armistice, a Holiday. Delmore Schwartz. TrJP
Today is Candlemas, and by the light. Simeon's Light Remembered. John W. Simons. JKCP (1955 ed.)
"Today is hard. Tomorrow will/ Be harder still." The Kindly Screen. Belle Chapman Morrill. MaRV
To-day is here, and from the sullen skies. To-Day. William James Price. LPS-1
Today Is Ours. Abraham Cowley. *See* Epicure, The ("Fill the bowl with rosy wine").
Today, looking at the flowering peach. To My Father. James K. Baxter. AnNZ
Today, Muse, you must stand by the side of a friend. For Arkesilas of Kyrene. Pindar. *Fr.* Pythian Odes. GrL
To-day my friend is seventy-five. Felix Antonius. Sir Henry Newbolt. PtOT
To-day my heart is heavy. Cologne. John Bate. NeBP
To-day my tall broad-shouldered lad. On a Seventeenth Birthday. Anne P. L. Field. MOAH
To day my thoughts/ Are swift and cool. To-Day. Sister Mary Philip. GoBC
Today, new-born from all my yesterdays. Today. Ozora Stearns Davis. OQP; QP-2
Today, O Lord. Maltbie D. Babcock. OQP; QP-2
(Not to Be Ministered To.) PraP; TrPWD
To-day the axe has almost touched my being at its source. José Moreno Villa, *tr. from Spanish by* Eleanor L. Turnbull. CoSP
Today, the fifth moon, there are rice shoots at Chun-k'u. Song of Chun-k'u. Li Ho. WhP
Today the journey is ended. A Soul's Soliloquy. Wenonah Stevens Abbott. BLPA; NeHB
Today the Nazi Forces Marched. Melech Ravitch, *tr. fr. Yiddish by* Sarah Zweig Betsky. OnCuPl
Today the peace of autumn pervades the world. Autumn. Rabindranath Tagore. WGRP
To-day "the pines of Ramoth wood." John Greenleaf Whittier. John Cameron Grant. DD; GA
Today the rain. Rain. Frank Marshall Davis. GoSl
Today the seasons halted in their swing. Masquerade. Faith Baldwin. MuM
To-day the sense of spring fills all my frame. A Violin Mood. Robert Haven Schauffler. ADAH
Today the swards of heaven are merry. The First of April. Geoffrey Johnson. PoRL
Today the woods are trembling through and through. Corn. Sidney Lanier. CoBA; CoV; LaNeLa; TCAP
Today the world is bound in blue. First Geography. Gladys McKee. JKCP (1955 ed.)
To-day the world is wide and fair. April in the Hills. Archibald Lampman. CPG
Today this town is dull, my world confin'd. The Wilderness. Gyula Juhasz. LiTW
Today unnumbered church bells ring. Easter. John Van Brakle. ChIP
To-day was a sea-gull day, dear heart, to-day was a sea-gull day. Sea-Song. Martha Haskell Clark. NLK
Today we carted home the last brown sheaf. Load. John Hewitt. OnYI
Today we have naming of parts. Yesterday. Naming of Parts. Henry Reed. Lessons of the War, I. HoPM; LiTB; LiTM (rev. ed.); MoAB; MoVE; SeCePo; ShBV-3; SiTL; TrGrPo (rev. ed.); ViBoPo (1958 ed.); WaP
Today we think of that great man. For February Twelfth. Muriel M. Gessner. YeAr
To-day, what is there in the air. Carpe Diem. Théophile Marzials. VA
Today, whatever may annoy. Today. John Kendrick Bangs. PoToHe
Today when I heard. Retrospect. "An Pilibin." OnYI
To-day you shall have but little song from me. Irradiations, X [XXXII]. John Gould Fletcher. MAPA; TwAmPo
To-day's house makes to-morrow's road. The Survival. Edmund Blunden. OBEV (new ed.); OBMV
To-day's the Sabbath Holiday. Max Elskamp, *tr. fr. French by* Alan Conder. TrFP
Todlen Butt, and Todlen Ben. *Unknown.* EBSV; OBS
Todlin' Hame. *Unknown.* HBV
Toe Tipe. *Unknown.* OxNR
Toe, trip and go. *Unknown.* OxNR
Together. Ludwig Lewisohn. HBMV; PoToHe; TBM; TrJP
Together. Siegfried Sassoon. AlDL
Together arise the associated warriors. The Lost Legion. Aneirin. LyMA
Together in infinite shade. Too Much Coffee. E. A. Robinson. MAP; MoAmPo
Together in this grave lie Benjamin Pantier, attorney at law. Benjamin Pantier. Edgar Lee Masters. *Fr.* Spoon River Anthology. AlBD
"Together with my dead body shall they arise." Easter Tuesday. Christina Rossetti. MeRV
Together with my wife I passed. Passing the Cape. Otomo Tabito. OnPM
Toil. *Unknown.* PEDC; PEOR
Toil and grow rich. The Witch. W. B. Yeats. FaBoTw
Toil Away. John Jay Chapman. BAP; HBMV; LPS-1
Toil is the Sun-god's portion. The Sun's Golden Bowl. Mimnermus. GrL; LiTW
Toil of day is ebbing, The. Before Sleep. Prudentius. LiTW; TriL
Toil of the march is over, The. The Rappahannock Army Song. John C. M'Lemore. BlG
Toil of the Trail, The. Hamlin Garland. HBV; NLK; SN
Toil on, poor muser, to attain that goal. The Ideal. Francis Saltus Saltus. AA
Toil on! toil on! ye ephemeral train. The Coral Insect. Lydia Huntley Sigourney. LPS-2
Toil, trouble, praise and blame through office won. Seneca's Epitaph. Hildebert of Lavardin. LaP
Toiler, The, *sel.* Edwin Markham.
"Behold, O world, the toiling man." PGD
Toiler, Canst Thou Dream? Lulu W. Mitchell. DD
Toilet, The. Pope. *Fr.* The Rape of the Lock. CoEV; LPS-2; OBEC
("And now, unveil'd, the toilet stands display'd.") BCEP, *longer sel.;* BrBE; LEAP
(Belinda's Morning.) ExPo
Toilette, The; a Town Eclogue. John Gay. CEP
Toiling in the naked fields. The Laborer. John Clare. LPS-2

Toiling in Town now is "horrid." In Town. Austin Dobson. InP
Toiling of Felix, The, *sels.* Henry van Dyke.
Angler's Reveille, The. BBV (1923 ed.); GN; PYM; StVeCh
Envoy to "The Toiling of Felix." BLPA
"Never in a costly palace did I rest on golden bed." ChIP
Toils Are Pitched, The. Sir Walter Scott. *See* Song: "Toils are pitched, The."
Token, The. John Donne. *See* Sonnet: "Send me some token . . ."
Token, The. F. T. Prince. FaBoTw
Tokens. William Barnes. PoEL-4
Tokens. John Richard Moreland. IHA
Tokens, The. Francis Thompson. *Fr.* Daisy. OtMeF
Tokyo Imperial University Students. Shigeharu Nakano, *tr. fr. Japanese by* Takamichi Ninomiya *and* D. J. Enright. PoLJ
Told by Seafarers. Galway Kinnell. NePoAm-2
Told in the Market-Place. Edwina Stanton Babcock. StJW
Toledo ("Perched on its yellow peak"). Antonio Gómez Restrepo, *tr. fr. Spanish by* Thomas Walsh. CAW
Toledo ("No more the jousts"). José Zorrilla, *tr. fr. Spanish by* Thomas Walsh. CAW
Toledo Captured by the Franks. Al-Assal, *tr. fr. Arabic by* A. J. Arberry. MooP
Toledo, July 1936. Roy Campbell. FaBoTw; MoBrPo
Tolerance. Sir Lewis Morris. OBVV
Toll-a-Winker, *with music.* *Unknown.* OuSiCo
Toll for the Brave! William Cowper. *See* On the Loss of the *Royal George.*
Toll-Gate Man, The. Wilson MacDonald. CaP; OCL
Toll no bell for me, dear Father, dear Mother. TheChangeling. Charlotte Mew. CH; MPB
Toll of the Desert, The. Arthur W. Monroe. PoOW
Toll! Roland, toll! The Great Bell Roland. Theodore Tilton. PAH
Toll the Bell for Damon. Maxwell Anderson. InMe
Toll the lilies' silver bells! Dirge on the Death of Oberon, the Fairy King [*or* The Death of Oberon]. George Walter Thornbury. CBPC; HOAH
"Tollable Well!" Frank L. Stanton. FaFP
Tolling. Lucy Larcom. GA; LBAH; OHIP
Tolling Bells. Lady Kasa, *tr. fr. Japanese by* Ishii *and* Obata. OnPM
Tom a Bedlam. *Unknown.* *See* Tom o' Bedlam's Song.
Tom-a-Bedlam's Poem. *Unknown.* *See* Tom o' Bedlam's Song.
Tom Agnew, Bill Agnew. Dante Gabriel Rossetti. ChTr
Tom and Dick were in love with the fair Mrs. Brown. The Foolish Husband. Johannes Secundus. LaP
Tom Bolyn[n], *with music.* *Unknown.* OuSiCo; TrAS
Tom Bowling. Charles Dibdin. EtS; EV-3; HBV; LPS-2; SG; TVSH
(Perfect Sailor, The.) LH
(Poor Tom Bowling.) CBOV
(Poor Tom, or the Sailor's Epitaph.) OBEC; OxBoLi
(Tom Bowline, *with music.*) AmSS
Tom Brainless at College. John Trumbull. *Fr.* The Progress of Dulness. AmPP (3d ed.); ATP (1935 ed.); IAP
(Tom Brainless as Student and Preacher.) AmPP (4th ed.)
Tom Brainless Seeks a Wife. John Trumbull. *Fr.* The Progress of Dulness. AmPP (3d ed.)
(Amorous Temper, An.) AmPP (4th ed.)
Tom Brown's two little Indian boys. *Unknown.* OxNR
Tom Dansey was a famous whip. John Masefield. *Fr.* Reynard the Fox. OtMeF
Tom Dixon, *with music.* *Unknown.* ShS
Tom Dooley. *Unknown.* ViBoFo
Tom Dunstan; or, The Politician. Robert Buchanan. HBV; PoFr, *abr.*
Tom Gage's Proclamation. Thomas Flucker. PAH
Tom—garlanded with squat and surly steel. Tom's Garland. Gerard Manley Hopkins. EmBrPo; ViP
Tom he was the [*or* a *or* Tom, Tom, the] piper's son. Over the Hills and Far Away [*or* Tom, the Piper's Son]. *Unknown.* GaP; GoBP; OnHT; OTPC; OxNR; PCH; PPL; RIS; TiPo (1952 ed.)
Tom Hight is my name, an old bachelor I am. Greer County. *Unknown.* ABF; CoSo; CSF
Tom Joad, *with music.* Woody Guthrie. TrAS
Tom Mooney. William Ellery Leonard. PreP; TCPD
Tom o' Bedlam's Song (*diff. versions*). *Unknown.* AnFE; AtBAP; ChTr; EG; HoPM; InvP; LiTB; LiTG; OtMeF, *sl. abr.;* PoEL-2; PoFS; RiBV; SeCeV; ShBV-4; TrGrPo; ViBoPo, *at. to* Giles Earle
(Loving Mad Tom.) EnSB
(Mad Song; or, Tom o' Bedlam's Song.) BLV
(Tom a Bedlam.) SeEP
(Tom-a-Bedlam's Poem.) BCEP; HBV
(Tom o' Bedlam.) BoW; CH, *much abr.;* CoEV; FaBoCh; LoGBV; KN; NBE; OxBoLi; SiTL; WaKn
"Moon's my constant mistress, The," *sel.,* 5 *ll.* LO
Tom of Bedlam ("From the top of high Caucasus"). *Unknown.* SiTL
Tom, old fellow, I grieve to see. The Empty Sleeve. J. R. Bagby. BlG
Tom O'Roughley. W. B. Yeats. ChMo; CMP
Tom Paine. Byron. BoHiPo
"Tom Pearse, Tom Pearse, lend me your gray mare." Widdicombe [*or* Widdecombe] Fair. *Unknown.* BBV (1951 ed.); CH; MoShBr; MuP; OBB; OnSP; PoMS; WP
Tom Potts. *Unknown.* ESPB
Tom Pringle. Louis Simpson. NePoAm-2
Tom Tatter's Birthday Ode. Thomas Hood. LoBV; RO
Tom the Lunatic. W. B. Yeats. OnYI
Tom, the Piper's Son. *Unknown.* *See* Over the Hills and Far Away.
Tom the Porter. John Byrom. CEP
Tom Thomson. Arthur S. Bourinot. CaP
Tom Thumbkin. *Unknown.* OxNR
Tom Thumb's Alphabet. *Unknown.* HBV; HBVY; OTPC; SiTL
("A was an archer, who shot at a frog.") OxNR
Tom told his dog called Tim to beg. Tom's Little Dog. Walter de la Mare. TiPo
Tom-tom sun awakens day's jungle with heat beats, A. Midsummer Morn. Frank Marshall Davis. GoSl
Tom, Tom, the Piper's Son. John Crowe Ransom. ViBoPo
Tom, Tom, the piper's son/ Stole a pig and away he run. Mother Goose. BoChLi; OTPC; OxNR; RIS; SiTL
Tom, Tom, the piper's son,/ He learned to play when he was young. Over the Hills and Far Away. *Unknown.* *See* Tom he was the piper's son.
Tom Twist. William Allen Butler. OTPC (1946 ed.)
Tom Tyler and His Wife, *sel.* *Unknown.*
"Proverb reporteth, no man can deny, The." EIL; ElSeCe; SiCE; TuPP
Tomah Stream, *with music.* Larry Gorman. ShS
Tomato Juice. A. P. Herbert. WhC
Tomb, The. Matthew Arnold. *Fr.* The Church of Brou. PoVP; TriL
Tomb/ A hollow hateful word. Agamemnon's Tomb. Sacheverell Sitwell. LiTB; OBMV
Tomb at Akr Çaar, The. Ezra Pound. APA; CoAnAm; TwAmPo
Tomb by the Sea, A. Archias, *tr. fr. Greek by* Sir William Marris. OxBG
Tomb by the Sea, A. Asclepiades, *tr. fr. Greek by* Walter Leaf. OxBG
(Tomb of a Lost Mariner.) GrR
Tomb of a shipwrecked mariner am I. Pass On. Theodorides. OxBG; WoL
Tomb of Charles Baudelaire, The. Stéphane Mallarmé, *tr. fr. French by* Joseph Bennett. AnFP
Tomb of Crethon, The. Leonidas of Tarentum, *tr. fr. Greek by* John Herman Merivale. AWP; JAWP; WBP
Tomb of Diogenes, The. *Unknown, tr. fr. Greek by* John Addington Symonds. AWP; JAWP; OnPM; WBP
Tomb of Edgar Poe, The. Stéphane Mallarmé, *tr. fr. French.* AnFP, *tr. by* Daisy Aldan; TrFP, *tr. by* Alan Conder
Tomb of God before us, The. Crusader Chorus. Charles Kingsley. *Fr.* The Saint's Tragedy. VA
Tomb of Honey Snaps Its Marble Chains, The. Derek Stanford. NeBP
Tomb of Lieutenant John Learmonth, A.I.F., The. John S. Manifold. BoAV; LiTM; NeLNL
Tomb of Michael Collins, The. Denis Devlin. OxBI
Tomb [of Paul Verlaine]. Stéphane Mallarmé, *tr. fr. French by* Kate Flores. AnFP
Tomb of Sardanapalus, The. *Unknown, tr. fr. Greek by* Sir William Marris. OxBG
Tomb of the Brave, The. Joseph Hutton. PAH
Tomb, thou shalt not hold Him longer. Easter Morning. Phillips Brooks. MaRV
Tombe, The. Thomas Stanley. OBS
Tombless Epitaph, A, *sel.* Samuel Taylor Coleridge.
"Sickness 'tis true." OBRV
Tomboy, The. William Burford. NePA
Tombs. Louise Webster. ChIP
Tombstone Told When She Died, The. Dylan Thomas. FaBoTw; TriL
Tombstone with Cherubim. Horace Gregory. NAMP
Tomcat, The. Don Marquis. BAP; CIV; DDA; LEAP; PoeMoYo; PoMa; PoRA
Tomlinson. Kipling. BeLS; ChMo; OtMeF, *abr.;* PIR; PoVP; VLEP
Tommies in the Train. D. H. Lawrence. NP
Tommy. Kipling. BPN: EnLi-2 (1949 ed.); EnLit; MBP; MoBrPo; NeMA; PoVP; PTA-2; TreFS; ViPP
Tommy for his evening game. *Unknown.* WhC
Tommy kept a chandler's shop. *Unknown.* OxNR
Tommy O'Linn was a Scotsman born. *Unknown.* OxNR
Tommy Tibule. *Unknown.* OxNR
Tommy Trot, a man of law. *Unknown.* OxNR
Tommy was a silly boy. Kate Greenaway. TiPo
Tommy's Dead. Sydney Dobell. HBV; VA

Tommy's Gone to Hilo, *with music.* *Unknown.* AmSS; SG; ShS
(Tom's Gone to Hilo, *with music.*) SoAmSa
Tommy's Prayer. John F. Nicholls. PTA-2
Tommy's tears and Mary's fears. Mother Goose. HBV; HBVY
To-Morrow. Florence Earle Coates. AA
To-Morrow. John Collins. GTBS; GTBS-D; GTBS-W; GTSE; GTSL; HBV
Tomorrow. Charles Cotton. BCEP
Tomorrow. Kenneth Fearing. ChMo
Tomorrow. Samuel Johnson. *Fr.* Irene, III, iii. LPS-3
Tomorrow. Lope de Vega, *tr. fr. Spanish by* Longfellow. AnSpL-1; AWP; CAW; MeRV; TeCS; TrPWD
To-Morrow. Martial. *See* Procrastination.
Tomorrow. John Masefield. MBP; MoBrPo; NeMA; OtMeF; POTE; StaSt; TrGrPo; YT
Tomorrow. Regino Pedroso, *tr. fr. Spanish by* Dudley Fitts. AnCL; PoFr
To-Morrow. E. A. Robinson, *after the Greek of* Macedonius. (Variations of Greek Themes, IX.) MOAP
Tomorrow. Shakespeare. *See* Tomorrow and Tomorrow and Tomorrow.
To-Morrow. Shelley. BPN; EmBrPo; EPN
Tomorrow and Tomorrow Sir William Davenant, *revision of* Shakespeare. UnPo
Tomorrow and Tomorrow and Tomorrow. Shakespeare. *Fr.* Macbeth, V, v. BLP; BrBE; FaFP; LiTB; OQP; PFE; PG; PIR; QP-1; TrGrPo; WHA
(Empty Life, The.) MaRV
(Macbeth Learns of His Wife's Death.) TreF
(Macbeth on His Wife's Death.) CoEV
(Out, Out, Brief Candle!) ChTr
(She Should Have Died Hereafter.) FiP
("She should have died hereafter.") InP; NBE
(Tomorrow.) BCEP
(Tomorrow and Tomorrow.) NeHB; UnPo
(Way to Dusty Death. The.) EV-1
Tomorrow and Tomorrows. "Stuart Sterne." BPP
Tomorrow at dawn. A Soldier's Wife. Li Po. OnPM
Tomorrow didst thou say? Tomorrow. Charles Cotton. BCEP
"Tomorrow, friend, will be another day." Faith for Tomorrow. Thomas Curtis Clark. PoToHe
Tomorrow I was/ Going to the Spring meadows. Yamabe no Akahito, *tr. fr. Japanese by* Kenneth Rexroth. OnPJ
Tomorrow Is a Birthday. Gwendolen Haste. GoYe
"To-Morrow Is a New Day." Palladas, *tr. fr. Greek by* F. L. Lucas. GrPE
Tomorrow Is [*or* Good Morrow, 'Tis] Saint Valentine's Day. Shakespeare. *Fr.* Hamlet, IV, v. EnLoPo; InPo; ViBoPo
(Saint Valentine's Day.) LiTB; LiTG
(Song.) FaPON; HH; MPB; SiSoSe
Tomorrow let loveless, let lover tomorrow make love. The Vigil of Venus (Pervigilium Veneris). *Unknown.* LaP; LiTW
"Tomorrow, Pa, I'm sweet sixteen, and Billy Grimes the drover." The Courtship of Billy Grimes. *Unknown.* ABS
To-Morrow Shall Be My Dancing Day. *Unknown.* AnEC; PoEL-1
(My Dancing Day.) OxBoLi
To-morrow? Then your one word left is always now the same. Variations of Greek Themes, IX: To-Morrow. E. A. Robinson, *after* Macedonius. MOAP
Tomorrow, tomorrow's the circus parade! The Circus Parade. Olive Beaupré Miller. GFA
Tomorrow when I go to shop. Pretense. Helen Welshimer. PoMa
Tomorrow you are born again. December Twenty-fourth. Eleanor Slater. ChIP; MaRV; OQP; QP-2
To-morrow you will live, you always cry. Procrastination [*or* To-Morrow]. Martial. AWP; JAWP; LiTW; OnPM; OuHeWo; WBP
Tomorrow's action can that hoary wisdom. Tomorrow. Samuel Johnson. *Fr.* Irene. LPS-3
Tomorrows and tomorrows stretch a gray. Tomorrow and To-morrows. "Stuart Sterne." BPP
Tomorrow's Men. Georgia Douglas Johnson. GoSl
Tomorrow's News. "George Klingle." OQP; QP-1
Tom's album was filled with the pictures of belles. The Unattainable. Harry Romaine. BOHV
Tom's Angel. Walter de la Mare. POTE
Tom's Garland. Gerard Manley Hopkins. EmBrPo; ViP
Tom's Gone to Hilo. *Unknown. See* Tommy's Gone to Hilo.
Tom's Little Dog. Walter de la Mare. TiPo
Tone de Bell Easy, *with music. Unknown.* ABF
Tone of Voice, The. *Unknown.* PoToHe (new ed.)
Tone's Grave. Thomas Osborne Davis. OnYI
Tongue, The. *Unknown.* PoToHe (new ed.); WBLP
Tongue hath not told it. Paraclete. Alfred Noyes. LBBV
Tongue of England, that which myriads, The. Shakespeare and Milton. Walter Savage Landor. BPN; MeRV; PtP; VA
Tongues. T. Sturge Moore. HBMV
Tongues of dying men, The. Dying Men. Shakespeare. King Richard II, *fr.* II, i. MaRV
Tongues there are that naught can say. Tongues. T. Sturge Moore. HBMV
Tonight. Franklin P. Adams. FiBHP
To-Night. Louise Chandler Moulton. AA; OBAV
Tonight. *Unknown. See* For All Who Need.
Tonight/ when the moon comes out. Proposition. Nicolás Guillén. FaPON; PoNe
Tonight a blackout. Christmas Eve under Hooker's Statue. Robert Lowell. NePA; OxBA
Tonight and forever I shall be yours so says the oleo king. Some Stories of the Beauty Wapiti. Ebbe Borregaard. NeAP
To-night eternity alone is near. Dusk at Sea. Thomas S. Jones, Jr. BAP; OBAV; SBMV
To-night from deeps of loneliness I wake in wistful wonder. Bluebells. Lucia Clark Markham. HBMV
Tonight, grave sir, both my poor house and I. Inviting a Friend to Supper [*or* Epigram]. Ben Jonson, *after* Martial. AWP; ElSeCe; JAWP; LiTB; LoBV; MaPo; MyFE; OAEP; OBS; OxBoLi; Po; PoE; PoEL-2; ReEn; RiBV; SeCV-1; SeEP; TuPP; WBP
To-night her lids shall lift again, slow, soft, with vague desire. Heart's Wild-Flower. William Vaughn Moody. LEAP; TOP
Tonight I also came, sweet brother of Nazareth. Jesus. Joseph Eliyia. MoGP
To-night I do not come to conquer thee. Anguish. Stéphane Mallarmé. AWP
To-night I lay with fever in my veins. 104° Fahrenheit. Francis Brett Young. PoP
Tonight I may die. Rain, wind, sun. The Impossible. Jules Laforgue. AnFP
To-night I sing, though all mankind forbid it. Night Piece to Another Julia. Paul Fearon. CIV
To-night I stay at the Summit Temple. The Summit Temple. Li Po. OnPM
To-night I will lie between silver sheets. In Bed. Jacqueline Green. CAG
To-night in million-voiced London I. The Telephone. Hilaire Belloc. MoVE
Tonight is so coarse with chocolate. Ode. Louis MacNeice. ChMo
Tonight is the night. Hallowe'en. Harry Behn. FaPON; GBV (1952 ed.); SiSoSe; StVeCh (1955 ed.); TiPo; YeAr
Tonight our ship is anchored where. Labrador Night. Leo Cox. BoCaPo (1943 ed.)
To-night retir'd the queen of heaven. Ode to the Evening Star [*or* The Nightingale *or* To the Evening Star]. Mark Akenside. CEP; EV-3; HBV; OBEC; OBEV; PoEL-3
Tonight the Christmas landscape of the skull. Carol for His Darling on Christmas Day. Derek Stanford. NeBP
Tonight, the country wine was clear. Hugh, the Carter, Tarries. Willard Wattles. PR
To-night, the gaudy auditorium. After the Show. Sam Harrison. NeIP
Tonight the hut grows menacing, the walls. This Is My Song. Norma Davis. NeLNL
To-night the little nun-girl died. Cloistered. Mary Carolyn Davies. LEAP
Tonight the moon is high, to summon all. Elegy XII. William Bell. FaBoTw
Tonight the rain sheets down. After an hour. Cheshire Cat. Kenneth Allott. NeBP
Tonight the schools disperse. On the Breaking-up of a School. Tadhg O'g O'Huiginn AnIL; SiB
Tonight the stars lean close, as though aware. The Stars Lean Close. Lucille Evans. MuM
To-night the stranger city and the old. The Cruel Solstice. Sidney Keyes. POTE
Tonight the very horses springing by. Winter Evening. Archibald Lampman. BoCaPo; CPG; PeCV
To-night the wind is lyrical again. South Wind. George O'Neil. PFE
Tonight the winds begin to rise. In Memoriam A. H. H., XV. Tennyson. AnFE; CaAE; CoEV; EmBrPo; EnLi-2; EnSW; EPN; FaBoEn; GEPC; GTBS-D; LiTB; OAEP; OBEV (1st ed.); PoEL-5; PoFS; ReaPo; ShBV-4; ViPo; VLEP
Tonight this city seated on a hill. Midnight Mass. Sister Mary Madeleva. Christmas in Provence, II. WHL
To-night this city seems delirious. The air. London Squares. Sir Osbert Sitwell. LBBV
To-night this sunset spreads two golden wings. Sunset Wings. Dante Gabriel Rossetti. EmBrPo; HBV; RO
To-night ungathered let us leave. In Memoriam A. H. H., CV. Tennyson. EM-2; EmBrPo; EnLi-2; EPN; GEPC; OAEP; ViPo; VLEP
To-night we strive to read, as we may best. Prologue. Longfellow. *Fr.* John Endicott. PAH

Tonight when the hoar frost falls on the wood. Christmas in the Woods. Frances Frost. BrR; ChBR; TiPo (1952 ed.)
To-night when you sit in the deep hours alone. The Vision on the Brink. Francis Ledwidge. VOD
To-night's a moonlit cup. The Offensive. Keith Douglas. NeBP
Tons upon tons the brown-green fragrant hay. In an Old Barn. Sir Charles G. D. Roberts. BoCaPo
Tonversation with Baby, A. Morris Bishop. FiBHP; WhC
Tony O! Colin Francis. CH
Tony's Grave. "Seumas O'Sullivan." PoC
Too Anxious for Rivers. Robert Frost. MoPW
Too avid of earth's bliss, he was of those. Byron the Voluptuary. Sir William Watson. VA
Too beautiful this earth is! Weep I must. The Troubled Unquickening. William Baylebridge. *Fr.* Sextains. BoAV
Too big the sky too big I don't know where to go. The Sick Man. Jules Supervielle. MiCF
Too Busy? Ralph S. Cushman. PraP
Too Busy. *At. to* Paul Laurence Dunbar. *See* Get Somebody Else.
Too Candid by Half. John Godfrey Saxe. HBV
Too cold this night for Hugh Maguire. Hugh Maguire. Eochadh O'Hussey. AnIL; KiLC
Too dearly had I bought my green and youthful years. Earl of Surrey. SiPS
Too Early Death. L. F. Gerlach. PtPa
Too fair, I may not call thee mine. Parting. Gerald Massey. HBV
Too far for you to see. The Welsh Hill Country. R. S. Thomas. PoN
Too far, too far, though hidden in thine arms. Pandora's Song. William Vaughn Moody. *Fr.* The Fire-Bringer. MOAP
Too Fragmentary Is Life in the Main. Heine, *tr. fr. German by* Vernon Watkins. AnGP
Too green the springing April grass. Spring in New Hampshire. Claude McKay. BANP; GoSl; PoNe
Too honest for a gypsy, too lazy for a farmer. Shepherd's Holiday. Elinor Wylie. CrMA; HBMV; PoTo
Too Late. Robert Browning. EmBrPo; PoVP
Too Late. Dinah Maria Mulock Craik. *See* Douglas, Douglas, Tender and True.
Too Late. Emily Dickinson. *See* Delayed till she had ceased to know.
Too Late. "Michael Field." MBP
Too Late. William James Linton. VA
Too Late? Longfellow. WBLP
Too Late. Fitzhugh Ludlow. BOHV; LPS-3
Too Late. Nora Perry. PoToHe
Too Late. Tennyson. *Fr.* Idylls of the King: Guinevere. MaRV; OQP; QP-2
Too Late, *with music.* *Unknown.* BoAN-2
Too late, alas! I must confess. Song. Earl of Rochester. HBV; LPS-1
Too-late Born, The. Archibald MacLeish. AmP; AnFE; APA; ChMo; CMP; CoAnAm; GTBS-W; LiTM; MAP; MoAB; MoAmPo; NAMP; OxBA; PreP; ReaPo; SeCeV; TBM; TwAmPo; TwHP; WaP
(Silent Slain, The.) CoBMV; ExPo; MoVE; NePA
Too Late for Love. Christina Rossetti. *See* Bride Song.
Too Late I Stayed. William Robert Spencer. LoPo; LPS-1; PIR
Too Late, My Love. Conon de Béthune, *tr. fr. French* by Claude C. Abbott. LyMA
Too late, too late! I did not know my fairness. A Beauty's Soliloquy during Her Honeymoon. Thomas Hardy. PoVP
Too late, too late, sinnah. Too Late. *Unknown.* BoAN-2
Too long it seems e'er I shall view. Virelay. Jean Froissart. LyMA
Too long outside your door I have shivered. The Terrible Door. Harold Monro. EnLoPo; FaBoTw
Too long the silent South, untaught to sing. Utterance. James Larkin Pearson. NoCaPo
Too long, too long. Spring Song in Winter. Michael Hamburger. PoN
Too long we have cheated our bellies with crumbs of tradition. An Oration. Kenneth Porter. *Fr.* To the Younger Old-Americans. PoFr
Too many of the dead—some I knew well. In the Backs. Frances Cornford. DiM
Too Many Songs ("Too many pretty songs are sung"). Amanda Benjamin Hall. TBM
Too many summers out of the way of a trowel. The Lawn Roller. Robert Layzer. NePoEA
Too Much. Edwin Muir. LiTB
Too Much Coffee. E. A. Robinson. MAP; MoAmPo
Too Much for One: Not Enough to Go Around. R. P. Blackmur. Scarabs for the Living, I. CrMA
Too much good luck no less than misery. Joy May Kill [*or* Fearful Joy]. Michelangelo. AWP; JAWP; OnPM; WBP
Too much of charity's a sin! Jealous Doggerel. Burges Johnson. AlBD
Too much thought. Proverbs: Day-Dreamer. *Unknown.* RIS; TiPo
Too Near the Sea. Harold Monro. CoEV
Too Near the Waves. Poseidippus, *tr. fr. Greek.* OnPM
Too poor for a bribe, and too proud to importune. Sketch of His Own Character. Thomas Gray. BEL; CEP; EnLit; TOP
Too popular is tragic poesy. Joseph Hall. *Fr.* Virgidemiarum. ReEn; SiCE
Too powerful a drug is Hope. "Bottle Should Be Plainly Labeled 'Poison.'" Sara Henderson Hay. GoYe
Too solemn for day, too sweet for night. William Sidney Walker. OBEV
Too Soon the Lightest Feet. Amanda B. Hall. HBMV; TBM
(Too Soon.) BAP
Too soon the winter cold and heavy frost. Sonnet. Fernando de Herrera. TeCS
Too soothe and mild your lowland airs. Margaret's Song. Lascelles Abercrombie. *Fr.* The New God; a Miracle. GTBS; LBBV; PoeT
Too swiftly my coracle flies on her way. On His Exile to Iona. St. Columcille. CAW; LiTW
Too Versatile. Archilochus, *tr. fr. Greek by* F. L. Lucas. GrPE
Too warm, my friend, your anger waxes. The Peace. Henry Luttrell. *Fr.* Advice to Julia. OBRV
Too wearily had we and song. To a Poet Breaking Silence. Francis Thompson. EmBrPo; VA
Too well, O Christ, we know Thee; on our eyes. He Is Not Risen. W. S. Handley Jones. MaRV
Too Wonderful. Proverbs, XXX: 18–19, Bible, *O.T.* TrJP
Took Bladyn then his crowth, anew, and toucht. Bladyn's Song of Cloten. Charles M. Doughty. *Fr.* The Dawn in Britain. PoEL-5
Tool of Fate, The. "Yehoash," *tr. fr. Yiddish by* Isidore Goldstick. TrJP
Tools must tap in the quarry. The Building of the Sea-Wall. Lyon Sharman. CPG
Tools with the comely names. A Saxon Song. V. Sackville-West. MBP; MoBrPo (1943 ed.)
Toothache. *Unknown.* PA
Toothpick, The. Al-Hajjam, *tr. fr. Arabic by* A. J. Arberry. MooP
Top Hand. *Unknown.* CoSo; CSF
Top o' the mornin' to you, Mick, The. Seed-Time. Patrick James Coleman. TIP
Top of Day, The. Anne Blackwell Payne. GFA
Tophet; an Epigram. Thomas Gray. MyFE
Toponymy. Ralph Gustafson. BoCaPo (1943 ed.)
Topsails shiver in the wind, The. Song to Mary. —— Thomson. SG
Topside Galah! *Unknown.* PA
Topsy-turvy Land. Phyllis M. Stone. BoTP
Topsy-turvy Land. H. E. Wilkinson. BoTP
Topsy-turvy World. William Brighty Rands. MPB; OTPC (1946 ed.); TSW; TSWC; VA
Sels.
"Ba-ba, black wool." BoN
(Chorus: "Ba-ba, black wool.") PIAE
"Carry and Kate." BoN
"If black was white." BoN
"If the butterfly courted the bee." BoN
Tor House. Robinson Jeffers. AnAmPo; LA; LoBV
Tora's Song. Knut Hamsun, *tr. fr. Norwegian by* Charles W. Stork. AnNoLy
Torben's Daughter. *Unknown, tr. fr. Danish by* E. M. Smith-Dampier. BoDaBa
Torch, The. Arthur B. Dale. OQP; QP-2
Torch, The. Theodosia Garrison. BLPA
Torch-Bearers, *sel.* Arlo Bates.
America. AA; PaA
("America, last hope of man and truth," 8 *ll.*) PGD
Torch Bearers, The. Alfred Noyes. *See* Last Voyage, The, *and* Watchers of the Sky.
Torch-Light in Autumn. John James Piatt. AA; LEAP
Torch of Liberty, The. Thomas Moore. DD; IDAH; PEDC
Torches Are Bright, The. *Unknown, tr. fr. Chinese.* WhP
Torches beat out, to your dark body's rhythm, the shadows of the world. Nocturne of Sin and Its Accusation. José Miguel Ferrer. AnCL
Torches Have Gone Out, The. Putinas, *tr. fr. Lithuanian by* W. K. Matthews. LiTW
Tord Foleson. Per Sivle, *tr. fr. Norwegian by* Charles W. Stork. AnNoLy
Torii. Dorothy Choate Herriman. CPG
Tormented by the World. Lascelles Abercrombie. POTE
Tormented with incessant pains. To Stella; March 13, MDCCXXIII-IV. Swift. Po
Torn between hunger and maternal cares. A Mother with Young Kittens. Richard Hart. CIV
Torn book we burn, and the dead tree, The. The Broken One. John Holmes. MiAP
Torn from his country bed. The Settler. Roy Macnab. BoSA

Torn Hat, The. Nathaniel P. Willis. AA
Torn upon Thy wheel. Out of the Depths. Frederic Lawrence Knowles. TrPWD
Tornado, The. Charles de Kay. EtS
Toro. W. S. Merwin. NePA
Toronto Crossing. Robert Finch. TwCaPo
Torquatus four miles from the city. Outclassed. Martial. RoL
Torqued warriors turned their galley's crimson prow. The Blessing of Columcille. Thomas S. Jones, Jr. Sonnets of the Saints, II. TBM
Torrent, The. E. A. Robinson. MaPo; NePa
Torrismond, *sels.* Thomas Lovell Beddoes.
In a Garden by Moonlight. VA
Song: "How many times do I love thee, dear?" *fr.* sc. iii. AnFE; CaAE; LiTB; LiTG; LiTL; LoPo; OBEV (1st ed.); OBRV; PCD; PoEL-4; TrGrPo; VA; ViBoPo
(How Many Times.) TSW; TSWC
(How Many Times Do I Love Thee, Dear?) EnRP; ERP; GTBS-D; NeHB
Torso of an Archaic Apollo. Rainer Maria Rilke. *See* Archaic Torso of Apollo.
Tortoise, The. Herbert Asquith. RIS
Tortoise. Sakutaro Hagiwara, *tr. fr. Japanese by* Takamichi Ninomiya *and* D. J. Enright. PoLJ
Tortoise Family Connections. D. H. Lawrence. ChMP; HaMV
Tortoise in Eternity, The. Elinor Wylie. ChMo; FaPON; ImOP
Tortoise Shell. D. H. Lawrence. ExPo
Tortoise-Shell, The, *abr.* *Unknown, tr. fr. Greek by* Shelley. *Fr.* Homeric Hymns. OxBG
(Singing Tortoise, The.) GrR
Tortoiseshell Cat, The. Patrick Reginald Chalmers. CenHV
Tortoise Shout. D. H. Lawrence. LiTM
Torture. Sigbjörn Obstfelder, *tr. fr. Norwegian by* Charles W. Stork. AnNoLy
Tortured body, lie at rest alone. Unknown Man in the Morgue. Merrill Moore. MAP; MoAmPo
Toshie Norrie. Alexander Anderson. EBSV
Toss your delicate spun flowers of crystal high. The Fountain. Herbert S. Gorman. NV
Tossed by the seas of love how have I striven. Four Sonnets to Helen, 1. Pierre de Ronsard. *Fr.* Sonnets pour Hélène. LitW
Tossed on a sea of troubles, Soul, my Soul. Equanimity. Archilochus. GrPo; GrR
Tossing his mane of snows in wildest eddies and tangles. In Earliest Spring. William Dean Howells. AA; FaBoBe; PFY
Total Abstainer, A. Martial, *tr. fr. Latin by* Paul Nixon. LiTW; RoL
Total Love. Vicente Aleixandre, *tr. fr. Spanish by* Eleanor L. Turnbull. CoSP
Total Revolution, A. Oscar Williams. LiTM; SiTL
T'other day as I was twining. Cupid Swallowed [*or* Cupid Drowned]. Leigh Hunt. BCEP; HBV; LPS-1; PECK
Tottenham Court, *sel.* Thomas Nabbes.
Song: "What a dainty life the milkmaid leads!" EG; SeCL
Totus Mundus in Maligno Positus. *Unknown.* SiCE; TuPP
Touch. Joseph Auslander. MAP; MoAmPo (1942 ed.)
Touch, The. James Graham, Marquess of Montrose. *See* My Dear and Only Love
Touch, A, a kiss! The charm was snapped. The Revival [*or* The Sleeping Beauty, II]. Tennyson. *Fr.* The Day-Dream. CG; LPS-1
Touch and Go. Stevie Smith. DiM
Touch but thy lire (my Harrie) and I heare. To M. Henry Lawes, the Excellent Composer, of His Lyrics. Robert Herrick. OAEP
"Touch him ne'er so lightly, into song he broke." Epilogue to "Dramatic Idyls." Robert Browning. BPN; PoVP
Touch me, and you shall see. Come on: come on! Peleus. Euripides. *Fr.* Andromache. GrR
Touch me, touch me. Grass Fingers. Angelina W. Grimké. CDC
Touch Not a Leaf. Rietta Trimm. CAG
Touch not that maid. Salopia Inhospitalis. Douglas B. W. Sladen. VA
Touch of cold in the Autumn night, A. Autumn. T. E. Hulme. FaBoMo; LoBV; MBP; MoBrPo (1942 ed.); SeCePo; ViBoPo
Touch of Human Hands, The. Thomas Curtis Clark. OQP; PoToHe; QP-1
Touch of Nature, A. Thomas Bailey Aldrich. ADAH; SN
Touch of the gold of thy tresses, A. A Love Song. Steingrimur Thorsteinsson IcP
Touch of the Master's Hand, The. Myra Brooks Welch. BLPA; PoToHe (new ed.)
Touch once more a sober measure. Lament for Capt. Paton [*or* Captain Paton's Lament]. John Gibson Lockhart. EBSV; OBRV
Touch our bodies, wind. A House in Taos: Wind. Langston Hughes. CDC
Touch sets free the prisoned rage, A. The Camp-Fire. W. Harry Clemons. CAG
Touch us gently, Time! A Petition to Time. "Barry Cornwall." BCEP; VA
Touché. Jessie Fauset. CDC
Touched by the sunlight of the evening hour. Noel T. Carrington. *Fr.* My Native Village. EnSW
Touched with a certain silver light. In My Time. Edmund Blunden. MoPW
Touched with some divine repose. The Sleeper. Duncan Campbell Scott. BoCaPo (1948 ed.)
Touches of man's modern speech. The Singer Saith of His Song. Francis Thompson. VLEP
Touching Shoulders. *Unknown.* BLPA; MaRV
Touchstone, The. William Allingham. LPS-3
Touch-Stone, The. Samuel Bishop. *See* Maiden's Choice, The.
Touchstone, The, *sels.* Kalonymos ben Kalonymos, *tr. fr. Hebrew by* Joseph Chotzner. TrJP
Hypocrite, The.
Unfortunate Male, The
Yoke, The.
Touchstone on a Bus, *sel.* Alfred Noyes.
New Duckling, The. BoTP; FaPON; MPB
Tough Cuss from Bitter Creek, A. James Barton Adams. PoOW
Tough hand closes gently on the load, The. Man Carrying Bale. Harold Monro. MBP; MoBrPo; MoP; PoeMoYo; TCEP; TCPD
Tough Luck. *Unknown.* LauV
Toujours Amour. Edmund Clarence Stedman. HBV; OBAV; PR
T'our tale.—The feast was over, the slaves gone. Ave Maria. Byron. *Fr.* Don Juan, III. ERP
Touring. David Morton. TrPWD
Tourist. Mark Van Doren. NePoAm-2
Tourist Time. F. R. Scott. BoCaPo; WhC
Tourists. Howard Moss. FiBHP
Tourists in a Sacred Place. Sir Herbert Read. MBP; MoBrPo (1942 ed.)
Tourists in the courtyard. Sightseers in a Courtyard. Nicolás Guillén. PoNe
Tournament, The. Sidney Lanier. PECK
Tournament of Man, The. Ernest Crosby. PGD
Tournament of Tottenham, The. *Unknown.* OxBoLi
Toussaint L'Ouverture. E. A. Robinson. PoNe
Toussaint, the most unhappy man of men! To Toussaint L'Ouverture. Wordsworth. AnEmPo; BCEP; BEL; BPN; CBE; EM-2; EmBrPo; EnL; EnLi-2; EnLit; EnLP; EnRP; EPP; ERP; ES; ExPo; GEPC; LoBV; LPS-3; OAEP; OBRV; PeBoSo; PoNe; PoRA; TrGrPo
Toute la Lyre, *sel.* Victor Hugo, *pr. tr. fr. French. Fr.* A Théophile Gautier.
"Let us pass on, for it is the law which no one can evade." LiA
Toutouie la, la, my little child. The Love and Protection of Mother and Father—Breton. *Unknown.* BOL
"Towanda Winooski? Gowanda!" Sing a Song of the Cities. Morris Bishop. WhC
Toward a True Peace. Lucia Trent *and* Ralph Cheyney. *See* True Peace, A.
Toward God in heaven spacious. The Child in Our Soul. Björnstjerne Björnson. WoL
Toward Jerusalem. Amy Carmichael. MaRV
Toward the doors of lonely folk. Holly Carol. Margaret Widdemer. SDH
Toward the Piraeus. Hilda Doolittle ("H. D."). TBM
Toward the sea turning my troubled eye. The Huge Leviathan. Spenser. *Fr.* Visions of the World's Vanity. ChTr
Toward Which. Thomas Wolfe. *See* Something Has Spoken to Me in the Night.
Towards France a maiden went. The French Princess. *Unknown.* AnSpL-1
Towards nightfall when the wind. Winter Mask. Allen Tate. NePA; OxBA
Towards the end he sailed into an extraordinary mildness. Herman Melville. W. H. Auden. GTBS-W; LiTA; LiTM (rev. ed.); NePA; OAEP (2d ed.); OxBA
Towards the North Star. John Gould Fletcher. LaNeLa
Towards the Past. Henri de Régnier, *tr. fr. French by* Alan Conder. TrFP
Towards the South. Guillaume Apollinaire, *tr. fr. French by* Glauco Cambon. OnPM
Towards your brow where an autumn dreams. Sigh. Stéphane Mallarmé. AnFP
Tower, The. Agnes Lee. NP
Tower, The. Albert Samain, *tr. fr. French by* Alan Conder. TrFP
Tower, The. Mark Van Doren. MoPo
Tower, The. W. B. Yeats. ChMo; CMP; CoBMV; FaBoMo; HoPM; LiTB; LiTM (rev. ed.); MoPo; OAEP (2d ed.); SeCeV
It Is Time That I Wrote My Will, *sel.* MoVE; TCPD

Tower high, The. Butterfly. Kwaso. OnPM
Tower of David, Chinese wall. Everywhere. "A. Almi." OnCuPl
Tower of Genghis Khan, The. Hervey Allen. TCPD
Tower of Ivory. Leonard Bacon. WhC
Tower of Iznajar, The. Rafael Alberti, *tr. fr. Spanish by* Eleanor L. Turnbull. CoSP
Tower of Lowliness, The. Sister Miriam. PraNu
Towering it stood. Starvation Peak Evening. David O'Neil. AnAmPo; LA
Towering o'er the Wrecks of Time. Sir John Bowring. *See* In the Cross of Christ I Glory.
Towers at Evening, The. Frank Wilmot. *Fr.* Melbourne and Memory. NeLNL
Towers of New York, The. Joseph Auslander. MuM
Towers of Song. Malcolm Cowley. NP
Towery city and branchy between towers. Duns Scotus's Oxford. Gerard Manley Hopkins. CoBE; MaPo; NAMP; OBMV; PoE; PoEL-5; TriL; ViP
Towie Castle, Towie Castle. Prologue to Towie Castle. Gordon Bottomley. MM
Town and Country. William Cowper. *See* God Made the Country.
Town and the Country Mouse, The, *sl. abr.* Horace, *tr. fr. Latin by* Francis Howes. Satires, II, 6. WoL
Town Child. Andrew Hewitt. NoCaPo
Town Child, The. Irene Thompson. BoTP
Town Child. Barbara Young. PoMa
Town Damascus and the lands about, The. Armida, the Sorceress. Tasso. *Fr.* Jerusalem Delivered. EnLi-1
Town down the River, The. E. A. Robinson. ChMo; CMP; CoBA; CV; IAP
Town is old and very steep, The. Ken. Charlotte Mew. TCPD
Town lies in the valley, A. The Silent Town. Richard Dehmel. AWP; JAWP; WBP
Town Lights. Clark Ashton Smith. MuM
Town Maid. Clifford Bax. POTE
Town Meeting. John Hay. NePoAm
Town Meeting, The, *abr.* John Trumbull. *Fr.* M'Fingal, I *and* II. AnNE
Town Meeting, A.M., The, *fr.* I. IAP; TCAP
Town Meeting, P.M., The, *fr.* II. TCAP
Town of Don't-You-Worry, The. I. J. Bartlett. BLPA; WBLP, *st.* 1
Town of France. Henri de Régnier, *tr. fr. French by* Alan Conder. TrFP
Town of Hay, The. Sam Walter Foss. AA
Town of Nice, The. Herman C. Merivale. BOHV
Town of Nogood, The. William Edward Penney. BLPA
Town of Passage, The. *Unknown.* OxBoLi
Town of Passage, The/ Is both large and spacious. The Attractions of a Fashionable Irish Watering-Place. Francis Sylvester Mahony. IrPN
Town, The, our hero's scene of action. The Town Meeting. John Trumbull. *Fr.* M'Fingal. AnNE
Town Pictures, *sel.* Ernest Crosby.
"It is an August evening." PC
Town-Rakes, The. *At. to* P. A. Motteux. CoMu
Town visitor's easy talk flows in an endless stream, The. To a Talkative Guest. Po Chü-i. TrCh
Town was full of bells, where I grew up, The. The Childhood Church. Pat Wilson. AnNZ
Town Window, A. John Drinkwater. BoTP; GTBS; NeMA; PoeT; POT; PoTo
Town without a Market, The. James Elroy Flecker. MBP; MoBrPo
Towneley Plays. *Unknown. See* Second Shepherds' Play, The.
Town's fast asleep as a child, The. Deep Night, Summer. Thad Stem, Jr. NoCaPo (rev. ed.)
Townsman on his yielding bed, The. Note-Book of a European Tramp, XI. Michael Hamburger. NePoEA
Tow'rds the lofty walls of Balbi, lo! Durand of Blonden here hies. Durand of Blonden. Ludwig Uhland. AWP; JAWP; WBP
Towser Shall Be Tied Tonight. *Unknown.* AlBD; BLPA; PTA-2
Toy Band, The. Sir Henry Newbolt. BoTP
Toy-bewitched. Samuel Taylor Coleridge. *Fr.* Religious Musings. WGRP
Toy Cross, The. Roden Noel. VA
Toy Horse, The. Edwin Muir. FaBoMo
Toy-Seller, The. Laurence Binyon. BMEP
Toys, The. Coventry Patmore. The Unknown Eros, I, x. ACP; AnFE; BeLS; BLV; BMEP; BPP; CAW; EnLit; EPN; EPP; FaFP; FAOV; GoBC; GTBS; GTBS-W; GTML; GTSL; HBV; JKCP; LEAP; MaRV; OBEV; OBVV; PC; PG; PoToHe (new ed.); POTT; PoVP; ReaPo; ReTS; TreFS; TrGrPo; TrPWD; VA; ViBoPo; ViP; VLEP; WP; YT
Toys, and treats, and pleasures pass. Love and the Child. William Brighty Rands. PRWS
Toys of a Tutankhamen, The. The Playbox. Nathalia Crane. TBM
Trace-horse, watch her move, The. Duchess. Lilian Bowes-Lyon. AlDL; HaMV; POTE
Traces. Rafael Estrada, *tr. fr. Spanish by* Donald Devenish Walsh. AnCL
Trachiniae [*or* Trachinian Maidens], *sels.* Sophocles, *tr. fr. Greek.*
Childhood's Immunity from Inward Sorrows, *tr. by* Lewis Campbell. GrR
Deianira's Love Charm, *tr. by* Sir George Young. GrR
Deianira's Wooing, *pr. tr. by* Gilbert Murray. OxBG
Heracles, *tr. by* Robert Whitelaw. OxBG
(Heracles' Errant Love.) GrR
Paean of Joy, *tr. by* Lewis Campbell. GrR
Pity the Captive Maiden's Lot, *tr. by* Robert Whitelaw. GrR
Wanderings of Heracles, The, *tr. by* Lewis Campbell. GrR
Track into the Swamp, The. Samuel French Morse. CrMA
Trackless Deeps, The. Shelley. *Fr.* The Daemon of the World, Pt. II. EtS
Tracks. John Farrar. GFA
Tracks in the Snow. Marchette Chute. SiSoSe
Tracks in the Snow. Elizabeth J. Coatsworth. BoChLi (1950 ed.)
Tract. William Carlos Williams. AmP; AmPP; CoBMV; LiTA; LiTM; MoAB; MoAmPo; MOAP; NePA; OnAP; TrGrPo; WoL
Tract for Autos, A. Arthur Guiterman. MPB
Tractor. William Hart-Smith. AnNZ
Trade, *abr.* Edwin James Brady. TVSH
"Trade" Rat. Eleanor Glenn Wallis. NePoAm
Trade Winds. John Masefield. FaBoCh; OBMV; ShBV-4
Trades. Amy Lowell. OTPC (1946 ed.)
Tradesman, The. *Unknown.* PCH
Tradition. Dryden. *Fr.* Religio Laici. OBS; PoLi
Tradition of Conquest. Sara Morgan Bryan Piatt. AA
Traditional Tune. Robert D. Fitzgerald. BoAV
Traditions. Ramón Campoamor, *tr. fr. Spanish by* Thomas Walsh. OnPM
Trafalgar. William Canton. TVSH
Trafalgar. Thomas Hardy. *See* Night of Trafalgar, The.
Trafalgar. Francis Turner Palgrave. BeLS; FaBoBe
Trafalgar. *Unknown.* SG
Trafalgar Day, 1940. "Clemence Dane." NeTW
Trafalgar Square. Rose Fyleman. UTS
Tragedia de Heraclio Bernal, *with music. Unknown, tr. fr. Spanish.* ABF
Tragedie of Edward the Second, The. Christopher Marlowe. *See* Edward the Second.
Tragedie of Philotas, The, *sels.* Samuel Daniel.
Chorus: "How does thou wear and weary out thy days." OBSC
Writer's Tragedy, The. LiA
Tragedienne, The. Zoë Akins. NP
Tragedies that entertained the burghers of antiquity, The. The New Hellas. Irwin Edman. InMe
Tragedy. "Æ." MoBrPo
Tragedy, The. Thomas Curtis Clark. ChIP
Tragedy, A. Théophile Marzials. BMEP; HBV; LEAP
Tragedy. Howard Moss. NePoEA
Tragedy, A. Edith Nesbit. HBV
Tragedy. Jill Spargur. BLPA; DDA
Tragedy. Mark Van Doren. NePoAm-2
Tragedy of Caesar and Pompey, The, *sels.* George Chapman.
"As nature works in all things to an end." NBE
"Poor slaves, how terrible this Death is to them!" ViBoPo
Tragedy of Charles, Duke of Byron, The, *sels.* George Chapman.
"And so, farewell for ever." MyFE
Last Words of Byron, *fr.* V, i. CoEV
Tragedy of Cleopatra, The. Samuel Daniel. *See* Cleopatra.
Tragedy of Cleopatra, The, *sel.* Thomas May.
Not He That Knows. SeCL
("Not he that knows how to acquire.") TuPP
(Song, A: "Not he, that knows how to acquire.") SeEP
Tragedy of Dido, The, *sels.* Christopher Marlowe *and* Thomas Nashe.
I Have an Orchard. ChTr
"So much have I received at Dido's hands." SG
Tragedy of Nero, The, *sel.* Nathaniel Lee.
Very Dark. BeR
Tragedy of Orestes, The, *sel.* Thomas Goffe.
"Lullaby, lullaby baby." TuPP
Tragedy of Pete, The. Joseph Seamon Cotter, Sr. CDC; PoNe
Tragedy of Pompey the Great, The, *sels.* John Masefield.
Chanty. BMEP
Chief Centurions, The. POTE; TCPD
("Man is a sacred city, built of marvellous earth.") WGRP
Tragedy of Rollo, Duke of Normandy, The. John Fletcher, *and others. See* Bloody Brother, The.
Tragedy of the Deep, A. Don Marquis. LHV

Tragedy of the Duchess of Malfy, The. John Webster. *See* Duchess of Malfi, The.
Tragedy of the Sparrow and the Cursing of the Cat, The. John Skelton. *Fr.* Phyllyp Sparowe. EV-1
(O Cat of Carlish Kind.) ChTr
Tragedy of Valentinian, The, *sels.* John Fletcher.
Care-charming Sleep, *fr.* V, ii. BEL; BLV; KN; OnPM; PC; TrGrPo; ViBoPo
("Care-charming sleep, thou easer of all woes.") AtBAP; BrBE; OAEP; SeEP; TuPP
(Into Slumbers.) SeCePo
(Invocation to Sleep.) AnEnPo; EPP; WHA
(Sleep.) EV-2
(Song.) LoBV (2d ed.); PoEL-2
(Song for the Sick Emperor.) FaBoEn
(Song to Sleep.) OxBoLi
(To Sleep.) EnLi-1
God Lyaeus, *fr.* V, viii. LEAP; OBEV
("God Lyaeus, ever young.") ElSeCe; OnPM; TuPP; ViBoPo
(Song to Bacchus.) BEL; EPP; EV-2; TOP
Hear, Ye Ladies [That Despise], *fr.* II, v. BCEP; ElL; LiTG; OAEP; OBEV; PoEL-2; ViBoPo
(Mighty Love.) TrGrPo
(Power of Love, The.) HBV
"Now the lusty spring is seen," *fr.* II, v. EG; ElSeCe; ViBoPo
(Love Song.) FaBoEn
(Love's Emblems.) ElL; HBV; LEAP; OBEV
(Song.) SeEP
Tragic Books. Lizette Woodworth Reese. TBM
Tragic Guilt. Keidrych Rhys. MoWP; WaP
Tragic Love. W. J. Turner. LO; LoPS; OBMV
Tragic Mary Queen of Scots, The. "Michael Field." GTML; MBP; OBMV; TCPD
("Ah me, if I grew sweet to man.") EnLoPo
Tragic Memory. George Meredith. *See* Modern Love: "In our old shipwrecked days . . ."
Tragic Memory. *Unknown, tr. fr. Japanese by* Ishii *and* Obata. *Fr.* Manyo Shu. OnPM
Tragic poet's a happy man, The. Antiphanes, *tr. fr. Greek by* Charles H. Kahn. GrPo
Tragic Story, A. Adelbert von Chamisso, *tr. fr. German by* Thackeray. BoChLi (1950 ed.); BOHV; BoTP; FaPON; GaP; GoTP; HBV; HBVY; MoShBr; MPB; OTPC; RIS; StVeCh (1940 ed.)
Tragic Tale. Boris Pasternak, *tr. fr. Russian by* Jack Lindsay. RuPo
Tragic Tale of Hooty the Owl, The. *Unknown. See* Owl and the Fox, The.
Tragic Verses. *Unknown.* CoMu
Tragical History of Dr. Faustus, The. Christopher Marlowe. *See* Dr. Faustus.
Tragiques, Les, *sel.* Théodore Agrippa d'Aubigné, *pr. tr. fr. French.*
Cain. LiA
Trail, The. Percy MacKaye. *Fr.* Ourselves. AOAH
Trail, The. Edward Weismiller. WaP
Trail All Your Pikes. Countess of Winchilsea. *See* Soldier's Death, The.
Trail End. *Unknown, at. to* Everett Chatham. *See* Blood on the Saddle.
Trail Makers, The. H. H. Knibbs. OBAV
Trail of Life, The. George W. Caldwell. PoP
Trail of the Bird, The. William John Courthope. HBVY
Trail to Lillooet, The. Pauline Johnson. CaP; OCL
Trail to Mexico, The. *Unknown.* AS, *with music;* CoSo (A *and* B *vers., with music*); CSF; IHA
Trailing Arbutus. Henry Abbey. SN
Trailing Arbutus, The. Whittier. AnAmPo; BLP; CoBA; IAP; LA; PEOR; PTA-2; REAL; TCAP
Trailing Clouds of Glory. Wordsworth. Ode: Intimations of Immortality, *st.* 8. GrCo-2
Trail's End. Beulah May. MuM
Trails of Smoke. Rowena Bennett. MPB (1956 ed.)
Train, The. Mary Elizabeth Coleridge. BoTP
Train, The. Emily Dickinson. *See* I like to see it lap the miles.
Train, The. Gerardo Diego, *tr. fr. Spanish by* Eleanor L. Turnbull. CoSP
Train Butcher, The. Thomas Hornsby Ferril. GoYe
Train Dogs, The. E. Pauline Johnson. OCL; TwCaPo
Train in the Night, The. Elizabeth Riddell. NeLNL
Train is a dragon that roars through the dark, A. A Modern Dragon. Rowena Bastin Bennett. GFA; TiPo; UTS
Train-Mates. Witter Bynner. MAP; MoAmPo (1942 ed.); PFY; TCAP
Train pulled out of Palestine, eighteen coaches long. Dirty Mistreatin' Women. *Unknown.* ABF
Train Ride. John Wheelwright. AnFE; CoAnAm; MoPo; TriL; TwAmPo
Train stands still, The. The Child in the Train. Eleanor Farjeon. AlDL
Train, The! The twelve o'clock for paradise. Week-End, I. Harold Monro. CP; MoBrPo (1950 ed.); PIAE; YT
Train Tune. Louise Bogan. NePoAm
Train was passing overhead, The. Late Autumn. Sakutaro Hagiwara. PoLJ
Train-whistles have a lonesome sound. Who-o-o-o-o! Harry Silleck Grannatt. StaSt
Train Will Fight to the Pass, The. Ruth Pitter. HaMV
Train Window. Robert Finch. BoCaPo; PeCV
Training. Demetrio Herrera S., *tr. fr. Spanish by* Dudley Fitts. AnCL
Training-ship *Eurydice,* The. The Last of the *Eurydice.* Sir Joseph Noel Paton. VA
Trains, The. "Seumas O'Sullivan." BoTP
Trains. Hope Shepherd. BoTP
Trains. James S. Tippett. FaPON; GFA; OTPC (1946 ed.); SUS; TiPo
Trains are for going. Things. William Jay Smith. TiPo (1959 ed.)
Trains at Night. Frances Frost. BrR; TiPo
Trains of thought, The. La Bête Humaine. James Kirkup. NeBP
Trains that scream past every day, The. Traveler. Frances Frost. BoChLi
Trainwrecked Soldiers. John Frederick Nims. MiAP; ReMP
Traitors. Shakespeare. King Henry V, *fr.* II, ii. BHV
Traitors, The. Morton Dauwen Zabel. NP
Tramp. Richard Hughes. MBP; MoBrPo
Tramp Sings, The. Ridgely Torrence. *Fr.* Eye-Witness. PFY
Tramp squares with rebellious treading! Our March. Vladimir Mayakovsky. BoR
Tramp! Tonight the night is so fine, so fine. Epilogue. Tefcros Anthias. MoGP
Tramp, Tramp, Tramp. George Frederick Root. FOAH; MDAH; OlF; TreFS
Tramp, Tramp, Tramp, Keep on a-Tramping, *with music. Unknown.* AS
Tramping the right-of-way. Beaver Sign. Kenneth Porter. NePoAm
Trample! trample! went the roan. The Cavalier's Escape. George Walter Thornbury. FaBoBe; GN; HBV; MW; OTPC; ShGoBo
Tramp's Prayer, A. Harry Kemp. QS
Tramp's Song, The. Mary Devenport O'Neill. AnIV
Trampwoman's Tragedy, A. Thomas Hardy. AtBAP; BeLS; HBMV; MoVE
Trance, The. Konstantin Simonov, *tr. fr. Russian by* Jack Lindsay. RuPo
Trance, The. Stephen Spender. ChMP; CoBMV
Trance and Transformation. Goethe, *tr. fr. German by* Carol North Valhope *and* Ernst Morwitz. LiTW
Trance of Time, The. Cardinal Newman. OxBoCh
Tranquil Sea. Claire Aven Thomson. EtS
Tranquil Soul, A. John Oldham. *Fr.* To the Memory of Mr. Charles Morwent. EV-3
(Quiet Soul, A.) OBEV
Tranquility. *Unknown, tr. fr. Sanskrit by* Joseph Nadin Rawson. *Fr.* The Upanishads. OnPM
Tranquillity, the winter night. Sherry. Mokutaro Kinoshita. PoLJ
Tranquillity! thou better name. Ode to Tranquillity. Samuel Taylor Coleridge. BPN; EmBrPo
Trans Canada. Francis Reginald Scott. BoCaPo (1948 ed.); PeCV
Transaction on the Roman Exchange. Henrietta A. Burke. JKCP (1955 ed.)
Transcendence. Richard Hovey. OQP; QP-1; WGRP
Transcendence of God, The. Milton. *Fr.* Samson Agonistes. OBS
Transcendent beauty though thou art. *Unknown.* SeCSL
Transcendentalism. *Unknown.* BOHV; NA
Transcendentalism; a Poem in Twelve Books. Robert Browning. PoVP; VLEP
Transcontinental Bus. Daniel Smythe. NeTW
Transfiguration. Louisa May Alcott. MOAH
Transfiguration, The. St. Matthew, XVII: 1–8, Bible, *N.T.* GrCo-2
Transfiguration, The. James M. Hayes. JKCP
Transfiguration, The. Edwin Muir. FaBoMo
Transfiguration. Swinburne. PeBoSo
Transfiguration, The. *Unknown, tr. fr. Sanskrit by* Sir Edwin Arnold. *Fr.* Bhagavad Gita. OuHeWo
Transfiguration, *sel.* Sergei Aleksandrovich Yesenin, *tr. fr. Russian by* Babette Deutsch.
"Ho, Russians," *fr.* III. TrRV
Transfiguration of Beauty, The. Michelangelo, *tr. fr. Italian by* John Addington Symonds. AWP
Transfigured. Sarah Morgan Bryan Piatt. AA
Transfigured Bird. James Merrill. MoAB
Transfigured Life. Dante Gabriel Rossetti. The House of Life, LX. BPN; PoVP; ViPo
Transfigured Swan. Louis Untermeyer. MAP

Transfiguring Love. Theocritus. *See* In Praise of Bombyca.
Transformation. Lewis Alexander. CDC; PoNe
Transformation. Catullus, *tr. fr. Latin by* Horace Gregory. LiTW
("There was a time, O Lesbia, when you said Catullus.") RoL
Transformation. Jessie B. Rittenhouse. HBMV
Transformation of a Texas Girl, The. James Barton Adams. SCC
Transformation of the Furies, The. Aeschylus, *tr. fr. Greek by* G. M. Cookson. *Fr.* Eumenides. GrR
Transformation Scene. Constance Carrier. GoYe
Transformations. Thomas Hardy. ChMo; CMP; NV; TwCV
Transience. Sarojini Naidu. MCCG
Transience. Theocritus, *tr. fr. Greek by* F. L. Lucas. *Fr.* Idylls, XXIII. GrPE
Transient Beauty. Basho, *tr. fr. Japanese by* H. G. Henderson. OnPM
Transient Beauty. Byron. *Fr.* The Giaour. LPS-1
Transit city, A, marvellously fair. Buffalo. Florence Earle Coates. PAH
Transition. Hermann Hesse, *tr. fr. German by* Herman Salinger. TwGV
Transition. May Sarton. NePoAm
Transitional Poem, *sel.* C. Day Lewis.
"When nature plays hedge-schoolmaster." EnLit
Translat. ex Martial. Martial, *tr. fr. Latin by* John Weever. TuPP
Translated out of Horace Which Begins Rectius Vives. Horace, *tr. by* Sir Philip Sidney. *See* To Licinius.
Translated Way, The. Franklin P. Adams. BOHV; FiBHP
Translated, won't the operatic word. Opera in English? Benjamin M. Steigman. WhC
Translation. Roy Fuller. ChMP
Translation. Anne Spencer. BANP
Translation, The. Mark Van Doren. TCPD
Translation from Du Bellay ("Happy, who like Ulysses or that lord"). *Tr. by* G. K. Chesterton. *See* Heureux qui, comme Ulysse . . .
Translation from Petrarch ("Mine old dear enemy, my froward master"). *Tr. fr. Italian by* Sir Thomas Wyatt. SiPS
Translation from Petrarch, A ("What a grudge I am bearing . . ."). *Pr. tr. fr. Italian by* J. M. Synge. Sonnets to Laura: To Laura in Death, XXXII. MBP; MoBrPo; NeMA
(He Is Jealous of the Heavens and Earth.) TwCV
Translation from Villon, A ("Mother of God that's Lady of the Heavens"). *Pr. tr. fr. French by* J. M. Synge. *See* Two Translations from Villon.
Translation from Virgil's Aeneid. *Tr. by* the Earl of Surrey. *See* Certain Books of Virgil's Aeneis.
Translation from Walther von der Vogelweide ("I never set my two eyes . . ."). *Tr. fr. German by* J. M. Synge. MoBrPo
Translation is man's deep, continual task. Required Course. Frances Stoakley Lankford. GoYe
Translation of Horace. *Tr by* Samuel Johnson. *See* Spring's Return.
Translations from Modern Japanese Poetry. Tabubokee Ishikawa, Takeko Kujo, Akiko Yanagiwara, *and* Akiko Yosano, *tr. fr. Japanese by* Glenn Hughes *and* Yozan T. Iwasaki. PFE
Translator who rhymed the Iliad, The. Epigram. Jean Baptiste Rousseau. LiA
Translucent in the flawless pond. Lost World. Louis Ginsberg. MuM
Transmigration. Empedocles, *tr. fr. Greek by* Frances Cornford. OxBG
Transmutation, The. Edwin Muir. FaBoEn
Transparent and ethereal above the Sea of Time. The Two Bells. Viktor Rydberg. AnSL
Transparent still in the far distance. Meganom. Osip Mandelstam. BoRS
Transplanted. Helen Hunt Jackson. EOAH
Transport. Stefan George. *See* Rapture.
Transport. William Meredith. WaP
Transport *Dorchester* set forth upon her dangerous mission north, The. The Four Men of God. Edgar A. Guest. OHFP (1958 ed.)
Transportation Problem. Richard Armour. WhC
Transvaal Morning, A. William Plomer. BoSA
Trapped. Adelaide Crapsey. MCCG
Trapped Dingo. Judith Wright. NeLNL
Traps. Mary Carolyn Davies. HBMV
Trash. Robert Haven Schauffler. TCAP
Traubel, Traubel, boil and bubble. I Like to Sing Also. John Updike. FiBHP
Traümerei at Ostendorff's. "William Laird." HBMV
Travel. Edna St. Vincent Millay. FaPON; LaNeLa; MoShBr; MoSiPe; MPB; NP; PFY; StVeCh; TCAP; TiPo
Travel. Robert Louis Stevenson. FaBoCh; FaPON; GoBP; GoTP; LoGBV; MoShBr; MPB; OnHT; PoVP; StVeCh (1940 ed.); TiPo; WaKn
Travel Bureau, The. Ruth Comfort Mitchell. HBMV; PoeMoYo; VOD
Travel Song. Hugo von Hofmannsthal. *See* Travelers' Song.
Travel Song. Anne Glenny Wilson. BoAu
Traveller, The. W. H. Auden. ReMP
Traveler. Frances Frost. BoChLi
Traveller, The. Goldsmith. CEP; EiPP; EV-3; OAEP
Sels.
France. OBEC
Happiness Dependent on Ourselves. OBEC
Home. LPS-1
(First, Best Country, The.) GN
Real Happiness. OBEC
"Remote, unfriended, melancholy, slow." ViBoPo
"To men of other minds." BHV
Traveler, The. Vachel Lindsay. MAP; MoAmPo; NeMA
Traveler, The. Joseph Corson Miller. UnW
Traveller, The. Ono no Komachi, *tr. fr. Japanese by* Mabel Lorenz Ives. PFE
Traveller, The. Cicely Fox Smith. POT; PoTo
Traveler, The. Joseph C. Sonneborn. CAG
Traveler, The. Allen Tate. LiTM; MM
Traveler. Sister Mary Thérèse. JKCP (1955 ed.)
Traveller, A. *Unknown.* WGRP
Traveller came from across the seas, A. Taoism and Buddhism. Po Chü-i. TrCh
Traveler Caught in a Storm, A. Kiokusui, *tr. fr. Japanese.* GaP
Traveller for many long years I have been, A. The Widow That Keeps the Cock Inn. *Unknown.* CoMu
Travel[l]er on a dusty road, A. Little and Great [*or* Small Beginnings]. Charles Mackay. HBV; HBVY; LPS-3; PECK; PTA-2; TVSH
Traveler once, A, when skies were rose and gold. I Am the Door. *Unknown.* BLP; OQP; QP-1
Traveler, pluck a stem of moly. Moly. Edith M. Thomas. HBV; PECK
Traveller take heed for journeys undertaken in the dark of the year. October Journey. Margaret Walker. PoNe
Traveller the long way wearies, under my poplars seat thee. The Wayside Fount. Nicias. GrPE
Travel[l]er wended the wilds among, A. The Quaker's Meeting. Samuel Lover. BOHV; CenHV; OnYI
"Traveler, what lies over the hill?" Over the Hill. George Macdonald. GaP
Traveller who crossed Les Halles at summer's end, The. Sunflower. André Breton. LiTW
Traveller who walks a temperate zone, A. Against Romanticism. Kingsley Amis. NePoEA
Travellers. Arthur St. John Adcock. BoTP
Travellers, The. Mark A. De Wolfe Howe. AA
Traveller's Curse after Misdirection, The. Robert Graves, *fr. the Welsh.* ExPo; FiBHP; HoPM; LiTM; MBP; MoAB; MoBrPo; NeMA; SiTL
Traveller's Ditty. Miriam Allen deFord. HBMV
Traveller's Hope. Charles Granville. HBV; OBVV
Traveller's Joy. Arthur Ketchum. NLK
Traveler's Rest. Ogden Nash. InMe
Traveller's Rest. Cicely Fox Smith. NLK
Traveller's Return, The. Robert Southey. BoTP; OTPC
Travelers' Song. Hugo von Hofmannsthal, *tr. fr. German by* Michael Hamburger. AnGP
(Travel Song, *tr. by* Charles Wharton Stork.) TrJP
Travellers' Song. George Macdonald. BSV
Traveller's Tale, A. William Plomer. BoSA
Travelers who came that day to Pisa's Baptistry. Echo. Elizabeth Stanton Hardy. GoYe
Traveling. Chu Tun-ru, *tr. fr. Chinese by* Ching Ti. ChLP; WhP
Travelling. Dorothy Gradon. BoTP
Travelling. Henry David Thoreau. CoV
Travelling America. "Jan Struther." NeTW
Travelling Light. Minnie Leona Upton. PCH
Travelling Northward. Tu Fu, *tr. fr. Chinese by* Kenneth Rexroth. OnPC
Travelling south, leaves overflow the farms. The Puritan on His Honeymoon. Robert Bly. NePoEA
Traveling South toward Italy. Elizabeth Barrett Browning. *Fr.* Aurora Leigh, VII. BCEP
Traveling Storm. Mark Van Doren. MoSiPe
Travelogue, A; Clovelly. Carolyn Wells. InMe
Travelogue for Exiles. Karl Shapiro. AnFE; CoAnAm; MoAmPo (1950 ed.); NeMA; PG (1945 ed.); TrJP; TwAmPo
Travelogue in a Shooting-Gallery. Kenneth Fearing. PoLFOT
Travels. W. W. Gibson. PtOT
Travel's End. May Folwell Hoisington. TBM
Travels with a Donkey, *sel.* Robert Louis Stevenson.
Camp, A. VLEP
(Camper's Night Song.) BBV
(God's Green Inn.) MW
Traverse not the globe for lore! The sternest. Advice against Travel. James Clarence Mangan. OBVV

Travesty of Miss Fanshawe's Enigma. Horace Mayhew. *See* Cockney Enigma on the Letter H.
Trawlers. Hilton Brown. NeTW
Tray. Robert Browning. BPN
Tray, The. Thomas Cole. NePoAm
Tray, The. Gerardo Diego, *tr. fr. Spanish by* Eleanor L. Turnbull. CoSP
Tray's Epitaph. "Peter Pindar." TreFS
Treachery. Ibn Khafaja, *tr. fr. Arabic by* A. J. Arberry. MooP
Tread back—and back, the lewd and lay! Horace. Odes, III, 1. LaP
Tread lightly here, for here, 'tis said. An Epitaph on a Robin Redbreast [*or* The Robin's Grave]. Samuel Rogers. CG; EV-3; OTPC (1923 ed.); PRWS
Tread lightly, she is near. Requiescat. Oscar Wilde. BLV; BMEP; CaAE; EnLit; GTIV; GTSL; HBV; InvP; LEAP; MBP; MoBrPo; NeMA; OBVV; OnYI; OxBI; PIAE; PoVP; TreF; TrGrPo; ViPP; VLEP; WHA
Tread Not the Snow. Mikata Shami, *tr. fr. Japanese by* Ishii *and* Obata. OnPM
Tread softly. Warning. W. H. Gerry. CAG
Tread Softly! All the Earth Is Holy Ground. Christina Rossetti. Later Life, X. PeBoSo; VLEP
Tread softly, bow the head. The Pauper's Death-Bed. Caroline Anne Bowles. LPS-1
Tread softly, for here you stand. On Ithaca Standing. Lawrence Durrell. FaBoTw
Tread softly here. The Woodpecker. Richard Church. HaMV
Tread Softly, Sorrow. Robert Nathan. MuM
Tread the Green Grass, *sel.* Paul Green.
Young Davie's Song. NoCaPo
Treade Junos steps who list for me. *Unknown.* SeCSL
Treadmill prisoner of that century, The. Scene with Figure. Babette Deutsch. TrJP
Treason. Lora Dunetz. NePoAm
Treason doth never prosper [*or* Treason never prospers]—what's the reason? Of Treason [*or* Epigram]. Sir John Harington. ALV; BCEP; ExPo; FiBHP; HBV; InvP; LiTG; OtMeF; OxBoLi; SiCE; SiTL; TuPP
Treason of Ganelon, The. Elise Aylen. NeTW
Treason's Last Device. Edmund Clarence Stedman. PAH
Treasure, The. Rupert Brooke. VOD
Treasure. Lucilius, *tr. fr. Greek by* William Cowper. AWP; LiTW
("They call thee rich; I deem thee poor.") GrPo
Treasure, The. Dorothy Frances McCrae. BoAu
Treasure, A. Reed Whittemore. NePoEA
Treasure House, A. Mark Antony De Wolfe Howe. PC
"Treasure Island." Patrick R. Chalmers. ReTS
Treasure not so the forlorn days. Behind the Line. Edmund Blunden. ChMP
Treasure of Our Tongue, The. Samuel Daniel. *See* English Poetry.
Treasures, The. Job, XXXVIII: 22–32, Bible, *O.T.* BoW
Treasures. St. Matthew, Bible, *N.T. See* Treasures in Heaven.
Treasures. Mary Dixon Thayer. MPB
Treasures. *Unknown.* PoToHe (new ed.)
Treasures in Heaven. St. Matthew, VI: 19–21, Bible, *N.T.* GoTP
(Treasures.) TrGrPo
Treasures of the Deep, The. Felicia Dorothea Hemans. LPS-2
Treat well the living. Vanity of Vanities. Euripides. OxBG
Treatie of Human Learning, A. Fulke Greville. *See* Of Humane Learning.
Treatment for Old Jades and Janes, The. Pope. *Fr.* An Essay on Criticism. BeR
Trebetherick. John Betjeman. AlDL; ExPo
Tree, The. Björnstjerne Björnson, *tr. fr. Norwegian.* ADAH; DD; FaPON; HH; MPB; OHIP; OTPC (1946 ed.); PCH; PRWS; PTA-1; RAR
Tree, The. Ilya Ehrenburg, *tr. fr. Russian by* Babette Deutsch. TrJP; TrRV
Tree, The. John Freeman. BoTP
Tree, The. Alfred Kreymborg. BAP; HBMV; TSW; TSWC
Tree, The. John Masefield. GTML
Tree, The. Ezra Pound. APA; ChMo; CMP; CoAnAm; InPo; MOAP; TwAmPo
Tree, A. *Unknown, wr. at. to* Christina Rossetti. RIS
("In spring I look gay.") BoTP; OxNR
Tree, The. Jones Very. ADAH; AnAmPo; AnNE; APW; DD; GN; GoTP; HBV; LA; OHIP; PEDC; PoRL
Tree, The. Pat Wilson. AnNZ
Tree, The. Countess of Winchilsea. CEP; CoBE; DiM; EiPP; OBEC; RiBV
Tree and Sky. Siegfried Sassoon. TSW
Tree and the Chaff, The. Psalms, I, Bible, *O.T. See* Godly and the Ungodly, The.
Tree and the Lady, The. Thomas Hardy. MBP; MOAB; MoBrPo
Tree ascending there, O pure transcension, A! Rainer Maria Rilke. Sonnets to Orpheus, Pt. I, I. UnS
Tree at Dusk, A. Winifred Welles. MPB; SP; TSW; TSWC
Tree at My Window. Robert Frost. AmPP; AnNE; BLV; BoLiVe; FaBoBe; FaBoEn; MAP; MoAB; MoAmPo; MoVE; NePA; OxBA; TrGrPo; TwHP
Tree at Post 4, The. Kenneth Mackenzie. MoAuPo
Tree Birthdays. Mary Carolyn Davies. OHIP
Tree Buds, The. Kate L. Brown. BOL; TVC; TVSH
Tree-building. Franklin Cable. OQP; PGD; QP-2
Tree Design, A. Arna Bontemps. CDC
Tree Feelings. Charlotte Perkins Gilman. GFA; MW; NLK; PGD
Tree Felling. George Woodcock. NeBP
Tree has entered my hands, The. A Girl. Ezra Pound. MAP; MoAB; MoAmPo; MoPW; NeMA
Tree in December. Melville Cane. MAP; MoAmPo
Tree in the Desert, The. Friedrich Hebbel, *tr. fr. German by* Herman Salinger *and* Marion Salinger. LiTW
Tree in the Garden, The. Christine Chaundler. BoTP
Tree is built of many things, A. Tree-building. Franklin Cable. OQP; PGD; QP-2
Tree is more than a shadow, A. A Tree Design. Arna Bontemps. CDC
Tree is such a sacred thing, A. The Cross and the Tree. William L. Stidger. ChIP; PGD
Tree leaves are murmuring hua-la-la, The. *Unknown.* BOL
Tree-leaves labour up and down. Nobody Comes. Thomas Hardy. MoVE; PoFS; ViPP
Tree may be laughter in the spring, A. Winter Night. Collister Hutchison. TiPo (1952 ed.)
Tree of deepest root is found, The. The Three Warnings. Hester Thrale. BeLS; HBV; LPS-3
Tree of Faith its bare dry boughs must shed, The. Adjustment. Whittier. WGRP
Tree of knowledge we in Eden prov'd, The. Hope. Countess of Winchilsea. TriL
Tree of life my soul hath seen, The. Jesus Christ the Apple-tree. *Unknown.* BeR
Tree of Love, The. Ramon Lull. CAW
Tree of my treasure and longing, The. Two Songs in Praise of Steingerd [*or* Three Songs to Steingerd]. Cormac Ogmundarson. LiTW; LyMA
Tree of Starlings, The. Grace Hazard Conkling. BLA
Tree of the Cross, The. "Angelus Silesius," *tr. fr. German.* CAW
Tree on the Hill. *Unknown.* OTPC; PPL
Tree-planting. Samuel Francis Smith. OHIP
Tree Planting. *Unknown* OHIP
Tree Purge. George Rostrevor Hamilton. POTE
Tree rose up, A. O clear transcendency! Rainer Maria Rilke. Sonnets to Orpheus, Pt. I, I. ReMP
Tree Shadows. *Unknown, tr. fr. Japanese.* GFA
Tree, sky and star my teachers. Autumn Hour. George Chapman. JKCP (1955 ed.)
Tree Stands Very Straight and Still, The. Annette Wynne. SUS
Tree still bends over the lake, The. Winter. Sheila Wingfield. EnLoPo
Tree stretched high, The. The Apricot Tree. Ibn A'isha. MooP
Tree Tag. Mary E. Caragher. GoYe
Tree that fell last year, The. Our Calvary. Constance Holm. OQP; QP-1
Tree, the Serpent, and the Star, The. A. P. Gray. BIG
Tree the tempest with a crash of wood, The. On a Tree Fallen across the Road. Robert Frost. TwP
Tree-Toad. Hilda Conkling. GBV (1922 ed.); RG
Tree-Toad, The. Orrick Johns. HBMV; NP; PoeMoYo
Tree Toad, The. Monica Shannon. FaPON; MPB; TiPo (1952 ed.)
Tree-Toad is a small gray person. Tree-Toad. Hilda Conkling. GBV (1922 ed.); RG
Tree unto which you reached, The. Ancient Sorrow. Giosuè Carducci. OnPM
Tree, whereon the pitying skies. The Dying Eusebio's Address to the Cross. Calderón de la Barca, *tr. by* D. F. MacCarthy. OuHeWo
Tree, which heaven has willed to dower. The Cross. Calderón de la Barca, *tr. by* Richard Chenevix Trench. CAW; LiA; TeCS
Tree will prove a blessing all life long, A. Upon the Hearth. Lloyd Mifflin. POT; PoTo
Tree will soon be hewn, The. Issa, *tr. fr. Japanese by* Lois J. Erickson. SoLD
Tree Woman. Dorothy Quick. DaM
Trees. Harry Behn. SiSoSe; TiPo; YeAr
Trees. Bliss Carman. ChPo; DD; NLK; OHIP; PoRL
Trees. Thomas Curtis Clark. OQP; PGD; QP-2
Trees, The. Samuel Valentine Cole. NLK; OHIP
Trees. Sara Coleridge. BoTP; DD; MeMeAg; MPB; OHIP; PCH; RAR; TVC
Trees. Walter de la Mare. GTBS; OHIP
Trees. Nikolai Gumilev, *tr. fr. Russian by* Y. Hornstein. BoRS
Trees. Joyce Kilmer. BAP; BAV; BBV (1923 ed.); BLPA; BTP; CP; CV; DD; FaBoBe; FaFP; FaPON; HBV; HBVY; HH; InP; JKCP; LEAP; MAP; MaRV;

Trees (*continued*)
MCCG; MPB; NeHB; NeMA; NP; NV; OBAV; OHFP; OlF; OTPC (1946 ed.); PEDC; PoMa; POT; PoTo; PYM; SBMV; TCAP; TreF; UnPo; VOD; WBLP; WGRP; YT
Trees, The. Lucy Larcom. NLK; OHIP
Trees, *sel.* Harold Monro.
"There are some men, of course, some men, I know." PtOT; TwCV
Trees, The. Christopher Morley. OHIP
Trees. William Haskell Simpson. *Fr.* In Arizona. NP
Trees, The. Herbert Trench. *See* O Dreamy, Gloomy, Friendly Trees.
Trees. Henry van Dyke. *See* Salute to the Trees.
Trees alone possess the gift sublime, The. Trees. Nikolai Gumilev. BoRS
Trees along our city streets, The. City Trees. Vere Dargan. OQP; PGD; QP-2
Trees along this city street, The. City Trees. Edna St. Vincent Millay. FaPON; LaNeLa; PoMa
Trees and Fairies. Rose Fyleman. RAR
Trees and herbage, as the seasons wane, The. Flowers of the Sea. Yasuhide. OnPM
Trees and the Master, The. Sidney Lanier. *See* Ballad of Trees and the Master, A.
Trees and the menace of night. Rhymes and Rhythms, XXI. W. E. Henley. Po
Trees and Waves. Al-Isra'ili, *tr. fr. Arabic by* A. J. Arberry. MooP
Trees are all wonderful yellow and red, The. Autumn. Arthur A. Knipe. GFA
Trees are bare, their branches high over the pool where we drink, The. Exile. Tu Fu. OnPM
Trees are brilliant with flowers, The. Spring Walk to the Pavilion of Good Crops and Peace. Ou-yang Hsiu. OnPC
Trees Are Down, The. Charlotte Mew. MBP; MoAB; MoBrPo; PoTo
Trees are God's great alphabet, The. A B C's in Green. Leonora Speyer. DD; HBMV; HBVY; NLK; OHIP; OQP; QP-1
Trees are humming a lazy song, The. Interlude. Holger Lundbergh. PoMa
Trees are hung with crystal lamps, the world lies still and white, The. A Christmas Carol. Christian Burke. COAH
Trees are in their autumn beauty, The. The Wild Swans at Coole. W. B. Yeats. BLA; BLV; BoLiVe; ChMo; ChTr; CMP; CP; EnLi-2 (1949 ed.); EnLP; GTBS-D; GTIV; MaPo; MBP; MoAB; MoBrPo; MoVE; NP; OAEP (2d ed.); OnYI; Po; PoVP; ReMP; TCEP; TwCV; TwHP; TyEnPo; VLEP; WHA
Trees are the kindest things I know. Trees. Harry Behn. SiSoSe; TiPo; YeAr
Trees are tracing in the waning haze, The. Evening. Victor van Vriesland. TrJP
Trees are waving to and fro, The. Just like This. D. A. Olney. BoTP
Trees' Choice, The. Grace B. Carter. PEOR
Tree's early leaf-buds [*or* buds] were bursting their brown, The. The Tree. Björnstjerne Björnson. ADAH; DD; FaPON; HH; MPB; OHIP; OTPC (1946 ed.); PCH; PRWS; PTA-1; RAR
Trees growing,—right in front of my window. Pruning Trees. Po Chü-i. TrCh
Trees in groves. Saadi. Emerson. AmP; IAP; LEAP; OxBA
Trees in Sherwood forest are old and good, The. Sonnet to ——. John Hamilton Reynolds. OBRV
Trees in the Garden, The. Stephen Crane. War Is Kind, XXVI. AmPP
Trees in the Garden. D. H. Lawrence. MBP; MoAB; MoBrPo; Po
Trees learn music from the birds they hold, The. Wood Music. Ethel King. GoYe
Trees, like great jade elephants, The. John Gould Fletcher. Irradiations, VII [X]. MAP; MAPA; NeMA; NePA; PFE; TwAmPo
Trees of the elder lands, The. St. Anthony's Township. Gilbert Sheldon. CH
Trees of the Garden, The. Dante Gabriel Rossetti. The House of Life, LXXXIX. BPN; PoVP; ViPo
Trees of the Lord are full of sap, The. The Rich Earth. *Fr.* Psalm CIV, Bible, *O.T.* GoTP
Trees shake gentle skaters out. Cadenza. Miriam Waddington. CaP
Trees So High, The. *Unknown.* OBB; OxBoLi; PoD; SiTL
Trees That Shade a House. Katharine Worth. PoMa
Trees Used in Games and Sports. Mary Isabel Curtis. GFA
Trees were taller than the night, The. The Robber. W. J. Turner. MBP; MoBrPo
Trees, Who Are Distant. Bertram Warr. CaP
Tree-Top Road, The. May Riley Smith. HBV; MaRV; NLK
Treetops sway rustling and shudder, The. Beautiful Foreign Land. Joseph von Eichendorff. AnGP
Treizaine. Sir Thomas Wyatt. *See* If in the World There Be More Woe.
Trelawny. Robert Stephen Hawker. *See* Song of the Western Men, The.
Trelawny Lies by Shelley. Charles L. O'Donnell. HBMV
Tremble, be fearful. A Warning by the Emperor Yao. *Unknown.* *Fr.* The Fountain of Old Poems. WhP
Tremble before your [*or* thy] chattels. Cry of the People. John G. Neihardt. BAP; CP; MAP; PoeMoYo; PoFr
Trembling before thine awful throne. Forgiveness of Sins a Joy unknown to Angels. Augustus Lucas Hillhouse. AA
Trembling I write my dream, and recollect. A Vision. Philip Freneau. *Fr.* The House of Night. AnFE; APA; CoAnAm; IAP; TCAP
Trembling old men are stamm'ring. Lines on Carmen Sylva. Emma Lazarus. TrJP
Trembling, the god Kneph shook the universe. Horus. Gérard de Nerval. TrFP
Trembling train clings to the leaning wall, The. Moonrise in the Rockies. Ella Higginson. AA
Trembling with grief came Mary Magdalene. Mary Knew. Ida Norton Munson. ChIP
Tremendous. marching through smashed buildings, trees. Pieta. Guy Butler. BoSA
Tremor, like magnitude, shook the world, A. Coup d'Etat. Ruth Herschberger. LiTA
Trench Blues, *with music.* *Unknown.* OuSiCo
Trencher Chaplain, The. Joseph Hall. *Fr.* Virgidemiarum. EV-2
("Gentle squire would gladly entertain, A.") SiCE; ViBoPo
(Satire: "Gentle squire would gladly entertain, A.") ReIE; TuPP
Trenches, The. Frederic Manning. MCCG
Trenton and Princeton. *Unknown.* PAH
Tress, The. Al-Husri, *tr. fr. Arabic by* A. J. Arberry. MooP
Tress of Cloud, A! Thinking of My Love. Prince Li Yü. ChLP
Tresses. Baudelaire, *tr. fr. French by* Alan Conder. TrFP
Tresses of thy glossy hair, The. To Harriett. John Clare. AtBAP
Tretis of the Tua Mariit Wemen and the Wedo. William Dunbar. *See* Tua Maritt Wemen and the Wedo, The.
Triad. Adelaide Crapsey. BAP; BLV; CBOV; InP; MAP; MCCG; MoAmPo (1942 ed.); NeMA; NP; PFE; PFY; VOD (1935 ed.)
Triad of Things Not Decreed. The. Alice Furlong. AnIV
Triads. Swinburne. BPN; PoVP; VLEP
Triads of Ireland, The, *sels.* *Unknown, tr. fr. Old Irish.*
"Three accomplishments well regarded in Ireland: a clever/verse," *tr. by* Thomas Kinsella. OxBI
"Three slender things that best support the world," *tr. by* Kuno Meyer. OnYI
Trial, The. W. H. Auden. NePA
Trial, The. Longfellow. *Fr.* Giles Corey of the Salem Farms. PAH
Trial, The. Muriel Rukeyser. NAMP; PoNe
Trial and Error. Phyllis McGinley. SiTL
Trial by Existence, The. Robert Frost. CoBA
Trial by Jury, *sels.* W. S. Gilbert.
Judge's Song, The. PoVP
Rover's Apology, The. ALV
Trial of Orthodoxy, A. Sir William Watson. ArmLP
Trial of the Dog, The. Aristophanes. *See* Mock Trial.
Trial of Treasure, The, *sels.* *Unknown.*
"Hey ho, care away, let the world pass." TuPP
My Dear Lady. EIL
("Am not I in blessed case.") TuPP
Triangles are commands of God. The Starfish. Robert P. Tristram Coffin. ImOP
Tribal Lay. "Pablo de Rokha," *tr. fr. Spanish by* H. R. Hays. TwSpPo
Tribe prophetic with their ardent eyes, The. Gypsies on the March. Baudelaire. OnPM
Tribes, The. Roy Fuller. BoSA
Tributary wish, to be a part, The. Great Zimbabwe. Peter Jackson. BoSA
Tribute. Aline Kilmer. TBM
Tribute, The. Coventry Patmore. The Angel in the House, I, iv, 2. HBV; LPS-1
Tribute, A ("Lincoln, the man who freed the slave"). *Unknown.* PGD
Tribute of Grasses, A (to W. W.). Hamlin Garland. AA; AnAmPo; LA
Tribute on the Passing of a very Real Person. *Unknown.* PoToHe (new ed.)
Tribute to America. Shelley. PaA
Tribute to Dante, A ("Dante Alighieri, a dark oracle"). Boccaccio. *See* Inscription for a Portrait of Dante.
Tribute to Dante, A ("If Dante mourns, there wheresoe'er he be"). Boccaccio. *See* To One Who Had Censured His Public Exposition of Dante.

Tribute to Grass. John J. Ingalls. WBLP
Tribute to Our Soldiers. Marion Kennedy. PEDC
Tribute to the Angels, *sels.* Hilda Doolittle ("H. D.").
Ah (You Say), This Is Holy Wisdom. CrMA; MeRV
Hermes Trismegistus. FaBoTw
Swiftly Relight the Flame. FaBoTw
"We have seen her." MeRV
Tribute to Washington. *Unknown.* OHIP
Tribute to Wyatt ("Wyatt resteth here"). Earl of Surrey. *See* On the Death of Sir Thomas Wyatt.
Trick, The. W. H. Davies. ChMP
Trick that everyone abhors, A. Rebecca. Hilaire Belloc. BoChLi (1939 ed.); RIS; StaSt
Trickling tears that falls along my cheeks, The. A Lover Rejected Complaineth. Edward de Vere, Earl of Oxford. ReIE
Tricks of Imagination, The. Shakespeare. *See* Lunatic, the Lover, and the Poet, The.
Tricksters. William Rose Benét. HBMV
Tri-colored Ribbon, The. Peadar Kearney. OnYI
Trico's Song. John Lyly. *Fr.* Alexander and Campaspe, V, i. OBSC; RiBV; TrGrPo
(Spring, The.) CH
(Spring's Welcome.) AnEnPo; BCEP; BEL; EPP; OBEV; TOP
(To Welcome in the Spring.) EV-1
(What Bird So Sings.) EG; ElL; SiCE; ThWaDe; TuPP; ViBoPo
Trifle, A. Henry Timrod. HBV
Trifles. *Unknown.* HBV
Trilby. Alice Brown. AA
Trilby, *sel.* George Du Maurier.
Little Work, A, *after the French of* Leon van Montenaeken, *fr.* Pt. VIII. FaBoBe; HBV; NeHB; OQP; QP-2
(Little, A.) MaRV
(Little Work, a Little Play, A.) PoToHe (new ed.); TreFS
Trilce, XVIII, XXVIII, XLIV. César Vallejo, *tr. fr. Spanish by* H. R. Hays. TwSpPo
Trilobite, Grapholite, Nautilus pie. Boston Nursery Rhymes. Joseph Cook. BoHV; InMe; PA
Trimmed Lamp, The. Laura Simmons. ChIP; MaRV
(Vigil.) LPS-1
Trindad Market. Ronald de Carvalho, *tr. fr. Portuguese by* Dudley Poore. AnCL
Trinity. Struthers Burt. NoCaPo (1941 ed.)
Trinity, The. Marian Osborne. CaP; CPG
Trinity, The. *Unknown.* ACP
Trinity [*or* Trinitee] blessed, deity coequal. A Prayer to the Trinity [*or* To the Trinity]. Richard Stanyhurst. CoBE; ElL; OxBoCh; PoEL-2; TuPP
Trinket. Winifred Welles. NP
Triolet: "All women born are so perverse." Robert Bridges. ChMo; CMP; HBV; PoVP; SeCePo
Triolet, The: "Easy is the triolet." W. E. Henley. *See* Easy Is the Triolet.
Triolet, The: "Gesture in space, A." Michael Lewis. PIAE
Triolet: "I intended a handspring." Margaret Hoover. PCD
Triolet: "I intended an Ode." Austin Dobson. *See* "Urceus Exit."
Triolet: "I love you, my lord!" Paul T. Gilbert. BOHV
Triolet: "Night is full of the crying, The." Alexander K. Laing. PIAE; YT
Triolet: "When first we met we did not guess." Robert Bridges. ChMo; CMP; PoVP
(When First We Met) Po
Triolet, The: "Your triolet should glimmer." Don Marquis. PFE
Triolet on a Downhill Road. Margaret Fishback. WhC
Triolets. Patrick Carey. AEV
Triomphe de Pétrarque, Le, *sel.* Théophile Gautier, *pr. tr. fr. French.*
"Let the flame be fed on the altar of the ideal." LiA
Trip, The. "Lambros Porphyras," *tr. fr. Modern Greek by* Rae Dalven. MoGP
Trip and go, heave and ho! A-Maying, a-Playing [*or* A Clownish Song]. Thomas Nashe. *Fr.* Summer's Last Will and Testament. ElL; OBSC
Trip down to Bangor, the Fourth of July, A. The Red Light Saloon. *Unknown.* ShS
Trip It, Gipsies [Trip It Fine]. Thomas Middleton *and* William Rowley. *Fr.* The Spanish Gipsy, III, i. OAEP; SeCL
(Song: "Trip it gipsies, trip it fine.") OBS
Trip on the Erie, A. *Unknown.* ABF; IHA
Trip; San Francisco. Langston Hughes. GoSl
Trip to Cambridge, The. *Unknown.* PAH
Trip to Rome, A—great pains and little gain! *Unknown. Fr.* Four Short Poems. LyMA
Trip to the Grand Banks, A. *with music. Unknown.* ShS
Trip upon trenchers, and dance upon dishes. *Unknown.* OxNR
Tripe. J. B. Morton. InMe
Triple-decker and the double-cone, The. Saturday Sundae. Francis Reginald Scott. BoCaPo (1948 ed.); CaP
Triple Dream, The. Mikhail Lermontov, *tr. fr. Russian by* Vladimir Nabokov. LiTW
Triple Fool, The. John Donne. CenL; CoBE; ElSeCe; EPS (1942 ed.); OAEP; Po
Triplet on the Reign of the Great Sultan, A. James Clarence Mangan. IrPN
Trippers. Sir Osbert Sitwell. HaMV
Tripping down the Field-Path. Charles Swain. HBV; VA
Tristan. August, Graf von Platen, *tr. fr. German by* Mabel Cotterell. AnGP
Tristan and Iseult are dead. Bird of Time. Gustav Davidson. MuM
Tristan and Isolda. Newman Levy. InMe
Tristan da Cunha. Roy Campbell. CoEV; MBP; MM; MoBrPo; MoVE; OnHM; TwCV
Tristia. Osip Mandelstam, *tr. fr. Russian by* C. M. Bowra. BoR
Tristia, *sels.* Ovid, *tr. fr. Latin.* LaP
"Now the zephyrs diminish the cold, and the year being ended," III, 12, *tr. by* Longfellow.
"Should any one there in Rome remember Ovid the exile," III, 10, *tr. by* Longfellow.
Time Is No Remedy, *fr.* IV, 6, *tr. by* Geoffrey Johnson.
To His Wife, *fr.* III, 3, *tr. by* Geoffrey Johnson.
Tristram against the heathen hound. The Ballad of Tristram. *Unknown.* PaOS
Tristram and Iseult. Matthew Arnold. PoVP; ViPo; ViPP; VLEP
Sels.
Iseult of Brittany, III. GEPC
"Raise the light, my Page, that I may see her," *fr.* II. ReTS
Tristram and Iseult. Swinburne. Tristram of Lyonesse: Prelude. TCEP; VLEP
(From Prologue to "Tristram of Lyonesse.") LEAP
(Love, That Is First and Last.) LiTL
(Prelude to "Tristram of Lyonesse.") BMEP; POTT
(Prelude: Tristram and Iseult.) PoVP; ViP
Tristram and Isolt. Don Marquis. HBMV
Tristram lies sick to death. Tristram's End. Laurence Binyon. EnLit; OBMV
Tristram of Lyonesse, *sels.* Swinburne.
Death of Urgan, The, *fr.* The Last Pilgrimage. WHA
Sunrise at Sea, *br. sel. fr.* The Sailing of the Swallow. EtS
Swimming. GN
Tristram and Iseult. Prelude. PoVP; TCEP; ViP; VLEP
(From Prologue to "Tristram of Lyonesse.") LEAP
(Love, That Is First and Last.) LiTL
(Prelude to "Tristram of Lyonesse.") BMEP; POTT
Tristram's End. Laurence Binyon. EnLit; OBMV
Trit trot to market to buy a penny doll. *Unknown.* OxNR
Tritemius of Herbipolis, one day. The Gift of Tritemius. Whittier. TVSH
Triton in the ilex-wood, The. Castello. Agnes Mary Frances Robinson. LBBV
Triumph. H. C. Bunner. OBAV
"As a gray rose-leaf," *sel.* BAP
Triumph, The. Ben Jonson. *See* Triumph of Charis, The.
Triumph, The. Sidney Lanier. *Fr.* The Psalm of the West. PAH
Triumph. John Crowe Ransom. HBMV
Triumph. Kathryn White Ryan. TBM
Triumph. L. D. Stearns. BLRP
Triumph America! Thomas Burke. NoCaPo
Triumph may be of several kinds, A. Emily Dickinson. NePA
Triumph of Beauty, The, *sel.* James Shirley.
"Cease, warring thoughts, and let his brain." TuPP
(Lullaby, A.) BOL
Triumph of Charis, The. Ben Jonson. *Fr.* A Celebration of Charis. BEL; ElSeCe; EPP; EV-2; ExPo; GoBC; LiTB; LoBV; SeCeV; TCEP; TOP; WHA
(Her Triumph.) AEV; AtBAP; ElL; EPS; FaBoEn; HBV; InPo; LiTL; MaPo; OAEP; Po; PoEL-2; SeCV-1; SeEP; TuPP; TwHP; TyEnPo; ViBoPo
("See the Chariot at hand here of Love.") InvP; SiCE
(Triumph, The.) AnFE; CoEV; OBEV
"Have you seen but a bright lily grow," *sel.* EG
(From "Love's Chariot.") LEAP
(Have You seen a Bright Lily Grow.) OTPC (1923 ed.)
(She.) BCEP
(So Sweet Is She.) GN
(So White, So Soft, So Sweet.) TrGrPo
(Triumph, The.) LoPS; PG, 8 *ll.*
Triumph of Chastity, The Barbara Howes. NePoAm-2
Triumph of Civilization, The. Edward Carpenter. EPP
Triumph of Death, The. Barbara Howes. NePoAm-2
Triumph of Death, The. Shakespeare. *See* Sonnets, LXXI.
Triumph of Dulness, The. Pope. *Fr.* The Dunciad. CoEV; OBEC
("O muse! relate [for you can tell alone].") EPP; EV-3
Triumph of Forgotten Things, The. Edith M. Thomas. HBV
Triumph of Freedom, The. William Lloyd Garrison. PoFr
Triumph of His Grace. Charles Wesley. BePJ

Triumph of Ignorance, The. Pope. *See* Conclusion: "In vain, in vain . . ."

Triumph of Infidelity, The, *sel.* Timothy Dwight.
Smooth Divine, The. AA; AnAmPo; IAP; LA; TCAP; WGRP
(Minister, New Style, A.) AmPP (3d ed.)

Triumph of Joseph, The. Charles Jeremiah Wells. *Fr.* Joseph and His Brethren. VA

Triumph of Life, The. Shelley. ChER; ERP; PoEL-4
"Old anatomies, The," *sel* CoEV

Triumph of Love. John Hall Wheelock. MAP; MoAmPo
(Triumph of the Singer, The.) NP

Triumph of Peace, The, *sel.* James Shirley.
"Come away, away, away." TuPP

Triumph of Sensibility. Sylvia Townsend Warner. MBP; MoAB; MoBrPo

Triumph of Spring, The. Mary Bayard Clarke. NoCaPo

Triumph of the Defeated. Byron. MaRV

Triumph of the Singer, The. John Hall Wheelock. *See* Triumph of Love.

Triumph of the Whale. Charles Lamb. EtS; OBRV
"Io! Paean! Io! sing," *sel* ImOP

Triumph of Time, The. Sophocles. *See* Decay, Earth's Universal Law.

Triumph of Time, The. Swinburne. EmBrPo; EtPaEn; PoVP; ViPo; ViPP; VLEP
Sels.
"I have put my days and dreams out of mind." ViBoPo
"I will go back to the great sweet mother." GTSL; LEAP; MBP; POTT
(Disappointed Lover, The, *abr.*) LPS-2
(Return, The.) NLK
(Sea, The.) BLV; BoLiVe; PIAE; TrGrPo; TSW
(Stanzas.) HBV
(Triumph of Time, The.) BMEP, *longer sel.;* OAEP
"There lived a singer in the France of old." GTSL
(Farewell, A.) GTML

Triumphal arch, that fill'st the sky. To the Rainbow [*or* The Rainbow]. Thomas Campbell. ERP; HBV; PECK; SN

Triumphal Chant. Exodus, XV: 1-13, 18, Bible, *O.T.* TrGrPo
(Song of Moses, The, XV: 1-18.) LiTW
(Then Sang Moses, XV: 1-18.) TrJP
("Then sang Moses and the children of Israel this song," XV: 1-27.) PoFr
(War Song of the Red Sea, XV: 1-10.) BHV

Triumphal March. T. S. Eliot. *Fr.* Coriolan. KN; PoLFOT; ShBV-4; SoV; WaaP

Triumphal Ode MCMXXXIX. George Barker. LiTB; WaP

Triumphal Song of the Roman Army. *Unknown, tr. fr. Latin by* Poe. *Fr.* Aurelian (*by* Flavius Vopiscus). LaP

Triumphalis. Bliss Carman. HBMV; PG

Triumphant amid the many realms of this life. Linford Newman. Edgar Lee Masters. GrCo-2

Triumphant Entry, The. Henry Vaughan. *Fr.* Palm-Sunday. MaRV; StJW

Triumphs of Owen, The. Thomas Gray, *after the Welsh of* Meilir ap Gwalchmai. CEP; EnRP; EV-3; LiTW; PoEL-3; PrWP

Triumphs of Thy Conquering Power, The. William H. Bathurst. BePJ

Trivia; or, The Art of Walking the Streets of London, *sels.* John Gay.
I: Of the Implements for Walking the Streets, and Signs of the Weather. CEP
Origin of Pattens, The. BeR
II: Of Walking the Streets by Day. CEP; EiPP
Dangers of Football, The. EnLi-1 (1949 ed.)
Death at the Thames Ice Fair. BeR
Great Frost, The. OBEC; SeCePo
Of Narrow Streets. EnLi-1 (1949 ed.)
On Walking the Streets by Day. TOP
(Morning, The, *shorter sel.*) EnLi-1 (1949 ed.)
Pell Mell Celebrated, The. EnLi-1 (1949 ed.)
Pleasure of Walking through an Alley, The. EnLi-1 (1949 ed.)
"Thus far the muse has traced in useful lays." EnLi-1 (1949 ed.)
III: Of Walking the Streets by Night.
"Consider, reader, what fatigues I've known." EnLi-1 (1949 ed.)
Evening, The. EnLi-1 (1949 ed.)
"O Trivia, Goddess, leave these low abodes." EnLi-1 (1949 ed.)
Of Ballad-Singers. EnLi-1 (1949 ed.)
Of Crossing the Street. EnLi-1 (1949 ed.)
Of Pick-Pockets. EnLi-1 (1949 ed.)
Of Watchmen. EnLi-1 (1949 ed.)

Triviality, A. Waring Cuney. CDC

Troades. Euripides. *See* Trojan Women.

Trochee trips from long to short. Metrical Feet [*or* Lessons for a Boy]. Samuel Taylor Coleridge. ExPo; HBV; LPS-3; PCD

Troelus a Chresyd, *sel. Unknown, tr. fr. Welsh by* Gwyn Williams.
Prayer of Calcas, The. PrWP

Troia Fuit. Reginald Wright Kauffman. HBV

Troilus and Cressida. Chaucer. *See* Troilus and Criseyde.

Troilus and Cressida. Aubrey Thomas De Vere. IrPN

Troilus and Cressida, *sels.* Dryden.
"Can life be a blessing." ATP (1953 ed.); ElSeCe; SeCePo; SeCL; ViBoPo
(Song.) CEP; SeCV-2; SeEP
Dulness Is Decent, *fr.* Prologue. BeR
Prologue: "See my lov'd Britons, see your Shakespeare rise." CEP; SeCV-2

Troilus and Cressida, *sels.* Shakespeare.
Agamemnon and Nestor, *fr.* I, iii. EV-1
Portrait of Cressida, *fr.* IV, v. TrGrPo
Portrait of Helen, *fr.* II, ii, and IV, i. TrGrPo
Single Famished Kiss, A, *fr.* IV, iv. LiA
"This she? No, this is Diomids Cressida," *fr.* V, ii. NBE
Time, *fr.* III, iii. CoEV
(Good Deeds Past.) LiA
(Ulysses Advises Achilles [Not to Let Slip Opportunity].) LiTB; LiTG
(Ulysses; the Instant Way.) EV-1
Ulysses; on Degree, *fr.* I, iii. EV-1
("Heavens themselves, the planets and this center.") ImOP
(On Degree.) ExPo
"We two, that with so many thousand sighs," *fr.* IV, iv. EtPaEn

Troilus and Criseyde, *sels.* Chaucer.
"As proude Bayard ginneth for to skip," *fr.* I. MyFE
Assumption of Troilus, The, *fr.* V. CoEV
At the Gate. SeCePo
But Whan the Cok, *fr.* III. AtBAP
Complaint of Troilus, The, *fr.* V. OBEV (new ed.)
Death of Troilus, The, *fr.* V. PoD
Despair of Troilus, The, *fr.* IV. LoBV
"Go, litel book, go litel myn tragedie," *fr.* V. MyFE; ViBoPo
(Envoy, The.) FiP
(From the Epilogue to "Troilus and Criseyde.") NBE
"If no love is, O god, what fele I so?" *fr.* I. LO
(Canticus Troili.) AtBAP
(Song of Troilus.) AWP; LoPS
(Troilus Soliloquizes.) EG
"Morwe com, and goostly for to speke, The," fr. V. EPP
"O younge freshe [*or* yonge fresshe] folkes, he or [*or* and] she," *fr.* V. CAW; ExPo; LO
(Exhortation to Youth.) PoLi
(Love Unfeigned, The.) OBEV
"Owt of thise blake wawes for to sayle," II. EnLi-1
Sorrow of Troilus, The, *fr.* V. PoEL-1
"Therewith when he was ware, and gan behold," *fr.* V. LO
"With this he tok his leve and home he wente," *fr.* II. EPP
"With-inne the temple he went him forth pleyinge," *fr.* I. LO
Wooing of Criseide, The, III. PoEL-1
(O Blissful Light, *shorter sel.*) AtBAP

Trojan Camp-Fires, The. Homer, *tr. fr. Greek. Fr.* The Iliad, VIII. GrR, *tr. by* the Earl of Derby; OxBG, *tr. by* Tennyson

Trojan Women, *sels.* Euripides, *tr. fr. Greek by* Gilbert Murray.
Arraignment of Helen. GrR
Cassandra. GrR
Child-Burial; Sequel to Battles. GrR
End of Troy, The. OxBG
Fate of Astyanax, The. GrR
(Andromache Learns of Her Son's Fate, *longer sel., tr. by* Arthur S. Way.) LiA
"Lift your foot high in the dance," *tr. by* G. M. A. Grube. GrPo
Troy. OxBG; WoL
(Song of Troy.) GrR

Trojans. C. P. Cavafy, *tr. fr. Modern Greek by* Rae Dalven. MoGP

Trojans and Greeks. Homer. *See* Advance of the Trojans.

Trojans Encamp before the Achaean Wall, The. Homer, *tr. fr. Greek by* F. L. Lucas. *Fr.* The Iliad, VIII *and* IX. GrPE
("So Hector spake; the Trojans roared applause," *shorter sel., fr.* VIII, *tr. by* Tennyson.) GrPo

Trojans outside the Walls, The. Homer. *See* Camp at Night, The.

Troll Sat Alone on His Seat of Stone. J. R. R. Tolkien. LiL

Troll the Bowl! Thomas Dekker. *See* Cold's the Wind.

Trolley cars are very swift. How to Catch a Trolley. *Unknown.* DDA

Troop home to silent grots and caves! The Mermaidens' Vesper-Hymn [*or* Siren Chorus]. George Darley. Syren Songs, VI. BLV; ChTr; FaBoEn; GTIV; KN; LoBV; OBRV; OxBI; PoEL-4; RO; ViBoPo

Troop of the Guard, A. Hermann Hagedorn. HBV; OHIP

Troop Train. Karl Shapiro. OxBA; WaaP; WaP

Trooper and Maid, The. *Unknown.* BaBo

Trooper Temple Pulvermacher. William Branford. BoSA

Trooper's Death, The. *Unknown, tr. fr. German by* R. W. Raymond. LPS-2
Troops, The. Siegfried Sassoon. ChMo; CMP; POTE
(Prelude: "Dim, gradual thinning of the shapeless gloom.") GTSL
(Prelude: Troops, The.) ChMP; GTBS-D
Troops Returning from Milan. Niccolò degli Albizzi. *See* Prolonged Sonnet: When the Troops Were Returning from Milan.
Troopship in the Tropics. Alun Lewis. WaP
Troop-Ship Sails, The. Robert W. Chambers. MDAH
Troparion. Aleksey Konstantinovich Tolstoy, *tr. fr. Russian by* Maurice Baring. *Fr.* John Damascene. BoR
Trophies. Samuel Daniel. *See* To Delia: "Let others sing of knights . . ."
Trophy, The. Erycius, *tr. fr. Greek by* F. L. Lucas. GrPE
Trophy, The. Edwin Muir. LiTM; NeTW; POTE
Tropic Siesta. Luis Carlos López, *tr. fr. Spanish by* Donald Devenish Walsh. AnCL; WoL
Tropic Storm. Walter Adolphe Roberts. *Fr.* Boyhood Etchings. PoNe
Tropic Sunset. Walter Adolphe Roberts. *Fr.* Boyhood Etchings. PoNe
Tropic village night: the hours. Village Night. Luis Carlos López. AnCL
Tropical Girl to Her Garden. Genevieve Taggard. NP
Tropical mid-day. Indolence. Heat. Gilberto González y Contreras. AnCL
Tropical Morning at Sea, A. Edward Rowland Sill. EtS; PIAE
Tropical Pool. Muna Lee. NV
Tropical Tempest. Arthur Davison Ficke. Sonnets of a Portrait Painter, XVI.
("I have seen beauty where light stabs the hills.") AnAmPo; LA
Tropical Town. Salomón de la Selva. BAP; HBV
Tropical Weather. Epes Sargent. EtS
Tropics, The. Douglas Brooke Wheelton Sladen. VA
Tropics in New York, The; New York. Claude McKay. GoSl; PoNe
Trosachs, The. Wordsworth. BPN; EM-2; EmBrPo; EnLi-2; EPN; ES; GTSL; HBV; OBEV; OBRV; SeCePo
Trot Along, Pony. Marion Edey. TiPo
Trot, and a canter, a gallop, and over, A. *Unknown.* OxNR
Trot, Trot! Mary Frances Butts. HBV; HBVY
("Every evening Baby goes.") PPL
(Trot, Trot to Town.) SAS
Troth ladye Ile not court ye too't. *Unknown.* SeCSL
Trotting flocks had left their winter folds, The. The Shepherd Boy's Day. Stefan George. AnGP
Troubadour Alba: "'Neath leafy hawthorn in a garden gay." *Unknown, tr. fr. French by* Frances Winwar. EnLi-1
Troubadour of Eze, The, *sel.* Paul Engle.
"High on this point of rock, this mighty needle." PoeMoYo
Troubadour of God, The. Charles Wharton Stork. WGRP
Troubadour Song: "'Tis no wonder if my songs." Bernart of Ventadorn, *tr. fr. French by* Bernard D. N. Grebanier. EnLi-1
Troubadour who plucks the oboe's strings, The. Diavolina. Fielding H. Garrison. PoP
Troubadours. Arthur Davison Ficke. Sonnets of a Portrait Painter, X. HBMV
Trouble. David Keppel. FaFP; TreF; WBLP
Trouble at Sea. Thomas Prys, *tr. fr. Welsh by* Gwyn Williams. PrWP
Trouble at the Farm. Ivy O. Eastwick. BoTP
Trouble in the Amen Corner. T. C. Harbaugh. BLPA; PTA-2
Trouble, not of clouds, or weeping rain, A. On the Departure of Sir Walter Scott from Abbotsford, for Naples. Wordsworth. EnRP
Trouble Not the Maiden's Soul. Johan Ludvig Runeberg, *tr. fr. Swedish by* Charles W. Stork. AnSL; LiTW
Trouble, Trouble, *with music.* *Unknown.* OuSiCo
Trouble with a kitten is, The. The Kitten. Ogden Nash. FaPON; MoShBr; WhC
Trouble with you is, The. Denunciation: or, Unfrock'd Again. Philip Whalen. NeAP
Troubled Friar, The. *Unknown, tr. fr. Irish by* Douglas Hyde. GTIV
Troubled Jesus. Waring Cuney. BANP; GoSl
Troubled long with warring notions. Near the Spring of the Hermitage. Wordsworth. BPN
Troubled man turned head away, The. Country Life. Frank Kendon. POTE
Troubled Soldier, The. *Unknown. See* Rebel Soldier, The.
Troubled Unquickening, The. William Baylebridge. *Fr.* Sextains. BoAV
Troubled with the Itch, and Rubbing with Sulphur. George Moses Horton. NoCaPo
Troubles. Dorothy Aldis. StVeCh
Troubles, they say, are sent us to grow wise on. Dream and Image. Heinrich von Morungen. LiTW; LyMA
Trout-fishing on Tweed. Andrew Lang. *See* April on Tweed.
Trout Map, The. Allen Tate. FaBoMo
Trouting. John Townsend Trowbridge. SN
Troy ("In Salamis, filled with the foaming"). Euripides, *tr. fr. Greek by* Gilbert Murray. *Fr.* Trojan Women. OxBG; WoL
(Song of Troy.) GrR
Troy ("My Fatherland, O my Troy!"). Euripides. *See* Ilion overthrown.
Troy. Robin Flower. MM; SeCePo
Troy. Thomas Sackville. *Fr.* Induction to "The Mirror for Magistrates." SeCePo
Troy Depicted. Shakespeare. *Fr.* The Rape of Lucrece. OBSC
Troy rac'd, Greece wrack'd, who mourns? Ye both may boast. To the Ruins of Troy and Greece. George Chapman. ReIE
Troy Restored. Hadrianus, *tr. fr. Greek by* Sir William Marris. OxBG
Troy Town. Dante Gabriel Rossetti. BEL; BPN; EmBrPo; PoVP; ViP; ViPo; ViPP; VLEP
Troy Town is covered up with weeds. Fragments. John Masefield. PoeT
Troylus and Criseyde. Chaucer. *See* Troilus and Criseyde.
Troynovant ("Troynovant is now no more a city"). Thomas Dekker. *Fr.* Entertainment to James. ChTr; LoBV; OBSC
Truants, The. Walter de la Mare. ChMo; CMP; InP; MBP; MoBrPo
Truants from love, we dream of wrath. Our Father's Door. Oliver Wendell Holmes. *Fr.* The Professor at the Breakfast Table. OQP; QP-2
Truce. Sara Teasdale. ChMo; CMP
Truce, gentle love, a parley now I crave! Idea, LXIII. Michael Drayton. ReIE; TuPP
Truce with a Southern Neighbor. Helen Bevington. NoCaPo (rev. ed.)
Trucks. James S. Tippett. FaPON; GFA
Truculentus, *sel.* Plautus, *tr. fr. Latin by* F. A. Wright.
"These courtesans are like the sea." LaP
Trudge, Body. Robert Graves. MoAB
True. Andrew Hewitt. NoCaPo
True and False Glory. Milton. *Fr.* Paradise Regained, III. LiTB; OBS
True and False Singing. *Unknown. See* Ballata: Of True and False Singing.
True and Perfecte Newes of the Worthy Enterprises of Sir Francis Drake, 1586, The, *sel.* Thomas Greepe.
Taking of Cartagena, The. SG
True Apostolate, The. Ruby T. Weyburn. BLRP
True Aristocrat, The. W. Stewart. WBLP
Aristocrats of Labor, *sel.* OQP; PGD; PSO; QP-1
True as the church clock hand the hour pursues. John Clare. *Fr.* The Cottager. OBRV
True Balm. Ben Jonson. *See* Ode, An: "High-spirited friend."
True bard and simple, as the race. To Campbell. Thomas Moore. LPS-3
True Beauty. Francis Beaumont. ElL; HBV
True Beauty, The. Thomas Carew. *See* Disdain Returned.
True Bible, The. Sam Walter Foss. *Fr.* The Higher Catechism. BPP
True-born Englishman, The, *sels.* Defoe.
"England unknown as yet, unpeopled lay," *fr.* I. NBE
English Race, The, *fr.* I. OBEC
Introduction. BEL
Part I. BEL; CEP
"Satire be kind, and draw a silent veil," *fr.* I. TOP
"Wherever God erects a house of prayer," *fr.* I. BeR; NBE; TreF
True Brahmin, in the morning meadows wet. Gardener. Emerson. *Fr.* Quatrains. APW; OxBA
True Britons all of each degree. Admiral Rodney's Triumph on the 12th of April. *Unknown.* SG
True Brotherhood. Ella Wheeler Wilcox. OQP; QP-1; WBLP
True cherubs never run in debt. On Cherubs. Arthur Guiterman. LauV
True Christian hearts cease to lament. The Song of a Happy Rising. John Thewlis. ACP
True Confession of George Barker, The, *sel.* George Barker.
"I sent a letter to my love." FaBoTw
"True culture is not for the masses." The Goldfish. William F. Kirk. LHV
True Description of Love, A. *Unknown.* TuPP
True ease in writing comes from art, not chance. The Craft of Verse [*or* Sound and Sense]. Pope. *Fr.* An Essay on Criticism. BLV; BoLiVe; CBOV; ExPo; TrGrPo; UnPo
True Fair, The. Spenser. *See* Amoretti, LXXIX.
True Form and Shape of a Monsterous Child, The. William Elderton. ReIE
True Freedom. Charles Mackay. PGD
True Freedom. *Unknown, at. to* Lao-tzu, *tr. fr. Chinese by* Witter Bynner. *Fr.* Tao Teh King. OnPM
True Freedom breaks the yokes that gall. Ferdinand Freiligrath. *Fr.* Black, Red and Gold. PoFr
True Friendship. *Unknown, tr. fr. Sanskrit by* Arthur Ryder. *Fr.* The Panchatantra. AWP; JAWP; WBP

True Friendship (*continued*)
("'Tis hard to find in life.") LiTW
True friendship unfeigned. A Plain Description of Perfect Friendship. *At. to* Henry Cheke. ElL; TuPP
True genius, but true woman! dost deny. To George Sand [*or* Recognition]. Elizabeth Barrett Browning. *Fr.* Sonnets to George Sand. EmBrPo; LPS-3
True Gift, The. *Unknown.* ChIP; MaRV
True Greatness. "Owen Meredith." MaRV
True Greatness. Isaac Watts. MaRV
True Happiness. Morris Talpalar. PoToHe (new ed.)
True Heaven, The. Paul Hamilton Hayne. WGRP
True Heroism. *Unknown.* PEOR
True Hymn, A. George Herbert. GrCo-2; InvP; OxBoCh
True is it that Ambrosio Salerino. Epitaphs, V. Gabriello Chiabrera. AWP
True Knight, The. Stephen Hawes. *Fr.* The Pastime of Pleasure, *ch.* 27. ACP; AnEnPo; OBEV
(True Knighthood.) TrGrPo
True Knowledge. Panatattu. WGRP
True Knowledge, The. Oscar Wilde. VLEP
True Lent, A. Robert Herrick. *See* To Keep a True Lent.
True Love. *See also* Truelove.
True Love. Phoebe Cary. PoToHe
True Love. Waring Cuney. CDC
True Love, A. Nicholas Grimald. ElL; OBEV; TuPP
(Truelove, A.) OBSC
True Love. James Russell Lowell. *Fr.* Love. LiTL; MaRV; OQP; QP-2
True Love. Ernest Rhys. POTE
True Love. Sir Walter Scott. *Fr.* The Lay of the Last Minstrel, V. EV-4
("True love's the gift which God has given.") OBRV
True Love. Shakespeare. *See* Sonnets, CXVI.
True Love. Shelley. *Fr.* Epipsychidion. LoBV
True Love. Sir Philip Sidney. *See* My True Love Hath My Heart.
True Love. *Unknown, tr. fr. Japanese by* Lois J. Erickson. SoLD
True-Love, an Thou Be True. Sir Walter Scott. *Fr.* The Bride of Lammermoor. BPN
True Love at Length United. *Unknown.* *See* Wandering Maiden, The.
True Love Ditty, A. Thomas Middleton. *Fr.* Blurt, Master Constable. ElL
True Love in this differs from gold and clay. Shelley. *Fr.* Epipsychidion. LO
True love is but a [*or* an] humble, low-born thing. True Love. James Russell Lowell. *Fr.* Love. LiTL; MaRV; OQP; QP-2
True Love is founded in rocks of Remembrance. Love and Law. Vachel Lindsay. OQP; QP-1
True Loveliness. George Darley. TIP
True Lover, The. Abbie Huston Evans. NP
True Lover, The. A. E. Housman. A Shropshire Lad, LIII. ATP; BLV; BoLiVe; DaM; LiTL; PoVP; TwP
True Lover's Farewell, The ("Farewell, farewell, my pretty maid"). *Unknown.* *See* Lass of Lochroyan, The.
True love's own talisman, which here. A Footnote to a Famous Lyric. Louise Imogen Guiney. AA
True love's the gift which God has given. True Love. Sir Walter Scott. *Fr.* The Lay of the Last Minstrel, V. EV-4; OBRV
True Maid, A. Matthew Prior. ALV; LiTG
True Martyr, The. Thomas Wade. EPN; OBVV
True Messiah now appears, The. Christ Is the Substance of the Levitical Priesthood. Isaac Watts. BeR
True mirth resides not in the smiling skin. Mirth. Robert Herrick. LiTB
True Need, The. Thomas Curtis Clark. OQP; QP-1
True or False. Catullus, *tr. fr. Latin by* Walter Savage Landor. AWP; JAWP; OuHeWo; WBP
(Love's Madness.) LiA
True, our converse a stranger is to speech. Walden. Henry David Thoreau. CoV
True Paddy's Song, The, *with music.* *Unknown.* OuSiCo
True Peace, A. Lucia Trent *and* Ralph Cheyney. *Fr.* Ten Years After. PSO
(Toward a True Peace.) PGD
True Preacher, The. William Cowper. *Fr.* The Task, II. MaRV
True Rest. Goethe, *tr. fr. German by* John S. Dwight. LPS-2
"Rest is not quitting," *sel.* OQP; QP-2; WBLP
(True Rest.) MaRV
True Riches. *Unknown.* MaRV
True Riches. Isaac Watts. OBEC
True Romance. Edwin Honig. SiTL
True Romance, The. Herbert Jones. HBMV
True Royalty. Kipling. *Fr.* Just-so Stories. PECK
True Story, A. *Unknown.* *See* There Was a Little Rabbit Sprig.
True Story of Skipper Ireson, The. Charles Buxton Going. YT
True Story of Web-Spinner, The. Mary Howitt. OTPC (1923 ed.)
True Sufi, The. Jalal ed-Din Rumi, *tr. fr. Persian by* R. A. Nicholson. PeP
True Tale of Robin Hood, A. *Unknown.* ESPB
True, the Good and the Beautiful, The, *abr.* Delmore Schwartz. MiAP
True Thomas. *Unknown.* *See* Thomas the Rhymer.
"True 'tis P T, and P T 'tis, 'tis true." O D V. *Unknown.* BOHV
True to his trade—the slave of fortune still. The Argonaut; or, Lost Adventurer. Philip Freneau. MOAP
True to Poll. F. C. Burnand. *See* His Heart Was True to Poll.
True to the Best. Benjamin Keech. PoToHe
True until Death. Burns. *See* Farewell, The: "It was a' for our rightfu' king."
True Vine, The. St. John, XV: 1-27, Bible, *N.T.* WoL
True Vine. Elinor Wylie. AnFE; APA; CoAnAm; LiTA; MOAP; TwAmPo
True, we must tame our rebel will. Courage. Matthew Arnold. ReTS
True Weather for Women, The. Louis Simpson. NePoAm
True Wisdom. *Unknown.* BePJ
True wit is nature to advantage dress'd. Pope. *Fr.* An Essay on Criticism. ShBV-3
True Woman. Dante Gabriel Rossetti. The House of Life, LVI-LVIII.
Her Heaven. BMEP; BPN; EmBrPo; EPN; GTML; PoVP; ViPo
Her Love. BPN; EmBrPo; EPN; PoVP; ViPo
Herself. BPN; EmBrPo; EPN; POTT; PoVP; ViPo; ViPP
True Work Is Worship. Edwin Markham. *Fr.* The Angelus. MaRV
True Worth. Pope. *See* Worth Makes the Man.
True worth is in being, not seeming. Nobility [*or* The Noble Life]. Alice Cary. MaRV; OHFP; OQP; PTA-1; QP-2; WBLP
Truelove, A. Nicholas Grimald. *See* True Love, A.
Truelove. *Unknown, tr. fr. German by* Jethro Bithell. AWP
Truest of Sages Are You to Me. August, Graf von Platen, *tr. fr. German by* Edwin Morgan. AnGP
Truest poet is not one, The. The Poet. T. A. Daly. JKCP
Trull came out of nothing and was there, The. Visitation. Vincent Starrett. DaM
Truly buzzards/ Around my sky are circling! Glyph. *Unknown.* LiTA
Truly Great. W. H. Davies. ChMo; CMP; HBV; OBMV; OBVV; PCN; POTT
Truly I want to die. Parting. Sappho. GrL; OxBG
Truly, My Satan, thou art but a Dunce. To the Accuser Who Is the God of This World [*or* Epilogue]. Blake. *Fr.* The Gates of Paradise. FaBoEn; NBE; TrGrPo; UnPo (1st ed.); ViBoPo
Truly the light is sweet. The Light Is Sweet. Ecclesiastes, Bible, *O.T.* FaPON
Truly, the light is sweet. A Man's Bread. Josephine Preston Peabody. YeAr
Truly, the South Mountain. *Unknown, tr. fr. Chinese.* WhP
Truly, there is no beauty in Fort Worth, no song. Beauty Is Elsewhere. Boyce House. HiLiAm
Truly these women are like birds; they take. Birds. "Seumas O'Sullivan." OxBI
Trumbull Stickney. George Cabot Lodge. LBMV
Trump hath blown, The. The Lonely Bugle Grieves. Grenville Mellen. *Fr.* Ode on the Celebration of the Battle of Bunker Hill, June 17, 1825. AA; BAP; IDAH; LEAP
Trumpet, The. Ilya Ehrenburg, *tr. fr. Russian by* Y. Hornstein. BoRS; TrJP
Trumpet, The. Edward Thomas. BLV; HBMV; MBP; MoBrPo; OHIP; POTE; TSW
Trumpet, The. *Unknown, tr. fr. Arabic by* Sir Edwin Arnold. OnPM
Trumpet and Flute. Gunnar Hernaes, *tr. fr. Norwegian by* Martin S. Allwood. LiTW
Trumpet Call, The. Dmitry Sergeyevich Merezhkovsky, *tr. fr. Russian by* Babette Deutsch. TrRV
Trumpet for Yuletide. Louis J. Sanker. JKCP (1955 ed.)
Trumpet of a prophecy, The! O wind. The West Wind. Shelley. *Fr.* Ode to the West Wind. PCH
Trumpet of the Dawn, The. Clinton Scollard. NLK
Trumpet Song. Tennyson. *Fr.* Idylls of the King: The Coming of Arthur. BPN
(War Song, The.) BHV
Trumpet sounds it in my soul, De. Moanin'. *Unknown.* ABF
Trumpet-Vine Arbour, The. Amy Lowell. *Fr.* 1777. MAPA; NP
Trumpeter, The. Ai Ching, *tr. fr. Chinese.* WhP
Trumpeter, The. Thomas Wentworth Higginson. BLP; LBAP
Trumpeter, The. *Unknown.* CoMu
Trumpets. Enter a King, in the sunset glare. Stage Directions. William Rose Benét. ShBV-2
Trumpet's loud clangor, The. The Instruments [*or* Fife and Drum]. Dryden. *Fr.* Song for St. Cecilia's Day. BLV; GN

Trumpets of Doolkarnein, The. Leigh Hunt. LPS-2
Trumpets of the Mind, The. Victor Hugo, *tr. fr. French.* WoL
Trumpets were curled away, the drum beat no more, The. The Swan. Stephen Spender. UnS
Trundled from/ the strangeness of the sea. The Sea-Elephant. William Carlos Williams. LiTA
Trus' an' Smile. B. Y. Williams. BLRP
Trust. Frances Anne Kemble. *See* Faith.
Trust. Lizette Woodworth Reese. AA; OBAV
Trust. Christina Rossetti. Monna Innominata, XIII. HiLiEn; VA
("If I could trust mine own self with your fate.") EmBrPo; ViPo
Trust; a Song. Eben E. Rexford. BLRP
Trust and Obedience. *Unknown.* BLRP
Trust in God. Addison. *See* Pastoral Hymn.
Trust in God and Do the Right, *sel.* Norman Macleod.
Trust in God. BLRP
Trust in Jesus. Josiah Conder. BePJ
Trust in the Lord: So shalt thou dwell. Psalm XXXVII, Bible. *O.T. Paraphrased by* Charles Frederic Sheldon. BLRP
Trust in Women. *Unknown.* BOHV; NA
("When nettles in winter bring forth roses red.") LO
Trust me, I have not earned your dear rebuke. Christina Rossetti. Monna Innominata. VI. EmBrPo; ViPo
Trust not his wanton tears. Wily Cupid [*or* Aeliana's Ditty *or* Of Cupid]. Henry Chettle. *Fr.* Piers Plainness' Seven Years' Prenticeship. ALV; EG; EIL; OBSC
Trust not the treason of those smiling [*or* smyling] look[e]s. Amoretti, XLVII. Spenser. BLV; BoLiVe; LO; PeBoSo; TrGrPo
Trust not to tears, Philaenis, nay. Posidippus, *tr. fr. Greek by* J. A. Pott. GrPo
Trust not too much, fair youth, unto thy feature. White Primit Falls. *Unknown.* ChTr; EG
Trust the Form of Airy Things. Henry Harington. ElSeCe; LO
(Song: "Trust the form of airy things.") SeCL
Trust the Great Artist. Thomas Curtis Clark. WBLP
Trust Thou Thy Love. Ruskin. OBEV; OBVV; VA
Trust Thy Last Friend against the World. *Unknown, tr. fr. Chinese by* William Jennings. BoFr
Trusting Jesus. Grace B. Renfrow. BePJ
Trusty, Dusky, Vivid, True. Robert Louis Stevenson. *See* My Wife.
Trusty Learning A. B. C. Eliza Lee Follen. SAS
Truth. "Æ." AnIL; BMEP; GTML; GTSL; MoBrPo; TOP
Truth. W. H. Auden. MaRV
Truth. Erik Blomberg, *tr. fr. Swedish by* Charles W. Stork. AnSL
Truth. Robert Browning. *Fr.* A Death in the Desert. MaRV
Truth. Chaucer. *See* Balade de Bon Conseyl.
Truth, *sel.* William Cowper.
Simple Faith. OBEC
Truth, The. W. H. Davies. FaBoTw
Truth. John Donne. *See* Satire III: "Kind pity chokes my spleen . . ."
Truth. Max Eastman. *See* Invocation: "Truth, be more precious to me than the eyes."
Truth. Ben Jonson. *See* To James Warre.
Truth, The. Archibald Lampman. CaP; CPG; OCL
Truth. Cecil Francis Lloyd. CaP; OCL
Truth. John Masefield. WGRP
Truth. Howard Nemerov. MoVE
Truth. Jessica Nelson North. HBVY; NP
Truth. Coventry Patmore. *See* Magna Est Veritas.
Truth, The? John Cowper Powys. BAP
Truth about B. F., The. Albert Stillman. InMe
Truth about Horace, The. Eugene Field. BOHV; InMe; InP; LHV
Truth—and let us then restrain. Pedro Calderón de la Barca. *Fr.* Life's a Dream. TeCS
Truth and Love Abide. James Russell Lowell. *Fr.* Elegy on the Death of Dr. Channing. MaRV
Truth, be more precious to me than the eyes. Invocation [*or* Truth]. Max Eastman. BAP; CP; MaRV; NV; OQP; QP-1; WGRP
Truth, Beauty, Love, in these are formed a ring. The Trinity. Marian Osborne. CaP; CPG
Truth, Crushed to Earth. Bryant. *Fr.* The Battlefield. BAP; MaRV; NeHB; OQP; QP-2
(Truth, the Invincible.) TreF
Truth Doth Truth Deserve. Sir Philip Sidney. *Fr.* Arcadia. HBV; LiTL
(Advice to the Same.) SiPS
Truth for him was like a tree, The. Exaggerator. Mark Van Doren. AnFE; CoAnAm
Truth Has Perished. Ulma Seligman, *tr. fr. Yiddish by* Joseph Leftwich. TrJP
Truth in Poetry. George Crabbe. *Fr.* The Village. OBEC; SeCePo
Truth is a golden sunset far away. Threnody. I. O. Scherzo. HoPM
Truth is as old as God. Emily Dickinson. MoAmPo
Truth is enough for prose. At the Mermaid Cafeteria. Christopher Morley. BAP; PFY; PoeMoYo
Truth Is Great, The. Coventry Patmore. *See* Magna Est Veritas.
Truth is love and love is truth. Mendacity. A. E. Coppard. GTBS-W; LiTL; LiTM; OBMV
Truth is that there comes a time, The. Sad Strains of a Gay Waltz. Wallace Stevens. OxBA
Truth is the trial of itself. To James Warre [*or* Truth]. Ben Jonson. EV-2; PG
Truth Is Within. Robert Browning. *Fr.* Paracelsus, Pt. I. MaRV
Truth it is, few doubt but fewer trust, A. This Life and the Next. Edward Young. *Fr.* Night Thoughts. GrCo-1
Truth-loving Persians do not dwell upon. The Persian Version. Robert Graves. LiTB; LiTM (rev. ed.); SiTL
Truth needs no champions: in the infinite deep. Truth and Love Abide. James Russell Lowell. *Fr.* Elegy on the Death of Dr. Channing. MaRV
Truth Never Dies. *Unknown.* OQP; QP-2; WBLP
Truth of It, The. Theognis, *tr. fr. Greek by* J. M. Edmonds. GrR
Truth of Two. Pedro Salinas, *tr. fr. Spanish by* Eleanor L. Turnbull. CoSP
"Truth Shall Make You Free, The." Chaucer. *See* Balade de Bon Conseyl.
Truth, so far, in my book; the truth which draws. Elizabeth Barrett Browning. *Fr.* Aurora Leigh, VII. WGRP
Truth, the Invincible. Bryant. *See* Truth Crushed to Earth.
Truthful James. Bret Harte. CenHV
Truth's Complaint over England. Thomas Lodge. ACP (1952 ed.)
Truth's Integrity. *Unknown.* *See* Love Will Find Out the Way.
Truths That Never Can Be Proved, The. Tennyson. In Memoriam A. H. H., CXXIX, CXXX, CXXXI. MaRV
Truxton's Victory. *Unknown.* PAH
Try Again. Eliza Cook. *See* King Bruce and the Spider.
Try Again. *Unknown.* *See* Try, Try Again.
Try Smiling. *Unknown.* BLPA; FaFP; WBLP
Try the Uplook. *Unknown.* BLRP
Try This Once. *Unknown.* WBLP
Try Tropic. Genevieve Taggard. MAP; MoAmPo
Try, Try Again. *Unknown, at. to* William Edward Hickson, *also to* T. H. Palmer. FaFP; FaPON, *st.* 1; PTA-2; TreF
(Try Again.) TVC
Trying to Forget. Emily Dickinson. *See* Bereaved of all . . .
Trylle the ball, again, my Jacke. *Unknown.* BOL
Tryst, The. Valery Yakovlevich Bryusov, *tr. fr. Russian by* Babette Deutsch. TrRV
Tryst, The. E. V. Knox. CenHV
Tryst, The. Li Yu, *tr. fr. Chinese by* Ch'u Ta'kao. ChLP
Tryst, The. Whitney Montgomery. BLA
Tryst, The. Christopher Morley. ALV; BOHV; HBMV
Tryst, A. Louise Chandler Moulton. HBV
Tryst. Stepan Petrovich Shchipachev, *tr. fr. Russian by* Jack Lindsay. RuPo
Tryst, The. Shen Yüeh, *tr. fr. Chinese by* Henry H. Hart. PoHN
Tryst, The. William Soutar. GoTS; GTBS-D; NeBP
Tryst, The. Lauchlan MacLean Watt. MaRV
Tryst after Death, The, *abr. Unknown, tr. fr. Old Irish by* Kuno Meyer. LiTW; OnYI
(Tryst with Death, The, *tr. by* Seán O'Faoláin.) SiB
Tryst of Queen Hynde, The. "Fiona Macleod." BMEP
Tryst of the Night, The. May C. G. Byron. VA
Tryst with Death, The. *Unknown.* *See* Tryst after Death, The.
Tryste Noël. Louise Imogen Guiney. HBV; JKCP; LBMV; LEAP; OBVV; SDH
(Five Carols for Christmastide, I.) ISi
Tryste with Morfudd true I made, A. The Mist. *Unknown, formerly at. to* Dafydd ap Gwilym. PrWP
Trysting, A. Richard Dehmel, *tr. fr. German by* Jethro Bithell. AWP
Trysting Path, The. Albert E. S. Smythe. CPG
Tsar Lazar and Tsaritsa Militsa, *sel. Unknown, tr. fr. Serbian by* George Rapall Noyes *and* Leonard Bacon.
"And when he was himself again, she questioned him withal." PoFr
Tségihi. A Prayer of the Night Chant. *Unknown, tr. fr. Navajo Indian by* Washington Matthews. ExPo
Tsigane's Canzonet, The. Edward King. AA
Tsoqalem, the Cowichan Monster, *sel.* Lionel Haweis.
"And so the wrinkled squaw." CPG
Tsu Mei is early dead. Reading the Poems of an Absent Friend. Ou-yang Hsiu. OnPC
"Tu Non Se' in Terra, Si Come Tu Credi . . ." Kathleen Raine. NeBP
Tu Quoque. Austin Dobson. BOHV
Tu-Whit To-Who. *See* When Icicles Hang by the Wall.

Tu-whit, tu-whit, tu-whee! *See* Te-whit! te-whit! te-whee!
"Tu-whitt, Tu-whitt, Tu-whoo, Tu-whoo." "Good Night," Says the Owl. Lady Erskine-Crum. BoTP
Tua Mariit Wemen and the Wedo, The. William Dunbar. GoTS
Sels.
"Thus drave they out that dear night with dances full noble." BSV
"Upon the midsummer even, merriest of nichtis." BSV
Widow Speaks, The. PoEL-1
Tub, The. George S. Chappell. DDA
Tubal Cain. Charles Mackay. BMEP; GTBS; LPS-2; MPB; PIR; TVSH; WBLP
Tubby Hook. Arthur Guiterman. TSWC
Tuberculosis. Victor Robinson. PoP
Tuberose. Louis James Block. AA
Tuck the earth, fold the sod. Dirge. William Alexander Percy. HBMV
Tucked-up Skirts. *Unknown, tr. fr. Chinese by* E. D. Edwards. ChLP
Tucking the Baby In. Curtis May. HBV
Tudor Aspersions. R. A. Piddington. FiBHP
Tudor Church Music. Sylvia Townsend Warner. UnS
Tudor indeed is gone and every rose. Ezra Pound. *Fr.* The Pisan Cantos. FaBoTw
Tudor Rose, The. Sebastian Brant, *tr. fr. German by* Alexander Barclay. *Fr.* The Ship of Fools. ACP
Tudur Aled. Davies Aberpennar. MoWP
Tuft of Flowers, The. Robert Frost. AmP; AmPP; AnNE; AtBAP; AWP; CoBMV; CV; GoYe; HBV; HBVY; IAP; InP; JAWP; LaNeLa; LiTA; MAP; MoAB; MoAmPo; MoPW; NeMA; OxBA; PC; ReaPo; SeCeV; TSW; TSWC; TwP; WBP
Tuft of Kelp, The. Herman Melville. ChTr; RO
Tug-of-War, A. M. M. Hutchinson. BoTP
Tug pulls, tightening the steel strand, The. From Le Havre. Charles G. Bell. NePoAm
Tugged Hand, The. W. H. Davies. MoPW
Tugs. James S. Tippett. FaPON; GFA
Tulip. Humbert Wolfe. BLV; MBP; MoBrPo; NP; TSW
Tulip Garden, A. Amy Lowell. VOD
Tulip Queens. Hilda Mary Hooke. CPG
Tulip Tree. Sacheverell Sitwell. MBP; MM; MoBrPo
Tulips. Padraic Colum. ImOP
Tulips. Margaret Bell Houston. LS
Tulips, The. Thomas Tickell. *Fr.* Kensington Garden. BeR
Tulips in the window. Tulips. Margaret Bell Houston. LS
Tulips now are pushing up, The. April. Eunice Tietjens. YeAr
Tullie's Love, *sels.* Robert Greene.
Mars and Venus. OBSC
(Song: "Mars in a fury 'gainst love's brightest queen.") CaAE
(Sonnet or Dittie: "Mars in a fury . . .") LoBV
Shepherd's Ode, The. OBSC
When Gods Had Fram'd the Sweet of Women's Face. ReIE
(Love and Jealousy.) ElL
Tullochgorum. John Skinner. BSV; EBSV; GoTS; OBEC
Tumadir al-Khansa For Her Brother. *Unknown, tr. fr. Arabic by* E. Powys Mathers. *Fr.* The Thousand and One Nights. AWP; JAWP; PG (1945 ed.); WBP
Tumble, The. Ann Taylor. HBVY
Tumble me down, and I will sit. To Fortune. Robert Herrick. SeCV-1
Tumbling Doggie. *Unknown.* SAS
Tumbling Jack goes clickety-clack. *Unknown.* RIS
Tumult. Charles Enoch Wheeler. PoNe
Tumult Ends, The. Roland Robinson. NeLNL
Tumult in a Syrian town had place, A. The Great Physician. Sadi. *Fr.* The Bustan. AWP; OuHeWo
Tumult of death, dizziness hath seized me, The. Elegy. Moses Rimos of Majorca. TrJP
Tumult of my fretted mind, The. Self-Analysis. Anna Wickham. BLV; MBP; MoBrPo; TrGrPo (1942 ed.)
Tumult, weeping, many new ghosts. Snow Storm. Tu Fu. OnPC
Tumultous sea, whose wrath and foam are spent. Eumares. Asclepiades. AWP, JAWP; WBP
Tumultuously move against my heart. Invasion. Hubert Witheford. AnNZ
Tumultuously void of a clean scheme. Octavus, II. E. A. Robinson. CoV
Tune me for life again, oh, quiet Musician. A Prayer after Illness. Violet Alleyn Storey. TrPWD
Tune Me, O Lord, into One Harmony. Christina Rossetti. TrPWD
Tune of [the] Seven Towers, The. William Morris. PoVP; ViPP; VLEP
Tune on my pipe the praises of my Love. In Praise of His Daphnis. Sir John Wotton. ElL
Tune on my pipe the praises of my Love. Of His Mistress [*or* Melicertus' Description of His Mistress]. Robert Greene. *Fr.* Menaphon. ElL; ReIE
Tune persists in nature, ever new, A. Song of Nature. Elizabeth Selden. BoFr
Tune thy music to thy heart. Heart's Music. *Unknown.* OBEV (new ed.)
Tunnel, The. Hart Crane. *Fr.* The Bridge. AmP; LiTA; LiTG; MAP; MoAB; MoAmPo; MoVE; NePA; OxBA; PoFS; TCPD
Tunnel Beach. James K. Baxter. AnNZ
Tunnelled in solid blackness creeps. Mole. Aldous Huxley. LBBV
Tunning [*or* Tunnyng] of Elinour Rumming, The. John Skelton. *See* Elinor Rumming.
Tuppence Coloured. Babette Deutsch. PFY
Turbine, The. Harriet Monroe. NP
Turbulent Waters, The. *Unknown, tr. fr. Chinese.* WhP
Turf Stacks. Louis MacNeice. *See* Among These Turf-Stacks.
Turin beneath, on the green banks of the Po. At the Tombs of the House of Savoy. William Jay Smith. NePoAm-2
Turk and Pope. Robert Wisdom. ReIE
Turk by the name of Haroun, A. *Unknown.* SiTL
Turk in Armenia, The. Sir William Watson. BMEP; PoFr
Turkey and the Ant, The. John Gay. OTPC (1923 ed.)
Turkey-Buzzards. Mark Van Doren. BLA
Turkey-Cock. D. H. Lawrence. AnEnPo
Turkey in the Straw. *Unknown.* AS (A *vers., with music;* B *and* C *vers.*); FaFP; TrAS, *with music;* TreFS; YaD
Turkey is my favorite bird, The. Thanksgiving. Margarete Münsterberg. GFA
Turkey Time. *Unknown.* PCH
Turkish Lady, The. *Unknown. See* Young Beichan.
Turkish Legend, A. Thomas Bailey Aldrich. GN; HBV; HBVY; OTPC (1946 ed.); YT
Turkish Ode of Mesihi, A. *Tr. by* Sir William Jones. RO
Turkish Tradition, A. *Unknown.* PEOR
Turkish Trench Dog, The. Geoffrey Dearmer. HiLiEn; LBBV; ShGoBo
Turn Again to Life. Mary Lee Hall. MaRV
Turn All Thy Thoughts to Eyes. Thomas Campion. LiTL; ViBoPo
Turn, and we stand in the heart of things, A. By the Fireside. Robert Browning. BMEP; EV-5; SN; VLEP
Turn apple blooms to silver. Magic. John Farrar. LEAP
Turn Back, O Man. Clifford Bax. MaRV
Turn back the leaves of history. On yon Pacific shore. The Sunset City. Isabel Ambler Gilman. PTA-2
Turn Back, You Wanton Flyer. Thomas Campion. EnLi-1
(Basia.) GTSL
Turn, Fortune, Turn Thy Wheel. Tennyson. *Fr.* Idylls of the King: The Marriage of Geraint. TVSH; VLEP
(Enid's Song.) BPN; LPS-3
(Fortune.) BHV
Turn from that girl. I Shall Laugh Purely. Robinson Jeffers. CrMA; LiTA; LiTM (rev. ed.); WaP
"Turn, gentle hermit of the dale." Edwin and Angelina [*or* The Hermit]. Goldsmith. *Fr.* The Vicar of Wakefield. CEP; EV-3; LPS-1; OTPC
Turn I my looks unto the skies. Rosader's Second Sonetto [*or* Rosader's Sonnet]. Thomas Lodge. *Fr.* Rosalynde; or, Euphues' Golden Legacy. EPP; OBSC; SiCE; TuPP
Turn Me to My Yellow Leaves. William Stanley Braithwaite. BANP
Turn not aside, Shepherd, to see. Help, Good Shepherd. Ruth Pitter. OxBoCh
Turn not to the prophet's page, O Son! For the Holy Family by Michelangelo. Dante Gabriel Rossetti. GoBC
Turn, now, tired mind unto your rest. Forests. Walter de la Mare. ChMo; CMP
Turn o' the Year. Katharine Tynan. HBV; NLK
Turn o'er thy outward man, and judge aright. The Outward Man Accused. Edward Taylor. *Fr.* God's Determinations. LiTA
Turn of a Dragonfly's Wing, The. Simonides, *tr. fr. Greek by* T. F. Higham. GrL; OxBG
(Wingèd Change, *tr. by* John Herman Merivale.) GrR
Turn of the Road, The. Alice Rollit Coe. HBV
Turn of the Road, The. Fannie Stearns Davis. HBMV
Turn on Your Side and Bear the Day to Me. George Barker. AtBAP
Turn out more ale, turn up the light. Dum Vivimus Vigilamus [*or* Vigilemus]. Charles Henry Webb. AA; LEAP
Turn over world! O monstrous world! Universe into Stone. A. J. M. Smith. PeCV
Turn to the Grass. Mary Gilmore. MoAuPo
Turn, turn, for my cheeks they burn. The Milkmaid's Song. Sydney Dobell. LPS-1
Turn, turn, my wheel! Turn round and round. The Potter's Song. Longfellow. *Fr.* Kéramos. PoEL-5; ReTS; YT
Turn, Turn Thy Beauteous Face Away. Beaumont *and* Fletcher. *Fr.* Love's Cure. AtBAP
(Song: "Turn, turn thy beauteous face away.") PoEL-2
Turn, turn your rein. Night of Joy. Ibn Abi Ruh. MooP
Turn under, plow. Plowman's Song. Raymond Knister. CaP
Turn, Willie Macintosh. Willie Macintosh. *Unknown.* ESPB; OBB; OxBoLi; ViBoFo
Turn with me from the city's clamorous street. Thomas à Kempis. Richard Rogers Bowker. AA
Turn Ye to Me. "Christopher North." EBSV

Turncoat, The. LeRoi Jones. NeAP
Turned from the "eau-forte/ Par Jaquemart." Mauberley. Ezra Pound. *Fr.* Hugh Selwyn Mauberley. CoBMV; CoV; LiTA; LiTM (rev. ed.); MoPo
Turned to jade are the boy's rosy cheeks. Poems in Depression, at Wei Village, 2. Po Chü-i. TrCh
Turners Dish of Lentten Stuffe; or, A Galymaufery. William Turner. CoMu
Turnimspike, The. Dougal Graham. EBSV
Turning, The. Philip Booth. NePoAm-2
Turning, The. Philip Murray. NePoAm
Turning and turning in the widening gyre. The Second Coming. W. B. Yeats. AtBAP; CoBMV; CoEV; EnL; EnLP; ExPo; FaBoEn; FaBoMo; GTBS-W; HoPM; InPo; LiTB; LiTG; LiTM; LoBV; MaPo; MoAB; MoVE; OAEP (2d ed.); OxBI; Po; PoE; PoFS; PoLFOT; ReaPo; ReMP; RiBV; SeCePo; SeCeV; TwHP; TwP; UnPo (3d ed.); WaP
Turning Aside from Battles. Sextus Propertius, *tr. fr. Latin by* Ezra Pound. WaaP
Turning Dervish, The. Arthur Symons. MBP; MoBrPo
Turning down, goatherd, by the oaks, you'll see. The Prayer in the Bower. Leigh Hunt. ERP
Turning from Plato to the rocky sergeant. Apocalypse. John Frederick Nims. MiAP
Turning from Shelley's sculptured face aside. On a Grave in Christ-Church, Hants. Oscar Fay Adams. AA
Turning from these with awe, once more I rais'd. Keats. *Fr.* The Fall of Hyperion, I. CBE; NBE
Turning, I found the gauze grow thin. Vision of St. Obadiah. *Unknown.* CAG
Turning my chariot I yoke my horses and go [*or* drive]. The Nineteen Han Poems, XI [*or* Seventeen Old Poems, 10]. *Unknown, tr. fr. Chinese.* TrCh; WhP
Turning of the Babies in the Bed, The. Paul Laurence Dunbar. MAP; MoAmPo (1942 ed.); MotAn; NeMA
Turning of the Leaves, The. Vernon Watkins. FaBoMo; NeBP
Turning of the year, The. Rain. Ch'en Fu Liang. PoHN
Turning the secrets from her pack of cards. A Fortune-Teller. Witter Bynner. HBMV; TCAP
Turning to go, she feels her hand in his. Reconciliation. Frank M. Towne. PreP
Turning Year, The. Su T'ung-po, *tr. fr. Chinese by* Kenneth Rexroth. OnPC
Turnip Seller, The. Samuel Johnson. *See* If the Man Who Turnips Cries.
Turnstile, The. William Barnes. CH; OBVV
Turpin and the Lawyer. *Unknown.* ABS
(Dick Turpin and the Lawyer.) ViBoFo
Turquoise Bowl, The. Kathryn White Ryan. BAP
Turris Eburnea. Aubrey Thomas De Vere. *Fr.* May Carols. PoVP
Turris Eburnea. *Unknown.* GoBC
Turtle, The. Ogden Nash. FaFP; FiBHP; LiTM; NePA; SiTL; WhC
(Autres Bêtes, Autres Mœurs.) NaMP; TreFS
Turtle, The. James Schevill. FiMAP
Turtle, The. *Unknown.* PAH
Turtle and Flamingo, The. James Thomas Fields. BOHV; HBV
(Song of the Turtle and Flamingo.) GN
Turtle, clam, and crab as well, The. Covering the Subject. Richard Armour. WaKn
Turtle-Dove, The ("Oh! don't you see the turtle-dove"). *Unknown.* OxBoLi
("Oh, don't you see the turtle-dove.") LO
Turtle Dove, The. Geoffrey Hill. NePoEA
Turtle-Dove's Nest, The. *Unknown, sometimes at. to* Ann Hawkshaw. HBVY, *abr.*; OTPC (1923 ed.); SAS
("High in the pine-tree.") BoTP
Turtle is a simple byrde, The. *Unknown.* SeCSL
Turtle lives 'twixt plated decks, The. The Turtle [*or* Autres Bêtes, Autres Mœurs]. Ogden Nash. FaFP; FiBHP; LiTM; NAMP; SiTL; TreFS; WhC
Turtle on yon withered bough, The. Song of Thyrsis. Philip Freneau. *Fr.* Female Frailty. AA; AnFE; APA; APW; CoAnAm; HBV; LBAP; LEAP; LiTA; OnPM; PR; ViBoPo
Turtle Soup. "Lewis Carroll." *Fr.* Alice's Adventures in Wonderland, *ch.* 10. BrR; InMe; PA
Turtle-tortle, what dost thou there? Play-Song. *Unknown.* LiTW
Turtle Town. Helen Wing. GFA
Turvey Top. William Sawyer. BOHV; NA
Tuscan Cypress, *sels.* Agnes Mary Frances Robinson.
"Ah love, I cannot die," XV
(Rispetto.) AV; HBMV
"Ah me, you well might wait," VIII. VA
"Let us forget we loved each other," XII.
(Rispetto.) AV; HBMV
"Love me today and think not," IV. VA
"What good is there, ah me," II.
(Rispetto.) AV; HBMV
"When I am dead," VII. VA
Tuscan Folk Songs. *Unknown, tr. fr. Italian into Scottish by* Edwin Morgan. LyPI
Tuscan, that wanderest through the realms of gloom. Dante. Longfellow. AA; AnNE; BAV; CoBA; IAP; ReaPo; TCAP
Tuscany. V. Sackville-West. PtOT
Tush hang it, have at all, says Curio. Henry Parrot. SiCE
Tusitala. Andrew Lang. VOD
Tuskegee. Leslie Pinckney Hill. BANP; PoNe
Tusks of Blood, The. Samuel Greenberg. MoPo
Tusks that clashed in mighty brawls, The. On the Vanity of Earthly Greatness. Arthur Guiterman. HoPM; NAMP; TrJP; WhC
Tutelage, The. Robert Mowry Bell. AA
Tutor Who Tooted the Flute, A. Carolyn Wells. *See* Limerick: "Tutor who tooted the flute, A."
Tutto è Sciolto. James Joyce. MM; OBMV; OxBI; TriL
Twa Brothers, The (*diff. versions*). *Unknown.* ATP; BaBo (A *and* B *vers.*); Ch; Em-1; ESPB (A *and* B *vers.*); EV-2; OBB; PreP; ViBoFo (A *and* B *vers.*)
(Two Little Boys.) ABS; BaBo
Twa Corbies, The. *Unknown.* AnFE; BCEP; BoLiVe; BSV; CaAE; CBOV; CH; CoEV; DaM; EBSV; EnL; EnLi-1; EnLit; EnSB; ESPB; EV-2; ExPo; FaBoCh; GoTS; GTBS; GTBS-D; GTBS-W; GTSE; GTSL; HBV; InP; InPo; LEAP; LH; LiTL; LoGBV; OBB; OBEV; SeCePo; SeCeV; ShBV-2; StPo; TOP
("As I was walking all alane.") LO
(Three Ravens, The, B *vers.*) BaBo; ViBoPo
(Two Corbies, The.) Po
Twa Dogs, The. Burns. CEP
Borrowing Trouble, *sel.* BLP
Twa Knights, The. *Unknown.* ESPB
Twa Magicians, The. *Unknown.* BaBo; ESPB
Twa race doon by the Gatehope-Slack. Solway Sands. Elizabeth Craigmyle. VA
Twa Sisters, The. *Unknown. See* Two Sisters, The.
Twain that, in twining, before in the twine, The. A Twister. *Unknown.* SiTL
Twain that were foes, while Mary lived, are fled. His Lady's Death. Pierre de Ronsard. *Fr.* Amours de Marie. AWP; PrPoCR
Twanging Gold. Winifred Welles. MuM
'Twas a balmy summer evening, and a goodly crowd was there. The Face on [*or* upon] the Floor. H. Antoine D'Arcy. BeLS; BLPA; FaBoBe; FaFP; HBV; NeHB; PTA-1; TreF; YaD
'Twas a balmy summer morning. The Dawning of the Day. James Clarence Mangan. GoBC; TIP
'Twas a busy day in the courtroom, and a curious crowd was there. The Bank Thief. J. R. Farrell. BeLS; BLPA
'Twas a calm and peaceful evening in a camp called Arapahoe. Buckskin Joe [*or* Araphoe]. *Unknown.* CoSo; CSF
'Twas a Christmas morning. Stagolee. *Unknown.* ABF
'Twas a dangerous cliff, as they freely confessed. A Fence or an Ambulance. Joseph Malins. BLPA; PTA-1
'Twas a fierce night when old Mawgan died. Mawgan of Melhuach. Robert Stephen Hawker. EPN; VA
'Twas a Friday morn when we set sail. The Mermaid. *Unknown.* LiTG; SiTL; TreF
'Twas a grand display was the prince's ball. Baron Renfrew's Ball. Charles Graham Halpine. PAH
'Twas a Jacqueminot rose. A Rose. Arlo Bates. HBV; PR
'Twas a jolly old pedagogue, long ago. The Jolly Old Pedagogue. George Arnold. HBV; LPS-2; OnPP; TreFS
Twas a Jubilee Day, our first Mother's first Daughter. Mother Mary Xavier. Benjamin Dionysius Hill. PraNu
'Twas a little sermon preached to me. The Little Messenger of Love. *Unknown.* PEOR
'Twas a long journey lay before us. Journey to Brundusium. Horace. WoL
'Twas a Marechal of France, and he fain would honour gain. The Bold Dragoon. Sir Walter Scott. BHV
'Twas a new feeling—something more. Did Not [*or* Quantum Est Quod Desit]. Thomas Moore. ALV; EnLoPo
'Twas a pleasant summer's morning. As I'd Nothing Else to Do. Herbert Fry. TreFS
'Twas a pretty little maiden. The Lost Pleiad. Arthur Reed Ropes. BOHV
'Twas a sage said it, and the saying's good. Scevola de Sainte-Marthe. *Fr.* The Art of Bringing Up Children. PoP
'Twas a stylish congregation, that of Theophrastus Brown. Trouble in the Amen Corner. T. C. Harbaugh. BLPA; PTA-2
'Twas a terrible moment! Lee at the Wilderness. Mary Evelyn Moore Davis. BIG
'Twas a tough task, believe it, thus to tame. Upon Dr. Davies' British Grammar. James Howell. PrWP
'Twas a wonderful brave fight. The Fight at Sumter [*or* Fort Sumter]. *Unknown.* BIG; PAH
'Twas after a supper of Norfolk brawn. Turvey Top. William Sawyer. BoHV; NA
'Twas after dread Pultowa's day. Mazeppa. Byron. EmBrPo; EnRP

'Twas all along the Binder Line. Sensitive Sydney. Wallace Irwin. FiBHP
'Twas all on board a ship down in a southern sea. The Golden Vanity. *Unknown.* BaBo
'Twas all prepared; and from the rock. The Fiery Cross. Sir Walter Scott. *Fr.* The Lady of the Lake, III. ERP
'Twas an ancient legend they used to tell. The Demon on the Roof. Josephine Pollard. PEOR
'Twas an evening in November. *Unknown.* CenHV
'Twas April when she came to town. Bessie Brown, M.D. Samuel Minturn Peck. BOHV; LauV; PR
'Twas at Assisi, of a summer's eve. A Sermon of Saint Francis. Edward F. Garesché. SaFP
'Twas at thatt hour of beauty when the setting sun. Robert Bridges. *Fr.* The Testament of Beauty. MoVE; OxBoCh
'Twas at the Bridal Time of Flowers. Johannes Jørgensen, *tr. fr. Danish by* Charles W. Stork. BoDS
'Twas at the Cimarron Crossing. Oliver Wiggins. "Stanley Vestal." IHA
'Twas at the close of that dark morn. Trafalgar. *Unknown.* SG
'Twas at the landing-place that's just below Mount Wyse. Port Admiral. Frederick Marryat. SG
'Twas at the Matin Hour. *Unknown.* OHIP
'Twas at the Pictures, Child, We Met. A. P. Herbert. LauV; WhC
'Twas at the royal feast, for Persia won. Alexander's Feast; or, The Power of Music. Dryden. ACP; AEV; AnFE; ATP; BCEP; BLV; BoLiVe; BrBE; CaAE; CEP; CoBE; EiPP; EM-1; EnL; EnLi-1; EnLit; EPP; EPS; EV-3; FiP; GEPC; GN; GoBC; GTBS; GTBS-D; GTBS-W; GTSE; GTSL; HBV; LEAP; LH; LiA; LiTB; LoBV; LPS-3; OAEP; OBS; OtMeF; OuHeWo; PIAE; PoE; PreP; REAL; SeCeV; SeCV-2; SeEP; TCEP; TOP; TrGrPo; TwCrTr; TyEnPo; WHA
'Twas at the season when the Earth upsprings. Shelley. *Fr.* Prince Athanese. CBE
'Twas at the silent, solemn hour. William and Margaret. David Mallet. BSV; CEP; EBSV; EPP; EV-3; OBEC
'Twas at thy door, O friend! and not at mine. The Two Angels. Longfellow. UnW
'Twas August, and the fierce sun overhead. East London. Matthew Arnold. BMEP; BPN; EM-2; EmBrPo; EPN; MaRV; OAEP; OHIP; PoVP; StJW; VLEP; WGRP
'Twas autumn daybreak gold and wild. The Three Beggars. Walter de la Mare. RIS
'Twas battered and scarred, and the auctioneer. The Touch of the Master's Hand. Myra Brooks Welch. BLPA; PoToHe (new ed.)
'Twas Bedford Special Assize, one daft Mid-summer's Day. Ned Bratts. Robert Browning. VLEP
'Twas beyond at Macreddin. at Owen Doyle's weddin'. Herself and Myself. Patrick Joseph McCall. TIP
'Twas brillig, and the slithy toves. Jabberwocky. "Lewis Carroll." *Fr.* Through the Looking Glass. AIDL; ALV; BLV; BoChLi; BoN; EnLi-2 (1949 ed.); FaBoBe; FaFP; FaPON; FiBHP; GoTP; HBV; HoPM; InP; LBN; LEAP; LiTB; LiTG; MBP; NA; NAMP; OnSP; OTPC; PIAE; PoRA; PoVP; PreP; PYM; RAR; RIS; SeCeV; ShBV-2; SiTL; TiPo; TreF; TrGrPo; ViP; WhC
'Twas brussels, and the loos liège. Somewhere-in-Europe-Wocky. F. G. Hartswick. BOHV
'Twas but a poor little room: a farm servant's loft in a garret. Dorothy's Room. Arthur Joseph Munby. *Fr.* Dorothy; a Country Story. VA
'Twas but a single rose. Upon a Virgin Kissing a Rose. Robert Herrick. SeCV-1
'Twas but last night I traversed the Atlantic's furrow'd face. To Duffy in Prison. Thomas D'Arcy McGee. TIP
'Twas by the bank of beating sea we stood. The Ride to Doom. Euripides. *Fr.* Hippolytus. GrR
'Twas Captain Church, bescarred and brown. King Philip's Last Stand. Clinton Scollard. PAH
'Twas Christmas Eve, the snow lay deep. When the Christ Child Came. Frederic E. Weatherly. OHIP
'Twas down at Dan McDevitt's at the corner of this street. Throw Him Down M'Closkey. John W. Kelly. TreF
'Twas early on a May morning. Lady Isabel. *Unknown.* BaBo; ESPB
'Twas eighteen hundred years ago. The Day of Days. *Unknown.* PEOR
'Twas Euclid, and the theorem pi. Plane Geometry. Emma Rounds. ImOP
'Twas eve, and Time, his vigorous course pursuing. Akinetos. Richard Henry Horne. *Fr.* Orion. VA
'Twas even: the dewy fields were green. The Lass of Ballochmyle. Burns. EBSV
'Twas evening, though not sunset, and the tide [*or* springtide]. The Nymph [*or* Tamar and the Nymph *or* Tamar's Wrestling]. Walter Savage Landor. *Fr.* Gebir. EnRP; NBE; RO; VA
'Twas Ever Thus. Henry S. Leigh. BOHV; HBV; PA
'Twas Ever Thus. *Unknown.* PA
'Twas ever thus from childhood's hour! Disaster. Charles Stuart Calverley. BOHV; CenHV; HBV; LPS-3; PA
'Twas fifty quatrains: and from unknown strands. Fifty Quatrains. "Michael Field." TwCV
'Twas five wild swans in silver plumage dressed. The Swans from the North. Hans Hartvig Seedorff Pedersen. BoDS
'Twas Friday morn: the train drew near. Through Baltimore. Bayard Taylor. PAH
'Twas Friday morn when we set sail. The Mermaid (B *vers.*). *Unknown.* ViBoFo
'Twas Fultah Fisher's boarding-house. The Ballad of Fisher's Boarding-House. Kipling. PIR
'Twas gilbert. The kchesterton. The Jabberwocky of Authors. Harry Persons Taber. BOHV
'Twas going to snow—'twas snowing! Curse his luck! The Drove-Road. W. W. Gibson. EnLit
'Twas good to live when all the range. Way Out West. *Unknown.* CoSo
'Twas Goosey Goosey Gander. Goosey Goosey Gander—by Various Authors (Macaulay's Version). William Percy French. CenHV
'Twas homeward bound one night on the deep. Lady Franklin's Lament, *vers.* II. Unknown. ShS
'Twas hurry and scurry at Monmouth town. Molly Pitcher. Kate Brownlee Sherwood. GA; GoTP; MC; OTPC (1946 ed.); PAH
'Twas in eighteen hundred and fifty-three. The Greenland Whale Fishery [*or* Greenland Fishery]. *Unknown.* SoAmSa; ViBoFo
'Twas in eighteen hundred and sixty-four. Abraham Lincoln's Christmas Gift. Nora Perry. LBAH
'Twas in green-leafy springtime. Rose Adair. Malachy Ryan. TIP
'Twas in heaven pronounced, and 'twas muttered in hell. *See* 'Twas whispered in heaven . . .
'Twas in mid autumn, and the woods were still. Death as the Teacher of Love-Lore. Frank T. Marzials. VA
'Twas in that place o' Scotland's isle. The Twa Dogs. Burns. CEP
'Twas in that pleasant season, when the year. Consolation. George Darley. TriL
Twas in the dawn. Mother Saint Urban. James M. Hayes. PraNu
'Twas in the dying of the day. The Lone Sentry. James R. Randall. BIG
'Twas in the good ship *Rover*. The Greenwich Pensioner. *Unknown.* CBPC; SG
'Twas in the lonely stable whence the Holy Babe had gone. The Murmur from the Stable. Rubén Darío. CAW
'Twas in the merry month of May. Barbara Allen. *Unknown.* TrAS
'Twas in the middle of the night. Mary's Ghost. Thomas Hood. FiBHP
'Twas in the month of August, or the middle of July. She Said the Same to Me. *Unknown.* AS
'Twas in the month of February 'way down in the Southern Seas. Blow Ye Winds, 2. *Unknown.* SoAmSa
'Twas in the month when lilacs bloom. Dutchman's Breeches. Arthur Guiterman. YT
'Twas in the moon of winter time when all the birds had fled. Jesous Ahatonhia. Jesse Edgar Middleton, *after* Jean de Brébeuf. CaP; ChrBoLe; OCL
'Twas in the prime of summer time. The Dream of Eugene Aram. Thomas Hood. BCEP; BeLS; CG; DaM; EnRP; ERP; EV-4; HBV; LPS-3; ShGoBo; StPo; UnW; VA
'Twas in the reign of George the Third. A New Song Called the Gaspee. *Unknown.* PAH
'Twas in the schooner *Kandahar*. The Schooner *Kandahar*. *At. to* Sepley Collin. ShS
'Twas in the town of Jacksboro in the spring [*or* year] of seventy-three [*or* '73]. The Buffalo Skinners. *Unknown.* ABF; AS; BaBo
'Twas in the year of eighty-five. A Woodsman Goes to Sea. Charles R. Knapp. IHA
'Twas in the year of forty-nine. The Whale. *Unknown.* ChTr
'Twas in the year two thousand and one. The Last Man. Thomas Hood. ERP; NBE; OBRV; RO
'Twas in this shade. Song. Pope. CaAE
'Twas Jolly, Jolly Wat. C. W. Stubbs. OHIP
'Twas Juet spoke—the *Half Moon*'s mate. The Death of Colman. Thomas Frost. PAH
'Twas June on the face of the earth, June with the rose's breath. The Eve [*or* On the Eve] of Bunker Hill. Clinton Scollard. DD; MC; PAH; PEDC; PoRL
'Twas just as dawn rose o'er the North Sea. The Golden Willow Tree. *Unknown.* SoAF
'Twas just at gnat and cobweb-time. The Rift. Thomas Hardy. BoFr
'Twas just at sunrise, and a glorious day. The Battle of Erie. *Unknown.* GA; PAH
'Twas Just before the Hay Was Mown. Charles Swain. VA
'Twas just before the last fierce charge. The Last Fierce Charge. *Unknown.* ViBoFo
'Twas late, and the gay company was gone. The Declaration. Nathaniel Parker Willis. BOHV

'Twas late in my long journey, when I had clomb to where. Introduction. Robert Bridges. *Fr.* The Testament of Beauty. MoVE
'Twas late last night when my lord came home. The Raggle Taggle Gypsies. *Unknown.* GoTP
'Twas later when the summer went. Cricket. Emily Dickinson. OnPM
'Twas like a maelstrom, with a notch. Emily Dickinson. ExPo; SeCeV
(Final Inch, The.) LiTA; LiTM; NePA
'Twas long ago—ere ever the signal gun. How He Saved St. Michael's. Mary A. P. Stansbury. BLPA; PTA-1
'Twas May upon the mountains, and on the airy wing. The Surprise at Ticonderoga. Mary A. P. Stansbury. GA; MC; PAH
'Twas Maytime, and the lawyer coves. Waggawocky. Shirley Brooks. PA
'Twas merry then in England. A Bow-Meeting Song. Reginald Heber. BCEP
'Twas midsummer; cooling breezes all the languid forests fanned. The Death of Jefferson. Hezekiah Butterworth. GA; PAH
'Twas more than a million years ago. Annabel Lee. Stanley Huntley. BOHV; PA
'Twas morn, and beautiful the mountain's brow. On the Rhine. William Lisle Bowles. LPS-2
'Twas morning, and the Lord of day. The Lesson of the Flowers. Hafiz. PeP
'Twas my Beloved spake. Canticle. John Norris. SeCL; SeEP
Twas my pleasure to walk in the river meadows. The Midnight Court. Brian Merriman, *tr. by* Frank O'Connor. AnIL
'Twas my wont to wander beside the stream. The Midnight Court. Brian Merriman, *tr. by* Arland Ussher. OnYI
'Twas Night. *Unknown.* OBS
'Twas night; nor yet had either wearied host. Tasso. *Fr.* Jerusalem Delivered, XII. PrPoCR
'Twas night; the noise and bustle of the day. Bologna and Byron. Samuel Rogers. *Fr.* Italy. OBRV
'Twas night upon the Darro. The Thanksgiving for America. Hezekiah Butterworth. PAH
'Twas noontide of summer. Evening Star. Poe. AmP
'Twas not enough to kneel in prayer. When Saint Chrysostom Prayed. Margaret J. Preston. PraP
'Twas not his person nor his partes. *Unknown.* SeCSL
'Twas not in him to deal with cringing touch. Roosevelt. T. E. Thomas. PEDC
'Twas not my wish. About the Shelleys. *Unknown, quoted by* Wordsworth. WhC
'Twas not the brown of chestnut boughs. Gwendoline. Bayard Taylor. PA
'Twas November the fourth, in the year of ninety-one. Sainclaire's Defeat. *Unknown.* PAH
'Twas now the blooming season of the year. Luis de Góngora. *Fr.* Solitudes. AnSpL-1
'Twas now the hour that turneth back desire. Dante. *Fr.* Divina Commedia: Purgatorio. CAW
Twas of a gay young cavalier. Riddles Wisely Expounded. *Unknown.* BaBo (C *vers.*); ViBoFo (B *vers.*)
'Twas of a lofty ship, boys, and she put out to sea. The *Golden Vanity.* *Unknown.* SoAmSa
'Twas of a maiden both young and fair. The Dark-eyed Sailor. *Unknown.* ShS
'Twas on a cold and frosty morning. Ye Noble Old Pine Tree. *Unknown.* APW
'Twas on a cold winter's night. Mary of the Wild Moor. *Unknown.* ABS
'Twas on a Holy Thursday, their innocent faces clean. Holy Thursday. Blake. *Fr.* Songs of Innocence. AnFE; CEP; CH; CoBE; EG; EiPP; EnL; EnRP; EV-3; HBV; OAEP; OBEC; OTPC; PoE; PoFS
'Twas on a lofty vase's side. Ode on [*or* On] the Death of a Favourite Cat, Drowned in a Tub of Goldfishes [*or* On a Favourite Cat Drowned . . .]. Thomas Gray. ATP; BEL; BeLS; BOHV; CaAE; CEP; CG; CIV; EM-1; EnLi-2 (1949 ed.); EnLit; EV-3; ExPo; FaBoBe; GBV (1952 ed.); GN; GTBS; GTBS-D; GTBS-W; GTSE; GTSL; HBV; HoPM; InMe; InvP; KN; LiTB; LITG; MCCG; NeHB; OAEP; OBEC; OBEV; OnSP; OTPC (1923 ed.); PoC; PoE; PoEL-3; PoRA; SeCeV; ShBV-2; TOP; TyEnPo; WP
'Twas [*or* It was] on a merry time,/ When Jenny Wren was young. Mother Goose. BoChLi (1939 ed.); MeMeAg
'Twas on a Monday morning. Charlie, He's [*or* Is] My Darling. Burns. EV-3; HBV; ViBoPo. *See also* An' Charlie he's my darling.
'Twas on a Monday morning. Charlie Is My Darling. James Hogg. OTPC (1946 ed.)
'Twas on a Monday morning. Charlie Is My Darling. Lady Nairne. DiM
'Twas on a Monday morning, the first I saw my darling. Hanging Out the Linen Clothes. *Unknown.* AS
'Twas on a night, an evening bright. Proud Lady Margaret. *Unknown.* BaBo; ESPB
'Twas on a night not long gone by. Alcoholic Goblins. Thomas Jefferson Savage. PoP
'Twas on a pleasant morning all in the bloom of spring. William Reilly's Courtship. *Unknown.* ABS
'Twas on a pleasant mountain. The Battle of King's Mountain. *Unknown.* PAH; SPP
'Twas on a simmer's afternoon. The Lass o' Gowrie. Lady Nairne. HBV
'Twas on a summer evening. *See* It was a summer . . .
'Twas on a windy night. The Sabine Farmer's Serenade. Francis Sylvester Mahony. BOHV; HBV
'Twas on an early day of spring. Aleksey Konstantinovich Tolstoy, *tr. fr. Russian by* Sir Cecil Kisch. WaL
'Twas on an evening fair I went to take the air. Willie's Fatal Visit. *Unknown.* BaBo; ESPB
'Twas on board the sloop of war *Wasp*, boys. The *Wasp*'s Frolic. *Unknown.* PAH
'Twas on Lake Erie's broad expanse. John Maynard. Horatio Alger, Jr. BeLS; BLPA; FaBoBe; PTA-2
'Twas on one dark and cheerless night to the south-'ard of the Cape. The *Flying Dutchman.* *Unknown.* ShS
'Twas on the famous trotting-ground. How the Old Horse Won the Bet. Oliver Wendell Holmes. AnNE; IAP; TCAP
'Twas on the first of February from Lunenburg we set sail. The *Donzella* and the *Ceylon.* *At. to* Daniel Smith. ShS
'Twas on the fourteenth day of April we sailed from the land. The Bold *Princess Royal, vers.* II. *Unknown.* ShS
'Twas on the glorious day. The Death of General Pike. Laughton Osborn. PAH
'Twas on the shores that round our coast. The Yarn of the *Nancy Bell.* W. S. Gilbert. ATP (1935 ed.); BBV; BeLS; BLPA; BoChLi; BOHV; CenHV; EtS; FaBoBe; FaBoCh; FaFP; GBV; GoTP; HBV; HoPM; InMe; LauV; LEAP; LoGBV; LPS-3; MCCG; MoShBr; MW; OTPC; (1946 ed.); PCD; PCN; PFE; PIR; PoeMoYo; PoVP; PYM; ShBV-1; StVeCh; TreFS; TrGrPo; TSW; TSWC
'Twas on the twelfth of April. Sumter—a Ballad of 1861. *Unknown.* PAH
'Twas once upon a time, when Jenny Wren was young. When Jenny Wren Was Young. Mother Goose. MPB (1956 ed.)
'Twas one October mornin'. Bigerlow. *Unknown.* AS
'Twas one of the charmed days. The Guide [*or* The Heart of All the Scene]. Emerson. *Fr.* Woodnotes, I. AA; APW
'Twas out upon mid ocean that the *San Jacinto* hailed. The Death of the Lincoln Despotism. *Unknown.* PAH
'Twas raw, and chill, and cold outside. An Old Bachelor. Tudor Jenks. BOHV; LHV
'Twas said of one "he wrote no line." Markham. Robert Underwood Johnson. BAP
'Twas so; I saw thy birth. That drowsy lake. The Shower [*or* Showre]. Henry Vaughan. LiTB; MePo; ViBoPo
'Twas spring, and dawn returning breathed new-born. Idyll of the Rose. Decimus Magnus Ausonius. AWP
'Twas stinging, blustering winter weather. The Game of Chess. David Skaats Foster. PR
'Twas such a saucy little brook. And O the Wind. Witter Bynner. VOD
'Twas summer, and the spot a cool retreat. A Dream. Elizabeth Clementine Kinney. AA
'Twas summer, and the sun had mounted high. Margaret; or, The Ruined Cottage. Wordsworth. *Fr.* The Excursion, I. EnRP; ERP
'Twas Summer I recall. Elegies, III. Philippe Thoby-Marcelin. PoNe
'Twas summer time, the radiant world of June. John Francis O'Donnell. *Fr.* Happy Christmases. IrPN
'Twas sure a luckless planet. Out of Luck. Abraham ibn Ezra. TrJP
'Twas taussig, and the bushnell hart. Jabberwocky. R. C. Evarts. CAG
'Twas the body of Judas Iscariot. The Ballad of Judas Iscariot. Robert Buchanan. BMEP; DaM; HBV; VA
'Twas the day beside the Pyramids. The Old Grenadier's Story. George Walter Thornbury. VA
'Twas the dead of the night. By the pineknot's red light. New England's Chevy Chase. Edward Everett Hale. DDA; HBV; HBVY; PAH; PoRL; YaD
'Twas the deep mid-watch of the silent night. The Cid's Rising. Felicia Dorothea Hemans. OBRV
'Twas the dream of a God. Ireland. Dora Sigerson Shorter. BMEP; GTIV; LBBV; LEAP; OBEV; OBVV; OxBI
'Twas the end of round-up, the last day of June. Whose Old Cow? *Unknown.* CoSo; CSF
'Twas the eve before Christmas. "Good night," had been said. Annie and Willie's Prayer. Sophia P. Snow. BeLS; BLPA; PTA-2
'Twas the first leisure of my life. Samuel Taylor Coleridge. *Fr.* The Piccolomini. SoV
'Twas the Frogge in the well. The Marriage of the Frog and the Mouse. *Unknown.* EV-1

'Twas the gray of early morning when the dreadful cry of fire. The Milwaukee Fire. *Unknown.* ABS
'Twas the heart of the murky night, and the lowest ebb of the tide. Wayne at Stony Point. Clinton Scollard. GA; MC; PAH
" 'Twas the last fight at Fredericksburg." "Bay Billy." Frank H. Gassaway. PTA-1; TVSH
'Twas the lean coyote told me, baring his slavish soul. The Desert. Henry Herbert Knibbs. SCC
'Twas the night after Christmas in Santa-Claus land. The Night after Christmas. Anne P. L. Field. COAH
'Twas the night before Christmas, when all through the house. A Visit from St. Nicholas [*or* The Night before Christmas]. Clement C. Moore. AA; BeLS; BLPA; BoChLi; BOHV; ChBR; COAH; DD; FaBoBe; FaFP; FaPON; GaP; GFA; GoTP; HBV; HBVY; HH; LHV; LPS-1; MeMeAg; MPB; NeHB; OHFP; OnHT; OTPC; PCH; PECK; PEDC; PoRH; PRWS; PTA-1; RAR; RIS; SAS; SDH; SiSoSe; StVeCh; TiPo; TreF; TVC; TVSH; WBLP; YaD
'Twas the proud Sir Peter Parker came sailing in from the sea. The Boasting of Sir Peter Parker. Clinton Scollard. PAH
'Twas the soul of Judas Iscariot. Judas Iscariot. Robert Buchanan. *Fr.* The Ballad of Judas Iscariot. LEAP; OBVV; OxBoCh
'Twas the valiant knight, Sir Aager. Aager and Eliza. *Unknown.* LyMA
'Twas the very verge of May. Dewey at Manila. Robert Underwood Johnson. GA; HBV; MC; PAH
'Twas the year of the famine in Plymouth of old. Five Kernels of Corn. Hezekiah Butterworth. DD; MC; PAH
'Twas then I thought I'd have some fun. Breaking in a Tenderfoot. *Unknown.* ABS; IHA
'Twas three an' thirty year ago. The Rivals. Paul Laurence Dunbar. IHA
'Twas twelve o'clock, not twelve at night. Pompey's Ghost. Thomas Hood. DaM
'Twas twilight, and the sunless day went down. The Shipwreck. Byron. *Fr.* Don Juan. BPN; OBRV; WHA
'Twas warm at first like us. Emily Dickinson. CoV; ExPo; LiTA; RiBV
'Twas when at last the million flags were stacked. Saecla Ferarum. William Ellery Leonard. AOAH
'Twas when the fields had shed their golden grain. Autumn. Mary Leapor. *Fr.* Colinetta. BeR
'Twas when the rain fell steady an' the Ark was pitched an' ready. The Legends of Evil, II. Kipling. MoShBr
'Twas when the sea's tremendous roar. My Father's at the Helm. *Unknown.* BePJ
'Twas when the seas were roaring. Ballad. John Gay. *Fr.* The What D'ye Call It. CEP; EV-3; HBV; ViBoPo
'Twas When the Spousal Time of May. Coventry Patmore. *Fr.* The Angel in the House. EV-5
'Twas when the wan leaf frae the birk tree was fa'in'. Lucy's Flittin'. William Laidlaw. EBSV
'Twas whispered in Heaven [*or* in heaven pronounced], 'twas muttered in Hell. A Riddle [*or* Enigma on the Letter H]. Catherine M. Fanshawe. BCEP; BOHV; ChTr; GN; GoTP; LiTG; LPS-3; OTPC; RIS; SiTL
'Twas yesterday He made me and tomorrow I shall die. Song of the Gulf Stream. Francis Alan Ford. EtS
Tweed and Till. *Unknown.* FaBoCh
Tweedledum and Tweedledee. Mother Goose. NA; OTPC; OxNR; RIS; SiTL
Tweedmouth Bar. Will H. Ogilvie. TVSH
Tweedside. Lord Yester. EBSV
'Tween Earth and Sky. Augusta Webster. *See* Seeds.
"Tweet" pipes the robin as the cat creeps by. The Firetail's Nest. John Clare. EnRP
Twelfth day of Christmas, The. The Twelve Days of Christmas. *Unknown.* LiTL; OxBoLi
Twelfth Night. John Peale Bishop. UnPo (3d ed.)
Twelfth Night. Philip Booth. NePoEA
Twelfth Night. Elizabeth J. Coatsworth. *See* Song of the Camels.
Twelfth Night, *sels.* Shakespeare.
  "Come away, come away, death," *fr.* II, iv. AnFE; AtBAP; CenL; EG; ElL; ElSeCe; EM-1; EnLi-1 (1949 ed.); EPP; ExPo; InPo; KN; MaPo; OAEP; OBSC; PoEL-2; SiCE; TCEP; TOP; TwHP; TwP; ViBoPo; WHA
    (Come Away, Death.) BLV; PoRA; SeCeV
    (Dirge.) OBEV
    (Dirge for Love.) CBOV
    (Dirge of Love.) GTBS; GTBS-D; GTBS-W; GTSE; GTSL
    (Feste's Songs, 2.) CoEV
    (Lover's Lament.) EV-1
    (Love's Despair.) TrGrPo
    (Song: "Come away, come away death.") CaAE; FiP
    (Two of Feste's Songs.) BoLiVe
  "Come hither, boy: if ever thou shalt love," *fr.* II, iv. LO
  "Give me some music.—Now, good morrow, friends," II, iv. MyFE
  If Music Be the Food of Love, *fr.* I, i. BCEP; EV-1; PoFS; UnS
    (Food of Love, The.) TrGrPo
    (Music.) TreFS
  "O Mistress mine, where are you roaming," *fr.* II, iii. AEV; AnFE; BEL; EG; ElL; ElSeCe; EnL; EnLi-1; EnLit; EPP; ExPo; LoBV; OAEP; OBSC; OuHeWo; PIR; PoE; SiCE; TOP; TwHP; WHA
    (Carpe Diem.) GTBS; GTBS-D; GTBS-W; GTSE; GTSL
    (Clown's Song: "O mistris mine where are you roming?") FaBoEn
    (Feste's Song from Twelfth Night.) ALV
    (Feste's Songs, 1.) CoEV
    (Mistress Mine.) CBOV
    (O Mistress Mine.) BLV; EM-1; EV-1; FaFP; HH; InMe; InPo; KN; LiA; LiTB; LoPo; LPS-1; MCCG; OtMeF; PoFS; PoRA; PreP, *with music;* SeCeV; ShBV-2; TrGrPo; TyEnPo; ViBoPo
    (Song: "O mistress mine, where are you roaming?") CaAE; FiP; HBV; PG (1945 ed.)
    (Song from "Twelfth Night.") LEAP
    (Songs from the Plays.) AWP; JAWP; WBP
    (Sweet-and-twenty.) LiTG; LiTL; OBEV
    (Two of Feste's Songs.) BoLiVe
  Olivia, *fr.* I, v. LPS-1
  She Never Told Her Love, *fr.* II, iv. BCEP
    (Love Concealed.) TreFS
    (Patience on a Monument.) TrGrPo
    (Unrequited Love, *longer sel.*) LPS-1
  "When that I was and a little tiny boy," *fr.* V, i. AnFE; AtBAP; CH; EG; ElL; ExPo; FaBoCh; HBV; InPo; KN; LiTB; LoBV; LoGBV; MyFE; OAEP; OBSC; PoEL-2; PoRA; ReaPo; SiCE; SiTL; ViBoPo; WaKn
    (Feste's Song.) OxBoLi
    (Rain It Raineth Every Day, The.) OTPC (1923 ed.)
    (Song: "When that I was and a little tiny boy.") FiP; LiTG
Twelfth Night. Elinor Wylie. MM
Twelfth Night Carol. *Unknown.* *See* Here We Come a-Whistling.
Twelfth Night Song. Stephen Sennett. SDH
12th Raga: For John Wieners. David Meltzer. NeAP
Twelve, The. Aleksandr Aleksandrovich Blok, *tr. fr. Russian.* AWP, *abr., tr. by* Babette Deutsch *and* Avrahm Yarmolinsky; BoRS, *tr. by* C. M. Bowra; LiTW, *tr. by* Babette Deutsch; PoFr, *abr., tr. by* Babette Deutsch *and* Avrahm Yarmolinsky; TrRV, *tr. by* Babette Deutsch
Twelve Articles. Swift. BOHV; InMe
Twelve Blades of Grass. Mikhail Isakovsky, *tr. fr. Russian by* Jack Lindsay. RuPo
Twelve by the Clock. Jorge Guillén, *tr. fr. Spanish.* CoSP, *tr. by* Eleanor L. Turnbull; WoL, *tr. by* Frances Avery Pleak
Twelve Days of Christmas, The ("The first day of Christmas"). *Unknown.* FaFP; LiTL; OxBoLi; OxNR; SiTL
  (First Day of Christmas, The.) ChBR; GoBP
Twelve Days of Christmas, The ("The first day of Yule"). *Unknown.* *See* Make We Mirth for Christès Birth.
Twelve-Elf, The. Christian Morgenstern, *ad. fr. German by* Louis Untermeyer. StaSt
Twelve good friends. Peter and John. Elinor Wylie. HBMV; MaC; MAP; MoAB; MoAmPo; StJW
Twelve Good Joys. *Unknown.* OBB
  (Joys Seven, *older vers.*) SDH
Twelve little figures around me. A Clock. *Unknown.* OTPC (1946 ed.)
Twelve months ago this morning. To My Sister. Hsi P'ei Lan. BoFr; PoHN
Twelve Moons, The. Li Ho, *tr. fr. Chinese by* Ho Chih-yuan. WhP
Twelve o'clock./ Along the reaches of the street. Rhapsody on a Windy Night. T. S. Eliot. AmP; ExPo; InPo; MAP; MoAmPo (1942 ed.); MOAP; TwP
Twelve o'clock—a misty night. The Highwayman's Ghost. Richard Garnett. DaM; StPo
Twelve o'Clock Boat. J. A. R. McKellar. BoAV; MoAuPo
Twelve Oxen. *Unknown.* *See* I Have Twelve Oxen.
Twelve pairs hanging high. *See* Twelve pears hanging high.
Twelve palaces of gold palling on me. The Tower. Albert Samain. TrFP
Twelve pears [*or* pairs] hanging high. Mother Goose. BoChLi; OxNR
XII Properties or Condicyons of a Lover, The, *sels.* Sir Thomas More.
  VII Properte, The. CoBE
  X Properte, The. CoBE
Twelve Songs of the Gypsy, The, *sels.* Kostes Palamas, *tr. fr. Modern Greek by* Rae Dalven. MoGP
  Arrival, The.
  Fair of Kakava, The.
  Love.
  Prophet, The.

Twelve stars upon the brow of her. Our Lady of the Skies. James M. Hayes. ISi
Twelve years ago I made a mock. School and Schoolfellows. Winthrop Mackworth Praed. EV-4; OBRV
Twelve years ago, when I could face. The Voice in the Wild Oak. Henry Clarence Kendall. VA
Twentie are making for me head tyres and gownes. George Chapman. *Fr.* The Blind Beggar of Alexandria. NBE
Twentieth-Century Blues. Kenneth Fearing. ChMo
Twentieth Century Love-Song. Richard Church. HaMV
Twentieth Century Psalter, *sel.* Richard Church.
Twenty-fourth Day—Evening. SoV
Twentieth Century Songs. Elsa Gidlow. PreP
Twentieth year is well nigh past, The. To Mary [*or* My Mary *or* To the Same]. William Cowper. BEL; BoFr; EiPP; EM-1; EnLi-2 (1949 ed.); EnLoPo; EnRP; EV-3; FiP; GTBS; GTBS-D; GTBS-W; GTSE; GTSL; LiTL; LO; OAEP; OBEC; OBEV; TreFS
Twenty. Albert Durrant Watson. CPG
Twenty abreast down the Golden Street ten thousand riders marched. Riders of the Stars. Henry Herbert Knibbs. SCC
Twenty Below. R. A. D. Ford. CaP
Twenty-eight young men bathe by the shore. Song of Myself, XI. Walt Whitman. CoV; ExPo; MaPo
Twenty Foolish Fairies. Nancy Byrd Turner. SUS
Twenty, forty, sixty, eighty. Then. Walter de la Mare. GaP; TVC; TVSH
Twenty-four Years. Dylan Thomas. LiTM; MoAB
Twenty-fourth Day—Evening. Richard Church. *Fr.* Twentieth Century Psalter. SoV
Twenty-fourth of December, The. *Unknown.* PCH
Twenty-fourth Psalm, The. Psalms, XXIV, Bible, *O.T.* PreP
(Antiphonal, An.) CBOV
(Earth Is the Lord's, The.) FaPON; TrJP
(Lift Up Your Heads [O Ye Gates].) PCD; PCH; TrGrPo
(Psalm XXIV.) AWP; EnLi-1; JAWP; OHIP; OnPM; OuHeWo; TiPo (1952 ed.); WoL
Twenty Froggies. George Cooper. *See* Frogs at School.
Twenty Golden Years Ago. James Clarence Mangan. IrPN, *abr.*; OnYI
Twenty-ninth Ode of the Third Book of Horace, The. Horace. *See* To Maecenas.
Twenty-one miles of boys in blue. The Last Review. Emily J. Bugbee. BLPA
Twenty Poems of Love, *sel.* "Pablo Neruda," *tr. fr. Spanish by* H. R. Hays.
No. XVII: "Thinking, entangling shadows . . ." TwSpPo
Twenty-second of August, The. Bold Hawthorne [*or* The Cruise of the *Fair American*]. *Unknown.* IAP; PAH
Twenty-second of December, The. Bryant. GN
Twenty-second of February, The. Bryant. DD; GA; HH; MPB; OTPC (1946 ed.); PEOR; PoRL
Twenty-seven Sonnets, *sels.* Feng Chih, *tr. fr. Chinese by* Chu K'an.
Sonnets (I–VIII). WhP
Twenty Stars to Match His Face. William Stanley Braithwaite. HBMV
Twenty-third Psalm, The. Psalms, XXIII, Bible, *O.T.* *See* Lord Is My Shepherd, The.
Twenty white horses. *See* Thirty white horses upon a red hill.
Twenty Years After. Evan V. Shute. CaP
Twenty Years Ago. *Unknown.* *See* Forty Years Ago.
Twenty years ago. Mud. Richard Church. MoBrPo (1942 ed.); MoP
Twenty years are gone. Palinode. Oliver St. John Gogarty. OBMV; PG (1955 ed.); PoP
Twenty Years Hence. Walter Savage Landor. EmBrPo; EPN; EV-4; OBEV (1st ed.); PCD; TOP; TrGrPo; ViBoPo
(Lyrics and Epigrams, VIII.) ERP
(Poems, LVIII.) PG
("Twenty years hence my eyes may grow.") BPN
Twenty Years Old. Aleksey Surkov, *tr. fr. Russian by* Jack Lindsay. RuPo
'Twere a dree night, a dree night, as the squire's end drew nigh. The Dree Night. *Unknown.* ChTr
'Twere an ill world, I'll swear, for every friend. Abraham Cowley. *Fr.* Friendship in Absence. EPS (1942 ed.)
'Twere frenzy of his every frantic feat. Ariosto. *Fr.* Orlando Furioso, XXIX. PrPoCR
'Twere Long to Tell. Wordsworth. *Fr.* The Prelude. AtBAP
'Twere time that I died too, now she is dead. The Lady Venetia Digby. Ben Jonson. GoBC
Twice. M. M. Hutchinson. BoTP
Twice. Christina Rossetti. GTML; GTSL; OBEV; OBVV; TyEnPo; ViBoPo
Twice a day. The Great Tides. Lyon Sharman. CPG
Twice a week the winter thorough. A. E. Housman. A Shropshire Lad, XVII. PoVP; VLEP
Twice a year,/ Chatty and blithe. Alma Mater, Forget Me. William Cole. FiBHP
Twice Fed. A. A. Bassett. HBV
Twice forty months ot wedlock I did stay. Little Hector Philips. Katherine Philips. DiM
Twice had Diana bent her golden bowe. Giles Fletcher. *Fr.* Christ's Victory and Triumph: Christ's Victory on Earth. SeEP
Twice happy Violets! that first had birth. Violets in Thaumantia's Bosome. Sir Edward Sherburne. OBS
"Twice have I sought Clan-Alpine's glen." Roderick Dhu. Sir Walter Scott. *Fr.* The Lady of the Lake, V. OBRV
Twice nineteen years, dear Nancy, on this day. On Our Thirty-ninth Wedding Day. Jonathan Odell. CaP
Twice one are two. Twice. M. M. Hutchinson. BoTP
Twice or thrice had I loved thee. Aire [*or* Air] and Angells [*or* Angels]. John Donne. AtBAP; BoW; EG; MeLP; MePo; MeRV; OBS; PoFS; SeCV-1; TuPP
Twice thirty centuries and more ago. The First Spousal. Coventry Patmore. *Fr.* The Unknown Eros. OBVV
Twice welcome, disrupter of stillness! Night Express. MacKnight Black. NP
Twickenham Ferry. Théophile Marzials. HBV; VA
Twickenham Grotto. Robin Skelton. PoN
Twicknam Garden. John Donne. EnLoPo; EPS; MeLP; MePo; OBS; PoEL-2; PoFS; ReIE; SeEP; TuPP
(Twickenham Garden.) CaAE; LoBV
Twig, The, turned in her hand and the diviner said: "Water." The Water-Witch. Martha Eugenie Perry. CaP
Twigs of the birch imprint the December sky, The. The Prospect. Thomas Hardy. NeMA
Twilight. Ch'en Yün, *tr. fr. Chinese by* Henry H. Hart. LiTW
Twilight. Olive Custance. CAW; HBV; JKCP; VA
Twilight. Olive Tilford Dargan. LS; NoCaPo
Twilight. Eileen Duggan. JKCP (1955 ed.)
Twilight. Rafael Estrada, *tr fr. Spanish by* Donald Devenish Walsh. AnCL
Twilight. Gerald Gould. MBP; MoBrPo (1942 ed.)
Twilight. Hazel Hall. AnAmPo; HBMV; LA
Twilight. Charles Heavysege. VA
Twilight. Heine, *tr. fr. German by* Louis Untermeyer. AWP; JAWP; WBP
(Fisher's Cottage, The, *tr. by* Charles G. Leland.) LPS-2
Twilight. Jules Laforgue, *tr. fr. French by* William Jay Smith. AnFP
Twilight. D. H. Lawrence. OBMV
Twilight. Longfellow. CH
Twilight. Virginia McCormick. HBMV
Twilight. John Masefield BoFr; PoeT
Twilight. Joaquin Arcadio Pagaza, *tr. fr. Spanish by* Alice Stone Blackwell. CAW
Twilight. Agnes Mary Frances Robinson. HBV
Twilight. Margaret Ryan. GTIV
Twilight. Arthur Symons. POTT
Twilight. Feodor Ivanovich Tyutchev, *tr. fr. Russian by* Babette Deutsch. OnPM; TrRV
Twilight. Wordsworth. *See* Written in Very Early Youth.
Twilight, a timid fawn, went glimmering by. Refuge. "Æ." CaAE; ChMo; CMP; GTIV; HBV; OnYI; POTE
Twilight. And on a dusty ribboned way. The Road to Emmaus. Ida Norton Munson. ChIP
Twilight: and pine trees keep the blessed enclosure. Convent Cemetery, Mount Carmel. Sister Mary St. Virginia. GoBC
Twilight at Sea. Amelia B. Welby. AA; BAP; HBV; LPS-2; NLK; OTPC
Twilight at the Heights. Joaquin Miller. AA; BAP; LEAP
Twilight Calm. Christina Rossetti. GTSE
"Oh pleasant eventide!" *sel.* AlDL
Twilight comes down the mountain to. Night in the Villa by the River. Tu Fu. WhP
Twilight comes, The; the sun. June Twilight. John Masefield. GoYe
Twilight falls on the hill. Vespers. Odell Shepard. TrPWD
Twilight floods the darkening skies. Sowing Season. Victor Hugo. TrFP
Twilight . . . From the houses I pass come the smell of cooking. Twilight. Jules Laforgue. AnFP
Twilight hours, like birds, flew by, The. Twilight at Sea. Amelia B. Welby. AA; BAP; HBV; LPS-2; NLK; OTPC
Twilight in Middle March, A. Francis Ledwidge. GTIV; OnYI; OxBI; TCEP; WHA
Twilight is here and the baby is weary. The Sand-Man. Elmer Ruán Coates. BOL
Twilight is sad and cloudy, The. Twilight. Longfellow. CH
Twilight is spacious, near things in it seem far. Miracles. Conrad Aiken. HBMV; MAP; MoAmPo; NeMA
Twilight it is, and the far woods are dim, and the rooks cry and call. Twilight John Masefield. BoFr; PoeT
Twilight leaned mirrored in a pool. The Old Angler. Walter de la Mare. GoTL (1949 ed.); OAEP (2d ed.); POTT
Twilight Musing. Mabel Langdon. CAG
Twilight of Earth, The. "Æ." AnIL; ChMo; CMP; TOP
Twilight of Liberty, The. Osip Emilyevich Mandelstamm, *tr. fr. Russian by* Babette Deutsch. TrRV
Twilight of Love. Shakespeare. *See* Sonnets, LXXIII.

Twilight of Thanksgiving, The. William D. Kelly. TOAH
Twilight of the Outward Life. Hugo von Hofmannsthal. *See* Ballad of the Outer Life.
Twilight of the Wood. Léonie Adams. NLK (1947 ed.)
Twilight on Sumter. Richard Henry Stoddard. PAH; PAP
Twilight on Tweed. Andrew Lang. EBSV; OBVV; POTT; PoVP
Twilight over the sea and no ship in sight. Alone. Stella Gibbons. AlDL
Twilight People, The. "Seumas O'Sullivan." OnYI
Twilight. Red in the West. The Wild Duck. John Masefield. BEL; ShBV-2; WP
Twilight Song. John Hunter-Duvar. *Fr.* De Roberval. VA
Twilight Song. E. A. Robinson. HBV
Twilight twiles in the vernal vale, The. In the Gloaming. James C. Bayles. NA
Twilight's inner flame grows blue and deep, The. Sappho. Sara Teasdale. LBMV
Twilit Revelation. Léonie Adams. AV; MAP; MoAB; MoAmPo
'Twill not be long before they hear. Away Down Home. John Charles McNeill. NoCaPo
" 'Twill overtask a thousand men." The Two Houses. Charles Mackay. BSV
Twin Brothers. Pindar. *See* Castor and Polydeuces.
Twin songs there are, of joyance, or of pain. Morton Luce. *Fr.* Thysia. HBV
Twin stars through my purpling pane. Dusk. Angelina Weld Grimké. CDC
Twine laurels to lay o'er the Blue and the Gray. Memorial Day, 1889. S. E. Kiser. DD; HH; MDAH; PEDC
Twine then the rays. Psycholophon. Gelett Burgess. CenHV; NA
Twined together and, as is customary. Never Such Love. Robert Graves. FaBoEn
Twining a wreath, I found, one day. Love and Wine. Julianus. OnPM
Twinkle, Little Star. Jane Taylor. *See* Twinkle, Twinkle, Little Star.
Twinkle, Twinkle, Little Bat! *parody.* "Lewis Carroll." *Fr.* Alice's Adventures in Wonderland, *ch.* 7. WhC
(Bat, The.) PA
Twinkle, twinkle, Little Star. Jane Taylor. BoTP; GFA; GoBP; OxNR; PECK; PTA-1; SAS; SiTL; TVC; TVSH
(Little Star, The.) OTPC; StVeCh
(Star, The.) BoChLi; CBPC; FaBoBe; FaFP; FaPON; HBV; HBVY; MPB; OnHT; OxNR, *st.* 1; PCH, *abr.*; PPL; RAR; RIS; TiPo, *st.* 1; TreF
(Twinkle, Little Star.) OlF
Twinkling Gown. Dorothy Vena Johnson. GoSl
Twins, The. Henry Sambrooke Leigh. BOHV; CenHV; FaPON; GaP; GoTP; HBV; HBVY; MaC; OTPC (1946 ed.); PoeMoYo; PoMa; PYM; StaSt; StVeCh (1940 ed.); TiPo; TSW; TSWC; WaKn
Twins, The. Elizabeth Madox Roberts. TiPo
Twins, The. Karl Shapiro. AnFE; CoAnAm; MiAP; MoAmPo (1950 ed.); Po; TrJP; TwAmPo
Twirl about, dance about. Dreidel Song. Efraim Rosenzweig. TiPo (1952 ed.)
Twirling your blue skirts, traveling the sward. Blue Girls. John Crowe Ransom. AmP; AnFE; APA; ChMo; ChTr; CoAnAm; HoPM; LiTA; LiTL; MAP; MoAB; MoAmPo; MoPW; MoVE; NP; ReMP; SPP; TBM; TwAmPo
Twist about, turn about. *Unknown.* OxNR
Twist Me a Crown. Christina G. Rossetti. *Fr.* Sing-Song. VA
(Sing-Song.) MBP
Twist of fresh flowers on your dark hair, A. Ballade of Muhammad Din Tilai. *Unknown.* PG (1945 ed.)
Twist the tinsel. Round and Round. Dorothy Brown Thompson. ChBR
Twist thou and twine! in light and gloom. Featherstone's Doom. Robert Stephen Hawker. VA
Twist Ye, Twine Ye! Even So. Sir Walter Scott. *Fr.* Guy Mannering, *ch.* 3. BPN; EmBrPo; EnRP; TOP
Twisted apple, with rain and magian fire, The. June Morning. Hugh McCrae. BoAV
Twister Twisting Twine. *Unknown, at. to* John Wallis. ChTr
(Twister, A.) SiTL
("When a twister a-twisting will twist him a twist.") OTPC; OxNR
Twisting curl, A. The Tress. Al-Husri. MooP
Twisting little street, lined with trees. Praise of Saccarello Street. Hipólito Sánchez Quell. AnCL
Twitched strings, the clang of metal, beaten drums. Javanese Dancers. Arthur Symons. POTT; PoVP; VA
Twitter of Swallows. Merrill Moore. PIAE
'Twixt Carrowbrough Edge and Settlingstones. Old Skinflint. W. W. Gibson. OBMV
'Twixt clouded heights Spain hurls to doom. The *Brooklyn* at Santiago. Wallace Rice. PAH
'Twixt Cup and Lip. Mark Hollis. FiBHP
'Twixt death and doubtfulness. To His Lady, of Her Doubtful Answer. Thomas Howell. TuPP
Twixt devil and deep sea, man hacks his caves. Arachne. William Empson. InvP; MoVE; OBMV
'Twixt failure and success the point's so fine. Don't Give Up. *Unknown.* FaFP; PoToHe (new ed.)
'Twixt Fréron and La Beaumelle me! On His Portrait between Two Others. Voltaire. LiA
Twixt hope & feare the best affection sits. *Unknown.* SeCSL
'Twixt kings and tyrants there's this difference known. Kings and Tyrants. Robert Herrick. PoFr
'Twixt optimist and pessimist. The Difference. *Unknown.* GoTP
'Twixt Paris fair and Saint-Denis. Entre Paris et Saint-Denis. *Unknown.* BoCaPo (1948 ed.)
Twixt the Girthhead and Langwood-end. The Lads of Wamphray. *Unknown.* BaBo; ESPB
'Twixt the sunlight and the shade. Hands. William Morris. BPN
'Twixt those twin worlds—the world of Sleep. Percy Bysshe Shelley. Dante Gabriel Rossetti. Five English Poets, 5. BPN; EmBrPo; PoVP; PtP
Two. Ralph Cheyney. PR
Two, The. Hugo von Hofmannsthal, *tr. fr. German by* Ludwig Lewisohn. AWP; JAWP; WBP; TrJP, *tr. by* Jethro Bithell
Two. Gerasimos Markoras, *tr. fr. Modern Greek by* Rae Dalven. MoGP
Two aged matrons, daughters of one sire. Epitaph on Two Aged Priestesses. Diotimus of Miletus. LiA
Two-an'-six. Claude McKay. BANP; GoSl
Two Anchors, The. Richard Henry Stoddard. BeLS
Two and One Are a Problem. Ogden Nash. FiBHP
Two Angels, The. Rafael Alberti, *tr. fr. Spanish by* Eleanor L. Turnbull. CoSP
Two Angels, The. Longfellow. PTA-2
" 'Twas at thy door, O friend! and not at mine," *sel.* UnW
Two Angels. Richard Monckton Milnes. OBRV
Two Angels, The. Whittier. AA
Two angels came through the gate of heaven. A Song of Two Angels. Laura E. Richards. AA
Two angels, one of Life and one of Death. The Two Angels. Longfellow. PTA-2
Two angels stood with dawn beside my bed. The Choice. Dora Hagemeyer. MuM
Two Apple-howling Songs. *Unknown.* *See* Apple Howling Songs.
Two apples, a book. Autumn Eve. Amelia Andriello. SiSoSe
Two April Mornings, The. Wordsworth. BPN; EmBrPo; EnRP; ERP; GEPC; GTBS; GTBS-D; GTBS-W; GTSE; GTSL
Two Argosies. Wallace Bruce. AA
Two Armies, The. Oliver Wendell Holmes. TCAP
Two Armies. Stephen Spender. ChMP; CoBMV; SeCeV; WaP
Two Armies, The. Henry Timrod. BIG
Two armies covered hill and plain. Music in Camp. John R. Thompson. AA; BLPA; HBV; IAP; PaA; PAP; TCAP
Two as One. Bhartrihari, *tr. fr. Sanskrit by* Paul Elmer More. OnPM
Two Asses, The. Christian Morgenstern, *tr. fr. German by* Lola Gruenthal. AnGP
Two at a Fireside. Edwin Markham. OQP; QP-2
Two at Norfolk. Wallace Stevens. FaBoMo
Two bards met on the deep mid-sea. The Meetings of the Ships. Felicia Dorothea Hemans. LPS-1
Two basins, one above the other, soaring. Roman Fountain. Ranier Maria Rilke. AnGP
Two beings stood on the edge of things. Supernal Dialogue. Harriet Monroe. NP
Two Bells, The. Viktor Rydberg, *tr. fr. Swedish by* Charles W. Stork. AnSL
Two birds within one nest. Home. Dora Greenwell. HBV
Two black heifers and a red. Drinking Time. D. J. O'Sullivan. OnYI
Two blind mice/ See how they run! Paul Dehn. *Fr.* Rhymes for a Modern Nursery. FiBHP
Two bloated bodies in rotted rags. War. Sulamith Ish-Kishor. GoYe
Two bodies have I. *Unknown.* OxNR
Two Boxers, The. Theocritus, *tr. fr. Greek by* Henry Harmon Chamberlin. *Fr.* Idylls, XXII. GrR
Two Boys, The. Mary A. Lamb. OBRV
Two Brides and One Groom. *Unknown, tr. fr. Danish by* E. M. Smith-Dampier. BoDaBa
Two bright heads in the corner. Grandpa and Bess. Emily Huntington Miller. PEOR
Two Brothers, The. Theodosia Garrison. UnW
Two brothers we are. *Unknown.* OxNR
Two brown heads with tossing curls. Katie Lee and Willie Grey. *Unknown, at. to* Josie R. Hunt *and to* J. H. Pixley. BeLS; BLPA; PTA-1
Two, by themselves, each other, love, and fear. Pyramus and Thisbe. John Donne. ReIE
Two Cantos of Mutabilitie. Spenser. *Fr.* The Faerie Queene. ReEn; SiCE

Two Captains, The. William Johnson Cory. *See* Ballad for a Boy, A.
Two Carols to Our Lady. *Unknown. See* I Sing of a Maiden *and* Rosa Mystica.
Two caterpillars crawling on a leaf. Immortality. Joseph Jefferson. BLPA; DDA; NeHB
Two cats/ One up a tree. Diamond Cut Diamond. Ewart Milne. FaBoCh; LoGBV; NeIP
Two Cats on the Hearth. Bernice Kenyon. CIV
Two Chalices. Edwin McNeill Poteat. ChIP
Two Children, The. Emily Brontë. PoEL-5
Two Children. Nicolás Guillén, *tr. fr. Spanish by* H. R. Hays. AnCL; LiTW
Two children in two neighbor villages. Circumstance. Tennyson. BPP; CG
Two Christmas-Cards. Robinson Jeffers. NeTW
"For an hour on Christmas eve," II. MeRV
Two Christs were at Golgotha. Early Lynching. Carl Sandburg. MAP; MoAmPo
Two Chronometers, The. Kenneth Slessor. *Fr.* Five Visions of Captain Cook. MoAuPo; SeCePo
("Two chronometers the captain had.") NeLNL
Two Coffees in the Español. Conrad Aiken. Preludes to Attitude, I. LiTA; LiTG; TwAmPo
Two Confessions. William Langland, *mod. by* Henry W. Wells. *Fr.* The Vision of Piers Plowman. WoL
Two Corbies, The. *Unknown. See* Twa Corbies, The.
Two Crosses. Addie M. Hedrick. ChIP
Two Days. T. A. Daly. LHV
Two Days, The. Bernhard Severin Ingemann, *tr. fr. Danish by* Charles W. Stork. BoDS
Two days a woman's best—the day she's wed. Misogynist. Hipponax. GrPE
Two days ago the wild-rose buds. Puzzles. John Drinkwater. WaKn
Two days are the best of a man's wedded life. Best Days. Pseudo-Hipponax. OxBG
Two Deserts, The. Coventry Patmore. The Unknown Eros, I, xviii. PoVP; VA
Two Dogs. F. Hey. SAS
Two Dogs, The. *Unknown.* OTPC (1946 ed.); PCH
("Two little dogs.") OxNR
Two Doves, The. La Fontaine, *tr. fr. French by* Elizur Wright. OuHeWo
Two doves upon the selfsame branch. Christina Rossetti. EG
Two Drinking Songs. Alcaeus. *See* Drinking Songs.
Two drummers sat at dinner, in a grand hotel one day. My Mother Was a Lady [*or* The Two Drummers]. Edward B. Marks. ABS; TreF; YaD
Two Easter Lilies. John Banister Tabb. StJW
Two XI. E. E. Cummings. *See* My Sweet Old Etcetera.
Two empires by the sea. International Hymn [*or* Peace Hymn for England and America]. George Huntington. MaRV; PaA
Two Epigrams. J. V. Cunningham.
"Elders at their services begin, The," I. SiTL
(Epigram.) NePoAm
"You ask me how Contempt who claims to sleep," II. SiTL
(Epigram.) NePoAm
Two Epigrams. James Kenneth Stephen.
Cynicus to W. Shakespeare [*or* Shakspere]. BOHV; CenHV; WhC
Senex to Matt. Prior. BOHV; CenHV; FiBHP; WhC
Two Epigrams. Sir William Watson. TrGrPo
Love.
Poet, The.
Two Epitaphs. *Unknown.* PEOR
Two evils, monstrous either one apart. Winter Remembered. John Crowe Ransom. MoAB; MoPW; OxBA; UnPo
Two Eyes Our Souls Possess. "Angelus Silesius," *tr. fr. German by* Paul Carus. OnPM
Two Families, The. Joyce L. Brisley. BoTP
Two Festivals. Lucy Larcom. DD; TOAH
Two Figures in Dense Violet Light [*or* Night]. Wallace Stevens. CoV; MAP; MoAB; MoAmPo; OnPM
Two Fires. Meleager, *tr. fr. Greek by* Robert Guthrie MacGregor. OnPM
Two Fishers. *Unknown.* BOHV
Two fleets have sailed from Spain. The one would seek. The Sailing of the Fleet. *Unknown.* PAH
Two flower-enfolding crystal vases. Grace and Love. George Meredith. EmBrPo
Two flowers I love, the March-flower and the rose. Sonnet. Pierre de Ronsard, *tr. by* Henry F. Cary. RO
Two Folk Songs. *Unknown, tr. fr. Finnish by* L. R. Lind. LiTW
"Blue and white are the heavens."
"Kukkuu, kukkuu, sounds the distant voice."
Two foot-companions once in deep discourse. The Nimmers. John Byrom. EV-3
Two forms inseparable in unity. Robert Southey. *Fr.* The Curse of Kehama. OBRV
Two Foscari, The, *sel.* Byron.
Swimming. GN; LPS-2
Two Foxes, The. *Unknown.* FTB
Two Friends, The. Charles Godfrey Leland. AA; BLP; LBAP; LEAP
Two Funerals. Eden Phillpotts. BMEP
Two Fusiliers. Robert Graves. BoFr
Two Garden Scenes. Charles Burgess. NePoAm-2
Two gaz'd into a pool, he gaz'd and she. An Echo from Willowwood. Christina Rossetti. VA
Two Generations. L. A. G. Strong. GTIV; OBMV
Two Gentlemen of Soho, *parody, sel.* A. P. Herbert.
Recipe. WhC
Two Gentlemen of Verona, The, *sels.* Shakespeare.
This Spring of Love, *fr.* I, iii. ChTr
"Who is Silvia [*or* Sylvia]? what is she," *fr.* IV, ii. AnFE; ATP; BEL; CoBE; EG; ElL; ElSeCe; EM-1; EnL; EnLi-1; EnLit; EPP; FaBoBe; FaFP; GN; InPo; KN; LiTB; NeHB; OAEP; OIF; OTPC; OuHeWo; PFE; PIR; PreP, *with music,* ReaPo; RiBV; SeCeV; SiCE; SiTL; TOP; TreF; TrGrPo; TwP; TyEnPo
(Silvia.) BLV; EV-1; HBV; OBEV; OnPP; WP
(Song: "Who is Silvia [*or* Sylvia]?") LiTG; REAL; ViBoPo; WHA
(Song from "Two Gentlemen of Verona.") LEAP
(Song of the Musicians.) BoLiVe
(Song to Silvia.) OBSC
(Sylvia.) BCEP
(To Silvia.) MCCG
Two gentlemen their appetite had fed. Saying Not Meaning. William Basil Wake. BOHV
Two German officers crossed the Rhine, parley voo. Mademoiselle from Armentières [*or* Hinky, Dinky Parlee-Voo]. *Unknown.* AS; SiTL; SoAmSa
Two gifts I gave you, Love and Sorrow. The Wife's Song. Anna Wickham. LBBV
Two girls of Ukraine. Mikhail Isakovsky, *tr. fr. Russian by* V. de S. Pinto. BoRS
Two Glasses, The. Ella Wheeler Wilcox, *wr. at. to* "C. B. A." BLPA; PEOR; PTA-1
Two glowing roses, fresh from Paradise. Petrarch. *Fr.* Sonnets to Laura: To Laura in Life. PrPoCR
Two Gods. Sam Walter Foss. MaRV
Two Gods devise the scene. Chess. John Thompson. BoAu
Two Graces. *Unknown.* FaBoCh; LoGBV
"Hurly, hurly, roon the table."
"Some hae meat that canna eat."
Two hands lie still, the hairy and white. Love for a Hand. Karl Shapiro. FiMAP
"Two hands upon the breast." Now and Afterwards. Dinah Maria Mulock Craik. LPS-1; WGRP
Two Harvests, The. Francisco de Medrano, *tr. fr. Spanish by* Longfellow. OnPM
Two Heads Are Better than One. Joseph Jekyll. WhC
Two Heavens. Leigh Hunt. GN
Two heavy trestles, and a board. My Table. W. B. Yeats. Meditations in Time of Civil War, III. LiTB
Two Heroes. Harriet Monroe. *Fr.* The Commemoration Ode. OHIP
Two Highwaymen, The. Wilfrid Scawen Blunt. The Love Sonnets of Proteus, LXXI. MBP; MoBrPo (1942 ed.); OBEV (1st ed.)
Two honder year ago de worl' is purty slow. Two Hundred Years Ago. William Henry Drummond. HBV
Two honest tradesmen meeting in the Strand. The Three Black Crows. John Byrom. BOHV
Two Horses. W. S. Merwin. NePA
Two Hosts, The. Homer, *tr. fr. Greek by* W. E. Gladstone. *Fr.* The Iliad, IV. OxBG
(Strife, War's Sister Urges On the Host, *longer sel., tr. by* Pope.) GrR
Two hours, or more, beyond the prime of a blithe April day. The Battle of Charleston Harbor. Paul Hamilton Hayne. MOAH; PAH
Two Houses, The. Thomas Hardy. NP
Two Houses, The. Charles Mackay. BSV
Two Houses. Edward Thomas. ChMP; FaBoCh; LoGBV
221B. Vincent Starrett. DaM
Two hundred wagons, rolling out to Oregon. The Oregon Trail. Arthur Guiterman. FaPON; MPB
Two Hundred Years Ago. William Henry Drummond. HBV
Two Hunters. Harvey Wagner Flink. DaM
Two Illustrations That the World Is What You Make of It. Wallace Stevens. NePoAm
Two immortalities has the Volga. Soldier's Tale. Aleksey Nedogonov. RuPo
Two in August. John Crowe Ransom. AWP; InPo; LoPS; MOAP; MoPo; NePA; OxBA
Two in Bed. Abram Bunn Ross. FaPON; MPB; TiPo
Two in One. Earl of Stirling. *See* To Aurora.
Two in the Campagna. Robert Browning. BLV; BMEP; BoLiVe; BPN; CoEV; EM-2; EmBrPo; EnLi-2 (1949 ed.); EPN; EtPaEn; ExPo; FaBoEn; GEPC; GTBS-D; GTML; HBV; OAEP; PoEL-5; PoVP; SeCePo; SeCeV; TOP; TrGrPo; TyEnPo; ViPo; ViPP; VLEP; WHA
Two Infinities. Edward Dowden. VA

Two Inscriptions for the Christmas Candle. Anna Hempstead Branch. MaRV
Two Invocations of the Virgin. Chaucer. *See* Invocatio ad Mariam *and* Invocation. "O mother-maid!"
Two Italian Gentlemen. *Tr. by* Anthony Munday. *See* Fedele and Fortunio.
Two kinds of courage are there in the creed. Courage. Arthur Adams. BoAu
Two Kinds of People. Ella Wheeler Wilcox. *See* Lifting and Leaning.
Two Kinds of Riches. Blake. EPP
Two Kings. Andrew Marvell. *See* Horatian Ode upon Cromwell's Return from Ireland, An.
Two Kisses. Mary Fleming. JKCP (1926 ed.)
Two Kisses. Stephen Spender. ChMo; LoPo; LoPS
Two Kites, The. James Reaney. TwCaPo
Two ladies to the summit of my mind. Sonnet: Of Beauty and Duty [*or* Beauty and Duty]. Dante. AWP; JAWP; PIAE; WBP
Two Lean Cats. Myron O'Higgins. PoNe
Two leaps the water from its race. The [*or* A] Mill. William Allingham. ChTr; IrPN; SeCePo
Two Legs Sat upon Three Legs. *Unknown.* OTPC; OxNR; PPL; RIS; SiTL
(Riddles.) HBV; HBVY
Two lengths has every day. Emily Dickinson. MoPo
Two little beaks went tap! tap! tap! To Let. D. Newey-Johnson. BoTP
Two little birdies, one wintry day. The Birdies' Breakfast. *Unknown.* BoTP
Two little birds one Autumn day. *Unknown.* GFA
Two Little Blackbirds. *Unknown.* BoTP
Two little blackbirds sat upon a hill. *Unknown.* SAS
Two little blackbirds singing in the sun. Two Little Blackbirds. *Unknown.* BoTP
Two little boats sail side by side. Hochi, *ad. fr. Japanese by* Lois J. Erickson. SoLD
Two little bowls. Pudding and Milk. *Unknown.* MeMeAg
Two Little Boys. *Unknown.* *See* Twa Brothers, The.
Two little boys with frowsy head. Tit for Tat. Esther Antin. RIS
Two little clouds, one summer's [*or* April] day. The Rainbow Fairies. Lizzie M. Hadley. BoTP; GFA; OTPC (1946 ed.); TVC; TVSH
Two little creatures. Monkeys. Padraic Colum. AnFE; PoeMoYo
Two little dicky birds/ Sitting on a wall. *Unknown.* OxNR
Two little dicky-birds/ Sitting on a twig. Dicky-Birds. Natalie Joan. BoTP
Two little dogs/ Sat by the fire. The Two Dogs. *Unknown.* OTPC (1946 ed.); OxNR; PCH
Two little dogs went out for a walk. D'Arcy Wentworth Thompson. *Fr.* Nursery Nonsense. BoN
Two little elves/ Were lost one night. A Fairy Dream. Dorothy Gradon. BoTP
Two little feet, so small that both may nestle. Little Feet. Elizabeth Akers Allen. HBV; LPS-1
Two little girls are better than one. One and One. Mary Mapes Dodge. HBV; HBVY; PPL
Two Little Kittens. *Unknown, at. to* Jane Taylor. BoTP; CIV; RAR; SAS; UTS
(One Stormy Night.) PCH
Two little niggers lyin' in bed. Shortenin' Bread. *Unknown.* ABF
Two Little Sisters. *Unknown.* *See* Two Sisters, The.
Two Little Skeezucks, The. Eugene Field. MPB
Two Little Stockings, The. Sara Keables Hunt. PTA-6
Two Little Toadies. *Unknown.* RAR
Two Lives, *sels.* William Ellery Leonard. AnAmPo, *7 sonnets fr.* Pt. III: AnEnPo, *12 sonnets fr.* Pt. II: LA, *7 sonnets fr.* Pt. III: MOAP, *32 sonnets fr.* Pt. III
"Death hath two hands to slay with," *fr.* Pt. III. MOAP
(Sonnets from "Two Lives.") TBM
"How little do they know of sorrow," *fr.* Pt. III. MOAP; MuM
Indian Summer, *fr.* Pt. III. AnAmPo; HBMV; LA; MOAP; MuM; NP; NV; PG (1945 ed.); SBMV
"O Earth-and-Autumn," *sel.* BAP
"Mid-morning of mid-June: her sudden whim," *fr.* Pt. I. BAP
(Sonnet from "Two Lives.") PFE
"My boat lies waiting where the willow stirs," *fr.* Pt. I. BAP
"This afternoon on Willow-Walk alone," *fr.* Pt. III.
(Sonnets from "Two Lives.") TBM
"Thrice summer and autumn passed into the west," *fr.* Pt. III. MOAP
(Sonnets from "Two Lives.") TBM
Two Long Vacations; Grasmere. Arthur Gray Butler. OBVV
Two Look at Two. Robert Frost. AnAmPo; CoBA; CoBMV; CrMA; LA; LiTL; MAP; MoAB; MoAmPo
Two Lovers. "George Eliot." HBV
Two Lovers, The. Richard Hovey. HBV
Two Lovers. Aline Kilmer. AV
Two Lovers, The. *Unknown.* *See* Elfin Knight, The.
Two lovers by a moss-grown spring. Two Lovers. "George Eliot." HBV
Two Lovers Discoursing, *with music.* *Unknown.* ShS
Two lovers in the north. The Admirable New Northern Story of Two Constant Lovers. *Unknown.* SG
Two Lovers in the Toils of Honor. Corneille, *tr. fr. French by* Paul Landis. *Fr.* The Cid. LiTW
Two Loves. Richard Eberhart. FiMAP
Two Loves, The. Laurence Housman. HBMV
Two loves had I. Now both are dead. Dead Love. Mary Matthews Adams. AA
Two Loves, Hyacinth! José Moreno Villa, *tr. fr. Spanish by* Eleanor L. Turnbull. CoSP
Two loves I have of comfort and despair [*or* dispaire]. Sonnets, CXLIV. Shakespeare. EM-1; InvP; LoBV; OAEP; PeBoSo; PoEL-2; ReEn; ReIE
Two Magicians, The. *Unknown.* ChTr; OxBoLi
Two Magpies Sat on a Garden Rail. D'Arcy W. Thompson. MoShBr
Two Married (I–IV). Helen Frazee-Bower. HBMV
Two Married Women and the Widow, The. William Dunbar. *See* Tua Mariit Wemen and the Wedo, The.
Two Masks, The. George Meredith. VA
Two Men. E. A. Robinson. BOHV; GoTP; LaNeLa; OBAV; WhC
Two Men in Armour. John Heath-Stubbs. NeBP
Two men stood thigh-deep in the sea. The Fishers. Brian Vrepont. MoAuPo
Two men went up into the temple to pray. Parable of the Pharisee and the Publican. St. Luke, Bible, *N.T.* GrCo-1
Two men went up to pray; and one gave thanks. The Newer Vainglory. Alice Meynell. JKCP; MaRV; OQP; QP-2; QS
Two men wrote a lexicon, Liddell and Scott. *Unknown.* CenHV
Two 'Mericana Men. T. A. Daly. CV; MPB
Two Mice, The Pope. *Fr.* An Imitation of the Sixth Satire of the Second Book of Horace. BeR
Two minutes' rest till the next man goes in! A Cricket Bowler. Edward Cracroft Lefroy. OBVV
Two mirrors, face to face, is all I need. World beyond World. Arthur Davison Ficke. NP
Two mites, two drops (yet all her house and land). The Widow's Mites. Richard Crashaw. LPS-2; OxBoCh
Two moonbeams flung across a chair. The Mode Atmospheric. Claire Wallis. DDA
Two Morsels of Profundity from the Minor Pre-Socratics. John Simon. SiTL
Two Mothers. Richard Burton. MOAH
Two Mothers, The. Shane Leslie. ISi
Two Mountains Men Have Climbed. Pauline Starkweather. GoYe
Two Musics. Norman McCaig. NeBP
Two Mysteries, The. Mary Mapes Dodge. AA; HBV; LPS-1; MaRV; WGRP
Two neighbours, who were rather dense. Parable. William Soutar. HaMV
Two Nests, The. Francis Carlin. BLA; PFY; TBM
Two noble dukes of great renown. A Song of the Banishment of Two Dukes. Thomas Deloney. SiCE
Two Noble Kinsmen, The, *sels.* Fletcher *and* Shakespeare.
Funeral Song: "Urns and odors, bring away," *fr.* I, v. AtBAP; ChTr; OBS; UnPo (1st ed.)
(Dirge of the Three Queens.) OBEV
(Song: "Urnes and Odours bring away!") BoW
(Urns and Odours Bring Away!) ElL; SiCE
"Hail Sovereign Queen of secrets, who hast power," *fr.* V, i. PoEL-2
"Roses, their sharp spines being gone," *fr.* I, i. BrBE; CenL; EG; ElSeCe; EV-1; MyFE; SiCE; ViBoPo
(Bridal Song.) CBOV; ElL; OBEV; OBSC
Two Nocturnes. Katherine Mansfield. HBMV
Arabian Shawl, The.
Sleeping Together.
Two nudists of Dover. Third Limick. Ogden Nash. NePA
Two Nut Trees. Edith Sitwell. *See* King of China's Daughter, The.
Two of a Trade. Samuel Willoughby Duffield. AA
Two of far nobler shape, erect and tall. Adam and Eve in the Garden [*or* Man and Woman Made One Unity *or* Satan Looks upon Adam and Eve in Paradise]. Milton. *Fr.* Paradise Lost, IV. BCEP; EV-2; LPS-2; TreFS
Two of Feste's Songs. Shakespeare. *See* Come Away, Come Away Death *and* O Mistress Mine . . .
Two of Thy children one summer day worked in their garden, Lord. The Garden. Rose Parkwood. WGRP
Two of us are left! Two Gerasimos Markoras. MoGP
Two of You. Mark Van Doren. UnPo (1st ed.)
Two Old Bachelors, The. Edward Lear. BeLS; BOHV; FiBHP
Two Old Kings, The. Lord De Tabley. ES; OBEV (new ed.); OBVV; VA
Two Old Lenten Rhymes. *Unknown.* ACP
"Lenten has brought us, as I understand," II.
"Lenten stuff is come to the town," I.

Two Old Men. Louise Driscoll. NLK
Two old men, The/ Sit in silence together. Old Friends. Hsü Chi. BoFr; PoHN
Two Old Men Look at the Sea. J. R. Hervey. AnNZ
Two-ones is the name for it, The. The Twins. Elizabeth Madox Roberts. TiPo
Two or three angels. The Black Riders, XXXII. Stephen Crane. AnAmPo; LA
Two or thee minutes—two or three hours. Minutes of Gold. *Unknown.* PoToHe
Two Others, on Either Side. Edith Mirick. ChIP
Two pale old men. Distance. Babette Deutsch. PoMa; VOD
Two Parents, The. "Hugh MacDiarmid." FaBoTw
Two Parodies. *Unknown.* CoSo
"Backward, turn backward, film guy, in your flight."
"Backward, turn backward, O Time with your wheels."
Two Pastorals, *sel.* Sir Philip Sidney.
Upon His Meeting with His Two Worthy Friends and Fellow-Poets. SiCE
("Join mates in mirth to me.") TuPP
Two Paths. Julia C. R. Dorr. AA; LEAP
Two Pewits. Edward Thomas. CH; MM; WhBS
Two Pictures. "Marian Douglas." LPS-1
Two Pictures, The ("It was a bright and lovely summer's morn"). *Unknown.* PTA-2
Two Pictures ("Two pictures hung on the dingy wall"). *Unknown.* BeLS; BLPA; FaBoBe
Two Pigeons, The. *Unknown, tr. fr. Russian by* W. R. S. Ralston. OnPM
Two pilgrims from the distant plain. Love and Time. Denis Florence MacCarthy. LPS-1
Two pilgrims on the sand espied. The Oyster and the Litigants. La Fontaine. WoL
Two Poems. Frances Cornford. EnLoPo
"I am a lamp, a lamp that is out," I.
"My love came back to me," II.
Two Poems against His Rival. Catullus, *tr. fr. Latin by* Jack Lindsay. LiTW
"If ever there was man who justly stank," I.
"Rufus, I trusted you. How vain that trust," II.
Two Poems on the Catholic Bavarians. Edgar Bowers. PtPa
"Fierce and brooding holocaust of faith, The," I.
"I know a wasted place high in the Alps," II.
Two Poets, The. Alice Meynell. OBVV
Two Poets of Croisic, The, *sels.* Robert Browning.
Epilogue: "What a pretty tale you told me." BPN
Such a Starved Bank of Moss. EPN; LoPo; VLEP
(Apparitions.) EPP; TSW; TSWC
(Prologue: "Such a starved bank of moss.") BMEP; BPN
(Prologue to "The Two Poets of Croisic.") HiLiEn
Two Points of View. Lucian B. Watkins. BANP
Two Prayers. Andrew Gillies. BLRP; MaRV; PoToHe
Two Prayers. Charlotte Perkins Gilman. OQP; QP-2; WGRP
Two pretty rills do meet, and, meeting, make. George Wither. *Fr.* Fair Virtue, the Mistress of Philarete. EPP; EPS
Two Pursuits. Christina Rossetti. EmBrPo; EPN; POTT
Two Rabbins, The. Whittier. EV-5
Two Red Roses across the Moon. William Morris. BLV; BPN; EmBrPo; EnLit; PoRA; PoVP; ViP; VLEP
Two Red Towers, The. Po Chü-i, *tr. fr. Chinese by* Arthur Waley. TrCh
Two regiments surround the throne. Dingaan and Retief. Charles Barter. *Fr.* Stray Memories of Natal and Zululand. BoSA
Two Remember Dawn. Heinrich von Morungen, *tr. fr. German by* Margaret R. Richey. LyMA
Two rival consorts ne'er can I approve. Monogamy. Euripides. *Fr.* Andromache. GrR
Two Rivers. Emerson. AmPP; AnNE; APW; CoBA; DDA; IAP; MOAP; OBAV; OxBA; TrGrPo
Two Rivers. *Unknown. See* Rivers Till and Tweed, The.
Two roads diverged in a yellow wood. The Road Not Taken. Robert Frost. AmPP; AnFE; AnNE; APA; BAP; BrBE; ChMo; ChTr; CMP; CoAnAm; CoBA; CoBMV; CV; FaBoCh; FaFP; GTBS-D; GTBS-W; InP; LEAP; LiTA; LiTG; LiTM; LoGBV; MAP; MAPA; MM; MoAB; MoAmPo; MOAP; NePA; OBAV; OxBA; PG; PoE; PreP; ReMP; SBMV; SeCeV; TwAmPo; TwP
Two Robin Red-Breasts built their nest. The Robin Red-Breasts [*or* I'll Try]. Ann Hawkshaw. OTPC (1923 ed.); PPL; SAS
Two Rossettis, The (brothers they). The P.R.B. Christina Rossetti. ViP
Two rows of cabbages. In the Ambulance. W. W. Gibson. BMEP
Two Rural Sisters. Charles Cotton. *See* Resolution in Four Sonnets . . .
Two sailors, when the vessel sank. Antipater of Thessalonica, *tr. fr. Greek by* the Earl of Cromer. GrPo
Two Sayings, The. Elizabeth Barrett Browning. MaRV
Two Sea Nymphs. William Diaper. *Fr.* Nereides; or, Sea-Eclogues. BeR
Two Seas. Abus Salt, *tr. fr. Arabic by* A. J. Arberry. MooP
Two Selves, The. Elsa Barker. UnW
Two separate divided silences. Severed Selves. Dante Gabriel Rossetti. The House of Life, XL. BPN; EmPrPo; PoVP; ViPo
Two Sermons. Austin Dobson. VLEP
Two Sewing. Hazel Hall. MoSiPe; NP
Two shall be born, the whole wide world apart. Fate. Susan Marr Spalding. AA; BBV (1951 ed.); BLPA; DDA; HBV; LEAP; NeHB; PoToHe
Two Ships, The. Bret Harte. MaRV
Two Short Ballettes . . . Made for His Pastime While He Was Prisoner in the Tower of London. Sir Thomas More.
Davy, the Dicer. TuPP
Lewis, the Lost Lover. OBSC; TuPP
(Fortune.) GoBC; PoLi
Two sides to a story! One of mine. Messalina Speaks. Charles Pelham Mulvany. TIP
Two Silences. Robert Haven Schauffler. AOAH
Two [*or* Twa] Sisters, The (*diff. versions*). *Unknown.* ABS; BaBo (A, B, *and* C *vers.*); BEL; CH; CoBE; EM-1; EnLit; ESPB (A *and* B *vers.*); EV-2; HBV; OuHeWo; PoMa; REAL; TOP; ViBoFo (A, B, *and* D *vers.*; C *vers.*, *with music*)
(Binnorie.) AnFE; BoLiVe; BSV; CBOV; EBSV; LEAP; OBB; OBEV; OnSP; ShBV-1; TrGroPo; WHA
(Cruel Sister, The.) BaBo
(Two [*or* Twa] Sisters of [*or* o'] Binnorie, The.) BLV; EnSB; GBV (1952 ed.); PCN; StaSt
Two slender stalks of black bamboo. Shi-ei, *tr. fr. Japanese by* Lois J. Erickson. SoLD
Two soldiers, lying where they fell. Death the Peacemaker. Ellen H. Flagg. MDAH
Two Solitudes. Evelyn Ames. GoYe
Two Somewhat Different Epigrams. Langston Hughes. NePoAm-2
"I look with awe upon the human race," II.
"Oh, God of dust and rainbows, help us see," I.
Two Songs, The. Blake. *See* Angel Singing, An.
Two Songs. C. Day Lewis. OAEP (2d ed.)
Love Was Once Light as Air.
Oh Light Was My Head.
Two Songs. Heine, *tr. fr. German by* Sir Theodore Martin. WoL
"Immovable, unchanging," I.
"People have teased and vexed me," II.
Two Songs. Kabir. *See* Songs of Kabir.
Two Songs. Abraham Reisen, *tr. fr. Yiddish by* Marie Syrkin. LiTW
"On with another new love," II.
"Sweetest Melody, The," I.
Two Songs. *Unknown, tr. fr. Spanish by* Richard Beaumont. LyMA
"All are asleep, heart so true."
"Moon, moon shining bright."
Two Songs by Amiens. Shakespeare. *See* Blow, Blow, Thou Winter Wind *and* Under the Greenwood Tree.
Two Songs for General Chao. Ts'en Ts'an, *tr. fr. Chinese by* Wang Sheng-chih. WhP
"Coat of squirrel fur, A," I.
"Wind on Tien Shan slashes the autumn, The," II.
Two Songs from a Play. W. B. Yeats. *Fr.* The Resurrection.
"I saw a staring virgin stand," I. CoBMV; EnLP; ExPo; LiTB; MoPo; PoFS; RiBV; SeCeV; UnPo
(Song from a Play.) FaBoTw
"In pity for man's darkening thought," II. EnLP; ExPo; LiTB; MoPo; PoFS; RiBV; SeCeV; UnPo
Two Songs in Praise of Steingerd. Cormac Ogmundarson, *tr. fr. Old Norse by* W. G. Collingwood *and* Jón Stefánsson. LiTW
"Moon of her brow, The, it is beaming," I.
"Tree of my treasure and longing, The," II.
Two Songs in Spring. Thomas S. Jones, Jr.
"At hint of spring I have you back again," II. VOD
"O little buds all bourgeoning with spring," I. VOD
(Song in Spring, A.) LBMV; POT; PoTo
Two Songs of a Fool, *sel.* W. B. Yeats.
"Speckled cat and a tame hare, A." AlDL
Two Songs of Advent. Yvor Winters. NP
"Coyote, on delicate mocking feet," II.
"On the desert, between pale mountains," I.
Two Songs on the Economy of Abundance. James Agee. MAP; MoAmPo
Red Sea.
Temperance Note; and Weather Prophecy.
Two Songs to Celia. Ben Jonson. *See* Come, My Celia, Let Us Prove *and* To Celia ("Drink to me only with thine eyes").
Two Sonnet-Songs. Frank T. Marzials. VA
"Fleet, fleet and few," II.
"Hist, hist, ye winds," I.
Two Sonnets. David P. Berenberg. HBMV
"Antigone and Helen—would they laugh."
"Or is it all illusion? Do the years."
Two Sonnets. *sel.* John Crowe Ransom.
"It was beside the fire that I had lit," I. LO
(Yea.) LoPS

Two Sonnets. Charles Hamilton Sorley.
"Saints have adored the lofty soul of you," I. HBMV; MBP; MoBrPo; NeMA; TrGrPo (1942 ed.)
"Such, such is Death: no triumph: no defeat," II. HBMV; MBP; MoBrPo; NeMA; TrGrPo (1942 ed.)
(Such Is Death.) BLV
Two Sonnets. Dylan Thomas.
"Altarwise by owl-light in the halfway-house." MoAB; MoBrPo (1950 ed.)
(Sonnets, I.) LiTM
"Death is all metaphors, shape in one history." MoAB; MoBrPo (1950 ed.)
(Sonnets, II.) LiTM
Two Sonnets. James Thomson.
"Striving to sing glad songs, I but attain," II. EmBrPo; PoVP
"Why are your songs all wild and bitter sad," I. EmBrPo; PeBoSo; PoVP
Two Sonnets. Frederick Goddard Tuckerman. OnAP
"Yes, the dead pines and deersfoot on the ground."
"Young Silas Long, a carrier through these woods."
Two Sonnets, *sel.* Hans Zinsser.
"Now is Death merciful. He calls me hence," II. LoPS
Two Sonnets for a Lost Love. Samuel A. DeWitt. GoYe
"If I were less the man, I might have kept," II.
" 'There is no permanence,' you sagely said," I.
Two Sonnets from a Sequence. Edgar Holt. BoAV
"This side of madness, while the flames abate," I.
"Under the midnights' iron rain, under," II.
Two Sonnets on Death. Charles Hamilton Sorley. *See* Two Sonnets.
Two Sonnets on Fame. Keats.
"Fame, like a wayward girl, will still be coy," I. EmBrPo; EnRP
(Fame.) EM-2
(On Fame.) BPN; EnLit; ERP
"How fevered is the man, who cannot look," II. EmBrPo; EnL; EnRP
(Fame.) EM-2; ES
(On Fame.) BPN; EnLit; EPN; ERP
Two Sonnets; to a Spiritual Entity. Helen Pinkerton. PtPa
"I did not see you even when I went," I.
"If I had stood, waiting for you to come," II.
Two Sons. Robert Buchanan. TVSH; VA
Two souls diverse out of our human sight. On the Deaths of Thomas Carlyle and George Eliot. Swinburne. BEL; BMEP; BPN; EmBrPo; HBV; PoVP; TOP; VA; VLEP
Two Sparrows. Humbert Wolfe. TSWC; TwCV
Two Spirits, The. James Benjamin Kenyon. AA
Two Spirits, The; an Allegory. Shelley. CH; EmBrPo; EPN; ERP
Fatal Vision, The, *sel.* RO
("Some say, when nights are dry and clear.") LO
Two Springs. Li Ch'ing-chao, *tr. fr. Chinese by* Kenneth Rexroth. OnPC
Two springs she saw—two radiant Tuscan springs. Mimma Bella, II. Eugene Lee-Hamilton. HBV
Two Stanzas about Eve. Herman Wildenvey, *tr. fr. Norwegian by* Charles W. Stork. AnNoLy
Two Stars, The. W. H. Davies. ChMo; CMP; MBP; MoBrPo
Two stars alone of primal magnitude. Washington and Lincoln. Wendell Phillips Stafford. PGD; PSO
Two stars once on their lonely way. Orbits. Richard Le Gallienne. VA
Two States of Prayer. Thomas Merton. JKCP (1955 ed.)
Two statesmen met by moonlight. What the Moon Saw. Vachel Lindsay. CrMA
Two steps from my garden rail. Hayyim Nahman Bialik. Songs of the People, I. AWP; JAWP; WBP
Two Streams, The. Oliver Wendell Holmes. *Fr.* The Professor at the Breakfast Table. PEOR
Two Streams, The. Thomas Moore. *Fr.* Evenings in Greece. GoBC
Two stubborn beaks. Argument. Mildred Weston. PoMa; WhC
Two summers since, I saw at Lammas fair. Phoebe Dawson. George Crabbe. GoTL
Two sunnes at once from one fair heaven there shinde. Rosaders Sonnet, Sent to Rosalynde. Thomas Lodge. *Fr.* Rosalynde; or, Euphues' Golden Legacy. BrBE
Two Suns. Al-Dabbaj, *tr. fr. Arabic by* A. J. Arberry. MooP
Two Swans, The. Thomas Hood. CH
Two swans break, The. The Love of Swans. Leonard Mann. MoAuPo
Two Swede families live downstairs. House. Carl Sandburg. ChMo; CMP
Two Taverns. Edwin Markham. TSW
Two that could not have lived their single lives. Two in August. John Crowe Ransom. AWP; InPo; LoPS; MOAP; MoPo; NePA; OxBA
Two thieves, pursuing their profession. The Thieves and the Ass. La Fontaine. OnPM
Two Things. Donald C. Babcock. NePoAm
Two things have I asked of Thee. Neither Poverty nor Riches. Proverbs, Bible, *O.T.* TrJP
Two Things Have Met in Me. Solomon ibn Gabirol, *tr. fr. Hebrew by* Israel Zangwill. LiTW
Two things make woman slow, we find. Good Reasons. Keith Preston. WhC
"Two things," said Kant, "fill me with breathless awe." The Third Wonder [*or* Breathless Awe]. Edwin Markham. MAP; MaRV
Two things there are with Memory will abide. Memories. Thomas Bailey Aldrich. AA
Two things were set. Two things. Donald C. Babcock. NePoAm
Two Thoughts of Death. Christina Rossetti. DiM
Two thousand feet beneath our wheels. Cockpit in the Clouds. Dick Dorrance. FaPON; PoMa; TiPo
Two thousand years ago a flower. Resurrection. Sarah H. Bradford. EOAH
Two thousand years are far enough! It Isn't Far to Bethlehem. Arthur R. Macdougall, Jr. PGD
Two thousand years of the Christian creed, and a thousand years before. Trade. E. J. Brady. TVSH
Two top-knots not yet plaited into one. Going to the Mountains with a Little Dancing Girl, Aged Fifteen. Po Chü-i. TrCh
Two Towns. Ralph Linton. DDA
Two Tramps in Mud Time. Robert Frost. AmPo; AmPP; AnNE; BoLiVe; ChMo; CoBA; CoBMV; CoV; LiTA; LiTM; MAP; MoAB; MoAmPo; NaMP; NePA; PoFS; PoLFOT; TrGrPo; TwP; UnPo (3d ed.)
Two Translations from Villon. *Pr. tr. fr. French by* J. M. Synge.
"Man I had a love for, The." MoBrPo
(Old Woman's Lamentations, An.) OBMV; TwCV
"Mother of God that's Lady of the Heavens." MoBrPo
(Translation from Villon, A.) NeMA
Two Travelers. C. Day Lewis. EnLit
Two Trees, The. W. B. Yeats. MaPo; POTE; TIP
Two Triolets ("I ran over a pig"). *At. to* Maurice Baring. AlDL
Two Triolets. Harrison Robertson. HBV
What He Said. PR
What She Thought. PR
Two Truths. Helen Hunt Jackson. PR
2 Variations: All About Love. Philip Whalen. NeAP
Two vases stood on the Shelf of Life. Vases. Nan Terrell Reed. BLPA
Two Veterans. Walt Whitman. *See* Dirge for Two Veterans.
Two Victories. Wordsworth. *Fr.* Song at the Feast of Brougham Castle. LH
Two Views of a Cadaver Room. Sylvia Plath. GoYe
Two Villages, The. Rose Terry Cooke. HBV
Two Voices. Valery Yakovlevich Bryusov, *tr. fr. Russian by* C. M. Bowra. BoR
Two Voices. Alice Corbin. HBMV; NP; NV
Two Voices, The. Tennyson. EmBrPo; PoVP
Sels.
Dragon-Fly, The. SN
Life Not Death ("Whatever crazy sorrow saith"), *2 sts.* MaRV
Two Voices. Paul Verlaine, *tr. fr. French by* Alan Conder. TrFP
Two voices are there: one is of the deep. A Sonnet [*or* Wordsworth]. James Kenneth Stephen. CenHV; EnLi-2 (1949 ed.); FiBHP; HBV; PC; VA; WhC
Two voices are there; one is of the sea. Thought of a Briton on the Subjugation of Switzerland [*or* Sonnet *or* England and Switzerland, 1802]. Wordsworth. BEL; BoLiVe; BPN; ChER; EM-2; EmBrPo; EnL; EnLi-2; EnRP; EPN; EPP; ERP; ES; GEPC; GTBS; GTBS-D; GTBS-W; GTSE; GTSL; HiLiEn; MCCG; OBRV; PC; PeBoSo; PoFr; REAL; ReaPo; SeCeV; ShBV-3; TOP; TwHP
Two Voices in a Meadow. Richard Wilbur. NePoAm-2; UnPo (3d ed.)
Two-Volume Novel. Dorothy Parker. InMe
Two Voyages. Maurice James Craig. NeIP
Two Waitings, The. John White Chadwick. LPS-1
Two War Sonnets. E. H. W. Meyerstein. NeTW
Thoughts of a Briton in the Fourth Year of War.
Thus Answered.
Two Ways. John V. A. Weaver. HBMV; LoPS; NP
Two Ways of Visiting. Timothy Dwight. *Fr.* Greenfield Hill. AmPP (4th ed.)
Two webfoot brothers loved a fair. That Gentle Man from Boston Town. Joaquin Miller. BOHV
Two Weeks. Nicolás Guillén, *tr. fr. Spanish by* Langston Hughes. PoNe
Two weeping for beauty perished, husband. Exhortation to the Artists. Hyam Plutzik. FiMAP
Two Went Up to [*or* into] the Temple to Pray. Richard Crashaw. ALV; CAW; GrCo-1; LPS-2; MaRV
Two were silent in a sunless church, The. Her Dilemma. Thomas Hardy. EmBrPo; Po
Two white heads the grasses cover. Louise Imogen Guiney. Two Epitaphs, I. OBAV

Two White Horses, *with music*. *Unknown*. AS
Two wild duck of the upland spaces. Duck. John Lyle Donaghy. OxBI
Two Winds. Victor Starbuck. LS
Two winds, one calm, another fierce to see. Robert Tofte. *Fr*. Laura. ReIE
Two winged genii in the air. Love and Youth. William James Linton. VA
Two Witches, *sel*. Robert Frost.
Witch of Coös, The. AmP; AnNE; AtBAP; CoBMV; DaM; ExPo; LiTM (rev. ed.); MoAB; NePA; ReMP; ViBoPo (1958 ed.)
Two Witnesses, The. Pierre Jean Jouve, *tr. fr. French by* David Gascoyne. MiFP
Two Wives, The. William Dean Howells. AA
Two Women. Nathaniel Parker Willis. *See* Unseen Spirits.
Two women had these words engraved. Epitaphs; for a Fickle Man. Mark Van Doren. ViBoPo
Two women loved him, shapes of Heaven. Thomas Caulfield Irwin. *Fr*. Swift. IrPN
Two women on the lone wet strand. The Watchers. William Stanley Braithwaite. PoNe
Two words from China: "Ku li"—bitter strength. Ku Li. "Robin Hyde." AnNZ
Two worlds hast thou to dwell in, Sweet. The First Skylark of Spring. Sir William Watson. VA
Two Yankee wags, one summer day. Here She Goes, and There She Goes. James Nack. BOHV
Two Years Later. W. B. Yeats. GTIV
Two years the blank walls stared at him. A History. John Williams. NePoAm-2
Two years thus spent in gathering knowledge. Tom Brainless at College [*or* as Student and Preacher]. John Trumbull. *Fr*. The Progress of Dulness. AmPP; ATP (1935 ed.); IAP
'Twon't do to linger here. Lampoon: In the School of Socrates. Aristophanes. *Fr*. The Clouds. GrR
'Twould be too bad to keep my flowers. My Flowers. Shizu Moki. SoLD
'Twould ring the bells of Heaven. The Bells of Heaven. Ralph Hodgson. BoTP; ChMo; CMP; GTBS-W; LiTM; MBP; MoAB; MoBrPo; OBEV (new ed.); OtMeF; PC; QS; ShBV-1; SiSoSe; SP; TwCV; UTS; WP
Twy-horn Pan, the ridgy hills. To Pan. *Unknown*. OxBG
Tyburn and Westminster. John Heywood. ACP
Tyburn, lament, in pensive sable mourn. The Execution Chaplain, Mr. Sam Smith, Ordinary of Newgate. Tom Brown. *Fr*. An Elegy on That Most Orthodox and Painstaking Divine, Mr. Sam Smith, Ordinary of Newgate. BeR
Tydes-Well, the Third Wonder of the Peak. Charles Cotton. *Fr*. The Wonders of the Peake. BeR
Tyger, The. Blake. *See* Tiger, The.
Tygers. Thomas Chatterton. *Fr*. The Death of Nicou. RO
Tying a Knot in the Devil's Tail. *Unknown*. ABF
Tying her bonnet under her chin. The Love-Knot. Nora Perry. AA; BOHV; HBV; LPS-1; PR
Tyl it was noon, they stoden for to se. At the Gate. Chaucer. *Fr*. Troilus and Criseyde. SeCePo
Tymes Goe by Turnes. Robert Southwell. *See* Times Go by Turns.
Tyne Dock. Francis Scarfe. NeBP
Tyneside Widow, The. Swinburne. PoVP; ViP
Type of the antique Rome! Rich reliquary. The Coliseum. Poe. AmPP (3d ed.); IAP; SPP; TCAP
Typewriter, The. Mariana Griswold Van Rensselaer. GFA
Tyrannicide. Walter Savage Landor. PoFr
Tyrannick [*or* Tyrannic] Love; or, The Royal Martyr, *sels*. Dryden.
Ah, How Sweet It Is to Love, *fr*. IV, i. EnLi-1; HBV; HoPM; LEAP; LiTL; LPS-1; MaPo; OBEV (1st ed.); ViBoPo
(Song: "Ah, how sweet it is to love.") EiPP; EPS (1942 ed.); FaBoEn
Epilogue. OAEP; ViBoPo
(Epilogue to "Tyrannick Love.") SeCV-2
Prologue. OAEP; ViBoPo
"You pleasing dreams of love and sweet delight," *fr*. IV, i. ElSeCe
Tyranny and Law. Samuel Butler. *Fr*. Hudibras. BeR
Tyrant Apple Is Eaten, The. Norman McCaig. NeBP
Tyrant Cat, A, by surname Nibblelard. The Council Held by the Rats. La Fontaine. CIV
Tyrant has fallen, The. Vincenzo Monti. *Fr*. Ode on Superstition. PoFr
Tyrant's Death, The. Judith, XIII, Bible, Apocrypha. BHV (6–19); PoFr (6–15)
Tyrants of the Golden City tremble, The. Shelley. *Fr*. The Revolt of Islam. PoFr
Tyrants when they come to die. King David. Heine. PoFr
Tyr'd with all these for restfull death I cry. *See* Tired with all these . . .
Tyre. Nonnus, *tr. fr. Greek by* F. L. Lucas. *Fr*. Dionysiaca. GrPE
Tyre. Bayard Taylor. LBAP
Tyre brought me up, who born in thee had been. Of Himself. Meleager. AWP
Tyre of the farther West! be thou too warned. United States. John Keble. CoBE
Tyre of the West, and glorying in the name. England. Cardinal Newman. ACP; CAW; GOBC; JKCP; PoVP; VA
Tyrian dye why do you wear. To His Mistress [*or* Ode to His Mistress]. Abraham Cowley. CaAE; EG; EV-2; SeCL
Tyrle, Tyrlow, Tyrle, Tyrlow. *Unknown*. AnEC; MeRV
Tywater. Richard Wilbur. GTBS-W; LiTA; LiTM (rev. ed.); MiAP; MoAB; NePA; ReMP
"Tzu-yeh" Song, A: "All night I could not sleep." *Unknown, tr. fr. Chinese by* Arthur Waley. OnPM; TrCh
(Five Songs.) ChLP
"Tzu-yeh" Song, A: "At the time when blossoms." *Unknown, tr. fr. Chinese by* Arthur Waley. TrCh
(Five Songs.) ChLP
"Tzu-yeh" Song, A: "I have brought my pillow and am lying at the northern window." *Unknown, tr. fr. Chinese by* Arthur Waley. TrCh
(Five Songs.) ChLP
"Tzu-yeh" Song, A: "I heard my love was going to Yang-chou." *Unknown, tr. fr. Chinese* by Arthur Waley. OnPM; TrCh
(Five Songs.) ChLP
"Tzu-yeh" Song, A: "I will carry my coat and not put on my belt." *Unknown, tr. fr. Chinese by* Arthur Waley. TrCh
(Five Songs.) ChLP

U

U is for Umbrellas. Phyllis McGinley. *Fr*. All Around the Town. TiPo
USA. Paul Engle. SiTL
U.S.A. Recruit, The. *Unknown*. CSF
U.S. Air Force, The. Robert Crawford. PoRL
U.S. Sailor with the Japanese Skull, The. Winfield Townley Scott. FiMAP; MiAP; PreP; WaP
U-S-U Range, The. *At. to* G. W. Barr. CoSo; CSF
Ubasti. Gelett Burgess. CIV
Ubi Sunt Qui ante Nos Fuerunt? *Unknown*. CBOV; CoBE; EnLi-1; EPP, *Middle and mod. Eng.*; OAEP; SeCeV
Ubique. *At. to* Joshua Sylvester. *See* Were I as Base as Is the Lowly Plain.
Uccello. Gregory Corso. NeAP
Uccello on the Heath. Geoffrey Grigson. WaP
Uffia. Harriet R. White. BOHV; NA
Ug was a hairy but painstaking artist. The Story of Ug. Edwin Meade Robinson. HBMV; YaD
Ugliness. Ibn Shakil, *tr. fr. Arabic by* A. J. Arberry. MooP
Ugolino. Dante, *tr. fr. Italian by* Laurence Binyon. *Fr*. Divina Commedia: Inferno, XXXIII. LiA
Uh—go down, go down, you little red. Go Down, You Little Red Rising Sun. *Unknown*. OuSiCo
"Ukraina is sad for that she has no place to dwell in." Fragment. *Unknown*. PoFr
Ukrainian Song. Ivan Surikov, *tr. fr. Russian by* V. de S. Pinto. BoR
Ulalume. Poe. AA; AmP; AmPo; AmPP; AnAmPo; AnEnPo; AnFE; APA; APW; ATP; AWP; BAP; BAV; CoAnAm; CoBA; CoV; DaM; IAP; JAWP; LA; LEAP; LiTA; LiTG; LO; MOAP; NePA; OBAV; OuHeWo; OxBA; PoFS; REAL; SPP; TCAP; TOP; TreF; UnPo; ViBoPo; WBP; WHA
Ulf in Ireland. Charles De Kay. AA
Ulla, mine Ulla, to thee may I proffer. To Ulla at a Window in Fishertown, Noon of a Summer Day. Karl Mikael Bellman. AnSL
Ulric Dahlgren. Kate Brownlee Sherwood. BIG; PAH
Ulsterman, An. "Lyn Doyle." OnYI
Ultima in mortis hora. The Benedictine Ultima. *Unknown*. CAW
Ultima Ratio Regum. Stephen Spender. BBV (1951 ed.); EnLi-2 (1949 ed.): FaFP; LiTB; LiTM; MaRV; PoLFOT; SeCePo; SoV; WaaP; WaP
Ultima Thule. *sel*. Longfellow.
Dedication: "With favoring winds, o'er sunlit seas." CoV; ViBoPo
("With favouring winds, o'er the sunlit seas.") AlDL
Ultima Veritas. Washington Gladden. MaRV; OQP; QP-1
Ultimate Atrocity, The. Siegfried Sassoon. ChMo; CMP
Ultimate Exile, *sel*. R. N. Currey.
"How lovely are the waters of Babylon." BoSA
Ultimate Joy, The. *Unknown*. BOHV
Ulysses. Robert Graves. ChMP; FaBoTw; OxBI

Ulysses, *sel.* Stephen Phillips.
"Slowly the mist fades! Ah! the cypress tree." ReTS
(Homecoming of Ulysses, The.) MW
Ulysses. Tennyson. AEV; ATP; AWP; BEL; BHV; BLV; BMEP; BoLiVe; BPN; CaAE; CBOV; CoBE; CoEV; EM-2; EmBrPo; EnL; EnLi-2; EnLit; EPN; EPP; EV-5; ExPo; FiP; GDAH; GEPC; GTSE; HBV; HoPM; InP; InPo; LEAP; LiTB; LoBV; MaPo; MCCG; MyFE; NBE; OAEP; OnPP; OuHeWo; PIAE; PIR; Po; PoE; PoeMoYo; PoFS; PoRA; PoVP; PreP; REAL; ReaPo; ReTS; SeCePo; SeCeV; ShBV-4; TCEP; TOP; TreF; TrGrPo; TriL; TwCrTr; TwHP; TyEnPo; UnPo; VA; ViBoPo; ViPo; ViPP; VLEP; WHA; YT
Sels.
Challenge of Life, The. MaRV
(Experience.) OQP; QP-2
"Lights begin to twinkle from the rocks, The." MuP
"Old age hath yet his honor and his toil." BLP
"There lies the port; the vessel puffs her sail." ETS; MaRV; OQP; OTPC; PC; QP-2
(Work May Yet Be Done.) GrCo-1
Ulysses Advises Achilles Not to Let Slip Opportunity. Shakespeare. *See* Time ("Time hath, my lord").
Ulysses and His Dog. Homer, *tr. fr. Greek by* Pope. *Fr.* The Odyssey, XVII. FiP; OBEC
("And a dog, lying there, lifted its head," *pr. tr. by* Martin Johnson.) LO
(Death of Argus, The, *tr. by.* F. L. Lucas.) GrPE
(Dog Argos, The, *pr. tr. by* T. E. Lawrence.) OxBG
("Dog lying near lifted his head and ears, A," *pr. tr. by* George H. Palmer.) GrPo
(Old Hound Argos, The, *pr. tr. by* Samuel Butler.) GrR
Ulysses and the Siren [*or* Syren]. Samuel Daniel. ElL; EV-1; LiA; LoBV; OBEV; OBSC; PoEL-2; ReaPo; ReEn; ReIE; SiCE; TuPP; TwCrTr; ViBoPo
Ulysses and the Sirens. Homer, *tr. fr. Greek by* George Chapman. *Fr.* The Odyssey, XII. ReEn
Ulysses answered, "I hope you may be as dear to the gods as you are to me." An Heroic Answer to the Servant Problem. Homer. *Fr.* The Odyssey, XV. GrR
Ulysses has come back to me again! Ulysses Returns, I. Roselle Mercier Montgomery. BAP; HBMV; LPS-1; LS; TBM
Ulysses Hears the Prophecies of Tiresias. Homer, *tr. fr. Greek by* George Chapman. *Fr.* The Odyssey, XI. LoBV
Ulysses in Autumn. Joseph Auslander. MAP; MoAmPo (1942 ed.); PoeMoYo
Ulysses in the Waves. Homer, *tr. fr. Greek by* George Chapman. *Fr.* The Odyssey, V. OBS
Ulysses; on Degree. Shakespeare. *See* On Degree.
Ulysses Returns, I–IV. Roselle Mercier Montgomery. BAP; HBMV; LPS-1; LS; TBM
Ulysses S. Grant. Paul Southworth Bliss. StaSt
Ulysses; the Instant Way. Shakespeare. *See* Time ("Time hath, my lord").
"Ulysses!" (with a sigh she thus began). Homer. *Fr.* The Odyssey, V. GroPo
Umber slant lands under the Apennines, The. To the South. Brewster Ghiselin. LiTA; LiTM (rev. ed.); NePA
Umbrella Brigade, The. Laura Richards. SUS; TiPo
Umbrella Jim. Cotton Noe. LS
Umbrellas. Rowena Bennett. TiPo (1959 ed.)
Umpire, The. Walker Gibson. NePoAm
Un, Deux, Trois, *with music.* *Unknown, tr. fr. French.* ABF
Un Médecin Malgré Eux. Martial, *tr. fr. Latin by* Paul Nixon. RoL
Una Anciana Mexicana. Alice Corbin. *See* Muy Vieja Mexicana.
Una and the Lion. Spenser. The Faerie Queene, I, 3. BCEP, *mod vers.;* LPS-3
("One day, nigh wearie of the yrkesome way.") BoLiVe
Una and the Red Cross Knight. Spenser. The Faerie Queene, I, 1. LPS-3 (*7 sts.*)
("Gentle Knight was pricking on the plaine, A.") ATP; BoLiVe, *abr.;* CoBE; EPP (*fr.* 1 *and* 3); ExPo; PIAE (*5 sts.*); TyEnPo
(Red-Cross Knight, The, *2 sts.*) GoBC
Una Bhan. Robert Farren, *ad. fr. Gaelic.* JKCP (1955 ed.)
Unable by Long and Hard Travel to Banish Love, Returns Her Friend. George Turberville. TuPP
Unable to breathe, I inhaled the classic Aegean. Small Perfect Manhattan. Peter Viereck. MiAP
Unaltered aisles that wait and wait forever. The Answer. "Katherine Hale." CPG
Unanswered. Martha Dickinson Bianchi. AA
Unanswered encores, rue, and requiems sung. Requiescat. Otto Freund. MuM
Unanswered Prayer[s]. Oliver Huckel. MaRV; PraP
(I Thank Thee, Lord.) BLRP; WBLP
Unanswered Prayers. Ella Wheeler Wilcox. WGRP
Unanswered Question, An. Leonard Bacon. MuM
Unanswered yet the prayer your lips have pleaded. Sometime, Somewhere [*or* Pray without Ceasing]. Ophelia Guyon Browning. BLPA; BLRP; NeHB; PraP
Unarme Eros, the long dayes task is done. Shakespeare. *Fr.* Antony and Cleopatra, IV, xii. NBE
Unarmed Combat. Henry Reed. Lessons of the War, III. LiTB
Unarmed she goeth, yet her hands. Charity. George Parsons Lathrop. CAW; JKCP
Unattainable, The. Harry Romaine. BOHV
Unattained, The. David Gascoyne. MoP
Unattained, The. Henry Jerome Stockard. NoCaPo
Unawares. Emma A. Lent. PTA-2
Unawkward Singers, The. David Ferry. NePoAm-2
Unbark'd and leafless, passenger, you see. Alcaeus of Messene. Philip V, King of Macedon. OXBG
Unbearable is the sickness that invades old age. Old Age. Lu Yu. WhP
Unbelief. Elizabeth York Case. *See* There Is No Unbelief.
Unbelievable, The. Edwin Markham. MaRV; PSO
Unbeliever, The. Elizabeth Bishop. FiMAP; LiTA
Unbeliever, An. Anna Hempstead Branch. MaRV; NV; PFY; WGRP
Unbeliever. Dorothy Dow. HBMV
Unbeseechable, The. Frances Cornford. MBP; MoBrPo
Unborn, The. Julia Neely Finch. AA
Unborn. Irene Rutherford McLeod. HBMV
Unborn, The. Judith Wright. MoAuPo
Unborn Eternal Self. *Unknown, tr. fr. Sanskrit by* Joseph Nadin Rawson. *Fr.* The Upanishads. OnPM
Unbounded is thy range, with varied style. William Collins. *Fr.* Ode on the Popular Superstitions of the Highlands. BCEP
Unbowed. Margaret R. Richter. MuM
Unbridled Now. Laura Lourene LeGear. GoYe
Unc' Si, de Holy Bible say. The Difference. John Banister Tabb. BAP; BPP; PC
Uncalled the cattle did at evening go. The Cow Herd. Diotimus. OxBG
Uncaptured is essential death, III. Frances Crawford. PtPa
Uncertain Battle, The. David Gascoyne. SoV
Uncertain State of a Lover, The. *Unknown.* ElL
Uncertain still, new-mated birds. Wild Apple. Elise Aylen. TwCV
Uncertainty of Life, The. Barnabe Googe. SiCE
Uncessant Minutes, whil'st you move you tell. To His Watch, When He Could Not Sleep. Lord Herbert of Cherbury. MePo; PoEL-2
Unchangeable, The. Shakespeare. *See* Sonnets, CIX.
Unchanged, The. Isabel Ecclestone Mackay. OCL
Unchanged. Martial. *See* Shopper, The.
Unchanged, O lovely lamp, you still adorn. On a Lamp. Eduard Mörike. AnGP
Unchanging, The. Sara Teasdale. ChMo; CMP
Unchanging Jesus. Karl Johann Philipp Spitta, *tr. fr. German by* R. Massie. BLRP
Uncivil sickness, hast thou no regard. Henry Constable. *Fr.* Diana. ReIE
Uncivilized. Edmund Vance Cooke. BAP
Unclaimed. Florida Watts Smyth. StaSt
Uncle, The. Whittier. *Fr.* Snow-bound. GoTP
Uncle Ananias. E. A. Robinson. AnNE; BAV; BoLiVe (1945 ed.); IAP; LaNeLa; MaPo; MoAmPo (1950 ed.); NePA; PoeMoYo; TwP
Uncle Andy and I. Leroy F. Jackson. GaP
Uncle Bud, *with music.* *Unknown.* StDa
Uncle Eph's Banjo Song. James Edwin Campbell. BANP
Uncle Frank. Monica Shannon. GaP
Uncle Gabe's White Folks. Thomas Nelson Page. AA; OBAV
Uncle Jim. Alice Corbin. *Fr.* Echoes of Childhood. PoNe
Uncle Jim. Countee Cullen. BANP
Uncle or Sun. Vladimir Kazin, *tr. fr. Russian by* Jack Lindsay. RuPo
Uncle Remus and His Friends, *sel.* Joel Chandler Harris.
My Honey, My Love. AA; FaBoBe
Uncle Remus, His Songs and His Sayings, *sels.* Joel Chandler Harris.
Big Bethel Church, De. LEAP
Plantation Play-Song. MCCG
Plough-Hands' Song, The. AA; LHV
Revival Hymn. HBV; MCCG
Time Goes by Turns. IHA
Uncle Simon and Uncle Jim. "Artemus Ward." BOHV; NA
Unclose Those Eyelids. Henry Glapthorne. SeCL
Uncommon. Callimachus, *tr. fr. Greek by* Robert Guthrie MacGregor. OnPM
Unconcern. Virginia Moore. TBM
Unconcerned, The. Thomas Flatman. CEP; FaBoCh
Unconquerable Love. Sophocles. *See* Love, Conquering and Unconquerable.
Unconquerably, men venture on the quest. The Polar Quest. Richard Burton. AA
Unconquer'd captive—close thine eye. Virginia Capta. Margaret Junkin Preston. PAH
Unconquered Air, The. Florence Earle Coates. LBMV; PoMa

Unconscious, The. Merrill Moore. PoP
Unconscious, The. Alfred Noyes. *See* You That Sing in the Blackthorn.
Unconscious Cerebration. W. E. H. Lecky. *See* Say Not That the Past Is Dead.
Unconscious is incredibly wise, The. The Unconscious. Merrill Moore. PoP
Unconscious of amused and tolerant eyes. Portrait of a Child. Louis Untermeyer. BAP; FAOV; HBMV
Unconstant Lover, The, *with music*. *Unknown*. TrAS
Uncourtly Love. Walther von der Vogelweide, *tr. fr. German by* Jethro Bithell. LiTW
Uncouth, unconquered, unafraid. The Trail. Percy MacKaye. *Fr.* Ourselves. AOAH
Uncover for the majesty of Death. Death. Agnes Lindsay Carnegie. EBSV
Uncover to the Flag. Edward C. Cheverton. FOAH
Uncrowned. Alfred G. Bailey. BoCaPo
Uncuddled Baby, The. Elsie Duncan Yale. DDA
Undedicated. Jean Starr Untermeyer. TBM
Under. J. C. Squire. FaBoTw
Under a bridge of stone the river shuddered by. The Dreamer. Clifford Bax. TCPD
Under a budding hedge I hid. While April Rain Went By. Shaemas O'Sheel. HBMV
Under a daisied bank. The Milkmaid. Thomas Hardy. SiTL
Under a grey October sky. Conclusion. W. J. Turner. *Fr.* Death's Men. TCPD
Under a Lady's Picture. Edmund Waller. EnLoPo
Under a Laurel. Anyte, *tr. fr. Greek by* R. A. Furness. OxBG
Under a lonely sky a lonely tree. On a Lonely Spray. James Stephens. AnFE; ChMo; CMP; OnYI
Under a sky of azure. O, Fair New Mexico. Elizabeth Garrett. PoRL
Under a southern wind. Song. Theodore Roethke. CrMA
Under a Spell. Catullus, *tr. fr. Latin*. OnPM
Under a splintered mast. A Talisman. Marianne Moore. AnFE; APA; CoAnAm; MAP; MoAB; MoAmPo; NP; TCPD; ViBoPo
Under a spreading chestnut-tree. The Village Blacksmith. Longfellow. AA; AnNE; CoBA; FaBoBe; FaFP; FaPON; GoTP; HBV; HBVY; IAP; LEAP; LPS-2; NeHB; OnPP; OTPC; PECK; PIR; PTA-1; PYM; StVeCh; TCAP; TreF; TVSH; WBLP
Under a spreading gooseberry bush the village burglar lies. The Village Blacksmith. *Unknown*. FiBHP
Under a stagnant sky. To James McNeill Whistler. W. E. Henley. PoVP
Under a sultry, yellow sky. Mercedes. Elizabeth Stoddard. AA; LBAP
Under a Telephone Pole. Carl Sandburg. PoeMoYo; PoTo; VOD (1935 ed.)
Under a throne I saw a virgin sit. Sonnet. Fulke Greville. Caelica, LXXXI [LXXXII]. ReIE; SiCE; TuPP
Under a toadstool/ Crept a wee elf. The Elf and the Dormouse. Oliver Herford. AA; BoChLi; FaBoBe; FaPON; GFA; GoBP; GoTP; HBV; HBVY; MPB; OnHT; OTPC (1946 ed.); PCH; PoRh; PRWS; RAR; SP; TiPo; TSW; TSWC; TVC; TVSH; UTS
Under a tree I read a Latin book. Connoisseurs. Dugald Sutherland MacColl. PoC
Under a tree, in sporting me. A Song upon, "Now Must I Sing." *Unknown*. AnEC
Under a tree in the shade sits a toad. The Toad. Louis Kent. WaKn
Under a wall of bronze. The Swan. John Gould Fletcher. MM; OTPC (1946 ed.); PoeMoYo; SPP; TwCV
Under a Wiltshire Apple Tree. Anna de Bary. CH
Under All This Slate. James Hayford. NePoAm-2
Under an aged oak was Willie laid. Fourth Eclogue. William Browne. *Fr.* The Shepherd's Pipe. EPS
Under an Eastern sky. For Me. *Unknown*. ChIP; OQP; QP-1
Under an elm tree where the river reaches. Captured. Archibald MacLeish. HBMV
Under an undermined [*or* undermin'd], and shot-bruised [*or* bruis'd] wall. Fall of a Wall. John Donne. ReIE; TwP
Under and over forever. Death at Sea. Coleman Rosenberger. DaM
Under Arcturus. Madison Cawein. LBMV
Under Ben Bulben. W. B. Yeats. AnIV; CoBMV; LiTM (rev. ed.); LoBV; OxBI
For His Own Epitaph, *sel.* AnFE
Under cool trees the City tombs. Bunhill's Fields. Anne Ridler. NcBP
Under der Linden. Walther von der Vogelweide. *See* Tandaradei.
Under Dusky Laurel Leaf. Margaret Widdemer. *See* Cyprian Woman, A; Greek Folk Song.
Under enormous and cemented cliffs. The Second Iron Age (1939–1945). Michael Harrington. CaP
Under Glass. Alfred Kreymborg. AnAmPo; LA; MAPA
Under great yellow flags and banners of the ancient Cold. The Shadow of Cain. Edith Sitwell. CoBMV
Under green/ I have seen. Vidi Viridi Phyllida sub Tilia. *Unknown*. *Fr.* Carmina Burana. LaP
Under green apple boughs. Madonna Mia. Swinburne. HBV; MBP; VLEP
Under her gentle seeing. On a Young Poetess's Grave. Robert Buchanan. VA
Under his helmet, up against his pack. Asleep. Wilfred Owen. POTE
Under Leafy Bowers. Judah Al-Harizi, *tr. fr. Hebrew*. TrJP
Under Milk Wood, *sel.* Dylan Thomas.
Johnnie Crack and Flossie Snail. FaPON
(Song.) FiBHP
Under Mr. Milton's Picture. Dryden. *See* Lines Printed under the Engraved Portrait of Milton.
Under Monadnock. A New Hampshire Boy. Morris Bishop. HBMV
Under my feet the moon. Brimming Water. Tu Fu. OnPC
Under my keel another boat. A Shadow Boat. Arlo Bates. HBV
Under My Window. Thomas Westwood. HBV; HBVY; LPS-1; OTPC (1923 ed.)
Under my window Dolores sings. Spanish Song. Charles Divine. HBMV
Under my window-ledge the waters race. Coole and Ballylee, 1931. W. B. Yeats. ChMo; CMP; OBMV
Under One Blanket. James Barron Hope. TCAP
Under one star, now, or under two? A Double Star. David McCord. MAP
Under our curtain of fire. The White Comrade. Robert Haven Schauffler. AOAH; SBMV; StJW
Under our hedge there is a pleasant nook. Little Folk. Carrie Ward Lyon. HOAH
Under Sail. Maximilian Aleksandrovich Voloshin, *tr. fr. Russian by* Babette Deutsch. TrRV
Under Sea. *See* Undersea.
Under Sirius. W. H. Auden. NePA
Under Song *See* Undersong.
Under the after-sunset sky. Two Pewits. Edward Thomas. CH; MM; WhBS
Under the almond tree. In Kensington Gardens. Arthur Symons. EnLoPo
Under the apple bough. Remembrance. George Parsons Lathrop. AA; LEAP
Under the arch of life, where love and death. Soul's Beauty [*or* Sibylla Palmifera]. Dante Gabriel Rossetti. The House of Life, LXXVII. BMEP; BPN; CoBE; EmBrPo; EnLit; EV-5; GTML; OAEP; OBEV (new ed.); OBVV; POTT; PoVP; ViP; ViPo; ViPP; VLEP
Under the arch of summer. Heyst-sur-Mer. Richard Middleton. BMEP; LEAP
Under the azure where the noon sun totters. Antony and Cleopatra. José Maria de Heredia, *tr. by* Henri Coulette. NePoEA
Under the bark remembers now my heart. Sonnet. Roy Daniells. PeCV
Under the bed. Saturday Towels. Lysbeth Boyd Borie. UTS
Under the big 500-watted lamps, in the huge sawdusted government inspected slaughter-house. The Slaughter-House. Alfred Hayes. LiTA; LiTM
Under the blossoms. Greetings! Wang An Shih. PoHN
Under the Blue. Francis Fisher Browne. AA
Under the bronze crown. A Baroque Wall-Fountain in the Villa Sciarra. Richard Wilbur. NePoEA
Under the bronze leaves a colt was foaled. Song. "St.-J. Perse." *Fr.* Anabasis. AtBAP; LiTW
Under the Cliff. Geoffrey Grigson. WaP
Under the crosses white on a foreign meadow. Silent Testimony. Catherine Parmenter. PGD
Under the dark industrial sky. Kirkland Lake. James Wreford Watson. BoCaPo
Under the Drooping Willow Tree. *Unknown*. OxBoLi
Under the dying sun. The Reaper. L. H. Allen. MoAuPo; NeLNL
Under the Eaves. Celia Thaxter. MW
Under the eaves, out of the wet To a Phoebe Bird. Witter Bynner. BAP; BLA; CP; HBMV; PoeMoYo; VOD; WhBS; YT
Under the flag of this pneumatic moon. Noctambule. A. J. M. Smith. BoCaPo (1948 ed.)
Under the Frontier Post. Wang Chang-ling, *tr. fr. Chinese by* Rewi Alley. ChTr
Under the Goal Posts. Arthur Guiterman. BBV (1951 ed.)
Under the great hill sloping bare. The King's Missive. Whittier. PAH; TCAP
Under the green hedges, after the snow. Violets. John Moultrie. BoTP; CG
Under the green lamp-light her letter there. Letter of a Mother. Robert Penn Warren. MAP; MoAmPo
Under the Greenwood Tree. Shakespeare. *Fr.* As You Like It, II, v. ADAH; AnFE; BBV (1923 ed.); BCEP; BEL; BLV; BoTP; CBE; CBOV; CH; EG; EIL; ElSeCe; EM-1; EnLi-1; EnLit; EPP; ExPo; FaBoBe; FaFP; FaPON; GBV; GN; GTBS; GTBS-D; GTBS-W; GTSE; GTSL; HoPM; InPo; KN; LiTB; LiTG; MCCG; MPB; OAEP; OBEV; OBSC; OHIP; OTPC; OuHeWo; PCH;

Under the Greenwood Tree (*continued*)
PFE; PIR; PYM; RG; SeCeV; ShBV-2; SiCE; TCEP; TiPo; TOP; TreFS; TVSH; TyEnPo; ViBoPo; WHA; **WoL**
(Call of the Woods, The.) CBPC
(Greenwood, The.) EV-1
(Greenwood Tree, The.) RIS
(In the Greenwood.) AnEnPo
(Song: "Under the greenwood tree.") CG; FiP; REAL
(Songs from the Plays.) AWP; JAWP; WBP
(Songs of the Greenwood.) TrGrPo
(Two Songs by Amiens, 2.) BoLiVe
Under the Harvest Moon. Carl Sandburg. NP; OBAV; OQP; QP-2
Under the heather. *Unknown.* RIS
Under the high-arching bridge. Arches. Helen Hoyt. NP
Under the hill the old horse stands. Second Coming 1942. Henry Treece. MoWP
Under the hive-like dome the stooping haunted readers. The British Museum Reading Room. Louis MacNeice. LiTM; MoAB; MoBrPo; SeCePo; WaP
Under the Holly Bough. Charles Mackay. COAH; DD
(Holly Bough, The.) OBVV
(Reconciliation.) MaRV
Under the leafless arches. Song from Portugal, II. Frederic Prokosch. LoPo
Under the Leaves. Albert Laighton. HBV; OHIP; SN
Under the Leaves Green. *Unknown.* OxBoLi
("Who shall have my fair [*or* fayre] lady?" AtBAP; EG; EnLoPo; EPP; Lo; PoEL-1
Under the light, yet under. Emily Dickinson. Po
Under the lily shadow. The Swan. F. S. Flint. NP
Under the Lime Tree. Walther von der Vogelweide. *See* Tandaradei.
Under the Linden. Walther von der Vogelweide. *See* Tandaradei.
Under the linden the music is gay. A Meeting. Heine. PoMS
Under the Lindens. Walter Savage Landor. HBV
Under the lindens on [*or* linden by] the heather. Tandaradei. Walther von der Vogelweide. AWP; LiA; LiTW; LyMA
Under the Locusts. John Crowe Ransom. LS
Under the long dark boughs, like jewels red. Cherry Robbers. D. H. Lawrence. MBP; MoAB; MoBrPo
Under the long fell's stony eaves. The Ploughman. Gordon Bottomley. POTE
Under the long grass. Their Thanksgiving Day. Louise Driscoll. PCH
Under the low dark sky and the sodden leaves. Wet Summer; Botanic Gardens. Nan McDonald. BoAV
Under the manycoloured showcase of the sky. Twilight. Rafael Estrada. AnCL
Under the Mirabeau Bridge the Seine. The Mirabeau Bridge. Guillaume Apollinaire. AnFP
Under the Mistletoe. Countee Cullen. GoSl
Under the Mistletoe. George Francis Shults. BOHV
Under the mock-oranges the children spy. The People in the Park. Léonie Adams. MoVE
Under the Moon. W. B. Yeats. EG
Under the Mountain. Frederick Goddard Tuckerman. PeBoSo
Under the Oak. D. H. Lawrence. OnHM
Under the oak tree, oak tree. *Unknown. Fr.* Four Songs. LyMA
Under the oak tree stretched, in the youthful leaf of the greenwood. Forest Idyll. Eduard Mörike. AnGP
Under the Old Elm, *sels.* James Russell Lowell.
Great Virginian, The, *fr.* VII. PGD; PSO
Imperial Man, *fr.* VIII. PGD
Unwasted Days, *abr., fr.* VI. MCCG
Washington ("Beneath our consecrated elm"), *abr., fr.* III, V, *and* VI. LPS-3
(New-come Chief.) GA (*fr.* III *and* VII); MC (*fr.* III)
Washington ("Soldier and statesman, rarest union"), *fr.* V. DD; GN; HH; MC; MW, *abr.;* OHIP; OQP, *abr.;* OTPC; PSO, *abr.;* QP-1, *abr.*
(George Washington.) GrCo-2
(Ours, and All Men's.) PGD
(Washington under the Old Elm.) PEDC
Washington ("What figure more immovably august"), *fr.* V. GA
Whom We Revere, *fr.* III. PGD
Under the Open Sky. Albert Durrant Watson. CPG
Under the pale October sun I was wandering. The Swans. Catulle Mendès. OnPM
Under the parabola of a ball. How to Kill. Keith Douglas. ChMP
Under the pent-house branches the eight swans have come. A Dark World. E. J. Scovell. MoVE
Under the Pillars of the Sky. Sir Charles G. D. Roberts. CPG
Under the Pines. Arthur S. Bourinot. BoCaPo
Under the pines and hemlocks. The Deer. Mary Austin. FaPON; PoTo
Under the pines I asked the boy. Searching for the Hermit in Vain. Chia Tao. WhP
Under the Pondweed. *Unknown, tr. fr. Chinese by* Helen Waddell. *Fr.* Shi King. AWP
Under the poplar tree, sweetheart. From Gumiel de Hizán to Gumiel del Mercado. Rafael Alberti. CoSP
Under the Portrait of John Milton. Dryden. *See* Lines Printed under the Engraved Portrait of Milton.
Under the Pyrenees. Alfred Noyes. *Fr.* The Last Voyage. GoBC
Under the Red Cross. Chauncey Hickox. AA
"Under the roots of the roses." Mors et Vita. Richard Henry Stoddard. AA
Under the Rose. Richard Hen y Stoddard. PR
Under the sea, which is their sky, they rise. Submarine Mountains. Cale Young Rice. EtS
Under the Shade of the Trees. Margaret Junkin Preston. BlG; BoHiPo; DD; GA; MC; PAH
(Shade of the Trees, The.) SPP; TCAP
Under the shadows of a clift. A Rise. Ernest McGaffey. AA
Under the shape of his sail, Ulysses. Presence of an External Master of Knowledge. Wallace Stevens. NePA
Under the sky of blue, that seems now. February Morning on the Gulf. Nils Collett Vogt. AnNoLy
Under the slanting light of the yellow sun of October. The Modern Romans. Charles Frederick Johnson. AA; LHV
Under the Snow. Robert Collyer. AA
Under the Stars. Wallace Rice. AA; MDAH; OBAV; OHIP
Under the Stars and Stripes. Madison Cawein. FOAH
Under the Sun. Henry Charles Beeching. OTPC (1946 ed.); YT
Under the sun, groaned Solomon. Solomon. Hermann Hagedorn. GoBC
Under the sun on the gray hill. The Man on the Hill. Maurice Hewlett. *Fr.* The Song of the Plow. POTE
Under the surface of flux and of fear there is an underground movement. Louis MacNeice. *Fr.* The Kingdom. LiTM
Under-the-Table Manners. *Unknown.* DDA
Under the Tent of the Sky. Rowena Bastin Bennett. UTS
Under the thin green sky, the twilight day. Country Sale. Edmund Blunden. NV
Under the tree the farmer said. Cherries. Frederic E. Weatherly. SAS
Under the trees I sat, under the blue. William Ellery Leonard. *Fr.* Two Lives, Pt. III. AnAmPo; LA; MOAP
Under the viaduct, by the hot canal. Plaque. Bruce Ruddick. CaP
Under the Violets. Oliver Wendell Holmes. *Fr.* The Professor at the Breakfast Table. AA; IAP
Under the Violets. Edward Young. AA
Under the walls of Monterey. Victor Galbraith. Longfellow. EV-5; IAP; PAH; TCAP
Under the Washington Elm, Cambridge. Oliver Wendell Holmes. PEOR
Under the Waterfall. Thomas Hardy. LiTB; PoVP
Under the Wattle. Douglas Brook Wheelton Sladen. OBVV
Under the weight and depth of the brightness of the clear sapphire sky. High Summer. Shuzo Hishiyama. PoLJ
Under the wide and starry sky. Requiem. Robert Louis Stevenson. AnFE; ATP; BBV; BMEP; BTP; CaAE; CBE; CBOV; DD; EBSV; EPN; EPP; EV-5; GoTP; GoTS; GTML; GTSL; HBV; HBVY; HiLiEn; InP; LBBV; LEAP; LiTG; MaRV; MBP; MCCG; MoBrPo; MPB; NeHB; NeMA; OBEV; OBVV; OQP; OtMeF; OTPC; PCD; PFE; PIAE; PIR; PoeMoYo; PoeT; PoFS; PoRA; POTT; PoVP; PreP; PYM; QP-1; ReaPo; ShBV-2; TCEP; TOP; TreF; TrGrPo; TSW; TSWC; TVSH; VA; ViBoPo; VOD; WaKn; WGRP; WHA; WP; YT
Under the willow the willow. Recruiting Drive. Charles Causley. NePoEA
Under the Willows, *sel.* James Russell Lowell.
May and June. APW
Under the winter, dear. Song. Eugene Lee-Hamilton. OBVV
Under the Woods. Edward Thomas. CH; LoBV
Under the yellow moon, when the young men and maidens pass in the lanes. The Last Fairy. Rosamund Marriott Watson. OBVV
Under the yellow sun. A White Tree in Bloom. John Richard Moreland. PGD
Under the yew-tree's heavy weight. Les Hiboux. Baudelaire. AWP; JAWP; WBP
Under these brooding skies. Reflections on the Fall of France, June, 1940. Eiluned Lewis. POTE
Under this beech why sittest thou here so sad. An Eglogue to Mr. Johnson. Thomas Randolph. SeEP
Under this crust. *Unknown.* WhC
Under this elm, the wandering Wyandots trod. Ohio Farmstead. Minnie Hite Moody. MuM
Under this loop of honeysuckle. The Caterpillar. Robert Graves. TSW
Under this shade of crimson wings abhorred. The World in Armor. Sir William Watson. PoVP
Under this sod and beneath these trees. An Epitaph. *Unknown.* MoShBr
Under this sod lies a great bucking hoss. To Midnight. *Unknown.* CoSo

Under this stone, reader, survey. On [*or* Epitaph on] Sir John Vanbrugh [Architect]. Abel Evans. FiBHP; OBEC; ViBoPo
Under this stone there lieth at rest. An Epitaph of Sir Thomas Gravener, Knight. Sir Thomas Wyatt. OBSC; SiPS
Under thy shadow may I lurk awhile. St. Peter's Shadow. Richard Crashaw. ACP
Under Which Lyre. W. H. Auden. MoAB; MoBrPo (1950 ed.); PoLFOT
Under white eyelids. The Sleeper. "Isobel Hume." HBMV
Under yonder beech-tree single on the green-sward. Love in the Valley. George Meredith. AEV; AnEnPo; AWP; BEL; BMEP; EmBrPo; EnL; EnLi-2; EPN; GTBS-D; GTBS-W; GTSL; HBV; InPo; LEAP; LiTB; LiTG; LiTL; LoPS; OBEV; OBVV; OnPP; PIAE; POTT; PoVP; ShBV-4; TOP; TrGrPo; TriL; TyEnPo; ViBoPo; ViP; ViPo; VLEP; WHA
Underfoot on the hill the water spurts. Sunday on Hampstead Heath. George Woodcock. NeBP
Underground, The. Guy Boas. CenHV
Underground. Ian Mudie. BoAV; MoAuPo
Underground grower, blind and a common brown, An. Potato. Richard Wilbur. CrMA; LiTA; MoAB; TrGrPo (rev. ed.)
Underground Rumbling. James S. Tippett. GFA
Underground there is a rustle. The Trumpet Call. Dmitry Sergeyevich Merezhkovsky. TrRV
Underneath an old [*or* a huge] oak tree. The Raven [and the Oak]. Samuel Taylor Coleridge. CG; OTPC (1923 ed.)
Underneath My Window Sir Philip Sidney. *See* Astrophel and Stella: Eleventh Song.
Underneath the boardwalk, way, way back. The Secret Cavern. Margaret Widdemer. FaPON; MPB
Underneath the Clothes. Madeleine Nightingale. RIS
Underneath the growing grass. The Bourne. Christina Rossetti. BLV; FaBoEn; HBV; LoBV; MBP; PIAE; POTT; VLEP
Underneath the leaves of life. The Riddle. W. H. Auden. EnLi-2 (1949 ed.)
Underneath the water-weeds. The Tadpole. Elizabeth Gould. BoTP
Underneath their eider-robe. The Poetry of a Root Crop. Charles Kingsley. LoBV
Underneath this ancient pew. *Unknown.* WhC
Underneath this greedy stone. Erotion [*or* Epitaph on Erotion]. Martial. OBRV; OnPM
Underneath this marble hearse. *See* Underneath this sable hearse.
Underneath this marble stone. Epitaph. Abraham Cowley. EnLoPo
Underneath this myrtle shade. The Epicure. Abraham Cowley. AWP; EG; EV-2; OBEV; PG (1945 ed.); PoP; SiTL
Underneath this sable [*or* marble] hearse [*or* herse]. On the Countess Dowager of Pembroke [*or* Epitaph on . . .]. William Browne, *wr. at to* Ben Jonson. AWP; BCEP; BEL; BoFr; CaAE; CenL; CoEV; EG; ElSeCe; EnLi-1; EPP; EV-2; HBV; InP; InvP; JAWP; LEAP; LoBV; LPS-3; MyFE; OBEV; OBS; OnPP; PoEL-2; ReEn; SeCeV; SeCL; SeEP; TOP; TreFS; TriL; UnPo (1st ed.); ViBoPo; WBP; WHA; WoL
Under Sea. Konstantin Balmont, *tr. fr. Russian by* C. M. Bowra. BoRS
Undersea Fever. William Cole. FiBHP
Undersong, The. Emerson. *Fr.* Woodnotes. AA
Undersong, The. "Fiona Macleod." NLK
Under Song, The. *Unknown.* ACP (1926 ed.)
Undersong. Robert Kelley Weeks. PR
Understanding. H. W. Bliss. PoToHe
Understanding. Margaret E. Bruner. AlBD
Understanding. *Unknown.* PoToHe (new ed.)
Understanding. Nixon Waterman. *See* "To Know All Is to Forgive All."
Understanding Heart, The. Georgia Harkness. MaRV
Understanding of a medical man, The. Sonnet. Rex Warner. ChMP
Undertaker's Advertisement, An. Ernest G. Moll. WhC
Undertaking, The. John Donne. AnFE; BLV; BoLiVe; EPS; MePo; ReEn; SeEP; TuPP
Undertone. William Bedell Stanford. NeIP; OnYI
Underway, my pockets split only with fist. My Bohemia. Arthur Rimbaud. ReMP
Underwood. Howard Moss. NePA
Undeveloped Lives. W. E. H. Lecky. TIP
Undiscouraged God, The. *Unknown.* MaRV
Undiscovered Country, The. Thomas Bailey Aldrich. AA
Undiscovered Country, The. William Dean Howells. MaRV; OQP; PraP; QP-2
(Our Thanksgiving Accept.) PEOR
(Prayer, A: "Lord, for the erring thought.") WGRP
(Thanksgiving, A.) HBV; TrPWD
Undiscovered Planet, The. Norman Nicholson. ChMP; FaBoMo; PoN
Undistinguished buttercup. Advice to a Buttercup. Maxwell Bodenheim. LEAP
Undisturbed the Autumn grass grows by the deserted door. On Passing a Friend's House. Wang Wei. OnPM
Undoubtedly the Kangaroos. Nature Note. Arthur Guiterman. SUS
Undress. Robert Desnos, *tr. fr. French by* Wallace Fowlie. MiCF
Undue significance a starving man attaches. Emily Dickinson. LiTA; LiTM (rev. ed.)
Undulating country, where the roads, An. Fields of Soria, III. Antonio Machado. AnSpL-2; TeCS
Undulations of precision harass the mind. Kochia. Thomas Hornsby Ferril. NePoAm-2
Undying Law, The. Sophocles. *See* State versus Conscience, The.
Undying Love, whose beams forever glow. Love One Another. Bedros Tourian. ArmLP
Undying Soul, The. Whittier. *Fr.* On a Fly-Leaf of Longfellow's Poems. MaRV; OQP; QP-2
Undying Thirst. Antipater of Sidon, *tr. fr. Greek by* Robert Bland. AWP; OuHeWo
("This rudely sculptured porter-pot.") GrPo
Une Idole du Nord. Francis Stuart. NeIP
Une Marquise. Austin Dobson. BPN
Une petite pêche dans un orchard fleurit. The Little Peach. *Unknown.* NA
Unearned Increment. Christopher Morley. SiTL; WhC
Unearth. Alfred Barrett. GoBC
Uneasy Lies the Head. Shakespeare. *See* Henry IV's Soliloquy on Sleep.
Unemployed. Ralph Cheyney. ChIP
Unemployed, The. LeVan Roberts. PGD
Unemployment. Richard X. Evans. CAG
Unequal Distribution. Samuel Hoffenstein. TrJP
Unerring Guide, The. Anna Shipton. BLRP
Unexpected Fact, An. Edward Cannon. *See* Unsuspected Fact, An.
Unexpected Fortune. Abul Qasim of Silves, *tr. fr. Arabic by* A. J. Arberry. MooP
Unexpected Visit, An. Tu Fu, *tr. fr. Chinese by* Chi Hwang Chu *and* Edna Worthley Underwood. OnPM
Unexplorer, The. Edna St. Vincent Millay. MoShBr; SUS
Unexpress'd, The. Walt Whitman. NePA
Unfading Beauty, The. Thomas Carew. *See* Disdain Returned.
Unfading Hope! when life's last embers burn. Hope. Thomas Campbell. *Fr.* Pleasures of Hope. LPS-3
Unfailing Friend, The. Joseph Scriven. BLRP
("What a friend we have in Jesus") OlF
Unfailing One, The. Phillips Brooks. *See* Our Burden Bearer.
Unfaith. Ted Robinson. MaRV
Unfaithful, The. Genevieve Taggard. AV
Unfaithful Shepherdess, The. *Unknown. See* Faithless Shepherdess, The.
Unfaithful Shepherds. Ezekiel, XXXIV: 1-28, Bible, *O.T.* WoL
Unfamiliar Air, An. Zinaida Shishova, *tr. fr. Russian by* Babette Deutsch. TrRV
Unfamiliar Quartet. Stephen Vincent Benét. WhC
Unfathomable Sea! Shelley. *See* Time.
Unfathomable sea, and time, and tears, The. To N. V. de G. S. Robert Louis Stevenson. VA
Unfathomable sea! whose waves are years. Time. Shelley. BEL; BPN; CBE; EM-2; EmBrPo; EnLi-2; EPN; EtS; EV-4
Unfinished Portrait. Elinor Wylie. CoBA
Unfit die, The—the fit both live and thrive. The Survival of the Fittest. Sarah N. Cleghorn. BAP; HBMV
Unflinching Dante of a later day. To an Imperilled Traveller. Nathan Haskell Dole. AA
Unflinching foot 'gainst foot was set. Bannockburn. Sir Walter Scott. *Fr.* The Lord of the Isles. BSV
Unfold unfold/ Thou beaten-gold. In Grato Jubilo. David McCord. UnS
Unfold, unfold! take in His light. The Revival. Henry Vaughan. BLV; BoLiVe. MaPo; OBS; OxBoCh; PoEL-2; PrWP; SeCL; SeEP; TrGrPo; TriL
Unfolde thyne armes & let me goe. *Unknown.* SeCSL
Unforeseen. Richard Hovey. PR
Unforeseen, The. Conrado Nalé Roxlo, *tr. fr. Spanish by* Milton Ben Davis. AnCL; LiTW
Unforgettable September is strewn about Spasskoye. Spasskoye. Boris Pasternak. BoRS
Unforgivable and Unforgiven. C. D. B. Ellis. SiTL
Unforgiven, The. E. A. Robinson. ChMo; CMP
Unforgotten, The, II. Robert Louis Stevenson. VLEP
Unforgotten voices call at twilight, The. The Call. Katharine Tynan. BMEP
Unfortunate Coincidence. Dorothy Parker. ALV; TreF; WhC
Unfortunate Lovers, The, *sels.* Sir William Davenant.
Love ("'Tis, in good truth, a most wonderful thing"). SeCL
Song: "Roses and pinks will be strewn where you go." ViBoPo

Unfortunate Male, The. Kalonymos ben Kalonymos, *tr. fr. Hebrew by* Joseph Chotzner. TrJP
Unfortunate Miller, The. A. E. Coppard. FaBoTw; POTE
Unfortunate Miller, The; or, The Country Lasses Witty Invention. *Unknown.* CoMu
Unfortunate Miss Bailey. George Colman, the Younger. BOHV; FiBHP; ViBoFo
(Miss Bailey's Ghost.) OxBoLi
Unfortunate Mole, The. Mary Kennedy. GoYe
Unfortunate Rake, The. *Unknown. See* Cowboy's Lament, The.
Unfriendly, friendly universe. The Child Dying. Edwin Muir. ChMP; FaBoTw; GTBS-D
Unfrocked Priest, The. Joseph Campbell. AnIL; OnYI
Unfulfilled. Corinne Roosevelt Robinson. AV
Unfulfilment. Frances Louisa Bushnell. AA
Unfurl the flag of Freedom. Hymn of Freedom. Mary Perry King. OBAV
Unfurling of the Flag, The. Clara Endicott Sears. PEDC
Ungar and Rolfe. Herman Melville. *Fr.* Clarel. OxBA
Ungentle Alice, thy sorrow is my sore. *Unknown. Fr.* Arden of Feversham. LO
Ungrateful Beauty Threatened. Thomas Carew. *See* Ingrateful Beauty Threatened.
Ungrateful Cupid, The. John Hughes, *after the Greek of* Anacreon. CG
Unguarded. Ada Foster Murray. HBV
Unguarded Gates. Thomas Bailey Aldrich. AA; AnNE; MC; PAH
Unhappie light. *See* Unhappy light.
Unhappie verse, the witness of my unhappie state. *See* Unhappy verse, the witness of my unhappy state.
Unhappily married beauty. *Unknown. Fr.* Four Songs. LyMA
Unhappy about some far off things. The Stars Go over the Lonely Ocean. Robinson Jeffers. GTBS-W; LiTA; LiTM (rev. ed.); NePA; WaP
Unhappy Boston. Paul Revere. PAH
Unhappy country what wings you have. Eagle Valor, Chicken Mind. Robinson Jeffers. LiTA; OxBA; WaP
Unhappy dreamer, who outwinged in flight. On the Death of a Metaphysician. George Santayana. AA; AnFE; APA; CoAnAm; LEAP; MAP; MoAmPo; OBAV; ViBoPo
Unhappy East (not in that awe). Reply. Sidney Godolphin. OBS
Unhappy Erin, what a lot was thine! National Presage. John Kells Ingram. OnYI
Unhappy, I observe the Ass. A Rondeau of Remorse. Burges Johnson. HBMV
Unhappy is Bo-Peep. Bo-Peep. Anthony C. Deane. PA
Unhappy [*or* Unhappie] light. Madrigal. William Drummond of Hawthornden. AtBAP; EPS; OBS
Unhappy Lover, The. Judah al-Harizi, *tr. fr. Hebrew by* Joseph Chotzner. TrJP
Unhappy Man, An. *Unknown, tr. fr. Greek by* T. F. Higham. OxBG
Unhappy sight, and hath she vanisht by. Astrophel and Stella, CV. Sir Philip Sidney. SiPS
Unhappy [*or* Unhappie] verse, the witness of my unhappy state. Iambicum Trimetrum [*or* Iambica]. Spenser. ElL; OBEV (new ed.); OxBoLi; PoEL-1; ReIE; SiTL
Unhearing all, who would have loved my song. To Me and Not to Them. Alma Ellis Hoernecke. MuM
Unheeded Vocation. Eleanore L. Perry. PraNu
Unherded came the cattle from the hills with falling even. Lightning. *At. to* Diotimus *and to* Leonidas of Tarentum. GrPE
Unhistoric Story, The. Allen Curnow. AnNZ
Unholy Garden. Leila Jones. PIAE
Unhous'd, unfriended, solitary, slow. Tears. Jami. PeP
Unhurried as a snake I saw Time glide. On Time. Richard Hughes. MBP; MoBrPo
Unicorn, The. George Darley. *Fr.* Nepenthe. ChTr; FaBoEn; PoEL-4
("Lo! in the mute, midwilderness.") NBE; OBRV
Unicorn, The. Ruth Pitter. LO; MoBrPo; MoVE
Unicorn, The. Philippe de Thaon, *tr. fr. French by* Richard Beaumont. LyMA
Unicorn, The. Ella Young. FaPON; TiPo
Unicorn and the Hippogrif, The. Martha Ostenso. BAP
Unicorn's hoofs, The! Dance Song. *Unknown.* FaBoCh; LoGBV; WhP
Unicorns move furtively among. Lemon Sherbet. Marvin Solomon. NePoAm
Unillumined Verge, The. Robert Bridges. AA
Uninfected, The. E. L. Mayo. MiAP
Uninscribed Monument on One of the Battle-Fields of the Wilderness, An. Herman Melville. AA
Uninterruptedly falls the snow. The Snow. Emile Verhaeren. MiFP
Union and Liberty. Oliver Wendell Holmes. FOAH; OHIP
Union Jack, The. Jeannie Kirby. BoTP
Union of Love. Jami, *tr. fr. Persian by* F. Hadland Davis. OnPM
Union of the World, A. Joel Barlow. *Fr.* The Columbiad, X. IAP
(League of Nations, A.) CoBA
Union with the Eternal. *Unknown, tr. fr. Sanskrit by* Charles Johnston. *Fr.* Bhagavad-Gita. GrCo-1
Unison, A. William Carlos Williams. SeCeV
Unit. Mary Fullerton. BoAV
Unite, unite, let us all unite. The Padstow Night Song. *Unknown.* ChTr
United. Paulus Silentiarius, *tr. fr. Greek by* W. H. D. Rouse. AWP
United States. John Keble. CoBE
United States and *Macedonian,* The ("The Banner of Freedom high floated unfurled"). *Unknown.* PAH
United States and *Macedonian,* The ("How glows each patriot bosom"). *Unknown.* PAH
United States are rich, they're powerful and great, The. Rubén Darío. *Fr.* To Theodore Roosevelt. PoFr
Unity. "Æ." *See* Secret, The.
Unity. Emerson. APW
Unity. Eva Gore-Booth. DiM
Unity. Lloyd Frank Merrell. ChIP
Unity. Alfred Noyes. HBV; InP; VOD
Unity of God, The. Panatattu. *See* God Is One.
Unity of Nature, The. Pope. *Fr.* An Essay on Man, Epistle I. CBOV
Unity of the North, The. Parmo Carl Ploug, *tr. fr. Danish by* Charles W. Stork. BoDS
Universal Change. Sophocles. *See* Ajax! to All Farewell.
Universal Favorite, The. Carolyn Wells. InMe
Universal Fire, The. *Unknown, tr. fr. Sanskrit by* Joseph Nadin Rawson. *Fr.* The Upanishads. OnPM
Universal Hallelujah, The, *sel.* Isaac Watts, *paraphrased from* Psalm CXLVIII, Bible, *O.T.*
"Thunder and hail, and fire and storms." BeR, 5 *sts.*
Universal Heart of Man, The. Wordsworth. *Fr.* The Prelude, XIII. TOP
Universal Language. Josephine Robinson. BoHiPo
Universal Language, The. Ella Wheeler Wilcox. ChIP; OQP; QP-1
Universal Peace, The. Tennyson. *See* Prophecy.
Universal Prayer, The. Pope. AEV; BCEP; BEL; CEP; EiPP; EnLit; EV-3; FaBoBe; GoBC; HBV; LPS-2; MaRV; OAEP; RiBV; TCEP; TOP; WGRP
"Teach me to feel another's woe," *sel.* BPP
Universal Republic, The. Victor Hugo, *tr. fr. French.* OQP; PGD; QP-1
(Republic of the World.) MaRV
Universal Self, The. *Unknown, tr. fr. Sanskrit by* F. Max Müller. *Fr.* The Upanishads. WoL
Universalism. Kathleen Sutton. MuM
Universe into Stone. A. J. M. Smith. PeCV
Universe is deathless, The. Endless Self. *Unknown, at. to* Lao-tzu. *Fr.* Tao Teh King. OnPM
Universe of Death, A. Milton. *Fr.* Paradise Lost, II. CoEV
Universe-Solitude, *sel.* Paul Eluard, *tr. fr. French by* Samuel Beckett.
"Woman every night, A/ Journeys secretly. MiFP
University. Karl Shapiro. AmPP (4th ed.); CoBA; LiTA; OxBA
University Examinations in Egypt. D. J. Enright. MoPW
Unkind spring sun, to wake me all too soon! Butterfly in April. Eduard Mörike. AnGP
Unkind was he, the first who sang. A Girl's Song. Aubrey Thomas De Vere. GTBS-D
Unkindness. George Herbert. HBV
Unknowable Power is o'er me. The Visitor Abhorred. Sir William Watson. PoVP
Unknown, The. John Davidson. MBP; MoBrPo
Unknown, The. Harry Kemp. AOAH
Unknown, The. E. O. Laughlin. AOAH; BLPA; BoHiPo
Unknown. Ono no Yoshiki, *tr. fr. Japanese by* Basil Hall Chamberlain. *Fr.* Kokin Shu. OnPM
("My love/ Is like the grasses," *tr. by* Arthur Waley.) AWP
Unknown, The. Edward Thomas. BMEP; LEAP
Unknown Beloved, The. John Hall Wheelock. HBMV; SBMV
Unknown Bird, The. Edward Thomas. FaBoEn; MoP
Unknown Citizen, The. W. H. Auden. ChMP; LiTA; LiTM; MoAB; NePA; PoRA; ShBV-4; SiTL
Unknown City, The. Sir Charles G. D. Roberts. CaP; CPG; OCL
Unknown Color, The. Countee Cullen. FaPON; GoSl
"Unknown" Dead, The. John R. Rathom. DD; HH; VOD (1931 ed.)
Unknown Dead, The. Henry Timrod. AmP; MDAH; MOAP; SPP
Unknown Eros, The. Coventry Patmore. *Poems indexed separately by titles and first lines.*
Unknown God, The. "Æ." ChMo; CMP; EPP; GTSL; MBP; MoBrPo; NeMA; PFE; TOP; WGRP
Unknown God, The. Charles G. Blanden. OQP; QP-1

Unknown God, The. Henry Francis Lyte. MaRV
Unknown God, The. Sir William Watson. WGRP
Unknown God, The—alas! His feet. The Unknown God. Charles G. Blanden. OQP; QP-1
Unknown in history or in time they stand. Speakers, Columbus Circle. Raymond Souster. CaP
Unknown love/ Is as bitter a thing. The Lady of Sakanoye. *Fr.* Manyo Shu. AWP; JAWP
Unknown Man in the Morgue. Merrill Moore. MAP; MoAmPo
Unknown Poets. Wordsworth. *Fr.* The Excursion, I. LPS-3
Unknown Reporter, The. Lee Shippey. DDA
Unknown Sculptor, The. Stanton A. Coblentz. MaRV
Unknown, she was the form I preferred. Loss. Paul Eluard. OnPM
Unknown Shepherd's Complaint, The. Richard Barnfield. ElL; ElSeCe; TuPP
(Shepherd's Complaint, A.) OBSC
Unknown Soldier, The. Conrad Aiken. *Fr.* The Soldier. WaaP; WaP
Unknown Soldier. Alta Booth Dunn. PGD; PSO
Unknown Soldier, The. Virginia Eaton. BoHiPo
Unknown Soldier, The. Arthur B. Rhinow. OQP; QP-2
Unknown Soldier, The. Billy Rose. BLPA
Unknown Soldier, The. Charles A. Wagner. AnAmPo; LA
Unknown Sword-Maker, The. Rachel Annand Taylor. EBSV
"Unknown to fame"—believe me—that's on earth a blessing. Monologue. Mikhail Yurevich Lermontov. WaL
Unknown to her the maids supplied. Imogen. Richard Henry Stoddard. IAP
Unknown to me, brave boy, but still I wreathe. Our Confederate Dead. Henry Marvin Wharton. BlG
Unknown Warrior Sings and Curses in the Street, The. Herbert Palmer. FaBoTw
Unknown Wind, The. "Fiona Macleod." BoTP
Unknown Woman. Josef Weinheber, *tr. fr. German by* Herman Salinger. TwGV
Unless. Ella Maria Deitz Glynes. AA
Unless I am Careful. W. W. Gibson. NP
Unless I learn to ask no help. Lessons. Sara Teasdale. Interlude: Songs Out of Sorrow, III. PC
Unless I Learn to Walk Upright. Sophie Himmell. MuM
Unless that kitty shines again in heaven. To a Black Dog, Bereaved. Elizabeth J. Coatsworth. PCD
Unless there were consent 'twixt hell and heaven. Thomas Campion. LO
Unless you come of the gipsy stock. Gipsy Vans. Kipling. OtMeF; VLEP
Unless you knew just where to look. The Cobbler in Willow Street. George O'Neil. HBMV; VOD
Unlike are we, unlike, O princely Heart! Sonnets from the Portuguese, III. Elizabeth Barrett Browning. AnFE; BPN; EmBrPo; EnLi-2; ES; EV-4; GTSL; HBV; LEAP; OAEP; OBEV; OBVV; PIAE; TCEP; TrGrPo; ViPo; VLEP
Unlike Virgil's verse on the *Troiae bella.* The Bachelor's Ballade. David Fisher Parry. InMe
Unlikely Rebel, The. Franklin D. Elmer, Jr. ChIP
Unloading Hay. Emyr Humphreys. MoWP
Unlooked-for Bargain, The. Simonides. *See* Cretan Merchant, The.
Unloved, The. Arthur Symons. PoVP; VLEP
Unloved to His Beloved, The. William Alexander Percy. HBMV; LS
Unmanifest Destiny. Richard Hovey. AA; AnAmPo; CBOV; HBV; HBVY; LA; MAP; MaRV; MoAmPo (1942 ed.); NeMA; OBAV; PaA; PFY; PoFr; WGRP
Unmarried Mother Sings, An. F. R. Higgins. POTE
Unmindful of gray January skies. January Jasmine. Zoe Kincaid Brockman. NoCaPo
Unmindful of my low desert. The Quiet Nights. Katharine Tynan. HBV
Unmoored, unmanned, unheeded on the deep. The Derelict. Lucius Harwood Foote. AA
Unmourn'd, unburied, traveller, we lie. Alcaeus of Messene, *tr. fr. Greek by* J. H. Merivale. GrPo
Unnamed Lake, The. Frederick George Scott. BoCaPo; CaP; CPG; OCL
Unnamed Sonnets (I–V), *sels.* Edna St. Vincent Millay.
Thou Art Not Lovelier Than Lilacs, I. BLV; BoLiVe; ChMo; CMP
Time Does Not Bring Relief, II. LoPo
Unnamed Sonnets (I–XII), *sels.* Edna St. Vincent Millay.
"And you as well must die, belovèd dust," VIII. BAP; GTBS-W; NP; PoRA
Cherish You Then the Hope I Shall Forget, XII. AV; NP; TCPD
"Into the golden vessel of great song," II. NP
"Not with libations, but with shouts and laughter," III. HBMV; NP
(Not with Libations.) WHA
"Oh, my beloved, have you thought of this," X. HBMV
Unnatural, Unusual and Unfair. James Schevill. FiMAP
Unnoted as the setting of a star. Mulford. Whittier. AA
Unnumber'd suppliants crowd Preferment's gate. The Rise and Fall. Samuel Johnson. *Fr.* The Vanity of Human Wishes. BeR; PoFr
Unpalatable Truths. Sophocles, *tr. fr. Greek by* Lewis Campbell. *Fr.* Ajax. GrR
Unparalleled Autumn, An. "Anna Akhmatova," *tr. fr. Russian by* Babette Deutsch. TrRV
Unpardonable Sin, The. Vachel Lindsay. ChMo; CMP; LiTM (rev. ed.); MaRV; NePA; QS
Unpathed Haunts. Lucretius, *tr. fr. Latin by* William Ellery Leonard. *Fr.* Of the Nature of Things (De Rerum Natura), IV. LiA
Unpetalled Rose, The. St. Thérèse of Lisieux, *tr. fr. French by* Prioress Augustine of the Mother of God. CAW
Unplait the braided dark. To the Spring Sun. Freda Laughton. NeIP
Unplumbed the wellhead of this pantomime. Greek Vase. Margaret R. Richter. MuM
Unpopular youth of Cologne, An. Limerick. *Unknown.* TSWC
Unpraised Picture, An. Richard Burton. AA
Unprofitableness. Henry Vaughan. AtBAP; EPS; SeCV-1
Unpunished. Mary Elizabeth Coleridge. BMEP
(He Knoweth Not That the Dead Are Thine.) PoVP
Unpurged images of day recede, The. Byzantium. W. B. Yeats. BrBe; CoBMV; CoEV; EnLP; FaBoEn; FaBoMo; GTBS-W; LiTM; LoBV; MaPo; MoAB; MoP; MoPo; OAEP (2d ed.); OnYI; PoE; PoLFOT; ReaPo; SeCePo; SeCeV; TwHP
Unquestionable Questions. Hy Sobiloff. SiTL
Unquestioning. Blake. *See* Eternity.
Unquiet Grave, The. *Unknown.* AnFE; AtBAP; BaBo; CH; EnL; EnSB, *longer vers.;* ESPB; ExPo; LoBV; OBB; PoD; PoEL-1; ViBoFo, *with music;* ViBoPo
("Wind doth blow to-day, my love, The.") LO
Unquiet thought! whom at the first I bred. Amoretti, II. Spenser. PeBoSo
Unravelling from the rags of the clouds, a tangle. Wild Geese in Midwinter. Stanley E. Babb. HiLiAm
Unreal!/ Unreal are both creation. Facing Death. Chih Ming. OnPM; PoHN; WoL
Unrealities, The. Schiller, *tr. fr. German by* James Clarence Mangan. AWP; WoL
Unrealized Ideal, The. Frederick Locker-Lampson. EPP; LEAP; TSW
(My Love Is Always Near.) BMEP
Unreaped Field, The. Nikolai Nekrasov, *tr. fr. Russian by* J. S. Phillimore. BoR
Unreasoning Heart. Louis Untermeyer. MAP; MoAmPo (1942 ed.)
Unregarding. Walter de la Mare. ChMo
Unregenerate. Jacqueline Embry. HBMV
Unrelated paragraphs of morning, The. Schoolroom on a Wet Afternoon. Vernon Scannell. HaMV
Unremembered, The. Hermann Hagedorn. CAG
Unremitting Voice of Nightly Streams, The. Wordsworth. BPN; EmBrPo
Unrequited Love. Shakespeare. *See* She Never Told Her Love.
Unrequited Love on the Back Piazza. Margaret Fishback. CIV
Unrequited Lover, The. T'ai Wang-shu, *tr. fr. Chinese by* Harold Acton *and* Ch'en Shih Hsiang. ChLP
Unrest. Don Marquis. BAP; HBMV; MaRV; OQP; PC; PoeMoYo; PoFr, *abr.;* QP-1
Unresting as the pulse of arteries. Steel Mills after Midnight. Louise Crenshaw Ray. JKCP (1955 ed.)
Unreturning, The. Bliss Carman. LBMV
Unreturning, The. Wilfred Owen. MBP; MoBrPo
Unreturning, The. Clinton Scollard. DD; PAH
Unreturning. Elizabeth Stoddard. AA
Unrewarded Lover, The. William Walsh. EV-3
(Elegy: Unrewarded Lover, The.) CEP
Unrewarded, my will to serve the State. Planting Bamboos. Po Chü-i. TrCh
Unriddle me my riddle. Winter Rune. Elizabeth J. Coatsworth. SUS
Unrighteous Lord of love, what law is this. Amoretti, X. Spenser. PeBoSo
Unripe Orange, The. Al-Asamm, *tr. fr. Arabic by* A. J. Arberry MooP
Unromantic Song. Anthony Brode. FiBHP
Unsaid. Josephine Preston Peabody. PR
Unsatisfactory. *Unknown.* LPS-1
Unsatisfied. Oliver Wendell Holmes. AnNE; APW
Unsatisfied Yearning. R. K. Munkittrick. AlBD; BOHV; InMe; LauV; PoMa; YT
Unscarred Fighter Remembers France, The. Kenneth Slade Alling. HBMV
Unschooled as yet the yoke to wear. Horace. Odes, II, 5. LaP
Unseasonable/ as bees in April. Vermont; Indian Summer. Philip Booth. NePoEA
Unseen. Fanny Crosby. TrPWD

Unseen, The. Sara Teasdale. TCAP
Unseen and unknown. The Sylph. Paul Valéry. TrFP
Unseen Bridge, The. Gilbert Thomas. HBMV; MaRV; PraP
Unseen Playmate, The. Robert Louis Stevenson. OnHT; PCH
Unseen Power, The. Jalal ed-Din Rumi, *tr. fr. Persian by* R. A. Nicholson. PeP
Unseen Riches. Bianor, *tr. fr. Greek by* Walter Leaf. OxBG
Unseen Spirits. N. P. Willis. AA; AnAmPo; APW; BAV; HBV; IAP; LA; LBAP; LEAP; LPS-1; OBAV; TCAP
(Two Women.) BAP; BeLS; OBVV
Unseen World, The. Craven Langstroth Betts. OQP; QP-1
Unsettled Soul, The. Francis Quarles. *See* Like to the Arctic Needle.
Unsexed by the Cold Sea. Winfield Townley Scott. FiMAP
Unshaken by the storms that rage. Jesus of Nazareth Passes By. George T. Liddell. ChIP
Unshrinking Faith. William Hiley Bathurst. BLRP
Unshunnable is grief; we should not fear. Grief and God. Stephen Phillips. WGRP
Unsolved Mystery. George Ryan. WhC
Unstable Dream, According to the Place. Sir Thomas Wyatt. *See* Lover Having Dreamed of Enjoying of His Love, The.
Unstable monster, formless, vast, alone. Ocean. Louis Lavater. BoAu
Unstooping. Walter de la Mare. UTS
Unsubdued. S. E. Kiser. MaRV; PoToHe
Unsullied Spring, O just-about-to-begin. To Spring. Virginia Moore. AnEnPo
Unsullied temple, heavenly light enshrining. The Assumption. St. Nerses. CAW
Unsung. Thomas Bailey Aldrich. UnW
Unsung. Nettie Palmer. BoAu
Unsung Heroes, The, *abr.* Paul Laurence Dunbar. PoFr
Unsung, unsigned upon the dust of time. A Wreath for Ashes. Hildegarde Flanner. MuM
Unsuspected Fact, An. Edward Canon. BOHV; NA
(Unexpected Fact, An.) BoN
Untended Field, The. Robert Hillyer. AnNE
Unthrift. Coventry Patmore. The Angel in the House, I, iii, 3. HBV; POTT
(Preludes, I.) GoBC
(Wasteful Woman.) BMEP
Unthrifty loveliness, why dost thou spend. Sonnets, IV. Shakespeare. PeBoSo
Untidy, squat, and soft old body slack. The Old Woman. *Unknown.* DDA
Until Death. Elizabeth Akers Allen. HBV
Until, finally,/ after aching, laming stages. Report. A. Fleming MacLiesh. *Fr.* The Jungle. NAMP
Until I caught the rhythm of his life. The Rhythm of His Life. Mary Hallet. ChIP
Until I helped. Gethsemane, Illinois. Martin S. Allwood. LiTW
Until I lose my soul and lie. A Prayer. Sara Teasdale. HBMV; TrPWD
Until I Reach-a Ma Home, *with music. Unknown.* BoAN-1
Until I was a roustabout. Animal Fair. Philip Booth. NePoAm-2
Until Jove let it be, no colonist. Georgic I. Virgil. *Fr.* Georgics. LaP; LiTW
Until my lamp and I. Discovery. Hildegarde Flanner. HBMV; TBM
Until the birth of my thirtieth birthday. Confidential Data on the Loyalty Investigation of Herbert Ashenfoot. James Schevill. FiMAP
Until the day the world shall die. Comrades of the Trail. Mary Carolyn Davies. NLK
Until the day when thou and I are wed. The Maid in the Rice-Fields. Viola Meynell. MBP; MoBrPo (1942 ed.)
Until the desert knows. Emily Dickinson. MaPo; MoPo
Until the poet hears Apollo's. The Poet. Pushkin. BoR
Until thine hands clasp girdlewise the waist of the Belov'd. Ode. Sadi. AWP
Until this poem is over, I shall not leave. Windfall. F. R. Scott. CaP
Until We Built a Cabin. Aileen Fisher. TiPo (1959 ed.)
Until yesterday I was polite and peaceful. Opinions of the New [Chinese] Student. Regino Pedroso. AnCL; PoNe
Until You Pass. A. Newberry Choyce. BoHiPo
Until your laughter. Tumult. Charles Enoch Wheeler. PoNe
Untimely End, The. Chidiock Tichborne. *See* Elegy: "My prime of youth is but a frost of cares."
Untimely Thought. Thomas Bailey Aldrich. AnNE
Unto a Child in Bethlehem-town. Eugene Field. *Fr.* Bethlehem-Town. PGD
Unto a heavenly course decreed. Star Morals. Nietzsche. AWP
Unto all poets I do me excuse. The Excusation of the Auctor. Stephen Hawes. *Fr.* The Pastime of Pleasure. ReIE
Unto Each [Man] His Handiwork. Swinburne. *Fr.* Super Flumina Babylonis. OQP, *2 sts.;* QP-2, *2 sts.*
("Whoso Loseth His Life," *4 sts.*) MaRV
Unto God let praise be brought. And It Came to Pass at Midnight. Yannai. TrJP
Unto me, the All-controlling. Bird-Pastoral. Aristophanes. *Fr.* The Birds. GrR
Unto my faith as to a spar, I bind. Adrift. Elizabeth Dickinson Dowden. WGRP
Unto my friends I give my thoughts. Legacies. Ethelwyn Wetherald. CPG; MaRV; OQP; QP-2
Unto my thinking, thou behold'st all worth. Sonnet: To Dante Alighieri (He Interprets Dante's Dream). Guido Cavalcanti. AWP
Unto Myself I Reared a Monument. Pushkin, *tr. fr. Russian by* Babette Deutsch. TrRV
(Monument, *tr. by* C. M. Bowra.) BoR
Unto salvation's spring. The Holy Eclogue. Sister Francisca Josefa del Castillo. CAW
Unto the blithe and lordly Fellowship. Sonnets of the Months [*or* Of the Months]: Dedication. Folgore da San Gemignano. AWP; LyPI
Unto the boundless ocean of thy beauty. To Delia, I. Samuel Daniel. LiTL; LoBV; OAEP; OBSC; ReIE; SiCE
Unto the deep the deep heart goes. The Place of Rest. "Æ." CMP; PC; WGRP
Unto the End. Jessie B. Rittenhouse. MuM
Unto the Hills. John Campbell, *paraphrased from* Psalm CXXI, Bible, *O.T.* MaRV
Unto the Least. St. Matthew, XXV: 32–40, Bible, *N.T.* GrCo-1
Unto the prison house of pain none willingly repair. The House of Pain. Florence Earle Coates. BPP; HBV; LBAP; OQP; QP-1
Unto the silver night. Revelation. Sir Edmund Gosse. BMEP; OBEV; OBVV; TCPD
Unto the soundles vaultes of Hell below. *Unknown.* SeCSL
Unto the temple of thy beauty. *Unknown.* OBSC
Unto the Upright Praise, *sel.* Moses Hayyim Luzzatto of Padua, *tr. fr. Hebrew by* Nina Davis Salaman.
Chorus: "All ye that handle harp and viol and pipe." TrJP
Unto Thee. Thomas Curtis Clark. PraP
Unto this altar, rich with thine own spice. To My Friend, Master John Ford. James Shirley. PtP
Unto this moving tide, into this deep. Sonnet of the Sea. Florence La Bau. CAG
Unto thy favor, which when nature formed. Robert Tofte. *Fr.* Laura. TuPP
Unto Us a Boy Is Born, *with music. Unknown.* YaCaBo
Unto Us a Child Is Born. Agnes H. Begbie. BOL
Unto Us a Son Is Given. Alice Meynell. ChIP; GTBS; JKCP; OQP; PoRL; QP-1; SDH; StJW
Untold Want, The. Walt Whitman. MoAmPo (1950 ed.)
Untouched by Adam's curse—our Mary's soul! Hymn for Second Vespers; Feast of the Apparition of Our Lady of Lourdes. *Unknown.* ISi
Untrammelled giant of the West. The Parting of the Ways. Joseph B. Gilder. AA; HBV; PAH
Untremulous in the river clear. Summer Storm. James Russell Lowell. LPS-2
Untried Door, The. Edward Shillito. ChIP
Untrodden Ways. Agnes Maule Machar. CaP; OCL
Untutored Giraffe, The. Oliver Herford. PoMa
Untutored Mind, An. Frank Dempster Sherman. PR
Untwine those ringlets! Ev'ry dainty clasp. Frangipanni. *Unknown.* NA
Unusual Chum, An. James W. Foley. FAOV
Unutterable Beauty, The. G. A. Studdert-Kennedy. TrPWD
Unutterable silence here is spread. The Lake of Van. Raffi. ArmLP
Unvanquished. Grace Hoffman White. PC
Unwarmed by any sunset light. The World Transformed [*or* The Snow-Storm]. Whittier. *Fr.* Snow-bound. AA; BBV; GBV; MW
Unwasted Days, *abr.* James Russell Lowell. *Fr.* Under the Old Elm, VI. MCCG
Unwatch'd the garden bough shall sway. In Memoriam A. H. H., CI. Tennyson. BrBE; CaAE; EmBrPo; EnLi-2; EnSW; EPN; GEPC; GTBS-D; OBEV (1st ed.); PoEL-5; SeCeV; ViPo; VLEP
Unwedded. Ada Foster Murray. AV
Unwelcome. Mary Elizabeth Coleridge. BMEP; CH; GTBS; GTBS-D; OBEV (new ed.); OBVV; PoVP
Unwelcome child. The Child Compassion. Margot Ruddock. OBMV
Unwept, unburied, traveller, we lie here. Philip, King of Macedon. Alcaeus of Messene. OxBG
Unwilling Guest, The; an Urban Dialogue. Horace Gregory. CrMA
Unwilling Gypsy, The. Josephine Johnson. HBMV
Unwinking frog of malachite, The. Museum-Piece. Audrey Alexandra Brown. CaP
Unwound the long evolvement. A Dream. Mary Fullerton. BoAV
Unwritten Poems. William Winter. AA
Unwritten Song, The. Ford Madox Ford. BoTP

Up a Hill and a Hill. Fannie Stearns Davis. NLK; NV; VOD
Up a river of sweet milk. *Unknown. Fr.* The Land of Cokaigne. CAW
Up above, a passing breeze. Fir Forest. Ethel Romig Fuller. PGD
Up aloft amid the rigging. Rolling Home. *Unknown.* AmSS
Up amang Yon Cliffy Rocks. William Dudgeon. EBSV
Up, Amaryllis! Wake, little sweeting! Of Fishing. Karl Mikael Bellman. AnSL
Up among the grey clouds. Grey. Karle Wilson Baker. LS
"Up among those top leaves, what do you see." Magnolia Tree. Sacheverell Sitwell. NV
Up and away through the drifting rain! The Little Tower. William Morris. POTT
Up and away, thy Saviour's gone before. The Resurrection, or Easter-Day. George Herbert. EOAH
Up and down/ Runs arrowy fire. How a Poet's Soul Comes into Play. Robert Browning. *Fr.* Sordello. MyFE
Up and down he goes. America. Alfred Kreymborg. NP
Up and down, o'er hill and valley. Triumph. L. D. Stearns. BLRP
Up and down, the air you float. The Butterfly. Clinton Scollard. GFA
Up and down the City Road. Pop Goes the Weasel. *Unknown.* BoN; OxNR
Up and down, up and down. A Nursery Hour. Lady Anne Lindsay. BOL
Up and rejoice, and know thou hast matter for revel, my heart! Edith M. Thomas. *Fr.* Sursum Corda. PC
Up and up, the Incense-Burner Peak! Having Climbed to the Topmost Peak of the Incense-Burner Mountain. Po Chü-i. TrCh
Up at a Villa—Down in the City. Robert Browning. BEL; BPN; EM-2; EmBrPo; EnLi-2 (1949 ed.); EnLit; EPN; GEPC; HBV; InP; PoRA; PoVP; SeCeV; TCEP; TOP; ViPo; ViPP; VLEP; WoL
Up at Forclaz, on the Pass. Bouton d'Or. Jessie B. Rittenhouse. PR
Up at Piccadilly oh! *Unknown.* OxNR
Up boy! arise, and saddle quick. The Message. Heine. AWP; JAWP; WBP
Up, Fairy! quit thy chick-weed bower. The Second Quest. Joseph Rodman Drake. *Fr.* The Culprit Fay. AA
Up, for mercy, and be going. A Love Song. *Unknown.* OxBG
Up from Earth's Center through the Seventh Gate. The Master-Knot. Omar Khayyám, *tr. by* Edward Fitzgerald. *Fr.* The Rubáiyát. OnPM
Up from my golden saucer in the dawn. Domine Jesu! John Duffy. JKCP (1955 ed.)
Up from the darkness on the laughing stage. Villiers de l'Isle-Adam. Aldous Huxley. HBMV
Up from the desert desolate and bleak. The Organ Cactus. Dorothy Scarborough. HiLiAm
Up from the Egg; the Confessions of a Nuthatch Avoider. Ogden Nash. FiBHP
Up from the Jordan straight his way he took. The Wilderness. Caroline Hazard. ChIP; StJW
Up from the low-roofed dockyard warehouses. Grain Elevator. A. M. Klein. CaP; TwCaPo
Up from the man's cottage. The Lady Elgin. *Unknown.* ABS
Up from the meadows rich with corn. Barbara Frietchie. Whittier. AmPP (3d ed.); AnNE; BAV; BBV; BeLS; BoTP; DD; EV-5; FaBoBe; FaFP; FaPON; GA; GN; GoTP; HBV; HBVY; IAP; LEAP; LH; LPS-2; MaC; MC; MW; NeHB; OnHT; OnSP; OTPC; PaA; PAH; PAP; PECK; PTA-1; PYM; REAL; RIS; ShGoBo; StVeCh (1940 ed.); TreF; TrGrPo; TVSH; WBLP; YaD; YT
Up from the sea a flaky, dank. The Fishermen. Emile Verhaeren. WoL
Up from the south, at break of day. Sheridan's Ride. Thomas Buchanan Read. BBV; BeLS; BIG; BoHiPo; CBPC; CoBA; DD; FaBoBe; FaFP; GA; GN; HBV; HBVY; IAP; LPS-2; MC; MDAH; OBAV; OHFP; OHIP; OnHT; OnSP; OTPC; PaA; PAH; PAP; PECK; PTA-1; PYM; TCAP; TreF; TVSH; WBLP; YaD
Up from the Wheelbarrow. Ogden Nash. FaBoBe
Up from Toulouse, September in the air. Le Cœur de l'Immaculée. Benjamin Francis Musser. WHL
Up heart, away heart. A Road Song. Duncan Campbell Scott. PC
Up, Heart of mine. Wayfarer of Earth. Sir Charles G. D. Roberts. CPG
Up here in Arkansaw the weather's colder. Exile. Rex Browne. DDA
Up-Hill [*or* Uphill]. Christina Rossetti. BLP; BLPA; BMEP; BrBE; CaAE; CBOV; CH; CoBE; EmBrPo; EnLi-2; EV-5; FaBoBe; GTBS; HBV; LEAP; LoBV; LPS-2; MaRV; MCCG; NeHB; NLK; OAEP; OBEV; OBVV; OQP; OtMeF; OTPC (1946 ed.); PCD; Po; PoFS; PoMa; PoRA; POTT; PoVP; PreP; QP-1; ShBV-2; TCEP; TOP; TreFS; TrGrPo; TSW; TSWC; TyEnPo; VA; ViBoPo; ViP; ViPo; VLEP; WGRP; WHA
("Does the road wind up-hill all the way?") EG
Up hill and down dale. *Unknown.* OxNR
Up, in free-born hardihood. Marching Song. Tyrtaeus. GrL; OxBG
Up in the Air. Allan Ramsay. BSV; CEP
Up in the Air. James S. Tippett. BoChLi; SUS; TiPo
Up in the attic, down in the cellar, and under. A Treasure. Reed Whittemore. NePoEA
Up in the barn where they keep the hay. The Hayloft. Luella Markley Mockett. BrR
Up in the Mornin' Early. John Hamilton. EBSV
(Cold Blows the Wind, *sl. abr.*) CH
Up in the Morning Early. Burns. OTPC; PCH
Up in the morning early. The Sun Is First to Rise. Elizabeth J. Coatsworth. StVeCh (1955 ed.)
Up in the morning's no' for me. Up in the Morning Early. Burns. OTPC; PCH
Up in the mountains, it's lonesome all the time. The Mountain Whippoorwill. Stephen Vincent Benét. HiLiAm; IHA; MOAP; OnAP; PoeMoYo; StPo; TBM; TrGrPo; YaD; YT
Up in the North. *Unknown.* LiTG; OxBoLi; SiTL
Up in the north an island lies. Iceland. Andreas Munch. AnNoLy
Up in the woodland where Spring. A Ballade of Spring's Unrest. Bert Leston Taylor. PoMa; YT
Up into the cherry tree. Foreign Lands. Robert Louis Stevenson. ADAH; BoTP; GFA; HBV; HBVY; MPB; OTPC; PCH; PoVP; RIS; TiPo (1952 ed.); TVC; VA
Up Johnie [*or* Johnnie] raise [*or* rose] in a May morning. Johnie [*or* Johnnie] Cock. *Unknown.* ESPB (D *vers.*); TCEP
Up leapt Achilles dear to Zeus, and Pallas flung. Achilles over the Trench. Homer. *Fr.* The Iliad, XVIII. GrPE
Up my brothers! Set all men free! Goethe. *Fr.* The Awakening of Epimenides. PoFr
Up, my dogs, merrily. The Nor'-west Courier. John E. Logan. VA
Up, O ye lovers, and away! 'Tis time to leave the world for aye. Departure. Jalal ed-Din Rumi. PeP
Up on de Mountain, *with music. Unknown.* BoAN-1
Up on the Downs. John Masefield. FaBoEn
Up on their brooms the Witches stream. The Ride-by-Nights. Walter de la Mare. FaPON; SiSoSe; TiPo
Up over windy wastes and up. G. K. Chesterton. *Fr.* The Ballad of the White Horse. BMEP; LEAP
Up! quit thy bower! late wears the hour. Good Morning [*or* Morning Song *or* Wake, Lady]. Joanna Baillie. HBV; LPS-2; OTPC (1923 ed.)
Up rose [*or* Uprose] the king of men with speed. The Descent of Odin; an Ode from the Norse Tongue. Thomas Gray. CEP; EiPP
Up rose the sun; the mists were curl'd. Byron. *Fr.* Mazeppa. OBRV
Up-Set, The. Corey Ford. WhC
Up She Goes, *with music. Unknown.* SoAmSa
Up soared the lark into the air. Saint Francis' Sermon to the Birds. Longfellow. SaFP
Up spake the King to Stig the Knight. The Death of Knight Stig. *Unknown.* BoDaBa
Up spoke the man of our gallant ship. Three Sailor Boys. *Unknown.* ABS
Up spring the spirits of the waves. War under Water. Joseph Rodman Drake. *Fr.* The Culprit Fay. APW
Up springs the lark. The Songsters. James Thomson. *Fr.* The Seasons: Spring. LPS-2
Up street and down street. *Unknown.* OxNR
Up sun and merry weather. A Ballad against Long-loving. *Unknown.* TMEV
Up tails all! Down and under! Undersea Fever. William Cole. FiBHP
Up the Airy Mountain. William Allingham. *See* Fairies, The.
Up the ash tree climbs the ivy. Upper Lambourne. John Betjeman. FaBoTw; GTBS-D
Up the crag/ In the screaming wind. Weapons. Anna Wickham. MBP; MoBrPo
Up the dale and down the bourne. Song of the Summer Winds [*or* Summer Winds]. George Darley. LPS-2; VA
Up the dark-valleyed river stroke by stroke. The Dawn on the Lievre. Archibald Lampman. CaP; OCL
Up the hillside, down the glen. Texas. Whittier. PAH
Up the Noran Water/ In by Inglismaddy. Shy Geordie. Helen B. Cruickshank. GoTS
Up the old hill to the old house again. The Long Race. E. A. Robinson. CrMA
Up the pound path. Betty Perrin. A. E. Coppard. MBP; MoBrPo (1942 ed.)

Up the sea-sadden'd valley at evening's decline. Dirge of Rory O More. Aubrey Thomas De Vere. IrPN; TIP
Up the slope and over the crest. The Stormy Petrel. James Harold Manning. CPG
Up the Spout. Swinburne. BOHV; PA
Up the steep slopes of morning. The Steep Slopes of Morning. Mary Weedan. MuM
Up the street,/ Down the street. The Old Man's Toes. Eleanor Farjeon. PoRh
Up the streets of Aberdeen. Barclay of Ury. Whittier. IAP; LPS-2; TCAP
Up the wooden hill. *Unknown.* OxNR
Up then, Melpomene, thou mournfulst [*or* mournefulst] Muse of nine. Dido My Dear, Alas, Is Dead. Spenser. *Fr.* The Shepheardes Calender. AtBAP; ChTr
Up then spake our noble cabin boy. The Lowlands Low. *Unknown.* ABS
Up this beaten pathway poured a long and weaving queue. W. E. Bard. *Fr.* Mesa Trail. HiLiAm
Up through a cloudy sky, the sun. The Battle of Bennington. Thomas P. Rodman. GA; MC; PAH
Up through the air, over land, over ocean. Chorus of the Winds. Per Daniel Amadeus Atterbom. AnSL
Up through the hyaline ether-sea. The Chaplet of Cypress. Thomas Holley Chivers. APW; MOAP; SPP
Up through the rocky pastures. Queen Anne's Lace. Georgia Benedict. CAG
"Up, Timothy, up with your staff and away!" The Childless Father [*or* Timothy]. Wordsworth. CG; CH
Up to both sweet-spoken Nestor stood. Nestor's Speech to Achilles and Agamemnon. Homer. *Fr.* The Iliad, I. ReEn
Up to her chamber window. Nocturne. Thomas Bailey Aldrich. HBV; PR
Up to my lips and over my gums. Toast. *Unknown.* CoSo
Up to the bed by the window, where I be lyin'. Old Shepherd's Prayer. Charlotte Mew. MBP; MoAB; MoBrPo
Up to the breeze of the morning I fling you. Flag o' My Land. T. A. Daly. HH
Up to the top of the haunted turf. Mother Goose Up-to-Date. Louis Untermeyer. MoAmPo
Up! Up! let us a voyage take. Northern Seas. William Howitt. GN; OTPC (1923 ed.); TVSH
Up, up, my drowsie Soule, where thy new eare. Our Company in the Next World. John Donne. *Fr.* Of the Progresse of the Soule. OBS
Up! Up! My Friend, and Quit Your Books. Wordsworth. *See* Tables Turned, The.
Up! Up! the sky's afloat. Song for a Camper. John Farrar. YeAr
Up! Up! the time for sleep is past! The Expensive Wife. Judah ibn Sabbatai. *Fr.* The Gift of Judah the Woman-Hater. TrJP
Up, Up! Ye Dames and Lasses Gay. Samuel Taylor Coleridge. *See* Hunting Song.
Up where the white bluffs fringe the plain. Prairie Wolves. Robert V. Carr. PoOW
Up with me! up with me into the clouds! To a Sky-Lark. Wordsworth. BEL; BLA; BPN; DD; EM-2; EmBrPo; GEPC; HBV; MCCG; REAL; SN; TCEP; TOP
Up with the banner of the free! The Flag. Henry Lynden Flash. FOAH; MC; PEOR
Up with the rafters high. Wedding Song. Sappho. GrR
Up with windows, up with hearts. The Coming of Spring. Wilhelm Müller. PEOR
Up with you, lazybones! Getting Out of Bed. Eleanor Farjeon. SiSoSe
Up with your heads, ye sylvan lords! The Forest Trees. Eliza Cook. PEOR
Up yonder on the mountain. The Shepherd's Lament. Goethe. AWP; JAWP; WBP
Up, youths and virgins, up and praise. Ben Jonson. *Fr.* Epithalamium. LEAP
Upanishads, The, *sels.* *Unknown, tr. fr. Sanskrit.*
All, The, *tr. by* Joseph Nadin Rawson. OnPM
As Pure Water, *tr. by* Joseph Nadin Rawson. OnPM
God, *tr. by* Dhan Ghopal Mukerji. MW
"He, being one, rules over all and everything," *tr. by* F. Max Müller. PoFr
Inner Vision, *tr. by* Joseph Nadin Lawson. OnPM
No Peace, *tr. by* Joseph Nadin Rawson. OnPM
Omnipresent Self, *tr. by* Joseph Nadin Rawson. OnPM
Self, The, *tr. by* Joseph Nadin Rawson. OnPM
Story of Svetaketu, The, *tr. by* F. Max Müller. WoL
Tranquility, *tr. by* Joseph Nadin Rawson. OnPM
Unborn Eternal Self, *tr. by* Joseph Nadin Rawson. OnPM
Universal Fire, The, *tr. by* Joseph Nadin Rawson. OnPM
Universal Self, The, *tr. by* F. Max Müller. WoL
Yoga, *tr. by* Joseph Nadin Rawson. OnPM
Upas Tree, The. Pushkin, *tr. fr. Russian.* LiTW, *tr. by* Frances Cornford *and* E. P. Salaman; TrRV, *tr. by* Babette Deutsch
Upbroke the sun. The Poor Old Cannon. Elinor Wylie. LHV
Uphead an' Scatter, Boys, *with music.* *Unknown.* StDa
Upheld by His Hand. Grace B. Renfrow. BePJ
Uphill. Christina Rossetti. *See* Up-Hill.
Uphill path, sun-gleams between the showers, An. The Pilgrims. John McCrae. CPG
Upland of Nirvana. *Unknown, tr. fr. Japanese by* Ishii *and* Obata. OnPM
Uplifted and waved until immobilized. Elephants. Marianne Moore. FaBoMo
Uplifting suddenly slim fiery-golden anthers. Charcoal Sketch. Michael Scot. PoC
Upon a Bank. Michael Drayton. EV-1
Upon a Braid of Hair in a Heart. Henry King. EnLoPo
Upon a Child ("Here a pretty baby lies"). Robert Herrick. LoBV; OBS; PIAE; SeCV-1; TrGrPo
(Another.) OBEV
(Two Epitaphs upon a Child That Died.) CBOV
Upon a Child. Swinburne. *See* Children.
Upon a Child That Died. Robert Herrick. *See* Epitaph upon a Child That Died.
Upon a cloud among the stars we stood. The Flight. Lloyd Mifflin. AA; AnAmPo; HBV; LA; LBMV; LEAP
Upon a cock-horse to market I'll trot. *Unknown.* OxNR
Upon a dark ball spun in Time. Giraffe and Tree. W. J. Turner. CH
Upon a dark, light, gloomy, sunshine day. A Messe of Nonsense. *Unknown.* OBS
Upon a darksome night. The Dark Night of the Soul [*or* Songs of the Soul]. St. John of the Cross. AnSpL-1; LiTW; TeCS
Upon a Day. Spenser. OAEP
Upon a day, came sorrow in to me. Sonnet: On the 9th of June 1290. Dante. AWP
Upon a day in Ramadan. The Caliph's Draught. Sir Edwin Arnold. VA
Upon a Dead Man's Head. John Skelton. CoBE; SeCePo; SiCE; UnPo (1st ed.)
(Gift of a Skull, The.) ACP
(Skelton Laureate, upon a Dead Man's Head.) ReIE
Upon a Diamond Cut in Form[e] of a Heart . . . Sent in a New Year's [*or* Yeares] Gift. Sir Robert Ayton. EIL; OBS
Upon a Drawing. Lionel Johnson. VLEP
Upon a Dying Lady (I–VII). W. B. Yeats. LiTB; UnPo (3d ed.)
Upon a Favour Offered. William Walsh. SeCL
Upon a fool's provocation. A Fool's Tongue. John Heywood. SiCE
Upon a Friend's Pet Cat, Being Sick. John Winstanley. PoC
Upon a Gloomy Night. St. John of the Cross. *See* Obscure Night of the Soul, The.
Upon a Great Black Horse-ily. *Unknown, tr. fr. German.* MeMeAg; OTPC; PPL; SAS
Upon a great ship's tilted deck. In a Storm. Harry Kemp. PFY
Upon a high balcony I lean alone. Thinking of Her. Liu Yung. ChLP
Upon a Hill. Miriam LeFevre Crouse. ChIP
Upon a Hill. Keats. *See* I Stood Tiptoe.
Upon a jolting wagonseat she rode. The Pioneer Mother. Ethel Romig Fuller. PGD
Upon a Lady Fair and Bright, *in mod. Eng.* *Unknown.* TMEV
Upon a letter old I came to-day. A Faded Letter. William J. Fischer. CAW
Upon a life I have not lived. He Took My Place. Horatius Bonar. BePJ
Upon a lonely road at shut of day. The Blind Preacher. Yakov Polonsky. BoR
Upon a Maid ("Here she lies, in bed of spice"). Robert Herrick. ChTr; ElSeCe; FaBoCh; KN; LoGBV; OxBoLi; SeEP
Upon a Maid That Died the Day She Was Married. Meleager, *tr. fr. Greek by* Robert Herrick. AWP
("That morn which saw me made a bride.") GrPo
Upon a mountain's height, far from the sea. The Wanderer. Eugene Field. BLP; PoOW; TVSH
Upon a noon I pilgrimed through. Her Immortality. Thomas Hardy. VLEP
Upon a Passing Bell. Thomas Washbourne. SeCL
Upon a Patch Face. Thomas, Lord Fairfax. SeCL
Upon a poet's page I wrote. Her Initials. Thomas Hardy. EmBrPo; InP
Upon a Rare Voice. Owen Felltham. SeCL
Upon a Ribbon Tied about His Arm by a Lady. Thomas Carew. EPS
Upon a Ring of Bells. Bunyan. CH
Upon a rock that, high and sheer. The Hunter's Vision. Bryant. UnW
Upon a rock, yet uncreate. The Cosmic Egg. *Unknown.* BOHV; LPS-3
Upon a Sabbath-Day it fell. The Eve of Saint Mark. Keats. BPN; CH; EM-2; EmBrPo; EnRP; ERP; GEPC; NBE; OBRV

Upon a showery night and still. Dandelions. Helen Gray Cone. ADAH; DD; GFA; HBV; NLK; PRWS; SN
Upon a Sickly Lady. *At. to* Charles Burnaby *and to* William Burnaby. *Fr.* The Reformed Wife. SeCL
Upon a simmer Sunday morn. The Holy Fair. Burns. BEL; CEP; EiPP; EnRP; OAEP
Upon a Spider Catching a Fly. Edward Taylor. AmP; AmPP (4th ed.); CoV; GTBS-W; NePA; OxBA; PoEL-3
Upon a sultry, yellow sky. Mercedes. Elizabeth Stoddard. AA; LBAP
Upon a summer Sunday: sweet the sound. The Runaways. Mark Van Doren. PoRA
Upon a summer's time. A Pleasant New Court Song. *Unknown.* CoMu
Upon a Sweet-Briar. Walter Savage Landor. *Fr.* The Citation and Examination of Shakespeare. BPN
Upon a tall piano stool. Learning to Play. Abbie Farwell Brown. HH; PPL
Upon a time a neighing steed. The Council of Horses. John Gay. BoChLi; CG; GN
Upon a time, before the faery broods. Lamia. Keats. BEL; EM-2; EmBrPo; EnLi-2; EnRP; EPN; ERP; GEPC; OAEP; PIR; TwCrTr
Upon a time I had a heart. A Song of a Heart [*or* A Song]. Oliver Herford. PA; PR
Upon a tuffet of most soft and verdant moss. Little Miss Muffet. *Unknown.* PA
Upon a Virgin Kissing a Rose. Robert Herrick. SeCV-1
Upon a Wasp Chilled with Cold. Edward Taylor. AmPP (4th ed.); AtBAP; FaBoEn; GTBS-W; PoEL-3
Upon an eve I sat me down and wept. Error and Loss. William Morris. BPN
Upon an everlasting tide. The Epicurean. Sir Francis Hastings Doyle. EPN; OBVV
Upon an Honest Man's Fortune, *sel.* John Fletcher.
Man Is His Own Star, 6 *ll.* OQP; QP-2
(Destiny: "An honest and a perfect man," 7 *ll.*) MaRV
(Man His Own Star.) EV-2
Upon an island, all alone. The Converted Cannibals. G. E. Farrow. BOHV
Upon an obscure night. The Obscure Night of the Soul. St. John of the Cross, *tr. by* Arthur Symons. AWP; CAW; MeRV; OBMV; OuHeWo; TriL; VLEP
Upon an old estate from ancient sires descended. The Portraits. Anna Maria Lenngren. AnSL
Upon an upland orchard's sunny side. Sonnet. Thomas Caulfield Irwin. IrPN
Upon ane stormy Sunday. The Plaidie. Charles Sibley. BOHV; HBV; LPS-1
Upon Appleton House, *abr.* Andrew Marvell. ReEn; SeCV-1
Sels.
"And now to the abbyss I pass." AtBAP
Carrying Their Coracles. ChTr
Hewel, or Woodpecker, The. ChTr
In a Forest. EV-2
Kingfisher, The. AtBAP; ChTr; FaBoEn
"Oh thou, that dear and happy isle." OxBoLi
"See how the flowers, as at parade." TrGrPo
(Garden, A.) CEP; EPS (1942 ed.); HBV; OBEV; ShGoBo
"Within this sober frame expect." NBE
Upon Being Awakened at Night by My Four Year Old Daughter. Dachine Rainer. NePoAm-2
Upon Being Obliged to Leave a Pleasant Party. Thomas Moore. BOHV
Upon Ben. Johnson. Edmund Waller. SeCV-1
Upon Ben Jonson. Robert Herrick. BEL; BoFr; OAEP; OBS; PtP; SeCV-1
Upon Bishop Andrewes His Picture before His Sermons. Richard Crashaw. OBS
Upon Black Eyes, and Becoming Frowns. James Howell. SeCL
Upon Castara's Departure. William Habington. *Fr.* Castara. SeCL
Upon Combing Her Hair. Lord Herbert of Cherbury. *See* Breaking from under That Thy Cloudy Veil.
Upon Consideration of the State of This Life He Wisheth Death. *Unknown.* SiCE; TuPP
Upon de Mountain, *with music. Unknown.* TrAS
Upon Differences of Opinion. Hy Sobiloff. SiTL
Upon Discovering One's Own Intolerance. Sara Henderson Hay. MaRV
Upon Dr. Davies' British Grammar. James Howell. PrWP
Upon Drinking in a Bowl. Earl of Rochester. CEP; EPS; OBS; OxBoLi; SeCV-2
(Bowl, The.) EV-3
Upon Eckington Bridge, River Avon. Sir Arthur Quiller-Couch. OBVV; PoeT; POTE
Upon Ford's Two Tragedies, "Loves Sacrifice" and "The Broken Heart." Richard Crashaw. OBS
Upon green hills in droves the horses graze. Droves. Sergei Aleksandrovich Yesenin. TrRV
Upon her eyes they gazed. Beauty. Abu Hafs. MooP
Upon Her Feet. Robert Herrick. *See* Upon Mistress Susanna Southwell, Her Feet.
Upon her hair, with brilliants grac'd. Imagination. Christopher Smart. *Fr.* Reason and Imagination. BeR
Upon her head she weares a crowne of starres. An Angel Describes Truth. Ben Jonson. *Fr.* Hymenaei. OBS
Upon Her Play Being Returned to Her Stained with Claret. Mary Leapor. DiM
Upon Himself. Robert Herrick. SeEP
Upon himself a miracle he wrought. Eugenio Pacelli. Francis Neilson. GoYe
Upon His Departure Hence. Robert Herrick. PCD; PIAE; PreP
Upon His Leaving His Mistress. Earl of Rochester. EnLoPo; ViBoPo
(Upon Leaving His Mistress.) TrGrPo
Upon His M. Dancing. James Shirley. *See* Upon His Mistress Dancing.
Upon His Meeting with His Two Worthy Friends and Fellow-Poets. Sir Philip Sidney. *Fr.* Two Pastorals. SiCE
("Join mates in mirth to me.") TuPP
Upon His Mistress Dancing. James Shirley. SeCL
(Upon His M. Dancing.) SeEP
Upon His Picture. Thomas Randolph. ElSeCe; MePo; SeCL; SeEP
Upon His Sister in Law. Robert Herrick. SeEP
Upon His Timorous Silence in Her Presence. Francis Davison. TuPP
("Are lovers full of fire?") EG
Upon his tractor's steady seat. The Plowman of Today. Hamlin Garland. StVeCh
Upon his will he binds a radiant chain. The Peacemaker. Joyce Kilmer. CAW; MaRV; PoFr
Upon Julia Weeping. Robert Herrick. ExPo
Upon Julia's Clothes. Robert Herrick. AEV; AnFE; AtBAP; AWP; BEL; BLV; BoLiVe; CaAE; ChTr; CoBE; CoEV; ElSeCe; EM-1; EnL; EnLi-1; EnLit; EnLoPo; EPP; EPS (1942 ed.); EV-2; ExPo; FaFP; HBV; HoPM; InPo; JAWP; LiTB; LiTG; LoBV; LoPS; MaPo; OAP; OBEV; OBS; OuHeWo; PG (1945 ed.); Po; PoEL-3; PoFS; ReaPo; RiBV; SeCeV; SeCV-1; SeEP; TOP; TreF; TrGrPo; TwHP; TyEnPo; ViBoPo; WBP
(As in Silks My Julia Goes.) BLP
(Poetry of Dress, The, II.) GTBS; GTBS-D; GTBS-W; GTSE; GTSL
(Whenas in Silks My Julia Goes.) BCEP; BLPA; EG; InP; LEAP; LiTL; LoPo; LPS-1; NeHB; PIAE; ShBV-4
Upon Julia's Hair[e] Filled [*or* Fill'd] with Dew. Robert Herrick. AtBAP; EG
Upon Julia's Recovery. Robert Herrick. AtBAP
Upon Julia's Voice. Robert Herrick. AtBAP; BoW; ExPo; MyFE; SeCePo; SeCL
Upon Kind[e] and True Love. Aurelian Townsend. MeLP; MePo; OBS; SeCL
("'Tis not how witty, nor how free.") EG
Upon Kings. Robert Herrick. PoFr
Upon Lazarus His Teares. Richard Crashaw. SeCV-1
Upon Leaving His Mistress. Earl of Rochester. *See* Upon His Leaving His Mistress.
Upon Lesbia—Arguing. Alfred Cochrane. HBV
Upon Lesbia's Abuse. Catullus. *See* Lesbia Railing.
Upon Love ("Love brought me to a silent grove"). Robert Herrick. BLV; BoLiVe; TrGrPo
Upon Love ("Love scorch'd my finger, but did spare"). Robert Herrick. SeCV-1
Upon Love, by Way of Question and Answer ("I bring ye Love"). Robert Herrick. Po
Upon M. Ben Jonson, Epigram. Robert Herrick. HoPM; OAEP; PtP
Upon Manassa's bloody plain a soldier boy lay dying! The Dying Soldier Boy. A. B. Cunningham. BIG
Upon Master Fletchers Incomparable Playes. Robert Herrick. OBS; PtP
Upon Master W. Montague. Thomas Carew. SeEP
Upon Mr. Fletchers Playes, Published, 1647. Henry Vaughan. PtP
Upon Mr. John Fletcher's Playes. Edmund Waller. PtP
Upon Mrs. Eliz. Wheeler, under the Name of Amarillis. Robert Herrick. EV-2
Upon Mistress Susanna Southwell, Her Feet. Robert Herrick. EnLi-1; PoFS
(Upon Her Feet.) ViBoPo
Upon my bier no garlands lay. Now. Mary Barker Dodge. AA
Upon my breast. Once in a Lonely Hour. John Hall Wheelock. LoPS; NP
Upon my darling's beaming eyes. Auf meiner Herzliebsten Augelein. Heine. AWP
Upon My Lap My Sovereign Sits. Richard Verstegan. *See* Lullaby: "Upon my lap . . ."
Upon my mantel-piece they stand. A Moral in Sèvres. Mildred Howells. AA; HBV; PR

Upon my ryght syde y me leye. An Evening Prayer. *Unknown.* AtBAP
Upon New Year's Eve. Sir Arthur Quiller-Couch. OBVV
Upon Nirwána's brink the ráhat stood. The Ráhat. John Jerome Rooney. AA; BAP
Upon Nothing. Earl of Rochester. AtBAP; BLV; MePo; NBE; OBS; Po; PoEL-3; SeEP; TrGrPo, *abr.;* ViBoPo
Upon our country roads have stood. Wooden Crosses. Paul Gérardy. TrFP
Upon our eyelids, dear, the dew will lie. Before Dawn in the Woods. Marguerite Wilkinson. HBMV; LEAP; PC
Upon our fullness shines the dawning day. Sonnet. Francis Lyman Windolph. MaRV
Upon Our Late Loss of the Duke of Cambridge. Edmund Waller. Po
Upon our Vain Flattery of Ourselves that the Succeeding Times Will Be Better than the Former. Robert Gomersal. SeCL
Upon Pagget. Robert Herrick. FaBoCh; LoGBV
Upon Paul's steeple stands a tree. *Unknown.* OxNR
Upon Phillis [*or* Phyllis] Walking in a Morning before Sunrising. John Cleveland. EPS; LiTL; MeLP
("Sluggish morn as yet undrest.") EG
Upon Prudence Baldwin Her Sicknesse. Robert Herrick. OAEP; SeCV-1
Upon Prue [*or* Prew] His Maid. Robert Herrick. EM-1; EPS; OAEP; SeCV-1; SeEP; TyEnPo
Upon Reading an Old Book. Pearce Young. PtPa
Upon Returning a Silk Handkerchief. Herbert P. Horne. LEAP
Upon St. Michael's Isle. The Burial of Robert Browning. "Michael Field." VA
Upon Scarlet and Blush-coloured Ribbands, Given by Two Ladies. James Shirley. GoBC
Upon Sibilla. Robert Herrick. SeCePo
Upon Sir Francis Drake's Return from His Voyage about the World, and the Queen's Meeting Him. *Unknown.* CoMu; EIL; FaBoCh
Upon that night, when fairies light. Hallowe'en. Burns. HOAH; OBEC
Upon the anvil of my heart. The Unknown Sword-Maker. Rachel Annand Taylor. EBSV
Upon the arid shoulder. The Broom. Giacomo Leopardi. LiTW
Upon the Author's First Seven Years' Service. Thomas Tusser. *See* Sonnet upon the Author's First Seven Years' Service, A.
Upon the barren sand. Pocahontas. George Pope Morris. GA; MC; PAH
Upon the Beach. Ilo Orleans. RIS; TiPo (1952 ed.)
Upon the beach are thousands of crabs. Crustaceans. Roy Fuller. NeBP
Upon the black brow of a cliff where no life ever stirred. Eagles. Vasily Vasilyevich Bashkin. TrRV
Upon the black horse of midnight I ride. Night Musick for Thérèse. Dachine Rainer. NePoAM-2
Upon the Bleeding Crucifix. Richard Crashaw. *See* On the Bleeding Wounds of Our Crucified Lord.
Upon the Body of Our Blessed Lord, Naked and Bloody. Richard Crashaw. ACP; EnLi-1; InvP; OAEP; OBS; Po; RiBV
(On Our Crucified Lord Naked, and Bloody.) SeCV-1
Upon the Book and Picture of the Seraphical Saint Teresa. Richard Crashaw. *See* Flaming Heart, The.
Upon the borders of the desert is a town. The Loves of the Lions. Charles Madge. MoP
Upon the bridge the blind man stands alone. Pont du Carrousel. Rainer Maria Rilke. OnPM
Upon the Burning of Our House. Anne Bradstreet. AmP; AmPP (4th ed.); OxBA
Upon the Crucifix. William Alabaster. PoEL-2
"Upon the day thou weariest of me." William Morris. *Fr.* The Life and Death of Jason. LoPS
Upon the Death of George Santayana. Anthony Hecht. NePA
Upon the Death of King Charles I. James Graham, Marquess of Montrose. *See* Epitaph on King Charles I.
Upon the Death of My Ever-desired Friend, Doctor Donne [Dean] of Paul's. Henry King. EPS (1942 ed.); NBE
Upon the Death of Sir Albert Morton's Wife. Sir Henry Wotton. CaAE; CBOV; EnLoPo; Ev-2; OBEV; OBS; OnPM; SeEP; ViBoPo; WoL
(On the Death of Sir Albert Morton's Wife.) BLV; TrGrPo
(On the Death of Sir Albertus and Lady Morton.) PIAE
Upon the Death of the Earl of Dundee. Dryden. *See* Upon the Death of the Viscount of Dundee.
Upon the Death of the Lord Hastings. Dryden. CEP; SeCV-2 ("Must noble Hastings immaturely die.") ReEn
Upon the Death of the Viscount of [*or* Earl of] Dundee. Dryden. ACP; OBS; PoFr
Upon the Downs. Sir George Etherege. ViBoPo
Upon the Dramatick Poems of Mr. John Fletcher. William Cartwright. OBS
Upon the ecstatic diving board the diver. Lone Bather. A. M. Klein. TwCaPo
Upon the eighteenth day of June. Bonny John Seton. *Unknown.* BaBo; ESPB
Upon the Ensignes of Christes Crucifyinge. William Alabaster. MePo
Upon the everlasting element. Ideal Passion, XIV. George Edward Woodberry. MOAP
Upon the eyes, the lips, the feet. Extreme Unction. Ernest Dowson. ACP; CAW; JKCP; LEAP; MBP; MoBrPo; OBMV; POTT; VLEP
Upon the far-drifting flood of grey. Sapporo City. Kenji Miyazawa. PoLJ
Upon the first new morn of May. Encounter. *Unknown.* LyMA
Upon the flowery forefront of the year. Thalassius. Swinburne. PoVP; VLEP
Upon the gale she stooped her side. The Gallant Ship. Sir Walter Scott. BoTP
Upon the gates of the prison. Prison. *Unknown.* OnPM
Upon the grass no longer hangs the dew. Hay Making. Joanna Baillie. EV-3
Upon the Hard Crest. "Anna Akhmatova," *tr. fr. Russian by* Babette Deutsch. TrRV
Upon the Hearth. Lloyd Mifflin. POT; PoTo
Upon the Heavenly Scarp. A. M. Klein. *See* Psalm VI: "And on that day . . ."
Upon the highest hill of all. The Apple Tree. Beatrice Curtis Brown. SiSoSe
Upon the Hill before Centreville. George Henry Boker. PAH
Upon the hill he turn'd. The Soldier's Tear. Alexander Lee. BHV
Upon the hills of Phrygie near a teyle there stands a tree. Philemon and Baucis. Ovid, *tr. by* Arthur Golding. *Fr.* Metamorphoses. OBSC
Upon the house a crooked sign. For Sale or Rent. *Unknown.* PoToHe (new ed.)
Upon the Image of Death. Robert Southwell. CH; CoBE; EIL; OBSC; ReEn; ReIE; SiCE; TuPP
(Before My Face the Picture Hangs.) OxBoCh; PoLi
Upon the incoming ship, with sails full set. On Tsukuda-Isle in July. Munetake. OnPM
Upon the lake. The Gramophone. James Reaney. CaP; TwCaPo
Upon the Lark and the Fowler. Bunyan. CH
Upon the lonely shore I lie. By the Sea. Mary Clemmer. LPS-3
Upon the Loss of His Mistresses. Robert Herrick. BEL; EM-1; EnLi-1 (1949 ed.); EPS; OAEP; ReEn; SeCV-1; SeEP
Upon the low brine-sprinkled shore stand we. A Temple. Mnasalcas. OxBG
Upon the marsh mud, dank and foul. Love's Miracle. Lucy Maud Montgomery. MaRV
Upon the Midlands now th' industrious muse doth fall. The Thirteenth Song. Michael Drayton. *Fr.* Polyolbion. ReEn; ReIE; TuPP
Upon [*or* Apon] the midsumme even, merriest [*or* evin, mirriest] of nichtis. The Tua Maritt Wemen and the Wedo. William Dunbar. BSV; GoTS
Upon the Most Useful Knowledge, Craft or Cunning, Which Is More Wisdom, as 'Tis Less Wit. William Wycherley. SeCV-2
Upon the New-built House at Appleton. Thomas, Lord Fairfax. SeCL
Upon the Nipples of Julia's Breast. Robert Herrick. LiTL; ViBoPo
Upon the patch of earth that clings. Public Aid for Niagara Falls. Morris Bishop. InMe
Upon the platform Croker. Martial, *tr. fr. Latin by* "T.W.M." Epigrams, IV, 41. LaP
Upon the Plymouth shore the wild rose blooms. The Wild Rose of Plymouth. Jones Very. TCAP
Upon the point/ Of the descending steep I stand. William Lisle Bowles. *Fr.* Sketch from Bowden Hill after Sickness. EnSW
Upon the poop the captain stands. The Shipwreck. E. H. Palmer. BOHV; NA
Upon the Priory Grove, His Usual Retirement. Henry Vaughan. TriL
Upon the road to Romany. From Romany to Rome. Wallace Irwin. HBV
Upon the road which I have trod so long. Sunset. *Unknown.* SoLD
Upon the sadness of the sea. The Sunrise Never Failed Us Yet. Celia Thaxter. PEOR
Upon the Same ("I yearn more hungrily to see your face"). Joachim du Bellay, *tr. fr. French by* Alan Conder. Les Amours, XXVII. TrFP
Upon the Savior's Tomb. Richard Crashaw. StJW
(To Our Blessed Lord upon the Choice of His Sepulchre.) ACP
Upon the shadowy sunset bound of sleep. Home. Homer C. House. MuM

Upon the Shore. Robert Bridges. EtS; VA
(After the Gale.) LoBV
Upon the shore of Argolis there stands. Atalanta's Race. William Morris. *Fr.* The Earthly Paradise. BMEP
Upon the sides of Latmos was outspread. The Forest. Keats. *Fr.* Endymion. BCEP
Upon the Sight of a Beautiful Picture. Wordsworth. BPN
Upon the skyline [glows] i' the dark. The Universal Republic [*or* Republic of the World]. Victor Hugo. MaRV; OQP; PGD; QP-1
Upon the Snail. Bunyan. ChTr
Upon the sober sky thy robes are spread. Hesperus. James Stephens. GTIV
Upon the Stair I See My Lady Stand. Clinton Scollard. PFE
Upon the street they lie. The Children. William Soutar. POTE
Upon the Sudden Restraint of the Earl[e] of Somerset, Then Falling from Favor [*or* Favour]. Sir Henry Wotton. MePo; OBS
Upon the sunny summer hill. Clover for Breakfast. Frances Frost. StVeCh (1955 ed.)
Upon the terrace where I play. The Fountain. Rose Fyleman. GFA
Upon the Thought of Age and Death. William Habington. AEV
Upon the threshold ot another year. New Year. Thomas Wearing. MaRV
Upon the threshold of the year we stand. The New Year. Homera Homer-Dixon. BLRP; PraP
Upon the Tomb of John Cotton. Benjamin Woodbridge. BAV
Upon the topmost branches dies. Doubt. Fernand Gregh. WGRP
Upon the tree of time. A Harvest to Seduce. Melville Cane. PG (1955 ed.)
Upon the utmost corners of the warld. In Orkney. William Fowler. GoTS
Upon the Valley's Lap. Francis W. Bourdillon. BPP
Upon the walls the graceful ivy climbs. Ivy. Frank Dempster Sherman. MAP
Upon the Whirlwind. Antero de Quental, *tr. fr. Portuguese by* S. Griswold Morley. UnW
Upon the white sea sand there sat a pilgrim band. The Greatest Loss [*or* Losses]. Frances Brown. LPS-1; MaRV
Upon the wreckage of thy yesterday. Building. Ella Wheeler Wilcox. OQP; QP-1
Upon these dreary bars the ocean rolls. In the Lighthouse at Point Lookout, North Carolina. Henry Jerome Stockard. NoCaPo
Upon these words of Telemachus, Pallas Athene fired. The Vision of Theoclymenus. Homer. *Fr.* The Odyssey, XX. OxBG
Upon this greying page you wrote. On Looking at a Copy of Alice Meynell's Poems, Given Me, Years Ago, by a Friend. Amy Lowell. BoFr; NP; PtP
Upon this leafy bush. The Linnet. Walter de la Mare. BLA; BMEP; BrBE; GTML; HBMV; LiTB; LoBV; NP
Upon this marble bust that is not I. The Pioneer. Edna St. Vincent Millay. PoFr
Upon This Rock. James L. Duff. JKCP
Upon This Rock. Robert Whitaker. ChIP
Upon this seal Love whom none e'er withstands. Marcus Argentarius, *tr. fr. Greek by* Norman Douglas. GrPo
Upon this shore which I follow to Shibutani. Gazing at the Moon while Journeying Homewards. Otomo Yakamochi. OnPM
Upon this trouble shall I whet my life. Grief. Angela Morgan. PC
Upon This Wild Headland. Apollon Nikolayevich Maikov, *tr. fr. Russian by* Babette Deutsch. TrRV
Upon those who defy authority. True Freedom. *Unknown. Fr.* Tao Teh King. OnPM
Upon Thought Castara May Die. William Habington. *Fr.* Castara, I. ACP
Upon thy bended knees, thank God for work. The Sacrament of Work [*or* Gratitude for Work]. John Oxenham. MaRV; PGD
Upon thy lips now lies. Song to Isa Singing. Thomas Holley Chivers. APW; MOAP; SPP
Upon thy tomb 'tis graven "Here lies one." Keats. John Banister Tabb. AmP
Upon Time. Robert Herrick. EV-2; OBS
Upon us vagabonds who take. Vagabonds. Sara Hamilton Birchall. NLK
Upon Visiting His Lady by Moonlight. "A. W." OBSC; ReIE; TuPP
Upon Westminster Bridge. Wordsworth. *See* Composed upon Westminster Bridge, Sept. 3, 1802.
Upon What Base. Edward Taylor. OnAP
Upon what manner man is bound to man. Community. Iqbal. PeP
Upon your brow the shining star of hope. A Sonnet to That Great Mother Schumann-Heink. Marian Leland. MotAn
Upon your heart, which is the heart of all. Sonnets from "One Person." Elinor Wylie. NP
Upper Air. Frank Ernest Hill. AnAmPo; LA; MAP; MoAmPo (1942 ed.)
Upper Chamber, An. Frances Bannerman. HBV; OBEV
Upper Chamber in a Darkened House, An. Frederick Goddard Tuckerman. AnNE
Upper Lake, The. Francis Stuart. NeIP
Upper Lambourne. John Betjeman. FaBoTw; GTBS-D
Upper Room, An. Daniel Lawrence Kelleher. NeIP
Upper Room, The. Belle F. Owens. ChIP
Upper Skies, The. Robert Bridges. BoTP
Upright and shrewd, more woo'd of fame. Henry Charles Beeching. *Fr.* The Masque of Balliol. CenHV
Upright Life, The. Thomas Campion. *See* Man of Life Upright, The.
Uprising See the Fitful Lark. *Unknown.* NA
Uproar, An,/ a spruce-green sky. The Butterfly. Margaret Avison. BoCaPo; ExPo
Uprose the king of men with speed. *See* Up rose the king of men with speed.
Upside-down World, The. Hamish Hendry. BoTP
Upstairs Downstairs. Hervey Allen. HBMV; PoNe
Upstairs on the third floor. Bottled; New York. Helene Johnson. CDC; GoSl
Upstart Courtier. Samuel Rowlands. SiCE
Upstood upstaffed passing sinuously away. Poem. Russell Atkins. PoNe
Upstream. Carl Sandburg. HBV; MAP; MoAB; MoAmPo; NeMA; PoFr; SAS; TBM
Upward and back to their fountains the sacred rivers are stealing. Chorus. Euripides. *Fr.* Medea. PoFr
Upward Pass, The. Henry Bellamann. LS
Ur Burial. Richard Eberhart. NePoAm
Ur ol' Hyar lib in ur house on de hill. Ol' Doc' Hyar. James Edwin Campbell. BANP
Urals for the First Time, The. Boris Pasternak, *tr. fr. Russian by* Babette Deutsch. TrRV
Urania. Matthew Arnold. HBV
Urania. Aubrey Thomas De Vere. IrPN
Urania. Ruth Pitter. MoVE
Urania speaks with darken'd brow. In Memoriam A. H. H., XXXVII. Tennyson. EmBrPo; EPN; GEPC; ViPo; VLEP
Uranium cumulus mushrooms bursting sores. Exodus. Roy Basler. SiTL
Uranus. Arthur Hugh Clough. ViPP
Urban History. Chester Kallman. CrMA
Urbs Beata. Thomas S. Jones, Jr. UnW
"Urceus Exit." Austin Dobson. *Fr.* Rose-Leaves. ATP (1935 ed.); BPN; GTSL; HBV; MBP; MoBrPo (1942 ed.); PreP; TCEP; TOP; VLEP
(I Intended an Ode.) OBEV; PIAE
(Triolet.) BMEP; LEAP
Urchins' Dance, The. *Unknown. See* By the Moon We Sport and Play.
"Urge not, divine Achilles, me to sit." Homer. *Fr.* The Iliad, XXIV. GrPo
Urge of the seed, The: the germ. Cleanthus Trilling. Edgar Lee Masters. *Fr.* The New Spoon River. LEAP; OQP; QP-1
Uriel. Emerson. AnFE; AnNE; APA; APW; CoAnAm; IAP; LiTA; MOAP; NePA; OBEV (1st ed.); OxBA; PFY
Uriel. Percy MacKaye. LBMV
Uriel. "Owen Meredith." UnW
Uriel, *sels.* William Force Stead.
"I thought the night without a sound was falling." TrPWD
(How Infinite Are Thy Ways.) OBMV
"Praise, then, to Uriel, who in unlikely places," *fr.* Pt. IV, iii. OxBoCh
"Reach forth Thy hand!" *fr.* Pt. V, i. OxBoCh
Uriel, you that in the ageless sun. Uriel. Percy MacKaye. LBMV
Urn, The. Malcolm Cowley. *Fr.* Blue Juniata. AnAmPo; LA; MoVE; NP
Urns and Odours Bring Away! Fletcher *and* Shakespeare. *See* Funeral Song.
Ursa Major. James Kirkup. ImOP
Ursula. Robert Underwood Johnson. HBV
Us boys ain't scared o' pa so much. We Ain't Scared o' Pa. James W. Foley. FAOV
Us Potes. Franklin P. Adams. WhC
Us the lot chose; so soon must we seek a new home. Departure of the First-born. Stefan George. AnGP
Us Two. A. A. Milne. TiPo
Us two was pals, the Kid and me. The Kid's Last Fight. *Unknown.* TreF
Us two wuz boys when we fell out. Our Two Opinions. Eugene Field. AA; CP; IHA; MAP; MoAmPo (1942 ed.); PFY
Use all your hidden forces. Do not miss. Attainment. Ella Wheeler Wilcox. OQP; QP-2; WGRP

Use me, God, in Thy great harvest field. Send Me. Christina Rossetti. MaRV
Use of Flowers, The. Mary Howitt. LPS-2
Use up thy store, for thou must die. A Rule of Life. Lucian. OxBG
Use Well the Moment. Goethe, *tr. fr. German by* John Stuart Blackie. MaRV; OQP; QP-2
(Day's Work, The, *longer sel.*) GrCo-1
Useful, The. W. H. Auden. *Fr.* The Quest. ChMo
Useful Plough, The. *Unknown.* CG; DD; HBV; LPS-2; OTPC (1923 ed.); RIS; TVSH
Useless Flight, The. Juan Meléndez Valdés, *tr. fr. Spanish by* Eleanor L. Turnbull. TeCS
Uselessness. Ella Wheeler Wilcox. TrPWD
Uses of Adversity, The. Shakespeare. *Fr.* As You Like It, II, i. LiTB; TreFS; TrGrPo
(Banished Duke [Living in the Forest] Speaks to His Retainers, The.) CBE; LiTG
(Forest of Arden, The, *sl. abr.*) EV-1
(Good in Everything, *much abr.*) PoToHe
("Now, my co-mates and brothers in exile.") PIR
(Sermons in Stones.) GrCo-1
(Sweet Are the Uses of Adversity, 6 *ll.*) MaRV
Uses of Ocean, The. Sir Owen Seaman. ALV; FiBHP
Usk. T. S. Eliot. Landscapes, III. CoBE; FaBoCh; KN; LoGBV
Usless pipe stop I have been, A. *Unknown.* SeCSL
Usual Way, The. Frederic E. Weatherly. BOHV
Usually hateful crows, The! They Also. Basho. OnPM
Usurper, The. Theognis, *tr. fr. Greek by* J. M. Edmonds. GrR
Utah Carroll. *Unknown.* CoSo, *with music;* CSF
Utah, We Love Thee. Evan Stephans. PoRL
Ute Lover, The. Hamlin Garland. AA; OBAV; PFY
Ute Pass. Ernest Whitney. PoOW
Utile canons, the set codes of priests, The. Love Redeemed, XXXIII. William Baylebridge. BoAV
Utmost, The. "Owen Meredith." VA
Utmost island of Europe, loveliest land. Ireland Weeping. William Livingston. GoTS
Utopia, Limited, *sel.* W. S. Gilbert.
Sir Bailey Barre. PCD
Utopian Journey, A. Randall Jarrell. FiMAP
Utter is the quietude of this golden day. Elis. Georg Trakl. AnGP
Utter Silence. Jorge Guillén, *tr. fr. Spanish by* Eleanor L. Turnbull. CoSP; OnPM
Utterance. Donald Davidson. TBM
Utterance. Emily Dickinson. *See* I found the phrase to every thought.
Utterance. James Larkin Pearson. NoCaPo

V

V. A. D. *Unknown.* AOAH
V. D. F. *Unknown.* HBV
V Is for Victory, as You Can Plainly See. Marsden Hartley. LiTM
V-J. Day. John Ciardi. MiAP
V-Letter. Karl Shapiro. CoBMV; FiMAP; MiAP; TrJP; WaP
V-Letter to Karl Shapiro in Australia. Selden Rodman. WaP
Vacant Cage, The. Charles Tennyson Turner. VA
Vacant Chair, The. Henry Stevenson Washburn. BlG; OIF; TreFS
Vacant Farmhouse, The. Walter de la Mare. HaMV
Vacant Lot, The. Nathalia Crane. LPS-1
Vacant Lots. Molly Anderson Haley. BAP
Vacation. Nixon Waterman. *See* Far from the Madding Crowd.
Vacation Exercise. M. K. Joseph. AnNZ
"Vacation is coming, where shall we go?" Compromise. Laurence McKinney. InMe
Vacation Song. Edna St. Vincent Millay. YeAr
Vacation Time. Rowena Bennett. SiSoSe
Vacation Time. Frank Hutt. BoTP
Vacation Time. Margaret E. Sangster. DD
Vacation Trip. Donald C. Babcock. NePoAm
Vacationing at Baiae, where the Herculean Way extends. The Watering Place. Propertius. LiTW
Vachel Lindsay. Sydney King Russell. MuM
Vacillation. W. B. Yeats. EnLP; MoVE
"Must we part, Von Hügel," *sel.* OBMV
Vacuum, The. Howard Nemerov. NePoEA
Vae Soli. Sappho. *See* Night.
Vagabond, The. Edgar A. Guest. NLK
Vagabond. John Masefield. OtMeF
Vagabond, The. Robert Louis Stevenson. AlDL; AnFE; BBV; BMEP; CBE; EV-5; GTSL; HBV; HBVY; HiLiEn, *abr.;* MCCG; OnPP; OTPC (1946 ed.); PCN; PoeMoYo; PoeT; PoMa; PoRL; POTT; PYM; ShBV-1; TCEP; ViBoPo; VLEP
Vagabond at Home, The. Ruth Wright Kauffman. NLK
Vagabond House. Don Blanding. BLPA
Vagabond Song, A. Bliss Carman. BTP; FaPON; GBV; GN; GoTP; HBV; HBVY; HOAH; LBMV; MAP; MCCG; MM; MoAmPo (1942 ed.); MPB; NeMA; NLK; OTPC (1946 ed.); PoMa; POT; PoTo; StaSt; StVeCh (1940 ed.); TCAP; YT
(Autumn Song, An.) VOD
(Vagabond's Song, A.) PoeMoYo
Vagabondia, *abr.* Richard Hovey. PC
Vagabonds. Sara Hamilton Birchall. NLK
Vagabonds, The. E. Pauline Johnson. VA
Vagabonds, The. John Albert Macy. CAG
Vagabonds, The. John Townsend Trowbridge. AA; AlBD; BAP; BeLS; BLPA; LEAP; LPS-2; OBAV; OnPP; PCD; PTA-2; TreFS
Vagabond's Song, A. Bliss Carman. *See* Vagabond Song, A.
Vagrant, A. Erik Axel Karlfeldt, *tr. fr. Swedish by* Charles W. Stork. AnSL
Vagrant, The. John Crowe Ransom. NV
Vagrant, The. Pauline Slender. HBMV; NLK; PoTo
Vagrant of Time, The. Sir Charles G. D. Roberts. OCL
Vague immutable contour of the earth, The. Grass. Edwin Muir. MBP
Vague in plot but clear in style. Review of a Cook Book. Louise Dyer Harris. WhC
Vague sea thuds against the marble cliffs, The. Time. Robert Graves. AtBAP; CoEV; FaBoMo; LiTM (rev. ed.); MoP
Vague Story, A. Walter Parke. BOHV
Vague winds of sorrow blow. Wandering. Hortense Flexner. HBMV
Vaguely I hear the purple roar of the torn-down 3rd Avenue El. You Are Gorgeous and I'm Coming. Frank O'Hara. NeAP
Vailima. Robert Louis Stevenson. *See* To S. R. Crockett.
Vain Britons, boast no longer with proud indignity. War and Washington. Jonathan Mitchell Sewall. *Fr.* Cato. GA; PAH
Vain Cry; Lydian Campaign, 1941. Glauco Cambon, *tr. fr. Italian by* Glauco Cambon. OnPM
Vain, delusive world, adieu. Only Jesus Will I Know. Charles Wesley. BePJ
Vain Desire, A. Theodore Wratislaw. VA
Vain Farewell, The. Paulus Silentiarius, *tr. fr. Greek by* A. J. Butler. OxBG
Vain, frail, short liv'd and miserable Man. Vanity of Vanities. Michael Wigglesworth. AnNE; APW; BAV
Vain Gratuities. E. A. Robinson. MaPo; NePA
Vain is the chiming of forgotten bells. Poets. Joyce Kilmer. AnAmPo; LA; NP; SBMV; WGRP
Vain is the dream! However hope may rave. The White Pacha. Andrew Lang. LH
Vain is the effort to forget. On the Rhine. Matthew Arnold. LO
Vain is the fleeting wealth. Of [*or* On] the Vanity of Man's Life. *Unknown.* EG; OBSC; SiCE; TuPP
Vain-Love, The, *sel.* Abraham Cowley.
"I sought not from thee a return." LO
Vain Love, why dost thou boast of wings. Jealousy. Countess of Winchilsea. SeCL
Vain man, born to no happiness. Chorus. Sidney Godolphin. LoBV
Vain men, whose follies make a god of love. Thomas Campion. LO
Vain Quest of Beauty. Viktor Rydberg, *tr. fr. Swedish by* Charles W. Stork. AnSL
Vain Questioning. Walter de la Mare. MoVE
Vain Resolves. Ernest Dowson. VLEP
Vain, sinful Art! who first did fit. The Daughter of Herodias. Henry Vaughan. MeRV
Vain the ambition of kings. Vanitas Vanitatum. John Webster. *Fr.* The Devil's Law Case. PoFr
Vain thing, A/ is the thing that I have done. Liadain and Cuirithir. *Unknown.* SiB
Vain, very vain, my weary search to find. Happiness Dependent on Ourselves. Goldsmith. *Fr.* The Traveller. OBEC
Vain Virtues. Dante Gabriel Rossetti. The House of Life, LXXXV. EmBrPo; EnLi-2; EPP; HBV; PoVP; ViPo; ViPP
Vain Wish, A. Philip Bourke Marston. VA
Vain Wish. Otomo Yakamochi, *tr. fr. Japanese by* Ishii *and* Obata. OnPM
Vain wits and eyes. Holy Fire. Henry Vaughan. MeRV
Vain worldly yearnings in my breast. At Parting. Heine. AnGP
Vainglorious Oak and the Modest Bulrush, The. Guy Wetmore Carryl. TSW; TSWC
Vainly doth Pallas strive to appease great Zeus of Olympus. The Wooden Walls of Athens. Delphic Oracle. OxBG

Vainly for us the sunbeams shine. Casa's Dirge. David Macbeth Moir. VA
Vainly we crave for some divine Redeemer. In a Troubled World. Stanton A. Coblentz. ChIP
Vainly were the words of parting spoken. Hermotimus. William Edmondstoune Aytoun. OBVV
Vala; or, The Four Zoas, sels. Blake.
　Arts of Death, The. CoEV
　"Cities, The, send to one another . . ." fr. Night I. ViBoPo
　Enitharmon's Song. ChTr
　It Is Not So with Me. SeCePo
　Night. BoW
　"O Lord wilt thou not look . . ." Fr. Night II. ViBoPo
　Price of Experience, The. EnRP; RO
Valdemar and Tove. Unknown, tr. fr. Danish by E. M. Smith-Dampier. BoDaBa (A and B vers.); PaOS
Vale. "Æ." ChMo; CMP
Vale. Maurice Baring. JKCP (1955 ed.)
Vale. John Ciardi. MiAP
Vale! Roden Noel. OBVV
Vale. Patrick Mary Plunkett. JKCP (1955 ed.)
Vale. Unknown. CAG
Vale, Amor! "Fiona Macleod." PoVP
Vale—atque Salve. Mark Antony De Wolfe Howe. AOAH
Vale from Carthage (Spring, 1944). Peter Viereck. MiAP; MoAmPo (1950 ed.)
Vale of Avoca, The. Thomas Moore. See Meeting of the Waters, The.
Vale of Cashmere, The, much abr. Thomas Moore. Fr. Lalla Rookh. LPS-2
　(Light of the Haram, The.) EnRP
Vale of Indolence, The. James Thomson. Fr. The Castle of Indolence. CBOV; EBSV
　(Enchanted Ground.) BSV
　("In lowly dale, fast by a river's side.") EnRP; EPP; ViBoPo
　(Land of Indolence.) OBEC; SeCePo
Vale of Tempe had in vain been fair, The. Ideality. Hartley Coleridge. VA
Vale of the waterfalls! The Call of the Morning. George Darley. OnYI
Valediction, A. Elizabeth Barrett Browning. HBV
Valediction, A. William Cartwright. ElSeCe; OBS; SeCL; SeEP
　("Bid me not go where neither suns nor showers," abr.) EG
Valediction. Louis MacNeice. AnIL; MoVE
Valediction. John Hall Wheelock. NePoAm
Valediction Forbidding Mourning, A. John Donne. CoBE; CoEV; ElSeCe; EM-1; EnL; EnLi-1; EnLit; EnLP: EPS; EtPaEn; ExPo; FaBoEn; HoPM; LEAP; LiTB; MaPo; MeLP; MePo; NBE; OAEP; OBS; Po; PoEL-2; PoFS; ReaPo; ReEn; ReIE; RiBV; SeCeV; SeCV-1; SeEP; TCEP; TuPP; TwP; TyEnPo; UnPo
Valediction, A; Liverpool Docks. John Masefield. FaBoTw; OBMV
Valediction, A; of the Booke. John Donne. NBE
Valediction, A; of Weeping. John Donne. AtBAP; ATP; EG; EnLP; MeLP; MePo; OBS; ReIE; TuPP
Valediction to My Contemporaries. Horace Gregory. MAP; MoAmPo
　(To My Generation, 1919–1933, sl. abr.) ChMo
Valedictory. Adam Lindsay Gordon. VA
Valedictory. Wrenne Jarman. DiM
Valedictory. Tennyson. See In Memoriam—W. G. Ward and In the Garden at Swainston.
Valedictory Sonnet to the River Duddon. Wordsworth. See After-Thought.
Valedictory Stanza to Kemble, sel. Thomas Campbell. Taste. BCEP
Valentine, A. Matilda Barbara Betham-Edwards. OBVV
Valentine. Charles G. Blanden. DD
Valentine. Mary H. Blodgett. CAG
Valentine, A. Eugene Field. PoRL
Valentine, A. Jeannette Bliss Gillespy. Fr. Cameos. AA
Valentine, A. Eleanor Hammond. GFA; TiPo; YeAr
Valentine, A. Laura E. Richards. AA; DD; HH; MPB; YeAr
Valentine, A. Hal Summers. ChMP
Valentine. Hollis Summers. GoYe
Valentine. "C. W. T." YeAr
Valentine. Edith M. Thomas. PR
Valentine for a Lady, A. Lucilius, tr. fr. Greek by Dudley Fitts. LiTW
Valentine for My Mother. Harry Lee. MPB
Valentine to a Little Girl. Cardinal Newman. GoBC
Valentine to My Mother, A (1882). Christina Rossetti. See Valentines to My Mother (1876–1886).
Valentine to One's Wife. John Erskine. BAP; PR; TBM
Valentine Verses. Thomas Nelson Page. DD
Valentine's Day. Aileen Fisher. YeAr
Valentine's Day. Charles Kingsley. BoTP
Valentine's Message, The. Mildred J. Hill. GFA

Valentines to My Mother (1876–1886). Christina Rossetti. MOAH Sels.
　1879 ("Mother mine"). BoChLi
　1880 ("More shower than shine"). DD
　1882 ("My blessed mother").
　(Valentine to My Mother, A.) MotAn; OHIP
　1885 ("All the Robin Redbreasts"). BoChLi; DD
Valentinian. John Fletcher. See Tragedy of Valentinian, The.
Valerius on Women. Thomas Heywood. Fr. The Rape of Lucrece. HBV
　("She that denies me, I would have.") LO
Valhalla for the Living. Léonie Adams. MOAP
Valiant-for-Truth. Corinne Roosevelt Robinson. DD; GA; HH; PEDC
Valley Brook, The. John Howard Bryant. LPS-2
Valley familiar with my desperate din. Petrarch. Fr. Sonnets to Laura: To Laura in Death. PrPoCR
Valley Forge. Thomas Buchanan Read. Fr. The Wagoner of the Alleghanies. MC; PAH
Valley Harvest, The. H. L. Davis. NP
Valley lay smiling before me, The. The Song of O'Ruark, Prince of Breffni. Thomas Moore. OnYI
Valley of ancient life, how many visions died. The Other Journey. Katherine Garrison Chapin. MoVE
Valley of Decision, The. John Oxenham. PGD
Valley of mine, sweet valley! The Girl and the Cuckoo. Unknown. OnPM
Valley of Pale Blue Flowers, The. "Fiona Macleod." PoVP
Valley of pines unclosed its gates, The. Orphic Interior. Leonardo Sinisgalli. LiTW
Valley of Shanganagh, The. John Martley. TIP
Valley of Silence, The. "Fiona Macleod." PoVP
Valley of Sleep, The. Hendrik Marsman, tr. fr. Dutch by A. J. Barnouw. Fr. The Zodiac. LiTW
Valley of the Black Pig, The. W. B. Yeats. ChTr
Valley of the Heavens, The. Luis de León, tr. fr. Spanish by Thomas Walsh. CAW
Valley of the Shadow. John Galsworthy. HiLiEn; MaRV; OHIP; QS; TrPWD
Valley of the Shadow, The. E. A. Robinson. TCPD
Valley of the Shadow of Death, The. William Cowper. TriL
Valley of Unrest, The. Poe. AmPo; AmPP; APW; IAP; KN; LBAP; MOAP; PoEL-4; TriL; ViBoPo
Valley of Vain Verses, The. Henry van Dyke. HBV
Valley of White Poppies, The. "Fiona Macleod." MoSiPe; PoVP
Valley Song. Carl Sandburg. SBMV
Valley That God Forgot, The. Henry Herbert Knibbs. PCD; PFE
Valley Wind, The. Lu Yün, tr. fr. Chinese by Arthur Waley. OnPM; TrCh
Valley with a silver-grayish mist, The. A Vision. Hugo von Hofmannsthal. TrJP
Valley's Singing Day, The. Robert Frost. UnS
Valleys, splendid as her womb, The. Sarah. "Robin Hyde." AnNZ
Valleys that we knew in sunlit hours, The. Three Nocturns. Sir Osbert Sitwell. POTE
Valmondois. Clark Mills. NeTW
Valour. Shakespeare. Fr. Coriolanus, II, ii. BHV
Valour and Innocence. The Queen's Men. Kipling. AtBAP
Valor of Ben Milam, The. Clinton Scollard. HBV; MC; PAH
Valorous Acts Performed at Gaunt by the Brave Bonny Lass, Mary Ambree, The. Unknown. See Mary Ambree.
Valraven and the Danish King. Unknown, tr. fr. Danish by E. M. Smith-Dampier. BoDaBa
Valse des Fleurs. Denis Hudson. NeTW
Valse Jeune. Louise Imogen Guiney. AA
Valse Triste. Ruth Guthrie Harding. MuM
Value of Elemental Remedies. Charles Anson Ingraham. PoP
Values. Leslie Savage Clark. ChIP
Values. Dorothy Mitchell. CAG
Values in Use. Marianne Moore. NePoAm-2
Vamp Passes, The. James J. Montague. HBMV
Vampire, The. Conrad Aiken. HBMV
Vampire, The [as Suggested by the Painting by Philip Burne-Jones]. Kipling. BLPA; BMEP; EnLit; HBV; LEAP; NeHB
Vampire, The. Efrén Rebolledo, tr. fr. Spanish by Samuel Beckett. AnMP
Vampire, The. Unknown, tr. fr. Modern Greek by Rae Dalven. MoGP
Van Amburgh's Menagerie. Unknown. RLPA
Vance Song, The, with music. Abner Vance. OuSiCo
Vancouver Lights. Earle Birney. CaP; TwCV
Van Dieman's Land. Unknown. BaBo; CoMu
Vane on Hughley steeple, The. Hughley Steeple. A. E. Housman. A Shropshire Lad, LXI. PoVP; ViPo; VLEP
Vane, young in yeares, but in sage counsell old. To Sir Henry Vane the Younger. Milton. ES; OBS
Van Elsen. Frederick George Scott. HBV; VA

Vanessa Vanessa. Ewart Milne. NeIP
Vanguard of Liberty, ye men of Kent. To the Men of Kent. Wordsworth. BPN
Vanished. Emily Dickinson. *See* She died—this was the way she died.
Vanished Fay, The. Bert Leston Taylor. FAOV
Vanished house that for an hour I knew, A. Souvenir. E. A. Robinson. InP
Vanished Night, The. Niall MacMurray, *tr. fr. Irish by* Frank O'Connor. KiLC
Vanishers, The. Whittier. AA; IAP
Vanishing Boat, The. Sir Edmund Gosse. TCPD
Vanitas Vanitatum. Byron. *Fr.* Don Juan, VII. GEPC
Vanitas Vanitatum. John Webster. *See* All the Flowers of the Spring.
Vanitas Vanitatum. Israel Zangwill. TrJP
Vanitie. George Herbert. *See* Vanity.
Vanities. Paulus Silentiarius. *See* No Matter.
Vanity. Ecclesiastes, I: 12–II: 26, Bible, *O.T.* OuHeWo
Vanity. Robert Graves. CoEV
Vanity. George Herbert. EPS (1942 ed.); MeRV; ReEn
(Vanitie.) MePo; SeCV-1
Vanity. Harriet Prescott Spofford. LPS-3
Vanity. Anna Wickham. FaBoTw
Vanity Fair. Victor Starbuck. LS
Vanity of Existence, The. Philip Freneau. CoV
Vanity of Human Learning, The. Sir John Davies. *See* Man.
Vanity of Human Wishes, The. Juvenal, *tr. fr. Latin.* Satires, X. LaP, *tr. by* L. R. Lind; RoL, *tr. by* William Gifford
Vanity of Human Wishes, The; the Tenth Satire of Juvenal Imitated. Samuel Johnson. ATP; CoBE; EiPP; LaA; LoBV, *abr.;* Po; PoE; PoEL-3; PoFS; TriL; UnPo (1st ed.), *abr.*
Sels.
Ambition, *abr.* BHV
"Let observation with extensive view." ATP; BEL; CEP; EPP, *abr.;* EV-3; TOP, *abr.*
Life's Last Scene. OBEC; SeCePo
(Burden of Age, The.) BeR
"On what foundations stands the warrior's pride." ViBoPo
(Charles XII [of Sweden].) BCEP; CoEV; LPS-3; OBEC; PIR
Scholar's Life, The. FaBoEn; OBEC; SeCePo
"Unnumbered suppliants crowd Preferment's gate." PoFr
(Rise and Fall, The.) BeR
"What gave great Villiers to th' assasin's knife." NBE
"Where then shall Hope and Fear their objects find?" EnLi-1 (1949 ed.)
(Prayer.) CoEV; OBEC
Vanity of Kissing. Bonefonius, *tr. fr. Latin by* John Nott. OnPM
Vanity of Riches ("Non ebur neque aureum"). Horace, *tr. fr. Latin by* T. Rutherford Clark. Odes, II, 18. RoL; WoL
Vanity of Spirit. Henry Vaughan. EPS; ReEn
Vanity of the Beautiful, The. George Gascoigne. LPS-2
Vanity of the World, The. Francis Quarles. *Fr.* Emblems. BCEP; LEAP; LPS-3
(False World, Thou Ly'st.) ElSeCe; SeCePo; SeEP
(Wilt Thou Set Thine Eyes upon That Which Is Not?) OBS
(World's Fallacies.) EV-2
Vanity of Vanities. Ecclesiastes, Bible, *O.T.* *See* Words of the Preacher, The.
Vanity of Vanities. Euripides, *tr. fr. Greek.* OxBG
Vanity of Vanities. Palladas. *See* Naked I Came.
Vanity of Vanities. Christina Rossetti. POTT
Vanity of Vanities. *Unknown, at. to* Philip Rosseter. *See* All Is Vanity.
Vanity of Vanities. Michael Wigglesworth. AnNE; APW
("Vain, Frail, short liv'd and miserable man," *7 sts.*) BAV
"Vanity of Vanities; All Is Vanity." Sophocles, *tr. fr. Greek by* Gilbert Murray. *Fr.* Oedipus Rex. GrR
Vanity of vanities, saith Koheleth. Vanity of Vanities. Ecclesiastes, Bible, *O.T.* TrJP
Vanity of vanities, saith the Preacher, vanity of vanities; all is vanity. The Words of the Preacher. Ecclesiastes, Bible, *O.T.* TreFS
Vanity of vanities, the Preacher saith. One Certainty. Christina Rossetti. EmBrPo
"Vanity, Saith the Preacher." Josephine Preston Peabody. InP
Vanity, saith the preacher, vanity! The Bishop Orders His Tomb at Saint Praxed's Church. Robert Browning. ATP; AWP; BEL; BMEP; BoLiVe; BPN; CoEV; CP; EM-2; EmBrPo; EnL; EnLi-2; EnLit; EPN; ExPo; FiP; GEPC; GTSE; HBV; MaPo; MyFE; OAEP; OtMeF; Po; PoD; PoE; PoVP; SeCeV; ShBV-4; TwCrTr; TwP; VA; ViBoPo; ViPo; ViPP; VLEP
Vanquished. Francis Fisher Browne. AA; DD; HBV; MDAH
Vanquished. Katherine E. Conway. PraNu
Vanquished, The. Charles Eglington. BoSA
Vanquished and weary was my soul in me. Sonnet: A Trance of Love. Cino da Pistoia. AWP
Vantage Point, The. Robert Frost. CoBMV; MaPo; OxBA; PoLFOT
Van Winkle. Hart Crane. *Fr.* The Bridge: Powhatan's Daughter. AmP; AmPP; CrMA; LiTA; MAP; MoAB; MoAmPo; ReMP
Vanya's house has a roof of iron. Maiden Meditation. Mikhail Isakovsky. RuPo
Vapour and Blue. Wilfred Campbell. CaP; OCL
Vaquero. Edward Dorn. NeAP
Vaquero. Joaquin Miller. AA; BAP; PFY
Variation: Ode to Fear. Robert Penn Warren. FiMAP
Variation on a Line by Emerson. W. S. Merwin. NePA
Variation on a Sentence. Louise Bogan. ImOP
Variation on a Theme. G. T. Hellman. CAG
Variation on a Theme by Francis Kilvert. Rolfe Humphries. UnS
Variation on a Theme by John Lyly. Sacheverell Sitwell. ViBoPo
Variation on Ronsard. T. Sturge Moore. OBMV
Variations, *sels.* Conrad Aiken.
"Beautiful body made of ivory," XIV. PG (1945 ed.)
"Green light from the moon." II. NV
Queen Cleopatra, X. HBMV
"Wind, wind, wind in the old trees," XII. ChMo; CMP; PG (1933 ed.)
"You are as beautiful as white clouds," VI. NV
Variations (I–IV). Randall Jarrell. MiAP
Variations, *sel.* Apostolos Melachrinos, *tr. fr. Modern Greek by* Rae Dalven.
Magic Refrains. MoGP
Variations Done for Gerald van de Wiele. Charles Olson. NeAP
Variations of Greek Themes. E. A. Robinson. MOAP
Variations on a Still Morning. Thomas Cole. NePoAm
Variations on a Theme. Alfred G. Bailey. BoCaPo
Variations on a Theme. John Hay. NePoAm
Variations on a Theme. Robert Hillyer. MAP; MoAmPo
Variations on a Theme, *parody.* Joseph G. E. Hopkins. JKCP (1955 ed.)
Variations on a Theme. Oscar Williams. LiTA; NePA
Variations on a Theme by George Herbert. Marya Zaturenska. TrPWD
Variations on a Theme by Sidney Keyes. Eithne Wilkins. NeBP
Variations on a Time Theme, *sel.* Edwin Muir.
"At the dead centre of the boundless plain." MoVE
(Riders, The.) MoP
Variations on an Air. G. K. Chesterton. InP
Variations on an Old Nursery Rhyme. Edith Sitwell. *See* King of China's Daughter, The.
Variations: The Air Is Sweetest That a Thistle Guards. James Merrill. NePoEA
Varied colours are a fitful heap, The. The Year's Sheddings. George Meredith. POTT
Varied Effects of Love. Lope de Vega, *tr. fr. Spanish by* Marguerite Gamble. AnSpL-1
Various Ends. Ruthven Todd. NeBP; SeCePo
Various the Roads of Life. Walter Savage Landor. BPN; EmBrPo; EnRP; OQP; QP-2; TOP
Various voices are his poem now, The. Glaucus. Sidney Keyes. FaBoMo
Varitalk. Weare Holbrook. SiTL
Varium et Mutabile. Sir Thomas Wyatt. *See* Is It Possible?
Varuna, The. George Henry Boker. PAH
Varus took me to call upon his sweetheart. Catullus, *tr. fr. Latin by* Myron H. Broomell. LaP
Varus, whom I chanced to meet. A Fib Detected. Catullus. AWP
Vasari tells that Luca Signorelli. An Episode. John Addington Symonds. PoVP; VA
Vase, The. Victor Hugo. *See* More Strong than Time.
Vase, The. Henri de Régnier, *pr. tr. fr. French by* Amy Lowell. LiA
V-a-s-e, The. James Jeffrey Roche. BOHV; HBV; LHV; PreP
Vase, The. Terence Tiller. ChMP
Vase of Life, The. Dante Gabriel Rossetti. The House of Life, XCV. PoVP; ViPo
Vase of Myrrh, The. Thomas S. Jones, Jr. MuM
Vase of Tears, The. Stephen Spender. AtBAP; LO; POTE
Vase which holds all fat'ning liquor, The. *Unknown. Fr.* Riddles. CoBE
Vases. Nan Terrell Reed. BLPA
Vashti, *sel.* Lascelles Abercrombie. *Fr.* Emblems of Love, I.
Woman's Beauty. MBP; MoBrPo; PG
Vast and grey, the sky. The Desolate Field. William Carlos Williams. MOAP
Vast and immaculate; no pilgrim bands. The Sea Cathedral. E. J. Pratt. CaP; OCL
Vast and solemn company of clouds, The. After Sunset. William Allingham. IrPN

Vast bodies of philosophy. To Mr. Hobbes. Abraham Cowley. LoBV; ReEn; SeCV-1
Vast canopies across its crater bloat. Vespasian's Circus. John Myers O'Hara. BAP
Vast Chaos, of eld, was God's dominion. He Made the Night. Lloyd Mifflin. HBV
Vast corridor through Nature's roofless halls. Ute Pass. Ernest Whitney. PoOW
Vast occasion of our time, The. War. Mary Fullerton. NeLNL
Vast Superstition! Glorious style of weakness! Chorus Quintus: Tartarorum. Fulke Greville. *Fr.* Mustapha. OBS
Vast world, The. Alone. Li Lung Yü. PoHN
Vastness. Jorge Guillén, *tr. fr. Spanish by* Eleanor L. Turnbull. CoSP
Vastness. Tennyson. BMEP; BPN; EM-2; EmBrPo; GEPC; PoVP; TCEP; VA; VLEP
"Spring and summer," *sel.* OQP; QP-2
"Vasty Halls of Death, The." Damascius, *tr. fr. Greek by* F. L. Lucas. GrPE
Vaticide. Myron O'Higgins. OnHM
Vaudeville Dancer. John Hall Wheelock. UnS
Vaudracour and Julia. Wordsworth. *See* Prelude, The: "Among that band of Officers was one."
Vault inside the Castle at Goito, A. Robert Browning. *Fr.* Sordello. MyFE
Vault on the opal carpet of the sun. To Potapovitch. Hart Crane. UnS
Vault, A, see; thick/ Black shade about the ceiling. And What Sordello Would See There. Robert Browning. *Fr.* Sordello. MyFE
Vaulting Ambition. Shakespeare. *See* Duncan's Murder.
Vaunting Oak. John Crowe Ransom. OxBA
Vaunts of Tamburlaine, The. Christopher Marlowe. *Fr.* Tamburlaine the Great, Pt. I *and* Pt. II. BCEP
Vedic Hymns, *sels.* *Unknown, tr. fr. Vedic.*
Brahma, the World Idea. Rig-Veda. WGRP
Charm to Quell a Rival, *tr. by* R. T. H. Griffith. Rig-Veda. LiTW
Creation Hymn, The, *tr. by* R. T. H. Griffith. Rig-Veda, Bk. X, Hymn 129. OuHeWo
(Hymn of Creation, *tr. by* Arthur A. Macdonnell.) LiTW
Funeral Hymn, *tr. by* Arthur A. Macdonnell. Rig-Veda. LiTW
Hymn to Night, *tr. by* R. T. H. Griffith. Rig-Veda. LiTW
Hymn to Varuna, God of Fire and Light, *tr. by* R. T. H. Griffith. Rig-Veda. LiTW
Indra, the Supreme God, *tr. by* Romesh Dutt. Rig-Veda. AWP
Pushan, God of Pasture, *tr. by* Romesh Dutt. Rig-Veda. AWP; JAWP; WBP
Reverence to Prana, *tr. by* Maurice Blomfield. Atharva-Veda, Hymn 10. GrCo-1
To Liberality, *tr. by* R. T. H. Griffith. Rig-Veda, Bk. X, Hymn 117. PoFr
To the Unknown God, *tr. by* Max Müller. Rig-Veda, Bk. X, Hymn 121. GrCo-1; OuHeWo
Veery, The. Archibald Rutledge. MuM
Veery, The. Henry van Dyke. AA; BLA; LBAP; OBAV
Veery-Thrush, The. Joseph Russell Taylor. AA
Vegetable Fantasies. Helen Hoyt. RIS
Vegetable Loves. Erasmus Darwin. *Fr.* The Botanic Garden: The Loves of the Plants, I. OBEC; SeCePo
Vegetables. Eleanor Farjeon. FaPON; TiPo (1959 ed.)
(Country Vegetables.) PCH
Vegetables. Rachel Field. GFA
Vehicles. Alba Zizzamia. CAG
Veil, The. Anne Abbott. UnW
Veil, The. Walter de la Mare. ChMo; CMP; MM
Veil, The. Ferid ed-Din Attar, *tr. fr. Persian by* A. J. Arberry. PeP
Veil, I think, is thinner than we know, The. The Veil. Anne Abbott. UnW
Veil not thy mirror, sweet Amine. To Amine. James Clarence Mangan. OBEV (new ed.); OBVV
Veil of cloud, A/ O'er men and horses all around is spread. Ajax Prays for Light. Homer. *Fr.* The Iliad, XVII. LiA
Veil thine eyes, O belovéd, my spouse. The Bridegroom of Cana. Marjorie Pickthall. BoCaPo; CaP; CPG; OCL
Veil white as whale's bone, A. Grey Eyes. *Unknown.* TMEV
Veiled are the heavens, veiled the throne. Dawn on Mid-Ocean. John Hall Wheelock. EtS
Veiled in that light amazing. The Dispraise of Absalom. *Tr. fr. Irish by* Robin Flower. OxBI
Velasquez took a pliant knife. Castilian. Elinor Wylie. AnAmPo; HBMV; LA; NAMP; TBM; TCAP; VOD (1935 ed.)
Veld Eclogue, A; the Pioneers, *sel.* Roy Campbell.
"But 'nameless somethings' and 'unbounded spaces.'" BoSA
Velvet beautiful and dark, A. Peace by Night. Sister Mary Madeleva. GoBC
Velvet Shoes. Elinor Wylie. AV; CH; ChMo; FaPON; MAP; MoAB; MoAmPo; MPB; NeMA; NP; NV; OTPC (1946 ed.); PCH; PFY; PG; PIAE; PoeMoYo; PoTo; ReaPo; SiSoSe; SP; StVeCh; TCPD; TiPo (1952 ed.); TreFS; TrGrPo; TSW; TSWC; WHA
Velvet Sonneteers, The. Tom MacInnes. CaP
Venadito Song. *Unknown.* *See* Lo Que Digo.
Venantius Fortunatus. *Tr. fr. Latin by* Helen Waddell. TriL
Vendémiaire. Guillaume Apollinaire, *tr. fr. French by* Dudley Fitts. AnFP
Vendetta. Theognis, *tr. fr. Greek by* F. L. Lucas. GrPE
Vendor's Song. Adelaide Crapsey. AnFE; APA; CoAnAm; HBV; MAP; MoAmPo (1942 ed.); OBAV
Venemous toung, tipt with vile adders sting. *See* Venomous tongue, tipped . . .
Venerable Bede, with age grown blind, The. The Amen of the Rocks. Christian Gellert. PEOR
Venerable Bee, The. A. M. Klein. TrJP
Venerable Mother Toothache. A Charm against the Toothache. John Heath-Stubbs. NePoEA
Veneration of Images. Alice Meynell. GTBS
Veneta Marina. Arthur Symons. VLEP
Venetian Epigrams, *sel.* Goethe, *tr. fr. German by* F. Melian Stawell *and* Nora Purtscher-Wydenbruck.
"All the apostles of freedom." PoFr
Venetian Night, A. Hugo von Hofmannsthal, *tr. fr. German by* Ludwig Lewisohn. AWP; JAWP; WBP
Venetian Pastoral, A. Dante Gabriel Rossetti. *See* For "A Venetian Pastoral" by Giorgione.
Venetian Serenade, The. Richard Monckton Milnes. OBRV
Venetian Sonnets, *sels.* August, Graf von Platen, *tr. fr. German by* Edwin Morgan. AnGP
"At last I left the open sea behind," I.
"Here, I admit, there are no green fields to see," VI.
"I love you, as the sum of all those forms," VIII.
"I seem to hear a long, undying 'alas,'" V.
"This labyrinth of bridges and cramped streets," II.
"Venice lies in a dream landscape today," IV.
"What is it life lets us win in the end?" IX
"What joy it is when the hot day grows cool," III.
"When I am deeply burdened, desolate," VII.
Venez ici, mon cher ami, an' sit down by me—so. Le Vieux Temps. William Henry Drummond. BoCaPo
Vengeance. Euripides, *tr. fr. Greek by* F. L. Lucas. *Fr.* Medea. OxBG
Vengeance is God's: he will repay. Hagesichora. Alcman. GrL; OxBG
Vengeance of Finn, The, *sel.* Austin Clarke.
Awakening of Dermuid, The. AnIV
Vengeance of the Duchess, The. John Davidson. VLEP
Vengeance of the Nymphs, The. Antipater of Sidon, *tr. fr. Greek by* F. L. Lucas. GrPE
Vengeance was once her nation's lore and law. Watkwenies. Duncan Campbell Scott. PeCV
Vengeaunce must fall on thee, thou filthie whore. Against the Court of Rome. Petrarch. Sonnets to Laura: To Laura in Life, CVII. LiTW; LyMA
Vengeful across the cold November moors. The Pity of the Leaves. E. A. Robinson. AA; MoAmPo (1950 ed.)
Veni, Coronaberis. *Unknown.* AtBAP; BoW; TMEV
Veni Creator ("Lord of my heart's elation"). Bliss Carman. *See* Lord of My Heart's Elation.
Veni Creator ("Lord of the grass and hill"). Bliss Carman. *See* Overlord.
Veni Creator Spiritus. *Unknown, at. to* St. Gregory the Great *and to* Charlemagne, *paraphrased fr. Latin by* Dryden. AWP; CAW; CEP; CoBE; EV-3; GoBC; HBV; LPS-2; LyMA; MaRV; OuHeWo; SeCV-2; WBP; WGRP; WHL, *abr., tr. unknown*
Veni, Domine Jesu! Henry Augustus Rawes. WHL
Veni Sancte Spiritus. *Unknown, at. to* Robert II, King of France, *tr. fr. Latin by* Catherine Winkworth. HBV; LPS-2; WHL, *tr. unknown*
Venice. Byron. *Fr.* Childe Harold's Pilgrimage, IV. BEL; EV-4; HBV; TCEP, *abr.*
("I stood in Venice on the Bridge of Sighs.") BPN, *abr.;* OAEP, *abr.;* OBRV, *abr.;* ViBoPo, 3 *sts.*
(Refuge in Venice.) ERP
(Venice and Rome, *abr.*) MCCG
(Venice and Sunset, *abr.*) EPN
Venice. Longfellow. AmPP
Venice. Howard Moss. MoAB
Venice. Samuel Rogers. *Fr.* Italy. LPS-2
Venice. John Addington Symonds. *Fr.* Stella Maris. HBV; PIAE; VA
("Venice, thou Siren of sea-cities, wrought.") PoVP
Venice. Wordsworth. *See* On the Extinction of the Venetian Republic.
Venice and Rome. Byron. *See* Venice.
Venice and Sunset. Byron. *See* Venice.
Venice lies in a dream landscape today. Venetian Sonnets, IV. August, Graf von Platen. AnGP

Venice Preserved, *sels.* Thomas Otway.
Bankrupt, The. EV-3
Jaffier Parting with Belvidera. LPS-1
O Woman! Lovely Woman! EV-3
Venice Recalled. Bruce Boyd. NeAP
Venice, thou Siren of sea-cities, wrought. Venice. John Addington Symonds. *Fr.* Stella Maris. HBV; PIAE; PoVP; VA
Venite Adoremus. Margery Cannon. GoBC
Venite Descendamus. Ernest Dowson. POTT
Veniunt Spectentur ut Ipsi. Henry Parrot. SiCE
Venomous tongue, tipped [*or* Venemous toung, tipt] with vile adder's sting. Amoretti, LXXXV. Spenser. PeBoSo; ReEN
'Vention did in Boston meet, The. Convention Song. *Unknown.* PAH
Venture of Faith, The. Francis Greenwood Peabody. MaRV
Venus. Edgar Bowers. PtPa
Venus Abandoned. Shakespeare. *Fr.* Venus and Adonis. OBSC
("Nay then," quoth Adon, "you will fall again," *abr.*) LO
Venus, again thou mov'st a war. To Venus. Horace. Odes, IV, 1. AWP
Venus and Adonis. William Browne. *Fr.* Britannia's Pastorals, II. ElL
("Venus, by Adonis' side.") SeEP
Venus and Adonis. Shakespeare. BeLS
Sels.
"But if thou needs wilt hunt, be rul'd by me." SiCE
Courser and the Jennet, The. LoBV
(Courser, The.) OBSC
Death of Adonis, The. WHA
Horse, A. ExPo
Lo! Here the Gentle Lark. ChTr
"Looke how a bird lyes tangled in a net." BrBE
" 'Nay then,' quoth Adon, 'you will fall again.' " LO
(Venus Abandoned.) OBSC
Poor Wat. OBSC; UnPo (1st ed.)
"Thus hoping that Adonis is alive." EPP
Venus and the young new moon. Serenade. Leon W. Kellogg. CAG
Venus, and [*or* with] Young Adonis Sitting by Her. Bartholomew Griffin. Fidessa, More Chaste than Kind, III; *sl. diff. vers. in* The Passionate Pilgrim, XI. PeBoSo; ReIE; ViBoPo
Venus, by Adonis' side. Venus and Adonis. William Browne. *Fr.* Britannia's Pastorals. ElL; SeEP
Venus fair did ride. The Shepherd's Song of Venus and Adonis. Henry Constable. TuPP
Venus has lit her silver lamp. The Lamp in the West. Ella Higginson. AA; HBV
Venus, if men at sea you save. Shipwrecked Heart. *Unknown.* OnPM
Venus in Search of Cupid, Coming to Diana. Spenser. *Fr.* The Faerie Queene, III, 6. BCEP
Venus of Bolsover Castle, The. Sacheverell Sitwell. HBMV
Venus of the Louvre. Emma Lazarus. AA; AnAmPo; LA; LBAP; LEAP
Venus on a Sea Horse. Maurice Carpenter. FaBoTw
Venus Poised. Rafael López, *tr. fr. Spanish by* Samuel Beckett. AnMP
Venus' Runaway. Ben Jonson. *See* Beauties, Have Ye Seen This Toy.
Venus Shines Out. James Thomson. *Fr.* The Seasons: Summer. BeR
Venus' Speech. Louis MacNeice. ChMo
Venus, take my votive glass. The Lady Who Offers Her Looking-Glass to Venus [*or* A Farewell *or* Lais' Mirror]. Matthew Prior, *after the Greek of* Plato. AWP; CaAE; OBEV; OnPM; PIAE; ViBoPo; WoL
Venus the Goddess. Virgil, *pr. tr. fr. Latin by* H. R. Fairclough. *Fr.* The Aeneid, I. LiA
Venus Transiens. Amy Lowell. MM; NP; OBAV; SBMV
Venus Verticordia. Dante Gabriel Rossetti. EmBrPo
Venus Victrix. Dante Gabriel Rossetti. The House of Life, XXXIII. BPN; PoVP; ViPo
Venus, when her son was lost. Cupid. Emerson. *Fr.* The Initial Love. APW
Venus, with Young Adonis Sitting by Her. Bartholomew Griffin. *See* Venus, and Young Adonis . . .
Ver and Hiems. Shakespeare. *See* When Daisies Pied and Violets Blue.
Ver Redit Optatum. *Unknown, tr. fr. Latin by* George F. Whicher. *Fr.* Carmina Burana. LaP
Vera Cruz/ The neighbourhood of the sea is abolished. Gulf of Mexico. Alfonso Reyes. AnCL
Veracious people, The. Dante, *tr. fr. Italian by* Longfellow. *Fr.* Divina Commedia: Purgatorio. CAW
Verazzano. Hezekiah Butterworth. PAH
Verbal Critics. Pope. *Fr.* Epistle to Dr. Arbuthnot. CoEV; OBEC
Verbs. *Unknown.* DDA
Verbum Patris Hodie Processit ex Virgine. *Unknown.* AnEC
Verbum Supernum. *At. to* St. Ambrose, *tr. fr. Latin by* H. T. Henry. CAW
Verdant branch was swinging here, A. So Long Ago. Morris Rosenfeld. TrJP
Verdict, The. Norman Cameron. SeCePo
Vergidemiarum. Joseph Hall. *See* Virgidemiarum.
Vergissmeinnicht. Keith Douglas. ChMP
(Vergissmeinicht.) NePoEA; PoN
Verification. Christopher Morley. PC
Verily God is guard! Guardian of All. *Unknown.* OnPM
Verily the new day. Salute, Czechoslovakia! William Rose Benét. NeTW
Verily there is a vengeance from on high. Alcman, *pr. tr. fr. Greek by* J. M. Edmonds. GrPo
Verily, verily, I say unto you, He that entereth not by the door. The Good Shepherd. St. John, Bible, *N. T.* WoL
Verily, verily that day shall come. The Final Conflagration. *Unknown.* OxBG
Verily Vertue dothe all thinges excelle. Vertue. Plautus. *Fr.* Amphitryon. LiA
Veritable night, The. Rigmarole. William Carlos Williams. AnAmPo; LA
Verlaine. E. A. Robinson. PtP
Vermin only tease and pinch, The. On Fleas. Swift. TreFS
Vermont. Sarah N. Cleghorn. HBMV; PoeMoYo; VOD
Vermont; Indian Summer. Philip Booth. NePoEA
Vern. Gwendolyn Brooks. TiPo (1959 ed.)
Vernal Equinox. Amy Lowell. MAPA
Vernal hours are sweet as clover. The Sweetness of Spring. *Unknown.* LyMA
Vernal Paradox. Kim Kurt. NePoAm-2
Vernal Sentiment. Theodore Roethke. MiAP
Vernal Showers. David O'Neil. AnAmPo; LA
Vernon Castle. Harriet Monroe. HBMV
Vers la Vie. Arthur Upson. HBV
Vers Nonsensiques. George Du Maurier. HBV; NA
Versailles. Godfrey Fox Bradby. TVSH
Versailles. Stopford Brooke. VA
Versailles. Adrienne Cecile Rich. NePoEA
Versailles!—Up the chestnut alley. The Pompadour. George Walter Thornbury. BeLS
Verse: "Past ruined Ilion Helen lives." Walter Savage Landor. *See* Past Ruin'd Ilion . . .
Verse: "What should we know." Oliver St. John Gogarty. AnIL; FaBoCh; LO; LoGBV; OBMV; PoRA
Verse, a breeze mid blossoms straying. Youth and Age. Samuel Taylor Coleridge. BEL; BPN; EM-2; EmBrPo; EnLi-2 (1949 ed.); EnRP; ERP; EV-4; FiP; GTBS; GTBS-D; GTBS-W; GTSE; GTSL; HBV; LiA; OBEV; OBRV; ReTS; TCEP; TVSH
Verse? But verse signed his long indenture. Song's Indenture. Humbert Wolfe. MM
Verse for a Certain Dog. Dorothy Parker. AlBD
Verse in Praise of Lord Henry Howard, Earl of Surrey. George Turberville. ReIE; SiCE; TuPP
Verse is a chalice; place within it only. Art. José Asuncion Silva. CAW
Verse makes heroick vertue live. To Mr. Henry Lawes, Who Had Then Newly Set a Song of Mine in the Year 1635. Edmund Waller. EPS; SeCV-1
Verse-making was least of my virtues. Robert Browning. *Fr.* Ferishtah's Fancies. BPN
Verse Written in the Album of Mademoiselle ——. Pierre Dalcour, *tr. fr. French by* Langston Hughes. PoNe
Verses: "Clean is the autumn wind." Li Po, *tr. fr. Chinese.* WhP
Verses: "I am old, sick, and lonely." Su T'ung-po, *tr. fr. Chinese by* Yu Min-chuan. WhP
Verses: "What hopes, what terrors does thy gift create." Samuel Johnson. CaAE
Verses: "When pride and envy, and the scorn." Henry Kirke White. ERP
Verses: "Who strives to mount Parnassus hill." Richard Bentley. ViBoPo
(Reply to an Imitation of the Second Ode in the Third Book of Horace, A.) OBEC
Verses: "You who come from the old village." Wang Wei, *tr. fr. Chinese.* WhP
Verses Composed on the Eve of His Execution. James Graham, Marquess of Montrose. ChTr; EBSV
(On Himself, upon Hearing What Was His Sentence.) OBS; SeCePo
Verses Copied from the Window of an Obscure Lodging-House, in the Neighborhood of London. *Unknown.* LiTL; ViBoPo
Verses Expressing the Feelings of a Lover. Sister Juana Inés de la Cruz, *tr. fr. Spanish by* Samuel Beckett. AnMP
Verses for a First Birthday. George Barker. *Fr.* Second Cycle of Love Poems. MoAB; MoBrPo (1950 ed.)
Verses for Fruitwomen, *sels.* Swift.
Apples. AnIV; OnYI
Herrings. AnIV; OnYI
Onions. AnIV; OnYI

Verses for the 60th Birthday of T. S. Eliot. George Barker. ChMP
Verses Found in His Bible in the Gate-House at Westminster. Sir Walter Ralegh. *See* Conclusion, The.
Verses from the Shepherds' Hymn. Richard Crashaw. *See* Hymn Sung as by the Shepherds, A.
Verses Intended to Be Written below a Noble Earl's Picture. Burns. HoPM
Verses Made by Sir Walter Raleigh the Night Before He was Beheaded. Sir Walter Ralegh. *See* Passionate Man's Pilgrimage, The.
Verses Occasioned by the Death of Dr. Aikman. James Thomson. *Fr.* On the Death of Mr. William Aikman the Painter. CoEV; OBEC
(Finis: "As those we love decay.") BSV
(On the Death of a Particular Friend.) OBEV
Verses Occasioned by the Sudden Drying Up of St. Patrick's Well, *sel.* Swift.
English in Ireland, The. BeR
Verses of Mans Mortalitie, with an Other of the Hope of His Resurrection. *At. to* Simon Wastell. *See* Man's Mortality.
Verses on a Cat. Charles Daubeny. CIV; HBV
Verses on a Cat. Shelley. CIV; PoC
Verses on Blenheim. Swift. *See* On Blenheim.
Verses on Daniel Good. *Unknown.* CoMu
Verses on Games, *sel.* Kipling.
Boxing. OtMeF
Verses on Sir Joshua Reynolds's Painted Window at New-College, Oxford. Thomas Warton, the Younger. CEP; OBEC; PoEL-3
Verses on the Death of Dr. Swift. Swift. CEP, *abr.;* CoBE, *abr.;* EiPP; LoBV; NBE; PoEL-3; PoFS, *abr.;* TriL
Sels.
"Dean, if we believe report, The." FaBoEn
"From Dublin soon to London spread." WHA
"Had he but spar'd his tongue and pen." FaBoEn
"He never thought an honour done him." PoFr
"My female friends, whose tender hearts." SeCePo
"Perhaps I may allow the Dean." FaBoEn; OnYI
"Time is not remote, when I, The." BCEP; OBEC; OxBoLi; PoD; SiTL; ViBoPo; WoL
Verses on the Prospect of Planting Arts and Learning in America. George Berkeley. *See* On the Prospect of Planting . . .
Verses Placed over the Door at the Entrance into the Apollo Room at the Devil Tavern. Ben Jonson. HBV
(Over the Door at the Entrance into the Apollo.) ReEn
Verses Prefixed to the "Lay of St. Gengulphus." "Thomas Ingoldsby." *Fr.* The Ingoldsby Legends. EV-4
Verses Supposed to Be Written by Alexander Selkirk, During His Solitary Abode in the Island of Juan Fernandez. William Cowper. CaAE; CEP; CG; HBV; LPS-3; PoEL-3
(Alexander Selkirk.) FiP
(Alexander Selkirk during His Solitary Abode in the Island of Juan Fernandez.) CBE
(I Am Monarch of All I Survey.) OnPP
(Monarch, The.) TreFS
(Solitude of Alexander Selkirk, The.) BCEP; EV-3; GTBS; GTBS-D; GTBS-W; GTSE; GTSL; LiTB; LiTG; MCCG; PECK
Verses to Mr. Vaughan of Hengwrt. Evan Evans. PrWP
Verses to St. Cecilia. David Wright. POTE (1959 ed.)
Verses to the Memory of an Unfortunate Lady. Pope. *See* Elegy to the Memory of an Unfortunate Lady.
Verses Why Burnt. Walter Savage Landor. VA
Verses Written after an Ecstasy of High Exaltation. St. John of the Cross, *tr. fr. Spanish by* Roy Campbell. AnSpL-1
(Verses Written upon an Ecstasy of High Contemplation, *tr. by* E. Allison Peers.) TeCS
Verses Written at the Hermitage of Braid, near Edinburgh, *abr.* Robert Fergusson. EV-3
Verses Written during a Sleepless Night. Pushkin, *tr. fr. Russian by* Babette Deutsch. OnPM; TrRV
(Night Piece, *tr. by* V. de S. Pinto.) BoR
Verses Written during the War 1756–1763. Thomas Osbert Mordaunt. OBEC
Verses Written in a Lady's Sherlock "Upon Death." Earl of Chesterfield. CEP; OBEC
Verses Written in an Album. Thomas Moore. LPS-1
Verses Written in 1872. Robert Louis Stevenson. *See* Resurgence.
Verses Written in His Bible. Sir Walter Ralegh. *See* Conclusion, The.
Verses Written in the Tower the Night before He Was Beheaded. Chidiock Tichborne. *See* Elegy: "My prime of youth . . ."
Verses Written upon an Ecstasy of High Contemplation. St. John of the Cross. *See* Verses Written after an Ecstasy of High Exaltation.
Versos de Montalgo, *with music.* *Unknown, pr. tr. fr. Spanish by* Frank L. Dobie. AS
Vert-Vert, the Parrot. Louis Gresset, *tr. fr. French by* Francis Sylvester Mahony. CAW
Vertical light. You Light. Juan Ramón Jiménez. TeCS
Vertue. George Herbert. *See* Virtue.
Vertue. Plautus, *tr. fr. Latin by* Sir Thomas Elyot. *Fr.* Amphitryon. LiA
Very acme of my woe, The. Little Son. Georgia Douglas Johnson. CDC; FAOV
Very afraid. The Dalliance of Leopards. *Unknown.* OnPM
Very bitter weeping that ye made, The. Dante. *Fr.* La Vita Nuova. AWP
Very careless child indeed, A. Sally Centipede. Helen Cowles LeCron. GFA
Very Dark. Nathaniel Lee. *Fr.* The Tragedy of Nero. BeR
Very dark the autumn sky. A Belated Violet. Oliver Herford. AA
Very earth will disown you, The. God Wills It. "Gabriela Mistral." AnCL
Very Fair My Lot. Jacob David Kamzon, *tr. fr. Hebrew by* Sholom J. Kahn. TrJP
Very Far Away. William Alexander. TIP
Very first bluebird of Spring, The. The First Bluebird. James Whitcomb Riley. CV
Very gentlest of all human natures, The. Joseph Sturge. Whittier. BHV
Very Grail I Elevate, A. Christian Morgenstern, *tr. fr. German by* R. G. L. Barrett. AnGP
Very grandiloquent Goat, A. The Grandiloquent Goat. Carolyn Wells. LiL; MoShBr
Very Happy Family, A. Joseph G. Francis. CIV
Very heart went out of me, The. To a Lady Going Veiled. Gómez Manrique. AnSpL-1
Very high in the pine-tree. The Turtle-Dove's Nest. *Unknown, at. to* Ann Hawkshaw. HBVY; OTPC (1923 ed.); SAS
Very like a Whale. Ogden Nash. ShBV-3; TrGrPo
Very Little Sphinx, A, *sel.* Edna St. Vincent Millay.
Wonder Where This Horseshoe Went. SUS; TiPo (1952 ed.)
(Horseshoe, The.) StVeCh
(Wonder Where.) PoRh
Very Lovely. Rose Fyleman. GFA; TiPo
Very Minor Poet Speaks, A. Isabel Valle. BLPA
Very Model of a Modern College President, The, *parody.* Harold A. Larrabee. WhC
Very Mournful Ballad on the Siege and Conquest of Alhama, A. *Unknown.* *See* Alhama.
Very Names of Things Beloved, The. Robert Bridges. The Growth of Love, IV. ChMo; CMP; PoVP
Very natural girl I hate, A. Rufinus, *tr. fr. Greek by* Elsie Spoerl. GrPo
Very Nearly. Queenie Scott-Hopper. FaPON; GoBP; MeMeAg; MPB; OTPC (1946 ed.); RAR; TVC; TVSH
Very old are the woods. All That's Past. Walter de la Mare. AnFE; BrBE; CaAE; CoBE; CoEV; GTML; InP; MM; MoAB; NP; OAEP (2d ed.); OBMV; PG (1945 ed.); PoeMoYo; PoeT; POTE; POTT; SeCeV; ShBV-4; ThWaDe; TrGrPo; TwCV; ViBoPo; WHA
Very Old Song, A. "William Laird." HBV
Very pitiful lady, very young, A. Dante. *Fr.* La Vita Nuova. AWP; JAWP; WBP
Very Popular Prayer, A. *Unknown.* TMEV
Very Pretty Maid of This Town, and the Amorous 'Squire Not One Hundred Miles from the Place, The. *Unknown.* CoMu
Very pulse of ocean now was still, The. Evening in Gloucester Harbor. Epes Sargent. EtS
Very quickly will it be over with thee here. Imitation of Christ: The Thoughts of Death. Thomas à Kempis. OuHeWo
Very Seldom. C. P. Cavafy, *tr. fr. Modern Greek by* Rae Dalven. MoGP
Very small children in patched clothing, The. The Study in Aesthetics. Ezra Pound. ChMo; CMP; NP
Very solid rascals. Several have exploited your worlds. Bally. Arthur Rimbaud. AnFP
Very sounding of her name, The. Undedicated. Jean Starr Untermeyer. TBM
Very Torch, The. Erinna, *tr. fr. Greek by* John Herman Merivale. OnPM
Very Tree. Stanley J. Kunitz. NP
Very True, the Linnets Sing. Walter Savage Landor. TrGrPo
(Autumnal Song.) RO
Very ungraceful dog is Sandy, A. Sandy—a Small Dog. Alan Anderson. PCD
"Very, very queer things have been happening to me." Queer Things. James Reeves. PoMS
Very well, you liberals. Thomas Rhodes. Edgar Lee Masters. *Fr.* Spoon River Anthology. NP
Vespasian's Circus. John Myers O'Hara. BAP
Vesper. Alcman, *tr. fr. Greek by* F. L. Lucas. GrPE
Vesper Bells. Dwight Edwards Marvin. PraP
Vesper Sparrow, The. Edith M. Thomas. SN
Vesperal. Ernest Dowson. OBMV

Vesperal. S. Weir Mitchell. *See* Vespers.
Vespers. Claribel Weeks Avery. PraP
Vespers. Thomas Edward Brown. BLV; BMEP; BoTP; EnLit; MBP; PIAE; VLEP; YT
Vespers. Georgios Drossinis, *tr. fr. Modern Greek by* Rae Dalven. MoGP
Vespers, *sels.* Vyacheslav Ivanovich Ivanov, *tr. fr. Russian.*
"Clear the fountain waters glowing," *fr.* III, *tr. by* Babette Deutsch. TrRV
"Now the golden leafage is beggared," *fr.* V, *tr. by* Babette Deutsch. TrRV
("Now the golden leaves have been beggared," *tr. by* C. M. Bowra.) BoRS
Vespers. Luis Carlos López, *tr. fr. Spanish by* Donald Devenish Walsh. AnCL
Vespers. Ian Maxwell. MoAuPo
Vespers. Louis Mercier, *tr. fr. French by* Joseph T. Shipley. CAW
Vespers. S. Weir Mitchell. OQP; QP-1; WGRP
(Evening.) LBAP
(From Dark to Light.) MaRV
(Vesperal.) BPP
Vespers. Odell Shepard. TrPWD
Vessel that rests here at last, The. The Yacht. Walter Savage Landor. OBVV
Vessels. Francis Carlin. JKCP (1955 ed.)
Vesta. Sarah Trousdale Mallory. DDA
Vesta. Whittier. OBEV (1st ed.); TrPWD; WHA
Vestal, The. Nathalia Crane. AnAmPo; LA; MAP; MoAmPo (1942 ed.); TrJP
Vestal, The. Pope. *See* Nun's Lot, The.
Vestal Virgin, The, *sel.* John Plummer Derwent Llwyd.
"Night is soft with summer; yon faint arch, The." CaP
Vestal Virgins. Yiannis Griparis, *tr. fr. Modern Greek by* Rae Dalven. MoGP
Vestiges. Denis Devlin. OnHM
Vestigia. Bliss Carman. CaP; GrCo-2; MaRV; OCL; OQP; QP-1; QS; WGRP
Vesting of Aphrodite, The. *Unknown, tr. fr. Greek by* Arthur S. Way. *Fr.* Homeric Hymns. GrR
(Aphrodite on Ida, *tr. by* Jack Lindsay.) OxBG
Vestments in your church, they say, The. To a Prince of the Church. Kenneth W. Porter. MaRV
Veteran, The. Louis O. Coxe. MoVE
Veteran Cowboy's Ruminations, A. John M. Kuykendall. PoOW
Veteran of Heaven, The. Francis Thompson. HBV; MaRV; PoLi
"O Captain of the wars, whence won Ye so great scars?" *sel.* ChIP
Veteran Sirens. E. A. Robinson. AnAmPo; AnNE; BLV; BoLiVe; LA; OnHM; TwP
Veterans, The. Denis A. McCarthy. PEDC
Veterans, The. Donagh MacDonagh. JKCP (1955 ed.); OnYI
Veteran's Grave, The. Mikhail Lermontov, *tr. fr. Russian by* J. S. Phillimore. BoR
Vex no man's secret soul—if that can be. Help. Sadi. *Fr.* The Gulistan. AWP; JAWP; OnPM; WBP
Vex not thou the poet's mind. The Poet's Mind. Tennyson. ViPP
Vexational. The Monk of Montaudon, *tr. fr. Provençal by* Hubert Creekmore. LyMA
Vexed by the distant. God's-Eye View. Robert Haven Schauffler. TCAP
Vexilla Regis. Venantius Fortunatus, *tr. fr. Latin by* John Mason Neale. CAW; WHL
(Hymn to the Holy Cross, *tr. by* John Mason Neale.) LiA; LiTW; LyMA
(Vexilla Regis Prodeunt, *tr. by* Albert Cook.) LaP
Vezzosi Augelli. Thomas Watson, *tr. fr. Italian.* TuPP
Via Amoris. Sir Philip Sidney. *See* Astrophel and Stella, LXXXIV.
Via Crucis, Via Lucis. T. H. Hedge. BePJ
Via Dolorosa. Phoebe Smith. PGD
Via, et Veritas, et Vita. Alice Meynell. JKCP; MaRV; OQP; QP-1; WGRP
Via Longa. Patrick McDonough. HBMV
Via Lucis. Charles G. Blanden. OQP; QP-1
Via Lucis. Howard Chandler Robbins. MaRV; OQP; QP-2
Vial, The. Baudelaire, *tr. fr. French by* Kate Flores. AnFP
Viaticum. Herbert S. Gorman. TBM
Viaticum. Ethna MacCarthy. NeIP
Vibrations. Siegfried Sassoon. CaAE
Vicar, The. George Crabbe. *Fr.* Inebriety. AnFE
Vicar, The. Winthrop Mackworth Praed. Every-Day Characters, I. BCEP; EnRP; EPN; ERP; EV-4; HBV; InMe; OBEV (new ed.); OBRV; OBVV; PoEL-4; VA
Vicar at the table's front presides, The. The Vicar. George Crabbe. *Fr.* Inebriety. AnFE
Vicar of Bray, The. *Unknown.* ALV; CEP; EV-4; HBV; LPS-3; OxBoLi; ViBoPo
(In Good King Charles's Golden Days.) InvP; OBEC
Vicar of Wakefield, The, *sels.* Goldsmith.
Edwin and Angelina, *fr. ch.* 8. CEP; EV-3; OTPC
(Hermit, The.) LPS-1
Elegy [*or* Elegie] on the Death of a Mad Dog, *fr. ch.* 17. AlBD; ALV; BeLS; BLPA; BOHV; BTP; CEP; CG; EV-3; FaBoBe; FaBoCh; FaFP; GN; GTIV; HBV; HBVY; HiLiEn; LBN; LiTG; LoGBV; LPS-3; MaC; MCCG; NA; NeHB; OAEP; OBEC; OnSP; OTPC; PFE; PIR; PoeMoYo; RIS; SiTL; TreF; WaKn; WP
Song: "When lovely woman stoops to folly," *fr. ch.* 24. AWP; BEL; CEP; EiPP; EV-3; GTBS; GTSE; GTSL; JAWP; LiTL; OBEC; PoFS; SeCePo; TOP; TrGrPo; TyEnPo; ViBoPo; WBP
(On Woman.) CaAE; LPS-1
(Stanzas on Woman.) EnLit; ExPo; OnYI; OxBI
(When Lovely Woman Stoops to Folly.") EnLi-1; GTBS-D; GTBS-W; HBV; InP; TreF
(Woman.) LEAP; LiTB; LiTG; OBEV; PIR; PoP
Vicarious Atonement. Richard Aldington. MBP; MoBrPo; WGRP
Vice. Pope. *Fr.* Essay on Man, Epistle II. BLP
Vice, from privation of that sacred grace. Satire IV. John Marston. *Fr.* The Scourge of Villainy. ReIE
Vice Versa. Christian Morgenstern, *tr. fr. German by* R. F. C. Hull. AnGP
Viceroy they made him, Admiral and Don. Columbus. Florence Earle Coates. DD; MC
Vices be wild and virtues lame. "So Runs the World Away." *Unknown.* TMEV
Vichy. Dudley G. Davies. NeTW
Vicious winter finally yields, The. W. D. Snodgrass. Heart's Needle, X. NePoEA
Vicissitudes of the Creator. Archibald MacLeish. NePA
Vicisti. Elliott Coleman. NoCaPo (1941 ed.)
Vickery's Mountain. E. A. Robinson. MAP; MoAmPo
Vicksburg—a Ballad. Paul Hamilton Hayne. AA; BIG; MC; MDAH; PAH; SPP; TCAP
Vicksburg 'round the Bend, *with music. Unknown.* StDa
Vicomte is wearing a brow of gloom, The. Chez Brébant. Francis Alexander Durivage. AA
Victim Invisible. Sister Miriam. PraNu
Victimae Paschali, *abr.* Wipo, *tr. fr. Latin.* WHL
(Victimae Paschali Laudes, *tr. by* Charles Kent.) CAW
Victor, The. Theodosia Garrison. UnW
Victor, The. Milton. *Fr.* Paradise Lost, VI. BCEP
("So spake the Son, and into the terrour chang'd.") NBE
Victor, The. Sydney King Russell. StaSt
Victor, The. William Young. HBMV
Victor and Vanquished. Longfellow. CoBA; CoV
Victor Galbraith. Longfellow. EV-5; IAP; PAH; TCAP
Victor in drama [*or* poesy], Victor in romance. To Victor Hugo. Tennyson. LPS-3; PtP
Victor of Antietam, The. Herman Melville. GA, *abr.*; MC; PAH
Victor stood beside the spoil, and by the grinning dead, The. Omar and the Persian. Sarah Williams. VA
Victor was a little baby. Song. W. H. Auden. AnFE
Victoria. Sir Arthur Quiller-Couch. SG
Victoria Dancing. Anne Welsh. BoSA
Victoria Falls, The. William Plomer. BoSA
Victoria Market. Francis Brabazon. BoAV
Victoria Markets Recollected in Tranquillity, The, *abr.* Frank Wilmot. BoAV; NeLNL
"Winds are bleak, stars are bright," *sel.* MoAuPo
Victorian Song. John Farrar. GoYe
Victorious beauty, though your eyes. To the Countesse of Salisbury [*or* Loves Victory]. Aurelian Townsend. MeLP; MePo; OBS
Victorious knights without reproach or fear. To the Returning Brave. Robert Underwood Johnson. PAH
Victorious Men of Earth. James Shirley. *Fr.* Cupid and Death. EV-2; OBS; TrGrPo
(Death, the Conqueror.) GoBC
(Death's Emissaries.) LoBV
(Death's Subtle Ways.) HBV
(Last Conqueror, The.) GTBS; GTBS-D; GTBS-W; GTSE; GTSL
(More Ways to Kill.) BLV
(Song: "Victorious men of earth, no more.") FaBoEn; SeCL
("Victorious men of earth, no more.") TuPP
Victorious Time. *Unknown.* ElSeCe
Victorious Titus, rue the tears I shed. Shakespeare. *Fr.* Titus Andronicus, I, i. MotAn
Victorious Wrong, with vulture scream. The Final Chorus from "Hellas." Shelley. EnLi-2
Victors, The, *abr.* Charles Hanson Towne. OQP; QP-1
Victory. Roger Axford. PGD
Victory. Eileen Duggan. AnNZ
Victory. Ibn Hani, *tr. fr. Arabic by* A. J. Arberry. MooP
Victory. Aline Kilmer. MaRV
Victory. Alfred Noyes. BEL
Victory. Arthur B. Rhinow. MaRV
Victory, The. Laura Riding. MoP

Victory. Sir Owen Seaman. BPP; OQP; QP-1; WGRP
(Between Midnight and Morning.) MaRV
("Ye that have faith to look with fearless eyes.") PoToHe
Victory. Shelley. *See* Promethean Ideal, The.
Victory. Miriam Teichner. BLP
Victory ("I am a youthful lady"). *Unknown.* CoMu
Victory ("The strife is o'er"). *Unknown.* *See* Strife Is O'er, The.
Victory, The. John Hall Wheelock. NP
Victory. Marguerite Wilkinson. ChIP
Victory at Salamis. Aeschylus. *See* Salamis.
Victory Ball, A. Alfred Noyes. EnLit
Victory Bells. Grace Hazard Conkling. AOAH; HBV; MC; PaA; PAH
Victory comes. The New Victory. Margaret Widdemer. AOAH; WGRP
Victory in Defeat. Edwin Markham. CV; MaRV; OQP; PC; PoeMoYo; QP-2; StaSt
Victory in Hungary, The. Thomas Shadwell. *Fr.* The Squire of Alsatia. SeCL
Victory in the Cabarets. Louis Untermeyer. HBMV
Victory March. M. K. Joseph. AnNZ
Victory of Guernica. Paul Eluard, *tr. fr. French by* Wallace Fowlie. MiCF
Victory over Aggressors. Sophocles, *tr. fr. Greek by* Gilbert Murray. *Fr.* Antigone. GrR
(Thebes of the Seven Gates, *longer sel., tr. by* Dudley Fitts *and* Robert Fitzgerald.) WaaP
Victory Parade. George Edward Hoffman. PGD
Victory! Victory!—Yes! ah, yes, thou republican Zion. Arthur Hugh Clough. *Fr.* Amours de Voyage, II. SoV
Victory Which Is Peace, The. Frederic Lawrence Knowles. *See* New Age, The.
Victus. Quentin Stevenson. POTE (1959 ed.)
Vide Astra. Julia Cooley Altrocchi. LEAP
Videantur Quae Non Sunt. Henry Parrot. SiCE
Vidi Viridi Phyllida sub Tilia. *Unknown, tr. fr. Latin by* Rolfe Humphries. *Fr.* Carmina Burana. LaP
Vieux Carré. Walter Adolphe Roberts. PoNe
View across the Roman Campagna, A. Elizabeth Barrett Browning. LPS-2
View at Gunderson's. Joseph Warren Beach. NP
View from Heights. Arthur Davison Ficke. *See* I Am in Love with High, Far-seeing Places.
View from the Euganean Hills, North Italy. Shelley. *See* Lines Written among the Euganean Hills.
View Me, Lord, a Work of Thine. Thomas Campion. MaRV; OxBoCh; SiCE
(View Mee, Lord.) TrPWD
View not my tomb with pity, passer-by. A Full Life. Carphyllides. OnPM
View now the winter storm! Above—one cloud. The Winter Storm at Sea. George Crabbe. *Fr.* The Borough. EtS
View of Jersey, A. Edward Field. NeAP
View of Montreal, A, *sel.* Francis Webb.
Cartier at St. Malo. BoAV
View of Rangitoto, A. Charles Brasch. AnNZ
View of T'ai-shan, A. Tu Fu, *tr. fr. Chinese by* Witter Bynner *and* Kiang Kang-hu. OuHeWo
View of the Brooklyn Bridge, A. William Meredith. MoVE
View of the Capitol from the Library of Congress. Elizabeth Bishop. FiMAP
View of the Sea, A. Mabuchi, *tr. fr. Japanese by* Asataro Miyamori. OnPM
View of the sky. Solo. Bocho Yamamura. PoLJ
Viewless thing is the wind, A. Love Is Strong. Richard Burton. AA; HBV
Viewpoints. Arthur Guiterman. UTS
Views of Boston Common and Nearby. R. P. Blackmur. MoVE
Views of the Favorite Colleges. John Malcolm Brinnin. LiTA; MoAB; OnHM
Vigil. Katharine Lee Bates. PCD
Vigil. Faith Baldwin. MaRV; MuM
Vigil, The. Abbie Farwell Brown. CV
Vigil. Marjorie Freeman Campbell. CaP
Vigil. Richard Dehmel, *tr. fr. German by* Ludwig Lewisohn. AWP; JAWP; LiTW; WBP
Vigil. W. E. Henley. In Hospital, VII. LoBV; POTT
Vigil, The. T. Sturge Moore. POTE
Vigil. Laura Simmons. *See* Trimmed Lamp, The.
Vigil. Mabel Simpson. BAP
Vigil and Remorse. Apollonius Rhodius. *See* Remorse.
Vigil of Joseph, The. Elsa Barker. NV; StJW
Vigil of the Assumption. Gertrude von Le Fort, *tr. fr. German by* Margaret Chanler. ISi
Vigil of the Immaculate Conception. Maurice Francis Egan. CAW; JKCP
Vigil of Venus, The. *Unknown, sometimes at. to* Catullus, *tr. fr. Latin by* Thomas Stanley. AWP; OuHeWo
——*Tr. by* Allen Tate. LaP; LiTW
——*Tr. by* Thomas Parnell. WoL
Vigil Strange I Kept on the Field One Night. Walt Whitman. AmPo; CoBA; IAP; KN; LoBV; MoAmPo (1950 ed.); MOAP; OnAP; WaaP; WHA
Vigilance. André Breton, *tr. fr. French by* Wallace Fowlie. MiCF
Vigilantes, The. Margaret Ashmun. SCC
Vigils. Aline Kilmer. PFE; PoTo
Vigils. Siegfried Sassoon. ChMo; CMP
"Down the glimmering staircase, past the pensive clock," *sel.* AlDL
Vignette of Ancient Peace. Aristophanes, *tr. fr. Greek by* Benjamin Bickley Rogers. *Fr.* The Peace. GrR
Vigor, vitality, vim and punch. "Pep." Grace G. Bostwick. WBLP
Viking, The. Whitley Stokes. OnYI
Viking Ship, The. Norreys Jephson O'Conor. NeTW
Viking Terror, The. *Unknown, tr. fr. Old Irish by* F. N. Robinson. AnIL; OnYI; KiLC, *tr. by* Frank O'Connor
(Vikings, The, *tr. unknown.*) ChTr
Vilest work of vilest man, The. Nature the False Goddess. James Jeffrey Roche. JKCP
Villa Borghese. Sophus Michaëlis, *tr. fr. Danish by* Charles W. Stork. BoDS
Villa by the Bosphorus, A. Arabius Scholasticus, *tr. fr. Greek by* F. L. Lucas. GrPE
Villa Sciarra; Rome. Christine Turner Curtis. GoYe
Villafranca de Córdoba. Pedro Garfias, *tr. fr. Spanish by* Kenneth Porter. PoFr
Village, The. George Crabbe. CEP
Sels.
"Here, wand'ring long, amid these frowning fields." NBE
Parish Workhouse, The. BCEP; LEAP
(Parish Poor-House, The, *longer sel.*) OBEC
Pauper's Funeral, The. CoEV; FaBoEn
"Thus groan the old, till, by disease oppress'd." PoFS; PreP
Truth in Poetry. OBEC; SeCePo
"Village Life, and every care that reigns, The." BEL; CoBE; EiPP; EnLi-2; EnRP; NBE; Po; PoE
(Village Life.) PoEL-4
Village, The ("Sweet Auburn! loveliest village of the plain"). Goldsmith. *Fr.* The Deserted Village. TrGrPo
(Auburn.) OBEC; SeCePo
(From "The Deserted Village.") LEAP
(Sweet Auburn.) LiTB
("Sweet Auburn! loveliest village of the plain.") OTPC; TreFS; ViBoPo
Village, The ("Sweet was the sound"). Goldsmith. *Fr.* The Deserted Village. GTIV
(Evening.) ShBV-2
("Sweet was the sound, when oft at evening's close.") BrBE; EnSW; FaBoEn
Village, The. R. S. Thomas. HaMV
Village and Factory. Alexander Ilyich Bezymensky, *tr. fr. Russian by* Babette Deutsch. TrJP; TrRV
Village and the River, The. Tu Fu, *tr. fr. Chinese.* WhP
Village Atheist, The. Edgar Lee Masters. *Fr.* Spoon River Anthology. AmP; ChMo; CMP; LiTA; MaRV
Village Barber, The. Luis Lopez, *tr. fr. Spanish by* Thomas Walsh. OnPM
Village before Sunset. Frances Cornford. LoGBV
Village Bell, The. Alphonse de Lamartine, *tr. fr. French by* Alan Conder. TrFP
Village Blacksmith, The. Longfellow. AA; AnNE; CoBA; FaBoBe; FaFP; FaPON; GoTP; HBV; HBVY; IAP; LEAP; LPS-2; NeHB; OnPP; OTPC; PECK; PIR; PTA-1; PYM; StVeCh; TCAP; TreF; TVSH; WBLP
Village Blacksmith, The. *Unknown.* FiBHP
Village Choir. *Unknown.* BOHV; PA
Village church, so small it has hardly shrunk, The. The Return. L. A. G. Strong. HaMV
Village Curate, The, *sels.* James Hurdis.
"I love to meet/ A sudden turn like this." EnSW
"Then let the village bells, as often wont." EnSW
Village-folk told me, saying, The. Foreboding. *Unknown. Fr.* Manyo Shu. OnPM
Village is submerged, houses and creatures, The. Ashokan. Dachine Rainer. NePoAm
Village knew her as a faithful wife, The. The Stay-at-Home. Marjorie Charles Driscoll. DDA
Village lies in Sabbath heat, The. Sanna. Alan Paton. BoSA
Village Life. George Crabbe. *Fr.* The Village. PoEL-4
("Village life, and every care that reigns, The.") BEL; CoBE; EiPP; EnLi-2; EnRP; NBE; Po; PoE
Village Loves outside the Gate. *Unknown, tr. fr. Chinese by* E. D. Edwards. ChLP
Village maid was leaving home, with tears her eyes were wet, A. Heaven Will Protect the Working Girl. Edgar Smith. FaFP; TreF
Village Night. Luis Carlos López, *tr. fr. Spanish by* Donald Devenish Walsh. AnCL
Village Noon; Mid-Day Bells. Merrill Moore. MAP; MoAmPo
Village of Erith, The. *Unknown.* ChTr

Village of Love, The. "Petros Vlastos," *tr. fr. Modern Greek by* Rae Dalven. MoGP
Village of Winter Carols. Laurie Lee. ChMP
Village Oracle, The. *Unknown.* DDA
Village Parson, The. Goldsmith. *See* Village Preacher, The.
Village pedagogue announced one day, A. The Snuff-Boxes. *Unknown.* StPo
Village Portrait. Thomas W. Duncan. MoSiPe
Village Preacher, The. Goldsmith. *Fr.* The Deserted Village. CBOV; GrCo-1; MaRV; TrGrPo, *shorter sel.*
(Country Parson, The.) OTPC (1923 ed.)
(Village Parson, The.) CoEV; OBEC; WGRP
Village School, The. Longfellow. *Fr.* Christus; a Mystery, Pt. II, 3. APW
Village Schoolmaster, The. Goldsmith. *Fr.* The Deserted Village. BTP; OBEC; TrGrPo
(Schoolmaster, The.) CBOV; OTPC (1946 ed.); ShBV-2; TVSH
Village Schoolmistress, The. William Shenstone. *Fr.* The Schoolmistress. LPS-2
Village sleeps, a name unknown, till men, The. Distinction. M. A. De Wolfe Howe. AA
Village Stork, The. Bayard Taylor. BLA; PFY
Village where they ring, A. Dusk. Basho. OnPM; WoL
Village wine is sweet and sour, the town wine rotten, The. Autumn. Lu Yu. WhP
Villagers all, this frosty tide. Carol [*or* Christmas Carol]. Kenneth Grahame. *Fr.* The Wind in the Willows. FaPON; MPB; OHIP
Villagers who gather round. Spiel of the Three Mountebanks. John Crowe Ransom. MAP; MoAB; MoAmPo
Villain, The. W. H. Davies. MBP; MoBrPo; NeMA; POTE; WHA
Villain, The, *sel.* Thomas Porter.
Serenade, to Two Ladies. SeCL
Villain shows his indiscretion. Curtain! Paul Laurence Dunbar. CenHV
Villancico. *Unknown, tr. fr. Spanish by* Thomas Walsh. AWP; JAWP; OnPM; WBP
Villancico for His Three Daughters. Marqués de Santillana, *tr. fr. Spanish by* Richard Beaumont. LyMA
Villanelle. W. H. Auden. LoPo; MoAB; MoBrPo
(Time Will Say Nothing but I Told You So.) LiTA
Villanelle. Philippe Desportes, *tr. fr. French by* Alan Conder. TrFP
Villanelle. William Empson. ChMP; EnLoPo
Villanelle. W. E. Henley. InP; MBP; TOP
Villanelle. Walter H. Kerr. NePoAm-2
Villanelle. Jean Passerat, *tr. fr. French by* John Payne. LiA
Villanelle W. W. Skeat. FiBHP; SiTL
Villanelle. A. M. Sullivan. OQP; QP-2
Villanelle of a Villaness. Edwin Meade Robinson. HBMV
Villanelle of His Lady's Treasures. Ernest Dowson. HBV
Villanelle of Light. A. M. Sullivan. JKCP (1955 ed.)
Villanelle of Marguerites. Ernest Dowson. EnLi-2; MBP; MoBrPo; PIAE; POTT
Villanelle of Poor Pierrot. Walter Adolphe Roberts. PFE
Villanelle of the Living Pan. Walter Adolphe Roberts. LEAP; PoNe
Villanelle of the Poet's Road. Ernest Dowson. OBMV; PoVP; TrGrPo; ViPP
Villanelle of Things Amusing. Gelett Burgess. BOHV
Villanelle of Washington Square. Walter Adolphe Roberts. PFE; PoNe
Villanelle; the Psychological Hour. Ezra Pound. MOAP; NP
Villanelle, with Stevenson's Assistance. Franklin P. Adams. PC
Villeins clustered round the bowl, The. Brawn of England's Lay. John Hunter-Duvar. VA
Villiers de l'Isle-Adam. Aldous Huxley. HBMV
Villkins and His Dinah (A *and* B *vers.*). *Unknown.* BaBo
Villon among the birds is he. The Blue Jay. Louise Driscoll. BLA; VOD
Villon Strolls at Midnight. Vincent Starrett. BAP; LEAP
Villon's Ballade. Andrew Lang, *after* Villon. HBV
Villon's Epitaph in Ballade Form. Villon. *See* Epitaph in Form of a Ballad, The, Which Villon Made for Himself and His Comrades . . .
Villon's Good-Night. W. E. Henley, *after* Villon. CenHV
Villon's Straight Tip to all Cross Coves. W. E. Henley, *after* Villon. AWP; BOHV; CenHV; HBV; InMe; InvP; NA; SeCePo
Vinco. Elliot Field. ChIP
Vincula Sponte Decidunt. Richard Crashaw, *tr. fr. Latin by* D. C. Allen. Epigrammata Sacra, I, 31. LaP
Vindictive Staircase, The; or, The Reward of Industry. W. W. Gibson. AnFE; POTT
Vine, The. Mu'tamid, King of Seville, *tr. fr. Arabic by* A. J. Arberry. MooP
Vine, The. James Thomson. Sunday up the River, XVIII. HBV; LEAP; LoPS; MBP; OBEV; OBVV
("Wine of Love is music, The.") EmBrPo; POTT; PoVP; ViBoPo; VLEP
Vine and the Goat, The. Aesop, *rhymed tr. fr. Greek by* William Ellery Leonard. AWP
Vine I see, and though 'tis time to glean, A. Overripe Fruit. Kasmuneh. TrJP
Vine Out of Egypt, A. Psalms, LXXX: 8-15, Bible, *O.T.* LiA
Vine to the Goat, The. Euenus, *tr. fr. Greek.* LiTW, *tr. by* L. R. Lind; OxBG, *tr. by* Sir William Marris
Vinegar Man, The. Ruth Comfort Mitchell. MPB; SP
Vines branching stilly. A Carol [*or* Five Carols for Christmastide, II]. Louise Imogen Guiney. CAW; ISi; OBVV
Vines tougher than wrists. Forcing House. Theodore Roethke. AtBAP
Vingtaine. Alice Learned Bunner. AA
Immutabilis, II.
Separation, I.
Vintage, The. Belle Cooper. GoBC
Vintage, The. Mary Carolyn Davies. *Fr.* A Girl's Song. SBMV
Vintage, The. Kostas Krystallis, *tr. fr. Modern Greek by* Rae Dalven. MoGP
Vintage. V. Sackville-West. *Fr.* The Land. TwCV
Vintage to the Dungeon, The. Richard Lovelace. SeCV-1
Vinum Daemonum. Lionel Johnson. POTT
Violet. Ibn A'isha, *tr. fr. Arabic by* A. J. Arberry. MooP
Violet, The. Bryant. *See* Yellow Violet, The.
Violet, The. Sir Walter Scott. BPN; EmBrPo; EnRP; EPN
Violet, The. William Wetmore Story. HBV; LPS-2
Violet, The. Jane Taylor. BoChLi; HBV; HBVY; OTPC; PECK; PRWS; RIS; TreF; TVC; TVSH
Violet, The. Wordsworth. *Fr.* She Dwelt among the Untrodden Ways. PCH
Violet and the Rose, The. Joseph Skipsey. OBVV
Violet and the Rose, The. Augusta Webster. HBV
Violet Bank, A. Shakespeare. *Fr.* A Midsummer Night's Dream, II, i. FaPON; OTPC (1946 ed.); PRWS
(I Know a Bank.) ADAH
(Titania's Bower.) PCH
(Where the Wild Thyme Blows.) TrGrPo
Violet by a mossy stone, A. The Violet. Wordsworth. *Fr.* She Dwelt among the Untrodden Ways. PCH
Violet in her green-wood bower, The. The Violet. Sir Walter Scott. BPN; EmBrPo; EnRP; EPN
Violet in Her Hair, A. Charles Swain. LPS-1
(Song: "Violet in her lovely hair, A.") HBV
Violet in the wood, that's sweet to-day, The. The Violet and the Rose. Augusta Webster. HBV
Violet invited my kiss, The. The Violet and the Rose. Joseph Skipsey. OBVV
Violet is much too shy, The. A Song the Grass Sings. Charles G. Blanden. HBV; NLK
Violet loves a sunny bank, The. Proposal. Bayard Taylor. PR
Violet Star, The. Eugene Fitch Ware. DDA
Violet under the Snow, The. Rachel Capen Schauffler. ADAH
Violet, violet, sparkling with dew. The Wild Violet. Hannah Flagg Gould. PEOR
Violets. Dinah Maria Mulock Craik. PRWS
Violets, The. Stephen Crane. War Is Kind, XXIII. AA
(War Is Kind, III: "There was a land where lived no Violets.") AnAmPo; LA
Violets. Robert Herrick. *See* To Violets.
Violets. Lucy Larcom. ADAH
Violets. John Moultrie. BoTP; CG
(Dear Little Violets.) PRWS
Violets. Josephine O'Conner. CAG
Violets. P. A. Ropes. BoTP
Violets ("I know, blue modest violets"). *Unknown.* BoTP
Violets and Roses. *Unknown.* *See* Sweet Violets, Love's Paradise.
Violets are like shy little children. Violets. Josephine O'Conner. CAG
Violets blue of the eyes divine, The. The Withered Heart [*or* Die blauen Veilchen der Augelein]. Heine. AWP; OnPM
Violets, daffodils. Eilzabeth J. Coatsworth. TiPo (1959 ed.)
Violets in Thaumantia's Bosome. Sir Edward Sherburne. OBS
Violets, violets, sweet March violets. Violets. Dinah Maria Mulock Craik. PRWS
Violin, The. Richard Watson Gilder. PoRL
Violin Calls, The. Florence Randal Livesay. CaP; CPG; OCL
Violin Mood, A. Robert Haven Schauffler. ADAH
Violinist, A. Francis William Bourdillon. OBVV; VA
Violinist, The. Archibald Lampman. CaP; OCL
Violin's Complaint, The. William Roscoe Thayer. AA
Violins, too. The Old Amati. Oliver Wendell Holmes. BPP
Viper, The. Hilaire Belloc. BOHV; RIS
Viper, The. Ruth Pitter. AlDL; FaBoTw
Viper stung a Cappadocian's hide, A. The Snake It Was That Died. Demodocus. OxBG

Vipers bugloss beckons me, The. Song to My Love. Laurence McKinney. InMe
Virelay: "Am I, am I beautiful?" Eustache Deschamps, *tr. fr. French by* Ralph N. Currey. FoS
Virelay: "Thou cruel fair, I go." Charles Cotton. LO; LoPS; SeCL
Virelay: "Too long it seems e'er I shall view." Jean Froissart, *tr. fr. French by* Louisa S. Costello. LyMA
Virgidemiarum, *sels.* Joseph Hall.
"Another scorns the homespun thread of rhymes," Bk. I, Satire VI. SiCE; TuPP
Coxcomb, A, *fr.* Bk. III, Satire V. EV-2
"Gentle squire would gladly entertain, A," Bk. II, Satire VI. ReIE; SiCE; TuPP; ViBoPo
(Trencher Chaplain, The.) EV-2
"Great is the folly of a feeble brain," Bk. I, Satire VII. ReIE
(Love-sicke Poet, The.) FaBoEn
"Great Osmond knows not how he shall be known," Bk. III, Satire II. ReIE
"Hence, ye profane; mell not with holy things," Bk. I, Satire VIII. SiCE
"I first adventure, with foolhardy might," Prologue, Bk. I. ReEn; ReIE; SiCE; ViBoPo
"I wot not how the world's degenerate," Bk. IV, Satire VI. ReIE
"Nor ladies' wanton love, nor wandering knight," Bk. I, Satire I. SiCE; TuPP
"Satire should be like the porcupine, The," Bk. V, Satire III. ReEn
"Seest thou how gayly my young master goes," Bk. III, Satire VII. SiCE
"Some say my satires over-loosely flow," Prologue, Bk. III. SiCE
"Time was, and that was termed the time of gold," Bk. III, Satire I. SiCE
(Olden Days, The.) OBSC
"Too popular is tragic poesy," Bk. I, Satire IV. ReEn; SiCE
"With some pot-fury, ravished from their wit," Bk. I, Satire III. ReEn; SiCE
Virgil from Homer, th' Italian from him. Of Spenser's *Faerie Queene* [*or Fairy Queen*]. Thomas Freeman. SiCE; TuPP
Virgilia. Edwin Markham. BAP
"What was I back in the world's first wonder?" *sel.* EtS
Virgil's Farewell to Dante. Dante, *tr. fr. Italian by* Laurence Binyon. *Fr.* Divinia Commedia: Purgatorio, XXVII. FaBoTw
Virgil's Tomb. Robert Cameron Rogers. AA
Virgin. Padraic Fallon. OnYI
Virgin, The. Ibn Sa'id of Alcala la Real, *tr. fr. Arabic by* A. J. Arberry. MooP
Virgin, The. Katherine Philips. LO
Virgin, The. Wordsworth. CAW; CoBE; GoBC
(Sonnet to the Virgin.) ISi
Virgin and Unicorn. John Heath-Stubbs. NeBP
Virgin, Bright, and Beautiful To-Day, The. Stéphane Mallarmé, *tr. fr. French by* G. S. Fraser. MiFP
Virgin calm and gentle, in thine eyes. To Joseph. Harriet Hoock. WHL
Virgin Country. Roy McFadden. NeIP
Virgin, daughter of Locrine. Milton. *Fr.* Comus. ElSeCe
Virgin Declares Her Beauties, A. Francesco da Barberino, *tr. fr. Italian by* Dante Gabriel Rossetti. AWP; LyPI; MeRV
Virgin Earth. Ibn al-Bain, *tr. fr. Arabic by* A. J. Arberry. MooP
Virgin is not humble, but her son, The. In Beatae Virginis Verecundiam. Richard Crashaw. Epigrammata Sacra, II, 11 LaP
Virgin Martyrs, The. Sigebert of Gembloux, *tr. fr. Latin by* Helen Waddell. MeRV
Virgin Mary, The. Edgar Bowers. NePoEA; PtPa
Virgin Mary, The. Robert Herrick. NBE
Virgin Mary, The. Erik Axel Karlfeldt, *tr. fr. Swedish by* Charles W. Stork. *Fr.* Poems on Dalecarlian Paintings. AnSL
Virgin Mary cannot enter into, The. And in Her Morning. Jessica Powers. ISi
Virgin Mary to Christ on the Cross, The. Robert Southwell. ViBoPo
Virgin Mary to the Child Jesus, The. Elizabeth Barrett Browning. BOL; ISi, *abr.*
Holy Night, The, *sel.* CLS
Virgin Mary's Conception, The. Robert Southwell. ReIE
Virgin most lovely, who clothed with the sun. To the Virgin. Petrarch, *tr. by* Anna Maria Armi. *Fr.* Sonnets to Laura. LiA
Virgin Mother, The. "Æ." ChMo; CMP
Virgin Mother, The, *sel.* D. H. Lawrence.
"I kiss you good-bye, my darling." ViBoPo
"Virgin mother, daughter of thy son, lowly and uplifted more than any creature." Love. Dante, *tr. by* Philip Henry Wicksteed. *Fr.* Divina Commedia: Paradiso. LiA
Virgin Mother, thou hast known. Latin Hymn to the Virgin [*or* Latin Hymn]. Winthrop Mackworth Praed. CoBE; ERP
Virgin pure, this is full sure, A. Now Let Us Sing, Both More and Less. *Unknown.* AnEC
Virgin Queen, The; an Anagram. Sir John Davies. *See* Of Astraea.
Virgin stills the crying, The. A Cradle-Song of the Virgin. *Unknown.* BOL
Virgin thus to Jesus did sing, The. The Virgin's Lullaby. *Unknown.* BOL
Virgin Truly Full of Wonder. St. Ephrem, *tr. fr. Syriac by* W. H. Kent. *Fr.* Christmas Hymn. ISi
(Christmas Hymn, The.) CAW
Virginal, A. Ezra Pound. AmPP; APA; ChMo; CMP; CoAnAm; CoBMV; MAP; MoAB; MoAmPo; MOAP; NeMA; NePA; OxBA; PR; TCPD; TwAmPo
Virginia. Hart Crane. *Fr.* The Bridge: Three Songs. LiTA
Virginia. Vachel Lindsay. ATP (1935 ed.)
Virginia Britannia. Marianne Moore. MoVE
Virginia Capta. Margaret Junkin Preston. PAH
Virginia gave us this imperial man. Imperial Man. James Russell Lowell. *Fr.* Under the Old Elm. PGD
Virginia Song, The. *Unknown.* PAH
Virginian Voyage, The. Michael Drayton. *See* To the Virginian Voyage.
Virginiana. Mary Johnston. HBMV
Virginians Are Coming Again, The. Vachel Lindsay. NP
Virginians of the Valley, The. Francis Orrery Ticknor. AA; AnAmPo; BlG; DD; HBV; LA; PaA; PAH; SPP; TCAP
Virgins. Francis Carlin. HBMV
Virgins as I advise forbeare. *Unknown.* SeCSL
Virgin's Complaint, The. *Unknown.* *See* Quia Amore Langueo ("In a tabernacle").
Virgin's Cradle-Hymn, The. *Unknown, tr. fr. Latin by* Samuel Taylor Coleridge. AnEC; BOL
Virgins, in vain you labour to prevent. Christopher Marlowe. *Fr.* Tamburlaine the Great, Pt. I. MyFE
Virgin's Lullaby, The. Nora Hopper. BOL
Virgin's Lullaby, The ("Sleep, oh sleep, dear Baby mine"). *Unknown, tr. fr. Piedmontese lullaby.* BOL
Virgin's Lullaby, The ("The Virgin thus to Jesus did sing"). *Unknown, tr. fr. Sicilian lullaby.* BOL
Virgins promis'd when I dy'd. An Epitaph upon a Child. Robert Herrick. SeCV-1
Virgins, sing the Virgin Huntress. Horace. Odes, I, 21. LaP
Virgin's Slumber Song, The. Francis Carlin. BOL; ISi; NV; YeAr
Virgin's Song, The. *Unknown.* *See* Our Lady's Song.
Virgins with T-squares. The Angel of Numerals. Rafael Alberti. AnSpL-2; CoSP
Virgo, Rosa Virginum. *Unknown.* AnEC
Virile Christ, A. Rex Boundy. ChIP; MaRV; OQP; QP-1; WGRP
Virtue. Theodore Beza, *tr. by* Nicholas Grimald. *See* Description of Virtue.
Virtue. George Herbert. ATP; AWP; BCEP; BEL; BLV; BoLiVe; CaAE; CBOV; CenL; CH; CoBE; CoEV; ElSeCe; EM-1; EnLi-1; EnLit; EOAH; EPP; EPS; EV-2; ExPo; HBV; InPo; InvP; JAWP; LEAP; LoBV; LPS-1; OBEV; OnPM; PG (1955 ed.); PIAE; Po; PoE; PoFS; PoRA; SeCeV; SeCL; SeEP; ShBV-4; TCEP; TOP; TrGrPo; TVSH; TwCrTr; TwHP; TyEnPo; UnPo (1st ed.); ViBoPo; WBP; WGRP; WHA
(Memento Mori.) LH
("Sweet day, so cool, so calm, so bright.") EG
(Vertue.) AtBAP; FaBoEn; MeLP; MePo; OBS; SeCV-1
(Virtue Immortal.) LPS-1
Virtue. Immanuel di Roma, *tr. fr. Hebrew by* Joseph Chotzner. *Fr.* Machberoth. TrJP
Virtue. *Unknown, tr. fr. Greek by* T. F. Higham. OxBG
Virtue, alas, now let me take some rest. Astrophel and Stella, IV. Sir Philip Sidney. MaPo; ReEn; SiPS
Virtue and Vice. Pope. *Fr.* Epilogue to the Satires, Dialogue I. BeR
Virtue, beauty, and speech did strike, wound, charm. An Excellent Sonnet of a Nymph. Sir Philip Sidney. ReIE
Virtue dwells rarely in the bright eyed and fair. Virtue. Immanuel di Roma. *Fr.* Machberoth. TrJP
Virtue dwells, so runs the tale. The Climb to Virtue. Simonides. GrL; OxBG
Virtue Immortal. George Herbert. *See* Virtue.
Virtue may chuse the high or low degree. Virtue and Vice. Pope. *Fr.* Epilogue to the Satires. BeR
Virtue may unlock hell, or even. Epilogue. Francis Thompson. *Fr.* A Judgment in Heaven. EmBrPo; PoLi
Virtue, so hardly pursued by men. To Virtue. Aristotle. OxBG

Virtue the Safest Guide. George Chapman. *Fr.* Bussy d'Ambois, I, i. CoEV
Virtue to an upgrowing life lends grace. Fragment. Bacchylides. GrR
Virtue, to men thou bringest care and toil. Aristotle, *tr. fr. Greek by* John Addington Symonds. GrPo
Virtue's branches wither, virtue pines. A Priest's Song [*or* Song *or* O Pittie]. Thomas Dekker. *Fr.* Old Fortunatus. AtBAP; EIL; OBSC; SiCE
Virtuosa. Mary Ashley Townsend. AA
Virtuoso, The. Mark Akenside. BCEP; LPS-3, *abr.*
Virtuous Clam, The. Winifred Fry Webster. DDA
Virtuous Wife, The. Proverbs, Bible, *O.T. See* Good Housewife, The.
Virtuous Wife, The, *sel.* Thomas D'Urfey.
"Sawney was tall." OAEP
Virtuous Wife, The. Süsskind von Trimberg, *tr. fr. Middle High German.* TrJP
Virtuous Woman, The. Proverbs, Bible, *O.T. See* Good Housewife, The.
Viscous air, wheres'ere she fly, The. The Kingfisher. Andrew Marvell. *Fr.* Upon Appleton House. ChTr
Visible and Invisible. Helen Pinkerton. PtPa
Vision, The. William Stanley Braithwaite. OQP; QP-2
Vision. Robert Bridges. ChMo; CMP
Vision, A. William Browne. *See* Rose, The.
Vision, The ("As I stood by yon roofless tower"). Burns. PoFr
(As I Stood by Yon Roofless Tower.) EBSV
Vision, The ("The sun had closed the winter day"), *sels.* Burns.
Muse of Burns, The, *last* 12 *sts.* RO
"Sun had clos'd the winter day, The," *first* 5 *sts.* BSV
Vision. Giosuè Carducci, *tr. fr. Italian by* Glauco Cambon. OnPM
Vision, A. John Clare. *See* I Lost the Love of Heaven.
Vision, A, *sel.* "Barry Cornwall."
"First, I saw a landscape fair." OBRV
Vision, A. Geoffrey Dearmer. HBMV
Vision. Edward Dowden. ChIP; OQP; QP-1
Vision, The. Virginia Moran Evans. UnW
Vision. John Gould Fletcher. LEAP; TBM
Vision, A. Philip Freneau. *Fr.* The House of Night. IAP; TCAP
("Trembling I write my dream, and recollect.") AnFE; APA; CoAnAm
Vision. Rose Fyleman. PCH
Vision, The. Walter Greenough. DD; GA
Vision. Elizabeth N. Hauer. PoToHe
Vision, A. Hugo von Hofmannsthal, *tr. fr. German by* Charles Wharton Stork. TrJP
Vision. William Dean Howells. AA; AnAmPo; LA
Vision, The. Lounkianos, *tr. fr. Armenian by* Thomas Walsh. CAW
Vision, The. "Fiona Macleod." *Fr.* Sospiri di Roma. BMEP; VLEP
Vision. Ida Norton Munson. ChIP
Vision, A. Arthur Rimbaud, *tr. fr. French by* Alan Conder. TrFP
Vision, The. Shakespeare *and probably* John Fletcher. King Henry VIII, Act IV, sc. ii. LiA
Vision, A. Tennyson. *See* Prophecy.
Vision, A. Ts'ao Chih, *tr. fr. Chinese by* Arthur Waley. TrCh
Vision, A. Henry Vaughan. *Fr.* The World. BBV; GTSL
("I saw eternity the other night," *first* 7 *ll.*) BCEP; CBOV; EPP; ImOP; PC; PoeMoYo; TCEP
Vision, A. Yvor Winters. MoVE
Vision, A, *sel.* W. B. Yeats.
All Souls' Night. MoVE; ReMP
Vision. Israel Zangwill. TrJP
Vision and Prayer. Dylan Thomas. LiTG; LiTM (rev. ed.); MoPo
"I turn the corner of prayer and burn," *sel.* MeRV
Vision as of crowded city streets, A. Shakespeare. Longfellow. AWP; IAP; InPo; MOAP; TOP
Vision by Sweetwater. John Crowe Ransom. CoBMV; CrMA; FaBoMo; MoAB; OxBA
Vision Clear, The. J. M. Westrup. BoTP
Vision Concerning Piers Plowman, The. William Langland(?). *See* Vision of Piers Plowman, The.
Vision of a Queen of Fairyland, A. The First Vision. Tadhg Dall O'Huiginn. AnIL
Vision of Athens. Milton. *See* Athens.
Vision of Beauty, A. Ben Jonson. *See* It Was a Beauty That I Saw.
Vision of Belshazzar, The. Byron. GN; HBV; OTPC; ShGoBo; TOP
Vision of Beulah. Blake. *See* Nightingale and Flowers.
Vision of Children, A. Thomas Ashe. VA
Vision of Christ that thou dost see, The. Blake. *Fr.* The Everlasting Gospel. OBRV
Vision of Columbus, The. Joel Barlow. *Fr.* The Columbiad, Bk. IX. APW
Vision of Connaught in the Thirteenth Century, A. James Clarence Mangan. AnIL; IrPN; TIP
(King Cahal Mór of the Wine-red Hand.) AnIV; GoBC
Vision of Delight, The. Presented at Court in Christmas, 1617. Ben Jonson. PoEL-2; SeCV-1
Fantasy, *sel.* LPS-3
Vision of God, The. Dante, *tr. fr. Italian by* Laurence Binyon. *Fr.* Divina Commedia: Paradiso, XXXIII. ExPo
Vision of her girlhood glinted by, The. Margaret Roper's Vision of Her Father, Sir Thomas More. Francis Turner Palgrave. *Fr.* London Bridge. FAOV
Vision of Ita, The. *Unknown. See* Jesukin.
Vision of Jesus, The. William Langland(?). *Fr.* The Vision of Piers Plowman. ACP; CAW
Vision of Judgment, A, *sel.* Robert Southey.
Absolvers, The, Pt. VI. EnRP; ERP
Vision of Judgment, The. Byron. BPN; EM-2, *abr.*; EmBrPo; EnRP; ERP; GEPC; NBE; OxBoLi, *first* 15 *sts.*; ReaPo; TOP
Sels.
At the Gate of Heaven, *abr.* OBRV
(Archangel, The.) LoBV
(Where He Gazed a Gloom Pervaded, *br. sel.*) LiA
George the Third. FiP
"He ever warred with freedom and the free." PoFr
"Saint Peter sat by the celestial gate." CoEV
Vision of Lazarus, The, *sel.* Fenton Johnson. BANP
"Another sate near him." BANP
Vision of MacConglinne, The. MacConglinne, *tr. fr. Middle Irish.* CAW, *abr., tr. by* George Sigerson; CH, *tr. by* Kuno Meyer
(Vision That Appeared to Me, A, *tr. by* Kuno Meyer.) OnYI
Vision of Moth-eaten Pianos Falling to Pieces. "César Moro," *tr. fr. Spanish by* Muna Lee. AnCL
Vision of Nature, A. William Langland(?). *Fr.* The Vision of Piers Plowman. PoEL-1
Vision of Oxford, A, *sel.* William Alexander.
"Methought I met a Lady yester even." OBVV
Vision of Peace, The. Nathan Haskell Dole. PSO
Vision of Piers Plowman, The, *sels.* William Langland(?).
Average Man, The, *fr.* Passus XIII (B *text*), *mod. by* Henry W. Wells. PoLi
Covetousness, *fr.* Passus V (B *text*). CoEV
(Avarice, *mod. by* Henry W. Wells.) PoLi
Crucifixion and the Harrowing of Hell, The, *fr.* Passus XXI (C *text*), *mod.* MeEV
Descent into Hell, The, *fr.* Passus XXI (C *text*). PoEL-1
Dream, A, *fr.* Passus VIII (B *text*). CoEV
Fable of Belling the Cat, The, *fr.* Prologue (B *text*), *Middle English and mod. vers.* EPP
Glutton and Bat the Brewer, *fr.* Passus V (B *text*), *mod. by* Grover Cronin, Jr. CoBE
(Glutton, The.) ACP
(Gluttony, *shorter sel.*) CoEV
Holy Church, *fr.* Passus I (B *text*), *mod.* MeEV
(Field Full of Folk, A, *mod. by* Grover Cronin, Jr.) CoBE
Holy Church Speaks, *fr.* Passus I (B *text*), *mod. by* Henry W. Wells. PoLi
Human Soul Speaks, The, *fr.* Passus XV (B *text*), *mod. by* Henry W. Wells. PoLi
"'I have no penny,' quoth Piers, 'pullets to buy,'" *fr.* Passus IX (C *text*). MyFE
Incarnation, The, *fr.* Passus II (C *text*). PoEL-1
("For trewthe telleth that loue is triacle of hevene," *fr.* Passus II, B *text.*) OBEV (new ed.)
"King and his knights went to church, The," *fr.* Passus V (A *text*). BEL
(Confession of the Deadly Sins, The, *mod.*) MeEV
(Confessions of the Seven Deadly Sins, The, *mod. by* W. A. Neilson *and* K. G. T. Webster.) EnLi-1 (1949 ed).
Langland's Life, *fr.* Passus VI (C *text*), *mod.* MeEV
Love We as Brothers, *fr.* Passus XI (B *text*), *mod. by* Henry W. Wells. PoLi
Maiden Meed, The, *fr.* Passus II (A *text*), *mod. by* Grover Cronin, Jr. CoBE
(Lady Meed, *fr.* Passus II, B *text, mod. by* Albert C. Baugh.) EnLit
Palace of Truth, The, *fr.* Passus V (B *text*). ACP
Palmer, The, *fr.* Passus VI (A *text*). ACP; CAW
Poverty Not All Loss, *fr.* Passus XI (B *text*), *mod. by* Henry W. Wells. PoLi
Prayer for the Poor, *fr.* Passus XIV (B *text*), *mod. by* Henry W. Wells. PoLi
("But beggars about midsummer go breadless to supper," *mod. by* Henry W. Wells.) PoFr
Preaching and Not Doing, *fr.* Passus X (B *text*), *mod. by* Henry W. Wells. PoLi
Prologue: "In a somer sesun [*or* summer season]," A *text,* BCEP, B *text, much abr.*; BEL, B *text*; CoBE, *opening ll. original, mod. by* Grover Cronin, Jr.; EnLi-1, *mod. by* W. A. Neilson *and* K. G. T. Webster; EnLit, B *text, mod.*

by Albert C. Baugh; EPP, *Middle English and mod. vers.;* TCEP, B *text, abr.*
(Field Full of Folk, The, *mod.*) MeEV
(Field of Folk, The, B *text.*) PoEL-1
(Induction, The: "In a summer season," *mod. by* Henry W. Wells.) PoLi
Providence, *fr.* Passus XIV (B *text*), *mod. by* Henry W. Wells. PoLi
Search for St. Truth, The, *fr.* Passus V–VII, *mod.* MeEV
Sufferings of the Poor, The, *fr.* Passus X (C *text*), *mod. by* Henry W. Wells. PoLi
("Needy are our neighbors, The," *mod. by* Henry W. Wells.) PoFr
(Poor, The.) PoEL-1
Theology, *fr.* Passus X (B *text*), *mod. by* Henry W. Wells. PoLi
(Grace for Theology.) GoBC
"This I trow be truth—who can teach thee better," *fr.* Passus I (A *text*). EG
Two Confessions, *fr.* Passus V (B *text*), *mod. by* Henry W. Wells. WoL
Vision of Jesus, The, *fr.* Passus XIX (B *text*). ACP; CAW
Vision of Nature, A, *fr.* Passus XIV (C *text*). PoEL-1
Vision of Poets, A, *sel.* Elizabeth Barrett Browning.
". . . These were poets true." PtP
Vision of Rome's Destiny. Virgil, *tr. fr. Latin by* Dryden. *Fr.* The Aeneid, VI. RoL
Vision of St. Bernard, The. M. Whitcomb Hess. ISi
Vision of St. Obadiah. *Unknown.* CAG
Vision of Sin, The. Tennyson. BPN; EmBrPo; LiA; PoVP; ViPo; ViPP; VLEP
Song at the Ruin'd Inn, *sel.* PoEL-5
Vision of Sir Launfal, The. James Russell Lowell. AnNE; IAP; MCCG; TCAP
Sels.
"'For Christ's sweet sake, I beg an alms,'" *fr.* Pt. II. WGRP
He Gives Nothing ("He gives nothing but worthless gold"), *fr.* Pt. I. MaRV
Joys, *br. sel. fr.* Prelude to Pt. I. BoTP
June, *fr.* Prelude to Pt. I. BBV; BTP; DD; EV-5; GoTP; HBV; HBVY; LPS-2; OHFP; PECK; PIR; PoRL; PTA-1; StaSt
("And what is so rare as a day in June?") OBAV
(Day in June, A.) FaPON; GrCo-1; HiLiAm; PoeMoYo; PYM; StVeCh (1955 ed.)
("Earth gets its price for what Earth gives us.") TreF
("For a cap and bells our lives we pay.") AA; LEAP
(June Weather.) GN
(Now Is the High-Tide of the Year.) TreFS
(What Is So Rare as a Day in June.) FaBoBe; FaFP; NePA
"Lo, it is I, be not afraid!" *fr.* Pt. II. OQP; QP-1; TreF
("And the voice that was softer [*or* calmer] than silence said," *longer sel.*) ChIP; MaRV
"Not only around our infancy," *fr.* Prelude to Pt. I. BLV; FaFP; GTBS-W; NePA
Not What We Give, 4 *ll., fr.* Pt. II. GrCo-1
Over His Keys, *fr.* Prelude to Pt. I. PoRL
(Prelude to Part First.) LiTA
(Prelude: "Over his keys the musing organist.") APW; BAP
(Prelude from "The Vision of Sir Launfal.") LiTG
Sir Launfal and the Leper, *fr.* Pt. I. GN; OTPC
Winter Morning, A, *fr.* Pt. II. GN
(January.) PoRL
Winter Pictures, Prelude to Pt. II, *incl. st.* 1 *of* Pt. II. BAP; LPS-2
(Brook in Winter, The, *shorter sel.*) GN; OTPC
(December.) GoTP
("Down swept the chill wind," *shorter sel.*) TreF
Vision of Sorrow. Thomas Sackville. *Fr.* Induction to "The Mirror for Magistrates." LoBV
Vision of Spring in Winter, A. Swinburne. PoVP; VLEP
Vision of the Day of Judgment. Isaiah, LXIII, Bible, *O.T.* (*Moulton, Modern Reader's Bible*). WGRP
Vision of the Divine Mystery. Dante. *See* St. Bernard's Prayer to Our Lady.
Vision of the Future, A. Pope. *Fr.* Messiah. MuP
Vision of the Mermaids, A, *sel.* Gerard Manley Hopkins.
"Rowing, I reach'd a rock—the sea was low." ChTr
Vision of the Milk-white Doe, The. Benjamin Sledd. NoCaPo
Vision of the Sea, A. Shelley. EmBrPo
Vision of the Snow, The. Margaret Junkin Preston. AA
Vision of the World, The. Tennyson. *See* Prophecy.
Vision of the World's Instability, A. Richard Verstegan. EIL
Vision of Theoclymenus, The. Homer, *tr. fr. Greek. Fr.* The Odyssey, XX. GrPE, *tr. by* F. L. Lucas; OxBG, *pr. tr. by* T. E. Lawrence
Vision of Twilight, A. Archibald Lampman. UnW
Vision of War, A. Thomas Sackville. *Fr.* Induction to "The Mirror for Magistrates." FaBoEn
Vision of William Concerning Piers the Plowman, The. William Langland(?). *See* Vision of Piers Plowman, The.
Vision on the Brink, The. Francis Ledwidge. VOD
Vision Splendid, The, *sel.* John Oxenham.
"'Mid all the traffic of the ways." MaRV
Vision That Appeared to Me, A. MacConglinne. *See* Vision of MacConglinne.
Vision to Electra, The. Robert Herrick. ALV
Vision upon This Conceit of the Faerie [*or* Faery] Queene, A. Sir Walter Ralegh. BCEP; BEL; CoBE; ElSeCe; EnLi-1 (1949 ed.); EnLit; OBSC; PoFS; PtP; SiCE; TuPP
(Faerie Queen, The.) LEAP
(Faery Queen, The.) ViBoPo
("Methought I saw the grave where Laura lay.") ReEn
(Of Spenser's Faery Queen.) SiPS
(Vision upon the Faery Queen, A.) ES; TOP
Visionary, The. Emily Brontë *and* Charlotte Brontë. EmBrPo; EnLi-2; GTBS-D; LiTB; LO; LoBV; NBE; OAEP; TriL; UnW
(Silent Is the House.) CH
Visionary and not believed. The Frozen City. Howard Nemerov. FiMAP
Visions, *sels.* William Browne.
"Down in a valley, by a forest's side," VI. ElSeCe; EPS (1942 ed.); PeBoSo
"Rose, as fair as ever saw the north, A," V. CenL; ViBoPo
(Rose, The.) CH; ES; EV-2; HBV; OBEV; OTPC (1923 ed.)
(Vision, A.) SeCL; SeEP
Visions, *sel.* Joachim du Bellay, *tr. fr. French by* Spenser.
"It was the time, when rest, soft sliding downe." AWP
(Sonnet.) OnPM
Visions. William Noel Hodgson. UnW
Visions. Lionel Johnson. MeRV
Visions. Edmund Leamy. BBV; GBV (1922 ed.); JKCP
Visions of days outworn, why do ye grow. To Teresa. José de Espronceda. TeCS
"Visions of glory, crowd not on my soul." Lycophron. *Fr.* Alexandra. GrPo
Visions [of Petrarch, The]. Petrarch, *tr. fr. Italian by* Spenser. *Fr.* Sonnets to Laura: To Laura in Death, Canzone III. AWP; EnLi-1; JAWP, *abr.;* WBP, *abr.*
I Saw a Phoenix in the Wood Alone, *sel.* ChTr
Visions of the Daughters of Albion, *sels.* Blake.
"Father of Jealousy, be thou accursed from the earth!" ViBoPo
I Cry: Love, Love! RO
Marigold, The. AtBAP
Take Thy Bliss, O Man. EnRP
Visions of the Night. Job, IV: 13–17, Bible, *O.T.* LiA
Visions of the World's Vanity, *sel.* Spenser.
Huge Leviathan, The. ChTr
Visit, The. Ogden Nash. FiBHP
Visit, A. Wang Chien, *tr. fr. Chinese by* Henry H. Hart. PoHN
Visit by Water. Floris Clark McLaren. BoCaPo (1948 ed.)
Visit from Abroad, A. James Stephens. PoMS
Visit from Mr. Fox, A. *Unknown.* *See* Fox, The.
Visit from St. Nicholas, A. Clement Clarke Moore. AA; BeLS; BLPA; BoChLi; BOHV; ChBR; COAH; DD; FaBoBe; FaFP; FaPON; GaP; GFA; GoTP; HBV; HBVY; HH; LHV; LPS-1; MeMeAg; MPB; NeHB; OTPC; PCH; PECK; PEDC; PoRh; PRWS; PTA-1; RAR; RIS; SAS; SDH; SiSoSe; StVeCh; TiPo; TreF; TVC; TVSH; YaD
(Night before Christmas, The.) OHFP; OnHT; WBLP
Visit from the Sea, The. Robert Louis Stevenson. GN; YT
Visit from Wealth, A. Hipponax, *tr. fr. Greek by* A. D. Knox. OxBG
Visit of the Wise Men, The. St. Matthew, II: 1–12, Bible, *N.T.* ChrBoLe; CLS
Visit of Thetis to Hephaistos. Homer. *See* Thetis and Hephaestus.
Visit the Sick. James J. Metcalfe. PoToHe (new ed.)
Visit to a Hospital. Jean Valentine Chace. GoYe
Visit to a Tenement. Nicolás Guillén, *tr. fr. Spanish by* Dudley Fitts. AnCL
Visit to the Lambs, A. *Unknown.* OTPC (1923 ed.); SAS
Visit to the Sea, A. Edgar Lee Masters. BoFr
Visit with a Woodpecker, A. Charles Commerford. BLA
Visit with Yang Chi, A. Cheng Hsieh, *tr. fr. Chinese by* Henry H. Hart. PoHN
Visitant, The. Walter de la Mare. UnW
Visitant, The. Theodore Roethke. UnPo (3d ed.)
Visitation, A. Hesiod, *tr. fr. Greek by* Sir William Marris. *Fr.* Eoiae. OxBG
Visitation. Max Jacob, *tr. fr. French by* Wallace Fowlie. MiCF
Visitation, The. Calvin Le Compte. ISi
Visitation. David Morton. PFE
Visitation. Vincent Starrett. DaM

Visitations. Lawrence Durrell. *Fr.* Eight Aspects of Melissa. NeBP
Visiting Sea, The. Alice Meynell. GTML; LoPS
Visiting the Chou Family Tombs. T'ao Yuan-ming, *tr. fr. Chinese* by Henry H. Hart. PoHN
Visiting the Hermit Cheng. Po Chü-i, *tr. fr. Chinese* by Ching Ti. WhP
Visiting the Hsi-lin Temple. Po Chü-i, *tr. fr. Chinese* by Arthur Waley. TrCh
Visiting the Ruins. Chang Ch'ien, *tr. fr. Chinese* by Arthur Christy. OnPM
Visiting Tsan, Abbot of Ta-yun. Tu Fu, *tr. fr. Chinese* by Kenneth Rexroth. OnPC
Visitor, The. Patrick R. Chalmers. DD; HBV; HBVY
Visitor, The. Rachel Field. TiPo (1952 ed.)
Visitor. W. E. Henley. *Fr.* In Hospital, XX. PIAE
Visitor Abhorred, The. Sir William Watson. PoVP
Visitors. Sir John Davies. ES
Visitors. Tu Fu, *tr. fr. Chinese* by Kenneth Rexroth. OnPC
Visitors to the Waterfall. James Reeves. MoP
Vista. Alfred Kreymborg. MAPA
Vista. Marguerite Wilkinson. *Fr.* Songs of an Empty House. SBMV
Vistas. Odell Shepard. HBMV; NV; QS
Visual Memory. Harry Martinson, *tr. fr. Swedish* by Erik Wahlgren *and* Martin S. Allwood. LiTW
Vita Benefica. Alice Wellington Rollins. AA
Vita Magistra. Walter Stanley Senior. MM
Vita Nuova, La, *sels.* Dante, *tr. fr. Italian* by Dante Gabriel Rossetti.
  "All my thoughts always speak to me of Love," VI. AWP
  (Divided Thoughts.) OnPM
  "All ye that pass along Love's trodden way," II. AWP; JAWP; LiTW; LyMA; WBP
  "At whiles (yea oftentimes) I muse over," IX. AWP; JAWP; WBP
  "Beyond the sphere which spreads to widest space," XXIX. AWP; JAWP; OnPM; OuHeWo; WBP
  (Sonnet.) LyPI
  "Canst thou indeed be he that still would sing," *fr.* XIII. AWP
  "Day agone, as I rode sullenly, A," IV. AWP
  "Death, always cruel, Pity's foe in chief," *fr.* III. AWP; JAWP; LiTW; WBP
  "Even as the others mock, thou mockest me," VII. AWP; LiTW
  "Eyes that weep for pity of the heart, The," XIX. AWP; OuHeWo; WGRP
  (Canzone.) LyMA; LyPI
  "For certain he hath seen all perfectness," XVII. AWP
Frae the Second Canzone o Dante's "Vita Nuova," *tr. into Scottish* by Douglas Young. LyPI
  "Gentle thought there is will often start, A," XXVI. AWP; JAWP; OuHeWo; WBP
  "I felt a spirit of love begin to stir," XV. AWP; JAWP; PreP; WBP
  "Ladies that have intelligence in love," X. AWP; LiTW; OuHeWo; WoL
  (Canzone.) LiA; LyPI
  "Love and the gentle heart are one same thing," XI. AWP; OuHeWo
  "Love hath so long possessed me for his own," XVIII. AWP; OuHeWo
  "Love's pallor and the semblance of deep ruth," XXIV. AWP; JAWP; WBP
  "Mine eyes beheld the blessed pity spring," XXIII. AWP; LiTW
  (Sonnet.) LyMA
  "My lady carries love within her eyes," XII. AWP; JAWP; OnPM; WBP
  (Sonnet.) LyPI
  (Within Her Eyes.) LiTW
  "My lady looks so gentle and so pure," XVI. AWP; JAWP; WBP
  (Sonnet.) LyPI
On the Death of Beatrice: The Dream. MeRV
  "Song, 'tis my will that thou do seek out Love," V. AWP
Sonnet: "Beatrice is gone up into high Heaven," *fr.* XIX. GoBC
Sonnet: "With sighs my bosom always laboureth," *fr.* XIX, *sl. abr.* GoBC
Sonnet: "Wonderfully out of the beautiful form," *fr.* XIX. GoBC
  "Stay now with me, and list to my sighs," XX. AWP
  "That lady of all gentle memories," XXII. AWP
  "Thoughts are broken in my memory, The," VIII. AWP; JAWP; WBP
  "To every heart which the sweet pain doth move," I. AWP; OnPM
  (Sonnet.) LyPI
  "Very bitter weeping that ye made, The," XXV. AWP
  "Very pitiful lady, very young, A," XIV. AWP; JAWP; WBP

  "Weep, Lovers, sith Love's very self doth weep," *fr.* III. AWP
  (On the Death of Beatrice, 2.) MeRV
  "Whatever while the thought comes over me," XXI. AWP; JAWP; WBP
  "Woe's me! by dint of all these sighs that come," XXVII. AWP
  "Ye pilgrim-folk, advancing pensively," XXVIII. AWP; JAWP; WBP
  (Sonnet.) LyPI
  ("Ye pilgrims, who with pensive aspect go," *tr.* by Louise I. Guiney.) CAW
  "You that thus wear a modest countenance," *fr.* XIII. AWP
Vita Nuova. Sir William Watson. OBVV
Vitae Summa Brevis Spem Nos Vetat Incohare Longam. Ernest Dowson. AWP; BLV; CBOV; ChTr; HBV; InPo; JAWP; LBBV; OBEV (new ed.); OQP; POTT; PoVP; SBA; TOP; TrGrPo; ViBoPo; ViPP; VLEP; WBP; WGRP; WHA
  (Envoy: "They are not long, the weeping and the laughter.") MBP; MoBrPo; NeMA
  (They Are Not Long.) EnLit; PoRA
Vitai Lampada. Sir Henry Newbolt. BLPA; MaRV; NeHB; OQP; PCN; PoeT; PoMa; POT; QP-2; TCEP; TCPD; TreF; TVSH; YT
  (Play the Game.) BBV; BTP
Vital Spark of Heavenly Flame! Pope. *See* Dying Christian to His Soul, Tne.
Vivamus Mea Lesbia atque Amemus. Thomas Campion. *See* My Sweetest Lesbia.
Vivamus Mea Lesbia atque Amemus. Ben Jonson. *See* Come, My Celia, Let Us Prove.
"Vive Hodie." Theognis, *tr. fr. Greek* by F. L. Lucas. GrPE
Vive Hodie. Unknown, *tr. fr. Greek* by F. L. Lucas. *Fr.* Anacreontea. GrPE
Vive la France. Charlotte Holmes Crawford. BoHiPo; POT
Vivérols. David Starr Jordan. AA
Vivian's Speech. John Davidson. BSV
Vivid, alone, against the wide expanse. Pedro. Phoebe W. Hoffman. GoVe
Vivien's Song. Tennyson. *See* In Love, if Love Be Love.
Vixen Woman, The. Harold Monro. *Fr.* Natural History. OBMV
Vixi. At. to Charles Mackay. HBV
Vixi Puellis Nuper Idoneus. Sir Thomas Wyatt. *See* Lover Showeth How He Is Forsaken of Such as He Sometime Enjoyed, The.
Vizier's Apology, The. Arthur Guiterman. PoeMoYo
Vladimir Ilyich-Lenin, *sel.* Vladimir Mayakovsky, *tr. fr. Russian* by Jack Lindsay.
Death of Lenin, The. RuPo
Vobiscum Est Iope. Thomas Campion. *See* When Thou Must Home.
Vocation. W. H. Auden. *Fr.* The Quest. ChMo
Vocation. Sister Mary David. PraNu
Vocation. John Drinkwater. BMEP
Vocation. Rabindranath Tagore. FaPON; GaP
Vocation of St. Francis, The. Sister Mary Eleanore. SaFP; WHL
Vocation of the Mirror. Jorge Carrera Andrade, *tr. fr. Spanish* by Muna Lee. AnCL
Vogue of the Tar-Brush. Aristophanes, *tr. fr. Greek* by Benjamin Bickley Rogers. *Fr.* The Wasps. GrR
Voice, The. Matthew Arnold. GEPC; GTML; ViPP
Voice, A. Samuel Valentine Cole. OQP; QP-1
Voice, The. Norman Gale. HBV; OHIP
Voice. Zona Gale. OQP; QP-2
Voice, The. W. W. Gibson. CV; TCPD
Voice, The. Thomas Hardy. CoEV; EnLoPo; FaBoEn; MoVE; NP; OAEP (2d ed.); PoEL-5; ViPP
Voice, The. Richard Mansfield. POTE
Voice, The. Sister Maris Stella. GoBC
Voice, The. Henri de Régnier, *tr. fr. French* by Alan Conder. TrFP
Voice, The. Vissarion Sayanov, *tr. fr. Russian* by C. M. Bowra. BoRS
Voice. Harriet Prescott Spofford. AA
Voice, The. Sara Teasdale. ChMo; CMP; NV
Voice, A. Tennyson. *See* Voice by the Cedar Tree, A.
Voice, The. Edmund Wilson. TwAmPo
Voice, The. W. B. Yeats. *See* Fairy Song.
Voice, a voice, that is borne on the Holy Way, A! When Pestilence Strikes. Sophocles. *Fr.* Oedipus Rex. GrR
Voice and Nothing Else, A. Unknown. LPS-3
Voice and the Dusk, The. Duncan Campbell Scott. CPG; OCL
Voice and the Peak, The. Tennyson. BPN; EmBrPo; EPN; PoVP; VLEP
Voice before April, A. Briton Niven Busch. CAG
Voice by the Cedar Tree, A. Tennyson. Maud, Pt. I, v. AtBAP; HBV
  (Voice, A.) BLV
  ("Voice by the cedar tree, A.") BPN; GEPC

Voice from a Grave, A. A. E. Housman. *See* Is My Team Ploughing?
Voice from Galilee, The. Horatius Bonar. *See* I Heard the Voice of Jesus Say.
Voice from heaven was heard on earth, A. St. Andrew's Voyage to Mermedonia. *Unknown. Fr.* Andreas. AnOE
Voice from the Chorus. Aleksandr Blok, *tr. fr. Russian by* C. M. Bowra. BoR
Voice from the dark is calling me, A. Divorce. Anna Wickham. MBP; MoBrPo
Voice from the Invisible World, A. Goethe, *tr. fr. German by* James Clarence Mangan. AWP; JAWP; WBP
Voice from the Nile, A. James Thomson. EmBrPo
Voice from the sea to the mountains, A. The Great Voices. Charles Timothy Brooks. HBV
Voice from the Waters, A. Thomas Lovell Beddoes. *See* Dirge: "Swallow leaves her nest, The."
Voice from the Well of Life Speaks to the Maiden, The. George Peele. *See* Song at the Well, The.
Voice from the West, A. Alfred Austin. *See* To America.
Voice from the Whirlwind, The; God's Majesty. Job, Bible, *O.T. See* Voice Out of the Whirlwind Answers Job, The.
Voice from under the Table, A. Richard Wilbur. NePoEA
Voice in a Cathedral. Thomas Curtis Clark. ChIP
Voice in Darkness. Richard Dehmel, *tr. fr. German by* Margarete Münsterberg. AWP; JAWP; WBP
Voice in the Air [Singing]. Shelley. *See* Life of Life.
Voice in the Scented Night, A. Austin Dobson. PFE
Voice in the Wild Oak, The. Henry Clarence Kendall. VA
Voice, Marvellous voice. Circe. Alfred Kreymborg. MAPA
Voice of a Bird, The. Alice Meynell. TCPD
Voice of an Alumnus, The. S. N. Whitney. CAG
Voice of Beauty Drowned, The. *Unknown.* PtOT
Voice of Christmas, The. Harry Kemp. HBV; MaRV; OQP; POT; PoTo; QP-1
Voice of D. G. R., The. Sir Edmund Gosse. VA
Voice of England is a trumpet tone, The. England. George Edgar Montgomery. AA
Voice of Enlightenment, The. Euripides, *tr. fr. Greek by* Arthur S. Way. *Fr.* Suppliants. GrR
Voice of God, The. Katherine R. Barnard. BLRP; WBLP
Voice of God, The. Louis I. Newman. OQP; PoToHe; QP-2; TreF
Voice of God, The. James Stephens. WGRP
Voice of God Is Calling, The. John Haynes Holmes. MaRV
Voice of God Out of the Whirlwind, The. Job, Bible, *O.T. See* Voice Out of the Whirlwind Answers Job, The.
Voice of Heraclitus, The—"Why fret me with disputations." Heraclitus to His Popular Critics. *Unknown.* GrPE
Voice of Hypocrisy, The. Euripides, *tr. fr. Greek by* Hugh Owen Meredith. *Fr.* Orestes. GrR
Voice of my beloved, The. Arise, My Love, My Fair One [*or* Love Lyrics]. Song of Solomon, Bible, *O.T.* EnLi-1; LiTW; LoPo; OuHeWo
Voice of Nature, The. Robert Bridges. ChMo; CMP; PoVP
Voice of Song. Steingrímur Thorsteinsson, *tr. fr. Icelandic by* Jakobina Johnson. IcP
Voice of sorrow and a sound of weeping, A. Ode on the Death of Don Sebastian. Fernando de Herrera. TeCS
Voice of Spring, The. Felicia Dorothea Hemans. OTPC (1946 ed.); PECK; PEOR; PTA-2
Voice of Spring, The. Mary Howitt. *See* Coming of Spring, The.
Voice of summer, keen and shrill. To a Cricket. William Cox Bennett. BoTP; GN; HBV; OTPC
Voice of the Announcer. Archibald MacLeish. *Fr.* The Fall of the City. HoPM
Voice of the Bard, The. Blake. *See* Hear the Voice of the Bard.
Voice of the deeps thou art! But not the wild. Emerson. Craven Langstroth Betts. GA
Voice of the Dove, The. Joaquin Miller. AA
Voice of the Grass, The. Sarah Roberts Boyle. AA; DD, *abr.;* HBV; HBVY, *abr.;* LPS-2; PCH, *abr.;* PRWS, *abr.;* SN
(Song of the Grass, The, *abr., wr. at. to* Leigh Hunt.) BoTP
Voice of the Hills, The. Satyrus, *tr. fr. Greek by* F. L. Lucas. GrPE
Voice of the last cricket, The. Splinter. Carl Sandburg. FaPON; SUS; TiPo; UTS
Voice of the Last Trumpet Blown by the Seventh Angel, The, *sel.* Robert Crowley.
"Ye robbed, ye spoiled, ye bought, ye sold." PoFr
Voice of the Lobster, The. "Lewis Carroll." *Fr.* Alice's Adventures in Wonderland, *ch.* 10. SAS; SiTL
(Lobster, The.) BoN
Voice of the Pine, The. Richard Watson Gilder. ADAH; SN
Voice of the Poor, The. Lady Wilde. VA
Voice of the river running through Chamonix. Chamonix. George Hookham. OBVV
Voice of the Studio Announcer. Archibald MacLeish. *Fr.* The Fall of the City. HoPM
Voice of the Void, The. George Parsons Lathrop. AA
Voice of the Western Wind. Edmund Clarence Stedman. HBV
Voice of Thought, The. Thomas Holley Chivers. AnAmPo; APW; LA; MOAP; SPP
Voice of Toil, The. William Morris. AnFE; BMEP; BPN; CoBE; EmBrPo; EPN; HBV; POTT; PoVP; TCEP; VLEP
Voice of Webster, The, *sel.* Robert Underwood Johnson.
"Silence was envious of the only voice." AA
Voice on the winds, A. To Morfydd. Lionel Johnson. AnIV; GTIV; LBBV; MBP; MoBrPo; OBMV; POTT; PoVP; ThWaDe; ViPP; VLEP
Voice Out of the Whirlwind Answers Job, The. Job, XXXVIII–XLII, Bible, *O.T.* EM-1
(God Replies, XXXVIII: 2–41.) TrGrPo
(Inscrutable Mystery, The, *sels. fr.* XXXVIII–XL.) GrCo-2
(Job, XXXIX: 19–XL: 2.) InP
(Out of the Whirlwind, XL: 7–24, XLI.) AWP; JAWP; WBP
(Then the Lord Answered, XXXVIII: 2–24, XXXIX.) AWP; JAWP; WBP
(Then the Lord Answered Job Out of the Whirlwind, XXXVIII: 1–16.) ShBV-4
(Voice from the Whirlwind, The; God's Majesty, XXXVIII: 1–41.) PG (1955 ed.)
(Voice of God Out of the Whirlwind, The, XXXVIII–XL.) CBOV
(Voice Out of the Whirlwind, The.) MaRV (XXXVIII: 2–XL: 2, *Moulton, Modern Reader's Bible*); OuHeWo (XXXVIII: 2–XLII: 6)
("Where wast thou when I laid the foundations of the earth?" XXXVIII: 4–38, *abr.*) ImOP
Voice peals in this end of night, A. A Thrush before Dawn. Alice Meynell. BLA; BMEP; HBMV; MBP; MoBrPo; POTT; TCEP
Voice resounds like thunder-peal, A. The Watch on the Rhine. Max Schneckenburger. HBV
Voice, A, said, "Follow, follow"; and I rose. Two Pursuits. Christina Rossetti. EmBrPo; EPN; POTT
Voice, The, said, "Hurl her down!" The Lovely Shall Be Choosers. Robert Frost. AmP; CoBMV; CoV; MAP; MoAB; MoAmPo; OxBA
Voice Sings, A. Samuel Taylor Coleridge. *See* Invocation, An: "Hear, sweet spirit."
Voice Speaks from the Well, A. George Peele. *Fr.* The Old Wives' Tale. FaBoCh; LoGBV; OBSC; OxBoLi; RiBV; SiTL
Voice That Beautifies the Land, The. *Tr. fr. Navajo Indian by* Washington Matthews. AWP; JAWP; WBP
Voice that breathed o'er Eden, The. Holy Matrimony. John Keble. HBV; MaRV; VA
Voice that resounds from pole to pole, The. Sonnet. Jean Ogier de Gombauld. LiA
Voice was speaking, known to many ears, A. "The Spoken Word." Christopher Morley. PoFr
Voice went over the waters, A. Cuba to Columbia. Will Carleton. MC; PAH
Voice, with what emulous fire thou singest free hearts of old fashion. To-Day. Helen Gray Cone. LBMV
Voiceless, The. Oliver Wendell Holmes. *Fr.* The Autocrat of the Breakfast Table, *ch.* 12. AA; BAP; CoBA; IAP; TCAP; ViBoPo
Voiceless my robe when I dwell on the earth. A Swan. *Unknown.* BEL
Voices. Witter Bynner. MAP; MoAmPo (1942 ed.); PCH; PoeMoYo; TSW; TSWC
Voices. Walter de la Mare. UnPo (3d ed.)
Voices. James S. Hearst. MoSiPe
Voices. Homer C. House. MuM
Voices. Alexander M. Stephen. CPG
Voices, The. *Unknown.* BoHiPo; MCCG; PoMa
Voices. Louis Untermeyer. PC
Voices are crying from the dust of Tyre. No Nation Liveth unto Itself. *Unknown.* MaRV
Voices at the Window. Sir Philip Sidney. *See* Astrophel and Stella: Eleventh Song.
Voices moving about in the quiet house. Falling Asleep. Siegfried Sassoon. MBP; MCCG; MoBrPo; MoVE
Voices of Hellas, The. Laurence Binyon. NeTW
Voices of Heroes. Horace Gregory. PoFr; TrGrPo (1942 ed.)
Voices of Nature, The. Thomas Edward Brown. PoVP
Voices of Pine Trees, The. Rengetsu, *tr. fr. Japanese by* Asataro Miyamori. OnPM
Voices of the Air. Katherine Mansfield. HBMV
Voices of the Loved and Lost. Gerald Massey. MotAn
Voices of Women. Frank Prewett. MBP
Void Between, The. John Lancaster Spalding. *Fr.* God and the Soul. AA
Void, damned weed! that hell's dry sweetmeats art. On Tobacco. Thomas Pestel. EIL

Void of a Joyless Heart, The. Sophocles, *tr. fr. Greek by* Gilbert Murray. *Fr.* Antigone. GrR
Void that's highly embraceable, The. Chorus. Jack Kerouac. *Fr.* Mexico City Blues. NeAP
Vois loude in that light to Lucifer seide, A. The Descent into Hell. William Langland. *Fr.* The Vision of Piers Plowman. PoEL-1
Vo'k a-Comen into Church. William Barnes. OxBoCh
Vole, The. Marvin Solomon. NePoAm-2
Volo Virum Vivere Viriliter. *Unknown, tr. fr. Latin by* Helen Waddell. *Fr.* Carmina Burana. LaP
Volpone, *sels.* Ben Jonson.
"Come, my Celia, let us prove," *fr.* III, vii. AtBAP; EiL; ElSeCe; EnLi-1 (1949 ed.); MaPo; ReaPo; SiCE; WHA
(Come, My Celia.) TrGrPo
(Song to Celia.) EnL; OBS; SeCeV; SeCV-1; SiTL; TuPP
(To Celia.) FaBoEn; LoBV; ReEn; ReIE; TyEnPo
(Two Songs to Celia.) TwHP
(Vivamus Mea Lesbia atque Amemus.) EG
(Volpone's Song: To Celia.) PreP
"Good morning to the day; and, next, my gold," *fr.* I, i. AtBAP; NBE
"If thou hast wisdom, hear me, Celia," *fr.* III, vii. ViBoPo
Nano's Song, *fr.* I, ii. BoLiVe; LoBV; TrGrPo
(Fools.) ElL; TuPP
("Fools, they are the only nation.") CenL; InvP
(Fortunate Fool.) BLV
Parasite, The, *fr.* III, i. CoEV
Voltaire and Gibbon. Byron. *Fr.* Childe Harold's Pilgrimage, III. CoEV; OBRV
Voltaire at Ferney. W. H. Auden. GTBS-W; LiTA; LiTM; NePA; PoE
Voltaire, Cobbett, and Gastronomy. Winthrop Mackworth Praed. *Fr.* A Preface. RO
Volto Sciolto e Pensieri Stretti. James Clarence Mangan. IrPN
Volucre Ferrum. John Heath. SiCE
Volume II (Kinsey). David Daiches. SiTL
Voluntaries. Emerson. IAP; TCAP
Sels.
Duty ("In an age of fops and toys"), III. AnNE
(In an Age of Fops and Toys.) LiTA; MaRV; PoeMoYo
(So Nigh Is Grandeur.) HBVY; TreFS; YT
Duty ("So nigh is grandeur"), *last 4 ll. of* III. FaFP; GN; HBV; TreF; YaD
(Heroism.) BAP; OQP; QP-2
(Quatrains, II.) CBOV
"Freedom all winged expands," II. PoFr
"Stainless soldier on the walls," *fr.* IV *and* V. WGRP
Voluntarily every evening of/ Ephemeral death. The Man Closes the Shutters. Lionello Fiumi. LiTW
Volunteer, The. Herbert Asquith. LBBV; MM; OtMeF
Volunteer, The. Eldridge Jefferson Cutler. AA; IDAH; MDAH
Volunteer, The. Sir Henry Newbolt. CBE; PoeT
Volunteer, The. Frank L. Stanton. MDAH
Volunteer Organist, The. Sam Walter Foss. PTA-2
Volunteer Song, A. Joanna Baillie. DiM
Volunteers, The. William Haines Lytle. MC; PAH
Volunteer's Grave, A. William Alexander Percy. HBMV
Volunteer's Reply to the Poet, The. Roy Campbell. *Fr.* Talking Bronco. ViBoPo (1958 ed.)
Volunteers, The! the Volunteers! The Volunteers. William Haines Lytle. MC; PAH
Voluspo. *Unknown. See* Beginning and the End, The.
Voortrekker, The. Kipling. HBV
Vor a Gauguin Picture zu Singen. Kurt M. Stein. FiBHP
Vorobyev Hills. Boris Pasternak, *tr. fr. Russian.* OnHM, *tr. by* J. M. Cohen; RuPo, *tr. by* Jack Lindsay
(Sparrow Hills, *tr. by* C. M. Bowra.) BoRS
Vos Non Vobis. Edith M. Thomas. AV
Votary to His Goddess, A. Euripides, *tr. fr. Greek by* F. W. Pember. *Fr.* Hippolytus. GrR
(Garland, The, *tr. by* C. M. Bowra.) OxBG
Votary to publick zeal. To the Right Honourable Robert Walpole, Esq. Ambrose Philips. CEP
Vote, A, *sel.* Abraham Cowley.
Of Myself. ElSeCe; LPS-3; OAEP; OBS; SeCL
("This only grant me, that my means may lie.") SeEP
(Wish, A.) ReTS; WP
Votive Ode. Erasmus, *tr. fr. Greek by* J. T. Walford. ISi
Votive Song. Edward Coote Pinkney. AA; AnFE; APA; APW; CoAnAm; LEAP; OBAV
(Widow's Song, The.) BAV; IAP; MOAP; SPP
Vouchsafe, O Lord, Thy consolation. Feodor Tyutchev, *tr. fr. Russian.* BoR
Vouchsafe, O Lord, to be our guide. A Prayer for Gentlewomen and Others to Use. Nicholas Breton. SiCE
Vouchsafe to grace these rude, unpolish'd rimes. To the Dear Child of the Muses and His Ever Kind Maecenas, Master Anthony Cooke, Esquire. Michael Drayton. *Fr.* Idea's Mirrour. ReIE; SiCE; TuPP
Vouchsafe to me. The Shield. Hafsa. MooP
Vouchsafe to those that have not read the story. Agincourt [*or* England at War]. Shakespeare. King Henry V, Prologue to Act V. BHV; EV-1; LH
Vow, The. Anthony Hecht. NePoEA
Vow, The. Meleager. *See* Writ in Water.
Vow, The. Sir Edward Sherburne. SeCL
Vow-Breaker, The. Henry King. OBS; SeEP
Vow Breaker, The, *sel.* William Sampson.
"When from the wars I do return." TuPP
Vow for New Year's, A. Mary Carolyn Davies. PoToHe
Vow of the European. Ulrich Becher, *tr. fr. German by* Herman Salinger. TwGV
Vow of Vengeance, The. Homer, *tr. fr. Greek by* William Cowper. *Fr.* The Iliad, XVIII. GrR
Vow of Washington, The. Whittier. DD, *abr.*; GA, *abr.*; MC; PAH
Washington's Vow, *sel.* OHIP
Vow to Cupid, The. *Unknown, tr. fr. Latin by* John Addington Symonds. LyMA
Vow to Heavenly Venus, A. Joachim du Bellay, *tr. fr. French by* Andrew Lang. AWP
Vow to Love Faithfully [Howsoever He Be Rewarded], A. Petrarch, *tr. fr. Italian by* the Earl of Surrey. Sonnets to Laura: To Laura in Life, CXIII. BLV; EIL; ElSeCe; EnLi-1 (1949 ed.); EnLit; ES; LiTL; PIAE; PoFS; SiCE; TrGrPo; TuPP; ViBoPo
(Love's Fidelity.) AWP; JAWP; WBP
("Set me whereas the sun doth parch the green.") OnPM; PeBoSo; ReEn; SiPS
(To His Lady.) OBSC; RiBV
Vowel Englyn to the Spider. *Unknown, tr. fr. Welsh by* George Borrow. LiTW
Vowels. Arthur Rimbaud, *tr. fr. French.* AnFP, *tr. by* Louise Varèse; TrFP, *tr. by* Alan Conder
(Voyels, *tr. by* Norman Cameron.) MiFP
Vowels, The; a Riddle. Swift. *See* Riddle, A: "We are little airy creatures."
Vows. Leonard Cline. PR
Vows are vain. No suppliant breath. Upon Castara's Departure. William Habington. *Fr.* Castara. SeCL
Vox Populi. Dryden. *Fr.* The Medal. OBS
Vox Ultima Crucis. John Lydgate. OBEV; OxBoCh; StJW
"Voy wawm" said the dustman. Hymn to the Sun. Michael Roberts. FaBoCh; LoGBV
Voyage, The. Baudelaire, *tr. fr. French.* AnFP, *tr. by* Barbara Gibbs; LiTW, *tr. by* C. F. MacIntyre
Voyage. Hart Crane. *See* Voyages.
Voyage. John Lyle Donaghy. OxBI
Voyage, The. W. W. Gibson. ChMo; CMP
Voyage, The. Heine, *tr. fr. German by* John Todhunter. AWP
Voyage, The. Vachel Lindsay. MAP; MoAmPo
Voyage, The. Edwin Muir. GTBS-W; LiTM (rev. ed.)
Voyage. Vincent Starrett. LPS-1
Voyage, The. Tennyson. BPN; EmBrPo; PoVP; ViPP; VLEP
Voyage à l'Infini. Walter Conrad Arensberg. AnAmPo; LA; SBMV
Voyage of Bran, The, *sel. Unknown, tr. fr. Old Irish by* Kuno Meyer.
"Branch of the apple-tree from Emain, A." AnIL
Voyage of Democracy, The. Walt Whitman. *Fr.* Thou Mother with Thy Equal Brood. GrCo-1
Voyage of Life, The. Cynewulf, *tr. fr. Anglo-Saxon by* Charles W. Kennedy. *Fr.* Christ 2. AnOE
Voyage of Life, The. Matthew Green. *See* On Even Keel.
Voyage of Love, The. Cercidas, *tr. fr. Greek by* Gilbert Highet. GrL; OxBG
Voyage of Maeldune, The. Tennyson. PoEL-5
Voyage of the soul is simply, The. The Helmsman; an Ode. J. V. Cunningham. MoVE
Voyage of the Sun. Stesichorus, *tr. fr. Greek by* John Herman Merivale. GrR
(Setting Sun, The, *tr. by* "H. M.") OxBG
Voyage to Africa, A, *sel.* David Wright.
"Adamastor, whom Camoens and the sea." BoSA
Voyage to Cythera, A. Baudelaire, *tr. fr. French.* AnFP, *tr. by* Frederick Morgan; LiTW, *tr. by* Hubert Creekmore
Voyage to Lullaby Land, The. E. A. Brininstool. BOL
Voyage West. Archibald MacLeish. CoV
Voyage with the Nautilus, The. Mary Howitt. TVSH
Voyager upon life's sea. Paddle Your Own Canoe. Sarah K. Bolton. FaFP
Voyagers. Henry van Dyke. MaRV; PraP
(Thy Sea Is Great, Our Boats Are Small.) OQP; QP-1
Voyager's Prayer, A. *Tr. fr. Ojibwa Indian by* Tanner. WGRP
Voyager's Song, The. Edward Coote Pinkney. APW; SPP
Voyager's Song. Clement Wood. HBMV
Voyages, *sels.* Hart Crane.
"Above the fresh ruffles of the surf," I. ChMo; OxBA; Po; ReaPo
(Sea, The.) CrMA
"And yet this great wink of eternity," II. AnFE; BLV; BoLiVe (1939 ed.); CoAnAm; CoBMV; ExPo; FaBoEn;

GTBS-W; LiTM; MAP; MoAB; MoAmPo; MoPo; MoVE; NAMP; NePA; OxBA; ReaPo; Po; PoFS; TwAmPo; UnPo (3d ed.); ViBoPo (1958 ed.) (Voyage.) NP

"Infinite consanguinity it bears," III. MoPo; MoVE; OxBA; Po

"Meticulous, past midnight in clear rime," V. ChMo; MoPo; MoVE

"Where icy and bright dungeons lift," VI. AnFE; ChMo; CoAnAm; MAP; MoAB; MoAmPo; MoVE; SeCeV; TBM; TwAmPo; UnPo (3d ed.)

Voyageur. S. Frances Harrison. *Fr.* Down the River. CPG

Voyageur. R. E. Rashley. CaP

Voyaging on our way. Sailors. Théophile Gautier. TrFP

Voyels. Arthur Rimbaud. *See* Vowels.

Vulcan begat me; Minerva me taught. Description of a Gun. Pandolphus, *tr. by* Sir Thomas Wyatt. ReIE; TuPP

Vulcan contrive me such a cup. Upon Drinking in a Bowl [or The Bowl]. Earl of Rochester. CEP; EPS; EV-3; OBS; OxBoLi; SeCV-2

Vulcan Forges the Shield of Achilles. Homer. *See* Shield of Achilles, The.

Vulcan! hear your glorious task. Odes of Anacreon. *tr. by* Thomas Moore. OuHeWo

Vulcan Oh Vulcan my deare. *Unknown.* SeCSL

Vulcan's Song. John Lyly. *See* Song in Making of the Arrows, The.

Vulgar of manner, overfed. Owed to New York. Byron Rufus Newton. BLPA; NeHB; TreFS

Vulture, The. Hilaire Belloc. BMEP; HBVY; LiL; OTPC (1946 ed.); PYM; RAR; RIS; StaSt

Vulture. Aleksandr Blok, *tr. fr. Russian by* C. M. Bowra. BoR

Vulture and the Husbandman [or Husband-Man], The. Arthur Clement Hilton. CenHV; PA

Vulture eats between his meals, The. The Vulture. Hilaire Belloc. BMEP; HBVY; LiL; OTPC (1946 ed.); PYM; RAR; RIS; StaSt

Vultures. Al-Hajjam, *tr. fr. Arabic by* A. J. Arberry. MooP

W

W. James Reeves. ChTr

W. H. Davies Simplifies the Simplicities He Loves. Louis Untermeyer. WhC

WPA Worker Reflects on Suicide, A. Stewart Atkins. *See* Relief Worker Reflects on Suicide, A.

W. resteth here, that quick could never rest. *See* Wyatt resteth here . . .

Waal, yass, stranger, them's fine cows. The Branding Iron Herd. Ralph Rigby. PoOW

Wabanaki Song. *Unknown.* BoCaPo, *tr. by* Charles G. Leland; PeCV, *tr. by* Mrs. Wallace Brown

Wacs and Waves will win the war, The. World War II. *Unknown.* SiTL

Wade/ through black jade. The Fish. Marianne Moore. AnFE; APA; CoAnAm; MAP; MoAB; MoAmPo; MoVE; OnAP; OxBA; TwAmPo

Wade in de Water. *Unknown. See* God's a-Gwineter Trouble de Water.

Wading at Wellfleet. Elizabeth Bishop. AmP

Waes-hael for knight and dame. King Arthur's Waes-Hael. Robert Stephen Hawker. ISi; JKCP; OBEV; OBVV; OxBoCh; SDH

Wae's Me for Prince Charlie. William Glen. EBSV

Wae's me! wae's me! The Cauld Lad of Hilton [or The Ghost's Song *or* The Wandering Spectre]. *Unknown.* AtBAP; CH; ChTr; FaBoCh; LoGBV; OxBoLi

Wag a leg, wag a leg. *Unknown.* OxNR

Wage-Slaves to War-Makers. Ralph Cheyney. QP-2

Wages. Ibn Kharuf, *tr. fr. Arabic by* A. J. Arberry. MooP

Wages, The. Don Marquis. MaRV

Wages. Tennyson. BPN; EmBrPo; EPN; EPP; OAEP; OQP; PoVP; QP-2; TCEP; VLEP

Waggawocky. Shirley Brooks. PA

Waggoner, The. Edmund Blunden. AnFE; MM

Waggoner, The, *sel.* Wordsworth.

"'Tis spent—this burning day of June!" EnSW

Wagner. Rupert Brooke. NAMP

Wagon in the Barn, The. John Drinkwater. MoSiPe

Wagon of Life, The. Pushkin. *See* Coach of Life, The.

Wagon of the Little Sisters, The. Hugh Francis Blunt. SaFP

Wagon Train. E. L. Mayo. MiAP

Wagon Wheel Gap is a place I never saw. Localities. Carl Sandburg. Po

Wagoner of the Alleghanies, The, *sels.* Thomas Buchanan Read.

Brave at Home, The. BLP; HBV; LBAP; LPS-2; MDAH; PAP

Rising. PAH; TreFS

Valley Forge. MC; PAH

Wagoner's Lad, The (A *vers.*). *Unknown.* BaBo (Old Smoky, B *vers.*) BaBo

Wagtail and Baby. Thomas Hardy. HBMV

Waif, The. A. C. Smith. VA

Waif from days of puffs and patches. Belinda's Fan. Samuel Minturn Peck. PR

Waifs and Strays. Arthur Rimbaud, *tr. fr. French by* Jethro Bithell. WoL

Wail, element tossed by the tempest. Russia. "Andrei Bely." BoRS

Wail for Hector, The. Homer. *See* Lamentations, The.

Wail, let me hear you wail, ye woodland glades. The Lament for Bion. Moschus, *tr. by* Andrew Lang. GrL; LiA

Wail me a sad lament, ye dells and Dorian water. A Lament for Bion. Moschus, *tr. by* J. H. Hallard. EnLi-2

Wail of a waking wind in a wide-flung wheat field, The. Sea Hunger. John Hanlon Mitchell. EtS

Wail of an Editor, The. Bramwell T. Main. DoReMi

Wail of Archy, The, *sel.* Don Marquis. *Fr.* Archy and Mehitabel.

"Gods I am pent in a cockroach." FiBHP

Wail of Irish winds, The. The Parnell. Lionel Johnson. POTT

Wail of Prometheus Bound, The. Aeschylus, *tr. fr. Greek by* Elizabeth Barrett Browning. *Fr.* Prometheus Bound. WGRP

("O holy Aether, and swift-winged Winds.") GrPo

Wail of the Well, The. *Unknown.* DDA

Wail, wail, Ah for Adonis! He is lost to us, lovely Adonis! Lament for Adonis. Bion. AWP; JAWP; LiA; WoL

Wail! wail ye o'er the dead! Dirge. George Darley. *Fr.* Sylvia; or, The May Queen. OBRV

Wail'd the sweet warbler to the lonely shade. Petrarch, *tr. fr. Italian by* John Langhorne. Sonnets to Laura: To Laura in Death, XI. RO

Wailful sweetness of the violin, The. Ode to the Setting Sun. Francis Thompson. EmBrPo; GoBC; VLEP

Wailing diminutive of me, be still. Diminutivus Ululans. Francis MacNamara. OxBI

Wailing Lynx. Lew Sarett. NP

Wailing, wailing, wailing, the wind over land and sea. Rizpah. Tennyson. BEL; BMEP; BPN; DaM; EM-2; EmBrPo; EnLi-2; EPN; MotAn; PIAE; PoEL-5; PoVP; TCEP; TOP; VA; VLEP

Waillie, Waillie! *with music. Unknown, arr. by* Daniel Read and Isadora Bennett Read. AS

Wails of slow music move along the street. Honors of War. John James Piatt. BIG

Waist high sea was rolling, The. Tunnel Beach. James K. Baxter. AnNZ

Waistcoat, The. Padraic Fallon. OxBI

Wait a minute. The Green Bus. James S. Tippett. GFA

Wait, and I'll be home again. Konstantin Simonov, *tr. fr. Russian by* C. M. Bowra. BoRS

Wait but a little while. Song. Norman Gale. HBV VA

Wait! Church of God! in quiet contemplation. The Charter of Salvation. George Arthur Clarke. MaRV

Wait for Death, The. Jules Supervielle, *tr. fr. French by* Alan Conder. TrFP

Wait for the Hour. William Soutar. NeBP

Wait for the Wagon. *Unknown.* PAH

Wait here, and I'll be back, though the hours divide. Three Star Final. Conrad Aiken. OxBA

Wait! It would be insane to call. Do What You Will. Dorothy Hobson. GoBC

Wait, Kate! You skate at such a rate. To Kate, Skating Better than Her Date. David Daiches. FiBHP

"Wait. Let me think a minute," you said. The Wit. Elizabeth Bishop. NePoAm-2

Wait On. Dnyanodaya. MaRV

Wait till the Sun Shines, Nellie. Andrew B. Sterling. TreFS

Waitaki Dam. Denis Glover. AnNZ

Waiting. Harry Behn. SiSoSe; TiPo

Waiting. John Burroughs. AA; AnAmPo; AnFE; APA; BAP; BLPA; BTP; CoAnAm; DD; DDA; FaBoBe; HBV; LA; LBAP; LEAP; MaRV; NeHB; OBAV; OHFP; OQP; PC; QP-1; TreF; WGRP (My Own Shall Come to Me.) PECK

Waiting. John Davidson. ViBoPo

Waiting. John Freeman. CH

Waiting. W. E. Henley. In Hospital, II. BPN; PoVP; VLEP

Waiting. Dorothy Choate Herriman. CPG

Waiting. Alan Hodge. LO; MoP

Waiting. Victor Hugo, *tr. fr. French by* Alan Conder. TrFP

Waiting. Masaaki Shiki, *tr. fr. Japanese by* H. G. Henderson. OnPM

Waiting. Lizette Woodworth Reese. SPP

Waiting. Ts'ui Ying Ying, *tr. fr. Chinese by* Henry H. Hart. ChLP; PoHN

Waiting. Katharine Tynan. TIP

Waiting. *Unknown, tr. fr. Greek by* W. H. D. Rouse. OxBG
Waiting, The. Whittier. APW; BLV; IAP
Waiting and Peeking. V. R. Lang. NePA
Waiting Both. Thomas Hardy. ChMo; CMP; MBP; MoAB; MoBrPo; NeMA; OxBoLi; WaKn; WHA
Waiting by the Gate. Bryant. TCAP
Waiting Chords, The. Stephen Henry Thayer. AA
Waiting for Audience on a Spring Night. Tu Fu, *tr. fr. Chinese by* Kenneth Rexroth. OnPC
Waiting for Dawn. Toyohiko Kagawa, *tr. fr. Japanese by* Lois J. Erickson. SoLD
Waiting for Death. Mordecai Gebirtig, *tr. fr. Yiddish by* Joseph Leftwich. TrJP
Waiting for Death. Michelangelo, *tr. fr. Italian by* John Addington Symonds. OnPM
Waiting for Father. Mary Mapes Dodge. FAOV
Waiting for News. Richard Church. ChMP
Waiting for News. Ou-yang Hsiu, *tr. fr. Chinese.* ChLP
Waiting for news! What news? Waiting for News. Richard Church. ChMP
Waiting for Sunrise. Zygmunt Krasinski, *tr. fr. Polish by* Watson Kirkconnell. PoFr
Waiting for the Dawning. *Unknown.* BLRP
Waiting for the end, boys, waiting for the end. Just a Smack at Auden. William Empson. FaBoTw; LiTM (rev. ed.); SiTL; UnPo (3d ed.)
Waiting for the Grapes. William Maginn. LPS-1
Waiting for the Kings. Richard Lawson Gales. SDH
Waiting for the Wind. Alex Comfort. POTE
Waiting Harp, The. Gustavo Adolfo Bécquer, *tr. fr. Spanish by* Thomas Walsh. CAW
Waiting Mothers. Anne Zuker. PEDC
Waiting Soul, The. William Cowper. NBE
Waiting to Grow. *Unknown.* PEDC
Waiting today while planes roar over the seacoast. 1944—On the Invasion Coast. Jack Beeching. WaP
Waiting Watchers, The. Henry Treece. NeBP
Waitress. Karl Shapiro. FiMAP; TwAmPo
Waits, The. Margaret Deland. COAH; DD; HH
Waits, The. John Freeman. BoTP
Waits, The. Madeleine Nightingale. SDH; SUS
Waits are whining in the cold, The. From "A Vigo-Street Eclogue." Sir Owen Seaman. WhC
Wait's Carol: "Give ye good-den." Barbara Young. MoSiPe
Waiwera. Kendrick Smithyman. AnNZ
Wake, The. Robert Avrett. UnW
Wake, The. Robert Herrick. ElSeCe; EPS; EV-2
Wake, The. Tsurayuki, *tr. fr. Japanese by* Arthur Waley. WoL
Wake All the Dead! What Ho! What Ho! Sir William Davenant. *Fr.* The Law against Lovers. FaBoCh; LoGBV; PoD; SeCePo; SeCL (Song: "Wake all the dead! What hoa! What hoa!") LoBV
Wake, Awake, for Night Is Flying, *with music.* Philip Nicolai, *tr. fr. German by* Catherine Winkworth. YaCaBo
Wake Cry. Waring Cuney. BANP
Wake for Papa Montero. Nicolás Guillén, *tr. fr. Spanish by* Langston Hughes. AnCL; PoNe
Wake! for the hack can scatter into flight. Extracts from the Rubaiyat of Omar Cayenne. Gelett Burgess. BOHV
Wake! for the sun has driven in equal flight. The Golfer's Rubaiyat. H. W. Boynton. PA
Wake! For the Sun, who scatter'd into flight. Rubáiyát of Omar Khayyám. *Tr. by* Edward Fitzgerald. AtBAP; AWP; BCEP; BEL; BPN; EmBrPo; EnL; EnLi-2; EPN; EPP; EV-5; FaBoBe; FaFP; FaPON; GTBS; GTSL; HBV; JAWP; LiA; LiTB; LiTG; NeHB; OtMeF; OuHeWo; PIAE; PeP; PIR; PoEL-5; PoVP; PYM; REAL; ReaPo; SeCeV; TCEP; TOP; TrGrPo; UnPo (1st ed.); VA; ViBoPo; ViP; ViPo; ViPP; VLEP; WBP; WHA; WoL. *See also* Awake! for Morning in the bowl of Night.
Wake from thy slumbering, Heart of the Lion! Allenby Enters Jerusalem! Stephen Chalmers. PoMa
Wake her with the voice of cannon—give her colors to the morn! Freedom's Natal Day. Elizabeth M. Griswold. PEOR
Wake, Isias, lips of fragrance, lips ten times sweeter, tasted. Serenade. Marcus Argentarius. GrPE
Wake, Israel, wake! Recall today. The Banner of the Jew. Emma Lazarus. AA; OBAV; TrJP
Wake, Lady! Joanna Baillie. *See* Good Morning.
Wake Me Tomorrow. Sergei Yesenin, *tr. fr. Russian by* Jack Lindsay. RuPo
Wake me to-night, my mother dear. Christmas Bells. John Keble. COAH
Wake not, but hear me, love! Song. Lew Wallace. *Fr.* Ben-Hur. AA
Wake not for the world-heard thunder. A. E. Housman. Last Poems, XXIX. ChMo
Wake not the imprisoned power that sleeps. The Atom. Thomas Thornely. QS
Wake oh my Soule awake & raise. *Unknown.* SeCSL
Wake of the Absent, The. Gerald Griffin. TIP
Wake of Tim O'Hara, The. Robert Buchanan. VA
Wake of William Orr, The. William Drennan. GTIV; OnYI; OxBI; TIP
Wake: the silver dusk returning. Reveille. A. E. Housman. A Shropshire Lad, IV. AlDL; BEL; BMEP; BPN; ChMo; CMP; CoBE; CP; EmBrPo; EnLi-2; EnLit; EPN; FaFP; GTBS-W; LiTB; LiTM (rev. ed.); MBP; MoAB; MoBrPo; NeMA; OAEP; OuHeWo; PG; PoeMoYo; PoLFOT; PoMA; PoTo; PoVP; PYM; TCEP; TreF; TwCV; TyEnPo; ViP; ViPo
Wake thou much afflicted man. *Unknown.* SeCSL
Wake up, Jacob, day's a-breakin'. Cowboy's Gettin'-up Holler. *Unknown.* ABF; CoSo; TrAS
Wake Up, Marie. Pierre de Ronsard, *tr. fr. French by* Alan Conder. *Fr.* Amours de Marie. TrFP ("Marie, arise, my indolent sweet saint!" *tr. by* Curtis Hidden Page.) PrPoCR
Wake up, wake up, darling Corey. Darling Corey. *Unknown.* OuSiCo
Wake Up, Wake Up, Ye Drowsy Sleepers. *Unknown. See* Who's That at My Bedroom Window?
"Wake up! Wake up! you bloomin' lot." Song of the Leadville Mine Boss. Don Cameron. PoOW
"Wake up, wake up, you drowsy sleeper." The Drowsy Sleeper (A *vers.*). *Unknown.* BaBo
Wakeful all night I lay [*or* I lay all night] and thought of God. Renunciation. Wathen Mark Wilks Call. OBVV; WGRP
Wakeful, vagrant, restless thing. The Power of Fancy. Philip Freneau. AmPP; CoBA; IAP
"Waken from your sleep." The Summons. W. W. E. Ross. CaP
Waken, Lords and Ladies Gay. Sir Walter Scott. *See* Hunting Song.
Waken, O world, if you would glimpse the wonder. Resurrection. Angela Morgan. OQP; QP-1
Wakening, The. *Unknown. See* On a Time.
Wakening bugles cut the night, The. A Good-by. Ednah Proctor Clarke. AA
Wakers, The. John Freeman. HBMV; MBP; TSW
Wakeupworld, The. Countee Cullen. GoSl
Waking. John Le Gay Brereton. BoAu
Waking. Patrick MacDonogh. NeIP
Waking, The. Theodore Roethke. CoBMV; CrMA; FiMAP; Po
Waking alone in a multitude of loves when morning's light. The Marriage [*or* On the Marriage] of a Virgin. Dylan Thomas. EnLoPo; LiTM; PoE
Waking at morn, with the accustomed sigh. On the Death of His Son Vincent. Leigh Hunt. ERP
Waking by Night. Charles Brasch. *Fr.* The Estate. AnNZ
Waking from Drunkenness on a Spring Day. Li Po, *tr. fr. Chinese by* Arthur Waley. TrCh
Waking from sleep we heard the Great Lakes' tide. Horace Gregory. *Fr.* Chorus for Survival. AtBAP
Waking, he found himself in a train, andante. Slow Movement. Louis MacNeice. FaBoMo
Waking I look to Jesus on the Rood. Waking Thought. Marguerite Wilkinson. ChIP; OQP; QP-1
Waking, my eyes, and in the night. Petronius, *tr. fr. Latin by* Kenneth Rexroth. LaP
Waking of Angantyr, The. *Unknown, tr. fr. Old Norse by* Lee M. Hollander. PaOS
Waking of Spring, The. Olive Custance. VA
Waking of the Lark, The. Eric Mackay. VA
Waking Song. Thomas Heywood. *See* Pack, Clouds, Away.
Waking this morning to a glory. Something Private. Richard Church. NeTW
Waking Time. Ivy O. Eastwick. SiSoSe; TiPo (1959 ed.)
Waking Thought. Marguerite Wilkinson. ChIP; OQP; QP-1
Waking Up ("Millons of cradles up in the trees"). *Unknown.* TVC
Waking Up ("Pretty little crocus, in your cosy bed"). *Unknown.* BoTP
Waking with morning, I note the empty. The Landscape of Love. Thomas Cole. NePoAm
Waking World, The. Frank Mason North. MaRV
Waking Year, The. Emily Dickinson. *See* Lady red upon the hill, A.
Wal, no! I can't tell whar he lives. *See* Wall, no! I can't tell . . .
Wal, you see, it's a queer story, Missy. The Miner's Protégée. *Unknown.* IHA
Walam Olum. *Unknown. See* Walum-Olum.
Wald my gude [*or* gud] lady luve me best. The Garmount of Gude Ladies. Robert Henryson. EBSV; GoTS
Waldeinsamkeit. Emerson. AmPP (3d ed.); APW; HBV; IAP; OBAV; SN; WGRP
Walden (*poem*). Henry David Thoreau. CoV
Walden, *sel.* Henry David Thoreau.
Smoke, *fr. ch.* 13. AA; AmPP; AnAmPo; AnFE; AnNE; APA; AWP; BAV; CoAnAm; CoBA; IAP; InPo;

JAWP; LA; LBAP; LPS-2; MOAP; OxBA; PIR; SN; TOP; WBP
(Light-winged Smoke.) ViBoPo
(Light-winged Smoke, Icarian Bird.) CoV; OnPM
Waldere I: ". . . heard him gladly." *Unknown, tr. fr. Anglo-Saxon by* Charles W. Kennedy. AnOE
Waldere II: "Waldere addressed him, the warrior brave." *Unknown, tr. fr. Anglo-Saxon by* Charles W. Kennedy. AnOE
Wales. Norman Nicholson. ChMP
Wales—a Mourning. Walter Dowding. MoWP
Wales England wed; so I was bred. An Autobiography. Ernest Rhys. OBEV (new ed.); OBVV; POTE; PrWP; VA
Walk, The. Leonard Clark. AtBAP
Walk, The. Thomas Hardy. PoEL-5
Walk, A. Hedwig Lachmann, *tr. fr. German by* Jethro Bithell. TrJP
Walk. Rainer Maria Rilke, *tr. fr. German by* Herman Salinger. TwGV
Walk, The. W. W. E. Ross. PeCV
Walk after Dark, A. W. H. Auden. MaPo
Walk at Sunset, A. Bryant. BAV
Walk by the Charles, A. Adrienne Cecile Rich. NePoEA
Walk fast in snow. A Devonshire Rhyme. *Unknown.* BrR; MPB; SiSoSe
Walk in Jerusalem Jus' like John, *with music. Unknown.* BoAN-2
Walk in Kyoto, A. Earle Birney. GoYe
Walk in Meditation. Wordsworth. *See* Inner Vision, The.
Walk in Spring, A. K. C. Lart. BoTP
Walk in the Country, A. Galway Kinnell. NePoAm
Walk in the Country, A. Su T'ung-po, *tr. fr. Chinese by* Kenneth Rexroth. OnPC
Walk in the half light of rain. Monsoon. Kenneth Slade Alling. NePoAm
Walk in the Precepts. Moses ibn Ezra, *tr. fr. Hebrew by* Solomon Solis-Cohen. TrJP
Walk into the dark room. Halloween. Carrie Ward Lyon. HOAH
Walk into the world. Possession. Jean Starr Untermeyer. AV
Walk, Jaw-Bone, *with music.* S. S. Steele. TrAS
Walk, Mary, down de Lane, *with music. Unknown.* BoAN-2
Walk on a Winter Day. Sara Van Alstyne Allen. YeAr
Walk on Snow, A. Peter Viereck. MiAP; OnHM
Walk Past Those Houses on a Sunday Morning. Kendrick Smithyman. AnNZ
"Walk right in, Brother Wilson—how you feelin' today?" The Rain Song. Alex Rogers. BANP
Walk Slowly. Adelaide Love. BLPA
Walk to Church. John Keble. EnSW
Walk to Emmaus, The. William Cowper. StJW
Walk Together Children, *with music. Unknown.* BoAN-2
Walk with the sun. Dream Song. Lewis Alexander. PoNe
Walk with thy fellow-creatures: note the hush. Fragment. Henry Vaughan. WGRP
Walker, The. Arturo Giovannitti. AnAmPo; LA
"I hear footsteps over my head all night," *sel.* PoFr
Walker, The. Yvor Winters. NP
Walker in Nicaragua. Joaquin Miller. *See* With Walker in Nicaragua.
Walker of the Snow, The. Charles Dawson Shanly. BoCaPo (1943 ed.); OnYI; UnW; VA
Walking. Grace Ellen Glaubitz. GFA; TiPo
Walking. Thomas Traherne. BLV; ElSeCe; SeCL; TrGrPo, *abr.*
Walking alone, all only full of grief. The Most Pithy and Pleasant History of Glaucus and Scylla. Thomas Lodge. *Fr.* Scylla's Metamorphosis. ReIE
Walking along beside the beach. The Sea Bird. Keith Douglas. ChMP
Walking along the streets the other day. John Taylor. SiCE
Walking Around. "Pablo Neruda," *tr. fr. Spanish by* H. R. Hays. AnCL; LiTW
Walking at Leisure. Wang Wei, *tr. fr. Chinese.* WhP
Walking at Night. Amory Hare. NLK
Walking at Night. Henry Treece. WaP
Walking at night alone. Mozart Perhaps. John Hall Wheelock. UnS
Walking besides the lank sea-shore in February. Poem in February. Ormond Thomas. MoWP
Walking between the ruined walls. Walking in London. Wrey Gardiner. NeBP
Walking Home. *Unknown, tr. fr. Chinese by* Robert Bridges. EPP
Walking in a grove of pines. A Leisurely Indulgence. Sakutaro Hagiwara. PoLJ
Walking in a valley greene. The Shepherd's Ode. Robert Greene. *Fr.* Tullie's Love. OBSC
Walking in Beech Leaves. Andrew Young. MoVE
Walking in bright Phoebus' blaze. Dispraise of a Courtly Life. Sir Philip Sidney. LoBV; OAEP; SiCE
Walking in Bush. Basil Dowling. AnNZ
Walking in London. Wrey Gardiner. NeBP
Walking into the shadows, walking alone. Lee in the Mountains. Donald Davidson. MoVE; SPP; UnPo
Walking Next Day upon the Fatal Shore. Cyril Tourneur. *Fr.* The Atheist's Tragedy, II, i. ViBoPo; WaaP
(Drowned Soldier, A.) BHV
Walking on the step of the shingle, here. Wales. Norman Nicholson. ChMP
Walking out in morning snow. The Game. Winfield Townley Scott. AnAmPo
Walking Road, The. Richard Hughes. OBMV
Walking Sampford Way. Paul L. Grano. BoAu
Walking Song. Charles Williams. AlDL; BoTP, *abr.*; TCPD
Walking, striving. Melancholy. August Straum. OnPM
Walking through trees to cool my heat and pain. Not Dead. Robert Graves. HBMV; LBBV; LEAP
Walking to Dedham. David Wright. NeBP
Walking to the Museum. Bone Thoughts on a Dry Day. George Starbuck. GoYe
Walking to-day in your garden, O gracious lady. The Moss-Rose. Sir Henry Newbolt. HBV
Walking under the Tour. James I, King of Scotland. *See* Dawn of Love, The.
Walking with God. William Cowper. BEL; EiPP; EnLi-2 (1949 ed.); EnRP; MaRV; OAEP; OBEC; PoEL-3; PreP; TOP
(Oh! for a Closer Walk with God.) FiP; OlF; OxBoCh
(Olney Hymns.) CEP
Walking with God. *Unknown.* BLRP
Walking with Him in White. Charles Wesley. BePJ
Walking Woman, The. Sidney Keyes. *Fr.* Against a Second Coming. AtBAP; POTE
Walkley. Ebenezer Elliott. EnSW
Walks in a Forest, *sels.* Thomas Gisborne. EnSW
Summer—Noon.
Winter—Frost.
Winter—Thaw.
Walky-talky Jenny, *with music. Unknown.* AS
Wall, The. Homer. *See* Wall of the Greeks, The.
Wall, The. Eve Merriam. TrJP
Wall. Elizabeth Morrow. MaRV
Wall, The. Octavio Paz, *tr. fr. Spanish by* Dudley Fitts. AnCL
Wall, The. Arthur L. Phelps. CaP; OCL
Wall, The. Henry Reed. LiTB
Wall, The. Isidor Schneider. PG
Wall, a bony finger, The. The Sea Wall. W. Wesley Trimpi. PtPa
Wall-Flower, The. Walter Savage Landor. *See* Place Where Soon, The.
Wall-Flower, The, *abr.* John Langhorne. *Fr.* The Fables of Flora. RO
Wall-Flower, The. Henrik Wergeland. *See* To My Gillyflower.
Wall [*or* Wal], no! I can't tell whar he lives. Jim Bludso [of the Prairie Belle]. John Hay. AA; AmPP (3d ed.); AnAmPo; BAP; BAV; BBV; BeLS; BOHV; CoBA; DDA; FaBoBe; FaFP; HBV; HiLiAm; IHA; LA; LEAP; MaC; MCCG; MoAmPo (1942 ed.); NeMA; OBAV; PaA; PCD; PFY; PoeMoYo; PoMa; TreFS; YaD
Wall of his environment, The. Walls. Hervey Allen. HBMV
Wall of the Greeks, The. Homer, *tr. fr. Greek by* William Cowper. *Fr.* The Iliad, XII. GrR
(Wall, The.) OxBG
Wall of Weeping, The, *sels.* Edmond Fleg, *tr. fr. French by* Humbert Wolfe. TrJP
End of Sorrow, The.
Wandering Jew Comes to the Wall, The.
Wall should be low, as to say, The. The Wall. Arthur L. Phelps. CaP; OCL
Wallace, The, *sels.* Henry the Minstrel.
Description of Wallace, A, *fr.* IX. EBSV; GoTS
Wallace's Lament for the Graham, *fr.* X. EBSV; GoTS
War Summons the Lover, *fr.* VI. EBSV
Wallam Olum. *Unknown.* *See* Walum-Olum.
Wallet, The. La Fontaine, *tr. fr. French by* Alan Conder. TrFP
Walloping Window-Blind, The. Charles Edward Carryl. *See* Nautical Ballad, A.
Wallowing in this bloody sty. The Drunken Fisherman. Robert Lowell. AmP; CrMA; FiMAP; LiTA; LiTM (rev. ed.); MoPo; MoVE; OxBA; SeCeV
Walls. Hervey Allen. HBMV
Walls. C. P. Cavafy, *tr. fr. Modern Greek by* Rae Dalven. MoGP; TrJP
Walls. Robert Francis. CrMA
Walls. Eva Gore-Booth. MBP
Walls. Marjorie Meeker. PC
Walls. Myriam Page. ChIP
Walls and Arches, The. Giacomo Leopardi, *tr. fr. Italian by* Lorna de' Lucchi. PoFr
Walls cannot save the cities from their fate. Civitas Dei. Edith Lovejoy Pierce. MaRV

Walls have been shaded for so many years, The. The Soldier Walks under the Trees of the University. Randall Jarrell. OxBA; WaP
Walls of a house are not built of wood, brick or stone, but of truth and loyalty, The. Your House. *Unknown.* PoToHe (new ed.)
Walls of Jericho, The. Blanche Taylor Dickinson. CDC
Walls unbroken rise. It Might Be Avila. Pedro Salinas. AnSpL-2
Walnut, The. Ibn al-Qutiya, *tr. fr. Arabic by* A. J. Arberry. MooP
Walrus and the Carpenter, The. "Lewis Carroll." *Fr.* Through the Looking-Glass. BeLS; BMEP; BoChLi; BOHV; BoN; FaBoBe; FaFP; FaPON; FiBHP; GN; GoBP; HBV; HBVY; InMe; LBN; LiTB; LiTG; MaC; MBP; MCCG; NA; NeHB; OnSP; OTPC; PFE; PIR; PoRA; PoRh; PoVP; PTA-1; PYM; SAS; ShBV-1; StVeCh; TVC; TVSH; YT
"'Time has come, The,' the Walrus said," *sel.* TiPo
Walsinghame. *Unknown, at. to* Sir Walter Ralegh. *See* As You Came from the Holy Land.
Walt Whitman. Zona Gale. GA
Walt Whitman. Edwin Honig. NePA
Walt Whitman. Harrison Smith Morris. AA; DD; GA
Walt Whitman. E. A. Robinson. AmP; CoV; NePA; OxBA
Walt Whitman. Walt Whitman. *See* Song of Myself.
Walt Whitman. Francis Howard Williams. AA; DD; GA
Walt Whitman, a kosmos, of Manhattan the son. Walt Whitman. Song of Myself, XXIV. BAV; PoFr
Walter and His Dog. Eliza Lee Follen. SAS
Walter de la Mare Tells the Listener about Jack and Jill, *parody.* Louis Untermeyer. MoAmPo
Walter Lesly. *Unknown.* BaBo; ESPB
Walton's Book of Lives. Wordsworth. *Fr.* Ecclesiastical Sonnets, V. LPS-3
Waltz. Edith Sitwell. *Fr.* Façade. OAEP (2d ed.)
Waltz in, waltz in, ye little kids, and gather round my knee. The Spelling Bee at Angels. Bret Harte. StPo
Waltz in Yungay Square. "Winétt de Rokha," *tr. fr. Spanish by* H. R. Hays. AnCL
Waltzing It. William Thomas Moncrieff. UnS
Waltzing Matilda. A. B. Paterson. ChTr; StPo; WaKn; WhC (*orig. text and popular vers.*)
Waltzing Mice. David McCord. RIS
Walum [*or* Walam *or* Wallam]-Olum. *Unknown, tr. fr. Lenape Indian.*
(Walam Olum, The, *tr. by* Daniel G. Brinton.) WoL
Sels.
Deluge, The, *tr. by* C. S. Rafinesque. LiTA
On the Creation and Ontogony, *tr. by* C. S. Rafinesque. LiTA
Waly, Waly [Love Be Bonnie]. *Unknown.* BCEP; BSV; CBOV; CoEV; EV-2; LEAP; LPS-1; OBEV; ViBoPo
(Forsaken.) GTSE; GTSL; HBV
(Forsaken Bride, The.) GTBS; GTBS-D; GTBS-W
(Jamie Douglas, A *and* B *vers.*) BaBo; ViBoFo
(Jamie Douglas: Lament of Barbara, Marchioness of Douglas.) OBB; WHA
(O, Waly, Waly.) EBSV; EnSB; GoTS; OBS
("O, waly, waly, up the bank.") EG, *abr.*; EnLoPo; LO
(Waly, Waly, Gin Love Be Bonny.) BaBo
Wan/ Swan. The Bereaved Swan. Stevie Smith. FaBoTw
Wan-cheeked girl with faded eyes, A. Roses in the Subway. Dana Burnet. BAP; NV; POT; PoTo
Wan from the wild and woful West. A Song of Sorrow. Charles Battell Loomis. BOHV
Wan sun westers, faint and slow, The. Echoes, XIV. W. E. Henley. BPN
Wan-visaged Azrael, in a darkened room. Their Victory Won. Florence Earle Coates. PEDC
Wander-Lovers, The. Richard Hovey. AA; HBV; LEAP; OBAV; TCAP
Wander Lure, The. Kendall Banning. NLK
Wander-Lure. Hermann Ford Matin. DDA
Wander, oh, wander, maiden sweet. Goethe and Frederika. Henry Sidgwick. HBV
Wander-Thirst. Gerald Gould. BMEP; NLK; PoMa; POT; PoTo; StaSt; TiPo; TSW; TSWC; TVSH
(Wanderlust.) HBV
Wandered from the Antrim hills. Saint Patrick. Edwin Markham. HH
Wanderer, The. Zoë Akins. BAP; HBMV; LEAP; NLK; NP; SBMV
Wanderer, The, *sel.* Christopher Brennan.
"When window-lamps had dwindled, then I rose." MoAuPo
Wanderer, The. Austin Dobson. HBV; InP; TOP
(Rondel; the Wanderer.) Austin Dobson. MBP; MoBrPo (1942 ed.)
Wanderer, The. Eugene Field. BLP; PoOW; TVSH
Wanderer, The. Amanda Benjamin Hall. HBMV
Wanderer, The ("All day they loitered by the resting ships"). John Masefield. MCCG; TCEP
Wanderer, The, *sel.* "Owen Meredith."
Portrait, The, *fr.* II. HBV; LPS-1
Wanderer, The. William Alexander Percy. LS; SPP
Wanderer, The. Julius Polyaenus, *tr. fr. Greek by* F. L. Lucas. GrPE
Wanderer, The, *sels.* Richard Savage. BeR
Cliff and Cloud, *fr.* V.
King-Cups and a Stream, *fr.* V.
Northern Lights, *fr.* III.
Sunset and Landscape, *fr.* V.
Wintry Sunrise, A, *fr.* I.
Wanderer, The. Theognis, *tr. fr. Greek by* F. L. Lucas. GrPE
Wanderer, The. *Unknown, tr. fr. Anglo-Saxon by* Charles W. Kennedy. AnOE; EnL; LiTW; EnLi-1 (1949 ed.), *tr. by* Stith Thompson
Wanderer, The. William Carlos Williams. MAPA; TwAmPo
Wanderer, The. Wordsworth. *Fr.* The Excursion, I. EnRP; GEPC
Wanderer, The. "Yehoash," *tr. fr. Yiddish by* Isidore Goldstick. TrJP
Wanderer from the Fold, The. Emily Brontë. EmBrPo; EnLit
Wanderer is man from his birth, A. The Future. Matthew Arnold. BPN; EM-2; EmBrPo; EOAH; EPP; EV-5; GTBS; OAEP; PoVP; ViPo; VLEP
Wanderers, The. Robert Browning. *See* Song: "Over the sea our galleys went."
Wanderers. Charles Stuart Calverley. CenHV
Wanderers. Thomas Curtis Clark. ChIP; OQP; QP-1; TrPWD
Wanderers. Walter de la Mare. AlDL; CP
Wanderers. James Hebblethwaite. BoAu; NeLNL
Wanderers. Rose Myra Phillips. BPP
Wanderers, The. Arthur Symons. PoVP
Wanderers. George Sylvester Viereck. LBMV
Wanderers, chosen of God. Chosen of God. Stefan Zweig. *Fr.* Jeremiah. TrJP
Wanderer's First Night-Song, The. Goethe. *See* Wanderer's Night-Songs.
Wanderer's Grave, The. Rufus B. Sage. PoOW
Wanderer's Litany. Arthur Stringer. WGRP
Wanderer's Night-Song. Nigel Heseltine. MoWP
Wanderer's Night-Songs. Goethe, *tr. fr. German by* Longfellow.
"O'er all the hill-tops," II. AWP; InP; JAWP; LiA; WBP; WoL
(Wanderer's Second Night-Song, The.) OnPM
"Thou that from the heavens art," I. AWP; InP; JAWP; WBP; WoL
(Wanderer's First Night-Song, The.) OnPM
Wanderers outside the gates [*or* gate]. The Urn. Malcolm Cowley. AnAmPo; LA; MoVE; NP
Wanderer's Second Night-Song, The. Goethe. *See* Wanderer's Night-Songs.
Wanderer's Song, A. John Masefield. AlDL; BMEP; MBP; MCCG; MoAB; MoBrPo; NLK; PoeMoYo; PYM; TSW; TSWC
Wanderer's Song. Arthur Symons. BMEP; MBP; MoBrPo; POTT; ViBoPo
Wanderers, wanderers we are. Emigrant Song. "S. Ansky." TrJP
Wanderin' (A *and* B *vers.*), *with music. Unknown.* AS
Wandering. Hortense Flexner. HBMV
Wandering above a sea of glass. Down on My Luck. A. R. D. Fairburn. AnNZ
Wandering Ant, The. Corydon Bell. RAR
Wandering Armenian to the Swallow, The. C. A. Dodochian, *tr. fr. Armenian by* Alice Stone Blackwell. ArmLP
Wandering at Night. K'ung P'ing Chung, *tr. fr. Chinese by* Henry H. Hart. PoHN
Wandering Cowboy, The. *Unknown.* CoSo
Wandering, ever wandering. The Wanderers. Arthur Symons. PoVP
Wandering Jack. Emile Jacot. BoTP
Wandering Jew, The. *Unknown.* RO
Wandering Jew Comes to the Wall, The. Edmond Fleg, *tr. fr. French by* Humbert Wolfe. *Fr.* The Wall of Weeping. TrJP
Wandering Jew once met a man, A. The Eternal Jew. Jacob Cohen. TrJP
Wandering Knight's Song, The. *Unknown, tr. fr. Spanish by* John Gibson Lockhart. ChTr, HBV, RO
(Constancy, *tr. by* Sir John Bowring.) TeCS
(Knight's Song, The, *tr. by* Sir John Bowring.) OnPM
("My ornaments are arms.") AnSpL-1, *tr. by* Sir John Bowring; EG, *tr. by* John Gibson Lockhart
Wandering lost upon the mountains of our choice. W. H. Auden. *Fr.* In Time of War. ChMo; EnLit
Wandering Lunatic Mind, The. Edward Carpenter. WGRP
Wandering Maiden, The; or, True Love at Length United. *Unknown.* CoMu
Wandering Outlaw, The. Byron. *Fr.* Childe Harold's Pilgrimage, III. FiP
Wandering Rats, The. Heine, *tr. fr. German by* Charles Issawi. AnGP

Wandering Spectre, The. *Unknown.* *See* Cauld Lad of Hilton, The.
Wandering theatres of the seasons which have played my life, The. Curtain Curtain. André Breton. MiCF
Wandering tribe called the Siouxs, A. Prevalent Poetry. Charles Follen Adams. CenHV
Wandering up and down one day. The Cobbler. *Unknown.* BoTF
Wandering Void, The. *Unknown.* CAG
Wandering Willie. Burns. EBSV
Wandering Willie. Robert Louis Stevenson. *See* Home No More Home to Me.
Wanderings of Cain, The, *sel.* Samuel Taylor Coleridge.
Fruit Plucker, The. CH; SeCeV
(Boy in the Wilderness.) OTPC (1923 ed.)
(Fragment: "Encinctur'd with a twine of leaves.") RO
(In a Moonlight Wilderness.) FaBoCh; LoGBV
Wanderings of Heracles, The. Sophocles, *tr. fr. Greek by* Lewis Campbell. *Fr.* Trachiniae. GrR
Wanderings of Oisin, The, *sels.* W. B. Yeats.
Island of Sleep, The. TIP
"We galloped over the glossy sea." SeCePo
Wanderlust. Gerald Gould. *See* Wander-Thirst.
Wanderlust. Isabel Ecclestone Mackay. NLK
Wanderlust. Alba Zizzamia. CAG
Wand'ring Minstrel, A. W. S. Gilbert. *Fr.* The Mikado. OlF; TreFS
Wang Peng, Famous Sociologist. Paul Eldridge. PoeMoYo
Waning Moon, The. P'an Shih, *tr. fr. Chinese by* Henry H. Hart. PoHN
Waning Moon, The. Shelley. *See* Moon, The ("And like a dying lady").
Waning moon looks upward, this grey night, The. Nostalgia. D. H. Lawrence. LBBV; NP
Waning Summer. Thomas Nashe. *See* Fair Summer Droops.
Want any papers, Mister? The Newsboy. Mrs. E. T. Corbett. PTA-2
Want of You, The. Ivan Leonard Wright. BLPA; FaBoBe; NeHB
Want quickens wit: Want's pupils needs must work. The Fishermen. Theocritus. Idylls, XXI. AWP
Want to go to heab'n, when I die. To See God's Bleedin' Lam'. *Unknown.* BoAN-2
Want to trade me, do you, mistah? Oh, well, now, I reckon not. Dat Ol Mare o' Mine. Paul Laurence Dunbar. MW
Wanted. Josiah Gilbert Holland. *See* God Give Us Men.
Wanted—a Man. Edmond Clarence Stedman. IAP; PAH
Wanted, a Minister's Wife. *Unknown.* BLPA; TreFS
Wanted: Men. Ad. Kenneth Fearing. ChMo
Wanted: One Cave Man with Club. Margaret Fishback. WhC
Wanting His Desire, He Complaineth. Richard Edwards. ReIE
Wanting Is—What? Robert Browning. BPN; EmBrPo; EPN; EPP; PoVP; TCEP; VLEP
Wanton drole [*or* droll], whose harmless play. The Kitten. Joanna Baillie. CIV; DiM; PoC
Wanton Trick, The. *Unknown.* CoMu
Wanton troopers riding by, The. The Nymph Complaining for the Death of Her Fawn [*or* The Death of the White Fawn]. Andrew Marvell. AtBAP; BrBE; CH; EPS; EV-2; GoTL; HBV; LoBV; LPS-1; MePo; OBS; PoEL-2; ReEn; SeCV-1
Wanton with long delay the gay spring leaping cometh. April, 1885. Robert Bridges. BrBE; ChMo; CMP
Wantoning. Sadi, *tr. fr. Persian by* R. A. Nicholson. PeP
Wanton's Death, The. Norman Cameron. FaBoTw
Wants of Man, The. John Quincy Adams. LPS-3; PR, *sl. diff.*
Wapentake. Longfellow. AA; PtP
Wapiti, The. Ogden Nash. MoShBr
War. Guillaume Apollinaire, *tr. fr. French by* Jessie Degen *and* Richard Eberhart. WaaP
War. Blake. *See* War Song to Englishmen, A.
War. Herbert Cadett. BHV
War. Grace Ellery Channing. AA
War. Patric Dickinson. NeTW; SoV
War. Dryden. *Fr.* Alexander's Feast. TreFS
War. Sam Walter Foss. MDAH
War. Mary Fullerton. NeLNL
War. J. C. Hall. HaMV; PoN
War. Sulamith Ish-Kishor. GoYe
War. Chief Joseph. PGD
War. Joseph Langland. NePoEA
War. J. Gilchrist Lawson. WBLP
War. Richard Le Gallienne. *See* This Is War.
War. Li Po, *tr. fr. Chinese by* Rewi Alley. ChTr
War ("Ez fer war, I call it murder"). James Russell Lowell. *Fr.* The Biglow Papers, 1st Series, No. 1. MaRV
War. E. Merrill Root. OQP; QP-2
War. Shelley. *Fr.* Queen Mab, IV. LPS-2
War. Arthur Stringer. BoCaPo (1943 ed.); OCL; TwCaPo
War. Tu Fu, *tr. fr. Chinese* by Henry H. Hart. PoHN
(White Horse, The, *tr. by* Rewi Alley.) ChTr
War, The. Jones Very. IAP; TCAP
War. Hedd Wyn, *tr. fr. Welsh by* Gwyn Williams. PrWP
War:/ And the heavy hand. In Prison. Tamiko Yamamuro. SoLD
War/ I abhor,/ And yet how sweet. This Is War [*or* Illusion of War *or* War]. Richard Le Gallienne. BMEP; MaRV; OQP; QP-1
War, The: A–Z. John R. Edwards. BOHV
War and Peace. Alexander Petofi, *tr. fr. Hungarian by* Alice Stone Blackwell. PoFr
War and Washington. Jonathan Mitchell Sewall. *Fr.* Cato. GA, *much abr.*; PAH
War and Wine. Jean Le Houx, *formerly at. to* Olivier Basselin, *tr. fr. French by* Ralph N. Currey. FoS
War at Home, The. Willard Wattles. OQP; QP-2
War Bird's Burlesque, A, *with music.* *Unknown.* AS
War Cat. Dorothy L. Sayers. PoC
War Comes. Zalman Schneour, *tr. fr. Yiddish by* Joseph Leftwich. TrJP
War Cry: To Mary. Pope Leo XIII, *tr. fr. Latin by* Raymond F. Roseliep. ISi
War Dance, The. Robert V. Carr. PoOW
War Dead. Patrick Anderson. BoCaPo (1943 ed.)
War drum booms, The: all roads are bare. Thinking of My Brothers. Tu Fu. OnPM
War Drum is beating, prepare for the fight, The. We Conquer or Die. James Pierpont. MC; PAH
War Films, The. Sir Henry Newbolt. MaRV; MM
War for the Sake of Peace. James Thomson. *Fr.* Britannia. LPS-2
War God, The. Stephen Spender. BoFr; NeTW
War God wakened drowsily, The. The Awakened War God. Margaret Widdemer. WGRP
War God's Horse Song, The. *Unknown, tr. fr. Navajo by* Dane Coolidge *and* Mary Roberts Coolidge. LiTA; LoGBV
War, he sung, is toil and trouble. War. Dryden. *Fr.* Alexander's Feast. TreFS
War-Horse, The. Job, Bible, *O.T.* *See* Horse, The.
War-Horse, The. Macaulay. *Fr.* Lays of Ancient Rome: The Battle of Lake Regillus. BHV
War husks its rumours, and the yellow scurf. Steel Valley, 1938. George Woodcock. MoWP
War Hymn. Rhigas Pheraios, *tr. fr. Modern Greek by* Rae Dalven. MoGP
War in Heaven. Milton. *Fr.* Paradise Lost, VI. ExPo; PoF, *shorter sel.*
War in the Dark, The. Rolfe Humphries. NeTW
War Is Kind, *sels.* Stephen Crane.
Candid Man, The, IX. MAP; MoAmPo
Hymn: "Slant of sun on dull brown walls, A," XIV. BAP; MAP; MoAmPo
(Slant of Sun, A.) AmPP; TCAP
I Explain, VI. AA; AmP; TCAP
"In the night/ Gray, heavy clouds," XVIII.
(Peaks, The.) AA; AmP; HBV; TCAP; WGRP
"Little ink more or less, A," IV. AmPP (3d ed.); AnAmPo; LA
"Man said to the universe, A," XXI. AmPP; AnAmPo; CoBA; ImOP; InP; LA; YaD
(Man, The.) BOHV
"Newspaper is a collection of half-injustices, A," XII. AmP; CoBA; TCAP; ViBoPo
"There was a land where lived no violets," XXIII. AnAmPo; LA
(Violets, The.) AA
There Was a Man with a Tongue of Wood, XVI. LiTA; MoAmPo (1950 ed.); NePA
Trees in the Garden, The, XXVI. AmPP
War Is Kind, I (title poem). AmPP; AnAmPo; AnFE; APA; CoAnAm; HBV; InPo; LA; MOAP; OnAP; ViBoPo; WaaP
("Do not weep, maiden, for war is kind.") CoBA; LiTA
(If War Be Kind.) BAP, *abr.*
Wayfarer, The, XIII. AA; AmPP (3d ed.); BAP; CoBA; LiTA; MAP; MoAmPo; NeMA; NePA; PoMA
What? You Define Me God, *fr.* IV. AmPP (3d ed.)
War lords perish with the millions slain, The. "One World." Brent Dow Allinson. MaRV
War makes the vulgar multitude to drink. Dialogue betwixt Peace and War. Margaret Cavendish, Duchess of Newcastle. DiM
War of time O it seizes the soul tonight. Easter Eve, 1945. Muriel Rukeyser. MiAP
War-path is true and straight, The. Just One Signal. *Unknown.* PAH
War Poem. Henry Treece. MaRV
War Relief. Oliver Herford. BOHV
War Ship. *See* Warship.
War shook the land where Levi dwelt. The Field of Glory. E. A. Robinson. ChMo; CMP; HBV; MAP; MoAmPo; TBM
War Song, A. Blake. *See* War Song to Englishmen, A.
War Song, The. Tennyson. *See* Trumpet Song.

War Song. *Unknown.* ABF
War-Song of Dinas Vawr, The. Thomas Love Peacock. *Fr.* The Misfortunes of Elphin. ALV; AWP; BCEP; CBOV; EnRP; ERP; ExPo; FaBoCh; GTBS; InvP; JAWP; KN; LEAP, *abr.*, LiA; LiTG; LoBV; MuP; MyFE; OBRV; OtMeF; PIAE; ShBV-2; SoV; StPo; TOP; TVSH; ViBoPo, 4 *ll.*; WaaP; WBP; WhC
War Song of Kishon. Judges, Bible, *O.T.* *See* Song of Deborah and Barak, The.
War Song of O'Driscol. Gerald Griffin. OnYI
War Song of the Red Sea. Exodus, Bible, *O.T.* *See* Triumphal Chant.
War Song of the Saracens, The. James Elroy Flecker. *Fr.* Hassan, III, iii. GTML; MBP; MM; MoBrPo; MuP; OBVV; OtMeF; ShBV-2; WHA
War Song to Englishmen, A. Blake. *Fr.* King Edward the Third. CH; MeRV; RO; WaaP
(War.) BHV
(War Song, A.) OHIP
War Summons the Lover. Henry the Minstrel. *Fr.* The Wallace, VI. EBSV
War Swaggers. Emanuel Litvinoff. WaP
War, that for a space did fail, The. Flodden; the Last Stand. Sir Walter Scott. *Fr.* Marmion, VI. EV-4
War that we have carefully for years provoked, The. Black-out. Robinson Jeffers. LiTA; LiTM (rev. ed.); NePA; WaP
War-Time. *See* Wartime.
War-Token, The. Longfellow. *Fr.* The Courtship of Miles Standish, IV. PAH
War under Water. Joseph Rodman Drake. *Fr.* The Culprit Fay. APW
War Widow. Bertram Warr. BoCaPo (1948 ed.)
War will not always be. Prospect. Thomas Curtis Clark. PoRL
War with the Weeds, The. Keith Sinclair. AnNZ
Waradgery Tribe, The. Mary Gilmore. BoAV; NeLNL
Warblers. Marsden Hartley. AnFE; CoAnAm; TwAmPo
Ward, A, and still in bonds, one day. Regeneration. Henry Vaughan. AEV; ExPo; KN; LoBV; MeLP; MePo; OBS; SeEP
Ward has no heart, they say; but I deny it. On J. W. Ward. Samuel Rogers. ALV
Ward in the States, A. Randall Jarrell. FiMAP
Warden at ocean's gate. Liberty Enlightening the World. Edmund Clarence Stedman. PAH
Warden of the Cinque Ports, The. Longfellow. AA; AmPP (3d ed.); HBV; IAP; TCAP; WHA
Warden spoke of him as "Ninety-four," The. Five Peas on a Barrelhead. Lew Sarett. PoMa
Warden's Watch, 2 A.M., The. Robert W. Cumberland. NeTW
Warder, from his watch-tower high, The. Matin-Song. *Unknown.* WoL
Wardrobe. Sister Mary Madeleva. GoBC
Warehouses. Frederick Mortimer Clapp. VOD (1935 ed.)
Waring. Robert Browning. OtMeF; PoEL-5
Warm air blew, A,/ My wintry slothfulness beyond the stars. With Energy Renewed. Louis Untermeyer. *Fr.* Summons. GrCo-2
Warm and buoyant in his oily mail. The Whale. Erasmus Darwin. GoTP
Warm are the still and lucky miles. Song. W. H. Auden. FaBoMo; GTBS-D; POTE
Warm as a little mouse he lay. Christ Child. Henry Treece. MaRV
Warm Babies. Keith Preston. FiBHP; HBMV; WhC
Warm below us lay the desert, blue the moonlight overhead. Sunrise over the Pyramids. Lorentz Dietrichson. AnNoLy
Warm Cradle, The. Laurence Alma-Tadema. BOL
Warm flute on the cold snow. Nine Variations in a Chinese Winter Setting. Charles Tomlinson. PoN
Warm Front and the Cold, The. James Wreford Watson. BoCaPo (1948 ed.)
Warm hands, warm, daddy's gone [*or* the men have gone] to plough. *Unknown.* OxNR; PPL
Warm mist and the fitful dripping of sodden eaves. Birth. George Burt Lake. PoP
Warm of heart shall never lack a fire, The. Elizabeth J. Coatsworth. TiPo
Warm rain and pure wind, The. Alone in the Night. Li Ch'ing-chao. OnPC
Warm rain sighs and throbs upon my roses, The. Roses and Rain. Archibald T. Strong. BoAu
Warm rain whispers, A, but the earth knows best. Sonnet. Kenneth Leslie. *Fr.* By Stubborn Stars. BoCaPo; PeCV; TwCaPo
Warm summer sun. Epitaph Placed on His Daughter's Tomb [*or* Requiem]. Robert Richardson, *ad. by* "Mark Twain." BMEP; MaRV; TreF
Warm sun is failing, the bleak wind is wailing, The. Autumn; a Dirge. Shelley. AEV; CG; CH; HBV; OTPC; WP
Warm sunshine came down. Crocus. *Unknown.* GFA
Warm, weary day was departing, The. The Battle Rainbow. John Reuben Thompson. BlG
Warm, wild, rainy wind, blowing fitfully. May Morning. Celia Thaxter. AA; OBAV
Warm with the wind and sun, he said, "Today." November Furrow. Ruth Kennon. CAG
Warmed by her hand and shadowed by her hair. The Love-Letter. Dante Gabriel Rossetti. The House of Life, XI. BPN; EmBrPo; PoVP; REAL; ViPo; VLEP
Warning, The. Thomas Brown. PoP
Warning, The. Robert P. Tristram Coffin. DaM
Warning. Harold Lewis Cook. AnAmPo
Warning, The. Aldelaide Crapsey. AnAmPo; BAP; BAV; BLV; CBOV; InP; LA; MAP; MCCG; MoAmPo (1942 ed.); NeMA; NP; NV; PFE; PIAE; SBMV
Warning, The. Robert Creeley. NeAP
Warning. Jesse Douglas. WhC
Warning. W. H. Gerry. CAG
Warning. Sara Henderson Hay. MaRV
Warning, A. Heine, *tr. fr. German by* Louis Untermeyer. PoFr
Warning, The. Longfellow. CoBA
Warning, A. Coventry Patmore. EnLoPo
Warning. Clark Ashton Smith. DaM
Warning ("Let no one say he is adored"). *Unknown.* APW
Warning, A ("Thow thou be kyng of tour and town"). *Unknown.* EnLit
Warning. Margaret Widdemer. PR
Warning and Reply. Emily Brontë. GTIV; OBVV; OxBI; PoVP; TriL; VA; VLEP
Warning by the Emperor Yao, A. *Unknown, tr. fr. Chinese. Fr.* The Fountain of Old Poems. WhP
Warning for Abraham Lincoln, A. Jacinto Fombona Pachano, *tr. fr. Spanish by* Angel Flores. AnCL; PoFr; WoL
Warning to a Guest. John Holloway. NePoEA
Warning to Children. Robert Graves. FaBoCh; FaFP; GTBS-W; LoGBV; SiTL
Warning to Conquerors, A. Donagh MacDonagh. OxBI
Warning to One. Merrill Moore. MAP; MoAmPo; NP; PIAE; TrGrPo; YaD
Warnings, The. Alice Furlong. AnIV
Warp and Woof. Harry Halbisch. BLRP
Warren's Address [to the American Soldiers]. John Pierpont. AA; AnNE; APW; BoHiPo; DD; GA; GN; IDAH; LEAP; LPS-2; MC; PaA; PAH; PAP; PECK; PEDC; PTA-2
(General Joseph Warren's Address.) WBLP
(Warren's Address at Bunker Hill.) FaBoBe; HBV; HBVY; PoFr; TreF
Warrior at Nightfall, A. *Unknown, tr. fr. Japanese.* GaP
Warrior Bold, A. Edwin Thomas. OlF
Warrior bowed his crested head, and tamed his heart of fire, The. Bernardo del Carpio. Felicia Dorothea Hemans. PTA-2
Warrior Maid, The. Anna Hempstead Branch. HBV; LoEn
Warrior Passes, The. Hubert Kelley. DD; GA; LPS-1
Warrior so bold and a virgin so bright, A. Alonzo the Brave and Fair Imogine. Matthew Gregory Lewis. *Fr.* The Monk. LPS-3
Warrior to His Dead Bride, The. Adelaide Anne Procter. DiM; OBVV
Warriors and chiefs! should the shaft or the sword. Song of Saul before His Last Battle. Byron. BPN; Po
Warrior's Lament, The. Sir Owen Seaman. FiBHP
Warrior's Prayer, A. Paul Laurence Dunbar. MaRV; OQP; QP-1
Warriors, tigers, flowers of Delacroix, The. Lightning for Atmosphere. Marya Zaturenska. TwAmPo
Wars, The. Conrad Aiken. *Fr.* The Soldier. WaaP
"Wars are to be," they say, they blindly say. The Lament of the Voiceless. Laura Bell Everett. OQP; PGD; QP-2
War's Clown in the Proscenium. Gene Derwood. *See* In the Proscenium.
Wars end, and men come back from them. Legacy. Frederick Ebright. NeTW
War's Folly. Anacreon, *tr. fr. Greek by* F. L. Lucas. GrPE
Wars of Germany, The. *Unknown.* CSF
Wars we wage, The. Robert Gould Shaw. William Vaughn Moody. *Fr.* An Ode in Time of Hesitation. AA; MDAH
Wars worse then civil on Thessalian plains. Lucan. *Fr.* Pharsalia. ReIE
Warsaw, 27 September, 1939. Leo Minster. NeTW
Warsaw's last champion from her height surveyed. Poland. Thomas Campbell. *Fr.* The Pleasures of Hope. LPS-2
Warship *Dixie*, The. Frank L. Stanton. MDAH
Warship *Mari*, The. Fuyue Anzai, *tr. fr. Japanese by* Takamichi Ninomiya *and* D. J. Enright. PoLJ
War Ship of Peace. The. Samuel Lover. PAH
Warship, which bore the name *Mari*, lay at anchor again, The. The Warship *Mari*. Fuyue Anzai. PoLJ
Wartime Dawn, A. David Gascoyne. MoVE
War-Time Prayer, A. Anna Bunston de Bary. MaRV
Wartons, The. Edmund Blunden. PtP

Warty Bliggens, the Toad. Don Marquis. *Fr.* Archy and Mehitabel. FiBHP
Warum sind denn die Rosen so blass. Heine, *tr. fr. German by* Richard Garnett. AWP; JAWP; WBP
Wary of time O it seizes the soul tonight. Easter Eve. Muriel Rukeyser. NePA
Was a soule from farre away. Five Carols for Christmastide, IV. Louise Imogen Guiney. ISi
. . . was broken./ He bade a warrior abandon his horse. The Battle of Maldon. *Unknown.* AnOE
Was ever such vision to mortals sent. Northern Lights. Einar Benediktsson. IcP
Was Galahad hired. Folkways. Isabella Gardner. SiTL
Was hunting bigger prey and came upon her. Sarah Lorton. Mary Finnin. BoAV
Was I a Samurai renowned. Ballade of a Toyokuni Color-Print. W. E. Henley. BPN; PoVP
Was I to blame to trust thy lovelike teares. *Unknown.* SeCSL
Was, Is, and Yet-to-be. Ella Wheeler Wilcox. PoToHe
Was it a constancy of wind that kept. My Father. Virginia Moore. FAOV
Was it a dream, or did I see it plain? Amoretti, LXXVII. Spenser. PeBoSo; ReIE
Was it a dream? The books were men. The Wounded. Louise Louis. GoYe
Was it a dream? We sailed, I thought we sailed. A Dream. Matthew Arnold. SeCePo
Was It a Form [a Gate, a Grace]? Henry Reynolds. *See* Song: "Was it a form, a gait, a grace."
"Was it a little baby." A Tonversation with Baby. Morris Bishop. FiBHP; WhC
Was it a mirror then across a room. Mirrors. Elizabeth Jennings. NePoEA
Was it at Nazareth/ of the marvellous breath? Joy's Peak. Robert Farren. ISi
Was it because the breast had bruised the breast. Leda, the Lost. Eda Lou Walton. AnAmPo
Was it fancy, sweet nurse. Don Marquis. Grotesques, I. FiBHP
Was It for This? Rene Verlon. ChIP
Was it for this I braved a pathless, dark. A Mother before a Soldier's Monument. Winnie Lynch Rockett. PGD
Was it hundreds of years ago, my love. James Thomson. Sunday at Hampstead, III. EmBrPo
Was it I, was it I who dallied there. Ulysses Returns, III. Roselle Mercier Montgomery. BAP; HBMV; LPS-1; LS; TBM
Was it in Greece, was it in Crete. Romance. Mavis Clare Barnett. BAP
Was it Sappho's voice upon the wind to-day. In an Alameda Field. Anna Catherine Markham. BAP
Was it the proud full sail of his great verse. Sonnets, LXXXVI. Shakespeare. EM-1; InvP; NBE; OAEP; PeBoSo; PtP; ReEn; ReIE; SiCE; TwP
Was it the wind I heard starting the leaves athrill? The Hamadryad. Theodore Goodridge Roberts. CPG
Was It the Wind That Stirred? Florence Wilson Roper. UnW
Was it the wind they followed? The Mountain in the Sky. Howard McKinley Corning. MuM; NP
Was it the work[e] of Nature or of Art. Amoretti, XXI. Spenser. LiTL; PeBoSo; ReaPo
Was it worth while to paint so fair. The Morning-Glory. Florence Earle Coates. BAP; HBV
Was it wrong, dear Lady Abbess. Marcela. George Henry Miles. PraNu
Was It You? Stewart I. Long. WBLP
Was Jesus chaste? Blake. *Fr.* The Everlasting Gospel. OBRV
Was Jesus just a boy like me. Christmas "Good Night." Ethel Robb. GFA
Was never day came on my head. George Turberville. *Fr.* The Lover Abused Renounceth Love. EIL
Was never file yet half so well yfiled. The Abused Lover Seeth His Folly and Entendeth to Trust No More. Sir Thomas Wyatt. ReIE
Was never in Scotland heard nor seen. Christis Kirk of the Green *Unknown.* EBSV
Was never none other. Carol Naïve. John McClure. HBMV
Was She a Witch? Laura E. Richards. MPB
Was sorrow ever like unto our sorrow? The Voice of the Poor. Lady Wilde. VA
Was stronger than the light this heart which beat in her. Woman and Earth. Pierre Jean Jouve. MiFP
Was that the cuckoo's song? The Cuckoo's Song. Josui. MPB
Was that the landmark? What—the foolish well. The Landmark. Dante Gabriel Rossetti. The House of Life, LXVII. BPN; EmBrPo; EPN; EPP; PoVP; TCEP; ViPo
"Was that the wind?" she said. A Moment. John Todhunter. GTIV
Was There a Summer? *abr.* Irene Rathbone. DiM
Was There Another Spring? Helen Hay Whitney. AA
Was there ever message sweeter. A Message. Elizabeth Stuart Phelps Ward. PAH
Was there love once? I have forgotten her. Fulfilment. Robert Nichols. BMEP; HBMV; MBP; PtOT
Was this His coming! I had hoped to see. Ave Maria Gratia Plena. Oscar Wilde. ACP (1926 ed.); CAW; ChIP; ISi; JKCP (1926 ed.); StJW
Was this his face, and these the finding eyes. On a Portrait of Columbus. George Edward Woodberry. AA
Was This the Face. Christopher Marlowe. *Fr.* Dr. Faustus. LiTL; TrGrPo
(Faustus to Helen.) NeHB
(Faustus to the Apparition of Helen.) ReTS
(From the Tragical History of Dr. Faustus.) BoHiPo
(Helen.) BCEP; FaFP; GTBS-W; LiTB; LiTG; WHA
(Helen of Troy.) CoEV; EV-1; LiA
("Was this the face that launched [*or* lancht] a thousand ships [*or* shippes]?") AtBAP; EtPaEn; InP; LEAP; LoPS; PIAE; TreF; ViBoPo
Was this the flaming thunderbolt of Jove. The Meteorite. Arthur Guiterman. MuM
Was Worm. May Swenson. GoTP
Was yon a charger, or. Meteor. Al-Haitham. MooP
Was you ever down in Mobile bay? Mobile Bay. *Unknown.* SoAmSa
Was you ever in Quebec? Highland Laddie. *Unknown.* SoAmSa
Wash-Day. *See* Washday.
Wash Dolly Up like That. "Eleanor Kirk." PEOR
Wash, hands, wash. A Rhyme for Washing Hands. *Unknown.* BoTP
Wash is hanging on the line, The. Windy Wash Day. Dorothy Aldis. TiPo
Wash Me Whiter than Snow. Charles Wesley. BePJ
Wash of Cold River. Hilda Doolittle ("H. D."). ChMo; CMP
Wash the dishes, wipe the dishes. Mother Goose. BrR; OxNR
Wash your hands, or else the fire. Christmas Eve—Another to the Maids. Robert Herrick. OHIP
Wash-Day. Lilian McCrea. BoTP
Washday. Elizabeth F. Upson. GFA
Washed by the rain, dust and grime are laid. Starting Early from the Ch'u-ch'eng Inn. Po Chü-i. TrCh
Washed in the blood of the brave and the blooming. God Save the Flag. Oliver Wendell Holmes. FaFP; OHFP
Washer of the Ford, The. "Fiona Macleod." LBBV; PoVP
Washers of the Shroud, The. James Russell Lowell. CoBA; HBV; IAP; PAH; PAP; TCAP
Washer-Woman, The. Otto Leland Bohanan. BANP
Washerwoman's Song. L. A. G. Strong. YT
Washing. John Drinkwater. FaPON; StVeCh
Washing and Dressing. Ann Taylor. SAS
Washing Day. *Unknown.* CoMu
Washing hanging from the lemon tree, The. The Five-Day Rain. Denise Levertov. NeAP
Washing hangs upon the line, A. Songs for a Colored Singer. Elizabeth Bishop. MiAP; PoNe
Washing the Corpse. Rainer Maria Rilke, *tr. fr. German by* Randall Jarrell. AnGP
Washing-up Song, The. Elizabeth Gould. BoTP
Washington. Bryant. PTA-2
Washington. Byron. Ode to Napoleon Buonaparte, *st.* 19. BoHiPo; DD; GA; MC; OHIP; PaA; PAH
(Cincinnatus of the West, The.) PoRL
Washington ("Land of the West!"). Eliza Cook. WOAH
Washington. Mae Winkler Goodman. PGD
Washington ("Beneath our consecrated elm"). James Russell Lowell. *Fr.* Under the Old Elm, III. LPS-3 (*abr.*, *fr.* III, V, *and* VI)
(New-come Chief.) GA (*fr.* III *and* VII); MC (*fr.* III)
Washington ("Soldier and statesman, rarest union"). James Russell Lowell. *Fr.* Under the Old Elm, V. DD; GN; HH; MC; MW, *abr.;* OHIP; OQP, *abr.;* OTPC; PSO, *abr.;* QP-1, *abr.*
(George Washington.) GrCo-2
(Ours, and All Men's.) PGD
(Washington under the Old Elm.) PEDC
Washington ("What figure more immovably august"). James Russell Lowell. *Fr.* Under the Old Elm, V. GA
Washington. Geraldine Meyrich. OHIP
Washington. Harriet Monroe. *Fr.* Commemoration Ode. AA; FaBoBe; MaRV; OQP; PoRL; QP-1; WOAH
Washington. Denis O'Crowley. OHIP; PoRL
Washington. John A. Prentice. OHIP
Washington. James Jeffrey Roche. GA; MC; PAH
Sels.
First Citizen. PGD
"No angel led our Chieftain's steps aright." DD
Washington. Robert Haven Schauffler. PaA
Washington. Nancy Byrd Turner. FaPON; MPB; TiPo; YeAr
Washington. B. Y. Williams. OQP; PGD; QP-1

Washington. Mary Wingate. HH; OHIP; PSO; WOAH
(When Shall We See Thy Like Again?) PGD
Washington and Lincoln. Wendell Phillips Stafford. PGD; PSO
Washington at Trenton. Richard Watson Gilder. WOAH
Washington at Valley Forge. R. G. Sutherland. WOAH
Washington Cathedral. Karl Shapiro. MiAP
Washington led armies. Footnote to History. Elizabeth J. Coatsworth. SiSoSe
Washington, Lincoln, and the American Flag, *sel. Unknown.* Patriotic Band, The. FOAH
Washington McNeeley. Edgar Lee Masters. *Fr.* Spoon River Anthology. SBMV
Washington, man of mystery. *Unknown.* RIS
Washington-Month. Will Carleton. WOAH
Washington Monument, The. Alma Adams Wiley. PEDC
Washington Monument by Night. Carl Sandburg. ChMo; CMP; FaPON; OHIP
Washington Sequoia, The, *sel.* Milicent Washburn Shinn. Yosemite. AA
Washington, the brave, the wise the good. Inscription at Mount Vernon. *Unknown.* PoRL
Washington under the Old Elm. James Russell Lowell. *See* Washington ("Soldier and statesman, rarest union").
Washington's Birthday. Arthur J. Burdick. OHIP
Washington's Birthday. Hezekiah Butterworth. PTA-2
Washington's Birthday. Charles S. Davis. HH
Washington's Birthday. Oliver Wendell Holmes. *See* Ode for Washington's Birthday.
Washington's Birthday. George Howland. WOAH
Washington's Birthday. Margaret E. Sangster. GA; HH; PEDC; PEOR; WOAH
Washington's Last Birthday. Alfred Noyes. PoMa
Washington's Monument. *Unknown.* OHIP; PAH
Washington's Name in the Hall of Fame. Margaret E. Sangster. WOAH
Washington's Song. Edmond S. Meany. PoRL
Washington's Statue. Henry T. Tuckerman. AA; WOAH
Washington's Tomb. Ruth Lawrence. OHIP
Washington's Vow. Whittier. *See* Vow of Washington, The.
Wasn't it pleasant, O brother mine. Out to Old Aunt Mary's. James Whitcomb Riley. BPP; FaFP; OHFP
Wasn't this the site, asked the historian. House and Land. Allen Curnow. AnNZ
Wasp, The. "Fiona Macleod." BMEP; BoTP; FaPON; PCH; TSW
Wasp, The. Eden Phillpotts. BMEP
Wasp Bite Nobi on Her Conch-Eye, A, *with music. Unknown.* OuSiCo
Wasp nests and yaller jackets. Cowboy Boasting Chants. *Unknown.* ABF
Wasps, The, *sels.* Aristophanes, *tr. fr. Greek.*
"Amateur, driving too fast, An," *ad. by* F. A. Wright. LiBL
Mock Trial, *tr. by* Benjamin Bickley Rogers. GrR
(Trial of the Dog, The, *tr. by* George Allen.) OxBG
Politics and Perquisites, *tr. by* Benjamin Bickley Rogers. GrR
Vogue of the Tar-Brush, *tr. by* Benjamin Bickley Rogers. GrR
Wasps. Homer, *tr. fr. Greek by* F. L. Lucas. *Fr.* The Iliad, XII. GrPE
Wasp's Frolic, The. *Unknown.* PAH
Wassail. John Bale. *See* Wassail, Wassail.
Wassail, The. Robert Herrick. AnEC; EPS
Wassail Chorus at the Mermaid Tavern. Theodore Watts-Dunton. BMEP; OBEV (1st ed.)
Wassail Song, The ("Here we come a-wassailing"). *Unknown. See* Here We Come a-Wassailing.
Wassail Song ("Wassail! Wassail! all round the town"). *Unknown. See* Wassail, Wassail, All over the Town.
Wassail, Wassail. John Bale. *Fr.* King John. ChTr
(Wassail.) AnEC
("Wassail, wassail, out of the milk-pail.") TuPP
Wassail, Wassail, All over the Town. *Unknown.* AnEC; YaCaBo, *with music, diff. vers.*
(Wassail Song, *diff. vers.*) OHIP
Wassail! wassail! all over the town. Wassailer's Song. Robert Southwell. COAH; OHIP
Wassail! Wassail! all round the town. Wassail Song. *Unknown.* OHIP
Wassail, wassail, out of the milk pail. Wassail, Wassail [*or* Wassail]. John Bale. *Fr.* King John. AnEC; ChTr; TuPP
Wassail, Wassail, Wassail, Sing We. *Unknown.* AnEC
Wassailers' Carol, The. *Unknown. See* Here We Come a-Wassailing.
Wassailer's Song. Robert Southwell. COAH; OHIP
Wassell wassell wassell wassell. *Unknown.* SeCSL
Waste. Harry Graham. LiTG; SiTL
(Aunt Maud.) MoShBr
Waste. Edward Shanks. LBBV
Waste Land, The. T. S. Eliot. AmPo; AmPP; AtBAP; ATP (1953 ed.); CoBMV; EnLit; FaBoMo; LiTA; LiTM; MoAB; MoAmPo (1950 ed.); MoPo; MoVE; NePA; OAEP (2d ed.); OxBA; ReaPo; ReMP; UnPo (3d ed.)
Sels.
Death by Water, IV. CaAE; PoD
Game of Chess, A, II. PreP
Waste Not Your Hour. Omar Khayyám, *tr. fr. Persian by* Edward Fitzgerald. *Fr.* The Rubáiyát. OnPM
Waste of land, a sodden plain, A. Death the Peacemaker. Ellen H. Flagg. BIG; MDAH
Waste of War, The. William L. Stidger. PGD
Waste Places, The. James Stephens. CBOV; ChMo; CMP; GTML; HBV; NP; NV; ReaPo
(In Waste Places.) GTSL; MBP; MoAB; MoBrPo; MoVE; PoFr; TCPD
Wasted Ammunition. Stoddard King. InMe
Wasted Day, A. Frances Cornford. HBMV; MBP; MoBrPo; NeMA; TSW; TSWC
Wasted Hours. Medora Addison. NLK
Wasted Hours. W. H. Davies. PoTo
Wasted Sympathy, A. Winifred Howells. AA
Wasted, Weary, Wherefore Stay. Sir Walter Scott. *Fr.* Guy Mannering, *ch. 27.* BPN; EmBrPo; EnRP
(Dying Gipsy's Dirge, The.) BHV
(Gipsy's Dirge, The.) BSV
Wasteful Woman. Coventry Patmore. *See* Unthrift.
Wastes of Time, The. Lord Alfred Douglas. ES
Wasting thistle whitens on my crest, The. The Wild Knight. G. K. Chesterton. WGRP
Wastrel, The. Reginald Wright Kauffman. HBV
Wat Tyler, *sel.* Robert Southey.
"When Adam delved and Eve span," *fr.* II, i. BCEP
Watch, The. Frances Cornford. HBMV; LiTM; MBP; MoBrPo
Watch, America. Robert Nathan. WaKn
Watch Any Day [His Nonchalant Pauses]. W. H. Auden. ChMo; FaBoMo; TwCV
Watch before Dawn ("Come out, old man"). Euripides. *Fr.* Iphigenia in Aulis. *See* In the Stillness of Dawn.
Watch before Dawn, The ("Say, whose is the watch?"). Euripides. *Fr.* Rhesus. *See* Night Watch.
Watch her an' catch her an' jump her juberju. Ten Thousand Miles from Home. *Unknown.* AS
Watch Long Enough, and You Will See the Leaf. Conrad Aiken. Preludes for Memnon, XIX. ChMo; CMP; NePA; OxBA
Watch of a Swan, The. Sarah Morgan Bryan Piatt. AA
Watch on the Rhine, The. Max Schneckenburger, *tr. fr. German.* HBV
Watch on the Rhine, The. Gertrude Stein. *Fr.* Accents in Alsace. AtBAP
Watch over me while I'm asleep. To the Guardian Angel. Mme Tastu. BOL
Watch, please, this painted ballet of the fed. Uccello on the Heath. Geoffrey Grigson. WaP
Watch that near my midriff ticks, The. Pocket and Steeple. Mark Antony De Wolfe Howe. WhC
Watch the Lights Fade. Robinson Jeffers. ChMo
Watch thou and fear; tomorrow thou shalt die. The Choice, 2. Dante Gabriel Rossetti. The House of Life, LXXII. ATP; BEL; BPN; EmBrPo; EnL; EnLi-2; EPP; HBV; MyFE; OBVV; PIAE; POTT; PoVP; PreP; TOP; ViPo; VLEP
Watch-Tower of the Soul. Anna Hempstead Branch. MOAP
Watch well the poor in this late hour. Temperance Note; and Weather Prophecy. James Agee. *Fr.* Two Songs on the Economy of Abundance. MAP; MoAmPo
Watch will tell the time of day, A. Mr. Coggs [Watchmaker]. E. V. Lucas. BoTP; FaPON; GaP; GFA; HBV; HBVY; MPB
Watch Yourself Go By. Strickland Gillilan. BLPA; PoToHe
(Cure for Fault-finding, A, *abr.*) WBLP
Watcher, The. Sarah Josepha Hale. AA
Watcher, The. James Stephens. HBV; MBP; MoBrPo; OBEV (new ed.); OBVV
Watcher, The. Margaret Widdemer. CV; DD; HBMV; MaRV; OHIP; TCAP; TSW; TSWC
(Watcher, The—Mother.) OQP; QP-1
Watcher, who watchest by the bed of pain. Jesus of Nazareth Passeth By. Lydia Huntley Sigourney. BePJ; StJW
Watchers, The. Arlo Bates. AA
Watchers, The. W. S. Braithwaite. PoNe
Watchers, The. Charles Spear. AnNZ
Watchers of the Sky, *sels.* Alfred Noyes. The Torch Bearers, I.
Music of the Spheres, The. GrCo-1
Song of Jeppe, The. EPP
"This music leads us far." MaRV; OQP; QP-2
Torch Bearers, The. GrCo-1
Celeste and Galileo.
Copernicus.
Epilogue, 3 *ll.*
Herschel.
Newton.

("Fools have said/ That knowledge drives out wonder.") MaRV
Tycho Brahe.
Wotton to Kepler.
Watching. "Fanny Forester." AA; LPS-3
Watching and Wishing. Charlotte Brontë. DiM
Watching Angels. Christina Rossetti. *Fr.* Sing-Song. PPL
("Angels at the foot.") EmBrPo
Watching by a Sick-Bed. John Masefield. NP
Watching Clouds. John Farrar. StVeCh
Watching Post. C. Day Lewis. AlDL
Watching the Moon. David McCord. YeAr
Watching the night contract the viridian fields. O Rose, O Rainbow. Nicholas Moore. NeBP
Watching the Reapers. Po Chü-i, *tr. fr. Chinese by* Arthur Waley. TrCh
Watching You Walk. Ruthven Todd. LiTL; NeBP
Watchmaker's Shop, The. *Unknown.* BoTP
Watchman, The. Abraham Reisen, *tr. fr. Yiddish by* Joseph Leftwich. TrJP
Watchman, Tell Us of the Night. Sir John Bowring. OlF; TreFS
(What of the Night?) VA
Watchman, watchman on your height. The Watchman. Abraham Reisen. TrJP
Watchman, What of the Night? Isaiah, XXI: 11-15, Bible, *O.T.* AWP
Watchman, what of the night? A Ballad of the War. George Herbert Sass. BlG
Watchman, what of the night? Prologue to Morning. Hermann Hagedorn. MaRV
Watchmen have waited on Capitol Hill, The. Signal Fires. Edward Everett Hale. From Potomac to Merrimac, II. PAH
Watchmen of the Night. Cecil Roberts. VOD (1931 ed.)
Water. Hermann Claudius, *tr. fr. German by* Herman Salinger. TwGV
Water. Hilda Conkling. ExPo; NP; TiPo
Water. John R. Crossland. BoTP
Water. Emerson. PoEL-4
Water. Ibn Saad al-Khair, *tr. fr. Arabic by* A. J. Arberry. MooP
Water. Christian Morgenstern, *tr. fr. German by* Lola Gruenthal. AnGP
Water, *sel.* Kathleen Raine.
"There is a stream that flowed before the first beginning." ImOP
Water and Air. Robert Browning. *Fr.* Pauline. OBRV
Water Babies, The, *sels.* Charles Kingsley.
Clear and Cool. GN; PC
(Song of the River.) LPS-2; SN
(Tide River, The.) HBV; PoVP
Lost Doll, The. FaPON; MoShBr; MPB; OTPC; PRWS; TVC; TVSH
("I once had a sweet little doll, dears.") TiPo
Young and Old. AlDl; EV-5; FaBoBe; FaFP; FAOV; GTBS; GTBS-W; GTSL; HBV; InP; LiTG; MCCG; OTPC; PoMa; PoVP; SiTL; TreF; TSW; TSWC
(Old, Old Song, The.) BTP; MaRV; PYM
(Old Song, The.) NeHB; OBVV; PFE; PG; TOP; WaKn
(When All the World Is Young.) BBV (1923 ed.); BoTP; LiTL; ViBoPo
Water-Boy. *Unknown.* APW; SPP; TrGrPo
Water brimmed against the shore. Lake, Mountain, Tree. Dennis Glover. AnNZ
Water bring, and bring me wine. Nunc Est Bibendum. Anacreon. GrL; OxBG
Water, cease singing on the height. Song of Babek. Ilya Selvinsky. *Fr.* The Man with an Eagle on His Shoulder. RuPo
Water clangs, the crystal flies in shivers, The. The Centaur's Bath. Luis G. Urbina. AnMP
Water-Colour of Venice, A. Lawrence Durrell. FaBoMo
Water-Cooler, The. Sharaf al-Din, *tr. fr. Arabic by* A. J. Arberry. MooP
Water does not sing on the wheel, The. Perpetual Motion. Gerardo Diego. CoSP
Water down the rocky wall, The. The Bunyip. Douglas Stewart. MoAuPo
Water-Drinker, The. Edward Johnson. LPS-2
Water Fantasy. Fannie Stearns Davis. LBMV
Water, for anguish of the solstice—nay. For "A Venetian Pastoral" by Giorgione. Dante Gabriel Rossetti. BPN; ES; GTML; POTT; PoVP; VA; ViBoPo; ViP; VLEP
Waterfront. Oliver Jenkins. EtS
Water Front. Jennie M. Palen. MuM
Water-Front. Cecil ffrench Salkeld. OnYI
Water has no color. Ilo Orleans. RIS
Water has no taste at all. Water. John R. Crossland. BoTP
Water hen is hopping, A. May Evening. Eileen Brennan. NeIP
Water-Images. Mary Elizabeth Osborn. NePoAm-2
Water in the creek glides by, The. Friction. Esther Pinch. PoMa
Water Is Burred with Rain, The. Allen Curnow. *Fr.* Not in Narrow Seas. AnNZ
Water is close to the gunwale's brink, The. The Life-Boat. Erik Lindorm. AnSL
Water is cool, there is a faint smile, The. A Bather in a Painting. Ashton Greene. NePoAm
Water Jewels. Mary Frances Butts. *See* Million Little Diamonds, A.
Water Lady, The. Thomas Hood. CH; HBV; RO; VA; ViBoPo
Water-Lilies. Felicia Dorothea Hemans. OTPC
Water-Lilies. Ibn Hamdis, *tr. fr. Arabic by* A. J. Arberry. MooP
Water-Lilies. Sara Teasdale. MAP; MoAmPo; NeMA
Water-lilies in myriads rocked on the slight undulations. On the Atchafalaya. Longfellow. *Fr.* Evangeline. AA
Water lilies of summer are gone, The. They are no more. Autumn. Su T'ung-po. OnPC
Water Lily. John Farrar. GFA
Water-Lily, The. Robert Nichols. TCPD
Water-Lily, The. John Banister Tabb. AA; ACP; ADAH; GoBC; SN
Water-Lion is the God verray, The. King Arthur's Dream. *Unknown.* ACP
Water Mill, A. Antipater of Thessalonica, *tr. fr. Greek by* Sir William Marris. OxBG
Water Mill, The. Sarah Doudney. *See* Lesson of the Water Mill, The.
Water Mill, The. Ann Hawkshaw. OTPC (1923 ed.)
Water murmurs, The. A Happy Old Man. Liu Tzu Hui. PoHN
Water Music. Alun Lewis. ChMP; GTBS-D
Water Music. "Hugh MacDiarmid." GoTS
Water Noises. Elizabeth Madox Roberts. GFA; GoBP; NP; RAR; SP; VOD
Water-Nymph and the Boy, The, *sel.* Roden Noel.
I Flung Me Round Him. HBV
("I flung me round him.") OBEV (1st ed.); OBVV
(Song of the Water-Nymph.) BMEP
Water-Nymphs. Hermocreon, *tr. fr. Greek by* Sir William Marris. OxBG
Water of Dirce, The. Edith M. Thomas. TBM
Water of life no prophet could divine. A Christening Remembered. Vernon Watkins. FaBoMo
Water of the Mirror Lake, The. A Woman of Yueh. Li Po. OnPM
Water-Ousel, The. Mary Webb. CH
Water Ouzel. William H. Matchett. NePoEA
Water Ouzel, The. Harriet Monroe. BLA; CP; NP; OTPC (1946 ed.); SBMV
Water-Party, The. Robert Bridges. CaAE
Water plunges to devour us. Travel Song. Hugo von Hofmannsthal. TrJP
Water pulls nervously whispering satin across cool roots, cold stones. Interval. Joseph Auslander. MAP; MoAmPo (1942 ed.)
Water sings along our keel, The. Armistice. Sophie Jewett. AA
Water Song. Solomon ibn Gabirol, *tr. fr. Hebrew by* Israel Abrahams. TrJP
Water still flows. Illegitimate Things. William Carlos Williams. MoAB; MoAmPo
Water-still is the shade of old Coppelius. Dr. Coppelius. Wrey Gardiner. NeBP
Water the fair lad went to seek and bring. Hylas. Theocritus. *Fr.* Idylls. OxBG
Water the first of elements we hold. To Hiero the Syracusan. Pindar. Olympian Odes, I. EnLi-2; OuHeWo
Water the ground with his tears. The Light. John Holloway. NePoEA
Water, The! the Water! William Motherwell. OTPC; PRWS
Water understands, The. Water. Emerson. PoEL-4
Water, water, wild-flower. *Unknown.* RIS
Water-Wheel, The. Abu Abd Allah, *tr. fr. Arabic by* A. J. Arberry. MooP
Water-Wheel, The. Jack R. Clemo. ChMP
Water Witch, The, *sel.* James Fenimore Cooper.
My Brigantine, *fr. ch.* 15. AA; EtS; LEAP; LPS-2
Water-Witch, The. Martha Eugenie Perry. CaP
Water, with lidless stare. Narcissus. Charles Gullans. NePoEA
Waterbirds sailing upon the darkness. Petron, the Desert Father. Lawrence Durrell. *Fr.* Eight Aspects of Melissa. NeBP
Waterdrop. Sergei Smirnov, *tr. fr. Russian by* Jack Lindsay. RuPo
Watered Lilies, The. *Unknown.* *See* For the Master's Use.
Waterfall, The. Arthur Davison Ficke. UnW
Waterfall, The. Kristján Jónsson, *tr. fr. Icelandic by* Runólfur Fjeldsted. IcP

Waterfall, The. Frank Dempster Sherman. BoChLi; OTPC (1946 ed.); PRWS
Waterfall [or Water-Fall], The. Henry Vaughan. CoBE; ElSeCe; EPS; MaPo; MeLP; MePo; MeRV; OAEP; OBS; PoE; PoEL-2; PoFS; ReaPo; SeCV-1; TwCrTr; TwHP; ViBoPo, st. 1
Waterfall and the Eglantine, The. Wordsworth. OTPC
Waterfalls of Stone. Louis Ginsberg. PIAE; PoMa
Waterfront. See Water Front.
Watergaw, The. "Hugh MacDiarmid." GoTS; NeBP
Watering Place, The. Propertius, tr. fr. Latin by Frances Fletcher. LiTW
Watering Rhyme, A. P. A. Ropes. BoTP
Waterloo ("There was a sound of revelry by night"). Byron. Fr. Childe Harold's Pilgrimage, III. BHV, abr., BLV, abr.; EPP; EV-4; FiP; LPS-2, abr.; MCCG; OBRV; PIR; TCEP; TrGrPo; WaaP; WHA
(Battle of Waterloo, The.) FaFP; HiLiEn; TreF
(Eve of the Battle of Waterloo, The.) OTPC
(Eve of Waterloo, The.) BBV, abr.; BCEP, abr.; BeLS, abr.; CBPC; FaBoBe; FaBoCh; FaBoEn; HBV; OnSP; OtMeF; PECK, abr.; PTA-2, abr.; PYM, abr.; ShBV-3
(Night before the Battle of Waterloo, The, abr.) WBLP
(Night before Waterloo.) BoHiPo; GN, abr.
("There was a sound of revelry by night.") AnFE; ViBoPo
Waterloo. Sir Aubrey De Vere. HBV
Waterloo. Winthrop Mackworth Praed. SoV
Waters. Elder Olson. NP
Waters. Kenneth Slessor. NeLNL
Waters above! Eternal springs! The Shower. Henry Vaughan. AtBAP; ChTr; OBS
Waters are flashing, The. The Fugitives. Shelley. PCH
Waters chased him as he fled, The. Emily Dickinson. PoEL-5
Waters dance on the ocean crest, The. The Conger Eel. Patrick MacGill. OnYI
Waters ill-fated, sad spinsters. Manuel Altolaguirre, tr. fr. Spanish by Eleanor L. Turnbull. CoSP
Waters in the gorge, The. Doubt. Wang Chin Chu. PoHN
Waters, The—O the waters! wild and glooming. Spanish Point. Sir Aubrey De Vere. TIP
Waters of Babylon. Louis Untermeyer. AnAmPo; LA
Waters of church windows vaulted in silence. Cathedral by Sea. Norman Levine. PeCV
Waters of Life, The. Humbert Wolfe. MBP; MoBrPo; NP
Waters of Lung-t'ou, The. Hsü Ling, tr. fr. Chinese by Arthur Waley. TrCh
Waters of Mirror Lake are white like the moon, The. A Girl of Yueh. Li Po. WhP
Waters of the Boyne. W. B. Yeats. Fr. Responsibilities. LiA
Waters of the Grand Canal, The. The Grand Canal. Wang Chih Huan. PoHN
Waters of the Sea. Cecil Goldbeck. EtS
Waters of the world in their cold chasm, The. Waters. Elder Olson. NP
Waters of Wei, The. Homesick. Ts'en Ts'an. PoHN
Waters purled, the waters swelled, The. The Fisher. Goethe. LPS-3
Waters slept, The. Night's silvery veil hung low. David's Lament for Absalom. Nathaniel P. Willis. PTA-2
Waters were Thy path, The. The Ship in the Midst of the Sea. Christopher Wordsworth. BePJ
Waters whisper softly, The. Autumn Sunset. Wang Shih Cheng. PoHN
Watershed, The. Alice Meynell. POTE; POTT
Waterspout. Luís de Camões, tr. fr. Portuguese. EtS
Waterwall Blues. Howard Moss. MoPo; NePA
Wathers o'Moyle an' the white gulls flyin'. Lookin' Back. "Moira O'Neill." TIP
Watkwenies. Duncan Campbell Scott. PeCV
Wattle and Myrtle. James Lister Cuthbertson. BoAu
Wattles were sweet with September's rain, The. Beneath the Wattle Boughs. Frances Gill. VA
Waukin' o' the Fauld, The. Allan Ramsay. See My Peggy.
Wave, The. Nordahl Grieg, tr. fr. Norwegian by Charles W. Stork. AnNoLy
Wave, The. John Curtis Underwood. EtS
Wave after wave of greenness rolling down. Perished. Mary Louise Ritter. LPS-1
Wave after wave successively rolls on. Newport Beach. Henry T. Tuckerman. LPS-2
Wave-born Queen of the Cyprian foam. Horace. Odes, I, 3. LaP
Wave high in glory over. Dannebrog (The Danish Flag). Bernhard Severin Ingemann. BoDS
Wave knows no contentment, The. L'Onda dal Mar' Divisa. Vladimir Soloviev. TrRV
Wave of Cliona, The. James Stephens, after the Irish of Egan O'Rahilly. ChMo; CMP
(Clann Cartie.) GTIV
Wave of coldness, A. Translations from Modern Japanese Poetry. Akiko Yosano. PFE
Wave plunges and the sea-birds cry, The. Power. Duncan Campbell Scott. TwCaPo
Wave, wave your glorious battle-flags, brave soldier of the North. Gettysburg. Edmund Clarence Stedman. PAH
Wave Wing. Ibn Sa'id of Alcala la Real, tr. fr. Arabic by A. J. Arberry. MooP
Wave withdrawing, The. "Dover Beach"—a Note to That Poem. Archibald MacLeish. ReaPo
"Wave ye, dark tresses! clust'ring, or apart." Not Gone Yet. John Swanwick Drennan. IrPN
Waverley, sels. Sir Walter Scott.
David Gellatley's Song, fr. ch. 14. BSV
False Love, fr. ch. 9. ViBoPo
Hie Away! fr. ch. 12. BoTP; EnRP; MoShBr; MPB; OTPC; PCD; PCH; PRWS; RAR; ViBoPo
(Gellatley's Song to the Deerhounds.) AlDL; OBRV
(Hie Away, Hie Away.) BPN; EmBrPo; EV-4; TiPo
Late When the Autumn Evening Fell, fr. ch. 5. EBSV
St. Swithin's Chair, fr. ch. 13. HOAH
Waves. Emerson. AA
Waves, sels. Boris Pasternak, tr. fr. Russian by Babette Deutsch. TrRV
"Caucasus lay spread before our gaze, The," II.
"We were in Georgia. You can get this land," I.
Waves about Iona dirge, The. To William Sharp. Clinton Scollard. HBV; LBMV
Waves are still, and touched with crimson light, The. The Sea-Bird's Cry. Edith F. Parsons. CAG
Waves are stirring, winds are playing. Adagio. Bo Bergman. AnSL
Waves come rolling, and the billowes rore, The. Sea-Monsters. Spenser. Fr. The Faerie Queene, II, 12. AtBAP; FaBoEn
Waves crowd away, The. James Macpherson. Fr. Temora. BCEP
Waves forever move, The. The Sisters. John Banister Tabb. AA; BAP; LEAP; MaRV
Waves Gleam in the Sunshine, The. Heine, tr. fr. German by Emma Lazarus. Fr. Songs to Seraphine. TrJP
Waves, grey-green as brittle glass. Midwinter Monochrome. Stanley E. Babb. HiLiAm
Waves lay down their trail, The. Evening Scene. E. J. Scovell. FaBoMo
Waves of Breffny, The. Eva Gore-Booth. See Little Waves of Breffny, The.
Waves of the ocean toll a bell, The. The Shepherdess of the Shell. Stanley Pillsbury. CAG
Waves on the Sea-Shore, The. Ann Hawkshaw. OTPC (1923 ed.)
Waves that danced about the rock have gone, The. Grandmother and Child. Ruth Dallas. AnNZ
Waves unbuild the wasting shore, The. Faith Shall Build a Fairer Throne. Oliver Wendell Holmes. MaRV
Waving a Bough. Boris Pasternak, tr. fr. Russian by Babette Deutsch. TrJP; TrRV
Waving of the Corn, The. Sidney Lanier. CoV; MOAP
Waving ripe fields glow with gold, The. Basho, tr. fr. Japanese by Lois J. Erickson. SoLD
Waxen and the false grace of tulips, The. Elegy. G. S. Fraser. NeBP
Way, The. William Stanley Braithwaite. Sandy Star and Willie Gee, IV. BANP
Way, The. Leslie Savage Clark. PGD
Way, The. Robert Creeley. NeAP
Way, The. Sidney Henry Morse. HBV
Way, The. Laura Simmons. ChIP
Way, The. Henry van Dyke. MaRV; OQP; QP-1
Way a crow, The. Dust of Snow [or Snow Dust]. Robert Frost. AmPP; BAP; ChMo; CMP; InP; MoShBr; MoSiPe; OxBA; TiPo; TwP; UnPo
Way-ah, we'll pay Paddy Doyle for his boots! Paddy Doyle. Unknown. ShS
Way Back, The. Thomas S. Jones, Jr. VOD
Way can only return, The. Tao Teh Ching, II. Unknown, tr. fr. Chinese. WhP
'Way Down in Cuba. Unknown. AmSS
Way Down in Mexico. Unknown. CoSo; CSF
Way down in the lonely valley. The Jealous Lover. Unknown. ABS
Way down in the meadow where the lily first blows. Evalina. Unknown. ABS
Way down in yonder valley/ Where the weeping willows wave. The Weeping Willow. Unknown. ABS
Way down South in Dixie. Song for a Dark Girl. Langston Hughes. CDC; PoNe
Way Down South in Mississippi. Verne Barnes. PoRL
Way down South in the land of cotton, I wrote this song. Crazy Song to the Air of "Dixie." "Andy Lee." AS
Way down South where bananas grow. The Elephant and the Flea. Unknown. TrAS
Way down South where I was born. Roll the Cotton Down, vers. III. Unknown. ShS
Way Down the Ohio, with music. Unknown. TrAS

Way down the rivuh an' I couldn't stay long. B'y Sara Burned Down. *Unknown.* StDa
Way down upon de Swanee [*or* Suwanee] Ribber [*or* River]. Old Folks at Home [*or* Swanee River]. Stephen Collins Foster. AA; APW; BAV; FaBoBe; FaFP; HBV; IAP; InP; LEAP; MotAn; OBAV; OIF; PECK; PoRL; TreF; WBLP
Way down upon the Wabash. El-a-noy. *Unknown.* AS; TrAS
Way down yonder in the maple swamp. *Unknown.* GoTP
Way, hay, there she rises. Early in the Morning. *Unknown.* AmSS
Way He Used to Do, The. James W. Foley. FAOV
'Way high up in the Mokiones, among the mountain tops. High Chin Bob. *Unknown.* SCC
Way high up in the Syree Peaks. Tying a Knot in the Devil's Tail. *Unknown.* ABF
'Way high up [*or* 'Way up high in] the Mogollons. The Glory Trail. Badger Clark. CP; IHA; PoeMoYo; SCC; SoAF; StPo
Way I read a letter's this, The. Emily Dickinson. MOAP (Letter Received, A.) CoBA
Way I would look at the world, the houses, The. Statute. Josephine Miles. FiMAP
Way is eternal and has no name, The. Tao Teh Ching, X. *Unknown, tr. fr. Chinese.* WhP
Way is long and dreary, The. The Pilgrims. Adelaide Anne Procter. UnPo
Way is long, the body overburdened, The. On Meeting a Sick Soldier. Lu Lun. WhP
Way My Ideas Think Me, The. José Garcia Villa. AnFE; CoAnAm; TwAmPo
Way O Christ Thou Art, The. Ernest De Witt Burton. MaRV
Way of a Cat, The. Margaret E. Bruner. CIV
Way of a Man, The. Lois Halderman. FAOV
Way of Cape Race, The. E. J. Pratt. CoBE; EtS
Way of Daily Living, The, *mod.* *Unknown.* TMEV
Way of Happiness, The. Bacchylides, *tr. fr. Greek by* Arthur S. Way. GrR
Way of It, The. John Vance Cheney. HBV
Way of Knowledge, The. Parmenides, *tr. fr. Greek by* T. F. Higham. OxBG
Way of Life, The. Aesopus, *tr. fr. Greek by* A. J. Butler. OxBG
Way of Life, The. *Unknown, at. to* Lao-tzu. *See* Tao Teh King.
Way of Looking, A. Elizabeth Jennings. NePoEA
Way of Perfect Love, The, *sel.* Georgiana Goddard King.
Song: "Something calls and whispers, along the city street." HBV; NLK
Way of the Air, The. Laura Riding. *Fr.* Three Sermons to the Dead. LiTA
Way of the Cross, The. Joseph I. C. Clarke. CAW
Way of the Cross, The. Leonard Feeney. WHL
Way of the Master, The. Albert E. S. Smythe. CPG
Way of the Sage, The. *At. to* Lao-tzu, *tr. fr. Chinese by* Walter Gorn Old. *Fr.* Tao Teh King. GrCo-2
Way of the Wind, The. Swinburne. VLEP
Way of the World, The. George Frederick Cameron. BoCaPo; CPG
Way of the World, The, *sel.* Congreve.
Song: "Love's but the frailty of the mind," *fr.* III. EnLi-1; SeCL; SeEP
Way of the World, The. James Jeffrey Roche. CAW; ChIP; JKCP; WBLP
Way of the World, The. Ryota, *tr. fr. Japanese by* H. G. Henderson. OnPM
Way of the World, The. Ella Wheeler Wilcox. *See* Solitude.
Way out in Californy. Stewball. *Unknown.* ABF
Way Out in Idaho ("Come all you jolly railroad men"), *with music.* *Unknown.* OuSiCo
Way Out in Idyho ("Remember what I promised you"), *with music.* *Unknown.* CoSo
'Way out in the land of the setting sun. Home Means Nevada. Bertha Raffetto. PoRL
Way out in western Texas, where the Clear Fork's waters flow. The Cowboy's Christmas Ball. Larry Chittenden. CoSo; CSF; SCC; SoAF
Way out upon the Platte, near Pike's Peak we were told. A Hit at the Times. A. O. McGrew. PoOW
Way Out West. LeRoi Jones. NeAP
Way Out West. *Unknown.* CoSo
Way Over in the Blooming Garden, *with music.* *Unknown.* ABF
Way Over in the New Buryin' Groun', *with music.* *Unknown.* AS
'Way Over in the Promised Land, *with music.* *Unknown.* SoAF
(Where O Where Is Old Elijah? *with music.*) AS
Way ran under boughs of checkered green, The. Wood Witchery. Richard Burton. AnAmPo; LA
Way the Baby Slept, The. James Whitcomb Riley. AA
Way the Baby Woke, The. James Whitcomb Riley. AA
Way, the Truth, and the Life, The. Theodore Parker. ChIP; HBV; LPS-2; MaRV; OQP; QP-2; TrPWD; WGRP
(Jesus.) GrCo-1
Way, the Truth, and the Life, The. *Unknown.* BePJ
Way, the Truth, and the Life, The—Love One Another. St. John, XIV, 1–19, XV, 12–17, Bible, *N.T.* EM-1
Way, the Truth, the Life, The. George Washington Doane. *See* Christ, the Way.
Way, The; the Truth; the Life. Samuel Judson Porter. BLRP
Way they scrub, The. An Indignant Male. A. B. Ross. BrR; MPB
Way Through, The. Denise Levertov. NeAP
Way through the Woods, The. Kipling. CH; FaBoCh; FaPON; GTBS-D; LoGBV; MCCG; MM; MoVE; OBEV (new ed.); OBVV; Po; POTE; SeCeV; ShBV-2; ThWaDe; TwCV
Way to a Happy New Year, A. Robert Brewster Beattie. OQP; PSO; QP-1
Way to Arcady, The. H. C. Bunner. AA; BOHV; InMe; OBAV; PFY
Way to Bethlehem, The. Clinton Scollard. OQP; PSO; QP-1
Way to Dusty Death, The. Shakespeare. *See* Tomorrow and Tomorrow and Tomorrow.
Way to Fairyland, The. Eunice Close. BoTP
Way to Hades, The. *Unknown, tr. fr. Greek by* W. C. Lawton. OxBG
Way to Have Hansome Children, The, *sel.* Claude Quillet, *tr. fr. French, in part by* N. Rowe.
"You now, who are dispos'd to learn our arts." PoP
Way to Heaven, The. Charles Goodrich Whiting. AA
Way to Hump a Cow, The. E. E. Cummings. AmP; OxBA
Way to Know a Father, The. Robert P. Tristram Coffin. PoRL
Way to Poverty, The. *Unknown, tr. fr. Greek* by H. Wellesley. OxBG
Way to Power, The. Tennyson. *Fr.* Oenone. MaRV; OQP; QP-2
'Way up high in the Mogollons. *See* 'Way high up the Mogollons.
Way Up on Clinch Mountain. *Unknown.* *See* Rye Whisky.
Way up on de mountain, Lord! Up on de Mountain. *Unknown.* BoAN-1
Way Up on Old Smoky, *with music.* *Unknown.* TrAS
Way was long, the wind was cold, The. The [Last] Minstrel. Sir Walter Scott. *Fr.* The Lay of the Last Minstrel. EV-4; OTPC; TreFS
Way was rocky, rough, and steep, The. Upheld by His Hand. Grace B. Renfrow. BePJ
Way We Wonder, The. Robert Pack. NePoEA
Wayfarer, The. Stephen Crane. War Is Kind, XIII. AA; AmPP (3d ed.); BAP; CoBA; LiTA; MAP; MoAmPo; NeMA; NePA; PoMa; WaKn
Wayfarer, The. Verna Loveday Harden. PSO
Wayfarer, The. Keats. *See* Keen, Fitful Gusts Are Whisp'ring Here and There.
Wayfarer, The. Padraic Pearse. OxBI
Wayfarer, The. Sara Teasdale. ChMo; CMP
Wayfarer, The/ Perceiving the pathway to truth. The Wayfarer. Stephen Crane. War Is Kind, XIII. AA; AmPP (3d ed.); BAP; CoBA; LiTA; MAP; MoAmPo; NeMA; PoMa; WaKn
Wayfarer of Earth. Sir Charles G. D. Roberts. CPG
Wayfarers. Dana Burnet. EtS
Wayfarers. Harvey Wagner Flink. DaM
Wayfarers on the dusty road. By Shaded Wells. Bhartrihari. OnPM
Wayfaring. Francisco A. de Icaza, *tr. fr. Spanish by* Samuel Beckett. AnMP
Wayfaring. Richard Le Gallienne. TVSH
Wayfaring. Georg Trakl, *tr. fr. German by* Christopher Middleton. AnGP
Wayfaring Fools. Frances Beatrice Taylor. CPG
Wayfaring Stranger, The. *Unknown.* *See* Poor Wayfaring Stranger.
Wayfaring, to the Valley of the Dove, *sel.* Charles Doughty. "In these fresh meadows." TCPD
Wayland learned bitterly banishment's ways. Deor's Lament. *Unknown.* BEL
Wayne at Stony Point. Clinton Scollard. GA; MC; PAH
Ways, The. John Oxenham. HBMV; MaRV; PoMa
(High Way and a Low, A.) OQP; QP-1
Ways and Means. "Lewis Carroll." *See* White Knight's Song, The.
Ways o' Men, The. Angelina Weld Grimké. CDC
Ways of Death, The. W. E. Henley. BPP; OQP; QP-1
Ways of God to Men, The. Milton. *Fr.* Samson Agonistes. OBS
(Choruses from "Samson Agonistes.") SeCeV
Ways of Love. Elizabeth Barrett Browning. *See* Sonnets from the Portuguese: "How do I love thee . . ." *and* "If thou must love me . . ."

Ways of Love, The. Jami, *tr. fr. Persian by* F. Hadland Davis. OnPM
Ways of Regard, *sels.* Ebenezer Jones.
"Seer saw on, The." NBE
"Sharks' jaws are glittering, The." NBE
Ways of the Gods, The. Stanton A. Coblentz. OQP; QP-2
Ways of Time, The. W. H. Davies. ChMo; CMP
Ways of Trains, The. Elizabeth J. Coatsworth. BoChLi (1950 ed.); TiPo
Ways of Traveling. Alice Wilkins. GFA
Ways of War. Lionel Johnson. AnIV; GTIV; TIP
Wayside, The. James Herbert Morse. AA
Wayside cherry tree, A. Hokku. Basho. InP
Wayside Cross, The. Frederick George Scott. BoCaPo; OCL
Wayside Epigram. Leonidas of Tarentum, *tr. fr. Greek by* Robert Allason Furness. GrR
Wayside Fount, The. Nicias, *tr. fr. Greek by* F. L. Lucas. GrPE
Wayside Grave, A. Leonidas of Tarentum, *tr. fr. Greek by* E. R. Bevan. OxBG
Wayside Inn, The. Longfellow. Tales of a Wayside Inn: Prelude, Pt. I. CoBA; TCAP
Wayside Inn, The. *Unknown, tr. fr. German.* TVSH
(Wayside Inn, The—an Apple Tree.) ADAH
Wayside Music. Charles Henry Crandall. SDH
Wayside Shrine. Gertrude Ryder Bennett. ChIP
Wayside Station, The. Edwin Muir. FaBoTw; MoVE
Wayside Virgin, The. Langdon Elwyn Mitchell. AA; OBAV; PoTo
Way-Side Well, The. Joseph Seamon Cotter, Sr. CDC; PoNe
Wayward Desire. *Unknown, tr. fr. Greek by* T. F. Higham. OxBG
Wayworn and weary. The Good Companion. Belle F. Owens. ChIP
Wayworn pilgrim from a distant shore, A. Knowest Thou Isaac Jogues? Francis W. Grey. CAW
Wayzgoose, The, *sel.* Roy Campbell.
"Attend my fable if your ears be clean." BoSA
Wazir Dandan for Prince Sharken, The. *Unknown, tr. fr. Arabic by* E. Powys Mathers. *Fr.* The Thousand and One Nights. AWP; JAWP; WBP
We. Hervey Allen. PC
We. Mary Carolyn Davies. GaP
We. Vladimir Kirillov, *tr. fr. Russian by* Alexander Kaun. LiTW
We?/ Whee! The Next Next Shortest Poem in the World. Martha Salemme. SiTL
We Achieve Our Joy. *Unknown, tr. fr. Chinese by* Bernhard Karlgren. *Fr.* Shi King. ChLP
We ain't no saints on the Bar-Z ranch. Bar-Z on a Sunday Night. Percival Combes. SCC
We Ain't Scared o' Pa. James W. Foley. FAOV
We all are [*or* are all] blind, until we see. Man-making. Edwin Markham. MaRV; OQP; PGD; QP-1
We All Do Fail as a Leaf. Mimnermus, *tr. fr. Greek by* J. A. Pott. GrL; OxBG
We all look on with anxious eyes. When Father Carves the Duck. E. V. Wright. FaFP; PTA-2; TreF
We already and first of all discern him making this thing. Rite and Fore-Time. David Jones. *Fr.* The Anathemata. AtBAP
We always drive along until. The Harper's Farm. Dorothy Aldis. RIS
We always had to do our work at night. Before Action. Leon Gellert. BoAV
We always like a rainy day. A Rainy Day. Emily Blackmore Stapp. GFA
We Am Clim'in' Jacob's Ladder, *with music. Unknown.* BoAN-1
We and the little cheerful goldfinch. Two Angels. Richard Monckton Milnes. OBRV
We Are. Paul Eluard, *tr. fr. French by* Wallace Fowlie. MiCF
We are a band of brothers, and native to the soil. The Bonnie Blue Flag. Harry McCarthy. BlG; SPP
We are a band of shanty boys. The Merry Shanty Boys. *Unknown.* IHA
We are a part of all things that we see. Sonnet. William Gilmore Simms. SPP
We are a people living in shells and moving. The British. A. S. J. Tessimond. ChMP
We are airy little creatures. *See* We are little airy creatures.
We are all blind until we see. *See* We all are blind . . .
We are all here. The Family Meeting. Charles Sprague. HBV
We are all in the dumps. *Unknown.* OxNR; SiTL
We are all near to death. But in my friends. One Who Watches. Siegfried Sassoon. TrJP
We Are All Nodding, *with music. Unknown.* FTB
We are all of us dreamers of dreams. Dreamer[s] of Dreams. William Herbert Carruth. BTP; MaRV; OQP; QP-2
We are almost come to Hsün-yang: how my thoughts are stirred. Arriving at Hsün-yang, 2. Po Chü-i. TrCh
We are as clouds that veil the midnight moon. Mutability. Shelley. BCEP; BEL; BoLiVe; BPN; CoBE; EM-2; EmBrPo; EPN; ERP; HBV; TOP
We are as leaves in jewelled springtime growing. We All Do Fail as a Leaf. Mimnermus. GrL; OxBG
We are as mendicants who wait. The Mendicants. Bliss Carman. HBV; NLK; VA
We are blushing roses. Songs and Chorus of the Flowers. Leigh Hunt. ADAH
We are born and pass on so quickly! Man. Marvin Stevens. MaRV
We Are Born Every Day. Palladas, *tr. fr. Greek by* R. A. Furness. OxBG
We are born, then cry. Life. "N. C." SeCL
We are born; we laugh; we weep. Life. "Barry Cornwall." VA
We Are Brethren A'. Robert Nicoll. HBV; LPS-1
We are bringing back some canceled notes. Dividends. Hubert Creekmore. WaP
We are building in sorrow or joy. Building for Eternity. N. B. Sargent. BLPA
"We are but clay," the preacher saith. Clay. E. V. Lucas. HBV
We are but two—the others sleep. The Brothers. Charles Sprague. AA
We Are Children. Robert Buchanan. VA
We are children of the sun. Children of the Sun. Fenton Johnson. BANP
We are climbing Jacob's ladder. Jacob's Ladder. *Unknown.* MaRV
We are coming, Cuba, coming; our starry banner shines. The Gathering. Herbert Swett. PAH
We are coming, Father Abraham, three hundred thousand more. Three Hundred Thousand More. James Sloan Gibbons. MDAH; PaA; PAH; PoFr
We are crescent moons, whose light. On Taking Up a Humble Place at Court. Ibn Adha. MooP
We are done with little thinking. The Bigger Day. G. E. Bishop. WBLP
We are eating nuts, Hyacinth. Eating Nuts and Oranges. José Moreno Villa. CoSP
We are false and evanescent, and aware of our deceit. The False Gods. E. A. Robinson. CP; NV
We Are Four Bums, *with music. Unknown.* AS
We are friends. My Mind and I. Hilda Conkling. NP
We are gazing now on old Tom Moore. *See* You are gazing now . . .
We are ghost-ridden. The Dead Moon. Danske Bedinger Dandridge. AA
We are going on a journey. The Journey. Aidan Clarke. BoTP
We are growing old together, you and I. Old Age. Po Chü-i. TrCh
We are here in a wood of little beeches. The Sign. Frederic Manning. LBBV; NP
We are here on the central plaza. Voice of the Announcer. Archibald MacLeish. *Fr.* The Fall of the City. HoPM
We are ill of a new wind. Panic. Rosamund Dargan Thomson. NeTW
We are in love's land to-day. Love at Sea. Swinburne, *after* Gautier. AWP; BPN; HBV; TOP; VA; VLEP
We are little airy creatures. A Riddle [*or* The Vowels *or* The Five]. Swift. GN; MeMeAg; OnYI; OTPC; RIS
We are living, we are dwelling. The Present Age. Arthur Cleveland Coxe. BLPA; MaRV
We are na fou, we're nae that fou. Willie Brewed a Peck o' Maut. Burns. AWP; BEL; CEP; ESBV; EM-1; EnLit; JAWP; REAL; TOP; WBP
We Are Never Old. Emerson. *Fr.* The World-Soul. OQP; PoRL; QP-1
We are no other than a moving row. Fatalism. Omar Khayyám, *tr. by* Edward Fitzgerald. *Fr.* The Rubáiyát. MaRV; PC
We are not called to love that old, one way. Friendship. Florence Converse. BoFr
We Are Not Cast Away. Plotinus, *tr. fr. Greek.* MaRV
We are not come to wage a strife. The Daybreakers. Arna Bontemps. CDC; GoSl; PoNe
We are not free: Freedom doth not consist. James Russell Lowell. *Fr.* Freedom. BHV
We are not in the world at all, but somewhere. Second Canzone. Nikolai Stepanovich Gumilev. TrRV
We are not sure of sorrow. Swan Song. Swinburne. OtMeF
We are not wholly blest who use the earth. Charles Mair. *Fr.* Dreamland. CaP; OCL
We Are Old. Edith M. Thomas. TBM
We are old. Sons of Belial. Lola Ridge. BAP; PFY; TCPD
We are old—it must be so. We Are Old. Edith M. Thomas. TBM
We are our fathers' sons: let those who lead us know! No Hint of Stain. William Vaughn Moody. *Fr.* An Ode in Time of Hesitation. AA
We are poor and lowly born. The Child's Hymn. Mary Howitt. GoTP

We are quite sure. He Will Give Them Back. "George Klingle." BLRP
"We are ready for work." Song of the Steamer Engine. Caroline B. Le Row. PEOR
We are resting here in the twilight. Compline. Duncan Campbell Scott. GoBC
We are sailing away in a Wonder-Boat. The Dream Boat. Louise Ayres Garnett. BOL
We Are Seven. Wordsworth. BLPA; BPN; EM-2; EmBrPo; EnLi-2; EnRP; EPN; EPP; ERP; GEPC; GN; HBV; HiLiEn; LPS-1; NeHB; OnPP; PIR; PoE; PTA-1; TCEP; TreF; WBLP
We are sighing for you, far land. The Far Land. John Hall Wheelock. WGRP
We are sitting in a swimming air. Arion Anadyomenos. Ronald Bottrall. CoEV; MoP
We are so lonely—all of us. Each in His Inmost Heart. John D. Sheridan. JKCP (1955 ed.)
We are so soon dead. Mask. Ken Etheridge. MoWP
We are so stupid about death. We will not learn. Death. William Croswell Doane. EOAH
We are sons of mighty Manitou. The Red Ghosts Chant. Lilian White Spencer. PoOW
We are souls in hell, who hear no gradual music. A Prayer from 1936. Siegfried Sassoon. TrPWD
We are standing in the great dawn of a day they did not know. Odell Shepard. *Fr.* In the Dawn. MaRV
We are such little men when the stars come out. Starry Night. Hermann Hagedorn. MaRV
We Are Such Stuff as Dreams. Petronius Arbiter, *tr. fr. Latin by* Howard Mumford Jones. AWP
We are such stuff as dreams are made of, and these. Poem. Hugo von Hofmannsthal. LiTW
We are the abandoned roads. Abandoned Roads. Amy May Rogers. DDA
We are the age predestined to lie fallow. The Young Dead Speak. Sister Mary Irma. JKCP (1955 ed.)
We are the Ancient People. The Song of the Ancient People. Edna Dean Proctor. AA
We Are the Burden-Bearers! *abr.* William L. Stidger. PGD
We are the children of Science that mated with Vision. The Flyers. Frank Ernest Hill. PoeMoYo
We are the fallen, who, with helpless faces. The Prayer of Beaten Men. William Hervey Woods. *Fr.* The House of Broken Swords. HBV
We are the flute, our music is all Thine. The Unseen Power. Jalal ed-Din Rumi. PeP
We are the hollow men. The Hollow Men. T. S. Eliot. APA; BAV; BoLiVe (1945 ed.); ChMo; CoAnAm; CoBE; CoBMV; EnL; LiTA; LiTM; MAP; MAPA; MoAB; MoAmPo; MoP; NAMP; NeMA; OBMV; Po; PoLFOT; POTE; PreP; TwAmPo; TwCV; TwHP; TwP
We are the homeless, even as you. To Poets. Charles Hamilton Sorley. GTML; LO
We are the laborers who water the earth. The Laborers. Kostes Palamas. MoGP
We are the lovers of Local 1. Theme Song for a Songwriters' Union. Al Graham. WhC
We are the Magians of old. The Veil. Ferid ed-Din Attar. PeP
We Are the Music-Makers. Arthur O'Shaughnessy. *See* Ode: "We are the music-makers."
We are the only ones who will remember. Secret. Catherine Haydon Jacobs. GoYe
We are the partly real ones. The Moon Worshippers. Eric Robertson Dodds. GTIV; POTE
We are the Pilgrims, master; we shall go. The Golden Road. James Elroy Flecker. *Fr.* Hassan. OtMeF
We are the poor children, come out to see the sights. The Carol of the Poor Children. Richard Middleton. QS
We are the puppets of a shadow-play. Prologue: Before the Curtain. Arthur Symons. POTT
We are the roadside flowers. Roadside Flowers. Bliss Carman. CPG; CV; HBMV
We are the singing shadows beauty casts. Eagle Sonnets, XX. Clement Wood. HBMV
We are the singing troubadours of God. Franciscans. Hyacinth Blocker. SaFP
We are the toilers whom God hath barred. The Song of the Unsuccessful. Richard Burton. LBMV; OQP; QP-2; WGRP
We are the trees. Song of the Trees. Mary Colborne-Veel. BoAu
We Are the Voices of the Whispering Wind. Sir Edwin Arnold. LEAP
We are the whirlwinds that winnow the West. The Vigilantes. Margaret Ashmun. SCC
We are they that go, that go. The Fugitives. Florence Wilkinson Evans. LBMV; NV; OQP; QP-2
We are they who come faster than fate. The War Song of the Saracens. James Elroy Flecker. *Fr.* Hassan. GTML; MBP; MM; MoBrPo; MuP; OBVV; OtMeF; ShBV-2; WHA
We are thine, O Love, being in thee and made of thee. Hymn to Love. Lascelles Abercrombie. *Fr.* Emblems of Love. OBEV (new ed.); OBVV
We are things of dry hours and the involuntary plan. Kitchenette Building. Gwendolyn Brooks. PoNe
We are those same children who amazed. Prelude XXIII. Stefan George. WaaP
We Are Three. *Unknown. See* Catch, A: "Wisemen were but seven, The."
We are three brethren come from [*or* out of] Spain. Three Knights from Spain. *Unknown.* AtBAP; CH; OxNR; RIS
We are tired who follow after. Natural Magic. "Æ." BEL
We are trained and quiet intellectuals. On Being Invited to a Testimonial Dinner. William Stafford. NePoAm-2
We are travelling west of Alice Springs, and Sam is at the wheel. West of Alice. W. E. Harney. NeLNL
We are trying to carry this timber to the building. Timber. *Unknown.* AS
We are two eagles. The Flight. Sara Teasdale. BAP; ChMo; CMP; HBMV; LEAP; MAP; MoAmPo; NP; TBM; WHA
We are two phantoms haunting man. Phantoms. Frances Kiely. CAG
We are two travellers, Roger and I. The Vagabonds. John Townsend Trowbridge. AA; AlBD; BAP; BeLS; BLPA; LEAP; LPS-2; OBAV; OnPP; PCD; PTA-2; TreFS
We are used to the murmur. Engine Failure. Timothy Corsellis. WaP
We are very little creatures. A E I O U. Swift. BoTP. *See also* We are little airy creatures.
We are very slightly changed. A General Summary. Kipling. HBV
We Are Weary. "Feodor Sologub," *tr. fr. Russian by* Babette Deutsch. TrRV
We are weary of little words. The Little Words. Edith Daley. BAP
We are weary of steering a course. We Are Weary. "Feodor Sologub." TrRV
We are what suns and winds and waters make us. Regeneration [*or* Invocation]. Walter Savage Landor. BPN; ERP; VA; ViBoPo
We are what we are made; each following day. Written in Naples. Emerson. CoBA; IAP
We are yesterday's catch. Fish! Ch'en Te Chien. PoHN
We ask for peace. We, at the bound. Surrender. Angelina Weld Grimké. CDC
We Ask No Shield. William Rose Benét. MOAP
We ask not that the slave should lie. Abolitionist Hymn. *Unknown.* TrAS
We ask not to be born: 'tis not by will. Contentment in the Dark. William Bell Scott. EBSV
We ask that Love shall rise to the divine. Which. Corinne Roosevelt Robinson. SBMV
We asked for rain. It didn't flash and roar. Our Hold on the Planet. Robert Frost. PreP
We ate our breakfast lying on our backs. Breakfast. W. W. Gibson. NV; OBMV
We ate with steeps of sky about our shoulders. The Terrace. Richard Wilbur. MiAP
We be simple shepherds. Shepherds' Song. Norah M. Holland. ChrBoLe
We Be Soldiers Three. *Unknown.* ChTr
We be the King's men, hale and hearty. Men Who March Away. Thomas Hardy. *Fr.* The Dynasts, Pt. I. CH
We Be Three Poor Mariners. *Unknown.* AmSS, *with music;* ElSeCe
We bear sealed orders o'er life's weltered sea. Sealed Orders. Richard Burton. HBV; OQP; QP-2
We bear the strain of earthly care. Our Brother Christ. Ozora Stearns Davis. MaRV
We being so hidden from those who. The Children Look at the Parents. A. S. J. Tessimond. ChMP
We bless Thee for Thy peace, O God. Thy Peace, O God. *Unknown.* PraP
We bless you, cicada. Cicada. *Unknown.* GrL; OxBG
We both were five and we both were wild. The Chronicle of Meola Creek. Keith Sinclair. AnNZ
We Break New Seas Today. John Oxenham. OQP; QP-1
We break the glass, whose sacred wine. Song. Edward Coote Pinkney. APW; HBV; LBAP; MOAP; SPP
We brought a rug for sitting on. The Picnic. Dorothy Aldis. TiPo (1952 ed.)
We brought him home, I was so pleased. My New Rabbit. Elizabeth Gould. BoTP
We brought the wagons home at dusk. A Silly Song. Louis How. PR
We built a hut, my brother and I. The Hut. Hilda Van Stockum. BrR
We built a ship upon the stairs. A Good Play. Robert Louis Stevenson. FaPON; GFA; MoShBr; MPB; OTPC; StVeCh (1940 ed.); TiPo; VLEP
We built our love up like a work of art. Dirge. Louis Johnson. AnNZ

We buried the mouse that was caught in a trap. Funerals. *Unknown.* DDA
We by no shining Galilean lake. Vision. Edward Dowden. ChIP; OQP; QP-1
We call them wrong! God pity us, the blind. In Defense of Youth. Robbins Wolcott Barstow. QP-2
We Call This Life. Douglas Malloch. BPP
We call this Time, and gauge it by the clock. But This Is Also Everlasting Life. Sarah N. Cleghorn. QS
We call up the green to hide us. Summer Wish. Louise Bogan. AnFE; CoAnAm; TwAmPo
We call you Mother of our Lord and Savior. Hymn for Laudes; Feast of Our Lady, Help of Christians. *Unknown.* ISi
We called him "Rags," he was just a cur. Rags. Edmund Vance Cooke. AIBD; BLPA
We came at dawn to a market place. The Market Place. J. Corson Miller. MuM
We came by boat in the late arctic twilight. Visit by Water. Floris Clark McLaren. BoCaPo (1948 ed.)
We came that way by choice. A Traveller's Tale. William Plomer. BoSA
We came to a wood and within it, where dark its shadows run. Love Lies Sleeping. Plato. GrPE
We came to Tamichi in 1880. Song. Scott Judy *and* "Doc" Hammond. PoOW
We came to the high cliffs of Bonaventure. Long-billed Gannets. Frances D. Emery. GoYe
We came to the islands. We came saying. The Quest. Harold Vinal. GoYe
We can no longer stay on shore. The Greenland Whale Fishery. *Unknown.* BaBo
We can only see a little of the ocean. God's Love. *Unknown.* BLRP
We can sing a different tune from the "Song of Desolation?" Boredom. Nalan Hsinteh. ChLP
We can slide. Sliding. Myra Cohn. SiSoSe
We cannot all be Washingtons. Like Washington. *Unknown.* DD; GA; HH; MeMeAg
We cannot die, for loveliness. Song. Mary Carolyn Davies. TBM
We cannot kindle when we will. Morality [*or* Tasks in Hours of Insight Willed]. Matthew Arnold. BLP; BMEP; BPN; EM-2; EmBrPo; EPN; EPP; GEPC; GrCo-1; GTBS; GTSL; HBV; LEAP; MaRV; OQP; PoVP; QP-2; TOP; ViPo; ViPP; VLEP
We cannot look beyond. Light. Grace Wilkinson. OQP; QP-2
We cannot rest, whose hearts are like the breakers. Architects of Dream. Lucia Trent. PGD
We cannot retrace our steps. Gertrude Stein. *Fr.* The Mother of Us All. CrMA
We can't tonight! We're overworked and busy. Tonight. Franklin P. Adams. FiBHP
We care not for money, riches or wealth. Drinking Song. Thomas Randolph. *Fr.* Aristippus. SeCL
We Cared for Each Other. Heine, *tr. fr. German by* John Todhunter. AWP
We carve His Cross into an amulet. Good Friday. Hugh O. Isbell. PSO
We caught the tread of dancing feet. The Harlot's House. Oscar Wilde. LEAP; MBP; MoBrPo; PIR; PoVP; ViPP
We chanced in passing by that afternoon. The Black Cottage. Robert Frost. AmPo; AmPP; CoBA; CV; OnAP
We charged at Vimy—zero was at four. The Hero of Vimy. Brent Dow Allinson. AOAH
We checked our pace—the red road sharply rounding. The Hawk's Nest. Bret Harte. BAV
We clear the grasses and trees. Clearing the Fields. *Unknown.* WhP
We climb'd the steep where headless Edwin lies. The Old Parish Church, Whitby. Hardwicke Drummond Rawnsley. OBVV
We climbed the steps of air with motor roaring. Flying. Florence Ripley Mastin. VOD (1935 ed.)
We climbed to it by secret flights. The Enchanted Castle. Jeanne D'Orge. AnAmPo; LA
We climbed to the top of Goat Point hill. Forty Years After. H. H. Porter. BOHV
We cobblers lead a merry life. The Cobblers' Song [*or* Strumbo, Dorothy, Trumpart, Cobbling Shoes]. *At. to* George Peele, *also at. to* Charles Tilney. *Fr.* Locrine. ElSeCe; OBSC; TuPP
We come by a terrible gate. Eden; or One View of It. Theodore Spencer. LiTM; NePA
We come in arms, we stand ten score. School Fencibles. William Cory. LH
We come to music for defense. Night Concert. Virginia Earle. JKCP (1955 ed.)
We come to your doorstep. A Carol for Christmas Eve. Eleanor Farjeon. BoChLi
We come, we come, we come. A Hymn of Unity. Robert Freeman. OQP; QP-1
We Conquer or Die. James Pierpont. MC; PAH
We conquer'd France, but felt our captive's charms. Pope on Dryden. Pope. *Fr.* The First Epistle of the Second Book of Horace. BeR
We could hang my Chartres upon a lamplit wall. Budget. "Elspeth." PR
We could have crossed the road but hesitated. The Interrogation. Edwin Muir. LiTB; SeCePo
We could not pause, while yet the noontide air. Obsequies of Stuart. John Reuben Thompson. BIG; GA; PAH
We count the broken lyres that rest. The Voiceless. Oliver Wendell Holmes. *Fr.* The Autocrat of the Breakfast Table. AA; BAP; CoBA; IAP; TCAP; ViBoPo
We cover thee, sweet face. Emily Dickinson. BoFr
We crazed for you, aspired and fell for you. The Knights to Chrysola. Rachel Annand Taylor. OBVV
We Creators. Olive Tilford Dargan. LS; NoCaPo
We cried: Good luck! and watched them go. The Last Ascent. John Lehmann. ChMP
We cross a stream and my horse. Under the Frontier Post. Wang Chang-ling. ChTr
We cross sulphurous land. Desolation. Ann Louise Hayes. PtPa
We cross the prairie as of old. The Kansas Emigrants. Whittier. CoBA; MC; PaA; PAH
We crossed Brook Cedron to Gethsemane. Malchus. Ida Norton Munson. ChIP
We crown'd the hard-won heights at length. After the Battle. Richard Chenevix Trench. VA
We curl into your eyes. The Female God. Isaac Rosenberg. FaBoTw
We dance on gossamer wings. The Dance of the Fairies. *Unknown.* WGEM
. . . We danced/ Shyly, not speaking, more as partial friends. Christopher Hassall. *Fr.* Soliloquy to Imogen. LO
We deck to-day each soldier's grave. Decoration Day. Wallace Bruce. PEOR
We dedicate a church today. Dedication. Ethel Arnold Tilden. MaRV; OQP; PraP; QP-2
We did not believe. This anger is surprise. The Hosting. Brooke Byrne. NeTW
We did not dare to breathe a prayer. Hope. Oscar Wilde. Fr. The Ballad of Reading Gaol. MaRV
We did not know his unfamiliar head. Archaic Torso of Apollo. Rainer Maria Rilke. LiTW
We died in the glen of Dirphys; here by our country's giving. The Dead of Athens at Chalcis. Simonides. GrPE
We digged our trenches on the down. Song of the Dark Ages. Francis Brett Young. HBMV
We do accept thee, heavenly Peace! Acceptation. Margaret Junkin Preston. MC; PAH
We Do Lie beneath the Grass. Thomas Lovell Beddoes. *See* Sibylla's Dirge.
We do not find Him on the difficult earth. Christmas Night. Alice Meynell. POTT; StJW
We do not know the ports from which we sail. The Stars Are True. *Unknown.* MaRV
We do not know this thing. Vale, Amor! "Fiona Macleod." PoVP
We do not know—we can but deem. The Hero. Ambrose Bierce. OQP; PoRL; QP-2
We do not know who made them. Negro Spirituals. Rosemary Benét *and* Stephen Vincent Benét. FaPON
We do not play on graves. Emily Dickinson. MoVE; PoEL-5
We don't forget—while in this dark December. To the School at War. Cyril Argentine Alington. ShGoBo
We Don't Get No Justice Here in Atlanta, *with music.* *Unknown.* OuSiCo
We doubted our God in secret. Resurgam. Theodosia Garrison. MaRV
We Drifted to Each Other like Two Birds. Maurice Baring. MM
We drink the cup of life while yet. The Cup of Life. Mikhail Lermontov. BoR
"We dwell in Him"—oh, everlasting Home. In Him. Annie Johnson Flint. BLRP
We eat and drink and laugh and energize. Death's Transfiguration. Israel Zangwill. TrJP
We enter our earthly bodies. A Dirge. *Unknown.* PoHN
We enter the dismal wood where boughs black. The Wood of the Self-Destroyers. Samuel Yellen. NePoAm-2
We entered the city at noon! High bells. The radio on. One Night Stand. LeRoi Jones. NeAP
We face the nations with one hand outstretched. Armistice. Eunice Mitchell Lehmer. PGD; PSO
We fancied he'd share in our cause. What's in It for Me? Edgar A. Guest. PoToHe (new ed.)
We feed the birds in winter. Joe. David McCord. TiPo (1959 ed.)
We feed the chickens every day. Off We Go to Market. Gwen A. Smith. BoTP
We fell in Dirphys' straits. At public cost. Sacrifice of Youth. Simonides. OnPM

We fidgeted. The school-clock drawled its chimes. Greece. Lord Vansittart. NeTW
We Fish. Herman Melville. *Fr.* Mardi. GoTP
We follow where the Swamp Fox guides. The Swamp Fox. William Gilmore Simms. AA; BeLS; DD; FaBoBe; GA; MC; PaA; PAH; SPP; TCAP
We followed them into the west. The West. Edwin Muir. MoVE
We fought you once—but that was long ago! Britons and Guests. Edith M. Thomas. PaA
We found a hill all green with grass. Pete's Holiday. Don Marquis. AlBD
We galloped over the glossy sea. W. B. Yeats. *Fr.* The Wanderings of Oisin. SeCePo
We gather together to ask the Lord's blessing. *Unknown.* OlF
We gave her a discardment. The Discardment. Alan Paton. BoSA
We gazed on Corryvrekin's whirl. Iona. Arthur Cleveland Coxe. AA
We get no good/ By being ungenerous. Reading [*or* "Good from a Book"]. Elizabeth Barrett Browning. *Fr.* Aurora Leigh, I. GN; HH; PoRL
We git up in de mornin' so dog-gone soon. Levee Camp "Holler." *Unknown.* ABF
We Give Thee but Thine Own. William Walsham How. MaRV
We give Thee thanks, O Lord! Thanksgiving Day. Robert Bridges. MaRV; OHIP
We Go. Karl Wolfskehl, *tr. fr. German by* Carol North Valhope *and* Ernst Morwitz. TrJP
We go from God to God—then though. Journey's End. Evelyn H. Healey. MaRV
We go no more to Calverly's. Calverly's. E. A. Robinson. LBMV; MOAP
We Go No More to the Forest. Mary Colborne-Veel. BoAu
We Go Out Together. Kenneth Patchen. MoAmPo (1950 ed.)
We go to the Golden Palace. The Golden Palace. *Unknown.* TrCh
We go wading in the winter. Four Kinds of Wading. Mildred D. Shacklett. GFA
We got a necho at our house since we moved out beside the hill. The Necho. Samuel Ellsworth Kiser. DDA
We grant, altho' he had much wit. Samuel Butler. *Fr.* Hudibras. EPP
"We grasp our battle spears: we don our breast-plates of hide." The Battle. Chu Yuan, *tr. by* Arthur Waley. TrCh; WaaP
We grasp our *wu-k'o* shields; we put on rhinoceros hides. The Patriots Who Died in Battle. Chu Yuan, *tr. by* Shen Yu-ting. *Fr.* The Nine Songs. WhP
We Grow Out of Iron. Aleksey Kapitonovich Gastev, *tr. fr. Russian by* Babette Deutsch *and* Avrahm Yarmolinsky. TrRV, *rev. tr. by* Babette Deutsch; WoL
We grow to the sound of the wind. Dates. *Unknown. Fr.* The Thousand and One Nights. AWP; FaPON; JAWP; LiTW; WBP
We had a circus in our shed. Our Circus. Laura Lee Randall. GFA; TiPo (1952 ed.); UTS
We had a female passenger who came. September 1, 1802. Wordsworth. BPN; EmBrPo
We had a Goblin party on the night of Hallowe'en. Hallowe'en. Helen Wing. GFA
We had a parade for the lady near Livorno. Snapshot: Ambassadress. George Garrett. NePoAm-2
We had a pleasant walk to-day. The Spring Walk. Thomas Miller. OTPC (1923 ed.)
We had battered their weakening rush line till it gave like a wisp of grass. Under the Goal Posts. Arthur Guiterman. BBV (1951 ed.)
We had been long in mountain snow. The Greeting of the Roses. Hamlin Garland. AA
We had climbed the last steep flight of stairs. The Bead Mat. Walter de la Mare. MoPW
We had crackers/ And cambric tea. Tea Party. Aileen Fisher. GoBP
We had expected everything but revolt. Nightmare Number Three. Stephen Vincent Benét. DaM; MaC; MoAmPo (1950 ed.)
We had forgotten You, or very nearly. Christ in Flanders. Lucy Whitmell. PTA-1; QS
We had gone down to Tabor, to the door. Balloon over the Rhondda. Roland Mathias. MoWP
We had no need of faith in those young days. The Test of Faith. Sidney Royse Lysaght. GrCo-2
We had no sword for strife. We Shall Survive. Arnulf Överland. AnNoLy
We had ridden [*or* rode] long and were still far from the inn. Sleeping on Horseback. Po Chü-i. LiTW; TrCh
We had to fire/ Our housemaid Nan. Reference. *Unknown.* LauV
We had to wait for the heat to pass. August Night. Elizabeth Madox Roberts. YeAr
We had waffles-with-syrup for breakfast. Birthdays. Marchette Chute. SiSoSe; StVeCh
We hail your "stripes" and lessened "Stars." Over the River. Jane T. H. Cross. BIG
We hang the holly up once more. Christmas Singing. Elsie Williams Chandler. ChBR; SiSoSe
We hate the Saxon and the Dane. Celts and Saxons. Thomas Osborne Davis. TIP
We have a bed, and a baby too. The Laborer. Richard Dehmel. AWP; JAWP; WBP; WoL
We Have a Day. Marion Strobel. NP
We have a flash packet, she's a packet of fame. The Clipper Ship *Dreadnaught. Unknown.* IHA
We have a little garden. The Garden. Esther Antin. *Fr.* On Our Farm. RIS
We have a mountain at the end of our street. In a Desert Town. Lionel Stevenson. StVeCh
We have a pretty witty King. Impromptu on Charles II. Earl of Rochester. ChTr
We have a secret, just we three. The Secret. *Unknown.* BoChLi; MPB (1956 ed.); OTPC (1946 ed.); RAR; StVeCh (1940 ed.); TiPo; UTS
We have all, one time or another, met a famous figure. Back Room Joys. Justin Richardson. FiBHP
We have an old mother that peevish is grown. The Mother Country. Benjamin Franklin. PAH
We have bags and bags of whitest down. Keeping Store. Mary Frances Butts. GFA; OTPC (1946 ed.); PCH; PPL
We have bathed where none have seen us. Bridal Song to Amala [*or* Epithalamia *or* Song at Amala's Wedding]. Thomas Lovell Beddoes. *Fr.* Death's Jest Book. ChER; FaBoEn; LoBV; OBVV; PoE; PoEL-4
We Have Been Believers. Margaret Walker. PoNe
We have been cruel in thought. Life's not so sweet. Frank Wilmot. *Fr.* To God, from the Warring Nations. BoAV
We have been dead, our shroud enfolds the sea. To God, from the Warring Nations. Frank Wilmot. BoAu
We have been deeply interested in the words of the song. Alsace or Alsatians. Gertrude Stein. *Fr.* Accents in Alsace. AtBAP
We Have Been Friends Together. Caroline Elizabeth Sarah Norton. LPS-1; VA
We Have Been Happy. Max Eastman. AnEnPo
We have been helping with the cake. Day before Christmas. Marchette Chute. ChBR
We Have Been Here Before. Morris Bishop. FiBHP; InMe; WhC
We have come with joyful greeting. Song of Arbor Day. Sara J. Pettinos. PEOR
We have cried in our despair. When Helen Lived. W. B. Yeats. ViBoPo
We have dreamed dreams beyond our comprehending. Beyond the Farthest Horizon. Sidney Royse Lysaght. GrCo-2
We have faith in old proverbs full surely. Where There's a Will There's a Way. Eliza Cook. BLPA; FaFP; TreF
We have fed you all for a thousand years. Labor. *Unknown.* OQP; PGD; QP-1
We have forgot what we have been. Stanzas. Thomas William Parsons. UnW
We have found our peace, and move with the turning globe. Epithalamium. A. R. D. Fairburn. AnNZ
We have fulfilled our apprehension, hope. Flight into Darkness. Ralph Gustafson. PeCV
We have gone around the field. Charm to Save Cattle. *Unknown.* OnPM
We have heard no nightingales singing. Working Class. Bertram Warr. BoCaPo (1948 ed.); WaP
We have heard the trumpets calling Youth. Katharine Lee Bates. PGD
We have kept faith, ye Flanders' dead. In Flanders Now. Edna Jaques. CaP; MaRV
We have known sins and evils every day and death we have known. Rabindranath Tagore. *Fr.* The Oarsmen. MaRV
We Have Lived and Loved Together. Charles Jefferys. FaBoBe; NeHB; PoToHe
We have lived long enough to know. Storm over Rockefeller Center. Raymond Holden. AnAmPo
We have loitered and laughed in the flowery croft. A Garden Lyric. Frederick Locker-Lampson. HBV
We Have Lost Our Little Hanner. "Max Adeler." FiBHP
"We have made them fools and weak!" said the Strong Ones. God and the Strong Ones. Margaret Widdemer. CP; HBMV; HiLiAm; PoFr; QS
We have met late—it is too late to meet. A Denial. Elizabeth Barrett Browning. LEAP
We have minted her beauty in multiple golden medallions. Ox-Bone Madonna. John Duffy. ISi
We have much sand along our beach. Fun on the Beach. Alice Wilkins. GFA
We have neither summer nor winter. Nature. H. D. Carberry. PoNe

We have no heart for the fishing, we have no hand for the oar. The Dykes. Kipling. ChMo
We have no land for which to fight. Wage-Slaves to War-Makers. Ralph Cheyney. QP-2
We have opened the door. The Dead Feast of the Kol-Folk. Whittier. PoEL-4
We have our hopes and fears that flout us. A New Heaven. John Gould Fletcher. MAP; MoAmPo
We Have Paid Enough Long Since in Our Own Blood. Virgil, *tr. fr. Latin by* Richmond Lattimore. *Fr.* Georgics. WaaP
We have picked the pocket of silence. Radio. Therese Lindsey. BAP; PoeMoYo; VOD (1935 ed.)
We Have Planted a Tree. Laurence Binyon. LBBV
We have rested our limbs. Mutations of the Phoenix. Sir Herbert Read. BrBE
We have sailed many months, we have sailed many weeks. "Lewis Carroll." *Fr.* The Hunting of the Snark. NA
We have saved the soul of the man who killed. What Our Lord Wrote in the Dust. *Unknown.* ChIP; OQP; QP-2
We have scarcely time to tell thee. Shelly. James McIntyre. FiBHP
We have scotched [*or* scotch'd] the snake, not kill'd it. Shakespeare. *Fr.* Macbeth, III, ii. AtBAP; NBE
We have seen her. Hilda Doolittle ("H. D."). Tribute to the Angels, XXIX. MeRV
We Have Seen His Star in the East. Molly Anderson Haley. ChIP; PGD
We Have Seen Thee, O Love. Swinburne. *Fr.* Atalanta in Calydon. BEL; PoVP; VLEP, *abr.* (Chorus: "We have seen thee, O Love.") VA (Choruses from "Atalanta in Calydon.") EnLi-2; LiA (Love and Love's Mates.) BMEP, *abr.*; BPN, *abr.*; EmBrPo
We have seen thee, queen of cheese. Queen of Cheese. James McIntyre. FiBHP
We have seen worlds together, you and I. Reminiscence. Jeanne Gidding. CAG
We have sent him seeds of the melon's core. Ku-Klux. Madison Cawein. AA; PAH
We have shared already our father's goods; and besides thy share. The Fall of Man and the Early Ages of the Earth. Hesiod. *Fr.* Works and Days. GrPE
We have shared beauty and have shared grief, too. A Prayer for a Marriage. Mary Carolyn Davies. TrPWD
We have short time to stay as you. Daffodils. Robert Herrick. *Fr.* To Daffodils. PEOR
We have shot the last whiskey cup from the trapper's head. The Last Whiskey Cup. Paul Engle. ATP; YaD
We have spent the whole day until dusk. The Love Cave. Seami Motokiyo. LiTW
We have sweat our share. Stable-Talk. Raymond Knister. BoCaPo; CaP
We have talent. People call us. To Pi Ssu Yao. Tu Fu. OnPC
We have the smallest house of all. We. Mary Carolyn Davies. GaP
We have tomorrow. Youth. Langston Hughes. GoSl
We have tried words before—always in vain. The Knife. Milton Kaplan. TrJP
We have two gardens. One is sweet. Our Two Gardens. Richard Kirk. TSWC
We Have Unlearned. Nikolai Tikhonov, *tr. fr. Russian by* Babette Deutsch. TrRV ("We have unlearned to give when beggars cry," *tr. by* C. M. Bowra.) BoRS
We have walked in Love's land a little way. April Love. Ernest Dowson. PG
We have walked, looking at the actual trees. Leaves before the Wind. May Sarton. NePoAm
"We Have with Us Tonight." Bert Leston Taylor. PFE
We have worked our claims. '49. Joaquin Miller. BAV
We hear thee speak of the thyroid gland. The Thyroid Gland. "R. M." PA
We heard her speaking of Chinese musicians. The Woman Who Disapproved of Music at the Bar. Horace Gregory. MoPo
We heard it calling, clear and low. The Cuckoo. Frederick Locker-Lampson. HBV
We heard the corncrake's call from close at hand. First Corncrake. John Hewitt. NeIP
We heard the dead leaves rustle. Wayfarers. Harvey Wagner Flink. DaM
We heard the little hen was black. The Little Black Hen. Armel O'Connor. SaFP
We heard the thrushes by the shore and sea. In Kerry. J. M. Synge. AWP; JAWP; MBP; MoBrPo; WBP
We heard them like besiegers down the street. Subway Builders. Lawrence Lee. PoMa
We helped to save her from the life. A New Year Bride. Tamiko Yamamuro. SoLD
We, Hermia. Helena and Hermia. Shakespeare. *Fr.* A Midsummer Night's Dream, III, ii. GN
We hold not in our power. Odes, V, 16. Pierre de Ronsard. PrPoCR
We humbly ask, dear Master. New Year's Morning. *Unknown.* PraP
We hunted that day in the forest: I started an antlered buck. Two Hunters. Harvey Wagner Flink. DaM
We in our wandering. A Song of the Open Road. John Addington Symonds. AWP; JAWP; WBP; WHA
We in this radiant circle looked so long. Macias in the Circle of Venus. Juan de Mena. *Fr.* Labyrinth of Fortune. AnSpL-1
We, innumerable dread legions of labor. We. Vladimir Kirillov. LiTW
We invoke holy Patrick, Ireland's chief apostle. Prayer to St. Patrick. Ninine. OnYI
We is gathered hyeah, my brothahs. An Ante-Bellum Sermon. Paul Laurence Dunbar. YT
We jogged along slowly. Granada. Mikhail Svetlov. RuPo
We journey to Eleusis, you and I. The Greater Mystery. John Myers O'Hara. TBM
We journeyed through broad woodland ways. A Spring Journey. Alice Freeman Palmer. HBV
We Keep Memorial Day. Kate Brownlee Sherwood. HH
We Kiss'd Again with Tears. Tennyson. *See* As thro' the Land at Eve We Went.
We kissed at the barrier; and passing through. On the Departure Platform. Thomas Hardy. ChMo; CMP; LO
We knew it would rain, for all the morn. Before the Rain. Thomas Bailey Aldrich. GN; LPS-2
We knew so much; when her beautiful eyes could lighten. Sagacity. William Rose Benét. MAP; MoAmPo; NeMA
We knew that he was not a model cat. Elegy. Margaret E. Bruner. CIV
We know as we grow older. Whatever Is—Is Best. Ella Wheeler Wilcox. PoToHe
We know him now: all narrow jealousies. Albert the Good. Tennyson. *Fr.* Idylls of the King: Dedication. BMEP
We know not through what trackless space of night. The Star. Ida Norton Munson. ChIP
We know not what it is, dear, this sleep so deep and still. The Two Mysteries. Mary Mapes Dodge. AA; HBV; LPS-1; MaRV; WGRP
We know not where horizons end. On a Ship at Sea. Ann Stanford. MuM
We know not yet what life shall be. Mors et Vita. Samuel Waddington. HBV
We know she lives upon that thorny hill. Jezebel. Scudder Middleton. HBMV; TBM
We know the paths wherein our feet should press. A Prayer [*or* Purpose]. John Drinkwater. OQP; PraP; QP-1
We know Thee, each in part. All in All. John Banister Tabb. OQP; QP-2
We labor and are heavy-laden. Come unto Me. Katharine Lee Bates. ChIP
We lack, yet cannot fix upon the lack. Later Life, VI. Christina Rossetti. VA
We, lads and lasses pure. Hymn to Diana. Catullus. LiA
We lay in the trenches we'd dug in the ground. The Ballad of Bunker Hill. Edward Everett Hale. MC; PAH
We Lay Us Down to Sleep. Louise Chandler Moulton. AA; OBAV
We learn in the retreating. Emily Dickinson. BoFr
We learned to laugh. Although the flying bombs. Rackheath. Coman Leavenworth. *Fr.* Norfolk Memorials. LiTA
We leave the well-beloved place. In Memoriam A. H. H., CII. Tennyson. BPN; EM-2; EmBrPo; EnLi-2; EPN; GEPC; PoEL-5; ViPo; VLEP
We left behind the painted buoy. The Voyage. Tennyson. BPN; EmBrPo; PoVP; ViPP; VLEP
We left the city, street and square. John Francis O'Donnell. *Fr.* A July Dawn. IrPN
We left the homestead at break of day. In the Day's Work. Jessie Litchfield. MoAuPo
We left the silent forest. Charles Mair. *Fr.* Tecumseh, IV, vi. BoCaPo
We lie by towering hollyhocks. August Night, 1953. Elizabeth B. Harrod. NePoEA
We lie in the King's Hall at Winchester. The Player Queen. "Sagittarius" (Olga Katzin). DiM
We lift our glad hearts, Lord, in thankfulness. Youth's Thankfulness. Edgar Daniel Kramer. PEDC; PGD
We lift our standard to the mountain top. Manuel María Flores. *Fr.* Ode to the Fatherland. PoFr
We, like the leaves of many-blossomed Spring. Mimnermus, *tr. fr. Greek by* C. A. Elton. GrPo
We like to go to Granny's house. Taking Turns. Emilie Blackmore Stapp. GFA
We like you, Glorious Dead. The Glorious Survivors. A. E. Coppard. FaBoTw
We listen, wind from where. The Runner with the Lots. Léonie Adams. MoPo; NePA
We live a little while. Old People. Richard R. Kirk. LS
We Live by Faith. Whittier. OQP; QP-1 (Requirement.) GrCo-2

We Live in a Rickety House. Alexander McLachlan. BoCaPo
We Live in Deeds. Philip James Bailey. *See* Aim of Life, The.
We live in separate worlds. I cannot pierce. On "Shep," a Pet Dog. Stanton A. Coblentz. AlBD
We live in so complete and full a world. Worlds. Michael Stern. CAG
We live in the oblivion of our changes. Movement. Paul Eluard, *tr. by* Wallace Fowlie. MiCF
We live oblivious of our transformations. Our Movement. Paul Eluard, *tr. by* Stephen Spender *and* Frances Cornford. LiTW
We live, while we see the sun. Pedro Calderón de la Barca. *Fr.* Life Is a Dream. AWP; JAWP; LiTW; PoFr; WBP
We Long to See Jesus. Anna E. Hamilton. BePJ
We look before and after. Our Sweetest Songs. Shelley. *Fr.* To a Skylark. MaRV
We looked, we loved, and therewith instantly. Pure Death. Robert Graves. CoBMV; MoAB; MoPo; PoD
We Love the Venerable House. Emerson. MaRV
We love thee, Ann Maria Smith. The Editor's Wooing. "Orpheus C. Kerr." BOHV
We loved our Nightjar, but she would not stay with us. The Nightjar. Sir Henry Newbolt. MBP
We loved the wild clamor of battle. The Song of the Flags. S. Weir Mitchell. PAH
We loved thee, Swordy Well, and love thee still. Swordy Well. John Clare. WHA
We lying by seasand, watching yellow. Poem. Dylan Thomas. MoWP
We made ourselves a castle. September. Katharine Pyle. PCH
We make both mead and garden gay. Daffodils. P. A. Ropes. BoTP
We make our meek adjustments. Chaplinesque. Hart Crane. ChMo; CrMA; LiTG; LiTM (rev. ed.); OxBA; ReMP
We make ourselves a place apart. Revelation. Robert Frost. InPo; MOAP; TwP
We make that lovely sighing sound. The Name. Eileen Duggan. ISi
We make the world in which we live. The World We Make. Alfred Grant Walton. PoToHe (new ed.)
We may go through the world, but it will be slow. People Will Talk. *Unknown.* TreFS
We may live without poetry, music and art. What We May Live Without. "Owen Meredith." *Fr.* Lucile. PoToHe (new ed.); TreF
We may not abide, even with what is most. To Hölderlin. Rainer Maria Rilke. AnGP
We may not climb the heavenly steeps. Whittier. *Fr.* Our Master. BePJ; ChIP; OQP; QP-1
We may not know. In the Time of Strife. Frank L. Stanton. FOAH
We may not say. Siege Conditions. Robert Herring. MoWP
We may raise our voices even in this still glade. The Glade. Edward Shanks. LO
We may shut our eyes. Joys. James Russell Lowell. *Fr.* The Vision of Sir Launfal: Prelude to Pt. I. BoTP
We may well wonder at those froward hermits. The Eremites. Robert Graves. LiTB
We meet and part now over all the world. The Company of Lovers. Judith Wright. BoAV; MoAuPo
We meet in joy, though we part in sorrow. Martyrs' Song. Christina Rossetti. EmBrPo
We Meet at Morn. Hardwicke Drummond Rawnsley. POT; PoTo
We meet 'neath the sounding rafter. The Revel [*or* Revelry for the Dying *or* Stand to Your Glasses *or* Our Last Toast]. Bartholomew Dowling. AnIV; BLPA; HBV; LPS-3; OnYI; PIR; TreF; VA; YaD
We meet—one another, and friendship expands. The Prayer Meeting. Amos R. Wells. PraP
We meet upon the Level and we part upon the Square. The Level and the Square. Robert Morris. BLPA
We Men Are of Two Worlds. Mary Elizabeth Colman. CaP
We men of Earth have here the stuff. Earth Is Enough. Edwin Markham. MaRV; OQP; PoTo; QP-1; TreFS
We men of Hellas live now turned to dust. The End. Palladas. GrPE
We met after a year. Marionettes. "Michael Field." TCPD
We met but in one giddy dance. To ——. Winthrop Mackworth Praed. ERP; HBV
We met in a bushel of paradise birds. A Night Full of Nothing. Keith Sinclair. AnNZ
We Met on Roads of Laughter. Charles Divine. FaBoBe; HBMV
We met the *Flying Dutchman.* The *Flying Dutchman.* Charles Godfrey Leland. DaM; PoMS
We Met Them on the Common Way. Elizabeth C. Cardozo. MaRV
We met upon a crowded street one day. Casual Meeting. Margaret E. Bruner. PoToHe
We might, if you had willed, have conquered Heaven. On a Lost Opportunity. Wilfrid Scawen Blunt. The Love Sonnets of Proteus, LVII. EtPaEn
We mind not how the sun in the mid-sky. Cleone to Aspasia. Walter Savage Landor. *Fr.* Pericles and Aspasia. BPN
We miss her, not because we see. Emily Dickinson. BoFr
We more than others have the perfect right. Song of the Moderns. John Gould Fletcher. AWP; InPo; MOAP
We move, the wheel must always move. Politics. Tennyson. CoBE; PoRL
We muse on miracles who look. Miracle. Edith Daley. BAP; MaRV
We must admire her perfect aim. The Colder the Air. Elizabeth Bishop. MiAP
We must affirm the supernatural. On the Supernatural. W. W. E. Ross. BoCaPo
We must be free or die, who speak the tongue. Faith and Freedom. Wordsworth. *Fr.* It Is Not to Be Thought Of. GN
We must be nobler for our dead, be sure. The Watchers. Arlo Bates. AA
We must have silence where we go. There Must Be Silence. Anne Tansey. JKCP (1955 ed.)
We must not hope to be mowers. As a Man Soweth. Goethe. MaRV
We Must Not Part [as Others Do]. *Unknown.* ElSeCe; EV-1; SeCL
We must pass like smoke or live within the spirit's fire. Immortality. "Æ." AnIV; AWP; GTIV; JAWP; OBMV; VA; WBP; WGRP
We must uprise O my people. Lynette Roberts. *Fr.* A Heroic Poem. MoWP
We mustered at midnight, in darkness we formed. Bethel. A. J. H. Duganne. PAH
We name us a name. To Björnstjerne Björnson. Knut Hamsun. AnNoLy
We Need a King. Arthur R. Macdougall, Jr. PGD
We need a new patriotism. A New Patriotism. Chauncey R. Piety. PGD
We need him now—his rugged faith that held. Abraham Lincoln, the Master [*or* The Master]. Thomas Curtis Clark. OHIP; OQP; PEDC; QP-2
We Need Not Bid, for Cloistered Cell. John Keble. HBV
We need you now, strong guardians of our hearts. The Poets. Scudder Middleton. HBMV
We Needs Must Be Divided in the Tomb. George Santayana. Sonnets, XXXV. LBMV; OBAV; ViBoPo
We Needs Must Love the Highest. Tennyson. *Fr.* Idylls of the King: Guinevere. MaRV
We never half believed the stuff. James Wetherell. E. A. Robinson. MoAmPo
We never knew the touch of fur and feather. Timber Line Trees. Jamie Sexton Holme. PoOW
We never know how high we are. Emily Dickinson. AmP; AmPo; AmPP; AnFE; APA; CoAnAm; WaKn (Aspiration.) CV (Self-Reliance.) CoBA
We never know we go—when we are going. Emily Dickinson. TCAP
We never meet, yet we meet day by day. Thoughts in Separation. Alice Meynell. ACP; GoBC; MeRV; POTT
We Never Speak as We Pass By. *Unknown.* TreFS
We, not content with naming distant views. Country Walk. Geoffrey Taylor. OxBI
We now mid hope vor better cheer. Jeane. William Barnes. LO
We numbered many in the ship. Arion. Pushkin. TrRV
We often read with new delight. Sir Orfeo. *Unknown.* MeEV
We old men. The Old Men. Ernest Rhys. POTE
We only ask for sunshine. Song. Helen Hay Whitney. HBV
We open here our treasures and our gifts. A Christmas Prayer. Herbert H. Hines. ChIP; MaRV; OQP; PGD; PSO; QP-1
We park and stare. A full sky of the stars. The Death of the Sheriff [*or* Noli Me Tangere]. Robert Lowell. FiMAP; MoAB; MoAmPo (1950 ed.)
We parted, but my heart still wears. Mikhail Lermontov, *tr. fr. Russian by* Maud F. Jerrold. BoR
We Parted in Silence. Julia Crawford. LPS-1
We pause beside this door. January. Lucy Larcom. OQP; QP-1
We pity; we should dread. The Terrible Dead. Mary Carolyn Davies. HBMV
We place Thy sacred name upon our brows. Still Thou Art Question. *Unknown.* ChIP; PGD; StJW
We plant the trees on Memorial Day. Memorial Day. Rose Florence Levy. MeMeAg
We planted a garden. Flowers. Harry Behn. FaPON
We play at paste. Emily Dickinson. TCAP
We play now very lightly, on the strings. Rondel for Middle Age. Louise Townsend Nicholl. NePoAm
We pledge ourselves. Facing the New Year. *Unknown.* PGD; PSO

We pledged our hearts, my love and I. The Exchange. Samuel Taylor Coleridge. EmBrPo; ERP; FiBHP; HBV; LPS-1; OAEP; WhC
We plough and sow—we're so very, very low. The Song of the Lower Classes. Ernest Charles Jones. CoMu; OBVV
We Plow the Fields. Matthias Claudius, *tr. fr. German by* Jane M. Campbell. MaRV
(We Plough the Fields.) OTPC (1946 ed.)
We praise not now the poet's art. Bryant on His Seventieth Birthday. Whittier. DD; GA
We praise thee, O God; we acknowledge thee to be the Lord. Te Deum Laudamus. *Unknown.* MaRV; WGRP; WHL
We pray for pity, Lord, not justice, we. Frank Wilmot. *Fr.* To God, from the Warring Nations. BoAV; NeLNL
We pray Thee, have mercy on Zion! Prayer for Redemption. *Unknown.* TrJP
We prayed for miracles: the prairie dry. Epilogue to the Outrider. Dorothy Livesay. CaP
We prowl through midnight streets. Night. Tamiko Yamamuro. SoLD
We pulled for you when the wind was against us. Song of the Galley-Slaves. Kipling. *Fr.* Many Inventions. ChTr; PoEL-5; PoFr
We put him to bed in his little nightgown. After the Fourth of July. M. Phelps Dawson. DD
We put more coal on the big red fire. Father's Story. Elizabeth Madox Roberts. FaPON; MPB
We put out from Sunderland loaded down with rails. The Ballad of the *Bolivar.* Kipling. EPP; TCEP
We quarreled that morning. Julia Miller. Edgar Lee Masters. *Fr.* Spoon River Anthology. MoVE
We ranging down this lower track. In Memoriam A. H. H., XLVI. Tennyson. EmBrPo; EnLi-2; EPN; GEPC; ViPo; VLEP
We reach the utmost limit of the earth. Prometheus Bound. Aeschylus, *tr. by* Elizabeth Barrett Browning. EnLi-2 (1939 ed.)
We Reached Out Far. Peretz Markish, *tr. fr. Yiddish by* Jacob Sonntag. TrJP
We read of kings and gods that kindly took. A Cruel Mistress. Thomas Carew. ElSeCe; EPS
We Reason of These Things. Wallace Stevens. *Fr.* Notes toward a Supreme Fiction. CrMA
We rode at a trot. Grenada. Mikhail Svetlov. WaaP
We rode hard, and brought the cattle from brushy springs. Proud Riders. H. L. Davis. AnAmPo; LA; NP
We rode out with the pealing day before us. N. H. Brettell. *Fr.* Wind and an Eagle Owl. BoSA
We rode the tawny Texan hills. That Texan Cattle Man. Joaquin Miller. BOHV
We rode together. Winter Weather. William Morris. BPN; EmBrPo; EPN; PFE; TOP
We said: there will surely be hawthorn out. Spring Snow and Tui. Mary Ursula Bethell. AnNZ
We said *We understand,* and for a while. Urban History. Chester Kallman. CrMA
We sail toward evening's lonely star. Song. Celia Thaxter. AA; PR
We sailed and sailed upon the desert sea. Hope. William Dean Howells. AA; OBAV
We sailed by the old world's tideways, down through the long sea-lanes. The Secret of the Deeps. Sidney Royse Lysaght. EtS
We sailed to and fro in Erie's broad lake. Perry's Victory. *Unknown.* PAH
We sat among the stalls at Bethlehem. *See* We sate among the stalls . . .
We sat and talked. It was June, and the summer light. Horse in a Field. Walter de la Mare. HBMV
We sat at the hut of the fisher. Twilight. Heine, *tr. by* Louis Untermeyer. AWP; JAWP; WBP
We Sat at the Window. Thomas Hardy. EPP
We sat by the fisher's cottage. The Fisher's Cottage. Heine, *tr. by* Charles G. Leland. LPS-2
We sat debating many things together. Notation on Immortality. Nancy Byrd Turner. AlBD
We sat together at one summer's end. Adam's Curse. W. B. Yeats. CoBMV; Po
We sat together close and warm. The Young Mystic. Louis Untermeyer. TSW; TSWC
We sat, two children, warm against the wall. The Gate. Edwin Muir. LiTM (rev. ed.)
We sat within the farm-house old. The Fire of Drift-Wood. Longfellow. AmPP (4th ed.); CoV; HBV; IAP; LBAP; OxBA
We sate [*or* sat] among the stalls at Bethlehem. The Holy Night. Elizabeth Barrett Browning. *Fr.* The Virgin Mary to the Child Jesus. CLS
We saw a bloody sunset over Courtland. Remembering Nat Turner. Sterling A. Brown. PoNe
We saw and woo'd [*or* wooed] each others eyes. To Castara [*or* The Reward of Innocent Love]. William Habington. *Fr.* Castara. ACP; EV-2; LoBV
We saw him go, rifles on either side. The Crime Took Place at Granada. Antonio Machado. PoFr
We Saw Him Sleeping. Gerald Bullett. *See* Carol: "We saw Him sleeping in His manger bed."
We saw one first and thought it was the only one. Bloody Cranesbill on the Dunes. E. J. Scovell. ChMP
We saw that city on the inland sea. Archibald MacLeish. *Fr.* Conquistador: Bernal Diaz' Preface. AtBAP
We saw the dark birds fly. The Ninth of April. Otto Gelsted. BoDS
We saw the light shine out a-far. The Golden Carol. *Unknown.* OHIP; SDH; YT
We saw the slow tides go and come. A Sea Dream. Whittier. IAP; TCAP
We saw the swallows gathering in the sky. Modern Love, XLVII. George Meredith. AnFE; BEL; BMEP; BoLiVe; CaAE; CoEV; EmBrPo; EnLi-2; EnLoPo; EtPaEn; FaBoEn; GTBS-D; GTML; GTSL; LEAP; LiA; POTT; SeCeV; TyEnPo; VA; ViBoPo; ViPo; WHA
We saw thee come in, a wee naked babe. Farewell to the Old Year. Eleanor Farjeon. SiSoSe
We saw Thee in Thy balmy nest. Shepherds' Hymn [*or* A Hymn Sung as by the Shepherds]. Richard Crashaw. *Fr.* In the Holy Nativity of Our Lord God. ACP; CAW; EG; GoBC; OBEV; TrGrPo
We saw truth shining through the shabby compromise. Rededication. Emanuel Litvinoff. WaP
We say it for an hour, or for years. Good-by. Grace Denio Litchfield. PoToHe
We say the sea is lonely; better say. The Open Sea. William Meredith. NePoEA; UnPo (3d ed.)
We scatter seeds with careless hand. The Effect of Example [*or* Example]. John Keble. HBV; HBVY; LPS-3; MaRV
We seamen are the bonny boys. The Saylor's Song. *Unknown.* SG
We search the world for truth. The Bible [*or* The Book Our Mothers Read *or* Knowledge]. Whittier. *Fr.* Miriam. BLRP; MaRV; NeHB; OQP; PoToHe (new ed.); QP-1
We see Him come, and know Him ours. Robert Herrick. *Fr.* A Christmas Carol: "What sweeter music can we bring." MyFE
We see him sculptured in each ruined hall. The Assyrian Lion. Leah Bodine Drake. MuM
We See Jesus. Annie Johnson Flint. BLRP
We see not, know not; all our way. Thy Will Be Done. Whittier. LPS-2
We see Orestes and his Phocian friend. To Friendship. Don Juan de Arguijo. BoFr
We see them not—we cannot hear. Are They Not All Ministering Spirits? [*or* Angels of the Spring]. Robert Stephen Hawker. CoBE; EPN; EV-4; GoBC; HBV; NLK; OBEV (1st ed.)
We seek the saloons and the wenches. The Sailors. Karel van de Woestijne. OnPM
We seek to know, and knowing seek. In Immemoriam [*or* In Memoriam]. "Cuthbert Bede." BOHV; NA; PA
We seek to know the moving of each sphere. Sir John Davies. *Fr.* Nosce Teipsum. MyFE
We seek what no man has perceived by light. Chant of the Old Men in the Woods. Charles Norman. BAP
We seem to tread the self-same street. Florence MacCarthy's Farewell to His English Love. Aubrey Thomas De Vere. IrPN
We serve no weak and timid Christ. The Christ Militant. Thomas Curtis Clark. ChIP
We set up tents. So Cold. Tamiko Yamamuro. SoLD
We Shall Attain. James B. Kenyon. OQP; QP-2
We shall build it again though it caves in. Lost City. Marion Strobel. NP
We Shall Build On! G. A. Studdert-Kennedy. MaRV; OQP; QP-2
We Shall Come Back. Nordahl Grieg, *tr. fr. Norwegian by* Charles W. Stork. AnNoLy
We shall come to-morrow morning, who were not to have her love. Emily Hardcastle, Spinster. John Crowe Ransom. ChMo; LS; NV
We shall do so much in the years to come. What Have We Done Today? [*or* Today]. Nixon Waterman. OQP; PTA-1; QP-1; WBLP
We shall grow old apace, and die. Robert Herrick. *Fr.* Corinna's Going a-Maying. PoD
We shall have everything we want and there'll be no more dying on the pretty plains or in the supper clubs. Ode to Joy. Frank O'Hara. NeAP
We Shall Have Far to Go. James Wreford Watson. CaP
We shall have music. Love in Age. Charles G. Bell. NePoAm-2
We shall live, maybe, till our world turns grey. Love Looks to the Future. Gerald Gould. POTE
We shall meet, but we shall miss him. The Vacant Chair. Henry Stevenson Washburn. BlG; OlF; TreFS

We shall never know, never. The Case of the Murdered Bird. Luis Cernuda. CoSP
We shall not always plant while others reap. From the Dark Tower. Countee Cullen. BANP; CDC; NeMA; PoNe
We shall not cease from exploration. T. S. Eliot. *Fr.* Four Quartets: Little Gidding. ImOP
We Shall Not Dwell Forever in These Yellow Lands. "St. J. Perse," *tr. fr. French by* T. S. Eliot. *Fr.* Anabasis. AtBAP
We shall not go up against you. This Be Our Revenge. Saul Tchernichowsky. TrJP
We shall not miss thee less but more. R. S. S. Wendell Phillips Stafford. GrCo-2
We Shall Not Overcome Our Sorrows. Karolina Karlovna Pavlova. *tr. fr. Russian by* Babette Deutsch. TrRV
We shall not travel by the road we make. Pioneers [*or* Road Makers]. *Unknown, at. to* V. H. Friedlaender. BMEP; MaRV; PoTo
We shall not wholly die. To Poets All. Thomas Curtis Clark. MaRV
We shall remember him. John Butler Yeats. Jeanne Robert Foster. GoYe
We Shall Remember Them. James Terry White. PEDC
We Shall Say. Miriam Allen deFord. GoYe
We Shall Survive. Arnulf Överland, *tr. fr. Norwegian by* Charles W. Stork. AnNoLy
We sha'n't see Willy any more, Mamie. To a Bull-Dog. J. C. Squire. AlBD; ReTS
We shape ourselves the joy or fear. Destiny. Whittier. *Fr.* Raphael. MaRV
We should stay longer if we durst. *See* Ye should stay longer if we durst.
We show no monstrous crocodile. Jasper Mayne. *Fr.* The City Match. CenL
We shut them out, the houses. Time Out. Oliver Jenkins. GoYe
We sighed and said, The world's high purpose falters. The Lyric Deed. John G. Neihardt. DD; GA; TBM
We, sighing, said, "Our Pan is dead." Thoreau's Flute. Louisa May Alcott. AA; DD; GA; HBV; LBAP
We sink within this earth's dark waters: we. To Him Who Walks the Water. E. Merrill Root. ChIP
We sit and talk, and kiss away the hours. James Randolph. LO
We sit indoors and talk of the cold outside. There Are Roughly Zones. Robert Frost. ChMo; PoLFOT
We Sit Solitary. *Unknown.* TrJP
We sleep and wake and sleep, but all things move. The Golden Year. Tennyson. PSO
We smile at astrological hopes. For the Conjunction of Two Planets. Adrienne Cecile Rich. ImOP
We sneer and we laugh with the lip—the most of us do it. The Way of the World. George Frederick Cameron. BoCaPo; CPG
We sow the glebe, we reap the corn. Mystery. Elizabeth Barrett Browning. OBVV; UnPo
We spend six hours. Hours. *Unknown.* OxBG
We spin along, we pass and see. A Spiritual Song. Franz Werfel. BoFr
We spoke of a rest in a fairy knowe of the North, but he. Tusitala. Andrew Lang. VOD
We squander health in search of wealth. Health and Wealth. *Unknown.* PTA-2
We stand apart. The Priesthood. Yvor Winters. NP
We stand talking in the cave whose walls are. On Meeting a Stranger in a Bookshop. Oscar Williams. LoPo; NePA
We stand unbroken in our places. The Song of the Siberian Exiles. Nikolai Alekseyevich Nekrasov. PoFr
We stand upon the moorish mountain side. The Pine Woods. John, Lord Hanmer. VA
We started speaking. The Meeting. Katherine Mansfield. AV; LoPS
We stay/ as the leaves. The Soldiers. Giuseppe Ungaretti. OnPM
We stayed the night in the pathless gorge of Ventana Creek, up the east fork. Oh, Lovely Rock. Robinson Jeffers. Po
We steamed into New York harbor the other day. The Statue of Liberty. Sheila Jane Crooke. DDA; YaD
We stood beside an opening grave. "I Am the Resurrection and the Life," Saith the Lord! Robert Stephen Hawker. GoBC
We stood by a pond that winter day. Neutral Tones. Thomas Hardy. ChMo; CMP; CoBMV; CoEV; LiTL; LoPo; MaPo; MBP; MoBrPo; PoFS; PoVP; RiBV; ViPP; VLEP
We stood on the haunted island. The Phantom Ship. J. W. De Forest. EtS
We stood so steady. Crossing the Blackwater. Robert Dwyer Joyce. VA
We stood still in the bright sunlight. The Parade. Marjorie Seymour Watts. PCH
We stood up before day. In the Dordogne. John Peale Bishop. AnAmPo
We stood upon the ragged rocks. Cape-Cottage at Sunset. William Belcher Glazier. LPS-2
We stood where the wooden piers. Dora Markus. Eugenio Montale. OnHM
We strain toward Heaven and lay hold on Hell. Battle-Song of Failure. Amelia Josephine Burr. HBMV
We stride together in the rich brocade. After Harvest. Stefan George. *Fr.* Das Jahr der Seele. TwGV
We stumble down the pocked and cratered road. Madonna of the Exiles. James Edward Tobin. ISi
We summoned not the Silent Guest. The Skeleton at the Feast. James Jeffrey Roche. AA; LEAP
We Survive! Hirsch Glick, *tr. fr. Yiddish by* Ruth Rubin. TrJP
We swing ungirded hips. The Song of the Ungirt Runners. Charles Hamilton Sorley. EnLit; HBMV; MBP; MoBrPo; MuP; NeMA; OBEV (new ed.); PIAE; PreP; ShBV-2; TrGrPo (1942 ed.); TSW; TSWC; TVSH
We talked all morning, she said. A Walk in the Country. Galway Kinnell. NePoAm
We talked together in the Yung-shou Temple. The Letter. Po Chü-i, *tr. by* Arthur Waley. BoFr; LoBV; TrCh
We talked [*or* talk'd] with open heart, and tongue. The Fountain. Wordsworth. BPN; EmBrPo; EnRP; ERP; EV-3; GEPC; GTBS; GTBS-D; GTBS-W; GTSE; GTSL; OBRV; SeCePo
We Thank Thee ("For glowing autumn's brimming yield"). Thomas Curtis Clark. PGD
We Thank Thee ("Not for our lands"). Thomas Curtis Clark. OQP; PEDC; PGD, *abr.*; PoToHe (1941 ed.), *abr.*; QP-1
We Thank Thee. Grenville Kleiser. PraP
We Thank Thee. Carmen Malone. MeMeAg
We Thank Thee ("For all life's beauties"). John Oxenham. *See* For Beauty, We Thank Thee.
We Thank Thee ("For all thy ministries"). John Oxenham. *See* We Thank Thee, Lord ("For all thy ministries").
We Thank Thee. Mattie M. Renwick. HH; MeMeAg; OTPC (1946 ed.); PEDC
We Thank Thee ("For flowers that bloom about our feet"). *Unknown, sometimes at. to* Emerson. HH, *abr.*; TOAH, *abr.*
(Father, We Thank Thee.) PraP; PSO, *sl. abr.*
(Spring Prayer.) BoTP
We Thank Thee ("For gainful hours of pain and loss"). *Unknown.* TOAH
We Thank Thee ("For mother-love and father-care"). *Unknown.* FaPON; MPB; OTPC (1946 ed.)
We thank Thee for the joy of common things. A Prayer for Thanksgiving. Joseph Auslander. TrPWD
We thank Thee for the morning light. Table Graces, or Prayers. *Unknown.* BLRP
We thank Thee for the sun and rain. We Thank Thee. Carmen Malone. MeMeAg
We thank Thee, God, for eyes to see. Social Hymn for Children. Jeanette E. Perkins. PraP
We thank Thee, Heavenly Father. A Thankful Heart. *Unknown.* PraP
We thank Thee, Heavenly Father. Thanks to Spring. Mary Anderson. BoTP
We Thank Thee, Lord ("For all thy ministries"). John Oxenham. WBLP
(We Thank Thee.) PGD
We Thank Thee, Lord ("We thank Thee, Lord,/ For all Thy golden silences"). John Oxenham. OQP; PSO; QP-1
We thank Thee, Lord, for food and drink. Table Blessing. Bernice Ussery. MeMeAg
We thank Thee, Lord, for quiet upland lawns. Grace and Thanksgiving. Elizabeth Gould. BoTP
We thank Thee, Lord, for strength to serve. An Aged Couple Gives Thanks. Lois Givens Vaughan. PraP
We thank Thee, Lord, for this our food. Table Graces, or Prayers. *Unknown.* BLRP
We thank Thee, now, O Father. The Most Acceptable Gift. Matthias Claudius. BLRP
We Thank You! L. E. Cox. BoTP
We That Are Old. Stephen Gwynn. NeTW
We that are sick. Looking Up. Hiromi. SoLD
We, that did nothing study but the way. A Renunciation. Henry King. OBEV
We that look on, with God's goodwill. For the Blinded Soldiers. Austin Dobson. BPN
We that with like hearts love, we lovers twain. A Vow to Heavenly Venus. Joachim du Bellay. AWP
We, the fairies, blithe and antic. Fairies' [*or* Fairy] Song [*or* Song of Fairies Robbing an Orchard]. Thomas Randolph, *tr. by* Leigh Hunt. *Fr.* Amyntas. ALV; EPP; HBV; LPS-3; OBRV; PoMS
We, the maids of New-York city. Petition of the Maids of New-York. *Unknown.* LauV
We the proper ancients speak not out of turn. Choral. Marcus Adeney. *Fr.* Mansong. BoCaPo (1943 ed.)
We, the symmetrians, seek justice here. N.B., Symmetrians Gene Derwood. LiTA; NePA

We think to create festivals. Poems, 4. Antonio Machado. AWP; LiTW
We thirst at first—'tis nature's act. Thirst. Emily Dickinson. WGRP
We thought at first, this man is a king for sure. Blue Blood. James Stephens, *after* O'Bruaidar. MBP; MoAB; MoBrPo; OBMV; OxBI
We thought that we had tricked you, Poverello. Saint Francis. Horace Shipp. SaFP
We three are on the cedar-shadowed lawn. Modern Love, XXI. George Meredith. EmBrPo; OAEP; POTT; ViPo
We Three Kings of Orient Are. John Henry Hopkins, Jr. OHIP; OlF; YaCaBo, *with music*
(Three Kings of Orient.) ChrBoLe
We told of him as one who should have soared. Discovery. E. A. Robinson. ChMo; CMP
We too (one cried), we too. To the Mother of Christ, the Son of Man. Alice Meynell. ISi
We too take ship, O soul. Be Not Afraid. Walt Whitman. *Fr.* Song of the Open Road. MaRV
We too, we too, descending once again. The Too-late Born [*or* The Silent Slain]. Archibald MacLeish. AmP; AnFE; APA; ChMo; CMP; CoAnAm; CoBMV; ExPo; GTBS-W; LiTM; MAP; MoAB; MoAmPo; MoVE; NAMP; NePA; OxBA; PreP; ReaPo; SeCeV; TBM; TwAmPo; TwHP; WaP
We took it to the woods, we two. Emerson. Mary Mapes Dodge. AA; DD; GA; PoRL
We took our work, and went, you see. Recreation. Jane Taylor. OBRV; OxBoLi
We trample filial obedience. October. Anatoly Borisovich Marienhof. TrRV
We travelled empty-handed. The Enchanted Traveller. Bliss Carman. DDA
We trees were chopping down the monsters in the/ Street to count their rings. The Slacker Apologizes. Peter Viereck. MiAP
We trekked into a far country. Translation. Anne Spencer. BANP
We twain with one will and one heart were united. Alexandrian Erotic Fragment. *Unknown.* GrPo
We two have got a master. Political Cartoon. Aristophanes. *Fr.* The Knights. GrR
We two kept house, the Past and I. The Ghost of the Past. Thomas Hardy. BrBE
We two, O true-heart, who have learned so well. Sonnet. Odell Shepard. CAG
We two, that with so many thousand sighs. Shakespeare. *Fr.* Troilus and Cressida, IV, iv. EtPaEn
We used to be ten brothers. Ten Brothers. *Unknown.* MaC
We used to picnic where the thrift. Trebetherick. John Betjeman. AlDL; ExPo
We used to shadow-box on the shining grass. Dimidium Animae Meae. Charles A. Brady. GoYe
We used to talk of so many things. Before and after Marriage. Anne Campbell. PoToHe (new ed.)
We Visit My Estate. Richard R. Kirk. BPP; LS
We waged a war within a war. Karl Shapiro. Recapitulations, XI. PoNe
We waited in the quivering heat for his return. Lazarus. Ursula Wood. DiM
We waited out the lion weeks. Vernal Paradox. Kim Kurt. NePoAm-2
We wake to hear the storm come down. The Storm. Edward Shanks. AlDL; PtOT
We walked along, while bright and red. The Two April Mornings. Wordsworth. BPN; EmBrPo; EnRP; ERP; GEPC; GTBS; GTBS-D; GTBS-W; GTSE; GTSL
We Walked among the Whispering Pines. John Henry Boner. AA
We walked in that green field. Fossil. Paul Engle. ReMP
We walked together in the dusk. The Metropolitan Tower. Sara Teasdale. ChMo; CMP
We wander now who marched before. Old Soldier. Padraic Colum. OBMV; POTE
We wandered to the Pine Forest. Shelley. *Fr.* The Recollection. CH
We, wandering to death. Marching Song. Ernst Toller. MaRV
We wanted Li Wing. Lapsus Linguae. Keith Preston. WhC
We was camped on the plains at the head of the Cimarron. Zebra Dun. *Unknown.* ViBoFo
We watch for the light of the morn to break. Song of the Bees. Hannah Flagg Gould. OTPC
We watch the only eagles in the world. At a Parade. F. T. Prince. NeBP; WaP
We watch'd [*or* watched] her breathing thro' [*or* through] the night. The Death-Bed. Thomas Hood. BCEP; BEL; EnRP; EV-4; GTBS; GTBS-D; GTBS-W; GTSE; GTSL; HBV; MaRV; MCCG; OBEV; OBRV; OBVV; PG; TCEP; TreFS; VA
We watched/ a red rooster. Calypso. William Carlos Williams. NePoAm-2
We watched our love burn with the lumberyard. The Lumberyard. Ruth Herschberger. LiTA; LiTL; LiTM (rev. ed.)
We watched the rain come pouring down. Rainbows. Dixie Willson. GFA
We watched thy spirit flickering in the dark. In Memoriam; John Davidson. Ronald Campbell Macfie. GoTS
We Wear the Mask. Paul Laurence Dunbar. CDC
We weep, how often, I and you. Voice from the Chorus. Aleksandr Blok. BoR
We went down to the river's brink. Explanation, on Coming Home Late. Richard Hughes. ThWaDe
We went to a circus in the town. Magic Lariat. Glenn Ward Dresbach. BrR
We were able to weave from the ant to the loftiest star. Plenitude. Otto D'Sola. AnCL
We were apart; yet, day by day. Isolation; to Marguerite. Matthew Arnold. Switzerland, IV. BPN; GEPC; PoVP; ViPP; VLEP
We were born of night and terror in a wilderness of fear. The Weak. John Curtis Underwood. BAP
We Were Boys Together. George Pope Morris. AA
We were camped on the plains at the head of the Cimarron. The Zebra Dun. *Unknown.* CoSo; CSF; StPo; StVeCh
We were closed, each to each, yet dear. Each to Each. Melville Cane. GoYe
We were crowded in the cabin. Ballad of the Canal. Phoebe Cary. BOHV
We were crowded in the cabin. Ballad of the Tempest [*or* The Captain's Daughter *or* The Tempest]. James Thomas Fields. BeLS; EtS; FaBoBe; FaFP; HBV; HBVY; LPS-2; PECK; PTA-2; TreF; YaD
We were driving the down express. The Engine Driver's Story. William Wilkins. BeLS
We were forty miles from Albany. The Erie. *Unknown.* ABF; AS
We were hunting for wintergreen berries. Sister and I. *Unknown.* PTA-1
We were in bed by nine, but she did not hear the clock. All Night Long. Stephen Vincent Benét. LoPo; LoPS
We were in Georgia. You can get this land. Boris Pasternak. *Fr.* Waves. TrRV
We were laying the road to a Riddle. The Riddle. Dana Burnet. OBAV
We were lying on a prairie on Slaughter's ranch one night. Home, Sweet Home. *Unknown.* CoSo
We were not made for refuges of lies. Mary Elizabeth Coleridge. GTML
We were not many, and no bronze asserts. Epitaph. Brooke Byrne. NeTW
We were not many, we who stood. Monterey. Charles Fenno Hoffman. AA; FaBoBe; HBV; LBAP; LEAP; LPS-2; MC; OTPC (1923 ed.); PaA; PAH; PAP; PTA-2
We were often separated. A Meeting. Tu Fu. WhP
We were ordered to Samoa from the coast of Panama. An International Episode. Caroline Duer. AA; PAH
We were playing on the green together. "Is It Nothing to You?" May Probyn. GoBC; JKCP; OBEV (new ed.); OBVV; VA
We were schooner-rigged and rakish, with a long and lissome hull. A Ballad of John Silver. John Masefield. BoChLi (1939 ed.); CV; MPB; PtOT; TSW; TSWC
We were settin' there an' smokin' of our pipes discussin' things. What We Need. Edgar A. Guest. LPS-1
We were shut off from the street. Crossroads. Miguel Otero Silva. WoL
We were sitting idly gazing on the varied scene before us. A September Violet. *Unknown.* PEOR
We were so many children small. Torben's Daughter. *Unknown.* BoDaBa
We were spawned in lava mountains, from the surf line of the sea. The Strong. John Curtis Underwood. BAP; MaRV
We were taken from the ore-bed and the mine. The Secret of the Machines. Kipling. PoMa; PoTo; StVeCh
We were together. Otomo no Yakamochi, *tr. fr. Japanese by* Kenneth Rexroth. LiTW; OnPJ
We were together since the War began. A Servant. Kipling. *Fr.* Epitaphs of the War. PoVP
We were told that wars are made by the makers of munition. The Attitude of Youth. John Gould Fletcher. NeTW
We were twin brothers, tall and hale. A Flight Shot. Maurice Thompson. AA; AnAmPo; LA; OBAV
We were two daughters of one race. The Sisters. Tennyson. InvP; ReTS
We were two pretty babes, the youngest she. Childhood Fled. Charles Lamb. EnRP
We were very tired, we were very merry. Recuerdo. Edna St. Vincent Millay. FaFP; LiTA; LiTL; LiTM; NP; OxBA
We were waiting for the storm. The Storm. "Robin Christopher." RIS
We were walking and talking on the roof of the world. End of the Seers' Convention. Kenneth Fearing. LiTA

We were young, we were merry, we were very very wise. Unwelcome. Mary Elizabeth Coleridge. BMEP; CH; GTBS; GTBS-D; OBEV (new ed.); OBVV; PoVP
We Who Are about to Die ("We who are about to die salute each other in the old way"). Harold E. Fey. PGD
We, who are borne on one dark grain of dust. The Music of the Spheres. Alfred Noyes. *Fr.* Watchers of the Sky. GrCo-1
We Who Are Dead. Paul L. Benjamin. PGD
We Who Are Left. George Whalley. CaP
We who are left, how shall we look again. Lament. W. W. Gibson. BMEP; CaAE; ChMo; CMP; PtOT; TwCV
We who are old, old and gay. A Faery Song. W. B. Yeats. CBE; POTE; ViBoPo
We Who Build Visions. Stanton A. Coblentz. PGD
We who have come all ways into the city. The Trail. Edward Weismiller. WaP
We who have come back from the war. We. Hervey Allen. PC
We who have no perfection but to die. And Only Our Shadow Walks with Us. Eithne Wilkins. NeBP
We who play under the pines. Song of the Rabbits [*or* The Rabbits' Song] outside the Tavern. Elizabeth J. Coatsworth. AnNE; PoMa; RIS; SUS; TiPo
We who went where Dante went. Revisitants. Margaret Widdemer. TBM
We Who Were Born. Eiluned Lewis. *See* Birthright, The.
We who were prophets and priest-men. Joseph Auslander. *Fr.* The Poets. PoeMoYo
We who with songs beguile your pilgrimage. Prologue to "The Golden Journey to Samarkand." James Elroy Flecker. AlDL; GTBS; MM; OBMV; ReTS; TwCV
We [He, *wr.*] Whom the Dead Have Not Forgiven. Sara Bard Field. MuM; PGD
We will go no more to Shaemus, at the Nip. Shaemus. Conrad Aiken. OxBA
We will go to the wood, says Robin to Bobbin. *Unknown.* OxNR
We will have angels and men for sons. The Angel Sons. Vachel Lindsay. TCAP
We Will Not Die, These Lovers Say. Richard Burke, *tr. fr. Irish by* Robin Flower. GTIV
We will not speak of years to-night. James Russell Lowell's Birthday Festival. Oliver Wendell Holmes. PEOR
We will not whisper, we have found the place. Sonnets, XIX. Hilaire Belloc. MBP; MoBrPo
We will return, O Lord, before the snows. "Our Father Who Art." Virginia French. QS
We Will Speak Out. James Russell Lowell. PoFr
We will wait by the chestnut and the ilex tree. Orion Seeks the Goddess Diana. Sacheverell Sitwell. *Fr.* Landscape with the Giant Orion. MoVE
We wind wreaths of holly. For Randolph Bourne. James Oppenheim. AnAmPo; LA
We wish to declare how the birds of the air. The Trail of the Bird. William John Courthope. HBVY
We wish to the new child. For C. K. at His Christening. Daniel Lawrence Kelleher. NeIP
We with our Fair pitched among the feathery clover. The Individualist Speaks. Louis MacNeice. MoVE; OBMV
We Woke Together. Christopher Brennan. BoAV
We wonder whether the dream of American liberty. Archibald MacLeish. *Fr.* Land of the Free. MoAB; MoAmPo; NeMA
We wondered why he always turned aside. Inheritance. Mary Potter Thatcher Higginson. AA; LBAP
We work when the sun rises. Song of the Peasants. *Unknown. Fr.* The Fountain of Old Poems. WhP
We worship the Spirit that walks unseen. The Arctic Indian's Faith. Thomas D'Arcy McGee. BoCaPo (1943 ed.)
We worship Thee, O Sun of God. The Perfect Gift. Julia Benson Parker. BePJ; PraP
We would be building; temples still undone. Builders. Purd E. Deitz. MaRV
We would have inward peace. Matthew Arnold. *Fr.* Empedocles on Etna. LEAP
We Would See Jesus. John Edgar Park. MaRV
We Would See Jesus. W. J. Suckow. ChIP; MaRV; OQP; QP-1
We Would See Jesus ("We would see Jesus—for the shadows lengthen"). Anna B. Warner. BePJ
(Let Us See Jesus.) MaRV
We would see Jesus; lo! His star is shining. We Would See Jesus. John Edgar Park. MaRV
We would see Jesus! we have longed to see Him. We Long to See Jesus. Anna E. Hamilton. BePJ
We would see Jesus! We would look upon. We Would See Jesus. W. J. Suckow. ChIP; MaRV; OQP; QP-1
We wreathed about our darling's head. The Morning-Glory. Maria White Lowell. AA; HBV; LPS-1
We, Wystan Hugh Auden and Louis MacNeice. Their Last Will and Testament. Louis MacNeice. NAMP
We zealots made up of stiff clay. Let Us All Be Unhappy on Sunday. Charles Neaves. EBSV
Weak, The. John Curtis Underwood. BAP
Weak and irresolute is man. Human Frailty. William Cowper. HBV
Weak is th' assurance that weak flesh reposeth. Amoretti, LVIII. Spenser. PeBoSo
Weak Is the Will of Man, His Judgment Blind. Wordsworth. EnRP
Weak Monk, The. Stevie Smith. FaBoTw
Weak princes flatter when they want the power. The Oak of State. Dryden. *Fr.* Don Sebastian. BeR
Weak-winged is song. Ode Recited at the Harvard Commemoration, July 21, 1865 [*or* The Commemoration Ode]. James Russell Lowell. AA; AmPP; AnAmPo; BIG; CoBA; HBV; IAP; LA; LEAP; PaA; REAL; TCAP; TOP
Weaker the Wine, The. Su T'ung-po, *tr. fr. Chinese by* Kenneth Rexroth. OnPC
Weakest Thing, The. Elizabeth Barrett Browning. HBV
Weakling, The. Arthur Adams. BoAu
Weakness of Nature. Richard Hurrell Froude. OBRV
Weal, thou art a crooked thing, ever in thy serving! Fortune. *Unknown.* TMEV
Wealth. Emerson. BAV; ImOP
Wealth. Joyce Kilmer. LEAP; LoPo; VOD
Wealth. Sadi, *tr. fr. Persian by* Sir Edwin Arnold. *Fr.* The Gulistan. AWP; OuHeWo
Wealth came by water to this farmless island. Delos. Bernard Spencer. FaBoMo; PoN
Wealth can never produce a king. Seneca. *Fr.* Thyestes. LaP
Wealth, my good fellow, is the wise man's god. A Cyclops' Philosophy [*or* Fair Exchange]. Euripides, *tr. by* Shelley. *Fr.* Cyclops. GrR; OxBG
Wealth, my lad, was made to wander. Samuel Johnson. *Fr.* One-and-twenty. OtMeF; ViBoPo
Wealth of gold-abounding Croisos, The. Archilochus, *tr. fr. Greek by* N. H. Dole. GrPo
Wealthy Man, A. William Allingham. IrPN
Wealthy Moore, that in the Easterne rockes, The. Precious Stones. Christopher Marlowe. *Fr.* The Jew of Malta, I, i. EV-1
Wealthy Shepherd, The. Louise Morey Bowman. CPG
Wealthy young squire of Tamworth we hear, A. The Golden Glove. *Unknown.* MaC
Weapon shapely, naked, wan. Song of the Broad-Axe [*or* The Broad-Ax]. Walt Whitman. APW; MAP; MoAmPo; WoL
Weapon that comes down as still, A. The Ballot. John Pierpont. AA; InP; LEAP; PoRL
Weapon that you fought with was a word, The. Unpunished [*or* He Knoweth Not That the Dead Are Thine]. Mary Elizabeth Coleridge. BMEP; PoVP
Weapons. Anna Wickham. MBP; MoBrPo
Weapons of Evil. *Unknown, at. to* Lao-tzu, *tr. fr. Chinese by* Lin Yutang. *Fr.* Tao Teh King. MaRV
Wear and Tear. *At. to* Robert Louis Stevenson. *See* Limerick: "There was an old man of the cape."
Wear it as a bangle on your arm. Fame. Eleanor Hollister Cantus. GoYe
Wear the gown, and wear the hat. On Hearing Miss Thrale Deliberate about Her Hat. Samuel Johnson. BeR
Wear your gold and silken garments. Wise Age to Youth. Tu Chiu Niang. PoHN
Wearie Wayfarer, Ye, *sels.* Adam Lindsay Gordon.
Chase and the Race, The, *fr.* Fytte VII. OtMeF
Question Not, *fr.* Fytte VIII. PoToHe
(Man's Testament.) OtMeF
Risks of the Game, The, *fr.* Fytte II. OtMeF
Wearied arm and broken sword. Pocahontas. Thackeray. DD; FaPON; GA; GN; GoTP; MC; MPB; OTPC; PAH; TVSH
Wearily, drearily,/ Half the day long. In Prison [*or* The Knight in Prison]. William Morris. AtBAP; BPN; PoVP; SoV; ViP
Wearily, still in her dressing gown. Eliza Telefair. Jocelyn Macy Sloan. GoYe
Wearin' o' [*or* of] the Green, The. *Unknown, add. words by* Dion Boucicault. AnIL; AnIV; AWP; DD; HBV; HH; JAWP; OnYI; PoFr; TIP; TreF; WBP
(Wearing of the Green, The.) FaFP; OIF; OxBoLi; SiTL
Weariness. Longfellow. IAP
Weariness. William Alexander Percy. *Fr.* In New York. SPP
Weariness has aggravated since the year. Melancholy. Li Yu. WhP
Weariness of life that has no will, The. Everyman. Siegfried Sassoon. BLV; BoLiVe; MBP; MoBrPo
Weariness of the bones. Lament. "Pablo de Rokha." OnPM; TwSpPo
Wearing of the Green. Aileen Fisher. YeAr
Wearing of the Green, The. *Unknown. See* Wearin' o' the Green, The.

Wearing worry about money like a hair shirt. Worry about Money. Kathleen Raine. FaBoTw
Weary. George A. Chadwick. GTIV
Weary. Sir Henry Parkes. BoAu
Weary and wet-shod I went forth afterwards. The Crucifixion and the Harrowing of Hell. William Langland. *Fr.* The Vision of Piers Plowman. MeEV
Weary are the hours of a sailor boy. The Sailor Boy. *Unknown.* BaBo
Weary at heart with winter yesterday. April. Obadiah Cyrus Auringer. AA
Weary Blues, The. Langston Hughes. PoNe; TCPD; UnS
Weary day rins down and dies, The. A Jacobite's Exile, 1746 [*or* A Jacobite in Exile]. Swinburne. LH; OBVV; OtMeF
Weary in Well-doing. Christina Rossetti. RiBV; SeCePo; TrPWD; ViPo; VLEP
Weary Lot Is Thine, A. Sir Walter Scott. *Fr.* Rokeby, III. BSV; CH; EG; EmBrPo
(Rover, The.) GTBS-D; GTBS-W; GTSE; GTSL
(Rover's Adieu, The.) EBSV; HBV; OBEV
(Rover's Farewell, The.) PoE
(Song: "Weary lot is thine, fair maid, A.") EnLoPo; EV-4; OBRV; ViBoPo
Weary men, what reap ye?—"Golden corn for the stranger." The Famine Year. Lady Wilde. OnYI; PoFr; TIP
Weary night is o'er at last, The! The Trooper's Death. *Unknown.* LPS-2
Weary of Bitter Ease. Stéphane Mallarmé, *tr. fr. French by* Hubert Creekmore. AnFP
Weary of erring in this Desert Life. To Our Ladies of Death. James Thomson. BSV; GoTS
Weary of myself, and sick of asking. Self-Dependence. Matthew Arnold. BBV; BEL; BLP; BPN; EM-2; EmBrPo; EnLi-2; EnLit; EPN; GEPC; HBV; MCCG; OAEP; OQP; Po; PoVP; QP-1; ReTS; TCEP; TreFS; ViPP; VLEP; WGRP
Weary of the ceaseless war. Weary. Sir Henry Parkes. BoAu
Weary of vainly seeking happiness. Happiness. Arschag Tchobanian. ArmLP
Weary one had rest, the sad had joy, The. The Secret [*or* Because We Do Not See]. *Unknown.* BLRP; PraP
Weary Peddlers. Elias Lieberman. BAP
Weary Ploughman, The. *Unknown. See* Little Farm, The.
Weary souls, that wander wide. Fly to Jesus. Charles Wesley. BePJ
Weary Task, The. Emily Brontë. *See* Little While, a Little While, A.
Weary teacher sat alone, The. The Teacher's Dream. William Henry Venable. BeLS; PTA-1
Weary the cry of the wind is, weary the sea. Sorrow of Mydath. John Masefield. MBP; MoBrPo
Weary Traveler, *with music. Unknown.* BoAN-1
Weary way-wanderer, languid and sick at heart. The Soldier's Wife. Robert Southey. OBEC
Weary, weary, desolate. Yuma. Charles Henry Phelps. AA
Weary, weary lies the soldier. In His Blanket on the Ground. Caroline H. Gervais. BlG
Weary weed, tossed to and fro, A. Gulf-Weed. Cornelius George Fenner. EtS; LPS-2
Weary Willie and tired Tim. *Unknown.* BoN
Weary with running long, though she is fleet. Daphne. Ann Louise Hayes. PtPa
Weary with serving where I nought could get. Diella, XXVIII. Richard Lynche. TuPP
Weary with toil, I haste me to my bed. Sonnets, XXVII. Shakespeare. OBSC; PeBoSo; PoFS; ReEn; SiCE
Weary year[e] his race now having run, The. Amoretti, LXII. Spenser. OBSC; PeBoSo; ReaPo; ReIE; SiCE
Wearyin' for You. Frank L. Stanton. BAP; HBV
(Just a Wearyin' for You.) TreF
Weasel, The. *Unknown.* ChTr
Weasel and the wren consort, The. Mole Talk. Leo Kennedy. PeCV
Weasel, by a person caught, A. The Man and the Weasel. Phaedrus. AWP; OnPM
Weasel thieves in silver suit, The. Somewhere. John Vance Cheney. LBMV
Weather. Mary Ursula Bethell. AnNZ
Weather. Hilda Conkling. TiPo
Weather. Thomas Hardy. *See* Weathers.
Weather. Archibald MacLeish. *See* Cook County.
Weather, The. Nancy Byrd Turner. POT; PoTo
Weather bothered him, and the delicate muscular. Mr. Pollington Remembers a Poet. Hyam Plutzik. FiMAP
Weather Factory, The. Nancy Byrd Turner. SUS
Weather in London and Stratford-on-Avon was so, The. Shakespeare, Possibly, in California. Reed Whittemore. MoVE
Weather is fair after the fall of a few snowflakes, The. On Hearing the Flute. Lu Yu. WhP
Weather is getting cold, The. Yearnings of Love. Nalan Hsinteh. ChLP
Weather is mild, The. The Death of a Zulu. William Plomer. BoSA
Weather is the answer. Weather. Hilda Conkling. TiPo
Weather-leech of the topsail shivers, The. Tacking Ship off Shore. Walter Mitchell. AA; EtS; FaBoBe; GN; HBV; LPS-2; OBAV; PFY; PoeMoYo
Weather-man has promised snow and sleet, The. The Humble Bumble Bee. Vachel Lindsay. UTS
Weather Signs. *Unknown.* OTPC (1946 ed.)
(Rhymes about the Weather.) FaBoBe
(Weather Rule, A.) MPB (1956 ed.); OTPC (1923 ed.)
(Weather Wisdom.) HBV; HBVY; TreF
Weather Vanes. Frances Frost. SiSoSe
Weather wept, and all the trees bent down, The. "The Shimmer of Evil." Theodore Roethke. NePoAm-2
Weather Wisdom. *Unknown. See* Weather Signs.
Weather Words. David McCord. ImOP
Weathercock, The. H. H. Abbott. TVSH
Weathercock, The. Rose Fyleman. BoTP
Weathercock. Elizabeth Jennings. NePoEA
Weathers. Thomas Hardy. AlDL; ALV; AnEnPo; BLV; BoLiVe; BoTP; CBE; CBOV; CBPC; CH; FaBoCh; GTSL; LoGBV; MBP; MoAB; MoBrPo; MuP; OBMV; OtMeF; POTE; ReMP; SeCePo; ShBV-1; TCEP; VOD; YT
(Weather.) WHA
Weave garlands, maiden, from the strands. Flowers for the Graces. Sappho. GrL; OxBG
Weave In, My Hardy Life. Walt Whitman. IAP; TCAP
Weave no more silks, ye Lyons looms. Our Orders. Julia Ward Howe. AA; APW
Weave the dance, and raise again the sacred chorus. Hymn to Demeter. Louis V. Ledoux. *Fr.* The Story of Eleusis. LEAP
Weave the warp, and weave the woof. Curse upon Edward. Thomas Gray. *Fr.* The Bard. BCEP; OBEV
Weave the Weird dance—behold the hour. The Chorus of the Furies. Aeschylus. *Fr.* Eumenides. LiA
Weaver, The. William H. Burleigh. BLPA
Weaver, The. "Fanny Forester." BLPA
Weaver, The. Eloise Hamilton. MuM
Weaver, The ("I sat at my loom in silence"). *Unknown.* BLRP
Weaver, The ("I was a bachelor, I lived by myself"). *Unknown. See* Foggy, Foggy Dew.
Weaver at his loom is sitting, The. The Mystic Weaver. *Unknown.* PTA-2
Weaver of Snow, The. "Fiona Macleod." PoVP
Weaver sat by the side of his loom, A. The Weaver. "Fanny Forester." BLPA
Weavers, The. Heine, *tr. fr. German.* PoFr, *tr. by* Louis Untermeyer; TrJP
Weaver's Apprentice, The. Al-Rusafi, *tr. fr. Arabic by* A. J. Arberry. MooP
Weavers' Song, The. Thomas Deloney. *Fr.* Jack of Newbury. EV-2; SiCE
Weaving, The. Harold Lewis Cook. MoSiPe
Weaving. Tzu Yeh, *tr. fr. Chinese by* Henry H. Hart. PoHN
Weaving soft garlands. A Wreath for Persephone. Marie Emilie Gilchrist. RAR
Weazen planet Mercury, The. Around the Sun. Katharine Lee Bates. NV
Web, The. Witter Bynner. *Fr.* Chapala Poems. NP
Web, The. Homer, *tr. fr. Greek by* Sir William Marris. *Fr.* The Odyssey, II. OxBG
Web flew out and floated wide, The. For All Ladies of Shalott. Aline Murray Kilmer. NP; TBM
Web of Eros, The. Edith Sitwell. BMEP; HBMV; LBBV
Web of intrigue round me forms, A. Paranoia. Louis J. Karnosh. PoP
Web-spinner was a miser old. The True Story of Web-Spinner. Mary Howitt. OTPC (1923 ed.)
Webster. Epes Sargent. GA
Webster, an Ode, *sel.* William Cleaver Wilkinson.
At Marshfield. AA
Webster Ford. Edgar Lee Masters. *Fr.* Spoon River Anthology. NP
Webster was much possessed by death. Whispers of Immortality. T. S. Eliot. APA; ATP (1953 ed.); CaAE; ChMo; CMP; CoAnAm; CoEV; LiTA; LiTG; MAPA; NePA; NP; OBMV; PtP; TwAmPo; TwP
We'd ever so many kinds of cake. The Pirates' Tea-Party. Dorothy Una Ratcliffe. BoTP
We'd face, I'm sure, with more aplomb. Unsolved Mystery. George Ryan. WhC
We'd found an old Boche dug-out, and he knew. The Sentry. Wilfred Owen. AnEnPo; SoV
We'd gained our first objective hours before. Counter-Attack. Siegfried Sassoon. EnLit; HiLiEn; MBP; MoBrPo; PIAE; PreP; TCEP; WaP
We'd rather have the iceberg than the ship. The Imaginary Iceberg. Elizabeth Bishop. LiTM; MoAB; MoAmPo (1950 ed.); MoVE; ReMP

Weddase Maryam. *Unknown, tr. fr.* Ethiopian MS. *by* Sir E. A. Wallis Budge. ISi
Wedded. Isaac Rosenberg. FaBoEn; LO
Wedded Bliss. Charlotte Perkins Gilman. HBV
Wedded light and heat, The. Wind and Wave. Coventry Patmore. *Fr.* The Unknown Eros, I, ii. VLEP
Wedded Love. Milton. *Fr.* Paradise Lost, IV. OBS; PoFS (Their Wedded Love.) SeCePo
Wedded to a Tartar. Liu Hsi Chün, *tr. fr. Chinese by* Henry H. Hart. PoHN
Wedding, The. Conrad Aiken. AnAmPo; ChMo; CMP; LA; TCPD
Wedding, The. Tom Hood. BOHV; InMe
Wedding, A. Sir John Suckling. *See* Ballad upon a Wedding, A.
Wedding, A ("Rosy apple"). *Unknown. See* Rosy Apple, Lemon or Pear.
Wedding, The ("Thus sang she:/ One, two, three"). *Unknown, tr. fr. German.* SAS
Wedding and hanging. John Heywood. SiCE
Wedding Anniversary. Margaret E. Bruner. PoToHe
Wedding bells were ringing on a moonlit [*or* moonlight] winter's night, The. The Fatal Wedding. W. H. Windom. ABS; TreFS
Wedding Chant, The. Aristophanes, *tr. fr. Greek by* T. F. Higham. *Fr.* The Birds. OxBG
Wedding Garment, The. Rowland Watkyns. AEV
Wedding Gift, The. Minna Irving. BLPA
Wedding Hymn, A. Luis de Góngora, *tr. fr. Spanish by* Edward Meryon Wilson. *Fr.* The Solitudes. TeCS
Wedding-Hymn. Sidney Lanier. *See* Prayer at a Wedding.
Wedding Hymn, A, *sel.* Thomas Tiplady.
"O Thou, Who love in mercy hast created." MaRV
Wedding Hymn, A ("Jesus, stand beside them"). Thomas Tiplady. MaRV
Wedding Is Great Juno's Crown. Shakespeare. *Fr.* As You Like It, V, iv. ViBoPo
Wedding Morn. D. H. Lawrence. MBP; MoAB; MoBrPo
Wedding Morning, The. Francis Ledwidge. TCPD
Wedding of Alcmane and Mya, The. George Chapman. *See* Epithalamion Teratos.
Wedding of Rane Jonson, The. *Unknown, tr. fr. Danish by* E. M. Smith-Dampier. BoDaBa
Wedding of Shon Maclean, The. Robert Buchanan. EBSV
Wedding of the Clans, The. Aubrey Thomas De Vere. AnIL; GTIV; IrPN; TIP
Wedding Ring, The. Donald F. Drummond. PtPa
Wedding Ring, The. John Gould Fletcher. CMP
Wedding Sermon, The. Coventry Patmore. *Fr.* The Angel in the House. PoVP
Wedding-Song, A. John White Chadwick. AA
Wedding Song ("Up with the rafters high"). Sappho, *tr. fr. Greek by* J. M. Edmonds. GrR
Wedding Song ("My lord is all a-glow"). *Unknown, tr. fr. Chinese by* Arthur Waley. *Fr.* Shi King. LiTW
Wedding Song, The ("The sun fell in love"). *Unknown, tr. fr. Modern Greek by* Rae Dalven. MoGP
Wedding Songs. Sappho, *tr. fr. Greek.* GrL; OxBG
"Bridegroom dear," *tr. unknown.*
"Maidenhood, O Maidenhood," *tr. by* C. M. Bowra. (Farewell to Maidenhood, *tr. by* H. De Vere Stacpoole.) GrR
Wedgwood Bowl, A. Frances Beatrice Taylor. CaP; OCL
Wedlock. Jenny Grahame. LiTL
Wedlock. *Unknown. See* When Adam Was Created.
Wednesbury Cocking. *Unknown.* EnSB
Wednesday. "Elspeth." WhC
Wednesday in Holy Week. Christina Rossetti. ChIP; PGD
Wee bird came to our ha' door, A. Wae's Me for Prince Charlie. William Glen. EBSV
Wee doe account that musique good. *Unknown.* SeCSL
Wee Folk, The. Donald A. MacKenzie. EBSV
Wee folk will be tripping, The. When a Ring's around the Moon. Mary Jane Carr. BrR; TiPo
Wee, glossy, cowering, timorous beastie. To a Mouse. Burns, *ad. by* William Kean Seymour. WaKn
Wee gods with whom I live, who share. To My Household Gods. Jean François Ducis. TrFP
Wee Hughie. Elizabeth Shane. HBMV
Wee little nut lay deep in its nest, A. Among the Nuts. *Unknown.* BoTP; TVC; TVSH
Wee little worm in a hickory-nut, A. It. James Whitcomb Riley. *Fr.* A Session with Uncle Sidney. MeMeAg
Wee man o' leather. Riddle. *Unknown.* ChTr
Wee, modest, crimson-tippèd flow'r. To a Mountain Daisy. Burns. ADAH; AnEnPo; ATP; BCEP; BEL; CEP; EBSV; EiPP; EM-1; EnLi-2; EnLit; EnRP; EPP; EV-3; GN; HBV; LiA; LPS-2; MPB; OAEP; OTPC (1923 ed.); PECK; PIAE; PIR; REAL; SN; TCEP; UnPo (1st ed.); WBLP
Wee Sandy in the corner. The Still Small Voice. Alexander Smart. PRWS
Wee, sightless thing. To a Blind Bird. Hubbard Fulton Page. NoCaPo
Wee sing, wee feast, wee daunce, wee play. *Unknown.* SeCSL
Wee, sleekit, cow'rin', tim'rous beastie. To a Mouse. Burns. AnEnPo; AnFE; ATP; BBV (1923 ed.); BCEP; BEL; BLV; BoLiVe; BSV; BTP; CaAE; CBE; CEP; CoBE; EBSV; EiPP; EM-1; EnL; EnLi-2; EnLit; EnRP; EPP; EV-3; FaFP; GoTS; GTBS; GTBS-D; GTBS-W; GTSE; GTSL; HBV; HBVY; LiTG; LoBV; LPS-2; MCCG; MPB; OAEP; OBEC; OTPC; OuHeWo; PECK; PIR; PoeMoYo; PoFS; PoMa; PreP; PYM; RG; SeCeV; ShBV-2; SN; TCEP; TOP; TreFS; TrGrPo; TyEnPo; WHA
Wee sprites have followed mistletoe. Mistletoe Sprites. Solveig Paulson Russell. ChBR
Wee Tammy Tyrie. *Unknown.* OxNR
Wee, Wee German Lairdie, The. Allan Cunningham. EBSV
Wee Wee Man, The. *Unknown.* BaBo; CH; DaM; ESPB; FaBoCh; OBB; OTPC (1946 ed.)
Wee Willie Gray. Burns. CBE
Wee Willie Winkie rins [*or* runs] through the town. Willie Winkie. William Miller. BoChLi; BOL; FaFP; GaP; HBV; HBVY; LPS-1; OxNR; PCH; PECK; RIS; SAS; SiSoSe; StVeCh; TiPo; VA
Wee Willy Winkie,/ Runs through the town. Willy Winkie. Daniel Henry Holmes. TSW
Weed, The. Elizabeth Bishop. MoPo
Weed Month. V. Sackville-West. *Fr.* The Land. MBP; MoBrPo (1942 ed.)
Weeds. Edna St. Vincent Millay. TCPD
Weehawken and the New York Bay. Fitz-Greene Halleck. *Fr.* Fanny. LPS-2 (Weehawken.) BAV
Week ago to-day, when red-haired Sally, A. Done For. Rose Terry Cooke. AA
Week-End, *sels.* Harold Monro.
"Be staid; be careful; and be not too free," IX. SeCePo
"Contented evening; comfortable joys," III. CP; YT
"Key will stammer, and the door reply, The," II. CP; MoBrPo (1950 ed.); YT
"Morning! Wake up!" VI. CP; YT
"Train, The! The twelve o'clock for paradise," I. CP; MoBrPo (1950 ed.); PIAE; YT
Week-End by the Sea. Edgar Lee Masters. MoAmPo
Week had gloomily begun, The. A Penitential Week. Carolyn Wells. PC
Week is dealt out like a hand, The. Hope. Randall Jarrell. MoAB; MoAmPo (1950 ed.)
Week of Doodle, A. Reed Whittemore. NePoEA
Week on the Concord and Merrimack Rivers, A, *sels.* Henry David Thoreau.
All Things Are Current Found. AnNE; OnPM; ViBoPo, WoL
Atlantides, The. MOAP; ViBoPo
Conscience. AnNE; HBV; OnAP
Haze. AmPP (3d ed.); CoBA; InPo; MOAP; OnAP (Woof of the Sun [Ethereal Gauze].) AnNE; OnPM; ViBoPo
Mist. AA; AmPP (4th ed.); AWP; DDA; HBMV; InPo; JAWP; LEAP; LPS-2; MOAP; OxBA; SN; WBP (Low-anchored Cloud.) ImOP; ViBoPo
Weel May the Keel Row. *Unknown. See* Keel Row, The.
Weeng; an Indian Slumber Song. Lew Sarett. GaP
Weep, ah weep love's losing. Weep Love's Losing [*or* Ode]. Imr el Kais. *Fr.* The Mu'allaqát. AWP; LiTW
Weep balm and myrrh, you sweet Arabian trees. Stanzas from "Saint Peter's Complaint." Robert Southwell. ACP; CAW
Weep, daughter of a royal line. Lines to a Lady Weeping. Byron. ERP
Weep eyes, break heart! Parting. Thomas Middleton. *Fr.* A Chaste Maid in Cheapside. EIL; TuPP
Weep for me, friends, for now that I am hence. Tears of the World. Mu'tamid, King of Seville. AWP
Weep for the one so strong to slay, whom One has taken at last! Saul. George Sterling. HBMV; TBM
Weep for Youth's Passing. Theognis, *tr. fr. Greek by* T. F. Higham. GrL; OxBG
Weep, gentle halcyons, by the moaning deep. The Young Tarentine. André Chénier. LiA
Weep him dead and mourn as you may. Keen. Edna St. Vincent Millay. HBMV
Weep, Israel! your tardy meed outpour. Bar Kochba. Emma Lazarus. TrJP
Weep, little shrinking spirits of the woods. Our Little Sister. Laura E. McCully. CPG
Weep, lovers, sith Love's very self doth weep. On the Death of Beatrice. Dante. *Fr.* La Vita Nuova. AWP; MeRV
Weep Love's Losing. Imr el Kais, *tr. fr. Arabic by* Lady Anne Blunt *and* Wilfrid Scawen Blunt. *Fr.* The Mu'allaqát. LiTW
(Ode: "Weep, ah weep love's losing.") AWP
Weep me not long, but truly. The Last Request. Philetas. OxBG
Weep No More. John Fletcher, *and others. Fr.* The Queen of Corinth, III, ii. AtBAP; BEL; CH; EIL; EPP; EV-2;

Weep No More (*continued*)
LiTG; OBEV; OnPM; TOP; TriL; ViBoPo
(Mourn No More.) BLV; TrGrPo
("Weep no more, nor sigh, nor groan.") TuPP
Weep No More. Margaret L. Woods. DiM
Weep no more for what is past. What Is Past. Sir William Davenant. *Fr.* The Cruel Brother. TrGrPo
Weep no more, for why should sorrow. Weep No More. Margaret L. Woods. DiM
Weep no more, nor sigh nor groan. Weep [*or* Mourn] No More. John Fletcher, *and others. Fr.* The Queen of Corinth, III, ii. AtBAP; BEL; BLV; CH; ElL; EPP; EV-2; LiTG; OBEV; OnPM; TOP; TrGrPo; TriL; TuPP; ViBoPo
Weep no more, woful Shepherds, weep no more. Immortality. Milton. *Fr.* Lycidas. MaRV
Weep not,/ You who love her. Burial of the Young Love. Waring Cuney. PoNe
Weep not, beloved friends! nor let the air. Epitaphs, I [*or* Francesco Ceni]. Gabriello Chiabrera. AWP; JAWP; OnPM; WBP
Weep not beside his tomb. Arthur Hugh Clough. *Fr.* Easter Day. PGD
Weep Not, My Wanton. Robert Greene. *See* Sephestia's Song to Her Child.
Weep not, nor backward turn your beams. The Lover Consults with Reason. Thomas Carew. TrGrPo
Weep Not! Sigh Not! William James Linton. VA
Weep not that you no longer feel the tide. Lost Youth. Roger Casement. CAW; JKCP (1926 ed.)
Weep not the Brave Dead! Cean-Salla. James Clarence Mangan. OnYI
Weep Not To-Day. Robert Bridges. OBMV; OBVV
Weep not, weep not. Go Down Death. James Weldon Johnson. AnAmPo; LA; MaRV; PoeMoYo; TCPD
Weep not, you who love her. Burial of the Young Love. Waring Cuney. BANP
Weep! Weep! Weep! Tumadir al-Khansa for Her Brother. *Unknown. Fr.* The Thousand and One Nights. AWP; JAWP; PG (1945 ed.); WBP
Weep, weep, weep and weep. Alton Locke's Song, 1848 [*or* People's Song, 1849]. Charles Kingsley. *Fr.* Alton Locke. BMEP; PoFr
Weep, Weep, Ye Woodmen. Anthony Munday *and* Henry Chettle. *Fr.* Death of Robert, Earl of Huntingdon. CH
(Dirge: "Weep, weep, ye woodmen, wail.") OBSC
(Dirge for Robin Hood.) TriL
(Song: "Weep, weep, ye woodmen! wail.") ElL; ThWaDe
("Weep, weep, ye woodmen, wail.") ElSeCe
Weep [*or* Weepe] with me, all you that read. [An] Epitaph on S. P. [Salamon *or* Salomon *or* Salathiel Pavy], a Child of Q. El.'s [Queen Elizabeth's] Chap[p]el. Ben Jonson. BEL; BoFr; CBOV; CenL; CoBE; CoEV; ElL; ElSeCe; EM-1; EPP; EPS; FaBoEn; GoBC; HBV; InP; LoBV; MaPo; MePo; OAEP; OBEV; OBS; PIAE; PoE; PoEL-2; PoFS; ReEn; ReIE; SeCV-1; SeEP; TrGrPo; TuPP; TwHP; UnPo (1st ed.); ViBoPo
Weep, wooded glens; weep, Dorian wave; ye rivers, weep. Lament for Bion. *Unknown.* GrPE
Weep You No More, Sad Fountains. *Unknown.* CaAE; CenL; CH; CoEV; EG; ElL; ElSeCe; EnLoPo; ExPo; LoBV; OAEP; ReEn; ReIE; RiBV; ShBV-4; SiCE; TrGrPo; TuPP; ViBoPo
(Lullaby: "Weep you no more . . .") CBOV
(Rest Sad Eyes.) BLV
(Sleep.) LPS-3
(Sleep Is a Reconciling.) ChTr
(Song for Music, A.) GTSL; TOP
(Tears.) EV-1; OBEV; PG
(Weepe You No More, Sad Fountaines.) AtBAP; PoEL-2
Weepe O Mine Eyes. *Unknown.* AtBAP; PoEL-2
Weepe with me all you that read. *See* Weep with me . . .
Weepe You No More, sad Fountaines. *Unknown. See* Weep You No More . . .
Weeper, The. Richard Crashaw. MePo; OBEV, *abr.*; ViBoPo, *abr.*
(Saint Mary Magdalene.) AtBAP; MeLP; PoFS; ReEn; SeCV-1; SeEP
"Dew no more will weep, The," *sel.* EV-2
Weepest thou?/ Nay, why, my little one? The Fate of Astyanax. Euripides. *Fr.* Trojan Women. GrR
Weeping, The. Federico García Lorca, *tr. fr. Spanish by* Eleanor L. Turnbull. CoSP; OnPM
Weeping and Kissing. Sir Edward Sherburne. ElSeCe; SeCL; SeEP
Weeping and Singing. César Tiempo, *tr. fr. Spanish by* Donald Devenish Walsh. AnCL
Weeping and wakeful all the night I lie. Rhodanthe. Agathias Scholasticus. AWP; GrPo
Weeping Cherry, The. Robert Herrick. AtBAP
Weeping I came to life, weeping I go. Lacrimae Rerum. Palladas. OxBG
Weeping, I still regret the years that went. Petrarch. *Fr.* Sonnets to Laura: To Laura in Death. PrPoCR
Weeping, Sad and Lonely. Charles Carroll Sawyer. *See* When This Cruel War Is Over.
Weeping sorely as he journeyed. The Canadian Exile. Antoine Gerin-Lajoie. CaP
Weeping Water. Ruth Pitter. POTE
Weeping Willow. Richard Aldridge. NePoAm-2
Weeping Willow, The. *Unknown. See* Jealous Lover, The.
Weeps out of Kansas country something new. The Birth in a Narrow Room. Gwendolyn Brooks. PoNe
Weevily Wheat, *with music. Unknown.* ABF, *2 vers.*; AS; TrAS
'Weh Down Souf. Daniel Webster Davis. BANP
Weighing the Baby. Ethel Lynn Beers. HBV; PoToHe (new ed.)
Weighing the ste[a]dfastness and state. Man. Henry Vaughan. AnEnPo; CoEV; EPS; EV-2; FaBoEn; HBV; MeLP; MePo; OBEV (new ed.); OBS; PoEL-2; PoFS; SeCV-1; TwCrTr
Weight distributed. One Down. Richard Armour. WhC
Weight Gainer. Edgar A. Guest. OnHT
Weird Lady, The. Charles Kingsley. DaM
Weird wife of Bein-y-Vreich! horo! horo! Cailleach Bein-y-Vreich. John Campbell Shairp. VA
"Wel seyd, by *corpus dominus*," quod our hoste. The Prioress's Prologue. Chaucer. *Fr.* The Canterbury Tales. EM-1; OAEP
Weland experienced exile in Wermland. Deor's Lament. *Unknown, tr. by* Harold S. Stine. EnLit
Weland for a woman learned to know exile. Deor's Lament. *Unknown, tr. unknown.* TCEP
Weland knew fully affliction and woe. Deor's Lament. *Unknown, tr. by* Charles W. Kennedy. AnOE
Welcome, A. William Browne. EV-2; HBV; LiTL; OBEV
(Welcome, Welcome, Do I Sing.) LPS-1; ViBoPo
Welcome, The. Abraham Cowley. *Fr.* The Mistress. SeCV-1
Welcome, The. Thomas Osborne Davis. HBV; LPS-1; VA
"Come in the evening, or come in the morning," *sel.* IrPN
Welcome, The. Leonard Feeney. WHL
Welcome, A. Charles Kingsley. *See* Ode to the North-east Wind.
Welcome, The. Freda Laughton. NeIP
Welcome, The. Nettie Palmer. BoAu
Welcome, The. Arthur Powell. NLK; OQP; POT; QP-1
Welcome. Rose Waldo. MPB
Welcome all who lead or follow. Verses Placed over the Door at the Entrance into the Apollo Room at the Devil Tavern [*or* Over the Door at the Entrance into the Apollo]. Ben Jonson. HBV; ReEn
Welcome! all Wonders in one sight! The Coming Child. Richard Crashaw. MaRV
Welcome, baby, to the world of swords. News of a Baby. Elizabeth Riddell. BoAV
Welcome [*or* Wolcum] be Thou, Heavenly King [*or* thu, hevene kyng]. Welcome Yule. *Unknown.* CAW; CH
Welcome Bonny Brid! Samuel Laycock. VA
Welcome, boy, to these green fields. Alma Mater. Mary Elizabeth Osborn. NePoAm
Welcome, Christmas! heel and toe. Stocking Song on Christmas Eve. Mary Mapes Dodge. ChBR; OHIP
Welcome, dear Wanderer, once more! Upon Her Play Being Returned to Her Stained with Claret. Mary Leapor. DiM
Welcome Death. Juan Escrivá, *tr. fr. Spanish by* Sir John Bowring. AnSpL-1; OnPM
(Song to Death, *tr. by* E. Allison Peers.) LiTW
Welcome Eild. *Unknown.* GoTS
Welcome Every Guest, *with music. Unknown.* TrAS
Welcome, fayre chylde, what is thy name? Dalyaunce. *Unknown.* AtBAP; CH
Welcome, Fortune. *Unknown.* BSV, *abr.*; TMEV
Welcome freshness over the garden lay, A. Suspended Moment. Mariana B. Davenport. GoYe
Welcome, friend. Newton to Einstein. Jeannette Chappell. GoYe
Welcome, happy Easter day! Easter Praise. Rodney Bennett. BoTP
Welcome, Happy Morning. Venantius Fortunatus. EOAH
Welcome Home. Louella C. Poole. AlBD
Welcome Home! Su Ch'an I, *tr. fr. Chinese by* Henry H. Hart. PoHN
Welcome, little Robin. *Unknown.* BoTP
Welcome, maids of honour [*or* honor]. To Violets [*or* Violets]. Robert Herrick. EG; EV-2; HBV; LPS-2; MyFE; OBEV; OBS; OTPC (1923 ed.); RG; TrGrPo; ViBoPo
Welcome me, if you will. For James Dean. Frank O'Hara. NeAP
Welcome, my old friend. To an Old Danish Song-Book. Longfellow. OBVV
Welcome My World. Denis Devlin. AnIV
Welcome now, Victoria! Queen Victoria. *Unknown.* CoMu
Welcome of the Young Cacique, The. Alonso de Ercilla y Zúñiga, *tr. fr. Spanish by* Elizabeth Selden. *Fr.* La Araucana. BoFr

Welcome, old friend! These many years. To Age. Walter Savage Landor. BEL; BPN; EmBrPo; EnRP; EPN; ERP; HBV; OQP; QP-1; TreFS; VA
Welcome over the Door of an Old Inn. *Unknown. See* America Greets an Alien.
Welcome, pale morning. Cellach's Poem to the Dawn. *Unknown.* SiB
Welcome, pale primrose! starting up between. To a Primrose [*or* The Primrose]. John Clare. BCEP; GTSE; OTPC (1923 ed.)
Welcome, precious stone of the night. Welcome to the Moon. *Unknown.* ChTr
Welcome, Queen Sabbath. Zalman Schneour, *tr. fr. Hebrew by* Harry H. Fein. TrJP
Welcome, red and roundy sun. The Wood-Cutter's Night Song. John Clare. EnRP; ERP; GTML; GTSE; OBRV
Welcome, spirit borne on wings of rapture. My Saint. Johan Sebastian Cammermeyer Welhaven. AnNoLy
Welcome the lord of light, and lamp of day. Welcome to the Sun. Virgil, *tr. by* Gawin Douglas. *Fr.* The Aeneid. ACP
Welcome, thou festal morn! Washington's Birthday Ever Honored. George Howland. WOAH
Welcome, Thou Safe Retreat! William Habington. OxBoCh; PoLi
Welcome, thrice welcome to this shady green. The Forest's Queen. Philip Massinger. GoBC
Welcome to Agamemnon. Aeschylus, *tr. fr. Greek by* Walter Headlam. *Fr.* Agamemnon. LiA; OxBG (Clytemnestra, *longer sel., tr. by* G. M. Cookson.) GrR
Welcome to Alexandra, A. Tennyson. PoVP
Welcome to Bliss Carman, A. Dorothy Choate Herriman. CPG
Welcome to "Boz," A. William Henry Venable. LPS-3
Welcome to Day. Thomas Heywood. *See* Pack, Clouds, Away.
Welcome to Dr. Benjamin Apthorp Gould, A. Oliver Wendell Holmes. ImOP
Welcome to Margaret Tudor. William Dunbar. *See* Now Fair, Fairest of Every Fair.
Welcome to May. *Unknown.* EBSV
Welcome to May. Ballata. Angelo Poliziano. LyPI
Welcome to My Heart. *Unknown.* BePJ
Welcome to our wond'ring [*or* wondering] sight. Chorus [*or* A Hymn of the Nativity]. Richard Crashaw. *Fr.* In the Holy Nativity of Our Lord God. ChIP; MeRV
Welcome to Sack, The. Robert Herrick. SeCV-1
Welcome to Spring. Irene Thompson. BoTP
Welcome to the day returning. Ode for Washington's Birthday. Oliver Wendell Holmes. DD; GA; PEDC; PSO
Welcome to the Moon. *Unknown, tr. fr. Gaelic.* ChTr
Welcome to the Nations. Oliver Wendell Holmes. IDAH; PAH
Welcome to the New Year. Eleanor Farjeon. MoSiPe; YeAr
Welcome to the Prince of Ossory. William Heffernan the Blind, *tr. fr. Irish by* James Clarence Mangan. IrPN
Welcome to the Sun. Virgil, *tr. fr. Latin by* Gawin Douglas. *Fr.* The Aeneid, XII. ACP
Welcome to this flowery place. Thomas Campion. *Fr.* A Relation of the Late Royal Entertainment Given by the Lord Knowles. SiCE
Welcome to us Holy Child. Christmas Night. Hugh MacCawell. KiLC
Welcome to you, rich autumn days. Rich Days. W. H. Davies. BoTP; TwCV
Welcome Visitors. Emilie Blackmore Stapp. GFA
Welcome, Welcome, Do I Sing. William Browne. *See* Welcome, A.
Welcome, welcome, ev'ry guest. Welcome Every Guest. *Unknown.* TrAS
Welcome, wild North-easter! Ode to the North-east Wind [*or* A Welcome]. Charles Kingsley. EV-5; GN; GTBS; LH; OTPC; TVSH
Welcome Yule. *Unknown.* AnEC; CAW; CH
Weldon House. August Derleth. DaM
Well, The. Luis Palés Matos, *tr. fr. Spanish by* Donald Devenish Walsh. AnCL
Well, The. Manuel de la Parra, *tr. fr. Spanish by* Samuel Beckett. AnMP
Well, A. Aleksey Konstantinovich Tolstoy, *tr. fr. Russian by* Babette Deutsch. OnPM; TrRV ("Well, A, and the cherry-trees blowing," *tr. by* C. M. Bowra.) BoR
We'll A' Go Pu' the Heather. Robert Nicoll. VA
We'll All Feel Gay. Winfield Townley Scott. MiAP
We'll All Go Down to Rowser's. *Unknown.* ABS
Well, *alter ego,* Time has trudged. Why Do We Live? Israel Zangwill. TrJP
Well and/ If day on day. Trapped. Adelaide Crapsey. MCCG
Well, A, and the cherry trees swaying [*or* blowing]. A Well. Aleksey Konstantinovich Tolstoy. BoR; TrRV
Well, as you say, we live for small horizons. Palimpsest; a Deceitful Portrait. Conrad Aiken. *Fr.* The House of Dust. ChMo; CMP
We'll aye be friens, but mair sae frae this day. Tuscan Folk Songs, 3. *Unknown, tr. into Scottish by* Edwin Morgan. LyPI
Well begun. Well-packed Wisdom. Benjamin Franklin. *Fr.* Poor Richard's Almanac. StaSt
Well-beloved, The. Thomas Hardy. ViP
Well Belovéd House, The. Antonio Machado, *tr. fr. Spanish by* Eleanor L. Turnbull. TeCS
Well boss did it/ ever strike you. The Hen and the Oriole. Don Marquis. Fr. Archy and Mehitabel. FiBHP; TwCV
Well boss I met. Cheerio My Deario. Don Marquis. *Fr.* Archy and Mehitabel. ShBV-4
Well boss mehitabel the cat. Mehitabel Sings a Song. Don Marquis. *Fr.* Archy and Mehitabel. InMe
Well-bred Man, A. William Cowper. BPP
Well, come along boys, and listen to my tale. The [Old] Chisholm Trail. *Unknown.* CoSo (D *vers.*); TrAS
Well; come to me to-morrow. Shakespeare. *Fr.* Measure for Measure, II, ii. LO
We'll cut the cackle about attainment. Preamble to a Great Adventure. Ronald Bottrall. MoP
Well Done. James Montgomery. MaRV
Well, don't cry, my little tiny boy. A Dreary Song. Shirley Brooks. PA
Well dost thou, Love, thy solemn feast to hold. Saint Valentine's Day. Coventry Patmore. *Fr.* The Unknown Eros. EV-5; FaBoEn; GoBC; GTML; PoLi
Well-drest woman in the costly car, The. Toronto Crossing. Robert Finch. TwCaPo
Well dy'd the World, that we might live to see. An Anatomie of the World. John Donne. EPS; NBE
Well, Emily Sparks, your prayers were not wasted. Reuben Pantier. Edgar Lee Masters. *Fr.* Spoon River Anthology. BoFr
Well, ev'ry Monday mornin'. John Henry. *Unknown.* OuSiCo
We'll fill a Provence bowl and pledge us deep. Growing Old. Francis Ledwidge. LEAP
We'll Fling the Starry Banner Out. William F. Knott. HH
Well fought Timocritus, and has this grave. On a Slain Warrior. Anacreon. GrL
Well from the first I knew how long deferred. Ideal Passion, XXI. George Edward Woodberry. MOAP
"Well, General Grant, have you heard the news?" Lee's Parole. Marion Manville. BIG; GA; PAH
We'll Go No More a-Roving. Byron. *See* So We'll Go No More a-Roving.
We'll Go No More a-Roving. W. E. Henley. Echoes, VIII. MBP; MoBrPo
We'll Go to Sea No More. *Unknown.* ChTr; EtS
We'll go to the meadows, where cowslips do grow. The Meadows. Ann *or* Jane Taylor. BoTP
Well, God don't like it, no, no. God Don't Like It. *Unknown.* OuSiCo
Well, good-by, Jim; take keer yerself. To James Whitcomb Riley. Bide Dudley. BLP
Well hast thou stood, my country! To Britain—after War. Sir Walter Scott. *Fr.* The Field of Waterloo: Conclusion. ShGoBo
Well hath the powerful hand of majesty. To Sir Thomas Egerton. Samuel Daniel. OBSC
We'll Have Another Drink before the Boat Shoves Off, *with music.* *Unknown.* ShS
Well! have I acted right at last, my lady? Schiller. *Fr.* Mary Stuart. ReTS
"We'll have the sun now." Confidence. Marsden Hartley. AnFE; CoAnAm
Well he slumbers, greatly slain. The Mighty Denier. Sir William Watson. LBBV
We'll heave him up from down below. Susiana. *Unknown.* ShS
Well, Heaven's hard to understand. Dick Said. Louis Untermeyer. TSW; TSWC
Well, he's come home, this younger son of mine. The Father. Sara Henderson Hay. StaSt
Well, honour is the subject of my story. Cassius Poisons Brutus' Mind. Shakespeare. *Fr.* Julius Caesar, I, ii. TreFS
Well, I am thinking this may be my last. Canoe. Keith Douglas. NeBP
Well, I am young and the world is wide. Ysolte. George Frederick Cameron. BoCaPo
Well, I confess, I did not guess. I'm Not a Single Man [*or* Lines in a Young Lady's Album]. Thomas Hood. ALV; HBV
Well, I have thought on't, and I find. The Retirement. John Norris. OBS
. . . Well, I looked at the camel. At the Zoo. Anne May Smith. PCH
Well I looked upon each face. Guillaume de Lorris *and* Jean de Meun. *Fr.* The Romance of the Rose. EnLi-1

Well; I may now receive, and die; my sinne. John Donne. Satires, IV. SeEP
Well, I must go. Why keep on loitering here? Socrates' Experiments. Aristophanes. *Fr.* The Clouds. OxBG
Well I never, did you ever. *Unknown.* FaBoCh; LoGBV
Well I recall how first I met. Mark Twain; a Pipe Dream. Oliver Herford. BOHV
Well I Remember How You Smiled. Walter Savage Landor. *Fr.* Ianthe. BCEP; BPN; EmBrPo; FaBoEn; GTBS; LoBV; TrGrPo; ViBoPo
(Epigram.) EV-4
(Her Name.) OBVV
Well I remember that bleak day of snow. Alone. Carolyn Spencer. MuM
Well, I went down in Hell-Town. Johnny, Won't You Ramble? *Unknown.* OuSiCo
"Well, I would have it so. I should have known." André Chénier. *Fr.* Elegies. AWP
Well, if a King's a lion, at the least. Ten Per Cent; Then as Now. Pope. *Fr.* The First Epistle of the First Book of Horace Imitated. BeR
Well; if ever I saw such another Man since my Mother bound my head. Mary the Cook-Maid's Letter to Dr. Sheridan. Swift. LoBV; OnYI; OxBoLi
Well! If the Bard was weather-wise, who made. Dejection; an Ode. Samuel Taylor Coleridge. AnEnPo; BEL; BPN; EM-2; EmBrPo; EnL; EnLi-2; EnLit; EnRP; EPN; ERP; EV-4; FaBoEn; FiP; HBV; LiTB; LoBV; MaPo; NBE; OAEP; OBRV; PoE; PoEL-4; PoFS; ReaPo; SeCePo
Well, if the thing is over, better it is for me. Mary, Helper of Heartbreak [*or* Irish Love Song]. Margaret Widdemer. BAP; HBMV; SBMV
Well, I'm a wild cowboy, I've roved the West o'er. Wild Bronc Peeler. *Unknown.* CoSo
Well, it makes no difference. Hard to Be a Nigger. *Unknown.* ABF
Well, it's Mamma, Mamma, O Lawd, you don't know. Mamma, Mamma. *Unknown.* OuSiCo
Well, it's partly the shape of the thing. Limerick. *Unknown.* WhC
Well, las' Monday mornin'. De Grey Goose. *Unknown.* ABF
Well! Let him sleep! Time enough to awake. Danger. S. Frances Harrison. *Fr.* Down the River. CPG
Well, mates, I don't like stories. California Joe. "Captain Jack" Crawford. CoSo; CSF
Well may sure hope at times, on wings elate. Sonnet LIX. Michelangelo. BoFr
Well may'st thou halt—and gaze with brightening eye! Admonition to a Traveller. Wordsworth. GTBS; GTSE; GTSL
Well-meaning readers, you that come as friends. The Flaming Heart. Richard Crashaw. CAW; GoBC; LiTB; LoBV; MeRV; OxBoCh; PoEL-2; SeCePo; SeCL; SeCV-1
We'll meet beside the dusky glen, on yon burn side. By Yon Burn Side. Robert Tannahill. HBV
We'll meet nae mair at sunset, when the weary day is dune. Durisdeer. Lady John Scott. EBSV
Well met, pretty Betty, my joy and my dear. Gallant Seaman's Song at His Meeting of Betty. *Unknown.* SG
Well met, pretty nymph, says a jolly young swain. The Country Wedding. *Unknown.* HBV
"Well met, well met, my own true love." The Demon Lover [*or* The House Carpenter]. *Unknown.* ABS; BaBo (B *and* D *vers.*)
"Well met, well met," said an old true love. James Harris (B *vers.*). *Unknown.* ViBoFo
Well, Mrs. Rogers,/ I hear you're taking lodgers. Coals of Fire. A. P. Herbert. ALV
Well my heart warns me, saying: "Flee, flee from Heliodora!" The Coquette. *At. to* Meleager *and to* Philodemus. GrPE
Well, My Heart, We Have Been Happy. *Unknown.* DDA
We'll not weep for summer over. After Summer. Philip Bourke Marston. HBV; VA
Well now, these mariners—sailors, captains. The End. Tristan Corbière. AnFP
We'll o'er the water and o'er the sea. O'er the Water to Charlie. Burns. EBSV; FaBoCh
Well of freshness, A. Juxta. Grover Jacoby. GoYe
Well of Living Water, The. Charles Wesley. BePJ
Well of Pity, The. Chaucer. *Fr.* An A. B. C. PoLi
Well of St. Keyne, The. Robert Southey. BeLS; BoChLi (1939 ed.); BOHV; EPP; EV-4; FaBoBe; HBV; LPS-3; NeHB; OTPC; PCN; PECK; ShGoBo
Well-packed Wisdom. Benjamin Franklin. *Fr.* Poor Richard's Almanac. StaSt
Well, Peter, dost thou wield thy active sword. Malchus' Ear. Richard Crawshaw. StJW
We'll plant a corn-flower on his grave. The Lark's Grave. Thomas Westwood. TVC; TVSH
Well Pleaseth Me the Sweet Time of Easter. Bertrand de Born, *tr. fr. Provençal by* Ezra Pound. InvP
(Song of Battle.) AWP; WaaP
We'll Roll the Golden Chariot Along, *with music.* *Unknown.* ShS
(Roll the Chariot: "We'll roll, we'll roll the chariot along," *diff. vers., with music.*) AS
We'll run all night till the morning. Run with the Bullgine. *Unknown.* SoAmSa
We'll sail from hence to Greece, to lovely Greece. The Song of Ithamore. Christopher Marlowe. *Fr.* The Jew of Malta. WHA
We'll sing a song, a soldier's song. The Soldier's Song. Peadar Kearney. OnYI
Well Sir, 'tis granted, I said D[ryden's] rhymes. An Allusion to Horace; The Tenth Satire of the First Book. Earl of Rochester. OBS; SeEP
Well, So That Is That. W. H. Auden. *See* After Christmas.
Well, some may hate, and some may scorn. Stanzas to ——. Emily Brontë. EmBrPo; LoBV
Well, son, I'll tell you. Mother to Son. Langston Hughes. BoChLi (1950 ed.); CDC; FAOV; GoSl; IHA; PoNe; StVeCh
Well; tell me now, what lady is the same. Shakespeare. *Fr.* The Merchant of Venice, I, i. BoFr
Well then! I now do plainly see. The Wish. Abraham Cowley. *Fr.* The Mistress. BEL; BLV; CBOV; CoBE; ElSeCe; EnLi-1; EnLit; EPP; EPS; EV-2; GTBS-W; HBV; LEAP; LiTB; LiTG; OAEP; OBEV; OBS; SeCL; SeCV-1; SeEP; TOP; TrGrPo; ViBoPo; WHA
Well, then, the last day the sharks appeared. The Sharks. Denise Levertov. NeAP
Well then, the promised hour is come at last. To My Dear Friend, Mr. Congreve, on His Comedy Called "The Double-Dealer." Dryden. CEP; EiPP; FiP; GEPC; NBE; OBS; PoE; PoEL-3; PtP; SeCV-2; SeEP
Well there is in the west country, A. The Well of St. Keyne. Robert Southey. BeLS; BoChLi (1939 ed.); BOHV; EPP; EV-4; FaBoBe; HBV; LPS-3; NeHB; OTPC; PCN; PECK; ShGoBo
Well! there you lie already . . . on the board. Before a Corpse. Manuel Acuña. AnMP
Well, they are gone, and here must I remain. This Lime-Tree Bower My Prison. Samuel Taylor Coleridge. BPN; EM-2; EmBrPo; EnRP; ERP; LoBV; PoEL-4; ShBV-4
Well! Thou Art Happy. Byron. ERP
"Well, though it seems." Liddell and Scott; on the Completion of Their Lexicon. Thomas Hardy. OxBoLi
We'll to the woods and gather may. Alons au bois le may cueillir [*or* Rondeau of Spring]. Charles d'Orléans. AWP; JAWP; LyMA; PreP; WBP
We'll to the Woods No More. A. E. Housman. PoRA
We'll wander to the woods no more. The Woods No More. Jay Macpherson. PeCV
Well was dry beside the door, The. Going for Water. Robert Frost. HBMV; NP
Well, we will do that rigid thing. To a Friend before Taking a Journey. Katherine Philips. EV-2
"Well, well,—Heaven bless you all from day to day." Arthur Hugh Clough. *Fr.* "Blank Misgivings of a Creature Moving About in Worlds Not Realized." VLEP
Well, well, my dear! So you thought you could cheat me! To Heliodora; a Fretful Monody. Meleager. LiTW
Well, well, 'tis true. Plain Dealing. Alexander Brome. OBS
Well, when all is said and done. Epilogue. "Æ." MoBrPo
Well, when I first infested this retreat. First Settler's Story. Will Carleton. IHA
Well, wife, I've found the model church! The Old Man in the Model Church. John H. Yates. PTA-2
Well-wishing to a Place of Pleasure, A. *Unknown.* SeCL
Well worthy the mongoose, though wanting in size. The Ichneumon. Oppian. *Fr.* Cynegetica. OxBG
Well worthy to be magnified are they. The Pilgrim Fathers. Wordsworth. PAH; PoRL
Well, yes, I calkerlate it is a little quiet here. When the Train Comes In. Nixon Waterman. IHA
Well, yes, I've lived in Texas, since the spring of '61. A Spool of Thread. Sophie E. Eastman. PAH
Well, yes, sir, dat am a comical name. Ashcake. Thomas Nelson Page. AA; OBAV
"Well, you may believe me or may not believe me." Mountain Trolls. Gustaf Fröding. AnSL
Well, you wake up in de mornin'. De Midnight Special. *Unknown.* ABF
Well-a, jumpin', Jumpin' Judy. Drive It On. *Unknown.* OuSiCo
Well-a, Shorty George he ain' no friend of mine. Shorty George. *Unknown.* ABF
Welladay, welladay, poor Colin, thou art going to the ground. Dirge [*or* The Shepherd's Dirge]. George Peele. *Fr.* The Arraignment of Paris. EIL; OBSC
Well-a-way; and so you pass. Epithalamion for Amaryllis. John Farrar. PR
Wellington. Byron. *Fr.* Don Juan, IX. GEPC; OBRV

("Oh Wellington or 'Villainton'—for fame.") OxBoLi
(On Wellington, *abr.*) FiP
Wellington. Benjamin Disraeli. EPN; OBVV; VA
Wellnigh a year, swift-running Brook, is past. The Early Spring Brook. Richard Henry Dana. BAV
Wells of air pour down, The. Pour Down. John Holmes. NePoAm
Wells of Our Fathers, The. Inez Barclay Kirby. MuM
Welsh harp has no silver string, The. Variation on a Theme by Francis Kilvert. Rolfe Humphries. UnS
Welsh Hill Country, The. R. S. Thomas. PoN
Welsh Incident. Robert Graves. ShBV-3
Welsh Lullaby, A. John Ceiriog Hughes, *fr. the Welsh.* BOL
Welsh Lullaby. *Unknown. See* All through the Night ("Sleep, my babe, lie still and slumber").
Welsh Marches, The. A. E. Housman. A Shropshire Lad, XXVIII. FaBoTw; POTT; PoVP; TCPD; ViPo; VLEP
Welshmen of Tirawley, The. Sir Samuel Ferguson. OBVV; OnYI; PoVP
Welt. Georgia Douglas Johnson. BANP
Welt ist dumm, die Welt ist blind. Heine, *tr. fr. German by* James Thompson. AWP
(World Is Dull, The.) OnPM
Welter upon the waters, mighty one. Sonnet to the Sea Serpent. John G. C. Brainard. EtS
Weltering London ways where children weep, The. John Keats. Dante Gabriel Rossetti. Five English Poets, 4. BPN; EmBrPo; EPN; PoVP; PtP
W'en de colo'ed ban' comes ma'chin' down de street. The Colored Band. Paul Laurence Dunbar. MPB
W'en de evenin' shadders. The Boogah Man. Paul Laurence Dunbar. VOD
"Wen Gott Betrügt, Ist Wohl Betrogen." Arthur Hugh Clough. PoVP; ViP; VLEP
(Is It True, Ye Gods, Who Treat Us.) ViPP
W'en I was young boy on de farm, dat's twenty year ago. How Bateese Came Home. William Henry Drummond. IHA
W'en Spreeng Ees Com'. T. A. Daly. CV
W'en you see a man in woe. Hullo! Sam Walter Foss. CenHV; PTA-2
Wendell Phillips. Amos Bronson Alcott. AA; GA; LEAP; PoFr
Wendell Phillips. James Russell Lowell. IAP; PEOR
Wendell Phillips, *sel.* John Boyle O'Reilly.
"What shall we mourn? For the prostrate tree?" AA; DD; GA
Wendling. Coman Leavenworth. *Fr.* Norfolk Memorials. LiTA
Wenlock. A. E. Housman. A Shropshire Lad, XXXIX. SeCePo
("'Tis time, I think, by Wenlock town.") BPN; LBBV; PoVP
Wenlock Edge. A. E. Housman. *See* On Wenlock Edge.
Wenn ich in deine Augen seh'. Heine. *See* I Love but Thee.
Went down to New Orleans, got on a fence, Tom Turkey in de buckwheat straw. Turkey in the Straw (B *vers.*). *Unknown.* AS
Went down to St. Joe's infirmary. Those Gambler's Blues (B *vers.*). *Unknown.* AS
Went into a shoestore to buy a pair of shoes. Sale. Josephine Miles. FiMAP
Went to sleep, babe, last night in a snow-white feather bed. I'm Worried Now but I Won't Be Worried Long. *Unknown.* OuSiCo
Went to the river, couldn't get across. *Unknown.* GoTP
Went weeping little bones. But where? I Cry, Love! Love! Theodore Roethke. MoVE
Went you to conquer? and have so much lost. H: W: In Hiber: Belligeranti. John Donne. BoFr
"*Werden* and *Sein,* the old dichotomy!" Faustus. Hyam Plutzik. Horatio, III. FiMAP
We're All Bound to Go. *Unknown. See* Heave Away.
We're all dry with drinking on't. *Unknown.* OxNR; SiTL
We're all in the dumps. In the Dumps. *Unknown.* BoN; NA; SiTL
We're all inclined to bore our friends. Ballade of a Summer Hotel. "Junia." WhC
Were all the tributes of Scotia. The Praise of Derry. St. Columcille. CAW
Were all the world a paradice of ease. Thomas Traherne. *Fr.* Christian Ethics. MeRV
We're alone, Doney Gal, in the rain [*or* wind] and hail. Doney Gal. *Unknown.* CoSo; OuSiCo
Were beth they that biforen us weren. Ubi Sunt Qui ante Nos Fuerunt? *Unknown.* CoBE; CBOV; EnLi-1; EPP; OAEP; SeCeV
We're bound for blue water where the great winds blow. A Valediction. John Masefield. OBMV
Were But My Spirit Loosed upon the Air. Louise Chandler Moulton. AA; HBV; LEAP; OBAV
Were but that sigh a penitential breath. Melancholy. William Habington. *Fr.* Castara. LoBV
We're crossing the bar of another year. "I Am with Thee." Ernest Bourner Allen. BLRP
We're Few. Boris Pasternak, *tr. fr. Russian by* Babette Deutsch. TrRV
("We're few, perhaps not more than three," *tr. by* C. M. Bowra.) BoRS
Were Flowers There? George William Allison. ChIP
We're foot—slog—slog—slog—sloggin' over Africa! Boots. Kipling. BLPA; BPN; MBP; MoBrPo; PFE; PoVP; ShBV-2; WHA
We're going down to Dixie, to Dixie, to Dixie. Hold On, Abraham. *Unknown.* ABF
We're going to have a party. The Christmas Party. Adeline White. BoTP
We're going to the fair at Holstenwall. Holstenwall. Sidney Keyes. FaBoTw
Were half the power that fills the world with terror. When War Shall Be No More [*or* Message of Peace *or* Peace]. Longfellow. *Fr.* The Arsenal at Springfield. MaRV; OQP; PEDC; PGD; PSO; QP-1; WBLP
We're having a lovely time to-day! Fun in a Garret. Emma C. Dowd. GFA; SUS; TiPo
We're here a-marching on to old Quebec. A-Marching to Quebec. *Unknown.* APW
"We're homeward bound," I hear them say. Homeward Bound, *vers.* II. *Unknown.* ShS
"We're homeward bound," I heard our captain say. Homeward Bound, *vers.* III. *Unknown.* ShS
"We're homeward bound!" I've heard them say. Homeward Bound, *vers.* I. *Unknown.* ShS
Were I a happy bird. Faith Trembling. "Madeline Bridges." AA
Were I a King. Edward de Vere, Earl of Oxford. ElSeCe
(Choice, A.) OBSC
(Doubtful Choice. A.) ElL
(Epigram.) PoE; TuPP
Were I a Lark So Gay. Thor Lange, *tr. fr. Danish by* Charles W. Stork. BoDS
Were I a painter I'd paint only skies. Heaven Tree. Henry Morton Robinson. JKCP (1955 ed.)
Were I a real poet, I would sing. Sunday up the River, X. James Thomson. OAEP
Were I as Base as Is the Lowly Plain. *At. to* Joshua Sylvester. HBV; LPS-1; TOP
(Amor Ineluctabilis.) ES
(Constancy.) PG
(Love Omnipresent.) CBOV
(Love's Omnipresence.) GTBS; GTBS-D; GTBS-W; GTSE; GTSL
(Sonnet: "Were I as base as is the lowly plain.") AEV; ElL; ElSeCe; EV-1; OBSC; TuPP; ViBoPo
(Ubique.) OBEV
Were I but able to rehearse. The Ewie wi' the Crookit Horn. John Skinner. EBSV
Were I But His Own Wife. Ellen Mary Patrick Downing. VA
Were I immortal only I would proffer. October Birthday. Sister Mary Madeleva. JKCP (1955 ed.)
Were I in the Province of Yamato. Kyukin Susukida, *tr. fr. Japanese by* Takamichi Ninomiya *and* D. J. Enright. PoLJ
Were I Laid on Greenland's Coast. John Gay. *See* Song: "Were I laid on Greenland's coast."
Were I possessed of an alchemy rare. Love's Magic. Clara Carson LeLand. PSO
Were I Reborn. Juan Ramón Jiménez, *tr. fr. Spanish by* Eleanor L. Turnbull. TeCS
Were I so tall to reach the pole. True Greatness. Isaac Watts. MaRV
Were I the red-brushed fox, I should go warier. December [*or* November] Fugitive. Henry Morton Robinson. AnEnPo; GoYe
Were I to hate the one who injures me. The Scales of Love. Hartmann von Aue. LiTW; LyMA
Were I to Mount Beyond the Field. Sidney Keyes. The Foreign Gate, V. MoPo
Were I to name, out of the times gone by. The Dearest Poets [*or* The Poets]. Leigh Hunt. BCEP; ERP; HBV; OTPC (1923 ed.); PtP
Were I to Take Wife. John Wilson. *Fr.* Belphegor; or, The Marriage of the Devil. SeCL
Were I transported to some distant star. A Plain Man's Dream. Frederick Keppel. AA
Were I west in green Arran. The Cup of O'Hara [*or* When Kian O'Hara's Cup Was Passed to Turlough O'Carolan]. Turlough Carolan. AnIV; OnYI
Were I, who to my cost already am. A Satire [*or* Satyr] against Mankind. Earl of Rochester. CEP; CoEV; EiPP; FaBoEn; LiTB; LiTG; NBE; OBS; PoEL-3; SeCV-2; SiTL
Were I with You, or You with Me. Arthur Hugh Clough. Songs in Absence, XII. EmBrPo
We're in from a voyage where the sea is deep. The Call of the Sea. Howard James Savage. CAG

Were it mine to repose for one night on thy bosom. Reproach. Firdausi. LiTW
Were it not for the fragile rose. The Shore. Pedro Salinas. CoSP
Were it table, trunk or stool. The Carpenter of Nazareth. Walter Smith. ChIP
Were it undo that is y-do. A Forsaken Maiden's Lament. *Unknown.* SeCePo
We're making sail on the Yankee Clipper. Yankee Clipper. Leonard Bacon. NeTW
Were My Heart as Some Men's Are. Thomas Campion. EV-2; HBV
Were Na My Heart Light I Wad Dee. Lady Grizel Baillie. EBSV
(There Ance Was a May.) BSV
(Werena My Heart's Licht I Wad Dee.) OBEV
Were not the eye itself a sun. Godlike Heart. Goethe. OnPM
Were Not the Gael Fallen. Peadar O'Mulconry, *tr. fr. Early Modern Irish by* Robin Flower. AnIL
Were Not the Sinful Mary's Tears. Thomas Moore. StJW
Were pain a simple stab. Strange Guest. Gertrude Jane Codd. JKCP (1955 ed.)
We're queer folks here. Just Folks. Edgar A. Guest. FaFP; TreFS
We're sailing down the river from Liverpool. Santy Anno. *Unknown.* OuSiCo
Were 't aught to me I bore the canopy. Sonnets, CXXV. Shakespeare. PeBoSo
We're Tenting Tonight. Walter Kittredge. *See* Tenting on the Old Camp Ground.
Were thanks with every gift expressed. Thanksliving. Chauncey R. Piety. OQP; PGD; QP-1
Were the bright day no more to visit us. *Unknown.* LO
Were the burned sands of Aeaea. Coasts. Beatrice Ravenel. *Fr.* Tidewater. LS
We're the children of the open and we hate the haunts o' men. Ridin' up the Rocky Trail from Town. *Unknown.* SCC
Were the whole known, that we uncouth suppose. Cliff and Cloud. Richard Savage. *Fr.* The Wanderer. BeR
Were the whole world good as you—not an atom better. The Question. *Unknown.* WBLP
Were there lovers in the lanes of Atlantis. Song at Santa Cruz. Francis Brett Young. HBMV; PtOT
Were there no crowns on earth. The Dead President. Edward Rowland Sill. PAH
Were there one whose fires. Addison. Pope. *Fr.* Epistle to Dr. Arbuthnot. BCEP
Were this impossible, I know full well. A House and Grounds. Leigh Hunt. OBRV
We're up in the morning ere breaking of day. The Railroad Corral. *Unknown.* TrAS
We're very small, we're very small. Song of the Snowflakes. Annette Wynne. GFA
Were you a leper bathed in wounds. Proving. Georgia Douglas Johnson. CDC
Were you and I to play this fugue again. Fugue. Harold Lewis Cook. NP
Were You Ever in Dumbarton? *with music. Unknown.* ShS
Were you ever in sweet Tipperary, where the fields are so sunny and green. Tipperary. Mary Kelly. TIP; VA
Were You There When They Crucified My Lord? *Unknown.* BoAN-2, *with music;* OIF
Were You with Me, or I with You. Arthur Hugh Clough. Songs in Absence, X *and* XIII. BPN; EmBrPo
(Were You with Me.) VLEP
Were-bear, why are you not in hell? Chant to a Were-Bear. *Ad. by* Hermia Harris Fraser. BoCaPo
Werena My Heart's Licht I Wad Dee. Lady Grizel Baillie. *See* Were Na My Heart Light I Wad Dee.
Were-Wolf. Julian Hawthorne. AA
Werewolf. Arthur Inman. DaM
Were-Wolves, The. Wilfred Campbell. VA
Werfel dead? Hark. The forest is empty. The Shooting of Werfel. Vernon Watkins. WaP
Wersh an drumlie are the lees. Sang: Recoll o Skaith. Sidney Goodsir Smith. NeBP
Wert thou a king, yet not command content. Answered Thus by Sir P. S. Sir Philip Sidney. TuPP
Wert thou but blind, O Fortune, then perhaps. Poems, XCVIII. Walter Savage Landor. PG
Werther had a love for Charlotte. The Sorrows of Werther. Thackeray. ALV; BLPA; BMEP; BOHV; CenHV; EnLi-2; FiBHP; HBV; InMe; InP; LEAP; LiTL; NA; NeHB; OnSP; PoVP; SiTL; TOP; TreF; VA
Wessex Guidebook. Louis MacNeice. HaMV
Wessex Heights. Thomas Hardy. FaBoEn; PoEL-5; UnPo
West, The. A. E. Housman. Last Poems, I. POTT
West, The. Edwin Muir. MoVE
West and away the wheels of darkness roll. Revolution. A. E. Housman. Last Poems, XXXVI. CaAE; ImOP
West and East. Matthew Arnold. *See* Pagan World, The.
West-Country Damosel's Complaint, The. *Unknown.* ESPB
West-Country Lover, A. Alice Brown. HBV; LBMV; LEAP; PR
West-Eastern Divan, *sels.* Goethe, *tr. fr. German by* Edward Dowden.
"Behramgur first discovered rhyme." BoFr
Gingo Biloba. BoFr
"Honour the salutation of the unknown!" BoFr
Zuleika. BoFr
West Indies, The, *sels.* James Montgomery.
Columbus. PEDC
(Inspiration, The.) PAH
Lust of Gold, The, *abr.* PAH
West is lost in space that rosy pallors fill. Aleksey Konstantinovich Tolstoy, *tr. fr. Russian by* Sir Cecil Kisch. WaL
West is purple, and a golden globe, The. Harvest. John Addington Symonds. PoVP
West London. Matthew Arnold. BMEP; BPN; EmBrPo; EPN; MCCG; OAEP; PeBoSo; PoFr; PoVP; VLEP
West of Alice. W. E. Harney. NeLNL
West River, The. Yü Hsüan Chi, *tr. fr. Chinese by* Henry H. Hart. PoHN
West road for my father, A. Legacy. Gladys McKee. JKCP
West-running Brook. Robert Frost. AmP; MAP; MoAB; MoAmPo; PoLFOT; ReaPo
West Sussex Drinking Song. Hilaire Belloc. MoBrPo
West Texas. *At. to* Leona Mae Austin. CoSo
West Virginia Hills, The. Ellen King *and* H. E. Engle. PoRL
West was white, the east was black, as if, The. At Nightfall, on the Wall of Paris. Victor Hugo. TrFP
West Wind, The. John Masefield. BEL; ChMo; CMP; CV; EnLi-2 (1949 ed.); EnLit; FaFP; GTBS-W; GTSL; InP; LiTB; LiTM; MBP; MoAB; MoBrPo; PG; POT; PoTo; TOP; TreF; TSW; TSWC; VOD
West Wind, The. Shelley. *Fr.* Ode to the West Wind, *2 ll.* PCH
West wind, blow from your prairie nest. The Song My Paddle Sings. E. Pauline Johnson. CaP; CPG; FaPON; HBV; OCL; OTPC; PoRL; POT; PoTo; VA
West wind, come from the west land. To the West Wind. George Frederick Cameron. CPG
West wind dances down the lane and sets the robins winging, The. Spring Wind. Nancy Byrd Turner. SiSoSe
West Wind's Secret, The. Mary Jane Carr. BrR
Westering. Douglas V. Kane. GoYe
Western Emigration. David Humphreys. AnAmPo; LA
Western Formula. *Unknown.* PoOW
Western Sun withdraws the shorten'd Day, The. Moonlight in Autumn. James Thomson. *Fr.* The Seasons; Autumn. OBEC
Western Town. David Wadsworth Cannon, Jr. PoNe
Western Trail, The. Robert V. Carr. PoOW
Western Wagons. Stephen Vincent Benét. WaKn
Western Waves of Ebbing Day. The. Sir Walter Scott. *Fr.* The Lady of the Lake, I. OTPC; PoEL-4
Western Wind. *Unknown. See* Western Wind, When Wilt Thou Blow?
Western wind has blown but a few days, The. The Cranes. Po Chü-i. MBP; MoBrPo (1942 ed.); TrCh
Western wind is blowing fair, The. Serenade. Oscar Wilde. HBV
Western Wind, When Wilt [*or* Will] Thou Blow? *Unknown.* AnFE; EG; EnLoPo; ExPo; FaBoCh; LiTL; LO; LoGBV; Po; ReaPo; RiBV; SeCeV; ViBoPo
(Absence.) LoPS; OBSC
(Drouth.) BLV
(Lover in Winter Plaineth for the Spring, The.) EnLi-1 (1949 ed.); LiTG; OBEV
(O Western Wind.) GTBS-W; HoPM; LiTB; SiTL; TrGrPo
(Song: "Western wind, when will thou blow.") LyMA
(Song: "Westron wynde when wyll thou blow.") BrBE; SeCePo
(Western Wind.) BCEP; CoEV; ElSeCe; KN; LoPo; OnPM; TuPP; UnPo (3d ed.)
(Westron Winde, When Will Thou Blow?) AtBAP; InvP; PoEL-1
Westgate-on-Sea. John Betjeman. OxBoLi
Westland Row. James Stephens. HBMV
Westminster Abbey. Matthew Arnold. ViPo
Westminster Bridge. Wordsworth. *See* Composed upon Westminster Bridge, Sept. 3, 1802.
Westminster is gray at midnight. A Christmas Thought about Dickens. Bertha S. Scranton. PEOR
Westminster Wedding, A; or, Like unto Like, Quoth the Devil to the Collier. *Unknown.* CoMu
Westphalian Song. *Unknown, tr. fr. German by* Samuel Taylor Coleridge. AWP; JAWP; LiTW; LyMA; WBP
Westron Winde, When Will Thou Blow? *Unknown. See* Western Wind, When Wilt Thou Blow?
West's Asleep, The. Thomas Osborne Davis. OnYI
Westward. Lionel Johnson. POTT

Westward at even . . . yet never, never to die! The Birds Go By. Shaw Neilson. MoAuPo
Westward Ho! Joaquin Miller. AA; FaBoBe; OBAV
Westward Ho. *Unknown.* CoSo; CSF
Westward I watch the low green hills of Wales. Clevedon Church. Andrew Lang. BSV; GoTS
Westward, much nearer by south-west, behold. Satan's Survey of Greece. Milton. *Fr.* Paradise Regained, IV. EV-2
Westward on the high-hilled plains. A. E. Housman. A Shropshire Lad, LV. BPN; BrBE; MCCG; PoVP
Westward the course of empire takes its way. George Berkeley. *Fr.* On the Prospect of Planting Arts and Learning in America. BCEP
Westward, under a wild wood side. Mercy Passeth All Things. *Unknown.* TMEV
Wet almond-trees, in the rain. Bare Almond Trees. D. H. Lawrence. MoP
Wet are the roads in the dew. The Roads in the Dew. *Unknown.* WhP
Wet day on the road, A: the slim blades cutting. Windshield. Robert Fitzgerald. CrMA
Wet Earth. Ramón López Velarde, *tr. fr. Spanish by* Samuel Beckett. AnMP
Wet leaves fall in a pattern of rusty yellows, The. Rainy Morning. Jessica Nelson North. NP
Wet Litany, The. Kipling. TriL
Wet Morning, The. Thomas Warton, the Younger. *Fr.* The Pleasures of Melancholy. BeR
Wet or Fine. Amory Hare. HBMV
Wet sands were grey-blue that afternoon, The. The Onset. Jessie B. Rittenhouse. BLA
Wet Sheet and a Flowing Sea, A. Allan Cunningham. BCEP; BHV; BTP; EBSV; EG; EnRP; ERP; EtS; EV-4; GoTS; GTBS; GTBS-D; GTBS-W; GTSE; GTSL; HBV; HBVY; LPS-2; MCCG; NeHB; NLK; OBRV; OTPC; PoMa; PYM; TiPo; TreFS; TVSH; WaKn; WP
(At Sea.) GBV (1922 ed.)
(Sea Song, A.) BBV; BoTP; FaBoBe; GN; LH; NeHB; RG; RIS
(Wet Sheet and a Flowing Sail, A.) PCH
Wet Summer. May Williams Ward. GoYe
Wet Summer; Botanic Gardens. Nan McDonald. BoAV
Wet Through. Hal Summers. HaMV
Wet, wayward fingers of the west wind wave the wheat. Corn Cañon. Patric Stevenson. NeIP
Wet your feet, wet your feet. To an Irish Blackbird. James MacAlpine. BLA; HBMV; HBVY
We've been visited by men across the seas. Fuzzy Wuzzy Leaves Us. "E. P. C." PA
We've despatched, *pour la guerre.* Message to General Montgomery. H. F. Ellis. WhC
We've Done Our Hitch in Hell. *Unknown.* ABF
We've formed our band and we are well manned. Sacramento. *Unknown.* TrAS
We've fought with many men acrost the seas. Fuzzy-Wuzzy. Kipling. BEL; CV; EnLi-2 (1949 ed.); EnLit; HBV; MBP; MCCG; MoBrPo; PoVP; PYM; StaSt; TrGrPo; VA; ViPP; VLEP; YT
We've foxgloves in our garden. Foolish Flowers. Rupert Sargent Holland. GFA; MeMeAg; OTPC
We've kept the faith. Our souls' high dreams. To Our Friends. Lucian B. Watkins. BANP
We've lived for forty years, dear wife. The Ideal Husband to His Wife. Sam Walter Foss. BOHV; InMe
We've lived owre lang, my jar and I. The Empty Jar. William Stenhouse. AnNZ
We've ploughed our land, we've sown our seed. The Bird-Scarer's Song. *Unknown.* CBPC
We've put a fine addition on the good old church at home. The Ladies' Aid. *Unknown.* DDA
We've reached the land of desert sweet. Dakota Land. *Unknown.* ABS; AS; CoSo
We've smashed the tablets and the songs, forsworn. Frank Wilmot. *Fr.* To God, from the Warring Nations. BoAV
We've trod the maze of error round. Late Wisdom. George Crabbe. *Fr.* Reflections. EV-3; HBV; OBEV; OBRV; TrGrPo
We've wandered all about the upland fallows. A Lullaby. Ford Madox Ford. BOL
Wexford Girl, The. *Unknown.* ShS (*2 vers., with music*); ViBoFo
Weyla's Song. Eduard Mörike, *tr. fr. German by* Mabel Cotterell. AnGP
Wh-wh—wh-wh—wh-where's he. The Building of Cloudcuckoocity. Aristophanes. *Fr.* The Birds. OxBG
Wha Has Gude Malt. *Unknown.* EBSV
Wha Is Perfyte. Alexander Scott. GoTS
Wha Is That at My Bower Door? Burns. InvP; RO
Wha lies here? Johnny Dow. *Unknown.* FiBHP; SiTL; WhC
Wha the deil hae we got for a King. The Wee, Wee German Lairdie. Allan Cunningham. EBSV
Wha wad na be in love. Maggie Lauder. Francis Sempill. EBSV; OBS
Whack Fol the Diddle. Peadar Kearney. FiBHP; OnYI
Whale. William Rose Benét. EtS; MAP; MoAmPo; TBM
Whale, The. Erasmus Darwin. GoTP
Whale. Geoffrey Dearmer. BoTP
Whale, The. John Donne. *Fr.* The Progress of the Soul. ChTr
Whale, The. Herman Melville. *See* Father Mapple's Hymn.
Whale, The ("It was in the year of . . ."). *Unknown. See* Greenland Fishery, The.
Whale, The ("Now I will fashion the tale of a fish"). *Unknown, tr. fr. Anglo-Saxon by* Charles W. Kennedy. *Fr.* Physiologus. AnOE
Whale, The (" 'Tis a hundred years"). *Unknown.* EtS
Whale and the *Essex*, The. A. M. Sullivan. EtS
Whale and the Tiger, The. John W. Simons. JKCP (1955 ed.)
Whale butting through scarps of moving marble, The. Explorations. Louis MacNeice. ChMP; CoBMV
Whale of great porosity, A. A Fish Story. Henry A. Beers. BOHV
Whaleman's Song, The. *Unknown.* EtS
Whalen's Fate, *with music. Unknown.* ShS
Whaler's Confession, A. Harry Kemp. NV
Whales, The. Marguerite Young. ReMP
Whale's Nature, The. *Unknown, tr. fr. Middle English. Fr.* The Bestiary. MeEV
Whalin' up the Lachlan. Louis Esson. NeLNL
Whaling for continents suspected deep in the south. The Unhistoric Story. Allen Curnow. AnNZ
Wha'll Be King but Charlie. Lady Nairne. EBSV; EV-3
Wha'll buy caller herrin'. Caller Herrin'. Lady Nairne. EBSV; EV-3; HBV; MCCG; OBRV
Wham at his birth wi' mournfu' smile. Quem Tu, Melpomene. J. Logie Robertson. EBSV
Whan bells war rung, an mass was sung. Sweet William's Ghost (B *vers.*). *Unknown.* ESPB
Whan father Adie first pat spade in. Robert Fergusson. *Fr.* Caller Water. EPP
Whan gloamin' [*or* gloming] grey out-owre the welkin keeks. The Farmer's Ingle. Robert Fergusson. BSV; CEP
Whan my faither's faither was a bairn. The Star. William Soutar. NeBP
Whan Phoebus ent'red was in Gemine. How Grand Amour Walked in a Meadow and Met with Fame . . . Stephen Hawes. *Fr.* The Pastime of Pleasure. ReIE
Whan seyd was al this miracle, every man. Sir Thopas. Chaucer. *Fr.* The Canterbury Tales. BEL; EM-1
Whan that Aprille with his shoures sote [*or* soote]. Prologue. Chaucer. *Fr.* The Canterbury Tales. ATP; BEL; BLV; BoLiVe; CaAE; CBOV; ChTr; CoBE; EM-1; EnL; EnLi-1; EnLit; EPP; EV-1; FiP; GEPC; GoBC; InP; LiA; LPS-2; MaPo; OAEP; PIAE; PreP; REAL; SeCeV; TCEP; TOP; TrGrPo; TyEnPo; ViBoPo
Whan that Arcite to Thebès comen was. Chaucer. *Fr.* The Canterbury Tales: The Knight's Tale. LiA
Whan That the Month of May. Chaucer. *Fr.* The Legend of Good Women: Prologue. AtBAP
Whan the Hert Is Laich. Sidney Goodsir Smith. NeBP
Whango Tree, The. *Unknown.* BOHV; NA
Whanne autumpne blake and sonne-brente doe appere. Autumn Fruits. Thomas Chatterton. *Fr.* Aella. RO
Whanne I this Supplicacioun. The Parting of Venus and Old Age. John Gower. *Fr.* Confessio Amantis. PoEL-1
"Whar hae ye been a'day—my boy Tammy?" My Boy Tammy. Hector MacNeill. CH; LO
Whar you goin', buzzard. Jump Jim Crow. *Unknown.* APW
Whar y'u from, little stranger, little boy? A Cowboy's Son *Unknown.* SCC
"Wharefore sou'd ye talk o' love." Willie and Helen. Hew Ainslie. ESBV; HBV; OBEV (1st ed.)
Wharf of Dreams, The. Edwin Markham. HBV
Wharton ("Wharton! the scorn and wonder of our days"). Pope. *See* Characters from the Satires: Wharton.
What?/ You define me God with these trinkets. What? You Define Me God. Stephen Crane. *Fr.* War Is Kind, IV. AmPP (3d ed.)
What a big nose Mrs. Mother has. Mrs. Mother Has a Nose. James Broughton. SiTL
What a blow that of the knocker. Manuel Altolaguirre, *tr. fr Spanish by* Eleanor L. Turnbull. CoSP
What a calamity! What dreadful loss! Honesty at a Fire. J. C. Squire. FiBHP
What a commanding power. Prayer. Thomas Washbourne. WGRP
What a Court Hath Old England, *with music. Unknown.* TrAS, *incl.* You Simple Bostonians
What a dainty life the milkmaid leads! Song. Thomas Nabbes. *Fr.* Tottenham Court. EG; SeCL
What a fearful battle. The Chickens. Rose Fyleman. TiPo (1952 ed.)
What a fine cow your predecessor was! To a Sacred Cow. *Unknown.* WGRP

What a fine life is the farmer's in the open air. *Unknown, tr. fr. Italian by* L. R. Lind. LyPI
What a fluffy little kitty! Dog Meets Cat. Margaret Mackprang Mackay. AlBD
What a friend we have in Jesus. The Unfailing Friend. Joseph Scriven. BLRP; OlF
What a gay/ September day! School Begins. Nell Goodale Price. BrR
What a great battle you and I have fought! The Marriage. Anna Wickham. BMEP
What a grudge I am bearing the earth. A Translation from Petrarch [*or* He Is Jealous of the Heavens and Earth]. Petrarch, *tr. by* J. M. Synge. Sonnets to Laura: To Laura in Death, XXXII. MBP; MoBrPo; NeMA; TwCV
What a liar/ Was the tinker woman. Outside Dunsandle. Sacheverell Sitwell. ChMP
What a line of them, brave and bright. The Tattered Flag. James Buckham. FOAH
"What a lovely world," said the baby chick. An Easter Chick. Thirza Wakley. BoTP
What a moment, what a doubt! Sneezing. Leigh Hunt. HBV; LPS-3
What a Piece of Work Is a Man. Sophocles. *See* Choral Ode: "Wonders are many . . ."
What a piece of work is [a] man! Man. Shakespeare. *Fr.* Hamlet, II, ii. InP; TreF
What a pity, when you are made. Satrapy. C. P. Cavafy. MoGP
What a plague is this o' mine. Jenny wi' the Airn Teeth. Alexander Anderson. BOL; HBV
What a pleasure, what a treasure. Vignette of Ancient Peace. Aristophanes. *Fr.* The Peace. GrR
What a pretty tale you told me. Epilogue. Robert Browning. *Fr.* The Two Poets of Croisic. BPN
What a Proud Dreamhorse. E. E. Cummings. InvP
What a sharp little fellow is Mister Fly. Mister Fly. Thomas Miller. OTPC (1923 ed.)
What a sorrowful sunset we had tonight! Winter Sunset. Jules Laforgue. AnFP
What a stir in the harbor! Palos, Spain, 1492. Annette Wynne. HH
What a thin life the girl. Constantino Suasnavar. *Fr.* Numbers. AnCL
What a thing to come upon relations sitting at their food! The Family Dinner-Party. Menander. OxBG
What a wonderful bird the frog are. The Frog. *Unknown.* DDA; MoShBr; SiTL; WhC; YaD
What a wondrous day I passed. Sun and Cloud. Abus Salt. MooP
What a world that was you planned us. John o' Dreams. Theodosia Garrison. HBMV
What! After your six-month drowsing and indolent sleeping. At the Edge of the Bay. Thomas Caldecot Chubb. EtS
What ails John Winter, that so oft. John Winter. Laurence Binyon. PtOT; SG; TCPD
What Ails This Heart o' Mine? Susanna Blamire. LPS-1
"What ails you that you look so pale." A Ballad of Marjorie. Dora Sigerson Shorter. TIP
What alchemist could in one hour so drain. A Prairie Sunset. E. J. Pratt. MM; NLK (1947 ed.)
What! alive and so bold, O Earth? Lines Written on Hearing the News of the Death of Napoleon. Shelley. ChER
What Am I? Dorothy Aldis. OTPC (1946 ed.); RIS; StVeCh (1955 ed.)
What am I? how produc'd? and for what end? John Arbuthnot. *Fr.* Know Yourself. PoP
What Am I, Life? John Masefield. *Fr.* Sonnets ("Long long ago"). ImOP; NP
(Sonnet: "What am I, Life? A thing of watery salt.") PoeMoYo
What am I? O thou sea, with all thy noise. Theseus. T. Sturge Moore. TCPD
"What am I to do with my Sister?" Prince Yuhara. *Fr.* Manyo Shu. AWP; JAWP; WBP
What Am I Who Dare to Call Thee, God! William Habington. OxBoCh
(What Am I Who Dare.) PoLi; TrPWD
What America Means to Me. Letta Eulalia Thomas. HiLiAm
What? an English sparrow sing? Did You Ever Hear an English Sparrow Sing? Bertha Johnston. BLPA
What an evening! Streamlets run. Afanasi Fet, *tr. fr. Russian by* C. M. Bowra. BoR
What an image of peace and rest. Old St. David's at Radnor. Longfellow. MeRV
What Answer? Baudelaire, *tr. fr. French by* Alan Conder. TrFP
What answer shall we make to them that seek. Lincoln. Florence Kiper Frank. PGD
What are earthly honors. Henry Shirley. *Fr.* The Martyred Soldier. TuPP
What are heavy? Sea-sand and sorrow. Sea-Sand and Sorrow. Christina Rossetti. ChTr
What are little boys made of, made of? Mother Goose. ABF; BoN; BoChLi; FaFP; OxNR; LiTG; OTPC; PPL; RIS; SAS; SiTL; TreF
What are men's lives, but labyrinths of error. An Inquisition upon Fame and Honor. Fulke Greville. SiCE
What are our light afflictions here. Our Light Afflictions. *Unknown.* BLRP
What Are Outward Forms? Isaac Bickerstaffe. OnYI
What are poets? Are they only drums commanding? No Armistice in Love's War. Ralph Cheyney. PGD
What are stars but hieroglyphics of God's glory writ in lightning. Apollo. Thomas Holley Chivers. APW; MOAP; SPP
"What are the bugles blowin' for?" said Files-on-Parade. Danny Deever. Kipling. AnFE; BBV (1923 ed.); BEL; BPN; ChMo; CoEV; EnLi-2 (1949 ed.); EPP; ExPo; HBV; InP; LEAP; LiA; LiTB; LiTM (rev. ed.); MaC; MCCG; MBP; MoBrPo; NeMA; OAEP (2d ed.); OxBoLi; PFE; PoE; PoFS; PoVP; PYM; SeCePo; ShBV-3; TOP; TreFS; TrGrPo; TSW; TSWC; UnPo (3d ed.); VA; WaaP
What are the falling rills, the pendent shades. A Fragment. Pope. CaAE
What are the islands to me. The Islands. Hilda Doolittle ("H. D.") AV; MAP; MoAmPo; PG; TBM
What are the lays of artful Addison. The Charms of Nature. Joseph Warton. SeCePo
What are the long waves singing so mournfully evermore? Olivia. Edward Pollock. AA
What are the tears upon your pleated dress? The White Curtains. W. G. Archer. PoN
What are the thoughts that are stirring his breast? Under the Shade of the Trees [*or* The Shade of the Trees]. Margaret Junkin Preston. BlG; BoHiPo; DD; GA; MC; PAH; SPP; TCAP
What are the Vision and the Cry. The Confused Dawn. William Douw Lighthall. VA
What are the voices that harass their dreaming? Last Cargo. Silence Buck Bellows. EtS
What are the youngsters saying. The Old Boys. Arthur Guiterman. FAOV
What are these, angels or demons. Skyscrapers. John Gould Fletcher. ChMo; CMP; VOD (1935 ed.)
What are these words that beat their wings in vain. The Gaelic. Blanche Mary Kelly. CAW
What Are They Thinking. Bryan Guinness. OxBI
What are they? Why, only qualities of light. Time and Motion Study. Iain Fletcher. PoLFOT; PoN
"What are those Golden Builders doing?" Blake. *Fr.* Jerusalem, I. OBRV
What Are We? Thomas Wolfe. QS
What Are We First? George Meredith. Modern Love, XXX. AnEnPo; LiTL
(Modern Love, XXX.) PoEL-5; ViBoPo; ViP; ViPo
What are we set on earth for? Say, to toil. Work. Elizabeth Barrett Browning. PC
What Are Years? Marianne Moore. AmP; CoBMV; LiTA; MoAB; MoAmPo (1950 ed.); MoPo; OxBA; ReMP; TrGrPo (rev. ed.)
What are you able to build with your blocks? Block City. Robert Louis Stevenson. FaPON; MPB; OnHT; PCH; TiPo
What are you carrying Pilgrims, Pilgrims? Atlantic Charter, A.D. 1620–1942. Francis Brett Young. TiPo (1952 ed.)
What Are You Doing for Jesus? Martha Snell Nicholson. BePJ
What are you doing like a naughty child. To a Poet. Walter Conrad Arensberg. AnAmPo; LA
What are you doing, little day-moon. The Runaway. Cale Young Rice. VOD
What are you doing, my lady, my lady. *Unknown.* OxNR
What are you doing now. To Thomas Moore. Byron. BoFr; EmBrPo; PtP
What are you doing out here in the snow. Welcome Visitors. Emilie Blackmore Stapp. GFA
"What are you doing there, Robin a Bobbin." "Talents Differ." Laura E. Richards. TiPo
What, are you drop't? John Webster. *Fr.* The White Devil, V, vi. PoEL-2
What, are you hurt, Sweet? So Am I. To a Hurt Child. Grace Denio Litchfield. AA; BLP; LBAP; OBAV
What are you, Lady?—naught is here. Portrait of a Lady in the Exhibition of the Royal Academy. Winthrop Mackworth Praed. *Fr.* Every-Day Characters. PoEL-4
What are you, rose?—lips that lean back to meet. The Rose and God. Charles Wharton Stork. HBMV
What are you singing of, soft and mild. The Song of the Wood. Frederic Edward Weatherly. OTPC (1946 ed.)
What are you . . . ? they ask, in wonder. Cold Colloquy. Patrick Anderson. *Fr.* Poem on Canada. CaP; PeCV; TwCaPo
What are you waiting for, George, I pray? Tardy George. *Unknown.* GA; PAH
What art thou, balmy sleep? Sleep. John Banister Tabb. PC

What art thou, Life? The shadow of a dream. Sonnet on Life. Sir Brooke Boothby. ViBoPo
What Art Thou, Love? Jacob Allestry. SeCL; SeEP
What art Thou saying, Lord, to me. Thanksgiving. Gene H. Osborne. PGD; PSO
What art thou what wouldst thou have? *Unknown.* SeCSL
What Artifice. George Dillon. NP
What artist took in hand this ship to frame? An Epigram upon His Majestie's Great Ship (the *Sovereign of the Seas*) Lying in the Docks at Woolwich. Thomas Heywood. SG
What asks the Bard? He prays for nought. After Horace. A. D. Godley. BOHV
What avails it, when shipwreck'd, that error appears? Reflections. George Crabbe. TriL
What awful perspective! while from our sight. The Same —King's College Chapel. Wordsworth. *Fr.* Ecclesiastical Sonnets. EnLP; GEPC
"What bait do you use," said a Saint to the Devil. The Lure. John Boyle O'Reilly. HBV; LauV
What bark impelled by autumn's freshening gale. Geese in Autumn. *Unknown.* OnPM
What Became of Them? *Unknown.* *See* Old Rat's Tale, An.
What beck'ning ghost, along the moonlight shade. Elegy [*or* Verses] to the Memory of an Unfortunate Lady. Pope. ACP; CEP; CoEV; EiPP; EV-3; FiP; HBV; LO; OBEC; OBEV; PoE; SeCeV; TriL
What Becomes of a Strain of Music. Juan Ramón Jiménez, *tr. fr. Spanish by* John Crow. WoL
What Best I See in Thee. Walt Whitman. IAP
What Bids Me Leave. Herbert Trench. HBMV
What bird are you in the grass-tops? Grass-Tops. Witter Bynner. MAP; MoAmPo (1942 ed.); NP
What bird is that, with voice so sweet. A Creole Slave-Song. Maurice Thompson. AA
What Bird So Sings. John Lyly. *See* Trico's Song.
What blast of Fate, melodious mocker, say. To a Skylark, Singing above Barnhill Poorhouse, Glasgow. Roger Quin. EBSV
"What bluid's that on thy coat lap." Edward (A *vers.*). *Unknown.* BaBo; ESPB
What body can be ploughed. Chanson un Peu Naive. Louise Bogan. HBMV
What bond was this, of life or doom. Strange Girl. Clark Ashton Smith. MuM
What Booker can prognosticate. When the King Enjoys His Own Again. Martin Parker. FaBoCh; OBS; OxBoLi; TuPP
What boots it me to see this verdure fair. Pierre de Ronsard, *tr. fr. French by* Curtis Hidden Page. PrPoCR
What bright soft thing is this? The Tear. Richard Crashaw. EnLi-1; GTBS-W; LiTB; OAEP; UnPo
What bring ye me, O camels, across the southern desert. Caravans. Josephine Preston Peabody. AA
What bring[s] you, sailor, home from the sea. Luck. W. W. Gibson. EtS; MoShBr; OBMV
What brought you to my frozen solitude. Wild Idyll. Manuel José Othón. AnMP
What bullet [could have] killed him? Dead Soldier. Nicolás Guillén. AnCL; PoNe
What came before and afterward. The Queen Forgets. George Sterling. MOAP; TCPD; UnW
What came ye out for to seek, O Maker of Words? Out-of-Doors. Ethel E. Mannin. NLK
What can a mother give her children. The Beautiful Gift. Grace Noll Crowell. PEDC
What Can an Old Man Do but Die? Thomas Hood. *See* Ballad: "Spring it is cheery."
What can be better than to let the screen of years. Lowlands Low. Kenneth Leslie. BoCaPo
What can be the matter. The Wind. Dorothy Gradon. BoTP
What can console for a dead world? Believe and Take Heart. John Lancaster Spalding. AA; JKCP
What can forgive us for. Failure. Eithne Wilkins. NeBP
What Can I Do? Horace Traubel. *Fr.* Chants Communal. TrJP
What can I do in Poetry. The Departure of the Good Daemon. Robert Herrick. NBE
What can I give Him. My Gift [*or* A Birthday Gift]. Christina Rossetti. *Fr.* A Christmas Carol: "In the bleak mid-winter." BrR; ChBR; FaPON; MaRV; MeMeAg; OTPC (1946 ed.); PRWS; SiSoSe
What can I give my dear. Doubt. Elinor Chipp. HBMV
What can I give thee back, O liberal. Elizabeth Barrett Browning. Sonnets from the Portuguese, VIII [*or* The Gift]. BPN; BrBE; EV-4; GTBS; GTSL; HBV; OBVV; ViPo
What can I write in thee, O dainty book. In a Lady's Album. Marcus Clarke. BoAu
What can it avail. John Skelton. *Fr.* Colin Clout. SiCE; TuPP
What can it mean? Is it aught to Him. God Cares [*or* He Careth]. "Marianne Farningham." BLRP; WBLP
What can lambkins do. A Chill. Christina Rossetti. BoTP; PRWS
What, can these dead bones live, whose sap is dried. The New Ezekiel. Emma Lazarus. AA; AnAmPo; LA
What can we give in return. Australia. Dowell O'Reilly. BoAu
What Can We Poor Females Do. *Unknown.* SeCL
(Song for Two Voices, A.) SeEP
What can you do, sir, pray let me see? Two Dogs. F. Hey. SAS
What can't be cured. *Unknown.* FaFP; SiTL
What Care I. George Wither. *See* Shall I, Wasting in Despair.
What care I for caste or creed. Creed and Deed. Robert Loveman. MaRV; OQP; QP-1
What care I how black I be? *Unknown.* OxNR
What care I, so they stand the same. Merops. Emerson. AnFE; APA; CoAnAm; FaBoEn; IAP; MOAP; OxBA
What care I tho' beauty fading. Spiritual Love. William Caldwell Roscoe. OBVV
What care I though she be fair. The Choice. Thomas Beedome. SeCL
"What care I, what cares he." The Cowboy. John Antrobus. AA; FaBoBe; FaPON; OTPC (1946 ed.); PoRL
What care if the day. The Good Inn. Herman Knickerbocker Viele. *Fr.* The Inn of the Silver Moon. HBV
What celebration should there be? Holiday. Horace. AWP; JAWP; WBP
What change has made the pastures sweet. A Maiden with a Milking Pail. Jean Ingelow. LPS-2
What charlatans in this later day. The Deathless. Ednah Proctor Clarke. AA
What Cheer? Good Cheer! Good Cheer! Good Cheer! *Unknown.* AnEC
What Child Is This? William Chatterton Dix. MaRV
(What Child Is This, Who, Laid to Rest, *with music.*) YaCaBo
What Christ Is to Us. *Unknown.* BLRP
What Christ Said. George Macdonald. *See* Obedience.
What cities these! What a people. Cities. Arthur Rimbaud. AnFP
What color [*or* colour] are they now, thy quiet waters? Evening on the Moselle. Decimus Magnus Ausonius. AnEnPo; LiTW
What color is Thy face, Lord. In Thine Image; a Negro Speaks. Fania Kruger. QS
What comes from your willing hands I will take. The Disciple Speaks. W. F. Maxwell. CAG
What cometh here from west to east a-wending? A Death Song. William Morris. EmBrPo; PoVP; VA; VLEP
What comfort! through conditioned air. Parlor Car. Dorothy Brown Thompson. PoMa
What, comrade of a night. Life. Alice Brown. AA
What conscience, say, is it in thee. To Aenone [*or* Oenone]. Robert Herrick. HBV; OBEV
What Constitutes a State? Sir William Jones. BCEP; BLPA; LPS-2; MCCG, *abr.;* NeHB; PEDC, *abr.;* PGD
(Ode in Imitation of Alcaeus, An.) HBV; PoFr
(State, The.) BHV; LEAP
What could be done? The inn was full of folks! The Inn That Missed Its Chance. Amos Russell Wells. ChrBoLe
What Could Be Lovelier than to Hear. Elizabeth J. Coatsworth. BrR; SiSoSe
What could be nicer than the spring. A Walk in Spring. K. C. Lart. BoTP
What could be viler. Malcolm Bryler. *Unknown.* SiTL
What could he know of sky and stars, or heaven's all-hidden life. The Sooth-Sayer. Sadi. *Fr.* The Gulistan. AWP
What could make me more morose. The Ovibos. Robert Hale. FiBHP
What could thus high thy rash ambition raise? Honest Fame. Pope. *Fr.* The Temple of Fame. OBEC
What Counsel Has the Hooded Moon. James Joyce. Chamber Music, XII. OnYI; OxBI
What country maiden charms thy heart. E'en the Country Maid. Sappho. GrR
What courier could arrive thus rapidly? The Beacons. Aeschylus. *Fr.* Agamemnon. OxBG
What course of life should wretched mortals take? *At. to* Posidippus, *tr. fr. Greek by* John Beaumont. GrPo
What cry—from out the moonlit blue of wood. Wailing Lynx. Lew Sarett. NP
What Cunning Can Express. Edward de Vere, Earl of Oxford. ElL; ReEn; SiCE; TuPP
(White and Red.) OBSC
What curious things we said. Intra Sepulchrum. Thomas Hardy. MaPo
What curled and scented sun-girls, almond-eyed. On a Lute Found in a Sarcophagus. Sir Edmund Gosse. GTML; GTSL; VA
"What danger, Mary." Carol of Jesus Child. Francis Macnamara. BOL
What dawn-pulse at the heart of heaven, or last. Beauty's

What dawn-pulse at the heart of heaven, or last (*continued*)
Pageant. Dante Gabriel Rossetti. The House of Life, XVII. BPN; PoVP; ViPo
What days await this woman, whose strange feet. A Forecast. Archibald Lampman. VA
What death is worse than this. Sir Thomas Wyatt. SiPS
What delightful hosts are they. A Parting Guest. James Whitcomb Riley. BLP; CP; HBV; IAP; LBMV; LEAP; MAP; MoAmPo (1942 ed.); NeMA; PoMa; POT; PoTo; VA
What dewdrops or what tears. Madrigal. Tasso. LyPI
What did he have in his wagon? Little Black Man with a Rose in His Hat. Audrey Wurdemann. YaD
What did I do on my blooming vacation? The Jokesmith's Vacation. Don Marquis. ALV; FiBHP
What did she resemble, my God, tell me? Fleeting Return. Juan Ramón Jiménez. TeCS
What did she see—oh, what did she see. The Cats Have Come to tea [*or* All the Cats]. Kate Greenaway. OTPC (1946 ed.); PCH; SAS
What did the captain say to the cook. A Capstan Chantey. Edwin James Brady. HBMV
What did the day bring? Letter from a Coward to a Hero. Robert Penn Warren. MAP; MoAmPo
What did thy song boad lady? Shakespeare. *Fr.* Othello, V, ii. AtBAP
What did you build the trophy of, soldier, soldier? Victory March. M. K. Joseph. AnNZ
What did you do with the world that you bade us to bow to anew? William Rose Benét. *Fr.* Arraignment. MaRV
What did you see, Soldier? What did you see at war? Soldier, What Did You See? Don Blanding. BBV (1951 ed.); MaRV
What different dooms our birthdays bring! Miss Kilmansegg's Birth. Thomas Hood. OxBoLi
What Dim Arcadian Pastures. Alice Corbin. HBMV; LEAP; NP; NV
What dire offence [*or* offense] from amorous [*or* am'rous] causes springs. The Rape of the Lock. Pope. AtBAP; ATP; BEL; BLV; BoLiVe; CEP; CoBE; EiPP; EM-1; EnL; EnLi-1; EnLit; EPP; EV-3; GEPC; LiA; MaPo; OAEP; OuHeWo; Po; PoE; PoEL-3; PoFS; REAL; ReaPo; RiBV; SeCeV; TCEP; TOP; TrGrPo; TwHP; TwP; TyEnPo
What discord at the heart of things. The Search for Truth. Boethius. LyMA
What distant thunders rend the skies. On the Death of Captain Nicholas Biddle. Philip Freneau. PAH
What Do I Care? Sara Teasdale. NP
What Do I Care for Morning. Helene Johnson. CDC
What do I care for sorrow. Flail. Power Dalton. HBMV
What do I here! what's beauty? 'las. John Hall. *Fr.* Of Beauty. LO
What Do I Know? Christopher Brennan. BoAV; NeLNL
What do I owe to you. Debt. Sara Teasdale. BAP; LEAP; LoPS; NP
What do I see and hear of an April morning? Shore Roads of April. Bill Adams. EtS
What do the old men say. Under the Locusts. John Crowe Ransom. LS
What do the robins whisper about. Three o'Clock in the Morning. R. S. Palfrey. DD; MPB
What do the stars do. The Stars. Christina Rossetti. *Fr.* Sing-Song. MeMeAg; OTPC (1946 ed.)
What do they care for your books, will they ever read. The Enemies. Raymond Souster. BoCaPo (1948 ed.)
What Do They Do? Christina Rossetti. *See* What Does the Bee Do?
What do they do in Bylo-land. Bylo-land. James B. Kenyon. BOL
What do they here then. Cairn Builders. "An Pilibin." GTIV
What do they here, these denizens of the deep. Gulls over Great Salt Lake. Ross Sutphen. BLA
What do they mean—the stripes of red? The Flag We Fly. Aileen Fisher. YeAr
What do they matter, our headlong hates, when we take the toll of our Dead? The Song of the Pacifist. Robert W. Service. ReTS
What do we earn for all our gentle grace? The Worms' Contempt. W. H. Davies. ChMo
What do we hear? What majesty, what force. Vittorio Alfieri. *Fr.* The First Brutus. PoFr
What Do We Plant? Henry Abbey. DD; FaPON; HBV; HBVY; MPB; NLK; OHIP; PGD; TiPo; WBLP
(What Do We Plant when We Plant the Tree? ADAH; HH; OTPC (1946 ed.); PEOR
What do you call it, bobsled champion. Twentieth-Century Blues. Kenneth Fearing. ChMo
What do you care for Caesar, who yourself. Peter at Fourteen. Constance Carrier. NePoAm
What do you do? Why, everything. Asides. Paul Valéry. AnFP
What do you here, O golden voyager? A City Butterfly. Victor Starbuck. LS
What do you look for, what do you seek? Wishes. Norman Ault. HBMV; HBVY
What do you owe me, Love of all my years? Debt. Corinne Roosevelt Robinson. BoFr
"What do you paint, when you paint a wall?" I Paint What I See. E. B. White. LiTM; NAMP; OnAP; PoFr
What do you remember thinking back? Ever Since. Archibald MacLeish. NePA
What do you see now, my child and offering? The Binding of Isaac. Itzik Manger. OnCuPl
What do you seek within, O Soul, my Brother? Introversion. Evelyn Underhill. MaRV; WGRP
"What do you sell, John Camplejohn." Ballad of John Camplejohn. Bliss Carman. LEAP
What do you sell, O ye merchants? In the Bazaars of Hyderabad. Sarojini Naidu. FaPON; GaP; MoSiPe
What do you think endures? The Great City [*or* What Endures]. Walt Whitman. BHV; GrCo-1
What do you think I saw to-day. The Fairy Cobbler. A. Neil Lyons. BoTP
What do you think? Last night I saw. The Dragon. Mary Mullineaux. BoTP
"What do you with your rifle, son?" I clean it every day. The Hipe. Patrick MacGill. VOD
What Does a Man Think About. John Holmes. CrMA
What Does Easter Mean to You? May Ricker Conrad. OQP; PGD; QP-1
What does he plant who plants a tree? The Heart of the Tree. H. C. Bunner. ADAH; DD; HH; OHFP; OHIP; OQP; PGD; QP-2
What Does It Avail Me? Louise Labé, *tr. fr. French by* Frederic Prokosch. LiTW
What Does It Matter Now. Sydney King Russell. PR
What does it mean? I look across the years. What Does It Mean to Be American? Roselle Mercier Montgomery. MC
What does it mean? Tired, angry, and ill at ease. Beauty. Edward Thomas. NP
What Does It Mean to Be American? Roselle Mercier Montgomery. MC
What does it take to make a day? A Day. William L. Stidger. PoToHe
What Does Little Birdie Say? Tennyson. *Fr.* Sea Dreams. GFA; HBV; HBVY; HH; LPS-1; MeMeAg; MPB; OTPC
(Baby-Song.) BOL
(Cradle Song: "What does little birdie say.") BoTP; PPL; TVC; TVSH
(Little Birdie.) PTA-1; SAS
What does not change/ is the will to change. The Kingfishers. Charles Olson. NeAP
What Does the Bee Do? Christina Rossetti. *Fr.* Sing-Song. BoTP; RIS; SUS; TiPo
(What Do They Do?) FaPON
What does the eye see? The Rose. Kathleen Raine. DiM
What does the farmer in the spring? Spring Work at the Farm. Thirza Wakley. BoTP
What does the hangman think about. The Hangman at Home. Carl Sandburg. ChMo; CMP
What does the train say? The Baby Goes to Boston. Laura E. Richards. GoBP; SAS; TiPo
What does this pure rose child of chastity. This Pure Child. Jules Supervielle. MiCF
What domes and pinnacles of mist and fire. Evening in Tyringham Valley. Richard Watson Gilder. AA; NLK (1947 ed.)
What domination of what darkness dies this hour. The City. "Æ." WGRP
What dost thou fear? Within the Canopy of Leaves. Earl of Rochester. *Fr.* A Pastoral Courtship. BeR
What dost thou here. Moth-Song. Ellen Mackay Hutchinson Cortissoz. AA
What dost thou here, thou shining, sinless thing. A Butterfly in Church. George Marion McClellan. BANP
What! dost thou pray that the outgone tide be rolled back on the strand. A Far Cry to Heaven. Edith M. Thomas. AA; PFY; WGRP
What doth it serve to see sun's burning face. Sonnet. William Drummond of Hawthornden. EIL; ElSeCe
What Doth the Lord Require? Micah, Bible, *O.T. See* Acceptable Sacrifice, The.
What Doth the Lord Require of Thee. Allen Eastman Cross. MaRV
What! doubt the Master Workman's hand. Ridgely Torrence. *Fr.* The House of a Hundred Lights. PC
What drinks the dragon fly, that dart of blue light. Dragon Flies. W. J. Turner. GTBS-D
What Ducks Require. John Crowe Ransom. FaBoMo
What D'ye Call It, The, *sel.* John Gay.
Ballad: "'Twas when the seas were roaring," *fr.* II, viii. CEP; EV-3; HBV; ViBoPo

What ecstasies her bosom fire! To a Lady on Her Passion for Old China. John Gay. EiPP; FaFP; LiTB; LoBV; OBEC; PoE; SiTL

"What else/ Is love, but the most noble, pure affection." Ben Jonson. *Fr.* The New Inn. LO

What else no speech could utter. The Soul of Poetry. Johan Sebastian Cammermeyer Welhaven. AnNoLy

What end the gods may have ordained for me. To Leuconoë. Horace. AA

What Endures? Walt Whitman. *See* Great City, The.

What essences from Idumean palm. Mimma Bella, XX. Eugene Lee-Hamilton. HBV

What ever 'tis, whose beauty here below. The Starre. Henry Vaughan. MePo

What Every Gardener Knows. *Ad. by* Louis Untermeyer. StaSt

What Faire Pompe Have I Spide of Glittering Ladies. Thomas Campion. *See* Love's Pilgrims.

"What fairings will ye that I bring?" The Singing Leaves. James Russell Lowell. GN; LoEn; MPB; OnSP; OTPC; PTA-2; StVeCh

What fancy, or what flight of wingèd thought. George Henry Boker. *Fr.* Sonnets. MOAP

What Far Kingdom. Arthur S. Bourinot. CaP

What Father Knows. *Unknown, at. to* Edgar A. Guest. BAP

What faut had he done that was hang'd yesterday? Of One Hanged. John Heywood. ReIE

What feet she has, what legs, what waist, what thighs. Philodemus, *tr. fr. Greek by* F. A. Wright. GrPo

What fettle, mate? to me he said. The Greeting. W. W. Gibson. POTE

What figure more immovably august. Washington. James Russell Lowell. *Fr.* Under the Old Elm. GA

What flecks the outer gray beyond. The Dead Ship of Harpswell. Whittier. EtS; UnW

What flower is my lady like? Of His Lady. *Unknown.* EIL

What flower is this that greets the morn. The Flower of Liberty. Oliver Wendell Holmes. DD; FOAH; HBVY; MC; PEOR; PoRL; PTA-2

What Followed. Josephine Miles. FiMAP

What folly for any man on earth. Man and Bird and God. *Unknown.* LyMA

What fools men are to weep the dead and gone! Weep for Youth's Passing. Theognis. GrL; OxBG

What! for a term so scant. Westminster Abbey. Matthew Arnold. ViPo

What for an amethyst sea. A Bargain. Abbie Farwell Brown. CV

What force, what sudden impulse, thus can make. Hymn to Apollo. Callimachus. GrPo

What foreland fledged with myrrh. Lord De Tabley. *Fr.* Hymn to Astarte. LEAP

What forms of anguish might this pattern show. Melanie Hyman. PtPa

What fragrant-footed comer. The Little Knight in Green. Katharine Lee Bates. AA

What frenzy has of late possess'd the brain! Sir Samuel Garth. SiTL

What from the founder Aesop fell. The Purpose of Fable-writing. Phaedrus. AWP

What froward will of man, O Zeus! can check thy might? As It Was in the Beginning Is Now and Ever Shall Be. Sophocles. *Fr.* Antigone. GrR

What fun it is. Carefree. Po T'ing. PoHN

What fun to be a baby swan. A Swan Boat. Robert Palfrey Utter. PCH

What gave great Villiers to th' assassin's knife. Samuel Johnson. *Fr.* The Vanity of Human Wishes. NBE

What gentle looks! On Seeing a Beautiful Woman Ride By in a Cart. Hsüan Ti. PoHN

What ghost of an old room comes, goes at will. Lilac Dusk. Lizette Woodworth Reese. VOD

What gifts of speech a man may own. The Sincere Man. Alfred Grant Walton. PoToHe (new ed.)

What girl but, having gathered flowers. Humility. Robert Browning. PoVP

What gives us that fantastick fit. Natura Naturata. Sir John Denham. CEP

What gnarlèd stretch, what depth of shade, is his! The Oak. James Russell Lowell. ADAH

What! go to see the kittens drowned. The Cruel Boy and the Kittens. Ann *or* Jane Taylor. PoC

What god forbid, that made me first your slave. Sonnets, LVIII. Shakespeare. PeBoSo

What God gives, and what we take. Grace for Children [*or* Another Grace for a Child]. Robert Herrick. EV-2; OxBoCh

What God Hath [*or* Has] Promised. Annie Johnson Flint. BLRP; MaRV; WBLP

What God never sees. *Unknown.* OxNR

What god will choose me from this labouring nation. Odes, I. George Santayana. AnFE; APA; CoAnAm; TwAmPo

What gods have met in battle to arouse. Shadows and Lights. "Æ." PoeT

What gods or heroes, whose brave deeds none can dispute. At the Ball Game. Roswell Martin Field. InMe

What golden rabbits do you chase. To a Dog Dreaming. Lord Dunsany. AlBD

What good is there, ah me, what good in love? Rispetto. Agnes Mary Frances Robinson. Tuscan Cypress, II. AV; HBMV

What Grandpa Mouse Said. Vachel Lindsay. UTS

What great yoked brutes with briskets low. Crossing the Plains. Joaquin Miller. AA; AmPP (3d ed.); AnAmPo; BAP; CBOV; GN; LA; LEAP; MAP; MoAmPo (1942 ed.); PaA

What greater torment ever could have been. Lonely Beauty. Samuel Daniel. *Fr.* The Complaint of Rosamond. OBSC

What Greece, when learning flourished, only knew. Prologue and Epilogue to the University of Oxford. Dryden. EV-3; OBS

What grief keeps company with love! O Comes Amoris, Dolor. *Unknown.* *Fr.* Carmina Burana. LaP

What grieves my bones and makes my body faint? In His Extreme Sickness. Thomas, Lord Vaux. ReIE

What Guardian Counsels? Auzias March, *tr. fr. Spanish by* Thomas Walsh. CAW

What guile [*or* guyle] is this, that those her golden tresses. Amoretti, XXXVII. Spenser. ElSeCe; EV-1; InP; LiTL; LoPS; OBSC; PeBoSo; ReEn; SiCE; TCEP; TrGrPo

What hand trimmed these strident feathers for flight. Night Flight. George Whalley. CaP

What hangs in the balance is nowise in doubt. Courage. "Anna Akhmatova." TrRV

What happier fortune can one find. Exile. *Unknown.* KiLC

What happiness you gave to me. The Yew-Tree. *Unknown.* ChTr

What happy mortal sees that mountain now. The White Cascade. W. H. Davies. NeMA

What happy secret fountain. The Dwelling Place. Henry Vaughan. MaRV; MeLP; OBS; OxBoCh; SeEP; TrPWD; WGRP

What happy time? For God's sake, for man's sake. Robert Browning. *Fr.* Paracelsus. EmBrPo

What harm have I done to the stars? Without My Friends the Day Is Dark. Moses ibn Ezra. TrJP

What harvest half so sweet is. Thomas Campion. EG

What has become of our astonishment. The Way We Wonder. Robert Pack. NePoEA

What has become of the good ship *Kite?* Of the Lost Ship. Eugene Richard White. AA; DDA; OBAV

What has bent you. The Pine at Timber-Line. Harriet Monroe. NP

What has happened in the night? The Primroses. W. Graham Robertson. ADAH

What has that woman done to you, my dear! Tea. Jacqueline Embry. HBMV; YaD

What has the sea swept up? The Shell. Mary Webb. AlDL

What has this bugbear Death that's worth our care? Sonnet on Death [*or* Death; a Sonnet]. William Walsh. SeCL; SeEP; ViBoPo

What has this bugbear Death to frighten man. Against the Fear of Death. Lucretius, *tr. by* Dryden. *Fr.* De Rerum Natura. AWP; JAWP; WBP

What has this man got? A sack. The Sand-Man. *Unknown.* BOL

What hast thou learnt today? After a Retreat. Robert Hugh Benson. JKCP

What, hast thou run thy race? Art going down? Of the Going Down of the Sun. Bunyan. CH

What have I done for you. England, My England [*or* Pro Rege Nostro]. W. E. Henley. BMEP; BPN; EnLi-2 (1949 ed.); EV-5; LBBV; MBP; MoBrPo; OBEV; OBVV; OTPC (1923 ed.); PoVP; TreF; VOD (1931 ed.); YT

"What have I earned for all that work," I said. The People. W. B. Yeats. ChMo

What have I gained by the toil of the trail? The Toil of the Trail. Hamlin Garland. HBV; NLK; SN

What, have I 'scaped love-letters. Shakespeare. *Fr.* The Merry Wives of Windsor, II, ii. LO

What, have I thus betrayed my liberty [*or* libertie]? The Yoke of Tyranny. Sir Philip Sidney. Astrophel and Stella, XLVII. AtBAP; PoEL-1; ReEn; SiPS; TrGrPo

What have I to give? In the Far Years. Wilson MacDonald. CaP; OCL

What have I to say to you. Love Song. William Carlos Williams. LoPS; NP; TCPD

What have the years left us? Song. Charles G. Blanden. OQP; QP-1

What Have We Done Today? Nixon Waterman. WBLP (Today.) OQP; PTA-1, *sts.* 1-2; QP-2

What, have ye kithed you a knight, Sir Douglas the Doughty. Against Garnesche. John Skelton. ViBoPo

"What have you looked at, Moon." To the Moon. Thomas Hardy. ChTr; CoBE

What, he on whom our voices unanimously ran. The Pope and the Net. Robert Browning. BOHV

What He Said. Harrison Robertson. *Fr.* Two Triolets. PR
(Two Triolets.) HBV

What He Took. Tom Hood. *See* Takings.

What, Heard Ye Not. *Unknown.* AnEC

What heart could have thought you? To a Snowflake. Francis Thompson. AlDL; BLV; BMEP; BoLiVe; CP; GoTP; HBV; HiLiEn; ImOP; InP; LEAP; LoBV; MBP; MoAB; MoBrPo; NeMA; PIAE; PIR; PoeMoYo; PoeT; POTT; SeCePo; TCEP; ThWaDe; TrGrPo; TSW; TSWC; TVSH; VLEP; VOD (1935 ed.)

What heartache—ne'er a hill! From the Flats. Sidney Lanier. AmP; CoBA; IAP; NePA; OxBA; TCAP

What heartbeats, lisping like a lizard in a broken cistern. Ode to the Present Century. Thomas Merton. JKCP (1955 ed.)

What heave of grapnels will resurrect the fabric. "S.S.R., Lost at Sea."—The *Times.* Ralph Gustafson. PeCV

What heaven-entreated [*or* heav'n-intreated *or* heaven-besiegèd] heart is this. To the Noblest and Best of Ladies [*or* Ladyes], the Countess[e] of Denbigh [*or* Against Irresolution]. Richard Crashaw. EPS; MeLP; MePo; OxBoCh; ReEn

What heavy-hoofed coursers the wilderness roam. The Fall of Tecumseh. *Unknown.* PAH

What held the bones together? Not belief. No Faith. Mark Van Doren. AnFE; CoAnAm; TwAmPo

What helps it now, that Byron bore. Matthew Arnold. *Fr.* Stanzas from the Grande Chartreuse. PtP

What helps it those,/ Who skill in song have found. For [*or* To] a Musician. George Wither. OBS; OxBoCh [*wr. at. to* William Austin]

What! here again, indomitable pest! To a Troublesome Fly. Thomas MacKellar. SN

What heroes from the woodland sprung. Seventy-six. Bryant. DD; HBV; MC; PAH

What hideous noyse was that? John Webster. *Fr.* The Dutchess of Malfi, IV, ii. AtBAP; PoEL-2

What hid'st thou in thy treasure-caves and cells? The Treasures of the Deep. Felicia Dorothea Hemans. LPS-2

What high adventure, in what world afar. Captain Guynemer. Florence Earle Coates. AOAH

What Highway? George N. Shuster. JKCP (1955 ed.)

What ho! my shepherds, sweet it were. A Sylvan Revel. Edward Cracroft Lefroy. Echoes from Theocritus, XXV. AWP; JAWP; WBP

What holds her fixed far eyes nor lets them range? Dürer's "Melancholia" [*or* On Dürer's "Melencolia"]. Sir William Watson. CBOV; VA

What hope is here for modern rhyme. In Memoriam A. H. H., LXXVII. Tennyson. CoBE; EmBrPo; EnLi-2; EPN; GEPC; LPS-1; ViPo; VLEP

What hopes, what terrors does thy gift create. Verses. Samuel Johnson. CaAE

What Horace says is. Eheu Fugaces. "Thomas Ingoldsby." OxBoLi

What hours I spent of precious time. Poetical Economy. Harry Graham. CenHV; SiTL; TreFS

What hubbub rocks the nest? What panic-freighted. Some Lines in Three Parts, III. Peter Viereck. MoAmPo (1950 ed.)

"What hundred books are best, think you?" I said. John Kendrick Bangs. CenHV

What hurrying human tides, or day or night! Broadway. Walt Whitman. DDA

What I Am, I Cannot Avoide. Shakespeare. *Fr.* The Merry Wives of Windsor, III, v. LiA

What I Do Is Me. Gerard Manley Hopkins. *See* As Kingfishers Catch Fire, Dragonflies Draw Flame.

What I Expected. Stephen Spender. CoBMV; MBP; MoAB; MoBrPo; OAEP (2d ed.); ReMP
(What I Expected Was.) MoPo

What I gave, I have. On a Gravestone. *Unknown.* PCD

What I Have. Robert Farren. JKCP (1955 ed.)

What I Have Wrote. Julia Moore. SiTL
("And now, kind friends, what I have wrote.") FiBHP

What I like about Clive. Lord Clive. E. C. Bentley. *Fr.* Biography for Beginners. BOHV; CenHV; MoShBr; OxBoLi; ShBV-3; WhC

What I liked best in Sicily. Goats. Charles Erskine Scott Wood. AnEnPo; PoTo

What I Live For. George Linnaeus Banks. BLPA; FaBoBe; MaRV; NeHB; PTA-1; TreFS
(My Aim.) WBLP
(Why Do I Live? 1 *st., wr. at. to* Thomas Guthrie.) PoToHe (new ed.)

What I love best in all the world. Robert Browning. *Fr.* De Gustibus. PoeMoYo

What I need is lots of money. Take I, 4: II: 58. Philip Whalen. NeAP

What I saw was just one eye. The Bird at Dawn. Harold Monro. BLA; BoTP; GoTP; MoBrPo (1950 ed.)

What I shall leave thee none can tell. To His Son, Vincent [Corbet]. Richard Corbet. ElSeCe; EV-2; FaBoCh; FAOV; LoGBV; SeCL; SeEP; TrGrPo

What I speak, my fair Chloe, and what I write, shews. Chloe. Matthew Prior. LEAP

What I will ask, if one free wish comes down. A Boon. William Meredith. NePoEA

What I will say today. Lo Que Digo. *Unknown.* AS

What If. Gertrude B. Gunderson. OQP; QP-1

What if a Day or a Month or a Year. Thomas Campion. ElL; ElSeCe; ReEn; TuPP
(Chance and Change.) BEL

What If a Much of a Which of a Wind. E. E. Cummings. FaFP; GTBS-W; LiTA; LiTM; MoPo; MoPW; MoVE; NePA; OxBA; PoRA; ReMP; ViBoPo (1958 ed.); WaP

What if but yesterday. Yesterday. Nora Perry. PR

What if his glance is bold and free. To a Brown Girl. Countee Cullen. TBM

What if I bade you leave. Those Images. W. B. Yeats. POTE

What if I coasted near the shore. Voyager's Song. Clement Wood. HBMV

What if I dye for love of thee. *Unknown.* SeCSL

What if I say—/ "The Bible is God's Holy Word." Faith. Maud Frazer Jackson. MaRV

What if my vision shows a curving pond. The Ocean. Florence Wilson Roper. MuM

What If Remembrance? Richard Eberhart. FiMAP

What if small birds are peppering the sky. It Is Winter, I Know. Merrill Moore. MAP; MoAmPo

What if Some Little Paine the Passage Have. Spenser. *Fr.* The Faerie Queene, I, 9. CH
(Death.) MaRV
(Port after Stormie Seas.) EtS

What If Some Lover in a Far-off Spring. Arthur Davison Ficke. Sonnets of a Portrait Painter, XLIII. TBM

What if some morning, when the stars were paling. A Morning Thought. Edward Rowland Sill. UnW

What if the air has a nipping tooth! A Skater's Valentine. Arthur Guiterman. SiSoSe

What if the back be stooped and the skin be dried. Farmers. Helene Mullins. BPP; WGRP

What if the clouds are from the left! *Unknown.* *Fr.* Sea Snatches. SiB

What if the soul her real life elsewhere holds. The Soul in the Body. Edith M. Thomas. AA

What if the sun comes out. Boy Remembers in the Field. Raymond Knister. CaP

What if the winds sang softly the whole night long. The Poet Tells about Nature. Merrill Moore. NP

What if there is no "someday" in God's ken. Three Sonnets, I. Cathleen Keegan. MuM

What if these mountains lift their pride. Mountain Interval. Robert Nathan. MuM

What if this present were the world's last night? Holy Sonnets, XIII. John Donne. ElSeCe; ExPo; GTBS-W; LiTB; MeLP; MeRV; OAEP; OBS; SeCeV; SeEP; TuPP

What? If thou hast need of me, let it be said. Pylades [*or* By Friendship's Ties]. Euripides. *Fr.* Iphigenia in Tauris. GrR; OxBG

What if to edge of dream. The Owl. Walter de la Mare. BrBE

What if we carved truth in the graveyards? What If. Gertrude B. Gunderson. OQP; QP-1

What in these lines doth ripened stand. Prelude. Clemens Brentano. AnGP

What inn is this. Emily Dickinson. NePA; TCAP

What instinct forces man to journey on. The Poet. Amy Lowell. WGRP

What! Irving? thrice welcome, warm heart and fine brain. Irving. James Russell Lowell. *Fr.* A Fable for Critics. AnNE; CoBA

What Is a Brook? Lucy Sprague Mitchell. PCH

What is a day, what is a year of vain delight and pleasure? *Unknown.* OBSC

What is a forest with nothing terrible there. To My Fellow Writers. Aleksandr Yashin. RuPo

What is a friend? I'll tell you. A Friend. *Unknown.* PoToHe (new ed.)

What is a modern poet's fate? The Poet's Fate. Thomas Hood. FiBHP

What is a poet's love? The Poet's Lot. Oliver Wendell Holmes. PoEL-5

What is a sonnet? 'Tis the pearly shell. The Sonnet. Richard Watson Gilder. AA; HBV

What Is a Woman Like? *Unknown.* BOHV

What is a woman that you forsake her. Harp Song of the Dane Women. Kipling. AtBAP; FaBoEn; OAEP (2d ed.).; OtMeF; PoRA; POTE; SeCePo; ShBV-3; TwCV

What is a yielded life? The Yielded Life. "W. A. G." BLRP

What is Africa to me. Heritage. Countee Cullen. BANP; MAP; MoAmPo; PoNe; TBM; TCPD

What is all this washing about. Washing. John Drinkwater. FaPON; StVeCh

What Is an Epigram. Samuel Taylor Coleridge. PreP (Epigram, An: "What is an epigram? a dwarfish whole.") GoTP; HBV; InP

What is beauty, saith my sufferings, then? Tamburlaine on Poetry. Christopher Marlowe. *Fr.* Tamburlaine the Great, Pt. I. CoEV; MyFE; ReaPo

What Is Charm? Louisa Carroll Thomas. BLPA; NeHB

What is death? 'Tis to be free. The Genius of Death. George Croly. HBV; LPS-3

What is earth, sexton? A place to dig graves. Questions with Answers. *Unknown.* BOHV

What Is Excellent Is Permanent. Emerson. *Fr.* Threnody. GrCo-1

What is fairer than the river. The River. Ellis M. Potter. VOD

What is fame? an empty bubble. James Grainger. *Fr.* Solitude. PoP

What is Freedom? Ye can tell. Slavery. Shelley. BCEP

What is freinshipp? but a pleasure. *Unknown.* SeCSL

"What is funny?" you ask, my child. The Anatomy of Humor. Morris Bishop. InMe; WhC

What is gold worth, say. Child's Song. Swinburne. BPN; GTML; GTSL; OBVV; PoVP

What Is Good? John Boyle O'Reilly. HBV; HBVY; LBAP; OQP; OTPC (1946 ed.); PoToHe; PTA-1; QP-2; TreF; WBLP

What is Greece to us now? Salute to Greece. "Clemence Dane." NeTW; PoFr

What is he buzzing in my ears. Confessions. Robert Browning. BPN; EmBrPo; EPN; GEPC; GTBS-D; GTML; PoVP; ViBoPo; ViPo; VLEP

What is home without a Bible? A Home without a Bible. Charles D. Meigs. WBLP

What Is Home without a Mother? Septimus Winner. PEDC

What is hope? a smiling rainbow. Cui Bono? Thomas Carlyle. HBV; OBRV; WGRP

What is house and what is home. House and Home [*or* Home]. Joseph Beaumont. GoTL; OBS

What Is It? Marie Louise Allen. TiPo

What Is It? H. E. Wilkinson. BoTP

What is it fades and flickers in the fire. By the Fireside. Lucy Larcom. LPS-1

What Is It Jesus Saith? Christina Rossetti. ChIP; EPN

What is it life lets us win in the end? Venetian Sonnets, IX. August, Graf von Platen. AnGP

What is it like (you ask perplexed), this fear? William Ellery Leonard. *Fr.* Two Lives, Pt. III. MOAP

What is it men in women do require? The Question Answer'd. Blake. ViBoPo

What is it, O dear country of our pride. For Remembrance. Basil Ebers. DD; HH

What is it so transforms the boulevard? Another Spirit Advances. Jules Romains. AWP; JAWP; MiFP; WBP

What is it that a-billowing there. First Fruits in 1812. Wallace Rice. GA; MC; PAH

What is it that is gone we fancied ours? Aeolian Harp. William Allingham. TIP

"What is it then,"—some Reader asks. Epilogue to Eighteenth Century Vignettes, 2d Series. Austin Dobson. *Fr.* Eighteenth-Century Vignettes. BPN

What is it, then, to die, that it should be. What Is It to Die? Pliny Earle. PoP

"What is it to be dead?" O Life. A Child's Question. Emma Huntington Nason. AA

What Is It to Die? Pliny Earle. PoP

What is it to grow old? Growing Old. Matthew Arnold. BPN; EmBrPo; EPN; EnLi-2; EnLit; FaFP; FiP; GEPC; HBV; OuHeWo; PoEL-5; PoVP; VLEP

What is it you remember?—the summer mornings. To Any Member of My Generation. George Barker. WaP

What is joy of life apart from Venus the golden? Mimnermus, *tr. fr. Greek by* N. H. Dole. GrPo

What Is Life? Samuel Taylor Coleridge. FiP

What Is Life? Euripides, *tr. fr. Greek.* OxBG

What Is Life? Keats. *Fr.* Sleep and Poetry. CBE (From "Sleep and Poetry.") EV-4 ("Stop and consider.") OBRV; SeCePo

What is life if, full of care. *See* What is this life . . .

What is life? It is a faded rose. Life. T. P. Cameron Wilson. VOD

What Is Love? Beaumont *and* Fletcher. *See* Tell Me, Dearest, What Is Love?

What Is Love? "A. J. T." CAG

What is love besides the name. *Unknown.* SeCSL

What is love but the desire. Batte's Song. Michael Drayton. *Fr.* The Shepherd's Garland. LoBV

What is love of one's land. Footsloggers. Ford Madox Ford. LBBV; NP

What is lovelier than the gold. Casual Gold. Maud E. Uschold. YeAr

What Is Man? Psalms, VIII, Bible, *O.T.* EM-1; MaRV; TrGrPo

(How Glorious Is Thy Name.) TrJP

(O Lord, How Excellent Is Thy Name.) TreFS

(Psalm VIII.) AWP; JAWP; OnPM; OuHeWo; PFE; PG (1955 ed.)

(Psalm of Praise, A.) CBOV

(Song of Praise, A.) EnLi-1

What Is Man? Palladas, *tr. fr. Greek by* C. M. Bowra. OxBG

What is more gentle than a wind in summer? Sleep and Poetry. Keats. AtBAP; ATP; EmBrPo; EnRP; EV-4

What is my fate to suffer, my Cyrnus, knows no cure. The Stoic. Theognis. GrPE

What is my mast? A pen. The Voyage. Vachel Lindsay. MAP; MoAmPo

What is our innocence. What Are Years? Marianne Moore. AmP; CoBMV; LiTA; MoAB; MoAmPo (1950 ed.); MoPo; OxBA; ReMP; TrGrPo (rev. ed.)

What Is Our Life? Sir Walter Ralegh. *See* On the Life of Man.

What Is Past. Sir William Davenant. *Fr.* The Cruel Brother, V, i. TrGrPo

What is pink? a rose is pink. Color. Christina Rossetti. *Fr.* Sing-Song. GoBP; RAR; SUS; TiPo

What Is Poetry? Eleanor Farjeon. YeAr

What is poetry? Is it a mosaic. Fragment. Amy Lowell. WGRP

What is poetry, you say. Rimas, XXI. Gustavo Adolfo Bécquer. AnSpL-2; TeCS

What Is Prayer? Marie Barton. PraP

What Is Prayer? James Montgomery. BLRP; MaRV; PraP; WGRP

(Prayer.) GrCo-1

What is prayer but listening in. What Is Prayer? Marie Barton. PraP

What is required of us is the recognition of the frontiers between the centuries. Geography of This Time. Archibald MacLeish. CoV; PG (1945 ed.); PoLFOT

"What is she making?" asked the mate. The Ballad of the *Ivanhoe.* Bill Adams. BBV; PYM

What is so nice in the dining room. Eunice in the Evening. Gwendolyn Brooks. TiPo (1959 ed.)

What Is So Rare as a Day in June ("And what is so rare as a day in June?"). James Russell Lowell. *See* June.

What Is So Rare as a Day in June? ("No price is set on the lavish summer"). James Russell Lowell. *Fr.* The Vision of Sir Launfal. NePA

What is so rare as a day in June? Question and Answer. Samuel Hoffenstein. FiBHP

What is so wondrous as mother's knee? Mother's Knee. Edgar A. Guest. MotAn

What is song's eternity? Song's Eternity. John Clare. BLV; FaBoCh; LoGBV; PG; WaKn

What Is Terrible. Roy Fuller. WaP

What is that beyond thy life. That. Charles Weekes. GTIV

What is that book you read? Stephen Phillips. *Fr.* Paolo and Francesca. ReTS

What is that light, which points the way for me. Providence. Matthias Jochumsson. IcP

What is the boy now, who has lost his ball. The Ball Poem. John Berryman. MoAmPo (1950 ed.)

What Is the Church? Sam Walter Foss. OQP; QP-1

What is the course of the life. Matthew Arnold. *Fr.* Rugby Chapel. MaRV

What is the cross on Golgotha to me. Golgotha's Cross. Raymond Kresensky. ChIP; OQP; QP-2

What is the end of fame? 'tis but to fill. Fame. Byron. *Fr.* Don Juan, I *and* III. GEPC

What is the Eternal? What is the highest Self? The Eternal Self. *Unknown. Fr.* Bhagavad-Gita. WoL

What is the existence of man's life. The Dirge. Henry King. EV-2

What is the fair to whom so long I plead? Coelia, XV. William Percy. ReIE

What is the gold of all this world but dross. Nicholas Breton. *Fr.* The Soul's Harmony. SiCE

What Is the Grass? Walt Whitman. *See* Grass, The.

What is the heart of a girl? The Heart of a Girl Is a Wonderful Thing. *Unknown.* BLPA

What is the horn that the dawn holds. The Horn. James Reaney. PeCV

What is the life of a man. D'Arcy Singer. Edgar Lee Masters. *Fr.* The New Spoon River. ChMo; CMP

What is the little one thinking about? Cradle Song. Josiah Gilbert Holland. *Fr.* Bitter-sweet. AA; BOL; HBV; LPS-1; PCD

What is the matter with Grandpapa? Poor Dear Grandpapa. D'Arcy W. Thompson. BOHV; NA

What is the matter with Mary Jane? After Reading Milne. Ruth Powell. PCD

What is the meaning of the song. I Love My Love. Charles Mackay. NeHB

What is the metre of the dictionary? Sonnets, IV. Dylan Thomas. LiTM

What is the moral? Who rides may read. L'Envoi [*or* The Winners]. Kipling. *Fr.* The Story of the Gadsbys. BLPA; MoBrPo; NeMA; TrGrPo
What is the name of King Ringang's daughter? Beauty Rohtraut. Eduard Mörike. AWP; JAWP; WBP; WoL
What is the Old Year? 'Tis a book. The Old Year. Clarence Urmy. OQP; PGD; PoToHe; PSO; QP-1
"What is the real good?" What Is Good? John Boyle O'Reilly. HBV; HBVY; LBAP; OQP; OTPC (1946 ed.); PoToHe; PTA-1; QP-2; TreF; WBLP
What is the rhyme for porringer? Mother Goose. OxNR; RIS; SiTL
What is the road to Slumberland? And when does the baby go? The Road to Slumberland. Mary Dow Brine. BOL
"What is the song I am singing?" The Founts of Song. "Fiona Macleod." WGRP
What is the song the stars sing? New Year's Chimes. Francis Thompson. AIDL
What is the sorriest thing that enters Hell? Vain Virtues. Dante Gabriel Rossetti. The House of Life, LXXXV. EmBrPo; EnLi-2; EPP; HBV; PoVP; ViPo; ViPP
What is the sound of the earth spinning? The Natural History of Pliny. Vincent McHugh. NePoAm-2
What Is the Use? *sel.* Erastus Wolcott Ellsworth.
"I saw a man, by some accounted wise." AA
What is the use of time and rhyme? Vladislav Khodasevich. *See* It Scarcely Seems Worth While.
What is the voice I hear. To America [*or* A Voice from the West]. Alfred Austin. GN; HBV; PAH; PECK; POT; PoTo; TVSH
What is the word for "death." Flowers for Luis Bunuel. Stuart Z. Perkoff. NeAP
"What is the world, O soldiers?" Napoleon. Walter de la Mare. FaBoCh; FaBoTw; LoGBV; MoVE; OtMeF; SoV
What is the world's true Bible—'tis the highest thought of man. The True Bible. Sam Walter Foss. *Fr.* The Higher Catechism. BPP
What is there hid in the heart of a rose. Song. Alfred Noyes. CH
"What is there in thee, Moon! that thou shouldst move." Address to the Moon. Keats. *Fr.* Endymion, III. ERP
What is there left to be said? A Farewell. A. R. D. Fairburn. AnNZ
What is there wanting in the Spring? The Wistful Days. Robert Underwood Johnson. AA; ADAH; BAP; LEAP; SN
What is this?/ The white and crumbling clouds. Rapture; an Ode. Richard Watson Dixon. OxBoCh
What is this atom which contains the whole. John Masefield. *Fr.* Sonnets ("Long, long ago"). GTML
What Is This Coming Year? William Olney. PSO
What is this crying that I hear in the wind? The Lament of Ian the Proud. "Fiona Macleod." VLEP
What is this dream I have, between sleeping and waking? Dream. Marion Ethel Hamilton. MuM
What is this grandeur I see up in heaven. The Grandeurs of Mary. Frederick William Faber. JKCP
What is this image in the clouded mirror. Image in a Mirror. Mae Winkler Goodman. GoYe
What is this knowledge but the sky-stolen fire. Much Knowledge, Little Reason [*or* Knowledge and Reason]. Sir John Davies. *Fr.* Nosce Teipsum. ChTr; OBSC
What Is This Life? William Dunbar. EBSV
What is this life, if, full of care. Leisure. W. H. Davies. AnFE; AWP; BLV; BMEP; BoTP; CaAE; CH; ChMo; CMP; EnLit; FaBoBe; FaFP; FaPON; GTSE; HBV; HiLiEn; JAWP; LBBV; LiTB; LiTM; MBP; MoShBr; NBE; OBEV (new ed.); OBMV; OBVV; OtMeF; PC; PoeMoYo; PoeT; PoTo; POTT; PYM; SeCePo; ShBV-1; TCPD; TiPo; TOP; TrGrPo; TSW; TSWC; TVSH; WaKn; WBP; WHA; WoL; WP
What is this man, thy darling kissed and cuffed. Francis Thompson. *Fr.* An Anthem of Earth. BrBE
What is this mystery that men call death? Mystery. Jerome B. Bell. MaRV
What is this recompense you'd have from me? From a Woman to a Greedy Lover. Norman Cameron. Three Love Poems, I. FaBoTw
What is this that I can see. O Death. *Unknown.* TrAS
What is this that I have heard? Dawn Has Yet to Ripple In [*or* Before Dawn]. Melville Cane. MAP; MoAmPo; PIAE
What is this that roareth thus? The Motor Bus. A. D. Godley. OtMeF
What is this, the sound and rumour? What is this that all men hear. The March of the Workers. William Morris. *Fr.* Chants for Socialists. BMEP; ViP
What is this thing that keeps me tirelessly waiting. Love Song. Sophia Mavroidi Papadaky. MoGP
What is this whisper of homelessness, good my heart. If the Heart Be Homeless. Annemarie Ewing. NePoAm-2
What is thy joy, O heart of man? Question. Nikolaus Lenau. AnGP
What Is Time? William Marsden. BCEP; LPS-3
What Is to Be Given. Delmore Schwartz. FiMAP
What Is to Come [We Know Not]. W. E. Henley. EtPaEn; HBV; NeMA; PoVP
What is to start? As Many Questions as Answers. Laura Riding. MoP
What Is Truth? *sel.* James Harold Manning.
"I have been,/ Three separate times, in war." CaP
What Is Veal? Mary Elliott. OTPC (1923 ed.)
What Is White? Thomas MacDonagh. CAW; JKCP
What Is Winter? Edmund Blunden. ChMP; GTBS-D
What Is Worth the Singing? Cecil French. GTIV
What is your name? and your father's? A Boxer. Simonides. OxBG
What is your substance, whereof are you made. Sonnets, LIII. Shakespeare. AtBAP; EIL; EtPaEn; EV-1; FaFP; GTBS-W; LiTB; LiTG; LiTL; OAEP; OBEV; OBSC; PeBoSo; RiBV; ViBoPo
What? Is't not folly for to dread. That Death Is Not So Much to Be Feared as Daily Diseases Are. George Turberville. ReIE
What is't to me (a passenger God wot). Has Life No Sourness? Pope. *Fr.* The Second Epistle of the Second Book of Horace. BeR
What Is't to Us? Charles Churchill. *Fr.* Night. SeCePo
What joy attends the fisher's life. The Fisher's Life. *Unknown.* ChTr; EtS
What joy does earthly life possess. Troparion. Aleksey Konstantinovich Tolstoy. *Fr.* John Damascene. BoR
What joy hath yon glad wreath of flowers that is. The Garland and the Girdle. Michelangelo. AWP
What joy it is when the hot day grows cool. Venetian Sonnets, III. August, Graf von Platen. AnGP
What, Kaiser dead? The heavy news. Kaiser Dead. Matthew Arnold. AIBD; TCEP
What! kill a partridge in the month of May! On Mr. Partridge. *Unknown.* WhC
What Kin' o' Pants Does the Gambler Wear, *with music.* *Unknown.* AS
What kind of men are these. Shiki, *tr. fr. Japanese by* Lois J. Erickson. SoLD
What Kind of Mistress He Would Have. Robert Herrick. TrGrPo
What kind of trees. Lamp Posts. Helen Hoyt. YT
What know I,/ As I bite the blue veins of the throbbing sky. The Song of the Arrow. Isabella Valancy Crawford. *Fr.* Gisli, the Chieftain. BoCaPo
What Know We Greater than the Soul? Tennyson. *Fr.* Ode on the Death of the Duke of Wellington. MaRV
"What Lack We?" *abr.* Gudmundur Fridjónsson, *tr. fr. Icelandic by* Jakobina Johnson. IcP
What land of Silence. Beata Solitudo. Ernest Dowson. POTT; PoVP
What large, dark hands are those at the window. Love on the Farm. D. H. Lawrence. MBP; MoAB; MoBrPo; TrGrPo
"What length of verse can serve brave Mopsa's good to show." Sir Philip Sidney. *Fr.* Arcadia. ReIE
What lewd, naked and revolting shape is this? Shopping for Meat in Winter. Oscar Williams. GTBS-W; LiTA; LiTM; NePA
What life can compare with the jolly town-rakes. The Town-Rakes. *At. to* P. A. Motteux. CoMu
What light ill-omened shone. Evadne. Euripides. *Fr.* Suppliants. GrR
What light of unremembered skies. The Song of the Pilgrims. Rupert Brooke. QS
What lightning shall light it? What thunder shall tell it? Martin Luther at Potsdam. Barry Pain. ALV; BOHV; NA
What links are ours with orbs that are. Meditation under Stars. George Meredith. EmBrPo; OAEP; POTT; ViP; VLEP
What Lips My Lips Have Kissed. Edna St. Vincent Millay. AnFE; APA; AV; CaAE; CoAnAm; GTBS-W; LiTA; MAP; MoAB; MoAmPo; PeBoSo; PIAE; PreP; ReaPo; TBM; TwAmPo
(Sonnet: "What lips my lips have kissed, and where, and why.") HBMV; LiTG; ViBoPo
What Literature Needs. John Holmes. InMe
What little Roman maiden loved you so? To a Roman Doll. Mahlon Leonard Fisher. MuM
What little throat. The Blackbird by Belfast Lough. *Unknown.* KiLC
What lively lad most pleasured me. A Last Confession. W. B. Yeats. LiTL; LO; TwP
What living being. Hymns to the Night, I. "Novalis." AnGP
What long-forgotten gleam is this? Aleksandr Blok, *tr. fr. Russian by* Oliver Elton. BoRS
What lookest thou herein to have? A Preface to the Buyer of This Book. Thomas Tusser. SiCE; TuPP
What loud wave-motioned hooves awaken. The Blue Horses. J. P. McAuley. BoAV

What love do these men give their women. Structural Iron Workers. MacKnight Black. NP
What Love Is This. Edward Taylor. *Fr.* Sacramental Meditations. AmPP (4th ed.); AnNE
("What Love is this of thine, that cannot bee.") PoEL-3
What lovelier home could gentle Fancy choose? Between Namur and Liége. Wordsworth. EPN; MCCG
What lovely names for girls there are! Girls' Names. Eleanor Farjeon. SUS; TiPo
What lovely things. The Scribe. Walter de la Mare. AnFE; AtBAP; ChMo; CMP; FaBoCh; LoGBV; OBMV; QS; TCPD; TrPWD
What luck had Peter! For he took a fish. The Shekel in the Fish's Mouth. Francis Quarles. StJW
What made thee then so keen to look on Rome? Virgil. *Fr.* Eclogues, I. PoFr
What madly whirling universe is this. Dance of the Gnats. Marguerite Steffan. MuM
What magic halo rings thy head. Aucassin and Nicolete. Francis William Bourdillon. HBV
"What make you so late at the trysting?" The Fetch. Dora Sigerson Shorter. DaM
What Makes a City. *Unknown.* MaRV
What makes a city great? Huge piles of stone. The City's Crown. William Dudley Foulke. GrCo-1; HBMV; MaRV; OQP; QP-2; WGRP
What Makes a Friend. *Unknown, tr. fr. Greek by* H. H. Milman. OxBG
What makes a garden? The Garden. Caroline Giltinan. HBMV
What Makes a Happy Life. Martial. *See* Means to Attain Happy Life, The.
What makes a hero? not success, not fame. The Hero. Sir Henry Taylor. VA
What Makes a Home? *Unknown.* PoToHe (new ed.)
What makes a knave a child of God. Rules of Life. Samuel Butler. *Fr.* Hudibras. BeR
What Makes a Nation Great? Alexander Blackburn. OQP; QP-2; WBLP
What makes a nation's pillars high. A Nation's Strength. Emerson. MaRV; PGD
What makes a plenteous harvest, when to turn. Prelude. Virgil. *Fr.* Georgics. AWP
What makes life worth the living. Giving and Forgiving. Thomas Grant Springer. PoToHe
What makes me disinclined. Pretences. Ibn Rashiq. MooP
What makes men live but honor? I have felt. Andrew Jackson. Donald Davidson. *Fr.* The Tall Men. SPP
What makes my bed seem hard, seeing it is soft? A Captive of Love. Ovid. AWP
What makes the cornfields happy, under what constellation. Virgil. Georgics, I. RoL
What makes the crickets "crick" all night. Crickets. Helen Wing. GFA
What makes the dog's nose always cold? Why the Dog's Nose Is Always Cold. *Unknown.* PTA-2
What makes the ducks in the pond, I wonder, go. In the Park. Rose Fyleman. StVeCh (1955 ed.)
What Makes the Man. Euripides, *tr. fr. Greek by* R. Potter. *Fr.* Electra. GrR
What makes the Sufi? Purity of heart. The True Sufi. Jalal ed-Din Rumi. PeP
What makes you come here fer, Mister. Prior to Miss Belle's Appearance. James Whitcomb Riley. BOHV
What makes you write at this odd rate? Epigram on Miltonicks. Samuel Wesley. OBEC
What makes your lip so strange? Thomas Middleton. *Fr.* The Changeling, III, iv. AtBAP; PoEL-2
What man first forged the terrifying blade? Tibullus. Elegies, I, 10. LaP
What Man Has Made of Man. Wordsworth. *See* Lines Written in Early Spring.
What man is he that yearneth. Chorus [*or* Old Age]. Sophocles. *Fr.* Oedipus at Colonus. AWP; JAWP; LiTW; OxBG; WBP
What man is so clever, so crafty of mind. A Storm, I. *Unknown. Fr.* Riddles. OuHeWo
What man is there so bold that he should say. Liberty. John Hay. AA; PoFr
What Man May Choose. Priscilla Leonard. MaRV
What man of you, having an hundred sheep. The Lost Sheep. St. Luke, Bible, *N.T.* TreF
What man so wise, what earthly wit so ware. Spenser. The Faerie Queene, I, 7. CoBE
What man that sees the ever-whirling wheele. Two Cantos of Mutabilitie. Spenser. *Fr.* The Faerie Queene. ReEn; SiCE
What man, what man is he whom the voice of Delphi's cell. The Outlaw. Sophocles. *Fr.* Oedipus Rex. GrR
What man would sojourne heer. *Unknown.* SeCSL
What manner of man's flower-viewing! Issa. Satirical Poems on Daimyos, III. PoFr
What man's land is the graveyard? The Graveyard. *Unknown.* Burial Songs, II. TrCh
What matter how the night behaved? Faith in Time of Darkness. Whittier. GrCo-2
What matter if the sun be lost? Daffodil's Return. Bliss Carman. CaP; OCL
What matter though my room be small. The Solace of Books. *Unknown.* MOB
What matter where the apple grows. The Journey. Scudder Middleton. HBMV
What matters all his love for me? A Sailor's Wife. Clara Bernhardt. CaP
What Matters It? George Frederick Cameron. CPG; VA
What May Happen to a Thimble. "B." PRWS
What may the woman labor to confess? Modern Love, XXII. George Meredith. EmBrPo; ViPo
What may we take into the vast Forever? The Future. Edward Rowland Sill. AnNE; HBV
What may words say, or what may words not say. Astrophel and Stella, XXXV. Sir Philip Sidney. ReIE; SiCE; SiPS; TuPP
What mean these peals from every tower. The Fall of Richmond. Herman Melville. MC; PAH
What meane these mortall children of mine owne. Chorus Tertius: Of Time: Eternitie. Fulke Greville. *Fr.* Mustapha. OBS
What meanest thou, my fortune. *Unknown.* EnLoPo
What meaneth this? When I lie alone. Sir Thomas Wyatt. SiPS
"What means this glory 'round our feet." A Christmas Carol. James Russell Lowell. ChIP
What meant the poets in invective verse. Robert Greene. *Fr.* A Groatsworth of Wit Bought with a Million of Repentance. LO
What measure Fate to him shall mete. Love Serviceable. Coventry Patmore. *Fr.* The Angel in the House. EnLoPo; MaRV
What message brings the New Year sun? New Year's Hymn. Matthias Jochumsson. IcP
What Might Be Done. Charles Mackay. VA
What mind shall fathom Russia? None. Feodor Ivanovich Tyutchev, *tr. fr. Russian by* Sir Cecil Kisch. WaL
What mist hath dimmed that glorious face! The Virgin Mary to Christ on the Cross. Robert Southwell. ViBoPo
What Mr. Robinson Thinks. James Russell Lowell. The Biglow Papers, 1st Series, No. III. AA; AmPP; AnNE; APW; BAP, *abr.*; BOHV; DDA; HBV; IAP; IHA; InMe; LHV; LPS-3; PAH; TOP; YaD
(Biglow Papers, The) LEAP
What moan is made of the mountain, what sob of the hillside. Jack and Jill. Elisabeth Cavazza Pullen. PA
What mockery is this? How many times. Not Here. D. S. Leonard. UnW
What more? Where is the third Calixt. Ballad of the Lords of Old Time. Villon. AWP; JAWP; WBP
What mortal, when he saw. Human Life. Matthew Arnold. EmBrPo; EPN
What most is certain. Faith of Appearances. Mark Van Doren. TBM
What motley cares Corilla's mind perplex. The Literary Lady. Sheridan. BOHV
What mournful metamorphosis. Variations on a Theme by John Lyly. Sacheverell Sitwell. ViBoPo
What moved me, was the way your hand. Lament. Dorothy Livesay. CaP
What moves at Cardiff, how a man. Per Omnia Deus. Thomas Edward Brown. MBP
What moves that lonely man is not the boom. The Hermit. W. H. Davies. MBP; MoBrPo
What musical numbers float over the breeze. Petrillo. "Gilbertulus." WhC
What, must my lord be gone? Lord Vyet. A. C. Benson. OBVV
What My Father Was to Me. D. G. Bechers. FAOV
What My Little Brother Thinks. *Unknown.* MeMeAg
What My Lover Said. Homer Greene. AA; HBV; TreFS
What nation, tell me, in the older day. Ode to Spain—after the Revolution of March. Manuel José Quintana. AnSpL-2
What Need Have I for Memory? Georgia Douglas Johnson. CDC
What need I say how it doth wound my breast. Sonnet VII: Of His Lady's Weeping. Walter Davison. ReIE
What need I travel, since I may. Home Travell. John Hall. AEV; EG
What need you, being come to sense. September 1913. W. B. Yeats. ChMo; CMP; CoBMV; MoPW; PoRA; TCPD
What needest thou?—a few brief hours of rest. Vain Questioning. Walter de la Mare. MoVE
What Needeth All This Travail. *Unknown.* EIL
What needs complaints. Comfort to a Youth That Had Lost His Love. Robert Herrick. EV-2; OBEV
What needs my Shakespeare for his honored bones. On Shakespeare [*or* An Epitaph on the Admirable Dramatic Poet, William Shakespeare]. Milton. BCEP; BEL; BLV; BoLiVe; CaAE; CoBE; ElSeCe; EM-1; EnLit; GTBS-W; HBV; InvP; LEAP; LoBV; LPS-3; MePo; OAEP;

What needs my Shakespeare for his honored bones (*continued*) MeLP; PG (1945 and 1955 eds.); PIR; PoRA; PtP; SeCePo; SeCL; SeEP; TCEP; TOP; TrGrPo; TyEnPo; ViBoPo; WHA
"What new mob disturbs the days?" These Are the Young. Vachel Lindsay. ATP (1935 ed.); TCAP
What news, what news, thou pilgrim gray, what news from the southern land? The Laureate's Tourney. William Aytoun. PA
What No Man Knoweth. Hugh Francis Blunt. CAW
What No, Perdy. Sir Thomas Wyatt. *See* Rondeau: "What? No perdie!"
What noble courage must their hearts have fired. The Rising Village. Oliver Goldsmith, the Younger. BoCaPo; PeCV
What noise of viols is so sweet. Beggars. Francis Davidson. CH
What northern hive pour'd out these foes to wit? The Animal Critics. Swift. *Fr.* To Mr. Congreve. BeR
What! not know our Clean Clara? Clean Clara. William Brighty Rands. BOHV; HBV; HBVY
What nothing earthly gives, or can destroy. The Soul's Calm Sunshine. Pope. *Fr.* An Essay on Man. BeR
What now avails the pageant verse. Camoens in the Hospital. Herman Melville. PtP; ViBoPo
What now? the Lido shall it be? Arthur Hugh Clough. *Fr.* Dipsychus. ViP
What now? Thou look'st surprised. Charles Heavysege. *Fr.* Saul. PeCV
What nudity as beautiful as this. Portrait of a Machine. Louis Untermeyer. ShBV-3
What nymph should I admire or trust. The Question to Lisetta. Matthew Prior. OBEV
What of all the will to do? Sung on a By-Way. "Æ." TOP
What of earls with whom you have supt. The Toad-Eater. Burns. RO
What of her glass without her? Without Her. Dante Gabriel Rossetti. The House of Life, LIII. BPN; CoBE; EmBrPo; GTBS-W; PoEL-5; PoVP; ReaPo; VA; ViBoPo; ViP; ViPo; VLEP
What of it, that the realms of this epoch. The Animal Howl. "M. J." TrJP
What of That? ("I reason, earth is short"). Emily Dickinson. OnPM
What of That? *Unknown.* PEOR
What of the bow? The Song of the Bow. Sir Arthur Conan Doyle. *Fr.* The White Company. BHV; HBV; MCCG; MuP
What of the Darkness? Richard Le Gallienne. HBV; LEAP; OQP; QP-2
What of the empires that are built on beds of dead men's bones. The Reddened Road. H. M. Tickener. PSO
What of the faith and fire within us. Men Who March Away. Thomas Hardy. BEL; EPP; PoFr; SoV
What of the Night? Sir John Bowring. *See* Watchman, Tell Us of the Night.
What of the Night? *sel.* John Richard Moreland.
"Arrogant Kings, with envious lust." ChIP
(Coins of Love, The.) MaRV
What of the night? The Torches Are Bright. *Unknown.* WhP
What of this fabulous country. Canoe-Trip. Douglas Le Pan. CaP; PeCV; TwCaPo
"What of vile dust?" the preacher said. The Praise of Dust. G. K. Chesterton BLV; MBP; MoBrPo; OtMeF; PoeT; POTE
What old man has not in his mournful keeping. Home-Land. Verner von Heidenstam. AnSL
What one art thou, thus in torn weed[s] yclad? Description of Virtue. Theodore Beza, *tr. by* Nicholas Grimald. CenL; OBSC; SiCE; TuPP
What One May and May Not Call a Woman. *Unknown.* TreF
What ordinary gallant now but goes. Quot Bipedes Aurum. Thomas Freeman. SiCE
What other form were worthy of your praise. Foreword. Muna Lee. *Fr.* Sonnets. HBMV
"What other men have dared, I dare." The Kiss. Tom Masson. BOHV; LauV
What Other Name Had Half Expressed. Elinor Wylie. ChMo
What other woman could be loved like you. Soul-Light. Dante Gabriel Rossetti. The House of Life, XXVIII. CoBE; EPP; PoVP; ViPo; VLEP
What Our Lord Wrote in the Dust. *Unknown.* ChIP; OQP; QP-2
What padded feet rustle the dead leaves? Druidic Gums. T. I. Moore. MoAuPo
What painter has not with a careless smutch. Accident in Art. Richard Hovey. HBV; PreP
What palace-temple of the mystic East. Turris Eburnea. *Unknown.* GoBC
What passing-bells for these who die as cattle? Anthem for Doomed Youth. Wilfred Owen. AnFE; BLV; BoLiVe; CBOV; ChTr; CoBMV; EnLi-2 (1949 ed.); ES; FaBoMo; FaFP; GTBS-D; GTBS-W; GTML; GTSL; HBMV; LBBV; LiTM; MaRV; MBP; MoAB; MoBrPo; MoPW; MoVE; NeMA; NP; OAEP (2d ed.); OBEV (new ed.); PoE; PoeMoYo; POTE; SeCePo; ShBV-4; TrGrPo; ViBoPo; VOD (1931 ed.); WaP; WHA
What path list you to tread? What trade will you assay? Man's Life, after Posidonius or Crates. Nicholas Grimald. ReIE; SiCE; TuPP
What pen can well report the plight. A Ballad of Sea Fardingers, Describing Evil Fortune. *Unknown.* SG
What perfumed, pozie-dizened sirrah. To Mistress Pyrrha. Horace. PR
What phantom is this that appears. Helen of Tyre. Longfellow. MeRV
What Piggy-Wig Found. Enid Blyton. BoTP
What pity-driven angel proved his speed. Petrarch. *Fr.* Sonnets to Laura: To Laura in Death. PrPoCR
What place is this? what ayre? what rhegion? George Chapman. *Fr.* The Conspiracy of Charles, Duke of Byron, I, i. NBE
What place so strange—though unrevealed snow. Memorial Thresholds. Dante Gabriel Rossetti. The House of Life, LXXXI. BPN; EmBrPo; PoVP; ReaPo; ViPo
What Pleasure Have Great Princes. *Unknown.* *See* Quiet Life, The.
What poet wrote these lovely lines? Intermission, Please! Irwin Edman. SiTL; WhC
What poets feel not, when they make. A Caution to Poets. Matthew Arnold. PoVP
What poets mean by what they mean. The Reader Writes. Carl Crane. WhC
What poets sang in Atlantis? Who can tell. Atlantis. Gordon Bottomley. AEV; POTE; PtOT; TCPD
What Poor Astronomers Are They. *Unknown.* OBSC; ReIE
What poor short-sighted worms we be. K. K. Can't Calculate. Frances Miriam Whitcher. BOHV
What potions have I drunk of Siren tears. Sonnets, CXIX. Shakespeare. EtPaEn; EV-1; NBE; PeBoSo; ReIE; WHA
What power is this released in man's dark night. Earth Bows to the New Bomb. Aline Badger Carter. ChIP
What precious thing are you making fast. Art, I. James Thomson. EmBrPo; EnLi-2; OBVV; PoVP
What presses about here in the evening. Waters of Babylon. Louis Untermeyer. AnAmPo; LA
What Price. Lulu Minerva Schultz. GoYe
What Profit? Immanuel di Roma, *tr. fr. Hebrew by* Joseph Chotzner. TrJP
What profits it, O England, to prevail. The Turk in Armenia. Sir William Watson. BMEP; PoFr
What put the wiggle in a little dog's tail. My Dog's Tail. Arthur Wallace Peach. AlBD
What Rabbi Jehosha Said. James Russell Lowell. BAP
What race of life run you? what trade will you assay? Metrodorus' Mind to the Contrary. Metrodorus, *tr. by* Nicholas Grimald. SiCE; TuPP
What rage is this? what furor [*or* furour] of what kind? Sir Thomas Wyatt. EnLoPo; SiPS
What ragged beggar stalks the dusty road. Saint Francis of Assisi. Pierson Ricks. SaFP
What ran under the rosebush? Could It Have Been a Shadow? Monica Shannon. FaPON; GaP; StVeCh (1955 ed.); TiPo
What reck we of the creeds of men? What Matters It? George Frederick Cameron. CPG
What Remains but Only Dying? *Unknown.* EIL
What Reward? Winifred M. Letts. BMEP
What Riches Have You? George Santayana. Sonnets, XXIX. BAP; HBV; LEAP; POT; PoTo; TrGrPo
What Riddle Asked the Sphinx. Archibald MacLeish. HoPM
What? rise again with all one's bones. Giles's Hope [*or* Epigrams]. Samuel Taylor Coleridge. BOHV; HBV
What roar the seas would make that lie. Elemental. George Dillon. AnAmPo; LA
What Robin Told. George Cooper. FaPON; GFA; MPB; TiPo
What! Roses growing in a meadow. Wild Roses. Mary Effie Lee Newsome. CDC
What! Roses on thy tomb; and was there then. Ave! Nero Imperator. Duffield Osborne. AA
What ruined shapes of feudal pomp are there. Kilmallock. Sir Aubrey De Vere. IrPN
What Rules the World. William Ross Wallace. *See* Hand That Rules the World, The.
What rumoured heavens are these. To the Unknown Eros. Coventry Patmore. LO; NBE; OxBoCh; PoEL-5
What said John Paul Jones on the brave *Bon Homme Richard.* The Countersigns. *Unknown.* SoAmSa
"What!" said the king. The Song of Jeppe. Alfred Noyes. *Fr.* Watchers of the Sky. EPP
What saies my brother? *See* What says my brother.
What saintly features do abound in the Vatican Museum and Church. The Church of the Sacred Heart. Ashton Greene. NePoAm

What saith the river to the rushes grey. Aeolian Harp. William Allingham. OnYI
What Sanguine Beast? LeRoy Smith, Jr. NePoAm
What saw you in your flight to-day. The Vagabonds. E. Pauline Johnson. VA
"What sawest thou, Orion, thou hunter of the starlands." Singing Stars. Katharine Tynan. VA
What say the Bells of San Blas. The Bells of San Blas. Longfellow. AmP; AmPP (3d ed.); IAP; OxBA
What says [*or* saies] my brother?/ Death is a fearful thing. On Death [*or* Let Me Live *or* Fear of Death]. Shakespeare. *Fr.* Measure for Measure, III, i. CoEV; FiP; LiA
What scenes appear where-e'er I turn my view. Eloisa. Pope. *Fr.* Eloisa to Abelard. SeCePo
What sculptor carved the arches of a tree. The Unknown Sculptor. Stanton A. Coblentz. MaRV
What seas what shores what grey rocks and what islands. Marina. T. S. Eliot. AmP; BrBE; ChMo; ChMP; CoEV; EnLit; FaBoMo; GTBS-D; InPo; LiTA; MM; MoP; NP; PoE; PoFS; ReaPo; TwAmPo
What secret thing of splendor or of shade. Swinburne. *Fr.* A Sequence of Sonnets on the Death of Robert Browning. BPN
What seek'st thou at this madman's pace? His Quest. Lewis Frank Tooker. AA
What Semiramis Said. Vachel Lindsay. TwAmPo
(Poems about the Moon.) MAPA
What shall be added to your praises? Lines for a Feast of Our Lady. Sister Maris Stella. ISi
What shall be said between us here. Félise. Swinburne. BeLS; EmBrPo; LoPS
What shall be said of this embattled day. Parted Love. Dante Gabriel Rossetti. The House of Life, XLVI. PoVP; ViPo
What shall become of Man so wise. Lycophron, *tr. by* Sir Charles Sedley. *Fr.* Alexandra. BeR
What shall become of the ancient race. Ancient Race. Michael Tormey. JKCP (1926 ed.); TIP
What Shall Endure? Ethelyn M. Hartwich. OQP; QP-2
What Shall He Have That Kill'd the Deer? Shakespeare. *Fr.* As You Like It, IV, ii. KN; OBSC; ViBoPo
What shall her silence keep. Dirge. Madison Cawein. AA; OBAV
"What shall I ask for the voyage I must sail to the end alone?" The Helmsman. Mark Antony De Wolfe Howe. PC
What Shall I Do? *At. to* Dryden *and to* Thomas Betterton. *Fr.* The Prophetess; or, The History of Dioclesian. SeCL
What Shall I Do? Frances Anne Kemble. *Fr.* Absence. PoToHe (new ed.)
What shall I do in Denmark? Young Danneved and Swain Trust. *Unknown.* BoDaBa
What shall I do, my mother? Mozarabic Songs, 2. *Unknown.* TeCS
What shall I do this afternoon? Half Holiday. Olive Enoch. BoTP
What shall I do to be just? The Cry of the Age. Hamlin Garland. OQP; QP-2; WGRP
What shall I do to show how much I love her? What Shall I Do? *At. to* Dryden *and to* Thomas Betterton. *Fr.* The Prophetess; or, The History of Dioclesian. SeCL
What shall I do? what could I do, if I could find these criminals? Blake. *Fr.* Jerusalem, II. NBE
What shall I do, what will become of me? Mozarabic Songs, 3. *Unknown.* TeCS
What shall I do, who may not be. The Skeptic. Witter Bynner. PR
What shall I do with all the days and hours. Absence [*or* What Shall I Do?]. Frances Anne Kemble. LPS-1; NeHB; PoToHe (new ed.)
What shall I do with this absurdity. The Tower. W. B. Yeats. ChMo; CMP; CoBMV; FaBoMo; HoPM; LiTB; LiTM (rev. ed.); MoPo; OAEP (2d ed.); SeCeV
What shall I doe I've lost my hart. *Unknown.* SeCSL
What Shall I Give? Edward Thomas. CP; FaBoCh; LoGBV
What shall I leave my son. Testament. Langston Hughes. NePoAm-2
What? Shall I ne'er more see those halcyon days. *Unknown.* *Fr.* Zepheria. TuPP
What shall I render to thy Name. In Thankfull Remembrance for My Dear Husband's Safe Arrivall Sept. 3, 1662. Anne Bradstreet. TrPWD
What shall I say more than I have inferred? The Address of Richard III to His Army. Shakespeare. King Richard III, *fr.* V, iii. UnPo (1st ed.)
What shall I say of the Great Peak? A View of T'ai-shan. Tu Fu. OuHeWo
What shall I say to you, Old Flag? Old Flag. Hubbard Parker. DD; FOAH; HH; OTPC (1946 ed.); PoRL; PSO; PTA-2
What shall I send my love to-day. A Valentine. Matilda Barbara Betham-Edwards. OBVV
What shall I sing to thee, babe, on my back? The Wild Woman's Lullaby. Constance Lindsay Skinner. BOL; CPG
What shall I sing when all is sung. All Sung. Richard Le Gallienne. OBVV
What shall I teach in the vivid afternoon. Going to School. Karl Shapiro. TrJP
What shall I wish thee this New Year? A New Year Wish. *Unknown.* BLRP
What shall I wish thee? Treasures of earth? New Year's Wishes. Frances Ridley Havergal. BLRP
What shall I your true-love tell. Messages. Francis Thompson. CH; OtMeF; PoeT; UnW
What Shall It Profit? William Dean Howells. *See* Faith.
What shall it profit a man. Anastasis. Albert E. S. Smythe. CaP; CPG; OCL
What shall my gift be to the dead one lying. Lilian Adelaide Neilson. Clement Scott. VA
What! shall that sudden blade. Custer. Edmund Clarence Stedman. GA; PAH
What shall we be like when. Seeds. John Oxenham. WGRP
What shall we count to cool our angry pride? Count Ten. Bonaro Overstreet. PoToHe (new ed.)
What shall we do for Love these days? Epilogue. Lascelles Abercrombie. *Fr.* Emblems of Love. AnFE; GTML; HBV; MBP; MoBrPo; OBVV; TCPD
What shall we do for timber? Kilcash. *Tr. by* Frank O'Connor. KiLC; OBMV; OxBI; ThWaDe
What shall we do, my soul, to please the King. The City of the Soul. Lord Alfred Douglas. HBV; LBBV
What shall we do now, Mary being dead. Mary Booth. Thomas William Parsons. AA; OBAV
What shall we do—what shall we think—what shall we say? Prelude XXIX. Conrad Aiken. *Fr.* Preludes for Memnon. FaBoMo
What shall we do with the [*or* a] drunken sailor. The Drunken Sailor [*or* A Runaway Chorus]. *Unknown.* SG; SoAmSa
What shall we fear, son, now that the stars go down. Psalm against the Darkness. A. M. Sullivan. MaRV
What shall we mourn? For the prostrate tree that sheltered the young green wood? John Boyle O'Reilly. *Fr.* Wendell Phillips. AA; DD; GA
What Shall We Render. *Unknown.* BLRP
What shall we say, now, of our gentle knight. John Pegram. William Gordon McCabe. BIG
What shall we say of her. An Old Tale. Marya Zaturenska. NP; TBM
What shall we sing? sings Harry. Themes. Denis Glover. AnNZ
What shape so furtive steals along the dim. A Faun in Wall Street. John Myers O'Hara. LBM
What sharpe assaultes of cruell Cupids flame. Chorus. Seneca. *Fr.* Medea. LaP
What she fears in her child is what. Mother of a Daughter. Louis Johnson. AnNZ
What She Is. Ludvig Bødtcher, *tr. fr. Danish by* Charles W. Stork. BoDS
What She Said about It. Charles Henry Webb. PR
What She Thought. Harrison Robertson. *Fr.* Two Triolets. PR
(Two Triolets.) HBV
What should a man desire to leave? Pro Mortuis. Francis Turner Palgrave. VA
What Should a Man Want? Wang Chi. *See* Tell Me Now.
What should be said of him cannot be said. Dante [*or* Sonnet: Dante]. Michelangelo. AWP; JAWP; LyPI; WBP
What should I be but a prophet and a liar. The Singing-Woman from the Wood's Edge. Edna St. Vincent Millay. HBMV
What should [*or* shulde] I say. Farewell [*or* Farewell, Unkist *or* A Revocation]. Sir Thomas Wyatt. AtBAP; CaAE; CoEV; GoBC; LO; LoBV; LoPS; OBEV; OBSC; PoEL-1; ReEn; SiCE; SiPS; UnPo (1st ed.)
What should I speak in praise of Surrey's skill. Verse in Praise of Lord Henry Howard, Earl of Surrey. George Turberville. ReIE; SiCE; TuPP
What should we be without the sexual myth. Men Made Out of Words. Wallace Stevens. MoAB
What should we know. Verse. Oliver St. John Gogarty. AnIL; FaBoCh; LO; LoGBV; OBMV; PoRA
What should you know at last. Elegy. Robert Fitzgerald. AnAmPo
What sight so lured him through the fields he knew. Far—Far—Away. Tennyson. BPN; EmBrPo; GEPC; PoVP; ViPo; VLEP
What silences we keep, year after year. Too Late. Nora Perry. PoToHe
What silks endued with time's own balms. In Thought. Stéphane Mallarmé. TrFP
What sin was mine, sweet, silent boy-god, Sleep. Sleep. Statius. AWP
What sky more lovely than this azure night! Night of the Immaculate Conception. Juan Maragall. CAW
What slender youth bedew'd with liquid odours. The Fifth Ode of Horace [*or* For Whom, Pyrrha? *or* To a Flirt].

What slender youth bedew'd with liquid odours (*continued*)
Horace, *tr. by* Milton. *Fr.* Odes. AWP; EnLoPo; JAWP; LiA; LiTW; PoEL-3; RoL
What slender youth, with perfumed locks. To Pyrrha. Horace, *tr. by* Goldwyn Smith. *Fr.* Odes. EnLi-1; OuHeWo
What slim elegant youth, drenched in effusive scent. Horace, *tr. by* Gilbert Highet. *Fr.* Odes. LaP
What slim youth, moistened with liquid perfumes. Horace, *tr. by* Joseph Bennett. *Fr.* Odes. LaP
What smouldering senses in death's sick delay. The Kiss. Dante Gabriel Rossetti. The House of Life, VI. PoVP; ViPo
What snakes! long, lithe and beautiful. Joaquin Miller. *Fr.* With Walker in Nicaragua. BAP
What! soar'd the old eagle to die at the sun! The Death of Harrison. Nathaniel Parker Willis. GA; PAH
What soft, cherubic creatures. Emily Dickinson. AnNE; CoBA; MoAB; MoAmPo; TCAP
What song is that in the airless night? The Toad. Tristan Corbière. TrFP
What song of mine will live? A Song from Old Spain. Alice Corbin. NP
What song sang the twelve with the Savior. The Last Supper. Joaquin Miller. StJW
What songs found voice upon those lips. Helen Hunt Jackson. Ina Donna Coolbrith. AA
What sorrowful sounds do I hear. Pastoral Elegy. *Unknown.* ABS
What sort of a church would our church be. Just like Me. P. W. Sinks. BLRP
What soul would bargain for a cure that brings. Modern Love, XIV. George Meredith. ViPo
"What sound awakened me, I wonder." The Deserter. A. E. Housman. OBMV; POTT; SeCeV
What spendthrifts are we of the day. The Casket. Nathaniel Wanley. SeCL
What sphinx of cement and aluminum bashed open their skulls and ate up their brains and imagination? Allen Ginsberg. *Fr.* Howl. NeAP
What spirit of what tree. Coal. Dorothy E. Hanbury Rowe. MM
What spirit touched the faded lambrequin? The Ilex Tree. Agnes Lee. NP
What splendid names for boys there are! Boys' Names. Eleanor Farjeon. SUS; TiPo
What stands 'tween me and her that I adore? Echo Poem. M. Allan. FiBHP
What Star is This? *Unknown, tr. fr. Latin by* J. Chandler. MaRV
What Stillness around a God! Rainer Maria Rilke, *tr. fr. German by* Jessie Lemont. OnPM
What strange perversity is this of man! To Dr. Plot. John Norris. NBE
What strength! what strife! what rude unrest! Westward Ho! Joaquin Miller. AA; FaBoBe; OBAV
What stronger breastplate than a heart untainted! Thrice Armed. Shakespeare. King Henry VI, Pt. II, *fr.* III, ii. BTP; MaRV
What substitute for mouse and rat. There May, of Course, Be Mice. Richard Kirk. LS
What sudden bugle calls us in the night. Reveille. Louis Untermeyer. HBV; OBAV; NLK (1947 ed.); PaA; SBMV
What sugared terms, what all-persuading art. Diella, IV. Richard Lynche. ElSeCe; ReEn; TuPP
What summons do I hear? The Graduate Leaving College. George Moses Horton. NoCaPo
What sweet relief the showers to thirsty plants we see. A True Love. Nicholas Grimald. EIL; OBEV; TuPP
What sweeter music [*or* musick] can we bring. A Christmas Carol. Robert Herrick. AnEC; CBPC; EV-2; MeRV; MPB; TriL
What tell you me of such a peasant groom. Henry Parrot. SiCE
What th' English bed, the Welch call sepulcher. The Bed. John Owen. *Fr.* Four Epigrams. PrWP
What that man is, I often was: but in time, perhaps. Propertius. Elegies, II, 9. LaP
What the Auld Fowk Are Thinkin. George Macdonald. BSV
What the Birds Say. Samuel Taylor Coleridge. *See* Answer to a Child's Question.
What the Bones Know. Carolyn Kizer. NePoAm-2
What the Bullet Sang. Bret Harte. AA; BAV; LEAP; LH; MAP; MDAH; MoAmPo (1942 ed.); OBEV; OBVV; PFY
What the Chimney Sang. Bret Harte. BTP
What the Choir Sang about the New Bonnet. M. T. Morrison. BLPA; PTA-2
What the Christmas Tree Thinks. Mary Carolyn Davies. PCH
What the Devil Said. James Stephens. ChMo; CMP
What the diuel hast thou brought there? The Tavern. Shakespeare. King Henry IV, Pt. II, Act II, sc. iv. LiA
What the eye gazes at and cannot see is called "beyond vision." Tao Teh Ching, VI. *Unknown, tr. fr. Chinese.* WhP
What the eyes do not admire. Well-packed Wisdom. Benjamin Franklin. *Fr.* Poor Richard's Almanac. StaSt
What the Gray Cat Sings. Arthur Guiterman. MoShBr; MPB; PoMS; PoRL
What the King Has. Ethel Romig Fuller. PoToHe (new ed.)
What the Laborer Says Is Always beside the Point. Paul Eluard, *tr. fr. French by* Wallace Fowlie. MiCF
What the Madman Sees Looking in the Window. Kay Smith. BoCaPo (1948 ed.)
What the Moon Saw. Vachel Lindsay. CrMA
What the Old Man Said. Cicely Fox Smith. EtS
What the people learn out of lifting and hauling and waiting and losing and laughing. Carl Sandburg. The People, Yes, Sec. 32. CoV
What the Prince of I Dreamt. Henry Cholmondeley-Pennell. NA
What the Rattlesnake Said. Vachel Lindsay. TSW; TSWC
What the Serpent Said to Adam. Archibald MacLeish. NePA
What the Shuiler Said as She Lay by the Fire in the Farmer's House. Padraic Colum. TwCV
What the Sonnet Is. Eugene Lee-Hamilton. HoPM; OBVV; VA
What the Swallows Say. Théophile Gautier, *tr. fr. French by* Alan Conder. TrFP
What the Thrush Said. Keats. PIR
What the Thrush Says. Queenie Scott-Hopper. BoTP
What the Toys Are Thinking. ffrida Wolfe. GoBP; TiPo
What the Trumpeter Said. Sebastian Evans. VA
What the Village Bell Said. John G. M'Lemore. BIG
What the Weather Does. Hamish Hendry. BoTP, *st.* 1
What the wind harried, the fire worried. Deadfall. Martha Keller. GoYe
What the Winds Bring. Edmund Clarence Stedman. DD; GoBP; LPS-2; PRWS; RAR; SN
What Then? W. B. Yeats. ChMo; POTE
What Then, Dancer? Kay Smith. CaP
What then: if the roses wither? The Enduring World. Audrey Wurdemann. QS
What then is love but mourning? Thomas Campion. FaBoEn
What then is Merlyn's message, his word to thee weary of pain. The Wisdom of Merlyn. Wilfrid Scawen Blunt. ViBoPo
What, then, were my emotions, when in arms. Wordsworth. *Fr.* The Prelude, X. NBE
"What then, what if my lips do burn." Ulf in Ireland. Charles De Kay. AA
What there is once may not be twice. No Laws. Brian Allwood. WaP
What they undertook to do. Gratitude to the Unknown Instructors. W. B. Yeats. TwP
What thing insistent urges me away. Star-Fear. Leonora Speyer. AnEnPo
What Thing Is Love? George Peele. *Fr.* The Hunting of Cupid. EIL; OAEP; RiBV; SeCePo
(Love.) OBSC
("What thing is love? for, well I wot, love is a thing.") ReEn; TuPP
What thing shall be held up to woman's beauty? Women's Beauty. Lascelles Abercrombie. *Fr.* Emblems of Love: Vashti. MBP; MoBrPo; PG
What thing unto mine ear. The Stream's Secret. Dante Gabriel Rossetti. EmBrPo
What things have we seen. Francis Beaumont. *Fr.* Master Francis Beaumont's Letter to Ben Jonson. EnLit
"What Think Ye of Christ?" Geraldine Farrar. StJW
What this mountain meaneth [*or* betokens] and the murky [*or* and what this dark] dale. Holy Church [*or* A Field Full of Folk]. William Langland. *Fr.* The Vision of Piers Plowman. CoBE; MeEV
What tho', Valclusa, the fond bard be fled. Sonnet to Valclusa. Thomas Russell. CEP; OBEC
What Thomas an Buile Said in a Pub. James Stephens. *See* What Tomas an Buile Said in a Pub.
What thou art, if thou wouldst know. These Stones. Menander. LiTW
What thou hast done, thou hast done; for the heavenly horses are swift. Irrevocable. Mary Wright Plummer. WGRP
What thou lovest well remains. Ezra Pound. *Fr.* Canto LXXXI. FaBoTw; GTBS-D; MoAB; NePA; OxBA; SeCeV; UnPo (3d ed.); ViBoPo (1958 ed.)
What though, for showing truth to flatter'd state. Sonnet: Written on the Day that Mr. Leigh Hunt Left Prison. Keats. ChER; EM-2; GEPC; PoFr
What though he spoke in words and accents fair. The Quack Vendor. Augustus Peck Clarke. PoP
What though life conspire to cheat you. Pushkin, *tr. fr. Russian by* C. M. Bowra. BoRS
What though my harp, and viol be. To God, on His Sickness. Robert Herrick. OxBoCh
What though my mistress frowne one me. *Unknown.* SeCSL

What though the axe an oak-tree's branches clove. Great Heart. Pindar. *Fr.* Pythian Odes, IV. GrR

What Though the Dark! Archie Edwards. BePJ

What though the field be lost? Satan's Adjuration. Milton. *Fr.* Paradise Lost, I. FaBoEn

What though the flowers in Joseph's garden grew. The Sepulcher in the Garden. John Finley. ChIP

What Though the Green Leaf Grow? Maybury Fleming. AA

What though the moon should come. Dilemma. Orrick Johns. LEAP; MAP; SBMV

What though the spirit of man, by Plato taught. Pierre de Ronsard. *Fr.* Sonnets pour Hélène. PrPoCR

What though thy Muse the singer's art essay. To America. Richard Garnett. VA

What though thy way is often dark. To a Dejected Friend. Morton Bryan Wharton. BlG

What though unmarked the happy workman toil. Honors. Jean Ingelow. OQP; QP-2

What though with figures I should raise. On a Mistress of Whose Affections He Was Doubtful. Thomas Nabbes. *Fr.* The Spring's Glory. EG; SeCL

What thought ye to burn, when ye kindled the pyre. Epigram IV. *Unknown. Fr.* Duel with Verses over a Great Man. TrJP

What thoughts I have of you tonight, Walt Whitman. A Supermarket in California. Allen Ginsberg. NeAP

What Tidings? *Unknown.* AnEC

What tidings of reverent gladness are voiced by the bells that ring. On Easter Morning. Eben E. Rexford. BLRP

What time I hear the storming sea. Thrustararorum. Henry Nehemiah Dodge. EtS

What time I see you passing by. Popular Songs of Tuscany. *Unknown.* AWP

What time in his hand the bowl he shaketh. Swimming. Hafiz. PeP

"What time is it?" said the one. The Chronometer. A. M. Sullivan. WaKn

What time soft night had silently begun. Fame and Fortune. Michael Drayton. *Fr.* The Legend of Robert, Duke of Normandy. OBSC

What time soft zephyrs fan the trees. Ibycus, *tr. fr. Greek by* J. H. Merivale. GrPo

What time the earth takes on the garb of Spring. Incipit Vita Nova. William Morton Payne. AA

What time the gifted lady took. George Sand. Dorothy Parker. FiBHP

What time the Lord drew back the sea. Panama. Amanda Theodosia Jones. PAH

What time the mighty moon was gathering light. Love and Death. Tennyson. PIR

What time the noble Lovewell came. Lovewell's Flight. *Unknown.* PAH

What time the poet hath hymned. "Oh, Hollow! Hollow! Hollow!" W. S. Gilbert. *Fr.* Patience. PoVP

What time the rose of dawn is laid across the lips of night. The Angler's Reveille. Henry van Dyke. *Fr.* The Toiling of Felix. BBV (1923 ed.); GN; PYM; StVeCh

What time the weatherbeaten flocks. The Ninth Eglog. Michael Drayton. *Fr.* The Shepherd's Garland. ReIE

What time this world's great Workmaster did cast. Beauty [*or* Soul Is Form]. Spenser. *Fr.* An Hymne in Honour of Beautie. EPP; GoBC; OBSC

What time with brow the loveliest gins to scowl. Robert Tofte. *Fr.* Laura. ReIE

What to a man who loves the air. Riches. Robert Loveman. OQP; QP-2

What to Do. John Wesley. *See* John Wesley's Rule.

What to Do. William Wise. TiPo (1959 ed.)

What to the maiden has happened? Old Russian Song. Ippolit Bogdanovich. BoRS

What to Us, My Heart. Arthur Rimbaud, *tr. fr. French by* Louise Varèse. AnFP

What Tomas [*or* Thomas] an Buile Said in a Pub. James Stephens. AnFE; BMEP; CMP; EPP; LBBV; LiTM; MBP; MoAB; MoBrPo; NeMA; NP; TCPD; TrGrPo; WGRP

(What Tomas Said in a Pub.) ChMo; GTSL; TwCV

What Tongue Can Her Perfections Tell? Sir Philip Sidney. *Fr.* Arcadia. SiPS

What treasure greater than a friend. A Friend. Santob de Carrion. TrJP

What trees were in Gethsemane. Song. Charles G. Blanden. ChIP; OQP; QP-1

What Trinkets? Thomas Hornsby Ferril. NePoAm-2

What Troubled Poe's Raven. John Bennett. PA

What tuneful bard of auld lang syne. The Bard of Auld Lang Syne. James Main Dixon. POT

What utter loneliness he knew. Before Pilate. Leslie Savage Clark. ChIP

What vaileth troth, or by it to take pain? Complaint for True Love Unrequited. Sir Thomas Wyatt. ReIE

What veilèd form sits on that ebon throne? Shelley. *Fr.* Prometheus Unbound, II, iv. NBE

What vigor raised those spires; what joyful hand. Portrait of an Old Cathedral. Louis Untermeyer. QS

What voice did on my spirit fall. Peschiera. Arthur Hugh Clough. BPN; HBV; PoVP; VA; ViPo; VLEP

What voice has stilled the tumult, stayed the might. Glacier. Mary Sinton Leitch. BAP

What voice revisits me this night? What face. Revisitation. Siegfried Sassoon. BoFr

What voice, what harp, are those we hear. The Minstrel. Goethe. AWP

What wad na be in love. Maggie Lauder. Francis Sempill. EBSV; OBS

What wage, what guerdon, Life, asked I of you? Arraignment. Lizette Woodworth Reese. VOD

What wants thee, thou that art in this sad taking? London Sad London. *Unknown.* OBS

What Was a Cure for Love? Thomas Godfrey. AnAmPo; LA

What was he doing, the great god Pan. A Musical Instrument. Elizabeth Barrett Browning. BEL; BCEP; BPN; EmBrPo; EnLi-2; EPP; EV-4; FaBoBe; FaPON; GBV; GoTP; GTBS; GTML; GTSL; HBV; HBVY; HiLiEn; LEAP; LPS-3; MCCG; OAEP; OBEV; OBVV; OTPC (1946 ed.); PECK; PFE; PIR; PoRL; PoVP; ReTS; ShBV-3; TOP; TVSH; TwCrTr; TyEnPo; VA; ViPo; VLEP; YT

What was his creed? He Lived a Life. H. N. Fifer. BPP; PoToHe (new ed.)

What was his name? I do not know his name. The Nameless Saints. Edward Everett Hale. MaRV; OQP; QP-1; WGRP

What was I back in the world's first wonder? Edwin Markham. *Fr.* Virgilia. EtS

What, was it a dream? am I all alone. Left on the Battle-Field. Sarah Tittle Bolton. LPS-2

What was it Colin gave to thee? I Lay My Lute beside Thy Door. Clarence Urmy. HBMV

What was it first began their voyaging? The Coming of Jason to Iolcus. Pindar. *Fr.* Pythian Odes, IV. GrPE

What was it you remember?—the summer mornings. To Any Member of My Generation. George Barker. LiTM (rev. ed.); ViBoPo (1958 ed.)

What Was Lost. W. B. Yeats. POTE

What was my crime, youthful most gentle god. Statius. *Fr.* Silvae. LaP

What Was My Dream? Joseph O'Connor. AA

What was our trust, we trust not. E = MC². Morris Bishop. ImOP

What Was Solomon's Mind. Geoffrey Scott. OBMV

What was that glinting. A Signature. Robert A. Davis. GA

"What was that sound we heard." Why Must You Know? John Wheelwright. CrMA; MeRV

What was the beginning of their voyage? The Tale of the Golden Fleece. Pindar. *Fr.* Pythian Odes, IV. GrL

What was the first prophetic word that rang. Peace. Edwin Markham. WBLP

"What was the hardest hour," you ask. The *Mary Ross.* Blanche Edith Baughan. BoAu

What was the name you called me? Evening Waterfall. Carl Sandburg. NP; OTPC (1946 ed.); TSW

What Was Your Dream, Doctor Murricombe? Sir Osbert Sitwell. AtBAP

What Was Your Name in the States? *with music. Unknown.* AS

What waspish whim of Fate. To a Portrait of Whistler in the Brooklyn Art Museum. Eleanor Rogers Cox. HBMV; LEAP; SBMV

What watch, what woe, what want, what wrack. The Shipmen [*or* No Pains Comparable to His Attempt]. William Hunnis. OBSC; TuPP

What way does the Wind come? What way does he go? The Wind. Dorothy Wordsworth. *Fr.* Address to a Child During a Boisterous Winter Evening. BoTP; OTPC (1923 ed.)

What we have done, is done; and I have learned. Wisdom. Evelyn Werner Barkins. MuM

What we know to be not possible. Nones. W. H. Auden. CoBMV; PoLFOT

What We May Live Without. "Owen Meredith." *Fr.* Lucile, Pt. I, Canto 2. TreF ("We may live without poetry, music and art.") PoToHe (new ed.)

What We Need. Edgar A. Guest. LPS-1

What! We of Spear-Danes in spent days. *Unknown. Fr.* Beowulf. ViBoPo

What We, When Face to Face We See. Arthur Hugh Clough. *See* Through a Glass Darkly.

What wear thy thoughts sadd Dido on that day. Sad Dido. Virgil. *Fr.* The Aeneid, IV. LiA

What Weariness Is Mine. Guillaume Apollinaire, *tr. fr. French by* Alan Conder. TrFP

What weight of ancient witness can prevail. Private Judgment Condemned [*or* A Prayer]. Dryden. *Fr.* The Hind and the Panther. FiP; OBS

"What Went Ye Out for to See?" Arthur Hugh Clough. PoVP; StJW
What Went Ye Out to See? John Keble. *Fr.* The Christian Year. ViP
What went you forth to find? Everest. Horace Shipp. HaMV
What went you, Pilgrim, for to see? Traveller's Joy. Arthur Ketchum. NLK
What were his dreams who wove this colored shawl. The Paisley Shawl. W. W. Gibson. ChMo; CMP; VOD
What were you carrying, Pilgrims, Pilgrims? Atlantic Charter; 1942. Francis Brett Young. *Fr.* The Island. BBV (1951 ed.)
What were you saying while we sat. Lucid Interval. George O'Neil. TBM
What, what, is virtue, but repose of mind? A Witching Song. James Thomson. *Fr.* The Castle of Indolence. OBEC
What, what, what,/ What's the news from Swat. A Threnody [*or* The Ahkoond of Swat]. George Thomas Lanigan. AA; BoCaPo; BOHV; CaP; CenHV; FiBHP; HBV; InMe; LauV; LEAP; LHV; NA; PeCV; TreFS
What Wight He Loved. William Browne. *See* Shall I Tell You Whom I Love?
What will be left when my life is over? Song. Audrey Alexandra Brown. TwCV
What, will he come for me. Microcosmos, XVI. Nigel Heseltine. NeBP
What will it please you, my darling, hereafter to be? A Child's Future. Swinburne. BPN; EmBrPo; EnLi-2
What Will the Stars Remember? Lilith Lorraine. ChIP
What will they give me, when journey's done? Journey's End. Humbert Wolfe. TrJP; TwCV; YT
What Will We Do? Robert J. Burdette. BOHV
What will you do. What Then, Dancer? Kay Smith. CaP
What Will You Do, God, When I Die? Rainer Maria Rilke, *tr. fr. German by* Babette Deutsch. LiTW
What Will You Do, Love? Samuel Lover. OnYI
What Will You Give Me If I Get Up? *Unknown.* ABS
What will you give to a barefoot lass. A Song of Riches. Katharine Lee Bates. AA
"What will you have for your birthday?" Birthday Gifts. Herbert Asquith. SiSoSe
What will you ride on? Hey! My Pony! Eleanor Farjeon. FaPON
What wind is this across the roofs so softly makes his way. Quod Semper. Lucy Lyttelton. VOD
What winter holiday is this? The Man of Peace. Bliss Carman. DD; HH; OHIP
What wisdom have I that I surely know. Certainty. Evelyn Hardy. HBMV
What wisdom more, what better life, than pleaseth God to send? Posies for Thine Own Bedchamber. Thomas Tusser. SiCE
What wish you, immortality? Florence Wilkinson Evans. *Fr.* The Things That Endure. OQP; QP-2
What without speech we knew and could not say. Preludes to Definition, IV. Conrad Aiken. TwAmPo
What wonders now I have to pen, sir. The Female Husband, Who Had Been Married to Another Female for Twenty-one Years. *Unknown.* CoMu
What wondrous life is this I lead! Thoughts in a Garden. Andrew Marvell. *Fr.* The Garden. CBOV; CH; ChTr
What wondrous love is this, Oh! my soul, oh, my soul! Wondrous Love. *Unknown.* TrAS
What wondrous sermons these seas preach to men! Along Shore. Herbert Bashford. AA
What word have you, interpreters, of men. Of Heaven Considered as a Tomb. Wallace Stevens. AnFE; AnNE; APA; CoAnAm
What word is that, that changeth not. Of His Love Called Anna. Sir Thomas Wyatt. ElSeCe; ReIE; TuPP
What words are these have fall'n from me? In Memoriam A. H. H., XVI. Tennyson. CoBE; EmBrPo; EnLi-2; EPN; GEPC; ViPo; VLEP
What work of honour and eternal name. De Guiana, Carmen Epicum. George Chapman. OBSC
What worlds of wonder are our books! Books. Eleanor Farjeon. YeAr
What Would He Say? Stanton A. Coblentz. ChIP
What would it mean for you and me. The Miracle of the Dawn. Madison Cawein. HBV
What Would She More? *in mod. Eng. Unknown.* TMEV
What would the world be, once bereft. Wildness. Gerard Manley Hopkins. *Fr.* Inversnaid. OtMeF
What would we do in this world of ours. The Dreams Ahead. Edwin Carlile Litsey. PoToHe
What would you do. The Artist. Henry Bellamann. LS
What! would you have the fatal sister lend. For the Dead Gregorians. Ignacio Ramirez. AnMP
What Would You See? George Macdonald. PRWS
What would'st thou have for easement after grief. Comfort of the Fields. Archibald Lampman. CaP; OCL
What wouldst thou have, O soul. The Sacred Heart. Adelaide Anne Procter. JKCP
What wrote he on the parched and dusty ground. Contrast. Aubert Edgar Bruce. ChIP
What Yo' Gwine to Do When Yo' Lamp Burn Down? *with music. Unknown.* BoAN-1
What you are I cannot say. Siegfried Sassoon. *Fr.* The Heart's Journey. LoPS
"What, you are stepping westward?" Stepping Westward. Wordsworth. BEL; BPN; CH; EmBrPo; EnLi-2; EnRP; ERP; ExPo; GEPC; HBV; OBRV; PoEL-4; SeCeV; ShBV-4
What? You Define Me God. Stephen Crane. *Fr.* War Is Kind, IV. AmPP (3d ed.)
What you desire not starlight nor tearose. In the Web. E. L. Mayo. MiAP
What you do/ Still betters what is done. Shakespeare. *Fr.* The Winter's Tale, IV, iii. LoPS; NBE
What you give me I cheerfully accept. To Rich Givers. Walt Whitman. AnAmPo; LA
What you gonna do when the liquor gives out, sweet thing? Sweet Thing. *Unknown.* OuSiCo
What you gwain to do when the meat gives out, my Baby? What Kin' o' Pants Does the Gambler Wear. *Unknown.* AS
"What you will to your father, Jimmy Randolph, my son?" Jimmy Randolph. *Unknown.* ABS
Whate'er I be, old England is my dam! The Old Chartist. George Meredith. EmBrPo; PoFr
Whate'er is born of mortal birth. To Tirzah. Blake. *Fr.* Songs of Experience. EiPP; EnRP; LO; MeRV; OxBoCh
Whate'er of woe the Dark may hide in womb. The Breath of Avon. Theodore Watts-Dunton. VA
Whate'er the passion—knowledge, fame, or pelf. Human Folly [*or* Man]. Pope. *Fr.* An Essay on Man, Epistle II. BLV; BoLiVe; CBE; FiP; TrGrPo
Whate'er thou art, where'er thy footsteps stray. This, Too, Shall Pass Away. *Ad. by* A. L. Alexander. PoToHe
Whate'er thy countrymen have done. Written in the Beginning of Mezeray's History of France. Matthew Prior. CEP; OBEC; PoE; PoEL-3; PoFS
Whate'er we leave to God, God does. Inspiration, *proem.* Henry David Thoreau. CBOV; IAP; MOAP; OxBA; TriL
Whate'er You Dream with Doubt Possest. Arthur Hugh Clough. *See* All Is Well.
Whatever Aunt Eliza wants to hear. Aunt Eliza's Slow Ear. Winifred Welles. GaP
Whatever brawls disturb the street. Love between Brothers and Sisters. Isaac Watts. CaAE; PECK
Whatever crazy sorrow saith. Life Not Death. Tennyson. *Fr.* The Two Voices. MaRV
Whatever doubt the eye might have imposed. E. J. Pratt. *Fr.* Behind the Log. TwCaPo
Whatever else be lost among the years. Let Us Keep Christmas [*or* Eternal Values]. Grace Noll Crowell. MaRV; PoToHe (new ed.)
Whatever good is naturally done. Sonnet: Of Love, in Honor of His Mistress Becchina [*or* In Honor of His Mistress]. Cecco Angiolieri da Siena. AWP; OnPM
Whatever I do, and whatever I say. Aunt Tabitha. Oliver Wendell Holmes. CenHV; PTA-1
Whatever I have said or sung. In Memoriam A. H. H., CXXV. Tennyson. BPN; EmBrPo; EPN; GEPC; OAEP; TCEP; ViPo; VLEP
Whatever I said and whatever you said. Husband and Wife. Arthur Guiterman. PoToHe (new ed.)
Whatever intentions. The Meadow Brook Runs Over. Howard McKinley Corning. MAP; MoAmPo (1942 ed.)
Whatever Is—Is Best. Ella Wheeler Wilcox. BLPA; PoToHe; TreFS
Whatever Is, Is Right. Laman Blanchard. BOHV
Whatever Is, Is Right. Pope. *Fr.* An Essay on Man, Epistle I. OBEC
Whatever is shrunk. *Unknown, tr. fr. Chinese.* Tao Teh Ching, XI. WhP
Whatever it was she had so fiercely fought. The Recognition of Eve. Karl Shapiro. *Fr.* Adam and Eve. MoAB
Whatever its function. The Purist to Her Love. Margaret Fishback. WhC
Whatever place is poor and small. The Hut. Ruth Pitter. AlDL
Whatever ripened in these lines. Prelude. Clemens Brentano. LiTW
Whatever the books may say, or the plausible. December: Of Aphrodite. W. S. Merwin. NePoEA
Whatever the worth of a man, yet poverty can bring him. Poverty. Theognis. GrPE
Whatever while the thought comes over me. Dante. *Fr.* La Vita Nuova. AWP; JAWP; WBP
Whatever you do, whatever you say. Old German Mottos. *Unknown.* StaSt
"Whatever you want is yours." The Lay of the Battle of Tombland. Dunstan Thompson. LiTA; NePA

Whatever's lost, it first was won. Elizabeth Barrett Browning. *Fr.* De Profundis. TrPWD
What'll Be the Title? Justin Richardson. *See* Titles.
What're you gonna do with the pretty Bessie Larkin. Callahan. *Unknown.* OuSiCo
What's a cuckold learne of me. *Unknown.* SeCSL
"What's all this rich land," said I to the Meath man. The Boyne Walk. F. R. Higgins. OxBI
What's become of Waring. Waring. Robert Browning. OtMeF; PoEL-5
What's come? The end of Nikon's nose. Old Greek Nonsense Rhymes. Nicarchus. BoN
What's Fame? a fancied life in others' breath. Fame. Pope. *Fr.* An Essay on Man. LPS-3; ViBoPo
What's hallowed ground? Has earth a clod. Hallowed Ground. Thomas Campbell. BLPA; HBV; LPS-3; MaRV
What's he that wishes so? Agincourt (Battle of Saint Crispian's Day). Shakespeare. King Henry V, *fr.* IV, iii. BHV
What's in a Name? Helen F. More. GA; PAH
What's in a Name? R. K. Munkittrick. BOHV; InMe
What's in It for Me? Edgar A. Guest. PoToHe (new ed.)
What's in the brain, that ink may character. Sonnets, CVIII. Shakespeare. PeBoSo
What's in the Cupboard? *Unknown.* ChTr; OxNR
What's in the net? O feel. Girl's Love Song. Eduard Mörike. AnGP
What's in There? *Unknown.* CH; OxNR
What's life but full of care and doubt. Domestic Didactics by an Old Servant. Thomas Hood. OBRV
What's life or pleasure wanting Aphrodite? Among the Embers. Mimnermus. GrR
What's love, when the most is said? When the Most Is Said. "Madeline Bridges." AA; HBV
What's my sweetheart? A laundress is she. Jeannette. Otto Julius Bierbaum. AWP
What's My Thought Like? Thomas Moore. BOHV; OBRV
"What's new?"—What's old? what's anything. S. T. Coleridge Dismisses a Caller from Porlock. Gerard Previn Meyer. GoYe
What's she, so late from Penshurst come. On Her Coming to London. Edmund Waller. HBV
What's silver and a house to me. Her First Song. James K. Baxter. Cressida, V. AnNZ
What's that shining in the leaves. Songs for a Colored Singer, IV. Elizabeth Bishop. PoNe
"What's that stain on your shirt sleeve?" Edward (C *vers.*). *Unknown.* BaBo
"What's that that hirples at my side?" Heriot's Ford. Kipling. PoRA
What's that we see from far? the spring of Day. A Nuptiall Song, or Epithalamie, on Sir Clipseby Crew and His Lady. Robert Herrick. AtBAP; PoEL-3; SeCV-1
What's that, which, ere I spake, was gone. Life of Life. Coventry Patmore. *Fr.* The Angel in the House. EPP
What's the best thing in the world? The Best. Elizabeth Barrett Browning. OBVV
What's the brightness of a brow? Evanescence. Harriet Prescott Spofford. AA; PR
What's the good [*or* use] of breathing. The Frost Pane. David McCord. BrR; RIS; StaSt; StVeCh
What's the greeting for a rajah riding on an elephant? Some Questions to Be Asked of a Rajah, Perhaps by the Associated Press. Preston Newman. FiBHP
What's the gud of these Pazons? They're the most despard rubbage goin'. The Pazons. Thomas Edward Brown. In the Coach, V. POTT
What's the Lesson for To-Day. *Unknown.* PEOR
What's the Matter, Haven't You Got Any Sense of Humor? Ogden Nash. SiTL
What's the matter with you—ain't I always been your friend? A Boy and His Stomach. Edgar A. Guest. OnHT; PTA-1
What's the news of the day. *Unknown.* OxNR
What's the point of having your radio set set. Sonnet on a Somewhat Inferior Radio Outfit. Cary Ross. AnAmPo; LA
What's the Railroad to Me? Henry David Thoreau. PoEL-4
What's this? A dish for fat lips. The Shape of the Fire. Theodore Roethke. AmP; LiTA; MiAP; MoAB; OnAP
What's this dull town to me? Robin Adair. Lady Caroline Keppel. BCEP; FaBoBe; HBV; LPS-1; OlF
What's this morn's bright eye to me. Morning Hymn. Joseph Beaumont. OxBoCh; TrPWD
What's This of Death. Edna St. Vincent Millay. BLV; BoLiVe
What's this vain world to me? Rest Is Not Here. Lady Nairne. HBV
What's Wrong, Little Blonde. *Unknown.* *See* Qu'avec-vous, oui, belle blonde.
"What's your most vexing parasite." The Same Complaint. Norman Gale. PIAE
What's your name? Pudden Tame. *Unknown.* ChTr; GoTP
Whatsoe'er/ The form of building or the creed professed. The Sovereign Emblem. James Russell Lowell. *Fr.* The Cathedral. ChIP; MaRV
"Whatsoe'er He bids you—do it!" Leave the Miracle to Him. Thomas H. Allan. BLRP
Whatsoever I Do. Mary Louise Hector. GoBC
Whatsoever things are true. Think on These Things. Philippians, Bible, *N.T.* GrCo-1; TiPo (1952 ed.)
Whaup o' the Rede, *sel.* Will H. Ogilvie.
Blades of Harden, The. GoTS
Whaups, The. Robert Louis Stevenson. *See* To S. R. Crockett.
Whaur? Heine. *See* Where?
Whaur yon broken brig hings owre. Song. William Soutar. GoTS
Wheatlet Son of Milklet. MacConglinne, *tr. fr. Middle Irish by* Kuno Meyer. OnYI
Whee hee lo, whee hee. Evening on Howth Head. Eileen Brennan. NeIP
Whee—oop! Whoop—eee! In Town. *Unknown.* ABF
Wheel, The. Ibn al-Abbar, *tr. fr. Arabic by* A. J. Arberry. MooP
Wheel, The. Sully-Prudhomme, *tr. fr. French by* William Dock. ImOP
Wheel, The. W. B. Yeats. MoVE; TwP
Wheel me into the sunshine. Home, Wounded. Sydney Dobell. LPS-1
Wheel, oh, wheel,/ Wheel in de middle of a wheel. 'Zekiel Saw de Wheel. *Unknown.* BoAN-2; OlF
Wheel of the quivering meat, The. Chorus. Jack Kerouac. *Fr.* Mexico City Blues. NeAP
Wheel turns with a will, The. Water. Ibn Saad al-Khair. MooP
Wheelbarrow. Eleanor Farjeon. FiBHP
Wheeler at Santiago. James Lindsay Gordon. PAH
Wheeler's Brigade at Santiago. Wallace Rice. MC
Wheelgoround, The. Robert Clairmont. PoMS
Wheels flee on silky steel. We are seated. To the Shore. May Swenson. NePoAm-2
Wheel's inventor, nameless demigod, The. The Wheel. Sully-Prudhomme. ImOP
Wheer 'asta beän saw long and meä liggin' 'ere aloän? Northern Farmer; Old Style. Tennyson. BEL; BPN; EM-2; EmBrPo; EPN; EV-5; GEPC; OAEP; PoVP; TCEP; VA; ViPo; VLEP
Wheesht, wheesht, my foolish hert. "Hugh MacDiarmid." LO
Whelp that nipped its mother's dug in turning from her breast, The. The Lion's Cub. Maurice Thompson. AA
When. "Æ." ATP; BEL; ChMo; CMP; GTIV; OnYI; POTE; TOP
When. Dorothy Aldis. SiSoSe
When. "Susan Coolidge." HBV; LPS-2
When? José Moreno Villa, *tr. fr. Spanish by* Eleanor L. Turnbull. CoSP
When,/ Halting in front of it. Hitomaro. *Fr.* Shui Shu. AWP; JAWP; PFE; WBP
When/ Sir/ Beelzebub. Sir Beelzebub. Edith Sitwell. *Fr.* Façade. CoBMV; FaBoMo; HoPM; MBP; MoAB; MoBrPo
When/ Dr./ Edith. A Thin Façade for Edith Sitwell. John Malcolm Brinnin. FiBHP
When a bare hundred thousand was all that you had. Sealed Bags of Ducats. Martial. LiTW
When a Beau Goes In. Gavin Ewart. WaP
When a brass sun staggers above the sky. Tramp. Richard Hughes. MBP; MoBrPo
When a certain great king, whose initial is G. An Ancient Prophecy. Philip Freneau. PAH
When a daffodil [*or* daffadil] I see. Divination by a Daffodil. Robert Herrick. OBS; SeCV-1; SeEP
When a deed is done for freedom. The Present Crisis. James Russell Lowell. BAP; CoBA; GrCo-1; IAP; MaRV; OHFP; OQP; PSO; QP-1
When a dream is born in you. A Pinch of Salt. Robert Graves. HBMV; LBBV; MBP; MoBrPo; PtOT
When a feller hasn't got a cent. Fellowship. *Unknown.* BLPA
When a feller's feelin' lazy—when the springtime's comin' 'round. Just Keep Fishin'. Harry M. Dean. DDA
When a fellow loves a maiden. La Cucaracha. *Unknown.* AS; TrAS
When a felon's not engaged in his employment. The Policeman's Lot. W. S. Gilbert. *Fr.* The Pirates of Penzance. ALV; NeHB; PoVP; TrGrPo
When a friend calls to me from the road. A Time to Talk. Robert Frost. CoBA; LaNeLa
When a friend starts on a journey of a thousand miles. The End of the Year. Su T'ung-po. OnPC
When a Girl Looks Down. Kay Smith. CaP; PeCV
When a goose meets a moose. Zhenya Gay. TiPo (1959 ed.)
When a great tree falls. To Be Answered in Our Next Issue. *Unknown.* WaKn
When a jolly young fisher named Fisher. Limerick. *Unknown.* LiBL

When a maid is sweet and fair. If a Maid Be Fair. Laura Goodman Salverson. CaP
When a man ain't got no money. Let's Go Fishin'. Robert S. Holmes. DDA
When a man has cast out fear. The End of Fear. Ruth Pitter. POTE
When a Man Has Married a Wife. Blake. *See* Marriage.
When a Man Hath No Freedom [to Fight for at Home]. Byron. EnLi-2 (1949 ed.); EnRP; EPN; PoFS; TrGrPo
(Impromptus.) BPN
(Stanza[s].) PoFr; SoV
When a Man Turns Homeward. Daniel Whitehead Hicky. PoToHe
When a Man's Busy. Robert Browning. WhC
When a mounting skylark sings. Skylark and Nightingale [*or* Heaven Is Heaven]. Christina Rossetti. *Fr.* Sing-Song. MBP; RIS; YeAr
When a' other bairnies are hushed to their hame. The Mitherless Bairn. William Thom. EV-4; HBV; LPS-1; VA
When a patterned stuff will so flutter. A Minute. Innokenti Annenski. BoR
When a Ring's around the Moon. Mary Jane Carr. BrR; TiPo
When a sighing begins/ In the violins. Chanson[s] d'automne [*or* Song of Autumn]. Paul Verlaine. AWP; JAWP; LiA; OnPM; WBP; WoL
When a squash ball. The Scientific Attack. Frederick Bertolet. CAG
When a twister a-twisting will twist him a twist. Twister Twisting Twine. *Unknown, at. to* John Wallis. ChTr; OTPC; OxNR
When a Warlock Dies. Isabella Gardner. NePA
When a Woman Blue. *Unknown. See* Blue Woman.
When a young man, passion-laden. A Poem of Privacy. *Unknown.* ALV
When Abraham Lincoln was shoveled into the tombs. Cool Tombs. Carl Sandburg. AmP; AmPP; AnFE; AtBAP; BAP; BLV; BoLiVe; CaAE; ChMo; CMP; CoAnAm; CoBA; CP; HBMV; IAP; MAP; MoAB; MoAmPo; MOAP; MoVE; NeMA; NV; TBM; TrGrPo; TwAmPo; TwCV; ViBoPo; WHA
When Abraham Went Out of Ur. Nancy Byrd Turner. QS
When Abu Amir pardoned me. Forgiveness. Al-Jaziri. MooP
When Adam Day by Day. A. E. Housman. FiBHP; WhC
When Adam delved and Eve span. Robert Southey. *Fr.* Wat Tyler. BCEP
When Adam first did from his dust arise. The World. Thomas Traherne. AlDL
When Adam found his rib was gone. The Lady's-Maid Song. John Hollander. NePoEA
When Adam named in days of old. The Burro. J. J. Gibbons. PoOW
When Adam quitted the Garden. The Dog. Don Marquis. AlBD; PoeMoYo
When Adam Was Created, *with music. Unknown.* TrAS
(Wedlock, *sl. diff., with music.*) ABF
When Admonition's hand essays. Rebuke. Ambrose Bierce. BAP
When Advent dawns with lessening days. The Golden Flower. Oliver Wendell Holmes. PEOR
When, after all, you come to Love and lay. After All. Arthur Upson. PR
When after many battles past. After Battle. *Unknown.* MaRV
When, after storms that woodlands rue. A Requiem for Soldiers Lost in Ocean Transports. Herman Melville. GTBS-D; PoEL-5
When against earth a wooden heel. Winter Sleep. Elinor Wylie. BAV; NePA
When age hath made me what I am not now. Upon His Picture. Thomas Randolph. ElSeCe; MePo; SeCL; SeEP
When Ah was young Ah use' to wait. De Blue-Tail Fly. *Unknown.* SoAF
When Ahab saw his white leviathan. The Whale and the Tiger. John W. Simons. JKCP (1955 ed.)
When Alexander Our King Was Dead. *Unknown.* GoTS
(Cantus.) BSV
(Quhen Alysandyr Our King Was Dede.) AtBAP
(When Alysandyr Our King Was Dede.) FaBoCh
When Alexander Pope. E. C. Bentley. FiBHP
When Alexander Pope strolled in the city. Mr. Pope. Allen Tate. MAP; MoAB; MoAmPo; MOAP; PtP; ReaPo; SPP; TBM
When all around grew drear and dark. Stanzas to Augusta. Byron. ERP
When all besides a vigil keep. The West's Asleep. Thomas Osborne Davis. OnYI
When all but her were sleeping fast. The Little Dead Child. Josephine Daskam Bacon. DaM
When All Is Done. Paul Laurence Dunbar. MaRV
When all is done and said, in the end thus shall you find. Of [*or* On] a Contented Mind [*or* Content]. Thomas, Lord Vaux. CoBE; ElL; EV-1; GoBC; HBV; MaRV; OBSC; ReIE; SiCE; TuPP
When All Is Said. John Dynham Cornish Pellow. PtOT
When all is said and done, I urge again. Put Grief Away. Robert K. Ekvall. *Fr.* Tibetan Comforter. MaRV
When all is still within these walls. The Man's Prayer [*or* A Father's Prayer]. T. A. Daly. PraP; TrPWD
When all is written and sung. Food. Ruby Weyburn Tobias. OQP; QP-2
When All My Five and Country Senses See. Dylan Thomas. MaPo; MoAB; MoBrPo; SeCePo
When All My Heavy Heart. Bilhana, *formerly at. to* Chauras, *tr. fr. Sanskrit by* E. Powys Mathers. *Fr.* Black Marigolds. OnPM
When all my will drops from me like a shroud. Where No Thoughts Are. Anna Hempstead Branch. MOAP
When all night long a chap remains. The Contemplative Sentry. W. S. Gilbert. *Fr.* Iolanthe. ALV; EnLi-2; FiBHP; PoVP
When all of us wore smaller shoes. Ancient Lights. Austin Clarke. OxBI
When all our hopes are sown on stony ground. A Note of Humility. Arna Bontemps. PoNe
When all our lovely words are blown away. Arbor Una Nobilis. Sister Thomas Aquinas. JKCP (1955 ed.)
When all our troubled errantries are done. Nocturne in a Library. Arthur Davison Ficke. AOAH
When all that matters shall be written down. All That Matters. Edgar A. Guest. ATP
When all the altar lights were dead. Resurrection. Alfred Noyes. EOAH
When all the days are hot and long. Swimming. Clinton Scollard. FaPON; GFA; MPB; UTS
When all the Greeks were closely throng'd around. The Reconciliation of Achilles and Agamemnon. Homer. *Fr.* The Iliad, XIX. GrR
When all the ground with snow is white. The Snow-Bird. Frank Dempster Sherman. SiSoSe; TiPo; UTS
When all the ice and cold and snow. Canso. Giraut de Bornelh. LyMA
When all the leaves are off the boughs. Thanksgiving Time. *Unknown.* MeMeAg; OTPC (1946 ed.); PCH
When all the little birds have gone to rest. Lullaby-O, By-O, Babe. Harry Noyes Pratt. BOL
When all the night is horrible with clamour. All in All. Edith Nesbit. PoFr
When all the other leaves are gone. Oak Leaves. Elizabeth J. Coatsworth. StVeCh
When all the over-work of life. The Heart Knoweth Its Own Bitterness. Christina Rossetti. EmBrPo
When all the powers have fallen. Eclogue. Hal Summers. POTE
When all the sky is pure. Canticle. Thomas Edward Brown. VLEP
When all the soul has been inhaled. Poetry. Stéphane Mallarmé. TrFP
When all the West is fold on fold. The Boats of Slumberland. *Unknown.* BOL
When All the World Is Young, Lad. Charles Kingsley. *See* Young and Old.
When all the world would keep a matter hid. The Fabulists. Kipling. ChMP
When All the Young Were Dying. Edmund Wilson. AnAmPo; LA
When all this life is suddenly quite done. A Sinner Contemplates. Frances Boal Mehlek. DDA
When All Thy Mercies. Addison. OxBoCh
(Hymn: "When all thy mercies, O my God.") OBEC
(Providence.) EV-3
When all were dreaming but Pastheen Power. The Song of the Ghost. Alfred Perceval Graves. AnIV; DaM
When all within is dark. "From Thee to Thee." Solomon ibn Gabirol. TrJP
When all works that have. The Fool by the Roadside. W. B. Yeats. MoVE
When all your bitter grief is gone. The Mourner. W. H. Davies. POTE
When Almonds Bloom. Milicent Washburn Shinn. AA
When along the light ripple the far serenade. The Venetian Serenade. Richard Monckton Milnes. OBRV
When Alysandyr Our King Was Dede. *Unknown. See* When Alexander Our King Was Dead.
When Amaryllis Bowls. John Farrar. LEAP; PR
When and how shall I earliest meet her? My Queen. *Unknown.* HBV
When André rode to Pont-du-lac. André's Ride. Augustus Henry Beesly. HBV
When Angel Death comes knocking at my door. Resignation. Mother Francis d'Assisi. WHL
When apple boughs are dim with bloom. Sacrifice. Ada Foster Murray. NV
When April comes, and pelts with buds. Reed Call. Madison Cawein. PR
When April, one day, was asked whether. April Weather. Jessie McDermott. OTPC (1946 ed.); PCH

When April pours the colours of a shell. Wild Peaches, III. Elinor Wylie. LiTA; NAMP; OxBA

When April rains make the flowers bloom. The Shamrock. Maurice Francis Egan. AA; DD; HBV; HH

When April skies are bright with sun. The Spectre Ship. Thomas Stephens Collier. EtS

When April with his showers sweet with fruit. The Prologue to The Canterbury Tales, *mod.* Chaucer. OuHeWo

When arms and numbers both have failed. Aguinaldo. Bertrand Shadwell. PAH

When Art goes bounding, lean. Art and Life. Lola Ridge. HBMV

When Arthur first in court began. Sir Lancelot du Lake. *Unknown.* CG

When as. *See also* Whenas.

When as a Lad. Isabel Ecclestone Mackay. HBV; OCL

When as a young and budding pote. De Senectute. Franklin P. Adams. HBMV; TCAP

When as black night, her vaile displayes. *Unknown.* SeCSL

When as in Silks My Julia Goes. Robert Herrick. *See* Upon Julia's Clothes.

When as King Henry ruled this land. Fair Rosamund. Thomas Deloney. CG

When as man's life, the light of human lust. *See* Whenas man's life . . .

When as the chill Charokko blows. *See* Whenas the chill sirocco blows.

When, as the garish day is done. The New Moon. Bryant. OTPC

When as the nightingale chanted her vespers. *See* Whenas the nightingale . . .

When as the Rye Reach to the Chin. George Peele. *See* Whenas the Rye . . .

When as the sheriff of Nottingham. Robin Hood and the Golden Arrow. *Unknown.* ESPB

When at close of winter's night. Birdcatcher's Song. William John Courthope. *Fr.* The Paradise of Birds. VA

When at home alone I sit. The Little Land. Robert Louis Stevenson. GoBP; OnHT; PoVP; PRWS; StVeCh (1955 ed.); TVC; TVSH

When at last he was well enough to take the sun. A Leg in a Plaster Cast. Muriel Rukeyser. MoAmPo

When, at the end of it all. Henry Spaulding. Donald Burnie. PaA

When at the sun we stare too fixedly. The Black Dot. Gérard de Nerval. TrFP

When at Thy footstool, Lord, I bend. Forgiveness. Henry Francis Lyte. BePJ; PraP

When at thy love a lamp we light. Gamble. Iraqi. PeP

When at your desk you sit with studious look. Books and Love. Carl David af Wirsén. AnSL

When Atlantis sank into the sea. America. Raúl Otero Reiche. AnCL

When, Atlas-born, the Pleiad stars arise. Works and Days. Hesiod. WoL

When Aunt Selina comes to tea. Aunt Selina. Carol Haynes. HBMV; HBVY; MPB

When Aurelia First I Courted. *Unknown.* OBS

When autumn wounds the bough. Autumnal Spring Song. Vassar Miller. NePoEA

When Autumn's here and days are short. Lydia. Madison Cawein. PR

When awful darkness and silence reign. The Dong with a Luminous Nose. Edward Lear. CenHV; ChTr; KN; LBN; PoEL-5; PoMS; SiTL; TOP

When Baby Hurts Her Hand. *Unknown, tr. fr. German.* SAS
("Pat it, kiss it.") PPL

When baby woke in woolly spread. Where Is My Butterfly Net? David McCord. FiBHP

When baby's first tooth hove in view. The Teeth Called Straight. Fairfax Downey. LauV

When bairns on pillows lay their heids. The Land o' Nae Surprise. John Stevenson. BOL

When Banners Are Waving. *Unknown.* GN; HBV

When beasts could speak (the learned say). The Beasts' Confession. Swift. ATP (1935 ed.); CEP; EiPP; EV-3; PIAE; TOP

When beauty grows too great to bear. Song at Capri. Sara Teasdale. ChMo; CMP

When beechen [*or* birchen] buds begin to swell. The Yellow Violet [*or* The Violet]. Bryant. AmPP; AnNE; BAV; CoBA; DDA; IAP; OBAV; PEOR; ReaPo

When bees come hither in the fair springtide. A Bee-Keeper. *Unknown.* OxBG

When before the cloud-white throne. The Judgment. Katharine Lee Bates. OQP; QP-2

When Bill gives me a book, I know. The Christmas Exchange. Arthur Guiterman. BrR; ChBR

When Bill was a lad he was terribly bad. Those Two Boys. Franklin P. Adams. ALV; FiBHP; MAP; MoAmPo (1942 ed.); PFE; TrJP

When birchen buds begin to swell. *See* When beechen buds . . .

When birds and brittle leaves come down. Poem. John Prichard. MoWP

When birds came to set the leaves in motion. The High Sailboat. Salvatore Quasimodo. LiTW

When birds of passage 'neath wet skies are lost. To Madame N. Ménessier. Alfred de Musset. TrFP

When biting Boreas, fell and doure. Burns. *Fr.* A Winter Night. BSV; MCCG

When Bob Got Throwed. *Unknown.* SCC

When Boreas at the autumn's end. Protinus Extremo cum Jam Boreas Autumno. Politian. LaP

When bosoms quivering. Fruit Tree. Ibn Qadi Mila. MooP

When bosses grow censorious. The Gay Wag. Berton Braley. AlBD

When both hands of the town clock stood at twelve. Village Noon; Mid-Day Bells. Merrill Moore. MAP; MoAmPo

When both side lights you see ahead. Rules of the Road. *Unknown.* SoAmSa

When Boys Go a-Courting, *with music. Unknown.* TrAS

When Bradbury sang, "The Roast Beef of Old England." Dissent; a Fable. Donald Davie. PoN

When brambles vex me sore and anguish me. The Fellowship. Katharine Lee Bates. OQP; QP-2

When brave Van Rensselaer cross'd the stream. The Battle of Queenstown. William Banker, Jr. PAH

When breezes are soft and skies are fair. Green River. Bryant. AmPP (4th ed.); CoBA; IAP; OxBA; PEOR; TCAP

When Britain first, at heaven's command. Rule, Britannia! [*or* An Ode]. James Thomson. *Fr.* Alfred, a Masque (*by* Thomson *and* David Mallet). AEV; BEL; BHV; CaAE; CEP; EiPP; EnLi-2 (1949 ed.); EnLit; EPP; EV-3; GTBS; GTBS-D; GTBS-W; GTSE; GTSL; HBV; LEAP; LPS-2; OAEP; OBEC; PoFr; TCEP; TreF; WBLP

When Britain *really* ruled the waves. The House of Peers [*or* The House of Lords *or* Song]. W. S. Gilbert. *Fr.* Iolanthe. InMe; InP; MBP; TrGrPo

When Britain, with envy and malice inflamed. Capture of Little York. *Unknown.* PAH

When British troops first landed here. Cornwallis's Surrender. *Unknown.* PAH

When brother takes me walking. The Ordinary Dog. Nancy Byrd Turner. AlBD; TiPo

When brother teaches her to skate. Learning to Skate. Emilie Blackmore Stapp. GFA

When Bunyan swung his whopping axe. Folk-Tune. Richard Wilbur. OnHM

When Burbadge Played. Austin Dobson. InP; PFE; PoVP

When by me in the dusk my child sits down. John Berryman. *Fr.* Homage to Mistress Bradstreet. CrMA; ReMP

When, by pronouncement of almighty powers. Benediction. Baudelaire. AnFP

When by the marbled lake I lie and listen. Hymn. Wathen Mark Wilks Call. OBVV

When by their sev'ral chiefs the troops were rang'd. Trojans and Greeks. Homer. *Fr.* The Iliad, III. GrR

When by thy scorn[e], O murd'ress [*or* murderess *or* murdresse] I am dead. The Apparition. John Donne. AtBAP; ElSeCe; EnLoPo; EnLP; ExPo; LoBV; MePo; OBEV (new ed.); OBS; ReEn; SeCV-1; SeEP; ViBoPo

When by Zeus relenting the mandate was revoked. Phoebus with Admetus. George Meredith. EnLi-2; OBEV; OBVV; ViP

When C. J. G. Arden goes out in the garden. To His Godson Gerald C. A. Jackson. A. E. Housman. WhC

When Cain killed Abel to end a perfect day. A Curse for the Saxaphone. Vachel Lindsay. ATP (1935 ed.)

When calm is the night, and the stars shine bright. Sleighing Song. John Shaw. AA

When came the priest thy father to recapture. Chryseis. Walter Conrad Arensberg. AnAmPo; LA

When Captain O'Bruadir shook a sword across the sea. The Ballad of O'Bruadir. F. R. Higgins. EtS

When captains [*or* captain] courageous, whom death could not daunt. Mary Ambree [*or* The Valorous Acts Performed at Gaunt . . .]. *Unknown.* OBB; OTPC (1923 ed.); TuPP

When Carolina's hope grew pale. Sumter's Band. James Wright Simmons. GA; PAH

When Cats Run Home. Tennyson. *See* Owl, The.

When, Celia, I Intend. *Unknown.* ElSeCe; TuPP
(To Celia.) SeCL
("When Celia I intend to flatter you.") SeEP

When, Celia [*or* Coelia], must my old day set. To Celia [*or* To Coelia]. Charles Cotton. EV-2; HBV; OBS

When chapman [*or* chapmen] billies leave the street. Tam o' Shanter. Burns. AEV; BCEP; BEL; BeLS; BLV; BOHV; BoLiVe; BSV; CBOV; CEP; DaM; EBSV; EiPP; EM-1; EnL; EnLi-2; EnLit; EnRP; EPP; EV-3; GoTL; GoTS; HBV; HOAH; LPS-3; OAEP; OBEC; OnSP; OuHeWo; PIAE; PoE; RiBV; SeCePo; ShBV-3; TCEP; TOP; TrGrPo; TyEnPo; UnPo (1st ed.); ViBoPo; WHA

When cherry flowers begin to blow. Yuki. Mary McNeil Fenollosa. AA
When children are playing alone on the green. The Unseen Playmate. Robert Louis Stevenson. OnHT; PCH
When children, blundering on their fathers' guns. Prayer for Light. Stanton A. Coblentz. TrPWD
When children lay them down to sleep. *Unknown.* BOL
When chill November's surly blast. Man Was Made to Mourn. Burns. CEP; LPS-1
When chinks in April's windy dome. Love in the Calendar. Robert Underwood Johnson. PR
When, Chloe, I your charms survey. To Chloe. Thomas Cheek. SeCL
When Christ the Babe was born. The Lamb-Child. John Banister Tabb. ChBR; SDH
When Christ was born in Bethlehem. Christmas Carol. *Unknown, tr. by* Longfellow. ChrBoLe; CLS; OHIP
When Christ was born in Bethlehem, Pan left his Sussex-Downs. Ballad of the Epiphany. Charles Dalmon. HBMV; TSW
When Christ Was Born of Mary Free. *Unknown. See* In Excelsis Gloria.
When Christ was taken from the rood. Robin Redbreast. John Banister Tabb. StJW
When Christ went up to Calvary. Recognition. John Banister Tabb. ChIP; JKCP; OQP; QP-1
When Christmas-Eve is ended. The Dutch Patrol. Edmund Clarence Stedman. OBAV
When Christmas trees at last are burned. Ashes of the Christmas Tree. Yetza Gillespie. ChBR
When circle round the board the cups refilled. Dreams out of a Wine-Cup. Bacchylides. GrR
When cities prod me with demands. Return to Birds. Louis Untermeyer. BLA
When civil dudgeon [*or* fury] first grew high. Description of Hudibras and His Equipments. Samuel Butler. *Fr.* Hudibras. BCEP; CEP; EiPP; EPS; EV-2; SeCV-2; SeEP; TOP; ViBoPo
When Claudius was emperor and grandeur still was Roman. Rise and Fall of Valentines. Fairfax Downey. InMe
When clerks and navvies fondle. For X. Louis MacNeice. EnLoPo
When closed are all the jaws. Magic. José Moreno Villa. CoSP
When clouds appear like rocks and towers. Weather Wisdom. *Unknown.* GoTP; HBVY; OxNR; TreF
When cockle shells turn silver bells. Waillie, Waillie! *Unknown.* AS
When, Coelia, must my old day set. *See* When, Celia, must . . .
When Coldness Wraps This Suffering Clay. Byron. EmBrPo; ERP; UnW
(Immortal Mind, The.) WGRP
When colds and frosts and snows were wont to reign. De Mense Januarii Quae Fuit An. Do. 1595. Thomas Bastard. SiCE
When colour goes home into the eyes. The Treasure. Rupert Brooke. VOD
When coltsfoot withers and begins to wear. Cuckoos. Andrew Young. ChTr; MoPW
When comes in May, with what we call long hours. Fair Erembor. *Unknown.* LyMA
When comes the ghostly gallery. The Ghostly Gallery. Jessie B. Rittenhouse. TBM
When comes the Spring? The Seasons. John Vance Cheney. DD
When Congress sent great Washington. The Trip to Cambridge. *Unknown.* PAH
When conquering love did first my heart assail. To the Senses. Michael Drayton. Idea, XXIX. OAEP
When consciousness came back he found he lay. Between the Lines. W. W. Gibson. HiLiEn; MCCG
When consummate the day hangs before you. Three Variations, I. Boris Pasternak. TrJP; TrRV
When Contemplation, like the night-calm felt. Books. Wordsworth. *Fr.* The Prelude. ERP
When country hills are soft with snow. Les Chasse-Neige. Ralph A. Lewin. FiBHP
When Crassus died, his friends, to grace his hearse. In Epitaphium Pingui Minerva Compositum. Thomas Freeman. TuPP
When, cruel fair one, I am slain. The Tombe. Thomas Stanley. OBS
When Cuckoo First. Frank Prewett. MBP
When Cupid did his grandsire Jove intreat. On Mrs. Biddy Floyd. Swift. CEP
When Cupid first instructs his darts to fly. The Prophecy of Famine; a Scots Pastoral. Charles Churchill. EiPP
When Cupid sees how thickly now. Thou'st Had Thy Day. Anacreon. OnPM
When curfew-bells begin. The Two Loves. Laurence Housman. HBMV
When Dad Takes Me. Douglas Malloch. FAOV
When Daddy/ Walks. Walking. Grace Ellen Glaubitz. GFA; TiPo
When Daddy shaves and lets me stand and look. Daddy. Rose Fyleman. FAOV; SiSoSe
When Daddy Sings. Burges Johnson. FAOV
When Daffodils Begin to Peer. Shakespeare. *Fr.* The Winter's Tale, IV, ii. ChTr; ElL; ExPo; FaBoBe; FaBoCh; HBV; InPo; KN; LoBV; LoGBV; OBSC; SiCE; ViBoPo; WhC
(Autolicus's Song.) FaBoEn
(Autolycus.) EG; EV-1
(Pedlar's Song, The.) OxBoLi
(Song: "When daffodils [*or* daffadils] begin to peer[e].") FiP; PoEL-2
(Song from "The Winter's Tale.") LEAP
(Songs of Autolycus.) OTPC (1923 ed.)
When Daisies Pied and Violets Blue. Shakespeare. *Fr.* Love's Labour's Lost, V, ii. AnFE; EG; EM-1; MyFE; OBEV; OBSC; PoEL-2; PoRA; SeCeV; SiCE; TyEnPo
(Song: Spring and Winter.) LoBV
(Song: "When daisies pied and violets blue.") FiP; HBV; TwHP
(Songs: Spring and Winter.) ExPo
(Songs from "Love's Labour's Lost," 1.) LEAP
(Spring.) BoTP; ElL; ElSeCe; EV-1; InPo; MaPo; PoFS; PreP; ReaPo; SeCePo; SiTL; TrGrPo; UnPo; ViBoPo
(Spring and Winter.) KN; OBEV; ThWaDe
(Ver and Hiems.) ALV
When Dandy Dandelion wakes. Dandy Dandelion. Christopher Morley. GFA
When dangers press, a mind sustain. To Quintus Dellius. Horace. OuHeWo
When Daniel Boone goes by at night. Daniel Boone. Stephen Vincent Benét. NAMP
When Darby saw the setting sun. Darby and Joan. St. John Honeywood. AA; LHV
When dark December glooms the day. Sir Walter Scott. *Fr.* Marmion, *Introd. to* V. OBRV
When, darkly brooding on this Modern Age. Standardization. A. D. Hope. BoAV
When darkness prevail'd and aloud on the air. The Tomb of the Brave. Joseph Hutton. PAH
When darkness was three hours beyond its noon. Bridal Night. Don Marquis. TBM
When Dawn Comes to the City; New York. Claude McKay. GoSl
When dawn no longer, with the hunters use. For Omar. Humbert Wolfe. PtP
When day follows inarticulate day. Wait for the Hour. William Soutar. NeBP
When day is done and work is o'er. Romance. *Unknown.* DDA
When day is ended, and grey twilight flies. The Slumber Angel. Virna Sheard. CPG
When day is hushed and hidden. The Veery. Archibald Rutledge. MuM
When daylight was yet sleeping under the billow. Ill Omens. Thomas Moore. PoEL-4
When days were vaster and the dark more tragic. Tuppence Coloured. Babette Deutsch. PFY
When de Co'n Pone's Hot. Paul Laurence Dunbar. BANP; MotAn
When de fiddle gits to singin' out a ol' Vahginny reel. Angelina. Paul Laurence Dunbar. HBV; VOD
When de golden trumpets sound. A Group of Negro Songs. *Unknown.* NAMP
When de Good Lord Sets You Free, *with music. Unknown.* ABF
When de Whale Get Strike, *with music. Unknown.* OuSiCo
When de whippo'will cry. Whippoorwill. John Richard Moreland. IHA
When, Dearest, I but Think of [*or* on] Thee. *At. to* Sir John Suckling *and to* Owen Felltham. HBV; OBEV; OBS; SeCL; SeEP
(Song: "When, dearest, I but think of [*or* on] thee.") BrBE; EPS; LO; MePo; SeCeV
When Death claimed Helen of the golden hair. Helen. Cecil Francis Lloyd. OCL
When Death comes near to grimly claim his toll. May God Give Strength. Peter van Wynen. BLRP
When Death Shall Come. Helen Frazee-Bower. *See* Who Goeth Hence.
When Death, the angel of our higher dreams. The Journey. Thomas Curtis Clark. MaRV
When Death to Either Shall Come. Robert Bridges. EtPaEn; HBV; OBEV; PoP
When Death was young and bleaching bones were few. Edna St. Vincent Millay. Epitaph for the Race of Man, II. AmP
When Death's pale angel comes to me. My Death. Bedros Tourian. ArmLP
When Delia on the plain appears. Song [*or* Tell Me, My Heart, if This Be Love]. George Lyttelton. CEP; HBV; LoPS; LPS-1; OBEC; OBEV (1st ed.)
When descends on the Atlantic. Seaweed [*or* The Equinox].

Longfellow. APW; CoBA; CoV; EtS; HBV; IAP; LPS-2; MOAP; OxBA; PCD
When Diana lighteth/ Late her crystal lamp. Dum Diane Vitrea. *At. to* Peter Abelard, *tr. by* Helen Waddell. LiA
("When Diana's gleaming lamp," *tr. by* George F. Whicher.) LyMA
When Did the World Begin. Robert Clairmont. *See* Answers, The.
When did these gray ones. Duel in the Park. Lisa Grenelle. GoYe
When did you sink to your dreamless sleep. The Sleeping Giant. E. Pauline Johnson. OCL
When did you start your tricks. The Mosquito. D. H. Lawrence. SiTL
When Dido found Aeneas would not come. Dido [*or* On the Latin Gerunds]. Richard Porson. BOHV; PIAE; SiTL
When disappointment saddens you. Trusting Jesus. Grace B. Renfrow. BePJ
When do I see thee most, beloved one? Lovesight. Dante Gabriel Rossetti. The House of Life, IV. BEL; BLV; BMEP; BoLiVe; BPN; CaAE; CoBE; EmBrPo; EnLi-2; EnLit; EPN; EPP; ES; EV-5; FaBoEn; GTBS-D; GTSL; HBV; LEAP; OAEP; OBVV; PIAE; POTT; PoVP; ReaPo; TCEP; TOP; TrGrPo; TyEnPo; VA; ViBoPo; ViPo; ViPP; VLEP; WHA
When Dobbin and Robin, unharnessed from the plow. The Circus-postered Barn. Elizabeth J. Coatsworth. MAP; MoAmPo; PoeMoYo
When doctrines meet with general approbation. Epigram. David Garrick. HBV
When Doris took her milking pail. Her Milking Pail. "Madeline Bridges." PR
When Dorothy and I took tea, we sat upon the floor. Small and Early. Tudor Jenks. AA; PCD
When down the loud streets I go straying. Stanzas. Pushkin. BoR
When down the stair at morning. My April Lady. Henry van Dyke. HBV
When down the windy vistas of the years. Clement Wood. Eagle Sonnets, XI. HBMV
When Dragon-fly would fix his wings. The Flower of Mending. Vachel Lindsay. LEAP; OBAV; SBMV
When dreaming kings, at odds with swift-paced time. Washington. Harriet Monroe. *Fr.* Commemoration Ode. AA; FaBoBe; MaRV; OQP; QP-1; WOAH
When droning summer earth had slewed the shadows. Woodcut. V. Sackville-West. ChMP
When Dutchy Plays the Mouth Harp. Robert V. Carr. PoOW
When Duty comes a-knocking at your gate. Duty. Edwin Markham. HBMV; HBVY; OQP; QP-1; TSW
When Each Bright Star Is Clouded. Jeremiah Joseph Callanan. IrPN
When early summer called us back. The Whip-poor-will. *Unknown.* BLA
When earth was finished and fashioned well. The Choristers. Bliss Carman. OCL
When Earth's Last Picture Is Painted. Kipling. *See* L'Envoi: "When Earth's last picture . . ."
When Erin [*or* Eire] first rose from the dark-swelling flood. Erin [*or* Eire]. William Drennan. OnYI; TIP
When Eve brought woe to all mankind. Woman. *Unknown.* LPS 3
When Eve first saw the glistering day. Song with Words. James Agee. MAP; MoAmPo
When Eve had led her lord away. Album Verses. Oliver Wendell Holmes. *Fr.* The Autocrat of the Breakfast-Table. AmPP
When Eve upon the first of men. Epigram. Thomas Moore. HBV
When Eve walked in her garden. First Rain. Zoë Akins. HBMV; PoeMoYo
When Evelyn Ann/ Moved down our way. Rich. Aileen Fisher. GaP; MPB
When Even Cometh On. Lucy Evangeline Tilley. AA
When evening came and the warm glow grew deeper. The Buzzards. Martin Armstrong. BLA; HBMV; POTE; TwCV
When evening comes. Yakamochi, *tr. fr. Japanese by* Arthur Waley. *Fr.* Manyo Shu. AWP; JAWP; LiTW; WBP
When evening winds, with ghostly violining. Evening by the Sea, the Plovers Fly. Richard Leon Spain. MuM
When every least commander's will best soldiers had obeyed. Homer. *Fr.* The Iliad, III. ReEn
When every lip invokes young loveliness. To L. C. Lucy Hawkins. HBMV
When Fabre took his children locust hunting. The Locust Hunt. Philip Murray. NePoAm-2
When face to face we stand. Paradox. Angelina W. Grimké. CDC
When Faction in league with the treacherous Gaul. The Lords of the Main. Joseph Stansbury. IAP; PAH
When fair Columbia was a child. The Daughter's Rebellion. Francis Hopkinson. PAH
When faith and love, which parted from thee never. On the Religious Memory of Mrs. Catherine Thomson [*or* Sonnet]. Milton. ES; OBS; PeBoSo
When faith in friends bear fruit and foolish fancies fade. Davy Dicar's Dream. Thomas Churchyard. ReIE
When faith in God goes, man, the thinker, loses his greatest thought. Have You Lost Faith? *Unknown.* WBLP
When Faithorne heard that his friend was dead. Fult Faithorne. William Aspenwall Bradley. BAP
When fallen I lay on the torn field. The Nurse. Iosif Utkin. RuPo
When falls the snow, lo! every herb and tree. Flowers of Snow. Tsurayuki. OnPM
When falls the soldier brave. Sentinel Songs. Abram J. Ryan. DD; GA; HBV; LPS-2
When far-spent night persuades each mortal eye. Astrophel and Stella, XCIX. Sir Philip Sidney. MaPo; OBSC; ReEn; SiPS
When Fate equips her sons, us fools, to take. The Road of Life. Yevgeny Abramovich Boratynsky. TrRV
When Father Carves the Duck. Ernest V. Wright. FaFP; PTA-2; TreF
When father comes from Gunjiwump. He Comes. Sam Walter Foss. *Fr.* Father's Journey. FAOV
When father goes to Gunjiwump. He Goes. Sam Walter Foss. *Fr.* Father's Journey. FAOV
When Father goes to town with me to buy my Sunday hat. When Polly Buys a Hat. E. Hill. BoTP
When Father Played Baseball. Edgar A. Guest. PEDC
When father takes his spade to dig. The Robin. Laurence Alma-Tadema. BoTP; GFA; OTPC (1946 ed.)
When Father's birthday comes around. Father's Birthday Cake. Ada Lorraine Jex. GFA
When Father's come from some long trip. 'Round Father's Grip. Strickland Gillilan. FAOV
When February sun shines cold. Late Winter. Philip Henry Savage. PCH
When fell thy dreadful shadow and it seemed. Sorrow. Reginald C. Eva. OQP; QP-2
When fiddlers play their tunes, you may sometimes hear. Fairy-Music. Rose Fyleman. HH; TSW; TSWC
When fields here lose their colour, when the wood. The Hedge-Row Story. Lilian Bowes-Lyon. POTE
When fierce political debate. Jolly Jack. Thackeray. HBV
When first a gentle kiss. A Sum of Kisses [*or* Nisé]. Juan Meléndez Valdés. AnSpL-2; OnPM
When First by Force of Fatal Destiny. *Unknown.* ReIE
When first, descending from the moorlands. Extempore Effusion upon the Death of James Hogg. Wordsworth. BPN; EmBrPo; FiP; MyFE; OBRV; PoD; PtP; TriL
When first Diana leaves her bed. The Progress of Beauty. Swift. RiBV
When first eternity stooped to nought. The Choice. Thomas Traherne. EPS
When First I Came Here. Edward Thomas. UnPo (3d ed.)
When first I came to be a man, of twenty years, or so. John o' Badenyon. John Skinner. EBSV
When first I came to Frisco, boys, I went upon a spree. Off to Sea Once More, *vers.* II. *Unknown.* ShS
When first I drew the breath of life. The Distressed Sailor's Garland. *Unknown.* SG
When first I ended, then I first began. The Paradox. Michael Drayton. Idea, LXII, *also in* Idea's Mirrour, L. BLV; PIAE; TrGrPo
When first I looked into thy glorious eyes. To Edgar A[llan] Poe. Sarah Helen Whitman. Sonnets from the Series Relating to Edgar Allan Poe, II. AA; DD; GA
When first I made. Summer Vacation. Wordsworth. *Fr.* The Prelude. ERP; OBRV
When First I Saw Her. George Edward Woodberry. Wild Eden, V. AA; BAP; HBV
When first I saw our banner wave. Astraea at the Capitol. Whittier. PAH
When first I saw sweet Peggy. The Low-backed Car. Samuel Lover. HBV; LPS-1
When first I saw you at my door. The Way of a Cat. Margaret E. Bruner. CIV
When first I saw you in the curious street. German Prisoners. Joseph Johnston Lee. BLP; MaRV
When first I started out cow-driving, I drove them on the square. The Rustler. *Unknown.* CoSo
When first I thee beheld, in colors black and white. The Lover Declareth His Affection, Together with the Cause Thereof. George Gascoigne. TuPP
When first I took to cutlass, blunderbuss and gun. The Ballad of O'Bruadir. F. R. Higgins. OBMV
When first mine eyes did view and mark. Sir Thomas Wyatt. SiPS
When first mine Infant-Ear. Christendom. Thomas Traherne. PoEL-2
When first my brave Johnnie lad. Johnnie, Cock Up Your Beaver. Burns. AtBAP; CBE
When first my verse of heavenly joys made mention. Jordan. George Herbert. ATP; EPS; MePo; OBS; PoFS; SeEP

When First My Way [to Fair I Took]. A. E. Housman. Last Poems, XXXV. EmBrPo; EnLi-2 (1949 ed.); EnLit; MoPW; TCPD; TwP
When first that horse, within whose populous womb. Death's Songsters. Dante Gabriel Rossetti. The House of Life, LXXXVII. PoVP; ViPo
When first the bride and bridegroom wed. At Last. Richard Henry Stoddard. HBV
When first the busy, clumsy tongue is stilled. Supersensual. Evelyn Underhill. WGRP
When first the college rolls receive his name. The Scholar's Life. Samuel Johnson. *Fr.* The Vanity of Human Wishes. FaBoEn; OBEC; SeCePo
When First the Coppered Ramparts Were Aglow. Stefan George, *tr. fr. German by* David Luke. AnGP
When first the crocus thrusts its point of gold. A Touch of Nature. Thomas Bailey Aldrich. ADAH; SN
When first the fiery-mantled Sun. Ode to Winter. Thomas Campbell. BSV; EBSV; EV-4; GTBS; GTBS-D; GTBS-W; GTSE; GTSL
When first the magic [*or* magick] of thine eye. The Vow-Breaker. Henry King. OBS; SeEP
When first the Pleiads, children of Atlas, arise. The Sign of the Pleiads. Hesiod. *Fr.* Works and Days. OxBG
When first the post arrived at my tent. King Henry to Rosamond. Michael Drayton. *Fr.* England's Heroical Epistles. OBSC
When first the unflowering fern-forest. Darwinism. Agnes Mary Frances Robinson. VA
When first these eyes beheld with great delight. Thomas Watson. *Fr.* Hecatompathia. ReIE
When first thou camest, gentle, shy, and fond. The Mother's Heart. Caroline Elizabeth Sarah Norton. LPS-1; MOAH
When first thou didst entice to thee my heart. Affliction. George Herbert. CoEV; EPS; EV-2; LiTB; MaPo; MeLP; MePo; NBE; OBS; OxBoCh
When first Thou on me, Lord, wroughtest Thy sweet print. The Ebb and Flow. Edward Taylor. AmP; AmPP; AnNE; CoV
When first thy eyes unveil, give thy soul leave. Early Rising and Prayer. Henry Vaughan. EV-2
When first thy sweet and gracious eye. The Glance. George Herbert. EPS
When First to This Country a Stranger I Came, ***with music.*** *Unknown.* OuSiCo
When first we hear the shy-come nightingales. John Clare. EG
When First We Met. Robert Bridges. *See* Triolet: "When first we met we did not guess."
When first we met, our souls stood up. Prelude I. Jamie Sexton Holme. LoPS
When first we parted, she. The Camomile. Al-Buqaira. MooP
When first you learn to read a clock. Clock. Harold Monro. MoP
When first you look upon her face. Leila. George Hill. APW
When first you sang a song to me. Your Songs. Gwendolyn B. Bennett. CDC
When first your glory shone upon my face. Commemoration. Claude McKay. BANP
When fishes flew and forests walked. The Donkey. G. K. Chesterton. ACP (1952 ed.); BLV; BMEP; CaAE; CBOV; GoBC; GTBS-D; MaRV; MBP; MM; MoBrPo; NeHB; NeMA; OBEV (new ed.); PIAE; PoMa; PoRL; POT; POTE; PoTo; QS; ShBV-1; StaSt; StJW; TCEP; TCPD; TOP; TwCV; WGRP; WP
When fishes set umbrellas up. Sing-Song Verses. Christina Rossetti. *Fr.* Sing-Song. BoN
When flighting-time is on I go. The Birdcatcher. Ralph Hodgson. AtBAP; MBP; MoBrPo; NeMA
When Flora Had O'erfret the Firth. *Unknown.* EBSV; OBEV
"When Flora with her fragrant flowers." Sir Andrew Barton. *Unknown.* SG
When flowers thrust their heads above the ground. Bloom. Alfred Kreymborg. HBMV; TSW
When foolish kings, at odds with swift-paced Time. Two Heroes. Harriet Monroe. *Fr.* Commemoration Ode. OHIP
When for love it was fain of. In As Much . . . "Æ." ChMo; CMP
When for the thorns with which I long, too long. The Coronet. Andrew Marvell. CenL; CoEV; ElSeCe; LoBV; MeLP; MePo; OBS; OxBoCh; SeCV-1
When forced to wait and wait for luncheon. Assorted Relishes. Richard Armour. WhC
When, forehead full of torments hot and red. Les Chercheuses de poux. Arthur Rimbaud. AWP
When formed our band, we are all well manned. California. *Unknown.* AS
When fortune's blind goddess. Bonnie Black Bess. *Unknown.* CoSo; CSF
When Fortune's shield protects thee, then beware. Fortune's Treachery. Judah Halevi. TrJP
When forty winters shall besiege thy brow. Sonnets, II. Shakespeare. EG; EM-1; LiTB; OBSC; PeBoSo; ReEn; ReIE; SiCE; TwP
When foxes eat the last gold grape. Escape. Elinor Wylie. AnFE; APA; CoAnAm; GBV (1952 ed.); LiTA; MAP; MoAmPo; MOAP; PFY; TBM; ThWaDe; TwAmPo
When frail nature can no more. What Is Excellent Is Permanent. Emerson. GrCo-1
When frank, straightforward hearts defile. The Best Way. Walter C. Smith. EBSV
When Freedom, dressed in bloodstained vest. Freedom's War Song [*or* Ode to Liberty]. Thomas Chatterton. *Fr.* Goddwyn. BLV; PoFr; TrGrPo
When Freedom, fair Freedom, her banner display'd. Truxton's Victory. *Unknown.* PAH
When freedom from her home was driven. The Hills Were Made for Freedom. William Goldsmith Brown. PoFr
When Freedom, from her mountain height. The American Flag. Joseph Rodman Drake. AA; APW; BAP; BAV; DD; DDA; FaBoBe; FaFP; FOAH; GN; HBV; HBVY; HH; IAP; LBAP; LEAP; LPS-2; MaRV; MC; OBAV; OnHT; OTPC; PaA; PAH; PAP; PEOR; PGD; PIR; PoFr; PTA-1; TCAP; TreF; TVSH; WBLP
When Freedom, on her natal day. The Moral Warfare. Whittier. AnNE; CoV; IAP; PEOR; PoFr
When fresh grass-blades and leaves appear. Canzo. Bernard de Ventadour. LiTW
When friends are met o'er merry cheer. Song. Sir Walter Scott. *Fr.* The Doom of Devorgoil. EmBrPo
When from afar these mountain tops I view. Sonnet of the Mountain. Mellin de Saint-Gelais. AWP
When from Eternity were separate. Ceremonial Ode Intended for a University. Lascelles Abercrombie. OBVV
When from her winter-prison. Spring. *Unknown.* SUS
When from His throne the Godhead bowed. A Christmas Song. Laurence Housman. SDH
When from my fumbling hand the tired pen falls. The Scribe's Prayer. Robert Service. TrPWD
When from my lips the last faint sigh is blown. An Epicurean's Epitaph. Aubrey Thomas De Vere. VA
When from the Calyx-Canopy of Night. Freda Laughton. NeIP
When from the chrysalis of the tomb. On John Grubb. *Unknown.* WhC
When from the gloom of earth we see the sky. The Void Between. John Lancaster Spalding. *Fr.* God and the Soul. AA
When from the hush of this cool wood. The Cell. George Rostrevor Hamilton. GTML; TrPWD
When from the tower, like some big flower. The Child in the House. Madison Cawein. FAOV
When, from the tower whence I derive love's heaven. Sonnet. *Unknown.* *Fr.* Zepheria. ElL
When from the vaulted wonder of the sky. Faith's Vista. Henry Abbey. AA
When from the wanderer's lips these words had fallen. The Parsonage. Wordsworth. *Fr.* The Excursion. ERP
When from the wars I do return. William Sampson. *Fr.* The Vow Breaker. TuPP
When from the West dark shadows creep. The Journey's End. Henry Lee Smith. PoP
When from the world I shall [*or* should] be ta'en. Sing No Sad Songs for Me. *Unknown.* LO; TriL
When from this good world I depart. The Epitaph. John Alexander Bouquet. MaRV
When from this prison drear. Ode to Felipe Ruiz. Luis de León. TeCS
When frost is shining on the trees. At Mrs. Appleby's. Elizabeth Upham McWebb. BrR; SiSoSe; StVeCh (1955 ed.); TiPo
When, full of warm and eager love. Snowdrop. William Wetmore Story. HBV; PR
When furrowed fields of shaded brown. The Canadian Rossignol. Edward William Thomson. CaP; CPG; OCL
When fury sings like nothing, like a war. Variations on a Theme. John Hay. NePoAm
When gadding snow makes hill-sides white. Winter. Charles Mair. PeCV
When Gathering Clouds. Sir Robert Grant. MaRV (Faith and Hope.) BPP
When gentle winds are blowing. Land and Sea. Moschus. GrR
When George the King would punish folk. How We Became a Nation. Harriet Prescott Spofford. MC; PAH
When George the Third was reigning a hundred years ago. A Ballad for a Boy [*or* The Two Captains]. William Johnson Cory. LH; PECK
When George's Grandmamma was told. George. Hilaire Belloc. FiBHP; GoTP; YT
When God at first made man. The Pulley [*or* The Gifts of God]. George Herbert. AnFE; AtBAP; ATP; AWP; BCEP; BEL; BLV; BoLiVe; CaAE; CBOV; CenL; CoBE; CoEV; ElSeCe; EM-1; EnL; EnLi-1; EPS; EV-2; ExPo; FaBoEn; GTBS; GTBS-D; GTBS-W; GTSE;

GTSL; HBV; InPo; LiTB; LiTG; LPS-3; MaRV; MePo; OAEP; OBEV; OBS; OtMeF; OuHeWo; OxBoCh; PoFS; PreP; ReaPo; ReEn; RiBV; SeCeV; SeCL; SeCV-1; SeEP; TCEP; TrGrPo; TwCrTr; TwHP; TyEnPo; UnPo (1st ed.); ViBoPo; WHA
When God gave to all men. Ship-Love. Ethel E. Mannin. NLK
When God had finished Master Messerin. Sonnet: Of the Making of Master Messerin [*or* The Making of Master Messerin]. Rustico di Filippo. AWP; JAWP; LiTW; LyMA; OnPM; WBP
When God had finished the stars and whirl of coloured suns. Frederick W. Harvey. Ducks, III. PC; QS; YT
When God Lets My Body Be. E. E. Cummings. ChMo; MAP; MoAB; MoAmPo
When God of old came down from Heaven. Whitsunday. John Keble. OBRV
When God ordained the restless life of man. The First Chorus. George Gascoigne. *Fr.* The Glass of Government. Po
"When God put man in a garden." King Alfred Answers the Danes. G. K. Chesterton. *Fr.* The Ballad of the White Horse. HBV; OxBoCh
When God reveals his plans to men. An Eclipse. Pindar. OxBG
When God sends out His company to travel through the stars. The Wrestler. Sir Charles G. D. Roberts. BMEP
When God was born of Mary free. Psallite Gaudentes. *Unknown.* AnEC
When God was making the world. The World in Making. Sir Gilbert Parker. CaP; CPG; OCL
When God, who is forever free. Liberty. Michael Chazarian Nalbandian. PoFr
When Gods Had Fram'd the Sweet of Women's Face. Robert Greene. *Fr.* Tullie's Love. ReIE (Love and Jealousy.) ElL
When gold was found in forty-nine [*or* forty-eight] the people thought 'twas gas. The Fools of Forty-nine. *Unknown.* CoSo; CSF
When golden Autumn, wreath'd in ripen'd corn. Autumn and Winter. Thomas Chatterton. *Fr.* Elegy to the Memory of Mr. Thomas Philips of Fairford. RO
When Golden Flies upon My Carcass Come. Richard Eberhart. FiMAP
When golden Phoebus moved from the Ram. Anno Domini. John Bellenden. ACP (1926 ed.)
When golden ritual and scarlet rite. Akhnaton. Thomas S. Jones, Jr. AnAmPo; LA
When good King Arthur ruled this land. Mother Goose. BOHV; BoTP; HBV; HBVY; NA; OTPC; OxNR; PCH; PPL; RIS; SAS
When good-nights have been prattled, and prayers have been said. The Dance. Rudolph Chambers Lehmann. HBMV
When Good Queen Elizabeth Governed the Realm. Joseph Stansbury. IAP
When good St. David, as old writs record. In Honour of St. David's Day. *Unknown.* PrWP
When good St. Francis feeds his flock. In My Garden. Alma L. Gray. SaFP
When Goody O'Grumpity baked a cake. Goody O'Grumpity. Carol Ryrie Brink. FaPON; GaP
When gooseberries grow on the stem of a daisy. To Mollidusta. James Robinson Planché. NA
When Grandma, so very old, was near death. Grandma, May She Rest in Peace, Died. Moyshe Kulbak. OnCuPl
When Grandmother comes to our house. The Grandmother. Elizabeth Madox Roberts. GaP; MPB
When Grandmother Polly had married and gone. The Wolves. Elizabeth Madox Roberts. UTS
When Grandpa Was a Little Boy. Malcolm Douglas. PEOR
When Granite mines employed a thousand men. Granite. John C. Fröhlicher. DDA
When Grasshopper, chirping late. Fall of the Year. Henry Ellison. OBVV
When green as a river was the barley. Daphne. Edith Sitwell. HBMV
When Green Buds Hang in the Elm. A. E. Housman. More Poems, IX. MoP
When gripping grief the heart doth wound. Music's Silver Sound. Shakespeare. *Fr.* Romeo and Juliet, IV, v. GN; HH
When groping farms are lanterned up. A Country God. Edmund Blunden. MBP; MoBrPo
When Handiman shaves Herr von Wolf. Martial, *tr. fr. Latin by* "T. W. M." Epigrams, VII, 83. LaP
When hard luck overtakes you. Hard Luck. Langston Hughes. NP
When, hardly moving, you decorate night's hush. The Waters of Life. Humbert Wolfe. MBP; MoBrPo; NP
When, having watched for a long time the trees. Grove and Building. Edgar Bowers. NePoEA
When hawthorn buds are creaming white. The Chimney-Sweeps of Cheltenham. Alfred Noyes. VOD
When He appoints to meet thee, go thou forth. Specula. Thomas Edward Brown. OQP; QP-1
When he came to the sweet flower of his growth. Pelops. Pindar. *Fr.* Olympian. Odes. OxBG
When he entered on my heart. The House of the Heart. Siraj. MooP
When He Goes to Play with the Boys. Strickland W. Gillilan. PEDC
When he had cut down the ardent youth in his spacious courts. Nicholas Kazantzakis. *Fr.* The Odyssey. MoGP
When he had left the mountains and received. Childhood. Wordsworth. *Fr.* The Prelude, I. CoBE
When he is a little chap. Sleep. John Banister Tabb. PC
When he killed the Mudjokivis. The Modern Hiawatha. George A. Strong. *Fr.* The Song of Milkanwatha. BBV (1951 ed.); FaFP; LiTG; ShBV-1; SiTL. *See also* He killed the noble Mudjokivis.
When he measured out the spirit tower. The Spirit Tower. *Unknown.* WhP
When he protested, not too solemnly. Erasmus. E. A. Robinson. TwP
When he pushed his bush of black hair off his brow. Sicilian Cyclamens. D. H. Lawrence. ChMP; MoVE
When He returns, and finds the world so drear. When We Are All Asleep. Robert Buchanan. VA
When he runs hunting the chipmunk stretches. Chipmunk. Marie de L. Welch. PoeMoYo
When he saw the multitude [*or* people] he went up into a mountain. St. Matthew, Bible, *N.T.* ReIE
When he sees red lanterns. Fisherman of the Moon. José Gorostiza. TwSpPo
When he stepped within. The Murder of Neoptolemus. Euripides. *Fr.* Andromache. GrR
When he takes a bath, the Antelope. Antelope. William Jay Smith. TiPo (1959 ed.)
When He Thought Himself Contemned. Thomas Howell. ElL, *3 sts.*; ReIE; TuPP
When he was a lad he served a term. President Garfield. *Unknown.* PA
When he was shot he toppled to the ground. Shot Who? Jim Lane! Merrill Moore. MAP; MoAmPo; MOAP; SPP
When he was young and beautiful and bold. Peer Gynt. Charles Hamilton Sorley. HBMV
When he was young, and clad in green. Why Sould Nocht Allane Honorit Be? *Unknown.* EBSV
When he was young, his parents saw (as parents by the million see). How He Turned Out. Edwin Meade Robinson. PCN
When he went blundering back to God. Of [*or* To] One Self-slain. Charles Hanson Towne. BAP; BPP; LEAP; SBMV; WGRP
When He Who Adores Thee. Thomas Moore. *See* Pro Patria Mori.
When he, who is the unforgiven. The Unforgiven. E. A. Robinson. ChMo; CMP
When He Would Have His Verses Read. Robert Herrick. EnL; NBE; OAEP; OBS; SeCV-1; SeEP
When, head high in corn, I walked with my mother the long, golden meadows. The Walk. Leonard Clark. AtBAP
When hearts have once mingled. The Nest of Love. Shelley. *Fr.* Lines: "When the lamp is shattered." RO
When heaven with a cheek's red hue. The Girdle. Paul Valéry. TrFP
When heaven would strive to do the best she can. Michael Drayton. LO
When heavy, dark, continued, a'-day rains. Burns. *Fr.* The Brigs of Ayr. MCCG
When Helen first saw wrinkles in her face. Wrinkles [*or* Lyrics to Ianthe]. Walter Savage Landor. BPN; EnLoPo; VA
When Helen Lived. W. B. Yeats. ViBoPo
When her soul flies to the predestined dancing-place. Her Courage. W. B. Yeats. Upon a Dying Lady, VI. LiTB
When Heracles was nearly ten months old. Domestic Scene. Theocritus. *Fr.* Idylls. GrR
When Hercules did use to spin. The Weavers' Song. Thomas Deloney. *Fr.* Jack of Newbury. EV-2; SiCE
When he's returned I'll tell him—oh. A. J. J. A. E. Housman. BoFr
When hills and plains are powdered white. The Shepherd Wind. Virna Sheard. CPG
When his bones are as seaweed, when his sweet tongue is parched. The White Rainbow. Starr Nelson. GoYe
When Hitler was the Devil. The Silent Generation. Louis Simpson. NePoAm-2
When Hölderlin started from Bordeaux. Hölderlin's Journey. Edwin Muir. PtP; TriL
When Hsüang Tsung, great emperor. Poisoned in Search of the Medicine of Immortality. Sheila Wingfield. PoN
When Human Folk put out the light. Kitten's Night Thoughts. Oliver Herford. BoChLi; MPB
When I a Lover Pale Do See. *Unknown.* SeCL
When I a verse shall make. His Prayer to Ben Jonson. Robert Herrick. AEV; BLV; BoLiVe; ElSeCe; EM-1; EnL; EnLit; EPS; OAEP; OBS; OxBoLi; PtP; ReEn; SeCeV; SeCV-1; SeEP; TrGrPo; UnPo; WP

When I admire the rose. The Rose [*or* A Fancy]. Thomas Lodge. *Fr.* The Life and Death of William Longbeard. EIL; OBSC
When I adore thee. *Unknown.* SeCSL
When I adore you and you have me in scorne. *Unknown.* SeCSL
When I am a man and can do as I wish. The Conjuror. E. V. Lucas. BoChLi; PoMS
When I am alone, and quite alone. Hide and Seek. "Robin Christopher." RIS; StaSt
When I am alone, to dream. Nocturne. Shahriyar. PeP
When I am asked by some rich man to dine. Diphilus, *tr. fr. Greek by* F. A. Paley. GrPo
When I am buried, all my thoughts and acts. Biography. John Masefield. ChMo; CMP
When I Am Dead. Georgia Douglas Johnson. CDC
When I Am Dead. John G. Neihardt. HBMV; MAP
When I Am Dead. Sir Rennell Rodd. VA
When I am Dead. Christina Rossetti. *See* Song: "When I am dead, my dearest."
When I Am Dead. Albert Stillman. InMe
When I Am Dead. *Unknown.* OxBoLi
When I am dead, ah, shall I then remember. If a Man Die [*or* Conjecture]. Florence Hamilton. BAP; MaRV
When I am dead and deep in dust. Reconciliation. J. U. Nicolson. HBMV
When I am dead and gone to dust. When I Am Dead. Albert Stillman. InMe
When I am dead and I am quite forgot. Tuscan Cypress, VII. Agnes Mary Frances Robinson. VA
When I am dead and nervous hands have thrust. When I Am Dead. John G. Neihardt. HBMV; MAP
When I am dead and over me bright April. I Shall Not Care. Sara Teasdale. AnEnPo; BAP; BTP; ChMo; CMP; HBV; LBMV; MAP; MoAmPo; NeMA; PFY; TCPD; TrGrPo; TwCV
When I Am Dead and Sister to the Dust. Elsa Barker. BAP; HBV; LBMV
When I am dead & thou would'st try. *Unknown.* SeCSL
When I am dead, I hope it may be said. On His Books [*or* Epigram]. Hilaire Belloc. ACP (1952 ed.); MBP; MoBrPo; OtMeF; OxBoLi; SiTL; WhC
When I am dead I want you to dress me. When I Am Dead. *Unknown.* OxBoLi
When I Am Dead, My Dearest. Christina Rossetti. *See* Song: "When I am dead, my dearest."
When I am dead, my spirit. When I Am Dead. Sir Rennell Rodd. VA
When I am dead, no pageant train. Dirge of Alaric the Visigoth. Edward Everett. BeLS; LPS-3
When I am dead unto myself, and let. De Profundis. George Macdonald. EPN
When I am dead, withhold, I pray, your blooming legacy. When I Am Dead. Georgia Douglas Johnson. CDC
When I am dead you'll find it hard. He and She. Eugene Fitch Ware. BOHV; YaD
When I am deeply burdened, desolate. Venetian Sonnets, VII. August, Graf von Platen. AnGP
When I am drinking, drink with me. What Makes a Friend. *Unknown.* OxBG
When I am fed, with no occupation or care, I am glad. Drinking at the Village. Lu Yu. WhP
When I am gone and all my songs are still. Here Lies . . . Michael Lewis. YT
When I am gone, brook no complaining. Last Words. Annette von Droste-Hülshoff. CAW
When I am grown an *hombre.* Ambition. Edith Agnew. GaP; TiPo
When I am grown to man's estate. Looking Forward. Robert Louis Stevenson. CenHV; InP; OTPC (1946 ed.); PoVP; VLEP
When I am in a great city, I know that I despair. City-Life. D. H. Lawrence. OAEP (2d ed.)
When I am in my grave. Grave. Waring Cuney. PoNe
When I am listening to the sweet, tuneful airs of my country. I'r hen iaith a'i chaneuon. Walter Dowding. MoWP
When I am living in the Midlands. The South Country. Hilaire Belloc. ACP (1952 ed.); EPP; GoBC; HBV; JKCP; LBBV; MBP; MoBrPo; OBVV; PoeT; POTE; ShBV-3; TCPD; TwCV
When I am lost in the deep body of the mist on a hill. Lines. Yone Noguchi. NP
When I am lying cold and dead. What No Man Knoweth. Hugh Francis Blunt. CAW
When I am lonely. The Monk Ryozen, *tr. fr. Japanese by* Kenneth Rexroth. OnPJ
When I am lying under. What If Remembrance? Richard Eberhart. FiMAP
When I Am Old. Caroline Atherton Briggs Mason. BLPA; NeHB
When I Am Old. Marjorie Meeker. TBM
When I am old—and O, how soon. When I Am Old. Caroline Atherton Briggs Mason. BLPA; NeHB
When I am old and passionless. To the Woman I Will Be Fifty Years Hence. Virginia Moore. BAP
When I am old, and sadly steal apart. In Tempore Senectutis. Ernest Dowson. POTT; VLEP
When I am old and think of the old days. The Last Memory. Arthur Symons. HBV
When I am old and tutored by. A Franciscan Prayer. Enid Dinnis. CAW; SaFP
When I am old and you are young. When I Am Old. Marjorie Meeker. TBM
When I am old, I'll sit within my room. Twilight Musing. Mabel Langdon. CAG
When I am overmatched by petty cares. The Comfort of the Stars. Richard Burton. AnAmPo; LA; NLK
When I Am Plagued. Aleksey Konstantinovich Tolstoy, *tr. fr. Russian by* Babette Deutsch. TrRV
When I am playing by myself. Water Noises. Elizabeth Madox Roberts. GFA; GoBP; NP; RAR; SP; VOD
When I am safely laid away. My Last Will. Sir Walter Raleigh. MM
When I am sore beset I seek some quiet place. Meditation. Antoinette Goetschius. MaRV
When I am standing on a mountain crest. Love in the Winds. Richard Hovey. AA; HBV; LEAP; LoPo; MAP; MoAmPo (1942 ed.); PoeMoYo; PoMa
When I am the President. *Unknown.* GoTP
When I am tired of earnest men. Martin. Joyce Kilmer. BAP; CP; DDA; LBMV; MAP; NeMA; NV; OBAV; OnPP; PFY; PoeMoYo; PYM; VOD
When I am tired, the Bible is my bed. The Bible. *Unknown.* OQP; QP-1
When I am turned to moulding dust. George Henry Boker. *Fr.* The Book of the Dead. MOAP
When I am very earnestly digging. Pause. Mary Ursula Bethell. AnNZ
When I am walking down the street. New Shoes. Marjorie Seymour Watts. PCH
When I am walking sadly or triumphantly. The Shadow. Arthur Symons. OBVV
When I am weary, throng'd with the cares of the vain day. Day's End. Laurence Binyon. OBVV
When I asked you for a kiss. The Third Kiss: Butterfly Kisses. Johannes Secundus. LaP
When I Awake, I Am Still with Thee. Harriet Beecher Stowe. *See* Still, Still with Thee.
When I awoke in the night I heard the trees sighing. The Seas. Stella Gibbons. AlDL
When I began my love to sow. Husbandry. William Hammond. SeCL
When I began to enquire. The Universal Heart of Man. Wordsworth. *Fr.* The Prelude. TOP
When I beheld the poet blind, yet bold. On [Mr. Milton's] "Paradise Lost." Andrew Marvell. OAEP; PtP; SeEP
When I Behold. *Unknown.* ElSeCe
(Song: "When I behold my mistress' face.") SeCL
When I behold a for[r]est spread. Art above Nature; to Julia. Robert Herrick. BrBE; EM-1
When I behold Becchina in a rage. Sonnet: Of Becchina in a Rage. Cecco Angiolieri da Siena. AWP; JAWP; WBP
When I behold how black, immortal ink. Silet. Ezra Pound. MAP; MoAB; MoAmPo
When I behold my mistress' face. When I Behold [*or* Song]. *Unknown.* ElSeCe; SeCL
When I behold that beauty's [*or* beauties] wonderment. Amoretti, XXIV. Spenser. BEL; HBV; PeBoSo
When I behold the bier, my last and posting horse. The Latter Day [*or* Bethinking Himself of His End, Writeth Thus]. Thomas, Lord Vaux. PoLi; SiCE
When I behold the heaven of thy face. To Cynthia. Sir Francis Kynaston. AEV
When I behold the heavens as in their prime. Anne Bradstreet. *Fr.* Contemplations. BAV; MaRV
When I behold the lacelike tracery. To a Fossil Fern. John A. Foote. CAG
When I behold the sky. Night of Stars. Luis de León. TeCS
When I behold thee, blameless Williamson. Sonnet: True Ambition. Benjamin Stillingfleet. OBEC
When I beneath the cold red earth am sleeping. Last Verses. William Motherwell. HBV
When I bethink me of the care. Precarious Life of Man. Euripides. *Fr.* Hippolytus. GrR
When I bethink[e] me on that speech whilere. Mutability. Spenser. *Fr.* The Faerie Queene, VII. CoEV; OxBoCh; ReEn; TwCrTr
When I but hear her sing, I fare. Upon a Rare Voice. Owen Felltham. SeCL
When I but think upon the great dead days. Piere Vidal Old. Ezra Pound. MoAB
When I buy a bun. Buns for Tea. Dorothy M. Richardson. VOD (1935 ed.); YT
When I Buy Pictures. Marianne Moore. OxBA
When I came back to my hills. Returning. Olive Tilford Dargan. NoCaPo
When I Came from Colchis. W. S. Merwin. NePoEA

When I came home at evening. The Chaplet. Witter Bynner. PFY; PoeMoYo
When I came into Witches' Town. Witches' Town. *Unknown.* CAG
When I came last to Ludlow. Friends. A. E. Housman. A Shropshire Lad, LVIII. EmBrPo; PoVP; SeCePo
When I can hold a stone within my hand. Rumination. Richard Eberhart. FiMAP; LiTA; LiTM (rev. ed.)
When I can make my thoughts come forth. Thoughts. Sara Teasdale. ChMo; CMP; PoTo
When I can read my title clear/ to mansions in the skies. The Saint's Delight. *Unknown.* TrAS
When I carefully consider the curious habits of dogs. Meditatio. Ezra Pound. FaBoCh; LoGBV
When I climb up. Drinking Fountain. Marchette Chute. TiPo (1959 ed.)
When I come back from secret dreams. The Name. Anna Hempstead Branch. SBMV
When I come down to sleep death's endless night. My City. James Weldon Johnson. BANP; CDC; PoNe
When I come groping back through mists of sleep. Mortal Combat. Alice Fay di Castagnola. GoYe
When I come in f'om de co'n-fiel' aftah wo'kin' ha'd all day. At Candle-lightin' Time. Paul Laurence Dunbar. HOAH; IHA
When I come to die. Memento. Federico García Lorca. CoSP; OnPM
When I compare. Loss and Gain. Longfellow. PEOR; PTA-2
When I consider. Milton. *See* On His Blindness.
When I consider every thing that grows. Sonnets, XV. Shakespeare. AWP; BEL; CoBE; EM-1; EnLi-1; EPP; EtPaEn; OAEP; OBSC; OuHeWo; PeBoSo; PoFS; ReEn; ReIE; SiCE; TrGrPo; TwP; TyEnPo
When I Consider How My Light Is Spent. Milton. *See* On His Blindness.
When I consider how proud nations fall. One Who Dared to Die. Thomas Curtis Clark. ChIP
When I Consider Life. Dryden. *Fr.* Aureng-Zebe, IV, i. FiP
(Life a Cheat.) BCEP
When I consider life and its few years. Tears. Lizette Woodworth Reese. AA; BAP; BLP; BLV; CBOV; CP; HBV; HBVY; InP; LBMV; LEAP; LS; MAP; MaRV; MCCG; MM; MoAmPo; NeMA; OBAV; OQP; PC; PFY; PYM; QP-2; SPP; TCPD; TreFS; VOD; WGRP; WHA
When I consider life, 'tis all a cheat. When I Consider Life [*or* Life a Cheat]. Dryden. *Fr.* Aureng-Zebe. BCEP; FiP
When I consider, Thérèse. Upon Being Awakened at Night by My Four Year Old Daughter. Dachine Rainer. NePoAm-2
When I consider this, that bare. Life. Francis Burrows. PtOT
When I consider thy heavens, the work of thy fingers. *Fr.* Psalm VIII, Bible, *O.T.* FaPON; ImOP; InP
When I consider Thy heavens, the work of Thy fingers, the moon and the stars, which Thou hast ordained. James Oppenheim. *Fr.* Night. NV
When I consider Time and Space. Fences. Rebecca McCann. PoMa
When I considered it too closely. Meditation on Saviours. Robinson Jeffers. ChMo; CMP
When I contemplate all alone. In Memoriam A. H. H., LXXXIV. Tennyson. EmBrPo; EPN; GEPC; ViPo; VLEP
When I contemplate o'er me. The Night Serene. Luis de León. CAW; TrJP; WoL
When I could savour manna from the skies. On His Deafness. Joachim du Bellay. Les Amours, XXVI. TrFP
When I crept over the hill, broken with tears. The Comforters. Dora Sigerson Shorter. BMEP; CH; DiM; GTIV; HBMV; LBBV
When I decide I shall assemble you. Identity. Elizabeth Jennings. NePoEA
When I did part from thee the other night. Robert Tofte. *Fr.* Laura. ReIE
When I did wake this morn from sleep. Early Morn. W. H. Davies. CH; PoeT
When I Die. Fenton Johnson. CDC; PoNe
When I died [*or* dyed] last [*or* When last I died], and dear, I die. The Legacy. John Donne. AtBAP; EPS; TrGrPo
When I died, the circulating library. Seth Compton. Edgar Lee Masters. *Fr.* Spoon River Anthology. ChMo; CMP; LiTA; NP
When I do count the clock that tells the time. Sonnets, XII. Shakespeare. AWP; BEL; EG; EIL; ElSeCe; EM-1; EnLi-1; EV-1; FaFP; InPo; JAWP; LPS-3; OBSC; OuHeWo; PeBoSo; Po; REAL; ReEn; ReIE; SiCE; TOP; TwP; ViBoPo; WBP
When I dream of reading alone on the highest terrace. The Composition of Distances. Pien Chih-lin. LiTW
When I drift out on the Silver Sea. The Great Divide. Lew Sarett. BAP; HBMV
When I drive cab. After Anacreon. Lew Welch. NeAP
When I dyed last, and, deare, I dye. *See* When I died last . . .
When I Fall on My Knees, *with music.* *Unknown.* BoAN-2
When I first came here a dozen years ago. Old Mr. So-and-So. Malville Haller. NV
When I first put this uniform on. Song: Colonel. W. S. Gilbert. *Fr.* Patience. PoVP
When I first went a-wagoning, a-wagoning did go. The Jolly Wagoner. *Unknown.* TrAS
When I forsook my homely town. The Prodigal Son. A. E. Coppard. MBP; MoBrPo (1942 ed.)
When I forth fare beyond this narrow earth. After Death. Charles Francis Richardson. AA
When I from schools came to the city first. Misacmos of Himself, Who Loves to Be Worst in the Company. Sir John Harington. SiCE
When I gather the herbs in the land of Mei. The Philanderer. *Unknown.* *Fr.* Shi King. PoHN
When I gaze on the glistening faucets. Evolution. *Unknown.* DDA
"When I get rich" the children dream. Horizons. Rebecca McCann. PoMa
When I Get Time. Thomas L. Masson. BLPA
When I get up in the morning. Getting Up. Lilian McCrea. BoTP
Well I go a-courtin'. Liza Jane. *Unknown.* ABF
When I go away from you. The Taxi. Amy Lowell. AV; MAP; MoAmPo
When I go back to earth. The Answer. Sara Teasdale. LEAP; NP; NV; TCPD
When I go free. The Little Salamander. Walter de la Mare. BMEP; LBBV; NP
When I Go Home. Milton Lee. OQP; QP-2
When I Go Home. John Charles McNeill. NoCaPo
When I go [*or* goe] musing all alone. The Author's Abstract of Melancholy. Robert Burton. *Fr.* The Anatomy of Melancholy. OBS; SeCL
When I go riding. Dahlias. Edith Agnew. GaP
When I go to bed at night. At Night. Anne Blackwell Payne. GFA; UTS
When I go walking down the street. Food. Marchette Chute. BrR
When I goe musing all alone. *See* When I go musing all alone.
When I, good friends, was called to the Bar. The Judge's Song. W. S. Gilbert. *Fr.* Trial by Jury. PoVP
When I grew tired of gypsying. A Little House. Abigail Cresson. DDA
When I grow old and my quick blood is chilled. To ——. Muriel Stuart. AV
When I grow old I hope to be. Growing Old. Rose Henderson. BoChLi (1950 ed.)
When I grow old, if I should live till then. The Contented Bachelor. John Kendall. InMe
When I Grow Up. Rupert Sargent Holland. OTPC
When I grow up I'll carry a stick. Growing Up. Marchette Chute. GoBP
When I had a little leisure. The Flute. Wang Mou Fang. PoHN
When I had dreamed and dreamed what woman's beauty was. The Body. John Freeman. TCPD
When I had firmly answered "No." The Last Ride Together (from Her Point of View). James Kenneth Stephen. BOHV; CenHV; PA
When I had met my love the twentieth time. Her Merriment. W. H. Davies. EnLoPo
When I had money, money, O! Money. W. H. Davies. OBEV (new ed.); OBMV; OBVV
When I Had Need of Him. S. E. Kiser. BLRP
When I had turned Catullus into rhyme. Sonnet. Thomas Caulfield Irwin. IrPN
When I had wings, my brother. To a Seamew. Swinburne. BLA; EtS; MBP
When I ha'e a saxpence under my thoom. Todlin' Hame. *Unknown.* HBV
When I have a flask well laden. A Nota Bene. Karl Mikael Bellman. AnSL; OnPM
When I have a house—as I sometime may. Vagabond House. Don Blanding. BLPA
When I Have Borne in Memory [What Has Tamed]. Wordsworth. BPN; EM-2; EmBrPo; EnLit; EnRP; GTBS; GTBS-D; GTBS-W; GTSE; GTSL; MaPo; OBRV; PoFr; TyEnPo
(England, 1802, V.) OBEV; HBV
(London, 1802, IV.) ES
When I have ceased to break my wings. Wisdom. Sara Teasdale. *Fr.* Interlude: Songs Out of Sorrow. InP
When I have done consider. Advice to Leesome Merriness. Sir Richard Maitland. EBSV
When I have ended, then I see. Dedication. Laurence Housman. TrPWD

When I Have Fears [That I May Cease to Be]. Keats. ATP; AWP; BEL; BoLiVe; BPN; CBOV; CoBE; EM-2; EmBrPo; EnL; EnLi-2 (1949 ed.); EnLit; EnLP; EnRP; EPN; EPP; ERP; EV-4; GoTP; HBV; HoPM; InP; InPo; JAWP; KN; LEAP; LiTB; MaPo; MaRV; MCCG; OAEP; OBEV; OBRV; OnPM; OuHeWo; PeBoSo; PIAE; Po; PoE; PoFS; PoP; PoRA; PreP; ReaPo; SeCeV; TCEP; TOP; TreFS; TrGrPo; TwHP; TwP; TyEnPo; WBP; WHA
(Reflection.) PIR
(Sonnet: "When I have fears that I may cease to be.") CaAE; FiP; PoD; REAL
(Sonnet: Written in January, 1818.) ChER
(Terror of Death, The.) GTBS; GTBS-D; GTBS-W; GTSE; GTSL
When I have finished with this episode. When I Have Gone Weird Ways. John G. Neihardt. HBV; LBMV; OBAV
When I have folded up this tent. The Last Word. Frederic Lawrence Knowles. HBV
When I have forgotten your lips. The Desolate Lover. Eileen Shanahan. NeIP
When I have gone away. Sugawara Michizane, *tr. fr. Japanese by* I. W. Furukami. LiTW
When I Have Gone Weird Ways. John G. Neihardt. HBV; LBMV; OBAV
When I have heard small talk about great men. Grandeur of Ghosts. Siegfried Sassoon. AnFE; HaMV; MBP; MM; MoBrPo; OBMV; PtOT; TwCV
When I have lain an hour watching the skies. Clouds. John Jay Chapman. EtS
When I have lost my temper I have lost my reason, too. Temper. *Unknown.* PoToHe (new ed.)
When I have lost the power to feel the pang. Strangeness of Heart. Siegfried Sassoon. PtOT; TrJP
When I have rested dead a thousand years. Erosion. James Larkin Pearson. NoCaPo
When I have seen by Time's fell hand defaced. Sonnets, LXIV. Shakespeare. AWP; BEL; CoEV; ElL; ElSeCe; EM-1; EnL; EnLi-1 (1949 ed.); EnLit; EnLoPo; ES; Ev-1 FaFP; GTBS; GTBS-D; GTBS-W; GTSE; GTSL; InP; InPo; JAWP; LiTB; LiTL; LO; MCCG; OGSC; OuHeWo; PeBoSo; PFE; PoFS; PoRA; ReaPo; ReEn; ReIE; SeCeV; SiCE; TCEP; TOP; TwHP; TwP; ViBoPo; WBP
When I have sung the sweet songs and the sad. The Song You Love. William Alexander Percy. *Fr.* In New York. SPP
When I have told you all I know. In Limine. Struthers Burt. NoCaPo (1941 ed.)
When I have touched the end of days. The Gift of Work. Edwin Markham. DD
When I, having finished with things below. A Tired Doctor's Prayer. George David Stewart. PoP
When I hear laughter from a tavern door. Wilfrid Scawen Blunt. *Fr.* Esther; a Young Man's Tragedy. MBP; MoBrPo (1942 ed.); OBEV; OBMV; OBVV; TrGrPo; ViBoPo
When I hear the old men. A Song of Greatness. *Tr. by* Mary Austin. BoChLi; FaPON; TiPo
When I Heard at the Close of the Day. Walt Whitman. AmPP (4th ed.); AnEnPo; IAP; LEAP; NePA; OBAV; OxBA
When I Heard the Learn'd [*or* Learned] Astronomer. Walt Whitman. AlDL; AmPP; APW; ATP (1935 ed.); BLV; BoLiVe; CBOV; CV; IAP; InP; LoGBV; MAP; MaRV; MCCG; MoAmPo; MOAP; NeMA; OnPM; OQP; OuHeWo; OxBA; PFE; PG (1955 ed.); PoLFOT; PoMa; PreP; QP-2; TrGrPo; WHA; WoL; YT
When I in wild defiance fled. In Tribute. Vernal House. CaP
When I kneel down. Saying a Prayer. Rowena Bennett. MPB (1956 ed.)
When I Kneel down my prayers to say. Prayers. Flora Hastings. OTPC (1923 ed.)
When I Knew a Little Bit. Bhartrihari, *tr. fr. Sanskrit by* Arthur W. Ryder. OnPM
When I lay dead in Thessaly. In Thessaly. Clark Ashton Smith. DaM
When I leaned over a pool of black water. The King o' Spain's Daughter. Jeanne Robert Foster. BAP; HBMV
When I left Missouri River. A Forty-Niner Tells His Story. *Unknown.* IHA
When I left my girl. Hitomaro, *tr. fr. Japanese by* Kenneth Rexroth. OnPJ
When I lie burning in thine eye. Song. Thomas Stanley. ViBoPo
When I lie where shades of darkness. Fare Well. Walter de la Mare. CoBMV; GTBS-D; MoVE; OBEV (new ed.); POTE; TwCV
When I lived in Singapore. In Foreign Parts. Laura E. Richards. HBV; HBVY; LiL
When I look back across the waste of years. The Poet. Anita Grannis. HBMV
When I look back and say, of all our hours. A Prairie Ride. William Vaughn Moody. AnEnPo
When I look back upon my early days. Sonnets; a Sequence of Profane Love, XVII [XLV]. George Henry Boker. MOAP
When I look back upon my life nigh spent. A Prayer. George Macdonald. BSV; TrPWD
When I look forth at dawning, pool. Nature's Questioning. Thomas Hardy. BEL; CoBMV; EPN; InPo; MoPo; PoFS; ViP; ViPo
When I look in the mirror. Hysteria. Chu Shu Chen. OnPC
When I look into a glass. A Thought [*or* The Mirror]. W. H. Davies. GTML; GTSL; MoShBr; MoSiPe; POTE
When I look into my sons' eyes I see. Beyond Connecticut, beyond the Sea. John Peale Bishop. SPP
When I looke backe, and in my selfe behold. Youth. Thomas, Lord Vaux. EV-1
When I looked into your eyes. Reflections. Amy Lowell. *Fr.* Chinoiseries. AnAmPo; LA; NP
When I Loved Thee. Thomas Stanley. *See* Deposition from Beauty, A.
When I Loved You. Thomas Moore. ALV; HBV
(To ——.) EnLoPo
When I Loved You. Charles A. Wagner. InMe
When I loved you, I can't but allow. When I Loved You [*or* To ——]. Thomas Moore. ALV; EnLoPo; HBV
When I made answer, I began: "Alas!" Francesca da Rimini. Dante, *tr. by* Dante Gabriel Rossetti. *Fr.* Divina Commedia: Inferno. EmBrPo; EPN; EPP
When I marched away to war. Colleen Oge Asthore. *Unknown.* OnYI
When I meet the morning beam. The Immortal Part. A. E. Housman. A Shropshire Lad, XLIII. BrBE; MBP; MoBrPo; Po; POTT; PoVP; UnPo (3d ed.); VLEP
When I meet you, I greet you with a stare. The Silence. Anna Wickham. NP
When I more large thy praises forth shall show. Chloris, XLIV. William Smith. TuPP
When I move. Eventide. Yang Kuei-fei. PoHN
When I no more as now can find. Laughter and Tears. Tertius van Dyke. MaRV
When I opened your letter. A Thought of Marigolds. Janice Farrar. GoYe
When I pass down the street and see. Love, like a Drop of Dew. W. H. Davies. ChMo; CMP
When I pause before my mirror. Kakinomoto no Asomi Hitomaro, *tr. fr. Japanese by* I. W. Furukami. LiTW
When I Perceive the Sable of Your Hair. Elinor Wylie. *Fr.* One Person. ChMo; PeBoSo
(Sonnet: "When I perceive the sable of your hair.") LoPS; NP
When I Peruse the Conquer'd Fame. Walt Whitman. GTBS-W; MCCG; PoEL-5; PoMa
When I play on my fiddle in Dooney. The Fiddler of Dooney. W. B. Yeats. AlDL; BEL; FaBoCh; GTML; HBV; InP; LoGBV; MM; NeMA; OBVV; PoMa; TCPD; TiPo; TwCV; UnS; YT
When I, poor Lais, with my crown. Lais to Aphrodite. E. A. Robinson. MOAP
When I reflect how good a wife I've been. Sonnet for Myself. Mildred Plew Meigs. DDA
When I remark her golden hair. Jessie. Eugene Field. InMe
When I remember again. The Sparrow's Dirge. John Skelton. *Fr.* Phyllyp Sparowe. FaBoCh; LoGBV; SeCePo
When I remember them, those friends of mine. Three Friends of Mine. Longfellow. BAV; IAP
When I return I search for myself. On Going Home. Marjorie L. Agnew. GoYe
When I returned at sunset. Great City. Harold Monro. NP
When I ride into the mountains on my little broncho bird. A Cowboy Alone with His Conscience. James Barton Adams. SCC
When I ride my bicycle. Different Bicycles. Dorothy W. Baruch. FaPON; SUS; TiPo
When I run about all day. Night and Day. Mary Mapes Dodge. PRWS
When I Sail Away. Elizabeth Clark Hardy. *See* Some Time at Eve.
When I sailed out of Baltimore. A Child's Pet. W. H. Davies. CH; POT
When I saw that clumsy crow. Night Crow. Theodore Roethke. AmP; MoVE
When I saw the grapefruit drying, cherries in each center lying. Arrogance Repressed. John Betjeman. FiBHP
When I saw the woman's leg on the floor of the subway train. The Leg in the Subway. Oscar Williams. AnFE; CoAnAm; LiTM; NePA; TwAmPo
When I Saw You Last, Rose. Austin Dobson. BPN; CBOV; HBV; InP; YT
When I saw you, your hair newly put up. First Love. Toson Shimazaki. PoLJ
When I see a prairie schooner. The Prairie Schooner. William Everett Dale. HiLiAm

When I see a young tree. My Lady Is Compared to a Young Tree. Vachel Lindsay. ChMo; CMP
When I See Another's Pain. Mani Leib, *tr. fr. Yiddish by* Joseph Leftwich. TrJP
When I see birches bend to left and right. Birches. Robert Frost. AmPo; AmPP; AnNE; ChMo; CMP; CoBA; CoV; CP; CV; HaMV; HBMV; HiLiAm; IAP; LEAP; LiTA; LiTM; LoGBV; MAP; MAPA; MCCG; MoAB; MoAmPo; MoVE; NeMA; OxBA; PFY; PIAE; PoFS; PoRA; PreP; SBMV; TCPD; TOP; TreF; TrGrPo; TwAmPo; TwCV; UnPo (3d ed.)
When I See carved so clearly on your face. Two Solitudes. Evelyn Ames. GoYe
When I see childhood on the threshold seize. The Growth of Love, CXLIII [XLII]. Robert Bridges. GTML
When I see high on the tip-top twig. The Indigo Bird. Ethelwyn Wetherald. CPG
When I See Old Men. Raymond Souster. CaP
When I see the falling bombs. Conflict. F. R. Scott. BoCaPo; CaP; PeCV
When I see the first. Otomo no Yakamochi, *tr. fr. Japanese by* Kenneth Rexroth. LiTW; OnPJ
When I see the life of day. Nightfall. Siraj. MooP
When I Set Out for Lyonnesse. Thomas Hardy. GTSE; MBP; MoBrPo; NeMA; Po; PoTo; PoVP; SeCePo; ShBV-2; TCPD; TwCV; ViPo
When I shall answer Charon's call. Post-Mortem. Richard Hoffman. PIAE
When I shall come before Thy gate and stand. The Password. Reginald C. Eva. ChIP
When I shall die, the wind and rain will squander. The Impossible. Jules Laforgue. TrFP
When I shall go to sleep and wake again. At Waking. Ethelwyn Wetherald. CPG
When I Shall Hear You Coming. Barbara Young. BAP
When I sit up to bread and milk. At Breakfast. I. M. Mills. BoTP
When I some antique jar behold. To a Lady. John Gay. OBEV (new ed.)
When I spin round without a stop. Spinning Top. Frank Dempster Sherman. GFA
When I stand in the center of that man's madness. Reflection by a Mailbox. Stanley Kunitz. TrJP; WaP
When I step thimble heeled at an end of day. River Sawdde. Keidrych Rhys. MoWP
When I stepped homeward to my hill. Home-coming. Léonie Adams. HBMV; MAP; MoAmPo; MOAP; NeMA; NV; PoeMoYo; TSW; TSWC
When I Survey the Bright. William Habington. *See* Nox Nocti Indicat Scientiam.
When I Survey the Wondrous Cross. Isaac Watts. BePJ; EV-3; MaRV; OlF; WGRP
(Cross, The.) TriL
(Crucifixion to the World by the Cross of Christ.) BeR, *last 3 sts.*; EiPP; OBEC
When I think of all you've got. A Father's Heart Is Touched. Samuel Hoffenstein. FiBHP
When I think of it all I am so sad. Choucoune. Oswald Durand. PoNe
When I think of my kindness which is tentative and quiet. Kind. Josephine Miles. FiMAP
When I Think of the Hungry People. O-Shi-O, *tr. fr. Japanese.* MaRV
When I think of the last great round-up. The Cowboy's Dream [*or* The Great Round-up]. *Unknown.* ABF; CoSo; CSF
When I think of things denied me. Oh, No Cross That I May Carry! Alice Mortenson. BePJ
When I think on the happy days. Absence. *Unknown.* GTSL; LPS-1
When I think upon things three. Three Sorrowful Things. *Unknown.* MeEV
When I to you sometimes make friendly motion. To the Lady Rogers, of Her Unprofitable Sparing. Sir John Harington. SiCE
When I try to skate. Skating. Herbert Asquith. BoChLi; BrR; FaPON; StVeCh; SUS; TiPo
When I verse shall make. *See* When I a verse shall make.
When I Walk Alone. Charles Erskine Scott Wood. BAP
When I walk forth into the woods. Ode. Barnabe Barnes. *Fr.* Parthenophil and Parthenophe. TuPP
When I was a bachelor [*or* little boy],/ I lived by myself,/ And all the bread and cheese I got. Mother Goose. BoTP; GFA; HBV; OTPC; OxNR; Po; PPL; RIS; SAS
When I was a bachelor, brisk and young. Blue Bottle. *Unknown.* OuSiCo
When I was a bachelor, I lived by myself [*or* batchelor early and young]. Foggy, Foggy Dew [*or* The Foggy Dew]. *Unknown.* AS; CoMu; LiTB; LiTG; OxBoLi; SiTL
When I was a beggarly boy. Aladdin. James Russell Lowell. AnNE; APW; BAV; BBV (1951 ed.); BLP; HBV; MW; NeHB; OBAV; PoMS; PYM; StVeCh (1940 ed.); WaKn
When I was a boy. The Piper's Progress. Francis Sylvester Mahony. FiBHP
When I was a boy I heard the sea upstairs in a shell. Old Men Are Facts. Vivian Smith. NeLNL
When I was a boy I lived by myself. Posey-Boy. *Unknown.* APW
When I was a boy my mother often said to me. I Want a Girl. Will Dillon. TreFS
When I was a boy on the old plantation. The Grapevine Swing. Samuel Minturn Peck. POT
When I Was a Brave Cowboy, *with music. Unknown.* CoSo
When I was a burst of thunder. Memnon. Leslie Holdsworth Allen. BoAu
When I was a child I lay in dread. To the Wind. Vicente Riva Palacio. AnMP
When I was a child I saw. To a Child. Judith Wright. BoAV
When I was a child, my eldest cousin. Takis Plumis. Miltiades Malakassis. MoGP
When I was a child there was nothing. City Childhood. Selma Robinson. PIAE
When I Was a Cowboy, *with music. Unknown.* ABF
(Leadbelly's Chisholm Trail, *longer vers., with music.*) CoSo
When I was a cowboy I learned to throw the line. The Sporting Cowboy. *Unknown.* OuSiCo
When I was a cowboy way out on de western plains. When I Was a Cowboy [*or* Leadbelly's Chisholm Trail]. *Unknown.* ABF; CoSo
When I Was a Greenhorn and Young. Charles Kingsley. *Fr.* The Saint's Tragedy. PoVP
When I Was a Lad, *with music.* W. S. Gilbert. *Fr.* H. M. S. Pinafore. PreP
(First Lord of the Admiralty, The.) LiA
(First Lord's Song, The.) TreFS
(Ruler of the Queen's Navee, The.) OlF
(Sir Joseph's Song.) CoBE; LiTB; SiTL
When I was a lad and so was my dad. *Unknown.* OxNR
When I was a lad of twenty. I Was a Bustle-Maker Once, Girls. Patrick Barrington. WhC
When I was a lad there were hansoms in London. Hansom Cabbies. Wilfrid Thorley. HBMV
When I was a little boy as fat as I could roll. Toll-a-Winker. *Unknown.* OuSiCo
When I was a little boy, I followed hope. Hope. Gamaliel Bradford. HBMV
When I was a little boy I had but little wit. *Unknown.* OxNR; RIS
When I was a little boy I lived by myself. Mother Goose. *See* When I was a bachelor.
When I was a little boy I washed my mammy's dishes. *Unknown.* OxNR
When I was a little boy my mammy kept me in. *Unknown.* OxNR
When I Was a Little Girl. Alice Milligan. DiM; GTIV; OnYI; OxBI
When I was a little girl,/ About seven years old. *Unknown.* OxNR
When I was a little lad. Duna. Marjorie Pickthall. BMEP; HBV; MCCG; POT; PoTo; VOD
When I was a live man. Matter. Louis Untermeyer. YT
When I was a maid. The Old Story Over Again. James Kenney. OnYI
When I was a passenger in the barque *Windrush.* The Sun's over the Foreyard. Christopher Morley. EtS
When I was a serving maid, down in Drury Lane. Bell-Bottom Trousers. *Unknown.* AmSS
When I Was a Tree. Vachel Lindsay. ATP (1935 ed.)
When I was a young man I lived upon [*or* on] the square. The Bad Boy [*or* Root Hog or Die]. *Unknown.* CoSo; CSF
When I was alive, I wandered in the streets of the Capital. Bearer's Song. Miu Hsi. TrCh
When I was almost forty. Golden Bells. Po Chü-i. TrCh
When I was as high as that. A Memory. L. A. G. Strong. SiTL; WhC
When I was a-stealin' cross the deep blue sea. Trench Blues. *Unknown.* OuSiCo
When I was at the funeral. Snapshot: Politician. George Garrett. NePoAm-2
"When I was at the party." Betty at the Party. Mary E. Bradley. BoTP
When I was born. The Day's Ration. Emerson. BAV; IAP
When I was born, my mother taped my ears. Youth's Progress. John Updike. FiBHP
When I was born on Amman hill. The Collier. Vernon Watkins. FaBoTw; MoVE; MoWP
When I was bound apprentice in famous Lincolnshire. The Lincolnshire Poacher. *Unknown.* CH; OxBoLi
When I was but a child, I liked to press. The Traveler. Joseph C. Sonneborn. CAG
When I was but a lad of eight. An Untutored Mind. Frank Dempster Sherman. PR

When I was but thirteen or so. Romance. Walter James Turner. AlDL; BMEP; CH; HBMV; HBVY; LBBV; LiTM; MBP; MoBrPo; OBMV; PoMS; PoRA; POTE; PtOT; ShBV-1; TCEP; ThWaDe; TrGrPo; TwCV; VOD (1935 ed.); WHA; WP
When I Was Christened. David McCord. Perambulator Poems, V. RIS; WhC
When I was coming down from the country. The Forgotten City. William Carlos Williams. LiTA; NePA
When I was dead, my spirit turned. At Home. Christina Rossetti. PoVP; UnW; VA; VLEP
When I was down beside the sea. At the Seaside. Robert Louis Stevenson. FaPON; GFA; MPB (1956 ed.); OTPC; StVeCh (1940 ed.); SUS; TiPo
When I Was Fair and Young. Elizabeth I, Queen of England. ElSeCe; EnLi-1; PoRA; ReEn; TuPP
(Importune Me No More.) ElL
(Youth and Cupid.) OBSC
When I was far from the sea's voice and vastness. Providence. Cale Young Rice. WGRP
When I was forced from Stella ever dear. Astrophel and Stella, LXXXVII. Sir Philip Sidney. SiPS
When I was happy in my youth. I Stand Corrected. Margaret Fishback. WhC
When I was home de. Po' Boy Blues. Langston Hughes. BANP
When I was ill in the long ago. The Market Town. Frances Carlin. HBMV
When I was in the garden. The Queen Bee. Mary K. Robinson. BoTP
When I was just a little boy. The Ships of Yule. Bliss Carman. CaP; CPG; HBVY; OCL
When I was just a tiny chap. The Gypsy Heart. Harry Noyes Pratt. BAP; PoMa; POT; PoTo
When I was just as far as I could walk. The Telephone. Robert Frost. AnFE; APA; CoAnAm; HBV; OBAV
When I was little, oh a very small boy. So Long Folks, Off to the War. Anthony Ostroff. NePoAm-2
When I was making myself a game. Little Rain. Elizabeth Madox Roberts. PoRh; SUS; TiPo (1952 ed.)
When I was marked for suffering, Love forswore. Sonnet. Cervantes. AWP; PoFr
When I was once in Baltimore. Sheep. W. H. Davies. BMEP; ChMo; CMP; LiTM; MBP; MoBrPo; PoTo; PrWP; StPo
When I was one. The End. A. A. Milne. SiSoSe
When I was one. Sophisticate. Barbara Young. SiSoSe
When I Was One-and-twenty. A. E. Housman. A Shropshire Lad, XIII. AnFE; BBV; BLV; BoLiVe; BPN; ChMo; CMP; CoBE; EmBrPo; EnLi-2; EnLit; FaFP; FAOV; GTBS-W; GTSL; HBV; LiTB; LiTL; LiTM; LoPo; LoPS; MBP; MoAB; MoBrPo; NeMA; OAEP; OtMeF; OuHeWo; PFE; PG; PoeMoYo; PoLFOT; PoVP; PYM; TreF; TrGrPo; TwP; ViBoPo; ViP; VLEP; WHA
When I was one and twenty. A Shropshire Lad. David McCord. PIAE
When I was only six years old. When I Was Six. Zora Cross. BoAu; FaPON; HBVY
When I was seven. Growing Up. Harry Behn. SiSoSe
When I was seventeen I heard. To Critics. Walter Learned. AA; AnAmPo; HBV; LA; LEAP
When I was sick and lay a-bed. The Land of Counterpane. Robert Louis Stevenson. BoChLi; FaBoBe; FaFP; FaPON; GoBP; HBV; HBVY; MPB; NeHB; OTPC; PCH; PoVP; RIS; StVeCh; TreF; VA
When I Was Single (A *and* B *vers.*), *with music. Unknown.* ABF
(I Wish I Was Single Again.) ABS; AS, *with music*
(Single Girl, The.) TrAS
When I Was Six. Zora Cross. BoAu; FaPON; HBVY
When I was small, a woman died. Along the Potomac. Emily Dickinson. OnPM
When I was small I hated rain. For April Showers. Emily Rose Burt. GFA
When I was small, my mother's clothes. My Mother's Clothes. Anna Hempstead Branch. MotAn
When I was still a boy and mother's pride. False Friends —Like. William Barnes. CG
When I was ten and she fifteen. Time's Revenge. Walter Learned. HBV
When I was thirteen or fourteen. Speaking My Mind. Yüan Chi. WhP
When I was tiny she was tall and fair. A Young Man. André Chénier. TrFP
When I was told he had been learning. The Young Carpenter. Al-Rusafi. MooP
When I was told of your death, Heraclitus. Callimachus to Heraclitus. Callimachus. OnPM
When I was twenty inches long. The New-born Baby's Song. Frances Cornford. DiM
When I was very young. Dimple Diggers. "Robin Christopher." RIS
When I was wandering far from home. The Bust. W. H. Davies. MoPW
When I was yet a child. Of Love's Awakening [*or* Juvenilities]. Juan Meléndez Valdés. AnSpL-2; TeCS
When I Was Young. Aubrey Thomas De Vere. *See* Song: "When I was young . . ."
When I Was Young. Alun Llywelyn-Williams, *tr. fr. Welsh by* Gwyn Williams. PrWP
When I was young/ I dared to sing. The Pit of Bliss. James Stephens. AnFE; ChMo; CMP
When I Was Young and Foolish, *with music. Unknown.* AS
When I was young and full o' pride. Blow Me Eyes! Wallace Irwin. BOHV; HBMV; InMe; StPo
When I was young and in my prime. A Long Time Ago, *vers.* III. *Unknown.* ShS
When I was young and slender, a spender, a lender. Song for a Cracked Voice. Wallace Irwin. InMe
When I was young I felt so small. Height. Anne Morrow Lindbergh. BAP
When I was young, I had a bed. The Ship o' Bed. Robert P. Tristram Coffin. TSW; TSWC
When I was young I had a care. Soliloquy. Francis Ledwidge. EnLit
When I was young, I had no sense. The Fiddle. Neil Munro. BoTP
When I was young, I had no taste for worldly affairs. Return to the Country. Tao Yuan-ming. WhP
When I was young I heard a tune. For the Eightieth Birthday of a Great Singer. Edward Shanks. UnS
When I was young I learnt fencing. Regret. Yüan Chi. TrCh
When I was young I played with a soft brush. Day Dreams. Tso Ssu. TrCh
When I was young I remained aloof from worldly affairs. Retrospect. Tao Yuan-ming. WhP
When I was young, I said to Sorrow. Song. Aubrey Thomas De Vere. GTBS-D; GTIV; TIP
When I was young I strove to glean. Experience. Eden Phillpotts. LBBV
When I was young I used to wait. The Blue-Tail Fly. *Unknown.* FaFP; SiTL; ViBoFo
When I was young, I was out of tune with the herd. Returning to the Fields. T'ao Ch'ien [Tao Yuan-ming]. LiTW; PoFr; TrCh
When I was young I'd little sense. The Mysteries. L. A. G. Strong. HaMV
When I was young my heart and head were light. Memory. Siegfried Sassoon. ChMo; NLK (1947 ed.)
When I was young the days were long. The Flying Wheel. Katharine Tynan. WGRP
When I was young the twilight seemed too long. Twilight. Agnes Mary Frances Robinson. HBV
When I was young, throughout the hot season. Satire on Paying Calls [in August]. Ch'eng Hsiao. TrCh; WoL
When I was young unapt for use of man. *Unknown.* SeCSL
When I was young, with sharper sense. A Summer Commentary. Yvor Winters. LiTM; UnPo (3d ed.)
When I was younger. Pastoral. William Carlos Williams. OxBA
When I was younger, and more wise. Values. Dorothy Mitchell. CAG
When I Watch the Living Meet. A. E. Housman. A Shropshire Lad, XII. AnFE; ChMo; CMP; MBP; MoBrPo; OAEP; PoVP; TrGrPo; TwP; ViPo; WHA
When I watched an elm, a Grenstone tree. A Grenstone Elm. Witter Bynner. VOD
When I went out. A Spike of Green. Barbara Baker. AlDL
When I went out/ In the Spring meadows. Akahito, *tr. fr. Japanese by* Kenneth Rexroth. OnPJ
When I went out in/ The Spring fields. The Emperor Koko, *tr. fr. Japanese by* Kenneth Rexroth. OnPJ
When I went to bed at night. Through the Porthole. Marjorie Wilson. BoTP
When I went to the Bar as a very young man. Said I to Myself, Said I. W. S. Gilbert. *Fr.* Iolanthe. PoVP
When I Went to the Circus. D. H. Lawrence. LiTB
When I went up the minster tower. At Lincoln. Oscar Fay Adams. AA
When I went up to Nazareth. The Lilies of the Field. Daniel Henderson. MaRV; StJW
When I wooed Carinda first. Of His Mistress Grown Old. William Hicks. SeCL
When I would get me to the upper fields. Climbing. Thomas Edward Brown. VLEP
When I Would Image. George Meredith. UnW
When I would muse in boyhood. A. E. Housman. Last Poems, XXXII. CBE; EmBrPo
When I would pray. The Thorn. *Unknown.* SoLD
When I would send you rimes that could relate. The Effigy [*or* Sonnet: The Effigy]. Guido Cavalcanti. LiTW; LyPI
When I would think of you, my mind holds only. The Kestrels. Sidney Keyes. FaBoMo; POTE

When ice is thawed and snow is gone. The Bluebird. Maurice Thompson. BLA
When Icicles Hang by the Wall. Shakespeare. *Fr.* Love's Labour's Lost, V, ii. AEV; AnFE; ATP; BBV (1923 ed.); BEL; CoBE; EG; EM-1; EnLi-1; EnLit; EPP; FaPON; GN; LiTB; LPS-2; MyFE; OBSC; OTPC; OuHeWo; PIR; PoEL-2; PoRA; SeCeV; SiCE; TOP; TyEnPo
(Hiems.) FaBoCh; LoGBV
(Song: "When icicles hang by the wall.") FiP; HBV; WP
(Songs: Spring and Winter.) ExPo
(Songs from "Love's Labour's Lost," 2.) LEAP
(Songs from the Plays.) AWP; JAWP; WBP
(Spring and Winter, 2.) OBEV
(Tu-Whit To-Who.) CH
(Winter.) BCEP; BLV; CBE; CBOV; CenL; CG; ChTr; EIL; ElSeCe; EnL; EV-1; GBV (1952 ed.); GTBS; GTBS-D; GTBS-W; GTSE; GTSL; InPo; LiTG; MaPo; MCCG; MPB; PCD; PCH; PIAE; PoE; PoFS; PreP; ReaPo; RG; SeCePo; ShBV-1; TreFS; TrGrPo; UnPo; ViBoPo; WaKn; WHA
(Winter Song.) BoLiVe
(Winter's Song.) FaBoEn
When I'm a big man, then I'll buy me a gun. A Plan. John Alden Carpenter. RIS
When I'm a little older. My Plan. Marchette Chute. BrR; FaPON
"When I'm alone"—the words tripped off his tongue. Alone [*or* When I'm Alone]. Siegfried Sassoon. BLV; BoLiVe; MBP; MoBrPo; OBMV; POTE; ShBV-3; TrGrPo (1942 ed.); YT
When I'm an angel, I'll covet news from North Carolina. News from Home. Thad Stem, Jr. NoCaPo (rev. ed.)
When I'm an aviator. Trails of Smoke. Rowena Bennett. MPB (1956 ed.)
When I'm an old alumnus. My Alma Mater. "T. M. M." CAG
When I'm asleep, dreaming and lulled and warm. Sick Leave. Siegfried Sassoon. LBBV; MM; NP
"When I'm big I'll be a soldier." The Little Soldier. J. L. Molloy. BIG
When I'm in bed at night. Night Watchmen. Jimmy Garthwaite. BrR
When I'm in bed at night. Noises in the Night. Lilian McCrea. BoTP
When I'm in health and asked to choose between the This and That, alas! Carpe Diem. Ridgely Torrence. *Fr.* The House of a Hundred Lights. AA
When imperturbable the gentle moon. Dedication. John Erskine. PC
When in Celia's heav'nly eye. Song. Thomas Godfrey. NoCaPo
When in death I shall calm recline. Legacy. Thomas Moore. AS
When in dim dreams I trace the tangled maze. To Olive. Lord Alfred Douglas. OBVV
When in disgrace with fortune and men's eyes. Sonnets, XXIX. Shakespeare. AEV; AnFE; AtBAP; ATP; AWP; BCEP; BEL; BLV; BoLiVe; BrBE; CaAE; CBE; CoBE; CoEV; EIL; ElSeCe; EM-1; EnL; EnLi-1; EnLit; EPP; ES; EtPaEn; EV-1; ExPo; FaBoEn; GrCo-2; GTBS; GTBS-D; GTBS-W; GTSE; GTSL; HBV; HiLiEn; InP; InPo; InvP; JAWP; LEAP; LiTB; LiTG; LiTL; LoBV; LoPo; LoPS; MaPo; MaRV; OAEP; OBEV; OBSC; OuHeWo; PeBoSo; PFE; PG; PIR; Po; PoE; PoEL-2; PoFS; PoMa; PoRA; REAL; ReaPo; ReEn; ReIE; SeCeV; SiCE; TCEP; TOP; TreF; TrGrPo; TwHP; TwP; TyEnPo; ViBoPo; WBP; WHA; WP
When in her face mine eyes I fix. Madrigal. Earl of Stirling. Aurora, Madrigal I. EIL
When in her fifteenth year Louise was ta'en. The Funeral of a Poor Girl. Auguste Brizeux. TrFP
When in his father's arms he lay. Timomachus. Simonides. GrL; OxBG
When in mid-air, the Golden Trump shall sound. Poet's Resurrection [*or* The Last Day]. Dryden. *Fr.* To the Pious Memory of the Accomplished Young Lady, Mrs. Anne Killigrew. BeR; WHA
When in My Arms. Pushkin, *tr. fr. Russian by* Babette Deutsch. TrRV
When in my dreams thy lovely face. Dream Land. Frances Ann Kemble. OBVV
When, in my effervescent youth. Who'd Be a Hero (Fictional)? Morris Bishop. FiBHP
When in my walks I meet some ruddy lad. A Proem. Samuel Ward. AA
When in my youth I travellèd. The Grey Squirrels. William Howitt. TVC; TVSH
When in Sad and Weary Hour. "Novalis," *tr. fr. German by* Eileen Hutchins. Sacred Songs, III. AnGP
When in spring they viewed the blossoms from the turret. The Moon on the Ruined Castle. Bansui Tsuchii. PoLJ
When in summer thou walkest. Thou Flower of Summer [*or* Spring]. John Clare. LO; LoPS
When in the affluent splendour of the day. Day and Night. Helena Coleman. CPG
When in the ardent spells. Echoes. José Peón y Contreras. AnMP
When in the bedded dark of night. Marriage. Donald Hall. NePoEA
When in the blue dusk of a summer night. Visions. William Noel Hodgson. UnW
When, in the carven chest. Danaë [*or* The Lamentation of Danaë]. Simonides. BOL; GrPo; GrR; LiA
When in the chronicle of wasted time. Sonnets, CVI. Shakespeare. AnFE; AWP; BCEP; BEL; BLV; BoLiVe; CaAE; CoBE; EG; EIL; ElSeCe; EM-1; EnL; EnLi-1; EnLit; EnLoPo; EPP; ES; EtPaEn; EV-1; ExPo; FaBoCh; FaBoEn; FiP; GTBS; GTBS-D; GTBS-W; GTSE; GTSL; HBV; InPo; JAWP; LEAP; LiTB; LiTG; LiTL; LoBV; LoGBV; LPS-1; MaPo; MCCG; OAEP; OBEV; OBSC; OuHeWo; PeBoSo; PIAE; Po; PoE; PoFS; PoRA; REAL; ReaPo; ReEn; ReIE; SeCeV; ShBV-3; SiCE; TOP; TrGrPo; TwCrTr; TwHP; TwP; TyEnPo; ViBoPo; WBP; WHA; WP
When in the Crowd I Suddenly Behold. Robert Nathan. MAP
When in the dim beginning of the years. The Testing. Edwin Markham. LPS-1; MaRV; OQP; QP-1
When in the down I sink my head. In Memoriam A. H. H., LXVIII. Tennyson. EmBrPo; EPN; GEPC; OAEP; ViPo; VLEP
When in the Eastern skies the wondrous Star did rise. The Birds Praise the Advent of the Saviour. *Unknown.* SDH
When in the festival of August heat. Horas Tempestatis Quoque Enumero; the Sundial. John Hollander. NePoEA
When in the First Great Hour. Edith M. Thomas. *Fr.* The Inverted Torch. AA
When, in the frozen dawn. Mexican Soldiers. Rafael Estrada. AnCL
When, in the gold October dusk, I saw you near to setting. Arcturus in Autumn. Sara Teasdale. AV; MOAP; NP; NV; TBM
When, in the hour of lonely woe. Trust in Jesus. Josiah Conder. BePJ
When in the mazes of a dream. Even to the Dead. Whitney Montgomery. UnW
When in the mirror of a permanent tear. Elegy on Gordon Barber, Lamentably Drowned in His Eighteenth Year. Gene Derwood. FaFP; GTBS-W; LiTA; LiTG; LiTM; NePA
When, in the morning, fresh from sleep. In the Morning. Cecilia Loftus. GFA
When in the morning hour you rise. Prayer. W. T. Pearman. PraP
When in the Night We Wake and Hear the Rain. Robert Burns Wilson. SN
When in the parlor car we speed. The Ballade of Fact and Fiction. Brander Matthews. PFE
When in the spring the swallows all return. Sappho, XCIII. Bliss Carman. PeCV
When in the starry gloom. Easter. Richard Watson Gilder. DD
When in the storm on Albion's coast. The Minute-Gun. R. S. Sharpe. LPS-2
When in the sun the hot red acres smoulder. The Zulu Girl. Roy Campbell. AtBAP; BoSA; ChMP; JKCP (1955 ed.); MoPW; MoVE; OBMV; POTE
When in the Woods I Wander All Alone. Edward Hovell-Thurlow. HBV; HBVY
When in thy glass thou studiest thy face. Afternoon. Wendell Phillips Garrison. *Fr.* Post-Meridian. AA
When indoor young ones club their wicked wits. The First of April. William Hone. PoRL
When infinite space, without outline, sums/ Up in a cloud. Slender Spring. Jorge Guillén. CoSP
When insect wings are glistening in the beam. A Walk at Sunset. Bryant. BAV
When is He nearest to all of us. Gethsemane's Gift. Katherine Brégy. MaRV; StJW
When is the Muse most lustily acclaimed? Song's Apostasy. Sir William Watson. EPN
When Israel Came Forth Out of Egypt. Psalms, CXIV, Bible, *O.T.* TrJP
(Psalm CXIV.) LiTW
When Israel, of the Lord beloved. Rebecca's Hymn. Sir Walter Scott. *Fr.* Ivanhoe. BPN; EmBrPo; EnRP; LPS-2; ViBoPo
When Israel Out of Egypt Came. A. E. Housman. LiTB
When Israel was in Egypt's land. Go Down, Moses. *Unknown.* AmPP
When it behoves me to go to you, O my God, let. Prayer to Go to Paradise with the Donkeys. Francis Jammes. LiTW; MiFP

When it comes to a question of trusting. The Average Man. Margaret E. Sangster. WBLP
When it comes to saddle hawses, there's a difference in steeds. The Ol' Cow Hawse. Earl Alonzo Brininstool. SCC
When it is finally ours, this freedom, this liberty. Frederick Douglass. Robert E. Hayden. PoNe
When It Is Given You to Find a Smile. Enrique González Martínez, *tr. fr. Spanish by* Samuel Beckett. AnMP
When It Is Over. Edna St. Vincent Millay. PreP
When it is the winter time. Ice. Dorothy Aldis. GFA; SUS; TiPo
When it rained in Devon. London Rain. Nancy Byrd Turner. MoSiPe
When it was dark in Martin Place. Cenotaph. Brian Fitzpatrick. MoAuPo
When it was said that she was dead. A Conversational Neighbor. Richard R. Kirk. LS; PoMa
When It's Iris Time in Tennessee. Willa Mae Waid. PoRL
When it's just past April. The Flower-Cart Man. Rachel Field. SiSoSe
When its rays fall on its cheeks the cat licks them, thinking them milk. The Moon. Bhasa. LiTW
When I've a saxpence under my thumb. Todlen Butt, and Todlen Ben. *Unknown.* EBSV; OBS
When I've hoed and dug my garden. My Garden. Frederic E. Weatherly. OTPC (1946 ed.)
When Jack Frost comes—oh! the fun. Jack Frost. *Unknown.* GFA
When Jack the King's commander. The Fate of John Burgoyne. *Unknown.* PAH
When Jacob from the land of Canaan down. The Exodus from Egypt. Ezekielos of Alexandria. TrJP
When Jacky's a good boy [*or* very good boy]. Mother Goose. BrR; OxNR; PPL
When Januar' wind was blawing cauld [*or* cold]. The Lass That Made the Bed to Me. Burns. InvP; RO
When Jean Renaud returned from war. Song of Renaud. *Unknown.* LiA
When Jemmy the Second, not Jemmy the First. A New Song Entitled the Warming Pan. *Unknown.* CoMu
When Jesse Holmes came among the people. The Fool Killer. Helen Bevington. NoCaPo (rev. ed.)
When Jessie comes with her soft breast. Jessie. Thomas Edward Brown. EtPaEn; HBV; OBEV
When Jesus came to Golgotha they hanged Him on a tree. Indifference [*or* The Crucifixion]. G. A. Studdert-Kennedy. BPP; ChIP; MaRV; OQP; PGD; QP-1; QS; StJW
When Jesus Christ was four years old. The Birds. Hilaire Belloc. JKCP
When Jesus lay on Mary's knee. The Winds at Bethlehem. Winifred M. Letts. StJW
When Jesus walked upon the earth. The Greatest. Marion Brown Shelton. MaRV
When Jesus was a little Child. Mother and Child. Ivy O. Eastwick. SiSoSe
When Jesus was a little thing. His Mother in Her Hood of Blue. Lizette Woodworth Reese. ISi; OHIP
When Jesus Wept, *with music.* William Billings. TrAS
When Jim and Bill and I were boys a many years ago. Ashes on the Slide. Eugene Field. BBV (1923 ed.)
When Jo was young he used to hate the land. La Terre. Frank Oliver Call. CPG
When John Henry was a baby [*or* little boy]. John Henry. *Unknown.* APW; BaBo (A *vers.*); SPP
When John Henry was about three days old. John Henry. *Unknown.* TiPo (1959 ed.)
When John Henry was nothin' but a baby. John Henry. *Unknown.* FaBoBe
When John the Baptist was so young. Apocrypha. Babette Deutsch. HBMV
When Johnny Comes Marching Home. Patrick Sarsfield Gilmore. OIF; PaA; PAH; TrAS, *with music;* TreF
When Johnson sought (as Shakespear says) that bourn. Introduction and Anecdotes. "Peter Pindar." *Fr.* Bozzy and Piozzi. PoEL-3
When Johnson's Ale Was New, *with music.* *Unknown.* ShS
When Jonathan Bing was young, they say. Jonathan Bing Does Arithmetic. Beatrice Curtis Brown. GaP; RIS
When Joseph was an old man, an old man was he. The Cherry-Tree Carol. *Unknown.* ABS; BaBo (B *vers.*)
When Joshua Peabody drives to town. Joshua Peabody. John A. Holmes. BPP
When Juan woke he found some good things ready. Byron. *Fr.* Don Juan, II. EnLit
When Julius Caesar went to town. The Same Old Story. James J. Montague. HBMV
When Julius Fabricius, Sub-Prefect of the Weald. The Land. Kipling. MBP; MoBrPo; ViPP
When June Is Come. Robert Bridges. PoeT
When June was cool and clover long. The Song-Sparrow. Percy MacKaye. BLA
When Justice Dwelt on Earth. Aratus, *tr. fr. Greek by* George Allen. *Fr.* Phaenomena. OxBG
When Kian O'Hara's Cup Was Passed to Turlough O'Carolan. Turlough Carolan. *See* Cup of O'Hara, The.
When kindly Christ walked in our way. Beati Oculi Qui Vident. Richard Crashaw. Epigrammata Sacra, I, 76. LaP
When kings knelt to a Maid and a Child. A Song of Women. Anna Wickham. QS
When klingle, klangle, klingle. When the Cows Come Home. Agnes E. Mitchell. PTA-1
When la bella Simonetta was born forth on her black bier. Simonetta. Angelo Poliziano. LaP
When lads have done with labor. A. E. Housman and a Few Friends. Humbert Wolfe. FiBHP; WhC
When lads were home from labour. Fancy's Knell. A. E. Housman. AnFE; BMEP; EG; FaBoCh; MM; MoPW; PoRA; POTT; ShBV-4; TwCV
When Lady Jane refused to be. Save the Tiger! A. P. Herbert. OnSP
When land is gone and money spent. *Unknown.* OxNR
When languor and disease invade. Rejoicing in Hope. Augustus Montague Toplady. BePJ
When languorous noons entreat the summer sky. The Humming Bird. Ivan Swift. BLA
When last I died, and, dear, I die. *See* When I died last, and, dear, I die.
When last I hear your nimble fingers play. To Lucia Playing on Her Lute. Samuel Pordage. SeCL
When late I attempted your pity to move. An Expostulation. Isaac Bickerstaffe. FiBHP
When late I heard the trembling cello play. The Cello. Richard Watson Gilder. AA
When late in summer the streams run yellow. A Song of Early Autumn. Richard Watson Gilder. DD; HBV; NLK (1947 ed.); SN
When late the trees were stript by Winter pale. On Bathing. Thomas Warton, the Younger. ES
When late we followed, in her coffin laid. Which Was Most Truly Dead? Charles Augustin Sainte-Beuve. PoP
When lately Pym descended into hell. On the Death of Pym. William Drummond of Hawthornden. ALV
When laughing Ann trips down the street. Laughing Ann. A. P. Herbert. OnPP
When Lazarus left his charnel-cave. In Memoriam A. H. H., XXXI. Tennyson. BPN; EM-2; EmBrPo; EPN; EPP; GEPC; ViPo; VLEP
When Learning's triumph o'er her barbarous [*or* barb'rous] foes. Prologue Spoken by Mr. Garrick at the Opening of the Theatre Royal in Drury Lane, 1747 [*or* Shakespeare and Jonson]. Samuel Johnson. BCEP; CBOV; CEP; EiPP; EV-3; LPS-3; NBE; OBEC; PoFS; PtP; SeCeV
When leaves are dressed in red and brown. Autumn Races. Emilie Blackmore Stapp. GFA
When leaves grow sear all things take sombre hue. Indian Summer. *Unknown.* LPS-2
When leaves of April glisten. The Concert. Phyllis McGinley. YeAr
When leaves turn outward to the light. Poet and Lark. "Madeline Bridges." AA; HBV
When leäzers wi' ther laps o' carn. Night a-Zettèn In. William Barnes. RO
When legislators keep the law. Latter-Day Warnings. Oliver Wendell Holmes. *Fr.* The Autocrat of the Breakfast-Table. BAP; IAP; OnAP; PCD
When Lesbia first I saw, so heavenly fair. Lesbia [*or* Silly Fair]. Congreve. BCEP; LPS-2
When Letty had scarce pass'd her third glad year. Letty's Globe. Charles Tennyson Turner. BTP; EPN; ES; HBV; OBEV; OBVV; PECK; VA
When life and matter keep their ancient tryst. Unbowed. Margaret R. Richter. MuM
When Life has borne its harvest from my heart. A Prayer in Late Autumn. Violet Alleyn Storey. TrPWD
When life hath run its largest round. Birthday of Daniel Webster. Oliver Wendell Holmes. DD; GA
When Life Is Done. Edgar A. Guest. MaRV
When life is hard, your soul possess. Life Is Short. Horace. Odes, II, 3. RoL
When life is quite through with. E. E. Cummings. CrMA
When Life's Day Closes. Thomas Tiplady. MaRV
When life's oppressive hour is mine. Prayer. Mikhail Lermontov. BoR
When lights are low, and the day has died. Song of the Open Country. Dorothy Parker. PC
When like a bud my Julia blows. To Julia under Lock and Key. Sir Owen Seaman. BOHV
When, like the early rose. Eileen [*or* Aileen] Aroon. Gerald Griffin. AnIV; GoBC; HBV; IrPN; OBVV; OnYI; PCD; TIP
When like the rising day. Gerald Griffin. *Fr.* Eileen Aroon. OBEV (new ed.)
When Lilacs Last in the Dooryard Bloom'd. Walt Whitman. *Fr.* Memories of President Lincoln. AmP; AmPo; AmPP (3d ed.); AnAmPo; AnEnPo; APW; ATP; AWP; BAP; BAV; BLV; BoLiVe; CoBA; CoV; EV-5; ExPo; FaBoEn,

abr.; GTBS-D, *sts.* 1–6; HBV; IAP; InPo; JAWP; LA; LBAH; LEAP; LiTA; LoBV; MAP; MaPo; MoAmPo; MOAP; NeMA, *sts.* 1–6; OBAV; OuHeWo; OxBA; PaA; PFE, *much abr.;* PIAE; Po; PoE; PoEL-5; PoFS; PoLFOT; PoRA; REAL; RiBV; SeCeV; TCAP; TOP; TreF; TrGrPo; TriL; ViBoPo; WHA; WoL; YT
Death Carol: "Come lovely and soothing Death," XIV. AnFE; APA; CoAnAm; LBAP; LEAP; MaRV
(Come Lovely and Soothing Death.) PoD
When lilies by the river fill with sun [*or* snow]. The Wood-Thrush. John Vance Cheney. BLA; WhBS
When Lincoln Came to Springfield. Vachel Lindsay. GA; MAP; MoAmPo; NeMA
When Lion sends his roaring forth. The Lion. Mary Howitt. FaPON
When lions roar, the beasts with terrour hear. Lions and Dragons. Oppian, *tr. by* William Diaper. *Fr.* Halieuticks. BeR
When Little Birdie Bye-bye Goes. *Unknown.* OTPC; PPL
(Bye-bye.) SAS
(Lullaby: "When little birdie . . .") BOL
When little boys grow patient at last, weary. Death of Little Boys. Allen Tate. LiTA; MAP; MoAB; MoAmPo; MOAP
When little boys with merry noise. Reinforcements. Thomas Toke Lynch. OBVV
When little Calathine was brought to bed. Little Calathine. *Unknown.* OnPM
When little daily winds have died away. Winter; Two Sonnets, II. Malcolm Cowley. *Fr.* Blue Juniata. MAP; MoAmPo (1942 ed.)
When little Fred/ Was called to bed. Little Fred. Mother Goose. HBV; HBVY
When little heads weary have gone to their bed. The Plum-puppets. Christopher Morley. FaPON; GaP; MPB; TiPo
When little John Hardy was four years old. John Hardy (A *vers.*). *Unknown.* ViBoFo
When little lights in little ports come out. Evening. V. Sackville-West. DiM
When little things would irk me, and I grow. Morning Prayer. *Unknown.* PoToHe
When long the shadows of the wind had rolled. The Sheaves. E. A. Robinson. ReMP
When, looking on the present face of things. October 1803. Wordsworth. BPN; EmBrPo; EnRP; PeBoSo
When lordly Saturn in a sable robe. Eurymachus's Fancy. Robert Greene. *Fr.* Francesco's Fortunes. OBSC
When, Lost in Thought. Pushkin, *tr. fr. Russian by* Babette Deutsch. TrRV
When, lov'd by poet and painter. The Ivory Gate. Mortimer Collins. VA
When Love arose in heart and deed. The Flowers. William Brighty Rands. OBEV; OBVV
When love at first did move. Song. Ben Jonson. *Fr.* The Masque of Beauty. GoBC
When love begins with Ganymede, he gathers. Ganymede. Witter Bynner. AnFE; CoAnAm; TwAmPo
When Love, born first of thought and will. Divorce. Charles Williams. POTE
When Love Comes Knocking. William Henry Gardner. AA
When Love cools down, ice forms upon the heart. Sentences of Wisdom. Thomas Lake Harris. BAP
When Love disputes/ He carries his battles! Love, Conquering and Unconquerable [*or* The Power of Love *or* Unconquerable Love]. Sophocles. *Fr.* Antigone. GrR; LiA; OxBG
When Love ensnares my mind unbidden. Composition in Late Spring. Irving Layton. PeCV
When Love had strove us to subdue. Love. Joseph Beaumont. OBS
When love has passed its limits. Chorus. Euripides. *Fr.* Medea. LiTW
When Love his flaming image on her brow. Petrarch. *Fr.* Sonnets to Laura: to Laura in Life. PrPoCR
When love in the faint heart trembles. Song of Eros. George Edward Woodberry. *Fr.* Agathon. AA; HBV
When Love Meets Love. Thomas Edward Brown. OBVV; UnPo
When love on time and measure makes his ground. Song [*or* False Love *or* Love, Time and Measure]. *At. to* John Lilliat. BLV; EIL; LO; OBSC
When Love, our great Immortal. The Rose of Stars. George Edward Woodberry. *Fr.* Wild Eden. AA; HBV; LBMV
When Love suddenly grows jealous. Embarrassment of Eyes. *Unknown.* PIAE
When love with inordinate might. Sweetest in Measure, Each Pleasure. Euripides. *Fr.* Medea. GrR
When Love with unconfinèd wings. To Althea from Prison [*or* From Prison]. Richard Lovelace. AEV; AnEnPo; AnFE; ATP; AWP; BCEP; BEL; BLPA; BLV; CaAE; CBOV; CoBE; ElSeCe; EM-1; EnL; EnLi-1; EnLit; EPP; EV-2; FaBoBe; FaBoEn; GTBS; GTBS-D; GTBS-W; GTSE; GTSL; HBV; InPo; JAWP; LEAP; LH; LiTB; LiTG; LiTL; LoBV; LPS-1; MCCG; MeLP; MePo; NeHB; OAEP; OBEV; OBS; OuHeWo; PCD; PG (1945 ed.); PIAE; PIR; PoE; PoFS; PoRA; PreP; ReEn; SeCeV; SeCL; SeCV-1; SeEP; TCEP; TOP; TreF; TrGrPo; TVSH; TwHP; TyEnPo; ViBoPo; WBP; WHA
When Lovely Woman, *parody.* Phoebe Cary. ALV; BOHV; FaBoBe; HBV; PA; PR; TreFS
(When Lovely Woman Wants a Favor.) InP
When Lovely Woman [Stoops to Folly]. Oliver Goldsmith. *See* Song: "When lovely woman stoops to folly."
When Lovely Woman Wants a Favor. Phoebe Cary. *See* When Lovely Woman.
When lovers in the spring contend. Vows. Leonard Cline. PR
When love's brief dream is done. Remember. Georgia Douglas Johnson. PoNe
When Lucinda's blooming beauty. Lucinda. *Unknown.* SeCL
When lyart leaves bestrow the yird. The Jolly Beggars; a Cantata. Burns. BEL; CEP; EiPP; EM-1; EnRP; OAEP; PoEL-4
When Lynus meets me, after salutations. Of Lynus, Borrowing. Sir John Harington. SiCE
When Madelon comes tripping by our table. Madelon. *Unknown.* BoHiPo
When maidens are young, and in their spring. Serenade. Aphra Behn. *Fr.* The Emperor of the Moon. SeCL
When maidens such as Hester die. Hester. Charles Lamb. EnRP; ERP; EV-4; GTBS; GTBS-D; GTBS-W; GTSE; GTSL; HBV; LEAP; LoBV; LPS-1; OBEV; OBRV; OTPC (1923 ed.); PoE; TriL
When Malindy Sings. Paul Laurence Dunbar. MCCG; PoNe; VOD
When man and woman die, as poets sung. The Difference. Benjamin Franklin. WhC
When man has conquered space. Earth's Bondman. Betty Page Dabney. GoYe
When Man rose up out of the red mountains. The Return of Eve. G. K. Chesterton. ISi; PoLi
When many a day had come and fled. Kilmeny. James Hogg. *Fr.* The Queen's Wake. OtMeF
When many years we'd been apart. Reminiscence. Wallace Irwin. FiBHP
When Marathonis in this chest of stone. On a Stone at Salonica. *Unknown.* OxBG
When March doth into April merge. Alisoun. *Unknown.* MeEV
When Mary Ann Dollinger got the skule daown thar on Injun Bay. Courting in Kentucky. Florence E. Pratt. BOHV; PTA-2
When Mary bids Thee sleep, Thou sleepest. Jesus, Child and Lord. Frederick William Faber. BePJ
When Mary came to Bethlehem. Mary of Bethlehem. Mary King. ISi
When Mary Goes Walking. Patrick R. Chalmers. BoTP; HBVY
When Mary thro' the Garden Went. Mary Elizabeth Coleridge. BoTP
When [*or* While] May bedecks the naked trees. The Maryland Yellow-Throat. Henry van Dyke. BAP; DDA; HBV; OBAV
When May has come, and all around. The Archer. Clinton Scollard. FaPON; GaP
When May is here, and every morn. Fairy Music. Francis Ledwidge. YeAr
When May is in his prime, then may each heart rejoice. May [*or* M. Edwards' May]. Richard Edwards. OBSC; SiCE; TuPP
When May-time comes I love to feel. May-Time. Margaret Gant. PCH
When Me an' my Ma an' Pa went to the Fair. Going to the Fair. James Whitcomb Riley. IHA
When Meggy and me were acquaint. Tweedside. Lord Yester. EBSV
When men a dangerous disease did 'scape. To Doctor Empiric. Ben Jonson. BOHV; TuPP
When men betray the cause they smiled upon. Prayer for This Our Time. Thomas Moult. QS
When men describe a happy lot. The Day of My Profession. Sister Mary Christina. PraNu
When men discovered freedom first. The Ash and the Oak. Louis Simpson. NePoAm
When men go down to the sea in ships. Beyond the Horizon. Robert Freeman. BPP; MaRV; OQP; QP-2
When men must labor that the wheels may grind. History of the Modern World. Stanton A. Coblentz. PGD
When men of old, O Thrasybulus, drove. Before the Laureate's Day. Pindar. *Fr.* Isthmian Odes, II. GrR
When men shall find thy flower [*or* flow'r], thy glory, pass. To Delia, XXXVI [XXXVIII]. Samuel Daniel. BLV; CaAE; EG; EIL; ES; HBV; LEAP; LiTL; LO; OBEV; OBSC; PIAE; PoE; ReEn; SiCE; TrGrPo; TuPP
When [*or* While] men were all asleep the snow came flying. London Snow. Robert Bridges. AlDL; AnFE; CBOV; CBPC; CH; ChMo; ChTr; CMP; CoBMV; EPP; EV-5;

When men were all asleep the snow came flying (*continued*) GTBS-W; GTML; GTSE; LiTB; LiTG; LiTM (rev. ed.); LoBV; MBP; MM; MoAB; MoBrPo; PIAE; Po; PoE; PoEL-5; PoeMoYo; PoeT; PoMa; PoVP; ReMP; SeCePo; SeCeV; ShBV-3; TCEP; TrGrPo; VLEP; VOD (1935 ed.)
When Merche was with variand windis past. The Thrissil and the Rose. William Dunbar. EBSV
When Mercy Seasons Justice. Shakespeare. *See* Quality of Mercy, The.
When merry Christmas day is done. Christmas-Night in the Quarters. Irwin Russell. SPP
When 'mid the budding elms the bluebird flits. Blood-Root. "E. S. F." SN
When 'mid the tempests, livid, clad in skin. Conscience. Victor Hugo. TrFP
When Mid-Years come our joys to rout. The Widow. William B. Wheelwright. CAG
When Midget [*or* Midgit] was a puppy. A Puppy['s] Problem. Emilie Poulsson. AlBD; PPL
When midnight comes a host of dogs [*or* boys] and men. Badger. John Clare. EnRP; ExPo; LiTB; PoE; PoEL-4; UnPo (3d ed.)
When midnight has come to the desolate fen. The Reeds. Konstantin Dmitreyevich Balmont. BoR
When, midst their panic at our Loveliest. William Ellery Leonard. *Fr.* Two Lives, Pt. III. MOAP
When mighty roast beef was the Englishman's food. The Roast Beef of Old England [*or* Song in Praise of Old English Roast Beef]. Richard Leveridge. BHV; LPS-2; OBEC
When mighty Rome was conqueror. On the Bad Government of Toledo. Gómez Manrique. WoL
When mighty rost beef was the Englishman's food. The Roast Beef of Old England. Henry Fielding. *Fr.* Don Quixote in England, I. CEP; LPS-2; OBEC
When mild Favonius breathes, with warbling throat. Hoc Cygno Vinces. Henry Hawkins. ACP
When milder autumn summer's heat succeeds. Field Sports. Pope. *Fr.* Windsor Forest. OBEC; SeCePo
When mine hour is come. When. "Æ." ATP; BEL; ChMo; CMP; GTIV; OnYI; POTE; TOP
When mirth is full and free. Reverses. Cardinal Newman. VA
When Mr. Apollinax visited the United States. Mr. Apollinax. T. S. Eliot. OnHM
When Mrs. Evans died they sang. Sympathy Explained. Emyr Humphreys. MoWP
When moiling seems at cease. "According to the Mighty Working." Thomas Hardy. ChMo; OnPM; ReMP
When Molly Smiles. *Unknown.* HBV
(Molly.) CBOV
"When moonlight/ Near midnight." The Fairies in New Ross. *Unknown.* OnYI
When Moonlight Falls. Hilda Conkling. BoChLi; YT
When Moonlike ore [*or* o'er] the Hazure Seas. Thackeray. BOHV; InMe; NA; WhC
When Morning Gilds the Skies. *Unknown, tr. fr. German by* Edward Caswall. MaRV; OlF
When morning is early, is early. Early Light. Lilian Bowes-Lyon. AlDL
When morning moves in slow processional. The Hills Keep Holy Ground. Hellene Seaman. MaRV
When Moses an' his soldiers, f'om Egypt's lan' did flee. He's Jus' de Same Today. *Unknown.* BoAN-1
When Moses and his people. Just the Same To-Day. *Unknown.* BLRP; WBLP
When Moses, musing in the desert, found. The Burning Bush. Norman Nicholson. NeBP; SeCePo
When Moses wuz leadin' the Israelites. Red Sea. *Unknown.* StDa
When most I wink, then do mine eyes best see. Sonnets, XLIII. Shakespeare. PeBoSo
When mother comes each morning. Mother. Rose Fyleman. DD; HH; MPB; SiSoSe
When mother-love makes all things bright. A Christmas Song. Tudor Jenks. COAH
When Mother Reads Aloud. *Unknown.* DDA; FaPON; HH; MPB; OTPC (1946 ed.)
When Mother Scrubs. *Unknown.* PEDC
When mother takes me calling. The Extraordinary Dog. Nancy Byrd Turner. AlBD; TiPo
When mother takes the Fairy Book. The Fairy Book. Abbie Farwell Brown. HBV; HBVY; MPB
When Mountain Ash in Clusters Reddens. Aleksandr Aleksandrovich Blok, *tr. fr. Russian by* Babette Deutsch. TrRV
When mountain rocks and leafy trees. Nature's Lineaments. Robert Graves. FaBoTw
When mountains crumble and rivers all run dry. The Line of Beauty. Edward Dowden. OnYI
When music, heav'nly maid, was young. The Passions; an Ode for Music. William Collins. BCEP; BEL; CEP; CoBE; EiPP; EM-1; EnLi-2 (1949 ed.); EPP; EV-3; GoTL; GTBS; GTBS-D; GTBS-W; GTSE; GTSL; HBV; LoBV; LPS-3; OBEC
When music sounds, gone is the earth I know. Music. Walter de la Mare. AlDL; HH; PoRL; VOD
When my abode's prefixèd time is spent. Amoretti, XLVI. Spenser. PeBoSo; PoFS
When my arms wrap you round I press. Michael Robartes [*or* He] Remembers Forgotten Beauty. W. B. Yeats. PoVP; TIP; TyEnPo
When My Beloved Sleeping Lies. Irene Rutherford McLeod. HBV
When my birthday was coming. Little Brother's Secret. Katherine Mansfield. FaPON; MoSiPe; TiPo
When My Blood Runs Chilly and Col', *with music. Unknown.* ABF
When my brother Tommy. Two in Bed. Abram Bunn Ross. FaPON; MPB; TiPo
When my Clorinda walks in white. Her Confirmation. Selwyn Image. VA
When my devotions could not pierce. Denial [*or* Deniall]. George Herbert. EnL; EPS (1942 ed.); FaBoEn; InPo; LoBV (1949 ed.); MePo; PoEL-2
When My Eye Loses Its Hue. Kadie Molodowsky, *tr. fr. Yiddish by* Sarah Zweig Betsky. OnCuPl
When my eyes descried thee. Moon and Venus. Abul Mughira. MooP
When my father/ Needs water. Irrigation. Ann Nolan Clark. StVeCh (1955 ed.)
When my feet have wander'd. Litany. John S. B. Monsell. VA
When my gloomy hour comes on me. Alexander McLachlan. *Fr.* Woman. CaP
When my good angel guides me to the place. Astrophel and Stella, LX. Sir Philip Sidney. SiPS
When my grave is broke up again [*or* againe]. The Relic [*or* The Relique]. John Donne. AnFE; AtBAP; CaAE; EIL; ElSeCe; EPS; EtPaEn; LiTB; LiTG; LoBV; MaPo; MeLP; MePo; MyFE; OAEP; OBS; PoEL-2; ReEn; ReIE; SeCeV; SeCV-1; SeEP; TuPP; TwP; TyEnPo; ViBoPo; WHA
When my gray city wavers from her sleep. City Asleep. Maurice Lesemann. NP
When my heart was the amorous worms' meat. The Amorous Worms' Meat. Petrarch. Sonnets to Laura: To Laura in Death, XXXVI. LiTW
When my house was bare of skins and pots of meal. Hungry Master and Hungry Cat. Abu Shamaqmaq. PoC
When my last song is sung and I am dead. Requiem. Theodore Maynard. GoBC
When my life has enough of love, and my spirit enough of mirth. A Wanderer's Litany. Arthur Stringer. WGRP
When my love swears [*or* sweares] that she is made of truth. Sonnets, CXXXVIII. Shakespeare. AWP; InPo; JAWP; OAEP; PeBoSo; PoEL-2; ReEn; TrGrPo; TwP; ViBoPo; WBP
When my love was away. Absence. Robert Bridges. EG; LO; OBEV (1st ed.)
When my mother died I was very young. The Chimney Sweeper. Blake. *Fr.* Songs of Innocence. AtBAP; BCEP; BoW; CEP; CH; EiPP; EnRP; KN
When my Nana lets me run. With Peter Pan. Robert Haven Schauffler. HOAH
When My Ship Comes In ("Somewhere, out on the blue sea sailing"). Robert Jones Burdette. FaFP; PTA-2
When My Ship Comes In, *sel.* Frank Sidgwick, *wr. at. to* Robert Jones Burdette
"One room I'll have that's full of shelves." DDA
When my sun of life is low. Sundown. Bert Leston Taylor. OQP; QP-1
When my time came. The Eagle's Song. Mary Austin. NP
When my young brother was killed. War. Joseph Langland. NePoEA
When nations at their Christmas Feast. Christmas Encyclical. Joseph Auslander. QS
When native Britons British lands possess'd. Belvoir Castle. George Crabbe. CaAE
When Nature bids us leave to live, 'tis late. To William Roe. Ben Jonson. SeCV-1
When Nature formed Cassandra, who should move. Pierre de Ronsard. *Fr.* Amours de Cassandre. PrPoCR
When Nature, from her lavish urn. Our Heroes' Graves. *Unknown.* PEOR
When Nature had made all her birds. The Bobolinks. Christopher Pearse Cranch. AA; GN; OTPC
When Nature Hath Betrayed the Heart That Loved Her. Sophie Jewett. AA
When nature made her chief work, Stella's eyes. Astrophel and Stella, VII. Sir Philip Sidney. ElSeCe; ReEn; ReIE; SiCE; SiPS; TuPP
When Nature once in lustful hot undress. Giantess. Baudelaire. MiFP
When nature plays hedge-schoolmaster. C. Day Lewis. *Fr.* Transitional Poem. EnLit
When Nature Wants a Man. Angela Morgan. CV
When navies are forgotten. The New Age [*or* The Victory

Which Is Peace]. Frederic Lawrence Knowles. MaRV; OQP; QP-1
When Neptune from his billows London spied. Of London Bridge, and the Stupendous Sight, and Structure Thereof. James Howell. ChTr
When nettles in winter bring forth roses red. Trust in Women. *Unknown.* BOHV; LO; NA
When next appear'd a dam—so call the place. The Lover's Journey. George Crabbe. *Fr.* Tales. EnSW
When next we met, she bade me turn. Apostasy. Aus of Kuraiza. TrJP
When Night Comes. Henry Vaughan. OQP; QP-1
When night comes down on the children's eyes. At [*or* A] Night in the Wood. Nancy M. Hayes. BoTP; TVC; TVSH
When night comes, list thy deeds; make plain the way. When Night Comes. Henry Vaughan. OQP; QP-1
When night comes on and the chills creep in. Autumn Healing. Jean Ward. LaNeLa
When night drifts along the streets of the city. Solitaire. Amy Lowell. LaNeLa; MAP; MAPA; MoAmPo; NeMA; NP
When night first bids the twinkling stars appear. The Evening. John Gay. *Fr.* Trivia; or, The Art of Walking the Streets of London, III. EnLi-1 (1949 ed.)
When night is come, and all around is still. Safe in His Keeping. Edgar Cooper Mason. BLRP
When night is o'er the wood. The White Owl. F. J. Patmore. PoMS
When night plows the meadows of darkness. Lonely Are the Fields of Sleep. Mary Newton Baldwin. GoYe
When night stirred at sea. The Planter's Daughter. Austin Clarke. OxBI
When night unfoldeth her dusky veil. Freya's Spinning Wheel. Adam Oehlenschläger. BoDS; LiTW
When Noah, perceiving 'twas time to embark. The Dog's Cold Nose. Arthur Guiterman. AlBD; StPo; TiPo (1959 ed.)
When noisy day at last is quieted. Remembrance. Pushkin. TrRV
When None Shall Rail. David Lewis. OBEC
When noon is warm, old Pensioners. Out of Soundings. Padraic Fallon. NeIP
When North first began. Lord North's Recantation. *Unknown.* PAH
When nothing remains of me but a tree. Sowing. Miguel Otero Silva. AnCL
When nothing whereon to lean remains. The Time to Trust. *Unknown.* BLRP
When November's night comes down. Hearth Song. Robert Underwood Johnson. YeAr
When now the end of agony was come. Apostrophe to Death. Caelius Sedulius. *Fr.* Carmen Paschale [*or* Easter Song]. OnYI
When Numbers, Figures, No More Hold the Key. "Novalis," *tr. fr. German by* Mabel Cotterell. AnGP
When nuns were spitted and poets fell. Karl Shapiro. Recapitulations, XIII. FiMAP
When ocean-clouds over inland hills. Misgivings. Herman Melville. AmP; GTBS-D; NePA; OxBA
When October horns are blowing. October. Nancy Birckhead. StaSt
When o'er the crested wood the sun, uprising. Tears. Johan Ludvig Runeberg. AnSL
When o'er the Fields. Carsten Hauch, *tr. fr. Danish by* Charles W. Stork. BoDS
When o'er the hill the eastern star. The Lea Rig [*or* My Ain Kind Dearie, O]. Burns. BSV; EBSV; GoTS
When o'er the mountain steeps. Rêve du Midi. Rose Terry Cooke. LPS-2
When, o'er the silent seas alone. The Meeting of the Ships. Thomas Moore. EtS
When o'er the waters' azure trail. Earth and Sea. Pushkin. WaL
When o'er the yellowing corn a fleeting shadow rushes. Mikhail Yurevich Lermontov. *See* When the Yellow Rye-Field Billows.
When Ol' Sis' Judy Pray. James Edwin Campbell. BANP
When old Gutenberg, inventor of the printing press, and mentor. The Song of the Press. William Hurd Hillyer. PoeMoYo
When old heads felt to-day. On Hearing a Broadcast of Ceremonies in Connection with Conferring of Cardinals' Hats. Denis Wrafter. NeIP
When Olympian Hera was given. The Wedding Chant. Aristophanes. *Fr.* The Birds. OxBG
When 'Omer Smote 'Is Bloomin' Lyre. Kipling. OtMeF
When on a razor's edge all Hellas stood. The Saviors. *Unknown.* OnPM
When, on an autumn evening, with closed eyes. Exotic Perfume. Baudelaire. TiFP
When on Mine Eyes. *Unknown.* ElSeCe
When on my bed the moonlight falls. In Memoriam A. H. H., LXVII. Tennyson. BPN; EM-2; EmBrPo; EnL; EPN; GEPC; LoBV; NeHB; OAEP; PoE; ReaPo; SeCePo; SeCeV; TOP; UnW: ViPo; VLEP
When on my country walks I go. Amico Suo. Herbert P. Horne. VA
When on my day of life the night is falling. At Last [*or* To Paths Unknown]. Whittier. MaRV; NeHB; OQP; PraP; QP-2; TreFS; TrPWD; WGRP
When on my day the evening shadows fall. When Life's Day Closes. Thomas Tiplady. MaRV
When on my sick bed I languish. A Thought of Death. Thomas Flatman. CEP; OBS
When on my soul in nakedness. The Quiet Pilgrim. Edith M. Thomas. AA; BAP; LEAP; OBAV
When, on our casual way. The Shakespearean Bear. Arthur Guiterman. BOHV; CenHV
When, on Ramillies' bloody field. Clare's Dragoons. Thomas Osborne Davis. OnYI
When on the barn's thatch'd roof is seen. Signs of Christmas. Edwin Lees. OHIP; SDH
When on the breath of autumn [*or* autumn's] breeze. Mary Howitt. *Fr.* Cornfields. PRWS; SN; VA
When on the green the rag-tag game had stopt. Sheet Lightning. Edmund Blunden. HaMV
When on the level summer seas. Nature's Key-Notes. Thomas Caulfield Irwin. IrPN
When on the Marge of Evening. Louise Imogen Guiney. AV; OBAV
When on the primal peaceful blank profound. Uranus. Arthur Hugh Clough. ViPP
When once a chic busts through a egg. Gettin' Born. Anthony Euwer. WhC
When once I knew the Lord. Hymn of Sivaite Puritans. *Unknown.* WGRP
When once I rose at morning. Lament for the Woodlands. *Unknown.* KiLC
When once the scourging prophet, with his cry. The Disused Temple. Norman Cameron. ChMP
When once the sun sinks in the west. Evening Primrose. John Clare, *wr. at. to* Emily Brontë. CH; EG; RO; TrGrPo
When once thy foot enters the Church, be bare. On Worship. George Herbert. *Fr.* The Church Porch. MaRV
When one calls on the Quinks they always say. The Quinks. Don Marquis. YaD
When one is wounded in the strife. George W. Caldwell. *Fr.* The Doctor. PoP
When One Knows Thee. Rabindranath Tagore. *See* Divine Companion, The.
When One Loves Tensely. Don Marquis. FiBHP
When Orpheus died, some Muse the lyre still fingered. Plato, a Musician. Leontius. OxBG; UnS
When Orpheus Went Down. Samuel Lisle. ALV
When Oscar came to join his God. Oscar Wilde. *At. to* Swinburne. SiTL
When other ladies to the shades go down. Epigram. Pope. PoEL-3
When other lips and other eyes. Self-evident. James Robinson Planché. PA
When Other Lips and Other Hearts. Alfred Bunn. *Fr.* The Bohemian Girl. TreF
(Then You'll Remember Me, *wr. at. to* Charles Henry Webb.) OlF
When other lovers in arms across. Earl of Surrey. *Fr.* Complaint of the Absence of Her Lover Being upon the Sea. LO
When other wits and other bards. A Yule-Tide Parody. *Unknown.* PA
When our babe he goeth walking in his garden. Garden and Cradle. Eugene Field. AA
When our banner went down. Song. *Unknown.* FOAH
When our brother Fire was having his dog's day. Brother Fire. Louis MacNeice. AtBAP; FaBoMo; MoAB; MoPW; OAEP (2d ed.); WaaP
When our children cried in the shadow of the gallows. Nathan Alterman. *Fr.* From All Peoples. TrJP
When our ducks waddle to the pond. The Ducks. Alice Wilkins. GFA; TiPo
When our heads are bow'd with woe. Hymn for the Sixteenth Sunday after Trinity. Henry Hart Milman. VA
When Our Lady sings the heavens. Madonna's Lullaby. St. Alphonsus Liguori. JS
When our rude and unfashion'd words, that long. To a Lady Who Did Sing Excellently. Lord Herbert of Cherbury. OBS
When our two souls have left this mortal clay. Birds. W. H. Davies. ChMo; CMP
When our two souls stand up erect and strong. Sonnets from the Portuguese, XXII. Elizabeth Barrett Browning. AnFE; BEL; BPN; CBOV; EmBrPo; EnLi-2; EnLit; EPN; EPP; ES; EtPaEn; GTML; GTSE; GTSL; HBV; LiTL; LoPo; LoPS; OAEP; OBEV; PIAE; ReaPo; TCEP; TrGrPo; ViBoPo; ViP; ViPo; WHA
When out by Shellbrook, round by stile and tree. Shellbrook. William Barnes. EnSW
When, out of an intact sea rose terrible. Cataclysm. Louis Johnson. AnNZ

When out of the West long shadows creep. Bylo Land. *Unknown.* BOL
When, over-arched by gorgeous night. The Unknown God. Sir William Watson. WGRP
When, over-burdened with its care. Lincoln's Birthday—1918. John Kendrick Bangs. DD; HH
When over the fair fame of friend or foe. Let Something Good Be Said. James Whitcomb Riley. MaRV
When over the flowery, sharp pasture's/ edge. Flowers by the Sea. William Carlos Williams. AnEnPo; ExPo; MoAB; MoAmPo; Po
When Pa Was a Boy. S. E. Kiser. FAOV
When paint or steel or wood are wearing thin. Docks. Dorothy Wellesley. ShBV-3
When panting sighs the bosom fill. Love and Reason. Arthur Hugh Clough. VLEP
When Papa Was a Boy. Earl Alonzo Brininstool. FAOV; PTA-2
When partners with each other don't agree. The Swan, the Pike, and the Crab. Ivan Andreievich Krylov. BoChLi
When Passion's Trance [Is Overpast]. Shelley. EmBrPo; LoPo
(To ——: "When passion's trance is overpast.") EnRP; ERP
When pavements were blown up, exposing nerves. Epilogue to a Human Drama. Stephen Spender. EnLit
When pensive on that Portraiture I gaze. Sonnet on a Family Picture. Thomas Edwards. CEP; OBEC
When people aren't asking questions. More about People. Ogden Nash. Po
When people call this beast to mind. The Elephant. Hilaire Belloc. BoTP; LiL; RAR; TiPo; UTS
When people's ill they come[s] to I. On [a] Dr. [*or* Doctor Named] Isaac Letsome [*or* Self-composed Epitaph on a Doctor by the Name of I. Letsome]. *Unknown.* GoTP; LiTG; WhC
When Pershing's men go marching into Picardy. Marching Song. Dana Burnet. AOAH; MC; PAH
When Pestilence Strikes. Sophocles, *tr. fr. Greek by* Gilbert Murray. *Fr.* Oedipus Rex. GrR
When Peter Wanderwide was young. The Death and Last Confession of Wandering Peter. Hilaire Belloc. OtMeF
When Petrarch Peck, aged twenty-three. Polite Petrarch Peck. Horatio Winslow. LauV
When Phoebe form'd a wanton smile. Sonnet. William Collins. EnLoPo
When Phoebus bright the azure skies. Leader-Haughs and Yarrow. *Unknown.* EBSV
When Phoebus had melted the sickles of ice. Robin Hood and the Ranger. *Unknown.* ESPB; StVeCh
When Phoebus in the rainy cloud. Welcome Eild. *Unknown.* GoTS
When Phoebus lifts his head out of the Winter's wave. Michael Drayton. *Fr.* Polyolbion, Thirteenth Song. OBS
When Plaintively and Near the Cricket Sings. Nora May French. AV
When Planes Outsoar the Spirit. Lilith Lorraine. MaRV; MuM
When poetry walked the live, spring wood. Kingcups. Sacheverell Sitwell. BLV; MBP; MoBrPo
When poets wrote and painters drew. Protogenes and Apelles. Matthew Prior. GoTL
When Polly Buys a Hat. E. Hill. BoTP
When Polly lived back in the old deep woods. Stranger. Elizabeth Madox Roberts. MAP; MoAmPo
When Pontius wished an edict might be passed. Epigram. Matthew Prior. ALV
When Poor Mary Came Wandering Home. *Unknown. See* Mary of the Wild Moor.
When prayers have been offered, and good-nights are said. The Voyage to Lullaby Land. Earl Alonzo Brininstool. BOL
When President John Quincy. John Quincy Adams. Stephen Vincent Benét. NAMI
When pride and envy, and the scorn. Verses. Henry Kirke White. ERP
When Priests Are More in Word. Shakespeare. *Fr.* King Lear, III, ii. ViBoPo
When primroses are out in spring. Days Too Short. W. H. Davies. MBP; MoBrPo; NeMA; NV; POTE; TCEP
When Psyche's friend becomes her lover. Friend and Lover. "Madeline Bridges." AA; HBV
When quacks with pills political would dope us. Canopus. Bert Leston Taylor. ALV; FiBHP; HBMV; InMe; PIAE; WhC
When Queen Djenira slumbers through. Queen Djenira. Walter de la Mare. BMEP; LEAP
When raging love with extreme [*or* extreeme] pain. The Lover Comforteth Himself with the Worthiness of His Love. Earl of Surrey. EnLoPo; EV-1; PoE; SiCE; SiPS; TuPP
When rain falls, I say. Chanty. Ronald McCuaig. MoAuPo
When Reason, giving way to heat of blood. Ariosto. *Fr.* Orlando Furioso, XXX. PrPoCR
When rebullient the brine. A Sea-Fight. Timotheus. *Fr.* The Persae. OxBG
When red hath set the beamless sun. The Shepherd [*or* The Shepherd in Winter]. Sir Walter Scott. *Fr.* Marmion, *Introd. to* IV. ERP; OTPC (1923 ed.)
When red sun fox steals down the sky. The Hunting. Eden Phillpotts. MBP
When Reedisdale and Wise William. Redesdale and Wise William. *Unknown.* ESPB
When rhymes were yet but rude, thy pen endeavored. An Epitaph in Commendation of George Turberville, a Learned Gentleman. Sir John Harington. SiCE
When Richard Cory went down town. *See* Whenever Richard Cory went down town.
"When rites and melodies began." The Trial. W. H. Auden. NePA
When Robin Hood, and his merry men all. Robin Hood and the Valiant Knight. *Unknown.* ESPB
When Robin Hood and Little John. Robin Hood's Death [*or* The Death of Robin Hood]. *Unknown.* EM-1; ESPB; OnSP; TrGrPo; ViBoFo
When Robin Hood in the green-wood livd. Robin Hood Rescuing Will Stutly. *Unknown.* BaBo; ESPB
When Robin Hood was about twenty [*or* eighteen *or* was twenty] years old. Robin Hood and Little John. *Unknown.* BaBo (A *vers.*); BHV; ESPB; OTPC (1946 ed.); StaSt; StVeCh; ViBoFo
When Robin now three days had married been. Prudence. Benjamin Franklin. LauV
When Roland saw that life had fled. *Unknown. Fr.* The Song of Roland. EnLi-1; OuHeWo
When rolling thunders shake the skies. Lines Written after a Very Severe Tempest, Which Cleared Up Extremely Pleasant. Mercy Warren. BAV
When rosy plumelets tuft the larch. In Memoriam A. H. H., XCI. Tennyson. EmBrPo; EPN; FaBoEn; GEPC; ViBoPo; ViPo; VLEP
When round the earth the Father's hands. Rest. George Macdonald. BSV
When rowan leaves are dank and rusting. Autumn Love. Aleksandr Blok. BoR
When russet beech-leaves drift in air. Autumn Memories. George Francis Savage-Armstrong. VA
When Ruth was left half desolate. Ruth; or, The Influence of Nature. Wordsworth. ChER; EnRP; ERP; GEPC; GTBS; GTBS-D; GTBS-W; GTSE; GTSL; PoEL-4; REAL
When Ruth was old. The Immigrant. Frank Kendon. MBP; MoBrPo (1942 ed.); POTE
When ruthful time the South's memorial places. The Stricken South to the North. Paul Hamilton Hayne. PAH
When Sadness Fills a Journey. John Waller. NeBP
When sage Ulysses sailed by. Beware of Sirens. —— Bewe. ReIE; SiCE
When Saint Chrysostom Prayed. Margaret J. Preston. PraP
When Saint Stephen was at Jerusalem. Now Sing We, Both All and Some. *Unknown.* AnEC
When Sam goes back in memory. Sam. Walter de la Mare. MBP; MoAB; MoBrPo; NeMA; PoMS; TiPo; TwCV
When sane men gather in to talk of Love. Irene Rutherford McLeod. *Fr.* Sonnets. HBMV
When Santa Claus Comes. *Unknown.* ChBR
When Santa Claus has trimmed our Christmas tree. At Christmas Time. Mary Brennan Clapp. GFA
When sap ebbed low and your green days were over. To My Blackthorn Stick. F. R. Higgins. POTE
When Sarah Pierrepont let her spirit rage. Address to the Scholars of New England. John Crowe Ransom. AmPP; LiTM (rev. ed.); NePA
When Sarah's papa was from home a great way. The Letter. Elizabeth Turner. *Fr.* Mrs. Turner's Object-Lessons. OTPC (1923 ed.)
When school is out, we love to follow. Sniff. Frances Frost. BrR; SiSoSe; TiPo (1959 ed.)
When scribblers of the Saxon brood. Verses to Mr. Vaughan of Hengwrt. Evan Evans. PrWP
When sense of taste controls the route. Thoughts on Choosing. George MacBeth. PoN
When Serpents Bargain. E. E. Cummings. PoLFOT
When seven years were come and gane. Sweet William's Ghost (F *vers.*). *Unknown.* ESPB
When shades of night have come. Domestic Scenes. Miguel de Unamuno. WoL
When Shakespeare Laughed. Christopher Morley. PFE
When Shakespeare leads the mind a dance. The Critic's Rules. Robert Lloyd. *Fr.* Shakespeare; an Epistle to Mr. Garrick. OBEC
When shall disunion and estrangement end? The Mock Caliph. *Unknown.* EnLi-1
When shall I expel you from my blood? The Knife. "J. R." MoAuPo
When shall I, Lord, this mortal load untied. To Our Saviour. Agostinho da Cruz. CAW

When shall I make a song for you, my love? Unsung. Nettie Palmer. BoAu
When shall I see the half-moon sink again. End of Another Home Holiday. D. H. Lawrence. FaBoMo; MoVE
When shall the Island Queen of Ocean lay. The Bower of Peace. Robert Southey. *Fr.* Ode Written during the War with America, 1814. MC; PAH
When shall the panting fox. Prayer for the Hunted. Daniel Henderson. SaFP
When shall the tale of wandering years be done? "Cursed Be He Who First Taught Grecians War." Sophocles. *Fr.* Ajax. GrR
When shall we be married. *Unknown.* OxNR; SiTL, *st.* I
When shall we learn, what should be clear as day. Canzone. W. H. Auden. LiTA; LiTM; MoVE
When Shall We See Thy Like Again? Mary Wingate. *See* Washington.
When shall we three meet again. The Witches' Meeting. Shakespeare. *Fr.* Macbeth, I, i, *and* IV, i. CG
When shaven crown, and hallow'd girdle's power. Satyr III. John Oldham. *Fr.* Satires upon the Jesuits. SeCV-2
When shawes beene sheene, and shradds full fayre. Robin Hood and Guy of Gisborne. *Unknown.* ATP (1935 ed.); BaBo; BEL; CoBE; EM-1; EPP; ESPB; OAEP; OBB; PFE; TOP
When She a Maiden Slim. Maurice Hewlett. OHIP
When She Cam Ben, She Bobbed. Burns. EBSV
When she came suddenly in. The Door. Robert Graves. LiTB
When she carries food to the table and stoops down. Part of Plenty. Bernard Spencer. LiTB; LiTL; LiTM
When She Comes Home. James Whitcomb Riley. AA; BAP; FaBoBe; HBV; LBAP
When she fed the/ child. The Feeding. Joel Oppenheimer. NeAP
When she floated into sight. Two Suns. Al-Dabbaj. MooP
When she her crimson lips uncloses. Afanasi Fet, *tr. fr. Russian by* Oliver Elton. BoRS
When she in other writing had displayed. Ariosto. *Fr.* Orlando Furioso, XXXV. PrPoCR
When she is far, I only want to see her. Love Grows by What It Feeds On. Bhartrihari. OnPM
When she knew the day was come. Alcestis' Final Hour. Euripides. *Fr.* Alcestis. GrR
When She Plays upon the Harp or Lute. Moses ibn Ezra, *tr. fr. Hebrew by* Solomon Solis-Cohen. TrJP
When she rises in the morning. Gloire de Dijon. D. H. Lawrence. EnLoPo; LBBV; OAEP (2d ed.)
When she sleeps, her soul, I know. Doubts. Rupert Brooke. CH
When She Smiles. Spenser. *See* Amoretti, XL.
When she spoke to me. Pearls. Al-Mushafi. MooP
When she, that soul of fire, appears. Portrait. Pushkin. OnPM; TrRV
When she was born she came with smiling eye. Robert Tofte. *Fr.* Laura. ElSeCe; ReIE; TuPP
When she was set in her carven chest. Danaë Adrift. Simonides. GrPE
When she was still alive. Hitomaro, *tr. fr. Japanese by* Kenneth Rexroth. OnPJ
When shepherds pipe on oaten straws. Spring, 2. Shakespeare. *Fr.* Love's Labour's Lost, V, ii. UnPo
When Shrill Winds Shriek. Wright Thomas. ReaPo
When, sick of all the sorrow and distress. The City. Charles Hanson Towne. *Fr.* Manhattan, XIV. CV; SBMV
When Silence Divests Me. Henry Birnbaum. GoYe
When silent I. Thomas Traherne. *Fr.* The Salutation. AlDL
When silver Diane full of beames bright. A Starscape. John Bellenden. ACP
When, sin-stricken, burdened, and weary. "My Grace Is Sufficient for Thee." *Unknown.* BLRP; PraP
When Sir Beelzebub. Edith Sitwell. *See* Sir Beelzebub.
When Sir Joshua Reynolds died. Sir Joshua Reynolds [*or* Epigram]. Blake. FiBHP; LiTG; OxBoLi; SiTL
When Sir Ulrich's widow in church knelt to pray. The Fair Agnete. Agnes Miegel. CAW
When skies are blue and days are bright. The Choice. Katharine Tynan. CP; PoeT
When ski-ing in the Engadine. Patience. Harry Graham. FiBHP; MoShBr; WhC
When sleep forsook my open eye. My Mother. Ann Taylor. MeMeAg
When sleep, the supposed guardian. Dead Morning. Raymond Holden. MAP; MoAmPo (1942 ed.)
When slumbering in my convict cell my childhood days I see. The Convict. *Unknown.* CoSo; CSF
When Smoke Stood Up from Ludlow. A. E. Housman. A Shropshire Lad, VII. AnFE; ChMo; CMP; EnLit; MBP; MoBrPo; OuHeWo; POTT; PoVP; TyEnPo; VLEP
(Blackbird, The.) BLA; HBV
When snow-balls [pack] on the horses' hoofs. Sugar Weather. Peter McArthur. CaP; CPG; OCL
When snow like sheep lay in the fold. In Memory of Jane Frazer. Geoffrey Hill. NePoEA
When snow, like silence visible. The Snowbird. John Banister Tabb. SPP
When snowdrifts have melted to rillet and run. Cotter's Song. Johan Skjoldborg. BoDS
When soft winds and sunny skies. Fragment. Shelley. EmBrPo; ERP
When softly gathering shades of ev'n. To My Soldier Brother. Sallie M. Ballard. BlG
When Sol did cast no light. The Seaman's Happy Return. *Unknown.* ChTr; SG
When Solomon was reigning in his glory. Solomon and the Bees. John Godfrey Saxe. GN; GoTP; OTPC
When some belovèd voice that was to you. Substitution. Elizabeth Barrett Browning. MaRV; WGRP
"When some great oak-tree, glorious in men's gaze." Courage in Exile. Pindar. *Fr.* Pythian Odes, IV. GrPE
When some great sorrow, like a mighty river. This, Too, Shall Pass Away. Lanta Wilson Smith. BLPA; NeHB
When some grim sorceress, whose skill. To Helen. Winthrop Mackworth Praed. LoBV
When some mad bard sits down to muse. Love at a Rout. Winthrop Mackworth Praed. ERP
When some proud son of man returns to earth. Epitaph to a Dog. Byron. AlBD
When someone beat a dog, he stopped and said. Pythagoras and the Dog. Xenophanes. GrR
When Sorrow moves with silent tread. Peace Be Thine. Winthrop Mackworth Praed. ERP
When Sorrow, using mine own fire's might. Astrophel and Stella, CVIII. Sir Philip Sidney. SiPS
When sorrowe singes a litle a litles enough. *Unknown.* SeCSL
When souls that have put off their mortal gear. Recognition. John White Chadwick. AA
When sporgles spanned the floreate mead. Uffia. Harriet R. White. BOHV; NA
When spring begins, the maids in flocks. Spring. Edith Sitwell. OAEP (2d ed.)
When spring came on with fresh delight. Anacreontic. Thomas Parnell. GTIV
When spring came tiptoe up the hill. The Dress of Spring. May Justus. YeAr
When Spring Came to Nazareth. Mary Sinton Leitch. ChIP
When Spring Comes Back to England. Alfred Noyes. HBV
(World's May-Queen, The.) OBVV
When spring comes laughing. A Song of the Four Seasons. Austin Dobson. BMEP; HBV; POTT; VLEP
When spring comes on with freshness of new leaves. To Men Unborn. David Osborne Hamilton. HH; PEDC
When spring fires with sweet rage. Moschatel. A. J. Young. MM
When spring grows old, and sleepy winds. Atalanta. Maurice Thompson. OBAV
When spring in sunny woodland lay. Love's Forget-Me-Not. Isabella Valancy Crawford. CPG
When spring is in the fields that stained your wing. To a Linnet in a Cage. Francis Ledwidge. OnYI; TIP
When spring revives in Arun's veins. Kingcups. Eleanor Farjeon. GBV (1952 ed.)
When spring, to woods and wastes around. The Murdered Traveller. Bryant. CoBA
When spring unbound comes o'er us like a flood. In April. Ethelwyn Wetherald. CaP; OCL
When spring was running through the woods. Camelot. Charles Dalmon. TCPD
When spring-time flushes the desert grass. The Ballad of the King's Jest. Kipling. GBV
When spurred by tasks unceasing or undone. Rest Where You Are. Charles Poole Cleaves. OQP; QP-2
When starry legions gleam on. Moonbeams. Carl David af Wirsén. AnSL
When Stars Are in the Quiet Skies. Sir Edward Bulwer-Lytton. *Fr.* Ernest Maltravers. VA
(Night and Love.) HBV
When Stars Are Shrouded. "I. T." ElL
When stars begin softly to spatter. Milking Kraal. F. C. Slater. BoSA
When stars pursue their solemn flight. Music in the Night. Harriet Prescott Spofford. AA
When stars ride in on the wings of dusk. Refuge. Lew Sarett. HBMV; MaRV
When stealthy age creeps on me unaware. A Litany for Old Age. Una W. Harsen. TrPWD
When stone-hewn storms knock against our cottage. Third and Fourth. Keidrych Rhys. NeBP
When storms arise Hymn. Paul Laurence Dunbar. TrPWD
When storms blow loud, 'tis sweet to watch at ease. Suave Mari Magno. Lucretius. *Fr.* De Rerum Natura. AWP
When storms go growling off to lonely places. The Whale and the *Essex.* A. M. Sullivan. EtS
When, stricken by the freezing blast. Daniel Webster. Oliver Wendell Holmes. LPS-3; PAH

When strong and rich the wicked ones you see. Prudence. Sadi. PeP
When stubble-lands were greening, you came among the stooks. The Green Autumn Stubble. *Tr. fr. Irish by* Patrick Browne. OxBI
When suddenly at midnight. God Forsakes Anthony. C. P. Cavafy. MoGP
When Sue Wears Red. Langston Hughes. GoSl
When summer came, we locked up our lives and fled. The Gentle Snorer. Mona Van Duyn. NePA
When summer comes I like to stay. On the Beach. Emilie Blackmore Stapp. GFA
When summer comes, the swains on Tweed. Cowdenknowes. Robert Crawford. EBSV
When summer o'er her native hills. On a Picture. Anne C. Lynch Botta. LPS-1
When summer took in hand the winter to assail. Love's Rebel [*or* Complaint of a Lover That Defied Love and Was by Love After the More Tormented]. Earl of Surrey. OBSC; ReIE; SiCE; SiPS
When Summer's End Is Nighing. A. E. Housman. MoVE
When summer's in the city. The Ice-Cream Man. Rachel Field. BoChLi; FaPON; GaP; SiSoSe
When Summer's sunny hues adorn. Evergreens. Edward Coote Pinkney. BAV
When sun has set behind the hill. Finis. Eden Phillpotts. LBBV
When sunny clouds sail over Kent. Green and Black. Sir Charles Scott Sherrington. PoP
When sunny hills are draped in velvet shadows. At Close of Day. Stephan G. Stephansson. IcP
When suns are low, and nights are long. The Queen of the Year. Edna Dean Proctor. DD
When suns are set, and stars in view. On the Sleep of Plants. Philip Freneau. IAP
When sunset flows into golden glows. Star Song. Robert Underwood Johnson. HBV
When sunshine met the wave. In the Beginning. Harriet Monroe. AA
When supper time is almost come. Milking Time. Elizabeth Madox Roberts. BoChLi; FaPON; LS; OTPC (1946 ed.); RIS; SUS; UTS
When Susanna Jones wears red. When Sue Wears Red. Langston Hughes. GoSl
When Susan's work was done, she'd [*or* she would] sit. Old Susan. Walter de la Mare. ChMo; CMP; InP; MBP; MoBrPo; NeMA; OnPP; PoeMoYo; PoRL; POT; PoTo; TCEP; TreFS; TwCV; VOD
When swallows Northward flew. Lord Guy. George F. Warren. BOHV
When sycamore leaves wer a-spreaden. Woak Hill. William Barnes. GTML; GTSL
When Tayis Bank. *Unknown.* EBSV
When tempest winnowed grain from bran. The Victor of Antietam. Herman Melville. GA; MC; PAH
When tender ewes, brought home with evening sun. Menaphon's Roundelay. Robert Greene. *Fr.* Menaphon. WP
When that Abe Lincoln was a boy. Prairie. K. N. Llewellyn. YeAr
When that Arthur was King. King Arthur. Layamon. *Fr.* The Brut. LEAP
When that body loved/ As no other was. Death and Transfiguration. Marya Zaturenska. QS
When that brave honor of the Latin name. Ruins of Rome, V. Joachim du Bellay OnPM
When that career was ended, from the steed the Cid got down. Arrival of the Family at Valencia. *Unknown. Fr.* The Cid. TeCS
When that day comes, whose evening sayes I'm gone. His Sailing from Julia. Robert Herrick. PoEL-3
"When that dead face, bowered in the furthest years." The Love-Moon. Dante Gabriel Rossetti. The House of Life, XXXVII. PoVP; ViPo
When that great Kings return to clay. The Burial. Kipling. BoSA
When that huge serpent, night. Daybreak. Ibn Burd. MooP
When that I, poor soul, was born. The Nymph Diana's Song. Jorge de Montemayor, *tr. by* Bartholomew Young. *Fr.* Diana. ReIE
When That I Was and a Little Tiny Boy. Shakespeare. *Fr.* Twelfth Night, V, i. AnFE; AtBAP; CH; EG; EiL; ExPo; FaBoCh; HBV; InPo; KN; LiTB; LoBV; LoGBV; MyFE; OAEP; OBSC; PoRA; ReaPo; SiCE; SiTL; ViBoPo; WaKn
(Feste's Song.) OxBoLi
(Rain It Raineth Every Day, The.) OTPC (1923 ed.)
(Song: "When that I was . . .") FiP; LiTG; PoEL-2
When that my days were fewer. Middle Age. Rudolph Chambers Lehmann. HBV
When that my mood is sad, and in the noise. The Shaded Water. William Gilmore Simms. LPS-2
When that old joke was new. Old Fashioned Fun. Thackeray. BOHV; InMe; PA
When that our English tongue. "That Did in Luve So Lively Write." Georgine M. Adams. InMe
When that our gentle Lord was born. A Ballad of Wise Men. George M. P. Baird. ChrBoLe; SDH
When that rich Soul[e] which to her heaven is gone. An Anatomie [*or* Anatomy] of the World: The First Anniversary. John Donne. EnLP; SeCV-1; SeEP
When That St. George Had Slain His Dragon. *Unknown.* SiTL
(Limerick: "When that Seint George hadde Sleyne ye dragone.") NA
When that sweet April showers with downward shoot. Chaucer. Prologue to "The Canterbury Tales." BCEP; WoL
When that the chill Charocco blows. *See* Whenas the chill sirocco blows.
When that the Eternal deigned to look. Ballade of Illegal Ornaments. Hilaire Belloc. ACP (1952 ed.)
When that which is divine in us doth try. The Model and the Statue. Michelangelo. OnPM
When that your sail bent to the ocean-swell. Pierre de Ronsard, *tr. fr. French by* Curtis Hidden Page. PrPoCR
When the air of October is sweet and cold as the wine of apples. Johnny Appleseed. Edgar Lee Masters. CP
When the *Alabama's* keel was laid. The *Alabama. Unknown.* ShS, *vers.* I; SoAmSa
When the allegorical man came calling. The Inflatable Globe. Theodore Spencer. LiTA; LiTM; NePA; WaP
When the anchors that faith has cast. Ultima Veritas. Washington Gladden. MaRV
When the anchor's weigh'd and the ship's unmoored. Jack the Guinea Pig. *Unknown.* AmSS
When the angry passion gathering in my mother's face I see. The Patter of the Shingle. *Unknown.* BLPA
When the anxious hearts say "Where?" Missing. *Unknown.* WGRP
When the *Ark* and *Dove* within the glassy wave. The *Ark* and the *Dove.* Daniel Sargent. EtS
When the Arts in their infancy were. The Magpie's Nest. Charles *and* Mary Lamb. OTPC (1923 ed.); PRWS
When the Assault Was Intended to the City. Milton. EM-1; EPP; ES; EV-2; GTBS; GTBS-D; GTBS-W; GTSE; GTSL; OuHeWo: TCEP
(Arms and the Muse.) LH
(Sonnet: "Captain or Colonel, or Knight in Arms.") SeEP
When the Atlantic upsloped itself. Winter Tryst. Mark Van Doren. LiTA; LiTM (1946 ed.)
When the band comes along the street. The Band. —— John. GFA
When the bat's on the wing and the bird's in the tree. The Starlighter. Arthur Guiterman. GaP; MoSiPe; SiSoSe
When the battle is long, and I am weary with strife. Your Prayers. *Unknown.* PraP
When the beauteous Spring I see. Pierre de Ronsard. *Fr.* Amours de Marie. PrPoCR
When the bird flew from the Columbus hull. Jeremiad. Oscar Williams. LiTA
When the black car came thundering from its pale. Proserpine at Enna. Ronald Bottrall. SeCePo
When the black herds of the rain were grazing. The Lost Heifer. Austin Clarke. OxBI
When the black-lettered list to the gods was presented. Wife, Children, and Friends. William Robert Spencer. LPS-1
When the blue-black waves are tipped with white, and the balmy trade-winds blow. In Action. *Unknown.* MDAH
When the boat touches on the other side. A Masque of Loved Ladies. Anne Goodwin Winslow. LS
When the breath of twilight blows to flame the misty skies. By the Margin of the Great Deep. "Æ." CaAE; HBMV; OBEV; OBVV; PoVP
When the breeze from the bluebottle's blustering blim. To Marie. John Bennett. BOHV; NA
When the breeze of a joyful dawn blew free. Recollections of the Arabian Nights. Tennyson. EV-5; PoVP; VLEP
When the bright eyes of the day. Day and Night. James Stephens. BoTP
When the British warrior queen. Boadicea. William Cowper. BCEP; BeLS; BHV; CG; EV-3; HBV; LEAP; LH; LPS-2; OTPC
When the bubble moon is young. June. Harrison S. Morris. BAP; HBV
When the buds began to burst. The Three Roses. Walter Savage Landor. BPN; EmBrPo
When the candles burn again in the Kowhai tree. Kowhai. A. R. D. Fairburn. MM
When the Cannon Booms No More. William Herbert Carruth. PEDC
When the cardoon flowers, and the loud cicada sings. Cicada Days. Hesiod. *Fr.* Works and Days. OxBG
When the cat's away. Well-packed Wisdom. Benjamin Franklin. *Fr.* Poor Richard's Almanac. StaSt
When the charge of the passionate gale beats the billows to foam. Song of the Storm. Albert Durrant Watson. CPG

When the Child Appears. Victor Hugo, *tr. fr. French by* Alan Conder. TrFP
When the children have been good. Heinrich Hoffmann, *tr. fr. German at. to* J. R. Planché. BoN
When the child's brow, with torment flushing red. The Louse-Catchers. Arthur Rimbaud, *tr. by* Roy Campbell. LiTW; MiFP
When the child's forehead full of red torments. The Lice Seekers. Arthur Rimbaud, *tr. by* Kenneth Koch *and* Georges Guy. AnFP
When the chill Charoko blows. *See* Whenas the chill sirocco blows.
When the Christ Child Came. Frederic E. Weatherly. OHIP
When the Church Is No Longer Regarded. T. S. Eliot. *Fr.* The Rock. MaRV
When the Clans of the Open Hand convene. Rebecca and Abigail. Katharine Lee Bates. CV
When the Clocks Strike. Rainer Maria Rilke, *tr. fr. German by* Herman Salinger. TwGV
When the Cloud Comes down the Mountain. Sir Charles G. D. Roberts. CPG
When the clouds are upon the hills. *Unknown.* OxNR
When the clouds shake their hyssops, and the rain. A Rainy Day in April. Francis Ledwidge. MBP
When the clouds' swoln bosoms echo back the shouts. In Tenebris, II. Thomas Hardy. BrBE; ChMo; CMP; LiTM (rev. ed.); PoLFOT; ViPo
When the cock in the dish. The Innocents. Elinor Wylie. StJW
When the cocks craw. The Deserted Maiden. Eduard Mörike. LiA
When the cold comes. Where? When? Which? Langston Hughes. NePoAm-2
When the cold wind visits you from the corners of the earth. To Li Po. Tu Fu. WhP
When the Cows Come Home. Agnes E. Mitchell. PTA-1
When the Cows Come Home. Christina Rossetti. *Fr.* Sing-Song. OTPC (1946 ed.); RAR; UTS
(Do You Know?) StVeCh (1940 ed.)
(Milking Time) GFA; MPB; PRWS
When the Crane Flies South. Hesiod. *See* Crane's Flight, The.
When the creeping vine blooms and spreads her tendrils. The Vintage. Kostas Krystallis. MoGP
When the crop is fair in the olive-yard. The Cocooning. Frédéric Mistral. *Fr.* The Mirèio. AWP; JAWP; WBP; WoL
When the curtains of night are pinned back by the stars. I'll Remember You, Love, in My Prayers. *Unknown.* AS; BLPA; FaBoBe; NeHB
When the Dark Comes Down. L. M. Montgomery. CPG
When the dark-eyed lad, Columbus. Dark-eyed Lad Columbus. Nancy Byrd Turner. SiSoSe
When the dawn comes. *Unknown. Fr.* Kokin Shu. AWP
When the dawn flames in the sky. At Dawning. Nelle Richmond Eberhart. OIF
When the day and the night do meete. Cobbe's Prophecies. *Unknown.* NA
When the Day Comes. Manuel Gutiérrez Nájera, *tr. fr. Spanish by* Samuel Beckett. AnMP
When the day darkens. The Unknown Wind. "Fiona Macleod." BoTP
When the day is stormy, and no sun shines through. Trust; a Song. Eben E. Rexford. BLRP
When the Daylight Wanes. Thomas Tiplady. MaRV
When the days begin to lengthen. *Unknown.* GoTP; RIS
When the Days Shall Grow Long. Hayyim Nahman Bialik, *tr. fr. Hebrew by* A. M. Klein. TrJP
When the Dead Men Die. Rose O'Neill. HBMV
When the dentist adjusts his drill. Variation: Ode to Fear. Robert Penn Warren. FiMAP
When the departing, great sun stands. A Presence. Kenneth Slade Alling. QS
When the devil was sick, the devil a monk would be. Epigram. *Unknown.* ALV
When the dew is on the grass. *Unknown.* OxNR
When the Dews Are Earliest Falling. Arthur Hugh Clough. OAEP
When the diplomats cease from their capers. The Song of the Cannon. Sam Walter Foss. IDAH
When the donkey saw the zebra. A Surprise. Malcolm Douglas. MeMeAg
When the Drive Goes Down. Douglas Malloch. StVeCh
When the Duke of Leeds shall have made his choice. *Unknown.* LO
When the dumb Hour, clothed in black. The Silent Voices. Tennyson. BMEP; EPP; LEAP; MaRV; OQP; QP-2; VA
When the dying flame of day. Hymn of the Moravian Nuns of Bethlehem. Longfellow. PAH
When the eager squadrons of day are faint and disbanded. The Cult of the Celtic. Anthony C. Deane. PA
When the earth is turned in spring. The Worm. Ralph Bergengren. FaPON; SiSoSe; UTS
When the Ecstasy Has Passed. Euripides, *tr. fr. Greek by* Gilbert Murray. *Fr.* Bacchae. GrR
When the Ecstatic Body Grips. Eric Robertson Dodds. GTIV; POTE; ViBoPo
When the enemy doth throw. Love the Foe. Sadi. PeP
When the enemy is near thee. Arthur Hugh Clough. *Fr.* Dipsychus, II. BPN
When the evening came my love said to me. Prothalamion. Francis Brett Young. HBMV
When the fair one was here, the house was adorned with flowers. To ——. Li Po. WhP
When the fair year. The Jews. Henry Vaughan. OBS
When the Fairies. Edward Dorn. NeAP
When the fairies are all for their dances drest. The Nightingale and the Lark. Ernest Whitney. ATP (1935 ed.)
When the fairies come back to Santa Fe. When the Fairies. Edward Dorn. NeAP
When the far south glittered. Pilgrimage. Austin Clarke. OxBI
When the farmer comes to town with his wagon broken down. The Farmer Comes to Town [*or* The Farmer]. *Unknown.* AS; TrAS
When the farmer's day is done. The Barnyard. Maud Burnham. PCH; PPL; TiPo
When the feud of hot and cold. December. Joel Benton. SN
When the fiddlers play their tunes, you may sometimes hear. Fairy-Music. Rose Fyleman. HH; TSW; TSWC
When the fields catch flower. April. Vidame de Chartres. AWP
When the fierce North-wind with his airy forces. The Day of Judgement [*or* Judgment]. Isaac Watts. BCEP; CEP; CoEV; EiPP; EV-3; LoBV; OBEV; SeCePo; TriL
When the fight begins within himself. Robert Browning. *Fr.* Bishop Blougram's Apology. MaRV
When the firelight, red and clear. Alfred Noyes. *Fr.* The Flower of Old Japan. AIDL
When the first faint stars come peeping out. My Bess. Raymond W. Walker. CAG
When the first larks began to soar. After Battle. Duncan Campbell Scott. AOAH; TwCV
When the first man who wasn't quite an ape. The Ultimate Atrocity. Siegfried Sassoon. ChMo; CMP
When the first opal presage of the morn. Dawn in the Desert. Clinton Scollard. POT; PoTo
When the first silent frost has trod. The Ghost-Yard of the Goldenrod. Bliss Carman. TwCaPo
When the flower of the sun, the rose of Lahore. Immortal Perfume. Leconte de Lisle. TrFP
When the flush of a newborn sun fell first on Eden's green and gold. The Conundrum of the Workshops. Kipling. BMEP; HBV; MBP; MoBrPo; PoVP; VA
When the foe came in numbers. Granny Tassia. "Markos Avgeris." MoGP
When the foes, in conflict heated. On the Heights of Mission Ridge. J. Augustine Signaigo. BlG
When the folk of my household. Lament. *Tr. by* Edward Walsh. OBVV
When the formless infinite enshrouds. Slender Spring. Jorge Guillén. AnSpL-2
When the foundations quaked and the pillars shook. Rejoice in the Abyss. Stephen Spender. OnHM
When the fox talks about peace. Country Proverbs. *Unknown.* StaSt
When the French fleet lay. Running the Blockade. Nora Perry. PAH
When the frost did so long a time persevere. De Gelu Diutino, Anno Dom. 1607. John Heath. SiCE
When the Frost Is on the Punkin. James Whitcomb Riley. BAV; BOHV; CP; DD; DDA; FaBoBe; FaFP; HBV; HBVY; IAP; MAP; MCCG; MoAmPo (1942 ed.); MPB; NeMA; OTPC; PFY; PoeMoYo; PoMa; TreF; VOD
When the frost is white on the fodder-stack. In the Barn-Yard's Southerly Corner. Sir Charles G. D. Roberts. BoCaPo; TwCaPo
When the full-bosomed and free-limbed spring. Exultation. Shaemus O'Sheel. PC
When the funereal shadow and black drape. A Jovino: El Melancólico. Juan Meléndez Valdés. BoFr
When the game began between them for a jest. Stage Love. Swinburne. PoEL-5; ViPP
When the gay sun first breaks the shades of night. Dawn and Night. John Gay. *Fr.* A Contemplation on Night. BeR
When the glory of the Lord comes, it's like a mighty wind. The Prophet. Sherard Vines. LBBV; OS
When the glow of fading sunlight. The Man of the Open West. Arthur W. Monroe. PoOW
When the God of Liberty. Liberty. Mikael Nalbandian. ArmLP
When the God of Merry Love. Thomas Campion. ReIE
When the golden sun he knelt. The Good Day. Henry Howarth Bashford. HBV
When the gong sounds ten in the morning. Vocation. Rabindranath Tagore. FaPON; GaP

When the Grass Shall Cover Me. Ina Donna Coolbrith. AA; CP; HBV; LBAP
When the grass was closely mown. The Dumb Soldier. Robert Louis Stevenson. GoTP; OnHT
When the Great Gray Ships Come In. Guy Wetmore Carryl. AA; EtS; FaBoBe; GDAH; HBV; LBAP; MC; PAH
When the great hero, adding to the charms. The Damnation of Byron. A. D. Hope. MoAuPo
When the great man hears of Tao. *Unknown, tr. fr. Chinese.* Tao Teh Ching, XXIV. WhP
When the great wind sets things whirling. The Popular Poplar Tree. Blanche Willis Howard. ADAH
When the Green Gits Back in the Trees. James Whitcomb Riley. ADAH
When the Green Lies over the Earth. Angelina Weld Grimké. CDC; PoNe
When the Green Woods Laugh. Blake. *See* Laughing Song.
When the grey lake-water rushes. The Solitary Woodsman. Sir Charles G. D. Roberts. BoCaPo; CaP; OCL; TwCV
When the grey night is pierced. Afterwards. Peter Baker. NeTW
When the Gulls Come In. Helen Merrill Egerton. CPG
When the gunner spoke in his sleep the hut was still. The Gunner Francis Webb. BoAV
When the Hand that sprinkles midnight. The Victory Which Is Peace. Frederic Lawrence Knowles. BoHiPo
When the hands that scattered. Dionysios Solomos. *Fr.* The Dream. MoGP
When the head of Bran. The Head of Bran. George Meredith. LH
When the Heart Is Full of Love. *Unknown.* MaRV
When the heart wanders, seeking endless change. The Darweesh. Sadi. PeP
When the heat of the summer. A Dragon-Fly. Eleanor Farjeon. FaPON
When the heathen trumpet's clang. The Monks of Bangor's March. Sir Walter Scott. CAW
When the herds [*or* herd] were watching. Carol [*or* Bethlehem]. William Canton. BoTP; DD; HBVY; OHIP; SDH; YeAr
When the hero had made an end of speaking. Phaeacian Nights —Demodocus. Homer. *Fr.* The Odyssey, VIII. OxBG
When the heron's in the high wood and the last long furrow's sown. Mary Shepherdess. Marjorie Pickthall. ISi; VOD; WHL
When the hero's task was done. The Hero. Roy Fuller. FaBoMo
When the high heart we magnify. Greatness Passing By. John Drinkwater. MaRV
When the hills of Spring. Girls in Spring. Owari. OnPM
When the Himalayan peasant meets the he-bear in his pride. The Female of the Species. Kipling. BLPA; BPN; HBV; OtMeF; TreFS; VLEP
When the hornet hangs in the hollyhock. A Fragment. Madison Cawein. BAP
When the hot sun smiles on the endless miles. The Stampede. *Unknown.* CoSo
When the Hounds of Spring [Are on Winter's Traces]. Swinburne. *Fr.* Atalanta in Calydon. BLV; BoLiVe; CoBE; EnL; FaBoBe; HBV; LiTB; MBP; PIAE; PoFS; PoVP; TreF; TrGrPo; TyEnPo; ViPP; VLEP
(Chorus: "When the hounds of spring are on winter's traces.") AnFE; AWP; CaAE; CBOV; CoEV; EnLit; EPN; EPP; ExPo; FaBoEn; InPo; JAWP; LEAP; LPS-2; OBEV; OuHeWo; PIR; Po; REAL; RG, *abr.;* SeCeV; ShBV-4; TCEP; TOP; VA; ViP; WBP
(Chorus from "Atalanta.") EV-5; GTSL
(Choruses from "Atalanta in Calydon.") EnLi-2; LiA; ViBoPo
(Hounds of Spring, The.) BEL; BMEP; YT
(Huntsmen's Chorus.) GTML
(Youth of the Year, The.) BPN; EmBrPo
When the hours of Day are numbered. Footsteps of Angels. Longfellow. IAP; LPS-1
When the house is silent. Song for a Little Cuckoo Clock. Elizabeth J. Coatsworth. SiSoSe
When the humid shadows hover [*or* gather]. Rain on the Roof [*or* The Patter of the Rain]. Coates Kinney. BLP; HBV; LPS-1; PTA-2
When the hunter sets traps only for rabbits. To His Three Friends. Li Po. BoFr
When the hunter-star Orion. Retrospection. Sir Arthur Quiller-Couch. CenHV
When the hurricane unfolds. The Hurricane. Luis Palés Matos. FaPON
When the jar is just begun. Spending and Sparing. Hesiod. *Fr.* Works and Days. OxBG
When the King Enjoys His Own Again. Martin Parker. FaBoCh; OxBoLi; TuPP
(King Enjoys His Own Again, The.) OBS
When the Kye Comes Hame. James Hogg. BLP; EBSV; EV-3; HBV; LPS-1
When the Lad for Longing Sighs. A. E. Housman. A Shropshire Lad, VI. MBP; MoBrPo; PoVP; ViPo
When the Lamp Is Shattered. Shelley. *See* Lines: When the Lamp Is Shattered.
When the landfolk of Galway converse with a stranger. Undertone. William Bedell Stanford. NeIP; OnYI
When the landlord wants the rent. Pensées de Noël. A. D. Godley. BOHV; InMe
When the last bitterness was past, she bore. Actea. Sir Rennell Rodd. VA
When the last day is ended. The Survivor. Frederic L. Knowles. OQP; QP-2
When the last dread hour is o'er us. The Benedictine Ultima. *Unknown.* CAW
When the last great and solemn act was played. Pushkin. *See* Secular Power.
When the last H-bomb blast has done its stuff. Brave Old World. Elisabeth Lambert. FaFP; SiTL
When the last hope of trampled France had failed. Shelley. *Fr.* The Revolt of Islam. MyFE
When the last hound has wearied of his race. The Last Hound. Howard McKinley Corning. MuM
When the last of gloaming's gone. The Shadow. Walter de la Mare. BoChLi (1950 ed.)
When the last sea is sailed and [*or* when] the last shallow [*or* shallow's] charted. Prayer [*or* D'Avalos' Prayer]. John Masefield. GTSL; LEAP; POTT; TrPWD; VOD
When the last voyage is ended. Requiem. Joseph Lee. DD; OHIP
When the last weariness. Humbly. Ramón López Velarde. AnMP
When the lean, gray grasses. Give Love To-Day. Ethel Talbot. HBV
When the least whistling wind begins to sing. Her Hair. Sir Robert Chester. *Fr.* Love's Martyr. EIL
When the leaves in autumn wither. Autumnus. Joshua Sylvester. EIL; LO; OBS; SeEP; UnPo (1st ed.)
When the lessons and tasks are all ended. The Children. Charles Monroe Dickinson. AA; BAP; HBV; LPS-1; PTA-1; PTA-2
When the Light Goes Out. Harry S. Chester. PTA-2
When the lights are lit. The Sandman. Mary White Slater. BOL
When the lights come on at five o'clock on street corners. For Futures. Josephine Miles. FiMAP
When the lights come out in the cottages. Sir Charles G. D. Roberts. *Fr.* Hill-Top Songs. CP; CPG
When the little armadillo. Mexican Serenade. Arthur Guiterman. BOHV; FiBHP
When the Little Boy Ran Away. *Unknown.* BTP
When the little children die. Notre Dame des Petits. Louis Mercier. ISi
When the little children sleep. *Unknown.* BOL
When the little Grecian cities went a-warring each with each. Little Songs. Marjorie Pickthall. CaP; OCL
When the little spent winds are at rest in the tamarack tree. In the Night Watches Sir Charles G. D. Roberts. PeCV
When the Lord brought back those that returned to Zion. Like unto Them That Dream. Psalm CXXVI, Bible, *O.T.* TrJP
When the Lord fashioned man, the Lord his God. The Mother. Catulle Mendès. TrJP
When the Lord turned again the captivity of Zion. Psalm CXXVI, Bible, *O.T.* OnPM
When the low flying wind, awake. Slumber Song. Marie van Vorst. BOL
When the many move, the man. Isolationist. P. K. Page. BoCaPo
When the Martian Maid knocked on my door. The Martian Maid. Brian Lazarus. SiTL
When the master sits at ease. Friend Cato. Anna Wickham. MBP; MoBrPo
When the May has culled her flowers for the summer waiting long. We Keep Memorial Day. Kate Brownlee Sherwood. HH
When the merry lark doth gild. A Song for the Seasons. "Barry Cornwall." HBV
When the mighty Maccabean led the armies of the Lord. The Snarlers. Arthur Guiterman. PaA
When the mild gold stars flower out. A Humming Bird. Edgar Fawcett. BLA
When the mild weather came. Sunrise at Sea. Epes Sargent. EtS
When the Minister Comes to Tea. Joseph C. Lincoln. DDA; PTA-1
When the Minister Comes [*or* Came] to Tea. Juliet Tompkins. DDA
When the Mississippi Flowed in Indiana. Vachel Lindsay. Three Poems about Mark Twain, II. ChMo; CMP
When the mists grow bright with the morning light. Morning and Evening. Philip P. Frost. CAG
When the mole goes digging. The Mole. E. L. Mayo. WaKn
When the monkey in his madness. The Monkey's Glue. Goldwin Goldsmith. NA
When the moon comes over Brooklyn. The Moon of Brooklyn. Nathalia Crane. AnAmPo; LA

When the moon is afloat. Norman Cradle Song. Vincent O'Sullivan. BOL
When the Moon Is in the River of Heaven. Ou-yang Hsiu, *tr. fr. Chinese by* Kenneth Rexroth. OnPC
When the moon is on the wave. An Incantation. Byron. *Fr.* Manfred. OBRV; UnW
When the moon lights up. The Moon's Orchestra. John Gould Fletcher. Down the Mississippi, IV. ChMo; CMP; LaNeLa; LiTA; MOAP; NP; SPP; TCAP
When the moon shines o'er the corn. The Field Mouse. "Fiona Macleod." FaPON; GBV; MoShBr
When the moon was horned the mother died. The Mother's Soul. Isabella Valancy Crawford. CPG
When the moon's immortal glow. Eclipse. Al-Ghassani. MooP
When the moon's splendour shines in naked heaven. To His Friend in Absence. Walafrid Strabo. LiTW; LyMA
When the morning was waking over the war. Among Those Killed in the Dawn Raid Was a Man Aged One Hundred. Dylan Thomas. InPo; MoPo
When the morning whistles blow in the factory districts. Factory Whistles. Aleksey Kapitonovich Gastev. TrRV
When the Most Is Said. "Madeline Bridges." AA; HBV
When the night her visions is weaving. The Harp of David. "Yehoash." TrJP
When the night is cloudy. In the Hours of Darkness. James Flexner. FaPON; MPB
When the night is still and far. The Highway. William Channing Gannett. WGRP
When the night kneels down by your bed. Faith. Preston Clark. HBMV; MaRV
When the night raven finds our hearth and fans. Entropy. Roy G. Pearce. PoP
When the night shall lift from Erin's hills, 'twere shame if we forget. The Hedge Schoolmasters. Seumas MacManus. CAW
When the night wind howls in the chimney cowls, and the bat in the moonlight flies. Sir Roderic's Song. W. S. Gilbert. *Fr.* Ruddigore. GBV (1952 ed.); PoMS; WhC
When the nightingale chanted her vespers. Mark Anthony. John Cleveland. SeEP
When the nightingale singeth the woods waxen green. Spring. *Unknown.* TMEV
When the nights are long and the dust is deep. Thistledown. Lizette Woodworth Reese. YeAr
When the Norn Mother saw the whirlwind hour. Lincoln, the Man of the People. Edwin Markham. BAP; BoChLi; CP; CV; DDA; GA; GN; GrCo-2; HBV; HH; HiLiAm; LBAH; LBMV; LEAP; MAP; MC; MCCG; MoAmPo; NeMA; NV; OHFP; OHIP; OnPP; PaA; PAH; PFY; PIAE; PoeMoYo; PoMa; POT; PoTo; PTA-2; PYM; TCAP; TreFS; TrGrPo; VOD; YT
When the nursery corners are creepy dim. The Muffin-Man. Madeleine Nightingale. GaP
When the Nyhtegale Singes [The Wodes Waxen Grene]. *Unknown.* BrBE; NBE
(Spring, *mod. vers.*) TMEV
(When the Nightingale Sings.) EnLit
When the old flaming Prophet climb'd the sky. On a Virtuous Young Gentlewoman That Died Suddenly. William Cartwright. OBEV
When the old, long-preserved wine stands at the repast. Five Arabic Verses in Praise of Wine, II. *Unknown.* TrJP
When the one o'clock cock begins to crow. The Milkman. Leonard J. Feeney. MoSiPe
When the oppressive sky weighs like a cover. Spleen. Baudelaire. AnFP
When the opulence of summer unto wood and meadow comes. The Smallest of the Drums. James Buckham. MDAH
When the other children go. The Invisible Playmate. Margaret Widdemer. FaPON; MPB; RAR
When the "Our Father" I have said. Afterwards. Mary Dixon Thayer. GFA
When the outlook is dark, try the uplook. Try the Uplook. *Unknown.* BLRP
When the pale moon hides and the wild wind wails. The Wolf. Georgia R. Durston. GFA; UTS
When the people and horses have gone. The Hour before Dawn. John Cowper Powys. BAP
When the picnic was over. Beach Fire. Frances M. Frost. TiPo
When the pine tosses its cones. Woodnotes, I. Emerson. AmPP (4th ed.); BAV; CoBA; IAP; MOAP; NePA; OxBA. *See also* For this present, hard.
When the pines have fallen on the hillside. An August Mood. Duncan Campbell Scott. PC
When the Pleiades, daughters of Atlas, are rising at morning-prime. The Sign of the Pleiades. Hesiod. *Fr.* Works and Days. GrR
When the pocket flasks are opened. A Pugilistic Parody. *Unknown.* CAG
When the pods went pop on the broom, green broom. A Runnable Stag. John Davidson. AnFE; EBSV; EV-5; GoTS; GTML; GTSL; HBV; LiTG; OBEV (new ed.); OBVV; OnSP; PoVP; ShBV-2; VLEP
When the Preacher Comes to Tea. S. R. Huiatt. DDA
When the present has latched its postern behind my tremulous stay. Afterwards. Thomas Hardy. AnFE; BEL; CaAE; CH; ChMP; ChTr; EG; EnLi-2 (1949 ed.); EPP; FaBoEn; KN; LiTB; LiTG; LiTM (rev. ed.); MBP; MM; MoAB; MoBrPo; MoVE; NAMP; PoEL-5; PoLFOT; POTE; ReTS; SeCeV; ShBV-3; TrGrPo; TwCV; ViBoPo; ViPP; VLEP; VOD; YT
When the prime mover of my many sighs. To Vittoria Colonna. Michelangelo. AWP; JAWP; MeRV; WBP
When the Proficient Poison of Sure Sleep. E. E. Cummings. MOAP
When the proud World does most my world despise. Sonnets to Aurelia, I. Robert Nichols. OBMV
When the Puritans came over A Song for the Centennial Celebration of Harvard College, 1836. Oliver Wendell Holmes. TCAP
When the rain comes tumbling down. The Story of Flying Robert. Heinrich Hoffmann. BoN; RIS
When the rain is raining. Umbrellas. Rowena Bennett. TiPo (1959 ed.)
When the rains of November are dark on the hills. Storm Lines. Bayard Taylor. BAV
When the reaper's task was ended, and the summer wearing late. The Swan Song of Parson Avery [*or* Parson Avery]. Whittier. AA; BHV
When the red moon hangs over the fold. The Shepherd Boy. Marjorie Pickthall. CPG
When the ripe pears droop heavily. The Wasp. "Fiona Macleod." BMEP; BoTP; FaPON; TSW
When the roads are heavy with mire and rut. The Ballade of Prose and Rhyme. Austin Dobson. PIAE
When the ropes droop and loosen, and the gust. For My Grandfather. Francis Webb. BoAV
When the rose came I loved the rose. Song. Arthur O'Shaughnessy. PoVP
When the rose is brightest. To Giulia Grisi. Nathaniel Parker Willis. AA; IAP
When the Rose Is Dead. *Unknown, tr. fr. Greek by* R. A. Furness. OxBG
When the Rose Is Faded. Walter de la Mare. LoPS; NP
When the rose of morn through the dawn was breaking. The Dream of Ængus Og. Eleanor Rogers Cox. HBMV; SBMV
When the runner's whistle lights the last miles of darkness. Soldier (T. P.). Randall Jarrell. WaP
When the sap runs up the tree. A-Roving. Victor Daley. BoAu
When the scarlet cardinal tells. July [*or* It Is July]. Susan Hartley Swett. GN; OTPC (1946 ed.); PoRL; StVeCh (1940 ed.); YeAr
When the sea has devoured the ships. My Light with Yours. Edgar Lee Masters. ChMo; CMP; LoPS; NP; NV; TBM
When the seasons clothed with purple have flung their chamber wide. Spring. Pindar. GrPE
When the shades of night are falling, and the sun goes down. The Dustman. *Unknown.* BOL; BoTP
When the Shades of Night Have Come. Miguel de Unamuno, *tr. fr Spanish by* Thomas Walsh. OnPM
When the sheen on tall summer grass is pale. The Gazelles. T. Sturge Moore. OBMV; PtOT
When the sheep are in the fauld, and the kye [*or* cows] at hame. Auld Robin Gray. Lady Anne Lindsay. AV; BCEP; BeLS; BSV; CBE; CBOV; CH; DiM; EBSV; EV-3; GoTS; GTBS; GTBS-D; GTBS-W; GTSE; GTSL; HBV; LPS-1; OBEC; OBEV; OnPP; TCEP; ViBoPo
When the ship drives on through the tumbling sea. The Clinker. *Unknown.* PEDC; StVeCh (1940 ed.)
When the shy, slender thrush. Spring Doggerel. Rhoda Coghill. NeIP
When the siege and assault ceased at Troy. Sir Gawain and the Green Knight. *Unknown, tr. fr. Middle English.* EnLi-1; MeEV; OuHeWo
When the sky starts in a-rainin'. Let Be. *Unknown.* WBLP
When the Sleepy Man Comes. Sir Charles G. D. Roberts. *Fr.* The Book of the Native. HBV; HBVY; MPB
(Sleepy Man.) BOL
When the Snail Climbs. Hesiod, *pr. tr. fr. Greek by* Samuel Butler. *Fr.* Works and Days. OxBG
(Snail's Moving Day, The, *tr. by* Arthur S. Way.) GrR
When the snail crawls over the bare flag-stone. Omens. James H. Cousins. OnYI
When the snow has gone away. The Procession. Margaret Widdemer. YeAr
When the snow is on the ground. *Unknown.* SAS
When the soft winds did blow The Goddesses' Glory. *Unknown.* SeCL
When the Son of Man Shall Come in His Glory. St. Matthew, XXV: 31-46, Bible, *N.T.* TreF
When the soul sought refuge in the place of rest. Self-Discipline. "Æ." MoBrPo; VA
When the southern gale is blowing hard. At Sea. D. H. Rogers. AnNZ

When the spent sun throws up its rays on cloud. Acceptance. Robert Frost. ChMo; CMP; MOAP; OxBA
When the spinning-room was here. The Maids of Elfin-Mere. William Allingham. GTIV; IrPN; OnYI
When the Spring comes laughing. A Song of the Four Seasons. Austin Dobson. BMEP; HBV; POTT; VLEP
When the spring is fresh from the hand of God. The Tryst. Whitney Montgomery. BLA
When the springtime does come. Hallelujah, Bum Again. *Unknown.* ABF
When the stars are shining bright. Look and See. Tom Robinson. BoChLi (1950 ed.)
When the Stars of Morning Sang. Anne P. L. Field. COAH
When the still fire burns like roses. Baffled. Rose Macaulay. AlDL
When the storm was fiercely raging. It Is I, Be Not Afraid. A. B. Simpson. BePJ
When the storm was in the sky. The Beloved. May Probyn. GoBC
When the Sultan Goes to Ispahan. Thomas Bailey Aldrich. AA; BAP; BAV; BeLS; FaBoBe; HBV
When the sun goes down and the world is still. Jock o' Dreams. Rose Fyleman. BoTP
When the sun has left the hill-top. A Blessing for the Blessed [*or* Sunset]. Laurence Alma-Tadema. BOL; BoTP; GFA; PRWS
When the sun has slipped away. The Skunk. Robert P. Tristram Coffin. FaPON; TiPo
When the sun is shining overhead. Shady Woods. E. M. Adams BoTP
When the sun rises I go to work. Creativity. *Tr. by* Y. S. Han. OQP; QP-1
When the sun rises on another day. Litany. Charles Angoff. TrPWD
When the sun rose I was still lying in bed. Hearing the Early Oriole. Po Chü-i. TrCh; UnS
When the sun set, I came to the village of Shi-kao. The Recruiting Officer. Tu Fu. WhP
When the sun sets behind a cloud. Rules of the Road. *Unknown.* SoAmSa
When the sun shouts and people abound. Summer Holiday. Robinson Jeffers. CrMA; MAP; MoAmPo; MoVE; OxBA
When the sun was sinking. Sunshine. Ibn Abi Bishr. MooP
When the sun's perpendicular rays. Beginning of an Undergraduate Poem. *Unknown.* SiTL
When the sun's red fiery ball. Sea Song. Stefan George. AnGP; LiTW
When the supreme event had come to pass, and He. Secular Power. Pushkin. TrRV
When the surf licks with its tongues. Indian Point. Marsden Hartley. TwAmPo
When the Swallows Homeward Fly. Carl Herlossohn, *tr. fr. German.* OlF
When the swans turned my sister into a swan. The Black Swan. Randall Jarrell. FiMAP
When the sweet showers of April follow March. Prologue to The Canterbury Tales, *mod.* Chaucer. BLV; TrGrPo
When the tall bamboos are clicking to the restless little breeze. In a Southern Garden. Dorothea Mackellar. BoAu
When the tea is brought at five o'clock. Milk for the Cat. Harold Monro. BoTP; FaBoBe; FaFP; GoTP; HBVY; MBP; MoBrPo; OBMV; PoC; ShBV-1; SiTL; ThWaDe; TwCV; VOD; YT
When the teacher asks you to bound Texas. Texas. James Daugherty. TiPo (1959 ed.)
When the Teacher Gets Cross. *Unknown.* PTA-1
When the thin fountains are again. Quan lo ruis de la fontana. Jaufré Rudel. LiTW
When the tide is at the turning, and the wind is fast asleep. The Blue Men of the Minch. Donald A. MacKenzie. EBSV
When the Tigers claw the Bulldogs. College Song. Ed Anthony. InMe
When the time comes for me to die. Night. Thomas William Rolleston. HBV
When the Tom-Tom Beats. Jacques Roumain, *tr. fr. French by* Langston Hughes AnCL; PoNe
When the toys are growing weary. The Dustman. Frederic Edward Weatherly. BOL; HBV; OTPC
When the Train Comes In. Nixon Waterman. IHA
When the Tree Bares. Conrad Aiken. MAP; MoAmPo
When the Troops Were Returning from Milan. Niccolò degli Albizzi. *See* Prolonged Sonnet.
When the trumpet shall sound. The Trumpet. *Unknown.* OnPM
When the Turf Is Thy Tower. *Unknown, tr. fr. Middle English by* Mabel Van Duzee. MeEV
(Grave The.) ChTi
(When the Turuf Is Thi Tuur.) SeCePo
When the veil from the eyes is lifted. Si Jeunesse Savait [*or* Why?]. Edmund Clarence Stedman. AA; BLP
When the vengeance wakes, when the battle breaks. Battle Song. Robert Burns Wilson. MC; PAH
When the voices of children are heard on the green/ And laughing. Nurse's Song. Blake. *Fr.* Songs of Innocence. AWP; BoChLi; BOL; CBE; CEP; CH; EiPP; EnRP; EV-3; FaBoBe; FaPON; GaP; GoTP; HBV; HBVY; InPo; KN; MPB; OBEC; OnPM; OTPC (1923 ed.); RG; ThWaDe; TiPo (1952 ed.); WoL; WP
When the voices of children are heard on the green/ And whisp'rings. Nurse's Song. Blake. *Fr.* Songs of Experience. CEP; EiPP; EnLi-2 (1949 ed.); EnRP; PoFS; TOP
When the volcano with stone lips drawn back. Silent. Iwan Goll. OnPM
When the wain of the first heaven which setting nor rising never knew. Dante Sees Beatrice in Glory. Dante. *Fr.* Divina Commedia: Purgatorio. LiA
When the war-cry of Liberty rang through the land. The Death of Warren. Epes Sargent. GA; MC; PAH
When the War Will End. Reginald Arkell. InMe
When the warl's couped roun' as a peerie. Munestruck. "Hugh MacDiarmid." NeBP
When the warm sun, that brings. April. Longfellow. ADAH
When the water's countenance. The Wet Litany. Kipling. TriL
When the waves of trouble roll. Show Me Thyself. Margaret E. Sangster. TrPWD
When the ways are heavy with mire and rut. The Ballade [*or* Ballad] of Prose and Rhyme. Austin Dobson. LEAP; MBP; MoBrPo (1942 ed.); PIAE; POTT
When the wayside tangles blaze. Goldenrod. Elaine Goodale Eastman. HBV
When the weather is rough, said the anxious child. Contemporary Song. Theodore Spencer. LiTA
When the weather suits you not. Try Smiling. *Unknown.* BLPA; FaFP; WBLP
When the white feet of the baby beat across the grass. Baby Running Barefoot. D. H. Lawrence. MoPW
When the white flame in us is gone. Dust. Rupert Brooke. ALV; HBV; MBP; MoBrPo; OBVV; TwCV
When the white iris folds the drowsing bee. Evening. Marjorie Pickthall. OCL
When the white wave of a glory that is hardly I. Sinfonia Domestica. Jean Starr Untermeyer. HBMV; LEAP; MAP; MoAmPo; NP
When the Wild Geese were flying to Flanders away. The Sailor Girl. Alfred Perceval Graves. RIS
When the wind blows. *Unknown.* OxNR
When the wind blows, walk not abroad. To the Maids Not to Walk in the Wind. Oliver St. John Gogarty. AnIL
When the wind is in the east. Weather Signs [*or* Country Proverbs *or* The Wind and the Fisherman]. *Unknown.* BoTP; CBPC; GoTP; OTPC; OxNR; PCH; PPL; RIS; StaSt
When the Wind Is Low. Cale Young Rice. LBMV
When the wind, Mother. Letrilla. *Unknown.* TeCS
When, the wind stirring the Carpathian main. A Little Garment. Diodorus. OnPM
When the wind swells the canvas and the anchor's a-trip. Believe Me, Dearest Susan. *Unknown.* SoAmSa
When the wind works against us in the dark. Storm Fear. Robert Frost. DDA; HBV; NP; OBAV; OXBA; TCAP; ViBoPo
When the Wise Physiognomist Looked at Me. Ariake Kambara, *tr. fr. Japanese by* Takamichi Ninomiya *and* D. J. Enright. PoLJ
When the woods are green again. Midsummer Moon. "E. M. G. R." BoTP
When the words rustle no more. Stillness. James Elroy Flecker. BLV; CH; GTBS-D; MBP; MoBrPo; POTT
When the Work's All Done This Fall. *Unknown, at. to* D. J. O'Malley *or* D. J. White. AS, *with music;* CoSo, *with music;* IHA
When the World Ends. Mark Van Doren. GoYe
When the World Is Burning. Ebenezer Jones. OBEV; OBVV; PrWP
When the world turns completely upside down. Wild Peaches, I. Elinor Wylie. AmP; LiTA; LiTM (rev. ed.); NAMP; OxBA
When the wounded seaman heard the ocean daughters. Legend. Ridgely Torrence. EtS
When the Year Grows Old. Edna St. Vincent Millay. SBMV; YT
When the years grew worse, and the tribe longed sore. Thunderchild's Lament. Edward William Thomson. CPG
When the yellow bird's note was almost stopped. Rejoicing at the Arrival of Ch'en Hsiung. Po Chü-i. AWP; TrCh
When the Yellow Rye-Field Billows. Mikhail Yurevich Lermontov, *tr. fr. Russian by* Babette Deutsch. TrRV
(Composed While under Arrest, *tr. by* Max Eastman.) AWP
("When o'er the yellowing corn . . . ," *tr. by* W. A. Morison.) BoR
When the young Augustus Edward. On the Beach. Charles Stuart Calverley. ALV; FiBHP
When the young hand of Darnley locked in hers. Mary Queen of Scots. Charles Tennyson Turner. HBV

When theaters pour down exotic light. Rainy Night. Samuel Schrieber. CAG
When Thee (O holy sacrificed Lamb). To the Blessed Sacrament. Henry Constable. ACP; CAW
When Theo: Roos: unfurled his bann. The Conversational Reformer. Harry Graham. InMe; YaD
When there are no distances in music. Desolate Scythia. Edgar Lee Masters. ChMo; CMP; NP
When there are so many we shall have to mourn. In Memory of Sigmund Freud. W. H. Auden. AtBAP; CoBMV; FaBoMo; LiTB; OxBA
When there are whitecaps on the ocean. Stormy Sea. Janet Vaughn. PCD
When There Is Music. David Morton. HBMV; LPS-1
When there is nothing left but darkness. Any Woman. Hazel Hall. MAP; MoAmPo (1942 ed.)
"When There Is Peace." Austin Dobson. AOAH; PAH
When there is peace again, soldier, what will you do? Retreat. Virginia Graham. NeTW
When there was heard no more the war's loud sound. The Death of Ailill. Francis Ledwidge. OnYI
When there was not one moment left to us. By Return Mail. Richard Aldridge. NePoAm-2
When these assaults proove vain, the Enemy. Stanzas. Edward Taylor. *Fr.* Difficulties Arising from Uncharitable Cariages of Christians. OnAP
When, these eyes closed in death, you look on me. Rispetto. Angelo Poliziano. LyPI
When these graven lines you see. A Happy Man [*or* Variations of Greek Themes, I]. E. A. Robinson, *after* Carphyllides. AWP; JAWP; LiTW; MOAP; WBP
When these old woods were young. Under the Woods. Edward Thomas. CH; LoBV
When these the steely flocks of Death returning. "Reported Missing." Audrey Alexandra Brown. NeTW
When these things following be done to our intent. Trust in Women. *Unknown.* BOHV; NA
When these were carried down the road no friends went on ahead. Dissecting Room. John Fallon. PoP
When these were past, thus gan the Titanesse. Mutability. Spenser. *Fr.* The Faerie Queene, VII. PoEL-1
When they begin the Beguine. Begin the Beguine. Cole Porter. PreP
When they found Giotto. Allan M. Laing. FiBHP
When They Grow Old. Nathan Ralph. CaP
When they had passed all those troubled ways. Tasso, *tr. by* Edward Fairfax. *Fr.* Jerusalem Delivered, XVI. TuPP
When they had pitched their smoked tepees. Indian Dance. Frederick Niven. CaP; OCL
When They Have Lost. C. Day Lewis. EnLit; MoAB; MoBrPo (1950 ed.); NeMA
When They Have Made an End. Gerald H. Crow. BoFr
When they heard Sigmund the Saviour in these coasts. The Return from the Freudian Islands. A. D. Hope. MoAuPo
When they heard the Captain humming and beheld the dancing crew. The Post Captain. Charles Edward Carryl. BOHV; PCD
When they him fand, and gude Wallace him saw. Wallace's Lament for the Graham. Henry the Minstrel. *Fr.* The Wallace, X. EBSV; GoTS
When they in throngs a safe retirement seek. The Shoal of Slime-Fish. Oppian, *tr. by* William Diaper. *Fr.* Halieuticks. BeR
When they killed my mother it made me nervous. The State. Randall Jarrell. MiAP
When they said the time to hide was mine. The Rabbit. Elizabeth Madox Roberts. BAP; BoChLi; GoTP; MPB; TiPo; TSW; TSWC; UTS
When they threw him overboard. Historical Incidents. Clarence Day. InMe
When they togidder murnit had full lang. Robert Henryson. *Fr.* The Testament of Cresseid. NBE
When thick and fast the snow flies. A Winter's Tale. Frank Dempster Sherman. PR
When thin-strewn memory I look through. Miss Loo [*or* Miss Lou]. Walter de la Mare. ChMo; CMP; EPP; HBV; NV; TVSH; VOD
When things forget their form and their colour. Vocation of the Mirror. Jorge Carrera Andrade. AnCL
When things go wrong, as they sometimes will. Don't Quit [*or* You Mustn't Quit]. *Unknown.* BLPA; PoToHe
When think you comes the Wind. The Rose and the Wind. Philip Bourke Marston. OBVV; VA
When This American Woman. Leonard Cohen. PeCV
When This Cruel War Is Over. Charles Carroll Sawyer. BlG; TrAS, *with music.*
When this crystal shall present. The Looking Glass. James Shirley. LiTL; LO
When this old cap was new. Time's Alteration. *Unknown.* EV-2
When This Old World Was New. Austin Dobson. VLEP
When this, our rose, is faded. Amantium Irae. Ernest Dowson. HBV
When This Tide Ebbs. Verna Loveday Harden. CaP
When this yokel comes maundering. The Plot against the Giant. Wallace Stevens. OxBA
When thistle-blows do lightly float. November. C. L. Cleaveland. DD; HBV; SN
When those renownèd noble peers of Greece. Amoretti, XLIV. Spenser. PeBoSo; ReIE
When thou approachest to the One. Approaching God. Amos Bronson Alcott. IAP
When thou art dead, and thinkst to com. *Unknown.* SeCSL
When thou art happy, thou dear heart of pleasure. They Shall Not Know. Wilfrid Scawen Blunt. VLEP
When thou art near to me, it seems. To Anne. Clément Marot. OnPM; WoL
When thou arte callde at anye time. John Halle. *Fr.* Goodlye Doctrine and Instruction. PoP
When Thou Did Thinke I Did Not Love. Sir Robert Ayton. *See* When Thou Didst Think I Did Not Love.
When thou didst give thy love to me. Robert Bridges. EG
When Thou Didst Think I Did Not Love. Sir Robert Ayton. ElL
(When Thou Did Thinke I Did Not Love.) OBS
When Thou Dost Dance. *Unknown.* SeCL
When thou dost eat from off this plate. Inscription for My Little Son's Silver Plate. Eugene Field. FAOV; PPL
When thou faire Celia like the settinge sunn. *Unknown.* SeCSL
When thou hast spent the lingering day in pleasure and delight. Gascoigne's Good-Night. George Gascoigne. ReEn; ReIE; SiCE
When thou hast taken thy last applause, and when. Sonnet. E. E. Cummings. NP
When Thou Must Home [to Shades of Underground]. Thomas Campion, *after the Latin of* Propertius. AtBAP; AWP; BEL; CenL; CoEV; ElL; ElSeCe; EM-1; EnL; EnLi-1; EnLoPo; FaBoEn; InPo; JAWP; LO; LoBV; OBSC; OnPM; PoE; PoEL-2; PoRA; ReEn; ReIE; RiBV; SeCeV; SiCE; TuPP; ViBoPo; WBP
(Conjuration.) CBOV
(His Lover's Triumphs.) BLV
(O Crudelis Amor.) GTSL
(Tell, O Tell.) TrGrPo
(To Shades of Underground.) ChTr
(Vobiscum Est Iope.) BCEP; HBV; LEAP; OBEV
When Thou Passest through the Waters. Henry Crowell. BLRP
"When thou passest through the waters." Passing Through. Annie Johnson Flint. BLRP
When thou, poor[e] excommunicate. To My Inconstant Mistress [*or* Mistris]. Thomas Carew. BrBE; EG; ElSeCe; EnLit; EnLoPo; EPS; EV-2; HBV; LO; LoBV; MeLP; MePo; OBEV; OBS; SeCePo; SeCL; SeCV-1; SeEP; TrGrPo
When thou shalt be dispos'd to set me light. Sonnets, LXXXVIII. Shakespeare. BoFr; PeBoSo
When thou shalt sleep, my fair Tenebrous. Remorse after Death. Baudelaire. OnPM
When thou to my true-love com'st. Westphalian Song. *Unknown.* AWP; JAWP; LiTW; LyMA; WBP
When thou turn'st away from ill. Approaches. George Macdonald. MaRV; OQP; QP-1
When thou wakest in the morning. Tell Jesus. *Unknown.* BePJ
When thou wouldst know thyself, what man thou art. Aid to Self-Knowledge. Menander. GrR
When thro' life unblest we rove. On Music. Thomas Moore. TIP
When through a thousand eyes. A Faery Song. Madeleine Nightingale. TVSH
When through the heaviness and clamouring throng. To a Grosbeak in the Garden. Ivan Swift. BLA
When through the Whirl of Wheels. G. A. Studdert-Kennedy. MaRV
When through valley and o'er mountain. Lays of Tom-Cat Hiddigeigei. Joseph Viktor von Scheffel. PoC
When thus I had implored. Odysseus in Hades. Homer. *Fr.* The Odyssey, XI. GrR
When thy [*or* your] beauty appears. Song [*or* Angel or Woman]. Thomas Parnell. CBOV; EiPP; EV-3; LO; LoPS; LPS-1; OBEC; OBEV
When thy heart, with joy o'erflowing. Thy Brother. Theodore Chickering Williams. GrCo-1; MaRV
When thy soft round form was lying. To Allegra Florence in Heaven. Thomas Holley Chivers. APW; SPP
When tides were neap, and, in the sultry day. Sea Marsh. George Crabbe. *Fr.* The Borough. RO
When Tim and I stumbled/ On the rough Tarras track. Tarras Moon. James K Baxter. AnNZ
When time seems short, and death is near. He Died for Me. George Washington Bethune. BePJ
When Time shall stalk contemptuous through this wood. To Edwin Arlington Robinson. Winfield Townley Scott. CAG
When time wears thin. Forgetful Hour. Yetza Gillespie. DaM

When Time, who steals our years away. Song. Thomas Moore. TreFS
When, to a cheap and tawdry tune, the orchestra cried out. Vaudeville Dancer. John Hall Wheelock. UnS
When to a nation's loss, the virtuous die. To My Old, and Most Worthy Friend, Mr. Izaak Walton. Charles Cotton. SeEP
When to any saint I pray. Saint Peray. Thomas William Parsons. HBV
When to Be Born. *Unknown.* *Fr.* Old Wives' Sayings. StaSt
When to Cut Your Nails. *Unknown.* *Fr.* Old Wives' Sayings. StaSt
When to Her Lute Corinna Sings. Thomas Campion. AtBAP; CenL; EG; ElSeCe; EnLi-1; EV-2; ExPo; OBSC; ReEn; ReIE; SeCeV; SiCE; TuPP
(Corinna.) ElL; EM-1; TrGrPo; UnS
(Of Corinna's Singing.) BEL; EnLit; HBV
When to My Deadly [*or* Deadlie] Pleasure. Sir Philip Sidney. AtBAP; EnLoPo; MaPo; PoEL-1
When to my eyes. Midnight. Henry Vaughan. OAEP
When to my lone soft bed at eve returning. Povre Ame Amoureuse. Louise Labé. AWP; EPP
When to My Serene Body. Freda Laughton. NeIP
When to New Zealand first I cam. New Zealand Comforts. John Barr of Craigielee. AnNZ
When to Sneeze. *Unknown.* *Fr.* Old Wives' Sayings. StaSt
When to soft sleep we give ourselves away. Sleep. Thomas Bailey Aldrich. AA; IAP
When, to the Attractions of the Busy World. Wordsworth. ERP
When to the flowers so beautiful. The Forget-Me-Not. *Unknown.* BoTP
When to the garden of untroubled thought. The Child in the Garden. Henry van Dyke. FAOV; HBV; MaRV
When to the sessions of sweet silent thought. Sonnets, XXX. Shakespeare. AEV; AnFE; ATP; BCEP; BEL; BLV; BoFr; BoLiVe; CBE; CoBE; EG; ElL; ElSeCe; EM-1; EnL; EnLi-1; EnLit; EPP; ES; EtPaEn; EV-1; ExPo; FaBoEn; FaFP; GTBS; GTBS-D; GTBS-W; GTSE; GTSL; HBV; InPo; JAWP; KN; LEAP; LiTB; LiTG; LoBV; LPS-1; MaPo; NeHB; OAEP; OBEV; OBSC; OuHeWo; PeBoSo; PFE; PIAE; PIR; PoE; PoEL-2; PoeMoYo; PoFS; PoRA; REAL; ReaPo; ReEn; ReIE; SeCeV; ShBV-4; SiCE; TCEP; TOP; TreFS; TrGrPo; TwHP; TwP; TyEnPo; ViBoPo; WBP; WHA; WoL; WP
When toils are ended and the task complete. A Colonial Song. Albert Durrant Watson. CPG
When Tom and Elizabeth took the farm. The Magpies. Denis Glover. AnNZ
When tongues will tax me in the public ear. William Baylebridge. *Fr.* A Wreath. BoAV
When, Tossed upon the Stormy Waters. "Feodor Sologub," *tr. fr. Russian by* Babette Deutsch. TrRV
When trade and traffic and all the noise of town. Remembrances. Pushkin. BoR
When trees are haggard and winter-bare. The Windmill. Geoffrey Johnson. HaMV
When trees did bud, and fields were green. Down the Burn, Davie. Robert Crawford. EBSV
When trees have lost remembrance of the leaves. Crocus. Alfred Kreymborg. HBMV; MAP
When, tremulous on the sand and on the seas. Morgana. Gabriele d'Annunzio. LiTW
When trouble comes your soul to try. The Friend Who Just Stands By. B. Y. Williams. PoToHe
When trouble haunts me, need I sigh? The Stranger. John Clare. OxBoCh
When troubled in spirit, when weary of life. The Horseback Ride. "Grace Greenwood" LPS-2
When Trout Swim down Great Ormond Street. Conrad Aiken. Priapus and the Pool, III [IV]. AnAmPo; InPo; LA; MaPa; MOAP; PFY; TBM
(Whim.) TSW
When Tulips Bloom. Henry van Dyke. *See* Angler's Wish, An.
When twilight comes to Prairie Street. The Winning of the TV West. John T. Alexander. WaKn
When Two Are Parted. Heine, *tr. fr. German by* Louis Untermeyer. AWP; JAWP; WBP
When two lovers love each other well. Young Bearwell. *Unknown.* ESPB
When two men hate, my Cyrnus, they find traps hard to lay. Love's Blindness. Theognis. GrPE
When Two Suns Do Appear. Sir Philip Sidney. *Fr.* Arcadia. SiPS
When two who love are parted. When Two Are Parted. Heine. AWP; JAWP; WBP
When tyranny's pampered and purple-clad minions. Extermination. Richard D'Alton Williams. OnYI
When under Edward or Henry the English armies. Now as Then. Anne Ridler. WaP
When unto heaven the souls elect take flight. The Vision. Lounkianos. CAW
When unto Nights of Autumn Do Complain. E. E. Cummings. MOAP
When vain desire at last and vain regret. The One Hope. Dante Gabriel Rossetti. The House of Life, CI. BEL; BPN; EmBrPo; EnLi-2; EnLit; EPN; EPP; HBV; NBE; POTT; PoVP; REAL; ViPo; ViPP
When veins congeal/ And gesture is confounded. For Federico García Lorca. Dorothy Livesay. BoCaPo
When Very was a celibate. Varitalk. Weare Holbrook. SiTL
When Vice triumphant holds her sov'reign sway. Byron. *Fr.* English Bards and Scotch Reviewers. TCEP
When wake-robin is white in shady dells. It Is Spring and All Is Well. Charles Erskine Scott Wood. PFY
When walking in a tiny rain. Vern. Gwendolyn Brooks. TiPo (1959 ed.)
When walking through the woods. Four-Leaf Clover. Wesley Curtright. GoSl
When War Shall Be No More. Longfellow. *Fr.* The Arsenal at Springfield. MaRV; OQP; PSO; QP-1
(Message of Peace.) WBLP
(Peace.) PEDC
("Were half the power that fills the world with terror.") PGD
When warfare blusters at high Lucifer's command. War Cry: To Mary. Pope Leo XIII. ISi
When wars and ruined men shall cease. Prayer against Indifference. Joy Davidman. AnAmPo; AnEnPo; TrPWD
When was the redman's summer? Indian Summer. Lydia Huntley Sigourney. BAV
When waves invade the yellowing wheat. Composed While under Arrest. Mikhail Yurevitch Lermontov. AWP
When We Are All Asleep. Robert Buchanan. VA
When we are dead, some Hunting-boy will pass. The Statue. Hilaire Belloc. ACP (1952 ed.); MoVE
When we are gone, love. Wood-Song. Eugene Lee-Hamilton. OBVV
When We Are Men. E. Stella Mead. BoTP
When We Are No More. Lucretius, *tr. fr. Latin by* William Ellery Leonard. *Fr.* Of the Nature of Things (De Rerum Natura), III. LiA
When we are older and the hidden fires. Vera Wainwright. LO
When We Are Parted. Hamilton Aidé. HBV; VA
When We Are upon the Seas. George Wither. *Fr.* Hallelujah. BEL
When we are young and wake from sleep. The Snow-flake. W. H. Davies. ChMo; CMP
When we behold. Dahlias. Padraic Colum. NePoAm
When we buried old Bill at the church far away. Two Funerals. Eden Phillpotts. BMEP
When we come to that dark house. Edith Sitwell. *Fr.* The Sleeping Beauty. MoVE
When we count out our gold at the end of the day. Service. Georgia Douglas Johnson. CDC
When we dwelt long ago on the hills. Memory. Victor Hugo. TrFP
When we entered into the eastern gate. The Second Walk in the Garden. John Gould Fletcher. MAPA
When we for age could neither read nor write. Of the Last Verses in the Book [*or* Of His Divine Poems *or* On the Foregoing Divine Poems]. Edmund Waller. BEL; CEP; CoBE; ElSeCe; EPS; FaBoEn; HBV; LoBV; MePo; OAEP; OBS; PoD; PoE; PoFS; SeCL; SeCV-1; SeEP; TriL; ViBoPo
When we fought campaigns (in the long Christmas rains). Many Sisters to Many Brothers. Rose Macaulay. PoeT
When we have thrown off this old suit. The Question Whither. George Meredith. BPN; EPN; HBV; OQP; POTT; QP-2; WGRP
When we, in kind embracements, had agreed. *Unknown.* *Fr.* Zepheria. ReEn; ReIE; TuPP
When we lay where Budmouth Beach is. Budmouth Dears [*or* Hussar's Song]. Thomas Hardy. *Fr.* The Dynasts. CH; LO; MoVE; PoVP; TCPD
When we lived in a city. Until We Built a Cabin. Aileen Fisher. TiPo (1959 ed.)
When we met first and loved, I did not build. Sonnets from the Portuguese, XXXVI. Elizabeth Barrett Browning. BPN
When we, my love, are gone to dust. A Song of Dust. Lord De Tabley. EnLoPo
When We Plant a Tree. Warren P. Landers. GFA
When we remember that dear childhood day. A Nun's Diamond Jubilee. Gertrude Jane Codd. PraNu
When We Shall Be Dust. Muna Lee. AV
When we told you minus twenty. A Correction. Robert Frost. WhC
When we travel back in summer to the old house by the sea. Little Girl That Mother Used to Be. Nancy Byrd Turner. HH
When we two, friends from childhood, wanderers are. The Madonna's Lamp. Wilhelm, Prince of Sweden. CAW

When We Two Parted. Byron. AnFE; BCEP; BEL; BLV; BoLiVe; BPN; CaAE; ChER; EM-2; EmBrPo; EnLi-2; EnLit; EnRP; EPN; ERP; EV-4; FiP; GTBS; GTBS-D; GTBS-W; GTSE; GTSL; HBV; HoPM; LiTL; LoBV; LoPS; OAEP; OBEV; OBRV; PG; PoFS; REAL; TOP; TreFS; TrGrPo; TyEnPo; ViBoPo; WHA
When We Went Gathering Cat-Tails. Rachel Field. GFA
When we went to the circus. A Ballad of the Circus. Charles Hanson Towne. CV
When we were building Skua Light. The Dancing Seal. W. W. Gibson. HBMV; PoMS; WP
When we were girl and boy together. Ballad of Human Life. Thomas Lovell Beddoes. BeLS; VA
When we were idlers with the loitering rills. To a Friend [*or* Friendship]. Hartley Coleridge. BoFr; ES; HBV; OBEV; OBRV; PeBoSo
When we were little childer we had a quare wee house. Grace for Light. "Moira O'Neill." CP; PoRh; SP; WHL
When we were little, wandering boys. Fratri Dilectissimo. John Buchan. OtMeF
When We Were Poor in Paris. Charles Hanson Towne. PR
When we were silly sisters seven. Fair Mary of Wallington. *Unknown.* ESPB; OBB
When we would reach the anguish of the dead. Near an Old Prison. Frances Cornford. OBMV
When weakness now do strive wi' might. Withstanders. William Barnes. OxBoCh
When weary with the long day's care. To Imagination. Emily Brontë. VLEP
When wee were parted. *Unknown.* SeCSL
When weight of all the garnered years. Love's Lord. Edward Dowden. HBV
When we're at the tavern we. In Taberna Quando Sumus. *Unknown. Fr.* Carmina Burana. LaP
When wert thou born, Desire? Of the Birth and Bringing Up of Desire. Edward de Vere, Earl of Oxford. OBSC; ReIE; SiCE; TuPP
When Wesley died, the Angelic orders. The Organist in Heaven. Thomas Edward Brown. LoBV (1949 ed.); OBVV; POTT
When West Comes East. Corey Ford. InMe
When Westwall Downes I 'gan to tread. On Westwall Downes. William Strode. FaBoEn; PoEL-2; SeCL; SeEP
When whelmed are altar, priest and creed. Epigram. Sir William Watson. WGRP
When, when, and whenever death closes our eyelids. Ezra Pound. *Fr.* Homage to Sextus Propertius. MoAB; OBMV
When whispering strains do softly steal [*or* with creeping wind]. In [*or* The] Commendation of Music. William Strode. OBEV (new ed.); SeCL
When Whistler's Mother's Picture's frame. Don Marquis. *Fr.* To a Lost Sweetheart. FiBHP
When Whistler's strongest colors fade. The Durable Bon Mot. Keith Preston. HBMV
When white man git to worryin'. Farmers of the South. *Unknown.* OuSiCo
When will He come? A Christmas Question. Minot J. Savage. PEOR
When Will Love Come? Pakenham Beatty. HBV
When will men again. The Leaping Laughers. George Barker. OBMV
When will the bright moon come? Thinking of My Brother. Su T'ung-po. WhP
When will the fountain of my tears be dry? Give Me Leave [*or* Petition to Have Her Leave to Die]. "A. W." EG; OBSC; TrGrPo
When will violence shake, when break me. The House. Winfield Townley Scott. MiAP
When will you dream,/ You Germans. Giovanni Battista Niccolini. *Fr.* Barbarossa. PoFr
When will you ever, Peace, wild wooddove, shy wings shut. Peace. Gerard Manley Hopkins. AtBAP; GTBS-D; OAEP (2d ed.); POTT
"When will you marry me, William." The West-Country Damosel's Complaint. *Unknown.* ESPB
When William asked, how veal was made. What Is Veal? Mary Elliott. OTPC (1923 ed.)
When Wilt Thou Save the People? Ebenezer Elliott. BLPA; EV-4; MaRV; NeHB
(God Save the People.) WBLP
(People's Anthem, The.) BCEP; PoFr
(Social Religion, *st.* 1.) QS
When window-lamps had dwindled, then I rose. Christopher Brennan. *Fr.* The Wanderer. MoAuPo
When winds are locked along the tropic shore. The *Flying Dutchman.* A. M. Sullivan. EtS
When winds are raging o'er the upper ocean. Hymn. Harriet Beecher Stowe. PoToHe
When winds go organing through the pines. The Wind in the Pines. Madison Cawein. AA; ADAH
When winds that move not its calm surface sweep. The Ocean [*or* The Gleaming Sea *or* The Landsman]. Moschus. AWP; CBE; JAWP; OxBG; WBP
When Windsor walls sustained my wearied arm. How Each Thing save the Lover in Spring Reviveth to Pleasure. Earl of Surrey. ReIE; SiPS
When winter came the land was lean and sere. Summer Drought. J. P. Irvine. SN
When winter full of lusty might. Song in Time of Plague. Pushkin. *Fr.* The City of the Plague. BoRS
When winter hoar no longer holds. The Lover's Song. Alfred Austin. OBVV
When winter is gone and spring comes. Goodness of Age. *Unknown.* OnPM
When Winter on Forgotten Woods. Stéphane Mallarmé, *tr. fr. French by* Frederick Morgan. AnFP
When winter pipes in the poplar tree. A Ballade of Busy Doctors. James Newton Matthews. PoP
When winter scourged the meadow and the hill. Ice. Sir Charles G. D. Roberts. BoCaPo; ExPo
When winter snows upon thy sable [*or* golden] hairs. To Delia, XXXIX. Samuel Daniel. OBSC; ReIE; TuPP
When winter's cold tempests and snows are no more. The Blue-Bird. Alexander Wilson. AA; HiLiAm
When winter-time grows weary, I lift my eyes on high. Winter Branches. Margaret Widdemer. CP
When wintry days are dark and drear. The Light'ood Fire. John Henry Boner. AA
When wise Minerva still was young. The Origin of Didactic Poetry. James Russell Lowell. IAP; PoEL-5
When wisps of smoke from the guns were flying. Happiness. Mikhail Lvovich Matusovsky. TrRV
When with a serious musing I behold. The Marigold. George Wither. OBS; SeCL
When with eyes closed as in an opium dream. Exotic Perfume [*or* Parfum exotique]. Baudelaire. AWP; OnPM
When with fingers all uncertain, tiny stars have torn the curtain. Moon-Children. Michael Lewis. TSW
When with May the air is sweet. Love, Whose Month Was Ever May. Ulrich von Lichtenstein. AWP; JAWP; WBP
When, with my little daughter Blanche. Presence of Mind. Harry Graham. WhC
When with the cannon's mighty voice. The Girondins. Alexandre Dumas. *Fr.* Le Chevalier de maison rouge. PoFr
When with the thorns with which I long, too long. The Coronet. Andrew Marvell. OBS; StJW
When within my arms I hold you. Aurelia. Robert Nichols. OBMV; POTE
When women first Dame Nature wrought. Of Women. Richard Edwards. EIL
When Work Is Done This Fall. *Unknown.* CSF
When world is water and all is flood, God said. Noah's Ark. Marguerite Young. MoPo
When Yankies, skilled in martial rule. The Town-Meeting, A.M. John Trumbull. *Fr.* M'Fingal, I. IAP; TCAP
When Yon Full Moon. W. H. Davies. LiTM (1946 ed); MBP; MoBrPo
When you and I. When You and I Grow Up. Kate Greenaway. MPB; PCH
When you and I are apart (Alas!). Idas Te Diliget Unam. Seaforth Mackenzie. MM
When you and I behind the Veil are past. The Long While. Omar Khayyám, *tr. by* Edward Fitzgerald. *Fr.* The Rubáiyát. OnPM
When you and I go down. Midnight Lamentation. Harold Monro. BSV; ChMo; ChMP; CMP; Lo; ViBoPo
When You and I Grow Up. Kate Greenaway. MPB; PCH
When you and I have play'd the [*or* this] little hour. Reunited [*or* Envoy]. Sir Gilbert Parker. *Fr.* A Lover's Diary. OBVV; OQP; QP-2; VA
When You and I Were Young, Maggie. George W. Johnson. OlF; TreF
When you and my true lover meet. The Lady's Third Song. W. B. Yeats. *Fr.* The Three Bushes. FaBoTw
When you are caught breathless in an empty station. This Is the Place to Wait. Horace Gregory. The Passion of M'Phail, V. MoAmPo
When you are dead some day, my dear. In Pace. Arthur Reed Ropes. VA
When you are discouraged. Try This Once. *Unknown.* WBLP
When you are gone. Translations from Modern Japanese Poetry. Akiko Yanagiwara. PFE
When You Are Old. W. E. Henley. PoVP
When You Are Old. John McClure. LS
When You Are Old. Pierre de Ronsard, *tr. fr. French by* Alan Conder. *Fr.* Sonnets pour Hélène. TrFP
(Four Sonnets to Helen, 4, *tr. by* Humbert Wolfe.) LiTW
("When you are very old, by the hearth's glare," *tr. by* Curtis Hidden Page.) PrPoCR
When You Are Old. W. B. Yeats. AWP; BLV; BMEP; BoLiVe; CaAE; ChMo; CMP; EnL; EnLi-2 (1949 ed.); EPP; EtPaEn; FaFP; GTSE; GTSL; HBV; InP; InvP; JAWP; LEAP; LiTG; LiTL; LiTM (rev. ed.); LoPo; LoPS; MaRV; MBP; MM; MoAB; MoBrPo; NeMA; OBEV; OBVV; OtMeF; PFE; PoE; PoeT; POTT;

When You Are Old (*continued*)
PoVP; PtOT; ReaPo; TCPD; TIP; TreFS; TwCV; TwP; TyEnPo; WBP
When you are old, and I am passed away. When You Are Old. W. E. Henley. PoVP
When you are old, and I—if that should be. After Ronsard. Charles Williams. GTBS; TCPD
When you are old and sit by candle-light. When You Are Old. Pierre de Ronsard. *tr. by* Alan Conder. *Fr.* Sonnets pour Hélène. TrFP
When you are old, at evening candle-lit. Four Sonnets to Helen, 4. Pierre de Ronsard, *tr. by* Humbert Wolfe. *Fr.* Sonnets pour Hélène. LiTW
When you are really quite grown up. To a Certain Little Boy. Charles Hanson Towne. FAOV
When you are tall and old and far too wise. For an Argonaut, Age Seven. Ted Olson. FAOV
When you are tired of the long road and the open sky. Traveller's Rest. Cicely Fox Smith. NLK
When you are very old, at evening. Of His Lady's Old Age [*or* To Helen]. Pierre de Ronsard, *tr. by* Andrew Lang. *Fr.* Sonnets pour Hélène. AWP; JAWP; OuHeWo; POTT; WBP
When you are very old, by the hearth's glare. Pierre de Ronsard, *tr. by* Curtis Hidden Page. *Fr.* Sonnets pour Hélène. PrPoCR
When you awake. The Sleeper. Sydney Clouts. BoSA
When you buy clothes on easy terms. Cotton-Mill Colic. *Unknown.* OuSiCo
When you call me home, let it be, dear God. Fisherman's Prayer. Ethel Romig Fuller. DDA
When You Came. Ada Foster Murray. LEAP
When you came and you talked and you read. To William Carlos Williams. Galway Kinnell. NePoAm
When you came, you were like red wine and honey. A Decade. Amy Lowell. ChMo; CMP; LoPS; MAP; MoAmPo; NeMA; ReaPo
When You Come. Mary Aldis. NP
When You Come. Vilhelm Krag, *tr. fr. Norwegian by* Charles W. Stork. AnNoLy
When you come to the end of a perfect day. A Perfect Day. Carrie Jacobs Bond. PTA-1; TreF; WBLP
When you come tonight. When You Come. Mary Aldis. NP
When you dance. Creole Girl. Leslie M. Collins. PoNe
When you destroy a blade of grass. To Iron-Founders and Others. Gordon Bottomley. GTML; GTSL; OBEV (new ed.); OBMV; OBVV
When You elect to call me, God, O call. Prayer to Go to Paradise with the Asses. Francis Jammes. LO; TrFP
When you feel like saying something. The Most Vital Thing in Life. Grenville Kleiser. PoToHe (new ed.)
When you find you're a broken-down critter. Out of Sorts. W. S. Gilbert. *Fr.* The Grand Duke. ALV
When you get hard knocks and buffets. Keep the Glad Flag Flying. *Unknown.* FaFP
When you go to a store in Ascutney. Limerick. Richard H. Field. WhC
When You Go to Fairyland. *Unknown.* PCD
When you ground the lenses and the moons swam free. The Emancipators. Randall Jarrell. WaP
When you had played with life a space. To a Young Poet Who Killed Himself. Joyce Kilmer. YT
When you hark to the voice of the knocker. The Quarrelsome Trio. "L. G." WBLP
When you have come, the house is emptied quite. Evening. Mary Matheson. CaP
When you have tidied all things for the night. Solitude. Harold Monro. CMP; MBP; MoBrPo; StaSt; TrGrPo; TSW
When you hear dat Ise a-dyin'. Tone de Bell Easy. *Unknown.* ABF
When you imagine trumpet-faced musicians. Homage to Literature. Muriel Rukeyser. NAMP
When you know you love a sweetheart. Cantiga de Amigo. Martín Códax. LyMA
When you look/ into a mirror. Mirror. John Updike. WaKn
When you look back at me with surprise. The Reflection in the Mirror. Annette von Droste-Hülshoff. AnGP
When you look way 'cross dat lonesome stream. Dat Lonesome Stream. *Unknown.* ABF
When you perceive these stones are wet. Epitaph. Sir William Davenant. ACP
When You Reach the Hilltop the Sky Is on Top of You. Etta Blum. GoYe
When you reach the top of Aigle. *Unknown.* *Fr.* Eulogistic Snatches. SiB
When you said you were coming it was but empty words. Melancholy. Li Shang-yin. ChLP
When you see a man in woe. Hullo! Sam Walter Foss. PTA-2
When You Send a Valentine. Mildred J. Hill. GFA
When you set forth on the voyage to Ithaca. Ithaca. C. P. Cavafy. LiTW
When you shake loose [*or* free] your hair from all controlling. Lisa's [*or* On Lisa's] Golden Hair. Francisco de Quevedo. AtBAP; TeCS
When you shall see me in the toils of Time. She, to Him. Thomas Hardy. BEL; ES; OBVV; TOP
When you shall sleep, my faithless one, under. Posthumous Remorse. Baudelaire. AnFP
When you sing. Shakespeare. *Fr.* The Winter's Tale, IV, iii. UnS
When you slice a Georgy melon you mus' know what you is at. How to Eat Watermelons. Frank L. Stanton. BOHV
When you slowly emerged from the den of Time. A Plaint to Man. Thomas Hardy. ChMo; CMP
When you so wildly loved her, she was cold. Six Sonnets. Mary Queen of Scots. DiM
When you speak of dauntless deeds. Ballad [*or* Deed] of Lieutenant Miles. Clinton Scollard. MC; PAH
When you start for San Francisco. Humbug Steamship Companies. *Unknown.* IHA
When you start your voyage to Ithaca Ithaca. C. P. Cavafy. MoGP
When you think of the hosts without No. Limerick. *Unknown.* SiTL; TSWC
When you to Acheron's ugly water come. Sonnets, XVIII. Hilaire Belloc. TCPD
When you to Telephus devote. Horace. Odes, I, 13. LaP
When You Touch. William Hart-Smith. BoAV
When you waken in the morning. Tell It to God. Dorothy Dix Porges. PraP
When You Walk. James Stephens. WaKn
When you watch for. Feather or Fur. John Becker. FaPON; TiPo (1959 ed.)
When you were a tadpole and I was a fish. Evolution. Langdon Smith. BAP; BeLS; BLPA; BoHiPo; DDA; FaBoBe; FaFP; HBV; TreF; YaD
When you were alive, my Leukothea. Leukothea. Keith Douglas. NeBP
When you were Jacob's favorite son. Woman. Nyleen Newton. CAG
When you were there, and you, and you. Dining-Room Tea. Rupert Brooke. MBP; MoBrPo; POTE
When you were weary, roaming the wide world over. The Betrayal. Alice Furlong. AnIV
When You Will Walk in the Field. Leah Goldberg, *tr. fr. Hebrew by* Simon Halkin. TrJP
When young-ey'd Spring profusely throws. Invocation to Fancy. Joseph Warton. *Fr.* Ode to Fancy. OBEC
When Young Hearts Break. Heine, *tr. fr. German by* Louis Untermeyer. AWP
(Stars Look at Love, The.) LiTW
When Young Melissa Sweeps. Nancy Byrd Turner. FaPON; GaP; OTPC (1946 ed.)
When young Nils Jonson, god of girded steel. Shadow of Smoke. Andrew Hewitt. NoCaPo (1941 ed.)
When Young Rogero goes to see a play. Veniunt Spectentur ut Ipsi. Henry Parrot. SiCE
When Your Beauty Appears. Thomas Parnell. *See* Song: "When thy beauty appears."
When your feet are like lead. Consolatory! St. John Emile Clavering Hankin. CenHV
When your lips have turned to dust, and your hands. You Need Not Fear. Frances Frieseke. JKCP (1955 ed.)
When your perfections to my thoughts appear. Henry Constable. *Fr.* Diana. SiCE
When your teeth decay you cannot. I Get Up at Dawn. Lu Yu. OnPC
When You're Away. Samuel Hoffenstein. FiBHP
("When you're away, I'm restless, lonely.") InP
When you're lying awake with a dismal headache. The Lord Chancellor's Song [*or* Nightmare]. W. S. Gilbert. *Fr.* Iolanthe. CoBE; CoEV; LiTM; OxBoLi; PCD; ShBV-3; SiTL; YT
When You're Throwed. *Unknown.* SCC
When you're tired and worn at the close of day. Confide in a Friend. *Unknown.* PoToHe (new ed.)
When Youth and Beauty Meet Togither. *Unknown.* EIL
When youth and strength had changed my blood to fire. Clown Pondi. Sir Osbert Sitwell. PtOT
When youth had led me half the race. Earl of Surrey. SiPS
When Youth no more goes faring. A Song against the Evil Days. Edgar McInnis. MM
When Youth observes with pitying smile. In Praise of Commonplace. Sir Owen Seaman. InMe
When youth still made my spirit bold. Peter Vyazemsky, *tr. fr. Russian by* C. M. Bowra. BoRS
When youth was lord of my unchallenged fate. On a Boy's First Reading of "King Henry V." S. Weir Mitchell. AA; LEAP; PFY
When Youthful Faith Hath Fled. John Gibson Lockhart. *See* Lines: "When youthful faith hath fled."
When you've failed with ordered people, when you've sunk neck-deep again. The Remedy. Harry Kemp. POT
When you've something hard to do. Making a Man. Carolyn R. Freeman. FAOV

When-a my blood runs chilly an' col', Ise got to go. When My Blood Runs Chilly and Col'. *Unknown.* ABF
Whenas. *See also* When as.
Whenas a royal fleet, with joyful minds. The Last Voyage of Sir Francis Drake, and Sir John Hawkins. Charles Fitzgeffrey. *Fr.* Sir Francis Drake. SG
Whenas her lute is tuned to her voice. Licia, XXXI. Giles Fletcher. TuPP
Whenas in Jeans. Paul Dehn. FiBHP
Whenas in Silks My Julia Goes. Robert Herrick. *See* Upon Julia's Clothes.
Whenas [*or* When as] man's life, the light of human lust. Caelica, LXXXVII [LXXXVIII]. Fulke Greville. ElSeCe; GTBS-W; LiTB; MePo; OBS; OxBoCh; PoD; PoEL-1
Whenas—methinks that is a pretty way. They Answer Back; to His Ever-worshipped Will from W. H. "Francis." FiBHP
Whenas [*or* When as *or* When that] the chill sirocco [*or* charocco] blows. In Praise of Ale [*or* Give Me Ale *or* Pipe and Can]. *Unknown.* ALV; CenL; ElSeCe; EV-2; FaBoCh; HBV; OBEV; OBS; SeCL; SeEP; ViBoPo
Whenas the mildest month. The Rose [*or* The Red Rose]. Thomas Howell. ElL; ElSeCe; OBSC; PrWP; ReIE; TuPP
Whenas [*or* When as] the nightingale chanted [*or* chaunted] her vespers. Mark Antony. John Cleveland. ALV; EG; ElSeCe; EPS; InvP; LiTL; ReaPo; SeCL; ViBoPo
Whenas [*or* When as] the Rye Reach to the Chin. George Peele. *Fr.* The Old Wives' Tale. ElSeCe; EM-1; EnLoPo; FaBoCh; InvP; LO; LoGBV; SeCePo; SiTL; TuPP; ViBoPo
(Song: "Whenas [*or* When as] the rye reach to the chin.") ALV; AtBAP; ElL; FaBoEn; LoBV; OBSC; OxBoLi; PoEL-2
(Summer Song, A.) OBEV (new ed.)
Whenas the swarming flood of night. Moon in Eclipse. Ibn Hamdis. MooP
Whenas to shoot my Julia goes. To Julia in Shooting Togs. Sir Owen Seaman. BOHV
Whence and what art thou, execrable shape. Satan's First Meeting with Death. Milton. *Fr.* Paradise Lost, II. CBE
Whence and Whither. Hayyim Nahman Bialik, *tr. fr. Hebrew by* Helena Frank. TrJP
Whence are ye, vague desires. Sehnsucht. Arthur Hugh Clough. EPN; VLEP
"Whence are you, learning's son?" The End of Clonmacnois. *Unknown.* KiLC
Whence came his feet into my field, and why? He and I. Dante Gabriel Rossetti. The House of Life, XCVIII. PoVP; ViPo
Whence came this man? As if on the wings. Abraham Lincoln. Samuel Valentine Cole. OHIP; PEDC
Whence came this purple color not its own? Aquae in Vinum Versae. Richard Crashaw. Epigrammata Sacra, I, 96. LaP
Whence came ye; and the people of the groves. The Light of Life. *Unknown.* OnPM
Whence come those shrieks so wild and shrill. The Polish Boy. Ann S. Stephens. PTA-2
Whence come ye, Cherubs? from the moon? The Chanting Cherubs—a Group by Greenough. Richard Henry Dana. AA
Whence come you, all of you so sorrowful? Sonnet: To Certain Ladies. Dante. AWP
Whence comes my love? A Sonnet Made [*or* Lines] on Isabella Markham. John Harington. ElL; ElSeCe; LPS-1; OBEC; TuPP
Whence comes the sound of the jade flute. On Hearing the Sound of Flutes at Loyang on a Spring Night. Li Po. WhP
Whence Comes This Rush of Wings? *Unknown.* *See* Carol of the Birds.
Whence comest thou, Gehazi. Gehazi. Kipling. OtMeF
Whence comest thou, my moon, gentle and still. The Nightingale of Avarair. Leo Alishan. ArmLP
Whence Cometh My Help. P. L. Montgomery. OQP; QP-2
Whence Cometh My Help. Odell Shepard. OBAV
Whence Cometh War? Robert Whitaker. OQP; QP-2
Whence com'st thou, Beauty? Heaven, or the abyss? Hymn to Beauty. Baudelaire. TrFP
Whence deathless Kit-Cat took its name. Epigram on the Toasts of the Kit-Kat Club, Anno 1716. Pope. CEP
Whence is it, Glaucus, that in Lycian land. Homer. *Fr.* The Iliad, XII. GrPo
Whence, O fragrant form of light. The Water-Lily. John Banister Tabb. AA; ACP; ADAH; GoBC; SN
Whence the sudden stir that roars through my vitals? Epithalamium for Mary Stuart and the Dauphin of France. George Buchanan. GoTS
Whence thou returnst, and whither wentst, I know. Leave Taking. Milton. *Fr.* Paradise Lost, XII. FaBoEn
Whence, whence this heat of the brain? The Confinement. Mark Van Doren. MOAP
Whence you have come, it puzzles me. Unknown Woman. Josef Weinheber. TwGV
Whenceness of the Which. *Unknown.* BOHV
Whene'er [*or* Where'er] a noble deed is wrought. Santa Filomena. Longfellow. PEDC; PoRL; PTA-2
Whene'er across this sinful flesh of mine. The Sign of the Cross. Cardinal Newman. GoBC; JKCP; PoVP; VA
Whene'er bitter foe attack thee. Advice to Hotheads. Samuel ben Elhanan Isaac Archevolti of Padua. TrJP
Whene'er Don Juan has a feast at home. Satirical Letrilla IV. Manuel Bretón de los Herreros. AnSpL-2
Whene'er I come where ladies are. Love at Large. Coventry Patmore. *Fr.* The Angel in the House. HoPM; PoVP
Whene'er I quote I seldom take. The Bards We Quote. Bert Leston Taylor. HBMV; WhC
Whene'er I see soft hazel eyes. The Lapful of Nuts. *Unknown.* GTIV; IrPN; WP
Whene'er I take my walks abroad. More Walks. "Thomas Ingoldsby." BOHV
Whene'er my mind the dawn of life recalls. Dejection. Gaspar Núñez de Arce. AnSpL-2
Whene'er the old exchange of profit rings. Francis Quarles. Emblems, IV, 3. EPS
Whene'er there comes a little child. "That They All May Be One." Roden Noel. VA
Whene'er with haggard eyes I view. Song [*or* Song of One Eleven Years in Prison]. George Canning, George Ellis, *and* John Hookham Frere. *Fr.* The Rovers. ALV; BOHV; CEP; FiBHP; OBEC; TOP
Whenever a Little Child Is Born. Agnes Louisa Carter Mason. AA
Whenever a man has arisen to fame. Fame. James J. Montague. LPS-1
Whenever a snowflake leaves the sky. Snowflakes [*or* The Snowflake *or* Winter]. Mary Mapes Dodge. AA; GFA; HBV; OTPC (1946 ed.); PRWS
Whenever Auntie moves around. Auntie's Skirts. Robert Louis Stevenson. MPB (1956 ed.); PoVP
Whenever he observes me purchasing. Sextus the Usurer. Martial. AWP
Whenever I am prone to doubt and wonder. God and Man. S. A. Nagel. MaRV
Whenever I come on kelp-stained nets. Beacon Light. Leslie Savage Clark. ChIP; PGD
Whenever I get angry. Translations from Modern Japanese Poetry. Tabubokee Ishikawa. PFE
Whenever I look in her kind eyes. Mother. *Unknown.* DD
"Whenever I plunge my arm, like this." Under the Waterfall. Thomas Hardy. LiTB; PoVP
Whenever I ride on the Texas plains. Texas Trains and Trails. Mary Austin. TiPo
Whenever I Say "America." Nancy Byrd Turner. YeAr
Whenever I see old garrets I think of mice and cheese. Old Garrets. Morris Abel Beer. LEAP
Whenever I see waves surging. Barcarola. Roy Fernández. LyMA
Whenever I see you pass, dear indolent one. The Love of Deceit. Baudelaire. AnFP
Whenever I start out to walk, our dog he seems to know. Sympathetic. Burges Johnson. AIBD
Whenever I walk in a London street. Lines and Squares. A. A. Milne. BoN
Whenever I walk to Suffern along the Erie track. The House with Nobody in It. Joyce Kilmer. BLPA; DDA; MPB; MW; PTA-2; SP; StVeCh
Whenever I'm walking in a wood. Which? Joyce L. Brisley. GFA
Whenever [*or* When] Richard Cory went down town. Richard Cory. E. A. Robinson. AmP; AmPP; AnNE; BAP; CaAE; ChMo; CMP; CoBA; CoV; ExPo; FaFP; GTBS-W; IAP; LiTA; LiTG; LiTM; LoGBV; MAP; MM; MoAB; MoAmPo; MoVE; NeMA; NePA; NP; NV; OnPP; OxBA; PFE; PFY; PoLFOT; PoMa; PoRA; ReaPo; SBMV; StPo; TCPD; TOP; TreF; TrGrPo; TwP
Whenever the bright blue nails would drop. Nails. Leonard Feeney. WHL
Whenever the days are cool and clear. The Sandhill Crane. Mary Austin. TiPo
Whenever the moon and stars are set. Windy Nights. Robert Louis Stevenson. AlDL; BLP; BoChLi; BoTP; EPP; PoRA; PoRh; PRWS; RIS; ShBV-1; SiSoSe; StaSt; TiPo
Whenever the Presbyterian bell. J. Milton Miles. Edgar Lee Masters. *Fr.* Spoon River Anthology. CrMA
Whenever the rain comes gently down. The Leaves Drink. Alice Wilkins. GFA
Whenever there is music, it is you. When There Is Music. David Morton. HBMV; LPS-1
Whenever there is silence around me. There Is a Man on the Cross. Elizabeth Cheney. ChIP; MaRV; OQP; PGD; QP-1
Whenever troublous hours I find. Happiness amidst Troubles. Immanuel di Roma. TrJP
Whenever [*or* Wherever] war, with its red woes. The Red

Whenever war, with its red woes (*continued*)
Cross [Spirit Speaks]. John Huston Finley. BoHiPo; LPS-1; PEDC
Whenever we touched, I thought of the Lying-in Hospital. Elegy. Robert Layzer. NePoEA
Wher One Would Be. Sir Edward Dyer. PoEL-1
Wher shall a man an object finde. *Unknown.* SeCSL
Where? Heine, *tr. fr. German by* Kate Flores. AnGP
(Whaur? *tr. into Scottish by* Edwin Morgan.) AnGP
Where? José Moreno Villa, *tr. fr. Spanish by* Eleanor L. Turnbull. CoSP
Where a Roman Villa Stood, above Freiburg. Mary Elizabeth Coleridge. BoHiPo; PoeT; PoMa; TCPD
Where a twisted tree. The Possum and the Moon. David Campbell. MoAuPo; NeLNL
Where Alcis keeps her state, shrill grasshopper. A Dead Locust. Aristodicus. OxBG
Where all the winds are tranquil. A Pine-Tree Buoy. Harrison Smith Morris. AA
"Where am I from?" From the green hills of Erin. A Broken Song. "Moira O'Neill." BMEP; MBP; OBVV; PG (1945 ed.)
Where am I, O awesome friend? Yitzhak Lamdan. *Fr.* For the Sun Declined. TrJP
Where ancient forests round us spread. Hymn for the Dedication of a Church. Andrews Norton. AA
Where ancient hovels stood so close. The Esplanade Method. August Strindberg. AnSL
Where angel trumpets hail a brighter sun. My Own Hereafter. Eugene Lee-Hamilton. WGRP
Where Are All Thy Beauties Now. Thomas Campion. OBSC; PoD
Where are Elmer, Herman, Bert, Tom and Charley. The Hill. Edgar Lee Masters. *Fr.* Spoon River Anthology. AmP; ExPo; LiTA; LiTM; NePA; NP; OxBA; ReMP; SeCeV; ViBoPo
Where are my laurel leaves? The Pharmaceutria. Theocritus, *tr. by* Andrew Lang. Idylls, II. GrL
Where are my leaves of laurel? Quick—lay them in my hand. The Sorceress. Theocritus, *tr. by* F. L. Lucas. Idylls, II. GrPE
Where are my roses, where are my violets. Songs of Play. *Unknown.* OxBG
Where are now the Captains. A Ballad of the Captains. E. J. Brady. EtS
Where are our sweethearts? The Cydalises. Gérard de Nerval. AnFP
Where are the bay-leaves, Thestylis? Simaetha. Theocritus, *tr. by* Jack Lindsay. Idylls, II. OxBG
Where are the bay-leaves, Thestylis, and the charms? The Incantation [*or* The Sorceress]. Theocritus, *tr. by* Charles Stuart Calverley. Idylls, II. AWP; GrPo; JAWP; LiA; WBP
Where are the bay-leaves, Thestylis? where are the love-charms? The Second Idyll. Theocritus, *tr. by* Jack Lindsay. *Fr.* Idylls. LiTW
Where are the cats? Rain. Elizabeth J. Coatsworth. CIV
Where are the cities of the plain? Ballade of Dead Cities. Sir Edmund Gosse. BMEP
Where are the friends that I knew in my Maying. Comrades. George Edward Woodberry. BoFr; HBV; LBMV; PFY
Where are the great, whom thou would'st wish to praise thee? Isolation. Arthur Hugh Clough. *Fr.* Dipsychus. BPN; EPN; OBVV
Where are the loves that we have loved before. L'Envoi. Willa Cather. HBV
Where are the lumberjacks who came from the woods for Christmas. River Song. Elizabeth Brewster. CaP
Where Are the Men? "Talhaiarn," *tr. fr. Welsh by* Thomas Oliphant. LPS-2
Where are the men who at the call. The Southern Dead. Morton Bryan Wharton. BIG
Where are the men who went forth in the morning. Where Are the Men? "Talhaiarn." LPS-2
Where are the opium ships—gulls of the Indian seas? Opium Clippers. Daniel Henderson. EtS
Where are the passions they essayed. Ballade of Dead Actors. W. E. Henley. ALV; InP; OBMV; PFE; PoVP; POTT; VLEP
Where are the ships I used to know. The Ships of Saint John. Bliss Carman. EtS
Where are the stones that mark the bones. The Men of Oyster Bay. *Unknown.* DDA
Where are the swallows fled? A Doubting Heart. Adelaide Anne Procter. HBV; LPS-1; VA
Where are the tidings of union? that I may arise. Tidings of Union. Hafiz. PeP
Where are the towers that crowned thee, the wealth that filled thy portals. The Sea-Birds Crying above the Ruins of Corinth. Antipater of Sidon. GrPE
Where are they gone, and do you know. The Little Ghosts. Thomas S. Jones, Jr. HBV
Where are they gone, the old familiar faces? The Old Familiar Faces. Charles Lamb. EnRP; ERP. *See also* I have had playmates, I have had companions.
Where are they that lived of yore? Ubi Sunt Qui ante Nos Fuerunt? *Unknown.* CBOV; EPP
Where are those laurels? Bring them, Thestylis—and the love-charms too. Love-Magic. Theocritus, *tr. by* R. C. Trevelyan. *Fr.* Idylls. GrR
Where are those legs with which you run. Johnny, I Hardly Knew Ye: In Dublinese. *Unknown.* OnYI
Where are we going? where are we going? Song of [the] Slaves in the Desert. Whittier. AmPP; AnAmPo; LA; OBVV; OxBA; PFY
Where are we to go when this is done? Sonnet. Alfred A. Duckett. PoNe
"Where are you [*or* Where you] coming from, Lomey Carter." Old Christmas [Morning]. Roy Helton. DaM; MaC; MAP; MoAmPo; NeMA; PoMS
Where are you? Drunk and drowsy, my soul is filled. Sunset. Friedrich Hölderlin. AnGP
Where are you, ever-youthful, that day by day. The Blind Singer. Friedrich Hölderlin. LiA; LiTW
"Where are you from?" A Broken Song. "Moira O'Neill." BMEP; MBP; OBVV
Where are you going. Holiday. Ella Young. TiPo (1952 ed.)
Where are you going,/ My little cat? Eliza Lee Follen. *Fr.* The Little Kittens. BoTP
Where are you going,/ My little kittens? The Little Kittens. Eliza Lee Follen. BoTP; GFA; TiPo; UTS
Where Are You Going, Great-Heart? John Oxenham. BLPA; PGD; POT; PoTo
(Great Heart.) MaRV
"Where are you going, Master mine?" Whither Away? Mary Elizabeth Coleridge. CH
"Where are you going, Mrs. Cat." Country Cat. Elizabeth J. Coatsworth. GoTP
"Where are you going [to], my pretty maid?" The Milkmaid [*or* The Pretty Maid]. Mother Goose. ABS; GaP; HBVY; LPS-3; OTPC; OxNR; RIS; SiTL; WP
"Where are you going?" said the false knight, false knight. The False Knight. *Unknown.* ABS
Where are you going to, Hywel and Blodwen. Hywel and Blodwen. Idris Davies. MoWP
Where are you going to, my pretty maid? The Rio Grande. *Unknown.* SG
Where are you going? To Scarborough Fair? Scarborough Fair. *Unknown.* LO; OxBoLi
Where are you going to, you little pig? Precocious Piggy [*or* The Little Piggies]. Thomas Hood. BoTP; MeMeAg
"Where are you going to-night, to-night." John Evereldown. E. A. Robinson. AmPP (4th ed.); MOAP; NePA; OBAV; OxBA
Where are you going, winsome maid. Arrows of Love. Bhartrihari. OnPM
"Where are you going, young fellow my lad." Young Fellow My Lad. Robert W. Service. CV
Where are you hid from me, belovèd one. Legend. John Hall Wheelock. LiTL
Where are you, my friend? Letter. Olga Berggolts. *Fr.* Parting. RuPo
Where are your ancient waves, O river. Home-coming. Albert Ehrenstein. TrJP
Where are your oranges? The Children's Bells. Eleanor Farjeon. BoTP; CH
Where art thou, belovèd To-Morrow? To-Morrow. Shelley. BPN; EmBrPo; EPN
Where art thou gone, light-ankled youth? To Youth. Walter Savage Landor. BEL; BPN; EmBrPo; EnRP; EPN; ERP; HBV; VA
Where art thou lingering, tell me, thou fair one? Nikolai Karamzin, *tr. fr. Russian by* Sir John Bowring. BoRS
Where art thou, Muse, that thou forget'st so long. Sonnets, C. Shakespeare. OBSC; PeBoSo
Where art thou, my beloved son. The Affliction of Margaret. Wordsworth. BPN; EmBrPo; EnRP; ERP; EV-3; GEPC; GTBS; GTBS-D; GTBS-W; GTSE; GTSL; MotAn; OBRV; PoEL-4
Where art thou, my darling? Two Voices. Valery Yakovlevich Bryusov. BoR
"Where art thou wandering, little child?" The Little Maid and the Cowslips. John Clare. BoTP
Where Athanase once hankered for a star. Letter to Karl Shapiro. E. L. Mayo. MiAP
Where Ausonian summers glowing. To the Nautilus. Hartley Coleridge. VA
Where Avalanches Wail. *Unknown.* NA
Where balsams droop their fragrant boughs. Little Ponds. Arthur Guiterman. HBMV
Where be those roses gone which sweetened so our eyes? Astrophel and Stella, CII. Sir Philip Sidney. SiPS
Where Be You Going, You Devon Maid. Keats. HBV; LiTL
(Devon Maid, The.) TwP

Where beth they that biforen us weren. *See* Were beth they that . . .
Where Billy the Kid Still Rides. S. Omar Barker. HiLiAm
Where blood once quenched the camp-fire's brand. Between the Graves. Harriet Prescott Spofford. PEOR
Where boughs above the pool are swinging. Aleksey Konstantinovich Tolstoy, *tr. fr. Russian.* BoR
Where broods the Absolute. Quest. Edmund Clarence Stedman. *Fr.* Corda Concordia. AA
Where Cadmus, old Agenor's son, did rest and plant his reign. The Fate of Narcissus. William Warner. *Fr.* Albion's England, IX. OBSC
Where Calydon on rocky mountains stands. Battle of the Curetes and Aetolians. Homer. *Fr.* The Iliad, IX. LiA
Where can I hide you, my dear son. The Pains of the Virgin Mary. Kostas Varnalis. MoGP
Where can the good, the beautiful, the great. The Freedom of the Press. Henrik Wergeland. PoFr
Where Cape Delgado strikes the sea. E. J. Pratt. *Fr.* The Cachalot. CaP
Where chimneys cut the sky. The Black Boys. James Boyd. MuM
Where Claribel low-lieth. Claribel. Tennyson. AtBAP; BPN; EmBrPo; PoVP; ViPo; VLEP
Where close the curving mountains drew. Untrodden Ways. Agnes Maule Machar. CaP; OCL
Where [*or* Whence] comes this rush of wings afar. Carol of the Birds. *Unknown.* ChrBoLe; OHIP; SDH
Where, Corinth, are thy glories now. The Ruins of Corinth. Antipater of Sidon, *tr. by* Goldwin Smith. LiA
Where, Corinth, is the glory of thy keep. The Ruins of Corinth. Antipater of Sidon, *tr. by* Walter Leaf. OxBG
Where Covent Garden's famous temple stands. The Dangers of Football. John Gay. *Fr.* Trivia; or, The Art of Walking the Streets of London, II. EnLi-1 (1949 ed.)
Where cross the crowded ways of life. Christ in the City [*or* The City]. Frank Mason North. MaRV; OlF; WGRP
Where Dawn Is Sprinkling. Sergei Aleksandrovich Yesenin, *tr. fr. Russian by* Babette Deutsch. TrRV
Where did I find this measure quaint? The Quail. Alcman. GrR
Where did Momotara go. Momotara. Rose Fyleman. TiPo
Where did the little boy go, you say. The Runaway. Daniel Whitehead Hicky. BrR
Where Did You Borrow That Last Sigh? Sir William Berkeley. *Fr.* The Lost Lady. SeCL; TuPP
Where Did You Come From? George Macdonald. *See* Baby, The.
Where did you come from. Cotton Eye Joe. *Unknown.* OuSiCo
Where Did You Get That Hat? Joseph J. Sullivan. TreF
Where didst Thou tarry, Lord, Lord. In the Silence. Josephine Preston Peabody. QS
Where dips the rocky highland. The Stolen Child. W. B. Yeats. BEL; EnLi-2 (1949 ed.); GTIV; GTML; MPB; OnYI; OxBI; PoMS; POTE; PoVP; TVSH
Where Do All the Daisies Go? *Unknown.* PPL
Where Do I Love You, Lovely Maid? Raymond F. Roseliep. ISi
Where Do the Gipsies Come From? Henry Howarth Bashford. ALV; CH
"Where do the stars grow, little Garaine?" Little Garaine. Sir Gilbert Parker. FaPON; OTPC (1946 ed.); PRWS
Where do these voices stray. The Eccho. Richard Leigh. MePo
Where Do They Come From? W. H. Auden. *See* Crisis.
Where do we go, my love, who have been led. The Bed. James Merrill. NePoEA
Where do you come from. *See* Oh, where do you come from.
Where do you come from, Mr. Jay? Strange Lands. Laurence Alma-Tadema. DD; HBVY; OTPC; PRWS
Where do you sing your hymns. Lament for Richard Rolston. Sir Osbert Sitwell. ChMP
Where do you think I've been to-day? The Pigeon's Story. Jeannie Kirby. BoTP
Where do you think the Fairies go? The Fairies' Shopping. Margaret Deland. HBVY; PRWS
Where do you wait, coming Huns. The Coming Huns. Valery Yakovlevich Bryusov. TrRV
Where do you walk this moment that I fall? Next of Kin. H. B. Mallalieu. WaP
Where does my sweetheart baby go. Lullaby Song. William P. M'Kenzie. BOL
Where does Pinafore Palace stand? Lilliput Levee. William Brighty Rands. CenHV; TSW; TSWC
Where dost [*or* do'st] thou careless[e] lie. An Ode to Himself. Ben Jonson. AtBAP; EV-2; ExPo; FaBoEn; LiTB; NBE; OAEP; OBS; PoEL-2; PoFr; SeCePo; SeCeV; SeCL; SeCV-1; SeEP; TuPP
Where Dreams Are Sold. Jean Graham. OCL
Where dwell the dear dream people who fly at break of day? Dream People. Isabel Ecclestone Mackay. UnW
Where dwell the lovely, wild white women folk. The White Women. Mary Elizabeth Coleridge. TCPD
Where e'er my flatt'ring passions rove. *See* Where-e'er My Flatt'ring Passions Rove.
Where Englands Damon us'd to keep. The Pastoral on the King's Death. Written in 1648. Alexander Brome. OBS
Where e're thy navy spreads her canvas wings. To the King on His Navy. Edmund Waller. CEP
Where finds philosophy her eagle eye. City and Country Life. William Cowper. *Fr.* The Task. CoBE
"Where floating shapes of stars and leaves." The Deep. Gladys Cromwell. PC
Where, for this within. Interior of the Rose. Rainer Maria Rilke. AnGP
Where Forlorn Sunsets Flare and Fade. W. E. Henley. *See* Over the Hills and Far Away.
Where Foyle his swelling waters rolls northward to the main. The Maiden City. Elizabeth Tonna. HBV
Where Gadie Rins. John Park. EBSV
Where girt with orchard and with olive-yard. An Etruscan Ring. John William Mackail. VA
Where glows the Irish hearth with peat. Cois na Teineadh. T. W. Rolleston. AnIV
Where Go the Boats? Robert Louis Stevenson. AlDL; BoChLi; FaBoBe; FaBoCh; GoBP; LoGBV; MPB; PRWS; RAR; StVeCh (1940 ed.); SUS; TiPo
Where God had walked. The First Autumn. Marshall Schacht. CAG; YT
Where Goest Thou? Victor Hugo. *See* Poet's Simple Faith, A.
Where got ye the mandrake, old grannie Gyp? Mandrake. Leland Davies. BAP
Where great Pike's Peak his summit rears. Old Balaam. *Unknown.* PoOW
Where green Earth from azure sky. Declivities of Heaven. George Darley. *Fr.* Nepenthe. RO
Where had I heard this wind before. Bereft. Robert Frost. AnFE; AtBAP; CoAnAm; LiTM; MAP; MoAB; MoAmPo; OxBA; TwAmPo
Where hae ye been a' the day. *Unknown.* OxNR
Where has he of race divine. Chorus of Satyrs Driving Their Goats. Euripides. *Fr.* The Cyclops. AWP; GrPo; JAWP; WBP
Where hast been toiling all day, sweetheart. The Child on the Judgment Seat. Elizabeth Rundle Charles. BLPA; PEOR
Where hast thou floated, in what seas pursued. To the Immortal Memory of the Halibut, on Which I Dined This Day, Monday, April 26, 1784. William Cowper. CaAE; NBE; SeCePo
Where hast Thou hidden Thyself. Song of the Soul and the Bridegroom. St. John of the Cross. LiA
Where have all the colours gone? The Darkening Garden. *Unknown.* BoTP
Where have our loved ones gone? The Glorified. Gérard de Nerval. TrFP
Where have these hands been. Musician. Louise Bogan. UnS
Where have they gone. The Saint John. George Frederick Clarke. CaP
Where have we laid him now. The Lost Christ. Franklin E. Elmer, Jr. ChIP
Where have ye [*or* you] been all the day, Billy Boy, Billy Boy? Billy Boy. *Unknown.* LO; OxNR; SiTL
Where have ye been, ye ill woman. The Witch of Fife. James Hogg. *Fr.* The Queen's Wake, I. BCEP; BSV
"Where have you been,/ Miss Marjorie Keen?" Banbury Fair. Edith G. Millard. BoTP
"Where have you been all the day." The Young Thing. *Unknown.* MeMeAg; RIS
Where have you been all the day, Billy boy, Billy boy? *See* Where have ye been . . .
"Where have you been all the day, Randall, my son?" Lord Randall. *Unknown.* MaC
"Where have you been Billy boy, Billy boy." Billy Boy. *Unknown.* ABF, *with music;* ABS; BLPA; IHA
Where have you been, my canny honey? Captain Bover. *Unknown.* SG
Where Have You Been, My Good Old Man? *with music. Unknown.* OuSiCo
Where have you been, South Wind, this May-day morning? South Wind. Siegfried Sassoon. BoTP; NLK (1947 ed.)
Where have you been to, Randall my son? Lord Randall. *Unknown.* ReaPo
Where have you gone to, Yesterday. Yesterday. Hugh Chesterman. BoTP; SiSoSe
"Where have you hidden them?" I asked the sea. Lost Ships. Thomas Hornsby Ferril. EtS
Where He Gazed a Gloom Pervaded. Byron. *See* At the Gate of Heaven.
Where Helen Comes. John Jerome Rooney. AA
Where Helen Sits. Laura E. Richards. AA

Where hidest thou from me. Spiritual Canticle between the Soul and Christ. St. John of the Cross. TeCS
Where hills and valleys crowd toward Ching-men. On a Historic Landmark. Tu Fu. WhP
Where hints of racy sap and gum. Wild Honey. Maurice Thompson. AnFE; APA; CoAnAm; HBV; OBAV
Where His Lady Keeps His Heart. "A. W." *See* Sweet Love, Mine Only Treasure.
Where honor or where conscience does not bind. Liberty. Abraham Cowley. *Fr.* Ode upon Liberty. GrCo-1
Where Hudson's Wave. George Pope Morris. AA
Where I go are flowers blooming. Les Planches-en-Montagne. Michael Roberts. OBMV
Where I, Mycenae, stood in state. Mycenae. Pompeius. OxBG
Where I spat in the harbor the oranges were bobbing. The Metamorphoses. Randall Jarrell. FiMAP
Where I was born, near Stepney Green. Stepney Green. John Singer. WaP
Where icy and bright dungeons lift. Voyages, VI. Hart Crane. AnFE; ChMo; CoAnAm; MAP; MoAB; MoAmPo; MoVE; SeCeV; TwAmPo; UnPo (3d ed.)
Where Ignorance Is Bliss. Thomas Gray. Ode on a Distant Prospect of Eton College. TreF
Where in its old historic splendor stands. The Hudson. George Sidney Hellman. AA
Where in the attic the dust encumbers. Mournful Numbers. Morris Bishop. WhC
Where in the summer-warm woodlands with the sweet wind. Iphione. Thomas Caulfield Irwin. EnLoPo; IrPN
Where in the valley the summer rain. Summer Rain. Laurie Lee. MoVE
Where? In what secret. April. Jaime Torres Bodet. AnCL
Where, in whichever blissfully watered gardens, on which. Sonnets to Orpheus, Pt. II, XVII. Rainer Maria Rilke. AnGP
Where innocent bright-eyed daisies are. Daisies. Christina Rossetti. *Fr.* Sing-Song. MBP; RIS
Where is a golden goblet fill'd so deep. The Golden Elegy. Leopold Staff. LiTW
Where is a holier thing. Flos Virginum. Maurice Hewlett. BMEP; LEAP
Where is Australia, singer, do you know? Last Stanzas of "The Bush." Bernard O'Dowd. *Fr.* The Bush. BoAu; PoFr
Where Is Dominga? Francisco de Sá de Miranda, *tr. fr. Spanish by* Sir John Bowring. OnPM
Where is every piping lad. Dawn of Day. William Browne. *Fr.* The Shepherd's Pipe. EIL; WP
Where Is Fancy Bred. Shakespeare. *See* Tell Me Where Is Fancy Bred.
Where Is God? Minot J. Savage. OQP; QP-2
"Where is God!" inquired the mind. Evidence. Thomas Curtis Clark. MaRV
Where is he gone, the queer little man. Bill Manning. Joseph I. C. Clarke. JKCP (1926 ed.)
Where Is Heaven? Bliss Carman. *Fr.* Here and Now. GoTP; MaRV; OQP; QP-2
Where is it now? Look, there it flies in merry sport. The Swallow's Flight. Louis Levy. TrJP
Where is it that these frail adventurers go. Moths. David Morton. MuM
Where is my boy, my boy. Emily Sparks. Edgar Lee Masters. *Fr.* Spoon River Anthology. BoFr
Where Is My Butterfly Net? David McCord. FiBHP
Where is my chief, my master, this bleak night, mavrone? O'Hussey's Ode to the Maguire [*or* Ode to the Maguire]. *Unknown, at. to* Eochadh O'Hussey. AnIV; ERP; GTIV; IrPN; OnYI; OxBI; SeCePo; TIP
Where is my golden palace? Blake. *Fr.* Lament of Ahania. LoPS
Where is my kingdom? I would be a king. Kingdoms. Charles Oluf Olsen. OQP; QP-2
"Where is my little basket gone?" Kitty in the Basket. Eliza Lee Follen. SAS
Where is my ruined life, and where the fame. Odes. Hafiz. AWP
Where Is My Wandering Boy Tonight? *Unknown.* FaFP; TreF
"Where is now Elijah's God?" A Martyr's Death. Menahem ben Jacob. TrJP
Where is one that, born of woman, altogether can escape. The Making of Man. Tennyson. EPN
Where Is Paris and Heleyne? Thomas of Hales. *Fr.* The Luve Ron. ChTr
Where is she now? Where all must be. *Unknown.* LO
Where is that good, which wise men please to call. Excellence. Amos Bronson Alcott. IAP
Where is that sugar, Hammond? Early Evening Quarrel. Langston Hughes. HoPM
Where is the beauteous majesty of Denmark? Shakespeare. *Fr.* Hamlet, IV, v. AtBAP
Where is the Cat with the Fiddle gone? Ballad of the Cats of Bygone Time. Michael Scot. PoC
Where is the Grand Duke Ruffanuff, who stole the Czar's first wife? And When They Fall. James J. Montague. HBMV
Where is the grave of Sir Arthur O'Kellyn. The Knight's Tomb. Samuel Taylor Coleridge. AEV; BCEP; BHV; EM-2; EmBrPo; EnRP; EPN; ERP; EV-4; FaBoCh; GN; InP; LEAP; LoGBV; LPS-2; ShBV-1; TCEP; TVSH
Where is the hand to trace. With a Coin from Syracuse. Oliver St. John Gogarty. OBMV
Where is the home for me? Song of the Bacchanals [*or* The Home of Aphrodite]. Euripides. *Fr.* Bacchae. AWP; GrR
Where is the Jim Crow section. Merry-go-round. Langston Hughes. PoNe
Where is the keeper of the temple-gates. Stratagem. Euripides. *Fr.* Iphigenia in Tauris. GrR
"Where is the Kingdom?" asked the solemn [*or* pompous] priest. The Kingdom. Thomas Curtis Clark. ChIP; MaRV
Where is the love that, both soon and late. My Mother. Zakarias Topelius. AnSL
Where is the man who has been tried and found strong and sound? A Degenerate Age. Solomon ibn Gabirol. TrJP
Where is the nightingale. Songs [*or* Second Song *or* A Song] from Cyprus. Hilda Doolittle ("H. D."). CBOV; MAP; MoAmPo; NeMA; TCPD; TriL; TwCV
Where is the nymph, whose azure eye. Song. Thomas Moore. EnLoPo
Where is the port of grey St. John? The Port of St. John. H. A. Cody. CPG
Where is the prisoner fellow? won't he catch it! Mock Trial. Aristophanes. *Fr.* The Wasps. GrR
Where Is the Real Non-Resistant? Vachel Lindsay. OQP; QP-1; StJW
Where Is the Sea? Felicia Dorothea Hemans. EtS
Where is the true man's fatherland? The Fatherland. James Russell Lowell. BHV; GDAH; GN; HBV; HBVY; MaRV; OTPC; PGD; PoRL; TVSH
Where is the word of Your youth and beauty. To the Young Man Jesus. Annie Charlotte Dalton. CaP
Where is the world we roved, Ned Bunn? To Ned. Herman Melville. PoEL-5; ViBoPo
Where is there an end of it, the soundless wailing. T. S. Eliot. *Fr.* Four Quartets: The Dry Salvages. FaBoTw
Where is there happiness today? Whither? Po Chü-i. PoHN
Where is this blessed Babe. Hymn for Christmas Day. Jeremy Taylor. AnEC
Where is this stupendous stranger. The Nativity of Our Lord. Christopher Smart. LoBV; PoEL-3; RO
Where is thy beauty, Dorian Corinth, where. On Corinth Fallen. Antipater of Sidon. GrPo
Where Is Thy Brother? *Unknown.* MaRV
Where Is Thy God? J. Lewis Milligan, *paraphrased fr.* Psalm XLII, Bible, *O.T.* MaRV
Where Is Thy God, My Soul? Thomas T. Lynch. MaRV
Where is thy lovely perilous abode? To the Leanán Shee [*or* Sidhe]. Thomas Boyd. GTIV; OnYI; TIP
Where is your far-famed beauty, Corinth town? Lament for Corinth. Antipater of Sidon. GrR
"Where is your home, Sir?" Such the question posed. On the Frontier. Nathaniel Micklem. NeTW
Where It Is Winter. George O'Neil. HBMV
Where Kensington high o'er the neighb'ring lands. The Tulips. Thomas Tickell. *Fr.* Kensington Garden. BeR
Where Late the Sweet Birds Sang. Shakespeare. *See* Sonnets, LXXIII.
Where leap the long Atlantic swells. The Cod-Fisher. Joseph C. Lincoln. EtS
Where leaves are glassy green. The Air in Spring. Basil Dowling. AnNZ
Where Lies the Land [to Which the Ship Would Go]? Arthur Hugh Clough. Songs in Absence, VII. AlDL; AWP; BEL; BMEP; BoTP; ChTr; EmBrPo; EtS; EV-5; FaBoBe; FaBoCh; GN; HBV; JAWP; LoGBV; MCCG; NLK (1947 ed.); OBVV; OTPC (1946 ed.); TOP; TVSH; VA; ViPo; ViPP; VLEP; WBP; WGRP
(Songs in Absence.) OQP; QP-2
(Two Ships, 2.) ES
("Where lies the land to which the ship would go.") BPN; EPN; GTBS; GTBS-D; GTSL
Where Lies the Land to Which Yon Ship Must Go? Wordsworth. EnRP; ERP EtS; GEPC; OBRV; PeBoSo; PoEL-4
(Sonnet: "Where lies the land to which yon ship must go?") AlDL; ChER
Where life and death try friendships. A Farewell to Ho Yung on His Leaving Min Valley for the Capital. Tu Fu. WhP
Where life's road through the waste is driven. Three Roses. Dmitri Venevitinov. BoRS
Where, like a pillow on a bed. The Ecstasy [*or* The Extasie]. John Donne. AnFE; ATP; BLV; CaAE; CoEV; EM-1; EnLoPo; EnLP; EPS; ExPo; FaBoEn; LiTB; LiTG; LO; LoBV; MaPo; MeLP; MePo; OBEV; OBS; PoEL-2;

PoFS; ReaPo; ReEn; ReIE; RiBV; SeCePo; SeCeV; SeCV-1; SeEP; TrGrPo; TuPP; TwP; TyEnPo; ViBoPo
Where limpid waters lie between. Deep unto Deep. John Banister Tabb. PFE
Where Lincoln wide extends her fenny soil. The Origin of Pattens. John Gay. *Fr.* Trivia. BeR
Where lives the man that never yet did hear. Orchestra [*or* Of Homer's Odyssey]. Sir John Davies. EG; OBSC; ReIE; SiPS; TuPP
Where long the shadows of the wind had rolled. The Sheaves. E. A. Robinson. AWP; CoBMV; InPo; JAWP; MAP; MaPo; MoAB; MoAmPo; MOAP; NePA; OxBA; ReaPo; RiBV; TBM; TOP; TwP; WBP; WHA; YT
Where Love Is. Amelia Josephine Burr. HBV; SBMV
Where Love Is King. Hilda Doolittle ("H. D."). *Fr.* Hymen. BAP; ChMo; CMP; HBMV
Where Love Once Was. James Oppenheim. SBMV
Where lovely Avon winds her rippling train. Recompense. Agnes Aston Hill. NeTW
Where man was all too marred with sin. Bethlehem. Katharine Tynan. SDH
Where many an eagle builds her nest. On Mount Tsukuba. Mushimaro. OnPM
Where may the wearied eye repose. Washington [*or* The Cincinnatus of the West]. Byron. *Fr.* Ode to Napoleon Bonaparte. BoHiPo; DD; GA; MC; OHIP; PaA; PAH; PoRL
Where men have held the vision clear. The Seekers. Lucia Trevitt Auryansen. OQP; QP-2
Where Mortals Dwell. Schiller, *tr. fr. German by* Benjamin W. Wells. *Fr.* Die Braut von Messina, IV, iv. LiA
Where mountains round a lonely dale. The Mowers. William Allingham. IrPN
Where murdered Mumford lies. Mumford. Ina M. Porter. PAH
Where My Books Go. W. B. Yeats. OBEV; OBVV
Where, my childhood's home, art thou. Sergei Yesenin, *tr. fr. Russian by* C. M. Bowra. BoR
Where, my days, are you. Song. Aleksey Koltsov. BoRS
Where my fathers stood. Devon to Me. John Galsworthy. HBMV
Where My Step Falters. Marjorie Meeker. BAP; NP
Where No Seeds Grow. Dorothy Dow. TBM
Where No Thoughts Are. Anna Hempstead Branch. MOAP
Where none but Nature is the guide, Minerva hath no part. To the Reader. Thomas Howell. SiCE
Where None Intrudes. Byron. *See* Ocean, The.
Where not a breeze the silence raids. The Garden. Roy Campbell. TriL
Where nothing is, a little thing doth ease. Of Nothing and Althing. John Heywood. SiCE
Where now he roves, by wood or swamp whatever. Proem to "The Kid." Conrad Aiken. *Fr.* The Kid. MoAB
Where now lies Mustolphus? Everywhere. Why? Against Mustolphus His Lying. John Davies of Hereford. SiCE
Where now these mingled ruins lie. Stanzas Occasioned by the Ruins of a Country Inn [*or* On the Ruins of a Country Inn]. Philip Freneau. AA; APW; DDA; IAP; MOAP; OxBA; TCAP
Where nowadays the Battery lies. Peter Stuyvesant's New Year's Call. Edmund Clarence Stedman. PaA; PAH
Where, O, Where? Elinor Wylie. LoPS
Where, Oh Where Are the Hebrew Children. *Unknown.* BLPA
Where O Where Is Old Elijah? *Unknown. See* 'Way Over in the Promised Land.
Where old-time ships came, canvas seagull-white. Sea-Chronicles. Rex Ingamells. BoAV
Where, on the mountain peaks high up. On the Mountains. Alcman. GrL; LiTW; OxBG
Where on the wrinkled stream the willows lean. The Water-Ousel. Mary Webb. CH
Where once the sun had dragged its humid breath. Homage. George O'Neil. AnAmPo; LA
Where once we danced, where once we sang. An Ancient to Ancients. Thomas Hardy. AEV; BMEP; ChMo; ChMP; CMP; CoBMV; LiTM (rev. ed.); MoPo; MoVE; PoVP; TCPD; TOP; TriL; TwCV
Where ought youth to be. Winged Heels. Harry Lee. BBV (1923 ed.)
Where parsley and lilies lie. Saint Francis to the Birds. Clement Cook. SaFP
Where Potomac's stream is flowing. Mount Vernon's Bells. M. B. C. Slade. PTA-1
Where poverty strikes pavement—there is found. Englyn. Lynette Roberts. MoWP
Where Quair Rins Sweet amang the Flowers. James Nicol. EBSV
Where rain-wet crosses know the dawn that gleams. Songs above the Dust. Grantland Rice. DDA; PaA
Where Runs the River. Francis William Bourdillon. BPP; HBV; WGRP
Where San Juan and Chacabuco intersect. Houses like Angels. Jorge Luis Borges. AnCL
Where shall a diaphanous dream find spaces. Children of Francis, 1953. Sister Mary Francis. SaFP
Where shall Celia fly for shelter. Song. Christopher Smart. EnLoPo
Where Shall I Be When de Firs' Trumpet Soun'? *with music. Unknown.* BoAN-1
Where shall I find you. Sub Terra. William Carlos Williams. NP
"Where shall I gang, my ain true love?" The Duke of Athole's Nurse. *Unknown.* ESPB
Where shall I go then. R. P. Blackmur. Sea Island Miscellany, XIV. MoVE
Where shall I have at mine own will. Sir Thomas Wyatt. SiPS
Where shall I learn to get my peace again? Keats. *Fr.* Lines to Fanny. ChER
Where shall I seek a guide? where shall I meet. On Psalm CXIX, 5. Francis Quarles. EV-2
Where shall my troubled soule at large discharge. *Unknown.* SeCSL
Where shall once the wanderer weary. Exile. Heine. OnPM
Where Shall the Baby's Dimple Be? Josiah Gilbert Holland. BLPA; BOL
Where shall the eyes a darkness find. Back in the Return. Huw Menai. MoWP
Where Shall the Lover Rest. Sir Walter Scott. *Fr.* Marmion, III. CBE; CBOV; CH, *abr.*; EBSV; EmBrPo; EnRP; GTBS; GTBS-D; GTBS-W; GTSE, 4 *sts.*; GTSL (Song: "Where shall . . .") EV-4; OBRV; PoEL-4; ViBoPo
Where Shall We Dance? "Gabriela Mistral," *tr. fr. Spanish by* Alice Stone Blackwell. OnPM
Where shall we find a perfect life whereby. The Perfect Life. Charles Francis Richardson. BePJ
Where shall we find Thee—where art Thou, O God? Search. Margaret Widdemer. TrPWD
Where shall we get religion? Beneath the open sky. Nature and Religion. Sam Walter Foss. *Fr.* The Higher Catechism. OQP; QP-2
Where shall we go? August Afternoon. Marion Edey. YeAr
Where shall we go? The Hounded Lovers. William Carlos Williams. LoPS; TrGrPo
"Where shall we go for our garlands glad." A Song of Autumn. Adam Lindsay Gordon. BoAu
Where shall we learn to die? Teach Us to Die. Arthur Penrhyn Stanley. VA
Where shall we seek for a hero, and where shall we find a story? Crispus Attucks. John Boyle O'Reilly. PAH
Where Shall Wisdom Be Found? *abr.* Euripides, *tr. fr. Greek by* Gilbert Murray. *Fr.* Bacchae. OxBG ("This Is Alone Life, Joy, Empire and Victory.") GrR "Will they ever come to me, ever again," *sel.* UnS
Where she fell swearing, hand to side. Epitaph. L. A. G. Strong. GTIV
Where She Her Sacred Bower Adorns. Thomas Campion. LoBV (Her Sacred Bower.) HBV
Where shelved the lifeless clouds are lying. A Daisy in an Alien Land. Nikolay Novosyolov. TrRV
Where ships of Purple gently toss. Emily Dickinson. AmP; AmPP
Where should he seek, to go away. The Mark. Louise Bogan. MOAP; MoPo; MoVE; NP
Where should this music be? I' the air, or the earth? Shakespeare. *Fr.* The Tempest, I, ii. UnS
Where sleeps the north wind when the south inspires. To Castara: Of the Knowledge of Love. William Habington. *Fr.* Castara. EV-2
Where southern suns and winds prevail. The Nautilus. Charlotte Smith. OTPC (1923 ed.)
Where Sugarloaf with bare and ruinous wedge. On Great Sugarloaf. George Arthur Greene. TIP
Where sunless rivers weep. Dream Land. Christina Rossetti. EmBrPo; EnLi-2; GTML; MBP; POTT; PoVP; ViPo
Where swell the songs thou shouldst have sung. A Soldier Poet. Rossiter Johnson. AA; MDAH
Where tender love had laid him down to sleep. Thomas Watson. *Fr.* Hecatompathia. ReIE
Where the bare brown slope of the hill goes down. My House. Harry Noyes Pratt. PoTo
Where the bee sucks, there suck I. Ariel's Song. Shakespeare. *Fr.* The Tempest, V, i. AnEnPo; AnFE; AWP; BCEP; BEL; BoTP; CaAE; CBE; CBPC; CH; EG; EIL; EM-1; EnLi-1; EnLit; EPP; EV-1; GN; GTSL; HBV; HBVY; HOAH; InPo; JAWP; KN; LEAP; MCCG; MPB; OBEV; OBSC; OTPC; PCD; PCH; PFE; PIR; PoRh; RAR; ReaPo; RIS; SeCeV; SiCE; ThWaDe; TiPo; TOP; TyEnPo; UTS; ViBoPo; WBP; WHA
Where the Blessed Feet Have Trod. "Michael Field." OxBoCh; StJW
Where the bluebells and the wind are. Bluebells. Walter de la Mare. MPB

Where the bog ends, there, where the ground lips, lovely. Landscape of Love. P. K. Page. BoCaPo (1943 ed.)
Where the Buddha sleeps and dreams. Oblivion. *Unknown.* MM
Where the buttercups so sweet. The Little Herd-Boy's Song. Robert Buchanan. BoTP
Where the cedar leaf divides the sky. Passage. Hart Crane. ExPo; MoVE
Where the Cedars. Jacob Glatstein, *tr. fr. Yiddish by* Joseph Leftwich. TrJP
Where the cement-lined bowels of the city. The Hunt. Babette Deutsch. AnAmPo; LA
Where the city's ceaseless crowd moves on the livelong day. Sparkles from the Wheel. Walt Whitman. FaBoEn
Where the columned cliffs far out have planted. Ghosts. Margaret L. Woods. UnW
Where the cowboys roost on the green rolling prairie. A Kansas Cowboy. *Unknown.* CoSo
Where the crumbling pathway descends in the shadow of autumn elms. On the Mönchsberg. Georg Trakl. AnGP
Where the dark green hollows lift. Sea-Gulls. Norah M. Holland. MCCG
Where the Dead Men Lie. Barcroft Henry Boake. BoAu; BoAV; NeLNL
Where the dews and the rains of heaven have their fountain. The Battle in the Clouds. William Dean Howells. PAH
Where the dim paths wind and creep. The Old Garden. Arthur Stringer. CPG
Where the dreaming Tiber wanders by the haunted Appian Way. The Magpie's Song. Frank S. Williamson. BoAu
Where the drift went the waters answered it. "Final Status Never Ascertained." Lloyds Registry. Merrill Moore. MAP; MoAmPo (1942 ed.)
Where the Dropwort Springs Up Lithe and Tall. John Lyle Donaghy. NeIP
Where the flowers lean to their shadows on the wall. Shadows of Chrysanthemums. E. J. Scovell. MoVE
Where the fountain murmurs in the shade. Love in Age. Ethel Anderson. MoAuPo
Where the graves were many, we looked for one. In Clonmel Parish Churchyard. Sarah Morgan Bryan Piatt. AA
Where the gray sea lay sad and vast. By the Gray Sea. John Hall Wheelock. TBM
Where the Grizzly Dwells. James Fox. SCC
Where the hare-bells are ringing. The Lily of the Valley. Thomas Lovell Beddoes. EG
Where the huge Atlantic swings heavy water eastward. Mater Severa. Stephen Lucius Gwynn. TIP
Where the ironbarks are hanging leaves disconsolate and pale. The Lonely Woman. M. Forrest. BoAu
Where the lazy wall is down. Sierran Vigil. Ewart Milne. NeIP
Where the lotus pool. Cups of Jade. Huang Pien. PoHN
Where the Mind Is without Fear. Rabindranath Tagore. Gitanjali, XXXV. MM; PoFr
(My Free Country.) GrCo-2
Where the mob gathers, swiftly shoot along. Of Pick-Pockets. John Gay. *Fr.* Trivia; or, The Art of Walking the Streets of London, III. EnLi-1 (1949 ed.)
Where the Moosatockmaguntic. Hiram Hover. Bayard Taylor. BOHV; PA
Where the northern ocean darkens. Watch, America. Robert Nathan. WaKn
Where the Northern Ocean in vast whirls. Sea-Birds. James Thomson. EtS
Where the orange-branches mingle on the sunny garden-side. The Demon of the Mirror. Bayard Taylor. BeLS
Where the patient oxen were, by the ass's stall. A Country Carol. Margaret Widdemer. SDH
Where the Pecos River winds and turns in its journey to the sea. The Pecos Queen. *Unknown.* CSF
Where the Picnic Was. Thomas Hardy. MoPW
Where the pools are bright and deep. A Boy's Song. James Hogg. AlDL; BoChLi; BoTP; BSV; CBPC; CH; EBSV; EV-3; FaPON; GaP; HBV; HBVY; LEAP; LiTG; MoShBr; OBEV; OnHT; OTPC (1946 ed.); PCH; PECK; PoRh; PRWS; PTA-1; RIS; StVeCh (1940 ed.); TVC; TVSH; WaKn; WP
Where the quiet-colored end of evening smiles. Love among the Ruins. Robert Browning. BEL; BoLiVe; BPN; CoBE; EM-2; EmBrPo; EnL; EnLi-2 (1949 ed.); EnLit; EPN; EtPaEn; GEPC; GTML; GTSE; HBV; MaPo; MCCG; OAEP; OBEV (new ed.); OBVV; PoEL-5; PoVP; ReTS; TOP; UnPo (1st ed.); ViPo; ViPP; VLEP
Where the Rainbow Ends. Robert Lowell. AmP; AnNE; CoBMV; FiMAP; MoAB; MoAmPo (1950 ed.); NePoEA; OnHM; TrGrPo (rev. ed.)
Where the ramparts tower in flame or shadow. Epitaph in Anticipation. Leonard Bacon. WhC
Where the Red Lion, flaring o'er the way. His Bedchamber. Goldsmith. RO
Where the remote Bermudas ride. Bermudas [*or* Song of the Emigrants in Bermuda]. Andrew Marvell. AlDL; AtBAP; AWP; BrBE; CaAE; CEP; CH; ChTr; CoBE; CoEV; ElSeCe; EnL; EPS; EV-2; ExPo; FaBoCh; FaBoEn; GN; GTBS; GTBS-D; GTBS-W; GTSE; GTSL; HBV; InPo; KN; LH; LoBV; LoGBV; LPS-2; MePo; OAEP; OBEV; OBS; OTPC; OxBoCh; PAH; PoE; PoFS; ReEn; RiBV; SeCeV; SeCV-1; SeCL; SeEP; ShBV-3; TriL; TwHP; TyEnPo; ViBoPo
Where the ripe pears droop heavily. The Wasp. "Fiona Macleod." BMEP; PCH; TSW
Where the salt creek broadens to a brown lagoon. The Hermit. James K. Baxter. AnNZ
Where the sea gulls sleep or indeed where they fly. The Ballet of the Fifth Year. Delmore Schwartz. MoAB; OxBA
Where the short-legged Esquimaux. An Arctic Vision. Bret Harte. PAH; MC
Where the Single Men Go in Summer. Nina Bourne. FiBHP
Where the slanting forest eves. To Nature Seekers. Robert W. Chambers. MoShBr
Where the slow river. Leda. Hilda Doolittle ("H. D."). HBMV; InPo; MOAP; TCPD
Where the small heads of violets. Seed Pods. John Wheelwright. MeRV
Where the snowy peaks gleam in the moonlight. Land Where the Columbines Grow. Arthur J. Fynn. PoOW
Where the streams wind and the wind is always sighing. Jade Flower Palace. Tu Fu. LiTW; WhP
Where the sun shines in the street. Seeking [*or* Feet]. Mary Carolyn Davies. OQP; QP-1; WGRP
Where the thistle lifts a purple crown. Daisy. Francis Thompson. AEV; AnEnPo; AWP; BeLS; BMEP; EnLit; GoBC; GTBS-D; GTML; HBV; LBBV; LEAP; MBP; MoAB; MoBrPo; NeMA; OBEV (new ed.); OBVV; PoeT; POTT; VA; VLEP; WHA
Where the waves are lapping, lapping softly o'er the pearly pebbles. Indian Lullaby. Sarah Comstock. BOL
Where the waves of burning cloud are rolled. Ballade of the Dreamland Rose. Brian Hooker. HBMV
Where the West Begins. Arthur Chapman. PTA-1
Where the western zun, unclouded. Zun-zet. William Barnes. PoEL-4
Where the wheel of light is turned. Pole Star for This Year. Archibald MacLeish. AmPP; CoBMV; NAMP; NePA; OxBA
Where the Wild Thyme Blows. Shakespeare. *See* Violet Bank, A.
Where the wild wave, from ocean proudly swelling. Fort Bowyer. Charles L. S. Jones. PAH
Where the Wood-Thrush Calls. Jessie Wallace Hughan. TSW
Where then shall Hope and Fear their objects find? Prayer. Samuel Johnson. *Fr* The Vanity of Human Wishes. CoEV; EnLi-1 (1949 ed.); OBEC
Where there is life, there must be death. An Elegy for Myself. Tao Yuan-ming. WhP
"Where There Is No Vision," *abr.* Elizabeth Barrett Browning. *Fr.* Aurora Leigh, II. MaRV
Where there is nothing more to see. The Secret Wood. Andrew Young. POTE
Where there is personal liking we go. The Hero. Marianne Moore. *Fr.* Part of a Novel, Part of a Poem, Part of a Play. OnHM; OxBA
Where there is the Way under heaven. Tao Teh Ching, IX. *Unknown, tr. fr. Chinese.* WhP
Where There's a Will There's a Way. Eliza Cook. BLPA; FaFP; TreF
Where There's a Will There's a Way. John Godfrey Saxe. (Find a Way.) PEDC
(On Fort Sumter, *ad., with add. st. by unknown author.*) PAH
Where these low walls run fast to desert sand. The Seventh City of Cibola. Harry Noyes Pratt. MuM
Where they once dug for money. The Old Marlborough Road. Henry David Thoreau. PoEL-4
Where They Were. *Unknown. See* If You Want to Know Where the Privates Are.
Where thou dwellest, in what grove. The Birds. Blake. CH; OBRV
Where through entangling bays. Freedom the Goddess. Arthur Wilberforce Jose. BoAu; PoFr
Where to begin I do not know. The Poet's Poverty. Rutebeuf. LyMA
Where tom-tom drummed. The Inheritors. Dorothy Livesay. CaP
Where troops of virgins follow the lamb. O Glory of Virgins. Fortunatus. ISi
Where Truest Pleasure Is. *Unknown. See* Fain Would I Change That Note.
Where under Loughrigg, the stream. Haworth Churchyard. Matthew Arnold. VLEP
Where unimaginably Bright. Oliver Hale. GoYe
Where Venta's Norman castle still uprears. Sonnet: On King Arthur's Round Table at Winchester. Thomas Warton, the Younger. Sonnets, VIII. EiPP
Where voices vanish into dream. Elected Silence. Siegfried Sassoon. MBP; MoBrPo

Where wards are weak and foes encount'ring strong. Scorn Not the Least. Robert Southwell. ElSeCe; SiCE
Where was a jewel and pretty. Rewards and Punishments—English. *Unknown.* BOL
"Where was you last night, Johnny Randall, my son?" Johnny Randall. *Unknown.* ABS
Where wast thou when I laid the foundations of the earth? The Voice of God Out of the Whirlwind. Job, Bible, *O.T.* CBOV; ImOP
Where water folds across the stones. Heritage. A. M. Sullivan. JKCP (1955 ed.)
Where water-grass grows overgreen. The Blue Heron. Maurice Thompson. BLA
Where we made the fire. Where the Picnic Was. Thomas Hardy. MoPW
Where We Must Look for Help. Robert Bly. NePoEA
Where we walk to school each day. Indian Children. Annette Wynne. BoChLi; GaP; GFA; MPB; OTPC (1946 ed.); PCH; StVeCh; SUS; TiPo
Where we went in the boat was a long bay. The Mediterranean. Allen Tate. AmP; ExPo; FaBoMo; InPo; LiTA; LiTG; LiTM; MAP; MoAB; MoAmPo; MoVE; NePA; PoFS; ReMP; SeCeV
Where Wealth Accumulates. Goldsmith. *See* Common Man, The.
Where weary folk toil, black with smoke. The Dream-Bearer. Mary Carolyn Davies. BAP
Where were the greenhouses going. Big Wind. Theodore Roethke. InvP; ViBoPo (1958 ed.)
Where were the pathways that your childhood knew? First Pathways. Sidney Royse Lysaght. OBVV
Where were ye, birds, that bless His name? The Child, II. John Banister Tabb. AA
Where were you, Baby? Mother to a Baby. Mary Elizabeth Coleridge. GTML
Where wert thou, Soul, ere yet my body born. Soul and Body. Samuel Waddington. OBVV; VA
Where, when weary with wandering. Where? Heine. AnGP
Where? When? Which? Langston Hughes. NePoAm-2
Where, where but here have Pride and Truth. On Hearing That the Students of Our New University Have Joined the Agitation against Immoral Literature. W. B. Yeats. FaBoTw
Where, where—O where, where, where. The Building of Cloudcuckoobury. Aristophanes. *Fr.* The Birds. GrR
Where, where will be the birds that sing. A Hundred Years to Come. Hiram Ladd Spencer, *wr. at. to* William Goldsmith Brown. HBV
Where White Creek Goes. Clinton Scollard. PoTo
Where white, stares, smokes or breaks. Aegean Islands 1940–41. Bernard Spencer. NeBP
Where will the girl be. Our Lives Are Pendulums. Ramón López Velarde. TwSpPo
Where will they stop, those breathing powers. Devotional Incitements. Wordsworth. OxBoCh
Where will your training lead. The Boy Washington. Dorothy Brown Thompson. SiSoSe
Where wilt thou go my harassed heart? Emily Brontë. *Fr.* I Am the Only Being. LO
Where wit is over-ruled by will. Desire's Government. "A. W." ElL
Where, with unruffled surface wide. Flowers in Ashes. James Matthew Legaré. SPP
Where, without bloodshed, can there be. Long Feud. Louis Untermeyer. AnAmPo; AnFE; APA; CoAnAm; LA; MAP; MoAmPo; NeMA
Where woods of ash, and beech. Charlotte Smith. *Fr.* Beachy Head. EnSW
Where Wuz You Las' Night? *with music. Unknown.* StDa
Where yet was ever found a mother. John Gay. *Fr.* The Mother, the Nurse, and the Fairy. MotAn
Where yonder ancient willow weeps. Alexander McLachlan. *Fr.* A Backwoods Hero. CaP
Where you can go farther and see less. West Texas. *At to* Leona Mae Austin. CoSo
"Where you coming from, Lomey Carter?" *See* "Where are you coming from, Lomey Carter?"
Where you (in this saying) lag in the waving woods. Love Poem. W. S. Graham. FaBoMo
Where You Passed. Amelia Josephine Burr. HBMV
Whereas Adam caused by sin. Tidings, Tidings That Be True. *Unknown.* AnEC
Whereas Aongus, the philosophic. On a Cock Which Was Stolen from a Good Priest. Egan O'Rahilly. OnYI
Whereas, on certain boughs and sprays. The Lawyer's Invocation to Spring. Henry Howard Brownell. BOHV; LPS-3; PR
Whereas the rebels hereabout. Tom Gage's Proclamation. Thomas Flucker. PAH
Whereas we twain, who still are bound for life. A Separation Deed. Sir Lewis Morris. OBVV
Whereat Erewhile I Wept, I Laugh. Robert Greene. *Fr.* Arbasto. ElL
Where-e'er My Flatt'ring Passions Rove. Isaac Watts. *See* Hazard of Loving the Creatures, The.
Where'er a noble deed is wrought. *See* Whene'er a noble deed is wrought.
Where'er have trod Thy sacred feet. With Thee to Soar to the Skies. *Unknown.* BePJ
Where'er spreads Heaven's arch, my home declare! My Home. Mikhail Yurevich Lermontov. WaL
Where'er there's a thistle to feed a linnet. Poets and Linnets. Tom Hood. CenHV; HBV
Where'er You Walk. Congreve. OlF
Wherefore Hidest Thou Thy Face, and Holdest Me for Thy Enemie? Francis Quarles. *See* Why Dost Thou Shade Thy Lovely Face?
Wherefore, O fair one, dost withhold thy messengers. Parted Lovers. Judah Halevi. LiTW
Wherefore sou'd ye talk o' love. Willie and Helen. Hew Ainslie. EBSV; HBV; LO; OBEV
"Wherefore starts my bosom's lord?" Comfort in Affliction. William E. Aytoun. BOHV; InMe
Wherefore these revels that my dull eyes greet? The Royal Mummy to Bohemia. Charles Warren Stoddard. AA; OBAV
Wherefore this busy labor without rest? Tuskegee. Leslie Pinckney Hill. BANP; PoNe
"Wherefore thy woe these many years." Ballad of Two Seas. George Sterling. MOAP
Wherefore to-night so full of care. Dejection. Robert Bridges. TCPD
Wherefore, Unlaurelled Boy. George Darley. *See* Solitary Lyre, The.
Wherefore was that cry? She Should Have Died Hereafter. Shakespeare. *Fr.* Macbeth, V, v. FiP
Wherein Lies Happiness. Keats. *Fr.* Endymion, I. ERP
Where's an old woman to go when the years. The Riddle. "H. E. H." PoToHe
Where's Commander All-a-Tanto? Herman Melville. *Fr.* Bridegroom Dick. OnAP; PoEL-5, *longer sel.*
Where's he that died o' Wednesday? Falstaff's Song. Edmund Clarence Stedman. AA; BAP; DDA; HBV; LEAP; OBAV
Where's Mary? Ivy O. Eastwick. TiPo
Where's now the object of thy fears. Resolution. Henry More. OxBoCh
Where's Peace? I start, some clear-blown night. Mr. Hosea Biglow to the Editor of the Atlantic Monthly. James Russell Lowell. Fr. The Biglow Papers, 2d Series, No. X. AA
"Where's the need of singing now?" Momus. E. A. Robinson. ViBoPo
Wheresoe'er I turn mine eyes. God Everywhere. Abraham ibn Ezra. TrJP
Wheresoe'er I turn my view. Lines Written in Ridicule of Certain Poems Published in 1777. Samuel Johnson. EiPP
Wheresoever you may walk. The High Road. *Unknown.* BPP
Whereto Art Thou Come. Francis Thompson. VLEP
Whereto Should I Express. Henry VIII, King of England. TuPP
(To His Lady.) OBSC
Whereupon I told,/ That once in the stillness of a summer's noon. Books. Wordsworth. *Fr.* The Prelude, V. PoEL-4
Wherever dark pines lift their plumes against a sunset sky. The Stay at Home. Martha Haskell Clark. VOD
Wherever God erects a house of prayer. Daniel Defoe. *Fr.* The True-born Englishman, I. BeR; NBE; TreF
Wherever I Am, and Whatever I Do. Dryden. *Fr.* The Conquest of Granada. MaPo
(Phyllis.) SeCL
(Song: "Wherever I am, and whatever I do.") EPS (1942 ed.)
Wherever I am, there's always Pooh. Us Two. A. A. Milne. TiPo
Wherever I go, I do no wrong. William Baylebridge. *Fr.* Moreton Miles. BoAV
Wherever I walk there are only little deaths. The Deaths. Solveig von Schoultz. LiTW
Wherever may the mollusk roam. The Mollusk. James J. Montague. PoMa
Wherever on Italian ground. Italian Poppies. Joel Elias Spingarn. HBMV
Wherever she may turn her ravished eyes. A Girl. Viola Meynell. MBP; MoBrPo (1942 ed.)
Wherever smoke wreaths. Home. Stephen Chalmers. HBMV
Wherever souls of men have worshiped, there. Holy Places. Herbert D. Gallaudet. MaRV
Wherever the wind's head walks. The Wind's Head. John L. Sweeney. JKCP (1955 ed.)
Wherever war, with its red woes. *See* Whenever war, with its red woes.
Wherever we are found. All. Antoni Slonimski. PoFr
Wherever you go there is autumn and evening. To Sister. Georg Trakl. *Fr.* Rosary Songs. AnGP

Wherewith shall I come before the Lord. The Acceptable Sacrifice [*or* What Doth the Lord Require?]. Micah, Bible, *O.T.* GrCo-1; MaRV
Whet up yo' knife an' whistle up yo' dog. Ground-Hog. *Unknown.* APW
Whethen is it yourself, Mister Hagan? an' lookin' right hearty you are. A Curlew's Call. Jane Barlow. VA
Whether a cheerful air does rise. On Mary, Duchess of Richmond. Richard Flecknoe. SeCL
"Whether all towns and all who live in them." Tasker Norcross. E. A. Robinson. ChMo; CMP
Whether amid the gloom of night I stray. A Contemplation on Night. John Gay. CEP
Whether away my sweetest deerest. *Unknown.* SeCSL
Whether conditioned by God, or their neural structure, still. Truth. W. H. Auden. MaRV
Whether day my spirit's yearning. The Thought Eternal. Goethe. AWP; JAWP; WBP
Whether dinner was pleasant, with the windows lit by gunfire. No Credit. Kenneth Fearing. ChMo; PoLFOT
Whether for rope to hang my love. Night-Labour. Quentin Stevenson. POTE (1959 ed.)
Whether I find thee bright with fair. Love in Her Hair [*or* Changeful Beauty]. *Unknown, tr. by* Andrew Lang. EnLoPo; OxBG
Whether I live, or whether I die. Mary Elizabeth Coleridge. GTML
"Whether is her beauty by her words divine?" *Unknown. Fr.* Edward the Third. LO
Whether it be that we in letters trace. Prototypes. Madison Cawein. SPP
Whether men do laugh or weep. All Is Vanity [*or* Vanity of Vanities]. *Unknown, at. to* Philip Rosseter. BLV; ElSeCe; HBV; OBSC
Whether on Ida's shady brow. To the Muses. Blake. AnFE; BCEP; BLV; BoLiVe; CEP; ChER; ChTr; CoBE; EiPP; EM-1; EnLi-2; EnLit; EnRP; EV-3; GTBS-W; GTSL; HBV; LiTB; LiTG; LoBV; OAEP; OBEC; OBEV; OnPM; OuHeWo; PoFS; RO; SeCeV; TCEP; TrGrPo; TwCrTr; TyEnPo; ViBoPo; WHA
Whether or Not. D. H. Lawrence. MBP; MoBrPo
Whether the moorings are invisible. Conversation. John Berryman. LiTA; LiTM; NePA; WaP
Whether the time be slow or fast. To Any One. Witter Bynner. SBMV
Whether the Turkish new moon minded be. Astrophel and Stella, XXX. Sir Philip Sidney. ReEn; ReIE; SiPS; TuPP
Whether the weather be fine, or whether the weather be not. *Unknown.* BoTP
Whether they delve in the buried coal, or plow the upland soil. The Glory of Toil. Edna Dean Proctor. PGD
Whether 'twas in that dome of evening sky. Reverie. Edward Rowland Sill. UnW
Whether we climb, whether we plod. Heroism. Lizette Woodworth Reese. LS; MaRV; PC
Whether winding idly on or roaring ravaging downward. The River. Sir Ronald Ross. BSV
Whether with reason or with instinct blest. Reason and Instinct. Pope. *Fr.* An Essay on Man, III. LPS-3
Whether you live by hut or throne. Certainties. Margaret Widdemer. HBMV
Whether you love me. Canción. Marqués de Santillana. AnSpL-1
Which? Joyce L. Brisley. GFA
Which? Hsi P'ei Lan, *tr. fr. Chinese by* Henry H. Hart. PoHN
Which. Corinne Roosevelt Robinson. SBMV
Which are the living? We who stride unyielding earth in engine fumes. Three City Cantos. Charles A. Wagner. GoYe
Which I wish to remark. The Heathen Pass-ee. A. C. Hilton. CenHV; PA
Which I wish to remark. Plain Language [*or* Talk] from Truthful James [*or* That Heathen Chinee]. Bret Harte. AmPP; AnAmPo; BAP; BAV; BeLS; BLPA; BOHV; CenHV; CoBA; DD; DDA; EV-5; FaBoBe; HBV IAP; InMe; LA; LEAP; LHV; LPS-3; MAP; MoAmPo (1942 ed.); OBAV; OnSP; PFY; PoE; PoeMoYo; PYM; TreF; WhC; YaD
Which Is a Proud, and Yet a Wretched Thing. Sir John Davies. *See* Man.
Which Is Me? Edward Sandford Martin. *See* My Name Is Legion.
Which is more sweet—the slow mysterious stream. Izaak Walton to River and Brook. Eugene Lee-Hamilton. VA
Which is of greater value, prythee, say. A Conjugal Conundrum. *Unknown.* BOHV
Which is the best to hit your taste. Epigram on Two Ladies. Lady Burrell. DiM
Which Is the Favourite? Charles *and* Mary Lamb. OTPC (1923 ed.)
Which is the German's fatherland. The German Fatherland. Ernst Moritz Arndt. HBV
Which is the lovelier scene. Felicia's Song. Per Daniel Amadeus Atterbom. AnSL
"Which is the way to Baby-land?" Baby-Land. George Cooper. BoTP; HBV; HBVY; OTPC; PPL
Which is the way to Fairyland. The Way to Fairyland. Eunice Close. BoTP
"Which is the way to London Town,/ To see the King." Mother Goose. BoTP
Which is the way to London Town?/ Over the hills. *Unknown.* BoTP
"Which is the way to the nearest town." Conversation with an April Fool. Rowena Bennett. SiSoSe
Which is the weakest thing of all. The Weakest Thing. Elizabeth Barrett Browning. HBV
Which is the wind that brings the cold? What the Winds Bring. Edmund Clarence Stedman. DD; GoBP; LPS-2; PRWS; RAR; SN
Which Is Which? John Byrom. *See* Jacobite Toast, A.
Which is you, old two-in-one? What the Serpent Said to Adam. Archibald MacLeish. NePA
Which Loved Best? "Joy Allison." WBLP
(Which Loved Her Best?) HH; OHIP; PEDC
Which of the aims that spurred me to unite. Solon, *tr. fr. Greek by* Martin Ostwald. GrPo
Which of the Angels sang so well in Heaven. On the Death of Mrs. Browning. Sydney Dobell. VA
Which of those rebell Spirits adjudg'd to Hell. Gabriel Meets Satan. Milton. *Fr.* Paradise Lost, IV. LoBV
Which of your waves is it that comes so childlike. Atlantic. Eugenio Florit. TwSpPo
Which road, which road did you take. Exaltation. Franz Werfel. TrJP
Which Shall It Be? Ethel Lynn Beers. BLPA; PTA-2; TreF
(Not One to Spare.) LPS-1
Which Side Am I Supposed to Be On? W. H. Auden. CoBMV
(Ode: To My Pupils.) MBP; MoBrPo
Which Sword? Jason Noble Pierce. PGD; PSO
Which the best way of life? The forum rings. No Way Is Good. Poseidippus. OnPM
Which things being so, as we said when we studied. Good-bye Now, Plato and Hegel. Louis MacNeice. *Fr.* Autumn Journal. OnHM
Which Was Most Truly Dead? Charles Augustin Sainte-Beuve, *tr. fr. French by* Henry Carrington. PoP
Which way, and whence the lightning flew. Apollo's Song. Ben Jonson. *Fr.* The Masque of Augurs. LoBV
Which Way Does the Wind Blow? Lucy Aikin. OTPC
Which will he choose? Both call their challenge. The Centaur. Poul Sørensen. BoDS
Which Will Scarcely Be Understood. Robert Ervin Howard. DaM
Which will you have, a ball or a cake? Choosing. Eleanor Farjeon. TiPo
Whichever Way the Wind Doth Blow. Caroline Atherton Briggs Mason. *See* En Voyage.
Whiff of forest scent, A. The Creed of the Wood. Katharine Lee Bates. PC
Whiffaree an' a-whiffo'rye. Honey Take a Whiff on Me. *Unknown.* ABF
Whiffs of the Ohio River at Cincinnati. Carl Sandburg. MOAP
While Adam slept, from him his Eve arose. Epigram. *Unknown.* ALV. *See also* Whilst Adam slept, Eve from his side arose.
While all to this auspicious day. To Mrs. Leigh upon Her Wedding-Day. George Canning. ALV
While April Rain Went By. Shaemus O'Sheel. HBMV
While at her bedroom window once. The Keys of Morning. Walter de la Mare. AtBAP; MoVE
While at the stook the shearers cow'r. To the Rev. John M'Math. Burns. EiPP
While back St. Peter was callèd Simon, A. How Holy Church Is Underfoot. *Unknown.* TMEV
While blue-eyed children, goggle-faced and giggling. An Old-World Effect. Siegfried Sassoon. ChMo; CMP
While briers an' woodbines budding green. Epistle to John Lapraik [an Old Scottish Bard]. Burns. BEL; CEP; CoEV; EiPP; Em-1; EnL; EnLi-2; EnRP; MCCG; OAEP; PIR
While Butler, needy wretch! was yet alive. On the Setting Up [of] Mr. Butler's Monument in Westminster Abbey. Samuel Wesley. ALV; BOHV; CoEV; InvP; OBEC; WhC
While cleaning my old six-branched candelabrum. Cleaning the Candelabrum. Siegfried Sassoon. HaMV
While crabapple now is a windfall. The Wilding. Philip Booth. NePoEA
While crouds of princes your deserts proclaim. The Campaign. Addison. CEP
While cruel Nero only drains. Picture of Seneca Dying in a Bath. Matthew Prior. CEP

While deepening shades obscure the face of day. Gilbert White. *Fr.* The Natural History of Selborne. LO
While down the meads wound slow. Good Night. William Barnes. RO
While far along the eastern sky. After the Fire. Oliver Wendell Holmes. MC; PAH
While fates permit us, let's be merry. To Enjoy the Time. Robert Herrick. EM-1
While going the road to sweet Athy. Johnny, I Hardly Knew Ye. *Unknown.* AnIV; GTIV; OnYI; OxBoLi; TIP; WaaP
While hastening through his pilgrimage on earth. Saint Francis of Assisi. Tom Sweeney. SaFP
While he says Mass, Carmelo's sins. Fra Carmelo's Morning Sacrifice. Gervase Toelle. JKCP (1955 ed.)
While he to whom her vexing thoughts still clung. Seven Sad Sonnets, III. Mary Aldis. HBMV
While homeward bound across the deep. Franklin's Crew. *Unknown.* SoAmSa
"While I am quick in the body," quoth he, "I am called Anima." The Human Soul Speaks. William Langland. *Fr.* The Vision of Piers Plowman. PoLi
While I Have Vision. Peter Quennell. ChMP
While I, here in this rented room, under. The Imitation of Faust. Alfred Hayes. LiTM (1946 ed.)
While I linger in her room. Undersong. Robert Kelley Weeks. PR
While I of summum bonum was disputing. Of Summum Bonum. Sir John Harington. SiCE
While I recline. The Cotton Boll. Henry Timrod. AA; AmPP; HiLiAm; IAP; SPP; TCAP
While I Sang My Song. Jacinto Fombona Pachano, *tr. fr. Spanish by* Angel Flores. AnCL
"While [*or* Whilst] I sit at the door." Eve. Christina Rossetti. CH; NBE; OxBoCh; PoEL-5; SeCeV
While I stood listening, discreetly dumb. The Growth of Lorraine. E. A. Robinson. NP
While I walked in the moonlight. Lady Murasaki Shikibu, *tr. fr. Japanese by* I. W. Furukami. LiTW
While I was all absorbed in seeing him. Dante. *Fr.* Divina Commedia: Inferno. CAW
While I was wandering, foot-loose, in the Forum. Catullus, *tr. fr. Latin by* Horace Gregory. RoL
While I watch the Christmas blaze. The Reminder. Thomas Hardy. ChMo; CMP
While Immortality Endures. Ernest Briggs. NeLNL
While in dark and deadly places. Karolina Pavlova, *tr. fr. Russian by* C. M. Bowra. BoRS
While in the park I sing, the listning deer. At Penshurst. Edmund Waller. EPS; OAEP
While joy gave clouds the light of stars. The Villain. W. H. Davies. MBP; MoBrPo; NeMA; POTE; WHA
While larks with little wing. Phillis the Fair. Burns. EV-3
While life is running out in me through time. Madrigal 86. Michelangelo. LyPI
While life is vigorous and bright. In the Days of Thy Youth. Bhartrihari. OnPM
While Life Sits Idly. Cullen Jones. *Fr.* Sonnets in Wartime. MuM
While life was mine, the little hour. Epigram. Thomas Moore. ALV
While Loveliness Goes By. Anna Hempstead Branch. MAP; MoAmPo (1942 ed.)
While mad Ophelia we lament. On a Pretty Madwoman. Matthew Prior. CEP
While malice, Pope, denies thy page. When None Shall Rail. David Lewis. OBEC
While Mary and the Christ-Child. The Windflowers and the Sage. Laura Spencer Portor. StJW
While May bedecks the naked trees. *See* When May bedecks the naked trees.
While men perversely waste the hours. First Smile of Spring. Théophile Gautier. TrFP
While men were all asleep the snow came flying. *See* When men were all asleep.
While midnight clung to every shore. Natura in Urbe. E. B. White. WaKn
While Morpheus thus doth gently lay. Song. Henry Killigrew. CH
While my hair was still cut straight across my forehead. The River-Merchant's Wife; a Letter. Li Po, *tr. by* Ezra Pound. AmP; AmPP; AnAmPo; AWP; CoAnAm; InPo; LA; LiTA; LiTL; LiTW; MoAB; MoAmPo (1950 ed.); MOAP; MoPo; NAMP; NP; OBMV; OxBA; PG (1945 ed.); TwAmPo; WBP
While my lady sleepeth. Serenade. John Gibson Lockhart. OBRV
While nations rage, while empires rock and fall. Loyalty Hymn. Edith Lovejoy Pierce. ChIP; MaRV
While Northward the hot sun was sinking o'er the trees. The Psalm. Robert Bridges. FaBoTw; LiTB
While not a leaf seems faded, while the fields. Sonnet: September, 1815 [*or* September, 1815]. Wordsworth. ChER; PEOR
While now the Pole Star sinks from sight. Crossing the Tropics. Herman Melville. AA
While now the Rising Village claims a name. Oliver Goldsmith, the Younger. *Fr.* The Rising Village. CaP
While o'er the deep Thy servants sail. The Heavenly Breeze. George Burgess. BePJ
While o'er the globe, fair nymph! your searches run. To Lady Jane Wharton, on Her Studying the Globe. Nicholas Rowe. LO
While on a [*or* the] cliff with calm delight she kneels. On a [*or* the] Picture of an Infant Playing near a Precipice. Leonidas of Alexandria. LPS-1; MOAH
While on Those Lovely Looks I Gaze. Earl of Rochester. SeCL
While people hunt for what can satisfy their wants. Shelter. Gene Derwood. NePA
While rain, with eve in partnership. Beyond the Last Lamp. Thomas Hardy. MoVE; PoVP; TwCV
While riding down that greenwood road. John of Hazelgreen (C *vers.*). *Unknown.* BaBo
While riding toward Jerusalem. The Syrian's Tale. Leslie Savage Clark. ChIP
While round the armed bands. The Execution of King Charles. Andrew Marvell. *Fr.* An Horatian Ode upon Cromwell's Return from Ireland. AnEnPo; PoRA
While sauntering through the crowded street. Pre-Existence. Paul Hamilton Hayne. HBV; LPS-3; UnW
While she darns her children's socks, The. Prayer Time. Ruby Weyburn Tobias. PraP
While Shepherds Watched Their Flocks by Night. Margaret Deland. COAH; DD; GN; HBVY; StJW
(First Best Christmas Night, The.) SDH
While Shepherds Watched Their Flocks by Night. Nahum Tate. DD; GN; HBV; HBVY; HH; MaRV; OlF; OnYI; OTPC; OxBI; PCH; TreFS; YaCaBo, *with music*
(Christmas.) COAH; MW; OHIP; PEDC
(Song of the Angels.) BePJ
(While Shepherds Watch'd.) SDH
While Sherman stood beneath the hottest fire. Before Vicksburg. George Henry Boker. PAH
While sleeping in your clothes. This Needle. Kurahashibe Otome. OnPM
While [*or* Whilst] some affect the sun, and some the shade. The Grave. Robert Blair. CoBE; EiPP; EnRP
While some go dancing reels. Three Old Brothers. Frank O'Connor. OnYI
While star-shells fell in showers of constellations. The Anonymous Lieutenant. Clark Mills. NeTW
While Stars of Christmas Shine. Emilie Poulsson. OHIP
While strengthened by its roots the oak. Dum Librata Suis Haeret Radicibus Ilex. George Herbert. LaP
While strolling down the street one eve upon mere pleasure bent. Just Tell Them That You Saw Me. Paul Dresser. TreFS
While strolling out one evening. The Banks of the Pamanaw. *Unknown.* ABF
While sways the restless sea. Sleep. "Fiona Macleod." GBV; TSW
While that my soul repairs to her devotion. Church Monuments. George Herbert. MaPo; RiBV; TriL
While [*or* Whyle] that the sun with his beams hot. The Faithless Shepherdess [*or* Philon *or* Adieu Love, Untrue Love]. *Unknown.* ALV; ElL; ElSeCe; EV-1; GTBS; GTBS-D; GTBS-W; GTSE; GTSL; OBEV; OBSC; SiCE
While the angels sang hosannas. Unto Us a Child Is Born. Agnes H. Begbie. BOL
While the Bells Ring. Lora Dunetz. NePoAm
While the Billy Boils. David McKee Wright. AnNZ
While the blue is richest. Fairies' Recall. Felicia Dorothea Hemans. OTPC
While the blue moon above us arches. Annihilation. Conrad Aiken. BLV; CrMA; LO; MAP; MoAB; MoAmPo
While the cobbler mused, there passed his pane. How the Great Guest Came [*or* The Great Guest Comes]. Edwin Markham. BeLS; BLPA; WBLP
While the dawn on the mountain was misty and gray. The Cavalier [*or* Song: The Cavalier]. Sir Walter Scott. *Fr.* Rokeby. EV-4; TVSH
While the Days Are Going By. George Cooper. BLRP; WBLP
While the evening here is approaching the mountain paths. Overnight in the Apartment by the River. Tu Fu. ChTr
While the fair morning's beauty held, and day increased in height. The Scales of Zeus. Homer. *Fr.* The Iliad, VIII. GrR
While the flute played on the edge of the water. Beside the Lake. Wang Wei. WhP
While the form's tingling in your fingers. Craftsmanship. Nikolai Ushakov. RuPo
While the lily dwells in the earth. The Lily of the Resurrection. Lucy Larcom. EOAH
While the shot and shell were screaming on the battlefield. Break the News to Mother. Charles Kassell Harris. TreFS

While the station of light was passing, on the highway. Fugue. Alfonso Gutiérrez Hermosillo. AnCL
While the Summer Trees Were Crying. Valentin Iremonger. *See* Evening in Summer.
While the Tragedy's afoot. Colophon. Oliver St. John Gogarty. OBMV
While the tremulous leafy haze on the woodland is spreading. Henry van Dyke. *Fr.* God of the Open Air. ADAH
While the West Is Paling. W. E. Henley. Echoes, XVI. VLEP
While the world lay round me sleeping. Isadore. Thomas Holley Chivers. APW; SPP
While their route they silent made, A. Lake Coriskin. Sir Walter Scott. *Fr.* The Lord of the Isles, III. EV-4
While there He hung, the scoffing Levites cried. The Priests and Soldiers. *Unknown.* PSO
While thir hearts were jocund and sublime. Samson Hath Quit Himself. Milton. *Fr.* Samson Agonistes. LoBV
While this America settles in the mould of its vulgarity, heavily thickening to empire. Shine, Perishing Republic. Robinson Jeffers. AmP; AmPP; AnAmPo; ChMo; CMP; InP; LA; LiTA; LiTM; MAP; MoAB; MoAmPo; MoVE; NAMP; NePA; NP; OxBA; PoLFOT; PreP; ReaPo; UnPo (3d ed.); ViBoPo
While this night I read, I'm battleground. Invalid. Audrey McGaffin. NePoAm-2
While thus, of power and fancy'd empire vain. Crusty Critics. George Crabbe. *Fr.* The Library. OBEC
While to Bethlehem We Are Going. Sister Violante do Ceo, *tr. fr. Portuguese by* Sir John Bowring. CAW
While walking down [*or* Whilst walking] a crowded city street the other day. If I Only Was the Fellow [*or* Just Try to Be the Fellow . . .]. Will S. Adkin. BLPA; WBLP
While we are still drowsing. The Little One Smiles. Oscar Stjerne. AnSL
While we in night lie hidden, there in the world below. Elysium. Pindar. GrPE
While we sail and laugh, joke and fight, comes death. In Memoriam; Ingvald Bjorndal and His Comrade. Malcolm Lowry. BoCaPo (1948 ed.)
While We Slept. David Wolff. AnAmPo; TrJP
While we slumber and sleep. A Song of Flight. Christina Rossetti. CAW; GTML
While we wandered, A (thus it is I dream!). Gray Nights. Ernest Dowson. PoVP
While winds frae off Ben Lomond blaw. Epistle to Davie, a Brother Poet. Burns. EBSV; OBEC
While wise men, long beset by doubt. The Victor. Sydney King Russell. StaSt
While [*or* Whilst] with a strong, and yet a gentle hand. Edmund Waller. *Fr.* A Panegyrick to My Lord Protector. EV-2; SeCV-1
While with labour assiduous due pleasures I mix. The Secretary. Matthew Prior. CEP; PoE; PoFS
While words of learned strength and thundering sound. Still the Wonder Grew. Goldsmith. *Fr.* The Deserted Village. TreF
While working sadly by my window. Prose Poem: The Red Flower. Judith Gautier. OnPM
While yesterevening, through the vale. Haw-Blossoms. James Matthew Legaré. SPP
While yet I speak the winged galley flies. The Sirens, Scylla and Charybdis. Homer. *Fr.* The Odyssey, XII. LiTW
While yet in time our last intent. Yet in Time. Pearce Young. PtPa
While yet the grapes were green, thou didst refuse me. Grapes. *Unknown.* AWP
While yet the Morning Star. The Unicorn. Ella Young. FaPON; TiPo
While you converse with lords and dukes. A Bookworm's Content. Thomas Sheridan. MOB
While you, dear Tom, are forced to roam. Ode to My Ingenious Friend, Mr. Thomas Godfrey. Nathaniel Evans. IAP
While you, great Patron of Mankind! sustain. The First Epistle of the Second Book of Horace [*or To* Augustus]. Pope. CEP; EiPP; GEPC; PtP
While you, my Lord, bid stately piles ascend. A Journey to Exeter. John Gay. WoL
While you, my lord, the rural shades admire. A Letter from Italy. Addison. CEP
While you nurse at your mother's breast. Lines for Those Invited in T. Stefan George. AnGP
While you that in your sorrow disavow. A Christmas Sonnet. E. A. Robinson. CoV; MaRV
While young John runs to greet. Lines on the Celebrated Picture by Leonardo da Vinci, Called the Virgin of the Rocks. Charles Lamb. ISi
While your veil lay floating still around me. To Nature. Friedrich Hölderlin. LiTW
While you're all so frisky I'll sing a little song. Top Hand. *Unknown.* CoSo; CSF
Whiles in my Soul I feel the soft warm hand. Visitors. Sir John Davies. ES
Whiles in the early winter eve. The Days That Were. William Morris. BPN
Whiles some one did chant this lovely lay, The. Gather the Rose. Spenser. *Fr.* The Faerie Queene, II. EIL
Whilom [*or* Whylom], as olde stories tellen us. The Knightes [*or* Knight's] Tale. Chaucer. *Fr.* The Canterbury Tales. BEL; GEPC; GoTL; TOP
Whilom by silver Thames's gentle stream. The Virtuoso. Mark Akenside. BCEP; LPS-3
Whilom in the winter's rage. The Penitent Palmer's Ode. Robert Greene. *Fr.* Francesco's Fortunes. LoBV; OBSC
Whilom ther was dwellinge in my contree. The Friar's Tale. Chaucer. *Fr.* The Canterbury Tales. BLV
Whilom [*or* Whylom] ther was dwellynge at Oxenford. The Carpenter's Young Wife. Chaucer. *Fr.* The Canterbury Tales: The Miller's Tale. ExPo; OxBoLi
Whilst Adam slept, Eve from his side arose. Epigram. *Unknown.* HBV. *See also* While Adam slept, from him his Eve arose.
Whilst echo cries, "What shall become of me?" Henry Constable. *Fr.* Diana. OBSC; ReEn; ReIE; SiCE; TuPP
Whilst human kind/ Throughout the lands lay miserably crushed. Lucretius. *Fr.* De Rerum Natura: Beyond Religion. AWP; PoFr
Whilst I alone did call upon thy aid. Sonnets, LXXIX. Shakespeare. EM-1; PeBoSo
Whilst I beheld the neck o' the dove. Hymn. Patrick Carey. SeCL
"Whilst I sit at the door." *See* "While I sit at the door."
Whil'st I, the Sun's bright face may view. The Marigold. George Wither. SeEP
Whilst I was dear and thou wert kind. The Reconciliation. Horace. *Fr.* Odes. OuHeWo
Whilst in peaceful quarters lying. The Battle of Monmouth. "R. H." PAH
Whilst in this cold and blust'ring clime. To My Dear and Most Worthy Friend, Mr. Isaac Walton. Charles Cotton. BoFr; FaBoEn
Whilst, Lydia, I was lov'd of thee. Reconciliation of Lovers. Horace. *Fr.* Odes. LiA; RoL
Whilst my souls eye beheld no light. A Dialogue betwixt God and the Soul. *At. to* Sir Henry Wotton. MeLP; OBS; OxBoCh
Whilst on Septimus panting bre[a]st. Acme and Septimius. Catullus, *tr. by* Abraham Cowley. AWP; LiA
Whilst on thy head I lay my hand. A Spell of Invisibility. *At. to* Christopher Marlowe. ChTr
Whilst some affect the sun and some the shade. *See* While some affect the sun
Whilst Talbot, whose fresh spirit hauing got. The Death of Talbot. Samuel Daniel. *Fr.* The Civil Wars. EV-1
Whilst the red spittle of the grape-shot sings. Evil. Arthur Rimbaud. WaaP
Whilst thus his wrath with threats the Tyrant fed. Abraham Cowley. *Fr.* Davideis. SeEP
Whilst thus in fervent toil the artisan. Tasso. *Fr.* Jerusalem Delivered, IV. PrPoCR
Whilst thus my pen strives to eternize thee. Idea, XLIV. Michael Drayton. BEL; OBSC; ReEn; SiCE; TuPP; ViBoPo
Whil'st thy weigh'd judgements. Egerton, I heare. To Thomas Lord Chancellor. Ben Jonson. OBS
Whilst walking a crowded city street the other day. *See* While walking down a crowded city street
Whilst we sing the doleful knell. Ding Dong. *Unknown.* *Fr.* Swetnam, the Woman-Hater. EIL
Whilst what I write I do not see. Written in Juice of Lemmon. Abraham Cowley. Fr. The Mistress. SeCV-1
Whilst with a strong and yet a gentle hand. *See* While with a strong, and yet a gentle hand.
Whilst yet to prove. Farewell to Love. John Donne. BrBE; ReEn
Whim. Conrad Aiken. *See* When Trout Swim down Great Ormond Street.
Whim Alley. Hervey Allen. AnAmPo; CBOV; LA; MAP; NV
Whim of Time, A. Stephen Spender. MBP; MoAB; MoBrPo (In 1929.) MoP
Whimper of Sympathy. George Meredith. EPN
Whip, The. Robert Creeley. NeAP
Whip-crack of a Union Jack, The. The Boer War. William Plomer. BoSA
Whip cracks on the plough-team's flank, The. Rural Evening. Lord De Tabley. EnSW
Whip of Anger, The. Mary Ross. ChIP
Whipped On by December. Aleksey Aleksandrovich Surkov, *tr. fr. Russian by* Babette Deutsch. TrRV
Whippoorwill, The. Madison J. Cawein. MW
Whip-Poor-Will. Philip Cummings. BLA
Whippoorwill. John Richard Moreland. IHA
Whip-Poor-Will, The. *Unknown.* BLA
Whippoorwill, The. Henry van Dyke. WhBS
Whip-poor-will, through the crystal starlight, The. Whip-Poor-Will. Philip Cummings. BLA

Whipp'will's singin' to de moon. Go Sleep, Ma Honey. Edward D. Barker. AA; BOL; MOAH

Whirl-Blast from behind the Hill, A. Wordsworth. BPN; EmBrPo; ERP

(Whirl-Blast.) OTPC

Whirl, snow, on the blackbird's chatter. Eager Spring. Gordon Bottomley. AlDL; BMEP; CP; MBP; MoBrPo; POTE

Whirl up, sea. Oread. Hilda Doolittle ("H. D."). AWP; BLV; ExPo; InP; JAWP; MAP; MoAmPo; MOAP; MoVE; NeMA; OxBA; PoeMoYo; PoTo; TCPD; TSW; WBP

Whirligig Beetle. C. Lindsay McCoy. GFA

Whirling year, ah, friend! the whirling year, The. Death Inevitable. Horace. Odes, II, 14. RoL

Whirling your deep and gloomy tresses pour. The Vampire. Efrén Rebolledo. AnMP

Whirlpool, The ("He was caught in the whirlpool of dismay"). *Unknown.* PoToHe (new ed.)

Whirlpool. *Unknown, tr. fr. Japanese by* Arthur Waley. WoL

("They say there is.") LiTW

Whirlwind Road, The. Edwin Markham. AA

Whirring spindles spun swiftly under the blue electric night-time daylight. Love in a Cotton Mill. Stewart Atkins. NoCaPo

Whiskey Bill; a Fragment. *Unknown.* SCC

Whiskey for My Johnny. *Unknown. See* Whisky Johnny.

Whiskey here and whiskey there. Whiskey, Johnny, *vers.* I. *Unknown.* ShS

Whiskey is the life of man. Whiskey Johnny. *Unknown.* ShS, *vers.* III; SoAmSa

Whiskey Johnny. *Unknown. See* Whisky Johnny.

Whiskey on your breath, The. My Papa's Waltz. Theodore Roethke. AmP; CrMA; HoPM; MiAP; MoAB

Whisky, Drink Divine. Joseph O'Leary. OnYI

Whisky Frisky. *Unknown.* See Squirrel, The.

Whisky [*or* Whiskey] Johnny. *Unknown.* ABF, *with music;* AS, *with music;* SG; ShS, 3 *vers., with music;* SoAmSa, *with music*

(Whiskey for My Johnny, *with music.*) AmSS

Whisper half reveal'd her to herself, A. Tennyson. *Fr.* Aylmer's Field. EnSW

Whisper in Agony. Jules Supervielle, *tr. fr. French.* MiCF, *tr. by* Wallace Fowlie; MiFP, *tr. by* James Kirkup; TrFP, *tr. by* Alan Conder

Whisper of Earth, The. Edward J. O'Brien. NLK

Whisper on the heath I hear, A. Spring. Robert Loveman. AA

Whisper, whisper out of the west. Come, O Wind. James B. Kenyon. BOL

Whisper woke the air, A. Calumny. Frances Sargent Osgood. AA; HBV

Whispered to the Afternoon. Georg Trakl, *tr. fr. German by* Glauco Cambon. OnPM

Whisperer, The. Arthur Bullen. HBMV

Whisperer, The. James Stephens. WGRP

Whisperer, The. Mark Van Doren. AnFE; CoAnAm; LoPS; MAP; MoAmPo; TwAmPo

Whisperers, The. W. W. Gibson. CMP; HBV

Whispering. A timid sigh. Afanasi Afanasievich Fet, *tr. fr. Russian by* R. M. Hewitt. BoR

Whispering Palms. Lope de Vega. *See* Madonna, to Her Sleeping Child, The.

Whispering Pine Tree, The. Mariana Griswold Van Rensselaer. PCH

Whisperings in Wattle-Bough. Adam Lindsay Gordon. BoAu; OBVV

Whispers. Afanasi Afanasievich Fet, *tr. fr. Russian by* Babette Deutsch. TrRV

("Whispering. A timid sigh," *tr. by* R. M. Hewitt.) BoR

Whispers of Heavenly Death. Walt Whitman. AnFE; APA; CoAnAm; IAP; LiTA; NePA; TOP

Whispers of Immortality. T. S. Eliot. APA; ATP (1953 ed.) CaAE; ChMo; CMP; CoAnAm; CoEV; LiTA; LiTG; MAPA; NePA; NP; OBMV; PtP; TwAmPo; TwP

Whispers. Timid breathing. Whispers. Afanasi Afanasievich Fet. TrRV

Whist. Eugene Fitch Ware. DDA

Whist-Players Soliloquy, The. Carolyn Wells. PA

Whist-Whee Wilson MacDonald CPG

Whistle. Dorothy Aldis. *See* Whistles.

Whistle, The. Charles Murray. EBSV; GoTS; ShBV-1

Whistle, The. Robert Story. *See* Whistler, The.

Whistle Aloud, Too Weedy Wren. Wallace Stevens. LiTA

Whistle an' I'll Come to Ye [*or* You], My Lad. Burns. BLV; BoLiVe; EV-3; LiTL; LPS-1; OtMeF; OxBoLi; ViBoPo

(O Whistle an' I'll Come to Ye [*or* You] My Lad.) BSV; EBSV; GoTS; PoEL-4

Whistle and Wheels. Alfred G. Bailey. PeCV

Whistle, daughter, whistle. *Unknown.* OxNR

Whistle-Fantasy. Margaret Widdemer. VOD

Whistle, Laddie, whistle. To Laddie. Anne Robinson. SUS

Whistle o'er the Lave o't. Burns. BSV; CEP; EBSV; TCEP

Whistle under the water. Amy Lowell. *Fr.* Flute-Priest Song for Rain. UnS

Whistler, The. Robert Story. BOHV

(Whistle, The.) LPS-1

Whistles. Dorothy Aldis. GFA; TiPo (1952 ed.)

(Whistle.) BoChLi (1950 ed.)

Whistles. Rachel Field. GFA; StVeCh (1955 ed.); TiPo

Whistling Boy, The. George Crabbe. PoFS; TrGrPo

Whistling Girls. *Unknown.* APW

Whistling in Heaven. *Unknown.* PTA-1

Whistling Jack, The. John Shaw Neilson. NeLNL

Whistling Marmot, The. Hamlin Garland. SN

Whistling postman swings along, The. The Postman. *Unknown.* FaPON

Whistling strangely, whistling sadly, whistling sweet and clear. The Seven Whistlers. Alice E. Gillington. VA

Whit Sunday. *See* Whitsunday.

Whit wee wee things o the yerth, yet nane sae bonny! Tuscan Folk Songs, 11. *Unknown, tr. into Scottish by* Edwin Morgan. LyPI

Whit wey is my hert sae eerie? The Lorelei. Heine, *tr. into Scottish by* Edwin Morgan. AnGP

White. George Woodcock. NeBP

White Alder, The. *Unknown.* CAG

White an' Blue. William Barnes. RO

White and Black. Ibn al-Attar, *tr. fr. Arabic by* A. J. Arberry. MooP

White and crimson, cheek and breast. Cantiga. Gil Vicente. CAW; ISi

White and delicate, like white lilies. The Phantom. Salvador Díaz Mirón. AnMP

White and gold theatre, The. Mother's Boy. Patrick Anderson. BoCaPo (1948 ed.)

White and Red. Edward de Vere, Earl of Oxford. *See* What Cunning Can Express.

White and ruddy is my Beloved. A Song of White and Red. Sister Mary Benvenuta. JKCP (1926 ed.)

White Anemone. Lucille Evans. MuM

White Anemone, The, *sel.* "Owen Meredith."

"Tis the white anemone, fashioned so." GN; OTPC

White are the far-off plains, and white. Snow. Archibald Lampman. PeCV

White are the heavens. This Yuletide morning. Snow at Christmas. Sten Granlund. AnSL

White Armour. Jean Starr Untermeyer. NLK (1947 ed.)

White arms, Love, you have, and thin fingers with glittering nails. She-Devil. Douglas Goldring. HBMV

White as a lily, redder than a rose. Rondeau. Guillaume de Machault, *tr. by* Ralph N. Currey. FoS

White as her hand fair Julia threw. The Snow Ball. Petronius Arbiter. LiTW

White as Snow. *Unknown. See* Blanche comme la neige.

White as the great white dusk through which he moves. The Hunter. Eleanor Glenn Wallis. NePoAm-2

White Asters, The. *Unknown, tr. fr. Chinese.* WhP

White Azaleas. Harriet McEwen Kimball. AA; HBV

White beard and pink face. Myself. Po Chü-i. WhP

White-bearded Dr. Yamada goes home with books under his arm. Orchard. Kenji Miyazawa. PoLJ

White billows and huge waves block the river crossing. Kept Waiting in the Boat at Chiu-k'ou Ten Days by an Adverse Wind. Po Chü-i. TrCh

White Bird, The. "Anna Akhmatova," *tr. fr. Russian by* Frances Cornford *and* E. P. Salaman. LiTW

White Bird, The. Roy McFadden. NeIP

White bird featherless. Riddle [*or* Snow]. *Unknown.* ChTr; OxNR; RIS

White bird floats down through the air, A. Riddle. *Unknown.* ChTr

White bird of the tempest! oh, beautiful thing. Lines Addressed to a Seagull. Gerald Griffin. OnYI; TIP

White Birds, The. W. B. Yeats. EnL; VA

White birds over the grey river. Another Spring. Tu Fu. OnPC

White Blossom, A. D. H. Lawrence. MBP; MoBrPo; NeMA

White blossom, white, white shell; the Nazarene. Music of Colours—White Blossom. Vernon Watkins. FaBoMo; LiTM; WaP

White Blossom's off the Bog, The. Alfred Perceval Graves. VA

White Brigade, The. John Macy. MDAH

White Butterflies. Swinburne. FaPON; MeMeAg; MPB; OTPC; PCD; PCH; RAR; StaSt; UTS

(Envoi: "Fly, white butterflies, out to sea.") SUS

White Camellia, A. Edgar Fawcett. SN

White Canoe, The. Alan Sullivan. CaP; OCL

White-capped Waves. James Freeman Clarke. EtS

White Captain of my soul, lead on. Prayer [*or* A Soldier's Prayer]. Robert Freeman. ChIP; MaRV; OQP; QP-1; TrPWD

White Carnation, The. Margaret E. Sangster. PEDC

White Cascade, The. W. H. Davies. NeMA
White cat, The. Cat Ballerina Assoluta. Emilie Glen. GoYe
White Cat and the Student, The. *Unknown. See* Monk and His Pet Cat, The.
White cats of the duchess, The. The Duchess's White Cats. Rafael Méndez Dorich. AnCL
White Charger, The. Abus Salt, *tr. fr. Arabic by* A. J. Arberry. MooP
White chocolate jar full of petals, The. Chez Jane. Frank O'Hara. NeAP
White Christmas. W. R. Rodgers. ChMP; GTBS-W; LiTM; MoAB; MoBrPo (1950 ed.); SeCePo
White Christs, The. Guy Fitch Phelps. OQP; QP-2
White chrysanthemum, The. Oshikochi no Mitsune, *tr. fr. Japanese by* Kenneth Rexroth. LiTW; OnPJ
White Chrysanthemum, The. Ryota, *tr. fr. Japanese by* H. G. Henderson. OnPM
White church on the hill, The. A New England Church. Wilson Agnew Barrett. WGRP
"White City, The." Richard Watson Gilder. PAH
White Cliffs, The, *sels.* Alice Duer Miller.
"I have seen much to hate here," 3 *ll.* OtMeF
"Young and in love—how magical the phrase!" MaRV
White cloud drifts to meet a sail at sea, A. The Old Sailor. Glenn Ward Dresbach. EtS
White clouds/ (White stallions, white horses tethered). Centaurs and Lapithae. Sacheverell Sitwell. *Fr.* Battles of the Centaurs. AtBAP
White clouds are in the sky, The. The Ditty of the White Clouds. *Unknown.* BoFr
White clouds float over the mountains of Chu, The. A Farewell Song of White Clouds. Li Po. BoFr
White clouds, whose shadows haunt the deep. Summer by the Lakeside. Whittier. IAP
White Cockade, The ("King Charles he is King James's son"). *Unknown, tr. fr. Modern Irish by* James Joseph Callanan. OnYI
White Cockade, The ("O he's a ranting roving blade!"). *Unknown.* EBSV
White cock's tail, The. Ploughing on Sunday. Wallace Stevens. FaPON; ThWaDe
White columns of towering masonry. Monserrat. William Edwin Collin. CaP
White Company, The, *sel.* Sir Arthur Conan Doyle.
Song of the Bow, The. BHV; HBV; MCCG; MuP
White Comrade, The. Robert Haven Schauffler. AOAH; SBMV; StJW
White Curtains, The. W. G. Archer. PoN
White daisies are down in the meadows. Alone. John Farrar. BoChLi; GaP; GFA; MPB; YeAr
White delightful swan, The. The Dying Swan. *Unknown.* ChTr
White Devil [*or* Divel], The, *sels.* John Webster.
"Banisht!/ It greev'd me much to heare the sentence," *fr.* I, i. AtBAP
Call for the Robin Redbreast [and the Wren], *fr.* V, iv. AtBAP; BrBE; CenL; ChTr; ElSeCe; ExPo; FaBoCh; LoGBV; OAEP; PoE; PoEL-2; PoRA; ReaPo; ReEn; SeCePo; SeCeV; SiCE; TuPP; ViBoPo
(Cornelia's Song.) CoEV; OBS; TrGrPo
(Dirge, A: "Call for the robin-redbreast and the wren.") AEV; BCEP; BEL; CBOV; EIL; EnLi-1; EV-2; FaBoEn; GTBS; GTSE; GTSL; HBV; KN; LEAP; LiA; LiTB; OBEV; RiBV; ThWaDe; UnPo; WHA
(Funeral Dirge for Marcello.) AnFE
(Land Dirge, A.) BLV; CH; GTBS-D; GTBS-W; LoBV
(Song: "Call for the robin redbreast and the wren.") CaAE; ShBV-3
"How now my noble cossin—what in blacke!" *fr.* III, ii. AtBAP
"I am i'th way to study a long silence," *fr.* V, vi. PoD
"Indeede I am studying alcumye," *fr.* I, ii. AtBAP
"O thou soft naturall death, thou art joint-twin,' *fr,* V, iii. AtBAP
"Then here's an end of me: fare-well day-light," *fr.* V, vi. AtBAP
"What, are you dropt?" *fr.* V, vi. PoEL-2
White Dove of the Wild Dark Eyes. Joseph Mary Plunkett. BLA; HBMV
White doves of Cytherea, by your quest. The Pledge. Adelaide Crapsey. NP; TOP
White Dream, The. May Doney. HBMV
White Dress, The. Humbert Wolfe. LoPS; NP
White Dress, The. Marya Zaturenska. MoAmPo; TwAmPo
White Dusk. Marion Margaret Boyd. HBMV
White Dust, The. W. W. Gibson. MoBrPo; NeMA
White England shouldering from the sea. Fair England. Helen Gray Cone. AA
White Fear. Winifred Welles. BAP; HBMV; MW; TBM
White Fields. James Stephens. BoTP; FaPON; MoShBr; SiSoSe; SUS
White Fisher, The. *Unknown.* ESPB
White Flag, The. John Hay. HBV; PR
White flag I never surrendered, The. Aleksandr Blok, *tr. fr. Russian by* C. M. Bowra. BoRS
White flame of a candle, The. Blue Larkspur. Sister Mariella. JKCP (1955 ed.)
"White folks is white," says Uncle Jim. Uncle Jim. Countee Cullen. BANP
White-footed Deer, The. Bryant. AnNE; PTA-1
White for Mourning. Al-Fata al-Kafif, *tr. fr. Arabic by* A. J. Arberry. MooP
White founts falling in the courts of the sun. Lepanto. G. K. Chesterton. AIDL; AnFE; BEL; BMEP; CAW; CoBE; CP; GDAH; GoBC; GoTL (1949 ed.); HBMV; HBVY; InP; JKCP (1955 ed.); LBBV; MBP; MoBrPo NeMA; NV; OBMV; OnSP; OtMeF; PC; PFE; PoRA; POT; POTE; PoTo; PYM; ShBV-3; TreFS; TwCV; WHA
White Fox. Elizabeth Alsop Shepard. GoYe
White Frost, The. Wang Chi, *tr. fr. Chinese by* E. Powys Mathers. ChLP
White frost comes. October Night. Agnes Louise Dean. YeAr
White frost covers all the arbute-trees, The. The White Frost. Wang Chi. ChLP
"White Galatea, why disdain thy love?" The Giant's Wooing. Theocritus. *Fr.* Idylls, XI. GrR
White gleam the gulls across the darkling tide. In Absence. Tu Fu. OuHeWo
White goat Amaryllis, The. The Visitor. Patrick R. Chalmers. DD; HBV; HBVY
White Goat, White Ram. W. S. Merwin. NePoEA
White gowned doctor holds the charming arm, The. In the Hospital. Patrick Anderson. BoCaPo
White gulls wheeled above the cliffs, the air was slashed with foam, The. Solomon Kane's Home-coming. Robert Ervin Howard. DaM
White-habited, the mystic Swan. The Swan. Jay Macpherson. PeCV
White Hair. Ibn Ghaiyath, *tr. fr. Arabic by* A. J. Arberry. MooP
White hair covers my temples. Blaming Sons. T'ao Ch'ien. Twelve Poems, 5. TrCh
White hair of the sea is shaken, The. *Unknown. Fr.* Sea Snatches. SiB
White hands of languorous grace. He Praises His Wife When She Has Left Him [*or* When She Had Gone from Him]. *Unknown.* AnIL; OxBI
White hen sitting, A. Christina Rossetti. *Fr.* Sing-Song. SAS
White Horse, The. Mary Mills. NePoAm
White Horse, The. Tu Fu. *See* War.
White Horse with a Crimson Flash, A. Ibn Abdus, *tr. fr. Arabic by* A. J. Arberry. MooP
White Horses. Eleanor Farjeon. PoRh
White Horses. Winifred Howard. BrR; SUS; UTS
White Horses. Irene F. Pawsey. BoTP
White House Blues, The, *with music. Unknown.* OuSiCo
White-housed village, The. Inquisitive Barn. Frances Frost. BrR
White Houses. Claude McKay. PoNe
White in her woven shroud. Dies Ultima. Frank Dempster Sherman. LBAP
White in the Moon the Long Road Lies. A. E. Housman. A Shropshire Lad, XXXVI. AWP; BEL; ChMo; EmBrPo; EnLi-2; JAWP; LiTB; LoPo; PoVP; ReaPo; TOP; TwHP; TwP; WBP
(Long Road, The.) TSW
White Iris, A. Pauline B. Barrington. NV
White iris, The. Translations from Modern Japanese Poetry. Akiko Yosano. PFE
White is the evening nature of my thought. White. George Woodcock. NeBP
White is the sail and lonely. A Sail. Mikhail Yurevich Lermontov. AWP; JAWP; WBP
White is the skimming gull on the sombre green of the fir-trees. Standards. Charles Wharton Stork. BLP; NV; TBM
White Island, The; or, Place of the Blest. Robert Herrick. ChTr; EPS; EV-2; HBV; MeRV; OBS; OxBoCh; SeCL; SeEP
White Isle of Leuce, The. Sir Herbert Read. BrBE; FaBoTw
White Jessamine, The. John Banister Tabb. HBV
White Kite, The. *Unknown, tr. fr. Aztec by* John Hubert Cornyn. *Fr.* Song of Quetzalcoatl. LiTW
White Kitten, The. "Marian Douglas." SAS
White Knight's Song, The. "Lewis Carroll." *Fr.* Through the Looking-Glass, *ch.* 8. EnLi-2; FaBoCh; GoTP; LoGBV; ViP
(Aged, Aged Man, The.) BoN; CoEV; OnPP
(A-Sitting on a Gate.) PoE
(I'll Tell Thee Everything I Can.) InvP
(Ways and Means.) BOHV; FiBHP; NA
(White Knight's Ballad, The.) PoRh
(White Knight's Tale, The.) RIS; ShBV-4

White lambs leap. Through miles of snow. The Fire in the Snow. Vernon Watkins. GTBS-W; LiTM (rev. ed.); MoVE
White Land within the West. Westward. Lionel Johnson. POTT
White lilacs blossom by his cottage gate. Spinoza. Thomas S. Jones, Jr. MuM
White Lily. Luis de Sandoval y Zapata, *tr. fr. Spanish by* Samuel Beckett. AnMP
White lily hammered out of steel. Manhattan. John Gould Fletcher. VOD (1935 ed.)
White Lily, thou who wast, unfurling wide. White Lily. Luis de Sandoval y Zapata. AnMP
White little hands! Mother-Song. Alfred Austin. *Fr.* Prince Lucifer. BOL; HBV; MOAH; VA
White Magic. Tom MacInnes. CPG
White Magic. Arthur Symons. POTT; VLEP
White Magic; an Ode. William Stanley Braithwaite. PoNe
"White man, pause and gaze around, for we tread on haunted ground." The Legend of Grand Lake. Joseph L. Westcott. PoOW
White-maned, wide-throated, the heavy-shouldered children of the wind. Granite and Cypress. Robinson Jeffers. AnAmPo; LA
White Man's Burden, The. Kipling. BPN; EnLi-2 (1949 ed.); InP; PoVP; ViP
White Man's Road, The. Arthur Chapman. PoMa
White mares of the moon rush along the sky, The. Night Clouds. Amy Lowell. BAP; MAP; MoAmPo; MoSiPe; NeMA; NP; PreP; WHA
White Monster, The. W. H. Davies. LiTB
White Moon, The. Paul Verlaine, *tr. fr. French by* Kate Flores. AnFP
(Celestial Hour, *tr. by* Alan Conder.) TrFP
White moon is rising, The. The Moon Is Rising. *Unknown.* WhP
White Morfydd through the woods. Sylvan Morfydd. Lionel Johnson. VLEP
White Moth, The. Sir Arthur Quiller-Couch. VA
White moth is wooing his chosen mate, The. The Priest Is Come and the Candles Burn. John Richard Moreland. PR
White moth to the closing bine [*or* vine], The. The Gipsy Trail. Kipling. HBV; InP; NLK; PoeMoYo; PoRA
White nymph wandering in the woods by night, A. Elegies, 2. André Chénier. AWP; JAWP; WBP
White ocean birds that seek the land. Gulls and Dreams. Lionel Stevenson. CaP; OCL
White of cherry bloom, The. Two Cinquains, I. Louise Owen. PFE
White of the first light snow. Basho, *tr. fr. Japanese by* Lois J. Erickson. SoLD
White Opal, The. "R. K. K." CAG
White Owl, The. George Meredith. *Fr.* Love in the Valley. ChTr
White Owl, The. F. J. Patmore. PoMS
White Owl, The. Tennyson. *See* Owl, The.
White Pacha, The. Andrew Lang. LH
White Paper. Sydney Jephcott. BoAu
White Paternoster, The. *Unknown. See* Matthew, Mark, Luke, and John.
White Peace, The. "Fiona Macleod." EPN; FaBoBe; HBV; OQP; PoVP; QP-2
White Peacock. Brenham McKay. BLA
White Peacock, The. "Fiona Macleod." *Fr.* Sospiridi Roma. PoVP; VA
White Peacock, The. Mary Mills. NePoAm
White Peacocks. Jessie B. Rittenhouse. BLA
White pebbles jut from the river stream. In the Hills. Wang Wei. WhP
White pennant on the wing. Departure. Ibn Mujbar. MooP
White, Pillared Neck. Richard Watson Gilder. PR
White pinnace on lactic waves, The. Birth by Anesthesia. George Scarbrough. GoYe
White plum tree, where can my loved one be? Fujiwara, *tr. fr. Japanese by* Lois J. Erickson. SoLD
White Pony, The. *Unknown, tr. fr. Chinese.* ChLP; WhP
White Presence, The. Joseph Fort Newton. ChIP; MaRV
("Follow Me.") OQP; QP-1
White Primit Falls. *Unknown, after the Latin of* Virgil. ChTr
("Trust not too much, fair youth, unto thy feature.") EG
White Princess, The, *sel.* William Brighty Rands.
Kitty: What She Thinks of Herself. CBPC, *abr.*; MoShBr
(Cat of Cats, The.) CIV
(Kitten Speaks, The.) RIS
White Rainbow, The. Starr Nelson. GoYe
White ram rears against a wall, A. The Ram. Robert P. Tristram Coffin. AnAmPo; LA
White Rat, The. Marguerite Young. MoPo
White River was flooded, and I, in the midst, The. Acheloos (the River-God). Angelos Sikelianos. MoGP
White Rooster, The. George O'Neil. PoeMoYo; TCPD
White Rose, A. John Boyle O'Reilly. AA; ACP; AnAmPo; HBV; LA; LBAP; LEAP; OBAV; OBEV; OBVV; OnYI; PR
White Rose, The. *Unknown.* LPS-1
White-rose garland at her feet, The. E. B. B. James Thomson. HBV; PtP; VLEP
White rose had a sorrow, A. The Betrayal of the Rose. Edith M. Thomas. AA
White rose in red rose-garden. Before the Mirror. Swinburne. OBVV
White Rose over the Water, The. George Walter Thornbury. VA
White rose tree that spent its musk, The. Old Gardens. Arthur Upson. HBV
White Roses. Cora Randall Fabbri. AA
White Roses. Ernest Rhys. VA
White, said Worsley, and glistening, the ridgy plain. Douglas Stewart. *Fr.* Worsley Enchanted, II. NeLNL
White sail upon the ocean verge. Arthur. William Winter. AA
White Sand, The. Edmund Wilson. NePoAm
White sand and cedars; cedars, sand. Sandy Hook. George Houghton. AA
White seagull on the breast of the sea, A. The Seagull. Dafydd ap Gwilym. LyMA
White Seal, The, *sel.* Kipling. *Fr.* The Jungle Book.
"Oh! hush thee, my baby, the night is behind us," 8 *ll.* CaAE
(Seal['s] Lullaby.) FaPON; NV; PoRA; PRWS; TiPo (1959 ed.)
(White Seal's Lullaby, The.) RAR
White Season. Frances Frost. FaPON; TiPo
White Sheep. *Unknown. See* Clouds.
White sheep, white sheep. Clouds [*or* White Sheep]. *Unknown, wr. at. to* Christina Rossetti *and to* W. H. Davies. BoTP; BrR; OTPC (1946 ed.); PCH; StVeCh; TiPo
White sheet on the tail-gate of a truck, A. Elegy for a Dead Soldier. Karl Shapiro. AmPP (4th ed.); CoBMV; MiAP; OnAP; OxBA; WaaP; WaP
White shields they carry in their hands. The Hosts of Faery. *Unknown.* OnYI
White Ship, The. Dante Gabriel Rossetti. EmBrPo; OnSP; POTT; PoVP
White Ships and the Red, The. Joyce Kilmer. CV; MC; PAH
White Sisters of Culion, The. Wilbur Underwood. PraNu
White sky, over the hemlocks bowed with snow. The Buck in the Snow. Edna St. Vincent Millay. CrMA; NP
White Snow. Guillaume Apollinaire, *tr. fr. French by* Dudley Fitts. AnFP
White soul of England's glory, sovereign star! Nelson. Archibald T. Strong. *Fr.* Sonnets of the Empire. BoAu
White Splendor. Leslie Savage Clark. ChIP
White Squall, The. "Barry Cornwall." LPS-2
White Squall, The, *sel.* Thackeray.
After the Storm. PRWS
White, stamen-shadowed petals of wild rose. Dogrose. Patric Stevenson. NeIP
White stars falling gently. Winter Joys. Dorothy Gradon. BoTP
White Steed of the Prairies, The. *Unknown.* CoSo
White Sun and Bright Moon. Li Po, *tr. fr. Chinese by* Nee Wen Yei. WhP
White swan of cities, slumbering in thy nest. Venice. Longfellow. AmPP
White Symphony. John Gould Fletcher. AnFE; APA; ChMo; CMP; CoAnAm; MAPA; SPP; TwAmPo
White-tailed Hornet, The. Robert Frost. CoV; OxBA
White Thorn. Rose Darrough. PoTo
White though ye be, yet, lilies, know. Robert Herrick. EG
White-Throat, The. *Unknown.* BLA
White-Throat Sings, A. Walter Prichard Eaton. DD; HBMV
White-throated Sparrow, The. A. West. SN
White Tintoretto clouds beneath my naked feet. The Strand. Louis MacNeice. AnIV
White tomb in the desert, A. From a Felucca. Cale Young Rice. LS; SPP
White Tree in Bloom, A. John Richard Moreland. PGD
White Veil, The. Grace Fallow Norton. PraNu
White Violet. Marian Osborne. CaP; CPG
White Violets. Benjamin R. C. Low. HBMV
White Water Lily, The. Stéphane Mallarmé, *tr. fr. French by* Bradford Cook AnFP
White Wave Following, The. Alice Milligan. GTIV
White way is the wind's way, A. The Wind's Way. Grace Hazard Conkling. HBV
White Whippet, The. W. W. Gibson. MM
White wide wonder of a cloud, The. Assuagement. Sister Claude of Jesus. JKCP (1955 ed.)
White wind whispers of the woes, The. The Four Winds. Shane Leslie. OnYI
White Window, The. James Stephens. StVeCh; SUS; TiPo
White wings of commerce sailing far. In Memory of General Grant. Henry Abbey AA
White Witch, The. James Weldon Johnson. BANP; CDC

White with daisies and red with sorrel. Weeds. Edna St. Vincent Millay. TCPD
White Women, The. Mary Elizabeth Coleridge. TCPD
Whitely the Lily Wavers. August, Graf von Platen, *tr. fr. German by* Edwin Morgan. AnGP
Whitely, while benzine. Lachrymae Christi. Hart Crane. ReMP
Whiteness. "Isobel Hume." HBMV
Whiteness of faintly roseate milk. Dayspring. Luis G. Urbina. AnMP
Whiteness of the lily once was thine, The. The Maid. Katherine Brégy. CAW; GoBC
Whiteness, or Chastity. Joseph Beaumont. LiTL; LoBV
Whiter than White. Swift. RIS
Whiter there is not nor rosier. Peggy. Blanaid Salkeld. OnYI
Whitewinged circus/ of kittiewaking. Spring, St. Stephen's Green. Leslie Daiken. OnYI
Whither. John Vance Cheney. AA
Whither? Hartley Coleridge. *See* Whither Is Gone.
Whither. Philip Becker Goetz. AA
Whither? Wilhelm Müller, *tr. fr. German by* Longfellow. AWP
Whither? Po Chü-i, *tr. fr. Chinese by* Henry H. Hart. PoHN
Whither Away? Mary Elizabeth Coleridge. CH
Whither Away? Euripides, *tr. fr. Greek by* T. F. Higham. *Fr.* Hecuba. OxBG
Whither away is the Spring to-day? The World's May-Queen [*or* When Spring Comes to England]. Alfred Noyes. HBV; OBVV
Whither away, O Sailor! say? Outward. John G. Neihardt. HBV
Whither away, Robin. The Flight of the Birds. Edmund Clarence Stedman. GN
Whither, curs'd rabble, do you rush? Why show. Horace. Epodes, VII. LaP
Whither depart the souls of the brave that die in the battle. Arthur Hugh Clough. *Fr.* Amours de Voyage, V. OAEP
Whither doth now this fellow flee. March. Robert Loveman. AA
Whither fled, wild deer? Wild Deer. Hafiz. PeP
Whither Is Gone [the Wisdom and the Power]. Hartley Coleridge. EPN; HBV; OBRV
(Whither.) VA
Whither is she gone, wing'd by the evening airs. Laurence Binyon. *Fr.* The Sirens. MM; TwCV
Whither leads the path. The Harvard Commemoration Ode. James Russell Lowell. *Fr.* Ode Recited at the Harvard Commemoration, July 21, 1865. MDAH
Whither leads this pathway, little one? Whither. John Vance Cheney. AA
Whither, mad maiden, wilt thou roame? To His Muse. Robert Herrick. OAEP
Whither [*or* Wither], midst falling dew. To a Waterfowl. Bryant. AA; AmP; AmPP; AnAmPo; AnFE; AnNE; APA; APW; AWP; BAP; BAV; BLA; BLV; BoLiVe; BTP; CG; CH; CoAnAm; CoBA; DD; DDA; EV-4; ExPo; FaBoBe; FaBoEn; FaFP; GN; GTBS; GTBS-D; HBV; HBVY; HiLiAm; HoPM; IAP; InP; LA; LBAP; LEAP; LiTA; LiTG; LPS-2; MaRV; MCCG; MOAP; NeHB; NePA; OBAV; OBRV; OHFP; OQP; OTPC; OxBA; PFE; PG (1945 ed.); PIAE; PIR; Po; PoE; PoEL-4; PoeMoYo; PTA-1; PYM; QP-1; REAL; RiBV; SeCeV; SN; TCAP; TOP; TreF; TrGrPo; TVSH; UnPo (1st ed.); WBLP; WGRP
Whither, Moeris, your haste? By the usual road to the city? Virgil. Eclogues, IX. LaP
Whither, O splendid ship, thy white sails crowding. A Passer-by. Robert Bridges. AlDL; BLV; ChMo; CMP; CoBMV; CoEV; EnLit; EPP; EtS; EV-5; GTBS-W; GTML; GTSE; GTSL; HBV; LEAP; LiTB; LiTM; MBP; MoAB; MoBrPo; OAEP; OBVV; POTT; PoVP; SeCeV; SG; ShBV-3; TCEP; TwCV; TyEnPo; VA; VLEP
Whither, O whither didst Thou fly? The Eclipse. Henry Vaughan. HBV
Whither, oh! whither wilt thou wing thy way? Flight of the Spirit. Felicia Dorothea Hemans. ES; UnW
Whither shall I, the fair maiden, flee from Sorrow? Sorrow. *Unknown.* AWP
Whither So Fast? *Unknown.* EIL
"Whither thus hastes my little book so fast?" The Writer to His Book. Thomas Campion. OAEP
Whither, with blue and pleading eyes. The Ashes in the Sea. George Sterling. LBMV
Whiting and the Snail, The. "Lewis Carroll." *See* Lobster Quadrille, The.
Whitman's Mother. Walt Whitman. *Fr.* Faces. APW
(Justified Mother of Men, The.) OHIP
Whitman's Ride for Oregon. Hezekiah Butterworth. GA, *abr.*; PAH
Whit Sunday. Joseph Beaumont. OxBoCh
Whitsunday. George Herbert. AtBAP
Whitsunday. John Keble. OBRV
Whitsuntide. *Unknown.* *See* In Summer.
Whittier. James Russell Lowell. *Fr.* A Fable for Critics. AmPP (4th ed.); AnNE; APW; OxBA
("There is Whittier, whose swelling and vehement heart.") CoBA; PtP
Whittier. Margaret E. Sangster. AA; DD; GA
Whittier Alphabet, A. *Comp. by* Caroline B. Le Row, *fr. various poems by* Whittier. PEOR
Whittington and His Cat. *Unknown.* CIV
Whittling. John Pierpont. GN; LPS-3
Who. Moishe-Leib Halpern, *tr. fr. Yiddish by* Joseph Leftwich. TrJP
Who? Florence Hoatson. BoTP
Who/ Are you/ Who is born. Vision and Prayer. Dylan Thomas. LiTG; LiTM (rev. ed.); MoPo
Who all time dodgin' en de cott'n en de corn? Mammy's Li'l' Boy. Harry Stillman Edwards. BOL
Who am I? Imitation of Walt Whitman. "Judy." BOHV; PA
Who Are My People? Rosa Zagnoni Marinoni. BLPA; PoToHe
Who Are the Dead? Euripides, *tr. fr. Greek by* James Adam. MaRV
Who Are the Dead? Lilith Lorraine. UnW
Who are the nobles of the earth, the true aristocrats. The True Aristocrat. W. Stewart. WBLP
"Who are the winds? Who are the winds?" The Winds. "John Eglinton." GTIV; OnYI
Who Are the Wise Men? B. Y. Williams. ChIP; MaRV
Who are these among you. The Decision. Owen Dodson. PoNe
Who are these? Why sit they here in twilight? Mental Cases. Wilfred Owen. FaBoMo; LiTM (rev. ed.); WaP
"Who are we waiting for?" "Soup burnt?" . . . Eight. The Feckless Dinner Party. Walter de la Mare. FaBoTw; MoPW
Who are ye, spirits that stand. The Blazing Heart. Alice Williams Brotherton. AA
"Who are ye with clustered light." The Pleiads. John Banister Tabb. UTS
Who are you? Death Speaks. Pedro Calderón de la Barca. TeCS
"Who are you and whence do you come?" A Vagrant. Erik Axel Karlfeldt. AnSL
"Who are you?" asked the cat of the bear. Elizabeth J. Coatsworth. TiPo
Who are you dusky woman, so ancient hardly human. Ethiopia Saluting the Colors. Walt Whitman. AmP; BAV; GTBS-D; IAP; PAH; PoNe; TCAP
Who are you, gray mysterious visitors. Cats. William Wallace Whitelock. CIV
"Who are you, Sea Lady." Santorin. James Elroy Flecker. FaBoTw; OBMV
"Who are you that so strangely woke." The Princess of Scotland. Rachel Annand Taylor. GoTS
Who art thou, girl, in such mean garb arrayed? Religion. Vauquelin de la Fresnaye, *tr. by* Wilfrid Thorley. CAW
Who art thou, lady, 'neath this carven stone? Asked the Traveller of the Tomb. Leonidas of Tarentum. GrR
Who art thou, so penuriously clad? Religion. Jean Vauquelin de la Fresnaye, *tr. by* Alan Conder. TrFP
Who Art Thou, Starry Ghost? Herbert Trench. GTIV
Who art thou? Whose relics, I wonder. A Wayside Grave. Leonidas of Tarentum. OxBG
Who beckons the green ivy up. The Miracle. Walter de la Mare. CoBE; GTML; LiTB; UnPo (3d ed.)
Who bids for the little children. The Children's Auction. Charles Mackay. BMEP
Who bids us have a care, lads. Song of Youth. Austin Melvin Works. CAG
Who Bids Us Sing? Rhys Carpenter. WGRP
Who borrows all your ready cash. A Friend. Marguerite Power. FaFP; SiTL
Who braves it now as doth young Histrio. Ortus Novus Urbe Britannus. Henry Parrot. TuPP
Who builds a church within his heart. Piety [*or* The Church in the Heart]. Morris Abel Beer. MaRV; PFE; PoToHe
Who builds him a house of stone or brick. Builders. Hortense Flexner. HBMV
Who builds of stone a shrine to bear his name. The Glory of Lincoln. Thomas Curtis Clark. PGD
Who builds the state? Builders of the State. Richard Watson Gilder. PoRL
"Who burst the barriers of my peaceful grave?" The Lament of the Damned in Hell. Edward Young. OxBoCh
Who but the wind. The Wind. Betty Miller. BrR
Who by himself hath come hither on isle? The Waking of Angantyr. *Unknown.* PaOS
Who by Searching Can Find Out God? Eliza Scudder. *See* Quest, The.
"Who called?" I said, and the words. Echo. Walter de la Mare. MoVE; OBMV; SeCeV; ShBV-4
Who Calls? Frances Clarke. HH; PoRh; SiSoSe; StaSt; TSW; TSWC

Who calls me bold because I won my love. Song. Cosmo Monkhouse. VA
Who calls? Who calls? Who? For a Mocking Voice. Eleanor Farjeon. AlDL; CH; PoMS; TiPo (1959 ed.)
Who came in the quiet night. The Little Fox. Marion Edey. TiPo
Who Can Be Happy and Free [*or* Who Lives Happily] in Russia? *sels.* Nikolai Alekseyevich Nekrasov, *tr. fr. Russian.*
Hungry One, The, *tr. by* Juliet M. Soskice. BoR
"Oh tread not the road," *tr. by* Juliet M. Soskice. BoR
Salt Song, The, *tr. by* Babette Deutsch. TrRV
Wife's Lament, The, *tr. by* Juliet M. Soskice. BoR
Who can be that somber fellow. Catbird. Stephen Crombie. BLA; WhBS
Who can bear/ The wail of a young orphan? Rabbi Yussel Luksh of Chelm. Jacob Glatstein. TrJP
Who can bring back the magic of that story. The Descent of the Child. Susan L. Mitchell. DiM; GTIV
Who can find a virtuous woman? The Virtuous Wife [*or* The Good Wife]. Proverbs, Bible, *O.T.* MaRV; TrGrPo
Who Can Forget? Leslie Savage Clark. ChIP
Who Can Forget—Never to Be Forgot. Giles Fletcher. AnEC
Who can live in heart so glad. The Merry Country Lad [*or* Pastoral]. Nicholas Breton. *Fr.* The Passionate Shepherd. CH; EIL; ElSeCe; EV-1; LoBV; OBSC; PoE; ReEn; SiCE; TuPP; ViBoPo
Who can love you, January? January. Rosaline Jones. PEOR
Who can make a delicate adventure. Advice to a Blue-Bird. Maxwell Bodenheim. HBMV; MAP; MoAmPo (1942 ed.)
Who can make a poem of the depths of weariness. Carl Sandburg. *Fr.* The People, Yes. MaRV; NAMP
Who Can Say. Alastair Reid. NePoEA
Who can say. Song. Tennyson. FaBoCh; LoGBV
Who can scape his bow? George Herbert. EG
Who can see her. Youth. Tzu Yeh. ChLP
Who can strip off his outer garment? Leviathan, the Crocodile. Job, Bible, *O.T.* MuP
Who can support the anguish of love? Ode. Ibn al-Arabi. AWP; LiTW
Who can surrender to Christ, dividing his best with the stranger. Where Is the Real Non-Resistant? Vachel Lindsay. OQP; QP-1; StJW
"Who Cannot Weep Come Learn of Me." *Unknown.* TMEV (Sodenly Afraide.) EnLit
Who cantereth forth in the night so late. The Witch of Erkmurden. James Whitcomb Riley. DaM
Who comes dancing over the snow. The New Year. Dinah Maria Mulock Craik. BrR; DD; HH; MeMeAg; MPB; OTPC (1946 ed.); PCH; PTA-2; YeAr
Who Comes Here? *Unknown.* OTPC (1923 ed.) ("Who comes here?/ A grenadier.") OxNR
Who comes to England not to learn. England. Grace Ellery Channing. AA
Who comforts flesh unreconciled, II. Frances Crawford. PtPa
Who copies Yours or Oxford's better part. The Man of Ross. Pope. *Fr.* Moral Essays, Epistle III. CoBE
Who could be sad in April. One April Day. John Richard Moreland. ChIP
Who could forget her wild black eyes? Lois Malone. August Derleth. DaM
Who counsels peace at this momentous hour. Ode, Written during the Negociations with Buonaparte, in January, 1814. Robert Southey. LiA
"Who," cried the elders on the Trojan wall. Pierre de Ronsard. *Fr.* Sonnets pour Hélène. PrPoCR
Who cries that the days of daring are those that are faded far. Deeds of Valor at Santiago. Clinton Scollard. HBV; PAH
Who crieth: "Woe"? who: "Alas"? The Drunkard. Proverbs, Bible, *O.T.* TrJP
Who danced Saturday mornings. Roots. Harold Telemaque. PoNe
Who dare complain or be ashamed. Celebrations. Austin Clarke. OxBI
Who dares play a flute so early. Despair. Chu Shu Chen. PoHN
Who Dat a-Comin' ovah Yondah? *with music. Unknown.* BoAN-1
Who dat knockin' at de do'? Encouragement. Paul Laurence Dunbar. PTA-2; YT
Who does not love the juniper tree? Juniper. Eileen Duggan. CAW; ChBR; MoSiPe
Who Does Not Love True Poetry. Henry Clay Hall. LPS-1; PoToHe (new ed.)
Who Does Not Love Wine, Women and Song. J. H. Voss. FaFP; SiTL
Who doth behold my mistress' face. The Fairest of Her Days. *Unknown.* EIL
Who doth desire that chaste his wife should be. Truth Doth Truth Deserve [*or* Advice to the Same]. Sir Philip Sidney. *Fr.* Arcadia. HBV; LiTL; SiPS
Who doubts has met defeat ere blows can fall. Columbus the World-Giver. Maurice Francis Egan. OQP; PGD; QP-1
Who doubts there are classes. Every-Day Botany. Katherine H. Perry. PEOR
Who dreamed that beauty passes like a dream? The Rose of the World. W. B. Yeats. BoLiVe; CBOV; ChMo; CMP; EnLi-2 (1949 ed.); EnLit; FaBoEn; HBV; MBP; MoAB; MoBrPo; OBVV; PoLFOT; PoVP; TIP; TwCV; VA; VLEP
Who Dreams Shall Live. Dana Burnet. OBAV
Who drives the horses of the sun. The Happiest Heart. John Vance Cheney. AA; AnAmPo; AnFE; APA; BAP; CoAnAm; HBV; HBVY; LA; LBMV; LEAP; MaRV; OBAV; OQP; PoMa; POT; QP-1; TreFS; WGRP
Who e'er. *See* Whoe'er.
Who even dead, yet hath his mind entire! Canto XLVII. Ezra Pound. CrMA; MoPo
Who ever. *See* Whoever.
Who fears to speak of Easter Week. Easter Week. *Unknown.* OnYI
Who fears to speak of Ninety-Eight? The Memory of the Dead. John Kelly Ingram. AnIV; GTIV; HBV; OnYI; OxBI; PoFr; TIP; VA
Who feasts tonight? The Fairies Feast. Charles M. Doughty. CH
Who fed me from her gentle breast. My Mother. Ann Taylor. BLPA; DD; MaRV; MOAH; MotAn; OHIP; PEDC; PTA-1; TreF
Who feels not, when the Spring once more. Aubrey Thomas De Vere. *Fr.* May Carols. IrPN
Who findeth comfort in the stars and flowers. L'Envoi. Thomas Lovell Beddoes. *Fr.* Death's Jest Book. LO
Who finds a woman good and wise. Song. George Wither. AEV
Who first invented work, and bound the free. Work. Charles Lamb. NBE; PeBoSo
Who first reform'd our stage with justest laws. An Elegy on Ben Jonson. *At. to* John Cleveland, *also at. to* James Cleyton. ElSeCe; EPS; MeLP; OBS; SeEP
Who Follow the Flag. Henry van Dyke. FOAH
Who Follows in His Train? Reginald Heber. *See* Son of God Goes Forth to War, The.
Who for the hungry spreads a bounteous board. Beneficence. Sadi. PeP
Who forced the Muse to this alliance? On Professor Drennan's Verse. Roy Campbell. WhC
Who friendship with a knave hath made. The Old Woman and Her Cats. John Gay. BeR
Who gave Love wings? Love Is Not Winged. Eubulus. OxBG
Who gave thee, O Beauty. Ode to Beauty. Emerson. IAP; MOAP; PoEL-4
Who God Possesseth. St. Theresa of Avila, *tr. by* Longfellow. *See* Santa Teresa's Book-Mark.
Who Goes By. Clinton Scollard. TBM
Who Goes By Lightly. Gertrude Callaghan. JKCP (1955 ed.)
Who Goes Home, *br. sel.* G. K. Chesterton. "Men that are men again; who goes home." OtMeF
Who Goes There? Grace Duffie Boylan. HH
Who goes there? God knows. I'm nobody. How should I answer? 'Ετώσιον ἄχθος ἀρούρης. Robert Bridges. FaBoTw
Who goes there? hankering, gross, mystical, nude. Song of Myself, XX. Walt Whitman. CoV; TrGrPo
Who goes there, in the night. Apparitions [*or* It Shall Not Be Again]. Thomas Curtis Clark. BPP; MaRV; OQP; PEDC; PGD; PoRL; PSO; QP-1
Who goes there? No sound on all the air. Qui Vive. Anne Goodwin Winslow. LS
Who Goes with Fergus? W. B. Yeats. CoEV; FaBoCh; LoGBV
Who Goeth Hence. Helen Frazee-Bower. OQP; QP-1 (When Death Shall Come.) MaRV
Who governs his own course with steady hand. Portrait of a Freeman. Abraham Cowley. Fr. Of Liberty; an Essay PoFr
Who grace, for zenith had, from which no shadowes grow. Despair. Fulke Greville. Caelica, LXXXIII [LXXXIV]. OBSC; PoEL-1
Who grafted quince on Western may. The Avengers. Robert Graves. HBMV
Who had seen them, the mystic sprites. The Miracle-Workers. Elizabeth Allen. SN
Who hail us from the hill. Homage to Mürren. Morton Dauwen Zabel. NP
Who harbors Hatred, sees a small. Horizons. Clinton Scollard. OQP; QP-2
Who, harnessed in his mail of Self, demands. Self-Mastery. Bayard Taylor. MaRV
Who has a thing to bring. L'Ancien Régime. James Thomson. PoVP
Who has but dighted his tricks in a bed. This Is What the

Who has but dighted his tricks in a bed (*continued*)
Watchbird Sings, Who Perches in the Lovetree. Bruce Boyd. NeAP
Who has described the wave. Thoughts in the Gulf Stream. Christopher Morley. EtS
Who has e'er been at Paris, must needs know the Grève. The Thief and the Cordelier. Matthew Prior. EV-3
Who Has Ever Held Life in His Hand. August, Graf von Platen, *tr. fr. German by* Edwin Morgan. AnGP
Who has ever stopped to think of the divinity of Lamont Cranston? In Memory of Radio. LeRoi Jones. NeAP
Who Has Gone through the Wood. Floris Clark McLaren. BoCaPo
Who Has Known Heights. Mary Brent Whiteside. BLPA; MaRV; NeHB
Who has not ceased from evil ways. No Peace. *Unknown. Fr.* The Upanishads. OnPM
Who has not dreamed a world of bliss. Summer Noon. William Howitt. LPS-2
Who has not heard of the dauntless *Varuna?* The *Varuna.* George Henry Boker. PAH
Who has not heard of the Vale of Cashmere. The Vale of Cashmere [*or* The Light of the Haram]. Thomas Moore. *Fr.* Lalla Rookh. EnRP; LPS-2
Who has not marveled at the might of kings. Kings. John Richard Moreland. ChIP; MaRV
Who has not seen the spring, is blind, is dead. The Land: Spring. V. Sackville-West. MoP
Who has not thought, when scuffing shells. Lower Forms of Life. Mary Winter. GoYe
Who has not walked upon the shore. Upon the Shore [*or* After the Gale]. Robert Bridges. EtS; LoBV; VA
Who has robbed the ocean cave. Song. John Shaw. AA; HBV; PR; SPP
Who has seen Echidna. Echidna. Mary Elizabeth Counselman. DaM
Who has seen the pageant. Argumentum ad Hominem. Hyam Plutzik. FiMAP
Who Has Seen the Wind? Christina Rossetti. *Fr.* Sing-Song. BoTP; BPN; BrR; CoBE; FaPON; GoBP; HBV; HBVY; MPB; NLK; OnHT; OTPC; OuHeWo; PCH; PoRh; PoVP; PPL; PTA-1; RAR; StVeCh; SUS; TiPo; TSW; TSWC
(Sing-Song.) MBP
(Wind, The.) BoChLi; FaBoBe; GFA; MaRV; NeHB; RIS
Who hasn't heard of London Bridge? Hay's Wharf. Richard Church. HaMV
Who Hath a Book. Wilbur D. Nesbit. BLPA; MOB; NeHB; SiSoSe; TiPo (1959 ed.); TreFS
Who hath believed our report? The Man of Sorrows. Isaiah, Bible, *O.T.* EM-1
Who hath believed that which we have heard. The Servant of God [*or* Behold, My Servant]. Isaiah, Bible, *O.T.* GrCo-1; OuHeWo
Who hath desired the sea?—the sight of salt water unbounded. The Sea and the Hills. Kipling. OtMeF
Who hath despised the day of little things. Jabesh Gilead. Victor Starbuck. *Fr.* Saul, King of Israel. MuM
Who hath gathered the wind in his fists? The Words of Agur. Proverbs, Bible, *O.T.* TrGrPo
Who hath given man speech? or who hath set therein. Choruses from Atalanta in Calydon, 3. Swinburne. ViBoPo
Who hath heard of such cruelty before? Epigram. Sir Thomas Wyatt. SiPS
Who Hath His Fancy [*or* Fancie] Pleasèd. Sir Philip Sidney. AtBAP; ElL; OAEP; PoEL-1; RiBV; SiCE
(Immortality.) OBSC
(Song: "Who hath his fancy pleasèd.") OBEV; SiPS
Who hath not kissed the rose's tender leaf. George Edward Woodberry. *Fr.* Ideal Passion. MOAP
Who hath restored my sense, given me new breath. John Fletcher. *Fr.* The Faithful Shepherdess, III, i. LO
Who hath woe?/ Who hath sorrow? Wine and Woe. Proverbs, Bible, *O.T.* MaRV
Who have been lonely once. Careless Love. Stanley Kunitz. WaP
Who have no heaven come. String Quartet. Babette Deutsch. UnS
Who hears in the night. The Train in the Night. Elizabeth Riddell. NeLNL
Who Hold the Steps To-Night? James Cresse, Jr. CAG
Who hurts his heel upon a stone. After Disaster. Lizette Woodworth Reese. TBM
Who, in his tenderest years. Only a Dream-Shadow [*or* Human Life]. Pindar. *Fr.* Pythian Odes, VIII. GrR; OxBG
Who in One Lifetime. Muriel Rukeyser. Po
Who, in the brief, incredible northern spring. Let Him Return. Leona Ames Hill. PoToHe (new ed.)
Who, in the dark, has cast the harbor-chain? Putting to Sea. Louise Bogan. LiTM
Who, in the garden-pony carrying skeps. Horses. Dorothy Wellesley. AIDL; ChMP; OBMV; ShBV-4
Who in this desert calls on Paris? Laurence Binyon. *Fr.* Paris and Oenone. ReTS
Who in this small urn reposes. Ad Cinerarium. Victor Plarr. MBP
Who Is at My Window? *Unknown.* BLV; GTBS-W; LiTG; TrGrPo
("Quho is at my windou, quho, quho?") EG
Who Is Drunk? Thomas Love Peacock. *See* Not Drunk Is He.
Who Is Free? Philemon, *tr. fr. Greek by* T. F. Higham. OxBG
Who is in love with loveliness. Miracle. Lizette Woodworth Reese. MAP; MoAmPo
Who Is It? José Gorostiza, *tr. fr. Spanish by* H. R. Hays. TwSpPo
Who Is It? *Unknown.* PEOR
Who is it calling by the darkened river. Voices. Walter de la Mare. UnPo (3d ed.)
"Who is it knocking in the night." The Ballad of the Angel. Theodosia Garrison. HBV
Who is it opens her blue bright eye. Andalusian Cradle-Song. Thomas Bailey Aldrich. *Fr.* Mercedes. BOL
Who is it runs through the many-storied mansion of myth. Dwarf of Disintegration. Oscar Williams. LiTM (rev. ed.); MoPo; NePA; TwAmPo
Who is it stands on the polished stair. A Ballade of Old Loves. Carolyn Wells. COAH
Who Is It Talks of Ebony? Manmohan Ghose. OBMV
Who is it that says most, which can say more. Sonnets, LXXXIV. Shakespeare. PeBoSo
Who is it [*or* this] that sits by the way, by the wild wayside. Mater Dolorosa. Swinburne. BMEP; VLEP
Who is it that this dark [*or* darke] night. Eleventh Song [*or* A Dialogue *or* Lovers' Dialogue *or* Voices at the Window]. Sir Philip Sidney. *Fr.* Astrophel and Stella. AtBAP; CBOV; EG; ElL; EnLi-1; EV-1; OBEV; OBSC; PoEL-1; ReEn; ReIE; SeCePo; SiCE; SiPS; TuPP; ViBoPo; WoL
Who is like unto thee who teachest knowledge. Hymn of Unity. *Unknown.* TrJP
Who is lord of lordly fate. Song. Charles Heavysege. *Fr.* Count Filippo. PeCV
Who is lovelier than she? Alone in Her Beauty. Tu Fu. ChLP
Who Is My Neighbor? St. Luke, Bible, *N.T. See* Good Samaritan, The.
Who Is on the Lord's Side? Frances Ridley Havergal. MaRV
Who Is She? Félix Arvers, *tr. fr. French by* Alan Conder. TrFP
Who is she coming, whom all gaze upon. Sonnet: A Rapture concerning His Lady. Guido Cavalcanti. AWP
Who is she here that now I see. To Little Renee on First Seeing Her Lying in Her Cradle. William Aspenwall Bradley. HBV
Who is she that ascends so high. The Assumption. Sir John Beaumont. ACP (1952 ed.); CAW; GoBC
Who is she that comes, makyng turn every man's eye. Sonnet [*or* Chi è questa]. Guido Cavalcanti. LyMA; ReMP
Who Is Silvia [*or* Sylvia]? Shakespeare. *Fr.* The Two Gentlemen of Verona, IV, ii. ATP; ElL; EM-1; EnL; FaBoBe; FaFP; GN; InPo; KN; LiTB; NeHB; OAEP; OlF; OTPC; PFE; PreP, *with music;* ReaPo; RiBV; SeCeV; SiTL; TreF; TrGrPo; TwP; TyEnPo
(Silvia.) BLV; EV-1; HBV; OBEV; OnPP; WP
(Song: "Who is Silvia? what is she.") LiTG; REAL; ViBoPo; WHA
(Song from "Two Gentlemen of Verona.") LEAP
(Song of the Musicians.) BoLiVe
(Song to Silvia.) OBSC
(Sylvia.) BCEP
(To Silvia.) MCCG
("Who is Silvia? what is she?") AnFE; BEL; CoBE; EG; ElSeCe; EnLi-1; EnLit; EPP; OuHeWo; PIR; SiCE; TOP
Who is skilled to read. The Question. R. S. Thomas. MoWP
Who Is So Low. S. Ralph Harlow. MaRV
Who is so proud. The Performing Seal. Rachel Field. *Fr.* A Circus Garland. StVeCh; TiPo (1959 ed.); UTS
Who is softly calling whom. Noonday Ghosts. Geoffrey Johnson. UnW
Who Is That a-Walking in the Corn? Fenton Johnson. GoSl; NP; PoNe
Who is that calling through the night. Christmas at Indian Point. Edgar Lee Masters. ChMo; CMP; NP
Who is that goddess to whom men should pray. The Virgin Mother. "Æ." ChMo; CMP
Who is that sad-eyed slave. The Slave. Wu Shang Yeh. PoHN
Who Is the Angel That Cometh? Adelaide Anne Procter. MaRV
Who is the happy warrior? Who is he. Character of the Happy Warrior [*or* The Happy Warrior]. Wordsworth. BEL; BHV; BLV; BoLiVe; BPN; CBE; EM-2; EmBrPo; EnLit; EnLP; EnRP; EPN; ERP; EV-3; FaBoBe; FaFP;

GDAH GePC; GrCo-1; HBV; HBVY; HiLiEn; LiTB; LiTG; LoBV; MaRV; OBRV; OHFP; OQP; PTA-1; QP-2; TOP; TreF
Who is the honest man? Constancy. George Herbert. CBE; EV-2
Who Is the Man? *with music.* *Unknown.* TrAS
Who is the man in sterile white. The Surgeon. George W. Caldwell. PoP
Who is the man, that life doth will. Who Is the Man? *Unknown.* TrAS
Who is the pioneer? Leonora Speyer. *Fr.* Of Mountains. PC
Who is the runner in the skies. The Runner in the Skies. James Oppenheim. AnEnPo; BAP; CP; LEAP; MAP; MoAmPo (1942 ed.); NP; NV; PFY; SBMV; TrJP
Who is the sleeping giant. Giant's Tomb in Georgian Bay. "Katherine Hale." CaP
Who is the voyager in these leaves? America Was Promises. Archibald MacLeish. ChMo; PoLFOT
Who is this host of folk this fair spread day? The Bystanders. Mark Van Doren. MOAP
Who is this I hear?—Lo, this is I, thine heart. The Dispute of the Heart and Body of François Villon. Villon. AWP
"Who is this maid in wild array." A Theme with Variations III Barry Pain. PA
Who is this that comes to break the lethargy of night? Morning Song. Johan Skjoldborg. BoDS
Who is this that cometh from Edom. Vision of the Day of Judgment. Isaiah, Bible. *O.T.* WGRP
Who is this that cometh up not alone. The Bride Song. Christina Rossetti. *Fr.* The Prince's Progress. EPP; OBEV; OBVV; TOP
Who is this that darkeneth counsel by words without knowledge? The Voice Out of the Whirlwind [*or* The Inscrutable Mystery *or* God Replies]. Job, Bible, *O.T.* AWP; GrCo-2; JAWP; MaRV; OuHeWo; TrGrPo; WBP
Who is this that sits by the way, by the wild wayside. *See* Who is it that sits by the way
Who is this whose feet. The Swan's Feet. E. J. Scovell. FaBoMo
Who is this ye say is slain? Ellsworth. *Unknown.* PAH
Who is thy neighbor? He whom thou. Thy Neighbor. *Unknown.* OQP; QP-1
Who is vouchsafed to traffic with the truth. Prescience. Harold Vinal. MuM
Who is waiting at the doorstep now? Threshold. Charles David Webb. NePoAm-2
Who is, who is the rider there. Who. Moishe-Leib Halpern. TrJP
Who is wise?/ He who learns from everyone. The Good Man. *Fr.* The Talmud. TrJP
Who is yonder poor maniac, whose wildly-fixed eyes. Mary, the Maid of the Inn. Robert Southey. CG
Who is yonder siren so distressed. An Old Burden. Amado Nervo. AnMP
Who is your lady of love, O ye that pass. The Pilgrims. Swinburne. BPN; PoVP; TCEP; VLEP
Who journeying when the days grow shorter, stops. Historic Time. Walter Savage Landor. *Fr.* The Impious Feast. OBRV
Who keeps Saint Angel gates? A Letter to Rome. Steven Peele. ReIE
Who Kill'd [*or* Killed] John Keats? Byron. BPN; EnRP; HiLiEn; SiTL
Who killed Cock Robin? The Death and Burial of Cock Robin. Mother Goose. BoN; GoTP; HBV; HBVY; OTPC; OxNR; PPL; RIS. *See also* Here lies Cock Robbin . . .
Who Killed John Keats? Byron. *See* Who Kill'd John Keats.
Who killed Kildare? Who dared Kildare to kill? Epigram. Swift. HBV; TreFS
Who knocks at the Geraldine's door to-night. Ballad of the Little Black Hound. Dora Sigerson Shorter. OnYI; StPo
"Who knocks?" "I, who was beautiful." The Ghost. Walter de la Mare. CaAE; ChMo; ChMP; CoEV; DaM; EnLoPo; HaMV; HBMV; MBP; MoAB; MoBrPo; MoP; MoVE; POTT
Who Know Thee Best ("Who know her but as children do"). Sister Mary Catherine. JKCP (1955 ed.)
Who Knows? Nora Perry. AA
Who Knows a Mountain? Ethel Romig Fuller. OOP; QP-1
Who knows if in the world beneath the ground. Who Are the Dead? Euripides. MaRV
Who knows if living after all is death. What Is Life? Euripides. OxBG
Who Knows if the Moon's. E. E. Cummings. PoMS
Who knows the quiet road beyond the silence? Resurrection. Blodwen Davies. PSO
Who knows the thoughts of a child. Who Knows? Nora Perry. AA
Who knows this or that? Limits. Emerson. PoEL-4
Who knows what days I answer for to-day? The Young Neophyte. Alice Meynell. ACP; CAW; GoBC
Who knows, when raindrops are descending. Rain. Einar Benediktsson. IcP; LiTW
Who knows when the tiger passes. Color. Rowena Bennett. MPB (1956 ed.)
Who Knows Where. Detlev von Liliencron, *tr. fr. German by* Ludwig Lewisohn. AWP
Who lags from dread of daily work. Noble Work. Charles Mackay. PSO
Who Learns My Lesson Complete? Walt Whitman. AmPP (3d ed.)
"Who lifteth up the spirit." Jalal ed-Din Rumi, *tr. fr. Persian by* A. J. Arberry. PeP
Who Likes the Rain? Clara Doty Bates. BoTP; GFA; GoBP; OTPC (1946 ed.); PCH; PPL; RAR; TiPo
Who Likes to Love, Let Him Take Heed. *Unknown.* ReIE
Who list the Roman greatness forth to figure. Ruins of Rome, VI. Joachim du Bellay. OnPM
Who lists to see whatever nature, art. Ruins of Rome, II. Joachim du Bellay. OnPM
Who lit the furnace of the mammoth's heart. The Sun. Francis Thompson. *Fr.* Ode to the Setting Sun. MBP; MoAB; MoBrPo
Who Live under the Shadow. Stephen Spender. TwCV
Who Lives Happily in Russia? Nikolai Alekseyevich Nekrasov. *See* Who Can Be Happy and Free in Russia?
Who lives in suit of armor pent. Chant Royal of High Virtue. Sir Arthur Quiller-Couch. HBV
Who Liveth Well. Horatius Bonar. *See* He Liveth Long Who Liveth Well.
Who living but daily discern it he may. A Description of Life and Riches. Thomas Tusser. SiCE
Who, long before she left her teens. An Old Song Resung. Charles Larcom Graves. CenHV
Who looking back upon his troubled years. Disillusion. Bessie B. Decker. PoToHe (new ed.)
Who love would seek. Silent Love. *Unknown.* LiTW
Who Loves a Garden. Louise Seymour Jones. BLPA; NeHB
Who loves like me for his friend's eye to frame. Epistle to Boscán. Garcilaso de la Vega. BoFr
Who loves not Knowledge? Who shall rail. In Memoriam A. H. H., CXIV. Tennyson. BPN; EmBrPo; EPN; GEPC; OAEP; ViPo; VLEP
Who Loves the Rain. Frances Shaw. BPP; BrR; HBMV; LEAP; MPB; MW; NP; NV; OQP; PoToHe (new ed.); QP-2; SP
Who loves the sea has found its waters blue. Chameleon Gordon LeClaire. EtS
Who loveth a little mountain stream. A Mountain Stream *Unknown.* CAG
Who made the world, sir? Ants. Alfred Kreymborg. MAPA
Who makes the past, a pattern for next year. To Sir Henry Goodyere. John Donne. SeEP
Who Maketh the Grass to Grow. Psalms, CXLVII, Bible. *O.T.* FaPON (Psalm CXLVII.) TiPo (1952 ed.)
Who masquerades behind the winds? Moods. Leib Kwitko. TrJP
Who may praise her? Olive. Swinburne. GTBS
Who may quench the god-born fire. Isabella Valancy Crawford. *Fr.* The Helot. CPG; PeCV
Who, mid the grasses of the field. Dante. Bryant. PtP; ViBoPo
Who minds if the wind whistles and howls. Windy Morning. Harry Behn. TiPo (1959 ed.)
Who Minds to Bring His Ship to Happy Shore. Jasper Heywood. SiCE
Who money has, well wages the campaign. Money. Jehan du Pontalais. BOHV
Who Mou'n fo' Me? *with music.* *Unknown.* SoAF
Who must be blamed for the young head. The Landscape of the Heart. Geoffrey Grigson. LiTB; LiTM; WaP
Who nearer Nature's life would truly come. Thoreau. Amos Bronson Alcott. AA; GA; LBAP; OBAV
Who needs words in autumn woods. Gloria Mundi. Siegfried Sassoon. MoPW
Who Never Ate [*or* Broke] with Tears His Bread. Goethe. *See* Sorrow.
Who never wept knows laughter but a jest. Compensation. E. M. Brainard. PoToHe
Who, not to trifle with his days or blood. The Ampler Circumscription. William Baylebridge. BoAV
Who Not with Others Bides. "Angelus Silesius," *tr. fr. German by* Paul Carus. OnPM
Who now dare longer trust thy mother hand? San Francisco. John Vance Cheney. PAH
Who now remembers Almack's balls. Reminiscences of a Dancing Man. Thomas Hardy. MoVE
Who now remembers General Galliéni. General Galliéni. Robert Hillyer. PG (1955 ed.)
Who Now Shall Sneer? James Russell Lowell. PAP
Who of the eternal future will read. Courage. Emyr Humphreys. NeTW
Who of the gods set on those two to strife? The Beginning of the Wrath. Homer. *Fr.* The Iliad, I. OxBG

Who often found their way to pleasant meadows. Elegy for Minor Poets. Louis MacNeice. HaMV
Who on your breast pillows his head now. A Lost Jewel. Robert Graves. EnLoPo
Who or why, or which, or what. The Akond [*or* Ahkond] of Swat. Edward Lear. ALV; BOHV; CenHV; FaBoCh; FiBHP; GoTP; LauV; LiL; NA; OnPP; RIS; SiTL
Who owns the moonlit skies, the purple dawn. Owning. Wilmot B. Lane. CaP
Who owns these cattle, Corydon? Philondas? Prythee say. The Herdsmen. Theocritus. Idylls, IV. AWP
"Who owns these lands?" the Pilgrim said. The Staff and Scrip. Dante Gabriel Rossetti. OAEP; POTT; PoVP; VLEP
Who passes down the wintry street? Daffodil. Katharine Tynan. TIP
Who Pilots Ships. Daniel Whitehead Hicky. BrR; MoSiPe
Who Plants a Dogwood Tree. Mabel Brown. NLK (1947 ed.)
Who pleasure follows pleasure slays. Sensuality. Coventry Patmore. *Fr.* The Angel in the House. OBVV
Who Ponders National Events Shall Find. Wordsworth. EPN
Who praises God the most, what says he more than he. Richard Chenevix Trench. *Fr.* A Century of Couplets. OBRV
Who prises the blue mountain is stumbled by a hair. Animus et Corpus. Ralph Gustafson. BoCaPo (1948 ed.)
Who prop, thou ask'st, in these bad days, my mind? To a Friend. Matthew Arnold. BPN; EM-2; EmBrPo; EnLi-2; EPN; GEPC; OAEP; PoVP; PtP; TCEP; TwCrTr; ViPo; ViPP; VLEP
Who puts off shift. My Naked Aunt. Archibald MacLeish. NePA
Who questions if the punctual sun unbars. Love Redeemed, LXXXII. William Baylebridge. BoAV
Who reach their threescore years and ten. Threescore and Ten. Richard Henry Stoddard. HBV; LEAP
Who readeth much, and never meditates. Surcloying the Stomach. Joshua Sylvester. *Fr.* Tetrasticha. MOB
Who reaps the grain and plows the sod. Countryman's God. Roger Winship Stuart. MaRV
Who refuses to die is tormented. To Die. Paul Eluard. OnPM
Who Reigns? Shelley. *Fr.* Prometheus Unbound. SeCePo ("Who reigns? There was the Heaven and Earth at first.") BHV
Who remains in London Spring Song in the City. Robert Buchanan. HBV; OTPC (1923 ed.); SN; VA
"Who Ride?" Stella Kobrin. GA
Who ride by night through the woodland so wild? The Erl-King. Goethe, *tr. by* Sir Walter Scott. MaC
Who rides with such fury. Winter. Bjarni Thorarensen. IcP
Who rideth so fast as a fleet Navajo? Song of the Navajo. Albert Pike. PoOW
Who rideth so late through the night-wind wild? The Erl King. Goethe, *tr. by* Frederic H. Hedge. DaM
Who rideth through the driving rain. The King's Son. Thomas Boyd. AnIV; GTIV; OBMV; OxBI
Who rings New England's Angelus? The Hermit Thrush. Nelly Hart Woodworth. SN
Who rose up like a goddess from the sea. The Museum. William Abrahams. WaP
Who Runs May Read. John Keble. VA
Who said, "Peacock Pie"? The Song of the Mad Prince. Walter de la Mare. AtBAP; FaBoCh; LBBV; LoGBV; MoVE; OAEP (2d ed.); POTT; ShBV-4
Who saw the toad cross a street? Love of One's Neighbor. Max Jacob. MiCF
Who says/ That it's by my desire. People Hide Their Love. Wu Ti. ChLP; LiTW; TrCh
Who say[e]s that fictions on[e]ly and false hair. Jordan. George Herbert. CoEV; ElSeCe; FaBoEn; LiTB; MeLP; MePo; OBS; Po; PoEL-2; PoFS; PrWP; ReEn; SeEP; TriL; TwCrTr
Who says that the dead do not think of us? In Broad Daylight I Dream of My Dead Wife. Mei Yao Ch'en. OnPC
"Who says that the Irish are fighters be birth?" The Peaceable Race. T. A. Daly. HBV
Who sculptured Love beside this fountain?—Fool! A Statue of Love. *At. to* Zenodotus. OxBG
Who seeks for heaven alone to save his soul. The Way. Henry van Dyke. MaRV; OQP; QP-1
Who seeks perfection in the art. Perfection. Francis Carlin. FaFP; HBMV
Who seeks the way to win renown. Sir Richard Grenville's Farewell. *Unknown.* SG
Who Seeks to Please All Men. Lord Holland. MaRV
Who sees my face so pale & sad with greife. *Unknown.* SeCSL
Who sees the first marsh marigold. A Charm for Spring Flowers. Rachel Field. TiPo (1959 ed.)
Who sees the panic unconfessed, XI. Frances Crawford. PtPa
Who sees with equal eye, as God of all. Pope. *Fr.* An Essay on Man. FaBoEn
Who sees you, sins. Who has not seen you, therefore. Propertius. Elegies, II, 32. LaP
Who serves his country best? The Better Way. "Susan Coolidge." PaA
Who shall contend with his lords. Atalanta in Calydon: Final Chorus. Swinburne. BPN
Who shall declare the joy of the running! A Winter Ride. Amy Lowell. LBMV
Who Shall Deliver Me? Christina Rossetti. OxBoCh (Battle Within, The.) MaRV
Who shall doubt, Donne, where I a poet be. To John Donne. Ben Jonson. MaPo; ReIE; SeCV-1; TuPP
Who shall have my fair [*or* fayre] lady? Under the Leaves Green. *Unknown.* AtBAP; EG; EnLoPo; EPP; LO; OxBoLi; PoEL-1
Who shall invoke when we are gone. Tragic Love. Walter James Turner. LO; LoPS; OBMV
Who shall receive my new-born book. Catullus, *tr. fr. Latin by* Horace Gregory. RoL
Who Shall Speak for the People? Carl Sandburg. The People, Yes, Sec. 24. CoV; OxBA
Who shall succor me in my extremest hour. Sonnet: In Absence. Gaspara Stampa. LyPI
Who shall tell the lady's grief. On the Death of a Cat, a Friend of Mine Aged Ten Years and a Half. Christina Rossetti. CIV; PoC
Who shall tell what did befall. Wealth. Emerson. BAV; ImOP
Who shall thy gay buffoonery describe? To the Mocking-Bird. Richard Henry Wilde. AnAmPo; LA; LEAP. *See also* Winged mimic of the woods!
Who shall understand the mysteries of Thy creations? The Royal Crown, XXIV. Solomon ibn Gabirol. AWP
Who shall welcome home. The Hosts. George M. Brady. NeIP
Who sings not when the wine-cups throng. Nikolai Yazykov, *tr. fr. Russian by* C. M. Bowra. BoRS
Who sings upon the pinnacle of night? A Bird Sings at Night. Hildegarde Flanner. BLA
Who sits alone by the bright window? To the Tune of "Like a Dream." Li Ch'ing-chao. WhP
Who sits within the house and spins and spins. Lonely. Lizette Woodworth Reese. MOAP
Who Sleeps by Day and Walks by Night. Henry David Thoreau. PoEL-4
Who smoke-snorts toasts o' My Lady Nicotine. Variations on an Air: After Robert Browning. G. K. Chesterton. InP
Who so late. At the Garden Gate. David McCord. FaPON; RIS; StaSt
Who So List to Hount. Sir Thomas Wyatt. *See* Hind, The.
Who so valiant to decide? Young Woman at a Window. Mark Van Doren. LiTA; MoPo; MoVE
Who so wary and so wise of the warriors lives. Riddle. *At. to* Cynewulf. TCEP
Who sought for death, some gold espying. An Exchange of Fortune. Statyllius Flaccus. OxBG
Who sows the seas, or ploughs the easy shore? Woman's Inconstancy. Phineas Fletcher. *Fr.* Sicelides. ElL; ElSeCe
Who spurs his horse against the mountain-side. Fond Youth. Samuel Rogers. *Fr.* Human Life. OBRV
Who stands before me on the stairs. Body and Spirit. W. H. Davies. AtBAP
Who Stole the Bird's Nest? Lydia Maria Child. OTPC; PRWS; PTA-2; SAS
Who storms the moss-grown walls of eld. The Wages. Don Marquis. MaRV
Who strives to mount Parnassus hill. Verses [*or* Reply to an Imitation . . . of Horace]. Richard Bentley. OBEC; ViBoPo
Who strolls so late, for mugs a bait. French Lisette; a Ballad of Maida Vale. William Plomer. LiTM (rev. ed.); SiTL
"Who stuffed that white owl?" No one spoke in the shop. The Owl-Critic. James Thomas Fields. BLPA; BOHV; CenHV; GoTP; HBV; MW; PoeMoYo; PTA-1; RIS; StPo; TreFS; WBLP; YaD
Who tamed your lawless Tartar blood? To Russia. Joaquin Miller. AA; AnAmPo; LA
Who tames the lion now? Song. Thomas Lovell Beddoes. PoE; ViBoPo
Who tarried in Jericho. In Jericho. *Unknown.* SiTL
Who Taught Thee First to Sigh? Edward de Vere, Earl of Oxford. CoBE; TuPP
Who taught this pleading to unpractised eyes? To a Gipsy Child by the Sea-Shore. Matthew Arnold. ViPP
Who that once has seen/ How truth leads on to truth. The Torch Bearers: Herschel. Alfred Noyes. GrCo-1
Who that trusts his mind could believe the man of Lindos, Cleobulus. Simonides, *tr. fr. Greek by* Richmond Lattimore. GrPo
Who Then Extends His Arms to Me. David Einhorn, *tr. fr. Yiddish by* Sarah Zweig Betsky. OnCuPl

Who then is "he"? The Voice of a Bird. Alice Meynell. TCPD
Who, then, was Cestius. Rome. Thomas Hardy. EmBrPo; EnLi-2; MoAB
Who thinks that he has sufficience. Of Content. William Dunbar. EBSV
Who Thou art I know not. God the Architect [or To God, the Architect]. Harry Kemp. HBMV; MaRV; TrPWD; WGRP
Who thought of the lilac? The Lilac. Humbert Wolfe. FaPON; HBVY; MBP; MoBrPo; NeMA; OTPC (1946 ed.); YT
Who took me from my mother's arms. My Father. William Drennan. TIP
Who travels by the weary wandering way. Despair. Spenser. *Fr.* The Faerie Queene, I, 9. SeCePo
Who walked between the violet and the violet. T. S. Eliot. *Fr.* Ash Wednesday. BrBE
Who Walks by the Dockside. R. G. G. Price. SiTL
Who Walks with Beauty. David Morton. BLPA; FaBoBe; GBV (1952 ed.); HBMV; NeHB; PoTo
Who wanders near that palmy glade. Kais in the Desert. Nizami. *Fr.* Laili and Majnún. PeP
Who wants a gown. George Darley. *Fr.* Sylvia. LEAP
Who wants my jellyfish? The Jellyfish. Ogden Nash. FaPON
Who Wants to Travel All Over Europe and See Nothing but a Lot of American Tourists? I Do. Ogden Nash. SiTL
Who wants Wednesday? Who wants that day? Auction. John Holmes. WaKn
Who was ever sped by fortune. Count Arnaldos. *Unknown.* TeCS
Who was he that said. Jalal ed-Din Rumi, *tr. fr. Persian by* A. J. Arberry. PeP
Who Was It, Tell Me. Heine. *See* Sag' mir wer einst die Uhren erfund.
Who was it then that lately took me in the wood? Faun-taken. Rose O'Neill. AnAmPo; HBMV; LA; LEAP
Who was there had seen us. The Dark Girl's Rhyme. Dorothy Parker. InMe
Who weeps now anywhere in the world. Solemn Hour. Rainer Maria Rilke. TrJP
Who went to sleep in the flower-bed? The Song of the Dumb Waiter. James Reeves. AlDL
Who Were before Me. John Drinkwater. OBMV
Who were the builders? Question not the silence. The Nameless Doon [or Dun]. William Larminie. AnIL; GTIV; IrPN; OnYI; OxBI
Who were the Wise Men in the long ago? Who Are the Wise Men? B. Y. Williams. ChIP; MaRV
"Who Wert and Art and Evermore Shalt Be." William Channing Gannett. TrPWD
Who? Who? *Unknown.* CH
Who, who from Dian's feast would be away? The Feast of Dian. Keats. *Fr.* Endymion. BPN
"Who—Who—the bride will be?" Who? Who? *Unknown.* CH
Who, who will be the next man to entrust his girl to a friend? Ezra Pound. *Fr.* Homage to Sextus Propertius. FaBoMo
Who will away to Athens with me? Thrasymedes and Eunoe. Walter Savage Landor. BPN; EmBrPo
Who will believe my verse in time to come. Sonnets, XVII. Shakespeare. AEV; EM-1; EnLi-1; EPP; PeBoSo; SiCE
Who Will Buy a Poem? Mahon O'Heffernan, *tr. fr. Early Modern Irish by* Kenneth Jackson. AnIL
Who Will Buy Me an Orange? José Gorostiza, *tr. fr. Spanish by* H. R. Hays. TwSpPo
Who will endure. Poems, XXV. W. H. Auden. CaAE
Who will feed the dicky-birds on the garden wall? Who? Florence Hoatson. BoTP
Who will go drive with Fergus now. Who Goes with Fergus? W. B. Yeats. CoEV; FaBoCh; LoGBV
Who will in fairest book of Nature know. Astrophel and Stella, LXXI. Sir Philip Sidney. MaPo; ReEn; ReIE; SiCE; SiPS
Who Will Mend Them? *Unknown, tr. fr. Japanese by* Ishii *and* Obata. OnPM
Who will protect you from the thrust of wings. To My Friend, behind Walls. Carolyn Kizer. NePoAm-2
Who will remember, passing through this Gate. On Passing the New Menin Gate. Siegfried Sassoon. AnEnPo; OBMV
Who will say a word for a country town of a sultry summer night? Not without Beauty. John A. B. McLeish. CaP
Who Will Shoe Your Pretty Little Foot? *Unknown. See* Lass of Lochroyan, The.
Who will show us where. At the Doors. "Der Nistor." TrJP
Who will watch thee, little mound. The Long Night. Harry Bache Smith. AA
Who wins his Love shall lose her. Lost Love. Andrew Lang. BMEP; BSV; HBV; LEAP
Who Wishes to Behold. Petrarch, *tr. fr. Italian by* Lord Charlemont. WoL
Who with the soldiers was stanch danger-sharer. The Daughter of the Regiment. Clinton Scollard. BIG; PAH
Who Won the War? Woodbury Pulsifer. PTA-1
Who would be/ A mermaid fair. The Mermaid. Tennyson. BoTP; BPN; FaPON; GN; GoTP; MPB; OTPC (1946 ed.); PCH; PoMS; TSW
Who would be/ A merman bold. The Merman. Tennyson. BoTP; BPN; FaPON; GN; GoTP; OTPC (1946 ed.); PCD; PCH; PoMS
Who would be loved, let him possess. Perfect Love. Sanai. PeP
Who would care to pass his life away. Comfort. Mortimer Collins. LPS-3
Who would have dreamed, hearing the wind at night. After a Symphony Concert. Katharine Shepard Hayden. MuM
Who Would Have Thought? George Herbert. PG (1955 ed.) ("Who would have thought my shrivelled heart.") EG; LO
Who Would Have Thought. Thomas Howell. *Fr.* The Lover Deceived Writes to His Lady. ElL
Who would have thought there could have bin. Of Tears. *Unknown.* LoPS
Who would linger idle. The Swimmer. Roden Noel. OBVV
Who would not be. The Laureate. William Aytoun. PA
Who would not love to go. Adventure. William Alexander Percy. LS
Who would please all, and himself, too. Well-packed Wisdom. Benjamin Franklin. *Fr.* Poor Richard's Almanac. StaSt
Who would true valour see. The Pilgrim [or The Pilgrim Song]. Bunyan. *Fr.* The Pilgrim's Progress. BoTP; CoMu; EV-2; GN; HBV; MaRV; OBS; OtMeF; OTPC; PCH; RG; TiPo (1952 ed.); WaKn
Who would wish back the saints upon our rough. At the Goal. Christina Rossetti. OQP; QP-1
Who writes by rule must please himself alone. The New Art of Making Plays. Lope de Vega. AnSpL-1
Who'd Be a Hero (Fictional)? Morris Bishop. FiBHP
Who'd believe me if. The Third Dimension. Denise Levertov. NeAP
Who'd love again on this old rambling star. Wisdom. Padraic Fallon. OnYI
Whoe'er she be. Wishes to His [or for the] Supposed Mistress. Richard Crashaw. AEV; AnFE; ATP; BCEP; BEL; BLV; CoBE; EnLit; EPS; EV-2; GoBC; GTBS; GTBS-D; GTBS-W; GTSE; GTSL; HBV; LEAP; LiTG; LiTL; LPS-1; MeLP; MePo; OAEP; OBEV; OBS; PoEL-2; ReEn; SeCL; SeCV-1; SeEP; ViBoPo; WHA
Whoe'er thou art, who walkest there. New England. Philip Henry Savage. OBAV
Whoe'er you are, your master see. Inscription for a Statue of Love. Voltaire. LiTW
Whoever [or Who ever] comes to shroud me, do not harm[e]. The Funeral[l]. John Donne. ATP; AWP; BrBE; CoBE; ElSeCe; EM-1; EnLi-1 (1949 ed.); EnLoPo; EPP; EPS; EV-2; InPo; JAWP; KN; LEAP; LiTL; LO; MeLP; OBEV; OBS; PoE; PoEL-2; PoRA; ReaPo; ReEn; SeCV-1; SeEP; TCEP; TOP; TuPP; TwHP; TwP; WBP
Whoever could have had such fortune. Count Arnaldos. *Unknown.* LyMA
Whoever [or Who ever] guesses, thinks, or dreames he knowes. The Curse. John Donne. EnLP; OAEP
Whoever hath her wish, thou hast thy "Will." Sonnets, CXXXV. Shakespeare. PeBoSo; ReEn
Whoever hath washed his hands of living. Courage. Sadi. *Fr.* The Gulistan. AWP; JAWP; OnPM; WBP
Whoever is washed ashore at that place. Legend. Ralph Gustafson. CaP
Whoever lives true life, will love true love. England [or The Sweetness of England]. Elizabeth Barrett Browning. *Fr.* Aurora Leigh, I. EV-4; VA
Who Ever Loved, That Loved Not at First Sight? Christopher Marlowe. *See* It Lies Not in Our Power to Love or Hate.
Whoever loves, if he do not propose. Love's Progress. John Donne. Elegies, XVIII. LiTB; LiTG; ViBoPo
Who ever saw so fair a sight. Constancy. Samuel Daniel. *Fr.* Hymen's Triumph. OBSC
Whoever sees my friend's, my Cato's cottage. Cato's Way of Life. Furius Bibaculus. LaP
Whoever weeps somewhere out in the world. Silent Hour. Rainer Maria Rilke. AWP; OnPM; WoL
Whoever with the compasses of his eyes. Waitress. Karl Shapiro. FiMAP; TwAmPo
Whoever without money is in love. Sonnet: Of Why He Is Unhanged. Cecco Angiolieri da Siena. AWP
Whoever you are: at evening step forth. Eingang (Prelude). Rainer Maria Rilke, *tr. by* M. D. Herter Norton. Po
Whoever you are, go out into the evening. Initiation. Rainer Maria Rilke, *tr. by* C. F. MacIntyre. TrJP
Whoever You Are Holding Me Now in Hand. Walt Whitman. InvP; PoEL-5

Whoever you are, I fear you are walking the walks of dreams. To You. Walt Whitman. APW; IAP
Whoever you are who wander near. The Poet's Father. Callimachus. OxBG
Whole assembly of elders gathered at the pier agreed, The. Kanaris. Alexandros Pallis. MoGP
Whole day have I followed in the rocks, The. Fergus and the Druid. W. B. Yeats. CoBE
Whole day long, under the walking sun, The. The Sleeping Giant. Donald Hall. NePoEA
Whole Duty of a Poem, The. Arthur Guiterman. PoToHe (new ed.)
Whole Duty of Berkshire Brooks, The. Grace Hazard Conkling. HBMV; HBVY; NLK; OBAV; PoTo
Whole Duty of Children. Robert Louis Stevenson. HBV; HBVY; NeHB; OTPC; PoVP; SAS; TreFS
Whole Duty of Man, The. Henry Vaughan. OQP; QP-1
Whole earth is at rest, and is quiet, The. Death of the King of Babylon. Isaiah, Bible, *O.T.* PoD
Whole health resides with peace. Description of Elysium. James Agee. CrMA
Whole showers of tears to Chloris I will pour. Chloris, IV. William Smith. TuPP
Whole Story, The. "Madeline Bridges." PR
Whole vast concourse of the Achaean host, The. Euripides. *Fr.* Hecuba. GrPo
Whole, wide world, turned selfless for a day, The. Alchemy. Adelaide Love. PGD
Whole world came to hear him speak that day, The. Lincoln at Gettysburg. Thomas Curtis Clark. PSO
"Whole World Kin, The." *Unknown, tr. fr. Greek by* F. L. Lucas. GrPE
Wholesome Strife. Hesiod, *tr. fr. Greek by* Sir William Marris. *Fr.* Works and Days. OxBG
Who'll Be a Witness for My Lord? *Unknown.* APW; BoAN-1, *with music;* OIF
Who'll buy my laces? I've laces to sell! The Lace Pedlar. Catherine A. Morin. BoTP
Who'll Buy My Valley Lilies? Eleanor Farjeon. BrR
Who'll come and play with me here under the tree. Employment. Jane Taylor. OTPC (1923 ed.); PPL
Who'll have the crumpled pieces of a heart? Laurana's Song. Richard Hovey. AA
Who'll Help a Fairy? *Unknown.* BoTP
Who'll Ride with Me? Wade Oliver. PFE
Who'll That Be. Kenneth Patchen. WaKn
Who'll Toll the Knell? Alfred Alvarez. PoN
Who'll walk the fields with us to town. Market Day. Mary Webb. CH
Whom answer'd thus Achilles, swift of foot. Achilles Unreconciled. Homer. *Fr.* The Iliad, IX. GrR
Whom does he love the most. The Hungry. Caroline Giltinan. OQP; QP-2
Whom I lay down for dead rises up in blood. In All the Argosy of Your Bright Hair. Dunstan Thompson. WaP
"Whom I shall kiss," I heard a Sunbeam say. Betrayal. John Banister Tabb. ACP
Whom Lesbia Loved. Catullus, *tr. fr. Latin by* Horace Gregory. LiTW
("Caelius, my Lesbia, that one, that only Lesbia.") RoL
"Whom lovest thou the best, enigmatical man." Prose Poem: The Stranger. Baudelaire. OnPM
Whom Shall One Teach. Isaiah, XXVIII: 9-13, Bible, *O.T.* TrJP
"Whom the Gods Love." Mark A. De Wolfe Howe. AA
Whom the gods love, die young; that man is blest. The Passing Show. Menander. GrPo; GrR
"Whom the gods love die young." The thought is old. I Die, Being Young [*or* In the Shadows]. David Gray. BMEP; VA
"Whom the gods love die young" was said of yore. Byron. *Fr.* Don Juan, IV. EnLit
Whom the untaught Shepherds call. Songs of the Pixies. Samuel Taylor Coleridge. OBEC
Whom thus answered the Arch Fiend now undisguised. Satan's Guile. Milton. *Fr.* Paradise Regained, I. LiTB; OBS
Whom We Revere. James Russell Lowell. *Fr.* Under the Old Elm, III. PGD
Whomsoe'er look I upon. Love-Song. *Unknown.* APW
Whomsoever among the heaven-fostered princes of earth. Gift of the Muses. Hesiod. *Fr.* Theogony. GrR
Who-o-o-o-o! Harry Silleck Grannatt. StaSt
Whoop! the Doodles have broken loose. "Call All." *Unknown.* BoHiPo; PAH
Whoopee, Ti Yi Yo, Git Along, Little Dogies. *Unknown.* ABS; AmPP; AS, *sl. abr., with music;* CoSo, *incl.* Owen Wister's *vers., with music;* CSF, *with music;* FaPON; IHA; InP; MPB; StVeCh (1940 ed.); TiPo; TreF; TSW, *abr.;* TSWC, *abr.;* WaKn
(Git Along, Little Dogies.) ABF, *with music;* MoShBr; StVeCh (1955 ed.)
(Run Along, You Little Dogies, *diff. vers., with music.*) OuSiCo
(Whoopie Ti Yi Yo, Git Along Little Dogies.) OTPC (1946 ed.)
Whoopin' up cattle. Clear Rock's Chisholm Trail. *Unknown.* CoSo
Whoppers. John A. Lomax, Jr. OuSiCo
Whore on the Snow Crust, The. *Unknown.* OnAP
Who's coming there, who's riding there? He prances with a zest! The City Lieutenant. Gustaf Fröding. AnSL
Who's crouching by the screen there. The Stonebreaker. Jeppe Aakjaer. BoDS
Who's In? Elizabeth Fleming. BoTP; BrR; MoSiPe
Who's in the Next Room? Thomas Hardy. PoEL-5
Who's knocking at the door? The Guide Within. Menander. *Fr.* Epitrepontes. GrR
Who's learned the lure of trodden ways. Highways. Leslie Nelson Jennings. NLK
Who's Most Afraid of Death? Thou. E. E. Cummings. SeCeV
Who's That a-Knocking? Emile Jacot. BoTP
Who's that a-knocking at my door? Rollicking Bill the Sailor. *Unknown.* AmSS
Who's That at My Bedroom Window? *with music.* *Unknown.* ShS
(Drowsy Sleeper, The.) ABS; BaBo (A *and* B *vers.*)
(Wake Up, Wake Up, Ye Drowsy Sleepers.) HiLiAm
(Willie and Mary.) ABS
Who's that beggar-man? Come and see. Caw, Caw. F. Hey. SAS
Who's That Calling So Sweet? —— Deveen. SCC
Who's that knocking at my door? Abram Brown. *Unknown.* SoAmSa
Who's that ringing at my door bell? *Unknown.* FaBoCh; LoGBV; OxNR
"Who's that ringing at the front door bell?" *Unknown.* BoTP
Who's the Fool Now? *Unknown. See* Martin to His Man.
Who's the Pretty Girl Milkin' the Cow? *with music.* *Unknown.* AS
Who's there? Shakespeare. *Fr.* Hamlet, I, i, iv, *and* v. ExPo
Who's this that comes, as each man looks at her. Sonnet. Guido Cavalcanti. LyPI
Who's Who. W. H. Auden. CoBMV; MoAB; MoBrPo (1950 ed.); MoPW; NeMA; ReMP
("Shilling life will give you all the facts, A.") CaAE; ChMo
Whose absolute dumbness circumscribed by sound. On First Hearing Beethoven. George Barker. UnS
Whose after-supper tattle's ever bent. For Choice. Anacreon. GrR
Whose candles light the tulip tree? Tulip Tree. Sacheverell Sitwell. MBP; MM; MoBrPo
Whose doorway was it, in the sordid street. The Rainbow. Vine Colby. AV; HBMV
Whose eye has marked his gendering? On his throne. The Tornado. Charles de Kay. EtS
Whose eyes have pierced that tragic East. Falcon. William Rose Benét. MOAP
Whose freedom is by suff'rance, and at will. William Cowper. *Fr.* The Task, V. EnRP; PoFr
Whose furthest footstep never strayed. Envoy. Richard Hovey. AA; HBV; LEAP; OBAV
Whose Hand. *Unknown, tr. fr. Hebrew by* Arthur Davis. TrJP
Whose is that noble dauntless brow? Verses Intended to Be Written below a Noble Earl's Picture. Burns. HoPM
Whose is the love that, gleaming through the world. To Harriet ——. Shelley. Queen Mab: Dedication. EmBrPo; EPN
Whose is the river, Excellency, whose the fish. The Geographers. Karl Shapiro. OxBA
Whose is the speech. The Two Poets. Alice Meynell. OBVV
Whose is this horrifying face. Ecce Homo. David Gascoyne. *Fr.* Miserere. ChMP; FaBoMo; FaBoTw; LiTM (rev. ed.); NeBP; OnHM
Whose little lanterns are those. The Automobile and the Cat. Elizabeth J. Coatsworth. DDA
Whose little pigs are these, these, these? *Unknown.* OxNR
Whose love's a broad highway. The Cul-de-Sac. "Jan Struther." LO
Whose minds like horse or ox. The Learned Men. Archibald MacLeish. MoAB; MoAmPo (1950 ed.)
Whose Old Cow? *Unknown.* CoSo; CSF
Whose powers shed round him in the common strife. Wordsworth. *Fr.* Character of the Happy Warrior. PC
Whose there, what light is that, wherefore comes thou? Edward's Death. Christopher Marlowe. *Fr.* Edward the Second. LiA
Whose voice shall say him nay? Siva, Destroyer. George Perry. OBAV
Whose were they those voices? What footsteps came near me? Dirge. Aubrey Thomas De Vere. IrPN
Whose whips are those cracking up the river? The Last Night of Winter. Winifred Welles. NP
Whose woods these are I think I know. Stopping by Woods

on a Snowy Evening. Robert Frost. AmP; AmPo; AmPP; AnFE; AnNE; APA; BLV; BoLiVe; CaAE; CBOV; ChMo; CMP; CoAnAm; CoBA; CoBMV; CoV; DDA; ExPo; FaBoCh; FaFP; FaPON; GBV (1952 ed.); GTBS-W; HBMV; HoPM; IAP; InP; InPo; LiTA; LiTG; LiTM; LoGBV; MAP; MaPo; MoAB; MoAmPo; MOAP; MoShBr; MoVE; MW; NeMA; NePA; NP; OTPC (1946 ed.); OxBA; PCD; PG (1955 ed.); PoE; PoeMoYo; PoFS; PoLFOT; PoRA; PoTo; PreP; ReMP; RiBV; ShBV-1; SiSoSe; StaSt; StVeCh; SUS; TBM; ThWaDe; TiPo; TreFS; TrGrPo; TSW; TSWC; TwAmPo; TwCV; TwP; UnPo (3d ed.); UTS; ViBoPo (1958 ed.); WaKn; WHA
Whose work could this be, Chapman, to refine. To My Worthy and Honoured Friend, Mr. George Chapman, on His Translation of Hesiod's Works and Days. Ben Jonson. PtP
Whoso Draws Nigh to God. *Unknown.* MaRV
Whoso has felt the Spirit of the highest. Knowledge. Frederic W. H. Myers. *Fr.* Saint Paul. OQP; QP-1
Whoso List to Hunt. Sir Thomas Wyatt. *See* Hind, The.
"Whoso Loseth His Life." Swinburne. *See* Unto Each His Handiwork.
Whoso That Will. Henry VIII, King of England. TuPP
Whoso the path of law would tread. The Inflamed Disciple. Arthur Kramer. InMe
Whoso thy witty writings thoroughly knows. In Senecam. John Heath. SiCE
Whoso to marry a minion wife. A Minion Wife. Nicholas Udall. *Fr.* Ralph Roister Doister. ElL
Whoso walks in solitude. Emerson. *Fr.* Woodnotes, II. OBVV
Whoso would see me by a God assaulted. Blissful Bane. Pierre de Ronsard. TrFP
Whosoe'er had look'd upon the glory of that day. Palermo. Harriet Eleanor Hamilton King. *Fr.* The Disciples. VA
Whosoever adapteth himself shall be preserved to the end. Paradoxes. Lao-tzu. *Fr.* Tao Teh King. GrCo-2
"Who've ye got there?"—Only a dying brother. "The Brigade Must Not Know, Sir!" *Unknown.* GA; MC; PAH; SPP
Whummil Bore, The. *Unknown.* CH; ESPB
Why. "Madeline Bridges." PR
Why. Bliss Carman. LBMV; OBEV (1st ed.); OBVV
Why? Stephen Crane. The Black Riders, XXV. AA; LEAP
Why. Adelaide Crapsey, *fr. the French.* MaRV
Why? Walter de la Mare. FiBHP
Why? Emily Dickinson. *See* Murmur of a bee, The.
Why. Robert Freeman. *See* Peace on Earth.
Why. Walter Savage Landor. *See* Why Do Our Joys Depart.
Why. Mikhail Lermontov, *tr. fr. Russian by* J. Pollen. BoR
Why? Robert Norwood. OQP; QP-1
Why? Mary Louise Ritter. LPS-1
Why? Edmund Clarence Stedman. *See* Si Jeunesse Savait!
Why. H. P. Stevens. BOHV
Why? *Fr.* The Talmud. TrJP
Why? Mary Webb. DiM
Why/ Is the sky? Questions at Night. Louis Untermeyer. FaPON; GoTP; OTPC (1946 ed.); RIS
Why Adam Sinned. Alex Rogers. BANP
Why all these fears and feigned alarms. Catalogue. Louis Untermeyer. HBMV
Why all this toil for triumphs of an hour? Life. *Unknown.* BOHV
Why am I if I am uncertain reasons may inclose. Stanzas in Meditation VI (1940). Gertrude Stein. OnAP
Why am I not an epigrammatist? Me Quoque Vatem. Thomas Freeman. SiCE; TuPP
Why am I silent from year to year? Why Silent. Henry Timrod. SPP
Why am I so specially happy? In the Train. Bodil Bech. BoDS
Why and Wherefore set out one day. Metaphysics. Oliver Herford. NA
Why are doors brass. Unquestionable Questions. Hy Sobiloff. SiTL
Why are her eyes so bright, so bright. Any Lover, Any Lass. Richard Middleton. HBV; OBVV
Why are not women fair. Peter Parasol. Wallace Stevens. NP
Why are the things that have no death. Irony. Louis Untermeyer. NP; TrJP
Why are these pipples taking their hets off? ? E. E. Cummings. FiBHP
Why are those hours, which Heaven in pity lent. To Cynthia Weeping and Not Speaking. Congreve. LiTL; LO; NBE
Why are thy looks so blank, grey friar? The Grey Friar. Thomas Love Peacock. ALV
Why are we [*or* wee] by all creatures waited on? Holy Sonnets, XII. John Donne. MaPo; OBS; PeBoSo; PoEL-2; TuPP
Why are we forever speaking. The Legion of Honor. H. L. Flash. BlG
"Why are we waiting, assembled in the public square?" Awaiting the Barbarians. C. P. Cavafy. MoGP
Why Are Ye Afraid, O Ye of Little Faith? Richard Crashaw. MeRV
Why are you always glad to me? A Guilty Father to His Daughter. James Schevill. FiMAP; Po
Why are you doing it this year, Spring? Spring Sows Her Seeds. Mary Carolyn Davies. NV
Why are you dragged to be stoned? Why? *Fr.* The Talmud. TrJP
Why are your eyes like dry brown flower-pods. Factory Girl. Maxwell Bodenheim. MAP; MoAmPo (1942 ed.)
Why Are Your Songs All Wild and Bitter Sad. James Thomson. Two Sonnets, I. PeBoSo
(Two Sonnets, I.) EmBrPo; PoVP
Why art thou bound and mayst go free? Shall reason yield to raging will? He Persuadeth His Friend from the Fond Affects of Love. Thomas Churchyard. ReIE
Why Art Thou Silent? Wordsworth. ERP; HBV; LoPo; OBRV
(Speak!) LoPS; OBEV
(To a Distant Friend.) BoFr; GTBS; GTBS-D; GTBS-W; GTSE; GTSL
("Why art thou silent? Is thy love a plant.") ES; LO
Why art thou slow, thou rest of trouble, Death. Song [*or* A Sad Song *or* Death Invoked]. Philip Massinger. *Fr.* The Emperor of the East. ACP (1952 ed.); ElSeCe; EV-2; OBS; SeCL; SeEP; TuPP; ViBoPo
Why art thou troubled, Herod? what vain fear. Herod's Suspicions. Richard Crashaw. StJW
Why, as to that, said the engineer. The Ghost That Jim Saw. Bret Harte. PoMS
Why be afraid of death, as though your life were breath? Death [*or* Emancipation]. Maltbie D. Babcock. BLRP; MaRV; OQP; QP-2; WBLP; WGRP
"Why?" Because all I haply can and do. Why I Am a Liberal. Robert Browning. BPN; EmBrPo; EnLi-2; EnLit; EPN; GEPC; HiLiEn; PoFr; PoVP; TCEP
Why bowest thou, O soul of mine. Heredity. Lydia Avery Coonley Ward. HBV
Why, Caelia, is your spreading waist. The Poet and His Patron. Edward Moore. Fables for the Ladies, V. CEP
Why call the miser miserable? The Power of Money. Byron. *Fr.* Don Juan, XII. CoEV
Why came I so untimely forth. To a Very Young Lady [*or* To My Young Lady Lucy Sidney]. Edmund Waller. EG; EV-2; LO; MePo; OAEP; OBS; PoFS; SeCL; SeEP; TrGrPo; ViBoPo
Why came the rose? Because the sun, in shining. Why? Mary Louise Ritter. LPS-1
Why cannot the Ear be closed to its own destruction? Blake *Fr.* The Book of Thel. FaBoEn
Why cannot the one good. The War God. Stephen Spender. BoFr; NeTW
Why Canst Thou Not. *Unknown.* EG; ElL; ElSeCe
(Song: "Why canst thou not, as others do.") LiTL
(Why Canst Thou Not, as Other Do.) OnPM
Why come ye hither, stranger? The Rifleman's Song at Bennington. *Unknown.* PAH
"Why coom ye hame sae soon, my son." The Ballad of the Prodigal Son. "W. H. S." CAG
Why, Cow, art thou so satisfied. Ode to a Cud-chewing Cow. *Unknown.* DDA
Why crack up our sires of aforetime. Drinking Song. Knud Lyhne Rahbek. BoDS
Why, cruel Herod, dost thou fear? The Magi Visit Herod. Caelius Sedulius. *Fr.* Carmen Paschale. CAW
Why, Damon, with the forward day. The Dying Man in His Garden George Sewell. GTBS; GTBS-D; GTBS-W; GTSE
Why, dear Cousin,/ why. Monks. Cardinal Newman. GoBC
Why, Death, what does thou here. On One Who Died in May. Clarence Chatham Cook. AA; LEAP
Why did I kiss you, sweet? Unforeseen. Richard Hovey. PR
Why Did I Laugh To-Night? Keats. ERP
(Sonnet: "Why did I laugh to-night?") AEV; NBE
Why did I print upon myself the names. Requiem—for the Death of a Boy. Rainer Maria Rilke. AnGP
Why did I sell you plated silver. Levy Silver. Edgar Lee Masters. *Fr.* The New Spoon River. ChMo; CMP
Why Did I Write ("Of all mad creatures"). Pope. *Fr.* Epistle to Dr. Arbuthnot. OBEC
Why did I write? what sin to me unknown. Pope. *Fr.* Epistle to Dr. Arbuthnot. BeR; ChTr; FiP; ViBoPo
Why did my parents send me to the schools. Of Human Knowledge. Sir John Davies. *Fr.* Nosce Teipsum. EV-2; ReIE; SiCE; SiPS; TuPP
Why did Perico kiss me? *Unknown, tr. fr. Spanish by* Eleanor L. Turnbull. TeCS
Why Did They Dig Ma's Grave So Deep? George Cooper. TreFS
Why did you come, with your enkindled eyes. Why? Mary Webb. DiM
Why did you die? I died of everything. Epitaphs, I. Lady Margaret Sackville. MM

Why did you give no hint that night. The Going. Thomas Hardy. EtPaEn; LiTB; MaPo; UnPo (3d ed.); ViPP
Why did you grow so big, Daddy. Playmates. Mary White Slater. FAOV
Why did you hate to be by yourself. As to Being Alone. James Oppenheim. PoMa; TrJP
Why did you lay there asleep. Fragment from "Clemo Uti—the Water Lilies." Ring Lardner. FiBHP
"Why did you melt your waxen man." Sister Helen. Dante Gabriel Rossetti. BEL; BeLS; BMEP; BPN; CBOV; DaM; EmBrPo; EnL; EnLi-2; EnLit; EPN; EPP; OAEP; PIAE; PoE; POTT; PoVP; REAL; ShBV-2; TCEP; TOP; TyEnPo; ViPo; ViPP; VLEP
Why didst thou carve thy speech laboriously. Father Gerard Hopkins, S.J. Joyce Kilmer. PtP
Why didst thou choose that cursèd sin. Saintship versus Conscience. Samuel Butler. *Fr.* Hudibras. BCEP
Why didst thou come into my life so late? To a Late Comer. Julia C. R. Dorr. AV; LBAP
Why didst thou promise such a beauteous day. Sonnets, XXXIV. Shakespeare. OBSC; PeBoSo; PoE
"Why do/ You thus devise." Susanna and the Elders. Adelaide Crapsey. AnAmPo; LA; MAP; MoAmPo (1942 ed.); NP
Why do bells for Christmas ring? *See* Why do the bells of Christmas ring?
Why Do I? Thomas Hardy. ChMo; CMP
Why do I curse the jazz of this hotel? The Jazz of This Hotel. Vachel Lindsay. ATP
Why do I deny manna to another? Sather Gate Illumination. Allen Ginsberg. NeAP
Why do I go on doing these things? Why Do I? Thomas Hardy. ChMo; CMP
Why do I languish thus, drooping and dull. Dullness. George Herbert. McRV; TriL
Why Do I Live? George Linnaeus Banks, *wr. at. to* Thomas Guthrie. *See* What I Live For.
Why do I love our flag? The Flag. Edward A. Horton. HH
Why do I love thee, Sir? Emily Dickinson. CoBA
Why Do I Love You? *At. to* Roy Croft. See Love.
Why do I praise a peach. The Genius of Greece. Walter Savage Landor. EmBrPo
Why do I sleep amid the snows. Roger Williams. Hezekiah Butterworth. PAH
Why Do I Use My Paper, Ink, and Pen. *Unknown.* ReIE
Why do men smile when I speak. Is It Because I Am Black? Joseph Seamon Cotter, Jr. BANP
Why Do Our Joys Depart. Walter Savage Landor. EmBrPo (Why.) EPP
Why do poets like to die. More Letters Found near a Suicide. Frank Horne. BANP
Why do the bells of [*or* do bells for] Christmas ring? Song [*or* Christmas Song]. Eugene Field, *wr. at. to* Lydia Avery Cooney Ward. BoTP; COAH; DD; GaP; GFA; HH; OHIP; PCH; PRWS; RAR; TiPo (1952 ed.); YeAr
Why do the houses stand. Song. George Macdonald. OBVV
Why do the wheels go whirring round. The Shadow Child. Harriet Monroe. BAP; HBV; LBAP
Why do they come? What do they seek. On a Replica of the Parthenon. Donald Davidson. MoVE
Why do they whistle so loud, when they walk past the graveyard late at night? Thirteen o'Clock. Kenneth Fearing. ExPo
Why do we follow, like a flock of sheep. Why? Robert Norwood. OQP; QP-1
Why do we greet thee, O blithe New Year! A New Year. Margaret E. Sangster. DD; PEDC; PEOR
Why do we labor at the poem. Reasons for Music. Archibald MacLeish. NePA
Why Do We Live? Israel Zangwill. TrJP
Why Do We Love. Sir Benjamin Rudyerd. ElL; ElSeCe
Why do [*or* doe] ye weep, sweet babes? To Primroses Filled with Morning Dew Robert Herrick. BCEP; EG; ElSeCe; EPS; EV-2; HBV; OBS; SeCL; SeCV-1; SeEP; ViBoPo
Why do you always stand there shivering. The Poplar. Richard Aldington. HBMV; NP; PoTo
"Why do you clasp me." Love and the Child. Francis Thompson. VLEP
Why do you cry out, why do I like to hear you. Sound of Breaking. Conrad Aiken. AnAmPo; AWP; InPo; LA; MAPA; MOAP
Why do you dig like long-clawed scavengers. Verlaine. E. A. Robinson. PtP
Why do you flutter in my arms and scream. Clipped Wings. Lew Sarett. PoMa
Why do you frown on me, you puritans. Petronius, *tr. fr. Latin by* Kenneth Rexroth. LaP
Why do you hide, O dryads! when we seek. Chant for Reapers. Wilfrid Thorley. OBEV (new ed.); OBVV
Who Do You Howl So Madly, Wind of Night? Feodor Ivanovich Tyutchev, *tr. fr. Russian by* Babette Deutsch. TrRV
Why do you lean beside the window, Will? Schoolroom: 158. James E. Warren, Jr. GoYe
Why do you lie with your legs ungainly huddled. The Dugout. Siegfried Sassoon. AtBAP; CH; MBP; MCCG; MoBrPo; MoVE; NeMA; OHIP; POTE; WaaP; WaP
Why do you listen, trees? Archibald MacLeish. *Fr.* The Farm. ChMo; CMP
"Why do you look so pale, my son William?" The Image. Sylvia Townsend Warner. BLV; BoLiVe (1939 ed.); InP; PIAE
"Why do you seek the sun." The Dreamer. Vachel Lindsay. LBMV
"Why do you stand in the dripping rye." The Woman in the Rye. Thomas Hardy. VLEP
Why do you tear from me my darling son. The Mothers' Lament at the Slaughter of the Innocents. *Unknown.* OnYI
Why do you tempt me, accursed roses. Torture. Sigbjörn Obstfelder. AnNoLy
Why Do You Walk through the Fields with Gloves? Frances Loveland. DDA
"Why do you wear your hair like a man." After Dilettante Concetti. Henry Duff Traill. BOHV; CenHV; HBV
Why do you, whenever you are addressed. Poet. Merrill Moore. MOAP
Why do ye weep, sweet babes? *See* Why do ye weep, sweet babes?
Why does a fire eat big sticks of wood? A Fire. Rachel Field. GFA
Why Does it Snow? Laura E. Richards. BrR; SiSoSe
Why does my husband beat me? Poor Me. *Unknown.* LyMA
Why does the crocodile weep, Mamma? The Crocodile. Laura E. Richards. UTS
Why does the fire burn so bright? The Nursery. Mrs. Motherly. SAS
Why does the king not pay. The Toothpick. Al-Hajjam. MooP
Why does the thin grey strand. Sorrow. D. H. Lawrence. OBMV
Why does the wind so want to be. The Wind. Elizabeth Rendall. BoTP; HBVY
"Why does [*or* dois] your brand sae [*or* sword so] drap wi[th] bluid [*or* blude *or* blood]." Edward [*or* Edward, Edward]. *Unknown.* ABS; AnFE; AtBAP; ATP; BaBo (B *vers.*); BBV; BEL; BLV; BoLiVe; BSV; CaAE; CBOV; CH; CoEV; EBSV; EM-1; EnLi-1; EnLit; EnRP; ESPB; ExPo; GoTS; HBV; HoPM (A *vers.*); LiTB; LiTG; MaC; OAEP; OBB; OBEV; OnSP; OuHeWo; PCN; PG (1955 ed.); PIAE; PoEL-1; PoRA; SeCeV; ShBV-3; TOP; TreFS; TrGrPo; TwHP; UnPo (1st ed.); ViBoFo (A *vers.*); WHA
Why Don't the Men Propose? Thomas Haynes Bayly. BOHV
Why don't you go back to the sea, my dear? Light Lover. Aline Kilmer. HBMV; LEAP
Why dost thou grieve, as rises from the sea. The Cloud. Salvador Díaz Mirón. PoFr
Why dost thou hail with songful lips no more. Memnon. Clinton Scollard. AA; BAP; OBAV
Why dost thou haste away. Madrigal. Sir Philip Sidney. *Fr.* Arcadia. EG; OBSC; SiPS
Why dost thou leave thy flowers, bee, to settle. Heliodora and the Bee. Meleager. GrR
Why dost thou lie in hushed surprise. The Little Lake. Bedros Tourian. ArmLP
Why dost thou like a Roman vestal make. Patrick Moloney. Sonnets—Ad Innuptam, V. BoAu
Why Dost Thou Shade Thy Lovely Face? Francis Quarles. *Fr.* Emblems. EV-2; MeLP; OxBoCh; SeCL; SeEP; TriL; TrPWD
(God Who Hides, The.) MaRV
(Wherefore Hidest Thou Thy Face, and Holdest Me for Thine Enemy?) MePo; OBS
Why dost thou shade thy lovely face? O, why. To His Mistress. Earl of Rochester. EPP; LEAP; LO; OBEV
Why dost thou weep, my child? Hottentot Cradle-Song. Fanny Raymond Ritter. BOL
Why dost thou wildly rush and roar. Mad River. Longfellow. PTA-2
Why Doth a Pussy Cat? Burges Johnson. BOHV
Why doth heaven bear a sun. An Ode. Barnabe Barnes. *Fr.* Parthenophil and Parthenophe. ElL; OBSC
Why doth the world study vain glory to attain. A Song. Thomas Ingelend. *Fr.* The Disobedient Child. CaAE
Why Doubt God's Word? A. B. Simpson. BLRP
Why East Wind Chills. Dylan Thomas. AtBAP; MaPo
Why fadest thou in death. Song. Richard Watson Dixon. CBE; ChTr
Why Fear to Die? Sir Philip Sidney. *Fr.* Arcadia. SiPS
Why fear to-morrow, timid heart? To-Day. Lydia Avery Coonley Ward. HBV; MaRV
Why fearest thou thy outward foe. That Each Thing Is Hurt of Itself. *Unknown.* ElL
Why from the danger did mine eyes not start. Sonnet: Of His Pain from a New Love. Guido Cavalcanti. AWP
"Why from the world," Ferishtah smiled. Robert Browning. *Fr.* Ferishtah's Fancies. BPN

Why get a chip on your shoulder. Big-lipped Negro. Nicolas Guillén. TwSpPo
Why groaning so, thou solid earth. Earth's Burdens. Ernest Charles Jones. VA
Why, Grubbinol, dost thou so wistful seem? Friday; or, The Dirge. John Gay. *Fr.* The Shepherd's Week. CEP; EiPP
Why has our poetry eschewed. Food and Drink. Louis Untermeyer. MAP; MoAmPo
Why hast thou breathed, O God, upon my thoughts. The Poet. Angela Morgan. TrPWD; WGRP
Why hast thou nothing in thy face? Ερως (Eros). Robert Bridges. ExPo; GTML; LiTB; LO; PoEL-5; RiBV; SeCeV; ViP
Why have/ I thought the dew. Why. Adelaide Crapsey. MaRV
Why have I come hither, after all? To Tu Fu from Sand Hill City. Li Po. BoFr
Why have the mighty lived—why have they died? Waterloo. Sir Aubrey De Vere. HBV
Why have ye no ruth of my dear child? Mater Dolorosa. J. Grimstone. TMEV
Why have you come if for a moment only. Imperatrix. Gustav Davidson. TBM
Why have you lit so bright a fire. The Last Guest. Frances Shaw. HBMV; NP
Why have you risen, to stand with naked feet. With the Dawn. Thomas Caulfield Irwin. EnLoPo; IrPN
Why, having won her, do I woo? The Married Lover. Coventry Patmore. *Fr.* The Angel in the House. EG; EPN; EV-5; GoBC; GTBS; HBV; LiTL; LoPS; OBEV; PIAE; POTT; PoVP; TrGrPo; VA
Why He Stroked the Cats. Merrill Moore. MOAP
Why He Was There. E. A. Robinson. ChMo; CMP
Why here, on this third planet from the Sun. Tellus. William Reed Huntington. AA
Why hoard your maidenhood? There Is No Loving After Death [*or* Carpe Diem]. Asclepiades. GrL; GrR; OxBG
Why how now, Babel? Whither wilt thou build? Quo Ruis ab Demens? London's Progress. Thomas Freeman. SiCE
Why how now, Cupid, grown so wild? Cupid Ungodded. James Shirley. GoBC
Why, hullo, Sextus! Left the farm? From the West. Martial. RoL
Why hurry, little river. The River. Frederick George Scott. CPG
Why I Am a Liberal. Robert Browning. BPN; EmBrPo; EnLi-2; EnLit; EPN; GEPC; HiLiEn; PoFr; PoVP; TCEP
Why I Am Not a Painter. Frank O'Hara. NeAP
Why I Drink. Henry Aldrich. ALV; LauV
("If on my theme I rightly think.") WhC
Why I Love Her. Alexander Brome. HBV; LO
Why I No Longer Travel. Laura E. Richards. MPB
Why I tie about thy wrist. The Bracelet to Julia. Robert Herrick. EG; EV-2; HBV; OBEV; TrGrPo
Why I Write Not of Love. Ben Jonson. ElSeCe; EnLit; OAEP; TuPP
Why, if Becchina's heart were diamond. Sonnet: Of Becchina, the Shoemaker's Daughter. Cecco Angiolieri da Siena. AWP
Why, if one should win a victory in the foot-race. Xenophanes, *tr. fr. Greek by* Emily Ann Wolff. GrPo
Why, if the seasons of life could be passed as a laurel. The Ninth Duino Elegy. Rainer Maria Rilke. *Fr.* The Duino Elegies. AnGP
Why, if 'tis dancing you would be. The Power of Malt. A. E. Housman. *Fr.* A Shropshire Lad, LXII. HBV; LEAP
Why, in Drunken Blend of Flute and Bugle. Stefan George, *tr. fr German by* Peter Viereck. AnGP
Why is a pump like Viscount Castlereagh. What's My Thought Like? Thomas Moore. BOHV; OBRV
Why is his name unsung. O minstrel host? Infelix Felix. Thomas D'Arcy McGee. TIP
Why Is It? Conrad Aiken. Priapus and the Pool, VII [VIII]. MOAP
"Why is it," Queen Edain said. Deirdre. W. B. Yeats. ViBoPo
Why is it that I cannot rest? Sleeplessness. Dwight Edwards Marvin. PraP
Why is it that the poets tell. Smells. Christopher Morley. PoeMoYo; PoMa; POT; PoTo; ShBV-1; YT
Why is it the children don't love me. Little Mamma. Charles Henry Webb. BOHV; FAOV
Why is it, when I am in Rome. On Being a Woman. Dorothy Parker. BOHV
Why is my daughter standing thus to-day? The Mystic Union. *Unknown.* OnPM
"Why is my district death-rate low?" Municipal. Kipling. WhC
Why is my verse so barren of new pride. Sonnets, LXXVI. Shakespeare. AEV; EnLi-1 (1949 ed.); InvP; NBE; PeBoSo; ReEn; ReIE; SiCE
Why Is Pussy in Bed? *Unknown.* OTPC (1923 ed.)
(Pussy in Bed.) CIV
Why is she not with you upon this feast. Sonnet for Selvaggia. Cino da Pistoia. LyPI
Why is there in the least touch of her hands. Quid Non Speremus, Amantes? Ernest Dowson. HBV
Why is your forehead deep-furrowed with care? Call Me Not Back from the Echoless Shore. *Unknown.* BLPA
Why It Was Cold in May. Henrietta Robins Eliot. AA
Why it's Mary—yes it must be. Spring. Jean Föyen. AnNoLy
Why, let the stricken deer go weep. Shakespeare. *Fr.* Hamlet, III, ii. CoBE
Why, let them rail! God's full anointed ones. Invincible. Sir Gilbert Parker. *Fr.* A Lover's Diary. VA
Why, Liquor of Life? Turlough Carolan, *tr. fr. Modern Irish by* John D'Alton. OnYI
Why listen, even the water is sobbing for something. The Maid's Thought. Robinson Jeffers. BAV
Why, little charmer of the air. To the Nightingale. Philip Ayres. CEP
Why look the distant mountains. The Refusal of Charon. William E. Aytoun. EBSV
Why look'st so solemn and so thought-absorbed? Hospitality. Euripides. *Fr.* Alcestis. GrPo; OxBG
Why, Lord. Mark Van Doren. TrPWD
Why, Love, beneath the fields of asphodel. George Edward Woodberry. Ideal Passion, XXXIII. HBMV; MOAP
Why, lovely charmer, tell me why. Song. Sir Richard Steele. *Fr.* The Tender Husband. HBV; LiTL; LPS-1; ViBoPo
Why loves my flower, the sweetest flower. The Wall-Flower. John Langhorne. *Fr.* The Fables of Flora. RO
Why make your lodging here in this spent lane. Wild Cherry. Lizette Woodworth Reese. AnAmPo; LA; MAP; MoAmPo
Why, man, he doth bestride the narrow world. Portrait of Caesar [*or* A Shakespeare Gallery: Caesar]. Shakespeare. *Fr.* Julius Caesar, I, ii. MaC; PIR; TrGrPo
Why mourn thy dead, that are the world's possession? To the Canadian Mothers. Duncan Campbell Scott. AOAH
Why must I be hurt? Pain. Elsie Robinson. PoToHe (new ed.)
Why Must You Know? John Wheelwright. CrMA; MeRV
Why, my heart, do we love her so? W. E. Henley. BPN
Why My Poems Died. Bhartrihari, *tr. fr. Sanskrit by* Arthur W. Ryder. OnPM
Why need a pretty woman chat. Why. "Madeline Bridges." PR
Why Not? *Unknown.* WhC
Why not come and see. An Invitation. Basho. OnPM
"Why not open your eyes." Foolish Emily and Her Kitten. Adelaide O'Keeffe. OTPC (1923 ed.)
Why, O willow, to the river. Feodor Tyutchev, *tr. fr. Russian by* W. A. Morison. BoR
"Why of the sheep do you not learn peace?" An Answer to the Parson [*or* Epigram]. Blake. OxBoLi; SiTL
Why pay more for your funeral when. An Undertaker's Advertisement. Ernest G. Moll. WhC
"Why, Phoebe, are you come so soon." The Blackberry Girl. Nancy Dennis Sproat. BLPA
Why Plague Me, Loves? Asclepiades, *tr. fr. Greek by* J. S. Phillimore. OxBG
Why practise, love, this small economy. To One on Her Waste of Time. Wilfrid Scawen Blunt. The Love Sonnets of Proteus, LVIII. ViBoPo
Why pray, of late, do Europe's kings. The Kings of Europe; a Jest. Robert Dodsley. CEP
Why, pretty rogue! do you protest. To Emma. Lady Burrell. DiM
Why puts our Grandame Nature on. On the Unusual Cold and Rainie Weather in the Summer, 1648. Robert Heath. OBS
Why Read a Book? Colette M. Burns. UTS
Why reproach me. Farewell to Po Chü I. Yüan Chen. PoHN
Why rouse from thy long winter sleep? A Queen Wasp. Walter de la Mare. AtBAP
Why, ruthless shepherds, from my dewy spray. The Cicada. *Unknown.* OxBG
Why say "death"? Death is neither harsh nor kind. The Presence. Robert Graves. ChMP
Why seraphim like lutanists arranged. Evening without Angels. Wallace Stevens. MoPo
Why shou'd I thus employ my time. An Ode on Miss Harriet Hanbury at Six Years Old. Sir Charles Hanbury Williams. OBEC
Why Should a Foolish Marriage Vow. Dryden. *Fr.* Marriage-a-la-Mode, I, i. InPo; LiTL; ViBoPo
(Song: "Why should a foolish marriage vow.") AWP; CEP; EiPP; SeCV-2
(Songs from the Plays.) OAEP
Why Should a Man. Shakespeare. *See* Let Me Play the Fool.
Why should a man. The Rose. Humbert Wolfe. MBP; MoBrPo; NP

Why should I blame her that she filled my days. No Second Troy [*or* Courage Equal to Desire]. W. B. Yeats. ChMo; EnLoPo; LiA; MaPo; NP; PoE; PoEL-5; SeCePo
Why should I care for the Ages. A Novelty. G. K. Chesterton. AlDL
Why Should I Care for the Men of Thames? Blake. ChTr; PoFr
Why Should I Grieve? Moses ibn Ezra, *tr. fr. Hebrew by* Solomon Solis-Cohen. TrJP
Why should I hate you, love, or why despise. In Answer to a Question. Wilfrid Scawen Blunt. The Love Sonnets of Proteus, XXVIII. ViBoPo
Why should I keep holiday. Compensation. Emerson. AnFE; AnNE; APA; CoAnAm; LiTA; TCAP
Why should I know or care what month it is? Calendar. Witter Bynner. *Fr.* Chapala Poems. NP
Why should I let the toad work. Toads. Philip Larkin. NePoEA
Why should I long for what I know. Prayer for Courage. Louis Untermeyer. OQP; PraP; QP-1
Why should I longer long to live. Being Forsaken of His Friend He Complaineth. "E. S." EIL; SiCE
Why should I say I see the things I see not? The Music of the World and of the Soul. Arthur Hugh Clough. VLEP
Why should I sing in verse, why should I frame. To Delia, XVII. Samuel Daniel. TuPP
Why should I sing of women. Song against Women. Willard Huntington Wright. HBV
Why should I stay? Nor seed nor fruit have I. The Bubble. John Banister Tabb. AA
Why should I think that heaven hears my prayer. Sonnet. Ariosto. LyPI
Why Should I Wander Sadly. Süsskind von Trimberg, *tr. fr. Middle High German.* TrJP
Why should I wish to see God better than this day? Beholding God. Walt Whitman. *Fr.* Song of Myself. GrCo-1
Why should my daily pathway seem. The Hills of God. Takamoto. SoLD
"Why should not Wattle do." Under the Wattle. Douglas Brook Wheelton Sladen. OBVV
Why should not we all be merry. *Unknown.* OBS
Why should she wait Death's bidding to begin. The Contemplative. Sister Mary Benvenuta. PraNu
Why Should the Spirit of Mortal Be Proud! William Knox. *See* Oh! Why Should the Spirit of Mortal Be Proud?
Why should this a desert be? Orlando's Rhymes. Shakespeare. *Fr.* As You Like It, III, ii. OBSC
Why should this flower delay so long. The Last Chrysanthemum. Thomas Hardy. ChMo; CMP; LiTB; PG (1955 ed.); PoVP; TwCV; ViP
Why should this Negro insolently stride. August. Elinor Wylie. AnEnPo; BAV; MAP; MoAB; MoAmPo; NeMA; PIAE; PoeMoYo
Why should those birds disturb us as they walk. The Night Walkers. Kendrick Smithyman. AnNZ
Why should thy look requite so ill. A Paradox. William Herbert, Earl of Pembroke. EIL
Why should vain mortals tremble at the sight of. The American Hero [*or* Bunker Hill]. Nathaniel Niles. IAP; PoFr; TrAS; WaaP
Why should we argue with the falling dust. Romance. Scudder Middleton. SBMV
Why Should We Mourn? *Unknown.* BPP
Why should we tremble to convey. The Dead. Isaac Watts. *Fr.* The Death and Burial of a Saint. BeR
Why should we waste and weep? Fledglings. Thomas Lake Harris. AA
Why Should We Weep for Those Who Die. Charles Tennyson Turner. MaRV
Why should you be so full of spight. *Unknown.* SeCSL
Why should you [*or* shouldst thou] swear I am forsworn. The Scrutiny [*or* Song]. Richard Lovelace. BOHV; EG; ElSeCe; EnLit; EnLoPo; EPS; InMe; LO; MeLP; MePo; OBS; ReEn; SeEP; TrGrPo
Why should you thinke me so unwise. *Unknown.* SeCSL
Why should your fair eyes with such sovereign [*or* sovran] grace. Against Knowledge in Loving. Michael Drayton. Idea, XLIII. ES; OBSC
Why shouldst thou cease thy plaintive song. To an Obscure Poet Who Lives on My Hearth. Charles Lotin Hildreth. AA
Why shouldst thou swear I am forsworn. *See* Why should you swear I am forsworn.
Why Silent. Henry Timrod. SPP
Why, silly Man! so much admirest thou. George Wither. *Fr.* A Collection of Emblemes, Ancient and Moderne. SeCV-1
Why sing the legends of the Holy Grail. The Frozen Grail. Elsa Barker. LBMV; LEAP
Why sits she thus in solitude? Her heart. The Old Maid. Amelia B. Welby. LPS-3
Why Sitt'st [*or* Sit'st] Thou by That Ruined Hall. Sir Walter Scott. *See* Time.
Why slander we the times? Bad Times. Joseph Beaumont. MaRV
Why so impatient, my heart? He Cares. Kabir. MaRV
"Why so often, silent one." The Musing Maiden. Thomas Hardy. BEL
Why So Pale and Wan [Fond Lover]? Sir John Suckling. *Fr.* Aglaura, IV, ii. AEV; ALV; AnFE; AWP; BBV (1923 ed.); BCEP; BEL; BLV; CenL; CoBE; EG; ElSeCe; EM-1; EnL; EnLi-1; EnLit; EPP; HoPM; InPo; JAWP; LiTG; LiTL; LoPo; LPS-1; MCCG; OBEV; OBS; OtMeF; OuHeWo; PoFS; PoMa; PoRA; ReaPo; RiBV; SeCePo; SeCL; ShBV-4; TOP; TreFS; TrGrPo; TyEnPo; ViBoPo; WBP; WHA
(Advice to a Lover.) CBOV
(Constant Lover, The.) NeHB; PG
(Encouragements to a Lover.) BTP; FaFP; GTBS; GTBS-D; GTBS-W; GTSE; GTSL; PYM
(Orsames' Song.) AnEnPo
(Song: "Why so pale and wan, fond lover?") CaAE; EnLoPo; EPS; EV-2; HBV; InP; LEAP; LoBV; MePo; PoE; PoEL-3; PoeMoYo; ReEn; SeCV-1; SeEP; TCEP; TwHP
(Why So Pale?) OnPM
Why so triumphs the world in pomp and glory vain. Saint Bernard's Verses. *At. to* St. Bernard of Clairvaux. SiCE
"Why so young, and set." The Young Pilgrim. Ibn Faddal. MooP
Why Sould Nocht Allane Honorit Be? *Unknown.* EBSV
Why stand ye, nurslings of Earth, before my gates. The Over-Song of Niagara. John Daniel Logan. CPG
"Why stand you, gentle mother." Premonition. Laura Goodman Salverson. CaP
Why, Star of Morning, foe to Love. Favoritism. Meleager. GrR
Why stayes my Floramell where love. *Unknown.* SeCSL
Why the British Girls Give In So Easily. Nicholas Moore. WaP
Why the Dog's Nose Is Always Cold. *Unknown.* PTA-2
Why the Robin's Breast Was Red. James Ryder Randall. AA; CAW; JKCP
Why the unbroken spiral, Virtuoso. Apple Peeler. Robert Francis. CrMA; NePoAm
Why, then, let Pholegandros or Sikinos be my city. The Shame of Losing Salamis. Solon. GrPE
Why then (quod I) old proverbs never fail. George Gascoigne. LO
Why, then thou canst not break her to the lute? Shakespeare. *Fr.* The Taming of the Shrew, II, i. UnS
Why, then, 'tis time to arm and give direction. Shakespeare. King Richard III, *fr.* V, iii. PoFr
Why this flower is now called so. How the Wallflower Came First and Why So Called. Robert Herrick. EV-2
Why those knit brows, ye Catos of the age? All the Heaven. Petronius. OnPM
Why Thus Longing? Harriet Winslow Sewall. AA; LPS-2
Why thy Round Table dost to a Square prefer? King Arthur's Round Table. John Ower. *Fr.* Four Epigrams. PrWP
Why Tomas Cam Was Grumpy. James Stephens. ChMo; CMP; WhC
Why Travel. Patience Eden. DDA
Why wait we for the torches' lights? Let Us Drink. Alcaeus. AWP
Why was Cupid a boy. Cupid. Blake. BOHV
Why was I born into this dismal age. War. Hedd Wyn. PrWP
Why was my breeding order'd and prescrib'd. Milton. *Fr.* Samson Agonistes. PoFr
"Why weep ye by the tide, ladie?" Jock of [*or* o'] Hazeldean. Sir Walter Scott. BEL; BeLS; BPN; CoBE; EBSV; EmBrPo; EnLi-2; EnLit; EnRP; EPN; ERP; EV-4; GN; GTBS; GTBS-D; GTBS-W; GTSE; GTSL; HBV; HiLiEn; MCCG; OAEP; OBRV; OTPC; TCEP; TOP
"Why weep ye [*or* 'e] by the tide, ladye." John of Hazelgreen [*or* Haselgreen]. *Unknown.* BaBo; ESPB (E *vers.*)
Why weep you, Conan of Fortingall. Conan of Fortingall. J. Corson Miller. TBM
Why weeping, mother? and why veil your eyes. Chivalry. Euripides. *Fr.* Suppliants. OxBG
Why Were Ye Calliope Embrawdred with Letters of Golde? John Skelton. CaAE
Why were you born when the snow was falling? A Dirge. Christina Rossetti. ChTr; LoBV; ViPo
Why were you hailed a sacred thing. Ibis. *Unknown.* BLA
Why what's the world and time? a fleeting thought. Insignificance of the World. Thomas Lovell Beddoes. *Fr.* Fragments Intended for the Dramas. ERP
"Why, when the world's great mind." The World and the Quietest. Matthew Arnold. VA
Why, whenever she can spy me. To Chloe [*or* Time to Choose a Lover]. Horace. Odes, I, 23. LiTW; OnPM
Why, where have you been? I go a-Walking. Barbara Young. DDA
Why, who makes much of a miracle? Miracles. Walt Whitman. APW; BBV (1951 ed.); CaAE; CoBA; GoTP; GrCo-1; HBVY; LaNeLa; NeMA; OQP; PoMa; QP-2. StVeCh; VOD (1935 ed.); WaKn; YT

Why, Why Repine. Walter Savage Landor. BPN; EmBrPo; EPN; LEAP
(Lyrics and Epigrams.) ERP
(Resignation.) HBV; OBEV (1st ed.); TyEnPo; WP
Why will they never sleep. Ode. John Peale Bishop. LiTA; LiTM; MoPo; MoVE; NePA
Why will ye ever/ With unjust hatred. King Alfred's Metres of Boethius: Metre XXVII. Boethius. BoFr
Why will you haunt me unawares. Mathilde Blind. *Fr.* Love in Exile. VA
Why will you haunt my sleep? A Dream. Andrew Lang. BSV
"Why, William, on that old gray [*or* grey] stone." Expostulation and Reply. Wordsworth. BEL; BPN; EM-2; EmBrPo; EnL; EnLi-2; EnLit; EnRP; EPN; EPP; ERP; GEPC; HBV; OAEP; OBRV; PoE; TwP; UnPo
"Why wilt thou cast the roses from thine [*or* thy] hair?" Mary Magdalene at the Door of Simon the Pharisee. Dante Gabriel Rossetti. BPN; EmBrPo; GoBC; PoVP; VA
Why with scorn-reverting eye. Anacreon, *tr. fr. Greek by* Addison. GrPo
Why ye Blossome Cometh before ye Leafe. Oliver Herford. AA; ADAH
Why, yes, dear, we can put it by. It does seem out of place. Grandmother's Quilt. *Unknown.* PTA-2
Whyle that the sunne with his beames hot. *See* While that the sun with his beams hot.
Whylom, as olde stories tellen us. *See* Whilom, as olde stories tellen us.
Whylom ther was dwellinge at Oxenford. *See* Whilom ther was dwellynge at Oxenford.
Whylome, as antique stories tellen us. Spenser. *Fr.* The Faerie Queene, IV, 2. PtP
Whym Chow. "Michael Field." BoFr
Wi' a hundred pipers an' a', an' a'. The Hundred Pipers. Lady Nairne. CBOV; EBSV
Wick of my lamp, The. The Bell in the Night. Hsi P'ei Lan. PoHN
Wicked barons laid the landscape waste, The. The Middle Ages: Two Views. Leah Bodine Drake. NePoAm-2
Wicked one lies buried here, A. An Epitaph. *Unknown.* ShGoBo
Wicked Polly. *Unknown.* ABF; ABS (A *and* B *vers.*)
Wicked witch, A. Poison Ivy! Katharine Gallagher. SiSoSe
Wickedest Man in Memphis, The. Alex J. Brown. BeLS
Wickedness of Poets. Xenophanes, *tr. fr. Greek by* F. L. Lucas. GrPE
Wicklow. George Francis Savage-Armstrong. *Fr.* De Verdun of Darragh. TIP
Wicklow Scene, A. George Francis Savage-Armstrong. *Fr.* Lugnaquillia. TIP
Wid his di'mond blade. Long Gone. *Unknown.* ABF
Wid Thady's Pipe beside the Door. "Madeline Bridges." JKCP (1926 ed.)
Widdicombe [*or* Widdecombe] Fair. *Unknown.* BBV (1951 ed.); CH; MoShBr; MuP; OBB; OnSP; PoMS; WP
Widdy-widdy-wurkey. The Family. *Unknown.* TiPo (1959 ed.)
Wide acres you inherit. Beauty's Nomads. Vyacheslav Ivanov. BoR
Wide amorphous sea, The. Form. Polly Chase Boyden. NP
Wide and curling ocean, The. By the Sea. Marchette Chute. StVeCh (1955 ed.)
Wide and shallow, in the cowslip marshes. Vermont. Sarah N. Cleghorn. HBMV; PoeMoYo; VOD
Wide and wider spreads the vale. John Dyer. *Fr.* Grongar Hill. EnSW
Wide are the meadows of night. Wanderers. Walter de la Mare. AlDL; CP
Wide as this night, old as this night is old. Lullaby. Kenneth Fearing. ChMo
Wide desolate river, the low bare shore, The. Niagara. J. C. Squire. PtOT
Wide door into sorrow, The. The Narrow Doors. Fannie Stearns Davis. HBMV; SBMV
Wide-eyed all night in the weatherworn inn. Mountain Hamlet. Lew Sarett. PoMa
Wide fields of corn along the valleys spread. Lo, I Am with You Always. John Charles Earle. ChIP; MaRV; OQP; QP-1
Wide flocks of narrow birds have fled. Light the Lamp Early. Raymond Holden. MAP; MoAmPo (1942 ed.)
Wide Front Porch. Leslie N. Jennings. DDA
Wide gates swung open, The. Little Nan. *Unknown.* MDAH; PEOR
Wide green earth is mine in which to wander, The. The Unwilling Gypsy. Josephine Johnson. HBMV
Wide Haven. Clement Wood. SBMV
Wide is the world and wide its open seas. The Keeper. Arthur Stringer. MaRV
Wide Missouri [*or* Mizzoura], The. *Unknown.* *See* Shenandoah.
Wide mouth, no ears nor eyes, A. *Unknown.* *Fr.* Riddles. CoBE
Wide o'er the fields, in rising moisture strong. Robert Bloomfield. *Fr.* The Farmer's Boy. EnSW
Wide o'er the valley the pennons are fluttering. The Siege of Chapultepec. William Haines Lytle. MC; PAH
Wide open and unguarded stand our gates. Unguarded Gates. Thomas Bailey Aldrich. AA; AnNE; MC; PAH
Wide Open Spaces, The. Oscar H. Lear. InMe
Wide pastures, thatch of turf, and ancient spire. George Herbert. Thomas S. Jones, Jr. PtP
Wide sleeves sway. Dancing. Yang Kuei-fei. FaPON
Wide-spreaded Night. Keats. *Fr.* Lamia. LiA
Wide sun stares without a cloud, The. Written in Australia. Arthur Adams. BoAu
Wide Walls. *Unknown.* PoToHe (new ed.)
Wide was the land. The Coming of the White Man. Patrick Anderson. *Fr.* Poem on Canada. CaP
Wide waters in the waste; or, out of reach. "Rivers Unknown to Song." Alice Meynell. HBMV; NP
Wide, Wide World, The. Kipling. *Fr.* In the Neolithic Age. OtMeF
Widely is flung, warning of slaughter. The Song of the Norns [*or* The Song of the Valkyries]. *Unknown.* LiTW; PaOS; WaaP
Widen the circle, O. Christmas Tree. V. Lebedev-Kumach. RuPo
Widow, The, *sel.* Thomas Middleton.
"Give me fortune, give me health." TuPP
Widow, The. Allan Ramsay. HBV
Widow, The. Robert Southey. OBEV
Widow, The ("Oi! beneath the wooden hill-top"). *Unknown, tr. fr. Ukrainian by* Florence Randal Livesay. CPG
Widow, The ("Sweet, my child"). *Unknown, tr. fr. Sicilian song.* BOL
Widow, The. William B. Wheelwright. CAG
Widow and Child. Tennyson. *See* Home They Brought Her Warrior Dead.
Widow at Windsor, The. Kipling. OAEP (2d ed.)
Widow Bedott Papers, The, *sel.* Frances Miriam Whitcher.
Widow Bedott to Elder Sniffles. BOHV; LPS-3
Widow Bell's Pictures, *sel.* Al Hall.
"Whenever the last of the year fades into darkening night." FeBoPe
Widow Bird [Sate Mourning], A. Shelley. *Fr.* Charles the First, sc. v. AtBAP; BoTP; CG; CH; EPN; EV-4; FaPON; MPB; OBRV; OTPC (1946 ed.); SeCeV
(Song: "Widow bird sate mourning for her love, A.") BPN; FaBoEn; KN; LoBV; PoEL-4; ShBV-1; ThWaDe; WP
("Widow bird sate [*or* sat] mourning for her love, A.") CBE; GTBS; GTBS-D; GTBS-W; GTSE; LO
(Winter.) BLV; CBOV; PIAE; StaSt
Widow Brown's Christmas. John Townsend Trowbridge. BeLS
Widow can bake and the widow can brew, The. The Widow. Allan Ramsay. HBV
Widow Machree. Samuel Lover. *Fr.* Handy Andy. HBV; LPS-1; TIP; VA
Widow Malone, The. Charles Lever. *Fr.* Charles O'Malley, the Irish Dragoon. BOHV; HBV; LPS-3; TIP; TreFS
Widow-Mother. Ada Jackson. NeTW
Widow of Drynam, The. Patrick MacDonogh. NeIP; OnYI; OxBI
Widow-ology. Charles Graham Halpine. PR
Widow poor, somewhat advanced in age, A. The Nun's Priest's Tale, *mod.* Chaucer. *Fr.* The Canterbury Tales. OuHeWo
Widow, A—she had only one! The Widow's Mite. Frederick Locker-Lampson. HBV; LPS-1; MOAH; VA
Widow Speaks, The. William Dunbar. *Fr.* The Tua Mariit Wemen and the Wedo. PoEL-1
Widow That Keeps the Cock Inn, The. *Unknown.* CoMu
Widow, well met; whither go you today? A Contention betwixt a Wife, a Widow, and a Maid. Sir John Davies. OBSC; SiPS
Widowed Heart, The. Albert Pike. AA
Widows. Edgar Lee Masters. MoAmPo
Widows be woeful whose husbands be taken, The. A Ballad of the Rising in the North. *Unknown.* ACP
Widow's Hymn, A. George Wither. *See* Hymn for a Widower or a Widow . . .
Widow's Lament in Springtime, The. William Carlos Williams. CoBMV; NP
Widow's Lullaby, The. Sydney Dobell. BOL
Widow's Lullaby, The. *Unknown, tr. fr. Welsh and arr. by* Alma Strettel. BOL
Widow's Mite, The. Frederick Locker-Lampson. HBV; LPS-1; MOAH; VA
Widow's Mites, The. St. Luke, XXI: 2-4, Bible, *N.T.* GrCo-1
Widow's Mites, The. Richard Crashaw. LPS-2; OxBoCh
Widow's Solace, The. Thomas Deloney. SiCE
Widow's Song, The. Edward Coote Pinkney. *See* Votive Song.

Widow's Weeds, A. Walter de la Mare. AtBAP
Widsith, *sels.* *Unknown, tr. fr. Anglo-Saxon.*
Anglian Tradition, The, *tr. by* Francis B. Gummere. PaOS
Lone Man, The. PoLi
Widsith, the Minstrel, *tr. by* Charles W. Kennedy. AnOE
Wie langsam kriechet sie dahin. Heine, *tr. fr. German by* Richard Monckton Milnes. AWP
Wife, The. Phoebe Cary. BOHV
Wife, The. Anna Peyre Dinnies. AA
Wife, The. Theodosia Garrison. HBV
Wife, The. William Livingston. BAV
Wife, A. Sheridan. BOHV
Wife, A. Sir Henry Taylor. *Fr.* Philip van Artevelde. LPS-1
Wife, The. *Unknown, tr fr. Chinese by* Henry H. Hart. OnPM; PoHN; WoL
Wife a-Lost, The. William Barnes. EnLoPo; EV-4; GTBS; GTBS-D; OBEV; OBVV
Wife and servant are the same. A Caveat to the Fair Sex. Lady Mary Wortley Montagu. DiM
Wife at daybreak I shall be, A. Emily Dickinson. CoBA; CoV; IAP; OnAP
Wife at Usher's Well, The. *Unknown. See* Wife of Usher's Well, The.
Wife, Children, and Friends. William Robert Spencer. LPS-1
Wife for a Month, A, *sel.* John Fletcher.
To the Blest Evanthe. SeCL; SeEP
Wife from Fairyland, The. Richard Le Gallienne. HBV; LBMV
Wife-Hater, The. *Unknown.* CoMu
Wife I Do Hate, A. William Wycherley. SeCL
Wife of Aed mac Ainmirech, King of Ireland, Laments Her Husband, The. *Unknown, tr. fr. Old Irish by* Myles Dillon. AnIL
Wife of Auchtermuchty, The. *Unknown.* EBSV; GoTS
Wife of Bath [and the Parson], The. Chaucer. *See* Canterbury Tales, The: Prologue.
Wife of Bath's Prologue, The. Chaucer. *Fr.* The Canterbury Tales. EnL, *mod. by* Theodore Morrison; EnLi-1 (1949 ed.); OxBoLi, *abr.*
(Prologue to the Wife of Bath's Tale, The.) PoEL-1
"My fifthe housbonde, god his soule blesse," *sel., abr.* FiP
Wife of Bath's Tale, The. Chaucer. *Fr.* The Canterbury Tales. EnL, *mod. by* Theodore Morrison; EnLit
(Tale of the Wyf of Bathe, The.) REAL
(Wife of Bath, The.) LiA
"In th' olde dayes of the Kyng Arthour," *25 ll.* ViBoPo
Wife of Judas Iscariot, The. Cale Young Rice. BAP; StJW; TBM
Wife of Kelso, The, *with music.* *Unknown.* ShS
Wife of Llew, The. Francis Ledwidge. LBBV; LEAP; MBP; PoMS
Wife of Loki, The. Lady Charlotte Elliot. VA
Wife of Usher's Well, The. *Unknown.* AnFE; AtBAP; AWP; BaBo (A *and* B *vers.*); BEL, *abr.*; BLV; BoLiVe; BrBE; BSV; CBE; CBOV; CH; ChTr; DaM; EBSV; EM-1; EnLi-1; EnRP; EnSB; ESPB (A, B, C, *and* D *vers.*); EV-2; ExPo; GoTS; HBV; InP, *sl. abr.*; InPo; JAWP; LiTB; LoBV, *sl. abr.*; OAEP; OBB; OBEV; OuHeWo; PoEL-1; REAL; ReaPo; RiBV; SeCeV; ShBV-2; TCEP; TiPo (1952 ed.); TOP; TreF; TrGrPo; TwHP; UnPo; UnW; ViBoFo (A, B, *and* C *vers.*); WBP
(Wife at Usher's Well, The.) EnL
Wife Speaks, The. Mary Stanley. AnNZ
Wife to a Husband, A. Hsi P'ei Lan, *tr. fr. Chinese by* Henry H. Hart. PoHN
Wife to Her Husband, The. *Unknown.* HBV; LPS-1
Wife to Husband. Christina Rossetti. VA; ViPo
Wife Waits, A. Thomas Hardy. At Casterbridge Fair, VI. BEL; EmBrPo; EnLi-2 (1949 ed.); EnLit; PoVP
Wife was sitting at her ree' ae night, A. The Strange Visitor. *Unknown.* ChTr; FaBoCh
Wife who is charming, obedient, and chaste, A. The Good Wife. Sadi. PeP
Wife-Woman, The. Anna Spencer. BANP
Wife Wrapt [*or* Wrapped] in Wether's Skin. *Unknown.* ABS; BaBo (A, B, *and* C *vers.*); ESPB (A, B, D, *and* F *vers.*); ViBoFo (A *and* B *vers.*)
(Dandoo.) ABS; TrAS, *with music*
Wife's Grave, A. Damagetus, *tr. fr. Greek by* R. A. Furness. OxBG
Wife's Lament, The. Nikolai Nekrasov, *tr. fr. Russian by* Juliet M. Soskice. *Fr.* Who Can Be Happy and Free in Russia? BoR
Wife's Lament, The. *Unknown, tr. fr. Anglo-Saxon by* Charles W. Kennedy. AnOE; LiTW; LyMA
Wife's Prayer, The. Antipater of Thessalonica, *tr. fr. Greek by* F. L. Lucas. GrPE
Wife's Song, A. William Cox Bennett. HBV
Wife's Song, The. Elizabeth J. Coatsworth. DDA
Wife's Song, The. Anna Wickham. LBBV
Wil the Merry Weaver, and Charity the Chamber-Maid; or, A Brisk Encounter between a Youngman and His Love. *Unknown.* CoMu
Wilbur Wright and Orville Wright. Rosemary Benét *and* Stephen Vincent Benét. PoMa
Wild air, world-mothering air. The Blessed Virgin Compared to the Air We Breathe. Gerard Manley Hopkins. ISi; MoPo; OxBoCh; PoLi
Wild and plunging seas have smote our sides, The. Columbus. Percy Hutchison. EtS
Wild and wet, and windy wet falls the night on Hamilton. Hamilton. Marie E. J. Pitt. MoAu
Wild and windy morning is lit with lurid fire, The. Tyre. Bayard Taylor. LBAP
Wild and woeful race he ran, A. The Outlaw. Robert W. Service. AlBD; CV
Wild Animals. Elizabeth Fleming. StVeCh
Wild Apple. Elise Aylen. TwCV
Wild Ass. Padraic Colum. MBP; MoBrPo; NP
Wild Beast. Pierre de Ronsard, *tr. fr. French by* Alan Conder. TrFP
Wild Beasts. Evaleen Stein. MPB (1956 ed.); RAR; UTS
Wild Bees. James K. Baxter. AnNZ
Wild bird filled the morning air, A. The Fowler. W. W. Gibson. BMEP; HBMV; PoTo
Wild bird, whose warble, liquid sweet. In Memoriam A. H. H., LXXXVIII. Tennyson. BEL; BPN; EM-2; EmBrPo; EPN; GEPC; OAEP; ViPo; VLEP
Wild birds flying across the moon. If There Be Any Gods. "Seumas O'Sullivan." BMEP
Wild birds on the roof are bitterly complaining to man, The. Seeking Spring beyond the City. Su T'ung-po. WhP
Wild Blossoms. W. H. Davies. MeRV
Wild Bronc Peeler. *Unknown.* CoSo
Wild Carthage held her, Rome. A Puritan Lady. Lizette Woodworth Reese. AnAmPo; InP; LA; MAP; MoAmPo; NP
Wild Cats. Vachel Lindsay. MAP; MoAmPo
Wild Cherry. Jeanne Robert Foster. TBM
Wild Cherry. Louise Townsend Nicholl. NePoAm
Wild Cherry. Lizette Woodworth Reese. AnAmPo; LA; MAP; MoAmPo
Wild Colonial Boy, The. *Unknown.* NeLNL; OuSiCo, *with music;* ViBoFo
(Wild Montana Boy, The, *diff. vers.*) CoSo
Wild Common, The. D. H. Lawrence. CoBMV
Wild Deer. Hafiz, *tr. fr. Persian by* A. J. Arberry. PeP
Wild Duck, The. Leroy McLeod. BLA
Wild Duck, The. John Masefield. BEL; ShBV-2; WP
Wild Duck and Her Brood, The. James Grahame. EnSW
Wild Duck's Nest, The. Wordsworth. EnSW
(Sonnet: Wild Duck's Nest, The.) ChER
Wild Eden, *sels.* George Edward Woodberry.
Child, The, XXX. AA
Divine Awe, XVI. AA; LBAP
Homeward Bound, XXV. AA
O, Inexpressible as Sweet, VII. AA; BAP; HBV; PFY
(Song: "O, inexpressible as sweet.") InMe
O, Struck beneath the Laurel, XXXIII. AA; PFY; TCPD
Rose of Stars, The, IX. AA; HBV
Seaward, XLI. AA
Secret, The, VI. AA; BAP; HBV; LBMV
So Slow to Die, XXXVIII. AA
When First I Saw Her, V. AA; BAP; HBV
Wild Eden, III. HBV
Wild eyes—and faces ashen grey. Stars. Dowell O'Reilly. BoAu
Wild Flower Man, The. Lu Yu, *tr. fr. Chinese by* Kenneth Rexroth. OnPC
Wild Flowers. Peter Newell. NA
Wild Flowers and Potted Plants. Ibsen, *tr. fr. Norwegian by* Charles W. Stork. AnNoLy
Wild Flower's Song. Blake. BoTP
Wild Geese. Elinor Chipp. BLA; FaPON; HBMV; MPB; TiPo
Wild Geese. Grace Noll Crowell. BLA
Wild Geese. Ise, *tr. fr. Japanese by* Basil Hall Chamberlain. OnPM
Wild Geese, The. James Herbert Morse. AA
Wild Geese. Frederick Peterson. BLA; DDA; HBV; HBVY; OBAV; OTPC (1923 ed.)
Wild Geese. Celia Thaxter. PRWS; SN; UTS
Wild Geese Katharine Tynan. GoTP
Wild Geese, The. *Unknown, tr. fr. Chinese by* Henry H. Hart. PoHN
Wild Geese Come Over No More, The. Cale Young Rice. BLA
Wild geese, flying in the night, behold, The. The Wild Geese. James Herbert Morse. AA
Wild Geese in Midwinter. Stanley E. Babb. HiLiAm
Wild Goat, The. Claude McKay. CDC
Wild goose, wild goose. Haiku Issa. LiTW; OnPJ
Wild heart in me that frets and grieves. Primrose Hill. Olive Custance. JKCP

Wild Home-Pussy, The. Emma Rounds. RIS
Wild Honey. Maurice Thompson. AnFE; APA; CoAnAm; HBV; OBAV
Wild Honeysuckle, The. Philip Freneau. AA; AmP; AmPP; AnAmPo; APW; BAP; BAV; CoBA; CoV; HBV; HiLiAm; IAP; LA; LEAP; LiTA; MOAP; OxBA; PoEL-4; RiBV; TCAP; TrGrPo
Wild Horse Jerry's Story. Sarah Elizabeth Howard. PoOW
Wild Huntsman, The, *abr.* Gottfried A. Bürger, *tr. fr. German by* Sir Walter Scott. CG
Wild Huntsmen, The. Philip Gilbert Hamerton. VA
Wild Idyll. Manuel José Othón, *tr. fr. Spanish by* Samuel Beckett. AnMP
Wild Iron. Allen Curnow. AnNZ
Wild is its nature, as it were a token. Song of the Palm. Tracy Robinson. AA
Wild Joys of Living, The. Robert Browning. *Fr.* Saul, IX. BLV; MuP
(David Sings to Saul.) GTML
(David's Song.) BoLiVe
(Joy of Living, The.) ShBV-2
(Saul: "Oh, our manhood's prime vigor!") OtMeF
(Saul: "Oh, the wild joys of living.") PC
(Youth.) BoTP
Wild Knight, The. G. K. Chesterton. WGRP
"So, with the wan waste grasses on my spear," *br. sel.* MaRV
Wild Larkspur. Annie Charlotte Dalton. CPG
Wild March. Constance Fenimore Woolson. YeAr
Wild Marjorie. "Jean Lorrain," *tr. fr. French by* Wilfrid Thorley. CAW
Wild Miz-zou-rye, The. *Unknown. See* Shenandoah.
Wild Montana Boy, The. *Unknown. See* Wild Colonial Boy, The.
Wild nights—Wild nights! Emily Dickinson. AmP; AmPP (4th ed.); LoPS; OxBA
Wild Old Wicked Man, The. W. B. Yeats. AnIL; AtBAP
Wild Past. Paul Verlaine, *tr. fr. French by* Alan Conder. TrFP
Wild Peaches (I-IV). Elinor Wylie. AmP; LiTA; LiTM (rev. ed.); NAMP; OxBA
"Down to the Puritan marrow of my bones," *sel.* InP; PIAE
(Puritan Sonnet.) MAP; MoAB; MoAmPo; NeMA; TrGrPo
(Sonnet: "Down to the Puritan marrow of my bones.") PoeMoYo
Wild pear trees shout up Tinges Lane. Roads. Lizette Woodworth Reese. DaM
Wild Philomela. William Rose Benét. NP
Wild pigeon of the leaves. Birds. *Unknown. Fr.* The Thousand and One Nights. AWP; LiTW
Wild Plum. Orrick Johns. DDA; HBMV; LEAP; MAP; NP; PG (1945 ed.); PoeMoYo; TBM
Wild Rattling Cowboy, A. *Unknown.* CoSo
Wild Red Wine, The. Holger Drachmann, *tr. fr. Danish by* Charles W. Stork. BoDS
Wild Ride, The. Louise Imogen Guiney. AA, *abr.*; BAP; CAW; CBOV; CP; HBV; JKCP; MAP; MoAmPo (1942 ed.); NV; OBAV; PC; PFY; POT; PoTo; TCAP
Wild Rippling Water, The, *with music. Unknown.* CoSo
Wild Romantic Dell, A. William Julius Mickle. *Fr.* The Concubine, II. OBEC
(Wyld Romantic Dell, A.) RO
Wild Rose. William Allingham. GN, *abr.*; OTPC
Wild Rose, The. Hermann Hagedorn. PFY
Wild Rose of Alloway! my thanks. Burns. Fitz-Greene Halleck. AA; LPS-3; TCAP
Wild Rose of Plymouth, The. Jones Very. TCAP
Wild Roses. Edgar Fawcett. HBV
Wild Roses. Mary Effie Lee Newsome. CDC
Wild Rovers. *Unknown.* CSF
Wild scream, and the vortex whirls him down, A. The Death of the Eagle. José Maria de Heredia. *Fr.* Les Trophées. LiA
Wild sea, A. Haiku. Basho. OnPJ
Wild Strawberries. Robert Graves. FaBoCh; LoGBV
Wild strawberries, gooseberries, trampled. Ave Eva. John Wheelwright. MoPo
Wild stream the clouds, and the fresh wind is singing. The Hunt. Harriet Prescott Spofford. AA
Wild Swan, The. D. S. Savage. NeBP
Wild Swan. *Unknown, tr. fr. Anglo-Saxon by* Charles W. Kennedy. *Fr.* Riddles. AnOE
Wild Swans. Edna St. Vincent Millay. BAP; MAP; MM; MoAmPo
Wild Swans at Coole, The. W. B. Yeats. BLA; BLV; BoLiVe; ChMo; ChTr; CMP; CP; EnLi-2 (1949 ed.); EnLP; GTBS-D; GTIV; MaPo; MBP; MoAB; MoBrPo; MoVE; NP; OAEP (2d ed.); OnYI; Po; PoVP; ReMP; TCEP; TwCV; TwHP; TyEnPo; VLEP; WHA
Wild the sea clamors from its echoing caves. All Souls' Eve. Mary E. Mannix. GoBC
Wild Thyme. Eleanor Farjeon. SiSoSe
Wild Thyme. Joyce Sambrook. BoTP
Wild Trees, The. Laurie Lee. GTBS-D
Wild Violet, The. Hannah Flagg Gould. PEOR
Wild was the day; the wintry sea. The Twenty-second of December. Bryant. DD; GA; HH; MPB; PEOR
Wild was the night, yet a wilder night. The Death of Napoleon. Isaac McLellan. BAP; PECK
Wild was Vingthor when he awoke. The Lay of Thrym [*or* Thrymskvitha]. *Unknown. Fr.* The Elder Edda. LiA; LiTW; OuHeWo
Wild Weather. Katharine Lee Bates. PGD
Wild Weather. Dryden. *Fr.* All for Love, I, i. BoW
("Portents and Prodigies are grown so frequent.") AtBAP
Wild white camel, camel wild, what behind. Camel. Gene Derwood. NePA
Wild White Rose, The. Ellen H. Willis. PTA-1
Wild, wild the storm, and the sea high running. Patrolling Barnegat. Walt Whitman. GTSE; LoBV; NePA
Wild, wild wind, wilt thou never cease thy sighing? The Dead Church. Charles Kingsley. VA
Wild Willow. James Wreford Watson. TwCaPo
Wild wind batters/ Window-panes. Aleksandr Blok, *tr. fr. Russian by* C. M. Bowra. BoR
Wild wind blows, the sun shines, the birds sing loud, The. *See* Wind blows, the sun shines . . . , The.
Wild Winds. Mary Frances Butts. OTPC; PRWS
Wild winds weep, The. Mad Song. Blake. BCEP; BEL; CEP; EiPP; EM-1; EnLi-2; EnLit; EnRP; NBE; PoE; PoEL-4; PoRA; TrGrPo
Wild Wishes. Ethel M. Hewitt. HBV
Wild with passion, sorrow-beladen. Song on the Water. Thomas Lovell Beddoes. EG; ERP
Wild Woman's Lullaby, The. Constance Lindsay Skinner. BOL; CPG
Wild Wreath, The. *Unknown.* OTPC (1923 ed.)
Wildebeest, The. June Daly. FaPON
Wilderness, The. Caroline Hazard. ChIP; StJW
Wilderness. Leslie Nelson Jennings. MuM
Wilderness, The. Gyula Juhasz, *tr. fr. Hungarian by* Watson Kirkconnell. LiTW
Wilderness, The. Sidney Keyes. LiTB; LiTM (rev. ed.); NeBP
Wilderness, The. E. A. Robinson. BAV; POT; PoTo
Wilderness. Carl Sandburg. AnAmPo; LA
Wilderness. Katsumi Tanaka, *tr. fr. Japanese by* Takamichi Ninomiya *and* D. J. Enright. PoLJ
Wilderness a secret keeps, The. Ecce in Deserto. Henry Augustin Beers. AA; AnFE; APA; CoAnAm; OBAV
Wilderness Is Tamed, The. Elizabeth J. Coatsworth. *See* Axe Has Cut the Forest Down, The.
Wildgrave winds his bugle horn, The. The Wild Huntsman. Gottfried A. Bürger. CG
Wilding, The. Philip Booth. NePoEA
Wildly round our woodland quarters. The Lumbermen. Whittier. BHV; WoL
Wildness. Gerard Manley Hopkins. *Fr.* Inversnaid. OtMeF
Wildness. Blanche Shoemaker Wagstaff. BAP; HBMV
Wildwest. Archibald MacLeish. Frescoes for Mr. Rockefeller's City, II. ReaPo; ReMP; UnPo
Wilful waste brings woeful want. *Unknown.* OxNR
Wilhelm Meister, *sels.* Goethe, *tr. fr. German.*
Mignon, *fr.* Wilhelm Meister's Apprenticeship, *Bk.* III, *ch.* 1. LiA, *tr. by* Edgar A. Bowring; LiTW, *tr. by* Anthony Hecht; LPS-3, *tr. by* Felicia Dorothea Hemans
(Mignon's Song, *tr. by* James Elroy Flecker.) AWP; JAWP; WBP
Sorrow, *fr.* Wilhelm Meister's Apprenticeship, *Bk.* II, *ch.* 13, *tr. by* Gretchen Warren. MaRV
(Who Never Ate with Tears His Bread, *tr. by* Farnsworth Wright.) WGRP
Will, The. John Donne. ATP (1935 ed.); EM-1; EnLP; EPS (1942 ed.); LiA; LiTB; LiTG; LPS-3; MePo; SeEP; TOP; TuPP
Will. Tennyson. BHV; BPN; EmBrPo; EPN
Will. Ella Wheeler Wilcox. BLPA; NeHB; PoToHe
Will Beauty Come. Robert Nathan. HBMV
Will came back from school that day. Dunkirk. Robert Nathan. MaC; NeTW; OnSP
Will days, indeed, yet come in forgiveness and grace. When You Will Walk in the Field. Leah Goldberg. TrJP
Will dissolves, the heart becomes excited, The. Soliloquy in an Air-Raid. Roy Fuller. LiTM
Will Ever? Walter de la Mare. GBV
Will ever the perilous dip of a plane's wing. Twentieth Century Songs. Elsa Gidlow. PreP
Will he always love me? Lady Horikawa, *tr. fr. Japanese by* Kenneth Rexroth. OnPJ
Will he ever be weary of wandering. Will Ever? Walter de la Mare. GBV
"Will He Give Him a Stone?" Abbie Huston Evans. QS
Will he love me forever? Lady Horikawa, *tr. fr. Japanese by* I. W. Furukami. LiTW

Will He No Come Back Again? *Unknown.* OBEC; OBEV (new ed.), *abr.*
Will I cease to be. Lady Izumi Shikibu, *tr. fr. Japanese by* Kenneth Rexroth. OnPJ
Will It Be So? Edith M. Thomas. *Fr.* The Inverted Torch. AA
Will it be whole of limb and clear of brain. Au Revoir. Alexander Robertson. MM
Will it ne'er be morning? Will that promised light. Sweet Phosphor, Bring the Day. Francis Quarles. EPS (1942 ed.)
Will lightning strike me if I take. Thoughts of Loved Ones. Margaret Fishback. FiBHP
Will Love again awake. Muse and Poet. Robert Bridges. OBMV
Will mortals never know each other's station. Milton. Walter Savage Landor. NBE; RO
Will night already spread her wings and weave. Night-Thoughts. Solomon ibn Gabirol. TrJP
Will not Fear, Favor, Bribe, and Grutch. Tyranny and Law. Samuel Butler. *Fr.* Hudibras. BeR
Will not our hearts within us burn. The White Presence [*or* "Follow Me"]. Joseph Fort Newton. ChIP; MaRV; OQP; QP-1
Will-o'-the-Wisp. Sumako Fukao, *tr. fr. Japanese by* Takamichi Ninomiya *and* D. J. Enright. PoLJ
Will-o'-the-Wisp, The. Annie Campbell Huestis. CPG
Will o' the Wisp. George Meredith. BMEP
Will of God, The. Frederick William Faber. MaRV; VA
Will of God be done by us, The. Blessed Be the Holy Will of God. *Unknown.* OnYI
Will of God we must obey, The. The Death of King Edward VII. *Unknown.* OxBoLi
Will of Writing, The. James Schevill. FiMAP
Will people accept them? Tenzone. Ezra Pound. CoV
Will seeing Concan make a dog a lion? Ritual Not Religion. *Unknown.* WGRP
Will Shakespeare, *sel.* "Clemence Dane."
Him I Follow. QS
Will Shakespeare's out like Robin Hood. Alfred Noyes. *Fr.* Tales of the Mermaid Tavern. POTT
Will sprawl, now that the heat of day is best. Caliban upon Setebos. Robert Browning. AWP; BPN; EM-2; EmBrPo; EPN; GEPC; OAEP; PoVP; ViPo; VLEP; WGRP
Will Stewart and John. *Unknown.* ESPB
Will the wolves lie down with the lambs and feed them? The End of Sorrow. Edmond Fleg. *Fr.* The Wall of Weeping. TrJP
Will there come a day. Prayer to St. Francis. Frances Frost. SaFP
Will there never come a season. The Pedestrian's Plaint. E. V. Lucas. CenHV
Will there never come a season. To R. K. [*or* Lapsus Calami *or* The Millennium]. James Kenneth Stephen. BOHV; CenHV; EnLi-2 (1949 ed.); OtMeF; VA; WhC
Will there really be a morning? Emily Dickinson. SiSoSe
(Child's Question, The.) WGRP
(Morning.) AA; BoChLi; FaPON
Will they ever come to me, ever again. "This Is Alone Life, Joy, Empire and Victory" [*or* Where Shall Wisdom Be Found?]. Euripides. *Fr.* Bacchae. GrR; OxBG; UnS
Will they fight? They say so. Arthur Hugh Clough. *Fr.* Amours de Voyage, II. SoV
Will they never fade or pass! The Farmer Remembers the Somme. Vance Palmer. MoAuPo
Will they stop. Requiem. Kenneth Fearing. ChMo; TriL
Will to Serve, The. Joseph B. Gilder, *wr. at. to* Jeannette L. Gilder. *Fr.* The Parting of the Ways. OQP; QP-2
("Be thou guardian of the weak.") MaRV
Will Warner. William Aspenwall Bradley. BAP
Will winter never be over? February. Adeline D. T. Whitney. YeAr
Will ye gang wi' me and fare. The Bush aboon Traquair. John Campbell Shairp. EBSV; OBVV
"Will ye gang wi' me, Lizzy Lindsay." *See* "Will you gang wi' me, Leezie Lindsay."
Will ye go to the ewe-bughts, Marion. Ewe-Bughts, Marion. *Unknown.* EBSV
Will Ye No Come Back Again? Lady Nairne. DiM; EBSV; ShBV-1
Will ye see what wonders love hath wrought. Sir Thomas Wyatt. SiPS
Will ye that I should sing. A Lady of High Degree. *Unknown.* AWP
Will You Be as Hard? Douglas Hyde, *tr. fr. Irish by* Lady Gregory. GTIV; OBMV
Will You Be My Little Wife. Kate Greenaway. MoShBr
(Will You?) MeMeAg; SiSoSe
Will You Buy Any Tape? Shakespeare. *Fr.* The Winter's Tale, IV, iii. GaP; OBSC; SiCE; ViBoPo
(Songs of Autolycus, The, 3.) OTPC (1923 ed.)
Will You Come? Edward Thomas. AlDL; CH; LoBV; MM
Will you come a boating, my gay old hag. The Gay Old Hag. *Unknown.* IrPN
Will you come as of old with singing. Winter Night Song. Sara Teasdale. ChMo; CMP; MOAP; TwCV
Will you come back? 1536–1936. Emyr Humphreys. MoWP
Will you come to the bower I have shaded for you? Walter Savage Landor. *Fr.* A Reply to Lines by Thomas Moore. ChTr
Will you come to Turvy Land. Topsy-turvy Land. Phyllis M. Stone. BoTP
"Will you [*or* ye] gang wi' me, Leezie [*or* Lizzy] Lindsay." Leezie [*or* Lizzy] Lindsay. *Unknown.* EBSV; FaBoCh; LoGBV
Will you glimmer on the sea? Moonrise. Hilda Doolittle ("H. D."). NP
Will you hear a Spanish lady. The Spanish Lady's Love. *Unknown.* CG; OBB
Will you hear of a bloody battle? The Downfall of Piracy [*or* Teach the Rover]. *At. to* Benjamin Franklin. PAH; SG
Will you heare a tale of Robin Hood. Robin Hood and the Pedlars. *Unknown.* ESPB
Will you know. *Unknown.* SeCSL
Will you knowe my mistris face. *Unknown.* SeCSL
Will you lend me your mare to ride but a mile? *Unknown.* OxNR
Will you, like other men. Impulsive Dialogue. Maxwell Bodenheim. NP
Will You Love Me When I'm Old? *Unknown.* BLPA; FaBoBe; NeHB
Will You, One Day. Marian Ramié. HBMV
Will You Perhaps. Delmore Schwartz. *See* "Mentrechè il Vento, Come Fa, Si Tace."
Will you take a sprig of hornbeam? Forester's Song. A. E. Coppard. FaPON; MPB
"Will you take a walk with me." The Clucking [*or* Clocking] Hen. Ann Hawkshaw. BoTP; HBVY; OTPC; PPL; SAS
"Will you trot a little quicker?" said a Lily to a Fox. Dolly's Dogs. "Lewis Carroll." BoN
"Will you walk a little faster?" said a whiting to a snail. The Lobster Quadrille [*or* The Mock Turtle's Song *or* The Whiting and the Snail]. "Lewis Carroll." *Fr.* Alice's Adventures in Wonderland. BoChLi; BoTP; ChTr; EnLi-2; FaPON; HBV; HBVY; MoShBr; MPB (1956 ed.); OTPC (1946 ed.); PA; PCD; PCH; PoVP; PRWS; RAR; RIS; SAS; StVeCh; TiPo (1952 ed.); UTS
"Will you walk into my parlor?" said the Spider to the Fly. The Spider and the Fly. Mary Howitt. BeLS; FaFP; FaPON; GFA; HBV; HBVY; OHFP; OnHT; OnSP; OTPC; RIS; TreFS; TVC; TVSH; WBLP
Will you wear white, O my dear, O my dear? Jennie Jenkins. *Unknown.* OuSiCo
William and Agnes Pringle. W. W. Gibson. CMP
William and Helen. Sir Walter Scott, *imitated fr.* Lenore (*by* Gottfried August Bürger). BPN; EmBrPo; EnRP; ERP; OAEP
William and Margaret. David Mallet. BSV; CEP; EBSV; EPP; EV-3; OBEC
William and Marjorie. *Unknown.* *See* Sweet William's Ghost.
William and Mary. *Unknown.* OxNR
William Blake. Dante Gabriel Rossetti. Five English Poets, 2. BPN; EmBrPo; PoVP; PtP
(Two English Poets.) BMEP
William Blake. James Thomson. EmBrPo; HBV; OAEP; OBVV; POTT; PoVP; PtP; VLEP
William Blake Sees God. Roy McFadden. NeIP
William Bond. Blake. MyFE
"I thought love lived in the hot sunshine," *sel.* LO
William Brown of Oregon. Joaquin Miller. BOHV
William Cullen Bryant. Fitz-Greene Halleck. PEOR
William Dewy, Tranter Reuben, Farmer Ledlow late at plough. Friends Beyond. Thomas Hardy. CoBMV; MaPo; OBEV (new ed.); OBVV; PoD; POTT; PoVP; TCPD; ViP
William I—1066. Eleanor Farjeon. BBV (1951 ed.)
William Glen. *Unknown.* BaBo
(Captain Glen.) SG
William Grismond's Downfall, *sel.* *Unknown.*
"There in the broom I killed her." SG
William H. Herndon. Edgar Lee Masters. *Fr.* Spoon River Anthology. NP; SBMV; TOP
William Jake Hall. Campfire and Bunkhouse. *Unknown.* CoSo
William Jones. Edgar Lee Masters. *Fr.* Spoon River Anthology. ImOP
William Lloyd Garrison. James Russell Lowell. LPS-3
William Longbeard. Thomas Lodge. *See* Life and Death of William Longbeard, The.
William McTrimbletoe. *Unknown.* OxNR
William Morris. Idris Davies. MoWP
William of Nassau, scion. Ballad to William of Nassau. *Unknown.* PoFr
William O'Kelly. James Stephens, *after the Irish of* Raftery. BoFr
William P. Frye, The. Jeanne Robert Foster. MC; PAH
William Reilly's Courtship. *Unknown.* ABS
William Shakespeare. Swinburne. *Fr.* Sonnets on English

Dramatic Poets. BMEP; BPN; PIAE; PoVP; TrGrPo; VLEP
William Shakespeare to Mrs. Anne, Regular Servant to the Rev. Mr. Precentor of York. Thomas Gray. CEP
William Tell, *sel* James Sheridan Knowles.
Switzerland. LPS-2; PoFr
William Tell, *poem.* Schiller, *tr. fr. German by* Sir Edward Bulwer-Lytton. PoFr
William the Bastard. "Lakon." FiBHP
William the Conqueror long did reign. England's Sovereigns in Verse. *Unknown.* BLPA
William the Conqueror, ten sixty-six. *Unknown.* OxNR
William the First was the first of our kings. William I—1066. Eleanor Farjeon. BBV (1951 ed.)
William Wilson. Malcolm Cowley. *Fr.* Blue Juniata. AnAmPo; LA; MoVE
William Wordsworth. Sidney Keyes. ChMP; GTBS-D; POTE; SeCePo
William Wordsworth. Francis Turner Palgrave. PtP; VA
Willie and Earl Richard's Daughter. *Unknown. See* Birth of Robin Hood, The.
Willie and Helen. Hew Ainslie. EBSV; HBV; OBEV (1st ed.)
("Wherefore sou'd ye talk o' love.") LO
Willie and Lady Maisry (A *and* B *vers.*). *Unknown.* ESPB
Willie and Mary ("O who is at my bedroom window"). *Unknown. See* Who's That at My Bedroom Window.
Willie and Nellie, one evening sat. Willie's and Nellie's Wish. Julia A. Moore. FiBHP
Willie [*or* Willy] boy, Willie boy, where are you going? Mother Goose. BoTP; OxNR; RIS; SAS; StVeCh
Willie Brew'd [*or* Brewed] a Peck o' Maut. Burns. AWP; BEL; CaAE; CEP; EBSV; EM-1; EnLi-2; EnLit; EnRP; InPo; JAWP; REAL; TOP; ViBoPo; WBP
(O, Willie Brew'd a Peck o' Maut.) EnL
(Willie Brewed.) EV-3; OAEP
Willie Drowned in Yarrow. *Unknown. See* Willy Drowned in Yarrow.
Willie, fold your little hands. By the Alma River. Dinah Maria Mulock Craik. LPS-2
"Willie has taen him o'er the fame." Willie's [*or* Willy's] Lady. *Unknown.* BaBo; ESPB; OBB
Willie in his roguish way. *Unknown.* WhC
"Willie is fair, and Wille's rair." Rare Willie Drowned in Yarrow (D *vers.*). *Unknown.* ESPB
Willie Leonard; or, The Lake of Cold Finn. *Unknown.* BaBo
Willie Macintosh. *Unknown.* ESPB (A *and* B *vers.*); OBB; OxBoLi; ViBoFo
Willie o Douglas Dale. *Unknown.* BaBo; ESPB
Willie o Winsbury. *Unknown.* BaBo; ESPB (A *and* D *vers.*)
Willie Reilly. *Unknown. See* Willy Reilly.
Willie saw some dynamite. Little Willie. *Unknown.* FaPON
Willie stands in his stable-door. The Mother's Malison; or, Clyde's Water. *Unknown.* BaBo; BSV
Willie, take your little drum. Burgundian Carol [*or* Patapan]. Bernard de la Monnoye. ChBR; UnS
Willie the Weeper. *Unknown.* ABF, *with music;* APW; BeLS; BLPA; SoAF, *with music;* TrAS, *diff. vers., with music;* YaD
(Willy the Weeper, *diff vers., with music.*) AS
Willie Was a Wanton Wag. William Hamilton. EBSV
Willie was a widow's son. Willie and Lady Maisry. *Unknown.* ESPB
Willie was an onion. Vegetable Fantasies. Helen Hoyt. RIS
Willie Wastle dwalt on Tweed. Sic a Wife as Willie Had. Burns. GoTS
"Willie, Willie, I'll learn you a wile." Willie's Lyke-Wake. *Unknown.* ESPB
"Willie, Willie, what makes you sae sad?" Willie's Lyke-Wake. *Unknown.* OBB
Willie Winkie. William Miller. BOL; FaFP; HBV; HBVY; LPS-1; PECK; VA
(Wee Willie Winkie.) BoChLi, *st.* 1; GaP, *st.* 1; PCH; RIS, *st.* 1; SAS; SiSoSe, *st.* 1; StVeCh, *st.* 1
("Wee Willie Winkie runs through the town," *st.* 1.) OxNR; TiPo
Willie, with a thirst for gore. Careless Willie. *Unknown.* FaPON
Willie Wolf. Helen Cowles LeCron. GFA
Willie's and Nellie's Wish. Julia A. Moore. FiBHP
"Willie's fair, an Willie's rare." Rare Willie Drowned in Yarrow; or, The Water o Gamrie. *Unknown.* BaBo
Willie's Fatal Visit. *Unknown.* BaBo; ESPB
Willie's Gane to Melville Castle, *with music. Unknown.* SaSa
Willie's Lady. *Unknown.* BaBo; ESPB; ViBoFo
(Willy's Lady.) OBB
Willie's Lyke-Wake. *Unknown.* BaBo; ESPB; OBB, *diff. vers.*
Willie's taen him o'er the fame. Willie's Lady. *Unknown.* ViBoFo
Willing Couple, The. *Unknown. See* Jovial Tinker, The.
Willing Mistress, The. Aphra Behn. *See* Amyntas Led Me to a Grove.
Willis, The. David Law Proudfit. AA
Willobie His Avisa, *sel. At. to* Henry Willoby.
To Avisa. ElL
Willoughby liked being Willoughby. The Contentment of Willoughby. Frances Alexander. GoYe
Willow, The. Walter de la Mare. CBE
Willow. Richard Watson Dixon. *See* Song: "Feathers of the willow, The."
Willow, The. Tu Fu, *tr. fr. Chinese by* Kenneth Rexroth. OnPC
Willow. Sylvia Townsend Warner. DiM
Willow and Water. Edward Davison. *See* Lovers, The.
Willow Bend and Weep. Herbert Clark Johnson. PoNe
Willow Bottom, The. Madison Cawein. VOD
Willow-Boughs, The. Aleksandr Blok. *See* Little Catkins.
Willow by the River, The. Po Chü-i, *tr. fr. Chinese by* Henry H. Hart. PoHN
Willow Cats, The. Margaret Widdemer. BrR; OTPC (1946 ed.); RIS
Willow Garland, The. Robert Herrick. OAEP
Willow Leaf, The. Tchan Tiou-lin, *tr. into English by* James Whitall *fr. the Chinese-to-French translation of* Judith Gautier. ChLP
Willow-Man, The. Juliana Horatia Ewing. TVC; TVSH
Willow Poem. William Carlos Williams. NP
Willow, Titwillow. W. S. Gilbert. *See* Suicide's Grave, The.
Willow-Tree, The, *parody.* Thackeray. BOHV; CenHV; HBV; InMe; PA
Willow tree leans far over the brook, A. Pastorale. Robert A. Davis. GoSl
Willow Whistle. Ethel Romig Fuller. DDA
Willow Whistles. Grace Noll Crowell. LS
Willow: Why do you bend so low. Springtime. Alfred Kreymborg. MAPA
Willow, willow, willow, sing all of green willow. A Lover Approving His Lady Unkind Is Forced Unwilling to Utter His Mind. *Unknown.* ReIE
Willows, The. Walter Prichard Eaton. DD; FaPON; HBMV; MPB; MW; OHIP
Willows, The, *parody.* Bret Harte. BOHV; InMe
Willows. Joseph Langland. NePoEA
Willows and willows in two gust-worn rows. A Chesapeake Marsh. Lizette Woodworth Reese. LS
Willows are taking the old river road, The. Old River Road. Blanche Whiting Keysner. GoYe
Willows are trees of life. They ride. Willows. Joseph Langland. NePoEA
Willows at the East Gate. *Unknown, tr. fr. Chinese.* WhP
Willows carried a slow sound, The. Repose of Rivers. Hart Crane. AWP; CoBMV; ExPo; InPo; LiTM (rev. ed.); MM; MoAB; MoAmPo (1950 ed.); MOAP; NP; OxBA; SeCeV
Willows in the Snow. Tsuru, *tr. fr. Japanese by* William N. Porter. MPB; SUS
Willowwood. Dante Gabriel Rossetti. The House of Life, XLIX–LII. BPN; EmBrPo; OAEP; POTT; PoVP; ReaPo; TCEP; ViP; ViPo; VLEP
"I sat with Love," XLIX. HBV; PoEL-5; TyEnPo; WHA
"O ye, all ye that walk in Willowwood," LI. BrBE; ViPP
Will's at the dance in the Club-room below. A Wife Waits. Thomas Hardy. At Casterbridge Fair, VI. BEL; EmBrPo; EnLi-2 (1949 ed.); EnLit; PoVP
Wills Dies in Solitude. Colin Thiele. *Fr.* Burke and Wills. NeLNL
Will's under the willow. True. Andrew Hewitt. NoCaPo
Willy and the Lady. Gelett Burgess. HBMV
Willy boy, Willy boy, where are you going? *See* Willie boy, Willie boy . . .
Willy Drowned in Yarrow. *Unknown.* GTBS; GTBS-D; GTBS-W; GTSE; GTSL; HBV
(Rare Willy Drowned in Yarrow.) BaBo; BSV; EBSV; ESPB (A, B, *and* D *vers.*); GoTS; OBB
(Willie Drowned in Yarrow.) EV-2
Willy nilly, he comes or goes, with the clown's logic. Come Away Death. E. J. Pratt. BoCaPo; PeCV
Willy Reilly. *Unknown.* HBV; OnYI; OuSiCo, *with music;* TIP
(Sweet Riley, B *vers.*) BaBo
(Willie Riley, A *vers.*). BaBo
Willy Smith at the Ball Game. George Sterling. BAP
Willy the Weeper. *Unknown. See* Willie the Weeper.
Willy, Willy Wilkin. *Unknown.* OxNR
Willy Winkie. Daniel Henry Holmes. TSW
Willy's Lady. *Unknown. See* Willie's Lady.
"Willy's rare, and Willy's fair." Rare Willy Drowned in Yarrow. *Unknown.* BSV; EBSV; ESPB; GoTS; OBB
Wilson. Percy MacKaye GA
Wilson and Pilcer and Snack stood before the zoo elephant. Elephants Are Different to Different People. Carl Sandburg. MAP; MoAmPo
Wilt thou accept not. Worship. Shelley. *Fr.* One Word Is Too Often Profaned. MaRV

Wilt thou be gone? It is not yet near day. Shakespeare. *Fr.* Romeo and Juliet, III, v. LoPS
Wilt thou bee gon thou hartless man? *Unknown.* SeCSL
Wilt thou forgive that sin [*or* sinne] where I begun [*or* begunne]. A Hymn [*or* Hymne] to God the Father [*or* To Christ *or* For Forgiveness]. John Donne. AnFE; AtBAP; AWP; BEL; CaAE; CenL; CoBE; EG; ElSeCe; EnLi-1; EnLit; EnLP; EPS; EV-2; GoBC; GTSE; HBV; InPo; JAWP; LiTB; LiTG; LoBV; MaRV; MeLP; MePo; OBEV (1st ed.); OBS; OxBoCh; PG (1945 ed.); Po; PoE; PoEL-2; PoFS; PoRA; PreP; ReEn; RiBV; SeCeV; SeCL; SeCV-1; SeEP; ShBV-4; TOP; TrGrPo; TrPWD; TuPP; TwCrTr; TwHP; TyEnPo; ViBoPo; WBP; WGRP
"Wilt thou forsake me? and wilt thou leave me." *Unknown.* *Fr.* "My dear, adieu! my sweet love, farewell!" LO
Wilt thou hear, O sailor, what this people say? *Unknown.* *Fr.* The Battle of Maldon. PoFr
Wilt thou lend me thy mare to ride a mile. *Unknown.* OBS
Wilt thou? Let us make a dream. The Palace. Humbert Wolfe. HOAH
Wilt thou love God, as he thee? then digest. Holy Sonnets, XV. John Donne. EnLP; OBS
Wilt thou not ope thy heart to know. Emerson. *Fr.* Threnody. MaRV
Wilt thou not visit me? The Prayer. Jones Very. APW; MaRV; OxBA; TriL; TrPWD
Wilt Thou Set Thine Eyes upon That Which Is Not? Francis Quarles. *See* Vanity of the World, The.
Wilt Thou steer my frail black bark. The Heavenly Pilot. Cormac. *Fr.* Book of Leinster. CAW; OnYI
Wilt Thou Yet Take All. Swinburne. *Fr.* Hymn to Proserpine. UnPo (1st ed.)
Wiltshire Downs. Andrew Young. AlDL; ChMP; GTBS-D
Wily Auld Carle, The. *Unknown.* *See* Wife of Kelso, The.
Wily Beguiled, *sel.* *Unknown.*
"Old Tithon must forsake his dear." TuPP
Wily Cupid. Henry Chettle. *Fr.* Piers Plainness' Seven Years' Prenticeship. EG
(Aeliana's Ditty.) ALV; OBSC
(Of Cupid.) ElL
Wily Cupid. *Unknown, tr. fr. Spanish by* James Young Gibson. TeCS
Win at First and Lose at Last; or a New Game at Cards. Laurence Price. OxBoLi
Winander Lake. Wordsworth. *See* There Was a Boy.
Winchelsea Fight, or the Humbling of the Spaniards. Laurence Minot. SG
Winchester. Lionel Johnson. OBVV
Wind, The. W. H. Davies. SeCePo
Wind, The. Emily Dickinson. *See* Of all the sounds despatched abroad *and* Wind tapped like a tired man, The.
Wind, The. Eleanor Farjeon. TVSH
Wind. Leonard Feeney. GoTP
Wind. John Galsworthy. NLK; VOD
Wind, The. Louis Ginsberg. RIS
Wind, The. Dorothy Gradon. BoTP
Wind. Langston Hughes. *Fr.* A House in Taos. CDC
Wind, The. Ibn Sa'id of Alcala la Real, *tr. fr. Arabic by* A. J. Arberry. MooP
Wind, The. Letitia Elizabeth Landon. OTPC; PRWS
Wind, The. Betty Miller. BrR
Wind, The. Harold Monro. *See* Wind in the Dusk.
Wind, The. William Morris. DaM; PoVP; VLEP
Wind. Phyllis Reid. DiM
Wind, The. Elizabeth Rendall. BoTP; HBVY
Wind, The. Christina Rossetti. *See* Who Has Seen the Wind?
Wind, The. Edward Shanks. AlDL
Wind, The. Victor Starbuck. NoCaPo
Wind, The. James Stephens. AnIL
Wind, The. Robert Louis Stevenson. BoTP; BTP; GBV (1922 ed.); GFA; GN; HBVY; MPB; OnHT; OTPC; PCH; PoVP; RAR; StVeCh; SUS; TiPo; YT
Wind, The. John Banister Tabb. AnAmPo; LA
Wind, The. *Unknown.* FaBoCh; LoGBV
("Arthur O'Bower has broken his band.") OxNR
(High Wind, The.) ChTr
Wind, The. Dorothy Wordsworth. *Fr.* Address to a Child during a Boisterous Winter Evening. BoTP
Wind/ flattening its gaunt furious self. The Wind Our Enemy. Anne Marriott. BoCaPo; CaP; TwCV
Wind among the Reeds, The. Nora Hopper. DiM; GTIV
Wind and an Eagle Owl, *sel.* N. H. Brettell.
"We rode out with the pealing day before us." BoSA
"Wind and Fire, Wind and Fire." Burn the Stubble! Sidney Lanier. CoV
Wind and Silver. Amy Lowell. MAP; MoAmPo; NeMA; ReaPo
Wind and the beam loved the rose, The. Nydia's Song. Sir Edward Bulwer-Lytton. *Fr.* The Last Days of Pompeii. OBVV
Wind and the Fisherman, The. *Unknown.* *See* When the wind is in the east.
Wind and the Moon, The. George Macdonald. GoTP; HBV; HBVY; MoShBr; OnHT; OTPC; PECK; PTA-1; StVeCh (1940 ed.); SUS; TreFS; TVC; TVSH
Wind and the Rain, The. Lu Yu, *tr. fr. Chinese by* Pai Chwen-yu. WhP
Wind and the Rain, The. *Unknown, tr. fr. Chinese.* WhP
Wind and the Wires, The. Benjamin Sledd. NoCaPo
Wind and Violent Weather. *Unknown, tr. fr. Chinese by* Bernhard Karlgren. *Fr.* Shi King. ChLP
Wind and Wave. Coventry Patmore. The Unknown Eros, I, ii. VLEP
Wind and Wave. Charles Warren Stoddard. AA; BAP
Wind and Window-Flower. Robert Frost. YT
Wind at the Door, The. William Barnes. AtBAP; EV-4; LO; PoEL-4; RO
Wind billowing out the seat of my britches, The. Child on Top of a Greenhouse. Theodore Roethke. AtBAP; MiAP
Wind blew fresh and seaward made, The. The Danaë. Simonides. GrL; LiTW; OxBG
Wind, The, blew out from Bergen from the dawning to the day. The Last Hero. G. K. Chesterton. OtMeF
Wind blew strongly like the voice of fate, The. Christoph. Charles Spear. AnNZ
Wind blew, the wind blew, The! The Wind. Eleanor Farjeon. TVSH
Wind blew wide the casement, and within, The. Mother and Child. William Gilmore Simms. LPS-1; MOAH
Wind Blew Words, The. Thomas Hardy. EPN; NV
Wind Blow East, The, *with music.* *Unknown.* OuSiCo
Wind Bloweth Where It Listeth, The. Countee Cullen. NP
Wind Bloweth Where It Listeth, The. Susan L. Mitchell. AnIV
Wind Blows, The. Donagh MacDonagh. NeIP
Wind blows cold from a storm, The. The Dead City. Clinch Calkins. AnAmPo; LA
Wind blows east, the wind blows storm, The. A Bee Sets Sail. Katharine Morse. UTS
Wind blows east, The—the wind blows west. A Salem Witch. Ednah Proctor Clarke. PAH
Wind blows from the north, The. A Complaint. Chwang Këang. OuHeWo
Wind blows hot, The. English and foreign birds. Christmas Eve: Australia. Karl Shapiro. ReMP
Wind blows in the night, A. John Drinkwater. *Fr.* Abraham Lincoln. MM
Wind blows out of the gates of the day, The. Fairy Song [*or* Song *or* The Voice]. W. B. Yeats. *Fr.* The Land of Heart's Desire. BEL; ChMo; CMP; CP; GBV; GTSL; InP; MBP; MoBrPo; OnYI; PtOT; TSW; ViBiPo
Wind blows the line out from his fishing pole, The. Fisherman. Ou-yang Hsiu. OnPC
Wind [*or* Wild wind] blows, the sun shines, the birds sing loud, The. Wild Geese. Celia Thaxter. PRWS; SN; UTS
Wind blows tonight, The. Pause. Henry Bellamann. LS
Wind blows wild on Bos'n Hill, The. Bos'n Hill. John Albee. AA
Wind breaks bound, tossing the oak and chestnut, The. Gale Warning. Michael Roberts. AlDL
Wind came up out of the sea, A. Daybreak. Longfellow. AnNE; APW; BoTP; HBV; LPS-2; MOAP; PIR; SN; WaKn
Wind carries me on its wings, The. Aristotelis Valaoritis. *Fr.* Kera Phrosini. MoGP
Wind charged every way and fled, The. The Wind's Word. Archibald Lampman. OCL
Wind comes from the north, The. Suspense. D. H. Lawrence. MBP; MoBrPo
Wind comes, singing, The. Glad Earth. Ella C. Forbes. YeAr
Wind comes up across the hill, the wind goes laughing by, The. September. Sara Hamilton Birchall. NLK
Wind cracked his whip, The Under the Tent of the Sky. Rowena Bastin Bennett. UTS
"Wind doth blow today, my love, The." The Unquiet Grave. *Unknown.* AnFE; AtBAP; BaBo; CH; EnL; ExPo; LO; LoBV; OBB; PoD; PoEL-1; ViBoPo
Wind doth wander up and down, The. Destiny. Nathalia Crane. GoTP; MAP; NeMA
Wind exultant swept, The. A Mood. Winifred Howells. AA
Wind-Fiend, The. W. E. Henley. *See* Scherzando.
Wind flapped loose, the wind was still, The. The Woodspurge. Dante Gabriel Rossetti. AnFE; AtBAP; BLV; BoLiVe; BPN; BrBE; EmBrPo; EPN; EtPaEn; FaBoEn; GTBS-D; GTML; LoBV; OAEP; OBEV (new ed.); PoEL-5; PoVP; TCEP; UnPo (3d ed.); VA; ViPP; VLEP; WHA
Wind-flicked and ruddy her young body glowed. Sea-Change. W. W. Gibson. ChMo; CMP
Wind from out the west is blowing, The. The Woods That Bring the Sunset Near. Richard Watson Gilder. LBAP
Wind from the east, oh, lapwing of the day. Odes. Hafiz. AWP
Wind from the north: the young spring day. The Song of the

Four Winds. Thomas Love Peacock. *Fr.* The Misfortunes of Elphin. OBRV
Wind, gentle evergreen, to form a shade. On the Tomb of Sophocles. Simmias. GrPo; OnPM
Wind gently, ivy, o'er the tomb. Sophocles' Tomb [*or* On Sophocles]. Simmias, *tr. by* Walter Leaf. GrR; OxBG
Wind Harbour, The. Norman Levine. PeCV
Wind has a language I would I could learn, The. The Wind. Letitia Elizabeth Landon. OTPC; PRWS
Wind has at last got into the clock, The. The Wind, the Clock, the We. Laura Riding. LiTA
Wind has blown the rain away and blown, A. Sonnet. E. E. Cummings. AmPP; AnNE; MAP; MoAB; MoAmPo
Wind has fallen asleep, The; the bough that tost. Initiation. Laurence Binyon. GTML
Wind has stopped, The. Harumichi no Tsuraki, *tr. fr. Japanese by* Kenneth Rexroth. OnPJ
Wind has such a rainy sound, The. Christina Rossetti. *Fr.* Sing-Song. BrR; PoVP; TiPo
(Sing-Song.) MBP
(Sound of the Wind, The.) BoTP
Wind, The, has swept from the wide atmosphere. A Summer Evening Churchyard. Shelley. EmBrPo; EnSW
Wind in a Frolic, The. William Howitt. CBPC; MoShBr; OTPC; PRWS; StVeCh (1940 ed.)
Wind in the Alleys. Lola Ridge. MAP; MoAmPo (1942 ed.); OnYI
(Wind Rising in the Alleys.) PoeMoYo
Wind in the bush and bird-calls loud. Spring Day. Hermann Hesse. TwGV
Wind in the Dusk. Harold Monro. NeMA; VOD
(Wind, The.) OBVV
Wind in the Elms, The. J. Corson Miller. HBMV
Wind in the Grass, The. Emerson. *Fr.* To Ellen at the South. BoTP
Wind-in-the-Hair and Rain-in-the-Face. Arthur Guiterman. POT; PoTo
Wind in the Pine. Lew Sarett. BAP; MaRV; MW; OTPC (1946 ed.); QS; TrPWD
Wind in the Pines, The. Madison Cawein. AA; ADAH
Wind in the Pines, The. Sir Henry Taylor. *Fr.* Edwin the Fair. VA
Wind, The, in the plane trees shakes my heart, alas! Departure of Autumn. Li Ho. WhP
Wind in the Poplars. Sophocles, *tr. fr. Greek by* John Addington Symonds. OxBG
Wind in the street, and sadness of unknown walkers. Epithalamion. Terence Tiller. POTE
Wind in the Willows, The, *sels.* Kenneth Grahame.
Carol: "Villagers all, this frosty tide." OHIP
(Christmas Carol.) MPB
Duck's [*or* Ducks'] Ditty BoTP; FaPON; MoShBr; MPB; OTPC (1946 ed.); PCH; PoRh; RAR; SUS; TiPo; UTS; WaKn; WhBS
World Has Held Great Heroes, The. LiL
(Song of Mr. Toad, The.) FaPON; FiBHP
Wind in the Wood. Paul Verlaine, *tr. fr. French by* Alan Conder. LO; TrFP
Wind Is a Cat. Ethel Romig Fuller. MoSiPe; MPB; UTS
Wind is a teasing hunger, The. Captive. John Richard Moreland. PoMa
Wind is awake on the mountain's breast, The. A Morning Lullaby. J. A. Coll. BOL
Wind is awake, pretty leaves, pretty leaves, The. The Way of It. John Vance Cheney. HBV
Wind Is Blind, The. Alice Meynell. MBP; MoBrPo; SeCePo
Wind is blowing east, The. Out to Sea. Richard Henry Stoddard. TCAP
Wind is blowing from the hill, The. Nocturne. H. A. Vaughan. PoNe
Wind is brushing down the clover, A. On Malvern Hill. John Masefield. TCPD; WP
Wind is east but the hot weather continues, The. American Letter. Archibald MacLeish. AmPP; CoV; OxBA; PoLFOT
Wind is east, the wind is west, The. A Stave of Roving Tim. George Meredith. EmBrPo
Wind is Howling through the Winter Night, The. Avetis Isahakian, *tr. fr. Armenian by* Zabelle C. Boyajian. ArmLP
Wind Is Ill, The. John Malcolm Brinnin. LiTA
Wind is low in air, The. The Cool of Evening. Lizette Woodworth Reese. LS
Wind is pushing against the trees, The. March Wind. Helen Wing. GFA
Wind is rising on the sea, The. Before the Squall. Arthur Symons. PoVP; VLEP
Wind is sewing with needles of rain, The. Two Sewing. Hazel Hall. MoSiPe; NP
Wind is such an optimist, The. The Wind. Louis Ginsberg. RIS
Wind is tapping the window-pane, The. A Lullabye. William Noble Roundy. BOL
Wind is to show. Wind. Leonard Feeney. GoTP
Wind is up, The: Hark! how it howls! The Church of Graves. Robert Blair. *Fr.* The Grave. BeR
Wind it blew, and the ship it flew, The. The Earl o' Quarterdeck. George Macdonald. BeLS; EtS; LoEn; LPS-2
Wind it blew from sou' sou'-east, it blew a pleasant breeze, The. The Light on Cape May. *Unknown.* ShS
Wind It Blew up the Railroad Track, The, *with music. Unknown.* AS
Wind it wailed, the wind it moaned, The. Alec Yeaton's Son. Thomas Bailey Aldrich. EtS; FAOV
Wind keen, the sky high, the gibbons wailing, The. On Climbing the Heights on the Ninth Day of the Ninth Moon. Tu Fu. WhP
Wind King from the North came down, The. Hatteras. Joseph William Holden. NoCaPo
Wind like this tonight, A. Exile. Audrey Beecham. NeBP
Wind-Litany. Margaret Widdemer. NLK
Wind Me a Summer Crown. Menella Bute Smedley. HBV; OBVV
Wind mutters thinly on the sagging wire. Prairie Graveyard. Anne Marriott. BoCaPo; CaP; PeCV
Wind of April softly stole, A. The Song of the Pine. James Buckham. PEOR
Wind of Death, The. Ethelwyn Wetherald. CPG; VA
Wind of Fall, A. Léonie Adams. YT
Wind of Hampstead Heath still burns my cheek, The. Breath of Hampstead Heath. Edith M. Thomas. AA
Wind of January, The. Christina Rossetti. *See* Year's Windfalls, A.
Wind of Night, The. George Sterling. *Fr.* Sonnets by the Night Sea. UnW
Wind of September in the Poplars. Luis Cernuda, *tr. fr. Spanish by* Eleanor L. Turnbull. CoSP
Wind of Sorrow, The. Henry van Dyke. LBAP; PC
Wind of Summer. "Michael Field." VA
Wind of the city streets. To a June Breeze. H. C. Bunner. AA
Wind of the North. The Four Winds. Charles Henry Luders. AA; HBV; LBAP; OBAV
Wind of the Prairie. Grace Clementine Howes. GoYe
Wind of the West, that fans with fragrant wing. To the Western Wind. Judah Halevi. TrJP
Wind of the winter, drive the ships home. To the Winter Wind. John Gould Fletcher. TSW; TSWC
Wind on the Hills, The. Dora Sigerson Shorter. HBMV; JKCP
Wind on the waters blowing. Whither Away? Euripides. *Fr.* Hecuba. OxBG
Wind on the Wold, The. W. E. Henley. VOD
Wind on Tien Shan slashes the autumn like a knife, The. Two Songs for General Chao, II. Ts'en Ts'an. WhP
Wind one morning sprang up from sleep, The. The Wind in a Frolic. William Howitt. CBPC; MoShBr; OTPC; PRWS; StVeCh (1940 ed.)
Wind Our Enemy, The. Anne Marriott. BoCaPo; TwCV, *abr.*
"Wind/ flattening its gaunt furious self against," *sel.* CaP
Wind passes over the lake. Autumn Evening beside the Lake. Li Ch'ing-chao. OnPC
Wind Rising in the Alleys. Lola Ridge. *See* Wind in the Alleys.
Wind roars and the river roars, The. The Sounding Portage. Annie Charlotte Dalton. CaP
Wind rose, and the wind fell, The. The Day That Was That Day. Amy Lowell. ChMo; CMP
Wind Rose in the Night, A. Aline Kilmer. HBMV; SBMV
Wind rustles the bamboos, The. Yakamochi, *tr. fr. Japanese by* Kenneth Rexroth. OnPJ
Wind sang to the cornfields, The. August. Eunice Fallon. BoTP
Wind shakes the mists, The. Mutability. John Gould Fletcher. ChMo; CMP
Wind shall lull us yet, The. From the Antique. Christina Rossetti. EnLoPo
Wind sings of a breed of men who taught the wind to sing, The. Men of America, Answering the Call. Hal Borland. PoFr
Wind slammed shut the door and he remembered, The. A Prisoner Freed. Geoffrey Dutton. BoAV
Wind—snow—ice—and sleet. Cold. Margaret Parton. PCD
Wind Song. *Tr. fr. Pima Indian Song by* Natalie Curtis. SUS
Wind Song. Carl Sandburg. GBV (1952 ed.); MAP; MoAB; MoAmPo; MoShBr; NeMA; TwAmPo; YT
Wind Song. *Unknown.* GFA
Wind Sprang Up at Four o'Clock, The. T. S. Eliot. LiTB; NePA
Wind, stirring in the dark foliage, brings, The. God's Harp. Gustav Falke. AWP; JAWP; WBP
Wind stood up, and gave a shout, The. The Wind. James Stephens. AnIL
Wind Suffers, The. Laura Riding. AnAmPo; FaBoMo
Wind sways the pines, A. Dirge in [the] Woods. George Meredith. AEV; BLV; BMEP; BoLiVe; CaAE; CBOV;

Wind sways the pines, A (*continued*)
EG; EmBrPo; EPN; EPP; GTML; LiA; LoBV; OAEP; OBEV (new ed.); OBVV; POTT; PoVP; SeCeV; TOP; TwCV; VLEP; WHA
Wind sweeps down the mountain side, The. A Deserted Temple. Yüan Chen. PoHN
Wind-swept and fire-swept and swept with bitter rain. The Homesteader. Isabel Ecclestone Mackay. CPG
Wind-swept Wheat, The. "Madeline Bridges." AA
Wind takes the moon riding, The. Round. Vicente Huidobro. AnCL
Wind tapped like a tired man, The. Emily Dickinson. MoAB; MoAmPo (1950 ed.); NePA
(Wind, The.) NeMA
Wind tears a leaf from the willow tree, The. The Leaf on the Water. Ouan-tsi. ChLP
Wind that blows in my own land hath a pleasant sound, The. Two Winds. Victor Starbuck. LS
Wind that dies on the meadows lush, A. The Dreamer. Alice Furlong. TIP
Wind that speeds the bee and plucks the bee-line. Awake! W. R. Rodgers. LiTM (rev. ed.); WaP
Wind, the Clock, the We, The. Laura Riding. LiTA
Wind tramping along the clouds. Child and Wind. Lola Ridge. BAP
Wind voice calls and calls you, The. The Summons. Elizabeth Roberts MacDonald. CaP; OCL
Wind was a torrent ot darkness among the gusty trees, The. The Highwayman. Alfred Noyes. ATP; BBV; BEL; BeLS; BMEP; ChMo; CMP; CP; CV; EnLit; FaFP; FaPON; GoTP; GTSL; HBV; HBVY; HiLiAm; InP; LBBV; LoEn; MaC; MCCG; MW; OHFP; OnSP; PCD; PFE; PoeMoYo; PoMa; POT; PoTo; PYM; ShBV-2; TCEP; TOP; TreFS; TSW; TSWC; TwCV; YT
Wind Was Cold, the Sky Steel Gray, The. John Richard Moreland. LS
Wind was in another country, The. Mirage. R. P. Blackmur. *Fr.* Sea Island Miscellany. GTBS-W; LiTM; MoVE
Wind was rising easterly, the morning sky was blue, The. The Old *Superb*. Sir Henry Newbolt. BBV (1923 ed.)
Wind-washed and free, full-swept by rain and wave. Joyous-Gard. Thomas S. Jones, Jr. LBMV
Wind waves the lotoses in the scented palace by the water, The. For the Dancer of the King of Wu, When She Is Half Drunk. Li Po. WhP
Wind Weather. Virginia Brasier. StVeCh (1955 ed.)
Wind went forth a little after dawn, A. A Wind of Fall. Léonie Adams. YT
Wind went wooing the rose, The. A Summer Wooing. Louise Chandler Moulton. HBV
Wind whines and whines the shingle. On the Beach at Fontana. James Joyce. AnEnPo; LO; MBP; MoBrPo; NP; OBMV; TwCV
Wind whistled loud at the window-pane, The. Lullaby. William Brighty Rands. BOL; BoTP
Wind: why do you play. Improvisation. Alfred Kreymborg. MAP
Wind, Wind. Kenneth Slade Alling. VOD
Wind, wind—heather gipsy. Wind. John Galsworthy. NLK; VOD
Wind, wind, wind in the old trees. Variations, XII. Conrad Aiken. ChMo; CMP; PG (1933 ed.)
Wind, Wind, you like to go in silver best. Wind, Wind. Kenneth Slade Alling. VOD
Wind with foetid muzzle sniffed its feast, The. African Moonrise. Roy Campbell. CoBE
Wind-Wolves. William D. Sargent. MPB; TiPo; UTS
Windfall. F. R. Scott. CaP
Windflower, A. Bliss Carman. VA
Wind-Flower, The. Jones Very. AnNE; APW
Windflowers and the Sage, The. Laura Spencer Portor. StJW
Windhover, The. Gerard Manley Hopkins. ACP; AnFE; AtBAP; ATP (1953 ed.); BrBE; CAW; ChMo; CoBE; CoBMV; CoEV; EmBrPo; EnL; EnLi-2 (1949 ed.); EnLit; ExPo; FaBoEn; FaBoMo; InvP; LiTB; LiTM; LoBV; MaPo; MoAB; MoBrPo; MoP; MoPo; MoPW; MoVE; OAEP; Po; PoE; PoEL-5; PoF; PoRA; POTT; PoVP; PreP; ReaPo; ReMP; SeCeV; ShBV-4; TwHP; UnPo (3d ed.); ViP; ViPo; ViPP; VLEP
Winding Banks of Erne, The. William Allingham. AnIV; IrPN; TIP
(Adieu to Belashanny.) GTIV; OxBI
Winding road lies white and bare, The. The Footpath Way. Katharine Tynan. HBV
Winding way the serpent takes, The. Norembega. Whittier. PAH
Windlass Song. William Allingham. BBV (1923 ed.); GN; OTPC
Windle-Straws. Edward Dowden. HBV
Windmill, The. Robert Bridges. ChMo; CMP; PoTo; TCPD; WP
Windmill, The. John Farrar. GFA
Windmill, The. Geoffrey Johnson. HaMV
Windmill, The. Longfellow. MoShBr; TVSH
Windmill, The. E. V. Lucas. BoTP
Windmill, The. Allen Upward. *Fr.* Scented Leaves from a Chinese Jar. NP
Windmill on the Cape. William Vincent Sieller. GoYe
Windmill stands up like a flower on the hill, The. The Windmill. John Farrar. GFA
Windmills, The. John Gould Fletcher. Arizona Poems, IV. CrMA; NV; PoMa; PoTo; TCPD
Windmills of Holland are turning again, The. The Battle of Peace. Wilson MacDonald. MaRV
Window, The. Edwin Muir. LiTM (rev. ed.)
Window, The. Francis Scarfe. NeBP
Window, a Table, on the North, A. Ralph Gustafson. PeCV
Window Boxes. Eleanor Farjeon. FaPON
Window Cleaner, The. Elizabeth Fleming. BoTP
Window-Glance, The. Heine, *tr. fr. German by* John Todhunter. AWP
Window has four little panes, The. The Window Pain. Gelett Burgess. HBV; HBVY; PIAE; TSW; TSWC
Window in the Breast, A. *Unknown, tr. fr. Greek by* Walter Headlam. OxBG
Window Pain, The. Gelett Burgess. PIAE
(Nonsense Rhymes.) HBVY; TSW; TSWC
(Nonsense Verses.) HBV
Window Sill, The. Robert Graves. AtBAP; EnLoPo
Window Song, A. Thomas Caulfield Irwin. TIP
Window, The, was born of a desire for sky. Biography. Jorge Carrera Andrade. TwSpPo
Windowed Habitations. Charles G. Bell. NePoAm-2
Windows. Abbie Farwell Brown. POT; PoTo
Windows, The. George Herbert. CoBE; ElSeCe; MaPo; MeLP; OAEP; SeCV-1
(Church Windows, The.) EPS; OBS
Windows. Stéphane Mallarmé, *tr. fr. French by* Daisy Aldan. AnFP
Windows for My Soul. Angela Morgan. OQP; QP-2
Windows of heaven were open wide, The. A Ballad of the Conemaugh Flood. Hardwicke Drummond Rawnsley. PAH
Windows of the place wherein I dwell, The. Windows. Abbie Farwell Brown. POT; PoTo
Windows of the Soul. Ella Wheeler Wilcox. *Fr.* Progress. OQP; QP-1
Winds, The. Madison Cawein. CP; MAP; NV; PIAE; SPP
Winds, The. "John Eglinton." GTIV; OnYI
Winds, The. Swinburne. POTT; TOP; VLEP
Winds, The. William Carlos Williams. AnAmPo; LA
Winds a-Blowing. May Justus. BrR
Wind's an old woman in front of the rain, The. Wind Weather. Virginia Brasier. StVeCh (1955 ed.)
Winds are bleak, stars are bright. The Victoria Markets Recollected in Tranquillity. Frank Wilmot. BoAV; MoAuPo; NeLNL
Winds are blowing. Woman's Song. Aleksey Koltsov. BoR
Winds are high on Helle's wave, The. Byron. *Fr.* The Bride of Abydos. OBRV
Winds are roaring out of the West, The. Inisgallun. Darrell Figgis. OnYI
Winds are whispering over the sea, The. Cradle Song. Merle St. Croix Wright. BOL; MotAn
Winds at Bethlehem, The. Winifred M. Letts. StJW
Winds gathered deep in the winter night, The. City Birds. "Spud" Johnson. PoMa
Winds go down in peace, dear child, The. At the Dreamland Gate. Mary E. Freeman. BOL
Winds have talked with him confidingly, The. Longfellow. James Whitcomb Riley. AA; DD; PoRL
Wind's Head, The. John L. Sweeney. JKCP (1955 ed.)
Wind's in the heart of me, a fire's in my heels, A. A Wanderer's Song. John Masefield. AIDL; BMEP; MBP; MCCG; MoAB; MoBrPo; NLK; PoeMoYo; PYM; TSW; TSWC
Wind's Life, The. Harry Kemp. NLK
Winds of Angus, The. "Æ." ChMo; CMP
Winds of autumn, winters dipped in mud. Mists and Rain. Baudelaire. OnPM
Winds of Eros. "Æ." HBMV
Winds of Fate, The. Ella Wheeler Wilcox. BLPA; DDA; MaRV; WBLP
(One Ship Drives East.) OQP; QP-1
Winds of God, The. Clinton Scollard. PoRL
Winds of Heaven, The. Saul's Faithfulness. Charles Heavysege. *Fr.* Saul, a Drama. BMEP
Winds of March, come sweeping through the long, brown valley. March Dreams. Rose Henderson. MoSiPe
Winds of the morning. Nobody Knows. Helen Coale Crew. GFA
Winds of the People. Miguel Hernández, *tr. fr. Spanish by* Willard Maas. PoFr
Winds of the West, Arise. George Darley. AtBAP
Winds of the world for a little season, The. The Wind's Way. Richard Le Gallienne. HBMV
Winds of the worlds, give answer! They are whimpering to and

fro. The English Flag [or The Flag of England]. Kipling. LH; PECK
Wind's on the wold, The. Inscription for an Old Bed [or For the Bed at Kelmscott or Lines for a Bed at Kelmscott Manor]. William Morris. CH; EmBrPo; OBEV (new ed.); OBVV; PoEL-5; PoVP; ViP; WP
Winds out of the west land blow, The. A. E. Housman. A Shropshire Lad, XXXVIII. PoVP
Winds ride bareback, The. Bareback. William Haskell Simpson. *Fr.* In Arizona. NP
Wind's Song, The. Eduard Mörike, *tr. fr. German by* William R. Hughes. AnGP
Wind's Song, The. "Gabriel Setoun." HBV; HBVY; OTPC; PPL
Winds That Blow across the Wild Moor, The. *Unknown. See* Mary of the Wild Moor.
Winds that bring the swans are racing. "Anna Akhmatova," *tr. fr. Russian by* C. M. Bowra. BoRS
Winds that change against the sun. Rules of the Road. *Unknown.* SoAmSa
Winds that once the Argo bore, The. Heroes. Edna Dean Proctor. GA; HBV; TVSH
Winds that sweep the southern mountains. Allatoona. *Unknown.* PAH
Winds they did blow, The. The Squirrel. *Unknown.* BoTP; OxNR
Winds through [or thro'] the olive trees. Long, Long Ago [or A Christmas Song]. *Unknown.* BoTP; BrR; ChBR; DD; FaPON; GFA; MPB; OHIP; OTPC (1946 ed.); PEDC; RAR; TiPo (1952 ed.)
Winds transferred into the friendly sky, The. The Camp at Night. Homer. *Fr.* The Iliad, VIII. LPS-2
Wind's Way, The. Grace Hazard Conkling. HBV
Wind's Way, The. Richard Le Gallienne. HBMV
Wind's way in the deep sky's hollow, The. The Way of the Wind. Swinburne. VLEP
Winds were yelling, the waves were swelling, The. The Last Buccaneer. Macaulay. EtS; EV-4; HBV; LH; SG
Winds whisper gently whilst she sleeps. Laura Sleeping. Charles Cotton. ElSeCe; FaBoEn; LoBV; OBS; SeCL; ViBoPo
Wind's Word, The. Archibald Lampman. OCL
Wind's Work. T. Sturge Moore. AlDL; HBMV; HBVY; TVSH
Windshield. Robert Fitzgerald. CrMA
Windsor Forest, *sels.* Pope.
Field Sports. OBEC; SeCePo
Glitter, 4 *ll.* BeR
"Groves of Eden, The, vanish'd now so long." BEL; OBEC
"See! from the brake the whirring pheasant springs." FaBoEn; PoEL-3
(Flames of Death, The.) BeR
(Pheasant, The.) GoTP
"Time shall come, when, free as seas or wind, The." PoFr
"With slaught'ring guns th' unwearied fowler roves." EnSW
Windy and waste and battered by the sea. To Delos [or Delos]. Callimachus. GrR; OxBG
Windy Bill. *Unknown.* CoSo, *with music;* CSF
Windy City, The, *sel.* Carl Sandburg.
"Night gathers itself into a ball of yarn." PIAE
Windy Day, A. Winifred Howard. FaPON
Windy Day, A. Andrew Young. GoTP; MoPW; ThWaDe
Windy evening drops a grey [or gray], The. The Evening in February. Francis Ledwidge. AlDL; TCPD; VOD
Windy forest is checkered, The. Banquet at the Tso Family Manor. Tu Fu. OnPC
Windy Morning. Harry Behn. TiPo (1959 ed.)
Windy Night, The. Thomas Buchanan Read. GN
Windy Night, A. Lizette Woodworth Reese. DaM
Windy night was blowing on Rome, A. The Rider at the Gate. John Masefield. POTT; ShBV-2
Windy Nights. Robert Louis Stevenson. AlDL; BLP; BoChLi; BoTP; EPP; PoRA; PoRh; PRWS; RIS; ShBV-1; SiSoSe; StaSt; TiPo
Windy toss of blood-red banners, The. Red Square. Nikolai Poletayev. TrRV
Windy trammel of her dress, The. Grace of the Way. Francis Thompson. EmBrPo
Windy Wash Day. Dorothy Aldis. TiPo
Windy Weather. Jorge Carrera Andrade, *tr. fr. Spanish by* H. R. Hays. TwSpPo
Wine. Francis Carlin. JKCP (1926 ed.)
Wine. Dakiki, *tr. fr. Persian by* R. A. Nicholson. LiTW
Wine. Micah Joseph Lebensohn, *tr. fr. Hebrew by* A. M. Klein. LiTW; TrJP
Wine. Nikolai Ushakov, *tr. fr. Russian by* Jack Lindsay. RuPo
Wine and cakes for gentlemen. *Unknown.* OxNR
Wine and Citron. Abu Abd Allah, *tr. fr. Arabic by* A. J. Arberry. MooP
Wine and Dew. Richard Henry Stoddard. AA
Wine and Grief. Solomon ibn Gabirol, *tr. fr. Hebrew by* Emma Lazarus. LiTW; TrJP
Wine and Song. Nicaenetus, *tr. fr. Greek by* T. F. Higham. OxBG
Wine and the Moon. *Unknown, tr. fr. Japanese by* Ishii and Obata. *Fr.* Manyo Shu. OnPM
Wine and Water. G. K. Chesterton. *Fr.* The Flying Inn. ACP (1952 ed.); CenHV; FiBHP; GoBC; HBMV; InMe; LiTM; MBP; MoBrPo; ShBV-4; ViBoPo
Wine and Woe. Proverbs, XXIII: 29-35, Bible, *O.T.* (*Moulton, Modern Reader's Bible*). MaRV
Wine and woman and song. Villanelle of the Poet's Road. Ernest Dowson. OBMV; PoVP; TrGrPo; ViPP
Wine at Dawn. Ibn Sa'id of Alcala la Real, *tr. fr. Arabic by* A. J. Arberry. MooP
Wine at Morning. Ibn Safar, *tr. fr. Arabic by* A. J. Arberry. MooP
Wine-Bearer, The. Habib, *tr. fr. Arabic by* A. J. Arberry. MooP
Wine comes in at the mouth. A Drinking Song. W. B. Yeats. TwP
Wine-Cup, The. Richard Aldington. LBBV
Wine-cup is glad, The: dear Zenophile's lip. The Draught of Love. Meleager. OnPM
Wine divinely cool. Magian Wine. Abu Jaafar. MooP
Wine Jelly. *Unknown.* WhC
Wine Menagerie, The. Hart Crane. OxBA
Wine, My Love. Abu Jaafar, *tr. fr. Arabic by* A. J. Arberry. MooP
Wine of Cyprus, *sel.* Elizabeth Barrett Browning.
"Our Euripides, the human," 4 *ll.* PtP
Wine of Love Is Music, The. James Thomson. *See* Vine, The.
Wine of Song, The. Charles Sangster. CPG
Wine of the grapes. Maid of Wu. Li Po. ChLP
Wine Press, The, *sel.* Alfred Noyes.
Dawn of Peace, The, *fr.* Epilogue. MaRV; QS
Wine-Press of Los, The. Blake. *Fr.* Milton. EnRP
Wine-red sedges stain the rolling hills, The. Tipsiness. Clement Wood. VOD
Wine Shop, The. Chu Miao Tuan, *tr. fr. Chinese by* Henry H. Hart. PoHN
Wine-Songs, *sels.* Moses ibn Ezra, *tr. fr. Hebrew by* Solomon Solis-Cohen. TrJP
Awake, My Soul.
Bring Me the Cup.
Drink, Friends.
Rosy Days Are Numbered, The.
Wine taken with excess. Temperance. *Unknown.* ACP; CAW
Wine they drink in Paradise, The. A Cider Song. G. K. Chesterton. MM
Wine, to a gifted bard. Wine and Song. Nicaenetus. OxBG
Wine to the weak and to those unsound. Wine. Francis Carlin. JKCP (1926 ed.)
Wine's Sting. Alcaeus, *tr. fr. Greek by* Walter Petersen. GrR
Wing by wing the wild geese fly. *Unknown, tr. fr. Japanese by* Kenneth Rexroth. LiTW
Wing of Separation, The. Ibn Darraj al-Andalusi, *tr. fr. Arabic by* J. B. Trend. AWP; JAWP; WBP
Wing Tee Wee. J. P. Denison. BOHV
Wing Wang Waddle Oh. *Unknown. See* Swapping Song, The.
Wing'd company, for you. From a Winnower of Corn to the Winds. Joachim du Bellay. TrFP
Wing'd seeds with decaying wings, The. Fragment. William Allingham. IrPN
Wingèd Change. Simonides. *See* Turn of a Dragonfly's Wing, The.
Wingèd death has smitten dumb thy bells. A. Rheims Cathedral. Grace Hazard Conkling. AOAH
Winged Heels. Harry Lee. BBV (1923 ed.)
Winged Horse, The. Hilaire Belloc. AlDL
Winged Horseman, The. Joseph Auslander. PoTo
Winged horses descend to drink, The. On a Bas-Relief. Wesley Trimpi. NePoEA
Winged Hours. Dante Gabriel Rossetti. The House of Life, XXV. EmBrPo; EPN; PoVP; ViPo
Winged Man. Stephen Vincent Benét. MAP; MoAmPo; VOD
Winged Mariner. Grace Clementine Howes. EtS
Winged mimic of the woods! thou motley fool! To the Mocking Bird. Richard Henry Wilde. AA; APW; BLA; HiLiAm; IAP; SN; SPP; TCAP. *See also* Who shall thy gay buffoonery describe?
Winged rocket curving through, A. The Humming Bird. Maurice Thompson. BLA
Winged Victory. Harold Trowbridge Pulsifer. BAP
Winged wonder of motion. The Dragonfly. Theodore Harding Rand. CaP; CPG; OCL
Winged Words. Robert Crawford. BoAu
Winged Worshipers, The. Charles Sprague. AA; HBV; LPS-2; SN
Wings. William Rose Benét. PoMa
Wings. Charles G. Blanden. PoTo

Wings. Victor Hugo. *See* Be like the Bird.
Wings. Joseph Easton McDougall. MM
Wings. Psalms, LV: 6-7, Bible, *O.T.* FaPON; PCD; PCH
Wings. Blanche W. Schoonmaker. DD; GA
Wings and the boy I sing, who, braving fate. Our Boy. Oliver Herford. GA
Wings and Wheels. Nancy Byrd Turner. StVeCh (1955 ed.); SUS; TiPo
Wings at Dawn. Joseph Auslander. BAP; HBMV
Wings Have We. Wordsworth. Personal Talk, III. CBOV
("Wings have we—and as far as we can go.") EM-2; EmBrPo; PeBoSo
Wings in the Dark. John Gray. SG
Wings of Azrael, The. Edwin Björkman. NoCaPo (1941 ed.)
Wings of Love, The. James H. Cousins. AnIV
Wings of the Dragonfly. *Unknown, tr. fr. Chinese.* WhP
Wings of the windmill rustle no longer. Nocturne. Sigbjörn Obstfelder. AnNoLy
Wings of Time are black and white, The. Compensation. Emerson. IAP; RiBV; TCAP
Wings of Wine. Ibn al-Yamani *tr. fr. Arabic by* A. J. Arberry. MooP
Wings over Europe, *abr.* Maria Olimpia de Obaldía, *tr. fr. Spanish by* Milton Ben Davis. BoFr
Wings the seaweed and the waves, The. Sleepless Palinurus. Silvina Ocampo. AnCL
Winifred Waters. John Daniel Logan. CPG
Winifred White. Nonsense Verses, III. Laura E. Richards. RIS
Winifreda. *Unknown.* EV-2; HBV; OBEV (new ed.)
(Translation from the Ancient British.) OBEC
Winked too much and were afraid of snakes. The Monkeys [*or* My Apish Cousins]. Marianne Moore. AnFE; APA; CoAnAm; LiTA; NAMP; OxBA; SeCeV; TwAmPo
Winky, Blinky. *Unknown.* PCH
Winner of the Pentathlon, A. Simonides, *tr. fr. Greek by* Gilbert Highet. OxBG
Winners, The. Kipling. *See* L'Envoi: "What is the moral?"
Winnie the Pooh, *sel.* A. A. Milne.
Hums of Pooh. BoN
Winning of Cales, The. Thomas Deloney. CoMu; SG, *sl. diff.*
Winning of the TV West, The. John T. Alexander. WaKn
Winning way, a pleasant smile, A. Little Annie Rooney. Michael Nolan. TreF
Winnipeg at Christmas. Rose Fyleman. ChBR
Winnow me through with thy keen clear breath. The Sea-Wind. Arthur Ketchum. NLK
Winnower of Wheat to the Winds, A. Joachim du Bellay. *See* Hymn to the Winds.
Winnowers, The. Robert Bridges. OAEP; POTT; TVSH
Winny, *abr.* William Allingham. OTPC (1923 ed.)
Winsome Torment rose from slumber, rubbed his eyes, and went his way. The Hammam Name. James Elroy Flecker. FaBoTw
Winter. Enid Blyton. BoTP
Winter. John Howard Bryant. LPS-2
Winter. John Clare. ATP
Winter. Charles Cotton. BrBE
Winter's Troops, *sel.* ChTr
Winter. William Cowper. *Fr.* The Task, IV. OBEC
("O winter, ruler of the inverted year," *longer sel.*) TyEnPo
Winter. Maurice James Craig. OnYI
Winter. Adelaide Crapsey. MPB; PFE
Winter. Walter de la Mare. ChTr; MoVE; OBMV; YeAr
Winter. Aubrey Thomas De Vere. *Fr.* The Year of Sorrow: Ireland—1849. IrPN; TIP
(Year of Sorrow, A, *abr.*) ACP
Winter. Mary Mapes Dodge. *See* Snowflakes ("Whenever a snowflake").
Winter. Gawin Douglas. *Fr.* Prologues to the Aeneid, Prologue to Bk. VII. EBSV; SeCePo
Winter. Hesiod, *tr. fr. Greek. Fr.* Works and Days. GrPE, *tr. by* F. L. Lucas; OxBG, *pr. tr. by* T. F. Higham
("Beware the January month; beware," *tr. by* C. A. Elton.) GrPo
Winter. Horace. *See* To Thaliarchus.
Winter. Richard Hughes AlDL; OBMV; ThWaDe
Winter. Issa, *tr. fr. Japanese by* H. G. Henderson. OnPM
Winter. Joso, *tr. fr. Japanese by* H. G. Henderson. OnPM; WoL
Winter. Kalidasa, *tr. fr. Sanskrit by* Arthur W. Ryder. *Fr.* The Seasons. AWP
Winter. W. D. Landor. BoTP
Winter. Dorothy Livesay. TwCaPo
Winter. Charles Mair. PeCV
Winter. Tosaburo Ono, *tr. fr. Japanese by* Takamichi Ninomiya *and* D. J. Enright. PoLJ
Winter. Coventry Patmore. The Unknown Eros, I, iii. LEAP; NBE; POTT; VLEP
("I, singularly moved.") LO
Winter ("Bread and milk . . ."). Christina Rossetti. *Fr.* Sing-Song. PCH
("Bread and milk for breakfast.") EmBrPo; SAS
Winter ("Sweet blackbird . . ."). Christina Rossetti. BoTP
Winter. Thomas Sackville. *See* Approach of Winter, The.
Winter. V. Sackville-West. *Fr.* The Land. AlDL
Winter. Shakespeare. *See* When Icicles Hang by the Wall.
Winter. Shelley. *See* Widow Bird, A.
Winter. Robert Southey. PEOR
Winter. Spenser. *Fr.* The Faerie Queene, VII, 7. GN; OTPC
Winter. J. M. Synge. OBMV
Winter. Tennyson. PCH
Winter ("See, Winter comes, to rule the varied year"). James Thomson. *Fr.* The Seasons. BEL, *sl. abr.*; CEP; EiPP; EM-1, *shorter sel.*; EnL, *shorter sel.*; EnLi-2, *shorter sel.*; EnLit, *shorter sel.*; OAEP, *abr.*; PIAE, *abr.*; Po, *abr.*; TyEnPo, *shorter sel.*
Sels.
Approach of Winter. OBEC
"Clear frost succeeds, and thro' the blew serene." FaBoEn
Frost at Night. CoEV; OBEC
"Late, in the louring sky, red, fiery, streaks." FaBoEn
"Lo! from the livid East or piercing North." AtBAP; FaBoEn
Lost Shepherd, The. CoBE
"Now, solitary, and in pensive guise." FaBoEn
"Now when the cheerless empire of the sky." BSV
Storm, The. CoBE
Winter ("As thus the snows arise, and, foul and fierce"). SeCePo
Winter ("The keener tempests come: and, fuming dun"). EnRP; ViBoPo
(Snow Scene, A.) EPP
(Storm in Winter, A.) EV-3
(Winter Scenes.) LPS-2
(Winter Storm, A.) TOP
Winter Scene, A. OBEC
Winter Winds. UnPo (1st ed.)
Winter. Bjarni Thorarensen, *tr. fr. Icelandic by* Vilhjalmur Stefansson. IcP
Winter. Meta E. B. Thorne. *Fr.* Songs of the Seasons. PEOR
Winter ("Chill, chill!"). *Unknown, tr. fr. Irish by* Frank O'Connor. KiLC
Winter ("Keen is the wind, bare the hill, it is difficult to find shelter"). *Unknown, tr. fr. Welsh by* Kenneth Jackson. *Fr.* The Black Book of Carmarthen. PrWP
Winter ("Old Winter is a sturdy one.") *Unknown.* DD
Winter ("Winter is a dreary season"). *Unknown, tr. fr. Irish by* Frank O'Connor. KiLC
Winter. Sheila Wingfield. EnLoPo
Winter; a Dirge. Burns. HBV
Winter afternoon, The. A Moment. L. A. G. Strong. NeMA
Winter all in branches and hard as a corpse, A. What the Laborer Says Is Always beside the Point. Paul Eluard. MiCF
Winter among the Days. Raymond Holden. MAP; MoAmPo (1942 ed.)
Winter and night, the white frost and the darkness. Urania. Ruth Pitter. MoVE
Winter and Red Berries. Nicholas Moore. NeBP
Winter and Spring. *Unknown.* BoTP
Winter and Summer. Stephen Spender. MoAB; MoBrPo (1950 ed.); MoPo
Winter, and the sky is a land of gray fiords. Grisaille with a Spot of Red. Samuel Yellen. NePoAm-2
Winter Apples. Winifred Welles. AnAmPo; LA
Winter at Tomi. Ovid, *tr. fr. Latin by* F. A. Wright. AWP; JAWP; WBP
Winter be greeted by lads and lasses. A Dance Song. Burkhard von Hohenfels. LiTW
Winter Being Over. The. Anne Collins. LPS-2
Winter Birds. Elinor MacArthur. BLA; WhBS
Winter blows on my eaves. Solstitium Saeculare. Robert Fitzgerald. MoVE
Winter Branches. Margaret Widdemer. CP
Winter Breath. Edward Weismiller. PoMa
Winter, by whom our stumbling feet were caught. Winter. Dorothy Livesay. TwCaPo
Winter Circus. Aileen Fisher. YeAr
Winter clenched its fist, The. The Redwing. Patric Dickinson. HaMV
Winter Coats. Dorothy Aldis. RIS
Winter comes; I walk alone, The. The Winter's Spring. John Clare. AtBAP
Winter Dawn. Tu Fu, *tr. fr Chinese by* Kenneth Rexroth. OnPC
Winter Day. Whittier. *Fr.* Snow-bound. TrGrPo
(Lines from "Snowbound.") BBV
(Snow, The, *longer sel.*) StVeCh
(Sun That Brief December Day, The.) OnAP
Winter Days. Henry Abbey. AA; SN
Winter days and spring and summer still the yearly round renew. Flute Song. *Unknown.* OxBG

Winter days are drawin' nigh, De. Winter Is Coming. Waverly Turner Carmichael. BANP
Winter Dusk. Walter de la Mare. AnEnPo; UnW
Winter Dusk. Richard Kendall Munkittrick. BOHV
Winter Eden, A. Robert Frost. MOAP
Winter Evening ("Come, Evening"). William Cowper. *Fr.* The Task, IV. CoBE
(Evening.) OBEC
Winter Evening, The ("Hark! 'tis the twanging horn"). William Cowper. The Task, IV. EiPP; EnLi-2; EnLit; EV-3, *sel.;* OAEP; SeCePo; TOP, *sel.*
(Post-Boy, The.) FiP
(Postman, The.) CoBE; CoEV
Winter Evening. Archibald Lampman. BoCaPo; CPG; PeCV
Winter Evening. Pushkin, *tr. fr. Russian.* BoR, *tr. by* C. M. Bowra; TrRV, *tr. by* Babette Deutsch; WoL, *tr. by* C. Fillingham Coxwell
Winter Evening. Katharine Tynan. TIP
Winter Evening Hymn to My Fire, A, *abr.* James Russell Lowell. LPS-1
Winter evening settles down, The. Preludes, I. T. S. Eliot. AmP; AmPP; AnAmPo; BAV; BoLiVe (1945 ed.); CoBA; ExPo; GBV (1952 ed.); GTBS-W; InP; LA; LiTA; LiTM; MAP; MoAmPo (1942 ed.); MoShBr; MoVE; NeMA; OBMV; PoFS; ReMP; SeCePo; ShBV-3; TiPo (1952 ed.); TwP; UnPo; VOD (1935 ed.)
Winter Feast. Frances Frost. YeAr
Winter Feathers. Mildred D. Shacklett. GFA
Winter Field. A. E. Coppard. MBP; MoBrPo (1942 ed.)
Winter Fire, The. Mary Howitt. OTPC (1923 ed.)
Winter Flood, The. Pearce Young. PtPa
Winter flood is out, dully glasing the weald, The. The Flood. Andrew Young. ChMP
Winter for a Moment Takes the Mind. Conrad Aiken. Preludes for Memnon, I. LiTA; LiTM; MoPo; MoVE; NP; OxBA
(Preludes to Attitude, IV.) TwAmPo
Winter forests mutely standing. In the Winter Woods. Frederick George Scott. CPG
Winter—Frost. Thomas Gisborne. *Fr.* Walks in a Forest. EnSW
Winter Galaxy, The. Charles Heavysege. BoCaPo
(Stars Are Glittering in the Frosty Sky, The.) CaP; PeCV
Winter Garden. David Gascoyne. ChMP; GTBS-D
Winter garden in an alder swamp, A. A Winter Eden. Robert Frost. MOAP
Winter Glass, The. Charles Cotton. HBV
Winter has a joy for me. I Will Praise the Lord at All Times. William Cowper. CEP
Winter has at last come. Minamoto no Shigeyuki. *Fr.* Shui Shu. AWP
Winter Has Come. *Unknown.* CBPC
Winter Has Come ("Winter has come with scarcity"). *Unknown, tr. fr. Old Irish by* Kenneth Jackson. AnIL
Winter has come; fierce is the cold. Hot Cake. Shu Hsi. AlDL; AtBAP; BoW; MBP; MoBrPo (1942 ed.)
Winter has come with pinching dearth. *Unknown. Fr.* Four Short Poems. LyMA
Winter has come with scarcity. Winter Has Come. *Unknown.* AnIL
Winter has grown so still, The. Lute and Furrow. Olive Tilford Dargan. LS; SPP; TBM
Winter has no cold teeth to crumble these. Rainbow Lands. Howard McKinley Corning. NP
Winter has planted the field black with crows. Serfs. Cale Young Rice. BLA
Winter has reached thee once again at last. To Hampstead. Leigh Hunt. OBRV
Winter has wrecked the legend of your wings. To the Ghost of a Kite. James Wright. NePoEA
Winter Heavens. George Meredith. BLV; BoLiVe; Po; ViP
Winter, her life was past. To her charmed sill. Death of Saint Therese of Lisieux. Jessica Powers. PraNu
Winter hurts me not. *Unknown. Fr.* Eulogistic Snatches. SiB
Winter in Castile. John Dos Passos. VOD (1935 ed.)
Winter in Durnover Field. Thomas Hardy. MBP; MoBrPo
Winter in Lower Canada Standish O'Grady. *Fr.* The Emigrant. BoCaPo
Winter in Montreal. Patrick Anderson. BoCaPo (1948 ed.)
Winter in the Wood. Ivy O. Eastwick. YeAr
Winter in the world it is. Meeting in Winter. William Morris. EnLi-2 (1949 ed)
Winter is a dreary season. Winter. *Unknown.* KiLC
Winter is cold-hearted. Summer Days [*or* Summer]. Christina Rossetti. AlDL; BPN; MCCG; OTPC; PRWS
Winter Is Coming. Waverly Turner Carmichael. BANP
Winter Is Coming. Jules Laforgue. *See* Approach of Winter, The.
Winter is dead, and the spring is a-dying, The. The Balliol Rooks. Frederick S. Boas. BLA
Winter Is Gone. Alfred Austin. LiTG; SiTL
Winter is gone, and spring returns. Spring Returns. Li Ch'ing-chao. WhP
Winter is here. Brother Beasts. Cale Young Rice. MW
Winter is icumen [*or* icummen] in. Ancient Music. Ezra Pound. CoV; LiTM; NePA; OxBA; PoE; ReaPo; SiTL
Winter is passing, and the bells. Spring in the Students' Quarter. Henry Murger. AWP
Winter Is Past, The. Song of Solomon, Bible, *O.T. See* For, Lo, the Winter Is Past.
Winter is past, The. My Love Is like the Sun. *Unknown.* AnIV
Winter is too cold fer work. Nothin' Done. Sam S. Stinson. LHV
Winter is upon us, not the snow, The. Before the Snow. Andrew Lang. VOD
Winter is wroth, with reason! Spring. Feodor Tyutchev. BoRS
Winter Joys. Dorothy Gradon. BoTP
Winter Juniper. Joseph Langland. NePoEA
Winter Lakes, The. Wilfred Campbell. BoCaPo
Winter Landscape. John Berryman. LiTA; LiTG; MoAmPo (1950 ed.)
Winter Landscape. Stephen Spender. MBP; MoAB; MoBrPo
Winter Life and Scenery. Thomas Caulfield Irwin. IrPN
Winter Lightning [for Paul], The. Howard Nemerov. FiMAP; MoVE
Winter Love. Elizabeth Jennings. NePoEA
Winter Love Song. *Unknown. See* De Ramis Cadunt Folia.
Winter Lullaby, A. Madeleine Sweeny Miller. BOL
Winter Madrigal, A. Morris Bishop. InMe
Winter Mask. Allen Tate. NePA; OxBA
Winter Memories. Henry David Thoreau. AmPP (4th ed.); NePA; OxBA
(Within the Circuit of This Plodding Life.) CoV
Winter midnight. Otsuji, *tr. fr. Japanese by* Kenneth Rexroth. LiTW
Winter Moonlight. Gillespie Evans. CAG
Winter Morning. William Cowper. *See* Winter Morning Walk, The.
Winter Morning, A. James Russell Lowell. *Fr.* The Vision of Sir Launfal, Pt. II. GN
(January.) PoRL
Winter Morning. Pushkin, *tr. fr. Russian by* C. M. Bowra. BoR
Winter Morning Walk, The ("'Tis morning"). William Cowper. *Fr.* The Task, V. PoEL-3
("'Tis morning; and the sun, with ruddy orb.") EnSW; EPP
(Winter Morning, *abr.*) LPS-2
Winter Morning Walk, The ("Whose freedom is by suff'rance, and at will"). William Cowper. *Fr.* The Task, V. EnRP
Winter Night, A. William Barnes. ChTr
Winter Night, A, *sel.* Burns.
"When biting Boreas, fell and doure." BSV; MCCG
Winter Night. Mary Frances Butts. OTPC; PRWS; RAR; TiPo (1952 ed.)
Winter Night. Emperor Ch'ien Wen-ti, *tr. fr. Chinese by* Arthur Waley AtBAP; BoW; OnPM; TrCh
Winter Night. A. R. D. Fairburn. AnNZ
Winter Night. Gustaf Fröding, *tr. fr. Swedish by* Charles W. Stork. AnSL
Winter Night. Roy Fuller. NeBP
Winter Night. Collister Hutchison. TiPo (1952 ed.)
Winter Night. Edna St. Vincent Millay. BAP; PoRL
Winter Night. Po Chü-i, *tr. fr. Chinese by* Arthur Waley. TrCh
Winter Night. Georg Trakl, *tr. fr. German by* David Luke. AnGP
Winter Night ("As night drew on"). Whittier. *Fr.* Snow-bound. TrGrPo
("As night drew on.") YT
(Fireside, The.) MW
Winter night is cold and drear, The. Across the Delaware. Will Carleton. MC; PAH
Winter-Night Song. Ford Madox Ford. NP
Winter Night Song. Sara Teasdale. ChMo; CMP; MOAP; TwCV
Winter Nightfall. Robert Bridges. GTBS-D; MBP; MM; MoAB; MoBrPo; NeMA; OBEV; PoVP
Winter Nightfall. J. C. Squire. GTML; ShBV-3
Winter Nights. Thomas Campion. *See* Now Winter Nights Enlarge.
Winter 1939. George Ewart Evans. MoWP
Winter 1939–1940. Laurie Lee. PoN
Winter Noon. William Cowper. *See* Winter Walk at Noon, The.
Winter Noon. James Rorty MOAP
Winter Noon. Sara Teasdale. YeAr
Winter Noon in the Woods, *sel* Thomas Caulfield Irwin.
"With witchlike branches, barren, bleak, and drear." IrPN
Winter, now thy spite is spent. The Vow to Cupid. *Unknown.* LyMA
Winter Oak. Mary Sinton Leitch. MuM

Winter of Our Discontent Shakespeare. King Richard III, *fr.* I, i. LiA
(Evil Designs.) TreF
(Hate the Idle Pleasures.) TrGrPo
Winter of '73, The, *with music.* Larry Gorman. ShS
Winter of the soul . . . the living sun, The. Vyacheslav Ivanovich Ivanov. *Fr.* Winter Sonnets, III. TrRV
Winter Offering. D. S. Savage. LiTB; LiTM; NeBP
Winter on Black Mingo, *sel.* *Unknown.*
"Cold, deserted and silent." FiBHP
Winter owl skirts hemlock tree. Winter Sketch. Arthur S. Bourinot. CaP
Winter Pictures. James Russell Lowell. *Fr.* The Vision of Sir Launfal: Prelude to Pt. II, *incl. st.* 1 *of* Pt. II. BAP; LPS-2
(Brook in Winter, The, *shorter sel.*) GN; OTPC
(December.) GoTP
("Down swept the chill wind.") TreF
Winter Piece, A. Bryant. AmPP (4th ed.); CoBA; MOAP; OxBA
Winter Piece, A. Ambrose Philips. CEP; OBEC; SeCePo
Sels.
Glittering Frost. BeR
Ocean of Ice, The. BeR
Winter, Plague and Pestilence. Thomas Nashe. *See* Autumn.
Winter Remembered. John Crowe Ransom. MoAB; MoPW; OxBA; UnPo
Winter Revery. Sara Bard Field. BAP; PoeMoYo
Winter Ride, A. Amy Lowell. LBMV
Winter Road. Pushkin, *tr. fr. Russian by* Oliver Elton. BoRS
Winter Rune. Elizabeth J. Coatsworth. SUS
Winter Saturday. Earle Birney. TwCaPo
Winter Scene, The. Bliss Carman. VOD
Winter Scene. William Cowper. *Fr.* The Task. *See* Winter Walk at Noon, The.
Winter Scene [*or* Scenes]. James Thomson. *See* Winter.
Winter Shower, A. Harumi, *tr. fr. Japanese by* Asataro Miyamori. OnPM
Winter Sketch. Arthur S. Bourinot. CaP
Winter Sleep. Edith M. Thomas. AA; EOAH; LBMV
Winter Sleep. Elinor Wylie. BAV; NePA
Winter Solstice, *sel.* Gerald Bullett.
So Still the World. POTE
Winter Solstice. Sara Teasdale. *See* December Day, A.
Winter Song, A. William Cox Bennett. PCH
Winter Song, A. Pauline Frances Camp. BOL
Winter Song. Ludwig Hölty, *tr. fr. German by* Charles T. Brooks. LPS-2
Winter Song. V. Sackville-West. *Fr.* The Land. MBP; MoBrPo (1942 ed.)
Winter Song. Shakespeare. *See* When Icicles Hang by the Wall.
Winter Song ("Drop down, drop down, white snowflakes!"). *Unknown, tr. fr. Czech.* PCH
(Winter's Song.) BoTP
Winter Song, A ("Oh, summer has the roses"). *Unknown.* PEOR
Winter-Song for Pan. John Erskine. CAG
Winter Sonnets, *sel.* Vyacheslav Ivanovich Ivanov, *tr. fr. Russian by* Babette Deutsch.
"Winter of the soul . . . the living sun, The," *fr.* III. TrRV
Winter Spring. Richard Wilbur. FiMAP
Winter Stalks. Bertram J. Warr. TwCaPo
Winter Starset. Elliott Coleman. NoCaPo (1941 ed.)
Winter Storm, A. James Thomson. *See* Winter.
Winter Storm at Sea, The. George Crabbe. *Fr.* The Borough, Letter I. EtS
(Winter Storm, The, *longer sel.*) EV-3
Winter Storms, The. Sir William Davenant. SeCL
Winter Streams. Bliss Carman. YeAr
Winter Sunrise, *sel.* Laurence Binyon.
"It is early morning within this room; without." ChMP
Winter Sunset. Jules Laforgue, *tr. fr. French by* Kate Flores. AnFP
Winter Swan. Louise Bogan. AnAmPo; LA
Winter Sweetness. Langston Hughes. GoSl
Winter, that coils in the thickets now. Deciduous Branch. Stanley Kunitz. HoPM
Winter—Thaw. Thomas Gisborne. *Fr.* Walks in a Forest. EnSW
Winter the Huntsman. Sir Osbert Sitwell. AlDL; AtBAP; BoW; POTE; ShBV-2
Winter-Time. *See* Wintertime.
Winter to Spring. Horace, *tr. fr. Latin by* Louis MacNeice. Odes, I, 4. LiTW
("Winter to Spring: the west wind melts the frozen rancour.") LaP
Winter Treats. Mildred D. Shacklett. GFA
Winter Trees. William Carlos Williams. NP
Winter Tryst. Mark Van Doren. LiTA; LiTM (1946 ed.)
Winter Twilight, A. Arlo Bates. AA
Winter Twilight. George Tracy Elliot. AA
Winter Twilight, A. Angelina W. Grimké. CDC; PoNe
Winter; Two Sonnets. Malcolm Cowley. *Fr.* Blue Juniata. MAP; MoAmPo (1942 ed.)
Winter Walk at Noon, The. William Cowper. *Fr.* The Task, VI. EV-3
("Night was winter in his roughest mood, The.") BrBE; EnRP; EnSW; NBE
(Winter Noon, *abr.*) LPS-2
(Winter Scene.) OBEC
Winter was so late in coming. The Discouraged Cherry Tree. Kathleen Millay. PEDC
Winter, we are by thy might. Winter-Time. Neidhart von Reuental. WoL
Winter Weather. William Morris. BPN; EmBrPo; EPN; PFE; TOP
Winter Weather. James Wreford Watson. BoCaPo
Winter Westerlies. James Devaney. BoAV; MoAuPo
Winter wheat is fair to see. Autumnal. Marie Emilie Gilchrist. TBM
Winter: When Icicles Hang by the Wall. Shakespeare. *See* When Icicles Hang by the Wall.
Winter Will Follow. Richard Watson Dixon. *See* Heaving Roses of the Hedge Are Stirred, The.
Winter will not let go of earth. In Defense of Felons. Robert Mezey. NePoEA
Winter wind is loud and wild, The. Faith and Despondency. Emily Brontë. EmBrPo
Winter Winds. James Thomson. *See* Winter.
Winter winds howled and the great barn creaked. The Barn in Winter. Claire Harris MacIntosh. CaP
Winter Wish, A. Robert Hinckley Messinger. AA; LEAP; ViBoPo
(Give Me the Old.) HBV; LPS-1
Winter with the Gulf Stream. Gerard Manley Hopkins. ExPo; ViP
Winter, you're nothing but a lout. Rondel. Charles d'Orléans. FoS
Wintering time and weather. Winter Weather. James Wreford Watson. BoCaPo
Winter's Beauty. W. H. Davies. ChMo; CMP
Winter's Cold. W. R. Rodgers. EnLoPo
Winter's End. Howard Moss. NePoEA
Winters know. Nature. Emerson. GBV (1952 ed.); MOAP
Winter's Morning Muse, A. Thomas Howell. SiCE
Winter's Song. Shakespeare. *See* When Icicles Hang by the Wall.
Winter's Song. *Unknown.* *See* Winter Song ("Drop down, drop down . . .")
Winter's Spring, The. John Clare. AtBAP
Winter's Tale, A. D. H. Lawrence. MBP; MoAB; MoBrPo
Winter's Tale, The, *sels.* Shakespeare.
"But shall I go mourn for that, my dear?" 4 *ll., fr.* IV, ii. PoD
Flowers ("Out, alas!"), *fr.* IV, iii. UnPo (1st ed.)
Flowers of Perdita, The ("Here's flowers for you"), *fr.* IV, iii. FiP
(Flowers of Middle Summer.) YeAr
Jog On, Jog On [the Footpath Way], *fr.* IV, ii. CBE; EG; FaBoCh; GN; HBV; HBVY; LoGBV; OBSC; SiCE; TiPo (1952 ed.); TVC; TVSH; ViBoPo
(Autolycus.) EV-1
(Autolycus' Song.) WhC
(Footpath Way, The.) RIS
(Merry Heart, The.) BoTP; EIL; PCH; ShGoBo; SiTL; TrGrPo
(Songs of Autolycus, The.) OTPC (1923 ed.)
"Lawn as white as driven snow," *fr.* IV, iii. ElSeCe; EM-1; EV-1; OAEP; OBSC; SiCE; ViBoPo; WP
(Autolycus' Song.) KN; LoBV
(Come Buy! [Come Buy]) EIL; GaP
(Pedlar's Song.) CH
(Songs of Autolycus, The.) OTPC (1923 ed.)
"Now/ My fair'st friend," *fr.* IV, iii. NBE
(Some Flowers o' the Spring.) ChTr
"O Proserpina!/ For the flowers now," *fr.* IV, iii. LEAP
(Daffodils.) CBPC
(Flowers.) ADAH; EV-1; SN
(Perdita's Garden.) WHA
(Spring Flowers.) BCEP
". . . daffodils/ That come before the swallow dares," 3 *ll.* TiPo
"Sir, welcome," *fr.* IV, iii. AtBAP
"What you do/ Still betters what is done," *fr.* IV, iii. LoPS; NBE
When Daffodils [*or* Daffadils] Begin to Peer, *fr.* IV, ii. ChTr; EIL; ExPo; FaBoBe; FaBoCh; HBV; InPo; KN; LoBV; LoGBV; OBSC; PoEL-2; SiCE; ViBoPo; WhC
(Autolicus's Song.) FaBoEn
(Autolycus.) EG; EV-1
(Pedlar's Song, The.) OxBoLi
(Song: "When daffodils begin to peer.") FiP
(Song from "The Winter's Tale.") LEAP
(Songs of Autolycus, The.) OTPC (1923 ed.)
"When you sing," *fr.* IV, iii. UnS

Will You Buy Any Tape?, *fr.* IV, iii. GaP; OBSC; SiCE; ViBoPo
(Songs of Autolycus, The.) OTPC (1923 ed.)
Winter's Tale, A. Frank Dempster Sherman. PR
Winter's Tale, A. Dylan Thomas. AtBAP; FaBoMo; LiTB; PoLFOT; SeCeV
Winter's thunder. *Unknown.* GoTP; RIS
Winter's Tree, *sel.* Marjorie Allen Seiffert.
"Grieve not too much for April." BAP
Winter's Troops. Charles Cotton. *Fr.* Winter. ChTr
Winter's Turning. Amy Lowell. CV
Winter-Time. Neidhart von Reuental, *tr. fr. German by* Jethro Bithell. WoL
Winter-Time. Robert Louis Stevenson. GFA; GoTP; MBP; MoBrPo; StVeCh
Winter time is bleak, the wind. Caoilte. *Unknown.* KiLC
Wintertime nighs. In Tenebris, I. Thomas Hardy. FaBoEn; LiTB; OAEP (2d ed.); SeCePo; TreFS; UnPo; ViP; ViPo
Wintry blast goes wailing by, The. Christmas Night of '62. William Gordon McCabe. AA
Wintry Day. *Unknown.* PCH
Wintry Lullaby, A. Laurence Alma-Tadema. BOL
Wintry month of storm and cold, The. Some Years in Washington's Life. M. Lizzie Stanley. WOAH
Wintry Sunrise, A. Richard Savage. *Fr.* The Wanderer, I. BeR
Wintry west extends his blast, The. Winter; a Dirge. Burns. HBV
Wintry winds have ceased to blow, The. Resurrection. George Crabbe. OxBoCh
Wir Sind Alle Verloren. Michael Roberts. *Fr.* Elegy for the Fallen Climbers. MoP
Wire, briar, limber-lock. *Unknown.* RIS
Wireless. Rodney Bennett. BoTP
Wires Are So Still and High, The. Annette Wynne. GFA; PCH
Wires spread out far and wide, The. The Telegraph. Annette Wynne. GFA
Wires strung with diamonds. Snowfall. "I.V.S.W." InMe
Wirra, wirra! ologone! Fan Fitzgerl. Alfred Perceval Graves. TIP
Wisdom. Evelyn Werner Barkins. MuM
Wisdom. Bible, Apocrypha. *See* Wisdom of Solomon, The.
Wisdom ("But where shall wisdom"). Job, XXVIII: 12–28, Bible, *O.T.* BHV
Wisdom ("Length of days"). Proverbs, III: 16–18, Bible, *O.T.* BPP
Wisdom. George Frederick Cameron. CPG
Wisdom. William Cowper. *Fr.* The Task, VI. MaRV
Wisdom. Padraic Fallon. OnYI
Wisdom. Ford Madox Ford. HBV
Wisdom. Phyllis Hanson. GoYe
Wisdom. Daniel Whitehead Hicky. OQP; QP-2
Wisdom? "Laurence Hope." *Fr.* The Teak Forest. OtMeF
Wisdom. Langston Hughes. TiPo
Wisdom. Virginia Lawrence. PR
Wisdom. Scudder Middleton. HBMV
Wisdom. Jay Paul. CAG
Wisdom. Christina Rossetti. OBVV; TOP
Wisdom ("It was a night"). Sara Teasdale. BAP; LoPo; MAP; MoAmPo; MuM
Wisdom ("When I have ceased"). Sara Teasdale. Interlude; Songs Out of Sorrow, IV. InP
Wisdom and Spirit of the universe! Influence of Natural Objects [*or* Boyhood *or* Nature's Ministry]. Wordsworth. *Fr.* The Prelude. AtBAP; AWP; BPN; CoEV; GrCo-2; InPo; JAWP; LoBV; MCCG; OBRV; RO; WBP; WHA
Wisdom be Thou. A Prayer for St. Innocent's Day. Helen Parry Eden. CAW
Wisdom Cometh with the Years. Countee Cullen. TBM
Wisdom found no place where she might dwell. Wisdom's Plight. Enoch, Bible, Pseudepigrapha. TrJP
Wisdom has no end and folly no ornament. Poem. Nathan Alterman. LiTW
Wisdom hath builded her house. The House of Wisdom. Proverbs, Bible, *O.T.* TrGrPo
Wisdom immortal from immortal Jove. Wisdom. George Frederick Cameron. CPG
Wisdom in Winter. *Unknown, tr. fr. Welsh by* Gwyn Williams. *Fr.* The Black Book of Carmarthen. PrWP
Wisdom is better than bread. Nevertheless. Gustav Davidson. GoYe
Wisdom of Folly. Ellen Thorneycroft Fowler. BLP; HBV
Wisdom of Insecurity, The. Richard Eberhart. NePA
Wisdom of Merlyn, The, *sels.* Wilfrid Scawen Blunt.
"What then is Merlyn's message" ViBoPo
"Wouldst thou be wise, O Man?" OBMV
Wisdom of Solomon, The, *sels.* Bible, Apocrypha.
Wisdom ("For she is a vapour"), VII: 25–26 (*Douay vers.*). ISi
Wisdom ("I called upon God"), VII: 7–14, 22–27. GrCo-1
Wisdom of the Gazelle. George P. Solomos. GoYe
Wisdom of the World, The. Siegfried Sassoon. MBP; MoBrPo; NeMA
Wisdom of the world said unto me, The. Sapientia Lunae. Ernest Dowson. EnLi-2; HBV; POTT
Wisdom, out of Anguish by Denial. Pedigree. Mary Mills. NePoAm
Wisdom 'tis and courtesy. The Highest Wisdom. Jacopone da Todi. CAW
Wisdom warns me to shun that once I sought for. Phaleuciacs II. *Unknown.* SiCE
Wisdom with better thoughts prevailed; aloof. The Jew's Home. Robert Eyres. *Fr.* The Impious Feast. OBRV
Wisdom's Plight. Enoch, XLII: 1–3, Bible, Pseudepigrapha. TrJP
Wise, The. Countee Cullen. PoNe
Wise. Lizette Woodworth Reese. HBV; LBAP
Wise, The. *Unknown, tr. fr. Sanskrit by* Sir Edwin Arnold. *Fr.* Bhagavad-Gita. OQP; QP-2
Wise Age to Youth. Tu Chiu Niang, *tr. fr. Chinese by* Henry H. Hart. PoHN
Wise and Foolish Virgins, The. St. Matthew, XXV: 1–13, Bible, *N.T.* TreF
Wise Colonist who in this storied place. Champlain; First Canadian. John Daniel Logan. CPG
Wise counsel is not always wise. The Boy and the Schoolmaster. La Fontaine. WoL
Wise emblem of our politick world. The Snayl. Richard Lovelace. AtBAP; NBE; PoEL-3
Wise forget, dear heart, The. A Valentine. Jeannette Bliss Gillespy. *Fr.* Cameos. AA
Wise guys, The/ tell me. Kid Stuff. Frank Horne. PoNe
Wise Johnny. Edwina Fallis. SiSoSe; SUS; TiPo
Wise king crowned [*or* dowered] with blessings on his throne, The. The Trophy. Edwin Muir. LiTM; NeTW; POTE
Wise man holds himself in check, A. Wisdom. Scudder Middleton. HBMV
Wise man, the fourfold wise. Serenade at the Window of the Wise Man. Zacharias Papondoniou. MoGP
Wise Man, Wise Man. Louis Ginsberg. YT
Wise may bring their learning, The. A Child's Offering. *Unknown.* MaRV
Wise Men, The. Edgar Bowers. NePoEA; PtPa
Wise Men and Shepherds. Sidney Godolphin. *See* Lord, When the Wise Men Came from Far.
Wise men, The, ask, "What language did Christ speak?" The Universal Language. Ella Wheeler Wilcox. ChIP; OQP; QP-1
Wise Men in Their Bad Hours. Robinson Jeffers. AnAmPo; LA
Wise men, indeed, to know a new-born star. A Different Way. Esther Lloyd Hagg. ChIP
Wise men love the cats for their perversity, The. The Cats. Baudelaire. OnPM
Wise Men of Gotham, The ("In a bowl to sea went wise men three"). Thomas Love Peacock. BoN
Wise Men of Gotham, The ("Seamen three! What men be ye?"). Thomas Love Peacock. *See* Three Men of Gotham.
Wise men patience never want. Thomas Campion. SiCE
Wise Men Seeking Jesus. James East. MaRV
Wisemen to glossators unknown. Apocryphal Apocalypse. John Wheelwright. MoVE
Wise men [*or* Wisemen] were but seven, ne'er more shall be for me, The. A Catch [*or* We Are Three]. *Unknown.* AlDL; SeCL; SeEP
Wise Men, Wise Men. The Gifts. Odell Shepard. ChrBoLe
Wise Misogynist, The. Bhartrihari, *tr. fr. Sanskrit by* Arthur W. Ryder. OnPM
Wise, O Man, thou only shalt become. At the End of the Way. Verner von Heidenstam. AnSL
Wise Old Owl, The. Edward Hersey Richards. BLPA; FaBoBe; FaFP; NeHB; SiTL; TreF; YaD
(Question & Answer, *with add. st.*) LiTG
("Wise old owl sat in an oak, A.") OxNR
Wise Penelope. Homer, *pr. tr. fr. Greek by* A. T. Murray. *Fr.* The Odyssey, XIX. LiA
Wise Rochefoucauld a maxim writ. The Life and Genuine Character of Dean Swift. Swift. EiPP
Wise Sarah and the Elf. Elizabeth J. Coatsworth. PoMS
Wise self is not born and does not die, The. Unborn Eternal Self. *Unknown.* *Fr.* The Upanishads. OnPM
Wise Thrush, The. Robert Browning. *Fr.* Home Thoughts from Abroad. BLA; WhBS
Wise to have gone so early to reward. The Wazir Dandan for Prince Sharkan. *Unknown.* *Fr.* The Thousand and One Nights. AWP; JAWP; WBP
Wise wind surely could never have sown, A. Chance-fallen Seed. Marie Emilie Gilchrist. BAP
Wise with the wisdom of ages. Lincoln. Thomas Curtis Clark. BAP; HH
Wise Woman, The. Louis Untermeyer. ALV; HBMV; PR; TBM
Wisely a woman prefers to a lover a man who neglects her. Distichs. John Hay. BOHV

Wisely he spoke, a plan for both to accept. The Meeting. Apollonius Rhodius. *Fr.* Argonautica. OxBG
Wisemen. *See* Wise men.
Wiser than the Children of Light. Monk Gibbon. NeIP
Wisest men are glad to die, The; no fear. Death. Thomas May. *Fr.* Continuation of Lucan. MaRV
Wisest of dogs was Vigi, a tawny-coated hound. Vigi. Katharine Lee Bates. PCD
Wisest of sparrows that sparrow which sitteth alone. Wisdom. Christina Rossetti. OBVV; TOP
Wisest of the wise, The. One White [*or* Grey] Hair. Walter Savage Landor. HBV; LPS-3; VA
Wisest scholar of the wight most wise, The. Astrophel and Stella, XXV. Sir Philip Sidney. ReEn; SiPS
Wish, A. Matthew Arnold. BPN; EmBrPo; EPN; HBV; PoVP; VLEP
Wish, A ("This only grant me"). Abraham Cowley. *See* Of Myself.
Wish, The ("Well then; I now do plainly see"). Abraham Cowley. *Fr.* The Mistress. BEL; BLV; CBOV; CoBE; ElSeCe; EnLi-1; EnLit; EPP; EPS; EV-2; GTBS-W; HBV; LEAP; LiTB; LiTG; OAEP; OBEV; OBS; SeCL; SeCV-1; SeEP; TOP; TrGrPo; ViBoPo; WHA
Wish, The. John Dancer. SeCL
Wish, A. Robert Devereux, Earl of Essex. *See* Happy Were He.
Wish, The. Thomas Flatman. SeCL
Wish, A. Hamlin Garland. AA
Wish, The. Thomas Godfrey. IAP; NoCaPo
Wish, A. Elizabeth Gould. BoTP
Wish, A. "Jazbo of Old Dubuque." DDA
Wish, A. Ben Jonson. *See* Gipsy Song ("The faery beam upon you").
Wish, A. Omar Khayyám, *tr. fr. Persian by* Edward Fitzgerald. *Fr.* The Rubáiyát. OnPM
Wish, The. Mikhail Yurevich Lermontov, *tr. fr. Russian by* Sir Cecil Kisch. WaL
Wish, The. Walter Pope. *See* Old Man's Wish, The.
Wish, A. Samuel Rogers. BoTP; BPP; CBPC; EnSW; EPN; ERP; EV-3; GTBS; GTBS-D; GTBS-W; GTSE; GTSL; HBV; LPS-1; MCCG; OBEC; OBEV (new ed.); OBVV; OTPC (1923 ed.); PECK; RIS; TreFS; WP
Wish, A. Christina Rossetti. BPN
Wish, A. Haruo Sato, *tr. fr. Japanese by* Takamichi Ninomiya *and* D. J. Enright. PoLJ
Wish, A. Frank Dempster Sherman. TVC; TVSH
(Kite, A.) BoChLi (1950 ed.); PCH
Wish, A. Walter C. Smith. TVSH
Wish, The. Thomas Stanley, *after the Greek of* Anacreon. AWP; JAWP; WBP
Wish ("I hope you'll never get"). *Unknown.* DDA
Wish, A ("I wish I was a little egg"). *Unknown.* DDA
Wish, A ("Now, Jesus, Mary's Son, be unto thee"). *Unknown.* CAW
Wish at Meal-Time. John Farrar. BoChLi
Wish Is Quite a Tiny Thing, A. Annette Wynne. MPB; SP
Wish no word unspoken, want no look away! Robert Browning. *Fr.* Ferishtah's Fancies. BPN
Wish of Manchin of Liath, The. *Unknown, tr. fr. Old Irish by* Kenneth Jackson. AnIL
(Hermit's Song, The.) KiLC, *tr. by* Frank O'Connor; OnYI, *tr. by* Kuno Meyer
Wish of the Aged Bard, The. *Unknown, tr. fr. Gaelic by* Hugh Macmillan. EBSV
Wish, that of the living whole, The. In Memoriam A. H. H., LV. Tennyson. AnFE; AtBAP; BEL; BPN; EM-2; EmBrPo; EnL; EnLi-2; EnLit; EPN; GEPC; HBV; LoBV; MaPo; OAEP; OBEV (1st ed.); OQP; OuHeWo; PIAE; PoFS; QP-1; ReaPo; SeCeV; TCEP; TOP; UnPo; ViPo; VLEP
Wished morning's come! And now upon the plains. Morning. Thomas Otway. *Fr.* The Orphan. EV-3
Wishes. Norman Ault. HBMV; HBVY
Wishes. Callistratus, *tr. fr. Greek by* John Herman Merivale. OnPM
Wishes. A. C. Child. PoToHe
Wishes. Richard Crashaw. *See* Wishes to His (Supposed) Mistress.
Wishes. Kate Greenaway. BoChLi (1950 ed.)
Wishes. Semyon Kirsanov, *tr. fr. Russian by* Jack Lindsay. RuPo
Wishes. F. Rogers. BoTP
Wishes. Robert Louis Stevenson. *See* Go, Little Book.
Wishes ("O that a lovely lyre were!"). *Unknown, tr. fr. Greek by* F. E. Garrett. OxBG
Wishes ("Said the first little chicken"). *Unknown.* *See* Five Little Chickens.
Wishes. Edna Kingsley Wallace. MoSiPe
Wishes for My Son. Thomas MacDonagh. AnIV; CP; FAOV; GoBC; HBMV; JKCP; LBBV; MBP; NV; TSW
Wishes for the Supposed Mistress. Richard Crashaw. *See* Wishes to His (Supposed) Mistress.
Wishes for William. Winifred M. Letts. OnYI
Wishes of an Elderly Man, The. Sir Walter Raleigh. FaBoCh; FiBHP; LoGBV; SiTL; WhC
("I wish I loved the human race.") CenHV
(Wishes of an Elderly Man at a Garden Party.) ShBV-4
Wishes of Youth. Laman Blanchard. ES
Wishes on this child's mouth, The. Helga. Carl Sandburg. ChMo; CMP; NP; TSW; TSWC
Wishes to His (Supposed) Mistress. Richard Crashaw. AnFE, *sl. abr.*; ATP, *sl. abr.*; BCEP, *abr.*; BEL; CoBE; EPS; EnLit; EV-2, *sl. abr.*; HBV; LEAP; LiTL, *sl. abr.*; LPS-1, *abr.*; MeLP; MePo; OBEV, *sl. abr.*; OBS; PoEL-2; SeCL; SeCV-1; SeEP; ViBoPo, *abr.*; WHA
(Wishes.) AEV; OAEP; ReEn
(Wishes for the Supposed Mistress.) BLV, *abr.*; GoBC, *abr.*; GTBS; GTBS-D; GTBS-W; GTSE; GTSL, *abr.*; LiTG, *abr.*
Wishful to add to my mental power. Ballade of Schopenhauer's Philosophy. Franklin P. Adams. HBMV
Wishing. William Allingham. BoChLi (1939 ed.); BoTP; CBPC; DD, *abr.*; FaPON; GFA; HBV; HBVY; MPB; NLK; OHIP; OTPC; PCH; PRWS; PTA-1; RAR; TVC; TVSH
Wishing. John Charles McNeill. NoCaPo
Wishing Bridge, The. Whittier. PTA-2
Wishing-Caps, The. Kipling. OtMeF
Wishmakers' Town, *sels.* William Young.
Bells, The. AA
Bridal Pair, The. AA
Conscience-Keeper, The. AA
Flower-Seller, The. AA
Pawns, The. AA
(Losers, The.) HBMV
Wistaria Blossoms. Charles Dalmon. *Fr.* Three Pictures. TSW; TSWC
Wistaria blossoms trail and fall. At the Convent Gate. Austin Dobson. VLEP
Wisteria. M. Kathleen Ahern. CAG
Wistful Days, The. Robert Underwood Johnson. AA; ADAH; BAP; LEAP; SN
Wistful One, The. Abigail Cresson. MW
Wistfully shimmering, shamelessly wise and weak. Epicede. Donald Evans. NP
Wiston Vault. Katherine Philips. DiM
Wit, The. Elizabeth Bishop. NePoAm-2
Wit. Mark Van Doren. MOAP
Wit and Wisdom. Ambrose Philips. EV-3
Wit is the only wall. Wit. Mark Van Doren. MOAP
Wit Predominant. Thomas Rymer. *Fr.* Edgar. SeCL
Wit, Whither Wilt Thou? *Unknown.* EIL
Wit ye well, all that be here. Testamentum Domini. *Unknown.* TMEV
Witch, A. William Barnes. CG; PoMS
(Country Witch, A.) GoTP
Witch, The. Louise Morey Bowman. CPG
Witch, The. Mary Elizabeth Coleridge. GTBS-D; PoVP
Witch, The. Lord Alfred Douglas. HBMV
Witch, The. Robert Herrick. *See* Hag, The.
Witch, The. Percy H. Ilott. BoTP
Witch, The. Katharine Tynan. OnYI
Witch, The. W. B. Yeats. FaBoTw
Witch Bride, The. William Allingham. DaM
Witch Cat. Rowena Bennett. SiSoSe
Witch-elms that counterchange the floor. In Memoriam A. H. H., LXXXIX. Tennyson. EmBrPo; EPN; GEPC; ViPo; VLEP
Witch in the Glass, The. Sarah Morgan Bryan Piatt. AA; LEAP; PR
Witch is astride, The. The Witch. Robert Herrick. ReTS
Witch-Mother, The. Swinburne. TOP
Witch of Atlas, The. Shelley. EmBrPo
"And every beast of beating heart grew bold," *sel.* MyFE
Witch of Coös, The. Robert Frost. *Fr.* Two Witches. AmP; AnNE; AtBAP; CoBMV; DaM; ExPo; LiTM (rev. ed.); MoAB; NePA; ReMP; ViBoPo (1958 ed.)
Witch of Endor, The, *sel.* Robert Norwood.
"One word!" CPG
Witch of Erkmurden, The. James Whitcomb Riley. DaM
Witch of Fife, The. James Hogg. *Fr.* The Queen's Wake, Night I. BCEP; BSV
Witch of King Charles's Time, A. Karl Jonas Love Almquist, *tr. fr. Swedish by* Charles W. Stork. AnSL
Witch of Willowby Wood, The. Rowena Bennett. PoMS
Witch that came, The (the withered hag). Provide, Provide. Robert Frost. AmP; AtBAP; MoAB
Witch-Wife, The. Mary Eleanor Roberts. BAP
Witchcraft. Edmund Clarence Stedman. PR
Witchcraft by a Picture. John Donne. PoFS
Witchcraft; New Style. Lascelles Abercrombie. MBP; MoBrPo
Witchery. Frank Dempster Sherman. LBMV
Witchery, watch out for witchery! Ballad of the Güije. Nicolas Guillén. TwSpPo
Witches. Ted Hughes. GoYe
Witches, The. *Unknown.* *See* Hallowe'en.

Witches' Brew, The. E. J. Pratt. BoCaPo (1948 ed.)
Witches' Charm. Shakespeare. *See* Witches' Song.
Witches' Charms, The. Ben Jonson. *Fr.* The Masque of Queens. EIL; PoMS, *abr.;* ThWaDe; TwHP
Witches' Charm, III: "Owl is abroad, The." FaBoCh; LoBV; LoGBV; ReEn
(Charm, A.) KN
Witches' Meeting, The. William Shakespeare. Witches' Song, The.
Witches' Song. Elizabeth J. Coatsworth. PoMS
Witches' Song, The. Ben Jonson. CH
Witches' Song, The. Shakespeare. *Fr.* Macbeth, IV, i. OnHT
(Charm, The.) EIL
("Thrice the brinded cat hath mewed.") ElSeCe; InvP; MyFE
(Witches' Charm.) SiTL
(Witches' Meeting, The, *fr.* I, i, *and* IV, i.) CG
(Witches' Spell, The.) PoMS
Witches' Steeds, The. Will H. Ogilvie. TVSH
Witches' Town. *Unknown.* CAG
Witching Song, A. James Thomson. *Fr.* The Castle of Indolence, I. OBEC
Witch's Ballad, The. William Bell Scott. AnFE; BMEP; BSV; CH; EBSV; OBEV; OBVV
Witch's Broomstick Spell, The. *Unknown.* ChTr
Witch's Daughter, The. *Unknown, tr. fr. Modern Greek by* Rae Dalven. MoGP
Witch's Daughter, The, *abr.* Whittier. *Fr.* Mabel Martin; a Harvest Idyl. PTA-2
Witch's Moon, The. Eleanor Osborne Scheier. CAG
Witch's Ride, The. Adelheid Wette, *tr. fr. German. Fr.* Hansel and Gretel. PCH
Witch's Spell, A. *Unknown.* ChTr
Witch's Whelp, The. Richard Henry Stoddard. AA; AnAmPo; LA; LEAP
Witchwood. May Justus. SiSoSe
With a Coin from Syracuse. Oliver St. John Gogarty. OBMV
With a conscience we're able to see. The Conscience. Anthony Euwer. *Fr.* The Limeratomy. HBMV
With a Copy of Herrick. Sir Edmund Gosse. PtP; TCEP; TCPD; VA; WP
With a Daisy ("A science—so the savants say"). Emily Dickinson. ImOP
With a First Reader. Rupert Hughes. HBMV
With a Flower ("I hide myself within a flower"). Emily Dickinson. LiTL
With a gentle hand. The Irish. Francis Carlin. JKCP (1926 ed.)
With a Guitar, to Jane. Shelley. BEL; BPN; EmBrPo; EnRP; EPN; ERP; EtPaEn; HBV
(To a Lady with a Guitar.) GTBS; GTBS-D; GTBS-W; GTSE; GTSL
With a gull's beak I cry. The Bright Hillside. Rhoda Coghill. NeIP; OxBI
With a jar of wine I sit by the flowering trees. Three with the Moon and His Shadow. Li Po. WoL
With a Kiss I Die. Shakespeare. *Fr.* Romeo and Juliet, V, iii. LiTL
With a Lifting of the Head. "Hugh MacDiarmid." MoBrPo
With a Little Bit of Luck. Alan Jay Lerner. FaFP
With a long heavy heave, my very famous men. Old Anchor Chanty. Herbert Trench. AnFE
With a Nantucket Shell. Charles Henry Webb. AA
With a Nosegay. Henrik Wergeland, *tr. fr. Norwegian by* Charles W. Stork. AnNoLy
With a pert moustache and a ready candid smile. The Mixer. Louis MacNeice. FaBoTw
With a pick and with a shovel, and with a hoe. Words for Army Bugle Calls: Fatigue Call. *Unknown.* TreF
With a rocking. Prince Yuke, *tr. fr. Japanese by* Arthur Waley. LiTW
With a Rod No Man Alive. Walther von der Vogelweide, *tr. fr. German by* Jethro Bithell. AWP; JAWP; WBP
With a Rose from Conway Castle. Julia C. R. Dorr. AA
With a shout by the hearth let the palace-roof ring. Paean of Joy. Sophocles. *Fr.* Trachiniae. GrR
With a skill that knows no measure. Old New Hampshire. John F. Holmes. PoRL
With a Spray of Apple Blossoms. Walter Learned. AA; ADAH
With a thunder-driven heart. The Conquest of the Air. Harold T. Pulsifer. PFE
With a very big yawn. Mr. Beetle. Emily Hover. BoTP
With a Water Lily. Ibsen, *tr. fr. Norwegian by* Charles W. Stork. AnNoLy
With a wet slap the red road hit the plain. Senchi Ferry; Gold Coast. L. D. Lerner. BoSA
With a whirl of thought[s] oppress'd. The Day of Judgement [*or* On the Day of Judgement *or* On the World]. Swift. AnIV; BeR; CEP; FaBoEn; NBE
With a yellow lantern. Glow-Worms. P. A. Ropes. BoTP
With all a woman's virtues but the pox. Fufidia (Lady Mary Wortley Montagu). Pope. *Fr.* Sober Advice from Horace to the Young Gentlemen about Town. BeR
With all her eyes the goddess Night looks forth approaching many a spot. Hymn to Night. *Unknown. Fr.* The Rigveda. LiTW
With all its sinful doings, I must say. Italy. Byron. *Fr.* Beppo. OBRV; SeCePo
With all my heart, in truth, and passion strong. The Pride of a Jew. Judah Halevi. TrJP
With all my will, but much against my heart. A Farewell. Coventry Patmore. The Unknown Eros, I, xvi. ACP; AnFE; BLV; EnLoPo; EtPaEn; FaBoEn; HBV; LiTL; LO; OBEV; OBVV; PoEL-5; POTT; PoVP; TrGrPo
With all of us nursing you. Silent Wail. Kenji Miyazawa. PoLJ
With all that's ours, together let us rise. Western Emigration. David Humphreys. AnAmPo; LA
With all the drifting race of men. Léonie Adams. *Fr.* April Mortality. TrGrPo
With all the fairest angels nearest God. Ad Matrem Amantissimam et Carissimam Filii in Aeternum Fidelitas. John Myers O'Hara. SBMV
With all the powres my poor heart hath. The Hymn of Saint Thomas [*or* Hymn] in Adoration of the Blessed Sacrament. Richard Crashaw. MeLP; OBS; PoLi
With an alarming big voice. Will-o'-the-Wisp. Sumako Fukao. PoLJ
With an effort Grant swung the great block. Blocking the Pass. Charles Madge. MoP
With an heavy heart Envy asked pardon. Two Confessions. William Langland. *Fr.* The Vision of Piers Plowman. WoL
With an honest old friend and a merry old song. Harry Carey's General Reply, to the Libelling Gentry, Who Are Angry at His Welfare. Henry Carey. HBV
With an inexpensive jennet. The Poor Man. Francis Carlin. PR
With Antecedents. Walt Whitman. IAP
With aspect wild, in ranting strain. The Millennium. To a Ranting Field Orator Philip Freneau. MOAP
With awful walls, far glooming, that possessed. The Trumpets of Doolkarnein. Leigh Hunt. LPS-2
With Bacchus' shower soak us all. Posidippus, *tr. fr. Greek by* W. R. Paton. GrPo
With banners furled, the clarions mute. The Night-March. Herman Melville. AnFE; CoAnAm; LiTA
With base-born men let not thy converse be. On Choosing Friends. Theognis, *tr. by* C. T. Murphy. GrL
With base men, boy, do not communicate. Choosing Friends. Theognis, *tr. by* A. E. Crawley. OxBG
With blackest moss the flower-plots [-pots, *wr.*]. Mariana. Tennyson. AWP; BLV; BMEP; BPN; CH; ChER; EmBrPo; EV-5; GEPC; GTML; GTSL; HBV; InPo; JAWP; LiTL; MaPo; MyFE; OAEP; OBEV; OBRV; OBVV; OnPP; Po; PoE; PoEL-5; PoFS; PoVP; ShBV-4; TOP; TrGrPo; TwHP; UnPo (3d ed.); ViBoPo; ViPo; ViPP; VLEP; WBP
With book forgotten. Evening at the Inn of Yün Meng. Liu Tzu Hui. PoHN
With breath indrawn and every nerve alert. To a Pet Cobra. Roy Campbell. AtBAP
With breath of thyme and bees that hum. To a Greek Girl. Austin Dobson. HBV; VA; VLEP
With buds embalmed alive in ice. A Mile from Eden. Anne Ridler. MoPo
With burning fervour. The Crystal. George Barker. LiTM; OBMV; POTE
With button eyes and cotton skin. The Cotton Cat. Mary Effie Lee Newsome. GoSl
With calm the seas grow purple now. No storm-winds sunder. Spring Sailing. Agathias Scholasticus. GrPE
With camel's hair I clothed my skin. Dream. Richard Watson Dixon. LoBV; NBE
With cannon ten on port and starboard. Pirate's Song. José de Espronceda. AnSpL-2; TeCS
With cassock black, baret and book. Little Gray Songs from St. Joseph's, XXX. Grace Fallow Norton. LBMV
With caverned bole and twisted limb they bide. Olive Trees. Padraic Colum. NePoAm
With changeful sound life beats upon the ear. Silence. Walter de la Mare. BrBE
With Child Genevieve Taggard. AnAmPo; AnEnPo; LA; MAP; MoAmPo
With chocolate-cream that you buy in the cake. Chocolate-Cream. E. V. Lucas. *Fr.* Counsel to Those That Eat. BOHV
With Christopher Smart. Robert Browning. *Fr.* Parleyings with Certain People of Importance. PtP
With cicada's nymphal skin. The Largess. Richard Eberhart. LiTA; LiTM (rev. ed.); TwAmPo
With coat like any mole's, as soft and black. Mole Catcher. Edmund Blunden. CaAE; OBMV
With Corse at Allatoona. Samuel H. M. Byers. GA; PAH
With Cortez in Mexico. Wilfred Campbell. PAH

With courage seek the kingdom of the dead. The Last Journey. Leonidas of Tarentum. AWP; JAWP; WBP
With crafty brooding life turned to Jack Rose. Jack Rose. Maxwell Bodenheim. HBMV
With dead figures of heroes. Evening. Georg Trakl. AnGP
With deadly drive Your grim advance. To a Revolutionist. Harold E. Fey. ChIP
With death doomed to grapple. Epigram. Byron. HBV
With deep affection/ And recollection. The Bells of Shandon [*or* The Shandon Bells]. Francis Sylvester Mahony. ACP; AnIV; BCEP; CAW; CH; ChTr; EV-4; GoBC; GTBS; HBV; IrPN; LPS-2; OBEV; OBRV; OBVV; OnYI; ShBV-2; TIP; TreFS; UnPo; VA
With delicate mad hands behind his sordid bars. To One in Bedlam. Ernest Dowson. ACP; BLV; EnLi-2; LBBV; MBP; MoBrPo; NeMA; OBMV; PoVP; ViPP; WHA
With delicate, rosy assaults the dawn was giving you names. The Name-giving Aurora. Rafael Alberti. CoSP
With Donne, whose muse on dromedary trots. On Donne's Poetry. Samuel Taylor Coleridge. InvP; OAEP; PtP; SeCePo
With doubt and dismay you are smitten. Opportunity. Berton Braley. FAOV; WBLP
With Dreams of Wealth and Fame. Giuseppe Parini, *tr fr. Italian by* Lorna de' Lucchi. WoL
With drooping sail and pennant. The White Ships and the Red. Joyce Kilmer. CV; MC; PAH
With due condescension, I'd call your attention. The Origin of Ireland. *Unknown.* BOHV
With dying fire and light. Immortal. Richard Church. MoBrPo (1942 ed.)
With eager heart and will on fire. Peace. Henry van Dyke. MaRV
With earth's first clay they did the last man knead. Predestination. Omar Khayyàm, *tr. by* Edward Fitzgerald. *Fr.* The Rubáiyát. OnPM
With echoing step the worshippers. Give Me Thy Heart. Adelaide Anne Procter. ACP; CAW; GoBC
With elbow buried in the downy pillow. Clarimonde. Théophile Gautier. AWP; JAWP; UnW; WBP
With endles teares, that never cease. *Unknown.* SeCSL
With Energy Renewed. Louis Untermeyer. *Fr.* Summons. GrCo-2
With Esther. Wilfrid Scawen Blunt. *See* Esther; a Young Man's Tragedy.
With every movement, the soft particles. The Dusting of the Books. Dorothy Hughes. GoYe
With every rising of the sun. You and To-Day. Ella Wheeler Wilcox. OQP; QP-2
With every rolling stone place me in the breach. Place Me in the Breach. Yehuda Karni. TrJP
With evil omens from the harbour sails. Arnold's Departure. Philip Freneau. MOAP
With expectation faint & blind; yett still. *Unknown.* SeCSL
With eyes hand-arched he looks into. Comradery. Madison Cawein. AA; OBAV
With faces bright, as ruddy corn. A Dream of Youth. Lionel Johnson. VLEP
With fainting soul athirst for grace. The Prophet. Pushkin. BoR
With fair Ceres, Queen of Grain. Praise of Ceres. Thomas Heywood. *Fr.* The Silver Age. ElL
With fame in just proportion envy grows. Fame and Envy. Edward Young. *Fr.* Epistles to Mr. Pope. BCEP
With Farmer Allan at the farm abode. Dora. Tennyson. BPN; CG; GEPC; PFE; VLEP
With favour and fortune fastidiously blest. The Character of Sir Robert Walpole. Swift. BeR
With favoring [*or* favouring] winds, o'er [the] sunlit seas. Dedication. Longfellow. *Fr.* Ultima Thule. AlDL; CoV; ViBoPo
With favoure in hir face far passyng my reason. Sodenly Afraide. *Unknown.* EnLit
With fifteen-ninety or sixteen-sixteen. On an Anniversary. J. M. Synge. OBMV
With fingers weary and worn. The Song of the Shirt. Thomas Hood. BCEP; BEL; BTP; CoBE; EnLi-2; EnLit; EnRP; EPN; EPP; ERP; EV-4; HBV; LEAP; LPS-1; MaC; MCCG; OBVV; OHFP; OnHT; OTPC (1946 ed.); PCD; PoFr; PreP; PTA-1; PYM; StaSt; TCEP; TreF; VA; WBLP
With fire and desolation the Moors are in Castile. The Cid and the Five Moorish Kings. *Unknown.* AnSpL-1
With flintlock[ed] guns and polished stocks. In Hardin County, 1809. Lulu E. Thompson. BoHiPo; PoMa; StPo
With floods and storms thus we be tossed. God Our Help. *Unknown.* OxBoCh
With Flowers ("If recollecting were forgetting"). Emily Dickinson. AA
With flowers fair adorn thy lustrous hair. To Mnesidice. Sappho. GrR
With focus sharp as Flemish-painted face. The [*or* A] Dome of Sunday. Karl Shapiro. CoBMV; LiTM; MoAB; MoAmPo (1950 ed.); MoPo; NePA; OxBA; WaP
With folded claws, with eyes unblinking. Blue Ribbon Cats. Lalia Mitchell Thornton. CIV
With fore-cloth smoothed by careful hands. Allah's Tent. Arthur Colton. HBV
With forehead bent. Wordsworth. *Fr.* The Prelude, XIV. NBE
With Fragrant Flowers We Strew the Way. Thomas Watson. *Fr.* The Honourable Entertainment Given to the Queen's Majesty in Progress at Elvetham, 1591. ElL
(Ditty of the Six Virgins, The.) OBSC
(Ditty of the Six Virgins' Song, The.) SiCE
With Freedom's Seed. Pushkin, *tr. fr. Russian by* Babette Deutsch. OnPM, *rev. tr.*; PoFr; TrRV, *rev. tr.*; WoL, *rev. tr.*
With frontier strength ye stand your ground. Mountains. Henry David Thoreau. MOAP
With frost again the thought is clear and wise. Frost. John Hewitt. NeIP
With full-leav'd lillies I will stick. Michael Drayton. *Fr.* The Muses' Elysium: The Second Nimphall. AtBAP
"With future hope I oft would gaze." The Muse of Burns. Burns. *Fr.* The Vision. RO
With ganial foire. The Crystal Palace. Thackeray. BOHV; InMe
With gentle step I came at last. Afterward. Mary Matheson. CaP
With gladness hail the dawning year. The New Year. *Unknown.* PEDC
With glass like a bull's eye. Mrs. MacQueen. Walter de la Mare. BoTP
With God. *Unknown.* PraP
With God Conversing. Gene Derwood. LiTA; LiTM; NePA
With grave/ Aspect he rose. Milton. *Fr.* Paradise Lost, II. ATP
With great good cheer the bells ring out. Bells of New Year. Arthur Gordon Field. PGD
With grief and mourning I sit to spin. The Girl's Lamentation. William Allingham. IrPN; SeCePo
With hairs, which for the wind to play with, hung. On Lydia Distracted. Philip Ayres. EnLoPo
With half a heart I wander here. In the States. Robert Louis Stevenson. PoVP; VA; VLEP
With half the Western world at stake. Sea and Land Victories. *Unknown.* PAH
With Happiness Stretched across the Hills. Blake. EnRP
With heart and breast of brimstone, flesh of flax. Sonnet. Michelangelo. LyFI
With heart at rest I climbed the citadel's steep height. Epilogue [*or* Epilogue to Prose Poems]. Baudelaire. AWP; OnPM
With hearts of poor men it is so. The Poor. Emile Verhaeren. AWP; JAWP; WBP; WoL
With hearts responsive. John Oxenham. *Fr.* A Little Te Deum of the Commonplace. TrPWD
With heavenly, with quietly resounding. Celebration of Peace. Friedrich Hölderlin. AnGP
With heaviness this wingless wind is cursed. Evening. Nikolai Stepanovich Gumilev. TrRV
With heaving breast the fair-haired Eileen sang. Edmund John Armstrong. *Fr.* Fionnuala. TIP
With heavy blows I have made fast the axles of my chariot. The Chariot Axles *Unknown.* ChLP
With heavy doleful clamor, hour on hour. The Groundswell. John Gould Fletcher. ChMo; CMP; TBM
With heavy groans did I approach my friends. Wine and Grief. Solomon ibn Gabirol. LiTW; TrJP
"With her basket of apples comes Nora McHugh." The Ould Apple Woman. T. A Daly. CV
With Her Beauty. Tu Fu, *tr. fr. Chinese by* Witter Bynner *and* Kiang Kang-hu. OuHeWo
With her, her sister went, a warlike maid. Parthenia. Phineas Fletcher. *Fr.* The Purple Island. EV-2
With Hermione the witching as I played once, she was wearing. Light Love. Asclepiades. GrPE
With hey, ho, the wind and the rain. Shakespeare. *Fr.* King Lear, III, ii. TiPo (1952 ed.)
With him there was his son, a youthful Squire. Seven Pilgrims [*or* Three Canterbury Pilgrims: A Squire *or* A Squire]. Chaucer. *Fr.* The Canterbury Tales: Prologue. GoTP; MaC; TrGrPo
With Him who sets the lily on the stem. Prayer. Hildegarde Flanner. NV; VOD (1935 ed.)
With His kind [*or* kinde] mother, who partakes thy woe. Temple [*or* Jesus in the Temple]. John Donne. OBS; StJW
With his lean, ragged levies, undismayed. Washington at Valley Forge. R. G. Sutherland. WOAH
With his unspent youth. Bargain. Louise Driscoll. HBMV
With honeysuckle, over-sweet, festoon'd. Arbor Vitae. Coventry Patmore. The Unknown Eros, II, iii. GoBC; LoBV; SeCePo; ViP
With Hopeless Love. Moses ibn Ezra, *tr. fr. Hebrew by* Solomon Solis-Cohen. TrJP
With horns and [with] hounds I waken the day. Diana's

Hunting-Song. Dryden. *Fr.* The Secular Masque. ElSeCe; InPo; SeCePo; SeCL
With How Sad Steps [O Moon]. Sir Philip Sidney. Astrophel and Stella, XXXI. AnEnPo; BLV; BoLiVe; CBOV; CH; ChTr; InvP; LiTL; PoE; PoeMoYo; PoRA; RiBV; SeCeV; WHA
(His Lady's Cruelty.) OBEV
(Moon, The.) ES; LoBV
(Sonnet: "With how sad steps, O Moon . . .") AEV; AtBAP; CoEV; ElL; LPS-1
(Sonnets from "Astrophel and Stella.") LEAP
(To the Moon.) LiTG; PIAE
("With how sad steps, O Moon, thou climb'st the skies!") AnFE; AWP; BEL; CaAE; CoBE; EG; ElSeCe; EnL; EnLi-1; EnLit; EnLoPo; EPP; EV-1; FaBoEn; GTSL; HBV; JAWP; MaPo; OAEP; OBSC; PeBoSo; PoEL-1; ReaPo; ReEn; ReIE; SiCE; SiPS; TCEP; TOP; TrGrPo; TuPP; TwHP; ViBoPo; WBP
With How Sad Steps ("With how sad steps, O Moon, thou climb'st the sky"). Wordsworth. ERP
With humble and discouraged mien. Alessandro Manzoni. *Fr.* Soffermati sull' arida sponda. PoFr
With Husky-haughty Lips, O Sea. Walt Whitman. PIAE; TCAP
With Inky Sails. Heine, *tr. fr. German by* Sir Theodore Martin. WoL
With instruments in ill-accord a hundred men. The Symphony. Herman W. Stillman. PEDC
With its baby rivers and little towns, each with its abbey or its cathedral. England. Marianne Moore. CrMA; LiTA; MAP; MoAB; MoAmPo
With its cloud of skirmishers in advance. An Army Corps on the March. Walt Whitman. AmPo; APW; CoBA; IAP; MOAP; TCAP
With its rat's tooth the clock. The Alarum. Sylvia Townsend Warner. MBP; MoBrPo
With joy he saw that city which the Shaker of the Earth. Tyre. Nonnus. *Fr.* Dionysiaca. GrPE
With kisses across your breast, as when a pitcher pours. Vorobyev Hills. Boris Pasternak. RuPo
With klingle, klangle, klingle. When the Cows Come Home. Agnes E. Mitchell. PTA-1
With leaden foot Time creeps along. Absence. Richard Jago. BCEP; HBV; OBEV
With leering looks, bull-fac'd, and freckl'd fair. Jacob Tonson, His Publisher. Dryden. BeR; ChTr
With Life and Death I walked when Love appeared. Hymn to Color. George Meredith. EmBrPo; PoVP
With lifted feet, hands still. Going down Hill on a Bicycle. Henry Charles Beeching. BBV (1951 ed.); CP; GN; HBV; HBVY; OBEV; OBVV; OTPC (1923 ed.)
With light of magic India shines afar. India the Magic. H. A. Jules-Bois. CAW
With Lilacs. Charles Henry Crandall. AA
With Lilacs in My Eye. Lucile Coleman. GoYe
With link-boys running on before. My Lady Goes to the Play. Arthur Ketchum. PR
With lips painted lightly pink. Woman! Sakutaro Hagiwara. PoLJ
With Little Boy Blue. Sara Beaumont Kennedy. PTA-2
With little here to do or see. To the Daisy [*or* To the Same Flower]. Wordsworth. BPN; EmBrPo; EnRP; EPN; ERP; GEPC; GTBS; GTBS-D; GTBS-W; GTSE; GTSL; HBV; HBVY
With little white leaves in the grasses. The Daisy. Sir Rennell Rodd. VA
With loitering step and quiet eye. In November. Archibald Lampman. BoCaPo
With louder plaints the mother spoke her woes. Goldsmith. *Fr.* The Deserted Village. MotAn
With Love among the haycocks. A Song. Ralph Hodgson. AlDL
With love exceeding a simple love of the things. Melampus. George Meredith. EmBrPo; EnLi-2; OBVV; PoEL-5; ViP
With love he shaped the limbs, her breasts arose. Pygmalion. Louis Johnson. AnNZ
With Love I garnered mirth and dreams, and shame. Retractions, VI. James Branch Cabell. HBMV
With love is come to town the spring. Springtime (*mod. vers.*). *Unknown.* EPP
With love that counted not the cost. Mary. Thomas Curtis Clark. ChIP
With love, with highest worth, with every grace. The Nonpareil of All Mortality. Joachim du Bellay. Olive, II. TrFP
With loveliness the little princess. Figurines. Manuel Machado. AnSpL-2
With Lullay, Lullay, like a Child. John Skelton. *See* Lullay, Lullay.
With margerain [*or* marjoram] gentle. To Mistress Margery Wentworth. John Skelton. *Fr.* The Garlande of Laurell. CoEV; EG; EnLoPo; EV-1; LoBV; OBEV; OBSC; TrGrPo; ViBoPo
With Mary, ere dawn in the garden. Woman's Easter. Lucy Larcom. EOAH
With mask well fitted for your chosen role. Denouement. Sister Mary Eulalia. JKCP (1955 ed.)
With Me in Paradise. Alexander Harvey. ChIP
With Me My Lover Makes. C. Day Lewis. OBMV
With me youth led . . . I will speak now. Robert Browning. *Fr.* By the Fireside. LoPS
With Merry Glee and Solace. *Unknown.* AnEC
With merry lark this maiden rose. Old-Time Service. Thomas Churchyard. *Fr.* A Fayned Fancye between the Spider and the Gowte. OBSC
With Metaphor. Sarah Wingate Taylor. GoYe
With mighty hand the Holy Lord. The Temptation and Fall of Man. *Unknown. Fr.* Genesis. AnOE
With much ado you fail to tell. A Critic. Walter Savage Landor. ChTr
With murder and rebellion drunk, their flight. Centaurs' Flight. José Maria de Heredia. TrFP
With Music Strong I Come. Walt Whitman. Song of Myself, XVIII. AtBAP; TrGrPo
With My Fancy I Grasped. Konstantin Dmitreyevich Balmont, *tr. fr. Russian by* Babette Deutsch. TrRV
With my love my life was nesled. *Unknown.* SeCSL
With my sleeping beloved huddled beside me, why do I lie awake. Prologue: In Darkness. J. C. Squire. MBP
With narrow eyes below soft chains, a slave. Interior. Paul Valéry. AnFP
With nerves all shattered and worn. The Dripping Sheet. *Unknown.* PA
With no irreverent voice or uncouth charm. Alvar's Address to the Spirits of the Dead. Samuel Taylor Coleridge. *Fr.* Remorse. EmBrPo
With no wrought roof of ivory and gold. Horace. Odes, II, 18. LaP
With nought to hide or to betray. L'Amitié et L'Amour. John Swanwick Drennan. IrPN
With nuts and sweets and dainty fare. The Parrot's Song. Raffi. ArmLP
With oh such peculiar branching and over-reaching of wire. St. Saviour's, Aberdeen Park, Highbury, London, N. John Betjeman. MoVE
With oaken staff and swinging lantern bright. The Andalusian Sereno. Francis Saltus Saltus. AA
With omens oft I strove to warn thy swains. The English in Ireland. Swift. *Fr.* Verses Occasioned by the Sudden Drying Up of St. Patrick's Well. BeR
With one black shadow at its feet. Mariana in the South. Tennyson. GEPC; PoVP; VLEP
With one consent, on no man's bidding. London. Maurice Hewlett. *Fr.* The Song of the Plow. PoFr
With One Swift Thought. Sister Maryanna. JKCP (1955 ed.)
With other women I beheld my love. Ballata [*or* Ballata: Of His Lady among Other Ladies]. Guido Cavalcanti. AWP; OnPM
With paste of almonds, Syb her hands doth scoure. Upon Sibilla. Robert Herrick. SeCePo
With paws in firelight dipped, and drowsy ears. Old Hound. Florence Ripley Mastin. DDA; PoMa
With Pegasus upon a day. To John Taylor. Burns. WhC
With pensive eyes the little room I view. The Garret. Pierre Jean de Béranger, *tr. by* Thackeray. HBV
With Persian cat beside my cheek. My Cat and I. Edna Gearhart. CIV
With Peter I refuse to dine. Unforgivable and Unforgiven. C. D. B. Ellis. SiTL
With Peter Pan. Robert Haven Schauffler. HOAH
With Petrarch's Sonnets. Walter Savage Landor. InP
With pious mien, a Fox and a Tom-cat. The Cat and the Fox. La Fontaine. PoC
With Pipe and Flute. Austin Dobson. EPN; PC; VA; VLEP
With porcupine locks. The Katzenjammer Kids. James Reaney. PeCV; TwCaPo
With pretty speech accost both old and young. To the Stall Holders at a Fancy Fair. W. S. Gilbert. PA
With primal void and cosmic night. Earth's Story. Thomas Curtis Clark. OQP; QP-2
With proud thanksgiving, a mother for her children. For the Fallen. Laurence Binyon. AnFE; CaAE; GTBS; InP; MaRV; MM; MuP; OBEV (new ed.); PoeT; PoFr; POTE; ShBV-3; TVSH; TwCV
With prune-dark eyes, thick lips, jostling each other. Refugees. Louis MacNeice. LiTB; TwHP; WaP
With pure nails brightly flashing their onyx. Pure Nails Brightly Flashing. Stéphane Mallarmé. LiTW
With purple glow at even. To the Lakes. Wilfred Campbell. VA
With rakish eye and 'plenished crop. The Crow. William Canton. BMEP; GoTP; HBV
With reeds and bird-lime from the desert air. On a Fowler. Isidorus. AWP
With Regard to Dogs. Nancy Byrd Turner. AlBD
With restless step of discontent. Balboa. Nora Perry. PAH

With reverence to your worships, 'tis our fate. Demos and His Flatterer. Aristophanes. *Fr.* The Knights. OxBG
With Roses. Beatrix Demarest Lloyd. AA
With Rosy Hand. Walter Savage Landor. EmBrPo; EPN
(Cowslips.) VA
(Lyrics to Ianthe.) BPN
With Rue My Heart Is Laden. A. E. Housman. A Shropshire Lad, LIV. AnFE; AWP; BEL; BMEP; BoFr; BPN; CaAE; CBOV; ChMo; CMP; EmBrPo; EnL; EnLi-2; EnLit; EPN; FaFP; GTBS-W; GTSL; HoPM; JAWP; LBBV; LEAP; LiTB; LiTL; LiTM; MBP; MoAB; MoBrPo; OAEP; OuHeWo; PG; PIAE; PoE; PoMa; POTT; PoVP; ReaPo; TCPD; TOP; TrGrPo; ViP; ViPo; VLEP; WBP; WoL
With sable-draped banners, and slow-measured tread. You Put No Flowers on My Papa's Grave. C. E. L. Holmes. PTA-2
"With sacrifice before the rising morn." Laodamia. Wordsworth. BEL; BPN; EM-2; EmBrPo; EnRP; EPN; ERP; EV-3; GEPC; OAEP; TwCrTr
With saddened face and battered hat. Essex Junction. E. J. Phelps. DDA
With Sa'di in the Garden, *sels.* Sir Edwin Arnold.
Mahmud and Ayaz; a Paraphrase on Sa'di. VA
Song without a Sound. VA
With sails full set, the ship her anchor weighs. Emigravit. Helen Hunt Jackson. AA; AnFE; APA; CoAnAm; OBAV
With saintly grace and reverend tread. Presentiment. Ambrose Bierce. AA
"With salt and potatoes and meal for bread." Margie's Thanksgiving. Eudora S. Bumstead. TOAH
With secrets in their eyes the blue-winged Hours. A Tree at Dusk. Winifred Welles. MPB; SP; TSW; TSWC
With Seed the Sowers Scatter. A. E. Housman. *See* Stinging Nettle, The.
With Self Dissatisfied. Frederick L. Hosmer. TrPWD
With separated phrase and smothered word. Burial at Sea. E. J. Pratt. *Fr.* The *Roosevelt* and the *Antinoe.* TwCV
With Serving Still. Sir Thomas Wyatt. EG; EIL; LoBV; RiBV; SiPS; WHA
(His Reward.) OBSC
With Shakespeare's [*or* Shakspeare's] manhood at a boy's wild heart. Thomas Chatterton. Dante Gabriel Rossetti. Five English Poets, I. BMEP; BPN; EmBrPo; PoVP; PtP
With sharp white teeth the mountains tore his shroud. Lazarus Walks in the Alps. Ernest Walsh. MeRV
With sharpened pen and wit, one tunes his lays. The Praise of New Netherland. Jacob Steendam. PAH
With shattered panes the grassy court was starred. Thomas Hood. *Fr.* The Haunted House. BCEP
With Ships the Sea Was Sprinkled [Far and Nigh]. Wordsworth. EnRP; HBV
(Two Ships, I.) ES
With shirt burst open wide, it stands. Definition of Creativeness. Boris Pasternak. RuPo
With shot and shell, like a loosened hell. The Charge at Santiago. William Hamilton Hayne. MC; PAH
With sick and famisht eyes. Longing. George Herbert. SeCV-1
With sighing and with sorrow all my nights are bitter. The Swallows. Agathias Scholasticus. GrPE
With sighs my bosom always laboureth. Sonnet. Dante. GoBC
With silent awe I hail the sacred morn. The Sabbath Morn. John Leyden. LPS-2
With silver soundes derived from deepest skill. *Unknown.* SeCSL
With six small diamonds for his eyes. The Spider. Robert P. Tristram Coffin. ImOP; OTPC (1946 ed.); PoeMoYo
With slaught'ring guns th' unwearied fowler roves. Pope. *Fr.* Windsor Forest. EnSW
With slender arms outstretching in the sun. The Hay Field. Ethelwyn Wetherald. CPG
With slender rod, and line, and reel. Trouting. John Townsend Trowbridge. SN
With slower pen men used to write. On the Hurry of This Time. Austin Dobson. HBV; PoVP
With snakes of rubber and glass thorax. Filling Station. A. M. Klein. TwCaPo
With snort and pant the engine dragged. The Song of the Engine. H. Worsley-Benison. BoTP
With snow-white veil and garments as of flame. Divina Commedia, IV. Longfellow. AmP; AmPP; AnAmPo; AnFE; APA; APW; CoAnAm; CoBA; CoV; ES; IAP; LA; LPS-2; MOAP; NePA; OBAV; OxBA; PIAE; PtP; ReaPo; TCAP; TOP
With sobbing sighs and trickling tears. The Lamentation of Beckles. Thomas Deloney. SiCE
With sober pace an heav'enly maid walks in. Abraham Cowley. *Fr.* Davideis. SeCV-1
With solemn benediction at the end. The Secret. José Joaquin Casas. CAW
With some pot-fury, ravished from their wit. Joseph Hall. *Fr.* Virgidemiarum. ReEn; SiCE
With song and sun-burst comes the Easter morn. Easter. Robert Whitaker. ChIP; PGD; PSO
With songs and honors sounding loud. Isaac Watts. OlF
With sorrow and heart's distress. Eve to Adam. Milton. *Fr.* Paradise Lost, XII. LPS-1
With sorrowing voice begin the strain. Ode on the Death of Don Sebastian. Fernando de Herrera. AnSpL-1
With spangles gay and candle light. The Christmas Tree. Isabel de Savitzsky. BoTP
With steadfast heart and true. "Go Forward." "A. R. G." BLRP
With stedfast and unwavering faith, with hard and patient toil. Thanksgiving Day. James J. Montague. HH; PEDC
With Strawberries. W. E. Henley. HBV; POT; PoTo
With subtle poise he grips his tray. Atlantic City Waiter. Countee Cullen. BAP
With subtlest mimicry of wave and tide. By the Bridge. Arthur W. H. Eaton. CPG
With such a throb does blood. Joy of Knowledge. Isidor Schneider. TrJP
With such compelling cause to grieve. In Memoriam A. H. H., XXIX. Tennyson. EmBrPo; EnLi-2; EPN; GEPC; OAEP; ViPo; VLEP
With such unseemly caution have I taken heed. Saint Francis and the Cloud. Marie de L. Welch. SaFP
With sweetest milk and sugar first. The Girl and Her Fawn. Andrew Marvell. *Fr.* The Nymph Complaining for the Death of Her Fawn. BoTP; FaBoCh; GTSL; LoGBV; OTPC (1923 ed.)
With tangled brushwood overgrown. L'Ile Sainte Croix. Arthur W. H. Eaton. CPG
"With tears thy grief thou dost bemoan." Stanzas. Solomon ibn Gabirol. TrJP
With tentive list'ning each wight was settled in hark'ning. Virgil. *Fr.* The Aeneid, II. ReIE
With that a thundring noise seem'd shake the skie. The Overthrow of Lucifer. Phineas Fletcher. *Fr.* The Purple Island. OBS
With that he gave the thralls his battle-gear. Laertes. Homer. *Fr.* The Odyssey, XXIV. OxBG
With that low cunning, which in fools supplies. A Critical Fribble [*or* A Criticaster]. Charles Churchill. *Fr.* The Rosciad. FaBoEn; OBEC
With that pathetic impudence of youth. The Family of Nations. Willard Wattles. PAH
With that ran there a route of ratones at ones. The Fable of Belling the Cat. William Langland. *Fr.* The Vision of Piers Plowman: Prologue (B *text*). EPP
With that she rose, Athene at her side. Eros and His Mother. Apollonius Rhodius. *Fr.* Argonautica. OxBG
With that (such power was given him then), he took. Milton. *Fr.* Paradise Regained, III *and* IV. StJW
With the Ages. Longfellow. *See* Oft Have I Seen at Some Cathedral Door.
With the apples and the plums. The Dessert. Charles *and* Mary Lamb. OTPC (1923 ed.)
With the Caravan. Donna Coolbrith. BAP
With the Dawn. Thomas Caulfield Irwin. EnLoPo; IrPN
With the evening/ the two or three colours of the patio grew weary. Patio. Jorge Luis Borges. AnCL
With the fierce rage of winter deep suffus'd. Frost at Night. James Thomson. *Fr.* The Seasons: Winter. CoEV; OBEC
With the first bright, slant beam. Awakening. Rose Terry Cooke. EOAH
With the first drop of rain, the summer was killed. Helen. "Odysseus Elytis." MoGP
With the gulls' hysteria above me. Galway Bay. George Barker. FaBoMo
With the hooves of a doe. Lenox Avenue. Sidney Alexander. PoNe
With the Mallard Drake. *Unknown.* BLA
With the Most Susceptible Element, the Mind, Already Turned under the Toxic Action. Walter Benton. WaP
With the old kindness, the old distinguished grace. Upon a Dying Lady. W. B. Yeats. LiTB; UnPo (3d ed.)
With the preserved fruit of your voice. Klare von Reuter. Jorge Carrera Andrade. AnCL
With the shrewd and upright man. Fool and False. *Unknown.* *Fr.* Panchatantra. AWP; JAWP; WBP
With the smell of the meads in his plaiden dress. Dave. James Logie Robertson. EBSV
With the third part of day's diminishing. Jason's Sowing and Reaping. Apollonius Rhodius. *Fr.* Argonautica. OxBG
With the Tide. Edith Wharton. PEDC
With the treason of mingled love and wine. Girl Betrayed. Hedylos. LiTW
With the wanderer's staff in hand. Exile Song. Morris Jacob Rosenfeld. LiTW
With the Winds. Matilda Hutchinson Turner. RAR
With Thee a moment! Then what dreams have play! Desire. "Æ." GTIV; OBMV; TrPWD
With thee conversing I forget all time. Eve to Adam [*or* Eve

Speaks to Adam]. Milton. *Fr.* Paradise Lost, IV. BrBE; CBE; ChTr; FaBoEn; LoPS; TreFS; TrGrPo
With thee, O Christ, I fain would walk. The Way O Christ Thou Art. Ernest De Witt Burton. MaRV
With Thee to Soar to the Skies. *Unknown.* BePJ
With their feet in the earth. Tall Trees. Eileen Mathias. BoTP
With their harsh leaves old rhododendrons fill. The Mountain Cemetery. Edgar Bowers. NePoEA; PtPa
With their trunks the elephants. The Elephants. Dorothy Aldis. *Fr.* At the Circus. UTS
With Them that Rest. Milton. *Fr.* Samson Agonistes. LiA
With these heaven-assailing spires. New York. "Æ." OBMV
With these words Hermes sped away for lofty Olympos. Priam and Achilles. Homer. *Fr.* The Iliad, XXIV. OxBG
With this ambiguous earth. Christ in the Universe. Alice Meynell. ACP; CAW; EV-5; GoBC; HBMV; JKCP; MBP; MeRV; MoBrPo; StJW
With this he took his leve, and hoom he wente. Chaucer. *Fr.* Troilus and Criseyde, II. EPP
With this worde he, right anoon. Chaucer. *Fr.* The Hous of Fame, III. NBE
With those proud birds that feed not. The Snares. Nahab Koutchak. CAW
With those swathing bands/ Which death unbinds. Moral Responsibility. Dante. *Fr.* Divina Commedia: Purgatorio. GrCo-2
With three great snorts of strength. The Night Express. Cosmo Monkhouse. OBVV
With thy black hen and thy trim green grass. The Old House. Tristan Klingsor. TrFP
With tiger pace and swinging head. The Known World. Brewster Ghiselin. MoVE
". . With Timbrels." Judith, XVI: 2–17, Bible, Apocrypha. TrJP
With tingling eyes he stares into the dense. The Coast-Watch. W. W. Gibson. NeTW
With tonsured hair and figure spare. Portrait. Máire Cotter. SaFP
With treble vivas and limp hedgerow flags. The Vanquished. Charles Eglington. BoSA
With trembling fingers did we weave. In Memoriam A. H. H., XXX. Tennyson. BPN; CoBE; EM-2; EmBrPo; EnL; EnLi-2; EnLit; EPN; GEPC; OAEP; RiBV; ViPo; VLEP
With troubled heart and trembling hand I write. In Memory of My Dear Grandchild. Anne Bradstreet. BAV
With twilight passing her silken window. Spring Heart-break. Liu Fang-p'ing. ChLP
With twinkling stars the sky is crowned. A Day. Verner von Heidenstam. AnSL
With Two Fair Girls. *Unknown, tr. fr. Greek by* Robert Guthrie MacGregor. ALV
With two strange fires of equal heat possest. Love and Jealousy. Sir Philip Sidney. *Fr.* Arcadia. SiPS
With Usura/ With usura hath no man a house of good stone. Canto XLV. Ezra Pound. LiTM (rev. ed.); MoPo; NePA; OnAP; ReMP
With vineyards and with woodlands, with gardens and with rivers. A Villa by the Bosphorus. Arabius Scholasticus. GrPE
With virtue such as yours had Eve been arm'd. Written in a Lady's Milton. Matthew Prior. InP
With visionary care. Summer Noon, 1941. Yvor Winters. CrMA
With Walker in Nicaragua, *sels.* Joaquin Miller.
Monkeys ("How ran live monkeys"). PCH
"What snakes, long, lithe and beautiful."
(Walker in Nicaragua.) BAP
With Wavering Feet I Walked. Vladimir Soloviev, *tr. fr. Russian by* Babette Deutsch. TrRV
("Once in the misty dawn with timid foot," *tr. by* R. M. Hewitt.) BoR
With weary steps I loiter on. In Memoriam A. H. H., XXXVIII. Tennyson. EmBrPo; EPN; GEPC; ViPo; VLEP
With weed and with sea-barley crowned. The Drowned Wife. Robert Horan. OnHM
With weight of years and yoke forspent. The Pensioned Ox [*or* An Ox Past Service]. Addaeus. GrR; OxBG
With what a childish and short-sighted sense. Danger. Helen Hunt Jackson. AnFE; APA; CoAnAm
With what a glory comes and goes the year! Autumn. Longfellow. BAV
With what anguish of mind I remember my childhood. The Old Oaken Bucket, *parody. Unknown.* BLPA; FaFP; WBLP
With what attractive charms this goodly frame. Mark Akenside. The Pleasures of Imagination, I. EiPP; EnRP
With what contentment in its ordered ways. Mathematical. Jessie Nelson North. NP
With what deep murmurs through time's silent stealth. The Waterfall [*or* The Water-Fall]. Henry Vaughan. CoBE; ElSeCe; EPS; MaPo; MeLP; MePo; MeRV; OAEP; OBS; PoE; PoEL-2; PoFS; ReaPo; SeCV-1; TwCrTr; TwHP; ViBoPo
With what good canst thou supply mankind. The Gifts of Poverty. Aristophanes. *Fr.* Plutus. OxBG
With what sharp checks I in myself am shent. Astrophel and Stella, XVIII. Sir Philip Sidney. ReEn; SiPS
With what smug elegance the small goat minces. Nosegay for a Young Goat. Winifred Welles. PoeMoYo
With what thou gavest me, O Master. Equipment. Paul Laurence Dunbar. TrPWD
With whitened scalp and nose bedaubed with red. The Circus Clown. John Ferguson. MW
"With Whom Is No Variableness, neither Shadow of Turning." Arthur Hugh Clough. BMEP; BPN; BPP; EmBrPo; EnLi-2; EnLit; EPN; EPP; GTML; MaRV; PC; PoVP; TOP; TreFS; ViPo; VLEP; WGRP
(It Fortifies My Soul to Know.) OAEP
(Steadfast.) OQP; QP-1
With whom shall I find perfect ease. "Thou Shalt Purge Me with Hyssop and I Shall Be Clean." Anna Bunston de Bary. MaRV
With whomsoever I share the spring. Song. Jan Burroway. NePoAm-2
With wild surprise/ Four great eyes. The Christmas Tree in the Nursery [*or* Sery]. Richard Watson Gilder. COAH; DD; HBVY; OHIP
With willing arms I row and row. The Barcarole of James Smith. Herbert S. Gorman. HBMV
With wine I did not notice the approach of evening. Amusing Myself. Li Po. WhP
With wings held close and slim neck bent. Swans. Leonora Speyer. BLA
With witchlike branches, barren, bleak, and drear. Thomas Caulfield Irwin. *Fr.* Winter Noon in the Woods. IrPN
With women and apples both Paris and Adam. Epigram. Thomas Moore. ALV
With words as counters, talk of day and night. Epilogue. Edward Thompson. MM
With Wordsworth at Rydal. James Thomas Fields. AA
With Wound Still Fresh. Virgil, *pr. tr. fr. Latin by* H. R. Fairclough. *Fr.* The Aeneid, VI. LiA
With wrath-flushed cheeks, and eyelids red. Ahmed. James Berry Bensel. AA
With wrinkled hide and great frayed ears. A Circus Garland: The Elephant. Rachel Field. StVeCh
With yellow pears. Life Half Lived. Friedrich Hölderlin. ChTr
With You a Part of Me. George Santayana. To W. P., II. TrGrPo
(To W. P., II.) OBAV
With you first shown to me. William Barnes. EnLoPo
With you I wander the Nine Rivers. The God of the River. Chu Yuan. *Fr.* The Nine Songs. WhP
With your A B C book under your arm. Since Tomorrow Is Sunday. Jacinto Fombona Pachano. TwSpPo
With your beautiful hair and seemly. Petronius, *tr. fr. Latin by* Kenneth Rexroth. LaP
With your fair eyes a charming light I see. Love, the Light-Giver. Michelangelo. AWP; LiTW
With your head-cloth knotted and your shawl pinned tight. Mary Salome, Widow. Anne Ryan. JKCP (1926 ed.)
With your kind attention, a song I will trill. Down, Down, Down. William Keating. OuSiCo
With youth, is deade the hopes of loves returne. Sir Walter Ralegh. *Fr.* The Last Book of the Ocean to Scinthia. FaBoEn
Withal a meagre man was Aaron Stark. Aaron Stark. E. A. Robinson. MoAB; MoAmPo (1950 ed.); TwP
Withdraw thee, soul, from strife. Sleep. Alice Brown. AA
Withdrawal. Eduard Mörike, *tr. fr. German by* Kate Flores. AnGP
Withdrawal from Crete. Audrey Alexandra Brown. NeTW
Withdrawing from the amorous grasses. The Snake. Kenneth Mackenzie. BoAV
Withdrawn on this warm ledge I lie. Summer Afternoon. Elizabeth B. Harrod. NePoEA
Wither, midst falling dew. *See* Whither, midst falling dew.
Wither'd pansies faint and sweet. Requiem. Sir Joseph Noel Paton. VA
Withered Crown, The. Marceline Desbordes-Valmore, *tr. fr. French by* Alan Conder. TrFP
Withered Heart, The. Heine, *tr. fr. German by* James Thomson. OnPM
(Blauen Veilchen der Augelein, Die.) AWP
Withered leaves that drift in Russell Square, The. Drilling in Russell Square. Edward Shanks. OBMV
Withered Rose, A. "Yehoash," *tr. fr. Yiddish by* Isidore Goldstick. TrJP
Withered Tree, The. Sten Selander, *tr. fr. Swedish by* Charles W. Stork. AnSL
Withering grass knows not its needs, The. After the Rain. Edward A. Collier. BLRP
Withhold all eulogies when I am dead. Today and Tomorrow. Edward N. Pomeroy. MaRV; OQP; QP-2

Withhold not good from them to whom it is due. Proverbs, Bible, *O.T.* BoFr
Withhold your breath! Tropical Girl to Her Garden. Genevieve Taggard. NP
Within. Sydney Clouts. BoSA
Within a budding grove. The Lover and Birds. William Allingham. GTIV; OBVV
Within a chamber of a tower Quia Amore Langueo. *Unknown.* ISi
Within a copse I met a shepherd-maid. Ballata: Concerning a Shepherd-Maid. Guido Cavalcanti. AWP
Within a Dainty Garden-Close. *Unknown, tr. fr. French by* Arthur Symons. VLEP
Within a gloomy dimble she doth dwell. Mother Maudlin the Witch. Ben Jonson. *Fr.* The Sad Shepherd. ChTr
Within a low-thatch'd hut, built in a lane. The Net-Braiders. Thomas Wade. VA
Within a narrow span of time. Shelley's Centenary. Sir William Watson. BMEP; PoVP; TCPD
Within a native hut, ere stirred the dawn. Nativity. Gladys May Casely Hayford (Aquah Laluah). CDC; PoNe
Within a poor man's squalid home I stood. Vision. William Dean Howells. AA; AnAmPo; LA
Within a splendid home is missed a frank and joyous smile. Sister Agatha. Mary A. McMullen. PraNu
Within a thick and spreading hawthorn bush. The Thrush's Nest. John Clare. AlDL; BCEP; BoTP; CG; GoTP; PoRL; ThWaDe; WP
Within an Emerald. Salvador Díaz Mirón, *tr. fr. Spanish by* Samuel Beckett. AnMP
Within an English village yesterday. Nora. Dora Sigerson Shorter. HBMV
Within and Without, *sel.* George Macdonald.
"My soul leans toward Him." WGRP
Within Fancy's halls I sit and quaff. The Wine of Song. Charles Sangster. CPG
Within Heaven's circle I had not guessed at this. The Flight into Egypt. Peter Quennell. LiTB; LiTM
Within Her Eyes. Dante. *See* My Lady Carries Love.
Within her hair Venus and Cupid sport them. Emaricdulfe, VI. "E. C." ElL; TuPP
Within her heart o'erflowing care was preying. The Mother. Nikolai Alekseyevich Nekrasov. WaL
Within his hut he lay at flaming noon. Gauguin. Marion Ethel Hamilton. MuM
Within his [*or* the] sober realm of leafless trees. The Closing Scene. Thomas Buchanan Read. AA; HBV; LBAP; LPS-2; SN
Within how many metamorphoses. To Primal Matter. Luis de Sandoval y Zapata. AnMP
Within its belly dark. The Galley. Ibn Hariq. MooP
Within King's College Chapel, Cambridge. Wordsworth. *See* Inside of King's College Chapel, Cambridge.
Within mankind's duration, so they say. The Birds. J. C. Squire. BLA; BMEP; HBMV
Within me are two souls that pity each. Duality. Arthur Sherburne Hardy. AA
Within me I bear my solitude. Manuel Altolaguirre, *tr. fr. Spanish by* Eleanor L. Turnbull. CoSP
Within my bosom stirs once more tonight. Lament. Princess Zeb-un-Nissa. LiTW
Within my earthly temple there's a crowd. My Name Is Legion [*or* Which is Me?]. Edward Sandford Martin. MaRV; OQP; QP-2
Within my garden rides a bird. Emily Dickinson. TiPo (1952 ed.)
Within my hand I hold. Magic. Hamlin Garland. PoeMoYo; VOD
Within my head, aches the perpetual winter. Winter and Summer. Stephen Spender. MoAB; MoBrPo (1950 ed.); MoPo
Within my heart I long have kept. Blondel. Clarence Urmy. AA; HBMV; PFY
Within My Heart. Judah al-Harizi, *tr. fr. Hebrew.* TrJP
Within my house of patterned horn. The Tortoise in Eternity. Elinor Wylie. ChMo; FaPON; ImOP
Within my mind. The Prophecy of Taliesin. Taliesin. PoFr
Within my twenty yer of age. The Dream of the Romaunt of the Rose. Guillaume de Lorris, *tr. by* Chaucer. *Fr.* The Romance of the Rose LoBV
Within myself, this bit of dying dust. Flame against the Wind. Florence Wilson Roper. MuM
Within our happy Castle there dwelt One. Stanzas Written in My Pocket Copy of Thomson's "Castle of Indolence." Wordsworth. EnRP
Within our orchard's walls I saw thee. Fatal Blindness. Virgil. *Fr.* Eclogues, VIII. LiA
Within that awful [*or* this ample] volume lies. The Book of Books [*or* The Bible]. Sir Walter Scott. *Fr.* The Monastery, *ch.* 12. BLRP; MaRV; NeHB; OQP; QP-1; WBLP
Within that semi-circle formed by mounds. Old Earthworks. Thomas Sweeney. OQP; QP-2
Within the Alamo. Karle Wilson Baker. HiLiAm
Within the cage he ramped and raged! The Caged Mongoose. Constance Hollar. PoNe
Within the Canopy of Leaves. Earl of Rochester. *Fr.* A Pastoral Courtship. BeR
Within the Circuit of This Plodding Life. Henry David Thoreau. *See* Winter Memories.
Within the city's midst a grove there stood. Sunt Lacrimae Rerum. Virgil. *Fr.* The Aeneid, I. LiA
Within the cloister blissful of thy sides. Two Invocations of the Virgin, I. Chaucer. *Fr.* The Canterbury Tales: The Second Nun's Tale. ACP
Within the covert of a shady grove. Love Sleeping. Plato. AWP; OnPM; WoL
Within the crib that stands beside my bed. Maternity. Anne P. L. Field. MOAH
Within the darkened room he gently stept. The Healing Hands. Victor Robinson. PoP
Within the dim museum room. Thomas Caulfield Irwin. *Fr.* Caesar. TIP
Within the flower there lies a seed. Spell of Creation. Kathleen Raine. FaBoCh; LoGBV; WaKn
Within the garden of Beaucaire. Provençal Lovers; Aucassin and Nicolette. Edmund Clarence Stedman. HBV; LBAP
Within the garden-plot of thy fair face. To a Fair Gentlewoman, False to Her Friend. George Turberville. TuPP
Within the garden's deepness filled of light. Goose à la Mode. Elisabeth Cavazza Pullen. PA
Within the Gates. David W. Foley. MaRV
Within the gates ere a man shall go. The Sayings of the High One. *Unknown. Fr.* The Elder Edda. PaOS
Within the gentle heart Love shelters him. Canzone: Of the Gentle Heart. Guido Guinicelli. AWP; GoBC; LiTW; LyMA; LyPI; WoL
"Within the gold square of the proscenium arch." An Opera House. Amy Lowell. CV
Within the Gorges there is no lack of men. Invitation to Hsiao Chü-shih. Po Chü-i. TrCh
Within the grave lies the king whom autumn winds have swept away. Song for the Bronze God. Li Ho. WhP
Within the great wall's perfect round. The Window. Edwin Muir. LiTM (rev. ed.)
Within the iron cities. The Garden of God. "Æ." WGRP
Within the isle, far from the walks of men. In Forest Depths. Richard Henry Horne. *Fr.* Orion. VA
Within the letter's rustling fold. Spring Flowers from Ireland. Denis Florence MacCarthy. ACP; GoBC; TIP
Within the mind strong fancies work. The Pass of Kirkstone. Wordsworth. HBV
Within the navel of this hideous wood. The Haunt of the Sorcerer. Milton. *Fr.* Comus. BCEP; LPS-3
Within the night, above the dark. Mary Gilmore. *Fr.* Swans at Night. MoAuPo
Within the oak a throb of pigeon wings. A Twilight in Middle March. Francis Ledwidge. GTIV; OnYI; OxBI; TCEP; WHA
Within the pale blue haze above. The Storm. Coventry Patmore. EnLoPo
Within the precincts of this yard. The Beasts in the Tower. Charles *and* Mary Lamb. OTPC (1923 ed.)
Within the ring o' sallies. The Sally Ring. Patrick Kelly. GTIV
Within the sand of what far river lies. Shadows of His Lady. Jacques Tahureau. AWP
Within the silence of a cloistered court. Only Then. Frances Revett Wallace. MuM
Within the sober realm of leafless trees. *See* Within his sober realm . . .
Within the Soul a Faculty Abides. Wordsworth. *Fr.* The Excursion, IV. OBRV
Within the spring's bright shell of dawn, XIII. Frances Crawford. PtPa
Within the still, white room that gave me birth. Alien. Helen Frazee-Bower. HBMV
Within the timeless wood In the Forest. Jules Supervielle. TrFP
"Within the town, of whose huge walls so monstrous high and thick." Pyramus and Thisbe. Ovid. *Fr.* Metamorphoses. LiTW; ReIE
Within the unchanging twilight. The Norns Watering Yggdrasill. William Bell Scott. VA
Within the Veil. Margaret E. Sangster. BLRP
Within the window of this white. A Window Song. Thomas Caulfield Irwin. TIP
Within the wires of the post, unloading the cans of garbage. Prisoners. Randall Jarrell. OxBA; WaP
Within the wood behind the hill. The Satyrs and the Moon. Herbert S. Gorman. HBV; PFY; TSW; TSWC
Within the world a second world. The Hidden Tide. Roderic Quinn. BoAu
Within the year of Christ our Lord. Queen Elizabeth at Tilbury. Thomas Deloney. SiCE
Within these gray walls Life begins and ends. Inscription for a Hospital E. O. Laughlin. PoP

Within these walls of rustic wood. A Country Church. Pearce Young. PtPa
Within these woods of Arcadie. Sir Philip Sidney. Matthew Royden. *Fr.* An Elegy, or Friend's Passion for His Astrophil. LPS-3
Within this ample volume lies. *See* Within that awful volume lies.
Within this black hive to-night. Beehive. Jean Toomer. PoNe
Within this grave do lie. *Unknown.* WhC
Within this gray substantial rock. Time at Timberline. Donald F. Drummond. PtPa
Within this humble thatched-roof place. Peace. Beatrice Plumb. PraP
Within this lowly grave a Conqueror lies. The Conqueror's Grave. Bryant. AA
Within this nation-hallowed tomb. Epitaph for the Unknown Soldier. Annette Kohn. DD
Within this place lies Abraham the Civil. In Tumulum Abrahami Simple. John Weever. SiCE; TuPP
Within this sepulcher. Adelheid. Paul the Deacon. LaP
Within this silent palace of the Night. Moonrise. Frank Dempster Sherman. AA
Within this sober frame expect. Upon Appleton House. Andrew Marvell. NBE; ReEn; SeCV-1
Within this stumbling ground for bulls. Conflict. Lincoln Fitzell. AnAmPo; LA
Within this termitary. By an Ant-Heap. Terence Heywood. BoSA
Within this windless covert silence drops. Scarabs for the Living, IV. R. P. Blackmur. TwAmPo
Within this wood, out of a rocke did rise. The Visions of Petrarch. *Tr. by* Spenser. Sonnets to Laura: To Laura in Death, Canzone III. EnLi-1
Within those halls where student zeal. The College Cat. Alfred Denis Godley. CenHV
Within unfriendly walls. Waiting. John Davidson. ViBoPo
Within what weeks the melilot. Sweet Clover. Wallace Rice. HBV
Within your heart. Hold Fast Your Dreams. Louise Driscoll. TiPo
Within your magic web of hair lies furled. The Web of Eros. Edith Sitwell. BMEP; HBMV; LBBV
Within your silent words what nets pass secretly. Pisces Multiplicati. Richard Crashaw. Epigrammata Sacra, II, 29. LaP
With-inne the temple he went him forth pleyinge. Chaucer. *Fr.* Troilus and Criseyde, I. LO
Without an accoucheuse, in darkness. The Urals for the First Time. Boris Pasternak. TrRV
Without and Within. Norman Ault. MaRV; StJW
Without and Within. James Russell Lowell. BOHV; HBV; PR; TOP
Without and Within. Pierre A. B. D. Metastasio. LPS-3
Without avail the flocks of sparrows try. Eagles and Sparrows. José Santos Chocano. PoFr
Without contraries is no progression. Heaven and Hell. Blake. *Fr.* The Marriage of Heaven and Hell. RO
Without dressmakers to connect. Because of Clothes. Laura Riding. LiTA
Without haste! Without rest! Haste Not, Rest Not. Goethe. MaRV; OQP; QP-1
Without Her. Dante Gabriel Rossetti. The House of Life, LIII. BPN; CoBE; EmBrPo; GTBS-W; PoEL-5; PoVP; ReaPo; VA; ViBoPo; ViP; ViPo; VLEP
Without him still this whirling earth. Egotism. Edward Sandford Martin. AA
Without how small, within how strangely vast! On the Skull of Shakespeare. George Sterling. PFE
Without Light. Vicente Aleixandre, *tr. fr. Spanish by* Eleanor L. Turnbull. CoSP
Without love's charm, both wild and rude. Boredom. Ramón de Campoamor. OnPM
Without meaning to, they watch him play. The Child. Rainer Maria Rilke. AnGP
Without millions of pennies and millions of men. The Victory. Laura Riding. MoP
Without My Friends the Day Is Dark. Moses ibn Ezra, *tr. fr. Hebrew by* Solomon Solis-Cohen. TrJP
Without Name. Pauli Murray. PoNe
Without Regret. Lilith Lorraine. PGD
Without Sleep. Glenway Wescott. NP
Without surprise, on that not distant shore. Delusions VI. Charles Madge. NeBP
Without Syncopation. Joyce Rowe. DiM
Without That Once Clear Aim. Stephen Spender. ChMo; PeBoSo
Without the evening dew and showers. Ode. Charles Cotton. ViBoPo
Without the Herdsman. Diotimus. *See* Cow Herd, The.
Without, the lonely night is sweet with stars. Martyrdom. "Rufus Learsi." TrJP
Without the Moon. Jules Laforgue, *tr. fr. French by* Hart Crane. LiTW
Without the slightest basis. How Jack Found That Beans May Go Back on a Chap. Guy Wetmore Carryl. ALV; HoPM; MAP; MoAmPo (1942 ed.)
Without, the sullen noises of the street! Benedictio Domini. Ernest Dowson. CAW; JKCP; POTT
Without the Way, there can be no going. The Way; the Truth; the Life. Samuel Judson Porter. BLRP
Without Thee What Are Song and Dance to Me? Sayat Nova, *tr. fr. Armenian by* Zabelle C. Boyajian. ArmLP
Without thought, without remorse, without shame. Walls. C. P. Cavafy. MoGP; TrJP
"Withouten Time is no erthely thinge." Time and Eternity. Stephen Hawes. *Fr.* The Pastime of Pleasure. PoEL-1
Withouten you/ No rose can grow. Little Elegy. Elinor Wylie. BoFr
Withstanders. William Barnes. OxBoCh
Witlaf, a king of the Saxons. King Witlaf's Drinking-Horn. Longfellow. CoBA; TCAP
Witless alike of will and way divine. Epilogue to Dramatis Personae. Robert Browning. BPN
Witless Gallant, A. Michael Drayton. Idea, XXI. PeBoSo ("Witless gallant, a young wench that wooed, A.") SiCE; TuPP
Witness of God. James Russell Lowell. *Fr.* The Cathedral. OQP; QP-2
Witness then the all-pervading fog. Autumn. Rietta Trimm. CAG
Witness, ye days and nights, and all ye hours. Dryden. *Fr.* All for Love, II. LoPS
Witnesses, The. W. H. Auden. MoP; ShBV-4
Witnesses, The. Longfellow. AtBAP
Wits, The. Samuel Johnson. *Fr.* Prologue Spoken at the Opening of the Theatre in Drury-Lane, 1747. BeR
Wit's a feather and a chief a rod, A. An Honest Man. Pope. *Fr.* An Essay on Man, Epistle IV. TreF
Wit's End Corner. Antoinette Wilson. BLRP
Wits of Charles found easier ways to fame, The. The Wits. Samuel Johnson. *Fr.* Prologue Spoken at the Opening of the Theatre in Drury-Lane, 1747. BeR
Wit's perfection, Beauty's wonder. Three Epitaphs upon the Death of a Rare Child of Six Years Old, 1. Francis Davison. OBSC; ReIE
Witty Fair One, The, *sel.* James Shirley.
Love, a Thousand Sweets Distilling. SeCL
(Song: "Love a thousand sweets distilling.") SeEP
Wives are a curse. Palladas, *tr. fr. Greek by* F. A. Wright. GrPo
Wives in the Sere. Thomas Hardy. TyEnPo; VLEP
Wizard Frost. Frank Dempster Sherman. YeAr
Wizard of the Nile, The, *sel.* Harry B. Smith.
My Angeline. BOHV; InMe
Wizard of the woods is he. The. The Woodpecker. John Banister Tabb. UTS
Wizard Oil, *with music.* *Unknown.* AS
Wizards. Alfred Noyes. POT
Wizard's Funeral, The. Richard Watson Dixon. GTBS-D; LoBV
Wo' his purple an' linen, too Dives and Laz'us. *Unknown.* ABF
Woak Hill. William Barnes. GTML; GTSL
Woe, a man cast askew on a mossy mound. Gethsemane Now. Bobb Hamilton. MeRV
Woe Be unto You, *with music.* *Unknown.* ABF
Woe for the brave ship *Orient!* The Brave Old Ship, the *Orient.* Robert Traill Spence Lowell. AA; FaBoBe
Woe having made, with many fights, his own. Astrophel and Stella, LVII. Sir Philip Sidney. ReEn; SiPS
Woe, he went galloping into the war. Rosny. Robert Browning. BPN
Woe is he who sees vanish and then melt away. Juan Díaz Covarrubias. *Fr.* A Selection. PoP
Woe Is Me! Micah, VII: 1-6, Bible, *O.T.* TrJP
Woe is me that I from Israell. *Unknown.* SeCSL
Woe is me! what am I like? The Lament of Saint Ann. *Unknown.* *Fr.* The Protevangelium of James. CAW
Woe to Him ("Woe to him that has not known the woe of man"). Laurence Binyon. MaRV
Woe to the South Mountain! Meditation. Li Ho. WhP
Woe to thee that spoilest. Isaiah, Bible, *O.T.* PoFr
Woe unto them/ That rise up early. Intemperance. Isaiah, Bible, *O.T.* (*Moulton, Modern Reader's Bible*). MaRV
Woe, woe for Adonis, he hath perished. The Lament for Adonis. Bion. GrL
Woe, woe, unto the fallen city! Sorrow. Jóhann Sigurjónsson. IcP
Woe worth thee, woe worth thee, false Scottlande! Earl Bothwell. *Unknown.* ESPB
Woeful spirit in my heart may not, The. Arcite's Farewell. Chaucer. *Fr.* The Canterbury Tales: The Knight's Tale. LiTL
Woefully Arrayed. John Skelton. ChTr; LoBV; OxBoCh
Woes me alas unblest unhappy I. *Unknown.* SeCSL
Woe's me! by dint of all those sighs that come. Dante. *Fr.* La Vita Nuova. AWP

Wofle New Ballad of Jane Roney and Mary Brown, The. Thackeray. BOHV
Wofully araid [*or* Woefully arrayed]/ My blode [*or* blood] man for thee ran. Woefully Arrayed. John Skelton. ChTr; LoBV; OxBoCh
Woggly bird sat on the whango tree, The. The Whango Tree. *Unknown.* BOHV; NA
Woke up this mo'nin'. Young Woman's Blues. *Unknown.* OnAP
Woken, I lay in the arms of my own warmth and listened. First Things First. W. H. Auden. NePoAm-2
Wol ze here a wonder thynge. Riddles Wisely Expounded. *Unknown.* BaBo (A *vers.*); ESPB
Wolcum be thu, hevene kyng. *See* Welcome be Thou, Heavenly King.
Wolf, The. Donald Davidson. AnAmPo; LA; LS
Wolf, The. Georgia R. Durston. GFA; UTS
Wolf, a hornet and a nightingale, A. The Wolf, the Hornet and the Nightingale. Stanton A. Coblentz. BAP
Wolf also shall dwell with the lamb, The. The Peaceable Kingdom. Isaiah, Bible, *O.T.* FaPON; LiTW
Wolf and the Dog, The. La Fontaine, *tr. fr. French by* Elizur Wright. AnSpL-2 (Félix María de Samaniego, *wr.*); LiA; LiTW; PoFr; TrFP, *tr. by* Alan Conder
Wolf and the Lamb, The. La Fontaine, *tr. fr. French by* Elizur Wright. OuHeWo
Wolf and the Lambs, The. Ivy O. Eastwick. BoTP
Wolf Cry, The. Lew Sarett. FaPON; PoMa
Wolf in the Kennels, The. Ivan Andreyevich Krylov, *tr. fr. Russian by* Frances Cornford *and* E. P. Salaman. LiTW
Wolf of Gubbio, The. Hyacinth Blocker. SaFP
Wolf of Gubbio Speaks to Saint Francis, The. Sister Mary Monica. SaFP
Wolf of Gubbio to Saint Francis, The. Anna McClure Sholl. SaFP
Wolf of the winter wind is swift, The. An Indian Wind Song. Peter McArthur. CPG
Wolf, the Goat, and the Kid, The. La Fontaine, *tr. fr. French by* Alan Conder. TrFP
Wolf, the Hornet and the Nightingale, The. Stanton A. Coblentz. BAP
Wolf who was a bag of skin and bone, A. The Wolf and the Dog. La Fontaine. TrFP
Wolf, with hunger fierce and bold, A. The Shepherd Dog and the Wolf. John Gay. AlBD
Wolfram's Dirge. Thomas Lovell Beddoes. *See* Dirge: "If thou wilt ease thine heart."
Wolfram's Song. Thomas Lovell Beddoes. *See* Song: "Old Adam, the carrion crow."
Wolsey's Farewell to Cromwell ("Cromwell, I did not think"). Shakespeare, *and probably* John Fletcher. King Henry VIII, *fr.* III, ii. EV-1
("Cromwell, I did not think to shed a tear.") InP; PIR
(Wolsey.) OTPC (1923 ed.)
(Wolsey's Advice to Cromwell.) LPS-1
(Wolsey's Regrets.) TreFS
Wolsey's Farewell to His Greatness. Shakespeare, *and probably* John Fletcher. King Henry VIII, *fr.* III, ii. OHFP; PTA-2
(Cardinal Wolsey's Farewell.) LiTB; MaRV; TreF
("Farewell, a long farewell, to all my greatness!") PIR
(Farewell to All My Greatness.) BCEP; LiTG
(Farewell to Greatness.) TrGrPo
(Wolsey, on His Downfall.) TVSH
(Wolsey's Fall.) LPS-1
Wolves. Louis MacNeice. BrBE
Wolves, The. Elizabeth Madox Roberts. UTS
Wolves, The. Allen Tate. LiTA; LiTG; LiTM; MOAP; OxBA
Wolves in dim the forest prowl. A Christmass Carol for Saint Francis' Ears. Raymond E. F. Larsson. SaFP
Wolves of Egremont, The. Dorothy Quick. DaM
Woman. Eaton Stannard Barrett. HBV; OnYI; OxBI; PIAE
Woman. Isabel Fiske Conant. TBM
Woman. Zora Cross. BoAu
Woman. C. D. B. Ellis. SiTL
Woman. Fu Hsüan, *tr. fr. Chinese by* Arthur Waley. TrCh; WoL
Woman. Goldsmith. *See* Song: "When lovely woman stoops to folly."
Woman! Sakutaro Hagiwara, *tr. fr. Japanese by* Takamichi Ninomiya *and* D. J. Enright. PoLJ
Woman. Fitz-Greene Halleck. PR
Woman. Kalidasa, *tr. fr. Sanskrit by* Horace H. Wilson. HBV; LPS-3
Woman, A. Thomas MacDonagh. TIP
Woman, *sel.* Alexander McLachlan.
"When my gloomy hour comes on me." CaP
Woman, A. Scudder Middleton. BAP; NV; PC
Woman. Milton. *Fr.* Samson Agonistes. OBS
Woman. Nyleen Newton. CAG
Woman. Thomas O'Hagan. CAW
Woman. Coventry Patmore. *See* Foreign Land, The.
Woman. Earl of Rochester. *Fr.* The Nature of Women. BeR
Woman, A. Mary Dixon Thayer. HBMV
Woman ("A clever man builds a city"). *Unknown, tr. fr. Chinese by* H. A. Giles. *Fr.* Shi King. AWP; LiTW
Woman ("When Eve brought woe to all mankind"). *Unknown.* LPS-3
Woman Always Pays, The. "H. T. R." CAG
Woman and Cat. Paul Verlaine. *See* Femme et chatte.
Woman and Earth. Pierre Jean Jouve, *tr. fr. French by* David Gascoyne. MiFP
Woman and Her Dead Husband, A. D. H. Lawrence. NP
Woman and Man, *abr.* Tennyson. *Fr.* The Princess, Pt. VII. BMEP; OQP; QP-2
Woman at the Piano. Marya Zaturenska. MoAmPo
Woman at the Washington Zoo, The. Randall Jarrell. UnPo (3d ed.)
Woman, bathe this head of mine. The Bathing of Oisin's Head. *Unknown.* AnIL
Woman, beguiling man, herself beguiles. Woman. C. D. B. Ellis. SiTL
Woman Blue, *with music.* *Unknown.* ABF
Woman-Captain, The, *sel.* Thomas Shadwell.
Let Some Great Joys Pretend to Find. OAEP
Woman Clothed with the Sun, A. Apocalypse (Revelation) XII: 1, 2, 5, 10, Bible, *N.T.* (*Douay vers.*). ISi
Woman every night, A/ Journeys secretly. Paul Eluard. *Fr.* Universe-Solitude. MiFP
Woman! experience might have told me. To Woman. Byron. HBV; ViBoPo
Woman from Samos. Alexandros Pallis, *tr. fr. Modern Greek by* Rae Dalven. MoGP
Woman full of wile. Growing Old [*or* Autumn]. *Unknown, tr. by* Frank O'Connor. KiLC; OBMV
Woman, give him alms. For the Poor Blind Man. Francisco A. de Icaza. AnMP
Woman had I seen, as I rode by, A. Bogac Bán. Darrell Figgis. AnIV
Woman-Hater, The, *sel.* Beaumont *and* Fletcher.
"Come, Sleep, and with thy sweet deceiving," *fr.* III, i. EG; ElL; SiCE
(Invocation to Sleep.) LPS-3
(Lullaby.) FaBoEn
(Sleep.) EV-2; HBV; OBEV (1st ed.); PC
Woman I Am, The. Glen Allen. BLPA
Woman I Met, The. Thomas Hardy. AtBAP
Woman in Sunshine, The. Wallace Stevens. CoV; MoVE
Woman in the garden. Duo. Olive Tilford Dargan. HBMV
Woman in the Rye, The. Thomas Hardy. VLEP
Woman in the Wagon, The. Clyde Robertson. PoOW
Woman in Winter Costume, A. John Gould Fletcher. ChMo; CMP
Woman Is a Branchy Tree, A. James Stephens. ChMo; CMP; POTE
Woman is a foreign land, A. The Foreign Land [*or* Woman]. Coventry Patmore. The Angel in the House, II, ix, 2. HBV; OBVV
Woman Looking at a Vase of Flowers. Wallace Stevens. CrMA
Woman, meanwhile, from strawberry lips, The. The Metamorphoses of a Vampire. Baudelaire. ReMP
Woman much missed, how you call to me, call to me. The Voice. Thomas Hardy. CoEV; EnLoPo; FaBoEn; MoVE; NP; OAEP (2d ed.); PoEL-5; ViPP
Woman named Tomorrow, The. Four Preludes on Playthings of the Wind, I. Carl Sandburg. AnAmPo; AnFE; BLV; BoLiVe; CoAnAm; CoBA; InP; LA; MAP; MoAB; MoAmPo; NePA; NP; SeCeV
Woman of Beare, The. *Unknown, tr. fr. Middle Irish by* Stephen Gwynn. AnIV; GTIV
(Hag of Beare, The, *tr. by* Seán O'Faoláin.) SiB
(Old Woman of Beare, The, *tr. by* Frank O'Connor.) AnIL; KiLC; OnYI, *abr., tr. by* Kuno Meyer
(Old Woman of Beare Regrets Lost Youth, The, *tr. by* Frank O'Connor.) OBMV
Woman of Llyn y Fan's Call to Her Cattle, The. *Unknown, tr. fr. Welsh by* Gwyn Jones. PrWP
Woman of Samaria, The, *sel.* Edmond Rostand, *tr. fr. French by* Henderson Daingerfield Norman.
"Curses upon this land; till plague devours," Pt. I, iv. StJW
Woman of the North, The. Jens Christian Hostrup, *tr. fr. Danish by* Charles W. Stork. BoDS
Woman of This Earth, *sels.* Frances Frost. AnAmPo
"Before sheep came."
"History of earth is a moving of leaves in the sun, The."
Woman of Three Cows, The. *Unknown, tr. fr. Late Middle Irish or fr. Modern Irish by* James Clarence Mangan. AnIL; EnRP; GTIV; IrPN; OnYI; OxBI; TIP
Woman of Words, A. Amanda B. Hall. HBMV
Woman of Yueh, A. Li Po, *tr. fr. Chinese by* Shigeyoshi Obata. OnPM
Woman on the Walls, The. H. A. Cody. CPG

Woman or her shadow of ivy, A. Elegy to the Invented Woman. Xavier Abril. AnCL
Woman Passes the Door, A. George O'Neil. NP
Woman sings across the wild, A. The Christ-Child. Agnes Lee. BPP
Woman, speak not with me! The Tryst with Death. *Unknown.* SiB
Woman Standing by a Gate with an Umbrella, A. John Gould Fletcher. ChMo; CMP
Woman supremely blest. Mulier Amicta Sole. Fray Angelico Chavez. ISi
"Woman, take away my tunic." Goll's Parting with His Wife. *Unknown.* AnIL
Woman That Had More Babies than That, The. Wallace Stevens. LiTA
Woman, though undependable. Experts on Woman. Arthur Guiterman. InMe
Woman to Man. Judith Wright. BoAV; MoAuPo
Woman walking the street adown, A. Two Mothers. Robert Burton. MOAH
Woman was old and ragged and gray, The. Somebody's Mother. Mary Dow Brine. BeLS; BLPA; FaFP; OTPC (1946 ed.); PTA-1; TreF; WBLP
Woman watches her husband rubbing his nose, The. Twenty Below. R. A. D. Ford. CaP
Woman weak and woman mortal. Streets of Baltimore. *Unknown.* BLPA; BoHiPo
Woman Who Came behind Him in the Crowd. George Macdonald. StJW
Woman Who Disapproved of Music at the Bar, The. Horace Gregory. MoPo
Woman who has borne a child, The. The Mothers of the Earth. Grace Noll Crowell. PEDC
Woman who has grown old, The. The Crows. Louise Bogan. TBM; YT
Woman who lived in Holland, of old, A. Going Too Far. Mildred Howells. TiPo
Woman who walked home on the arm of John. Chant of Departure; a Missionary's Prayer. Alfred J. Barrett. GoBC; ISi
Woman with Child, The. Freda Laughton. OnYI
Woman with no face walked into the light, A. Homage to Hieronymus Bosch. Thomas McGreevy. OnYI
Woman with the Baby to the Philosopher, The. Frances Cornford. PoMa
Woman with the Serpent's Tongue, The. Sir William Watson. BMEP; HBV
Woman without Fear. George Dillon. AnEnPo
Woman without Tears, A. Euripides, *tr. fr. Greek by* Witter Bynner. *Fr.* Iphigenia in Tauris. GrR
Woman, Woman, I Seen Yo' Man, *with music. Unknown.* StDa
Woman wrapped her coat, A. Isador and Ida Strauss. E. J. Pratt. *Fr.* The *Titanic.* TwCaPo
Woman Wrapped in Silence, A, *sel.* John W. Lynch.
"Little girl, A/ Had wandered," V. ISi
Womankind. Sophocles, *tr. fr. Greek by* C. M. Bowra. OxBG
Woman's Answer, A. Adelaide Anne Procter. LPS-1
Woman's Answer, A. *At. to* the Earl of Surrey. SiPS
Woman's Answer to "The Vampire," A. Felicia Blake. BLPA; NeHB
Woman's Antidote for War, A. Aristophanes, *tr. fr. Greek by* Benjamin Bickley Rogers. *Fr.* Lysistrata. GrR
Woman's Beauty. Lascelles Abercrombie. *Fr.* Emblems of Love: Vashti. MBP; MoBrPo; PG
Woman's beauty is like a white, A. Song from "The Only Jealousy of Emer." W. B. Yeats. MoAB
Woman's Beloved, A. Marguerite Wilkinson. NP
Woman's cause is man's, The: they rise or sink. Woman and Man. Tennyson. *Fr* The Princess, Pt. VII. BMEP; OQP; QP-2
Woman's Constancy. John Donne. ElSeCe; EnLit; EnLP; EPS; LiTL; PoE; PoFS; ReIE; SeCV-1; SeEP; TuPP
Woman's Easter. Lucy Larcom. EOAH
Woman's Execution, A. Edward King. AA; LEAP
Woman's face is full of wiles, A. Song. Humphrey Gifford. *Fr.* A Delectable Dream. EIL; ElSeCe; SiCE; TuPP
Woman's face with Nature's own hand painted, A. Sonnets, XX. Shakespeare. InvP; PeBoSo; ReEn
Woman's Faith ("Woman's faith and woman's trust"). Sir Walter Scott. *Fr.* The Betrothed, *ch.* 20. ViBoPo
Woman's Hand, A. Sir Gilbert Parker. *Fr.* A Lover's Diary. VA
Woman's hands with polished finger-nail, A. Hands on a Card-Table. Polly Chase Boyden. NP
Woman's Heart, *br. sel* Frances Anne Kemble.
"Maids must be wives and mothers." MotAn
Woman's Inconstancy. Sir Robert Ayton. *See* I Loved Thee Once.
Woman's Inconstancy. Phineas Fletcher. *Fr.* Sicelides, II, ii. EIL
("Who sows the seas, or ploughs the easy shore?") ElSeCe
Woman's Jealousy. Baltasar del Alcázar, *tr. fr. Spanish by* Sir John Bowring. OnPM
Woman's Last Word, A. Robert Browning. BEL; BLPA; BMEP; BoLiVe; BPN; EmBrPo; EPN; EV-5; FaBoBe; FaFP; GEPC; GTBS; GTBS-D; HBV; InPo; LiTL; LO; LoPS; OAEP; PIR; PoVP; TreFS; TrGrPo; ViBoPo; ViPo; VLEP
Woman's Looks, A. *Unknown.* OBSC; ReEn; SiCE; TrGrPo
Woman's Love, A. John Hay. HBV; LPS-1
Woman's Love. Robert Mannyng. *See* Praise of Women.
Woman's Love. *Unknown.* WBLP
Woman's Prayer, A. *Unknown.* PraP
Woman's Pride, A. Helen Hay Whitney. AA
Woman's Question, A. Lena Lathrop, *wr. at. to* Elizabeth Barrett Browning. BLPA; PoToHe; PTA-1; WBLP
Woman's Question[s], A. Adelaide Anne Procter. AV; BMEP; HBV; LiTL; LO; LPS-1; VA
Woman's Ruling Passions. Pope. *Fr.* Moral Essays, Epistle II. OBEC
Woman's sho' a cur'ous critter, an' dey ain't no doubtin' dat. The Turning of the Babies in the Bed. Paul Laurence Dunbar. MAP; MoAmPo (1942 ed.); MotAn; NeMA
Woman's Shortcomings, A. Elizabeth Barrett Browning. BLPA; HBV; NeHB
Woman's Song. Aleksey Koltsov, *tr. fr. Russian.* BoR
Woman's Song, A. Muna Lee. NP
Woman's Song. Edward Shanks. LO
Woman's Song. Judith Wright. BoAV
Woman's Thought, A. Richard Watson Gilder. BAP; HBV
Woman's Tongue Tree, The. Arthur Guiterman. PoMS
Woman's Will. John Godfrey Saxe. BOHV; FaFP; HBV; LauV; LPS-3; SiTL
("Men, dying, make their wills; but wives.") InP
Woman's Will. *Unknown.* HBV
Woman's Wit, *sel.* Colley Cibber.
Celia and Belinda. SeCL
Wombat, The. Ogden Nash. CenHV
Women. Louise Bogan. HBMV; LiTA; LiTL; MAP; MoAB; MoAmPo; MOAP; WHA
Women. José Gorostiza, *tr. fr. Spanish by* Donald Devenish Walsh. AnCL
Women. —— Heath. *See* These Women All.
Women. Lizette Woodworth Reese. MAP; MoAmPo; MOAP; NP
Women. Semonides. *See* Some Women.
Women and poets see the truth arrive. Letter to the Front. Muriel Rukeyser. WaP
Women and Roses. Robert Browning. EmBrPo; EPN; ViBoPo
Women and the Wolf, The. Avianus, *tr. fr. Latin by* Jack Lindsay. LaP
Women and wine and baths bring life's decline. *Unknown. Fr.* Carmina Epigraphica. LaP
Women are door-mats and have been. Door-Mats. Mary Carolyn Davies. BAP; BPP; HBMV; YaD
Women are timid, cower and shrink. Betty Zane. Thomas Dunn English. GA; PAH
Women at the Corners Stand, The. Louis Golding. TrJP
Women Beware of Women, *sel.* Thomas Middleton.
"How near am I now to a happiness." LO; LoPS
Women Folk, The. James Hogg. HBV; LPS-3
Women have no wilderness in them. Women. Louise Bogan. HBMV; LiTA; LiTL; MAP; MoAB; MoAmPo; MOAP; WHA
Women He Liked. Edward Thomas. HaMV
Women Men's Shadows. Ben Jonson. *See* Song: That Women Are but Men's Shadows.
Women, my mind is clear. I go to slay. Heart, Steel Thyself! Euripides. *Fr.* Medea. GrR
Women, of kinde, have conditions three. John Lydgate. *Fr.* A Ballad Warning Men to Beware of Deceitful Women. LO
Women of Mumbles Head, The. Clement Scott. PTA-2
Women of Suli. "Myrtiotissa," *tr. fr. Modern Greek by* Rae Dalven. MoGP
Women of the Better Class, The. Oliver Herford. HBMV
Women of Yueh, The. Li Po, *tr. fr. Chinese by* Shigeyoshi Obata. ChLP
Women Pleased, *sels.* John Fletcher.
Song: "O fair[e] sweet face, O eyes celestial[l] bright," *fr.* III, iv. OBS; PoEL-2
Women's Longing, *fr.* V, i. HBV
Women Singing. Sir Henry Taylor. OBVV
Women sit or move to and fro, some old, some young. Beautiful Women. Walt Whitman. LEAP
Women tell me every day, The. Odes of Anacreon. *Tr. by* Thomas Moore. GrPo; LoBV; OuHeWo
Women that are loved are more than lovable. The Colours of Love. Denis Devlin. OxBI
Women there are on earth, most sweet and high. Of Those Who Walk Alone. Richard Burton. HBV
Women through the years have stood. The Fire Tenders. Grace Noll Crowell PEDC
Women Toilers, The. Grace Bowen Evans. OQP; QP-2

Women who do not love are free. The Free Woman. Theodosia Garrison. BAP; HBMV
Women Who Wait. Homer, *tr. fr. Greek by* Maurice Hewlett. *Fr.* The Iliad, VI. GrR
Women Will Soon Knit Again, The. Roger Burlingame. NeTW
Women's Eyes. Bhartrihari. *tr. fr. Sanskrit by* Arthur W. Ryder. OnPM
Women's Festival of Demeter. Aristophanes. *See* Thesmophoriazusae, The.
Women's Longing. John Fletcher. *Fr.* Women Pleased, V, i. HBV
Women's Loveliness. Paul Verlaine, *tr. fr. French by* James Kirkup. MiFP
Wonder. John Galsworthy. QS
Wonder, The. Kipling. *Fr.* Epitaphs of the War. PoVP
Wonder. Bernard Raymund. MW
Wonder. Thomas Traherne. AtBAP; CH; EPS; LiTB; LiTG; LoBV; PoE; ReaPo; SeCePo; SeCeV; SeCL; SeCV-2; SeEP; TrGrPo; TriL; TwHP; WHA
Wonder and a Thousand Springs. William Alexander Percy. HBMV
Wonder and Joy. Robinson Jeffers. BAP; PoTo
Wonder Books. Carrie Ward Lyon. MOB
Wonder-Child, The. Richard Le Gallienne. VA
Wonder is not precisely knowing. Emily Dickinson. MoPo
Wonder of It. Harriet Monroe. NP
Wonder of the world is o'er, The. The Twilight of Earth. "Æ." AnIL; ChMo; CMP; TOP
Wonder of these, glory of other times. To the Right Honorable, the Lady Mary, Countess of Pembroke. Samuel Daniel. *Fr.* Delia. SiCE; TuPP
Wonder stranger ne'r was known, A. The Suffolk Miracle. *Unknown.* BaBo (A *vers.*); CG; ESPB; OBB
Wonder was on me in Curraghmacall, The. The Two Nests. Francis Carlin. BLA; PFY; TBM
Wonder Where This Horseshoe Went. Edna St. Vincent Millay. *Fr.* A Very Little Sphinx. SUS; TiPo (1952 ed.)
(Horseshoe, The.) StVeCh
(Wonder Where.) PoRh
Wonder-working Providence of Sions Saviour in New England, 1628–1651, The, *sel.* Edward Johnson.
Cry unto the Lord to Stay His Hand, A ("From silent night true register of moans"), *fr. ch.* 9. BAV
Wonderer, The. Robert W. Service. BBV
Wonderful are thy works, as my soul overwhelmingly knoweth. Solomon ibn Gabirol. *Fr.* The Royal Crown. AWP
Wonderful bears that walked my room all night. Bears. Adrienne Cecile Rich. NePoEA
Wonderful bird is the pelican, A. Limerick. Dixon Lanier Merritt. CenHV; LiBL; LiTG
Wonderful Country. Miriam Waddington. PeCV
Wonderful Crocodile, The, *with music. Unknown.* ABF
Wonderful Derby Ram, The. *Unknown. See* Derby Ram, The.
Wonderful family is Stein, A. Limerick. *Unknown.* LiBL. *See also* There is a wonderful family called Stein.
Wonderful lass was Marie, petite, A. An Old Song by New Singers: How Andrew Lang Sings It. A. C. Wilkie. BOHV; NA
Wonderful Man, A. Aileen Fisher. SiSoSe
Wonderful Meadow, The. "Olive A. Wadsworth." *See* Over in the Meadow.
Wonderful night, that sent to me. Aubade. Ibn Hani. MooP
Wonderful Old Man, The. *Unknown.* NA
Wonderful "One-Hoss Shay," The. Oliver Wendell Holmes. *See* Deacon's Masterpiece, The.
Wonderful scarcity will shortly ensue, A. Thomas Bastard. SiCE
Wonderful way is the King's Highway, A. The King's Highway. John Masefield. BLRP
Wonderful Weaver, The. George Cooper. BoChLi; OTPC (1946 ed.); StVeCh (1940 ed.)
Wonderful World, The. William Brighty Rands. BoChLi; DD; FaPON; GFA; HBV; HBVY; MPB; OnHT; PRWS; PTA-1; RAR; StVeCh (1940 ed.); TiPo (1959 ed.); TVC; TVSH
(Child's World, The.) OHIP
(World, The.) BoTP; OTPC; PCH, *abr.*
(World, The; a Child's Song.) OBVV
Wonderfully out of the beautiful form. Sonnet. Dante. GoBC
Wonderland. Harry Thurston Peck. AA
Wonders. *Unknown.* ElL
(Madrigal.) CoEV
("Thule, the period of cosmography.") CenL
"Andalusian merchant, that returns, The," *sel.* FaBoCh
Wonders are many, and none is more wonderful than man. Choral Ode. Sophocles, *pr. tr. by* R. C. Jebb. *Fr.* Antigone. PreP
Wonders are many, but none there be. Man; Creation's Masterpiece. Sophocles, *tr. by* Gilbert Murray. *Fr.* Antigone. GrR
Wonders are many, but there is no wonder. What a Piece of Work Is a Man. Sophocles, *tr. by* F. L. Lucas. *Fr.* Antigone. OxBG
Wonders of Nature. *Unknown.* BOHV
Wonders of the Peake, The, *sels.* Charles Cotton.
Cave, A; Pool's Hole, Derbyshire. BeR
Tydes-Well, the Third Wonder of the Peak. BeR
Wondrous Apple Tree, The, *with music. Unknown, tr. fr. French by* Alice M. G. White. SaSa
Wondrous beauty, thinks Bran, A. Mananaan to Bran. *Unknown.* SiB
Wondrous is the wall-stone, by Wyrd broken. The Ruin. *Unknown, tr. by* Harold S. Stine. EnLit
Wondrous Love. Countess of Pembroke. BePJ
Wondrous Love, *with music. Unknown.* TrAS
Wondrous Motherhood. *Unknown.* PGD; PSO
Wondrous Show, A. James Thomson. *Fr.* The Castle of Indolence, I. OBEC
Wondrous things have come to pass. Wizard Frost. Frank Dempster Sherman. YeAr
Wondrous this masonry wasted by Fate! The Ruin. *Unknown, tr. by* Charles W. Kennedy. AnOE
Wondrously wrought and fair its wall of stone. The Ruined City. *Unknown, tr. by* Chauncey B. Tinker. EPP
Won't somebody please take care of Spot? On Parting with Spot. Helen Welshimer. AlBD
"Won't you look out of your window, Mrs. Gill?" The Mocking Fairy. Walter de la Mare. GBV; MBP; MoBrPo; MoShBr
Woo Not the World. Mu'tamid, King of Seville, *tr. fr. Arabic by* Dulcie L. Smith. AWP; JAWP; LiTW; WBP
Wood. Thomas Hornsby Ferril. PoRA
Wood and Hill. Andrew Young. HaMV
Woo'd and Married and A'. Alexander Ross. EBSV
Woo'd and Married and A'. *Unknown, wr. at. to* Alexander Ross. EBSV; EV-3
(Wooed and Married and A'.) HBV
Wood by the Sea, The. Duncan Campbell Scott. CPG
Wood-Dove's Note, The. Emily Huntington Miller. BLA; HBV
Wood Finches. Boethius, *tr. fr. Latin by* Martin F. Tupper. WhBS
Wood Flower. Richard Le Gallienne. HBMV
Wood-Gatherers, The. F. C. Slater. BoSA
Wood, The, is bare: a river-mist is steeping. Elegy. Robert Bridges. CaAE; ChMo; CMP; OAEP; POTT; PoVP; VLEP
Wood is one blue flame of love, The. Derbyshire Bluebells. Sacheverell Sitwell. ChMP
Wood-Lot Hill. Frances Frost. BAP
Wood louse sits on a splinter, The. Archygrams. Don Marquis. *Fr.* Archys Life of Mehitabel. WhC
Wood-Mouse, The. Mary How tt. RAR; TVC
Wood Music. Ethel King. GoYe
Wood of Flowers, The. James Stephens. BoTP
Wood of Tara, The. Harry Noyes Pratt. MuM
Wood of the Cross. Violet Alleyn Storey. StJW
Wood of the Self-Destroyers, The. Samuel Yellen. NePoAm-2
Wood-Path, A. Bliss Carman. MM
Wood-Pigeons. John Masefield. ChMP
Wood-Raven, The. *Unknown, tr. fr. Danish by* E. M. Smith-Dampier. BoDaBa
Wood Song, A. Ralph Hodgson. HBV; TCPD
Wood-Song. Eugene Lee-Hamilton. OBVV
Wood-Song. Josephine Preston Peabody. AA; ADAH
Wood Song. Sara Teasdale. Interlude: Songs Out of Sorrow, VI. BAP; BLA; PoeMoYo; PYM
Wood, swollen with mushrooms, The. The Circle. Jean Garrigue. LiTA; MoPo
Wood, the Weed, the Wag, The. Sir Walter Ralegh. BLV; Po; PoD; SiPS; TrGrPo
(Sir Walter Raleigh to His Son.) ReIE
(Three Thinges There Bee That Prosper Up Apace.) PoEL-2
(To His Son.) EnL; PoE; TuPP
Wood Thrush, The. John Vance Cheney. BLA; WhBS
Wood-Thrush. Clinton Scollard. BLA
Wood-Thrush. John Hall Wheelock. NePoAm
Wood to Burn and Not to Burn. *Unknown. See* Song of the Forest Trees.
Wood was rather old and dark, The. The Little Boy Lost. Stevie Smith. FaBoTw
Wood-Weasel, The. Marianne Moore. Po
Wood Wife. Leah Bodine Drake. DaM
Wood wind warbled wisely, The. A Beethoven Andante. Grace Hazard Conkling. PFY
Wood Witchery. Richard Burton. AnAmPo; LA
Woodbines in October. Charlotte Fiske Bates. AA
Woodbird. Charles G. Bell. NePoAm
Woodbox, The. Joseph C. Lincoln. DDA; PTA-2
Woodchuck told it all about, The. On Knowing When to Stop. L. J. Bridgman. BOHV
Woodchucking. *Unknown.* DDA
Woodchuck's very very fat, The. The Jolly Woodchuck. Marion Edey. FaPON; TiPo

Woodcock of the Ivory Beak. Elizabeth Madox Roberts. MAP; MoAmPo
Wood-cut. V. Sackville-West. ChMP
Woodcut. R. N. D. Wilson. OxBI
Woodcutter and the Fisherman Turn Home, The. Bilhana, *formerly at. to* Chauras, *tr. fr. Sanskrit by* E. Powys Mathers. *Fr.* Black Marigolds. OnPM
Woodcutter's Hut, The. Archibald Lampman. BoCaPo (1948 ed.)
Wood-Cutter's Night Song, The. John Clare. EnRP; ERP; GTML; GTSE; OBRV
Woodcutter's Wife, The. William Rose Benét. AnAmPo; AWP; InPo; LA; MOAP
Wooden Christ, The. Martha Foote Crow. ChIP; StJW
Wooden Christ within a wayside shrine, A. Wayside Shrine. Gertrude Ryder Bennett. ChIP
Wooden Crosses. Paul Gérardy, *tr. fr. French by* Alan Conder. TrFP
Wooden Fence, The. Christian Morgenstern, *tr. fr. German by* Babette Deutsch *and* Avrahm Yarmolinsky. LiTW
Wooden Horse of Myth, The. Oscar Williams. PeBoSo
Wooden Ships. David Morton. EtS; NV
Wooden Tiger, The. Samuel Yellen. NePoAm
Wooden Walls of Athens, The. Delphic Oracle, *tr. fr. Greek by* A. D. Godley. OxBG
Woodland. Sister Margaret Teresa. JKCP (1926 ed.)
Woodland Choir, The. James Thomson. *Fr.* The Seasons: Spring. CoBE
Woodland Grave, A. Lord De Tabley. VA
Woodland Magic. S. Omar Barker. HiLiAm
Woodland Mass, The. Dafydd ap Gwilym, *tr. fr. Welsh by* Gwyn Williams. PrWP
Woodland Peace. George Meredith. POTT; TwCV
Woodland Revel, A. Clarence Urmy. HBMV
Woodland Singer, The. John Jerome Rooney. MaRV
Woodland sprite of the rakish kind, A. A Scandal among the Flowers. Charles S. Taylor. BLPA
Woodland Worship. Ethelwyn Wetherald. CaP; OCL
Woodlanders, The, *sel.* Thomas Hardy.
In a Wood. InP; OAEP; POTT; ViP
Woodlands, The. William Barnes. GTBS-D; LEAP; OBVV; PoVP
Woodlore. Kim Kurt. NePoAm-2
Woodman and the Nightingale, The. Shelley. *See* Fragment, A: Woodman and the Nightingale, The.
Woodman, Spare That Tree. George Pope Morris. AA; ADAH; BAV; BLPA; DD; FaBoBe; FaFP; FaPON, *abr.*; HBV; HH; LEAP; LPS-1; MPB (1956 ed.); NeHB; OBAV; OHIP; OIF; OTPC; PECK; PIR; PTA-1; PYM; TCAP; TreF; WBLP
Woodman, A, whose rough heart was out of tune. A Fragment: The Woodman and the Nightingale. Shelley. EmBrPo
Woodman's Ax, The. *Unknown, tr. fr. Chinese.* WhP
(Ode II/I/5: "On the trees go the blows," *st.* 1, *tr. by* James Legge.) BoFr
Woodman's Dog, The. William Cowper. *Fr.* The Task. BoTP; OTPC (1946 ed.); PCD; PCH
("Shaggy, and lean, and shrewd, with pointed ears.") AlDL
Wood-Man's Walk, The. Anthony Munday. EV-1
Woodnotes, I ("When the pine tosses its cones"). Emerson. AmPP (4th ed.); AnNE; BAV; CoBA; IAP; MOAP; NePA; OxBA
Sels.
"For Nature ever faithful is," *br. sel.* OBAV
Guide, The. APW
(Heart of All the Scene, The.) AA
Woodnotes, II ("As sunbeams stream through liberal space"). Emerson. IAP; MOAP
Sels.
"All the forms are fugitive." WGRP
"As [the] sunbeams stream through liberal space." ADAH; OHIP
God ("As the bee through the garden ranges"). OQP; QP-2
God Hide the Whole World in Thy Heart, *br. sel.* OQP; QP-2
Immanent God, The. MaRV
Mighty Heart, The. AA
Undersong, The. AA
"Whoso walks in solitude." OBVV
Woodpecker, The. Richard Church. HaMV
Woodpecker, The. Elizabeth Madox Roberts. BoChLi; FaPON; GFA; GoBP; MPB; StVeCh; TiPo; UTS; WhBS
Woodpecker, The. Joyce Sambrook. BoTP
Woodpecker, The. John Banister Tabb. UTS
Woodpecker and a horned owl call on me, A. Country Pastor. Mitsuko Inoue. LiTW
Woodpecker pecked out a little round hole, The. The Woodpecker. Elizabeth Madox Roberts. BoChLi; FaPON; GFA; GoBP; MPB; StVeCh; TiPo; UTS; WhBS
Woodpeckers here are redheaded, The. Ornithology in Florida. Arthur Guiterman. InMe
Woodpeckers' Song. Po Chü-i, *tr. fr. Chinese by* Ching Ti. WhP
Wood-Pile [*or* Woodpile], The. Robert Frost. AmP; BrBE; CoBMV; LiTA; MAPA; MOAP; SeCeV; TwAmPo; YT
Woodrow Wilson. S. Omar Barker. DD; GA
Woodrow Wilson. Katharine Lee Bates. GA
Woodrow Wilson. Edward Parker Davis. LPS-1
Woodrow Wilson. Donald Gillies. DD; GA
Woodrow Wilson. Robert Underwood Johnson. DD; GA
Woodrow Wilson. Roselle Mercier Montgomery. GA
Woodruffe, The. Isa Craig Knox. VA
Woods. W. H. Auden. NePA; NePoAm
Woods, The. Manuel Bandeira, *tr. fr. Portuguese by* Dudley Poore. AnCL
Woods and coppice [*or* coppices] by tempests lashed. Epping Forest. John Davidson. *Fr.* November. CP; GTSL
Woods and downs have caught the mid-December, The. Stanzas Written on Battersea Bridge during a Southwesterly Gale. Hilaire Belloc. GoBC
Woods and Kestrel. Julian Bell. ChMP
Woods are full of fairies, The. The Child and the Fairies. *Unknown.* MeMeAg; OTPC (1946 ed.); PCH; PRWS; StVeCh (1940 ed.)
Woods are purple with the haze, The. Autumn Color. Tom Robinson. YeAr
Woods Are Still, The. "Michael Field." OBVV
Woods decay, the woods decay and fall, The. Tithonus. Tennyson. BPN; EmBrPo; EnL; EPN; FaBoEn; GEPC; GTBS-D; KN; LiTB; LoBV; NBE; OAEP; PoE; PoEL-5; PoFS; PoVP; ReaPo; TOP; TwCrTr; ViPo; ViPP; VLEP; WHA
Woods have stored the rain, and slow comes the smoke, The. My Lodge at Wang-ch'uan after a Long Rain. Wang Wei. LiTW
Woods have their secrets but I know one of them, The. The Secret. Mary Sinton Leitch. LS
Woods have wakened, birch and oak are gay, The. Spring. Hannes Hafstein. IcP
Woods No More, The. Jay Macpherson. PeCV
Woods of Arcady are dead, The. The Song of the Happy Shepherd. W. B. Yeats. PoFS
Woods of my fathers, sovereign deity. Sylvan Ode. José Santos Chocano. WoI
Woods of Westermain, The. George Meredith. BEL; EmBrPo; ViPo; ViPP
Enter these enchanted woods," *first 2 sts.* BMEP; ShBV-3; WaKn
Woods, rocks, & mountaynes, & ye desart places. *Unknown.* SeCSL
Woods stretch wild [*or* deep] to the mountain side, The. The Man Hunt. Madison Cawein. AnAmPo; LA; MAP; PoeMoYo; SPP
Woods That Bring the Sunset Near, The. Richard Watson Gilder. LBAP
Woods that wave o'er Delphi's steep. Thomas Gray. *Fr.* The Progress of Poesy. BCEP
Woods, The, toss and whirl and writhe and shake themselves from end to end! The Woods. Manuel Bandeira. AnCL
Woods we're lost in aren't real, The. Villanelle. Walter H. Kerr. NePoAm-2
Woodsman Goes to Sea, A. Charles R. Knapp. IHA
Woodspurge, The. Dante Gabriel Rossetti. AnFE; AtBAP; BLV; BoLiVe; BPN; BrBE; EmBrPo; EPN; EtPaEn; FaBoEn; GTBS-D; GTML; LoBV; OAEP; OBEV (new ed.); PoEL-5; PoVP; TCEP; UnPo (3d ed.); VA; ViPP; VLEP; WHA
Woodstock, *sel.* Sir Walter Scott.
Here's a Health to King Charles, *fr. ch.* 20. BPN; EmBrPo; TCEP
(Glee for King Charles.) CoBE; EPN
Woodville Mound. *Unknown. See* Springfield Mountain.
Woodworkers' Ballad. Herbert Edward Palmer. HaMV; OBEV (new ed.)
Woodyards in the Rain. Anne Marriott. CaP; TwCaPo; TwCV
Wooe then the heavens (gentle love). *Unknown.* SeCSL
Wooed and Married and A'. *Unknown. See* Woo'd and Married and A'.
Wooed and married and a', Woo'd and Married and A'. Alexander Ross. EBSV
Wooer's Song, The. Richard Brathwaite. *See* Of Maids' Inconstancy.
Woof of the Sun [Ethereal Gauze]. Henry David Thoreau. *See* Haze.
Woof! Woof! Woof! Little Brown Bear. Alice Wilkins. GFA
Wooin' at her, pu'in' at her. Tibbie Fowler. *Unknown.* EBSV
Wooing Lady, The. William Jay Smith. NePoEA
Wooing Maid, The. Martin Parker. CoMu

Wooing of Criseide, The. Chaucer. Troilus and Criseyde, III. PoEL-1
(O Blisful Light.) AtBAP
Wooing of Cyrene, The. Pindar, *tr. fr. Greek by* C. J. Billson. *Fr.* Pythian Odes, IX. GrR
(Cyrene, *shorter sel., tr. by* H. T. Wade-Gery *and* C. M. Bowra.) OxBG
Wooing of Daphnis, The. Theocritus, *pr. tr. fr. Greek by* Andrew Lang. *Fr.* Idylls, XXVII. GrL
Wooing of Saint Francis, The. Hyacinth Blocker. SaFP
Wooing Rogue, The. *Unknown.* CoMu
Wooing Song. Giles Fletcher. *Fr.* Christ's Victory and Triumph: Christ's Victory on Earth. EIL; EV-2; HBV; OBEV
("Love is the blossom where there blows.") ElSeCe; LO; ViBoPo
Wooing Stuff. Sir Philip Sidney. BCEP; ElSeCe
Wool-box, roll-box, cards and wheel. The Last Spinning Wheel. Hubbard Fulton Page. NoCaPo
Wool Trade, The. John Dyer. *Fr.* The Fleece, III. OBEC; SeCePo
Woolly Lambkins. Christina Rossetti. *See* On the Grassy Banks.
Woone Smile Mwore. William Barnes. VA
Wops came down to the port, The. The City of Beggars. Alfred Hayes. WaP
Word, The. St. John, Bible, *N.T.* *See* In the Beginning Was the Word.
Word, A ("A word is dead"). Emily Dickinson. TCAP
Word, The. John Masefield. MaRV
Word, The. Richard Realf. *See* World, The.
Word. Stephen Spender. FaBoTw
Word, The. Tennyson. *See* In Memoriam A. H. H.: "Tho' truths in manhood darkly join."
Word, The. Edward Thomas. NP
Word, The. Allen Upward. *Fr.* Scented Leaves from a Chinese Jar. NP
Word, a Word, A. Dialogue. Sister Mary Madeleva. CAW
Word about Woodpiles, A. Nancy Byrd Turner. BrR
Word at St. Kavin's, The, *sel.* Bliss Carman.
"Therefore my friends, I say." PC
Word bites like a fish, The. Word. Stephen Spender. FaBoTw
Word Fitly Spoken, A. Proverbs, XXV: 11, Bible, *O.T.* FaPON
Word for the Innkeeper, A. Paul Grano. MoAuPo
Word has come to May Marjorie. Jellon Grame (B *vers.*). *Unknown.* ESPB
Word has gane thro a' this land. The Bonny Lass of Anglesey (B *vers.*). *Unknown.* ESPB
Word Incarnate, The. Tennyson. *See* In Memoriam A. H. H.: "Tho' truths in manhood darkly join."
Word is dead, A. A Word. Emily Dickinson. TCAP
Word is framework where the Thing, The. The Word Was with God. Donald F. Drummond. PtPa
Word Made Flesh, The. W. J. Turner. OBMV
Word of Encouragement, A. J. R. Pope. FiBHP; SiTL
Word of God, The. Bernard Barton. PraP
Word of God, The. Annie Johnson Flint. BLRP
Word of God came unto me, The. In the Garden of the Lord. Helen Keller. BPP; MaRV; OQP; QP-2; WGRP
Word of God to Leyden Came, The. Jeremiah Eames Rankin. AA; DD, *abr.*; HBV; MC; OBAV; OTPC; PoRL
Word of mystery is told, A. A Rime of the Rood. Charles L. O'Donnell. GoBC
Word of the ever-lasting God. The Word of God. Bernard Barton. PraP
Word of the Lord by night, The. Boston Hymn. Emerson. AnNE; BAP; DD; IAP; LaNeLa; LPS-2; MC; PaA; PAH; TCAP; TOP; WGRP
Word of the Lord came unto me, saying, The. Chorus from "The Rock"—III. T. S. Eliot. *Fr.* The Rock. LiTB
Word of the Lord from Havana, The. Richard Hovey. HBV; PAH
Word of the sun to the sky, The. Triads. Swinburne. BPN; PoVP; VLEP
Word of Warning, A. *Unknown.* *See* Pilgrim at Rome, The.
Word over All. C. Day Lewis. CaAE; OAEP (2d ed.)
Word over all, beautiful as the sky. Reconciliation. Walt Whitman. AnAmPo; AnEnPo; APW; BLV; BoLiVe; CBOV; CoBA; CoV; FaBoEn; GTBS-D; IAP; LA; MAP; MaRV; MoAmPo; MOAP; NeMA; OxBA; PoE; SoV; TCAP; TrGrPo; WaaP
Word sticks in the wind's throat, A. Apology. Richard Wilbur. NePoAm
Word, The, that came to Jeremiah from the Lord, saying, Stand in the gate of the Lord's house. A Call for True Repentance. Jeremiah, Bible, *O.T.* WoL
Word to a Dictator. Adelaide Love. MaRV
Word to the Wise, A. Caroline Duer. AA
Word to the Wise, A. Louise M. Laughton. MeMeAg
Word was brought to the Danish king. The King of Denmark's Ride. Caroline E. S. Norton. BBV; BeLS; GN; HBV; LPS-1; VA
Word Was with God, The. Donald F. Drummond. PtPa
Word went down the moaning street, The. The Bread-Line. Dana Burnet. OBAV
Word, The, which came to Jeremiah from the Lord, saying, Arise, and go down to the potter's house. The Potter and the Clay. Jeremiah, Bible, *O.T.* WoL
Word with a Skylark, A. Sarah M. B. Piatt. BLA; JKCP (1926 ed.); NLK; SN
Word with the Wind, A. Swinburne. BPN
Words. Joseph Auslander. TBM; VOD
Words. Mary Josephine Benson. CPG
Words. Stella Benson. MBP; MoBrPo (1942 ed.)
Words. Will Carleton. OQP; QP-2
Words. Richard Eberhart. NePA
Words. Robert Finch. BoCaPo
Words. Charles Harpur. BoAu
Words. Sir Thomas Herbert Parry-Williams, *tr. fr. Welsh by* Gwyn Williams. PrWP
Words. Ernest Rhys. BMEP; HBMV; LBBV
Words. Robert Louis Stevenson. *See* Bright Is the Ring of Words.
Words. Nancy Byrd Turner. TSW
Words, The. Opal Whiteley. TSW; TSWC
Words are deeds. Words. Charles Harpur. BoAu
Words Are Never Enough. Charles Bruce. BoCaPo; CaP
Words are the silver notes. Two Cinquains, 2. Louise Owen. PFE
Words cannot speak. Response. Struthers Burt. NoCaPo (1941 ed.)
Words curl like fragrant smoke wreaths in the room. Interior. Marjorie Allen Seiffert. NP
Words fall, words fail, like rocks, like falling stones. The Castle. Michael Roberts. MoP
Words fell from your lips like flakes of snow, The. Like Flakes of Snow. B. Y. Williams. MuM
Words for a Resurrection. Leo Kennedy. BoCaPo; OCL; PeCV
Words, for alas my trade is words, a barren burst of rhyme. To M. E. W. G. K. Chesterton. HBV
Words for Army Bugle Calls. *Unknown.* TreF
Words for Artificers. Claude F. Koch. JKCP (1955 ed.)
Words for the Wind. Theodore Roethke. FiMAP
Words from a Wooden Image. John Oldham. *Fr.* Satyrs upon the Jesuits. BeR
Words from an Old Spanish Carol. *Unknown, tr. fr. Spanish by* Ruth Sawyer. BrR; ChBR; ChrBoLe
(On Christmas Morn.) FaPON
Word's gane to the kitchen. Mary Hamilton. *Unknown.* BaBo; CBOV; ESPB; LO; OAEP; OuHeWo; PoFS; ReaPo; ViBoFo
Words in the Wilderness. Sister Claude of Jesus. JKCP (1955 ed.)
Words in Time. Archibald MacLeish. CrMA; NePA; PoRA
Words, like fine flowers, have their colors too. Words. Ernest Rhys. BMEP; HBMV; LBBV
Words may well want, both ink and paper fail. Henry Lok. *Fr.* Sonnets of Christian Passions. ReEn; SiCE; TuPP
Words move, music moves. T. S. Eliot. *Fr.* Four Quartets: Burnt Norton. UnS; ViBoPo (1958 ed.)
Words of Agur, The. Proverbs, XXX: 4, 15-16, 18-19, 24-28, Bible, *O.T.* TrGrPo
Words of Faulconbridge, The. Shakespeare. *See* This England ("This England never did").
Words of Finn, The. *Unknown, tr. fr. Old Irish.* ChTr
Words of the Gods, The. Emerson. *Fr.* My Garden. OQP; QP-2
Words of the Last Inca. José Eusebio Caro, *tr. fr. Spanish by* Alice Stone Blackwell. PoFr
Words of the Preacher, The. Ecclesiastes, I: 2-11, Bible, *O.T.* TreFS
(Ecclesiastes, I: 1-XII: 14.) WoL
(Vanity of Vanities, I: 2-9.) TrJP
Words to Sleep Upon. Leonora Speyer. NP
Words were meant. Poet's Protest. Doris Hedges. CaP
Words Wherein Stinging Bees Lurk. Judah Halevi, *tr. fr. Hebrew by* Nina Davis Salaman. TrJP
Words with the freesia's wounded scent I know. Words. Joseph Auslander. TBM; VOD
Words without Music. Irving Layton. CaP
Words without Music. *Unknown.* WhC
Words! Words! Jessie Fauset. CDC
Words, words and words! What else, when men are dead. Correspondent. Witter Bynner. AnFE; CoAnAm; TwAmPo
Words, words, ye are like birds. Prelude. Josephine Preston Peabody. AA
Wordsworth. William Wilberforce Lord. *Fr.* Ode to England. AA
Wordsworth. James Kenneth Stephen. *See* Sonnet, A: "Two voices are there: one is of the deep."
Wordsworth upon Helvellyn! Let the cloud. On a Portrait of Wordsworth. Elizabeth Barrett Browning. DiM; LPS-3; PtP
Wordsworthian Reminiscence. *Unknown.* BOHV; TOP

Wordsworth's Early Reading. Wordsworth. *Fr.* The Prelude, V. MOB
Wordsworth's Grave. Sir William Watson. BMEP; EnLit; GoTL; HBV; PoVP
From "Wordsworth's Grave," I-II. LEAP
Work. Louis James Block. AA
Work. Abbie Farwell Brown. MaRV
Work. Elizabeth Barrett Browning. PC
Work. Kenyon Cox. OQP; PGD; PoRL; PSO; QP-1
Work. Toyohiko Kagawa *tr. fr. Japanese by* Lois J. Erickson. SoLD
Work. Charles Lamb. NBE; PeBoSo
Work. D. H. Lawrence. MM; MoP; OBMV; ShBV-3; TwCV
Work. James Russell Lowell. *See* Labor.
Work. Pushkin, *tr. fr. Russian by* Babette Deutsch *and* Avrahm Yarmolinsky. AWP; JAWP; WBP; TrRV, *rev. tr. by* Babette Deutsch
Work. Edwin L. Sabin. DD
Work. J. W. Thompson. PoToHe (new ed.)
Work. Henry van Dyke. *Fr.* The Three Best Things. BTP; MaRV; OQP; PoeMoYo; PoMa; PoRL; POT; PoTo; PYM; QP-1; SP; TCAP; YT
Work; a Song of Triumph. Angela Morgan. CV; GDAH; HH; PEDC; POT; PoTo; PTA-2; YaD
Work all week an' don't make enough. It's Hard on We Po' Farmers. *Unknown.* OuSiCo
Work and Days. Hesiod, *pr. tr. fr. Greek by* A. W. Mair. *Fr.* Works and Days. GrCo-1
Work-basket made of an old armadillo, A. The Caledonian Market. William Plomer. ChMP; HaMV
Work for a Cooper, *sel.* John Gay.
Bachelor's Maid. BeR
Work for Small Men, *sel.* Sam Walter Foss.
"Despise not any man that lives." PoToHe
Work, for the night is coming. Night Cometh. Sidney Dyer. HH
Work Gangs. Carl Sandburg. CoBA
Work is devout, and service is divine. Worship. Roy Campbell MacFie. OQP; QP-2
Work May Yet be Done. Tennyson. *Fr.* Ulysses. GrCo-1
("There lies the port; the vessel puffs her sail.") EtS; MaRV; OQP; OTPC; PC; QP-2
Work of Love, The. Margaret E. Sangster. BLRP
Work shaped from stuff perverse. Art. Théophile Gautier. TrFP
Work! That makes the red blood glow. Work. Abbie Farwell Brown. MaRV
Work, The, That Saves! Horatius Bonar. BePJ
Work that should to-day be wrought, The. Ourselves Alone. John O'Hagan. TIP
Work thou for pleasure. Work. Kenyon Cox. OQP; PGD; PoRL; PSO; QP-1
Work while the sun climbeth high in the heaven. A Song of Work. Mary Blake. HH
Work while you work. One Thing at a Time. M. A. Stodart. PoToHe (new ed.)
Work with might and main. For Hire. Morris Jacob Rosenfeld. LiTW
Work without Hope. Samuel Taylor Coleridge. BEL; BPN; EM-2; EmBrPo; EnLi-2; EnRP; EPN; ERP; ES; EV-4; FiP; HBV; LEAP; LoBV; OBEV; OBRV; OQP; PeBoSo; PG; QP-2; RO; TCEP
In Springtime, *sel.* BoTP
Work, work apace, you blessed sisters three. Fidessa, More Chaste than Kind, LI. Bartholomew Griffin. SiCE; TuPP
Worked-out Mine, The. Edward Dyson. BoAu; WoL
Worker Poet, The. Vladimir Mayakovsky, *tr. fr. Russian by* Babette Deutsch. TrRV
Workers. Arthur Rimbaud, *tr. fr. French by* Angel Flores. AnFP
Workers, The. Mary Blake Woodson. PEDC
Workers earn it. Money. Richard Armour. FaFP; TreFS; WaKn; WhC
Workers of Ireland, why crouch ye like cravens. New Words to the Tune of "O'Donnel Abu." Jim Connell. OnYI
Worker's Prayer, A. Frances Ridley Havergal. *See* Lord, Speak to Me . . .
Working Class. Bertram Warr. BoCaPo (1948 ed.); WaP
Working Man's Song, The. John Stuart Blackie. VA
Working Party, A. Siegfried Sassoon. ChMo; CMP; TCEP
Working with God. "George Eliot." *Fr.* Stradivarius. MaRV
Workman. *Unknown.* *See* From Break of Day.
Workman with a spade in half a day, A. Pompeian Quatrain: New Excavations. Leonora Speyer. InP
Workmen. Herbert Morris. NePoAm-2
Works and Days, *much abr.* Hesiod, *tr. fr. Greek by* Charles A. Elton. WoL
Sels.
Anatomy o Winter, The. *tr. into Scottish by* Robert Garioch. BoN
Autumn, *tr. by* F. L. Lucas. GrPE
Autumn Ploughing, *tr. by* F. L. Lucas. GrPE
"But they who never from the right have strayed," *tr. by* C. A. Elton. GrPo
Cicada Days, *tr. by* T. F. Higham. OxBG
Crane's Flight, The, *tr. by* Arthur S. Way. GrR
(When the Crane Flies South, *longer sel., tr. by* Jack Lindsay.) OxBG
Daemones, *tr. by* F. L. Lucas. GrPE
Fall of Man and the Early Ages of the Earth, The, *tr. by* F. L. Lucas. GrPE
Farmer's Year, The. OxBG
Five Ages, The, *tr. by* Jack Lindsay. LiTW; OxBG
(Five Ages of Man, *tr. by* Arthur S. Way.) GrR
Giving and Taking, *tr. by* Sir William Marris. OxBG
Good Days and Bad, *tr. by* Sir William Marris. OxBG
Marriage, *tr. by* Jack Lindsay. OxBG
Might and Right, *tr. by* Sir William Marris. OxBG
"Muses of Pieria who give glory through song," *pr. tr. by* H. G. Evelyn-White. GrL
Neighbours and Kinsfolk, *tr. by* Sir William Marris. OxBG
Pandora. LiA, *tr. by* H. G. Evelyn-White; OxBG, *tr. by* Jack Lindsay
(Creation of Pandora, *tr. by* Arthur S. Way.) GrR
"Pierian Muses whose songs glorify, hither!" *tr. by* Moses Hadas. GrPo
Plain Living, *tr. by* Sir William Marris. OxBG
Quoth a Hawk to a Nightingale, *tr. by* Arthur S. Way. GrR
("Once a hawk said this to a nightingale," *tr. by* Sir Edwin Arnold.) GrPo
Sailing Weather, *pr. tr. by* Samuel Butler. OxBG
Shame, *tr. by* Sir William Marris. OxBG
Sign of the Pleiades, The. GrR, *tr. by* Arthur S. Way; OxBG, *tr. by* T. F. Higham
Spending and Sparing, *tr. by* Sir William Marris. OxBG
(Golden Mean of Thrift, *tr. by* Arthur S. Way.) GrR
Spring Ploughing, *tr. by* F. L. Lucas. GrPE
Summer, *tr. by* F. L. Lucas. GrPE
When the Snail Climbs, *pr. tr. by* Samuel Butler. OxBG
(Snail's Moving Day, The, *tr. by* Arthur S. Way.) GrR
Wholesome Strife, *tr. by* Sir William Marris. OxBG
Winter. GrPE, *tr. by* F. L. Lucas; OxBG, *pr. tr. by* T. F. Higham
("Beware the January month: beware," *tr. by* C. A. Elton.) GrPo
Work and Days ("Fishes and beasts and winged birds"), *pr. tr. by* A. W. Mair. GrCo-1
Worldly Wisdom, *tr. by* F. L. Lucas. GrPE
"Zeus in the wrath of his hearth hath hidden the means of subsistence," *tr. by* W. C. Lawton. GrPo
Works of God, The. Moses ibn Ezra, *tr. fr. Hebrew by* Solomon Solis-Cohen. TrJP
Works of human artifice soon tire, The. Art and Nature. Francisco de Medrano. OnPM
World, The. Francis Bacon. *See* Life.
World, The. William Drummond of Hawthornden. OBS
World, The. George Herbert. BEL; OBS; SeCL; SeCV-1; SeEP; StJW; TOP
World, The. William Brighty Rands. *See* Wonderful World, The.
World, The. Richard Realf. *Fr.* Symbolisms. MaRV; OBAV
(Ever-present Spirit, The.) GrCo-1
(O Earth!) AnEnPo
(Symbolisms.) UnW
(Word, The.) AA; WGRP
World. The Thomas Traherne. AlDL
World, The ("This is the best world"). *Unknown.* ALV
World, The. Henry Vaughan. AtBAP; ATP; AWP; BEL; BLV; BoLiVe; CoBE; ElSeCe; EM-1; EnL; EnLi-1; EnLit; EPS; EV-2; ExPo; FaBoEn; GoTL; GTBS-W; HBV; InPo; LiTB; LiTG; LoBV; MaPo; MaRV; MePo; NBE; OAEP; OBS; OuHeWo; OxBoCh; Po; PoE; PoEL-2; PoFr, 3 *sts.*, PoFS; PreP; ReaPo; ReEn; SeCeV; SeCV-1; SeEP; TOP; TreFS; TrGrPo; TwCrTr; TwHP; TyEnPo; ViBoPo; WGRP; WoL
(Eternity, *abr.*) OBEV (new ed.)
"I saw eternity the other night," *first 7 ll.* BCEP; CBOV; EPP; ImOP; PC; PoeMoYo; TCEP
(Vision, A.) BBV; GTSL
World, The. Wordsworth. *See* World Is Too Much with Us, The.
World, The; a Child's Song. William Brighty Rands. *See* Wonderful World, The.
World a Game, The. William Drummond of Hawthornden. BSV; ElSeCe
("This world a hunting is.") CenL
(World a Hunt, The.) CoEV; OBS
(World a Hunting Is, The.) FaBoEn
World, The; a Ghazel. James Clarence Mangan. OBVV
World a Hunt, The. William Drummond of Hawthornden. *See* World a Game, The.
World a Hunting Is, The. William Drummond of Hawthornden. *See* World a Game, The.

World and Soul. George Macdonald. *See* This Infant World.
World and the Quietist, The. Matthew Arnold. VA
World as Meditation, The. Wallace Stevens. MoAB
World at the Bottom of the Lake. Karle Wilson Baker. LS
World Beautiful, The. Milton. *See* Sweet Is the Breath of Morn.
World believed the trap was sprung, The. In the Skies. E. J. Pratt. *Fr.* Dunkirk. BoCaPo
World below the Brine, The. Walt Whitman. NePA; PoE; SG
World-besieging storm, from horizon heaped and menacing. Laurence Binyon. The Sirens, III, 4. GoTL (1949 ed.)
World Beyond, A. Nathaniel Ingersoll Bowditch. AA
World beyond World. Arthur Davison Ficke. NP
World-Brotherhood. *Unknown.* *See* My Country Is the World.
World cheats those who cannot read, The. A Mad Poem Addressed to My Nephews and Nieces. Po Chü-i. TrCh
World Comes Galloping, The; a True Story. Robert Penn Warren. Mexico Is a Foreign Country, III. FiMAP
World Comes Not to an End, The. Robert Bridges. The Growth of Love, L. ChMo; CMP
World Conqueror. Laura Simmons. *See* I Have Overcome the World.
World, Defined. Edward Weismiller. AnAmPo
World did say to me, The. The Crazy World. William Gay. BoAu; BoAV
World feels dusty, The. Emily Dickinson. MAP; MoAmPo
World for Love, A. John Clare. PG
World goes up and the world goes down, The. Dolcino to Margaret. Charles Kingsley. PIR; PoVP
World grasps me in hands that wound, The. Forever. Halper Leivick. OnCuPl
World has brought not anything, The. Gladness. Anna Hempstead Branch. PC
World Has Held Great Heroes, The. Kenneth Grahame. *Fr.* The Wind in the Willows. LiL
(Song of Mr. Toad, The.) FaPON; FiBHP
World has room for the manly man, with the spirit of manly cheer, The. The Manly Man. *Unknown.* BLPA; WBLP
World hath conquered, the wind hath scattered like dust, The. Tara Is Grass. *Unknown, tr. by* Padraic Pearse. AnIL; AnIV
World hath its own dead, The; great motions start. Edith Cavell. George Edward Woodberry. HBMV
World Hymn, The. J. Gilchrist Lawson. WBLP
World I Am Passing Through, The. Lydia Maria Child. AA; HBV
World imprisons the truth of life, The. Eagles. Vicente Aleixandre. CoSP
World in Armor, The. Sir William Watson. PoVP
World in dreary darkness sleeps profound, The. Ode to the Lighthouse at Malta. Duque de Rivas. AnSpL-2
World in Making, The. Sir Gilbert Parker. CaP; CPG; OCL
World Is a Bundle of Hay, The. Byron. EnRP
(Impromptus.) BPN
World is a gift again, The. Spring Workman. Alan Creighton. CaP; TwCaPo
World is all orange-round, The. The Walking Road. Richard Hughes. OBMV
World is born ahead of me, The. O mine own twin! The First Born. Oscar Williams. GTBS-W
World is breaking, A. Midnight's bell rings down. World without End. Patric Dickinson. NeTW; SoV
World is charged with the grandeur of God, The. God's Grandeur. Gerard Manley Hopkins. AnFE; AWP; BBV (1951 ed.); CaAE; ChMo; CoBE; EmBrPo; EnLi-2; EnLit; ExPo; FaFP; GTBS-D; GTBS-W; InPo; InvP; LiTB; LiTG; LiTM; LoBV; MaPo; MBP; MoAB; MoBrPo; MoPo; MoVE; OxBoCh; PG (1955 ed.); PIAE; Po; PoE; PoLi; PoVP; ReMP; RiBV; SeCeV; TrGrPo; TwCV; ViP; ViPP; VLEP
World is dull, the world is blind, The. Die Welt ist dumm, die Welt ist blind. Heine. AWP; OnPM
World is fleeting; all things pass away, The. Passing Away. Lucian. OxBG; WoL
World is full of colour, The! Colour. Adeline White. BoTP
World, The, is full of loss; bring, wind, my love. Song. Muriel Rukeyser. MiAP
World is full of wistful ones who hoard their souvenirs, The. Ballad of Culinary Frustration. Phyllis McGinley. FiBHP
World is full of women's eyes, The. Women's Eyes. Bhartrihari. OnPM
World is full of wonderful smells, The. Zhenya Gay. TiPo (1959 ed.)
World is great, The: the birds all fly from me. I Am Lonely. "George Eliot." *Fr.* The Spanish Gypsy. GN; HBV
World is hollow like a pumpkin shell, The. Truth. Jessica Nelson North. HBVY; NP
World is in a mess today, The. Song about Whiskers. P. G. Wodehouse. FiBHP
World is in the Valley of Decision, The. The Valley of Decision. John Oxenham. PGD
World Is like a Woman of Folly, The. Moses ibn Ezra, *tr. fr. Hebrew by* Solomon Solis-Cohen. *Fr.* The World's Illusion. TrJP
World Is Mine, The. Florence Earle Coates. *See* Song: "For me the jasmine buds unfold."
World is no longer good, The. Chorus from a Tragedy. Leonard Bacon. ViBoPo
World Is One, The. Hinton White. MaRV; OQP; QP-2
World is ours till sunset, The. The Song of the Children. G. K. Chesterton. AlDL
World is Rome, The; Carnutum, on the Danube. Marcus Antoninus Cui Cognomen Erat Aurelius. Burns Singer. PoN
World is sick, and we sick men, The. Hospital Ward (of This Generation). George Rostrevor Hamilton. POTE
World is so full of a number of people, The. Happy Thought. Gertrude Pahlow. DDA
World is so full of a number of things, The. Happy Thought. Robert Louis Stevenson. BoTP; FaBoBe; HBV; HBVY; InP; LEAP; MeMeAg; OTPC; PoVP; RIS; SAS; TiPo; TreFS; VLEP
World is so full of a number of things, The. Villanelle, with Stevenson's Assistance. Franklin P. Adams. PC
World is something I must try, The. Tragedy. Mark Van Doren. NePoAm-2
"World is such a funny place, The." Relativity. Kathleen Millay. PoMa
World is the Inn at Bethlehem, The. Query. Lucia Trent. ChIP
World Is Too Much with Us, The. Wordsworth. AnFE; AWP; BEL; BoLiVe; BPN; CBE; CBOV; ChTr; CoBE; DD; EG; EM-2; EmBrPo; EnL; EnLi-2; EnLit; EnLP; EnRP; EPN; EPP; ERP; EV-3; ExPo; FaBoEn; FaFP; FiP; GEPC; GTBS; GTBS-D; GTBS-W; GTSE; GTSL; HBV; HBVY; HiLiEn; HoPM; InP; InPo; JAWP; LEAP; LiTB; LiTG; MaPo; MaRV; MCCG; NeHB; NLK; OAEP; OBRV; OQP; OTPC (1923 ed.); OuHeWo; PeBoSo; PECK; PoE; PoEL-4; PoeMoYo; PoFS; PoMa; PoRA; QP-1; REAL; ReaPo; SeCeV; SN; TCEP; TOP; TreF; TrGrPo; TVSH; TwCrTr; TwHP; TwP; TyEnPo; ViBoPo; WBP; WGRP; WHA
(Nature.) PIR
(Sonnet: "World is too much with us, The; late and soon.") BLP; ChER; CoEV; GBV; LoBV; LPS-2; OHFP; ShBV-4
(World, The.) BBV (1923 ed.); BCEP; BLV; CaAE; LiA, *last 6 ll.;* OBEV; PC; PIAE; PYM; WP
(Worldliness.) ES
World is very evil, The. The Celestial Country. Bernard of Cluny, *tr. by* John Mason Neale. *Fr.* De Contemptu Mundi. GoBC; LPS-2
World is very flat, The. Night Thought of a Tortoise Suffering from Insomnia on a Lawn. E. V. Rieu. FiBHP
World Is Waiting for You, The. S. S. Calkins. PEDC
World is weaned from this one dead by the thread of a shawl, The. The Spoils of War. Vernon Watkins. WaP
World is well amended with Sir Hugh, The. Asperius Nihil Est Humili Cum Surgat in Altum. Henry Parrot. SiCE
World is white with cherry-trees, The. June. Wilson MacDonald. CaP
World is wide, The. On Life's Way [*or* Worry]. Charles F. Deems. MaRV; OQP; QP-2
World is young to-day, The. Song. Digby Mackworth Dolben. LoBV
World-Man, The. Henry Victor Morgan. OQP; QP-1
World may like, for all I care, The. After Reading "Ajax." William Johnson Cory. PtP
World Morose, The. Frederick William Faber. *See* Mundus Morosus.
World Music. Frances Louisa Bushnell. AA
World-Nation, A. Earl B. Marlatt. MaRV
World Needs, The. *Unknown.* PoToHe (new ed.)
World, not hush'd, lay as in a trance, The. Old Souls. Thomas Gordon Hake. VA
World of Dream, The. Walter de la Mare. GaP
World of Dreams, The, *sel* George Crabbe.
Opium Dream. RO
World of fools has such a store, The. Epigram. *Unknown.* ALV
World of Ghosts Moves Closer Every Hour, The. Malcolm Lowry. BoCaPo (1948 ed.)
World of Light, The. Henry Vaughan. *See* They Are All Gone.
World of mightie kings and princes I could name, A. Michael Drayton. *Fr.* Polyolbion: Twentieth Song. OBS
World of the Seven Wells. Alfonsina Storni, *tr. fr. Spanish by* Donald Devenish Walsh. AnCL
World outside the World, The. Keats. *Fr.* Lines Written in the Highlands after a Visit to Burns's Country. RO

World Planners. Arvel Steece. PGD
World-Ruin. Hugh Wilgus Ramsaur. MaRV; MuM
World Secret. Hugo von Hofmannsthal, *tr. fr. German.* LiTW, *tr. by* Werner Heider; TrJP, *tr. by* Charles Wharton Stork
World shall want Phoebean light, The. An Ode of Johannes Secundus. Johannes Secundus. BoFr
World shines bright for inexperienced eyes, The. A Thought from Cardinal Newman. Matthew Russell. CAW; JKCP
World Sits at the Feet of Christ, The. Whittier. *Fr.* The Over-Heart. ChIP; MaRV
World-Soul, The. Emerson. IAP
We Are Never Old, *sel.* OQP; PoRL; QP-2
World-soul knows his own affair, The. Emerson. *Fr.* Monadnoc. BAV
World stands out on either side, The. Edna St. Vincent Millay. *Fr.* Renascence. MaRV
World State, The. G. K. Chesterton. CoBE
World still goeth about to show and hide, The. Robert Bridges. *Fr.* The Growth of Love. PoVP
World-Strangeness. Sir William Watson. BMEP; MBP; MoBrPo (1942 ed.); PoVP; TCPD; UnW
World Take Good Notice. Walt Whitman. APW; CoV
World, that all contains, is ever moving, The. Change. Fulke Greville. Caelica, VII. CoEV; OBSC; ReIE; SiCE; TuPP
World, that cannot deem of worthy things, The. Amoretti, LXXXIV. Spenser. PeBoSo; ReEn
World, the Times, The. Donald Hall. PoLFOT
World to Any Nun, The. Sister Mary Eleanore. PraNu
World Transformed, The. Whittier. *Fr.* Snow-bound. AA (Snow-Storm, The.) MW
("Unwarmed by any sunset light.") BBV; GBV
World Turned Upside Down, The. *Unknown.* PAH
World turns and the world changes, The. T. S. Eliot. *Fr.* The Rock. TiPo
World turns softly, The. Water. Hilda Conkling. ExPo; NP; TiPo
World under the sky, The. A Gone. Larry Eigner. NeAP
World uprose as a man to find Him, The. At the End of Things. Arthur Edward Waite. WGRP
World Wants Men, The. *Unknown.* PEDC
World War. Richard Eberhart. WaP
World War I. *Unknown.* FaFP; SiTL
World War III. *Unknown.* SiTL
World War II. *Unknown.* SiTL
World was at his feet, The. The Young Moses. Don Marquis. QS
World was first a private park, The. The Fisherman. Jay Macpherson. PeCV
World was made when a man was born, The. Experience. John Boyle O'Reilly. ACP; OBVV
World was wide when I was young, The. Troia Fuit. Reginald Wright Kauffman. HBV
World We Make, The. Alfred Grant Walton. PoToHe (new ed.)
World Well Lost, The. Dryden. *See* Conversion ("Be vengeance wholly left . . .").
World Well Lost. The. Edmund Clarence Stedman. AA; OBAV
World will find no pity in your pages, The. Siegfried Sassoon. *Fr.* On Reading the War Diary of a Defunct Ambassador. PoFr
World will not be understood, The. Comedy. Mark Van Doren. NePoAm-2
World will strive with hosts of men-at-arms, The. The Vaunts of Tamburlaine. Christopher Marlowe. *Fr.* Tamburlaine, Pt. I, Act II, sc. iii. BCEP
World within a War, A. Sir Herbert Read. MoPo
World without End. Catullus, *tr. fr. Latin by* E. A. Havelock. LiTW
World without End. Patric Dickinson. NeTW; SoV
World without Objects Is a Sensible Emptiness, A. Richard Wilbur. FiMAP; Po
World without Peculiarity. Wallace Stevens. CoV
World would be the better The. Japan Can Teach. Toyohiko Kagawa. SoLD
Worldliness. Wordsworth. *See* World Is Too Much with Us, The.
Worldly designes, feares, hopes, farewell! Triolets. Patrick Carey. AEV
Worldly Hope, The ("The worldly hope men set their hearts upon"). Omar Khayyám, *tr. fr. Persian by* Edward Fitzgerald. *Fr.* The Rubáiyát. MaRV
(Like Snow.) OnPM
Worldly matters again draw my steps [*or* body]. To Li Chien. Po Chü-i. BoFr; LiTW; TrCh
Worldly Place. Matthew Arnold. BMEP; BPN; EmBrPo; EPN; GrCo-1; PoVP; VLEP
Worldly possessions? 'twas easy to find them. Tora's Song. Knut Hamsun. AnNoLy
Worldly Prelates. John Skelton. *Fr.* Colyn Cloute. CoEV
Worldly prince doth in his scepter hold, The. Nicholas Breton. *Fr.* The Soul's Harmony. SiCE
Worldly Vanity. Dryden. *See* Conversion ("Be vengeance wholly left . . .").
Worldly Wisdom. Hesiod, *tr. fr. Greek by* F. L. Lucas. *Fr.* Works and Days. GrPE
Worldly Wisdom. Omar Khayyám, *tr. fr. Persian by* Edward Fitzgerald. *Fr.* The Rubáiyát. MaRV
(Great Argument.) OnPM
("Myself when young did eagerly frequent.") EG; WGRP
Worlds. Michael Stern. CAG
World's a bubble, and the Life of Man, The. Life [*or* The World]. Francis Bacon. EIL; ElSeCe; EV-1; GTBS; GTBS-D; GTBS-W; GTSE; HBV; LPS-1; OBSC; PIR; WHA
World's a prison, The; no man can get out. Distiches. Barten Holyday. EV-2
World's a Sea, The. Francis Quarles. ChTr
World's a sorry wench, akin, The. The Jester's Plea. Frederick Locker-Lampson. CenHV
World's a theater, the earth a stage, which God, The. The Author to His Booke. Thomas Heywood. *Fr.* An Apology for Actors. OBS
World's a very happy place, The. The World's Music. "Gabriel Setoun." FaBoBe; HBV; HBVY; HH; MPB; OTPC; PRWS; RAR; TVC; TVSH
World's a weary place, The. All thro' the Year. *Unknown.* BLRP
World's Advance, The. George Meredith. EPN
World's an orange, The—thou hast suck'd its juice. To a Foolish Wise Man. Sir William Watson. LEAP
Worlds at War. Robert Haven Schauffler. *See* Great Armistice, The.
World's Bright Comforter, The. Barnabe Barnes. *Fr.* A Divine Century of Spiritual Sonnets. OxBoCh
(God's Virtue.) OBSC
(Sonnet: "World's bright comforter, whose beamsome light, The.") EIL
("World's bright comforter, whose beamsome light, The.") SiCE
World's Centre, The. Ruth Dallas. AnNZ
World's Death-Night, The. James Chapman Woods. VA
World's Desire, The. William Rose Benét. TrPWD
World's End, The. William Empson. CoBMV; MoVE
World's End, The. Michael Roberts. FaBoMo
World's Fallacies, The. Francis Quarles. *See* Vanity of the World, The.
World's gone forward to its latest fair, The. The Moor. Ralph Hodgson. MBP; MoBrPo
World's Great Age Begins Anew, The. Shelley. *See* Chorus: "World's great age begins anew, The."
World's great heart. whence all things strange and rare, The. The Death of Richard Wagner. Swinburne. LoBV
World's Harmonious Plan, The. Aeschylus, *tr. fr. Greek by* Walter Headlam. *Fr.* Suppliants. LiA
World's Illusion, The. Moses ibn Ezra, *tr. fr. Hebrew by* Solomon Solis-Cohen. TrJP
All Ye That Go Astray, II.
He That Regards the Precious Things of Earth, IV.
In Vain Earth Decks Herself, VI.
Promises of the World, The, III.
World Is like a Woman of Folly, The, I.
Ye Anger Earth, V.
World's Justice, The. Emma Lazarus. HBV
World's Lone Lover, The. J. R. Perkins. ChIP
World's May-Queen, The Alfred Noyes. *See* When Spring Comes to England.
World's Miser, The. Theodore Maynard. CAW; JKCP; MBP; MoBrPo (1942 ed.); QS
World's Music, The. "Gabriel Setoun." FaBoBe; HBV; HBVY; HH; MPB; OTPC; PRWS; RAR; TVC; TVSH
World's Need, The. Ella Wheeler Wilcox. BLP; LBAP; PC
Worlds on Worlds Are Rolling Ever. Shelley. *See* Chorus: "Worlds on worlds . . ."
World's so wide I cannot cross it, The. Fond Affection. *Unknown.* AS
World's Stage, The. Palladas, *tr. fr. Greek by* F. L. Lucas. GrPE
World's Wanderers, The. Shelley. BEL; BPN; EmBrPo; EnLit; EPN; ERP; ViBoPo
World's Way, The. Thomas Bailey Aldrich. HBV; LHV
World's Way, The. Shakespeare. *See* Sonnets, LXVI.
World's Wonders, The. Robinson Jeffers. NePA
World's Worth. Dante Gabriel Rossetti. GoBC; PoVP
Worlds, you must tell me Round. Louis Untermeyer. WhC
Worm, The. Ralph Bergengren. FaPON; SiSoSe; UTS
Worm, The. Elizabeth Madox Roberts. BoChLi; GFA; PoeMoYo; UTS; VOD; YT
Worm, The. Ann Taylor. PCH; PPL; SAS
Worm cries not against the storm, The. Microcosmos, XVII. Nigel Heseltine. NeBP
Worm Fed on the Heart of Corinth, A. Isaac Rosenberg. AtBAP; MoPo
Worm in the Whirling Cross, The. John Malcolm Brinnin. MoPo

Worm unto his love, The: lo, here's fresh store. The Coffin-Worm. Ruth Pitter. MoBrPo; TrGrPo (1942 ed.)
Worm within a Rose, A. Tennyson. *Fr.* Idylls of the King: Pelleas and Etarre. VLEP
("Rose, A, but one, none other rose had I.") PoEL-5
Worms and the Wind. Carl Sandburg. WaKn
Worms at Heaven's Gate, The. Wallace Stevens. NP; TCPD
Worms begin to drop unceasingly. The Flesh. Tiroux Yamanaka. LitW
Worms' Contempt, The. W. H. Davies. CoMo
Worms of History, The. Robert Graves. MoPo
Worms would rather be worms. Worms and the Wind. Carl Sandburg. WaKn
Wormwood. Sappho, *tr. fr. Greek by* Randolph Shaffer, Jr. WoL
Worn is the winter rug of white. Footprints in the Snow. Frank Dempster Sherman. SN
Worn out with weeping my sad eyes I raise. Despair. Juan Meléndez Valdés. TeCS
Worn tokens that old tales repeat. A Ballad of College Days. *Unknown.* CAG
Worn Wedding-Ring, The. William Cox Bennett. LPS-1
Worn with the battle, by Stamford town. Saxon Grit. Robert Collyer. HBV; OTPC (1923 ed.)
Worried Skipper, The. Wallace Irwin. BLPA
Worries. Jules Supervielle, *tr. fr. French by* Glauco Cambon. OnPM
Worries. *Unknown.* PoToHe (new ed.)
Worry. Charles F. Deems. *See* On Life's Way.
Worry. *Unknown.* PoToHe (new ed.)
Worry about Money. Kathleen Raine. FaBoTw
Worry—is like a distant hill. Worry. *Unknown.* PoToHe (new ed.)
Worschippe ye that loveris bene this May. *See* Worshipe, ye that lovers been, this May.
Worse than despair. Beatrice Cenci in Her Cell. Shelley. *Fr.* The Cenci. ReTS
Worship. Emerson. IAP; MeRV; TCAP
Worship. Ruth Furbee. MaRV
Worship. Bob Jones, Jr. BePJ
Worship, *sel.* William Wilberforce Lord.
"For them, O God who only worship." AA
Worship. Roy Campbell MacFie. OQP; QP-2
Worship. Shelley. *Fr.* One Word Is Too Often Profaned. MaRV
Worship. Helen Welshimer. BPP
Worship. Robert Whitaker. TrPWD
Worship of Cotys, The. Aeschylus, *tr. fr. Greek. Fr.* Edoni. OxBG
Worship of Nature, The, *abr.* Whittier. GrCo-1
Worship the Lord in the Beauty of Holiness. John S. B. Monsell. MaRV
Worship the summer sun. Solstices. Richard Church. POTE
Worship We This Holy Day. *Unknown.* AnEC
Worshipe [*or* Worschippe], ye that lovers been [*or* loveris bene], this May. Spring Song of the Birds. James I, King of Scotland. *Fr.* The Kingis Quair. OBEV; TrGrPo
Worsley Enchanted, *sels.* Douglas Stewart.
"It's cold, says Crean at the tiller," VI. NeLNL
"White, said Worsley, and glistening, the ridgy plain," II. NeLNL
Worst, The. *Unknown, tr. fr. Spanish by* Havelock Ellis. OnPM
Worst burn is to come, The. Post-War. Eileen Duggan. AnNZ
Worst camp-life man ever lived, The. Monsieur Pipereau. James Whaler. MAP; MoAmPo (1942 ed.)
Worst Horror, The. Euripides, *tr. fr. Greek by* John Addington Symonds. OxBG
Worst Treason, The. Victor Hugo, *tr. fr. French by* Henry Carrington. PoFr
Worth Makes the Man. Pope. *Fr.* An Essay on Man, Epistle IV. CBOV; MaRV; PoeMoYo
(Greatness.) LPS-3
("Honor [*or* Honour] and shame from no condition rise.") PoFr; TrGrPo
(Man.) BoLiVe
(Pedigree.) BeR
(True Worth.) CBE
Worth Remembrance. Philip Bourke Marston. LBBV
Worth While. Ella Wheeler Wilcox. BLPA; PoToHe; TreF
Worthington, *with music.* *Unknown.* AS
Worthless Heart, The. Immanuel di Roma, *tr. fr. Hebrew.* TrJP
Worthy London prentice, A. The London Prentice. *Unknown.* CoMu
Worthy of adoration, The. The Angelic Vilancete. Gil Vicente. *Fr.* The Auto of the Four Seasons. CAW
Wotton, my little Bere dwells on a hill. Ad Henricum Wottonem. Thomas Bastard. SiCE
Wotton, the country and the country swain. Ad Henricum Wottonum. Thomas Bastard. SiCE
Woud ye hear of William Wallace. Gude Wallace (G *vers.*). *Unknown.* ESPB
Would a man lay siege to the whole world and make it his own? Tao Teh Ching, VIII. *Unknown, tr. fr. Chinese.* WhP
"Would a man 'scape the rod?" Ben Karshook's Wisdom. Robert Browning. BPN; PoVP
Would any deem Dacus were now the man. Henry Parrot. SiCE
Would-be-Goods, The, *sel.* Edith Nesbit.
Denny Misquotes. BoN
Would bounteous Heaven one more indulge, I'd choose. John Pomfret. *Fr.* The Choice. LO
Would God I Were the Tender Apple Blossom. Katharine Tynan. OlF
Would God my heart were greater; but God wot. Chastelard and Mary Stuart. Swinburne. *Fr.* Chastelard. VA
Would God my pen might be your trump of fame. The Praise of Our Soldiers. Thomas Churchyard. TuPP
Would God That It Were Holiday! Thomas Deloney. *Fr.* The Gentle Craft. ElL
Would God that men would see. Mutis Mutandis. *Unknown.* TMEV
Would God the route would come for home. The Frontier. John Masefield. NP
Would I again were with you!—O ye dales. That Delightful Time. Mark Akenside. *Fr.* The Pleasure of the Imagination. SeCePo
Would I Be Shrived? Villon, *tr. fr. French by* John Swain. BLPA
Would I could cast a sail on the water. The Collar-Bone of a Hare. W. B. Yeats. AtBAP; EnL; NP
Would I describe a preacher, such as Paul. Preachers: The True vs. the Insincere. William Cowper. *Fr.* The Task, II. MaRV
Would I Had Stayed. Princess Oku, *tr. fr. Japanese by* Ishii *and* Obata. OnPM
Would I Might Go Far over Sea. Marie de France, *tr. fr. French by* Arthur O'Shaughnessy. AWP; JAWP; OuHeWo; PoRA; WBP
Would I might mend the fabric of my youth. Welt. Georgia Douglas Johnson. BANP
Would I might rouse the Lincoln in you all. Lincoln. Vachel Lindsay. *Fr.* The Litany of the Heroes. MW; OHIP
Would I might wake Saint Francis in you all. St. Francis [*or* Franciscan Aspiration]. Vachel Lindsay. *Fr.* Litany of the Heroes. CAW; OQP; QP-1
Would I were a bird like the raven that flew. The Wish. Mikhail Yurevich Lermontov. WaL
Would I were a king of children. The Child-King. Morris Wintchevsky. TrJP
Would I Were a Rose. *Unkrown, tr. fr. Greek by* F. E. Garrett. OxBG
Would I were on the sea-lands. The Sea-Lands. Orrick Johns. HBV; LBMV
Would I Were the Wind. *Unknown, tr. fr. Greek by* F. A. Wright. OxBG
Would it had pleased the Lord that I never was born! *Unknown, tr. fr. Italian by* L. R. Lind. LyPI
Would my love were a bracelet! Love's Fancy. Tamuke. OnPM
Would some little joy today. A Song of Sighing. James Thomson. EnLit
Would that I had stayed. Would I Had Stayed. Princess Oku. OnPM
Would that I streamed like water. Like Water down a Slope. Zalman Schneour. TrJP
Would That I Were. Arthur Hugh Clough. TrPWD
Would that I were under the cliffs, in the secret hiding-places of the rocks. Euripides. *Fr.* Hippolytus. GrPo
Would that my father had taught me the craft of a keeper of sheep. The Craft of a Keeper of Sheep. Moschus. AWP
Would that our scrupulous sires had dared to leave. Church Decking at Christmas. Wordsworth. COAH
Would that swift ships had never been; for so. Loss at Sea. Callimachus. OnPM
Would that the structure brave, the manifold music I build. Abt Vogler. Robert Browning. BEL; BMEP; BPN; CoBE; EM-2; EmBrPo; EPN; GEPC; GoTL; HBV; OAEP; PoVP; TOP; TriL; VA; ViPo; ViPP; VLEP; WGRP
Would the lark sing the sweeter if he knew. An Open Secret. Caroline Atherton Briggs Mason. AA
Would they be envious, let them be great. Envy. Charles Jeremiah Wells. BCEP
Would we could coin for thee new words of praise. Washington's Tomb. Ruth Lawrence. OHIP
Would Wisdom for herself be wooed. The Joyful Wisdom. Coventry Patmore. The Angel in the House, I, x, 1. HBV
Would ye be taught, ye feathered throng. Anne Hathaway. *Unknown.* LPS-3
Would You Be a Man of [*or* in] Fashion? *Unknown.* ALV; SeCL; SeEP

Would you be young again? Heavenward. Lady Nairne. HBV
Would You End War? James Oppenheim. 1914—and After, IV. GrCo-1 (19 *ll.*)
(Create Great Peace.) MaRV
("Would you end war," 17 *ll.*) PSO
Would you extend your narrow span. Nathaniel Cotton. *Fr.* Health. PoP
Would you gather the liquorice, would you gather the liquorice. Ode I/X/12. *Unknown.* BoFr
Would you gaze upon. Such a Woman, the Principle of Life, the Ideal Questioner. Paul Eluard. MiFP
Would you hear of an old-time sea-fight? A Sea-Fight [*or* An Old-Time Sea-Fight]. Walt Whitman. Song of Myself, XXXV. CoBA; LH; MaC; SeCeV; TrGrPo; UnPo (3d ed.)
Would you hear of the River-Fight? Henry Howard Brownell. *Fr.* The River Fight. AA; EtS; GA; MDAH
"Would you kindly change into a fish for me." Palmström to a Nightingale Who Kept Him from Sleeping. Christian Morgenstern. AnGP
Would you know the baby's skies? Baby's Skies. Mary C. Bartlett. MOAH
Would you know what's soft? I dare. Song. Thomas Carew. BEL; EG; EnLi-1; EPP; TOP
Would you know why I summoned you together? Lucius Junius Brutus over the Dead Lucretia. John Howard Payne. *Fr.* Brutus; or, The Fall of Tarquin. LPS-3
Would you not be in Tryon. April—North Carolina. Harriet Monroe. SBMV
Would you relish a rural retreat. Verses Written at the Hermitage of Braid, near Edinburgh. Robert Fergusson. EV-3
Would you resembled the metal you work with. Reflections in an Iron Works. "Hugh MacDiarmid." NAMP
Would you see the little men. The Little Men. Flora Fearne. BoTP
Would you see the marks of the Roman scourge. Jesus of Nazareth. Ernest Cadman Colwell. ChIP; MaRV; QS
Would you tell me the way to Somewhere? Somewhere. Walter de la Mare. BrR
Would you win all the world for Christ? To Win the World. John Oxenham. MaRV
Would you wish me to sing to you. Song. *Unknown.* LyMA
Would you with us had sipped. The Nuptials. Ibn Sa'id of Alcala la Real. MooP
Wouldn't it be lovely if the rain came down. Very Lovely. Rose Fyleman. GFA; TiPo
Wouldn't it be wonderful to come across in cabaret. Unromantic Song. Anthony Brode. FiBHP
Wouldn't this old world be better. I Know Something Good about You. *Unknown.* BLPA; PoToHe
Wouldn't we have the nicest pets. Our Pets. Esther Antin. *Fr.* On Our Farm. RIS
Wouldn't you like to be a whale. Whale. Geoffrey Dearmer. BoTP
Wouldn't You Like to Know. John Godfrey Saxe. HBV
Wouldn't you say,/ Wouldn't you say: one day. One Almost Might. A. S. J. Tessimond. ChMP
Wouldst know the artist? Then go seek. Art. Lilla Cabot Perry. AA
Wouldst thou be wise, O Man? At the knees of a woman begin. Wilfrid Scawen Blunt. *Fr.* The Wisdom of Merlyn. OBMV
Wouldst thou fashion for thyself a seemly life? Live Each Day. Goethe. OQP; QP-1
Wouldst thou find my ashes? The Immortal Residue. Adelaide Crapsey. MaRV; MoAmPo (1942 ed.)
Wouldst Thou Have Me Love Thee? Alexander Beaufort Meek. BIG
Wouldst thou hear what man can say. Epitaph on Elizabeth, L. H. Ben Jonson. EIL; ElSeCe; EM-1; EnL; EnLi-1 (1949 ed.); EPP; EPS; HBV; InPo; LPS-3; OBEV; OBS; PoE; ReEn; ReIE; RiBV; SeCV-1; SeEP; TuPP; ViBoPo; WHA
Wouldst thou ken Nature in her better part? Eclogues, III. Thomas Chatterton. EV-3
Would'st thou know the way to lighten. Seek the Lord in Prayer. *Unknown.* PraP
Wouldst thou live long? The only means are these. He Lives Long Who Lives Well. Thomas Randolph. WBLP
Wound, The. Thom Gunn. NePoEA
Wound-Dresser, The. Walt Whitman. AmPo; CoBA; IAP; TCAP; ViBoPo
(Dresser, The.) LEAP
Wound is healed, but still the pain is there, The. Heart Wound. Otto Freund. MuM
Wound Love gave me th' other day, The. *Unknown.* SeCSL
Wound me, O Death! Far Over Yonder. Rafael Maya. AnCL
Wound which the dragon had dealt him began, The. Beowulf's Death. *Unknown.* *Fr.* Beowulf. AnOE
Wounded, The. Louise Louis. GoYe
Wounded Christ Heart, The. "George Klingle." PSO
Wounded Cupid, The. Robert Herrick, *after the Greek of* Anacreon. AWP
("Cupid, as he lay among.") GrPo
Wounded Daisy, The. *Unknown.* HOAH
Wounded deer leaps highest, A. Emily Dickinson. AWP; InPo; JAWP; MOAP; TwP; WBP
Wounded Eagle, The. Aeschylus, *tr. fr. Greek by* C. M. Bowra. *Fr.* Myrmidones. OxBG
Wounded Hare, The. *See* On Seeing a Wounded Hare . . .
Wounded Hawk, The. Herbert Palmer. FaBoTw; HaMV
Wounded Maiden, The. *Unknown, tr. fr. Danish by* E. M. Smith-Dampier. BoDaBa
Wounded Person, The. Walt Whitman. *Fr.* Song of Myself, XXXIII. PoNe
Wounded Prince, The. Douglas Le Pan. BoCaPo (1948 ed.)
Wounded, the steel-ribbed bird dipped to the sea. Remembrance. Hortense Flexner. VOD (1935 ed.)
Wounded to Death. John W. Watson. LPS-2
Wounded wilderness of Morris Graves, The. A Coney Island of the Mind, 11. Lawrence Ferlinghetti. NeAP
Wounded with love and piercing deep desire. Unable by Long and Hard Travel to Banish Love, Returns Her Friend. George Turberville. TuPP
Wow, but your letter made me vauntie! Epistle to Dr. Blacklock, Ellisland, Oct., 1789. Burns. OBEC
Wrack was dark an' shiny where it floated in the sea, The. Sea Wrack. "Moira O'Neill." OnYI
Wraggle Taggle Gipsies, The (*diff. versions*). *Unknown.* BLV; BoTP; CBOV; CH; LiTL; OnSP; OtMeF; PCD; ThWaDe
(Black Jack Davie [*or* Davy].) BaBo; OuSiCo, *with music*
("Gipsies came to the good Squire's gate, The.") LO
(Gipsy [*or* Gypsy] Laddie, The.) BaBo (A, B, *and* C *vers.*); ESPB; FaBoCh; LoGBV; OxBoLi; SiTL; ViBoFo (A *and* B *vers.*)
(Gypsy Davy, 2 *sts., with music.*) AS
(Jackie Faa.) ChTr
(Johnnie Faa.) EBSV
(Johnny Faa, the Gypsy Laddie.) AtBAP
(Johnny Faa, the Lord of Little Egypt.) EnSB
(Raggle, Taggle Gypsies, The.) FaPON; GoTP; MPB; StVeCh; TiPo (1952 ed.)
(Wraggle Taggle Gypsies, O, The.) SaSa, *with music;* ShBV-1
Wraith. Edna St. Vincent Millay. OBAV
Wraith-Friend, The. George Barker. OBMV
Wraith of Patroclus, The. Homer, *tr. fr. Greek by* F. L. Lucas. *Fr.* The Iliad, XXIII. GrPE
Wraith of Roanoke, The. Benjamin Sledd. NoCaPo
Wrangle up your mouth-harps, drag your banjo out. The Bunk-House Orchestra. Badger Clark. SCC
Wrap her hair in golden cloths. Of One Dead. Leo Kennedy. PeCV
Wrap Me Up in My Tarpaulin Jacket, *with music.* *Unknown.* AS
(Sailors.) OuSiCo
Wrapp'd up, O Lord, in man's degeneration. Caelica, XCIX. Fulke Greville. OxBoCh
Wrapped in a cloak. Fog, the Magician. Melville Cane. MoSiPe
Wrapped in a yielding air, beside. As He Is. W. H. Auden. MoPo
Wrapt in my careless cloak, as I walk to and fro. Earl of Surrey. SiPS
Wrapt up, O Lord, in man's degeneration. Caelica, XCVIII. Fulke Greville. SiCE
Wrath of Achilles, The. Homer, *tr. fr. Greek by* F. L. Lucas. *Fr.* The Iliad, I. GrPE
("Achilles' baneful wrath resound, O goddess that impos'd," *shorter sel., tr. by* George Chapman.) ReIE
("O Goddess! sing the wrath of Peleus' son," *shorter sel., tr. by* Bryant.) EnLi-1
(Quarrel, The, *longer sel., tr. by* Sir William Marris.) WoL
("Sing, goddess, the anger of Peleus' son Achilleus," *br. sel., tr. by* Richmond Lattimore.) GrPo
("Sing, goddess, the wrath of Achilles Peleus' song," *longer sel., pr. tr. by* Lang, Leaf, *and* Myers.) GrL
(Sing, O Muse, *br. sel., tr. by* the Earl of Derby.) LiA
Wrath of Achilles, The, *abr.* Homer, *tr. fr. Greek by* Bryant. *Fr.* The Iliad, XIX. BBV (1923 ed.)
Wrath of the people is dark, The. Eastern Front. Georg Trakl. AnGP
Wrath was Ving-Thor when he awakened. Thor Gets Back His Hammer. *Unknown.* *Fr.* The Elder Edda. PaOS
Wrathful winter, 'proaching on apace, The. Induction to "The Mirror for Magistrates" [*or* The Complaint of Henrie Duke of Buckinghame *or* Winter *or* The Approach of Winter]. Thomas Sackville. BEL; CoEV; EIL; OBSC; Po; PoEL-1; ReEn; ReIE; SeCePo; SiCE; TuPP
Wreath, A, *sel.* William Baylebridge
"When tongues will tax me in the public ear." BoAV
Wreath for Ashes, A. Hildegarde Flanner. MuM

Wreath for Heliodora. Meleager. *See* Garland for Heliodora, A.
Wreath for Persephone, A. Marie Emilie Gilchrist. RAR
Wreath Makers; Leeds Market. James Kirkup. PoN
Wreath that star-crowned Shelley gave, The. After a Lecture on Keats. Oliver Wendell Holmes. AA; OBAV; PtP; ViBoPo
Wreathe no more lilies in my hair. The Summer Is Ended. Christina Rossetti. HBV
Wreathe the Bowl. Thomas Moore. HBV
Wreathed in Storm-Clouds Overhanging. Stéphane Mallarmé, *tr. fr. French by* Ithell Colquhoun. MiFP
Wreaths of golden cloud are glancing. The Nixie. Erik Johan Stagnelius. AnSL
Wreaths shriveled and froze upon his grave, The. His Widow. Cale Young Rice. PR
Wreck, The. John Gould Fletcher. TCAP
Wreck, The. John Ruskin. VA
Wreck of Rivermouth, The. Whittier. IAP; MOAP
Wreck of the *Deutschland*, The. Gerard Manley Hopkins. AtBAP; CoBMV; FaBoMo; LiTB; LiTM (rev. ed.); MoVE; OAEP (2d ed.); PoEL-5; PoVP; ReMP; SeCeV; TriL; ViP; ViPP
Sels.
"On Saturday sailed from Bremen." SeCePo
"Thou mastering me," Pt. I. CoEV; OxBoCh
Wreck of the *Hesperus*, The. Longfellow. AnNE; ATP (1935 ed.); BeLS; BoChLi (1939 ed.); CBOV; CG; CoBA; EtS; FaBoBe; FaFP; FaPON; GN; HBV; HBVY; IAP; MOAP; MW; NeHB; OnSP; OTPC; PAH; PECK; TCAP; TreF; TVSH; WBLP
Wreck of the *Julie Plante*, The. William Henry Drummond. BoCaPo; BOHV; CaP; CP; CPG; FaPON; HBV; IHA; InMe; MM; NA; OCL; PeCV; StaSt; TreFS; WhC
(*Julie Plante*, The.) BeLS; BLPA; FaBoBe
Wreck of the Old 97, The. *Unknown.* ViBoFo
Wreck of the Six-Wheel Driver, The. *Unknown.* ABF
(Joseph Mica.) ViBoFo
Wreck of Walsingham, The. *Unknown. See* Lament for Our Lady's Shrine at Walsingham, A.
Wreck on the C. & O., The; or, The Death of Jack Hinton, *with music. Unknown.* ABF
Wreck on the Somerset Road, The, *with music. Unknown.* OuSiCo
Wrecker of the city's wall. A National Anthem. Lamprocles. OxBG
Wreckers' Prayer, The. Theodore Goodridge Roberts. BoCaPo (1948 ed.); PeCV
Wrens and Robins [in the Hedge]. Christina Rossetti. *Fr.* Sing-Song. GFA; SUS; TiPo
(Nesting-Time.) PCH
Wren's Nest, A. Wordsworth. CG
Wrestler, The. Stefan George, *tr. fr. German by* David Luke. AnGP
Wrestler, The. Sir Charles G. D. Roberts. BMEP
Wrestler, The. Sadi, *pr. tr. fr. Persian by* Sir Edwin Arnold. *Fr.* The Gulistan. OuHeWo
Wrestling. John Crowe Ransom. MoP
Wrestling Jacob. Charles Wesley. CEP; EiPP; LPS-2; NBE; OBEC; OBEV (new ed.); PoEL-3; SeCePo
("Come, O thou traveller unknown.") OxBoCh
Wrestling Match, The. Homer, *tr. fr. Greek by* George Chapman. *Fr.* The Iliad, XXIII. GrR
Wrestling Match, The. Robert Penn Warren. AnAmPo; LA; PreP
Wrestling with God. Genesis, XXXII: 22-30, Bible, *O.T.* GrCo-1
Wretch, The. Robert Graves. *See* Laureate, The.
Wretched Amintor with a flame. The Greater Trial. Countess of Winchilsea. BLV; TrGrPo
Wretched and foolish jealousy. Ben Jonson. LO
Wretched Catullus, play the fool no more. To Himself. Catullus. AWP; LiTW
Wretched life I live, The. Madrigal V: Allusion to the Confusion of Babel. Francis Davison. ReIE
Wretched Man. Earl of Rochester. *Fr.* A Satire against Mankind. SeCePo
Wretched thing it were, to have our heart, A. Retirement [*or* Sonnet]. Richard Chenevix Trench. EPN; OBVV; OQP; QP-2
Wretches, why sit ye here? Fly, fly to the ends of creation. Delphic Oracle, *tr. by* George Rawlinson. GrPo
Wretches, why tarry ye thus? The Army of Xerxes. Delphic Oracle, *tr. by* A. D. Godley. OxBG
Wring the Swan's Neck. Enrique González Martínez, *tr. fr. Spanish by* Samuel Beckett. AnMP
Wrinkled, crabbed man they picture thee, A. Winter. Robert Southey. PEOR
"Wrinkled ostler, grim and thin!" Song at the Ruin'd Inn. Tennyson. *Fr.* The Vision of Sin. PoEL-5
Wrinkles ("When Helen first saw wrinkles in her face"). Walter Savage Landor. VA
(Lyrics to Ianthe.) BPN
("When Helen first saw wrinkles . . .") EnLoPo
Wrinkling with laughter that made no sound. At a Country Fair. John Holmes. MoShBr
Writ in Water. Meleager, *tr. fr. Greek by* John Herman Merivale. OuHeWo
(Vow, The.) LPS-1
Writ of Loving Well, The. Love Suffereth Long. Sara Henderson Hay. ChIP; OQP; QP-2
Write a contract with the grass. Song for Government. Raymond Holden. PoFr
Write on my grave when I am dead. The Epitaph. Katharine Tynan. NLK; WGRP
Writer, The. Hildebrand Jacob. SiTL
Writer, attend no schools. The Teacher. Virginia Brady Young. GoYe
Writer owned an asterisk, A. The Asterisk. *Unknown.* DDA
Writer to His Book, The. Thomas Campion. OAEP
Writer's Tragedy, The. Samuel Daniel. *Fr.* The Tragedie of Philotas. LiA
Writing Letters. Rodney Bennett. BoTP
Writing on the Image, The. William Morris. *Fr.* The Earthly Paradise. EmBrPo
Writing on the Wall. Padraic Fallon. NeIP
Written after Swimming from Sestos to Abydos. Byron. ALV; BOHV; InMe; LauV; OBRV; PoE; PoeMoYo
Written after the Death of Charles Lamb, *sel.* Wordsworth.
"To a good man of most dear memory." CoBE
Written among the Euganean Hills, North Italy. Shelley. *See* Lines Written among the Euganean Hills.
Written at an Inn at Henley. William Shenstone. AWP; CEP; EiPP; EPP; EV-3; HBV; JAWP; LEAP; OBEC; OBEV (new ed.); OTPC (1923 ed.); PoE; TOP; ViBoPo; WBP
(Written in an Inn at Henley.) LoBV
Written at Cambridge. Charles Lamb. EnRP; OBRV
Written at Florence. Wilfrid Scawen Blunt. OBEV (1st ed.); OBVV
Written at Mr. Pope's House at Twickenham. George Lyttelton. CEP
Written at Rome. Emerson. IAP
Written at Sea, in the First Dutch War. Charles Sackville. *See* Song: "To all you ladies now at land."
Written at the End of a Book. Langdon Elwyn Mitchell. AA; OBAV
Written by the Authoress on Her Death Bed. Laetitia Pilkington. MeRV
Written 1811. Blake. *Fr.* Jerusalem, *ch.* 4. MaRV; StJW
("Jesus said: 'Wouldst thou love one who never died.'") NBE
Written Immediately after Reading the Speech of Robert Emmet. Robert Southey. ERP
(Emmet's Epitaph.) LPS-3
(On the Speech of Robert Emmet.) PoFr
Written in a Blank Leaf of Dugdale's "Monasticon." Thomas Warton, the Younger. *See* Sonnet: Written in a Blank Leaf . . .
Written in a Lady's Milton. Matthew Prior. InP
Written in a Little Lady's Little Album. Frederick William Faber. HBV; HBVY
Written in a Nunnery Chapel. James Clarence Mangan. *See* Lines Written in a Nunnery Chapel.
Written in a Song Book. Lizette Woodworth Reese. NP; VOD
Written in a Thunderstorm, 15 July 1841. John Clare. RO
Written in a Volume of Goethe. Emerson. IAP
Written in a Volume of "The Imitation of Christ." Marya Zaturenska. NV
Written in an Inn at Henley. William Shenstone. *See* Written at an Inn at Henley.
Written in an Old Cemetery. Mary Newton Baldwin. UnW
Written in Australia. Arthur Adams. BoAu
Written in Butler's Sermons. Matthew Arnold. MeRV
Written in Disgust of Vulgar Superstition. Keats. PeBoSo
Written in Early Spring. Wordsworth. *See* Lines Written in Early Spring.
Written in Edinburgh. Arthur Henry Hallam. VA
Written in Emerson's Essays. Matthew Arnold. EmBrPo; GEPC; VA; VLEP
Written in Flight from His Royal Patron. Al Mutanabbi, *tr. fr. Arabic by* Herbert Howarth *and* Ibrahim Shukrallah. LiTW
Written in Juice of Lemmon. Abraham Cowley. *Fr.* The Mistress. SeCV-1
Written in July, 1824. Mary Russell Mitford. OBRV
Written in London, September, 1802. Wordsworth. BoLiVe; BPN; EnLi-2; EPN; ERP; ES; GEPC; PeBoSo; TrGrPo
(England, 1802.) BCEP; BLV; HBV; LEAP; OBEV; PoeMoYo
(In London, September, 1802.) EM-2; EmBrPo; EnRP; MaRV
(London, 1802.) GTBS; GTBS-D; GTBS-W; GTSL
("O Friend! I know not which way I must look.") ReaPo
(Sonnet: Written in London, September, 1802.) ChER
Written in March. Wordsworth. AlDL; BLV; BoTP; BPN;

CG; DD; EmBrPo; EnRP; FaPON; GoTP; HBV; HBVY; HiLiEn; LiTG; MPB; MW; OnHT; OTPC; PCH; PoRL; RG; RIS; SUS; ThWaDe; TiPo; UnPo (3d ed.); WaKn; YeAr
(Cock Is Crowing, The.) ShBV-1
(In March.) StaSt
(March.) BoChLi. PRWS
(Merry Month of March, The.) CBPC; MoShBr
Written in Naples. Emerson. CoBA; IAP
Written in Northampton County Asylum. John Clare. CBE; EV-4; GTSE; GTSL; OBEV; OBVV; ViBoPo
(I Am.) CaAE; EnRP; FaBoEn; GTBS-W; LiTB; PG; PoE; PoEL-4; TrGrPo; TriL; WHA
(I Am: Yet What I Am Who Cares or Knows.) InvP
Written in the Album of a Child. Wordsworth. *See* To a Child.
Written in the Beginning of Mezeray's History of France. Matthew Prior. CEP; OBEC; PoE; PoEL-3; PoFS
Written in the Euganean Hills, North Italy. Shelley. *See* Lines Written among the Euganean Hills.
Written in the Heart. Deuteronomy, VI: 4-7, XXX: 11-14, 19-20, Bible, *O.T.* GrCo-2
Written in the Leaves of a Fan. Francis Atterbury. *See* Written on the Leaves of a White Fan.
Written in the Visitors' Book at the Birthplace of Robert Burns. George Washington Cable. AA
Written in Very Early Youth. Wordsworth. BPN; EmBrPo; EnRP
(Twilight.) ES
Written on a Blank Page in Shakespeare's Poems, Facing "A Lover's Complaint." Keats. *See* Bright Star, Would I Were Steadfast as Thou Art.
Written on a Fly-Leaf of Theocritus. Maurice Thompson. AA; BAP; LEAP
Written on a Looking-Glass. *Unknown.* HBV; LauV
Written on a Sunday Morning. Robert Southey. OBEC
Written on His Deathbed. Chaucer. *See* Balade de Bon Conseyl.
Written on the Banks of Wastwater during a Calm. "Christopher North." OBRV
Written on the Blank Space at the End of Chaucer's Tale of "The Floure and the Lefe." Keats. *See* Sonnet: Written at the End of "The Floure and the Lefe."
Written on the Day that Mr. Leigh Hunt Left Prison. Keats. *See* Sonnet: Written on the Day . . .
Written on the Eve of Execution. Chidiock Tichborne. *See* Elegy: "My prime of youth is but a frost of cares."
Written on the First of December, 1793. Robert Southey. EV-4
Written on the Leaves of a White Fan. Francis Atterbury. SeCL
(Written in the Leaves of a Fan.) SeEP
Written on the Sense of Isolation in Contemporary Ireland. Robert Greacen. NeIP
Written on the Wall at Chang's Hermitage. Tu Fu, *tr. fr. Chinese by* Kenneth Rexroth. HoPM; OnPC
Written on the Walls of His Dungeon. Luis de León, *tr. fr. Spanish by* Thomas Walsh. OnPM; TrJP
(Lines on the Wall of His Prison Cell.) CAW
Written the Night before His Execution. Chidiock Tichborne. *See* Elegy: "My prime of youth . . ."
Written to a Young Lady. Jeremiah Joseph Callanan. IrPN
Written under the Engraving of a Portrait of Rafael. Leigh Hunt. ERP
Written When Governor of Soochow. Po Chü-i, *tr. fr. Chinese by* Arthur Waley. TrCh
Written While a Student at Christ Church, Oxford. Thomas Brown. *See* I Do Not Love Thee, Doctor Fell.
Wrong about birds. I cannot call. Paradox: The Birds. Karl Shapiro. CrMA
Wrong is made and measured by, The. Shame. Coventry Patmore. *Fr.* The Angel in the House, I, ix, 2. OBVV
Wrong not, sweet [*or* dear] empress of my heart. The Silent Lover, II [*or* To the Queen]. Sir Walter Ralegh. BCEP; CaAE; ElL; ElSeCe; EPP; HBV; LiTB; LoPS; OAEP; OBEV; OBS, *sl. diff., at. to* Sir Robert Ayton; OBSC; PG; SiPS; ViBoPo
Wrong Road, The. Richard Church. POTE
Wronged Lover, The. Sir Philip Sidney. *Fr.* Arcadia. SiPS
Wry Rowan, The. *Unknown, tr. fr. Late Middle Irish by* Eoin MacNeill. OnYI
Wry Smile, A. Roy Fuller. WaaP; WaP
W's for Windows. Phyllis McGinley. *Fr.* All Around the Town. TiPo
Wulf and Eadwacer. *Unknown, tr. fr. Anglo-Saxon.* TrGrPo
Wulfstan and Venelil. *Unknown, tr. fr. Danish by* E. M. Smith-Dampier. BoDaBa
Wull ye come in early spring. Come! William Barnes. CH
Wunst I Had an Old Gray Mare, *with music. Unknown.* OuSiCo
Wunst I sassed my pa, an' he. The Runaway Boy. James Whitcomb Riley. MPB
Wunst they is a man 'at's got a lot o' little boys. The Small Boy Points a Moral Wilbur D. Nesbit. OnIIT
Wyatt Being in Prison, to Bryan. Sir Thomas Wyatt. SiCE; TuPP
(Epigram: "Sighs are my food, drink are my tears.") SiPS
Wyatt resteth here, that quick could never rest. On [*or* Of] the Death of Sir Thomas Wyatt [*or* A Tribute to Wyatt]. Earl of Surrey. BEL; EnLi-1 (1949 ed.); EnLit; FaBoEn; GoTL; PtP; ReEn; ReIE; SiCE; SiPS; TuPP
Wye and the Severn are offspring, The. The Playmates. Sir William Watson. PoVP
Wyld Romantic Dell, A. William Julius Mickle. *See* Wild Romantic Dell, A.
Wynken, Blynken, and Nod. Eugene Field. AA; AnAmPo; BAP; BAV; BeLS; BoChLi; BoTP; CBPC; FaBoBe; FaFP; FaPON; GoBP; GoTP; HBV; HBVY; LA; LBAP; LEAP; MPB; OTPC; PC; PCH; PECK; PoeMoYo; PoRA; PoRh; PRWS; RAR; StVeCh; TSW; TSWC; TVC; TVSH; VOD
(Dutch Lullaby, A.) BLPA; BOHV; LiTG; NeHB; PIR; TreF
Wynter Wakeneth Al My Care. *Unknown.* SeCePo
(This World's Joy.) OBEV
(Wynter Wakeneth.) OxBoCh
Wyoming. Charles E. Winter. PoRL
Wyoming Massacre, The. Uriah Terry. PAH
Wythin a garth, under a rede rosere. The Praise of Age. Robert Henryson. MeRV

X

X marks the spot where the body lies in time. USA. Paul Engle. SiTL
X-Ray. Leonora Speyer. ImOP
X shall stand for playmates Ten. *Unknown.* OxNR
Xanthias Phoceus, never mind your loving. Horace. Odes, II, 4. LaP
Xavier my name in the Gascon country till. John Sevier. Donald Davidson. *Fr.* The Tall Men. SPP
Xenokrates fell over a kettle. "Ecce Quomodo Moritur Justus." Diogenes Laertius. LiTW
Xenophanes. Emerson. AnNE; APW
Xerxes Defeated. Aeschylus. *See* Persia Prostrated.
Xylographer started to cross the sea, A. The Zealless Xylographer. Mary Mapes Dodge. BOHV

Y

Y Ddraig Goch. Henry Treece. MoWP
Y Y U R ("Too wise you are"). *Unknown.* BoN
Yacht, The. Catullus, *tr. fr. Latin by* John Hookham Frere. AWP; JAWP; WBP
Yacht, The. Walter Savage Landor. OBVV
Yachts, The. William Carlos Williams. AmPP; CoBMV; ExPo; InPo; LiTA; LiTM; MoAB; MoAmPo (1950 ed.); MoPo; MoVE; NAMP; NePA; OxBA; Po; PoFS; ReMP; SeCeV; ViBoPo (1958 ed.)
Yachts on the Nile. Bernard Spencer. ChMP
Yahoo. Palladas. *See* O Man, Remember.
Yak, The. Hilaire Belloc. ALV; BOHV; FaPON; HBVY; InMe; LauV; MBP; MoBrPo; MPB; NA; PCH; PoRh; StaSt; TreFS; TSW; TSWC; UTS
Yak, The. Nathalia Crane. StaSt
Yak, The. Oliver Herford. *Fr.* Child's Natural History. HBV; HBVY
Yak, The. Virna Sheard. CaP; PeCV
Yak. William Jay Smith. GoTP; TiPo (1959 ed.)
Yang-se-fu. "Yehoash," *tr. fr. Yiddish by* Isidore Goldstick. TrJP
Yankee boy, before he's sent to school, The. Whittling. John Pierpont. GN; LPS-3
Yankee Clipper. Leonard Bacon. NeTW
Yankee country churchyard holds, A. He Laughed Last. Francis Whiting Hatch. WhC
Yankee Doodle ("Once on a time old Johnny Bull"). George Pope Morris. PaA
Yankee Doodle (*diff. versions*). *Unknown, at. to* Richard Shuckburg *and to* Edward Bangs. ABF, *with music;* BoHiPo; ChTr; ExPo; FaFP; FaPON; OlF; OTPC (1946 ed.), 4 *ll.*; OxNR, 4 *ll.*; PaA, *with poem by* George Pope Morris; PoFr; PoRL, *sl. abr.*; SiTL; StVeCh (1955 ed.); TrAS, *with music;* TreF; YaD

Yankee Doodle (*continued*)
(Yankee's [*or* Yankeys'] Return from Camp, The.) IAP; MC; OxBoLi; PAH
Yankee Doodle sent to Town. The Last Appendix to "Yankee Doodle." *Unknown.* PAH
Yankee Doodle went to war. The Run from Manassas Junction. *Unknown.* PAH
Yankee Doodle's Expedition to Rhode Island. *Unknown.* PAH
Yankee Lyric, A. Hugh Peters. LauV
Yankee Man-of-War, The ("'Tis of a gallant Yankee ship"). *Unknown.* AA; AmSS, *with music;* EtS; FaBoBe; GA; LEAP; OBAV; PAH
(Stately Southerner, The, *with music.*) ShS; SoAmSa
("'Tis of a gallant Yankee ship.") LaNeLa
Yankee Privateer [The]. Arthur Hale. PaA; PAH
Yankee Ship and a Yankee Crew, A. *Unknown.* IHA
Yankee ship and a Yankee crew, A. The *Constitution's* Last Fight. James Jeffrey Roche. GA; MC; PAH
Yankee ship came [*or* comes] down the river, A. Blow, Boys, Blow [*or* Blow, Bullies, Blow]. *Unknown.* AmSS; SoAmSa; TrAS
Yankee Thunders. *Unknown* PAH
Yankee Volunteers, The. Thackeray. LauV
Yankee's [*or* Yankeys'] Return from Camp, The. *Unknown. See* Yankee Doodle.
Yanks. James W. Foley. PaA
Yaqui Dancers. Berta Hart Nance. *Fr.* Arizona Nights. HiLiAm
Yard in December, The. Arthur Davison Ficke. CAG
Yard Man. Andrew Hewitt. NoCaPo (rev. ed.)
Yardley-Oak. William Cowper. LaA
Y'are now transcrib'd, and publike view. To Mr. W. B. on the Birth of His First Child. William Cartwright. NBE
Yarn of the *Let-Her-Rip,* The. Thomas R. Ybarra. PFE
Yarn of the *Loch Achray,* The. John Masefield. CV; InP; SeCeV; StPo
Yarn of the *Nancy Bell,* The. W. S. Gilbert. ATP (1935 ed.); BBV; BeLS; BLPA; BoChLi; BOHV; CenHV; FaBoBe; FaBoCh; EtS; FaFP; GBV; GoTP; HBV; HoPM; InMe; LauV; LEAP; LoGBV; LPS-3; MCCG; MoShBr; OTPC (1946 ed.); PCD; PCN; PFE; PIR; PoeMoYo; PoVP; PYM; ShBV-1; StVeCh; TreFS; TrGrPo; TSW; TSWC
Yarns of the People. Carl Sandburg. *See* They Have Yarns.
Yarrow Revisited. Wordsworth. BPN; EM-2; EmBrPo; EnLi-2; EnRP; GEPC
Yarrow Unvisited. Wordsworth. BEL; BPN; EM-2; EmBrPo; EnLi-2; EnRP; ERP; GEPC; GTBS; GTBS-D; GTBS-W; GTSE; GTSL; HBV; PoRA
Yarrow Visited. Wordsworth. BEL; BPN; EM-2; EmBrPo; EnLi-2; EnRP; ERP; GEPC; GTBS; GTBS-D; GTBS-W; GTSL; HBV
Yasmin. James Elroy Flecker. *Fr.* Hassan, I, ii. LoPS; TCPD; TwCV
(Hassan's Serenade.) OBEV (new ed.)
Yattendon. Sir Henry Newbolt. HBMV; WP
"Yaup, yaup, yaup!" The Chorus of Frogs. Ann Hawkshaw. OTPC
Yaw, Dot Is So! Charles Follen Adams. HBV
Ye Alps audacious, through the heavens that rise. The Hasty Pudding. Joel Barlow. AmPP; CoBA; IAP; MOAP; OxBA; TCAP
Ye ancients of the earth, beneath whose shade. The Cedars of Lebanon. Letitia E. Landon. PEOR
Ye Angells bright, pluck from your wings a quill. Edward Taylor. *Fr.* Sacramental Meditations. PoEL-3
Ye Anger Earth. Moses ibn Ezra, *tr. fr. Hebrew by* Solomon Solis-Cohen. *Fr.* The World's Illusion. TrJP
Ye are God's messengers of love, O flowers! William Beans Magruder. *Fr.* Flowers. PoP
"Ye are the Duke of Athol's nurse." The Duke of Athole's Nurse (B *vers.*). *Unknown.* ESPB
Ye are the light of the world. Poems by the Roadside. St. Matthew, Bible, *N.T.* CAW
Ye are too young to bring me in. An Old Lover to a Young Gentlewoman. *Unknown.* TuPP
Ye are young, ye are young. An Old Man's Song. Richard Le Gallienne. HBV; VA
Ye Banks and Braes. Burns. *See* Banks o' Doon, The.
Ye banks and braes and streams around. Highland Mary. Burns. AEV; AnFE; ATP (1935 ed.); AWP; BCEP; BEL; BoLiVe; BTP; CaAE; CEP; EBSV; EiPP; EM-1; EnLi-2; EnLit; EnRP; EPP; EV-3; GTBS; GTBS-D; GTBS-W; GTSE; GTSL; HBV; InP; InPo; JAWP; LEAP; OAEP; OBEC; OBEV; OuHeWo; PTA-2; PYM; TCEP; TOP; TreFS; TrGrPo; TyEnPo; ViBoPo; WBLP; WBP
Ye Banks and Braes o' Bonnie Doon. Burns. *See* Banks o' Doon, The.
Ye barren hearts and bitter, steep'd in brine. Lyttelton Harbour, XXXVIII. D'Arcy Cresswell. AnNZ
Ye barren peaks, so mightily outlined. Altars. Bernard Freeman Trotter. MaRV
Ye beauties! O how great the sum. On a Bed of Guernsey Lilies. Christopher Smart. *Fr.* Ode to the Earl of Northumberland. OBEC
Ye [*or* Yee] blushing virgins happy are. To Roses in the Bosom of Castara. William Habington. *Fr.* Castara. ElSeCe; EnLoPo; EV-2; GoBC; HBV; LoBV; MeLP; OBEV; SeCL; SeEP; ViBoPo
Ye brave Columbian bands! a long farewell! On Disbanding the Army. David Humphreys. PAH
Ye brave sons of Freedom, come join in the chorus. The Times. *Unknown.* PAH
Ye bubbling springs that gentle music makes. Love's Limit. *Unknown.* EG; TrGrPo
Ye buds of Brutus' land, courageous youths, now play your parts! For Soldiers. Humphrey Gifford. CH; EIL; ElSeCe; SiCE; TriL; TuPP
Ye call Me Master and obey Me not. Thus Speaketh Christ Our Lord. *Unknown.* ChIP; PGD
"Ye Cannot Serve God and Mammon." Robert Herrick. *See* Neutrality Loathsome.
Ye cannot shut the trees in. They All Belong to Me. Eliza Cook. PGD
Ye captive souls of blindfold Cyprian's boat. My Love Is Past. Thomas Watson. *Fr.* Hecatompathia. ReIE
Ye cats that at midnight spit love at each other. An Appeal to Cats in the Business of Love. Thomas Flatman. EnLoPo
Ye children of man, whose life is a span. The Life of Men. Aristophanes, *tr. by* John Hookham Frere. *Fr.* The Birds. RO
Ye children of my fondest care. The Farmer's Advice to the Villagers. Timothy Dwight. *Fr.* Greenfield Hill. IAP
Ye Christian heralds, go, proclaim. Bourne H. Draper. OIF
Ye clerks that on your shoulders bear the shield. Preachment for Preachers. Sebastian Brant, *tr. by* Alexander Barclay. *Fr.* The Ship of Fools. ACP; CAW
Ye Clouds! that far above me float and pause. France; an Ode. Samuel Taylor Coleridge. ATP; BEL; BPN; EM-2; EmBrPo; EnLi-2 (1949 ed.); EnRP; EPN; ERP; LiA; OAEP; PoFr; TCEP; TOP
Ye clouds, who are the ornament of heaven. Clouds. James Gates Percival. APW
Ye Columbians so bold, attend while I sing. Hull's Surrender. *Unknown.* PAH
Ye columns and my Sirens, and thou funereal jar. Baucis. Erinna. OxBG
Ye Commons and Peers. Jack Frenchman's Lamentation. *Unknown.* CoMu
Ye congregated powers of heaven, who share. Shelley. *Fr.* Prometheus Unbound. EnLit
Ye coopers and hoopers, attend to my ditty. The Cooper o' Dundee. *Unknown.* CoMu
Ye Cupids, droop each little head. The Dead Sparrow. Catullus, *tr. by* Byron. EnLi-1; OuHeWo
Ye dainty [*or* dayntye] nymphs, that in this blessed brook[e]. Elisa [*or* Hobbinol's Lay of Fair Elisa]. Spenser. *Fr.* The Shepheardes Calender: April. AtBAP; CoEV; ElSeCe; OBSC
Ye dead and gone great armies of the world. The Ancient Sacrifice. Mahlon Leonard Fisher. AnAmPo; LA
Ye distant spires, ye antique towers. Ode on a Distant Prospect of Eton College. Thomas Gray. ATP (1935 ed.); BCEP; BEL; CaAE; CEP; CoBE; EiPP; EM-1; EnLi-2 (1949 ed.); EnLit; EPP; EV-3; ExPo; GTBS; GTBS-D; GTBS-W; GTSE; GTSL; HBV; LiTB; LiTG; OAEP; OBEC; OuHeWo; PoE; PoEL-3; SeCeV; TOP; TwHP; ViBoPo
Ye doctors all of every rank. Calomel. *Unknown.* ABS
Ye dreary plains, that round me lie. Summer on the Great American Desert. Rufus B. Sage. PoOW
Ye elms that wave on Malvern Hill. Malvern Hill. Herman Melville. AmPP; MC; PAH
Ye elves of hills, brooks, standing lakes, and groves. Magic [*or* Shakespeare's Fairies]. Shakespeare. *Fr.* The Tempest, V, i. AWP; CBPC; JAWP; WBP
Ye field flowers! the gardens eclipse you, 'tis true. Field Flowers. Thomas Campbell. OTPC (1923 ed.)
Ye Flags of Piccadilly. Arthur Hugh Clough. Songs in Absence, II. EmBrPo; PoVP; VLEP
Ye Flippering Soul[e]. An Address to the Soul Occasioned by a Rain. Edward Taylor. CoV; OxBA; Po; PoEL-3
Ye Flowery Banks [o' Bonnie Doon]. Burns. *See* Banks o' Doon, The.
Ye friends, who in the mighty city dwell. The Divine Philosopher. Empedocles. OxBG
Ye galleys of our land. Galleys of Spain. *Unknown.* TeCS
Ye gentlemen and ladies fair who grace this famous city. The Hunters of Kentucky. Samuel Woodworth. AS; PAH; TrAS
"Ye gie corn to [*or* unto] my hors[e]." Mother's Malison [*or* Clyde's Water]. *Unknown.* BSV; ESPB
Ye [*or* You] goat-herd [*or* gote-heard] gods, that love the grassy mountains [*or* grassie mountaines]. Double Sestine [*or* Sestina *or* Strephon and Klaius]. Sir Philip Sidney.

Fr. Arcadia. AtBAP; CoEV; LiTB; LiTG; PoEL-1; SiCE
Ye gods of love, look from above on a broken hearted maid. Young Billy Crane. Larry Gorman. ShS
Ye Gods, You Gave to Me a Wife, *Unknown.* ElSeCe; SeCL
Ye Golden Lamps of Heaven. Philip Doddridge. *See* Hymn: "Ye golden Lamps of Heav'n, farewel."
Ye good distressed!/ Ye noble few. Bear Up Awhile. James Thomson. MaRV
Ye graceful peasant-girls and mountain-maids. Ballata: His Talk with Certain Peasant Girls. Franco Sacchetti. AWP
Ye green-hair'd nymphs! Whom Pan allows. Ode to a Water Nymph. William Mason. Po
Ye green-rob'd Dryads, oft at dusky eve. The Enthusiast; or, The Lover of Nature. Joseph Warton. CEP; EiPP; EnRP; FaBoEn; Po; PoEL-3
Ye groves (the statesman at his desk exclaims). The Statesman in Retirement. William Cowper. *Fr.* Retirement. OBEC
Ye happy swains, whose hearts are free. Song. Sir George Etherege. ElSeCe; EV-3; HBV; LiTL; ViBoPo
Ye Hasten to the Grave! Shelley. PeBoSo
Ye have been fresh and green. To Meadows [*or* Meddowes]. Robert Herrick. AEV; AtBAP; AWP; CBE; CBOV; CenL; CH; EG; EPS; EV-2; FaBoEn; HBV; InPo; KN; LEAP; LoBV; MyFE; OBEV; OTPC (1923 ed.); PoEL-3; SeCL; SeCV-1; WP
Ye have heard that it was said, An eye for an eye. Love Your Enemies. St. Matthew, Bible, *N.T.* GrCo-1
"Ye have robbed," said he, "ye have slaughtered and made an end." He Fell among Thieves. Sir Henry Newbolt. BBV; CP; HBV; HBVY; OBEV; OBVV; PoeT; PCN; PoMa; ShBV-3; ShGoBo; TCEP; TwCV
Ye have seen a marvel in this town. The Lament for Yellow-haired Donough. *Unknown.* KiLC
Ye have sung me your songs, ye have chanted your rimes. The Song of the Derelict. John McCrae. EtS
Ye Heavens, Uplift Your Voices. *Unknown.* OHIP
Ye Highlands and ye Lawlands. The Bonny [*or* Bonnie] Earl of [*or* o'] Murray [*or* Moray]. *Unknown.* AnFE; BaBo (A *vers.*); BEL; BSV; EBSV; EnLit; ESPB; FaBoCh; GoTS; HBV; LoGBV; OBB; OBEV; OBS; ViBoFo; WP
Ye hours, then, but as minutes be. William Browne. *Fr.* Britannia's Pastorals, III, Song 1. LO
Ye Huntsmen Who Halloo and Wind the Horn. Joachim du Bellay, *tr. fr. French by* Alan Conder. Olive, LXXXII. TrFP
Ye intelligences, turning the third sphere. Dante. *Fr.* The Banquet. LyMA; LyPI
Ye jolly Yankee gentlemen, who live at home in ease. The C. S. A. Commissioners. *Unknown.* PAH
Ye jovial throng, come join the song. The Battle of Muskingum. William Harrison Safford. PAH
Ye Know My Heart. Sir Thomas Wyatt. LoBV
("Ye know, my heart, my lady dear.") SiPS
Ye know the ant that creeps upon the fig. The Dharra and the Date-Stone. *Unknown.* OnPM
Ye ladies, walking past me piteous-eyed. Sonnet: To the Same Ladies. Dante. AWP
Ye learnèd sisters, which have oftentimes. Epithalamion. Spenser. AEV; AtBAP; BCEP; BEL; BrBE; EIL; EM-1; EnL; EnLi-1 (1949 ed.); EPP; EV-1; GEPC; HBV; LEAP; LiA; LiTL; OAEP; OBEV; OBSC; PeBoSo; PIAE; Po; PoEL-1; PoFS; ReEn; ReIE; SeCeV; SiCE; TOP; TyEnPo; ViBoPo; WoL
Ye Little Birds That Sit and Sing. *At. to* Thomas Heywood. *Fr.* The Fair Maid of the Exchange. CBOV; EIL; ElSeCe; ViBoPo
(Go, Pretty Birds.) EPP
(Message, The.) HBV; OBEV (1st ed.)
(Ye Pretty Wantons, Warble.) EV-2
Ye little elves, who haunt sweet dells. Cecil. Walter de la Mare. BOL
Ye little household gods, that make. Lyrics and Epigrams, XVI. Walter Savage Landor. ERP
Ye little snails. Remonstrance with the Snails. *Unknown.* BMEP; LPS-2
Ye living lamps, by whose dear light. The Mower to the Glow-Worms. Andrew Marvell. ALV; AtBAP; AWP; BrBE; EG; ElSeCe; EnLoPo; EPS; InPo; InvP; KN; MePo; OBS; OnPM; OxBoLi; PoEL-2; ReaPo; ReEn; RIS; SeCL; TrGrPo
Ye living soldiers of the mighty war. The Burial of Grant. Richard Watson Gilder. MDAH
Ye mariners, by sea and land be yours a happy doom. A Seaman's Tomb. Plato. OnPM
Ye Mariners of England. Thomas Campbell. BCEP; BEL; BHV; BLPA; CaAE; CBE; CBPC; CoBE; EBSV; EnRP; EPN; EPP; ERP; EtS; EV-4; GN; GTBS; GTBS-D; GTBS-W; GTSE; GTSL; HBV; LEAP; LH; LPS-2; MuP; OBEV; OBRV; OTPC (1923 ed.); TCEP; TreF; TVSH
Ye mariners of Spain. The Song of the Galley. *Unknown.* AWP; PoFr
Ye marshes, how candid and simple and nothing-withholding and free. The Marshes. Sidney Lanier. *Fr.* The Marshes of Glynn. NLK; PG
"Ye maun gang to your father, Janet." Fair Janet. *Unknown.* BaBo; ESPB; OBB
Ye may simper, blush, and smile. To Cherry-Blossomes. Robert Herrick. SeCV-1
Ye may tramp the world over. Ould Doctor Mack. Alfred Perceval Graves. BOHV
Ye men who are dimly existing below. Chorus of Birds [*or* Hymn of the Birds]. Aristophanes. *Fr.* The Birds. GrR; WoL
Ye merry hearts that love to play. Win at First and Lose at Last; or, A New Game at Cards. Laurence Price. OxBoLi
"Ye midwives and women-kind, do one thing for me." The Death of Queen Jane (B *vers.*). *Unknown.* BaBo
Ye modern laureates, famous'd for your writ. Alli Veri Figlioli Delle Muse. *Unknown.* *Fr.* Zepheria. ReIE; TuPP
Ye morning-glories, ring in the gale your bells. The New God. James Oppenheim. SBMV; WGRP
Ye motions of delight, that haunt the sides. Nature's Healing. Wordsworth. *Fr.* The Prelude, XII. EPN
Ye Mountain Bluebells. Avetis Isahakian, *tr. fr. Armenian by* Zabelle C. Boyajian. ArmLP
Ye mountain valleys, pitifully groan. Lament for Bion. Moschus. AWP; JAWP; WBP
Ye Muses! dames of dignified renown. Two Ways of Visiting. Timothy Dwight. *Fr.* Greenfield Hill. AmPP (4th ed.)
Ye muses, pour the pitying tear. A Great Man. Goldsmith. NA
Ye Muses, sing of the fair-faced, wide-winded moon. To the Moon. *Unknown.* *Fr.* Homeric Hymns. GrL
Ye Naiads, ye high pastures, where the cold gusts go sweeping. The Old Bee-Master. *Unknown.* GrPE
Ye Noble Old Pine Tree. *Unknown.* APW
Ye nymphs and ye swains that trip over the plains. Black Thing. *Unknown.* CoMu
Ye nymphs, if e'er your eyes were red. On the Death of Mrs. (Now Lady) Throckmorton's Bullfinch. William Cowper. EV-3; HBV
Ye Nymphs of Solyma! begin the song. Messiah. Pope. OxBoCh
Ye Parliament of England. *Unknown.* AmSS, *with music;* PAH; SoAmSa
Ye people of great Murrough. On the Defeat of Ragnall by Murrough King of Leinster A.D. 994. *Unknown, tr. by* Kuno Meyer. OnYI
Ye people of great Murrough's band. Murrough Defeats the Danes, 994. *Unknown, tr. by* Frank O'Connor. KiLC
Ye people of Ireland, both country and city. A New Song of Wood's Halfpence. Swift. OxBoLi
Ye people that labour the world to measure. Geographers. Sebastian Brant, *tr. by* Alexander Barclay. *Fr.* The Ship of Fools. ACP
Ye pilgrim-folk, advancing pensively. Sonnet. Dante, *tr. by* Dante Gabriel Rossetti. *Fr.* La Vita Nuova. AWP; JAWP; LyPI; WBP
Ye pilgrims, who with pensive aspect go. Dante, *tr. by* Louise Imogen Guiney. *Fr.* La Vita Nuova. CAW
Ye poor little sheep, ah well may ye stray. The Enquiry. John Dyer. OBEC
Ye powers unseen, to whom the bards of Greece. Inscription. Mark Akenside. OBEC
Ye powers who rule the tongue, if such there are. Contradiction. William Cowper. *Fr.* Conversation. LPS-3
Ye Pretty Wantons, Warble. *At. to* Thomas Heywood. *See* Ye Little Birds That Sit and Sing.
Ye robbed, ye spoiled, ye bought, ye sold. Robert Crowley. *Fr.* The Voice of the Last Trumpet Blown by the Seventh Angel. PoFr
Ye sacred bands, ye knots that kept for me. Ion and Creusa; Recognition. Euripides. *Fr.* Ion. GrR
Ye sacred ruins and ye tragic sights. Ruins of Rome, IV. Joachim du Bellay. OnPM
Ye saw 't floueran in my breist. The Mandrake Hert. Sidney Goodsir Smith. AtBAP
Ye say the Injuns all alike. "The Injun." John E. Logan. BoCaPo (1943 ed.)
Ye say they all have passed away. Indian Names. Lydia Huntley Sigourney. BAP; BAV; FaPON; HBV; LEAP; MC; MPB; OTPC; PAH; PoRL; PTA-2
Ye servants of God, your Master proclaim. Charles Wesley. OIF
Ye shall know that in Atli's feast-hall on the side that joined the house. The Slaying of the Niblungs. William Morris. *Fr.* The Story of Sigurd the Volsung. LH
Ye Shall Live Also. Christian F. Gellert. *See* Jesus Lives, and So Shall I.

Ye shepherd so chearful and gay. Absence. William Shenstone. Pastoral Ballad in Four Parts, I. OBEC
Ye [or You or We] should stay longer if we durst. Francis Beaumont. *Fr.* The Masque of the Inner-Temple and Gray's Inne. GoBC; OBS; TrGrPo; ViBoPo
Ye smooth-faced sons of Jacob, hug close your ingleside. The Song of the Sons of Esau. Bertha Runkle. AA
Ye Sons of Columbia. Thomas Green Fessenden. PAH
Ye Sons of Columbia. *Unknown. See* Fuller and Warren.
Ye sons of Columbia, unite in the cause. Ye Sons of Columbia. Thomas Green Fessenden. PAH
Ye sons of Columbia, who bravely have fought. Adams and Liberty. Robert Treat Paine. MC; PAH
Ye sons of Columbia, your attention I do crave [or attention now I pray]. Fuller and Warren. *Unknown.* ABS; BeLS; CoSo; CSF; ViBoFo
Ye sons of freedom [or France or toil], wake [or awake] to glory! The Marseillaise. Claude Joseph Rouget de Lisle. BoHiPo; HBV; LPS-2; PoFr; TreFS; WBLP
Ye sons of Massachusetts, all who love that honored name. The Sudbury Fight. Wallace Rice. PAH
Ye sons of Sedition, how comes it to pass. On the Snake. *Unknown.* PAH
Ye sons of toil awake to glory! *See* Ye sons of freedom, wake to glory!
Ye Sorrowers. Franz Werfel, *tr. fr. German by* Ludwig Lewisohn. *Fr.* The Eternal Road. TrJP
Ye Spartan mothers, gentle ones. Matres Dolorosae. Robert Bridges. MOAH
Ye Spier Me. Sidney Goodsir Smith. AtBAP
Ye stately dames, whose beauties far excel. Thomas Watson. *Fr.* Hecatompathia. ReIE
Ye storm-winds of Autumn! Parting. Matthew Arnold. Switzerland, II. OAEP; ViPP
Ye swans that sail and lave. Swans, Lilies and Doves. Christopher Smart. RO
Ye Sylphs and Sylphids, to your chief give ear! Pope. *Fr.* The Rape of the Lock. ViBoPo
Ye sylvan Muses, loftier strains recite. The Birth of the Squire; an Eclogue. John Gay. BeR; PoEL-3
Ye That Do Live in Pleasures. *Unknown.* TuPP
Ye that dwell with cherub-turtles. Paradise. Christopher Smart. RO
Ye that for psalmody contend. Christopher Smart. *Fr.* Easter Day. KN
Ye [or You] that have faith to look with fearless eyes. Victory. Sir Owen Seaman. BPP; MaRV; OQP; PoToHe; QP-1; WGRP
Ye that have your portion beside the waters of Cephisus! For Asopichus of Orchomenus. Pindar. *Fr.* Olympian Odes, XIV. LiA
Ye that in love delight. On Clarastella Singing. Robert Heath. OBS
Ye that see in darkness. Nyctalops. Clark Ashton Smith. DaM
Ye that with me have fought and fail'd and fought. Sacramentum Supremum. Sir Henry Newbolt. CBE; GTML; GTSL
Ye tradeful merchants that, with weary toil. Amoretti, XV. Spenser. BLV; BoLiVe; LiTB; LiTG; LiTL; PeBoSo; ReEn; ReIE; SiCE; TCEP; TrGrPo
Ye two fair trees that I so long have known. Sonnet. Thomas Caulfield Irwin. IrPN
Ye valleys low, where the mild whispers rise. Flowers. Milton. *Fr.* Lycidas. ADAH
Ye walls! sole witnesses of happy sighs. Walter Savage Landor. EnLoPo
Ye wandering winds that from your threshing floor. Hubert Church. *Fr.* New Zealand. AnNZ
Ye Watchers and Ye Holy Ones. Athelstan Riley. OlF; YaCaBo, *with music*
Ye wha are fain to hae your name. Braid Claith. Robert Fergusson. BSV; CEP; EBSV; GoTS; OBEC
Ye white Sicilian goats, who wander. Little Theocritus. Caroline Wilder Paradise. AA
Ye, who Britain's soldiers be. A Volunteer Song. Joanna Baillie. DiM
Ye Who Fear Death Remember April. John Richard Moreland. MaRV
Ye who have passed Death's haggard hills. The Trees of the Garden. Dante Gabriel Rossetti. The House of Life, LXXXIX. BPN; PoVP; ViPo
Ye who have scorned each other. Under the Holly Bough [or Reconciliation]. Charles Mackay. COAH; DD; MaRV; OBVV
Ye, who may listen to each idle strain. Petrarch. *Fr.* Sonnets to Laura: To Laura in Life. PrPoCR
Ye who pass by and would raise your hand. To the Wayfarer. *Unknown.* SiSoSe
Ye Who Taste That Love Is Sweet. William Michael Rossetti. OQP; QP-2
Ye who would have your features florid. Moral Cosmetics. Horace Smith. LPS-2
Ye wild-eyed Muses, sing the twins of Jove. Hymn to Castor and Pollux. *Unknown. Fr.* Homeric Hymns. AWP
Ye winds, that in your hasty flight. To the Winds. Philip Ayres. CEP
Ye winds that sweep the grove's green tops. The Mariner. Allan Cunningham. EtS
Ye wise, instruct me to endure. On Censure. Swift. EV-3
Ye woods and wilds, receive me to your shade! God and His Creation. Elizabeth Rowe. DiM
Ye Yankee volunteers! The Yankee Volunteers. Thackeray. LauV
Ye young debaters over the doctrine. The Village Atheist. Edgar Lee Masters. *Fr.* Spoon River Anthology. AmP; ChMo; CMP; LiTA; MaRV
Yea. John Crowe Ransom. Two Sonnets, I. LoPS ("It was beside the fire that I had lit.") LO
Yea, and a good cause why thus should I plain. A Funeral Song upon the Decease of Annes, His Mother. Nicholas Grimald. ReIE; TuPP
Yea, as the west wind with its breath of day. Breath of Day. Catullus. LiA
Yea, black are the eyes that I bring ye. Three Songs to Steingerd, 2. Cormac Ogmundarson. LyMA
Yea, gold is son of Zeus: no rust. Gold [or Gold Is the Son of Zeus: Neither Moth nor Worm May Gnaw It or More Gold than Gold]. "Michael Field." LBBV; MBP; OBMV
Yea, Jubal?/ Nothing, mother. William Vaughn Moody. *Fr.* The Death of Eve. WoL
Yea, let me praise my lady whom I love. Sonnet: He Will Praise His Lady [or Praise]. Guido Guinicelli. AWP; OnPM
Yea, Lord, I too. "I Thirst." Katherine Brégy. CAW
Yea, love, I know, and I would have it thus. Love's Poor. Richard Le Gallienne. VA
Yea, Love is strong as Life; he casts out fear. Sonnet. Lady Blanche Elizabeth Lindsay. VA
"Yea, my King." Robert Browning. *Fr.* Saul. WGRP
Yea, she hath passed hereby and blessed the sheaves. Kore. Frederic Manning, *wr. at. to* Ezra Pound. HBV; LoBV
Yea [or Yes], the coneys are scared by the thud of hoofs. Before Waterloo [or Chorus or The Field of Waterloo]. Thomas Hardy. *Fr.* The Dynasts. FaBoCh; LoBV; LoGBV; WaaP
Yea, through life, death, through sorrow and through sinning. Alpha and Omega. Frederic William Henry Myers. *Fr.* Saint Paul. OQP; QP-1
Yea, vanquished am I—thralled at last and bound! Vanquished. Katherine E. Conway. PraNu
Yea, we have toiled all night. The Fishers. Josephine Preston Peabody. StJW
Year, The. Coventry Patmore. CaAE; GTSE; ThWaDe (Round the Year.) BoTP (Year's Round, The.) OTPC (1946 ed.); PoRL
Year, The. *Unknown.* MeMeAg; OTPC (1946 ed.)
Year, The/ An uncut jewel is. The New Year. Tsurue Miyauchi. SoLD
Year about to end, The. The Last Day of the Year. Su T'ung-po. OnPC
Year after year before my life began. The Tomb of Honey Snaps Its Marble Chains. Derek Stanford. NeBP
Year after year I linger round gold rivers and jade gates. Gold Rivers and Jade Gates. Tu Mu. WhP
Year after year I sit for them. A Model. Dollie Radford. VA
Year after year the leaf and the shoot. The Mystery. George Francis Savage-Armstrong. VA
Year after year unto her feet. The Sleeping Beauty. Tennyson. *Fr.* The Day Dream. CG; LPS-1
Year ago how often did I meet, A. Samuel Hoar. Franklin Benjamin Sanborn. AA
Year Ahead, The. Horatio Nelson Powers. WBLP
Year decays, November's blast, The. Thanksgiving Day. *Unknown.* TOAH
Year grows darker, but each day more lamps, The. Autumnal Consummation. Patric Stevenson. NeIP
Year had all the Days in charge, The. Why It Was Cold in May. Henrietta Robins Eliot. AA
Year had flown, and o'er the sea away, A. Iseult of Brittany. Matthew Arnold. *Fr.* Tristram and Iseult. GEPC
Year had gloomily begun, The. One Week. Carolyn Wells. LBN; PFE; PoeMoYo
Year has changed his mantle cold, The. Spring. Charles d'Orléans, *tr. by* Andrew Lang. AWP; JAWP; LiA; WBP
Year has put his cloak away, The. Rondel. Charles d'Orléans, *tr. by* R. N. Currey. FoS
Year Hath Doffed His Cloak To-Day, The. Charles d'Orléans, *tr. by* Alan Conder. *See* Spring.
Year his winter cloak lets fall, The. Rondeau. Charles d'Orléans, *tr. by* J. G. Legge. LiTW
Year In, Year Out. Kathleen Millay. NLK (1947 ed.)
Year is at its close, The. The Last Day of the Year. Annette von Droste-Hülshoff. AnGP

Year is dead, for Death slays even time, The. Year's End. Nathaniel A. Benson. CaP; OCL
Year is done, the last act of the vaudeville, The. Midnight Show. Karl Shapiro. OxBA
Year is gone, beyond all recall, The. The Opening Year. *Unknown.* BLRP
Year of Jubilo, *with music.* Henry Clay Work. TrAS
(Year of Jubilee, The.) PAH
Year of Sorrow, The; Ireland—1849. Aubrey Thomas De Vere. TIP
Sels.
Spring. IrPN
Winter. IrPN
(Year of Sorrow, A, *abr.*) ACP
Year of the Soul, The. Stefan George. *See* Jahr der Seele, Das.
Year stood at its equinox, The. The Milking-Maid. Christina Rossetti. BeLS; LPS-1
Year swings over slowly, like a pilot, The. Winter; Two Sonnets. Malcolm Cowley. *Fr.* Blue Juniata. MAP; MoAmPo (1942 ed.)
Year That Trembled and Reel'd beneath Me. Walt Whitman. AmPo; CoV
Year That's Awa', The. John Dunlop. HBV
Year turns, The. Summer blown from Europe. Waiting for the Wind. Alex Comfort. POTE
Year was the sixth of Constantine's sway, The. Constantine's Vision of the Cross. Cynewulf. *Fr.* Elene. AnOE
Year, with all its days, has come and gone, A. Autumn along the Beaches. John Hall Wheelock. AnAmPo; LA
Yearly thrilled the plum tree. Ballad of a Child. John G. Neihardt. SBMV
Yearning. Huang Pien, *tr. fr. Chinese by* Henry H. Hart. PoHN
Yearning. Alfred Kreymborg. MAPA
Yearning for Death. "Novalis," *tr. fr. German by* Mabel Cotterell. Hymns to the Night, VI. AnGP
Yearnings of Love. Nalan Hsinteh, *tr. fr. Chinese.* ChLP
Years. Walter Savage Landor. *See* Years, Many Parti-coloured Years.
Years, The. Theognis, *tr. fr. Greek by* F. L. Lucas. GrPE
Years, The. John Hall Wheelock. CrMA
Years After. Walter Savage Landor. *See* Do You Remember Me?
Years ago when I was at Balliol. To the Balliol Men Still in Africa. Hilaire Belloc. JKCP
Years and days had I been roaming. A Song of Sprats. Jørgen Vibe. BoDS
Years and years and man's thoughtful foot. The Lane. Andrew Young. HaMV
Years are but half a score, The. On the Big Horn. Whittier. PAH
Years Are Coming. *Unknown.* OQP; QP-1
Years are flowers and bloom within, The. God's Garden. Richard Burton. OQP; QP-1
Year's at the Spring, The. Robert Browning. *Fr.* Pippa Passes. AEV; BEL; BLPA; BoChLi; DD; EPN; EV-5; FaBoBe; GTBS; GTSL; HiLiEn; InP; NeHB; PoRL; PoToHe (new ed.); StVeCh; TSW; TSWC; YeAr
(Good Morning.) OnHT; PRWS
(Pippa.) PECK
(Pippa's Song.) ADAH; BBV (1923 ed.); BoTP; BrR; BTP; CaAE; EnLi-2; FaFP; FaPON; GTBS-W; LiTB; LiTG; MeMeAg; MPB; NLK; OBEV; OBVV; OHIP; OQP; OTPC; PC; PCH; PTA-1; QP-1; RAR; ShBV-1; SiTL; TreF; UnPo (3d ed.)
(Song: "Year's at the spring, The.") EnLit; HBV; HBVY; MaRV; MCCG; MW; PIR; RG; TCEP; TOP; TrGrPo; VA; WGRP
(Song from "Pippa Passes.") ATP; GBV; LEAP; PFE; WP
(Spring Song.) GoTP
Year's at the spring, and the birds do sing, The. Corinna Goes a-Singing. Frank Sidgwick. WhC
Year's Awakening, The. Thomas Hardy. ChMo; NLK
Years Between, The. Chiang Yün, *tr. fr. Chinese by* Henry H. Hart. PoHN
Year's Burden, A, 1870, *sel.* Swinburne.
"Are ye so strong, O kings, O strong men? Nay." PoFr
Years creep slowly by, Lorena, The. Lorena. H. D. L. Webster. BIG; BLPA
Years depart, The. The Mirror. Li Sui Ch'u. PoHN
Year's End. Nathaniel A. Benson. CaP; OCL
Year's End, The. Timothy Cole. HBV
Year's End, *sel.* Josephine Winslow Johnson.
"Now as the year closes and turns." QS
Years-End. Richard Wilbur. *See* At Year's-End.
Years had elapsed; the long room was the same. A Vision. Yvor Winters. MoVE
Years have flown since I knew thee first. Song. Richard Watson Gilder. *Fr.* The New Day. AA; BAP; LBAP
Years have risen and fallen in darkness or in twilight. The Last Oracle. Swinburne. BMEP; VLEP
Years I knew you cannot grow, The. At the Grave of My Grandfather. Pearce Young. PtPa
Years, Many Parti-coloured Years. Walter Savage Landor. BPN; ViBoPo
(Epigram: "Years, many parti-coloured years.") EV-4
(Years.) HBV; OBEV
Years of a lifetime do not reach a hundred, The. *Unknown, tr. fr. Chinese by* Arthur Waley. Seventeen Old Poems, 14. TrCh
Years of Discretion. Philodemus of Gadara, *tr. fr. Greek by* F. L. Lucas. GrPE
Years of the Modern. Walt Whitman. AmPP (3d ed.); CV, *abr.*; IAP; MaRV; PoLFOT
Years race by on padded feet, The. Invincible. Winnie Lynch Rockett. OQP; QP-2
Year's Round, The. Coventry Patmore. *See* Year, The.
Year's Sheddings, The. George Meredith. POTT
Years sped onward, The. He who forever sought. Mary Aldis. Seven Sad Sonnets, VI. HBMV
Years That Go to Make Me Man, The. Christopher Brennan. BoAV
Years that pass, The. Autumn Leaves. Lu Lun. PoHN
Years they come and go, The. Ad Finem. Heine. AWP; JAWP; WBP
Years they come, and the years they go, The. Cradle Song of Amy. Sydney Dobell. *Fr.* Balder. BOL
Years will bring their anodyne, The. The Devout Angler. *Unknown.* DDA
Year's Windfalls, A. Christina Rossetti. OTPC (1923 ed.); PRWS
"On the wind of January," 4 *ll.* BoTP
(Wind of January, The.) YeAr
Years, years ago, ere yet my dreams. The Belle of the Ball-Room. Winthrop Mackworth Praed. Every-Day Characters, III. ALV; BOHV; EnRP; EPP; ERP; HBV; InMe; LPS-3
Yeast, *sel.* Charles Kingsley.
Rough Rhyme on a Rough Matter, A, *fr. ch.* 11. BMEP; LPS-1; PIR
(Bad Squire, The.) EV-5
Yeats' Tower. Vernon Watkins. NeBP
Yee blushing virgins happy are. *See* Ye blushing virgins . . .
Yee powr's that guard loves silken throne. *Unknown.* SeCSL
Ye'll a' hae heard tell o' the Fusilier Jocks. In Praise of the Royal Scots Fusiliers. John Buchan. POT
Yell'ham-Wood's Story. Thomas Hardy. TOP
Yellow. Kenton Kilmer. GoYe
Yellow as flowers as dead fingers. Leave Train. Alan Ross. ChMP
Yellow Barn, The. John Dyer. *Fr.* The Country Walk. RO
Yellow-belly, yellow-belly, come and take a swim. Nursery Rhymes, 4. *Unknown.* OxBoLi
Yellow Bird, The. *Unknown, tr. fr. Chinese.* WhP
Yellow Bird Sings, The. Rabindranath Tagore. The Gardener, XVII. OBMV
Yellow Bittern, The. Cathal Buidhe MacElgun, *tr. fr. Modern Irish by* Thomas MacDonagh. OnYI; OxBI
Yellow butterflies. Korosta Katzina Song. *Tr. by* Natalie Curtis. AWP; JAWP
Yellow canary trilled, A. Jealous Adam. Itzig Manger. TrJP
Yellow chrysanthemum with furious hair, A. Dionysus. Winthrop Palmer. SiTL
Yellow Crane Tower, The. Li Po, *tr. fr. Chinese by* Henry H. Hart. PoHN
Yellow Dog, The. Edgar A. Guest. AlBD
Yellow Fairy, The. Charlotte Druitt Cole. BoTP
Yellow Girl. Nicolás Guillén, *tr. fr. Spanish by* H. R. Hays. TwSpPo
Yellow goldenrod is dressed, The. August. Helen Maria Winslow. YeAr
Yellow-hair'd Laddie, The. *Unknown.* EBSV
Yellow-hammer's rat-tat-too on the orchard bough. The Heart of Youth. *Unknown.* BLA
Yellow Horse with a Blaze, A. Ibn Sa'id of Alcala la Real, *tr. fr. Arabic by* A. J. Arberry. MooP
Yellow Horse with a Blaze and a Black Mane, A. Ibn Sa'id of Alcala la Real, *tr. fr. Arabic by* A. J. Arberry. MooP
Yellow Jessamine. Constance Fenimore Woolson. AA; HBV
Yellow leaf from the darkness, A. Brooding Grief. D. H. Lawrence. LoBV
Yellow Meal. *Unknown.* ShS
Yellow moon is a dancing phantom, The. On a Nightingale in April. "Fiona Macleod." HBV; OBVV; PoVP
Yellow Pansy, A. Helen Gray Cone. DD; GFA; HBMV; NLK; VOD
Yellow raft sails up the bluest stream, A. Spring. Louis Untermeyer. VOD
Yellow River, The. Lu Yu, *tr. fr. Chinese by* Pai Chwen-yu. WhP
Yellow River climbs amid the white clouds, The. Going beyond the Jade Gate Pass. Wang Chi-wen. WhP
Yellow Season, The. William Carlos Williams. MoAB; MoAmPo (1950 ed.)

Yellow sky grows vivid as the sun, The. The Singing Furies. Richard Hughes. PtOT
Yellow Spring. Juan Ramón Jiménez, *tr. fr. Spanish by* Eleanor L. Turnbull. TeCS
Yellow sun yellow. The Ballad of Red Fox. Melvin Walker La Follette. NePoEA
Yellow sunset has faded, The. Sundown. Chu Shu Chen. PoHN
Yellow Swan, The. Sir Gilbert Parker. CPG
Yellow the bracken. Autumn. Florence Hoatson. BoTP
Yellow Violet, The. Bryant. AmPP; AnNE; BAV; CoBA; DDA; IAP; OBAV; ReaPo
(Violet, The, *abr.*) PEOR
Yellow walls in the yellow sunlight. An Abandoned Adobe. Rose Henderson. VOD
Yellow Warblers. Katharine Lee Bates. NLK (1947 ed.); SBMV
Yellow waste of yellow sands, The. Empire (Persepolis). "Fiona Macleod." BMEP
Yellow Witch of Caribou, The. Clyde Robertson. PoOW
Yeoman, A. Edmund Blunden. NV
Yeomen of the Guard, *sel.* W. S. Gilbert.
Family Fool. ALV; InMe; SiTL
Yep, gold's where you find it. You betcha that's true. The Ol' Jinny Mine. Daisy L. Detrick. PoOW
"Yer know me little nipper." The Little Nipper an' 'Is Ma. George Fauvel Gouraud. AA
Yere yernes full yerne, and yeldes never like, A. The Passage of a Year. *Unknown. Fr.* Sir Gawain and the Green Knight. PoEL-1
Yes. Richard Doddridge Blackmore. HBV
Yes? H. C. Bunner. HBV
Yes/ Is made to bless. Yes and No. Louis Untermeyer. BoFr
Yes, all the world must sure agree. To His Mistress. William Walsh. EV-3
Yes, all your dutiful goodness I remember. Sick Room. Francis D. Clare. JKCP (1955 ed.)
Yes and No. Clément Marot, *tr. fr. French by* Leigh Hunt. OnPM
(Love Lesson, A, *tr. by* Leigh Hunt.) AWP; JAWP; WBP
(Of "Yea" and "Nay," *tr. by* Alan Conder.) TrFP
Yes and No. Ogden Nash. MaRV
Yes and No. Louis Untermeyer. BoFr
Yes and when the warm unseasonable weather. Memory Green. Archibald MacLeish. Po
Yes as alike as entirely. To My Father. W. S. Graham. FaBoTw
Yes, as I walk, I behold, in a luminous, large intuition. Arthur Hugh Clough. *Fr.* Amours de Voyage. GTBS-D
Yes! bear them to their rest. Hymn to Night. George Washington Bethune. LPS-3
Yes! Beauty still rebels! Art. Alfred Noyes. OBEV (new ed.)
Yes, by and by. But first a larger matter. God's Speech to Job. Robert Frost. *Fr.* A Masque of Reason. OnHM
Yes, Cara mine, I know that I shall stand. The Island of Shadows. Richard Garnett. VA
Yes, clean yer house, an' clean yer shed. Spring Cleaning. Sam Walter Foss. ADAH
Yes, come to my arms, little doves of iron. The Martyrdom of Saint Sebastian. Eugenio Florit. AnCL
Yes, Dear, lay bare thy lovely soul, nor fear. Confession. Elsa Barker. *Fr.* The Spirit and the Bride. HBMV
Yes, death is at the bottom of the cup. If. William Dean Howells. AA; LBAP; OBAV
Yes, ducks are valiant things. F. W. Harvey. *Fr.* Ducks. BoTP
Yes, every Poet is a Fool. Another [*or* Epigram]. Matthew Prior. CEP; LiA
Yes, faint was my applause and cold my praise. To a Friend. Joseph Rodman Drake. IAP
Yes, faith is a goodly anchor. After the Burial. James Russell Lowell. AA; BAP; CoBA; IAP; TCAP; TOP; UnPo
Yes, farewell, farewell forever. Lady Byron's Reply to Lord Byron's "Fare Thee Well." *Unknown.* BLPA
Yes! from mine eyes the tears unbidden start. Distant View of England from the Sea. William Lisle Bowles. EnRP
Yes, Gertrude, I remember well. St. John's Eve. Charles J. Kickham. TIP
Yes, give me the land where the ruins are spread. A Land without Ruins. Abram Joseph Ryan. SPP
Yes, he was that, or that, as you prefer. T. A. H. Ambrose Bierce. AA; AnAmPo; BAP; LA; LEAP; YaD
Yes, he's my dog. He knows a lot. His Dog. Ethel M. Kelley. AlBD
Yes! hope may with my strong desire keep pace. Love's Justification [*or* A Deathless Flower]. Michelangelo, *tr. by* Wordsworth. AWP; JAWP; LyPI; RO; WBP; WoL
Yes, I admit I've made a book. Ballade of a Conspicuous Omission from "The Book of Humorous Verse." Carolyn Wells. BOHV
Yes, I admit that Proust is rather good. A Ballade of Diminishing Control. J. C. Squire. WhC
Yes, I am in love. Mibu no Tadami, *tr. fr. Japanese by* Kenneth Rexroth. OnPJ
"Yes," I answered you last night. The Lady's "Yes." Elizabeth Barrett Browning. BPN; HBV; LiTL; LPS-1
Yes, I can understan' there's a sort o' pleasure collectin' old customs. A Dracula of the Hills. Amy Lowell. DaM
Yes, I come from another country. I and You. Nikolai Gumilev. BoR
Yes, I Could Love If I Could Find. *Unknown.* ALV
Yes, I have crushed them; yet a few more years. Aëtius at Châlons, September, 451. Arthur William Ryder. MuM
Yes, I have heard the nightingale. Hast Thou Heard the Nightingale? Richard Watson Gilder. AA
Yes, I have lied, and so must walk my way. Arthur Hugh Clough. "Blank Misgivings of a Creature Moving About in Worlds Not Realized," IV. VLEP
Yes, I have loved. And the mad glowing. Aleksandr Blok, *tr. fr. Russian by* C. M. Bowra. BoR
Yes, I have slain, and taken moving life. The Husband. Leon Gellert. BoAu
Yes, I have walked in California. Vachel Lindsay. *Fr.* The Golden Whales of California. AtBAP
Yes, I know what you say. Tempted. Edward Rowland Sill. AA
Yes, I love cats, I don't deny. Betsey Trotwood's Cat. Louella C. Poole. CIV
Yes, I love you. Hymeneal Chant of an Algonquin Maiden. *Tr. by* William T. Allison. CPG
Yes. I remember Adlestrop. Adlestrop. Edward Thomas. AlDL; CH; GTBS; GTBS-W; LBBV; LiTB; LiTM; MM; NP; OBEV (new ed.); PoeMoYo; ShBV-2; TCPD; TwCV
Yes! I swore to be true, I allow. Inconstancy. Joseph Rodman Drake. PR
Yes, I want God's heab'n to be mine. I Want God's Heab'n to Be Mine. *Unknown.* BoAN-2
Yes, I went down to the depot. Jesse James (*A vers.*). *Unknown.* BaBo
Yes, I Will Have Me a Heart's-beloved. Claus Pavels Riis, *tr. fr. Norwegian by* Charles W. Stork. AnNoLy
Yes, I will spend the livelong day. In May. W. H. Davies. OBVV; TCEP
Yes; I Write Verses. Walter Savage Landor. EmBrPo; EnLi-2; EnRP; EPN
(I Write Verses.) TOP
(Lyrics.) BPN
(Time to Be Wise.) HBV; InMe; VA
("Yes, I write Verses now and then.") ERP
Yes, I'm in love, I feel it now. The Je Ne Sais [*or* Sçay] Quoi. William Whitehead. LO; OBEC
Yes, I'm old and rough and gaunt. The Oak's Farewell. George H. Stover. CAG
Yes! in the sea of life enisled. To Marguerite. Matthew Arnold. Switzerland, V. BMEP; BPN; CoEV; EnL; EnLi-2; EPN; EPP; FaBoEn; FiP; GEPC; GTBS-D; GTML; HBV; MaPo; OAEP; OBEV; OBVV; PoEL-5; PoVP; ReaPo; RiBV; SeCeV; TOP; ViPo; ViPP; VLEP
Yes, injured Woman! rise, assert thy right! The Rights of Women. Anna Letitia Barbauld. DiM
Yes, it fell from the nipple of my breast and I did not see it. Frontispiece. Max Jacob. MiCF
Yes, It Was the Mountain Echo. Wordsworth. BPN; EmBrPo; EnRP; ERP
Yes, it's a quiet station, but it suits me well enough. The Station-Master's Story. George R. Sims. PTA-2
Yes, John, I was down thar at Memphis. Them Yankee Blankits. Samuel W. Small. MDAH
Yes, lads, I'm a poor old body. Granny's Story. Emily Huntington Miller. TOAH
Yes, leave it with Him; the lilies all do. Leave It with Him. *Unknown.* BLRP
Yes, "Let the tent be struck": Victorious morning. Gone Forward. Margaret Junkin Preston. DD; GA
Yes, let us speak, with lips confirming. Consolation. William Larminie. TIP
Yes, love, the Spring shall come again. Love's Autumn. John Payne. VA
Yes—loving is a painful thrill. *Unknown, tr. fr. Greek by* Thomas Moore. GrPo
Yes! mourn the soul, of high and pure intent. Sonnet. John Kells Ingram. TIP
Yes, muster them out, the valiant band. Muster Out the Ranger[s]. *Unknown.* CoSo; CSF
Yes, my ha't's ez ha'd ez stone. A Coquette Conquered. Paul Laurence Dunbar. MAP; MoAmPo (1942 ed.); NeMA
Yes, Nancy Hanks. A Reply to Nancy Hanks. Julius Silberger. TiPo
Yes, Nightingale, through all the summer-time. The Nightingale Unheard. Josephine Preston Peabody. BLA; LBMV
Yes, nothing seems changeless, but Change. Don Marquis *Fr.* The God-Maker, Man. MaRV

Yes, o'cose it's interestin' to a feller from the range. A Cowboy at the Carnival. *Unknown.* SCC
Yes—"on our brows we feel the breath." The Dawn of Peace. Alfred Noyes. *Fr.* The Wine Press: Epilogue. MaRV; OS
Yes, Poet, I am coming down to earth. To a Poet. Carolyn Wells. PoMa
Yes, quietly; drumbeat nor trumpet's peal. Cleveland. William Goldsmith Brown. DD; GA
"Yes, sir!" says Willy, "I was wild!" Responsible William. Keith Preston. FAOV
Yes! Steeple-chasing is stirring sport—and the most exciting events of all. Juniper Jim. "F. Anstey." YT
Yes, still I love thee! Time, who sets. Love Unchangeable. Rufus Dawes. AA
"Yes, stranger, them was red-hot times." Cow-Boy Fun. Wallace D. Coburn. PoOW
Yes, stranger! you well may say so. The Wickedest Man in Memphis. Alex J. Brown. BeLS
Yes; thank my stars! as early as I knew. Satire II. Pope. *Fr.* The Satires of Dr. John Donne, Versified. PoFS
Yes, that fair neck, too beautiful by half. Madame d'Albert's Laugh [*or* On Her Laugh]. Clément Marot. ALV; AWP; JAWP; OnPM; WBP
"Yes the book of Revelations will be brought forth dat day." A Group of Negro Songs. *Unknown.* NAMP
Yes, the candidate's a dodger, yes, a well known dodger. The Dodger. *Unknown.* OuSiCo
Yes, the coneys are scared by the thud of hoofs. *See* Yea, the coneys are scared by the thud of hoofs.
"Yes, the dead pines and deersfoot on the ground." Two Sonnets. Frederick Goddard Tuckerman. OnAP
Yes, the Year is growing old. Midnight Mass for the Dying Year. Longfellow. APW; GoBC; PoRL
Yes, theirs was a love that was tidal. Limerick. Paul Kieffer. LiBL
Yes, there is holy pleasure in thine eye! Admonition to a Traveller. Wordsworth. GTBS; GTBS-D; GTBS-W; GTSE; GTSL
Yes, these are the dog-days, Fortunatus. Under Sirius. W. H. Auden. NePA
Yes, they were kind exceedingly; most mild. Bitterness. V. Sackville-West. TCPD
Yes, this is Wicklow; round our feet. Wicklow. George Francis Savage-Armstrong. *Fr.* De Verdun of Darragh. TIP
Yes! thou art fair, and I had lov'd. Too Late. William James Linton. VA
Yes. Thus His Daemon. Aleksandr Aleksandrovich Blok, *tr. fr. Russian by* Babette Deutsch. TrRV
Yes—'tis decreed my Sword no more. A Runic Ode. Thomas Warton, the Elder. CEP
Yes, true, children will take advantage of. The Little Girl. Nicholas Moore. NeBP
Yes, utterly he loves his Nazareth. Young Man in a Galilean Doorway. Herbert D. Gallaudet. ChIP
Yes, we are fighting at last, it appears. Arthur Hugh Clough. *Fr.* Amours de Voyage, II. SoV
Yes, we did a heap o' riggin'. Old Ship Riggers. H. A. Cody. EtS
Yes, we do differ when we most agree. Religious Unity. Hartley Coleridge. MaRV
Yes, we have lost our way. No guiding star. Desert Wanderings. Thomas Curtis Clark. ChIP
Yes, we love this land together. Fatherland Song (Norwegian National Hymn). Björnstjerne Björnson. AWP; PoFr
Yes, we would honor our heroic dead. Let There Be No More Battles! Edwin Markham. PSO
Yes, we'll come to the table. Cowboy Grace. *Unknown.* CoSo
Yes, we'll rally round the flag, boys, we'll rally once again. The Battle Cry of Freedom. George F. Root. FaBoBe; FOAH; OlF; PaA; PAH; PoFr; TreFS; YaD
Yes; we'll wed, my little fay. The Conformers. Thomas Hardy. EnLi-2 (1949 ed.); TyEnPo; ViBoPo
Yes; when the ways oppose. Ars Victrix. Austin Dobson. BMEP; HBV; HBVY; MBP; MoBrPo (1942 ed.); POTT; PoVP; PreP; VA; VLEP
Yes. Why do we all, seeing of a soldier, bless him? The Soldier. Gerard Manley Hopkins. WaaP
Yes, write if you want to—there's nothing like trying. A Familiar Letter to Several Correspondents. Oliver Wendell Holmes. BOHV; InMe
"Yes, write it in the rock," Saint Bernard said. The Divinity. Matthew Arnold. EPN
Yes, yes, my boy, there's no mistake. McIlrath of Malate. John Jerome Rooney. PAH
Yes, yes, prepare the bed, the bed of luve. The Bed of Love. William Hamilton. *Fr.* The Braes of Yarrow. BeR
Yes, you despise the man to books confin'd. Pope. Moral Essays, Epistle I. CEP
"Yes, you did, too!" Little Words. Benjamin Keech. PoToHe
Yes, you have it; I can see. Partnership. E. A. Robinson. ChMo; CMP
Yes, you were loved, Sosicrates, when rich. The Poor Man Is Not Loved. Marcus Argentarius. OxBG
Yes, yours, my love, is the right human face. The Confirmation. Edwin Muir. POTE
Yesterday. Ethel Anderson. NeLNL
Yesterday. Hugh Chesterman. BoTP; SiSoSe
Yesterday. Frank Crane. OQP; QP-2
Yesterday. Nora Perry. PR
Yesterday!/ Betrayed, forsaken, crucified. The Conqueror. Ruth M. Williams. BePJ
Yesterday all the past. The language of size. Spain [1937]. W. H. Auden. EnLit; LiTB; LiTG; WaP
Yesterday as I lay nigh dead with toil. Isaac Rosenberg. *Fr.* Moses; a Play. FaBoMo
Yesterday, at dip of dusk. Old Man Long Ago. Nancy Byrd Turner. GaP
Yesterday Dr. Marcus went to see the statue of Zeus. On Marcus the Physician. Nicarchus. LiTW
Yesterday father said a prayer. Kiddush. Leah Rachel Yoffie. FAOV
Yesterday has slipped the perimeter of perfection. Meditation on Time. Sister Mary Athanasius. JKCP (1955 ed.)
Yesterday I heard that such-a-one was gone. Separation. Po Chü-i. TrCh
Yesterday I went to the yamen to pay my taxes. Heavy Taxes. Po Chü-i. WhP
Yesterday in Oxford Street. Rose Fyleman. OTPC (1946 ed.); PCH; RIS; TiPo
Yesterday it blew alway. To Petronilla Who Has Put Up Her Hair. Henry Howarth Bashford. HBV
Yesterday it seems you were acting on a stage. Legend. John Waller. NeBP
Yesterday my gun exploded. The Perils of Obesity. Harry Graham. FiBHP
Yesterday my pretty Nell. Marcus Argentarius, *tr. fr. Greek by* F. A. Wright. GrPo
Yesterday, Rebecca Mason. Rebecca's After-Thought. Elizabeth Turner. HBV; HBVY
Yesterday Rollin found me on the hillside gathering berries and he helped me. Rollin and Me. Charles Ballard. DDA
Yesterday the fields were only gray with scattered snow. A Winter's Tale. D. H. Lawrence. MBP; MoAB; MoBrPo
Yesterday the twig was brown and bare. The Miracle. Liberty Hyde Bailey. OHIP; OQP; QP-2; YeAr
Yesterday To-morrow. Spring. Gerardo Diego. CoSP
Yesternight I Walked Abroad. *Unknown, tr. fr. Armenian by* Zabelle C. Boyajian. ArmLP
Yestreen I had a pint o' wine. Anna. Burns. TrGrPo
Yestre'en the queen had four Maries. Mary Hamilton's Last Goodnight. *Unknown.* ViBoFo
Yet/ Ere the Season died a-cold. Ezra Pound. *Fr.* Canto LXXXI. MoVE
Yet a Little While. Christina Rossetti. BPN
Yet Ah, that Spring should vanish with the Rose. Omar Khayyám, *tr. by* Edward Fitzgerald. *Fr.* The Rubáiyát. SeCeV
Yet am I such that when the morning breaks. George Edward Woodberry. Ideal Passion, XXXVI. MOAP
Yet another great truth I record in my verse. The Viper. Hilaire Belloc. BOHV; RIS
"Yet Chloe sure was form'd without a spot." Chloe [*or* Characters from the Satires: Chloe]. Pope. *Fr.* Moral Essays, Epistle II. AWP; InPo; JAWP; WBP
Yet Do I Marvel. Countee Cullen. AnAmPo; BANP; CDC; LA; NP; PoNe
Yet Each Man Kills the Thing He Loves. Oscar Wilde. *Fr.* The Ballad of Reading Gaol, I. LO, 3 *sts.*; TrGrPo, 14 *sts. fr.* I *and* II; WHA, *br. sel.*
Yet for One Rounded Moment. Edith Wharton. AV
Yet Gentle Will the Griffin Be. Vachel Lindsay. SP; StVeCh; TSW; TSWC
(Poems about the Moon, 2.) MAPA; TwAmPo
Yet had his sun not risen; from his lips. The Final Struggle. Louis James Block. *Fr.* The New World. PAH
. . . Yet, hail to you. Retrospect—Love of Nature Leading to Love of Man. Wordsworth. *Fr.* The Prelude, VIII. ERP
Yet Homer has told of Ajax' worth, and sent his glory ringing. The Poet's Power. Pindar. *Fr.* Isthmian Odes, IV. GrPE
Yet howsoever changed or tost. The Undying Soul. Whittier. *Fr.* On a Fly-Leaf of Longfellow's Poems. MaRV; OQP; QP-2
Yet I knelt on my knees and begged her for grace. Passus II: Lady Meed. William Langland. *Fr.* The Vision of Piers Plowman. EnLit
Yet I recall/ Another Harvest. Vintage. V. Sackville-West. *Fr.* The Land. TwCV
Yet If His Majesty, Our Sovereign Lord. *Unknown.* CenL; ElSeCe; FaBoCh; LoGBV; SeEP; ViBoPo
(Coming of the King, The.) BLV; TrGrPo
(Guest, The.) CoEV; GoBC; MaRV; OBS; OxBoCh; SeCL; TyEnPo
(Guests.) CBOV; KN; OtMeF; StJW

Yet If His Majesty, Our Sovereign Lord (*continued*)
(Heavenlie Visitor, A.) CAW
(Preparations.) EV-1; MeRV; OBEV; WP
(Royal Guest, A.) CH
(Yet If His Majesty.) PoRA; TuPP
Yet if once we efface the joys of the chase. The Chase and the Race. Adam Lindsay Gordon. *Fr.* Ye Wearie Wayfarer. OtMeF
Yet if some voice that man could trust. In Memoriam A. H. H., XXXV. Tennyson. EmBrPo; EPN; GEPC; MaPo; OAEP; ViBoPo; ViPo; VLEP
Yet in spite/ Of pleasure won, and knowledge not withheld. Summer Vacation. Wordsworth. *Fr.* The Prelude, IV. PoEL-4
Yet in the end, you take us all, dear Sleep. Christopher Morley. *Fr.* Sleep. PC
Yet in their midst the Muses too are found. The Hyperboreans. Pindar. *Fr.* Pythian Odes, X. GrR; OxBG
Yet, in this lowly site, where all that charms. Making a Garden. William Mason. *Fr.* The English Garden. BeR
Yet in Time. Pearce Young. PtPa
Yet it forewarns you all. If once ye'll con. William Ellery Leonard. *Fr.* Two Lives, Pt. III. MOAP
Yet it is not all immaculate death. Not All Immaculate. Laura Riding. *Fr.* Three Sermons to the Dead. LiTA
Yet it was plain she struggled, and that salt. Modern Love, VIII. George Meredith. EnLit; GTBS-D; ViPo
Yet let me flap this bug with gilded wings. Pope. *Fr.* Epistle to Dr. Arbuthnot. ExPo
"Yet life," you say, "is life; we have seen and see." Personal Talk, II. Wordsworth. EM-2; EmBrPo; PeBoSo
Yet London, empress of the northern clime. Dryden. *Fr.* Annus Mirabilis. ViBoPo
Yet, love, mere love, is beautiful indeed. Sonnets from the Portuguese, X. Elizabeth Barrett Browning. BPN; EV-4; HBV; GTBS; GTML
Yet Love Was Born. Charles Hannibal Voss. BePJ
Yet Love Will Dream. Whittier. *See* Life and Love.
Yet nerve thy spirit to the proof. The Good Fight. Bryant. *Fr.* The Battlefield. BPP
Yet never heard I once hard speech from thee. Helen Unreproached by Hector. Homer, *tr. by* William Cowper. *Fr.* The Iliad, XXIV. LiA
Yet not in solitude if Christ anear me. Not in Solitude. Frederic William Henry Myers. *Fr.* Saint Paul. OQP; QP-2
Yet not ungrateful in the morn's approach. The Wet Morning. Thomas Warton, the Younger. *Fr.* The Pleasures of Melancholy. BeR
Yet Nothing Less. Louis Untermeyer. TBM
Yet now I think I have finished the tale of my inferno. Morning. Arthur Rimbaud. AnFP
Yet, O my friend—pale conjuror, I call. Bring Them Not Back. James Benjamin Kenyon. AA
Yet, O stricken heart, remember, O remember. In Memoriam F. A. S. Robert Louis Stevenson. GTBS
Yet often have I wandered from the good. George Edward Woodberry. Ideal Passion, XI. MOAP
Yet on fresh billows seaward wilt thou ride. Seek a Haven. Horace. *Fr.* Odes. OnPM
Yet, once again, Antinous did reply. Sir John Davies. *Fr.* Orchestra. LO
Yet once more, O ye laurels, and once more. Lycidas. Milton. AEV; AnEnPo; AnFE; AtBAP; ATP; AWP; BCEP; BEL; BLV; BoLiVe; CaAE; CBE; CBOV; ChTr; CoEV; EM-1; EnL; EnLi-1; EnLit; EPP; EPS; EV-2; ExPo; FaBoEn; FiP; GEPC; GTBS; GTBS-D; GTBS-W; GTSL; HBV; InPo; JAWP; LEAP; LH; LiA; LiTB; LiTG; LoBV; MaPo; MCCG; MyFE; OAEP; OBEV; OBS; OuHeWo; PIAE; PIR; Po; PoE; PoEL-3; PoFS; PreP; REAL; ReaPo; RiBV; SeCeV; SeEP; TCEP; TOP; TrGrPo; TriL; TwCrTr; TwHP; TyEnPo; UnPo; ViBoPo; WBP; WGRP; WHA; WoL
Yet one more hour, then comes the night. My Drinking Song. Richard Dehmel. AWP
Yet Ostia boasts of her regeneration. Regenerate London. Defoe. *Fr.* Reformation of Manners. BeR
Yet pity for a horse o'er-driven. In Memoriam A. H. H., LXIII. Tennyson. EmBrPo; EPN; GEPC; ViPo; VLEP
Yet pure its waters—its shallows are bright. Green River. Bryant. IAP; PEOR; TCAP
Yet shall the Highest, though stubborn be his will. Defiance. Aeschylus. *Fr.* Prometheus. GrR
Yet shall the prudent still find cause to fear. Pity the Captive Maiden's Lot. Sophocles. *Fr.* Trachiniae. GrR
Yet sighs, dear sighs, indeed true friends you are. Astrophel and Stella, XCV. Sir Philip Sidney. SiPS
Yet Still I Live. Thomas Campion. PoP
Yet still there whispers the small voice within. Conscience. Byron. MaRV
Yet there are watchmen, who with friendly light. Of Watchmen. John Gay. *Fr.* Trivia; or, The Art of Walking the Streets of London, III. EnLi-1 (1949 ed.)
"Yet there's one scruple with which I am much." Philip Massinger. *Fr.* The Renegado. ACP (1952 ed.)
Yet thou, they say, for marriage dost provide. Against Women: Satire VI. Juvenal. *Fr.* The Satires. LiTW
Yet, though a man have riches, and none so fair as he. Mortality. Pindar. *Fr.* Nemean Odes, XI. GrPE
Yet through the turmoil comfortless and loud. The Albatross. William Pember Reeves. AnNZ
Yet Vain, Perhaps, the Fruits. Frederick Goddard Tuckerman. AnNE
Yet was not Conrad thus by Nature sent. Byron. *Fr.* The Corsair, I. EV-4
Yet we have felt some ecstasy in time. Horizons. Struthers Burt. NoCaPo (1941 ed.); TBM
Yet, when I muse on what life is, I seem. To a Republican Friend, 1848, Continued [*or* Continued]. Matthew Arnold. EmBrPo; EPN; PoVP; ViPP; VLEP
Yet while my Hector still survives, I see. Hector and Andromache. Homer, *tr. by* Pope. *Fr.* The Iliad, VI. OBEC
Yet, yet a moment, one dim ray of light. Pope. *Fr.* The Dunciad. AtBAP; EiPP; PoEL-3
Yeux Glauques. Ezra Pound. *Fr.* Hugh Selwyn Mauberley. CoBMV; CoV; LiTA; LiTM (rev. ed.); MoPo
Yew in the Graveyard, The. Tennyson. *See* In Memoriam A. H. H.: "Old yew, which graspest at the stones."
Yew-Tree, The. *Unknown, tr. fr. Welsh.* ChTr
Yew-Tree, The. Vernon Watkins. LiTB
Yew-Trees. Wordsworth. BCEP; BEL; BPN; EmBrPo; EnLi-2; EnRP; ERP; UnPo (3d ed.)
"Y'expect to hear, at least, what Love has past." A Letter from Artemisa in the Town to Cloe, in the Country. Earl of Rochester. NBE
Y'heave ho! my lads, the wind blows free. Sailing. Godfrey Marks. OlF; TreFS
Yield not to temptation, for yielding is sin. Horatio R. Palmer. OlF
Yielded Life, The. "W. A. G." BLRP
Yip! Yip! Yip! Yip! tunin' up the fiddle. The Cowboys' [*or* Cowboy's] Ball. Henry Herbert Knibbs. PoOW; SCC
Ylen's Song. Richard Hovey. *Fr.* The Birth of Galahad. AA
Yo ho, ma hahties, da's a hurricane a-brewin'. Black Sailor's Chanty. Charles Keeler. EtS
Yoga. *Unknown, tr. fr. Sanskrit by* Joseph Nadin Rawson. *Fr.* The Upanishads. OnPM
Yogi. Benjamin De Casseres. BAP
Yoke, The. Kalonymos ben Kalonymos, *tr. fr. Hebrew by* Joseph Chotzner. *Fr.* The Touchstone. TrJP
Yoke of Steers, A. DuBose Heyward. LS; NP; TBM
Yoke of Tyranny, The. Sir Philip Sidney. *See* Astrophel and Stella, XLVII.
Yokes he made were true, The. My Yoke Is Easy. Gladys Latchaw. ChIP; MaRV
Yolp, Yolp, Yolp, Yolp. *Unknown.* ElL
Yom Kippur. Israel Zangwill. TrJP
Yon clouds that roam the deserts of the air. The Bedouins of the Skies. James Benjamin Kenyon. AA
Yon cottager who weaves at her own door. Simple Faith. William Cowper. *Fr.* Truth. OBEC
Yon Far Country. A. E. Housman. *See* Into My Heart an Air That Kills.
Yon goes a gallant which will get repute. In Rudionem. John Weever. SiCE; TuPP
Yon hanging woods, that touched by autumn seem. Lovely in Decay. Samuel Taylor Coleridge. *Fr.* Remorse. RO
Yon page being closed, my Shakespeare's let me ope. After Reading "Tamburlaine the Great." Sir William Watson. PtP. *See also* I close your Marlowe's page . . .
Yon silvery billows breaking on the beach. The Sonnet's Voice. Theodore Watts-Dunton. EtS; HBV; InP; PIAE; TOP; VA
Yon whey-faced brother, who delights to wear. The Moral Bully. Oliver Wendell Holmes. AnAmPo; AnNE; LA
Yonder come Roberta!/ Tell me how do you know? Midnight Special. *Unknown.* AS
Yonder comes a courteous knight. The Baffled Knight. *Unknown.* BaBo; ESPB
Yonder comes dat ole Joe Brown. Walky-talky Jennie. *Unknown.* AS
Yonder Comes My Pretty Little Girl. *Unknown.* *See* Roving Gambler, The.
Yonder Comes the High Sheriff, *with music.* *Unknown.* AS
Yonder doun dwynis the even sky away. An Evening and Morning in June. Gawin Douglas. *Fr.* Prologues to the Aeneid, Prologue to XIII. BSV
Yonder drifts a cloud. Night Storm. Al-Lama'i. MooP
Yonder great shadow—that blot on the passionate glare of the desert. The Dead of the Wilderness. Hayyim Nahman Bialik. AWP; JAWP; WBP
Yonder in the heather there's a bed for sleeping. In City Streets. Ada Smith. HBV; NLK; OTPC (1923 ed.); PoeT; PYM

Yonder is an old crow sitting on an oak. The Old Crow. *Unknown.* FTB
Yonder, lo! the tide is flowing. The Swimmer. Roden Noel. OBVV
Yonder Nether World. Milton. *Fr.* Paradise Lost, XI. LiA
Yonder see. Alchemy. Ibn Abil Khayal. MooP
Yonder See the Morning Blink. A. E. Housman. Last Poems, XI. ChMo; CMP; EmBrPo; EnLit; MaRV; MoShBr; PoE
Yonder sinks the sun; the wearied. Sedge Songs, I. Nikolaus Lenau. AnGP
Yonder stands a cottage all dark and alone. Fair Fannie Moore. *Unknown.* ABS; CSF
Yonder stands the orange-tree. Oranges. Ibn Sara. MooP
"Yonder there behold! a soul that stationed." Political Chaos in Italy. Dante. *Fr.* Divina Commedia: Purgatorio. WoL
Yonder, yonder see the fair rainbow. Corn-grinding Song. *Tr. by* Natalie Curtis. SUS
Yonder's a lanely fir-tree. Lone in the North a Pine Tree. Heine. AnGP
Yonder's the coach, all ready for the journey. Departure. Eduard Mörike. AnGP
Yonder's the man with his life in his hand. "Atkins." George Meredith. PoVP; SoV
Yond's the Cardinall's window: This fortification. John Webster. *Fr.* The Duchess of Malfi, V, iii. PoEL-2
Yonghy-Bonghy-Bo, The. Edward Lear. *See* Courtship of the Yonghy-Bonghy-Bo, The.
Yonnondio. Walt Whitman. MCCG
Yorkshire Bite, The. *Unknown.* BaBo
Yorkshire Moors, The. Hal Summers. HaMV
Yorktown Centennial Lyric. Paul Hamilton Hayne. PAH
Yorktown Road, The. Virginia McCormick. LS
Yosemite. Milicent Washburn Shinn. *Fr.* Washington Sequoia. AA
You. Edgar A. Guest. ATP
You. Ruth Guthrie Harding. SBMV
You. Kenneth Rexroth. *Fr.* A Bestiary. HoPM
You/ Who leap among words. Demosthenes to the Radio Announcer. David Ross. PG (1945 ed.)
You/ Over there. Echo. Mildred Weston. PoMa
You!—/ You stealing violets where the snail-tracks glisten. A Modern Endymion. Marjorie Pickthall. TwCV
You./ Boo! The Next Shortest Poem in the World. *Unknown.* SiTL
You abandon me, woman, because I am very poor. El Abandonado. *Unknown.* ABF; AS
You, after all, were good. Afterthoughts of Donna Elvira. Carolyn Kizer. NePoAm-2
You All Are Static; I Alone Am Moving. Peter Viereck. LiTA
You also, laughing one. A Girl. Babette Deutsch. BAP; HBMV
You and I. Henry Alford. BLPA; FaBoBe; NeHB
You and I. Thomas S. Jones, Jr. PR
You and I. Kuan Tao-sheng, *tr. fr. Chinese by* Ch'u Ta'kao. ChLP
You and I and Amyas. Latet Anguis. *Unknown, at. to* William Cornish. OBEV (new ed.)
You and I by this lamp with these. Together. Ludwig Lewisohn. HBMV; PoToHe; TBM; TrJP
You and I have found the secret way. The Secret Love. "Æ." HBV
You and Today. Ella Wheeler Wilcox. OQP; QP-2
You and You. Edith Wharton. PTA-1
You, Andrew Marvell. Archibald MacLeish. AmP; AmPP; AnAmPo; AnEnPo; AnFE; APA; AWP; BLV; BoLiVe; ChMo; CMP; CoAnAm; CoBA; CoBMV; CoV; GTBS-W; HoPM; InP; InPo; LA; LiTA; LiTM; MAP; MoAB; MoAmPo; MOAP; MoVE; NeMA; NP; OxBA; PoeMoYo; PoLFOT; PoMa; PoRA; ReaPo; TCPD; TrGrPo; TwAmPo; TwHP; ViBoPo; WoL
You appear/ Life is certain. You Come in the Night with the Fabulous Smoke of Your Hair. "César Moro." AnCL
You are a bugle blown for a weary bivouac. To a Pretty Woman. John Urban Nicholson. PR
You are a flower. Longing. Ch'ang Pi Lan. PoHN
You are a [*or* the] friend then, as I make it out. Ben Jonson Entertains a Man from Stratford. E. A. Robinson. AmPP; APA; ATP; CoAnAm; IAP; InP; MAP; MAPA; MoAB; MoAmPo; MOAP; MoPo; TwAmPo
You Are a Jew! Delmore Schwartz. *Fr.* Genesis. TrJP
You are a pacifist? So am I. Pacifists. M. A. De Wolfe Howe. AOAH
You are a riddle I would not unravel. Riddle. Josephine Miles. FiMAP
You are a sunrise. To a Golden-haired Girl in a Louisiana Town. Vachel Lindsay. MAP; MoAmPo; NeMA
You are a Treasure, Lord, beyond all price. Against Despair. Sister Mary Ada. JKCP (1955 ed.)
You are a tried and loyal friend. To My Setter, Scout. Frank H. Seldon. BLPA
You are a tulip seen to-day. A Meditation for His Mistress[e]. Robert Herrick. EV-2; OBEV; OBS; PIAE; TyEnPo
You Are Always New. "Anna Akhmatova," *tr. fr. Russian by* C. M. Bowra. LiTW
("You are always new and always hidden.") BoRS
You are as beautiful as white clouds. Conrad Aiken. Variations, VI. NV
You are as gold. Song. Hilda Doolittle ("H. D."). AnFE; APA; CoAnAm; CoBA; LiTA; LiTM; MAP; MAPA; MoAmPo; TwAmPo
You are beautiful and faded. A Lady. Amy Lowell. BAP; MAP; MAPA; MoAmPo; NeMA; NP; PoeMoYo; SBMV
You are blind like us. To Germany. Charles Hamilton Sorley. LBBV; MBP; MoBrPo
You are carried in a basket. Operation. W. E. Henley. *Fr.* In Hospital. EPP; LEAP; PoVP; ViP
You are clear,/ O rose, cut in rock. The Garden. Hilda Doolittle ("H. D."). AnFE; APA; AtBAP; CoAnAm; CoBA; LiTA; MAPA; NP; TwAmPo
"You are cold, Father William," the young man cried. The Old Man's Cold. *Unknown.* PA
You are coming to woo me, but not as of yore. The Lips That Touch Liquor Must Never Touch Mine. George W. Young. PTA-1
You are disdainful and magnificent. Sonnet to a Negro in Harlem. Helene Johnson. BANP; CDC
You are dull, Caska. Shakespeare. *Fr.* Julius Caesar, I, iii. NBE
You are earth, loam, actual fields. A Poet's Eye-View. Anne Wilkinson. TwCaPo
You are everywhere thought just too lovely to live. The Beau. Martial. RoL
You are far off, stranger mine. "Anna Akhmatova," *tr. fr. Russian by* C. M. Bowra. BoR
You are fayre and lovely too. *Unknown.* SeCSL
You [*or* We] are gazing [*or* looking] now on old Tom Moore. The Days of Forty-nine. *Unknown.* CoSo; CSF; IHA; PAH
You are going far away, far away from poor Jeannette. Jeannette and Jeannot. Charles Jeffries. BLPA
You are gone. The river is high at my door. Thoughts in the Cold. Li Shang-yin. BoFr
You Are Gorgeous and I'm Coming. Frank O'Hara. NeAP
You are here now,/ Who were so loud and feared. The Sleeping Fury. Louise Bogan. LiTM
You are, I think, assured I love you not. Bravery. Shakespeare. King Henry IV, Pt. I, *fr.* V, ii. BHV
You are kind beyond all emulation. Nikolai Alekseyevich Nekrasov, *tr. fr. Russian by* Sir Cecil Kisch. WaL
You are like startled song-wings against my heart. Songs to a Woman. Maxwell Bodenheim. NP
You are like the lightning. Love's Terror. *Unknown.* WoL
You Are like the Snow Only. E. E. Cummings. AtBAP
You are looking now on old Tom Moore. *See* You are gazing now . . .
You are millions. But we sweep an endless flood. The Scythians. Aleksandr Blok. RuPo
You are more beautiful than light. Marriage Song. William Thomas Walsh. JKCP (1955 ed.)
You are my companion. To F. W. Edith Wyatt. NP
You Are My Sisters. Georges Rodenbach, *tr. fr. French by* Thomas Walsh. CAW
You are my sky; beneath your circling kindness. Song. J. C. Squire. LBBV
You are my song come true. Reparation. Helen Hoyt. HBMV
You are no more, but sunken in a sea. Sea-Change. Genevieve Taggard. EtS; NP
You are not, Cynthia, better pleased than I. To the Unconstant Cynthia. Sir Robert Howard. SeCL
You are not dead—Life has but set you free! On the Death of an Aged Friend. Roselle Mercier Montgomery. MaRV
You are not merry, brother. Why not laugh. The Prodigal Son. E. A. Robinson. MAP; MoAmPo; TriL
You are not nearer God than we. Annunciation. Rainer Maria Rilke. MeRV
You are now/ In London, that great sea. Shelley. *Fr.* Letter to Maria Gisborne. ChER; OBRV
You are, O Life, the strangest friend I know. Prometheus Unbound. Sister Miriam. JKCP (1955 ed.)
"You are old, Father William," the young man cried. The Old Man's Comforts [*or* The Old Man's Comforts and How He Gained Them *or* Father William]. Robert Southey. CG; HBV; HoPM; LPS-2; OTPC
"You are old, Father William," the young man said. Father William [*or* You Are Old, Father William]. "Lewis Carroll." *Fr.* Alice's Adventures in Wonderland. ALV; BLV; BoChLi; BOHV; BTP; FaPON; FiBHP; GoTP; HBV; HoPM; InMe; KN; LBN; LiL; LiTB; LiTG; MBP; MW; OnPP; OTPC (1946 ed.); PA; PC; PCD; PECK; PIR; PoeMoYo; PoRA; PoVP; PYM; RIS; ShBV-2; SiTL; StaSt; TiPo; TOP; TreF; TrGrPo; TSW; TSWC; WaKn; WhC

"You are old, Father William," the young man said,/ "And your nose has a look of surprise." Father William. *Unknown.* BOHV; NA; SiTL
You are over there, Father Malloy. Father Malloy. Edgar Lee Masters. *Fr.* Spoon River Anthology. NP; OxBA
You are permitted to live so long as you have breath. Friedrich Hölderlin. *Fr.* The Death of Empedocles. LiA
You are Power. More Letters Found by a Suicide. Frank Horne. BANP
You are so fond of law, I hear. Disputes. Alonso Jerónimo de Salas Barbadillo. OnPM
You are so witty, profligate, and thin. Extempore to Voltaire Criticising Milton. Edward Young. ViBoPo
You are that legendary figure, never seen. Homage to Vaslav Nijinsky. James Kirkup. UnS
You are the buffalo-ghost, the broncho-ghost. America. Stephen Vincent Benét. *Fr.* John Brown's Body: Invocation. PoeMoYo
"You are the cake of my endeavour, and my jelly-roll forever." The Merry Pieman's Song. John Bennett. LiL
You are the Cardinal Acciaiuoli, and you. Guido. Robert Browning. *Fr.* The Ring and the Book. VLEP
You are the cause of this destruction, Lesbia. Catullus, *tr. fr. Latin by* Horace Gregory. RoL
You are the faintest freckles on the hide. Sonnet. Elinor Wylie. MuM
You are the fellow that has to decide. You. Edgar A. Guest. ATP
You Are the Future. Rainer Maria Rilke, *tr. fr. German by* Babette Deutsch. MaRV
You are the millions, we are multitude. The Scythians. Aleksandr Aleksandrovich Blok. AWP; TrRV; WaaP
You are the priest tonight. To Mary; at the Thirteenth Station. Raymond F. Roseliep. ISi
You are the spirit of earth, impalpable dust. Dust, Corpse of Time. Jorge Carrera Andrade. TwSpPo
You are the vision, you are the image of the dream. The Vision. William Stanley Braithwaite. OQP; QP-2
You are too fair to get for nothing. To Claire. Samuel Hoffenstein. LEAP
You Are Unhappy. Heine, *tr. fr. German by* Ralph Marcus. OnPM
You are where the dauntless wind in rebellion. Madrigal to a Streetcar Token. Rafael Alberti. LiTW
You are writing a Gospel. Your Own Version. Paul Gilbert. BLRP; MaRV
You ask a rhymeless sonnet since, you say. Rhymeless. John Freeman. MoP
You ask a sonnet? Well, it is your right. James Branch Cabell. *Fr.* Retractions. HBMV
You ask a verse, to sing (ah, laughing face!). To a Lady. John James Piatt. AA
You ask for fame or power? The Golden Text. George Frederick Cameron. VA
You ask me, fair Chloe, to strike the gay lyre. To Chloe. Thomas Burke. NoCaPo
You ask me, Fresher, who it is. Ballade of Andrew Lang. Dugald Sutherland MacColl. CenHV
You ask me how Contempt who claims to sleep. Epigram [*or* Two Epigrams, II]. J. V. Cunningham. NePoAm; SiTL
You ask me, Lydia, "whether I." To "Lydia Languish." Austin Dobson. PoVP
You ask me what—since we must part. Gifts. Juliana Horatia Ewing. AV
You ask me why I have no verses sent. To a Poetic Lover. Martial, *tr. by* W. Hay. ALV
You ask me "why I like him." Nay. Friends. E. V. Lucas. BoFr; HBV
You Ask Me, Why, tho' [*or* though] Ill at Ease. Tennyson. BEL; BPN; CoBE; EM-2; EmBrPo; EnLit; GEPC; OAEP; PoVP; TCEP; ViPo; ViPP; VLEP
You ask me why, upon my breast. A Knot of Blue and Gray. *Unknown.* PEDC
You ask my dearest treasure, and I come confessing. My Treasure. Egi. SoLD
You ask my love. What shall my love then be? On the Nature of Love. Wilfrid Scawen Blunt. The Love Sonnets of Proteus, XXII. ViBoPo
You ask what I have found, and far and wide I go. The Curse of Cromwell. W. B. Yeats. SeCePo
You ask what land I love the best. The Song of Iowa. S. H. M. Byers. PoRL
You ask what makes this darky weep. Kitty Wells. *Unknown.* ABS
You ask what place I like the best. The Kinkaiders [*or* The Kinkaider's Song]. *Unknown.* ABS; AS; CoSo
You ask when I shall come home [*or* return]. Sent to Home [*or* A Letter Home]. Li Shang-yin. ChLP; WhP
You ask why Mary was called contrary? Contrary Mary. Nancy Byrd Turner. HBMV; HBVY; TSW; TSWC
You asked me:/ Cannot youth save the world? To a Young Friend. Robert Nathan. NeTW
You, Atalanta, were so fleet. To Atalanta. Dorothy Dow. HBMV
You ax about dat music made. The Banjo of the Past. Howard Weeden. AA
You bad-eyed, tough-mouthed son-of-a-gun. Pardners. Berton Braley. SCC
You bad leetle boy, not moche you care. Little [*or* Leetle] Bateese. William Henry Drummond. BMEP; CaP; CPG; MW; OCL; POT; PoTo; PTA-2
You beat your pate, and fancy wit will come. To a Blockhead [*or* Epigram]. Pope. BOHV; HBV; SiTL
You beauteous ladies, great and small. The Lady Turned Serving-Man [*or* The Famous Flower of Serving-Men]. *Unknown.* CG; ESPB; OBB
You became. My Company. Sir Herbert Read. FaBoMo
You, being less than either dew or frost. Love Song Out of Nothing. Vassar Miller. NePoEA
You, being Southern, remember magnolia perhaps—the scent. The Passage Magnolia. Charles Edward Eaton. NoCaPo (rev. ed.)
You bells in the steeple, ring, ring out your changes. Songs of Seven: Seven Times Two. Jean Ingelow. GBV (1922 ed.); GN; HBV; LPS-1; OTPC (1923 ed.); PTA-1
You better sure shall live not evermore. The Golden Mean [*or* Translated Out of Horace Which Begins Rectius Vives]. Horace. *Fr.* Odes. ReIE; RoL
You bible-sharps that thump on tubs. Villon's Good-Night. W. E. Henley. CenHV
You bid me come into your solitude. The Lesson. Anne Goodwin Winslow. LS
You bid me hold my peace. The Poet to the Birds. Alice Meynell. NP
You Bid Me to Sleep. Arthur Stringer. LEAP
You Bid Me Try. Austin Dobson. *See* Rondeau, The: "You bid me try, Blue-Eyes, to write."
You birds whose warblings prove. Fernando de Rojas, *tr. by* James Mabbe. *Fr.* Celestina, XIX. ElSeCe
You Blessed Bowers. *Unknown.* EIL
You boast about your ancient line. Family Trees. Douglas Malloch. OHIP; PEDC
You Borgias among flowers, spilling so much blood. Carnations. Ken Etheridge. MoWP
You brave heroic [*or* heroique] minds. To [*or* Ode to] the Virginian Voyage. Michael Drayton. AtBAP; BHV; BrBE; CoBE; CoEV; ElSeCe; EnLi-1 (1949 ed.); EV-1; HBV; LoBV; MC; OAEP; OBEV; OBS; PaA; PAH; PoEL-2; PoFr; ReEn; ReIE; RiBV; SeCePo; SeEP; SG; TuPP; ViBoPo
You bring no joy, but strange regret. Sosei Hoshi, *tr. fr. Japanese by* I. W. Furukami. LiTW
You brought your childlike eyes to the capital. The Young Provincial. Michalis Stasinopoulos. MoGP
You built the new Court House, Spoon River. Benjamin Franklin Hazard. Edgar Lee Masters. *Fr.* The New Spoon River. TCAP
You burned the dawn. Wake for Papa Montero. Nicolás Guillén. AnCL; PoNe
"You butcher of cattle, cunning schemer, hard worker." *Unknown. Fr.* Homeric Hymns. GrPo
You buy some flowers for your table. Poems in Praise of Practically Nothing, I. Samuel Hoffenstein. BOHV; FiBHP; InMe; PFE; SiTL; TrJP
You buy yourself a new suit of clothes. Poems in Praise of Practically Nothing, IV. Samuel Hoffenstein. BOHV; InMe; SiTL
You called me a name on such and such a day. For T. S. E. Only. Hyam Plutzik. FiMAP
You came dressed in birds and guitars. America, My Sweet. Jacinto Fombona Pachano. TwSpPo
You came in out of the night. Francesca. Ezra Pound. MOAP
You came like the dawn. On the Death of a Child. Edward Silvera. PoNe
You came to me bearing bright roses. Crowned. Amy Lowell. HBV; LoPS
You came when roses were in bud. Roses. Dorothy Choate Herriman. CPG
You can find it only in attics or in ads. The Spinning Wheel. A. M. Klein. CaP
You can go in the stall. Unclaimed. Florida Watts Smyth. StaSt
You can pass on de worl' wherever you lak. De Nice Leetle Canadienne. William Henry Drummond. CPG
You cannot build again what you have broken. The Witch. Lord Alfred Douglas. HBMV
You cannot cage a field. Lives. Henry Reed. LiTB
You cannot choose but love, lad. To an Old Tune. William Alexander Percy. HBMV
You cannot choose your battlefields. The Colors [*or* Standards]. Nathalia Crane. GoTP; MAP; NeMA; StaSt
You cannot dream. Things Lovelier. Humbert Wolfe. LoPS; MBP; MoBrPo; TrJP
You cannot find comfort in ducks. The Bridge, St. James's Park. Virginia Graham. DiM

You cannot hope. The British Journalist. Humbert Wolfe. FiBHP
You cannot justly of the Court complain. To a Witty Man of Wealth and Quality; Who, after His Dismissal from Court, Said, He Might Justly Complain of It. William Wycherley. SeCV-2
You cannot leave a new house. The Strange Guest. Alfred Noyes. LBBV
You cannot undo Liver, you can take. Surgery of the Liver. Merrill Moore. PoP
You can't believe in mother much. God's Mothers. Douglas Malloch. PEDC
You can't do me lak you done po' Shine. Po' Shine. *Unknown.* StDa
You can't expect a cowboy to agitate his shanks. The Cowboy's Dance Song. James Barton Adams. CoSo; SCC
You can't see fairies unless you're good. Fairies. Marchette Chute. MoSiPe
You can't tell me God would have Heaven. A Malemute Dog. Pat O'Cotter. BLPA
You captains bold and brave, hear our cries, hear our cries. Captain Kidd [*or* Captain Robert Kidd]. *Unknown.* ABF; SoAmSa
You, Casey, long a baker. Martial, *tr. fr. Latin by* "T. W. M." Epigrams, VIII, 16. LaP
You charm when you talk, walk, or move. To Madame de Sévigné. Mathieu de Montreuil. LPS-3
You Charm'd Me Not. Dryden. *See* Song: "You charm'd me not with that fair face."
You close your book and put it down. Love. Louis Untermeyer. HBMV
You come along . . . tearing your shirt. To a Contemporary Bunkshooter. Carl Sandburg. CoBA; CoV; TCPD; WGRP
You Come in the Night with the Fabulous Smoke of Your Hair. "César Moro," *tr. fr. Spanish by* H. R. Hays. AnCL
You come not, as aforetime, to the headstone every day. Remember. William Johnson Cory. LEAP; OBVV; TOP
You come to fetch me from my work to-night. Putting in the Seed. Robert Frost. FaBoEn; OxBA
You could not give me toys in those bleak days. Your Gifts. DuBose Heyward. LS
You couldn't pack a Broadwood half a mile. The Song of the Banjo. Kipling. BPN; FaBoCh; OtMeF; PoVP; VLEP
You courtiers scorn us country clowns. A Contest between Court and Country. *Unknown.* SeCL
You crash over the trees. Storm. Hilda Doolittle ("H. D."). TiPo; TSW; TSWC
You cried in your sleep for your mother, dear. His Lullaby. Robert Healy. BOL
You criticise me, and declare. Spare. Ibn Ammar. MooP
You cry as the gull cries. The Contrary Experience. Sir Herbert Read. FaBoMo
You, Damon, covet to possess. The Lover's Choice. Thomas Bedingfield. HBV
You dare to say with perjured lips. Mare Liberum. Henry van Dyke. PaA; PAH
You dear swallow once a year. The Swallow. *Unknown.* GrR
You did late review my lays. To Christopher North. Tennyson. FiBHP
You did not come. A Broken Appointment. Thomas Hardy. CoEV; EPP; MoPW; OAEP (2d ed.); ViPo; ViPP
You did not deserve it. *Unknown, tr. fr. Modern Greek by* Rae Dalven. MoGP
You did not leave this fruited land. Evangeline. Norma E. Smith. CaP
You did not walk with me. The Walk. Thomas Hardy. PoEL-5
You died and I was born, O Christ. In Natales et Pascha Concurrentes. George Herbert. LaP
You died two thousand years ago, Catullus. To a Roman. J. C. Squire. HBMV
You disappoint no creditor, you say? To Sextus. Martial, *tr. by* J. A. Pott *and* F. A. Wright. ALV
You do look, my son, in a mov'd sort. Prospero. Shakespeare. *Fr.* The Tempest, IV, i. FiP
You do not come, and I wait. Fujiwara no Sadaie, *tr. fr. Japanese by* Kenneth Rexroth. OnPJ
You do not like my altar smoke. Defiance to False Gods. Bernice Kenyon. TBM
You do not listen. The Mother. Beatrice Redpath. CPG
You do not seem to realize that beauty is a liability. Roses Only. Marianne Moore. AnFE; CoAnAm; LiTM
You do not think it is because I do not share. Questions on a Nun's Habit. Sister Mary Madeleva. PraNu
"You don't bathe twice in the same river," said the philosopher Heraclitus. Ravignan Street. Max Jacob. MiCF
You don't see buffalo skulls very much any more. Something Starting Over. Thomas Hornsby Ferril. AnAmPo
You dowagers with Roman noses. The Witnesses. W. H. Auden. MoP; ShBV-4
You Drop a Tear. Aubrey Thomas De Vere. GTIV (Lines.) IrPN
You drove the nails in his white, white feet. Good Friday. Edgar Daniel Kramer. OQP; QP-1
You earthly Souls that court a wanton flame. La Belle Confidente. Thomas Stanley. FaBoEn; MeLP; MePo; OBS
You entered my life in a casual way. To a Friend. Grace Strickler Dawson. BLPA; NeHB
You Eyes, you large and all-inquiring Eyes. For Arvia. E. A. Robinson. TSW; TSWC
You fell; and on a distant field, shell-shatter'd. For Francis Ledwidge. Norreys Jephson O'Conor. PtP
You fell asleep in marble long ago. To an Attic Marble. Edna Worthley Underwood. VOD (1935 ed.)
You few, the one-time sharers of childhood's treasure. In Memoriam Egon von Rilke. Rainer Maria Rilke. BoFr
You Fight On, *with music. Unknown.* AS
You find him listless; of but little worth. A Mashona Husbandman. Arthur Shearly Cripps. MM
You fish for people. Aged Fisherman. Witter Bynner. GoYe
You fly away, O swallow, and then return. Sonnet: The Swallow. Tasso. LyPI
You fly the black flag. To a Child. Babette Deutsch. FAOV
You fools behind the panes who peer. Challenge. John Drinkwater. PoMa
You for every line I make. Kisses. Esaias Tegnér. AnSL
You found the green before the spring was sweet. Ave atque Vale. Thomas S. Jones, Jr. HBV; VOD
You from Givenchy, since no years can harden. V. D. F. *Unknown.* HBV
You gallants all, that love good wine. A Ballad to the Tune of Bateman. Sir Charles Sedley. CoMu
You gave me a farm—so you called it, at least. To Lupus. Martial. RoL
You gave me roses, love, last night. The Mystery. Lilian Whiting. AA
"You gave me the key of your heart, my love." Constancy. John Boyle O'Reilly. BOHV; OnYI
You gave to me a camel black. The Gift. Abul Arab. MooP
You gave us the bumble bee who has a soul. Letters to Dead Imagists. Carl Sandburg. AmPP (3rd ed.)
You gave your life, boy. What Reward? Winifred M. Letts. BMEP
You Gentlemen of England. Martin Parker. *See* Neptune's Raging Fury.
You get a girl; and you say you love her. Poems in Praise of Practically Nothing, III. Samuel Hoffenstein. BOHV; InMe; SiTL
You give but little when you give of your possessions. On Giving. Kahlil Gibran. *Fr.* The Prophet. MaRV
You give your cheeks a rosy stain. Artificial Beauty. Lucian. AWP; JAWP; OnPM; WBP
You go aboard a leaky boat and sail for San Francisco. A Ripping Trip. *Unknown.* CoSo; CSF
You Go, I'll Go wid You, *with music. Unknown.* BoAN-2
You go singing through my garden on little dancing feet. To Felicity Who Calls Me Mary. Frances Chesterton. HBMV
You go to high school, even college. Poems in Praise of Practically Nothing, XV. Samuel Hoffenstein. PFE
You go to your church, and I'll go to mine. Your Church and Mine. Phillips H. Lord. BLPA; MaRV
You goat-herd gods, that love the grassy mountains. *See* Ye goat-herd gods . . .
You gobble all and each. The Glutton. Al-Sumaisir. MooP
You good folks of Nottingham I would have you draw near. The Red Wig. *Unknown.* CoMu
You goodman Glutton, bellied like a butt. Glutton. Samuel Rowlands. SiCE
You Got a Right. *Unknown.* BoAN-1, *with music;* OIF
You Got to Cross It foh Yohself, *with music. Unknown.* AS
You gote-heard gods, that love the grassie mountaines. *See* Ye goat-herd gods . . .
You graves of grisly ghosts. The Lover Complaineth of His Lady's Unconstancy. *Unknown.* ReIE
You grottoes and you fountains. On the Choice of His Sepulchre. Pierre de Ronsard. TrFP
You guard your maidenhood, my girl; but why? To a Recalcitrant Virgin. Asclepiades. LiTW
You had a yellow steed. The Sport-Fellows. Li Po. BoFr
You had expected more. Now that I leave. The Departure. Robert Pack. NePoEA
You had no little maid, so I remember. A Nun Speaks to Mary. Sister Mary Madeleva. ISi; PraNu
You had two girls—Baptiste. At the Cedars. Duncan Campbell Scott. BoCaPo; CaP; CPG; OCL; PCN; VA
You have a most attractive pan. Poems of Passion, Carefully Restrained So as to Offend Nobody. Samuel Hoffenstein. InMe
You have a taste of storm on your lips—but where did you roam. Marina of the Rocks. "Odysseus Elytis." MoGP
You Have a Yellow Horse. Li Po, *tr. fr. Chinese.* WhP
You have asked me, "What am I?" Dick Diespecker. *Fr.* Between Two Furious Oceans. TwCaPo

You have been good to me, I give you this. Idolatry. Arna Bontemps. PoNe

You have beheld a smiling Rose. The Lilly [*or* Lily] in a Christall [*or* Crystal]. Robert Herrick. AtBAP; PoEL-3; SeCePo

You have coats and robes. You Will Die. *Unknown. Fr.* Shi King. AWP; JAWP; WBP

You have come from my native village? News from Home? Wang Wei. PoHN

You have come from very far, but what is distance. To the International Brigade. Rafael Alberti. PoFr

You have determined all that life should be. To an Old Friend. Arthur Davison Ficke. LEAP

You have gone, leaving my nights lonely. Parting Song. *Tr. by* Constance Lindsay Skinner. BAP

You have grown weary of a world effete. Zone. Guillaume Apollinaire. MiFP

"You have heard," said a youth to his sweetheart, who stood. The Whistler [*or* The Whistle]. Robert Story. BOHV; LPS-1

You have in you the flowers and the green grass. Sonnet. Guido Cavalcanti. LyPI

You Have Let the Beauty of the Day Go Over. Wilfrid Scawen Blunt. VLEP

You have loved forty women, but you have only one thumb. Personality. Carl Sandburg. CrMA

You have netted this dawn. The Archaeology of Love. Richard Murphy. EnLoPo; PoN

You have never hear de story of de young Napoleon Doré? 'Poleon Doré. William Henry Drummond. BBV (1923 ed.)

You Have Never Known the Tree of Tenderness. Vicente Huidobro, *tr. fr. Spanish by* Joseph Staples. AnCL

You have no enemies, you say? No Enemies. Charles Mackay. BLP; GoTP; MaRV

You have no mortal lineaments this day. Ordination. Sister Mary Immaculate. GoBC

You have not conquered me—it is the surge. Infidelity. Louis Untermeyer. NP; TrJP

You have not died, no. Love. Juan Ramón Jiménez. TeCS

You have not heard my love's dark throat. A Song of Praise. Countee Cullen. LoPS; NP

You have not left me usurer's black blood. Lines to My Father. Leslie Daiken. NeIP; OxBI

You have said, for certain. Confession. D. S. Savage. NeBP

You have seen the house built, you have seen it adorned. Chorus X. T. S. Eliot. *Fr.* The Rock. QS

You have stopped short of love, your May is over. The Old Saint. Muriel Stuart. HBMV

You have taken back the promise. Fidelis. Adelaide Anne Procter. BLPA; FaBoBe; NeHB

You have taught me laughter. The Masters. Margaret Widdemer. HBMV

You have the grit and the guts, I know. Message to America. Alan Seeger. LPS-1

You have thrust Nature out, to make. To Some Builders of Cities. Stanley Snaith. HaMV

You Have to Believe. Douglas Malloch. BLP

You have your hat and coat on and she says she will be right down. The Evening Out. Ogden Nash. MoAmPo (1950 ed.)

You have your water and your grain. My Little Birds. *Unknown.* FaPON

You haven't got so very far. Spring. Orrick Johns. InMe

You hear Youth laughing down green, budding aisles. Youth. Theresa Helburn. PFY

You hearken, fellows? Turned aside. At the Road-House. Bliss Carman. MOB

You hide your hand, Odysseus, underneath. Polyxena. Euripides. *Fr.* Hecuba. GrR

You Hire a Cook. Samuel Hoffenstein. WhC (Poems in Praise of Practically Nothing, V.) InMe

You hold a silver ship/ Upon your arm. Our Lady of Good Voyage. Lucy A. K. Adee. ISi

You hold your eager head. To a Romanticist. Allen Tate. MOAP

You husbandmen and ploughmen, of every degree. The Little Farm; or, The Weary Ploughman. *Unknown.* CoMu

You hymn of the woods that the pine trees sing. The Mountain Norther. Olav Aukrust. AnNoLy

You I dare not love. To One. Gustaf Munch-Petersen. LiTW

You I love, by all that's true. To Silvia. *Unknown.* SeCL

You, I presume, could adroitly and gingerly. How the Women Will Stop War. Aristophanes. *Fr.* Lysistrata. OxBG; WaaP

You, if you were sensible. Under the Oak. D. H. Lawrence. OnHM

You in whose veins runs the fire of loving. Voice. Zona Gale. OQP; QP-2

You in your school forever flog and flay us. On a Schoolmaster. *Unknown.* OnPM

You Kicked and Stomped and Beat Me, *with music. Unknown.* OuSiCo

You Kissed Me. Josephine Slocum Hunt. BLPA; FaBoBe

You kissed me in June. September. Dorothy Frances McCrae. BoAu

You kissed me! My head dropped low on your breast. You Kissed Me. Josephine Slocum Hunt. BLPA; FaBoBe

You knew her?—Mary the small. As Mr. Browning Has It. A. C. Wilkie. *Fr.* An Old Song by New Singers. BOHV; PA

You knew him? The Dark Forest. W. W. Gibson. ChMo; CMP

You knew—who knew not Astrophil? On Sir Philip Sidney. Matthew Royden. *Fr.* An Elegy, or Friend's Passion for His Astrophil. EIL

You know and I know what counts. Trinity. Struthers Burt. NoCaPo (1941 ed.)

You know, dear, that the gipsies strew. Patrins. Jessie B. Rittenhouse. NV

You know how we are wont to stand. "Bottoms Up" ad Finem. P. A. Hutchinson. CAG

You know it, too, the little beauteous land? My Home. Christian Winther. BoDS

"You know, my friends, with what a brave carouse." The Bride. Ambrose Bierce. AA; LHV

You know Orion always comes up sideways. The Star-Splitter. Robert Frost. ChMo; CMP; ImOP; PoLFOT

You know that day at Peach Tree Creek. Logan at Peach Tree Creek. Hamlin Garland. GA; MC; PAH

You know the answer to the last surmise. Sonnet for My Son. Melanie Gordon Barber. GoYe

You know the bloom, unearthly white. The Evening Primrose. Dorothy Parker. ALV; InMe

You know the password, then. Meeting of a Poetry Society. Henry Rago. AnAmPo

You know the school; you call it old. Country School. Allen Curnow. AnNZ

You know there goes a tale. The Modern Jonas. *Unknown.* PAH

You know those windless summer evenings, swollen to stasis. Cicadas [*or* Cigales]. Richard Wilbur. FiMAP; NePoEA

You know w'at for ees school keep out. Leetla Giorgio Washeenton. T. A. Daly. FaPON; MPB; OTPC (1946 ed.); TSW; TSWC

You know we French stormed [*or* storm'd] Ratisbon. Incident of the French Camp. Robert Browning. BBV; BEL; BeLS; BMEP; BPN; EmBrPo; EnLi-2 (1949 ed.); EPN; EV-5; GEPC; GN; GoTP; HBV; HBVY; HiLiEn; LPS-2; MaC; MCCG; MW; NeHB; OnSP; OTPC; PECK; PFE; PIR; PoeMoYo; PoVP; PTA-1; PYM; SoV; TCEP; TreF; TrGrPo; TSW; TSWC; TVSH; VA

You know we must be lonely, you and I. Souls. Paul Wertheimer. TrJP

You know your dad as a big, big, man. Your Dad. Strickland Gillilan. FAOV

You ladies all that are in fashion. A New Song Called The Curling of the Hair. *Unknown.* CoMu

You lads that are funny, and call maids your honey. Jenny from Ballinasloe. *Unknown.* TIP

You laughed at my toga, friend Zoilus, as worn. Tailor Bills. Martial. RoL

You lay a wreath on murdered Lincoln's bier. Abraham Lincoln. Tom Taylor. BMEP; BoHiPo; DDA; GA; LBAH; LPS-3; MCCG; PaA; PAH; PTA-1; VA

You leap out of bed; you start to get ready. Poems in Praise of Practically Nothing, VI. Samuel Hoffenstein. BOHV; InMe; SiTL

You leave us: you will see the Rhine. In Memoriam A. H. H., XCVIII. Tennyson. EmBrPo; EPN; GEPC; ViPo; VLEP

You left me when the weary weight of sorrow. Forgiven. Margaret E. Sangster. PoToHe

You left the field and no one heard. The Decision. E. J. Pratt. TwCV

You Light. Juan Ramón Jiménez, *tr. fr. Spanish by* Eleanor L. Turnbull. TeCS

You like it under the trees in autumn. The Motive for Metaphor. Wallace Stevens. MoAB; MoAmPo (1950 ed.)

You like not that French novel? Modern Love, XXV. George Meredith. ViPo

You like the country better than the town. To a Friend in the Country. Oliver St. John Gogarty. OnYI

You little, eager, peeping thing. The Awakening. Angela Morgan. OHIP

You little know the heart that you advise. In Answer to a Lady Who Advised Retirement. Lady Mary Wortley Montagu. DiM; OBEC

You Little Stars That Live in Skies. Fulke Greville. Caelica, IV. EIL
(His Lady's Eyes.) OBSC
(Sonnet.) ReIE
("You little stars [*or* starres] that live in skies [*or* skyes].") NBE; RiBV; SiCE; TuPP

You look at me. A Drop of Dew. Schmuel Halkin. TrJP

You look long about you. Within. Sydney Clouts. BoSA

You looked at me with eyes grown bright with pain. Parting

after a Quarrel. Eunice Tietjens. AV; HBMV; LEAP; LoPS; NP

You, love, and I. Counting the Beats. Robert Graves. Po; ViBoPo (1958 ed.)

You love me. That's a truth I know. Star. Vladimir Lugovskoi. RuPo

You love? that's high as you shall go. Attainment [*or* Preludes, II]. Coventry Patmore. *Fr.* The Angel in the House. GoBC; OBVV

You love the mountain tops; you lift your face. Ideal. Sister Miriam Clare. PraNu

You love the roses—so do I. Roses. "George Eliot." BoTP

You love us when we're heroes, home on leave. The Glory of Women. Siegfried Sassoon. TwCV

You loved me for a little. Midsummer. Sydney King Russell. BLPA; FaBoBe; NeHB

You loved me for an hour. The Hour. Jessie B. Rittenhouse. BAP

You loved the hay in the meadow. Her Way. William Rose Benét. HBMV

You lovely fisher-maiden. The Fisher Maiden. Heine. OnPM

You, Madam, may with safety go. The Fortune-Teller. Matthew Prior. CEP

You made your little lover kind. Little Lover. Leonora Speyer. BAP; HBMV

You Make Me Think of Loops of Water Lying. Grace Hazard Conkling. AV

You married men, whom Fate hath assign'd. The Merry Cuckold. *Unknown.* CoMu

You Masks of the Masquerade. Gustave Kahn, *tr. fr. French by* Jethro Bithell. TrJP

You, master of delays. Killing No Murder. Sylvia Townsend Warner. MBP; MoBrPo

You may be right, Lefroy, but, for my part. Enter General Brock and Lefroy. Charles Mair. *Fr.* Tecumseh. CPG

You may be very ugly and freckledy and small. Consolation. Rose Fyleman. GaP

You May Bury Me in de Eas'. *Unknown.* BoAN-1, *with music;* OIF

You may call a woman a kitten. What One May and May Not Call a Woman. *Unknown.* TreF

You may call the cowboy horned and think him hard to tame. The Cowboy at Work. *Unknown.* CSF

You may call, you may call. The Bad Kittens. Elizabeth J. Coatsworth. FaPON; MoSiPe; MPB; PoeMoYo; PoRL; YT

You may drink to your leman in gold. Wine and Dew. Richard Henry Stoddard. AA

You may fill the foreground with common stuff. Foreground and Background. Albert Teodor Gellerstedt. AnSL

You may get through the world, but 'twill be very slow. People Will Talk. Samuel Dodge. WBLP

You may give over plough, boys. Tommy's Dead. Sydney Dobell. HBV; VA

"You may have heard of an island called Syra." Eumaeus Tells the Story of His Life. Homer. *Fr.* The Odyssey, XV. GrR

You may lift me up in your arms, lad, and turn my face to the sun. The Famous Ballad of the Jubilee Cup. Sir Arthur Quiller-Couch. InMe; NA; OnSP; WhC; YT

You may never see rain, unless you see. A Dance for Rain. Witter Bynner. HiLiAm; MuM; PoTo; TBM

You may not believe it, for hardly could I. The Pumpkin. Robert Graves. PoMS

You may notch it on de palin's as a mighty resky plan. Rev. Gabe Tucker's Remarks. *Unknown.* BOHV

You may read in the paper of terrible crimes. Reverse English. *Unknown.* CAG

You may smile if you're a mind to, but perhaps you'll lend an ear. The Ghostly Crew, 2 *vers. Unknown.* ShS

You may talk about pleasures. A Trip on the Erie. *Unknown.* ABF; IHA

You may talk o' gin and beer. Gunga Din. Kipling. BBV; BEL; BPN; ChMo; CV; EnLi-2 (1949 ed.); EnLit; FaFP; HBV; HiLiEn; LiTB; LiTM (rev. ed.); MBP; MCCG; MoBrPo; NeMA; PoMa; PoVP; PTA-2; PYM; ShBV-2; TreF

You may talk of horses of renown. Bay Billy. Frank H. Gassaway. PTA-1; TVSH

You may tempt the upper classes. Edgar Smith. *Fr.* Heaven Will Protect the Working-Girl. FiBHP

You Mean My Mother. *Unknown.* PEDC

You meaner beauties of the night. On His Mistress, the Queen of Bohemia [*or* Elizabeth of Bohemia]. Sir Henry Wotton. AEV; BCEP; CaAE; CoEV; EG; EIL; ElSeCe; EnLoPo; EV-2; FaBoCh; GTBS; GTBS-D; GTBS-W; GTSE; GTSL; HBV; LEAP; LoBV; LPS-1; MeLP; MePo; MyFE; OBEV; OBS; OtMeF; PIAE; ReEn; SeEP; TrGrPo; ViBoPo

You meet a girl and you surrender. Poems in Praise of Practically Nothing, III. Samuel Hoffenstein. InMe

You mellow minstrel of a town. Old Nürnberg. Grace Hazard Conkling. PoeMoYo; VOD

You men of Angiers, open wide your gates. Citizens Defend Angiers. Shakespeare. *Fr.* King John, II, i. BHV

You—Mermaid! Your sea-green hair and sin-sweet singing. Fisherman's Blunder off New Bedford, Massachusetts. Annemarie Ewing. NePoAm-2

You messenger that comes from Rome. To an Anti-poetical Priest. Giolla Bridhde MacNamee. AnIV

You might have painted that picture. Rank and File. Edith M. Thomas. OBAV

You might have seen the ivy weeping blood. Elegy for Garcilaso. Rafael Alberti. CoSP

You Mus' Hab Dat True Religion, *with music. Unknown.* BoAN-2

You muses nurses of delights. *Unknown.* SeCSL

You must agree that Rubens was a fool. To English Connoisseurs [*or* Epigram]. Blake. OxBoLi; SiTL

You must be sad; for though it is to Heaven. To Two Bereaved. Thomas Ashe. OBEV

You must be troubled, Asthore. De Profundis. Katharine Tynan. VA

"You must be very old, Sir Giles." Old Love. William Morris. GTBS; ViPP; VLEP

"You must give back," her mother said. Gifts Returned. Walter Savage Landor. BOHV; OBVV

You must have been still sleeping, your wife there. The Sacred Hearth. David Gascoyne. FaBoTw

You must have heard it calling you, Ireland, your Ireland. Flying Charlie. Louise Ayres Garnett. GA

You must know that my uncle is a farmer. Down by the Old Mill Stream. John Read. TreFS

You must live through the time when everything hurts. The Double Shame. Stephen Spender. GTBS-W; LiTB; LiTL; LiTM (rev. ed.)

You must mean more than just this hour. Flos Aevorum. Richard Le Gallienne. BMEP; LBAP

You must not wonder, though you think it strange. For That He Looked Not upon Her. George Gascoigne. EIL

You must remember this, the cold turning year. Note from an Intimate Diary. Emanuel Litvinov. NeBP

You must wake and call me early, mother dear. The May Queen. Tennyson. BPN; DD; LPS-1; MPB; OTPC; PoRL

You Musn't Quit. *Unknown. See* Don't Quit.

You, my dearest swallow. Love's Nestlings. *Unknown. Fr.* Anacreontea. GrPE

You, my friends, and you strangers, all of you. The Sheep in the Ruins. Archibald MacLeish. CoV

You, my son,/ Have shown me God. The Open Door. Grace Coolidge. DDA; MaRV

You, my unrest, and night's tranquillity. To Stars. Francis Thompson. EmBrPo

You, Nebuchadnezzar, whoa, sah! Nebuchadnezzar. Irwin Russell. HBV; HiLiAm; IHA

You need no other death than this. Slow Death. Hazel Hall. MAP; MoAmPo (1942 ed.)

You need no torch to light your lamp. *Unknown, tr. fr. Greek by* Humbert Wolfe. PIAE

You Need Not Fear. Frances Frieseke. JKCP (1955 ed.)

You need not say one word to me, as up the hill we go. Comrades. Fannie Stearns Davis. AV

"You never attained to Him?" "If to attain." Via, et Veritas, et Vita. Alice Meynell. JKCP; MaRV; OQP; QP-1; WGRP

You never bade me hope, 'tis true. Maiden Eyes. Gerald Griffin. HBV

You Never Can Be Old. Shakespeare. *See* Sonnets, CIV.

You Never Can Tell. Ella Wheeler Wilcox. BLPA; NeHB; PoToHe; TreFS

You Never Have Cared. Ernst von der Recke, *tr. fr. Danish by* Charles W. Stork. BoDS

You never know what life means till you die. Robert Browning. *Fr.* The Ring and the Book, XI: Guido. OAEP

You never know with a doorbell. Doorbells. Rachel Field. FaPON; GaP; StVeCh (1955 ed.); TiPo

You never loved me, and yet to save me. Kashmiri Song by Juma. "Laurence Hope." DiM

You noble Diggers all, stand up now, stand up now. The Diggers' Song. Gerrard Winstanley. PoFr

You not alone, when you are still alone. Idea, XI. Michael Drayton. PoEL-2

You now, who are dispos'd to learn our arts. Claude Quillet. *Fr.* The Way to Have Hansome Children. PoP

You Nymphs, Call'd Naiads. Shakespeare. *Fr.* The Tempest, IV, i. ViBoPo

You, O lonely mountain-peak. The Artist. Oscar Levertin. AnSL

You, Oh Tityrus, lying at ease under the shelter of a beech tree. The Shepherd's Gratitude. Virgil. Eclogues, I. RoL

You of the crimson wing. A Marsh Blackbird. Harriet Sennet. BLA

You of the lyric, the ironic brow. Letter to Heine. Louis Ginsberg. MuM

You of the painted wagons, folk of the shimmering eye. Beggars. Rhys Carpenter. HBMV
You oft have heard of that dark night. The Easter Robin. Geraldine Farrar. StJW
You often have in dreams, I know. Joy and Dream. Goethe. LiTW
You open your timeless eyes. To Liane-Neila. Iwan Goll. OnPM
You oughta see my Uncla Joe. Da Greata Stronga Man. T. A. Daly. PYM; YT
You over there, young man with the guide-book. Home, Sweet Home, with Variations, V [VI]. H. C. Bunner. BOHV; CenHV; InMe; PA
You pace/ through my dusty rooms. Yiannis Ritsos. *Fr.* Spring Symphony. MoGP
You painted no Madonnas. To Mother. Thomas W. Fessenden. MaRV; MotAn
You Pictures Flying. Boris Pasternak, *tr. fr. Russian by* Babette Deutsch. TrRV
You play a fife. Elizabeth J. Coatsworth. RIS
You pleasing dreams of love and sweet delight. Dryden. *Fr.* Tyrannic Love, IV, i. ElSeCe
You practice every possible virtue. Poems in Praise of Practically Nothing, V. Samuel Hoffenstein. BOHV; InMe
You praise the firm restraint with which they write. On Some South African Novelists. Roy Campbell. AnFE; BoSA; ChMP; CoBE; MBP; MoBrPo; MoPW; MoVE; PIAE; SiTL; WhC
You Preach to Me of Laws. Iris Tree. HBMV
You prefer a buffoon to a scholar. Cynical Ode to an Ultra-cynical Public. Charles Mackay. BOHV
You promise heavens free from strife. Mimnermus in Church. William Johnson Cory. EPN; GTBS; GTML; GTSE; HBV; LO; OBEV; VA
"You promised to meet me at Adam's spring." Poor Omie. *Unknown.* ABS
You promised to send me some violets. Did you forget? Letter from Town; the Almond Tree. D. H. Lawrence. MoPW
You pure and nimble boy, like candle flame. David. Guy Butler. BoSA
You Put No Flowers on My Papa's Grave. C. E. L. Holmes. PTA-2
"You put the kid in my care.—He's dead." Letter from Mexico. Tristan Corbière. AnFP
You rambling [*or* ramblin'] boys of Liverpool, I'd [*or* I'll] have you [*or* ye's] to beware. The Banks of Newfoundland. *Unknown.* ShS; SoAmSa
You ramping girls which rage with wanton lust. Cressid's Complaint. George Whetstone. ReIE
You reek, swollen with hunger, blood and pus ooze from your open wounds. To Russia. Ilya Ehrenburg. TrRV
You Remember, Alyosha. Konstantin Simonov, *tr. fr. Russian by* Jack Lindsay. RuPo
You remember that pastoral frolic. Limerick. "R. K. B." LiBL
You remember the big Gaston, for whom everyone predicted a bad end? Monsieur Gaston. A. M. Klein. BoCaPo (1948 ed.)
You Repocrat squires in the Farm Bureau. Farmhands' Refrain. H. H. Lewis. LiTM
You rhymed like Lear for us when we were small. To My Father. William Rose Benét. FAOV
You ride dat horse, you call him Macadoni. Jesus, Won't You Come B'm-by. *Unknown.* AS
You Rise Up. Paul Eluard, *tr. fr. French by* Wallace Fowlie. MiCF
You root deep. Trees. William Haskell Simpson. *Fr.* In Arizona. NP
You roving young heroes of Prince Edward's Island. The Boys of the Island. *Unknown.* IHA
You ruffled black blossom. Turkey-Cock. D. H. Lawrence. AnEnPo
You rural goddesses. The Milkmaid's Life. Martin Parker. TuPP
You ruthless flea, who desecrate my couch. Song of the Flea. Judah Al-Harizi. TrJP
You said, "A sound can never die, you know." Summer Evening. Sara Henderson Hay. PoMa
You said, "I will go to another land, to another sea." The City. C. P. Cavafy. MoGP
You said so little that I had to guess. Remembering. Alice Hartich. PoeMoYo
You said the lodestar of the mind. St. Thomas Aquinas. J. Corson Miller. JKCP (1955 ed.)
You said to me:/ I shall become your comrade. Nudities. André Spire, *tr. by* Stanley Burnshaw. TrJP
You said to me: But I will be your comrade. Nudities. André Spire, *tr. by* Jethro Bithell. AWP
You said to me, "My father did not weep." Inheritance. Alfonsina Storni. OnPM
You sail and you seek for the Fortunate Isles. The Fortunate Isles. Joaquin Miller. PTA-2; WGRP
You sang me a song. Sing Again. Marie van Vorst. AA
You sang, Ronsard, in your imperial lay. Ronsard and Hélène. Humbert Wolfe. PtP
You saved the golden seeds of holy mirth. Saint Francis of Assisi. "Joan Ramsay." MaRV
You saw me staring at the girl. Songs of the Plains, II. Glenn Ward Dresbach. NP
You say, but with no touch of scorn. In Memoriam A. H. H., XCVI. Tennyson. BEL; BPN; EM-2; EmBrPo; EnL; EnLi-2; EnLit; EPN; EPP; GEPC; LEAP; OAEP; OQP; PIAE; QP-1; TOP; ViPo; VLEP; WGRP
You say I am frozen, and dry, and apart. Aleksandr Blok, *tr. fr. Russian by* C. M. Bowra. BoR
You say I have asked for the costliest thing. Reply to "A Woman's Question." Nettie H. Pelham. PTA-2
You Say I Love Not. Robert Herrick. LiTL
(To His Mistress Objecting to Him neither Toying or Talking.) EnLit
("You say I love not, 'cause I do not play.") EG
You say I touch the barberries. Barberries. Mary Aldis. HBMV
You say, "I will come." Lady Otomo no Sakanoye, *tr. fr. Japanese by* Kenneth Rexroth. LiTW; OnPJ
You say it's made of silver. The Moon. Robert Beverly Hale. SiTL
You say our ages are the same. My Contemporary. Pierre Jean de Béranger. TrFP
You say that I forget you, and you lie. To Celio. Sister Juana Inés de la Cruz. LiTW
You say that I'm asleep. Aleksandr Blok, *tr. fr. Russian by* C. M. Bowra. BoR
You say that in your eyes alone is all the world. Love Poem. Jiri Wolker. LiTW
You say, The things I like best to gaze on. Sonnets, VI. Feng Chih. *Fr.* Twenty-seven Sonnets. WhP
You Say There Is No Love. Grace Fallow Norton. AV; LoPS
You say this poppy blooms so red. Poppy Fields. William Alexander Percy. LS
You say, "Where goest thou?" I cannot tell. A Poet's Simple Faith [*or* Where Goest Thou?]. Victor Hugo. MaRV; OQP; QP-1; WGRP
You say you have no clothes. No Clothes. *Unknown.* WhP
You say you heard King Borborigmi laugh? King Borborigmi. Conrad Aiken. ChMo; CMP; MAPA; MOAP
You Say You Love. William King. SeCL
You say you love me, nay, can swear it too. Clarastella Distrusting. Robert Heath. SeCL
You say you love! Repeat again. You Say You Love. William King. SeCL
You say you saw a ghost, in the house, at night. Ghosts. Marguerite Wilkinson. CP
You Sea! Walt Whitman. *Fr.* Song of Myself, XXII. SN
You seamen, I have eaten your hard bread. To the Seamen. John Masefield. NeTW
You secret vales, you solitary fields. Henry Constable. *Fr.* Diana. OBSC
You see/ Nestled into a hollow of the downs. Fragment. William Allingham. *Fr.* By the Way. EnSW; IrPN
You see, merry Phyllis, that dear little maid. A Tea-Party. Kate Greenaway. MPB; OTPC; PPL
You see the evening fire coming out from its shell. We Are. Paul Eluard. MiCF
You see the goodly hair that Galla wears. Of Galla's Goodly Periwig. Sir John Harington. SiCE
You see this pebble-stone? It's a thing I bought. The Cock and the Bull. Charles Stuart Calverley. ALV; BOHV; InMe; LPS-3; NA; PA
You see us every morning. Pals. John E. Donovan. AlBD
You see, we three. Chums. Arthur Guiterman. GaP; MPB
You seek life, and a godly fire. Empedocles. Friedrich Hölderlin. AnGP
You seem to have lived, my lady. On Again Meeting a Lady. Otomo Miyori. OnPM
You seemed a caryatid melting. Love. Maxwell Bodenheim. NP
You send me apples hot with gold, Martia. Petronius, *tr. fr. Latin by* Jack Lindsay. LaP
You send me your love in a letter. Child and Poet. Swinburne. BPN; EmBrPo; EnLit; EPN; PoVP
You serve the best wine always, my dear sir. Martial, *tr. fr. Latin by* J. V. Cunningham. Epigrams, IV, 69. LaP
You Shall above All Things Be Glad and Young. E. E. Cummings. MoPW; NePA; OxBA
You shall hear how Hiawatha. The Legend of the Cornstalk. Longfellow. *Fr.* The Song of Hiawatha. GrCo-1
You shall hear how Pau-Puk-Keewis. Pau-Puk-Keewis. Longfellow. *Fr.* The Song of Hiawatha. CoBA
You shall not be overbold. The Titmouse. Emerson. BLA; IAP; PRWS
You shall not vanish into dust today. Funeral. Murray Bennett. GoYe
You should be the saint, St. Francis. Marionette. Fray Angelico Chavez. SaFP

You should have walked those cooler garden ways. Unheeded Vocation. Eleanore L. Perry. PraNu
You should have weighted my dream of you. Dream. Mary Austin. TBM
You should hear/ our brook in Spring! Rambunctious Brook. Frances Frost. BrR
You should stay longer if we durst. *See* Ye should stay longer if we durst.
You shrill mosquitoes, come away! Beware the Jealous Hand. Meleager. GrR
You shun me, Chloe, wild and shy. To Chloe. Horace. AWP; JAWP; WBP
You Simple Bostonians. *Unknown.* *See* What a Court Hath Old England.
You sing and sing, you talk and talk. Prelude to Hope. Vicente Huidobro. TwSpPo
You sit at your high windows, old men. The Old Men. Alexander Javitz. TrJP
You sit beside my chair. You gaze. My Dog and I. Isla Paschal Richardson. AlBD
"You sit on the bed there." "Andrei Bely." *Fr.* Requiem. TrRV
You sleep upon your mother's breast. A Rhyme of One. Frederick Locker-Lampson. HBV
You sleeping child asleep, away. To Ping-ku, Asleep. Lawrence Durrell. ChMP; NeBP
You smile and you smoke your cigar, my boy. My Boy. James Whitcomb Riley. FAOV
You Smile upon Your Friend To-Day. A. E. Housman. A Shropshire Lad, LVII. PoVP; TwP
You Smiled, You Spoke [and I Believed]. Walter Savage Landor. EmBrPo; OAEP
(Lyric, A: "You smiled, you spoke.") BCEP
(Lyrics to Ianthe.) BPN
(To Ianthe.) VA
You, so bravely splashing reds and blues! To a Portrait Painter Who Desired Him to Sit. Po Chü-i. TrCh
You sought forever for a phantom rose. The Phantom Rose. Mary Sinton Leitch. MuM
You speak; and my spirit to the soft breathing. Fantasy. Giosuè Carducci. LiTW
You splice together two broomsticks, then reef. Sonnet at Easter. Howard Nemerov. FiMAP
You spoke keys and looked. The Tyrant Apple Is Eaten. Norman McCaig. NeBP
You Spotted Snakes [with Double Tongue]. Shakespeare. *Fr.* A Midsummer Night's Dream, II, ii. AnFE; BoTP; EG; InvP; KN; LiTB; LiTG; OBSC; OTPC (1923 ed.); PoRA; ShBV-1; SiCE; ViBoPo
(Fairies' Lullaby, The.) ElL; WHA
(Fairies' Lullaby: "Come, now a roundel," *longer sel.*) LPS-3
(Fairies' Song, The.) EV-1; LoBV
(Fairy Land, 2.) OBEV
(Fairy Lullaby.) FaPON; GoTP; RIS
(Fairy Songs: "You spotted snakes with double tongue.") BLV; HBV; TrGrPo
(Lullaby for Titania.) BOL; CG; GN; RG
(Shakespeare's Fairies; They Sing Their Queen to Sleep.) CBPC
(Song: "You spotted snakes with double tongue.") FiP
(Song of the Fairies.) BoLiVe
(Songs from "A Midsummer-Night's Dream.") LEAP
You sprawl upon your special bed. Dog Asleep. Margaret Mackprang Mackay. AlBD
You stand atop your hill. New Hampshire Farm Woman. Rachel Graham. GoYe
You stared out of the window on the emptiness. To a Spanish Poet. Stephen Spender. ChMo; OAEP (2d ed.)
You stole my friend, a sneakthief manifest. A Faithless Friend. Theognis. GrL; OxBG
You strange, astonish'd-looking, angle-faced. The Fish, the Man, and the Spirit [*or* To Fish *or* To a Fish]. Leigh Hunt. ATP; ChTr; EnRP; EPN; FiBHP; OBEV (new ed.); PeBoSo; PIAE; PoEL-4; RO; SeCePo; ViBoPo
You suffered starvation in deserted villages. Sonnets, VIII [*or* For Tu Fu]. Feng Chih. *Fr.* Twenty-seven Sonnets. LiTW; WhP
You, Swallow, quit your twitterings. Tay Toy Babilarde Arondelle. Pierre de Ronsard, *tr. by* Jonathan Price. PoN
You take a bath, and sit there bathing. Poems in Praise of Practically Nothing, II. Samuel Hoffenstein. InMe
You take a town you cannot keep. Love's Spite. Aubrey Thomas De Vere. HBV; VA
You Take the First Street. Robert Desnos, *tr. fr. French by* Wallace Fowlie. MiCF
You Talk about Yo' Greenbacks, *with music.* *Unknown.* StDa
You talk about your harbor girls. Haul Away, My Rosy. *Unknown.* OuSiCo
You talk of the deeds of the old pioneers. A Cleary Pioneer. Fred Crewe. DDA; PaA
You taught me ways of gracefulness and fashions of address. To a Little Girl. Helen Parry Eden. HBV; OTPC (1923 ed.)
You tell me I'm handsome, I know not how true. Song the Ninth. Edward Moore. CEP
You tell me of my songs you cannot fit. To One Who Wanted a Philosophy from Me. "Æ." ChMo
You tell me that the day is fine. To My Hairdresser. Warham St. Leger. CenHV
You tell me you're promised a lover. A Letter of Advice. Winthrop Mackworth Praed. HBV; OBRV; OxBoLi; TOP; WhC
You Tell on Yourself. *Unknown.* PoToHe (new ed.)
You tender hearted Christians, I pray you lend an ear. The Millman Song. *Unknown.* ShS
You that a stranger in mid-Rome seek Rome. Rome. Ianus Vitalis Panormitanus. LaP
You that but seek your modest rolls and coffee. Rue Bonaparte. Joseph Warren Beach. NP
You that crossed the ocean old. Ponce de Leon. Edith M. Thomas. PAH
You that delight in concord liston all. *Unknown.* SeCSL
You that do search for every purling spring. Astrophel and Stella, XV. Sir Philip Sidney. CoBE; EPP; ES; EV-1; OBSC; ReEn; ReIE; SiCE; SiPS; TuPP
You that do see this child disfigured here. The True Form and Shape of a Monsterous Child. William Elderton. ReIE
You that extol the bliss of this our nation. Against an Extreme Flatterer That Preached at Bath on the Queen's Day the Fortieth Year of Her Reign. Sir John Harington. SiCE
You that have been this evenings light. Sir R. Hatton. SeCSL
You that have faith to look with fearless eyes. *See* Ye that have faith . . .
You that have spent the silent night. Gascoigne's Good Morrow. George Gascoigne. SiCE; TriL; TuPP
You that have that daintie eare. *Unknown.* SeCSL
You That in Love Find Luck and Abundance. Sir Thomas Wyatt. *See* Sonnet: "You that in love find luck . . ."
You that in music do delight. The Printer to the Reader. *At. to* Richard Jones. ElL; ReIE
You That Love England. C. Day Lewis. BrBE; FaBoMo; TwCV
You that make music from the seven voices of the lyre. Euripides. *Fr.* Ion. GrPo
You that nightly cross the straits. Crossing the Straits. Charles Brasch. AnNZ
You that on the four winds come. The Beautiful Land. Eric Chilman. TVSH
You that prophane our windows with a tongue. Beauty in Worship. *Unknown.* *Fr.* A Poem, in Defence of the Decent Ornaments of Christ-Church, Oxon. OBS
You that seek what life is in death. Time and Eternity. Fulke Greville. Caelica, LXXXIII. OBSC
You That Sing in the Blackthorn. Alfred Noyes. *Fr.* The Last Voyage, II. GoBC
(Bird Song.) BLA
(Tell Me You That Sing.) POTT
(Unconscious, The.) MM
You that think Love can convey. Celia Singing. Thomas Carew. EG; ElSeCe; EnLit; EPS (1942 ed.); EV-2; LiTL; LO; SeCL; SeEP
You that thus wear a modest countenance. Dante. *Fr.* La Vita Nuova. AWP
You that uphold the world. Pagan Prayer. Alice Brown. WGRP
You that with allegory's curious frame. Astrophel and Stella, XXVIII. Sir Philip Sidney. ReEn; ReIE; SiCE; SiPS; TuPP
You, the choice minions of the proud-lipped Nine. To Poets. George Darley. RO
You, the woman; I, the man; this, the world. The Character of Love Seen as a Search for the Lost. Kenneth Patchen. TwAmPo
You, the Young Rainbow. Edith Sitwell. MoVE
You, then, whose judgment the right course would steer, Homer. Pope. *Fr.* An Essay on Criticism. TwCrTr
You think, dear absent friend, that after you. Footprints. Ludvig Bødtcher. BoDS
You think Fuseli is not a great painter. I'm glad. To Hunt [*or* Epigram]. Blake. OxBoLi; SiTL
"You think I am dead." Talking in Their Sleep. Edith M. Thomas. ADAH; DD; OHIP; PEDC; PEOR
You think it's only a garden. The Secrets of Our Garden. Rupert Sargent Holland. OTPC
You think of him as one who fails. I Think of Him as One Who Fights. Anna Hempstead Branch. HBMV
You thought it was a falling leaf we heard. Rondel for September. Karle Wilson Baker. HBMV; PoTo; VOD
You thought my heart too far diseased. In Memoriam A. H. H., LXVI. Tennyson. EmBrPo; EPN; GEPC; ViPo; VLEP

You to the left and I to the right. At the Crossroads. Richard Hovey. BAP; BBV (1951 ed.); BLP; BoFr; CP; HBV; LBAP; MAP; MoAmPo (1942 ed.); NeMA; PFY; PoMa; PYM
You to whose soul a death propitious brings. An Elegy, for Father Anselm, of the Order of Reformed Cistercians. Helen Parry Eden. JKCP
You to your beech tree, Tityrus, withdraw. Eclogues, I. Virgil. LaP
You told me Age was a black wolf that lay. Comfort. Margaret Widdemer. GoYe
You told me, Maro, whilst you live. A Hinted Wish [or A Legacy]. Martial. AWP; JAWP; LiTW; OnPM; OuHeWo; WBP
You told me: My father did not weep. Ancestral Burden. Alfonsina Storni. AnCL
You too listless to examine. Lines to Our Elders. Countee Cullen. CDC
You too, of course, have counted sheep. Sheep Herders. Maurice Lesemann. NP
You, too, retire and sit you down again. Praxagora Rehearses Her Speech. Aristophanes. *Fr.* The Ecclesiazusae. GrR; OxBG
You, too, Tibullus, has unscrupulous Death sent. On the Death of Tibullus. Domitius Marsus. LaP
You tossed a blanket from the bed. Preludes, III. T. S. Eliot. AnAmPo; BoLiVe (1945 ed.); CoBA; InP; LiTA; LiTM; OBMV; ReMP; UnPo
You Turn for Sugar an' Tea, *with music.* *Unknown.* OuSiCo
You turn your eyes away, but still I have. Diversity. Frank Ernest Hill. TBM
You undergo before your time, my son. For My Son. Antoni Boguslawski. PoFr
You Understand. *Unknown.* SeCL
("You understand no tender vows.") SeEP
You, unique in human kind. The House. Ibn al-Hammara. MooP
You used to love the shining light. Lights. Mary Lanier Magruder. VOD
You, Vacerra, admire the ancients only. Martial, *tr. fr. Latin by* Robert R. Schnorr. Epigrams, VIII, 69. LaP
You very fine Miss Molly. The Daisies. Kate Greenaway. MPB; RAR
You vexed me with your vainness. Lines to Sigrún. Bjarni Thorarensen. IcP
You Virgins. James Shirley. *See* Piping Peace.
You vow you have no "parlor tricks." The Hallowe'en Party: Nonsense Rimes for the Maids. *Unknown.* HOAH
You, Voyager, with exile-heart that yearns. Speak to the Sun. Dedie Huffman Wilson. GoYe
You wait, expecting one alone. Remembrance. Rainer Maria Rilke. ReMP
You waken slowly. In your dream you're straying. Sonnet. William Bell. NePoEA
You walk above in the light. Hyperion's Song. Friedrich Hölderlin, *tr. by* Lola Gruenthal. AnGP
You Walk in a Strange Way. Gerald Gould. LBBV
You walk the floor of autumn where her corpse. Autumnall. Joseph Bennett. NePA
You walk the hills, blind in your dreaming. Warning. Harold Lewis Cook. AnAmPo
You walk unaware. Maeve. Mervyn Peake. LO
You walk up a deep roadbed to a hilltop. Variations on a Theme. Robert Hillyer. MAP; MoAmPo
You walk up there in the light. Song of Fate. Friedrich Hölderlin, *tr. by* Emery Neff. WoL
You want clear spectacles: your eyes are dim. The Accusation of the Inward Man. Edward Taylor. *Fr.* God's Determinations. LiTA
You wave your fan with such a graceful art. Ramón de Campoamor. *Fr.* Humoradas. AnSpL-2
You wear the morning like your dress. Song [or Song: Inviting the Influence of a Young Lady]. Hilaire Belloc. OBEV (new ed.); OBVV
You weep, you weep and look at me. Affinities. Heine. AnGP
You, weeping wide at war, weep with me now. The Coward. Eve Merriam. TrJP
You Went to the Verge, You Say, and Came Back Safely? Conrad Aiken. Preludes for Memnon, XIV. LiTA; LiTG; TwCV
(Preludes to Attitude, III.) TwAmPo
You were a foolish, though an amorous fellow. Foolish Leander. Mateo Vázquez de Leca. OnPM
You were a haughty beauty, Polly. Private Theatricals. Louise Imogen Guiney. PR
You were a pearl. A Lament for My Son Ts'ui. Po Chü-i. PoHN
You were a sophist. Advice. Gwendolyn B. Bennett. CDC
You were always a dreamer, Rose—red Rose. A Rose Will Fade. Dora Sigerson Shorter. HBV; TIP
You were amused to find you too could fear. Letter I. William Empson. ChMP; LiTB
You were before me. Vasili Zhukovsky, *tr. fr. Russian by* C. M. Bowra. BoRS
You were born; must die; were loved; must love. Sonnet: You Were Born; Must Die. Stephen Spender. EnLit; MoAB; MoBrPo (1950 ed.)
You were dawn on the Cuillin and benign day on the Clarach. Dain do Eimhir, LIV. Sorley Maclean. NeBP
You were glad to-night; and now you've gone away. Siegfried Sassoon. *Fr.* The Heart's Journey. CaAE; TwCV
You Were Much Too Near. Arnulf Överland, *tr. fr. Norwegian by* Charles W. Stork. AnNoLy
You were no more to me than many others. The Masquerader. Aline Kilmer. HBMV
You were praised, my books. Salutation the Second. Ezra Pound. OxBA
You were the clear Sicilian fluting. A Girl. Richard Aldington. *Fr.* Epigrams. PFE
You were the princess of the fairy-tale. One Voice. Winifred Welles. VOD
You were with me and it wasn't flying, exactly. A Dream as Reported. Virginia Earle. GoYe
"You! What d'you mean by this?" I rapped. Inspection. Wilfred Owen. WaP
You whispered, "Still the stars shine cold above me." Sonnet. William Bell. FaBoTw
You who are born of the hills. The Hill-born. Struthers Burt. MaRV; PC
You who are earth and cannot rise. To the World. William Habington. ElSeCe
You who are given to me to Time are given. Love in Time's Despite. Edwin Muir. LiTL
You who are inland born know not the pain. Sea Longing. Harold Vinal. PoMa
You who are slight/ and straight and true. To Someone in Berlin. Doris Peel. BoFr
You who come from the old village. Verses. Wang Wei. WhP
You who desired so much. To Emily Dickinson. Hart Crane. ChMo; PtP
You, who do breach mine eyes and touch the heart. Sonnet. Guido Cavalcanti. LyPI
You Who Dog My Footsteps. Leib Kwitko, *tr. fr. Yiddish by* Joseph Leftwich. TrJP
You who dread the cares and labors. The Last Landlord. Elizabeth Akers Allen. AA
You who dwell upon Helicon. Catullus, *tr. fr. Latin by* L. R. Lind. LaP
You who flee to escape a bloody death like mine. Propertius. Elegies, I, 21. LaP
You who flutter and quiver. Vision. John Gould Fletcher. LEAP; TBM
You who give ear to sorrow, as you scan. Sonnet. Petrarch. *Fr.* Sonnets to Laura: To Laura in Life. LyPI
You who go every Sunday to the Botanical Garden. Song for Afterwards. Francisco López Merino. AnCL
You, who have everything. Parable of Generosity. Antonio Spinetti Dini. BoFr
You who have felt the sting of dire defeat. Challenge. Harry W. Falconer. PoToHe (1941 ed.)
You who have grown so intimate with stars. To an Aviator. Daniel Whitehead Hicky. MoSiPe
You who have handed us life's torch, new kindled. To Our Forefathers. Frances Crosby Hamlet. PSO
You who have raised. Last Hill. Edith Mirick. ChIP
You who have spoken words in the earth. Reproach to Dead Poets. Archibald MacLeish. ChMo; CMP
You who have the horse can ride. Wanderer's Night-Song. Nigel Heseltine. MoWP
You, Who in April Laughed. Brenda Chamberlain. MoWP
(Poem: "You, who in April laughed, a green god in the sun.") NeBP
You, who in sultry weather. A Plea for a Plural. Rudolf Chambers Lehmann. CenHV
You who know unrequited love. Daphne and Apollo. George Macy. InMe
You who like a boulder stand. The Wildebeest. June Daly. FaPON
You who practise the four elegant occupations. Scroll-Section. Robert Finch. BoCaPo; PeCV
You who return from far Cathay. Paul Jean Toulet. *Fr.* Contrarimes. MiFP
You who seek the knightly order. The Knightly Code. Eustache Deschamps. CAW
You, who sought the great adventure. On an American Soldier of Fortune Slain in France. Clinton Scollard. MC
You who were once so careless, I can recall you now. The Beloved Vagabond. W. G. Tinckom-Fernandez. NLK
You Who Will Soon Be Unrecapturable. Louis MacNeice. ReaPo
You who with birch or laurel. To the Harpies. Arthur Davison Ficke. HBV; OBAV
You who would sorrow even for a token. Reciprocity. Vassar Miller. NePoEA

You, who would with wanton art. To the Cat-Bird. *Unknown.* BLA; SN
You whom I never knew. "The Sad Years." Eva Gore-Booth. HBMV
You whom the waters make fierce and the moon quiets. A Sestina for Cynthia. David Lougée. NePA
You, whose exploits the world itself admired. On Sir Francis Drake. Charles Fitzgeffrey. SG
You will ask how I came to be eavesdropping, in the first place. Confession Overheard in a Subway. Kenneth Fearing. LiTA; LiTM (rev. ed.); WaP
You will be enough for me. Little Serenade. Kenton Kilmer. WHL
You will be the color of water. Prophecy. Marjorie Meeker. NP
You will be what you will be. Will. Ella Wheeler Wilcox. BLPA
You will come back to me. Barren Stone. Nicolás Guillén. PoNe
You will come, my bird, Bonita? Juanita. Joaquin Miller. AA
You Will Die. *Unknown. Fr.* Shi King. AWP; JAWP; WBP
You will die and your friends with you and be forgotten. To the Rulers. John Frederick Nims. JKCP (1955 ed.)
You will end life just as you close a favorite book. Poise. Violet Alleyn Storey. BLP
You will find me drinking rum. The Logical Vegetarian. G. K. Chesterton. CenHV; LiTG; SiTL
You Will Grieve. Guillaume Apollinaire, *tr. fr. French by* Patricia Terry. OnPM
You will not find mention of her, sir. Tudur Aled. Davies Aberpennar. MoWP
You will not hear it as the sea. Hart Crane. *Fr.* The Bridge: The River. ViBoPo (1941 ed.)
You will not see the sorrow of no time. No Time. Terence Tiller. NeBP
You will print such books as these! A Warning. Heine. PoFr
You Will Remember Me. Sotiris Skipis, *tr. fr. Modern Greek by* Rae Dalven. MoGP
You will remember that the Twelfth was always dry. The Glorious Twelfth. Robert Greacen. NeIP
You will remember the kisses, real or imagined. Resurrection. Kenneth Fearing. ChMo
You will sail the dancing Aegean, Messalla, without me. Tibullus. *Fr.* Elegies, I, 3. LaP
You with shooting-sticks and cases for field-glasses. W. H. Auden. *Fr.* The Dog beneath the Skin. NAMP
You with the smooth round belly, and lofty neck ascendant. My Lady Wine-Pot. *Unknown.* GrPE
You within Love. Norman McCaig. NeBP
You Wi'yam, come 'ere, sah, dis instance. Kentucky Philosophy. Harrison Robertson. BOHV; HBV; IHA; PTA-1
You wonder why Drab sells her love for gold? Epigram. J. V. Cunningham. NePoAm
You won't even die like a dog. Postscript. Raymond Souster. PeCV
You Work and Work. Samuel Hoffenstein. WhC
You would give your red lips to press. A Woman. Mary Dixon Thayer. HBMV
You would have scoffed if we had told you yesterday. To a Child in Death. Charlotte Mew. MBP; MoAB; MoBrPo; POTE; QS
You Would Have Understood Me. Ernest Dowson. EnLit; MBP; MoBrPo; PoVP
(Lyric: "You would have understood me.") HBV
You would say that the streets flow sweetly in the night. Angel-Nocturne. Xavier Villaurrutia. AnCL
You would think the fury of aerial bombardment. The Fury of Aerial Bombardment. Richard Eberhart. AmP; ExPo; HoPM; LiTA; MiAP; Po; UnPo (3d ed.); WaP
You wouldn't believe. All Hallow Eve. Carolyn Wells. DD
You wrong me, Strephon, when you say. Song. "Ephelia." DiM; LiTL
You wrote a line too much, my sage. Cynicus to W. Shakspeare. James Kenneth Stephen. *Fr.* Two Epigrams. BOHV; CenHV; WhC
You yacht on the Hudson. The Erie Canal Ballad. *Unknown.* ABF
You—you/ Your shadow is sunlight. In Excelsis. Amy Lowell. MAP; MoAmPo
You, you are all unloving, loveless, you. The Sea. D. H. Lawrence. NAMP; POTE
You'd have men's hearts up from the dust. Near Perigord. Ezra Pound. FaBoMo; LiTA; LiTM (rev. ed.)
You'd scarce expect one of my age. Tall Oaks from Little Acorns Grow [*or* The Boy Reciter]. David Everett. BLPA; FaFP; TreF
You'd think I'd hate the hills?—well, this life brings. A Hill-Woman. John Farrar. OnPP; TBM
Youghall Harbor. *Unknown, tr. fr. Modern Irish by* Sir Samuel Ferguson. OnYI
You'l marvel when I tell ye o. Loudon Hill, or, Drumclog. *Unknown.* ESPB
You'll come to our ball;—since we parted. Our Ball. Winthrop Mackworth Praed. *Fr.* Letters from Teignmouth. EnRP; TCEP
You'll find it when you come to die. Emily Dickinson. TwP
You'll find the road is long and rough, with soft spots far apart. Grantland Rice. *Fr.* Alumnus Football. TreFS
"You'll have a son," the old man said. Telling Fortunes. W. H. Davies. ChMo
You'll have an eight-cylinder car in heaven. For a Modernist Sermon. Kenneth Burke. QS
You'll Know Love. F. T. Macartney. MoAuPo
You'll Love Me Yet! Robert Browning. *Fr.* Pippa Passes, sc. iii. BMEP; EPN; EV-5; HoPM; LoPo; OBEV (1st ed.)
(Song: "You'll love me yet!") HBV
You'll Travel Far and Wide. Sir Gilbert Parker. CPG
You'll wait a long, long time for anything much. On Looking Up by Chance at the Constellations. Robert Frost. ChMo; CMP; NePA; NP
Young Acacia, The. Hayyim Nahman Bialik, *tr. fr. Hebrew by* Helena Frank. TrJP
Young Allan. *Unknown.* BaBo; ESPB
Young America. Carolyn Wells. DD
Young and already satisfied. To a Careful Young Man. John Holmes. CAG
Young and in love—how magical the phrase! Alice Duer Miller. *Fr.* The White Cliffs. MaRV
Young and Old. Thomas Campion. PoP
("Though you are young, and I am old.") OBSC
Young and Old. Charles Kingsley. *Fr.* The Water Babies, *ch.* 2. AlDL; EV-5; FaBoBe; FaFP; FAOV; GTBS; GTBS-W; GTSL; HBV; InP; LiTG; MCCG; OTPC; PoMa; PoVP; SiTL; TreF; TSW; TSWC
(Old, Old Song, The.) BTP; MaRV; PYM
(Old Song, The.) NeHB; OBVV; PFE; PG; TOP; WaKn
(When All the World Is Young, Lad.) BBV (1923 ed.); BoTP; LiTL; ViBoPo
Young and Simple though I Am. Thomas Campion. EnL; FaBoEn; SeCeV; TuPP
Young and trusting, blithe and fair. Surrender. Ruth Guthrie Harding. HBMV
Young Andrew. *Unknown.* ESPB; OBB, *sl. diff.*
Young Apollo, golden-haired, A. Quatrain. Frances Cornford. WhC
Young as the youngest who donned the gray. The Southern Soldier Boy. Abram Joseph Ryan. BlG
Young Astronomer, The. Plato, *tr. fr. Greek by* F. L. Lucas. GrPE; GrR
Young Astronomer Dead, The. Plato, *tr. fr. Greek by* F. L. Lucas. GrPE; GrR
Young at his father's fire. Fathers and Sons. *Unknown.* KiLC
Young Bacon-nibbler, Cat of cats. The Rats Hold Council. La Fontaine. TrFP
Young Bearwell. *Unknown.* ESPB
Young Beichan (*diff. versions*). *Unknown.* BaBo (A *and* B *vers.*); EnSB; ESPB (A *and* C *vers.*); LoEn; OBB; ViBoFo
(Lord Bayham, *American vers.*) ABS
(Lord Beichan and Susie Pye.) GN
(Loving Ballad of Lord Bateman, The.) BeLS; BLPA; CoBE; OBB
(Turkish Lady, The.) BaBo; MaC
(Young Beichan and Susie Pye.) HBV
(Young Bekie.) FaBoCh; OBB
Young Ben he was a nice young man. Faithless Sally Brown. Thomas Hood. BEL; BOHV; ERP; HBV; LPS-3; TreFS
Young Benjie. *Unknown.* BaBo; EBSV; OBB, *abr.*
Young Billy Crane, *with music.* Larry Gorman. ShS
Young Birch, A. Robert Frost. LiTA
Young Blood. Lloyd Roberts. CPG
Young Boy, A. Jessica Nelson North. NP
Young Bride, A. Sappho. *See* One Girl.
Young Bride, The. *Unknown, tr. fr. Greek by* F. L. Lucas. GrPE
(Girl's Treasures, A, *tr. by* Lord Neaves.) OnPM
Young Bride's Dream, The. Rhoda Coghill. OxBI
Young Calidore is paddling o'er the lake. Calidore. Keats. EmBrPo
Young Calves, The. Robert P. Tristram Coffin. StVeCh (1955 ed.); TiPo
Young Canada; or, Jack's as Good as His Master. Alexander McLachlan. BoCaPo
Young Carpenter, The. Al-Rusafi, *tr. fr. Arabic by* A. J. Arberry. MooP
Young Charlotte. Seba Smith, *wr. at. to* William Lorenzo Carter. ABS; APW; BaBo; LoEn
(Frozen Girl, The.) AS, *with music;* IHA
(Young Charlottie.) BeLS; BLPA; CoSo, *with music;* CSF

Young child, Christ, is straight and wise, The. Child. Carl Sandburg. NV; OQP; QP-1; StJW
Young Colin Clout, a lad of peerless meed. The Ditty. John Gay. *Fr.* The Shepherd's Week. LoBV
Young Companions. *Unknown.* CoSo, *with music*; CSF
Young Coridon and Phillis. *At. to* Sir Charles Sedley. CoMu
Young Couple. Arthur Rimbaud, *tr. fr. French by* Louise Varèse. AnFP
Young Cupid strung his bow one day. Cupid at Court. Samuel Minturn Peck. PR
Young Dandelion, The ("I am a bold fellow"). Dinah Maria Mulock Craik. DD; GoTP; MPB; NLK
Young Dandelion ("Young Dandelion/ On a hedge-side"). Dinah Maria Mulock Craik. PRWS
Young Danneved and Swain Trust. *Unknown, tr. fr. Danish by* E. M. Smith-Dampier. BoDaBa
Young Davie's Song. Paul Green. *Fr.* Tread the Green Grass. NoCaPo
Young Dead, The. Struthers Burt. AOAH
Young Dead, The. Edith Wharton. AOAH
Young Dead Soldiers, The. Archibald MacLeish. MaRV; WaP
Young Dead Speak, The. Sister Mary Irma. JKCP (1955 ed.)
Young Death. Christina Rossetti. EmBrPo
Young deer lost on the mountain, A. Horace. Odes, I, 23. LaP
Young Democracy. Bernard O'Dowd. BoAu
Young Dove, The. Moses ibn Ezra, *tr. fr. Hebrew by* Solomon Solis-Cohen. TrJP
Young drunkards reeling, bayliffs dogging. In a London Street. Edward Ward. *Fr.* Hudibras Redivivus. BeR
Young Earl of Essex's Victory over the Emperor of Germany, The. *Unknown.* ESPB
Young Edwin in the Lowlands Low (A *and* B *vers.*). *Unknown.* BaBo
Young Endymion sleeps Endymion's sleep, The. Keats. Longfellow. AmP; IAP; MOAP
Young Engel. *Unknown, tr. fr. Danish by* E. M. Smith-Dampier. BoDaBa
Young Fellow My Lad. Robert W. Service. CV
Young Fellow Named Sydney, A. *Unknown. See* Limerick: "There was a young fellow named Sydney."
Young Firwood, A. Dante Gabriel Rossetti. GN; PoRL
Young folks, old folks, everybody come. Bible Stories. *Unknown.* LiTG
Young Forbest, *with music. Unknown.* ShS
Young Forest, The. "Demyan Bedny," *tr. fr. Russian by* Babette Deutsch. TrRV
"Young friend," 'e sez . . . Young friend! Well, spare me days! Pilot Cove. C. J. Dennis. WhC
"Young, gay, and fortunate!" Each yields a theme. Narcissa. Edward Young. *Fr.* Night Thoughts. LPS-1
Young Gazelle, The. Walter Parke. BOHV
Young Girl. Einar Solstad, *tr. fr. Norwegian by* Charles W. Stork. AnNoLy
Young girl dancing lifts her face, The. The Dancer. W. J. Turner. OBMV; POTE
Young girl of thirteen, A. The Cloak. Violet Anderson. CaP
Young girl stood beside me, The. The Orange Tree. John Shaw Neilson. BoAV; MoAuPo; NeLNL
Young girl, The, questions: "Whether were it better." Wisdom. Ford Madox Ford. HBV
Young girl, your heart prefers silence with us. Beauties Arouse Love. André Chénier. LiA
Young girls have gone down to the river, The. Prose Poem: By the River. Judith Gautier. OnPM
Young girls, if you'll listen. Pearl Bryan. *Unknown.* ViBoFo
Young Girl's Song, The. Vilhelm Krag, *tr. fr. Norwegian by* Charles W. Stork. AnNoLy
Young Girl's Song. *Unknown. See* Maidens Came, The.
Young Girl's Tomb, A. Rainer Maria Rilke, *tr. fr. German by* Vernon Watkins. AnGP
Young grass burnt up, so hot the air was, The. In the Field. Harold Lenoir Davis. NP
Young Gray Head, The. Caroline Anne Bowles. BeLS; LPS-3
Young head in sunlight! Not a woman born. No Woman Born. Robert Farren. OxBI
Young Helen's beauty has its source. Helen of Laughing Ledge. Robert Haven Schauffler. TCAP
Young Henry was as brave a youth. Love and Glory. Thomas Dibdin. CG
Young Hero, The. Tyrtaeus. *See* Pro Patria.
Young Hodge met Mog the miller's maid. Don't Be Foolish Pray. *Unknown.* CoMu
Young Hunting (*diff. versions*). *Unknown.* BaBo (A *vers.*); ESPB (3 *vers.*); OBB; OxBoLi; ViBoFo (Loving Henry, B *vers.*) BaBo
Young, I was unacquainted with sorrow. To the Tune of "The Ugly Slave." Hsin Ch'i-chi. WhP
Young is she, and slight to view. Dorothea. Sarah N. Cleghorn. HBMV
Young Janie was a strappin' lass. The Thocht. William Soutar. NeBP
Young Japanese son was in love with a servant boy, The. Dream Data. Robert Duncan. NeAP
Young Jemmy is a lad. England's Darling; or, Great Britain's Joy and Hope on That Noble Prince James, Duke of Monmouth. *Unknown.* CoMu
Young Jenny. John Clare. EnSW; ERP
Young Jesus. Leslie Savage Clark. ChIP
Young Jockey he courted sweet Mog the brunette. Mog the Brunette. *Unknown.* CoMu
Young John. *Unknown. See* False Lover Won Back, The.
Young Johnstone. *Unknown.* BaBo; ESPB
Young Kentucky. Jesse Stuart. SPP
Young Lady Named Bright, A. *Unknown, at. to* Arthur Buller. *See* Limerick: "There was a young lady named Bright."
Young lady of fair Mytilene, A. Limerick. *Unknown.* CenHV
Young Lady of Lynn, The. *Unknown. See* Limerick: "There was a young lady of Lynn/ Who was so exceedingly thin."
Young Lady of Niger, The. *Unknown. See* Limerick: "There was a young lady of Niger."
Young Lady of Norway, A. Edward Lear. *See* Limerick: "There was a young lady of Norway."
Young Lady of Spain, A. *Unknown. See* Limerick: "There was a young lady of Spain."
Young lady shows like a thing of light, The. A Morning Shower. J. S. Ling. ChLP
Young Lady, Whose Bonnet, A. Edward Lear. *See* Limerick: "There was a young lady whose bonnet."
Young Laird and Edinburgh Katy, The. Allan Ramsay. CEP; EiPP
Young Lambs. John Clare. GoTP; TrGrPo
Young lambs to sell! Mother Goose. OTPC
Young Lincoln. Edwin Markham. DD; GA; OHIP; OQP; PEDC; QP-2
Young Linnets, The. Ann Hawkshaw. OTPC
Young Lochinvar. Sir Walter Scott. *See* Lochinvar.
Young Lochinvar; the True Story in Blank Verse. *Unknown, at. to* J. J. Fay. BOHV; FiBHP; InMe; PA
Young lords o the north country, The. Lady Maisry. *Unknown.* BaBo (A *vers.*); ESPB; OBB; ViBoFo
Young Love. Lloyd Frankenberg. TwAmPo
Young Love. Andrew Marvell. EV-2
Young Love. Gerald Massey. OBVV
Young Love. Shakespeare. *See* Tell Me Where Is Fancy Bred.
Young Love lies sleeping. Dream-Love. Christina Rossetti. CH; GTBS-D; GTML; GTSL; MBP; PoEL-5
Young Love Storms like New Wine. "Angelus Silesius," *tr. fr. German by* Paul Carus. OnPM
Young love walks the countryside. Willow Whistles. Grace Noll Crowell. LS
Young Love, when tender mood beset him. L'Amour sans Ailes. Charles Fenno Hoffman. PR
Young Lovers, The. Ridgely Torrence. *Fr.* The House of a Hundred Lights. AA
Young McFee. *Unknown.* ABS
Young Man, A. André Chénier, *tr. fr. French by* Alan Conder. TrFP
Young man,/ Seize every minute. The Frost. Tzu Yeh. PoHN
Young man—/ Young man. The Prodigal Son. James Weldon Johnson. StJW
Young man, despite your hurry, mark this little stone's. His Own Epitaph. Pacuvius. LaP
Young man growing old, an old man aging, A. Cuban Voyage. Paul Engle. ReMP
Young Man in a Galilean Doorway. Herbert D. Gallaudet. ChIP
Young man lately in our town, A. The Maids Conjuring Book. *Unknown.* CoMu
Young man, methinks it has not dawned upon your mind. Defilement Cometh from Within. Menander. GrR
Young man on a journey had met her, A. Limerick. *Unknown.* LiBL
Young man once was sitting, A. Popular Ballad: "Never Forget Your Parents." Franklin P. Adams. BOHV
Young Man Thinks of Sons, The. R. A. K. Mason. AnNZ
Young Man Waited, The. Edmund Vance Cooke. PTA-1
Young man, you hold your head. Advice to a Young Romanticist. Allen Tate. TBM
Young Man's Exhortation, A. Thomas Hardy. ViPP
Young Man's Fancy, A. John Masefield. *See* Third Mate.
Young Man's Fancy. Ray Mathew. BoAV
Young Man's Song, A. William Bell. FaBoTw; NePoEA
Young Mary, loitering once her garden way. Mary and Gabriel. Rupert Brooke. ISi
Young May Moon, The. Thomas Moore. EnRP; EV-4; HBV; LEAP; OAEP; OBEV
Young men and maids, pray lend attention. The Silver Dagger. *Unknown.* BaBo
Young men and maids, pray tell your age. Locks and Bolts. *Unknown.* TrAS

Young men, The, come less often—isn't it so? Horace. Odes, I, 25. LaP
Young men dancing, and the old. Youthful Age. Thomas Stanley. AWP; JAWP; WBP
Young men die in battle, The. Scapegoats. Eleanor D. Breed. MaRV; PGD
Young men flash a brittle blade, The. The Old Men and the Young Men. Clement Wood. BAP
Young men give ear to me a while. The Maid's Complaint for Want of a Dil Doul. *Unknown.* CoMu
Young men go walking in the woods. The Pediment of Appearance. Wallace Stevens. Po
Young men have all the luck! The Girls' Lot. Agathias Scholasticus. OxBG
Young men walking the open streets. Remember Your Lovers. Sidney Keyes. WaP
Young men will love thee more fair and more fast. David Gellatley's Song. Sir Walter Scott. *Fr.* Waverley, *ch.* 14. BSV
Young Mistah Rooster Man planted him a gyarden. Miss Hen. Booth Lowrey. IHA
Young Molly Bawn. *Unknown.* OnYI
Young Molly, who lived at the foot of the hill. The Lass with the Delicate Air. Michael Arne. OlF
Young Monroe at Gerry's Rock. *Unknown. See* Jam on Gerry's Rock, The.
Young moon is white, The. A Japanese Love-Song. Alfred Noyes. LEAP; OBVV
Young Moses, The. Don Marquis. QS
Young Mother, A. Dioscorides, *tr. fr. Greek by* George Allen. OxBG
Young Mother, The. Lizette Woodworth Reese. LS; MOAP
Young Mouse, The. Jefferys Taylor. OnHT; OTPC (1923 ed.)
Young Mouse, A, small and innocent. The Old Cat and the Young Mouse. La Fontaine. CIV
Young Mystic, The. Louis Untermeyer. TSW; TSWC
Young Neophyte, The. Alice Meynell. ACP; CAW; GoBC
Young Night Thought. Robert Louis Stevenson. GaP; NeHB; RIS
Young Nun. Grace Noll Crowell. PraNu
Young oak greets thee at the water's edge, The. To the Connecticut River. John G. C. Brainard. APW
Young Paris. George Crabbe. *Fr.* Posthumous Tales. OBRV
Young Peach Trees, The. *Unknown, tr. fr. Chinese.* WhP
Young Peggy. *Unknown.* BaBo; ESPB
Young people in the bus began to sing. Girls and Soldiers Singing. Leonard Mann. BoAu
Young people who delight in sin. Wicked Polly. *Unknown.* ABF; ABS
Young Philosopher and His Friends, The. Félix María de Samaniego, *tr. fr. Spanish by* Lillian Resnick. AnSpL-2
Young Pilgrim, The. Ibn Faddal, *tr. fr. Arabic by* A. J. Arberry. MooP
Young Pithy, from your Djetis bed. Lines to Homo Somejerktensis. Earnest A. Hooton. WhC
Young Poet. Myron O'Higgins. PoNe
Young Priest to His Hands, The. Edward F. Garesché. CAW
Young Prince Peter suddenly, once. Prince Peter. Nancy Byrd Turner. GaP; RIS
Young Provincial, The. Michalis Stasinopoulos, *tr. fr. Modern Greek by* Rae Dalven. MoGP
Young Randal. Robert W. Chambers. EBSV
Young Reaper, The. Aleksey Koltsov, *tr. fr. Russian.* BoRS, *tr. by* C. M. Bowra; WoL, *tr. by* C. Fillingham Coxwell
Young Reynard. George Meredith. HoPM
Young Roger came tapping at Dolly's window. Roger and Dolly. Henry Carey. CoMu; OxNR, *st.* 1
Young Roger the miller, who courted of late. My Father's Gray Mare. *Unknown.* ABS
Young Romilly through Barden Woods. The Founding of Bolton Priory. Wordsworth. OTPC
Young Ronald. *Unknown.* ESPB
Young Rory O'More courted Kathleen Bawn. Rory O'More. Samuel Lover. BOHV; HBV; LPS-1; TIP; VA
Young Sea. Carl Sandburg. NLK (1947 ed.)
Young shepherd, turn aside and move. Melisea, Her Song in Scorn of Her Shepherd Narcissus. Jorge de Montemayor, *tr. by* Bartholomew Young. *Fr.* Diana. TuPP
Young Silas Long, a carrier through these woods. Two Sonnets. Frederick Goddard Tuckerman. OnAP
Young Silvia. —— De la Sale. SeCL
Young Sir Guyon proudly said. Queen's Song. Stopford Brooke. *Fr.* Riquet of the Tuft. VA
Young skull which the wind scrapes, which the sand. On the Relative Merit of Friend and Foe, Being Dead. Donald Thompson. WaP
Young Soldier, The. Wilfred Owen. BLV
Young soul, put off your flesh, and come. Thomas Lovell Beddoes. *Fr.* The Phantom-Wooer. PoD
Young Sten, all fear defying. A Song of Sten Sture. Edvard Bäckström. AnSL
Young sugar maples in a row. The Farm, 1800. Archibald MacLeish. ChMo; CMP
Young Svejdal. *Unknown, tr. fr. Danish by* E. M. Smith-Dampier. BoDaBa
Young Svend Dyre. *Unknown, tr. fr. Danish by* E. M. Smith-Dampier. BoDaBa
Young Tarentine, The. André Chénier, *tr. fr. French by* William Frederic Giese. LiA
Young Thing, The. *Unknown.* MeMeAg; RIS
Young thing in spring green slippers, A. Whiffs of the Ohio River at Cincinnati. Carl Sandburg. MOAP
Young things who frequent picture-palaces, The. The Jung Idea. "P. H." SiTL
Young Thyrsis with sighs often tells me his tale. A Song. Thomas Godfrey. IAP
Young to the end through sympathy with youth. James McCosh. Robert Bridges. AA
Young Warrior. George Edward Hoffman. ChIP
Young was Inge the maid. The Maiden at the Thing. *Unknown.* BoDaBa
Young was the woman. A Maiden Ring-adorned. Cynewulf. *Fr.* Christ. ISi
Young Washington. Arthur Guiterman. FaPON; MPB; OHIP
Young Waters. *Unknown.* EBSV; EnLit; ESPB; OBB; ReaPo; TOP
Young Widow, The. La Fontaine, *tr. fr. French by* Alan Conder. TrFP
Young Wife, A. D. H. Lawrence. ChMP; MBP; MoBrPo
Young Wife, The. Wang Ts'ang-ling, *tr. fr. Chinese.* WhP
Young Windebank. Margaret L. Woods. HBV; HBVY; VA
Young Witch, The—1698. George Sterling. BAP
Young Woman. Chaucer. *Fr.* The Canterbury Tales: The Miller's Tale. BoW
Young Woman. Howard Nemerov. FiMAP
Young Woman at a Window. Mark Van Doren. LiTA; MoPo; MoVE
Young Woman's Blues. *Unknown.* OnAP
Young women in their April moodiness. The True Weather for Women. Louis Simpson. NePoAm
Younger [*or* Snorra *or* Prose] Edda, The, *sel.* Snorri Sturluson, *tr. fr. Icelandic by* Arthur Gilchrist Brodeur. Frothi's Meal: The Lay of Grotti. *Unknown.* PaOS
Younger Van Eyck, The. E. C. Bentley. *Fr.* Biography for Beginners. FiBHP
Youngest of all three took her white hand, The. Blanche comme la neige. *Unknown.* OuSiCo
Youngster's 'mighty lucky, A. Dad 'n' Me. Stuart N. Lake. FAOV
Youpe! Youpe! River Along. *Unknown.* IHA
Your bark lies anchored in the peaceful bight. To W. P., III. George Santayana. BAP
Your Beauty and My Reason. *Unknown.* TrGrPo
("Like two proud armies marching in the field.") OBSC
Your beauty bids my spirit fare. My Songs. George Sterling. MuM
Your beauty is as timeless as the earth. Her Pedigree. Arthur Davison Ficke. Sonnets of a Portrait Painter, IX. HBMV
Your beauty, ripe and calm and fresh. The Philosopher and the Lover [*or* To a Mistress Dying]. Sir William Davenant. ACP; ElSeCe; FaBoEn; GoBC; LO; MePo; OBEV; PoD
Your birthday I wished to observe with a gift. To Quintus. Martial. RoL
Your body derns. Scunner. "Hugh MacDiarmid." FaBoTw
Your Body Drifting. Iwan Goll, *tr. fr. French by* Iwan Goll. OnPM
Your Body Is Stars. Stephen Spender. ChMo; FaBoTw
Your body's motion is like music. Like Music. John Hall Wheelock. NP
Your bony head, Jazbo, O dock walloper. Singing Nigger. Carl Sandburg. OnAP
Your bow swept over a string, and a long low note quivered to the air. Jan Kubelik. Carl Sandburg. NP
Your boy and my boy. Your Cross and My Cross. Emma Finty Cox. PEDC
Your brother has a falcon. Christina Rossetti. *Fr.* Sing-Song. EmBrPo
Your brother is a forfeit of the law. Mercy. Shakespeare. *Fr.* Measure for Measure, II, ii. EV-1
Your carol is a dewy, fragrant bloom that grows. Poet to Bird. Ralph Cheyney. BLA
Your cello was my voice and yours ascending. My Brother Played. Charles Ballard. MuM
Your Chase Had a Beast in View. John Peale Bishop. LiTA
Your cheeks were oh how fair. The Sprouting Beard. Al-Isra'ili. MooP
Your children are not your children. On Children. Kahlil Gibran. *Fr.* The Prophet. PoToHe (new ed.)
Your Church and Mine. Phillips H. Lord. BLPA; MaRV
Your Citron, Sir, who formerly would sleep. The Abandoned Dog. Théodore Agrippa d'Aubigné. BoFr

Your comedy I've read, my friend. To a Living Author. *Unknown.* SiTL
Your court contains. Riposte. Nazhun. MooP
Your courtiers scorn we country clowns. A Ballad of the Courtier and the Country Clown. *Unknown.* CoMu
Your Cross and My Cross. Emma Finty Cox. PEDC
Your Dad. Strickland Gillilan. FAOV
Your Death. Takamoto, *tr. fr. Japanese by* Lois J. Erickson. SoLD
Your door is shut against my tightened face. White Houses. Claude McKay. PoNe
Your downcast, harlequin, defenceless face. Lynched Negro. Maxwell Bodenheim. PoNe
Your dream/ Is beyond the horizon of peaks. The Frog. Shimpei Kusano. PoLJ
Your dream had left me numb and cold. Salutation. "Æ." OnYI
Your dusky shadow at the window lingers. Morning and Evening. Antoni Slonimski. TrJP
Your eyen [*or* yen] two wol slee me sodenly [*or* will slay me suddenly]. Merciles Beaute [*or* Captivity *or* Roundel]. Chaucer. ACP; AEV; AtBAP; CaAE; CoEV; EnLi-1 (1949 ed.); EnLoPo; LEAP; LiA; OBEV (1st ed.); OnPM; TrGrPo
Your eyes/ join hands. Nativity. "Martín Adán." AnCL
Your eyes and the valley are memories. Valley Song. Carl Sandburg. SBMV
Your eyes are sea-blue, and they hold. For a Very Little Boy. Edmund Leamy. FAOV
Your eyes are to-night so unusually thoughtful and sad. The Giraffe. Nikolai Gumilev. BoRS; LiTW
Your eyes drink of me. The Mystery. Sara Teasdale. HBMV
Your eyes of infinite kindness meeting mine. I Visit Carmel. Sister Mary Madeleva. PraNu
Your eyes open. Nothing. Barrie Reid. BoAV
Your eyes rejoiced in colour's ecstasy. Rupert Brooke, III. W. W. Gibson. PtP
Your eyes were made for laughter. Don't. James Jeffrey Roche. HBV
Your Face. Hugo von Hofmannsthal, *tr. fr. German by* Michael Hamburger. AnGP
Your face is stencilled with a pensiveness. Country Girl. Maxwell Bodenheim. MOAP
Your face was lifted to the golden sky. Rupert Brooke, I. W. W. Gibson. HBMV; POTT; PtOT; PtP
Your face was wholly laden down with dreams. Your Face. Hugo von Hofmannsthal. AnGP
Your Father Knoweth. *Unknown. See* God Knoweth Best.
Your feet tread no rhythms of the dance! The Reply. Sister Monica. PraNu
Your fine promises. Fujiwara no Mototoshi, *tr. fr. Japanese by* Kenneth Rexroth. OnPJ
Your Flag and My Flag. Wilbur D. Nesbit. FaFP; OnHT; OQP; PEDC; PoRL; PSO; QP-1; WBLP (Song of Our Flag, A.) PTA-1
Your flame nods. The Song of the Candle. Li Shih-ming. PoHN
Your friend is bidding you. The Party. Ibn al-Qabturnu. MooP
Your friends shall be the tall wind. For a Child. Fannie Stearns Davis. FaPON; MPB
Your ghost will walk, you lover of trees. "De Gustibus." Robert Browning. BPN; EmBrPo; EPN; GEPC; HBV; OAEP; PoVP; ReTS; VA; ViPo; VLEP
Your Gifts. DuBose Heyward. LS
Your glance is dark and your cheek is pale. At the End of Play. Bertel Gripenberg. AnSL
Your Glory, Lincoln. Mae Winkler Goodman. PGD
Your grieving moonlight face looks down. Reproach. Robert Graves. GTML; GTSL
Your hair has turned white. Hitomaro, *tr. fr. Japanese by* Kenneth Rexroth. LiTW; OnPJ
Your Hands. Ernest Dowson. LoPo (Ad Manus Puellae.) LoPS
Your Hands. Angelina Weld Grimké. CDC
Your hands lie open in the long fresh grass. Silent Noon. Dante Gabriel Rossetti. The House of Life, XIX. BEL; BLV; BoLiVe; BPN; EmBrPo; EnLi-2; EnLit; EPN; GTBS-D; HBV; LiTL; LO; LoPo; LoPS; OAEP; PIAE; PoEL-5; POTT; PoVP; RiBV; TCEP; TrGrPo; TwHP; TyEnPo; ViP; ViPo; ViPP; VLEP; WHA
Your hands, my dear, adorable. The Chilterns. Rupert Brooke. MBP; MoBrPo; POTT
Your hay it is mow'd, and your corn is reap'd. Harvest Song [*or* Song]. Dryden. *Fr.* King Arthur. BeR; CEP; SeCV-2
Your head is steel cut into drooping lines. To a Friend. Maxwell Bodenheim. LEAP
Your heart has trembled to my tongue. Echoes, XIX. W. E. Henley. BPN
Your heart is a music-box, dearest! Song. Frances Sargent Osgood. AA
Your heart is fickle. Impromptu. Ch'iu T'ung. PoHN
Your heart trembles in the shadows, like a face. When the Tom-Tom Beats. Jacques Roumain. AnCL; PoNe
Your hearts are lifted up, your hearts. To Women. Laurence Binyon. CP
Your Highness will excuse me; I will give you. George Chapman. *Fr.* The Conspiracy of Charles, Duke of Byron, III, i. NBE
"Your horse is faint, my King, my Lord! your gallant horse is sick." The Lord of Butrago. *Unknown.* LPS-2
Your hot mouth on mine is good. By an Iris-Shadowed Pool. Mary Carolyn Davies. TBM
Your House. *Unknown.* PoToHe (new ed.)
Your House of Happiness. B. Y. Williams. MaRV
Your joy, in flight. To the Dead Butterfly. Eugenio Florit. AnCL
Your kiss lies on my face. The Kiss. Mary Carolyn Davies. *Fr.* A Girl's Songs. SBMV
Your kisses, and the way you curl. Leves Amores. Arthur Symons. AnEnPo
Your Lad, and My Lad. Randall Parrish. MC; PAH
Your learning, James, in classics and romance. Letter to a Teacher of English. Robert Hillyer. AnFE; CoAnAm; TwAmPo
Your leaves bound up compact and fair. To an Author. Philip Freneau. AmPP; CoBA; CoV; OxBA
Your letter does not move me. Der Brief, den du geschrieben. Heine, *tr. by* Louis Untermeyer. ALV
Your Letter, Lady, Came Too Late. W. S. Hawkins. *See* More Cruel than War.
Your life was of the order true. The King Who Died Young. Ibn al-Khabbaza. MooP
Your Little Hands. Samuel Hoffenstein. ALV; FiBHP; TrJP
Your little words. Pebbles. May Brinkley. DDA
Your lively look that pierces them. Old-Clothes Woman. Stéphane Mallarmé. AnFP
Your looks so often cast. Sir Thomas Wyatt. SiPS
Your love and pity doth the impression fill. Sonnets, CXII. Shakespeare. PeBoSo
Your love is dead, lady, your love is dead. Madrigal. R. S. Thomas. EnLoPo
Your love to me appears in doubtful signs. George Henry Boker. *Fr.* Sonnets. MOAP
Your love was like moonlight. Mother. Lola Ridge. NV
Your loveliness was like a wave. Spent Wave. John Hall Wheelock. LiTM (1946 ed.)
Your lovely fair did first invite. The Excuse. Robert Heath. SeCL
Your lyre became your voice. Search for Perfection. W. Wesley Trimpi. PtPa
Your maidenhead—you grudge it?—for what? Beyond Death's river. The Coy Mistress. Asclepiades. GrPE
Your majesty shall shortly have your wish. And Ride in Triumph. Christopher Marlowe. *Fr.* Tamburlaine the Great, Pt. I. WHA
Your master grieved as though you'd savaged him. The Cat and the Partridge. Damocharis the Grammarian. PoC
Your milk-white maiden gown. The Maiden Gown. William Cavendish, Duke of Newcastle. SeCL
Your mind and you are our Sargasso Sea. Portrait d'une Femme. Ezra Pound. AnAmPo; APA; CoAnAm; HBMV; LA; MAP; MoAB; MoAmPo; MoVE; PoFS; ReaPo; TwAmPo
"Your mind is far, however light." Grandmother and Grandson. Hugo von Hofmannsthal. TwGV
Your Mission. Ellen M. Huntington Gates. BLPA; BLRP; NeHB; PTA-1
Your Mouth. Jenab Shehabuddin, *tr. fr. Turkish by* E. Powys Mathers. LiTW
Your name comes slowly like modest music. Mother. Carlos Oquendo de Amat. AnCL
"Your name is Achilles Deatheridge?" Achilles Deatheridge. Edgar Lee Masters. MaC; PoMa
Your Neighbor. H. Howard Biggar. PoToHe
Your neighbor, sir, whose roses you admire. My Neighbor's Reply. *Unknown.* PoToHe
Your northern grasses are as blue as jade. In Spring. Li Po. LiTW
Your old man's a sailor, I suppose? Cabin-Kid. Tristan Corbière. AnFP
Your Own Version. Paul Gilbert. BLRP; MaRV
Your park's like a gothic cathedral to me. To Madame la Duchesse de Bauffremont. Louis Morpeau. PoNe
Your peevish voice remarked "Oh, rats." To an Unknown Neighbor at the Circus. Rosemary Benét. InMe
Your pets, we know/ are so-called "dumb." The Home Brunt. Kay Riley. AlBD
Your piano is the better instrument. More Letters Found near a Suicide. Frank Horne. BANP
Your Place. John Oxenham. BLRP; MaRV; OQP; QP-2
Your plan I love not; with a number you. The Alms House. George Crabbe. *Fr.* The Borough. LO; NBE
Your Pleasures Spring like Daisies. Walter Savage Landor. *See* Ianthe: "From you, Ianthe, little troubles pass."

Your pocket-handkerchief is large enough. Metaphysical Poem. Maxwell Bodenheim. AnAmPo; LA; MOAP
Your poem must eternal be. An Eternal Poem. Samuel Taylor Coleridge. BOHV
Your Power. Spenser. *See* Amoretti, VIII.
Your Prayers. *Unknown.* PraP
Your proud eyes give me their wearied splendour. Disillusion. William Wilkins. TIP
Your radiance was the little light you had. Brief as the Snow. Gertrude MacGregor Moffat. CPG
Your rondeau's tale must still be light. The Rondeau. Don Marquis. PFE
Your Sanctuary. Walter Lyman French. MaRV
Your Shining Eyes. *Unknown.* ElSeCe; TuPP
Your silhouette against the dappled sky. Silhouette. Kathleen Hewitt. DiM
Your Sisters. Karl Asplund, *tr. fr. Swedish by* Charles W. Stork. AnSL
Your skill has fashioned stately creeds. The Lost Christ. Thomas Curtis Clark. ChIP; OQP; QP-2
Your sky is [a] hard and [a] dazzling blue. In Spain [*or* Spain]. Emily Lawless. AnIV; TIP
Your sloping forehead, your slender throat. To a Silhouette. Hans Hartvig Seedorff Pedersen. BoDS
Your smiles are not, as other women's be [*or* bee]. To the Lady May. Aurelian Townsend. MePo; SeCL; SeEP
Your smiling, or the hope, the thought of it. A Simile for Her Smile. Richard Wilbur. FiMAP; HoPM; MiAP
Your Songs. Gwendolyn B. Bennett. CDC
Your soul is a landscape rare. Moonlight. Paul Verlaine, *tr. by* Muriel Kittel. AnFP
Your soul is a sealed garden. Clair de lune. Paul Verlaine, *tr. by* Arthur Symons. AWP; LiA
Your soul is like a dove in flight. Bright Spirit. Josephine Royle. BAP
Your soul was lifted by the wings today. God Needs Antonio. "George Eliot." GrCo-2
Your soul's a charméd landscape wherein go. Moonlight. Paul Verlaine, *tr. by* Alan Conder. TrFP
Your spires are needles. Church. Gilberto González y Contreras. AnCL
Your steps, children of my still hours. The Steps. Paul Valéry. ReMP
Your swarthy, Grecian owner placed you there. To a Cafeteria Rubber-Plant. Philip Wrenn. CAG
Your Tears. Edwin Markham. BoFr; HBMV; TBM
Your Teeth. Ramón López Velarde, *tr. fr. Spanish by* Samuel Beckett. AnMP
Your thighs are appletrees. Portrait of a Lady. William Carlos Williams. OxBA
Your thoughts must be the sea-flowers. Sea-Flowers. Dorothy Livesay. OCL
Your threats how vain, Corregidor. A Ballad of Manila Bay. Sir Charles G. D. Roberts. GA; PAH
Your thunderous dirges strike a chord in me. The Sea. Ignace M. Ingianni. MuM
Your tiny picture makes me yearn. Christie's Portrait. Gerald Massey. VA
Your touch is a torch. Hardest It Is. F. R. Scott. BoCaPo (1943 ed.)
Your trail runs to the Westward. To James Whitcomb Riley. Kipling. YT
Your triolet should glimmer. The Triolet. Don Marquis. PFE
Your two great eyes will slay me suddenly. A Rondel of Merciless Beauty. Chaucer, *mod. by* Louis Untermeyer. TrGrPo
Your ugly token. Upon a Dead Man's Head [*or* The Gift of a Skull]. John Skelton. ACP; CoBE; ReIE; SeCePo; SiCE; UnPo (1st ed.)
Your verses, dear friend, I surmise. Limerick. *Unknown.* LiBL
Your Victory, *sel.* Margarita Aliger, *tr. fr. Russian by* Babette Deutsch.
Epilogue: "And lo! it shines upon the cities." TrRV
Your villa, Furius, is not placed. Cold Blast of Debt. Catullus. OnPM
Your voice is like bells over roofs at dawn. Prime. Amy Lowell. VOD
Your voice is the color of a robin's breast. To O. E. A. Claude McKay. BANP; PoNe
Your voice speaks:/ Little child out of Eternity. Christmas. Gertrude von Le Fort. ISi
Your voice speaks:/ The angel of the Lord came in unto Mary. Vigil of the Assumption. Gertrude von Le Fort. ISi
Your voice was the rugged. The Meeting of Sighs. Blanche Edith Baughan. BoAu
Your walk is lonely, blue-eyed Grace. Grace and Her Friends. Lucy Larcom. TVSH
Your wedding-ring wears thin, dear wife; ah, summers not a few. The Worn Wedding-Ring. William Cox Bennett. LPS-1
Your will is done. Its promise, that I fled. Oedipus to the Oracle. Wesley Trimpi. NePoEA
Your words came just when needed. Accept My Full Heart's Thanks. Ella Wheeler Wilcox. PoToHe
Your words dropped into my heart like pebbles into a pool. Absence. Claude McKay. CDC
Your words, my friend (right healthful caustics), blame. Astrophel and Stella, XXI. Sir Philip Sidney. PeBoSo; ReEn; ReIE; SiCE; SiPS; TuPP
Your yen two wol slee me sodenly. *See* Your eyen two wol slee me sodenly.
Your youth is like a water-wetted stone. Susan to Diana. Frances Cornford. MoVE
You're a good girl; you're gray with virtue. Poems in Praise of Practically Nothing, IV. Samuel Hoffenstein. InMe
You're a poet. *Unknown.* FaFP; SiTL
You're a traitor convicted, you know very well! Jefferson D. H. S. Cornwell. PAH
"You're clever at drawing, I own." The Coquette. John Godfrey Saxe. PR
You're going to leave the homestead, John. Leaving the Homestead. *Unknown.* PTA-2
You're in my mind. To My Wife. James Forsyth. WaP
You're kind to women, children, worms. Poems in Praise of Practically Nothing. Samuel Hoffenstein. InMe
You're late to-night; you should have let me come with you. The Operation. W. W. Gibson. CP
Youre love if vertuous will shew forth some fruitts of devotion. *Unknown.* SeCSL
You're my friend. The Flight of the Duchess. Robert Browning. VLEP
You're not alone when you are still alone. Idea, XI [*or* Give Me My Self]. Michael Drayton. BLV; LiTL; LO; LoPS; TrGrPo
You're Old, Anacreon. *Unknown, tr. fr. Greek by* J. M. Edmonds. GrL
You're So Kind. Groucho Marx. SiTL
You're surprised that I ever should say so? Whistling in Heaven. *Unknown.* PTA-1
You're the cook's understudy. Slip-Shoe Lovey. Edgar Lee Masters. NP
You're the Top. Cole Porter. Po
You're twenty-one to-day, Willie. A Consistent Anti to Her Son. Alice Duer Miller. FAOV
You're very well polished, I'm free to confess. The Cowboy to His Friend in Need. Burke Jenkins. SCC
You're worse than snails, who vote the whole world vicious. The Cautious Householder. Anaxilas. OxBG
Yours are the tranquil ways. The World to Any Nun. Sister Mary Eleanore. PraNu
Yours is the face that the earth turns to me. Love Poem. Kathleen Raine. LiTB; LoPS; MoAB; MoPo; NeBP
Yours is the sullen sorrow. Last Words to Miriam. D. H. Lawrence. CoBMV
Yours was a wondrous story. To the Flag of Stars. Thomas Curtis Clark. PEDC
Yourself. Jones Very. AA; LBAP; NePA; OxBA; PoEL-4
You's as stiff an' as cold as a stone. The Dead Pussy Cat. *Unknown.* CIV; PTA-1
You's Sweet to Yo' Mammy Jes' de Same. James Weldon Johnson. BOL
Youssouf. James Russell Lowell. *See* Yussouf.
Youth. Katharine Lee Bates. PGD
Youth. Robert Browning. *See* Wild Joys of Living, The.
Youth. Preston Clark. HBMV
Youth. Virginia Woodward Cloud. AA
Youth, A. Stephen Crane. *See* Content.
Youth. Euripides, *tr. fr. Greek by* George Allen. *Fr.* Heracles. OxBG
(Youth of All Blessings Best, *shorter sel., tr. by* Arthur S. Way.) GrR
Youth. Bartholomew Griffin. *See* Sonnet: "I have not spent the April of my time."
Youth. Bertel Gripenberg, *tr. fr. Swedish by* Charles W. Stork. AnSL
Youth. Theresa Helburn. PFY
Youth. Langston Hughes. GoSl
Youth, The. Ibn Sara, *tr. fr. Arabic by* A. J. Arberry. MooP
Youth. Georgia Douglas Johnson. BANP; GoSl; PoNe
Youth. Thomas S. Jones, Jr. BAP; OQP; QP-2
Youth. George Cabot Lodge. AA
Youth. Keidrych Rhys. MoWP
Youth. Jessie B. Rittenhouse. HBMV
Youth. Blanaid Salkeld. OxBI
Youth. Aline Thomas. MBP
Youth. Tzu Yeh, *tr. fr. Chinese by* Henry H. Hart. ChLP
Youth. *Unknown.* OBSC
Youth. Thomas, Lord Vaux. EV-1
Youth. R. Wever. *See* In Youth Is Pleasure.
Youth and Age. George Arnold. EPN; HBV
Youth and Age. Ecclesiastes, Bible, *O.T.* *See* Remember Now Thy Creator.
Youth and Age. Robert Browning. *Fr.* Rabbi Ben Ezra. GrCo-2

Youth and Age. Byron. *See* Stanzas for Music: "There's not a joy . . ."

Youth and Age. Samuel Taylor Coleridge. BEL; BPN; EM-2; EmBrPo; EnLi-2 (1949 ed.); EnRP; ERP; EV-4; FiP; GTBS; GTBS-D; GTBS-W; GTSE; GTSL; HBV; LiA; OBEV; OBRV; ReTS; TCEP; TVSH

Youth and Age. Mimnermus, *tr. fr. Greek* by John Addington Symonds. AWP; OnPM

Youth and Age. Vance Palmer. BoAu; NeLNL

Youth and Age. Sappho, *tr. fr. Greek* by H. De Vere Stacpoole. GrR

Youth and Age. William Bell Scott. VA

Youth and Age. Shakespeare. *See* Crabbed Age and Youth.

Youth and Age. Earl of Surrey. *See* How No Age Is Content.

Youth and Age. Ridgely Torrence. *Fr.* The House of a Hundred Lights. AA

Youth and Age. W. B. Yeats. TwP

Youth and Age on Beaulieu River, Hants. John Betjeman. ChMP; FaBoTw

Youth and Art. Robert Browning. BOHV; BoLiVe; BPN; EmBrPo; EV-5; GEPC; HBV; MaPo; PoVP; VA; ViBoPo; ViPo; VLEP

Youth and Beauty. Aurelian Townsend. MePo

Youth and Calm. Matthew Arnold. BPN; EmBrPo; PoVP; VLEP

Youth and Cupid. Elizabeth I, Queen of England. *See* When I Was Fair and Young.

Youth and Death. E. Merrill Root. OQP; PSO; QP-1

Youth and Love. Robert Louis Stevenson. BMEP; PoeT

Youth and Maidenhood. Sarah Williams. OBVV

Youth and Maturity. Fulke Greville. *See* Nurse-Life Wheat within His Green Husk Growing, The.

Youth and the Northwind, The. John Godfrey Saxe. StPo

Youth Autumnal. Raymond Roseliep. JKCP (1955 ed.)

Youth, Day, Old Age, and Night. Walt Whitman. AnAmPo; LA; TCAP

Youth Dreams, The. Rainer Maria Rilke, *tr. fr. German* by Ludwig Lewisohn. AWP; JAWP; TrJP; WBP

Youth fades; love droops. Oliver Wendell Holmes. *Br. sel. fr.* A Mother's Secret. PoToHe (1941 ed.)

Youth gone, and beauty gone if ever there. Monna Innominata, XIV. Christina Rossetti. EmBrPo; ViBoPo; ViPo

Youth Grows Old, *sel.* Robert Nathan. He Thinks of the Friend of His Youth, and of His Rooms at College. BoFr

Youth had a man's heart, The; he was a man in the din of battle. The Lovely Youth. Aneirin. LiTW

Youth hath many charms. Youth and Age. George Arnold. EPN; HBV

Youth in Age. George Meredith. EmBrPo; PoVP; VLEP

Youth in apparel that glittered, A. The Black Riders, XXVII [or A Youth or Content]. Stephen Crane. AA; AnAmPo; LA; LEAP; LiTA; MoAmPo (1950 ed.); NePA

Youth in Arms. Harold Monro. BMEP; LEAP; NP-1

Youth in the Landscape, The. Hugo von Hofmannsthal, *tr. fr. German* by Vernon Watkins. AnGP

Youth Is Sweet and Well. Lorenzo de' Medici, *tr. fr. Italian* by Lorna de' Lucchi. WoL

Youth, large, lusty, loving—youth full of grace, force, fascination. Youth, Day, Old Age, and Night. Walt Whitman. AnAmPo; LA; TCAP

Youth, Love, and Death. Philip James Bailey. *Fr.* Festus. VA

Youth Mowing, A. D. H. Lawrence. MBP; MoAB; MoBrPo; TrGrPo

Youth now flees on feathered feet. To Will. H. Low. Robert Louis Stevenson. PoeT

Youth of All Blessings Best. Euripides. *See* Youth.

Youth of Nature, The. Matthew Arnold. BPN; EmBrPo; GEPC; PoVP; VLEP

Youth of the Mountain. Walter Hard. AnNE

Youth of the Year, The. Swinburne. *See* When the Hounds of Spring.

Youth rambles on life's arid mount. The Progress of Poesy. Matthew Arnold. EnL; PoVP; VLEP

Youth Rides Forth. Li Po, *tr. fr. Chinese* by Henry H. Hart. PoHN

Youth Seekers, The. Dorothy Brown Thompson. DDA

Youth Sings a Song of Rosebuds. Countee Cullen. BANP; CaAE; PoNe

Youth that rides the wildest horse. Youth and Age. Vance Palmer. BoAu; NeLNL

Youth! thou wear'st to manhood now. Life. Sir Walter Scott. *Fr.* The Abbot. BPN

Youth was there, of quiet ways, A. Longfellow. *Fr.* Tales of a Wayside Inn: Prelude, Pt. I. LEAP

Youth with [the] Red-gold Hair, The. Edith Sitwell. FaBoTw; MoVE

Youthful Age. Thomas Stanley, *after the Greek of* Anacreon. AWP; JAWP; WBP

Youthful and buoyant and blithe they went into battle.
The Look in Their Eyes. Robert Haven Schauffler. AOAH

Youthful mouse, not up to trap, A. The Cockerel, the Cat, and the Young Mouse. La Fontaine. WoL

Youth's Antiphony. Dante Gabriel Rossetti. The House of Life, XIII. BPN; PoVP; TOP; ViPo

Youth's bright palace. A Lament. Denis Florence MacCarthy. JKCP (1926 ed.); OBVV

Youth's Flight. Hermann Hesse, *tr. fr. German* by Herman Salinger. TwGV

Youth's for an hour. Beauty's a Flower. "Moira O'Neill." BMEP; MBP

Youth's Prayer, A. Mary S. Edgar. MaRV (Prayer-Poem, A.) BLRP

Youth's Prayer. George W. Wiseman. PraP

Youth's Progress. John Updike. FiBHP

Youth's Spring-Tribute. Dante Gabriel Rossetti. The House of Life, XIV. BPN; PoVP; REAL; ViPo; VLEP

Youth's Thankfulness. Edgar Daniel Kramer. PEDC; PGD

Youth's the season made for joys. Song. John Gay. *Fr.* The Beggar's Opera. CEP; EV-3; OBEC

You've all heard of Larry O'Toole. Larry O'Toole. Thackeray. ALV

You've been a wanderer, you! The Quest. Gladys Cromwell. AWP

You've bestowed a suburban farm on me, Sir. Martial, *tr. fr. Latin* by Robert R. Schnorr. Epigrams, XI, 18. LaP

You've come early to see us this year. John Frost. William Miller. PCH

You've heard of Slattery's light dragoons. O'Duffy's Ironsides. "Tom Moore, Jr." OnYI

You've heard of the Turks and the Greeks. The Battle of Navarino. *Unknown.* CoMu

You've locked the doors and snecked the windows tight? William and Agnes Pringle. W. W. Gibson. CMP

You've never heard the voice of God? The Voice of God. Katherine R. Barnard. BLRP; WBLP

You've plucked a curlew, drawn a hen. On an Island. J. M. Synge. MBP; MoBrPo; OBVV

You've read of several kinds of Cat. The Ad-dressing of Cats. T. S. Eliot. GoTP

You've returned me my book all unrolled to the end. To Septicianus. Martial. RoL

"You've saved my life," the master said. The Three Wishes. *Unknown.* DDA

You've seen a pair of faithful lovers die. Epilogue to "Mithridates, King of Pontus." Dryden. OAEP

You've seen a strawberry. Nevertheless. Marianne Moore. MoAB; OxBA; SeCeV

You've seen men whose pipes keep going out? A Dog's Howl. Lowe W. Wren. AlBD

You've seen our entertainment through. Closing Address. *Unknown.* MeMeAg

Ys Yt Possyble. Sir Thomas Wyatt. *See* Is It Possible.

Ysolte, *abr.* George Frederick Cameron. BoCaPo

Ystrad Fflur. T. Gwynn Jones, *tr. fr. Welsh* by Alun Llywelyn-Williams. PrWP

Yt fell abowght the Lamasse tyde. *See* It fell about . . .

Yucca in the Moonlight. Glenn Ward Dresbach. HiLiAm

Yuki. Mary McNeil Fenollosa. AA

Yukon, The. Joaquin Miller. LBAP

Arctic Moon, The, *sel.* MAP; MoAmPo (1942 ed.)

Yule Days, The. *Unknown.* ChTr

Yule Log, The. William Hamilton Hayne. AA

Yuletide. Alice Furlong. JKCP

Yule-Tide Fires. *Unknown.* PCD; PCH; PoRL; SDH, *sl. diff.*

Yule-Tide Parody, A. *Unknown.* PA

Yuma. Charles Henry Phelps. AA

Yussouf. James Russell Lowell. BBV (1951 ed.); BeLS; BHV; BLPA; BoTP; FaBoBe; LPS-3; MPB; NeHB; OTPC (1946 ed.); PYM; TVSH (Youssouf.) PYM

Yvonne of Brittany. Ernest Dowson. PoVP

Z

Z, Y, X, and W, V. *Unknown.* OxNR

Zacchaeus in the Leaves. Vernon Watkins. FaBoTw

Zaccheus. Sister Julie. JKCP (1955 ed.)

Zack Bumstead useter flosserfize. A Philosopher. Sam Walter Foss. BOHV

Zagonyi. George Henry Boker. GA; PAH

Zainab, if you have departed. On the Death of His Wife. Ibn al-Hammara. MooP

Zalinka. Tom MacInnes. BoCaPo; PeCV

Zalka Peetruza. Ray Garfield Dandridge. BANP

Zambra Dance, The. Dryden. *See* Song of the Zambra Dance.
Zaph Describes the Haunts of Malzah. Charles Heavysege. *Fr.* Saul. BoCaPo
Zapolya, *sels.* Samuel Taylor Coleridge.
Glycine's Song, *fr.* Pt. II, Act II, sc. i. EmBrPo; ERP; OBEV; OTPC (1946 ed.)
(Song: "Sunny shaft did I behold, A.") BoTP; BPN; LO; TCEP; TwHP
(Sunny Shaft, A.) CEP
Hunting Song, *fr.* Pt. II, Act IV, sc. i. PRWS; ThWaDe
(Choral Song of Illyrian Peasants.) CG
(Up, Up! Ye Dames and Lasses Gay!) BoTP; OTPC (1923 ed.)
Zara's Ear-Rings. *Unknown, tr. fr. Spanish by* John Gibson Lockhart. LPS-1
Zarathustra. Thomas S. Jones, Jr. AnAmPo; LA
Zarian was saying: Florence is youth. A Water-Colour of Venice. Lawrence Durrell. FaBoMo
Zeal of Jehu, The. Cardinal Newman. OBRV
Zeal of Thy House, The. Dorothy L. Sayers. QS
Zealless Xylographer, The. Mary Mapes Dodge. BOHV
Zealots of Yearning. David Rokeah, *tr. fr. Hebrew by* I. M. Lask. TrJP
Zealous lock-smith dyed of late, A. On a Puritanicall Lock-Smith. William Camden. WhC
Zealous Platonist, The. Callimachus. *See* Cleomprotus.
Zealous Puritan, The. *Unknown.* OBS; SeEP
Zealously my Muse doth salute all thee. To Mr. R. W. John Donne. BoFr
Zebaoth. Else Lasker-Schüler, *tr. fr. German by* Jethro Bithell. TrJP
Zebra. William Jay Smith. TiPo (1959 ed.)
Zebra, The. Roland Young. StaSt
(Miscegeneous Zebra, The.) BOHV
Zebra Dun, The. *Unknown.* CoSo (A *and* B *vers., with music*); CSF; StPo; StVeCh; ViBoFo
Zebras, The. Roy Campbell. AnFE; BoSA; GTBS-D; LiTB; LiTM; MBP; MoBrPo; MoPW; ReMP; ShBV-4; ViBoPo
Zebras. S. H. Stackpole. CAG
Zechariah, *sels.* Bible, *O.T.*
I Return unto Zion, VIII: 3–5. TrJP
Open Thy Doors, O Lebanon, XI: 1–14. AWP
Zeenty, peenty, heathery, mithery. Counting-out Rhyme. *Unknown.* ChTr
Zeke. L. A. G. Strong. MBP; MoBrPo
'Zekiel Saw de Wheel. *Unknown.* BoAN-2, *with music;* OIF
Zek'l Weep, *with music. Unknown.* AS
Zelanto, the Fountain of Fame, *sel.* Anthony Munday.
Love. OBSC
Zempoalla's Dream. Sir Robert Howard *and* John Dryden. *Fr.* The Indian Queen. BeR
Zend Avesta. *See* Gathas.
Zenith/ All these regrets. Towards the South. Guillaume Apollinaire. OnPM
Zennor. Anne Ridler. MoVE
Zeno desirous of the idle fame. Of Zeno. Everard Guilpin. *Fr.* Skialetheia. SiCE
Zenocrate, lovelier than the Love of Jove. Tamburlaine to Zenocrate. Christopher Marlowe. *Fr.* Tamburlaine the Great, Pt. I. WHA
Zenophila. Meleager, *pr. tr. fr. Greek by* W. R. Paton. GrL
Zepheria, *sels. Unknown.*
Alli veri figlioli delle Muse, *introd.* ReIE; TuPP
"Illuminating lamps, ye orbs crystallite." ReIE
"Proud in thy love, how many have I cited." ReIE; TuPP
Sonnet: "When, from the tower whence I derive love's heaven." ElL
"Thy coral-colored lips, how should I portray." ReIE
"What? Shall I ne'er more see those halcyon days." TuPP
"When we, in kind embracements, had agreed." ReEn; ReIE; TuPP
Zephyr returns, and scatters everywhere. Sonnet. Petrarch. *Fr.* Sonnets to Laura: To Laura in Death. LyPI
Zephyr, should'st thou chance to rove. Slave. Hafiz. PeP
Zephyrus brings the time that sweetly scenteth. *Unknown.* ES
Zeppelin, The. Rowena Bastin Bennett. GFA
Zest of Life, The. Henry van Dyke. BLP; OQP; QP-1; WBLP
Zeus. Aeschylus, *tr. fr. Greek by* C. M. Bowra. *Fr.* Heliades. OxBG
Zeus,/ Brazen-thunder-hurler. The Faun Sees Snow for the First Time. Richard Aldington. MBP; MoBrPo; PFE
Zeus and the Titans. Hesiod, *tr. fr. Greek by* Jack Lindsay. *Fr.* Theogony. OxBG
(Doom of the Titans, The, *tr. by* Arthur S. Way.) GrR
Zeus, beginning of all things. To Zeus. Terpander. OxBG
"Zeus-born son of Laertes, thou wise and wileful Odysseus." Homer. *Fr.* The Odyssey, XVI. GrPo
Zeus—by what name soe'er. Hymn to Zeus. Aeschylus. *Fr.* Agamemnon. WGRP
Zeus Dances. Titanomachia, *tr. fr. Greek by* T. F. Higham. OxBG
Zeus, Father art thou called, and the Wise God. Pater Noster. Euripides. *Fr.* Helen. GrR
Zeus, father Zeus, the sky owns thy command. God Punishes. Archilochus. OxBG
Zeus in the wrath of his heart hath hidden the means of subsistence. Hesiod. *Fr.* Works and Days. GrPo
Zeus is the air, Zeus earth, and Zeus the sky. Zeus. Aeschylus. *Fr.* Heliades. OxBG
Zeus, my Father, once again. Sappho in Levkas. William Alexander Percy. LS
Zeus on Olympus. Homer, *pr. tr. fr. Greek by* A. T. Murray. *Fr.* The Iliad, I. LiA
Zeus rains; a storm comes in its might. Drinking Songs [*or* Two Drinking Songs]. Alcaeus, *tr. fr. Greek by* C. M. Bowra. GrL; LiTW; OxBG
Zeus rains upon us, and from the sky comes down. Alcaeus, *tr. fr. Greek by* Richmond Lattimore. GrPo
Zeus! since by Philip scal'd Macynus' wall. Alcaeus of Messene, *tr. fr. Greek by* R. G. MacGregor. GrPo
Zeus spake; and storm-foot Iris leapt forth to bear His word. Homer, *tr. by* F. L. Lucas. *Fr.* The Iliad, XXIV. GrPE
Zeus, the high God—whate'er be dim in doubt. Helen; and the Wages of War. Aeschylus. *Fr.* Agamemnon. GrR
Zeus Too Is a Victim. Asclepiades, *tr. fr. Greek by* Walter Leaf. OxBG
Zeus—whosoe'er He be, Whose state excels. The Sacrifice of Iphigenia. Aeschylus. *Fr.* Agamemnon. GrR
Zeuxis, the painter, strove in vain. Jean de Meun. *Fr.* The Romance of the Rose. WoL
Zig-zag bee, *zzz* and *zzz*-ing, came, A. The Bee. John Fandel. GoYe
Zigzag Boy and Girl, The. *Unknown.* GFA
Zig-zagging it went. The Old Line Fence. A. W. Bellaw. BOHV
Zimri. Dryden. *Fr.* Absalom and Achitophel, Pt. I. AnFE; AWP; BCEP; EV-3; JAWP; LPS-3; SeCePo; ShBV-4; WBP
(Characters from the Satires: Zimri.) InPo
(Duke of Buckingham, The.) CoEV
("How happy had he been, if Destiny," *longer sel.*) BrBE
("In the first rank of these did Zimri stand.") PoFS; ViBoPo
(Malcontents, The.) OBS
Zinnias, ochre, orange, chrome and amber, The. Transition. May Sarton. NePoAm
Zion Redeemed. Isaiah, LX, Bible, *O.T.* LiA
Zion, wilt thou not ask if peace's wing. Ode to Zion. Judah Halevi. TrJP
Zionist Marching Song. Naphtali Herz Imber, *tr. fr. Hebrew by* Israel Zangwill. TrJP
Zip Coon. *Unknown, at. to* Bob Farrell. YaD
(Old Zip Coon, *with music.*) TrAS
Zizi's Lament. Gregory Corso. NeAP
Zodiac, The, *sel.* Hendrik Marsman, *tr. fr. Dutch by* A. J. Barnouw.
Valley of Sleep, The. LiTW
Zola. E. A. Robinson. CoV; MoVE; NePA; OxBA; TwP
Zollicoffer. Henry Lynden Flash. BlG; PAH; SPP
Zone. Guillaume Apollinaire, *tr. fr. French.* AnFP, *tr. by* Dudley Fitts; MiFP, *tr. by* W. J. Strachan; OnHM, *tr. by* Selden Rodman
Zone Libre. Louis Aragon, *tr. fr. French by* Louis MacNeice. MiFP
Zones of warmth around his heart, The. Sculptured Worship. William Stanley Braithwaite. Sandy Star and Willie Gee, I. BANP
Zoo. Gonzalo Escudero, *tr. fr. Spanish by* Richard O'Connell. AnCL
Zoo, The. Gilbert Sorrentino. NeAP
Zoo, The. Humbert Wolfe. GBV (1952 ed.); MoShBr; WaKn
Zoo in the City, The. Sara Van Alstyne Allen. GoYe
Zoo Manners. Eileen Mathias. BoTP
Zooming across the sky. Up in the Air. James S. Tippett. BoChLi; TiPo
Zooming overhead . . . and steel-framed birds, A. Aladdin Throws Away His Lamp. Elias Lieberman. PoMa
Zoon, zoon, cuddle and croon. Moon Song. Mildrew Plew Meigs. GoBP
Zophiel; or, The Bride of Seven, *sels.* Maria Gowen Brooks.
"And this at intervals." BAV
Disappointment. LPS-1
Palace of the Gnomes. AA
("He sat upon a car," *longer sel.*) BAP
Respite, The. AA
Zoroaster Devoutly Questions Ormazd. *At. to* Zoroaster, *tr. fr. Persian by* A. V. Williams Jackson. *Fr.* Gathas. WGRP
(O Great Creator, *tr. by* L. H. Mills.) GrCo-1

Zoroaster Devoutly Questions Ormazd (*continued*)
(Sacred Book, The, *tr. by* A. V. Williams Jackson.) AWP
Zounds! how the price went flashing through. Israel Freyer's Bid for Gold. Edmund Clarence Stedman. PAH
Zu fragmentarisch ist Welt und Leben. Heine. *See* Philosophy.
Zuleika. Goethe, *tr. fr. German by* Edward Dowden. *Fr.* West-Eastern Divan. BoFr
Zuleika. Arthur O'Shaughnessy. PoVP
Zulia. Arthur Symons. CIV
Zuloaga. Charles Wharton Stork. TBM
Zulu Girl, The. Roy Campbell. AtBAP; BoSA; ChMP; JKCP (1955 ed.); MoPW; MoVE; OBMV; POTE
Zulu King, The; New Orleans. Josephine Copeland. GoSl
Zun-zet. William Barnes. PoEL-4
Zun'd a-zet back t'other night, The. The Motherless Child. William Barnes. BCEP

AUTHOR INDEX

"A." Child's Fancy, A.
Deaf and Dumb.
My Pony.
New Fern, A.
Spring and Summer.
"A., C. B." Two Glasses, The, *wr. at.* *See* Wilcox, Ella Wheeler.
"A., F. P." *See* Adams, Franklin Pierce.
"A. E." *See* "Æ."
"A. E. M." *See* "M., A. E."
"A. G." *See* "G., A."
"A. H. S." *See* "S., A. H."
"A. J. T." *See* "T., A. J."
"A. K." *See* "K., A."
"A. L. C." *See* "C., A. L."
"A. R. G." *See* "G., A. R."
"A. W." *See* "W., A."
"A. W. S." *See* "S., A. W."
Aakjaer, Jeppe. Oats, The.
Rye Field, The.
Stonebreaker, The.
Aarestrup, Emil. Evening Sigh.
Punishment.
To a "Friend."
Aaron, Madeleine. God Is Here.
Aaronson, Leonard [*or* Lazarus]. Baptism, The.
Homeward Journey, The.
In the Time of the Persecution.
Pesci Misti.
Aasen, Ivar. Old Mountains, The.
Others May Fuss and May Worry, The.
Abba Arika. *See* Rab.
Abbe, George. Horizon Thong.
New York City.
Abbey, Henry. Donald.
Draw-Bridge Keeper, The.
Faith's Vista.
In Memory of General Grant.
Trailing Arbutus.
What Do We Plant [When We Plant the Tree]?
Winter Days.
Abbott, Anne. Veil, The.
Abbott, Claude Colleer. Bunch, a Cat.
Encounter, *tr.*
Song: "Would you wish me to sing to you," *tr.*
Too Late, My Love, *tr.*
Abbott, Clifton. Just Keep On.
Abbott, Edgar Wade. Poppy-Land Limited Express, The.
Abbott, H. H. Weathercock, The.
Abbott, Samuel. My Baby Dear.
Abbott, Wenonah Stevens. Soul's Soliloquy, A.
Abd-ar-Rahman I. Palm-Tree, The.
À Beckett, Gilbert Abbott. Holiday Task, A.
Polka Lyric, A.
Abeita, Louise. *See* E-Yeh-Shure'.
Abelard, Peter. David's Lament for Jonathan.
Dum Diana [*or* Diane] Vitrea, *at.*
Good Friday [the Third Nocturn].
Rumor Laetalis, *at.*
To Gabriel of the Annunciation.
Abenatar Melo, David. Thanksgiving.
Abercrombie, Lascelles. All Last Night.
Balkis. *Fr.* Emblems of Love.
Ceremonial Ode Intended for a University.
Death of a Friar, The.
Emblems of Love, *sels.*
Epilogue: "What shall we do for Love these days?" *Fr.* Emblems of Love.
Epitaph: "Sir, you should notice me, I am the Man."
Epitaph: "These, who desired to live, went out to death."
Epitaph Written for the Liverpool University Roll of Honour.
Fear, The.
Fool's Adventure, The, *sel.*
Hope and Despair.
Hymn to Love. *Fr.* Emblems of Love.
Judith, *sel.* *Fr.* Emblems of Love.
Margaret's Song. *Fr.* The New God; a Miracle.
Marriage Song. *Fr.* Emblems of Love.
Mary and the Bramble.
New God, The; a Miracle, *sel.*
Ryton Firs.
Sale of Saint Thomas, The.
Sale of Saint Thomas, The, *sel.*
Seeker, The. *Fr.* The Fool's Adventure.
Small Fountains. *Fr.* Emblems of Love.
Song: "Balkis was in her marble town." *Fr.* Emblems of Love.
Stream's Song, The.
Tormented by the World. *Fr.* The Sale of Saint Thomas.
Vashti, *sel.* *Fr.* Emblems of Love.
Witchcraft; New Style.
Woman's Beauty. *Fr.* Emblems of Love.
Aberpennar, Davies. Beware, Wass.
For Gwenhwyfar and Blodeuwedd.
Poem for D. Robert Griffiths.
Poem for Gwyn and Käthe.
Poem for Keith Scott.
Poem for M. A. J. D.
Tudur Aled.
Abrahams, William. In the Henry James Country.
Museum, The.
Poem in Time of War.
Abril, Xavier. Elegy to the Invented Woman.
Elegy to the Lost and Already Blurred by Time.
Exaltation of Elementary Materials.
Nocturne: "How have you managed to enter so, like a mist."
Abse, Dannie. Game, The.
Inscription on the Flyleaf of a Bible.
Letter to Alex Comfort.
Abu Abd Allah. Scurvy Entertainment.
Water-Wheel, The.
Wine and Citron.
Abu Aiyub. Gift, The.
Abu Amr. Bad Company.
Abu Bakr (of Marrakesh). Sword, The.
Abu Bakr Muhammad. Panegyric.
Abu Dharr. Oranges, The.
Abu Hafs. Beauty.
Hips.
Sunburn.
Abu Ishaq. Changefulness.
Abu Jaafar. Magian Wine.
Wine, My Love.
Abu-l-Ala al-Maarri. Aweary Am I.
Cryptic Streets, The.
Draught of Life, The.
Man's Natural Element.
Summum Bonum.
This World.
Abul Arab. Gift, The.
Abu'l-Atahija. Atheist Buries His Son, The.
For Haroun Al Raschid.
Abul Bahr. Abstinent Lover, The.
Abulfadhel Ahmed. Blessed Spot, A.
Abul Fadl. Body and Soul.
Abul Hajjaj. Reed, The.
Abul Hasan of Badajoz. In Battle.
Abul Hasan of Santa Maria. Revel.
Abul Hasan of Seville. Dove, The.
Golden Glow.
Abul Mughira. Moon and Venus.
Abul Qasim of Alcira. Rider.
Abul Qasim of Silves. Unexpected Fortune.
Abu Nuwas. Great Offence, The.
Abur Rabi. Petition.
Abu Said ibn Abi-l-Khair [*or* Abi'l Khayr]. Six Rubaiyat.
Abu Shamaqmaq. Hungry Master and Hungry Cat.
Abus Salt. Bounty.
Incense Burner, The.
Sun and Cloud.
Two Seas.
White Charger, The.
Abu Yahya. Bloom of Age.
Moth, The.
Abu Zaid. Army, The.
Abu Zakariya. Bubbling Wine.
Spear, The.
Acharya, Ananda. My Faith.
Realization.
Ackerley, Joe Randolph. Ghosts.
Ackerly, W. C. Prayer of an Unemployed Man.
Ackerman, Zöe. My Canary's Rhapsody.
Ackerson, John. Bandage Is Red, The.
Ecce Homo.
Acton, Ellen M. V. Exodus from a Renaissance Gallery.
Acton-Bond, Marion. Sunset on an English Hill.
Acuña, Manuel. Before a Corpse.
Ada, Sister Mary. Against Despair.
Adair, Ivan. Real Presence.
Adam, Helen. I Love My Love.
Adam, Jean. Sailor's Wife, The, *at.*
There's Nae Luck about the House, *at.*
Adam of St. Victor. Eagle Swift, The.
Hail, Mother of the Savior.
Lux Advenit Veneranda.
Adams, Amy Belle. Annie McConkus.
Adams, Arthur. Australian, The.
Courage.
Fleet Street.
Pair of Lovers in the Street, A.
Pleiades, The.
Weakling, The.
Written in Australia.
Adams, Bill (Bertram Martin Adams). Ballad of the *Ivanhoe*, The.
Billy Peg-Leg's Fiddle.
Homeward Bound, The.
Peg-Leg's Fiddle.
Shore Roads of April.
Stowaway.
Adams, Charles Follen ("Yawcob Strauss"). Leedle Yawcob Strauss.
Prevalent Poetry.
Yaw, Dot Is So!
Adams, E. M. Action Rhyme.
Haymaking.
Paddling Pool, The.
Sea, The.
Shady Woods.
Snowman, The.
Adams, Francis P. To the Christians.
Adams, Franklin Pierce ("F. P. A.").
Ad Leuconoen, *after* Horace.
Ad Persephonen.
Ad Xanthium Phoceum, *after* Horace.
Amateur Botanist, The.
As to Eyes.
Ballade of 1933, A.
Ballade of Schopenhauer's Philosophy.
Baseball's Sad Lexicon.

AUTHOR INDEX

ADAMS, FRANKLIN PIERCE (*continued*)
Boston.
Christopher Columbus.
De Senectute.
Erring in Company.
February 14, 22 B.C., *after* Horace.
Garland of Recital Programs, A.
Georgie Porgie.
Happy Lifetime to You.
How?
"It Was a Famous Victory."
Jim and Bill.
Life.
Limerick: "Said a lady whose surname was Beaulieu."
Maud Muller Mutatur.
Metaphysics.
On the Day after Christmas.
Persicos Odi, *after* Horace.
Poetry and Thoughts on Same.
Popular Ballad: "Never Forget Your Parents."
Rarae Aves.
Regarding (1) the U.S. and (2) New York.
Rich Man, The.
Simplicity, *after* Horace.
Slump in Sybaris, The, *after* Horace.
Song: "Don't Tell Me What You Dreamt Last Night."
"Such Stuff as Dreams."
Those Two Boys.
Thoughts on the Cosmos.
To a Lady.
To a Lady Troubled by Insomnia.
To a Thesaurus.
To a Young Woman on the *World* Staff.
To His Lyre.
To the Polyandrous Lydia, *after* Horace.
Tonight.
Translated Way, The.
Us Potes.
Villanelle, with Stevenson's Assistance.
ADAMS, G. W. To November.
ADAMS, GEORGINE M. "That Did in Luve So Lively Write."
ADAMS, H. M. Johnny's Farm.
ADAMS, HENRY. Chanson: "There is no comfort to be found for pain," *tr.*
Death of Roland, The, *tr. Fr.* The Song of Roland.
Oh, Gentle Beauty, *tr.*
Prayer to the Virgin of Chartres.
Prison Song, *tr.*
Song of Roland, The, *sel., tr.*
ADAMS, JAMES BARTON. At a Cowboy Dance.
Billy, He's in Trouble.
Cowboy Alone with His Conscience, A.
Cowboy Toast, A.
Cowboy versus Broncho.
Cowboy's Dance Song, The.
Cowboy's Hopeless Love, A.
Cowboy's Life, The, *at.*
Cowboy's Worrying Love, A.
Dust of the Overland Trail, The.
Idaho Cowboy Dance, An.
Ruin of Bobtail Bend, The.
Tough Cuss from Bitter Creek, A.
Transformation of a Texas Girl, The.
ADAMS, JOHN QUINCY. Lip and the Heart, The.
Send Forth, O God, Thy Light and Truth.
To Sally, *tr.*
Wants of Man, The.
ADAMS, LÉONIE (Mrs. William Troy).
Alas, Kind Element.
April Mortality.
April Mortality, *sel.*
Bell Tower.
Caryatid.
Companions of the Morass.
Country Summer.
Death and the Lady.
Early Waking.
Figurehead, The.
Font in the Forest, The.
Ghostly Tree.
Grapes Making.
Home-coming.
Horn, The.
Kingdom of Heaven.
Lament of Quarry, The.
Light at Equinox.
Lullaby: "Hush, lullay."
Mount, The.
Never Enough of Living.
Night-Piece.
People in the Park, The.
Quiet.
Reminder, The.
River in the Meadows, The.
Runner with the Lots, The.
Said of the Earth and the Moon.
Send Forth the High Falcon.
Sundown.
This Measure.
Those Not Elect.
Thought's End.
Time and Spirit.
Twilight of the Wood.
Twilit Revelation.
Valhalla for the Living.
Wind of Fall, A.
ADAMS, MARGUERITE JANVRIN. American History.
They Who Possess the Sea.
ADAMS, MARY MATHEWS (Mrs. Charles Kendall Adams). Dead Love.
ADAMS, OSCAR FAY. At Lincoln.
On a Grave in Christ-Church, Hants.
ADAMS, SAMUEL HOPKINS. Centipede, The.
ADAMS, SARAH FLOWER (Mrs. William Bridges Adams). Hymn: "He sendeth sun, he sendeth shower."
Love.
Mourners Came at Break of Day, The.
Nearer, My God, to Thee.
ADAMS, WILLIAM HENRY DAVENPORT. Last Voyage of the Fairies, The.
"ADÁN, MARTÍN" (Rafael de la Fuente Benavides). Nativity.
ADCOCK, ARTHUR ST. JOHN. By Deputy.
Sam.
Travellers.
ADDAEUS [*or* ADDOEUS]. Draught-Ox, The.
Ox Past Service, An.
Ox, rewarded for his pains, The.
Pensioned Ox, The.
ADDAMS, JANE. There Is a River.
ADDISON, JOSEPH. Account of the Greatest English Poets, An, *sel.*
Blenheim. *Fr.* The Campaign.
Campaign, The.
Campaign, The, *sel.*
Cato, *sels.*
Cato's Soliloquy. *Fr.* Cato.
Cato's Soliloquy, *sel. Fr.* Cato.
Cicada, The, *tr.*
Confirmation of Faith, The.
Cowley.
How Are Thy Servants Blest.
Hymn: Confirmation of Faith, The.
Hymn: "Spacious firmament on high, The."
Hymn: "When all thy mercies, O my God."
Hymn to the Creation.
Immortality. *Fr.* Cato.
In All the Humors, *tr.*
Italy and Britain. *Fr.* A Letter from Italy.
Letter from Italy, A.
Letter from Italy, A, *sel.*
Lines: "Soul, secure in her existence, smiles, The." *Fr.* Cato.
Lord my pasture shall prepare, The.
Metamorphoses, *sel., tr.*
Narcissus, *tr. Fr.* Metamorphoses.
Ode: "How are thy servants blest, O Lord!"
Ode: "Spacious firmament on high, The."
Ode to Creation.
Pastoral Hymn.
Providence.
Psalm XIX.
Sempronius's Speech for War. *Fr.* Cato.
Soliloquy on Immortality. *Fr.* Cato.
Song: "Echo, tell me, while I wander."
Spacious Firmament on High, The.
Temperament, *tr.*
Thanksgiving after Travel.
To a Capricious Friend, *tr.*
Trust in God.
When All Thy Mercies.
Why with Scorn-reverting Eye, *tr.*
ADDISON, MEDORA (Mrs. Charles Read Nutter). Some Day.
Spell, The.
Wasted Hours.
ADDLESHAW, PERCY ("Percy Hemingway"). Happy Wanderer, The.
ADE, GEORGE. R-e-m-o-r-s-e.
ADEANE, LOUIS. Four Poems for April.
Night Loves Us, The.
Poem on Hampstead Heath.
ADEE, LUCY A. K. Let All the Earth Keep Silence.
Our Lady of Good Voyage.
"ADELER, MAX" (Charles Heber Clark). Out of the Hurly-Burly.
We Have Lost Our Little Hanner.
ADENEY, MARCUS. Choral: "We the proper ancients speak not out of turn." *Fr.* Mansong.
Mansong, *sel.*
ADKIN, WILL S. If I Only Was the Fellow.
Just Try to Be the Fellow That Your Mother Thinks You Are.
ADLER, FELIX. City of Light, The.
City of Our Hopes, The.
Hail! the Glorious Golden City.
ADLER, FREDERICK HERBERT. Song for May Day, A.
ADLER, FRIEDRICH. By the Waterfall.
ADLER, JACOB. Song of the Times.
ADY, ENDRE. Grape Hill, The.
Last Boats, The.
"Æ" (George William Russell). Ancient.
Aphrodite.
Babylon.
Burning-Glass, The.
By the Margin of the Great Deep.
Call, A.
Carrowmore.
Charge to Youth, A. *Fr.* On Behalf of Some Irishmen Not Followers of Tradition.
Chivalry.
Cities, The.
City, The.
Comfort.
Connla's Well.
Continuity.
Dana.
Dark Rapture.
Dawn.
Desire.
Dust.
Earth, The.
Earth Breath, The.
Epilogue: "Well, when all is said and done."
Exiles.
Farewell, A: "I go down from the hill in gladness."
Farewell, A: "Only in my deep heart I love you, sweetest heart."
Forgotten.
Frolic.
Garden of God, The.
Gates of Dreamland, The.
Gay, The.
Germinal.
Gift, The.
Gods of War.
Great Breath, The.
Hermit, The.
Holy Hill, A.
Hope in Failure.
Immortality.
In As Much . . .
Inheritance.
Innocence.
Irish Face, An.
Janus.
Krishna.
Leader, A.
Lonely, The.
Man to the Angel, The.
Memory of Earth, A.
Mountain Wind, A.
Murmur in the Grass, A.
Mutiny.

Natural Magic.
New York.
Om.
On Behalf of Some Irishmen Not Followers of Tradition.
On Behalf of Some Irishmen Not Followers of Tradition, *sel.*
Our Thrones Decay.
Outcast, The.
Oversoul.
Pain.
Parting.
Place of Rest, The.
Prisoner, A.
Promise.
Recollection.
Reconciliation.
Refuge.
Rest.
Resurrection.
Sacrifice.
Salutation.
Secret, The.
Secret Love, The.
Self-Discipline.
Shadows and Lights.
Silence of Love, The.
Summer Night, A.
Sung on a By-Way.
Symbolism.
Terence MacSwiney.
Three Counsellors, The.
Time.
To One Who Wanted a Philosophy from Me.
Tragedy.
Truth.
Twilight of Earth, The.
Unity.
Unknown God, The.
Vale.
Virgin Mother, The.
When.
Winds of Angus, The.
Winds of Eros.
AESCHYLUS. Achaians Have Got Troy, upon This Very Day, The. *Fr.* Agamemnon.
Aeschylus.
Agamemnon, *sels.*
Amphiaraus. *Fr.* Seven against Thebes.
Answer to Defiance; the Earthquake. *Fr.* Prometheus Bound.
Apollo Confounds the Furies. *Fr.* Eumenides.
Areiopagus, The; a Higher Justice Come to Dwell among Men. *Fr.* Eumenides.
Athena's Faith. *Fr.* Eumenides.
Battle of Salamis, The. *Fr.* Persians.
Beacons, The. *Fr.* Agamemnon.
Case for the Defense, A. *Fr.* Agamemnon.
Cassandra. *Fr.* Agamemnon.
Cassandra Prepares to Die. *Fr.* Agamemnon.
Cassandra's Lament. *Fr.* Agamemnon.
Choephoroe, *sels.*
Chorus: "Great fortune is an hungry thing." *Fr.* Agamemnon.
Chorus: "Now do our eyes behold." *Fr.* Seven against Thebes.
Chorus: "O Zeus our king and Night our friend." *Fr.* Agamemnon.
Chorus of the Furies, The. *Fr.* Eumenides.
Clytemnestra. *Fr.* Agamemnon.
Clytemnestra's Dream. *Fr.* Choephoroe.
Crime of Orestes, The. *Fr.* Choephoroe.
Danaides, *sel.*
Daughters of Atlas, The.
Death of Agamemnon, The. *Fr.* Agamemnon.
Defiance. *Fr.* Prometheus Bound.
"Dies Irae." *Fr.* Choephoroe.
Edoni, *sel.*
Epitaph for [*or* on] Himself, An.
Eumenides, *sels.*
Folly of Obstinacy. *Fr.* Prometheus Bound.
Furies' Prayer, The. *Fr.* Eumenides.
Gathering War Clouds. *Fr.* Seven against Thebes.
Ghost of Dareius [*or* Darius], The. *Fr.* Persians.
God of War, Money Changer of Dead Bodies, The. *Fr.* Agamemnon.
Gods' Children, The. *Fr.* Niobe.
Golden Mean, The. *Fr.* Eumenides.
Grave on Ossa, A.
Helen. *Fr.* Agamemnon.
Helen; and the Wages of War. *Fr.* Agamemnon.
Heliades, *sel.*
His Own Epitaph.
Hour of National Emergency. *Fr.* Seven against Thebes.
Human Responsibility. *Fr.* Agamemnon.
Hymn to Zeus. *Fr.* Agamemnon.
If I Were to Tell of Our Labours, Our Hard Lodging. *Fr.* Agamemnon.
Inexorable Death. *Fr.* Niobe.
Invocation of Agamemnon's Ghost. *Fr.* Choephoroe.
Io. *Fr.* Suppliants.
Justice Protects the Dead. *Fr.* Phryges.
Kilissa, the Nurse. *Fr.* Choephoroe.
Lament for the Two Brothers Slain by Each Other's Hand. *Fr.* Seven against Thebes.
Libation Bearers, *sels.*
Litany for Argos. *Fr.* Suppliants.
"Mad Scene, The." *Fr.* Choephoroe.
Marriage of Heaven and Earth, The. *Fr.* Danaides.
Menelaus Abandoned. *Fr.* Agamemnon.
Myrmidones, *sel.*
News of War. *Fr.* Seven against Thebes.
Niobe, *sels.*
O Zeus, Our Spirit Fails. *Fr.* Suppliants.
Orestes Goes Mad. *Fr.* Choephoroe.
Overthrow of Zeus, The. *Fr.* Prometheus Bound.
Persae, *sels.*
Persia Prostrated. *Fr.* Persians.
Persians, *sels.*
Philoctetes, *sel.*
Philoctetes Calls for Death. *Fr.* Philoctetes.
Phryges, *sel.*
Prayer for Deliverance. *Fr.* Suppliants.
Prometheus, *sels.*
Prometheus Bound.
Prometheus Bound, *sels.*
Prometheus Doomed. *Fr.* Prometheus Bound.
Prometheus' Gifts to Man. *Fr.* Prometheus Bound.
Prometheus in the Earthquake. *Fr.* Prometheus Bound.
Prometheus Liberatus, *sel.*
Prometheus the Teacher of Men. *Fr.* Prometheus Bound.
Prometheus Unbound, *sel.*
Prometheus Vinctus, *sels.*
Purple Carpet, The. *Fr.* Agamemnon.
Red Sea, The. *Fr.* Prometheus Unbound.
Sacrifice of Iphigenia, The. *Fr.* Agamemnon.
Salamis. *Fr.* Persians.
Seven against Thebes, *sels.*
Sin and Satiety. *Fr.* Agamemnon.
Suppliant Maidens, The, *sel.*
Suppliants, *sels.*
Thetis.
Transformation of the Furies, The. *Fr.* Eumenides.
Victory at Salamis. *Fr.* Persians.
Wail of Prometheus Bound, The. *Fr.* Prometheus Bound.
Welcome to Agamemnon. *Fr.* Agamemnon.
World's Harmonious Plan, The. *Fr.* Suppliants.
Worship of Cotys, The. *Fr.* Edoni.
Wounded Eagle, The. *Fr.* Myrmidones.
Xerxes Defeated. *Fr.* Persians.
Zeus. *Fr.* Heliades.
AESOP (6th century B.C.) Ass in the Lion's Skin, The.
Boy and the Wolf, The.
Frogs Who Wanted a King, The.
Greedy Fox and the Elusive Grapes, The.
Mountain in Labor, The.
Shepherd-Boy and the Wolf, The.
Swan and the Goose, The.
Vine and the Goat, The.
AESOP [*or* AESOPUS] (5th century A.D.). O Life, what refuge have we fleeing thee.
AESOPUS (1st century B.C.) Way of Life, The.
AGATHIAS SCHOLASTICUS [*or* AGATHIAS ASIANUS]. Best Memorial, The.
Chaeronean Plutarch, to thy deathless praise.
Dicing.
Girls' Lot, The.
Happy Woman, A.
"Here Lies a Most Beautiful Lady."
I love not wine, but shouldst thou wish.
Inscription for a Smyrna Privy.
Kiss within the Cup, A.
Leave a Kiss within the Cup.
Maid's Complaint, The.
Not Such Your Burden.
Plutarch.
Rhodanthe.
Spring Sailing.
Swallows, The.
To Pan.
Weeping and wakeful all the night I lie.
AGEE, JAMES. Description of Elysium.
I loitered weeping with my bride for gladness. *Fr.* Lyrics.
In Heavy Mind.
Let Us Now Praise Famous Men, *sel.*
Lullaby, A: "Sleep, child, lie quiet, let be."
Lyrics, *sels.*
Millions Are Learning How.
No doubt left. Enough deceiving. *Fr.* Lyrics.
Not met and marred with the year's whole turn of grief. *Fr.* Lyrics.
Now stands our love on that still verge of day. *Fr.* Sonnets.
Our doom is in our being. *Fr.* Sonnets.
Permit Me Voyage.
Prologue: "Against time and the damages of the brain." *Fr.* Let Us Now Praise Famous Men.
Rapid Transit.
Red Sea. *Fr.* Two Songs on the Economy of Abundance.
So It Begins. *Fr.* Sonnets.
Song with Words.
Sonnets, *sels.*
Temperance Note; and Weather Prophecy. *Fr.* Two Songs on the Economy of Abundance.
Those former loves wherein our lives have run. *Fr.* Sonnets.
Two Songs on the Economy of Abundance.
AGNES, SISTER. Our Lady's Assumption.
AGNEW, EDITH. Ambition.
Dahlias.
"Los Pastores."
Summer Comes.
AGNEW, JOAN. Freedom.
Sons of the King.
AGNEW, MARJORIE L. On Going Home.
AGOSTINHO DA CRUZ. To Our Saviour.
AHERN, M. KATHLEEN. Wisteria.
"AHMATOVA, ANNA." *See* "AKHMATOVA, ANNA."
AICARD, JEAN. In Provence.
AI CHING. Highway, The.
Snow Falls on China.
Trumpeter, The.
AÏDÉ, HAMILTON. Danube River, The.
Forsaken, The
Remember or Forget.
When We Are Parted.

AIKEN, A. HOLCOMBE. Slumber Song, A: "Beautiful bird at the casement sings, A."
AIKEN, CONRAD. A Is for Alpha: Alpha Is for A.
All Lovely Things [Will have an Ending].
And Already the Minutes. *Fr.* Priapus and the Pool.
And in the Hanging Gardens.
Annihilation.
At a Concert of Music.
Awakening, The. *Fr.* The Kid.
Beautiful body made of ivory. *Fr.* Variations.
Beloved, Let Us Once More Praise the Rain. *Fr.* Preludes to Attitude.
Bend as the Bow Bends.
Blind Date.
Bread and Music. *Fr.* Discordants.
But How It Came from Earth.
Carver, The. *Fr.* Priapus and the Pool.
Chance Meetings.
Chiaroscuro; Rose.
Cloister. *Fr.* Preludes to Attitude.
Dead Cleopatra Lies in a Crystal Casket. *Fr.* Discordants.
Discordants, *sels.*
Evening Song of Senlin. *Fr.* Senlin, a Biography.
Evensong.
Fade, Then. *Fr.* Priapus and the Pool.
First Note, Simple, The; the Second Note, Distinct. *Fr.* Preludes to Attitude.
Frostbite.
Green light from the moon. *Fr.* Variations.
Heaven, You Say, Will Be a Field in April.
House of Dust, The, *sels.*
If Man, That Angel of Bright Consciousness.
In the noisy street. *Fr.* Discordants.
Keep in the Heart the Journal [Nature Keeps]. *Fr.* Preludes for Memnon.
Kid, The, *sels.*
King Borborigmi.
Limberick.
Miracles.
Morning Song of Senlin. *Fr.* Senlin, a Biography.
Music I Heard [with You]. *Fr.* Discordants.
My heart has become as hard as a city street. *Fr.* Discordants.
Nameless Ones, The.
Nocturne of Remembered Spring.
Nothing to Say, You Say? *Fr.* Preludes to Attitude.
Nuit Blanche; North End.
Old Man Sees Himself, An.
One-eyed Calendar, The.
One Star Fell and Another. *Fr.* Preludes for Memnon.
Palimpsest; a Deceitful Portrait. *Fr.* The House of Dust.
Portrait of a Girl. *Fr.* Priapus and the Pool.
Portrait of One Dead. *Fr.* The House of Dust.
Prelude: "Rimbaud and Verlaine, precious pair of poets." *Fr.* Preludes for Memnon.
Prelude: "Stood, at the closed door, and remembered." *Fr.* Preludes for Memnon.
Prelude: "This is not you?" *Fr.* Preludes for Memnon.
Prelude: "What shall we do?" *Fr.* Preludes for Memnon.
Prelude: "Winter for a moment takes the mind." *Fr.* Preludes for Memnon.
Prelude: "You went to the verge, you say, and came back safely?" *Fr.* Preludes for Memnon.
Preludes for Memnon, *sels.*
Preludes to Attitude.
Preludes to Attitude, *sels.*
Preludes to Definition, *sels.*
Priapus and the Pool, *sels.*
Proem to "The Kid." *Fr.* The Kid.
Punch; the Immortal Liar, *sels.*
Puppet Dreams, The. *Fr.* Punch; the Immortal Liar.
Puppet Dreams, The, *sel. Fr.* Punch; the Immortal Liar.
Quarrel, The.
Queen Cleopatra. *Fr.* Variations.
Return, The.
Rimbaud and Verlaine, Precious Pair of Poets. *Fr.* Preludes for Memnon.
Road, The.
Room, The.
Samadhi.
Sea Holly.
See, as the Carver Carves the Rose. *Fr.* Priapus and the Pool.
Senlin, a Biography, *sels.*
Shaemus.
Sleep: and between the Closed Eyelids of Sleep. *Fr.* Preludes to Attitude.
Snowflake on Asphodel.
So, in the Evening, to the Simple Cloister. *Fr.* Preludes to Attitude.
Soldier, The, *sels.*
Sonnet, A: "Think, when a starry night of bitter frost."
Sound of Breaking.
Sounding, The.
South End.
Stepping Stones, The.
Sursum Corda.
Systole and Diastole.
Tetélestai.
Then Came I to the Shoreless Shore of Silence. *Fr.* Preludes for Memnon.
There is nothing moving there, in that desert of silence. *Fr.* Priapus and the Pool.
There Was an Island in the Sea. *Fr.* Priapus and the Pool.
This Is the Shape of the Leaf. *Fr.* Priapus and the Pool.
Three Star Final.
Time Has Come, the Clock Says Time Has Come, The. *Fr.* Preludes for Memnon.
Time in the Rock, *sels.*
Two Coffees in the Español. *Fr.* Preludes to Attitude.
Unknown Soldier, The. *Fr.* The Soldier.
Vampire, The.
Variations, *sels.*
Wars, The. *Fr.* The Soldier.
Watch Long Enough, and You Will See [the Leaf]. *Fr.* Preludes for Memnon.
Wedding, The.
When the Tree Bares.
When Trout Swim down Great Ormond Street. *Fr.* Priapus and the Pool.
Whim. *Fr.* Priapus and the Pool.
Why Is It? *Fr.* Priapus and the Pool.
Wind, wind, wind in the old trees. *Fr.* Variations.
Winter for a Moment Takes the Mind. *Fr.* Preludes for Memnon.
You are as beautiful as white clouds. *Fr.* Variations.
You Went to the Verge, You Say, and Came Back Safely? *Fr.* Preludes for Memnon.
AIKIN, ANNA LETITIA. *See* BARBAULD, ANNA LETITIA.
AIKIN, LUCY. Which Way Does the Wind Blow?
AINGER, A. C. God Is Working His Purpose Out.
AINGER, ALFRED. On Taine.
AINSLIE, DOUGLAS. Apprehension, *tr.*
Archer, The, *tr.*
Good Friday's Hoopoe.
Stirrup Cup, A [*or* The].
AINSLIE, HEW. I Left Ye, Jeanie.
Ingle-Side, The.
It's Dowie in the Hint o' Hairst. *Fr.* Mary.
Mary, *sel.*
Wherefore sou'd ye talk o' love.
Willie and Helen.
AINSWORTH, PERCY CLOUGH. "And the Life Everlasting."
Kingdom Within, The.
AINSWORTH, RUTH. Good Night.
AIRAS NÚÑEZ. Bailada: "Let's dance now, all of us, all of us, oh my maidens."
AIRD, THOMAS. Frank Sylvan, *sel.*
Swallow, The.
AIREY, PETER. Song of the Dial, The.
AI SHIH-TE. Human Mind, The.
AKAHITO (Yamabe no Akahito). I passed by the beach.
I wish I could lend a coat. *Fr.* Manyo Shu.
I wish I were close.
Love, that dwarfs our life.
Men of valor, The. *Fr.* Manyo Shu.
Mists rise over, The/ The still pools at Asuka.
On Fujiyama/ Under the midsummer moon.
Plum-blossom, The. *Fr.* Manyo Shu.
Tanka: "Men of Valor, The."
Tomorrow I was/ Going to the Spring meadows.
When I went out/ In the Spring meadows.
AKAZOME EMON, LADY. I should not have waited.
AKENSIDE, MARK. Against Suspicion, *sel.*
Amoret.
Benevolence. *Fr.* Against Suspicion.
Complaint, The.
Created Universe, The. *Fr.* The Pleasures of Imagination.
Delights of Fancy. *Fr.* The Pleasures of Imagination.
Early Influences. *Fr.* The Pleasures of Imagination.
England, Unprepared for War. *Fr.* An Ode to the Country Gentlemen of England.
For a Grotto.
For a Statue of Chaucer at Woodstock.
Hand of Nature, The.
Hymn to Science.
Inscription: "Ye powers unseen, to whom the bards of Greece."
Inscription for a Grotto.
Invocation to the Genius of Greece. *Fr.* The Pleasures of Imagination.
Nature. *Fr.* The Pleasures of Imagination.
Nature's Influence on Man. *Fr.* The Pleasures of Imagination.
Nightingale, The.
Ode: Allusion to Horace.
Ode: "On yonder verdant hillock laid."
Ode, on a Sermon against Glory.
Ode to the Country Gentlemen of England, An, *sel.*
Ode to the Evening Star.
Ode to the Evening Star, *sel.*
On Lyric Poetry, *sel.*
On the Winter Solstice, 1740.
Pleasures of Imagination, The, *sels.*
Poets. *Fr.* The Pleasures of Imagination.
Song: "Shape alone let others prize, The."
That Delightful Time. *Fr.* The Pleasures of Imagination.
To the Evening Star.
Virtuoso, The.
AKERMAN, JOHN YONGE. Harnet and the Bittle, a Wiltshire Tale, The.
AKERMAN, LUCY E. Nothing but Leaves.
AKERS, DANA KNEELAND. Mongol.
AKERS, ELIZABETH. *See* ALLEN, ELIZABETH AKERS.
"AKHMATOVA, ANNA" (Anna Andreyevna Gorenko). All Is Sold.
Broad Gold.
Confession.
Courage.
Here I have waited, none with me.
I said to the cuckoo: "Till I die."
In the Pioneer Camp.

Is our time worse than all the times that went before it.
It is simple, it is easy.
It's Good Up Here.
Like a White Stone.
Like this, unto a wounded crane.
Lime-trees by the open door, The.
Lot's Wife.
Maybe again the organ-music blaring.
Mistress of the House, The.
Muse, The.
No, no, I did not love you.
Not with Deserters.
Now All Is Sold.
Now is woven in my dark tresses.
Now we know well how each can bear the shock.
Oh, How Good.
Prayer: "Make me feverish, sleepless, and breathless."
Reject the Burden.
To awake when dawn is breaking.
Unparalleled Autumn, An.
Upon the Hard Crest.
White Bird, The.
Winds that bring the swans are racing.
You Are Always New.
You are far off, stranger mine.
AKINS, ZOË. Conquered.
Dead Aviator.
First Rain.
I Am the Wind.
Norah.
One Woman.
Rain, Rain.
Snow-Gardens, The.
This Is My Hour.
Tragedienne, The.
Wanderer, The.
ALABASTER, WILLIAM. Incarnatio Est Maximum Donum Dei.
On the Reed of Our Lord's Passion.
Upon the Crucifix.
Upon the Ensignes of Christes Crucifyinge.
ALAMANNI, LUIGI. Sonnet: To the River Seine.
ALARCÓN, JUAN RUIZ DE. Feast by the Manzanares. *Fr.* The Suspicious Truth.
AL-ASAMM. Excuses.
Unripe Orange, The.
ALASDAIR, ALASDAIR MACMHAIGHSTIR. *See* MACDONALD, ALEXANDER.
AL-ASSAL. Toledo Captured by the Franks.
AL-ASWAD, SON OF YA'FUR. Old Age. *Fr.* The Mufaddaliyat.
AL-BARRAQ. Inky Mouth, The.
Lyric: "Lo, as the thrushes' throats."
ALBEE, JOHN. At the Grave of Champernowne.
Bos'n Hill.
Dandelions.
Landor.
Music and Memory.
Soldier's Grave, A.
ALBERT, SAMUEL L. After a Game of Squash.
All of Her.
Honeymoon.
Near the Base Line.
One, Two, Three.
Rebuff.
Street-Walker in March.
ALBERTI, RAFAEL. Angel of Numerals, The.
Avaricious Angel, The.
Chaplin's Sad Speech.
Dead Angels.
Elegy for Garcilaso.
From Gumiel de Hizán to Gumiel del Mercado.
Good Angel, The.
Madrigal to a Streetcar Token.
Name-giving Aurora, The.
Open Letter.
Pirate of sea and sky.
Sea, The.
Sea, the Sea, The.
Street Cry
Street Cry Under Sea.
Three Memories of Heaven.
To Miss X, Buried in the West Wind.
To the International Brigade.
Tower of Iznajar, The.
Two Angels, The.
ALBERTSON, CHARLES CARROLL. Holy Child, The.
Prayer at a Wedding.
ALBERTSON, CYRUS E. Reflections.
ALBERTUS MAGNUS, SISTER (Marion McGrath). Prayer, A: "O Thou great Author of the World."
ALBRECHT VON JOHANNSDORF. Pilgrimage, The.
ALBRIGHT, MARY E. Let Me Go Back.
AL-BUQAIRA. Bow, The.
Camomile, The.
Singer, The.
ALCAEUS. After the Tyrant's Death.
Antidote.
Antimenidas.
Armory [*or* Armoury], The [*or* An].
Be with me now, leaving the Isle of Pelops.
Castor and Polydeuces.
Country's Greatness, A.
Drinking Songs.
Footsteps of Spring, The.
Glitters with brass my mansion wide.
Helen and Thetis.
I cannot understand how the winds are set.
Immortalia Ne Speres.
Let Us Drink.
Marigold and Myrrh.
Money Makes the Man.
Ship of State, The.
Song of Thirst.
Storm, The.
Storm at Sea.
Terrible Man, A.
To Athena.
To Castor and Pollux.
To His Brother in the Service of Nebuchadnezzar.
To Melanippus.
To Sappho.
Two Drinking Songs.
Wine's Sting.
Zeus rains upon us, and from the sky comes down.
ALCAEUS OF MESSENE. Breathe, Mountain Pan, a joyous note.
Philip, King of Macedon.
Unmourn'd, unburied, traveller, we lie.
Zeus! since by Philip scal'd Macynus' wall.
ALCAMO, CIULLO D'. *See* CIULLO D'ALCAMO.
ALCÁZAR, BALTASAR DEL. Jolly Supper, The.
Sleep.
Woman's Jealousy.
ALCMAN. Asleep.
Fragment: "Mountain summits sleep, The."
Hagesichora.
Halcyons, The.
Mountain brows, the rocks, the peaks are sleeping, The.
Night [and the Plain of Sparta].
No More, O Maidens.
Old Poet to His Maiden Choir, The.
On the Mountains.
Quail, The.
Sinner, The.
Sleep upon the World.
To His Maiden Quire.
Verily there is a vengeance from on high.
Vesper.
ALCOTT, AMOS BRONSON. Approaching God.
Bartol.
Channing.
Emerson.
Excellence.
Garrison.
Hawthorne.
Margaret Fuller.
Thoreau.
Wendell Phillips.
ALCOTT, LOUISA MAY. My Kingdom.
Thoreau's Flute.
To Mother.
Transfiguration.
ALCUIN. His Epitaph.
To a Run-away Pupil.
To the Cuckoo.
AL-DABBAJ. Two Suns.
ALDANA, FRANCISCO. Image of God, The.
ALDEN, ADA. *See* MURRAY, ADA FOSTER.
ALDEN, HENRY MILLS. Magic Mirror, The.
ALDERSON, ALETHEA TODD. In the Public Library.
ALDERSON, D. F. Montezuma.
AL-DHAHABI. Introduction, The.
ALDINGTON, HILDA DOOLITTLE. *See* DOOLITTLE, HILDA ("H. D.").
ALDINGTON, RICHARD. After Two Years.
Alcestis, *sel.*, *tr.*
All Lovely Things.
At the British Museum.
Ballata: Flowers and Love, *tr. Fr.* The Decameron.
Carnival Song: Song of the Girls and the Tattlers (Cicadas), *tr.*
Carnival Song: Triumph of Bacchus and Ariadne, *tr.*
Choricos.
Dawn.
Decameron, The, *sel.*, *tr.*
Elysia, *tr.*
Epigrams.
Epitaph for Giotto, the Painter, *tr.*
Evening.
Fannia, *tr.*
Faun Sees Snow for the First Time, The.
Girl, A. *Fr.* Epigrams.
Images.
Lesbia.
Lucia, *tr.*
Moment's Interlude, A.
New Love. *Fr.* Epigrams.
October. *Fr.* Epigrams.
Of the Dust in an Hour-Glass, *tr.*
Poplar, The.
Possession.
Prayer: "I am a garden of red tulips."
Simonetta, *tr.*
Sonnet: Dream, The, *tr.*
Sonnet: In Absence, *tr.*
Sonnet: To a Balcony, *tr.*
Sunsets.
Thyrsis, *tr.*
To Alcestis, *tr. Fr.* Alcestis.
To Demeter, *tr.*
To the Muse of Sirmio, *tr.*
Vicarious Atonement.
Wine-Cup, The.
ALDIS, DOROTHY. About Buttons.
At the Circus.
Balloon Man, The.
Bare-Back Rider. *Fr.* At the Circus.
Blum.
Brooms.
Elephants, The. *Fr.* At the Circus.
Everybody Says.
Feet.
Flies.
For Christmas.
Fourth of July Night.
Grasshoppers, The.
Hands.
Harper's Farm, The.
Hiding.
Hot Weather.
Ice.
Ice Man, The.
In the Barnyard.
Little.
Mister Carrot.
My Brother.
Names.
Night and Morning.
Not Any More.
Our Little Calf.
Our Silly Little Sister.
Picnic, The.
Radiator Lions.
Reason, The.
Seals, The. *Fr.* At the Circus.
Setting the Table.
Singing.
Skipping Ropes.
Snow.
Story of the Baby Squirrel, The.

ALDIS, DOROTHY (*continued*)
Troubles.
What Am I?
When.
Whistles.
Windy Wash Day.
Winter Coats.
ALDIS, MARY. Barberries.
Flash-Lights.
Seven Sad Sonnets.
When You Come.
ALDRICH, ANNE REEVE. April—and Dying.
Crowned Poet, A.
Death at Daybreak.
Eternal Justice, The.
Fanny.
Fraternity.
In November.
Little Parable, A.
Love's Change.
Music of Hungary.
Recollection.
Song about Singing, A.
Suppose.
ALDRICH, HENRY. Catch, A: "If all be true that I do think."
Christ Church Bells, *at.*
Five Reasons [for Drinking], The.
If All Be True That I Do Think.
If on my theme I rightly think.
Reasons for Drinking.
Why I Drink.
ALDRICH, JAMES. Death-Bed, A.
ALDRICH, THOMAS BAILEY. Act V (Midnight).
After the Rain.
Alec Yeaton's Son.
Andalusian Cradle-Song. *Fr.* Mercedes.
Andromeda.
Another Invitation.
Apparitions.
Appreciation.
Baby Bell.
Bayard Taylor.
Before the Rain.
Bells at Midnight, The.
Bluebird, The. *Fr.* Spring in New England.
By the Potomac.
Circumstance.
Comedy.
Cradle Song: "Ere the moon begins to rise."
Crescent and the Cross, The.
Difference, The.
Dirge: "Let us keep him warm."
Dressing the Bride.
Enamored Architect of Airy Rhyme.
Flight of the Goddess, The.
Forever and a Day.
Fredericksburg.
Great Captain, Glorious in Our Wars.
Guilielmus Rex.
Heredity.
Hesperides.
Hint from Herrick, A.
I Vex Me Not with Brooding on the Years.
Identity.
I'll Not Confer with Sorrow.
Kriss Kringle.
Lady of Castlenoire.
L'Eau Dormante.
Longfellow.
Maple Leaves.
Marjorie's Almanac.
Masks.
Memories.
Memory.
Mercedes, *sel.*
Metempsychosis, The.
Monastic Scribe, The.
Monody on the Death of Wendell Phillips.
No Songs in Winter.
Nocturne: "Up to her chamber window."
October.
Ode, An: On the Unveiling of the Shaw Memorial on Boston Common.
On an Intaglio Head of Minerva.
On Lynn Terrace.
On Reading.
Originality.
Outward Bound.
Palabras Cariñosas.
Pessimist and Optimist.
Petition, A.
Poet's Grave, A.
Prescience.
Quite like a Stocking.
Quits.
Realism.
Reminiscence.
Sargent's Portrait of Edwin Booth at "The Player's."
Sea Longings.
Shadow of the Night, A.
Sleep.
Sleepy Song.
Song from the Persian.
Spring in New England, *sel.*
Tennyson.
Thalia.
Thanksgiving Day.
Tiger-Lilies.
To Hafiz.
Touch of Nature, A.
Turkish Legend, A.
Undiscovered Country, The.
Unguarded Gates.
Unsung.
Untimely Thought.
When the Sultan Goes to Ispahan.
World's Way, The.
ALDRIDGE, RICHARD. By Return Mail.
Matter of Life and Death, A.
Pine Bough, The.
Serendipity of Love, A.
Spring Night.
To Himself.
Weeping Willow.
ALEICHEM, SHOLOM. Epitaph: "Here lies a simple Jew."
Sleep, My Child.
ALEIXANDRE, VICENTE. Beetle, The.
Come Always, Come.
Come, Come Thou.
Death.
Eagles.
I Would Know.
Light.
Song to a Dead Girl.
Total Love.
Without Light.
ALEPOUDELIS, ODYSSEUS. *See* "ELYTIS, ODYSSEUS."
ALEXANDER, MRS. Crow, The.
ALEXANDER, ALBERT LOUIS. This, Too, Shall Pass Away, *ad. fr. var. sources.*
ALEXANDER, CECIL FRANCES (Mrs. William Alexander). Adoration of the Wise Men, The.
All Things Bright and Beautiful.
Breastplate of St. Patrick, The, *tr.*
Burial of Moses, The.
Christmas Hymn, A: "Once in royal David's city."
Creation, The.
Dreams.
Evening Hymn.
Evening Song.
He Is Risen.
His Are the Thousand Sparkling Rills.
Irish Mother's Lament, The.
Jesus Calls Us o'er the Tumult.
Little Sister Left in Charge, The.
Morning Hymn.
Once in Royal David's City.
St. Patrick's Breastplate, *tr.*
St. Simon and St. Jude's Day.
Saw Ye Never in the Meadows.
Siege of Derry, The.
There Is a Green Hill Far Away.
ALEXANDER, FRANCES. Contentment of Willoughby, The.
Old Women.
ALEXANDER, JOHN T. Winning of the TV West, The.
ALEXANDER, JOSEPH ADDISON. Doomed Man, The. *Fr.* The Hidden Line.
Hidden Line, The.
ALEXANDER, LEWIS. Africa.
Dark Brother, The.
Day and Night.
Dream Song.
Japanese Hokku.
Negro Woman.
Nocturne Varial.
Tanka.
Transformation.
ALEXANDER, LILLA M. There Is Never a Day So Dreary.
ALEXANDER, S. J. To San Francisco.
ALEXANDER, SIDNEY. Castle, The.
Lenox Avenue.
Marine Cemetery, The, *tr.*
Plane, The.
ALEXANDER, SIR WILLIAM. *See* STIRLING, WILLIAM ALEXANDER, EARL OF.
ALEXANDER, WILLIAM, ARCHBISHOP OF ARMAGH. Among the Sand-Hills.
Birthday Crown, The.
Frost-Morning.
Inscription: "Oh, in the quiet haven, safe for aye."
Very Far Away.
Vision of Oxford, A, *sel.*
ALEXANDER, MRS. WILLIAM. *See* ALEXANDER, CECIL FRANCES.
ALEXANDER AETOLUS. Euripides.
ALEXIS. Confident Scientist, The.
"Flesh that hath life eat not," Pythagoras said.
AL-FATA AL-KAFIF. White for Mourning.
ALFIERI, VITTORIO. First Brutus, The, *sel.*
To Dante.
ALFONSO X, KING OF CASTILE AND LEON. Cantiga de Santa Maria.
ALFORD, HENRY. Bride, The.
Colonos.
Gypsy Girl, The.
Harvest Home.
Lady Mary.
Mendip Hills over Wells, The.
Sonnet: "Rise, said the Master, come unto the feast."
Ten thousand times ten thousand.
Thanksgiving Day.
You and I.
ALFORD, JANIE. Mother Love.
Thanks Be to God.
ALFORD, JOHN. Glory, Glory to the Sun.
ALFRED, KING OF ENGLAND (Alfred the Great). Consolation of Philosophy, *sel., tr., at.*
King Alfred's Metres of Boethius, *sel., tr.*
Opening Poem, *tr., at. Fr.* Consolation of Philosophy.
Proverbs of King Alfred, *sels., at.*
ALGER, HORATIO, JR. John Maynard.
AL-GHASSANI. Eclipse.
Roses.
AL-HADRAMI. Beauty's Armoury.
Departure.
AL-HAITHAM. Meteor.
Rich and Poor.
Rising Sun, The.
AL-HAJJAM. Broken Water-Wheel, The.
Candle, The.
False Friend.
Pen, The.
Stork, The.
Toothpick, The.
Vultures.
AL-HARIZI, JUDAH. Heavy-hearted.
Love Song.
Song of the Flea.
Song of the Pen, The.
Under Leafy Bowers.
Unhappy Lover, The.
Within My Heart.
AL-HUSRI. Breeze, The.
Tress, The.
ALI BEN ABU TALEB. Friends and Enemies [*or* Foes], *at.*
Make Friends, *at.*
ALIGER, MARGARITA. Epilogue: "And lo! it shines upon the cities." *Fr.* Your Victory.
Your Victory, *sel.*
ALIGHIERI, DANTE. *See* DANTE ALIGHIERI.
ALINGTON, CYRIL ARGENTINE. To the School at War.

ALISHAN, LEO. Easter Song.
Lily of Shavarshan, The.
Nightingale of Avarair, The.
AL-ISRA'ILI. Sprouting Beard, The.
Trees and Waves.
AL-JAZIRI. Forgiveness.
AL-JAZZAR. Moon of Grace.
ALKABEZ, SOLOMON HALEVI. Come, O Friend, to Greet the Bride.
AL-KASAD. Lost Angel, The.
AL-KUTANDI. Elegy for a Dead King.
River of Seville.
AL-LAMA'I. Night Storm.
ALLAN, EDWIN. Ass, The.
ALLAN, M. Echo Poem.
ALLAN, MABEL ESTHER. I Looked at England.
ALLAN, ROBERT. To a Linnet.
ALLAN, THOMAS H. Leave the Miracle to Him.
ALLEN, ALICE E. Life's Common Things.
My Mother's Garden.
Victory.
ALLEN, DON CAMERON. *For translations from Latin, see* LaP.
ALLEN, ELIZABETH AKERS ("Florence Percy"). Bird's Nest, A.
Bringing Our Sheaves.
Endurance.
In a Garret.
In April.
Last Landlord, The.
Left Behind.
Little Feet.
Lost Light.
Miracle-Workers, The.
"My Dearling."
My Ship.
Pipe of Pan, The.
Rock Me to Sleep.
Sea-Birds.
Snow.
Spring at the Capital.
Until Death.
ALLEN, ERNEST BOURNER. Hymn of Peace, A.
"I Am with Thee."
ALLEN, FLORENCE ELLENWOOD. Beethoven.
Old World to the New, The.
ALLEN, GEORGE. Chorus: Kings of Troy, The, *tr. Fr.* Andromache.
Cloister, The.
Lament for Adonis, *sel., tr.*
For other translations from Greek, see GrL; OxBG.
ALLEN, GEORGE LEONARD. Portrait.
To Melody.
ALLEN, GLEN. Woman I Am, The.
ALLEN, GRACE ELISABETH. Pinkletinks.
ALLEN, GRANT. Across the roaring ocean, with heart and with eye of flame, *tr.*
Ballade of Evolution.
First Idealist, The.
Prayer, A: "Crowned Caprice is god of this world, A."
ALLEN, HERVEY. Beyond Debate.
Carolina Spring Song.
Confession.
Funeral at High Tide.
Gargantua.
La Fayette Lands.
Moments.
Old Meadows.
Palmetto Town.
Priest and the Pirate, The.
Refuge.
Saga of Leif the Lucky, *sel.*
Shadow to Shadow.
Southward Sidonian Hanno.
Tower of Genghis Khan, The.
Upstairs Downstairs.
Walls.
We.
Whim Alley.
ALLEN, LESLIE HOLDSWORTH. Memnon.
Reaper, The.
ALLEN, LYMAN WHITNEY. Coming of His Feet, The.
Great American, The. *Fr.* The Star of Sangamon.
People's King, The.
Star of Sangamon, The.
Star of Sangamon, The, *sel.*
ALLEN, MARIE LOUISE. First Snow.
Mitten Song, The.
My Zipper Suit.
What Is It?
ALLEN, MARJORIE. *See* SEIFFERT, MARJORIE ALLEN.
ALLEN, PHILIP F. Horse and His Master, The.
ALLEN, SARA VAN ALSTYNE. Marble Statuette Harpist.
Walk on a Winter Day.
Zoo in the City, The.
ALLEN, WILLIAM S. Erie Canal, The.
Low Bridge, Everybody Down.
ALLEN, WILLIS BOYD. Cradle-Song of the Night Wind, A.
Thalatta.
ALLER, KATHARINE L. God of a Universe within Whose Bounds.
ALLERTON, ELLEN PALMER. Beautiful Things.
ALLESTRY, JACOB. What Art Thou, Love?
ALLFREY, PHYLLIS. Room under Bombardment.
ALLINE, HENRY. Christ Inviting Sinners to His Grace, *sel.*
ALLING, KENNETH SLADE. Beauty.
Dead Wasp.
Dr. Donne.
Duality.
First World War.
Iced Branches.
Monsoon.
On the Park Bench.
On the Passing of the Last Fire Horse from Manhattan Island.
Onion Skin in Barn.
Presence, A.
Rain.
Unscarred Fighter Remembers France, The.
Wind, Wind.
ALLINGHAM, WILLIAM. Abbey Asaroe.
Abbot of Inisfalen, The.
Adieu to Belashanny.
Aeolian Harp.
After Sunset.
Among the Heather.
Ballytullagh. *Fr.* Laurence Bloomfield in Ireland.
Ban-Shee, The.
Bird, The.
Blowing Bubbles.
Boy, The.
Bubble, The.
By the Way, *sel.*
Child's Song, A.
Day and Night Songs.
Death Deposed.
Dirty Old Man, The.
Dream, A.
Earth's Night.
Elf Singing, The.
Evening, An.
Fairies, The.
Fairies, The, *sel.*
Fairy Folk, The.
Fairy King, The.
Fairy Shoemaker, The.
Four Ducks on a Pond.
Fragment: "Near where the riotous Atlantic surge."
Fragment: "Wing'd seeds with decaying wings, The."
Fragment: "You see/ Nestled into a hollow of the downs." *Fr.* By the Way.
George Levison.
Girls Going to the Fair.
Girl's Lamentation, The.
Gravestone, A.
Half-waking.
Homeward Bound.
I Love You, Dear.
In a Spring Grove.
In Snow.
Irish History.
Kate o' Belashanny.
Late Autumn.
Laurence Bloomfield in Ireland, *sel.*
Leprecaun, or Fairy Shoemaker, The.
Little Men, The. *Fr.* The Fairies.
Lough, The.
Lovely Mary Donnelly.
Lover and Birds, The.
Lupracaun, or Fairy Shoemaker, The.
Maids of Elfin-Mere, The.
Memory, A.
Midsummer.
Milkmaid, The.
Mill, A [*or* The].
Mowers, The.
Nanny's Sailor Lad.
No Funeral Gloom.
Nobleman's Wedding, The.
Robin Redbreast.
Ruined Chapel, The.
Ruins at Sunset.
Sad Song, A.
Sailor, The.
Solitude.
Song: "I walk'd in the lonesome evening."
Song: "O spirit of the Summertime!"
Song: "Across the Sea."
Spring.
Sunday Bells.
Swing Song, A.
Therania.
These little songs.
Three Fragments.
Touchstone, The.
Up the Airy Mountain.
Wealthy Man, A.
Wild Rose.
Winding Banks of Erne, The.
Windlass Song.
Winny.
Wishing.
Witch Bride, The.
ALLINSON, BRENT DOW. Christmas, 1917.
De Profundis. *Fr.* Prayer in the Trenches.
Hero of Vimy, The.
"One World."
Prayer in the Trenches.
ALLISON, DRUMMOND. Brass Horse, The.
Dedication: "Had there been peace there never had been riven."
My Sister Helen.
ALLISON, GEORGE WILLIAM. Were Flowers There?
"ALLISON, JOY" (Mary A. Cragin). Which Loved [Her] Best?
ALLISON, WILLIAM TALBOT. Canadian Pine, The.
Cartier Arrives at Stadacona.
Hymeneal Chant of an Algonquin Maiden, *tr.*
O Amber Day, amid the Autumn Gloom.
Return to Nature, The.
ALLISON, YOUNG EWING. Buccaneers, The.
Dead Men's Song, The.
Derelict.
AL-LISS. Generosity.
Mountain, The.
Night.
Thimble, The.
ALLNUT, PHOEBE CROSBY. Colors.
ALLONBY, MARGARET. Book for Christmas, A.
Eurydice.
For Sheila.
Lustration of the Winter Tree, *sel.*
O Theophilus.
Reflection.
ALLOTT, KENNETH. Cheshire Cat.
Departure Platform.
Fête Champêtre.
ALLSTON, WASHINGTON. America to Great Britain.
Boyhood.
On the Late S. T. Coleridge.
Rosalie.
To Benjamin West.
ALLWOOD, BRIAN. No Laws.
ALLWOOD, MARTIN SAMUEL. Deaths, The, *tr.*
Dies Irae, *tr.*
Gethsemane, Illinois.
Journey: IV, *tr.*

Allwood, Martin Samuel (*continued*)
Life of Life, *tr.*
Man's Love, A, *tr.*
Trumpet and Flute, *tr.*
Allwood, Martin Samuel, *and* Sanford Kaufman. Swallow's Flight, The, *tr.*
Allwood, Martin Samuel, *and* Carl Nesjar. *See* Nesjar, Carl, *and* Martin S. Allwood.
Al-Mahdi. Preacher, The.
Alma-Tadema, Laurence. Bed-Time.
Blessing for the Blessed, A.
Gravel Path, The.
If No One Ever Marries Me.
Lambs in the Meadow.
Looking Forward.
Lullaby, A: "Baby, baby, hush-a-bye."
Playgrounds.
Robin, The.
Snowdrops.
Strange Lands.
Sunset.
Warm Cradle, The.
Wintry Lullaby, A.
"Almi, A." (Elias Sheps). Everywhere.
Almquist, Karl Jonas Love. Heart's Flower, The.
Witch of King Charles's Time, A.
Al-Munfatil. Enchantress.
Mole, The.
Al-Munsafi. Colloquy.
Skiff, The.
Al-Mushafi. Pearls.
Al-Mustazhir. Banished Lover, The.
Al-Mu'tamid. *See* Mu'tamid, King of Seville.
Al Mutanabbi. Shame Hitherto.
Written in Flight from His Royal Patron.
Al-Mutawakkil. Invitation.
Almy, Amy Bruner. Carpenter, The.
Al-Nashshar. Garden, The.
Al-Nasir. Royal Pride.
Alpheus [*or* Alphaeus]. Mycenae.
Mycenae Fallen.
Alpheus of Mitylene. Homer.
Life through Verse.
Alphonsa, Mother Mary. *See* Lathrop, Rose Hawthorne.
Alphonsus Liguori, Saint. Madonna's Lullaby.
Al-Qalami. Ramadan.
Alqamah. His Camel. *Fr.* The Mufaddaliyat.
Al-Radi Billah. Passers By, The.
Al-Ramadi. Shaven Beauty, The.
Al-Rusafi. Abode Divine.
Stream, The.
Weaver's Apprentice, The.
Young Carpenter, The.
Alsop, Richard. To the Shade of Washington.
Alston, Joseph Blynth. "Stack Arms!"
Al-Sumaisir. Glutton, The.
Mosquitoes.
Al-Taliq. Saki.
Altamirano, Ignacio Manuel. To the Atoyac.
Altenburg, Michael. Battle Hymn.
Battle-Song of Gustavus Adolphus, The.
Alterman, Nathan. From All Peoples, *sel.*
Poem: "Wisdom has no end and folly no ornament."
Saul.
Altolaguirre, Manuel. Along the sand of the beach.
Arches of a bridge my eyes.
He was master of self, master of nothing.
Hidden senses of the Universe.
How the ground escapes me!
I shall unsheathe my soul.
I would go to the white beach.
Meadow, The.
My body seems to me to-day.
On the Beach.
So high reached my sorrow.
Time is a flat even plain.
To a Cloud.
Waters ill-fated, sad spinsters.
What a blow that of the knocker.
Within me I bear my solitude.
Altrocchi, Julia Cooley (Mrs. Rudolph Altrocchi). Dreamers of Death, The.
Pigeon-Feeders in Battery Park, The.
Altrocchi, Rudolph. Insect Wives.
Al-Tulaitili. Ant, The.
Altun. Tchirek Song.
Al-Tutili. Battle.
Contentment.
Lion Fountain.
Sacrifice.
Seville.
Alvarez, Alfred. Catharsis, The.
Who'll Toll the Knell?
Alvarez Quintero, Serafín, *and* Joaquín Alvarez Quintero. Fan, The.
Alyea, Dorothy. Keepsake from Quinault.
Amaltheo, Girolamo. Of the Dust in an Hour-Glass.
Amarou. Drunken Rose, The.
Ambrose, Saint. Aeterne Rerum Conditor.
Before the ending of the day, *at.*
Verbum Supernum, *at.*
Amenhotep IV. *See* Ikhnaton.
Amergin. Aimirgin's Invocation, *at.*
Incantation, The, *at.*
Invocation to Ireland, *at.*
Mystery, The, *at.*
Ames, A. S. Abraham Lincoln.
Ames, Eleanor Maria Easterbrook. *See* "Kirk, Eleanor."
Ames, Evelyn. Because I Live.
Two Solitudes.
Ames, Mary Clemmer. *See* Clemmer, Mary.
Amici, Ruggieri d'. Canzone: Of Distance.
Amiel, Henri Frédéric. Each Thought of Ours Is Like a Flower.
Amir Khusrau. Goddess.
Amis, Kingsley. Against Romanticism.
Bookshop Idyll, A.
Departure.
Dream of Fair Women, A.
Masters.
Sources of the Past, The.
Amittai ben Shefatiah. Hymn of Weeping.
Ammianus. Morn follows morn, and day succeeds to day.
Omnes Eodem Cogimur.
Thou thinkest that beard of thine brains can create.
Ammonides. Secret Weapon.
Amon-Re. Hymn of Victory: Thutmose III.
Amoss, Harry (Harold Edwin Amoss). Pedagogical Principles.
Riding.
Amphis. Solace of Art, The.
Anacreon. As late I sought the spangled bowers. *Fr.* Odes.
Coy Mistress, The.
Drinking.
Envy-free.
For Choice.
Gentlemen Topers.
Give me the harp of epic song. *Fr.* Odes.
Golden Mean, The.
Grasshopper, The, *at.*
Horns to Bulls Wise Nature Lends.
I care not for the idle state. *Fr.* Odes.
I saw the smiling bard of pleasure. *Fr.* Odes.
Labuntur Anni.
Listen to the Muse's lyre. *Fr.* Odes.
Love.
Nunc Est Bibendum.
Odes, *sels.*
Old Age.
Old I Am, *at.*
On a Slain Warrior.
Sculptor, wouldst thou glad my soul. *Fr.* Odes.
Soldier's Grave, A.
Take Her, Break Her.
Tell Me Why.
Temperate Drinking.
Thou'st Had Thy Day.
To Artemis.
To Cleobulus.
To Dionysus.
To Eros.
To Himself.
Vulcan! hear your glorious task. *Fr.* Odes.
War's Folly.
Why with Scorn-reverting Eye.
Women tell me every day, The. *Fr.* Odes.
Anatolius. Fierce Was the Wild Billow.
Great and Mighty Wonder.
Jesus, Deliverer.
Peace on Earth.
Anaxandrides. Man who doubts if he should marry, A.
Anaxilas. Cautious Householder, The.
Human Worms.
"Ande" (Angela Milne). Coconut, The.
Andersen, Hans Christian. Little Match-Girl, The.
Pearl, The.
Rosebud, The.
Andersen, Johannes Carl. Summer.
Anderson, Alan. Lower Animals.
Sandy—A Small Dog.
Anderson, Alexander ("Surfaceman").
Cuddle Doon.
Jenny wi' the Airn Teeth.
Langsyne, When Life Was Bonnie.
Toshie Norrie.
Anderson, Ethel Louisa Mason. Flood.
Love in Age.
Migrants.
Yesterday.
Anderson, Hester L. American Girl and the War, The.
Anderson, John. Clipper Ships.
Shadows of Sails.
Anderson, John Redwood. Allotments.
Before Ararat.
Caravan, The.
Crane, The.
Fish-Cart, The.
Heat.
Mary O'Brian.
Anderson, Lee. Prevailing Winds.
Anderson, Margaret Steele. Breaking, The.
Somebody's Garden.
Song: "Bride, she wears a white, white rose—the plucking it was mine, The."
Anderson, Mary. In the April Rain.
Praise.
Thanks to Spring.
Anderson, Mary Louisa. Now, Lord, upon Thy Sea of Air.
Anderson, Maxwell. Full-Circle.
Holy City, A. *Fr.* The Star Wagon.
Journey to Jerusalem, *sel.*
Judith of Minnewaulken, *sel.*
Judith Remembers. *Fr.* Judith of Minnewaulken.
Prayer after Youth.
Star Wagon, The, *sel.*
Time When I Was Plowing, The.
Toll the Bell for Damon.
Anderson, Molly. *See* Haley, Molly Anderson.
Anderson, Patrick. Camp.
Capital Square.
Cold Colloquy. *Fr.* Poem on Canada.
Coming of the White Man, The. *Fr.* Poem on Canada.
Desert.
Drinker.
In the Hospital.
Mother's Boy.
My Bird-wrung Youth.
Poem on Canada, *sels.*
Portrait.
Ski Train.
Sleighride.
Summer's Joe.
War Dead.
Winter in Montreal.
Anderson, Persis Greely. Lengthy Symphony.
Melodie Grotesque.
Old Mandarin, The.

Penelope.
Question Mark, The.
Those Who Read in Bed.
ANDERSON, SHERWOOD. American Spring Song.
Chicago.
Evening Song.
Lame One, The.
Song of Industrial America.
ANDERSON, VIOLET. Cloak, The.
Through the Barber Shop Window.
ANDRADE, EDWARD NEVILLE DA COSTA. Song: "Nothing I have is worth a tear."
ANDRÉ, JOHN. Cow-Chace, The.
ANDREW, FATHER. Love's Argument.
ANDREW, HAROLD. Poem for the Living.
ANDREW OF CRETE, SAINT. Christian, Dost Thou See Them?
ANDREWES, FRANCIS. Phyllis Inamorata.
ANDREWS, ALBERT CHARLTON. Our Modest Doughboys.
ANDREWS, ARNOLD. Master Blacksmith, The.
ANDREWS, H. G. Give me of love my love to prove.
Take heed, my love.
ANDREWS, JOHN. Anatomy of Baseness, The, *sel.*
To the Detracted. *Fr.* The Anatomy of Baseness.
ANDREWS, JOHN WILLIAMS. La Madonna di Lorenzetti.
ANDREWS, MARY RAYMOND SHIPMAN. Baby, The.
Call to Arms, A.
ANDRIELLO, AMELIA. Autumn Eve.
ANDROS, R. S. Perseverance.
ANEIRIN [*or* ANEURIN]. Gododdin, *sel.*
Lost Legion, The.
Lovely Youth, The.
Of Manly Disposition.
ANGELINE, SISTER MARY. Laughter in Heaven.
ANGELITA, SISTER MARY. Dust.
Perpetual Vows.
Signum Cui Contradicetur.
Spinning Top, The.
To a Poet.
ANGELL, CHARLES R. Clouds.
ANGELL, WALTER FOSTER. To New Haven and Boston.
"ANGELUS SILESIUS" (Johannes Scheffler). Cherubic Pilgrim, The.
Death Is a Blessed Thing.
In Spirit Senses Are.
In Thine Own Heart.
Man Beholdeth God, A.
Nearest Way to God, The.
Not After nor Before.
Nothing Fair on Earth I See.
Rose, The.
Song of Praise to Mary.
Soul Wherein God Dwells, The.
They Say That Time Is Swift.
Thou Art Not in a Place.
Tree of the Cross, The.
Two Eyes Our Souls Possess.
Who Not with Others Bides.
Young Love Storms Like New Wine.
ANGERMAYER, FRANCES. Conversion.
ANGIOLIERI, CECCO, DA SIENA. *See* CECCO ANGIOLIERI DA SIENA.
ANGOFF, CHARLES. Litany: "When the sun rises on another day."
Little Girl, A.
ANGUITA, EDUARDO. Passage to the End.
Service.
ANGUS, MARION. Alas! Poor Queen.
Mary's Song.
"ANISE." *See* STRONG, ANNA LOUISE.
ANNAN, ANNIE RANKIN. Dandelion.
ANNAND, RACHEL. *See* TAYLOR, RACHEL ANNAND.
ANNENSKI [*or* ANNENSKY], INNOKENTI FYODOROVICH. Minute, A.
My Anguish.
October Myth.
Poppies.
ANSELM, SAINT. To Our Lord in the Sacrament.
"ANSKY, S." (Solomon Rappoport). Emigrant Song.
Tailor, The.
ANSTADT, HENRY. Little Rhyme and a Little Reason, A.
ANSTER, JOHN. Fairy Child, The.
If I Might Choose.
Sonnet: "If I might choose where my tired limbs shall lie."
ANSTEY, CHRISTOPHER. Letter Containing a Panegyric on Bath. *Fr.* The New Bath Guide.
Taste and Spirit. *Fr.* The New Bath Guide.
New Bath Guide, The, *sels.*
"ANSTEY, F." (Thomas Anstey Guthrie).
Burglar Bill.
Conscience-curst, The.
Juniper Jim.
Limerick: "There was an old man of Bengal."
Ordinary valour only works, The.
Select Passages from a Coming Poet.
ANT, HOWARD. Bucket of Sea-Serpents.
ANTARA. Abla. *Fr.* The Mu'allaqát.
ANTELLA, SIMONE DALL'. Prolonged Sonnet.
ANTHIAS, TEFCROS. Clown, The.
Epilogue: "Tramp! Tonight the night is so fine."
Hands Thrust in Pockets.
ANTHONY, ED. College Song.
ANTHONY, EDWARD ("A. C. Gate"). Advice to Small Children.
Bloodhound, The.
Bloodhound Speaks, The.
Bulldog Speaks, The.
Character Building.
Collies, The.
Dachshund, The.
Duty of the Student.
Fala.
Greyhound Speaks, The.
Let Others Share.
Oddity Land, *sels.*
ANTHONY OF PADUA, SAINT. Death-Bed Hymn of Saint Anthony of Padua.
ANTIN, ESTHER. Corn. *Fr.* On Our Farm.
Garden, The. *Fr.* On Our Farm.
Making Mushrooms.
On Our Farm.
Our Pets. *Fr.* On Our Farm.
Peter and Polly. *Fr.* On Our Farm.
Tit for Tat.
ANTIPATER OF SIDON. Aristeides.
Autumn.
Eagle on a Tombstone.
Erinna.
Greater Love.
Himself He Could Not Save.
Lament for Corinth.
Man at Peace.
Mournful Nut-Tree, The.
On Corinth Fallen.
Orpheus.
Pindar.
Poetess Erinna, The.
Preface to Erinna's Poems.
Ruins of Corinth, The.
Sea-Birds Crying above the Ruins of Corinth, The.
Terrifying Tell-Tale, The.
This rudely sculptured porter-pot.
To Anacreon.
To Sappho.
Undying Thirst.
Vengeance of the Nymphs, The.
ANTIPATER OF THESSALONICA. Amphipolis.
Desolation of the Cyclades, The.
Drachma and Europa's yours, A.
Drowned in Harbour.
Hero's Tower.
Thy Distaff Ply.
Two sailors, when the vessel sank.
Water Mill, A.
Wife's Prayer, The.
ANTIPHANES. No creature's so unlucky as a fish!
Not Dead, but Gone Before.
Profession of Flattery, The.
Tragic poet's a happy man, The.
ANTIPHILUS [*or* ANTIPHILOS] OF BYZANTIUM. Elms of Protesilaus, The.
Freshet, A.
Imaginary Dialogue.
Noontide Rest.
Old Ferryman, The.
On a ship's poop I'd like to lie, if I could have my way.
Once in a Way.
Simple Pleasures.
ANTISTIUS. Small Cleodemus.
ANTOKOLSKY, PAVEL GRIGORYEVICH. Hate!
ANTONINUS, BROTHER (William Everson). Advent.
Canticle to the Waterbirds, A.
Raid, The.
South Coast, The.
ANTROBUS, JOHN. Cowboy, The.
ANVARI. Tears of Khorassan, The.
ANYTE [*or* ANYTES]. Billy Goat, The.
By the Fountain.
Death the Leveller.
Dolphin's Tomb, The.
Goat, The.
Here in the orchard's breezy nook.
Maid Antibia, The.
On a Fountain.
Refreshment.
Seaward the gentle Cyprian loves to gaze.
Shepherd's Gift, A.
Spring of Hermes, The.
Statue of Cypris, A.
To a Dead Cockerel.
Under a Laurel.
ANZAI, FUYUE. Birthday Again.
Gulf of Tartary and a Butterfly, The.
Warship *Mari,* The.
APOLLINAIRE, GUILLAUME. Always.
Annie.
Autumn.
Bells, The.
Company Commander.
Departure.
Dusk.
Goodbye, The.
Hills.
Hunting Horns.
I Had the Courage.
I List.
Marizibill.
Mirabeau Bridge, The.
Poem to Lou.
Pont Mirabeau.
Porpoise.
Pretty Redhead, The.
Rhenish Autumn.
Rosamunde.
Salome.
Shadow.
Sick Autumn.
Song of the Ill-Beloved, The.
Star.
Towards the South.
Vendémiaire.
War.
What Weariness Is Mine.
White Snow.
You Will Grieve.
Zone.
APOLLINARIS SIDONIUS. Invitation to the Dance.
APOLLONIDES. Poor Farmer's Offering, The.
APOLLONIUS RHODIUS. Accordingly Medea Met Jason in the Temple of Hecate. *Fr.* Argonautica.
Amor Omnipotens. *Fr.* Argonautica.
Argonautica. *sels.*
Eros and His Mother. *Fr.* Argonautica.
Heart-Searchings of Medea, The. *Fr.* Argonautica.
Hylas. *Fr.* Argonautica.
Jason's Sowing and Reaping. *Fr.* Argonautica.
Medea Betrayed. *Fr.* Argonautica.
Medea's Dream. *Fr.* Argonautica.
Medea's Hesitation. *Fr.* Argonautica.
Medea's Parting Words. *Fr.* Argonautica.
Medea's Passion. *Fr.* Argonautica.
Meeting, The. *Fr.* Argonautica.
Meeting of Medea and Jason, The. *Fr.* Argonautica.
Moving Rocks, The. *Fr.* Argonautica.

Apollonius Rhodius (*continued*)
Remorse. *Fr.* Argonautica.
Sailing of the Argo, The. *Fr.* Argonautica.
She Tells Him How to Win the Fleece. *Fr.* Argonautica.
Slaying of the Earth-born, The. *Fr.* Argonautica.
Vigil and Remorse. *Fr.* Argonautica.
Appel, Benjamin. Talker, The.
Appleton, Everard Jack. Fighting Failure, The.
One, The.
Apukhtin, Aleksey Nikolayevich. Broken Vase, The.
Flies.
Apuleius, Lucius. Eros and Psyche, *sels.*
Aquinas, Saint Thomas. *See* Thomas Aquinas, Saint.
Arabius Scholasticus. Villa by the Bosphorus, A.
Aragon, Louis. Dirge for the Barrel-Organ of the New Barbarism.
Elsa's Eyes.
Tcheliabtraktrostroi Waltz, *sel.*
Zone Libre.
Aratus. Phaenomena, *sels.*
Proem. *Fr.* Phaenomena.
Signs of Rain. *Fr.* Phaenomena.
When Justice Dwelt on Earth. *Fr.* Phaenomena.
Arberry, A. J. *For translations from Arabic, see* MooP.
For translations from Persian, see PeP.
Arbuthnot, John. Godlike Brute, The. *Fr.* Know Yourself.
Know Yourself, *sels.*
Archer, Kate Rennie. Lairdless Place, The.
Archer, Sara F. Flag Song.
Archer, William George. White Curtains, The.
Archevolti, Samuel ben Elhanan Isaac, of Padua. Advice to Hotheads.
Archias. "Ah, Poor Faun, Poor Faun!"
Best Not to Be Born.
Dedication to Athene, A.
Echo.
Empty all your quiver on me.
I, Theris, who lie buried on this shore.
Imitatrix Ales.
Labour Lost.
Tomb by the Sea, A.
Archias of Byzantium. Sea Dirge.
Seaside Grave, A.
Archilochus. Be Still, My Soul.
Better Part of Valour, The.
Beware!
Blaming the bitterness of this sorrow, Perikles, no man.
Bows will not avail thee.
Come then, my friend, and seize the flask.
Equanimity.
Freelance, The.
General, A.
Girl, A.
Girlhood.
God Punishes.
God's Ways to Man.
I do not like a swagger captain.
Ideal General, The.
Knowledge.
Leave the gods to order all things.
Life and Art.
Miniature.
Naught, now, can pass belief; in Nature's ways.
On the Loss of His Shield.
Poet's Shield, The.
Poet's Spear, The.
Rough Sea.
Simple Tastes.
Some Thracian strutteth with my shield.
Staff of Life.
Sursum Corda.
Thasos.
There Is Nothing Strange.
Too Versatile.
Tossed on a sea of troubles, Soul, my Soul.
Wealth of gold-abounding Croisos, The.
"Archpoet of Cologne, the." Confession of Golias, The.
Confession of Golias, The, *sel.*
Drinking Song. *Fr.* The Confession of Golias.
Omnia Tempus Habent.
Arensberg, Walter Conrad. About an Allegory.
Chryseis.
Dialogue.
Inner Significance of the Statues Seated outside the Boston Public Library, The.
Masterpiece, The.
Out of Doors.
To a Poet.
To Hasekawa.
Voyage à l'Infini.
Aretino, Pietro. Serious Sonnets: Sleep, Ariosto!
Arévalo Martínez, Rafael. Clean Clothes.
Arey, John. To Becky in France.
Argensola, Bartolomé Leonardo de. Not of This World.
To Mary Magdalen.
Argentarius, Marcus. Blackbird, A.
Epigram: "Thou art in danger, Cincius, on my word."
"For All the Saints and Sages."
Love's Tyranny.
Lyre and the Crown, The.
Old Story, The.
Poor Man Is Not Loved, The.
Reading Hesiod.
"Rumoresque Senum Severiorum."
Serenade: "Wake, Isias, lips of fragrance."
Thin Diocleia I would see, for though.
Upon this seal Love whom none e'er withstands.
Yesterday my pretty Nell.
Arguijo, Don Juan de. To Friendship.
Argyll, 9th Duke of. *See* Campbell, John Douglas Sutherland.
Arion. Hymn to Poseidon, *at.*
Mighty master of the ocean! *at.*
Ariosto, Ludovico [*or* Lodovico]. Angelica and the Ork. *Fr.* Orlando Furioso.
Can I Believe.
Her Matchless Person. *Fr.* Orlando Furioso.
Lover's Prison, The.
Lunar Valley of Lost Things, The. *Fr.* Orlando Furioso.
Orlando Furioso, *sels.*
Rose, The. *Fr.* Orlando Furioso.
Satires: In the Service of the Duke.
Sonnet: "Why should I think that heaven hears my prayer."
Aristaenetus. Pleasing Constraint, The.
Aristodicus. Dead Locust, A.
Aristophanes. Acharnians, The, *sels.*
Aeschylean Chorus, An. *Fr.* The Frogs.
Bird-Pastoral. *Fr.* The Birds.
Birds, The, *sels.*
Birds' Life, The. *Fr.* The Birds.
Bounteous Poverty. *Fr.* Plutus.
Building of Cloudcuckoocity [*or* Cloudcuckoobury], The. *Fr.* The Birds.
Chorus: "Brekeke-kesh, koash, koash." *Fr.* The Frogs.
Chorus Hymeneal. *Fr.* The Birds.
Chorus of Birds. *Fr.* The Birds.
Chorus of [the] Clouds. *Fr.* The Clouds.
Chorus of Women. *Fr.* The Thesmophoriazusae.
Clouds, The, *sels.*
Communism? *Fr.* The Ecclesiazusae.
Demos and His Flatterer. *Fr.* The Knights.
Demos Rejuvenated. *Fr.* The Knights.
Demus; a Return to His Better Self. *Fr.* The Knights.
Demus Shriven. *Fr.* The Knights.
Dicaeopolis and the Case for the Enemy. *Fr.* The Acharnians.
Ecclesiazusae, The, *sels.*
Education vs. Fads. *Fr.* The Clouds.
Euripidean Chorus, A. *Fr.* The Frogs.
Euripides. *Fr.* The Thesmophoriazusae.
Fatal Oil-Flask, The. *Fr.* The Frogs.
Frogs, The, *sels.*
Frogs' Song, The. *Fr.* The Frogs.
Gifts of Poverty, The. *Fr.* Plutus.
Grand Chorus of Birds. *Fr.* The Birds.
Hark! the Hoopoe's Call. *Fr.* The Birds.
Hoopoe's Call, The. *Fr.* The Birds.
How the Women Will Stop War. *Fr.* Lysistrata.
Hymn of Peace. *Fr.* Lysistrata.
Hymn of the Birds. *Fr.* The Birds.
Hymn of the Initiates. *Fr.* The Frogs.
Initiates. *Fr.* The Frogs.
Knights, The, *sels.*
Lampoon: In the School of Socrates. *Fr.* The Clouds.
Life of Men, The. *Fr.* The Birds.
Lysistrata, *sels.*
Male Inconsistency. *Fr.* The Thesmophoriazusae.
Mock Trial. *Fr.* The Wasps.
Old Education, The. *Fr.* The Clouds.
Old-Time Virtues. *Fr.* The Knights.
Once More the Simple Things. *Fr.* The Peace.
Peace, The, *sels.*
Plea for the Enemy, A. *Fr.* The Acharnians.
Plutus, *sels.*
Poet and His Public, The. *Fr.* The Acharnians.
Poet and His Rivals, The. *Fr.* The Knights.
Poet and the People, The. *Fr.* The Acharnians.
Political Cartoon. *Fr.* The Knights.
Politics and Perquisites. *Fr.* The Wasps.
Praxagora Rehearses [Her Speech]. *Fr.* The Ecclesiazusae.
Rejoicings for Peace. *Fr.* Lysistrata.
Rival Poets, The. *Fr.* The Frogs.
Rivals, The. *Fr.* The Frogs.
Rogue, The. *Fr.* The Frogs.
Sausage-Seller's Triumph, The. *Fr.* The Knights.
Sky-riding on a Beetle. *Fr.* The Peace.
Slander! *Fr.* The Thesmophoriazusae.
Socrates' Experiments. *Fr.* The Clouds.
Song of the Clouds. *Fr.* The Clouds.
Symptoms of an Ailing Democracy. *Fr.* The Frogs.
Tell-Tale Tag, The. *Fr.* The Frogs.
Thesmophoriazusae, The, *sels.*
To Heaven on a Beetle. *Fr.* The Peace.
To the Fickle Gallery. *Fr.* The Knights.
Trial of the Dog, The. *Fr.* The Wasps.
Vignette of Ancient Peace. *Fr.* The Peace.
Vogue of the Tar-Brush. *Fr.* The Wasps.
Wasps, The, *sels.*
Wedding Chant, The. *Fr.* The Birds.
Woman's Antidote for War, A. *Fr.* Lysistrata.
Aristotle. To Virtue.
Virtue, to men thou bringest care and toil.
Ariwara no Yukihira. I must leave you.
Arkell, Reginald. When the War Will End.
Arkwright, John Stanhope. Supreme Sacrifice, The.
"Arkwright, Peleg." *See* Proudfit, David Law.
Armitage, Laura F. Prayer for the New Year, A.
Armknecht, Richard F. Crow's Nest.
Armour, Richard. Assorted Relishes.
Blurb, The.
Covering the Subject.

Horses.
Money.
Not a Cloud in the Sky.
One Down.
Pillow Cases.
Three Links of Light Armour.
To a Human Skeleton.
Transportation Problem.
Armstrong, Edmund John. Adieu.
Blind Student, The.
Fionnuala, *sel.*
Armstrong, George Francis Savage. *See* Savage-Armstrong, George Francis.
Armstrong, Hamilton Fish. Lines for the Hour.
Armstrong, J. A. Another Reply to "In Flanders Fields," *at.*
Armstrong, John. Art of Preserving Health, The, *sels.*
Blest Winter Nights. *Fr.* The Art of Preserving Health.
Building a Home. *Fr.* The Art of Preserving Health.
Home of the Naiads, The. *Fr.* The Art of Preserving Health.
Armstrong, Martin. Bird's Epitaph, A.
Buzzards, The.
Cage, The.
Envoy: "All the songs here sung."
Gold.
Honey Harvest.
Miss Thompson Goes Shopping.
Mrs. Reece Laughs.
On a Little Bird.
Armstrong, Mildred Bowers. Boredom.
Spring Signs.
Armstrong, Phyllis Eleanor. Form 1040A.
"Armytage, R." *See* Watson, Rosamund Marriott.
Arndt, Ernst Moritz. German Fatherland, The.
Arne, Michael. Lass with the Delicate Air, The.
Arnold, Sir Edwin. After Battle, *tr.* *Fr.* Bhagavad-Gita.
After Death in Arabia, *sel.* Fr. Pearls of the Faith.
Al-Maumin.
Allah, *tr.*
Allah, the Artificer, *tr.*
Almond Blossom.
Armageddon.
Bhagavad-Gita, *sels., tr.*
Black earth tipples rain, The, *tr.*
Bustan, The, *sels., tr.*
Caliph's Draught, The.
Courage, *tr.* *Fr.* The Gulistan.
Dancer, The, *tr.* *Fr.* The Bustan.
Darien.
Darweesh, The, *tr.*
Death, *tr.* *Fr.* Bhagavad-Gita.
Destiny.
Dharra and the Date-Stone, The, *tr.*
End Which Comes, The. *Fr.* The Light of Asia.
Forgiveness, *tr.*
From Slavery to Slavery, *tr.* *Fr.* The Gulistan.
Gita Govinda, The, *sels., tr.*
Great Journey, The, *tr.* *Fr.* Mahabharata.
Great Physician, The, *tr.* *Fr.* The Bustan.
Guardian of All, *tr.*
Gulistan, The, *sels., tr.*
He and She.
Help, *tr.* *Fr.* The Gulistan.
Hero and Leander, *sels., tr.*
His Face Is Forever, *tr.*
Hymn to Vishnu, *tr.* *Fr.* The Gita Govinda.
Light of Asia, The, *sels.*
Light of Life, The, *tr.*
Mahabharata, *sel., tr.*
Mahmud and Ayaz: A Paraphrase on Sa'di. *Fr.* With Sa'di in the Garden.
Mighty master of the ocean! *tr.*
Mountain brows, the rocks, the peaks are sleeping, The, *tr.*
Musmee.
Nimrud and the Gnat, *tr.*
Nirvana. *Fr.* The Light of Asia.
Ode to Aphrodite, *tr.*
Pearls of the Faith, *sel.*
Power That Moves to Good, The. *Fr.* The Light of Asia.
Proverbial Wisdom, *tr.*
Prudence, *tr.*
Purgatory May Be Paradise, *tr.* *Fr.* The Gulistan.
Raglan.
Secret of Death, The.
Shadows Worship, The, *tr.*
She and He.
Somewhere.
Song from "The Gita Govinda," A, *tr.* *Fr.* The Gita Govinda.
Song without a Sound. *Fr.* With Sa'di in the Garden.
Sooth-Sayer, The. *Fr.* The Gulistan.
Swallows, The.
Swallow's Nest, The.
Thou liest dead, and there will be no memory left behind, *tr.*
To a Pair of Egyptian Slippers.
Transfiguration, The, *tr.* *Fr.* Bhagavad-Gita.
Trumpet, The, *tr.*
We Are the Voices of the Whispering Wind.
Wealth, *tr.* *Fr.* The Gulistan.
Wise, The. *Fr.* The Bhagavad-Gita.
With Sa'di in the Garden, *sels.*
Works and Days, *sel., tr.*
Wrestler, The, *tr.* *Fr.* The Gulistan.
Arnold, Emily Gail. In April.
Arnold, George. Alone by the Hearth.
Beer.
Farewell to Summer.
Golden Fish, The.
In the Dark.
Jolly Old Pedagogue, The.
Jubilate.
Merry Christmas Time, The.
September.
Sweet September.
Youth and Age.
Arnold, Irene (Mrs. Major Arnold). Pray!
Thank God for the Country!
Arnold, Matthew. Absence. *Fr.* Switzerland.
Ah, Love, Let Us Be True. *Fr.* Dover Beach.
Apollo. *Fr.* Empedocles on Etna.
Atossa. *Fr.* Poor Matthias.
Austerity of Poetry.
Bacchanalia; or, The New Age.
Balder Dead, *sels.*
Better Part, The.
Buried Life, The.
Burning of Balder's Ship, The. *Fr.* Balder Dead.
Cadmus and Harmonia. *Fr.* Empedocles on Etna.
Calais Sands.
Callicles' Song. *Fr.* Empedocles on Etna.
Calm Soul of All Things. *Fr.* Lines Written in Kensington Gardens.
Canticle of the Creatures, *tr.*
Canticle of the Sun, *tr.*
Caution to Poets, A.
Church of Brou, The.
Church of Brou, The, *sel.*
Combat, The. *Fr.* Sohrab and Rustum.
Consolation.
Contagion of Courage. *Fr.* Rugby Chapel.
Courage.
Cuckoo's Parting Cry, The. *Fr.* Thyrsis.
Death of Sohrab, The. *Fr.* Sohrab and Rustum.
Departure of the Cuckoo, The. *Fr.* Thyrsis.
Desire.
Despondency.
Divinity, The.
Dover Beach.
Dream, A.
Early Death and Fame.
East, The. *Fr.* Obermann Once More.
East and West.
East London.
Empedocles on Etna.
Empedocles on Etna, *sels.*
Empedocles' Song. *Fr.* Empedocles on Etna.
Farewell, A. *Fr.* Switzerland.
Flee fro' the Press. *Fr.* The Scholar-Gipsy.
Forsaken Merman, The.
Fragment of Chorus of a "Dejaneira."
Future, The.
Geist's Grave.
Good Shepherd with the Kid, The.
Growing Old.
Haworth Churchyard.
Heine. *Fr.* Heine's Grave.
Heine's Grave.
Heine's Grave, *sel.*
Human Life.
Immortality.
In Harmony with Nature.
In Utrumque Paratus.
Incremation, The. *Fr.* Balder Dead.
Inward Peace. *Fr.* Lines Written in Kensington Gardens.
Iseult of Brittany. *Fr.* Tristram and Iseult.
Isolation. *Fr.* Switzerland.
Isolation: To Marguerite. *Fr.* Switzerland.
Jacopone da Todi.
Kaiser Dead.
Last Song of Callicles. *Fr.* Empedocles on Etna.
Last Word, The.
Leaders and Friends of Mankind. *Fr.* Rugby Chapel.
Life and Thought. *Fr.* Empedocles on Etna.
Lines Written in Kensington Gardens.
Lines Written in Kensington Gardens, *sel.*
Longing.
Lyric Stanzas of Empedocles. *Fr.* Empedocles on Etna.
Meeting. *Fr.* Switzerland.
Memorial Verses.
Modern Sappho, A.
Monica's Last Prayer.
Morality.
Morality, *sels.*
Mycerinus.
Neckan, The.
Obermann Once More.
Obermann Once More, *sels.*
On the Death of a Favorite Canary. *Fr.* Poor Matthias.
On the Rhine.
Oxus. *Fr.* Sohrab and Rustum.
Pagan World, The. *Fr.* Obermann Once More.
Palladium.
Parting. *Fr.* Switzerland.
Parting, *sel.* *Fr.* Switzerland.
Persistency of Poetry.
Philomela.
Pis-Aller.
Poor Matthias.
Poor Matthias, *sel.*
Progress.
Progress, *sel.*
Progress of Poesy, The.
Question, A.
Quiet Work.
Religious Isolation.
Requiescat.
Resignation.
Revolutions.
Rugby Chapel.
Rugby Chapel, *sels.*
Saint Brandan.
Scholar-Gipsy, The.
Second Asgard, The. *Fr.* Balder Dead.
Second Best, The.
Self-Deception.
Self-Dependence.
Separation.
Shakespeare [*or* Shakspeare].
Sick King in Bokhara, The.
Sohrab and Rustum.
Sohrab and Rustum, *sels.*

ARNOLD, MATTHEW (*continued*)
Sohrab's Death. *Fr.* Sohrab and Rustum.
Song for Apollo. *Fr.* Empedocles on Etna.
Song of Callicles, The ("Far, far from here"). *Fr.* Empedocles on Etna.
Song of Callicles [on Etna], The ("Through the black, rushing smoke-bursts"). *Fr.* Empedocles on Etna.
Song of the Creatures, The, *tr.*
Sonnet: Quiet Work.
Southern Night, A.
Stagirius.
Stanzas from the Grande Chartreuse.
Stanzas from the Grande Chartreuse, *sels.*
Stanzas in Memory of the Author of "Obermann."
Stanzas in Memory of the Author of "Obermann," *sel.*
Strayed Reveller, The.
Strayed Reveller, The, *sels.*
Strayed Reveller to Ulysses, The. *Fr.* The Strayed Reveller.
Summer Night, A.
Switzerland.
Switzerland, *sels.*
Tasks in Hours of Insight Willed. *Fr.* Morality.
Terrace at Berne, The. *Fr.* Switzerland.
Thyrsis.
Thyrsis, *sels.*
To a Friend.
To a Gipsy Child by the Sea-Shore.
To a Republican Friend, 1848.
To a Republican Friend, 1848, Continued.
To an Independent Preacher.
To Fausta.
To Marguerite. *Fr.* Switzerland.
Tomb, The. *Fr.* The Church of Brou.
Tristram and Iseult.
Tristram and Iseult, *sels.*
Urania.
Voice, The.
West and East. *Fr.* Obermann Once More.
West London.
Westminster Abbey.
Wish, A.
World and the Quietist, The.
Worldly Place.
Written in Butler's Sermons.
Written in Emerson's Essays.
Youth and Calm.
Youth of Nature, The.
ARNOLD, RICHARD K. Eight o'Clock.
Five o'Clock.
ARNOLD, SARAH LOUISE. Mother, The.
ARNSTEIN, FLORA J. Timers.
ARRIETA, RAFAEL ALBERTO. January Night.
ARTHUR, RUTH M. Snowflakes.
ARUNDEL, PHILIP HOWARD, 1ST EARL OF. *See* HOWARD, PHILIP, 1ST EARL OF ARUNDEL.
ARVERS, FÉLIX. Who Is She?
'ASA THE BLIND. Coat of Mail.
ASADI. Night and Day.
ASAYASU (Bunya no Asayasu). Across clear drops of dew.
In a gust of wind the white dew.
Jewels.
ASBAJE, JUANA DE. *See* JUANA INÉS DE LA CRUZ, SISTER.
ASBURY, ALBAN. If This Is All.
ASCLEPIADES. Archeanassa.
Better Eros, The.
Bitter-sweet.
Black but Comely.
Carpe Diem.
Coy Mistress, The.
Demetrios, go to the market.
Desire Knows.
Desolate Wreath, The.
Didyme.
Epitaph of a Courtesan.
Erinna's Poems.
Eumares.
"Fill the Can and Fill the Cup."
Flirt, The.
Glory to Cypris,
Hermione/ was roguishly.
I, Valour, wretched maid, sit here forlorn.
In less than two and twenty years.
Joy's Crown of Joy.
Light Love.
Love Is Best.
Plaything.
Power of Love, The.
Preface to Erinna's Poems.
Rain, Night, and Wine.
Snow and hail and flash and gloom.
There Is No Loving after Death.
This small, delightful book Erinna wrote.
To a Faithless Mistress.
To a Recalcitrant Virgin.
Tomb by the Sea, A.
Tomb of a Lost Mariner.
Why Plague Me, Loves?
Zeus Too Is a Victim.
ASEYEV, NIKOLAI. Blue Hussars.
To Shining Falcon.
ASGRÍMSSON, EYSTEINN. Author's Entreaty for His Lay. *Fr.* Lilya.
Lilya, *sel.*
ASH, SARAH LEEDS. Changeless Shore.
ASHBEE, CHARLES, *and* JANET ASHBEE. "Ich Stand auf Hohen Berge."
ASHBERY, JOHN. Boy, A.
How Much Longer Will I Be Able to Inhabit the Divine Sepulcher.
Instruction Manual, The.
ASHBY-STERRY, JOSEPH. Kindness to Animals.
King of the Cradle, The.
Little Rebel, The.
Marlow Madrigal, A.
Pet's Punishment.
Portrait, A.
Spring's Delights.
ASHE, THOMAS. By the Salpêtrière.
City Clerk, The.
Machine Hand, A.
Marian.
Meet We No Angels, Pansie?
No and Yes.
Phantoms.
Poeta Nascitur.
To Two Bereaved.
Vision of Children, A.
ASHLEY, LILLAH A. Soul, Mind, and Body.
ASHLEY, MARGARET LEE. In April.
ASHMOLE, ELIAS. Hermatic Poems.
ASHMUN, MARGARET. Vigilantes, The.
ASHTON, WINIFRED. *See* "DANE, CLEMENCE."
ASKEWE, ANNE. Fight of Faith, The.
"ASMUS." *See* CLAUDIUS, MATTHIAS.
ASPINWALL, ALICIA. Patrick Goes to School.
ASPLUND, KARL. Your Sisters.
ASQUITH, HERBERT. Aunt Jane.
Birthday Gifts.
Eggs.
Elephant, The.
Frowning Cliff, The.
Hairy Dog, The.
Nightfall.
Ship Sails Up to Bideford, A.
Skating.
Tortoise, The.
Volunteer, The.
ASQUITH, RAYMOND. In Praise of Young Girls.
ASTURIAS, MIGUEL ANGEL. Indians Come Down from Mixco, The.
ATHANASIUS, SISTER MARY. Meditation on Time.
ATHENOGENES, SAINT. Hymn for the Lighting of the Lamps, *at.*
ATHERSTONE, EDWIN. Sunrise at Sea.
ATKINS, RUSSELL. Poem: "Upstood upstaffed passing sinuously away."
ATKINS, STEWART. Cotton Mill Funeral.
Love in a Cotton Mill.
Relief Worker Reflects on Suicide, A.
Sharecropper.
To a Jazz Pianist, Dead.
To John Charles McNeill.
WPA Worker Reflects on Suicide, A.
ATKINSON, T. MOORE. Search.
ATO TOBIRA. Once Only.
ATTAR. *See* FERID ED-DIN ATTAR.
ATTERBOM, PER DANIEL AMADEUS. Chorus of the Winds.
Felicia's Song.
ATTERBURY, FRANCIS. Written on [*or* in] the Leaves of a White Fan.
ATTOWELL, GEORGE. Francis' New Jig.
ATTWOOD, A. A. Farmyard, The.
ATWELL, ROY. Some Little Bug.
AUBER, HARRIET. Holy Spirit, The.
AUBIGNÉ, THÉODORE AGRIPPA D'. Abandoned Dog, The.
Cain. *Fr.* Les Tragiques.
Psalm Eighty-eight, *par.*
Tragiques, Les, *sel.*
AUDEN, WYSTAN HUGH. Advent. *Fr.* For the Time Being.
After Christmas. *Fr.* For the Time Being.
Airman's Alphabet, The. *Fr.* Journal of an Airman.
Alonso to Ferdinand. *Fr.* The Sea and the Mirror.
Always the Following Wind.
And the Age Ended.
Another Time.
As He Is.
As I Walked Out One Evening.
At the Grave of Henry James.
Atlantis.
August for the People.
Autumn 1940.
Ballad: "O what is that sound which so thrills the ear."
Between Attention and Attention.
Bride in the '30's, A.
But in the evening the oppression lifted. *Fr.* In Time of War.
Canzone: "When shall we learn, what should be clear as day."
Capital, The.
Carry Her over the Water.
Casino.
Chorale: "Our Father, whose creative Will." *Fr.* For the Time Being.
Chorus: "He is the Way." *Fr.* For the Time Being.
Chorus: "Though he believe it, no man is strong." *Fr.* Paid on Both Sides.
Chorus: "To throw away the key and walk away." *Fr.* Paid on Both Sides.
Chorus from a Play.
Commentary, *sel.*
Composer, The.
Consider This and in Our Time.
Control of the Passes.
Crisis.
Cultural Presupposition, The.
Culture.
Dear, though the Night Is Gone.
Dedication: "Since the external disorder." *Fr.* Look, Stranger!
Dialogue between Mary and Gabriel. *Fr.* For the Time Being.
Diaspora, The.
Dog beneath the Skin, The, *sel.*
Doom is Dark [and Deeper than Any Sea-Dingle].
Edward Lear.
Epilogue: "'O where are you going?' said reader to rider." *Fr.* The Orators.
Family Ghosts.
Far from the Heart of Culture.
1st September 1939.
First Things First.
Fish in the Unruffled Lakes.
Flight into Egypt, The. *Fr.* For the Time Being.
For the Time Being; a Christmas Oratorio, *sels.*
Foxtrot from a Play.
Fugal Chorus. *Fr.* For the Time Being.
Get There if You Can and See the Land You Once Were Proud to Own.
Gonzalo's Song. *Fr.* The Sea and the Mirror.
Happy Ending.
He Is the Way. *Fr.* For the Time Being.

He stayed: and was imprisoned in possession. *Fr.* In Time of War.
Healthy Spot, A.
Hearing of Harvests Rotting in the Valleys.
Here on the Cropped Grass.
Here war is simple like a monument. *Fr.* In Time of War.
Herman Melville.
Herod. *Fr.* For the Time Being.
Hour-Glass Whispers, The.
If, on Account of the Political Situation. *Fr.* For the Time Being.
In Memory of Ernst Toller.
In Memory of Sigmund Freud.
In Memory of W. B. Yeats.
In Memory of W. B. Yeats, *sel.*
In Praise of Limestone.
In Schrafft's.
In Time of War, *sels.*
In War Time.
Island Cemetery, The.
It's No Use Raising a Shout.
Jew Wrecked in the German Cell, The.
Journal of an Airman, *sel.*
Journey to Iceland.
Jumbled in the Common Box.
Labyrinth, The.
Lady, Weeping at the Crossroads.
Lakes.
Law like Love.
Law, Say the Gardeners, Is the Sun.
Lay Your Sleeping Head [My Love].
Lesson, The.
Let the Florid Music Praise.
Letter to Lord Byron, *sels.*
Life of man is never quite completed, The. *Fr.* In Time of War.
Look, Stranger, *sel.*
Look, Stranger, on [*or* at] This Island Now.
Managers, The.
Miranda's Song. *Fr.* The Sea and the Mirror.
Mundus et Infans.
Munitions Expert.
Musée des Beaux Arts.
New Year Letter, *sel.*
Night Falls on China.
Night Mail.
Nones.
Note on Intellectuals.
Nothing Is Given: We Must Find Our Law.
Now the Leaves Are Falling Fast.
Now through Night's Caressing Grip.
Numbers and Faces, *sel.*
O for Doors to Be Open.
O Love, the Interest Itself in Thoughtless Heaven.
O Unicorn among the Cedars. *Fr.* New Year Letter.
O What Is That Sound [Which So Thrills the Ear].
O Where Are You Going? *Fr.* The Orators.
O Who Can Ever Gaze His Fill.
Objects.
Ode: To My Pupils.
Orators, The, *sel.*
Our Bias.
Our Hunting Fathers Told the Story.
Over the Heather [the Wet Wind Blows].
Paid on Both Sides, *sels.*
Paysage Moralisé.
Perhaps.
Petition.
Plains.
Poems: "Sir, no man's enemy, forgiving all."
Poems: "Who will endure."
Preface. *Fr.* The Sea and the Mirror.
Presumptuous, The. *Fr.* The Quest.
Prime.
Prologue: "O love, the interest itself in thoughtless Heaven."
Pur.
Quest, The, *sels.*
Refugee Blues.
Riddle, The.
Rimbaud.
Sea and the Mirror, The, *sels.*
September 1, 1939.
Shield of Achilles, The.
Shilling Life Will Give You, A.
Silly Fool, The.
Sing, Ariel, Sing. *Fr.* The Sea and the Mirror.
Sir, No Man's Enemy [Forgiving All].
Something Is Bound to Happen.
Song: "As I walked out one evening."
Song: "Fish in the unruffled lakes."
Song: "Lay your sleeping head, my love."
Song: "'O where are you going?' said reader to rider."
Song: "So large a morning, so itself, to lean."
Song: "Stop all the clocks."
Song: "Victor was a little baby."
Song: "Warm are the still and lucky miles."
Song for St. Cecilia's Day.
Song for the New Year.
Spain [1937].
Spring 1940.
Stop All the Clocks.
Strings' Excitement, The.
Taller Today, We Remember.
There Are Some Birds in These Valleys.
There Will Be No Peace.
This Lunar Beauty.
Time Will Say Nothing but I Told You So.
To Ask the Hard Question Is Simple.
To Chester Kallman.
To Throw Away the Key. *Fr.* Paid on Both Sides.
Traveller, The.
Trial, The.
Truth.
Under Sirius.
Under Which Lyre.
Unknown Citizen, The.
Useful, The. *Fr.* The Quest.
Villanelle.
Vocation. *Fr.* The Quest.
Voltaire at Ferney.
Walk after Dark, A.
Wandering lost upon the mountains of our choice. *Fr.* In Time of War.
Watch Any Day [His Nonchalant Pauses].
Well, So That Is That. *Fr.* For the Time Being.
Where Do They Come From?
Which Side Am I Supposed to Be On?
Who's Who.
Witnesses, The.
Woods.
AUDEN, WYSTAN HUGH, *and* CHRISTOPHER ISHERWOOD. Ascent of F 6, The, *sel.*
At Last the Secret Is Out. *Fr.* The Ascent of F 6.
AUERBACH, EPHRAIM. Grey Uncles.
AUGUSTINE, SAINT. Great Art Thou, O Lord.
Joys of Paradise, The.
Take my heart! for I cannot give it Thee.
AUKRUST, OLAV. Mountain Norther, The.
AULT, NORMAN. Clouds.
Ducks.
Father Time.
Pig's Tail, The.
Wishes.
Without and Within.
"AUNT EFFIE." *See* HAWKSHAW, ANN.
"AUNT MARY [*or* MAY]." *See* LATHBURY, MARY ARTEMISIA.
AURINGER, OBADIAH CYRUS. April.
Ballad of Oriskany, The.
Flight of the War-Eagle, The.
AURYANSEN, LUCIA TREVITT. Seekers, The.
AUS OF KURAIZA. Apostasy.
AUSLANDER, JOSEPH. Abraham Lincoln.
Berceuse for Birds.
Blackbird Suddenly, A.
Bough of Babylon.
César Franck.
Christmas Encyclical.
Covenant.
Dawn at the Rain's Edge.
Derricks and Rainbows.
Dragnet.
Elegy: "Fled is the swiftness of all the white-footed ones."
Enigma.
Gifts without Season.
He Is Risen, *sel.*
Hill Hunger.
I Come Singing.
I Will Leave This House.
Interval.
Is This the Lark!
Mardi Gras.
Near Dusk.
Pendulum.
Poets, The, *sel.*
Prayer for Thanksgiving, A.
Prayer to Jehanne of France.
Remember Me, Gulls!
Revenants.
Riveter, The.
Snow Advent.
Sonnets to Laura, *sels., tr.*
Spilled Flame.
Steel.
Sunrise Trumpets.
Three Things.
Touch.
Towers of New York, The.
Ulysses in Autumn.
Winged Horseman, The.
Wings at Dawn.
Words.
AUSONIUS, DECIMUS MAGNUS. Epigrams.
Evening on the Moselle.
Grave of Hector, The.
Idyll of the Rose.
Old Man near Verona Who Never Left His Farm, The.
On Newblown Roses.
On Scribe Pergamus, a Slave Who Vainly Fled.
Singing on the Moselle.
Sort of Girl He Prefers, The.
To His Wife.
To the Nymphs Pursuing Hylas.
AUSTIN, ADAM. For Lack of Gold.
AUSTIN, ALFRED. Agatha.
At His Grave.
Britannia to Columbia.
Elegy: "Crab, the bullace and the sloe, The."
Grave-Digger's Song. *Fr.* Prince Lucifer.
Haymakers' Song, The.
Is Life Worth Living?
Is Life Worth Living? *sel.*
Last Redoubt, The.
Lover's Song, The.
Love's Trinity.
Mother-Song. *Fr.* Prince Lucifer.
Primroses.
Prince Lucifer, *sels.*
To America.
Voice from the West, A.
Winter Is Gone.
AUSTIN, J. O. Nun, A.
AUSTIN, JOHN. Fain Would My Thoughts.
Hark, My Soul.
AUSTIN, LEONA MAE. West Texas, *at.*
AUSTIN, MARY. Ballad of Our Lady, *tr.*
Before Rain, *tr.*
Bravura, *tr.*
Brown Bear, The.
Buck and the Doe, The, *tr.*
Come Not near My Songs, *tr.*
Dance of the Maskers, *tr.*
Deer.
Do you long, my maiden, *tr.*
Dream.
Drouth.
Eagle's Song, The.
Early I rose, *tr.*
Feller I Know, A.
Forest Ranger, The.
Glyph, *tr.*
Grass on the Mountain, The, *tr.*
Grizzly Bear.
I Have Known Poets.
Lament of a Man for His Son, *tr.*
Little Song of Spring, A.
Love Song ("Early I rose"), *tr.*

AUSTIN, MARY (*continued*)
Navajo Prayer, *tr.*
Neither Spirit nor Bird, *tr.*
Penance by Whipping, *tr.*
Prairie-Dog Town.
Prayer to the Mountain Spirit, *tr.*
Rain-Songs from the Rio Grande Pueblos, *tr.*
Rathers.
Rhyming Riddles, *sels.*
Rocky Mountain Sheep, The.
Sandhill Crane, The.
Shepherds in Judea, The.
Song for the Passing of a Beautiful Woman, *tr.*
Song of Greatness, A, *tr.*
Sounds.
Texas Trains and Trails.
AUSTIN, WILLIAM. Carol: "All this night shrill chanticler."
Chanticleer.
Hymn: "All this night shrill chanticler."
Sun of Righteousness.
AUTOMEDON (1st century B.C.). Charcoal in sacks if you bring ten.
There's a girl just come to town.
AUTOMEDON OF AETOLIA (3d century B.C.?). Ill Merchandise, *at.*
AUXIER, SYLVIA TRENT. Breaking Point.
AVENZOAR. Drinking Song.
In Absence.
Revenge.
AVERILL, ANNA BOYNTON. Birch Stream.
AVERY, CLARIBEL WEEKS. Vespers.
"AVGERIS, MARKOS" (George Papadopoulo). Granny Tassia.
Plebeian Song.
AVIANUS. Crab, The.
Women and the Wolf, The.
AVIS, PATRICIA. Leper Island.
AVISON, MARGARET. Butterfly, The.
Christmas.
Knowledge of Age.
Maria Minor.
Meeting Together of Poles & Latitudes: In Prospect.
Neverness; or, The One Ship Beached on One Far Distant Shore.
Old Adam.
Perspective.
Rigor Viris.
Simple Horizontal, The.
Snow.
Tennis.
"AVOND, JAN VAN." *See* SLATER, FRANCIS CAREY.
AVRETT, ROBERT. I Think That There Is Laughter.
Renaissance.
Wake, The.
AWDLAY, JOHN. Flower of Jesse, The, *at.*
There Is a Flower, *at.*
There Is a Floure Sprung of a Tree, *at.*
AXFORD, ROGER. Victory.
AYER, ETHAN. Like a Whisper.
AYER, JEAN. Everyday Things.
AYER, WILLIAM WARD. Be Still.
AYLEN, ELISE (Mrs. Duncan Campbell Scott). Moon Spell.
Ode: "Here where a new life stirs and broods."
Treason of Ganelon, The.
Wild Apple.
AYRES, PHILIP. Complains, Being Hindered the Sight of His Nymph.
Cynthia on Horseback.
Describes the Place where Cynthia Is Sporting Herself.
Dream of His Lady, *tr.*
Emblems of Love, *sel.*
Endymion and Diana.
Invites His Nymph to His Cottage.
Madrigal: Restless Lover, The, *tr.*
On a Fair Beggar.
On Lydia Distracted.
On Old Rome.
To Love; a Sonnet.
To the Nightingale.
To the Winds.
AYSCOUGH, FLORENCE, *and* AMY LOWELL. *See* LOWELL, AMY, *and* FLORENCE AYSCOUGH.
AYTON [*or* AYTOUN], SIR ROBERT. I Loved Thee Once.
I'll Love No More.
Inconstancy Reproved, *at.*
Inconstant Mistress, The, *at.*
My Faggot and My Pipe.
On a Woman's Inconstancy.
On Love.
To an Inconstant Mistress, *at.*
To His Forsaken Mistress, *at.*
Upon a Diamond Cut in Form of a Heart . . . Sent in a New Year's Gift.
When Thou Did [*or* Didst] Think I Did Not Love.
Woman's Inconstancy.
Wrong Not Sweete Empress of My Heart.
AYTOUN, WILLIAM EDMONSTOUNE [*or* EDMONDSTOUNE *or* EDMONSTONE].
Battle of Killiecrankie, The.
Biter Bit, The.
Broken Pitcher, The.
Comfort in Affliction.
Execution of Montrose, The.
Heart of the Bruce, The.
Hermotimus.
Husband's Petition, The.
Laureate, The.
Laureate's Tourney, The.
Lay of the Levite, The.
Lay of the Lover's Friend, The.
Massacre of the Macpherson, The.
Milton.
O Child of Beauty Rare, *tr.*
Old Scottish Cavalier, The.
Refusal of Charon, The.
Sonnet to Britain.
AYTOUN, WILLIAM EDMONSTOUNE, *and* SIR THEODORE MARTIN. Cry of the Lovelorn, The.
Eastern Serenade.
Lay of the Love-Lorn, The.
AZUMAMARO. Moon, The.

B

"B." What May Happen to a Thimble.
"B., E. G." To Betty.
"B., E. R." Popcorn Party, The.
"B., L." Biologic Face, The.
"B., M. K." Four Sunbeams, The.
"B., R. K." Limerick: "Should a plan we suggest, just that minute."
Limerick: "You remember that pastoral frolic."
"B., W." Mary.
"B. A. D." *See* "D., B. A."
"B. A. T." *See* "T., B. A."
"B. H." *See* "H. B."
"B. I." *See* "I., B."
"B. L. T." *See* TAYLOR, BERT LESTON.
"B. V." ("Bysshe Vanolis"). *See* THOMSON, JAMES.
BAATH, ALBERT ULRIK. If I Were a Poet.
BABB, STANLEY E. High Noon; Galveston Beach.
Midwinter Monochrome.
Wild Geese in Midwinter.
BABBITT, CLARE HOUGH. Greetings!
BABCOCK, DONALD CAMPBELL. Adios.
America.
Anthill, The.
". . . Discourse Heard One Day . . ."
In a Garden.
Meditation by Mascoma Lake.
Migrant, The.
Neoplatonic Soliloquy.
Program Note on Sibelius.
Two Things.
Vacation Trip.
BABCOCK, EDWINA STANTON. Little Shade, The.
Told in the Market-Place.
BABCOCK, MALTBIE DAVENPORT. Be Strong!
Death.
Emancipation.
"Give Us This Day Our Daily Bread."
My Father's World.
No Distant Lord.
Not to Be Ministered To.
Our Daily Bread.
School Days.
This Is My Father's World.
Today, O Lord.
BABCOCK, WILLIAM HENRY. Bennington.
BABRIUS. Carter from the village drove his wain, A
Man of Athens on a summer's day, A.
BACCHYLIDES. Blessings of Peace.
Coming of Theseus toward Athens, The.
Croesus.
Dark-prowed ship through surges cleft her way, The.
Dreams Out of a Wine-Cup.
Eagle of Song, The.
Eagle, The (to Hiero of Syracuse).
Fecundi Calices.
For Alexidamus of Metapontum.
For Hiero of Syracuse.
Fragment.
Heracles and Meleager.
Heracles and the Wraith of Meleager.
On Wings of Song.
Peace.
Peace on Earth.
Song and Wine.
Theseus.
Theseus, *sels.*
To mortal men Peace giveth these good things.
Way of Happiness, The.
BACH, JOHANN SEBASTIAN. Herz und Mund, *sel.*
Jesu, joy of man's desiring. *Fr.* Herz und Mund.
Now let every tongue adore Thee! *Fr.* Sleepers, Wake!
Sleepers, Wake! *sel.*
BACHELDER, PHOEBE SMITH. Communion.
Holy Week.
BACHELLER, IRVING. Mocking Bird, The.
BÄCKSTRÖM, EDVARD. Song of Sten Sture, A.
BACKUS, BERTHA ADAMS. Then Laugh.
BACMEISTER, RHODA WARNER. Galoshes.
Stars.
BACON, ELEANOR KENLY. Luminous Hands of God, The.
BACON, SIR FRANCIS. Life.
Life of Man, The.
On the Life of Man.
World, The.
BACON, HELEN C. Song for Decoration Day.
BACON, JOSEPHINE DODGE DASKAM. Christmas Hymn for Children, A.
Little Dead Child, The.
Motherhood.
Omar for Ladies, An.
Prince.
Sleepy Song, The.
BACON, LEONARD. Afternoon in Artillery Walk, An.
Animula Vagula, *sels.*
Archaeologist of the Future, The.
Chorus from a Tragedy.
Day of the Slaves, The.
Easter Evening, 1942.
Epitaph in Anticipation.
Fame.
Hymn to Satan, *tr.*
I Saw That Shattered Thing.
Night Laughter.
Our Time.
Pilgrim Fathers, The.
Reason, The.
Richard Tolman's Universe.
Sonnets.
Tower of Ivory.
Unanswered Question, An.
Yankee Clipper.
BACON, LEONARD, *and* RIVERS BROWNE. Colorado Morton's Ride.
BACON, LEONARD, *and* R. SELDEN ROSE. Cid, The, *sels.*, *tr.*

BACON, PEGGY. Cobbler.
Darkness.
Hearth.
Hen-Party.
BADEN-POWELL, SIR ROBERT. Man, matron, maiden.
BADLEY, MARY ESTHER. Parade, The.
BAEDA. *See* BEDE, THE VENERABLE.
BAERLEIN, HENRY. Atheist Buries His Son, The, *tr.*
Fool, The.
BAGBY, J. R. Empty Sleeve, The.
BAGG, ROBERT. Ballad in Blonde Hair Foretold.
For Her on the First Day Out.
Oracle at Delphi.
Speak This Kindly to Her.
BAGGER, CARL CHRISTIAN. Departure, The.
BAGGESEN, JENS. Childhood.
"BAGRITSKY [*or* BAGRITZKY], EDUARD" (Eduard Dzyubin). Black Bread.
Fowler, The.
He Tries Out the Concords Gently.
My Honeyed Languor.
Piece of Black Bread, A.
Spring, the Vet, and I.
BAHA AD-DIN ZUHAYR. On a Blind Girl.
BAHAR. Miracle of Spring, The.
Random Thoughts.
BAÏF, JEAN ANTOINE DE. Loves.
Spring Song.
To Philippe Desportes.
BAILEY, ALFRED GOLDSWORTHY. Border River.
Colonial Set.
Ideogram.
Miramichi Lightning.
Shrouds and Away.
Tâo.
Uncrowned.
Variations on a Theme.
Whistles and Wheels.
BAILEY, CAROLYN SHERWIN. After Winter.
Christmas Party, A.
If.
Spider Silverlegs.
BAILEY, H. SEWALL. Sailor Man.
BAILEY, LANSING C. Eight Volunteers.
BAILEY, LIBERTY HYDE. Farmer.
Miracle.
BAILEY, PHILIP JAMES. Aim of Life, The. *Fr.* Festus.
Country Town, A. *Fr.* Festus.
Festus, *sels.*
Great Black Crow, The.
Helen's Song. *Fr.* Festus.
Lucifer and Elissa. *Fr.* Festus.
Lucifer's Song. *Fr.* Festus.
My Lady.
Poet, The. *Fr.* Festus.
Poet of Nature, The. *Fr.* Festus.
We Live in Deeds. *Fr.* Festus.
Youth, Love, and Death. *Fr.* Festus.
BAILLIE, LADY GRIZEL [*or* GRISELL]. There Ance Was a May.
Were Na My Heart Light I Wad Dee.
BAILLIE, JOANNA. Beacon, The, *sel.*
Country Inn, The, *sel.*
Fisherman's Song. *Fr.* The Beacon.
Good Morning.
Good-Night.
Hay Making.
Heath-Cock, The.
Kitten, The.
Morning Song.
Orra, *sel.*
Outlaw's Song, The. *Fr.* Orra.
Saw Ye Johnnie Comin'?
Shepherd's Song, The.
Song: "Oh welcome, bat and owlet gray."
Song: "Though richer swains thy love pursue." *Fr.* The Country Inn.
Song of the Outlaws. *Fr.* Orra.
Volunteer Song, A.
Wake, Lady!
BAIRAM AT TUNISIE. Autobiography, An.
BAIRD, GEORGE M. P. Ballad of Wise Men, A.
BAJZA, JOSEPH. Apotheosis.
BAKER, ANNA R. In His Sight.
BAKER, BARBARA. Spike of Green, A.
BAKER, DOROTHY. Castles in the Sand.
In the Woods.
BAKER, GEORGE AUGUSTUS. Le Dernier Jour d'un Condamné.
Thoughts on the Commandments.
BAKER, GEORGE M. Red Jacket, The.
Robber Kitten, *at.*
BAKER, GLEN. Simon the Cyrenian Speaks.
BAKER, SIR HENRY WILLIAMS. Christ the Consoler.
King of Love, The.
O God of Love, O King of peace.
BAKER, HOWARD. Letter from the Country, A.
Ode to the Sea.
BAKER, J. G. My Trundle Bed.
BAKER, JULIA ALDRICH. Mizpah.
BAKER, KARLE WILSON ("Charlotte Wilson"). Apple and Rose.
Beauty's Hands Are Cool.
Box-Car Letters.
Burning Bush.
Child's Game, A.
City Lights.
Courage.
Creeds.
Days.
Eagle Youth.
Friendly Faces of Old Sorrows, The.
Good Company.
Grey.
Growing Old.
Housewife, The; Winter Afternoon.
I Love the Friendly Faces of Old Sorrows.
I Shall Be Loved as Quiet Things.
Let Me Grow Lovely.
Lost One, The.
Morning Song.
Old Inn, The.
Ploughman, The.
Poet Songs.
Pronouns.
Rondel for September.
She Is Wise, Our Ancient Mother.
Silver Lantern, A.
Some Towns of Texas.
Song of the Forerunners.
Thrushes.
Within the Alamo.
World at the Bottom of the Lake, The.
BAKER, OLAF. Little Saling.
BAKER, PETER SHAW. Afterwards.
BAKER, ROWENA PORTER. Bandit, The.
Leaves.
BAKEWELL, JOHN. Hail, Thou Once Despised Jesus!
BALBUENA, BERNARDO DE. Grandeza Mexicana, *sel.*
Immortal Springtime and Its Tokens. *Fr.* Grandeza Mexicana.
BALBULUS, NOTKER. *See* NOTKER BALBULUS.
BALCH, EMILY GREENE. Flag Speaks, The.
BALDWIN, A. W. I. Ten Little Dicky-Birds.
BALDWIN, AUGUSTUS HENRY. New Year, The. *Fr.* On the Threshold.
On the Threshold.
On the Threshold, *sel.*
BALDWIN, FAITH. In These Dark Woods.
Masquerade.
Vigil.
BALDWIN, MARY NEWTON. Chapel in the Woods.
Lonely Are the Fields of Sleep.
Written in an Old Cemetery.
BALDWIN, WILLIAM. Beloved to the Spouse, The.
Christ, My Beloved.
Christ to His Spouse.
How Jacke Cade Traiterously Rebelling agaynst His Kyng, Was for His Treasons and Cruell Doinges Wurthely Punyshed, *at. Fr.* A Mirror for Magistrates.
Mirror for Magistrates, A, *sel., at.*
Spouse to the Beloved, The.
BALE, JOHN. King John [*or* Kynge Johan], *sel.*
Wassail, Wassail. *Fr.* King John.
BALFOUR, MARY. Dew Each Trembling Leaf Inwreath'd, The.
In Ringlets Curl'd Thy Tresses Flow.
BALL, CAROLINE A. Jacket of Gray, The.
BALL, JOHN. Sermon to the Rebels at Blackheath.
BALL, WILLIAM. Praise to Jesus!
BALLANTINE, JAMES. Castles in the Air.
Creep afore Ye Gang.
Its Ain Drap o' Dew.
Muckle-Mou'd Meg.
BALLANTYNE, GINA. Daffodils.
Native Land.
BALLARD, CHARLES. My Brother Played.
Rollin and Me.
BALLARD, COLIN ROBERT. Pacific Railway, The.
BALLARD, DOROTHY SCOTT. Father, The.
BALLARD, HARLAN HOGE. In the Catacombs.
BALLARD, SALLIE M. To My Soldier Brother.
BALMONT, KONSTANTIN DMITREYEVICH. I came into this world to see the sunlight.
Long Centuries of Centuries.
Morning.
Psalm of Silence, The.
Reeds, The.
She surrendered without complaining.
Under Sea.
With My Fancy I Grasped.
BALSDON, DACRE. Endurance Test.
BAMBERGER, AUGUSTUS WRIGHT. Each a Part of All.
Out of the Vast.
BAMPFYLDE, JOHN CODRINGTON. On a Wet Summer.
BANCROFT, CHARLES. Tadoussac.
BANCROFT, THOMAS. Cross, The.
BANDEIRA, MANUEL. Cactus, The.
Dead of Night.
Highway, The.
In Soapsuds Street.
Mozart in Heaven.
Salute to Recife.
Woods, The.
BANGHAM, MARY DICKERSON. Come, Holy Babe!
BANGS, EDWARD. Yankee Doodle, *at.*
Yankee's Return from Camp, *at.*
BANGS, JANET NORRIS. Design for Peace.
Reply.
BANGS, JOHN KENDRICK. Blind.
"Don't Care" and "Never Mind."
Hazard, The.
I Never Knew a Night So Black.
Lincoln's Birthday [—1918].
Line o' Cheer, A.
Little Elf, The.
Little Elfman, The.
May 30, 1893.
Mona Lisa.
My Dog.
On Being Good.
On File.
On Lincoln's Birthday.
Philosopher, A.
Philosophy.
Thanksgiving, A.
Thanksgiving Day.
To a Withered Rose.
Today.
"What hundred books are best, think you?" I said.
BANIM, JOHN. He Said That He Was Not Our Brother.
Irish Mother in the Penal Days, The.
Soggarth Aroon.
BANKER, WILLIAM, JR. Battle of Queenstown, The.
BANKO. Cattle.
BANKS, EMMA DUNNING. Flying Jim's Last Leap.
BANKS, GEORGE LINNAEUS. My Aim.
What I Live For.

BANNERMAN, FRANCES. Upper Chamber, An.
BANNING, KENDALL. Heart's Haven.
Lost Eden.
Once on a Time.
Sanctuary.
Wander Lure, The.
BANVILLE, THÉODORE FAULLAIN DE. Choose Flawless Marble, Sculptor.
Goddess, The.
No More We'll to the Wood.
Prose Poem: Angels, The.
Prose Poem: Harlequin.
To Font-Georges.
BARATYNSKY, EVGENI. Bare Days.
Complaint.
Death.
Dissuasion.
BARBAULD, ANNA LETITIA (Anna Letitia Aikin). Come.
Come, Says Jesus' Voice.
Doll's House, The.
Life! [I Know Not What Thou Art].
Mouse's Petition, The.
Ode to Spring.
Rights of Women, The.
Sabbath of the Soul, The.
Summer Evening's Meditation, A, sel.
To a Lady, with Some Painted Flowers.
To Mr. Barbauld.
BARBER, FRANCES. Play-acting.
BARBER, MELANIE GORDON. Sonnet for My Son.
BARBERINO [or BARBERINI], FRANCESCO DA. Of Caution.
Virgin Declares Her Beauties, A.
BARBOUR, GEORGE HURLBUT. Decoration Day.
BARBOUR, JOHN. Bannockburn. Fr. The Bruce.
Battle of Bannockburn, The. Fr. The Bruce.
Bruce, The, sels.
Bruce Addresses His Army. Fr. The Bruce.
Bruce Consults His Men. Fr. The Bruce.
Eve of Bannockburn, The. Fr. The Bruce.
Freedom. Fr. The Bruce.
Loyalty. Fr. The Bruce.
Sorrow of the Knights at Bruce's Death. Fr. The Bruce.
BARCLAY, ALEXANDER. Ballade to Our Lady, tr. Fr. The Ship of Fools.
Certain Eclogues, sel.
Fourth Egloge of Alexander Barclay, Entituled Codrus and Minalcas, Treating of the Behavior of Rich Men against Poets, The.
Geographers, tr. Fr. The Ship of Fools.
Preachment for Preachers, tr. Fr. The Ship of Fools.
Prologue, The: "Famous poets with the muses nine, The." Fr. Certain Eclogues.
Ship of Fools, The, sels., tr.
Star of the Sea, tr. Fr. The Ship of Fools.
Tudor Rose, The. tr. Fr. The Ship of Fools.
BARD, W. E. Mesa Trail, sel.
BARDEEN, CHARLES WILLIAM. Birds' Ball, The.
BARFIELD, OWEN. Sonnet: "Because the misery of some great men."
BARHAM, RICHARD HARRIS. See "INGOLDSBY, THOMAS."
BARING, MAURICE. Ballad: "Roses in my garden, The."
Beauty, The, tr.
Diffugere Nives, 1917.
Diffugere Nives, 1917, sel.
Do you remember, Mary, tr.
Dying Reservist, The.
Elegy: "As leaden as the aftermath of wine," tr.
Elegy on the Death of Juliet's Owl.
Good-bye! Forget the days of wane, tr.
I Dare Not Pray to Thee.
I. M. H.
I Too Have Travelled.

I've lived to bury my desires, tr.
John Damascene, sel., tr.
Julian Grenfell.
Λειριόεσσα Κάλυξ (Leirioessa Kalyx).
Moan in the Form of a Ballade.
Outside it is blowing and raining, tr.
Prayer, A: "Hermits and blameless women full of grace," tr.
Prophet, The, tr.
Rosy Wreath, The, tr.
Testament, The, tr.
Through the slush and the ruts of the highway, tr.
To——: "Bound for your far-off native shore," tr.
Troparion, tr. Fr. John Damascene.
Two Triolets, at.
Vale.
We Drifted to Each Other like Two Birds.
BARING-GOULD, SABINE. Child's Evening Hymn.
Evening Hymn.
Now the Day Is Over.
Olive Tree, The.
Onward, Christian Soldiers.
Pilgrim's Song, tr.
Three Kings' Song, tr.
BARKER, EDNA L. S. Child of the World.
BARKER, EDWARD D. Go Sleep, Ma Honey.
BARKER, ELSA. Breshkovskaya, sel.
Caresses. Fr. The Spirit and the Bride.
Confession. Fr. The Spirit and the Bride.
Consummation. Fr. The Spirit and the Bride.
Frozen Grail, The.
Fulfilment. Fr. The Spirit and the Bride.
I Know.
Inscription, The: "Sealed with the seal of Life, thy soul and mine." Fr. The Spirit and the Bride.
Love's Immortality. Fr. The Spirit and the Bride.
Prayer for Love, A.
Spirit and the Bride, The, sels.
Two Selves, The.
Vigil of Joseph, The.
When I Am Dead and Sister to the Dust.
BARKER, ERIC WILSON. Dark Inanimate, The.
Point Lobos, California.
To Lorna.
BARKER, GEORGE. Allegory of the Adolescent and the Adult.
And Now There Is Nothing Left.
Channel Crossing.
Crystal, The.
Death of Yeats, The.
Dog, Dog in My Manger.
Elegy: Separation of Man from God.
Elegy: "These errors loved no less than the saint loves arrows."
Elegy on the Eve.
Epistle I [or to Dylan Thomas].
Everywhere is our wilderness everywhere.
First Cycle of Love Poems (I-V).
First Cycle of Love Poems, sels.
Fourth Cycle of Love Poems, sel.
Galway Bay.
He Comes Among.
Holy Poems (I-III).
Just a Fishing Smack at Empson.
Leaping Laughers, The.
Letter to a Young Poet.
Love Poem: "Less the dog begged to die in the sky." Fr. Fourth Cycle of Love Poems.
Love Poem: "My joy, my jockey, my Gabriel." Fr. First Cycle of Love Poems.
Love Poem: "O Golden Fleece she is where she lies tonight."
Love Poem: "O tender under her right breast." Fr. Second Cycle of Love Poems.
Love Poem: "Then like the ship at rest in the bay." Fr. First Cycle of Love Poems.

Memorial (For Two Young Seamen Lost Overboard in a Storm in Mid-Pacific, January, 1940).
Munich Elegy No. 1.
My Joy, My Jockey, My Gabriel. Fr. First Cycle of Love Poems.
News of the World I ("Cold shuttered loveless star, skulker in clouds").
News of the World II ("In the first year of the last disgrace").
News of the World III ("Let her lie naked here, my hand resting").
O Golden Fleece [She Is].
O Tender under Her Right Breast. Fr. Second Cycle of Love Poems.
On First Hearing Beethoven.
Resolution of Dependence.
Sacred Elegy V: "These errors loved no less than the saint loves arrows."
Satan Is on Your Tongue.
Second Cycle of Love Poems, sels.
Shut the Seven Seas against Us. Fr. Third Cycle of Love Poems.
So in a one man Europe I sit here.
Sonnet of Fishes.
Sonnet to My Mother.
Summer Idyll.
Summer Song I.
Third Cycle of Love Poems, sels.
This is that month, Elizabeth. Fr. Third Cycle of Love Poems.
Three Dead and the Three Living, The.
Three Memorial Sonnets.
To Any Member of My Generation.
To My Mother.
Triumphal Ode MCMXXXIX.
True Confession of George Barker, The, sel.
Turn on Your Side and Bear the Day to Me.
Verses for a First Birthday. Fr. Second Cycle of Love Poems.
Verses for the 60th Birthday of T. S. Eliot.
Wraith-Friend, The.
BARKER, SHIRLEY. Clipper Captain.
Sonnets from a Sequence, sels.
BARKER, SQUIRE OMAR. Batchin'.
Code of the Cow Country.
Hot Ir'n!
Law West of the Pecos, The.
Rodeo Days.
Sheep Beezness, The.
To a Jack Rabbit.
Where Billy the Kid Still Rides.
Woodland Magic.
Woodrow Wilson.
BARKER, T. T. Cradle Song of a Soldier's Wife.
BARKINS, EVELYN WERNER. Wisdom.
BARLOW, GEORGE. Dead Child, The.
If Only Thou Art True.
Old Maid, The.
Soul, The.
Spiritual Passion.
BARLOW, JANE. Christmas Rede.
Curlew's Call, A.
End of Elfintown, The, sel.
Flitting of the Fairies, The. Fr. The End of Elfintown.
Misther Denis's Return. Fr. Th' Ould Master.
Ould Master, Th', sel.
Out of Hearing.
BARLOW, JOEL. Advice to a Raven in Russia, December, 1812.
Apparition of War. Fr. The Columbiad.
Choice in Spoons, A. Fr. The Hasty Pudding.
Columbiad, The, sels.
Creation. Fr. The Columbiad.
Eating of the Pudding, The. Fr. The Hasty Pudding.
First American Congress, The.
Freedom.
Hasty Pudding, The.
Hasty Pudding, The, sels.
Hasty Pudding Described, The. Fr. The Hasty Pudding.
Husking, The. Fr. The Hasty Pudding.
Hymn to Peace.

League of Nations, A. *Fr.* The Columbiad.
On the Discoveries of Captain Lewis.
Praise of the Pudding. *Fr.* The Hasty Pudding.
Pudding Prepared and Eaten, The. *Fr.* The Hasty Pudding.
To Freedom.
Union of the World, A. *Fr.* The Columbiad.
Vision of Columbus, The, *sels. Fr.* The Columbiad.
BARNARD, LADY ANNE. *See* LINDSAY, LADY ANNE.
BARNARD, CHARLOTTE ALINGTON ("Claribel"). Come Back to Erin.
I Cannot Sing the Old Songs.
BARNARD, KATHERINE R. Voice of God, The.
BARNEFIELD, RICHARD. *See* BARNFIELD, RICHARD.
BARNES, BARNABE. Ah, sweet Content, where is thy mild abode? *Fr.* Parthenophil and Parthenophe.
Blast of Wind, A, a Momentary Breath. *Fr.* A Divine Century of Spiritual Sonnets.
Burn on, sweet fire, for I live by that fuel. *Fr.* Parthenophil and Parthenophe.
Content. *Fr.* Parthenophil and Parthenophe.
Divine Century of Spiritual Sonnets, A, *sels.*
Fortress of Hope. *Fr.* A Divine Century of Spiritual Sonnets.
God's Virtue. *Fr.* A Divine Century of Spiritual Sonnets.
Gracious, Divine, and most omnipotent. *Fr.* A Divine Century of Spiritual Sonnets.
Jove for Europa's love took shape of bull. *Fr.* Parthenophil and Parthenophe.
Life of Man, The. *Fr.* A Divine Century of Spiritual Sonnets.
Madrigal: "Once in an arbor was my mistress sleeping." *Fr.* Parthenophil and Parthenophe.
Mistress, behold in this true-speaking glass. *Fr.* Parthenophil and Parthenophe.
No more lewd lays of lighter loves I sing. *Fr.* A Divine Century of Spiritual Sonnets.
O Powers Celestial, with what sophistry. *Fr.* Parthenophil and Parthenophe.
Ode: "When I walk forth into the woods." *Fr.* Parthenophil and Parthenophe.
Ode, An: "Why doth heaven bear a sun." *Fr.* Parthenophil and Parthenophe.
Parthenophil and Parthenophe, *sels.*
Soft, lovely, rose-like lips, conjoined with mine. *Fr.* Parthenophil and Parthenophe.
Sonnet: "Ah, sweet Content! where is thy mild abode?" *Fr.* Parthenophil and Parthenophe.
Sonnet: "Blast of wind, a momentary breath, A." *Fr.* A Divine Century of Spiritual Sonnets.
Sonnet: "World's bright comforter, whose beamsome light, The." *Fr.* A Divine Century of Spiritual Sonnets.
This careful head, with divers thoughts distressed. *Fr.* Parthenophil and Parthenophe.
To the Most Beautiful Lady, the Lady Bridget Manners.
World's Bright Comforter, The. *Fr.* A Divine Century of Spiritual Sonnets.
BARNES, RONALD GORELL. *See* GORELL, RONALD GORELL BARNES, 3D BARON.
BARNES, VERNE. Way Down South in Mississippi.
BARNES, WILLIAM. Blackbird, The.
Blackmwore Maidens.
Brisk Wind, A.
Broken Jug, The.
Castle Ruins, The.
Clote, The (Water-Lily).
Come!
Country Witch, A.
Cynddylan's Hall, *tr.*
Easter Monday.
Easter Zunday.
Evenen in the Village.
Evening, and Maidens.
Fall, The.
False Friends—Like.
Girt Woak Tree That's in the Dell, The.
Good Night.
Guy Faux's Night.
Harvest Hwome.
Head-Stone, The.
Heäre, The.
Hearth of Urien, The, *tr.*
Heedless o' My Love.
Hill and Dell.
In the Spring.
In Wintry Midnight, o'er a Stormy Main, *tr.*
Jeane.
Jeane's Wedden Day in Mornen.
Learning.
Leaves, The.
Liady-Day an' Ridden House.
Lilac, The.
Linden Lea.
Lost Little Sister, The.
Lullaby: "Rooks' nests do rock on the tree-top, The."
Mary-Ann's Child.
Mater Dolorosa.
May.
May, *sel.*
Motherless Child, The.
Mother's Dream, The.
My Love's Guardian Angel.
New House a-Gettèn Wold, The.
Night a-Zettèn In.
Oak-Tree, The.
Old House, The.
Readen ov a Head-Stwone.
Rwose in the Dark, The.
Sheep in the Shade.
Shellbrook.
Sky a-Clearèn, The.
Spring, The.
Surprise, The.
To Me.
Tokens.
Turnstile, The.
Vo'k a-Comen into Church.
White an' Blue.
Wife a-Lost, The.
Wind at the Door, The.
Winter Night, A.
Witch, A.
With you first shown to me.
Withstanders.
Woak Hill.
Woodlands, The.
Woone Smile Mwore.
Zun-zet.
BARNETT, MAVIS CLARE. Romance.
Silence.
BARNFIELD, RICHARD. Affectionate Shepherd, The, *sel.*
Against the Dispraisers of Poetry.
As It Fell upon a Day. *Fr.* The Passionate Pilgrim.
Comparison of the Life of Man, A.
Cynthia, *sels.*
Daphnis to Ganymede. *Fr.* The Affectionate Shepherd.
Epitaph upon the Death of Sir Philip Sidney, Knight, Lord-Governor of Vlissing, An.
If Music and Sweet Poetry. *Fr.* The Passionate Pilgrim.
In Praise of Music and Poetry. *Fr.* The Passionate Pilgrim.
Lady Pecunia; or, The Praise of Money, *sel.*
Nightingale, The. *Fr.* The Passionate Pilgrim.
Ode, An: "As it fell upon a day." *Fr.* The Passionate Pilgrim.
Philomel. *Fr.* The Passionate Pilgrim.
Remembrance of Some English Poets, A.
Shepherd's Complaint, A.
Sonnet: "But now my muse, toil'd with continual care."
Sonnet: "Sometimes I wish that I his pillow were."
Sonnet: "Stoics think (and they come near the truth), The."
To His Friend Master [*or* Maister] R. L., in Praise of Music and Poetry.
To His Mistress. *Fr.* Cynthia.
To the Learned and Accomplish'd Gentleman Maister Nicholas Blackleech of Gray's Inn.
To the Nightingale. *Fr.* The Passionate Pilgrim.
Unknown Shepherd's Complaint, The.
BARNOUW, ADRIAAN J. *For translations from Dutch, see* LiTW; LyMA; OnPM; TrJP.
BARON, ROBERT. To Eliza, upon May Day Morning, 1649.
"BARON IRELAND." *See* SALSBURY, NATE.
BAROZAI, GUI. Christmas Carols.
BARR, AMELIA EDITH HUDDLESTON. Poetic Responses.
Thanksgiving.
BARR, G. W. U-S-U Range, *at.*
BARR, ISABEL HARRISS. Madaket Beach.
Morning Concert—Nantucket.
BARR, JOHN, OF CRAIGIELEE. Bonny Harvest Moon, The.
New Zealand Comforts.
Rise Oot Your Bed.
There's Nae Place like Otago Yet.
To My Auld Dog Dash.
BARR, MARY A. I Wouldna Gie a Copper Plack.
BARR, MATTHIAS. Moon, So Round and Yellow.
Only a Baby Small.
BARR, NANCY. *See* MAVITY, NANCY BARR.
BARRATT, KEN. Burke and Wills.
BARRAUD, C. W. Saint Winefride.
BARRET, PRINGLE. Hint to the Wise, A.
Old Woman Who Lives in the Town, The.
Perhaps.
BARRETT, ALFRED JOSEPH. Chant of Departure; a Missionary's Prayer.
Martyr's Mass, A.
Mary's Assumption.
Mint by Night.
Rosebush and the Trinity, The.
Unearth.
BARRETT, DIANA. Beer and Skittles.
BARRETT, EATON STANNARD. Woman.
BARRETT, WILSON AGNEW. New England Church, A.
BARRICK, J. R. No Land like Ours.
BARRINGTON, MARGARET. Ships.
BARRINGTON, PATRICK. Air Sentry, The.
Diplomatic Platypus, The.
Here a Nit-Wit Lies.
I Had a Duck-billed Platypus.
I Had a Hippopotamus.
I Was a Bustle-Maker Once, Girls.
Take Me in Your Arms, Miss Moneypenny-Wilson.
BARRINGTON, PAULINE B. White Iris.
BARRIOS, MIGUEL DE. Epitaph: "Daniel and Abigail."
BARRIS, AMANDA. Pumpkin Speaks, A.
BARRIS, MARTHA. Guitar Song.
BARROW, RAYMOND. There Is a Mystic Splendor.
BARROWS, MARJORIE. Cricket, The.
Enchanted Garden, The.
May Morning.
BARRY, BEATRICE. Medical Corps, The.
BARRY, H. H. He Leadeth Me, *at.*
BARRY, L. E. F. Mad Girl's Song.
BARRY, MICHAEL JOSEPH. Sword, The.
BARSTOW, HENRY H. If Easter Be Not True.
BARSTOW, ROBBINS WOLCOTT. In Defense of Youth.
BARTER, CHARLES. Changes. *Fr.* Stray Memories of Natal and Zululand.
Dingaan and Retief. *Fr.* Stray Memories of Natal and Zululand.

BARTER, CHARLES (*continued*)
Stray Memories of Natal and Zululand, *sels.*
BARTHEL, MAX. Plow, The.
BARTLESON, F. A. New Year's Eve.
BARTLETT, ALICE HUNT. Gift of Poets, The.
Requiem.
BARTLETT, ELIZABETH. After the Storm.
Behold This Dreamer.
Cage, The.
Dark Angel.
Question Is Proof, The.
BARTLETT, I. J. Town of Don't-You-Worry, The.
BARTLETT, MARY C. Baby's Skies.
BARTLETT, RUTH FITCH. Belief.
BARTOLE, GENEVIEVE. Canadian Farmer.
BARTOLOMEO DI SANT' ANGELO. *See* SANT' ANGELO, BARTOLOMEO DI.
BARTON, BERNARD. Bruce and the Spider.
Caractacus.
Evening Prayer, An.
Not Ours the Vows.
Sea, The.
Squirrel, The.
Word of God, The.
BARTON, JANE. Grief Must Go.
BARTON, MARIE. Home of My Thoughts.
New Year.
Peace on Earth.
Thanksgiving Day.
There Was a Garden.
What Is Prayer?
BARUCH, DOROTHY WALTER. Automobile Mechanics.
Cat.
Different Bicycles.
Funny the Way Different Cars Start.
Lawn-Mower.
Merry-go-round.
On a Steamer.
Popcorn-Popper, The.
Rabbits.
Riding in a Motor Boat.
Riding in an Airplane.
Stop—Go.
BARUCH OF WORMS. Elegy: "Those reckless hosts rush to the wells."
BASHFORD, SIR HENRY HOWARTH. Good Day, The.
Lullaby in Bethlehem.
Parliament Hill.
To Petronilla Who Has Put Up Her Hair.
Where Do the Gipsies Come From?
BASHFORD, HERBERT. Alice.
Along Shore.
Arid Lands, The.
By the Pacific.
Morning in Camp.
Mount Rainier.
Night in Camp.
Song of the Forest Ranger, The.
Sunset.
BASHKIN, VASILY VASELYEVICH. Eagles.
BASHO (Matsuo Basho). Afterglow, The.
All That Is Left.
Crescent Moon.
Crow, A.
Dusk.
Even the Rocks of Futami.
Friend sparrow, do not eat, I pray.
Haiku: "Autumn evening."
Haiku: "New moon in the sky."
Haiku: "Old pond, An."
Haiku: "On this road."
Haiku: "Summer grass."
Haiku: "Wild sea, A."
Hail on the Pine Trees.
Hokku: "Cry of the cicada, The."
Hokku: "Wayside cherry tree, A."
Into the Darkness.
Invitation, An.
Island etched on a silver sky, An.
Lonely pond in age-old stillness sleeps, A.
Morning-Glories.
O cricket, from your cheery cry.
Old battle-field, fresh with spring flowers again.
Old men, white-haired, beside the ancestral graves.
Old pond, An.
On a Journey.
On Izumo Cliff.
On the Heights.
On this road.
Perfume of plum upon the air.
Plum Blossoms.
Quick-falling dew.
Rice Fields.
Roadside thistle, eager, The.
Spring Days.
Still chirp the crickets/ Cheerfully.
They Also.
This, then, the end of a dream of power.
Transient Beauty.
Waving ripe fields glow with gold, The.
White of the first light snow.
BASLER, ROY. Exodus.
BASSE, WILLIAM. Angler's Song, The.
Elegy on Mr. William Shakespeare.
Elegy on Shakespeare.
Epitaph, An: "Renownèd Spenser, lie a thought more nigh."
Hunter's Song, The.
Lines on the Tombs in Westminster, *at.*
Memento for Mortality [*or* Mortalitie], A, *at.*
On Mr. William [*or* Wm.] Shakespeare.
On the Tombs in Westminster Abbey, *at.*
On William Shakespeare.
Renownèd Spenser, lie a thought more nigh.
BASSELIN, OLIVIER. To His Nose, *at.*
War and Wine, *at.*
BASSETT, A. A. Twice Fed.
BASTARD, THOMAS. Ad Curiosum Lectorem.
Ad Eandem.
Ad Henricum Wottonem ("Wotton my little Bere dwells on a hill").
Ad Henricum Wottonum ("Wotton, the country and the country swain").
Ad Lectorem ("How quickly doth the reader pass away").
Ad Lectorem ("If my books easy of digestion be").
Ad Lectorem ("Reader, my book flies low, and comes not near").
Ad Lectorem ("Reader, there is no biting in my verse").
Ad Reginam Elizabetham ("Live long Elisa, that the wolf of Spain").
Ad Reginam Elizabetham ("Mother of England, and sweet nurse of all").
Ad Samuelem Danielem.
De Mense Januarii Quae Fuit An. Do. 1595.
De Microcosmo.
De Naevo in Facie Faustinae.
De Piscatione.
De Poeta Martiali.
De Subiecto Operis Sui.
First and riper world of men and skill, The.
Heywood goes down saith Davie, sikerly.
In Cacum.
In Caium.
In Philonem.
Laetus did in his mistress' quarrel die.
Methinks 'Tis Pretty Sport.
Nisus writes epigrams and so do I.
Our fathers did but use the world before.
They which read Horace, Virgil and the rest.
Wonderful scarcity will shortly ensue, A.
BATE, JOHN. Cologne.
BATES, ARLO. America. *Fr.* The Torch-Bearers.
Conceits.
Cyclamen, The.
In Paradise.
Kitty's Laugh. *Fr.* Conceits.
Kitty's "No." *Fr.* Conceits.
Like to a Coin.
On the Road to Chorrera.
Pool of Sleep, The.
Rose, A.
Shadow Boat, A.
Torch-Bearers, The, *sels.*
Watchers, The.
Winter Twilight, A.
BATES, MRS. ARLO. *See* "PUTNAM, ELEANOR."
BATES, BRAINARD L. *See* BATES, ESTHER WILLARD, *and* BRAINARD L. BATES.
BATES, CHARLOTTE FISKE. André.
Character, A.
Clue, The.
Delay.
Living Book, The.
Woodbines in October.
BATES, CLARA DOTY. Spring Questions.
Thistle-Down.
Who Likes the Rain?
BATES, DAVID. Speak Gently.
BATES, ESTHER WILLARD, *and* BRAINARD L. BATES. Ipswich Bar.
BATES, HARRIET LEONORA. *See* "PUTNAM, ELEANOR."
BATES, HERBERT. Heavens Are Our Riddle, The.
Prairie.
BATES, KATHARINE LEE. All the Road to Egypt.
Alone into the Mountain.
America the Beautiful.
Around the Sun.
At Nazareth.
By the Sea of Galilee.
Changing Road, The.
Christmas after War.
Christmas Island.
Come unto Me.
Creed of the Wood, The.
Debt, The.
Despised and Rejected.
Dogs of Bethlehem, The.
Earth Listens.
Ecco il Santo.
Fellowship, The.
First Voyage of John Cabot, The.
For Deeper Life.
Gypsy-Heart.
In His Steps.
Judgment, The.
Kings of the East, The.
Laddie.
Lame Shepherd, The.
Little Knight in Green, The.
Love Planted a Rose.
New Crusade, The.
Rebecca and Abigail.
Rima XI: "I am black and comely; my lips are glowing," *tr. Fr.* Rimas.
Rimas, *sel. tr.*
Robin's Secret.
Sarah Threeneedles.
Slumber Fairies.
Somebody's Boy.
Song of Riches, A.
Song of Waking, A.
Splendid Isolation.
Stranger in Scythopolis, A.
Tempted.
Thou Knowest.
Three Steps.
To Peace.
To Sigurd.
Vigi.
Wild Weather.
Woodrow Wilson.
Yellow Warblers.
Youth.
BATES, THEODORA. After.
Rondeau: "Land-locked I lie, in idleness."
BATHURST, WILLIAM HILEY. Triumphs of Thy Conquering Power, The.
Unshrinking Faith.
BATTERHAM, ERIC N. Once.
BATTERSBY, C. MAUD. Evening Prayer, *at.*
My Evening Prayer, *at.*
BATTLES, WILLIAM SNOWDEN. Doctor's Dream, The, *sel.*
BAUDELAIRE, CHARLES. Accursed, The.
Affinities.
Albatross, The.
All, All.

Anywhere Out of the World.
At One o'Clock in the Morning.
Balcon, Le.
Be Drunk.
Beatrice.
Beauté, La.
Beauty.
Benediction.
Blind Folk.
Carrion, A.
Cat, The.
Cats, The.
Clock, The.
Comes the Charming Evening.
Correspondences.
Cracked Bell, The.
Dawn.
Death of Artists, The.
Despair of the Old Woman, The.
Don Juan in Hell.
Elevation.
Enemy, The.
Epigraph for a Condemned Book.
Epilogue: "With heart at rest I climbed the citadel's."
Epilogue to Prose Poems.
Exotic Perfume.
Fair Dorothy, The.
Femmes Damnées, *sel.*
Former Life, The.
Ghost, The.
Giantess, The.
Gulf, The.
Gypsies on the March.
Harmonie du soir.
Harmonies of the Evening.
Heautontimoroumenos [*or* Heauton Timoroumenos].
Hiboux, Les.
Hymn: "To the Dearest One, to the Beauty divine."
Hymn to Beauty.
I Have Not Forgotten.
I Offer You This Verse.
In Her Entirety.
Invitation to the Voyage.
Invitation to Travel.
Jet Eyes.
King of the Rainy Country, The.
Landscape.
Lesbos.
Lethe.
Litanies of Satan, The.
Litany to Satan.
Little Old Women, The.
Love and the Skull.
Love of Deceit, The.
Lovers' Wine.
Meditation.
Metamorphoses of a Vampire, The.
Mists and Rain.
Morning Twilight.
Music.
My Cat.
Parfum exotique.
Pit, The.
Posthumous Remorse.
Prose Poem: Dog and the Flask, The.
Prose Poem: Stranger, The.
Prose Poem: Windows, The.
Ransom, The.
Rebel, The.
Remorse after Death.
Remorse of the Dead.
Sadness of the Moon.
Sed Non Satiata.
Seven Old Men, The.
Sight-Seer's Dream, A.
Sois sage o ma douleur.
Spleen ("The bored rain-god spills his irritation over").
Spleen ("When the oppressive sky weighs like a cover").
Spleen LXXV ("January, angry at the whole damned town").
Sun, The.
Swan, The.
Thee I Adore.
To Beauty.
To the Reader.
Tresses.
Vial, The.
Voyage, The.
Voyage to Cythera, A.
What Answer?
Woman and Cat, *wr. at.* *See* VERLAINE, PAUL.

BAUGHAN, BLANCHE EDITH. Five Prayers.
God's Acre.
Greatest Gift, The.
In Exile.
Mary Ross, The.
Meeting of Sighs, The.
Old Place, The (New Zealand).
On the Just and the Unjust.
Ship and the Sea, The.

BAUGHER, RUBY DELL. Christmas Prayer, A.

BAUM, PETER. Horror.
Psalms of Love.

BAX, SIR ARNOLD. *See* "O'BYRNE, DERMOT."

BAX, CLIFFORD. Berkshire Holiday, A.
Dreamer, The.
Excavation.
Fame.
Full Moon.
In the Train.
Migration.
Musician.
Town Maid.
Turn Back, O Man.

BAX, VERA (Mrs. Clifford Bax). April, 1941.
Christmas, 1943.
Suicides, The.
To Richard.

BAXTER, ELIZABETH. In Your Absence.

BAXTER, JAMES KEIR. Antelopes, The.
Cressida, *sels.*
Elegy for an Unknown Soldier.
Her Decision. *Fr.* Cressida.
Her First Song. *Fr.* Cressida.
Her Second Song. *Fr.* Cressida.
Hermit, The.
High Country Weather.
Homecoming, The.
In the Lecture Room. *Fr.* Cressida.
Lounge Bar. *Fr.* Cressida.
Mill Girl.
Never No More.
Parting, The. *Fr.* Cressida.
Poem in the Matukituki Valley.
Rocket Show.
Seraphion.
Sestina. *Fr.* Cressida.
Tarras Moon.
To My Father.
Tunnel Beach.
Wild Bees.

BAXTER, RICHARD. Entering by His Door.
Lord, It Belongs Not to My Care.
Preacher's Urgency, A.

BAYLEBRIDGE, WILLIAM. Ampler Circumscription, The.
Life's Testament, *sels.*
Love Redeemed, *sels.*
Master-Foe, The. *Fr.* Sextains.
Moreton Miles, *sel.*
Revelation. *Fr.* Life's Testament.
Sextains, *sels.*
Troubled Unquickening, The. *Fr.* Sextains.
Wreath, A, *sel.*

BAYLES, JAMES C. In the Gloaming.

BAYLISS, JOHN CLIFFORD. October.
To My Wife.

BAYLY, THOMAS HAYNES. Do You Remember.
I'd Be a Butterfly.
Long, Long Ago.
Mistletoe Bough, The.
Novel of High Life, A.
Oh! Where Do Fairies Hide Their Heads?
She Wore a Wreath of Roses.
Till Green Leaves Come Again.
Why Don't the Men Propose?

BEACH, JOSEPH WARREN. Rue Bonaparte.
View at Gunderson's, The.

"BEACHCOMBER." *See* MORTON, J. B.

BEACONSFIELD, EARL OF. *See* DISRAELI, BENJAMIN.

BEAGLEHOLE, JOHN CAWTE. Considerations on Certain Music of J. S. Bach, *sel.*

BEARDSLEY, AUBREY. Hail and Farewell, *tr.*
On the Burial of His Brother, *tr.*
Three Musicians, The.

BEATTIE, JAMES. But Who the Melodies of Morn Can Tell? *Fr.* The Minstrel.
Edwin, the Minstrel. *Fr.* The Minstrel.
Epitaph, An: "Escaped the gloom of mortal life, a soul."
Epitaph, An: "Like thee I once have stemm'd the sea of life."
Epitaph, Intended for Himself.
Hermit, The, *sel.*
Melodies of Morn, The. *Fr.* The Minstrel.
Minstrel, The, *sels.*
Morning. *Fr.* The Minstrel.
Nature and the Poets. *Fr.* The Minstrel.
Nature's Charms. *Fr.* The Minstrel.
Reasons for Humility.
Retirement, *sel.*
Solitude. *Fr.* Retirement.

BEATTIE, ROBERT BREWSTER. Way to a Happy New Year, A.

BEATTY, PAKENHAM. Charles Lamb.
Death of Hampden, The.
When Will Love Come?

BEAUMONT, FRANCIS. Dance, A. *Fr.* The Masque of the Inner-Temple and Gray's Inne.
Eies look off theires no beeholdinge, *at.*
Examination of His Mistress' Perfections, The.
Fie on Love.
Fit Only for Apollo. *Fr.* The Masque of the Inner-Temple and Gray's Inne.
In Westminster Abbey, *at.*
Indifferent, The.
Letter to Ben Jonson, A.
Lines on the Tombs in Westminster, *at.*
M. Francis Beaumont's Letter to Ben Jonson.
Masque of the Inner-Temple and Gray's Inne, The, *sels.*
Master [*or* Mr.] Francis Beaumont's Letter to Ben Jonson.
Master Francis Beaumont's Letter to Ben Jonson, *sel.*
Memento for Mortality, A, *at.*
On the Marriage of a Beauteous Young Gentlewoman with an Ancient Man.
On the Tombs in Westminster Abbey, *at.*
Shake Off Your Heavy Trance. *Fr.* The Masque of the Inner-Temple and Gray's Inne.
Song: "More pleasing were these sweet delights." *Fr.* The Masque of the Inner-Temple and Gray's Inne.
Song: "On blessed youths, for Jove doth pause." *Fr.* The Masque of the Inner-Temple and Gray's Inne.
Song: "Peace and silence be the guide." *Fr.* The Masque of the Inner-Temple and Gray's Inne.
Song: "Shake off your heavy trance." *Fr.* The Masque of the Inner-Temple and Gray's Inne.
Song: "You should stay longer if we durst." *Fr.* The Masque of the Inner-Temple and Gray's Inne.
Song for a Dance. *Fr.* The Masque of the Inner-Temple and Gray's Inne.
Songs from a Masque. *Fr.* The Masque of the Inner-Temple and Gray's Inne.
Superlative Dance and Song. *Fr.* The Masque of the Inner-Temple and Gray's Inne.
Three Songs. *Fr.* The Masque of the Inner-Temple and Gray's Inne.
True Beauty.
Ye should stay longer if we durst. *Fr.* The Masque of the Inner-Temple and Gray's Inne.

BEAUMONT, FRANCIS, *and* JOHN FLETCHER. Aspatia's Song. *Fr.* The Maid's Tragedy.
Away, Delights! *Fr.* The Captain.

BEAUMONT *and* FLETCHER (*continued*)
Better music ne'er was known. *Fr.* The Knight of the Burning Pestle.
Bridal Song ("Cynthia, to thy power"). *Fr.* The Maid's Tragedy.
Bridal Song ("Hold back thy hours"). *Fr.* The Maid's Tragedy.
Captain, The, *sels.*
Come, Sleep, and with thy sweet deceiving. *Fr.* The Woman-Hater.
Come, You Whose Loves Are Dead. *Fr.* The Knight of the Burning Pestle.
Cupid's Revenge, *sel.*
Cynthia, to thy power and thee. *Fr.* The Maid's Tragedy.
Dirge: "Come, you whose loves are dead." *Fr.* The Knight of the Burning Pestle.
Dirge: "Lay a garland on my hearse." *Fr.* The Maid's Tragedy.
Farewell, False Love! *Fr.* The Captain.
Farewell to Love, The.
Hold Back Thy Hours, Dark Night. *Fr.* The Maid's Tragedy.
I could never have the power. *Fr.* The Maid's Tragedy.
I Died True. *Fr.* The Maid's Tragedy.
Invocation to Sleep. *Fr.* The Woman-Hater.
Jillian of Berry. *Fr.* The Knight of the Burning Pestle.
Knight of the Burning Pestle, The, *sels.*
Laugh and Sing. *Fr.* The Knight of the Burning Pestle.
Lay a Garland on My Hearse. *Fr.* The Maid's Tragedy.
Lovers Rejoice! *Fr.* Cupid's Revenge.
Love's Cure, *sel.*
Lullaby: "Come sleep, and with the sweet deceiving." *Fr.* The Woman-Hater.
Maid's Tragedy, The, *sels.*
Merrythought's Song ("For Jillian of Berry"). *Fr.* The Knight of the Burning Pestle.
Merrythought's Song ("I would not be a servingman"). *Fr.* The Knight of the Burning Pestle.
Mirth. *Fr.* The Knight of the Burning Pestle.
Month of May, The. *Fr.* The Knight of the Burning Pestle.
Nose, nose, jolly red nose. *Fr.* The Knight of the Burning Pestle.
Sad Song, The. *Fr.* The Captain.
Sleep. *Fr.* The Woman-Hater.
Song: "Turn, turn thy beauteous face away." *Fr.* Love's Cure.
Tell Me, Dearest, What Is Love? *Fr.* The Captain.
Tell me, dearest, what is love? *Fr.* The Knight of the Burning Pestle.
'Tis mirth that fills the veins with blood. *Fr.* The Knight of the Burning Pestle.
Turn, Turn Thy Beauteous Face Away. *Fr.* Love's Cure.
What Is Love? *Fr.* The Captain.
Woman-Hater, The, *sels.*
BEAUMONT, SIR JOHN. Assumption, The.
Of His Dear Son, Gervase. *Fr.* Of My Dear Son Gervase Beaumont.
Of My Dear Son, Gervase Beaumont.
Of My Dear Son, Gervase Beaumont, *sels.*
Of Sir Philip Sidney.
Of True Liberty.
On the Coincidence of the Feasts of the Annunciation and the Resurrection in 1627.
To His Late Majesty, Concerning the True Form of English Poetry.
What course of life should wretched mortals take? *tr.*
BEAUMONT, JOSEPH. Ascension, The.
Bad Times.
Βιοθάνατος (Biothanatos).
Garden, The.
Gentle Check, The.
Gnat, The.
Home.
House and Home.
Love.
Morning Hymn.
Purification of the Blessed Virgin.
Snow, The.
Whit Sunday.
Whiteness, or Chastity.
BEAUMONT, THOMAS. His Despair.
To His Mistress.
To His Mistress; Sendng Her the Arcadia.
BECCADELLI, ANTONIO. Elysia.
BECH, BODIL. In the Train.
BECHER, ULRICH. Vow of the European.
BECHERS, D. G. What My Father Was to Me.
BECHTEL, LOUISE SEAMAN. Grandfather Frog.
BECK, CATHLEEN KEEGAN. *See* KEEGAN, CATHLEEN.
BECK, THOMAS. Bless, Dear Saviour, This Child.
BECK, VICTOR EMANUEL. Sifting.
BECKER, CHARLOTTE. Door-Bell, The.
BECKER, EDNA. Reflections.
BECKER, JOHN. Feather or Fur.
BECKETT, GILBERT ABBOTT À. *See* À BECKETT, GILBERT ABBOTT.
BECKETT, SAMUEL. *For translations from Spanish, see* AnMP.
BÉCQUER, GUSTAVO ADOLFO. Love Passing By.
Rimas, *sels.*
Shadowy Swallows.
Song: "I am a passion; I am a flame."
They Closed Her Eyes. *Fr.* Rimas.
Three Rimas.
Waiting Harp, The.
BEDA. *See* BEDE, THE VENERABLE.
BEDDOES, THOMAS LOVELL. Athulf's Death Song. *Fr.* Death's Jest Book.
Ballad of Human Life.
Beautiful Night, A. *Fr.* Fragments Intended for the Dramas.
Bridal Song to Amala. *Fr.* Death's Jest Book.
Bride's Tragedy, The, *sels.*
Carrion Crow, The. *Fr.* Death's Jest Book.
Crocodile, A. *Fr.* The Last Man.
Daisy and the Flood, The. *Fr.* The Second Brother.
Death's Jest Book, *sels.*
Dirge: "If thou wilt ease thine heart." *Fr.* Death's Jest Book.
Dirge: "Sorrow, lie still and wear."
Dirge: "Swallow leaves her nest, The." *Fr.* Death's Jest Book.
Dirge: "To her couch of evening rest."
Dirge for a Young Maiden.
Dirge for Wolfram. *Fr.* Death's Jest Book.
Dirge Written for a Drama.
Do Not Minute.
Dream, A.
Dream of Dying. *Fr.* Fragments Intended for the Dramas.
Dream-Pedlary.
Dream-Pedlary, *sels.*
Dreams to Sell. *Fr.* Dream-Pedlary.
Early Fragments, *sels.*
Epithalamia. *Fr.* Death's Jest Book.
Fragment: "All night a wind of music."
Fragment: "Or I will burst/ Damnation's iron egg, my tomb."
Fragments Intended for the Dramas, *sels.*
Ghosts' Moonshine, The.
Grief-in-Idleness. *Fr.* Early Fragments.
Has no one seen my heart of you?
Her Kisses. *Fr.* Early Fragments.
Her kisses are/ Soft as a snow-tuft in the dewless cup.
Hesperus Sings. *Fr.* The Bride's Tragedy.
Hist, oh hist!
How Many Times Do I Love Thee, Dear? *Fr.* Torrismond.
If There Were Dreams to Sell. *Fr.* Dream-Pedlary.
If Thou Wilt Ease Thine Heart. *Fr.* Death's Jest Book.
I'll Be as True. *Fr.* Early Fragments.
In a Garden by Moonlight. *Fr.* Torrismond.
Insignificance of the World. *Fr.* Fragments Intended for the Dramas.
Isbrand's Song. *Fr.* Death's Jest Book.
Ivory Gate, The, *sel.*
Lady, Was It Fair of Thee.
Last Man, The, *sel.*
L'Envoi: "Who findeth comfort in the stars and flowers." *Fr.* Death's Jest Book.
Lily of the Valley, The.
Lines Written at Geneva; July, 1824.
Lofty Mind, A. *Fr.* Fragments Intended for the Dramas.
Love Goes a-Hawking. *Fr.* The Bride's Tragedy.
Love-in-Idleness.
Mandrake's Song. *Fr.* Death's Jest Book.
Man's Anxious, but Ineffectual Guard against Death.
Mariners' Song. *Fr.* Death's Jest Book.
Mighty Thoughts of an Old World, The. *Fr.* The Ivory Gate.
Old Adam, the Carrion Crow. *Fr.* Death's Jest Book.
Phantom-Lover, The.
Phantom-Wooer, The.
Phantom-Wooer, The, *sel.*
Poor Old Pilgrim Misery. *Fr.* The Bride's Tragedy.
Reason Why, The.
Resurrection Song.
Sailor's Song. *Fr.* Death's Jest Book.
Sea, The. *Fr.* Death's Jest Book.
Sea Song. *Fr.* Death's Jest Book.
Second Brother, The, *sels.*
Sibylla's Dirge. *Fr.* Death's Jest Book.
Silenus in Proteus.
Song: "A ho! A ho!/ Love's horn doth blow." *Fr.* The Bride's Tragedy.
Song: "Hither haste, and gently strew."
Song: "How many times do I love thee, dear?" *Fr.* Torrismond.
Song: "Old Adam, the carrion crow." *Fr.* Death's Jest Book.
Song: "Strew not earth with empty stars." *Fr.* The Second Brother.
Song: "Under the lime-tree, on the daisied ground," *tr.*
Song: "We have bathed, where none have seen us." *Fr.* Death's Jest Book.
Song: "Who tames the lion now?"
Song at Amala's Wedding. *Fr.* Death's Jest Book.
Song from the Ship. *Fr.* Death's Jest Book.
Song of Thanatos, The. *Fr.* The Ivory Gate.
Song of the Stygian Naiades.
Song on the Water.
Song That Wolfram Heard in Hell, The. *Fr.* Death's Jest Book.
Songs at Amala's Wedding. *Fr.* Death's Jest Book.
Squats on a Toad-Stool under a Tree. *Fr.* Death's Jest Book.
Stanzas: "Mighty thought of an old world, The." *Fr.* The Ivory Gate.
Stanzas from "The Ivory Gate."
Strew Not Earth with Empty Stars. *Fr.* The Second Brother.
Subterranean City, A ("I followed once a fleet and mighty serpent").
Subterranean City. *Fr.* Fragments Intended for the Dramas.
Swallow Leaves Her Nest, The. *Fr.* Death's Jest Book.
Sybilla's Dirge. *Fr.* Death's Jest Book.
Threnody: "No sunny ray, no silver night."
To Night.
To Sea, to Sea! *Fr.* Death's Jest Book.

Torrismond, *sels.*
Under the Lime Tree, *tr.*
Voice from the Waters. *Fr.* Death's Jest Book.
We Do Lie beneath the Grass. *Fr.* Death's Jest Book.
Wolfram's Dirge. *Fr.* Death's Jest Book.
Wolfram's Song. *Fr.* Death's Jest Book.
Beddome, Benjamin. Glorious Gift of God, The.
Bede [*or* Beda *or* Baeda], the Venerable. Ascension Hymn.
Hymn, A: "Hymn of glory let us sing, A."
Hymn of Glory Let Us Sing, A.
Hymnum Canentes Martyrum.
"Bede, Cuthbert" (Edward Bradley). In Immemoriam.
In Memoriam.
Limerick: "There was a queer fellow named Woodin."
There was a queer fellow named Woodin.
Bedford-Jones, Henry James O'Brien. How Do You Do?
Bedingfield, Thomas. Lover's Choice, The.
'Bedny [*or* Byedny], Demyan" (Yefim Pridvorov). My Voice.
Nepman.
No One Knew.
None Knew.
Young Forest, The.
Bedregal de Cónitzer, Yolanda. Facing My Portrait.
Beecham, Audrey. Ditty.
Exile.
Beeching, Henry Charles. Accidian.
Bicycling Song.
Blackbird, The.
Boy's Prayer, A.
Bride, A, *tr.*
Fatherhood.
Going down Hill on a Bicycle.
Knowledge after Death.
Masque of Balliol, The, *sels.*
Prayers.
Summer Day, A.
To My Totem.
Under the Sun.
Beeching, Jack. 1944—On the Invasion Coast.
Beedome, Thomas. Broken Heart, The.
Choice, The.
To the Noble Sir Francis Drake.
Beeman, Katherine. Happiness.
Beer, Henry. Babe of Bethlehem, The.
Beer, Morris Abel. Achievement.
Book Is an Enchanted Gate, A.
Boy of Old Manhattan, A.
Candles Divine.
Church in the Heart, The.
Manhattan.
Old Garrets.
Piety.
Puddle, The.
Six Poets Gazed upon the Moon.
Subway, The.
Who builds a church within his heart.
Beer-Hofmann, Richard. "Evil Man, An!" *Fr.* Der Graf von Charolais.
Graf von Charolais, Der, *sel.*
Jacob's Destiny. *Fr.* Jacob's Dream.
Jacob's Dream, *sel.*
Beers, Carmen Brannon. *See* "Lars, Claudia."
Beers, Ethel Lynn. All Quiet along [*or* on] the Potomac.
Not One to Spare.
On the Shores of Tennessee.
Our Folks.
Picket-Guard, The.
Weighing the Baby.
Which Shall It Be?
Beers, Henry Augustin. Biftek aux Champignons.
Ecce in Deserto.
Fish Story, A.
Laye of ye Woodpeckore, Ye.
On a Miniature.
Posthumous.
Singer of One Song, The.
Beesly, Augustus Henry. André's Ride.
Began, Robert. As a Blossom Sweet and Rosy.
Begbie, Agnes H. Lullaby, A: "See how the poppies nod."
Song of Mary, A.
Unto Us a Child Is Born.
Behemb, Martin. I Shall Be Satisfied.
Behn, Aphra. Abdelazer, *sels.*
Amyntas Led Me to a Grove. *Fr.* The Dutch Lover.
City Heiress, The; or, Sir Timothy Treat-All, *sel.*
Coquet[te], The.
Defiance, The.
Dutch Lover, The, *sel.*
Emperor of the Moon, The, *sel.*
Jolly Swain, A. *Fr.* The City Heiress.
Libertine, The.
Love Armed. *Fr.* Abdelazer.
Love in Fantastic[k] Triumph [Sat]. *Fr.* Abdelazer.
Lucky Chance, The, *sel.*
Lycidus, *sel.*
O Love, that stronger art than wine.
Of Love, *at. Fr.* The Lucky Chance.
Serenade: "When maidens are young, and in their spring." *Fr.* The Emperor of the Moon.
Song: Love Arm'd. *Fr.* Abdelazer.
Song: "Love in fantastic triumph sate." *Fr.* Abdelazer.
Song: "Not to sigh and to be tender." *Fr.* Lycidus.
Song: "Oh love! that stronger art than wine."
Willing Mistress, The. *Fr.* The Dutch Lover.
Behn, Harry. Adventure.
Circles.
Easter Snowfall.
Evening.
Flowers.
Gnome, The.
Growing Up.
Hallowe'en.
Invitation.
Kite, The.
Lesson.
Mr. Pyme.
Others.
Spring.
Spring Rain.
Surprise.
This Happy Day.
Trees.
Waiting.
Windy Morning.
Behrend, Alice. Snowflakes.
Belitt, Ben. Drunken Boat, The, *tr.*
"Bell, Acton." *See* Brontë, Anne.
Bell, Arthur W. Case History.
Streamlined Stream-Knowledge.
Bell, Birdie. I Have Always Found It So.
Bell, Charles Dent. Solemn Rondeau.
Bell, Charles G. Banana.
Diretro al Sol.
From Le Havre.
Girl Walking.
Heraclitus in the West.
Island Dogs.
Love in Age.
On a Baltimore Bus.
Termites.
This Little Vigil.
Windowed Habitations.
Woodbird.
Bell, Clove. Change Is Sweetest of All.
Bell, Corydon. Wandering Ant, The.
"Bell, Currer." *See* Brontë, Charlotte.
"Bell, Ellis." *See* Brontë, Emily.
Bell, Gertrude Lowthian. Comfort, *tr.*
Desire, *tr.*
From the Garden of Heaven, *tr.*
Jewel of the Secret Treasury, The, *tr.*
Lady That Hast My Heart, *tr.*
Odes (*of* Hafiz), *sels., tr.*
Rose Bloom, *tr.*
Slaves of Thy Shining Eyes, *tr.*
Tidings of Union, *tr.*
To Hafiz of Shiraz.
Bell, H. W. Serenade: "Heart of my heart, awake! awake!"
Bell, Sir Harold Idris. Epilogue to Alun Mabon, *tr.*
For Little Dinogad, *tr.*
Love Poem, A, *tr.*
Ode to Rhys ap Maredudd of Tywyn, *tr.*
Snowy Day, A, *tr.*
To the Nun, *tr.*
Bell, Henry Glassford. Mary, Queen of Scots.
Bell, Jerome B. Mystery.
Bell, John Joy. "Blackie."
Lights, The.
On the Quay.
Ships, The.
Bell, Julian. Moths, The.
Pluviose.
Redshanks, The.
Woods and Kestrel.
Bell, Julian, *and* Charles Maurron. Drunken Boat, The, *tr.*
Bell, Mackenzie. At Stratford-on-Avon.
At the Grave of Dante Gabriel Rossetti.
Spring's Immortality.
Bell, Maurice. *Alabama,* The.
Men, The.
Bell, Robert Mowry. Second Volume, The.
Tutelage, The.
Bell, Thelma Harrington. Half-asleep.
Bell, Walker Meriwether. Jefferson Davis.
Bell, William. Elegy: "My dear, observe the rose! though she desire it."
Elegy: "Now Christendom bids her cathedrals call."
Elegy: "Silent is Orpheus now, and silent now."
Elegy: "Tonight the moon is high, to summon all."
On a Dying Boy.
Sonnet: "You waken slowly. In your dream you're straying."
Sonnet: "You whispered, 'still the stars shine cold above me.' "
To a Lady on Her Marriage.
Young Man's Song, A.
Bellamann, Henry. Artist, The.
Charleston Garden, A.
Cups of Illusion.
Deeper Seas, The.
Gulf Stream, The.
Pause.
Poppies.
Sound of Going in the Tops of the Mulberry Trees, A.
Upward Pass, The.
Bellamy, Claxson, *and* Harry Paulton. Erminie, *sel.*
Lullaby: "Dear mother, in dreams I see her." *Fr.* Erminie.
Bellaw, Americus Wellington. Conjugal Conjugations.
Old Line Fence, The.
Bellay, Joachim du. *See* Du Bellay, Joachim.
Belleau, Remy [*or* Remi]. April.
Grasshopper, The.
Sweet Month of April, The.
Bellenden, John. Address to Bellona and King James V.
Anno Domini.
Starscape, A.
Bellerby, Frances. It Is Not Likely Now.
Bellinger, Alfred Raymond. Angel and the Shepherds, The, *tr.*
Icarus.
Joseph and the Shopkeeper, *tr.*
Bellman, Carl Michael [*or* Karl Mikael]. Concerning Mollberg's Parade to Corporal Boman's Grave.
Cradle Song: "Lullaby, my little one."
Nota Bene, A.
Of Fishing.
Of Haga,

BELLMAN, CARL MICHAEL (*continued*)
Of Madame Bergström's Portrait at the Inn of Lilya in Torshälla.
To Old Movitz, Ill with Consumption.
To Ulla at a Window in Fishertown, Noon of a Summer Day.
BELLOC, ELIZABETH. Nightingale, The.
BELLOC, HILAIRE. Almighty God, Whose Justice like a Sun.
Ballad of Val-ès-Dunes, The, *sel.*
Ballade of Hell and of Mrs. Roebeck.
Ballade of Illegal Ornaments.
Ballade of the Heresiarchs.
Ballade to Our Lady of Czestochowa.
Because My Faltering Feet. *Fr.* Sonnets.
Big Baboon, The.
Birds, The.
Bison, The.
Charles Augustus Fortescue.
Courtesy.
Crusade.
Cuckoo!
Dawn Shall over Lethe Break.
Death and Last Confession of Wandering Peter, The.
Dedication: "Child! do not throw this book about!"
Dedication on the Gift of a Book to a Child.
Dedicatory Ode, *sel.*
Discovery.
Dodo, The.
Dromedary, The.
Duncton Hill.
Early Morning, The.
Elephant, The.
Elm, The.
Epigram: "When I am dead, I hope it may be said."
Epitaph on the Favourite Dog of a Politician.
Epitaph on the Politician [Himself].
False Heart, The.
Fatigue.
For False Heart.
Foreword, A: "Child! do not throw this book about."
Frog, The.
G.
Game of Cricket, The.
Garden Party, The.
George [Who Played with a Dangerous Toy].
Gnu, The. *Fr.* A Moral Alphabet.
Godolphin Horne.
Grandmamma's Birthday.
Greetings of the Season.
Ha'nacker Mill.
Henry King.
Her Faith.
Heretics All.
Hildebrand.
Hippopotamus, The.
I shoot the Hippopotamus.
In a Boat.
Jim.
Juliet.
Leader, The.
Lines to a Don.
Lion, The.
Llama, The.
Lord Finchley.
Lord Heygate.
Lord High-Bo.
Lord Lundy.
Matilda.
Microbe, The.
Modern Traveller, The, *sel.*
Moon's Funeral, The.
Moral Alphabet, A, *sel.*
Night, The.
Noël.
On a Dead Hostess.
On a General Election.
On a Great Election.
On a Politician.
On a Sleeping Friend.
On a Sundial.
On His Books.
On Hygiene.
On Lady Poltagrue, a Public Peril.
On Mundane Acquaintances.
Our Lord and Our Lady.
Pacifist, The.
Prophet Lost in the Hills at Evening, The.
Python, The.
Rebecca.
Rebel, The.
Rhinoceros, The.
Sarah Byng.
Song: Inviting the Influence of a Young Lady upon the Opening Year.
Song: "You wear the morning like your dress."
Sonnet: "Almighty God, whose justice like a sun."
Sonnet: "Because my faltering feet may fail to dare."
Sonnet: "Lift up your hearts in Gumber, laugh the Weald."
Sonnet: "Rise up and do begin the day's adorning."
Sonnet: "We will not whisper, we have found the place."
Sonnet: "When you to Acheron's ugly water come."
Sonnets, *sels.*
South Country, The.
Stanzas Written on Battersea Bridge during a Southwesterly Gale.
Statue, The.
Tarantella.
Telephone, The.
They Say, and I Am Glad They Say.
Tiger, The.
To Dives.
To the Balliol Men Still in Africa.
Viper, The.
Vulture, The.
West Sussex Drinking Song.
Winged Horse, The.
Yak, The.
BELLOWS, HENRY ADAMS. Attila the Hun, *tr. Fr.* The Elder Edda.
Beginning and the End, The, *tr. Fr.* The Elder Edda.
Death Song of Egil the Son of Grim, The.
Elder Edda, The, *sels., tr.*
Freyr's Courtship, *tr. Fr.* The Elder Edda.
Helgi Thrice Born, *tr. Fr.* The Elder Edda.
"Home They Brought Her Warrior Dead," *tr. Fr.* The Elder Edda.
Lay of Thrym, The, *tr. Fr.* The Elder Edda.
Lay of Wayland, The, *tr. Fr.* The Elder Edda.
On an Icelandic Skald.
Sayings of the High One, The, *tr. Fr.* The Elder Edda.
Sigurth and I, *tr. Fr.* The Elder Edda.
Thrymskvitha, *tr. Fr.* The Elder Edda.
Voluspo, *tr. Fr.* The Elder Edda.
BELLOWS, SILENCE BUCK. Last Cargo.
"BELY, ANDREI" (Boris Nikolayevich Bugayev). Bright Death.
Christ Is Risen, *sels.*
Fields.
Native Land.
Once More I Pray.
Requiem, *sel.*
Russia.
BEMIS, ARTHUR ROSZELLE, JR. Decoration Day Prayer.
BEMISS, J. M. Minister's Prayer, A.
BENEDICT, GEORGIA. Queen Anne's Lace.
BENEDICT, HESTER A. Good-Night.
BENEDIKTOV, VLADIMIR. Cold Confession.
BENEDIKTSDÓTTIR, UNNUR ("Hulda"). If the Moonbeam.
Lilies of White.
BENEDIKTSSON, EINAR. Northern Lights.
Rain.
BENÉT, LAURA. Adventure.
Bird of Paradise, The.
Cushy Cow.
Hedgehog, The.
Mountain Convent.
Penny, The.
Peter.
Rowers, The.
"She Wandered after Strange Gods."
Thrush, The.
BENÉT, ROSEMARY (Mrs. Stephen Vincent Benét). To an Unknown Neighbor at the Circus.
BENÉT, ROSEMARY, *and* STEPHEN VINCENT BENÉT. Abraham Lincoln.
Benjamin Franklin.
Christopher Columbus.
Clipper Ships and Captains.
Crawford Long and William Morton.
George Washington.
Johnny Appleseed.
Nancy Hanks.
Negro Spirituals.
Peregrine White and Virginia Dare.
Wilbur Wright and Orville Wright.
BENÉT, STEPHEN VINCENT. Aaron Burr.
All Night Long.
America. *Fr.* John Brown's Body.
American Names.
Andrew Jackson.
Ballad of William Sycamore, The.
Battle of Gettysburg, The. *Fr.* John Brown's Body.
Daniel Boone.
Death-Chant of the Centaurs, *sel.*
Enlistments, The. *Fr.* John Brown's Body.
Flood Tide.
For All Blasphemers.
Going Back to School.
Golden Corpse, The.
Invocation: "American muse, whose strong and diverse heart." *Fr.* John Brown's Body.
Invocation: "American muse, whose strong and diverse heart," *sel. Fr.* John Brown's Body.
John Brown. *Fr.* John Brown's Body.
John Brown's Body, *sels.*
John Brown's Body Lies a-Mouldering [in the Grave]. *Fr.* John Brown's Body.
John Brown's Prayer. *Fr.* John Brown's Body.
John Quincy Adams.
King David.
Lincoln Calls for Volunteers. *Fr.* John Brown's Body.
Litany for Dictatorships.
Lonely Burial.
Love Came By from the Riversmoke. *Fr.* John Brown's Body.
Metropolitan Nightmare.
Mortuary Parlors.
Mountain Whippoorwill, The.
Nightmare at Noon.
Nightmare Number Three.
1935.
Ode to Walt Whitman.
Out of John Brown's Strong Sinews. *Fr.* John Brown's Body.
Pickett's Charge. *Fr.* John Brown's Body.
Portrait of a Boy.
Rain after a Vaudeville Show.
Retort Discourteous, The.
Sad Song, A.
Significance of John Brown, The. *Fr.* John Brown's Body.
Slaver, The. *Fr.* John Brown's Body.
Soliloquy of Lincoln before Manassas. *Fr.* John Brown's Body.
Song of [the] Breath, The. *Fr.* John Brown's Body.
Song of the Riders. *Fr.* John Brown's Body.
Sparrow.
Thirteen Sisters, The. *Fr.* John Brown's Body.
Thomas Jefferson
To Rosemary.
Unfamiliar Quartet.
Western Wagons.
Winged Man.
BENÉT, WILLIAM ROSE. Army of the Dead, The.
Arraignment, *sel.*
Arrival, The.
At Warm Springs.
Bast.
Brazen Tongue.

Daughters.
Death of Robin Hood, The.
Debutantrum.
Eternal Masculine.
Falcon.
Falconer of God, The.
Fawn in the Snow, The.
Front Line.
Fugitive, The.
Gaspara Stampa.
Great Land, The.
Her Way.
His Ally.
Horse Thief, The.
House at Evening, The.
How to Catch Unicorns.
Inscription for a Mirror in a Deserted Dwelling.
Jesse James.
Judgment.
Last Ally, The.
Lullaby of the Catfish and the Crab.
Mad Blake.
Merchants from Cathay.
Moon Rider.
Night.
Old Adam, The.
Old Bill's Memory Book.
On Sunday in the Sunlight.
Oregon Trail, The.
Pearl Diver.
Question, The.
Red Country, The.
Roundhouse, The.
S. V. B.
Sagacity.
Salute, Czechoslovakia!
Skater of Ghost Lake, The.
Sky Writers.
Slings, *tr.*
Sorceress of the Moon, The.
Stage Directions.
Street of Cats.
Strong Swimmer, The.
There Lived a Lady in Milan.
Third Row, Centre.
To My Father.
To My Wife.
Tricksters.
We Ask No Shield.
Whale.
Wild Philomela.
Wings.
Woodcutter's Wife, The.
World's Desire, The.

BENEVIENI, GIROLAMO. Lauda.

BENHAM, IDA W. Little Brown Seed in the Furrow, The.

BENISON, H. WORSLEY-. *See* WORSLEY-BENISON, H.

BENJACOB, ISAAC. Epitaph, An: "Here lies Nachshon, a man of great renown."

BENJAMIN, PARK. Old Sexton, The.
To Arms.

BENJAMIN, PAUL L. We Who Are Dead.

BEN KALIR, ELEAZAR. O Hark to the Herald.
Palms and Myrtles.
Prayer for Dew.
Prophet Jeremiah and the Personification of Israel, The, *at.*
Terrible Sons, The.
To Him Who Is Feared.

BENLOWES, EDWARD. Evening Prayer. *Fr.* Theophila.
Life and Death. *Fr.* Theophila.
Theophila; or, Love's Sacrifice, *sels.*
To His Muse. *Fr.* Theophila.

BENNARD, GEORGE. On a hill far away stood an old rugged cross.

BENNETT, ANNA ELIZABETH. Candle Song.

BENNETT, ARNOLD. It Pays.
Limerick: "There was a young man of Montrose."

BENNETT, DOROTHY. Saint Francis.

BENNETT, GERTRUDE RYDER. Diary of a Raccoon.
Old Shoes.
These Times.
Wayside Shrine.

BENNETT, GWENDOLYN B. Advice.
Fantasy.
Hatred.
Heritage.
Lines Written at the Grave of Alexandre [*or* Alexander] Dumas.
Nocturne: "This cool night is strange."
Quatrains.
Secret.
Sonnet: "He came in silvern armour, trimmed with black."
Sonnet: "Some things are very dear to me."
Sonnets.
To a Dark Girl.
Your Songs.

BENNETT, HENRY. Saint Patrick.
St. Patrick Was a Gentleman.

BENNETT, HENRY HOLCOMB. Adventure.
Flag Goes By, The.

BENNETT, JOHN. Abbot of Derry, The.
Dead Pussy Cat, The, *at.*
God Bless You, Dear, To-Day!
Her Answer.
In a Rose Garden.
Ingenious Little Old Man, The.
Master Sky-Lark, *sels.*
Merry Pieman's Song, The.
Sky-Lark's Song, The. *Fr.* Master Sky-Lark.
Song of the Hunt, The. *Fr.* Master Sky-Lark.
Song of the Spanish Main, The.
Tiger's Tale, A.
To Marie.
What Troubled Poe's Raven.

BENNETT, JOSEPH DEERICKS. Autumnall.
Complaint.
Earthly Love.
Headsong.
On the Nativity of Christ Our Lord.
Pointillism.
Quatrina.
To C. T. C.
To Eliza, Duchess of Dorset.
For translations from French, see AnFP.

BENNETT, MURRAY. Funeral.

BENNETT, RODNEY. Christmas-Tree Song, A.
Easter Praise.
Fluttering Leaves.
Growing River, The.
Little Brown Seed.
Little Old Lady, The.
Merry Birds.
Mr. Brown.
Mrs. Jenny Wren.
My Dog, Spot.
Pigeons, The.
Postman's Knock.
Robin's Song.
Ten Little Christmas Trees.
Thank You for Friends, A.
There—and Back.
Three Little Men in a Boat.
Wireless.
Writing Letters.

BENNETT, ROWENA BASTIN. Airplane, The.
April Puddle.
Boats.
Christmas Brownie.
Color.
Come, Ride with Me to Toyland.
Conversation between Mr. and Mrs. Santa Claus.
Conversation with an April Fool.
Elfin Plane, The.
End-of-Summer Poem.
Four Seasons.
Golden Cobwebs.
Grumbling Truck, The.
Harvest Prayer.
If I Were a Pilgrim Child.
Jack-in-the-Pulpit.
Join the Caroling.
Lady Sleep.
Meeting the Easter Bunny.
Modern Dragon, A.
Motor Cars.
Mrs. C. (Or Any Other Too Practical Person).
Picture People.
Pussy Willows.
Remembering the Winter.
Rubber Boots.
Saying a Prayer.
Shell Castles.
Sunrise.
Thanksgiving Magic.
Trails of Smoke.
Umbrellas.
Under the Tent of the Sky.
Vacation Time.
Witch Cat.
Witch of Willowby Wood, The.
Zeppelin, The.

BENNETT, WILLIAM COX. Baby May.
Baby's Shoes.
Be Mine, and I Will Give Thy Name.
Christmas Song, A.
Invocation to Rain in Summer.
Lullaby, O Lullaby.
Right above the Wrong, The, 1857.
Summer Invocation, A.
To a Cricket.
Wife's Song, A.
Winter Song, A.
Worn Wedding-Ring, The.

BENOÎT, PIERRE. Diaduminius.

BENSEL, JAMES BERRY. Ahmed.
February.

BENSON, ARTHUR CHRISTOPHER. After Construing.
Amen.
English Shell, An.
Hawk, The.
Knapweed.
Lord Vyet.
Phoenix, The.
Prelude: "Hush'd is each busy shout."
Realism.

BENSON, EDWARD FREDERICK. Image in the Sand, The, *sel.*
Prayer: "Dawn of the everlasting day, The." *Fr.* The Image in the Sand.

BENSON, LOUIS FITZGERALD. Dedication: "O thou whose gracious presence blest."
Dedication for a Home.
Light of God is Falling, The.
Near the Cross, *tr.*
O Love That Lights the Evening Sky.
O Thou Whose Feet Have Climbed Life's Hill.
O Thou Whose Gracious Presence Blest.
Songs of Jesus.

BENSON, MARGARET. Once on a Time.

BENSON, MARY JOSEPHINE. Foam of Fancy.
Heredity and Ego.
Smoking Flax.
Song of the Moon-Spirit.
Sun-Song.
Words.

BENSON, NATHANIEL ANKETELL. Holy Night.
Year's End.

BENSON, ROBERT HUGH. After a Retreat.
At High Mass.
Priest's Lament, The.
Saint Francis and the Birds.
Teresian Contemplative, The.

BENSON, STELLA. Five Smooth Stones.
Thanks to My World for the Loan of a Fair Day.
Words.

BENT, O. M. Robin, The.

BENTLEY, EDMUND CLERIHEW. Biography for Beginners, *sels.*
Clerihews, *sels.*
Clive. *Fr.* Biography for Beginners.
"Dear me!" exclaimed Homer.
George III.
"I quite realized," said Columbus.
J. S. Mill. *Fr.* Biography for Beginners.
Liszt. *Fr.* Biography for Beginners.
Lord Clive. *Fr.* Biography for Beginners.
Miguel de Cervantes. *Fr.* Biography for Beginners.
People of Spain think Cervantes, The. *Fr.* Biography for Beginners.

BENTLEY, EDMUND CLERIHEW (*cont.*)
Savonarola.
Sir Christopher Wren. *Fr.* Biography for Beginners.
Sir Humphry Davy. *Fr.* Biography for Beginners.
When Alexander Pope.
Younger Van Eyck, The. *Fr.* Biography for Beginners.
BENTLEY, NICOLAS. On Mrs. W——.
BENTLEY, RICHARD. Reply to an Imitation of the Second Ode in the Third Book of Horace, A.
Verses: "Who strives to mount Parnassus hill."
BENTON, FRANK. Old Buck's Ghost.
BENTON, JOEL. Abraham Lincoln.
At Chappaqua.
December.
Grover Cleveland.
Hallowe'en.
Poet, The.
Scarlet Tanager, The.
BENTON, MYRON B. Midsummer Invitation.
Mowers, The.
There Is One Spot for Which My Soul Will Yearn.
BENTON, PATRICIA. Desert River.
BENTON, WALTER. Entry April 28.
Entry November 12.
Summary of the Distance between the Bomber and the Objective.
With the Most Susceptible Element, the Mind, Already Turned under the Toxic Action.
BENVENUTA, SISTER MARY. Contemplative, The.
Hawkesyard.
Mater Incognita.
Rich Man of Assisi, The.
Song of White and Red, A.
BÉRANGER, PIERRE JEAN DE. Frétillon.
King of Brentford, The.
King of Guzzlemuchgate, The.
King of Yvetot, The.
My Contemporary.
O Plaguy Spring.
Popular Recollections of Bonaparte.
BERCEO, GONZALO DE. Battle of Simancas, The. *Fr.* The Life of San Millán.
Life of San Millán, The, *sels.*
Miracles of Our Lady, The, *sels.*
Praise of Spring, The. *Fr.* The Miracles of Our Lady.
San Miguel de la Tumba. *Fr.* The Miracles of Our Lady.
BERCHAN. Fort of Rathangan, The.
BERENBERG, DAVID PAUL. Two Sonnets.
BERGENGREN, RALPH WILHELM. Apple Blossoms.
Book-Lover.
Dirigible, The.
Misfortune.
Thirst.
Worm, The.
BERGGOLTS, OLGA. Address to Tragedy.
Endpiece. *Fr.* Parting.
Letter. *Fr.* Parting.
Meeting. *Fr.* Songs of the Spanish Children.
Parting, *sels.*
Sisters. *Fr.* Songs of the Spanish Children.
Song: "O, I have been in the land where you were born." *Fr.* Parting.
Songs of the Spanish Children.
BERGIN, THOMAS G. *For translations from Italian, see* LyPI.
BERGMAN, ALEXANDER. Chronicler, The.
Letter.
BERGMAN, BO. Adagio.
BERGONZI, BERNARD. Anemones for Miss Austen.
Charing Cross Road.
BERGQUIST, BEATRICE. Song of the Robin, The.
BERKELEY, GEORGE. America. *Fr.* On the Prospect of Planting Arts and Learning in America.
On the Prospect of Planting Arts and Learning in America.
On the Prospect of Planting Arts and Learning in America, *sels.*
Verses on the Prospect of Planting Arts and Learning in America.
Westward the course of empire takes its way. *Fr.* On the Prospect of Planting Arts and Learning in America.
BERKELEY [*or* BERKLEY], SIR WILLIAM. Lost Lady, The, *sel.*
Where Did You Borrow That Last Sigh? *Fr.* The Lost Lady.
BERNARD DE VENTADOUR [*or* VENTADORN.] Canso: "I cannot see the bright sun's glow."
Canzo: "When fresh grass-blades and leaves appear."
No Marvel Is It.
Troubadour Song: "'Tis no wonder if my songs."
BERNARD OF CLAIRVAUX, SAINT. Conqueror Renowned, The.
Hail, Thou Head!
Iesu, Dulcis Memoria.
Jesu Dulcis.
Jesus, the Very Thought of Thee, *at.*
Jesus, Thou Joy of Loving Hearts, *at.*
King in His Beauty, The.
Of Our Lord's Passion, *sel.*
Saint Bernard's Verses, *at.*
Sweetest Name, The, *at.*
Thou Light of Life, *at.*
Thy Kingdom Come.
BERNARD OF CLUNY [*or* OF MORLAIX]. Celestial Country, The. *Fr.* De Contemptu Mundi.
De Contemptu Mundi, *sels.*
Jerusalem, the Golden. *Fr.* De Contemptu Mundi.
Mariale, *sel.*
BERNART OF VENTADORN. *See* BERNARD DE VENTADOUR.
BERNETTA, SISTER MARY. One Day at Rouen.
BERNHARDT, CLARA. Sailor's Wife, A.
BERNI, FRANCESCO. Portrait.
BERRIGAN, DANIEL. If Stones Can Dream.
Poet Prays Her, The.
BERRY, ANNABEL LEDLIE. Heaven and Earth.
BERRY, H. W. To an Egyptian Boy.
BERRYMAN, JOHN. Ball Poem, The.
Canto Amor.
Conversation.
Desires of Men and Women.
Homage to Mistress Bradstreet, *sels.*
Moon and the Night and the Men, The.
1 September 1939.
Parting as Descent.
Song of the Demented Priest, The.
Spinning Heart, The.
Statue, The.
Winter Landscape.
BERSOHN, ROBERT. Dignity of Labor, The.
BERTHOLD, ARTHUR. Aizmirstai Mihlai.
Thousands and Again Thousands.
BERTOLET, FREDERICK. Ode to Lowell House.
BERTRAM, JAMES. Epitaph for an American Bomber.
Rondeau in Wartime.
BERTRAND, SISTER MARY. Our Lady of Mercy.
Our Lady of the Apocalypse.
BERTRAND [*or* BERTRAN *or* BERTRANS] DE BORN. Disavowal.
Planh for the Young English King.
Protestation.
Song of Battle.
Well Pleaseth Me the Sweet Time of Easter.
BESANT, SIR WALTER. Day Is Coming, The.
To Daphne.
BESHIGTASHLIAN, MUGGURDICH. Spring.
BEST, CHARLES. Looke How the Pale Queene.
Moon, The.
Of the Moon.
Sonnet of the Moon, A.
BEST, SUSIE MONTGOMERY. Ich Dien.
Miracle Dreams, The.
Thanksgiving.
BETHAM-EDWARDS, MATILDA BARBARA. Child's Prayer, A.
Evening Hymn.
Gethsemane.
Pansy and the Prayer-Book, The.
Valentine, A.
BETHELL, MARY URSULA ("Evelyn Hayes"). Detail.
Garden-Lion.
Long Harbour, The.
Looking Down on Mesopotamia.
Pause.
Small Hours, The.
Spring Snow and Tui.
Weather.
BÉTHUNE, CONON DE. *See* CONON DE BÉTHUNE.
BETHUNE, GEORGE WASHINGTON. Blessed Name, The.
He Died for Me.
Hymn to Night.
It Is Not Death to Die.
My Mother.
O Jesus! When I Think of Thee.
BETHUNE, NORMAN. Compressionist's Creed, A.
Red Moon.
T. B.'s Progress, The.
BETJEMAN, JOHN. Archaeological Picnic, The.
Arrest of Oscar Wilde at the Cadogan Hotel, The.
Arrogance Repressed.
Before Invasion, 1940.
Before the Anaesthetic; or, A Real Fright.
Cottage Hospital, The.
East Anglian Bathe.
Hunter Trials.
In a Bath Teashop.
In Westminster Abbey.
Indoor Games near Newbury.
"New King Arrives in His Capital by Air . . ."——Daily Newspaper.
Norfolk.
Old Liberals, The.
Parliament Hill Fields.
Potpourri from a Surrey Garden.
St. Saviour's, Aberdeen Park, Highbury, London, N.
Shropshire Lad, A.
Subaltern's Love Song, A.
Sunday Afternoon Service in St. Enodoc Church, Cornwall.
Trebetherick.
Upper Lambourne.
Westgate-on-Sea.
Youth and Age on Beaulieu River, Hants.
BETSKY, SARAH ZWEIG. *For translations from Yiddish, see* OnCuPl.
BETTERTON, THOMAS. Prophetess, The; or, The History of Dioclesian, *sel., at.*
What Shall I Do?, *at.* *Fr.* The Prophetess; or, The History of Dioclesian.
BETTS, CRAVEN LANGSTROTH. Don Quixote.
Emerson.
Hollyhocks, The.
Longfellow.
To the Moonflower.
Unseen World, The.
BETTS, FRANK. Pawns, The.
BETTS, OTSIE VERNONA. Evangeline Trail, The, *ad. and abr. fr.* Longfellow's "Evangeline."
BEVINGTON, HELEN SMITH. Fool Killer, The.
Holly.
Lord Cornwallis and a Carolina Spring.
Sign of Fall in the Carolinas.
Tar Heel.
Truce with a Southern Neighbor.
BEWE,——. Actaeon, *at.*
Beware of Sirens.
I Would I Were Actaeon, *at.*
BEWSHER, PAUL. Nox Mortis.
BEYER, EVELYN. Jump or Jiggle.
BEZA, THEODORE. Description of Virtue.
Marcus Tullius Cicero's Death.

Marcus Tullius Cicero's Death, *sel.*
BEZRUC, PETR. Ostrava.
BEZYMENSKY, ALEXANDER ILYICH. Village and Factory.
BHAI VIR SINGH. Dream of Love.
Soul as a Plucked Flower, The.
BHARTRIHARI. Angler, The.
Arrows of Love.
Better in the Wild.
Better Part, The.
By Shaded Wells.
Dignity.
Dilemma.
Flaming Banners.
Friend or Stranger.
Half-Way Knowledge.
Heart in Brahma, The.
In the Days of Thy Youth.
Loaded Ass, The.
Love Grows by What It Feeds On.
Love in Moonlight.
Love, the Fisher.
Nothing and the Soul.
Peace.
Round Robin.
Sign, The.
Snake and the Mouse, The.
Struggling Fancies.
Stubborn Fool, The.
Sweet and Bitter.
Time.
Two as One.
When I Knew a Little Bit.
Why My Poems Died.
Wise Misogynist, The.
Women's Eyes.
BHASA. Dialogue from "The Dream Queen."
Dream Queen, The, *sel.*
Moon, The.
BIALIK, HAYYIM NAHMAN [*or* CHAIM NACHMAN]. Alone.
Beneath Thy Wing.
Blessing over Food.
City of Slaughter, The.
Dance of Despair, The.
Dead of the Wilderness, The.
Death of David, The.
For Hanukkah.
Grasshopper's Song, The.
Graveyard, The.
I Know on a Night Overcast.
If Thou Wouldst Know.
Mathmid, The.
Midnight Prayer.
Night.
On a hill there blooms a palm. *Fr.* Songs of the People.
Queen Sabbath.
Should I Be a Rabbi?
Songs of the People, *sels.*
Stars Are Lit, The.
Sunset.
Talmud Student, The.
Throbs the Night with Mystic Silence.
Two steps from my garden rail. *Fr.* Songs of the People.
When the Days Shall Grow Long.
Whence and Whither.
Young Acacia, The.
BIANCHI, MARTHA GILBERT DICKINSON. Forgiveness Lane.
Heaven.
Her Music.
One Day.
Priest's Prayer, A.
Reality.
Separation.
Twilight at Florence.
Unanswered.
What Heart But Fears a Fragrance?
BIANOR. "In Huts Where Poor Men Lie."
Loss after Loss.
Unseen Riches.
BIBACULUS, MARCUS FURIUS. Cato's Way of Life.
BIBLE, APOCRYPHA. Baruch, *sel.*
Blessed Is God. *Fr.* Tobit.
Dirge: "Her house is become like a man dishonored." *Fr.* First Maccabees.
Ecclesiasticus, *sels.*
First Maccabees, *sels.*
Great Mourning. *Fr.* First Maccabees.
Judas Maccabeus. *Fr.* First Maccabees.
Judith, *sels.*
Let Us Now Praise Famous Men. *Fr.* Ecclesiasticus.
Mother and Her Seven Sons, A. *Fr.* Second Maccabees.
Music. *Fr.* Ecclesiasticus.
O Death. *Fr.* Ecclesiasticus.
On Death—a Sonnet. *Fr.* Ecclesiasticus.
Our Fathers. *Fr.* Ecclesiasticus.
Path of Wisdom, The. *Fr.* Baruch.
Praise of Famous Men. *Fr.* Ecclesiasticus.
Second Maccabees, *sel.*
Simon, Son of Onias. *Fr.* Ecclesiasticus.
Test of Men, The. *Fr.* Ecclesiasticus.
Tobit, *sel.*
Tyrant's Death, The. *Fr.* Judith.
Wisdom ("For she is a vapour"). *Fr.* The Wisdom of Solomon.
Wisdom ("I called upon God"). *Fr.* The Wisdom of Solomon.
Wisdom of Solomon, The, *sels.*
". . . With Timbrels." *Fr.* Judith.
BIBLE, NEW TESTAMENT. Acts, The, *sels.*
Adoration of the Shepherds, The. *Fr.* St. Luke.
And there appeared a great wonder in heaven. *Fr.* Revelation.
Apocalypse, *sel.* (*Douay vers.*)
Be of Good Cheer. *Fr.* St. John.
Be of Good Cheer; I Have Overcome the World. *Fr.* St. John.
Beatitudes, The. *Fr.* St. Matthew.
Benedictus. *Fr.* St. Luke.
Birth of Jesus, The. *Fr.* St. Luke.
Blessed Are the Poor in Spirit. *Fr.* St. Matthew.
Charity. *Fr.* First Corinthians.
Child of Nazareth, The. *Fr.* St. Luke.
Christmas Eve. *Fr.* St. Luke.
Christmas Story, The. *Fr.* St. Luke.
Come unto Me. *Fr.* St. Matthew.
Death and the Resurrection of the Dead. *Fr.* First Corinthians.
Death of Jesus, The. *Fr.* St. Luke.
Death's Conqueror. *Fr.* First Corinthians.
Duties of Man, The. *Fr.* Romans.
Easter Morning. *Fr.* St. Matthew.
Ephesians, *sel.*
Fairness. *Fr.* St. Matthew.
Faith. *Fr.* Hebrews.
First Christmas, The. *Fr.* St. Luke.
First Corinthians, *sels.*
First Easter, The. *Fr.* St. Luke.
First John, *sel.*
Forgiveness. *Fr.* Ephesians.
Forgiveness. *Fr.* St. Matthew.
Glory of God Revealed in Jesus. *Fr.* Second Corinthians.
God Provides. *Fr.* St. Matthew.
Good Samaritan, The. *Fr.* St. Luke.
Good Shepherd, The. *Fr.* St. John.
Good Tidings. *Fr.* St. Luke.
Gospel of Love, The. *Fr.* First Corinthians.
Greatest Commandments, The. *Fr.* St. Matthew.
Greatest of These Is Love, The. *Fr.* First Corinthians.
Greatness of Love, The. *Fr.* First Corinthians.
Hebrews, *sel.*
Hymn of the Blessed Virgin, The. *Fr.* St. Luke.
I Am the Bread of Life. *Fr.* St. John.
In the Beginning Was the Word. *Fr.* St. John.
Jesus and Lazarus. *Fr.* St. John.
Jesus and the Children. *Fr.* St. Matthew.
Jesus Answers the Pharisees. *Fr.* St. John.
Jesus, Judas, and Peter. *Fr.* St. Luke.
Last Judgment, The. *Fr.* Revelation.
Last Supper, The. *Fr.* St. John.
Light of the World, The. *Fr.* St. John.
Living Sacrifice, A. *Fr.* Romans.
Lord's Prayer, The. *Fr.* St. Matthew.
Lost Sheep, The. *Fr.* St. Luke.
Love, Hate, Compassion. *Fr.* First John.
Love the Indispensable and Crowning Grace. *Fr.* First Corinthians.
Love Your Enemies. *Fr.* St. Matthew.
Magnificat, The. *Fr.* St. Luke.
Many Parts, One Body. *Fr.* First Corinthians.
Mary and Elizabeth. *Fr.* St. Luke.
Mary and Gabriel. *Fr.* St. Luke.
Mary and Simeon. *Fr.* St. Luke.
My Peace I Give unto You. *Fr.* St. John.
My Yoke Is Easy. *Fr.* St. Matthew.
Mystery of Death, The. *Fr.* First Corinthians.
Natural and Spiritual. *Fr.* First Corinthians.
Neither Do I Condemn Thee. *Fr.* St. John.
New Commandment, The ("He riseth from supper"). *Fr.* St. John.
New Commandment, The ("This is my commandment"). *Fr.* St. John.
New Jerusalem, The. *Fr.* Revelation.
Nunc Dimittis, The. *Fr.* St. Luke.
On Compassion ("And as ye would that men should do to you"). *Fr.* St. Luke.
On Compassion ("He, willing to justify himself"). *Fr.* St. Luke.
On the Road to Emmaus. *Fr.* St. Luke.
Parable of the Pharisee and the Publican. *Fr.* St. Luke.
Parable of the Talents, The. *Fr.* St. Matthew.
Parables from Nature. *Fr.* St. Mark.
Paul on the Road to Damascus. *Fr.* The Acts.
Peace of Christ, The. *Fr.* St. John.
Philippians, *sel.*
Poem of the Our Father, The. *Fr.* St. Matthew.
Poems by the Roadside. *Fr.* St. Luke *and* St. Matthew.
Prelude of the New Testament ("Hail Mary full of grace!"). *Fr.* St. Luke (*Douay vers.*)
Prodigal Son, The. *Fr.* St. Luke.
Pure Light, The. *Fr.* St. Matthew.
Revelation, *sels.*
Rich Man and the Kingdom of Heaven, The. *Fr.* St. Matthew.
Romans, *sels.*
St. John, *sels.*
St. Luke, *sels.*
St. Mark, *sel.*
St. Matthew, *sels.*
St. Paul on Charity. *Fr.* First Corinthians.
Second Corinthians, *sel.*
Second Timothy, *sel.*
Sermon on the Mount, The. *Fr.* St. Matthew.
Sparrow, The. *Fr.* St. Matthew.
Spiritual Gifts. *Fr.* First Corinthians.
There Shall Be No Night. *Fr.* Revelation.
Things That Are Caesar's, The. *Fr.* St. Matthew.
Tidings of Great Joy. *Fr.* St. Luke.
To His Disciples. *Fr.* St. Luke.
Transfiguration, The. *Fr.* St. Matthew.
Treasures [in Heaven]. *Fr.* St. Matthew.
True Vine, The. *Fr.* St. John.
Unto the Least. *Fr.* St. Matthew.
Visit of the Wise Men, The. *Fr.* St. Matthew.
Way, the Truth, and the Life, The—Love One Another. *Fr.* St. John.
When the Son of Man Shall Come in His Glory. *Fr.* St. Matthew.
Who Is My Neighbor? *Fr.* St. Luke.
Widow's Mites, The. *Fr.* St. Luke.

BIBLE, NEW TESTAMENT (*continued*)
Wise and Foolish Virgins, The. *Fr.* St. Matthew.
Woman Clothed with the Sun, A. *Fr.* Revelation.
Word, The. *Fr.* St. John.
BIBLE, OLD TESTAMENT. Abraham and Isaac. *Fr.* Genesis.
Acceptable Sacrifice, The. *Fr.* Micah.
Address of Ruth to Naomi. *Fr.* Ruth.
Affliction. *Fr.* Lamentations.
All Flesh Is Grass. *Fr.* Isaiah.
Amos, *sel.*
And There Shall Come Forth. *Fr.* Isaiah.
And They Shall Beat Their Swords into Plowshares. *Fr.* Micah.
Antiphonal, An. Psalms, XXIV.
Arise, My Love, My Fair One. *Fr.* The Song of Solomon.
As a Seal upon Thy Heart. *Fr.* The Song of Solomon.
As Fowlers Lie in Wait. *Fr.* Jeremiah.
As the Hart Panteth. Psalms, XLII.
Awake! *Fr.* The Song of Solomon.
Balaam's Blessing. *Fr.* Numbers.
Be Thankful unto Him. Psalms, C.
Behold, My Servant. *Fr.* Isaiah.
Behold, Thou Art Fair. *Fr.* The Song of Solomon.
Belshazzar's Feast. *Fr.* Daniel.
Benediction. *Fr.* Numbers.
Better Path, The. *Fr.* Ecclesiastes.
Bless the Lord, O My Soul. Psalms, CIV.
Blessed Is the Man. Psalms, I.
Blessed of the Lord Be His Land. *Fr.* Deuteronomy.
Blessing of the Priests. *Fr.* Numbers.
Burning Bush, The. *Fr.* Exodus.
But Fear Thou Not, O Jacob. *Fr.* Jeremiah.
By the Rivers of Babylon. Psalms, CXXXVII.
Call for True Repentance, A. *Fr.* Jeremiah.
Canticle of Canticles, *sels.*
Cast Thy Bread upon the Waters. *Fr.* Ecclesiastes.
Child Moses, The. *Fr.* Exodus.
Closing Doxology, The. Psalms, CL.
Comfort Ye [Comfort Ye] My People. *Fr.* Isaiah.
Creation, The. *Fr.* Genesis.
Cry in Distress, A. Psalms, XXII.
Cry of the Daughter of My People, The. *Fr.* Jeremiah.
Cursed Be the Day. *Fr.* Jeremiah.
Daniel, *sels.*
David and Bathsheba. *Fr.* Second Samuel.
David and Goliath. *Fr.* First Samuel.
David and Uriah, the Hittite. *Fr.* Second Samuel.
David Praiseth God for His Manifold and Marveilous Blessings. Psalms, XVIII.
David's Lament. *Fr.* Second Samuel.
David's Lament over [*or* for] Saul and Jonathan. *Fr.* Second Samuel.
De Profundis. Psalms, CXXX.
Death of the King of Babylon. *Fr.* Isaiah.
Deliverance of Jehovah, The. Psalms, XXVII.
Desolation in Zion. *Fr.* Lamentations.
Deuteronomy, *sels.*
Divine Compassion, The. *Fr.* Isaiah.
Downfall of the Tyrant. *Fr.* Isaiah.
Drunkard, The. *Fr.* Proverbs.
Earth Abideth Forever, The. *Fr.* Ecclesiastes.
Earth Is the Lord's, The. Psalms, XXIV.
Ecclesiastes, *sels.*
Eternal Quest, The. *Fr.* Job.
Everlasting Arms, The. *Fr.* Deuteronomy.
Everlasting Arms, The. Psalms, XCI.
Except the Lord Build the House. Psalms, CXXVII.
Exodus, *sels.*
Ezekiel, *sels.*
Fear of the Lord, The. *Fr.* Proverbs.
First Samuel, *sels.*
Floods Clap Their Hands, The. Psalms, XCVIII.
Fool Hath Said in His Heart, The. Psalms, XIV.
Foolish Woman, A. *Fr.* Proverbs.
For, Lo, the Winter Is Past. *Fr.* The Song of Solomon.
For Zion's Sake. *Fr.* Isaiah.
Four Things. *Fr.* Proverbs.
Fret Not Thyself Because of Evildoers. Psalms, XXXVII.
Garden of Eden, The. *Fr.* Genesis.
Genesis, *sels.*
Give Ear, O Ye Heavens. *Fr.* Deuteronomy.
Give Ear, Ye Heavens. *Fr.* Deuteronomy.
Glory of God, The. Psalms, XIX.
Go to the Ant [Thou Sluggard]. *Fr.* Proverbs.
God Is the Eternal Refuge of His People. Psalms, XLVI.
God, Our Dwelling Place. Psalms, XC.
God Our Refuge. Psalms, XCI.
God Replies. *Fr.* Job.
Godly and the Ungodly, The. Psalms, I.
God's Glory. Psalms, XIX.
God's Precepts Perfect. Psalms, XIX.
Golden Calf, The. *Fr.* Exodus.
Good Housewife [*or* Wife], The. *Fr.* Proverbs.
Habakkuk, *sels.*
Hallelujah. Psalms, CXLVI.
Hallelujah Chorus, A. Psalms, CXLVIII.
Hannah's Song of Thanksgiving. *Fr.* First Samuel.
Happy Is the Man. Psalms, I.
Happy Is the Man [That Findeth Wisdom]. *Fr.* Proverbs.
Hark! My Beloved! *Fr.* The Song of Solomon.
Hast Thou Given the Horse Strength? *Fr.* Job.
Hay Appeareth, The. *Fr.* Proverbs.
He That is Slow to Anger. *Fr.* Proverbs.
Hear the Word of the Lord. *Fr.* Isaiah.
Heathen Are Come into Thine Inheritance, The. Psalms, LXXIX.
Heavens [Above and the Law Within], The. Psalms, XIX.
Heavens Declare [the Glory of God], The. Psalms, XIX.
Here Am I—Send Me. *Fr.* Isaiah.
Ho, Everyone That Thirsteth. *Fr.* Isaiah.
Horse, The. *Fr.* Job.
Hosea, *sels.*
House of Wisdom, The. *Fr.* Proverbs.
How Are the Mighty Fallen. *Fr.* Second Samuel.
How Beautiful upon the Mountains. *Fr.* Isaiah.
How Glorious Is Thy Name. Psalms, VIII.
How Is the Gold Become Dim. *Fr.* Lamentations.
How Lovely Are Thy Tabernacles. Psalms, LXXXIV.
Hymn of the World Within. Psalms, CIII.
Hymn of the World Without. Psalms, CIV.
Hymns of Praise. *Fr.* Psalms.
I Am My Beloved's. *Fr.* The Song of Solomon.
I Am the Rose of Sharon. *Fr.* The Song of Solomon.
I Return unto Zion. *Fr.* Zechariah.
I Sleep, but My Heart Waketh. *Fr.* The Song of Solomon.
I Waste Away. *Fr.* Isaiah.
I Will Lift Up Mine Eyes [unto the Hills]. Psalms, CXXI.
I Will Sing Praise. Psalms, IX.
Immortality. *Fr.* Job.
In the End of Days. *Fr.* Isaiah.
Inscrutable Mystery, The. *Fr.* Job.
Intemperance. *Fr.* Isaiah.
Intreat Me Not to Leave Thee. *Fr.* Ruth.
Isaiah, *sels.*
Israel, My Servant. *Fr.* Isaiah.
It Is Better . . . *Fr.* Ecclesiastes.
Jehovah's Immovable Throne. Psalms, XCIII.
Jephthah's Daughter. *Fr.* Judges.
Jeremiah, *sels.*
Job, *sels.*
Job Complains. *Fr.* Job.
Job Cries Out. *Fr.* Job.
Job Longeth for Death. *Fr.* Job.
Job's Comforters. *Fr.* Job.
Job's Curse. *Fr.* Job.
Job's Entreaty. *Fr.* Job.
Job's Questions. *Fr.* Job.
Jonah, *sels.*
Jonah's Prayer. *Fr.* Jonah.
Joseph and His Brethren. *Fr.* Genesis.
Judges, *sels.*
Keep Not Thou Silence. Psalms, LXXXIII.
Lament in Exile. Psalms, CXXXVII.
Lament over Saul. *Fr.* Second Samuel.
Lamentation. *Fr.* Ezekiel.
Lamentation for the Fall of Jerusalem. *Fr.* Lamentations.
Lamentations, *sels.*
Laudate Dominum. Psalms, CL.
Law Within, The. Psalms, XIX.
Leader, The. *Fr.* Second Samuel.
Leave It All Quietly to God. Psalms, LXII.
Legacy, The. *Fr.* Proverbs.
Lest We Forget. *Fr.* Deuteronomy.
Let Me Sing of My Well-Beloved. *Fr.* Isaiah.
Let the Day Perish. *Fr.* Job.
Let the Nations Be Glad. Psalms, LXVII.
Leviathan. *Fr.* Job.
Leviticus, *sel.*
Life's Uncertainty. *Fr.* Ecclesiastes.
Lift Up Your Heads [O Ye Gates]. Psalms, XXIV.
Light Is Sweet, The. *Fr.* Ecclesiastes.
Like unto Them That Dream. Psalms, CXXVI.
Lips of the Wise, The. *Fr.* Proverbs.
Live Joyfully. *Fr.* Ecclesiastes.
Lo, The Winter Is Past. *Fr.* The Song of Solomon.
Lord Gave, The. *Fr.* Job.
Lord Is a Man of War, The. *Fr.* Exodus.
Lord Is My Shepherd, The. Psalms, XXIII.
Lord, Make Me to Know Mine End. Psalms, XXXIX.
Lord, who shall abide in thy tabernacle? Psalms, XV.
Love. *Fr.* The Song of Solomon.
Love Idyll, A. *Fr.* The Song of Solomon.
Love Lyrics. *Fr.* The Song of Solomon.
Man of Sorrows, The. *Fr.* Isaiah.
Man That Is Born of a Woman. *Fr.* Job.
Merry Heart, A. *Fr.* Proverbs.
Messiah, The. *Fr.* Isaiah.
Micah, *sels.*
Mighty Fortress, A. Psalms, XCI.
Misery of Jerusalem, The. *Fr.* Lamentations.
Mother of the House, The. *Fr.* Proverbs.
My Light and My Salvation. Psalms, XXVII.
My Soul Thirsteth for God. Psalms, XLII.
My Thoughts Are Not Your Thoughts. *Fr.* Isaiah.
Naomi and Ruth. *Fr.* Ruth.
Neither Poverty nor Riches. *Fr.* Proverbs.
New Covenant, A. *Fr.* Jeremiah.
Noah and the Flood. *Fr.* Genesis.
Not Flesh of Brass. *Fr.* Job.
Numbers, *sels.*

O come, let us sing unto the Lord. Psalms, XCV.
O Give Thanks. Psalms, CXVIII.
O Lord, How Excellent Is Thy Name. Psalms, VIII.
O Lord, How Long Shall I Cry? *Fr.* Habakkuk.
O Lord, our Lord, how excellent is thy name. Psalms, VIII.
O Lord, Thou Hast Enticed Me. *Fr.* Jeremiah.
O Sing unto the Lord a New Song. Psalms, XCVIII.
Oh That I Knew Where I Might Find Him. *Fr.* Job.
Oh That I Were in the Wilderness. *Fr.* Jeremiah.
O Ye That Would Swallow the Needy. *Fr.* Amos.
Ocean, The. Psalms, CVII.
On My Bed I Sought Him. *Fr.* The Song of Solomon.
Open Thy Doors, O Lebanon. *Fr.* Zechariah.
Our Refuge. Psalms, XLVI.
Out of the Depths. Psalms, CXXX.
Out of the Whirlwind. *Fr.* Job.
Peace! and There Is No Peace. *Fr.* Jeremiah.
Peaceable Kingdom, The. *Fr.* Isaiah.
Pilgrim's Song, The. Psalms, CXXI.
Potter and the Clay, The. *Fr.* Jeremiah.
Power to the Faint. *Fr.* Isaiah.
Praise Ye the Lord. Psalms, CXLVIII.
Prayer of Habakkuk, The. *Fr.* Habakkuk.
Price of Wisdom, The. *Fr.* Job.
Prince of Peace, The. *Fr.* Isaiah.
Prince of Peace, The. *Fr.* Micah.
Proclamation. *Fr.* Isaiah.
Protection of Jehovah, The. Psalms, XXIII.
Protection of the Lord, The. Psalms, XCI.
Proverbs, *sels.*
Psalm of David, A. Psalms, XXIII.
Psalm of Praise, A. Psalms, VIII *and* C.
Psalm of the Shepherd, The. Psalms, XXIII.
Psalme of Asaph, A. Psalms, L.
Psalms, *sels.*
Refuge, The. Psalms, XLVI.
Remember Now [*or* Also *or* Then] Thy Creator. *Fr.* Ecclesiastes.
Reproof, A. *Fr.* Proverbs.
Return, Return, O Shulammite. *Fr.* The Song of Solomon.
Rod of Jesse, The. *Fr.* Isaiah.
Ruth.
Ruth, *sels.*
Ruth, Naomi, and Boaz. *Fr.* Ruth.
Ruth to Naomi. *Fr.* Ruth.
Saul, David, and Jonathan. *Fr.* First Samuel *and* Second Samuel.
Search, The. Psalms, XLII *and* XLIII.
Searcher of Hearts [Is Thy Maker], The. Psalms, CXXXIX.
Second Samuel, *sels.*
Servant of God, The. *Fr.* Isaiah.
Set Me as a Seal. *Fr.* The Song of Solomon.
Seven Evils. *Fr.* Proverbs.
She of the Impudent Face. *Fr.* Proverbs.
Shepherd's Psalm, The. Psalms, XXIII.
Sing unto the Lord. Psalms, XCVIII.
Sluggard, The—a Sonnet. *Fr.* Proverbs.
Song of Deborah [and Barak], The. *Fr.* Judges.
Song of Exile, A. Psalms, CXXXVII.
Song of Hannah, The. *Fr.* First Samuel.
Song of Moses, The. *Fr.* Exodus.
Song of Praise, A. Psalms, VIII *and* CXLVIII.
Song of Safety, A. Psalms, CXXI.
Song of Solomon, The.
Song of Solomon, The, *sels.*
Song of Songs, The. *See* Song of Solomon, The.
Song of Supplication, A. Psalms, CXXX.
Song of the Harlot. *Fr.* Isaiah.
Song of the Well. *Fr.* Numbers.
Song of Trust, A. Psalms, CXXI.
Sower of Discord, A. *Fr.* Proverbs.
Span of Man, The. Psalms, XC.
Sparrow, The. Psalms, LXXXIV.
Spring. *Fr.* The Song of Solomon.
Story of Ruth, The. *Fr.* Ruth.
Strangers. *Fr.* Leviticus.
Swords and Plowshares. *Fr.* Isaiah.
Ten Commandments, The. *Fr.* Exodus.
Thanksgiving. Psalms, XCV, C, *and* CXXXVI.
Then Sang Deborah and Barak. *Fr.* Judges.
Then Sang Moses. *Fr.* Exodus.
Then the Lord Answered [Job Out of the Whirlwind]. *Fr.* Job.
They That Go Down to the Sea [in Ships]. Psalms, CVII.
Thou Art God. Psalms, XC.
Though the Earth Be Removed. Psalms, XLVI.
Thy Mother Was Like a Vine. *Fr.* Ezekiel.
Time for Everything, A. *Fr.* Ecclesiastes.
To Dwell Together in Unity. Psalms, CXXXIII.
Too Wonderful. *Fr.* Proverbs.
Treasures, The. *Fr.* Job.
Tree and the Chaff, The. Psalms, I.
Triumphal Chant. *Fr.* Exodus.
Twenty-fourth Psalm, The.
Twenty-third Psalm, The.
Unfaithful Shepherds. *Fr.* Ezekiel.
Vanity [of Vanities]. *Fr.* Ecclesiastes.
Vine Out of Egypt, A. Psalms, LXXX.
Virtuous Wife [*or* Woman], The. *Fr.* Proverbs.
Vision of the Day of Judgment. *Fr.* Isaiah.
Visions of the Night. *Fr.* Job.
Voice from the Whirlwind, The; God's Majesty. *Fr.* Job.
Voice [of God] Out of the Whirlwind, The. *Fr.* Job.
Voice Out of the Whirlwind Answers Job, The. *Fr.* Job.
War-Horse, The. *Fr.* Job.
War Song of Kishon. *Fr.* Judges.
War Song of the Red Sea. *Fr.* Exodus.
Watchman, What of the Night? *Fr.* Isaiah.
What Doth the Lord Require? *Fr.* Micah.
What Is Man? Psalms, VIII.
When I Consider Thy Heavens. Psalms, VIII.
When Israel Came Forth Out of Egypt. Psalms, CXIV.
Who Maketh the Grass to Grow. Psalms, CXLVII.
Whom Shall One Teach. *Fr.* Isaiah.
Wine and Woe. *Fr.* Proverbs.
Wings. Psalms, LV.
Winter Is Past, The. *Fr.* The Song of Solomon.
Wisdom. *Fr.* Job.
Wisdom. *Fr.* Proverbs.
Woe Is Me! *Fr.* Micah.
Word Fitly Spoken, A. *Fr.* Proverbs.
Words of Agur, The. *Fr.* Proverbs.
Words of the Preacher, The. *Fr.* Ecclesiastes.
Wrestling with God. *Fr.* Genesis.
Written in the Heart. *Fr.* Deuteronomy.
Youth and Age. *Fr.* Ecclesiastes.
Zechariah, *sels.*
Zion Redeemed. *Fr.* Isaiah.

BIBLE, PSEUDEPIGRAPHA. Enoch, *sels.*
Seven Metal Mountains, The. *Fr.* Enoch.
Wisdom's Plight. *Fr.* Enoch.

BICKERSTAFFE, ISAAC. Expostulation, An.
Jolly Miller. *Fr.* Love in a Village.
Love in a Village, *sels.*
Song: "How happy were my days." *Fr.* Love in a Village.
Song: "There was a jolly miller once." *Fr.* Love in a Village.
There Was a Jolly Miller. *Fr.* Love in a Village.
What Are Outward Forms?

BICKERSTETH, EDWARD HENRY, BISHOP OF EXETER. Give Us Men!
O God, the Rock of Ages.
Peace, Perfect Peace.
Prince of Peace, The.

BIDDLE, EUNICE K. My Song.

BIERBAUM, OTTO JULIUS. Blacksmith Pain.
Jeannette.
Kindly Vision.
Oft in the Silent Night.

BIERCE, AMBROSE. Another Way.
Bride, The.
Creation.
Death of Grant, The.
Hero, The.
Invocation, An, Read at the Celebration of Independence Day in San Francisco, in 1888.
Montefiore.
My country 'tis of thee.
Politician, The.
Presentiment.
Rebuke.
Religion.
T. A. H.
To a Critic of Tennyson.

BIGELOW, MARGUERITE OGDEN. *See* WILKINSON, MARGUERITE OGDEN BIGELOW.

BIGG, STANYAN. Night and the Soul, *sel.*

BIGGAR, H. HOWARD. Your Neighbor.

BILAC, OLAVO. To My Friends in São Paulo.

BILDERDIJK, WILLEM. Prayer: "Merciful God, who readst my inmost mind."

BILHANA. Black Marigolds.
Black Marigolds, *sels.*
Death Sends Me the Flickering of Powdery Lids. *Fr.* Black Marigolds.
Her Mouth Carelessly Scented. *Fr.* Black Marigolds.
I Have a Need. *Fr.* Black Marigolds.
I Have No Surety. *Fr.* Black Marigolds.
I Know My Princess. *Fr.* Black Marigolds.
I Know That I Have Savoured. *Fr.* Black Marigolds.
Love Long Black Eyes. *Fr.* Black Marigolds.
I Mind That I Went Round with Men and Women. *Fr.* Black Marigolds.
I Mind the Coming. *Fr.* Black Marigolds.
I Mind the Time of the Falling of Blossoms. *Fr.* Black Marigolds.
I See Her. *Fr.* Black Marigolds.
I See the Heavy Startled Hair. *Fr.* Black Marigolds.
I Seem to See My Prison Walls. *Fr.* Black Marigolds.
If I See in My Soul. *Fr.* Black Marigolds.
If My Girl with Lotus Eyes. *Fr.* Black Marigolds.
Love Is a God. *Fr.* Black Marigolds.
My Eyes That Hurry to See. *Fr.* Black Marigolds.
Pleased Intimacy, The. *Fr.* Black Marigolds.
She Swims Back in the Crowning Hour. *Fr.* Black Marigolds.
She with Young Limbs. *Fr.* Black Marigolds.
Spread We Our Nets. *Fr.* Black Marigolds.
Stainless Fair Appearance, The. *Fr.* Black Marigolds.
When All My Heavy Heart. *Fr.* Black Marigolds.

BILHANA (*continued*)
Woodcutter and the Fisherman Turn Home, The. *Fr.* Black Marigolds.
BILLER, MATTHEW. American Freedom, The.
BILLINGS, WILLIAM. Chester.
David's Lamentation.
When Jesus Wept.
BINDING, RUDOLF G. Love Song.
BINGHAM, G. CLIFTON. Love's Old Sweet Song.
BINGLEY, BARBARA. Anne Boleyn.
BINNEY, THOMAS. Eternal Light!
BINNS, ELSIE. Christmas Is Remembering.
Smallest Angel, The.
BINYON, LAURENCE. Amasis.
Bab-Lock-Hythe.
Beauty.
Belfry, The.
Burning of the Leaves, The.
Burning of the Leaves, The, *sel.*
Day That Is Boundless as Youth, A.
Day's End.
Dead to the Living, The.
Divina Commedia, *sels., tr.*
England.
English Earth.
Ezekiel.
Ferry Hinksey.
For Mercy, Courage, Kindness, Mirth.
For the Fallen.
For the Fallen, *sel.*
Glimpse of Time, A.
History.
House That Was, The.
Hunger.
In Misty Blue.
Inferno, *sel., tr. Fr.* Divina Commedia.
Initiation.
Invocation to Youth.
John Winter.
Lament: "Fall now, my cold thoughts, frozen fall."
Little Dancers, The.
Little Hands.
Magnets.
Midway the Journey, *tr. Fr.* Divina Commedia: Inferno.
Nature.
New Idol, A.
Nothing Is Enough.
O Summer Sun.
O World, Be Nobler.
Paolo and Francesca, *tr. Fr.* Divina Commedia: Inferno.
Paradiso, *sel., tr. Fr.* Divina Commedia.
Paris and Oenone, *sel.*
Prayer, A: "O Thou who seekest me."
Road Menders, The.
St. Bernard's Prayer to the Virgin Mary, *tr. Fr.* Divina Commedia: Paradiso.
Sirens, The.
Sirens, The, *sels.*
Song: "For Mercy, Courage, Kindness, Mirth."
Sowing Seed.
Statues, The.
There Is Still Splendour.
Thinking of Shores.
This Is England.
To Women.
Toy-Seller, The.
Tristram's End.
Ugolino, *tr. Fr.* Divina Commedia: Inferno.
Virgil's Farewell to Dante, *tr. Fr.* Divina Commedia: Purgatorio.
Vision of God, The, *tr. Fr.* Divina Commedia: Paradiso.
Vision of the Divine Mystery, *tr. Fr.* Divina Commedia: Paradiso.
Voices of Hellas, The.
We Have Planted a Tree.
Winter Sunrise, *sel.*
Woe to Him.
BION. Bion's Lament for Adonis.
Dream of Venus, A.
I Dreamt I Saw Great Venus.
I mourn for Adonis—Adonis is dead.
Lament for Adonis.
Lament for Adonis, *sel.*
Love Hunted.
Love's Tryst.
BIONDI, CLEMENTE. For a Blind Beggar's Sign.
BIRCHALL, SARA HAMILTON. A la Belle Etoile.
Answer, The.
Conversation, A.
Gipsy Song.
Gipsy Wedding, The.
September.
Sojourner, The.
Song of the Open.
Vagabonds.
BIRCHE, WILLIAM. Song between the Queen's Majesty and England, A.
BIRCKHEAD, NANCY. Everywhere.
Here I am.
October.
Strange Teeth, The.
To a Neglectful Lover.
BIRD, ROBERT MONTGOMERY. Fairy Folk, The.
BIRD, STEPHEN MOYLAN. May.
Silent Ranges, The.
BIRKENHEAD [*or* BERKENHEAD], SIR JOHN. Four-legg'd Elder, The; or, A Horrible Relation of a Dog and an Elder's Maid.
BIRNBAUM, HENRY. Room I Once Knew, A.
When Silence Divests Me.
BIRNEY, EARLE. Anglosaxon Street.
Bushed.
Canada: Case History.
Climbers.
David.
Dusk on English Bay.
For Steve.
Hands.
Man Is a Snow.
Mappemounde.
Monody on a Century.
North Star West.
On Going to the Wars.
Pacific Door.
Road to Nijmegen, The.
Slug in Woods.
This Page my Pigeon.
Time-Bomb.
Vancouver Lights.
Walk in Kyoto, A.
Winter Saturday.
BIRNIE, PATRICK. Auld Man's Mear's Dead, The.
BISHOP, ANNETTE. Rufflecumtuffle.
BISHOP, E. G. Echo.
BISHOP, ELIZABETH. Arrival at Santos.
At the Fishhouses.
Cirque d'Hiver.
Cold Spring, A.
Colder the Air, The.
Fish, The.
Florida.
From the Country to the City.
Imaginary Iceberg, The.
Invitation to Miss Marianne Moore.
Jeronimo's House.
Large Bad Picture.
Late Air.
Letter to New York.
Little Exercise.
Man-Moth, The
Map, The.
Miracle for Breakfast, A.
Monument, The.
Over 2000 Illustrations and a Complete Concordance.
Prodigal, The.
Roosters.
Seascape.
Sleeping on the Ceiling.
Songs for a Colored Singer.
Squatter's Children.
Unbeliever, The.
View of the Capitol from the Library of Congress.
Wading at Wellfleet.
Weed, The.
Wit, The.
BISHOP, G. E. Bigger Day, The.
BISHOP, JOHN PEALE. Admonition.
All Lovely Things I Love.
Apparition.
Beyond Connecticut, beyond the Sea.
Colloquy with a King-Crab.
Dream, The.
Fiametta.
Four Years Were Mine at Princeton.
Frieze, A.
Hours, The.
In the Dordogne.
Interlude, An.
Mothers, The.
Ode: "Why will they never sleep."
Peasant Declares His Love, The, *tr.*
Perspectives Are Precipices.
Protestation, *tr.*
Quan lo ruis de la fontana, *tr.*
Recollection, A.
Return, The.
Satyricon, *sel., tr.*
Speaking of Poetry.
Statue of Shadow, The.
Submarine Bed, The.
Then Twist the Neck of This Delusive Swan, *tr.*
This Dim and Ptolemaic Man.
Twelfth Night.
Your Chase Had a Beast in View.
BISHOP, MORRIS. Anatomy of Humor, The.
Canzone 129: "From thought to thought, from mountain-peak to mountain," *tr.*
Canzone: "It is the evening hour; the rapid sky," *tr.*
Complete Misanthropist, The.
Drinking Song for Present-Day Gatherings.
$E = MC^2$.
Ecclesiastes.
Epitaph for a Funny Fellow.
Eschatology.
How to Treat Elves.
Immoral Arctic, The.
It Rolls On.
Limerick: "Clergyman out in Dumont, A."
Limerick: "Said a girl from beyond Pompton Lakes."
Limerick: "Said old Peeping Tom of Fort Lee."
Limerick: "There's a vaporish maiden in Harrison."
Lines Written in a Moment of Vibrant Ill-Health.
Madrigal 52: "Diana, naked in the shadowy pool," *tr.*
Merry Old Souls.
Mournful Numbers.
Naughty Preposition, The.
New Hampshire Boy, A.
Ozymandias Revisited.
Perforated Spirit, The.
Public Aid for Niagara Falls.
Salute to the Modern Language Association, A, Convening in the Hotel Pennsylvania, December 28th–30th.
Sing a Song of the Cities.
Song of the Pop-Bottlers.
Sonnet and Limerick.
Sonnets to Laura, *sels., tr.*
Tales the Barbers Tell, The.
There's Money in Mother and Father.
Tonversation with Baby, A.
We Have Been Here Before.
Who'd Be a Hero (Fictional)?
Winter Madrigal, A.
BISHOP, ROY. Inefficacious Egg, The.
BISHOP, SAMUEL. Epigram: "Fool and knave with different views, A."
Maiden's Choice, The.
To His Wife on the Fourteenth [*or* Sixteenth] Anniversary of Her Wedding-Day, with a Ring.
To Mary.
Touch-Stone, The.
BISHOP, THOMAS BRIGHAM. John Brown's Body, *at.*
BISPHAM, GEORGE TUCKER, JR. Realm of Love, The.
BITHELL, JETHRO. *For translations from Flemish, French, and German, see* AWP; FaPON; JAWP; LiTW; LyMA; OnPM; PoMS; TrJP; WBP; WoL.

BITTON, W. NELSON. Resurgam.
BIXLER, WILLIAM ALLEN. Beautiful.
BJÖRKMAN, EDWIN. Atlantis Regained.
Beauty and the Beast.
Wings of Azrael, The.
BJÖRNSON, BJÖRNSTJERNE. Boy and the Flute, The.
Call, The.
Child in Our Soul, The.
Fatherland Song (Norwegian National Hymn).
I Love You, Ha! You Brown-Skin Devil.
Love Song.
Marie Stuart, *sel.*
My Troop.
National Song.
Olaf Trygveson.
Over the Lofty Mountains.
Princess, The.
Psalm II: "Hail to the springtime of deathless creation."
Sea, The.
Synnöve's Song.
Taylor's Song. *Fr.* Marie Stuart.
Tree, The.
BLACK, MACKNIGHT. Beside a Balance Wheel.
Corliss Engine-Wheel.
Express Trains.
Heart.
Night Express.
Poems of the Machine Age.
Rock, Be My Dream.
Structural Iron Workers.
BLACKBURN, ALEXANDER. What Makes a Nation Great.
BLACKBURN, GRACE. Chant of the Woman, The.
Cypress Tree, The.
Evening Star, The.
Sing Ho for the Herring.
BLACKBURN, PAUL. Assistance, The.
Continuity, The.
Encounter, The.
Night Song for Two Mystics.
Once-over, The.
Problem, The.
Sirventes.
BLACKBURN, THOMAS. Easter Hymn.
Muse, The.
Oedipus.
BLACKIE, JOHN STUART. Agamemnon, *sel., tr.*
Chorus of the Furies, *tr. Fr.* Eumenides.
Day's Work, The, *tr.*
Emigrant Lassie, The.
My Bath.
My Faithful Fond One, *tr.*
My Loves.
Seven against Thebes, *sel., tr.*
Working Man's Song, The.
BLACKMORE, SIR RICHARD. Creation, *sel.*
BLACKMORE, RICHARD DODDRIDGE. At the Last.
Dominus Illuminatio Mea.
Yes.
BLACKMUR, RICHARD P. All Things Are a Flowing.
Before Sentence Is Passed.
Dead Ride Fast, The.
Half-Tide Ledge.
In the Wind's Eye. *Fr.* Scarabs for the Living.
Mirage. *Fr.* Sea Island Miscellany.
Missa Vocis.
On Common Ground. *Fr.* Scarabs for the Living.
Rape of Europa, The.
Scarabs for the Living.
Scarabs for the Living, *sels.*
Sea Island Miscellany, *sels.*
Too Much for One: Not Enough to Go Around. *Fr.* Scarabs for the Living.
Views of Boston Common and Nearby.
BLACKSTOCK, WALTER. Old Voyager.
BLACKSTONE, SIR WILLIAM. Lawyer's Farewell to His Muse, The.
BLACKWELL, ALICE STONE. Chragan Palace, The, *tr.*
Christ-Child, The, *tr.*
Cloud, The, *tr.*
Cradle Song: "Nightingale, oh, leave our garden," *tr.*
Eagles and Sparrows, *tr.*
Easter Song, *tr.*
Epitaph to the Liberty of America, *tr.*
Good Comrade, A, *tr.*
Imprisoned Revolutionist, The, *tr.*
Liberty, *tr.*
Lily of Shavarshan, The, *tr.*
Little Lake, The, *tr.*
Ode to the Fatherland, *tr.*
Song of the General Strike, *tr.*
Song of the Storm-Finch, The, *tr.*
Talmud, The, *tr.*
Tears of Araxes, The, *tr.*
To Bolivar, *tr.*
Wandering Armenian to the Swallow, The, *tr.*
Where Shall We Dance? *tr.*
Words of the Last Inca, *tr.*
BLACKWELL, HARRIET GRAY. Forest.
BLACKWOOD, ALGERNON. Jack o' the Inkpot.
BLACKWOOD, HELEN SELINA SHERIDAN. *See* SHERIDAN, HELEN SELINA.
BLAIKIE, JOHN ARTHUR. Absence.
Love's Secret Name.
Song: "In thy white bosom."
BLAIR, GEORGE. Carpenter of Nazareth, The.
BLAIR, ROBERT. All Impelled Onward Alike. *Fr.* The Grave.
Church and Church-yard at Night. *Fr.* The Grave.
Church of Graves, The. *Fr.* The Grave.
Friendship. *Fr.* The Grave.
Grave, The.
Grave, The, *sels.*
Peace the End of the Good Man. *Fr.* The Grave.
BLAISDELL, JAMES ARNOLD. Beneath the Forms of Outward Rite.
BLAKE, FELICIA. Woman's Answer to "The Vampire," A.
BLAKE, JAMES VILA. In Him.
BLAKE, JAMES W. Sidewalks of New York, The.
BLAKE, MARIE. Barter.
BLAKE, MARY. Song of Work, A.
BLAKE, MARY ELIZABETH MCGRATH. Dawning o' the Year, The.
In Exile.
BLAKE, RODNEY. Hoch! Der Kaiser, *at.*
BLAKE, WILLIAM. Abstinence and Desire.
Abstinence sows sand all over. *Fr.* Gnomic Verses.
Ah, Sunflower [Weary of Time]. *Fr.* Songs of Experience.
Ah! weak and wide astray! *Fr.* Jerusalem.
America, *sels.*
Ancient Trees, The. *Fr.* Songs of Experience.
And Did Those Feet in Ancient Time. *Fr.* Milton.
Angel, The ("I asked a thief").
Angel, The ("I dreamt a dream!"). *Fr.* Songs of Experience.
Angel Singing, An.
Angel that presided o'er my birth, The. *Fr.* Gnomic Verses.
Answer to the Parson, An.
Apparition, The. *Fr.* America.
Arts of Death, The. *Fr.* Vala; or, The Four Zoas.
Auguries. *Fr.* Auguries of Innocence.
Auguries of Innocence.
Auguries of Innocence, *sels.*
Augury of Innocence, An.
Bard, The.
Beauty of Terror, The.
Birds, The.
Birdsong. *Fr.* Milton.
Blossom, The.
Book of Los, The, *sel.*
Book of Thel, The.
Book of Thel, The, *sels.*
Brotherhood. *Fr.* Jerusalem.
Building of Jerusalem, The. *Fr.* Milton.
Building of the New Jerusalem, The. *Fr.* Milton.
Character, A.
Chariot of Fire. *Fr.* Milton.
Child and the Piper, The.
Chimney Sweeper, The. *Fr.* Songs of Experience.
Chimney Sweeper, The. *Fr.* Songs of Innocence.
Choir of Day, The. *Fr.* Milton.
Clod and the Pebble, The. *Fr.* Songs of Experience.
Couplet: "Great things are done when men and mountains meet." *Fr.* Gnomic Verses.
Cradle Song: "Sleep, sleep, beauty bright."
Cradle Song, A: "Sweet dreams, form a shade." *Fr.* Songs of Innocence.
Cromek.
Cromek Speaks.
Crystal Cabinet, The.
Cupid.
Dedication of the Illustrations to Blair's "Grave," *sel.*
Divine Image, A ("Cruelty has a human heart").
Divine Image, The ("To Mercy, Pity, Peace, and Love"). *Fr.* Songs of Innocence.
Doctor Johnson. *Fr.* An Island in the Moon.
Door of Death, The. *Fr.* Dedication of the Illustrations to Blair's "Grave."
Dream, A. *Fr.* Songs of Innocence.
Earth's Answer. *Fr.* Songs of Experience.
Echoing Green, The. *Fr.* Songs of Innocence.
Empire Is No More. *Fr.* America.
England! awake! *Fr.* Jerusalem.
Enitharmon's Song. *Fr.* Vala.
Epigram: Answer to the Parson, An.
Epigram: Character, A.
Epigram: Sir Joshua Reynolds.
Epigram: To English Connoisseurs.
Epigram: To Flaxman.
Epigram: To Hunt.
Epilogue: "I am sure this Jesus will not do." *Fr.* The Everlasting Gospel.
Epilogue: "Truly, My Satan, thou art but a Dunce." *Fr.* The Gates of Paradise.
Epilogue to the Accuser Who Is the God of This World. *Fr.* The Gates of Paradise.
Eternity.
Ethinthus, Queen of Waters. *Fr.* Europe.
Europe, *sel.*
Everlasting Gospel, The, *sels.*
Fair Eleanor.
Fields from Islington to Marybone, The. *Fr.* Jerusalem.
Fly, The. *Fr.* Songs of Experience.
For the Sexes; the Gates of Paradise.
Four Zoas, The, *sel.*
Fragment: "Spirit, who lov'st Britannia's Isle."
French Revolution, The, *sel.*
From Islington to Marybone. *Fr.* Jerusalem.
Garden of Love, The. *Fr.* Songs of Experience.
Gates of Paradise, The, *sels.*
Gnomic Verses, *sels.*
Good English Hospitality. *Fr.* An Island in the Moon.
Great things are done when men and mountains meet. *Fr.* Gnomic Verses.
Grey Monk, The, *sels.*
Happy Piper, The. *Fr.* Songs of Innocence.
Happy Songs. *Fr.* Songs of Innocence.
He has observed the golden rule. *Fr.* Gnomic Verses.
He Who Binds [*or* Bends] to Himself [a Joy]
Hear the Voice [of the Bard].

BLAKE, WILLIAM (continued)
Holy Thursday. Fr. Songs of Experience.
Holy Thursday. Fr. Songs of Innocence.
How Sweet I Roamed from Field to Field.
How Sweet Is the Shepherd's Sweet Lot. Fr. Songs of Innocence.
Human Abstract, The. Fr. Songs of Experience.
Human Image, The, sel.
Humility and Doubt. Fr. The Everlasting Gospel.
I Asked a Thief.
I Cry: Love, Love! Fr. Visions of the Daughters of Albion.
I Give You the End of a Golden String. Fr. Jerusalem.
I laid me down upon a bank.
I love the jocund dance.
I Saw a Chapel All of Gold.
I Saw a Monk of Charlemain [or Charlemaine]. Fr. Jerusalem.
I told my love, I told my love. Fr. Love's Secret.
I was angry with my friend. Fr. Songs of Experience.
I Will Give You. Fr. Jerusalem.
Immortal, The. Fr. The Book of Los.
Immortal Tent. Fr. Milton.
In Deadly Fear. Fr. Jerusalem.
In Weary Night. Fr. The Gates of Paradise.
Infant Joy. Fr. Songs of Innocence.
Infant Sorrow. Fr. Songs of Experience.
Injunction. Fr. Gnomic Verses.
Introduction: "Hear the voice of the Bard!" Fr. Songs of Experience.
Introduction: "Piping down the valleys wild." Fr. Songs of Innocence.
Introduction to "Songs of Experience."
Introduction to "Songs of Innocence."
Island in the Moon, An, sel.
It Is Not So with Me. Fr. Vala; or, The Four Zoas.
Jerusalem ("And did those feet in ancient time"). Fr. Milton.
Jerusalem, sels.
Jesus Was Sitting in Moses' Chair. Fr. The Everlasting Gospel.
Joy in the Flowers. Fr. Milton.
King Edward the Third, sel.
Lamb, The. Fr. Songs of Innocence.
Lament of Ahania, sel.
Land of Dreams, The.
Lapwing, The.
Laughing Song. Fr. Songs of Innocence.
Liberty.
Life. Fr. Auguries of Innocence.
Little Black Boy, The. Fr. Songs of Innocence.
Little Boy Found, The. Fr. Songs of Innocence.
Little Boy Lost, A. Fr. Songs of Experience.
Little Boy Lost, The. Fr. Songs of Innocence.
Little Lamb. Fr. Songs of Innocence.
Little Vagabond, The.
London. Fr. Songs of Experience.
London. Fr. The Human Image.
London, sel. Fr. Songs of Experience.
Long John Brown and Little Mary Bell.
Los is by mortals nam'd Time. Fr. Milton.
Love to faults is always blind.
Love's Secret.
Love's Secret, sel.
Mad Song.
Marigold, The. Fr. Visions of the Daughters of Albion.
Marriage.
Marriage of Heaven and Hell, The.
Marriage of Heaven and Hell, The, sel.
Mayors, The. Fr. An Island in the Moon.
Memory, Hither Come.
Mental Traveller, The.
Milton, sels.
Mr. Cromek.
Mock On, Mock On, Voltaire, Rousseau.
Mockery.
Monk, The. Fr. Jerusalem.
Morning.
Morning Comes, The. Fr. America.
My Silks and Fine Array.
My Spectre around Me Night and Day.
Never Seek to Tell Thy Love.
New Jerusalem, A [or The]. Fr. Milton.
New Law, The. Fr. The Everlasting Gospel.
Night. Fr. Songs of Innocence.
Night, sel. Fr. Songs of Innocence.
Night—II. Fr. Vala; or, The Four Zoas.
Nightingale and Flowers. Fr. Milton.
Nurse's Song. Fr. Songs of Experience.
Nurse's Song. Fr. Songs of Innocence.
O Lapwing!
O Rose, thou art sick. Fr. Songs of Experience.
O thou with dewy locks, who lookest down.
On Another's Sorrow. Fr. Songs of Innocence.
Our Lesser Kindred. Fr. Auguries of Innocence.
Piper, The. Fr. Songs of Innocence.
Piping down the Valleys Wild. Fr. Songs of Innocence.
Play Time. Fr. Songs of Innocence.
Poet's Voice, The.
Poison Tree, A. Fr. Songs of Experience.
Preface to "Milton."
Price of Experience, The. Fr. Vala; or, the Four Zoas.
Prisoner of Love.
Proverbs of Hell. Fr. The Marriage of Heaven and Hell.
Question Answer'd, The.
Reason and Imagination. Fr. Milton.
Reeds of Innocence. Fr. Songs of Innocence.
Riches. Fr. Gnomic Verses.
Robin Redbreast, A. Fr. Auguries of Innocence.
Schoolboy, The. Fr. Songs of Experience.
Scoffers.
Seven of My Sweet Loves.
Shepherd, The. Fr. Songs of Innocence.
Sick Rose, The. Fr. Songs of Experience.
Silent, Silent Night.
Sir Joshua Reynolds.
Sleep, Sleep, Beauty Bright.
Smile, The.
Smile and Frown.
Soft Snow.
Song: "And did those feet in ancient time." Fr. Milton.
Song: "Fresh from the dewy hill, the merry year."
Song: "How sweet I roam'd [or roamed] from field to field."
Song: "I love the jocund dance."
Song: "Love and harmony combine."
Song: "Memory, hither come."
Song: "My silks and fine array."
Song: "Never seek to tell thy love."
Song: "Thou the golden fruit dost bear."
Song of Liberty, A.
Song of Singing, A.
Songs of Experience, sels.
Songs of Innocence, sels.
Spirit's Warfare, The.
Spring. Fr. Songs of Innocence.
Stanzas from "Milton."
Sunflower, The. Fr. Songs of Experience.
Sweet Dreams Form a Shade. Fr. Songs of Innocence.
Sword and the Sickle, The.
Sword sang on the barren heath, The. Fr. Gnomic Verses.
Take Thy Bliss, O Man. Fr. Visions of the Daughters of Albion.
Tear Is an Intellectual Thing, A. Fr. The Grey Monk.
Thel's Motto. Fr. The Book of Thel.
They said this mystery shall never cease. Fr. Gnomic Verses.
Things to Remember. Fr. Auguries of Innocence.
Thou hast a lap full of seed.
Thou hearest the nightingale. Fr. Milton.
Three Things to Remember. Fr. Auguries of Innocence.
Tiger, The. Fr. Songs of Experience.
Till We Have Built Jerusalem. Fr. Milton.
To English Connoisseurs.
To Flaxman.
To Hayley.
To Hunt.
To Mrs. Ann Flaxman.
To Morning.
To My Friend Butts I Write.
To see a world in a grain of sand. Fr. Auguries of Innocence.
To Spring.
To Summer.
To the Accuser Who Is the God of This World. Fr. The Gates of Paradise.
To the Christians. Fr. Jerusalem.
To the Evening Star.
To the Muses.
To the Queen.
To Tirzah. Fr. Songs of Experience.
To William Hayley.
To Winter.
'Twas on a Holy Thursday, their innocent faces clean. Fr. Songs of Innocence.
Two Kinds of Riches.
Two Songs, The.
Tyger, The. Fr. Songs of Experience.
Unquestioning.
Vala; or, The Four Zoas, sels.
Vision of Beulah. Fr. Milton.
Vision of Christ that thou dost see, The. Fr. The Everlasting Gospel.
Visions of the Daughters of Albion, sels.
Voice of the Bard, The. Fr. Songs of Experience.
War. Fr. King Edward the Third.
War Song [to Englishmen], A. Fr. King Edward the Third.
Was Jesus chaste? Fr. The Everlasting Gospel.
What are those Golden Builders doing? Fr. Jerusalem.
When a Man Has Married a Wife.
When the Green Woods Laugh. Fr. Songs of Innocence.
Why Should I Care For the Men of Thames?
Wild Flower's Song.
William Bond.
William Bond, sel.
Wine-Press of Los, The. Fr. Milton.
With Happiness Stretched across the Hills.
Written 1811. Fr. Jerusalem.
BLAMIRE, SUSANNA. Siller Croun, The.
What Ails This Heart o' Mine?
BLANCHARD, EDITH RICHMOND. Cats.
BLANCHARD, LAMAN. Art of Bookkeeping, The.
False Love and True Logic.
Hidden Joys.
Mother's Hope, The.
Nell Gwynne's Looking-Glass.
Ode to the Human Heart.
Whatever Is, Is Right.
Wishes of Youth.
BLANCHARD, SAMUEL LAMAN. See BLANCHARD, LAMAN.
BLAND, EDITH NESBIT. See NESBIT, EDITH.
BLAND, JAMES A. Carry Me Back to Old Virginny.

In the Evening by the Moonlight.
Oh! Dem Golden Slippers.
BLANDEN, CHARLES GRANGER. Ascent.
At Easter Time.
Enough.
"John Anderson, My Jo."
Paradise.
Passion Flower, The.
Quatrain: "Christ bears a thousand crosses now."
Rose Is a Royal Lady, The.
Song: "Life, in one semester."
Song: "What have the years left us?"
Song: "What trees were in Gethsemane."
Song the Grass Sings, A.
Songs I Sing, The.
To Silver Birches.
Unknown God, The.
Valentine.
Via Lucis.
Wings.
BLANDING, DON. Aloha Oe.
Childhood Reds.
Hollywood.
Journey Ends, A.
Soldier, What Did You See?
Vagabond House.
BLANKNER, FREDERIKA. Remainder.
BLASER, ROBIN. 4 Part Geometry Lesson, A.
Herons.
Poem: "And when I pay death's duty."
Poem: "For years I've heard."
Poem by the Charles River.
BLAU, ERNEST E. Christmas Day on the Aisne.
BLENKHORN, ADA. Heavenly Stranger, The.
BLEW, WILLIAM JOHN. O Lord, Thy Wing Outspread.
BLEWETT, JEAN. At Quebec.
Barley Fields, The.
Boy of the House, The.
Firstborn, The.
For He Was Scotch and So Was She.
In the Old Church.
She Just Keeps House for Me.
BLICHER, STEEN STEENSEN. Birds of Passage, *sel.*
Heather, The.
Jutlander, The.
Prelude: "Time draws nigh when I shall go forth, The." *Fr.* Birds of Passage.
To Sorrow.
BLIGHT, JOHN. Becalmed.
Cat-o'-Nine-Tails, The.
Crab.
Stonefish and Starfish.
BLIND, MATHILDE. April Rain.
Dare Quam Accipere.
Dead, The.
Hymn to Horus.
Love in Exile, *sels.*
"BLIND HARRY." *See* HENRY THE MINSTREL.
BLINN, LUCY MARION. Poor-House Nan.
BLISS, H. W. Understanding.
BLISS, PAUL SOUTHWORTH. Ulysses S. Grant.
BLITZSTEIN, MARC. Art for Art's Sake. *Fr.* The Cradle Will Rock.
Cradle Will Rock, The, *sel.*
BLOCH, JEAN-RICHARD. Idea of a Swimmer.
BLOCK, ALEXANDER ALEXANDROVICH. *See* BLOK, ALEKSANDR ALEKSANDROVICH.
BLOCK, LOUIS JAMES. Fate.
Final Struggle, The. *Fr.* The New World.
Garden Where There Is No Winter, The.
New World, The, *sel.*
Tuberose.
Work.
BLOCKER, HYACINTH. Franciscans.
Wolf of Gubbio, The.
Wooing of St. Francis, The.
BLODGETT, HARRIET F. December.
BLODGETT, MARY H. Counterpoint.
Valentine.
BLOEDE, GERTRUDE. *See* "STERNE, STUART."
BLOK, ALEKSANDR ALEKSANDROVICH. All that is finished, finished, finished.
Artist.
Autumn Love.
Aviator, The.
Dance of Death.
Dead roses and dying.
Demon.
Evening mist on the land was lying.
Glory and gallant deeds and fame forgetting.
Hawk, The.
Hours and days and years are fleeting, The.
How Narrow Is the Circle.
I have forebodings of Thee. Time is going.
I Have Foreknown Thee.
I Planted My Bright Paradise.
I seek salvation.
Little Black Man, A.
Little Catkins.
Maiden's song in the choir was telling, A.
My darling, be brave.
New America, The.
Night: the street, a foolish lamp giving.
Pipes on the bridge struck up to play.
Ravenna.
Russia.
Russia, my life! are we tied to one fate for us?
Scythians, The.
Season comes, a day comes, A.
Shadows on the Wall.
She Came Out of the Frost.
Steps of the Commander, The.
Stranger, The.
Those who were born in years of quiet.
To Sin, Unshamed.
Twelve, The.
Voice from the Chorus.
Vulture.
What long-forgotten gleam is this?
When Mountain Ash in Clusters Reddens.
White flag I never surrendered, The.
Wild wind batters/ Window-panes.
Willow-Boughs, The.
Yes, I have loved. And the mad glowing.
Yes. Thus His Daemon.
You say I am frozen, and dry, and apart.
You say that I'm asleep.
BLOMBERG, ERIK. Dead Gods.
Duet.
Night.
Truth.
BLOOD, HENRY AMES. Comrades.
Fighting Parson, The.
Shakespeare.
BLOOMFIELD, ROBERT. Abner and the Widow Jones.
Fakenham Ghost, The.
Farmer's Boy, The, *sels.*
Lambs at Play.
Moonlight in Summer.
Soldier's Return, The.
Thrush and Blackthorn. *Fr.* The Farmer's Boy.
BLOOMGARDEN [*or* BLUMGARTEN], SOLOMON. *See* "YEHOASH."
BLOUNT, EDWARD AUGUSTUS, JR. As They Fell.
Crew Poem, A.
Hunchback, The.
BLOUZ, HOVHANNES. Caravan, The.
BLUM, ETTA. When You Reach the Hilltop the Sky Is on Top of You.
BLUMENTHAL, WALTER HART. Da Silva Gives the Cue.
BLUNDELL, WILLIAM, OF CROSBY. England's Prayer.
BLUNDEN, EDMUND. Age of Herbert & Vaughan, The.
Almswomen.
Another Altar.
At the Great Wall of China.
Author's Last Words to His Students, The.
Barn, The.
Behind the Line.
Chinese Pond.
Cicada, *tr.*
Country God, A.
Country Sale.
Eastern Tempest.
Far East.
Fine Nature, The.
Forefathers.
Giant Puffball, The.
Idlers, The.
In Festubert.
In My Time.
In Wiltshire.
Infantryman, An.
Into the Salient.
Lark Descending.
Late Light.
Maltese Dog, A, *tr.*
May Day Garland, The.
Memorial, The; 1914-1918.
Memory of Kent, The.
Midnight Skaters, The.
Mole Catcher.
Odes (*of Horace*), *sel., tr.*
Old Homes.
Pike, The.
Poor Man's Pig, The.
Psalm, A: "O God, in whom my deepest being dwells."
Recovery, The.
Reliques, *sel.*
Report on Experience.
Sheet Lightning.
Shepherd.
Sick-Bed.
Silver Bird of Herndyke Mill, The.
Solutions.
Some Talk of Peace.
Spell of France, The.
Sunlit Vale, The.
Survival, The.
Thiepval Wood.
Threshold.
To Our Catchment Board.
Waggoner, The.
Wartons, The.
What Is Winter?
Yeoman, A.
BLUNT, LADY ANNE, *and* WILFRID SCAWEN BLUNT. Night Long, The, *tr.*
Weep Love's Losing, *tr.*
BLUNT, HUGH FRANCIS. Candlemas.
God's Handmaid.
Wagon of the Little Sisters, The.
What No Man Knoweth.
BLUNT, WILFRID SCAWEN. Alfred Tennyson.
As to His Choice of Her. *Fr.* The Love Sonnets of Proteus.
Camel-Rider, The, *tr.*
Chanclebury Ring.
Day in Sussex, A.
Days of Our Youth, The, *tr.*
Deeds That Might Have Been, The. *Fr.* In Vinculis.
Depreciating Her Beauty. *Fr.* The Love Sonnets of Proteus.
Desolate City, The, *tr.*
Esther; a Young Man's Tragedy, *sels.*
Falcon, The. *Fr.* The Love Sonnets of Proteus.
Farewell: "Farewell, then. It is finished." *Fr.* The Love Sonnets of Proteus.
Farewell to Juliet ("I see you, Juliet, still, with your straw hat"). *Fr.* The Love Sonnets of Proteus.
Farewell to Juliet ("Juliet, farewell. I would not be forgiven"). *Fr.* The Love Sonnets of Proteus.
Farewell to Juliet ("Lame, impotent conclusion . . ."). *Fr.* The Love Sonnets of Proteus.
Ghost of the Beautiful Past.
Gibraltar.
Grief of Love, The, *tr.*
Haunted House, The.

BLUNT, WILFRID SCAWEN (*continued*)
He Has Fallen from the Height of His Love. *Fr.* The Love Sonnets of Proteus.
He who has once been happy is for aye. *Fr.* Esther.
Honour Dishonoured.
How Shall I Build.
If We Had Met.
In Answer to a Question. *Fr.* The Love Sonnets of Proteus.
In Vinculis, *sels.*
Laughter and Death. *Fr.* The Love Sonnets of Proteus.
Liberty, Equality, Fraternity. *Fr.* In Vinculis.
Love Lyrics of Proteus, The, *sel.*
Love Secret, The, *tr.*
Love Sonnets of Proteus, The, *sels.*
Morte d'Arthur, The.
Nocturne, A: "Moon has gone to her rest, The."
Old Squire, The.
On a Lost Opportunity. *Fr.* The Love Sonnets of Proteus.
On the Nature of Love. *Fr.* The Love Sonnets of Proteus.
On the Shortness of Time. *Fr.* The Love Sonnets of Proteus.
Pleasures of Love, The.
Prison Sonnet.
St. Valentine's Day. *Fr.* The Love Sonnets of Proteus.
Sinner-Saint, The.
Song: "O fly not, Pleasure, pleasant-hearted Pleasure." *Fr.* The Love Lyrics of Proteus.
Sublime, The.
They Shall Not Know.
Think No More of Me.
To a Happy Warrior.
To Manon, as to His Choice of Her. *Fr.* The Love Sonnets of Proteus.
To Manon, Comparing Her to a Falcon. *Fr.* The Love Sonnets of Proteus.
To Manon, on Her Lightheartedness. *Fr.* The Love Sonnets of Proteus.
To Manon, on His Fortune in Loving Her. *Fr.* The Love Sonnets of Proteus.
To One on Her Waste of Time. *Fr.* The Love Sonnets of Proteus.
To One Who Would Make a Confession. *Fr.* The Love Sonnets of Proteus.
Two Highwaymen, The. *Fr.* The Love Sonnets of Proteus.
Venus of Milo, The.
When I hear laughter from a tavern door. *Fr.* Esther.
Wisdom of Merlyn, The, *sels.*
With Esther. *Fr.* Esther.
Written at Florence.
You Have Let the Beauty of the Day Go Over.
BLY, ROBERT. Barnfire during Church.
Man Whom the Sea Kept Awake, The.
Missouri Traveller Writes Home, A; 1830.
Puritan on His Honeymoon, The.
Where We Must Look for Help.
BLYTON, ENID. Fairy Music.
Field-Mouse, The.
What Piggy-Wig Found.
Winter.
BOAKE, BARCROFT HENRY. Where the Dead Men Lie.
BOAS, FREDERICK S. Balliol Rooks, The.
BOAS, GEORGE. House Dog.
BOAS, GUY. Underground, The.
BOBSTON, CHARLES A. Lovesick Cowboy, The.
BOCANEGRA, MATÍAS DE. Song on Beholding an Enlightenment.
BOCCACCIO, GIOVANNI. Apology for Love.
Ballata: Flowers and Love. *Fr.* The Decameron.
Decameron, The, *sel.*
Fiammetta.
Filostrato, Il.
Inscription for Portrait of Dante.
Of Fiammetta Singing.
Of His Last Sight of Fiammetta.
Of Three Girls and Their Talk.
Olympia.
Queen of the Angels, The.
Sonnet: "Now perish, Baia, root and stock and name."
Sonnet: "To that fair kingdom, o my gentle lord."
Sonnets, *sels.*
To Dante in Paradise.
To One Who Had Censured.
Tribute to Dante, A.
BODE, JOHN E. To the End.
BODENHEIM, MAXWELL. Advice to a Blue-Bird.
Advice to a Buttercup.
Advice to a Forest.
City Girl.
Country-Brook.
Country Girl.
Death.
Factory Girl.
Forgetfulness.
Here Is Your Realism.
Hill-Side Tree.
Impulsive Dialogue.
Interlude.
Interne, The.
Jack Rose.
King of Spain, The.
Landscape.
Love.
Lynched Negro.
Meditations on a Landscape.
Metaphysical Poem.
Miner, The.
Minna.
Negroes.
New York City.
Old Age.
Old Jew, The.
Old Poet to His Love, An.
Poem: "O men, walk on the hills."
Poem to Negro and Whites.
Poet to His Love.
Realism.
Rear Porches of an Apartment Building.
Short Story in Sonnet Form.
Sister Writes, A.
Soldiers.
Songs to a Woman.
To a Discarded Steel Rail.
To a Friend.
To an Enemy.
BØDTCHER, LUDVIG. Footprints.
What She Is.
BOESCH, RAYMOND. Life Is Leaving One Strange Port.
BOETHIUS (Anicius Manlius Severinus Boethius). Consolation of Philosophy, *sel.*
King Alfred's Metres of Boethius, *sel.*
O Qui Perpetua Mundum Ratione Gubernas.
O Thou Whose Pow'r.
Opening Poem. *Fr.* Consolation of Philosophy.
Search for Truth, The.
Si Vis Celsi Iura Tonantis.
This Discord in the Pact of Things.
Wood Finches.
BOGAN, LOUISE. After the Persian.
Alchemist, The.
Baroque Comment.
Cassandra.
Changed Woman, The.
Chanson un Peu Naïve.
Come, Break with Time.
"Come, Sleep . . ."
Crossed Apple, The.
Crows, The.
Decoration.
Dream, The.
Fiend's Weather.
For a Marriage.
Frightened Man, The.
Henceforth, from the Mind.
I Saw Eternity.
July Dawn.
Knowledge.
M., Singing.
March Twilight.
Mark, The.
Medusa.
Meeting, The.
Men Loved Wholly beyond Wisdom.
Musician.
Old Countryside.
Packet of Letters.
Portrait.
Putting to Sea.
Romantic, The.
Several Voices Out of a Cloud.
Simple Autumnal.
Single Sonnet.
Sleeping Fury, The.
Song: "Love me because I am lost."
Song for a Lyre.
Song for a Slight Voice.
Song for the Last Act.
Statue and Birds.
Summer Wish.
Tale, A.
To Be Sung on the Water.
Train Tune.
Variation on a Sentence.
Winter Swan.
Women.
BOGART, ELIZABETH ("Estelle"). He Came Too Late.
BOGDANOVICH, IPPOLIT. Old Russian Song.
BOGUSLAWSKI, ANTONI. Dawn.
For My Son.
BOHANAN, OTTO LELAND. Dawn's Awake, The.
Washer-Woman, The.
BOHUN-GREENE, MARIUS. Not One Thing Alone.
BOIARDO, MATTEO MARIA. Madrigal: "Sing with me, you little amorous birds."
Sonnet: "Give me, full-handed, lilies, give me the rose."
Sonnet: "Once in good hour there came in company."
Sonnet: "Poor drooping flowers and pallid violets."
Sonnet: "Song of birds which leaps from leaf to leaf, The."
Sonnet: To a Balcony.
BOILEAU-DESPRÉAUX, NICOLAS. Art of Poetry, The, *sels.*
Art Poétique, L', *sels.*
Fantastick Mind, The. *Fr.* L'Art Poétique.
BOILLEAU, JOAN. I Saw a Ghost.
BOKER, GEORGE HENRY. All the world's malice, all the spite of fate. *Fr.* Sonnets; a Sequence of Profane Love.
As some new ghost, that wanders to and fro. *Fr.* Sonnets; a Sequence of Profane Love.
Ballad of New Orleans, The.
Ballad of Sir John Franklin, A.
Battle of Lookout Mountain.
Before Vicksburg.
Black Regiment, The.
Book of the Dead, The, *sels.*
Countess Laura.
Crossing at Fredericksburg, The.
Cruise of the *Monitor,* The.
Death on his mission sought my lady's side. *Fr.* Sonnets; a Sequence of Profane Love.
Dirge for a Soldier.
Either the sum of this sweet mutiny. *Fr.* Sonnets.
Ferry, The.
Fever in My Blood Has Died, The.
Flag, The.
Here part we, love, beneath the world's broad eye. *Fr.* Sonnets.
Hooker's Across.
Hopes, on which our spirits live, The. *Fr.* The Book of the Dead.
I have been mounted on life's topmost wave. *Fr.* Sonnets.
I, sighing o'er the happy past. *Fr.* The Book of the Dead.
I strive to live my life in whitest time. *Fr.* Sonnets; a Sequence of Profane Love.
If any good may come to me. *Fr.* The Book of the Dead.
If dreaming of thee be a waste of

time. *Fr.* Sonnets; a Sequence of Profane Love.
I'll call thy frown a headsman, passing grim. *Fr.* Sonnets.
In this deep hush and quiet of my soul. *Fr.* Sonnets.
Lincoln. *Fr.* Our Heroic Times.
Love is that orbit of the restless soul. *Fr.* Sonnets.
Love sat at ease upon Time's bony knee. *Fr.* Sonnets; a Sequence of Profane Love.
My lady sighs, and I am far away. *Fr.* Sonnets.
Not when the buxom form which nature wears. *Fr.* Sonnets.
On Board the *Cumberland.*
Our Heroic Times, *sel.*
Perhaps in mercy is the future masked. *Fr.* Sonnets; a Sequence of Profane Love.
Prince Adeb.
Sir John Franklin.
Sometimes, in bitter fancy, I bewail. *Fr.* Sonnets.
Sonnet: "If dreaming of thee be a waste of time." *Fr.* Sonnets; a Sequence of Profane Love.
Sonnets, *sels.*
Sonnets; a Sequence of Profane Love, *sels.*
Thou who dost smile upon me, yet unknown. *Fr.* Sonnets.
Thus in her absence is my fancy cool. *Fr.* Sonnets; a Sequence of Profane Love.
To England.
To My Lady.
Today her Majesty was wroth and cold. *Fr.* Sonnets; a Sequence of Profane Love.
Upon the Hill before Centreville.
Varuna, The.
What fancy, or what flight of wingèd thought. *Fr.* Sonnets.
When I am turned to moulding dust. *Fr.* The Book of the Dead.
When I look back upon my early days. *Fr.* Sonnets; a Sequence of Profane Love.
Your love to me appears in doubtful signs. *Fr.* Sonnets.
Zagonyi.
BOKUJIN. Lightly, lightly,/ Summer breezes playing.
BOLD, HENRY. Chloris, Forbear Awhile.
BOLEYN, ANNE. Cruel Spite.
O Death, Rock Me Asleep [*or* on Sleep], *at.*
BOLEYN, GEORGE, VISCOUNT ROCHFORD. O Death, Rock Me Asleep [*or* on Sleep], *at.*
BOLLES, FRANK. Oven-Bird, The.
BOLTON, EDMUND. As withereth the primrose by the river.
Canzon Pastoral in Honor of Her Majesty, A.
Carol, A: "Sweet Music, sweeter far."
Palinode, A.
Shepherd's Song, The.
To Favonius.
BOLTON, SARAH KNOWLES. Faith.
Inevitable, The.
Live in the Present.
Live Today.
Paddle Your Own Canoe.
BOLTON, SARAH TITTLE. Left on the Battle-Field.
BOMKE, MARY COCKBURN. Roving Alley-Cat, A.
BONAR, HORATIUS. Abide with Us.
Be True.
Beyond the Smiling and the Weeping.
Bless the Blessed Morn.
Christ Is All.
Cross and Throne.
Fairest He, The.
First and the Last, The.
God's Way.
He Liveth Long Who Liveth Well.
He Took My Place.
Here, O my Lord, I see thee face to face.
His Glory Tell.
Honesty.
How We Learn.
I Heard the Voice of Jesus Say.
I Lay My Sins on Jesus.
I Was a Wandering Sheep.
It Is Finished.
Life.
Little While, A.
Lost but Found.
Love Is of God.
Master's Touch, The.
More of Thee.
My Prayer.
O Love that casts out fear.
Reappearing.
Reflection.
Same Forever, The.
This Do in Remembrance of Me, *sel.*
Thou Must Be True.
Thy Way, Not Mine.
Voice from Galilee, The.
Who Liveth Well.
Work, The, That Saves!
BONAVENTURE, SAINT. Adeste Fideles, *at.*
O Come All Ye Faithful, *at.*
Psalter of the Blessed Virgin Mary, *sels.*
BONCHO. Haiku: "Long, long river, The."
Long, long river, The.
BOND, CARRIE JACOBS. I Love You Truly.
Perfect Day, A.
Sleepy Song, A.
BONE, FLORENCE. Prayer for a Little Home, A.
BONE, GERTRUDE HELENA, LADY. Mystic, The.
BONER, JOHN HENRY. Boy in the Piney Woods, A.
Broken and Desolate.
Cliff, The.
Country House in the South, A.
Easter Advent.
Hunting Muscadines.
In the Organ-Loft with a Poetess.
Light 'ood Fire, The.
Poe's Cottage at Fordham.
Remembrance.
Stained-Glass Window, A.
We Walked among the Whispering Pines.
BONHAM, THOMAS. In Praise of Ale, *at.*
BONN, JOHN LOUIS. Admonition.
Madonna; 1936.
Resurgence.
BONNEFONS [*or* BONNEFONIUS], JEAN. Song: "Still to be neat, still to be drest." *Fr.* Epicoene; or, The Silent Woman.
Vanity of Kissing.
BØNNELYCKE, EMIL. My Soul.
BONTEMPS, ARNA. Black Man Talks of Reaping, A.
Blight.
Close Your Eyes!
Dark Girl.
Daybreakers, The.
Gethsemane.
God Give to Men.
Golgotha Is a Mountain.
Homing.
Idolatry.
Lancelot.
Length of Moon.
Miracles.
Nocturne at Bethesda.
Nocturne of the Wharves.
Note of Humility, A.
Return, The.
Southern Mansion.
To a Young Girl Leaving the Hill Country.
Tree Design, A.
BOODSON, ALISON. Carol: "Fire is what's precious now."
Night Alert.
Poem: "He lying spilt like water from a bowl."
Poem: "I do not want to be your weeping woman."
BOOMER, PAUL C. Life.
Mind.
BOOTH, BARTON. Song: "Sweet are the charms of her I love."
BOOTH, EVA GORE-. *See* GORE-BOOTH, EVA.
BOOTH, PHILIP. Animal Fair.
Barred Islands.
Catwise.
Cold Water Flat.
Heron.
North.
Siasconset Song.
Turning, The.
Twelfth Night.
Vermont; Indian Summer.
Wilding, The.
BOOTHBY, SIR BROOKE. Sonnet on Life.
BOOTHROYD, JOHN BASIL. "And Now . . ."
Holy Order.
Please Excuse Typing.
Sanctuary.
BORATYNSKY, YEVGENY ABRAMOVICH. Blessèd Are They.
Of What Use Are You, Days?
Phyllida.
Prayer: "King of Heaven, make me whole."
Road of Life, The.
BORGES, JORGE LUIS. Benares.
Butcher Shop.
Day's Run, A.
General Quiroga Rides to Death in a Carriage.
Houses like Angels.
July Avenue.
Love's Priority.
Natural Flow of Memory.
Night They Kept Vigil in the South, The.
Patio.
Recoleta, The.
Sepulchral Inscription.
To Rafael Cansinos Assens.
BORGESE, GIUSEPPE ANTONIO. Dream of a Decent Death.
Easter Sunday, 1945.
BORIE, LYSBETH BOYD. Five Years Old.
Greaty-great Grannie.
Just for Jesus.
Saturday Towels.
BORLAND, HAL. Caravans.
Men of America, Answering the Call.
BORN, BERTRAND DE. *See* BERTRAND DE BORN.
BORREGAARD, EBBE. Each Found Himself at the End of . . .
Some Stories of the Beauty Wapiti.
BORROW, GEORGE. Death the Great, *tr.*
French Princess, The, *tr.*
Invitation, The, *tr.*
Lavengro, *sel.*
Mist, The, *tr.*
Vowel Englyn to the Spider, *tr.*
BORTHWICK, JANE. Be Still, *tr.*
Light Shining Out of Darkness.
BOSCÁN ALMOGÁVER, JUAN. On the Death of Garcilaso.
Quarry, The.
BOSE, BUDDHADEVA. Burden of Everyday, The.
BOSMAN, HERMAN CHARLES. Luck in the Square Stone, The, *sel.*
Poet, The.
Recovery from Mental Illness.
Seed.
BOSSIDY, JOHN COLLINS. And this is good old Boston.
Boston.
Boston Toast, A.
On the Aristocracy of Harvard.
To Boston.
BOSTELMANN, CARL JOHN. Christ in the Andes.
BOSTWICK, GRACE G. "Pep."
Reward, The.
BOSTWICK, HELEN LOUISE BARRON. Little Dandelion.
BOSWELL, SIR ALEXANDER. Jenny Dang the Weaver.
Jenny's Bawbee.
BOSWELL, ARTHUR. Roughchin, the Pirate.
BOSWORTH, WILLIAM. Chaste and Lost Lovers, The, *sel.*

BOSWORTH, WILLIAM (*continued*)
See'st Not, My Love. *Fr.* The Chaste and Lost Lovers.
BOTKIN, BENJAMIN ALBERT. Gulls, The; Provincetown Harbor.
BOTREL, THEODORE. Little Gregory.
BOTTA, ANNE CHARLOTTE LYNCH. On a Picture.
BOTTOMLEY, GORDON. Atlantis.
Carol for Christmas Day before Dawn, A.
Dawn. *Fr.* Night and Morning Songs.
Eager Spring.
Eagle Song. *Fr.* Suilven and the Eagle.
Elegiac Mood. *Fr.* Night and Morning Songs.
End of the World, The.
Gruach.
I Am Tired of the Wind.
In January.
In Memoriam A. M. W.
Louse Crept Out of My Lady's Shift, A.
Maid of Arc, The.
My Moon. *Fr.* Night and Morning Songs.
Netted Strawberries.
New Year's Eve, 1913.
Night and Morning Songs, *sels.*
Ploughman, The.
Prologue to Towie Castle.
Song of Apple Gathering, A.
Suilven and the Eagle, *sel.*
To Iron-Founders and Others.
BOTTRALL, RONALD. Arion Anadyomenos.
Dream of His Lady, *tr.*
Future Is Not for Us, The.
Genesis.
Preamble to a Great Adventure.
Proserpine at Enna.
Rondeau: "Homage to change that scatters the poppy seed."
BOTWOOD, EDWARD. Hot Stuff.
"BOUCHER, ANTHONY" (William Anthony Parker White). Lazarus, *tr.*
Sonnet of the Unsleeping Dead.
BOUCICAULT, DION. Exiled Mother, The.
Peasant Woman's Song, A.
Wearing of the Green, *at.*
BOUFFLERS, STANISLAS JEAN, MARQUIS DE (Abbé Boufflers). Paying a Debt.
BOULTON, HAROLD. All through the Night.
BOUNDY, REX. Virile Christ, A.
BOUQUET, JOHN ALEXANDER. Epitaph, The: "When from this good world I depart."
Sorrow Turned into Joy.
BOURDILLON, FRANCIS WILLIAM. Aucassin and Nicolete.
Eurydice.
Heart-Cry, The.
Light.
Light and Love.
Lost God, A, *sel.*
Night Has a Thousand Eyes, The.
Old and Young.
Outwards and Homewards.
Song: "Night has a thousand eyes, The."
Upon the Valley's Lap.
Violinist, A.
Where Runs the River?
BOURINOT, ARTHUR STANLEY. Canadian Ski Song.
Dark Flows the River.
Enchantment.
Indian, The.
Johnny Appleseed.
Laurentians, The.
Nicolas Gatineau.
Only Silence.
Paul Bunyan.
Paul Bunyan, *sel.*
Sleeping Now in Coventry.
Snow Anthology.
Sonnets to My Mother.
To Suzette.
To the Ottawa.
Tom Thomson.
Under the Pines.
What Far Kingdom.
Winter Sketch.
BOURMAN, NICHOLAS. Epitaph upon the Death of the Right Reverent Father in God J. Jewel . . . , An.
BOURNE, DAVID. Parachute Descent.
BOURNE, NINA. Where the Single Men Go in Summer.
BOURNE, VINCENT. Cricket, The.
Familiarity Dangerous.
Housekeeper, The.
Jackdaw, The.
Snail, The.
BOUVÉ, THOMAS TRACY. *Shannon* and the *Chesapeake,* The.
BOWDITCH, NATHANIEL INGERSOLL. World Beyond, A.
BOWEN, ARNOLD VINCENT. Only Pretty Ringtime, The.
BOWEN, CHARLES SYNGE CHRISTOPHER BOWEN, BARON. Just & Unjust.
Rain It Raineth, The.
BOWEN, EDWARD ERNEST. Forty Years On.
Shemuel.
BOWEN, EUROS. Birds of Rhiannon, The.
BOWEN, JOHN ELIOT. Man Who Rode to Conemaugh, The.
BOWEN, MARY M. Cradle-Song: "Tis night on the mountain."
BOWEN, ROBERT ADGER. Gloaming.
BOWER, HELEN FRAZEE-. *See* FRAZEE-BOWER, HELEN.
BOWERS, E. Dear Mother, I've Come Home to Die.
BOWERS, EDGAR. Aix-la-Chappelle, 1945.
Epigram on the Passing of Christmas.
For W. A. Mozart.
From J. Haydn to Constanze Mozart (1791).
From William Tyndale to John Frith.
Grove and Building.
Mountain Cemetery, The.
Stoic, The; for Laura von Courten.
Two Poems on the Catholic Bavarians.
Venus.
Virgin Mary, The.
Wise Men, The.
BOWES-LYON, LILIAN. Allendale Dog.
Duchess.
Early Light.
Feather, The.
Hedge-Row Story, The.
Saturday Afternoon.
Shepherd's Coat, A.
Stars Go By, The.
BOWIE, WALTER RUSSELL. Continuing Christ, The.
Empty Soul, The.
God of the Nations.
Holy City, The.
O Love That Triumphs over Loss.
BOWKER, RICHARD ROGERS. Thomas à Kempis.
BOWLES, CAROLINE ANNE (Mrs. Robert Southey). April Day, An.
Birthday, The, *sels.*
Cuckoo Clock, The. *Fr.* The Birthday.
Evening Walk, The, *sel.*
Lady-Bird.
Pauper's Deathbed, The.
To Death.
To the Ladybird.
Young Gray Head, The.
BOWLES, CAROLINE ANNE, *and* ROBERT SOUTHEY. *See* SOUTHEY, ROBERT, *and* CAROLINE ANNE BOWLES.
BOWLES, FRED G. Song of the Road, A.
BOWLES, WILLIAM LISLE. At Dover Cliffs [July 20, 1787].
Avenue in Savernake Forest.
Bells of Ostend, The.
Bird in a Cage, The.
Butterfly and the Bee, The.
Come to These Scenes of Peace.
Distant View of England from the Sea.
Dover Cliffs.
Glow-Worm, The.
Go tell the Spartans, thou that passest by, *tr.*
Greenwood, The.
Healing.
Hope.
Influence of Time on Grief.
O Time! who know'st a lenient hand to lay.
On the Rhine.
Ostend, on Hearing the Bells at Sea.
Shepherd and His Dog, The.
Sketch from Bowden Hill after Sickness, *sel.*
Sonnet: At Dover Cliffs, July 20, 1787.
Sonnet: At Ostend, July 22, 1787.
Sonnet: "Evening, as slow thy placid shades descend."
Sonnet: "Languid and sad, and slow, from day to day."
Sonnet: Netley Abbey.
Sonnet: "O Time! who know'st a lenient hand to lay."
Sonnet: On a Distant View of England.
Sonnet, July 18th, 1787.
Time and Grief.
BOWMAN, LOUISE HOLLINGSWORTH. Quiet Hour, The.
BOWMAN, LOUISE MOREY. Deep Snow.
Green Apples.
Hyacinth.
Sea Lavender.
She Plans Her Funeral.
Wealthy Shepherd, The.
Witch, The.
BOWMAN, ROWLAND C. Pup Dog's Opinion of the Quick Tempered Man, The.
BOWRA, CECIL MAURICE. *For translations from Greek, see* GrL; LiTW; OxBG.
For translations from Russian, see BoR; BoRS; LiTW; TrJP.
BOWRING, SIR JOHN. Amaryllis, *tr.*
Chorus of Batavian Women, *tr.*
Clora! *tr.*
Come, Let Us Eat and Drink Today, *tr.*
Come, Wandering Sheep [O Come!], *tr.*
Constancy, *tr.*
Cooling Fountain, *tr.*
Count Arnaldos, *tr.*
Disputes, *tr.*
Faint Heart Never Won Fair Lady, *tr.*
Foolish Leander, *tr.*
Fount of Freshness, *tr.*
From the Recesses of a Lowly Spirit.
Galleys of Spain, *tr.*
God Is Love.
If She Frown My Heart Would Break, *tr.*
In the Cross of Christ I Glory.
Infinity of Wishes, *tr.*
Kiss, The, *tr.*
Knight's Song, The, *tr.*
Love's Extremes, *tr.*
Mortal Grief, *tr.*
My Ornaments Are Arms, *tr.*
Nightingale, The. *Tr. fr. the Portuguese of* Vicente.
Nightingale, The. *Tr. fr. the Dutch of* Visscher.
Not of This World, *tr.*
Penitence, *tr.*
Prayer to Jesus, *tr.*
Rose Song, The, *tr.*
Sleep, *tr.*
Sonnet: "Hard is yon rock, around whose head," *tr.*
Sorrow, *tr.*
Soul Eternal, The.
That's a Lie! *tr.*
To Liberty, *tr.*
Towering o'er the Wrecks of Time.
Watchman, Tell Us of the Night.
Welcome Death, *tr.*
What of the Night?
Where Is Dominga? *tr.*
Woman's Jealousy, *tr.*
BOYAJIAN, ZABELLE C. Armenia's Love to Shakespeare.
For translations from Armenian, see ArmLP.
BOYARS, ARTHUR. Poem: "Supremest fictions grow with fungus speed."
BOYCE, BURKE. Clam Man, The.
BOYD, BAIRD. Cowboy.
Drunken Desperado. The.

BOYD, BRUCE. Sanctuary.
This Is What the Watchbird Sings, Who Perches in the Lovetree.
Venice Recalled.
BOYD, JAMES. Black Boys, The.
Christmas, 1943.
Long Distance, 1944.
BOYD, MARION MARGARET. To One Older.
White Dusk.
BOYD, MARK ALEXANDER. Cupid and Venus.
Fra Bank to Bank.
Sonnet [*or* Sonet]: "Fra bank to bank, fra wood to wood I rin."
"BOYD, NANCY." *See* MILLAY, EDNA ST. VINCENT.
BOYD, THOMAS. Ballyvourney.
Heath, The.
King's Son, The.
Love on the Mountain.
To the Leanán Shee [*or* Sidhe].
BOYDEN, POLLY CHASE. Form.
Hands on a Card-Table.
Mud.
New Mexico.
Self-Control.
BOYESEN, HJALMAR HJORTH. Brier-Rose.
Earl Sigurd's Christmas Eve.
Thoralf and Synnöv.
BOYLAN, GRACE DUFFIE. Who Goes There?
BOYLE, KAY. Communication to Nancy Cunard, A.
Flying Foxes and Others.
Funeral in Hungary.
BOYLE, ROGER, EARL OF ORRERY. *See* ORRERY, ROGER BOYLE, BARON BROGHILL, 1ST EARL OF.
BOYLE, SARAH ROBERTS. Voice of the Grass, The.
BOYLE, VIRGINIA FRAZER. Abraham Lincoln.
I Kilt er Cat.
I Know That My Redeemer Liveth.
Lullaby: "They are fluttering and fluttering, like birds upon the tree."
Tennessee.
BOYNTON, HENRY WALCOTT. Golfer's Rubayyat, The.
BOYNTON, LUELLA. Plover.
BRABAZON, FRANCIS. Victoria Market.
BRABHAM, MOUZON W. Father's Prayer, A.
BRACKEN, THOMAS. Not Understood.
BRACKER, MILTON. P Is for Paleontology.
BRACKETT, ANNA CALLENDER. Benedicite.
In Hades.
BRACKLEY, JOHN. Carol: "I saw a sweet and seemly sight," *at.*
I Saw a Sweet and Silly Sight, *at.*
O Jesu Parvule, *at.*
BRADBURY, BIANCA. Coming Back to Mountains.
For the Quakers.
Nor'easter.
Old Major.
BRADBURY, RAY. Dublin Limerick, A.
BRADBURY, WILLIAM B. Marching Along.
BRADBY, GODFREY FOX. April.
"Could Ye Not Watch One Hour?"
Flowing Tide, The.
In Hoc Signo.
Kingdom.
Lyonesse.
Marsh Marigolds.
Versailles.
BRADDOCK, JOSEPH. Black Cat in Prunus-Tree.
BRADEN, CHARLES S. Cross, The.
BRADFORD, GAMALIEL. Ardor.
Can't You.
Exit God.
God.
Hope.
Illimitable.
Judas.
Love's Detective.
My Delight.
BRADFORD, SARAH H. Resurrection.
BRADFORD, WILLIAM (1590–1657). New England's Growth.
Plymouth Harvest, The.
BRADLEY, CHRISTINE E. Skippets, the Bad One.
BRADLEY, DWIGHT. Disciple, The.
BRADLEY, EDWARD. *See* "BEDE, CUTHBERT."
BRADLEY, KATHERINE, *and* EDITH COOPER. *See* "FIELD, MICHAEL."
BRADLEY, MARY EMILY NEELY. Betty at the Party.
Beyond Recall.
Chrysalis, A.
Frost Work.
In Death.
Spray of Honeysuckle, A.
BRADLEY, WILLIAM ASPENWALL. Fult Faithorne.
Garden Muse, The.
Island Tea.
Men of Harlan.
To Little Renée on First Seeing Her Lying in Her Cradle.
Will Warner.
BRADSTREET, ANNE. As Weary Pilgrim [Now at Rest].
Author to Her Book, The.
Contemplations.
Contemplations, *sel.*
Epitaph on My Dear and Ever Honoured Mother, An.
Flesh and the Spirit, The.
Four Seasons of the Year, The. *sel.*
In Memory of My Dear Grandchild Ann Bradstreet, Who Deceased June 20, 1669, Being Three Years and Seven Months Old.
In Thankfull Remembrance for My Dear Husband's Safe Arrivall Sept. 3, 1662.
Letter to Her Husband, A.
Letter to Her Husband, Absent upon Publick Employment, A.
Longing for Heaven.
Prologue, The: "To sing of wars, of captains, and of kings."
Spring. *Fr.* The Four Seasons of the Year.
To My Dear and Loving Husband.
Upon the Burning of Our House.
BRADY, CHARLES A. Ballad of St. Thomas, A.
Dimidium Animae Meae.
BRADY, EDWIN JAMES. Ballad of the Captains, A.
Capstan Chantey, A.
Great Grey Water, The.
Lost and Given Over.
Southerly.
Trade.
BRADY, GEORGE M. Autumn House, The.
Day, The.
Garden, The.
Generations, The.
Hosts, The.
Land-Fall.
Old Michael.
Settled Men, The.
BRAGANÇA NADEJDA DE. Prayer: "O God, I love Thee in the stars at night."
BRAGDON, CLAUDE. Beautiful Necessity, The, *sel.*
Point, the Line, the Surface, and Sphere, The. *Fr.* The Beautiful Necessity.
BRAINARD, E. M. Compensation.
BRAINARD, JOHN GARDINER CALKINS. Captain, The.
Deep, The.
Epithalamium: "I saw two clouds at morning."
Fall of Niagara, The.
I Saw Two Clouds at Morning.
If I Could Love.
Mr. Merry's Lament for "Long Tom."
On the Death of Commodore Oliver H. Perry.
Sonnet to the Sea Serpent.
Stanzas: "Dead leaves strew the forest walk, The."
To the Connecticut River.
BRAINARD, MARY GARDINER. Faith and Sight. *Fr.* Not Knowing.
Not Knowing, *sel.*
BRAINE, SHEILA. Apple-Elf, The.
Mr. Scarecrow.
BRAITHWAITE, WILLIAM CHARLES. Christ Our Contemporary.
BRAITHWAITE, WILLIAM STANLEY. Arsenal of the Lord, The.
Del Cascar.
Exit. *Fr.* Sandy Star and Willie Gee.
House of Falling Leaves, The.
I Am Glad Daylong.
Ironic: LL.D.
It's a Long Way.
Laughing It Out. *Fr.* Sandy Star and Willie Gee.
October XXIX, 1795 (Keats' Birthday).
Onus Probandi. *Fr.* Sandy Star and Willie Gee.
Rhapsody.
Rye Bread.
Sandy Star. *Fr.* Sandy Star and Willie Gee.
Sandy Star and Willie Gee.
Sandy Star and Willie Gee, *sels.*
Scintilla.
Sculptured Worship. *Fr.* Sandy Star and Willie Gee.
Sea Lyric.
Sea-Prayer, A.
Sic Vita.
Song of Living, A.
Turn Me to My Yellow Leaves.
Twenty Stars to Match His Face.
Vision, The.
Watchers, The.
Way, The. *Fr.* Sandy Star and Willie Gee.
White Magic; an Ode.
BRALEY, BERTON. At Your Service; the Panama Gang.
Business Is Business.
Do It Now.
Gay Wag, The.
Habit, The.
Hero Wanted.
Heroes.
Hills, The.
Loyalty.
Notice Given.
Once You Git the Habit, *at.*
Opportunity.
Pan in Pandemonium.
Pardners.
Prayer, A: "Lord, let me live like a Regular Man."
Preference.
Song of Power, A.
Start Where You Stand.
Success!
That's Success!
Thinker, The.
To a Photographer.
BRALEY, EPHRAIM. Canaday I. O.
BRAMSTON, JAMES. Art of Politicks, The, *sel.*
Time's Changes. *Fr.* The Art of Politicks.
BRAMWICH, JOHN. Hymn: "Britannia's sons, though slaves ye be."
BRANCH, ANNA HEMPSTEAD. Babel Falls. *Fr.* Nimrod.
Before the Fair.
Connecticut Road Song.
Dream.
Ere the Golden Bowl Is Broken.
Gladness.
Grieve Not, Ladies.
Her Hands. *Fr.* Songs for My Mother.
Her Words. *Fr.* Songs for My Mother.
I Think of Him as One Who Fights.
In the Beginning Was the Word.
Inheritance.
Mathematics or the Gift of Tongues.
Monk in the Kitchen, The.
Monk in the Kitchen, The, *sel.*
My Mother's Clothes.

BRANCH, ANNA HEMPSTEAD (*continued*)
My Mother's Hands. *Fr.* Songs for My Mother.
My Mother's Words. *Fr.* Songs for My Mother.
Name, The.
Nimrod, *sels.*
Nimrod Wars with the Angels. *Fr.* Nimrod.
Poet and His Song, The.
Service.
So I May Feel the Hands of God.
Song for My Mother, A—Her Hands. *Fr.* Songs for My Mother.
Song for My Mother, A—Her Stories. *Fr.* Songs for My Mother.
Song for My Mother, A—Her Words. *Fr.* Songs for My Mother.
Songs for My Mother, *sels.*
To a Dog.
To a New York Shop-Girl Dressed for Sunday.
Two Inscriptions for the Christmas Candle.
Unbeliever, An.
Warrior Maid, The.
Watch-Tower of the Soul, The.
Where No Thoughts Are.
While Loveliness Goes By.
BRANCH, MARY LYDIA BOLLES. Petrified Fern, The.
BRANCH, M. W. Schmaltztenor.
BRANDT, SEBASTIAN. *See* BRANT, SEBASTIAN.
BRANFORD, WILLIAM. Trooper Temple Pulvermacher.
BRANIGAN, JOHANNA RACHEL. Meditation on Jesus Christ.
BRANT [*or* BRANDT], SEBASTIAN. Ballade to Our Lady. *Fr.* The Ship of Fools.
Geographers. *Fr.* The Ship of Fools.
Preachment for Preachers. *Fr.* The Ship of Fools.
Ship of Fools, The, *sels.*
Star of the Sea. *Fr.* The Ship of Fools.
Tudor Rose, The. *Fr.* The Ship of Fools.
BRASCH, CHARLES. Crossing the Straits.
Discovery, The. *Fr.* Genesis.
Estate, The, *sel.*
Genesis, *sel.*
Henley on Taieri.
I Think of Your Generation.
In Memory of Robin Hyde, 1906–39.
Nineteen Thirty-nine, *sel.*
On Mt. Iron.
Poland, October. *Fr.* Nineteen Thirty-nine.
View of Rangitoto, A.
Waking by Night. *Fr.* The Estate.
BRASIER, VIRGINIA. Generosity.
Heartbeat of Democracy.
Wind Weather.
BRATHWAITE, RICHARD. English Gentlewoman, The, *sel.*
My Mistress. *Fr.* The English Gentlewoman.
Nature's Embassy, *sel.*
Nightingale, The. *Fr.* Nature's Embassy.
Of Maids' Inconstancy. *Fr.* A Strappado for the Devil.
Strappado for the Devil, A, *sels.*
To the Precision. *Fr.* A Strappado for the Devil.
Wooer's Song, The. *Fr.* A Strappado for the Devil.
BRAVO, MARIO. Song of the General Strike.
BRAWLEY, BENJAMIN. Chaucer.
My Hero.
My Hero; to Robert Gould Shaw.
BRAYTON, TERESA. Christmas Song, A.
BRAZELTON, ETHEL M. C. Poor Lil' Brack Sheep.
BREATHNACH, MICHAEL. Man-Child.
BRECHT, BERT [*or* BERTOLT]. In Memory of Marie A.
To Posterity.
BRECK, CARRIE ELLIS. Christmas Thought, A.
They Two.
BREED, ELEANOR D. Scapegoats.
BREGG, DOROTHY. Grandma's Tea.
BRÉGY, KATHERINE MARIE CORNELIA.
April Fools.
Franciscan.
Gethsemane's Gift.
"I Thirst . . ."
Japanese Cherries.
Maid, The.
BREINING, JUNE. Inexperience.
"BREITMANN, HANS." *See* LELAND, CHARLES GODFREY.
BREMER, FREDERIKA. Home, The, *sel.*
Song of the Dove. *Fr.* The Home.
Swedish Mother's Lullaby.
BREMSER, RAY. Blood.
Poem of Holy Madness, *sel.*
BRENAN, JOSEPH. Come to Me, Dearest.
BRENNAN, CHRISTOPHER. Burden of Tyre, The, *sel.*
Fire in the Heavens [and Fire along the Hills].
Grand Cortège, The.
How Old Is My Heart?
I Said, This Misery Must End.
Let Us Go Down.
My Heart Was Wandering in the Sands.
O Desolate Eves [along the Way, How Oft].
O White Wind, Numbing the World.
Pangs That Guard the Gates of Joy, The.
Point of Noon, The.
Sweet Silence after Bells.
Wanderer, The, *sel.*
We Woke Together.
What Do I Know?
Years That Go to Make Me Man, The.
BRENNAN, EILEEN. Evening on Howth Head.
May Evening.
One Kingfisher and One Yellow Rose.
Thoughts at the Museum.
BRENNAN, GERALD. Mornin's Mornin', The.
BRENNAN, JOSEPH PAYNE. Raccoon on the Road.
BRENNAN, MARY. Moira Dhu.
BRENT, HALLY CARRINGTON. I Think I Know No Finer Things than Dogs.
BRENTANO, CLEMENS MARIA. Cradle-song.
Lord! Within Thy Peace I Rest Me.
Lore Lay.
O Woodland Cool.
Peace, Heart! No Cry!
Prelude: "What in these lines doth ripened stand."
Prelude: "Whatever ripened in these lines."
Serenade: "Harken how the flute complains."
Speak from the Distance!
Spinner's Song, The.
Springtime—a Humble Cry from the Depths.
BRERETON, ETHEL C. Three Dogs.
BRERETON, JANE. On Beau Nash's Picture, Which Once Stood between the Busts of Newton and Pope.
BRERETON, JOHN LE GAY. Buffalo Creek.
Dead, The.
Robe of Grass, The.
Waking.
BRETHERTON, C. H. In Winter.
BRETON, ANDRÉ. Always for the First Time.
Curtain Curtain.
Hotel of Sparks.
In the Lovely Half-Daylight.
Marquis de Sade, The.
My Wife with Her Wood-Fire Hair.
Rano Raraku.
Sunflower.
Tiki.
Vigilance.
BRETON, NICHOLAS. Aglaia. *Fr.* The Passionate Shepherd.
Assurance, An.
Christmas Now Is Past, The.
Come, little babe, come silly soul.
Corydon's [*or* Coridon's] Supplication to Phyllis.
Country Song.
Cradle Song, A: "Come little babe, come silly soul."
Displeasure against Love, A.
Dolefull Passion, A.
Go, Muse, unto the Bower.
Happy Countryman, The. *Fr.* The Passionate Shepherd.
His Complaint against Love and Fortune.
His Wisdom. *Fr.* The Strange Fortunes of Two Excellent Princes.
Honourable Entertainment Given to the Queen's Majesty in Progress at Elvetham, 1591, The, *sels.*
I have neither plums nor cherries.
I Would I Were an Excellent Divine.
I Would Thou Wert Not Fair. *Fr.* The Strange Fortunes of Two Excellent Princes.
Invective against the Wicked of the World, An, *sel.*
Ipsa Quae.
Merry Country Lad, The. *Fr.* The Passionate Shepherd.
News from the Heavens!
Now Christmas Draweth Near.
Odd Conceit, An.
Olden Love-making.
Passionate Shepherd, The, *sels.*
Pastoral I: "Flora hath been all about." *Fr.* The Passionate Shepherd.
Pastoral, A: "In the merry month of May." *Fr.* The Honourable Entertainment Given to the Queen's Majesty in Progress at Elvetham.
Pastoral, A: "On a hill there grows a flower."
Pastoral, A: "Sweet birds, that sit and sing amid the shady valleys."
Pastoral: "Who can live in heart so glad." *Fr.* The Passionate Shepherd.
Pastoral of Phillis and Coridon, A.
Phillida and Coridon [*or* Phyllida and Corydon] ("In the merry month of May"). *Fr.* The Honourable Entertainment Given to the Queen's Majesty in Progress at Elvetham.
Phillis the Fair.
Phyllida and Corydon ("In the merry month of May"). *Fr.* The Honourable Entertainment Given to the Queen's Majesty in Progress at Elvetham.
Phyllida and Corydon ("On a hill there grows a flower").
Phyllis ("Sweet birds that sit and sing . . .").
Plowman's [*or* Ploughman's] Song, The. *Fr.* The Honourable Entertainment Given to the Queen's Majesty in Progress at Elvetham.
Prayer for Gentlewomen and Others to Use, A.
Preamble to N[icholas] B[reton] His Garden-Plot, The.
Pretty Twinkling Starry Eyes. *Fr.* The Passionate Shepherd.
Rare News.
Report Song, A.
Say That I Should Say I Love Ye.
Shepherd and Shepherdess. *Fr.* The Passionate Shepherd.
Shepherd's Dream, A.
Solemn Conceit, A.
Sonet to the Tune of A Hone a Hone, A.
Song: "Lovely kind and kindly loving."
Song of Phillida and Coridon.
Sonnet, A: "Those eyes that hold the hand of every heart."
Soul's Harmony, The, *sels.*
Strange Description of a Rare Garden-Plot, A.
Strange Fortunes of Two Excellent Princes, The, *sels.*
Supplication, A.
Sweet birds that sit and sing amid the shady valleys.
Sweet Lullaby, A.

Sweet Pastoral, A.
Third Pastor's Song, The. *Fr.* The Passionate Shepherd.
To His Muse.
Who Can Live in Heart So Glad.
BRETÓN DE LOS HERREROS, MANUEL. Satirical Letrilla III.
Satirical Letrilla IV.
BRETTELL, N. H. Cataclysm.
Elephant.
Giraffes.
Outside Kimberley.
Wind and an Eagle Owl, *sel.*
BREWER, EBENEZER COBHAM. Little Things, *wr. at. See* CARNEY, JULIA FLETCHER.
BREWSTER, ELIZABETH. East Coast—Canada.
Egoist Dead, The.
Eviction.
River Song.
BREYFOGLE, WILLIAM A. Greece.
BRICK, NORMAN. Of Snow.
"BRIDGES, MADELINE" (Mary Ainge De Vere). Breath, A.
Faith Trembling.
Farewell, A: "I put thy hand aside."
Friend and Lover.
God Keep You.
Her Milking Pail.
Life's Mirror.
Poet and Lark.
Spinner, The.
Third Proposition, The.
When the Most Is Said.
Whole Story, The.
Why.
Wind-swept Wheat, The.
BRIDGES [*or* BRYDGES], MATTHEW. And Jesus Wept.
Crown Him with Many Crowns.
Rise, Glorious Conqueror! Rise.
BRIDGES, ROBERT. Absence.
Achilles in Scyros, *sel.*
Aeneid, The, *sel., tr.*
Affliction of Richard, The.
After the Gale.
All Beauteous Things.
All Earthly Beauty Hath One Cause. *Fr.* The Growth of Love.
Angel Spirits of Sleep.
April, 1885.
Asian Birds.
At Eventide, *tr.*
Awake, My Heart [to Be Loved].
Cheddar Pinks.
Child to the Father, The.
Clear and Gentle Stream.
Cliff-Top, The.
Clouds Have Left the Sky, The.
Come Se Quando.
Country Music, *tr.*
Dear Lady, When Thou Frownest.
Dedication: "Christ and his Mother." *Fr.* Founder's Day.
Dejection.
Demeter, *sel.*
Democritus.
Dirge: "Man born of desire." *Fr.* Ode to Music.
Downs, The.
Elegy: "Clear and gentle stream!"
Elegy: "I have lov'd flowers that fade."
Elegy: Summer House on the Mound, The.
Elegy: "Wood, The, is bare: a river-mist is steeping."
Elegy on a Lady, Whom Grief for the Death of Her Betrothed Killed.
Ερως (Eros).
Eros and Psyche, *sels., tr.*
'Ετώσιον ἄχθος ἀρούρης.
Evening.
Evening Darkens Over, The.
First Spring Morning.
Flycatchers.
For beauty being the best of all we know. *Fr.* The Growth of Love.
Fortunatus Nimium.
Founder's Day.
Founder's Day, *sels.*
Friendship. *Fr.* The Testament of Beauty.
Full Moon from Her Cloudless Skies, The.
Garden in September, The, *sel.*
Gay Robin [Is Seen No More].
Ghosts.
Gird On Thy Sword.
Growth of Love, The, *sels.*
Hector in Hades. *Fr.* The Growth of Love.
Hill Pines Were Sighing, The.
How was November's melancholy endear'd to me. *Fr.* The Testament of Beauty.
Hymn of Nature, A.
I Have Loved Flowers That Fade.
I Heard a Linnet Courting.
I Love All Beauteous Things.
I Never Shall Love the Snow Again.
I Praise the Tender Flower.
I will be what God made me, nor protest. *Fr.* The Growth of Love.
I Will Not Let Thee Go.
I would be a bird, and straight on wings I arise. *Fr.* The Growth of Love.
Ibant Obscuri; Vision of Aeneas, *tr. Fr.* The Aeneid.
Idle Flowers, The.
Idle Life I Lead, The.
Iliad, The, *sel., tr.*
Immortality, *tr.*
Indolence, *sel.*
Introduction: " 'Twas late in my long journey, when I had clomb to where." *Fr.* The Testament of Beauty.
James McCosh.
Jesus. *Fr.* The Testament of Beauty.
Johannes Milton, Senex.
Last Week of February [1890].
Laus Deo.
Linnet, The.
London Snow.
Long Are the Hours the Sun Is Above.
Low Barometer.
Matres Dolorosae.
Melancholia.
Muse and Poet.
My Delight and Thy Delight.
My Eyes for Beauty Pine.
Nightingales.
Nimium Fortunatus.
Noel: Christmas Eve, 1913.
North Wind Came Up Yesternight, The.
North Wind in October.
November.
O Love, My Muse.
O Weary Pilgrims, Chanting of Your Woe. *Fr.* The Growth of Love.
O Youth Whose Hope Is High.
Ode to Music, *sels.*
On a Dead Child.
Our Lady.
Passer-by, A.
Pater Filio.
Philosopher to His Mistress, The.
Poor Poll.
Poor Withered Rose.
Poppy Grows upon the Shore, A.
Povre Ame Amoureuse, *tr.*
Priam and Achilles, *tr. Fr.* The Iliad.
Priam's Prayer to Achilles, *tr. Fr.* The Iliad.
Psalm, The.
Riding adown the Country Lanes.
Robin, A.
Screaming Tarn.
Since to Be Loved Endures.
Sky's unresting cloudland, that with varying play, The. *Fr.* The Testament of Beauty.
Snow Lies Sprinkled on the Beach, The.
So Sweet Love Seemed That April Morn.
Song: "Since thou, O fondest and tru est."
Spirits.
Spring Goeth All in White.
Starry Heavens Without, *tr.*
Storm Is Over, The.
Testament of Beauty, The, *sels.*
Thanksgiving Day.
There Is a Hill [beside the Silver Thames].
This world is unto God a work of art. *Fr.* The Growth of Love.
Thou Didst Delight My Eyes.
To Joseph Joachim.
To L. B. C. L. M.
To the United States of America.
Triolet: "All women born are so perverse."
Triolet: "When first we met we did not guess."
'Twas at thatt hour of beauty when the setting sun. *Fr.* The Testament of Beauty.
Unillumined Verge, The.
Upon the Shore.
Upper Skies, The.
Very Names of Things Beloved, The. *Fr.* The Growth of Love.
Vision.
Voice of Nature, The.
Walking Home, *tr.*
Water-Party, The.
Weep Not To-Day.
When Death to Either Shall Come.
When First We Met.
When I see childhood on the threshold seize. *Fr.* The Growth of Love.
When June Is Come.
When my love was away.
When thou didst give thy love to me.
Windmill, The.
Winnowers, The.
Winter Nightfall.
World Comes Not to an End, The. *Fr.* The Growth of Love.
World still goeth about to show and hide, The. *Fr.* The Growth of Love.
BRIDGES, ROBERT ("Droch"). Dedication: "Long years you've kept the door ajar." *Fr.* Overheard in Arcady.
Overheard in Arcady, *sel.*
Toast to Our Native Land, A.
BRIDGET [*or* BRIGID], SAINT. Feast of Saint Brigid of Kildare, The, *at.*
Heavenly Banquet, The, *at.*
I Should Like to Have a Great Pool of Ale, *at.*
BRIDGMAN, LEWIS JESSE. On Knowing When to Stop.
BRIDSON, D. G. Man, the Metal-Worker.
Sheffield Dawn.
BRIERRE, JEAN. Harlem.
BRIGGS, C. Framework-Knitters Petition, The.
BRIGGS, CAROLINE ATHERTON. *See* MASON, CAROLINE ATHERTON BRIGGS.
BRIGGS, ERNEST. Lonely Child, The.
While Immortality Endures.
BRIGGS, GEORGE WALLACE. Knowledge through Suffering.
BRIGGS, GRETA. London under Bombardment.
BRIGGS, OLGA HAMPEL. Brief History.
BRIGHT, VERNE. Comrade Christ.
Revelation.
BRIGID, SAINT. *See* BRIDGET, SAINT.
BRINCKMAN, ROSEMARY. Fish and Bird.
BRINE, MARY DOW NORTHAM. Road to Slumberland, The.
Somebody's Mother.
BRININSTOOL, EARL ALONZO. Disappointed Tenderfoot, The.
Ol' Cow Hawse, The.
Prairie Mother's Lullaby, A.
Range Rider's Soliloquy, The.
Stampede, The.
Voyage to Lullaby Land, The.
When Papa Was a Boy.
BRINK, CAROL RYRIE. Crèche, The.
Goody O'Grumpity.
BRINKLEY, MAY. Pebbles.
BRINNIN, JOHN MALCOLM. At the Airport.
Double Crucifixion, The.
Every Earthly Creature.
Fêtes, Fates.
Islands; a Song.
Late Summer, The.
Letter, A.
Marginal Dark, The.

BRINNIN, JOHN MALCOLM (*continued*)
Nuns at Eve.
Thin Façade for Edith Sitwell, A.
Views of the Favorite Colleges.
Wind Is Ill, The.
Worm in the Whirling Cross, The.
BRISLEY, JOYCE L. Two Families, The. Which?
BRISTOL, AUGUSTA COOPER. Pyxidanthera, The.
BRISTOL, GEORGE DIGBY, 2D EARL OF. Elvira, *sel.*
Song: "See, O see!/ How every tree." *Fr.* Elvira.
BRISTOL, JOHN DIGBY, 1ST EARL OF. Grieve Not, Dear Love.
BRIUSSOV, VALERII YACOVLEVICH. *See* BRYUSOV, VALERY YAKOVLEVICH.
BRIZEUX, AUGUSTE (Julien Auguste Pélage Brizeux). Funeral of a Poor Girl, The.
BRO, MARGUERITTE HARMON. Prayer: "God, listen through my words to the beating of my heart."
BROCK, DAVID. Natural Selection.
BROCK, HENRY IRVING. Limerick: "In this book every line has been clean."
BROCKMAN, ZOE KINCAID. Carolina Herons.
Christmas Eve.
Cold Wind Blows, A.
Dream Is Not Enough, The.
Grapevine, The.
January Jasmine.
This Fear.
BROD, MAX. Goldfish on the Writing Desk.
BRODE, ANTHONY. Breakfast with Gerard Manley Hopkins.
Calypsomania.
Obituary.
Unromantic Song.
BRODIE, HUGH R. Airman's Prayer, An.
Sergeant's Prayer, A.
BRODY, ALTER. Child-King, The, *tr.*
Cry of the Peoples, The.
Harp of David, The, *tr.*
Jephthah's Daughter, *tr.*
Lamentations.
Psalm CLI: "Praise ye the Lord, O Nations!"
Russian Cradle Song, A, *tr.*
Sleep, My Child, *tr.*
BROME, ALEXANDER. Ben Jonson's Sociable Rules for the Apollo, *tr.*
I Have Been in Love and in Debt.
Love, Drink and Debt.
Love's without Reason.
Mad Lover, The.
Mock Song, A.
Now I'm Resolved to Love no More.
Pastoral on the King's Death, The.
Plain Dealing.
Resolve, The.
Riddle, The: "No more, no more."
Tell me not of a face that's fair.
Why I Love Her.
BROME, RICHARD. Bonny, bonny bird I had, A. *Fr.* The Northern Lass.
Jovial Crew, A; or, The Merry Beggars, *sels.*
Northern Lass, The, *sels.*
Round, a round, a round, boys, a round, A. *Fr.* A Jovial Crew.
Song: "Peace, wayward barne! O cease thy moan!" *Fr.* The Northern Lass.
Song of the Beggars. *Fr.* A Jovial Crew.
BROMLEY, ISAAC H. Passenjare, The.
BRONOWSKI, JACOB. Take Your Gun.
BRONTË, ANNE ("Acton Bell"). Captain's Dream, The.
Doubter's Prayer, The.
He Doeth All Things Well.
Hope, A.
If This Be All.
Lines Composed in a Wood on a Windy Day.
Prayer, A: "My God (oh, let me call Thee mine)."
BRONTË, CHARLOTTE ("Currer Bell"). Christ in Introspect.
He Saw My Heart's Woe.
Life.
On the Death of Anne Brontë.
Stanzas: "Often rebuked, yet always back returning," *at.*
Watching and Wishing.
BRONTË, EMILY ("Ellis Bell"). All Hushed and Still within the House.
And when thy heart is resting.
Appeal, The.
At Castle Wood.
Ay—There It Is.
Bluebell, The.
Child of delight, with sun-bright hair.
Come, the wind may never again.
Day Dream, A.
Death.
Death-Scene, A.
Evening Primrose, The, *wr. at.*
Evening Sun, The.
Faith and Despondency.
Fall, Leaves, Fall.
God of Visions.
Harp of Wild and Dream-like Strain.
Heaven's Glory Shone.
Her Last Lines.
How Clear She Shines!
How Long Will You Remain?
I Am the Only Being, *sel.*
I Gazed upon the Cloudless Moon.
I Gazed Within.
I Know Not How It Falls on Me.
If grief for grief can touch thee.
I'm Happiest When Most Away.
Last Lines: "No coward soul is mine."
Lines: "Come hither, child—who gifted thee."
Lines: "No coward soul is mine."
Lines: "Shall earth no more inspire thee."
Lines by Claudia.
Linnet in the rocky dells, The.
Little While, A, a Little While.
Little While, A, a Little While, *sel.*
Love and Friendship.
Morning Star, The.
My Lady's Grave.
Night Is Darkening [round me], The.
Night Wind, The.
No Coward Soul Is Mine.
Oh, for the Time When I Shall Sleep.
Often Rebuked, Yet Always Back Returning, *at.*
Old Stoic, The.
Outcast Mother, The.
Philosopher, The.
Philosopher, The, *sel.*
Plead for Me.
Prisoner, The.
Prisoner, The, *sels.*
Remembrance.
Self-Interrogation.
Shall Earth No More Inspire Thee?
Sleep Brings No Joy.
Sleep Not, Dream Not, *sel.*
Song: "Linnet in the rocky dells, The."
Speak, God of Visions.
Stanzas: "I'll not weep that thou art going to leave me."
Stanzas [*or* Stanza]: "Often rebuked, yet always back returning," *at.*
Stanzas to ——: "Well, some may hate, and some may scorn."
Still let my tyrants know, I am not doom'd to wear.
Sun Has Set, The.
Sympathy.
Tell Me, Tell Me [Smiling Child].
That Dreary Lake.
That Wind [I Used to Hear].
There Let Thy Bleeding Branch Atone.
There Was a Time.
To a Bluebell.
To Imagination.
Two Children, The.
Wanderer from the Fold, The.
Wanderer from the Fold, The, *sel.*
Warning and Reply.
Weary Task, The.
BRONTË, EMILY, *and* CHARLOTTE BRONTË. Silent Is the House.
Visionary, The.
BRONTË, PATRICK. Cottager's Hymn, The.
Odes (*of Horace*), *sel., tr.*
Time to Choose a Lover, *tr.*
To Chloe, *tr.*
BROOKE, BRIAN. Smoke of the Camp Fire.
BROOKE, CARIS. Cradle Song: "O blue eyes close in slumber."
BROOKE, FULKE GREVILLE, 1ST BARON. *See* GREVILLE, FULKE, 1ST BARON BROOKE.
BROOKE, JOCELYN. Three Barrows Down.
BROOKE, RUPERT. All This Is Ended. *Fr.* 1914.
Busy Heart, The.
Channel Passage, A.
Charm, The.
Chilterns, The.
Clouds.
Day That I Have Loved, The.
Dead, The ("Blow out, you bugles"). *Fr.* 1914.
Dead, The ("These hearts were woven"). *Fr.* 1914.
Dear, They Have Poached the Eyes You Loved So Well.
Dining-Room Tea.
Doubts.
Dust.
Fish, The.
Fishes' Heaven.
Funeral of Youth, The; Threnody.
Great Lover, The.
Great Lover, The, *sel.*
Heaven.
Hill, The.
Little Dog's Day, The.
Mary and Gabriel.
Menelaus and Helen.
Mutability.
1914.
1914, *sels.*
Now, God be thank'd Who has match'd us with His Hour. *Fr.* 1914.
Oh! Death Will Find Me Long before I Tire.
Old Vicarage, Grantchester, The.
One before the Last, The.
Peace. *Fr.* 1914.
Pine-Trees and the Sky; Evening.
Retrospect.
Safety. *Fr.* 1914.
Second Best.
Soldier, The. *Fr.* 1914.
Song: "'Oh! Love,' they said, 'is King of Kings.'"
Song of the Pilgrims, The.
Song of the Pilgrims, The, *sel.*
Sonnet: "I said I splendidly loved you; it's not true."
Sonnet: "Not with vain tears, when we're beyond the sun."
Sonnet: "Oh! Death will find me, long before I tire."
There's Wisdom in Women.
These I have loved. *Fr.* The Great Lover.
Tiare Tahiti.
Treasure, The.
Wagner.
BROOKE, STOPFORD AUGUSTUS. Christ, *sel., tr.*
Courage.
Earth and Man, The.
Elene, *sel., tr.*
Jungfrau's Cry, The.
Lines: "In the day the sun is darkened."
Moment, A.
Noble Lay of Aillinn, The.
Prince Riquet's Song. *Fr.* Riquet of the Tuft.
Queen's Song. *Fr.* Riquet of the Tuft.
Riddle: "I a weaponed warrior was," *tr.*
Riddle: "I am all alone, with the iron wounded," *tr.*
Riddle: "Who so wary and so wise," *tr.*
Riquet of the Tuft, *sels.*
Versailles.
BROOKS, CHARLES TIMOTHY. Alpine Heights, *tr.*
Fisher, The, *tr.*
Good Night, *tr.*

Great Voices, The.
Harvest Song, *tr.*
Men and Boys, *tr.*
Nobleman and the Pensioner, The, *tr.*
Our Native Land, *tr.*
Plea for Flood Ireson, A.
Sword Song, *tr.*
Winter Song, *tr.*
BROOKS, ELBRIDGE STREETER. Rodney's Ride.
BROOKS, FRANCIS. Down the Little Big Horn.
Intaglios, *sels.*
On the Plains. *Fr.* Intaglios.
Tennessee. *Fr.* Intaglios.
BROOKS, FRED EMERSON. Lullaby: "Lay thy head upon this pillow."
Three Lullabies.
BROOKS, GWENDOLYN. Andre.
Birth in a Narrow Room, The.
Cynthia in the Snow.
Eunice in the Evening.
Kitchenette Building.
Love Note II: Flags.
Mentors.
Of DeWitt Williams on His Way to Lincoln Cemetery.
Old-Marrieds, The.
Piano after War.
Rudolph Is Tired of the City.
Vern.
BROOKS, JONATHAN HENDERSON. And One Shall Live in Two.
Last Quarter Moon of the Dying Year, The.
Muse in Late November.
My Angel.
Paean.
Resurrection, The.
She Said . . .
BROOKS, LOUISE UPHAM. Crowns.
BROOKS, MARIA GOWEN ("Maria del Occidente"). Day, in Melting Purple Dying.
Disappointment. *Fr.* Zophiel; or, The Bride of Seven.
Farewell to Cuba.
Palace of the Gnomes. *Fr.* Zophiel; or, The Bride of Seven.
Respite, The. *Fr.* Zophiel; or, The Bride of Seven.
Song of Egla.
Zophiel; or, The Bride of Seven, *sels.*
BROOKS, PHILLIPS. Christmas Carol: "Earth has grown old with its burden of care, The."
Christmas Carol, A: "Everywhere, everywhere Christmas to-night!"
Christmas Everywhere.
Easter Morning.
Everywhere, Everywhere Christmas Tonight.
O Little Town of Bethlehem.
Our Burden Bearer.
Unfailing One, The.
BROOKS, SHIRLEY. Dreary Song, A.
I paints and paints.
Philosopher and Her Father, The.
Practical Answer, A.
Waggawocky.
BROOKS, WALTER ROLLIN. Ode to the Pig: His Tail.
BROOKS, WILLIAM E. At the Lincoln Memorial.
Barabbas.
Inasmuch!
Memorial Day.
Spoil.
Three Wise Kings.
BROOME, SIR FREDERICK NAPIER. Leave-taking, A.
BROOME, WILLIAM. Belinda's Recovery from Sickness.
Rose-Bud, The.
BROOMELL, MYRON HENRY. Prayer for the Age.
Varus took me to call upon his sweetheart, *tr.*
BROPHY, LIAM. Assumpta Est Maria.
Notre Dame des Petits, *tr.*
Prayer to Saint Francis for Poverty.
BROTHERTON, ALICE WILLIAMS. Blazing Heart, The.
First Thanksgiving Day, The.
My Enemy.
Ragged Regiment, The.
Thanksgiving.
BROUGH, ROBERT BARNABAS. Early Christian, An.
Marquis of Carabas, The.
Marquis of Carabas, The, *sel.*
My Lord Tomnoddy.
BROUGHTON, JAMES RICHARD. Feathers or Lead?
Fruits of Experience.
Genesis of Vowels.
Lighthouse Keeper's Offspring, The.
Mrs. Mother Has a Nose.
BROWN, ABBIE FARWELL. All Wool.
Bargain, A.
Clothes.
Fairy Book, The.
Fisherman, The.
Friends.
Grandser.
Green Crosses.
Learning to Play.
Lizard, The.
Lost Playmate, The.
Music Box, A.
Names.
Nicest Story, The.
On Opening a New Book.
Peach, The.
Pirate Treasure.
Vigil, The.
Windows.
Work.
BROWN, ALAN. Street.
BROWN, ALEX J. Wickedest Man in Memphis, The.
BROWN, ALICE. Artisan, The.
Benedictine Garden.
Candlemas.
Cloistered.
Edwin Booth.
Farewell, A: "Thou wilt not look on me?"
Forewarned.
Hora Christi.
Life.
Pagan Prayer.
Revelation. *Fr.* The Road to Castaly.
Road to Castaly, The, *sel.*
Seaward Bound.
Sleep.
Sunrise on Mansfield Mountain.
To an Enchantress.
Trilby.
West-Country Lover, A.
BROWN, ALISON. If Ever Time Shall Come.
BROWN, AUDREY ALEXANDRA. Amber Beads.
Dark Cat, The.
Diana.
Goldfish, The.
Island, The.
King Philip's Men.
Laodamia, *sels.*
Museum-Piece.
Night Boat.
Phoenix, The.
Reed, The.
"Reported Missing."
Reveillé.
Song: "What will be left when my life is over?"
Withdrawal from Crete.
BROWN, BEATRICE CURTIS. Apple Tree, The.
Jonathan Bing.
Jonathan Bing Dances for Spring.
Jonathan Bing Does Arithmetic.
Jonathan Bing's Tea.
My Kite.
BROWN, CATHERINE BERNARD. Prayer for Pentecost, A.
BROWN, EARL BIGELOW. Daily Cross.
New Crucifixion.
BROWN, FORD MADOX. For the Picture, "The Last of England."
O. M. B.
BROWN, FRANCES. Greatest Loss, The.
Hope of the Resurrection, The.
Losses.
O, the Pleasant Days of Old!
BROWN, HARRY. Drill, The.
Parade.
Poem of Bunker Hill, The, *sel.*
BROWN, HILTON. Trawlers.
BROWN, IRENE FOWLER. Rear Guard, The.
BROWN, ISAAC HINTON. On the Other Train; a Clock's Story.
BROWN, IVOR. Stratford upon Avon.
BROWN, JOHN. Night.
BROWN, JOSEPH BROWNLEE. Thalatta!
BROWN, KATE LOUISE. Apple Blossom.
Christ Candle, The.
Christmas Candle, The.
Dandelion.
Five-fingered Maple, The.
In the Heart of a Seed.
Lady Moon, The.
Little Plant, The.
Pine Music.
Pussy Willow.
Tree Buds, The.
BROWN, MABEL. Who Plants a Dogwood Tree.
BROWN, MARGARET WISE. Little Black Bug.
BROWN, OLIVER MADOX. Before and After.
Laura's Song.
BROWN, PALMER. Dappled Duck, A.
Lucinda Prattle.
Spangled Pandemonium, The.
BROWN, PHOEBE HINSDALE. I Love to Steal Awhile Away.
Private Devotion.
BROWN, ROBERT CARLTON. I Am Aladdin.
BROWN, STERLING ALLEN. After Winter.
Challenge.
Effie.
Foreclosure.
Long Gone.
Maumee Ruth.
Memphis Blues.
Odyssey of Big Boy.
Old Lem.
Remembering Nat Turner.
Return.
Salutamus.
Sister Lou.
Slim Greer.
Southern Road.
Strong Men.
To a Certain Lady, in Her Garden.
BROWN, SUSIE DAWSON. First Trousers.
BROWN, T. CLARKE. Rhode Island.
BROWN, THERON. His Majesty.
BROWN, THOMAS (Tom) (1663–1704). Doctor Fell.
Elegy on That Most Orthodox and Pains-taking Divine, Mr. Sam Smith, Ordinary of Newgate, An, *sel.*
Execution Chaplain, Mr. Sam Smith, Ordinary of Newgate, The. *Fr.* An Elegy on That Most Orthodox and Pains-taking Divine, Mr. Sam Smith, Ordinary of Newgate.
I Do Not Love Thee, Doctor Fell.
No Reason Why.
Non Amo Te.
Written While a Student at Christ Church, Oxford.
BROWN, THOMAS (1778–1820). Warning, The.
BROWN, THOMAS EDWARD. Canticle.
Carol: "Three kings from out the Orient."
Catherine Kinrade.
Chalse A. Killey.
Clifton.
Climbing.
Dhoon, The.
Disguises.
Dora.
Dreams.
Garden, A.
I Bended unto Me.
In Memoriam.
In the Coach, *sel.*
Indwelling.
Intercepted Salute, The.
Jessie.
Juventa Perennis.

BROWN, THOMAS EDWARD (*continued*)
My Garden.
Norton Wood (Dora's Birthday).
O God to Thee I Yield.
Opifex.
Organist in Heaven, The.
Oxford Idyll, An.
Pazons, The. *Fr.* In the Coach.
Peggy's Wedding.
Per Omnia Deus.
ποιημάτιον (Poiemation).
Praesto.
Preparation.
Risus Dei.
Sad! Sad!
St. Bee's Head.
Salve!
Schooner, The.
Specula.
To E. M. O.
To K. H.
Vespers.
Voices of Nature, The.
When Love Meets Love.
BROWN, TOM (1663–1704). *See* BROWN, THOMAS.
"BROWN, VANDYKE" (Marc Eugene Cook). Growing Old.
BROWN, WILLIAM ADAMS. Prayer for Peace, A.
BROWN, WILLIAM GOLDSMITH. Cleveland.
Hills Were Made for Freedom, The.
Hundred Years to Come, A, *at.*
Mother, Home, Heaven.
Ne'er Shall I Forget.
BROWN, WILLIAM HILL. Lion and the Terrapin, The.
BROWN, WILLIAM LAIRD. *See* "LAIRD, WILLIAM."
BROWNE, CECIL. Reply, A.
BROWNE, CHARLES FARRAR. *See* "WARD, ARTEMUS."
BROWNE, FELICIA DOROTHEA. *See* HEMANS, FELICIA DOROTHEA.
BROWNE, FRANCIS FISHER. Santa Barbara.
Under the Blue.
Vanquished.
BROWNE, IRVING. At Shakespeare's Grave.
Man's Pillow.
My New World.
BROWNE, ISAAC HAWKINS. Fire Side, The; a Pastoral Soliloquy. *Fr.* The Foundling Hospital for Wit.
Foundling Hospital for Wit, The, *sel.*
In Imitation of Pope. *Fr.* A Pipe of Tobacco.
In Imitation of Young. *Fr.* A Pipe of Tobacco.
Pipe of Tobacco, A, *sels.*
"BROWNE, MATTHEW." *See* RANDS, WILLIAM BRIGHTY.
BROWNE, MOSES. Nocturnal Eclogue, The, *sel.*
BROWNE, REX. Exile.
BROWNE, RIVERS, *and* LEONARD BACON. *See* BACON, LEONARD, *and* RIVERS BROWNE.
BROWNE, SIR THOMAS. Colloquy with God, A. *Fr.* Religio Medici.
Evening Hymn. *Fr.* Religio Medici.
Religio Medici, *sel.*
BROWNE, WILLIAM. As Careful Merchants. *Fr.* Britannia's Pastorals.
Britannia's Pastorals, *sels.*
Caelia, *sel.*
Celadyne's Song. *Fr.* Britannia's Pastorals.
Celia Is Gone.
Complete Lover, The.
Dawn of Day. *Fr.* The Shepherd's Pipe.
Down in a Valley [by a Forest's Side]. *Fr.* Visions.
Epitaph: "May, be thou never graced with birds that sing."
Epitaph on the Countess Dowager of Pembroke.
Frolic Mariners of Devon, The. *Fr.* Britannia's Pastorals.
Gentle Nymphs, Be Not Refusing. *Fr.* Britannia's Pastorals.
Glide Soft, Ye Silver Floods. *Fr.* Britannia's Pastorals.
Hail, Thou My Native Soil. *Fr.* Britannia's Pastorals.
I oft have heard men say there be.
In Obitum M.S., X Maii, 1614.
Inner Temple Masque, The, *sels.*
Love Who Will [for I'll Love None].
Memory ("Marina's gone, and now sit I"). *Fr.* Britannia's Pastorals.
Memory ("So shuts the marigold her leaves"). *Fr.* Britannia's Pastorals.
My Choice. *Fr.* Britannia's Pastorals.
Near to this wood there lay a pleasant mead. *Fr.* Britannia's Pastorals.
Night.
Now was the Lord and Lady of the May. *Fr.* Britannia's Pastorals.
Ode, An: "Awake fair Muse for I intend."
On the Countess Dowager of Pembroke.
On the Death of Marie, Countess of Pembroke.
Praise of Poets. *Fr.* Britannia's Pastorals.
Praise of Spenser. *Fr.* Britannia's Pastorals.
Round, A: "Now that the spring hath filled our veins."
Round, A: "Shear sheep that have them, cry we still."
Shall I Love Again.
Shall I Tell You Whom I Love? *Fr.* Britannia's Pastorals.
Shepherd's Moan, A. *Fr.* Britannia's Pastorals.
Shepherd's Pipe, The, *sels.*
Since She Is Gone. *Fr.* Britannia's Pastorals.
Sirens' [*or* Siren] Song, The. *Fr.* The Inner Temple Masque.
So Shuts the Marigold Her Leaves. *Fr.* Britannia's Pastorals.
Son of Erebus and Night. *Fr.* The Inner Temple Masque.
Song: "For her gait, if she be walking."
Song: "Love, that looks still on your eyes."
Song: "Shall I tell you whom I love?" *Fr.* Britannia's Pastorals.
Song of the Sirens [*or* Syrens]. *Fr.* The Inner Temple Masque.
Sonnet: "Down in a valley, by a forest's side." *Fr.* Visions.
Sonnet: "Fairest, when by the rules of palmistry." *Fr.* Caelia.
Sonnet: "For her gait if she be walking."
Sonnet to Caelia.
Spring Morning.
"Steer hither, steer your wingèd pines." *Fr.* The Inner Temple Masque.
Thyrsis' Praise of His Mistress.
Time never can produce men to o'ertake. *Fr.* Britannia's Pastorals.
Underneath this sable hearse.
Venus and Adonis. *Fr.* Britannia's Pastorals.
Venus by Adonis' side. *Fr.* Britannia's Pastorals.
Vision, A.
Visions, *sels.*
Welcome, A.
Welcome, Welcome, Do I Sing.
What Wight He Loved. *Fr.* Britannia's Pastorals.
Ye hours, then, but as minutes be.
BROWNE, SIR WILLIAM. Epigram: "King to Oxford sent a troop of horse, The."
Oxford & Cambridge.
BROWNELL, AMANDA BENJAMIN HALL. *See* HALL, AMANDA BENJAMIN.
BROWNELL, FLORENCE KERR. Coin in the Fist.
BROWNELL, HENRY HOWARD. Abraham Lincoln.
Battle of Charlestown, The.
Bay Fight, The.
Burial of the Dane, The.
Bury Them.
Eagle of Corinth, The.
Lawyer's Invocation to Spring, The.
Night Quarters.
Old Cove, The.
River Fight, The.
River Fight, The, *sel.*
Sphinx, The.
Sumter.
BROWNING, ELIZABETH BARRETT. Accuse me not, beseech thee, that I wear. *Fr.* Sonnets from the Portuguese.
Ad Finem, *tr.*
And wilt thou have me fashion into speech. *Fr.* Sonnets from the Portuguese.
And yet, because thou overcomest so. *Fr.* Sonnets from the Portuguese.
Aurora Leigh, *sels.*
Aurora Leigh Discovers Books. *Fr.* Aurora Leigh.
Because thou hast the power and own'st the grace. *Fr.* Sonnets from the Portuguese.
Belovèd. *Fr.* Sonnets from the Portuguese.
Belovèd, my Belovèd, when I think. *Fr.* Sonnets from the Portuguese.
Belovèd, thou hast brought me many flowers. *Fr.* Sonnets from the Portuguese.
Best, The.
Bianca among the Nightingales.
Books. *Fr.* Aurora Leigh.
But only three in all God's universe. *Fr.* Sonnets from the Portuguese.
By Solitary Fires. *Fr.* Aurora Leigh.
Can it be right to give what I can give? *Fr.* Sonnets from the Portuguese.
Cares, *at.*
Casa Guidi Windows, *sels.*
Catarina to Camoens, *sel.*
Cheerfulness Taught by Reason.
Child's Thought of God, A.
Comfort.
Confessions.
Consolation.
Content.
Convinced by Sorrow. *Fr.* The Cry of the Human.
Court Lady, A.
Cowper's Grave.
Cry of the Children, The.
Cry of the Human, The.
Cry of the Human, The, *sel.*
Curse, The. *Fr.* A Curse for a Nation.
Curse for a Nation, A.
Curse for a Nation, A, *sels.*
Cyclops, The, *tr.*
De Profundis, *sel.*
Dead Pan, The.
Dead Rose, A.
Denial, A.
Deserted Garden, The.
Desire, A. *Fr.* Sonnets to George Sand.
Drama of Exile, A, *sels.*
Duty, *at.*
England. *Fr.* Aurora Leigh.
Face of all the world is changed, I think, The. *Fr.* Sonnets from the Portuguese.
False Step, A.
Farewells from Paradise.
Ferment of New Wine, The. *Fr.* Aurora Leigh.
First time he kissed me, he but only kissed. *Fr.* Sonnets from the Portuguese.
First time that the sun rose on thine oath, The. *Fr.* Sonnets from the Portuguese.
For Love's Sake Only.
Forced Recruit, The.
Gift, The. *Fr.* Sonnets from the Portuguese.
Glory in the Commonplace. *Fr.* Aurora Leigh.
Go from me. Yet I feel that I shall stand. *Fr.* Sonnets from the Portuguese.
"Good from a Book." *Fr.* Aurora Leigh.

Grief.

Heavy heart, Belovèd, have I borne, A. *Fr.* Sonnets from the Portuguese.

Hiram Powers's Greek Slave.

Holy Night, The.

How do I love thee? Let me count the ways. *Fr.* Sonnets from the Portuguese.

Hymn: "Since without Thee we do no good."

I lift my heavy heart up solemnly. *Fr.* Sonnets from the Portuguese.

I lived with visions for my company. *Fr.* Sonnets from the Portuguese.

I mourn for Adonis—Adonis is dead, *tr.*

I never gave a lock of hair away. *Fr.* Sonnets from the Portuguese.

I thank all who have loved me in their hearts. *Fr.* Sonnets from the Portuguese.

I thought once how Theocritus had sung. *Fr.* Sonnets from the Portuguese.

If I leave all for thee, wilt thou exchange. *Fr.* Sonnets from the Portuguese.

If thou must love me, let it be for nought [*or* naught]. *Fr.* Sonnets from the Portuguese.

In the Fields, *at.*

Inclusions.

Indeed this very love which is my boast. *Fr.* Sonnets from the Portuguese.

Insufficiency.

Irreparableness.

Is it indeed so? If I lay here dead. *Fr.* Sonnets from the Portuguese.

Juliet of Nations. *Fr.* Casa Guidi Windows.

Keep my riband, take and keep it. *Fr.* Catarina to Camoens.

Lady Geraldine's Courtship.

Lady's "Yes," The.

Lament for Adonis, *tr.*

Lessons from the Gorse.

Life and Love.

Little Mattie.

Live and Love. *Fr.* The Drama of Exile.

Look, The.

Lord Turned, and Looked upon Peter, The.

Lord Walter's Wife.

Lost Bower, The.

Love. *Fr.* Sonnets from the Portuguese.

Man. *Fr.* Aurora Leigh.

Man's Requirements, A.

Mask, The.

Meaning of the Look, The.

Mediator, The.

Mein Kind, wir waren Kinder, *tr.*

Mother and Poet.

Motherless. *Fr.* Aurora Leigh.

Mother's Prayer, The.

Mourning Mother, The.

Musical Instrument, A.

My Doves.

My future will not copy fair my past. *Fr.* Sonnets from the Portuguese.

My Heart and I.

My Kate.

My letters all dead paper, mute and white! *Fr.* Sonnets from the Portuguese.

My own belovèd, who has lifted me. *Fr.* Sonnets from the Portuguese.

My poet, thou canst touch on all the notes. *Fr.* Sonnets from the Portuguese.

Mystery.

Nevermore Alone. *Fr.* Sonnets from the Portuguese.

North and the South, The.

Nothing Small.

On a Portrait of Wordsworth.

Our Lady of the Passion, *tr.*

Out in the Fields with God, *at.*

Paris. *Fr.* Aurora Leigh.

Parting Lovers.

Patience Taught by Nature.

Pet Name, The.

Poet, The.

Poet and the Bird, The.

Poets, The. *Fr.* Aurora Leigh.

Poets, The. *Fr.* Lady Geraldine's Courtship.

Poet's Vow, The, *sel.*

Portrait, A.

Praise of Earth.

Proem: "Out of my own great woe," *tr.*

Prologue: "I heard an angel speak last night." *Fr.* A Curse for a Nation.

Prometheus Bound, *tr.*

Prometheus Bound, *sel., tr.*

Question and Answer.

Reading. *Fr.* Aurora Leigh.

Recognition, A. *Fr.* Sonnets to George Sand.

Reward of Service, *at.*

Rhyme of the Duchess May, *sels.*

Romance of the Swan's Nest, The.

Romney and Aurora. *Fr.* Aurora Leigh.

Rosalind's Scroll. *Fr.* The Poet's Vow.

Round Our Restlessness. *Fr.* Rhyme of the Duchess May.

Runaway Slave at Pilgrim's Point, The.

Say over again, and yet once over again. *Fr.* Sonnets from the Portuguese.

Sleep, The.

Sleep, The, *sel.*

Sleeping and Watching.

Sonnet: "Accuse me not, beseech thee, that I wear." *Fr.* Sonnets from the Portuguese.

Sonnet: "And wilt thou have me fashion into speech." *Fr.* Sonnets from the Portuguese.

Sonnet: "Belovèd, my Belovèd, when I think." *Fr.* Sonnets from the Portuguese.

Sonnet: "Belovèd, thou hast brought me many flowers." *Fr.* Sonnets from the Portuguese.

Sonnet: "Face of all the world is changed, I think, The." *Fr.* Sonnets from the Portuguese.

Sonnet: "First time he kissed me, he but only kissed." *Fr.* Sonnets from the Portuguese.

Sonnet: "Go from me. Yet I feel that I shall stand." *Fr.* Sonnets from the Portuguese.

Sonnet: "How do I love thee? Let me count the ways." *Fr.* Sonnets from the Portuguese.

Sonnet: "I lived with visions for my company." *Fr.* Sonnets from the Portuguese.

Sonnet: "I thank all who have loved me in their hearts." *Fr.* Sonnets from the Portuguese.

Sonnet: "I thought once how Theocritus had sung." *Fr.* Sonnets from the Portuguese.

Sonnet: "If thou must love me, let it be for nought." *Fr.* Sonnets from the Portuguese.

Sonnet: "My letters all dead paper, mute and white!" *Fr.* Sonnets from the Portuguese.

Sonnet: "Say over again, and yet once over again." *Fr.* Sonnets from the Portuguese.

Sonnet: "Unlike are we, unlike, O princely Heart!" *Fr.* Sonnets from the Portuguese.

Sonnet: "When our two souls stand up erect and strong." *Fr.* Sonnets from the Portuguese.

Sonnet: "Yet, love, mere love, is beautiful indeed." *Fr.* Sonnets from the Portuguese.

Sonnets from the Portuguese.

Sonnets from the Portuguese, *sels.*

Sonnets to George Sand, *sels.*

Soul's Rialto hath its merchandise, The. *Fr.* Sonnets from the Portuguese.

Substitution.

Sursum Corda. *Fr.* Casa Guidi Windows.

Swan's Nest among the Reeds, The.

Sweetest Lives, The, *at.*

Sweetness of England, The. *Fr.* Aurora Leigh.

Tears.

Thou comest! all is said without a word. *Fr.* Sonnets from the Portuguese.

Thou hast thy calling to some palace floor. *Fr.* Sonnets from the Portuguese.

Thought for a Lonely Death-Bed, A.

To Flush, My Dog.

To George Sand; a Recognition. *Fr.* Sonnets to George Sand.

To Sleep.

Traveling South toward Italy. *Fr.* Aurora Leigh.

Two Sayings, The.

Unlike are we, unlike, O princely Heart! *Fr.* Sonnets from the Portuguese.

Valediction, A.

View across the Roman Campagna, A.

Virgin Mary to the Child Jesus, The.

Vision of Poets, A, *sel.*

Wail of Prometheus Bound, The, *tr.*

Ways of Love. *Fr.* Sonnets from the Portuguese.

Weakest Thing, The.

What can I give thee back. *Fr.* Sonnets from the Portuguese.

When our two souls stand up erect and strong. *Fr.* Sonnets from the Portuguese.

When we met first and loved, I did not build. *Fr.* Sonnets from the Portuguese.

"Where There Is No Vision." *Fr.* Aurora Leigh.

Wine of Cyprus, *sel.*

Woman's Shortcomings, A.

Work.

Yet, love, mere love, is beautiful indeed. *Fr.* Sonnets from the Portuguese.

BROWNING, OPHELIA GUYON (Ophelia Guyon Browning Burroughs). Pray without Ceasing.

Sometime, Somewhere.

BROWNING, ROBERT. Abt Vogler.

Abt Vogler, *sels.*

Adam, Lilith, and Eve.

After.

Ah, Love, but a Day. *Fr.* James Lee's Wife.

Alcestis, *sels., tr.*

All-loving, The. *Fr.* An Epistle Containing the Strange Medical Experience of Karshish, the Arab Physician.

All service ranks the same with God. *Fr.* Pippa Passes.

Along the Beach. *Fr.* James Lee's Wife.

Among the Rocks. *Fr.* James Lee's Wife.

Amphibian.

Ancient Doctrine, The. *Fr.* James Lee's Wife.

And What Sordello Would See There. *Fr.* Sordello.

Andrea del Sarto.

Andromeda. *Fr.* Pauline.

Another Way of Love.

Any Wife to Any Husband.

Apparent Failure.

Apparent Failure, *sel.*

Apparitions. *Fr.* The Two Poets of Croisic.

Appearances.

April in England.

Artemis Prologizes.

Ask Not One Least Word of Praise. *Fr.* Ferishtah's Fancies.

Asolando, *sels.*

At Ecelin. *Fr.* Sordello.

At the Mermaid, *sel.*

Avenger Speaks, The.

Awakening of Man, The. *Fr.* Paracelsus.

Bad Dreams.

Balaustion's Adventure, *sel.*

Before, *sel.*

Ben Karshook's Wisdom.

BROWNING, ROBERT (*continued*)
Bishop Blougram's Apology.
Bishop Blougram's Apology, *sels.*
Bishop Orders His Tomb at Saint Praxed's Church, The.
Blot in the 'Scutcheon, A, *sels.*
Boot and Saddle. *Fr.* Cavalier Tunes.
Boy and the Angel, The.
By the Fireside.
By the Fireside, *sel.*
Caliban upon Setebos.
Cardinal and the Dog, The.
Cavalier Tunes.
Cavalier Tunes, *sels.*
"Childe Roland to the Dark Tower Came."
"Childe Roland to the Dark Tower Came," *sel.*
Christmas-Eve and Easter-Day, *sels.*
Cleon.
Cleon, *sel.*
Common Problem, The. *Fr.* Bishop Blougram's Apology.
Confessional, The.
Confessions.
Count Gismond.
Cristina.
Cristina, *sel.*
David Sings to Saul. *Fr.* Saul.
Day. *Fr.* Pippa Passes.
Day! Faster and more fast. *Fr.* Pippa Passes.
"De Gustibus."
"De Gustibus," *sel.*
Deaf and Dumb.
Death in the Desert, A.
Death in the Desert, A, *sels.*
Death the Enemy, *tr.* *Fr.* Alcestis.
Dedication: "O lyric love, half angel and half bird." *Fr.* The Ring and the Book.
Dedication to "The Ring and the Book," *sel.*
Development.
Development of Man, The. *Fr.* Paracelsus.
Dis Aliter Visum; or, Le Byron de Nos Jours.
Dramatic Idyls, *sel.*
Dramatis Personae, *sel.*
Dubiety.
Earl Mertoun's Song. *Fr.* A Blot in the 'Scutcheon.
Earth's Immortalities.
Echetlos.
Englishman in Italy, The.
Epilogue: "At the midnight in the silence of the sleep-time." *Fr.* Asolando.
Epilogue: "Oh, Love—no, Love! All the noise below, Love." *Fr.* Ferishtah's Fancies.
Epilogue: "On the first of the Feast of Feasts."
Epilogue: "Savage I was sitting in my house." *Fr.* Fifine at the Fair.
Epilogue: "What a pretty tale you told me." *Fr.* The Two Poets of Croisic.
Epilogue to "Dramatic Idyls."
Epilogue to "Dramatis Personae."
Epilogue to the Pacchiarotto Volume.
Epistle, An, Containing the Strange Medical Experience of Karshish, the Arab Physician.
Epistle, An, Containing the Strange Medical Experience of Karshish, the Arab Physician, *sels.*
Epitaph: "Thou whom these eyes saw never."
Escape Me?—Never.
Eurydice to Orpheus.
Evelyn Hope.
Face, A.
Faith. *Fr.* A Soul's Tragedy.
Fame. *Fr.* Earth's Immortalities.
Fears and Scruples.
Ferishtah's Fancies, *sels.*
Fifine at the Fair, *sels.*
Fire Is in the Flint. *Fr.* Ferishtah's Fancies.
Flight of the Duchess, The.
Flight of the Duchess, The, *sels.*
Flower's Name, The. *Fr.* Garden Fancies.
Forgiveness, A, *sel.*
Fra Lippo Lippi.
From the Pope's Speech. *Fr.* The Ring and the Book.
Garden Fancies.
Garden Fancies, *sels.*
Giuseppe Caponsacchi. *Fr.* The Ring and the Book.
Give a Rouse. *Fr.* Cavalier Tunes.
Give her but the least excuse to love me. *Fr.* Pippa Passes.
Glove, The.
God with Us. *Fr.* Saul.
Good Morning. *Fr.* Pippa Passes.
Grammarian's Funeral, A.
Greatest Tribute, The, *tr.*
Greece. *Fr.* Cleon.
Grow old along with me! *Fr.* Rabbi Ben Ezra.
Guardian-Angel, The.
Guidance. *Fr.* Paracelsus.
Guido. *Fr.* The Ring and the Book.
Gypsies. *Fr.* The Flight of the Duchess.
Heap Cassia, Sandal-Buds and Stripes. *Fr.* Paracelsus.
Hercules, *sel.*, *tr.*
Here's the garden she walked across. *Fr.* Garden Fancies.
Here's to Nelson's memory! *Fr.* Nationality in Drinks.
Heretic's Tragedy, The.
Hervé Riel.
Holy-Cross Day.
Home Thoughts from Abroad.
Home Thoughts from Abroad, *sels.*
Home Thoughts from the Sea.
Hospitality, *tr.* *Fr.* Alcestis.
House.
Householder, The. *Fr.* Fifine at the Fair.
How a Poet's Soul Comes into Play. *Fr.* Sordello.
How It Strikes a Contemporary.
How They Brought the Good News from Ghent to Aix.
Humility.
I Go to Prove My Soul. *Fr.* Paracelsus.
Illimitable God, The. *Fr.* A Death in the Desert.
In a Balcony.
In a Gondola.
In a Gondola, *sel.*
In a Year.
In Doubt of Doubt. *Fr.* Bishop Blougram's Apology.
In His Good Time. *Fr.* Paracelsus.
In Three Days.
Incident of the French Camp.
Instans Tyrannus.
Italian in England, The.
It's wiser being good than bad. *Fr.* Apparent Failure.
James Lee's Wife.
James Lee's Wife, *sels.*
Johannes Agricola in Meditation.
Joy of Living, The. *Fr.* Saul.
Karshish and Lazarus. *Fr.* An Epistle Containing the Strange Medical Experience of Karshish, the Arab Physician.
Karshish, the Arab Physician.
King Is Cold, The.
King lived long ago, A. *Fr.* Pippa Passes.
La Saisiaz, *sel.*
Laboratory, The; Ancien Régime.
Last Ride Together, The.
Life. *Fr.* Christmas-Eve and Easter-Day.
Life in a Love.
Light Woman, A.
Likeness, A.
Lost Leader, The.
Lost, Lost! Yet Come. *Fr.* Paracelsus.
Lost Mistress, The.
Love. *Fr.* Earth's Immortalities.
Love among the Ruins.
Love among the Ruins, *sel.*
Love in a Life.
Lovers' Quarrel, A.
Lyric Love. *Fr.* The Ring and the Book.
Magical Nature.
Man I Am and Man Would Be. *Fr.* Ferishtah's Fancies.
Man's Destiny. *Fr.* Paracelsus.
Marching Along. *Fr.* Cavalier Tunes.
May and Death.
Meeting at Night.
Memorabilia.
Misconceptions.
Mr. Sludge, "The Medium," *sel.*
Moth's Kiss, First, The. *Fr.* In a Gondola.
Muckle-Mouth Meg.
Music. *Fr.* Abt Vogler.
My Last Duchess.
My Lode-Star. *Fr.* Pauline.
My Star.
My Sun Sets to Rise Again. *Fr.* At the Mermaid.
Names, The.
Nationality in Drinks, *sel.*
Natural Magic.
Nay but you, who do not love her.
Ned Bratts.
Never the Time and the Place.
New Year's Hymn. *Fr.* Pippa Passes.
North Country, The. *Fr.* The Flight of the Duchess.
Now.
O good gigantic smile o' the brown old earth. *Fr.* James Lee's Wife.
O Lyric Love. *Fr.* The Ring and the Book.
Oft Have I stood by Thee. *Fr.* Pauline.
Old Pictures in Florence.
Old Pictures in Florence, *sels.*
On Deck. *Fr.* James Lee's Wife.
One Way of Love.
One Who Never Turned His Back. *Fr.* Epilogue to "Asolando."
One Word More.
One Word More, *sel.*
Ottima and Sebald, Two Lovers. *Fr.* Pippa Passes.
Our Known Unknown. *Fr.* The Ring and the Book.
Our Wars Are Wars of Life. *Fr.* Before.
Ours is a great wild country. *Fr.* The Flight of the Duchess.
Over the sea our galleys went. *Fr.* Paracelsus.
Pambo.
Paracelsus, *sels.*
Paracelsus Attains. *Fr.* Paracelsus.
Parleyings with Certain People of Importance in Their Day, *sels.*
Parting at Morning.
Patriot, The.
Pauline, *sels.*
Pearl, a Girl, A.
Phases of the Moon. *Fr.* One Word More.
Pheidippides.
Pictor Ignotus.
Pied Piper of Hamelin, The.
Pied Piper of Hamelin, The, *sel.*
Pippa. *Fr.* Pippa Passes.
Pippa Passes.
Pippa Passes, *sels.*
Pippa's Song. *Fr.* Pippa Passes.
Pisgah-Sights.
Poetics.
Pompilia. *Fr.* The Ring and the Book.
Pope, The. *Fr.* The Ring and the Book.
Pope and the Net, The.
Popularity.
Porphyria's Lover.
Progress is the law. *Fr.* Paracelsus.
Prologue: "Fancy I had to-day, The." *Fr.* Fifine at the Fair.
Prologue: "Poet's age is sad, The: for why?" *Fr.* Asolando.
Prologue: "Such a starved bank of moss." *Fr.* The Two Poets of Croisic.
Prologue to "Asolando."
Prologue to "La Saisiaz."

Prologue to "The Two Poets of Croisic."
Prospice.
Rabbi Ben Ezra.
Rabbi Ben Ezra, *sels.*
Religion. *Fr.* Mr. Sludge, "The Medium."
Rephan.
Respectability.
Rest Remaineth. *Fr.* Christmas-Eve and Easter-Day.
Ring and the Book, The, *sels.*
Rosny.
Round us the wild creatures, overhead the trees. *Fr.* Ferishtah's Fancies.
Rudel to the Lady of Tripoli.
Saul.
Saul, *sels.*
Scene in a Garden. *Fr.* Paracelsus.
Serenade at the Villa, A.
Service. *Fr.* Pippa Passes.
Shelley. *Fr.* Pauline.
Shop.
Sibrandus Schafnaburgensis. *Fr.* Garden Fancies.
So Sweet Love Seemed.
Soldier Relieved, The.
Soliloquy of the Spanish Cloister.
Something to Remember.
Song: "All service ranks the same with God." *Fr.* Pippa Passes.
Song: "Give her but a least excuse to love me!" *Fr.* Pippa Passes.
Song: "Heap cassia, sandal-buds and stripes." *Fr.* Paracelsus.
Song: "Lost, lost! yet come." *Fr.* Paracelsus.
Song: "Moth's kiss, first, The." *Fr.* In a Gondola.
Song: "Nay, but you, who do not love her."
Song: "Over the sea our galleys went." *Fr.* Paracelsus.
Song: "Thus the Mayne glideth." *Fr.* Paracelsus.
Song: "Year's at the spring, The." *Fr.* Pippa Passes.
Song: "You'll love me yet!—and I can tarry." *Fr.* Pippa Passes.
Song from "In a Gondola."
Song from "Paracelsus."
Song from "Pippa Passes."
Sordello, *sels.*
Sordello's Birth-Place. *Fr.* Sordello.
Speculative.
Spring Song. *Fr.* Pippa Passes.
Statue and the Bust, The.
Such a Starved Bank of Moss. *Fr.* The Two Poets of Croisic.
Summum Bonum.
Sunrise. *Fr.* Pippa Passes.
That One Face. *Fr.* Epilogue to "Dramatis Personae."
Then I tuned my harp. *Fr.* Saul.
Then the truth came upon me. *Fr.* Saul.
"There's a blessing on the hearth." *Fr.* The Ring and the Book.
There's a Woman like a Dewdrop. *Fr.* A Blot in the 'Scutcheon.
Through the Metidja to Abd-el-Kadr.
Thus the Mayne Glideth. *Fr.* Paracelsus.
Time's Revenges.
Toccata of Galuppi's, A.
Too Late.
Transcendentalism; a Poem in Twelve Books.
Tray.
Truth. *Fr.* A Death in the Desert.
Truth Is Within. *Fr.* Paracelsus.
Two in the Campagna.
Two Poets of Croisic, The, *sels.*
Up at a Villa—Down in the City.
Vault inside the Castle at Goito, A. *Fr.* Sordello.
Verse-making was least of my virtues. *Fr.* Ferishtah's Fancies.
Wanderers, The. *Fr.* Paracelsus.
Wanting Is—What?
Waring.
Water and Air. *Fr.* Pauline.
When a Man's Busy.
"Why from the world," Ferishtah smiled, "should thanks." *Fr.* Ferishtah's Fancies.
Why I Am a Liberal.
Wild Joys of Living, The. *Fr.* Saul.
Wise Thrush, The. *Fr.* Home Thoughts from Abroad.
Wish no word unspoken, want no look away! *Fr.* Ferishtah's Fancies.
With Christopher Smart. *Fr.* Parleyings with Certain People of Importance in Their Day.
Woman's Last Word, A.
Women and Roses.
Year's at the Spring, The. *Fr.* Pippa Passes.
You'll Love Me Yet! *Fr.* Pippa Passes.
Youth. *Fr.* Saul.
Youth and Age. *Fr.* Rabbi Ben Ezra.
Youth and Art.
BROWNJOHN, ALAN. Respects.
BROWNSON, WILLIAM GREEN. Consultation, The. *Fr.* The Country Doctor.
Country Doctor, The, *sel.*
Getting Gray.
BRUCE, AUBERT EDGAR. Contrast.
BRUCE, CHARLES. Alternative.
Attic, The. *Fr.* The Flowing Summer.
Back Road Farm.
Biography.
Dreaming Trout, The. *Fr.* The Flowing Summer.
Eastern Shore.
Fisherman's Son.
Flowing Summer, The, *sels.*
Hayfield, The. *Fr.* The Flowing Summer.
Immediates.
Steelyards, The.
Words Are Never Enough.
BRUCE, GEORGE. Kinnaird Head.
BRUCE, MICHAEL. Elegy: In Spring, *sel.*
Ode to the Cuckoo.
To the Cuckoo.
BRUCE, RICHARD. Cavalier.
Shadow.
BRUCE, WALLACE. Decoration Day.
Memorial Day.
Our Nation Forever.
Parson Allen's Ride.
Two Argosies.
BRUNER, MARGARET E. Angry Word, An.
Atonement.
Beggar, The.
Beyond the Grave.
Casual Meeting.
Christmas Eve Meditation.
Clown, The.
Cruelty.
Dog's Vigil, A.
Dreaded Task, The.
Elegy: "We knew that he was not a model cat."
Epitaph for a Cat.
Faithful Friend, The.
For One Lately Bereft.
For One Who Is Serene.
Gift, The.
God's Ways Are Strange.
Good-by.
Greater Gift, The.
Grocery Store Cat, The.
Hobo's Dog, The.
If Lincoln Should Return.
Lonely Dog, The.
Midwinter.
Monk and the Peasant, The.
Old Cat Meditates, An.
On City Streets.
Plea for Tolerance.
Prayer for Strength.
Rebirth.
Remembrance.
Retaliation.
Selfishness.
Sinner, The.
Something Sorto' Healing.
Sonnet: "There have been many cats I loved and lost."
Souvenirs.
There Is a Loneliness.
Time's Hand Is Kind.
Understanding.
Way of a Cat, The.
Wedding Anniversary.
BRUNINI, JOHN GILLAND. Assumption, The.
Descent of the Holy Ghost.
For a Young Idealist: "Godspeed!"
Repeated Pilgrimage.
Resurrection, The.
Silent Sufferer.
To Mary at Christmas.
BRUNO, ERIC. Libera Nos a Malo.
BRUNO, GIORDANO. Philosophic Flight, The.
Sonnet: Philosophic Flight, The.
Spurning the Earth.
BRUNS, JOHN DICKSON. Foe at the Gates, The.
BRYAN, CLAUDE. Indian Lullaby, An.
BRYAN, ELIZABETH MABEL. Father of the Man.
BRYAN, GEORGE SANDS. Modern Lochinvar, A.
BRYANT, JOHN H. At the Lincoln Tomb.
BRYANT, JOHN HOWARD. Indian Summer, The.
Little Cloud, The.
Valley Brook, The.
Winter.
BRYANT, M. ALICE. George Washington, *at.*
BRYANT, WILLIAM CULLEN. Abraham Lincoln.
African Chief, The.
Alexis Calls Me Cruel, *tr.*
Antiquity of Freedom, The.
Antiquity of Freedom, The, *sel.*
Autumn Woods.
Battlefield, The.
Battlefield, The, *sels.*
Be Ye Also Ready. *Fr.* Thanatopsis.
Caterpillar and the Butterfly, The, *tr.*
Centennial Hymn.
Christmas.
Conjunction of Jupiter and Venus, The.
Conqueror's Grave, The.
Dante.
Death of Lincoln, The.
Death of Schiller, The.
Death of Slavery, The.
Death of the Flowers, The.
Dedication: "Thou, whose unmeasured temple stands."
Earth.
Embargo, The, *sel.*
Evening Revery, An.
Evening Wind, The.
Farewell to My Mother, *tr.*
Fatima and Raduan, *tr.*
Flood of Years, The.
Forest Hymn, A.
Forest Hymn, A, *sel.*
Forest Maid, The.
Future Life, The.
Gladness of Nature, The.
Good Fight, The. *Fr.* The Battlefield.
Green Mountain Boys, The.
Green River.
Holy Star, The.
Home Mission Prayer, A.
How Amiable Are Thy Tabernacles!
Hunter of the Prairies, The.
Hunter's Vision, The.
Hurricane, The.
Hymn of the City.
Hymn of the Waldenses.
Hymn to Death.
Hymn to the North Star.
I Broke the Spell That Held Me Long.
I Cannot Forget with What Fervid Devotion.
I Would Not Always Reason. *Fr.* The Conjunction of Jupiter and Venus.
Iliad, The, *sels., tr.*
In Memory of John Lothrop Motley.
Indian at the Burial-Place of His Fathers, An.
Inscription for the Entrance to a Wood.
Invitation to the Country, An.
June.
Lapse of Time, The.
Life of the Blessed, The, *tr.*

BRYANT, WILLIAM CULLEN (*continued*)
Lifetime, A
Love and Folly, *tr.*
Love of God, The, *tr.*
March.
May Sun Sheds an Amber Light, The.
Mocking Bird and the Donkey, The.
Monument Mountain.
Murdered Traveller, The.
Mutation.
My Autumn Walk.
New Moon, The.
Night Journey of a River, The.
O Fairest of the Rural Maids.
O Goddess! sing the wrath of Peleus' son, *tr.* *Fr.* The Iliad.
Oh Mother of a Mighty Race.
October.
Odyssey, The, *sels., tr.*
On Jefferson.
Other Sheep I Have, Which Are Not of This Fold.
Our Country's Call.
Past, The.
Path, The.
Planting of the Apple Tree, The.
Poet, The.
Prairies, The.
Prairies, The, *sel.*
Robert of Lincoln.
Ruins of Itálica, The, *tr.*
Scene on the Banks of the Hudson, A.
Seventy-six.
Siesta, The, *tr.*
Snow-Shower, The.
So Live. *Fr.* Thanatopsis.
Song for New Year's Eve, A.
Song of Marion's Men.
Song of the Greek Amazon.
Spring in Town.
Stream of Life, The.
Summer Wind.
Thanatopsis.
Thanatopsis, *sels.*
Third of November, The.
Thou, Whose Unmeasured Temple Stands.
To a Mosquito.
To a Waterfowl.
To Cole, the Painter, Departing for Europe.
To Mary Magdalen, *tr.*
To the Evening Wind.
To the Fringed Gentian.
To the Memory of Abraham Lincoln.
Truth, Crushed to Earth. *Fr.* The Battlefield.
Truth, the Invincible. *Fr.* The Battlefield.
Twenty-second of December, The.
Twenty-second of February, The.
Violet, The.
Waiting by the Gate.
Walk at Sunset, A.
Washington.
White-footed Deer, The.
Winter Piece, A.
Wrath of Achilles, *tr.* *Fr.* The Iliad.
Yellow Violet, The.
BRYCE, HERBERT J. Dog That Howls at Night, The.
BRYDGES, MATTHEW. *See* BRIDGES, MATTHEW.
BRYDGES, SIR SAMUEL EGERTON. Echo and Silence.
On Echo and Silence.
BRYUSOV, VALERY YAKOVLEVICH. Benediction.
Coming Huns, The.
Eventide.
Inevitability.
Mowers in the Line of Fire.
Orpheus and Eurydice.
Radiant Ranks [of Seraphim].
Remote, in a Closed Space.
St. Sebastian.
Stonecutter, The.
To Comrade Intellectuals.
Tryst, The.
Two Voices.
BUCHAN, JOHN, 1ST BARON TWEEDSMUIR. Fratri Dilectissimo.
In Praise of the Royal Scots Fusiliers.
BUCHANAN, DUGALD. Day of Judgment, The.
Omnia Vanitas.
BUCHANAN, FRANK. Babel and Bethel.
I Must to Prayer.
BUCHANAN, GEORGE. Epithalamium for Mary Stuart and the Dauphin of France.
Of the Sad Lot of the Humanists in Paris.
BUCHANAN, J. A. Oregon State Song.
BUCHANAN, ROBERT WILLIAMS. Ballad of Judas Iscariot, The.
Book of Orm, The, *sel.*
Churchyard, The.
Dawn, The.
Dream of the World without Death, The. *Fr.* The Book of Orm.
Faery Foster-Mother, The.
Faery Reaper, The.
Fra Giacomo.
Green Gnome, The.
Image in the Forum, The.
Judas Iscariot.
Langley Lane.
L'Envoi: "I end as I began."
Little Herd-Boy's Song, The. *Fr.* The Pilgrim and the Herdboy.
Little Milliner, The.
O What Is This Moaning So Faint and Low?
On a Young Poetess's Grave.
Pilgrim and the Herdboy, The.
Pilgrim and the Herdboy, The, *sel.*
Spring Song in the City.
Summer Pool, The.
Tom Dunstan; or, The Politician.
Two Sons.
Wake of Tim O'Hara, The.
We Are Children.
Wedding of Shon Maclean.
When We Are All Asleep.
BUCHER, HELEN HALL. Pennsylvania.
BUCK, RICHARD HENRY. Kentucky Babe.
BUCKHAM, JAMES. Child of To-Day, A.
Heart's Proof, The.
Smallest of the Drums, The.
Song of the Pine, The.
Tattered Flag, The.
BUCKHURST, LORD. *See* SACKVILLE, THOMAS, 1ST EARL OF DORSET.
BUCKINGHAM, GEORGE VILLIERS, 2D DUKE OF. Prayer: "Lord God of the oak and the elm."
To His Mistress, *at.*
BUCKINGHAM AND NORMANBY, DUKE OF. *See* SHEFFIELD, JOHN, DUKE OF BUCKINGHAM AND NORMANBY.
BUCKLEY, VINCENT. Korea.
BUCKNER, SAMUEL O. Do It Right.
BUCKTON, ALICE M. At the Garden Rail.
At Welbedacht.
BUDGE, SIR ERNEST ALFRED THOMPSON WALLIS. Hymn to Ra, *tr.*
One God, The, *tr.*
Weddase Maryam, *tr.*
BUELL, HATTIE E. My Father is rich in houses and lands.
BUGAYEV, BORIS NIKOLAYEVICH. See "BELY, ANDREI."
BUGBEE, EMILY J. Last Review, The.
BULCKE, KARL. There Is an Old City.
BULFINCH, MARIA H. Easter-Tide Deliverance, A.D. 430, An.
BULKLEY, VIVIEN. Cat of Cats.
BULL, LUCY CATLIN. *See* ROBINSON, LUCY CATLIN BULL.
BULL, OLAF. Christmas Eve.
Ruin, The.
BULLEN, ARTHUR HENRY. Whisperer, The.
BULLER, ARTHUR. Limerick: "There was a young lady named Bright," *at.*
Relativity, *at.*
Young Lady Named Bright, A, *at.*
BULLER, MARGUERITE. Proud Hollyhock.
BULLETT, GERALD. Because I love her.
Carol: "We saw Him sleeping in His manger bed."
Exile, The.
Field in June, A.
Footnote to Tennyson.
October.
So Still the World. *Fr.* Winter Solstice.
Winter Solstice, *sel.*
BULLOCH, JOHN MALCOLM. To Homer.
BULLWINKLE, CHRISTINE WOOD. Night.
BULTEEL, JOHN. I Grant Your Eyes Are Much More Bright, *at.*
BULWER-LYTTON, EDWARD, BARON LYTTON. Absent Yet Present.
Ajax, *sel., tr.*
Cardinal's Soliloquy, The. *Fr.* Richelieu; or, The Conspiracy.
Christ's Sympathy.
Electra, *sel., tr.*
Ernest Maltravers, *sels.*
Friendship, *tr.*
Last Days of Pompeii, The, *sel.*
Night and Love. *Fr.* Ernest Maltravers.
Nydia's Song. *Fr.* The Last Days of Pompeii.
Odes (*of Horace*), *sel., tr.*
Richelieu; or, The Conspiracy, *sel.*
Rousseau, *tr.*
When Stars Are in the Quiet Skies. *Fr.* Ernest Maltravers.
William Tell, *poem, tr.*
BULWER-LYTTON, EDWARD ROBERT, 1ST EARL OF LYTTON. *See* "MEREDITH, OWEN."
BUMSTEAD, EUDORA S. Indian Summer.
Little Red Hen, The.
Margie's Thanksgiving.
Summer Lullaby, A.
Waiting for Santa Claus.
BUNIN, IVAN ALEKSEYEVICH. Flax.
Hops, The.
In an Empty House.
New Church, The.
Russian Spring.
Song, A: "I'm a plain girl whose hands are stained with earth."
BUNKER, JOHN. Old Woman, The.
Petition of Youth before Battle.
Remembrance.
Serenade: "Sometimes you seem a star."
BUNN, ALFRED. Bohemian Girl, The, *sels.*
I Dreamt That I Dwelt in Marble Halls. *Fr.* The Bohemian Girl.
Light of Other Days, The.
When Other Lips and Other Hearts. *Fr.* The Bohemian Girl.
BUNNER, ALICE LEARNED (Mrs. Henry Cuyler Bunner). Immutabilis. *Fr.* Vingtaine.
Separation. *Fr.* Vingtaine.
Vingtaine.
BUNNER, HENRY CUYLER. Appeal to Harold, The.
Behold the Deeds!
Candor.
Chaperon, The.
Da Capo.
Deaf.
Feminine.
Grandfather Watts's Private Fourth.
Heart of the Tree, The.
Home, Sweet Home, with Variations.
Imitation.
J. B.
Les Morts Vont Vite.
Lost Child, A.
Old Flag, The.
On Reading a Poet's First Book.
One, Two, Three.
Pitcher of Mignonette, A.
Ready for the Ride—1795.
Round-up, A.
Salute the Flag.
Shake, Mulleary and Go-ethe.
She Was a Beauty.
Strong as Death.
To a Dead Woman.
To a June Breeze.
Triumph.
Way to Arcady, The.
Yes?
BUNSTON, ANNA. *See* DE BARY, ANNA BUNSTON.

BUNYAN, JOHN. Enough! *Fr.* The Pilgrim's Progress.
He who would valiant be. *Fr.* The Pilgrim's Progress.
Hog, The.
My Little Bird.
Of the Child with the Bird at the Bush.
Of the Going Down of the Sun.
Pilgrim, The. *Fr.* The Pilgrim's Progress.
Pilgrim's Progress, The, *sels.*
Pilgrim's [*or* Pilgrim] Song. *Fr.* The Pilgrim's Progress.
Shepherd Boy Sings in the Valley of Humiliation, The. *Fr.* The Pilgrim's Progress.
Shepherd Boy's Song in the Valley of Humiliation, The. *Fr.* The Pilgrim's Progress.
Shepherd's Song, The. *Fr.* The Pilgrim's Progress.
Song of the Shepherd in the Valley of Humiliation, The. *Fr.* The Pilgrim's Progress.
Upon a Ring of Bells.
Upon the Lark and the Fowler.
Upon the Snail.
BUONARROTI. *See* MICHELANGELO BUONARROTI.
BURBIDGE, THOMAS. Eventide.
If I Desire.
Mother's Love.
She Bewitched Me.
To Imperia.
BURCH, LOREN W. Communion.
Into Thy Hands.
BURCHENAL, JOHN J. To My Children.
BURDETTE, ROBERT JONES. American Cradle-Song.
Bravest of the Brave.
Christ. *Fr.* My Guide.
Engineers' Making Love, The.
Limerick: "There was a young man of Cohoes."
My Guide.
My Guide, *sel.*
Orphan Born.
Romance of the Carpet, The.
"Soldier, Rest!"
"Songs without Words."
What Will We Do?
When My Ship Comes In.
BURDICK, ARTHUR J. Washington's Birthday.
BURFORD, WILLIAM. Christmas Tree, A.
Fire, The.
Tomboy, The.
BÜRGER, GOTTFRIED AUGUST. Wild Huntsman, The.
BURGESS, BANGS. Life's Finest Things.
BURGESS, CHARLES. Albatross.
Five Serpents.
Lady and Crocodile.
Two Garden Scenes.
BURGESS, GELETT. Abstemia.
Abstrosophy.
Adolphus Elfinstone.
Ah, Yes, I Wrote It.
Ah, Yes, I Wrote the "Purple Cow."
Bobby.
Cinq Ans Après.
Dighton Is Engaged.
Ego Sum.
Extracts from the Rubaiyat of Omar Cayenne.
Felicia Ropps.
Floorless Room, The.
Hair.
I Never Saw a Purple Cow.
I Wish That My Room Had a Floor.
I'd Rather Have Fingers than Toes.
Invisible Bridge, The.
Kitty Wants to Write.
Lament: "Ban of Time there is no disobeying, The."
Lazy Roof, The.
Limerick: "I wish that my room had a floor!"
Limerick: "I'd rather have fingers than toes."
Limerick: "I'd rather have habits than clothes."
Limerick: "Remarkable truly, is art!"
Magic Month, The.
Muse of Nonsense, The.
My Feet.
My house is made of graham bread.
My Legs Are So Weary.
Nonsense Quatrains.
On Digital Extremities.
Over the Hills with Nancy.
Protest of the Illiterate, The, *sel.*
Psycholophon.
Purple Cow, The.
Sestina of Youth and Age.
Sunset, The.
Ubasti.
Villanelle of Things Amusing.
Willy and the Lady.
Window Pain [*or* Pane].
BURGESS, GEORGE. Heavenly Breeze, The.
BURGESS, HELEN M. Mother's Petition, in Wartime.
BURGESS, STELLA FISHER. One There Was.
BURGH, HUGH DE. Punchinello.
BURGHLEY [*or* BURLEIGH], WILLIAM CECIL, 1ST BARON. To Mistress Anne Cecil, upon Making Her a New Year's Gift.
BURGON, JOHN WILLIAM. Pedra [*or* Petra].
BURGOYNE, ARTHUR G. "Everybody Works but Father" as W. S. Gilbert Would Have Written It.
BURKE, CHRISTIAN. Christmas Carol, A: "Trees are hung with crystal lamps, the world lies still and white, The."
BURKE, FRANCIS. Mediatrix of Grace, The.
Sequence, with Strophes in Paraphrase Thereof, A.
BURKE, HENRIETTA A. Transaction on the Roman Exchange.
BURKE, HENRY. Schooner *Blizzard,* The.
BURKE, KENNETH. For a Modernist Sermon.
BURKE, RICHARD. We Will Not Die, These Lovers Say.
BURKE, THOMAS. Piccadilly.
To Chloe.
Triumph America!
BURKET, GAIL BROOK. Columbus Never Knew.
February 12, 1809.
House in Springfield.
Noel.
Thought for a New Year.
BURKHARD VON HOHENFELS. Dance Song, A.
BURKHOLDER, CLARENCE M. Easter Beatitudes.
Prayer, A: "Lord, let not my religion be."
BURLEIGH, GEORGE S. Prayer for Life, A.
BURLEIGH, HARRY THACKER. Little Child of Mary.
BURLEIGH, WILLIAM H. Deborah Lee.
Lead us, O Father, in the paths of peace.
Weaver, The.
BURLIN, NATALIE CURTIS. *See* CURTIS, NATALIE.
BURLINGAME, ROGER. Women Will Soon Knit Again, The.
BURLINGHAM, ROBERT G. I Remember.
BURNABY, CHARLES *or* WILLIAM. Reformed Wife, The, *sel.*
Upon a Sickly Lady. *Fr.* The Reformed Wife.
BURNAND, SIR FRANCIS COWLEY. Faithful Lovers, The, *at.*
Fisherman's Chant, The.
His Heart Was True to Poll.
Oh, My Geraldine.
True to Poll.
BURNELL, FRITZ S. Isle of Apple-Trees, The.
Pool, The.
BURNET, DANA. Ballad of Dead Girls.
Bread-Line, The.
Homeland, The.
Laddie.
Marching Song.
Paper Roses.
Peace at Morning.
Ragged Piper, The.
Riddle, The: "We were laying the road to a Riddle."
Road to Vagabondia, The.
Roses in the Subway.
Sack of Old Panama, The.
Song: "Love's on the highroad."
Song for Youth.
Wayfarers.
Who Dreams Shall Live.
BURNET, W. HODGSON. Autumn Leaves.
BURNHAM, MAUD. Barnyard, The.
Five Little Fairies, The.
Pigeons, The.
BURNHAM, RICHARD. Friend of Sinners.
BURNIE, DONALD. Eliza Spaulding.
Henry Spaulding.
BURNS, COLETTE M. Why Read a Book?
BURNS, J. D. For England.
BURNS, JOHN DICKSON. O, Tempora! O Mores!
Our Christmas Hymn.
BURNS, ROBERT. Address to a Haggis.
Address to a Lady.
Address to the Deil.
Address to the Toothache.
Address to the Unco Guid, or the Rigidly Righteous.
Address to the Unco Guid, or the Rigidly Righteous, *sel.*
Address to the Woodlark.
Ae Fond Kiss [and Then We Sever].
Afton Water.
Again Rejoicing Nature Sees.
Anna.
As I Stood by Yon Roofless Tower.
As Others See Us. *Fr.* To a Louse.
Auld Lang Syne.
Ay Waukin, O.
Banks o' Doon, The.
Bannockburn.
Bard's Epitaph, A.
Before Bannockburn.
Before Parting.
Bess and Her Spinning Wheel.
Birks of Aberfeldie, The.
Bonie [*or* Bonnie] Doon.
Bonnie [*or* Bonie] Lesley.
Bonnie Wee Thing.
Book-Worms, The.
Borrowing Trouble. *Fr.* The Twa Dogs.
Braw Lads o' Galla Water.
Brigs of Ayr, The, *sel.*
Bruce to His Army.
Bruce to His Men at Bannockburn.
Bruce's Address to His Army at Bannockburn.
Bruce's March to Bannockburn.
Ca' the Yowes to the Knowes.
Charlie, He's My Darling.
Child's Grace, A.
Chloe.
Cock Up Your Beaver.
Comin' [*or* Coming] thro' the Rye.
Contented wi' Little.
Corn Rigs.
Cotter's Saturday Night, The.
Cotter's Saturday Night, The, *sels.*
Day Returns [My Bosom Burns], The.
Death and Doctor Hornbook.
Defiance.
De'il's Awa' wi' the Exciseman, The.
Devotion.
Drinking Song. *Fr.* The Jolly Beggars.
Duncan Gray.
Elegy on Captain Matthew Henderson.
Elegy on the Death of Peg Nicholson.
Epigram: "No more of your titled acquaintances boast."
Epistle to a Young Friend.
Epistle to Davie, a Brother Poet.
Epistle to Dr. Blacklock.
Epistle to James Smith.
Epistle to John Lapraik, an Old Scottish Bard.
Epistle to William Simpson, Ochiltree.
Epitaph for James Smith.

BURNS, ROBERT (*continued*)
Epitaph on a Friend.
Epitaph on John Dove.
Epitaph on My Father.
Excerpt, An.
Exciseman, The.
False Love.
Farewell, A: "Go fetch to me a pint o' wine."
Farewell, The: "It was a' for our rightfu' King."
Farewell, The: "It was a' for our rightfu' King," *sel.*
Farewell to Nancy.
Flow Gently, Sweet Afton.
For A' That an' A' That ("The bonniest lass that ye meet neist"), *at.*
For A' That and A' That ("Is there, for honest poverty").
For the Sake of Somebody.
From His First Song. *Fr.* O, Once I Lov'd a Bonie Lass.
Gie the Lass Her Fairin'.
Gloomy Night Is Gathering Fast, The.
Go Fetch to Me a Pint o' Wine.
Goal of Life, The.
Godly Girzie.
Green Grow the Rashes.
Hallowe'en.
Hark! the Mavis.
Here's a Health to Them That's Awa'.
Highland Balou, The.
Highland Mary.
Holy Fair, The.
Holy Willie's Prayer.
Hymn of Marriage.
I am my mammie's ae bairn.
I Love My Jean.
I Once Was a Maid.
I'll Aye Ca' In by Yon Town.
I'm Owre [*or* O'er] Young to Marry Yet.
Is There for Honest Poverty.
It Was A' for Our Rightfu' King.
Jean.
John Anderson, My Jo ("John Anderson, my jo, John/ I wonder what ye mean"), *at.*
John Anderson My Jo ("John Anderson my jo, John,/ When we were first acquent").
John Barleycorn.
Johnnie, Cock Up Your Beaver.
Jolly Beggars, The.
Jolly Beggars, The, *sels.*
Jolly Mortals, Fill Your Glasses. *Fr.* The Jolly Beggars.
Kirk's Alarm, The.
Lament for Culloden.
Lament of Mary Queen of Scots.
Lass o' Ballochmyle, The.
Lass That Made the Bed to Me, The.
Lassie wi' the Lint-white Locks.
Last May a Braw Wooer.
Lea Rig, The.
Let Not Woman E'er Complain.
Letter to a Young Friend.
Logan Braes.
Lovely Lass o' Inverness, The.
Macpherson's Farewell.
Man Was Made to Mourn; a Dirge.
Man Was Made to Mourn; a Dirge, *sel.*
Man's a Man for A' That, A.
Man's Inhumanity to Man. *Fr.* Man Was Made to Mourn.
Mary Morison.
Mary Queen of Scots.
Mother's Lament for the Death of Her Son, A.
Muse of Burns, The. *Fr.* The Vision.
My Ain Kind Dearie, O.
My Bonie [*or* Bonnie] Mary.
My Heart's in the Highlands.
My Jean.
My Love Is like a Red Red Rose.
My Love, She's But a Lassie Yet.
My Luve.
My Luve's like a Red, Red Rose.
My Nanie, O.
My Nannie's [*or* Nanie's] Awa.
My Wife's a Winsome Wee Thing.
Nobody.
November Evening. *Fr.* The Cotter's Saturday Night.
O, for Ane-and-twenty.
O Mally's Meek, Mally's Sweet.
O Mary, at thy window be.
O Merry Hae I Been Teethin' a Heckle.
O, My Luve is like a Red, Red Rose.
O, Once I Lov'd a Bonie Lass, *sel.*
O, Open the Door to Me, O!
O, Saw Ye Bonnie Lesley?
O Were My Love Yon Lilac Fair.
O, Wert Thou in the Cauld Blast.
O Whistle, and I'll Come to Ye [*or* You], My Lad.
O, Willie Brew'd a Peck o' Maut.
Ode, Sacred to the Memory of Mrs. Oswald of Auchencruive.
O'er the Water to Charlie.
Of A' the Airts [the Wind Can Blaw].
On a Wag in Mauchline.
On Seeing a Wounded Hare Limp by Me.
Open the Door to Me, O!
Parson's Looks, The.
Patriarch, The.
Phillis the Fair.
Poet's Grace, A.
Poet's Welcome to His Love-begotten Daughter, The.
Poor Mailie's Elegy.
Postscript to a Letter on the Excise Laws.
Prayer for My Native Land. *Fr.* The Cotter's Saturday Night.
Prayer in the Prospect of Death, A.
Prayer under the Pressure of Violent Anguish.
Rantin' Dog, the Daddie o't, The.
Red, Red Rose, A.
Rigs o' Barley, The.
Robert Bruce's Address to His Army, before the Battle of Bannockburn.
Robert Bruce's March to Bannockburn.
Robin.
Rosebud, A.
Saw Ye Bonie Lesley.
Scots Wha Hae [wi' Wallace Bled].
Scroggam.
See the Smoking Bowl before Us. *Fr.* The Jolly Beggars.
Selkirk Grace, The.
Sic a Wife as Willie Had.
Silver Tassie, The.
Simmer's a Pleasant Time.
Somebody.
Song: "Again rejoicing Nature sees."
Song: Green Grow the Rashes.
Song: Mary Morison.
Song: "My luve is like a red, red rose."
Song: My Nanie, O.
Song: "O my luve's like a red, red rose."
Spark o' Nature's Fire, A. *Fr.* Epistle to John Lapraik.
Sweet Afton.
Tam Glen.
Tam o' Shanter.
Tam Samson's Elegy.
There Was a Lad.
There'll Never Be Peace till Jamie Comes Hame.
Thou Lingering Star.
To a Field-Mouse.
To a Louse [on Seeing One on a Lady's Bonnet at Church].
To a Louse, *sel.*
To a Mountain Daisy [on Turning One Down with the Plow in April, 1786].
To a Mouse [on Turning Her Up in Her Nest with the Plough, November, 1785].
To James Smith.
To John Taylor.
To Mary in Heaven.
To Ruin.
To the Rev. John M'Math.
To the Unco Guid.
To William Simpson of Ochiltree.
Toad-Eater, The.
True until Death.
Twa Dogs, The.
Up in the Morning Early.
Verses Intended to Be Written below a Noble Earl's Picture.
Vision, The ("As I stood by yon roofless tower").
Vision, The ("The sun had closed the winter day"), *sels.*
Wandering Willie.
Wee Willie Gray.
Wha Is That at My Bower Door?
When She Cam Ben, She Bobbed.
Whistle, and I'll Come to Ye [*or* You], My Lad.
Whistle o'er the Lave o't.
Willie Brew'd [*or* Brewed] a Peck o' Maut.
Winter; a Dirge.
Winter Night, A, *sel.*
Wounded Hare, The.
Ye Banks and Braes [o' Bonnie Doon].
Ye Flowery Banks [o' Bonnie Doon].
BURNS, VINCENT GODFREY. If Jesus Came Back Today, *sel.*
Sonnet for Christmas.
BURNSHAW, STANLEY. Anonymous Alba, *tr.*
Bread.
End of the Flower-World (A.D. 2300).
Hear, O Israel! *tr.*
Now You're Content, *tr.*
Nudities, *tr.*
Strange.
BURR, AMELIA JOSEPHINE. Battle-Song of Failure.
Certainty Enough.
Deliver Us From.
Dog's Eye View, A.
Gorgio Lad.
In Deep Places.
Joyce Kilmer.
Kitchener's March.
Lynmouth Widow, A.
Mother Moon.
Mother of Judas, The.
Mothers of Men.
My Mother.
New Life.
Night Magic.
Nocturne: "All the earth a hush of white."
Pershing at the Tomb of Lafayette.
Perugia.
Rain in the Night.
Reality.
Romany Gold.
Song of Living, A.
Surrender.
To Her—Unspoken.
To Lovers.
Where Love Is.
Where You Passed.
BURR, WILLIAM NORRIS. God's Dream.
BURR, WINIFRED ADAMS. At Night.
BURROUGHS, ALETHEA S. Savannah.
"BURROUGHS, ELLEN." *See* JEWETT, SOPHIE.
BURROUGHS, JOHN. Crow, The.
Downy Woodpecker, The.
Golden Crown Sparrow of Alaska.
My Own Shall Come to Me.
Return, The.
Song of the Toad, The.
Swallow, The.
To the Lapland Longspur.
Waiting.
BURROWAY, JAN. Owed to Dickens, 1956.
Song: "With whomsoever I share the spring."
BURROWS, FRANCIS. Life.
BURSTEIN, ABRAHAM. Love of Hell, The.
BURT, EMILY ROSE. Escape, The.
For April Showers.
BURT, JEAN BROOKS. Things Divine, The.
BURT, MARY E. Flying Squirrel, The.
BURT, STRUTHERS. Beauty Persists.
Burial.
Element, The.

Fifty Years Spent.
Free Men.
Hill-born, The.
Horizons.
I Know a Lovely Lady Who Is Dead.
If Once the Great Archangel of Our Dreams.
In Limine.
Land, The.
Little House, The.
May.
No One Knows the Countryside.
Old Houses.
Pursuit, The.
Response.
Resurgam.
River, The.
To a Friend Recently Married.
Trinity.
Young Dead, The.
BURTIS, ELOISE. Ode to a Dawg.
BURTON, ERNEST DE WITT. Way O Christ Thou Art, The.
BURTON, HENRY. Jesus Himself.
Light upon the Mountains, A.
Pass It On.
BURTON, JOHN. Holy Bible, Book Divine.
Prayer: "I often say my prayers."
BURTON, KATHERINE. Epiphany.
Exile, The.
November Eleventh.
BURTON, RICHARD. Across the Fields to Anne.
Black Sheep.
City, The.
City of the Dead, The.
Comfort of the Stars, The.
Deserted Farms.
Dumb in June, *sel.*
Extras.
Factory Children.
Faithful Dog, A.
First Song, The.
Forefather, The.
Glorious Game, The.
God's Garden.
Human Touch, The.
Idols.
In a Library.
In Sleep.
In the Place de la Bastille.
Love Is Strong.
Mary Magdalene.
May-Lure.
Modern Saint, The.
Mortis Dignitas.
Of Those Who Walk Alone.
Old Santa Fé Trail, The.
On a Ferry Boat.
On Syrian Hills.
Plan, The.
Polar Quest, The.
Rhyme for Remembrance of May.
Roll a Rock Down.
Sealed Orders.
Shakespeare Reads the King James Version.
Song of the Sea.
Song of the Unsuccessful, The.
Strength in Weakness.
Summer. *Fr.* Dumb in June.
Two Mothers.
Unpraised Picture, An.
Wood Witchery.
BURTON, SIR RICHARD FRANCIS. Do What Thy Manhood Bids Thee Do.
Kasidah, The, *sel.*
Mock Caliph, The, *tr. Fr.* The Book of a Thousand Nights and a Night.
BURTON, ROBERT. Anatomy of Melancholy, The, *sels.*
Author's Abstract of Melancholy, The. *Fr.* The Anatomy of Melancholy.
BUSCH, BRITON NIVEN, JR. Voice before April, A.
BUSH, JOCELYN. Little Red Sled, The.
BUSHNELL, FRANCES LOUISA. In the Dark.
Unfulfilment.
World Music.
BUSHNELL, SAMUEL C. Boston, *at.*
On the Aristocracy of Harvard, *at.*
BUSON (Taniguchi Buson). Chums.
Fireflies massed upon the palm fronds, The.
Haiku: "Over the vast field of mustard flowers."
Mists of Daybreak.
Look! On the great bronze bell.
Spring rain! And as yet.
Summer night, A/ With breezes sweet.
BUSSE, CARL. In the Night of the Full Moon.
Quiet Kingdom, The.
BUSTAMANTE Y BALLIVIÁN, ENRIQUE. Telegraph Pole.
BUTCHART, ISABEL. Dawn.
BUTCHER, SAMUEL HENRY, *and* ANDREW LANG. Odyssey, The, *sels., tr.*
BUTLER, ARTHUR GRAY. Edith and Harold.
Two Long Vacations; Grasmere.
BUTLER, ELLIS PARKER. Secret Combination, The.
BUTLER, FRANCES ANNE KEMBLE. *See* KEMBLE, FRANCES ANNE.
BUTLER, GEORGE. Hallowe'en Meeting, A.
BUTLER, GUY. Cape Coloured Batman.
David.
Home Thoughts.
Myths.
Pieta.
Stranger to Europe.
BUTLER, HENRY MONTAGUE. Lift Up Your Hearts!
BUTLER, SAMUEL (1612–80). Art of Love, The. *Fr.* Hudibras.
Astral Fates, The. *Fr.* Hudibras.
Calf's Head Meeting, A. *Fr.* Hudibras.
Description of Hudibras and His Equipments. *Fr.* Hudibras.
Elephant in the Moon, The.
For All Fanatics. *Fr.* Hudibras.
How Men Write.
Hudibras, *sels.*
Hudibras' Sword and Dagger. *Fr.* Hudibras.
Hudibras, the Presbyterian Knight. *Fr.* Hudibras.
Hudibras the Sectarian. *Fr.* Hudibras.
Hypocrisy.
Lady's Answer, The. *Fr.* Hudibras.
Logic of Hudibras. *Fr.* Hudibras.
Love. *Fr.* Hudibras.
Maggots of Flattery.
Metaphysical Sectarian, The. *Fr.* Hudibras.
Poetry and Wine.
Portrait of Hudibras. *Fr.* Hudibras.
Portrait of Sidrophel. *Fr.* Hudibras.
Presbyterian Church Government. *Fr.* Hudibras.
Presbyterian Knight, The. *Fr.* Hudibras.
Presbyterian Knight and Independent Squire. *Fr.* Hudibras.
Religion of Hudibras, The. *Fr.* Hudibras.
Rules of Life. *Fr.* Hudibras.
Saintship versus Conscience. *Fr.* Hudibras.
Satire on the Royal Society, A.
Sidrophel, the Rosicrucian Conjurer.
Sir Hudibras. *Fr.* Hudibras.
Sir Hudibras's Religion. *Fr.* Hudibras.
Sir Sidrophel, the Conjuror. *Fr.* Hudibras.
Smatterers.
To His Mistress.
Tyranny and Law. *Fr.* Hudibras.
BUTLER, SAMUEL (1835–1902). Andromache, *tr. Fr.* The Iliad.
At-Home in Sparta, An, *tr. Fr.* The Odyssey.
At Sparta; Helen and Menelaus, *tr. Fr.* The Odyssey.
Eumaeus Plays Host to His Master, *tr. Fr.* The Odyssey.
Eumaeus Tells the Story of His Life, *tr. Fr.* The Odyssey.
Eumaeus the Swineherd, *tr. Fr.* The Odyssey.
Heroic Answer to the Servant Problem, An, *tr. Fr.* The Odyssey.
Iliad, The, *sels., tr.*
O God! O Montreal!
Odyssey, The, *sels., tr.*
Old Hound Argos, The, *tr. Fr.* The Odyssey.
Penelope Makes Trial of Odysseus, *tr. Fr.* The Odyssey.
Sailing Weather, *tr. Fr.* Works and Days (*of* Hesiod).
Thetis to Achilles, *tr. Fr.* The Iliad.
When the Snail Climbs, *tr. Fr.* Works and Days (*of* Hesiod).
Works and Days (*of* Hesiod), *sels., tr.*
BUTLER, WILLIAM ALLEN. All's Well.
Incognita of Raphael.
Nothing to Wear.
Tom Twist.
BUTLER, WILLIAM T. Gathering on the Plains, The.
BUTTERFIELD, FRANCES WESTGATE. Time Out.
BUTTERWORTH, HEZEKIAH. Bird with a Broken Wing, The.
Broken Pinion, The.
Church of the Revolution, The.
Crown Our Washington.
Death of Jefferson, The.
First Boston Thanksgiving—July, 1630, The.
Five Kernels of Corn.
Fountain of Youth, The.
Garfield's Ride at Chickamauga.
Immortal Morn.
Legend of Waukulla, The.
Ortiz.
Roger Williams.
Snowbird, The.
Star in the West, The.
Thanksgiving for America, The.
Thanksgiving in Boston Harbor, The.
Verazzano.
Washington's Birthday.
Whitman's Ride for Oregon.
BUTTS, ANTONY. Massenet/ Never wrote a Mass in A.
BUTTS, MARY FRANCES. Build a Fence of Trust.
Christmas Trees, The.
Every evening Baby goes.
Happy Hour, The.
In Galilee.
Keeping Store.
King, The.
Million Little Diamonds, A.
Night.
Sweetest Place, The.
That's July.
That's June.
To-Day.
Trot, Trot!
Trot, Trot to Town.
Water Jewels.
Wild Winds.
Winter Night.
BUXTON, ESTHER W. Putting the World to Bed.
"BYEDNY, DEMYAN." *See* "BEDNY, DEMYAN."
BYER, B. L. Ageless Christ, The.
BYERS, SAMUEL H. M. Sherman's March to the Sea.
Song of Iowa, The.
Song of Sherman's March to the Sea.
With Corse at Allatoona.
BYNNER, WITTER ("Emanuel Morgan").
Against the Cold.
Aged Fisherman.
Alone in Her Beauty, *tr.*
And O the Wind.
Asleep. *Fr.* Chapala Poems.
At the Last.
Autumn Walk, An.
Beforehand.
Birthday, The.
Bitter Love, A, *tr.*
Calendar. *Fr.* Chapala Poems.
Captain's Table.
Chapala Poems, *sels.*

BYNNER, WITTER (*continued*)
Chaplet, The.
Charioteer.
Chariots.
Consummation. *Fr.* To Celia.
Coquette, The.
Correspondent.
Dance for Rain, A.
Day, The.
Dream.
Drinking Alone with the Moon, *tr.*
During a Chorale by César Franck. *Fr.* To Celia.
Dynasty, A.
Ecce Homo.
Elegy, An: "O youngest, best-loved daughter of Hsieh," *tr.*
Endless Self, *tr. Fr.* Tao Teh King.
Endless Yearning, *tr.*
Epithalamium and Elegy.
Farmer Remembers Lincoln, A.
Fields, The.
Fortune-Teller, A.
Ganymede.
Garden of the Golden Valley, The, *tr.*
Gentle Touch, A, *tr. Fr.* Tao Teh King.
Ghost.
Ghosts of Indians.
God's Acre.
Golden Heart, The.
Grass-Tops.
Grenstone Elm, A.
Grenstone River.
Grieve Not for Beauty. *Fr.* The New World.
He Who Feels Punctured, *tr. Fr.* Tao Teh King.
Hey-Day.
Hills of Home.
Homeland, The, *tr.*
Horse-Chestnut Tree.
I Change.
In a Land, *tr. Fr.* Tao Teh King.
In Spring, *tr.*
Iphigenia in Tauris, *sels., tr.*
Iphigenia's Dream, *tr. Fr.* Iphigenia in Tauris.
Jeremiah.
Kids.
Knowledge Studies Others, *tr. Fr.* Tao Teh King.
Lesson of Water, *tr.*
Life, *tr. Fr.* Tao Teh King.
Looking at the Moon and Thinking of One Far Away, *tr.*
Lullaby: "I'll send you now sailing across the sea."
Masque of Life and Death, A.
Mocking Bird, A.
Montezuma. *Fr.* Chapala Poems.
My Lodge at Wang-Ch'uan after a Long Rain, *tr.*
My Retreat at Mount Chung-nan, *tr.*
Mystic, The.
Neighbors Help Him Build His House, The, *tr.*
New God, The. *Fr.* The New World.
New Life, The.
New World, The, *sels.*
Night. *Fr.* To Celia.
Night Vigil in the Left Court of the Palace, A, *tr.*
On a Moonlight Night, *tr.*
On Hearing a Flute at Night from the Wall of Shou-hsiang, *tr.*
On Hearing Her Play the Harp, *tr.*
On Meeting Li Kuei-nien down the River, *tr.*
Palace Poem, A, *tr.*
Parting, A, *tr.*
Poet, The.
Poet Lived in Galilee, A.
Prepare.
Property.
Republic to Republic.
Roofs.
Sandpiper, The.
Sentence.
She Sighs on Her Jade Lute, *tr.*
Sigh from a Staircase of Jade, A, *tr.*
Singing Huntsman, The.
Skeptic, The.
Song of a Pure-hearted Girl, A, *tr.*
Song of Dagger-dancing, A, *tr.*
Song of White Snow, A, *tr.*
Songs Ascending. *Fr.* To Celia.
Spectra, *sel.*
Spouse.
Spring Heart-break, *tr.*
Spring Rain, *tr.*
Spring Sigh, A, *tr.*
Stratagem, *tr. Fr.* Iphigenia in Tauris.
Tao Teh King, *sels., tr.*
Those Who Know Do Not Tell, *tr. Fr.* Tao Teh King.
To a Phoebe Bird.
To Anyone.
To Be, *tr.*
To Celia, *sels.*
To My Retired Friend Wei, *tr.*
To One Unnamed, *tr.*
To Robert Browning.
Train-Mates.
True Freedom, *tr. Fr.* Tao Teh King.
Vagrant.
Voices.
Way of Life, The, *sel., tr.*
Web, The. *Fr.* Chapala Poems.
Woman without Tears, A, *tr. Fr.* Iphigenia in Tauris.
BYNNER, WITTER, *and* KIANG KANG-HU.
After Missing the Recluse on the Western Mountain, *tr.*
Answering Vice-Prefect Chang, *tr.*
Beautiful Hsi-shih, The, *tr.*
Bringing in the Wine, *tr.*
Cicada, A, *tr.*
Home, *tr.*
Message to Meng Hao-jan, A, *tr.*
Moon at the Fortified Pass, The, *tr.*
On Leaving the Tomb of Premier Fang, *tr.*
Seeing Li Po in a Dream, *tr.*
Song of Ch'ang-kan, A, *tr.*
Stopping at a Friend's Farm-House, *tr.*
Taking Leave of Wang Wei, *tr.*
Thinking of a Friend Lost in the Tibetan War, *tr.*
Thoughts in the Cold, *tr.*
To a Friend Bound North after the Rebellion, *tr.*
To Chi Wu Ch'ien Bound Home after Failing in an Examination, *tr.*
To My Brothers and Sisters Adrift in Troubled Times This Poem of the Moon, *tr.*
View of T'ai-shan, A, *tr.*
With Her Beauty, *tr.*
BYRNE, BROOKE. Epitaph: "We were not many, and no bronze asserts."
Hosting, The.
BYRNE, DONN. Piper, The.
To the World's Edge.
BYRNE, WILLIAM A. Bog Lands, The.
BYROM, JOHN. Careless Content.
Careless Content, *sel.*
Christians, Awake [Salute the Happy Morn].
Colin and Phebe—a Pastoral.
Contentment; or, The Happy Workman's Song.
Desiderium.
Desponding Soul's Wish, The.
Epigram: "God bless the King—I mean the faith's defender!"
Epigram on Handel and Bononcini.
Epigram on the Feuds between Handel and Bononcini.
Extempore Verses Intended to Allay the Violence of Party-Spirit.
Extempore Verses upon a Trial of Skill between the Two Great Masters of the Noble Science of Defence, Messrs. Figg and Sutton.
Hymn for Christmas Day.
Hymn on the Omnipresence, An.
Intended to Allay the Violence of Party Spirit.
Jacobite Toast.
My Dog Tray.
My Spirit Longeth for Thee.
Nimmers, The.
On Clergymen Preaching Politics.
Pastoral, A: "My Time, O ye Muses, was happily spent."
Salutation of the Blessed Virgin, The.
Self-Righteousness.
Soul's Tendency towards Its True Centre, The.
Three Black Crows, The.
Toast, A.
Tom the Porter.
Which Is Which.
BYRON, GEORGE GORDON NOEL BYRON, 6TH BARON. Address to the Ocean. *Fr.* Childe Harold's Pilgrimage.
Adieu, Adieu! My Native Shore. *Fr.* Childe Harold's Pilgrimage.
Alhama, *tr.*
All for Love.
And I Have Loved Thee, Ocean! *Fr.* Childe Harold's Pilgrimage.
And Thou Art Dead, as Young and Fair.
And Thou Art Dead, as Young and Fair, *sels.*
Apostrophe to the Ocean. *Fr.* Childe Harold's Pilgrimage.
Appeal for Illumination, *tr. Fr.* Il Morgante maggiore.
Archangel, The. *Fr.* The Vision of Judgment.
Assault, The. *Fr.* The Siege of Corinth.
At the Gate of Heaven. *Fr.* The Vision of Judgment.
At Thirty Years. *Fr.* Don Juan.
Author's Purpose, The. *Fr.* Don Juan.
Ave Maria. *Fr.* Don Juan.
Ay de mi Alhama, *tr.*
Bard of Love, The, *tr.*
Battle of Waterloo, The. *Fr.* Childe Harold's Pilgrimage.
Beppo.
Beppo, *sels.*
Bitter Meditation. *Fr.* Childe Harold's Pilgrimage.
Bride of Abydos, The.
Bride of Abydos, The, *sels.*
Bright Be the Place of Thy Soul!
Byron's Farewell.
Byron's Latest Verses.
Calm and Storm on Lake Leman. *Fr.* Childe Harold's Pilgrimage.
Chain I Gave, The.
Childe Harold's Farewell to England. *Fr.* Childe Harold's Pilgrimage.
Childe Harold's Pilgrimage, *sels.*
Chillon. *Fr.* The Prisoner of Chillon.
Churchill's Grave.
Cincinnatus of the West, The. *Fr.* Ode to Napoleon Bonaparte.
Coliseum, The ("Arches on arches"). *Fr.* Childe Harold's Pilgrimage.
Coliseum, The ("The stars are forth"). *Fr.* Manfred.
Coliseum by Moonlight. *Fr.* Manfred.
Communion with Nature. *Fr.* Childe Harold's Pilgrimage.
Conscience.
Contemporary Poets. *Fr.* Don Juan.
Corsair, The, *sels.*
Corsair's Life, The. *Fr.* The Corsair.
Daniel Boone. *Fr.* Don Juan.
Darkness.
Dead Sparrow, The, *tr.*
Death of Haidée, The. *Fr.* Don Juan.
Dedication: "Bob Southey! You're a poet—Poet-laureate." *Fr.* Don Juan.
Dedication to the Poet Laureate. *Fr.* Don Juan.
Deep and Dark Blue Ocean. *Fr.* Childe Harold's Pilgrimage.
Deep in My Soul. *Fr.* The Corsair.
Defiance. *Fr.* Childe Harold's Pilgrimage.
Desire and Disillusion. *Fr.* Childe Harold's Pilgrimage.
Destruction of Sennacherib, The.
Devotion. *Fr.* Don Juan.
Disillusion. *Fr.* Don Juan.
Divina Commedia, *sel., tr.*
Don Juan, *sels.*
Don Juan and Haidee. *Fr.* Don Juan.
Don Juan's Education. *Fr.* Don Juan.
Donna Julia. *Fr.* Don Juan.

Dream, The.
Dying Gladiator, The. *Fr.* Childe Harold's Pilgrimage.
Elegy: "Oh! snatch'd away in beauty's bloom."
Elegy on Thyrza.
English Bards and Scotch Reviewers, *sels.*
Epigram: "With death doomed to grapple."
Epigrams on Castlereagh.
Epistle from Mr. Murray to Dr. Polidori.
Epistle to Augusta.
Epitaph: "With death doomed to grapple."
Epitaph to a Dog.
Epitaph to a Newfoundland Dog.
Eve of the Battle of Waterloo, The. *Fr.* Childe Harold's Pilgrimage.
Eve of Waterloo, The. *Fr.* Childe Harold's Pilgrimage.
Evening. *Fr.* Don Juan.
Existence May Be Borne. *Fr.* Childe Harold's Pilgrimage.
Fame. *Fr.* Childe Harold's Pilgrimage.
Fare Thee Well.
Farewell: "Farewell! if ever fondest prayer."
Farewell, The: "Oh, thou! in Hellas deem'd of heavenly birth." *Fr.* Childe Harold's Pilgrimage.
Farewell! If Ever Fondest Prayer.
Farewell to His Wife.
Farewell to Land, A. *Fr.* Childe Harold's Pilgrimage.
Filial Love. *Fr.* Childe Harold's Pilgrimage.
First Kiss of Love, The.
First Love. *Fr.* Don Juan.
For Music.
For Orford and for Waldegrave.
Fragment: "I would to heaven that I were so much clay." *Fr.* Don Juan.
Freedom's Hero. *Fr.* The Prisoner of Chillon.
Friendship.
From the Turkish ("The chain I gave").
George the Fourth in Ireland.
George the Third. *Fr.* The Vision of Judgment.
Giaour, The, *sels*
Glory That Was Greece, The. *Fr.* Don Juan.
Great Men. *Fr.* Don Juan.
Greece ("Clime of the unforgotten brave"). *Fr.* The Giaour.
Greece ("Fair Greece! sad relic"). *Fr.* Childe Harold's Pilgrimage.
Greek War-Song, *tr.*
Grief. *Fr.* And Thou Art Dead, as Young and Fair.
Gulbeyaz. *Fr.* Don Juan.
Haidee. *Fr.* Don Juan.
Hail and Farewell.
He Who Ascends to Mountain-Tops. *Fr.* Childe Harold's Pilgrimage.
Hesperus. *Fr.* Don Juan.
Hesperus the Bringer. *Fr.* Don Juan.
Highlands' Swelling Blue, The. *Fr.* The Island.
His Politics. *Fr.* Don Juan.
Hymn to Hesperus. *Fr.* Don Juan.
I have not loved the world. *Fr.* Childe Harold's Pilgrimage.
I Loved, I Love You.
I made a footing in the wall. *Fr.* The Prisoner of Chillon.
I stood in Venice. *Fr.* Childe Harold's Pilgrimage.
I want a hero: an uncommon want. *Fr.* Don Juan.
If That High World.
Illustrious Holland! *Fr.* English Bards and Scotch Reviewers.
Immortal Mind, The.
Incantation, An. *Fr.* Manfred.
Inferno, *sel., tr. Fr.* Divina Commedia.
Invocation: "Bob Southey! You're a poet—Poet-laureate." *Fr.* Don Juan.
Is thy face like thy mother's. *Fr.* Childe Harold's Pilgrimage.
Isles of Greece, The. *Fr.* Don Juan.
Isles of Greece, The, *sels. Fr.* Don Juan.
Isolation of Genius, The. *Fr.* Childe Harold's Pilgrimage.
It Is the Hush of Night. *Fr.* Childe Harold's Pilgrimage.
Italia! Oh Italia! *tr.*
Italy. *Fr.* Beppo.
Italy, *tr.*
Jephtha's Daughter.
John Keats. *Fr.* Don Juan.
Juan and Haidee; Ways of Love. *Fr.* Don Juan.
Juan in England. *Fr.* Don Juan.
Julia's Letter. *Fr.* Don Juan.
Kiss, Dear Maid, The.
Know Ye the Land. *Fr.* The Bride of Abydos.
Labuntur Anni. *Fr.* Don Juan.
Lachin y Gair.
Lady Adeline Amundeville. *Fr.* Don Juan.
Lake at Newstead, The. *Fr.* Don Juan.
Lake Leman. *Fr.* Childe Harold's Pilgrimage.
Lake Leman lies by Chillon's walls. *Fr.* The Prisoner of Chillon.
Lake Poets, The. *Fr.* Don Juan.
Lambro's Return. *Fr.* Don Juan.
Lament of Tasso, The.
Land of the Sun, The. *Fr.* The Bride of Abydos.
Lara, *sel.*
Learned Ladies. *Fr.* Don Juan.
Life. *Fr.* Don Juan.
Light broke in upon my brain, A. *Fr.* The Prisoner of Chillon.
Lines Inscribed upon a Cup Formed from a Skull.
Lines on Hearing That Lady Byron Was Ill.
Lines to a Lady Weeping.
Lines to Mr. Hodgson.
Lines Written in an Album at Malta.
London Literature and Society. *Fr.* Don Juan.
London Town. *Fr.* Don Juan.
Love. *Fr.* Childe Harold's Pilgrimage.
Love and the Poets. *Fr.* Don Juan.
Love of Women, The. *Fr.* Don Juan.
Love Unseen. *Fr.* Childe Harold's Pilgrimage.
Lovers, The.
Maid of Athens, Ere We Part.
Man and Nature. *Fr.* Childe Harold's Pilgrimage.
Man-o'-War, The. *Fr.* Childe Harold's Pilgrimage.
Manfred.
Manfred, *sels.*
Man's Love. *Fr.* Don Juan.
"Mary." *Fr.* Don Juan.
Mazeppa.
Mazeppa, *sel.*
Money. *Fr.* Don Juan.
Moorish King Who Lost Alhama, The, *tr.*
Morgante maggiore, Il, *sel., tr.*
Murat. *Fr.* Ode from the French.
My Boat Is on the Shore.
My Days of Love Are Over. *Fr.* Don Juan.
Napoleon. *Fr.* Childe Harold's Pilgrimage.
Napoleon's Farewell.
Nature. *Fr.* Childe Harold's Pilgrimage.
Newstead Abbey.
Night. *Fr.* Childe Harold's Pilgrimage.
Night and Storm in the Alps. *Fr.* Childe Harold's Pilgrimage.
Night before the Battle of Waterloo, The. *Fr.* Childe Harold's Pilgrimage.
Night before Waterloo. *Fr.* Childe Harold's Pilgrimage.
Night on Lake Leman. *Fr.* Childe Harold's Pilgrimage.
Norman Abbey. *Fr.* Don Juan.
Nothing so difficult as a beginning. *Fr.* Don Juan.
Oh! Snatched Away in Beauty's Bloom.
O Talk Not to Me.
Oh! Weep for Those.
Ocean, The. *Fr.* Childe Harold's Pilgrimage.
Ode: "Oh Venice! Venice! when thy marble walls."
Ode from the French, *sel.*
Ode on Venice.
Ode on Venice, *sels.*
Ode to Napoleon Buonaparte.
Ode to Napoleon Buonaparte, *sel.*
Ode to the Framers of the Frame Bill, An.
On a Nun, *tr.*
On Chillon. *Fr.* The Prisoner of Chillon.
On Jordan's Bank.
On My Thirty-third Birthday.
On Rome. *Fr.* Childe Harold's Pilgrimage.
On the Bust of Helen by Canova.
On the Castle of Chillon. *Fr.* The Prisoner of Chillon.
On the Soul, *tr.*
On This Day I Complete My Thirty-sixth Year.
On This Day I Complete My Thirty-sixth Year, *sel.*
On Wellington. *Fr.* Don Juan.
Orient, The. *Fr.* The Bride of Abydos.
Pantheon, The. *Fr.* Childe Harold's Pilgrimage.
Paolo and Francesca, *tr. Fr.* Divina Commedia: Inferno.
Picture of Death, A. *Fr.* The Giaour.
Pleasant Things. *Fr.* Don Juan.
Poems to Thyrza. *Fr.* And Thou Art Dead, as Young and Fair.
Poet and the World, The. *Fr.* Childe Harold's Pilgrimage.
Poetical Commandments. *Fr.* Don Juan.
Poet's Credo. *Fr.* Don Juan.
Poet's Impulse, The. *Fr.* Childe Harold's Pilgrimage.
Post-Obits and the Poets, *tr.*
Power of Money, The. *Fr.* Don Juan.
Prisoner of Chillon, The.
Prisoner of Chillon, The, *sels.*
Prometheus.
Prophecy of Dante, The.
Publisher to His Client, A.
Race with Death, The. *Fr.* Ode on Venice.
Refuge in Venice. *Fr.* Childe Harold's Pilgrimage.
Remember Thee! Remember Thee!
Remorse. *Fr.* On This Day I Complete My Thirty-sixth Year.
Rhine, The. *Fr.* Childe Harold's Pilgrimage.
Roll On, Thou Deep and Dark Blue Ocean. *Fr.* Childe Harold's Pilgrimage.
Romantic to Burlesque. *Fr.* Don Juan.
Rome. *Fr.* Childe Harold's Pilgrimage.
Rome and Freedom. *Fr.* Childe Harold's Pilgrimage.
Ruins of Athens, The. *Fr.* Childe Harold's Pilgrimage.
Ruins of Rome, The. *Fr.* Childe Harold's Pilgrimage.
Sceptic and His Poem, The. *Fr.* Don Juan.
Sea, The. *Fr.* Childe Harold's Pilgrimage.
Sennacherib.
She Walks in Beauty.
Shipwreck, The. *Fr.* Don Juan.
Siege of Corinth, The.
Siege of Corinth, The, *sel.*
Siege of Ismail, The. *Fr.* Don Juan.

BYRON, GEORGE GORDON (*continued*)
Sketch, A.
Sky, Mountains, River! *Fr.* Childe Harold's Pilgrimage.
So We'll Go No More a-Roving.
Solitude. *Fr.* Childe Harold's Pilgrimage.
Song: "Maid of Athens, ere we part."
Song: "So, we'll go no more a-roving."
Song for the Luddites.
Song of Saul before His Last Battle.
Song of the Corsairs.
Song of the Greek Poet [*or* Bard]. *Fr.* Don Juan.
Song of the Rover. *Fr.* The Corsair.
Sonnet: Addressed by a Father Mourning His Recently Deceased Married Daughter to the Father Whose Daughter Had Entered a Convent, *tr.*
Sonnet on Chillon. *Fr.* The Prisoner of Chillon.
Sonnet to Lake Leman.
Southey and Wordsworth. *Fr.* Don Juan.
Stanza: "When a man hath no freedom to fight for at home."
Stanzas: "Could Love for ever."
Stanzas: "Oh, talk not to me of a name great in story."
Stanzas: "When a man hath no freedom to fight for at home."
Stanzas for Music: "Bright be the place of thy soul!"
Stanzas for Music: "There be none of Beauty's daughters."
Stanzas for Music: "There's not a joy the world can give like that it takes away."
Stanzas for Music: "They say that Hope is happiness."
Stanzas to Augusta: "Though the day of my destiny's over."
Stanzas to Augusta: "When all around grew drear and dark."
Stanzas Written on the Road between Florence and Pisa.
Storming of Corinth, The. *Fr.* The Siege of Corinth.
Strahan, Tonson, Lintot of the times.
Summer. *Fr.* The Corsair.
Sun of the Sleepless!
Swimming. *Fr.* The Two Foscari.
There Be None of Beauty's Daughters.
There is a pleasure in the pathless woods. *Fr.* Childe Harold's Pilgrimage.
There Is Pleasure in the Pathless Woods. *Fr.* Childe Harold's Pilgrimage.
There was a sound of revelry by night. *Fr.* Childe Harold's Pilgrimage.
There's not a joy the world can give.
They Accuse Me.
They say that Hope is happiness.
Thou Art Not False, but Thou Art Fickle.
'Tis Sweet to Hear. *Fr.* Don Juan.
To Augusta.
To England. *Fr.* Childe Harold's Pilgrimage.
To Ianthe. *Fr.* Childe Harold's Pilgrimage.
To the Ocean. *Fr.* Childe Harold's Pilgrimage.
To Thomas Moore ("My boat is on the shore").
To Thomas Moore ("What are you doing now?").
To Woman.
To Woman, *sel.*
Tom Paine.
Transient Beauty. *Fr.* The Giaour.
Triumph of the Defeated.
Two Foscari, The, *sel.*
Vanitas Vanitatum. *Fr.* Don Juan.
Venice. *Fr.* Childe Harold's Pilgrimage.
Venice and Rome. *Fr.* Childe Harold's Pilgrimage.
Venice and Sunset. *Fr.* Childe Harold's Pilgrimage.
Very Mournful Ballad on the Siege and Conquest of Alhama, A, *tr.*
Vision of Belshazzar, The.
Vision of Judgment, The.
Vision of Judgment, The, *sels.*
Voltaire and Gibbon. *Fr.* Childe Harold's Pilgrimage.
Wandering Outlaw, The. *Fr.* Childe Harold's Pilgrimage.
Washington. *Fr.* Ode to Napoleon Buonaparte.
Waterloo. *Fr.* Childe Harold's Pilgrimage.
We'll Go No More a-Roving.
Well! Thou Art Happy.
Wellington. *Fr.* Don Juan.
When a Man Hath No Freedom to Fight for at Home.
When Coldness Wraps This Suffering Clay.
When We Two Parted.
Where He Gazed a Gloom Pervaded. *Fr.* The Vision of Judgment.
Where None Intrudes. *Fr.* Childe Harold's Pilgrimage.
Who Kill'd John Keats?
World Is a Bundle of Hay, The.
Written after Swimming from Sestos to Abydos.
Youth and Age.
BYRON, MAY CLARISSA GILLINGTON. Adventurers, The.
Fairy Thrall, The.
My Little House.
Pageant of Seamen, The.
Storm-Child, The.
Tryst of the Night, The.
BYSON, EVA. Now Bar the Door.

C

"C., A. L." To Him All Life Was Beauty.
"C., E." Emaricdulfe, *sels.*
I am enchanted with thy snow-white hands. *Fr.* Emaricdulfe.
My heart is like a ship on Neptune's back. *Fr.* Emaricdulfe.
Within her hair Venus and Cupid sport them. *Fr.* Emaricdulfe.
"C., E. M. H." Silent Grand Army, The.
"C., E. P." Fuzzy Wuzzy Leaves Us.
"C., F." Lines to a Book Borrower.
"C., H. B." New Liberty Bell, The.
"C., J." Alcilia, *sel.*
Frailty of Beauty, The. *Fr.* Alcilia.
"C., N." Life.
"C. B. A." *See* "A., C. B."
"C. G. L." *See* "L., C. G."
"C. H. W." *See* "W., C. H."
"C. N. S." *See* "S., C. N."
"C. W. T." *See* "T., C. W."
CABELL, JAMES BRANCH. Alone in April.
Although as yet my cure be incomplete. *Fr.* Retractions.
And therefore praise I even the most high. *Fr.* Retractions.
Cry Kismet and take heart. Eros is gone. *Fr.* Retractions.
Easter Eve.
Garden-Song.
I am contented by remembrances. *Fr.* Retractions.
It is in many ways made plain to us. *Fr.* Retractions.
Nightly I mark and praise, or great or small. *Fr.* Retractions.
One End of Love.
Retractions, *sels.*
So, let us laugh,—lest vain rememberings. *Fr.* Retractions.
Story of the Flowery Kingdom.
With Love I garnered mirth. *Fr.* Retractions.
You ask a Sonnet?—Well, it is your right. *Fr.* Retractions.
CABLE, FRANKLIN. Tree-building.
CABLE, GEORGE WASHINGTON. New Arrival, The.
Written in the Visitors' Book at the Birthplace of Robert Burns.
CADALSO VAZQUEZ, JOSÉ DE. Satirical Letrilla.
CADDEN, J. E. Embers.
Sunset on Sixth Avenue.
CADETT, HERBERT. War.
CADILLA, CARMEN ALICIA. Angelus.
Responsories.
Sad Air.
CÆDMON. Approach of Pharaoh, The. *Fr.* Genesis.
Beginning of Creation, The. *Fr.* Genesis.
Christ and Satan, *sels., at.*
Cloud by Day. *Fr.* Exodus.
Coming of Pharaoh, The. *Fr.* Exodus.
Creation, The.
Drowning of Pharaoh and His Army. *Fr.* Exodus.
Exodus, *sels.*
Fall of Satan, The. *Fr.* Genesis.
Fall of the Angels, The. *Fr.* Genesis.
Far and Wide She Went. *Fr.* Genesis.
Garden of Eden, The. *Fr.* Genesis.
Hymn of the World's Creator.
Lamentations of the Fallen Angels, *Fr.* Christ and Satan.
Satan's Presumption and Fall. *Fr.* Genesis.
CAHOON, HERBERT. Angleworm.
CAIN, MAUD LUDINGTON. To Omar Khayyám.
CALDERÓN DE LA BARCA, PEDRO. Cross, The. *Fr.* La Devocion de la Cruz.
Death Speaks.
Demon Speaks, The. *Fr.* El Magico prodigioso.
Devocion de la Cruz, La, *sel.*
Dream Called Life, The.
Dying Eusebio's Address to the Cross, The.
Holy Eucharist, The.
Life Is a Dream, *sel.*
Magico prodigioso, El, *sel.*
Sonnet: "These flowers that were resplendent, a delight."
Sonnet: "Those flakes of fire, brilliant sparks of light."
Thou Art of All Created Things.
CALDWELL, GEORGE W. Doctor, The, *sel.*
Surgeon, The.
Trail of Life, The.
CALDWELL, WILLIAM W. Robin's Come.
Rose-Bush, The, *tr.*
CALENBERG, CONNIE. I Love Thee, Lord.
Take My Hand, O Blessed Master.
CALHOUN, GEORGE. McKinley Brook.
Rufus's Mare.
CALHOUN, JOHN. Messenger Song, The, *at.*
Perigoo's Horse, *at.*
Peter Emberley.
CALKINS, CLINCH. Dead City, The.
CALKINS, S. S. World Is Waiting for You, The.
CALL, FRANK OLIVER. Blue Homespun. *Fr.* A Sonnet Series of French Canada.
Burned Forests.
Chinese Poet, A.
First Garden, The.
La Terre. *Fr.* A Sonnet Series of French Canada.
Maker of Toy Boats, The.
Old Habitant, An. *Fr.* A Sonnet Series of French Canada.
Oven, The.
Sonnet Series of French Canada, A, *sels.*
Sugar-Maker, The.
Through Arched Windows.
CALL, WATHEN MARK WILKS. Hymn: "When by the marbled lake I lie and listen."
People's Petition, The.
Renunciation.
Summer Days.

CALLAGHAN, GERTRUDE. Award.
I Shall Break a Heavy Bough.
Native Son.
New England Fog.
Sorrow's Ladder.
Who Goes By Lightly.
CALLANAN, JEREMIAH [*or* JAMES] JOHN [*or* JOSEPH]. Convict of Clonmel [*or* Clonmala], The, *tr.*
Dirge of O'Sullivan Bear, *tr.*
Girl I Love, The, *tr.*
Gougaune Barra.
Lament for [*or* of] O'Sullivan Bear[e], The, *tr.*
Lines to the Blessed Sacrament.
O Say, My Brown Drimin, *tr.*
Outlaw of Loch Lene, The, *tr.*
Pure Is the Dewy Gem.
Serenade: "Blue waves are sleeping, The."
Song: "Awake thee, my Bessy, the morning is fair."
To ——.
When Each Bright Star Is Clouded.
White Cockade, The, *tr.*
Written to a Young Lady.
CALLIMACHUS. Aesthete, The.
Artemis Visits the Cyclopes.
Bacchante's Offering, The.
Bathing of Pallas, The.
Battle of the Books, The.
Blinding of Tiresias, The.
Brother and Sister.
Callignotus and Ionis.
Callimachus to Heraclitus.
Cleombrotus.
Conopion.
Crethis.
Cyclops, The.
Daybreak in the City.
Dead Boy.
Dead Playmate, The.
Dead Poet, The.
Delos.
Dialogue with the Dead.
Don Juan.
Elegy on Herakleitos.
Epiphany of Apollo, The.
Epitaph on Himself.
Erysichthon.
Fastidious!
For the Bath of Pallas.
Good Live for Ever, The.
Heraclitus.
Here Dicon's son, Acanthian Saon lies.
Here lie, I, Timon; who, alive, all living men did hate.
His Son.
Hunting Code.
Hymn to Apollo.
Hymn to Zeus, *sel.*
In Memory of Saon of Acantus.
Loss at Sea.
Love's Capriciousness.
Love's Chase.
Misanthrope, The.
Nicoteles.
Now would to God swift ships had ne'er been made!
Odi Profanum Vulgus.
On the Tomb of Crethis.
Parnassian, The.
Poet's Father, The.
Poet's Own Epitaph, The.
"Pulvis et Umbra."
Rests Charidas beneath this tomb? "Here I."
Sacrilege of Tiresias, The.
Saon.
Saon of Acanthus.
Sinister Dialogue.
Sopolis.
Statue of Berenice, A.
This morning we beheld with streaming eyes.
Timon.
Timon's Epitaph.
To Apollo.
To Aratus.
To Archinus.
To Delos.
To Heracleitus.
To the Goddess of Childbirth.
Uncommon.
Zealous Platonist, The.
CALLINUS. Call to Action, A.
How long will ye slumber? when will ye take heart?
Rallying Song.
CALLISTRATUS. Harmodius Song, The.
In a wreath of myrtle I'll wear my glaive.
Patriotic Song.
Wishes.
CALLOWAY, R. C. Awful Lot to Fishin', An.
CALVERLEY, CHARLES STUART. A, B, C.
Ajax, *sel., tr.*
Alphabet, The.
Amycus, *tr.* *Fr.* Idylls.
Anno 1829, *tr.*
Arab, The.
Auld Wife, The.
Ballad: "Auld wife sat at her ivied door, The."
Bandusia, Stainless Mirror, *tr.*
Beer.
Beer, *sel.*
Cat, The. *Fr.* Sad Memories.
Changed.
Cock and the Bull, The.
Companions.
Contentment.
Disaster.
Dogs at the Homestead, The, *tr.* *Fr.* Idylls.
Eclogue I, *sel.* ("What made thee then so keen to look on Rome?"). *Fr.* Eclogues (*of* Virgil).
First Love.
"Forever."
Gemini and Virgo.
Gemini and Virgo, *sel.*
Giant's Wooing, The, *tr.* *Fr.* Idylls.
Harvest Home, *tr.* *Fr.* Idylls.
"Hic Vir, Hic Est."
Hylas, *tr.* *Fr.* Idylls.
Idylls (*of* Theocritus), *sels., tr.*
In the Gloaming, *parody.*
Lines on Hearing the Organ.
Lines Suggested by the Fourteenth of February.
Love.
Lovers, and a Reflection.
Mistrust To-Morrow, *tr.*
Morning.
Motherhood.
Ode to Tobacco.
Of Friendship.
Of Reading.
On the Beach.
On the Brink.
Peace.
Play.
Precious Stones.
Sad Memories.
Sad Memories, *sel.*
Schoolmaster, The.
Seek a Haven, *tr.*
Shelter.
Sorceress, The, *tr.* *Fr.* Idylls.
Striking.
To Leuconoë, *tr.*
Transfiguring Love, *tr.* *Fr.* Idylls.
Universal Change, *tr.* *Fr.* Ajax.
Wanderers.
CALVERLEY, SYBIL HORATIA. Midsummer.
CALVERT, GEORGE HENRY. Bunker Hill.
CALVIN, JOHN. Salutation to Jesus Christ.
CALVOS, ANDREAS. Lover of His Country, The.
Ocean, The.
To the Sacred Battalion.
CAMBON, GLAUCO. Vain Cry; Lydian Campaign, 1941.
For translations from French, German, and Italian, see OnPM.
CAMBRIDGE, ADA (MRS. George Frederick Cross). Honour.
CAMDEN, HARRIET PARKER. Oklahoma.
CAMDEN, WILLIAM. On a Puritanicall Lock-Smith [*or* Thieving Lock-smith].
CAMERON, C. C. Success.
CAMERON, DON. Drilling Missed Holes.
Song of the Leadville Mine Boss.
CAMERON, GEORGE FREDERICK. Ah Me! The Mighty Love.
Amoris Finis.
Answer, An.
Death.
Future, The.
Golden Text, The.
I Am Young.
In After Days.
My Political Faith.
Relics.
Standing on Tiptoe.
'Tis Strange, You Think.
To the West Wind.
Way of the World, The.
What Matters It?
Wisdom.
Ysolte.
CAMERON, NORMAN. Central Europe.
Disused Temple, The.
Drunken Boat, The, *tr.*
El Aghir.
Fight with a Water-Spirit.
Firm of Happiness, Limited, The.
From a Woman to a Greedy Lover. *Fr.* Three Love Poems.
Hook for Leviathan, A.
In the Queen's Room. *Fr.* Three Love Poems.
Invader, The.
Memory, *tr.*
Moonlight, Waterlight and Opal.
Seven-year-old Poet, *tr.*
Shepherdess. *Fr.* Three Love Poems.
Steep, Stone Steps.
Thespians at Thermopylae, The.
Three Love Poems.
Verdict, The.
Wanton's Death, The.
CAMETAS. On the Lawn.
CAMILLE, ROUSSAN. Nedjé.
CAMMAERTS, EMILE. Homeland, The.
CAMÕES [*or* CAMOENS], LUÍS [*or* LUIZ] DE. Babylon and Sion (Goa and Lisbon).
Blighted Love.
Cape of Tempests, The. *Fr.* The Lusiads.
Episode of Adamastor off the Cape of Good Hope. *Fr.* The Lusiads.
Lusiads, The, *sels.*
On Revisiting Cintra after the Death of Catarina.
On the Death of Catarina de Attayda.
Passage to India. *Fr.* The Lusiads.
Sonnet: "Leave me, all sweet refrains my lip hath made."
Sonnet: "Time and the mortal will stand never fast."
Waterspout.
CAMP, PAULINE FRANCES. Cradle Song: "There's a baby moon rocking far up in the sky."
Winter Song, A.
CAMPANA, DINO. Old Lines; a Fragment.
CAMPANELLA, TOMMASO [*or* TOMASSO]. People, The.
"CAMPASPE." To an Irish Setter Pup.
CAMPBELL, ALICE B. Sally and Manda.
CAMPBELL, ALISTAIR. At the Fishing Settlement.
Hut Near Desolated Pines.
Lie on the Sand.
Narcissus.
Now He Is Dead.
Now Sleeps the Gorge.
O Catch Miss Daisy Pinks.
CAMPBELL, ANNE. Before and after Marriage.
Shabby Old Dad.
There Is Always a Place for You.
To My Friend.
CAMPBELL, ARCHIBALD Y. Animula Vagula.
Dromedary, The.
There Are Still Kingfishers.
CAMPBELL, CALDER. Ossian's Serenade.
CAMPBELL, DAVID. Ariel.
Beach Queen.
End of Exploring, The.

CAMPBELL, DAVID (*continued*)
Harry Pearce.
Heart of Light.
Men in Green.
Monaro, The.
Night Sowing.
Possum and the Moon, The.
Soldier's Song.
Speak with the Sun.
Stockman, The.
CAMPBELL, ELIZABETH K. Psychology Class.
CAMPBELL, GEORGE. Litany.
CAMPBELL, JAMES EDWIN. Compensation.
Conjuh Man, De.
Negro Serenade.
Ol' Doc' Hyar.
Uncle Eph's Banjo Song.
When Ol' Sis' Judy Pray.
CAMPBELL, JOHN DOUGLAS SUTHERLAND, 9TH DUKE OF ARGYLL AND MARQUESS OF LORNE. Unto the Hills, *par.*
CAMPBELL, JOSEPH ("Seosamh MacCathmhaoil"). As I Came Over the Grey, Grey Hills.
At Harvest.
Besom-Man, The.
Blanaid's Song.
Blind Man at the Fair, The.
Chesspieces.
Ciaran, the Master of Horses and Lands.
Dancer, The.
Fighting-Man, A.
Gilly of Christ, The.
Go, Ploughman, Plough.
Herb-Leech, The.
Hills of Cualann, The.
I Am the Gilly of Christ.
I Am the Mountainy Singer.
I Will Go with My Father a-Ploughing.
Ninepenny Fidil, The.
O Glorious Childbearer.
Old Age Pensioner, The.
Old Woman, The.
On Waking.
Poet Loosed a Wingèd Song, The.
Shining Spaces of the South, The.
Three Colts Exercising in a Six-Acre.
Tinkers, The.
Unfrocked Priest, The.
CAMPBELL, LAURA. Peeny-Pen-Pone.
CAMPBELL, MARION SUSAN. Riding through Jerusalem.
CAMPBELL, MARJORIE FREEMAN. Only the Heart.
Vigil.
CAMPBELL, MARY, *and* ROY CAMPBELL. *See* CAMPBELL, ROY, *and* MARY CAMPBELL.
CAMPBELL, NANCY (Mrs. Joseph Campbell). Apple-Tree, The.
Like One I Know.
Monkey, The.
CAMPBELL, ROBERT BHAIN. Final Poem.
Task, The.
CAMPBELL, ROY. African Moonrise.
Autumn.
Buffel's Kop.
Choosing a Mast.
Dark Night of the Soul, The, *sel., tr.*
Death of Polybius Jubb, The.
Death of the Bull.
Dreaming Spires.
Fall of Satan, The. *Fr.* The Flaming Terrapin.
Familiar Daemon.
Flaming Terrapin, The, *sels.*
Garden, The.
Georgiad, The, *sel.*
Good Resolution, A.
Hialmar.
Horses on the Camargue.
Invocation to the African Muse. *Fr.* The Flaming Terrapin.
Limerick: "He died in attempting to swallow."
Lisa's Golden Hair, *tr.*
Louse-Catchers, The, *tr.*
Luis de Camões.
Mazeppa.
Mithraic Emblems, *sel.*
Noah. *Fr.* The Flaming Terrapin.
On Lisa's Golden Hair, *tr.*
On Professor Drennan's Verse.
On Some South African Novelists.
On the Death of a Journalist.
On the Same.
Palm, The.
Pomegranates.
Rounding the Cape.
Serf, The.
Sisters, The.
Sling, The.
Snake, The.
Talking Bronco, *sel.*
To a Pet Cobra.
To the Sun. *Fr.* Mithraic Emblems.
Toledo; July 1936.
Tristan da Cunha.
Upon a Gloomy Night, *tr. Fr.* The Dark Night of the Soul.
Veld Eclogue, A; the Pioneers, *sel.*
Verses Written after an Ecstasy of High Exaltation, *tr.*
Volunteer's Reply to the Poet, The. *Fr.* Talking Bronco.
Wayzgoose, The, *sel.*
Zebras, The.
Zulu Girl, The.
CAMPBELL, ROY, *and* MARY CAMPBELL. Somnambulistic Ballad, *tr.*
CAMPBELL, THOMAS. Adelgitha.
Battle of Hohenlinden, The.
Battle of the Baltic, The.
Beatific Sea, The.
Beech Tree's Petition, The.
Dead Eagle, The.
Dream, A, *sel.*
Earl March look'd on his dying child.
Evening Star, The.
Exile of Erin.
Field Flowers.
First Kiss, The.
Florine.
Fragment: "Mountain summits sleep, The," *tr.*
Freedom and Love.
Glenara.
Hallowed Ground.
Harper, The.
Hohenlinden.
Hope. *Fr.* The Pleasures of Hope.
How Delicious Is the Winning.
Irish Harper and His Dog, The.
Jilted Nymph, The.
Last Man, The.
Lochiel's Warning.
Lord Ullin's Daughter.
Maid of Neidpath, The.
Maid's Remonstrance, The.
Margaret and Dora.
Men of England.
Mighty Sea! Cameleon-like Thou Changest.
My Dog Tray.
My wealth's a burly spear and brand, *tr.*
Napoleon and the British Sailor.
Ode to the Germans.
Ode to Winter.
Parrot, The.
Pilgrim of a Day, The.
Pleasures of Hope, The, *sels.*
Poland. *Fr.* The Pleasures of Hope.
Poor Dog Tray.
Rainbow, The.
River of Life, The.
Sleep upon the World, *tr.*
Soldier and Sailor.
Soldier's Dream, The.
Soldier's Riches, A, *tr.*
Song: "Earl March looked on his dying child."
Song: "How delicious is the winning."
Song to the Evening Star.
Spectre Boat, The.
Star That Bringest Home the Bee.
Taste. *Fr.* Valedictory Stanza to Kemble.
Thought Suggested by the New Year.
To Mary Sinclair, with a Volume of His Poems.
To the Evening Star ("Gem of the crimson-colour'd even").
To the Evening Star ("Star that bringest home the bee").
To the Rainbow.
Valedictory Stanza to Kemble, *sel.*
Ye Mariners of England.
Young Hero, The.
CAMPBELL, WALTER STANLEY. *See* "VESTAL, STANLEY."
CAMPBELL, WILFRED (William Wilfred Campbell). Bereavement of the Fields.
Canadian Folk Song.
Children of the Foam, The.
England.
Harvest Slumber Song.
Higher Kinship, The.
Hills and the Sea, The.
How One Winter Came in the Lake Region.
Indian Summer.
Lake Memory, A.
Last Prayer, The.
Lazarus.
Lines on a Re-reading of Parts of the Old Testament, *sel.*
Manitou.
Mother, The.
Stella Flammarum.
To the Lakes.
Vapour and Blue.
Were-Wolves, The.
Winter Lakes, The.
With Cortez in Mexico.
CAMPIAN, THOMAS. *See* CAMPION, THOMAS.
CAMPION, MOTHER MARY. Cloister.
CAMPION [*or* CAMPIAN], THOMAS. Advice to a Girl.
Amaryllis.
And Would You See My Mistress' Face, *at.*
Author of Light.
Awake, Awake, Thou Heavy Spright.
Basia.
Beauty Is but a Painted Hell.
Beauty Is Not Bound.
Beauty Unbound.
Blame Not My Cheeks.
Chance and Change.
Cherry-ripe.
Come, Cheerful Day!
Come, Let Us Sound [*or* Sing] with Melody, the Praises.
Come, Oh, Come, My Life's Delight.
Come, You Pretty False-eyed Wanton.
Conjuration.
Content.
Corinna.
Cypress Curtain of the Night Is Spread, The.
Dance, The ("Robin is a lovely lad"), *at.*
Devotion ("Follow thy fair sun, unhappy shadow").
Devotion ("Follow your saint, follow with accents sweet!").
Dismissal. *Fr.* The Mountebank's Mask.
Fain Would I Wed.
First Love.
Follow, follow.
Follow Thy Fair Sun [Unhappy Shadow].
Follow Your Saint [Follow with Accents Sweet].
Fortunati Nimium.
Give Beauty All Her Right.
Hark, All You Ladies That Do Sleep!
Her Fair Inflaming Eyes.
Her Sacred Bower.
His Lover's Triumphs.
Hope and Fear.
Hours of Sleepy Night, The. *Fr.* The Mountebank's Mask.
Hymn in Praise of Neptune, A.
I Care Not for These Ladies.
I must complayne she doth enioye my love, *at.*
If Thou Longest So Much to Learn.
In Imagine Pertransit Homo.
Integer Vitae.

It Shall Suffice.
Jack and Joan.
Jack and Jone They Thinke No Ill.
Just Beguiler.
Kind Are Her Answers.
Kisses, *at.*
Lament for Prince Henry.
Lamentation, A.
Laura.
Life Upright, The.
Little Breath I'll Borrow, A.
Lo, when back mine eye.
Lord Hay's Mask, *sel.*
Lords' Mask, The, *sel.*
Lost Freedom.
Love Me or Not.
Love's Pilgrims.
Maids Are Simple.
Man of Life Upright, The.
Most Sweet and Pleasing Are Thy Ways.
Mountebank's Mask, The, *sel.*
My Life's Delight.
My Love Bound Me.
My Sweetest Lesbia.
Neptune.
Never Love unless You Can.
Never Weather-beaten Sail [More Willing Bent to Shore].
Night as Well as Brightest Day. *Fr.* A Relation of the Late Royal Entertainment Given by the Lord Knowles.
Now Hath Flora Robbed Her Bowers. *Fr.* Lord Hay's Mask.
Now Winter Nights Enlarge.
O Come Quickly!
O Crudelis Amor, *tr.*
O Sweet Delight.
Of Corinna's Singing.
Oft have I sigh'd for him that heares me not.
Out of My Soul's Depth.
Peaceful Western Wind, The.
Pilgrimage towards Loves Holy Land, A.
Proserpina.
Relation of the Late Royal Entertainment Given by the Lord Knowles, A, *sels.*
Renunciation, A.
Respect My Faith.
Rose-cheeked Laura [Come].
Roses. *Fr.* Lord Hay's Mask.
Seek the Lord.
Shall I come, if I swim? wide are the waves, you see.
Shall I Come, Sweet Love, to Thee.
Sic Transit.
Silly boy, 'tis full moon yet, thy night as day shines clearly.
Sing a Song of Joy, *sel.*
Sleep, Angry Beauty.
So Quicke, So Hot, So Mad Is Thy Fond Sute.
So sweet is thy discourse to me.
So Tir'd Are All My Thoughts.
Some hot, some cold.
Song: "Follow thy faire sunne, unhappy shadowe!"
Song: "Jack and Joan they think no ill."
Song: "Now winter nights enlarge."
Song: "O sweet delight, O more than human bliss."
Song: "Rose-cheekt Laura, come."
Song: To the Masquers Representing Stars. *Fr.* The Lords' Mask.
Song from a Booke of Ayres, A.
Spells.
Stars Dance, The. *Fr.* The Lords' Mask.
Tell, O Tell.
There Is a Garden in Her Face.
There Is None, Oh, None but You.
Think'st Thou to Seduce Me Then.
Thou Art Not Fair.
Thou Joy'st, Fond Boy.
Though you are young and I am old.
Thrice Toss These Oaken Ashes [in the Air].
To his sweet lute Apollo sung the motions of the spheres.
To Lesbia.
To Music Bent Is My Retired Mind.
To Shades of Underground.
Turn All Thy Thoughts to Eyes.
Turn Back, You Wanton Flyer.
Unless there were consent 'twixt hell and heaven.
Upright Life, The.
Vain men, whose follies make a god of love.
View Me, Lord, a Work of Thine.
Vivamus Mea Lesbia atque Amemus.
Vobiscum Est Iope.
Were My Heart as Some Men's Are.
What Faire Pompe Have I Spide of Glittering Ladies.
What harvest half so sweet is.
What if a Day, or a Month, or a Year.
What then is love but mourning?
When the God of Merry Love.
When Thou Must Home [to Shades of Underground].
When to Her Lute Corinna Sings.
Where Are All Thy Beauties Now.
Where She Her Sacred Bower Adorns.
Winter Nights.
Wise men patience never want.
Writer to His Book, The.
Yet Still I Live.
Young and Old.
Young and Simple though I Am.
CAMPOAMOR, RAMÓN DE. After Twenty Years. *Fr.* Doloras.
Boredom. *Fr.* Doloras.
Doloras, *sels.*
Great Banquet, The. *Fr.* Doloras.
Humoradas, *sel.*
If Only I Could Write! *Fr.* Doloras.
Traditions.
You wave your fan with such a graceful art. *Fr.* Humoradas.
CANÉ, LUIS. Prayer for Each Awakening.
CANE, MELVILLE. After Reading the Reviews of "Finnegans Wake."
Bed-Time Story.
Before Dawn.
Dawn Has Yet to Ripple In.
Each to Each.
Emily Dickinson.
Fog, the Magician.
Harvest to Seduce, A.
Hymn to Night.
Operatic Note.
Presence of Snow.
Snow toward Evening.
Tree in December.
CANFIELD, HARRY CLIFFORD. Elegy on the Loss of U.S. Submarine S4, *sel.*
CANNING, GEORGE. Cat and the Bird, The.
Dutch, The.
Elderly Gentleman, The.
Epitaph for the Tombstone Erected over the Marquis of Anglesea's Leg, Lost at the Battle of Waterloo.
Give me the avowed, the erect, the manly foe.
Ipecacuanha.
Progress of Man, The, *sel.*
Soldier's Friend, The.
To Mrs. Leigh upon Her Wedding-Day.
CANNING, GEORGE, GEORGE ELLIS, *and* JOHN HOOKHAM FRERE. Rovers, The, *sel.*
Song: "Whene'er with haggard eyes I view." *Fr.* The Rovers.
Song by Rogero the Captive. *Fr.* The Rovers.
Song of One Eleven Years in Prison. *Fr.* The Rovers.
CANNING, GEORGE, *and* JOHN HOOKHAM FRERE. Friend of Humanity and the Knife-Grinder, The.
Knife-Grinder, The.
Progress of Man, The, *sel.*
Sapphics.
CANNING, GEORGE, JOHN HOOKHAM FRERE, *and others.* New Morality.
CANNON, DAVID WADSWORTH, JR. Freedom in Mah Soul.
Western Town.
CANNON, EDWARD. Unexpected [*or* Unsuspected] Fact, An.
CANNON, MARGERY. Venite Adoremus.
CANTERBURY, GEORGE. New Mexico and Arizona.
CANTÓN, WILBERTO L. Island.
On Lake Llanquihue.
CANTON, WILLIAM. Bethlehem.
Bubble-blowing.
Carol: "When the herds were watching."
Child's Prayer, A.
Crow, The.
Heights and Depths.
Karma.
Laus Infantium.
New Poet, A.
Rhymes about a Little Woman.
She Was a Treasure.
Trafalgar.
CANTUS, ELEANOR HOLLISTER. Fame.
CANUTE [*or* CNUT], KING. Merie Sungen the Muneches, *at.*
Merrily sang the Monkes in Ely, *at.*
CAPE, FRED. Tin Gee Gee, The.
CAPELL, WILLIAM. I Saw Death Slain.
CAPERN, EDWARD. On a Snow Storm.
Rural Postman, The, *sel.*
CAPES, MOLLY. Hallowe'en.
CAPETANAKIS, DEMETRIOS. Abel.
CARAGHER, MARY E. Tree Tag.
CARBERRY, H. D. I Shall Remember.
Nature.
Return.
"CARBERY, ETHNA" (Anna Johnston MacManus). Hills o' My Heart.
In Tir-na'n-Og.
Love-Talker, The.
Mea Culpa.
Neece the Rapparee.
Other, The.
Sad Song of Finian, The.
Shadow House of Lugh, The.
CARDENAL, PEIRE. Sirventes: "Paramours, to those who would accuse, The."
CARDOZA Y ARAGÓN, LUIS. Ballad of Federico García Lorca.
CARDOZO, ELIZABETH C. We Met Them on the Common Way.
CARDUCCI, GIOSUÈ. Ancient Sorrow.
Fantasy.
First Snowfall.
Hymn to Satan.
Ox, The.
Petrarch.
Primo Vere.
Snowfall.
Vision.
CAREW, LADY ELIZABETH. Chorus: "'Tis not enough for one that is a wife." *Fr.* Mariam.
Mariam, *sels.*
Revenge of Injuries. *Fr.* Mariam.
CAREW, THOMAS. Ask Me No More [Where Jove Bestows].
Beautifull Mistress, A.
Boldness in Love.
Careless of love & free from feares, *at.*
Celia Singing ("Hark, how my Celia").
Celia Singing ("You that think love can convey").
Celia Threatened.
Compliment, The.
Cruel Mistress, A.
Deposition from Love, A.
Disdain Returned.
Elegie [*or* Elegy] upon the Death of the Dean[e] of Paul's, Dr. John Donne, An.
Epitaph, An: "This little vault, this narrow room."
Epitaph on a Young Girl.
Epitaph on Lady Salter.
Epitaph on Maria Wentworth.
Epitaph on the Lady Villiers.
Epitaph on the Lady Mary Villiers [*or* Villers].
Eternity of Love Protested.
Fear Not, Dear Love.
Give Me More Love or More Disdain.
Good Counsell to a Young Maid.
He That Loves a Rosy Cheek.
Her Sweet Voice.
How ill doth he deserve a lover's name.

Carew, Thomas (*continued*)
I Will Enjoy Thee Now.
If when the Sun at noon displays.
Ingrateful Beauty Threatened.
Inscription on the Tomb of the Lady Mary Wentworth, The.
Know, Celia, since thou art so proud.
Lover Consults with Reason, The.
Maria Wentworth [Thomae Comitis Cleveland, Filia Praemortua Prima Virgineam Animam Exhalavit].
Mark How the Bashful Morn.
Mediocrity in Love Rejected.
More Love or More Disdain.
Murdering Beauty.
Never-dying Fire.
Now That the Winter's Gone.
On Sight of a Gentlewomans Face in the Water.
Other, An ("The purest Soul that e're was sent").
Other, An ("This little Vault, this narrow room").
Pastoral Dialogue, A.
Persuasions to Enjoy.
Persuasions to Joy; a Song.
Persuasions to Love.
Persuasions to Love, *sel.*
Poore pensive I o're chargde with woe, *at.*
Protestation, The.
Psalm XCI ("Make the great God thy fort, and dwell").
Rapture, A.
Red and White Roses.
Secrecy Protested.
Song: "Ask me no more where Jove bestows."
Song: Beautiful Mistress, A.
Song: Celia Singing.
Song: Eternity of Love Protested.
Song: "Give me more love or more disdain."
Song: Perswasions to Enjoy.
Song: To My Inconstant Mistress.
Song: "Would you know what's soft? I dare."
Spring, The.
Steadfast Mind, The.
Sweetly Breathing, Vernal Air.
This little vault, this narrow room. *Fr.* Epitaph on a Young Girl.
To A. L.: Persuasions to Love.
To a Lady Resembling His Mistress.
To a Lady That Desired I Would Love Her.
To Ben Jonson.
To His Inconstant Mistress.
To His Mistress Confined, *at.*
To My Inconstant Mistress.
To My Worthy Friend Master [*or* Mr.] George Sands [on His Translation of the Psalmes].
To Saxham.
True Beauty, The.
Unfading Beauty, The.
Unfading Beauty, The, *sel.*
Ungrateful Beauty Threatened.
Upon a Ribbon Tied about His Arm by a Lady.
Upon Master W. Montague.
When thou poor excommunicate.
Would you know what's soft? I dare.
You that think Love can convey.
Carey, Henry. Ballad of Sally in Our Alley, The.
Contrivances, The, *sel.*
Drinking-Song, A.
God Save the King, *at.*
Happy Myrtillo.
Harry Carey's General Reply, to the Libelling Gentry, Who Are Angry at His Welfare.
Huntsman's Rouse, The.
Maiden's Ideal of a Husband, A. *Fr.* The Contrivances.
Namby Pamby.
Namby Pamby, *sel.*
Of all the girls that are so smart.
Roger and Dolly.
Sally in Our Alley.
Sally in our Alley, *sel.*
Sally Sweetbread.
Carey, Patrick. Chains.
Crucifixus pro Nobis.
Hymn: Crucifixus pro Nobis.
Hymn: "Whilst I beheld the neck o' the dove."
Nulla Fides.
Triolets.
Carleton, Emma. Faith.
Carleton, Sara King. Late October.
Carleton, Will. Across the Delaware.
Country Doctor, The.
Cuba to Columbia.
Doctor's Story, The.
First Settler's Story, The.
Flash—the Fireman's Story.
Little Black-eyed Rebel, The.
New Church Organ, The.
Out of the Old House, Nancy.
Over the Hill from the Poor-House.
Over the Hill to the Poor-House.
Prize of the Margaretta, The.
Ride of Jennie M'Neal, The.
Schoolmaster's Guests, The.
Second Settler's Story, The.
Washington-Month.
Words.
Carleton, William. Sigh for Knockmany, A.
Sir Turlough; or, The Churchyard Bride.
Carlin, Francis (James Francis Carlin MacDonnell). Alchemy.
Baby of Saint Brigid, The.
Ballad of Douglas Bridge.
Before I Stumbled.
Beyond Rathkelly.
Cuckoo, The.
Grey Plume, The.
Haymaker's Lullaby, The.
Hope's Song.
Irish, The.
Joy to You.
MacDiarmod's Daughter.
Market Town, The.
Perfection.
Plea for Hope.
Poor Man, The.
Provinces, The.
Solar Road, The.
Two Nests, The.
Vessels.
Virgins.
Virgin's Slumber Song, The.
Wine.
Carlin, George W. In Palestine.
Carlyle, Jane Welsh (Mrs. Thomas Carlyle). To a Swallow Building under Our Eaves.
Carlyle, Thomas. Adieu.
Cui Bono?
Music.
Sower's Song, The.
To-Day.
Carman, Bliss. April Morning, An.
April Weather.
Arnold, Master of the *Scud.*
At the Road-House.
Autumn.
Autumn Garden, An.
Autumn Song, An.
Ballad of John Camplejohn.
Behind the Arras, *sel.*
Bethlehem.
Camping Song.
Choristers, The.
Christmas Eve Choral, A.
Christmas Song.
Cry of the Hillborn, The.
Daffodil's Return.
Daisies.
Daphne.
Deserted Pasture, The.
Earth Voices, *sel.*
Eavesdropper, The.
Enchanted Traveller, The.
Enchantress, The.
Envoy: "Have little care that Life is brief."
Ghost-Yard of the Goldenrod, The.
Golden Rowan.
Grave-Tree, The.
Gravedigger, The.
Hack and Hew.
Hem and Haw.
Here and Now, *sel.*
Heretic, The.
I Loved Thee, Atthis, in the Long Ago.
In a Copy of Browning.
In October.
In Philistia.
In the House of Idiedaily.
Joys of the Road, The.
Juggler, The.
Lord of My Heart's Elation.
Lord of the Far Horizons.
Low Tide on Grand Pré.
Make Me Over, Mother April. *Fr.* Spring Song.
Man of Peace, The.
Man of the Marne, The.
Marian Drury.
Marigolds.
Mendicants, The.
Mr. Moon.
Moment Musicale.
More Ancient Mariner, A.
Mountain Gateway, A.
Northern Vigil, A.
Old Gray [*or* Grey] Wall, The.
On the Tomb of Bliss Carman.
Over the Shoulders and Slopes of the Dune.
Over the Wintry Threshold.
Overlord.
Rainbird, The.
Roadside Flowers.
St. Bartholomew's on the Hill.
Sappho, *sel.*
Sea Child, A.
Seamark, A.
Sending of the Magi, The.
Ships of Saint John, The.
Ships of Yule, The.
Son of the Sea, A.
Song: "Love, by that loosened hair."
Spring Song.
Spring Song, *sel.*
Spring's Saraband.
Staccato to O Le Lupe, A.
Tecumseh and the Eagles.
Threnody for a Poet.
To a Very Young Gentleman.
Trees.
Triumphalis.
Unreturning, The.
Vagabond Song, A.
Veni Creator ("Lord of my heart's elation").
Veni Creator ("Lord of the grass and hill").
Vestigia.
Where Is Heaven? *Fr.* Here and Now.
Why.
Windflower, A.
Winter Scene, The.
Winter Streams.
Wood-Path, A.
Carman, C. Kathleen (Mrs. L. M. Dodge). Song: "Sleep, O my darling, sleep."
Carmer, Carl. Antique Shop.
Black Boy.
Cathedral of St. Louis, The.
Slave Quarter.
Carmichael, Amy. In Acceptance Lieth Peace.
Last Defile, The.
Think It Not Strange.
Toward Jerusalem.
Carmichael, Waverly Turner. Keep Me, Jesus, Keep Me.
Winter Is Coming.
Carnegie, Agnes Lindsay. Death.
Carnegie, James, Earl of Southesk. Flitch of Dunmow, The.
November's Cadence.
Carnevali, Emanuel. His Majesty the Letter-Carrier.
In This Hotel.
Invocation to Death.
Serenade: "Come on, don't be afraid you'll spoil me."
Sermon.
Carney, Julia A. Fletcher. Kind Deeds

Little Things.
Little Things, *sel.*
CARO, JOSÉ EUSEBIO. Words of the Last Inca.
CARO, RODRIGO. Ruins of Itálica, The.
CAROLAN [*or* O'CAROLAN], TURLOUGH. Cup of O'Hara, The.
When Kian O'Hara's Cup Was Passed to Turlough O'Carolan.
Why, Liquor of Life?
CAROSSA, HANS. Mysterious Landscape.
Star-Song.
CARPENTER, AMELIA WALSTIEN JOLLS. Old Flemish Lace.
Recollection.
Ride to Cherokee, The.
CARPENTER, EDWARD. Among the Ferns.
Beethoven.
England, Arise!
Have Faith.
Love's Vision.
Over the Great City.
Songs of the Birds, The.
Stupid Old Body, The.
Triumph of Civilization, The.
Wandering Lunatic Mind, The.
CARPENTER, HENRY BERNARD. Mightier Church, A.
Reed, The.
CARPENTER, J. C. Her Bright Smile.
CARPENTER, JOHN ALDEN. Contemplation.
Plan, A.
Spring.
CARPENTER, JOSEPH EDWARD. Do They Think of Me at Home.
CARPENTER, LOIS R. At His Feet.
CARPENTER, MARGARET HALEY. September Afternoon.
CARPENTER, MAURICE. To S.T.C. on His 179th Birthday, October 12th, 1951.
Venus on a Sea Horse.
CARPENTER, RHYS. Beggars.
Master Singers, The.
Who Bids Us Sing?
CARPENTER, RUE. Stout.
CARPENTER, WILLIAM BOYD. Three Days.
CARPHYLLIDES. Full Life, A.
Happy Man, A.
CARR, ELIAS F. Ode to New Jersey.
CARR, MARY JANE. Big Swing-Tree Is Green Again, The.
Birthday of the Lord, The.
Castle in the Fire, The.
Pirate Wind.
Shop of Dreams.
West Wind's Secret, The.
When a Ring's around the Moon.
CARR, ROBERT VAN. Bill Haller's Dance.
Cowboy's Salvation Song.
Love Lyrics of a Cowboy.
Old Cowboy's Lament, The.
Prairie Wolves.
Rattlesnake, The.
Remember the Promise, Dakotah.
Romance of the Range.
Roundup Cook, The.
Silhouette in Sepia.
War Dance, The.
Western Trail, The.
When Dutchy Plays the Mouth Harp.
CARRANZA, EDUARDO. Sunday; Wherein a Man Laments like a Man.
CARRERA ANDRADE, JORGE. Anonymous Speech.
Biography.
Biography for the Use of the Birds.
Bulletin of Bad Weather.
Dining-Room Mirror.
Dust, Corpse of Time.
Election Handbill of Green.
Guest, The.
Hydrographic Poem.
Ill Humour.
Indian Rebellion.
It Rained in the Night.
Klare von Reuter.
Nameless Islands.
Nothing Belongs to Us.
Perfect Life, The.
Reaping the Barley.
Second Life of My Mother.
Sierra.
Spring & Co.
Stranger, The.
Stroke of One.
Sunday.
Vocation of the Mirror.
Windy Weather.
CARRIER, CONSTANCE. Colonel B.
Fugue.
Party.
Peter at Fourteen.
Pro Patria.
Seminary.
Transformation Scene.
CARRINGTON, HENRY. Inscription for a Statue of Love, *tr.*
Paroles sur la dune, *sel., tr.*
Rondeau: "By Jove, 'tis done with me, for Isabeau," *tr.*
Stanzas: "If, Marchioness, you can descry," *tr.*
CARRINGTON, JAMES BEEBE. I Planted Little Trees To-Day.
CARRINGTON, NOEL T. My Native Village, *sel.*
CARRIÓN, ALEJANDRO. Good Year, A.
CARROLL, A. B. "As Busy as I Tan Be."
"CARROLL, LEWIS" (Charles Lutwidge Dodgson). Aged, Aged Man, The. *Fr.* Through the Looking-Glass.
Alice's Adventures in Wonderland, *sels.*
A-Sitting on a Gate. *Fr.* Through the Looking-Glass.
Atalanta in Camden-Town.
Baker's Tale, The. *Fr.* The Hunting of the Snark.
Bat, The. *Fr.* Alice's Adventures in Wonderland.
Brother and Sister.
Carpette Knyghte, Ye.
Crocodile, The. *Fr.* Alice's Adventures in Wonderland.
Disillusioned.
Doll's Song.
Dolly's Dogs.
Evidence Read at the Trial of the Knave of Hearts. *Fr.* Alice's Adventures in Wonderland.
Father William. *Fr.* Alice's Adventures in Wonderland.
Gardener's Song, The. *Fr.* Sylvie and Bruno.
Ghost's Confession, The. *Fr.* Phantasmagoria.
He Thought He Saw. *Fr.* Sylvie and Bruno.
Hiawatha's Photographing.
How Doth the Little Crocodile. *Fr.* Alice's Adventures in Wonderland.
How to Recognize a Snark. *Fr.* The Hunting of the Snark.
Humpty Dumpty's Recitation [*or* Song]. *Fr.* Through the Looking-Glass.
Hunting of the Snark, The.
Hunting of the Snark, The, *sels.*
I'll Tell Thee Everything I Can. *Fr.* Through the Looking-Glass.
Important Evidence. *Fr.* Alice's Adventures in Wonderland.
Jabberwocky. *Fr.* Through the Looking-Glass.
King-Fisher Song, The. *Fr.* Sylvie and Bruno Concluded.
Landing, The. *Fr.* The Hunting of the Snark.
Limerick: "There was a young lady of station."
Little Birds Are Playing. *Fr.* Sylvie and Bruno Concluded.
Lobster, The. *Fr.* Alice's Adventures in Wonderland.
Lobster Quadrille, The. *Fr.* Alice's Adventures in Wonderland.
Long and a Sad Tale, A. *Fr.* Alice's Adventures in Wonderland.
Mad Gardener's Song, The. *Fr.* Sylvie and Bruno.
Maggie's Visit to Oxford, *sel.*
Manlet.
Melancholetta, *sel.*
Melancholy Pig, The. *Fr.* Sylvie and Bruno.
Metamorphoses. *Fr.* Sylvie and Bruno.
Mock Turtle's Song, The. *Fr.* Alice's Adventures in Wonderland.
Of Alice in Wonderland, *introd.* *Fr.* Alice's Adventures in Wonderland.
Outland Fare. *Fr.* Sylvie and Bruno.
Phantasmagoria, *sel.*
Pig-Tale, The. *Fr.* Sylvie and Bruno Concluded.
Poeta Fit, Non Nascitur.
Quadrille, A. *Fr.* Alice's Adventures in Wonderland.
Sea Dirge, A.
She's All My Fancy Painted Him.
Snark, The. *Fr.* The Hunting of the Snark.
Solitude, *sel.*
Some Hallucinations. *Fr.* Sylvie and Bruno.
Song of Love, A.
Speak Roughly to Your Little Boy. *Fr.* Alice's Adventures in Wonderland.
Stanza of Anglo-Saxon Poetry. *Fr.* Through the Looking-Glass.
Strange Wild Song, A. *Fr.* Sylvie and Bruno.
Sum, A.
Sylvie and Bruno, *sels.*
Sylvie and Bruno Concluded, *sels.*
There was a young lady of station.
There was once a Young Man of Oporta.
Through the Looking-Glass, *sels.*
Turtle Soup. *Fr.* Alice's Adventures in Wonderland.
Twinkle, Twinkle, Little Bat! *Fr.* Alice's Adventures in Wonderland.
Voice of the Lobster, The. *Fr.* Alice's Adventures in Wonderland.
Walrus and the Carpenter, The. *Fr.* Through the Looking-Glass.
Walrus and the Carpenter, The, *sel.* *Fr.* Through the Looking-Glass.
Ways and Means. *Fr.* Through the Looking-Glass.
White Knight's Song [*or* Tale *or* Ballad], The. *Fr.* Through the Looking-Glass.
Whiting and the Snail, The. *Fr.* Alice's Adventures in Wonderland.
You Are Old, Father William. *Fr.* Alice's Adventures in Wonderland.
CARROLL, PATRICK JOSEPH. Lady Day in Ireland.
St. Patrick's Treasure.
CARROLL, PAUL. Father.
CARROLL, VAUGHTIE. Child, The.
CARRUTH, LUCY. My Prayer.
CARRUTH, WILLIAM HERBERT. Autumn.
Dreamers of Dreams.
Each in His Own Tongue.
When the Cannon Booms No More.
CARRYL, CHARLES EDWARD. Admiral's Caravan, The, *sel.*
Alphabet, An.
Camel's Complaint [*or* Lament], The. *Fr.* The Admiral's Caravan.
Davy and the Goblin, *sels.*
Ferry to Nowhere, The.
My Recollectest Thoughts. *Fr.* Davy and the Goblin.
Nautical Ballad, A. *Fr.* Davy and the Goblin.
Plaint of the Camel, The. *Fr.* The Admiral's Caravan.
Post Captain, The.
Robinson Crusoe. *Fr.* Davy and the Goblin.
Robinson Crusoe's Story. *Fr.* Davy and the Goblin.
Song in the Dell, The.
Walloping Window-Blind, The. *Fr.* Davy and the Goblin.
CARRYL, GUY WETMORE. Arrogant Frog and the Superior Bull, The.
Ballad, A: "As I was walkin' the jungle round, a killin' of tigers an' time."

CARRYL, GUY WETMORE (*continued*)
Débutante, The.
Embarrassing Episode of Little Miss Muffet, The.
Gastronomic Guile of Simple Simon, The.
Harmonious Heedlessness of Little Boy Blue, The.
How a Cat Was Annoyed and a Poet Was Booted.
How a Fisherman Corked Up His Foe in a Jar.
How a Girl Was Too Reckless of Grammar [by Far].
How Jack Found that Beans May Go Back on a Chap.
How the Babes in the Wood Showed They Couldn't Be Beaten.
How the Helpmate of Blue-Beard Made Free with a Door.
Inhuman Wolf and the Lamb sans Gene.
Little Boy Blue.
Little Red Riding Hood.
Microscopic Trout and the Machiavelian Fisherman, The.
Red Riding Hood.
Singular Sangfroid of Baby Bunting, The.
Sycophantic Fox and the Gullible Raven, The.
Vainglorious Oak and the Modest Bulrush, The.
When the Great Gray Ships Come In.
CARSLEY, SARA E. Little Boats of Britain, The.
Portrait of a Very Old Man.
CARSON, MARY NEWLAND. My "Patch of Blue."
CARSTAIRS, CARROLL. Life and Death.
CARTAN, SHEMUS. Lament for Ireland.
CARTER, ALINE BADGER. Earth Bows to the New Bomb.
Give Our Conscience Light.
Immortal Words.
CARTER, ANN A. G. Nursery Song.
Robin to His Mate, The.
CARTER, ANN AUGUSTA. Rosy-Posy.
CARTER, D. Mrs. Indiarubber Duck.
CARTER, ELIZABETH. Ode to Wisdom.
CARTER, EMILY. Baby in the Basket, The.
CARTER, GRACE B. Trees' Choice, The.
CARTER, WILLIAM LORENZO. Young Charlottie, *wr. at.*
CARTWRIGHT, WILLIAM. Bid me not go where neither suns nor showers.
Come my sweet, whiles every strain.
Dead Sparrow, The.
Drinking Song. *Fr.* The Royal Slave.
Falsehood.
Good Eating Song, A. *Fr.* The Ordinary.
House Blessing, A.
New Year's Gift [to Brian Lord Bishop of Sarum], A.
No Platonic Love.
On a Virtuous Young Gentlewoman That Died Suddenly.
On the Queen's Return from the Low Countries.
Ordinary, The, *sel.*
Royal Slave, The, *sel.*
Seal Up Her Eyes, O Sleep. *Fr.* The Siege.
Siege, The, *sel.*
Song of Dalliance, A.
Tell me not of joy: there's none.
To Chloe.
To Chloe, *sel.*
To Chloe Who for His Sake Wished Herself Younger.
To Chloe Who Wished Her Self Young Enough for Me.
To Mr. W. B. on the Birth of His First Child.
Upon the Dramatick Poems of Mr. John Fletcher.
Valediction, A.
CARUS, PAUL. *For translations from German, see* OnPM.
CARUTHERS, MAZIE V. Fish-Day.
Matilda, Matriarch.
Matilda's Manners.
Mothering.
Prayer of a Tired Woman.
Prayer of Any Husband.
Threnody for a Pet Cat.
To a Dog, Grown Blind.
CARVALHO, RONALD DE. Brazil.
Interior.
Per Amica Silentia Lunae.
Trinidad Market.
CARVER, LOIS. For That Pale God of Silence Men Call Death.
CARVER, MABEL MACDONALD. Codicil.
CARY, ALICE. Among the Beautiful Pictures.
Balder's Wife.
Blackbird, The.
Cradle Song: "All by the sides of the wide wild river."
Dying Hymn, A.
Faded Leaves.
Gray Swan, The.
Her Mother.
Make Believe.
Mother's Picture, A.
My Creed.
Nobility.
Noble Life, The.
November.
Order for a Picture, An.
Pictures of Memory.
Spinster's Stint, A.
To Mother Fairie.
CARY, HENRY FRANCIS. Divina Commedia, *sels., tr.*
Fairest Thing in Mortal Eyes, The, *tr.*
Inferno, *tr. Fr.* Divina Commedia.
Paradise, *tr. Fr.* Divina Commedia.
Purgatory, *tr. Fr.* Divina Commedia.
Saints in Glory, The. *Fr.* Divina Commedia: Paradiso.
Sonnet: "Two flowers I love, the Marchflower and the rose," *tr.*
Sweet Month of April, The, *tr.*
CARY, LUCIUS, 2D VISCOUNT FALKLAND. Ben Jonson's Commonplace Book.
CARY, PHOEBE. Alas!
Ballad of the Canal.
Compensation.
Day Is Done, The.
Don't Give Up.
Dreams and Realities.
Dreams and Realities, *sel.*
Earth to Earth.
I Remember, I Remember.
In Extremity.
Jacob.
John Greenleaf Whittier.
John Thompson's Daughter.
Kate Ketchem.
Keep a Stiff Upper Lip.
Leak in the Dike, The.
Legend of the Northland, A.
Little Gottlieb.
Lovers, The.
Marriage of Sir John Smith, The.
Mother and Son.
Nearer Home.
Obedience.
Our Heroes.
Our Homestead.
Our Sun Hath Gone Down.
Peace.
Psalm of Life, A.
Ready.
Reuben.
Samuel Brown.
Suppose.
Thaddeus Stevens.
Thanksgiving.
There's a Bower of Bean-Vines.
True Love.
When Lovely Woman [Wants a Favor], *parody.*
Wife, The.
CARY, THOMAS. On His Mistress[e] Crossing the [*or* Going to] Sea.
CASA, GIOVANNI DELLA. To Sleep.
CASAL, JULIÁN DEL. Friar, The.
CASAS, JOSÉ JOAQUIN. Secret, The.
CASE, ELIZABETH [*or* LIZZIE] YORK. There Is No Unbelief.
Unbelief.
CASE, PHILA H. Nobody's Child.
CASEMENT, ROGER DAVID. Hamilcar Barca.
In the Streets of Catania.
Lost Youth.
CASEY, D. A. Spouse of Christ, The.
CASEY, JOHN KEEGAN. Maire My Girl.
Rising of the Moon A.D. 1798, The.
CASIMIR THE GREAT, KING OF POLAND. It Kindles All My Soul.
CASPARI, THEODOR. Hymn to Spring.
CASSIDY, ALICE CAROLINE COATES. *See* COATES, CAROL.
CASTERLINE, HELEN ANNIS. God Cares.
CASTIELLO, JAIME. Partners.
CASTILLA, ETHEL. Australian Girl.
CASTILLEJO, CRISTÓBAL DE. Kisses.
Some Day, Some Day.
CASTLE, MABEL WING. Irony.
CASTRO DE MURGUÍA, ROSALIA. Carillon, The.
CASTRO Z., OSCAR. Responsory for García Lorca.
"CASUAL." Dog's Life, A.
CASWALL, EDWARD. Come, Wandering Sheep.
Jesus the Very Thought of Thee, *tr.*
Light of the Soul, *tr.*
My God I Love Thee, *tr.*
Sleep, Holy Babe.
When Morning Gilds the Skies, *tr.*
CASWALL, EDWARD, *and* RICHARD MANT. *See* MANT, RICHARD, *and* EDWARD CASWALL.
CATER, CATHARINE. Here and Now.
CATHER, WILLA SIBERT. Grandmither, Think Not I Forget.
Hawthorn Tree, The.
In Media Vita.
In Rose Time.
L'Envoi: "Where are the loves that we loved before."
Palatine, The.
Poppies in Ludlow Castle.
Spanish Johnny.
CATLIN, ELLEN WESTON. Childlike Heart.
CATULLUS, CAIUS [*or* GAIUS] VALERIUS. Acme and Septimius.
Across the roaring ocean, with heart and with eye of flame.
Ad Lesbiam.
At once I hate and love as well.
Attis
Breath of Day.
Bridal Hymn.
Burdened as you are with misfortune and sorrow.
By strangers' coasts and waters, many days at sea.
Caelius, my Lesbia, that one, that only Lesbia.
Cataclysm.
Catullus' Translation of the Ode to Anactoria (*by* Sappho).
Cold Blast of Debt.
Colonia, you wish to have a long bridge built, I hear.
Come, Lesbia, let us live and love.
Come to me, my poems, all my far-flung armies.
Comparison, The.
Complaint, The.
Counting Kisses.
Dead Sparrow, The.
Dead Starling, The.
Dear brother, I have come these many miles, through.
Death of Lesbia's Bird, The.
Diana guardeth our estate.
Do please show me, if it's not too much trouble.
Do you know, my Lesbia, how many of your kisses.
Dress now in sorrow, O all.
Elegy on Quintilia.
Farewell to Bithynia.
Farewell to Lesbia.
Fib Detected, A.
For whom this pretty pamphlet, polished new.

From the Latin of Catullus ("Diana, mistress of the evening sky").
Furius and Aurelius, Catullus's comrades.
Furius, you've no slaves, no box to hold your money.
Grant Me Peace.
Hail and Farewell.
He is changed to a god who looks on her.
Her husband present, Lesbia lashes me with words.
Here is my relief at last.
Home to Sermio [*or* Sirmio].
Hymn to Diana.
I hate and love.
If a wished-for thing and a thing past hoping for.
If ever aching heart can speed across the years.
If I did not love you more than my very eyes.
If man can find rich consolation, remembering his good deeds.
If, to one who remembers his past beneficences.
In the old days, Lesbia, you said Catullus alone.
Inconsistency of Women's Love.
Lesbia.
Lesbia Railing.
Lesbia swears at me continually; she's never quiet.
Lesbia's Disgrace.
Lesbia's Vow.
Let us live, O my Lesbia, and go on loving!
Letter to Manlius Torquatus.
Love and Death.
Love and Hate.
Love Is All.
Love's Madness.
Love's Unreason.
Madame, whose nose is not of the smallest, greetings!
Miserable Catullus, stop being foolish.
My friend Cornificus, your friend Catullus.
My woman says she wants no other lover.
My woman says that she would rather wear the wedding-veil for me.
Now Spring brings back the tepid breeze.
O my little almost island, little island Sirmio.
Of all the sons of Romulus who walk the earth.
On an Unpleasant Woman.
On the Burial of His Brother.
Poor damned Catullus, here's no time for nonsense.
Prayer against Love.
Proud is Phasellus here, my friends, to tell.
Quarrel with Juventius.
Quintia is beautiful, many will tell you: to me.
Quintilia Dead.
Rendezvous, The.
Return to Sirmio.
Rite at a Brother's Grave.
Sappho.
Septimius held his Acme close.
Septimius with his arms entwined round his Acme.
Sir 'Arry, though lately created a knight.
Sirmio.
Sparrow, my mistress' pet.
Sparrow, O, sweet sparrow.
Spring Holidays.
That no fair woman will, wonder not why.
There are many who think of Quintia in terms of beauty.
There was a time, O Lesbia, when you said Catullus was.
This Suffenus, Varus, with whom you are acquainted.
This villa is raked of winds from fore and aft.
To Himself.
To His Cup Bearer.
To Lesbia.
To Quintius.
To the Garden God.
To Varus.
Transformation.
True or False.
Two Poems against His Rival.
Under a Spell.
Upon Lesbia's Abuse.
Varus took me to call upon his sweetheart.
Vigil of Venus, The, *at.*
While I was wandering, foot-loose, in the Forum.
Who shall receive my new-born book.
Whom Lesbia Loved.
World without End.
Yacht, The.
You are the cause of this destruction, Lesbia.
You who dwell upon Helicon.

"CAUDWELL, CHRISTOPHER" (Christopher St. John Sprigg). Classic Encounter.

CAUSLEY, CHARLES. At the British War Cemetery, Bayeux.
Ballad for Katharine of Aragon, A.
Cowboy Song.
On Seeing a Poet of the First World War on the Station at Abbeville.
Ou Phrontis.
Recruiting Drive.
Sailor's Carol.
To a Poet Who Has Never Travelled.

CAVAFY, CONSTANTINE P. Alexander Jannai.
Awaiting the Barbarians.
Body Remember.
City, The.
For Ammonis Who Died at 29 in 610.
God Forsakes Anthony.
Ionian Song.
Ithaca.
Manuel Komninos.
Morning Sea.
Of the Ship.
One of the Jews (50 A.D.).
Return.
Satrapy.
Since Nine o'Clock.
Trojans.
Very Seldom.
Walls.

CAVALCANTI, GUIDO. Ballata 7: "Being in thought of love I came upon."
Ballata: Concerning a Shepherd-Maid.
Ballata: He Reveals His Increasing Love for Mandetta.
Ballata: In Exile at Sarzana.
Ballata 11: Last Song; from Exile.
Ballata 5: "Light do I see within my Lady's eyes."
Ballata: Of a Continual Death in Love.
Ballata: Of His Lady among Other Ladies.
Ballata 12: Of Love's Power.
Ballata: "Since all my life out of my death derives."
Ballata 9: "There in a woodland, to my thought more bright."
Ballata: "With other women I beheld my love."
Ballata of Love's Power.
Canzone: Lady Asks Me, A.
Chi è questa.
Effigy, The.
Love's Assize.
Sonnet: "Beauty of ladies of compassionate heart."
Sonnet: Effigy, The.
Sonnet: He Compares All Things with His Lady.
Sonnet: He Speaks of a Third Love of His.
Sonnet: "I saw the eyes, where Amor took his place."
Sonnet: "If I should pray this lady pitiless."
Sonnet: Love's Assize.
Sonnet: "My Lady's face it is they worship there."
Sonnet: Of an Ill-favored Lady.
Sonnet: Of His Pain from a New Love.
Sonnet: Of the Eyes of a Certain Mandetta.
Sonnet: On the Detection of a False Friend.
Sonnet: Rapture concerning His Lady, A.
Sonnet: To a Friend Who Does Not Pity His Love.
Sonnet: To Dante Alighieri (He Interprets Dante's Dream).
Sonnet: To Dante Alighieri (He Mistrusts the Love of Lapo Gianni).
Sonnet: To Dante Alighieri (He Reports the Successful Issue of Lapo Gianni's Love).
Sonnet: To His Lady Joan, of Florence.
Sonnet: "Who is she that comes, makyng turn every man's eye."
Sonnet: "Who's this that comes, as each man looks at her."
Sonnet: "You have in you the flowers and the green grass."
Sonnet: "You, who do breach mine eyes and touch the heart."
To Dante.

CAVAZZA, ELISABETH JONES. *See* PULLEN, ELISABETH JONES CAVAZZA.

CAVENDISH, MARGARET, DUCHESS OF NEWCASTLE. *See* NEWCASTLE, MARGARET CAVENDISH, DUCHESS OF.

CAVENDISH, WILLIAM, DUKE OF NEWCASTLE. *See* NEWCASTLE, WILLIAM CAVENDISH, DUKE OF.

CAWEIN, MADISON. Abandoned.
Attainment.
Aubade.
Ballad of Low-lie-down.
Child in the House, The.
Comradery.
Covered Bridge, The.
Creek-Road, The.
Death.
Deserted.
Dirge: "What shall her silence keep."
Enchantment.
Flight.
Fragment, A: "When the hornet hangs in the hollyhock."
Here is the Place Where Loveliness Keeps House.
I Hear the Woodlands Calling.
Ku-Klux.
Love and a Day.
Lydia.
Man Hunt, The.
March.
"Mene, Mene, Tekel, Upharsin."
Miracle of the Dawn, The.
Moonshiner, The. *Fr.* The Mountain Still.
Morning Serenade.
Mosby at Hamilton.
Mountain Still, The, *sels.*
Old Bayou, The.
Old Home, The.
Old Man Rain.
Opportunity.
Path to the Woods, The.
Penetralia.
Proem: "There is no rhyme that is half so sweet."
Prototypes.
Rain-Crow, The.
Reed Call.
Sheriff, The. *Fr.* The Mountain Still.
Snow.
Soul, The.
To a Wind Flower.
Under Arcturus.
Under the Stars and Stripes.
Whippoorwill, The.
Willow Bottom, The.
Wind in the Pines, The.
Winds, The.

CAWOOD, JOHN. Hark! what mean those holy voices.

CAWTHORN, JOSEPH B. Cogitative Bass Crank, The.

CAYLEY, GEORGE JOHN. Epitaph, An:

CAYLEY, GEORGE JOHN (*continued*)
"Lovely young lady I mourn in my rhymes, A."
CECCO ANGIOLIERI DA SIENA. In Honor of His Mistress.
Love in Men and Devils.
Not Too Deeply in Love.
Of All He Would Do.
Past Help.
Sonnet: He Argues His Case with Death.
Sonnet: He Is Past All Help.
Sonnet: He Rails against Dante.
Sonnet: He Will Not Be Too Deeply in Love.
Sonnet: "If I were fire, I'd burn the world away."
Sonnet: In Absence from Becchina.
Sonnet: Of All He Would Do.
Sonnet: Of Becchina in a Rage.
Sonnet: Of Becchina, the Shoemaker's Daughter.
Sonnet: Of Love, in Honor of His Mistress Becchina.
Sonnet: Of Love in Men and Devils.
Sonnet: Of the 20th June 1291.
Sonnet: Of Why He Is Unhanged.
Sonnet: Of Why He Would Be a Scullion.
Sonnet: To Dante Alighieri (He Writes to Dante, Defying Him).
Sonnet: To Dante Alighieri (On the Last Sonnet of the "Vita Nuova").
CECH, SVATOPLUK. Songs of the Slave, *sel.*
CECIL, WILLIAM, 1ST BARON BURGHLEY. *See* BURGHLEY, WILLIAM CECIL, 1ST BARON.
"CEIRIOG." *See* HUGHES, JOHN CEIRIOG.
CELAN, PAUL. Death Fugue.
CELANO, TOMMÁSO DI. *See* THOMAS OF CELANO.
CENNICK, JOHN. Children of the Heavenly King.
CERCIDAS. Voyage of Love, The.
CERNUDA, LUIS. Case of the Murdered Bird, The.
Cathedral at Evening, The.
Fountain, The.
Graveyard in the City.
Hymn to Sorrow.
Impression of Exile.
Like the Light Sound.
Remorse in Garb of Night.
Spanish Elegy.
Wind of September in the Poplars.
CERVANTES SAAVEDRA, MIGUEL DE. Friendship.
Siege of Numancia, The, *sel.*
Sonnet: "When I was marked for suffering, Love forswore."
CÉSAIRE, AIMÉ. Memorandum on My Martinique, *sel.*
CESTRIAN, W. Because of You.
CETINA, GUTIERRE DE. Anacreon.
Madrigal: "Clear eyes, sweet and serene."
CHACE, JEAN VALENTINE. Visit to a Hospital.
CHADWICK, GEORGE A. Weary.
CHADWICK, HAL. Portrait.
CHADWICK, JOHN WHITE. Abiding Love, The.
Auld Lang Syne.
Divinity School Graduation Hymn.
Full Cycle.
Golden-Robin's Nest, The.
His Mother's Joy.
Hymn: "Eternal Ruler of the ceaseless round."
Hymn: "Father, we come not as of old."
It Singeth Low in Every Heart.
King Edwin's Feast.
Lullaby: "Day is ending; night is falling."
Making of Man, The.
Mugford's Victory.
O Love, That Dost with Goodness Crown.
Recognition.
Rise of Man, The.
Starlight.
Two Waitings, The.
Wedding-Song, A.
CHAEREMON. Maidens at Rest.
CHAFFEE, ELEANOR ALLETTA. Cobbler, The.
Cricket.
Nightingale.
CHA LIANG-CHENG. Hungry China, *sel.*
There Is No Nearer Nearness.
CHALKHILL, JOHN. Angler, The.
Coridon's Song.
Rhotus on Arcadia. *Fr.* Thealma and Clearchus.
Thealma and Clearchus, *sel.*
CHALMERS, ALLAN KNIGHT. Oh, Haunting Spirit of the Ever True.
CHALMERS, PATRICK REGINALD. Cuckoo, The.
Gardener's Cat, The.
Hay Harvest.
"Hold."
If I Had a Broomstick.
In an Old Nursery.
Lavender's for Ladies.
Little Young Lambs, The.
My Woodcock.
Pan-Pipes.
Puk- [*or* Pud-] Wudjies.
Road, The.
Roundabouts and Swings.
Tortoiseshell Cat, The.
"Treasure Island."
Visitor, The.
When Mary Goes Walking.
CHALMERS, STEPHEN. Allenby Enters Jerusalem.
Home.
New Physician, The.
Rebellion.
CHAMBERLAIN, BASIL HALL. *For translations from Japanese, see* OnPM.
CHAMBERLAIN, BRENDA. Dead Ponies.
First Woman's Lament.
Fisherman Husband.
Give No White Flower.
Lament: "My man is a bone ringèd with weed."
Poem: "You, who in April laughed, a green god in the sun."
Second Woman's Lament.
Song: "Bone-aged is my white horse."
Song: "Heron is harsh with despair."
Song-Talysarn.
To Dafydd Coed Mourning His Mountain-broken Dog.
You, Who in April Laughed.
CHAMBERLAIN, C. H. Illinois.
CHAMBERLAIN, ROBERT. Farewell this company. *Fr.* The Swaggering Damsel.
Swaggering Damsel, The, *sel.*
CHAMBERLAYNE, WILLIAM. Pharonnida, *sel.*
Strong Prophetick dream, A, *Fr.* Pharonnida.
CHAMBERS, ———. To Mistress Sarah Hickford.
CHAMBERS, ROBERT W. Officer Brady.
Recruit, The.
To Nature Seekers.
Troop-Ship Sails, The.
Young Randal.
CHAMISSO, ADELBERT [*or* ALBERT] VON. Tragic Story, A.
CHANDLER, ELLEN LOUISE. *See* MOULTON, LOUISE CHANDLER.
CHANDLER, ELSIE WILLIAMS. Christmas Singing.
CHANDLER, JOHN. Glad Tidings from the King of Kings, *tr.*
What Star is This? *tr.*
CHANDLER, MARY. Description of Bath, The, *sel.*
Rocky Landscape. *Fr.* The Description of Bath.
CHAN FANG-SHENG. Sailing Homeward.
CHANG CHI. Letter, A.
Old Temple in Mountains.
Song of a Modest Woman.
Thinking of a Friend Lost in the Tibetan War.
CHANG CH'IEN. Sanctuary in Po-shan Temple.
Visiting the Ruins.
CHANG CHIU-LING. Absence.
Looking at the Moon and Thinking of One Far Away.
CHANG CHUNG SU. Daydreams.
CHANG CHUNG-SUR. Spring, The.
CHANG HENG. Bones of Chuang Tzu, The.
CHANG HSU. Ravine of the Flowering Peach Tree, The.
CHANG JUNG. To One Afar.
CHANG MIAO CHING. Lost Happiness.
CH'ANG PI LAN. Longing.
CHANG SHOU. Green Spring.
CHANG TSAI. Desecration of the Han Tombs, The.
CHANG YUNG. Song of Parting, A.
CHANG YU SHU. Captive, The.
CHANLER, MARGARET. Christmas, *tr.*
Vigil of the Assumption, *tr.*
CHANNING, GRACE ELLERY (Mrs. Charles Walter Stetson). England.
Flag of Stars, The.
Judgment.
Song of Arno, A.
War.
CHANNING, WALTER. To Napoleon in Exile.
CHANNING, WILLIAM ELLERY. And Here the Hermit Sat, and Told His Beads.
Barren Moors, The.
Earth-Spirit, The.
Edith.
Flight of the Wild Geese.
Hymn of the Earth.
Mountain, The, *sel.*
Our Boat to the Waves.
Poet's Hope, A, *sel.*
Prayer, A: "To Thy continual Presence, in me wrought."
Tears in Spring.
CHANNING-STETSON, GRACE ELLERY. *See* CHANNING, GRACE ELLERY.
CHAO CHIA. South Arbor, The.
CHAO TZ'U. Midnight.
CHAO YING-TOU. Decrees of God, The.
CHAPIN, EDWIN H. Ocean Burial, The.
CHAPIN, KATHERINE GARRISON (Mrs. Francis Biddle). Other Journey, The.
Plain Chant for America.
Portrait in Winter.
CHAPLIN, KATHLEEN M. Merry Little Men.
CHAPLIN, RALPH. Mourn Not the Dead.
To France.
CHAPMAN, ARTHUR. Beecher Island.
Out Where the West Begins.
Where the West Begins.
White Man's Road, The.
CHAPMAN, E. W. Flowers for the Fallen Heroes.
CHAPMAN, ETHELYN BRYANT. Crisis, The.
CHAPMAN, GEORGE (1559?–1634). Achilles Goes Forth to Battle, *tr. Fr.* The Iliad.
Achilles' Shield, *tr. Fr.* The Iliad.
Achilles Shows Himself in the Battle by the Ships, *tr. Fr.* The Iliad.
Ad Deum.
Atrides Goes into Battle, *tr. Fr.* The Iliad.
Blind Beggar of Alexandria, The, *sel.*
Brave Spirit, A. *Fr.* Byron's Conspiracy.
Bridal Song. *Fr.* Hero and Leander.
Bridal Song. *Fr.* The Masque of the Middle Temple and Lincoln's Inn.
Bussy d'Ambois, *sels.*
Byron's Conspiracy, *sels.*
Byron's Tragedy, *sel.*
Caesar and Pompey, *sel.*
Calypso's Island, *tr. Fr.* The Odyssey.
Camp at Night, The, *tr. Fr.* The Iliad.
Chariot Race, The, *tr. Fr.* The Iliad.
Come, Night.
Conspiracy of Charles, Duke of Byron, The, *sels.*
Corinna Bathes. *Fr.* Ovid's Banquet of Sense.
Coronet for His Mistress Philosophy, A, *sel.*
De Guiana, Carmen Epicum.

Death of Hector, The, *tr.* *Fr.* The Iliad.
Descend, Fair Sun. *Fr.* The Masque of the Middle Temple and Lincoln's Inn.
End of the Suitors, The, *tr.* *Fr.* The Odyssey.
Epistle Dedicatory to Chapman's Translation of the Iliad, The, *sels.*
Epithalamion Teratus. *Fr.* Hero and Leander.
Escape from Cyclop, The, *tr.* *Fr.* The Odyssey.
Eugenia, *sel.*
Euthymiae Raptus; or, The Tears of Peace, *sels.*
Hector to Andromache, *tr.* *Fr.* The Iliad.
Helen, Menelaos, and Memories of Troy, *tr.* *Fr.* The Odyssey.
Herculean Silence. *Fr.* Euthymiae Raptus.
Hero and Leander, *sels.*
High and General Cause, The. *Fr.* The Revenge of Bussy d'Ambois.
Homeric Hymn to Neptune.
Homeric Hymns, *sel., tr.*
Hymn to Mars, *tr.* *Fr.* Homeric Hymns.
Hymne to Our Saviour on the Crosse, A.
Hymnus in Noctem. *Fr.* The Shadow of Night.
Iliad, The, *sels., tr.*
Invocation: "Give me a spirit that on this life's rough sea." *Fr.* The Conspiracy of Charles, Duke of Byron.
Invocation, An: "I long to know." *Fr.* Bussy d'Ambois.
Invocation to Spirit. *Fr.* Bussy d'Ambois.
Last Words of Byron. *Fr.* Byron's Tragedy.
Learning. *Fr.* Euthymiae Raptus; or, The Tears of Peace.
Love and Philosophy. *Fr.* A Coronet for His Mistress Philosophy.
Masque of the Middle Temple and Lincoln's Inn, The, *sels.*
Masque of the Twelve Months, The, *sel., at.*
Master Spirit, The. *Fr.* Byron's Conspiracy.
Muses That Sing Love's Sensual Empery. *Fr.* A Coronet for His Mistress Philosophy.
Natures Naked Jem. *Fr.* Ovid's Banquet of Sense.
Nausicaa, *tr.* *Fr.* The Odyssey.
Nausicaa and Odysseus, *tr.* *Fr.* The Odyssey.
Nestor's Speech to Achilles and Agamemnon, *tr.* *Fr.* The Iliad.
Night. *Fr.* The Shadow of Night.
Noman and the Cyclops; a Tale Told over Cups, *tr.* *Fr.* The Odyssey.
Now, Sleep, Bind Fast. *Fr.* The Masque of the Middle Temple and Lincoln's Inn.
O come, soft rest of cares! come, night! *Fr.* Hero and Leander.
Odyssey, The, *sels., tr.*
Ovid's Banquet of Sense, *sels.*
Parting of Hector and Andromache, The, *tr.* *Fr.* The Iliad.
Pilot, The. *Fr.* Bussy d'Ambois.
Plight of Wounded Aphrodite, The, *tr.* *Fr.* The Iliad.
Poetry and Learning. *Fr.* The Epistle Dedicatory.
Praise of Homer.
Presage of Storme. *Fr.* Eugenia.
Priam and Achilles, *tr.* *Fr.* The Iliad.
Repentance. *Fr.* Hero and Leander.
Revenge of Bussy d'Ambois, The, *sels.*
Rich Mine of Knowledge.
Sacrifice, The, *tr.* *Fr.* The Odyssey.
Sarpedon's Speech, *tr.* *Fr.* The Iliad.
Scales of Zeus, The, *tr.* *Fr.* The Iliad.
Scylla and Charybdis, *tr.* *Fr.* The Odyssey.
Seven Penitential Psalms, *sel., tr.*
Shadow of Night, The.
Shadow of Night, The, *sels.*
Shine Out, Fair Sun, with All Your Heat, *at.* *Fr.* The Masque of the Twelve Months.
Siren's Song, The, *tr.* *Fr.* The Odyssey.
Sixth Book of Homer's Iliad, The, *tr.* *Fr.* The Iliad.
Song: "O come, soft rest of cares!"
Song: "Shine out, fair Sun, with all your heat," *at.* *Fr.* The Masque of the Twelve Months.
Sonnet: "Muses that sing love's sensual empery." *Fr.* A Coronet for His Mistress Philosophy.
Such love is like a smoky fire.
Tears of Peace, The. *Fr.* Euthymiae Raptus.
Thersites Out of Bounds, *tr.* *Fr.* The Iliad.
To Mars, *tr.*
To the High-born Prince of Men, Henry. *Fr.* The Epistle Dedicatory.
To the Ruins of Troy and Greece.
To Young Imaginaries in Knowledge, *tr.* *Fr.* Seven Penitential Psalms.
Tragedy of Caesar and Pompey, The, *sel.*
Tragedy of Charles, Duke of Byron, The, *sel.*
Trojans outside the Walls, The, *tr.* *Fr.* The Iliad.
Ulysses and the Sirens, *tr.* *Fr.* The Odyssey.
Ulysses Hears the Prophecies of Tiresias, *tr.* *Fr.* The Odyssey.
Ulysses in the Waves, *tr.* *Fr.* The Odyssey.
Virtue the Safest Guide. *Fr.* Bussy d'Ambois.
Visit of Thetis to Hephaistos, *tr.* *Fr.* The Iliad.
Vulcan Forges the Shield of Achilles, *tr.* *Fr.* The Iliad.
Wedding of Alcmane and Mya, The. *Fr.* Hero and Leander.

CHAPMAN, GEORGE (20th century). Autumn Hour.
Knell.
CHAPMAN, JOHN ALEXANDER. Gipsy Queen.
CHAPMAN, JOHN JAY. Clouds.
Lines on the Death of Bismarck.
Song: "Old Farmer Oats and his son Ned."
Toil Away.
CHAPMAN, MARY BERRI. *See* HANSBROUGH, MARY BERRI CHAPMAN.
CHAPONE, HESTER (Mulso). To Stella.
CHAPPELL, GEORGE S. Innocence.
Tub, The.
CHAPPELL, JEANNETTE. Newton to Einstein.
CHAPPLE, BENNETT. Great Oak.
CHARASSON, HENRIETTE (Mme René Johannet). Ave Maria.
CHARLEMAGNE. Veni Creator Spiritus, *at.*
CHARLES I, KING OF ENGLAND. On a Quiet Conscience.
CHARLES II, KING OF ENGLAND. Song: "I pass all my hours in a shady old grove," *at.*
CHARLES, ELIZABETH RUNDLE. Ascension Hymn, *tr.*
Child on the Judgment Seat, The.
CHARLES, JACK. To Chuck—Concerning a Rendezvous in Siam.
CHARLES, MABEL MUNNS. Living Tithe, The.
CHARLES, MARY GRANT. Flood.
CHARLES, ROBERT E. Roundabout Turn, A.
CHARLES D'ORLÉANS. *See* ORLÉANS, CHARLES, DUC D'.
CHARTRES, VIDAME DE. April.
CHASE, FRANK. Tale of the Dixie-Belle, The.
CHASE, MARION MONKS. One.
CHASE, POLLY. *See* BOYDEN, POLLY CHASE.
CHATELAIN OF COUCY (Guy II of Coucy). Chanson: "My wand'ring thoughts awake to love anew."
CHATHAM, EVERETT. Trail End, *at.*
CHATTERTON, THOMAS. Accounte of W. Canynge's Feast, The.
Aella; a Tragycal Enterlude, *sels.*
African Song, An.
Autumn and Winter. *Fr.* Elegy to the Memory of Mr. Thomas Philips of Fairford.
Autumn Fruits. *Fr.* Aella.
Battle of Hastings, *sel.*
Bristowe Tragedie; or, The Dethe of Syr Charles Bawdin.
Cawna. *Fr.* Heccar and Gaira.
Coming Night, The. *Fr.* Elegy to the Memory of Mr. Thomas Philips of Fairford.
Death of Nicou, The, *sel.*
Eclogue: "Wouldst thou ken Nature in her better part?"
Elegy: "Why blooms the radiance of the morning sky?" *sel.*
Elegy to the Memory of Mr. Thomas Philips of Fairford, *sels.*
Excelente Balade of Charitie, An.
Flowers and Spice. *Fr.* Narva and Mored.
Freedom's War Song. *Fr.* Goddwyn.
Goddwyn, *sels.*
Heccar and Gaira, *sel.*
Hymn for Christmas Day, A.
Last Verses.
Minstrel's Roundelay, The. *Fr.* Aella.
Minstrel's [*or* Mynstrelles] Song[e]: "O! synge untoe mie roundelaie." *Fr.* Aella.
Mynstrelles Songe: "Angelles bee wrogte to bee of neidher kynde." *Fr.* Aella.
Mynstrelles Songe: "Boddynge flourettes bloshes atte the lyghte, The." *Fr.* Aella.
Narva and Mored, *sel.*
O Sing unto My Roundelay. *Fr.* Aella.
Ode to Liberty. *Fr.* Goddwyn.
Roundelay: "O sing unto my roundelay." *Fr.* Aella.
Song: "O sing unto my roundelay." *Fr.* Aella.
Song from "Aella."
Song of the Three Minstrels. *Fr.* Aella.
There Lackethe Somethynge Stylle.
Tygers. *Fr.* The Death of Nicou.
CHAUCER, GEOFFREY. A. B. C., An.
A. B. C., An, *sel*
Alisoun. *Fr.* The Canterbury Tales: The Miller's Tale.
And as for me. *Fr.* The Legend of Good Women.
Arcite's Farewell. *Fr.* The Canterbury Tales: The Knight's Tale.
Assumption of Troilus, The. *Fr.* Troilus and Criseyde.
At the Gate. *Fr.* Troilus and Criseyde.
Balade: "Hyd, Absolon, thy gilte tresses clere." *Fr.* The Legend of Good Women.
Balade de [*or* of] Bon Conseyl [*or* Conseil *or* Conseill].
Ballad[e] of Good Counsel.
Bill of Complaint, The.
Birds' Rondel, The. *Fr.* The Parlement of Foules.
Book of the Duchesse, The, *sel.*
Briddes that han left their song, The, *tr.* *Fr.* The Romaunt of the Rose.
But Whan the Cok. *Fr.* Troilus and Criseyde.
Canterbury Tales, The, *sels.*
Canticus Troili. *Fr.* Troilus and Criseyde.
Captivity. *Fr.* Merciles Beaute.
Carpenter's Young Wife, The. *Fr.* The Canterbury Tales: The Miller's Tale.
Chasing the Fox. *Fr.* The Canterbury Tales: The Nun's Priest's Tale.
Chaucer's Complaint to His Empty Purse.
Chaucer's Envoy to the Story of Patient Griselda. *Fr.* The Canterbury Tales: The Clerk's Tale.

CHAUCER, GEOFFREY (*continued*)
Chaucers Wordes unto Adam, His Owne Scriveyn.
Clerk of Oxenford [*or* Oxford], The. *Fr.* The Canterbury Tales: Prologue.
Clerk's Tale, The, *sel. Fr.* The Canterbury Tales.
Cock and the Fox, The. *Fr.* The Canterbury Tales: The Nun's Priest's Tale.
Complaint [*or* Compleint] of Chaucer to His [Empty] Purse, The.
Complaint of Troilus, The. *Fr.* Troilus and Criseyde.
Complaint unto Pity, The.
Counsel upon Marriage.
Croesus. *Fr.* The Canterbury Tales: The Monk's Tale.
Daisy, The. *Fr.* The Legend of Good Women.
Dawn. *Fr.* The Canterbury Tales: The Knight's Tale.
Death and the Ruffians. *Fr.* The Canterbury Tales: The Pardoner's Tale.
Death of Troilus, The. *Fr.* Troilus and Criseyde.
Despair of Troilus, The. *Fr.* Troilus and Criseyde.
Dream, The. *Fr.* The Book of the Duchesse.
Dream Garden, A. *Fr.* The Parlement of Foules.
Dream of the Romaunt of the Rose, The, *tr. Fr.* The Romaunt of the Rose.
Emily's Prayer to Diana. *Fr.* The Canterbury Tales: The Knight's Tale.
Envoy, The: "Go, litel book, go litel myn tregedie." *Fr.* Troilus and Criseyde.
Escape. *Fr.* Merciles Beaute.
Exhortation to Youth. *Tr.* Troilus and Criseyde.
Five Pilgrims. *Fr.* The Canterbury Tales: Prologue.
Foules Rondel. *Fr.* The Parlement of Foules.
Franklin's Prologue, The. *Fr.* The Canterbury Tales.
Franklin's Tale, The. *Fr.* The Canterbury Tales.
Friar's [*or* Freres] Tale, The. *Fr.* The Canterbury Tales.
Friar's Tale, The, *sel. Fr.* The Canterbury Tales.
Garden of Amour, The, *tr. Fr.* The Romaunt of the Rose.
General Prologue, The. *Fr.* The Canterbury Tales.
Gentilesse.
Good Counseil [*or* Counsel] of Chaucer.
Good Parson, The. *Fr.* The Canterbury Tales: Prologue.
Griselda. *Fr.* The Canterbury Tales: The Clerk's Tale.
Hous of Fame, The, *sels.*
Hyd, Absolon, Thy Gilte Tresses Clere.
Introduction to the Man of Law's Prologue. *Fr.* The Canterbury Tales.
Invocatio ad Mariam. *Fr.* The Canterbury Tales: The Prologue to the Second Nun's Tale.
Invocation: "O mother-maid! O maiden-mother free!" *Fr.* The Canterbury Tales: The Prologue of the Prioress's Tale.
Invocation to the Virgin. *Fr.* The Canterbury Tales: The Prioress's Tale.
Invocation to the Virgin. *Fr.* The Canterbury Tales: The Second Nun's Tale.
Knight, A. *Fr.* The Canterbury Tales: Prologue.
Knight's [*or* Knightes] Tale, The. *Fr.* The Canterbury Tales.
Knight's Tale, The, *sels. Fr.* The Canterbury Tales.
La Prière de Nostre Dame.
Lak [*or* Lack] of Stedfastnesse.
Lat Take a Cat. *Fr.* The Canterbury Tales: The Manciple's Tale.
Legend of Good Women, The, *sels.*
Love Unfeigned, The. *Fr.* Troilus and Criseyde.
Manciple's Tale, The, *sel. Fr.* The Canterbury Tales.
Merciles Beaute.
Merciles Beaute, *sels.*
Miller, A. *Fr.* The Canterbury Tales: Prologue.
Miller's [*or* Milleres] Tale, The, *sels. Fr.* The Canterbury Tales.
Monk's Tale, The, *sels. Fr.* The Canterbury Tales.
Morning in May. *Fr.* The Canterbury Tales: The Knight's Tale.
Murder Will Out. *Fr.* The Canterbury Tales: The Nun's Priest's Tale.
Nonne Preestes Tale, The. *Fr.* The Canterbury Tales.
Now Welcome, Somer [*or* Summer]. *Fr.* The Parlement of Foules.
Nun's Priest's Tale, The. *Fr.* The Canterbury Tales.
Nun's Priest's Tale, The, *sels. Fr.* The Canterbury Tales.
O Blisful Light. *Fr.* Troilus and Criseyde.
O Mooder Mayde. *Fr.* The Canterbury Tales: The Prioress's Tale.
O Yonge Fresshe Folkes. *Fr.* Troilus and Criseyde.
Of His Lady. *Fr.* The Legend of Good Women.
Pardoner's Tale, The. *Fr.* The Canterbury Tales.
Pardoner's Tale, The, *sels. Fr.* The Canterbury Tales.
Parish Priest, The. *Fr.* The Canterbury Tales: Prologue.
Parlement of Foules, The, *sels.*
Parson, The. *Fr.* The Canterbury Tales: Prologue.
Patient Griselda. *Fr.* The Canterbury Tales: The Clerk's Tale.
Poor Parson, The. *Fr.* The Canterbury Tales: Prologue.
Poor Widow's Cock, The. *Fr.* The Canterbury Tales: The Nun's Priest's Tale.
Poure Persoun, The. *Fr.* The Canterbury Tales: Prologue.
Prayer to the Blessed Virgin, A. *Fr.* The Canterbury Tales: The Prioress's Tale.
Prayer to Venus.
Prioress, The. *Fr.* The Canterbury Tales: Prologue.
Prioress's Prologue, The. *Fr.* The Canterbury Tales: The Prioress's Tale.
Prioress's Tale, The. *Fr.* The Canterbury Tales.
Prioress's Tale, The, *sel. Fr.* The Canterbury Tales.
Proem to "The Parlement of Foules."
Prologe of the Prioresses Tale. *Fr.* The Canterbury Tales.
Prologue: "This worthy limitour, this noble Frere." *Fr.* The Canterbury Tales: The Friar's Tale.
Prologue, The: "Thousand tymes have I herd men tell, A." *Fr.* The Legend of Good Women.
Prologue: "Whan that Aprille with his[e] shoures soote [*or* sote]." *Fr.* The Canterbury Tales.
Prologue: "When the sweet showers of April follow March." *Fr.* The Canterbury Tales.
Prologue of the Prioress's Tale, The, *sel. Fr.* The Canterbury Tales.
Prologue to Melibeus. *Fr.* The Canterbury Tales.
Prologue to Sir Thopas. *Fr.* The Canterbury Tales.
Prologue to "The Canterbury Tales."
Prologue to "The Canterbury Tales," *sels.*
Prologue to the Man of Law's Tale. *Fr.* The Canterbury Tales.
Prologue to the Pardoner's Tale. *Fr.* The Canterbury Tales.
Prologue to the Second Nun's Tale, The, *sel. Fr.* The Canterbury Tales.
Prologue to the Wife of Bath's Tale, The. *Fr.* The Canterbury Tales.
Quest for Death. *Fr.* The Canterbury Tales: The Pardoner's Tale.
Qui Bien Aime à Tard Oublie. *Fr.* The Parlement of Foules.
Reeve's Tale, The, *sel. Fr.* The Canterbury Tales.
Romaunt of the Rose, The, *sels., tr.*
Rondel of Merciles Beautè [*or* Merciless Beauty], A.
Roundel, A: "Now welcom, somer, with thy sonne [*or* sunne] softe." *Fr.* The Parlement of Foules.
Roundel: "Your eyën two will slay me suddenly."
St. Valentine's Rondel, A. *Fr.* The Parlement of Foules.
Second Nun's Tale, The, *sel. Fr.* The Canterbury Tales.
Seven Pilgrims. *Fr.* The Canterbury Tales: Prologue.
Shipman, The. *Fr.* The Canterbury Tales: Prologue.
Sir Thopas. *Fr.* The Canterbury Tales.
Some Characters from "The Canterbury Tales." *Fr.* The Canterbury Tales: Prologue.
Song of Troilus. *Fr.* Troilus and Criseyde.
Sorrow of Troilus, The. *Fr.* Troilus and Criseyde.
Squire, A. *Fr.* The Canterbury Tales: Prologue.
Story of Thisbe of Babylon, Martyr, The. *Fr.* The Legend of Good Women.
Tale of Hugelin, Count of Pisa, The. *Fr.* The Canterbury Tales: The Monk's Tale.
Tale of the Wyf of Bathe, The. *Fr.* The Canterbury Tales.
Than Longen Folk to Goon on Pilgrimages. *Fr.* The Canterbury Tales: Prologue.
Three Canterbury Pilgrims. *Fr.* The Canterbury Tales: Prologue.
To My Empty Purse.
To Rosemounde; a Balade.
Troilus and Criseyde, *sels.*
Troilus Soliloquizes. *Fr.* Troilus and Criseyde.
Truth.
Truth Shall Make You Free, The.
Two Invocations of the Virgin. *Fr.* The Canterbury Tales.
Well of Pity, The. *Fr.* An A. B. C.
Whan That Aprille with His Shoures Sote. *Fr.* The Canterbury Tales: Prologue.
Whan That the Month of May. *Fr.* The Legend of Good Women: Prologue.
Wife of Bath, The. *Fr.* The Canterbury Tales: Prologue.
Wife of Bath and the Parson, The. *Fr.* The Canterbury Tales: Prologue.
Wife of Bath's Prologue, The. *Fr.* The Canterbury Tales.
Wife of Bath's Prologue, The, *sel. Fr.* The Canterbury Tales.
Wife of Bath's Tale, The. *Fr.* The Canterbury Tales.
Wife of Bath's Tale, The, *sel. Fr.* The Canterbury Tales.
Wooing of Criseide, The. *Fr.* Troilus and Criseyde.
Written on His Deathbed.
Young Woman. *Fr.* The Canterbury Tales: The Miller's Tale.

CHAULIEU, GUILLAUME DE. On the Gout.

CHAUNDLER, CHRISTINE. Child's Christmas Carol, A.
Tree in the Garden, The.

CHAURAS. Black Marigolds, *sels., at.*
Death Sends Me the Flickering of Powdery Lids, *at. Fr.* Black Marigolds.
Her Mouth Carelessly Scented, *at. Fr.* Black Marigolds.
I Have a Need, *at. Fr.* Black Marigolds.

I Have No Surety, *at.* *Fr.* Black Marigolds.
I Know My Princess, *at.* *Fr.* Black Marigolds.
I Know That I Have Savoured, *at.* *Fr.* Black Marigolds.
I Love Long Black Eyes, *at.* *Fr.* Black Marigolds.
I Mind That I Went Round with Men and Women, *at.* *Fr.* Black Marigolds.
I Mind the Coming, *at.* *Fr.* Black Marigolds.
I Mind the Time of the Falling of Blossoms, *at.* *Fr.* Black Marigolds.
I See Her, *at.* *Fr.* Black Marigolds.
I See the Heavy Startled Hair, *at.* *Fr.* Black Marigolds.
I Seem to See My Prison Walls, *at.* *Fr.* Black Marigolds.
If I See in My Soul, *at.* *Fr.* Black Marigolds.
If My Girl with Lotus Eyes, *at.* *Fr.* Black Marigolds.
Love Is a God, *at.* *Fr.* Black Marigolds.
My Eyes That Hurry to See, *at.* *Fr.* Black Marigolds.
Pleased Intimacy, The, *at.* *Fr.* Black Marigolds.
She Swims Back in the Crowning Hour, *at.* *Fr.* Black Marigolds.
She with Young Limbs, *at.* *Fr.* Black Marigolds.
Spread We Our Nets, *at.* *Fr.* Black Marigolds.
Stainless Fair Appearance, The, *at.* *Fr.* Black Marigolds.
When All My Heavy Heart, *at.* *Fr.* Black Marigolds.
Woodcutter and the Fisherman Turn Home, The, *at.* *Fr.* Black Marigolds.

CHAVEZ, FRAY ANGELICO. Esther.
I Vowed.
In Extremis.
Lady of Lidice.
Lady of Peace.
Marionette.
Mary.
Mulier Amicta Sole.
Sea-Birds.
Southwestern Night.

CHAWNER, GEORGE F. Prayer, A: "Those who love Thee, may they find."

CHAZEAU, EUNICE DE. Only a Gambler Loves Peace.

CHEEK, THOMAS. To Chloe.

CHEETHAM, EVERETT. Blood on the Saddle, *at.*

CHEKE, HENRY. Of Perfect Friendship, *at.*
Plain Description of Perfect Friendship, A, *at.*

CHENEY, EDNAH DOW. Larger Prayer, The.

CHENEY, MRS. ELIZABETH (1859–). Overheard in an Orchard.

CHENEY, ELIZABETH. There Is a Man on the Cross.

CHENEY, JOHN VANCE. April.
Behind the hilltop drops the sun. *Fr.* Evening Songs.
Birds have hid, the winds are low, The. *Fr.* Evening Songs.
Days That Come and Go.
Evening Songs.
Every One to His Own Way.
Happiest Heart, The.
It is that pale, delaying hour. *Fr.* Evening Songs.
Kitchen Clock, The.
Lincoln.
Man with the Hoe, The; a Reply.
Now is Light, sweet mother, down the west. *Fr.* Evening Songs.
On a Picture of Lincoln.
One.
Rainbow, The.
San Francisco.
Seasons, The.
Skilful Listener, The.
Somewhere.
Song: "Birds of the air, they sing it, The."
Strong, The.
Way of It, The.
Whither.
Wood-Thrush, The.

CH'EN FU. Returning.

CH'EN FU LIANG. Rain.

CH'ENG HSIAO. Satire on Paying Calls.

CHENG HSIEH. Visit with Yang Chi, A.

CH'ENG-KUNG SUI. I sent out invitations.
Inviting Guests.

CH'ENG TSUNG LO. Morning Prayer.

CH'ENG WANG. Night Rain.

CHÉNIER, ANDRÉ MARIE DE. Beauties Arouse Love.
Bucoliques, *sel.*
Clytie.
Elegies.
Every man has his sorrows; yet each still. *Fr.* Elegies.
Flute, The.
Hymn to Night.
Néère. *Fr.* Bucoliques.
Satyr, The.
To Chromis.
Well, I would have it so. I should have known. *Fr.* Elegies.
White nymph wandering in the woods by night, A. *Fr.* Elegies.
Young Man, A.
Young Tarentine, The.

CH'EN SHENG CHI. Buddhist to His Soul, The.
Scholar, The.

CH'EN SHIH-TAO. Books.

CH'EN TE CHIEN. Fish!

CH'EN TZU-ANG. Ancients, The.
Business Men.
Evening.
Men of Affairs.

CH'EN TZU-LUNG. Little Cart, The.

CH'EN YÜ HUI. Lament, A: "Five long years."

CH'EN YÜN. Twilight.

CHERBURY, EDWARD HERBERT, 1ST BARON. *See* HERBERT OF CHERBURY.

CHERNICK, HANK. Situation Normal.

CHERRY, ANDREW. Bay of Biscay, The.
Green Little Shamrock of Ireland, The.
Shamrock, The.

CHERRY, EDITH E. Kept for Jesus.

CHERWINSKI, JOSEPH. Manhattan Menagerie.

CHESSON, NORA HOPPER. *See* HOPPER, NORA.

CHESTER, ANSON G. Tapestry Weavers, The.

CHESTER, HARRY S. When the Light Goes Out.

CHESTER, SIR ROBERT. Ditty: "O holy Love, religious saint!" *Fr.* Love's Martyr.
Her Hair. *Fr.* Love's Martyr.
Love's Martyr, *sels.*

CHESTER, THOMAS. Sir Launfal.

CHESTERFIELD, PHILIP DORMER STANHOPE, 4TH EARL OF. Advice to a Lady in Autumn.
Immortal Newton Never Spoke.
On a Full-Length Portrait of Beau Marsh.
To Miss Eleanor Ambrose on the Occasion of Her Wearing an Orange Lily at a Ball in Dublin Castle on July the 12th.
Verses Written in a Lady's Sherlock "Upon Death."

CHESTERMAN, HUGH. Bowman, The.
Coal Man, The.
Outside.
Rhyme Sheet of Other Lands, A.
Sir Nicketty Nox.
Yesterday.

CHESTERTON, FRANCES (Mrs. Gilbert Keith Chesterton). Alle Vögel Sind Schon Da.
Children's Song of the Nativity.
How Far Is It to Bethlehem?
To Felicity Who Calls Me Mary.

CHESTERTON, GILBERT KEITH. Antichrist, or the Reunion of Christendom; an Ode.
Ballad of the Battle of Gibeon, The.
Ballad of the White Horse, The, *sels.*
Ballade d'une Grande Dame.
Ballade of a Book-Reviewer, A.
Ballade of an Anti-Puritan, A.
Ballade of Suicide, A.
Ballade of the Grotesque, A.
Before the Roman Came to Rye.
Black Virgin, The.
Broad Minded Bishop Rebukes the Verminous Saint Francis, A.
By the Babe Unborn.
Christ-Child, The.
Christmas Carol, A: "Christ-child lay on Mary's lap, The."
Christmas Song for Three Guilds, A.
Cider Song, A.
Citizenship; Form 8889512, Sub-Section Q.
Commercial Candour.
Convert, The.
Dedication, A: "He was, through boyhood's storm and shower."
Donkey, The.
Ecclesiastes.
Elegy in a Country Churchyard.
Englishman, The.
Fantasia.
Feast of the Snow, The.
Feast on Wine or Fast on Water.
Flying Inn, The, *sel.*
Geography. *Fr.* Songs of Education.
Glencoe.
Grave of Arthur, The.
Happy Ulysses, The, *tr.*
Happy who like Ulysses, or that Lord, *tr.*
Harp of Alfred, The. *Fr.* The Ballad of the White Horse.
Heureux qui, comme Ulysse, a fait un beau voyage, *tr.*
Holy of Holies, The.
Home at Last.
House of Christmas, The.
Hymn, A: "From all that terror teaches," *sel.*
Hymn, A: "O God of earth and altar."
Hymn for the Church Militant.
King Alfred Answers the Danes. *Fr.* The Ballad of the White Horse.
Kingdom of Heaven, The.
Last Hero, The.
Lepanto.
Litany. *Fr.* A Hymn.
Logical Vegetarian, The.
Me Heart.
Music.
Myth of Arthur, The.
Novelty, A.
O God of Earth and Altar.
Old Song, The.
On a Prohibitionist Poem.
Praise of Dust, The.
Prayer: "O God of earth and altar."
Prayer in Darkness, A.
Regina Angelorum.
Return of Eve, The.
Rolling English Road, The.
Secret People, The.
Skeleton, The.
Song against Grocers, The.
Song against Songs, The.
Song of Quoodle, The.
Song of Right and Wrong, The.
Song of the Children, The.
Song of the Strange Ascetic, The.
Songs of Education, *sel.*
Songs of Guthrum and Alfred, The. *Fr.* The Ballad of the White Horse.
Strange Music, The.
Sword of Surprise, The.
To F. C., in Memoriam Palestine.
To M. E. W.
Translation from Du Bellay ("Happy, who like Ulysses or that lord"), *tr.*
Variations of [*or* on] an Air.
Who Goes Home, *sel.*
Wild Knight, The.
Wild Knight, The, *sel.*
Wine and Water. *Fr.* The Flying Inn.
World State, The.

CHETTLE, HENRY. Aeliana's Ditty. *Fr.* Piers Plainness' Seven Years' Prenticeship.

CHETTLE, HENRY (*continued*)
Damelus' Song of His Diaphenia, *at.*
Diaphenia, *at.*
Of Cupid. *Fr.* Piers Plainness' Seven Years' Prenticeship.
Piers Plainness' Seven Years' Prenticeship, *sels.*
Wily Cupid. *Fr.* Piers Plainness' Seven Years' Prenticeship.
CHETTLE, HENRY, *and* ANTHONY MUNDAY. *See* MUNDAY, ANTHONY, *and* HENRY CHETTLE.
CHEVERTON, EDWARD C. Uncover to the Flag.
CHEW, BEVERLY. Old Books Are Best.
CHEYNE, IRENE. Old Mr. Tatterlock.
CHEYNEY, EDWARD RALPH. *See* CHEYNEY, RALPH.
CHEYNEY, RALPH. Comrade Jesus.
Had I Not Loved Before.
Love, Give Me the Feel of Tomorrow.
Lover for Death, A.
Motion Picture Show.
Mountain Night.
No Armistice in Love's War.
Poet to Bird.
Two.
Unemployed.
Wage-Slaves to War-Makers.
CHEYNEY, RALPH, *and* LUCIA TRENT. *See* TRENT, LUCIA, *and* RALPH CHEYNEY.
CHIABRERA, GABRIELLO. Epitaphs.
Francesco Ceni.
CHIA CHI. Parting with Li Po on the Tung-ting Lake.
CHIANG YÜN. Years Between, The.
CHIA TAO. Searching for the Hermit in Vain.
CHICHESTER, BISHOP OF. *See* KING, HENRY.
CHIEN HSU. Stone Well, The.
CHIEN LIANG TSE. Glimpse of Beauty, A.
CH'IEN LIN. Coming of Autumn, The.
CHIEN T'ANG. Fifth Watch of the Night, The.
Old Garden, An.
CH'IEN WEN-TI, EMPEROR. Ferry, The.
Lo-yang.
Winter Night.
CHIH MING. Facing Death.
CHI HWANG CHU *and* EDNA WORTHLEY UNDERWOOD. *For translations from Chinese, see* ChLP; OnPM.
CHI K'ANG. Taoist Song.
CHI LAN YÜN. Dreams.
CHILD, A. C. Wishes.
CHILD, LYDIA MARIA. Apple-Seed John.
Thanksgiving Day.
Who Stole the Bird's Nest?
CHILD, O. C. A. Battle-Plane in France, A.
CHILD, PHILIP. Basilisk, The.
Dancing Partners.
Descent for the Lost.
Lyric: "I touched a shining mote of sand."
Macrocosm.
Oak.
CHILDE, WILFRED ROWLAND. Last Abbot of Gloucester, The.
Our Lady with Two Angels.
Shepherd of Meriador, The.
CHILMAN, ERIC. Beautiful Land, The.
CHILDRESS, W. LOMAX. Beautiful World, The.
Let Us Be Kind.
CHIN CH'ANG-HSÜ. Spring Sigh, A.
CH'IN CHIA. Ch'in Chia.
Ch'in Chia's Farewell.
To His Wife.
CHING. Odes of Ching, *sel.*
Shuh's Hunting. *Fr.* Odes of Ching.
CHIPP, ELINOR. Before Dawn.
Doubt.
Lullaby: "Sleep, little baby, sleep and rest."
Wild Geese.
CHISATO (Oe no Chisato). As I watch the moon.
Autumn Moon.
CHITTENDEN, "LARRY" (William Lawrence Chittenden). Cowboys' Christmas Ball, The.
Texas Types—"The Bad Man."
CHITWOOD, WILLIAM HANKINS. Gone to the Dogs.
CH'IU T'UNG. Impromptu.
CH'IU WEI. After Missing the Recluse on the Western Mountain.
CHIVERS, THOMAS HOLLEY. Apollo.
Avalon.
Burdens of Unrest.
Chaplet of Cypress, The.
Crucifixion, The.
Dying Beauty, The, *sel.*
Faith.
Georgia Waters.
Isadore.
Lily Adair.
Little Boy Blue.
Mary's Lament for Shelley Lost at Sea.
Oratio ad Dominum, *tr.*
Raising of Tabitha, The, *sel.*
Song: "On thy waters, thy sweet valley waters."
Song of Adoration to God.
Song to Isa Singing.
Sonnet: Grief.
To Allegra Florence in Heaven.
To Idealon.
Voice of Thought, The.
CHIYO NI. Small tendrils of a morning glory to the well ropes cling.
Smiles on my lips, while quick tears blind my eyes.
CHOCANO, JOSÉ SANTOS. Eagles and Sparrows.
Sylvan Ode.
CHOLMONDELEY, HESTER H. Betrayal.
Still as of Old.
CHOLMONDELEY-PENNELL, HENRY.
Bloated Biggaboon, The.
Ghostries.
How the Daughters Come Down at Dunoon.
I've Lost My ——.
Lay of the Deserted Influenzaed.
Our Traveller.
What the Prince of I Dreamt.
CHORLEY, HENRY FOTHERGILL. Brave Old Oak, The.
CHORLEY, HENRY FOTHERGILL, *and* JOHN LODGE ELLERTON. God, the Omnipotent.
CHOTZNER, JOSEPH. *For translations from Hebrew, see* TrJP.
CHOU SHANG JU. Night at Yen Chou.
CHO WEN-CHÜN. Song of Snow-white Heads.
CHOYCE, A. NEWBERRY. Come Michaelmas.
Let Me Love Bright Things.
Oblation.
Until You Pass.
CHRISTESEN, CLEMENT B. Dawn at Flying-Fish Point.
Reef Wrack.
Regent-Bird and Girl.
CHRISTIAN, MARCUS B. Craftsman, The.
Drums of Haiti.
McDonogh Day in New Orleans.
Song of Hannibal; Rome.
CHRISTIAN, SHELDON. Hunt, The.
CHRISTINA, SISTER MARY. Day of My Profession, The.
CHRISTINE DE PISAN. *See* PISAN, CHRISTINE DE.
CHRISTMAN, WILLIAM WEAVER. Deborah.
Fox Sparrow, The.
Mourning Dove, The.
Snow Lies Light, The.
CHRISTMAS, EDWIN. Ode to the West Wind.
CHRISTMAS, MARJORY. Blackbird Song, The.
"CHRISTOPHER, ROBIN" (Abraham B. Shiffrin). Dimple Diggers.
Hide and Seek.
One, Two, Three.
Rain.
Storm, The.
CH'ÜAN SHEN. Mountain Courtyard, The.
CHUBB, THOMAS CALDECOT. At the Edge of the Bay.
Praise of New England.
CHUDLEIGH, MARY, LADY. Resolve, The.
CHU HSI. Boats Are Afloat, The.
Farm by the Lake, The.
Spring Sun.
Thoughts while Reading.
CHULKOV, GEORGY IVANOVICH. Autumnal Love.
CHU MIAO TUAN. Butterflies.
Wine Shop, The.
CHURCH, BENJAMIN. Choice, The, *sel.*
To the Heirs of the Pilgrims.
CHURCH, EDWARD A. Cornerstone, The.
CHURCH, HUBERT. Favonius.
Fugue, A, *sel.*
New Zealand, *sel.*
Old Sandhills, Hobart, The.
Retrospection.
Rosalind.
Spring in New Zealand.
CHURCH, RICHARD. Cat, The.
Dandelion, The.
Edward Millington.
From an Upland Valley.
Hay's Wharf.
House in Wartime, A.
Immortal.
In a Woman's Face.
Lantern, The.
Londoner in the Country, The.
Man without Faith, The.
Mirage.
Mountain Lake, The.
Mud.
Nocturne: "See how the dying west puts forth her song."
On Hearing the First Cuckoo.
Portent.
Purification, The.
Riding up the Hill.
Road in the Weald, A.
Secret Service.
Ship, The.
Solstices.
Something Private.
Thinking of a Master.
Twentieth Century Love-Song.
Twentieth Century Psalter, *sel.*
Twenty-fourth Day—Evening. *Fr.* Twentieth Century Psalter.
Waiting for News.
Woodpecker, The.
Wrong Road, The.
CHURCHILL, CHARLES. At Least. *Fr.* The Times.
Bishop among the Plotters, The. *Fr.* The Duellist.
Conscience. *Fr.* The Conference.
Conference, The, *sel.*
Critical Fribble, A. *Fr.* The Rosciad.
Criticaster, A. *Fr.* The Rosciad.
Duellist, The, *sels.*
Farewell, The: "Farewell to Europe, and at once farewell."
Ghost, The, *sels.*
Gotham, *sels.*
Night; an Epistle to Robert Lloyd, *sels.*
Nut, a World, a Squirrel, and a King, A. *Fr.* Night.
On Himself. *Fr.* The Prophecy of Famine.
Pains of Education, The.
Prophecy of Famine, The; a Scots Pastoral.
Prophecy of Famine, The, *sel.*
Rosciad, The, *sel.*
Scotland. *Fr.* The Prophecy of Famine.
Times, The, *sel.*
What Is't to Us? *Fr.* Night.
CHURCHYARD, THOMAS. Davy Dicar's Dream.
Farewell to a Fondling, A.
Fayned Fancye betweene the Spider and the Gowte, A, *sel.*
Old-Time Service. *Fr.* Fayned Fancye betweene the Spider and the Gowte.
He Persuadeth His Friend from the Fond Affects of Love.
How Shore's Wife, Edward the Fourth's Concubine, Was by King

Richard Despoiled of All Her Goods . . . *Fr.* A Mirror for Magistrates.
How Thomas Wolsey Did Arise unto Great Authority and Government . . . *Fr.* A Mirror for Magistrates.
Lover Deceived by His Lady's Unconstancy Writeth unto Her as Followeth, The.
Mirror for Magistrates, A, *sels.*
Praise of Our Soldiers, The.
Sorrowful Verses Made on the Death of Our Most Sovereign Lady Queen Elizabeth My Gracious Mistress.
CHU SHU CHEN. Alone.
Despair.
Hysteria.
Morning.
Old Anguish, The.
Plaint.
Spring.
Stormy Night in Autumn.
Sundown.
CHUTE, MARCHETTE GAYLORD. Bees.
Birthdays.
By the Sea.
Christmas.
Day before Christmas.
Drinking Fountain.
Easter Parade.
Fairies.
Food.
Fourth of July.
Going to Bed.
Growing Up.
My Dog.
My Plan.
One Night.
Presents.
Secret, The.
Sliding.
Spring.
Spring Rain.
Tracks in the Snow.
CHU TUN-RU. Traveling.
CHU WAN. Retreat in the Mountains, A.
CHU YUAN. Battle, The.
Encountering Sorrow.
God of the River, The. *Fr.* The Nine Songs.
Great Summons, The.
Great Unity, the Sovereign of the East, The. *Fr.* The Nine Songs.
Lady of Hsiang, The. *Fr.* The Nine Songs.
Lord of Hsiang, The. *Fr.* The Nine Songs.
Lord of the East, The. *Fr.* The Nine Songs.
Lord Who Dwells in the Clouds, The. *Fr.* The Nine Songs.
Nine Declarations, The, *sel.*
Nine Songs, The [Chu K'o].
Patriots Who Died in Battle, The. *Fr.* The Nine Songs.
Sacrifice, The. *Fr.* The Nine Songs.
Senior Arbiter of Fate, The. *Fr.* The Nine Songs.
Spirit of the Mountain, The. *Fr.* The Nine Songs.
CHWANG KËANG. Complaint, A.
CHWOROWSKY, KARL M. Motherhood.
CIARDI, JOHN. Camptown.
Composition for a Nativity.
Divina Commedia, *sel., tr.*
Elegy Just in Case.
Evil Eye, The.
For My Twenty-fifth Birthday in Nineteen Forty-one.
Goodmorning with Light.
In the Year of Many Conversions and the Private Soul.
Morning in the Park.
My Father's Watch.
Mystic River.
Ode for the Burial of a Citizen.
On a Photo of Sgt. Ciardi a Year Later.
P-51.
Pier delle Vigne, *tr.* *Fr.* Divina Commedia: Inferno.
Pilot in the Jungle, The.
Poem for My Thirty-second Birthday.
Song: "Bells of Sunday rang us down, The."
To Judith Asleep.
V-J Day.
Vale.
CIBBER, COLLEY. Blind Boy, The.
Celia and Belinda. *Fr.* Woman's Wit.
Woman's Wit, *sel.*
CINO DA PISTOIA. At the Grave of Selvaggia.
Canzone: His Lament for Selvaggia.
Desperate.
In Great Bitterness.
Madrigal: To His Lady Selvaggia Vergiolesi.
On the Death of the Emperor Henry VII.
Sonnet: Death Is Not without but within Him.
Sonnet: Of the Grave of Selvaggia.
Sonnet: To Dante Alighieri (He Conceives of Some Compensation in Death).
Sonnet: To Dante Alighieri (He Interprets Dante's Dream).
Sonnet: To Love, in Great Bitterness.
Sonnet: Trance of Love, A.
Sonnet for Selvaggia.
CIULLO [*or* CIELO] D'ALCAMO. Dialogue; Lover and Lady.
CLAIRMONT, ROBERT. Answers, The.
Hero in the Land of Dough, A.
Wheelgoround, The.
When Did the World Begin.
CLANCY, LIAM P. Christmas Eve.
Gaelic Christmas, A.
CLANVOWE, SIR THOMAS. Cuckoo and the Nightingale, The.
CLAPP, FREDERICK MORTIMER. Bay, The; December.
Brooklyn Bridge.
Cancelled Itinerary.
Cattle.
Cicada, *tr.*
River Traffic.
Sky-Signs.
Snow at Midnight; the Elevated.
Steam.
Warehouses
CLAPP, MARY BRENNAN. At Christmas Time.
Gilead.
CLAPP, ROSS B. Mother's Love.
CLARE, FRANCIS D. Sick Room.
CLARE, JOHN. Address to Plenty, *sel.*
After Reading in a Letter Proposals for Building a Cottage.
Approach of Spring.
Autumn ("I love the fitful gust").
Autumn ("The thistledown's flying").
Autumn Evening.
Autumn Robin, The.
Badger.
Beanfield, The.
Birds' Lament.
Bonny Lassie O.
Clock-a [*or*-o']-Clay.
Cottager, The, *sel.*
Cowper.
Crows in Spring.
Daisy, The.
Death, *sel.*
Dying Child, The.
Early Nightingale.
Emmonsail's Heath in Winter.
Eternity of Nature.
Evening Primrose.
Evening Star, The.
Exile, The.
Fear of Flowers, The.
Fir trees taper into twigs and wear, The.
Firetail's Nest, The.
First Love.
Firwood.
Flitting, The, *sel.*
Fragment: "Hedgerow hips to glossy scarlet turn, The."
Fragment: "Language has not the power to speak what love indites."
Frightened Ploughman, The.
Gipsies.
Gipsy Camp, The.
Graves of Infants.
Hedgehog, The.
Honey Dew Falls from the Tree.
I Am.
I Dwell on Trifles. *Fr.* The Flitting.
I Feel I Am.
I Hid My Love.
I Lost the Love of Heaven.
I Love the Blue Violet.
I saw her crop a rose.
Invitation to Eternity.
July.
Laborer, The.
Little Maid and the Cowslips, The.
Little Trotty Wagtail.
Love.
Love Lives beyond the Tomb.
Love of Nature.
Love Scorned by Pride.
Maple Hangs Its Green Bee Flowers, The.
Mary.
Meet Me in the Green Glen.
Meet Me in the Primrose Lane.
Mole, The.
Morning.
Mouse's Nest.
My Early Home.
Nodding oxeye bends before the wind, The.
Noon.
November.
Old Cottagers, The.
Old Year, The.
On a Lane in Spring.
One Careless Look.
One gloomy eve I roam'd about.
Pale Sun, The.
Peasant Poet, The.
Ploughboy, The.
Primrose, The.
Ragwort, The.
Recollections after an Evening Walk.
Returned Soldier, The.
Schoolboys in Winter.
Secret Love.
Secret Love, *sel.*
Shepherd's Calendar, The, *sels.*
Shepherd's Tree, The.
Signs of Winter.
Silent Love.
Soldier, The.
Solitude.
Song: "Go with your tauntings, go."
Song: "Love lives beyond the tomb."
Song's Eternity.
Spring is coming by a many signs, The.
Spring Morning, A.
Stanzas: "Black absence hides upon the past."
Stone-Pit.
Stranger, The.
Sudden Shower.
Summer Evening.
Summer Images, *sels.*
Summer Moods.
Swallow, The.
Swordy Well.
Thou Flower of Spring.
Thou Flower of Summer.
Thrush's Nest, The.
To a Primrose.
To Harriett.
To Mary [It Is the Evening Hour].
Vision, A.
When first we hear the shy-come nightingales.
When once the sun sinks in the west.
Winter.
Winter's Spring, The.
Wood-Cutter's Night Song, The.
World for Love, A.
Written in a Thunderstorm, 15 July 1841.
Written in Northampton County Asylum.
Young Jenny.
Young Lambs.
CLARE, SISTER MIRIAM. Ideal.
"CLARIBEL." *See* BARNARD, CHARLOTTE ALINGTON.
CLARK, ANN NOLAN. Garden, The.
Irrigation.
Mountains.

CLARK, ARTHUR H. A-Working on the Railway.
Poor Reuben Ranzo.
CLARK, BADGER. Border Affair, A.
Bunk-House Orchestra, The.
Cottonwood Leaves.
Cowboy's Prayer, The.
Glory Trail, The.
God Meets Me in the Mountains.
Just a-Ridin'!
Legend of Boastful Bill, The.
Old Cowman, The.
Outlaw, The.
Pioneers.
Ranger, A.
Ridin'.
Sheep-Herder, The.
Smoke-blue Plains, The.
CLARK, CHARLES HEBER. *See* "ADELER, MAX."
CLARK, EUNICE (Mrs. John Knox Jessup). Fallow Land.
Impulses, *tr.*
People Has No Obituary, The.
CLARK, HENRY W. Far Distances.
Host and Guest.
CLARK, IMOGEN. Saint Francis Sings a New Song.
CLARK, JAMES GOWDY. Sleep, Robin, Sleep.
Song of the Indian Mother.
CLARK, LEONARD. Walk, The.
CLARK, LESLIE SAVAGE. Beacon Light.
Before Pilate.
Bread.
Carpenter.
Conquest.
Hands of Christ, The.
Hilltops.
Holier Night.
In Nazareth.
In the Time of Trouble.
Incense.
Litany for Peace.
Magi.
Of Things Not Seen.
Offering.
Remembrance.
Son of Man.
Sovereignty.
Syrian's Tale, The.
Temple Offering.
This Little Earth.
Values.
Way, The.
White Splendor.
Who Can Forget?
Young Jesus.
CLARK, LEWIS GAYLORD. Flamingo, The.
CLARK, MARTHA HASKELL. Black Ashes.
Changeless.
Chickadee.
Dreamers, The.
Hurdy-Gurdy Days.
Red Geraniums.
Sea Road, The.
Sea-Song.
Stay at Home, The.
To a Kitten.
CLARK, PRESTON. Faith.
Youth.
CLARK, THOMAS CURTIS. Abraham Lincoln, the Master.
Apparitions.
At Mount Vernon.
Blow, Bugle!
Bugle Song of Peace.
By an Ancient Sea.
Call, The.
Carry On!
Challenge.
Christ Militant, The.
Come, Follow Me!
Common Blessings.
Day Breaks, The.
Desert Wanderings.
Disillusioned.
Earth's Story.
Easter.
Evidence.
Faith and Science.
Faith for Tomorrow.
Faith of Christ's Freemen, The.
Farewell and Hail!
For Those Who Died.
Forgotten Star, The.
Friends.
God Give Me Joy.
Glory of Lincoln, The.
God's Dreams.
He Shall Speak Peace.
His Is the Way.
How Shall We Honor Lincoln.
I Am Still Rich.
In an Age of Science.
It Shall Not Be Again!
Journey, The.
Keep Love in Your Life.
Kingdom, The.
Knowledge.
Lincoln.
Lincoln at Gettysburg.
Lincoln, Come Back.
Lost Christ, The.
Master, The.
Mary.
Message of the Bells, The.
Mother.
My America.
My Country, Right!
Nazareth.
New Crucifixion.
New Dreams for Old.
O Sun of Life.
On a World War Battlefield.
One Who Dared to Die.
Poet's Call, The.
Prophet, The.
Prospect.
Repentance.
Requiem.
Search, The.
Song of Christian Workingmen.
Sonnet for My Dog.
Sons of Promise.
Take Time to Live.
There Lived a Man.
There Was a Man.
This Is America.
Thy Kingdom Come!
To Poets All.
To the Flag of Stars.
To the Master Poet.
Today.
Touch of Human Hands, The.
Tragedy, The.
Trees.
True Need, The.
Trust the Great Artist.
Unto Thee.
Voice in a Cathedral.
Wanderers.
We Thank Thee! ("For glowing autumn's brimming yield").
We Thank Thee ("Not for our lands").
CLARK, WILLIS GAYLORD. Remembrance, A.
CLARKE, AIDAN. Journey, The.
CLARKE, ANDREW STUART CURRIE. Prayer: "Bless Thou this year, O Lord!"
Prayer for a Happy New Year, A.
CLARKE, AUGUSTUS PECK. Physician's Advice.
Quack Vendor, The.
CLARKE, AUSTIN. Aisling.
Ancient Lights.
Awakening of Dermuid, The. *Fr.* The Vengeance of Finn.
Blackbird of Derrycairn, The.
Celebrations.
Celibacy.
Fair at Windgap, The.
Flower-quiet in the Rush-strewn Sheiling.
Jewels, The.
Lost Heifer, The.
Lucky Coin, The.
Marriage.
Night and Morning.
O Love, There Is No Beauty.
Pilgrimage.
Planter's Daughter, The.
Straying Student, The.
Tenebrae.
Vengeance of Finn, The, *sel.*
CLARKE, C. R. Song of the Mariner's Needle.
CLARKE, EDNAH PROCTOR. Dancer, The.
Deathless, The.
Good-by, A.
Humming Bird, The.
Salem Witch, A.
To a Wild Rose Found in October.
CLARKE, FRANCES (Frances Clarke Sayers). Who Calls?
CLARKE, GEORGE ARTHUR. Charter of Salvation, The.
CLARKE, GEORGE FREDERICK. Saint John, The.
CLARKE, GEORGE HERBERT. Child's Evening Hymn, A.
Christ before Pilate.
Fog-Horn.
Halt and Parley.
Off Duty.
On My Dog's Death.
Over Salève.
Santa Maria del Fiore.
CLARKE, HERBERT EDWIN. Age, The.
Cry, A.
In the Wood.
Lady Mine.
Life and Death.
CLARKE, JAMES FREEMAN. Caliph and Satan, The.
Cana.
Rabia, *tr.*
White-capped Waves.
CLARKE, JOSEPH IGNATIUS CONSTANTINE. Bill Manning.
Fighting Race, The.
Fret of Father Carty, The.
Pro Libra Mea.
Way of the Cross, The.
CLARKE, MARCUS. In a Lady's Album.
CLARKE, MARY BAYARD. Lines on an Album.
Racing Water.
Resurgam.
Swannanoa, *at.*
Triumph of Spring, The.
CLARKE, PHEBE ANN. Aliens.
CLARKSON, M. J. Secret of the Cross, The.
CLAUDE OF JESUS, SISTER. Assuagement.
More than the Moment.
Words in the Wilderness.
CLAUDEL, PAUL. Canticle for Three Voices, *sel.*
Five Grand Odes, *sel.*
Fourth Station.
Our Lady, Help of Christians.
Seventh Station.
Shadows.
CLAUDIAN (Claudius Claudianus). Epitaph: "Fate to beauty still must give."
Lonely Isle, The.
Old Man of Verona, The.
CLAUDIUS, HERMANN. Cherry Tree.
Rosebush.
Water.
CLAUDIUS, MATTHIAS ("Asmus"). At My Father's Grave.
Hen, The.
Most Acceptable Gift, The.
We Plough [*or* Plow] the Fields.
CLAUSSEN, SOPHUS. Abroad.
CLAYTOR, GERTRUDE. Grant at Appomattox.
CLEANTHES. God Leads the Way.
Hymn of Cleanthes, The.
Hymn to Zeus.
Stoic's Resignation, The.
CLEAR, GWEN. Goodwife Relents, The.
CLEAVELAND, C. L. November.
CLEAVELAND, ELIZABETH HANNAH JOCELYN. No Sects in Heaven.
CLEAVES, CHARLES POOLE. His Name.
Rest Where You Are.
CLEGHORN, SARAH NORCLIFFE. Air of Coolness Plays upon His Face, An.
Anodyne, The.
But This Is Also Everlasting Life.
Come, Captain Age!
Comrade Jesus.
Contented at Forty.
Dorothea.
Emilia.

For Sleep when Overtired [or Worried].
Golf Links [Lie So Near the Mill], The.
Hemlock Mountain.
Incentive, The.
Judge Me, O Lord.
O Altitudo!
Poltroon, The.
Portrait of a Lady.
Quatrain: "Golf links lie so near the mill, The."
St. Clare Hears St. Francis.
Saint R. L. S.
Saint's Hours, A.
Survival of the Fittest, The.
To Safeguard the Heart from Hardness.
Vermont.
CLELAND, WILLIAM, *and others*. Hallo My Fancy.
CLEMENS, JAMES R. Love of Books, The.
CLEMENS, SAMUEL LANGHORNE. *See* "TWAIN, MARK."
CLEMENT, BROTHER. Death of an Italian Beggar, The, *sel.*
CLEMENT OF ALEXANDRIA (Titus Flavius Clemens). Earliest Christian Hymn ("Curb for stubborn steed").
Earliest Christian Hymn, The ("Shepherd of tender youth").
Hymn to Christ the Saviour.
Shepherd of Eager Youth.
CLEMENTS, JOHN R. God's Trails Lead Home.
CLEMMER, MARY (Mary Clemmer Ames Hudson). By the Sea.
Nantasket, *sel.*
Something Beyond.
CLEMO, JACK R. Calvinist in Love, A.
Water-Wheel, The.
CLEMONS, W. HARRY. Camp-Fire, The.
CLEOBULUS OF LINDUS. Midas' Tomb, *at.*
CLEPHANE, ELIZABETH CECILIA. Beneath the Cross.
Lost Sheep, The.
Ninety and Nine, The.
There Were Ninety and Nine.
CLERK, SIR JOHN, OF PENICUIK. Miller, The.
O Merry May the Maid Be.
CLERKE, WILLIAM. Song: "So, so,/ Lo, lilies fade, before the roses show."
CLEVELAND, C. L. *See* CLEAVELAND, C. L.
"CLEVELAND, ELLEN KATE." *See* NICHOLS, REBECCA S. REED.
CLEVELAND, JOHN. Antiplatonick, The.
Elegy on Ben Jonson, An, *at.*
Epitaph on the Earl of Strafford.
Fuscara; or, The Bee Errant.
Here lies wise and valiant dust.
Mark Antony [*or* Anthony].
On Scotland.
On the Memory of Mr. Edward King, Drown'd in the Irish Seas.
Rebel Scot, The, *sel.*
Sluggish morn as yet undrest, The.
To the Memory of Ben Jonson.
To the State of Love; or, The Senses Festival.
Upon Phyllis Walking in a Morning before Sun-rising.
Whenas the Nightingale Chanted Her Vespers.
CLEVELAND, PHILIP JEROME. By Night.
I Yield Thee Praise.
CLEYTON, JAMES. On Ben Jonson, *at.*
CLIFFORD, ETHEL. Dark Road, The.
Harp of Sorrow, The.
Last Hour, The.
CLIFFORD, GEORGE, 3D EARL OF CUMBERLAND. My Thoughts Are Winged with Hopes.
To Cynthia.
CLIFFORD, JOHN. Anvil [of God's Word], The.
God's Word.
Hammers and Anvil.
CLIFFORD, MARGARET ROWE. Arizona.
CLIFFTON, WILLIAM. Mary Will Smile.
CLINE, LEONARD. Battery Park.
Vows.
CLINTON, J. E. Ode on Christmas.
CLIVE, CAROLINE MEYSEY-WIGLEY. Conflict.
CLOETE, STUART. La Femme de Quarante Ans.
CLOSE, EUNICE. Here We Come a-Haying.
Way to Fairyland, The.
CLOUD, FREDERICK. Hands.
CLOUD, VIRGINIA WOODWARD. Ballad of Sweet P, The.
Care.
Mother's Song, The.
Old Street, An.
Youth.
CLOUGH, ARTHUR HUGH. Academy at Venice, The.
Afloat; We Move. Delicious! *Fr.* Dipsychus.
Ah! Yet Consider It Again!
All Is Well.
Alteram Partem.
Am I with You, or You with Me? *Fr.* Songs in Absence.
Amours de Voyage.
Amours de Voyage, *sels.*
As I Sat at the Café, I Said to Myself. *Fr.* Dipsychus.
At Torcello. *Fr.* Dipsychus.
At Venice.
Autumn in the Highlands.
Bathers, The. *Fr.* The Bothie of Tober-na-Vuolich.
Bethesda.
"Blank Misgivings of a Creature Moving About in Worlds Not Realized."
"Blank Misgivings of a Creature Moving About in Worlds Not Realized," *sels.*
But That from Slow Dissolving Pomps of Dawn.
Bothie of Tober-na-Vuolich, The, *sel.*
Columbus.
Come Back, Come Back, Behold with Straining Mast. *Fr.* Songs in Absence.
Come Home, Come Home! And Where Is Home for Me. *Fr.* Songs in Absence.
Come, Poet, Come!
Currente Calamo. *Fr.* Mari Magno.
Dipsychus.
Dipsychus, *sels.*
Dipsychus Continued, *sel.*
Duty [—That's to Say Complying].
Easter Day.
Easter Day, *sels.*
Epi-Strauss-ium.
En Route. *Fr.* Amours de Voyage.
Envoi: "So go forth to the world." *Fr.* Amours de Voyage.
Evening Walk in Spring, An.
Farewell, Farewell! Her Vans the Vessel Tries. *Fr.* Songs in Absence.
Green Fields of England! *Fr.* Songs in Absence.
Help, Sure Help. *Fr.* Dipsychus.
Here am I yet, another twelvemonth spent. *Fr.* "Blank Misgivings of a Creature Moving About in Worlds Not Realized."
Hidden Love, The. *Fr.* Dipsychus.
Higher Courage, The.
Home, Rose, and Home, Provence and La Palie.
Hope.
Hope Evermore and Believe!
How Often Sit I. *Fr.* "Blank Misgivings of a Creature Moving About in Worlds Not Realized."
Ὕμνος Ἄυμνος (Hymnos Ahymnos).
I Have Seen Higher, Holier Things than These.
In a Lecture Room.
In a London Square.
In Controversial Foul Impureness.
In Stratis Viarum.
In the Depths.
In the Great Metropolis.
Is it illusion? or does there a spirit from perfecter ages. *Fr.* Amours de Voyage.
Is It True, Ye Gods, Who Treat Us.
Isolation. *Fr.* Dipsychus.
It Fortifies My Soul to Know.
Ite Domum Saturae, Venit Hesperus.
Jacob.
Juxtaposition. *Fr.* Amours de Voyage.
Keeping On.
Latest Decalogue, The.
Le Diner. *Fr.* Spectator ab Extra.
Les Vaches.
Letter from Rome, A. *Fr.* Amours de Voyage.
Life Is Struggle.
Love and Reason.
Love, Not Duty.
Mari Magno, *sel.*
Meeting, The. *Fr.* Songs in Absence.
Mighty Ocean Rolls and Raves, The. *Fr.* Songs in Absence.
Music of the World and of the Soul, The.
My Wind Is Turned to Bitter North.
Natura Naturans.
New Sinai, The.
Noli Aemulari.
O Let Me Love My Love unto Myself Alone. *Fr.* Dipsychus.
O Ship, Ship, Ship. *Fr.* Songs in Absence.
O Thou Whose Image.
Old Things Need Not Be Therefore True.
On Montorio's Height. *Fr.* Amours de Voyage.
Our gaieties, our luxuries. *Fr.* Dipsychus.
Over the great windy waters, and over the clear-crested summits. *Fr.* Amours de Voyage.
Pantheon, The. *Fr.* Amours de Voyage.
Parvenant. *Fr.* Spectator ab Extra.
"Perchè Pensa? Pensando S'Invecchia."
Peschiera.
Pleasure and Guilt. *Fr.* Dipsychus Continued.
Protest, A.
Put Forth Thy Leaf, Thou Lofty Plane.
Qua Cursum Ventus.
Questioning Spirit, The.
Qui Laborat, Orat.
Real Question, The. *Fr.* Amours de Voyage.
Revival.
Rome. *Fr.* Amours de Voyage.
Rome Is Fallen, I Hear. *Fr.* Amours de Voyage.
Say Not the Struggle Naught Availeth.
Sceptic Moods. *Fr.* Amours de Voyage.
Sehnsucht.
Serve in Thy Post.
Seven Sonnets, *sel.*
Sleeping Child, A.
So Pleasant It Is to Have Money. *Fr.* Dipsychus.
Some Future Day When What Is Now Is Not. *Fr.* Songs in Absence.
Song of Autumn, A.
Songs in Absence.
Songs in Absence, *sels.*
Sonnet: "But whether in the uncoloured light of truth." *Fr.* Seven Sonnets.
Spectator ab Extra.
Spectator ab Extra, *sels.*
Spirit's Song, The. *Fr.* Dipsychus.
Steadfast.
Stream of Life, The.
That Out of Sight Is Out of Mind. *Fr.* Songs in Absence.
That There Are Powers above Us I Admit.
"There is no God," the wicked saith. *Fr.* Dipsychus.
Thesis and Antithesis.
Though to the vilest things beneath the moon. *Fr.* "Blank Misgivings of a Creature Moving About in Worlds Not Realized."

Clough, Arthur Hugh (*continued*)
Through a Glass Darkly.
To a Sleeping Child.
Τὸ Καλόν.
To Spend Uncounted Years of Pain.
Uranus.
Well, well—Heaven bless you all from day to day. *Fr.* "Blank Misgivings of a Creature Moving About in Worlds Not Realized."
"Wen Gott Betrügt, Ist Wohl Betrogen."
Were You with Me, or I with You. Songs in Absence, X *and* XIII.
What We, When Face to Face We See.
"What Went Ye Out for to See?"
Whate'er You Dream with Doubt Possest.
When the Dews Are Earliest Falling.
When the enemy is near thee. *Fr.* Dipsychus.
Where are the great, whom thou would'st wish to praise thee? *Fr.* Dipsychus.
Where Lies the Land [to Which the Ship Would Go]? *Fr.* Songs in Absence.
"With Whom Is No Variableness, neither Shadow of Turning."
Would That I Were.
Ye Flags of Piccadilly. *Fr.* Songs in Absence.
Yes, I have lied, and so must walk my way. *Fr.* "Blank Misgivings of a Creature Moving About in Worlds Not Realized."
Clouts, Sydney. Hawk, The.
Of Thomas Traherne and the Pebble Outside.
Roy Kloof.
Roy Kloof Went Riding.
Sea and the Eagle, The.
Situation, The.
Sleeper, The.
Within.
Clover, Samuel T. Cadences.
Cnut, King. *See* Canute, King.
Coan, Titus Munson. Crystal, The.
Dream of Flowers, The.
Nihil Humani Alienum.
Coates, Carol (Alice Caroline Coates Cassidy). Choral Symphony Conductor.
Circle, The.
Country Reverie.
First Flight.
Light.
Coates, Elmer Ruán. Sand-Man, The.
Coates, Florence Earle. After.
America.
Angelus, The.
Be Thou My Guide.
Benjamin Franklin.
Buffalo.
By the Conemaugh.
Captain Guynemer.
Christ of the Andes, The.
Columbus.
Cradle Song: "Thy heart and mine are one, my dear."
Death.
Dream the Great Dream.
For Joy.
Hero, A.
His Face.
House of Pain, The.
Ideal, The.
Immortal.
India.
Lullaby: "Day is stealing down the west."
Morning-Glory, The.
Narrow Window, A.
New Mars, The.
Per Aspera.
Perdita.
Pilgrim Song.
Poetry of Earth, The.
Requiem for a Young Soldier.
Rhapsody.
Seeker in the Night, A.
Smile of Reims, The.
Song: "For me the jasmine buds unfold."
Song: "If love were but a little thing."
Song of Life.
Suppliant.
Survival.
Tennyson.
Thanksgiving.
Their Victory Won.
To-Morrow.
Unconquered Air, The.
World Is Mine, The.
Coats, Grace Stone. Prairie Birth.
Coats, Adelbert Sumpter. Common Lot, The.
Pentecost.
Coatsworth, Elizabeth Jane (Mrs. Henry Beston). After Christmas a Landlord Remembers.
All Goats.
Announcement.
April Fool.
August Smiles.
Automobile and the Cat, The.
Axe Has Cut the Forest Down, The.
Bad Kittens, The.
Barn, The.
Bed Is Too Small.
Calling in the Cat.
Cat and Northern Lights, The.
Ceremonial Hunt. *Fr.* The Painted Desert.
Circus-postered Barn, The.
Cold winter now is in the wood.
Complete Hen, The.
Conquistador.
Counters.
Country Cat.
Daniel Webster's Horses.
Down the Rain Falls.
Easter.
Ever Since.
Fields Are Spread, The.
Fireside Kitten, The.
Footnote to History.
Hard from the southeast blows the wind.
He who has never known hunger.
Horse would tire, A.
How gray the rain.
In Walpi. *Fr.* The Painted Desert.
January.
Kangaroo, The.
Labor of Fields.
Lady, The.
Lady Comes to an Inn, A.
Lullaby: "Sleep, mouseling, sleep."
March.
Mary's Lullaby.
Mice of Spain, The.
Mouse, The.
Navajo, The. *Fr.* The Painted Desert.
No Snake in Springtime.
November.
Oak Leaves.
Old Mare, The.
On a Night of Snow.
Painted Desert, The.
Pirates.
Plant cut down to the root, The.
Pleiades, The.
Pretty Futility.
Rabbits' Song outside the Tavern, The.
Rain.
Reminiscences of a Landlord.
Sea gull curves his wings, The.
Sitting Here.
Sleigh Bells at Night.
Snow.
Sometimes a Little House Will Please.
Song for a Hot Day.
Song for a Little Cuckoo Clock.
Song for Midsummer Night.
Song of the Camels.
Song of the Parrot.
Song of the Rabbits outside the Tavern.
Song of the Three Seeds in the Macaw's Beak.
Song to Night.
Storm Snapped Its Fingers, The.
Sun Is First to Rise, The.
Sunday.
Swan, The.
Swift Things Are Beautiful.
Syracuse.
This Air That Blows In from the Sea.
This Is the Hay That No Man Planted.
To a Black Dog, Bereaved.
To Think.
Tracks in the Snow.
Twelfth Night.
Violets, daffodils.
Warm of heart shall never lack a fire, The.
Ways of Trains, The.
What Could Be Lovelier than to Hear.
"Who are you?" asked the cat of the bear.
Wife's Song, The.
Wilderness is Tamed, The.
Winter Rune.
Wise Sarah and the Elf.
Witches' Song.
You play fife.
Cobb, Mabel Ruggles. Inarticulate.
Cobbes, John. To Chloris.
Coblentz, Catherine Cate. Boundaries.
Earth Worshiped, The!
God.
Housewife, The.
Nature's Sorrow Cure.
Our History.
Coblentz, Stanton Arthur. Better the Vase Be Broken.
Bringers of the Hemlock.
Calm.
Civilization.
Flesh Is Weak, The.
Heritage.
History of the Modern World.
In a Troubled Dream.
In a Troubled World.
In the Storm.
Land's End (Point Lobos, California).
Last Judgment.
Mountain Revery.
Nephree-ti-ta.
O Prophets and Redeemers!
Omnipresence.
On "Shep," a Pet Dog.
Pageant of Man, The, *sel.*
Patient Is Time. *Fr.* The Pageant of Man.
Prayer for Light.
Processional.
Second Coming, The.
To a Dog.
Unknown Sculptor, The.
Ways of the Gods, The.
We Who Build Visions.
What Would He Say?
Wolf, the Hornet and the Nightingale, The.
Coburn, Wallace David. Cow-Boy Fun.
Cowboy's Fate, The.
Stampede, The.
Cochrane, Alfred. Eight-Day Clock.
Omnia Vincit.
To Anthea, Who May Command Him Anything (New Style).
Upon Lesbia—Arguing.
Cochrane, Frances. Face to Face.
Cochrane, J. C. Somewhere.
Cockburn, Alison. Flowers of the Forest, The.
Cocke, Zitella. Doric Reed, A, *sel.*
Greek Mother's Lullaby. *Fr.* A Doric Reed.
Miss Nancy's Gown.
My Cross.
Cocteau, Jean. Angel Heurtebise, *sel.*
Crucifixion, The, *sel.*
Plain-Song.
Poem of Circumstance.
Codd, Gertrude Jane. Nun's Diamond Jubilee, A.
Song against Servants.
Strange Guest.
Cody, Alexander J. Saint Francis' Wood.
Sister of Charity, The.
Cody, Hiram Alfred. Old Figurehead Carver, The.
Old Ship Riggers.
Port of St. John, The.
Woman on the Walls, The.

COE, ALICE ROLLIT. Turn of the Road.
COE, ARTHUR C. For Fifty Years.
Hatred.
Song: "Here the sudden iron sound."
COFFIN, CHARLES. Glad Tidings from the King of Kings.
COFFIN, ROBERT BARRY ("Barry Gray"). Ships at Sea.
COFFIN, ROBERT PETER TRISTRAM. Alexander Graham Bell Did Not Invent the Telephone.
America Is Corn.
America Was Schoolmasters.
At the Lowest Ebb of Night.
At the Moon's Eclipse.
Country Church.
Cripple, The.
Crystal Moment.
Fire at Night, A.
First Flight.
Fog, The.
Getting Ready for Town.
Getting Through.
Golden Falcon.
Good Friday Song.
Hound on the Church Porch.
Humming-Bird.
Jelly Fish, The.
John Popham.
Joy Meets Boy.
Little Boys of Texas.
Mess of Clams, A.
New Englanders Are Maples.
Night-Hawk.
Old Cellar.
Old Farmer Alone.
Pheasant, The.
Ram, The.
Secret Heart, The.
Ship o' Bed, The.
Skunk, The.
Spider, The.
Star-Pudding.
Starfish, The.
Stone Crop, The.
Strange Holiness.
Sunrise; Maine Coast.
Tall Axe-Man, The.
Terrae Illuminatae.
Warning, The.
Way to Know a Father, The.
Young Calves, The.
COGHILL, RHODA. Bright Hillside, The.
Dead.
In Wicklow.
Plough-Horse, The.
Poem: "Is to love, this—to nurse a name."
Runaway.
Spring Doggerel.
Young Bride's Dream, The.
COHAN, CHARLES C. Montana.
COHEN, JACOB. Eternal Jew, The.
Harp of David, The.
Surely My Soul.
COHEN, LEONARD. Ballad: "He pulled a flower."
When This American Woman.
COHEN, SOLOMON SOLIS-. *See* SOLIS-COHEN, SOLOMON.
COHN, MYRA. Sliding.
COICOU, MASSILLON. Oblivion.
COIT, STANTON. Psalm of Confidence, A, *at.*
COKAYNE, SIR ASTON. Funeral Elegy on the Death of His Very Good Friend, Mr. Michael Drayton.
Know all to whom these few sad lines shall come.
Of a Mistress.
"COL. D. STREAMER." *See* GRAHAM, HARRY.
COLBORNE-VEEL, MARY. Blessing, The.
Cotswold Hills.
Empty Houses.
Song of the Trees.
We Go No More to the Forest.
COLBY, VINE. Rainbow, The.
COLCORD, LINCOLN. Fishing Fleet, The.
COLE, CHARLOTTE DRUITT. Christmas Eve.
Clothes-Line, The.
Dormouse, The.
Garden Path, The.
Green Lady, The.
Pimpernel.
Pudding Charms.
Spider's Web, The.
Sun and Moon.
Three Mice.
Yellow Fairy, The.
COLE, ELSIE. Song of the Foot-Track.
COLE, EUGENE ROGER. Oh, You Wholly Rectangular.
COLE, HARRIET. End of the Way, The.
COLE, HELEN WIEAND. Gifts.
Peace on Earth.
COLE, MAMIE GENE. Child's Appeal, The.
COLE, MARJORIE E. Reason.
COLE, ROBERT GERMAIN. Spiritus Intactus.
COLE, SAMUEL VALENTINE. Abraham Lincoln.
Roosevelt.
Satisfied.
Theodore Roosevelt.
Trees, The.
Voice, A.
COLE, THOMAS. By the Beautiful Sea.
La Grande Jatte; Sunday Afternoon.
Landscape of Love, The.
My Lady Takes the Sunlight for Her Gown.
Old Woman's Song.
Praise to Light.
Tray, The.
Variations on a Still Morning.
COLE, TIMOTHY. Year's End, The.
COLE, WILLIAM. Alma Mater, Forget Me.
Just Dropped In.
Undersea Fever.
COLEMAN, ELLIOTT. Eve of Revolution.
Night Dirge.
Passage.
Thorn of Somerset, The.
Vicisti.
Winter Starset.
COLEMAN, HELENA. As Day Begins to Wane.
Beyond the Violet Rays.
Day and Night.
Enlargement.
Indian Summer.
More Lovely Grows the Earth.
Prairie Winds.
To a Bluebell.
COLEMAN, HERBERT THOMAS JOHN. Cockle-Shell and Sandal-Shoon.
Poet Confides, The.
COLEMAN, LUCILE. Echoes of Jesus.
With Lilacs in My Eye.
COLEMAN, PATRICK JAMES. Seed-Time.
COLERIDGE, HARTLEY. Birth of Speech, The.
Early Death.
Friendship.
From Country to Town.
Hast Thou Not Seen an Aged Rifted Tower.
He Lived amidst th' Untrodden Ways.
Ideality.
Jesus Praying.
Lark and the Nightingale, The.
Lines ——: "I have been cherish'd and forgiven."
Long Time a Child [and Still a Child, When Years].
Lullaby: "O sleep, sweet infant, for we all must sleep."
May, 1840.
"Multum Dilexit."
November. *Fr.* Sonnets on the Seasons.
On Wordsworth.
Prayer: "Be not afraid to pray—to pray is right."
Religious Unity.
Reply.
Sense, if You Can Find It.
Shakespeare.
She Is Not Fair to Outward View.
She Was a Queen.
Solitary-hearted, The.
Song: "She is not fair to outward view."
Song: "'Tis sweet to hear the merry lark."
Sonnet: Long Time a Child.
Sonnets on the Seasons, *sel.*
There Was a Cot.
Three Sonnets.
To a Deaf and Dumb Little Girl.
To a Friend.
To a Lofty Beauty, from Her Poor Kinsman.
To Shakespeare.
To the Nautilus.
Whither Is Gone the Wisdom and the Power.
COLERIDGE, MARY ELIZABETH. After St. Augustine.
As I Went Singing Over the Earth.
Bird, The.
Blue and White.
Broken Friendship.
Change.
Chillingham.
Cut It Down.
Death, *sel.*
Dedication, A: "Life of my learning, fire of all my Art."
Depart from Me.
Deserted House, The.
Egypt's Might Is Tumbled Down.
Evening, *sel.*
Friends—with a Difference.
Gibberish.
Gifts.
Gone.
Good Friday in My Heart.
He Knoweth Not That the Dead Are Thine.
Huguenot, A.
I Saw a Stable.
In a Volume of Austin Dobson.
In Dispraise of the Moon.
Jealousy.
King, The.
L'Oiseau Bleu.
Lord of the Winds.
Moment, A.
Morning Dreams.
Mortal Combat.
Mother to a Baby.
Myrtle Bush Grew Shady, The.
Night Is Fallen.
Not Yet.
On Such a Day.
On the Hearth-Rug.
Our Lady.
Punctilio.
Shadow.
Street Lanterns.
There Was No Place Found.
To Memory.
Train, The.
Unpunished.
Unwelcome.
We were not made for refuges of lies.
When Mary thro' the Garden Went.
Where a Roman Villa Stood, above Freiburg.
Whether I live, or whether I die.
White Women, The.
Whither Away?
Witch, The.
COLERIDGE, SAMUEL TAYLOR. Alas! they had been friends in youth. *Fr.* Christabel.
All Seasons Shall Be Sweet. *Fr.* Frost at Midnight.
Alvar's Address to the Spirits of the Dead. *Fr.* Remorse.
Ancient Mariner, The. *See* Rime of the Ancient Mariner, The.
Answer to a Child's Question.
Apologia pro Vita Sua.
Ballad of the Dark Ladié, The.
Birds, The.
Boy in the Wilderness. *Fr.* The Wanderings of Cain.
Catullian Hendecasyllables.
Charity in Thought.
Child's Evening Prayer, A.
Choral Song of Illyrian Peasants. *Fr.* Zapolya.
Christabel.
Christabel, *sels.*

COLERIDGE, SAMUEL TAYLOR (*continued*)
Christmas Carol, A: "Shepherds went their hasty way, The."
Coleridge and His Child. *Fr.* Frost at Midnight.
Cologne.
Complaint.
Dead Starling, The, *tr.*
Death of Lesbia's Bird, The, *tr.*
Dejection; an Ode.
Dejection; an Ode, *sel.*
Dell, The. *Fr.* Fears in Solitude.
Desired Swan-Song, The.
Destiny of Nations, The, *sel.*
Desultory Poem, Written on the Christmas Eve of 1794, A, *sels.*
Dungeon, The. *Fr.* Remorse.
England. *Fr.* Fears in Solitude.
Eolian Harp, The.
Epigram ("What is an Epigram? A dwarfish whole").
Epigram: "Hoarse Maevius reads his hobbling verse."
Epigram: "In Köln [*or* Köhln], a town of monks and bones."
Epigram: "Sir, I admit your general rule," *at.*
Epigram: "Sly Beelzebub took all occasions."
Epigram: "Swans sing before they die."
Epigram: "What? rise again with all one's bones."
Epitaph: "Stop, Christian passer-by!—Stop, child of God."
Epitaph on an Infant.
Epitaph on Himself.
Eternal Poem, An.
Exchange, The.
Fancy in Nubibus, or the Poet in the Cloud.
Fears in Solitude.
Fears in Solitude, *sels.*
Fool and the Poet, The, *at.*
Fragment: "Encinctur'd with a twine of leaves."
Fragments on a Theme.
France; an Ode.
France; an Ode, *sel.*
Friendship. *Fr.* Christabel.
Frost at Midnight.
Frost at Midnight, *sels.*
Fruit Plucker, The. *Fr.* The Wanderings of Cain.
Garden of Boccaccio, The.
Genevieve.
Giles' Hope.
Glycine's Song. *Fr.* Zapolya.
Good, Great Man, The.
He Prayeth Best [*or* Well]. *Fr.* The Rime of the Ancient Mariner.
Hear, sweet spirit. *Fr.* Remorse.
House That Jack Built, The.
Human Life; on the Denial of Immortality.
Hunting Song. *Fr.* Zapolya.
Hymn before Sunrise, in the Vale of Chamouni.
I Asked My Fair, One Happy Day, *tr.*
If I Had but Two Little Wings.
In a Moonlight Wilderness.
In Springtime. *Fr.* Work without Hope.
Inscription for a Fountain on a Heath.
Invocation, An: "Hear, sweet spirit." *Fr.* Remorse.
Job.
Knight's Tomb, The.
Koskiusko.
Kubla Khan; or, A Vision in a Dream.
La Fayette.
Lessons for a Boy.
Lewti.
Life.
Life of Nature, The. *Fr.* Dejection; an Ode.
Limbo, *sel.*
Lines on an Autumnal Evening.
Lines Written in the Album at Elbingerode.
Little Child, a Limber Elf, A. *Fr.* Christabel.
Love.
Love, *sel.*
Lovely in Decay. *Fr.* Remorse.
Love's Apparition and Evanishment.
Metrical Feet.
Monody on the Death of Chatterton.
Names, *tr.*
Ne Plus Ultra.
Nightingale, The.
Nightingale, The, *sel.*
Nightingales. *Fr.* The Nightingale.
O, Lift One Thought.
Ode to the Departing Year.
Ode to Tranquillity.
On a Bad Singer.
On a Discovery Made Too Late.
On a Lord.
On Donne's Poetry.
On His Baptismal Birthday.
On My Joyful Departure from the City of Cologne.
On My Joyful Departure from the Same [City].
Opium Jottings.
Pains of Sleep, The.
Pantisocracy.
Phantom.
Phantom or Fact.
Piccolomini, The, *sels.*, *tr.*
Quarrel of Friends, The. *Fr.* Christabel.
Raven and the Oak, The.
Rebellion. *Fr.* France; an Ode.
Recollections of Love.
Reflections on Having Left a Place of Retirement.
Religious Musings, *sels.*
Remorse (Osorio), *sels.*
Rhymester, A.
Rime of the Ancient Mariner, The.
Rime of the Ancient Mariner, The, *sels.*
Romance. *Fr.* Kubla Khan.
Self-Knowledge.
Shepherds, The.
Snow-Drop, The.
Soldier's Return, The.
Something Childish, but Very Natural.
Song: "Hear, sweet spirit, hear the spell." *Fr.* Remorse.
Song: "Sunny shaft did I behold, A."
Song: "Though veiled in spires of myrtle-wreath."
Song, ex Improviso.
Songs of the Pixies.
Sonnet: Oft o'er My Brain.
Sonnet: To the River Otter.
Sonnet to a Friend Who Asked How I Felt When the Nurse First Presented My Infant to Me.
Swan Song.
Thekla's Song, *tr.* *Fr.* The Piccolomini.
This Lime-Tree Bower My Prison.
Three Graves, The, *sel.*
Time, Real and Imaginary.
To a Young Ass.
To a Young Friend, *sel.*
To Lesbia, *tr.*
To Nature.
To the Author of "The Robbers."
To the Reverend W. L. Bowles.
To William Wordsworth.
Tombless Epitaph, A, *sel.*
Trochee trips from long to short.
Up, Up! Ye Dames and Lasses Gay. *Fr.* Zapolya.
Virgin's Cradle-Hymn, The, *tr.*
Voice Sings, A. *Fr.* Remorse.
Wanderings of Cain, The, *sel.*
Westphalian Song, *tr.*
What Is an Epigram?
What Is Life?
What the Birds Say.
Work without Hope.
Work without Hope, *sel.*
Youth and Age.
Zapolya, *sels.*
COLERIDGE, SAMUEL TAYLOR, *and* ROBERT SOUTHEY. *See* SOUTHEY, ROBERT, *and* SAMUEL TAYLOR COLERIDGE.
COLERIDGE, SARA. Calendar, A.
Child, The.
Garden Year, The.
He Came Unlook'd For. *Fr.* Phantasmion.
I Thought by Tears.
I Tremble When with Looks Benign.
I Was a Brook. *Fr.* Phantasmion.
Months, The.
Mother, The.
O Sleep, My Babe. *Fr.* Phantasmion.
One Face Alone. *Fr.* Phantasmion.
Phantasmion, *sels.*
Song: "He came unlook'd for, undesir'd." *Fr.* Phantasmion.
Trees.
COLES, ABRAHAM. Dies Irae, *tr.*
Microcosm, The, *sel.*
Physician's Character and Aims; Science Progressive. *Fr.* The Microcosm.
Stabat Mater Dolorosa, *tr.*
COLESWORTHY, DANIEL CLEMENT. Don't Kill the Birds.
COLIN, MUSET. Complaint of the Minstrel's Life.
COLL, J. A. Morning Lullaby, A.
COLLESTER, CLINTON H. Morning Sprite, The.
Song of the Trip-Hammer.
COLLIER, EDWARD A. After the Rain.
COLLIER, THOMAS STEPHENS. Cleopatra Dying.
Compensation.
Disappointment.
Infallibility.
One Land, One Flag, One Brotherhood.
Power.
Spectre Ship, The.
These Are Not Lost, *at.*
Time.
COLLIN, SEPLEY. Schooner *Kandahar*, The, *at.*
COLLIN, WILLIAM EDWIN. Monserrat.
Samcho.
COLLINS, ANNE. Winter Being Over, The.
COLLINS, BETSEY MANN. Garden Visitor.
Prayer for Prince, A.
COLLINS, HELEN JOHNSON. To an Avenue Sport.
COLLINS, HENRY. Jesus, my Lord, my God, my all.
COLLINS, JOHN. To-Morrow.
COLLINS, LESLIE MORGAN. Creole Girl.
COLLINS, MORTIMER. Ad Chloen, M.A.
Chloe, M.A.
Comfort.
Darwin.
First of April, The.
Greek Idyl, A.
If.
Ivory Gate. The.
Kate Temple's Song.
Martial in London.
My Aunt's Spectre.
My Thrush.
Positivists, The.
Queen and Slave.
Salad.
Salad—after Tennyson.
Sky-making.
To F. C.
COLLINS, W. F. Lincoln Statue, The.
COLLINS, WILLIAM. Molly Maguire at Monmouth.
COLLINS, WILLIAM (1721–59). Dirge: "How sleep the brave, who sink to rest."
Dirge: "To fair Fidele's grassy tomb."
Dirge for Fidele.
Dirge in "Cymbeline."
Fidele's Dirge.
Hassan; or, The Camel Driver. *Fr.* Persian Eclogues.
How Sleep the Brave.
If aught of oaten stop, or pastoral song.
Lookout, The.
Ode: "How sleep the brave."
Ode on the Death of Mr. Thomson.
Ode on the Passions. *Fr.* The Passions.
Ode on the Poetical Character.
Ode on the Popular Superstitions of the Highlands of Scotland, An.
Ode on the Popular Superstitions of the Highlands of Scotland, An, *sels.*
Ode to Evening.
Ode to Fear.
Ode to Pity.

Ode to Simplicity.
Ode Written in 1746.
Ode Written in the Beginning of the Year 1746.
Passions, The; an Ode for [*or* to] Music.
Persian Eclogues, *sels.*
St. Kilda. *Fr.* Ode on the Popular Superstitions of the Highlands.
Sleep of the Brave, The.
Song from Shakespeare's "Cymbeline," A: "To fair Fidele's grassy tomb."
Sonnet: "When Phoebe form'd a wanton smile."
To Evening.
COLLOP, JOHN. Leper Cleansed, The.
Man a Microcosm.
To the Soul.
COLLUTHUS. Rape of Helen, *sel.*
COLLYER, ROBERT. Saxon Grit.
Under the Snow.
COLLYMORE, FRANK A. In Memoriam.
COLMAN, SAINT. Hymn against Pestilence, *sel., at.*
COLMAN, GEORGE, THE YOUNGER. Gluggity Glug. *Fr.* The Myrtle and the Vine.
Myrtle and the Vine, The, *sel.*
Sir Marmaduke.
Toby Tosspot.
Unfortunate Miss Bailey.
COLMAN, SISTER MARY. Prayer for a Silver Jubilee.
COLMAN, MARY ELIZABETH. Answer.
Cost, The.
We Men Are of Two Worlds.
COLOMBO, THEODORE. He Is Shy.
COLONNA, VITTORIA. Sonnet: "I write to soothe that inward grief alone."
Sonnet: "Like some small hungry bird that sees and hears."
COLONNE, GUIDO DELLE. *See* GUIDO DELLE COLONNE.
COLONY, HORATIO. Ghost Pet.
COLTON, ARTHUR WILLIS. Allah's Tent.
Concerning Tabitha's Dancing of the Minuet.
Harps Hung Up in Babylon.
Let Me No More a Mendicant.
Phillis and Corydon.
Sometime It May Be.
Song with a Discord, A.
To Faustine.
COLTON, BUEL P. Keep Thou My Heart.
COLTON, JAMES BYERS, 2D. Hymn to Truth.
COLUM, MARY M. Dirge of the Lone Woman.
COLUM, PADRAIC. Across the Door.
After Speaking of One Dead a Long Time.
At Ferns Castle.
Autumn Song, *tr.*
Ballad of Downal Baun, The.
Beggar's Child, The.
Belfast; High Street.
Burial of Saint Brendan, The.
Catalpa Tree.
Christ the Comrade.
Connachtman, A.
Cradle Song, A: "O men from the fields!"
Dahlias.
David ap Gwillam's Mass of the Birds.
Deer of Ireland, The.
Drover, A.
Dublin; the Old Squares.
Fair Hills of Eire, The.
Fourth Station.
Furrow and the Hearth, The.
Garadh.
Garland Sunday.
Her skin is so white as a lily, an' each.
I saw the wind to-day.
Idyll, An: "You stay for a while beside me."
Interior.
Islands of the Ever Living, The, *tr.*
Landing, The.
Lilies.
Men on Islands.
Mimosa.
Monkeys.
No Child.
Old Man Said, An.
Old Soldier.
Old Woman of the Roads, An.
Olive Trees.
On Not Hearing the Birds Sing in Ireland.
On the Death of Roger Casement.
Plougher [*or* Plower], The.
Polonius and the Ballad-Singer.
Poor Girl's Meditation, The, *tr.*
Poor Scholar of the Forties, A.
Poplar Tree.
River-Mates.
Sea Bird to the Wave, The.
Shall I Go Bound and You Go Free?
She Moved through the Fair.
Stag, The.
Stations of the Cross, The.
Terrible Robber Men, The.
Tin-Whistle Player, The.
Tulips.
What the Shuiler Said as She Lay by the Fire in the Farmer's House.
Wild Ass.
COLUMBA, SAINT. *See* COLUMCILLE, SAINT.
COLUMBA, MOTHER M. From My Window.
COLUMBAN [*or* COLUMBANUS], SAINT. Boating Song, *at.*
COLUMCILLE [*or* COLUMBA] SAINT. Columcille the Scribe, *at.*
Columcille's Greeting to Ireland, *at.*
Day of Wrath, The.
Farewell to Ireland, *at.*
On a Dead Scholar, *sel.*
On His Exile to Iona.
Praise of Derry, The.
St. Columcille the Scribe, *at.*
COLVIN, IAN G. Flanders Poppies.
Maria Bright, *tr.*
COLWELL, ERNEST CADMAN. Jesus of Nazareth.
COMBE, WILLIAM. Dr. Syntax in Search of the Picturesque, *sel.*
In Search of the Picturesque. *Fr.* Dr. Syntax in Search of the Picturesque.
COMBES, PERCIVAL. Bar-Z on a Sunday Night.
COMBS, ALONZO W. Ol' Man, De.
COMETAS. Country Gods.
COMFORT, ALEX. Atoll in the Mind, The.
Bullocks, The.
Epitaph: "One whom I knew, a student and a poet."
Fear of the Earth.
Fifth Elegy.
Hoc Est Corpus.
Lovers, The.
Notes for My Son. *Fr.* The Song of Lazarus.
Pick upon Pick.
Poem: "One whom I knew, a student and a poet."
Postures of Love, The.
Postures of Love, The, *sel.*
Song for the Heroes.
Song of Lazarus, The, *sel.*
Waiting for the Wind.
COMFORT, FLORENCE CROCKER. Make Way!
COMMERFORD, CHARLES. Meadow Lark Sang, A.
Visit with a Woodpecker, A.
COMSTOCK, MARY EDGAR. Gifts.
COMSTOCK, SARAH. Indian Lullaby.
COMYN, MICHAEL. Oisin in the Land of Youth.
CONANT, ISABEL [*or* ISABELLA] FISKE. Angler.
Answer.
Blue Persian.
Border.
Carpenter.
Casements.
Emergency.
Kind Sleep.
Many Wings.
Woman.
CONDER, ALAN. *For translations from French, see* LO; LyMA; OnPM; TrFP.
CONDER, JOSIAH. Trust in Jesus.
"CONDOL, F. KEVIN." *See* MIRIAM, SISTER.
CONE, HELEN GRAY ("Coroebus Green").
Arraignment.
Ballad of Cassandra Brown, The.
Chant of Love for England, A.
Common Street, The.
Contrast, The.
Dandelions.
Fair England.
Heartbreak Road.
Last Cup of Canary, The.
Lullaby, A: "Now while rest the happy herds."
Ride to the Lady, The.
Spark, The.
Spring Beauties, The.
Tender Heart, The.
Thisbe.
To-Day.
Yellow Pansy, A.
CONGER, KATHARINE JANEWAY. This Is America.
CONGER, MARION. Fall Days.
CONGREVE, WILLIAM. Aisle of a Temple, The. *Fr.* The Mourning Bride.
Among the Dead. *Fr.* The Mourning Bride.
Amoret.
Ancient Phyllis. *Fr.* The Double-Dealer.
Buxom Joan.
Death of a Queen, The. *Fr.* The Mourning Muse of Alexis.
Double-Dealer, The, *sel.*
False Though She Be.
Homeric Hymns, *sels., tr.*
Hue and Cry after Fair Amoret, A.
Lesbia.
Letter to Viscount Cobham.
Love for Love, *sels.*
Love's but the Frailty of the Mind. *Fr.* The Way of the World.
Metamorphoses, *sel., tr.*
Mourning Bride, The, *sels.*
Mourning Muse of Alexis, The, *sel.*
Music. *Fr.* The Mourning Bride.
Nil Admirari. *Fr.* Of Improving the Present Time.
Nymph and a Swain, A. *Fr.* Love for Love.
Of Improving the Present Time, *sel.*
Old Bachelor, The, *sel.*
Orpheus and Eurydice, *tr. Fr.* Metamorphoses.
Pious Selinda [*or* Celinda].
Silly Fair.
Soldier and a Sailor, A. *Fr.* Love for Love.
Song: "Ah stay! ah turn! ah whither would you fly." *Fr.* The Fair Penitent (*by* Nicholas Rowe).
Song: "False though she be to me and love."
Song: "Love's but the frailty of the mind." *Fr.* The Way of the World.
Song: "Pious Selinda goes to prayers."
Song: "See, see, she wakes! Sabina wakes!"
Song: Soldier and a Sailor, A. *Fr.* Love for Love.
Song: "Tell me no more I am deceived."
Song; Set by Mr. John Eccles. *Fr.* Love for Love.
Temple, The. *Fr.* The Mourning Bride.
To Cynthia.
To Cynthia Weeping and Not Speaking.
Way of the World, The, *sel.*
Where'er You Walk.
CONKLING, GRACE HAZARD. After Sunset.
Beethoven Andante, A.
Child's Song Overheard, A.
Different Day, The.
Elegy for the Irish Poet, Francis Ledwidge.
Francis Ledwidge.
Goatherd, The.
Guadalupe.
I Have Cared for You, Moon.
I Will Not Give Thee All My Heart.

CONKLING, GRACE HAZARD (*continued*)
Letter to Elsa, A.
Little Rose Is Dust, My Dear, The.
Maine Woods in Winter.
Mexican Lullaby, A.
Modern Sonnet.
Nightingales.
Nightingales of Flanders, The.
Old Nürnberg.
Pablo.
Proposed Barter.
Python.
Recuerdo.
Refugees.
Rheims Cathedral.
Road to the Pool, The.
Snail, The.
Star, The.
Tampico.
This Is Not Loneliness.
To a New-born Baby Girl.
To the Schooner *Casco*.
Tree of Starlings, The.
Victory Bells.
Whole Duty of Berkshire Brooks, The.
Wind's Way, The.
You Make Me Think of Loops of Water Lying.
CONKLING, HILDA. About Animals.
Bluebird.
Books.
Butterfly ("As I walked through my garden").
Butterfly ("Butterfly,/ I like the way you wear your wings").
Cellar, The.
Chickadee, The.
Daisies.
Dandelion.
Easter.
Fairies.
For You, Mother.
Hills.
I Am.
I Keep Wondering.
Joy.
Lilacs.
Little Papoose.
Little Snail.
Loveliness.
Moon Song.
Moonbeam.
Morning.
Mouse.
Music.
My Mind and I.
Old Bridge, The.
Pigeons Just Awake.
Poems.
Poplars.
Red Rooster, The.
Snow-flake Song.
Spring Song.
Thunder Shower.
Time.
Tired.
Tree-Toad.
Water.
Weather.
When Moonlight Falls.
"CONNELL, F. NORREYS." *See* O'RIORDAN, CONAL.
CONNELL, HUGH. Dream, A.
Erris Coast, 1943.
Mountain Tree, The.
CONNELL, JIM. New Words to the Tune of "O'Donnel Abu."
"CONNELL, NORREYS." *See* O'RIORDAN, CONAL.
CONNOLLY, FRANCIS X. For Having Thee.
No More Destructive Flame.
CONNOLLY, MYLES E. Lament for a Poor Poet.
Quo Vadis?
CONOLLY, LUKE AYLMER. Enchanted Island, The.
CONON DE BÉTHUNE. Too Late, My Love.
CONQUEST, ROBERT. Abolitionist, The.
Epistemology of Poetry.
Girl in the Snow, A.
Guided Missiles Experimental Range.
Humanities.
Level of Abstraction, A.
CONRAD, MAY RICKER. What Does Easter Mean to You?
CONRAD, SHERMAN. Circe Remembers.
Note for Navigators.
CONSTABLE, HENRY. Damelus' Song to [*or* of] His Diaphenia, *at.*
Dear to my soul, then leave me not forsaken! *Fr.* Diana.
Diana, *sels.*
Diaphenia, *at.*
Diaphenia, like the daffadowndilly, *at.*
Fair grace of graces, muse of muses all. *Fr.* Diana.
Fair sun, if you would have me praise your light. *Fr.* Diana.
Grace full of grace, though in these verses here. *Fr.* Diana.
Hope, like the hyena, coming to be old. *Fr.* Diana.
If ever sorrow spoke from soul that loves. *Fr.* Diana.
If This Be Love. *Fr.* Diana.
Love's Franciscan.
Mine eye with all the deadly sins is fraught. *Fr.* Diana.
Miracle of the world, I never will deny. *Fr.* Diana.
My lady's presence makes the roses red. *Fr.* Diana.
My tears are true, though others be divine. *Fr.* Diana.
Needs must I leave and yet needs must I love. *Fr.* Diana.
Not that thy hand is soft, is sweet, is white. *Fr.* Diana.
O Gracious Shepherd.
Of the Nativity of the Lady Rich's Daughter.
On Sir Philip Sidney.
On the Death of Sir Philip Sidney.
Ready to seek out death in my disgrace. *Fr.* Diana.
Shepherd's Song of Venus and Adonis, The.
Sonnet: "Dear to my soul! then leave me not forsaken!" *Fr.* Diana.
Sonnet: "If ever Sorrow spoke from soul that loves." *Fr.* Diana.
Sonnet: "My lady's presence makes the roses red." *Fr.* Diana.
Sonnet: "To live in hell, and heaven to behold." *Fr.* Diana.
Sun, his journey ending in the west, The. *Fr.* Diana.
To God the Father.
To God the Son.
To His Mistress.
To live in hell, and heaven to behold. *Fr.* Diana.
To Our Blessed Lady.
To Our Lady.
To Saint Catherine.
To Saint Margaret.
To Saint Mary Magdalen.
To St. Peter and St. Paul.
To Sir Philip Sidney's Soul.
To the Blessed Sacrament.
Uncivil sickness, hast thou no regard. *Fr.* Diana.
When your perfections to my thoughts appear. *Fr.* Diana.
Whilst Echo cries, "What shall become of me?" *Fr.* Diana.
You secret vales, you solitary fields. *Fr.* Diana.
CONSTABLE, THOMAS. Old October.
CONSTANTINE OF RHODES. Before the Ikon of the Mother of God.
CONTARDO, LUIS FELIPE. Calling, The.
CONTRACTUS, HERMANUS. Alma Redemptoris Mater, *at.*
Salve Regina, *at.*
CONVERSE, FLORENCE. Descend, O Dante.
Friendship.
Liberté, Egalité, Fraternité.
Rune of Riches, A.
They Have Blown the Trumpet.
To Vida D. Scudder.
CONWAY, KATHERINE ELEANOR. Annunciation Night.
Christ and the Mourners.
Heaviest Cross of All, The.
Saturninus.
Vanquished.
CONWAY, MARGARET DEVEREAUX. Annunciation, The.
COOGLER, J. GORDON. Poor South! Her books get fewer and fewer.
COOK, ——. So nigh is grandeur to man.
COOK, ALBERT JAY. There's About Two Million Fellows.
COOK, CLARENCE CHATHAM. On One Who Died in May.
COOK, CLEMENT. Saint Francis to the Birds.
COOK, ELIZA. A B C.
Christmas Holly, The.
Death of Master Tommy Rook, The.
Forest Trees, The.
George Washington ("Only a baby, fair and small").
Good By.
Hang Up His Harp; He'll Wake No More!
I Miss Thee, My Mother.
Indian Hunter, The.
King Bruce and the Spider.
Mouse and the Cake, The.
No!
Old Arm-Chair, The.
Old Arm-Chair, The, *sel.*
Quiet Eye, The.
Rook Sits High, The.
Sailor's Grave, The.
Sea-Child, The.
Song of the Seaweed, *sel.*
Star in the West, The.
They All Belong to Me.
Try Again.
Washington ("Land of the West!").
Washington ("Only a baby, fair and small").
Where There's a Will There's a Way.
COOK, HAROLD LEWIS. Coward.
Fugue.
Man.
Stag, The.
Starlight.
Warning.
Weaving, The.
COOK, JOSEPH. Boston Nursery Rhymes.
COOK, MARC EUGENE. *See* "BROWN, VANDYKE."
COOK, MILDRED ANNE. She Will Go Softly.
COOK, THEODORE P. Ode for Decoration Day.
COOK, WARREN F. Revelation.
COOKE, DONALD E. My Penguin Playmate.
New Year, The.
COOKE, EDMUND VANCE. Abraham.
Born without a Chance.
David.
Fin de Siècle.
How Did You Die?
Moo-Cow-Moo, The.
Off Manilly.
Rags.
Sin of the Coppenter Man.
Three Crosses, The.
Uncivilized.
Young Man Waited, The.
COOKE, JOHN ESTEN. Band in the Pines, The.
Broken Mug, The.
COOKE, PHILIP PENDLETON. Florence Vane.
Life in the Autumn Woods.
Power of the Bards, The, *sel.*
COOKE, ROSE TERRY. Abraham Lincoln.
Arachne.
Awakening.
Bluebeard's Closet.
Christmas.
Death of Goody Nurse, The.
Done For.
In Vain.
Lise.
Our Dead Heroes.
Rêve du Midi.
Segovia and Madrid.
Snow-filled Nest, The.
Then.
Two Villages, The.

Coolbrith, Ina Donna. Fruitionless.
Helen Hunt Jackson.
Mariposa Lily, The.
Memory, A.
Poet, The.
When the Grass Shall Cover Me.
With the Caravan.
Cooley, Julia. *See* Altrocchi, Julia Cooley.
Coolidge, Grace (Mrs. Calvin Coolidge). Open Door, The.
"Coolidge, Susan" (Sarah Chauncey Woolsey). Begin Again.
Better Way, The.
Calvary and Easter.
Child's Thought of Harvest, A.
Christ Has Risen.
Commonplace.
Commonplace, *sel.*
Easter Lilies.
Easter Song, An.
Forward.
God's Plan. *Fr.* Commonplace.
Gulf Stream.
He Cares.
Helen.
Hodge, the Cat.
How Does the Soul Grow?
How the Leaves Came Down.
In the Mist.
Little Christmas Tree, The.
Lost Days, The.
Mrs. June's Prospectus.
Old Stone Basin, The.
Patriotism.
Stone of the Sepulcher, The.
Time to Go.
When.
Coonley, Lydia Avery. *See* Ward, Lydia Avery Coonley.
Cooper, Alice Cecilia. San Juan Capistrano.
Cooper, Belle. Street Melody, A.
Vintage, The.
Cooper, Billy B. Salary.
Cooper, Courtney Ryley. My Old Dawg.
Cooper, Edith, *and* Katherine Bradley. *See* "Field, Michael."
Cooper, George. Babyland.
Bob White.
Christmas Bells.
Come, Little Leaves.
Frogs at School.
Merry Christmas and a Glad New Year, A.
Mother.
New Year, The.
October's Party.
Only One.
Only One Mother.
Sand-Man, The.
Summer Day, A.
Sweet Genevieve.
Swing, Cradle, Swing.
Twenty Froggies.
What Robin Told.
While the Days Are Going By.
Why Did They Dig Ma's Grave So Deep?
Wind and the Leaves, The.
Wonderful Weaver, The.
Cooper, James Fenimore (1789–1851). My Brigantine. *Fr.* The Water Witch.
Water Witch, The, *sel.*
Cooper, James Fenimore (1892–1918). Boston Symphony Orchestra, The.
Fate.
Cooper, Robert. In Youth, in Age.
Cooper, Thomas. Chartist Song.
Cooperman, Hasye. Mists Are Rising Now, The.
Copeland, Josephine. Zulu King, The; New Orleans.
Copland, Aaron. Lincoln Portrait.
Coplen, Grace Wilson. Fireflies.
My Swinging Shadow.
Coppard, Alfred Edgar. Apostate, The.
Betty Perrin.
Epitaph: "Like silver dew."
Forester's Song.
Glorious Survivors, The.
Mendacity.
Night Piece.
Oracle, The.
Prodigal Son, The.
Sluggard, The.
Stay, O Stay.
Unfortunate Miller, The.
Winter Field.
Coppée, François. Butterflies.
Promenades and Interiors, *sel.*
Coppinger, Matthew. To Clelia.
Corbet, Richard. Distracted Puritan, The.
Dreams.
Fairies' Farewell, The.
Fairies' Farewell, The, *sel.*
Farewell, Rewards and Fairies.
Farewell to the Fairies.
Great Tom.
Like to the Thundering Tone.
On Mr. Francis Beaumont Then Newly Dead.
Proper New Ballad, A, Intituled [*or* Entitled] The Fairies' Farewell; or, God-a-Mercy Will.
To His Son Vincent Corbet.
Corbett, Mrs. E. T. Inventor's Wife, The.
Newsboy, The.
Three Wise Couples, The.
Three Wise Women, The.
Corbière, Tristan (Edouard Joachim Corbière). After the Rain.
Blind Man's Cries.
Cabin-Kid.
Cries Out of Blindness.
End, The.
Epitaph; for Himself.
Epitaph for Tristan-Joachim-Edouard Corbière, Philosopher, Stray, Stillborn.
Evil Landscape.
His Epitaph.
Hours.
Insomnia.
Kazoo.
Landscape of Evil.
Letter from Mexico.
Paris at Night.
Rhapsody of the Deaf Man.
Rondel: "It's dark, child, snatcher of sparks!"
Sleep, Baby, Sleep.
Small Death to Laugh.
To Mount Aetna.
To My Mouse-colored Mare.
To Old Roscoff.
Toad, The.
Corbin, Alice (Alice Corbin Henderson). Apparitions.
Delphy. *Fr.* Echoes of Childhood.
Echoes of Childhood, *sels.*
Green Corn Dance, The.
Harvest, The.
Humoresque.
If War Is Right.
In the Desert.
Juan Quintana.
Love Me at Last.
Mandy's Religion. *Fr.* Echoes of Childhood.
Music.
Muy Vieja Mexicana.
Nodes.
O World.
On the Acequia Madre.
One City Only.
Pool, The.
Sand Paintings.
Song from Old Spain.
Star of Bethlehem, The.
Two Voices.
Una Anciana Mexicana.
Uncle Jim. *Fr.* Echoes of Childhood.
What Dim Arcadian Pastures.
Corbin, Richard K. Lines after Visiting a Cemetery.
Corder, W. Murder of Maria Marten, The.
Córdova y Bocanegra, Fernando de. Song to the Most Holy Name of Jesus.
Corinna. Daughters of Asopus, The.
Helicon and Cithaeron.
Pindarum Quisquis.
"Corinna." Sehnsucht; or, What You Will.
Corke, Hilary. Eden.
Corkery, Daniel. Call, The.
No Miracle.
Corkum, Alexander C. Minot's Beacon.
Cormac, King of Cashel. Instructions of King Cormac.
Cormac mac Cuilenan. Book of Leinster, *sel.*
Heavenly Pilot, The. *Fr.* Book of Leinster.
Cormac Ogmundarson. Three Songs to Steingerd.
Cormack, Barbara Villy. Reprieve.
Corneille, Pierre. Cid, The, *sel.*
Epitaph for Elizabeth Ranquet.
Stanzas: "If, Marchioness, you can descry."
Stanzas: "Lady fair, if on the page."
Stanzas to the Marquise.
Two Lovers in the Toils of Honor. *Fr.* The Cid.
Cornelius, Maxwell N. Some Time We'll Understand.
Cornell, Annette Patton. Sailor's Woman.
Cornford, Frances (Darwin). All Souls' Night. *Fr.* Two Poems.
At Night.
Autumn Morning at Cambridge.
Country Bedroom, The.
Dawn.
For M. S. Singing Frühlingsglaube in 1945.
For Nijinsky's Tomb.
Glimpse, A.
Grand Ballet.
Hills, The.
In France.
In the Backs.
Lincolnshire Remembered.
Little Dog, The.
London Despair.
Near an Old Prison.
New-born Baby's Song, The.
No Immortality.
Old Nurse, The.
Old Witch in the Copse, The.
On August Thirteenth, at the Mount, Marsden, Bucks.
On Maou Dying at the Age of Six Months.
Pre-Existence.
Princess and the Gypsies, The.
Quatrain: "Young Apollo, golden-haired, A."
She Warns Him. *Fr.* Two Poems.
Spring Morning.
Summer Beach.
Susan to Diana.
To a Fat Lady Seen from the Train.
Transmigration, *tr.*
Two Poems.
Unbeseechable, The.
Village before Sunset.
Wasted Day, A.
Watch, The.
Woman with the Baby to the Philosopher, The.
Cornford, Frances, *and* Esther Polianowsky Salaman. Crucifix, The, *tr.*
Hawk, The, *tr.*
Hay Harvest, The, *tr.*
Hymn, A: "Lord, give them freedom who are weak," *tr.*
I Come Again, *tr.*
I Planted My Bright Paradise, *tr.*
My Country, *tr.*
Upas Tree, The, *tr.*
White Bird, The, *tr.*
Wolf in the Kennels, The, *tr.*
Cornford, Frances, *and* Stephen Spender. *See* Spender, Stephen, *and* Frances Cornford.
Cornford, John. Huesca.
Poem: "Heart of the heartless world."
To Margot Heinemann.
Corning, Howard McKinley. Autumn Bird.
Farewell to Fields.
Green Councillors.
Judas.
Last Hound, The.

CORNING, HOWARD MCKINLEY (*cont.*)
Meadow Brook Runs Over, The.
Mountain in the Sky, The.
Pruning Vines.
Question.
Rainbow Lands.
Sagebrusher's Wife.
Song to Say a Farewell.
These People.
CORNISH, BUD. Extra at the House, The.
CORNISH, WILLIAM. Ah, Robin.
Ah! the Sighs.
Desire.
God's Blessings.
Gratitude.
Knight knock'd at the castle gate, The.
Latet Anguis, *at.*
Pleasure It Is.
Rutterkin.
Spring.
"CORNWALL, BARRY" (Bryan Waller Procter). Address to the Ocean.
Blood Horse, The.
Fate of the Oak, The.
Fisherman, The.
For a Fountain.
Golden Girl, A.
Golden-tressed Adelaide.
Hermione.
History of a Life.
Horned Owl, The.
Hunter's Song, The.
Inscription for a Fountain.
Is My Lover on the Sea?
Leveller, The.
Life.
Owl, The.
Peace! What Do Tears Avail.
Petition to Time, A.
Poet's Song to His Wife, The.
Poet's Thought, A.
Sea, The.
Sea, The—in Calm.
Sit Down, Sad Soul.
Softly Woo Away Her Breath.
Song for the Seasons, A.
Song of the Sea, A.
Song of Wood-Nymphs.
Stars, The.
Stormy Petrel, The.
Vision, A, *sel.*
White Squall, The.
CORNWALL, URSULA. Sowing Seeds.
CORNWALLIS, KINAHAN. Battle of Murfreesboro.
CORNWELL, HENRY SYLVESTER. Jefferson D.
May.
Sunset City, The.
CORRIDAN, FRANCES O'CONNELL. First Born.
Strong Arms.
CORRIGAN, WINIFRED. I Turn the Key.
CORROTHERS, JAMES DAVID. At the Closed Gate of Justice.
Black Cat Crossed His Luck, De.
Dream and the Song.
In the Matter of Two Men.
Indignation Dinner, An.
Negro Singer, The.
Paul Laurence Dunbar.
Road to the Bow, The.
CORSELLIS, TIMOTHY. Engine Failure.
Repression.
They Have Taken It from Me.
Thrush, The.
To Stephen Spender.
CORSO, GREGORY. Birthplace Revisited.
But I Do Not Need Kindness.
Dialogue—2 Dollmakers.
Dreamed Realization, A.
From Another Room.
Marriage.
Notes after Blacking Out.
Paranoia in Crete.
Poets Hitchhiking on the Highway.
Uccello.
Zizi's Lament.
CORTISSOZ, ELLEN MACKAY HUTCHINSON. April Fantasie.
Bride's Toilette, The.
Cry from the Shore, A.
Harvest.
Her Picture.
On Kingston Bridge.
Pamela in Town.
Praise-God Barebones.
Quaker Ladies.
Quest, The.
Sea-Way.
So Wags the World.
CORWIN, NORMAN. Man unto His Fellow Man. *Fr.* On a Note of Triumph.
On a Note of Triumph, *sel.*
CORY, DAVID. Miss You.
CORY, WILLIAM JOHNSON. After Reading "Ajax."
Amaturus.
Anteros.
Ballad for a Boy, A.
Dirge, A: "Naiad, hid beneath the bank."
Heraclitus, *after* Callimachus.
Invocation, An: "I never prayed for dryads, to haunt the woods again."
Mimnermus in Church.
Oh, Earlier Shall the Rosebuds Blow.
Parting.
Poor French Sailor's Scottish Sweetheart, A.
Remember.
School Fencibles.
They told me, Heraclitus, they told me you were dead, *after* Callimachus.
To Heracleitus, *after* Callimachus.
Two Captains, The.
COSMAS, SAINT. Menaion, *sel.*
Nativity Ode.
Purification, The. *Fr.* Menaion.
COSTANIANTZ, HOVHANNES. No Bird Can Reach the Mountain's Crest.
COSTANZO, ANGELO DI. Sonnet: Death of Virgil, The.
COTA DE MAGUAQUE, RODRIGO. Love ("Clouded vision, light obscure").
Such Is Love.
COTTER, JAMES F. Autumn Is a Season.
COTTER, JOSEPH SEAMON, SR. Tragedy of Pete, The.
Way-Side Well, The.
COTTER, JOSEPH SEAMON, JR. And What Shall You Say?
April Day, An.
Band of Gideon, The.
Deserter, The.
Is It because I Am Black?
Prayer, A: "As I lie in bed."
Rain Music.
Supplication.
COTTER, MÁIRE. Portrait.
COTTERELL, GEORGE. Autumn Flitting, An.
In the Twilight.
COTTERELL, MABEL. *For translations from German, see* AnGP.
COTTON, CHARLES. Alice. *Fr.* Resolution in Four Sonnets.
Amongst the mourners that attend his hearse.
Angler's Ballad, The.
Bee, the Ant, and the Sparrow, The.
Cave, A; Pool's Hole, Derbyshire. *Fr.* The Wonders of the Peake.
Celia, my fairest Celia, fell.
Concerning Four Rural Sisters.
Contentation; Directed to My Dear Father, and Most Worthy Friend Mr. Izaak Walton.
Day's grown old; the fainting sun, The.
Evening.
Evening Quatrains.
Joys of Marriage, The.
Laura Sleeping.
Les Amours.
Margaret. *Fr.* Resolution in Four Sonnets.
Montross.
New Year, The.
Noon Quatrains.
Ode: "Day is set did earth adorn, The."
Ode: "Good night, my Love."
Ode: "Without the evening dew and showers."
Ode of Johannes Secundus, An, *tr.*
Old Tityrus to Eugenia, *sel.*
Resolution in Four Sonnets, of a Poetical Question Put to Me by a Friend, Concerning Four Rural Sisters.
Retirement, The.
Retreat, The.
Rondeau: "Thou fool! if madness be so rife."
Song: "Join once again, my Celia, join."
Song: "See, how like twilight slumber falls."
Song; Set by Mr. Coleman.
Sonnet: "Chloris, whilst thou and I were free."
Summer Evening.
Tempest, The.
To Calista.
To Celia.
To Chloris.
To Mr. Izaak Walton, *sel.*
To My Dear [*or* Old] and Most Worthy Friend, Mr. Isaac [*or* Izaak] Walton.
Tomorrow.
Two Rural Sisters.
Tydes-Well, the Third Wonder of the Peak. *Fr.* The Wonders of the Peake.
Virelay: "Thou cruel fair, I go."
Winter.
Winter, *sel.*
Winter Glass, The.
Winter's Troops. *Fr.* Winter.
Wonders of the Peake, The, *sels.*
COTTON, HENRY. Fly, fly! The foe advances fast.
COTTON, NATHANIEL. Fireside, The.
Health, *sel.*
COULBY, MARGARET. Sudden Spring.
COULETTE, HENRI. Antony and Cleopatra, *tr.*
Intaglio.
COULTER, JOHN. Morning Bus.
COUNSELMAN, MARY ELIZABETH. Echidna.
Nostalgia.
COURTHOPE, WILLIAM JOHN. Birdcatcher's Song. *Fr.* The Paradise of Birds.
Dodoism. *Fr.* The Paradise of Birds.
In Praise of Gilbert White. *Fr.* The Paradise of Birds.
Ode: To the Roc. *Fr.* The Paradise of Birds.
Paradise of Birds, The, *sels.*
Trail of the Bird, The.
COURTNEY, MARGARET. Be Kind.
COUSENS, MILDRED. American Vineyard.
COUSINS, JAMES H. Behind the Plough.
Corn Crake, The.
Curse on a Closed Gate, A.
High and Low.
Omens.
Starling's Spring Rondel, A.
Wings of Love, The.
COUTTS, FRANCIS BURDETT MONEY. *See* MONEY-COUTTS, FRANCIS BURDETT.
COVERDALE, MILES. Of the Birth of Christ.
COVEY, LEONA. Easter Surprise, An.
COWARD, NOEL. Mad Dogs and Englishmen.
COWGILL, FRANK B. Final Armistice, The.
COWLEY, ABRAHAM. Acme and Septimius, *tr.*
Against Hope. *Fr.* The Mistress.
Age.
All-over Love. *Fr.* The Mistress.
Anacreontic on Drinking.
Annunciation, The. *Fr.* Davideis.
As I once in wanton play, *tr.*
Awake, Awake, My Lyre! *Fr.* Davideis.
Beauty.
But since I know thy falsehood and thy pride.
Change, The. *Fr.* The Mistress.
Cheer Up, My Mates.
Chronicle, The; a Ballad.
Clad All in White. *Fr.* The Mistress.
Creation, The. *Fr.* Davideis.

Cure, The.
Davideis, *sels.*
Destinie.
Drinking.
Ecstasy, The.
Elegie upon Anacreon.
Epicure, The ("Fill the bowl").
Epicure, The ("Underneath this myrtle shade").
Epitaph: "Underneath this marble stone."
Essay on Solitude, *sel.* *Fr.* Of Solitude.
Friendship in Absence, *sel.*
Garden, The, *sel.*
Grasshopper, The, *tr.*
Great Diocletian. *Fr.* The Garden.
Happy insect! what can be, *tr.*
Hell. *Fr.* Davideis.
Hymn to Light.
In Praise of Hope.
Inconstancy.
Invocation: "Awake, awake, my Lyre!" *Fr.* Davideis.
Liberty. *Fr.* Ode upon Liberty.
Life and Fame.
Love.
Love and Life. *Fr.* The Mistress.
Love's Absence in the Spring.
Love's Riddle, *sel.*
Mistress, The, *sels.*
Muse, The.
Music. *Fr.* Davideis.
My Diet. *Fr.* The Mistress.
Ode: Of Wit.
Ode to His Mistress.
Ode to the Royal Society, The, *sel.*
Ode upon Doctor Harvey.
Ode upon Liberty, *sel.*
Of Drinking.
Of Liberty; an Essay, *sel.*
Of Myself. *Fr.* A Vote.
Of Solitude.
Of Solitude, *sel.*
Of Wit.
Old Man of Verona, The, *tr.*
On Drinking.
On the Death of Mr. Crashaw.
On the Death of Mr. William Hervey.
On the Death of Mr. William Hervey, *sel.*
Platonic[k] Love. *Fr.* The Mistress.
Portrait of a Freeman. *Fr.* Of Liberty; an Essay.
Power of Numbers, The. *Fr.* Davideis.
Praise of Pindar, The.
Prayer: "For the few hours of life allotted me," *tr.*
Procrastination, *tr.*
Profane.
Prophet, The.
Resolved to Be Beloved.
Resolved to Love, *sel.*
Separation, The.
Sleep, *sel.*
Song: "Merry waves dance up and down, and play, The." *Fr.* Love's Riddle.
Sport. *Fr.* Love's Riddle.
Spring, The. *Fr.* The Mistress.
Supplication, A. *Fr.* Davideis.
Swallow, The.
Thief, The. *Fr.* The Mistress.
Thirsty Earth Soaks Up the Rain, The.
Thraldome, The. *Fr.* The Mistress.
To His Mistress.
To Mr. Hobbes [*or* Hobs].
To Sir William Davenant upon His Two First Books of Gondibert.
To the Royal Society.
Today Is Ours.
To-Morrow, *tr.*
Tyrian dye why do you wear?
Underneath this myrtle shade.
Vain-Love, The, *sel.*
Vote, A, *sel.*
Welcome, The. *Fr.* The Mistress.
Wish, A ("This only grant me, that my means may lie").
Wish, The ("Well, then, I now do plainly see"). *Fr.* The Mistress.
Written in Juice of Lemmon. *Fr.* The Mistress.

COWLEY, ABRAHAM, *and* RICHARD CRASHAW. On Hope, by Way of Question and Answer, betweene A. Cowley, and R. Crashaw.

COWLEY, MALCOLM. Blue Juniata, *sels.*
Eight Melons.
Farm Died, The. *Fr.* Blue Juniata.
Flower in the Sea, The.
For St. Bartholomew's Eve.
Hill above the Mine, The.
Lady from Harlem, The.
Long Voyage, The.
Mine No. 6. *Fr.* Blue Juniata.
Stone Horse Shoals.
Towers of Song.
Urn, The. *Fr.* Blue Juniata.
When little daily winds have died away. *Fr.* Winter; Two Sonnets.
William Wilson. *Fr.* Blue Juniata.
Winter; Two Sonnets. *Fr.* Blue Juniata.
Year swings over slowly, like a pilot, The. *Fr.* Winter; Two Sonnets.

COWPER, WILLIAM. Absence of Occupation. *Fr.* Retirement.
Address to Liberty.
Addressed to a Young Lady.
Advance of the Trojans, The, *tr.* *Fr.* The Iliad.
Ajax Covers the Flight of the Greeks, *tr.* *Fr.* The Iliad.
Ajax in the Fight, *tr.* *Fr.* The Iliad.
Alexander Selkirk.
Artificial Beauty, *tr.*
Beau's Reply.
Boadicea.
Briseis, the Slave Girl; Tears for Patroclus, *tr.* *Fr.* The Iliad.
Castaway, The.
Chaffinch's Nest at Sea, The.
City and Country Life. *Fr.* The Task.
Colubriad, The.
Comparison, A. Addressed to a Young Lady.
Contentment.
Contradiction. *Fr.* Conversation.
Contrite Heart, The.
Contrite Heart, The, *sel.*
Conversation, *sels.*
Cottager and His Landlord, The, *tr.*
Cricket, The, *tr.*
Discipline in Education. *Fr.* The Task.
Dispute between Nose and Eyes.
Diverting History of John Gilpin, The.
Dog and the Water-Lily, The.
Dreams, Empty Dreams. *Fr.* The Task.
Duelling. *Fr.* Conversation.
England. *Fr.* The Task.
Epigram: "Far happier are the dead," *tr.*
Epistle to Joseph Hill, Esq., An.
Epistle to Robert Lloyd, Esq., An.
Epitaph, An: "Here lies one who never drew."
Epitaph on a Hare.
Epitaph on Dr. Johnson.
Evening. *Fr.* The Task.
Expectation of Death, *tr.*
Faithful Bird, The.
Familiarity Dangerous, *tr.*
Flowering Shrubs. *Fr.* The Task.
Forbearance.
Fragment: "Pity, Religion has so seldom found." *Fr.* Table Talk.
Freeman, The. *Fr.* The Task.
Future Peace and Glory of the Church, The.
Garden, The. *Fr.* The Task.
Ghost of Patroclus, The. *Fr.* The Iliad.
God Made the Country. *Fr.* The Task.
God Moves in a Mysterious Way.
Golden Mean, The, *tr.*
Happy Change, The.
Happy Man, The. *Fr.* The Task.
Hark, My Soul! It Is the Lord.
Hector and Andromache, *tr.* *Fr.* The Iliad.
Heedless Cruelty. *Fr.* The Task.
Helen Unreproached by Hector, *tr.* *Fr.* The Iliad.
Human Frailty.
Humanity. *Fr.* The Task.
Hymn: "God moves in a mysterious way."
Hymn: On Opening a Place for Social Prayer.
I Am Monarch of All I Survey.
I Hate Their Empty Shows, *tr.*
I Was a Stricken Deer. *Fr.* The Task.
I Will Praise the Lord at All Times.
Iliad, The, *sels., tr.*
In Him Confiding.
Inscription.
Jackdaw, The, *tr.*
Jehovah-Shammah.
John Gilpin.
John Gilpin's Ride.
Journey to Brundusium, *tr.*
Landscape. *Fr.* The Task.
Last Journey of the Wooers, The, *tr.* *Fr.* The Odyssey.
Light Shining Out of Darkness.
Lines on a Bill of Mortality, 1790.
Lines on Receiving His Mother's Picture.
Lines Written during a Period of Insanity.
Lines Written under the Influence of Delirium.
Lord Will Happiness Divine, The.
Loss of the *Royal George.*
Love of England. *Fr.* The Task.
Lovest Thou Me?
Lovest Thou Me? *sel.*
Man, the Feeblest of Earth's Creatures, *tr.* *Fr.* The Odyssey.
Menelaos; Blasphemy under Duress, *tr.* *Fr.* The Iliad.
Minstrel Worthy of His Hire, The, *tr.* *Fr.* The Odyssey.
Miser, traversing his house, A, *tr.*
Moderation, *tr.* *Fr.* Odes.
Monarch, The.
My Former Hopes Are Fled.
My Mary.
My Mother's Picture.
My name, my country—what are they to thee? *tr.*
My Soul Thirsteth for God.
Narcissus.
Nature and God. *Fr.* The Task.
Nightingale and the Glowworm, The.
No Matter, *tr.*
Nose and the Eyes, The.
Nycilla dyes her locks, 'tis said, *tr.*
Oh! for a Closer Walk with God.
O Lord, My Best Desire Fulfil.
Odes (*of* Horace), *sels., tr.*
Odysseus in Hades, *tr.* *Fr.* The Odyssey.
Odyssey, The, *sels., tr.*
Of the Shade of Achilles, *tr.* *Fr.* The Odyssey.
On a Fowler, *tr.*
On a Goldfinch, Starved to Death in His Cage.
On a Spaniel Called Beau Killing a Young Bird.
On a True Friend.
On an Old Woman, *tr.*
On the Death of Mrs. (Now Lady) Throckmorton's Bullfinch.
On the Loss of the *Royal George.*
On the Receipt of My Mother's Picture Out of Norfolk.
On the Receipt of My Mother's Picture Out of Norfolk, *sel.*
Pairing-Time Anticipated.
Penelope's Constancy Rewarded, *tr.* *Fr.* The Odyssey.
Penelope's Dream, *tr.* *Fr.* The Odyssey.
Pernicious Weed.
Persian Fopperies, *tr.* *Fr.* Odes.
Persian Luxury, *tr.* *Fr.* Odes.
Persian Pomp, *tr.* *Fr.* Odes.
Phaeacian Nights—Odysseus' Tale, *sels., tr.* *Fr.* The Odyssey.
Playthings.
Pledge of Cheerfulness, The. *Fr.* Retirement.
Poetic Pains. *Fr.* The Task.

COWPER, WILLIAM (continued)
Poetry; Satire and Pulpit. *Fr.* The Task.
Poplar Field, The.
Post-Boy, The. *Fr.* The Task.
Postman, The. *Fr.* The Task.
Praise for the Fountain Opened.
Preachers; the True vs. the Insincere. *Fr.* The Task.
Providence.
Pursuit Round the Walls, The, *tr.* *Fr.* The Iliad.
Report of an Adjudged Case; Not to Be Found in Any of the Books.
Retired Cat, The.
Retirement.
Reunion of Ulysses and Telemachus, *tr.* *Fr.* The Odyssey.
Riches, *tr.*
Riddle, A.
Robin in Winter, The. *Fr.* The Task.
Rose, The.
Royal George, The.
Rural Walk, The. *Fr.* The Task.
Sarpedon and Glaucus; the Equation of Duty and Privilege, *tr.* *Fr.* The Iliad.
Scales of Zeus, The, *tr.* *Fr.* The Iliad.
Science and Prayer. *Fr.* The Task.
Self-Portrait. *Fr.* The Task.
Shrubbery, The.
Simple Faith. *Fr.* Truth.
Since God Is There, *tr.*
Slavery. *Fr.* The Task.
Slaves Cannot Breathe in England. *Fr.* The Task.
Snail, The, *tr.*
So Ends the Wrath of Achilles, *tr.* *Fr.* The Iliad.
Sofa, The. *Fr.* The Task.
Sofa, The, *sel.* *Fr.* The Task.
Solitude of Alexander Selkirk, The.
Sometimes a light surprises.
Sonnet to George Romney.
Sonnet to Mrs. Unwin.
Sonnet to William Hayley.
Sonnet to William Wilberforce, Esq.
Spirit's Light, The.
Squirrel, The.
Statesman in Retirement. *Fr.* Retirement.
Stream, The.
Stricken Deer, The. *Fr.* The Task.
Sum of Life, The. *Fr.* The Task.
Swallow, A, *tr.*
Sweet Stream, That Winds.
Table Talk, *sels.*
Task, The, *sels.*
Telemachus Finds His Father. *Fr.* The Odyssey.
They call thee rich; I deem thee poor, *tr.*
Time-Piece, The. *Fr.* The Task.
Time-Piece, The, *sel.* *Fr.* The Task.
To a Young Lady.
To Licinius Murena, *tr.*
To Mary.
To Mary Unwin.
To Mrs. Unwin.
To the Immortal Memory of the Halibut on Which I Dined This Day, Monday, April 26, 1784.
To the Rev. Mr. Newton.
To the Same (1793).
To William Wilberforce.
Toll for the Brave.
Town and Country. *Fr.* The Task.
Treasure, *tr.*
True Preacher, The. *Fr.* The Task.
Truth, *sels.*
Valley of the Shadow of Death, The.
Vanities, *tr.*
Verses: "I am monarch of all I survey."
Verses Supposed to Be Written by Alexander Selkirk.
Vow of Vengeance, The, *tr.* *Fr.* The Iliad.
Waiting Soul, The.
Walk to Emmaus, The.
Walking with God.
Wall, The, *tr.* *Fr.* The Iliad.
Wall of the Greeks, The, *tr.* *Fr.* The Iliad.
Well-bred Man, A.
Winter. *Fr.* The Task.
Winter Evening, The. *Fr.* The Task.
Winter Morning Walk, The. *Fr.* The Task.
Winter Noon. *Fr.* The Task.
Winter Scene. *Fr.* The Task.
Winter Walk at Noon, The. *Fr.* The Task.
Winter Walk at Noon, The, *sel.* *Fr.* The Task.
Wisdom. *Fr.* The Task.
Woodman's Dog, The. *Fr.* The Task.
Yardley-Oak.

COX, C. C. I Love Thee, Gracious Lord.
COX, DONALD. Meditation.
COX, ELEANOR ROGERS. At Benediction.
Death of Cuchulain.
Dream of Ængus Og, The.
Dreaming of Cities Dead.
Gods and Heroes of the Gael.
On Broadway.
Return, The.
Three White Birds of Angus.
To a Portrait of Whistler in the Brooklyn Art Museum.
To Barbary I Have Not Sailed.
COX, ELIZABETH. Mask.
COX, EMMA FINTY. Your Cross and My Cross.
COX, KENYON. Bumblebeaver, The. *Fr.* Mixed Beasts.
Herringdove, The. *Fr.* Mixed Beasts.
Kangarooster, The. *Fr.* Mixed Beasts.
Mixed Beasts.
Mixed Beasts, *sels.*
Octopussycat, The. *Fr.* Mixed Beasts.
Rhinocerostrich, The. *Fr.* Mixed Beasts.
Work.
Work Thou for Pleasure.
COX, L. E. We Thank You!
COX, LEO. Bells of Ste. Anne des Monts, The.
Birch-Wood.
Cornfield.
Easter Thought.
Father Point in August.
Labrador Night.
COX, LILIAN EDITH. Never Night Again.
COX, PALMER. Mouse's Lullaby, The.
COXE, ARTHUR CLEVELAND. America. *Fr.* England and America.
Body of Jesus.
Easter Chorus: "Christ is arisen," *tr.* *Fr.* Faust.
England and America, *sel.*
Faust, *sel.*, *tr.*
Hallowe'en.
He Standeth at the Door.
Iona.
O Where Are Kings and Empires Now.
Present Age, The.
Song: "I know, I know."
COXE, LOUIS O. Dead Marine.
Lake, The.
Pin-up Girl.
Red Right Returning.
Veteran, The.
COYLE, HENRY. She Made Home Happy.
CRABBE, GEORGE. "Age, with Stealing Steps . . ." *Fr.* Tales of the Hall.
Alms House, The. *Fr.* The Borough.
Ancient Mansion, The. *Fr.* Posthumous Tales.
Ancient Mansion, The, *sel.* *Fr.* Posthumous Tales.
Approach of Age, The. *Fr.* Tales of the Hall.
Belvoir Castle.
Books. *Fr.* The Library.
Borough, The, *sels.*
Burials. *Fr.* The Parish Register.
Caroline, The. *Fr.* The Borough.
Cathedral-Walk, The. *Fr.* Tales of the Hall.
Crusty Critics. *Fr.* The Library.
Dean's Lady, The.
Dejected Lover, The. *Fr.* Tales of the Hall.
Delay Has Danger. *Fr.* Tales of the Hall.
Demons of Opium, The. *Fr.* Sir Eustace Grey.
Drifting.
Foreshore, The. *Fr.* The Borough.
Frank Courtship, The, *sel.* *Fr.* Tales.
His Wife's Wedding Ring.
Inebriety, *sel.*
Jonas Kindred's Household. *Fr.* Tales.
Late Wisdom. *Fr.* Reflections.
Library, The, *sels.*
Life.
Lover's Journey, The. *Fr.* Tales.
Marriage Ring, A.
Meeting, *sel.*
Opium Dream. *Fr.* The World of Dreams.
Parish Poor-House, The. *Fr.* The Village.
Parish Register, The, *sels.*
Parish Workhouse, The. *Fr.* The Village.
Patron, The. *Fr.* Tales.
Pauper's Funeral, The. *Fr.* The Village.
Peter Grimes. *Fr.* The Borough.
Peter Grimes, *sel.* *Fr.* The Borough.
Phoebe Dawson.
Physic. *Fr.* The Borough.
Poor, The. *Fr.* The Borough.
Portrait of a Vicar. *Fr.* The Borough.
Posthumous Tales, *sel.*
Quack Medicines. *Fr.* The Borough.
Reflections, *sel.*
Resurrection.
Ring, so worn as you behold, The.
Sea, The. *Fr.* The Borough.
Sea Marsh. *Fr.* The Borough.
Sir Eustace Grey, *sel.*
Spring to Winter. *Fr.* The Ancient Mansion.
Suffolk Shore, The. *Fr.* The Borough.
Tales, *sels.*
Tales of the Hall, *sels.*
Truth in Poetry. *Fr.* The Village.
Vicar, The. *Fr.* Inebriety.
Village, The, *sels.*
Village as It Is, The. *Fr.* The Village.
Village Life. *Fr.* The Village.
Whistling Boy, The.
Winter Storm at Sea, The. *Fr.* The Borough.
World of Dreams, The, *sel.*
Young Paris. *Fr.* Posthumous Tales.
CRADDLE, W. Egoism.
Male and Female.
♂ and ♀.
On a Certain Scholar.
CRAFTON, ALLEN. St. Maixent.
CRAFTS, WILLIAM. On the Death of Decatur.
CRAGIN, MARY A. *See* "ALLISON, JOY."
CRAIG, ALEXANDER. Misery of Man, The.
Sonnet: "Go you, O winds that blow from north to south."
To His Pandora, from England.
To Pandora.
CRAIG, MAURICE JAMES. Address of Welcome. *Fr.* Three Cat Poems.
Ballad to a Traditional Refrain.
Book of Life, The. *Fr.* Three Cat Poems.
Fable: "Tale is every time the same, The."
From Burton the Anatomist.
Georgian Dublin.
High on a Ridge of Tiles.
Love Poem.
Occasion of Sin. *Fr.* Three Cat Poems.
Poem: "High on a ridge of tiles."
Three Cat Poems.
Two Voyages.
Winter.
CRAIG, ROBERT J. Evening.
CRAIGMYLE, ELIZABETH. Sir Olaf, *tr.*
Solway Sands.
CRAIK, DINAH MARIA MULOCK. Address to the New Year.
Autumn's Processional.
Blackbird, The.
Buried To-Day.
By the Alma River.

Christmas Carol, A: "God rest ye, merry gentlemen."
Dead Czar Nicholas, The.
Douglas, Douglas, Tender and True.
Four Years.
French Nun, A.
Friendship.
God Rest Ye, Merry Gentlemen.
Green Things Growing.
Her Likeness.
Highland Cattle, *sel.*
In Our Boat.
Lancashire Doxology, A.
Lettice.
New Year, The.
Now and Afterwards.
Only a Woman.
Philip, My King.
Plighted.
To the Memory of Fletcher Harper.
Young Dandelion, The ("I am a bold fellow").
Young Dandelion ("Young Dandelion/ On a hedge-side").

CRANCH, CHRISTOPHER PEARSE. After the Centennial.
Bobolinks, The.
Correspondences.
Gnosis.
Gnosis, *sel.*
I in Thee, and Thou in Me.
Pines and the Sea, The.
So Far, So Near.
Thought.

CRANDALL, CHARLES HENRY. Human Plan, The.
Stella.
Three Trees.
Wayside Music.
With Lilacs.

CRANE, CARL. Reader Writes, The.

CRANE, ELIZABETH GREEN. Gentian.

CRANE, FRANK. Because You Care.
Yesterday.

CRANE, HART. Aeroplane, The. *Fr.* The Bridge.
Air Plant, The.
And yet this great wink of eternity. *Fr.* Voyages.
At Melville's Tomb.
Atlantis. *Fr.* The Bridge.
Ave Maria. *Fr.* The Bridge.
Black Tambourine.
Bridge, The.
Bridge, The, *sels.*
Broken Tower, The.
Cape Hatteras. *Fr.* The Bridge.
Cape Hatteras, *sels.* *Fr.* The Bridge.
Chaplinesque.
Cutty Sark. *Fr.* The Bridge.
Dance, The. *Fr.* The Bridge.
Emblems of Conduct.
For the Marriage of Faustus and Helen.
Harbor Dawn, The. *Fr.* The Bridge.
Hurricane, The.
Idiot, The.
Imperator Victus.
In Shadow.
Indiana. *Fr.* The Bridge.
Island Quarry.
Key West.
Lachrymae Christi.
Legend.
My Grandmother's Love Letters.
National Winter Garden. *Fr.* The Bridge.
North Labrador.
O Carib Isle!
Old Song.
Paraphrase.
Passage.
Phantom Bark, The.
Power. *Fr.* The Bridge.
Powhatan's Daughter. *Fr.* The Bridge.
Praise for an Urn.
Proem: To Brooklyn Bridge. *Fr.* The Bridge.
Purgatorio.
Quaker Hill. *Fr.* The Bridge.
Recitative.
Repose of Rivers.
River, The. *Fr.* The Bridge.
Royal Palm.
Sea, The. *Fr.* Voyages.
Southern Cross. *Fr.* The Bridge.
Sunday Morning Apples.
Three Songs. *Fr.* The Bridge.
To Brooklyn Bridge. *Fr.* The Bridge.
To Emily Dickinson.
To Potapovitch.
To Shakespeare.
Tunnel, The. *Fr.* The Bridge.
Van Winkle. *Fr.* The Bridge.
Virginia. *Fr.* The Bridge.
Voyages.
Voyages, *sels.*
Wine Menagerie, The.
Without the Moon, *tr.*

CRANE, L. BURTON, JR. Spell of the Pool, The.

CRANE, NATHALIA. Alliances.
Blind Girl, The.
Colors, The.
Dead Bee, The.
Death of Poetry, The, *sel.*
Desire.
Destiny.
Discoverer, The.
Dust, The.
First Story, The.
Flathouse Roof, The.
Gossips, The.
History of Honey, The.
Janitor's Boy, The.
Moon of Brooklyn, The.
Playbox, The.
Poe Cottage, The.
Reading Boy, The.
Requiem. *Fr.* The Death of Poetry.
Song: "Great is the rose." *Fr.* Tadmor.
Spooks.
Standards.
Suffering.
Swinging Stair, The.
Tadmor, *sel.*
Vacant Lot, The.
Vestal, The.
Yak, The.

CRANE, STEPHEN. Ancestry. *Fr.* The Black Riders.
Black Riders, The, *sels.*
Blades of Grass, The. *Fr.* The Black Riders.
Book of Wisdom, The. *Fr.* The Black Riders.
Candid Man, The. *Fr.* War Is Kind.
Content. *Fr.* The Black Riders.
Eating. *Fr.* The Black Riders.
Heart, The. *Fr.* The Black Riders.
Hymn: "Slant of sun on dull brown walls, A." *Fr.* War Is Kind.
I Explain. *Fr.* War Is Kind.
I Saw a Man. *Fr.* The Black Riders.
I Stood upon a High Place. *Fr.* The Black Riders.
If War Be Kind. *Fr.* War Is Kind.
It Was Wrong to Do This, Said the Angel. *Fr.* The Black Riders.
Learned Man, A. *Fr.* The Black Riders.
Little Ink More or Less, A. *Fr.* War Is Kind.
Love met me at noonday. *Fr.* War Is Kind.
Man, The. *Fr.* War Is Kind.
Man Said to the Universe, A. *Fr.* War Is Kind.
Man Saw a Ball of Gold in the Sky, A. *Fr.* The Black Riders.
Many Workmen. *Fr.* The Black Riders.
Newspaper, A. *Fr.* War Is Kind.
Once I saw thee idly rocking. *Fr.* War Is Kind.
Peaks, The. *Fr.* War Is Kind.
Sage lectured brilliantly, The. *Fr.* The Black Riders.
'Scaped. *Fr.* The Black Riders.
Slant of Sun, A. *Fr.* War Is Kind.
There Was a Man [with a Tongue of Wood]. *Fr.* War Is Kind.
Trees in the Garden, The. *Fr.* War Is Kind.
Two or three angels. *Fr.* The Black Riders.
Violets. *Fr.* War Is Kind.
War Is Kind, *sels.*
Wayfarer, The. *Fr.* War Is Kind.
What? You Define Me God. *Fr.* War Is Kind.
Why? *Fr.* The Black Riders.
Youth, A. *Fr.* The Black Riders.
Youth in Apparel That Glittered, A. *Fr.* The Black Riders.

CRANE, WALTER. Across the Fields.
Crocus, The.
Seat for Three, A; Written on a Settle.

CRANMER-BYNG, LANCELOT. Alas, *tr.* *Fr.* The Gulistan.
Farewell to Chao Ta-lin, *tr.*
Friendship, *tr.* *Fr.* The Gulistan.
Gift of Speech, The, *tr.* *Fr.* The Gulistan.
Gulistan, The, *sels., tr.*
He Hath No Parallel, *tr.* *Fr.* The Gulistan.
In an Old Library, *tr.*
Little Rain, The, *tr.*
Love's Last Resource, *tr.* *Fr.* The Gulistan.
Maytime, *tr.* *Fr.* Shi King.
Mesnevi, *tr.* *Fr.* The Gulistan.
On the Deception of Appearances, *tr.* *Fr.* The Gulistan.
Persian Maxim, *tr.*
Riding by Moonlight, *tr.*
Take the Crust. *Fr.* The Gulistan.

CRANSTON, CLAUDIA. If I Were the Lord God.
In the Name of Jesus Christ.

CRAPSEY, ADELAIDE. Adventure.
Amaze.
Anguish.
Arbutus.
Cradle-Song: "Madonna, Madonna."
Dirge: "Never the nightingale."
Expenses.
Fate Defied.
Fiddling Lad, The.
Guarded Wound, The.
Immortal Residue, The.
Lonely Death, The.
Monk in the Garden, The.
Moon Shadows.
Niagara.
Night Winds.
November Night.
On Seeing Weather-beaten Trees.
Pledge, The.
Rose-Marie of the Angels.
Song: "I make my shroud but no one knows."
Susanna and the Elders.
Trapped.
Triad.
Vendor's Song.
Warning, The.
Why, *tr.*
Winter.

CRASHAW, RICHARD. Ad Judaeos Mactatores Stephani. *Fr.* Epigrammata Sacra.
Aethiopus Lotus. *Fr.* Epigrammata Sacra.
Against Irresolution.
And He Answered Them Nothing.
And Now Where're He Strays.
Answer for Hope.
Aquae in Vinum Versae. *Fr.* Epigrammata Sacra.
Beati Oculi Qui Vident. *Fr.* Epigrammata Sacra.
Charitas Nimia; or, The Dear Bargain.
Charitas Nimia, *sel.*
Chorus: "Welcome to our wond'ring sight." *Fr.* In the Holy Nativity of Our Lord God.
Christ Crucified.
Christ to Thomas.
Christ's Victory.
Christus Vitis ad Vinitorem Patrem. *Fr.* Epigrammata Sacra.
Coming Child, The.
Counting Kisses, *tr.*
Description of a Convent.
Dies Irae, *tr.*
Dives Asking a Drop.
Divine Love.
Easter Day.

CRASHAW, RICHARD (*continued*)
Ecstasy, An.
Epigrammata Sacra, *sels.*
Epitaph upon a Young Married Couple, An.
Epitaph upon Husband and Wife Which [*or* who] Died and Were Buried Together, An.
Epitaph upon Mr. Ashton.
Epithalamium: "Come, virgin tapers," *sel.*
Flaming Heart, The.
Flaming Heart, The, *sels.*
For Hope.
For Hope, *sel.*
Good Woman Made Welcome in Heaven, The.
Herod's Suspicions.
Holy Name of Jesus, The.
Holy Nativity of Our Lord God, The.
Hymn in Adoration of the Blessed Sacrament.
Hymn in Honor of Saint Teresa, a Carmelite Nun, A.
Hymn of Saint Thomas in Adoration of the Blessed Sacrament, The.
Hymn of the Holy Cross, The.
Hymn of the Nativity.
Hymn Sung as by the Shepherds, A. *Fr.* In the Holy Nativity of Our Lord God.
Hymn to St. Theresa.
Hymn to the Name and Honor of the Admirable Saint Teresa, A.
Hymn to the Name of Jesus.
I Am the Door.
In Asinum Christi Vectorem. *Fr.* Epigrammata Sacra.
In Beatae Virginis Verecundiam. *Fr.* Epigrammata Sacra.
In the Glorious Assumption of Our Blessed Lady.
In the Glorious Epiphanie of Our Lord God.
In the Holy Nativity [of Our Lord God].
In the Holy Nativity, *sels.*
Lesbia, *tr.*
Letter to the Countess of Denbigh against Irresolution and Delay in Matters of Religion, A.
Love's Horoscope.
Love's Nightingale.
M. Crashaw's Answer for Hope.
Malchus' Ear.
Music[k]s Duel[l].
Music's Duel, *sel.*
Nativity, The.
New Year's Day.
Nightingale's Song, The. *Fr.* Music's Duel.
On a Prayer Book Sent to Mrs. M. R.
On a Prayer Book Sent to Mrs. M. R., *sel.*
On a Young Married Couple.
On Dives.
On George Herbert's "The Temple" Sent to a Gentlewoman.
On Mr. G. Herbert's Book [Intituled the Temple of Sacred Poems, Sent to a Gentlewoman].
On Marriage.
On Our Crucified Lord Naked, and Bloody.
On the Assumption of the Virgin Mary.
On the Baptized Ethiopian [*or* Aethiopian].
On the Bleeding Wounds of Our Crucified Lord.
On the Blessed Virgin's Bashfulness.
On the Glorious Assumption of Our Blessed Lady.
On the Miracle of Loaves.
On the Water of Our Lord's Baptism.
On the Wounds of Our Crucified Lord.
Out of the Italian; a Song.
Piscatores Vocat. *Fr.* Epigrammata Sacra.
Pisces Multiplicati. *Fr.* Epigrammata Sacra.
Prayer: "Lo, here a little volume, but great book!"
Quaerit Jesum Suum Maria.
Qui Perdiderit Animam Suam.
Recommendation, The.
Richard Crashaw's Answer; for Hope.
Saint Mary Magdalene; or, The Weeper.
Saint Peter's Shadow.
Saint Teresa. *Fr.* The Flaming Heart.
Samson to His Delilah.
Sancta Maria Dolorum, or the Mother of Sorrows.
Shepherds' Hymn. *Fr.* In the Holy Nativity of Our Lord.
Si Filius Dei Es, Dejice Te. *Fr.* Epigrammata Sacra.
Song, A: "Lord, when the sense of Thy sweet grace."
Song of Divine Love, A.
Sospetto d'Herode, *sels.*
Tear, The.
Temperance, or the Cheap Physician.
To a Young Gentle-Woman, Councel Concerning Her Choice.
To Our Blessed Lord upon the Choice of His Sepulchre.
To Our Lord, upon the Water Made Wine.
To Pontius Washing His Hands.
To the Infant Martyrs.
To the Name above Every Name, the Name of Jesus a Hymn.
To the Noblest and Best of Ladies, the Countess of Denbigh.
"Two Went Up to [*or* into] the Temple to Pray."
Upon Bishop Andrewes His Picture before His Sermons.
Upon Ford's Two Tragedies, "Loves Sacrifice" and "The Broken Heart."
Upon the Bleeding Crucifix, *sel.*
Upon the Body of Our Blessed Lord, Naked and Bloody.
Upon the Book and Picture of the Seraphical Saint Teresa. *Fr.* The Flaming Heart.
Upon the Savior's Tomb.
Verses from "The Shepherds' Hymn."
Vincula Sponte Decidunt. *Fr.* Epigrammata Sacra.
Weeper, The.
Weeper, The, *sel.*
Why Are Ye Afraid, O Ye of Little Faith?
Widow's Mites, The.
Wishes to [*or* for] His [*or* the] Supposed Mistress.
CRASHAW, RICHARD, *and* ABRAHAM COWLEY. On Hope, by Way of Question and Answer, betweene A. Cowley, and R. Crashaw.
CRASTER, MRS. EDWARD. Centipede, A [*or* The].
Centipede Was Happy Quite, A.
Puzzled Centipede, The.
Quandary.
CRATES. Forethought.
Ledger, The.
Reliquiae.
CRATINUS. Pericles.
Poet's Inspiration, The.
CRAWFORD, "CAPTAIN JACK" (John Wallace Crawford). California Joe.
Death of Custer, The.
CRAWFORD, CHARLOTTE HOLMES. Vive la France.
CRAWFORD, DAN. Jesus and I.
CRAWFORD, FRANCES. Black Leopard, The.
He who would be reborn must seek.
I do not know if you will know.
Intensity abstracted in air, ready to break.
It is a secret sorrow.
Melody, from treble tones, The.
Mould sprouts in old shoes and empty heads.
Sanctuary in a maze, A.
Subtle evil that the mind engenders, The.
Supple body bends to will, The.
To face the arrows of the chance-drawn bow.
Uncaptured is essential death.
Who comforts flesh unreconciled.
Who sees the panic unconfessed.
Within the spring's bright shell of dawn.
CRAWFORD, FRANCIS MARION. New National Hymn.
CRAWFORD, ISABELLA VALANCY. Axe, The.
Canoe, The.
City Tree, The.
Epilogue: "Said the voice of Evil to the ear of Good." *Fr.* Gisli, the Chieftain.
Gisli, the Chieftain, *sels.*
Helot, The, *sel.*
Laughter.
Lily Bed, The.
Love's Forget-Me-Not.
Love's Land.
Malcolm's Katie, *sels.*
March.
Mother's Soul, The.
Rose, The.
Said the Daisy.
Song of the Arrow, The. *Fr.* Gisli, the Chieftain.
CRAWFORD, JOHN WALLACE. *See* CRAWFORD, "CAPTAIN JACK."
CRAWFORD, JULIA. We Parted in Silence.
CRAWFORD, LOUISA MACARTNEY. Kathleen Mavourneen.
CRAWFORD, PAULINE AVERY. Shut Doors along the Hall like Sleeping Eyes.
There Is No Sound save through the Sweltry Sheet.
To Me Wide-eyed throughout the Alien Night.
CRAWFORD, ROBERT (1695?–1733). Cowdenknowes.
Down the Burn, Davie.
CRAWFORD, ROBERT (1868–1930). Song: "Love, love me only."
Winged Words.
CRAWFORD, ROBERT MACARTHUR. U. S. Air Force, The.
CRAWFORD, VESTA PIERCE. Pioneer Woman.
CREECH, THOMAS. Death Inevitable, *tr. Fr.* Odes.
Flaming Torches, *tr. Fr.* Odes.
Odes (*of* Horace), *sels., tr.*
Times, The, *tr.*
To Manlius Torquatus, *tr. Fr.* Odes.
CREEKMORE, HUBERT. Artemis, *tr.*
Ballata 12: Of Love's Power, *tr.*
Ballata: "Since all my life out of my death derives," *tr.*
Ballata of Love's Power, *tr.*
Barbarian, *tr.*
Canso: "When all the ice and cold and snow," *tr.*
Canzo: "Can l'erba fresch'e lh folha par," *tr.*
Cerinthus Forgiven; Once More Tibullus Speaks for the Girl, *tr.*
Concert at Sea.
Dialogue of the Body with the Soul [Which Is] Leading It to Judgment, *tr.*
Dividends.
Effigy, The, *tr.*
Elegies (*of* Tibullus), *sels., tr.*
Funeral Toast, *tr.*
He Need Speak No Longer in Behalf of Sulpicia and Cerinthus, *tr.*
He Speaks for the Girl, on Cerinthus' Birthday, *tr.*
Intercession, on Sulpicia's Birthday, to Her Guardian Spirit, *tr.*
Lament of the Lovely Helmet-Dealer, *tr.*
Later, to Cerinthus, *tr.*
Love's Assize, *tr*
Matronalia, March 1, The, *tr.*
Mountain Song, *tr.*
Music in the Rec Hut.
No Harm to Lovers, *tr.*
On the Death of Tibullus, *tr.*
Orfeo, *sel., tr.*
Pale Is Death, *tr.*
Pastorela, *tr.*
Plea and Counsel, *tr.*
Pocket Guide for Servicemen.
Poem: "I'll write a poem, then sink to dreams," *tr.*

Poem to Lou, *tr.*
Sacrifice of the Bacchantes in Honor of Bacchus, *tr.* *Fr.* Orfeo.
Saint, *tr.*
Sirventes: "Paramours, to those who would accuse, The," *tr.*
Sonnet: Effigy, The, *tr.*
Sonnet: Love's Assize, *tr.*
Street Song, *tr.*
Sulpicia's Rival, *tr.*
To Cerinthus: "At last comes such a love that gossip that I conceal it," *tr.*
To Cerinthus: "Have you no tender thoughts, Cerinthus, for your sweetheart," *tr.*
To Cerinthus: "I thank you indeed that, sure of me, you assume such license," *tr.*
To Cerinthus: "May I be, dear love, no more a caution so glowing," *tr.*
To Cerinthus: "My hateful birthday is coming, and dismally I must spend it," *tr.*
Vexational, *tr.*
Voyage to Cythera, A, *tr.*
Weary of Bitter Ease, *tr.*
Creeley, Robert. Awakening, The.
Ballad of the Despairing Husband.
Counterpoint, A.
Door, The.
If You.
Immoral Proposition, The.
Innocence, The.
Just Friends.
Kind of Act of, The.
Marriage, A.
Three Ladies, The.
Warning, The.
Way, The.
Whip, The.
Creelman, Josephine Rice. Easter Day.
My Mother.
Creighton, Alan. Pastoral.
Return of a Reaper.
Spring Workman.
Crellin, Charles C. Ode to the Flag.
Crespo, Manuel. Song to the Soviet Union.
Cresse, James, Jr. Who Holds the Steps To-Night?
Cresson, Abigail. Cloak of Laughter.
Little Gods, The.
Little House, A.
Market Day.
Wistful One, The.
Cresswell, Walter D'Arcy. Impatient Poet, The.
Lyttelton Harbour, *sels.*
Time Lags Abed.
To L——.
Crew, Helen Coale. Bedtime.
In a Low Rocking-Chair.
Nobody Knows.
Crewe, Fred. Cleary Pioneer, A.
Crewe, Robert Offley Ashburton Crewe-Milnes, Marquess of. Harrow and Flanders.
Harrow Grave in Flanders, A.
Seven Years.
"Crichton, John" (Norman Gregor Guthrie). Bed of Campanula, A.
Bird's Nest in Winter, A.
Blue Hepatica.
Confluence, The.
Inspiration.
Red Trillium.
There's a Garden.
Crinagoras. Epitaph on an Infant.
How long, upon vain hopes intent.
Hunter's Thanksgiving.
Now to the right, now to the left I turn.
Parrot, bird that can, A.
Proclos, a silvern gift I send.
Sepulchral Imprecation.
Cripps, Arthur Shearly. Black Christ, The.
Essex.
Holy Poverty.
Lazarus.
"Les Belles Roses sans Mercie."
Love Pagan.
Lyke-Wake Carol, A.
Mashona Husbandman, A.
Pagan's Baptism, A.
Refrain, A: "Tell the tune his feet beat."
Resurgat.
Crisp, Lucy Cherry. After a Rain.
For Virginia Dare.
John Henry.
Peniny and the Silken Lady.
Crites, Lucile. Folks and Me.
"Croakers, The." *See* Halleck, Fitz-Greene, *and* Joseph Rodman Drake.
Croasdell, Anne. Muffin Man, The.
Croffut, W. F. Give Thanks for What?
Croffut, William Augustus. Dirge, A, Concerning the Late Lamented King of the Cannibal Islands.
Living Memory, A.
Croft, Roy. Love, *at.*
Why Do I Love You? *at.*
Croker, Henry. Evangelize!
Croly, George. A Fauxbourg. *Fr.* Paris in 1815.
Aestuary, An.
Approach of Evening.
Catiline, *sel.*
Catiline to the Roman Army. *Fr.* Catiline.
Death and Resurrection.
Death of Leonidas, The.
Genius of Death, The.
Leonidas.
Paris in 1815, *sel.*
Spirit of God [Descend upon My Heart].
Crombie, Stephen. Catbird.
Damascus Nightingale, A.
Indigo Bird.
Cromwell, Gladys. Crowning Gift, The.
Deep, The, *sel.*
Folded Power.
Mould, The.
Quest, The.
Renewal.
Cromwell, Henry. No, No! I Ne'er Shall Love Thee Less.
Cronyn, George. Palinurus.
Crooke, Sheila Jane. Statue of Liberty, The.
Cros, Charles. Smoked Herring, The.
Crosby, Ernest. Choir Practice.
Christianity and War.
How Did He Live?
In the Garden.
Life and Death.
Love Comes.
Rebels.
Search, The.
Soul of the World, The.
Tournament of Man, The.
Town Pictures, *sel.*
Crosby, Fanny (Frances Jane Crosby). All the way my Saviour leads me.
Best of All, The.
Blind.
Blind but Happy.
Jesus is tenderly calling thee home.
Jesus, keep me near the cross.
Keep Thou My Way, O Lord.
Pass me not, O gentle Saviour.
Rescue the perishing, care for the dying.
Safe in the arms of Jesus.
Saved by Grace.
State We Honor, The.
Suppose, *at.*
Thy Will Be Done in Me.
Unseen.
Cross, Allen Eastman. Hidden Years at Nazareth, The.
More Light Shall Break from Out Thy Word.
Pass on the Torch.
What Doth the Lord Require of Thee.
Cross, Mrs. George Frederick. *See* Cambridge, Ada.
Cross, Jane T. H. Confederacy, The.
Over the River.
Cross, Luther B. Thanksgiving Day Grace.
Cross, Mary Ann [*or* Marian] Evans Lewes. *See* "Eliot, George."
Cross, Zora. When I Was Six.
Woman.
Crossland, John R. Water.
Crossman, Samuel. I Said Sometimes with Tears.
Croswell, William. Clouds, The.
Crot, Robert J. Dead, The.
Crouch, Pearl Riggs. Snowstorm, The.
Story in the Snow, A.
Crouse, Miriam LeFevre. Dawn.
Lent.
Upon a Hill.
Crow, Gerald H. When They Have Made an End.
Crow, Martha Foote. Wooden Christ, The.
Crowe, William. Lewesdon Hill, *sel.*
Crowell, Albert. Joy of Incompleteness, The.
Crowell, Grace Noll (Mrs. Norman H. Crowell). Assurance.
Beautiful Gift, The.
Because of Thy Great Bounty.
Common Tasks, The.
Courage to Live.
Day Will Bring Some Lovely Thing, The.
Death.
Definition.
Eternal Values.
Fire Tenders, The.
I Do Not Like a Roof Tonight.
I Grieve for Beauty Wasted.
I Have Found Such Joy.
I Prayed Today.
I Think That God Is Proud.
Let Us Keep Christmas.
Mothers of the Earth, The.
Music-mad.
New Houses.
Poet, The.
Poet Prays, The.
Power.
Prayer for a Day's Walk.
Prayer for Courage, A.
Questioning.
Recompense.
Red Earth.
Shooting Stars.
Silver Poplars.
So Long As There Are Homes.
Someone Had Prayed.
Songs.
Sons.
Wild Geese.
Willow Whistles.
Young Nun.
Crowell, Henry. When Thou Passest through the Waters.
Crowell, Jane C. Saint Francis of Assisi, *sel.*
Crowell, Norman H. My Candidate.
Crowley, Robert. Voice of the Last Trumpet Blown by the Seventh Angel, The, *sel.*
Crowne, John. Calisto, *sel.*
Kind Lovers, Love on. *Fr.* Calisto.
Regulus, *sel.*
Song: "Kind lovers, love on." *Fr.* Calisto.
To Many Deaths Decreed. *Fr.* Regulus.
"Crowquill, Alfred." *See* Forrester, Alfred A.
"Cruger, Percy." *See* Winner, Septimus.
Cruickshank, Helen B. Shy Geordie.
Cruz, Juana Inés de la. *See* Juana Inés de la Cruz.
Cullen, Cornelius C. Battle of Somerset.
Cullen, Countee. Atlantic City Waiter.
Black Magdalens.
For a Lady I Know.
For a Pessimist.
For a Poet.
For a Virgin Lady.
For John Keats, Apostle of Beauty.
For My Grandmother.
For Paul Laurence Dunbar.
From the Dark Tower.
Fruit of the Flower.

CULLEN, COUNTEE (continued)
Heritage.
I Have a Rendezvous with Life.
I Have Wrapped My Dreams in a Silken Cloth.
Incident.
Incident; Baltimore.
Lady I Know. A.
Lines to My Father.
Lines to Our Elders.
Litany of the Black [or Dark] People.
Loss of Love, The.
Protest.
Red.
Saturday's Child
Simon the Cyrenian Speaks.
Song of Praise, A.
Tableau.
That Bright Chimeric Beast.
Timid Lover.
To a Brown Girl.
To an Unknown Poet.
To John Keats, Poet. At Springtime.
To Lovers of Earth: Fair Warning.
To One Who Said Me Nay.
Uncle Jim.
Under the Mistletoe.
Unknown Color, The.
Wakeupworld, The.
Wind Bloweth Where It Listeth, The.
Wisdom Cometh with the Years.
Wise, The.
Yet Do I Marvel.
Youth Sings a Song of Rosebuds.
CUMBERLAND, EARL OF. See CLIFFORD, GEORGE, EARL OF CUMBERLAND.
CUMBERLAND, ROBERT W. Warden's Watch, 2 A.M., The.
CUMMINGS, EDWARD ESTLIN. All Ignorance Toboggans into Know.
All in Green Went My Love Riding.
Always before Your Voice [My Soul].
Anyone Lived in a Pretty How Town.
As Freedom Is a Breakfastfood.
As Joe Gould says.
Being to Timelessness as It's to Time.
Buffalo Bill's/ defunct.
Buy Me an Ounce and I'll Sell You a Pound.
Cambridge Ladies, The. Fr. Sonnets —Realities.
Chanson Innocent[e].
Chaucer.
Come, Gaze with Me upon This Dome.
Come Nothing to My Comparable Soul.
Darling! Because My Blood Can Sing.
Four III.
Gee I Like to Think of Dead.
Here Is Little Effie's Head.
Hours Rise Up Putting Off Stars, The.
I Am a Little Church (No Great Cathedral).
I Am So Glad.
I Go to This Window.
I Like My Body.
I Sing of Olaf.
I Thank You God for Most This Amazing.
If I Have Made, My Lady.
If There Are Any Heavens.
If You Can't Eat [You Got To].
Impossibly, Motivated by Midnight.
Impression ("Stinging/ gold swarms").
Impression—IV ("The hours rise up putting off stars").
In Just-Spring When the World.
Is 5, sels.
It Is at Moments after I Have Dreamed.
It Is So Long Since My Heart.
It may not always be so. Fr. Sonnets —Unrealities.
It really must be nice. Fr. Is 5.
It Was a Goodly Co.
Item.
It's over a (See Just).
Jehovah Buried, Satan Dead.
La Guerre.
Lady Will You Come with Me into.
Life Is More True.
Listen.
Love Is More Thicker than Forget.
Love Is the Every Only God.
Maggie and Milly and Molly and May.

Man Who Had Fallen among Thieves, A.
May I Feel Said He.
May My Heart Always Be Open to Little.
Memorabilia.
Might these be thrushes climbing through almost.
Mr. U Will Not Be Missed.
Moon Is Hiding In, The.
My Father Moved through Dooms of Love.
My Love.
My Specialty Is Living Said.
My Sweet Old Etcetera. Fr. Is 5.
Next to of Course God [America I].
No Man, If Men Are Gods.
Nobody Loses All the Time.
Nonsun Blob A.
Noone and a Star Stand, Am to Am.
"Noone" autumnal this great lady's gaze.
O By the By.
O Sweet Spontaneous Earth.
O Thou to Whom the Musical White Spring.
Of Evident Invisibles.
Of Nicolette.
111.
147.
One X.
Orientale.
Paris; This April Sunset Completely Utters.
Pity This Busy Monster, Manunkind.
Plato Told.
Poem, or Beauty Hurts Mr. Vinal.
Poets yeggs and thirsties. Fr. Is 5.
Politician, A.
Ponder, Darling, These Busted Statues.
Portrait ("Buffalo Bill's/ defunct").
Portrait ("Here is little Effie's head").
Portrait ("Of evident invisibles").
Portrait ("Somebody knew Lincoln Somebody Xerxes").
Pretty a Day, A.
Salesman Is an It That Stinks Excuse, A.
Season 'Tis, My Lovely Lambs, The.
Serene Immediate Silliest and Whose.
She Being Brand.
Since Feeling Is First.
Somebody knew Lincoln Somebody Xerxes.
Somewhere I Have Never Travelled, Gladly Beyond.
Song: "All in green went my love riding."
Song: "Always before your voice my soul."
Song: "Thy fingers make early flowers."
Sonnet: "And what were roses."
Sonnet: "O Thou to whom the musical white spring."
Sonnet: "This is the garden: colours come and go."
Sonnet: "When thou hast taken thy last applause."
Sonnet: "Wind has blown the rain away and blown, A."
Sonnet Entitled How to Run the World.
Sonnets—Actualities, sel.
Sonnets—Realities, sel.
Sonnets—Unrealities, sel.
Space Being Curved.
Spring.
Spring Is Like a Perhaps Hand.
Spring Omnipotent Goddess.
Sunset.
Supposing I Dreamed This.
Sweet Spring Is Your.
These Children Singing.
This Is the Garden.
306.
Thy Fingers Make Early Flowers.
Two XI. Fr. Is 5.
Way to Hump a Cow, The.
What a Proud Dreamhorse.
What if a Much of a Which of a Wind.
When God Lets My Body Be.
When life is quite through with.

When Serpents Bargain.
When the Proficient Poison of Sure Sleep.
When unto Nights of Autumn Do Complain.
Wind has blown the rain away and blown, A.
Who Knows if the Moon's.
Who's Most Afraid of Death? Thou.
You Are Like the Snow Only.
You Shall above all Things Be Glad and Young.
CUMMINGS, PHILIP. Whip-Poor-Will.
CUNEY, WARING. Burial of the Young Love.
Conception.
Crucifixion.
Death Bed, The.
Dust.
Finis.
Grave.
I Think I See Him There.
Lame Man and the Blind Man.
No Images.
Radical, The.
Threnody: "Only quiet death."
Triviality, A.
Troubled Jesus.
True Love.
Wake Cry.
CUNNINGHAM, A. B. Dying Soldier Boy, The.
CUNNINGHAM, ALICE HATHAWAY. Syrian Lullaby.
CUNNINGHAM, ALLAN. At Sea.
Gone [or Gane] Were But the Winter Cold [or Cauld].
Hame, Hame, Hame.
John Grumlie.
Loyalty.
Mariner, The.
My Nanie, O.
Poet's Bridal-Day Song, The.
Rob Rool and Rattlin Willie.
Sea-Song, A.
Song of the Elfin Miller.
Spring of the Year, The.
Sun Rises Bright in France, The.
Thou Hast Sworn by Thy God, My Jeanie.
Wee, Wee German Lairdie, The.
Wet Sheet and a Flowing Sea, A.
CUNNINGHAM, JAMES VINCENT. Aeterne Rerum Conditor, tr.
Confession of Bishop Golias, The, tr.
Epigram: "And what is love? Misunderstanding, pain."
Epigram: "Arms and the man I sing, and sing for joy."
Epigram: "Elders at their services begin, The."
Epigram: "Friend, on this scaffold Thomas More lies dead."
Epigram: "Here lies my wife. Eternal peace."
Epigram: "I had gone broke, and got set to come back."
Epigram: "Man who goes for Christian resignation, The."
Epigram: "You ask me how Contempt who claims to sleep."
Epigram: "You wonder why Drab sells her love for gold?"
Helmsman, The; an Ode.
Horoscope.
Old Actor Addresses Julius Caesar, An, tr.
Rome, tr.
Silvae, sel., tr.
Two Epigrams.
CUNNINGHAM, JOHN. Contemplation; a Night Piece, sel.
Day; a Pastoral, sel.
Evening. Fr. Day; a Pastoral.
Fox and the Cat, The.
Kate of Aberdeen.
Landscape, A.
Miller, The.
Moonrise. Fr. Contemplation; a Night Piece.
Morning.
CUNNINGHAM, JOHN WILLIAM. Calvary's Cry.
CUNNINGHAM, NORA B. Feast, The.

Cunninghame-Graham, Robert. *See* Graham, Robert.
Curchod, Mary M. I Would Go Back.
Curl, Vega. Spendthrift.
Curnow, Allen. At Dead Low Water.
Attitudes for a New Zealand Poet, III.
Bishop Boundary-rides His Diocese, The. *Fr.* Not in Narrow Seas.
Country School.
Crash at Leithfield.
Elegy on My Father.
House and Land.
Landfall in Unknown Seas.
Magellan.
Not in Narrow Seas, *sels.*
Out of Sleep.
Stratagem.
Time.
Unhistoric Story, The.
Water Is Burred with Rain, The. *Fr.* Not in Narrow Seas.
Wild Iron.
Curran, Edwin. Autumn.
Clod, The.
First Frost.
Painted Hills of Arizona, The.
Curran, John Philpot. Cushla-Ma-Chree.
Deserter, The.
Deserter's Lamentation, The.
Deserter's Meditation, The.
Let Us Be Merry before We Go.
Currey, Ralph Nixon. Durban Revisited.
Epitaph on a Pet Cat, *tr.*
In Memoriam: Roy Campbell.
Landscape.
Man's Roots, *sel.*
Marshal Lyautey.
Morocco.
Song: "There is no joy in water apart from the sun."
Ultimate Exile, *sel.*
For other translations from French, see FoS.
Currie, Mary Montgomerie Currie, Baroness. *See* "Fane, Violet."
Currier, Ellen Bartlett. Silent Baby.
Curtis, Christine Turner. Villa Sciarra; Rome.
Curtis, George William. Ebb and Flow.
Egyptian Serenade.
Curtis, Natalie (Natalie Curtis Burlin). Corn-grinding Song, *tr.*
Flute-Song, *tr.*
Gone to War, *tr.*
Holy Song, *tr.*
Hunting-Song, *tr.*
Korosta Katzina Song, *tr.*
Love-Song, *tr.*
Navajo Hunting-Song, *tr.*
Song after Rain, *tr.*
Song of the Earth, *tr.*
Song of the Horse, *tr.*
Song of the Rain-Chant, *tr.*
Wind Song, *tr.*
Curtwright [*or* Curtright], Wesley. Close of Day, The.
Four-Leaf Clover.
Heart of the Woods.
Cushing, Anita Laurie. New Mother.
Cushman, Ralph Spaulding. Christmas Prayer.
His Presence Came like Sunrise.
I Shall Live On.
I Will Not Hurry.
Parson's Prayer, The.
Secret, The.
Too Busy?
Cushman, Rebecca. Homing Song.
Silhouette and Oil.
Cust, Henry. Non Nobis.
Custance, Olive (Lady Alfred Douglas). O! Do You Hear the Rain.
Parting Hour, The.
Primrose Hill.
Twilight.
Waking of Spring, The.
Cuthbertson, James Lister. Bush, The.
Corona Inutilis.
Wattle and Myrtle.
Cutler, Elbridge Jefferson. Law and Liberty.
Volunteer, The.
Cutler, Julian S. Angel of Dawn, The.
Through the Year.
Cutter, George W. Song of Steam, The.
Song of the Lightning.
Cutter, Walter A. Loyalties.
Cutts, John, Baron Cutts. Only Tell Her That I Love.
Song: "Only tell her that I love."
Cynewulf. Christ, *sels.*
Christ Tells of His Passion. *Fr.* Christ.
Constantine's Vision of the Cross. *Fr.* Elene.
Death of Saint Guthlac. *Fr.* Guthlac.
Dream of the Rood, A, *at.*
Elene, *sels.*
Fates of the Apostles, *sel.*
Guthlac, *sel.*
Heaven. *Fr.* Christ.
Helena Embarks for Palestine. *Fr.* Elene.
Human Race Comes to Be Judged, The. *Fr.* Christ.
Juliana, *sel.*
Last Judgment, The. *Fr.* Christ.
Maiden Ring-adorned, A. *Fr.* Christ.
Prayer to Christ Our Lord.
Riddle: "I a weaponed warrior was!"
Riddle: "I am all alone."
Riddle: "Who so wary and so wise."
Voyage of Life, The. *Fr.* Christ.

D

"D., B. A." On First Looking into a Circular for a Student's Around-the-World-Cruise.
"D., F. W." Only a Private.
"D., H." *See* Doolittle, Hilda.
"D., J." Essay on the Fleet Riding in the Downes, An.
"D., M. P." Little Mother.
Dabney, Betty Page. Earth's Bondman.
Dach, Simon. Friendship.
DaCosta, John Chalmers. Army of Despair, The.
Dacre, Harry. Daisy Bell.
Daeubler, Theodore. Beech, The.
Dafydd ap [*or* ab] Gwilym. He Desires Her Husband's Death.
Reproach to Morvyth, A.
Seagull, The.
Snowy Day, A.
To the Nun.
Woodland Mass, The.
"Dagonet." *See* Sims, George Robert.
"Dahl, Basil" (Joseph Ovshover). Revolution.
Dahlgren, Fredrik August. Sun-Parasol, The.
Daiches, David. Cosmogony.
Final Thoughts on the Weather in England during 1953.
Ostrava, *tr.*
Thoughts on Progress.
To Kate, Skating Better than Her Date.
Volume II (Kinsey).
Daigaku, Horiguchi. Muddy Rat, The.
Daihaku, Princess. Crossing the Mountain Alone. *Fr.* Manyo Shu.
How will you manage. *Fr.* Manyo Shu.
Path we have climbed has been steep and hard, The.
Daiken, Leslie. Bohernabreena.
June Song of a Man Who Looks Two Ways.
Larch Hill.
Lines to My Father.
Lines Written in a Country Parson's Orchard.
Nostalgie d'Automne.
Spring, St. Stephen's Green.
Dainty, Evelyn. Birds on the School Windowsill, The.
Dakiki [*or* Daqiqi]. On His Love.
Wine.
Dakin, Laurence. Pyramus and Thisbe, *sel.*
Song: "Peasant sun went crushing grapes, The." *Fr.* Tancred.
Tancred, *sels.*
Dakotsu. Through an old field.
Dalcour, Pierre. Verse Written in the Album of Mademoiselle ——.
Dale, Arthur B. Sound Thy Trumpet, God of Action.
Torch, The.
Dale, Edward Everett. Prairie Schooner, The.
Daley, Edith. Little Words, The.
Miracle.
Daley, Victor. A-Roving.
Day and Night.
Muses of Australia, The.
Dallas, Mary Kyle. He'd Nothing but His Violin.
Dallas, Ruth. Farmyard.
Grandmother and Child.
Milking before Dawn.
Roads.
World's Centre, The.
Dalliba, Gerda. To a Child.
Dalmon, Charles. Almond Blossoms. *Fr.* Three Pictures.
Ballad of the Epiphany.
Camelot.
Caterpillar's Apology for Eating a Favorite Gladiolus, A.
Cow at Sullington, A.
Early Morning Meadow Song.
Elegy for Edward Thomas, *sel.*
Legend of Cherries, A.
O What If the Fowler.
Separation.
She No Longer Loves Him.
Snowfall on Plum Trees after They Had Bloomed. *Fr.* Three Pictures.
Stanzas from "Elegy for Edward Thomas."
Sussex Legend, A.
Three Pictures.
Wistaria Blossoms. *Fr.* Three Pictures.
Dalton, Annie Charlotte. Flame and Adventure, *sel.*
For an Eskimo.
Incantations.
Lycosa, the Spider.
Neighing North, The.
Ode to a Garden.
Praying-Mantis, The.
Robin's Egg, The.
Sounding Portage, The.
To the Young Man Jesus.
Wild Larkspur.
Dalton, Power (Harold Caleb Dalton). Finite.
Flail.
Dalven, Rae. My Father.
Walls, *tr.*
For translations from Modern Greek, see MoGP.
Daly, Eugene Howell. Alpheus and Arethusa.
Daly, James. Eagle, The.
Daly, James Jeremiah. In Coventry.
Latin Tongue, The.
Nox Ignatiana.
October of the Angels.
Daly, John. Toast to the Flag, A.
Daly, June. Wildebeest, The.
Daly, Thomas Augustine. Between Two Loves.
Blossomy Barrow, The.
Boy from Rome, Da.
Child's Christmas Song, A.
Comica Man, Da.
Day of the Circus Horse, The.
Dixie Lullaby, A.
Een Napoli.
Father's Prayer, A.
Flag o' My Land.
For Old Lovers.
Greata Basaball, Da.
Greata Stronga Man, Da.
John Keats.

DALY, THOMAS AUGUSTINE (*continued*)
Leetla Boy, Da.
Leetla Giorgio Washeenton.
Leetla Giuseppina.
Man's Prayer, The.
Mia Carlotta.
October.
On the Road to Arden.
Ould Apple Woman, The.
Peaceable Race, The.
Perennial May.
Poet, The.
Pup een da Snow, Da.
Sanctum, The.
Song of the Thrush, The.
Song to One, A.
Tides of Love, The.
To a Plain Sweetheart.
To a Robin.
To a Thrush.
To th' Minstrel Girl.
Two Days.
Two 'Mericana Men.
W'en Spreeng Ees Com'.
DAMADIAN, MIHRAN. Imprisoned Revolutionist, The.
DAMAGETUS. Last Word, The.
Wife's Grave, A.
DAMAS, LÉON. Poems.
DAMASCENE, SAINT JOHN. *See* JOHN OF DAMASCUS, SAINT.
DAMASCIUS. Slave Girl, A.
"Vasty Halls of Death, The."
DAMOCHARIS THE GRAMMARIAN. Cat and the Partridge, The.
DAMON, SAMUEL FOSTER. At Memphis Station, *tr.*
Bridge.
Last Supper; Jesus to Judas.
DAMROSCH, ALICE BLAINE. Swimming by Night.
DANA, KATHERINE FLOYD. *See* "WADSWORTH, OLIVE A."
DANA, RICHARD HENRY. Buccaneer, The, *sel.*
Chanting Cherubs, The.
Early Spring Brook, The.
Husband and Wife's Grave, The.
I Saw Her Once
Immortality.
Island, The. *Fr.* The Buccaneer.
Little Beach-Bird, The.
Moss Supplicateth for the Poet, The.
Pleasure-Boat, The.
Soul, The.
DANCER, JOHN. Ha! now you think you've cheated me. Oh, no!
Wish, The.
DANDRIDGE, DANSKE BEDINGER. Dead Moon, The.
On the Eve of War.
Spirit of the Fall, The.
DANDRIDGE, RAY GARFIELD. Drum Majah, Da.
'Ittle Touzle Head.
Sprin' Fevah.
Time to Die.
Zalka Peetruza.
"DANE, BARRY." *See* LOGAN, JOHN EDWARD.
"DANE, CLEMENCE" (Winifred Ashton). Him I Follow. *Fr.* Will Shakespeare.
Salute to Greece.
Trafalgar Day, 1940.
Will Shakespeare, *sel.*
DANGERFIELD, GEORGE. To Ultima Thule.
DANIEL, ARNAUT. Bel m'es quan lo vens m'alena.
Canso: "Softly sighs the April air."
Canzo of Bird-Songs and Love.
Mot eran dous miei cossir.
DANIEL, GEORGE. Robin, The.
DANIEL, SAMUEL. Aminta, *sel.*, *tr.*
And yet I cannot reprehend the flight. *Fr.* To Delia.
Are They Shadows [That We See]? *Fr.* Tethys' Festival.
Beauty [*or* Beautie], sweet love, is like the morning dew. *Fr.* To Delia.
Beauty, Time, and Love. *Fr.* To Delia.
Beauty's Glass.
Beauty's Lease. *Fr.* To Delia.
But love whilst that thou mayst be loved again. *Fr.* To Delia.
Care-Charmer Sleep [Son of the Sable Night]. *Fr.* To Delia.
Chorus: "Behold what furies still." *Fr.* Cleopatra.
Chorus: "How dost thou wear and weary out thy days." *Fr.* Philotas.
Chorus: "Then thus we have beheld." *Fr.* Cleopatra.
Civil Wars, The, *sels.*
Cleopatra, *sels.*
Complaint of Rosamond, The.
Complaint of Rosamond, The, *sels.*
Constancy. *Fr.* Hymen's Triumph.
Death of Talbot. *Fr.* The Civil Wars.
Delia. *See* To Delia.
Description of Beauty, A, *sel.*
Eidola. *Fr.* Tethys' Festival.
English Poetry. *Fr.* Musophilus.
Enjoy Thy April Now. *Fr.* A Description of Beauty.
Epistle to the Lady Margaret, Countess of Cumberland, *sel.*
Eyes, Hide My Love. *Fr.* Hymen's Triumph.
Fair Is My Love. *Fr.* To Delia.
Had Sorrow Ever Fitter Place. *Fr.* Hymen's Triumph.
Half-blown Rose, The. *Fr.* To Delia.
Henry's Lament. *Fr.* The Complaint of Rosamond.
High Mind, The.
Hymen's Triumph, *sels.*
I must not grieve my love. *Fr.* To Delia.
If it so hap this offspring of my care. *Fr.* To Delia.
If this be love, to draw a weary breath. *Fr.* To Delia.
Let others sing of knights and paladins. *Fr.* To Delia.
Like as the lute delights or else dislikes. *Fr.* To Delia.
Lo, here the impost of a faith entire. *Fr.* To Delia.
Lonely Beauty. *Fr.* The Complaint of Rosamond.
Look, Delia, how we esteem the half-blown rose. *Fr.* To Delia.
Love. *Fr.* Hymen's Triumph.
Love Is a Sickness. *Fr.* Hymen's Triumph.
Most fair and lovely maid, look from the shore. *Fr.* To Delia.
Most Unloving One, The. *Fr.* To Delia.
Musophilus, or Defence of All Learning.
Musophilus, or Defence of All Learning, *sels.*
My cares draw on mine everlasting night. *Fr.* To Delia.
My spotless love hovers with purest wings. *Fr.* To Delia.
None other fame mine unambitious muse. *Fr.* To Delia.
O Fearfull, Frowning Nemesis. *Fr.* Cleopatra.
Ode, An: "Now each creature joys the other." *Fr.* To Delia.
Pastoral, A: "Oh happy golden age," *tr.* *Fr.* Aminta.
Pastoral of Tasso, A, *tr.*
Philotas, *sel.*
Poet and Critic. *Fr.* Musophilus.
Poetry of England, The. *Fr.* Musophilus.
Prayer to Sleep. *Fr.* To Delia.
Quand Vous Serez Bien Vieille. *Fr.* To Delia.
Reminiscence of Early Love, A. *Fr.* Hymen's Triumph.
Restore thy treasure [*or* tresses] to the golden ore. *Fr.* To Delia.
Richard II as Captive. *Fr.* The Civil Wars.
Rosamond's Appeal. *Fr.* The Complaint of Rosamond.
Secrecy. *Fr.* Hymen's Triumph.
Shadows. *Fr.* Tethys' Festival.
Sleep. *Fr.* To Delia.
Song: "Are they shadowes that we see?" *Fr.* Tethys' Festival.
Song: "Love is a sickness full of woes." *Fr.* Hymen's Triumph.
Sonnet: "Beauty, sweet love, is like the morning dew." *Fr.* To Delia.
Sonnet: "But love whilst that thou may'st be loved again." *Fr.* To Delia.
Sonnet: "Care-charmer Sleep, son of the sable night." *Fr.* To Delia.
Sonnet: "Drawn with th' attractive virtue of her eyes." *Fr.* To Delia.
Sonnet: "Fair and lovely maid, look from the shore." *Fr.* To Delia.
Sonnet: "Fair is my Love, and cruel as she's fair." *Fr.* To Delia.
Sonnet: "I must not grieve my Love, whose eyes would read." *Fr.* To Delia.
Sonnet: "I once may see when years shall wreck my wrong." *Fr.* To Delia.
Sonnet: "Let others sing of knights and paladins." *Fr.* To Delia.
Sonnet: "Look, Delia, how we esteem the half-blown rose." *Fr.* To Delia.
Sonnet: "O had she not been fair and thus unkind." *Fr.* To Delia.
Sonnet: "Reign in my thoughts, fair hand, sweet eye, rare voice!" *Fr.* To Delia.
Sonnet: "Star of my mishap impos'd this paining, The." *Fr.* To Delia.
Sonnet: "Unto the boundless ocean of thy beauty." *Fr.* To Delia.
Sonnet: "When men shall find thy flower, thy glory, pass." *Fr.* To Delia.
Sonnet: "When winter snows upon thy sable hairs [*or* golden hears]." *Fr.* To Delia.
Sonnets. *Fr.* To Delia.
Sorrow. *Fr.* Hymen's Triumph.
Star of my mishap imposed this pain, The. *Fr.* To Delia.
Tethys' Festival, *sel.*
Then and Now. *Fr.* To Delia.
These plaintive verse, the posts of my desire. *Fr.* To Delia.
Thou canst not die whilst any zeal abound. *Fr.* To Delia.
Time, cruel Time, come and subdue that brow. *Fr.* To Delia.
To Delia, *sels.*
To His Reader.
To Sir Thomas Egerton.
To the Lady Lucy, Countess of Bedford.
To the Lady Margaret, Countess of Cumberland.
To the Reader.
To the Right Honorable, the Lady Mary, Countess of Pembroke. *Fr.* To Delia.
To the Right Worthy and Judicious Favorer of Virtue, Master Fulke Greville. *Fr.* Musophilus.
Tragedie of Philotas, The, *sels.*
Tragedy of Cleopatra, The, *sels.*
Treasure of Our Tongue, The. *Fr.* Musophilus.
Trophies, The. *Fr.* To Delia.
Ulysses and the Siren.
Unto the boundless ocean of thy beauty. *Fr.* To Delia.
When Men Shall Find Thy Flower, Thy Glory, Pass. *Fr.* To Delia.
When winter snows upon thy sable hairs. *Fr.* To Delia.
Why should I sing in verse, why should I frame. *Fr.* To Delia.
Writer's Tragedy, The. *Fr.* The Tragedie of Philotas.
DANIEL BEN JUDAH. Living God, The.
Magnified Be the Living God.
DANIELL, EDITH. Inspect Us.
DANIELL, ERIC H. Silent Stars, The.
DANIELLS, ROY. Buffalo.
Deeper into the Forest.
Ducks.
Sonnet: "I never swung a staff and deep, oh deep."
Sonnet: "See the white stillness of the unicorn."

Sonnet: "Under the bark remembers now my heart."
Summer Days.
DANIELS, R. BALFOUR. Candlelight.
DANNECKER, HAZEL I. Balloon Man.
D'ANNUNZIO, GABRIELE. Evening in May.
Morgana.
September.
DANTE ALIGHIERI. Affinity with the Stars. *Fr.* Divina Commedia: Paradiso.
All my thoughts always speak to me of love. *Fr.* La Vita Nuova.
All Ye That Pass. *Fr.* La Vita Nuova.
At whiles (yea oftentimes) I muse over. *Fr.* La Vita Nuova.
Ballata: He Will Gaze upon Beatrice.
Banquet, The, *sel.*
Beatrice to Dante. *Fr.* Divina Commedia: Paradiso.
Beauty and Duty.
Being Underived. *Fr.* Divina Commedia: Paradiso.
Beyond the Sphere. *Fr.* La Vita Nuova.
Buonconte Relates His Fate. *Fr.* Divina Commedia: Purgatorio.
But not to deal/ Thus closely with thee longer. *Fr.* Divina Commedia: Paradiso.
Canst thou indeed be he that still would sing. *Fr.* La Vita Nuova.
Canzone: "Eyes that weep for pity of the heart, The." *Fr.* La Vita Nuova.
Canzone: He Beseeches Death for the Life of Beatrice.
Canzone: "Ladies that have intelligence in love." *Fr.* La Vita Nuova.
Canzone: To the Lady Pietra, of Sienna.
Celestial Pilot, The. *Fr.* Divina Commedia: Purgatorio.
Dante Enters the Gate of Hell. *Fr.* Divina Commedia: Inferno.
Dante Sees Beatrice in Glory. *Fr.* Divina Commedia: Purgatorio.
Day agone, as I rode sullenly, A. *Fr.* La Vita Nuova.
Death, Always Cruel. *Fr.* La Vita Nuova.
Divided Thoughts. *Fr.* La Vita Nuova.
Divina Commedia [*or* Divine Comedy], *sels.*
Even as the Others Mock. *Fr.* La Vita Nuova.
For certain he hath seen all perfectness. *Fr.* La Vita Nuova.
Frae the Second Canzone o Dante's "Vita Nuova."
Francesca da Rimini. *Fr.* Divina Commedia: Inferno.
Freedom of the Will. *Fr.* Divina Commedia: Purgatorio.
Gentle thought there is will often start, A. *Fr.* La Vita Nuova.
His Will Is Our Peace. *Fr.* Divina Commedia: Paradiso.
I Felt a Spirit of Love Begin to Stir. *Fr.* La Vita Nuova.
Incommunicable Glory, The. *Fr.* Divina Commedia: Paradiso.
Inferno, *sels.* *Fr.* Divina Commedia.
Ladies That Have Intelligence in Love. *Fr.* La Vita Nuova.
Love. *Fr.* Divina Commedia: Paradiso.
Love's pallor and the semblance of deep ruth. *Fr.* La Vita Nuova.
Marvel Ye Not. *Fr.* Divina Commedia: Purgatorio.
Midway the Journey. *Fr.* Divina Commedia: Inferno.
Mine Eyes Beheld the Blessed Pity. *Fr.* La Vita Nuova.
Moral Responsibility. *Fr.* Divina Commedia: Purgatorio.
My Lady Carries Love. *Fr.* La Vita Nuova.
My lady looks so gentle and so pure. *Fr.* La Vita Nuova.
On the Death of Beatrice. *Fr.* La Vita Nuova.
On the Death of Beatrice: The Dream. *Fr.* La Vita Nuova.
One World. *Fr.* Divina Commedia: Paradiso.
Paolo and Francesca. *Fr.* Divina Commedia: Inferno.
Paradiso, *sels.* *Fr.* Divina Commedia.
Pier delle Vigne. *Fr.* Divina Commedia: Inferno.
Political Chaos in Italy. *Fr.* Divina Commedia: Purgatorio.
Primal Cause, The. *Fr.* Divina Commedia: Paradiso.
Purgatorio, *sels.* *Fr.* Divina Commedia.
Saint Bernard's Prayer to Our Lady [*or* to the Virgin Mary]. *Fr.* Divina Commedia: Paradiso.
Saints in Glory, The. *Fr.* Divina Commedia: Paradiso.
Self-Guidance. *Fr.* Divina Commedia: Purgatorio.
Sestina; of the Lady Pietra degli Scrovigni.
Sestina; to the Lady Pietra of Siena.
Song, 'tis my will that thou do seek out love. *Fr.* La Vita Nuova.
Sonnet: "Beatrice is gone up into high Heaven." *Fr.* La Vita Nuova.
Sonnet: "Because mine eyes can never have their fill."
Sonnet: "Beyond the sphere which spreads to widest space." *Fr.* La Vita Nuova.
Sonnet: "Last All Saints' holy-day, even now gone by."
Sonnet: "Mine eyes beheld the blessed pity spring." *Fr.* La Vita Nuova.
Sonnet: "My lady carries love within her eyes." *Fr.* La Vita Nuova.
Sonnet: "My lady looks so gentle and so pure." *Fr.* La Vita Nuova.
Sonnet: Of Beatrice de Portinari.
Sonnet: Of Beauty and Duty.
Sonnet: On the 9th of June 1290.
Sonnet: To Brunetto Latini.
Sonnet: To Certain Ladies.
Sonnet: "To every heart which the sweet pain doth move." *Fr.* La Vita Nuova.
Sonnet: To Guido Cavalcanti.
Sonnet: To the Lady Pietra degli Scrovigni.
Sonnet: To the Same Ladies.
Sonnet: "With sighs my bosom always laboureth." *Fr.* La Vita Nuova.
Sonnet: "Wonderfully out of the beautiful form." *Fr.* La Vita Nuova.
Sonnet: "Ye pilgrim-folk, advancing pensively." *Fr.* La Vita Nuova.
Sonnet to the Lady Pietra.
Stay now with me, and listen to my sighs. *Fr.* La Vita Nuova.
That lady of all gentle memories. *Fr.* La Vita Nuova.
Thoughts are broken in my memory, The. *Fr.* La Vita Nuova.
To Beatrice on All Saints' Day.
To Every Heart. *Fr.* La Vita Nuova.
To Guido Cavalcanti.
Ugolino. *Fr.* Divina Commedia: Inferno.
Very bitter weeping that ye made, The. *Fr.* La Vita Nuova.
Very pitiful lady, very young, A. *Fr.* La Vita Nuova.
Virgil's Farewell to Dante. *Fr.* Divina Commedia: Purgatorio.
Vision of God, The. *Fr.* Divina Commedia: Paradiso.
Vision of the Divine Mystery. *Fr.* Divina Commedia: Paradiso.
Vita Nuova, La, *sels.*
Weep, Lovers, sith Love's very self doth weep. *Fr.* La Vita Nuova.
Whatever while the thought comes over me. *Fr.* La Vita Nuova.
Within Her Eyes. *Fr.* La Vita Nuova.
Woe's me! by dint of all these sighs that come. *Fr.* La Vita Nuova.
Ye pilgrim-folk, advancing pensively. *Fr.* La Vita Nuova.
You that thus wear a modest countenance. *Fr.* La Vita Nuova.
DANTE DA MAIANO. *See* MAIANO, DANTE DA.
DANYEL, JOHN. Can Doleful Notes to Mesur'd Accents Set.
DA PONTE, LORENZO. Capriccio Dramatico, Il, *sel.*
Don Giovanni, *sel.*
Giovinette, che fate all' amore. *Fr.* Don Giovanni.
To an Artful Theatre Manager. *Fr.* Il Capriccio Dramatico.
D'ARCY, HAL. Erris Fairy, An.
D'ARCY, HUGH ANTOINE. Face upon [*or* on] the Floor, The.
D'ARCY, JACK. Conservative Shepherd to His Love, The.
DARE, SHIRLEY. Lullaby: "Song for the baby, sweet little Bopeep, A."
DARGAN, OLIVE TILFORD. August Evening.
Cycle's Rim, The, *sel.*
Duo.
Evvie's Mother.
In the Blue Ridge.
It Will Be a Hard Winter.
Lute and Furrow.
New Freedom, The.
On Clingman Dome.
On the Mountain.
Path Flower.
Released.
Rescue.
Returning.
Sal's Gap.
Sonnet: "Pasture is a forest where we lie, The."
Sonnet: "Today I went among the mountain folk."
There's Rosemary.
These Latter Days.
To a Texas Primrose.
To William Blake.
Twilight.
We Creators.
DARGAN, VERE. City Trees.
DARÍO, RUBÉN (Félix Rubén García Sarmiento). Afternoon in the Tropics.
Murmur from the Stable, The.
Portico.
Slings.
Sonatina.
Symphony in Gray Major.
To Roosevelt.
To Theodore Roosevelt, *sel.*
DARLEY, GEORGE. Call of the Morning, The.
Chorus of Spirits. *Fr.* Sylvia.
Consolation.
Deadman's Dirge. *Fr.* Syren Songs.
Declivities of Heaven. *Fr.* Nepenthe.
Dirge: "Wail! Wail ye o'er the dead!" *Fr.* Sylvia.
Dreams of Flying.
Elfin Pedlar, The. *Fr.* Sylvia.
Enchanted Lyre, The.
Enchanted Spring, The.
Errors of Ecstasie, *sel.*
Ethelstan, *sel.*
Fallen Star, The.
Fight of the Forlorn, The, *sel.*
Flower of Beauty, The.
Gambols of Children, The.
Harvest Home, *sel.*
Have You Not Oft, in the Still Wind.
Hymn to the Sun.
It Is Not Beauty I Demand.
Last Night.
Lay of the Forlorn.
Lines: "Hurry me Nymphs! O, hurry me." *Fr.* Nepenthe.
List no more the ominous din. *Fr.* Nepenthe.
Listen to the Lyre!
Lo! in the mute, mid wilderness. *Fr.* Nepenthe.
Loveliness of Love, The.
Love's Likeness.
Mermaidens' Vesper-Hymn, The. *Fr.* Syren Songs.

DARLEY, GEORGE (*continued*)
Morning-Song. *Fr.* Sylvia.
Nepenthe, *sels.*
Nephon's Song. *Fr.* Sylvia.
O Blest Unfabled Incense Tree. *Fr.* Nepenthe.
O fast her amber blood doth flow. *Fr.* Nepenthe.
O'er the Wild Gannet's Bath. *Fr.* Ethelstan.
On the Death of a Recluse.
Over a bloomy land, untrod. *Fr.* Nepenthe.
Over hills and uplands high. *Fr.* Nepenthe.
Phoenix [*or* Phenix], The ("O blest unfabled incense tree"). *Fr.* Nepenthe.
Phoenix, The ("O fast her amber blood doth flow"). *Fr.* Nepenthe.
Robin's Cross.
Romanzo to Sylvia. *Fr.* Sylvia.
Runilda's Chant.
Sea, The. *Fr.* Nepenthe.
Sea-Ritual, The. *Fr.* Syren Songs.
Serenade: "Awake, thee, my lady-love." *Fr.* Sylvia.
Serenade of a Loyal Martyr.
Siren Chorus. *Fr.* Syren Songs.
Solitary Lyre, The.
Solitary Wayfarer! *Fr.* Nepenthe.
Song: "Down the dimpled green-sward dancing."
Song: "It is not Beauty I demand."
Song: "I've taught thee Love's sweet lesson o'er." *Fr.* Sylvia.
Song: "Sweet in her green dell the flower of beauty slumbers."
Song of the Mermaids. *Fr.* Syren Songs.
Song of the Summer Winds.
Summer Winds.
Sunset. *Fr.* Harvest Home.
Sylvia; or, The May Queen, *sels.*
Syren Songs, *sels.*
Thou, whose thrilling hand in mine. *Fr.* Nepenthe.
To Helene.
To My Egeria.
To Poets.
True Loveliness.
Unicorn, The. *Fr.* Nepenthe.
Wherefore, Unlaurelled Boy.
Winds of the West, Arise.
DARLING, ESTHER BIRDSALL. Friend, A.
DARLINGTON, JAMES HENRY. Joy Awaiting, The.
DARLOW, DAVID JOHN. Drought.
DARMESTETER, AGNES MARY FRANCES ROBINSON. *See* ROBINSON, AGNES MARY FRANCES.
DARROUGH, ROSE. Only Heaven Is Given Away.
White Thorn.
DARWIN, ERASMUS. Botanic Garden, The, *sels.*
French Revolution, The.
Fuseli's "Nightmare." *Fr.* The Botanic Garden: The Loves of the Plants.
Immortal Nature. *Fr.* The Botanic Garden: The Economy of Vegetation.
Of Good and Evil, *sel.*
Steam Power. *Fr.* The Botanic Garden: The Economy of Vegetation.
Vegetable Loves. *Fr.* The Botanic Garden: The Loves of the Plants.
Whale, The.
DARWIN, FRANCES. *See* CORNFORD, FRANCES.
DASKAM, JOSEPHINE DODGE. *See* BACON, JOSEPHINE DODGE DASKAM.
DAUBENY, CHARLES. Verses on a Cat.
DAUGHERTY, JAMES HENRY. Texas.
D'AURIA, GEMMA ABKAZOFF. Subject for Prophecy.
DAVENANT [*or* D'AVENANT], SIR WILLIAM. Aubade.
Awake! Awake!
Christians Reply to the Philosopher, The, *sel.*
Cruel Brother, The, *sel.*
Dream, The.
Dying Lover, The.
Endimion Porter and Olivia.
Epitaph: "When you perceive these stones are wet."
For the Lady Olivia Porter; A Present upon a New-Years Day.
Gondibert, *sels.*
History of Sir Francis Drake, The, *sel.*
Lark Now Leaves His Wat'ry [*or* Watery] Nest, The.
Law against Lovers, The, *sel.*
Life and Death. *Fr.* The Christians Reply to the Philosopher.
Love. *Fr.* The Unfortunate Lovers.
Lover and Philosopher.
Luminalia, *sel., at.*
Morning [Song].
News from Plymouth, *sel.*
Night's Song, *at. Fr.* Luminalia.
O Thou That Sleep'st like Pig in Straw. *Fr.* News from Plymouth.
Philosopher and the Lover, The; to a Mistress Dying.
Praise and Prayer. *Fr.* Gondibert.
Rivals, The, *sel.*
Siege of Rhodes, The, *sel.*
Sir Francis Drake Reviv'd. *Fr.* The History of Sir Francis Drake.
Soldier [*or* Souldier] Going to the Field, The.
Song: "Before we shall again behold."
Song: Endymion [*or* Endimion] Porter and Olivia.
Song: "Lark now leaves his watry nest, The."
Song: "My lodging it is on the cold ground." *Fr.* The Rivals.
Song: "O thou that sleep'st like pig in straw." *Fr.* News from Plymouth.
Song: "Roses and pinks." *Fr.* The Unfortunate Lovers.
Song: "Wake all the dead! What hoa! What hoa!" *Fr.* The Law against Lovers.
To a Mistress Dying.
To the Queen, Entertain'd at Night by the Countess of Anglesey.
Tomorrow and Tomorrow.
Unfortunate Lovers, The, *sels.*
Wake All the Dead! What Ho! What Ho! *Fr.* The Law against Lovers.
What Is Past. *Fr.* The Cruel Brother.
Winter Storms, The.
DAVENPORT, MARIANA B. Suspended Moment.
DAVENPORT, ROBERT. King John and Matilda, *sel.*
Requiem: "Matilda, now go take thy bed." *Fr.* King John and Matilda.
DAVID, SISTER MARY. Fourth Station, *tr.*
Our Lady, Help of Christians, *tr.*
Plain Chant of the Hill Country.
Vocation.
DAVID BEN MESHULLAM. Be Not Silent.
DAVIDA, SISTER. In Gusts of Music.
DAVIDMAN, JOY. Prayer against Indifference.
DAVIDSON, DONALD. Afternoon Call.
Andrew Jackson. *Fr.* The Tall Men.
Apple and Mole.
Avalon.
Cross Section of a Landscape.
David Crockett. *Fr.* The Tall Men.
Ecclesiasticus.
Epithalamion: "Come now, though Muses are not left to sing."
Fire on Belmont Street. *Fr.* The Tall Men.
John Darrow.
John Sevier. *Fr.* The Tall Men.
Lee in the Mountains.
On a Replica of the Parthenon.
Outland Piper, An.
Pavane.
Redivivus.
Southward Returning.
Spoken at a Castle Gate.
Tall Men, The, *sels.*
Utterance.
Wolf, The.
DAVIDSON, EDWARD. In This Dark House.
DAVIDSON, FRANCIS. Beggars.
DAVIDSON, GUSTAV. Ambushed by Angels.
Bird of Time.
Imperatrix.
Nevertheless.
Somewhere I Chanced to Read.
DAVIDSON, IRENE MARY. Little Towns, The.
DAVIDSON, JOHN. Ballad in Blank Verse of the Making of a Poet, A, *sels.*
Ballad of a Nun, A.
Ballad of Heaven, A.
Ballad of Hell, A.
Butterflies.
Chilterns, The.
Christmas Eve.
Cinque Port, A.
Eclogue: Merchantman, The.
Epping Forest. *Fr.* November.
Fleet Street Eclogues, *sels.*
Greenock. *Fr.* A Ballad in Blank Verse on the Making of a Poet.
Harvest-Home Song.
Holiday at Hampton Court.
I Haunt the Hills That Overlook the Sea. *Fr.* The Testament of a Man Forbid.
Imagination. *Fr.* New Year's Eve.
In Romney Marsh.
Last Journey, The. *Fr.* The Testament of John Davidson.
Last Rose, The.
London.
Man as God. *Fr.* A Ballad in Blank Verse of the Making of a Poet.
Merchantman, The.
New Year's Eve, *sel.*
Northern Suburb, A.
November, *sel.*
On Entering a Chapel.
Outcast, The.
Piper, Play!
Prescription for a Spring Morning, A. *Fr.* Fleet Street Eclogues.
Price, The.
Runnable Stag, A.
St. George's Day, *sel.*
St. Michael's Mount.
Song: "Boat is chafing at our long delay, The."
Song: "Closes and courts and lanes."
Spring Song.
Summer.
Testament of a Man Forbid, The, *sels.*
Testament of a Prime Minister, The, *sels.*
Testament of John Davidson, The, *sels.*
Thirty Bob a Week.
To the New Men.
To the New Women.
Unknown, The.
Vengeance of the Duchess, The.
Vivian's Speech.
Waiting.
DAVIDSON, MARGARET GILMAN GEORGE. Moritura.
DAVIDSON, THOMAS. And There Will I Be Buried.
Love's Last Suit.
Lullaby: "Hush thee, sweet baby."
DAVIE, DONALD. At Knaresborough.
Dissent; a Fable.
Evangelist, The.
Garden Party, The.
Homage to William Cowper.
On Bertrand Russell's "Portraits from Memory."
Remembering the 'Thirties.
DAVIES, BLODWEN. Resurrection.
DAVIES, CHARLES. Portrait of Several Selves.
There Is a Poem Everywhere.
DAVIES, CONSTANCE French Polisher, The.
New Triads.
Rhaiadr.
DAVIES, DUDLEY G. Migrants.
Vichy.
DAVIES, E. J. FRANCIS. To My Little Daughter.

Davies, Idris. From Ammanford to Fleur-de-Lys.
Gwalia Deserta, *sel.*
Hywel and Blodwen.
Interlude.
Lay Preacher Ponders, The.
Renaissance.
Sonnet: "I tossed my golden anchor to the sea."
William Morris.
Davies, John, of Hereford. Against Gaudy, Bragging, Undoughty Daccus.
Against Mustolphus His Lying.
Against the Fantastical Attire That Many Ladies Wear Nowadays.
Author Loving These Homely Meats, The.
Buttered Pippin-Pies.
Homely Meats.
Lies have short wings. He lies that so sings.
Little or nothing said soon mended is.
Of a Flatterer.
Of the Small Respect Had of Learned Men in General.
Sonnet: "It is as true as strange, else trial feigns."
Sonnet: "So shoots a star as doth my mistress glide."
Spend and God will send, but wot ye what follows?
To Old John Heywood, the Epigrammatist, Wheresoever.
To Our English Terence, Mr. Will. Shakespeare.
Davies, Sir John. Acclamation, An. *Fr.* Nosce Teipsum.
Ad Musam.
Affliction. *Fr.* Nosce Teipsum.
Contention between Four Maids Concerning That Which Addeth Most Perfection to That Sex.
Contention betwixt a Wife, a Widow, and a Maid, A.
Dance of Love, The. *Fr.* Orchestra.
Dancing of the Air, The. *Fr.* Orchestra.
Dancing Sea, The. *Fr.* Orchestra.
Dedication: "Strongest and the noblest argument, The." *Fr.* Nosce Teipsum.
Dedication: "To that clear majesty which in the north." *Fr.* Nosce Teipsum.
Dedications [*of* Orchestra].
Gulling Sonnets, *sels.*
Hardness of her heart and truth of mine, The. *Fr.* Gulling Sonnets.
Hymns of [*or* to] Astraea, *sels.*
I Know Myself a Man. *Fr.* Nosce Teipsum.
Immortality of the Soul, The ("All moving things to other things do move"). *Fr.* Nosce Teipsum.
Immortality of the Soul, The ("For why should we the busy soul believe"). *Fr.* Nosce Teipsum.
In Ciprium, *after* Martial.
In Dacum.
In Decium.
In Flaccum.
In Gerontem.
In Haywodum.
In Rufum.
In Severum.
In Titum.
In What Manner the Soul Is United to the Body. *Fr.* Nosce Teipsum.
Knowledge and Reason. *Fr.* Nosce Teipsum.
Lover, under burthen of his mistress' love, The. *Fr.* Gulling Sonnets.
Man. *Fr.* Nosce Teipsum.
Mariner's Song, The.
Meditations of a Gull.
Much Knowledge, Little Reason. *Fr.* Nosce Teipsum.
Muse Reviving, The.
My case is this: I love Zepheria bright. *Fr.* Gulling Sonnets.
Nosce Teipsum.
Nosce Teipsum, *sels.*
Of a Gull, *after* Martial.
Of Astraea. *Fr.* Hymns of Astraea.
Of Homer's Odyssey. *Fr.* Orchestra.
Of Human Knowledge. *Fr.* Nosce Teipsum.
Of Tabacco.
Of the Soul of Man and the Immortality Thereof. *Fr.* Nosce Teipsum.
On a Pair of Garters.
Orchestra; or, A Poem of Dancing.
Orchestra; or, A Poem of Dancing, *sels.*
Sacred muse that first made love divine, The. *Fr.* Gulling Sonnets.
Sea Danceth, The. *Fr.* Orchestra.
Sight.
Sonnets to Philomel, *sels.*
Soul and the Body, The. *Fr.* Nosce Teipsum.
That the Soul Is Immortal, and Cannot Die. *Fr.* Nosce Teipsum.
To Astraea. *Fr.* Hymns of Astraea.
To Envy. *Fr.* Hymns of Astraea.
To His Good Friend, Sir Anthony Cooke. *Fr.* Gulling Sonnets.
To His Lady.
To His Very Friend, Master Richard Martin. *Fr.* Dedications [*of* Orchestra].
To My Most Gracious Dread Sovereign. *Fr.* Nosce Teipsum.
To the Lark. *Fr.* Hymns of Astraea.
To the Month of September. *Fr.* Hymns of Astraea.
To the Prince. *Fr.* Dedications [*of* Orchestra].
To the Rose. *Fr.* Hymns of Astraea.
To the Spring. *Fr.* Hymns of Astraea.
Vanity of Human Learning, The, *sel.*
Virgin Queen, The; an Anagram. *Fr.* Hymns of Astraea.
Visitors.
Which Is a Proud, and Yet a Wretched Thing. *Fr.* Nosce Teipsum.
Davies, Leland. Mandrake, The.
Davies, Mary Carolyn. After All and After All.
Armistice Day.
Be Different [*or* Deferent] to Trees.
Being a Daughter.
Borrower. *Fr.* A Girl's Songs.
By an Iris-shadowed Pool.
Cloistered.
Comrades of the Trail.
David.
Day before April, The.
Dead Make Rules, The.
Discovery, The.
Door, The.
Door-Mats.
Dream-Bearer, The.
Easter.
Feet.
Fishing Pole, The.
Free. *Fr.* A Girl's Songs.
Honeymoon.
Hunger.
If I Had Known.
If I Were Santa's Little Boy.
I'll Wear a Shamrock.
June.
Kiss, The. *Fr.* A Girl's Songs.
Leading.
Left Out.
Let Me Be a Giver.
Let's Have a Picnic Out-of-Doors.
Love Song.
Men Are the Devil.
New Year, A.
Of Roses.
Out of the Earth.
Peak, The.
Prayer for a Marriage, A.
Prayer for a Sleeping Child, A.
Prayer for Every Day, A.
Rust.
Saturday's Party in Fairyland, The.
Sea Gull.
Seeking.
Smith of the Third Oregon, Dies.
Song: "Because I love, I weep."
Song: "We cannot die, for loveliness."
Spring Sows Her Seeds.
Stars, The.
Terrible Dead, The.
To Give One's Life.
Traps.
Tree Birthdays.
Vintage. *Fr.* A Girl's Songs.
Vow for New Year's, A.
What the Christmas Tree Thinks.
We.
Davies, Rhys. Louvre.
Seine.
Davies, William Henry. Ale.
Ambition.
Beautiful, The.
Bell, The.
Best Friend, The.
Bewitched.
Bird of Paradise, The.
Birds.
Body and Spirit.
Born of Tears.
Bust, The.
Captive Lion, The.
Charms.
Child and the Mariner, The.
Child's Pet, A.
Christ the Man.
Clouds.
Come, Let Us Find.
Days That Have Been.
Days Too Short.
Dog, The.
Dreams of the Sea.
Early Morn.
Early Spring.
East in Gold, The.
Elements, The.
Epitaph, An: "Beneath this stone lies one good man; and when."
Example, The.
Fancy's Home.
Flirt, The.
Fog, The.
Foliage, *sel.*
Forgiveness.
Great Time, A.
Greeting, A.
Happy Child, The.
Happy Wind.
Hawk, The.
Heap of Rags, The.
Her Merriment.
Hermit, The.
Hour of Magic, The.
I am the Poet Davies, William.
In May.
In Spring-Time.
In the Country.
In the Snow.
Jenny Wren.
Joy.
Joy and Pleasure.
Joy of Life, The.
Kingfisher, The.
Leaves.
Leisure.
Little Ones, The.
Love, like a Drop of Dew.
Lovely Dames.
Lovely Woman, A.
Love's Caution.
Mind's Liberty, The.
Mirror, The.
Money.
Moon, The.
Mother to Her Sick Child, A.
Mourner, The.
My Love Could Walk.
Nature's Friend.
No Master.
Oh, Sweet Content.
One Poet Visits Another.
One Token.
Pond, The.
Poor Kings.
Rabbit, The.
Rags and Bones.
Rain, The.
Rainbow, The.
Raptures.
Rich Days.
Rivals, The.
Sadness and Joy.
Sailor to His Parrot, The.
School's Out.
Sheep.

DAVIES, WILLIAM HENRY (*continued*)
Sleepers, The.
Sluggard, The.
Snowflake, The.
Songs of Joy.
Strong Moments.
Sweet Stay-at-Home. *Fr.* Foliage.
Telling Fortunes.
Thought, A.
Thunderstorms.
To a Lady Friend.
Trick, The.
Truly Great.
Truth, The.
Tugged Hand, The.
Two Stars, The.
Villain, The.
Wasted Hours.
Ways of Time, The.
When Yon Full Moon.
White Cascade, The.
White Monster, The.
White Sheep.
Wild Blossoms.
Wind, The.
Winter's Beauty.
World my guide, I lived to learn, The.
Worms' Contempt, The.
DAVIES-WOODROW, CONSTANCE. *See* WOODROW, CONSTANCE DAVIES.
DA VINCI, LEONARDO. *See* LEONARDO DA VINCI.
DAVIS, A. S., JR. Dawn Song—Pachayachachi's Gate.
DAVIS, ALBERT SAMUEL. Before the Storm.
DAVIS, CATHERINE W. After a Time.
Insights.
Nausea.
DAVIS, CHARLES S. Washington's Birthday.
DAVIS, CHESTER M. Easter Prayer, An.
DAVIS, DANIEL WEBSTER. Hog Meat.
'Weh down Souf.
DAVIS, DOROTHY MARIE. Roustabout Moon, The.
DAVIS, EDNA ETHEL. Lore.
DAVIS, EDWARD PARKER. Woodrow Wilson.
DAVIS, EMILY. *See* PFEIFFER, EMILY.
DAVIS, FANNIE STEARNS (Fannie Stearns Gifford). Afternoon.
Ancient Beautiful Things.
As in a Picture-Book.
Circus, The.
Comrades.
Evening Song.
For a Child.
Gipsy Feet.
Good-bye!
Lost Dream, The.
Moods, The.
Moon Folly. *Fr.* The Songs of Conn the Fool.
Narrow Doors, The.
Old Song, An.
Pupil Returns to His Master, The.
Pupil to His Master, The.
Sea Spell, A.
Songs of Conn the Fool, The, *sel.*
Souls.
Turn of the Road, The.
Up a Hill and a Hill.
Water Fantasy.
DAVIS, FLORENCE BOYCE. Legend of the Christmas Rose, The.
Sunsets.
This and That.
Three Wise Monkeys, The.
DAVIS, FRANCIS. Nanny.
DAVIS, FRANK MARSHALL. Flowers of Darkness.
Four Glimpses of Night.
I Sing No New Songs.
Midsummer Morn.
Rain.
Robert Whitmore.
Tenement Room; Chicago.
DAVIS, GUSSIE L. In the Baggage Coach Ahead.
DAVIS, HAROLD LENOIR. By the River.
In the Field.
My Step-Grandfather.
Old Are Sleepy, The.
Proud Riders.
Running Vines [in a Field].
Spirit, The.
Valley Harvest, The.
DAVIS, HELEN BAYLEY. Green Shawl.
Jack Frost.
DAVIS, J. C. Cowboy Race, A.
DAVIS, JOHN. Sun, The.
DAVIS, JOHN FRANCIS. Poems Translated from the Chinese, *tr.*
DAVIS, JULIA JOHNSON. Loss.
She Sews Fine Linen.
To My Little Son.
DAVIS, LELAND. Ballad of Adam's First, The.
DAVIS, MARY [*or* MOLLIE] EVELYN MOORE. Counsel.
Lee at the Wilderness.
DAVIS, NORMA L. Dry Time.
This Is My Song.
DAVIS, OZORA STEARNS. Brotherhood.
Courage.
Our Brother Christ.
Pathway to Paradise, The.
Today.
DAVIS, PHIL R. *See* "PHILARDEE."
DAVIS, ROBERT. I Thank Thee, Lord, for Strength of Arm.
DAVIS, ROBERT A. Dust Bowl.
Pastorale: "Willow tree leans far over the brook, A."
DAVIS, ROBERT H. Roosevelt.
Signature, A.
DAVIS, ROY. Retrospect.
Thoughts.
DAVIS, SAMUEL. Lines around Petersburg, The.
DAVIS, THOMAS OSBORNE. Battle Eve of the [Irish] Brigade, The.
Boatman of Kinsale, The.
Celts and Saxons.
Clare's Dragoons.
Fate of King Dathi, The.
Fontenoy.
Geraldines, The, *sel.*
Girl I Left behind Me, The.
Girl of Dunbwy, The.
Irish Hurrah, The.
Lament for the Death of Eoghan Ruadh [*or* Owen Roe] O'Neill.
My Grave.
My Land.
Nationality.
Oh! for a Steed.
O, the Marriage!
Sack of Baltimore, The.
This Native Land.
Tone's Grave.
Welcome, The.
Welcome, The, *sel.*
West's Asleep, The.
DAVISON, EDWARD. Don Juan's Dream.
Enchanted Heart, The.
I Heard the Old Men.
Judas.
Lovers, The.
Nocturne: "Be thou at peace this night."
Snare, The.
Willow and Water.
DAVISON, FRANCIS. Ah Cupid, I mistook thee.
Are lovers full of fire?
Are Women Fair? *at.*
Commendation of Her Beauty, Stature, Behavior, and Wit.
Her Commendation.
His Farewell to His Unkind and Unconstant Mistress.
In health and ease am I.
Like to the seely fly.
Love, if a god thou art.
Lovely boy, thou art not dead.
Madrigal V: Allusion to the Confusion of Babel.
Madrigal: "Some there are as fair to see to."
Madrigal: "Sound of thy sweet name, my dearest treasure, The."
Madrigal I: To Cupid.
My Only Star.
Ode V: His Farewell to His Unkind and Unconstant Mistress.
Ode VIII: That All Other Creatures Have Their Abiding . . .
Song: "Lady, you are with beauties so enriched."
Sonnet I: Dedication of These Rimes to His First Love.
Sonnet III: Upon His Absence from Her.
Sorrow seldom killeth any.
Sound of Thy Sweet Name, The.
Sweet, If You Like and Love Me Still.
Thou alive on earth, sweet boy.
Three Epitaphs upon the Death of a Rare Child of Six Years Old.
To Cupid.
To Samuel Daniel, Prince of English Poets.
Upon His Timorous Silence in Her Presence.
Wit's perfection, Beauty's wonder.
DAVISON, FRANCIS DOUGLAS. Bought.
DAVISON, WALTER. At Her Fair Hands.
How Can the Heart Forget Her.
Ode: "At her fair hands how have I grace entreated."
Ode II: Dialogue between Him and His Heart, A.
Sonnet I: He Demands Pardon for Looking, Loving, and Writing.
Sonnet VII: Of His Lady's Weeping.
To His Lady, Who Had Vowed Virginity.
DAWES, RUFUS. Love Unchangeable.
DAWLESS, SMITH. Conversation Piece.
DAWSON, DANIEL LEWIS. Seeker in the Marshes, The.
DAWSON, GRACE STRICKLER. To a Friend.
DAWSON, M. PHELPS. After the Fourth of July.
DAWSON, WILLIAM JAMES. Angel at the Ford, The.
Bird's Song at Morning.
Child's Portrait, A.
Deliverance.
House of Pride, The.
Ideal Memory.
Inspirations.
To a Desolate Friend.
DAY, BETH. Three Gates [of Gold].
DAY, CLARENCE. And/Or.
Historical Incidents.
Man Is But a Castaway.
Marco Polo.
Menelaus.
Might and Right.
Our Friend the Egg.
Sad Story.
DAY, DOROTHEA. Captain, The.
My Captain.
DAY, GEORGE EDWARD. Brothers.
Master of Laborers, The.
DAY, HOMAN F. Grampy Sings a Song.
DAY, JOHN. Ditty, A: "Peace, peace, peace, make no noise." *Fr.* Humour Out of Breath.
Humour Out of Breath, *sel.*
Parliament of Bees, The, *sels.*
DAY, JOHN, THOMAS DEKKER, *and* SAMUEL ROWLEY. *See* DEKKER, THOMAS, SAMUEL ROWLEY, *and* JOHN DAY.
DAY, PRICE. October Ending.
Theseus.
DAY, RICHARD EDWIN. England.
To Shakespeare.
DAY, SARAH J. Crocus.
DAY, THOMAS FLEMING. Clipper, The.
Coasters, The.
Main-Sheet Song, The.
Making Land.
DAY, WILLIAM. Mount Vernon, the Home of Washington.
DAY LEWIS, CECIL. Album, The.
All Gone.
As One Who Wanders into Old Workings.
Birthday Poem for Thomas Hardy.
Bombers.
But Two There Are . . .
Can the Mole Take.
Chiefly to Mind Appears.
Chorus: "Since you have come thus far." *Fr.* Noah and the Waters.
Christmas Tree, The.

Chrysanthemum Show, The.
Come, Live with Me and Be My Love.
Come Up, Methuselah.
Conflict, The.
Consider These, for We Have Condemned Them.
Departure in the Dark.
Desire Is a Witch.
Do Not Expect Again a Phoenix Hour.
Double Vision, The.
Eclogues (*of* Virgil), *sel., tr.*
Ecstatic, The.
Emily Brontë.
Few Things Can More Inflame.
Flight, The. *Fr.* A Time to Dance.
Flight to Australia. *Fr.* A Time to Dance.
Footsteps, The, *tr.*
From Feathers to Iron, *sels.*
Georgics, The, *sel., tr.*
Happy View, A.
Hard Frost, A.
Hornpipe.
In Heaven, I Suppose, Lie Down Together.
In Me Two Worlds.
In the Chaotic Age.
In the Heart of Contemplation.
In These Our Winter Days.
Is It Far to Go?
It Is Becoming Now to Declare My Allegiance.
I've heard Them Lilting at Loom and Belting.
Jig.
Let Us Be Off!
"Let Us Now Praise Famous Men."
Live You by Love Confined.
Love Was Once Light As Air. *Fr.* Two Songs (Written to Irish Airs).
Magnetic Mountain, The, *sels.*
Maple and Sumach.
Marriage of Two.
Moving In.
My Love Is a Tower.
Nabara, The.
Nearing Again the Legendary Isle.
Newsreel.
Noah and the Waters, *sel.*
Now She Is Like the White Tree-Rose. *Fr.* From Feathers to Iron.
O Dreams, O Destinations.
O Dreams O Destinations, *sel.*
Oh Light Was My Head. *Fr.* Two Songs (Written to Irish Airs).
On the Sea Wall.
One and One.
Overtures to Death.
Pegasus.
Poet, The.
Rest from Loving and Be Living.
Sitting, The.
Sky-wide an Estuary.
Sonnet: "To travel like a bird, lightly to view." *Fr.* O Dreams O Destinations.
Stand-to, The.
Statuette: Late Minoan.
Suppose That We, To-Morrow or the Next Day. *Fr.* From Feathers to Iron.
Tempt Me No More. *Fr.* The Magnetic Mountain.
Though Bodies Are Apart.
Though Winter's Barricade Delays. *Fr.* The Magnetic Mountain.
Time to Dance, A, *sels.*
Transitional Poem, *sel.*
Two Songs (Written to Irish Airs).
Two Travelers.
Watching Post.
When They Have Lost.
With Me My Lover Makes.
Word over All.
You That Love England.
DAYRE, SYDNEY. Remorse.
DAYTON, IRENE G. Ear Is Not Deaf.
DEAN, AGNES LOUISE. October Night.
DEAN, ELMA. Elder Brother, The (Poem for All Good and Loyal Dogs).
Old Men's Ward.
DEAN, HARRY M. Have You?
Just Keep Fishin'.
DEANE, ANTHONY C. Ballad of Jack and Jill.
Ballad of [*or* to] the *Billycock,* The.
Bo-Peep.
Cult of the Celtic, The.
Here Is the Tale.
Imitation.
Jack and Jill.
Little Jack Horner.
Ode, An: "I sing a song of sixpence."
Rural Bliss.
Rustic Song, A.
Three Mice, The.
DEARMER, GEOFFREY. Birds.
Giraffe, The.
Hands.
Turkish Trench Dog, The.
Vision, A.
Whale.
DEARMER, PERCY. Burgundian Carol (Patapan), *tr.*
Servants of the Great Adventure.
DE BARY, ANNA BUNSTON. As Rivers of Water in a Dry Place.
Bargain, The.
In the Heart.
Primrose by the Wayside, A.
Snowdrop, The.
"Thou Shalt Purge Me with Hyssop and I Shall Be Clean."
War-Time Prayer, A.
DE BÉRANGER, PIERRE JEAN. *See* BÉRANGER, PIERRE JEAN DE.
DE BRAGANÇA, NADEJDA. *See* BRAGANÇA, NADEJDA DE.
DE BRUCHÉ, COUNTESS. *See* STONER, WINIFRED SACKVILLE.
DE BURGH, H. J. Half Hours with the Classics.
DE CASSERES, BENJAMIN. Masses.
Moth-Terror.
Yogi.
DE CETINA, GUTIERRE. Madrigal: "Eyes that are clear, serene."
DE CHARMS, EDITH. Romany Lullaby, A.
DECIMUS MAGNUS AUSONIUS. *See* AUSONIUS, DECIMUS MAGNUS.
DECIUS, NICOLAUS. To God on high be thanks and praise.
DECK, JAMES G. King in His Beauty, The.
DECKER, BESSIE B. Disillusion.
DEEMS, CHARLES F. On Life's Way.
Worry.
DEEVES, M. Stonewall's Requiem.
DEFOE, DANIEL. City Magistrate. *Fr.* Reformation of Manners.
English Race, The. *Fr.* The True-born Englishman.
Kentish Petition, The, 1701, *sel.*
Reformation of Manners, *sels.*
Regenerate London. *Fr.* Reformation of Manners.
True-born Englishman, The, *sels.*
DEFORD, MIRIAM ALLEN. Carthage.
Life at Rome, *tr. Fr.* Satires.
Ronsard.
Satires (*of* Juvenal), *sel., tr.*
Traveller's Ditty.
We Shall Say.
DE FOREST, JOHN WILLIAM. Phantom Ship, The.
Sea-Maiden, The.
DE HEARN, NELLIE. Shut-In, The.
DEHMEL, RICHARD. Before the Storm.
Harvest Song.
Laborer, The.
My Drinking Song.
Silent Town, The.
Song before Night.
To ——? "I have baptized thee Withy."
Trysting, A.
Vigil.
Voice in Darkness.
DEHN, PAUL. Alternative Endings to an Unwritten Ballad.
At the Dark Hour.
Fern House at Kew.
Game of Consequences, A.
Government Official.
Ice on the Round Pond.
Lament for a Sailor.
Leaden Treasury of English Verse, A, *sel.*
Rhymes for a Modern Nursery, *sels.*
Whenas in Jeans.
DEISSLER, MARY LOUISE. Man of Galilee.
DEITZ, PURD EUGENE. Builders.
DE KAY, CHARLES. Arcana Sylvarum.
Draft Riot, The.
Peace.
Tornado, The.
Ulf in Ireland.
DEKKER, THOMAS. Brave iron! brave hammer! from your sound. *Fr.* London's Tempe.
Catch, A: "Cold's the wind." *Fr.* The Shoemaker's Holiday.
Christ's Coming to Judgment.
Cold's the wind, and wet's the rain. *Fr.* The Shoemaker's Holiday.
Drinking Song. *Fr.* The Shoemaker's Holiday.
Entertainment to James, *sel.*
First Three-Man's Song, The. *Fr.* The Shoemaker's Holiday.
First True Gentleman, The. *Fr.* The Honest Whore.
Fortune and Virtue. *Fr.* Old Fortunatus.
Fortune Smiles. *Fr.* Old Fortunatus.
Hey Derry Derry. *Fr.* The Shoemaker's Holiday.
Honest Whore, The, *sel.*
Hush, Hush, Hush!
King's Entertainment, The, *sel.*
London's Tempe; or, The Field of Happiness, *sel.*
Maytime. *Fr.* The Shoemaker's Holiday.
O Pittie. *Fr.* Old Fortunatus.
O, the Month of May. *Fr.* The Shoemaker's Holiday.
Old Fortunatus, *sels.*
Pleasant Comedie of Old Fortunatus, The, *sels.*
Portrait, A.
Priest's Song, A. *Fr.* Old Fortunatus.
Saint Hugh. *Fr.* The Shoemaker's Holiday.
Second Three-Man's Song, The. *Fr.* The Shoemaker's Holiday.
Shoemaker's Holiday, The, *sels.*
Song: "Fortune smiles: cry holiday." *Fr.* Old Fortunatus.
Song: "Virtue's branches wither, virtue pines." *Fr.* Old Fortunatus.
Song of the Cyclops, The. *Fr.* London's Tempe.
Troll the Bowl! *Fr.* The Shoemaker's Holiday.
Troynovant. *Fr.* The King's Entertainment.
Virtue's branches wither, virtue pines. *Fr.* Old Fortunatus.
DEKKER, THOMAS, *and* JOHN FORD. Cast away care, he that loves sorrow. *Fr.* The Sun's Darling.
Country Glee. *Fr.* The Sun's Darling.
Haymakers, rakers, reapers, and mowers. *Fr.* The Sun's Darling.
Live with Me Still. *Fr.* The Sun's Darling.
Song: "Haymakers, rakers, reapers, and mowers." *Fr.* The Sun's Darling.
Sun's Darling, The, *sels.*
DEKKER, THOMAS, SAMUEL ROWLEY, *and* JOHN DAY. Noble Soldier, The, *sel.*
O Sorrow, Sorrow. *Fr.* The Noble Soldier.
DEKKER, THOMAS, *and others.* Art thou poor, yet hast thou golden slumbers? *Fr.* The Pleasant Comedy of Patient Grissell.
Basket Maker's Song. *Fr.* The Pleasant Comedy of Patient Grissell.
Beauty, Arise! *Fr.* The Pleasant Comedy of Patient Grissell.
Bridal Song. *Fr.* The Pleasant Comedy of Patient Grissell.
Content. *Fr.* The Pleasant Comedy of Patient Grissell.
Cradle Song: "Golden slumbers kiss

Dekker, Thomas, *and others* (*cont.*)
your eyes." *Fr.* The Pleasant Comedy of Patient Grissell.
Golden Slumbers. *Fr.* The Pleasant Comedy of Patient Grissell.
Happy Heart, The. *Fr.* The Pleasant Comedy of Patient Grissell.
O Sweet Content. *Fr.* The Pleasant Comedy of Patient Grissell.
Patient Grissell, *sels.*
Pleasant Comedy of Patient Grissell, The, *sels.*
Sweet Content. *Fr.* The Pleasant Comedy of Patient Grissell.
Delafield, Harriet L. No Escape.
De la Mare, Walter ("Walter Ramal").
Alas, Alack!
All but Blind.
All That's Past.
Alone.
Alulvan.
Arabia.
As Lucy Went a-Walking.
As Soon as Ever Twilight Comes.
At Ease.
At the Keyhole.
Autumn.
Away.
Ballad of Christmas, A.
Bandog, The.
Barber's, The.
Bead Mat, The.
Bees' Song, The.
Before Dawn.
Berries.
Bewitched.
Bluebells.
Bones.
Bookworm, The.
Bottle, The.
Breughel's Winter.
Buckle, The.
Bunches of Grapes.
Burning-Glass, The.
Catechism, The.
Cecil.
Chart, The.
Chicken.
Child Asleep, A.
Child's Day Begins, A.
Clear Eyes.
Cupboard, The.
Dark Chateau, The.
Daybreak.
Dream-Song.
Dreamer, The.
Dreams, *sel.*
Dunce, The.
Dust to Dust.
Echo.
Eeka, Neeka.
End, The.
Englishman, The.
Epitaph, An: "Here lies a most beautiful lady."
Estranged.
Exile, The.
Faint Music.
Fare Well.
Farewell: "Look thy last on all things lovely."
Farewell: "When I lie where shades of darkness."
Feckless Dinner Party, The.
Fiddler, A.
Five Eyes.
Fly, The.
Forests.
Full Moon.
Funeral, The.
Galliass, The.
Ghost, The.
Go Far; Come Near.
Good-bye.
Happy, Happy It Is to Be.
Hare, The.
Haunted.
Hawthorn Hath a Deathly Smell, The.
Hidden Mermaids, The.
Holly, The.
Horn, The.
Horse in a Field.
Horseman, The.
How Sleep the Brave.
Huntsmen, The.
I Met at Eve.
I Saw Three Witches.
I Sit Alone.
In Memory of G. K. Chesterton.
In the Dock.
Isle of Lone, The.
Jim Jay.
Journey, The.
Keep Innocency.
Keys of Morning, The.
King David.
Kiph.
Last Chapter, The.
Last Coachload, The.
Linnet, The.
Listeners, The.
Little Green Orchard, The.
Little Salamander, The.
Lob Lie-by-the-Fire.
Lord of Tartary.
Lost Playmate, The.
Lost Shoe, The.
Lovelocks.
Lucy.
Lullaby: "Sleep, sleep, lovely white soul."
Macbeth.
Maerchen.
Many a Mickle.
Marionettes, The.
Martha.
Me.
Miracle, The.
Miss Loo.
Miss T.
Mrs. MacQueen.
Mocking Fairy, The.
Moonlight.
Moonshine.
Moth, The.
Music.
Napoleon.
Never More, Sailor.
Nicholas Nye.
Night.
No Bed.
Nod.
Nostalgia.
Not That Way.
O Dear Me!
O for a Moon to Light Me Home.
Off the Ground.
Old Angler, The.
Old Men, The.
Old Shellover.
Old Soldier, The.
Old Summerhouse, The.
Old Susan.
Owl, The.
Peace.
Peak and Puke.
Pollie.
Polonius.
Pooh!
Poor Henry.
Prince, The.
Quack!
Queen Djenira.
Queen Wasp, A.
Quiet Enemy, The.
Railway Junction, The.
Rainbow, The.
Remembrance.
Riddlers, The.
Ride-by-Nights, The.
Robin, A.
Ruinous Abbey, The.
Sam.
Sam's Three Wishes; or, Life's Little Whirligig.
Scarecrow, The.
Scribe, The.
Seeds.
Shadow, The.
Ship of Rio, The.
Silence.
Silver.
Silver Penny, The.
Sleeper, The.
Sleepyhead.
Slim Cunning Hands.
Snowflake, The.
Softly, Drowsily.
Solitude.
Someone [*or* Some One].
Somewhere.
Song of Enchantment, A.
Song of Finis, The.
Song of Shadows, The.
Song of Soldiers, The.
Song of the Mad Prince, The.
"Sooeep!"
Spectre, The.
Stranger, The.
Summer Evening.
Sunday, A.
Sunk Lyonesse.
Sunken Garden, The.
Suppose.
Sweep thy faint strings, Musician.
Tailor, The.
Tartary.
Then.
Then as Now.
There Blooms No Bud in May.
Three Beggars, The.
Three Cherry Trees, The.
Tillie.
Tired Tim.
Tit for Tat.
To a Candle.
Tom's Angel.
Tom's Little Dog.
Trees.
Truants, The.
Unregarding.
Unstooping.
Vacant Farmhouse, The.
Vain Questioning.
Veil, The.
Visitant, The.
Voices.
Wanderers.
When the Rose Is Faded.
Why?
Widow's Weeds, A.
Will Ever?
Willow, The.
Winter.
Winter Dusk.
World of Dream, The.
Deland, Margaret. Affaire d'Amour.
Bossy and the Daisy.
By One Great Heart.
Christmas Silence, The.
Clover, The.
Doubt.
Easter Music.
Fairies' Shopping, The.
First Best Christmas Night, The.
Life.
Love and Death.
Love's Wisdom.
Sent with a Rose to a Young Lady.
Waits, The.
While Shepherds Watched Their Flocks by Night.
Delaney, W. W. *See* "Lee, Andy."
Delany, Clarissa Scott. Interim.
Joy.
Mask, The.
Solace.
De la Sale, ——. Young Silvia.
Delavigne, Casimir. Columbus.
De Leeuw, Adèle Louise. Auction Sale—Household Furnishings.
De Lisle, Rouget. *See* Rouget de Lisle, Claude Joseph.
Delius, Anthony. Chameleon.
Coming, The.
Ethnic Anthem, The. *Fr.* The Great Divide.
Explorer, The.
Gamblers, The.
Great Divide, The, *sels.*
Pilgrims, The.
Del Medigo, Joseph Solomon. Epigram: "If men be judged wise by their beards and their girth."
Deloney, Thomas. Fair Rosamund.
Gentle Craft, The, *sels.*
Jack of Newbury, *sels.*
Joyful New Ballad, A.
Joyful New Ballad, A, *sel.*
Lamentation of Beckles, The.
Princely Ditty in Praise of the English Rose, A.

Queen Elizabeth at Tilbury.
Song: "Primrose in the green forest, The." *Fr.* The Gentle Craft.
Song of the Banishment of Two Dukes, Hereford and Norfolke, A.
Weavers' Song, The. *Fr.* Jack of Newbury.
Widow's Solace, The.
Winning of Cales, The.
Would God That It Were Holiday! *Fr.* The Gentle Craft.
DE LONG, JUANITA. My Hereafter.
DE LONGCHAMPS, JOANNE. Blind, I Speak to the Cigarette.
DELVIEG, ANTON. Romance.
Russian Song: "Ah, you night, you."
Russian Song: "Sang a little bird, and sang."
DEMAREST, MARY AUGUSTA. My Ain Countree.
DEMARU. Silly little fireflies, The.
DE' MEDICI, LORENZO. *See* MEDICI, LORENZO DE'.
DE MILLE, JAMES. Maiden of Passamaquoddy, The.
DEMIRJIAN, DERENIK. Eve of Ascension Day, The.
DEMIRJIBASHIAN, ELIA. Song of the Vulture, The.
DEMODOCUS. Snake It Was That Died, The.
DEMOREST, WILLIAM CURTIS ("Will Seedy"). Little Flag on Our House, The.
DE MORGAN, AUGUSTUS. Fleas, The.
Great Fleas.
On Fleas.
DEMOSTHENES. Epitaph on Those Who Fell at the Battle of Chaeronea.
DEMPSEY, MRS. S. L. Brown Eyes.
DENBY, EDWIN. Air.
First Warm Days.
Northern Boulevard.
DENHAM, SIR JOHN. Aeneid, The, *sel., tr.*
Cooper's Hill.
Cooper's Hill, *sels.*
Destruction of Troy, The, *tr. Fr.* The Aeneid.
Elegie upon the Death of the Lord Hastings, An.
Natura Naturata.
On Mr. Abraham Cowley, His Death and Burial amongst the Ancient Poets.
On Mr. Abraham Cowley, His Death and Burial amongst the Ancient Poets, *sel.*
On the Earl of Strafford's Trial and Death.
Reader, preserve thy peace; those busy eyes.
Somnus [the Humble God]. *Fr.* The Sophy.
Sophy, The, *sel.*
Thames, The. *Fr.* Cooper's Hill.
Thames from Cooper's Hill, The. *Fr.* Cooper's Hill.
DENIEHY, DANIEL HENRY. To His Wife.
DENISON, J. P. Wing Tee Wee.
DENMAN, ANNIE. For His Sake.
DENNEN, GRACE ATHERTON. Coming of Dawn, The.
Gold-of-Ophir Roses.
DENNEY, REUEL. Boxer Called Panther, A.
Elegy on the Pilot.
Hammer-Throw, The.
Laboratory Midnight, The.
DENNIS, CLARENCE JAMES. Ant Explorer, The.
Intro, The.
Joi, the Glug.
Pilot Cove.
Stoush o' Day, The.
DENNY, SIR EDWARD. Hope of Our Hearts.
DENNY, ERNEST. Julian the Apostate.
DENNYS, JOHN. Angler's Song, The. *Fr.* The Secrets of Angling.
Secrets of Angling, The.
Secrets of Angling, The, *sel.*
DENTON, CLARA JANETTA. Something Better.
Something to Be Thankful For.
DE PEYSTER, JAMES WATTS. Surrender of Burgoyne, The.
DERBY, EDWARD GEORGE GEOFFREY SMITH STANLEY, 14TH EARL OF. Ajax Prays for Light, *tr. Fr.* The Iliad.
Elders of Troy Behold Helen, The, *tr. Fr.* The Iliad.
Fall of Cleopatra, The, *tr. Fr.* Odes.
Iliad, The, *sels., tr.*
Odes (*of Horace*), *sel., tr.*
Shade of Patroclus, The, *tr. Fr.* The Iliad.
Sing, O Muse, *tr. Fr.* The Iliad.
DERHAM, ENID. Farewell: "I leave the world to-morrow."
Mountain Road, The.
O City, Look the Eastward Way.
Suburbs, The.
DERLETH, AUGUST. Bart Hinch.
Lois Malone.
Man at the Window.
Mark of Man, Mark of Beast.
Planetary Arc-Light, The.
Shores of Night, The.
Stranger in the Night.
Ted Birkett.
Weldon House.
DERMODY, THOMAS. Decayed Monastery, A.
John Baynham's Epitaph.
Ode to Myself, An.
Petition of Tom Dermody to the Three Fates in Council Sitting, The.
Shepherd's Despair, The.
"DER NISTOR" (Pinhas Kahanovitch). At the Doors.
DERWOOD, GENE. After Reading St. John the Divine.
Bird, Bird.
Camel.
Elegy: "When in the mirror of a permanent tear."
Elegy on Gordon Barber, Lamentably Drowned in His Eighteenth Year.
In Common.
In the Proscenium.
Innocent, The.
Mailed to G. B.
N. B., Symmetrians.
Rides.
Shelter.
So, Man?
Spring Air.
Star.
Third Madrigal.
To George Barker.
War's Clown in the Proscenium.
With God Conversing.
DERZHAVIN, GAVRIL ROMANOVICH. God.
O, Thou Eternal One!
On the Emperor's Departure, December 7, 1812.
Time's Long and Everflowing River.
DE SAVITZSKY, ISABEL. Christmas Tree, The.
DESBORDES-VALMORE, MARCELINE. Roses of Saadi, The.
Withered Crown, The.
DESCHAMPS, EUSTACHE. Knightly Code, The.
Virelay: "Am I, am I beautiful?"
DE SÉLINCOURT, MRS. AUBREY. *See* MCLEOD, IRENE RUTHERFORD.
DESHOULIÈRES, ANTOINETTE DU LIGIER DE LA GARDE. Grisette Dines.
DESNOS, ROBERT. Complaint of Fantomas.
Epitaph: "I have lived through these times and for a thousand years."
Meeting.
Neighborhood of Saint-Merri, The.
Poem to the Mysterious Woman.
Undress.
You Take the First Street.
DESPORTES, PHILIPPE. Beauty's Glass.
Conquest.
His Lady's Might.
Icarus.
Sonnet, A: "Icarus is fallen here, the marvelous boy."
Those Eyes Which Set My Fancy on Afire.
Villanelle.
DESPREZ, FRANK. Lasca.
DE STEIN, SIR EDWARD. Envoi: "How shall I say good-bye to you."
DE TABLEY, JOHN BYRNE LEICESTER WARREN, 3D BARON. Anticipation.
Chorus: "In wonder and time-mists." *Fr.* Philoctetes.
Chorus: "Sweet are the ways of death to weary feet." *Fr.* Medea.
Chorus from "Medea."
Churchyard on the Sands, The.
Churchyard on the Sands, The, *sel.*
Circe.
Conclusion.
Fortune's Wheel.
Frosty Day, A.
Hymn to Astarte, *sel.*
Medea, *sel.*
Nuptial Song.
Ode, An: "Sire of the rising day."
Orestes, *sel.*
Philoctetes, *sel.*
Rural Evening.
Simple Maid, A.
Song of Dust, A.
Song of Faith Forsworn, A.
Song of the Rolling Wind, A, *sel.*
Study of a Spider, The.
Two Old Kings, The.
Woodland Grave, A.
DETRICK, DAISY L. Little Johnny Mine, The.
Ol' Jinny Mine, The.
DETT, ROBERT NATHANIEL. Rubinstein Staccato Etude, The.
DEUTSCH, BABETTE (Mrs. Avrahm Yarmolinsky). Along the Noisy Streets, *tr.*
Apocrypha.
At the Top of My Voice, *sel., tr.*
Broad Gold, *tr.*
Candles.
Capriccio.
Dancers, The.
Definition of the Soul, *tr.*
Destruction of Letters.
Distance.
Earliness at the Cape.
Fire, the Rope, *tr.*
Flight.
Force, *tr.*
Fresh Paint, *tr.*
Girl, A.
Goldfish on the Writing Desk, *tr.*
Gratitude, *tr.*
Hate! *tr.*
Here the Trace, *tr.*
History.
Homage to the Philosopher.
Hound, The.
Hunt, The.
Immortality, *tr.*
Improvisation, *tr.*
In a Museum.
It Scarcely Seems Worth While, *tr.*
Long Roads, *tr.*
Marriage.
Maternity.
Morning Workout.
My Honeyed Languor, *tr.*
New Words for an Old Song.
New York—December, 1931.
Old Women.
Out of Superstition, *tr.*
Paradigm.
Piano Recital.
Pity.
Prophet, The, *tr.*
Put Out My Eyes, and I Can See You Still, *tr.*
Reflections in a Little Park.
Saffron Flower.
Sail, A, *tr.*
Scene with Figure.
Silentium, *tr.*
Solitude.
Songs.
Sons of Our Sons, The, *tr.*
Spring, *tr.*
String Quartet.
Suffering, *tr.*

DEUTSCH, BABETTE (*continued*)
They Came to the Wedding.
Three Variations, *tr.*
To a Child.
To My Son.
Tree, The, *tr.*
Tuppence Coloured.
Twelve, The, *tr.*
Village and Factory, *tr.*
Waving a Bough, *tr.*
What Will You Do, God, When I Die? *tr.*
You Are the Future, *tr.*
DEUTSCH, BABETTE, *and* AVRAHM YARMOLINSKY. *For translations from Russian, see* AWP; JAWP; OnPM; TrRV; WBP; WoL.
For translations from German, see LiTW; OnPM; TrJP.
DEVANEY, JAMES. Evening Gleam, The.
Mortality.
Winter Westerlies.
DEVEEN, ——. Who's That Calling So Sweet?
DE VEGA, LOPE. *See* LOPE DE VEGA CARPIO, FÉLIX.
DEVER, JOSEPH. Queen of Horizons.
DE VERE, SIR AUBREY. Castleconnell.
Children Band, The.
"Children's Crusade," The.
Christmas Carol, A: "They leave the land of gems and gold."
Gougane Barra.
Kilmallock.
Landrail, The.
Liberty of the Press.
Opening of the Tomb of Charlemagne, The.
Reality.
Right Use of Prayer, The.
Rock of Cashel, The.
Shannon, The.
Spanish Point.
Waterloo.
DE VERE, AUBREY THOMAS. Autumn. *Fr.* The Year of Sorrow: Ireland, 1849.
Ballad of Sarsfield, A.
Bard Ethell, The.
Cardinal Manning.
Coleridge.
Dei Genitrix.
Dirge: "Whose were they those voices? What footsteps came near me?"
Dirge of Kildare, The.
Dirge of Rory O'More.
Divine Presence, The. *Fr.* May Carols.
Early Friendship, *wr. at.*
Epicurean's Epitaph, An.
Epilogue: "At my casement I sat by night, while the wind remote in dark valleys."
Epitaph: "He roamed half-round the world of woe."
Evening Melody.
Fest. Puritatis. *Fr.* May Carols.
Festum Nativitatis. *Fr.* May Carols.
Florence MacCarthy's Farewell to His English Love.
Flowers I Would Bring.
Friendly Blight, The.
Girl's Song, A.
Glauce.
Human Life.
Hymn for the Feast of the Annunciation.
Implicit Faith. *Fr.* May Carols.
In Ruin Reconciled.
Incompatibility.
Ione.
Joy and Sorrow.
Lines: "Sights o'er yonder snowy range, The."
Lines: "You drop a tear for those that die."
Little Black Rose, The.
Love's Spite.
Mater Amabilis.
Mater Christi. *Fr.* May Carols.
May Carols, *sels.*
Mighty Mountain Plains, The.
Monasticism.
Parvuli Ejus.
Queen's Vespers, The.
Religio Novissima.
Roisin Dubh.
Sacraments of Nature, The.
Sad Is Our Youth.
Saint Frideswida, *sel.*
Scene in a Madhouse.
Sea-Watcher, The.
Serenade: "Softly, O midnight hours!"
Song: "He found me sitting among flowers."
Song: "Little Black Rose shall be red at last, The!"
Song: "Seek not the tree of silkiest bark."
Song: "Sing the old song, amid the sounds dispersing."
Song: "Softly, O midnight hours!"
Song: "When I was young, I said to Sorrow."
Sorrow.
Spring. *Fr.* The Year of Sorrow: Ireland, 1849.
Spring Song.
Stabat Mater, *tr.*
Summer. *Fr.* The Year of Sorrow: Ireland, 1849.
Sun God, The.
Three Woes, The.
Troilus and Cressida.
Turris Eburnea. *Fr.* May Carols.
Urania.
Wedding of the Clans, The.
When I Was Young.
Winter. *Fr.* The Year of Sorrow: Ireland, 1849.
Year of Sorrow, The: Ireland, 1849.
Year of Sorrow, The: Ireland, 1849, *sels.*
You Drop a Tear.
DE VERE, EDWARD, 17TH EARL OF OXFORD. *See* VERE, EDWARD DE.
DE VERE, MARY AINGE. *See* "BRIDGES, MADELINE."
DEVEREUX, ROBERT. *See* ESSEX, ROBERT DEVEREUX, 2D EARL OF.
DE VITO, ETHEL BARNETT. Birthday Gift.
Mother.
Soldier's Dog.
DEVLIN, DENIS. Amour, *sel., tr.*
Colours of Love, The.
Encounter.
Parsifal, *tr. Fr.* Amour.
Statue and the Perturbed Burghers, The.
Tomb of Michael Collins, The.
Vestiges.
Welcome My World.
DE VRIES, PETER. To My Friends.
DEWAR, A. W. Life and the Weaver.
DEWEY, BERENICE C. Conversation.
DEWEY, GEORGE WASHINGTON. Blind Louise.
DE WITT, SAMUEL AARON. Quatrains for a Bank Cashier.
Two Sonnets for a Lost Love.
DEZOUCHE, DOROTHY. Courage.
DIAMOND, LUCY. Eskimo Baby, An.
Fairy Umbrellas.
Greenland Winter, A.
Kayak Song, A.
DIAPER, WILLIAM. Beginnings of Day, The. *Fr.* Dryades.
Dryades; or, The Nymphs Prophecy, *sels.*
Eclogue: "Lycon begin—begin the mournful tale." *Fr.* Nereides.
Edges of the Sea. *Fr.* Nereides.
Eels, Tortoises, Soles, Lampreys, *tr. Fr.* Halieuticks.
Evening and Night and Meteors. *Fr.* Dryades.
Frost at Sea. *Fr.* Nereides.
Halieuticks, *sels., tr.*
How Sea-Calves Are Born, *tr. Fr.* Halieuticks.
Imitation of the Seventeenth Epistle of the First Book of Horace, An, *sel.*
Lions and Dragons, *tr. Fr.* Halieuticks.
Mr. Diaper Wants Advancement. *Fr.* An Imitation of the Seventeenth Epistle of the First Book of Horace.
Nereides; or, Sea-Eclogues, *sels.*
Prawn and Pearl. *Fr.* Nereides.
Roses and Lilies. *Fr.* Nereides.
Sea Eclogue: "Otys, begin." *Fr.* Nereides.
Shoal of Slime-Fish, The, *tr. Fr.* Halieuticks.
Submarine Landscape. *Fr.* Nereides.
Two Sea Nymphs. *Fr.* Nereides.
DÍAZ COVARRUBIAS, JUAN. Selection, A, *sel.*
DÍAZ LOYOLA, CARLOS. *See* "ROKHA, PABLO DE."
DÍAZ MIRÓN, SALVADOR. Cloud, The.
Corpse, The.
Example, The.
Grief.
Nox.
Phantom, The.
To an Araucaria.
Within an Emerald.
DIBDIN, CHARLES. Blow High, Blow Low.
Captain Wattle and Miss Roe.
Constancy.
Heaving of the Lead, The.
Jack's Fidelity.
Jolly Young Waterman, The.
Leadsman's Song, The.
Nongtongpaw.
Perfect Sailor, The.
Poor Jack.
Poor Tom Bowling.
Poor Tom, or the Sailor's Epitaph.
Sailor's Consolation, The, *wr. at.*
Tar for All Weathers, The.
Tom Bowling [*or* Bowline].
DIBDIN, THOMAS. All's Well. *Fr.* The British Fleet.
British Fleet, The, *sel.*
Child That Has a Cold, A.
Love and Glory.
Sir Sidney Smith.
DI CASTAGNOLA, COUNTESS ALICE FAY. Mortal Combat.
DICKENS, CHARLES. Cannibal Song. *Fr.* Holiday Romance.
Fine Old English Gentleman, The; New Version.
Goblins, The.
Holiday Romance, *sel.*
Ivy Green, The. *Fr.* The Pickwick Papers.
Merry Autumn Days.
Pickwick Papers, The, *sel.*
Things That Never Die.
DICKENSON, JOHN. Shepherd's Complaint, The, *sel.*
Tityrus to His Fair Phyllis. *Fr.* The Shepherd's Complaint.
DICKIE, E. P. "And I, If I Be Lifted Up, Shall Draw All Men."
"If I Be Lifted Up."
DICKINSON, BLANCHE TAYLOR. Four Walls.
Poem: "Ah, I know what happiness is!"
Revelation.
That Hill.
To an Icicle.
Walls of Jericho, The.
DICKINSON, CHARLES MONROE. Children, The.
DICKINSON, DOROTHY. There's a hole in the fence.
DICKINSON, EMILY. Afraid? Of whom am I afraid?
After a hundred years.
After great pain a formal feeling comes.
Along the Potomac.
Alter? When the hills do.
Altered look about the hills, An.
Although I put away his life.
Amherst Train, The.
Ample make this bed.
Apparently with no surprise.
April.
Arcturus is his other name.
Are friends delight or pain?
As by the dead we love to sit.
As imperceptibly as grief.
Aspiration.

At half-past three a single bird.
Auctioneer of parting, The.
Aurora.
Autumn.
Battle-Field, The.
Beauty and Truth.
Beauty crowds me till I die.
Beauty is not caused—it is.
Because I could not stop for Death.
Because that you are going.
Beclouded.
Bee, The ("Like trains of cars").
Bee is not afraid of me, The.
Before I got my eye put out.
Beggar lad, The—dies early.
Behind me dips eternity.
Bereaved ("If he were living").
Bereaved of all, I went abroad.
Besides the autumn poets sing.
Bird, A.
Bird, A, *sel.*
Bird came down the walk, A.
Bloom is result.
Bluebird, The.
Book, A.
Brain, The ("The brain within its groove").
Brain is wider than the sky, The.
Bring me the sunset in a cup.
Brook of the Heart, The.
Bustle in a house, The.
By the Sea.
Called Back.
Cemetery, A.
Certain Slant of Light, A.
Certainty.
Chariot, The.
Chariot, The, *sel.*
Chartless.
Child's Question, The.
Choice.
Clock stopped, A—not the mantel's.
Colloquy.
Constant.
Cricket.
Crumb for Robin.
Day, A ("I'll tell you how the sun rose").
Day came slow, The.
Dear March.
Death ("The bustle in a house").
Death ("Death is a dialogue").
Death and Life.
Death-blow is a life-blow to some, A.
Delayed till she had ceased to know.
Departed to the judgment.
Difference between despair, The.
Disillusioned.
Divinest Sense.
Dost Thou Remember Me?
Doubt me.
Drowning is not so pitiful.
Dying.
Dying Eye, A.
Dying! To be afraid of thee.
Early for God.
Elysium is as far as to.
Escape.
Eternity.
Evening.
Exclusion.
Exultation is the going.
Face we choose to miss, The.
Faded boy in sallow clothes, A.
Faith is a fine invention.
Farther in summer than the birds.
Feet of people walking home, The.
Final Inch, The.
Finding is the first act.
First day's night had come, The.
Floss won't save you from an abyss.
For Charlotte Brontë.
Forbidden Fruit, I ("Forbidden fruit a flavor has").
Forbidden Fruit, II ("Heaven is what I cannot reach").
Forever at his side to walk.
Forever cherished be the tree.
Forever is composed of Nows.
Four trees upon a solitary acre.
Fringed Gentian.
Frost, The.
Gentian weaves her fringes, The.
Glass was the street.
Go not too near a house of rose.
God made a little gentian.
Going to Him! Happy letter!
Good night! which put the candle out?
Grass, The.
Great streets of silence led away.
Grief is a mouse.
Have you got a brook in your little heart.
He ate and drank the precious words.
He preached upon "breadth" till it argued him narrow.
He scanned it, staggered, dropped the loop.
Heart asks pleasure first, The.
Heart, we will forget him!
"Heavenly Father," take to thee.
Helping the Handicapped.
Hemlock, The.
Her "Last Poems."
Hope is a subtle glutton.
Hope is the thing with feathers.
How happy is the little stone.
How many times these low feet staggered.
How the waters closed above him.
Hummingbird, The.
Hunger.
I am afraid to own a body.
I asked no other thing.
I cannot dance upon my toes.
I cannot live with you.
I died for beauty.
I dreaded that first robin so.
I dwell in Possibility.
I felt a cleavage in my mind.
I felt a funeral in my brain.
I found the phrase to every thought.
I got so I could hear his name.
I had been hungry all the years.
I had no time to hate.
I had not minded walls.
I have a king who does not speak.
I have never seen volcanoes.
I have not told my garden yet.
I heard a fly buzz when I died.
I held a jewel in my fingers.
I know a place where summer strives.
I know some lonely houses off the road.
I know that He exists.
I like a look of agony.
I like to see it lap the miles.
I make his crescent fill or lack.
I many times thought peace had come.
I meant to find her when I came.
I meant to have but modest needs.
I measure every grief I meet.
I never hear that one is dead.
I never lost as much.
I never saw a moor.
I read my sentence steadily.
I reckon, when I count at all.
I should not dare to be so sad.
I started early, took my dog.
I stepped from plank to plank.
I taste a liquor never brewed.
I tend my flowers for thee.
I thought that nature was enough.
I took my power in my hand.
I took one draught of life.
I went to heaven.
I would not paint a picture.
I years had been from home.
If anybody's friend be dead.
If I can stop one heart from breaking.
If I should die.
If I shouldn't be alive.
If my bark sink.
If you were coming in the fall.
I'll tell you how the sun rose.
I'm ceded.
I'm nobody! Who are you?
I'm wife.
Immortal is an ample word.
Immortality.
In a Library.
In lands I never saw, they say.
In the Garden.
In winter, in my room.
Indian Summer.
Inebriate of Air.
Intoxication.
Is Heaven a physician?
It dropped so low in my regard.
It is an honourable thought.
It sounded as if the streets were running.
It was a quiet way.
It was not death, for I stood up.
It would have starved a gnat.
It's such a little thing to weep.
I've known a Heaven like a tent.
I've seen a dying eye.
Jesus! thy Crucifix.
Joy in Insecurity.
Just lost when I was saved.
Keeping the Sabbath.
Lady red upon the hill, A.
Lamp burns sure, within, The.
Last night that she lived, The.
Letter Received, A.
Letter to the World.
Life.
Light exists in spring, A.
Lightly stepped a yellow star.
Lightning is a yellow fork, The.
Little Toil of Love, The.
Locomotive, The.
Lonely House, The.
Love can do all but raise the dead.
Love is that later thing than death.
Love's stricken "Why."
March.
Moon, The.
Morning.
Morns are meeker than they were, The.
Mountain sat upon the plain, The.
Mountains grow unnoticed, The.
Much madness is divinest sense.
Mushroom is the elf of plants, The.
Musicians wrestle everywhere.
My friend must be a bird.
My life closed twice before its close.
My life had stood a loaded gun.
My nosegays are for captives.
My triumph lasted till the drums.
Mysteries.
Mystery of Pain.
Narrow fellow in the grass, A.
New feet within my garden go.
No passenger was known to flee.
No rack can torture me.
No time to hate.
Nobody, A.
Not any sunny tone.
Not in vain.
Not what we did shall be the test.
Not with a club the heart is broken.
Of all the souls that stand create.
Of bronze and blaze.
Of course I prayed.
Of so divine a loss.
Once a Child.
One blessing had I, than the rest.
One crown not any seek.
One crucifixion is recorded only.
One dignity delays for all.
One sister have I in our house.
Only ghost I ever saw, The.
Only news I know, The.
Our journey had advanced.
Our little kinsmen after rain.
Our share of night to bear.
Pain has an element of blank.
Parting.
Peace.
Pedigree.
Poem: "I'll tell you how the sun rose."
Post Mortem.
Precious, mouldering pleasure 'tis, A.
Precious Words.
Presentiment is that long shadow on the lawn.
Proud of my broken heart.
Publication is the auction.
Purple Clover.
Railway Train, The.
Real.
Rearrange a wife's affection?
Remorse is memory awake.
Renunciation.
Resurgam.
Return, The.
Revery.
Revolution.
Robin, The.
Route of evanescence, A.

DICKINSON, EMILY (*continued*)
Safe in their alabaster chambers.
Said Death to Passion.
Savior! I've no one else to tell.
Sea, The.
Secret, The ("A fuzzy fellow without feet").
Secret, A ("A secret told").
Secret, The ("I have not told my garden yet").
Secret, The ("Somethings that fly there be").
Secrets.
Self-Reliance.
Service of Song, A.
Shady friend for torrid days, A.
She dealt her pretty words like blades.
She died—this was the way she died.
She lay as if at play.
She rose to his requirement, dropped.
Show, The ("The show is not the show").
Simplicity.
Sky is low, the clouds are mean, The.
Sleep.
Snake, The ("A narrow fellow in the grass").
Snake, A ("Sweet is the swamp with its secrets").
Snow, The.
So the eyes accost and sunder.
So well that I can live without.
Some keep the Sabbath [*or* Sunday] going to church.
Some things that fly there be.
Some we see no more, tenements of wonder.
Some wretched creature, savior take.
Sorrow.
Soul Alone, The.
Soul selects her own society, The.
Step lightly on this narrow spot!
Storm, The.
Struck was I, nor yet by lightning.
Success is counted sweetest.
Summer has two beginnings.
Sun, The.
Sunrise and Sunset.
Superiority to fate.
Surgeons must be very careful.
Suspense.
Tell all the truth but tell it slant.
Tempest, A.
Test, The.
That after horror that was Us.
That such have died enables us.
Their height in heaven comforts not.
There came a wind like a bugle.
There is a morn by men unseen.
There is a shame of nobleness.
There is a strength in knowing that it can be borne.
There is a word.
There is no frigate like a book.
There is no trumpet like the tomb.
There's a certain slant of light.
There's been a death.
These are the days when birds come back.
They called me to the window.
They dropped like flakes, they dropped like stars.
They might not need me; but they might.
They say that "time assuages."
Thirst.
This dirty little heart.
This is my letter to the world.
This quiet dust was gentlemen and ladies.
This world is not conclusion.
Those—dying, then.
Thought beneath so slight a film, The.
Thought went up my mind today, A.
"Till death" is narrow loving.
Tint I cannot take is best, The.
'Tis little I could care for pearls.
Title divine is mine.
To fight aloud is very brave.
To flee from memory.
To hear an oriole sing.
To know just how he suffered would be dear.
To make a prairie it takes a clover and one bee.
To my quick ear the leaves conferred.
Too late.
Train, The.
Triumph may be of several kinds, A.
Truth is as old as God.
Trying to Forget.
Twas like a maelstrom, with a notch.
'Twas warm at first like us.
Two lengths has every day.
Under the light, yet under.
Undue significance a starving man attaches.
Until the desert knows.
Utterance.
Vanished.
Waking Year, The.
Waters chased him as he fled, The.
Way I read a letter's this, The.
We cover thee, sweet face.
We do not play on graves.
We learn in the retreating.
We miss her, not because we see.
We never know how high we are.
We never know we go.
We play at paste.
What inn is this?
What of That?
What soft, cherubic creatures.
Where ships of purple gently toss.
Who robbed the woods?
Why?
Why do I love thee, Sir?
Wife at daybreak I shall be, A.
Wild nights! Wild nights!
Will there really be a morning?
Wind, The ("Of all the sounds despatched abroad").
Wind, The ("The wind tapped like a tired man").
With a Daisy.
With a Flower ("I hide myself").
With Flowers ("If recollecting were forgetting").
Within my garden rides a bird.
Wonder is not precisely knowing.
Word, A.
World feels dusty, The.
Wounded deer leaps highest, A.
You'll find it when you come to die.
DICKINSON, JOHN. Song of American Freedom, A.
DICKINSON, MARTHA GILBERT. *See* BIANCHI, MARTHA DICKINSON.
DICKINSON, PATRIC. Hounds, The.
I am no poet who can set.
Lament for the Great Yachts.
Redwing, The.
Sailors.
Swallows, The.
War.
World without End.
DICKINSON, PETER. By-Election Idyll.
DICKSON, DAVID. New Jerusalem, The, *at.*
O mother dear, Jerusalem, *at.*
DICKSON, SAMUEL HENRY. I Sigh for the Land of the Cypress and Pine.
DIEGO, GERARDO. Aesthetics.
Angelus, The.
Ballad of the River Duero.
Clouds.
Perpetual Motion.
Seesaw.
Spring.
Train, The.
Tray, The.
DIERS, THEODORE C. My Nebraska.
DIESPECKER, DICK. Between Two Furious Oceans, *sels.*
DIETMAR VON AIST. Bird Was Singing, A.
Dawn Song.
Lady Stood, A.
Linden Tree, The.
Parting at Morning.
DIETRICHSON, LORENTZ. Sunrise over the Pyramids.
DIETZ, HOWARD. On the Rising Generation.
DIGBY, GEORGE, 2D EARL OF BRISTOL. *See* BRISTOL, GEORGE DIGBY, 2D EARL OF.
DIGBY, SIR KENELM. On His Late Espoused Saint.
DIGBY, KENELM HENRY. Catholic Faith, The.
Erin.
DIGGES, LEONARD. If, of a wretched state and all forlorn.
Sonnet: "If, of a wretched state and all forlorn."
DILLENBACK, JOHN D. Colorado.
DILLER, JOHN IRVING. Lullaby Town.
DILLINGHAM, ELIZABETH T. Fairy Song, A.
DILLON, VISCOUNT. Donnybrook Jig, The, *at.*
DILLON, GEORGE. Address to the Doomed, *sel.*
Afternoon.
Albatross, The, *tr.*
All, All, *tr.*
April's Amazing Meaning.
Boy in the Wind.
Compliment to Mariners.
Elemental.
En Route.
Fall of Stars.
Hard Lovers, The.
Hours of the Day, The.
In Memory of Lake Superior.
In Two Months Now.
Kind Inn, A.
Memory of Lake Superior.
Noise of Leaves, The.
One Beauty Still.
Pigeons.
Remember, though the Telescope Extend.
Serenader.
To Losers.
What Artifice.
Woman without Fear.
DILLON, WENTWORTH. *See* ROSCOMMON, WENTWORTH DILLON, EARL OF.
DILLON, WILL, *and* HARRY VON TILZER. I want a Girl.
DIMMETTE, CELIA. Apology of the Young Scientists.
DIMOND, WILLIAM. Mariner's Dream, The.
DINI, ANTONIO SPINETTI. Parable of Generosity.
DINIS [*or* DINIZ], KING OF PORTUGAL. Alvorada: "Girl arose so lovely, The."
Cantiga de Amor: "Fair lady, I see you do complain."
Cossante: "Oh flowers, oh flowers of the tall green pine-tree."
Song: "Friend and lover mine."
DINNIES, ANNA PEYRE SHACKELFORD. Wife, The.
DINNIS, ENID. Cherub-Folk, The.
Ditty of Saint Clare, A.
Franciscan Dream, A.
Franciscan Prayer, A.
Mendicant, The.
DIODORUS. Gods Forget, The.
Little Garment, A.
DIOGENES LAERTIUS. "Ecce Quomodo Moritur Justus."
DIONYSIUS. No wasting sickness, but long years of peace.
DIONYSIUS THE SOPHIST. Rose-Girl, The.
DIOSCORIDES. Faithful Servant, A.
I, Thespis, in dramatic mould.
Lydian? Yes; to Timanthes foster father, and slave.
Old Slave, The.
Slave's Epitaph, A.
To a Spartan Mother.
Young Mother, A.
DIOTIMUS. Cow Herd, The.
Lightning, *at.*
Without the Herdsman.
DIOTIMUS OF ATHENS. Epitaph on a Flute-Player.
DIOTIMUS OF MILETUS. Epitaph on Two Aged Priestesses.
DIPHILUS. When I am asked by some rich man to dine.
DISMOND, HENRY BINGA. At Early Morn.
Status Quo.

DISRAELI, BENJAMIN, EARL OF BEACONSFIELD. Wellington.
DITLEVSEN, TOVE. Man's Love, A.
Mother Fear.
My Heart.
Snake in Paradise, The.
DITMARS, REMBRANDT WILLIAM B. Lincoln.
DIVALL, EDITH HICKMAN. Changeless.
In Whom Is No Variableness.
DIVINE, CHARLES. At the Lavender Lantern.
Little Senorita.
Look Not to Me for Wisdom.
Never Will You Hold Me.
Paris; the Seine at Night.
Spanish Song.
We Met on Roads of Laughter.
DIX, WILLIAM CHATTERTON. As with Gladness Men of Old.
Come unto me, ye weary.
Silver Lamps.
What Child Is This, Who, Laid to Rest.
DIXEY, WOLSTAN. Concert Rehearsal, The.
I Will Help You.
DIXON, GEORGE WASHINGTON. Turkey in the Straw, *at.*
DIXON, JAMES MAIN. Bard of Auld Lang Syne, The.
DIXON, RICHARD WATSON. Both Less and More.
Dream.
Feathers of the Willow, The.
Heaving Roses of the Hedge Are Stirred, The.
Holy Mother at the Cross, The.
Humanity.
If thou wast still, O stream.
Immortal Muse, The.
Love's Consolation, *sel.*
Mano; a Poetical History, *sels.*
November.
O Ubi? Nusquam.
Ode on Advancing Age.
Ode on Conflicting Claims.
Of a Vision of Hell, Which a Monk Had. *Fr.* Mano; a Poetical History.
Of Temperance in Fortune. *Fr.* Mano; a Poetical History.
Rapture; an Ode.
Skylark, The. *Fr.* Mano; a Poetical History.
Song: "Feathers of the willow, The."
Song: "Why fadest thou in death."
Sonnet: "Give me the darkest corner of a cloud."
To Fancy.
To Peace.
Why fadest thou in death.
Willow.
Winter Will Follow.
Wizard's Funeral, The.
DJELLALADIN PASHA, MAHMUD. Song: "If you love God, take your mirror between your hands and look."
DJIVAN. Good Comrade, A.
D'LETTUSO, HOMER. Old Houses.
DNYANODAYA. Wait On.
DOAK, HOUSTON LARMOUR. Beggar, The.
Scarecrow, The.
DOANE, GEORGE WASHINGTON. Banner of the Cross, The.
Bishop Doane on His Dog, *wr. at.*
Christ, the Way.
Evening.
Evening Contemplation.
Evening Hymn.
Life Sculpture.
Robin Redbreast.
Sculptors of Life.
Softly Now the Light of Day.
Way, the Truth, the Life, The.
"DOANE, JERRY." *See* MORSE, KATHARINE DUNCAN.
DOANE, WILLIAM CROSWELL. Ancient of Days.
Bishop Doane on His Dog ["Cluny"].
Death.
Hand That Rocks the Cradle, The.
Modern Baby, The.
Preacher's Mistake, The, *at.*
DOBELL, BERTRAM. Microcosm.
DOBELL, SYDNEY THOMPSON. Absent Soldier Son, The.
America.
America, *sel.*
Balder, *sels.*
Ballad of Keith of Ravelston, The. *Fr.* A Nuptial Eve.
Chanted Calendar, A. *Fr.* Balder.
Cradle Song of Amy. *Fr.* Balder.
Dante, Shakespeare, Milton. *Fr.* Balder.
Eden-Gate.
Epigram on the Death of Edward Forbes.
Even-Song, An.
Fragment of a Sleep- [*or* Sleepy] Song.
Home, in War-Time.
Home, Wounded.
How's My Boy?
Isabel.
Keith of Ravelston. *Fr.* The Nuptial Song.
Laus Deo.
Milkmaid's Song, The.
Monk's Song. *Fr.* The Roman.
Mother's Song, A. *Fr.* Balder.
Nuptial Eve, A, *sels.*
On the Death of Mrs. Browning.
Orphan's Song, The.
Procession of the Flowers, The. *Fr.* Balder.
Return!
Roman, The, *sel.*
Sea Ballad. *Fr.* Balder.
Spring's Procession. *Fr.* Balder.
This Dear English Land. *Fr.* Balder.
Tommy's Dead.
Widow's Lullaby, The.
DOBSON, AUSTIN. Ars Victrix.
At the Convent Gate.
Ballad of Antiquaries, A.
Ballad of Beau Brocade, The.
Ballad of Heroes, A.
Ballad of Imitation, The.
Ballad of the Armada, A.
Ballad of the Bore, The.
Ballad to Queen Elizabeth, A.
Ballade of Prose and Rhyme, The.
Ballade of the Pompadour's Fan.
Ballade of the Thrush.
Before Sedan.
Cap That Fits.
Child-Musician, The.
Circe. *Fr.* Rose-Leaves.
Clean Hands.
Cradle, The.
Curé's Progress, The.
Dance of Death, The.
Dead Letter, A.
Dialogue, A.
Dialogue from Plato, A.
Don Quixote.
Dora versus Rose.
Eighteenth-Century Vignettes, *sels.*
Epilogue to "Eighteenth-Century Vignettes."
Epitaph, An: "Here sleeps, at last, in narrow bed."
Fairy Tale, A.
Fame.
Fame and Friendship.
Fame Is a Food That Dead Men Eat.
Familiar Epistle, A.
Fancy from Fontanelle, A.
Farewell, Renown!
For a Charity Annual.
For a Copy of Herrick.
For a Copy of "The Vicar of Wakefield."
For a Copy of Theocritus.
For the Blinded Soldiers.
Forgotten Grave, The.
Fountain of Bandusia, The, *tr.*
Gage d'Amour, A.
Garden Song, A.
Gentleman of the Old School, A.
Glint of a Raindrop, The.
Good Luck to Your Fishing!
Good-Night, Babette!
Greek Gift, A. *Fr.* Rose-Leaves.
Greeting, A.
Growing Gray.
Henry Fielding.
Henry Wadsworth Longfellow.
Household Art.
I Intended an Ode. *Fr.* Rose-Leaves.
In After Days.
In Teacup Times.
In Town.
In Vain Today.
Incognita.
Jocosa Lyra.
Kiss, A. *Fr.* Rose-Leaves.
Ladies of St. James's, The.
Little Blue-Ribbons.
Maltworm's Madrigal, The.
Milkmaid, The.
My Books.
New and Old.
O Fons Bandusiae, *tr.*
O Navis.
On a Fan That Belonged to the Marquise de Pompadour.
On a Nankin Plate.
On the Future of Poetry.
On the Hurry of This Time.
Paradox of Time, The.
Postscript to "Retaliation," A.
Pot-Pourri.
Prodigals, The.
Prologue to "Eighteenth-Century Vignettes."
Rank and File.
Romaunt of the Rose, The.
Rondeau, The: "You bid me try, Blue-Eyes, to write."
Rondeau to Ethel, A.
Rondel; the Wanderer.
Rose and the Gardener, The.
Rose-Leaves.
Rose-Leaves, *sels.*
Song of Angiola in Heaven, A.
Song of the Four Seasons, A.
Sonnet in Dialogue, A.
Sun-Dial, The.
Tear, A. *Fr.* Rose-Leaves.
That Wooden Cross.
To a Greek Girl.
To a Missal of the Thirteenth Century.
To Brander Matthews.
To Daffodils.
To Laurence Hutton.
To "Lydia Languish."
To Q. H. F.
To Richard Watson Gilder.
To Rose. *Fr.* Rose-Leaves.
Triolet: "I intended an ode." *Fr.* Rose-Leaves.
Tu quoque.
Two Sermons.
Une Marquise.
"Urceus Exit." *Fr.* Rose-Leaves.
Voice in the Scented Night, A.
Wanderer, The.
When Burbadge Played.
When I Saw You Last, Rose.
When There Is Peace.
When This Old World Was New.
With Pipe and Flute.
You Bid Me Try.
DOBSON, ROSEMARY DE BRISSAC. Chance Met.
Cockerel Sun.
Detail from an Annunciation by Crivelli.
Devil and the Angel (1), The.
Devil and the Angel (6), The.
In a Convex Mirror.
In My End Is My Beginning.
Missal, The.
DODD, LEE WILSON. Comrade, The.
Escape, The.
Flower, The.
More Life . . . More!
Temple, The.
To Doris.
DODD, LEONARD. Compel Them to Come In.
DODD, P. Epigram: "Joe hates a sycophant. It shows."
On Joe.
DODDRIDGE, PHILIP. Amazing, Beauteous Change!
Awake, My Soul!
Dum Vivimus, Vivamus.

Doddridge, Philip (*continued*)
Hear Us, in This Thy House.
Hymn: "Ye golden lamps of heaven, farewell."
Jesus, I Love Thy Charming Name.
Live While You Live.
Prince of Peace, The.
Ye Golden Lamps of Heaven.
Dodds, Eric Robertson. Deathbed.
Iliad, The, *sel., tr.*
Moon Worshippers, The.
Patroclus' Body Saved, *tr. Fr.* The Iliad.
When the Ecstatic Body Grips.
Dodge, H. C. If.
Splendid Fellow, A.
Dodge, Henry Nehemiah. Spirit of Freedom, Thou Dost Love the Sea.
Thrustararorum.
Dodge, Josephine Daskam. *See* Bacon, Josephine Dodge Daskam.
Dodge, Mary Abigail ("Gail Hamilton"). Both Sides.
Dodge, Mary Barker. Now.
Dodge, Mary Mapes. Birdies with Broken Wings.
Bye, Baby, Night Is Come.
Christmas Eve.
Chrysanthemums.
Courtesy.
Emerson.
Frost-King, The.
Home and Mother.
In Trust.
Life in Laconics.
Little Dutchman, The.
Looking Back.
Mayor of Scuttleton, The.
Melons.
Minuet, The.
Mother.
Motherless.
Nearly Ready.
Night and Day.
Not Only in the Christmas-Tide.
Now the Noisy Winds Are Still.
Offertory.
Once Before.
One and One.
Over the Way.
Shadow-Evidence.
Snow-Flakes.
Stars, The.
Stocking Song on Christmas Eve.
Two Mysteries, The.
Waiting for Father.
Zealless Xylographer, The.
Dodge, Samuel. People Will Talk.
Dodgson, Charles Lutwidge. *See* "Carroll, Lewis."
Dodington, George Bubb, Baron Melcombe. Ode: "Love thy country, wish it well."
Shorten Sail.
Dodochian, C. A. Wandering Armenian to the Swallow, The.
Dodsley, Robert. Agriculture; a Poem, *sel.*
Epigram: "Cries Sylvia to a reverend Dean."
Kings of Europe, The; a Jest.
Song: "Man's a poor deluded bubble."
Dodson, Owen. Counterpoint.
Decision, The.
Epitaph for a Negro Woman.
Poems for My Brother Kenneth.
Rag Doll and Summer Birds.
Six o'Clock.
Doheny, Michael. A Cushla Gal Mo Chree.
Doherty, Kevin F. Astronomer, The.
Doherty, Lillian. Stella Matutina.
Dolben, Digby Mackworth. After Reading Homer.
April of the Ages, The.
Come to Me, Beloved.
Flowers for the Altar.
Garden, The.
He Would Have His Lady Sing.
Homo Factus Est.
I Asked for Peace.
Prayer, A: "From falsehood and error."
Requests.
Shrine, The.
Song: "World is young to-day, The."
Strange, All-absorbing Love.
Dole, Nathan Haskell. I do not like a swagger captain, *tr.*
Legend, A: "Christ, when a Child, a garden made," *tr.*
Lincoln's Birthday.
Man's Hidden Side.
O ye splendid children of Memory and Zeus the Olympian, *tr.*
Our Native Birds.
Patriot Hymn, The.
Russia.
Russian Fantasy, A.
To an Imperilled Traveller.
Vision of Peace, The.
Wealth of gold-abounding Croisos, The, *tr.*
What is joy of life apart from Venus the golden? *tr.*
Dollard, James Bernard ("Silav-Na-Mon"). At Dead o' the Night, Alanna.
Ballad of the Banshee.
Fairy Harpers, The.
Haunted Hazel, The.
Ould Kilkinny.
Passing of the Sidhe, The.
Rupert Brooke.
Song of the Little Villages.
Sons of Patrick, The.
Soul of Karnaghan Buidhe, The.
Dolliver, Clara G. No Baby in the House.
Dolmatovsky, Yevgeny Aronovich. Frost.
Dolson, Hildegarde. Platonic.
Religion.
Domett, Alfred. Christmas Hymn, A.
Christmas Hymn, A, *sel.*
Christmas Hymn, A: New Style, *sel.*
Christmas Hymn, A: Old Style, 1837.
Glee for Winter, A.
Maori Girl's Song, A.
Ranolf and Amohia, *sels.*
Dominici, Giovanni. Mother Most Powerful.
Domitius Marsus. On the Death of Tibullus.
Donaghy, John Lyle. At My Whisper.
Duck.
Ebb.
Fossil, The.
Glenarm.
Grave, The.
Heron, The.
Leitrim Woman, A.
Linota Rufescens.
Seeing.
Voyage.
Where the Dropwort Springs Up Lithe and Tall.
Donaghy, William Andrew. Ancestry.
Fourth Station.
He Falls. *Fr.* The Stations of the Cross.
He Is Buried. *Fr.* The Stations of the Cross.
He Is Condemned. *Fr.* The Stations of the Cross.
He Meets His Mother. *Fr.* The Stations of the Cross.
Stations of the Cross, The, *sels.*
Thirteenth Station. *Fr.* The Stations of the Cross.
Donahoe, D. J. Angelic Chorus, The.
Donaldson, Robert A. Night Road.
Donaldson, W. L. Our Village Eleven.
Doney, May. Comfort.
White Dream, The.
Donne, John. Absence, *at.*
Air[e] and Angel[l]s.
Anatomy of the World, An.
Anatomy of the World, An, *sels.*
Anniversary, The.
Anniversary, The, *sel.*
Annunciation.
Antiquary.
Apparition, The.
As due by many titles I resigne. *Fr.* Holy Sonnets.
Ascention.
At the round earth's imagin'd corners, blow. *Fr.* Holy Sonnets.
Autumnal[l], The. *Fr.* Elegies.
Bait, The.
Batter My Heart, Three-personed God. *Fr.* Holy Sonnets.
Blossom, The.
Blossom, The, *sel.*
Blow Your Trumpets, Angels. *Fr.* Holy Sonnets.
Break of Day.
Broken Heart, The.
Burnt Ship, A.
Busy old fool, unruly Sun.
But we by a love, so much refined.
Calm, The.
Canonization, The.
Change.
Community.
Computation, The.
Confined Love.
Contemplation of Our State in Our Deathbed. *Fr.* Of the Progresse of the Soule.
Crucifying.
Curse, The.
Daybreak.
Dear love, for nothing less than thee.
Death. *Fr.* Holy Sonnets.
Death, Be Not Proud. *Fr.* Holy Sonnets.
Devout Fits. *Fr.* Holy Sonnets.
Disinherited.
Dissolution, The.
Divine Sonnet. *Fr.* Holy Sonnets.
Doth Not a Tenarif, or Higher Hill. *Fr.* An Anatomy of the World.
Dream [*or* Dreame], The.
Ecstasy, The.
Elegie IX: Autumnall, The. *Fr.* Elegies.
Elegie XI: Bracelet, The. *Fr.* Elegies.
Elegie: Death, *sel.*
Elegie: Going to Bed. *Fr.* Elegies.
Elegie: His Picture. *Fr.* Elegies.
Elegie VI: "Oh, let mee not serve so, as those men serve." *Fr.* Elegies.
Elegie: On His Mistris [*or* Mistress]. *Fr.* Elegies.
Elegie on the Lady Marckham.
Elegie on the Lady Marckham, *sel.*
Elegies, *sels.*
Elegy V: His Picture. *Fr.* Elegies.
Elegy IX: "No spring nor summer beauty hath such grace." *Fr.* Elegies.
Elegy XVI: On His Mistress. *Fr.* Elegies.
Elegy on the L. C.
Epithalamion, An: "Haile Bishop Valentine, whose day this is."
Epithalamion Made at Lincolnes Inne.
Expiration, The.
Extasie [*or* Extasy], The.
Fall of a Wall.
Farewell to Love.
Father, part of his double interest. *Fr.* Holy Sonnets.
Fever [*or* Feaver], A.
First Anniversary, The, *sels.*
Flea, The.
Forget. *Fr.* Holy Sonnets.
From being anxious, or secure. *Fr.* The Litany.
Funeral[l], The.
Go and Catch a Falling Star.
Going to Bed.
Good Friday, 1613. Riding Westward.
Good-Morrow, The.
H: W: In Hiber: Belligeranti.
Hail,, Bishop Valentine. *Fr.* An Epithalamion.
Hero and Leander.
His Parting from Her. *Fr.* Elegies.
His Parting from Her, *sel. Fr.* Elegies.
His Picture. *Fr.* Elegies.
Holy Sonnets, *sels.*
Hymn[e] to Christ, at the Authors Last Going into Germany, A.
Hymn[e] to God My God, in My Sickness[e].
Hymn[e] to God My God, in My Sickness[e], *sel.*

Hymn[e] to God the Father, A.
I am a little world made cunningly. *Fr.* Holy Sonnets.
I can love both fair and brown.
I wonder, by my troth, what thou and I.
If faithful soules be alike glorifi'd. *Fr.* Holy Sonnets.
If poisonous minerals, and if that tree. *Fr.* Holy Sonnets.
Inconstancy. *Fr.* Holy Sonnets.
Indifferent, The.
Jeat Ring Sent, A.
Jesus in the Temple.
La Corona.
Lame Beggar, A.
Lecture upon the Shadow, A.
Legacy [*or* Legacie], The.
Letter to Sir H. Wotton at His Going Ambassador to Venice.
Litany [*or* Litanie], The.
Litany, The, *sels.*
Lover's Infiniteness[e].
Love's Alchemy [*or* Alchymie].
Love's Deity [*or* Deitie].
Love's Diet.
Love's Exchange.
Love's Growth.
Love's Infiniteness.
Love's Progress. *Fr.* Elegies.
Love's Usury.
Message, The.
Nativitie.
Negative Love.
New Philosophy, The. *Fr.* The First Anniversary.
Nocturnal[l] upon S. Lucies Day, A.
O how feeble is man's power.
O might those sighs and tears return again. *Fr.* Holy Sonnets.
Oh my black Soul! now thou art summoned. *Fr.* Holy Sonnets.
Oh, to vex me, contraries meet in one. *Fr.* Holy Sonnets.
Obscure Writer, An.
Obsequies of [*or* to] the Lord Harrington, The, *sel.*
Ode: "Absence, hear thou my protestation," *at.*
Of a Death in Winter, II. *Fr.* Elegie: Death.
Of the Progress[e] of the Soul[e].
Of the Progress[e] of the Soul[e], *sel.*
On His Mistress. *Fr.* Elegies.
Paradox, The.
Phryne.
Prayer for Violence. *Fr.* Holy Sonnets.
Present in Absence, *at.*
Progress of the Soul, The.
Progress of the Soul, The, *sels.*
Prohibition, The.
Pyramus and Thisbe.
Relic, The.
Religion. *Fr.* Satires.
Relique, The.
Resignation to God. *Fr.* Holy Sonnets.
Resurrection.
Satire: "Away, thou fondling motley humorist." *Fr.* Satires.
Satire III: "Kind pity chokes my spleen; brave scorn forbids." *Fr.* Satires.
Satire III: On Religion. *Fr.* Satires.
Satire: "Sir: though (I thank God for it) I do hate." *Fr.* Satires.
Satire IV: "Well; I may now receive, and die; my sinne." *Fr.* Satires.
Satires, *sels.*
Satyre: Of Religion.
Second Anniversary, The, *sels.*
Show me deare Christ, thy Spouse, so bright and clear. *Fr.* Holy Sonnets.
Since she whom I loved, hath paid her last debt. *Fr.* Holy Sonnets.
So, so, break off this last lamenting kiss.
Song: "Go and catch a falling star."
Song: "Sweetest love, I do not go."
Sonnet: "As due by many titles I resign." *Fr.* Holy Sonnets.
Sonnet: "At the round earth's imagined corners, blow." *Fr.* Holy Sonnets.
Sonnet: "Batter my heart, three-personed God, for you." *Fr.* Holy Sonnets.
Sonnet: "Death be not proud, though some have called thee." *Fr.* Holy Sonnets.
Sonnet: "I am a little world made cunningly." *Fr.* Holy Sonnets.
Sonnet: "If faithful souls be alike glorified." *Fr.* Holy Sonnets.
Sonnet: "If poysonous mineralls, and if that tree." *Fr.* Holy Sonnets.
Sonnet: "O might those sighs and tears return again." *Fr.* Holy Sonnets.
Sonnet: "O my black Soul! now thou art summonèd." *Fr.* Holy Sonnets.
Sonnet: "Oh, to vex me, contraryes meet in one." *Fr.* Holy Sonnets.
Sonnet: "Send me some token, that my hope may live."
Sonnet: "Show me deare Christ, thy spouse, so bright and cleare." *Fr.* Holy Sonnets.
Sonnet: "Since she whom I lov'd hath payd her last debt." *Fr.* Holy Sonnets.
Sonnet: "Spit in my face you Jews, and pierce my side." *Fr.* Holy Sonnets.
Sonnet: "This is my play's last scene, here heavens appoint." *Fr.* Holy Sonnets.
Sonnet: "Thou hast made me, and shall thy worke decay?" *Fr.* Holy Sonnets.
Sonnet: "What if this present were the world's last night?" *Fr.* Holy Sonnets.
Sonnet: "Why are we by all creatures waited on?" *Fr.* Holy Sonnets.
Soules Ignorance in This Life and Knowledge in the Next, The. *Fr.* Of the Progress of the Soul.
Spit in my face you Jews, and pierce my side. *Fr.* Holy Sonnets.
Stay, O sweet, and do not rise!
Storm, The.
Sun[ne] Rising, The.
Sweetest Love, I Do Not Go.
Take heed of loving me.
Temple.
That Time and Absence Proves Rather Helps than Hurts to Loves, *at.*
This Is My Body.
This is my play's last scene, here heavens appoint. *Fr.* Holy Sonnets.
Thou hast made me, and shall thy work[e] decay? *Fr.* Holy Sonnets.
'Tis true 'tis day; what though it be?
To Christ.
To His Mistress Going to Bed. *Fr.* Elegies.
To Mr. R. W. ("Zealously my Muse doth salute all thee").
To Mr. Roland Woodward ("Like one who'in her third widdowhood doth professe").
To Mr. T. W. ("At once, from hence, my lines and I depart").
To Mr. T. W. ("Pregnant again with th' old twins Hope, and Feare").
To Sir Edward Herbert at Julyers.
To Sir H. W. at His Going Ambassador to Venice.
To Sir Henry Goodyere.
To Sir Henry Wotton ("Here's no more news than virtue").
To Sir Henry Wotton ("Sir, more than kisses, letters mingle souls").
To the Countess of Bedford ("Reason is our soul's left hand").
To the Countesse of Bedford ("Honour is so sublime perfection").
To the Countesse of Bedford on New-Yeares Day.
Token, The.
Triple Fool, The.
Truth. *Fr.* Satires.
Twice or thrice had I loved thee.
Twicknam [*or* Twickenham] Garden.
Undertaking, The.
Valediction Forbidding Mourning, A.
Valediction, A; of the Booke.
Valediction, A; of Weeping.
Vision. *Fr.* An Anatomy of the World.
Whale, The. *Fr.* The Progress of the Soul.
What if this present were the world's last night? *Fr.* Holy Sonnets.
Why are we by all creatures waited on? *Fr.* Holy Sonnets.
Will, The.
Will, The, *sel.*
Wilt thou forgive that sin where I begun.
Wilt thou love God, as he thee! then digest. *Fr.* Holy Sonnets.
Witchcraft by a Picture.
Woman's Constancy.

DONNELLY, ELEANOR CECILIA. Ladye Chapel at Eden Hall.
Mary Immaculate.
Sister Mary Alphonsa.

DONNELLY, FRANCIS P. Mother Mary Xavier.

DONOHUE, JAMES J. God Said: Let There Be Sky.
Hymn: "Eternal Founder of the sky."
Last Antiphon: To Mary.
Praise of Engineers.

DONOVAN, JOHN E. Dachshund, The.
First Airing.
Pals.

DOOHER, MUREDACH J. Renascence.

DOOLITTLE, ESTHER HULL. Secret.

DOOLITTLE, HILDA ("H. D."). Adonis.
Ah (You Say), This Is Holy Wisdom. *Fr.* Tribute to the Angels.
At Baia.
At Ithaca.
Centaur Song.
Chance Meeting.
Choros: "Give me your poppies." *Fr.* Morpheus.
Chorus: "And Pergamos," *tr.* *Fr.* Iphigenia in Aulis.
Cities.
Claribel's Way to God, *sel.*
Cuckoo Song.
Egypt.
Evadne.
Evening.
Fragment 113: "Not honey,/ not the plunder of the bee."
Fragment Thirty-six: "I know not what to do."
Garden, The.
Garden, The, *sel.*
Gather for Festival. *Fr.* Songs from Cyprus.
Halcyon, *sel.*
Heat. *Fr.* The Garden.
Helen.
Heliodora.
Helmsman, The.
Hermes of the Ways.
Hermes Trismegistus. *Fr.* A Tribute to the Angels.
Hesperides.
Hippolytus Temporizes.
Holy Satyr.
Hymen, *sels.*
I would forgo.
Incident Here and There, An.
Iphigenia in Aulis, *sel., tr.*
Islands, The.
Keeper of the Orchards.
Lais.
Leda.
Let Zeus Record.
Let Zeus Record, *sel.*
Lethe.
Mid-Day.
Moonrise.
Morpheus, *sel.*
Never More Will the Wind. *Fr.* Hymen.
Not Honey.
O Heart, Small Urn.
Orchard.
Oread.
Pear Tree.
Pool, The.
Priapus.
Pygmalion.
Sea Gods.
Sea Gods, *sel.*
Sea Rose.

DOOLITTLE, HILDA (*continued*)
Second Song from Cyprus. *Fr.* Songs from Cyprus.
Sheltered Garden.
Shrine, The.
Simaetha.
Sitalkas.
Socratic.
Song: "Where is the nightingale." *Fr.* Songs from Cyprus.
Song: "You are as gold."
Songs from Cyprus.
Songs from Cyprus, *sels.*
Storm.
Swiftly Relight the Flame. *Fr.* A Tribute to the Angels.
There Is a Spell, for Instance.
Toward the Piraeus.
Tribute to the Angels, A, *sels.*
Wash of Cold River.
Where is the nightingale. *Fr.* Songs from Cyprus.
Where Love Is King. *Fr.* Hymen.
DOOP-SMITH, ETNA. Death.
DORAN, LOUISE A. Ship, The.
DORGAN, JOHN AYLMER. Beautiful, The.
Dead Solomon, The.
D'ORGE, JEANNE. Convent, The.
Enchanted Castle, The.
Portrait.
DORN, ALFRED. Challengers.
DORN, EDWARD. Air of June Sings, The.
Are They Dancing.
Hide of My Mother, The.
Rick of Green Wood, The.
Vaquero.
When the Fairies.
DORNEY, ELIZABETH. Chemistry of Character, The.
DOROTHY ANN, SISTER MARY. Exchange.
DORR, COLGATE. From the Latin of Catullus ("Diana, mistress of the evening sky"), *tr.*
Soliloquy of Cicero.
DORR, HENRY R. Comrades.
DORR, JULIA CAROLINE RIPLEY. Fallow Field, The.
Homesick.
Legend of the Organ-Builder, The.
Mother-Song, A.
No more the Thunder of Cannon.
O Earth! Art Thou Not Weary?
Outgrown.
Prayer for One Dead.
To a Late Comer.
Two Paths.
With a Rose from Conway Castle.
DORRANCE, DICK. Cockpit in the Clouds.
DORSET, CHARLES SACKVILLE, 6TH EARL OF. *See* SACKVILLE, CHARLES, 6TH EARL OF DORSET.
DORSET, THOMAS SACKVILLE, 1ST EARL OF. *See* SACKVILLE, THOMAS, 1ST EARL OF DORSET.
DOS PASSOS, JOHN. Calle de Toledo, Madrid. *Fr.* Winter in Castile.
Figures in the field against the sky! *tr.*
Four Poems, *tr.*
Frail sound of a tunic trailing, A, *tr.*
Naked is the earth, *tr.*
Paseo de la Castellana. *Fr.* Winter in Castile.
Plaza Santa Ana. *Fr.* Winter in Castile.
Poems, *tr.*
We think to create festivals, *tr.*
Winter in Castile.
DOTEN, ELIZABETH. In a Hundred Years.
Prayer, A: "God of the Granite and the Rose!" *Fr.* Reconciliation.
Reconciliation, *sel.*
DOTY, WALTER G. Best Firm, The.
DOUDNEY, SARAH. Christian's "Good-Night," The.
Lesson of the Water Mill, The. *Fr.* The Man o' Airlie.
Man o' Airlie, The, *sel.*
Sweet Surprises.
These Are Not Lost.
Water Mill, The. *Fr.* The Man o' Airlie.
DOUGHTY, CHARLES MONTAGU. Bladyn's Song of Cloten. *Fr.* The Dawn in Britain.
Dawn in Britain, The, *sels.*
Druids' Hymn to the Sun. *Fr.* The Dawn in Britain.
Fairies Feast, The.
Gauls Sacrifice Their Prisoners, The. *Fr.* The Dawn in Britain.
Roman Officer Writes Home, A. *Fr.* The Dawn in Britain.
Wayfaring, to the Valley of the Dove, *sel.*
DOUGHTY, LEGARDE S. Palimpsest.
To a King Snake.
DOUGLAS, LORD ALFRED BRUCE. Balcon, Le, *tr.*
Beauté, La, *tr.*
City of the Soul, The.
Dead Poet, The.
Each New Hour's Passage Is the Acolyte. *Fr.* The City of the Soul.
Green River, The.
Harmonie du soir, *tr.*
If He Should Come Again, *tr.*
Impression de Nuit; London.
Lighten Our Darkness.
Night Coming Out of a Garden.
Of a Dead Poet.
Plainte Eternelle.
Prayer, A: "Often the western wind has sung to me."
Sois sage o ma douleur, *tr.*
Song, A: "Steal from the meadows, rob the tall green hills."
Sonnet on the Sonnet.
Sphinx, The.
Summer Storm, A.
To Olive.
Wastes of Time, The.
Witch, The.
DOUGLAS, GAWIN [*or* GAVIN]. Aeneid, The, *sels., tr.*
Difficulties of Translation, The. *Fr.* Prologues to the Aeneid.
Entrance to Hell, The, *tr. Fr.* The Aeneid.
Entrance to Tartarus, The, *tr. Fr.* The Aeneid.
Evening and Morning in June, An. *Fr.* Prologues to the Aeneid.
Evening and Morning in Winter, An. *Fr.* Prologues to the Aeneid.
Hart's Castle. *Fr.* King Hart.
King Hart, *sel.*
Nightmare. *Fr.* The Palace of Honor.
Palace of Honor, The, *sel.*
Prologues to the Aeneid, *sels.*
Proloug of the Twelft Buik of the Aenead, The, *sel., tr. Fr.* The Aeneid.
Welcome to the Sun, *tr. Fr.* The Aeneid.
Winter. *Fr.* Prologues to the Aeneid.
DOUGLAS, GILEAN. Autumn in Wartime.
Children of Martha.
Last Leave.
DOUGLAS, JESSE. Warning.
DOUGLAS, KEITH CASTELLAIN. Aristocrats.
Cairo Jag.
Canoe.
Deceased, The.
Desert Flowers.
Enfidaville.
How to Kill.
Landscape with Figures.
Leukothea.
Mersa.
Offensive, The.
On a Return from Egypt.
Oxford.
Poem: "These grasses, ancient enemies."
Remember Me.
Round Number, A.
Sea Bird, The.
Simplify Me When I'm Dead.
Snakeskin and Stone.
Song: "Do I venture away too far."
Time Eating.
Vergissmeinnicht [*or* Vergissmeinicht].
DOUGLAS, MALCOLM. Surprise, A.
When Grandpa Was a Little Boy.
"DOUGLAS, MARIAN" (Annie Douglas Green Robinson). Canticle of Creatures, The, *tr.*
Good Thanksgiving, A.
Little Sorrow.
One Saturday.
Two Pictures.
White Kitten, The.
DOUGLAS, OLIVE, LADY. *See* CUSTANCE, OLIVE.
DOUGLAS, WILLIAM. Annie Laurie.
DOVETON, F. P. Some Day.
DOW, ALLEN. Street Hawker.
DOW, DOROTHY MINERVA (Mrs. James Edward Fitzgerald). Song: "I could make you songs."
Things.
To Atalanta.
Unbeliever.
Where No Seeds Grow.
DOWD, EMMA C. Fun in a Garret.
DOWDEN, EDWARD. Aboard the *Sea-Swallow.*
Autumn Song.
Communion.
Gingo Biloba, *tr. Fr.* West-Eastern Divan.
In the Cathedral Close.
Leonardo's "Monna Lisa."
Line of Beauty, The.
Love's Lord.
Mona Lisa.
New Hymns for Solitude, *sel.*
Oasis.
On the Heights.
Poet's Simple Faith, The, *tr.*
Renunciants.
Seeking God.
Singer, The.
Song: "Girls, when I am gone away."
Two Infinities.
Vision.
West-Eastern Divan, *sels., tr.*
Windle-Straws.
Zuleika, *tr. Fr.* West-Eastern Divan.
DOWDEN, ELIZABETH DICKINSON WEST (Mrs. Edward Dowden). Adrift.
DOWDING, WALTER. I'r hen iaith a'i chaneuon.
Wales—a Mourning.
DOWLING, BARTHOLOMEW. Our Last Toast.
Revel, The.
Revelry of [*or* for] the Dying.
Stand to Your Glasses.
DOWLING, BASIL CAIRNS. Air in Spring, The.
Canterbury.
Early Days, The.
Mortal Love.
Naseby; Late Autumn.
Shunting.
Summer Afternoon.
Walking in Bush.
DOWNEY, FAIRFAX. Rise and Fall of Valentines.
Teeth Called Straight, The.
DOWNING, ELEANOR. Mary.
On the Feast of the Assumption.
Pilgrim, The.
DOWNING, ELLEN MARY PATRICK. My Owen.
Old Church at Lismore, The.
Were I But His Own Wife.
"DOWNING, MAJOR JACK." *See* SMITH, SEBA.
DOWNMAN, HUGH. Infancy.
DOWNTON, HENRY. Lord, her watch thy Church is keeping.
DOWSON, ERNEST CHRISTOPHER. Ad Domnulam Suam.
Ad Manus Puellae.
Amantium Irae.
Amor Profanus.
April Love.
Beata Solitudo.
Benedictio Domini.
Carthusians.
Chanson sans Paroles.
Colloque sentimental, *tr.*
Cynara [*or* Cynarae].
De Amore, *sel.*
Dregs.
Envoy: "They are not long, the weeping and the laughter."

Epigram: "Because I am idolatrous and have besought."
Exchanges.
Extreme Unction.
Flos Lunae.
Garden of Shadow, The.
Gray Nights.
Il pleut doucement sur la ville, *tr.*
Impenitentia Ultima.
In Tempore Senectutis.
Last Word, A.
Lyric: "You would have understood me, had you waited."
My Lady April.
Non Sum Qualis Eram Bonae sub Regno Cynarae.
Nuns of the Perpetual Adoration.
O Mors! Quam Amara Est Memoria Tua Homini Pacem Habenti in Substantiis Suis.
Quid Non Speremus, Amantes?
Sagesse, *tr.*
Sapientia Lunae.
Seraphita.
Sky Is Up above the Roof, The, *tr.*
Sonnet of a Little Girl.
Spleen ("Let us go hence").
Spleen, *tr.*
Tears and Rain, *tr.*
Tears Fall within Mine Heart, *tr.*
They Are Not Long.
To Cynara.
To One in Bedlam.
Vain Resolves.
Venite Descendamus.
Vesperal.
Villanelle of His Lady's Treasures.
Villanelle of Marguerites.
Villanelle of the Poet's Road.
Vitae Summa Brevis Spem Nos Vetat Incohare Longam.
You Would Have Understood Me.
Your Hands.
Yvonne of Brittany.
DOYLE, SIR ARTHUR CONAN. Cremona.
Guards Came Through, The.
Little Billy.
Mind and Matter.
Song of the Bow, The. *Fr.* The White Company.
White Company, The, *sel.*
DOYLE, CAMILLA. Cuckoos, Larks, and Sparrows.
March.
Moon, The.
Prettiest Things, The.
Rabbit, The.
DOYLE, SIR FRANCIS HASTINGS CHARLES. Epicurean, The.
Loss of the *Birkenhead,* The.
Old Cavalier, The.
Private of the Buffs, The.
Red Thread of Honor, The.
DOYLE, KIRBY. Strange.
"DOYLE, LYNN" (Leslie Alexander Montgomery). Ulsterman, An.
DOYLE, MARION. Golden Month, The.
Month of the Thunder Moon, The.
DRACHMANN, HOLGER HENRIK HERHOLDT. Amber.
Dedication: "I've love songs of my springtime pride."
Drink the Sweet Scent!
I Sit as I Have Always Sat.
Parting in Autumn.
Wild Red Wine, The.
DRACONTIUS, BLOSSIUS AEMILIUS. Birds, The.
DRACOPOULOU, THEONI. *See* "MYRTIOTISSA."
DRAG, IAN. House-weary.
DRAKE, JOSEPH RODMAN. American Flag, The.
Assembling of the Fays, The. *Fr.* The Culprit Fay.
Bronx.
Culprit Fay, The.
Culprit Fay, The, *sels.*
Elfin Knight, An. *Fr.* The Culprit Fay.
Elfin Song. *Fr.* The Culprit Fay.
Fairy Dawn. *Fr.* The Culprit Fay.
Fairy in Armor, A. *Fr.* The Culprit Fay.
Fay Arms Himself, The. *Fr.* The Culprit Fay.
Fay's Crime, The. *Fr.* The Culprit Fay.
Fay's Departure, The. *Fr.* The Culprit Fay.
Fay's Sentence, The. *Fr.* The Culprit Fay.
First Quest, The. *Fr.* The Culprit Fay.
Gathering of the Fairies, The. *Fr.* The Culprit Fay.
Inconstancy.
King of the Doctors, The, *sel.*
Meeting.
Ode to the American Flag.
Second Quest, The. *Fr.* The Culprit Fay.
Throne of the Lily-King, The. *Fr.* The Culprit Fay.
To a Friend.
To the Defenders of New Orleans.
War under Water. *Fr.* The Culprit Fay.
DRAKE, JOSEPH RODMAN, *and* FITZ-GREENE HALLECK. *See* HALLECK, FITZ-GREENE, *and* JOSEPH RODMAN DRAKE.
DRAKE, LEAH BODINE. All-Saints' Eve.
Assyrian Lion, The.
Ballad of the Jabberwock, The.
Changeling.
Fantasy in a Forest.
Figures in a Nightmare.
Final Green, The.
Heard on the Roof at Midnight.
Honey from the Lion.
In the Shadows.
Middle Ages, The; Two Views.
On a Night of Stars.
Path through the Marsh, The.
Precarious Ground.
Rider, The.
Tenants, The.
Terror by Night.
Wood Wife.
DRANE, AUGUSTA THEODOSIA. *See* FRANCIS RAPHAEL, MOTHER.
DRANNAN, WILLIAM F. Old Scout's Lament, The.
DRAPER, A. S. Indian Summer.
DRAPER, BOURNE H. Ye Christian heralds, go, proclaim.
DRAPER, JANE. I Look into the Stars.
DRAPER, WILLIAM H. Hush, All Ye Sounds of War.
DRATT, FLORENCE EVELYN. Christmas Song, A.
DRAYSON, PHYLLIS. Blackbird, The.
Hide and Seek.
DRAYTON, MICHAEL. Against Knowledge in Loving. *Fr.* Idea.
Agincourt.
Arming of Pigwiggen, The. *Fr.* Nymphidia.
As in some countries, far remote from hence. *Fr.* Idea.
As other men, so I myself do muse. *Fr.* Idea.
Away yee barb'rous woods. *Fr.* Polyolbion.
Ballad of Agincourt.
Ballad of Dowsabell, The. *Fr.* The Shepherd's Garland.
Baron's War, The, *sel.*
Batte's Song ("Love is the heaven's fair aspect"). *Fr.* The Shepherd's Garland.
Batte's Song ("What is love but the desire"). *Fr.* The Shepherd's Garland.
Battle of Agincourt, The.
Beauty sometime, in all her glory crowned. *Fr.* Idea's Mirrour.
Birds in the Fens. *Fr.* Polyolbion.
Black pitchy night, companion of my woe. *Fr.* Idea's Mirrour.
Bright star of beauty, on whose eyelids sit. *Fr.* Idea.
Call Home the Heart.
Calling to mind since first my love begun. *Fr.* Idea.
Canzonet; to His Coy Love.
Cassamen and Dowsabell. *Fr.* The Shepherd's Garland.
Christopher Marlowe. *Fr.* To Henry Reynolds, of Poets and Poesy.
Clear Anker, on whose silver-sanded shore. *Fr.* Idea.
Cloris and Mertilla. *Fr.* The Muses' Elysium.
Come, Let Us Kiss and Part. *Fr.* Idea.
Court of Fairy, The. *Fr.* Nymphidia.
Crier [*or* Cryer], The.
Cupid, I hate thee, which I'd have thee know. *Fr.* Idea.
Daffodil. *Fr.* The Shepherd's Garland.
Dear [*or* Deere], why should you command me to my rest. *Fr.* Idea.
Death of Edward, The. *Fr.* Mortimeriados.
Description of Elysium, The. *Fr.* The Muses' Elysium.
Earl of Surrey to Geraldine, The. *Fr.* England's Heroical Epistles.
Earle Douglasse for this day, Th'. *Fr.* Polyolbion.
Eclogue: "Late 'twas in June." *Fr.* The Shepherd's Garland.
Eighth Eclogue, The. *Fr.* The Shepherd's Garland.
Elegy of His Lady's Not Coming to London.
Endimion [*or* Endymion] and Phoebe, *sels.*
Endymion's Convoy. *Fr.* Endimion and Phoebe.
England's Heroical Epistles, *sels.*
Evil spirit, your beauty haunts me still, An. *Fr.* Idea.
Fame and Fortune. *Fr.* The Legend of Robert, Duke of Normandy.
Farewell: "Since there's no help, come let us kiss and part." *Fr.* Idea.
Ferryman, Venus, and Cupid, The. *Fr.* The Muses' Elysium.
Fine Day, A. *Fr.* The Muses' Elysium.
First Song, The. *Fr.* Polyolbion.
Fools Gaze at Painted Courts. *Fr.* Polyolbion.
Forest of Arden, The. *Fr.* Polyolbion.
Fourth Song, The. *Fr.* Polyolbion.
Give Me My Self. *Fr.* Idea.
Glorious sun went blushing to his bed, The. *Fr.* Idea's Mirrour.
Gorbo and Batte. *Fr.* The Shepherd's Garland.
Guest, The. *Fr.* Idea.
Harmony of the Church, The, *sels.*
Heart, The.
Henry Howard, Earl of Surrey, to [the Lady] Geraldine. *Fr.* England's Heroical Epistles.
Her Fame. *Fr.* Idea.
His Ballad of Agincourt.
His Defense against the Idle Critic.
How many paltry, foolish, painted things. *Fr.* Idea.
I hear some say, "This man is not in love!" *Fr.* Idea.
I Pray Thee Leave, Love Me No More.
Idea, *sels.*
Idea; or, The Shepherd's Garland, *sels.*
Idea's Mirrour, *sels.*
If chaste and pure devotion of my youth. *Fr.* Idea's Mirrour.
Immortality in Song. *Fr.* Idea.
In pride of wit, when high desire of fame. *Fr.* Idea.
Into these loves who but for passion looks. *Fr.* Idea.
Jovial Shepherd's Song, The. *Fr.* The Shepherd's Sirena.
King Henry to Rosamond. *Fr.* England's Heroical Epistles.
Last Verses.
Laughing at Fortune. *Fr.* Idea.
Legend of Robert, Duke of Normandy, The, *sel.*
Letters and lines, we see, are soon defaced. *Fr.* Idea's Mirrour.
Like an adventurous sea-farer am I. *Fr.* Idea.
Lines: "Clear had the day been from

DRAYTON, MICHAEL (*continued*)
the dawn." *Fr.* The Muses' Elysium.
Love's Farewell. *Fr.* Idea.
Love's Parting. *Fr.* Idea.
Love's Proverbs. *Fr.* Idea.
Many there be excelling in this kind. *Fr.* Idea.
Methinks I see some crooked mimic jeer. *Fr.* Idea.
Moone-Calfe, The, *sel.*
Mortimeriados, *sels.*
Most Excellent Song Which Was Salomon's, The. *Fr.* The Harmony of the Church.
Muses' Elysium, The, *sels.*
My fair, look from those turrets of thine eyes. *Fr.* Idea's Mirrour.
My heart, imprisoned in a hopeless isle. *Fr.* Idea's Mirrour.
My heart the anvil where my thoughts do beat. *Fr.* Idea's Mirrour.
Near to the silver Trent. *Fr.* The Shepherd's Sirena.
Night and Day. *Fr.* Idea.
Ninth Eclogue, The. *Fr.* The Shepherd's Garland.
Noah's Floud, *sel.*
Nymphidia; or, The Court of Fairy.
Nymphidia; or, The Court of Fairy, *sels.*
Nymphs' Song, The. *Fr.* The Muses' Elysium.
Ode to the Cambrio Britons and their Harp, His Ballad of Agincourt.
Ode to the Virginian Voyage.
Ode Written in the Peak, An.
Of all the Beasts. *Fr.* Polyolbion.
Our floods' queen, Thames, for ships and swans is crowned. *Fr.* Idea.
Palace of the Fairies, The.
Paradox, The. *Fr.* Idea's Mirrour.
Parting, The. *Fr.* Idea.
Phoebe on Latmus. *Fr.* Endimion and Phoebe.
Pigwiggen. *Fr.* Nymphidia.
Pigwiggen Prepares for the Fight with King Oberon. *Fr.* Nymphidia.
Pigwiggin Arms Himself. *Fr.* Nymphidia.
Play with Proverbs, A. *Fr.* Idea.
Polyolbion, *sels.*
Queen Mab Visits Pigwiggen, the Fairy Knight. *Fr.* Nymphidia.
Queen Mab's Chariot. *Fr.* Nymphidia.
Queen Mab's Journey to Pigwiggen. *Fr.* Nymphidia.
Queen's Chariot, The. *Fr.* Nymphidia.
Read here (sweet maid) the story of my woe. *Fr.* Idea's Mirrour.
Roundelay, The: "Gorbo, as thou cam'st this way." *Fr.* The Shepherd's Garland.
Roundelay, A: "Tell me, thou skilful shepherd's swain." *Fr.* The Shepherd's Garland.
Rowland's Rhyme. *Fr.* The Shepherd's Garland.
Sacrifice to Apollo, The.
Second Nimphall, The, *sel.* *Fr.* The Muses' Elysium.
Severn, The. *Fr.* The Baron's War.
Shepherd's Anthem, The.
Shepherd's Daffodil, The. *Fr.* The Shepherd's Garland.
Shepherd's [*or* Shepheards] Garland, The, *sels.*
Shepherd's [*or* Shepheards] Sirena, The, *sel.*
Since there's no help, come let us kiss and part. *Fr.* Idea.
Sirena. *Fr.* The Shepherd's Sirena.
Sixth Nymphal, The. *Fr.* The Muses' Elysium.
Skeltoniad, A.
Soe Well I Love Thee.
Some men there be which like my method well. *Fr.* Idea.
Some misbelieving and profane in love. *Fr.* Idea.
Song: "Now are the Tritons heard, to Loving-land to call." *Fr.* Polyolbion.
Song of Jonah in the Whale's Belly, The. *Fr.* The Harmony of the Church.
Song to Beta. *Fr.* The Shepherd's Garland.
Song to Sirena. *Fr.* The Shepherd's Sirena.
Sonnet: "Black pitchy night, companion of my woe." *Fr.* Idea.
Sonnet: "Bright star of beauty, on whose eyelids sit." *Fr.* Idea.
Sonnet: "Cleere Ankor, on whose silver-sanded shore." *Fr.* Idea's Mirrour.
Sonnet: "Dear, why should you command me to my rest." *Fr.* Idea.
Sonnet: "Evil spirit, your beauty haunts me still, An." *Fr.* Idea.
Sonnet: "How many paltry, foolish, painted things." *Fr.* Idea.
Sonnet: "Into these loves, who but for passion looks." *Fr.* Idea.
Sonnet: "My heart the anvil where my thoughts do beat." *Fr.* Idea.
Sonnet: "Since there's no help, come let us kiss and part." *Fr.* Idea.
Sonnet: "To nothing fitter can I thee compare." *Fr.* Idea.
Sonnet: To the Critic. *Fr.* Idea.
Sonnet: "Witless gallant, a young wench that wooed, A." *Fr.* Idea.
Sonnet: "You're not alone when you are still alone." *Fr.* Idea.
Sonnets. *Fr.* Idea *and* Idea's Mirrour.
Stay, speedy Time, behold, before thou pass. *Fr.* Idea.
Stay, stay, sweet Time! Behold, or ere thou pass. *Fr.* Idea's Mirrour.
Sweet Secrecy, what tongue can tell thy worth? *Fr.* Idea's Mirrour.
Sylvia. *Fr.* The Shepherd's Garland.
There's nothing grieves me but that age should haste. *Fr.* Idea.
Third Eclogue, The, *sel.* *Fr.* The Shepherd's Garland.
Thirteenth Song, The, *sels.* *Fr.* Polyolbion.
To Cupid.
To Henry Reynolds, of Poets and Poesy, *sel.*
To Himselfe and the Harpe.
To His Coy Love.
To His Rival.
To His Valentine.
To Miracle. *Fr.* Idea.
To My Most Dearly Loved Friend, Henry Reynolds, Esquire, of Poets and Poesy.
To My Worthy Friend Mr. George Chapman, and His Translated Hesiod.
To nothing fitter can I thee compare. *Fr.* Idea.
To the Cambro-Britons [*or* Britans] and Their Harp [*or* Harpe], His Ballad of Agincourt.
To the Critic. *Fr.* Idea.
To the Dear Child of the Muses and His Ever Kind Maecenas, Master Anthony Cooke, Esquire. *Fr.* Idea's Mirrour.
To the Excellent and Most Accomplish'd Lady, Lucy, Countess of Bedford. *Fr.* Mortimeriados.
To the New Yeere.
To the Reader of These Sonnets. *Fr.* Idea.
To the River Anker. *Fr.* Idea.
To the Virginian Voyage.
To these, the gentle South. *Fr.* Polyolbion.
To Time. *Fr.* Idea.
Truce, gentle love, a parley now I crave! *Fr.* Idea.
Upon a Bank.
Virginian Voyage, The.
When conquering love did first my heart assail. *Fr.* Idea.
When first I ended, then I first began. *Fr.* Idea.
When heaven would strive to do the best she can.
When Phoebus lifts his head. *Fr.* Polyolbion.
Whilst thus my pen strives to eternize thee. *Fr.* Idea.
Why should your fair eyes with such sovereign grace. *Fr.* Idea.
Witless Gallant, A. *Fr.* Idea.
World of mightier kings, A. *Fr.* Polyolbion.
You're not alone when you are still alone. *Fr.* Idea.

DRENNAN, JOHN SWANWICK. Avaro.
Epigram: "Avaro sick is seen to shiver."
Epigram: "For Love is like a plant that clings."
Epigram: "Golden casket I designed, A."
Epigram: "Love signed the contract blithe and leal."
Epigram: "Metaphysic Sphynx that preys on us, The."
Epigram: "Of the divine and human thought."
Epigram: "With nought to hide or to betray."
L'Amitié et l'Amour.
Love.
Not Gone Yet.
On the Telescopic Moon.
Perdita.
Spinozaism, A.

DRENNAN, MARIE. Peace Must Come as a Troubadour.

DRENNAN, WILLIAM. Aspiration.
Branch of the Sweet and Early Rose.
Erin [*or* Eire].
My Father.
Wake of William Orr, The.

DRESBACH, GLENN WARD. Ant Battle.
Autumn Road, An.
Burro Bells in the Moonlight.
Desert Burial.
Dip your hand in the mountain water.
Early Morning in a Glade.
Fawn's First Snow, A.
Ghostly Battles.
I found in the arms of the valley.
If Scars Are Worth the Keeping.
In Western Mountains, *sel.*
Last Corn Shock, The.
Last Cowboy, The.
Life or Death. *Fr.* In Western Mountains.
Little Spring Flows Clear Again, The.
Magic Lariat.
O thrush, in what deep glades.
Old Sailor, The.
Requiem.
Since Youth Is All for Gladness.
Songs of the Plains.
To a Scarlet Tanager.
Yucca in the Moonlight.

DRESSER, PAUL. Just Tell Them That You Saw Me.
On the Banks of the Wabash, Far Away.

DREWRY, CARLETON. Evensong.

DREYFUS, LILIAN SHUMAN. Dedication: "Stumbling, we see the future as a cup." *Fr.* In Praise of Leaves.
In Praise of Leaves, *sel.*

"DRINAN, ADAM." *See* MACLEOD, JOSEPH GORDON.

DRINKWATER, JOHN. Abraham Lincoln, *sels.*
Bird's Nest, The.
Birthright.
Blackbird, The.
Bobby Blue.
Challenge.
Christ Child at Christmas, The.
Christmas Eve.
Christmas Night, A.
Cotswold Love.
Crowning of Dreaming John, The.
Deer.
Defenders, The.
Fairford Nightingales.
Feckenham Men, The.
For Thee They Died.
Gold.
Greatness Passing By.
Holiness.
I Want to Know.
In Lady Street.
Invocation: "As pools beneath stone arches take."

Last Confessional.
Mamble.
Man's Daughter, A.
May Garden.
Mrs. Willow.
Moonlit Apples.
Morning Thanksgiving.
My Estate.
Mystery.
Old Crow.
Petition.
Prayer, A: "Grant us the will to fashion as we feel."
Prayer: "Lord, as thou wilt, bestow," *tr.*
Prayer, A: "Lord, not for light in darkness do we pray."
Prayer, A: "We know the paths wherein our feet should press."
Prelude: "Though black the night, I know upon the sky."
Purpose.
Puzzles.
Reality.
Reciprocity.
Snail.
Sun, The.
Sunrise on Rydal Water.
Symbols.
Tiptoe Night.
To and Fro about the City.
To My Son.
Town Window, A.
Vocation.
Wagon in the Barn, The.
Washing.
Who Were before Me.
DRISCOLL, LOUISE. Banquet, The.
Bargain.
Blue Jay, The.
Bulbs.
Epitaph: "Here lies the flesh that tried."
Futility.
God's Pity.
Good Hour, The.
Grace for Gardens.
Harbury.
Highway, The.
Hold Fast Your Dreams.
Idol, The.
Indifference.
July Meadow.
Marigolds.
Metal Checks, The.
Mid-August.
My Garden Is a Pleasant Place.
November Garden.
Old Woman Rain.
Phlox.
Spring Market.
Thanksgiving.
Their Thanksgiving Day.
Two Old Men.
DRISCOLL, MARJORIE CHARLES. Stay-at-Home, The.
"DROCH." *See* BRIDGES, ROBERT.
DROMGOOLE, WILL ALLEN. Bridge Builder, The.
Building the Bridge for Him.
DROSSINIS, GEORGIOS. Almond Tree, The.
Greek Earth.
Vespers.
DROSTE-HÜLSHOFF, ANNETTE ELISABETH, BARONESSE VON. Gethsemane.
House in the Heath, The.
In the Grass.
Last Day of the Year, The.
Last Words.
Moonrise.
On the Tower.
Pond, The.
Reflection in the Mirror, The.
Sleepless Night.
DRUMMOND, DONALD F. Caution.
Endless Error, The.
Epitaph for a Reno Woman.
Five Times Zero.
Froward Gull, The.
Generation of Intention.
How Sleep the Brave.
Meek Shall Inherit, The.
On a Book by John Milton, Annotated.
Redemption of the Ridiculous.
Time at Timberline.
To My Father.
Wedding Ring, The.
Word Was with God, The.
DRUMMOND, WILLIAM, OF HAWTHORNDEN. Alexis, Here She Stay'd.
Angels [for the Nativity of Our Lord], The.
As in a Dusky and Tempestuous Night.
Baptist, The.
Baptist's Sonnet, The.
Book of the World, The.
Change Should Breed Change. *Fr.* Flowers of Sion.
Content and Resolute.
Doth Then the World Go Thus.
Fair Is My Yoke, Though Grievous Be My Pains.
Fair Moon, Who with Thy Cold and Silver Shine.
Flowers of Sion, *sel.*
For the Baptist.
For the Magdalene.
From a Cypress Grove, 1623.
Her Passing.
How Many Times Night's Silent Queen Her Face.
Hymn[e] of the Ascension, An.
I fear not henceforth death.
I Know That All beneath the Moon Decays.
If Crost with All Mishaps Be My Poor Life.
Inexorable.
Invocation: "Phoebus, arise!"
Invocation to Love.
Iōlas' Epitaph.
Jerusalem.
John the Baptist.
Kiss, A.
Kisses Desired.
Lament: "Chaste maids which haunt fair Aganippe's well." *Fr.* Tears on the Death of Meliades.
Lament, A: "My thoughts hold mortal strife."
Lessons of Nature, The.
Life, a Bubble.
Like the Idalian Queen.
Look How the Flower.
Love.
Love Vagabonding.
Love Which Is Here a Care.
Madrigal: "Beauty, and the life, The."
Madrigal: "Dear night, the ease of care."
Madrigal: "I fear not henceforth death."
Madrigal: "Ivory, coral, gold, The."
Madrigal: "Like the Idalian queen."
Madrigal: Love Vagabonding.
Madrigal: "My thoughts hold mortal strife."
Madrigal: "Sweet rose, whence is this hue."
Madrigal: "This life which seems so fair."
Madrigal: "Unhappy light."
My Lute, Be as Thou Wast When Thou Didst Grow.
My Thoughts Hold Mortal Strife.
Nativitie, The.
No Trust in Time.
Now while the Night her sable veil hath spread.
Of Phyllis.
Of this fair volume which we World do name.
On the Death of Pym.
On the Margin Wrought.
Permanency of Life, The.
Phoebus, Arise.
Phyllis.
Primitiae.
Redeem Time Past.
Regret [*or* Regrat].
Saint John Baptist.
Sextain.
Sleep, Silence' Child.
Sleeping Beauty.
Solitary Life, A.
Song: "It autumne was, and on our hemisphere."
Song: "Phoebus, arise!"
Song: "That Zephyr every year."
Song of the Ascension.
Sonnet: "Alexis, here she stayed among these pines."
Sonnet: "As in a duskie and tempestuous night."
Sonnet: "Dear quirister, who from those shadows sends."
Sonnet: "How that vast heaven intitled First is rolled."
Sonnet: "I know that all beneath the moon decays."
Sonnet: "In minds pure glasse when I my selfe beholde."
Sonnet: "Look how the flower which lingeringly doth fade."
Sonnet: "My lute, be as thou wast when thou didst grow."
Sonnet: "Of this fair volume which we World do name."
Sonnet: "Passing glance, a lightning long the skies, A."
Sonnet: "Sweet soul, which in the April of thy years."
Sonnet: "Sweet Spring, thou turn'st with all thy goodly train."
Sonnet: "That learned Grecian, who did so excel."
Sonnet: "Thrice happy he, who by some shady grove."
Sonnet: "Thy head with flames, thy mantle bright with flowers."
Sonnet: "What doth it serve to see sun's burning face."
Spring Bereaved ("Alexis, here she stayed").
Spring Bereaved ("Sweet Spring, thou turn'st with all thy goodly train").
Spring Bereaved ("That zephyr every year").
Spring, Wanting Her.
Stolen Pleasure.
Summons to Love.
Sweet nymphs, if, as ye stray.
Sweet Spring, Thou Turn'st.
Tears on the Death of Meliades, *sel.*
Tell Me No More.
This Life [a Bubble].
This Life, Which Seems So Fair.
This world a hunting is.
Thrice Happy He.
Thy Sun Posts Westward.
To a Nightingale.
To His Lute.
To Sir William Alexander.
To Sleep.
To the Nightingale ("Dear chorister who from these shadows sends").
To the Nightingale ("Sweet bird that sing'st away").
World, The.
World a Game, The.
World a Hunt, The.
World a Hunting Is, The.
DRUMMOND, WILLIAM HENRY. Doctor Hilaire, *sel.*
How Bateese Came Home.
Johnnie Courteau.
Johnnie's First Moose.
Julie Plante, The.
Le Vieux Temps.
Little [*or* Leetle] Bateese.
Madeleine Verchères.
Nice Leetle Canadienne, De.
'Poleon Doré.
Stove Pipe Hole, De.
Two Hundred Years Ago.
Wreck of the *Julie Plante*, The.
DRUMMOND DE ANDRADE, CARLOS. Childhood.
Fantasia.
Garden in Liberty Square.
DRUNINA, YULIA. Rye Unharvested, The.
DRYDEN, JOHN. Absalom and Achitophel, Pt. I.
Absalom and Achitophel, Pt. I, *sels.*
Absalom and Achitophel, Pt. II, *sels.*
Achitophel. *Fr.* Absalom and Achitophel, Pt. I.
Aeneid, The, *sels., tr.*
After the Pangs of a Desperate Lover. *Fr.* An Evening's Love.

Dryden, John (*continued*)
After the Rain, *tr.* *Fr.* Georgics.
Against the Fear of Death, *sels., tr.* *Fr.* De Rerum Natura.
Against Women: Satire VI, *tr.* *Fr.* The Satires (*of* Juvenal).
Ah, Fading Joy. *Fr.* The Indian Emperor.
Ah, How Sweet It Is to Love! *Fr.* Tyrannick Love.
Albion and Albanius, *sels.*
Alexander's Feast; or, The Power of Music.
Alexander's Feast, *sel.*
All. All of a Piece Throughout. *Fr.* The Secular Masque.
All for Love, *sels.*
Amphitryon, *sels.*
And welcom now (Great Monarch) to your own. *Fr.* Astraea Redux.
Annus Mirabilis, *sels.*
Apology for Love, *tr.*
Ars Amatoria, *sel., tr.*
Art of Love, The (Ars Amatoria), *sel., tr.*
Assignation, The, *sel.*
Astraea Redux.
Astraea Redux, *sels.*
Aureng-Zebe, *sels.*
Ave atque Vale. *Fr.* Sigismonda and Guiscardo.
Battle of Actium, *tr.* *Fr.* The Aeneid.
Baucis and Philemon, *tr.* *Fr.* Metamorphoses.
Bees. *Fr.* Annus Mirabilis.
Bright Vision, The. *Fr.* The Conquest of Granada.
Calm Was the Even. *Fr.* An Evening's Love.
Can Life Be a Blessing. *Fr.* Troilus and Cressida.
Catholic Church. *Fr.* The Hind and the Panther.
Chaeronean Plutarch, to thy deathless praise, *tr.*
Character of the Earl of Shaftesbury. *Fr.* Absalom and Achitophel, Pt. I.
Characters from the Satires: Achitophel. *Fr.* Absalom and Achitophel, Pt. I.
Characters from the Satires: Og and Doeg. *Fr.* Absalom and Achitophel, Pt. II.
Characters from the Satires: Zimri. *Fr.* Absalom and Achitophel, Pt. I.
Charm, A.
Chorus: "All, all of a piece throughout." *Fr.* The Secular Masque.
Church of England, The. *Fr.* The Hind and the Panther.
Churches of Rome and of England, The. *Fr.* The Hind and the Panther.
Church's Testimony, The. *Fr.* The Hind and the Panther.
Cleomenes, *sel.*
Cleopatra. *Fr.* All for Love.
Cleopatra and Antony. *Fr.* All for Love.
Confession of Faith. *Fr.* The Hind and the Panther.
Conquest of Granada, The, *sels.*
Conversion ("Be vengeance wholly left to powers divine"). *Fr.* The Hind and the Panther.
Conversion ("But, gracious God, how well dost Thou provide"). *Fr.* The Church's Testimony.
Corydon and Thyrsis, *tr.* *Fr.* Eclogues.
Country Life, *tr.*
Crowd and Buckingham, The. *Fr.* Absalom and Achitophel, Pt. I.
Cymon and Iphigenia, *sels.*
Damon and Celimena. *Fr.* An Evening's Love.
De Rerum Natura, *sel., tr.*
Death, *tr.* *Fr.* De Rerum Natura.
Death of Turnus, The, *tr.* *Fr.* The Aeneid.
Design. *Fr.* To My Honor'd Friend Sir Robert Howard.
Diana's Hunting-Song. *Fr.* The Secular Masque.
Dido among the Shades, *tr.* *Fr.* The Aeneid.
Don Sebastian, *sel.*
Duke of Buckingham, The. *Fr.* Absalom and Achitophel, Pt. I.
Dulness Is Decent. *Fr.* Troilus and Cressida.
Earl of Shaftesbury, The. *Fr.* Absalom and Achitophel, Pt. I.
Eclogues, *sel., tr.*
Elegy on the Death of Mr. Oldham, *sel.*
Eleonora, *sel.*
English in 1680, The. *Fr.* Absalom and Achitophel, Pt. I.
Enjoy the Hour, *tr.*
Epigram on Milton.
Epilogue: "Pretty task, A; and so I told the Fool." *Fr.* Aureng-Zebe.
Epilogue: "They, who have best succeeded on the stage." *Fr.* The Conquest of Granada.
Epilogue Spoken at Oxford by Mrs. Marshall.
Epilogue Spoken by Mrs. Boutell.
Epilogue to "Mithridates, King of Pontus."
Epilogue to "The Husband His Own Cuckold," *sel.*
Epilogue to the Second Part of "The Conquest of Granada by the Spaniards."
Epilogue to "Tyrannick Love."
Epitaph Intended for His Wife.
Epitaph on His Wife.
Epitaph on Mrs. Margaret Paston of Barningham, in Norfolk.
Evening's Love, An, *sels.*
Fable of Acis, Polyphemus and Galatea, The, *sel., tr.* *Fr.* Metamorphoses.
Fair Iris and Her Swain. *Fr.* Amphitryon.
Fair Iris I Love. *Fr.* Amphitryon.
Fair, Sweet, and Young.
False Achitophel, The. *Fr.* Absalom and Achitophel, Pt. I.
Farewell, Fair Armida, *at.*
Farewell, Ungrateful Traitor. *Fr.* The Spanish Friar.
Fear of Death, The, *tr.* *Fr.* De Rerum Natura.
Fife and Drum. *Fr.* Song for St. Cecilia's Day.
Finite Reason. *Fr.* Religio Laici.
Fire of London, The. *Fr.* Annus Mirabilis.
Flood, The, *tr.* *Fr.* Metamorphoses.
Fools in England. *Fr.* Epilogue to "The Husband His Own Cuckold."
Fourth Day's Battle, The. *Fr.* Annus Mirabilis.
Georgics, *sels., tr.*
Great Fire, The. *Fr.* Annus Mirabilis.
Happiness.
Happy the Man, *tr.*
Harvest Song. *Fr.* King Arthur.
Here lies my wife; here let her lie!
Heroic [*or* Heroique] Stanzas, Consecrated to the Memory of His Highness, Oliver, Late Lord Protector of This Commonwealth.
Heroic Stanzas . . . , *sel.*
Hidden Flame. *Fr.* Secret Love.
Hind and the Panther, The, *sels.*
Honey-Farm, The, *tr.* *Fr.* Georgics.
Horat. Ode 29. Book 3. Paraphras'd in Pindarique Verse, *tr.*
How Happy the Lover. *Fr.* King Arthur.
How Unhappy a Lover Am I. *Fr.* The Conquest of Granada.
Human Happiness. *Fr.* The Indian Emperor.
Hymn for St. John's Eve, *tr.*
I Feed a Flame Within. *Fr.* Secret Love.
I Heard the Ruffian-Shepherd Rudely Blow, *tr.* *Fr.* Metamorphoses.
Iliad, The, *sel., tr.*
In Saturn's Reign, *tr.*
Incantation in "Oedipus."
Indian Emperor, The, *sels.*
Instruments, The. *Fr.* Song for St. Cecilia's Day.
Introduction to a Text-Book on Love, *tr.* *Fr.* Ars Amatoria.
Jacob Tonson, His Publisher.
Kind Keeper, The, *sel.*
King Arthur, *sels.*
King James II. *Fr.* The Hind and the Panther.
Lady's Song, The.
Last Day, The. *Fr.* To the Pious Memory of the Accomplisht Young Lady Mrs. Anne Killigrew.
Last Parting of Hector and Andromache, The, *tr.* *Fr.* The Iliad.
Laureate of Dulness, The. *Fr.* MacFlecknoe.
Life a Cheat. *Fr.* Aureng-Zebe.
Limberham; or, The Kind Keeper, *sel.*
Lines beneath the Portrait of Milton.
Lines Printed under the Engraved Portrait of Milton, 1688.
London. *Fr.* Annus Mirabilis.
Long betwixt Love and Fear. *Fr.* The Assignation.
Lord Shaftesbury. *Fr.* Absalom and Achitophel, Pt. I.
Love. *Fr.* The Conquest of Granada.
Love Triumphant, *sel.*
Love's Despair. *Fr.* The Spanish Friar.
Lycidas and Moeris, *tr.* *Fr.* Eclogues.
MacFlecknoe; or, A Satire upon the True-Blue-Protestant Poet, T. S.
MacFlecknoe, *sels.*
Maiden Queen, The. *See* Secret Love; or, The Maiden Queen.
Malcontents, The. *Fr.* Absalom and Achitophel, Pt. I.
Marcellus, *tr.* *Fr.* The Aeneid.
Marriage a-la-Mode, *sel.*
Medal, The.
Medal, The, *sel.*
Mercury's Song to Phaedra. *Fr.* Amphitryon.
Messiah, The, *tr.* *Fr.* Eclogues.
Metamorphoses, *sels., tr.*
Midnight.
Milton.
Mood and Figure Bride, A, *tr.*
Must noble Hastings immaturely die.
Nat Lee's Images. *Fr.* To Mr. Lee, on His Alexander.
Nereids Rise Out of the Sea and Sing. *Fr.* Albion and Albanius.
New London, The. *Fr.* Annus Mirabilis.
No, No, Poor Suffering Heart. *Fr.* Cleomenes.
Now with a general peace the world was blest. *Fr.* Astraea Redux.
Oak, The.
Oak of State, The. *Fr.* Don Sebastian.
Ode to Thaliarchus, *tr.*
Ode, An, to the Pious Memory of the Accomplished [*or* Accomplisht] Young Lady, Mrs. Anne Killigrew.
Odes, (*of* Horace), *sel., tr.*
Oedipus, *sels.*
Og and Doeg. *Fr.* Absalom and Achitophel, Pt. II.
On the Death of Mr. Purcell.
On the Nature of Things, *sels., tr.*
One Happy Moment.
One Long Nuptial Day. *Fr.* Secret Love.
Paradise. *Fr.* The State of Innocence and the Fall of Man.
Phoenix Self-born, The, *tr.* *Fr.* Metamorphoses.
Phyllis. *Fr.* The Conquest of Granada.
Plant That Will Not Grow, A. *Fr.* Aureng-Zebe.
Plutarch, *tr.*
Poet Shadwell, The. *Fr.* MacFlecknoe.
Poet Shadwell's Coronation, The. *Fr.* MacFlecknoe.
Poet's Resurrection. *Fr.* To the Pious Memory of the Accomplished Young Lady, Mrs. Anne Killigrew.

Popish Plot, The. *Fr.* Absalom and Achitophel, Pt. I.
Portrait of Milton, The.
Power of Love, The. *Fr.* Cymon and Iphigenia.
Prayer, A: "What weight of ancient witness can prevail." *Fr.* The Hind and the Panther.
Prelude: "What makes a plenteous harvest when to turn," *tr. Fr.* Georgics.
Presbyterians, The. *Fr.* The Hind and the Panther.
Priestcraft and Private Judgement. *Fr.* Religio Laici.
Primacy of Dullness, The. *Fr.* MacFlecknoe.
Private Judgement Condemned. *Fr.* The Hind and the Panther.
Prologue: "If yet there be a few that take delight." *Fr.* The Loyal General.
Prologue: "Our Author by experience finds it true." *Fr.* Aureng-Zebe.
Prologue: "See my lov'd Britons, see your Shakespeare rise." *Fr.* Troilus and Cressida.
Prologue and Epilogue to the University of Oxford.
Prologue and Epilogue to "Tyrannick Love; or, The Royal Martyr."
Prologue to "Aureng-Zebe."
Prologue to "Love Triumphant."
Prologue to Nahum Tate's "The Loyal General," *sel.*
Prologue to "Secret Love; or, The Maiden Queen."
Prologue to the First Satire.
Prologue to "The Tempest."
Prologue to the University of Oxford, 1673, Spoken by Mr. Hart at the Acting of "The Silent Woman."
Prophetess, The; or, The History of Dioclesian, *sel.*
Pyrrha and Deucalion, *tr. Fr.* Metamorphoses.
Rang'd on the Line Opposed, Antonius Brings, *tr. Fr.* The Aeneid.
Reason and Religion. *Fr.* Religio Laici.
Reason and Revelation. *Fr.* Religio Laici.
Reason and the Soul. *Fr.* Religio Laici.
Religio Laici.
Religio Laici, *sels.*
Return of the Golden Age, with the Birth of Pollio, The, *tr. Fr.* Eclogues.
Revery of a Business Man, *tr.*
Rondelay [*or* Roundelay]: "Chloe found Amyntas lying."
Rude Militia, The. *Fr.* Cymon and Iphigenia.
Satires, The (*of* Juvenal), *sel., tr.*
Scriptures, The. *Fr.* Religio Laici.
Sea Battle, The. *Fr.* Annus Mirabilis.
Secret Love; or, The Maiden Queen, *sels.*
Secular Masque, The.
Secular Masque, The, *sels.*
Sex among Lions, *tr. Fr.* Georgics.
Shadwell. *Fr.* MacFlecknoe.
Shaftesbury. *Fr.* Absalom and Achitophel, Pt. I.
Sigismonda and Guiscardo, *sel.*
Sippets of Gruel. *Fr.* Prologue to Nahum Tate's "The Loyal General."
Sixth Book of the Aeneis, The, *tr. Fr.* The Aeneid.
Snake, The, *tr. Fr.* Georgics.
Song: "After the pangs of a desperate lover." *Fr.* An Evening's Love.
Song: "Ah fading Joy! how quickly art thou past!" *Fr.* The Indian Emperor.
Song: "Ah, how sweet it is to love." *Fr.* Tyrannick Love.
Song: "Calm was the even, and cleer was the sky." *Fr.* An Evening's Love.
Song: "Can life be a blessing." *Fr.* Troilus and Cressida.
Song: "Fair Iris I love, and hourly I die." *Fr.* Amphitryon.
Song: "Fair, sweet and young, receive a prize."
Song, A: "Farewell ungrateful Traitor." *Fr.* The Spanish Friar.
Song: "Hear, ye sullen Pow'rs below." *Fr.* Oedipus.
Song: "How happy the lover." *Fr.* King Arthur.
Song: "I feed a flame within, which so torments me." *Fr.* Secret Love.
Song: "Long betwixt love and fear Phillis tormented." *Fr.* The Assignation.
Song: "No, no, poor suff'ring heart." *Fr.* Cleomenes.
Song: "Sylvia the fair, in the bloom of fifteen."
Song: "Wherever I am, and whatever I do." *Fr.* The Conquest of Granada.
Song: "Why should a foolish marriage vow." *Fr.* Marriage a-la-Mode.
Song: "You charm'd me not with that fair face." *Fr.* An Evening's Love.
Song: "Your hay it is mowed and your corn is reaped." *Fr.* King Arthur.
Song for St. Cecilia's Day, 1687, A.
Song from the Italian, A. *Fr.* Limberham.
Song of Secret Love, The. *Fr.* Secret Love.
Song of Thamesis. *Fr.* Albion and Albanius.
Song of the River Thames, A. *Fr.* Albion and Albanius.
Song of the Zambra Dance. *Fr.* The Conquest of Granada.
Song of Venus. *Fr.* King Arthur.
Song Sung by Venus in Honor of Britannia. *Fr.* King Arthur.
Song to a Fair, Young Lady Going Out of the Town in the Spring.
Song to a Minuet. *Fr.* King Arthur.
Songs from "The Secular Masque": Diana.
Songs from "The Secular Masque": Momus.
Spanish Friar, The, *sel.*
Spanish Ships Reach Mexico, The. *Fr.* The Indian Emperor.
Stage Poets. *Fr.* The Conquest of Granada.
Stanzas on Oliver Cromwell. *Fr.* Heroic Stanzas.
State of Innocence and the Fall of Man, The, *sel.*
Sylvia the Fair.
Syren's Song. *Fr.* King Arthur.
Te Deum, The, *tr.*
Tears of Amynta, The, for the Death of Damon.
Tenth Satire of Juvenal, The, *tr.*
Theodore and Honoria.
Third Satire, The, *tr.*
Thomas Shadwell the Poet. *Fr.* Absalom and Achitophel, Pt. II.
Threnodia Augustalis, *sel.*
Titus Oates. *Fr.* Absalom and Achitophel, Pt. I.
To a Fair Young Lady Going Out of Town in the Spring.
To His Sacred Majesty, a Panegyrick on His Coronation, 1661, *sel.*
To Maecenas, *tr.*
To Maecenas, *sel., tr.*
To Mr. Lee, on His Alexander, *sel.*
To My Dear Friend, Mr. Congreve, on His Comedy Called "The Double-Dealer."
To My Honor'd Friend Dr. Charleton.
To My Honor'd Friend Sir Robert Howard, on His Excellent Poems.
To My Honor'd Friend Sir Robert Howard, *sel.*
To My Honour'd Kinsman, John Driden [*or* Dryden], of Chesterton, in the County of Huntingdon, Esq.
To Thaliarchus, *tr.*
To the Memory of Mr. Oldham.
To the Pious Memory of the Accomplished [*or* Accomplisht] Young Lady Mrs. Anne Killigrew.
To the Pious Memory of the Accomplished [*or* Accomplisht] Young Lady Mrs. Anne Killigrew, *sel.*
To the University of Oxford, 1674.
Today and Tomorrow.
Tradition. *Fr.* Religio Laici.
Troilus and Cressida, *sels.*
Twenty-ninth Ode of the Third Book of Horace, The, *par.*
Tyrannick [*or* Tyrannic] Love; or, The Royal Martyr, *sels.*
Under Mr. Milton's Picture.
Under the Portrait of John Milton.
Upon the Death of the Earl of Dundee.
Upon the Death of the Lord Hastings.
Upon the Death of the Viscount of Dundee.
Veni Creator Spiritus, *tr.*
Vision of Rome's Destiny, *tr. Fr.* The Aeneid.
Vox Populi. *Fr.* The Medal.
War. *Fr.* Alexander's Feast.
What Shall I Do? *at. Fr.* The Prophetess.
When I Consider Life. *Fr.* Aureng-Zebe.
Wherever I Am, and Whatever I Do. *Fr.* The Conquest of Granada.
Why Should a Foolish Marriage Vow. *Fr.* Marriage a-la-Mode.
Wild Weather. *Fr.* All for Love.
Winter, *tr. Fr.* Odes.
With horns and with hounds I waken the day. *Fr.* The Secular Masque.
World Well Lost, The. *Fr.* The Hind and the Panther.
Worldly Vanity. *Fr.* The Hind and the Panther.
You Charm'd Me Not. *Fr.* An Evening's Love.
You pleasing dreams of love and sweet delight. *Fr.* Tyrannick Love.
Zambra Dance, The. *Fr.* The Conquest of Granada.
Zimri. *Fr.* Absalom and Achitophel, Pt. I.

DRYDEN, JOHN, *and* SIR ROBERT HOWARD. *See* HOWARD, SIR ROBERT, *and* JOHN DRYDEN.
DRYDEN, JOHN, *and* SIR WILLIAM SOAMES. *See* SOAMES, SIR WILLIAM, *and* JOHN DRYDEN.
DRYDEN, JOHN, *and* NAHUM TATE. *See* TATE, NAHUM, *and* JOHN DRYDEN.
DRYDEN, MYRTLE MAY. Just Forget.
DSCHELLALEDDIN RUMI. *See* RUMI, JALAL ED-DIN.
D'SOLA, OTTO. Before the Coming of the Planes That Burn the Cities.
Last Song to a Girl of the Waterfront.
Plenitude.
"DUAN, JON." Rout of Belgravia, The.
DU AUTERMONT, HARRIET. Some Faith at Any Cost.
DU BELLAY, JOACHIM. Amours, Les, *sels.*
Antiquities of Rome, *sels.*
Autumn Fruits. *Fr.* Olive.
Blameless Kiss, The. *Fr.* Les Amours.
Contemplation. *Fr.* Les Amours.
Destruction. *Fr.* Antiquities of Rome.
Epitaph on a Pet Cat.
Epitaph on a Pet Dog.
Exile in Rome. *Fr.* Regrets.
From a Winnower of Corn to the Winds.
Happy Ulysses, The. *Fr.* Regrets.
Heureux qui, comme Ulysse, a fait un beau voyage. *Fr.* Regrets.
Home. *Fr.* Olive.
Hymn to the Winds.
I Hate. *Fr.* Regrets.
Immortality. *Fr.* Antiquities of Rome.
Kingship. *Fr.* Antiquities of Rome.
My House. *Fr.* Regrets.
Nonpareil of All Mortality, The. *Fr.* Olive.

DU BELLAY, JOACHIM (*continued*)
O France, Mother of Arts. *Fr.* Regrets.
Olive, *sels.*
On His Deafness. *Fr.* Les Amours.
Pale Is Death.
Regrets, *sels.*
Relics. *Fr.* Antiquities of Rome.
Returning Home. *Fr.* Regrets.
Revolt. *Fr.* Antiquities of Rome.
Rome. *Fr.* Ruins of Rome.
Ruined Glories. *Fr.* Antiquities of Rome.
Ruins of Rome, I-VIII.
Slave I Languish, A. *Fr.* Regrets.
Sonnet: "Happy as Ulysses, his voyage done." *Fr.* Regrets.
Sonnet: "He who would like to see what art and nature."
Sonnet: "I hate the money-lending avarice." *Fr.* Regrets.
Sonnet: "If life on earth be less than is a day." *Fr.* Olive.
Sonnet: "If of our life the span be not a day." *Fr.* Olive.
Sonnet: "It was the time, when rest, soft sliding downe." *Fr.* Visions.
Sonnet: "Newcomer, you who look in Rome for Rome."
Sonnet to Heavenly Beauty, A. *Fr.* Olive.
To Ceres.
To His Friend in Elysium.
Translation from Du Bellay ("Happy, who like Ulysses or that lord"). *Fr.* Regrets.
Upon the Same ("I yearn more hungrily to see your face"). *Fr.* Les Amours.
Visions, The, *sel.*
Vow to Heavenly Venus.
Winnower of Wheat to the Winds, A.
Ye Huntsmen Who Halloo and Wind the Horn. *Fr.* Olive.
DU BOIS, GERTRUDE. Meditation in St. Mary's.
DUBOIS, PATTERSON. Fatherhood.
DUBOIS, WILLIAM EDWARD BURGHARDT. Litany at [*or* of] Atlanta, A.
DUCAS, DOROTHY. Atheist's Wail, The.
DUCASSE, ISIDORE LUCIEN. *See* "LAUTRÉAMONT, COMTE DE."
DUCIC, JOVAN. Clock, The.
DUCIS, JEAN FRANÇOIS. To My Household Gods.
DUCK, STEPHEN. Thresher's Labour, The, *sel.*
DUCKETT, ALFRED A. Portrait Philippines.
Sonnet: "Where are we to go when this is done?"
DUCLAUX, AGNES MARY FRANCES. *See* ROBINSON, AGNES MARY FRANCES.
DUCLO, ESTELLE. Great Word, The.
DUDEK, LOUIS. Building a Skyscraper.
Dawn.
Europe, *sels.*
García Lorca.
I Have Seen the Robins Fall.
Improvisation.
Jungle, The.
Mountains, The.
Mouths.
Narrative.
O Contemporaries.
On Poetry.
Pomegranate, The.
Puerto Rican Side-Street.
Store-House, A.
Street in April, A.
DUDGEON, WILLIAM. Up amang Yon Cliffy Rocks.
DUDLEY, BIDE. To James Whitcomb Riley.
DUDLEY, DOROTHY. La Rue de la Montagne Sainte-Gèneviève.
DUDLEY, HELEN. Song: "Few more windy days, A."
To One Unknown.
DUDLEY, THOMAS. New England Gentleman's Epitaph, A.
DUER, ALICE. *See* MILLER, ALICE DUER.
DUER, CAROLINE. International Episode, An.
Portrait, A.
Word to the Wise, A.
DUER, CAROLINE, *and* ALICE DUER MILLER. How like a Woman.
DUERDEN, RICHARD. Dance with Banderillas.
Moon Is to Blood.
Musica No. 3.
DUFF, ESTHER LILIAN. Black and White.
Charles Gave Elizabeth a Dodo.
Lad's Love.
Not Three—but One.
Of a Certain Green-eyed Monster.
DUFFERIN, LADY. *See* SHERIDAN, HELEN SELINA.
DUFFETT, THOMAS. Celia.
DUFFIELD, GEORGE, JR. Stand Up for Jesus.
DUFFIELD, SAMUEL WILLOUGHBY. Two of a Trade.
DUFFIN, CELIA. Old Dog, An.
DUFFY, SIR CHARLES GAVAN. Irish Rapparees, The.
Muster of the North, The.
DUFFY, JOHN ALPHONSUS. Annunciation, The.
Domine Jesu!
Our Lady's Labor.
Ox-Bone Madonna.
Thrush, The.
DUFFY, NONA KEEN. Above the Stable.
Spring Is in the Making.
DU FRESNY, CHARLES RIVIERE. Next Day, The.
DUGAN, MRS. D. H. Christ Is Risen!
DUGAN, GERTRUDE ROBINSON. Our Airmen.
Secret Service.
DUGAN, MAURICE. *See* O'DUGAN, MAURICE.
DUGANNE, AUGUSTINE JOSEPH HICKEY. Bethel.
DUGGAN, EILEEN. After the Annunciation.
Aspiration.
Ballad of the Bushman.
Bushfeller, The.
Contrast.
Didymus.
Discipline of Consequences, The.
Epiphany.
Interlude.
Juniper.
Last Song, The.
Milker, The.
Musterer, The.
Name, The.
Peasantry.
Pilgrimage.
Plea.
Post-War.
Presumption.
St. Peter.
Tides Run up the Wairau, The.
Twilight.
Victory.
DUHAMEL, GEORGES. Flame and Clarity.
Meeting, The.
Stranger, The.
DUKE, DARYL. It Was My June.
DUKES, ASHLEY. Book I Held Grew Cold, The, *tr.*
O Heavy Step of Slow Monotony, *tr.*
O Master Masons, *tr.*
O My Swallows! *tr.*
DUMAS, ALEXANDRE. Chevalier de maison rouge, Le, *sel.*
Girondins, The. *Fr.* Le Chevalier de maison rouge.
DU MAURIER, GEORGE LOUIS PALMELLA BUSSON. Legend of Camelot, A.
Little, A. *Fr.* Trilby.
Little Work, A. *Fr.* Trilby.
Lost Illusion, A.
Music.
Trilby, *sel.*
Vers Nonsensiques.
"DUM-DUM." *See* KENDALL, JOHN KAYE.
DUMONT, HENRY. Bridge, The.
DUNBAR, ALDIS. Sic Semper Tyrannis.
DUNBAR, JENNIE. A-Hunting.
DUNBAR, PAUL LAURENCE. Accountability.
After the Quarrel.
Angelina.
Ante-Bellum Sermon, An.
At Candle-lightin' Time.
Boogah Man, The.
Boy's Summer Song, A.
Chrismus on the Plantation.
Colored Band, The.
Columbian Ode.
Compensation.
Conscience and Remorse.
Coquette Conquered, A.
Corn-Song, A.
Curtain!
Dat Ol' Mare o' Mine.
Dawn.
Death Song, A.
Deserted Plantation, The.
Differences.
Dinah Kneading Dough.
Discovered.
Dreamin' Town.
Encouragement.
Equipment.
Ere Sleep Comes Down to Soothe the Weary Eyes.
Get Somebody Else, *at.*
Harriet Beecher Stowe.
Haunted Oak, The.
He Had His Dream.
Hymn, A: "Lead gently, Lord, and slow."
Hymn: "O li'l' lamb out in de col'."
Hymn: "When storms arise."
In the Morning.
Keep a-Pluggin' Away.
Life.
Li'l' Gal.
Lincoln.
Little Black Sheep, The.
Little Brown Baby.
Lonesome.
Lover's Lane.
Lullaby: "Bedtime's come fu' little boys."
Master-Player, The.
Negro Love Song, A.
Ode for Memorial Day.
On the Road.
Opportunity.
Poet and His Song, The.
Prayer, A: "O Lord, the hard-won miles."
Retort.
Rivals, The.
Ships That Pass in the Night.
Song of Summer.
Sympathy.
Too Busy, *at.*
Turning of the Babies in the Bed, The.
Unsung Heroes, The.
Warrior's Prayer, A.
We Wear the Mask.
When All Is Done.
When de Co'n Pone's Hot.
When Malindy Sings.
DUNBAR, WILLIAM. Amends to the Tailors and Soutars.
Ane Ballat of Our Lady.
Ane Ballat of Our Lady, *sel.*
Ane Ballat of the Feignèd Friar of Tungland.
Ballad of Kynd [*or* Kind] Kittok, The.
Ballad of Our Lady.
Book of the Two Married Women and the Widow, The, *sels.*
Dance of the Seven Deadly Sins, The.
Done Is a Battle on the Dragon Black.
Flyting of Dumbar and Kennedie, The, *sel.*
Followis How Dumbar Wes Desyr to Be ane Freir.
Golden [*or* Goldyn] Targe, The.
Golden Targe, The, *sels.*
Hermes the Philosopher.
In Honour of the City of London.
Jerusalem, Rejoice for Joy!
Lament for the Makaris.
London.
Manere of the Crying of ane Playe, The.

Meditation in Winter.
New Year's Gift to the King, A.
Now Fair, Fairest of Every Fair.
O reverend Chaucer! rose of rhetoris all.
O Wretch, Beware.
Of Content.
Of the Changes of Life.
Of the Resurrection of Christ.
On the Nativity of Christ.
On the Resurrection of Christ.
Petition of the Grey Horse, Auld Dunbar, The.
Poet's Dream, The. *Fr.* The Golden Targe.
Quod Dunbar to Kennedy.
Rorate Coeli Desuper.
Sweet Rose of Virtue.
Thrissil and the Rose, The.
To a Lady.
To the City of London.
Tua Mariit Wemen and the Wedo, The.
Tua Mariit Wemen and the Wedo, The, *sels.*
Welcome to Margaret Tudor.
What Is This Life?
Widow Speaks, The. *Fr.* The Tua Mariit Wemen and the Wedo.
DUNCAN, MARY LUNDIE. Child's Evening Prayer, A.
Child's Morning Prayer, A.
Evening Prayer, An.
Jesus, Tender Shepherd, Hear Me.
My Little Brother.
Shadows, The.
Tender Shepherd, The.
DUNCAN, ROBERT EDWARD. Dance, The.
Dream Data.
Food for Fire, Food for Thought.
Hero Song.
Owl Is an Only Bird of Poetry, An.
Poem Beginning with a Line by Pindar, A.
Question, The.
Reaper, The.
Song of the Borderguard, The.
This Place Rumord to Have Been Sodom.
DUNCAN, THOMAS W. Village Portrait.
DUNETZ, LORA. Ailing Parent, The.
All That Summer.
"And All the While the Sky Is Falling . . ."
Black Cat.
Treason.
While the Bells Ring.
DUNLOP, JOHN. Dinna Ask Me.
Oh! Dinna Ask Me Gin I Lo'e Thee.
Year That's Awa', The.
DUNN, ALTA BOOTH. Unknown Soldier.
DUNN, MAXWELL WALTER DUMONT. Flower of Exile.
I Danced before I Had Two Feet.
DUNN, STANLEY GERALD. Havildar Ganga Singh, V.C.
DUNN, STEPHEN P. Prayer of the Young Stoic.
DUNNAM, OUIDA SMITH. Prayer of a Beginning Teacher.
DUNNING, EMERETTE H. Memorial Day.
DUNSANY, EDWARD JOHN MORETON DRAX PLUNKETT, 18TH BARON. Call to the Wild, A.
Deserted Kingdom, The.
Heterodoxy, A.
I met with Death in his country. *Fr.* Songs from an Evil Wood.
Memory, The.
Odes (*of Horace*), *sels., tr.*
On the Safe Side.
Refugee, The.
Snow on the East Wind.
Somewhere lost in the haze. *Fr.* Songs from an Evil Wood.
Song of Wandering, A.
Songs from an Evil Wood.
Songs from an Evil Wood, *sels.*
There is no wrath in the stars. *Fr.* Songs from an Evil Wood.
To a Dog Dreaming.
To a Lost Spirit.
To a Spirit Seen in a Dream.
To Keats.
DUPREE, EDGAR. Light of Faith, The.
DUPUY, J. Michael Met a White Duck.
DURAND, OSWALD. Black Man's Son, The.
Choucoune.
If.
DURANT, GILLES. Sunflower, The.
To His Mistress.
DURBIN, ELIZA W. Our Washington.
DURBIN, HARRIET WHITNEY. Little Dutch Garden, A.
DURELL, ANN. Cornish Magic.
D'URFEY [*or* DURFEY *or* D'URFÉ], THOMAS. Born with the Vices.
Bright Was the Morning.
Bully, The, *at.*
Campaigners, The; or, The Pleasant Adventures at Brussels, *sel.*
Chloe Divine.
Fisherman's Song, The.
Fool's Preferment, A, *sel.*
Hunting Song. *Fr.* The Marriage-Hater Match'd.
I'll Sail upon the Dog-Star. *Fr.* A Fool's Preferment.
Kingston Church.
Maid's Longing, The. *Fr.* Pills to Purge Melancholy.
Marriage-Hater Match'd, The, *sels.*
Pills to Purge Melancholy, *sel.*
Sawney Was Tall. *Fr.* The Virtuous Wife.
Scotch Song. *Fr.* The Campaigners.
Shepherd Kept Sheep on a Hill so High, A.
Solon's Song. *Fr.* The Marriage-Hater Match'd.
Virtuous Wife, The, *sel.*
D'URFEY, THOMAS, *and others.* All Hail to the Days That Merit More Praise.
DURHAM, RICHARD V. Dawn Patrol; Chicago.
DURIVAGE, FRANCIS ALEXANDER. Chez Brébant.
DURKAN, PATRICK F. Sisterhood of God, The.
DURLING, DWIGHT. *For translations from French, see* AnFP.
For translations from German, see AnGP.
DURRELL, LAWRENCE. Adepts, The. *Fr.* Eight Aspects of Melissa.
Alexandria.
At Epidaurus.
Ballad of the Good Lord Nelson, A.
By the Lake. *Fr.* Eight Aspects of Melissa.
Conon in Alexandria.
Coptic Poem.
Delos.
Eight Aspects of Melissa.
Encounter, The. *Fr.* Eight Aspects of Melissa.
Green Coconuts.
In a Time of Crisis.
In Arcadia.
In the Garden; Villa Cleobolus.
Nemea.
Night, The. *Fr.* Eight Aspects of Melissa.
On Ithaca Standing.
On Seeming to Presume.
Petron, the Desert Father. *Fr.* Eight Aspects of Melissa.
Prospect of Children, A. *Fr.* Eight Aspects of Melissa.
Rising Sun, The. *Fr.* Eight Aspects of Melissa.
Swans.
This Unimportant Morning.
To Argos.
To Ping-ku, Asleep.
Visitations. *Fr.* Eight Aspects of Melissa.
Water-Colour of Venice, A.
DURSTON, GEORGIA ROBERTS ("George Durston"). Hippopotamus, The.
Rabbit, The.
Wolf, The.
DURTAIN, LUC. Return of the Men, The.
DURWARD, BERNARD ISAAC. Good Night.
To My Firstborn.
DURWARD, JOHN T. Missed Again.
DURYEE, MARY BALLARD. Creation.
Father to Daughter.
Homestead—Winter Morning.
DUTHIE, WILLIAM. March of the Men of Harlech.
DUTT, ROMESH. Indra, the Supreme God, *tr. Fr.* The Rigveda.
Pushan, God of Pasture, *tr. Fr.* The Rigveda.
Rigveda, The, *sels., tr.*
DUTT, TORU. Our Casuarina Tree.
DUTTON, GEOFFREY. Mountain, The.
Nightflight and Sunrise.
Prisoner Freed, A.
DUVAL, PAUL. *See* "LORRAIN, JEAN."
DUVAR, JOHN HUNTER. *See* HUNTER-DUVAR, JOHN.
DWIGHT, THOMAS. To the Federal Convention.
DWIGHT, TIMOTHY. And when new regions prompt their feet to roam. *Fr.* Greenfield Hill.
Assault on the Fortress, The.
Battle of Ai, The. *Fr.* The Conquest of Canaan.
Church and School. *Fr.* Greenfield Hill.
Columbia.
Conquest of Canaan, The, *sel.*
Farmer's Advice to the Villagers, The. *Fr.* Greenfield Hill.
Greenfield Hill, *sels.*
I Love Thy Kingdom Lord.
Love to the Church.
Minister, New Style, A. *Fr.* The Triumph of Infidelity.
Smooth Divine, The. *Fr.* The Triumph of Infidelity.
Star of Columbia.
Sweet Simplicity. *Fr.* Greenfield Hill.
Triumph of Infidelity, The, *sels.*
Two Ways of Visiting. *Fr.* Greenfield Hill.
DYE, ROBERT. Alma Mater.
DYER, LADY CATHERINE. Epitaph on the Monument of Sir William Dyer at Colmworth, 1641.
DYER, SIR EDWARD. Alas, My Heart.
Another of the Same. Excellently Written by a Most Woorthy Gentleman, *at.*
Contentment.
Corydon to His Phyllis.
Cynthia.
Kingdom.
Love Is Love.
Lowest Trees Have Tops, The.
Man Whose Thoughts, The.
Modest Love, A.
My Mind to Me a Kingdom Is.
Prometheus When First from Heaven.
Shepherd's Conceit of Prometheus, The.
Wher One Would Be.
DYER, JOHN. British Commerce. *Fr.* The Fleece.
Country Walk, The.
Country Walk, The, *sel.*
English Fog, The. *Fr.* The Fleece.
English Weather. *Fr.* The Fleece.
Enquiry, The.
Epistle to a Famous Painter, *sel.*
Fleece, The, *sels.*
Grongar Hill.
Grongar Hill, *sels.*
Nation's Wealth, A. *Fr.* The Fleece.
Ruins of Rome, The, *sel.*
To a Famous Painter. *Fr.* Epistle to a Famous Painter.
To His Son.
Wool Trade, The. *Fr.* The Fleece.
Yellow Barn, The. *Fr.* The Country Walk.
DYER, SIDNEY. Night Cometh.
DYMENT, CLIFFORD. As a Boy with a Richness of Needs I Wandered.
Axe in the Wood, The.
Children, The.
Fox.
Pastoral: "In the old days the white gates swung."
Snow, The.
Swans, The.
Switch Cut in April, A.

DYMENT, CLIFFORD (*continued*)
Temple, The.
To London the Train Gallops, Its Shrill Steel Hooves.
DYSON, EDWARD. Peter Simson's Farm.
Worked-out Mine, The.
DYSON, WILL (William Henry Dyson). Death Is but Death.
Planet Moon, *sel.*
DZADOURIAN, ALEXANDER. Armenian Poet's Prayer, The.
DZYUBIN, EDUARD. *See* "BAGRITSKY, EDUARD."

E

"E." *See* FULLERTON, MARY ELIZABETH.
"E. C." *See* "C., E."
"E. G. B." *See* "B., E. G."
"E. H. K." *See* "K., E. H."
"E. H. R." *See* "R., E. H."
"E. M. G. R." *See* "R., E. M. G."
"E. M. H. C." *See* "C., E. M. H."
"E. O. G." *See* "G., E. O."
"E. P. C." *See* "C., E. P."
"E. R. B." *See* "B., E. R."
"E. S." *See* "S., E."
"E. S. F." *See* "F., E. S."
"E. W." *See* "W., E."
"EAGLE, SOLOMON." *See* SQUIRE, SIR JOHN COLLINGS.
EAKMAN, FLORENCE. Our Clock.
EARHART, AMELIA. Courage.
EARLE, GILES. Tom o' Bedlam's Song, *at.*
EARLE, JOHN CHARLES. Lo, I Am with You Always.
Onward and Upward.
Seeking and Finding God.
EARLE, PLINY. What Is It to Die?
EARLE, VIRGINIA. Dream as Reported, A.
Night Concert.
Receive, Beloved.
EARLS, MICHAEL. Autumn Rose-Tree, An.
Child's Play of Men, The.
From My Father.
To a Carmelite Postulant.
To a Nun of the Good Shepherd.
EARP, THOMAS WADE. Adventure.
EAST, JAMES. Wise Men Seeking Jesus.
"EASTAWAY, EDWARD." *See* THOMAS, EDWARD.
EASTER, MARGUERITE ELIZABETH. My Laddie's Hounds.
EASTMAN, BARRETT. How We Burned the *Philadelphia.*
Joy Enough.
Richard Somers.
EASTMAN, CHARLES GAMAGE. Dirge: "Softly! She is lying with her lips apart."
Picture, A.
Snow-Storm, A.
EASTMAN, ELAINE GOODALE. Ashes of Roses.
Baby.
Countrywoman of Mine, A.
Goldenrod.
EASTMAN, MAX. April Earth, The.
At the Aquarium.
Coming to Port.
Diogenes.
Egrets.
Hymn to God in Time of Stress, A.
Invocation: "Truth, be more precious to me than the eyes."
Message to Siberia, *tr.*
Rainy Song.
Thought, A. *tr.*
To a Tawny Thrush.
Truth.
We Have Been Happy.
EASTMAN, SOPHIE E. Spool of Thread, A.
EASTWICK, IVY O. And Dancing.
At Sunset.
Cherry Tree.
Dark Danny.
Elizabeth Ann Peabody.
Feather for My Cap, A.
First Snow.
Jack-in-the-Pulpit.
Jolly Days.
Larch Wood Secrets.
Lucy Lavender.
Mary's Lullaby.
May Mornings.
Mickleham Way.
Midsummer Magic.
Miller, Miller.
Morning.
Mother and Child.
My True Love.
Pretty Maid Marion.
Robber, The.
Scarf, The.
Shadow Dance.
Sing a Song of Moonlight.
Sing a Song of Sunshine.
Stay, Christmas!
Timothy Boon.
Trouble at the Farm.
Waking Time.
Where's Mary?
Winter in the Wood.
Wolf and the Lambs, The.
EASTWOOD, EARLE V. Barter.
EATON, ARTHUR WENTWORTH HAMILTON. By the Bridge.
Egyptian Lotus, The.
I Watch the Ships.
L'Ile Sainte Croix.
Lotus of the Nile, The.
Phantom Light of the Baie des Chaleurs, The.
Pray for the Dead.
EATON, BURNHAM. Technique.
EATON, CHARLES EDWARD. Burning Leaves.
House of the South, A.
Passage Magnolia, The.
Peony for Apollo, A.
Skull, The.
EATON, EVELYN SIBYL MARY. Gardener, The.
EATON, ISAAC F. Farmer John's Thanksgiving.
EATON, SIR JOHN. Song: "Tell me not I my time misspend," *at.*
EATON, VIRGINIA. My Neighbor.
Unknown Soldier, The.
EATON, WALTER PRICHARD. Birches, The.
White-Throat Sings, A.
Willows, The.
EBERHART, NELLE RICHMOND. At Dawning.
EBERHART, RICHARD. Advantage of the Outside, The.
At Lake Geneva.
Attic, The. *Fr.* Burr Oaks.
Brotherhood of Men, *sel.*
Burr Oaks, *sel.*
Cancer Cells, The.
Cold Fall.
Cover Me Over.
Dam Neck, Virginia.
Day-Bed, The.
Experience Evoked.
For a Lamb.
Forgotten Rock, The.
Forms of the Human.
From Four Lakes' Days.
Fury of Aerial Bombardment, The.
Go to the Shine That's on a Tree.
Goal of Intellectual Man, The.
Grave Piece.
Groundhog, The.
Horse Chestnut Tree, The.
Human Being Is a Lonely Creature, The.
I Walked Out to the Graveyard to See the Dead.
Idols of Imagination.
If I Could Only Live at the Pitch That Is Near Madness.
If This Be Love.
Imagining How It Would Be to Be Dead.
In a Hard Intellectual Light.
In the Garden.
It Is That Bane of Self in Love.
Largess, The.
Legend of Viable Women, A.
Lost Children, The.
Man of Sense, A.
Maze.
Meditation, A.
"Mysticism Has Not the Patience to Wait for God's Revelation."
New Hampshire, February.
1934.
Ode to the Chinese Paper Snake.
On a Squirrel Crossing the Road in Autumn, in New England.
On Shooting Particles beyond the World.
On the Lacedaemonian Dead at Plataea, *tr.*
Preacher Sought to Find Out Acceptable Words, The.
Reality! Reality! What Is It?
Rumination.
Sainte Anne de Beaupré.
Seals, Terns, Time.
Sestina: "I die, no matter what I do I die."
Soul Longs to Return Whence It Came, The.
Spring Mountain Climb.
Stone, A.
This Fevers Me.
Tobacconist of Eighth Street, The.
Two Loves.
Ur Burial.
What If Remembrance?
When Golden Flies upon My Carcass Come.
Wisdom of Insecurity, The.
Words.
World War.
EBERHART, RICHARD, *and* GARDNER TAPLIN. Odes (*of* Horace), *sel.*, *tr.*
EBERS, BASIL. For Remembrance.
EBRIGHT, FREDERICK. Legacy.
Memorial to the Great Big Beautiful Self-sacrificing Advertisers.
EDDY, MARY BAKER. Shepherd, show me how to go.
EDELMAN, KATHERINE. Irish Grandmother.
EDELSTEIN, HYMAN. Indian Night Tableau.
Last Mathematician.
Palimpsest.
EDEN, HELEN PARRY. Confessional, The.
Elegy, for Father Anselm, of the Order of Reformed Cistercians, An.
Four-Paws.
Phoenix Liberty, The.
Poet and the Wood-Louse, The.
Prayer for St. Innocent's Day, A.
Purpose of Amendment, A.
Sorrow.
To a Little Girl.
To Betsey-Jane, on Her Desiring to Go Incontinently to Heaven.
EDEN, PATIENCE. She Reports No Progress.
Song for a 'Fraid Cat.
Why Travel.
EDES, RICHARD. *See* EEDES, RICHARD.
EDEY, MARION. Ant Village, The.
August Afternoon.
Christmas Eve.
Jolly Woodchuck, The.
Little Fox, The.
Midsummer Night.
Open the Door.
Our Birthday.
So Many Monkeys.
Trot Along, Pony.
EDFELT, JOHANNES. Life of Life.
EDGAR, MARY S. Prayer-Poem, A.
Youth's Prayer, A.
EDGELOW, MARGUERITE. English Pastoral.
EDGERTON, JAMES ARTHUR. Tell Him So.
EDGETT, EDWIN FRANCIS. Old Books for New.
EDMAN, IRWIN. Advice to a Young Man (of Letters) Who Doesn't Know How to Take Care of Himself.

Curse of Faint Praise, The.
Flower for a Professor's Garden of Verses.
Intermission, Please!
Kiss-Fest, The.
La Donna E Perpetuum Mobile.
Little Bow to Books on How To, A.
Lux Aeterna.
New Hellas, The.
Peace.
Prayer for All Poets at This Time.
To Harold Jacoby.
To Henry David Thoreau.
EDMESTON, JAMES. Evening Blessing, An.
Hymn: "Lead us, heavenly Father, lead us."
Lead us, heavenly Father, lead us.
Prayer to the Trinity.
Saviour, Breathe an Evening Blessing.
EDMONDS, PAUL. Little Tommy Tiddler.
EDMUND, FATHER. *See* HILL, BENJAMIN DIONYSIUS.
EDSALL, FLORENCE SMALL. Stars.
To a Cat Purring.
EDSALL, RICHARD LINN. Resurgent.
EDSON, CHARLES L. Ravin's of Piute Poet Poe.
EDWARDES, RICHARD. *See* EDWARDS, RICHARD.
EDWARDINE, SISTER MARY. Ad Mariam.
At Palomar.
Disillusion.
For a Novice.
Madonna Remembers.
EDWARDS, AMELIA BLANDFORD. Give Me Three Grains of Corn, Mother.
EDWARDS, ARCHIE. What Though the Dark!
EDWARDS, DONALD EARL. Cross, The.
Faith.
EDWARDS, ETHEL ASHTON. Return, The.
EDWARDS, H. L. R. From Knees Up, Muvver Brown, *sels.*
Lugano, August 1937.
Museum Portico.
EDWARDS, HARRY STILLWELL. Mammy's Li'l Boy.
EDWARDS, JEANNETTE SLOCOMB. Hester MacDonagh.
EDWARDS, JOHN R. War, The: A–Z.
EDWARDS, MATHILDA C. Church Walking with the World, The.
EDWARDS, MATILDA BARBARA BETHAM. *See* BETHAM-EDWARDS, MATILDA BARBARA.
EDWARDS, OLIVER. Cat and the Man, The.
EDWARDS [*or* EDWARDES], RICHARD.
Amantium Irae.
Being Importunate, at the Length He Obtaineth.
Fortitude; a Young Man of Egypt and Valerian.
M. Edwards' May.
May.
Of Fortune's Power.
Of Women.
Wanting His Desire, He Complaineth.
EDWARDS, THOMAS. Sonnet on a Family Picture.
To Richard Owen Cambridge.
EEDES [*or* EDES], RICHARD. No Love, to Love of Man and Wife.
Of Man and Wife.
EELLS, MARION. Dirge for Beauty.
For a Young Musician.
EGAN, MAURICE FRANCIS. Canticle of the Sun, *tr.*
Columbus the World-Giver.
He Made Us Free.
Madonna of the Empty Arms.
Maurice de Guerin.
Old Violin, The.
Shamrock, The.
Vigil of the Immaculate Conception.
EGAR, J. H. Sing, Sing for Christmas.
EGBERT, ELLA ELIZABETH. Days like These.
EGERTON, HELEN MERRILL. Bluebirds.
Hill Song, A.
In Arcadie.
Sandpipers.
When the Gulls Come In.
EGI. Both Are Blessing.
My Treasure.
Thank Thee.
EGLINGTON, CHARLES. Arrival and Departure.
Cheetah.
Meeting.
Vanquished, The.
"EGLINTON, JOHN" (William Kirkpatrick Magee). Winds, The.
EGUREN, JOSÉ MARÍA. Abbey, The.
Girl with the Blue Lamp, The.
Lied V.
Marginal.
EHRENBURG, ILYA GRIGORYEVICH. Behold, newcomer, liberty is dead.
But Tell Me.
Day will come, The: our sufferings will be.
Our Children's Children Will Marvel.
Sons of Our Sons, The.
To Russia.
Tree, The.
Trumpet, The.
EHRENSTEIN, ALBERT. Ares.
Grief.
Home-coming.
Homer.
Suffering.
EHRMANN, MAX. Away.
Hate and the Love of the World, The.
I Ponder on Life.
If You Have Made Gentler the Churlish World.
Mother.
Prayer, A: "Let me do my work each day."
EICHENDORFF, JOSEPH, BARON VON. At Night.
Beautiful Foreign Land.
Broken Ring, The.
Conversation in the Forest.
Death's Delight.
Divining Rod, The.
Evening.
Hermit. The.
Moon-Night.
Night Blossoms.
Nocturne: "I wander through the silent night."
Old Age.
Old Garden, The.
On the Death of My Child.
Prague Students' Song.
Prayer: "God, I fain would pray with fervor."
Returning Home.
Returning Spring.
EIGNER, LARRY. B.
Do It Yrself.
Environs.
Fete, A.
Gone, A.
Keep Me Still, for I Do Not Want to Dream.
Noise Grimaced.
Open.
Passages.
EIKEI (the monk Eikei). Autumn has come.
EINHORN, DAVID. Evening Walk.
In Soft Moss, Muted Steps.
Who Then Extends His Arms to Me.
EISELEY, LOREN C. One Remembering the Marshes.
EISENBERG, EMANUEL. Abishag, *tr.*
Reflections in a Hospital.
EK, KARIN. Eye, An.
EKVALL, ROBERT K. Put Grief Away. *Fr.* Tibetan Comforter.
Tibetan Comforter, *sel.*
ELAM, WILLIAM C. Mecklenburg Declaration, The.
ELDERTON, WILLIAM. True Form and Shape of a Monsterous Child, The.
ELDRIDGE, JAY GLOVER. God of Years, Thy Love Hath Led Us.
ELDRIDGE, PAUL. Of China and Her Wisdom.
Wang Peng, Famous Sociologist.
ELDRIDGE, RICHARD BURDICK. Soul Remembers, The.
ELEANORE, SISTER MARY. Candles.
Lesson, The.
Missionary, The.
Soldier and the Nun, The.
Superannuation.
Vocation of Saint Francis, The.
World to Any Nun, The.
ELEAZAR. Thy Faithful Sons.
ELIJAH BEN MENAHEM HAZAKEN OF LE MANS. Precepts He Gave His Folk.
"ELIOT, GEORGE" (Mary Ann [*or* Marian] Evans Lewes Cross). At Set of Sun.
Brother and Sister.
Choir Invisible, The.
Count That Day Lost.
Dark, The. *Fr.* The Spanish Gypsy.
Day Is Dying. *Fr.* The Spanish Gypsy.
God Needs Antonio. *Fr.* Stradivarius.
I am Lonely. *Fr.* The Spanish Gypsy.
Life's Purpose. *Fr.* A Minor Prophet.
Making Life Worth While.
Minor Prophet, A, *sels.*
O May I Join the Choir Invisible.
Our Mother.
Roses.
Song of the Zincali. *Fr.* The Spanish Gypsy.
Spanish Gypsy, The, *sels.*
Spring Song. *Fr.* The Spanish Gypsy.
Stradivarius, *sel.*
Tide [*or* Tides] of Faith, The. *Fr.* A Minor Prophet.
Two Lovers.
Working with God. *Fr.* Stradivarius.
ELIOT, HENRIETTA ROBINS. Why It Was Cold in May.
ELIOT, HENRY RUTHERFORD. Laugh It Off.
ELIOT, HENRY W., JR. Life in the Chem. Lab.
ELIOT, THOMAS STEARNS. Ad-dressing of Cats, The.
Anabasis, *sels., tr.*
Animula.
Ash on an Old Man's Sleeve. *Fr.* Four Quartets: Little Gidding.
Ash Wednesday.
Ash Wednesday, *sels.*
Aunt Helen.
Battle of the Pekes and the Pollicles, The, and the Intervention of the Great Rumpus Cat.
Boston Evening Transcript, The.
Burbank with a Baedeker; Bleistein with a Cigar.
Burnt Norton. *Fr.* Four Quartets.
Burnt Norton, *sels.* *Fr.* Four Quartets.
Cape Ann. *Fr.* Landscapes.
Chorus: "Eagle soars in the summit of Heaven, The." *Fr.* The Rock.
Chorus: "It is hard for those who have never known persecution." *Fr.* The Rock.
Chorus: "Word of the Lord came unto me, The." *Fr.* The Rock.
Chorus: "You have seen the house built, you have seen it adorned." *Fr.* The Rock.
Circe's Palace.
Conversation Galante.
Cooking Egg, A.
Coriolan, *sels.*
Cousin Nancy.
Death by Water. *Fr.* The Waste Land.
Difficulties of a Statesman. *Fr.* Coriolan.
Dry Salvages, The. *Fr.* Four Quartets.
Dry Salvages, The, *sels.* *Fr.* Four Quartets.
Eagle Soars in the Summit of Heaven, The. *Fr* The Rock.
East Coker. *Fr.* Four Quartets.
Eyes That Last I Saw in Tears.
Four Quartets, *sels.*
Fragment of an Agon.
Game of Chess, A. *Fr.* The Waste Land.
Gerontion.
Growltiger's Last Stand.
Gus, the Theatre Cat.
Hippopotamus, The.

ELIOT, THOMAS STEARNS (*continued*)
His soul stretched tight across the skies. *Fr.* Preludes.
Hollow Men, The.
Hollow Men, The, *sel.*
I Have Built Myself, with Honour and Dignity, *tr. Fr.* Anabasis.
Journey of the Magi.
Knowledge without Wisdom. *Fr.* The Rock.
La Figlia Che Piange.
Landscapes.
Landscapes, *sels.*
Lines for an Old Man.
Lines for Cuscuscaraway and Mirza Murad Ali Beg.
Little Gidding. *Fr.* Four Quartets.
Little Gidding, *sel. Fr.* Four Quartets.
Love Song of J. Alfred Prufrock, The.
Love Song of J. Alfred Prufrock, The, *sels.*
Macavity, the Mystery Cat.
Marina.
Men Who Turn from God. *Fr.* The Rock.
Mr. Apollinax.
Mr. Eliot's Sunday Morning Service.
Morning at the Window.
Morning comes to consciousness, The. *Fr.* Preludes.
New Hampshire. *Fr.* Landscapes.
Old Gumbie Cat, The.
Portrait of a Lady.
Prelude: "Winter evening settles down, The." *Fr.* Preludes.
Preludes.
Preludes, *sels.*
Rannoch by Glencoe. *Fr.* Landscapes.
Rhapsody on a Windy Night.
Rock, The, *sels.*
Rum Tum Tugger, The.
Salutation.
Skimbleshanks, the Railway Cat.
Song: "I have halted my horse by the tree of the doves," *tr. Fr.* Anabasis.
Song: "Under the bronze leaves a colt was foaled," *tr. Fr.* Anabasis.
Song for Simeon, A.
Song of the Jellicles, The.
Soul of Man Must Quicken, The.
Such Is the Way of the World, *tr. Fr.* Anabasis.
Sweeney among the Nightingales.
Sweeney Erect.
There Shall Always Be the Church. *Fr.* The Rock.
Three Sections from "Anabasis," *tr.*
Thus Was the City Founded, *tr. Fr.* Anabasis.
Triumphal March. *Fr.* Coriolan.
Usk. *Fr.* Landscapes.
Waste Land, The.
Waste Land, The, *sels.*
We Shall Not Dwell Forever in These Yellow Lands, *tr. Fr.* Anabasis.
When the Church Is No Longer Regarded. *Fr.* The Rock.
Whispers of Immortality.
Wind Sprang Up at Four o'Clock, The.
Winter evening settles down, The. *Fr.* Preludes.
You tossed a blanket from the bed. *Fr.* Preludes.
ELIYIA, JOSEPH. Jesus.
Militarism.
Our Torah.
ELIZABETH, EMPRESS OF AUSTRIA-HUNGARY. Inscription on a Shrine near Ischl.
ELIZABETH I, QUEEN OF ENGLAND.
Daughter of Debate, The.
Doubt, The.
Doubt of Future Foes, The.
I grieve, and dare not show my discontent.
Importune Me No More.
Self and the Otherself.
When I Was Fair and Young.
Youth and Cupid.
ELIZABETH, QUEEN CONSORT OF HENRY VII. I Pray to Venus.
ELLERTON, JOHN LODGE. Evening.
God of the Living, The.
Living unto Thee.
Now the Laborer's Task Is O'er.
ELLERTON, JOHN LODGE, *and* HENRY FOTHERGILL CHORLEY. *See* CHORLEY, HENRY FOTHERGILL, *and* JOHN LODGE ELLERTON.
ELLIOT, LADY CHARLOTTE. Wife of Loki, The.
ELLIOT, GEORGE TRACY. Winter Twilight.
ELLIOT, SIR GILBERT. Amynta.
My Sheep I Neglected.
ELLIOT, JANE [*or* JEAN] (1727–1805). Flowers of the Forest, The.
Lament for Flodden.
ELLIOT, JEAN (*contemporary*). Exercise in a Meadow.
ELLIOTT, CHARLOTTE. Just as I Am.
Let Me Be with Thee.
My Soul Shall Cling to Thee.
Prayer: "My God, is any hour so sweet."
"Thy Will Be Done."
ELLIOTT, EBENEZER. Battle Song.
Builders, The.
Burns.
Corn-Law Hymn.
Elegy on William Cobbett.
God Save the People.
Land Which No One Knows, The.
Marching Song.
People's Anthem, The.
Plaint.
Poet's Epitaph, A.
Social Religion.
Song: "Child, is thy father dead?"
Spirits and Men, *sel.*
Splendid Village, The, *sel.*
Spring.
Walkley.
When Wilt Thou Save the People?
ELLIOTT, ELLEN COIT. Choice.
ELLIOTT, F. ANN. Pictures.
Snow, The.
ELLIOTT, MARY. Crocus, The.
Nest, The.
Oak, The.
Silkworms.
Think before You Act.
What Is Veal?
ELLIS, C. D. B. Head and Heart.
Unforgivable and Unforgiven.
Woman.
ELLIS, EDWIN JOHN. Himself, *sel.*
ELLIS, GEORGE. Rondeau Humbly Inscribed to the Right Hon. William Eden . . . , *at.*
ELLIS, GEORGE, GEORGE CANNING, *and* JOHN HOOKHAM FRERE. *See* CANNING, GEORGE, GEORGE ELLIS, *and* JOHN HOOKHAM FRERE.
ELLIS, H. F. Message to General Montgomery.
ELLIS, HAVELOCK. Folk Songs, *tr.*
Gospel of Consolation, The.
In the Strand.
Revelation, The.
For translations from Spanish, see OnPM.
ELLIS, RAY. Hunter, A.
ELLIS, VIVIAN LOCKE. At Common Dawn.
ELLISON, HENRY. Fall of the Year.
ELLISTON, GEORGE (Mrs. Augustus T. Coleman). April Morning.
ELLSWORTH, D. A. Pa's Soft Spot.
Piller Fights.
ELLSWORTH, ERASTUS WOLCOTT. *Mayflower,* The.
What Is the Use? *sel.*
ELLWANGER, WILLIAM DE LANCEY. To Jessie's Dancing Feet.
ELLWOOD, THOMAS. Prayer, A: "O that mine eyes might closèd be."
ELMER, FRANKLIN D., JR. Christmas Blessing.
Lost Christ, The.
Tale of One Hill.
Unlikely Rebel, The.
EL-REGISTAN *and* SERGEI MIKHALKOV. *See* MIKHALKOV, SERGEI, *and* EL-REGISTAN.
ELSKAMP, MAX. To-day's the Sabbath Holiday.
ELSON, LOUIS C. Lullaby, A: "Dollie, the night has come."
"ELSPETH" (Elspeth MacDuffie O'Halloran). Budget.
Forecast.
It's a Fib.
Possibly.
Sentimental Journey.
Wednesday.
ELTON, SIR CHARLES ABRAHAM. Boyhood, *sel.*
Brothers, The, *sel.*
Elegy, An: "Let others pile their yellow ingots high," *tr.*
Landscape of the Heart. *Fr.* The Brothers.
Naught, now, can pass belief; in Nature's ways, *tr.*
Pillars of death! carved sirens! tearful urn! *tr.*
Theogony, *sel., tr.*
This dust was Timas'; ere her bridal hour, *tr.*
To Lesbia, *tr.*
We, like the leaves of many-blossomed Spring, *tr.*
Works and Days, *tr.*
Works and Days, *sels., tr.*
ELTON, GODFREY. Lugete O Veneres Cupidinesque.
News.
ELUARD, PAUL All Life.
Death Is Dead.
First in the World.
Fish, The.
From Solitude to Solitude towards Life.
Loss.
Max Ernst.
Movement.
One for All Time, The.
Our Movement.
Such a Woman, the Principle of Life, the Ideal Questioner.
Through an Embrace.
To Die.
To Pablo Picasso.
To the Infinite.
Universe-Solitude, *sel.*
Victory of Guernica.
We Are.
What the Laborer Says Is Always beside the Point.
You Rise Up.
ELWES, RICHARD. After Hearing the Prime Minister, April 27th, 1941.
In a British Cemetery Overseas, May, 1940.
"ELYTIS, ODYSSEUS" (Odysseus Alepoudelis). Body of Summer, The.
Helen.
Mad Pomegranate Tree, The.
Marina of the Rocks.
EMANS, ELAINE V. Little Boy Speaks, A.
EMBRY, JACQUELINE. Tea.
Unregenerate.
EMBURY, EMMA CATHERINE. Love Unsought.
EMBURY, LUCY. Christmas Prayer, A.
EMERSON, CAROLINE D. Modern Ballad, A; the Ups and Downs of the Elevator Car.
EMERSON, CHESTER B. Quest, The.
EMERSON, RALPH WALDO. And When I Am Entombèd.
Anxiety, *sel.*
Apology, The.
April.
April and May. *Fr.* May-Day.
Art.
Astraea.
Atom from Atom. *Fr.* Fragments on Nature and Life.
Bacchus.
Berrying.
Blight.
Bohemian Hymn, The.
Borrowing.
Boston, *sel.*
Boston Hymn.
Brahma.
Celestial Love, *sel.*
Character.
Chickadee. *Fr.* The Titmouse.

Circles.
Compensation ("Why should I keep holiday").
Compensation ("The wings of time").
Concord Hymn.
Concord Hymn, *sel.*
Cupid. *Fr.* Initial Love.
Days.
Day's Ration, The.
Destiny.
Dirge: "Knows he who tills this lonely field."
Duty. *Fr.* Voluntaries.
Each and All.
Earth, The.
Enchanter, The.
Eros.
Experience.
Fable, A: "Mountain and the squirrel, The."
Faith.
Fate.
Father, We Thank Thee, *wr. at.*
Flower Chorus, *wr. at.*
Flute, The, *tr.*
Forbearance.
Forerunners.
Fragments.
Fragments on Nature and Life.
Fragments on Nature and Life, *sel.*
Fragments on the Poet and the Poetic Gift, *sels.*
Freedom.
Friends and Foes [*or* Enemies], *tr.*
Friendship ("A ruddy drop of manly blood").
From the Persian.
Gardener. *Fr.* Quatrains.
Gifts.
Give All to Love.
Give All to Love, *sel.*
God. *Fr.* Woodnotes.
God Hide the Whole World in Thy Heart. *Fr.* Woodnotes.
God's Altar.
God's Message to Men.
Good-bye [Proud World]!
Good-bye, *sel.*
Good Hope.
Grace.
Guide, The. *Fr.* Woodnotes.
Hamatreya.
Heart of All the Scene, The. *Fr.* Woodnotes.
Heroism.
History.
History, *sel.*
Holidays.
Humble-Bee, The.
Humble-Bee, The, *sel.*
Hush!
Hymn: "By the rude bridge that arched the flood."
Hymn Sung at the Completion of the Concord Monument, April 19, 1836.
I have an arrow that will find its mark.
I said to heaven that glowed above, *tr.*
Immanent God, The. *Fr.* Woodnotes.
In an Age of Fops and Toys. *Fr.* Voluntaries.
In the Woods. *Fr.* Good-bye.
Informing Spirit, The.
Initial Love, The, *sel.*
Intellect.
Journals, *sel.*
Let Me Go Where'er I Will. *Fr.* The Music.
Letter, A.
Letters.
Limits.
Lines to Ellen.
Love's Nobility. *Fr.* Celestial Love.
Make Friends, *tr.*
May-Day, *sel.*
Merlin.
Merlin, *sels.*
Merops.
Mighty Heart, The. *Fr.* Woodnotes.
Mithridates.
Monadnoc, *sels.*
Monument of Concord Fight, The.
Monumental Human Expressions. *Fr.* The Problem.
Mountain and the Squirrel, The.
Music.
Musketaquid.
My Garden.
My Garden, *sel.*
Nation's Strength, A.
Nature ("The rounded world is fair to see").
Nature ("She is gamesome and good").
Nature ("A subtle chain of countless rings").
Nature ("Winter knows").
Nemesis.
No Great, No Small. *Fr.* History.
Northman.
Ode: "O tenderly the haughty day."
Ode: "Though loath to grieve."
Ode Inscribed to W. H. Channing.
Ode Inscribed to W. H. Channing, *sel.*
Ode Sung in the Town Hall, Concord, July 4, 1857.
Ode to Beauty.
Oft have I said, I say it once more, *tr.*
Orator. *Fr.* Quatrains.
Pan.
Parks and Ponds.
Past, The.
Poet, The ("A moody child and wildly wise").
Poet, The ("Thy trivial harp"). *Fr.* Merlin.
Poet, The ("To clothe the fiery thought"). *Fr.* Quatrains.
Problem, The.
Problem, The, *sel.*
Quatrain: "Though love repine."
Quatrains, *sels.*
Rhodora, The.
Rhythm.
Romany Girl, The.
Rubies.
Saadi.
Sacrifice.
Sea, The. *Fr.* Sea-Shore.
Sea-Shore [*or* Seashore].
Shakespeare.
Shun Passion.
Singing World, The.
Snowstorm [*or* Snow-Storm], The.
Snowstorm, The, *sel.*
So Nigh Is Grandeur.
Song of Nature.
Sphinx, The.
Spring Prayer, *at.*
Stainless soldier on the walls. *Fr.* Voluntaries.
Teach me your mood, O patient stars.
Terminus.
Test, The.
Thanksgiving.
Thine Eyes Still Shine.
Thought.
Threnody: "South-wind brings, The."
Threnody, *sels.*
Titmouse, The, *sel.*
To Ellen at the South.
To Ellen at the South, *sel.*
To Eva.
To J. W.
To Rhea.
To the Humblebee.
Two Rivers.
Undersong, The. *Fr.* Woodnotes.
Unity.
Uriel.
Voluntaries.
Waldeinsamkeit.
Water.
Waves.
We Are Never Old. *Fr.* The World-Soul.
We Love the Venerable House.
We Thank Thee, *wr. at.*
Wealth.
What Is Excellent Is Permanent. *Fr.* Threnody.
Wind in the Grass, The. *Fr.* To Ellen at the South.
Woodnotes.
Woodnotes, *sels.*
Words of the Gods, The. *Fr.* My Garden.
World-Soul, The.
World-Soul, The, *sel.*
Worship.
Written at Rome.
Written in a Volume of Goethe.
Written in Naples.
Xenophanes.
EMERY, FRANCES D. Long-billed Gannets.
EMERY, GILBERT. Soldier-Dead.
EMERY, RICHARD W. Billy Goats Chew.
EMILIO, MARGUERITE. Prayer for Teachers, A.
EMMANUEL, KASSARIS. Dynasty of Chimeras, *sel.*
Haunted Ship, The.
EMMANUEL, PIERRE. Death Wedding.
Good Friday Rhapsody.
Nada.
EMMETT, DANIEL DECATUR. Dixie.
Dixie, *sel.*
Dixie's Land.
Old Dan Tucker.
EMORY, SUSAN L. Old Woman's Answer to a Letter from Her Girlhood, An.
EMORY, WILLIAM CLOSSON. Be Still.
EMPEDOCLES. Blood-Guilty, The.
I will report a twofold truth. Now grows.
Karma.
Limitations of Knowledge, The.
Nature the Artist.
Pre-Existence.
There is a word of Fate, an old decree.
Transmigration.
EMPSON, WILLIAM. Arachne.
Aubade.
Beautiful Train, The.
Camping Out.
Courage Means Running.
Doctrinal Point.
Flighting for Duck.
Four Legs, Two Legs, Three Legs.
High Dive.
Homage to the British Museum.
Ignorance of Death.
Invitation to Juno.
Just a Smack at Auden.
Legal Fiction.
Letter I ("You were amused to find you too could fear").
Letter IV ("Hatched in a rasping darkness of dry sand").
Manchouli.
Missing Dates.
Not Wrongly Moved.
Note on Local Flora.
Part of Mandevil's Travels.
Scales, The.
Sonnet: "Not wrongly moved by this dismaying scene."
This Last Pain.
To an Old Lady.
Villanelle: "It is the pain, it is the pain, endures."
World's End, The.
EMRICH, DUNCAN B. M. To Jean.
ENCINA, JUAN DEL. Come, Let Us Eat and Drink Today.
Mingo.
ENDICOFF, MAX. Excavation, The.
ENGELS, NORBERT. Ex Maria Virgine.
For an Old Man.
One Immortality.
ENGELS, VINCENT DAVID. At the Last.
ENGLE, H. E., *and* ELLEN KING. West Virginia Hills, The.
ENGLE, PAUL. America Remembers, *sel.*
Beasts, *sel.*
Break the Heart's Anger, *sel.*
Cat's Eye.
Chameleon.
Cuban Voyage.
Emily Dickinson.
Fossil.
If Everything.
Joseph's Suspicion, *tr.*
Last Whiskey Cup, The.
No Gull's Wings.
Orion.

ENGLE, PAUL (*continued*)
Panther, The, *tr.*
Remembrance, *tr.*
Troubadour of Eze, The, *sel.*
USA.
ENGLISH, THOMAS DUNN. Arnold at Stillwater.
Assunpink and Princeton.
At Seventy-two, *sel.*
Battle of Monmouth, The.
Battle of New Orleans, The.
Battle of the Cowpens, The.
Battle of the King's Mill.
Ben Bolt.
Betty Zane.
Burning of Jamestown, The.
Charge by the Ford, The.
Fall of Maubila, The.
Oh! Don't You Remember Sweet Alice.
Old Mill, The.
Sack of Deerfield, The.
ENGLISH, WILLIAM. Cashel of Munster, *at.*
ENGONOPOULOS, NIKOS. Hydra of Birds, The.
ENNIUS, QUINTUS. Annales, *sel.*
Like a Shower of Rain. *Fr.* Annales.
ENNODIUS, SAINT (Magnus Felix Ennodius). How of the Virgin Mother Shall I Sing? *Fr.* Hymnus Sanctae Mariae.
Hymnus Sanctae Mariae, *sel.*
ENOCH, OLIVE. Bluebells.
Half Holiday.
Laughter.
ENRIGHT, DENNIS JOSEPH. "Black" Country, The.
Laughing Hyena, by Hokusai, The.
Phoenix' Throne, The.
University Examinations in Egypt.
ENRIGHT, DENNIS JOSEPH, *and* TAKAMICHI NINOMIYA. *For translations from Japanese, see* PoLJ.
ENRIQUETA, MARÍA. Thoughts of a Little Girl.
ENZO, KING OF SARDINIA. On the Fitness of Seasons.
"EPHELIA" (Joan Philips?). Song: "You wrong me, Strephon, when you say."
EPHREM, SAINT. Christmas Hymn, *sel.*
Virgin Truly Full of Wonder. *Fr.* Christmas Hymn.
EPICHARMUS. Invite me to dinner, I'm sure to accept.
ERASMUS, DESIDERIUS. Votive Ode.
ERCILLA Y ZÚÑIGA, ALONSO DE. Araucana, La.
Araucana, La, *sel.*
Welcome of the Young Cacique, The. *Fr.* La Araucana.
ERICKSON, LOIS J. Day's End, *tr.*
For translations from Japanese, see SoLD.
ERINNA. Baucis.
Distaff, A.
Epitaph to Baucis.
Erinna to Her Friend.
Eternal Silence, The.
On a Portrait.
Pillars of death! carved sirens! tearful urn!
Very Torch, The.
ERLINGSSON, THORSTEINN. Snow-Bunting, The.
Terms, The.
ERMONAS. *See* "VLASTOS, PETROS."
ERSKINE, ANDREW. How Sweet This Lone Vale.
ERSKINE, FRANCIS ROBERT ST. CLAIR, EARL OF ROSSLYN. Bedtime.
Memory.
ERSKINE, SIR HENRY. In the Garb of Old Gaul.
ERSKINE, JOHN. Apparition.
Ash Wednesday.
At the Front.
Childhood.
De Gustibus.
Dedication: "When imperturbable the gentle moon."
Dialogue.
"Love That Never Told Can Be."
Modern Ode to the Modern School.
Shepherd Speaks, The.
Song, The: "Song lay silent in my pen, A."
Valentine to One's Wife.
Winter-Song for Pan.
ERSKINE, THOMAS, 1ST BARON ERSKINE. On Scott's "The Field of Waterloo."
ERSKINE, WILLIAM. Epigram: "This house, where once a lawyer dwelt."
This House Where Once a Lawyer Dwelt.
ERSKINE-CRUM, LADY. "Good Night," Says the Owl.
ERYCIUS. Trophy, The.
ERZINGATZI, HOVHANNES. Like an Ocean Is This World.
ESCHENBACH, WOLFRAM VON. *See* WOLFRAM VON ESCHENBACH.
ESCRIBA, COMENDADOR. *See* ESCRIVÁ, JUAN.
ESCRIVÁ, JUAN. Song to Death.
Welcome Death.
ESCUDERO, GONZALO. Dolmens, The.
God.
Zoo.
ESENIN, SERGEI. *See* YESENIN, SERGEI.
ESPAILLAT, RHINA P. From the Rain Down.
ESPINEL, VICENTE MARTÍNEZ. Faint Heart Never Won Fair Lady.
If She Frown My Heart Would Break.
ESPRONCEDA, JOSÉ DE. Condemned to Die, The.
Hymn to the Sun.
Pirate's Song.
Sonnet: "Luxuriant, fragrant, fresh the new-blown rose."
To Harifa, in an Orgy.
To Teresa.
ESSAYAN, ZABELLE. Incense.
ESSEX, EDWIN. Loneliness.
ESSEX, ROBERT DEVEREUX, 2D EARL OF. Change.
Change Thy Mind.
Content.
Happy Were He.
Passion, A.
To Plead My Faith.
Wish, A.
ESSON, LOUIS. Brogan's Lane.
Cradle Song: "Baby, O baby, fain you are for bed."
Old Black Billy an' Me, The.
Shearer's Wife, The.
Whalin' up the Lachlan.
"ESTELLE." *See* BOGART, ELIZABETH.
ESTELLE, SISTER MARY. From Desert to Metropolis.
ESTRADA, GENARO. Lament for Lost Love.
Little Song in the Air.
Paraphrase of Horace.
ESTRADA, RAFAEL. Mexican Soldiers.
Traces.
Twilight.
ESTRELLO, FRANCISCO E. Hands of Christ.
ETHEREGE, SIR GEORGE. Chloris, 'Tis Not in Your Power.
Comical Revenge, The, *sels.*
If She Be Not as Kind as Fair. *Fr.* The Comical Revenge.
Lines to a Lady, Who Asked of Him How Long He Would Love Her.
Love in a Tub, *sels.*
Man of Mode, The, *sels.*
She Would if She Could, *sel.*
Silvia.
Song: "If she be not as kind as fair." *Fr.* Love in a Tub.
Song: "Ladies, though to your conquering eyes." *Fr.* The Comical Revenge.
Song: "Pleasures of love, and the joys of good wine, The." *Fr.* The Man of Mode.
Song: "Ye happy swains, whose hearts are free."
To a Lady Asking [Him] How Long He Would Love Her.
To a Very Young Lady.
To Little or No Purpose I Spent Many Days. *Fr.* She Would if She Could.
Upon the Downs.
Ye Happy Swains, Whose Hearts Are Free.
ETHERIDGE, KEN. Annunciation.
Carnations.
Early Snow.
Mask.
Old Collier, An.
Spring Fragment.
EUBULUS. Love Is Not Winged.
EUENUS [*or* EVENUS]. Child of Athens, honey nurtured, wouldst thou for thy feathered brood.
Page-eater thou, the Muses' bitterest foe.
Swallow, A.
Vine to the Goat, The.
EUGENE, SISTER MARY. Convent Morning.
Maureen O'Reilly.
EUGENIUS III, POPE. Dedication: "Eugenius, thy son, who guards the Rock."
EULALIA, SISTER MARY. Denouement.
Mother.
Question of Sacrifice, A.
To Archbishop Stepinac.
EUPOLIS. Pericles.
Statesman who in speaking all surpassed, A.
EURIPIDES. Aeolus, *sel.*
Aethra's Intercession. *Fr.* Suppliants.
Aftermath, The. *Fr.* Iphigenia in Aulis.
Agamemnon's Children. *Fr.* Iphigenia in Tauris.
Alcestis, *sels.*
Alcestis' Final Hour. *Fr.* Alcestis.
Andromache, *sels.*
Andromache Learns of Her Son's Fate. *Fr.* Trojan Women.
Andromeda, *sel.*
Apollo the Betrayer. *Fr.* Ion.
Arraignment of Helen. *Fr.* Trojan Women.
Bacchae [*or* Bacchanals], *sels.*
Bereavement. *Fr.* Alcestis.
Beginning of Day, The.
Bellerophon, *sel.*
Bird of the Sea. *Fr.* Iphigenia in Tauris.
Birds of God, The. *Fr.* Hippolytus.
"Blot as Black as Death, A." *Fr.* Electra.
By Friendship's Ties. *Fr.* Iphigenia in Tauris.
Cassandra. *Fr.* Trojan Women.
Child-Burial; Sequel to Battles. *Fr.* Trojan Women.
Children.
Children of Heracles, *sels.*
Chivalry. *Fr.* Suppliants.
Chorus: "And Pergamus." *Fr.* Iphigenia in Aulis.
Chorus: "Could I take me to some cavern for mine hiding." *Fr.* Hippolytus.
Chorus: Kings of Troy, The. *Fr.* Andromache.
Chorus: Love Song. *Fr.* Cyclops.
Chorus: "Upward and back to their fountains the sacred rivers are stealing." *Fr.* Medea.
Chorus: "When love has passed its limits." *Fr.* Medea.
Chorus of Satyrs, Driving Their Goats. *Fr.* Cyclops.
Cyclops, *sels.*
Cyclops' Philosophy, A. *Fr.* Cyclops.
Cyclops' Views on Life, A. *Fr.* Cyclops.
Daughters of Troy, The, *sel.*
Dawn. *Fr.* Ion.
Dawn of Woman's Day, The. *Fr.* Medea.
Death of Rhesus, The. *Fr.* Rhesus.
Death the Enemy. *Fr.* Alcestis.
Democratic Way, The; Pro and Con. *Fr.* Suppliants.
Dirge: "I bring from funeral." *Fr.* Suppliants.
Divine Betrayal, The. *Fr.* Ion.
Divine Philosopher, The.
Doom of Hippolytus, The. *Fr.* Hippolytus.

Earth and Sky.
Electra, *sels.*
Electra and Orestes. *Fr.* Electra.
End of Troy, The. *Fr.* Trojan Women.
Epilogue to Fratricidal Folly. *Fr.* Phoenician Maidens.
Eros; Deus Catholicus. *Fr.* Hippolytus.
Escape. *Fr.* Hippolytus.
Eteocles and Polynices. *Fr.* Phoenician Maidens.
Evadne. *Fr.* Suppliants.
Fair Exchange. *Fr.* Cyclops.
Farewell: "Boat two-oared, upon water, A." *Fr.* Alcestis.
Fate of Astyanax, The. *Fr.* Trojan Women.
For Hellas! *Fr.* Iphigenia in Aulis.
Fortune's Wheel. *Fr.* Children of Heracles.
Friendship's Servitude. *Fr.* Hippolytus.
Furies, The. *Fr.* Orestes.
Garland, The. *Fr.* Hippolytus.
Gone Are Ilium's Kings. *Fr.* Andromache.
Guilt! *Fr.* Electra.
Heart, Steel Thyself! *Fr.* Medea.
Hecuba, *sels.*
Helen, *sels.*
"Hence Loathèd Melancholy . . ." *Fr.* Alcestis.
Henchman's Speech, The, *sel. Fr.* Hippolytus.
Heracles, *sels.*
Heraclidae, *sels.*
Hercules Furens, *sels.*
Hippolytus, *sels.*
His Death. *Fr.* Hippolytus.
Home of Aphrodite, The. *Fr.* Bacchae.
Hospitality. *Fr.* Alcestis.
Hymn to the Sirens. *Fr.* Helen.
"I Shame to Wear a Heart So White." *Fr.* Hecuba.
If Music Might but Assuage! *Fr.* Medea.
Ilion Overthrown. *Fr.* Hecuba.
In the Furies' Grasp. *Fr.* Orestes.
In the Stillness of Dawn. *Fr.* Iphigenia in Aulis.
Interlude. *Fr.* Medea.
Ion, *sels.*
Ion and Creusa; Recognition. *Fr.* Ion.
Iphigenia in Aulis, *sels.*
Iphigenia in Tauris, *sels.*
Iphigenia's Dream. *Fr.* Iphigenia in Tauris.
It Is a Gracious House and Ever Was. *Fr.* Alcestis.
Jocasta. *Fr.* Phoenician Maidens.
Kings of Troy, The. *Fr.* Andromache.
Leave-taking of Artemis, The. *Fr.* Hippolytus.
Longing. *Fr.* Hippolytus.
Love.
Love Is Idle.
Macaria and Iolaus. *Fr.* Children of Heracles.
Madness of Heracles, The. *Fr.* Heracles.
Medea, *sels.*
Medea's Resolve. *Fr.* Medea.
Monogamy. *Fr.* Andromache.
Murder of Neoptolemus, The. *Fr.* Andromache.
Necessity. *Fr.* Alcestis.
New Theology, A. *Fr.* Heracles.
Night Watch. *Fr.* Rhesus.
No More, O My Spirit. *Fr.* Hippolytus.
Not Peace at Any Price. *Fr.* Children of Heracles.
O for the Wings of a Dove. *Fr.* Hippolytus.
O Halcyon Bird. *Fr.* Iphigenia in Tauris.
Of the myriad afflictions that beset Hellas.
Old Age.
Old Men, The. *Fr.* Aeolus.
On Cithaeron. *Fr.* Bacchae.
Orestes, *sels.*
Orestes and Electra. *Fr.* Orestes.
Pater Noster. *Fr.* Helen.
Peace, deep and rich.
Peleus. *Fr.* Andromache.
Phoenician Maidens, *sels.*
Phoenissae, *sels.*
Plague the Meddling Female, A! *Fr.* Andromache.
Polyxena. *Fr.* Hecuba.
Powers of Darkness. *Fr.* Orestes.
Praise of a Heroine. *Fr.* Alcestis.
Prayer of Iphigenia, The. *Fr.* Iphigenia in Aulis.
Precarious Life of Man. *Fr.* Hippolytus.
Prelude to Revel. *Fr.* Bacchae.
Prophets Exposed. *Fr.* Helen.
Pure Love.
Pylades. *Fr.* Iphigenia in Tauris.
Rebuke. *Fr.* Rhesus.
Recrimination. *Fr.* Iphigenia in Aulis.
Refugee. *Fr.* Phoenician Maidens.
Revel, The. *Fr.* Bacchae.
Rhesus, *sels.*
Ride to Doom, The. *Fr.* Hippolytus.
Sacrifice of Polyxena, The. *Fr.* Hecuba.
Shifting Fortune. *Fr.* Medea.
Short Story, A. *Fr.* Electra.
Siren-Spirits. *Fr.* Helen.
Six Letters.
Solitary Mourner, The. *Fr.* Rhesus.
Song of the Bacchanals. *Fr.* Bacchae.
Song of the Initiated.
Song of Troy. *Fr.* Trojan Women.
Stratagem. *Fr.* Iphigenia in Tauris.
Strength of Fate, The. *Fr.* Alcestis.
Suppliants, *sels.*
Supplices, *sels.*
Sweetest in Measure, Each Pleasure. *Fr.* Medea.
Take Life as It Comes.
There Are No Gods. *Fr.* Bellerophon.
"This Is Alone Life, Joy, Empire and Victory." *Fr.* Bacchae.
This is true liberty.
Thou Shalt Not Die. *Fr.* Heracles.
Three Classes of Citizens. *Fr.* Suppliants.
Tidings of Home. *Fr.* Iphigenia in Tauris.
To Alcestis. *Fr.* Alcestis.
Troades, *sels.*
Trojan Women, *sels.*
Troy ("In Salamis"). *Fr.* Trojan Women.
Troy ("My fatherland"). *Fr.* Hecuba.
Vanity of Vanities.
Vengeance. *Fr.* Medea.
Voice of Enlightenment, The. *Fr.* Suppliants.
Voice of Hypocrisy, The. *Fr.* Orestes.
Votary to His Goddess, A. *Fr.* Hippolytus.
Watch before Dawn ("Come out, old man"). *Fr.* Iphigenia in Aulis.
Watch before Dawn, The ("Say, whose is the watch?"). *Fr.* Rhesus.
What Is Life?
What Makes the Man. *Fr.* Electra.
When the Ecstasy Has Passed. *Fr.* Bacchae.
Where Shall Wisdom Be Found? *Fr.* Bacchae.
Whither Away? *Fr.* Hecuba.
Who Are the Dead?
Woman without Tears, A. *Fr.* Iphigenia in Tauris.
Worst Horror, The.
Youth. *Fr.* Heracles.
Youth of All Blessings Best. *Fr.* Heracles.

EUSTACE, JOHN CHETWODE. Celestial Queen, *tr. Fr.* De Partu Virginis.
De Partu Virginis, *sel., tr.*

EUWER, ANTHONY. Cats and Humans—All the Same.
Face, The. *Fr.* The Limeratomy.
Gettin' Born.
Hands, The. *Fr.* The Limeratomy.
Limeratomy, The, *sels.*
Limerick: "As a [*or* For] beauty, I'm not a great star." *Fr.* The Limeratomy.
Limerick: "No matter how grouchy you're feeling."
My Face. *Fr.* The Limeratomy.
Smile, The. *Fr.* The Limeratomy.

EVA, REGINALD C. Password, The.
Sorrow.

EVALD, JOHANNES. *See* EWALD, JOHANNES.

EVANS, ABBIE HUSTON. By the Salt Margin.
Cock-crow.
Come to Birth.
Country Miracle.
Euroclydon.
First Concerns.
In Conclusion.
Jones's Pasture.
Mineral Collection, The.
Moonrise.
Return to Life.
Servant of the Prophet, The.
Sun-up in March.
This World.
True Lover, The.
"Will He Give Him a Stone?"

EVANS, ABEL. Epitaph on Sir John Vanbrugh.
For Sir John Vanbrugh, Architect.
On Blenheim House.
On Sir John Vanbrugh [Architect].

EVANS, C. ETHEL. Princess, The.

EVANS, DAVID. Poem I: "Cotton-still spire cracks in chimes on the, The."
Poem II: "Screamlight streams of gleaming waterbreasts smiling."
Sona Dialect.
Synthesis.
This Political Time-plotted Day.

EVANS, DONALD. Body of the Queen.
Bonfire of Kings.
Dinner at the Hotel de la Tigresse Verte.
En Monocle.
Epicede.
In the Gentlemanly Interest.
In the Vices.

EVANS, EVAN. Pastoral Poem, *sel., tr.*
Poet's Welcome, The, *tr. Fr.* Pastoral Poem.
Verses to Mr. Vaughan of Hengwrt.

EVANS, FLORENCE WILKINSON. At the Salon.
Don Juan in Portugal.
Flower Factory, The.
Fugitives, The.
Hawk Shadow.
Heart's Country, The.
Illuminated Canticle, The.
Memorial Tablet, A.
Our Lady of Idleness.
Students.
Things That Endure, The, *sel.*

EVANS, G. ESSEX. Australian Symphony, An.

EVANS, GEORGE EWART. At the Seaside.
Poem: "Progress in the peaceable blue of a sky in summer."
Winter 1939.

EVANS, GILLESPIE. Bacaote to Alexis.
Winter Moonlight.

EVANS, GRACE BOWEN. Women Toilers, The.

EVANS, JONATHAN. It Is Finished.

EVANS, LUCILLE. Stars Lean Close, The.
White Anemone.

EVANS, MARY ANN [*or* MARIAN]. *See* "ELIOT, GEORGE."

EVANS, NATHANIEL. Elegy to the Memory of My Beloved Friend, Mr. Thomas Godfrey.
Ode to My Ingenious Friend, Mr. Thomas Godfrey.

EVANS, PATRICK. At Morning an Iris.
Green Grass Growing.

EVANS, RICHARD X. Unemployment.

EVANS, SEBASTIAN. Dirge for Summer, A.
Seven Fiddlers, The.
Shadows.
What the Trumpeter Said.

EVANS, VIRGINIA MORAN. Vision, The.

EVARTS, R. C. Alice in Cambridge.
Jabberwocky.
EVE, MARIA LOUISA. New Dixie, The.
EVERAERTS, JAN NICOLAI. *See* JOHANNES SECUNDUS.
EVERETT, DAVID. Boy Reciter, The.
Tall Oaks from Little Acorns Grow.
EVERETT, EDWARD. Dirge of Alaric the Visigoth.
EVERETT, LAURA BELL. Death-Grapple.
Lament of the Voiceless, The.
Miser, The.
Resurgence.
EVERSLEY, MARY. Just to Be Needed.
EVERSON, WILLIAM. *See* ANTONINUS, BROTHER.
EVERTS, LILLIAN. Playmates.
"EVOE." *See* KNOX, EDMUND GEORGE VALPY.
EWALD [*or* EVALD], JOHANNES. King Christian.
Little Gunver.
Three Valkyries, The.
EWART, GAVIN. Bofors A. A. Gun, The.
Cigarette for the Bambino.
"For Whom the Bell Tolls."
Miss Twye.
Poem: "To go, to leave the classics and the buildings."
Sonnet: "Point where beauty and intelligence meet, The."
When a Beau Goes In.
EWEN, JOHN. Boatie Rows, The.
EWER, W. N. Chosen People, The.
Epigram: "How odd/ of God."
Five Souls.
EWING, ANNEMARIE. Ballad: "Mother mine, Mother mine, what do you see?"
Fisherman's Blunder off New Bedford, Massachusetts.
If the Heart Be Homeless.
Man Within, The.
Rhyme from Grandma Goose.
Sleep, Madame, Sleep.
EWING, JENNIE [*or* JEANNIE] PENDLETON. Inventor's Wife, An.
EWING, JULIANA HORATIA. Big Smith.
Bluebells.
Burial of the Linnet.
Dolly's Lullaby.
For Good Luck.
Friend in the Garden, A.
Gifts.
Kit's Cradle.
Little Kings and Queens of the May.
Willow-Man, The.
EXCELL, PATRICIA. Forgotten Objects on a Beach.
E-YEH-SHURE' (Louise Abeita). Beauty.
EYTINGE, MARGARET. Baby Louise.
EYVINDR FINSSON (*nicknamed* Skaldaspillir). Death Song of Haakon the Good.
Lay of Hakon, The.
EZEKIELOS [*or* EZECHIEL] OF ALEXANDRIA. Exodus from Egypt, The.
EZOBI, JOSEPH. Barren Soul, A. *Fr.* The Silver Bowl.
Silver Bowl, The, *sel.*

F

"F., E. S." Blood-Root.
"F. B. P." *See* "P., F. B."
"F. C." *See* "C., F."
"F. L. H." *See* "H., F. L."
"F. M." *See* "M., F."
"F. McK." *See* "McK., F."
"F. P. A." *See* ADAMS, FRANKLIN PIERCE.
"F. W. D." *See* "D., F. W."
FABBRI, CORA RANDALL. White Roses.
FABER, FREDERICK WILLIAM. Aged Cities.
All-embracing, The. *Fr.* God Our Father.
Cherwell Waterlily, The.
Ennerdale.
Expectation, The. *Fr.* Our Lady's Expectation.
Faith of Our Fathers.
God Our Father, *sels.*
God's Mercy. *Fr.* God Our Father.
Grandeurs of Mary, The.
He Satisfies.
Heart of the Eternal, The. *Fr.* God Our Father.
Jesus, Child and Lord.
Jesus, gentlest Saviour.
Jesus, My God and My All.
Larch Trees.
Mundus Morosus.
My God, How Wonderful Thou Art. *Fr.* Our Heavenly Father.
Nearest Friend, The.
O, How the Thought of God Attracts!
O Paradise! O Paradise!
Our Heavenly Father, *sel.*
Our Lady in the Middle Ages.
Our Lady's Expectation, *sel.*
Paradise.
Right Is Right.
Right Must Win, The.
Shadow of the Rock, The.
Sir Lancelot, *sel.*
There's a Wideness in God's Mercy. *Fr.* God Our Father.
Will of God, The.
World Morose, The.
Written in a Little Lady's Little Album.
FABYAN, ROBERT. Dedication of the Chronicles of England and France.
FADIMAN, CLIFTON. Jacobean.
Theological.
FAGIN, BRYLLION. On Rereading Shelley.
FAHY, FRANCIS A. Donovans, The.
Irish Molly O.
Little Mary Cassidy.
Ould Plaid Shawl, The.
FAIRBRIDGE, KINGSLEY OGILVIE. Song Maker, The.
FAIRBRIDGE, WOLFE SEYMOUR. Consecration of the House.
FAIRBURN, ARTHUR REX DUGARD. Beggar to Burgher.
Disquisition on Death, *sel.*
Down on My Luck.
Epithalamium.
Farewell, A: "What is there left to be said?"
Full Fathom Five.
Impetuous Lover, The.
Kowhai.
La Belle Dame sans Merci.
Landscape with Figures.
Night Song.
One Race, One Flag.
Song: "O lovers, this song I give to you." *Fr.* To Daphnis and Chloe in the Park.
Song at Summer's End.
To a Friend in the Wilderness, *sel.*
To Daphnis and Chloe in the Park, *sel.*
Winter Night.
FAIRFAX, EDWARD. Armida, the Sorceress, *tr. Fr.* Jerusalem Delivered.
Crusaders Reach Jerusalem, The, *tr. Fr.* Jerusalem Delivered.
Godfrey of Bulloigne, *sels., tr.*
Jerusalem Delivered, *sels., tr.*
Pluto's Council, *tr. Fr.* Jerusalem Delivered.
Prayer Brings Rain, A, *tr. Fr.* Jerusalem Delivered.
FAIRFAX, ROBERT. That Was My Woe.
FAIRFAX, THOMAS, 3D BARON. Upon a Patch Face.
Upon the New-built House at Appleton.
FAIRLESS, MICHAEL. Out of the Shadow.
FAIRTHORNE, DART. Early Autumn.
FALCONER, E. J. Cradle Song at Bethlehem.
Doves.
Elephant, The.
Little Finger Game, A.
Marketing.
FALCONER, EDMUND (Edmund O'Rourke). Killarney.
FALCONER, HARRY W. Challenge.
FALCONER, WILLIAM. All Hands Unmoor! *Fr.* The Shipwreck.
High o'er the Poop the Audacious Seas Aspire.
In vain the cords and axes were prepared. *Fr.* The Shipwreck.
It comes! the dire catastrophe draws near. *Fr.* The Shipwreck.
Shipwreck, The, *sels.*
Shortening Sail. *Fr.* The Shipwreck.
FALKE, GUSTAV. God's Harp.
Strand-Thistle.
FALKENBURY, FRANCIS E. South Street.
FALKLAND, LUCIUS CARY, 2D VISCOUNT. *See* CARY, LUCIUS, 2D VISCOUNT FALKLAND.
FALLIS, EDWINA H. Prairie Spring.
September.
Wise Johnny.
FALLON, DAVID. Nature's Miracle.
FALLON, EUNICE. August.
FALLON, JOHN. Dissecting Room.
Inscription for an Old Well.
FALLON, PADRAIC. Elegy for a Countryman.
Farmer.
Lady Day.
Long John.
Mary Hynes.
Out of Soundings.
River Walk, The.
Virgin.
Waistcoat, The.
Wisdom.
Writing on the Wall.
FALLSTRÖM, DANIEL. Oh, Never Ask!
Stockholm in White.
To a Sea-Gull in the Steamer's Wake.
"FALSTAFF, JAKE" (Herman Fetzer). Dick Johnson Reel, The.
FAN CH'ENG TA. Reverie.
FANDEL, JOHN. Bee, The.
Pulse of Darkness, The.
Synonym for God, A.
FANDEL, PETER. Roosevelt.
FANE, SIR FRANCIS. Cupid, I Scorn to Beg the Art. *Fr.* Love in the Dark.
Love in the Dark, *sel.*
FANE, JULIAN. Ad Matrem.
Apethorpe.
FANE, MILDMAY, EARL OF WESTMORLAND. *See* WESTMORLAND, MILDMAY FANE, 2D EARL OF.
"FANE, VIOLET" (Mary Montgomerie Singleton Currie, Baroness Currie). Afterwards.
Foreboding, A.
In Green Old Gardens.
May Song, A.
FANG CHE CHAI. Kite, The.
FANNING, ELLA AUGUSTA. Summer Cat, The.
FANSHAWE, CATHERINE MARIA. Enigma on the Letter H.
Fragment: "There is a river clear and fair."
Imitation of Wordsworth, An.
Letter for You, A.
Riddle, A: Letter "H," The.
Riddle: "'Twas whispered in heaven [*or* in heaven pronounced, and], 'twas muttered in hell."
FANSHAWE, SIR RICHARD. But, our Winter come, in vain.
Cape of Tempests, The, *tr. Fr.* The Lusiads.
Episode of Adamastor off the Cape of Good Hope, *tr. Fr.* The Lusiads.
Fall, The. *Fr.* Il Pastor Fido.
Golden Age, The. *Fr.* Il Pastor Fido.
Hope.
Il Pastor Fido, *sels.*
Lusiads, The, *sel., tr.*
Means to Attain Happy Life, The, *tr.*
Now War Is All the World About. *Fr.* Il Pastor Fido.
Ode, An, upon Occasion of His Majesties Proclamation in the Yeare 1630.
Of Beauty.
Of Time. *Fr.* Il Pastor Fido.

Rose, A. *Fr.* Il Pastor Fido.
Rose of Life, The.
Fan Tseng Hsiang. Fan, The.
Noonday.
Fan Yün. Joy.
Farber, Norma. Beyond the Tapestries.
Farbstein, W. E. Double Duty.
Fargo, Ruth Scofield. Perfection.
Fargue, Léon Paul. Aeternae Memoriae Patris, *sel.*
At Saint-Germain.
Home.
My Part of the City.
On the Thread of the Pale Hour.
Saint-Germain-des-Prés.
So Many Years Have Gone!
Farjeon, Eleanor. After Rain.
Annar-Mariar's Christmas Shopping.
Argus.
Bedtime.
Books.
Boys' Names.
Carol for Christmas Eve, A.
Child in the Train, The.
Children's Bells, The.
Choosing.
Circus.
City Show, The.
City Streets and Country Roads.
Coach.
Cock, The.
Country Vegetables.
Dance Ring, The.
Dancing.
Down! Down!
Dragon-Fly, A.
Earth and Sky.
Farewell to the Old Year.
Farm Cart.
Flower-Seller, The.
For a Cock.
For a Dewdrop.
For a Mocking Voice.
For Christmas Day.
For Snow.
For Them.
Fred.
Geography.
Getting Out of Bed.
Girls' Names.
Griselda.
Gypsy, The.
Heigh-ho, April!
Hey! My Pony!
In the Week When Christmas Comes.
Jenny White and Johnny Black.
Jill Came from the Fair.
Jim at the Corner.
Kingcups.
Kitten, A.
Light the Lamps Up, Lamplighter.
Milk-Cart Pony, The.
Minnie.
Mrs. Malone.
Mrs. Peck-Pigeon.
Moon-Come-Out.
Morning Song, A.
Music.
Narcissus Fields.
News! News!
Night Will Never Stay, The.
Now Every Child.
October's Song.
Old Man's Toes, The.
Old Shepherds, The.
On the Staircase.
Our Brother Is Born.
Our Mother's Tunes.
Outlet, The.
Over the Garden Wall.
People, Look East.
Picking Up Sticks.
Quarrel, The.
Rhyme for Francis, A; October 4th.
Riding of the Kings, The.
Sailor.
School-Bell.
Shall I to the Byre Go Down?
Shepherd and the King, The.
Shopman, The.
Sisters.
Six Green Singers.
Sonnet: "Farewell, you children that I might have borne."
Sounds in the Morning, The.
Sun and Wind.
There Are Big Waves.
There Isn't Time.
This Holy Night.
Three Little Puffins.
Through a Shop Window.
Tide in the river, The.
Vegetables.
Welcome to the New Year.
What Is Poetry?
Wheelbarrow.
White Horses.
Who'll Buy My Valley Lilies?
Wild Thyme.
William I—1066.
Wind, The.
Window Boxes.
Farjeon, Eleanor, *and* Herbert Farjeon. Henry VIII.
Rob Roy.
Sir Philip Sidney.
Farley, Corinne. Soul-feeding Hyacinths.
Farley, Henry. Bounty of Our Age, The. *Fr.* St. Paul's Church, Her Bill for the Parliament.
St. Paul's Church, Her Bill for the Parliament, *sel.*
To See a Quaint Outlandish Fowl. *Fr.* St. Paul's Church, Her Bill for the Parliament.
Farley, Robert E. Thinking Happiness.
Farnaby, Giles. Among the Daffadillies.
Farnham, Jessie. Garland for a Storyteller.
"Farningham, Marianne" (Mary Anne Hearn). Burden, The.
Daily Task, The.
God Cares.
He Careth.
Last Hymn, The.
Let Us Give Thanks.
People's Holidays, The.
"Farningham, Marianne," *and* James M. Gray. Pray One for Another.
Farnum, C. G. Let Me Live for a Time Way Back from the Road.
Farquhar, George. Love and a Bottle, *sel.*
Song: "How blest are lovers in disguise!" *Fr.* Love and a Bottle.
Farragut, David Glascoe. Through Fire in Mobile Bay, *at.*
Farrar, Geraldine. Easter Robin, The.
Legend of the Dogwood Tree, The.
Little Christmas Donkey, The.
Shepherd's Madrigal, The.
"What Think Ye of Christ?"
Farrar, Janice. Thought of Marigolds, A.
Farrar, John Chipman. Alone.
Ambitious Mouse, The.
Barge Wife, A.
Brest Left Behind.
Broom.
Bundles.
Catfish.
Chanticleer.
Choice.
Comparison, A.
Critic, The.
Cuckoo Clock, The.
Days of the Week, The.
Drum, The.
Epithalamion for Amaryllis.
Hillside Farmer, A.
Hill-Woman, A.
Magic.
Moral Song.
Morning at the Beach.
Parenthood.
Penny Problem.
Prayer: "Last night I crept across the snow."
Preference.
Roller Skates.
Serious Omission.
Shops.
Song for a Camper.
Song for a Forgotten Shrine to Pan.
Spring Wish.
Summer Wish.
Threnody: "Red leaves fall upon the lake, The."
Time Is Today, The.
Tracks.
Victorian Song.
Watching Clouds.
Water Lily.
When Amaryllis Bowls.
Windmill, The.
Wish at Meal-Time.
Farrell, Bob. Old Zip Coon, *at.*
Turkey in the Straw, *at.*
Farrell, J. R. Bank Thief, The.
Farren, Robert (Roibéard O'Farachåin).
All That Is, and Can Delight.
Beset Wife, The.
Cool Gold Wines of Paradise, The.
Finding of the Táin, The.
Immolation.
Island Boatman's Love-Croon, The.
Joy's Peak.
Lineage.
Mary.
Mason, The.
No Woman Born.
Pets, The.
To the Bell-Ringer.
Una Bhan, *ad.*
What I Have.
Farrington, Harry Webb. Airmen's Hymn, The.
As He Walked with Us.
Bethlehem.
Dear Lord, Who Sought at Dawn.
Our Christ.
Farrow, G. E. Converted Cannibals, The.
Retired Pork-Butcher and the Spook, The.
Farrukhi. Branding, The.
Faubion, Dorothy. Hump, the Escalator.
Faulds, Lena E. American Flag, The.
Faulkner, Sanford C. Arkansas Traveler, The, *at.*
Faulks, Theodosia. *See* Garrison, Theodosia Pickering.
Fauset, Jessie Redmond (Mrs. Herbert Harris). Christmas Eve in France.
Dead Fires.
Enigma.
Fragment: "Breath of life imbued those few dim days, The."
I Think I See Her.
La Vie C'est la Vie.
Noblesse Oblige.
Oblivion.
Oriflamme.
Rencontre.
Return, The.
Touché.
Words! Words!
Fawcett, Edgar. Fireflies.
Humming Bird, A.
January Is Here.
Old Beau, The.
Oriole.
Scholar's Sweetheart, The.
To an Oriole.
To the Evening Star.
Toad, A.
White Camellia, A.
Wild Roses.
Fawcett, John. Blest Be the Tie That Binds.
Lord, dismiss us with thy blessing.
Prayer before Execution, *tr.*
Fawkes, Francis. Argonautica, *sels., tr.*
Brown Jug, The.
Fay, J. J. Young Lochinvar; the True Story in Blank Verse, *at.*
Fay, Temple. Dedicated to Dr. Harvey Cushing.
These Hands of Ours.
Faydi. On the Death of His Child.
Fazio degli Uberti. Canzone: His Portrait of His Lady.
Of England, and of Its Marvels.
Fearing, Kenneth. A la Carte.
Ad.
American Rhapsody (4).
Any Man's Advice to His Son.

FEARING, KENNETH (*continued*)
C Stands for Civilization.
Confession Overheard in a Subway.
Cultural Notes.
Denouement.
Devil's Dream.
Dirge: "1-2-3 was the number he played."
End of the Seers' Convention.
Evening Song.
Homage.
John Standish, Artist.
Love 20¢ the First Quarter Mile.
Lullaby: "Wide as this night, old as this night is old."
Memo.
Minnie and Mrs. Hoyne.
No Credit.
Pact.
Pay-off.
People vs. the People, The.
Portrait.
Readings, Forecasts, Personal Guidance.
Reception Good.
Requiem.
Resurrection.
SOS.
These are the live.
Thirteen o'Clock.
Tomorrow.
Travelogue in a Shooting-Gallery.
Twentieth-Century Blues.
FEARNE, FLORA. Little Men, The.
FEARON, PAUL. Night Piece to Another Julia.
Serenade: "High in the dark the moon rides white."
FEDKOVICH, ——. Khustina—the Kerchief.
FEENEY, LEONARD. Altar Boy, The.
Because of Her Who Flowered So Fair. *Fr.* Song for a Listener.
Family Portrait.
Fledgling Robin, A.
Gift of Flowers, A.
Little Flower, The.
Lonely Crib, The.
Milkman, The.
Nails.
Noel.
Song for a Listener, *sel.*
Though art be on vacation.
Way of the Cross, The.
Welcome, The.
Wind.
FEINSTEIN, MARTIN. Burning Bush.
FELLTHAM, OWEN. Song: "When, dearest, I but think of [*or* on] thee," *at.*
Sympathy, The.
Upon a Rare Voice.
When, Dearest, I but Think of Thee, *at.*
FELSINKI, ALOIZY. Polish National Hymn.
FENG CHIH. For Tu Fu.
On a Puppy.
Room and the Windows, The.
Sonnets. *Fr.* Twenty-seven Sonnets.
Twenty-seven Sonnets, *sels.*
FENG YEN-CHI. Her Birthday.
FENNER, CORNELIUS GEORGE. Gulf-Weed.
FENNER, MARTHA DAY. My Lady Fair.
FENOLLOSA, ERNEST FRANCISCO. Golden Age, The.
Love-Cave, The, *tr.*
FENOLLOSA, MARY MCNEIL ("Sidney McCall"; Mrs. Ernest Francisco Fenollosa). Birth of the Flowers, The.
Blossoms.
Drifting Petal, A.
Flying Fish.
Iris Flowers.
Kite-Flying.
Miyoko San.
Morning Fancy.
Proud Vegetables, The.
Sunrise in the Hills of Satsuma.
Yuki.
FENTON, CORA D. Call, The.
FENTON, ELIJAH. Olivia.
To a Lady Sitting before Her Glass.
FERBER, EDNA. To William Allen White.
FERGUSON, JAMES. Auld Daddy Darkness.
FERGUSON, JOHN. Circus Clown, The.
FERGUSON, SIR SAMUEL. Abdication of Fergus Mac Roy, The.
Aideen's Grave, *sel.*
Bird and Brook, *sel.*
Boatman's Hymn, *tr.*
Burial of King Cormac, The.
Cashel of Munster, *tr.*
Ceann Dubh Deelish, *tr.*
Congal, *sels.*
Coolun, The, *tr.*
Cup of O'Hara, The, *tr.*
Dear Dark Head, *tr.*
Death of Dermid, The.
Deirdre, *sel.*
Deirdre's Farewell to Alba, *tr.*
Deirdre's Lament for the Sons of Usnach, *tr.*
Dinnshenchas, *sel., tr.*
Downfall of the Gael, The, *tr.*
Fair Hills of Ireland, The, *tr.*
Fair-haired Girl, The, *tr.*
Fairy Thorn, The.
Forging of the Anchor, The.
Hopeless Love, *tr.*
Lament for Corc and Niall of the Nine Hostages, *tr.*
Lament for the Death of Thomas Davis.
Lament for Thomas Davis.
Lament for Thomas Davis, *sel.*
"Land Is Ours, The." *Fr.* Congal.
Lapful of Nuts, The, *tr.*
Molly Asthore, *tr.*
Páistin Fionn [*or* Pastheen Finn], *tr.*
Paul Veronese; Three Sonnets.
Pretty Girl of Loch Dan, The.
Selections from "Congal," with an Argument. *Fr.* Congal.
Simile. *Fr.* Congal.
Story of Macha, The, *tr. Fr.* Dinnshenchas.
Welshmen of Tirawley, The.
When Kian O'Hara's Cup Was Passed to Turlough O'Carolan, *tr.*
Youghall Harbor, *tr.*
FERGUSSON, ELIZABETH. Heart, The.
FERGUSSON, ROBERT. Braid Claith.
Caller Water, *sel.*
Daft Days, The.
Elegy on the Death of Scots Music.
Farmer's Ingle, The.
Leith Races, *sels.*
My Winsome Dear. *Fr.* Leith Races.
Verses Written at the Hermitage of Braid, near Edinburgh.
FERID ED-DIN ATTAR. Attainment. *Fr.* The Bird-Parliament.
Bird-Parliament, The, *sels.*
Christian Child.
Excuses, The. *Fr.* The Bird-Parliament.
Nightingale, The. *Fr.* The Bird-Parliament.
Parrot, The. *Fr.* The Bird-Parliament.
Prelude: "Once on a time from all the Circles seven." *Fr.* The Bird-Parliament.
Ring-Dove, The. *Fr.* The Bird-Parliament.
Veil, The.
FERLINGHETTI, LAWRENCE. Coney Island of the Mind, A, *sels.*
He.
Pictures of the Gone World, *sels.*
FERNÁNDEZ, ROY. Barcarola; "Whenever I see waves surging."
FERNÁNDEZ DE ANDRADA, ANDRÉS. Epistle to Fabio, *at.*
FERNÁNDEZ DE LIZARDI, JOSÉ JOAQUÍN. Epitaph to the Liberty of America.
FERNÁNDEZ TORNEOL, NUÑO. Alvorada: "Arise, friend sleeping in the dawn so chilly."
FERNE, DORIS. Nijinsky.
Sounding.
FERO, GRACIA L. Sharing His Cross.
FERRER, JOSÉ MIGUEL. Nocturne of Sin and Its Accusation.
FERRIER, SUSAN. Laird o' Cockpen, The (*by* Lady Nairne), *add. sts.*
FERRIL, THOMAS HORNSBY. Basic Communication.
Kochia.
Lost Ships.
Man Who Thought He Was a Horse, The.
Something Starting Over.
Train Butcher, The.
What Trinkets?
Wood.
FERRIS, G. T. Chickamauga.
FERRITER, PIERCE. He Charges Her to Lay Aside Her Weapons.
Lamentation for the Death of Sir Maurice Fitzgerald, Knight of Kerry, A.
FERRY, DAVID. Antagonist, The.
On the Way to the Island.
Out of That Sea.
Poem about Waking.
Unawkward Singers, The.
FESSENDEN, THOMAS GREEN. Ye Sons of Columbia.
FESSENDEN, THOMAS WHITTEMORE. Mother.
To Mother.
FET [*or* FOETH], AFANASI AFANASIEVICH. Address to Death.
Aerial City, The.
All, all that was once mine is mine for ever.
At the Fireside.
Expect to-morrow to be fair.
For long I stood motionless, watching.
I Come Again.
I have come again with greeting.
I have come and brought you greeting.
I hear the stern decree: I bow to what is fated.
I stirred not, but stood long and pondered.
Last clouds in a throng above us sailing, The.
Magic Landscape, A.
May Night.
Morning Song.
Never.
Prisoner, The.
Skies again are deep and bare.
Storm in the skies in the evening.
Storm in the sky of an even.
Swallows.
To the Stars That Have Gone Out.
What an evening! Streamlets run.
When she her crimson lips uncloses.
Whispering. A timid sigh.
Whispers.
FETTER, GEORGE GRIFFITH. Name of Mother, The.
FETZER, HERMAN. *See* "FALSTAFF, JAKE."
FEWSTER, ERNEST. Cliff Rose, The.
Dawn.
Pearly Everlasting, The.
FEY, HAROLD E. To a Revolutionist.
We Who Are About to Die.
FFRENCH SALKELD, CECIL. Water-Front.
FIACC, PADRAIC. Boy and the Geese, The.
Deranged.
Poet, The.
Stolen Fifer, The.
FICHMAN, JACOB [*or* YAAKOV]. Abishag.
In the Old City.
Samarian Nights.
FICKE, ARTHUR DAVISON. Across the shaken bastions of the year. *Fr.* Sonnets of a Portrait Painter.
Alcibiades to a Jealous Girl.
Among Shadows.
April Moment. *Fr.* Sonnets of a Portrait Painter.
Beauty—what is it? A perfume without name. *Fr.* Epitaph for the Poet V.
Chrysanthemum Legend, The.
Come forth! for Spring is singing in the boughs. *Fr.* Sonnets of a Portrait Painter.
Dead Tree, The.
Don Quixote.
Epitaph for the Poet V., *sels.*
Fantasy for a Charming Friend.
Fate with Devoted . . .

Father.
Fathers and Sons.
For Beauty kissed your lips when they were young. *Fr.* Epitaph for the Poet V.
Her Pedigree. *Fr.* Sonnets of a Portrait Painter.
I Am in Love with High Far-seeing Places. *Fr.* Sonnets of a Portrait Painter.
I Am Weary of Being Bitter.
I have seen beauty where light stabs the hills. *Fr.* Sonnets of a Portrait Painter.
Immortals in Exile.
In That Dim Monument Where Tybalt Lies.
It is ordained—or so Politian said. *Fr.* Epitaph for the Poet V.
Last night I kissed you with a brutal might. *Fr.* Sonnets of a Portrait Painter.
Leaf-Movement.
Like Him Whose Spirit.
Long and Lovely.
Loreine, a Horse.
Meeting.
Mist.
My Love and I.
Nocturne in a Library.
November Dusk.
Oracle, The.
Out of the dusk into whose gloom you went. *Fr.* Sonnets of a Portrait Painter.
Peculiar ghost—great and immortal ghost! *Fr.* Epitaph for the Poet V.
Perspective of Co-ordination.
Portrait of an Old Woman.
Rue des Vents, *sel.*
So you go back—because they bid you come. *Fr.* Sonnets of a Portrait Painter.
Sonnet: "Across the shaken bastions of the year." *Fr.* Sonnets of a Portrait Painter.
Sonnet: "And what is beauty? It is a going-home."
Sonnet: "For I have dreamed a dream where Fate and God."
Sonnet: "He who loves life, and has the winging thought."
Sonnet: "I have seen beauty where light stabs the hills." *Fr.* Sonnets of a Portrait Painter.
Sonnet: "I walked, in meditation that was pain."
Sonnet: "In thousands toward the south the swallows fly."
Sonnet: "Last night I kissed you with a brutal might." *Fr.* Sonnets of a Portrait Painter.
Sonnet: "Mists on the mountain, mists far down the vale."
Sonnet: "Out of the dusk into whose gloom you went." *Fr.* Sonnets of a Portrait Painter.
Sonnet: "So you go back—because they bid you come." *Fr.* Sonnets of a Portrait Painter.
Sonnet: "There are strange shadows fostered of the moon." *Fr.* Sonnets of a Portrait Painter.
Sonnet: "Though not a hill be holy, and no spring." *Fr.* Sonnets of a Portrait Painter.
Sonnets of a Portrait Painter, *sels.*
Spring Landscape. *Fr.* Sonnets of a Portrait Painter.
Summons. *Fr.* Sonnets of a Portrait Painter.
There Stretch between Us Wonder-woven Bonds. *Fr.* Sonnets of a Portrait Painter.
They brought me tidings; and I did not hear. *Fr.* Sonnets of a Portrait Painter.
Three Sisters, The.
To an Old Friend.
To the Harpies.
Troubadours. *Fr.* Sonnets of a Portrait Painter.
View from Heights. *Fr.* Sonnets of a Portrait Painter.
Waterfall, The.
What if some lover in a far-off spring. *Fr.* Sonnets of a Portrait Painter.
World beyond World.
Yard in December, The.

FIELD, ANNE P. L. At Singing Time.
Christmas Fires, The.
Christmas Insurrection, A.
Maternity.
Night after Christmas, The.
On a Seventeenth Birthday.
Prayer at Bethlehem, A.
When the Stars of Morning Sang.

FIELD, ARTHUR GORDON. America Prays.
Bells of New Year.
Discoverer, The.
Name of Washington, The.
New Song, The.
Perpetual Christmas.

FIELD, EDWARD. Floor Is Dirty, The.
View of Jersey, A.

FIELD, EDWARD SALISBURY. Dedication: "I've gone about for years I find." *Fr.* The Quest.
Quest, The, *sel.*

FIELD, ELLIOT. Vinco.

FIELD, EUGENE. Always Right.
Apple-Pie and Cheese.
Ashes on the Slide.
Bachelor Hall.
Bench-legged Fyce, The.
Bethlehem-Town ("As I was going to Bethlehem-town").
Bethlehem-Town, *sel.*
Bibliomaniac's Prayer, The.
Casey's Table d'Hote.
Child and Mother.
Chipeta.
Christmas Eve.
Christmas Song.
Christmas Treasures.
Christmas Wish, A.
Clink of the Ice, The.
Colorado Sand Storm, A.
Contentment.
Death of Robin Hood, The.
Dibbin's Ghost.
Dinkey-Bird, The.
Duel, The.
Dutch Lullaby, A.
Epigram: "He is not drunk, who, from the floor."
Father's Letter.
Fiddle-dee-dee.
Fly-away Horse, The.
Garden and Cradle.
Horace to Pyrrha, *tr.*
In the Firelight.
Inscription for My Little Son's Silver Plate.
Jessie.
Jest 'fore Christmas.
Krinken.
Little Blue Pigeon.
Little Boy Blue.
Little Peach, The.
Long Ago.
Lover's Lane, Saint Jo.
Lyttel Boy, The.
Mother and I.
My Mother's Faith.
My Sabine Farm.
Night Wind, The.
Nightfall in Dordrecht.
Norse Lullaby.
Orkney Lullaby.
Our Two Opinions.
Our Whippings.
Piazza Tragedy, A.
Pioneer, The.
Play on Words, A.
Rock-a-by Lady, The.
Seein' Things.
Shut-Eye Train, The.
Sioux, The.
Some Time.
Song: "Why do the bells of [*or* bells for] Christmas ring?"
Song of the All-Wool Shirt.
Star of the East.
Sugar-Plum Tree, The.
Three Kings of Cologne, The.
To a Usurper.
To Leuconoe, *tr.*
To Mistress Pyrrha, *tr.*
To My Mother.
To Phyllis, *after* Horace.
To the Fountain of Bandusia, *tr.*
Truth about Horace, The.
Two Little Skeezucks, The.
Valentine, A.
Wanderer, The.
When Willie Wet the Bed, *at.*
Wynken, Blynken, and Nod.

"FIELD, MICHAEL" (Katherine Bradley *and* Edith Cooper). Aeolian Harp, An.
After Soufrière.
Ah me, if I grew sweet to man.
And on My Eyes Dark Sleep by Night.
Aridity.
Burial of Robert Browning, The.
Bury Her at Even.
But if Our Love Be Dying.
Canute the Great, *sel.*
Dancers, The.
David's Reconciliation with Absalom.
Descent from the Cross.
Earth to Earth.
Ebbtide at Sundown.
Eros Does Not Always Smite.
Fifty Quatrains.
Flaw, A.
Gold.
Gold is the son of Zeus; neither moth nor worm may gnaw it.
If they honored me, giving me their gifts.
Iris.
Lettice.
Marionettes.
Mete Me Out My Loneliness.
More Gold than Gold.
Nests in Elms.
Renewal.
Sweeter Far than the Harp, More Gold than Gold.
Thou Comest Down to Die.
Too Late.
Tragic Mary Queen of Scots, The.
Where the Blessed Feet Have Trod.
Whym Chow.
Wind of Summer.
Woods Are Still, The.

FIELD, MILDRED FOWLER. Carpenter Christ.

FIELD, NATHANIEL. Amends for Ladies, *sel.*
Matin Song. *Fr.* Amends for Ladies.
Rise, Lady Mistress, Rise! *Fr.* Amends for Ladies.
Song: "Rise Lady Mistress, rise." *Fr.* Amends for Ladies.

FIELD, RACHEL LYMAN (Mrs. Arthur Pederson). Almost.
Animal Store, The.
At the Theater.
Barefoot Days.
Birthday, A.
Busy Body, The.
Captain Enoch.
Charm for Spring Flowers, A.
Chestnut Stands.
Circus Garland, A.
City Lights.
City Rain.
Cranberry Road.
Dog Day, A.
Doorbells.
Eighth Street West.
Epitaph for a Scotch Terrier.
Fire, A.
Florist Shop, The.
Flower-Cart Man, The.
For Christmas.
For My Father.
Fourth of July.
General Store.
Good Green Bus.
Green Fiddler, The.
Gypsies.
Gypsy Children.
Hills, The.
Ice-Cream Man, The.
I'd Like to Be a Lighthouse.
If Once You Have Slept on an Island.
Islands.
Little Rose Tree, The.

FIELD, RACHEL LYMAN (*continued*)
Merry-go-round.
My Inside-Self.
New England Gothic.
New Year's Day.
Old Coach Road, The.
Old Gardener Time.
Old Music Box, The.
Performing Seal, The.
Picnic Day.
Piper, The.
Playhouse Key, The.
Pointed People, The.
Pushcart Row.
Rain in the City.
Roads.
Skyscrapers.
Snow in the City.
Some People.
Something Told the Wild Geese.
Song for a Blue Roadster.
Spring Signs.
Summer Morning, A.
Taxis.
Ticking Clocks.
Vegetables
Visitor, The.
When We Went Gathering Cat-Tails.
Whistles.
FIELD, RICHARD H. Limerick: "When you go to a store in Ascutney."
FIELD, ROSWELL MARTIN. At the Ball Game.
To Leuconoe, *tr.*
FIELD, SARA BARD (Mrs. Charles Erskine Scott Wood). Barabbas, *sels.*
Contemporary.
Could You Not Watch with Me One Little Hour?
I Had a Fair Young Son.
November 2 A.M. Conspiracy.
We Whom the Dead Have Not Forgiven.
Winter Revery.
FIELD, WALTER TAYLOR. Flag of the Free.
FIELDING, HENRY. A-Hunting We Will Go. *Fr.* Don Quixote in England.
Don Quixote in England, *sels.*
Hunting Song. *Fr.* Don Quixote in England.
Letter to Sir Robert Walpole, A.
Roast Beef of Old England, The. *Fr.* Don Quixote in England.
Song: A-Hunting We Will Go. *Fr.* Don Quixote in England.
FIELDS, ANNIE ADAMS. Cedar Mountain.
Little Guinever.
On Waking from a Dreamless Sleep.
Return, The.
Song, to the Gods, Is Sweetest Sacrifice.
Theocritus.
FIELDS, JAMES THOMAS. Alarmed Skipper, The.
Ballad of the Tempest.
Captain's Daughter, The.
Common Sense.
Don.
Mabel, in New Hampshire.
Nantucket Skipper, The.
On a Watchman Asleep at Midnight.
Owl-Critic, The.
Song of the Turtle and Flamingo.
Stars and Stripes, The.
Tempest, The.
Turtle and Flamingo, The.
With Wordsworth at Rydal.
FIELDS, MAURICE C. How Long till April?
FIFER, H. N. He Lived a Life.
He Lived a Life, *sel.*
FIGGIS, DARRELL ("Michael Ireland"). Bogac Bán.
Inisgallun.
FIGUEROA, FRANCISCO DE. Mortal Grief.
FIGUEROA, R. OLIVARES. Sower, The.
FIGUEROA, RODULFO. Surgical Art Versus Beauty.
FILICAJA [*or* FILICAIA], VINCENZO DA. Italia! Oh Italia!
Italy.
Providence.
Sonnet: "Italia, O Italia, upon whom."
FINCH, ANNE, COUNTESS OF WINCHILSEA. *See* WINCHILSEA, ANNE FINCH, COUNTESS OF.
FINCH, FRANCIS MILES. Blue and the Gray, The.
Nathan Hale.
FINCH, JULIA NEELY. Unborn, The.
FINCH, ROBERT. Alone.
Campers.
Egg-and-Dart.
History Class.
Jardin de la Chapelle Expiatoire.
Lost Tribe, The.
Mountain, The.
Network, The.
Nowell, Nowell.
Over.
Report.
Scroll-Section.
Shadows, The.
Sisters, The.
Statue, The.
Time's Bright Sand.
Toronto Crossing.
Train Window.
Words.
FINDLATER, MARY W. Annie Ferguson.
Ape and the Key, The.
Caterpillars' Conversation.
FINERTY, JOHN F. May-Day at Sea.
FINGER, CHARLES JOSEPH. Cowboy's Dream, The.
Roy Bean.
FINK, WILLIAM W. Larrie O'Dee.
FINKEL, DONALD. Clothing's New Emperor, The.
Esthetic of Imitation, An.
Hunting Song.
Juan Belmonte, Torero.
Sirens, The.
FINLEY, JOHN. Bachelor's Hall.
Birthday Prayer, A.
Matins.
Sepulcher in the Garden, The.
Tobacco.
FINLEY, JOHN HUSTON. Birthnight Candle, A.
"H. H."
Poor Poet's Lullaby.
Red Cross Spirit Speaks, The.
Road to Dieppe.
Three Wise Men, The.
FINNIN, OLIVE MARY. Sarah Lorton.
Three Trees at Solstice.
FIRDAUSI [*or* FIRDUSÍ] (Abul Kasim Mansur). Alas for Youth.
Birth of Rustem, The. *Fr.* Shah Namah.
Dream of Dakiki, The.
Kiumers. *Fr.* Shah Namah.
On the Sultan Mahmúd.
Reproach.
Rustem and Akwan Dev. *Fr.* Shah Namah.
Rustem Slays Sohráb. *Fr.* Shah Namah.
Satire on Mahmúd. *Fr.* Shah Namah.
Shah Namah [Book of Kings], *sels.*
Sohráb Is Born. *Fr.* Shah Namah.
FIRKINS, CHESTER. On a Subway Express.
"FIRTH." Britannia Rules of Orthography.
FISCHER, HELEN FIELD. Mystic Borderland, The.
There Is a Mystic Borderland.
FISCHER, JACOB. Lady Poverty, The, *at.*
FISCHER, WILLIAM J. Faded Letter, A.
In the Cloister.
FISHBACK, MARGARET. Brooklynese Champion.
I Stand Corrected.
I Take 'Em and Like 'Em.
In Extremis.
Lie of the Land, The.
On Viewing a Florist's Whimsy at Fifty-ninth and Madison.
Poem for Mother's Day.
Purist to Her Love, The.
Sentimental Lines to a Young Man Who Favors Pink Wallpaper, While I Personally Lean to the Blue.
Sprig Fever.
Strange Interlude, A.
This Way Out.
Thoughts of Loved Ones.
Triolet on a Downhill Road.
Unrequited Love on the Back Piazza.
Wanted: One Cave Man with Club.
FISHER, A. HUGH. Ceylon.
FISHER, AILEEN. Away We Go.
Bells of Peace, The.
Bug, A.
Christmas Shoppers.
Christmas Tree.
Coffeepot Face, A.
December.
Down in the Hollow.
Early, Early Easter Day.
Fall.
Flag We Fly, The.
Halloween Concert.
Holly Fairies.
January Snow.
Legends of Christmas.
Light in the Darkness.
Little Talk.
Moth Miller.
November.
Otherwise.
Outdoor Christmas Tree, The.
Race, The.
Rich.
Tea Party.
Until We Built a Cabin.
Valentine's Day.
Wearing of the Green.
Winter Circus.
Wonderful Man, A.
FISHER, CHARLES. Preoccupation with Death.
Some Prodigies.
FISHER, ED. Talk of the Town, The.
FISHER, I. H. *See* "HUME, ISOBEL."
FISHER, JASPER. Fuimus Troes, *sels.*
Morisco, A. *Fr.* Fuimus Troes.
So the silver-feathered swan. *Fr.* Fuimus Troes.
Song; a Morisko. *Fr.* Fuimus Troes.
Song to a Viol. *Fr.* Fuimus Troes.
FISHER, K. Story of the Corn.
FISHER, MAHLON LEONARD. Afterwards.
Ancient Sacrifice, The.
As an Old Mercer.
Immutabilis.
My Mother.
November.
Of Melodies Unheard.
Old Amaze.
On a Sculptured Head of the Christ.
Per Contra.
Poet to His Father, A.
Realization.
To a Roman Doll.
To Nature.
FISHER, PHILIP JOHN. "I Die Daily."
FISKE, FYNETTE. Brook, The.
FITGER, ARTHUR. Evening Prayer.
FITTS, DUDLEY. Imaginary Dialogue, *tr.*
Priam.
For translations from French, see AnFP.
For translations from Greek, see LiTW; LyMA.
For translations from Spanish, see AnCL; FaPON; LiTW; OnPM.
FITTS, DUDLEY, *and* ROBERT FITZGERALD. *For translations from Greek, see* LiTW.
FITZELL, LINCOLN. Conflict.
FITZGEFFREY [*or* FITZGEFFRY *or* FITZ-GEFFRY], CHARLES. Bee, The. *Fr.* Sir Francis Drake.
English Captains, The. *Fr.* Sir Francis Drake.
Holy Transportations, *sel.*
Last Voyage of Sir Francis Drake, and Sir John Hawkins, The. *Fr.* Sir Francis Drake.
On Sir Francis Drake. *Fr.* Sir Francis Drake.
Sir Francis Drake, *sels.*
Take Frankincense, O God. *Fr.* Holy Transportations.
FITZGERALD, EDWARD. Absál Tempts Salámán, *tr. Fr.* Salámán and Absál.

Attainment, *tr.* *Fr.* The Bird-Parliament.
Ball, The, *tr.* *Fr.* The Rubáiyát of Omar Khayyám.
Ballad of Jenny the Mare, The.
Because.
Bewildered Arab, The, *tr. Fr.* Salámán and Absál.
Bird of Time, The, *tr.* *Fr.* The Rubáiyát of Omar Khayyám.
Bird-Parliament, The, *sels., tr.*
Birth of Salámán, The, *tr.* *Fr.* Salámán and Absál.
Burning of Absál, The, *tr.* *Fr.* Salámán and Absál.
Careless Delight, *tr.* *Fr.* The Rubáiyát of Omar Khayyám.
Chivalry at a Discount.
Dream Called Life, The, *tr.*
Equity with God, *tr.* *Fr.* The Rubáiyát of Omar Khayyám.
Excuses, The, *tr.* *Fr.* The Bird-Parliament.
Fatalism, *tr.* *Fr.* The Rubáiyát of Omar Khayyám.
Fifteen Rubáiyát, *tr.* *Fr.* The Rubáiyát of Omar Khayyám.
Great Argument, *tr.* *Fr.* The Rubáiyát of Omar Khayyám.
Heaven and Hell, *tr.* *Fr.* The Rubáiyát of Omar Khayyám.
I Myself Am Heaven and Hell, *tr. Fr.* The Rubáiyát of Omar Khayyám.
If It Be Destined, *tr.* *Fr.* Sonnets to Laura.
Iram Indeed Is Gone, *tr.* *Fr.* The Rubáiyát of Omar Khayyám.
Like Snow, *tr.* *Fr.* The Rubáiyát of Omar Khayyám.
Long While, The, *tr.* *Fr.* The Rubáiyát of Omar Khayyám.
Lovers Flee, The, *tr.* *Fr.* Salámán and Absál.
Master-Knot, The, *tr.* *Fr.* The Rubáiyát of Omar Khayyám.
Meadows in Spring, The.
Minister of Wine, The, *tr.* *Fr.* The Rubáiyát of Omar Khayyám.
Moving Finger, The, *tr.* *Fr.* The Rubáiyát of Omar Khayyám.
New Year, The, *tr.* *Fr.* The Rubáiyát of Omar Khayyám.
Nightingale, The, *tr.* *Fr.* The Bird-Parliament.
Old Song.
Paradise, *tr.* *Fr.* The Rubáiyát of Omar Khayyám.
Parrot, The, *tr.* *Fr.* The Bird-Parliament.
Predestination, *tr.* *Fr.* The Rubáiyát of Omar Khayyám.
Prefer the Cash, *tr.* *Fr.* The Rubáiyát of Omar Khayyám.
Preliminary Invocation, *tr.* *Fr.* Salámán and Absál.
Prelude: "Once on a time from all the Circles seven," *tr.* *Fr.* The Bird-Parliament.
Quatrains, *tr.* *Fr.* The Rubáiyát of Omar Khayyám.
Ring-Dove, The, *tr.* *Fr.* The Bird-Parliament.
Ritual of the Grape, *tr.* *Fr.* The Rubáiyát of Omar Khayyám.
Rubáiyát of Omar Khayyám, The, *tr.*
Rubáiyát of Omar Khayyám, The, *sels., tr.*
Salámán and Absál, *sels., tr.*
Simple Arab, The, *tr.* *Fr.* Salámán and Absál.
Sleep Unbroken, *tr.* *Fr.* The Rubáiyát of Omar Khayyám.
So Red the Rose, *tr.* *Fr.* The Rubáiyát of Omar Khayyám.
Song of the Fire.
Sonnets to Laura, *sel., tr.*
Soul Is All, The, *tr.* *Fr.* The Rubáiyát of Omar Khayyám.
There Is No Sin, *tr.* *Fr.* The Rubáiyát of Omar Khayyám.
This Life Flies, *tr.* *Fr.* The Rubáiyát of Omar Khayyám.
Three Arrows, The.
Wake! *tr.* *Fr.* The Rubáiyát of Omar Khayyám.
Waste Not Your Hour, *tr.* *Fr.* The Rubáiyát of Omar Khayyám.
Wish, A, *tr.* *Fr.* The Rubáiyát of Omar Khayyám.
Worldly Hope, The, *tr.* *Fr.* The Rubáiyát of Omar Khayyám.
Worldly Wisdom, *tr.* *Fr.* The Rubáiyát of Omar Khayyám.
FITZGERALD, FRANCIS SCOTT. Obit on Parnassus.
FITZGERALD, GERALD MICHAEL JOSEPH CUSHING. *See* "PAGE, A."
FITZGERALD, MARY SCOTT. Rendezvous.
FITZGERALD, ROBERT. Ballade of the Hanged Men, *tr.*
By strangers' coasts and waters, many days at sea, *tr.*
Celestine.
Choral Poem from "Oedipus at Colonus," *tr.*
Cobb Would Have Caught It.
Colorado.
Elegy: "What should you know at last when spirit's."
Farewell to Lesbia, *tr.*
Furius and Aurelius, Catullus's comrades, *tr.*
Georgic I: "Until Jove let it be, no colonist," *tr.* *Fr.* Georgics.
Georgics, *sel., tr.*
History.
Music, *tr.*
Odes (*of* Horace), *sels., tr.*
Oedipus at Colonus, *sel., tr.*
Painter, The.
Portraits.
Solstitium Saeculare.
Souls Lake.
Windshield.
FITZGERALD, ROBERT, *and* DUDLEY FITTS. *See* FITTS, DUDLEY, *and* ROBERT FITZGERALD.
FITZGERALD, ROBERT DAVID. Copernicus, *sel.*
Envy Goes Groping.
Essay on Memory.
Face of the Waters, The.
Fifth Day.
1918–1941.
Traditional Tune.
FITZGERALD, ROBERT STUART. *For translations from Spanish, see* AnCL.
FITZPATRICK, BRIAN. Cenotaph.
FITZPATRICK, JOHN. Mater Dolorosa.
FITZSIMMONS, CAROLINE DARR. Spring and Mother.
FITZSIMON, HENRY. Swearing.
FIUMI, LIONELLO. Man Closes the Shutters, The.
FJELDSTED, RUNÓLFUR. Snow-Bunting, The, *tr.*
Waterfall, The, *tr.*
FLACCUS, AULUS PERSIUS. *See* PERSIUS.
FLACCUS, KIMBALL. Dance of Death.
Sonnet Sequence.
To Certain Men of Science.
FLACCUS, QUINTUS HORATIUS. *See* HORACE.
FLAGG, ELLEN H. Death the Peacemaker.
FLAGG, FRANCIS. Dreamer in the Desert, The.
Snake, The.
FLAGG, HANNAH. *See* GOULD, HANNAH FLAGG.
FLAGG, JAMES MONTGOMERY. Limerick: "Said the Reverend Jabez McCotton."
FLAGG, JAMES MONTGOMERY, *and* JULIAN STREET. *See* STREET, JULIAN, *and* JAMES MONTGOMERY FLAGG.
FLAGG, WILSON. O'Lincoln [*or* O'Lincon] Family, The.
FLAISCHLEN, CÄSAR. Most Quietly at Times.
FLAMINIO, MARC-ANTONIO. To the Muse of Sirmio.
FLANNER, HILDEGARDE (Mrs. Frederick Monhoff). Bird Sings at Night, A.
Birds.
Communion.
Daphne.
Discovery.
Flowers of Apollo, The.
Noon on Alameda Street.
Of Old Sat Freedom on the Heights.
Owl, The.
Pacific Winter.
Prayer: "With Him who sets the lily on the stem."
Prayer for This Day.
Sonnets in Quaker Language.
Spring's on the Curb.
This Morning.
To a Tree in Bloom.
To One of Little Faith.
Wreath for Ashes, A.
FLASH, HENRY LYNDEN. Flag, The.
Gallant Fifty-one, The.
Legion of Honor, The.
Stonewall Jackson.
Zollicoffer.
FLATMAN, THOMAS. Appeal to Cats in the Business of Love, An.
Bachelor's Song, The ("How happy a thing were a wedding").
Batchelors Song, The ("Like a Dog with a Bottle, fast ty'd to his tail").
Death.
Defiance, The.
Dooms-Day [*or* Doomsday] Thought, A.
Dooms-Day [*or* Doomsday] Thought, A, *sel.*
Hillocks of Mortality. *Fr.* A Dooms-Day Thought.
On Marriage.
Pastoral Dialogue, Castara and Parthenia.
Sad Day, The.
Slight, The.
Surrender, The.
Thought of Death, A.
Unconcerned, The.
Wish, The.
FLAVELL [*or* LAVELLE], THOMAS. County of Mayo, The, *at.*
FLECKER, JAMES ELROY. Ballad of Camden Town, The.
Ballad of Hampstead Heath, The.
Ballad of the Londoner.
Brumana.
Don Juan Declaims.
Don Juan in Hell, *tr.*
Dying Patriot, The.
Epilogue: "Away, for we are ready to a man!" *Fr.* The Golden Journey to Samarkand (*also in* Hassan).
Epithalamion: "Smile then, children, hand in hand."
Felo-de-Se.
For whom this pretty pamphlet, polished new, *tr.*
Gate of the Armies, The, *tr.*
Gates of Damascus.
Golden Journey to Samarkand, The.
Golden Journey to Samarkand, The, *sels.*
Golden Road, The. *Fr.* Hassan.
Hammam Name, The.
Hassan, *sels.*
Hassan's Serenade. *Fr.* Hassan.
In Phaeacia.
Lord Arnaldos.
Love, the Baby, *tr.*
November Eves.
Oak and Olive.
Old Ships, The.
Opportunity, *tr.*
Parrot, The.
Philomel, *tr.*
Prayer: Let me not know how sins and sorrows glide."
Prologue: "We who with songs." *Fr.* The Golden Journey to Samarkand.
Prologue to "The Golden Journey to Samarkand."
Proud is Phaselus here, my friends, to tell, *tr.*
Queen's Song, The.
Rioupéroux.
Saadabad.
Santorin.
Ship, A, an Isle, a Sickle Moon.
Stances, *sel., tr.*
Stillness.
Taoping.
Tenebris Interlucentem.
To a Poet a Thousand Years Hence.

FLECKER, JAMES ELROY (*continued*)
Town without a Market, The.
War Song of the Saracens, The. *Fr.* Hassan.
Yasmin. *Fr.* Hassan.
FLECKNOE, RICHARD. Invocation of Silence.
Noble Love.
On Mary, Duchess of Richmond.
Silence Invoked.
FLEG, EDMOND. End of Sorrow, The. *Fr.* The Wall of Weeping.
Wall of Weeping, The, *sels.*
Wandering Jew Comes to the Wall, The. *Fr.* The Wall of Weeping.
"FLEMING, ARCHIBALD." *See* MACLIESH, ARCHIBALD FLEMING.
FLEMING, ELIZABETH. Balloon Seller, The.
Chain of Princes Street, The.
Fires.
Hedgehog and His Coat, The.
Hurdy-Gurdy Man, The.
If I Were a Pig.
In the Mirror.
Lavender Bush, The.
My Barrow.
Old Mrs. Jarvis.
Patchwork Quilt, The.
Secret, The.
Shelling Peas.
Toadstools.
Who's In?
Wild Animals.
Window Cleaner, The.
FLEMING, MARJORY [*or* MARJORIE]. Melancholy Lay, A.
Sonnet to [*or* on] a Monkey.
Three Turkeys.
To a Monkey.
FLEMING, MARY. Two Kisses.
FLEMING, MAYBURY. To Demeter.
To Sleep.
What Though the Green Leaf Grow?
FLETCHER, ALICE CUNNINGHAM. Song to the Mountains, *tr.*
FLETCHER, FRANK. O Son of Man.
FLETCHER, GILES, THE ELDER. Elegy, An: "Down in a bed, and on a bed of down." *Fr.* Licia.
First did I fear, when first my love began. *Fr.* Licia.
I live, sweet love, whereas the gentle wind. *Fr.* Licia.
If sad complaint would show a lover's pain. *Fr.* Licia.
In Time the Strong and Stately Turrets Fall. *Fr.* Licia.
Licia, *sels.*
Like Memnon's rock, touched with the rising sun. *Fr.* Licia.
Love was laid down, all weary, fast asleep. *Fr.* Licia.
My love was mask'd and armed with a fan. *Fr.* Licia.
O sug'red talk, wherewith my thoughts do live. *Fr.* Licia.
Sad, all alone, not long I musing sat. *Fr.* Licia.
Seven are the lights that wander in the skies. *Fr.* Licia.
Sonnet: "Like Memnon's rock, touched with the rising sun." *Fr.* Licia.
Time. *Fr.* Licia.
Whenas her lute is tuned to her voice. *Fr.* Licia.
FLETCHER, GILES, THE YOUNGER. Celestial City, The. *Fr.* Christ's Victory and Triumph.
Christ's Triumph after Death, *sel.* *Fr.* Christ's Victory and Triumph.
Christ's Victory and Triumph, *sels.*
Christ's Victory in Heaven. *Fr.* Christ's Victory and Triumph.
Christ's Victory on Earth. *Fr.* Christ's Victory and Triumph.
Christ's Victory on Earth, *sel.* *Fr.* Christ's Victory and Triumph.
Description of Mercy. *Fr.* Christ's Victory and Triumph.
Easter Morn. *Fr.* Christ's Victory and Triumph.
Excellency of Christ. *Fr.* Christ's Victory and Triumph.
Heavenly Jerusalem, The. *Fr.* Christ's Victory and Triumph.
In Gethsemane.
Incarnation, The.
Love is the blossom where there blows. *Fr.* Christ's Victory and Triumph.
On the Crucifixion. *Fr.* Christ's Victory and Triumph.
Who Can Forget—Never to Be Forgot.
Wooing Song. *Fr.* Christ's Victory and Triumph.
FLETCHER, IAIN. Adolescents in the Dusk.
Giostra, La, *sel., tr.*
Simonetta, *tr.* *Fr.* La Giostra.
Time and Motion Study.
FLETCHER, JOHN. Arm, arm, arm, arm! *Fr.* The Mad Lover.
Beauty Clear and Fair. *Fr.* The Elder Brother.
Beggars' Bush, *sel.*
Bonduca, *sel.*
Care-charming Sleep [Thou Easer of All Woes]. *Fr.* The Tragedy of Valentinian.
Cast Our Caps and Cares Away. *Fr.* Beggars' Bush.
Come, Shepherds, Come! *Fr.* The Faithful Shepherdess.
Dead Host's Welcome, The. *Fr.* The Lover's Progress.
Dearest, Do Not You Delay Me, *at.* *Fr.* The Spanish Curate.
Destiny. *Fr.* Upon an Honest Man's Fortune.
Do not fear to put thy feet. *Fr.* The Faithful Shepherdess.
Elder Brother, The, *sel.*
Evening. *Fr.* The Faithful Shepherdess.
Evening Knell, The. *Fr.* The Faithful Shepherdess.
Evening Song. *Fr.* The Faithful Shepherdess.
Faithful Shepherdess, The, *sels.*
Folding the Flocks. *Fr.* The Faithful Shepherdess.
God Lyaeus [Ever Young]. *Fr.* The Tragedy of Valentinian.
God of Sheep, The. *Fr.* The Faithful Shepherdess.
Hear, Ye Ladies [That Despise]. *Fr.* The Tragedy of Valentinian.
Hymn to Pan. *Fr.* The Faithful Shepherdess.
Into Slumbers. *Fr.* The Tragedy of Valentinian.
Invocation by the Priest of Pan. *Fr.* The Faithful Shepherdess.
Invocation to Sleep. *Fr.* The Tragedy of Valentinian.
Joy of Battle, The. *Fr.* The Mad Lover.
Let the bells ring, and let the boys sing. *Fr.* The Spanish Curate.
Little French Lawyer, The, *sel.*
Love Song: "Now the lusty Spring is seen." *Fr.* The Tragedy of Valentinian.
Lover's Progress, The, *sel.*
Love's Emblems. *Fr.* The Tragedy of Valentinian.
Mad Lover, The, *sels.*
Man [Is] His Own Star. *Fr.* Upon an Honest Man's Fortune.
Mighty Love. *Fr.* The Tragedy of Valentinian.
Morning Song. *Fr.* The Faithful Shepherdess.
Music, *at.* *Fr.* Shakespeare's "King Henry VIII."
My man Thomas.
Night-Walker, The; or, The Little Thief, *sel.*
Now the lusty spring is seen. *Fr.* The Tragedy of Valentinian.
Orpheus I Am, Come from the Deeps Below.
Orpheus with His Lute, *at.* *Fr.* Shakespeare's "King Henry VIII."
Pan. *Fr.* The Faithful Shepherdess.
Power of Love, The. *Fr.* The Tragedy of Valentinian.
Prayer to Venus. *Fr.* The Mad Lover.
Priest's Chant, The. *Fr.* The Faithful Shepherdess.
River God, The. *Fr.* The Faithful Shepherdess.
River God's Song, The. *Fr.* The Faithful Shepherdess.
Rule a Wife and Have a Wife, *sel.*
Satyr, The ("Here be grapes"). *Fr.* The Faithful Shepherdess.
Satyr's Farewell, The. *Fr.* The Faithful Shepherdess.
Satyr's Leave-taking, The. *Fr.* The Faithful Shepherdess.
Satyr's Song, The. *Fr.* The Faithful Shepherdess.
Sing his praises. *Fr.* The Faithful Shepherdess.
Sleep. *Fr.* The Tragedy of Valentinian.
Song: "Care charming sleep, thou easer of all woes." *Fr.* The Tragedy of Valentinian.
Song: "Do not fear to put thy feet." *Fr.* The Faithful Shepherdess.
Song: "Heare ye ladies that despise." *Fr.* The Tragedy of Valentinian.
Song: "Let the bells ring, and let the Boys sing." *Fr.* The Spanish Curate.
Song: "Now the lusty spring is seen." *Fr.* The Tragedy of Valentinian.
Song: "Oh fair sweet face, oh eyes celestial bright." *Fr.* Women Pleased.
Song: "Sing his praises that doth keep." *Fr.* The Faithful Shepherdess.
Song for the Sick Emperor. *Fr.* The Tragedy of Valentinian.
Song in the Wood. *Fr.* The Little French Lawyer.
Song of the River-God to Amoret, The. *Fr.* The Faithful Shepherdess.
Song to Bacchus. *Fr.* The Tragedy of Valentinian.
Song to Pan. *Fr.* The Faithful Shepherdess.
Song to Sleep. *Fr.* The Tragedy of Valentinian.
Spanish Curate, The, *sels.*
'Tis Late and Cold. *Fr.* The Lover's Progress.
To Pan. *Fr.* The Faithful Shepherdess.
To Sleep. *Fr.* The Tragedy of Valentinian.
To the Blest Evanthe. *Fr.* A Wife for a Month.
Tragedy of Valentinian, The, *sels.*
Upon an Honest Man's Fortune, *sel.*
Valentinian, *sels.*
Wife for a Month, A, *sel.*
Women Pleased, *sels.*
Women's Longing. *Fr.* Women Pleased.
FLETCHER, JOHN, *and* FRANCIS BEAUMONT. *See* BEAUMONT, FRANCIS, *and* JOHN FLETCHER.
FLETCHER, JOHN, *and* PHILIP MASSINGER. Double Marriage, The, *sel.*
FLETCHER, JOHN, *and* (*at.*) THOMAS MIDDLETON. Hence All You Vain Delights. *Fr.* The Nice Valour.
Melancholy. *Fr.* The Nice Valour.
Nice Valour, The, *sels.*
O Sweetest Melancholy. *Fr.* The Nice Valour.
Passionate Man's Song, The. *Fr.* The Nice Valour.
Song: "Hence all you vain delights." *Fr.* The Nice Valour.
Sweetest Melancholy. *Fr.* The Nice Valour.
FLETCHER, JOHN, *and* WILLIAM ROWLEY. Come Follow Me, You Country Lasses. *Fr.* The Maid in the Mill.
Maid in the Mill, The, *sel.*
FLETCHER, JOHN *and* WILLIAM SHAKESPEARE. Bridal Song, A. *Fr.* The Two Noble Kinsmen.
Dirge of the Three Queens. *Fr.* The Two Noble Kinsmen.
Funeral Song. *Fr.* The Two Noble Kinsmen.

Roses, Their Sharp Spines Being Gone. *Fr.* The Noble Kinsmen.
Song: "Urnes and Odours bring away!" *Fr.* The Two Noble Kinsmen.
Two Noble Kinsmen, The, *sels.*
FLETCHER, JOHN, *and others.* Bloody Brother, The, *sels.*
Drink To-Day [and Drown All Sorrows]. *Fr.* The Bloody Brother.
Drinking Song. *Fr.* The Bloody Brother.
Hide, Oh, Hide Those Hills. *Fr.* The Bloody Brother.
Love Song: "Take, Oh take those lips away." *Fr.* The Bloody Brother.
Mourn No More. *Fr.* The Queen of Corinth.
Queen of Corinth, The, *sels.*
Song: "Take, oh take those lips away." *Fr.* The Bloody Brother.
Take, O Take Those Lips Away. *Fr.* The Bloody Brother.
Tragedy of Rollo, Duke of Normandy, The, *sels.*
Weep No More. *Fr.* The Queen of Corinth.
FLETCHER, JOHN GOULD. Ad Majorem Hominis Gloriam.
Advent.
Arizona Poems, *sels.*
Attitude of Youth, The.
Autobiography.
Autumnal Clouds.
Before Olympus.
Birth of Lucifer, The.
Black Rock, The.
Blake.
Blue Symphony, The.
Brahma.
Broadway's Canyon.
Caged Eagle, The.
Changing Love.
Clipper-Ships.
Clouds across the Canyon.
Crucifixion of the Skyscraper.
Down the Mississippi.
Down the Mississippi, *sels.*
Earth.
Ebb-Tide.
Elegy on a Nordic White Protestant.
Elegy on an Empty Skyscraper.
Embarkation. *Fr.* Down the Mississippi.
Enduring, The.
Evening Sky.
Exit.
Faith.
Fugitive Beauty.
Full Moon. *Fr.* Down the Mississippi.
Gale, The. *Fr.* Sand and Spray; a Sea Symphony.
Grand Canyon of the Colorado, The.
Green Symphony.
Groundswell, The
Heat. *Fr.* Down the Mississippi.
Hoopskirt, The.
House to the Man, The.
I Had Scarcely Fallen Asleep.
In the Open Air.
Irradiations, *sels.*
Last Frontier, The.
Last Judgment.
Life, A.
Lincoln.
Lincoln, *sel.*
Lofty House, The.
London Nightfall.
Lost Corner.
Manhattan.
Mexican Quarter. *Fr.* Arizona Poems.
Moon's Orchestra, The. *Fr.* Down the Mississippi.
Mutability.
My Father's Watch.
New Heaven, A.
Night Landing. *Fr.* Down the Mississippi.
Night of Stars.
Portrait, The.
Rain in the Desert.
Rebel, A.
Road, The.
Sand and Spray; a Sea Symphony, *sel.*
Silence, The. *Fr.* Down the Mississippi.
Skaters, The.
Skyscrapers.
Snow at Sea.
Song of the Moderns.
Song of the Old Man.
Stevedores, The. *Fr.* Down the Mississippi.
Swan, The.
To a Survivor of the Flood.
To Columbus.
To the Winter Wind.
Towards the North Star.
Vision.
Wedding Ring, The.
White Symphony.
Windmills, The. *Fr.* Arizona Poems.
Woman in Winter Costume, A.
Woman Standing by a Gate with an Umbrella, A.
Wreck, The.
FLETCHER, JULIA A. *See* CARNEY, JULIA A. FLETCHER.
FLETCHER, PHINEAS. Apollyonists, The, *sels.*
Brittain's Ida, *sel.*
Canto I: "Of Men, nay Beasts: worse, Monsters: worst of all." *Fr.* The Locusts, or Apollyonists.
Chromis. *Fr.* Piscatorie Eclogues.
Desiderium. *Fr.* The Purple Island.
Divine Wooer, The, *sel.*
Drop, Drop, Slow Tears.
Eclog. III: "Fisher-lad, A (no higher dares he look)." *Fr.* Piscatorie Eclogues.
Elisa, or an Elegy upon the Unripe Decease of Sir Antony Irby, *sel.*
Father's Testament, A, *sel.*
Fond Soul. *Fr.* A Father's Testament.
Hymn, An: "Drop, drop, slow tears."
Lines Written at Cambridge, to W. R., Esquire.
Litany, A: "Drop, drop, slow tears."
Locusts, or Apollyonists, The, *sels.*
Overthrow of Lucifer, The. *Fr.* The Purple Island.
Parthenia. *Fr.* The Purple Island.
Piscatorie Eclogues, *sel.*
Purple Island, The, *sels.*
Sicelides, *sels.*
Sin, despair, and Lucifer. *Fr.* The Locusts, or Apollyonists.
Song: "Fond men! whose wretched care the life soon ending," *at. Fr.* Brittain's Ida.
To My Soul.
To My Soul in Its Blindness.
Who sows the seas, or ploughs the easy shore? *Fr.* Sicelides.
Woman's Inconstancy. *Fr.* Sicelides.
FLETCHER, ROBERT. Epitaph on His Deceased Friend, An.
FLEURY, LEROY J. Kid and His Dog, A.
FLEXNER, HORTENSE (Mrs. Wyncie King). Builders.
French Clock.
Poets.
Remembrance.
Snuff Boxes.
Wandering.
FLEXNER, JAMES. In the Hours of Darkness.
FLINK, HARVEY WAGNER. Two Hunters.
Wayfarers.
FLINN, PATRICIA. November.
FLINT, ANNIE JOHNSON. Answered Prayer, The.
At the Place of the Sea.
Blessings That Remain, The.
By the Way.
Carpenter's Son.
Christ—and We.
Daily with You.
Everlasting Love, The.
He Giveth More.
His Will Be Done.
Hitherto and Henceforth.
I Look Not Back.
In Him.
Jesus Christ—and We.
Name of Jesus, The.
Old Year and the New, The.
Our Father's Hand.
Our High Priest.
Passing Through.
Place of Prayer, The.
Pray—Give—Go.
Prayer for a Friend.
Red Sea Place in Your Life, The.
Sentinel, The.
This Moment.
Thou Remainest.
Thy Strength and My Day.
We See Jesus.
What God Hath [*or* Has] Promised.
Word of God, The.
FLINT, F. BARRIE. Immanence.
FLINT, FRANCIS [*or* FRANK] STEWART. Beggar.
Chrysanthemums.
Cleopatra, *tr.*
Eau-forte.
Hats.
Houses.
In the Garden.
Lilac.
London.
Lunch.
Plane-Tree.
Prayer: "As I walk through the streets."
Sadness.
Swan, The.
FLOHR, NATALIE. Martyr, The.
FLORES, ANGEL. Almeria, *tr.*
Death Alone, *tr.*
Warning for Abraham Lincoln, A, *tr.*
For other translations from Spanish, see AnCL.
For translations from French, see AnFP.
FLORES, KATE. *For translations from French, see* AnFP.
For translations from German, see AnGP.
FLORES, MANUEL MARÍA. Eve.
Ode to the Fatherland, *sel.*
FLORIO, JOHN. Concerning the Honour of Books.
Of Books.
FLORIT, EUGENIO. Aquarium.
Atlantic.
Baby Girl, The.
Dead Nereid, The.
Death in the Sun.
Elegy for Your Absence.
Martyrdom of Saint Sebastian, The.
Nocturne: "Heart of my nights."
On Someone's Death.
Present Evening, The.
Signal, The.
Strophes to a Statue.
To the Dead Butterfly.
FLOWER, ALICE REYNOLDS. At All Times.
FLOWER, NEWMAN. Creed in a Garden, A.
FLOWER, ROBIN. At Mass, *tr.*
Death's Warning to Beauty, *tr.*
Dispraise of Absalom, The, *tr.*
Finis, *tr.*
Flight of the Earls, The, *tr.*
Good Tradition, The, *tr.*
He Praises His Wife When She Has Left [*or* Had Gone from] Him, *tr.*
He That Never Read a Line, *tr.*
In Praise of Aed [the Chieftain], *tr.*
In Tuaim Inbhir, *tr.*
Ivy Crest, The, *tr.*
My Christ Ever Faithful, *tr.*
No Sufferer for Her Love, *tr.*
Of Women No More Evil, *tr.*
On a Dead Scholar, *sel., tr.*
Open-Air Scriptorium, The, *tr.*
Over My Head the Forest Wall, *tr.*
Pangur Bán, *tr.*
Saint Ita's Fosterling, *tr.*
Saint Ite.
Say Not That Beauty.
Storm at Sea, A, *tr.*
Troy.
We Will Not Die, These Lovers Say, *tr.*
Were Not the Gael Fallen, *tr.*
White Cat and the Student, The, *tr.*

FLOWER, SARAH. *See* ADAMS, SARAH FLOWER.
FLUCKER, THOMAS. Tom Gage's Proclamation.
FLYNN, CLAIRE WALLACE. Glory of the Grass, The.
FLYNN, JOSEPH. Down Went McGinty.
FOCHT, MILDRED. David, Aged Four.
FOETH, AFANASI. *See* FET, AFANASI AFANASIEVICH.
FOGAZZARO, ANTONIO. Bells, The.
FOGEL, EPHIM G. Shipment to Maidenek.
FOLCACHIERO DE' FOLCACHIERI. Canzone: He Speaks of His Condition through Love.
FOLEY, DAN. Dyeing Prospector, The.
FOLEY, DAVID W. Within the Gates.
FOLEY, HELEN. Gorse.
FOLEY, JAMES WILLIAM. Chums.
Daddy Knows.
Drop a Pebble in the Water.
Echo of a Song, The.
Greetings for Two.
Jim Brady's Big Brother.
Lullaby: "Sleepy little, creepy little goblins in the gloaming."
My Wonderful Dad.
Nemesis.
North Dakota Hymn.
Passamquoddy's Apple Toddy.
Plain Bob and a Job.
Scientific Proof.
Song of Summer Days.
Story of Self-Sacrifice, A.
Unusual Chum, An.
Way He Used to Do, The.
We Ain't Scared o' Pa.
Yanks.
FOLEY, VIRGINIA J. Invalid, The.
FOLGORE DA SAN GEMINIANO. *See* SAN GEMINIANO, FOLGORE DA.
FOLLANSBEE, MITCHELL D. I Like to Quote.
FOLLEN, ELIZA LEE (Cabot). Annie's Garden.
Baby's Birthday, The.
Birdie.
Cock and Hens.
Ding Dong! Ding Dong!
Do You Guess It Is I?
Dog and the Cat, the Duck and the Rat, The.
Farm Yard, The.
Fiddlededee.
Follow Me!
Good Moolly Cow, The.
Kitty in the Basket.
Little Boy's Good-Night, The.
Little Kittens, The.
Little Kittens, The, *sel.*
Lullaby: "Sleep, my baby, sleep, my boy."
Moon, The.
New Moon, The.
Oh! Look at the Moon.
Ringely, Ringely.
Runaway Brook.
Three Little Kittens, The, *at.*
Trusty Learning A, B, C.
Walter and His Dog.
FOLWELL, ARTHUR H. Ode to City Snow.
FOMBONA PACHANO, JACINTO. America, My Sweet.
Clouds Have Already Told Me, The.
Coca Tree, The.
Complaint, The.
Dance of the Lost Key.
Death over the Air.
I Announce the Kingdom of the Star.
Puddle, The.
Since Tomorrow Is Sunday.
Warning for Abraham Lincoln, A.
While I Sang My Song.
FØNSS, OTTO C. Shooting Stars.
FONTAINE, JEAN DE LA. *See* LA FONTAINE, JEAN DE.
FONTAINE, LAMAR. All Quiet along [*or* on] the Potomac, *at.*
Picket-Guard, The, *at.*
FONTENELLE, BERNARD LE BOVIER DE. Daphne.
FOOTE, AGNES C. Annunciation to All Women.
FOOTE, JOHN A. To a Fossil Fern.
FOOTE, LUCIUS HARWOOD. Derelict, The.
Don Juan.
El Vaquero.
On the Heights.
Poetry.
FOOTE, SAMUEL. Great Panjandrum [Himself], The.
FORBES, ELLA C. Glad Earth.
FORD, CHARLES HENRI. Baby's in Jail; the Animal Day Plays Alone.
Plaint.
FORD, CHARLES L. Sacrament, The.
FORD, COREY. Up-Set, The.
When West Comes East.
FORD, FORD MADOX (*formerly* Ford Madox Hueffer). A Solis Ortus Cardine.
Children's Song.
Clair de Lune.
Footsloggers, *sels.*
Gray [*or* Grey] Matter.
House, A, *sel.*
Iron Music, The.
Lullaby, A: "We've wandered all about the upland fallows."
Old Houses of Flanders, The.
On Heaven, *sel.*
Tandaradei ("Under der Linden"), *tr.*
"There Shall Be More Joy."
To Christina at Nightfall.
Unwritten Song, The.
Winter-Night Song.
Wisdom.
FORD, FRANCIS ALAN. Song of the Gulf Stream.
FORD, JOHN. Broken Heart, A. *Fr.* The Broken Heart.
Broken Heart, The, *sels.*
Can You Paint a Thought. *Fr.* The Broken Heart.
Dawn. *Fr.* The Lover's Melancholy.
Dirge: "Glories, pleasures, pomps, delights, and ease." *Fr.* The Broken Heart.
Fly Hence, Shadows. *Fr.* The Lover's Melancholy.
Glories, pleasures, pomps, delights, and ease. *Fr.* The Broken Heart.
Lady's Trial, The, *sel.*
Lover's Melancholy, The, *sels.*
Matin Song. *Fr.* The Lover's Melancholy.
Musical Duel, The. *Fr.* The Lover's Melancholy.
Now Love Dies. *Fr.* The Broken Heart.
Oh. No More, No More, Too Late. *Fr.* The Broken Heart.
Pleasures, Beauty, Youth Attend Ye. *Fr.* The Lady's Trial.
Royall Lady. *Fr.* The Broken Heart.
Song: "Can you paint a thought? or number." *Fr.* The Broken Heart.
Song: "Fly hence, shadows, that do keep." *Fr.* The Lover's Melancholy.
Song: "Glories, pleasures, pomps, delights, and ease." *Fr.* The Broken Heart.
Song: "Oh no more, no more, too late." *Fr.* The Broken Heart.
'Tis Pity She's a Whore, *sel.*
FORD, JOHN, *and* THOMAS DEKKER. *See* DEKKER, THOMAS, *and* JOHN FORD.
FORD, MARY A. Hundred Years from Now, A.
FORD, R. A. D. Back to Dublin.
Delusion of Reference, A.
Lynx.
Roadside near Moscow.
Twenty Below.
FORD, RICHARD CLYDE. Forest Boat Song.
FORD, ROBERT. Bonniest Bairn in A' the Warl', The.
FORD, STEPHEN VAN RENSSELAER. Inasmuch.
FORD, THOMAS. There Is a Lady Sweet and Kind, *at.*
FORDE, THOMAS. Fond Love, No More. *Fr.* Love's Labyrinth.
Love's Labyrinth, *sel.*
FORESMAN, REBECCA. How to Forget.
If.
"FOREST, GREEN" (Samuel McP. Glasgow). Not My Will.
"FORESTER, FANNY" (Emily Chubbuck Judson). My Bird.
Watching.
Weaver, The.
FORREST, M. Lonely Woman, The.
FORREST, WILLIAM. Marigold, The.
New Ballade of the Marigolde, A.
FORRESTER, ALFRED A. ("Alfred Crowquill"). To My Nose.
FORRESTER, IZOLA LOUISE. And the Procession Moved On.
FORSSLUND, KARL ERIK. Hay-Making.
FORSYTH, JAMES. Artillery Shoot.
Soldier's Dove.
To My Wife.
FORSYTH, MARY ISABELLA. English Sparrow, The.
FORSYTH, P. T. Question, A.
FORT, JANETTA. *See* DENTON, CLARA JANETTA.
FORT, PAUL. Ballad of the Bells, *sel.*
Ballade: "Pretty maid, she died, she died, The."
Girl Is Dead, The.
Harmonious Vision of the Earth, The.
Joy.
Pan and the Cherries.
Philomel.
Pretty Maid, The.
Sailor and the Shark, The.
FORTUNATUS (Venantius Honorius Clementianus Fortunatus). Hail, Day of Days! In Peals of Praise.
Hymn to the Holy Cross.
O Glory of Virgins.
To Queen Radigunde with Herbs and Violets.
To the Noble and Patrician Iovinus, Governor of Provence.
Vexilla Regis [Prodeunt].
Welcome, Happy Morning.
FOSCOLO, UGO. To His Dead Brother.
FOSDICK, HARRY EMERSON. God of Grace and God of Glory.
O God, in Restless Living.
Prince of Peace, The.
FOSDICK, WILLIAM W. Maize, The.
FOSS, SAM WALTER. Boston.
Bring Me Men. *Fr.* The Coming American.
Calf-Path, The.
Coming American, The.
Coming American, The, *sel.*
Cosmopolitan Woman, A.
Country Summer Pastoral, A.
Creedless Love, The.
Father's Journey.
He Comes. *Fr.* Father's Journey.
He Goes. *Fr.* Father's Journey.
He Worried about It.
Higher Catechism, The, *sels.*
House by the Side of the Road, The.
Hullo!
Husband and Heathen.
Ideal Husband to His Wife, The.
Meeting of the Clabberhuses, The.
Nature and Religion. *Fr.* The Higher Catechism.
Philosopher, A.
Prayer of Cyrus Brown, The.
Song of the Cannon, The.
Spring Cleaning, The.
Then Ag'in.
Town of Hay, The.
Two Gods.
Volunteer Organist, The.
War.
What Is the Church?
Work for Small Men, *sel.*
FOSTER, DAVID SKAATS. Game of Chess, The.
FOSTER, FRANCIS M. Hunger.
FOSTER, JEANNE ROBERT. Bitter Herb, The.
John Butler Yeats.
King o' Spain's Daughter, The.
Pair of Lovers, A.
Song of Ballyshannon.
Tell Me, What Is Poetry.
Wild Cherry.

William P. Frye, The.
FOSTER, STEPHEN COLLINS. Beautiful Dreamer.
Camptown Races, De.
Come Where My Love Lies Dreaming.
Jeanie with the Light Brown Hair.
Massa's in de Cold, Cold Ground.
My Old Dog Tray.
My Old Kentucky Home.
Nelly Bly.
Nelly Was a Lady.
Oh! Susanna!
Old Black Joe.
Old Folks at Home, The.
Old Uncle Ned.
Swanee River.
FOSTER, WILLIAM A. Bonny Tweed for Me, The.
FOSTER, WILLIAM PRESCOTT. Icebergs.
Sea's Voice, The.
FOULKE, WILLIAM DUDLEY. Ad Patriam, *sel.*
Canzone: "Clear, fresh sweet waters," *tr.*
City's Crown, The.
Daughter's Love, A.
Life's Evening.
FOWLER, E. KATHRYN. Secrets.
FOWLER, ELLEN THORNEYCROFT. Wisdom of Folly, The.
FOWLER, ELSIE MELCHERT. Christmas Morning.
If You've Never.
Little Christ Child.
FOWLER, HAZEL J. Prayer: "Take from the earth its tragic hunger, Lord."
FOWLER, WILBUR HUMPHREY. Prayer, A: "Purge me, O God."
FOWLER, WILLIAM. If When I Die, *at.*
In Orknay.
Ship-broken Men Whom Stormy Seas Sore Toss.
FOWLIE, WALLACE. *For translations from French, see* MiCF; ReMP; TrJP.
FOX, GEORGE. County of Mayo, The, *tr.*
FOX, JAMES. Where the Grizzly Dwells.
FOX, MOIREEN. Fairy Lover, The.
Liadain to Curither.
FOX, WILLIAM JOHNSON. Barons Bold, The.
Life Is Love.
Martyrs' Hymn, The, *tr.*
FOX-SMITH, CICELY. *See* SMITH, CICELY FOX.
"FOXTON, E." (Sarah Hammond Palfrey). Pilgrim, The.
FÖYEN, JEAN. Spring.
FRANCES, EMMANUEL BEN DAVID. Price of Begging, The.
FRANCES, JACOB BEN DAVID. Song of Hate.
FRANCHINI, FRANCESCO. Lucia.
"FRANCIS." They Answer Back; to His Ever-worshipped Will from W. H.
FRANCIS, SAINT. *See* FRANCIS OF ASSISI, SAINT.
FRANCIS, COLIN. Tony O!
FRANCIS, JOSEPH G. Elephant, An.
Lion, A.
Musical Evening, A, *at.*
Very Happy Family, A.
FRANCIS, MARILYN. Neighbors.
FRANCIS, PHILIP. Art of Poetry, The, *tr.*
Bold Satirist, The, *tr.*
O Cruel Still, *tr.*
FRANCIS, ROBERT. Apple Peeler.
Beyond Biology.
Boy Riding Forward Backward.
Cold.
High Diver.
Picasso and Matisse.
Pitcher.
Seed-Eaters, The.
Swimmer.
Walls.
FRANCIS, THOMAS. Offspring, The, *sel.*
FRANCIS D'ASSISI, MOTHER. Resignation.
Samaritan Woman.
FRANCIS OF ASSISI, SAINT. Blessing of Saint Francis, The.
Cantica: Our Lord Christ, *at.*
Canticle of [the] Creatures.
Canticle of the Sun.
Lord, Make Me an Instrument of Your Peace.
Of Order in Our Lord Christ, *at.*
Order, *at.*
Praise of Created Things.
Prayer: "Lord, make me an instrument of Thy Peace."
Prayer for Peace.
St. Francis' Prayer.
Saint Francis' Salute to Our Lady.
Sermon to the Birds.
Song of the Creatures, The.
FRANCIS RAPHAEL, MOTHER (Augusta Theodosia Drane). Maris Stella.
Nun's Beloved, A.
FRANCIS XAVIER, SAINT. Hymn: "My God, I love thee, not because."
Hymn of Love.
My God I Love Thee.
O Deus Ego Amo Te.
FRANCISCA JOSEPHA DEL CASTILLO, SISTER. Christmas Carol: "Land grew bright in a single flower, The."
Holy Eclogue, The.
FRANCK, JOHANN. Peace and Joy in Jesus Christ.
FRANCO, LUIS L. Goat-Pen.
FRANK, EDGAR. Goshen!
FRANK, FLORENCE KIPER. Baby.
Jew to Jesus, The.
Jewish Conscript, The.
Lincoln.
Movies, The.
Now in the Bloom.
Sleep the Mother.
FRANK, JOHN FREDERICK. One No. 7.
FRANKENBERG, LLOYD. Existentialism.
Hide in the Heart.
Letter to the Night.
Roots Go Down.
Sea, The.
Young Love.
FRANKENSTEIN, ALFRED V. John Henry; an American Episode.
FRANKLIN, BENJAMIN. Difference, The.
Downfall of Piracy, The, *at.*
Epitaph on a Talkative Old Maid.
Here Skugg lies snug.
Jack and Roger.
Mother Country, The.
On Skugg.
Paper.
Poor Richard's Almanac, *sels.*
Poor Richard's Wisdom. *Fr.* Poor Richard's Almanac.
Prudence.
Quatrain: "Jack eating rotten cheese, did say."
Teach the Rover, *at.*
Well-packed Wisdom. *Fr.* Poor Richard's Almanac.
FRANKLIN, MICHAEL. Scarecrow, The.
FRANSEN, NATANAËL. Norwegian Cradle-Song.
FRANZ, WILLIS WALTON. Lullaby, A: "Close to the heart that is throbbing in love for you."
FRANZÉN, FRANZ MIKAEL. Champagne.
FRASER, ALEXANDER LOUIS. By Cobequid Bay.
Life's Illusion.
Rallying Hymn for the Church.
FRASER, CLAUD LOVAT. Robin's Song, The, *at.*
FRASER, GEORGE S. Ballata 11: Last Song; from Exile, *tr.*
Ballata 9: "There in a woodland, to my thought more bright," *tr.*
Bought Embrace, A.
Crisis.
Elegies (*of* Tibullus), *sels., tr.*
Elegy: "Waxen and the false grace of tulips, The."
Epode XV: "It was night with the shine of the moon amid the smaller stars shining," *tr. Fr.* Epodes.
Epodes (*of* Horace), *sel., tr.*
Lean Street.
Meditation of a Patriot.
Nilotic Elegy.
Odes (*of* Horace), *sel., tr.*
On a Memory of Beauty.
Poem about Love, A.
Rostov.
S.S. *City of Benares.*
Song for Music.
Sonnet: "Beauty of ladies of compassionate heart," *tr.*
Sonnet: "My simple heart, bred in provincial tenderness."
Sonnet: "Who's this that comes, as each man looks at her," *tr.*
Sonnet: "You have in you the flowers and the green grass," *tr.*
Summer and Winter.
Time, The.
FRASER, HERMIA HARRIS. Chant to a Were-Bear.
Copper Song, The.
Rousing Canoe Song, The.
Song of Welcome.
Song to the Wanderer.
FRASER, JAMES ANDERSON. Apprehension.
FRASER, JOHN. Maiden and the Lily, The.
FRAZEE-BOWER, HELEN. Alien.
Courage.
Fallen Tree.
I Bid You Keep Some Few Small Dreams.
Mother.
Song of Diligence, A.
This Is the Tragedy.
Two Married.
When Death Shall Come.
Who Goeth Hence.
FRAZER, JOHN DE JEAN. Song for July 12th, 1843.
FREDERICKS, JOSEPH PAGET-. *See* PAGET-FREDERICKS, JOSEPH.
FREDUGIS. Lament for Alcuin.
FREE, SPENCER MICHAEL. Human Touch, The.
Old-Time Family Doctor, The.
FREED, EDWARD M. Elusive Muse, The.
FREEMAN, CAROLYN R. Easter Airplane, The.
Making a Man.
FREEMAN, JOHN. Asylum.
Black Poplar-Boughs.
Body, The.
Caterpillars.
Crowns, The.
English Hills.
Evening Sky, The.
Fugitive, The.
Happy Death.
Home for Love.
Hounds, The.
It Was the Lovely Moon.
Knocking at the Door.
Merrill's Garden.
Moon-Bathers.
Music Comes.
Rhymeless.
Stone Trees.
To End Her Fear.
Tree, The.
Waiting.
Waits, The.
Wakers, The.
FREEMAN, MARY ELEANOR WILKINS. April Showers.
At the Dreamland Gate.
Christmas Tree, The.
Consolation.
Now Is the Cherry in Blossom.
Ostrich Is a Silly Bird, The.
FREEMAN, OLIVIA. Old Stone God, An.
FREEMAN, ROBERT. Beyond the Horizon.
Daddy.
Evening Prayer.
God Bless Our Home.
Hymn of Unity, A.
In My Father's House.
Peace on Earth.
Prayer: "White Captain of my soul, lead on."
Soldier's Prayer, A.
Why.
FREEMAN, THOMAS. Aliud.
In Christophorum.

FREEMAN, THOMAS (*continued*)
In Epitaphium Pingui Minerva Compositum.
In Marcellum.
In Owenni Epigrammata.
In Phaedram.
In Superbum.
Lectori Quomodo Legat.
Me Quoque Vatem.
O Tempora! O Mores!
Of Spenser's Fairy Queen.
Pity, oh pity! death had power.
Quo Ruis ab Demens? Londons Progress.
Quot Bipedes Aurum.
To George Chapman.
To Master W. Shakespeare.
To the Stationer.
FREEMAN, WALTER. Mother Church.
FREILIGRATH, FERDINAND. Black, Red, and Gold, *sel.*
Lion's Ride, The.
FRÉMONT, JOHN CHARLES. On Recrossing the Rocky Mountains after Many Years.
FRENCH, CECIL. What Is Worth the Singing?
FRENCH, FRANK. Waiting to Grow.
FRENCH, LUCY VIRGINIA SMITH. Palmetto and the Pine, The.
FRENCH, NORA MAY. I Must Not Yield.
Mission Graves, The.
Outer Gate, The.
When Plaintively and Near the Cricket Sings.
FRENCH, VIRGINIA. "Our Father Who Art."
FRENCH, WALTER LYMAN. Your Sanctuary.
FRENCH, WILLIAM PERCY. Fighting McGuire.
Goosey Goosey Gander—by Various Authors.
Queen's Afterdinner Speech, The, *sel.*
FRENEAU, PHILIP. Adventures of Simon Swaugum, a Village Merchant, The.
American Soldier, The.
Ancient Prophecy, An.
Argonaut, The; or, Lost Adventure.
Arnold's Departure.
Barney's Invitation.
Battle of Lake Champlain, The.
Battle of Stonington on the Seaboard of Connecticut, The.
Beauties of Santa Cruz, The, *sels.*
Bonhomme Richard and *Serapis*, The.
British Prison Ship, The, *sel.*
Columbus in Chains.
Columbus to Ferdinand.
Death. *Fr.* The House of Night.
Death's Epitaph. *Fr.* The House of Night.
Discovery.
Emancipation from British Dependence.
Epistle; from Dr. Franklin (Deceased) to His Poetical Panegyrists, on Some of Their Absurd Compliments.
Epitaph: "Here—for they could not help but die." *Fr.* The Fading Rose.
Eutaw Springs.
Fading Rose, The, *sel.*
Female Frailty, *sel.*
Hatteras.
Honey Bee, The.
Hospital Prison Ship, The. *Fr.* The British Prison Ship.
House of Night, The, *sels.*
How the British Fleet Bombarded New York.
Human Frailty.
Hurricane, The.
Indian Burying Ground, The.
Indian Student, The; or, Force of Nature.
Literary Importation.
Millennium, The. To a Ranting Field Orator.
Northern Soldier, The.
Occasioned by General Washington's Arrival in Philadelphia, on His Way to His Residence in Virginia.
Ode: "God save the Rights of Man!"
On a Book Called Unitarian Theology.
On a Hessian Debarkation.
On a Honey Bee [Drinking from a Glass of Wine and Drowned Therein].
On a Travelling Speculator.
On Mr. Paine's "Rights of Man."
On Retirement.
On the Anniversary of the Storming of the Bastille.
On the British Invasion.
On the British King's Speech.
On the Capture of the *Guerrière*.
On the Death of Captain Nicholas Biddle.
On the Death of Dr. Benjamin Franklin.
On the Departure of the British from Charleston.
On the Emigration to America.
On the Prospect of a Revolution in France.
On the Religion of Nature.
On the Ruins of a Country Inn.
On the Sleep of Plants.
On the Uniformity and Perfection of Nature.
On the Universality and Other Attributes of the God of Nature.
Parting Glass, The.
Plato to Theon.
Political Balance, The.
Political Litany, A.
Power of Fancy, The.
Progress of Balloons, The.
Republican Genius of Europe, The.
Retirement.
Royal Adventurer, The.
Sabbath-Day Chace.
Scurrilous Scribe, The.
Sir Henry Clinton's Invitation to the Refugees.
Song: On Captain Barney's Victory over the Ship *General Monk*.
Song of Thyrsis. *Fr.* Female Frailty.
Stanzas: "No tongue can tell, no pen describe."
Stanzas Occasioned by the Ruins of a Country Inn.
Stanzas to an Alien.
To a Caty-did.
To a Honey Bee.
To an Author.
To My Book.
To Sir Toby.
To the Memory of the Brave Americans.
Vanity of Existence, The.
Vision, A. *Fr.* The House of Night.
Wild Honey-Suckle, The.
FRERE, JOHN HOOKHAM. Acharnians, The, *sel.*, *tr.*
Bees and Monks. *Fr.* King Arthur and His Round Table.
Birds, The, *sels.*, *tr.*
Boy and His Top, The.
Boy and the Parrot.
Boy and the Wolf, The.
Cavern and the Hut, The.
Chorus: "Brekeke-kesh, koash, koash," *tr.* *Fr.* The Frogs.
Frogs, The, *sel.*, *tr.*
King Arthur and His Round Table, *sel.*
Life of Men, The, *tr.* *Fr.* The Birds.
Life of San Millan, *sel.*, *tr.*
Modern Improvements.
Piece of Glass, and the Piece of Ice, The.
Poverty, *tr.*
Showing How the Cavern Followed the Hut's Advice.
To rear a child is easy, but to teach, *tr.*
FRERE, JOHN HOOKHAM, *and* GEORGE CANNING. *See* CANNING, GEORGE, *and* JOHN HOOKHAM FRERE.
FRERE, JOHN HOOKHAM, GEORGE CANNING, *and* GEORGE ELLIS. *See* CANNING, GEORGE, GEORGE ELLIS, *and* JOHN HOOKHAM FRERE.
FRESNAYE, VAUQUELIN DE LA. *See* VAUQUELIN DE LA FRESNAYE.
FREUND, OTTO. Footsteps.
Heart Wound.
Isle of the Dead, The.
Music.
Requiescat.
FRIDJÓNSSON, GUDMUNDUR. "What Lack We?"
FRIEDLAENDER, VIOLET HELEN. Road Makers.
To a Blue Tit.
FRIEDRICH, RALPH. Even on a Night like This.
FRIEDRICH VON HAUSEN. Civil War.
FRIES, ANNERIKA. Soul Growth.
FRIESEKE, FRANCES. Armor the Bud.
You Need Not Fear.
FRIIS-MØLLER, KAI. Song of the Figurehead.
"FRIK" (Khachatur Kecharetzi). Reproaches.
FRINK, A. L. Rose Still Grows beyond the Wall, The.
FRISCH, ANTHONY. Convict, The.
Joan of Arc to the Tribunal.
Skiers, The.
FRISHMAN, DAVID. Messiah, The.
FRITSCH, H. S. Age, *at.*
How Old Are You? *at.*
FRÖDING, GUSTAF. Behold, This Dreamer Cometh!
City Lieutenant, The.
Dance by the Roadside, The.
Dreams in Hades.
Home-coming.
Idealism and Realism.
Little Joe-Johnny.
Love-Song, A.
Mountain Trolls.
Old Mountain Troll, The.
Old Room, An.
Pastoral.
Poor Monk of Skara, A.
Prayer-Meeting, The.
Prince Aladdin of the Lamp.
Sigh, Sigh, Rushes!
Spring-Time Sweetheart, A (If I Had Had One).
Winter Night.
FROHLICHER, JOHN C. Granite.
FROISSART, JEAN. Rondeau: "My heart enjoys the fragrance of the rose."
Rondel: "Love, love, what wilt thou with this heart of mine?"
Rondel: To His Mistress, to Succor His Heart.
Virelay: "Too long it seems e'er I shall view."
FROST, PHILIP P. Morning and Evening.
FROST, FRANCES MARY. Apple Season.
Apple Song.
Beach Fire.
Blue Smoke.
Christmas in the Woods.
Clover for Breakfast.
Counting-out Rhyme for March.
Cover.
Dandelions.
Easter in the Woods.
Father.
First Departure.
Girl in a Tree.
Hallowe'en.
Hydrographic Report.
Inquisitive Barn.
Kentucky Birthday.
Legend of Noël.
Little Whistler, The.
Long Night Moon, The; December.
Lost Fox.
Maple Feast.
New England Steeple.
Night of Wind.
Night Plane.
Of a Small Daughter Walking Outdoors.
Park Avenue Cat.
Prayer to St. Francis.
Proud, The.
Pup in the Snowstorm.
Purple Grackles.
Rambunctious Brook.
Refugee in New England.
School Is Out.
Sea Town.

Sniff.
Song for December Thirty-first.
Spring in Hiding.
Squirrel.
Trains at Night.
Traveler.
Weather Vanes.
White Season.
Winter Feast.
Woman of This Earth, *sels.*
Wood-Lot Hill.
FROST, ROBERT. Acquainted with the Night.
After Apple-picking.
Aim Was Song, The.
All Revelation.
Any Size We Please.
Armful, The.
At Woodward's Gardens.
Axe-Helve, The.
Bear, The.
Bereft.
Birches.
Birthplace, The.
Black Cottage, The.
Blue-Butterfly Day.
Blue Ribbon at Amesbury, A.
Bonfire, The.
Broken Drought, The.
Brook in the City, A.
Brown's Descent.
By Myself.
Canis Major. *Fr.* A Sky Pair.
Choose Something like a Star.
Christmas Trees.
Closed for Good.
Code, The.
Come In.
Considerable Speck, A.
Correction, A.
Cow in Apple-Time, The.
Death of the Hired Man, The.
Death of the Hired Man, The, *sels.*
Demiurge's Laugh, The.
Departmental.
Desert Places.
Design.
Directive.
Drumlin Woodchuck, A.
Dust in the Eyes.
Dust of Snow.
Early April.
Egg and the Machine, The.
Etherealizing.
Fear, The.
Fire and Ice.
Fireflies in the Garden.
For Once, Then, Something.
Freedom of the Moon, The.
From Plane to Plane.
Gift Outright, The.
God's Speech to Job. *Fr.* A Masque of Reason.
Going for Water.
Good-bye and Keep Cold.
Good Hours.
Grindstone, The.
Gum-Gatherer, The.
Happiness Makes Up in Height for What It Lacks in Length.
Hardship of Accounting, The.
Hill Wife, The.
Hill Wife, The, *sels.*
Hillside Thaw, A.
Home. *Fr.* The Death of the Hired Man.
Home Burial.
Home Defined. *Fr.* The Death of the Hired Man.
House Fear. *Fr.* The Hill Wife.
Hundred Collars, A.
Hyla Brook.
Impulse, The. *Fr.* The Hill Wife.
In a Poem.
Innate Helium.
Into My Own.
Investment, The.
Last Mowing, The.
Last Word of a Bluebird, The.
Leaf-Treader, A.
Lesson for Today, The.
Line-Storm Song, A.
Lockless Door, The.
Lodged.
Loneliness. *Fr.* The Hill Wife.
Lost in Heaven.
Lovely Shall Be Choosers, The.
Masque of Reason, A, *sel.*
Meeting and Passing.
Mending Wall.
Mending Wall, *sel.*
Middleness of the Road, The.
Minor Bird, A.
Misgiving.
Moon Compasses.
Most of It, The.
Mountain, The.
Mowing.
My November Guest.
My What-Is-It.
Need of Being Versed in Country Things, The.
Neither Out Far nor in Deep.
Never Again Would Birds' Song Be the Same.
Never ask of money spent.
New Hampshire.
Not Quite Social.
Not to Keep.
Nothing Gold Can Stay.
October.
Oft-repeated Dream, The. *Fr.* The Hill Wife.
Old Dog, The.
Old Man's Winter Night, An.
On a Tree Fallen across the Road.
On Looking Up by Chance at the Constellations.
On the Heart's Beginning to Cloud the Mind.
Once by the Pacific.
One Step Backward Taken.
Onset, The.
Our Hold on the Planet.
Our Singing Strength.
Out, Out.
Oven Bird, The.
Pan with Us.
Passing Glimpse, A.
Pasture, The.
Patch of Old Snow, A.
Paul's Wife.
Pauper Witch of Grafton, The.
Peaceful Shepherd, The. *Fr.* A Sky Pair.
Peck of Gold, A.
Prayer in Spring, A.
Provide, Provide.
Putting In the Seed.
Range-finding.
Record Stride, A.
Reluctance.
Revelation.
Road Not Taken, The.
Rose Family, The.
Runaway, The.
Sand Dunes.
Semi-Revolution, A.
Servant to Servants, A.
Silken Tent, The.
Sky Pair, A.
Sky Pair, A, *sel.*
Snow.
Snow Dust.
Soldier, A.
Sound of the Trees [*or* of Trees], The.
Span of Life, The.
Spring Pools.
Star-Splitter, The.
Stopping by Woods on a Snowy Evening.
Storm Fear.
Strong Are Saying Nothing, The.
Subverted Flower, The.
Telephone, The.
There Are Roughly Zones.
They Were Welcome to Their Belief.
Time to Talk, A.
To a Thinker.
To a Young Wretch.
To Earthward.
To the Thawing Wind.
Too Anxious for Rivers.
Tree at My Window.
Trial by Existence, The.
Tuft of Flowers, The.
Two Look at Two.
Two Tramps in Mud Time.
Two Witches, *sel.*
Valley's Singing Day, The.
Vantage Point, The.
West-running Brook.
White-tailed Hornet, The.
Wind and Window-Flower.
Winter Eden, A.
Witch of Coös, The. *Fr.* Two Witches.
Wood-Pile, The.
Young Birch, A.
FROST, THOMAS. Death of Colman, The.
Guns in the Grass, The.
FROTHINGHAM, NATHANIEL LANGDON. Crossed Swords, The.
FROUDE, RICHARD HURRELL. Weakness of Nature.
FRUG, SIMEON GRIGORYEVICH. Sail Peacefully Home.
Song: "Night is an ancient sorceress, The."
Talmud, The.
FRY, CHRISTOPHER. Boy with a Cart, The, *sel.*
FRY, HERBERT. As I'd Nothing Else to Do.
FRY, ROGER. Afternoon of a Faun, The, *tr.*
FU CHIH TAO. Sentry, The.
FUGUET, DOLLETT. Blithe Mask, The.
FU HSÜAN. Gentle Wind, A.
Woman.
FUJITA. New Year.
Sunshine.
FUJIWARA. White plum tree, where can my loved one be?
FUJIWARA IETAKA. Old Scent of the Plum Tree.
FUJIWARA NO ATSUTADA. I Think of the days.
FUJIWARA NO GO-KANESUKE. River Izumi, The.
FUJIWARA NO GO-KYOGOKU. Cricket cries, The.
FUJIWARA NO KAMATARI. I have got her.
FUJIWARA NO KIYOSUKE. I may live on until.
FUJIWARA NO MASATSUNE. From Yoshino.
FUJIWARA NO MICHINOBU. Day will soon be gone, The. *Fr.* The Hyaku-Nin-Isshu.
Hyaku-Nin-Isshu, The, *sel.*
In the dawn, although I know.
FUJIWARA NO MOTOTOSHI. Your fine promises.
FUJIWARA NO SADAIE. You do not come, and I wait.
FUJIWARA NO SADAYORI. As the mists rise in the dawn.
FUJIWARA NO SANESADA. Cuckoo calls, A.
FUJIWARA NO TADAMICHI. As I row over the plain.
FUJIWARA NO TOSHINARI. In all the world.
FUJIWARA NO TOSHIYUKI. Although it is not plainly visible to the eye. *Fr.* Kokin Shu.
Autumn has come invisibly.
Autumn Leaves.
In the Bay of Sumi.
Kokin Shu, *sel.*
FUKAO, SUMAKO. Dante's Scourge.
Will-o'-the-Wisp.
FULLER, EDWIN WILEY. Angel in the Cloud, The, *sels.*
Flight. *Fr.* The Angel in the Cloud.
Man Is a Prisoner. *Fr.* The Angel in the Cloud.
FULLER, ETHEL ROMIG. Airmail Arrives, The.
Diaries.
Diaries, *sel.*
Fir Forest.
Fisherman's Prayer.
Frost.
God Hears Prayer.
Man Speaks, A.
Mother—a Portrait.
Pioneer Mother, The.
Proof.
Today.
What the King Has.

FULLER, ETHEL ROMIG (*continued*)
Who Knows a Mountain?
Willow Whistle.
Wind Is a Cat.
FULLER, H. J. My Bonnie.
FULLER, MARGARET WITTER. Dryad Song.
Passion-Flower, The.
FULLER, ROY. Crustaceans.
Emotion of Fiction, The.
End of a Leave, The.
Epitaph on a Bombing Victim.
Giraffes, The.
Good-bye for a Long Time.
Green Hills of Africa, The.
Hero, The.
Image, The.
In Africa.
January, 1940.
Knole.
Letter to My Wife.
Meditation.
Native Working on the Aerodrome.
November, 1941.
October, 1942.
Petty Officers' Mess, The.
Plains, The.
Poem: "Pity, repulsion, love and anger."
Sadness, Glass, Theory.
Soliloquy in an Air-Raid.
Spring 1943.
Spring 1942.
Translation.
Tribes, The.
What Is Terrible.
Winter Night.
Wry Smile, A.
FULLER, VIOLET. Ring, Joyful Bells!
FULLERTON, MARY ELIZABETH ("E.").
Adventure.
Comet.
Dream, A.
Heart's Not Yet a Neighbour, The.
Independence.
Learning.
Lovers.
Passivity.
Selector's Wife, The.
Skull, The.
Unit.
War.
FUNAROFF, SOL. Dusk of the Gods, *sel.*
FUNK, WILFRED JOHN. From a Downtown Skyscraper.
Hospital.
Interior Decorator Gets in My House, An.
Surgeon, The.
FURBEE, RUTH. Worship.
FURIUS BIBACULUS, MARCUS. *See* BIBACULUS, MARCUS FURIUS.
FURLONG, ALICE. Betrayal, The.
Dreamer, The.
My Share of the World.
Slumber Song: "Shoheen sho! There's a new moon setting."
Triad of Things Not Decreed, The.
Warnings, The.
Yuletide.
FURLONG, THOMAS. John O'Dwyer of the Glen, *tr.*
FURNESS, WILLIAM HENRY. Evening Hymn.
Light of Stars, The.
FURSE, MARGARET CECILIA. Lamp Flower, The.
FURUKAMI, I. W. *For translations from Japanese, see* LiTW.
FU YÜAN. Other Days.
FYLEMAN, ROSE. Alms in Autumn.
At Dawn.
Attic, The.
Balloon Man, The.
Barge, The.
Best.
Best Game the Fairies Play, The.
Bingo Has an Enemy.
Birthday Child, The.
Boat, The.
Chickens, The.
Child Next Door, The.
Christmas-Time.
Christmas Wish, A.

Cock, The.
Consolation.
Conversation.
Cuckoo, The.
Daddy.
Dentist, The.
Differences.
Donkey, The.
Dormouse, The.
Fairies.
Fairies Have Never a Penny to Spend, The.
Fairy Flute, The.
Fairy Music.
Fairy Tailor, The.
Fairy Went a-Marketing, A.
Family, The, *tr.*
Fountain, The.
Frog, The.
Goblin, The.
Good Morning.
Grown-ups.
Have You Watched the Fairies?
Husky Hi.
If Only . . .
In the Park.
Jock o' Dreams.
Jonathan.
Little Shepherdess to Her Lambs, The.
Mary Middling.
Mice.
Mr. Minnitt.
Mrs. Barks.
Mrs. Brown.
Momotara.
Mother.
My Donkey.
My Policeman.
New Neighbor, The.
October.
Please.
Pretty Lady.
Primrose Hill.
Richard Has Something to Say.
Shop Windows.
Singing Fairy, The.
Singing-Time.
Sometimes.
Spring, The.
Temple Bar.
There Are No Wolves in England Now.
Timothy.
Trafalgar Square.
Trees and Fairies.
Very Lovely.
Vision.
Weathercock, The.
Winnipeg at Christmas.
Yesterday in Oxford Street.
FYNN, ARTHUR J. Land Where the Columbines Grow.

G

"G., A." Father, Hear Thy Children.
"G., A. R." "Go Forward."
"G., E. O." My Church ("My church has but one temple").
"G., L." Quarrelsome Trio, The.
"G., W. A." Yielded Life, The.
"G. S. O." *See* "O., G. S."
GABRIEL, CHARLES H. Evening Prayer, at.
My Evening Prayer, at.
GABRIEL Y GALÁN, JOSÉ MARÍA. Lord, The.
GADBURY, JOHN. Ballad upon the Popish Plot, A.
GAFFNEY, FRANCIS A. Our Lady of the Rosary.
GÁG, WANDA. A B C Bunny, The.
GALAI, BENYAMIN. To My Generation.
GALBRAITH, GEORGIE STARBUCK. Mist.
Neighbor's Dog.
GALBRAITH, W. CAMPBELL. Red Poppies in the Corn.
GALBREATH, CHARLES BURLEIGH. Another Reply to "In Flanders Fields."
In Flanders Fields; an Answer.

GALE, NORMAN. Bartholomew.
Bobby's First Poem.
Child of Loneliness.
Content.
Country Faith, The.
Creed, A.
Danger, The.
Dawn and Dark.
Dead Friend, A.
Dinah.
Fairy Book, The.
First Kiss, The.
Love-Song, A.
Mustard and Cress.
Pastoral, A: "Along the lane beside the mead."
Prayer, A: "Tend me my birds, and bring again."
Priest, A.
Question, The.
Same Complaint, The.
Second Coming, The.
Shaded Pool, The.
Song: "This peach is pink with such a pink."
Song: "Wait but a little while."
Spring.
Thanks.
To My Brothers.
To Sleep, *sel.*
Voice, The.
GALE, R. J. Teacher's "If," The.
GALE, VI. Shore Birds.
GALE, ZONA. Children of Tomorrow.
Credo.
North Star.
Sky-Goer, The.
Voice.
Walt Whitman.
GAL'ED, ZERUBAVEL. Chickory.
GALES, RICHARD LAWSON. Ballad of St. Christopher, A
Temptation of St. Anthony, The.
Waiting for the Kings.
GALINDEZ, BARTOLOMÉ. In the Azure Night.
GALL, RICHARD. Cradle Song: "Baloo, baloo my wee, wee thing."
Hazlewood Witch, The.
My Only Jo and Dearie, O.
GALLAGHER, DOROTHY HAMILTON. Morning.
GALLAGHER, F. O'NEIL. All Alone Tree, The.
GALLAGHER, JAMES F. As Always.
Love's Growing Pains.
GALLAGHER, KATHARINE. Chant for Skippers.
Poison Ivy!
GALLAGHER, MARGARET MIRIAM. *See* MIRIAM, SISTER.
GALLAGHER, WILLIAM DAVIS. August.
Autumn, The. *Fr.* Autumn in the West.
Autumn in the West.
Autumn in the West, *sel.*
Cardinal Bird, The.
Laborer, The.
Mothers of the West, The.
GALLAUDET, HERBERT D. Holy Places.
Young Man in a Galilean Doorway.
GALSWORTHY, JOHN. Courage ("Courage is but a word, and yet, of words").
Courage ("If on a spring night I went by").
Devon to Me.
Downs, The.
Limerick: "Angry young husband called Bicket, An."
Lost.
Mountain Air.
Never Get Out!
Past.
Peace in the World.
Prayer, The: "If on a spring night I went by."
Prayer for Gentleness to All Creatures.
Reminder.
To My Dog.
Valley of the Shadow.
Wind.
Wonder.

GALT, JOHN. Canadian Boat Song, *at.*
GALVAM, FRANCISCO. To Our Lord.
GALVIN, JAMES J. Lady of O.
Madonna's Lullaby, *tr.*
Morning Star.
Ox-Bone Madonna.
Photograph.
Spanish Alleluja.
GAMBARA, VERONICA. Sonnet: To the Emperor Charles V and to King Francis I of France.
GAMBLE, WILLIAM M. T. Medieval Appreciations.
GANNETT, WILLIAM CHANNING. A. L. G.
Consider the Lilies.
Dear Togetherness, The.
Highway, The.
Mary's Manger-Song.
Stream of Faith, The.
"Who Wert and Art and Evermore Shalt Be."
GANT, MARGARET. May-Time.
GARABRANT, NELLIE M. Dandelion.
Fairy Artist, The.
GARBORG, ARNE. Sunset Joy.
To a Mountain Fen.
GARCÍA LORCA, FEDERICO. Afterwards.
Arid Land.
Arrest of Antoñito el Camborio in the Streets of Seville, The.
Ballad of the Spanish Civil Guard.
Ballad Walking in Sleep.
Cazador (Hunter).
Cry, The.
Dagger, The.
Faithless Wife, The.
Guitar, The.
Lament: "Cry has left in the wind, The."
Lament for Ignacio Sanchez Mejias.
Lament for the Death of a Bull-Fighter.
Little Town.
Lola.
Memento.
Ode to Walt Whitman.
Red oxen/ in a field of gold.
Rider's Song.
Silence, The.
Six Strings.
Soledad.
Somnambulant [*or* Somnambule *or* Somnambulistic] Ballad.
Surprise.
Weeping, The.
GARCILASO [*or* GARCILASSO] DE LA VEGA.
Eclogue I: "Sweet lament of two Castilian swains, The."
Epistle to Boscán.
Song: "Now go I quietly."
Sonnet: "Fair Naiads of the river, that reside."
Sonnet: "I am for ever bathed in tears, I rend."
Sonnet: "In so much as the lily and the rose."
Sonnet: "Oh dear love tokens that did work me harm."
Sonnet: "O Fate, implacable in my pursuit."
Sonnet: "O precious locket, found by luckless me."
GARD, LILLIAN GILCHRIST. Her Allowance!
New Year, The.
GARD, WAYNE. Life.
GARDINER, WREY. Dr. Coppelius.
Our True Beginnings.
Poetry Is Happiness.
Walking in London.
GARDNER, ISABELLA. Folkways.
Masked Shrew, The.
Milkman, The.
That "Craning of the Neck."
When a Warlock Dies.
GARDNER, JO. Let Me Lift Jesus, Lord.
Lilies of the Valley.
Only One, The.
GARDNER, WILLIAM HENRY. When Love Comes Knocking.
GARESCHÉ, EDWARD FRANCIS. At the Leap of the Waters.
Niagara.
Nuns, The.
Sermon of Saint Francis, A.
Young Priest to His Hands, The.
GAREY, HANNAH E. Thanksgiving.
GARFIAS, PEDRO. Villafranca de Córdoba.
GARIOCH, ROBERT. Anatomy o Winter, The, *tr. Fr.* Works and Days.
Ghaisties.
Works and Days, *sel., tr.*
GARLAND, HAMLIN. Color in the Wheat.
Cry of the Age, The.
Do You Fear [the Force of] the Wind?
Eagle Trail, The.
Gift of Water, The.
Gold-Seekers, The.
Greeting of the Roses, The.
Herald Crane, The.
Horses Chawin' Hay.
In the Days When the Cattle Ran.
In the Grass.
Line Up, Brave Boys.
Logan at Peach Tree Creek.
Magic.
Massasauga, The.
Meadow Lark, The.
Mountains Are a Lonely Folk, The.
My Prairies.
O the Fierce Delight.
On the Mississippi.
Passing of the Buffalo, The.
Pioneers.
Plowing; a Memory.
Plowman of Today, The.
Prairie Fires.
Sport.
To a Captive Crane.
Toil of the Trail, The.
Tribute of Grasses, A.
Ute Lover, The.
Wish, A.
GARLICK, PHYLLIS L. Fairy Feet.
Fairy Shoemaker, The.
Lullaby: "Lullaby, Lullaby,/ Shadows creep across the sky."
GARNETT, LOUISE AYRES. Ballad of the Doorstone.
Dream Boat, The.
Flower of Hemp.
Flying Charlie.
Hello!
Hound at Night.
Jorridge and Porridge.
Li'l Jesus-Baby, De.
Li'l Yaller Cradle.
Moon, The.
Song of Liberty, *sel.*
GARNETT, RICHARD. Age.
Auf meiner Herzliebsten Augelein, *tr.*
Babylon and Sion (Goa and Lisbon), *tr.*
Ballad of the Boat, The.
Didactic Poem, The.
Epigram: "Amid all Triads let it be confest."
Epigram: "'I hardly ever ope my lips,' one cries."
Epigram: "Philosopher, whom dost thou most affect."
Epigram: "Thou art in danger, Cincius, on my word," *tr.*
Epigram: "'Tis highly rational, we can't dispute."
Es fällt ein Stern herunter, *tr.*
Fading-Leaf and Fallen-Leaf.
Fair Circassian, The.
Few There Be, *tr.*
Highwayman's Ghost, The.
Island of Shadows, The.
Lyrical Poem, The.
Marigold.
Menodotis, *tr.*
Mir träumte von einem Königskind, *tr.*
Nix, The.
Nocturne: "Keen winds of cloud and vaporous drift."
Not of Itself but Thee, *tr.*
On an Urn.
On Revisiting Cintra after the Death of Catarina, *tr.*
Rose, die Lilie, die Taube, die Sonne, Die, *tr.*
Sag' mir wer einst die Uhren erfund, *tr.*
Silence and Speech.
Sonnet: "Leave me, all sweet refrains my lip hath made," *tr.*
Sonnet: "Time and the mortal will stand never fast," *tr.*
Sonnet—Age.
To America.
Warum sind denn die Rosen so blas, *tr.*
Who Was It, Tell Me, *tr.*
GARNIER, ROBERT. Antigone, *sel.*
Antonius, *sel.*
Chorus: "Alas, with what tormenting fire." *Fr.* Antonius.
Oedipus. *Fr.* Antigone.
Of Death. *Fr.* Antonius.
GARRETT, ELIZABETH. O, Fair New Mexico.
GARRETT, GEORGE. Cædmon.
On Reading the *Metamorphoses.*
Snapshot: Ambassadress.
Snapshot: Politician.
Snapshot of a Pedant.
Tiresias.
GARRICK, DAVID. Epigram: "When doctrines meet with general approbation."
Heart of Oak.
Here lies Nolly Goldsmith.
To Mr. Gray.
GARRIGUE, JEAN. Apologia.
Circle, The.
Clovers, The.
Forest.
From Venice Was That Afternoon.
Lightly like Music Running.
Primer of Plato.
Stranger, The.
GARRISON, FIELDING H. Diavolina.
GARRISON, THEODOSIA PICKERING (Mrs. Frederic J. Faulks). April.
Ballad of the Angel, The.
Ballad of the Cross, The.
City Voice, A.
Closed Door, The.
Compensation.
Cynic, The.
Days, The.
Debt, The.
Dreamers, The.
Free Woman, The.
Great Cross of Mercy, The.
Green Inn, The.
Gypsying, The.
Hills, The.
John o' Dreams.
Kerry Lads, The.
Love Song, A.
May Flowers.
Memorial Day.
Monseigneur Plays.
Morning, A.
Neighbors, The.
One Fight More.
Poplars, The.
Prayer, A: "Let me work and be glad."
Red Cross Christmas Seal, The.
Resurgam.
Road's End, The.
Saint [*or* Sainte] Jeanne.
Shade.
Shepherd Who Stayed, The.
Sing Thou, My Soul.
Song in Autumn, A.
Song to Belinda, A.
Stains.
Tears of Harlequin, The.
Tears of Mary, The.
Torch, The.
Two Brothers, The.
Victor, The.
Wife, The.
GARRISON, WENDELL PHILLIPS. Afternoon. *Fr.* Post-Meridian.
Evening. *Fr.* Post-Meridian.
Post-Meridian, *sels.*
GARRISON, WILLIAM LLOYD. Freedom for the Mind.
Liberty for All.
Sonnet: "High walls and huge the body may confine."
Sonnet Written While in Prison for Denouncing the Domestic Slave-Trade.

GARRISON, WILLIAM LLOYD (*continued*)
Triumph of Freedom, The.
GARRISON, WINFRED ERNEST. At Carcassonne.
Book, The.
Easter Morning.
For an Hour.
Love and Life.
Quest, The.
Temptation.
Thy Sea So Great.
GARROD, HEATHCOTE WILLIAM. Thou should'st be living at this hour.
GARSTIN, CROSBIE. Callao.
Fantasy, A.
Figure-Head, The.
Nocturne: "Red flame flowers bloom and die, The."
Old Soldiers.
Spanish Ledges.
GARTH, SIR SAMUEL. Dispensary, The, *sels.*
What frenzy has of late possess'd the brain!
GARTHWAITE, JIMMY (Wymond Bradbury Garthwaite). Being Sick.
Night Watchmen.
Organ-Grinder, The.
Salt and Pepper Dance, The.
School after Christmas.
'Spress!
GARVIN, AMELIA BEERS (Warnock). *See* "HALE, KATHERINE."
GARVIN, JOHN W. Ancestral Ghosts.
Fatalist, A
Soul of Man Seeketh, The.
GARVIN, MARGARET ROOT. From All the Fools Who Went Before.
To Each His Own.
GARVIN, VIOLA GERARD. Gifts.
GASCOIGNE, GEORGE. Adventures of Master F. I., The, *sel.*
Amid my bale I bathe in bliss.
Anatomy of a Lover, The.
And If I Did, What Then? *Fr.* The Adventures of Master F. I.
Arraignment of a Lover, The.
Audaces Fortuna Iuvat.
Deep Desire Sung This Song.
Discourse of the Adventures Passed by Master F. J., A, *sels.*
Farewell, A: "And if I did, what then?" *Fr.* The Adventures of Master F. I.
Ferdinando Ieronimi's Sonnet.
Fie, Pleasure, Fie!
First Chorus, The. *Fr.* The Glass of Government.
For that He Looked Not upon Her.
Fruits of War, The.
Gascoigne's Arraignment.
Gascoigne's De Profundis.
Gascoigne's Good Morrow.
Gascoigne's Good-Night.
Gascoigne's Lullaby [*or* Lullabie].
Glass of Government, The, *sel.*
Grief of Joy, The, *sel.*
He Wrote to the Same Friend from Excester This Sonnet Following.
He Wrote unto a Scottish Dame Whom He Chose for His Mistress in the French Court as Followeth.
I Could Not though I Would.
I Tell Thee, Priest.
In Praise of a Gentlewoman Who, though She Were Not Very Fair, Yet Was She as Hard-favored as Might Be.
Inscription in a Garden.
Libel of Divorce, A.
Looks of a Lover Enamoured, The.
Lover Declareth His Affection, together with the Cause Thereof, The.
Lover's Lullaby, A.
Lullaby of a Lover, The.
My Worthy Lord, I Pray You.
Praise of Philip Sparrow, The.
Sing Lullaby, as Women Do.
Steel Glass, The, *sels.*
Strange Passion of a Lover, A.
Vanity of the Beautiful, The.
Why then (quod I) old proverbs never fail.
GASCOYNE, DAVID. Apologia.
Autumn Park, An.
De Profundis. *Fr.* Miserere.
Ecce Homo. *Fr.* Miserere.
Elegy, An: "Friend, whose unnatural early death."
Ex Nihilo. *Fr.* Miserere.
Gravel-Pit Field, The.
In Defence of Humanism.
Jardin du Palais Royal.
Kyrie. *Fr.* Miserere.
Lachrymae. *Fr.* Miserere.
Light of the Sun over Arctic Regions.
Miserere.
Miserere, *sels.*
On the Grand Canal.
Orpheus in the Underworld.
Pieta. *Fr.* Miserere.
Rex Mundi.
Sacred Hearth, The.
Sanctus. *Fr.* Miserere.
September Sun, 1947.
Snow in Europe.
Spring MCMXL.
Sudden Squall, A.
Tenebrae. *Fr.* Miserere.
Three Stars of Prophecy, The.
Unattained, The.
Uncertain Battle, The.
Wartime Dawn, A.
Winter Garden.
GASELEE, SIR STEPHEN. On China Blue.
Soul in the Kiss, The, *tr.*
GASETSU. Iris, The.
GASS, IRENE. Little King, The.
GASSAWAY, FRANK H. "Bay Billy."
Pride of Battery B, The.
GASTEV, ALEKSEY KAPITONOVICH. Factory Whistles.
We Grow Out of Iron.
GASTON, WILLIAM. Dream, A.
Epitaph on a Pet Mocking Bird.
Old North State, The.
"GATE, A. C." *See* ANTHONY, EDWARD.
GATES, ELLEN M. HUNTINGTON. Bars of Fate, The.
Beautiful Hands.
Home of the Soul.
I Shall Not Cry Return.
Sleep Sweet.
Your Mission.
GATES, JESSIE ROSE. Peace after Sorrow.
GATTO, ALFONSO. Grass and Milk.
Midnight at Mestre.
GAUTIER, JUDITH. Prose Poem: By the River.
Prose Poem: House in the Heart.
Prose Poem: Indifference.
Prose Poem: Mysterious Flute.
Prose Poem: Red Flower, The.
Prose Poem: Sadness of the Husbandman.
Prose Poem: Sages' Dance.
GAUTIER, THÉOPHILE. Art.
Blackbird, The.
Chinese Caprice.
Clarimonde.
During the Storm.
Escorial, The.
First Smile of Spring.
Novel.
Pastel.
Posthumous Coquetry.
Sailors.
Sierra Nevada.
Spring, The.
Triomphe de Pétrarque, Le, *sel.*
What the Swallows Say.
GAY, JOHN. Achilles, *sel.*
Acis and Galatea, *sels.*
Ay and No.
Bachelor's Maid. *Fr.* Work for a Cooper.
Ballad: "Of all the girls that e'er were seen."
Ballad: "'Twas when the seas were roaring." *Fr.* The What D'Ye Call It.
Ballad Monger, The. *Fr.* The Shepherd's Week.
Before the Barn-Door Crowing. *Fr.* The Beggar's Opera.
Beggar's Opera, The, *sels.*
Birth of the Squire, The.
Black-eyed Susan.
Blouzelinda's Death. *Fr.* The Shepherd's Week.
Blouzelinda's Funeral. *Fr.* The Shepherd's Week.
Butterfly and the Snail, The.
Contemplation on Night, A.
Contemplation on Night, A, *sel.*
Council of Horses, The.
Court of Death, The.
Damon and Cupid.
Dangers of Football, The. *Fr.* Trivia.
Dawn and Night. *Fr.* A Contemplation on Night.
Death at the Thames Ice Fair. *Fr.* Trivia.
Dione; a Pastoral Tragedy, *sel.*
Ditty, The. *Fr.* The Shepherd's Week.
Elegy on a Lap Dog, An.
Elephant and the Bookseller, The.
Epigram: "Life is a jest; and all things show it."
Epistle to the Right Honourable the Earl of Burlington, An, *sel.*
Epitaph: "Life is a jest, and all things show it."
Evening, The. *Fr.* Trivia.
Fan, The, *sel.*
Fox at the Point of Death, The.
Fox may steal your hens, Sir, A. *Fr.* The Beggar's Opera.
Friday; or, The Dirge. *Fr.* The Shepherd's Week.
Gardener and the Hog, The.
Great Frost, The. *Fr.* Trivia.
Hare and [*or* with] Many Friends, The.
His Epitaph.
His Own Epitaph.
Hound and the Huntsman, The.
How happy could I be with either. *Fr.* The Beggar's Opera.
If the Heart of a Man. *Fr.* The Beggar's Opera.
I'm like a skiff on the Ocean tost.
Journey to Exeter, A.
Jugglers, The.
Let Us Take the Road. *Fr.* The Beggar's Opera.
Linnet on the Bough, The. *Fr.* Dione; a Pastoral Tragedy.
Lion and the Cub, The.
Love in Her Eyes Sits Playing. *Fr.* Acis and Galatea.
Macheath and Polly. *Fr.* The Beggar's Opera.
Man may escape from rope and gun. *Fr.* The Beggar's Opera.
Mastiff, The.
Mr. Pope's Welcome from Greece.
Molly Mog.
Morning, The. *Fr.* Trivia.
Mother, Nurse, and Fairy, *sel.*
My Own Epitaph.
New Song, A.
O Polly, you might have toy'd and kist. *Fr.* The Beggar's Opera.
O Ruddier than the Cherry. *Fr.* Acis and Galatea.
Ode for the New Year, An, *at.*
Of Ballad-Singers. *Fr.* Trivia.
Of Crossing the Street. *Fr.* Trivia.
Of Narrow Streets. *Fr.* Trivia.
Of Pick-Pockets. *Fr.* Trivia.
Of Walking the Streets by Day. *Fr.* Trivia.
Of Walking the Streets by Day, *sels.* *Fr.* Trivia.
Of Walking the Streets by Night, *sels.* *Fr.* Trivia.
Of Watchmen. *Fr.* Trivia.
Old Woman and Her Cats, The.
On a Miscellany of Poems.
On His Dog.
Origin of Pattens, The. *Fr.* Trivia.
Over the Hills and Far Away. *Fr.* The Beggar's Opera.
Painter Who Pleased Nobody and Everybody, The.
Pell Mell Celebrated, The. *Fr.* Trivia.
Pleasure of Walking through an Alley, The. *Fr.* Trivia.
Poet and the Rose, The.
Polly, *sel.*
Rat-Catcher and Cats, The.

Ravens, the Sexton, and the Earth-worm, The.
Saturday; or, The Flights. *Fr.* The Shepherd's Week.
She who hath felt a real pain.
Shepherd and the Philosopher, The.
Shepherd Dog and the Wolf, The.
Shepherd's Week, The, *sels.*
Sick Man and the Angel, The.
Sleep, O Sleep. *Fr.* Polly.
Song: "Before the barn-door crowing." *Fr.* The Beggar's Opera.
Song: Black-eyed Susan.
Song: "Can love be controll'd by advice?" *Fr.* The Beggar's Opera.
Song: "If any wench Venus's girdle wear." *Fr.* The Beggar's Opera.
Song: "If the heart of a man is depressed with cares." *Fr.* The Beggar's Opera.
Song: "Love in her eyes sits playing." *Fr.* Acis and Galatea.
Song: "O ruddier than the cherry." *Fr.* Acis and Galatea.
Song: "Sleep, O sleep." *Fr.* Polly.
Song: "Think of dress in ev'ry light." *Fr.* Achilles.
Song: "Thus when the swallow, seeking prey." *Fr.* The Beggar's Opera.
Song: "Were I laid on Greenland's coast." *Fr.* The Beggar's Opera.
Song: "Youth's the season made for joys." *Fr.* The Beggar's Opera.
Spell, The.
Sweet William's Farewell to Black-eyed Susan.
Think of Dress in Every Light. *Fr.* Achilles.
Through all the employments of life. *Fr.* The Beggar's Opera.
Thursday; or, The Spell. *Fr.* The Shepherd's Week.
To a Lady.
To a Lady on Her Passion for Old China.
Toilette, The; a Town Eclogue.
Trivia; or, The Art of Walking the Streets of London, *sels.*
Turkey and the Ant, The.
Were I laid on Greenland's coast. *Fr.* The Beggar's Opera.
What D'Ye Call It, The, *sel.*
Work for a Cooper, *sel.*
Youth's the season made for joys. *Fr.* The Beggar's Opera.
GAY, WILLIAM. Australia, 1894.
Australian Federation.
Communion Hymn.
Crazy World, The.
To M.
GAY, ZHENYA. I was lying still in a field one day.
I'd like to be a worm.
When a goose meets a moose.
World is full of wonderful smells, The.
GAYLORD, TIMEUS. Owls, The.
GAYLORD, WILLIS. Lines Written in an Album.
GEARHART, EDNA. My Cat and I.
GEBIRTIG, MORDECAI. Waiting for Death.
GEDDES, ALEXANDER. Lewie Gordon.
Satire: "Satire, my friend ('twixt me and you)."
GEE, KENNETH. Come to the Park They Say Is Dead and See, *tr.*
Eve of the Festival, The, *tr.*
Sea Song, *tr.*
Stranger, The, *tr.*
GEIJER, ERIK GUSTAF. Charcoal-Burner's Son, The.
March, A, November Sixth, 1832.
Mignonette.
Music.
GELLERSTEDT, ALBERT TEODOR. Foreground and Background.
Isolation.
My Belief.
There Is a Laddie.
GELLERT, CHRISTIAN FÜRCHTEGOTT. Amen of the Rocks, The.
Jesus Lives, and So Shall I.
Ye Shall Live Also.
GELLERT, LAWRENCE. Ah'm Broke an' Hungry.
Ku Kluck Klan.
Look over Yonder.
GELLERT, LEON. Before Action.
Cross, The.
House-Mates.
Husband, The.
In the Trench.
These Men.
Through a Porthole.
GELSTED, OTTO. Drive, A.
Ninth of April, The.
GENEVIEVE, SISTER MARY. Divine Call, The.
GENOVEVA, SISTER MARY. Archers of the King.
Spendthrift.
GEOGHEGAN, ARTHUR GERALD. After Aughrim.
GEOGHEGAN, J. B. Down in a Coal Mine.
GEORGE, DANIEL. Ode to the Fourth of July.
GEORGE, MARGUERITE. I, Too, Have Known.
Prisoner.
GEORGE, STEFAN. After Harvest. *Fr.* Das Jahr der Seele.
After the Festival.
Anniversary.
Before You Now, My Tyrant-Sorrow.
Bird Omens.
Come to the Park They Say Is Dead and See.
Departure of the First-born.
Eve of the Festival, The.
From Glowing Purple Spoke the Wrath of Heaven.
From Nether Dark the Seed.
From out the Glow the Wrath of Heaven Spoke.
Incorporation, The.
Invocation and Prelude.
Jahr der Seele, Das, *sel.*
Lines for Those Invited in T.
Lord of the Isle [*or* Island], The.
My Boy's Come Home.
My Child Came Home.
None Are Wise That Savor to the Last.
None but Your Subtle Ear.
Now Once Your Garden in the Early Haze.
Poem for This Age.
Prelude XXIII: "We are those same children who amazed."
Rapture.
Sea Song.
Shepherd Boy's Day, The.
Stanzas concerning Love.
Star of the Covenant, The, *sel.*
Stop Pondering on Things Imponderable.
Stranger, The.
Streak of Blood, A.
Tapestry, The.
To a Young Leader of the First World War.
Transport.
When First the Coppered Ramparts Were Aglow.
Why, in Drunken Blend of Flute and Bugle.
Wrestler, The.
Year of the Soul, The, *sel.*
GEORGNS, ESTHER VALCK. Alley Cat.
GERALD, EARL OF DESMOND. Against Blame of Women.
GERALDY, PAUL (Paul Le Fèvre). Meditation.
Wooden Crosses.
GERASIMOV, MIKHAIL PROKOFYEVICH. Electric Poem, The, *sel.*
First Bulb Lights Up, The. *Fr.* The Electric Poem.
GERHARDT, PAUL. All My Heart This Night Rejoices.
Courage.
Dying Saviour, The.
O Sacred Head, Now Wounded, *tr.*
GERIN-LAJOIE, ANTOINE. Canadian Exile, The.
GERLACH, L. F. Algebra of Divorce.
Death of a Teacher.
Misogynist, The.
Seasonal Moraine.
Too Early Death.
GERMANUS, SAINT. Great and Mighty Wonder, A.
GERONDI, ABRAHAM. Hymn for the Eve of the New Year.
GERRY, W. H. Exchange.
Warning.
GERSHWIN, IRA. Babbitt and the Bromide, The. *Fr.* Funny Face.
Funny Face, *sel.*
GERVAIS, CAROLINE H. In His Blanket on the Ground.
GESSLER, CLIFFORD. Chart of the Pacific.
First Poem, The.
In Hawaiian Seas.
There Shall Be New Songs.
Timeless Island.
GESSNER, MURIEL M. For February Twelfth.
GETHING, PETER. Prayer: "I do not ask a truce."
GEZELLE, GUIDO. To the Sun.
GHIRALDO, ALBERTO. My Clarion Call.
GHISELIN, BREWSTER. Crotalus Rex.
Her Mood around Me.
Known World, The.
New World.
Of the New Prosody.
To the South.
GHOSE, MANMOHAN. Who Is It Talks of Ebony?
GIBBON, MONK. Babe, The.
Bees, The.
Being but Men.
Devil's Cauldron.
Discovery, The.
Dispossessed Poet.
Forebears.
French Peasants.
From Disciple to Master.
Salt.
Seaweed.
Shawls, The.
Song: "Singer within the little streets."
Wiser than the Children of Light.
GIBBON, PERCEVAL. Jim.
GIBBONS, J. J. Burro, The.
GIBBONS, JAMES SLOAN. Three Hundred Thousand More.
GIBBONS, STELLA. Alone.
Deer and Bracken.
Lullaby for a Baby Toad.
Seas, The.
GIBBS, BARBARA. *For translations from French, see* AnFP.
GIBBS, JESSIE WISEMAN. If We Believed in God.
GIBBS, MARGARET. On the Banisters.
Song of the Bath, The.
GIBBS, OPAL LEONORE. Interceding.
GIBRAN, KAHLIL. Crime and Punishment. *Fr.* The Prophet.
Night and the Madman.
Of Religion. *Fr.* The Prophet.
Of Work. *Fr.* The Prophet.
On Children. *Fr.* The Prophet.
On Friendship. *Fr.* The Prophet.
On Giving. *Fr.* The Prophet.
On Work. *Fr.* The Prophet.
Prophet, The, *sels.*
Said a Blade of Grass.
GIBSON, WALKER. Advice to Travelers.
Allergy.
Billiards.
Circus Ship *Euzkera,* The.
David.
Essay in Defense of the Movies.
Game, The.
In Memory of the Circus Ship *Euzkera,* Wrecked in the Caribbean Sea, 1 September 1948.
Love.
Thaw.
Umpire, The.
GIBSON, WILFRID WILSON. All Life Moving to One Measure.
Angus Armstrong. *Fr.* Casualties.
Back.
Battle: Hit.
Before Action.
Between the Lines.
Black.

GIBSON, WILFRID WILSON (*continued*)
Blind Rower, The.
Boy, The.
Breakfast.
By the Weir.
Casualties, *sels.*
Catch for Singing, A.
Coast-Watch, The.
Color.
Comrades.
Conscript, The.
Curlew Calling.
Daily Bread.
Dancing Seal, The.
Dark Forest, The.
December Daybreak.
Drove-Road, The.
Empty Purse, The.
Father, The.
Fear, The.
Fisherman's Luck.
Flannan Isle.
Flute, The.
For G.
Fowler, The.
Geraniums.
Girl's Song.
Going, The.
Golden Room, The.
Gorse, The.
Greeting, The.
Hands.
Henry Turnbull.
Her Death
Hill-born.
Hit.
Home.
Housewife, The.
I Heard a Sailor.
Ice, The.
Ice-Cart, The.
Immortality.
In a Restaurant.
In Course of Time.
In the Ambulance.
Inspiration.
John Pattison Gibson.
Katherine Veitch.
Lament: "We who are left, how shall we look again."
Lark, The.
Luck.
Machine, The.
Marriage.
Marriage, *sel.*
Messages, The.
Michael's Song.
Mugger's Song, The.
Noel Dark. *Fr.* Casualties.
Oblivion.
Old Bed, The.
Old Man Jobling.
Old Skinflint.
On Broadway.
On Hampstead Heath.
On the Embankment.
On the Road.
One Night.
Operation, The.
Orphans, The.
Paisley Shawl, The.
Parrot, The ("Long since I'd ceased to care").
Parrots, The ("Somewhere, somewhen I've seen").
Philip Dagg. *Fr.* Casualties.
Platelayer, The.
Ponies, The.
Prelude: "As one, at midnight, wakened by the call."
Proem: "As one, at midnight, wakened by the call."
Proem: "Snug in my easy chair."
Prometheus.
Puffin, The.
Question, The.
Quiet, The.
Ragtime.
Ralph Straker. *Fr.* Casualties.
Return, The.
Reveille.
Ridge, The, 1919.
Rupert Brooke.
Rupert Brooke, *sel.*
Scar, The.
Sea-Change.
Sentry, The.
Shop, The.
Sight.
Snow, The.
Snug in My Easy Chair.
So Long Had I Travelled.
Solway Ford.
Song: "If once I could gather in song."
Stone, The.
Swooping Wings, The.
Tenants.
Time, Gentlemen, Please!
To [the Memory of] Rupert Brooke.
Travels.
Unless I Am Careful.
Vindictive Staircase, The; or, The Reward of Industry.
Voice, The.
Voyage, The.
Whisperers, The.
White Dust, The.
White Whippet, The.
William and Agnes Pringle.
GIDDING, JEANNE. Reminiscence.
GIDLOW, ELSA. Twentieth Century Songs.
GIELOW, MARTHA SAWYER. Belgian Lullaby, A.
GIERASCH, GEORGIA B. Panacea.
GIFFORD, LADY. *See* SHERIDAN, HELEN SELINA.
GIFFORD, FANNIE STEARNS DAVIS. *See* DAVIS, FANNIE STEARNS.
GIFFORD, HUMPHREY [*or* HUMFREY].
Delectable Dream, A, *sel.*
For Soldiers.
Prayer, A: "O mighty God, which for us men."
Song: "Woman's face is full of wiles, A."
GIFFORD, WILLIAM. Baviad, The, *sel.*
Conditions in Rome, *tr. Fr.* Satires.
Della Cruscans, The. *Fr.* The Baviad.
Fair Field for Satire, A, *tr. Fr.* Satires.
New Woman, The, *tr. Fr.* Satires.
Rome a Greek City, *tr. Fr.* Satires.
Satires, The, *sels., tr.*
Vanity of Human Wishes, The, *tr. Fr.* Satires.
GILBERT, LADY. *See* MULHOLLAND, ROSA.
GILBERT, ANN TAYLOR. *See* TAYLOR, ANN.
GILBERT, ELLEN. Prodigal.
GILBERT, FRED. Man Who Broke the Bank at Monte Carlo, The.
GILBERT, SISTER MARY. Meditation on a March Wind.
GILBERT, MERCEDES. Friendless Blues.
GILBERT, MORRIS. Epitaph on a Madman's Grave.
GILBERT, NICOLAS JOSEPH LAURENT. Ode—Imitated from the Psalms.
GILBERT, PAUL. Your Own Version.
GILBERT, PAUL T. Triolet: "I love you, my lord!"
GILBERT, R. V. Great Victory, The.
GILBERT, RUTH. And There Shall Be No More Death, *sel.*
Li Po.
Rachel.
GILBERT, SIR WILLIAM SCHWENCK.
Aesthete, The. *Fr.* Patience.
Arac's Song. *Fr.* Princess Ida.
Bishop of Rum-ti-Foo, The.
British Tar, The. *Fr.* H.M.S. Pinafore.
Bunthorne's Recitative and Song. *Fr.* Patience.
Bunthorne's Song [the Aesthete]. *Fr.* Patience.
Captain and the Mermaids, The.
Captain Reece.
Contemplative Sentry, The. *Fr.* Iolanthe.
Darned Mounseer, The. *Fr.* Ruddigore.
Disagreeable Man, The. *Fr.* Princess Ida.
Discontented Sugar Broker, A.
Duke of Plaza-Toro, The. *Fr.* The Gondoliers.
Ellen McJones Aberdeen.
Emily, John, James, and I.
Etiquette.
Fable of the Magnet and the Churn, The. *Fr.* Patience.
Family Fool, The. *Fr.* Yeomen of the Guard.
Ferdinando and Elvira; or, the Gentle Pieman.
First Lord of the Admiralty, The. *Fr.* H.M.S. Pinafore.
First Lord's Song, The. *Fr.* H.M.S. Pinafore.
Folly of Brown, The.
General John.
Gentle Alice Brown.
Gondoliers, The, *sels.*
Grand Duke, The, *sel.*
H.M.S. Pinafore, *sels.*
Heavy Dragoon, The. *Fr.* Patience.
His Excellency, *sels.*
House of Lords, The. *Fr.* Iolanthe.
House of Peers, The. *Fr.* Iolanthe.
Humane Mikado, The. *Fr.* The Mikado.
I'm Called Little Buttercup. *Fr.* H.M.S. Pinafore.
Iolanthe, *sels.*
It Was the Cat. *Fr.* H.M.S. Pinafore.
Judge's Song, The. *Fr.* Trial by Jury.
King Goodheart. *Fr.* The Gondoliers.
King of Canoodle-Dum, The.
Ko-Ko's Song. *Fr.* The Mikado.
Ko-Ko's Winning Song. *Fr.* The Mikado.
Lady and an Ape, A.
Let the Punishment Fit the Crime. *Fr.* The Mikado.
Limerick: "There was an old [*or* a young] man of St. Bees."
Limerick in Blank Verse, A.
Little Buttercup. *Fr.* H.M.S. Pinafore.
Lord Chancellor's Song ("When you're lying awake"). *Fr.* Iolanthe.
Lost Mr. Blake, The.
Mad Margaret's Song. *Fr.* Ruddigore.
Major-General, The. *Fr.* The Pirates of Penzance.
Major-General's Song. *Fr.* The Pirates of Penzance.
Mighty Must, The. *Fr.* Princess Ida.
Mikado, The, *sels.*
Mikado's Song, The. *Fr.* The Mikado.
Mister William.
Modern Major-General, The. *Fr.* The Pirates of Penzance.
My Name Is John Wellington Wells. *Fr.* The Sorcerer.
Nightmare. *Fr.* Iolanthe.
Oh, Hollow! Hollow! Hollow! *Fr.* Patience.
Old Man of St. Bees.
Out of Sorts. *Fr.* The Grand Duke.
Patience, *sels.*
Perils of Invisibility, The.
Periwinkle Girl, The.
Pirates of Penzance, The, *sels.*
Played-out Humorist, The. *Fr.* His Excellency.
Policeman's Lot, The. *Fr.* The Pirates of Penzance.
Practical Joker, The. *Fr.* His Excellency.
Princess Ida, *sels.*
Pygmalion and Galatea, *sel.*
Recitation and Song: "Am I alone." *Fr.* Patience.
Recitative and Song: Bunthorne. *Fr.* Patience.
Rival Curates, The.
Rover's Apology, The. *Fr.* Trial by Jury.
Ruddigore, *sels.*
Ruler of the Queen's Navee, The. *Fr.* H.M.S. Pinafore.
Said I to Myself, Said I. *Fr.* Iolanthe.
Sing for the Garish Eye.
Sir Bailey Barre. *Fr.* Utopia, Limited.

Sir Guy the Crusader.
Sir Joseph's Song. *Fr.* H.M.S. Pinafore.
Sir Roderic's Song. *Fr.* Ruddigore.
Song: "When Britain really ruled the waves." *Fr.* Iolanthe.
Song: Bunthorne. *Fr.* Patience.
Song: Colonel. *Fr.* Patience.
Sorcerer, The, *sel.*
Story of Prince Agib, The.
Suicide's Grave, The. *Fr.* The Mikado.
Susceptible Chancellor, The. *Fr.* Iolanthe.
There Lived a King. *Fr.* The Gondoliers.
There Was an Old Man of St. Bees.
They'll None of 'em Be Missed. *Fr.* The Mikado.
Thomas Winterbottom Hance.
Thomson Green and Harriet Hale.
Three Little Maids from School. *Fr.* The Mikado.
Tit-Willow. *Fr.* The Mikado.
To Phoebe.
To Sit in Solemn Silence. *Fr.* The Mikado.
To the Stall-Holders at a Fancy Fair.
To the Terrestrial Globe.
Trial by Jury, *sels.*
Utopia, Limited, *sel.*
Wand'ring Minstrel, A. *Fr.* The Mikado.
When I Was a Lad. *Fr.* H.M.S. Pinafore.
Willow, Titwillow. *Fr.* The Mikado.
Yarn of the *Nancy Bell,* The.
Yeomen of the Guard, *sel.*

"GILBERTULUS." *See* HOWE, MARK ANTONY DE WOLFE.

GILCHRIST, MARIE EMILIE. Apples in New Hampshire.
Autumnal.
Chance-fallen Seed.
Springtime Theft.
Wreath for Persephone, A.

GILDER, JEANNETTE LEONARD. My Creed.

GILDER, JOSEPH B. Parting of the Ways, The.
Parting of the Ways, The, *sel.*
Will to Serve, The. *Fr.* The Parting of the Ways.

GILDER, RICHARD WATSON. After-Song. *Fr.* The New Day.
Ah, Be Not False.
Anger of Christ, The.
At the President's Grave.
Birds of Bethlehem, The.
Birthday Song, A.
Builders of the State.
Burial of Grant, The.
Call Me Not Dead.
Celestial Passion, The.
Cello, The.
Charleston.
Child, A.
Christmas Hymn, A.
Christmas Tree in the Nursery, The.
Comfort of the Trees, The.
Cost.
Cradle Song: "In the embers shining bright."
Credo, *sel.*
Dawn. *Fr.* The New Day.
Dead Comrade, The.
Decoration Day.
Doubter, The.
Easter.
Evening in Tyringham Valley.
God of the Strong, God of the Weak.
Great Nature Is an Army Gay.
Hast Thou Heard the Nightingale?
Heroic Age, The.
Holy Land.
How to the Singer Comes the Song?
Hymn: "God of the strong, God of the weak."
I Count My Time by Times That I Meet Thee.
Inauguration Day.
Invisible, The.
John Paul Jones.
Land That We Love.
Memorial Day.
Midsummer Song, A.
Motto for a Tree-planting.
My Love for Thee.
Navies nor armies can exalt the state.
New Day, The, *sels.*
New York.
Noël.
North to the South.
O, Love Is Not a Summer Mood.
Ode: "I am the spirit of the morning sea."
Of One Who neither Sees nor Hears.
On the Life-Mask of Abraham Lincoln.
Passing of Christ, The, *sel.*
Prelude: "Night was dark, though sometimes a faint star, The." *Fr.* The New Day.
Real Christ, The. *Fr.* The Passing of Christ.
Sery.
Sherman.
Song: "Because the rose must fade."
Song: "Not from the whole wide world I chose thee." *Fr.* The New Day.
Song, A: "Years have flown since I knew thee first." *Fr.* The New Day.
Song of a Heathen, The.
Song of Early Autumn, A.
Sonnet, The: "What is a sonnet? 'Tis the pearly shell."
Sonnets after the Italian.
To the Spirit of Abraham Lincoln.
Violin, The.
Voice of the Pine, The.
Washington at Trenton.
"White City, The."
White, Pillared Neck.
Woman's Thought, A.
Woods That Bring the Sunset Near, The.

GILES, HERBERT ALLEN. Do not forget your cotton days, *tr.*
Homeward, *tr.*
In Absence, *tr.*
Shi King, *sel., tr.*
Woman, *tr.* *Fr.* Shi King.
You Will Die, *tr.*

GILFILLAN, ROBERT. Exile's Song, The.
O Why Left I My Hame?
'Tis Sair to Dream.

GILI, J. L., *and* STEPHEN SPENDER. *See* SPENDER, STEPHEN, *and* J. L. GILI.

GILL, ERIC. Mutans Nomen Evae.

GILL, FRANCES. Beneath the Wattle Boughs.
Sœur Fidèle.

GILL, JULIA. Christ and the Little Ones.

GILL, MARY TERRY. To a Nun.

GILLESPIE, JEAN. Ain't Education Grand?

GILLESPIE, YETZA. Ashes of the Christmas Tree.
Forgetful Hour.
Haunted Stairs, The.
Specter's Tale, The.

GILLESPY, JEANNETTE BLISS. Cameos.
Forgiven? *Fr.* Cameos.
Seaward.
Valentine, A. *Fr.* Cameos.

GILLIES, ANDREW. Two Prayers.

GILLIES, DONALD. Woodrow Wilson.

GILLILAN, STRICKLAND. Are You There?
As I Go on My Way.
Be Hopeful.
Cure for Fault-finding, A.
Dixie Lullaby, A.
Finnigin to Flannigan.
Folks Need a Lot of Loving.
Her Great Secret.
Lines on the Antiquity of Microbes.
Mammy's Lullaby.
Need of Loving.
On the Antiquity of Microbes.
Other Fellow's Job, The.
Reading Mother, The.
'Round Father's Grip.
Talk to the Boy, A.
Watch Yourself Go By.
When He Goes to Play with the Boys.
Your Dad.

GILLINGTON, ALICE E. Doom-Bar, The.
Rosy Musk-Mallow, The.
Seven Whistlers, The.

GILLINGTON, MAY CLARISSA. *See* BYRON, MAY CLARISSA GILLINGTON.

GILLMAN, FREDERICK J. God Send Us Men.

GILLMAN, RICHARD. Bones of a French Lady in a Museum.
Moved by Her Music.
On a Very Young, Very Dead Soldier.
Snow Fell with a Will.

GILLOM, ARTHUR L. I Want You.

GILMAN, CAROLINE. To the Ursulines.

GILMAN, CHARLOTTE PERKINS STETSON. Beds of Fleur-de-Lys, The.
Child Labor.
Common Inference, A.
Conservative, A.
Flag of Peace, The.
For Us.
Give Way!
I Resolve.
Lion Path, The.
Living God, The.
"Man Must Live, A."
Obstacle, An.
Resolve.
Similar Cases.
To the Preacher, *sel.*
Tree Feelings.
Two Prayers.
Wedded Bliss.

GILMAN, ISABEL AMBLER. Our Presidents—a Memory Rhyme.
Sunset City, The.

GILMAN, SAMUEL. Fair Harvard.

GILMORE, ANNA NEIL. February, Tall and Trim.

GILMORE, JAMES ROBERTS ("Edmund Kirke"). Three Days.

GILMORE, JOSEPH HENRY. He Leadeth Me.

GILMORE, MARY. Baying Hounds, The.
Boolee, the Bringer of Life.
Dedicatory.
Dice Were Loaded, The.
Eve-Song.
I Saw the Beauty Go.
Marri'd.
Myall in Prison, The.
Nationality.
Never Admit the Pain.
Of Wonder.
Swans at Night, *sel.*
Sweethearts.
Tenancy, The.
They Called Her Sunshine.
Turn to the Grass.
Waradgery Tribe, The.

GILMORE, PATRICK SARSFIELD ("Louis Lambert"). When Johnny Comes Marching Home.

GILPIN, WILLIAM. Landscape Painting, *sel.*

GILTINAN, CAROLINE (Mrs. Leo P. Harlow). Alone in Spring.
Builder, The.
Communion.
Contrition across the Waves.
Courtyard Pigeons, The.
Garden, The.
Hungry, The.
Overnight, a Rose.
Spring.
Thirteenth Station, The.

"GINGER." *See* IRWIN, WALLACE.

GINSBERG, ALLEN. Howl.
Howl, *sels.*
Kaddish, *sel.*
Malest Cornifici Tuo Catullo.
Message.
Sather Gate Illumination.
Shrouded Stranger, The.
Sunflower Sutra.
Supermarket in California, A.

GINSBERG, LOUIS. Biography of an Agnostic.
Buttercups.
Childhood.
Clocks.
Coral Islands.
Defense against the Dark.
Dirt and Deity.
Fog.
Hounds of the Soul, The.
Hunger and Thirst.

GINSBERG, LOUIS (*continued*)
I Know That Any Weed Can Tell.
Letter to Heine.
Lost World.
Morning in Spring.
Mountain and River.
Ode to Machines.
Old Ships.
Prices.
Room, The.
Roots.
Song: "I know that any weed can tell."
Song: "Love that is hoarded, moulds at last."
Song: "Though your little word is light."
Song in Spring.
Soon at Last My Sighs and Moans.
Waterfalls of Stone.
Wind, The.
Wise Man, Wise Man.
GIOVANNITTI, ARTURO. Walker, The.
Walker, The, *sel.*
GIRAUT DE BORNELH. Canso: "When all the ice and cold and snow."
Glorious King.
GIRONDO, OLIVERIO. Las Sierpes Street.
GISBORNE, THOMAS. Summer—Noon. *Fr.* Walks in a Forest.
Walks in a Forest, *sels.*
Winter—Frost. *Fr.* Walks in a Forest.
Winter—Thaw. *Fr.* Walks in a Forest.
GÍSLASON, THORSTEINN. Spring.
Thorvaldur Thoroddsen.
GITTINGS, ROBERT. Parting.
GIUSTI, GIUSEPPE. Your Excellency.
GJELLERUP, KARL. Love Rides the Lion.
O, Let Me Kiss.
Pair, A.
GLADDEN, WASHINGTON. Ideal City, The.
My Pilot.
O Happy Soul.
O Master, Let Me Walk with Thee.
Service.
Ultima Veritas.
GLAENZER, RICHARD BUTLER. Ballad of Redhead's Day, A.
GLANZ-LEYELESS, A. Animal Howl, The, *tr.*
Castles.
Deportation, *tr.*
Funeral, The, *tr.*
Song of a Jewish Boy, *tr.*
GLAPTHORNE, HENRY. Unclose Those Eyelids.
GLASGOW, ELLEN. Creed, A.
GLASGOW, G. R. Lullaby, A: "Because some men in khaki coats."
GLASGOW, J. SCOTT. Pipes o' Gordon's Men, The.
GLASGOW, SAMUEL MCP. *See* "FOREST, GREEN."
GLATSTEIN, JACOB. Back to the Ghetto.
Ballad: "He did not kill."
Being. *Fr.* The Bratzlav Rabbi to His Scribe.
Biography.
Bratzlav Rabbi to His Scribe, The.
Bratzlav Rabbi to His Scribe, The, *sel.*
Ghetto Song.
I Have Never Been Here Before.
Jewishness.
Messenger, The.
Rabbi Yussel Luksh of Chelm.
Shining Fool, The.
Where the Cedars.
GLAUBITZ, GRACE ELLEN. Christmas Birthday.
Walking.
GLAUCUS. Cenotaph.
On the Cenotaph of One Lost at Sea.
Pan and Daphnis.
Pan the Lover.
GLAZIER, WILLIAM BELCHER. Cape-Cottage at Sunset.
GLEASON, HAROLD WILLARD. Comma Caution.
GLEASON, MADELINE. Once and Upon.
GLEN, EMILIE. Cat Ballerina Assoluta.
GLEN, WILLIAM. Wae's Me for Prince Charlie.
GLICK, HIRSCH. We Survive!
GLOAG, JOHN. Board Meets, The.
GLOVER, DENIS. Arrowtown.
Casual Man, The.
Drift.
Dunedin Revisited.
For a Child.
Home Thoughts.
I Remember.
If everywhere in the street. *Fr.* Songs.
In the Township.
Lake, Mountain, Tree.
Magpies, The.
Off Banks Peninsula.
Once the Days.
Security.
Songs.
Themes.
These songs will not stand. *Fr.* Songs.
Thistledown.
Threnody: "In Plimmerton, in Plimmerton."
To a Woman.
Waitaki Dam.
GLOVER, GUY. Lucifer, The.
GLOVER, JEAN. Owre the Muir amang the Heather.
GLOVER, R. W. It Isn't the Town, It's You.
GLOVER, RICHARD. Admiral Hosier's Ghost.
GLUCK, JOHANN CHRISTOPH VON. To Death.
GLYCON [*or* GLYCO]. All is dust, and all is laughter.
Futility.
Life's a Jest.
GLYN COTHI, LEWIS. On the Death of His Son.
Saxons of Flint, The.
"GLYNDON, HOWARD." *See* SEARING, LAURA CATHERINE REDDEN.
GLYNES, ELLA MARIA DIETZ. Unless.
GOCH, LLEWELYN. Elegy for Lucy Lloyd.
GODDARD, GLORIA (Mrs. Clement Wood). Pruned Trees.
To the Commonplace.
GODE, MARGUERITE. Nature's Wash Day.
GODFREY, THOMAS. Amyntor.
Dithyrambic on Wine, A.
Evanthe's Invitation. *Fr.* The Prince of Parthia.
Invitation, The.
Pastoral: "For Chloris long I sigh'd in vain."
Patriot, The.
Piece upon Masonborough.
Prince of Parthia, The, *sel.*
Song: "When in Celia's heav'nly eye."
Song, A: "Young Thyrsis with sighs often tells me his tale."
What Was a Cure for Love?
Wish, The.
GODLEY, ALFRED DENIS. After Horace.
Army of Xerxes, The, *tr.*
College Cat, The.
Eureka!
Football and Rowing—an Eclogue.
Lines on a Mysterious Occurrence.
Motor Bus, The.
Neutral Argos, *tr.*
Pensées de Noël.
Power of an Oath, The, *tr.*
Wooden Walls of Athens, The, *tr.*
GODLEY, ELIZABETH. Ragged Robin.
GODOLPHIN, SIDNEY. Aeneid, The, *sel.*, *tr.*
Chorus: "Doth not our chiefest bliss then lie."
Chorus: "Vain man, born to no happiness."
Constancye.
Hymn: "Lord when the wise men came from farr."
Lord When the Wise Men Came from Far[r].
Or Love Me Less or Love Me More.
Quatrains: "Noe more unto my thoughts appeare."
Reply.
Sad Dido, *tr.* *Fr.* The Aeneid.
Song: "Cloris, it is not thy disdaine."
Song: "Noe more unto my thoughts appeare."
Song: "Or love me less, or love me more."
To Chloris.
To the Tune of, In Fayth I Cannot Keepe My Fathers Sheepe.
Wise Men and Shepherds.
GODOY ALCAYAGA, LUCILA. *See* "MISTRAL, GABRIELA."
GODWHEN [*or* GODWIN], A. Continuance.
Now Would I Fain.
Song for My Lady.
GOETHE, JOHANN WOLFGANG VON. As a Man Soweth.
Awakening of Epimenides, The, *sel.*
Brothers, The.
Christ Is Arisen. *Fr.* Faust.
Day's Work, The.
Easter Chorus: "Christ is arisen." *Fr.* Faust.
Easter Hymn. *Fr.* Faust.
Epilogue of Schiller's "Song of the Bell," *sel.*
Erl-King, The.
Faust, *sels.*
Faust Struggles with His Soul. *Fr.* Faust.
Fisher, The.
Gentle Reminders.
Gingo Biloba. *Fr.* West-Eastern Divan.
Godlike, The.
Godlike Heart.
Haste Not! Rest Not!
Hermann and Dorothea.
Hermann and Dorothea, *sel.*
Irish Lamentation, An.
Joy and Dream.
King of Thule, The. *Fr.* Faust.
Lay of the Captive Count, The.
Live Each Day.
Lover Is Near, The.
Mignon. *Fr.* Wilhelm Meister.
Mignon's Song. *Fr.* Wilhelm Meister.
Minstrel, The.
Nor Will These Tears Be the Last.
O Child of Beauty Rare.
O'er all the hill-tops. *Fr.* Wanderer's Night-Songs.
Prayer: "Incline, O Maiden." *Fr.* Faust.
Prologue in Heaven. *Fr.* Faust.
Prometheus.
Rose, The.
Shepherd's Lament, The.
Soldier's Song. *Fr.* Faust.
Sorrow. *Fr.* Wilhelm Meister's Apprenticeship.
Thou that from the heavens art. *Fr.* Wanderer's Night-Songs.
Thought Eternal, The.
To a Golden Heart, Worn Round His Neck.
To the Parted One.
Trance and Transformation.
True Rest.
Use Well the Moment.
Venetian Epigrams, *sel.*
Voice from the Invisible World, A.
Wanderer's First Night-Song, The.
Wanderer's Night-Songs.
Wanderer's Night-Songs, *sel.*
Wanderer's Second Night-Song, The.
West-Eastern Divan, *sels.*
Who Never Ate with Tears His Bread. *Fr.* Wilhelm Meister.
Wilhelm Meister, *sels.*
Wilhelm Meister's Apprenticeship, *sel.*
Zuleika. *Fr.* West-Eastern Divan.
GOETSCHIUS, ANTOINETTE. Meditation.
GOETZ, PHILIP BECKER. Whither.
GOFFE, THOMAS. Courageous Turk, The, *sel.*
Drop Golden Showers, Gentle Sleep.
Lullaby, lullaby baby. *Fr.* The Tragedy of Orestes.
Tragedy of Orestes, The, *sel.*
GOGARTY, OLIVER ST. JOHN. After Galen.
Apple Tree, The.
Between Brielle and Manasquan.
Blackbird in the Town, The.

Boon Companion, The.
Colophon.
Conquest, The.
Crab Tree, The.
Death May Be Very Gentle.
Dedication: "Tall unpopular men."
Exorcism.
Forge, The.
Golden Stockings.
Good Luck.
I Tremble to Think.
Image-Maker, The.
Johnny, I Hardly Knew Ye: In Miltonese.
Kingdoms.
Leda and the Swan.
Marcus Curtius.
Non Dolet.
O Boys! O Boys!
On Troy.
Our Friends Go with Us.
Palinode.
Parable for Poetasters, A.
Per Iter Tenebricosum.
Perfection.
Plum Tree by the House, The.
Portrait with Background.
Ringsend.
Sung in Spring.
To a Boon Companion.
To a Friend in the Country.
To an Old Tenor.
To Death.
To Petronius Arbiter.
To the Liffey with the Swans.
To the Maids Not to Walk in the Wind.
To W. B. Yeats Who Says That His Castle of Ballylee Is His Monument.
Verse: "What should we know."
With a Coin from Syracuse.
GOING, CHARLES BUXTON. Armistice.
At the Top of the Road.
Blessed Road, The.
Columbus.
East Wind, The.
Great Master Dreamer.
Joan of Arc at Domremy.
Landlocked.
My Soul and I.
Rain in the Hills.
Sleepy Song, A.
Spring in England.
They Who Wait.
To Arcady.
True Story of Skipper Ireson, The.
GOLD, ALBERT REGINALD. Fishers.
GOLDBECK, CECIL. Waters of the Sea.
GOLDBERG, ISRAEL. *See* "LEARSI, RUFUS."
GOLDBERG, LEAH. Blade of Grass Sings to the River, The.
When You Will Walk in the Field.
GOLDING, ARTHUR. Metamorphoses, *sels.*, *tr.*
Philemon and Baucis, *tr. Fr.* Metamorphoses.
Pyramus and Thisbe, *tr. Fr.* Metamorphoses.
GOLDING, LOUIS. Broken Bodies.
Doom-devoted.
"I."
Is It Because of Some Dear Grace.
Jack.
Judaeus Errans.
Night on the Fields of Enna.
O Bird, So Lovely.
Ploughman [*or* Plowman] at the Plough [*or* Plow].
Prophet and Fool.
Quarries in Syracuse.
Second Seeing.
Singer of High State, The.
Women at the Corners Stand, The.
GOLDRICK, O. J. Grand Opening of the People's Theatre.
GOLDRING, DOUGLAS. Newport Street, E.
She-Devil.
Streets.
GOLDRING, MAUDE. Drowned Seaman, The.
GOLDSMITH, GOLDWIN. Monkey's Glue, The.
GOLDSMITH, OLIVER. Auburn. *Fr.* The Deserted Village.
Blest Retirement. *Fr.* The Deserted Village.
But the chaste blackbird, to its partner true.
Captivity, The; an Oratorio, *sels.*
Common Man, The. *Fr.* The Deserted Village.
Country Parson, The. *Fr.* The Deserted Village.
David Garrick. *Fr.* Retaliation.
Deserted Village, The.
Deserted Village, The, *sels.*
Edmund Burke. *Fr.* Retaliation.
Edwin and Angelina. *Fr.* The Vicar of Wakefield.
Elegy, An: "Good people all, with one accord."
Elegy on Mrs. Mary Blaize.
Elegy, An, on That [*or* the] Glory of Her Sex, Mrs. Mary Blaize.
Elegy on the Death of a Mad Dog, An. *Fr.* The Vicar of Wakefield.
Emma.
Epitaph on Dr. Parnell.
Evening. *Fr.* The Deserted Village.
Farewell to Poetry. *Fr.* The Deserted Village.
First, Best Country, The. *Fr.* The Traveller.
France. *Fr.* The Traveller.
Good-natur'd Man, The, *sel.*
Great Man, A.
Happiness Dependent on Ourselves. *Fr.* The Traveller.
Haunch of Venison, The.
Hermit, The. *Fr.* The Vicar of Wakefield.
His Bedchamber.
Home. *Fr.* The Traveller.
Hope. *Fr.* The Captivity; an Oratorio.
Memory. *Fr.* The Captivity; an Oratorio.
Mrs. Mary Blaize.
On a Beautiful Youth Struck Blind with Lightning.
On Woman. *Fr.* The Vicar of Wakefield.
Parson Gray.
Pitying Heart, The.
Real Happiness. *Fr.* The Traveller.
Retaliation.
Retaliation, *sels.*
Schoolmaster, The. *Fr.* The Deserted Village.
She Stoops to Conquer, *sel.*
Sir Joshua Reynolds. *Fr.* Retaliation.
Song: "Ah, me! when shall I marry me?"
Song: "Let schoolmasters puzzle their brains." *Fr.* She Stoops to Conquer.
Song: "O memory! thou fond deceiver."
Song: "When lovely woman stoops to folly." *Fr.* The Vicar of Wakefield.
Stanzas on Woman. *Fr.* The Vicar of Wakefield.
Still the Wonder Grew. *Fr.* The Deserted Village.
Sweet Auburn. *Fr.* The Deserted Village.
Three Jolly Pigeons, The. *Fr.* She Stoops to Conquer.
Thus, when soft love subdues the heart.
Traveller, The.
Traveller, The, *sels.*
Vicar of Wakefield, The, *sels.*
Village, The ("Sweet Auburn! loveliest village"). *Fr.* The Deserted Village.
Village, The ("Sweet was the sound"). *Fr.* The Deserted Village.
Village Preacher [*or* Parson], The. *Fr.* The Deserted Village.
Village Schoolmaster, The. *Fr.* The Deserted Village.
When Lovely Woman Stoops to Folly. *Fr.* The Vicar of Wakefield.
Where Wealth Accumulates. *Fr.* The Deserted Village.
Woman. *Fr.* The Vicar of Wakefield.
GOLDSMITH, OLIVER, THE YOUNGER. Rising Village, The, *sel.*
GOLL, CLAIRE. But All the Roses.
I Am the Wake, *tr.*
I Am Your Brook, *tr.*
I Look Forward.
John Landless beside the Road, *tr.*
Love Song, *tr.*
Prayer: "In the bright bay of your morning, O God."
Silent, *tr.*
Since My Birth, *tr.*
To Liane-Neila, *tr.*
To Sleep, to Sleep.
GOLL, IWAN [*or* YVAN]. Ages, *tr.*
From All the Queens.
I Am the Wake.
I Am Your Brook.
John Landless beside the Road.
John Landless Leads the Caravan.
Lay Your Head.
Love Song.
Pear-Tree, The.
Silent.
Since My Birth.
Song for a Jewess.
Sun.
To Liane-Neila.
Your Body Drifting.
GOMBAULD, JEAN OGIER DE. Sonnet: "Voice that resounds from pole to pole, The."
GOMEI. Baby's Hands.
GOMERSAL [*or* GOMERSALL], ROBERT. Upon Our Vain Flattery of Ourselves That the Succeeding Times Will Be Better than the Former.
GÓMEZ, ANTONIO ENRÍQUEZ. Elegy: "I die for Your holy word without regret."
GÓMEZ MANRIQUE. *See* MANRIQUE, GÓMEZ.
GÓMEZ RESTREPO, ANTONIO. Toledo.
GÓNGORA Y ARGOTE, LUIS DE. Come, Wandering Sheep, O Come!
Dedication to the Duke of Bejar. *Fr.* The Solitudes.
Let Me Go Warm.
Let Me Walk Alone Where Breaks the Sea.
Love Song of Polyphemus, The. *Fr.* Polyphemus and Galatea.
Loveliest Girl, The.
Nativity of Christ, The.
Not All Sweet Nightingales.
Polifemo y Galatea, *sels.*
Polyphemus and Galatea, *sels.*
Rose, A.
Rosemary Spray, The.
Roundelay: "They are not only nightingales."
Shipwrecked Youth Reaches Land, A. *Fr.* The Solitudes.
Solitudes, The, *sels.*
Sonnet: "Circean cup, and Epicurus' sty."
Streamlet Flows into the Sea, A. *Fr.* The Solitudes.
That's a Lie!
Wedding Hymn, A. *Fr.* The Solitudes.
GONZÁLEZ DE ESLAVA, FERNÁN. To the Nativity.
GONZÁLEZ LEÓN, FRANCISCO. Hours.
GONZÁLEZ [*or* GONZÁLES] MARTÍNEZ, ENRIQUE. Captive, The.
Condemned, The.
House with Two Doors.
Last Journey.
Pain.
Romance of the Living Corpse.
Then Twist the Neck of This Delusive Swan.
When It Is Given You to Find a Smile.
Wring the Swan's Neck.
GONZÁLEZ Y CONTRERAS, GILBERTO. Church.
Heat.
GOOD, JOHN MASON. Daisy, The.
GOODALE, DORA READ. April! April! Are You Here?
Bob White.
Feast Time of the Year, The.

GOODALE, DORA READ (*continued*)
Flight of the Heart, The.
High and Low.
Judgment, The.
May Basket, The.
Only a Little.
Ripe Grain.
Soul of Man, The.
GOODCHILD, JOHN ARTHUR. Firstborn, The.
Parable of the Spirit, A.
Schöne Rothraut.
GOODMAN, MAE WINKLER. And Who Shall Tell?
Image in a Mirror.
Memorial.
Washington.
Your Glory, Lincoln.
GOODMAN, PAUL. Little Prayer, A.
March, 1941.
GOODMAN, RYAH TUMARKIN. Silence Spoke with Your Voice.
GOODRICH, SAMUEL GRISWOLD ("Peter Parley"). Higglety, Pigglety, Pop!
Lake Superior.
Nonsense!
GOODWIN, HOOPER REYNOLDS. Parabola, The.
GOOGE, BARNABE. Coming Homeward Out of Spain.
Egloga Quinta: "Some doleful thing there is at hand."
Egloga Secunda: "My beasts, go feed upon the plain."
Epitaph of the Death of Nicholas Grimald, An.
Fly, The.
Going towards Spain.
Oculi Augent Dolorem (Out of Syght, Out of Mynd).
Of Edwards of the Chapel.
Of Money.
Oftener Seen, the More I Lust, The.
Once Musing as I Sat.
Out of Sight, Out of Mind.
To Doctor Bale.
To Master Henry Cobham of the Most Blessed State of Life.
Uncertainty of Life, The.
GORDON, A. M. R. *See* ROSE, ALEXANDER MACGREGOR.
GORDON, ADAM LINDSAY. After the Quarrel.
By Wood and Wold.
Chase and the Race, The. *Fr.* Ye Wearie Wayfarer.
Dedication, A: "They are rhymes rudely strung with intent less."
Fragment, A: "They say that poison-sprinkled flowers."
Gone.
How We Beat the Favo[u]rite.
Last Leap, The.
Man's Testament. *Fr.* Ye Wearie Wayfarer.
Question Not. *Fr.* Ye Wearie Wayfarer.
Risks of the Game, The. *Fr.* Ye Wearie Wayfarer.
Sick Stockrider, The.
Song of Autumn, A.
Valedictory.
Wearie Wayfarer, Ye, *sels.*
Whisperings in Wattle-Boughs.
GORDON, ADONIRAM JUDSON. O Holy Ghost, Arise.
GORDON, ALEXANDER GORDON, 4TH DUKE OF. Cauld Kail in Aberdeen.
GORDON, ALFRED. Dedication: "There was a time in boyhood, ere life ceased."
Innocence.
GORDON, ARMISTEAD CHURCHILL. Kree.
Roses of Memory.
GORDON, ARTHUR. Last Hour of Leave.
GORDON, DON. Laocoon.
Sea.
GORDON, GRACE. Mattie's Wants and Wishes.
GORDON, JAMES LINDSAY. Wheeler at Santiago.
GORDON, JUDAH LEIB. Simhat Torah.
GORDON, LESLEY. Armadillo, The.
GORDON, RUTH MCKEE. Summer Sky.
GORDON, WILLIAM STEWARD. Hymn for the New Age, A.
GORE-BOOTH, EVA. Cross, The.
Crucifixion.
Ecstasy.
Form.
Harvest.
Little Waves of Breffny, The.
Perilous Light, The.
Quest, The.
"Sad Years, The."
Unity.
Walls.
Waves of Breffny, The.
GORELL, RONALD GORELL BARNES, 3D BARON. England—June, 1940.
In the Fourth Year.
London to Paris, by Air.
Mother of God.
GORENKO, ANNA ANDREYEVNA. *See* "AKHMATOVA, ANNA."
GORING, J. H. English, The.
Home.
GORKI [*or* GORKY], MAXIM (Aleksey Maximovich Pyeshkov). Song of the Hawk.
Song of the Storm-Finch, The.
GORMAN, HERBERT SHERMAN. Barcarole of James Smith, The.
Birds, The.
Chanson de Chateaulaire.
Fountain, The.
Lèse-Majesté.
March-Patrol of the Naked Heroes.
Satyrs and the Moon, The.
Tartar Horse, A.
Viaticum.
GORMAN, LARRY (Lawrence E. Gorman).
Beware of Larry Gorman.
Boys of the Island, The.
Byrontown.
Gull Decoy, The.
History of Prince Edward Island, The.
Scow on Cowden Shore, The.
Tomah Stream.
Winter of '73, The.
Young Billy Crane.
GORODETSKY, SERGEI. Spring in the Convent.
GOROSTIZA, JOSÉ. Aquarium.
Autumn.
Bloom Hoists Its Banner, The.
Fisherman of the Moon.
Pauses.
Poor Little Conscience, A.
Prelude: "That word which never appears."
Who Is It?
Who Will Buy Me an Orange?
Women.
GORTER, HERMAN. Sea, The.
GOSSE, SIR EDMUND WILLIAM. Ballade of Dead Cities.
Boy and the Flute, The, *tr.*
Charcoal-Burner, The.
Chloë Is False.
Creation of My Lady, The, *tr.*
De Rosis Hibernis.
Epilogue: "If thou disdain the sacred muse."
Epithalamium: "High in the organ-loft with lilied hair."
Epitaph on the Duchess of Maine's Cat, *tr.*
Fear of Death, The.
Hans Christian Andersen.
Impression.
In the Orchard, *tr.*
Labor and Love.
Last Night I Woke.
Lying in the Grass.
Madrigal: "He comes again!"
Memory, *tr.*
Missive, The.
On a Lute Found in a Sarcophagus.
On the Death of a Pious Lady, *tr.*
On Yes Tor.
Philomel in London.
Pipe-Player, The.
Revelation.
Sestina.
Song for Music.
Sonnet: "And then I sat me down, and gave the rein," *tr.*
Sonnet: "Deep in a vale where rocks on every side," *tr.*
Sonnet: "When I was marked for suffering, Love forswore," *tr.*
Suppliant, The.
Theocritus.
To Austin Dobson.
Vanishing Boat, The.
Voice of D. G. R., The.
Wall-Flower, The, *tr.*
With a Copy of Herrick.
GOTTSCHALK, LAURA RIDING. *See* RIDING, LAURA.
GOUDGE, ELIZABETH. In the Stable.
Thanksgiving for the Earth.
GOUGH, JOHN BARTHOLOMEW. Famous Toast to Water.
GOULD, ALICE LAWRY. Small Rain.
GOULD, DOROTHY. Armistice Day Vow.
Dreamer, The.
His Task—and Ours.
In the Name of Our Sons.
Reconsecration.
GOULD, ELIZABETH. Grace and Thanksgiving.
Midsummer Night.
Mincemeat.
Mistress Comfort.
My New Rabbit.
Red in Autumn.
Shining Things.
Slumber in Spring.
Such a Blustery Day!
Tadpole, The.
Washing-up Song, The.
Wish, A.
GOULD, GERALD. Atonement, The.
Child's Song.
Clouds Have Wings, The.
Compensation.
Envoy: "God who made denial, The."
Fallen Cities.
Garden Is My Soul, A.
Happy Tree, The.
I Am Frightened.
Lancelot and Guinevere.
Little Things, The.
Love Looks to the Future.
Mortality.
Ode II: "I cannot thank you, Lord—because."
Overworked Horse, The.
Oxford.
Sea-Captain, The.
Some Lovers Make Comparison in Love.
Song: "She whom I love will sit apart."
'Tis But a Week.
Twilight.
Wander-Thirst.
Wanderlust.
You Walk in a Strange Way.
GOULD, HANNAH FLAGG. Frost, The.
Jack Frost.
Name in the Sand, A.
Song of the Bees.
Wild Violet, The.
GOULD, MARGARET R. Leviathan.
GOULD, MONA. This Was My Brother.
GOULD, ROBERT. Rival Sisters, The, *sel.*
Song: "Fair, and soft, and gay, and young." *Fr.* The Rival Sisters.
Song: Hopeless Comfort, The.
GOULD, T. H. Rhapsody, A.
GOULD, WALLACE. After Tschaikowsky.
Communion.
Drunken Heracles.
Moment Musicale.
Night Song.
GOULDSBURY, CULLEN. Councillor, The.
GOURAUD, GEORGE FAUVEL. Little Nipper an' 'Is Ma, The.
GOURGHINIAN, SHUSHANIK. Eagle's Love, The.
GOURMONT, REMY DE. Hair.
GOWER, JEAN MILNE. Big Thompson Canon.
Curtain, The (Old Tabor Grand Opera House).
GOWER, JOHN. Alexander and the Pirate. *Fr.* Confessio Amantis.
Ceix and Alceone, *sel.* *Fr.* Confessio Amantis.

Confessio Amantis, *sels.*
Florent and the Loathly Hag. *Fr.* Confessio Amantis.
House of Sleep, The. *Fr.* Confessio Amantis.
Jason and Medea. *Fr.* Confessio Amantis.
Jason and Medea, *sel.* *Fr.* Confessio Amantis.
Medea Goes to Gather Herbs for Her Incantations. *Fr.* Confessio Amantis.
Parting of Venus and Old Age, The. *Fr.* Confessio Amantis.
Poet Meets Venus and Her Priest, The. *Fr.* Confessio Amantis.
Prolog: "Books composed before our day, The." *Fr.* Confessio Amantis.
Story of Ulysses, The. *Fr.* Confessio Amantis.
Tale of Rosiphelee, The. *Fr.* Confessio Amantis.
GRACE, WILLIAM J. Suspense.
GRADE, CHAIM. In Wolfen Teeth.
Road of Suffering, The.
Sodom.
To Life I Said Yes.
GRADON, DOROTHY. Fairy Dream, A.
North Wind, The.
Travelling.
Wind, The.
Winter Joys.
GRADY, RICHARD F. God Wills It.
GRAFFLIN, MARGARET JOHNSTON. Like Mother, Like Son.
To My Son.
GRAHAM, A. M. Aconite, The.
GRAHAM, AL. Casey's Daughter at the Bat.
Folks, I Give You Science!
Football Is a Woman's Game.
Theme Song for a Songwriters' Union.
GRAHAM, CHARLES. Picture That Is Turned toward the Wall, The.
GRAHAM, DOUGAL. Turnimspike, The.
GRAHAM, ELEANOR. Judgment.
GRAHAM, HARRY ("Col. D. Streamer").
Aunt Eliza.
Aunt Maud.
Auntie, did you feel no pain.
Bath, The.
Billy.
Cockney of the North, The.
Common Sense.
Conversational Reformer, The.
Four Ruthless Rhymes.
Grandpapa.
Impetuous Samuel.
Lord Gorbals.
Misfortunes Never Come Singly.
Mr. Jones.
My First Love.
Nurse.
Patience.
Perils of Obesity, The.
Poetical Economy.
Presence of Mind.
Stern Parent, The.
Tact.
Tender-Heartedness.
Waste.
GRAHAM, JAMES, MARQUESS OF MONTROSE. Epitaph on King Charles I.
Heroic Love.
His Metrical Vow on the Death of King Charles I.
I'll Never Love Thee More.
Lines on the Execution of King Charles I.
Montrose to His Mistress.
My Dear and Only Love.
My Dear and Only Love, *sel.*
On Himself, upon Hearing What Was His Sentence.
On the Death of Charles I.
Proper New Ballad, A.
Touch, The. *Fr.* My Dear and Only Love.
Upon the Death of King Charles I.
Verses Composed on the Eve of His Execution.
GRAHAM, JEAN. Where Dreams Are Sold.
GRAHAM, RACHEL. New Hampshire Farm Woman.
GRAHAM, RAMONA. Circling Year, The.
GRAHAM, ROBERT (Robert Cunninghame-Graham). Cavalier's Song.
If Doughty Deeds [My Lady Please].
O Tell Me How to Woo Thee.
To His Lady.
GRAHAM, VIRGINIA. Bridge, St. James's Park, The.
October Boy.
Retreat.
GRAHAM, WILLIAM SYDNEY. At Whose Sheltering Shall the Day Sea.
Baldy Bane.
Children of Greenock, The.
Definition of My Brother.
Gigha.
Hill of Intrusion, The.
Letter II ("Burned in this element").
Letter V ("Lie where you fell and longed").
Letter VI ("A day the wind was hardly").
Listen. Put on Morning.
Love Poem.
Name Like a River, The.
Night's Fall.
Poem: "O gentle queen of the afternoon."
To My Father.
GRAHAME, JAMES. Sabbath, The, *sel.*
Sunday Morning. *Fr.* The Sabbath.
Wild Duck and Her Brood, The.
GRAHAME, JENNY. Wedlock.
GRAHAME, KENNETH. Carol [*or* Christmas Carol]: "Villagers all, this frosty tide." *Fr.* The Wind in the Willows.
Christmas-Trees.
Duck's Ditty. *Fr.* The Wind in the Willows.
Song of Mr. Toad, The. *Fr.* The Wind in the Willows.
Wind in the Willows, The, *sels.*
World Has Held Great Heroes, The. *Fr.* The Wind in the Willows.
GRAINGER, JAMES. Solitude.
Solitude, *sels.*
GRANICH, IRWIN. Little Children, The.
GRANLUND, STEN. Snow at Christmas.
GRANNATT, HARRY SILLECK. Happy Ending.
Who-o-o-o-o!
GRANNIS, ANITA. Poet, The.
GRANNISS, ANNIE J. Old Red Cradle, The.
GRANO, PAUL LANGTON. Pray Pity for Bill Smith.
Walking Sampford Way.
Word for the Innkeeper, A.
GRANT, ANNE (Mrs. Grant of Laggan). Bluebells of Scotland, The, *at.*
O Where, Tell Me Where, *at.*
GRANT, ELIZABETH (Mrs. Grant of Carron). Roy's Wife of Aldivalloch.
GRANT, GORDON. Last Gloucesterman, The.
Old Quartermaster, The.
GRANT, JOHN CAMERON. John Greenleaf Whittier.
GRANT, LILLIAN. Lines Written in a Mausoleum.
GRANT, SIR ROBERT. Faith and Hope.
Litany: "Saviour, when in dust to thee."
Majesty and Mercy of God, The.
O worship the King, all glorious above!
When Gathering Clouds.
GRANVILLE, CHARLES. Traveller's Hope.
GRANVILLE [*or* GRENVILLE], GEORGE, BARON LANSDOWNE. Chloe [*or* Cloe],
Happiest Mortals Once Were We, The.
I'll Tell Her.
Impatient with Desire.
Song: "Happiest mortals once were we, The."
Song: "I'll tell her the next time, said I."
Song: To Myra.
To Myra.
GRAVES, ALFRED PERCEVAL. As a Blossom Sweet and Rosy, *tr.*
Cradle of Gold, The.
Fairy Host, The, *tr.*
Fan Fitzgerl.
Father O'Flynn.
Girl with the Cows, The, *sel.*
Herring Is King.
Irish Lullaby: "I'd rock my own sweet childie to rest."
Irish Lullaby: "I've found my bonny babe a nest."
Irish Spinning-Wheel, The.
Limerick Lasses, The.
Little Red Lark, The.
Ould Doctor Mack.
Sailor Girl, The.
Song of the Ghost, The.
Song to the Wind, A, *tr.*
White Blossom's off the Bog, The.
GRAVES, CHARLES LARCOM. Horace, Book V, Ode III.
Old Song Resung, An.
GRAVES, JOHN WOODCOCK. John Peel.
GRAVES, ROBERT. Allie.
Assault Heroic, The.
Avengers, The.
Babylon.
Bards, The.
Blue-Fly, The.
Boy Out of Church, The.
Cat-Goddesses.
Caterpillar, The.
Certain Mercies.
Climate of Thought, The.
Cool Web, The.
Corner-Knot, The.
Counting the Beats.
Cruel Moon, The.
Cry Faugh!
Defeat of the Rebels.
Devil's Advice to Story-Tellers, The.
Door, The.
Double Red Daisies.
Down, Wanton, Down!
1805.
English Wood, An.
Epitaph on an Unfortunate Artist.
Eremites, The.
Escape.
Exile, The.
Fallen Tower of Siloam, The.
Finding of Love, The.
Florist Rose, The.
Flying Crooked.
Forced Music, A.
Foreboding, The.
Frosty Night, A.
Full Moon.
Great-Grandmother, The.
Haunted House, The.
History of Peace, A.
Homage to Texas.
I Wonder What It Feels Like to Be Drowned.
I'd Love to Be a Fairy's Child.
If ever against this easy blue and silver.
In Broken Images.
In the Wilderness.
Intercession in Late October.
Interruption.
It's a Queer Time.
King Stephen.
Kit Logan and Lady Helen.
Lament for Pasiphae.
Laureate, The.
Legs, The.
Like Snow.
Lollocks.
Lost Acres.
Lost Jewel, A.
Lost Love.
Love Story, A.
Love without Hope.
Lovers in Winter.
Lust in Song.
Mid-Winter Waking.
Mirror, Mirror.
Naked and the Nude, The.
Nature's Lineaments.
Neglectful Edward.
Never Such Love.
New Legends.
Nobody.
Not Dead.

GRAVES, ROBERT (*continued*)
O Love in Me.
Ogres and Pygmies.
On Dwelling.
On Portents.
One Hard Look.
Persian Version, The.
Pier-Glass, The.
Pinch of Salt, A.
Poets, The.
Pot and Kettle.
Presence, The.
Pumpkin, The.
Pure Death.
Quayside.
Recalling War.
Reproach.
Rocky Acres.
Sea Side.
She Tells Her Love while Half Asleep.
Sick Love.
Sirocco at Deyá.
Song: One Hard Look.
Star-Talk.
Straw.
Sullen Moods.
Survivor, The.
Thief.
Thieves, The.
Through Nightmare.
Time.
To an Ungentle Critic.
To Bring the Dead to Life.
To Juan at the Winter Solstice.
To Sleep.
To Walk on Hills.
To Whom Else?
Traveler's Curse after Misdirection, The.
Trudge, Body.
Two Fusiliers.
Ulysses.
Vanity.
Warning to Children.
Welsh Incident.
Wild Strawberries.
Window Sill, The.
Worms of History, The.
Wretch, The.
GRAY, A. P. Tree, the Serpent, and the Star, The.
GRAY, AGNES KENDRICK. Road to Firenze, A.
Shepherd to the Poet, The.
To My Terrier Rex.
GRAY, ALEXANDER. Epitaph on a Vagabond.
Kings from the East, The, *tr.*
Lassie, What Mair Wad You Hae? *tr.*
On a Cat, Ageing.
Scotland.
GRAY, ALMA L. In My Garden.
"GRAY, BARRY." *See* COFFIN, ROBERT BARRY.
GRAY, DAVID. Brooklet, The.
Corn-Crake, The.
Cross of Gold, The.
Dear Old Toiling One, The.
Die Down, O Dismal Day.
Divided.
Golden Wedding, The.
Homesick.
I Die, Being Young.
In the Shadows.
My Epitaph.
O Winter! Wilt Thou Never Go?
October, *sel.*
On Lebanon.
Sonnet: "If it must be; if it must be, O God!"
Sonnet: "October's gold is dim—the forests rot."
To a Friend.
GRAY, FRANCES ANGEVINE. Kaleidoscope.
GRAY, JAMES M., *and* "MARIANNE FARNINGHAM." *See* "FARNINGHAM, MARIANNE," *and* JAMES M. GRAY.
GRAY, JOHN. Complaint.
Crocuses in [the] Grass.
Flying Fish, The.
Gazelles and Unicorn. *Fr.* The Long Road.
Long Road, The, *sel.*
Lord, If Thou Art Not Present.
Night Nurse Goes Her Round, The.
Ox, The.
Wings in the Dark.
GRAY, LILLIAN. New Year's Thoughts.
GRAY, THOMAS. Agrippina, *sel.*
Alliance of Education and Government, The.
Bard, The.
Bard, The, *sel.*
Curse upon Edward. *Fr.* The Bard.
Descent of Odin, The.
Elegy Written in a Country Churchyard.
Elegy Written in a Country Churchyard, *sels.*
Epitaph, The: "Here rests his head upon the lap of Earth." *Fr.* Elegy Written in a Country Churchyard.
Epitaph on Mrs. William Mason.
Epitaph on Sir William Williams.
Fatal Sisters, The.
Gododdin, *sel., tr.*
Hymn to Adversity.
Impromptu, Suggested by a View, in 1766, of the Seat and Ruins of a Nobleman, at Kingsgate, Kent.
Ode on a Distant Prospect of Eton College.
Ode on the Death of a Favorite Cat, Drowned in a Bowl [*or* Tub] of Goldfishes.
Ode on the Pleasure Arising from Vicissitude.
Ode on the Spring.
On a Distant Prospect of Eton College.
On a Distant Prospect of Eton College, *sel.*
On [the Death of] a Favorite Cat, Drowned in a Tub of Goldfishes.
On Lord Holland's Seat near Margate, Kent.
On the Death of [Mr.] Richard West.
Progress of Poesy, The.
Progress of Poesy, The, *sel.*
Rape of Helen, The. *Fr.* Agrippina.
Sketch of His Own Character.
Song: "Thyrsis, when we parted, swore."
Sonnet on the Death of [Mr.] Richard West.
Spring.
Stanzas to Mr. Bentley.
Supreme Dominion. *Fr.* The Progress of Poesy.
Tophet; an Epigram.
Triumphs of Owen, The.
Where Ignorance Is Bliss. *Fr.* On a Distant Prospect of Eton College.
William Shakespeare to Mrs. Anne, Regular Servant to the Rev. Mr. Precentor of York.
GRAY, WILLIAM. Hunt Is Up, The.
King's Hunt Is Up, The.
GRAY, WILLIAM B. She Is More to Be Pitied than Censured.
GRAYER, ROSALIE. Altar Smoke.
GRAYSON, CAROLINE. After.
GRAYSON, ETHEL KIRK. Summer's End.
GREACEN, ROBERT. Bird, The.
Cycling to Dublin.
Far Country, The.
Glorious Twelfth, The.
Michael Walked in the Wood.
To a Faithless Lover.
Written on the Sense of Isolation in Contemporary Ireland.
GREEFF, ADELE. Sonnet XI: "Is God invisible? This very room."
GREEN, ANNE, *and* JULIAN GREEN. Night, *sel., tr.*
GREEN, BRENDA HELOISE. New England Is New England Is New England.
"GREEN, COROEBUS." *See* CONE, HELEN GRAY.
GREEN, HARRINGTON. Second Coming of Christ, The.
GREEN, HENRY MACKENZIE. Bush Goblins.
Enchanted Orchard, The.
GREEN, JACQUELINE. In Bed.
GREEN, JOSEPH. Elegy by Green for Byles's Cat.
GREEN, JULIAN. Passion of Our Lady, The, *sel., tr.*
GREEN, JULIAN, *and* ANNE GREEN. *See* GREEN, ANNE, *and* JULIAN GREEN.
GREEN, L. WORTHINGTON. Bull Fight.
GREEN, MARY MCB. Aeroplane.
Taking Off.
GREEN, MATTHEW. Cure for the Spleen, A. *Fr.* The Spleen.
Epigram, An, on the Reverend Mr. Laurence Echard's, and Bishop Gilbert Burnet's Histories.
Idyll: "There see the clover, pea, and bean." *Fr.* The Spleen.
On Even Keel [with Gentle Gale]. *Fr.* The Spleen.
Spleen, The.
Spleen, The, *sels.*
Voyage of Life, The. *Fr.* The Spleen.
GREEN, PAUL. Highland Call, The, *sel.*
Hymn to Democracy, A. *Fr.* The Highland Call.
Lost Colony, The, *sels.*
Old Tom's Song. *Fr.* The Lost Colony.
Plants in the Earth. *Fr.* Shroud My Body Down.
Prologue to "The Lost Colony."
Shroud My Body Down, *sel.*
Tread the Green Grass, *sel.*
Young Davie's Song. *Fr.* Tread the Green Grass.
GREEN, ROGER LANCELYN. My Garden.
On First Looking into the Dark Future.
GREEN, WILLIAM CHARLES. Loss of My Sons, The, *tr.*
GREENAWAY, KATE. All the Cats.
Alphabet, The.
Around the World.
Baby Mine.
Ball.
Blue Shoes.
Boat Sails Away, The.
Cats Have Come to Tea, The.
Child's Song.
Daisies, The.
Five Little Sisters Walking in a Row.
Five Sisters.
Happy Child, A.
Higgledy, piggledy! see how they run!
In go-cart so tiny.
In the pleasant green garden.
Jump—jump—jump.
Lamb, The.
Little Blue Shoes.
Little Jumping Girls, The.
Little Wind.
Naughty Blackbird, The.
O Ring the Bells.
Oh, Susan Blue.
On the Bridge.
Polly, Peg, and Poppety.
Prince Finikin.
Ring-a-Ring.
School is over.
Susan Blue.
Tea-Party, A.
To Baby.
Tommy was a silly boy.
When You and I Grow Up.
Will You?
Wishes.
GREENBERG, SAMUEL. Blank Book Letter, The.
Conduct.
Essence.
Essentials.
Glass Bubbles, The.
I Cannot Believe That I Am of Wind.
Immortality.
Killing.
Man.
Opponent Charm Sustained, The.
Peace.
Philosophic Apology, The.
Soul's Kiss.
Spirituality.
To Dear Daniel.
Tusks of Blood, The.
GREENBERG, URI ZVI. Jerusalem, *sel.*
Jerusalem the Dismembered. *Fr.* Jerusalem.

GREENE, ALBERT GORTON. Baron's Last Banquet, The.
Old Grimes.
GREENE, ASHTON. Bather in a Painting, A.
Church of the Sacred Heart, The.
Lagoon, The.
Parade, The.
GREENE, GEORGE ARTHUR. Arts Lough.
Lines: "Surely a Voice hath called her to the deep."
On Great Sugarloaf.
Return, The.
GREENE, GEORGE S. Shadow Line, The.
GREENE, HOMER. My Daughter Louise.
What My Lover Said.
GREENE, KATHLEEN CONYNGHAM. Old Joan.
GREENE, RICHARD L. Autolycus' Song (in Basic English).
Song to Imogen (in Basic English).
GREENE, ROBERT. Ah, were she pitiful as she is fair. Fr. Pandosto.
Ah what is love? It is a pretty thing. Fr. Greene's Mourning Garment.
Arbasto, sels.
Beauty, Alas, where Wast Thou Born, at.
Ciceronis Amor, sels.
Content. Fr. Farewell to Folly.
Coridon and Phillis. Fr. Perimedes.
Cupid Abroad Was Lated. Fr. Greene's Orpharion.
Description of a Shepherd and His Wife, The. Fr. Never Too Late.
Description of Sir Geoffrey Chaucer, The. Fr. Greene's Vision.
Doralicia's Song. Fr. Arbasto.
Doron's Description of Samela. Fr. Menaphon.
Doron's Jig. Fr. Menaphon.
Eurymachus's Fancy. Fr. Francesco's Fortunes.
Fair Is My Love for April in Her Face. Fr. Perimedes.
Farewell to Folly, sel.
Fawnia. Fr. Pandosto.
Fickle Seat Whereon Proud Fortune Sits, The. Fr. Morando, the Tritameron of Love.
Fie, Fie on Blind Fancy! Fr. Greene's Groatsworth of Wit.
Francesco's Fortunes, sels.
From His Flock Stray'd Coridon.
Greene's Farewell to Folly, sel.
Greene's Groatsworth of Wit, sels.
Greene's Mourning Garment, sels.
Greene's Never Too Late, sels.
Greene's Orpharion, sel.
Greene's Vision, sel.
Groatsworth of Wit Bought with a Million of Repentance, A, sels.
Hexametra Alexis in Laudem Rosamundi. Fr. Greene's Mourning Garment.
Ideals.
In Cypres Sat Fair Venus by a Fount.
In Praise of His Loving and Best-beloved Fawnia. Fr. Pandosto.
In Praise of Rosamund. Fr. Greene's Mourning Garment.
In Time We See That Silver Drops. Fr. Arbasto.
Infida's Song. Fr. Never Too Late.
Jig, A. Fr. Menaphon.
Lamilia's Song. Fr. Greene's Groatsworth of Wit.
Love and Jealousy. Fr. Tullie's Love.
Madrigal, A: "Swans, The, whose pens as white as ivory."
Maesia's Song. Fr. Farewell to Folly.
Mars and Venus. Fr. Tullie's Love.
Menaphon, sels.
Menaphon's Ditty. Fr. Menaphon.
Menaphon's Roundelay. Fr. Menaphon.
Menaphon's Song. Fr. Menaphon.
Mind Content, A. Fr. Farewell to Folly.
Morando, the Tritameron of Love, sel.
Never Too Late, sels.
Obscure and Dark Is All the Gloomy Air. Fr. Perimedes.
Of His Mistress. Fr. Menaphon.

Palinode, A. Fr. Greene's Groatsworth of Wit.
Palmer's Ode, The. Fr. Never Too Late.
Pandosto, sel.
Penitent Palmer's Ode, The. Fr. Francesco's Fortunes.
Perimedes, sels.
Phillis and Corydon. Fr. Perimedes.
Philomela, the Lady Fitzwater's Nightingale, sels.
Philomela's Ode That She Sung in Her Arbor. Fr. Philomela, the Lady Fitzwater's Nightingale.
Philomela's Second Ode. Fr. Philomela, the Lady Fitzwater's Nightingale.
Poor Estate, The. Fr. Farewell to Folly.
Samela. Fr. Menaphon.
Sephestia's Lullaby. Fr. Menaphon.
Sephestia's Song to Her Child. Fr. Menaphon.
Shepherd and the King, The. Fr. Greene's Mourning Garment.
Shepherd's Ode, The. Fr. Tullie's Love.
Shepherd's Wife's Song, The. Fr. Greene's Mourning Garment.
Sir Geoffrey Chaucer. Fr. Greene's Vision.
Song: "Mars in a fury 'gainst love's brightest queen." Fr. Tullie's Love.
Song: "Sweet are the thoughts that savour of content." Fr. Farewell to Folly.
Sonnet: "Fair is my love for April in her face." Fr. Perimedes.
Sonnet or Dittie: "Mars in a fury gainst love's brightest queen." Fr. Tullie's Love.
Sweet Are the Thoughts. Fr. Farewell to Folly.
Tullie's Love, sels.
Weep Not, My Wanton. Fr. Menaphon.
When Gods Had Fram'd the Sweet of Women's Face. Fr. Tullie's Love.
Whereat Erewhile I Wept, I Laugh. Fr. Arbasto.
GREENE, SARAH PRATT MCLEAN. Lamp, The.
Massa ob de Sheepfol', De.
Sheepfol', De.
GREENE, W. C. To William Morris.
GREENFIELD, MARJORIE H. Things I Like.
GREENLEAF, LAWRENCE N. Lodge Room over Simpkins' Store, The.
Pike's Peakers, The.
GREENOUGH, WALTER. Vision, The.
GREENWELL, DORA. Battle-Flag of Sigurd, The.
Content.
His Name.
Home.
Man with Three Friends, The.
Song of Farewell, A.
To Christina Rossetti.
"GREENWOOD, GRACE" (Sara Jane Clarke Lippincott). Horseback Ride, The.
Illumination for Victories in Mexico.
Poet of To-Day, The.
GREENWOOD, ROLAND R. Coward, The.
GREEPE, THOMAS. Taking of Cartagena, The. Fr. The True and Perfecte Newes of the Worthy Enterprises of Sir Francis Drake, 1586.
True and Perfecte Newes of the Worthy Enterprises of Sir Francis Drake, 1586, The, sel.
GREER, HILTON ROSS. Road of Midnight Pageants, The.
To a Bird on a Downtown Wire.
GREGAN, PAUL. Hush Song, A.
GREGG, A. Song: "Sun a-beatin' on the deck."
GREGH, FERNAND. Doubt.
GREGORIA FRANCISCA, SISTER. Envying a Little Bird.
GREGORY I, POPE. See GREGORY THE GREAT, SAINT.
GREGORY, AUGUSTA GREGORY, LADY. Army of the Sidhe, The.

Cold, Sharp Lamentation, tr.
Come ride and ride to the garden.
Donall Oge, tr.
Enchanted Mistress, The, tr.
Foretelling of Cathbad the Druid at Deirdre's Birth, The, tr.
Grief of a Girl's Heart, The, tr.
He Meditates on the Life of a Rich Man, tr.
I Am Ireland, tr.
Lament for Ireland, A, tr.
Mary Hynes, tr.
Old Woman Remembers, The.
Poem Written in Time of Trouble by an Irish Priest Who Had Taken Orders in France, A, tr.
Will You Be as Hard? tr.
GREGORY, HORACE. Ask No Return. Fr. Chorus for Survival.
Attis, tr.
Boy of Twenty, A.
Caelius, my Lesbia, that one, that only Lesbia, tr.
Cataclysm, tr.
Chorus for Survival, sels.
Come, Lesbia, let us live and love, tr.
Come to me, my poems, all my far-flung armies, tr.
Cymbalum Mundi.
Daemon & Lectern & a Life-Size Mirror.
Dear brother, I have come these many miles, through, tr.
Do you know, my Lesbia, how many of your kisses, tr.
Dress now in sorrow, O all, tr.
Elizabeth at the Piano.
Emerson; Last Days at Concord.
For You, My Son.
Fortune for Mirabel.
Furius, you've no slaves, no box to hold your money, tr.
Haunted Odysseus; the Last Testament.
He is changed to a god who looks on her, tr.
Here is my relief at last, tr.
Homage to Circe.
Homage to Columbus.
I hate and love, tr.
If man can find rich consolation, remembering his good deeds, tr.
Interior; the Suburbs.
Longface Mahoney Discusses Heaven.
My friend Cornificus, your friend Catullus, tr.
My woman says that she would rather wear the wedding-veil for me, tr.
No Cock Crows at Morning.
O Mors Aeterna.
O my little almost island, little island Sirmio, tr.
Of all the sons of Romulus who walk the earth, tr.
Passion of M'Phail, The, sels.
Poems for My Daughter, sel.
Poor damned Catullus, here's no time for nonsense, tr.
Postman's Bell Is Answered Everywhere, The.
Praise to John Skelton.
Prisoner's Song.
Return to Sirmio, tr.
Salvos for Randolph Bourne.
Septimius with his arms entwined round his Acme, tr.
Sparrow, O, sweet sparrow, tr.
Stanzas for My Daughter.
Tell her I love she will remember me. Fr. Poems for My Daughter.
There are many who think of Quintia in terms of beauty, tr.
There was a time, O Lesbia, when you said Catullus was, tr.
They Found Him Sitting in a Chair.
This Is the Place to Wait. Fr. The Passion of M'Phail.
Through Streets Where Crooked Wicklow Flows.
To My Generation (1919-1933).
Tombstone with Cherubim.
Transformation, tr.
Unwilling Guest, The.
Valediction to My Contemporaries.

GREGORY, HORACE (*continued*)
Voices of Heroes.
While I was wandering, foot-loose, in the Forum, *tr.*
Who shall receive my new-born book, *tr.*
Whom Lesbia Loved, *tr.*
Woman Who Disapproved of Music at the Bar, The.
You are the cause of this destruction, Lesbia, *tr.*
GREGORY, PADRAIC. Ballad of the Lady Lorraine, The.
Dream-Teller, The.
Shaun O'Neill.
GREGORY OF NAREK [*or* OF MAKAR], SAINT. Christ-Child, The.
GREGORY THE GREAT, SAINT. Darkness Is Thinning.
Morning Hymn.
Veni, Creator Spiritus, *at.*
GRENELLE, LISA. Duel in the Park.
GRENFELL, JULIAN. Into Battle.
To a Black Greyhound.
GRENVILLE, GEORGE. *See* GRANVILLE, GEORGE, BARON LANSDOWNE.
GRENVILLE, R. H. Pawnshop Window.
Praise.
GRESHAM, WALTER J. Crowded Ways of Life.
Let Me Walk with the Men in the Road.
GRESHOFF, JAN. I Beat the Drum.
GRESSET, LOUIS. Vert-Vert, the Parrot.
GREVILLE, FANNY MACARTNEY. Prayer for Indifference.
Prayer for Indifference, *sel.*
GREVILLE, FULKE, 1ST BARON BROOKE. Absence and Presence. *Fr.* Caelica.
All my senses, like beacon's flame. *Fr.* Caelica.
Another, of His Cynthia.
Away with these self-loving lads. *Fr.* Caelica.
Caelica, *sels.*
Caelica, I overnight was finely used. *Fr.* Caelica.
Change. *Fr.* Caelica.
Chorus: "O wearisome condition of humanity." *Fr.* Mustapha.
Chorus of Priests. *Fr.* Mustapha.
Chorus Primus: Wise Counsellors. *Fr.* Mustapha.
Chorus Quintus: Tartarorum. *Fr.* Mustapha.
Chorus Sacerdotum. *Fr.* Mustapha.
Chorus Tertius: Of Time: Eternitie. *Fr.* Mustapha.
Cupid, My Little Boy, Come Home Again. *Fr.* Caelica.
Cupid, my pretty Boy, leave off thy crying. *Fr.* Caelica.
Cupid, thou naughty boy, when thou wert loathed. *Fr.* Caelica.
Cynthia. *Fr.* Caelica.
Cynthia, because your horns look diverse ways. *Fr.* Caelica.
Cynthia, whose glories are at full forever. *Fr.* Caelica.
Despair. *Fr.* Caelica.
Down in the depth of mine iniquity. *Fr.* Caelica.
Earth, with thunder torn, with fire blasted, The. *Fr.* Caelica.
Epitaph on Sir Philip Sidney, *at.*
Epitaph upon the Right Honorable Sir Philip Sidney, An, *at.*
Eternal Truth, almighty, infinite. *Fr.* Caelica.
Farewell to Cupid. *Fr.* Caelica.
Fie, foolish earth, think you the heaven wants glory. *Fr.* Caelica.
His Lady's Eyes. *Fr.* Caelica.
I with whose colors Myra drest her head. *Fr.* Caelica.
Inquisition upon Fame and Honor, An.
Justice and Mercy. *Fr.* Mustapha.
Love and Fortune. *Fr.* Caelica.
Love and Honour. *Fr.* Caelica.
Love, the Delight of All Well-thinking Minds. *Fr.* Caelica.
Love's Glory. *Fr.* Caelica.
Malice and love in their ways opposite. *Fr.* Caelica.
Man's Service. *Fr.* Of Humane Learning.
Men that delight to multiply desire. *Fr.* Caelica.
More than Most Fair. *Fr.* Caelica.
Mustapha, *sels.*
Myra. *Fr.* Caelica.
Nurse-Life Wheat within His Green Husk Growing, The. *Fr.* Caelica.
O False and Treacherous Probability. *Fr.* Caelica.
O Wearisome Condition of Humanity. *Fr.* Mustapha.
Of His Cynthia. *Fr.* Caelica.
Of Humane Learning, *sel.*
Saving God, The. *Fr.* Caelica.
Selfe-pitties teares, wherein my hope lyes drown'd. *Fr.* Caelica.
Sion Lies Waste. *Fr.* Caelica.
Song to His Cynthia. *Fr.* Caelica.
Sonnet: "Away with these self-loving lads." *Fr.* Caelica.
Sonnet: "Downe in the depth." *Fr.* Caelica.
Sonnet: "Earth with thunder torn, with fire blasted, The." *Fr.* Caelica.
Sonnet: "Eternall Truth." *Fr.* Caelica.
Sonnet: "Fie, foolish earth, think you the heaven wants glory." *Fr.* Caelica.
Sonnet: "Man, dreame no more." *Fr.* Caelica.
Sonnet: "Men, that delight." *Fr.* Caelica.
Sonnet: "O false and treacherous probability." *Fr.* Caelica.
Sonnet: "Sion lies waste, and thy Jerusalem." *Fr.* Caelica.
Sonnet: "Three things there be." *Fr.* Caelica.
Sonnet: "Under a throne I saw a virgin sit." *Fr.* Caelica.
Sonnet: "Whenas [*or* When as] man's life." *Fr.* Caelica.
Sonnet: "World, that all contains, is ever moving, The." *Fr.* Caelica.
Sonnet: "You little stars that live in skies." *Fr.* Caelica.
Three Things There Be. *Fr.* Caelica.
Time and Eternity. *Fr.* Caelica.
To Cupid. *Fr.* Caelica.
To His Lady. *Fr.* Caelica.
To Myra. *Fr.* Caelica.
Treatie of Human Learning, A, *sel.*
Under a throne I saw a virgin sit. *Fr.* Caelica.
Whenas [*or* When as] man's life, the light of human lust. *Fr.* Caelica.
World, that all contains, is ever moving, The. *Fr.* Caelica.
Wrapp'd [*or* Wrapt] up, O Lord, in man's degeneration. *Fr.* Caelica.
You little stars that live in skies. *Fr.* Caelica.
Youth and Maturity. *Fr.* Caelica.
GREY, FRANCIS W. Knowest Thou Isaac Jogues?
GREY, LILLIAN. *See* GRAY, LILLIAN.
GREY OF FALLODON, PAMELA GREY, VISCOUNTESS (*formerly* Pamela Tennant). Echo.
Legend of the Saintfoin, The.
Legend of the Tortoise, The.
Moon Magic.
GRIEG, NORDAHL. Goodbye.
Norway in Our Hearts, *sel.*
Wave, The.
We Shall Come Back.
GRIER, ELDON. In Memory of García Lorca.
Minotaur, The.
Quebec.
GRIES, WALTER F. Cornish Miner, The.
GRIEVE, CHRISTOPHER MURRAY. *See* "MACDIARMID, HUGH."
GRIFFIN, BARTHOLOMEW. Arraigned, poor captive at the bar I stand. *Fr.* Fidessa, More Chaste than Kind.
Care-charmer sleep, sweet ease in restless misery. *Fr.* Fidessa, More Chaste than Kind.
Compare me to the child that plays with fire. *Fr.* Fidessa, More Chaste than Kind.
Fair is my love that feeds among the lilies. *Fr.* Fidessa, More Chaste than Kind.
Fidessa, More Chaste than Kind, *sels.*
Fly to her heart, hover about her heart. *Fr.* Fidessa, More Chaste than Kind.
Her Heart. *Fr.* Fidessa, More Chaste than Kind.
I have not spent the April of my time. *Fr.* Fidessa, More Chaste than Kind.
I see, I hear, I feel, I know, I rue. *Fr.* Fidessa, More Chaste than Kind.
If great Apollo offered as a dower. *Fr.* Fidessa, More Chaste than Kind.
My Love. *Fr.* Fidessa, More Chaste than Kind.
Sleep. *Fr.* Fidessa, More Chaste than Kind.
Sonnet: "Fair is my Love that feeds among the lilies." *Fr.* Fidessa, More Chaste than Kind.
Sonnet: "I have not spent the April of my time." *Fr.* Fidessa, More Chaste than Kind.
Striving is past. Ah, I must sink and drown. *Fr.* Fidessa, More Chaste than Kind.
Tell me of love, sweet Love, who is thy sire? *Fr.* Fidessa, More Chaste than Kind.
Venus, and [*or* with] Young Adonis Sitting by Her. *Fr.* Fidessa, More Chaste than Kind.
Work, work apace, you blessed sisters three. *Fr.* Fidessa, More Chaste than Kind.
Youth. *Fr.* Fidessa, More Chaste than Kind.
GRIFFIN, GERALD. Aileen Aroon.
Ancient Lullaby.
Céad Mile Fáilte, Elim!
Eileen Aroon.
Eileen Aroon, *sel.*
Gile Machree.
Gone! Gone! Forever Gone.
Hy-Brasail, the Isle of the Blest.
I Love My Love in the Morning.
Know Ye Not That Lovely River.
Lines Addressed to a Seagull.
Maiden Eyes.
Nightingale, The.
Nocturne: "Sleep that like the couched dove."
O Brazil, the Isle of the Blest.
Place in Thy Memory, A.
Sister of Charity, The.
Sleep That like the Couchèd Dove.
Song: "Place in thy memory, dearest, A."
To the Blessed Virgin Mary.
Wake of the Absent, The.
War Song of O'Driscol.
GRIFFIN, HOWARD. Suppose in Perfect Reason.
GRIFFIN, "SIN KILLER." Man of Calvary, The.
GRIFFITH, GEORGE BANCROFT. Before It Is Too Late.
GRIFFITH, WILLIAM. Aloha.
Autumn Song.
Canticle.
Encounter.
Hermit Thrush in the Catskills.
I, Who Fade with the Lilacs.
Loves and Losses of Pierrot, *sels.*
Pierrette in Memory. *Fr.* Loves and Losses of Pierrot.
Pierrot Makes a Song. *Fr.* Loves and Losses of Pierrot.
Pierrot the Conjuror.
Shadow.
Spring Song.
To the Least American, If Not the Greatest, of All American Poets.
GRIFFITH, WYN. All Saints.
Branwen, *sel.*
February Night.
Madam Rumour.
New Year's Eve.
Poem: "If there be time enough before the slaughter."
Silver Jubilee.

GRIGG, JOSEPH. Ashamed of Jesus.
Jesus, and shall it ever be.
GRIGORIS OF AGHTAMAR. Concerning the Rose and the Nightingale.
GRIGSON, GEOFFREY. Above the High.
Four, The.
June in Wiltshire.
Landscape of the Heart, The.
Meeting by the Gjulika Meadow.
New Dummy, The.
Uccello on the Heath.
Under the Cliff.
GRILLO, DON ANGELO. To Torquato Tasso.
GRIMALD, NICHOLAS. Concerning Virgil's Aeneids.
Description of Virtue, *tr.*
Funeral Song, upon the Decease of Annes, His Mother, A.
Garden, The.
Man's Life, after Posidonius or Crates, *tr.*
Marcus Tullius Cicero's Death, *tr.*
Metrodorus' Mind to the Contrary, *tr.*
Of Friendship.
To His Familiar Friend.
True Love, A.
Virtue.
GRIMARD, LUC. Amitié Amoureuse.
GRIMES, JOHN. Queen of Crete, The.
GRIMES, KATHARINE ATHERTON. Farm Boy, The.
GRIMES, MARIE. Kitten and Firefly.
GRIMES, WILLARD M. Piazza di Spagna.
GRIMESTONE, JOHAN DE. Luveli Ter of Loveli Eyghe, *at.*
GRIMKÉ, ANGELINA WELD. Black Finger, The.
Dusk.
Eyes of My Regret, The.
For the Candle Light.
Grass Fingers.
Greenness.
Hushed by the Hands of Sleep.
I Weep.
Mona Lisa, A.
Paradox.
Puppet Player, The.
Surrender.
Tenebris.
Ways o' Men, The.
When the Green Lies over the Earth.
Winter Twilight, A.
Your Hands.
GRIMSTONE, J. Love on the Cross.
Mater Dolorosa.
GRIPARIS, YIANNIS. Comrades in Death.
Mount Rhodope.
Reveille for the Dead.
Vestal Virgins.
GRIPENBERG, BERTEL. At the End of Play.
Drink.
Youth.
GRISSOM, ARTHUR. Artist, The.
Ballade of Forgotten Loves.
GRISWOLD, ELIZABETH M. Freedom's Natal Day.
GRISWOLD, MARIANA. *See* VAN RENSSELAER, MARIANA GRISWOLD.
GROESBECK, AMY. Momist.
GRÖNDAL, BENEDIKT. Regret.
GROSSETESTE, ROBERT. Little Song, A.
GROSSMAN, REUBEN. Therefore, We Thank Thee, God.
GROVE, ELIZA. Cat to Her Kittens, A.
Dancing Lesson, The.
Greedy Piggy That Ate Too Fast, The.
Little Hobby-Horse, A.
GROVE, MATTHEW. In Praise of His Lady. *Fr.* Pelops and Hippodamia.
Pelops and Hippodamia, *sel.*
GROVER, EDWIN OSGOOD. Banquet Song.
Down East and Up Along.
Knapsack Trail, The.
Spring's Answer.
To a Mocking Bird.
GRUBER, ABRAHAM L. My Neighbor's Roses.
GRUBER, EDMUND L. Caisson Song, The.
GRUDIN, LOUIS. Airborn.
Citizen.
GRUFFUDD AB YR YNAD COCH. Death of Llywelyn ap Gruffudd, The.
GRUNDTVIG, NIKOLAI FREDERIK SEVERIN. Niels Ebbesen.
Sabbath Morn.
GUARINI, GIOVANNI BATTISTA. Claim to Love.
Dream of His Lady.
Golden Age, The. *Fr.* Il Pastor Fido.
Il Pastor Fido, *sels.*
Madrigal: "This saith my Cloris bright."
Spring.
GUDMUNDSSON, GUDMUNDUR. Lament: "Snows cloaked."
Peace on Earth, *sel.*
Prologue from "Peace on Earth."
Rose, The.
GUÉRIN, CHARLES. In My Old Verses.
Out of the Deep.
Partings.
GUERNSEY, W. Alice Where Art Thou.
GUERZO DI MONTECANTI. Sonnet: He Is Out of Heart with His Time.
GUEST, BARBARA. Parachutes, My Love, Could Carry Us Higher.
Piazzas.
Santa Fe Trail.
Sunday Evening.
GUEST, EDGAR ALBERT. All That Matters.
Boy and His Stomach, A.
Call, The.
City-weary.
Creed, A.
Dr. Johnson's Picture Cow.
Dog, The ("I like a dog at my feet").
Dog, A ("'Tis pity not to have a dog").
Equipment.
Eternal Young, The.
Fellowship of Books.
Finest Fellowship, The.
Fishing.
Forgetful Pa.
Four Men of God.
Friend's Greeting, A.
God Made This Day for Me.
Grace at Evening.
Grandpa.
Home.
If I Had Youth.
It Couldn't Be Done.
Joy of a Dog, The.
Just Folks.
Kindly Neighbor, The.
Kindly Neighbor, The, *sel.*
Lines for a Friend's House.
Lord, Make a Regular Man Out of Me.
Lullaby: "Golden dreamboat's ready, all her silken sails are spread, The."
Mother Thought, A.
Mother's Knee.
My Bible. *Fr.* My Books and I.
My Books and I, *sel.*
My Creed.
My Paw Said So.
Myself.
Only a Dad.
Paging Mr. McGregor.
Prayer, A: "Grant me, O Lord, this day to see."
Prayer for the Home, *sel.*
Pup, The.
Radio, The.
Send Her a Valentine.
Sermons We See.
Sittin' on the Porch.
Stick to It.
Success.
Sunrise.
Vagabond, The.
Weight Gainer.
What Father Knows, *at.*
What We Need.
What's in It for Me?
When Father Played Baseball.
When Life Is Done.
Yellow Dog, The.
You.
GUEVARA, MIGUEL DE. I am not moved to love thee, my Lord God.
Raise Me Up, Lord.
Time and Account.
To Crucify the Son.
GUIDI, BENEDETTO. Love Enslaved.
GUIDICCIONI, GIOVANNI. To Italy.
GUIDO DELLE COLONNE. Canzone: To Love and to His Lady.
GUILDFORD, NICHOLAS DE. *See* NICHOLAS DE GUILDFORD.
GUILLAUME DE LORRIS *and* JEAN DE MEUN. Dream of the Romaunt of the Rose, The, *tr. by* Chaucer. *Fr.* The Romance of the Rose.
Garden of Amour, The, *tr. by* Chaucer. *Fr.* The Romance of the Rose.
Love vs. Marriage. *Fr.* The Romance of the Rose.
Romance of the Rose, The, *sels.*
Table Manners for the Hostess. *Fr.* The Romance of the Rose.
GUILLAUME DE MACHAULT. Rondeau: "White as a lily, redder than a rose."
GUILLAUME DE POITIERS (Guillem IX, Count of Poitou). Behold the Meads.
Poem: "I'll write a poem, then sink to dreams."
GUILLÉN, JORGE. Advent.
Ardor.
Departure.
Ecstasy of Bliss.
Elevation of Light.
Festivity.
Gardens.
Lighted Night.
Names.
Needed Word, The.
Nightingale, The.
Perfection.
Sand.
Slender Spring.
Snow.
Some One Attains to a Glimpse of Paradise.
Straying.
Swan, The.
Twelve by the Clock.
Utter Silence.
Vastness.
GUILLÉN, NICOLÁS. Ballad of the Güije.
Ballad of the Two Grandfathers.
Barren Stone.
Big-lipped Negro.
Cane.
Cantaliso in a Bar.
Dead Soldier.
Federico.
Proposition.
Reveille at Daybreak.
Sensemaya; Chant for Killing a Snake.
Sightseers in a Courtyard.
Soldier, I Can't Figure Why.
Two Children.
Two Weeks.
Visit to a Tenement.
Wake for Papa Montero.
Yellow Girl.
GUILPIN, EVERARD. De Ignoto. *Fr.* Skialetheia.
Of Cornelius. *Fr.* Skialetheia.
Of Pansa. *Fr.* Skialetheia.
Of Titus. *Fr.* Skialetheia.
Of Zeno. *Fr.* Skialetheia.
Proemium I: "As in the greatest of societies." *Fr.* Skialetheia.
Satira Prima. *Fr.* Skialetheia.
Satyra Quinta. *Fr.* Skialetheia.
Skialetheia, *sels.*
To Clodius. *Fr.* Skialetheia.
To Deloney. *Fr.* Skialetheia.
To Licus. *Fr.* Skialetheia.
To the Reader. *Fr.* Skialetheia.
GUINEY, LOUISE IMOGEN. Athassel Abbey.
Beati Mortui.
Cares, *at.*
Carol, A: "Vines branching stilly."
Cobwebs.
Deo Optimo Maximo.
Doves.
Five Carols for Christmastide.
Footnote to a Famous Lyric, A.
Friend's Song for Simoisius, A.
In Leinster.
In the Fields, *at.*
Irish Peasant Song.
John Brown; a Paradox.

GUINEY, LOUISE IMOGEN (*continued*)
Kings, The.
Knight Errant, The.
Lover Loquitur.
Martyr's Memorial.
Memorial Day.
Monochrome.
Nam Semen Est Verbum Dei.
Ode for a Master Mariner Ashore.
Of Joan's Youth.
On First Entering Westminster Abbey.
Open, Time.
Out in the Fields with God, *at.*
Outdoor Litany, An.
Pax Paganica.
Praise thou the Mighty Mother for what is wrought, not me.
Private Theatricals.
Rooks; New College Gardens.
Saint Francis Endeth His Sermon.
Sanctuary.
Song: "I try to knead and spin, but my life is low the while."
Song from "Sylvan," A, *at.*
Song in Leinster.
Talisman, A.
To a Dog's Memory.
Tryste Noël.
Two white heads the grasses cover.
Valse Jeune.
When on the Marge of Evening.
Wild Ride, The.
Ye pilgrims, who with pensive aspect go, *tr. Fr.* La Vita Nuova.
GUINICELLI, GUIDO. Canzone: He Perceives His Rashness in Love.
Canzone: Of the Gentle Heart.
Of the Gentle Heart.
Praise.
Sonnet: He Will Praise His Lady.
Sonnet: Of Moderation and Tolerance.
GUINNESS, BRYAN. Summer Is Coming, The.
What Are They Thinking.
GUITERMAN, ARTHUR. Afternoon Tea.
Ain't Nature Commonplace!
Ambiguous Dog, The.
Anthony Wayne.
Ballade of Dime Novels.
Bears.
Blessing on Little Boys.
Blue Hen's Chickens, The.
Boy and a Pup, A.
Call to the Colors, The.
Christmas Exchange, The.
Chums.
Coming of the Trees, The.
Comrades.
Constitution for a League of Nations.
Daniel Boone.
Death and General Putnam.
Design.
Dog Parade, The.
Dog's Cold Nose, The.
Dorlan's Home-Walk.
Dreamer, A.
Dutchman's Breeches.
Eagle, The.
Edinburgh.
Education.
Elegy: "Jackals prowl, the serpents hiss, The."
Epilogue to a Book of Verse.
Etiquette.
Experts on Woman.
Fashion.
First Thanksgiving, The.
Flying Dutchman of the Tappan Zee, The.
For a Good Dog.
Garden Song.
Haarlem Heights.
Habits of the Hippopotamus.
Harvest Home.
He Leads Us Still.
Hills.
House Blessing.
How Are You?
How the Feud Started.
Husband and Wife.
Idol-Maker Prays, The.
In Defense of Children.
In Praise of Llamas.
In the Hospital.
Independence Square, Christmas, 1783.
Indian Pipe and Moccasin Flower.
Indispensability.
Irreverent Brahmin, The.
Kit Carson.
Legend of the First Cam-u-el, The.
Little Lost Pup.
Little Ponds.
Man, A.
March.
Mascot, A.
Mavrone.
Messire Geoffrey Chaucer to His Editor.
Meteorite, The.
Mexican Serenade.
Motto for a Dog House.
Nature Note.
New York.
No King.
Ode to the Hayden Planetarium.
Of Courtesy.
Of Giving.
Of Quarrels.
Of Tact.
Offer, An.
Old Boys, The.
On Cherubs.
On the Vanity of Earthly Greatness.
Oregon Trail, The.
Ornithology in Florida.
Our Colonel.
Pilgrims' Thanksgiving Feast, The.
Pioneer, The.
Plea, A.
Poem on Spring, A.
Poet's Proverb, A.
Prologue for a Magician.
Pure Mathematician, A.
Pussy-Willows.
Quivira.
Reward of Virtue.
Rush of the *Oregon*, The.
School Days in New Amsterdam.
Scribe's Prayer, The.
Sea-Chill.
Shakespearean Bear, The.
Silver Canoe, The.
Skater's Valentine, A.
Sketch from the Life, A.
Snarlers, The.
Starlighter, The.
Storming of Stony Point, The.
Strictly Germ-proof.
Superstitious Ghost, The.
Tact.
This Is She.
Thunderstorm.
To the Littlest of All.
Tract for Autos, A.
Tubby Hook.
Under the Goal Posts.
Viewpoints.
Vizier's Apology, The.
What the Gray Cat Sings.
Whole Duty of a Poem, The.
Wind-in-the-Hair and Rain-in-the-Face.
Woman's Tongue Tree, The.
Young Washington.
GUITTONE D'AREZZO. Lady of Heaven.
GULCHIN. Curtain Fell, The.
GULICK, ALIDA CAREY. On Waking.
GULLANS, CHARLES. Autumn; an Ode.
First Love.
Narcissus.
Poema Morale.
To a Friend.
GUMILEV [*or* GUMILYOV], NIKOLAI STEPANOVICH. Black Diamond.
Captains, The.
Evening.
Forest, The.
Giraffe, The.
Giraffe, The, *sel.*
How Could We, Beforehand, Live in Quiet.
I and You.
Loneliness.
Memory.
Nature.
Night was drawing in, and the fire was low.
Reincarnation.
Second Canzone.
Sonnet: "I must be ill: my mind is dumb and bored."
Trees.
GUMMERE, FRANCIS BARTON. Anglian Tradition, The, *tr.*
Attack on Finnsburg, The, *tr.*
Beginning of Creation, The, *tr. Fr.* Genesis (*by* Cædmon).
Beowulf, *sels., tr.*
Death-going of Scyld, The, *tr. Fr.* Beowulf.
Deor's Lament, *tr.*
Genesis (*by* Cædmon), *sel., tr.*
Haunt of Grendel, The, *tr. Fr.* Beowulf.
John Bright.
Widsith, *sel., tr.*
GUNDERSON, GERTRUDE B. Pioneers.
Three Things.
What If.
GUNN, LOUISE D. Conversation with Rain.
GUNN, THOM. Before the Carnival.
Corridor, The.
Helen's Rape.
Incident on a Journey.
Light Sleeping.
Merlin in the Cave; He Speculates without a Book.
Mirror for Poets, A.
Nature of an Action, The.
On the Move.
St. Martin and the Beggar.
Tamer and Hawk.
Wound, The.
GUNSAULUS, FRANK WAKELEY. Goal, The.
GURI, HAIM. But We Shall Bloom.
Prayer: "Thy blessing on the boys—for time has come."
GURLEY, EDITH B. His Gift and Mine.
GURNEY, DOROTHY FRANCES. God's Garden.
In Memoriam.
Lord God Planted a Garden, The.
O Perfect Love.
GURNEY, IVOR. Love Song, The.
GURNEY, LAWRENCE. Nevada.
GUSTAFSON, RALPH. Animus et Corpus.
Dedication: " 'They shall not die in vain,' we said."
Epithalamium in Time of War.
Final Spring.
Fish, The.
Flight into Darkness.
Legend.
Mythos.
On Such a Wet and Blustery Night.
On the Road to Vicenza.
On the Struma Massacre.
"S.S.R., Lost at Sea."—The *Times.*
This Speaking Were Enough.
Toponymy.
Window, a Table, on the North, A.
GUTHRIE, CHARLES E. God's Will.
GUTHRIE, JAMES. Last Song.
GUTHRIE, NORMAN GREGOR. *See* "CRICHTON, JOHN."
GUTHRIE, THOMAS ANSTEY. *See* "ANSTEY, F."
GUTHRIE, WOODY. Tom Joad.
GUTIÉRREZ HERMOSILLO, ALFONSO. Earth.
Fugue.
GUTIÉRREZ NÁJERA, MANUEL. Dead Waters.
In the Depths of Night.
Non Omnis Moriar.
Pax Anima, *sel.*
To Be.
When the Day Comes.
GUTTERIDGE, BERNARD. Burma Hills.
Namkwin Pul.
Patrol; Buonamary.
GUY, GEORGES, *and* KENNETH KOCH. *See* KOCH, KENNETH, *and* GEORGES GUY.
GUYON, JEANNE MARIE BOUVIER DE LA MOTTE. Adoration.
By Thy Life I Live.
Little Bird I Am, A.
Prisoner's Song, A.
Since God Is There.
GWYNN, STEPHEN LUCIUS. Glencar.
Inscription for a Fountain.

Ireland.
Mater Severa.
Out in the Dark.
Stones of Greece.
We That Are Old.
Woman of Beare, The, *tr.*
Gwynne, J. Harold. Good Shepherd, The.
Gwynneth, John. My Love That Mourneth for Me.
Gyles, Althea. Sympathy.

H

"H., B." Anacreon to the Sophist.
"H., F. L." Father Knows, The.
"H., H." *See* Jackson, Helen Hunt.
"H., H. E." Riddle, The: "Where's an old woman to go when the years."
"H., J. B." Inventin'est Man, The.
"H., J. C. C., Jr." Horace à la Mode.
"H., J. P." Ode to a Side Car.
"H., M. K." Prayer Hymn.
"H., P." Jung Idea, The.
Li'l Pickanniny Coon.
"H., R." Battle of Monmouth, The.
"H., R. D." Lullaby: "Hush thee, hush."
"H. B. C." *See* "C., H. B."
"H. D." *See* Doolittle, Hilda.
"H. E. H." *See* "H., H. E."
"H. H." *See* Jackson, Helen Hunt.
"H. J. M." *See* "M., H. J."
"H. T. R." *See* "R., H. T."
Haaf, Katherine Maurine. Good Thoughts.
Haas, Elizabeth. Every Day.
Habergham, Mrs. Fleetwood. Seeds of Love, The, *at.*
Habib. Wine-Bearer, The.
Habington, William. Against Them Who Lay Unchastity to the Sex of Women. *Fr.* Castara.
Castara ("Like the violet, which alone"). *Fr.* Castara.
Castara, *sels.*
Cogitabo pro Peccato Meo.
Compliment, The.
Epistle to a Friend.
Fine Young Folly. *Fr.* The Queen of Aragon.
Love's Anniversary to the Sun.
Melancholy. *Fr.* Castara.
Nox Nocti Indicat Scientiam. *Fr.* Castara.
Paucitatem Dierum Meorum Nuncia Mihi. David.
Queen[e] of Ar[r]agon, The, *sel.*
Quoniam ego in flagella paratus sum.
Recogitabo tibi omnes annos meos.
Reward of Innocent Love, The.
Song: "Fine young folly, though you were." *Fr.* The Queen of Aragon.
Time! Where Didst Thou Those Years Inter.
To Castara: Of the Knowledge of Love. *Fr.* Castara.
To Castara: The Reward of Innocent Love. *Fr.* Castara.
To Castara Praying. *Fr.* Castara.
To Castara, upon Beauty. *Fr.* Castara.
To Roses in the Bosom of Castara. *Fr.* Castara.
To the World; the Perfection of Love.
Upon Castara's Departure. *Fr.* Castara.
Upon the Thought of Age and Death.
Upon Thought Castara May Die. *Fr.* Castara.
Welcome, Thou Safe Retreat!
What Am I Who Dare to Call Thee, God.
When I Survey the Bright. *Fr.* Castara.
Hackett, Eloise. Conventionality.
Hackett, Francis. Dead Aviator, The.
Sea Dawn.
Hadden, Maude Miner. Creative Force.
Hadewijch. Eighteenth Song, The: "New Year hath come in sight, The."
Nineteenth Song, The: "Great good fortune ere it is had."
Hadley, Lizzie M. Just like a Man, *at.*
Rainbow Fairies, The.
Rainbow Fairies, The, *sel.*
Thanksgiving Exercise.
Hadrian, Emperor (Publius Aelius Hadrianus). Adriani Morientis ad Animam Suam.
Animula Blandula Vagula.
On the Soul.
To His Soul.
Troy Restored.
Haenigsen, H. W. Listen, Pigeon, Bend an Ear.
Hafen, Ann Woodbury. Mountain Liars.
Hafiz. Beloved, The.
Comfort.
Desire.
Friendly Zephyr.
From the Garden of Heaven.
Full Fair.
Harvest.
I Cease Not from Desire. *Fr.* Odes.
Jewel of the Secret Treasury, The.
Lady That Hast My Heart.
Lawful Wine.
Lesson of the Flowers, The.
Love and Wine.
Love's Language.
My Bosom Grac'd.
Odes, *sels.*
Persian Song, A.
Persian Song of Hafiz, A.
Red Rose.
Revelation.
Rose Bloom.
Rose Is Not the Rose, The.
Slave.
Slaves of Thy Shining Eyes.
Strife.
Swimming.
Tidings of Union.
Wild Deer.
Hafsa. Exchange.
Shield, The.
Hafstein, Hannes. Nearing Cold-Dale.
Spring.
Hagarty, Sir John H. Funeral of Napoleon I.
Hagedorn, Hermann. Bomb That Fell on America, The.
Broadway.
Day's End. *Fr.* Songs from the Rockies.
Departure.
Discovery.
Doors.
Early Morning at Bargis.
Evening Prayer.
Eyes of God, The.
Flood Tide.
Ghost, The.
Greater Birth, The.
Heart of Youth, The, *sel.*
Hymn for the Victorious Dead.
Ladders through the Blue.
Lift Up the Curtain. *Fr.* The Heart of Youth.
Lincoln; an Ode, *sel.*
Master, Make Us One! *Fr.* Lincoln; an Ode.
Mother.
Mother in the House, The.
Prayer during Battle.
Prologue to Morning.
Service.
Solomon.
Song: "Song is so old."
Song Is So Old.
Song of the Grail Seekers.
Songs from the Rockies, *sel.*
Starry Night.
Troop of the Guard, A.
Unremembered, The.
Wild Rose, The.
Hagemeyer, Dora. Choice, The.
In the Pasture.
Parable of the Mustard Weed, The.
Hagen, John Milton. Cowboy and His Love, The.
Song of the Cattle Trail.
Hagerup, Inger. Dies Irae.
Hagg, Esther Lloyd. Different Way, A.
His Garments.
It Was Not Strange.
They Saw and Believed.
Haggard, J. Harvey. Dog Salesman, The.
Hagiwara, Sakutaro. Bar at Night, A.
Late Autumn.
Leisurely Indulgence, A.
Night Train.
Sick Face below the Surface of the Earth, A.
Tortoise.
Woman!
Hagthorpe, John. To Time.
Haight, Dorothy. New Orleans Balcony, A.
Hake, Thomas Gordon. Old Souls.
Sibyl, The.
Hakutsu. O pine-tree standing. *Fr.* Manyo Shu.
Halas, Frantisek. Again.
And Then There.
Halbisch, Harry. Warp and Woof.
Halderman, Lois. Way of a Man, The.
Hale, Arthur. Manila Bay.
Yankee Privateer, The.
Hale, Edward Everett. Adrian Block's Song.
Alma Mater's Roll.
Anne Hutchinson's Exile.
Ballad of Bunker Hill, The.
Columbus.
From Potomac to Merrimac.
Lamentable Ballad of the Bloody Brook, The.
Lend a Hand.
Look Up.
Marching Song of Stark's Men, The.
Merrimac Side, and Agiochook. *Fr.* From Potomac to Merrimac.
Nameless Saints, The.
New England's Chevy Chase.
Omnipresence.
Potomac Side. *Fr.* From Potomac to Merrimac.
Put It Through.
Signal Fires. *Fr.* From Potomac to Merrimac.
"Hale, Katherine" (Amelia Beers Warnock Garvin). Answer, The.
At Eighty.
Crimson Pool.
Cun-ne-wa-bum.
Eternal Moment.
Fourth Dimensional.
Giant's Tomb in Georgian Bay.
Lost Garden.
Northern Graveyards.
Old Lady, An.
Portrait of a Cree.
Hale, Marty. Example.
Friendship.
Mud.
My Dog.
"Old Bob"—"Friend."
Old Pal.
Only a Dog.
Quality.
Thanks.
To "Silk."
Hale, Oliver. Anniversary.
Where Unimaginably Bright.
Hale, Robert Beverly. Big Nasturtiums, The.
Moon, The.
Ovibos, The.
Hale, Sarah Josepha Buell. Alice Ray.
Mary and Her Lamb.
Mary Had a Little Lamb.
Mary's Lamb.
Watcher, The.
Hales, Thomas. *See* Thomas of Hales.
Halevi [*or* Ha-Levi], Judah [*or* Jehudah]. Asleep in the Bosom of Youth.

HALEVI, JUDAH (*continued*)
Awake, My Fair.
Dove, The.
Earth in Spring, The.
Fortune's Treachery.
God, Whom Shall I Compare to Thee?
Grey Hair, The.
He Cometh.
Hymn for Atonement Day.
Immortal Israel.
Israel's Duration.
Letter to His Friend Isaac, A.
Longing.
Longing for Jerusalem.
Lord, Where Shall I Find Thee?
Love Song, A: "Let my sweet song be pleasing unto Thee."
Love Song: "See'st thou o'er my shoulders falling."
Marriage Song.
Meditation on Communion with God.
Mirror, The.
My Heart Is in the East.
My Sweetheart's Dainty Lips.
Ode to Zion.
On Parting with Moses ibn Ezra.
Ophra.
Parted Lovers.
Parting.
Pride of a Jew, The.
Sabbath, My Love.
Song of Loneliness.
Time-Servers.
To the Western Wind.
To Zion.
Words Wherein Stinging Bees Lurk.
HALEY, MOLLY ANDERSON. "And Lo, the Star!"
Architect, The.
Christmas Prayer, A.
Faithless Generation Asked a Sign.
"He Is Our Peace."
Intolerance.
Prayer for Christian Unity, A.
River of Grace, A.
Thy Blessing, Lord, on All Vacation Days!
Vacant Lots.
We Have Seen His Star in the East.
"HALIBURTON, HUGH." *See* ROBERTSON, JAMES LOGIE.
HALKET, GEORGE. Logie o' Buchan.
HALKIN, SCHMUEL. Drop of Dew, A.
HALL, AGNES MAXWELL-. *See* MAXWELL-HALL, AGNES.
HALL, AMANDA BENJAMIN (Mrs. John Angell Brownell). Boy Fourteen.
For Madame Chiang Kai-shek.
Great Farewells, The.
I'll Build My House.
Joe Tinker.
Joy o' Living.
Saint Francis.
Stranger, The.
Too Many Songs.
Too Soon the Lightest Feet.
Wanderer, The.
Woman of Words, A.
HALL, ARTHUR VINE. Dad's Birthday.
Father.
Singsingetjie.
HALL, CAROLYN. Child upon the Stair, The.
Fireflies.
HALL, CHARLES SPRAGUE. Glory Hallelujah! or, John Brown's Body.
John Brown's Body.
HALL, CHRISTOPHER NEWMAN. My Times Are in Thy Hand.
HALL, DONALD. Abroad Thoughts from Home.
Beautiful Horses, The.
Body Politic, The.
Christmas Eve in Whitneyville, 1955.
Exile.
Five Epigrams.
Je Suis une Table.
Laocoon.
Marriage.
Morning Porches, The.
Munch's Scream.
My Son, My Executioner.
Second Stanza for Dr. Johnson, A.
Sestina.
Six Poets in Search of a Lawyer.
Sleeping Giant, The.
World, the Times, The.
"HALL, ELIZA CALVERT" (Eliza Calvert Obenchain). Enlisted.
HALL, EUGENE J. Engineer's Story, The.
Kate Shelly.
King and the Child, The.
HALL, GERTRUDE. Angels.
Dust, The.
How Dreary Looks the Ivied Cot.
How Shall We Tell an Angel.
In the Art Museum.
Mrs. Golightly.
My Old Counnselor.
One Distant April.
Rival, The.
HALL, HAZEL. Admonition before Grief.
Any Woman.
Flash.
Flight.
Footsteps.
Foreboding.
Here Comes the Thief.
Hunger.
Instruction.
June Night.
Late Winter.
Maker of Songs.
My Needle Says.
My Song.
On the Street.
One by One.
Slow Death.
Submergence.
Three Girls.
Twilight.
Two Sewing.
HALL, HELEN H. My House.
HALL, HENRY CLAY. Who Does Not Love True Poetry.
HALL, J. C. Crack, The.
Montgomery.
Responsibilities.
Telescope, The.
War.
HALL, JAMES NORMAN. Eat and Walk.
HALL, JOHN (1529?–1566?). *See* HALLE, JOHN.
HALL, JOHN (1627–56). Call, The.
Epicurean Ode, An.
Farewell, farewell, poor joys, let not my hearse.
Happy choristers of air.
Home Travell.
Lure, The, *sel.*
Morning Star, The.
Of Beauty, *sel.*
On an Hour-Glass.
On an Hour-Glass, *sel.*
Pastoral Hymn [*or* Pastorall Hymne], A.
Since that this thing we call the world.
To His Tutor.
What need I travel, since I may.
HALL, JOHN (*contemporary*). Metropolis.
HALL, JOSEPH. Coxcomb, A. *Fr.* Virgidemiarum.
For Christmas Day.
Gentle squire would gladly entertain, A. *Fr.* Virgidemiarum.
Golden Age, The. *Fr.* Virgidemiarum.
Love-sicke Poet, The. *Fr.* Virgidemiarum.
Olden Days, The. *Fr.* Virgidemiarum.
Prologue: "I first adventure, with foolhardy might." *Fr.* Virgidemiarum.
Satire: "Another scorns the homespun thread of rhymes." *Fr.* Virgidemiarum.
Satire: "Gentle squire would gladly intertain, A." *Fr.* Virgidemiarum.
Satire: "Great is the folly of a feeble brain." *Fr.* Virgidemiarum.
Satire: "Great Osmond knows not how he shall be known." *Fr.* Virgidemiarum.
Satire: "I wot not how the world's degenerate." *Fr.* Virgidemiarum.
Satire: "Nor lady's wanton love, nor wand'ring knight." *Fr.* Virgidemiarum.
Too popular is tragic poesy. *Fr.* Virgidemiarum.
Trencher Chaplain, The. *Fr.* Virgidemiarum.
Virgidemiarum, *sels.*
With some pot-fury, ravished from their wit. *Fr.* Virgidemiarum.
HALL, KAY DEBARD. Deer in Aspens.
HALL, MARY LEE. Turn Again to Life.
HALL, R. W. Last Longhorn, The, *at.*
HALL, SHARLOT MABRIDTH. Arizona.
Last Camp-Fire, The.
Song of the Colorado, The.
HALLACK, CECILY. Divine Office of the Kitchen, The.
HALLAM, ARTHUR HENRY. On the Picture of the Three Fates in the Palazzo Pitti, at Florence.
Written in Edinburgh.
HALLAR, SØREN. Denmark Speaks.
Song of Denmark, *sel.*
HALLE [*or* HALL], JOHN. Anatomye, *sel.*
Court of Virtue, The, *sels.*
Ditty of the Pen Inveighing against Usury and False Dealing, A. *Fr.* The Court of Virtue.
Example of the Praise of God for His Omnipotency, out of the CXIII Psalm, An. *Fr.* The Court of Virtue.
Goodlye Doctrine and Instruction, *sel.*
Song of the Lute in the Praise of God and Dispraise of Idolatry, A. *Fr.* The Court of Virtue.
HALLECK, FITZ-GREENE. Alnwick Castle.
Burns.
Elegy in Memory of Joseph Rodman Drake.
Fanny, *sels.*
Field of the Grounded Arms, The.
Fortune. *Fr.* Fanny.
Joseph Rodman Drake.
Marco Bozzaris.
On His Friend, Joseph Rodman Drake.
On the Death of Joseph Rodman Drake.
Red Jacket.
Weehawken and the New York Bay. *Fr.* Fanny.
William Cullen Bryant.
Woman.
HALLECK, FITZ-GREENE, *and* JOSEPH RODMAN DRAKE ("The Croakers").
Croaker Papers, The, *sels.*
Man Who Frets at Worldly Strife, The. *Fr.* The Croaker Papers.
National Paintings, The. *Fr.* The Croaker Papers.
Ode to Fortune. *Fr.* The Croaker Papers.
HALLER, SOEREN. *See* HALLAR, SØREN.
HALLET, MARY. Calvary.
My Saviour.
Rhythm of His Life, The.
HALLGRÍMSSON, JÓNAS. Golden Plover, The.
Greeting, A.
"HALLIBURTON, MAURINE" (Mrs. M. H. McGee). Incarnation.
HALLSTRÖM, PER. Inspiration.
HALPERN, MOISHE-LEIB [*or* MOYSHE LEYB]. Gingilee.
My Portrait.
Never Again Will I Say.
Restless as a Wolf.
Who.
HALPINE, CHARLES GRAHAM. Baron Renfrew's Ball.
Comrades Known in Marches Many.
Feminine Arithmetic.
Irish Astronomy.
Janette's Hair.
Lecompton's Black Brigade.
Mr. Johnson's Policy of Reconstruction.
Quakerdom.
Sambo's Right to Be Kilt.
Song of Sherman's Army, The.
Song of the Soldier.
Widow-ology.
HALSHAM, JOHN. My Last Terrier.

HAM, MARION FRANKLIN. O Lord of Life, Thy Kingdom Is at Hand.
Prayer, A: "I pray not for the joy that knows."
HAMBLETON, RONALD. Autumn, and I Would Go Back to You.
Comrades as We Rest Within.
Elegy on the Death of Virginia Woolf.
Last Night, When Fevered Minutes.
Lover and His Lass, A.
Sockeye Salmon.
That Strain Again.
HAMBURGER, MICHAEL. Ballad of the Outer Life, *tr.*
Death of an Old Man, The.
Emblem.
In October.
Infinite Time, *tr.*
Note-Book of a European Tramp, The, *sel.*
Poet's Progress, A.
Song about Great Men, A.
Spring Song in Winter.
Travelers' Song, *tr.*
Your Face, *tr.*
HAMDA. Beside a Stream.
Revenge.
HAMERTON, PHILIP GILBERT. Sanyassi, The.
Wild Huntsmen, The.
HAMILTON, ANN (Mrs. Daniel C. Sayre). Chanson d'Or.
Inscription: "It is not hard to tell a rose."
Pause.
HAMILTON, ANNA E. Christ's Giving.
Hem of His Garment, The.
Sympathy.
We Long to See Jesus.
HAMILTON, ANNE (1843–76). Deserts.
HAMILTON, BOBB. Gethsemane Now.
HAMILTON, CHARLES GRANVILLE. Contrast.
HAMILTON, CLAYTON. Lines Written on November 15, 1933 by a Man Born November 14, 1881 to Another Born November 15, 1881.
HAMILTON, DAVID OSBORNE. To Men Unborn.
HAMILTON, ELIZABETH. My Ain Fireside.
HAMILTON, ELOISE. Weaver, The.
HAMILTON, EUGENE LEE-. *See* LEE-HAMILTON, EUGENE.
HAMILTON, FLORENCE. April.
Conjecture.
If a Man Die.
"HAMILTON, GAIL." *See* DODGE, MARY ABIGAIL.
HAMILTON, GEORGE ROSTREVOR ("George Rostrevor"). Appollyon.
Atlantic.
Bodily Beauty.
Cell, The.
Hospital Ward (of this Generation).
Invocation: "O Thou, Creator from original Chaos."
Tears.
Three Cities.
Tree Purge.
HAMILTON, HAROLD. School of Sorrow, The.
HAMILTON, HARRIET ELEANOR. *See* KING, HARRIET ELEANOR HAMILTON.
HAMILTON, JOHN. Cold Blows the Wind.
Up in the Mornin' Early.
HAMILTON, MARION ETHEL. Bird at Night.
Dream.
Gauguin.
Rachel Laments.
HAMILTON, ROBERT BROWNING. Along the Road.
Pleasure and Sorrow.
HAMILTON, WILLIAM, of Bangour. Bed of Love, The. *Fr.* The Braes of Yarrow.
Braes of Yarrow, The.
Braes of Yarrow, The, *sel.*
HAMILTON, WILLIAM, of Gilbertfield. Last Dying Words of Bonnie Heck, The.
Willie Was a Wanton Wag.
HAMILTON, SIR WILLIAM ROWAN. O Brooding Spirit.
Prayer, A: "O brooding Spirit of Wisdom and of Love."
Spirit of Wisdom and of Love.
HAMLET, FRANCES CROSBY. But When Ye Pray.
Our Flag.
Prayer: "Thou who didst multiply, by Galilee."
To Our Forefathers.
HAMMEIRI, AVIGDOR. Hut, The.
HAMMERSTEIN, OSCAR, II. If I Loved You.
It Might as Well Be Spring.
HAMMITT, DEECORT. Hail! South Dakota.
HAMMON, JUPITER. Evening Thought, An.
HAMMOND, "DOC," *and* SCOTT JUDY. *See* JUDY, SCOTT, *and* "DOC" HAMMOND.
HAMMOND, ELEANOR. April Fool.
From a Street Corner.
Honest Mr. Robin.
In September.
Lonely Wind.
Magic Window, The.
March.
Rain in April.
St. Patrick's Day.
Sleepy Maple Trees, The.
Valentine, A.
HAMMOND, JAMES. Elegy: On Delia's Being in the Country. *Fr.* Love Elegies.
Elegy: To Delia. *Fr.* Love Elegies.
Love Elegies, *sels.*
HAMMOND, WILLIAM. Cruel Mistress, The.
Husbandry.
Man's Life.
Rose, The.
HAMPTON, EDGAR LLOYD. Peace Call, The.
HAMSUN, KNUT. God Punish You.
To Björnstjerne Björnson.
Tora's Song.
HANBY, BENJAMIN RUSSELL. Darling Nelly Gray.
HANCOCK, CAROLYN. Ninety-nine.
Stars.
HANDA. My Road.
HANDFORD, T. W. Easter Song, An.
HANDY, MRS. M. P. Only a Little Thing.
HANDY, WILLIAM CHRISTOPHER. Hesitating Blues, The.
St. Louis Blues.
HANES, LEIGH BUCKNER. Chipmunk.
Deserts.
Moon Magic.
Old Fence Post.
HAN HUNG. Farewell.
HANKEY, DONALD. Lord of Us All.
HANKEY, KATHERINE. I love to tell the story.
Tell me the old, old story.
HANKIN, ST. JOHN EMILE CLAVERING. Consolatory!
De Gustibus.
Editor's Tragedy, The.
Elegy on the Late King of Patagonia, An.
HANLINE, MAURICE A. Song of Pierrot, A.
HANMER, LORD JOHN. Pine Woods, The.
HANNA, EDWARD JUDSON. Three Gifts.
HANNAY, PATRICK. Maid Me Loved, A.
Song: "Now do the birds in their warbling words."
HANNSON, OLA. Songs of Home, *sel.*
HANNUM, ERLE REITER. Indian Summer.
HANRAHAN, AGNES I. Rosies.
HANSBROUGH, MARY BERRI CHAPMAN. Journey, The.
HANSCOM, BEATRICE. Old Collector, The.
HAN SHAN. House of Chung, The.
HANSHIN. Loneliness.
HANSON, GERTRUDE. Heart Is Bethlehem, The.
I Must Light a Candle.
This Holy Night.
HANSON, JOSEPH MILLS. Laramie Trail.
Springfield Calibre Fifty, The.
HANSON, PHYLLIS. Wisdom.
HAN WU. Descriptive Poem.
HARBAUGH, HENRY. Aloe Plant, The.
HARBAUGH, THOMAS CHALMERS. Trouble in the Amen Corner.
HARD, WALTER. Health Note, A.
Medical Aid.
Youth of the Mountain.
HARDEN, VERNA LOVEDAY. Post Mortem.
Wayfarer, The.
When This Tide Ebbs.
HARDENBERG, GEORG FRIEDRICH PHILIPP VON. *See* "NOVALIS."
HARDING, RUTH GUTHRIE. Call to a [*or* of the] Scot, The.
Daffodils.
From a Car-Window.
I Heard Her Whisper.
Lark Went Singing, A.
Madonna of the Carpenter Shop, The.
Night Pulse.
On a Fly-Leaf of Schopenhauer's "Immortality."
Peace Is Only an Interlude.
Returning.
Surrender.
Threnody: "There's a grass-grown road."
Valse Triste.
You.
HARDING, SAMUEL. Of Death. *Fr.* Sicily and Naples.
Sicily and Naples, *sel.*
HARDT, ERNST. Specter, The.
HARDY, ARTHUR SHERBURNE. Duality.
Immortality.
Iter Supremum.
Lullaby: "O Mary, mother, if the day we trod."
HARDY, ELIZABETH [*or* LIZZIE] CLARK. Message for the Year, A.
Some Time at Eve.
When I Sail Away.
HARDY, ELIZABETH STANTON. Echo.
Sea Shell.
HARDY, EVELYN. Certainty.
HARDY, JANE L. Lincoln.
HARDY, LIZZIE CLARK. *See* HARDY, ELIZABETH CLARK.
HARDY, THOMAS. Absolute Explains, The.
"According to the Mighty Working."
After a Journey.
After Jena. *Fr.* The Dynasts.
After Reading Psalms XXXIX, XL, etc.
After the Club-Dance. *Fr.* At Casterbridge Fair.
After the Fair. *Fr.* At Casterbridge Fair.
After the Visit.
Afterwards.
ΑΓΝΩΣΤΩι ΘΕΩι (Agnosto Theo: To an Unknown God).
Ah, Are You Digging on My Grave?
Albuera. *Fr.* The Dynasts.
Ancient to Ancients, An.
"And There Was a Great Calm."
At a Hasty Wedding.
At a House in Hampstead.
At a Lunar Eclipse.
At Casterbridge Fair.
At Casterbridge Fair, *sels.*
At Castle Boterel.
At Lulworth Cove a Century Back.
At Tea. *Fr.* Satires of Circumstance.
At the Altar-Rail. *Fr.* Satires of Circumstance.
At the Draper's. *Fr.* Satires of Circumstance.
August Midnight, An.
Autumn in King's Hintock Park.
Ballad-Singer, The. *Fr.* At Casterbridge Fair.
Barthélémon at Vauxhall.
Beauty's Soliloquy during Her Honeymoon, A.
Beeny Cliff.
Before Marching, and After.
Before Waterloo. *Fr.* The Dynasts.
Beyond the Last Lamp.
Birds at Winter Nightfall.

HARDY, THOMAS (*continued*)
Blinded Bird, The.
Boatman's Song, The. *Fr.* The Dynasts.
Broken Appointment, A.
Budmouth Dears. *Fr.* The Dynasts.
By Her Aunt's Grave. *Fr.* Satires of Circumstance.
By the Earth's Corpse.
Carrier, The.
Casterbridge Captains, The.
Channel Firing.
Chorus: "Yea, the coneys are scared by the thud of hoofs." *Fr.* The Dynasts.
Christmas Ghost-Story, A.
Church-Builder, The.
Church Romance, A.
Clock-Winder, The.
Comet at Yell'ham, The.
Coming of the End, The.
Conformers, The.
Contretemps, The.
Convergence of the Twain, The.
Curate's Kindness, The.
Curtains Now Are Drawn, The.
Dame of Athelhall, The.
Dark-eyed Gentleman, The.
Darkling Thrush, The.
Dead Quire.
Dead "Wessex," the Dog, to the Household.
Dissemblers, The.
Division, The.
Drummer Hodge.
During Wind and Rain.
Dynasts, The, *sels.*
Embarcation.
End of the Episode, The.
Epitaph: "I never cared for life: life cared for me."
Faintheart in a Railway Train.
Fallow Deer at the Lonely House, The.
Field of Waterloo, The. *Fr.* The Dynasts.
First or Last.
First Sight of Her and After.
Five Students, The.
For Life I Had Never Cared Greatly.
Former Beauties. *Fr.* At Casterbridge Fair.
Four Footprints.
Friends Beyond.
Garden Seat, The.
George Meredith.
Ghost of the Past, The.
God-forgotten.
God's Funeral.
Going, The.
Going and Staying.
Going of the Battery, The.
Great Things.
Hap.
Haunter, The.
Haunting Fingers.
He Abjures Love.
He Inadvertently Cures His Love-Pains.
Heiress and Architect.
Her Apotheosis.
Her Death and After.
Her Dilemma.
Her Immortality.
Her Initials.
Heredity.
His Country.
His Immortality.
House of Hospitalities, The.
Hussar's Song. *Fr.* The Dynasts.
I Found Her Out There.
I hate my beauty in the glass.
I Have Lived with Shades.
I Look into My Glass.
I Need Not Go.
I Said to Love.
I Was the Midmost.
I Watched a Blackbird.
Impercipient, The.
In a Cathedral City.
In a Museum.
In a Wood. *Fr.* The Woodlanders.
In Church. *Fr.* Satires of Circumstance.
In Tenebris.
In Tenebris, *sels.*
In the Days of Crinoline.
In the Evening.
In the Moonlight.
In the Restaurant. *Fr.* Satires of Circumstance.
In the Servants' Quarters.
In Time of "The Breaking of Nations."
Inquiry, The. *Fr.* At Casterbridge Fair.
Intra Sepulchrum.
Julie-Jane.
Lacking Sense, The.
Last Chrysanthemum, The.
Last Journey, A.
Last Leaf, The.
Last Words to a Dumb Friend.
Lausanne.
Let Me Enjoy.
Liddell and Scott; on the Completion of Their Lexicon.
Life Laughs Onward.
Man He Killed, The.
Man Was Drawing Near to Me, A.
Market-Girl, The. *Fr.* At Casterbridge Fair.
Men Who March Away ("We be the King's men"). *Fr.* The Dynasts.
Men Who March Away ("What of the faith and fire within us").
Midnight on the Great Western.
Milkmaid, The.
Minute before Meeting, The.
Missed Train, The.
Mongrel, The.
Musing Maiden, The.
Mute Opinion.
My Spirit Will Not Haunt the Mound.
Nature's Questioning.
Near Lanivet, 1872.
Neutral Tones.
New Year's Eve.
Newcomer's Wife, The.
Night of Trafalgar, The. *Fr.* The Dynasts.
1967.
No Buyers, a Street Scene.
Nobody Comes.
O I Won't Lead a Homely Life.
Old Furniture.
On a Midsummer Eve.
On an Invitation to the United States.
On Sturminster Foot-Bridge.
On the Departure Platform.
On the Doorstep.
On the Portrait of a Woman About to Be Hanged.
Overworld, The. *Fr.* The Dynasts.
Oxen, The.
Pedigree, The.
Phantom Horsewoman, The.
Pity of It, The.
Placid Man's Epitaph, A.
Plaint to Man, A.
Poet, A.
Postponement.
Postscript.
Prospect, The.
Puzzled Game-Birds, The.
Rain on a Grave.
Refusal, A.
Regret Not Me.
Reminder, The.
Reminiscences of a Dancing Man.
Respectable Burgher, The.
Revulsion.
Rift, The.
Roman Road, The.
Rome.
Ruined Maid, The.
Sacrilege, The.
Satin Shoes, The.
Satires of Circumstance, *sels.*
Second Night, The.
Self-unseeing, The.
Selfsame Song, The.
Seven Times, The.
Seventy-four and Twenty.
She Hears the Storm.
She, to Him.
Sheep Fair, The.
Shelley's Skylark.
Shiver, The.
Shut Out That Moon.
Shut Out That Moon, *sel.*
Sigh, The.
Singer Asleep, A.
Snow in the Suburbs.
Souls of the Slain, The.
Statue of Liberty, The.
Subalterns, The.
Superseded, The.
Surview.
Tess's Lament.
There Seemed a Strangeness.
Thought in Two Moods, A.
Thoughts of Phena at News of Her Death.
Thunderstorm in Town, A.
To a Lady Playing and Singing in the Morning.
To an Unborn Pauper Child.
To-be-forgotten, The.
To Life.
To Lizbie Browne.
To Shakespeare.
To the Moon.
Trafalgar. *Fr.* The Dynasts.
Trampwoman's Tragedy, A.
Transformations.
Tree and the Lady, The.
Two Houses, The.
Under the Waterfall.
Voice, The.
Wagtail and Baby.
Waiting Both.
Walk, The.
We Sat at the Window.
Weathers.
Well-beloved, The.
Wessex Heights.
When I Set Out for Lyonnesse.
Where the Picnic Was.
Who's in the Next Room?
Why Do I?
Wife Waits, A. *Fr.* At Casterbridge Fair.
Wind Blew Words, The.
Winter in Durnover Field.
Wives in the Sere.
Woman I Met, The.
Woman in the Rye, The.
Woodlanders, The, *sel.*
Year's Awakening, The.
Yell'ham-Wood's Story.
Young Man's Exhortation, A.
HARE, AMORY. After.
All Will Be Well.
Echo.
Life.
To a Little Girl.
Walking at Night.
Wet or Fine.
HARE, MAURICE EVAN. "There once was a man who said: 'Damn!'"
HARFORD, LESBIA. Beauty and Terror.
Experience.
I Have Golden Shoes.
Lovers Parted.
HARINGTON [*or* HARRINGTON], HENRY. Song: "Trust the form of airy things."
Trust the Form of Airy Things.
HARINGTON, JOHN (*fl.* 1550). Elegy Wrote in the Tower, 1554.
I See My Plaint, *at.*
Lines on Isabella Markham.
Sonnet Made on Isabella Markham, A.
HARINGTON, SIR JOHN (1561-1612). Against an Atheist, *after* Martial.
Against an Extreme Flatterer That Preached at Bath on the Queen's Day the Fortieth Year of Her Reign.
Against Feasting.
Against Paulus.
Against Writers That Carp at Other Men's Books, *after* Martial.
Angelica and the Ork, *tr. Fr.* Orlando Furioso.
Author to a Daughter of Nine Years Old, The, *after* Martial.
Author to Queen Elizabeth, in Praise of Her Reading, The.
Bought Locks, *tr.*
Comfort for Poor Poets, A.
Comparison of the Sonnet and the Epigram.

Critics [and Cooks], *after* Martial.
Epigram: "Treason doth never prosper."
Epitaph in Commendation of George Turberville, a Learned Gentleman, An.
Fair, Rich, and Young.
Gratulatory Elegy of the Peaceable Entry of King James, A.
Lesbia's Rule of Praise.
Lunar Valley of Lost Things, The, *tr. Fr.* Orlando Furioso.
Misacmos of Himself, Who Loves to Be Worst in the Company.
Of a Certain Man.
Of a Fair Shrew, *after* Martial.
Of a Precise Tailor.
Of Cinna's Election.
Of Clergymen and Their Livings.
Of Don Pedro and His Poetry, *after* Martial.
Of Faustus, a Stealer of Verses.
Of Friendship, *after* Martial.
Of Galla's Goodly Periwig, *after* Martial.
Of Good Sauce.
Of His Muse.
Of Honest Theft. To My Good Friend Master Samuel Daniel.
Of Inclosing a Common.
Of Lynus, Borrowing.
Of Summum Bonum.
Of the Pillars of the Church.
Of the Warres in Ireland.
Of Treason.
Of Two Religions.
On Treason.
Orlando Furioso, *sels., tr.*
Rule to Play, A.
To James the VI, King of Scotland.
To Master Bastard, a Minister That Made a Pleasant Book of English Epigrams.
To Master Bastard, Taxing Him of Flattery.
To Mr. [*or* Master] John Davies.
To Sextus, an Ill Reader.
To the Lady Rogers, of Her Unprofitable Sparing.
Treason.
HARKNESS, GEORGIA ELMA. Agony of God, The.
For God So Loved the World.
God Suffers.
Simon of Cyrene.
Swinging toward the Light.
Understanding Heart, The.
HARLOW, S. RALPH. Church Triumphant.
O Young and Fearless Prophet.
Who Is So Low.
HARMAN, ELIZABETH. Soldier's Dirge.
HARNEY, WILLIAM E. West of Alice.
HARNEY, WILLIAM WALLACE. Adonais.
Stab, The.
HARPER, CLARENCE S. Doris.
HARPER, FRANCES ELLEN WALKINS. Let the Light Enter.
Slave Auction, The.
HARPUR, CHARLES. Aboriginal Mother's Lament, An.
Midsummer['s] Noon in the Australian Forest, A.
Regret, A.
Similitude, A.
Sonnet: "She loves me! From her own bliss-breathing lips."
Words.
HARRELL, WILLIAM BERNARD. Ho! For Carolina!
"HARRIET ANNIE." Death of Gaudentis.
HARRIGAN, EDWARD. My Dad's Dinner Pail.
HARRIMAN, DOROTHY. Cat on the Porch at Dusk.
HARRINGTON, HENRY. *See* HARINGTON, HENRY.
HARRINGTON, JAMES. Treason Never Prospers, *wr. at.*
HARRINGTON, JOHN (*fl.* 1550). *See* HARINGTON, JOHN.
HARRINGTON, SIR JOHN. *See* HARINGTON, SIR JOHN.
HARRINGTON, MICHAEL. Gazeteer of Newfoundland.
Second Iron Age (1939–1945), The.
HARRINGTON, SARAH JANE S. Baby's Bath, The.
Happy Birds.
Lullaby: "Sleep, my little one, sleep."
My Little Boat.
My Pets.
HARRIS, CHARLES KASSELL. After the Ball.
Break the News to Mother.
HARRIS, G. W. Coat of Faded Gray, The.
HARRIS, HAZEL HARPER. Call to Freedom.
Hot Tamale Man, The.
My Little House.
Sailor's Song, A.
HARRIS, JOEL CHANDLER. Appile Tree, De.
Big Bethel Church, De. *Fr.* Uncle Remus, His Songs and His Sayings.
How Brer Tarrypin Learned to Fly.
My Honey, My Love. *Fr.* Uncle Remus and His Friends.
Plantation Play-Song. *Fr.* Uncle Remus, His Songs and His Sayings.
Plough-Hands' Song, The. *Fr.* Uncle Remus, His Songs and His Sayings.
Revival Hymn. *Fr.* Uncle Remus, His Songs and His Sayings.
Time Goes by Turns. *Fr.* Uncle Remus, His Songs and His Sayings.
Uncle Remus and His Friends, *sel.*
Uncle Remus, His Songs and His Sayings, *sels.*
HARRIS, JOSEPH U. *See* "UPPER, JOSEPH."
HARRIS, JUNE BROWN. Home.
HARRIS, LOUISE DYER. Crossing Boston Common.
Review of a Cook Book.
HARRIS, MARGUERITE. My Sun-killed Tree.
HARRIS, MAX. Lullaby: "Girl with eyes like dying flowers."
Mad Jasper.
Martin Buber in the Pub.
Plowman, The.
HARRIS, THOMAS LAKE. California.
Fledglings.
God Speaks in All Religions.
Sea-Sleep.
Sentences of Wisdom, *sel.*
Silent Tongue, *sel.*
HARRISON, ELIZABETH. Taking Off.
HARRISON, FLORENCE. Faerie Fair, The.
Summer Day, A.
HARRISON, GEORGE. Epitaph Acrostick on Robert Blake, The.
HARRISON, HENRY SYDNOR. Osculation.
HARRISON, SAM. After the Show.
Chez Madame.
Journey.
Meeting.
Poem: "This room is very old and very wise."
Rain.
HARRISON, SUSAN FRANCES ("Seranus").
At Ste. Thérèse.
Benedict Brosse. *Fr.* Down the River.
Catharine Plouffe. *Fr.* Down the River.
Château Papineau.
Danger. *Fr.* Down the River.
Down the River, *sels.*
Gatineau Point. *Fr.* Down the River.
Les Chantiers. *Fr.* Down the River.
Petite Ste. Rosalie. *Fr.* Down the River.
St. Jean B'ptiste. *Fr.* Down the River.
September.
Voyageur, The. *Fr.* Down the River.
HARRISON, VIRGINIA BIOREN. Lullaby: "Sleep, baby, sleep, waiting near."
Music of the Dawn.
One Gift I Ask.
HARROD, ELIZABETH B. August Night, 1953.
Calvinist Autumnal.
Sonnet against the Too-facile Mystic.
Summer Afternoon.
"HARRY, BLIND." *See* HENRY THE MINSTREL.
HARSEN, UNA W. Litany for Old Age, A.
Prayer before Meat.
Sacrament.
To Mary, Mother of Christ.
HART, ELIZABETH ANNA. Mother Tabbyskins.
Old Mother Tabbyskins.
Sweeping the Skies.
HART, HENRY HERSCH. *For translations from Chinese, see* BoFr; ChLP; OnPM; PoHN; WoL.
HART, JOSEPH. Come, ye sinners, poor and needy.
Pray with Faith.
HART, RICHARD. Inhibited Persian, An.
Mother with Young Kittens, A.
HART-SMITH, WILLIAM. Baiamai's Never-failing Stream.
Bathymeter.
Columbus Goes West.
Drama.
Holding-Paddock.
La Perouse.
Shag Rookery.
Shepherd and the Hawk, The.
Space.
Tractor.
When You Touch.
HARTE, BRET (Francis Bret Harte).
Aged Stranger, The.
Arctic Vision, An.
At the Hacienda.
Babes in the Woods, The.
Ballad of the Emeu, The.
Caldwell of Springfield.
Chicago.
Chiquita.
Crotalus.
Dickens in Camp.
Dow's Flat—1856.
Fate.
Ghost That Jim Saw, The.
Greyport [*or* Grayport] Legend, A.
Grizzly.
Hawk's Nest, The.
Heathen Chinee, The.
Her Letter.
"How Are You, Sanitary?"
Jessie.
Jim.
John Burns at Gettysburg.
Madroño.
Mrs. Judge Jenkins.
Mountain Heart's-Ease, The.
Personified Sentimental, The.
Plain Language [*or* Talk] from Truthful James.
Ramon.
Relieving Guard.
Return of Belisarius, The; Mud Flat, 1860.
Reveille, The.
Second Review of the Grand Army, A.
Serenade: "I'm a gay tra, la, la."
Society upon the Stanislaus [*or* Stanislow], The.
Spelling Bee at Angels, The.
Swiss Air.
That Heathen Chinee.
To a Sea-Bird.
To the Pliocene Skull.
Truthful James.
Two Ships, The.
What the Bullet Sang.
What the Chimney Sang.
Willows, The.
HARTE, WALTER. Soliloquy, A.
HARTICH, ALICE. Remembering.
HARTLEY, JOHN. To a Daisy.
HARTLEY, MARSDEN. Confidence.
Crucifixion of Noel, The.
In Robin Hood Cove.
Indian Point.
V Is for Victory, as You Can Plainly See.
Warblers.
HARTMAN, HELEN M. Moving Day.
HARTMAN, MARY R. Life's Made Up of Little Things.

HARTMANN VON AUE. None Is Happy.
Scales of Love, The.
HARTNOLL, PHYLLIS. Carpenter, The.
HARTSWICK, F. G. Somewhere-in-Europe-Wocky.
HARTSWICK, JENNIE BETTS. To St. Valentine.
HARTWICH, ETHELYN M. What Shall Endure?
HARUMI. Winter Shower, A.
HARUMICHI NO TSURAKI. Wind has stopped, The.
HARVEY, ALEXANDER. With Me in Paradise.
HARVEY, CHRISTOPHER. Comfort in Extremity.
HARVEY, FREDERICK WILLIAM. Bugler, The.
Ducks.
Ducks, *sels.*
Mole, The.
HARVEY, GABRIEL. Due Commendation of the Quipping Autor, A. *Fr.* Four Letters and Certain Sonnets.
Four Letters and Certain Sonnets, *sel.*
Greene's Memorial; or, Certain Funeral Sonnets, *sels.*
His Admonition to Greene's Companions. *Fr.* Greene's Memorial.
His Apology of His Good Father. *Fr.* Greene's Memorial.
To the Learned Shepheard.
HARWOOD, CHARLES W. Color Guard.
HARWOOD, RUTH. Shoe Factory, The.
"HASHIMURA TOGO." *See* IRWIN, WALLACE.
HASKIN, LESLIE L. Christ the Carpenter.
HASKINS, M. LOUISE. Gate of the Year, The, *sel.*
HASLEY, LOUIS. On Her Twenty-fifth Birthday.
HASLUCK, PAUL. Drunken Man on Highgate Hill, A.
HASSALL, CHRISTOPHER VERNON. No Clock with Numbered Eyes.
Soliloquy to Imogen, *sels.*
HASTE, GWENDOLEN. Daybreak Call, The.
Horizons.
Prayer of the Homesteader.
Tomorrow Is a Birthday.
HASTINGS, FANNY DE GROOT. Late Comer.
HASTINGS, LADY FLORA. Early Rising.
Prayers.
To a Butterfly.
HASTINGS, LADY T. "Exactly So."
HASTINGS, THOMAS. Be Hush'd.
Exhortation.
Gently, Lord, O gently lead us.
Hushaby.
In Sorrow.
Latter Day, The.
Sleep, O Sleep!
HATCH, EDWIN. Breathe on Me, Breath of God.
Heaven.
HATCH, FRANCIS WHITING. He Laughed Last.
So This Is Middle Age!
HATHAWAY, DONALD WING. Etchers of Eld.
HATTON, SIR R. You that have been this evenings light.
"HATZOPOULOS, KOSTES" (Petros Vasilikos). Let the Boat Go.
HAUCH, CARSTEN. Confession, *sel.*
When o'er the Fields.
HAUER, ELIZABETH N. Vision.
HAUK, WALTER. Nightfall before Syracuse.
HAUSGEN, MATTIE LEE. Her Choice.
Her Favorites.
Lovely Bed, A.
Spider Web, The.
HAUSHOFER, ALBRECHT. In Chains. *Fr.* Sonnets from Moabite Prison.
Rats, The. *Fr.* Sonnets from Moabite Prison.
Sonnets from Moabite Prison, *sels.*
HAUSTED, PETER. Have pity, grief, I cannot pay. *Fr.* The Rival Friends.
Have you a desire to see. *Fr.* The Rival Friends.
Of His Mistress. *Fr.* The Rival Friends.
Rival Friends, The, *sels.*
Song, The: "Have pity (Grief) I can not pay." *Fr.* The Rival Friends.
HAVENS, MRS. Ask and Ye Shall Receive.
HAVERGAL, FRANCES RIDLEY. Afterwards.
Another Year Is Dawning.
At the Portal.
Be Quiet; Fear Not.
Behold Your King!
Bells across the Snow.
Covenant, A.
Crown the Year.
Easter Dawn.
Easter Prayer.
For Easter.
For Every Day.
God Is Faithful.
Golden harps are sounding.
Happy Christmas, A.
I Gave My Life for Thee.
Increase Our Faith.
Life-Mosaic.
Lord, Speak to Me, That I May Speak.
New Year Wish, A.
New Year's Wishes.
O Saviour, precious Saviour.
Prayer, A: "Lord, in mercy pardon me."
Reality.
Take My Life.
Thanksgiving.
Thou Art Coming!
Thy life was given for me.
Thy Presence.
Who Is on the Lord's Side?
Worker's Prayer, A.
HAWEIS, HUGH REGINALD. Homeland, The.
HAWEIS, LIONEL. Tsoqalem, the Cowichan Monster, *sel.*
HAWEIS, THOMAS. Come and Welcome.
Remember Me!
HAWES, EDITH BENEDICT. Interruption.
HAWES, STEPHEN. Dame Music. *Fr.* The Pastime of Pleasure.
Epitaph, An: "O mortal folk, you may behold and see." *Fr.* The Pastime of Pleasure.
Epitaph of Graunde Amoure. *Fr.* The Pastime of Pleasure.
Excusation of the Auctor, The. *Fr.* The Pastime of Pleasure.
Here Begynneth the Passe Tyme of Pleasure. *Fr.* The Pastime of Pleasure.
His Epitaph. *Fr.* The Pastime of Pleasure.
How Grand Amour Walked in a Meadow . . . *Fr.* The Pastime of Pleasure.
Of the Great Marriage between Grand Amour and La Belle Pucelle. *Fr.* The Pastime of Pleasure.
Pastime of Pleasure, The, *sels.*
Seven Deadly Sins, The. *Fr.* The Pastime of Pleasure.
Time and Eternity. *Fr.* The Pastime of Pleasure.
True Knight, The. *Fr.* The Pastime of Pleasure.
True Knighthood. *Fr.* The Pastime of Pleasure.
HAWKER, ROBERT STEPHEN. Aishah Schechinah.
And Shall Trelawny Die?
Angels of the Spring.
Are They Not All Ministering Spirits?
Aunt Mary; a Christmas Chant.
Christ-Cross Rhyme, A.
Datur Hora Quieti.
Death Song.
Dirge, The: "Sing from the chamber to the grave!"
Featherstone's Doom.
First Fathers, The.
"I Am the Resurrection and the Life," Saith the Lord!
King Arthur's Waes-Hael.
Mawgan of Melhuach.
Modryb Marya.
Morwennae Statio.
Mystic Magi, The.
"Pater Vester Pascit Illa."
Queen Guennivar's Round.
Quest of the Sangraal, The, *sel.*
Rapture on the Cornish Hills, A.
Silent Tower of Bottreau[x], The.
Song of the Western Men, The.
Southern Cross, The.
To Alfred Tennyson.
Trelawny.
HAWKES, CLARENCE. Mountain to the Pine, The.
HAWKES, HENRY WARBURTON. "Thy Kingdom Come!" O Lord.
HAWKES, JACQUETTA. Moon Daisies.
HAWKES, WILLIAM. Christmas Still Lives.
HAWKINS, H. P. Good Shepherd, The.
HAWKINS, HENRY. Bee, The.
Hoc Cygno Vinces.
HAWKINS, LUCY. To L. C.
HAWKINS, W. S. More Cruel than War.
Your Letter, Lady, Came Too Late.
HAWKS, ANNIE SHERWOOD. I need Thee every hour.
Thine.
HAWKSHAW, ANN [*or* ANNE HAWKSHAWE] ("Aunt Effie"). Chorus of Frogs, The.
Clucking [*or* Clocking] Hen, The.
Common Things.
Dame Duck's First Lecture on Education.
Dame Duck's Lecture to Her Ducklings.
Freddie and the Cherry Tree.
Glow-Worms, The.
Great Brown Owl, The.
I'll Try.
Little Raindrops, *at.*
Moonlight, The.
Mother Duck.
Muffin-Man's Bell, The.
Old Kitchen Clock, The.
Pussy-Cat.
Robin Redbreasts, The.
Turtle-Dove's Nest, The, *at.*
Water Mill, The.
Waves on the Sea-Shore, The.
Young Linnets, The.
HAWLEY, CHARLES B. My Little Love.
HAWLING, MARY S. Futility.
Return.
"HAWTHORNE, ALICE." *See* WINNER, SEPTIMUS.
HAWTHORNE, HILDEGARDE. My Rose.
Song, A: "Sing me a sweet, low song of night."
HAWTHORNE, JULIAN. Were-Wolf.
HAWTHORNE, NATHANIEL. Star of Calvary, The.
HAWTHORNE, ROSE. *See* LATHROP, ROSE HAWTHORNE.
HAWTREY, EDWARD CRAVEN. Helen on the Walls of Troy Looking for Her Brothers, *tr.* *Fr.* The Iliad.
Iliad, The, *sel.*, *tr.*
HAY, CLARENCE LEONARD. Down and Out.
"HAY, ELIJAH." *See* SEIFFERT, MARJORIE ALLEN.
HAY, HELEN. *See* WHITNEY, HELEN HAY.
HAY, HENRY HANBY. Hymn for Arbor Day, A.
HAY, JOHN (1838–1905). Banty Tim.
Christine.
Distichs.
Enchanted Shirt, The.
Good and Bad Luck.
Jim Bludso [of the *Prairie Belle*].
Liberty.
Little Breeches.
Miles Keogh's Horse.
Not in Dumb Resignation.
Religion and Doctrine.
Sister Saint Luke.
Stirrup-Cup, The.
Surrender of Spain, The.
Thy Will Be Done.

White Flag, The.
Woman's Love, A.
HAY, JOHN (1915-). Aboriginal Sin.
Amor Mysticus, *tr.*
And Grow.
Bird Song.
Chickadees, The.
December Storm.
Energy of Light, The.
Five Grand Odes, *sel., tr.*
Life Must Burn.
Natural Architecture.
Old Man of Tennessee.
Railway Station.
Sent Ahead.
Silver Leaf, The.
To a Schoolmaster, *tr.*
Town Meeting.
Variations on a Theme.
HAY, PERONNEAN D. Phantom Host, The.
HAY, SARA HENDERSON. "Bottle Should be Plainly Labeled 'Poison.'"
Christmas, the Year One, A.D.
Cordial Soul.
Daily Manna, The.
Daily Paradox.
Entrance into Heaven.
Father, The.
For a Dead Kitten.
For a Little Bird That Blundered into Church.
Heresy Indeed.
Love Suffereth Long.
Man Named Legion, The.
Mary.
On Being Told That One's Ideas Are Victorian.
Prayer in April.
Prodigal, The.
Reflections on an Ideal Existence.
Search, The.
Shape God Wears, The.
Summer Evening.
Text.
To a Snail in the Cemetery.
Upon Discovering One's Own Intolerance.
Warning.
HAY, SARA HENDERSON, *and* RAYMOND HOLDEN. Detour—Gypsy Trail Closed.
HAYASHI, UTAKO. Morning Prayer ("A lowly woman").
Morning Prayer ("I waken in the early dawn").
My Task.
Not Alone.
Song of Daily Life, A.
HAYDEN, JOE. Hot Time in the Old Town, A.
HAYDEN, KATHARINE SHEPARD. After a Symphony Concert.
From the Cliffs at Puve, New Mexico.
HAYDEN, ROBERT EARL. Ballad of Remembrance, A.
Eine Kleine Nachtmusik.
Frederick Douglass.
Homage to the Empress of the Blues.
Letter from the South.
O Daedalus Fly Away Home.
Photograph of Isadora Duncan, A.
Runagate Runagate.
HAYES, ALFRED. Angel, The.
City of Beggars, The.
Death of the Craneman, The.
Epistle to the Gentiles.
Imitation of Faust, The.
Slaughter-House, The.
HAYES, ANN LOUISE. Alien.
Autumnal.
Daphne.
Desolation.
February.
Furlough.
In Description.
Poem: "Here poppies move beneath the sun."
Poem: "Take thy silent entity apart."
Poem: "They will not, then, with victory return."
Query.
Sonnet for a Marriage.

HAYES, DONALD JEFFREY. After All.
Appoggiatura.
Auf Wiedersehen.
Benediction.
Confession.
Haven.
Inscription: "He wrote upon his heart."
Night.
Nocturne: "Softly blow lightly."
Poet.
Prescience.
Sketch.
HAYES, EDNAH PROCTOR CLARKE. *See* CLARKE, EDNAH PROCTOR.
"HAYES, EVELYN." *See* BETHELL, MARY URSULA.
HAYES, J. MILTON. Green Eye of the Yellow God, The.
HAYES, JAMES M. Bleeding Heart Aflame, A.
But Two I Love.
Mother of the Rose, The.
Mother Saint Urban.
Old Nuns.
Our Lady of the Skies.
Sister Mary Philomena.
Transfiguration, The.
HAYES, JOHN RUSSELL. Old-fashioned Garden, The.
HAYES, NANCY M. At Night in the Wood.
Night in the Wood, A.
Shiny Little House, The.
HAYFORD, GLADYS MAY CASELY (Aquah Laluah). Baby Cobina.
Nativity.
Rainy Season Love Song.
Serving Girl, The.
Souls of Black and White, The.
HAYFORD, JAMES. Horn.
In a Closed Universe.
Overseer of the Poor.
Resident Worm, The.
Under All This Slate.
HAYLEY, WILLIAM. Card of Invitation to Mr. Gibbon, at Brighthelmstone, A.
HAYMAN, ROBERT. Of the Great and Famous Sir Francis Drake.
HAYNE, PAUL HAMILTON. Aspects of the Pines.
At Last.
Battle of Charleston Harbor, The.
Between the Sunken Sun and the New Moon.
Beyond the Potomac.
Bryant Dead.
Butler's Proclamation.
Charleston.
Heroes of the South.
In Harbor.
Little While I Fain Would Linger Yet, A.
Love Scorns Degrees. *Fr.* The Mountain of the Lovers.
Macdonald's Raid.
Mocking Bird, The.
Mocking-Birds, The.
Mountain of the Lovers, The, *sel.*
My Study.
Ode to Sleep.
Pine's Mystery, The.
Pre-Existence.
Rose and [the] Thorn, The.
Shelley.
Snow-Messengers, The.
South Carolina to the States of the North.
Storm in the Distance, A.
Stricken South to the North, The.
To Longfellow.
To O. W. Holmes.
To W. H. H.
True Heaven, The.
Vicksburg—a Ballad.
Yorktown Centennial Lyric.
HAYNE, WILLIAM HAMILTON. Autumn Breeze, An.
Charge at Santiago, The.
Cyclone at Sea, A.
Exiles.
Moonlight Song of the Mocking-Bird.
Night Mists.

Oliver Wendell Holmes.
Pine Needles.
Sea Lyric, A.
Sewing.
"Sleep and His Brother Death."
Southern Snow-Bird, The.
To a Cherokee Rose.
To My Father.
Yule Log, The.
HAYNES, CAROL. Any Husband or Wife.
Any Wife or Husband.
Aunt Selina.
HAYS, HOFFMAN REYNOLDS. For translations from German, see LiTW.
For translations from Spanish, see AnCL; LiTW; OnPM; TwSpPo.
HAYS, WILL S. O'Grady's Goat.
HAYWOOD, CAROLYN. Little Clown Puppet.
HAZARD, CAROLINE. Great Swamp Fight, The.
In Shadow.
Ninth Hour, The.
Out of Egypt Have I Called My Son.
Wilderness, The.
HAZARD, GRACE WALCOTT. *See* CONKLING, GRACE HAZARD.
HAZELTINE, ALICE ISABEL. Child at a Crèche, A.
Christmas Night.
HAZZARD, JOHN EDWARD. Ain't It Awful, Mabel?
HEAD, SIR HENRY. Died of His Wounds.
Seedtime and Harvest.
Songs of La Mouche.
HEADLAM, WALTER. For translations from Greek, see GrL; GrPo; GrR; OxBG; WoL.
HEADLAND, ISAAC TAYLOR. Bald Old Woman, The, *tr.*
Chinese Nursery Rhyme, A, *tr.*
Flour Fritters, *tr.*
Mouse, The, *tr.*
Old Chang, the Crab, *tr.*
Old Mother Wind, *tr.*
Rice Seller, The, *tr.*
Snail, The, *tr.*
HEALEY, EVELYN H. Journey's End.
HEALY, PATRICK. My Wishes.
HEALY, ROBERT. His Lullaby.
HEARN, LAFCADIO. All things change, we are told, in this world of change and sorrow, *tr.*
Clarimonde, *tr.*
Four Folk-Songs in Hokku Form, *tr.*
If with my sleeve I hide the faint color of the dawning sun, *tr.*
River of Heaven, The, *tr. Fr.* Manyo Shu.
Things never changed since the Time of the Gods, *tr.*
Thinking tomorrow remains, thou heart's frail flower-of-cherry, *tr.*
HEARN, MARIANNE. Consecration.
HEARN, MARY ANNE. *See* "FARNINGHAM, MARIANNE."
HEARST, JAMES S. Voices.
HEATH, ——. These Women All.
Women.
HEATH, ELLA. Poetry.
HEATH, JOHN. Ad Collegium Wintoniensem.
Ad Modernos Epigrammatistas.
Ad Tho. Bastardum Epigrammatistam.
Ad Zoilum.
De Gelu Diutino, Anno Dom. 1607.
Health is a jewell, true; which when we buy.
In Ariostum Orlandi Furiosi Autorem.
In Beatricem Praepropere Defunctam.
In Porcum.
In Senecam.
Parson, having a tithe pig or two, A.
Those which have travelld o'er the earth's round ball.
Volucre Ferrum.
HEATH, ROBERT. Clarastella Distrusting.
Excuse, The.
On Clarastella Singing.
On Clarastella, Walking in Her Garden.

HEATH, ROBERT (*continued*)
On the Unusual Cold and Rainie Weather in the Summer, 1648.
Seeing Her Dancing.
Song in a Siege.
To Clarastella on St. Valentines Day Morning.
HEATH-STUBBS, JOHN. Address Not Known.
Beggar's Serenade.
Broom, The, *tr.*
Canzone: Of Distance, *tr.*
Canzone: To the Lady Pietra, of Sienna, *tr.*
Charm against the Toothache, A.
Churchyard of St. Mary Magdalene, Old Milton.
Dance Song, *tr.*
Death of Digenes Akritas, The.
Don Juan Muses.
Epitaph: "Mr. Heath-Stubbs as you must understand."
Ghost in the Cellarage, The.
Infinito, L' (The Infinite), *tr.*
Maria Aegyptiaca.
Mermaid at Zennor, The.
Old King, The.
Quatrains: "Dog Star now, negating all desires, The."
Sestina 2: To the Lady Pietra of Siena, *tr.*
Two Men in Armour.
Virgin and Unicorn.
HEATON, JOHN LANGDON. Sea Irony.
HEAVYSEGE, CHARLES. Ages of Man, The.
Count Filippo, *sels.*
David Exorcizing Malzah, the Evil Spirit from the Lord. *Fr.* Saul, a Drama.
Dead, The.
Flight of Malzah, The. *Fr.* Saul, a Drama.
Hell's Road. *Fr.* Saul, a Drama.
How Great unto the Living Seem the Dead!
Jephthah's Daughter, *sel.*
"Lo! I Am Saul." *Fr.* Saul, a Drama.
Malzah and the Angel Zelehtha. *Fr.* Saul, a Drama.
Malzah Speaks. *Fr.* Saul, a Drama.
Malzah's Song. *Fr.* Saul, a Drama.
Night.
Saul, a Drama, *sels.*
Saul's Faithfulness. *Fr.* Saul, a Drama.
Song: "Who is lord of lordly fate." *Fr.* Count Filippo.
Stars Are Glittering in the Frosty Sky, The.
Twilight.
Winter Galaxy, The.
Zaph Describes the Haunts of Malzah. *Fr.* Saul, a Drama.
HEBBEL, FRIEDRICH. Tree in the Desert, The.
HEBBLETHWAITE, JAMES. Perdita.
Symbol, The.
Wanderers.
HEBER, REGINALD. Bow-Meeting Song, A.
Bread of the World.
Brightest and Best of the Sons of the Morning.
By Cool Siloam's Shady Rill.
Epiphany.
Evening Hymn.
From Greenland's Icy Mountains.
Holy, Holy, Holy.
If Thou Wert by My Side, My Love.
Lo, the Lilies of the Field.
Pitt.
Providence.
Son of God Goes Forth to War, The.
Sympathy.
Thrice Holy.
Who Follows in His Train?
HEBERT, ALBERT J., JR. Heart for All Her Children.
HÉBERT, ANNE. Someone Could Certainly Be Found.
HECHT, ANTHONY. Japan.
La Condition Botanique.
Mignon, *tr.*
Origin of Centaurs, The.
Ostia Antica.
Place of Pain in the Universe, The.
Samuel Sewall.
Upon the Death of George Santayana.
Vow, The.
HECTOR, MARY LOUISE. Whatsoever I Do.
HEDGE, FREDERIC HENRY. Erl King, The, *tr.*
Mighty Fortress Is Our God, A, *tr.*
Questionings.
HEDGE, T. H. Via Crucis, Via Lucis.
HEDGES, DORIS. Onwardness.
Poet's Protest.
Prayer: "O God of Goodness, Forwardness, and Fulness."
HEDRICK, ADDIE M. Two Crosses.
HEDYLUS [*or* HEDYLOS]. Crown high the cup and pass it round.
Girl Betrayed.
HEERMANS, MARY A. Arbor Day Song.
HEFFERNAN THE BLIND, WILLIAM. Welcome to the Prince of Ossory.
HEIBERG, JOHAN LUDVIG. Barcarole.
HEIDENSTAM, VERNER VON. Alone by the Lake.
At the End of the Way.
Burial of Gustaf Fröding, The.
Day, A.
Dove of Thought, The.
Fellow-Citizens.
Forest of Tiveden, The, *sel.*
Grant That We Die Young.
Home.
Home-Land.
How Easily Men's Cheeks Are Hot with Wrath.
Invocation and Promise.
Man's Last Word to a Woman, A.
Moonlight.
My Life.
Nameless and Immortal.
Prayer amid Flames.
Starting on the Journey.
Sweden.
Thoughts in Loneliness, *sel.*
HEIN, PIET. Dedication: "Mighty world's, The/ Eternity."
Literary Gruk.
HEINE, HEINRICH. Ad Finem.
Affinities.
Ah, Your White-as-Lily Fingers.
And When I Lamented. *Fr.* Homeward Bound.
Anno 1829.
Ashes.
At Parting.
At the Crossroad Lies Buried.
Auf meiner Herzliebsten Äugelein.
Azra, The.
Babylonian Sorrows.
Best Religion, The. *Fr.* Tannhäuser.
Blauen Veilchen der Äugelein, Die.
Brief, den du geschrieben, Der.
By the Waters of Babylon. *Fr.* Hebrew Melodies.
Choir Boys, The.
Coffin, The.
Come, O Friend, to Greet the Bride. *Fr.* Hebrew Melodies.
Dear Maiden.
Dearest Friend, Thou Art in Love. *Fr.* Homeward Bound.
Death Is at Hand.
Death Is the Chilly Night.
Doctrine.
Du bist wie eine Blume.
Du schönes Fischer-Mädchen.
Earth Is So Lovely, The.
Enfant Perdu.
Epilog: "Like the ears of the wheat." *Fr.* The North Sea.
Epilogue: "Like the stalks of wheat in the fields." *Fr.* The North Sea.
Es fällt ein Stern herunter.
Es stehen unbeweglich.
Evening Twilight. *Fr.* The North Sea.
Exile.
Farewell: "Linden blossomed, the nightingale sang, The."
Fichtenbaum steht einsam, Ein.
Firelight.
Fisher-Maiden, The.
Fisher's Cottage, The.
Forlornly.
Fresco-Sonnets to Christian Sethe.
Fürchte Nichts, geliebte Seele.
Gazelles.
Give me a mask, I'll join the masquerade. *Fr.* Fresco-Sonnets to Christian Sethe.
Good Fortune.
Grenadiers, The.
Hebrew Melodies, *sel.*
Heimkehr, Die, *sels.*
Homeward Bound, *sels.*
Hoo the Warld Wags.
I, a Most Wretched Atlas. *Fr.* Homeward Bound.
I Dreamt the Old, Old Dream Anew.
I laugh at each dull bore, taste's parasite. *Fr.* Fresco-Sonnets to Christian Sethe.
I Love a Flower.
I Love but Thee.
I Met by Chance.
I See a Star That Plummets.
I see ye like a flooer.
I Wept as I Lay Dreaming.
I Will Not Grieve.
Ich weiss nicht, was soll es bedeuten.
"If, Jerusalem, I Ever Should Forget Thee."
I'm Black and Blue.
Im Traum sah ich ein Männchen klein und putzig.
In Exile.
King David.
Kings from the East, The.
Lassie, What Mair Wad You Hae?
Lone in the North a Pine Tree.
Lonely Pine Is Standing, A.
Looking Back.
Lorelei [*or* Loreley], The.
Lost Child—Enfant Perdu.
Lotosblume ängstigt, Die.
Lotus-Flower, The.
Love Dead.
Lovely as a Flower.
Love's Résumé.
Mädchen mit dem rothen Mündchen.
Madonna, A.
Maiden Lies in Her Chamber, A.
Meeting, A.
Mein Herz, mein Herz, ist traurig.
Mein Kind, wir waren Kinder.
Mein Liebchen, wir sassen zusammen.
Mermaidens, The.
Message, The.
Mir träumte von einem Königskind.
Mir träumte wieder der alte Traum.
Mond ist aufgegangen, Der.
Mortal, Sneer Not at the Devil. *Fr.* Homeward Bound.
My Songs Are Poisoned!
New Jewish Hospital at Hamburg, The.
Night by the Sea, A. *Fr.* The North Sea.
Night on the Shore. *Fr.* The North Sea.
North Sea, The, *sels.*
Now Where To?
Oh Lovely Fishermaiden.
Philosophy.
Picture, The.
Pine Tree, The.
Prayer, A: "My darling, thou art flowerlike."
Princess Sabbath.
Proem: "Out of my own great woe."
Quiet Night, The.
Religion.
Rose, die Lilie, die Taube, die Sonne, Die.
Rose, the Fair Lily, the Dove, and the Sunlight, The.
Sag' mir wer einst die Uhren erfund.
Sag', wo ist dein schönes Liebchen.
Sea Hath Its Pearls, The.
Shadow-Love. *Fr.* Songs to Seraphine.
Shepherd Boy, The.
Slave Ship, The.
Solomon.
Song: "There stands a lonely pine-tree."
Songs to Seraphine, *sels.*

Sonnet to a Cat.
Sonnet to My Mother, A.
Stane wi Its Runes Rises frae the Sea, The.
Stars Look at Love, The.
Still the Emasculated.
Storm, The.
Superfluous Bite.
Tannhäuser, *sel.*
Tendency, The.
There Was an Aged Monarch.
This Mad Carnival of Loving. *Fr.* To Angélique.
Thou Hast Diamonds. *Fr.* Homeward Bound.
Thou Lovely Fishermaiden.
Thou Seemest like a Flower. *Fr.* Homeward Bound.
To Angélique, *sel.*
To Edom.
To His Mother.
To My Mother.
Too Fragmentary Is Life in the Main.
Twilight.
Two Songs.
Voyage, The.
Wandering Rats, The.
Warning, A.
Warum sind denn die Rosen so blass.
Waves Gleam in the Sunshine, The. *Fr.* Songs to Seraphine.
We Cared for Each Other.
Weavers, The.
Welt ist dumm, die welt ist blind, Die.
Wenn ich in deine Augen seh'.
Whaur?
When Two Are Parted.
When Young Hearts Break.
Where?
Who Was It, Tell Me.
Wie langsam kriechet sie dahin.
Window-Glance, The.
With Inky Sails.
Withered Heart, The.
World Is Dull, The.
You Are Unhappy.
Zu fragmentarisch ist Welt und Leben.
HEINER, JESSIE M. Mask, The.
HEINRICH VON MORUNGEN. Dream and Image.
Song: "Hast thou seen."
Two Remember Dawn.
HEINRICH VON RUGGE. He That Loves a Rosy Cheek.
HELBURN, THERESA. Mother.
Youth.
"HELEN." Another Cynical Variation.
HELEN, SISTER MARY. Identity.
HELLER, BINEM. Pesach Has Come to the Ghetto Again.
HELLINGS, PETER. Fairytales.
From Distant Lands.
Study; for Ezra Pound.
Swansea Market.
Synthesis, above Swansea.
HELLMAN, G. T. Variation on a Theme.
HELLMAN, GEOFFREY. Dynastic Tiff.
HELLMAN, GEORGE SIDNEY. Coleridge.
Hudson, The.
In a China Shop.
Sonnet: To the Hudson.
HELMER, CHARLES D. Battle of Oriskany.
HELMORE, THOMAS. Christmas Carol: "Christ was born on Christmas day," *at.*
HELTBERG, GRETHE. Happiness.
HELTON, ROY ADDISON. Glimpses.
In Passing.
Little More West.
Lonesome Water.
Miracles.
Old Christmas.
Old Christmas Morning.
Song of Dark Waters, The.
Street Car Symphony, A.
HEMANS, FELICIA DOROTHEA (Browne).
Bernardo del Carpio.
Birds of Passage, The.
Casabianca.
Child's First Grief, The.
Cid's Rising, The.
Cliffs of Dover, The.
Come to Me, Gentle Sleep.
Country Life, *tr.*
Death-Hymn, A. *Fr.* The Siege of Valencia.
Dirge: "Calm on the bosom of thy God."
Dirge, A: "Rest on your battlefields."
England's Dead.
Evening Song of the Weary.
Fairies' Recall.
Fairy Song.
First Grief, The.
Flight of the Spirit.
Foliage.
Graves of a Household, The.
He Never Smiled Again.
Homes of England, The.
Hour of Death, The.
Hymn for Christmas.
Landing of the Pilgrim Fathers.
Meetings of the Ships, The.
Mignon's Song, *tr.* *Fr.* Wilhelm Meister.
Palm Tree, The.
Pilgrim Fathers, The.
Prayer, A: "Father in Heaven! from whom the simplest flower."
Rome in Her Ruins, *tr.*
Sabbath Sonnet.
Siege of Valencia, The, *sel.*
Stately homes of England, The!
To My Mother.
Treasures of the Deep, The.
Voice of Spring, The.
Water-Lilies.
Where Is the Sea?
HEMENWAY, ABBY MARIA ("Marie Josephine"). Annunciation Night. *Fr.* Mary of Nazareth.
Mary of Nazareth, *sel.*
"HEMINGWAY, PERCY." *See* ADDLESHAW, PERCY.
HEMMER, JARL. Above the Dark.
HEMMINGER, GRAHAM LEE. This Smoking World.
Tobacco.
HEMPHREY, MALCOLM. Lanes in Summer.
HEMPSEED, ISABELL. Rufty and Tufty.
HEMSLEY, STUART. S.P.C.A. Sermon.
HENDERSON, ALICE CORBIN. *See* CORBIN, ALICE.
HENDERSON, DANIEL. Hard Rows to Hoe.
Homing Heart, The.
Hymn for a Household.
Lilies of the Field, The.
Nantucket Whalers.
Opium Clippers.
Poet, A.
Poet of Gardens, The.
Prayer for the Hunted.
Road to France, The.
St. Swithin.
Scarlet Thread, The.
Stranger, The.
Tea Trader, The.
HENDERSON, DOROTHY. Chinese Lullaby.
HENDERSON, E. H. March Wind, The.
HENDERSON, FLORENCE L. Garden That I Love, The.
HENDERSON, HAMISH. First Elegy.
HENDERSON, HAROLD GOULD. *For translations from Japanese, see* LiTW; OnPM; WoL.
HENDERSON, JOHN. Of Love and Time.
HENDERSON, ROSE. Abandoned Adobe, An.
Growing Old.
March Dreams.
Patio, The.
HENDERSON, RUTH EVELYN. My Spirit Will Grow Up.
HENDERSON, WILLIAM J. On a Hymn-Book.
HENDRICKSON, WILLIAM D. Spanish Cavalier, The.
HENDRY, HAMISH. Silver Bells.
Silver Road, The.
Upside-down World, The.
What the Weather Does.
HENDRY, J. F. Constant North, The.
Inverberg.
Orpheus.
Ship, The.
Tir-Nan-Og.
HENEY, THOMAS. Boundary Rider, The.
HENJO (the abbot Henjo). If the winds of heaven.
HENLEY, WILLIAM ERNEST. All in a Garden Green.
Allegro Maëstoso. *Fr.* London Voluntaries.
Alons au bois le may cueillir, *tr.*
And Lightly, like the Flowers, *tr.*
Apparition. *Fr.* In Hospital.
As Like the Woman as You Can.
Ave Caesar. *Fr.* In Hospital.
Ballade Made in the Hot Weather.
Ballade of a Toyokuni Color-Print.
Ballade of Dead Actors.
Ballade of Ladies' Names.
Ballade of Spring.
Ballade of Youth and Age.
Before. *Fr.* In Hospital.
Beside the idle summer sea.
Birds in April.
Blackbird, The.
Bowl of Roses, A.
Casualty. *Fr.* In Hospital.
Clinical. *Fr.* In Hospital.
Collige Rosas.
Culture in the Slums.
Desolate Shore, A.
Discharged. *Fr.* In Hospital.
Double Ballade of Life and Fate.
Easy Is the Triolet.
England, My England.
Enter Patient. *Fr.* In Hospital.
Epilogue: "These, to you now, O, more than ever now."
Epilogue to Rhymes and Rhythms.
Falmouth.
Fill a glass with golden wine.
Finale.
Fresh from His Fastnesses.
From a Window in Princes Street.
Full Sea Rolls and Thunders, The.
Good South-West on sea-worn wings, The. *Fr.* Hawthorn and Lavender.
Gulls in an Aëry Morrice.
Her Little Feet.
Home.
House-Surgeon. *Fr.* In Hospital.
I Am the Reaper.
I gave my heart to a woman.
I. M. Margaritae Sorori.
I. M.—R. T. Hamilton Bruce.
I Took a Hansom on To-Day.
I Was a King in Babylon.
In Fisherrow.
In Hospital, *sels.*
In Memoriam Margaritae Sororis.
In Memoriam R. T. Hamilton Bruce.
Inter Sodales.
Invictus.
Late Lark, A.
Late Lark Twitters, A.
London Voluntaries.
London Voluntaries, *sels.*
London Voluntary, A.
Look down, dear eyes, look down. *Fr.* Hawthorn and Lavender.
Madam Life.
Made in the Hot Weather.
Margaritae Sorori.
Midsummer Midnight Skies.
Music. *Fr.* In Hospital.
Night Cat, The. *Fr.* London Voluntaries.
Nocturne. *Fr.* In Hospital.
O, Falmouth Is a Fine Town.
O, Gather Me the Rose.
On the Way to Kew.
Operation. *Fr.* In Hospital.
Or Ever the Knightly Years Were Gone.
Orientale.
Out of the Night That Covers Me.
Out of Tune.
Over the Hills and Far Away.
Pastoral. *Fr.* In Hospital.
Pro Rege Nostro.
Prologue to "Rhymes and Rhythms."
R. T. Hamilton Bruce.
Rhymes and Rhythms, *sels.*
Romance. *Fr.* In Hospital.
Rondeau of Spring, *tr.*
Sands Are Alive with Sunshine, The

HENLEY, WILLIAM ERNEST (*continued*)
Scherzando. *Fr.* London Voluntaries.
Scrubber. *Fr.* In Hospital.
Since Those We Love and Those We Hate.
So Be My Passing.
So Let Me Hence.
Some starlit garden gray with dew.
Song of the Sword.
Space and Dread and the Dark.
Spirit of Wine, The.
Spring, my dear, The.
Staff-Nurse: New Style. *Fr.* In Hospital.
Staff-Nurse: Old Style. *Fr.* In Hospital.
Stanzas: "Where forlorn sunsets flare and fade."
Street Scene.
There's a Regret.
Thrush Sings, A.
To A. C.
To A. D.
To H. B. M. W.
To James McNeill Whistler.
To K. de M.
To My Mother.
To R. L. S.
To Robert Louis Stevenson.
To W. A.
Trees and the menace of night. *Fr.* Rhymes and Rhythms.
Triolet, The: "Easy is the triolet."
Vigil. *Fr.* In Hospital.
Villanelle.
Villon's Good-Night.
Villon's Straight Tip to All Cross Coves.
Visitor. *Fr.* In Hospital.
Waiting. *Fr.* In Hospital.
Wan sun westers, faint and slow, The.
Ways of Death, The.
We'll Go No More a-Roving.
West a glimmering lake of light, The.
What have I done for you?
What Is to Come.
When You Are Old.
Where Forlorn Sunsets Flare and Fade.
While the West Is Paling.
Why, my heart, do we love her so?
Wind on the Wold, The.
Wind-Fiend, The. *Fr.* London Voluntaries.
With Strawberries.
Your heart has trembled to my tongue.
HENLY, ANTHONY. Song: "No, no, no, no, resistance is but vain."
HENNELL, THOMAS. Mermaiden, A.
Queen Anne's Musicians.
Shepherd and Shepherdess.
HENNEQUIN, EMILE. Prose Poem: Irremediable, The.
Prose Poem: Words.
HENNESSY, DOYLE. And Left Me Stranded on a Hush.
HENNESSY, ROLAND BURKE. Lament of the Players.
HENRY VIII, KING OF ENGLAND. Alas! What Shall I Do for Love?
As the Holly Groweth Green.
Good Company.
Green Groweth the Holly.
Holly, The.
Pastime with Good Company.
To His Lady.
Whereto Should I Express.
Whoso That Will.
HENRY, NAT. Poet.
"HENRY, O." (William Sydney Porter). Options.
HENRY THE MINSTREL ("Blind Harry"). Description of Wallace, A. *Fr.* The Wallace.
Schir William Wallace. *See* Wallace, The.
Wallace, The, *sels.*
Wallace's Lament for the Graham. *Fr.* The Wallace.
War Summons the Lover. *Fr.* The Wallace.
HENRYSON, ROBERT. Abbey Walk, The.
Assembly of the Gods, The. *Fr.* The Testament of Cresseid.
Bludy Serk, The.
Cresseid's Lament. *Fr.* The Testament of Cresseid.
Cressida's Leprosy. *Fr.* The Testament of Cresseid.
Garment of Good Ladies, The.
Praise of Age, The.
Prologue: "Ane doolie, season to ane careful dyte." *Fr.* The Testament of Cresseid.
Robin and Makin.
Taill of the Uponlandis Mous and the Burges Mous, The.
Testament of Cresseid, The, *sels.*
To Our Lady.
HENSCHKE, ALFRED. *See* "KLABUND."
HENSLEY, LEWIS. Thy Kingdom Come, O God!
HENSLEY, SOPHIA ALMON. Because of You.
HENSON, PAULINE. On the Edge of the Copper Pit.
HENZE, HELEN ROWE. Etruscan Warrior's Head.
HEPBURN, ELIZABETH NEWPORT. Machines—or Men.
HEPBURN, MARY F. February Twelfth.
HEPBURN, THOMAS NICOLL. *See* "SETOUN, GABRIEL."
HEPPENSTALL, RAYNER. Actaeon.
Consolation in July.
Fleur de Lys.
Hagiograph.
St. Stephen's Word.
Spring Song.
Tammuz.
HERBERT, SIR ALAN PATRICK. At the Theater.
Bacon and Eggs.
Barnacle, The.
Bowline, The.
Centipede, The.
Chameleon, The.
Coals of Fire.
Come to Britain; a Humble Contribution to the Movement.
Cupid's Darts.
Farmer, The.
Finale. *Fr.* Perseverance; or, Half a Coronet.
Green Estaminet, The.
Hattage.
He Didn't Oughter.
I Can't Think What He Sees in Her.
I've Got the Giggles Today.
Laughing Ann.
Perseverance; or, Half a Coronet, *sel.*
Queen in Parliament, 1941, The.
Racing-Man, The.
Recipe. *Fr.* Two Gentlemen of Soho.
Save the Tiger!
Spider, The.
Stop, Science—Stop!
To a Junior Waiter.
Tomato Juice.
'Twas at the Pictures, Child, We Met.
Two Gentlemen of Soho, *sel.*
HERBERT, ALICE. Lullaby: "Sleep soft and long, no morn is worth the waking."
HERBERT, E. Balloon Man, The.
HERBERT, EDWARD. *See* HERBERT OF CHERBURY, EDWARD HERBERT, 1ST BARON.
HERBERT, GEORGE. Aaron.
Affliction.
Agonie, The.
Altar, The.
Antiphon: "Let all the world in every [*or* ev'ry] corner sing."
Artillery [*or* Artillerie].
Assurance.
Avarice.
Be Useful.
Bitter-sweet.
British Church, The.
Call, The.
Christmas.
Church-Floor, The.
Church Monuments.
Church-Music.
Church Porch, The, *sels.*
Church Windows, The.
Clasping of Hands.
Collar, The.
Confession.
Conscience.
Constancy.
Courage. *Fr.* The Church Porch.
Dare to Be True. *Fr.* The Church Porch.
Death.
Decay.
Dedication, The: "Lord, my first-fruits present themselves to thee."
Denial.
Dialogue.
Dialogue Anthem, A.
Discipline.
Doom's-Day.
Dullness.
Dum Librata Suis Haeret Radicibus Ilex.
Easter.
Easter, *sel.*
Easter Wings.
Elixir, The.
Employment ("He that is weary, let him sit").
Employment ("If as a flower doth spread and die").
Even-Song.
Flower, The.
Forerunners, The.
Frailty.
Gifts of God, The.
Glance, The.
Grace.
H. Baptisme.
Heaven.
Hoc, Genitrix, Scriptum Proles Tibi Sedula Mittit.
Holy Baptism.
Hope.
Horti, Deliciae Dominae, Marcescite Tandem.
I got me flowers to straw thy way.
I made a posie, while the day ran by.
Iesu [*or* Jesu].
Immortal Love, Author of This Great Frame.
In Natales et Pascha Concurrentes.
Invitation, The.
Jordan ("When first my lines of heav'nly joys made mention").
Jordan ("Who says that fictions only and false hair").
Judge Not the Preacher for He Is Thy Judge.
Life.
Longing.
Longing, *sel.*
Love ("Immortal Love, author of this great frame").
Love ("Love bade me welcome: yet my soul drew back").
Man.
Man's Medley.
Matins [*or* Mattens].
Maxims. *Fr.* The Church Porch.
Memento Mori.
Miserie.
Money, thou bane of bliss and source of woe.
Mortification.
My God, where is that ancient heat towards thee.
Nature.
Odour, The.
On Worship. *Fr.* The Church Porch.
Our Prayer.
Paradise.
Parodie, A.
Peace.
Pearl, The.
Pilgrimage, The.
Posy, The.
Praise.
Prayer: "Of what an easie quick accesse."
Prayer: "Prayer the church's banquet, angels' age."
Pulley, The.
Quidditie, The.
Quip, The.
Redemption.
Repentance.
Resolve, The.

Resurrection, or Easter-Day, The.
Rose, The.
Sacrifice, The.
Said I Not So?
Second Thanksgiving, or the Reprisal, The.
Sighs and Grones.
Sin.
Sins' Round.
Star, The.
Sunday.
Sweet day, so cool, so calm, so bright.
Temper, The.
Thou whose sweet youth and early hopes enhance. *Fr.* The Church Porch.
Throw away thy rod.
Time.
To All Angels and Saints.
To His Mother.
True Hymn, A.
Unkindness.
Vanity [*or* Vanitie].
Virtue [*or* Vertue].
Virtue Immortal.
Whitsunday.
Who can scape his bow?
Who would have thought my shrivelled heart.
Windows, The.
World, The.
HERBERT, HENRY WILLIAM. Come Back.
HERBERT, MARY, COUNTESS OF PEMBROKE. *See* PEMBROKE, MARY SIDNEY HERBERT, COUNTESS OF.
HERBERT, MOSS. Gentle Park, A.
HERBERT, WILLIAM, EARL OF PEMBROKE. *See* PEMBROKE, WILLIAM HERBERT, EARL OF.
HERBERT OF CHERBURY, EDWARD HERBERT, 1ST BARON. Another Sonnet to Black Itself.
Breaking from under That Thy Cloudy Veil.
Ditty in Imitation of the Spanish, A.
Echo to a Rock.
Elegy over a Tomb.
Epitaph on Sir Philip Sidney.
Innumerable Beauties.
Kissing.
La Gialletta Gallante; or, The Sunburn'd Exotique Beauty.
Madrigal: "Dear, when I did from you remove."
Madrigal: "How should I love my best?"
Now That the April of Your Youth.
Ode, An, upon a Question Moved, Whether Love Should Continue for Ever?
Ode, An, upon a Question Moved, Whether Love Should Continue for Ever, *sel.*
Of Black Beauty.
Platonic[k] Love.
Sonnet: "Innumerable Beauties, thou white haire."
Sonnet: "Thus ends my love, but this doth grieve me most."
Sonnet of Black Beauty.
Tears, Flow No More!
Thought, The.
To a Lady Who Did Sing Excellently.
To Her Eyes.
To Her Hair.
To His Watch, When He Could Not Sleep.
Upon Combing Her Hair.
HERBERTSON, AGNES GROZIER. Little Betty Blue.
Soldier, A.
There Is No Sanctuary for Brave Men.
There was a little goblin.
HERBIN, JOHN FREDERIC. Diver, The.
Haying.
HERDER, JOHANN GOTTFRIED VON. Esthonian Bridal Song.
Sir Olaf.
HEREDIA, JOSÉ MARIA DE. Antony and Cleopatra.
Centaurs' Flight.
Conquerors, The.
Death of the Eagle, The. *Fr.* Les Trophées.
Fire-Flowers.
Flute, The.
Laborer, The.
To a Triumpher.
Trophées, Les, *sel.*
HEREDIA, JOSÉ RAMÓN. My Poem to the Children Killed in the War in Spain.
HERFORD, BEATRICE. Old Man, The.
HERFORD, OLIVER. Ant, The.
Bashful Earthquake, The, *sel.*
Belated Violet, A.
Catfish, The.
Children, behold the Chimpanzee.
Child's Natural History.
Chimpanzee, The.
Christmas Legend, A.
Cloud, The.
Cow, The.
Dog, The (As Seen by the Cat).
Earth. *Fr.* The Bashful Earthquake.
Elf and the Dormouse, The.
Eve.
Fall of J. W. Beane, The.
Geese. *Fr.* Child's Natural History.
Godiva.
Hen, The.
Here Lies Bill.
Hippopotamus, The.
I Heard a Bird Sing.
Japanesque.
Kitten's Night Thoughts.
Kitten's Thought, A.
Laughing Willow, The.
Limerick: "There once was a sculptor called Phidias."
Limerick: "There once were some learned MD's."
Limerick: "There was a young lady of Twickenham."
Limerick: "There was a young man of Laconia."
Limerick: "There was a young man of the cape."
Limerick: "There was an old man of the Rhine."
Love Story, A.
Mark Twain; a Pipe Dream.
Metaphysics.
Milk Jug, The.
Missing Link, The.
Mrs. Seymour Fentolin.
Mon-goos, The. *Fr.* Child's Natural History.
Moon, The.
More Animals.
Music of the Future, The.
My Sense of Sight.
Our Boy.
Penguin, A.
Phyllis.
Poet's Proposal, The.
Proem: "If this little world tonight." *Fr.* The Bashful Earthquake.
Seal, A. *Fr.* Child's Natural History.
Silver Question, The.
Smile of the Goat, The.
Smile of the Walrus, The.
Snail's Dream, The.
Some Geese.
Song: "Gather kittens while you may."
Song, A: "Upon a time I had a heart."
Song of a Heart, A.
Stairs.
Telephone Girl's Prayer, The.
Thanksgiving Fable, A.
Untutored Giraffe, The.
War Relief.
Why Ye Blossome Cometh before Ye Leafe.
Women of the Better Class, The.
Yak, The. *Fr.* Child's Natural History.
HERFORD, WILL. That God Made.
HERIBERT, WILLIAM. "Behold Thy Mother and Thy Brother."
HERLOSSOHN, CARL. When the Swallows Homeward Fly.
"HERMES, PAUL." *See* THAYER, WILLIAM ROSCOE.
HERMOCLES. Demetrius Enters Athens.
Processional for Demetrius Poliorcetes.
HERMOCREON. Water-Nymphs.
HERNAES, GUNNAR. Trumpet and Flute.
HERNÁNDEZ, JOSÉ. Departure of Martin Fierro, The.
HERNÁNDEZ, MIGUEL. Winds of the People.
HERNDON, JOHN G. Fairies, The.
Friendly People.
HERODAS. Gentlemen of the jury, 'tis not birth.
Hark, girl! There's some one knocking at the door.
Look how the girl up there.
Low Trade, A.
HERRERA, FERNANDO DE. Disembodied Spirit, The.
Ideal Beauty.
Ode on the Death of Don Sebastian.
Ode to Sleep.
Sonnet: "Hard is yon rock, around whose head."
Sonnet: "Red sun, that with thy taper shining bright."
Sonnet: "Too soon the winter cold and heavy frost."
HERRERA S., DEMETRIO. Training.
HERRERA Y REISSIG, JULIO. Parish Church, The.
HERRICK, ROBERT. Age Not to Be Rejected.
Alms, *sel.*
Amber Bead, The.
Anacreontic.
Another Charm.
Another Grace for a Child ("Here a little child I stand").
Another Grace for a Child ("What God gives, and what we take").
Apparition of His Mistress Calling Him to Elysium, The.
Apron of Flowers, The.
Argument of His Book, The.
Argument of This Book, The.
Art above Nature; to Julia.
As in Silks My Julia Goes.
Bacchanalian Verse, A.
Bad Season Makes the Poet Sad, The.
Bag of the Bee, The.
Beggar, to Mab the Fairy Queen, The.
Bell-Man, The.
Bracelet to Julia, The.
Ceremonies for Candlemas [*or* Christmas] Day, The ("Kindle the Christmas brand").
Ceremonies for Candlemas[s] Eve ("Down with the rosemary and bays").
Ceremonies for Christmas [*or* Christmasse] ("Come bring with a noise").
Ceremony for Candlemas Day, A ("Down with the rosemary and so").
Charm, A ("If ye fear to be affrighted").
Charm, A ("In the morning when you rise").
Charm, or an Allay for Love, A ("If so be a toad be laid").
Cheat of Cupid, The; or, The Ungentle Guest.
Cherry-Pit.
Cherry [*or* Cherrie]-ripe.
Child's Grace, A.
Child's Present to His Child-Saviour.
Chop-Cherry.
Christ and We.
Christian Militant, The.
Christmas Carol, A: "What sweeter music can we bring."
Christmas Carol, A: "What sweeter music can we bring," *sel.*
Christmas Carol, Sung to the King in the Presence at White-Hall, A.
Christmas Eve.
Christmas Eve—Another Ceremony.
Christmas Eve—Another to the Maids.
Christ's Incarnation.
Clothes Do but Cheat and Cozen Us.
Cock-Crow.
Come Bring with a Noise.
Comfort to a Youth That Had Lost His Love.
Comming of Good Luck, The.
Conjuration, to Electra, A.
Corinna's Going a-Maying.
Corinna's Going a-Maying, *sel.*
Counsel to Girls.

HERRICK, ROBERT (*continued*)
Country Life, A; to His Brother, M. Tho: Herrick.
Cupid, as he lay among, *tr.*
Daffodils.
Dean-bourn, a Rude River in Devon, by Which Sometimes He Lived.
Death Ends All Woe.
Definition of Beauty, The.
Delight in Disorder.
Departure of the Good Daemon, The.
Dirge of Jephthah's Daughter, The; Sung by the Virgins.
Dirge upon the Death of the Right Valiant Lord, Bernard Stuart, A.
Discontents in Devon.
Divination by a Daffodil.
Dreams.
End-Piece for His Book, An.
Epitaph on a Virgin.
Epitaph upon a Child, An.
Epitaph upon a Child That Died.
Epitaph upon a Virgin.
Eternity.
Fair Days; or, Dawns Deceitful, *sel.*
Fairies, The.
Fame Makes Us Forward.
Five Wines.
Four Best Things, The, *tr.*
Four Sweet Months, The.
Funeral Rites of the Rose, The.
Gather Ye Rose-Buds.
Go, Pretty Child.
Going a-Maying.
Good Christians.
Good Friday; Rex Tragicus, or Christ Going to His Cross.
Good Men Afflicted Most.
Good-Night, or Blessing, The.
Grace, A.
Grace before Meat.
Grace for a Child.
Grace for Children.
Hag, The.
Here a little child I stand.
Herrick's Cavalier.
Hesperides ("I sing of brooks, of blossoms, birds and bowers").
His Answer to a Question.
His Charge to Julia at His Death.
His Content in the Country.
His Creed.
His Desire.
His Ejaculation to God.
His Farewell to Sack.
His Grange, or Private Wealth.
His Lachrimae or Mirth, Turn'd [*or* Turned] to Mourning.
His Litany, to the Holy Spirit.
His Parting with Mrs. Dorothy Kennedy, *sel.*
His Poetry [*or* Poetrie] His Pillar.
His Prayer for Absolution.
His Prayer to Ben Jonson.
His Request to Julia.
His Return to London.
His Sailing from Julia.
His Saviour's Words Going to the Cross.
His Tears to Thamesis.
His Theme.
His Winding Sheet.
His Wish to God.
Hock-Cart, The, or Harvest Home.
Hock-Cart, The, or Harvest Home, *sel.*
Holy Spirit, The.
How Marigolds Came Yellow.
How Roses Came Red.
How the Wallflower Came First and Why So Called.
How Violets Came Blue.
Humility.
I Call and I Call.
I dare not ask a kiss.
I sing of Brooks, of Blossomes, Birds, and Bowers.
In the Hour of My Distress.
Instead of Neat Inclosures. *Fr.* An Ode of the Birth of Our Saviour.
Invitation, The.
Julia.
July; the Succession of the Four Sweet Months.
Kings and Tyrants.
Kiss, The.
Kissing and Bussing.
Lady Dying in Childbed, A.
Lily [*or* Lilly] in a Crystal [*or* Christal], The.
Litany to the Holy Spirit.
Littles. *Fr.* A Ternary of Littles.
Love.
Lovers How They Come and Part.
Lyrick for Legacies.
Mad Maid's Song, The.
Meddow Verse, The; or, Anniversary to Mistris Bridget Lowman.
Meditation for His Mistress, A.
Mercy and Love.
Mirth.
Neutrality Loathsome.
New Charon, The.
New-Yeeres Gift, The, or Circumcisions Song, Sung to the King in the Presence at White Hall.
Night Piece, to Julia, The.
No Coming to God without Christ.
No Fault in Women.
No, no, the utmost share.
Not Every Day Fit for Verse.
Not to Love.
Nuptiall Song, or Epithalamie, on Sir Clipseby Crew and His Lady, A.
O Years!
Obedience.
Oberon's Feast.
Oberon's Feast, *sel.*
Ode for Ben Jonson, An.
Ode for Him [Ben Jonson], An.
Ode on the Birth of Our Saviour, An.
Ode on the Birth of Our Saviour, An, *sel.*
Ode to Ben Jonson.
Of Her Breath.
Of Love.
Old Wives Prayer, The.
Olive Branch, The.
On a Dark Road.
On Himself[e].
Only a little more.
Parting Verse, the Feast There Ended, The.
Pillar of Fame, The.
Poet Loves a Mistress, but Not to Marry, The.
Poetry of Dress, The.
Prayer to Ben Jonson.
Prayers Must Have Poise.
Primrose, The.
Rock of Rubies, The.
Rod, The.
Rosary [*or* Rosarie], The.
Rubies and Pearls.
Science in God.
Sins Loathed, and Yet Loved.
Soft Musick.
Star-Song, The; a Carol to the King.
Succession of the Four Sweet Months, The.
Sweet, Be Not Proud.
Sweet Disorder [in the Dress], A.
Sweetness in Sacrifice.
Temptation.
Ternary [*or* Ternarie] of Littles, A, upon a Pipkin of Jelly [*or* Jellie] Sent to a Lady.
Ternary of Littles, A, upon a Pipkin of Jelly Sent to a Lady, A, *sels.*
Thankful Heart, A.
Thanksgiving.
Thanksgiving to God for His House, A.
Thanksgiving to God for His House, A, *sel.*
That morn which saw me made a bride, *tr.*
There's pain in parting, and a kind of hell.
This Cross-Tree Here.
Though clock.
Time.
'Tis Hard to Find God.
To a Child.
To a Gentlewoman Objecting to Him His Gray Hairs.
To Aenone.
To Anthea ("Bid me to live").
To Anthea ("If deare Anthea").
To Anthea ("Now is the time").
To Anthea, Who May Command Him Anything.
To Ben Jonson.
To Blossoms.
To Cherry-Blossomes.
To Daffodils [*or* Daffadills].
To Daisies, Not to Shut So Soon.
To Death.
To Dianeme.
To Dianeme, Again.
To Electra.
To Enjoy the Time.
To Finde God.
To Fortune.
To Gather Flowers Sappha Went.
To God.
To God, on His Sickness.
To His Book, *tr.*
To His Book's End.
To His Conscience.
To His Dear God.
To His Dying Brother, Master William Herrick.
To His Ever-loving God.
To His Honoured Kinsman, Sir William Soame.
To His Lovely Mistresses.
To His Maid Prew.
To His Mistress.
To His Mistress Objecting to Him neither Toying or Talking.
To His Muse.
To His Saviour, a Child; a Present, by a Child.
To His Tomb-Maker.
To Keep a True Lent.
To Larr.
To Laurels.
To Live Merrily and to Trust to Good Verses.
To Live Merrily, and to Trust to Good Verses, *sel.*
To M. Henry Lawes, the Excellent Composer, of His Lyrics.
To Meadows [*or* Meddowes].
To Meadows, *sel.*
To Music [*or* Musique], to Becalm His Fever.
To Music, to Becalm His Fever, *sel.*
To Oenone.
To Perilla.
To Phillis.
To Phyllis [to Love and Live with Him].
To Primroses Fill'd with Morning-Dew.
To Robin Redbreast.
To the Lark.
To the Most Fair and Lovely Mistress, Anne Soame, Now Lady Abdie.
To the Most Learned, Wise, and Arch-Antiquary, M. John Selden.
To the Reverend Shade of His Religious Father.
To the Rose, a Song.
To the Sour Reader.
To the Virgins to Make Much of Time.
To the Water Nymphs, Drinking at the Fountain.
To the Western Wind.
To the Willow-Tree.
To Violets.
To Violets, *sel.*
To Virgins.
Tom o' Bedlam.
True Lent, A.
Upon a Child.
Upon a Child That Died.
Upon a Maid.
Upon a Maid That Died the Day She Was Married.
Upon a Virgin Kissing a Rose.
Upon Ben Jonson.
Upon Her Feet.
Upon Himself.
Upon His Departure Hence.
Upon His Sister in Law.
Upon Julia Weeping.
Upon Julia's Clothes.
Upon Julia's Hair[e] Fill'd [*or* Filled] with Dew.
Upon Julia's Recovery.
Upon Julia's Voice.

Upon Kings.
Upon Love.
Upon M. Ben Jonson, Epigram.
Upon Master Fletchers Incomparable Players.
Upon Mrs. Eliz. Wheeler, under the Name of Amarillis.
Upon Mistress Susanna Southwell, Her Feet.
Upon Pagget.
Upon Prue [*or* Prew] His Maid.
Upon Prudence Baldwin Her Sickness.
Upon Sibilla.
Upon the Loss of His Mistresses.
Upon the Nipples of Julia's Breast.
Upon Time.
Violets.
Virgin Mary, The.
Vision to Electra, The.
Wake, The.
Wassail, The.
Weeping Cherry, The.
Welcome to Sack, The.
What Kind of Mistress He Would Have.
What Love Is.
What Sweeter Music.
When He Would Have His Verses Read.
Whenas in Silks My Julia Goes.
White Island, The; or, Place of the Blest.
White though ye be, yet, lilies, know.
Why I tie about thy wrist.
Willow Garland, The.
Witch, The.
Wounded Cupid, The.
"Ye Cannot Serve God and Mammon."
You Say I Love Not.
HERRIMAN, DOROTHY CHOATE. Roses.
Spruce Tree, The.
Torii.
Waiting.
Welcome to Bliss Carman, A.
HERRING, ROBERT. Chelsea Crypt.
No Nice Girl's Song.
Poem of Quietness, *sels.*
Siege Conditions.
HERSCHBERGER, RUTH. Coup d'Etat.
In Panelled Rooms.
Love-grip, first excited by the eye, The.
Lumberyard, The.
Nature Poem.
HERSCHELL, WILLIAM. Kid Has Gone to the Colors, The.
Service Flag, The.
Soldier of the Silences, The.
HERSEY, HAROLD. Lay of the Last Frontier.
HERSHENSON, MIRIAM. Love Poem—1940.
HERVEY, JOHN RUSSELL. Carnival.
Hydro Works.
John Donne's Defiance.
Man of Crete.
Man Who Wanted to Be a Seagull, The.
Neighbour.
Sonnet of Departure.
Threnos.
Two Old Men Look at the Sea.
HERVEY, THOMAS KIBBLE. Cleopatra Embarking on the Cydnus.
Devil at Home, The. *Fr.* The Devil's Progress.
Devil's Progress, The, *sel.*
Grotto of Egeria, The.
I Think on Thee.
Love.
HERWEGH, GEORG. Dare to Be Free.
HESELTINE, NIGEL. At First.
Barter Our Northern Darkness.
Denbigh Eisteddfod.
Epithalamion.
Four-cornered Tower, The; Llanybri.
Gorse.
Hero of His Village.
Microcosmos.
Wanderer's Night-Song.
HESIOD. Ages of Man, The.
Anatomy o Winter, The. *Fr.* Works and Days.
Autumn. *Fr.* Works and Days.
Autumn Ploughing. *Fr.* Works and Days.
Battle-Piece. *Fr.* Shield of Heracles.
Birth of the Muses. *Fr.* Theogony.
Cicada Days. *Fr.* Works and Days.
Combat of Heracles and Cycnus. *Fr.* Shield of Heracles.
Coming of Aphrodite, The. *Fr.* Theogony.
Crane's Flight, The. *Fr.* Works and Days.
Creation of Pandora. *Fr.* Works and Days.
Daemones. *Fr.* Works and Days.
Doom of the Titans, The. *Fr.* Theogony.
Eoiae, *sels.*
Fall of Man and the Early Ages of the Earth, The. *Fr.* Works and Days.
Farmer's Year, The. *Fr.* Works and Days.
Five Ages, The. *Fr.* Works and Days.
Gift of the Muses. *Fr.* Theogony.
Giving and Taking. *Fr.* Works and Days.
Golden Mean of Thrift. *Fr.* Works and Days.
Good Days and Bad. *Fr.* Works and Days.
Length of Life. *Fr.* Precepts of Chiron.
Light-footed Iphiclus. *Fr.* Eoiae.
Marriage. *Fr.* Works and Days.
Might and Right. *Fr.* Works and Days.
Mountains. *Fr.* Theogony.
Muses' Gift, The. *Fr.* Theogony.
Neighbours and Kinsfolk. *Fr.* Works and Days.
Pandora. *Fr.* Works and Days.
Plain Living. *Fr.* Works and Days.
Poetry. *Fr.* Theogony.
Precepts of Chiron, *sel.*
Quoth a Hawk to a Nightingale. *Fr.* Works and Days.
Religion. *Fr.* Theogony.
Sailing Weather. *Fr.* Works and Days.
Shame. *Fr.* Works and Days.
Shield of Heracles, *sels.*
Sign of the Pleiades, The. *Fr.* Works and Days.
Snail's Moving Day, The. *Fr.* Works and Days.
Spending and Sparing. *Fr.* Works and Days.
Spring Called Parthenius, The.
Spring Ploughing. *Fr.* Works and Days.
Summer. *Fr.* Works and Days.
Theogony, *sels.*
Visitation, A. *Fr.* Eoiae.
When the Crane Flies South. *Fr.* Works and Days.
When the Snail Climbs. *Fr.* Works and Days.
Wholesome Strife. *Fr.* Works and Days.
Winter. *Fr.* Works and Days.
Works and Days, *sels.*
Worldly Wisdom. *Fr.* Works and Days.
Zeus and the Titans. *Fr.* Theogony.
HESKETH, PHOEBE. Fox, The.
HESS, M. WHITCOMB. First Grandchild.
Mirror, The.
Vision of St. Bernard, The.
HESSE, HERMANN. Alone.
Books.
Flower, Tree, and Bird.
Midsummer.
Night.
Spring Day.
Spring Song.
There Are Times.
Transition.
Youth's Flight.
HESSEY, VERA. Frog and the Bird, The.
HETHERINGTON, GEORGE. Charles at the Siege.
Palm House, Botanic Gardens.
Sonnet: "Now keep that long revolver at your side."
Sonnet: "Since I keep only what I give away."
HEWISON, R. J. P. Genius.
HEWITT, ANDREW. Grave Gentleman, The.
One.
Pigeons and Snow.
Shadow of Smoke.
Town Child.
True.
Yard Man.
HEWITT, ETHEL M. Wild Wishes.
HEWITT, JOHN. First Cornerake.
Frost.
Glens, The.
Leaf.
Little Lough, The.
Load.
Lyric: "Let but a thrush begin."
Once Alien Here.
Poem in May.
Swathe Uncut, The.
HEWITT, KATHLEEN. Silhouette.
HEWITT, LUISA. Plans.
Secrets.
HEWITT, MARY ELIZABETH. *See* STEBBINS, MARY ELIZABETH MOORE.
HEWLETT, MAURICE. Achilles' Reply to the Embassy, *tr. Fr.* The Iliad.
Dirge: "How should my lord come home to his lands?"
Flos Virginum.
Hektor and Andromache, *tr. Fr.* The Iliad.
Hodge in the Strife. *Fr.* The Song of the Plow.
Iliad, The, *sels., tr.*
London. *Fr.* The Song of the Plow.
Man on the Hill, The. *Fr.* The Song of the Plow.
Night-Errantry.
1914 Autumn and Winter. *Fr.* The Song of the Plow.
Old Thought, An. *Fr.* The Song of the Plow.
Poll Tax (1378). *Fr.* The Song of the Plow.
Rosa Nascosa.
Sarpedon and Glaucus, *tr. Fr.* The Iliad.
Song of the Plow, The, *sels.*
Thersites, *tr. Fr.* The Iliad.
When She a Maiden Slim.
HEY, F. Boy and the Squirrel, The.
Cat in the Snow, The.
Caw, Caw.
Fox and Goose.
Kittens, The.
Pug-Dog and Spitz.
Two Dogs.
HEYDUK, ADOLF. Three Fields.
HEYM, GEORG. Famine.
HEYRICK, THOMAS. On a Sunbeam.
On the Death of a Monkey.
HEYWARD, DUBOSE. Black Christmas.
Blockader, The.
Dusk.
Dusk in the Low Country.
Envoy: "So, at the last, I think that we must follow."
Epitaph for [*or* of] a Poet.
Equinox, The.
Evening in the Great Smokies.
Gamesters All.
I Stumbled upon Happiness.
Mountain Girl, The.
Mountain Woman, The.
Porgy, Maria, and Bess.
Prodigal.
Yoke of Steers, A.
Your Gifts.
HEYWARD, JANIE SCREVEN. Autumn Leaves.
Spirit's Grace, The.
HEYWOOD, JASPER. Easter Day.
If thou in surety safe wilt sit.
Look or You Leap.
Lookers-on, The.
Who Minds to Bring His Ship to Happy Shore.
HEYWOOD, JOHN. All a green willow, willow, willow.
Buying a Pig.
Cardinal Fisher.

HEYWOOD, JOHN *(continued)*
Cock and the Hen, The.
Description of a Most Noble Lady, A.
Dialogue Containing the Number of the Effectual Proverbs in the English Tongue, A, *sels.*
English Schoolboy, The. *Fr.* The Play of the Weather.
Epigram on This Book of Epigrams, An.
Fool's Tongue, A.
Four P's, The, *sels.*
Gloria Patri, The.
Green Willow Is My Garland, A.
How God Will Not Do for Us.
If Love, for Love of Long Time Had.
Jack and His Father.
Looking and Leaping.
Maister and the Man, The.
Of a Cat's Look.
Of a Husband Hang'd.
Of a Sheep's Eye.
Of Birds and Birders.
Of Common Meddlers.
Of Difference between Wise Men and Fools.
Of Enough and a Feast.
Of Heywood.
Of Holding of a Nose.
Of Late and Never.
Of Loving a Dog.
Of Nothing and Althing.
Of One Hanged.
Of Rebellion.
Of Taking Things Wrong.
Of the Senses.
On the Princess Mary.
One Driveth Out Another.
Palmer, The. *Fr.* The Four P's.
Play of the Weather, The, *sels.*
Portrait, The.
Praise of His Lady, A.
Spider and the Fly, The, *sel.*
Tyburn and Westminster.
Wedding and Hanging.
HEYWOOD, TERENCE. By an Ant-Heap.
Cactus.
Flamingo's Egg, A.
Grisaille.
Mantis.
Notes for a Bestiary.
HEYWOOD, THOMAS. Angry Kynges, The, *tr. Fr.* Hercules Furens.
Apology for Actors, An, *sel.*
Author to His Booke, The. *Fr.* An Apology for Actors.
Challenge for Beauty, A, *sel.*
Cherubim, The, *sel.*
Epigram upon His Majestie's Great Ship (the *Sovereign of the Seas*) Lying in the Docks at Woolwich, An.
Fair Maid of the Exchange, The, *sel., at.*
Go, Pretty Birds! *at. Fr.* The Fair Maid of the Exchange.
Golden Age, The, *sel.*
Good Morrow. *Fr.* The Rape of Lucrece.
Hence with Passion, Sighs and Tears. *Fr.* A Maidenhead Well Lost.
Hercules Furens, *sel., tr.*
Hierarchie of the Blessed Angels, *sel.*
Hymn to Diana. *Fr.* The Golden Age.
Maidenhead Well Lost, A, *sel.*
Matin Song. *Fr.* The Rape of Lucrece.
Message, The, *at. Fr.* The Fair Maid of the Exchange.
Morning. *Fr.* The Rape of Lucrece.
Pack, Clouds, Away. *Fr.* The Rape of Lucrece.
Passing Bell, The. *Fr.* The Rape of Lucrece.
Praise of Ceres. *Fr.* The Silver Age.
Rape of Lucrece, The, *sels.*
Search for God, The. *Fr.* Hierarchie of the Blessed Angels.
Silver Age, The, *sel.*
Song: "Pack clouds away, and welcome day." *Fr.* The Rape of Lucrece.
Valerius on Women. *Fr.* The Rape of Lucrece.
Waking Song. *Fr.* The Rape of Lucrece.
Welcome to Day. *Fr.* The Rape of Lucrece.
Ye Little Birds That Sit and Sing, *at. Fr.* The Fair Maid of the Exchange.
Ye Pretty Wantons, Warble, *at. Fr.* The Fair Maid of the Exchange.
HICKEY, AGNES MACCARTHY. Old Essex Door.
Shakespeare.
HICKEY, EMILY HENRIETTA. Beloved, It Is Morn.
Sea Story, A.
Song: "Belovèd, it is morn!"
HICKOK, ELIZA M. Prayer: "I know not by what methods rare."
This I Know.
HICKOX, CHAUNCEY. Under the Red Cross.
HICKS, GEORGE A. Mormon Immigrant Song, A, *at.*
HICKS, MABEL. Crosses.
HICKS, WILLIAM. Of His Mistress Grown Old.
HICKSON, WILLIAM EDWARD. Try, Try Again, *at.*
HICKSON, WILLIAM EDWARD, *and* SIEGFRIED AUGUST MAHLMANN. *See* MAHLMANN, SIEGFRIED AUGUST, *and* WILLIAM EDWARD HICKSON.
HICKY, DANIEL WHITEHEAD. Escape.
Machines.
No Friend like Music.
Polo Player.
Runaway, The.
Say That He Loved Old Ships.
Ship for Singapore, A.
Small Song.
To an Aviator.
When a Man Turns Homeward.
Who Pilots Ships.
Wisdom.
HIEBERT, PAUL GERHARDT. Farmer and the Farmer's Wife, The.
HIERS, LOIS SMITH. On Laying Up Treasure.
HIGGINS, FREDERICK ROBERT. Ballad of O'Bruadir, The.
Boyne Walk, The.
Cradle Song: "Out in the dark something complains."
Father and Son.
Gallows Tree, The.
Hermits.
Little Clan, The.
Old Air, An.
Old Jockey, The.
Padraic O'Conaire, Gaelic Storyteller.
Scribe, The.
Song for the Clatter-Bones.
Spanish Man, The.
To My Blackthorn Stick.
Unmarried Mother Sings, An.
HIGGINS, JOHN. Books.
HIGGINSON, ANNE. *See* SPICER, ANNE HIGGINSON.
HIGGINSON, ELLA. Beggars.
Beside the Sea.
Childless Mother's Lullaby, The.
Cradle-Song of the Fisherman's Wife.
Four-Leaf Clover.
Going Blind.
Grand Ronde Valley, The.
Helping Hand, A.
Lamp in the West, The.
Month of Falling Stars, The.
Moonrise in the Rockies.
Sweet, Low Speech of the Rain, The.
HIGGINSON, MARY POTTER THACHER. Changelings.
Ghost-Flowers.
In the Dark.
Inheritance.
HIGGINSON, NESTA. *See* "O'NEILL, MOIRA."
HIGGINSON, THOMAS WENTWORTH. Decoration.
Ode to a Butterfly.
Since Cleopatra Died.
Snowing of the Pines.
"Such Stuff as Dreams Are Made Of."
Things I Miss, The.
To Duty.
Trumpeter, The.
HIGHAM, THOMAS FARRANT. *For translations from Greek, see* FaBoCh; GrL; LiTW; LoGBV; OxBG; WoL.
HIGHET, GILBERT. *For translations from Greek, see* OxBG; *from Latin, see* LaP.
HILALI. Flute, The.
HILARY OF ARLES, SAINT. Thou Bounteous Giver of the Light.
HILDEBERT OF LAVARDIN [*or* OF LE MANS]. Oratio ad Dominum.
Prayer to the Holy Trinity, *sel.*
Roman Elegy.
Seneca's Epitaph.
HILDEBRANDT, KAREN. Romance.
HILDRETH, CHARLES LOTIN. At the Mermaid Inn.
Duet.
Implora Pace.
To an Obscure Poet Who Lives on My Hearth.
HILDRETH, HAROLD M. Silent Places.
HILEY, F. C. W. Mike.
To a Persian Cat.
HILL, AARON. Pulling Down St. Martin's Church. *Fr.* To Clelia, on the Pulling Down St. Martin's Church.
Strong Hand, A.
To Clelia, on the Pulling Down St. Martin's Church, *sel.*
HILL, AGNES ASTON. Recompense.
HILL, BENJAMIN DIONYSIUS (Father Edmund). Mother Mary Xavier.
Our Lady's Death.
To St. Mary Magdalen.
HILL, CLYDE WALTON. Byron.
Dying Year, The.
Lincoln.
HILL, E. When Polly Buys a Hat.
HILL, FRANK ERNEST. Autumn, Forsake These Hills.
Clouds.
Diversity.
Earth and Air.
Earth Will Stay the Same, The.
Flyers, The.
Snow Forest.
Snow Water.
This Is the City Children Made.
Upper Air.
HILL, GEOFFREY. Asmodai.
Genesis.
Gideon at the Well.
God's Little Mountain.
In Memory of Jane Frazer.
Re-Birth of Venus, The.
Turtle Dove, The.
HILL, GEORGE. Fall of the Oak, The.
Good-Night.
Leila.
Love and Reason.
Mariner's Adieu, The.
Oak, The.
Song of the Elfin Steersman.
HILL, HYACINTHE. Old Emily.
HILL, LEONA AMES. Let Him Return.
HILL, LESLIE PINCKNEY. Christmas at Melrose.
My Charge.
Of Greatness in Teaching.
So Quietly.
Summer Magic.
Teacher, The.
Tuskegee.
HILL, MARION. Lovelilts.
HILL, MILDRED J. Valentine's Message, The.
When You Send a Valentine.
HILL, THEOPHILUS HUNTER. Anacreontic.
St. Valentine's Day.
HILL, THOMAS. Bobolink, The.
HILLE, PETER. Beauty.
Maiden, The.
HILLHOUSE, AUGUSTUS LUCAS. Forgiveness of Sins a Joy Unknown to Angels.
HILLHOUSE, JAMES ABRAHAM. Demon-Lover, The. *Fr.* Hadad.

Hadad, *sel.*
HILLS, ELIJAH CLARENCE. To Pikes Peak.
HILLYER, ROBERT SILLIMAN. Adoration of the Disk, *tr.*
As One Who Bears beneath His Neighbor's Roof.
Assassination, The.
Bats, The.
Book of the Dead, *sels., tr.*
Christmas Pastoral.
Curtains Draw across the Brain, The.
Elegy on a Dead Mermaid Washed Ashore at Plymouth Rock.
Epigram: "Bring hemlock, black as Cretan cheese."
Eppur Si Muove?
For Maister Geoffrey Chaucer.
From the Foothills.
General Galliéni.
In the Shadowy Whatnot Corner.
In Time of Mistrust, XIII.
Intermezzo.
Letter to a Teacher of English.
Letter to Robert Frost, A.
Lullaby: "Long canoe, The."
Mentis Trist.
Mirrors of All Ages, The.
Moo!
Night Piece.
Nocturne: "If the deep wood is haunted, it is I."
Pastoral: "So soft in the hemlock wood."
Plants Stand Silent Round Me, The, *tr.*
Ponder the Tone; the Broken Theme.
Prelude: "Ponder the tone; the broken theme."
Prothalamion, *sel.*
Relic, The.
So Ghostly Then the Girl Came In.
Sonnet: "Even as love grows more, I write the less." *Fr.* Sonnets.
Sonnet: "Golden spring redeems the withered year, The." *Fr.* Sonnets.
Sonnet: "He who in spring's rebirth has put his trust."
Sonnet: "I will fling wide the windows of my soul." *Fr.* Sonnets.
Sonnet: "Let all men see the ruins of the shrine." *Fr.* Sonnets.
Sonnet: "Over the waters but a single bough." *Fr.* Sonnets.
Sonnet: "Quickly and pleasantly the seasons blow." *Fr.* Sonnets.
Sonnets, *sels.*
Spiritism.
There Is a Charming Land, *tr.*
Thermopylae.
Thermopylae and Golgotha.
To a Scarlatti Passepied.
Untended Field, The.
Variations on a Theme.
HILLYER, WILLIAM HURD. Lineman, The.
My Master's Face.
Song of the Press, The.
HILTON, ALFARATA. Busy Person, A.
HILTON, ARTHUR CLEMENT. Heathen Pass-ee, The.
Limerick: "There was a young critic of King's."
Limerick: "There was a young genius of Queens'."
Limerick: "There was a young gourmand of John's."
Limerick: "There was a young man of Sid. Sussex."
Limerick: "There was an old Fellow of Trinity."
Octopus.
Vulture and the Husband-Man, The.
HILTON, JOHN. Fair Oriana, Beauty's Queen.
Madrigal: "My mistress frowns when she should play," *at.*
My mistress frowns when she should play, *at.*
HIMES, ISAAC N. Doctor's Life, The, *sel.*
HIMMELL, SOPHIE. In the Month of Green Fire.
Pain of Stone, The.
Though Your Words Be Messengers of Hate.
Unless I Learn to Walk Upright.
HIMSTEDT, EDITH. Robin on da Fence.
HINCKLEY, J. Ambition.
HINDLEY, CHARLES. Mother Shipton's Prophecies, *at.*
HINDS, SAMUEL. Baby Sleeps.
HINE, DARYL. After the Agony in the Garden.
HINES, HERBERT HENRY. Christmas Prayer, A.
HINES, NELLIE WOMACK. Home.
HINKSON, KATHARINE TYNAN. *See* TYNAN, KATHARINE.
HIOKI NO KO-OKIMA. On the shore of Nawa. *Fr.* Manyo Shu.
HIPPONAX. Economy.
Misogynist.
Pugilist.
Visit from Wealth, A.
HIROMI. Looking Up.
HIRSHBEIN, PERETZ. Captive.
I Shall Weep.
Stars Fade.
HIRST, HENRY BECK. Fringilla Melodia, The.
Funeral of Time, The.
HISAKI. Dirge, A: "Looking on the peaceful face."
HISHIYAMA, SHUZO. High Summer.
HISLOP, CODMAN. Carnival.
These Things Have I Loved.
HITOMARO (Kakinomoto no Hitomaro).
Bay of Tsunu, The.
Colored leaves, The.
For my sister's sake. *Fr.* Manyo Shu.
Gossip grows like weeds.
Hills of autumn drop, The.
I sit at home.
I waited for my/ Lover until I could hear, *at.*
In the Autumn mountains.
In the empty mountains.
In the ocean of the sky.
In the sea of ivy clothed Iwami.
Lines from an Elegy on the Death of His Wife.
Manyo Shu, *sels.*
May the men who are born. *Fr.* Manyo Shu.
May those who are born after me. *Fr.* Manyo Shu.
Moon's Ship, The.
Mountain Top, The.
My girl is waiting for me.
My Love Who Loves Me Not.
O boy cutting grass. *Fr.* Manyo Shu.
On His Departed Wife.
On the moor of Kasuga. *Fr.* Manyo Shu.
On the shingle/ Beaten by the waves.
Pheasant of the mountain, The.
Plovers, The.
Plovers cry, The.
Shui Shu, *sel.*
Strange old man, A/ Stops me.
This morning I will not/ Comb my hair.
When,/ Halting in front of it. *Fr.* Shui Shu.
When I left my girl.
When I pause before my mirror.
When she was still alive.
Your hair has turned white.
HITTAN OF TAYYI. Hamasah, *sels.*
He Thinks of His Children. *Fr.* Hamasah.
His Children. *Fr.* Hamasah.
HOARE, FLORENCE. Pedlar Jim.
HOARE, PRINCE. *Arethusa,* The.
HOATSON, FLORENCE. Autumn.
Bird Bath, The.
Christmas Eve.
Fairy Frilly.
Who?
HOBART, MRS. CHARLES. Changed Cross, The.
HOBBS, VALINE. Change of Heart, A.
One Day When We Went Walking.
HOBERMAN, MARY ANN. It's fun to go out and buy new shoes to wear.
Slushy snow splashes and sploshes, The.
HOBSON, DOROTHY. Do What You Will.
Man Returns to the Gates of Eden.
Meditation.
HOBSON, KATHERINE THAYER. Duality.
HOCCLEVE [*or* OCCLEVE], THOMAS. De Regimine Principum, *sels.*
Hoccleve's Humorous Praise of His Lady.
Hoccleve's Lament for Chaucer and Gower. *Fr.* De Regimine Principum.
Lament for Chaucer. *Fr.* De Regimine Principum.
On Chaucer. *Fr.* De Regimine Principum.
Prologue: "Musing upon the restless bisinesse." *Fr.* De Regimine Principum.
Regiment of Princes, The. *See* De Regimine Principum.
To Chaucer. *Fr.* De Regimine Principum.
HOCH, EDWARD WALLIS. Good and Bad, *at.*
HOCHI. Two little boats sail side by side.
HO CHIH-FANG. Let Me Speak of Pure Things.
HODDER, EDWIN. Thy Word Is Like a Garden, Lord.
HODES, AUBREY. Jew Walks in Westminster Abbey, A.
HODGE, ALAN. Waiting.
HODGES, LEIGH MITCHELL. Give Them the Flowers Now.
Source.
HODGSON, FLORENCE B. How Can I Smile?
HODGSON, RALPH. After.
Babylon.
Bells of Heaven, The.
Birdcatcher, The.
Bride, The.
Bull, The.
Couplet: "God loves an idle rainbow."
Eve.
Ghoul Care.
Gipsy Girl, The.
Great Auk's Ghost, The.
Gypsy Girl, The.
Hammers, The.
Hymn of Being, The.
Hymn to Moloch.
Journeyman, The.
Late, Last Rook, The.
Linnet, The.
Moor, The.
Mystery, The.
Night, The.
Reason.
Reason Has Moons.
Riddle, The: "He told himself and he told his wife."
Silver Wedding.
Song, A: "With Love among the haycocks."
Song of Honour, The.
Song of Honour, The, *sels.*
Stupidity Street.
Swallow, The.
Thrown.
Time, You Old Gipsy [*or* Gypsy] Man.
Wood Song, A.
HODGSON, WILLIAM NOEL. Before Action.
Visions.
HOELDERLIN, FRIEDRICH. *See* HÖLDERLIN, FRIEDRICH.
HOERNECKE, ALMA ELLIS. He Has Fine Eyes.
To Me and Not to Them.
HOEY, GEORGE. Asleep at the Switch.
HOFF, CLAYTON. I Saw Two Lions.
HOFFENSTEIN, SAMUEL. As the Crow Flies, *sel.*
Bird, The.
Breathes There a Man.
Cloud.
Father's Heart Is Touched, A.
I Burned My Candle at Both Ends.
I'd rather listen to a flute.
If You Love Me.
Interlude, for a Solitary Flute, *sel.*
Let Our Love Be.
Little While to Love and Rave, A.

HOFFENSTEIN, SAMUEL (*continued*)
Lullaby: "Sleep, my little baby, sleep."
Mr. Walter de la Mare Makes the Little Ones Dizzy.
More Hair.
Observation.
Ocean Spills, The.
Poem Intended to Incite the Utmost Depression, A.
Poems in Praise of Practically Nothing, *sels.*
Poems of Passion, Carefully Restrained So as to Offend Nobody.
Primer.
Question and Answer.
Sheep.
Some Folks I Know.
Song of Fairly Utter Despair.
Sorrow That Cries.
To a Cat.
To Claire.
Unequal Distribution.
When You're Away.
Your Little Hands.
HOFFMAN, CHARLES FENNO. Calling-One's-Own, *tr.*
L'Amour sans Ailes.
Mint Julep, The.
Monterey.
Rio Bravo—a Mexican Lament, *tr.*
Sparkling and Bright.
HOFFMAN, DANIEL GERARD. Armada of Thirty Whales, An.
How We Logged Katahdin Stream.
In Humbleness.
HOFFMAN, GEORGE EDWARD. As It Began to Dawn.
December 26.
Hymn: "O world of love and beauty."
Refreshment.
Victory Parade.
Young Warrior.
HOFFMAN, O. S. Five Best Doctors, The.
HOFFMAN, PHOEBE. Cats of Baddeck, The.
HOFFMAN, PHOEBE W. Pedro.
HOFFMAN, RICHARD. Post-Mortem.
HOFFMANN, AUGUST HEINRICH. *See* HOFFMANN VON FALLERSLEBEN.
HOFFMANN, HEINRICH. Dreadful Story about Harriet and the Matches, The.
Dreadful Story of Pauline and the Matches, The.
Harriet and the Matches.
Shock-headed Peter.
Story of Augustus Who Would Not Have Any Soup, The.
Story of Cruel Frederick, The.
Story of Fidgety Philip, The.
Story of Flying Robert, The.
Story of Johnny Head-in-Air, The.
Story of Little Suck-a-Thumb, The.
Story of the Inky Boys, The.
Story of the Man That Went Out Shooting, The.
Story of the Wild Huntsman, The.
When the children have been good.
HOFFMANN VON FALLERSLEBEN (August Heinrich Hoffmann). Cradle Song: "To sleep the corn is sinking."
HOFMAN, VIKTOR VIKTOROVICH. Summer Ball.
HOFMANNSTHAL, HUGO VON. Ballad of the Outer Life.
Boy, A.
Evanescence.
Experience.
Grandmother and Grandson.
Infinite Time.
Many Indeed Must Perish in the Keel.
Many Truly.
Poem: "We are such stuff as dreams are made of, and these."
Ship's Cook, a Captive Sings, The.
Song of Life.
Stanzas on Mutability.
Travel Song.
Travelers' Song.
Twilight of the Outward Life.
Two, The.
Venetian Night, A.
Vision, A.
World Secret.
Your Face.
Youth in the Landscape, The.
HOFSTEIN, DAVID. My Thread.
HOGAN, MICHAEL ("Bard of Thomond").
O'Neill's War Song.
HOGG, JAMES ("The Ettrick Shepherd").
Athol Cummers.
Bonnie Prince Charlie.
Bonny Kilmeny Gaed up the Glen. *Fr.* The Queen's Wake.
Boy's Song, A.
Charlie Is My Darling.
Donald Macdonald.
Jock Johnstone, the Tinkler.
Kilmeny. *Fr.* The Queen's Wake.
Laird of Lamington, The.
Lament of Flora Macdonald, The.
Lark, The.
Last Cradle Song, The.
Lock the Door, Lariston.
Love is like a Dizziness.
M'Lean's Welcome.
Moggy and Me.
My Love She's But a Lassie Yet.
Queen's Wake, The, *sels.*
She's But a Lassie Yet.
Skylark, The.
There's Gowd in the Breast.
When the Kye Comes Hame.
Witch of Fife, The. *Fr.* The Queen's Wake.
Women Folk, The.
HO HUNG. Spring Wind, The.
HOISINGTON, MAY FOLWELL. Black Frost.
Travel's End.
HOLBERG, KAI. My Love.
HOLBROOK, FLORENCE. Prayer, A: "Not more of light I ask, O God."
HOLBROOK, WEARE. Varitalk.
HOLCROFT, THOMAS. Gaffer Gray.
HOLDEN, JOHN JARVIS. Mother and Home.
HOLDEN, JOSEPH WILLIAM. Hatteras.
Song: "O heart that gave its first sweet love!"
Tide, The.
HOLDEN, RAYMOND. Dead Morning.
Geese in the Running Water.
Light the Lamp Early.
March.
Mood.
Proud, Unhoped-for Light.
Song for Government.
Storm over Rockefeller Center.
Winter among the Days.
HOLDEN, RAYMOND, *and* SARA HENDERSON HAY. *See* HAY, SARA HENDERSON, *and* RAYMOND HOLDEN.
HOLDER, C. S. King's Wood, The.
HÖLDERLIN [*or* HOELDERLIN], FRIEDRICH. Ages.
Archipelago, The.
Blind Singer, The.
Celebration of Peace.
Death of Empedocles, The, *sel.*
Empedocles.
Evening Fantasy.
Half of Life, The.
Halves of Life.
Home.
Hyperion's Song.
Life Half Lived.
Life's Ways Are Devious.
Man.
Memories.
Patmos.
Public Acclaim.
Ripened the Fruit.
Song of Fate.
Source of the Danube, The.
Sunset.
To Nature.
To the Fates.
HOLFORD, MISS. Lines: "And this was she! the peerless and the bright."
HOLIDAY, BARTEN. *See* HOLYDAY, BARTEN.
HOLLAND, LORD. Who Seeks to Please All Men.
HOLLAND, HUGH. Lament: "Lo, now he shineth yonder."
Shakespeare Dead.
Sonnet to Shakespeare.
HOLLAND, JOSIAH GILBERT. Babyhood. *Fr.* Bitter-sweet.
Bitter-sweet, *sels.*
Christmas Carol, A: "There's a song in the air!"
Cradle Song: "What is the little one thinking about?" *Fr.* Bitter-sweet.
Daniel Gray.
Day's Demand, The.
Give Us Men.
God Give Us Men!
Gradatim.
Heaven Is Not Reached at a Single Bound.
Hymn: "For Summer's bloom and Autumn's blight." *Fr.* Bitter-sweet.
Invocation to Sleep, An.
Lullaby: "Rockaby, lullaby, bees in the clover!" *Fr.* The Mistress of the Manse.
Mistress of the Manse, The, *sel.*
Old and Blind.
Only in Dreams.
Rockaby, Lullaby. *Fr.* The Mistress of the Manse.
Song of Doubt, A.
Song of Faith, A. *Fr.* Bitter-sweet.
There's a Song in the Air!
To My Dog Blanco.
Wanted.
Where Shall the Baby's Dimple Be?
HOLLAND, NORAH M. First Christmas, The.
Kitty's Feet.
Little Dog-Angel, The.
Lost Shoe, The.
Mary Sings.
Sea-Gulls.
Sea Song.
Shepherds' Song.
Three Kings Came Riding.
HOLLAND, RUPERT SARGENT. Foolish Flowers.
Jack-in-the-Pulpit.
P's and Q's.
Secrets of Our Garden, The.
Teapot Dragon, The.
When I Grow Up.
HOLLANDER, JOHN. Fear of Trembling, The.
Horas Tempestatis Quoque Enumero; the Sundial.
Lady's-Maid Song, The.
Paysage Moralisé.
HOLLAR, CONSTANCE. Caged Mongoose, The.
HOLLEY, HORACE. Hill, The.
HOLLIDAY, CARL. Thus Speak the Slain.
HOLLINGSWORTH, L. M. Intercession.
HOLLIS, MARK. Careless Talk.
'Twixt Cup and Lip.
HOLLOWAY, ARIEL WILLIAMS. Northboun'.
HOLLOWAY, JOHN. Elegy for an Estrangement.
Gale.
Journey through the Night.
Light, The.
Warning to a Guest.
HOLLOWAY, JOHN WESLEY. Black Mammies.
Calling the Doctor.
Corn Song, The.
Miss Melerlee.
HOLLOWAY, WILLIAM. Scenes of Youth, *sel.*
HOLM, CONSTANCE. Our Calvary.
"HOLM, SAXE." *See* JACKSON, HELEN HUNT.
HOLMAN, MOSES CARL. And on This Shore.
Letter across Doubt and Distance.
Notes for a Movie Script.
Song: "Dressed up in my melancholy."
HOLME, JAMIE SEXTON. Mountain Evenings.
Prelude: "When first we met, our souls stood up."
Timber Line Trees.
HOLME, VINCENT. Good Friday.
HOLMES, C. E. L. You Put No Flowers on My Papa's Grave.
HOLMES, C. R. Abandoned Brothel.
Hotel Lobby.

Impression at Reno.
Island Battlefield.
Subway Engineer.
To John Fiorini.
HOLMES, CALVIN. Lilith.
HOLMES, DANIEL HENRY. Margery Daw.
Willy Winkie.
HOLMES, EDMOND GORE ALEXANDER.
Creed of My Heart, The.
Immanence.
HOLMES, F. S., *and* S. H. STACKPOLE.
Christmas: Past and Present.
HOLMES, GEORGE SANFORD. And Yet Fools Say.
HOLMES, GEORGIANA. *See* "KLINGLE, GEORGE."
HOLMES, JOHN. At a Country Fair.
Auction.
Being Young.
Broken One, The.
Bucyrus.
But Choose.
Carry Me Back.
Chance, The.
Core, The.
Council from a Poet, Middle-aged.
Evening Meal in the Twentieth Century.
Father, The.
Fear of Dying, The.
Flower, The.
Fortune Teller, The.
Good Night! Good Night!
Grass.
Having New England Fathers.
Herself.
Joshua Peabody.
Letter, The.
Man at Work.
Map of My Country.
Metaphor for My Son.
New View, The.
Old Men and Young Men.
Overgrown Back Yard, The.
Peter at His Mirror.
Pour Down.
Rhyme of Rain.
Spiral, The.
Table for One.
Take Home This Heart.
To a Careful Young Man.
What Does a Man Think About.
What Literature Needs.
HOLMES, JOHN F. Old New Hampshire.
HOLMES, JOHN HAYNES. All Hail, the Pageant of the Years.
God of the Nations.
Hymn: "Great Spirit of the speeding spheres."
Hymn: "Thou God of all, whose presence dwells."
Hymn of At-One-Ment.
O Father, Thou Who Givest All.
O God of Field and City.
O God, Whose Love Is over All.
O God, Whose Smile Is in the Sky.
Voice of God Is Calling, The.
HOLMES, LILIAN. Pipes and Drums.
HOLMES, MARGARET. Sister Veronica.
HOLMES, OLIVER WENDELL. Additional Verses to "Hail Columbia."
Aestivation. *Fr.* The Autocrat of the Breakfast Table.
After a Lecture on Keats.
After the Curfew.
After the Fire.
Album Verses. *Fr.* The Autocrat of the Breakfast Table.
All Here.
At the Pantomime.
At the Saturday Club.
Aunt Tabitha.
Autocrat of the Breakfast Table, The, *sels.*
Ballad of the Boston Tea-Party, A.
Ballad of the Oysterman, The.
Bill and Joe.
Birthday of Daniel Webster.
Boston Common—Three Pictures.
Boys, The.
Broomstick Train; or Return of the Witches.
Broomstick Train, The, *sel.*
Brother Jonathan's Lament for Sister Caroline.
Cacoëthes Scribendi.
Chambered Nautilus, The. *Fr.* The Autocrat of the Breakfast Table.
Chambered Nautilus, The, *sel.*
Contentment. *Fr.* The Autocrat of the Breakfast Table.
Crooked Footpath, The. *Fr.* The Professor at the Breakfast Table.
Daily Trials.
Daniel Webster.
Deacon's Masterpiece, The; or, The Wonderful "One-Hoss Shay." *Fr.* The Autocrat of the Breakfast Table.
Dilemma, The.
Dorchester Giant, The.
Dorothy Q.
Eggstravagance, An.
Epilogue to the Breakfast Table Series. *Fr.* The Poet at the Breakfast Table.
Faith Shall Build a Fairer Throne.
Familiar Letter to Several Correspondents, A.
Farewell to Agassiz, A.
Flower of Liberty, The.
Freedom, Our Queen.
God Save the Flag.
Golden Flower, The.
Grandmother's Story of Bunker Hill Battle.
Height of the Ridiculous, The.
How the Old Horse Won the Bet.
Hymn: "O Thou of soul and sense and breath."
Hymn of Trust, A.
International Ode.
Intramural Aestivation, or Summer in Town, by a Teacher of Latin.
Iris, *sel.*
J. D. R.
James Russell Lowell ("This is your month").
James Russell Lowell ("Thou shouldst have sung the swan-song").
James Russell Lowell's Birthday Festival.
La Grisette.
Last Leaf, The.
Latter-Day Warnings. *Fr.* The Autocrat of the Breakfast Table.
Lexington.
Limerick: "Reverend Henry Ward Beecher, The."
Limerick: "Said a great Congregational preacher," *at.*
L'Inconnue.
Living Temple, The. *Fr.* The Autocrat of the Breakfast Table.
Logical Story, A—The Deacon's Masterpiece; or, The Wonderful "One-Hoss Shay." *Fr.* The Autocrat of the Breakfast Table.
Lord of All Being. *Fr.* The Professor at the Breakfast Table.
Manhood. *Fr.* The Poet at the Breakfast Table.
Many Things.
Midsummer.
Moral Bully, The.
More Stately Mansions. *Fr.* The Chambered Nautilus.
Morning Visit, The, *sel.*
Mother's Secret, The. *Fr.* The Professor at the Breakfast Table.
Mother's Secret, The, *sel.*
Music Grinders, The.
My Aunt.
My Aviary.
No Time like the Old Time.
Non-Resistance.
O Lord of Hosts! Almighty King!
O Love divine, that stooped to share. *Fr.* The Professor at the Breakfast Table.
Ode for a Social Meeting.
Old Amati, The.
Old Hemlock, An. *Fr.* The Autocrat of the Breakfast Table.
Old Ironsides.
Old Man Dreams, The.
On Lending a Punch-Bowl.
On the Death of President Garfield.
"One-Hoss Shay," The; or, The Deacon's Masterpiece. *Fr.* The Autocrat of the Breakfast Table.
Our Father's Door. *Fr.* The Professor at the Breakfast Table.
Our Hymn.
Parody on "A Psalm of Life," *at.*
Ploughman, The.
Poem, A: Dedication of the Pittsfield Cemetery, September 9, 1850, *sel.*
Poem for the Meeting of the American Medical Association, A.
Poet at the Breakfast Table, The, *sels.*
Poet's Lot, The.
Professor at the Breakfast Table, The, *sels.*
Prologue to Songs in Many Keys.
Reverend Henry Ward Beecher, The.
Rudolph the Headsman. *Fr.* The Autocrat of the Breakfast Table.
Said a great Congregational Preacher, *at.*
Sea Dialogue, A.
September Gale, The.
September Gale, The, *sel.*
Sherman's in Savannah.
Song for the Centennial Celebration of Harvard College, 1836, A.
Strong Heroic Line, The.
Sun-Day Hymn, A. *Fr.* The Professor at the Breakfast Table.
Then As to Feasting.
To an Insect.
To My Readers.
To the Portrait of "A Gentleman."
Two Armies, The.
Two Streams, The. *Fr.* The Professor at the Breakfast Table.
Under the Violets. *Fr.* The Professor at the Breakfast Table.
Under the Washington Elm, Cambridge.
Unsatisfied.
Voiceless, The. *Fr.* The Autocrat of the Breakfast Table.
Washington's Birthday.
Welcome to Dr. Benjamin Apthorp Gould, A.
Welcome to the Nations.
When Eve had led her lord away. *Fr.* The Autocrat of the Breakfast Table.
Why They Twinkle.
Wonderful "One-Hoss Shay," The. *Fr.* The Autocrat of the Breakfast Table.
Youth fades; love droops. *Fr.* A Mother's Secret.
HOLMES, ROBERT S. Let's Go Fishin'.
HOLMES, RUTH. No Thoroughfare.
HOLMES, W. K. Dream Ship, The.
Old Brown Horse, The.
HOLSTEIN, LUDVIG. Apple Blossoms.
Father, Where Do the Wild Swans Go?
Forth, My Gallant Honey-Bees!
Thou Lovely One Far Distant.
HOLT, EDGAR. Two Sonnets from a Sequence.
HOLT, JESSIE. Dying.
HOLTHUSEN, HANS EGON. It Was My Blood. *Fr.* Lament for My Brother.
Lament for My Brother, *sel.*
Sacrifice.
HÖLTY, LUDWIG HEINRICH CHRISTOPH.
Harvest Song.
Winter Song.
HOLYDAY, BARTEN. Distiches.
Song: "O harmless feast." *Fr.* Technogamia.
Technogamia; or, The Marriage of the Arts, *sels.*
Tobacco's a musician. *Fr.* Technogamia.
HOLZ, ARNO. Buddha.
Leave-taking, A.
Phantasus ("Its roof among the stars projected").
Phantasus, I-8 ("On a mountain of sugar-candy").
Phantasus, VI-14 ("I wish you were real!").
Roses Red.
HOMAN, HELEN WALKER. Rain at Night.
HOME, ANNE. *See* HUNTER, ANNE.

"HOME, CECIL." *See* WEBSTER, AUGUSTA.

HOME, F. WYVILLE. Dover Cliff.
English Girl, An.
In a September Night.

HOME, JOHN. Douglas, *sel.*
Norval. *Fr.* Douglas.

HOMER. Achaeans Renew the Battle, The, *tr. by* F. L. Lucas. *Fr.* The Iliad.
Achilles and Agamemnon; the Fatal Feud, *tr. by* the Earl of Derby. *Fr.* The Iliad.
Achilles and Lycaon, *tr. by* the Earl of Derby *and by* C. M. Bowra. *Fr.* The Iliad.
Achilles and Patroclus, *tr. by* Sir William Marris. *Fr.* The Iliad.
Achilles and the Scamander, *tr. by* Sir William Marris. *Fr.* The Iliad.
Achilles and Thetis, *tr. by* Sir William Marris. *Fr.* The Iliad.
Achilles' Arms, *tr. by* F. L. Lucas. *Fr.* The Iliad.
Achilles Goes Forth to Battle, *tr. by* Chapman. *Fr.* The Iliad.
Achilles on the Rampart, *tr. by* Tennyson. *Fr.* The Iliad.
Achilles over the Trench, *tr. by* F. L. Lucas. *Fr.* The Iliad.
Achilles' Prayer, *tr. by* the Earl of Derby. *Fr.* The Iliad.
Achilles Refuses to Spare Lycaon's Life, *tr. by* A. T. Murray. *Fr.* The Iliad.
Achilles Rejects the Embassy, *tr. by* F. L. Lucas. *Fr.* The Iliad.
Achilles' Remorse, *tr. by* F. L. Lucas. *Fr.* The Iliad.
Achilles' Reply to the Embassy, *tr. by* Maurice Hewlett. *Fr.* The Iliad.
Achilles' Shield, *tr. by* Chapman. *Fr.* The Iliad.
Achilles' Shout, *tr. by* Tennyson. *Fr.* The Iliad.
Achilles Shows Himself in the Battle by the Ships, *tr. by* Chapman. *Fr.* The Iliad.
Achilles to Lycaon, *tr. by* Richmond Lattimore. *Fr.* The Iliad.
Achilles Unreconciled, *tr. by* the Earl of Derby. *Fr.* The Iliad.
Advance of the Trojans, The, *tr. by* William Cowper. *Fr.* The Iliad.
After the Chariot-Race, *tr. by* Pope. *Fr.* The Iliad.
Agamemnon; Peace Offerings to Achilles, *tr. by* Maurice Hewlett. *Fr.* The Iliad.
Ajax Covers the Flight of the Greeks, *tr. by* William Cowper. *Fr.* The Iliad.
Ajax in the Fight, *tr. by* William Cowper. *Fr.* The Iliad.
Ajax on the Decks, *tr. by* Lang, Leaf, *and* Myers. *Fr.* The Iliad.
Ajax Prays for Light, *tr. by* the Earl of Derby. *Fr.* The Iliad.
Andromache, *tr. by* Samuel Butler. *Fr.* The Iliad.
Andromache the Desolate, *tr. by* Lang, Leaf, *and* Myers. *Fr.* The Iliad.
Apollo Destroys the Wall, *tr. by* the Earl of Derby. *Fr.* The Iliad.
Appeal of Phoenix, The, *tr. by* George Ernle. *Fr.* The Iliad.
Arete; Portrait of a High-born Matron, *tr. by* Pope. *Fr.* The Odyssey.
At-Home in Sparta, An, *tr. by* Samuel Butler. *Fr.* The Odyssey.
At Pylos, *tr. by* J. W. Mackail. *Fr.* The Odyssey.
At Sparta; Helen and Menelaus, *tr. by* Samuel Butler. *Fr.* The Odyssey.
At Sparta; Menelaus and Proteus, *tr. by* Butcher *and* Lang. *Fr.* The Odyssey.
Atrides Goes into Battle, *tr. by* Chapman. *Fr.* The Iliad.
Barren Battlefield, The, *tr. by* F. L. Lucas. *Fr.* The Iliad.
Battle of the Curetes and Aetolians, *tr. by* Pope. *Fr.* The Iliad.
Beginning of the Wrath, The, *tr. by* Sir William Marris. *Fr.* The Iliad.
Blame Not the Gods! *tr. by* Butcher *and* Lang. *Fr.* The Odyssey.
Briseis, the Slave Girl; Tears for Patroclus, *tr. by* William Cowper. *Fr.* The Iliad.
Calypso's Island, *tr. by* Chapman. *Fr.* The Odyssey.
Camp at Night, The, *tr. by* Chapman. *Fr.* The Iliad.
Chariot Race, The, *tr. by* Chapman. *Fr.* The Iliad.
Circe, *tr. by* F. L. Lucas. *Fr.* The Odyssey.
Clouds upon Windless Peaks, *tr. by* F. L. Lucas. *Fr.* The Iliad.
Dead Is Patroclus, *tr. by* Pope. *Fr.* The Iliad.
Death of Argus, The, *tr. by* F. L. Lucas. *Fr.* The Odyssey.
Death of Gorguthion, The, *tr. by* F. L. Lucas. *Fr.* The Iliad.
Death of Gorgythian, The, *tr. by* Pope. *Fr.* The Iliad.
Death of Hector, The, *tr. by* Chapman. *Fr.* The Iliad.
Death of Patroclus [*or* Patroklos], The, *tr. by* Sir William Marris *and by* Lang, Leaf, *and* Myers. *Fr.* The Iliad.
Debate in Ithaca, The, *tr. by* F. L. Lucas. *Fr.* The Odyssey.
Demodocus Sings a Song of Troy, *tr. by* H. B. Cotterill. *Fr.* The Odyssey.
Dog Argos, The, *tr. by* T. E. Lawrence. *Fr.* The Odyssey.
Elders of Troy Behold Helen, The, *tr. by* the Earl of Derby. *Fr.* The Iliad.
End of the Suitors, The, *tr. by* Chapman. *Fr.* The Odyssey.
Escape from Cyclop, The, *tr. by* Chapman. *Fr.* The Odyssey.
Eumaeus Plays Host to His Master, *tr. by* Samuel Butler. *Fr.* The Odyssey.
Eumaeus Tells the Story of His Life, *tr. by* Samuel Butler. *Fr.* The Odyssey.
Eumaeus the Swineherd, *tr. by* Samuel Butler. *Fr.* The Odyssey.
Fallen Olive-Tree, The, *tr. by* F. L. Lucas. *Fr.* The Iliad.
Farewell to Kind Hosts and a Godspeed, *tr. by* William Morris. *Fr.* The Odyssey.
Farewell to Nausicaa, *tr. by* Butcher *and* Lang. *Fr.* The Odyssey.
Ghost of Patroclus, The, *tr. by* William Cowper. *Fr.* The Iliad.
Glaukos and Diomedes, *tr. by* Lang, Leaf, *and* Myers. *Fr.* The Iliad.
Hector and Andromache, *tr. by* F. L. Lucas *and by* Pope. *Fr.* The Iliad.
Hector and Andromache; the Parting, *tr. by* William Cowper. *Fr.* The Iliad.
Hector to Andromache, *tr. by* Chapman. *Fr.* The Iliad.
Hektor and Andromache, *tr. by* Maurice Hewlett. *Fr.* The Iliad.
Hektor to Andromache, *tr. by* Richmond Lattimore. *Fr.* The Iliad.
Helen, *tr. by* Maurice Hewlett *and by* William Cowper. *Fr.* The Iliad.
Helen, Menelaos, and Memories of Troy, *tr. by* Chapman. *Fr.* The Odyssey.
Helen on the Walls of Troy Looking for Her Brothers, *tr. by* E. C. Hawtrey. *Fr.* The Iliad.
Helen Seeks for Her Brothers among the Army of the Greeks before Troy, *tr. by* E. C. Hawtrey. *Fr.* The Iliad.
Helen; the Penitent, *tr. by* the Earl of Derby. *Fr.* The Iliad.
Helen Unreproached by Hector, *tr. by* William Cowper. *Fr.* The Iliad.
Heroic Answer to the Servant Problem, An, *tr. by* Samuel Butler. *Fr.* The Odyssey.
Home-coming, *tr. by* J. W. Mackail. *Fr.* The Odyssey.
Homeric Moonlight, A, *tr. by* Pope. *Fr.* The Iliad.
Horse Xanthus Warns Achilles, The, *tr. by* F. L. Lucas. *Fr.* The Iliad.
Horses of Achilles, The, *tr. by* the Earl of Derby *and by* F. L. Lucas. *Fr.* The Iliad.
Iliad, The, *sels.*
Immortal Steeds of Achilles, The, *tr. by* the Earl of Derby. *Fr.* The Iliad.
Kingdom of Death, The, *tr. by* F. L. Lucas. *Fr.* The Odyssey.
Laertes, *tr. by* William Morris *and by* Sir William Marris. *Fr.* The Odyssey.
Lamentations, The, *tr. by* Sir William Marris. *Fr.* The Iliad.
Lamentations of the Women, The, *tr. by* the Earl of Derby. *Fr.* The Iliad.
Last Fight, The, *tr. by* Lang, Leaf, *and* Myers. *Fr.* The Iliad.
Last Journey of the Wooers, The, *tr. by* William Cowper. *Fr.* The Odyssey.
Last Parting of Hector and Andromache, The, *tr. by* Dryden. *Fr.* The Iliad.
Last Stand at the Ships, The, *tr. by* F. L. Lucas. *Fr.* The Iliad.
Limbo; the Shades of the Suitors, *tr. by* William Cowper. *Fr.* The Odyssey.
Lotus-Land and the Cyclops' Cave, *tr. by* F. L. Lucas. *Fr.* The Odyssey.
Man of Many Devices, The, *tr. by* A. T. Murray. *Fr.* The Odyssey.
Man, the Feeblest of Earth's Creatures, *tr. by* William Cowper. *Fr.* The Odyssey.
Meeting of Priam and Achilles, The, *tr. by* F. L. Lucas. *Fr.* The Iliad.
Menelaos; Blasphemy under Duress, *tr. by* William Cowper. *Fr.* The Iliad.
Menelaus and Odysseus, *tr. by* William Cowper. *Fr.* The Iliad.
Menelaus; What Price Earthly Splendor! *tr. by* Butcher *and* Lang. *Fr.* The Odyssey.
Message of Hermes to Calypso, The, *tr. by* F. L. Lucas. *Fr.* The Odyssey.
Minstrel Worthy of His Hire, The, *tr. by* William Cowper. *Fr.* The Odyssey.
Nausicaa ("Having thus fulfilled . . ."), *tr. by* T. E. Lawrence. *Fr.* The Odyssey.
Nausicaa ("Now when at last . . ."), *tr. by* H. B. Cotterill. *Fr.* The Odyssey.
Nausicaa ("Now when they came to the bright running river"), *tr. by* Sir William Marris. *Fr.* The Odyssey.
Nausicaä ("So flashing-eyed Athene spoke"), *tr. by* F. L. Lucas. *Fr.* The Odyssey.
Nausicaa ("The servants then . . ."), *tr. by* Chapman. *Fr.* The Odyssey.
Nausicaa and Odysseus, *tr. by* Chapman. *Fr.* The Odyssey.
Nausicaa; the Ingenue, *tr. by* H. B. Cotterill. *Fr.* The Odyssey.
Nestor's Doubt, *tr. by* F. L. Lucas. *Fr.* The Iliad.
Nestor's Speech to Achilles and Agamemnon, *tr. by* Chapman. *Fr.* The Iliad.
Noman and the Cyclops; a Tale Told over Cups, *tr. by* Chapman. *Fr.* The Odyssey.
Odysseus and Demodocus, *tr. by* F. L. Lucas. *Fr.* The Odyssey.
Odysseus and Eurycleia, *tr. by* F. L. Lucas. *Fr.* The Odyssey.
Odysseus and His Father, *tr. by* F. L. Lucas. *Fr.* The Odyssey.
Odysseus and His Son, *tr. by* F. L. Lucas. *Fr.* The Odyssey.
Odysseus and Penelope Meet, *tr. by* A. T. Murray. *Fr.* The Odyssey.

Odysseus in Hades, *tr. by* William Cowper. *Fr.* The Odyssey.
Odysseus' Mother Speaks to Him in Hades, *tr. by* A. T. Murray. *Fr.* The Odyssey.
Odysseus Puts to Sea, *tr. by* J. W. Mackail. *Fr.* The Odyssey.
Odysseus' Return to Ithaca, *tr. by* F. L. Lucas. *Fr.* The Odyssey.
Odysseus Spurns Calypso, *tr. by* Butcher *and* Lang. *Fr.* The Odyssey.
Odysseus; the Shores of Scheria at Last, *tr. by* H. B. Cotterill. *Fr.* The Odyssey.
Odyssey, The, *sels.*
Of Circe, *tr. by* William Morris. *Fr.* The Odyssey.
Of Cyclops and the Ram, *tr. by* William Morris. *Fr.* The Odyssey.
Of His Mother's Shade, *tr. by* J. W. Mackail. *Fr.* The Odyssey.
Of Noman and Cyclops, *tr. by* William Morris. *Fr.* The Odyssey.
Of the Laestrygones, *tr. by* Sir William Marris. *Fr.* The Odyssey.
Of the Shade of Achilles, *tr. by* William Cowper. *Fr.* The Odyssey.
Of the Shade of Ajax, *tr. by* T. F. Higham. *Fr.* The Odyssey.
Old Hound Argos, The, *tr. by* Samuel Butler. *Fr.* The Odyssey.
Old Knight Phoenix, The, *tr. by* Lang, Leaf, *and* Myers. *Fr.* The Iliad.
Old Man of the Sea, The, *tr. by* F. L. Lucas. *Fr.* The Odyssey.
Old Traveller, The, *tr. by* F. L. Lucas. *Fr.* The Iliad.
Olympus, *tr. by* T. E. Lawrence. *Fr.* The Odyssey.
Palace of Alcinous, The, *tr. by* Pope. *Fr.* The Odyssey.
Paris Is Worsted by Menelaus and Returns to Helen, *tr. by* F. L. Lucas. *Fr.* The Iliad.
Paris Rescued by Aphrodite, *tr. by* Maurice Hewlett. *Fr.* The Iliad.
Parting of Hector and Andromache, The, *tr. by* Chapman *and by* William B. Smith *and* Walter Miller. *Fr.* The Iliad.
Passing Glimpse of Penelope, A, *tr. by* Butcher *and* Lang. *Fr.* The Odyssey.
Patroclus' Body Saved, *tr. by* E. R. Dodds. *Fr.* The Iliad.
Patroclus Goes to Battle, *tr. by* F. L. Lucas. *Fr.* The Iliad.
Patroclus Intercedes for the Achaeans, *tr. by* F. L. Lucas. *Fr.* The Iliad.
Patroclus to Achilles, *tr. by* the Earl of Derby. *Fr.* The Iliad.
Penelope Dreams ("But when her heart had had its fill of weeping"), *tr. by* Sir William Marris. *Fr.* The Odyssey.
Penelope Dreams ("So said he, and the crone went down the hall"), *tr. by* J. W. Mackail. *Fr.* The Odyssey.
Penelope Forlorn, *tr. by* J. W. Mackail. *Fr.* The Odyssey.
Penelope Makes Trial of Odysseus, *tr. by* Samuel Butler. *Fr.* The Odyssey.
Penelope; New Woes on Old, *tr. by* H. B. Cotterill. *Fr.* The Odyssey.
Penelope's Constancy Rewarded, *tr. by* William Cowper. *Fr.* The Odyssey.
Penelope's Dream, *tr. by* William Cowper. *Fr.* The Odyssey.
Phaeacian Nights—Demodocus, *tr. by* T. E. Lawrence. *Fr.* The Odyssey.
Phaeacian Nights—Odysseus' Tale, *sels.* *Fr.* The Odyssey.
Plight of Wounded Aphrodite, The, *tr. by* Chapman. *Fr.* The Iliad.
Prayer of Achilles, The, *tr. by* Lang, Leaf, *and* Myers. *Fr.* The Iliad.
Preparation of the Pyre for Patroclus, *tr. by* Pope. *Fr.* The Iliad.
Priam and Achilles, *tr. by* Robert Bridges, *by* Chapman, *and by* Pope. *Fr.* The Iliad.
Priam and Helen on the Wall, *tr. by* F. L. Lucas. *Fr.* The Iliad.
Priam at the Feet of Achilles, *tr. by* the Earl of Derby. *Fr.* The Iliad.
Priam's Prayer to Achilles, *tr. by* Robert Bridges. *Fr.* The Iliad.
Pursuit round the Walls, The, *tr. by* William Cowper. *Fr.* The Iliad.
Pyre of Patroclus, The, *tr. by* Pope. *Fr.* The Iliad.
Quarrel, The, *tr. by* Sir William Marris. *Fr.* The Iliad.
Rally, The, *tr. by* Sir William Marris. *Fr.* The Iliad.
Reconciliation of Achilles and Agamemnon, The, *tr. by* the Earl of Derby. *Fr.* The Iliad.
Reunion of Odysseus and Penelope, The, *tr. by* F. L. Lucas. *Fr.* The Odyssey.
Reunion of Ulysses and Telemachus, *tr. by* William Cowper. *Fr.* The Odyssey.
Sacrifice, The, *tr. by* Chapman. *Fr.* The Odyssey.
Sailing of Odysseus from Ogygia, The, *tr. by* F. L. Lucas. *Fr.* The Odyssey.
Sarpedon and Glaucus, *tr. by* Maurice Hewlett. *Fr.* The Iliad.
Sarpedon and Glaucus; the Equation of Duty and Privilege, *tr. by* William Cowper. *Fr.* The Iliad.
Sarpedon to Glaukos, *tr. by* Richmond Lattimore. *Fr.* The Iliad.
Sarpedon's Speech, *tr. by* Chapman. *Fr.* The Iliad.
Scales of War, The, *tr. by* F. L. Lucas. *Fr.* The Iliad.
Scales of Zeus, The, *tr. by* Chapman *and by* William Cowper. *Fr.* The Iliad.
Scamander the River God, *tr. by* the Earl of Derby. *Fr.* The Iliad.
Scylla and Charybdis, *tr. by* Chapman. *Fr.* The Odyssey.
Sequel to the Chariot Race, *tr. by* Lang, Leaf, *and* Myers. *Fr.* The Iliad.
Sere and Yellow Leaf, The, *tr. by* F. L. Lucas. *Fr.* The Iliad.
Shade of Patroclus, The, *tr. by* the Earl of Derby. *Fr.* The Iliad.
Shield of Achilles, The, *tr. by* F. L. Lucas *and by* Pope. *Fr.* The Iliad.
Silence of Ajax, The, *tr. by* T. E. Lawrence. *Fr.* The Odyssey.
Sing, O Muse, *tr. by* the Earl of Derby. *Fr.* The Iliad.
Sirens, The, *tr. by* Pope. *Fr.* The Odyssey.
Sirens, The; Scylla and Charybdis, *tr. by* F. L. Lucas *and by* Pope. *Fr.* The Odyssey.
Siren's Song, The, *tr. by* Chapman. *Fr.* The Odyssey.
Slaying, The, *tr. by* William Morris. *Fr.* The Odyssey.
Slaying of Hector, The, *tr. by* Lang, Leaf, *and* Myers *and by* F. L. Lucas. *Fr.* The Iliad.
Slaying of Patroclus, The, *tr. by* F. L. Lucas. *Fr.* The Iliad.
Slaying of the Suitors, The, *tr. by* F. L. Lucas *and by* William Morris. *Fr.* The Odyssey.
Sleep of Bronze, A, *tr. by* A. T. Murray. *Fr.* The Iliad.
Snow of Stones, The, *tr. by* Michael Balkwill. *Fr.* The Iliad.
So Ends the Wrath of Achilles, *tr. by* William Cowper. *Fr.* The Iliad.
Sound of Footsteps, The, *tr. by* A. T. Murray. *Fr.* The Odyssey.
Stag and Jackals, *tr. by* F. L. Lucas. *Fr.* The Iliad.
Steeds of Heaven, The, *tr. by* F. L. Lucas. *Fr.* The Iliad.
Storming of the Achaean Wall, The, *tr. by* F. L. Lucas. *Fr.* The Iliad.
Story of Bellerophon, The, *tr. by* Hallam Tennyson *and* Alfred Tennyson. *Fr.* The Iliad.
Strife, War's Sister Urges On the Host, *tr. by* Pope. *Fr.* The Iliad.
Struggle for Patroclus, The, *tr. by* F. L. Lucas. *Fr.* The Iliad.
Tale of Eumaeus, The, *tr. by* F. L. Lucas. *Fr.* The Odyssey.
Telemachus Finds His Father, *tr. by* William Cowper. *Fr.* The Odyssey.
Test of the Bow, The, *tr. by* William Morris. *Fr.* The Odyssey.
Thersites, *tr. by* Maurice Hewlett. *Fr.* The Iliad.
Thersites Out of Bounds, *tr. by* Chapman. *Fr.* The Iliad.
Thetis and Achilles, *tr. by* Sir William Marris. *Fr.* The Iliad.
Thetis and Hephaestus, *tr. by* Sir William Marris. *Fr.* The Iliad.
Thetis to Achilles, *tr. by* Samuel Butler. *Fr.* The Iliad.
Thunder of Zeus, The, *tr. by* Sir William Marris. *Fr.* The Iliad.
Trojan Camp-Fires, The, *tr. by* the Earl of Derby *and by* Tennyson. *Fr.* The Iliad.
Trojans and Greeks, *tr. by* the Earl of Derby. *Fr.* The Iliad.
Trojans Encamp before the Achaean Wall, The, *tr. by* F. L. Lucas. *Fr.* The Iliad.
Trojans outside the Walls, The, *tr. by* Chapman. *Fr.* The Iliad.
Two Hosts, The, *tr. by* Gladstone. *Fr.* The Iliad.
Ulysses and His Dog, *tr. by* Pope. *Fr.* The Odyssey.
Ulysses and the Sirens, *tr. by* Chapman. *Fr.* The Odyssey.
Ulysses Hears the Prophecies of Tiresias, *tr. by* Chapman. *Fr.* The Odyssey.
Ulysses in the Waves, *tr. by* Chapman. *Fr.* The Odyssey.
Vision of Theoclymenus, The, *tr. by* T. E. Lawrence *and by* F. L. Lucas. *Fr.* The Odyssey.
Visit of Thetis to Hephaistos, *tr. by* Chapman. *Fr.* The Iliad.
Vow of Vengeance, The, *tr. by* William Cowper. *Fr.* The Iliad.
Vulcan Forges the Shield of Achilles, *tr. by* Chapman. *Fr.* The Iliad.
Wail for Hector, The, *tr. by* F. L. Lucas. *Fr.* The Iliad.
Wall, The, *tr. by* William Cowper. *Fr.* The Iliad.
Wall of the Greeks, The, *tr. by* Cowper. *Fr.* The Iliad.
Wasps, *tr. by* F. L. Lucas. *Fr.* The Iliad.
Web, The, *tr. by* Sir William Marris. *Fr.* The Odyssey.
Wise Penelope, *tr. by* A. T. Murray. *Fr.* The Odyssey.
Women Who Wait, *tr. by* Maurice Hewlett. *Fr.* The Iliad.
Wraith of Patroclus, The, *tr. by* F. L. Lucas. *Fr.* The Iliad.
Wrath of Achilles, The, *tr. by* Bryant *and by* F. L. Lucas. *Fr.* The Iliad.
Wrestling Match, The, *tr. by* Chapman. *Fr.* The Iliad.
Zeus on Olympus, *tr. by* A. T. Murray. *Fr.* The Iliad.
HOMER-DIXON, HOMERA. New Year, The.
HONAN, DANIEL J. Dostoievsky to a Young Communist.
HONE, WILLIAM. First of April, The.
HONEYWOOD, ST. JOHN. Darby and Joan.
Radical Song of 1786, A.
HONIG, EDWIN. Happening.
Jane Retreat.
Tall Toms, The.
True Romance.
Walt Whitman.
HOOCK, HARRIET. Answer.
To Joseph.
HOOD, E. P. God, Who Hath Made the Daisies.
HOOD, THOMAS. Art of Book-keeping, The, *at.*
Autumn ("I saw old Autumn").

HOOD, THOMAS (*continued*)
Autumn ("The autumn is old").
Bachelor's Dream, The.
Ballad: "It was not in the winter."
Ballad: "Spring it is cheery."
Ballad: Time of Roses.
Bed-Time.
Ben Bluff.
Blank Verse in Rhyme.
Bridge of Sighs, The.
Bridge of Sighs, The, *sel.*
Death.
Death-Bed, The.
Death of Leander, The. *Fr.* Hero and Leander.
Death's Ramble.
Domestic Asides; or, Truth in Parentheses.
Domestic Didactics by an Old Servant.
Dream Fairy, The. *Fr.* Queen Mab.
Dream of Eugene Aram, The.
Dust to Dust.
Epicurean Reminiscences of a Sentimentalist.
Epigram: "After such years of dissension and strife."
Eugene Aram's Dream.
Fair Ines.
Faithless Nelly [*or* Nellie] Gray.
Faithless Sally Brown.
False Poets and True.
Farewell, Life!
Fewer Books, More Salad.
Flowers.
French and English.
Friendly Address, A.
Ghost, The.
Gold. *Fr.* Miss Kilmansegg and Her Precious Leg.
Good Night.
Haunted House, The.
Haunted House, The, *sels.*
Her Death. *Fr.* Miss Kilmansegg and Her Precious Leg.
Her Moral. *Fr.* Miss Kilmansegg and Her Precious Leg.
Hero and Leander, *sels.*
I Remember, I Remember.
I'm Not a Single Man.
It Is Not Death.
It Was Not in the Winter.
It Was the Time of Roses.
Lake and a Fairy Boat, A.
Last Man, The.
Lay of the Laborer, The.
Lear.
Lines in a Young Lady's Album.
Little Piggies, The.
Lost Heir, The.
Mary's Ghost.
Mermaid of Margate, The.
Miss Kilmansegg and Her Precious Leg, *sels.*
Miss Kilmansegg's Birth. *Fr.* Miss Kilmansegg and Her Precious Leg.
Morning Meditations.
Natural Tears.
No!
Nocturnal Sketch, A.
November [in England].
Ode: Autumn.
Ode to the Moon.
On a Royal Demise.
On Mistress Nicely, a Pattern for Housekeepers.
Our Village—by a Villager.
Pair'd, Not Match'd.
Parental Ode to My Son, Aged Three Years and Five Months, A.
Parental Ode to My Son, Aged Three Years and Five Months, A, *sel.*
Past and Present.
Plain Direction, A.
Plea of the Midsummer Fairies, The, *sels.*
Please to Ring the Belle.
Poet's Fate, The.
Poet's Portion, The.
Pompey's Ghost.
Precocious Piggy.
Queen Mab.
Queen Mab, *sel.*
Rhymes: "Still, for all slips of hers." *Fr.* The Bridge of Sighs.
Ruth.
Sailor's Apology for Bow-Legs, A.
Sally Simpkin's Lament.
Scylla's Lament. *Fr.* Hero and Leander.
Sea of Death, The.
Serenade: "Ah, sweet, thou little knowest how."
Serenade, A: "Lullaby, O, lullaby!"
Shakespeare. *Fr.* The Plea of the Midsummer Fairies.
Silence.
Song: "Lake and a fairy boat, A."
Song: "O lady, leave thy silken thread."
Song: "Stars are with the voyager, The."
Song of the Shirt, The.
Song of the Shirt, The, *sel.*
Sonnet: "It is not death."
Sonnet on Mistress Nicely, a Pattern for Housekeepers.
Sonnet to Vauxhall.
Stanzas: "Farewell, Life! my senses swim."
Stanzas Written in Sickness.
Stars Are with the Voyager, The.
Sun Was Slumbering in the West, The.
Sweated Labor. *Fr.* The Song of the Shirt.
Tender Babes. *Fr.* The Plea of the Midsummer Fairies.
Tim Turpin.
Time of Roses.
Titania. *Fr.* The Plea of the Midsummer Fairies.
To a Child Embracing His Mother.
To Minerva.
To My Infant Son.
To My Son, Aged Three Years and Five Months.
Tom Tatter's Birthday Ode.
Two Swans, The.
Water Lady, The.
What Can an Old Man Do but Die?
HOOD, TOM (Thomas Hood, Jr.). All in the Downs.
Cannibal Flea, The.
Catch, A: "If you were queen of bloaters."
From Nowhere to the North Pole, *sel.*
In Memoriam Technicam.
Little tigers are at rest, The.
Muddled Metaphors.
Poets and Linnets.
Quadrupedremian Song, A. *Fr.* From Nowhere to the North Pole.
Takings.
Tea, The.
Wedding, The.
What He Took.
HOOFT, PIETER CORNELISZOON. Thus Spoke My Love.
HOOK, THEODORE EDWARD. Cautionary Verses [to Youth of Both Sexes].
HOOKE, HILDA MARY (Mrs. Richard Tapscott Smith). Inspiration.
Iris.
King's Dancer, The.
Perfect Round, The.
Tulip Queens.
HOOKER, BRIAN. Ballade of the Dreamland Rose.
Cyrano de Bergerac, *sel., tr.*
Cyrano de Bergerac Discusses His Nose, *tr. Fr.* Cyrano de Bergerac.
From Life.
Ghosts.
Little Person, A.
Mother of Men.
Portrait, A.
Song: "Only a little while since first we met."
HOOKES, NICHOLAS. To Amanda Walking in the Garden.
HOOKHAM, GEORGE. Chamonix.
HOOLEY, TERESA. Christ in Woolworth's.
Legend of Gethsemane, A.
October.
To-day I saw a butterfly.
HOOPER, ELLEN STURGIS. Beauty and Duty.
Duty.
Straight Road, The.
To R. W. E.
HOOPER, LUCY HAMILTON. Three Loves.
HOOTON, EARNEST ALBERT. Fat-buttocked Bushmen, The.
Lines to Homo Somejerktensis.
Ode to a Dental Hygienist.
HOOVER, GENE BOARDMAN. Mountain Dawn.
HOOVER, MARGARET. Triolet: "I intended a handspring."
HOPE, A. D. Australia.
Conquistador.
Damnation of Byron, The.
Return from the Freudian Islands, The.
Standardization.
HOPE, HENRY. Now I Have Found a Friend.
HOPE, JAMES BARRON. Dreamers.
John Smith's Approach to Jamestown.
Oath of Freedom, The.
Our Anglo-Saxon Tongue.
Under One Blanket.
"HOPE, LAURENCE" (Adela Florence Cory Nicolson). Ashore.
Bride, The.
Carpe Diem. *Fr.* In the Early, Pearly Morning.
In the Early, Pearly Morning.
In the Early, Pearly Morning, *sel.*
Kashmiri Song.
Kashmiri Song by Juma.
Khristna and His Flute.
Less than the Dust.
Masters, The.
Request.
Reverie.
Sea Song.
Teak Forest, The, *sel.*
Wisdom? *Fr.* The Teak Forest.
HOPE, MARGARET. Through the Ages.
HOPEGOOD, OLIVE. Feathers.
HOPEGOOD, PETER. Dithyramb in Retrospect.
First Aid.
Free Martin.
Nicorn's Dower, The.
Protagonist, The.
There Sleeps in the Churchyard.
HO P'EI YÜ. Poem of Ten "Ones," The.
HOPKINS, ANNE. Hills Take Command.
HOPKINS, GERARD MANLEY. Abyss.
Andromeda.
As Kingfishers Catch Fire, Dragonflies Draw Flame.
At the Wedding March.
Barnfloor and Winepress.
Binsey Poplars (Felled 1879).
Blessed Virgin Compared to the Air We Breathe, The.
Brothers.
Bugler's First Communion, The.
Caged Skylark, The.
Candle Indoors, The.
Carrion Comfort.
Cuckoo, The.
Duns Scotus's Oxford.
Epithalamion.
Felix Randal.
Fragment: Furl of Fresh-leaved Dog-Rose Down, The.
Fragment, A: "Repeat that, repeat."
Fragment: "Strike, churl; hurl cheerless."
Glory be to God for dappled things.
God's Grandeur.
Golden Echo, The. *Fr.* The Leaden Echo and the Golden Echo.
Habit of Perfection, The.
Habit of Perfection, The, *sel.*
Harry Ploughman.
Heaven-Haven.
Henry Purcell.
Hurrahing in Harvest.
I Have Desired to Go.
I remember a house where all were good.
I Wake and Feel the Fell of Dark.
Iesu, Dulcis Memoria, *tr.*
Immanent, The.
In the Valley of the Elwy.
Inversnaid.
Inversnaid, *sel.*
Justus Quidem Tu Es, Domine.

Lantern Out of Doors, The.
Leaden Echo and the Golden Echo, The.
Life Death Does End.
Low Sunday and Monday, *sel.*
May Magnificat, The.
Moonrise.
My Own Heart Let Me More Have Pity On.
No Worst, There Is None.
Nothing is so beautiful as spring.
O Deus Ego Amo Te, *tr.*
Odes (*of* Horace), *sel., tr.*
Of a Death in Winter, I. *Fr.* That Nature Is a Heraclitean Fire and of the Comfort of the Resurrection.
On a Piece of Music.
Patience, Hard Thing!
Peace.
Pied Beauty.
Rhythmus ad SS. Sacramentum, *tr.*
Rosa Mystica.
St. Winefred's Well, *sel.*
Sea and the Skylark, The.
Six Epigrams, *sel.*
Soldier, The.
Sonnet: "I wake and feel the fell of dark, not day."
Sonnet: "No worst, there is none. Pitched past pitch of grief."
Sonnet: "Not, I'll not, carrion comfort, Despair, not feast on thee."
Sonnet: "Patience, hard thing! the hard thing but to pray."
Sonnet: "Thou art indeed just, Lord, if I contend."
Spelt from Sibyl's Leaves.
Spring.
Spring and Fall.
Starlight Night, The.
Summer Malison, The.
That Nature Is a Heraclitean Fire and of the Comfort of the Resurrection.
That Nature Is a Heraclitean Fire and of the Comfort of the Resurrection, *sel.*
Thou Art Indeed Just, Lord.
To His Watch.
To Oxford. *Fr.* Low Sunday and Monday.
To R. B.
To Seem the Stranger Lies My Lot.
To What Serves Mortal Beauty?
Tom's Garland.
Vision of the Mermaids, A, *sel.*
What I Do Is Me.
Wildness. *Fr.* Inversnaid.
Windhover, The.
Winter with the Gulf Stream.
Wreck of the *Deutschland,* The.
Wreck of the *Deutschland,* The, *sel.*
HOPKINS, JOHN HENRY, JR. We Three Kings of Orient Are.
HOPKINS, JOSEPH G. E. For a Child Who Died.
To a Baffled Idealist.
Variations on a Theme.
HOPKINS, LOUISA PARSONS. December. Nativity, The.
HOPKINS, MINNIE CASE. Autumn Leaves.
Heart Is a Strange Thing, The.
Life is a Lovely Thing.
HOPKINSON, FRANCIS. American Independence.
Battle of the Kegs, The.
British Valor Displayed.
Daughter's Rebellion, The.
New Roof, The.
On the Late Successful Expedition against Louisbourg.
Song: "My gen'rous heart disdains."
Song: "O'er the hills far away, at the birth of the morn."
HOPKINSON, JOSEPH. Hail, Columbia!
HOPPE, ANNA. Consecration.
HOPPER, EDWARD. Jesus, Saviour, Pilot Me.
HOPPER, NORA (Mrs. Wilfrid Hugh Chesson). Carol of Three Kings, The.
Connaught Lament, A.
Dark Man, The.
Fairy Fiddler, The.
June.
King of Ireland's Son, The.
March.
Marriage Charm, A.
Phyllis and Damon.
Sea, The.
Servian Lullaby, A.
'Tis I Go Fiddling, Fiddling.
Virgin's Lullaby, The.
Wind among the Reeds, The.
HOPPER, QUEENIE SCOTT. Amy Elizabeth Ermyntrude Annie.
HOPPIN, WILLIAM J. Charlie Machree.
HORACE (Quintus Horatius Flaccus). Ad Xanthium Phoceum. *Fr.* Odes.
Albi, Ne Doreas, *wr.* [Doleas]. *Fr.* Odes.
Art of Poetry, The [*or* Ars Poetica].
Bandusia, Stainless Mirror. *Fr.* Odes.
Bold Satirist, The.
Bore, The. *Fr.* Satires.
Carpe Diem. *Fr.* Odes.
Celebration for Neptune. *Fr.* Odes.
Coelo Tonantem. *Fr.* Odes.
Country Life. *Fr.* Epodes.
Death Inevitable. *Fr.* Odes.
Death of Cleopatra, The. *Fr.* Odes.
Endurance and Faithfulness. *Fr.* Odes.
Enjoy the Hour. *Fr.* Odes.
Epode XV: "It was night with the shine of the moon amid the smaller stars shining." *Fr.* Epodes.
Epode VII: "Whither, curs'd rabble, do you rush? Why show." *Fr.* Epodes.
Epodes, *sels.*
Extremum Tanain. *Fr.* Odes.
Fall of Cleopatra, The. *Fr.* Odes.
Fifth Ode of Horace, The.
Flaming Torches. *Fr.* Odes.
For Whom, Pyrrha? *Fr.* Odes.
Fountain of Bandusia. *Fr.* Odes.
Frippery. *Fr.* Odes.
Gift of Song, The. *Fr.* Odes.
Golden Mean, The. *Fr.* Odes.
Guardian of Hill and Woodland.
Happy the Man. *Fr.* Odes.
Holiday. *Fr.* Odes.
Horrors of Civil War, The.
I Hate Their Empty Shows. *Fr.* Odes.
Integer Vitae. *Fr.* Odes.
Invocation: "Maidens young and virgins tender." *Fr.* Odes.
Journey to Brundusium.
Life Is Short. *Fr.* Odes.
Martial Rage.
Mistrust To-Morrow. *Fr.* Odes.
Moderation. *Fr.* Odes.
Muses Love Me, The.
O Cruel Still.
O Fons Bandusiae. *Fr.* Odes.
Ode to Thaliarchus. *Fr.* Odes.
Odes, *sels.*
On Luxury. *Fr.* Odes.
Persian Fopperies. *Fr.* Odes.
Persian Luxury. *Fr.* Odes.
Persian Pomp. *Fr.* Odes.
Pine Tree for Diana, The. *Fr.* Odes.
Profane, The.
Proud Chloe's Heart. *Fr.* Odes.
Purity. *Fr.* Odes.
Questioning Lydia. *Fr.* Odes.
Reconciliation, The. *Fr.* Odes.
Reconciliation of Lovers. *Fr.* Odes.
Restorer, The. *Fr.* Odes.
Returned Warrior.
Revenge. *Fr.* Odes.
Revery of a Business Man.
Satires, *sels.*
Seek a Haven. *Fr.* Odes.
Ship of State, The. *Fr.* Odes.
Simplicity. *Fr.* Odes.
Spring. *Fr.* Odes.
Spring's Return. *Fr.* Odes.
Tell Me, Lydia. *Fr.* Odes.
This Is Thy Gift, O Muse. *Fr.* Odes.
Time to Choose a Lover.
Title to Fame. *Fr.* Odes.
To a Flirt. *Fr.* Odes.
To an Ambitious Friend. *Fr.* Odes.
To Aristius Fuscus. *Fr.* Odes.
To Chloe. *Fr.* Odes.
To Faunus. *Fr.* Odes.
To Fuscus Aristus.
To His Cup-Bearer. *Fr.* Odes.
To Leuconoë. *Fr.* Odes.
To Licinius [Murena]. *Fr.* Odes.
To Lucius Sestius. *Fr.* Odes.
To Maecenas. *Fr.* Odes.
To Manlius Torquatus. *Fr.* Odes.
To Mistress Pyrrha. *Fr.* Odes.
To Phidyle. *Fr.* Odes.
To Postumus. *Fr.* Odes.
To Pyrrha. *Fr.* Odes.
To Quintus Dellius. *Fr.* Odes.
To Sally. *Fr.* Odes.
To Thaliarchus. *Fr.* Odes.
To the Fountain of Bandusia. *Fr.* Odes.
To the Ship in Which Virgil Sailed to Athens. *Fr.* Odes.
To Venus. *Fr.* Odes.
Town and the Country Mouse, The. *Fr.* Satires.
Translated Out of Horace Which Begins Rectius Vives.
Translation of Horace. *Fr.* Odes.
Twenty-ninth Ode of the Third Book of Horace, The.
Vanity of Riches. *Fr.* Odes.
Winter. *Fr.* Odes.
Winter to Spring. *Fr.* Odes.
HORAN, ROBERT. Drowned Wife, The.
Emblems of Evening.
Little City.
HORIKAWA, LADY. How can one e'er be sure. *Fr.* Hyaku-Nin-Isshu.
Hyaku-Nin-Isshu, *sel.*
Will he always love me?
Will he love me forever?
HORNE, CYRIL MORTON. To My Unborn Son.
HORNE, FRANK. Immortality.
Kid Stuff.
Letters Found near a Suicide.
More Letters Found near a Suicide.
Nigger.
On Seeing Two Brown Boys in a Catholic Church.
To a Persistent Phantom.
To James.
Toast.
HORNE, HERBERT P. Amico Suo.
Et Sunt Commercia Coeli.
Formosae Puellae.
If She Be Made of White and Red.
Nancy Dawson.
Song, A: "Be not too quick to carve our rhyme."
Upon Returning a Silk Handkerchief.
HORNE, RICHARD HENRY [*or* HENGIST]. Akinetos. *Fr.* Orion.
Distraught for Merope. *Fr.* Orion.
Eos. *Fr.* Orion.
Genius.
In Forest Depths. *Fr.* Orion.
Meeting of Orion and Artemis. *Fr.* Orion.
Orion; an Epic Poem, *sels.*
Pelters of Pyramids.
Plough [*or* Plow], The.
Slave, The.
Solitude and the Lily.
HORNER, JOYCE MARY. Blackbirds in the Rain.
Public Holiday; Paris.
HORTON, EDWARD A. Flag, The.
HORTON, GEORGE. Night in Lesbos, A.
HORTON, GEORGE MOSES. George Moses Horton, Myself.
Graduate Leaving College, The.
Lines to My . . .
On Liberty and Slavery.
Slave's Complaint, The.
Troubled with the Itch, and Rubbing with Sulphur.
HORTON, PHILIP CLARK. Autumn Song.
HOSKING, ARTHUR NICHOLAS. Land of the Free.
HOSKINS, JOHN. Absence.
Epitaph on a Bellows-Maker, An.
Epitaph on a Man for Doing Nothing, An.
John Hoskins to His Little Child Benjamin, from the Tower.
Ode: "Absence, hear thou my protestation."
Of a Cozener.

HOSMER, FREDERICK LUCIAN. Cross and Flag.
Father, to Thee.
Forward through the Ages.
Friends Beyond.
Indwelling God, The.
My Dead.
New Year, The.
O Beautiful, My Country.
Our Country.
Prayer in Sorrow.
Prophecy Sublime, The.
Their Silent Ministry.
Thought of God, The.
Through Unknown Paths.
Thy Kingdom Come.
Thy Kingdom Come, O Lord.
With Self Dissatisfied.
HOSMER, WILLIAM HENRY CUYLER. Song of Texas.
HOSS, MARGARET MCBRIDE. Land Where the Taffy Birds Grow, The.
HOSTRUP, JENS CHRISTIAN. Woman of the North, The.
HOUGH, ALFRED J. Flag and Cross.
HOUGHTON, GEORGE WASHINGTON WRIGHT. Handsel Ring, The.
Legend of Walbach Tower, The.
Manor Lord, The.
March Winds, The.
Sandy Hook.
HOUGHTON, RICHARD MONCKTON MILNES, 1ST BARON. *See* MILNES, RICHARD MONCKTON, 1ST BARON HOUGHTON.
HOUSE, BEN D. Appomattox.
HOUSE, BOYCE. Beauty is Elsewhere.
Cities.
HOUSE, HOMER C. Home.
Insolence.
My Irish Great-Grandfather, Patrick O'Flyng.
Voices.
HOUSE, RICHARD. Sonnet: "Slow resistless flow of life goes on, The."
HOUSE, ROY TEMPLE. Three Magi, The.
HOUSE, VERNAL. In Tribute.
HOUSELANDER, CARYLL. Litany to Our Lady.
Mediocracy.
Reed, The.
HOUSMAN, ALFRED EDWARD. A. J. J.
Alcestis, *sel., tr.*
Along the Field as We Came By.
Alta Quies.
Amelia Mixed the Mustard.
As I Gird On for Fighting.
As through the Wild Green Hills of Wyre.
Away with Bloodshed.
Be Still, My Soul, Be Still.
Because I Liked You Better.
Blackbird, The.
Bredon Hill.
Bring, in this timeless grave to throw.
Carpenter's Son, The.
Cherry Trees.
Chestnut Casts His Flambeaux, The.
Chorus: "In speculation." *Fr.* Fragment of a Greek Tragedy.
Chorus: "What man is he that yearneth," *tr. Fr.* Oedipus at Colonus.
Clunton and Clunbury.
Could Man Be Drunk Forever.
Crossing Alone the Nighted Ferry.
Culprit, The.
Day of Battle, The.
Dedication: "They say my verse is sad: no wonder."
Deserter, The.
Easter Hymn.
Eight o'Clock.
1887.
Elephant, The, or the Force of Habit.
Epilogue: "Terence, this is stupid stuff."
Epitaph: "Here dead lie we because we did not choose."
Epitaph on an Army of Mercenaries.
Epithalamium: "He is here, Urania's Son."
Fairies Break Their Dances, The.
Fancy's Knell.
Far in a Western Brookland.
Farewell to Barn and Stack and Tree.
Farms of Home Lie Lost in Even, The.
First of May, The.
For My Funeral.
Fragment of a Greek Tragedy.
Fragment of a Greek Tragedy, *sel.*
Friends.
From Clee to Heaven the Beacon Burns.
From Far, from Eve and Morning.
Good-by, Young Man, Good-by.
Good Creatures, Do You Love Your Lives.
Grenadier.
Grizzly Bear is huge and wild, The.
Half-Moon Westers Low, My Love, The.
Hallelujah!
He Looked at Me with Eyes I Thought.
Hell Gate.
Her Strong Enchantments Failing.
Here Dead Lie We.
Ho, everyone that thirsteth.
How Clear, How Lovely Bright.
Hughley Steeple.
I Did Not Lose My Heart [in Summer's Even].
I Hoed and Trenched and Weeded.
I Knew a Cappadocian.
I lay me down and slumber.
I to My Perils.
If it chance your eye offend you.
If truth in hearts that perish.
Immortal Part, The.
In my own shire, if I was sad.
In the Morning, in the Morning.
In Valleys Green and Still.
In Valleys of Springs of Rivers.
Infant Innocence.
Inhuman Henry.
Into My Heart an Air That Kills.
Is My Team Plowing?
Isle of Portland, The.
It nods and curtsies and recovers.
Jar of Nations, The.
Lads in Their Hundreds, The.
Lancer.
Land of Biscay, The.
Laws of God, the Laws of Man, The.
Lent Lily, The.
Loitering with a vacant eye.
Long Road, The.
Look into Water, A.
Look Not in My Eyes, for Fear.
Loveliest of Trees [the Cherry Now].
March.
Merry Guide, The.
Mill-stream, now that noises cease, The.
My Dreams Are of a Field Afar.
New Mistress, The.
Night Is Freezing Fast, The.
Now Dreary Dawns the Eastern Light.
Now hollow fires burn out to black.
Oh Fair Enough Are Sky and Plain.
Oh Is It the Jar of Nations.
Oh, See How Thick the Goldcup Flowers.
Oh Stay at Home, My Lad [and Plow].
Oh, When I Was in Love with You.
Oh Who Is That Young Sinner.
Odes (*of* Horace), *sel., tr.*
Oedipus at Colonus, *sel., tr.*
Old Age, *tr. Fr.* Oedipus at Colonus.
Olive, The.
On Moonlit Heath and Lonesome Bank.
On the Idle Hill of Summer.
On Wenlock Edge [the Wood's in Trouble].
On your midnight pallet lying.
Oracles, The.
Others, I Am Not the First.
Parta Quies.
Power of Malt, The.
Rain, It Streams on Stone and Hillock, The.
Recruit, The.
Reveille.
Revolution.
Say, Lad, Have You Things to Do?
Seven against Thebes, The, *sel., tr.*
Shades of Night, The.
Shake Hands, We Shall Never Be Friends, All's Over.
Shot? so quick, so clean an ending?
Sigh That Heaves the Grasses, The.
Smooth between Sea and Land.
Soldier from the Wars Returning.
Stars Have Not Dealt Me, The.
Stars, I Have Seen Them Fall.
Stinging Nettle, The.
Street Sounds to the Soldiers' Tread, The.
Strength of Fate, The, *tr. Fr.* Alcestis.
Strong Love.
Summer Time on Bredon.
Tell Me Not Here [It Needs Not Saying].
Terence, This Is Stupid Stuff.
Then and Now.
There Is Hallelujah Hannah.
There pass the careless people.
They Say My Verse Is Sad.
Think No More, Lad.
This time of year a twelvemonth past.
'Tis time, I think, by Wenlock town.
To an Athlete Dying Young.
To His Godson Gerald C. A. Jackson.
To Stand Up Straight and Tread the Turning Mill.
To Think That Two and Two Are Four.
True Lover, The.
Twice a week the winter thorough.
Voice from a Grave, A.
Wake not for the world-heard thunder.
We'll to the Woods No More.
Welsh Marches, The.
Wenlock.
Wenlock Edge.
West and away the wheels of darkness roll.
Westward on the high-hilled plains.
When Adam Day by Day.
When First My Way to Fair I Took.
When Green Buds Hang in the Elm.
When I came last to Ludlow.
When I Was One-and-twenty.
When I Watch the Living Meet.
When I would muse in boyhood.
When Israel Out of Egypt Came.
When Smoke Stood Up from Ludlow.
When Summer's End Is Nighing.
When the Lad for Longing Sighs.
White in the Moon the Long Road Lies.
Winds out of the west land blow, The.
With Rue My Heart Is Laden.
With Seed the Sowers Scatter.
Yon Far Country.
Yonder See the Morning Blink.
You Smile upon Your Friend To-Day.
HOUSMAN, LAURENCE. All Fellows, *sel.*
"And the Word Was Made Flesh."
Annus Mirabilis.
Bonds.
Christmas Song.
Comrades.
Continuing City, The.
Cradle Song: "Sleep, my babe, your road of dreams."
Dead Warrior, A.
Dedication: "When I have ended, then I see."
Deus Noster Ignis Consumens.
Farewell to Town.
Gardener, The.
God's Mother.
Help-Givers, The.
Heroes.
Insets, *sel.*
Prayer for the Healing of the Wounds of Christ, A.
Resurrection. *Fr.* Rue.
Rue, *sel.*
Separation.
Settlers, The.
Spikenard.
To Thomas Hardy.
Two Loves, The.
HOUSTON, ELEANOR JORDAN. Glass Blower, The.
HOUSTON, MARGARET BELL. Admonitions.
Cerelle.
Song from the Traffic.
Tulips.

HOVELL-THURLOW, EDWARD, 2D BARON THURLOW. Beauty.
Heron, The.
May.
To a Bird.
When in the Woods I Wander All Alone.
HOVER, EMILY. Mr. Beetle.
HOVEY, RICHARD. Accident in Art.
Again among the Hills.
At the Crossroads.
At the End of the Day.
Barney McGee.
Battle of Manila, The.
Birth of Galahad, The, *sel.*
Call of the Bugles, The.
Chanson de Rosemonde.
Comrades.
Contemporaries.
Dartmouth Winter-Song.
Death Song in Taliesin. *Fr.* Taliesin.
Eleazar Wheelock.
Envoy: "Whose furthest footstep never strayed."
Faun, The, *sels.*
Hunting Song. *Fr.* King Arthur.
Immanence.
Kavanagh, The.
King Arthur, *sel.*
Laurana's Song.
Love in the Winds.
Love of a Boy, The.
Marriage of Guenevere, The, *sel.*
Mocking Bird, The.
New-born Year, The.
Sea. *Fr.* Seaward.
Sea Gypsy, The.
Seaward, *sel.*
Short Beach.
Song: "Flower-born Blodueda, The." *Fr.* The Marriage of Guenevere.
Spring.
Spring, *sels.*
Stein Song, A. *Fr.* Spring.
Taliesin, *sels.*
Thought of Her, The.
Three of a Kind.
Transcendence.
Two Lovers, The.
Unforeseen.
Unmanifest Destiny.
Vagabondia.
Wander-Lovers, The.
Word of the Lord from Havana, The.
Ylen's Song. *Fr.* The Birth of Galahad.
HOVHANNESSIAN, HOVHANNES. Araxes Came Devouringly.
Rock, The.
Spring.
HOW, LOUIS. Divina Commedia: Paradiso, *sel., tr.*
Saint Bernard's Prayer to Our Lady, *tr. Fr.* Divina Commedia: Paradiso.
Silly Song, A.
HOW, WILLIAM WALSHAM. Behold the Master passeth by!
For All the Saints.
Funeral Hymn.
Lord Jesus, When We Stand Afar.
O Jesus, thou art standing.
O Word of God Incarnate.
Soldiers of the cross, arise!
We Give Thee but Thine Own.
HOWARD, BLANCHE WILLIS. Popular Poplar Tree, The.
HOWARD, EDWARD. Now Having Proved Thy Fond Delays.
HOWARD, FRANCES MINTURN. Heron in Swamp.
Narcissus in a Cocktail Glass.
HOWARD, MRS. G. M. Secret, A.
HOWARD, GEOFFREY. Gratias Age.
HOWARD, HENRY. *See* SURREY, HENRY HOWARD, EARL OF.
HOWARD, JAMES. English Monsieur, The, *sel.*
Ladies, Farewell! *Fr.* The English Monsieur.
HOWARD, JOHN ZOLLIE. Solitaire.
HOWARD, PHILIP, 1ST EARL OF ARUNDEL. Hymn: "O Christ, the glorious Crown."
Lament for Our Lady's Shrine at Walsingham, A, *at.*
Though Here in Flesh I Be.
Through Thy Cross and Passion.
HOWARD, PHILIP E. Strength in Weakness.
HOWARD, SIR ROBERT. To the Unconstant Cynthia.
HOWARD, SIR ROBERT, *and* JOHN DRYDEN. Death like a Rose. *Fr.* The Indian Queen.
Indian Queen, The, *sels.*
Song of Aerial Spirits. *Fr.* The Indian Queen.
Zempoalla's Dream. *Fr.* The Indian Queen.
HOWARD, ROBERT ERVIN. Always Comes Evening.
Arkham.
Futility.
Ghost Kings, The.
Harp of Alfred, The.
King and the Oak, The.
Last Hour, The.
Lines Written in the Realization that I Must Die.
Moon Mockery.
Recompense.
Singer in the Mist, The.
Solomon Kane's Home-coming.
Which Will Scarcely Be Understood.
HOWARD, SARAH ELIZABETH. Round-up, The.
Wild Horse Jerry's Story.
HOWARD, WINIFRED. Fairy Wings.
Squirrels' Christmas, The.
White Horses.
Windy Day, A.
HOWARTH, ELLEN CLEMENTINE. 'Tis But a Little Faded Flower.
HOWARTH, ROBERT GUY. Elegy: "Here, awaiting what hereafter."
HOWE, D. N. Good Shepherd, The.
HOWE, JOSEPH. Acadia, *sels.*
Flag of Old England, The.
Indian Massacre, The. *Fr.* Acadia.
Song of the Micmac, The.
Toast, A.
HOWE, JULIA WARD. Battle Hymn of the [American] Republic.
Crown His Bloodstained Pillow.
Decoration Day.
Flag, The.
J. A. G.
Lincoln.
Message of Peace, The.
Our Country.
Our Orders.
Pardon.
Parricide.
Robert E. Lee.
Royal Guest, The.
HOWE, MARK ANTONY DE WOLFE ("Gilbertulus"). At the Heart.
Ben Franklin's Head (1728).
Distinction.
Helmsman, The.
Known Soldier, The.
Pacifists.
Petrillo.
Pocket and Steeple.
Travellers, The.
Treasure House, A.
Vale—atque Salve.
"Whom the Gods Love."
HOWELL, ELIZABETH LLOYD. Milton's Prayer [of Patience].
HOWELL, JAMES. Of London Bridge, and the Stupendous Sight, and Structure Thereof.
Stanzas for Lent.
Upon Black Eyes, and Becoming Frowns.
Upon Dr. Davies' British Grammar.
HOWELL, THOMAS. Jack Shows His Qualities and Great Good Will to Jone.
Lover Deceived Writes to His Lady, The, *sel.*
Man's Life Likened to a Stage Play.
Of Misery.
Of the Golden World.
Red Rose, The.
Reward Doth Not Always Answer Desert.
Rose, The.
To His Lady, of Her Doubtful Answer.
To One Who after Death Would Leave His Lively Picture.
To the Reader.
When He Thought Himself Contemned.
Who Would Have Thought. *Fr.* The Lover Deceived Writes to His Lady.
Winter's Morning Muse, A.
HOWELLS, MILDRED. Down a Woodland Way.
God's Will.
Going Too Far.
Moral in Sèvres, A.
Romance.
HOWELLS, WILLIAM DEAN. Barbarossa, *sel., tr.*
Battle in the Clouds, The.
Bewildered Guest, The.
Calvary.
Caprice.
Change.
Earliest Spring.
Faith.
From Generation to Generation.
Heredity.
Hope.
If.
In August.
In Earliest Spring.
Judgment Day.
Ode on Superstition, *sel., tr.*
Our Thanksgiving Accept.
Prayer, A: "Lord, for the erring thought."
Robin and the Cows, The.
Sometimes, When after Spirited Debate.
Song the Oriole Sings, The.
Thanksgiving.
Two Wives, The.
Undiscovered Country, The.
Vision.
What Shall It Profit?
HOWELLS, WINIFRED. Forthfaring.
Mood, A.
Past.
Poet and the Child, The.
Wasted Sympathy, A.
HOWES, BARBARA (Mrs. William Jay Smith). Light and Dark.
L'Ile du Levant; the Nudist Colony.
Triumph of Chastity, The.
Triumph of Death, The.
For translations from French, see AnFP; LyMA.
HOWES, GRACE CLEMENTINE. Wind of the Prairie.
Winged Mariner.
HOWITT, MARY. Barley-Mowers' Song, The.
Birds in Summer.
Broom Flower, The.
Buttercups and Daisies.
Child's Hymn, The.
Coming of Spring.
Cornfields.
Cornfields, *sel.*
Fairies of the Caldon Low, The.
Father Is Coming.
Flax Flower, The.
Hawking Party in the Olden Time, A.
Heron, The.
Humming Bird, The.
Lion, The.
Little Children.
Marien Lee.
Monkey, The.
Old Christmas.
Rose of May, The.
Sale of the Pet Lamb, The.
Sea Fowler, The.
Sea-Gull, The.
September.
Spider and the Fly, The.
Spring.
Spring Is Coming.
Spring Song, A.
Squirrel, The.

HOWITT, MARY (*continued*)
Swinging Song, A.
True Story of Web-Spinner, The.
Use of Flowers, The.
Voice of Spring, The.
Voyage with the Nautilus, The.
Winter Fire, The.
Wood-Mouse, The.
HOWITT, WILLIAM. Departure of the Swallow, The.
Grey Squirrels, The.
Northern Seas, The.
Summer Noon, A.
Wind in a Frolic, The.
HOWLAND, EDWARD. Condemned, The.
HOWLAND, GEORGE. Washington's Birthday.
HOWLAND, MARY WOOLSEY. First Spring Flowers.
In the Hospital.
Rest.
HOWLISTON, MARY H. Our Flag.
HOYLAND, JOHN SOMERVELL. For Family Love.
Prayer for Brotherhood, A.
Prayer for Family Love, A.
Prayer for Our Home.
Sacrament of Work, The.
HOYT, CHARLES HALE. Bowery, The.
HOYT, CHARLES SUMNER. Is This the Time to Halt?
Is This the Time to Sound Retreat?
HOYT, HELEN (Mrs. William W. Lyman). Arches.
Ellis Park.
Golden Bough.
Happiness Betrays Me.
Homage.
In the Park.
Lamp Posts.
Like a Cloud, like a Mist.
Lover Sings of a Garden, The.
Memory.
New-born, The.
Rain at Night.
Reparation.
Sense of Death, The.
Since I Have Felt the Sense of Death.
Stone-Age Sea, The.
HOYT, HELEN UNDERWOOD. Kate.
Vegetable Fantasies.
HOYT, HENRY MARTYN. Land of Dreams.
1917–1919.
Spell, The.
HOYT, RALPH. Old.
Snow—a Winter Sketch.
HSIANG SSU. Nightfall.
HSIAO WU TI. Loneliness.
HSI-CHÜN. Lament of Hsi-chün.
HSIEH HSIEH. To an Early Plum.
HSIEH T'IAO. Calm of Evening.
Song of the Men of Chin-ling.
HSIN CH'I-CHI. Drinking.
To the Tune of "The Ugly Slave."
HSING CH'E. To My Mother.
HSI P'EI LAN. Bell in the Night, The.
Morning Bell of Fang T'a, The.
To My Sister.
Which?
Wife to a Husband, A.
HSÜAN TI. On Seeing a Beautiful Woman Ride By in a Cart.
HSU CHAO. Locust Swarm, The.
HSÜ CHI. Old Friends.
HSÜ CHIEN. Just Sixteen.
HSÜ CHING FAN. Keepsake, The.
HSÜ CHU. From Exile.
HSÜEH FENG. Palace Poem, A.
HSÜEH LAN YING. Hu Chiu Shan.
HSÜEH T'AO. Home from the Wars.
HSU HUN. Song at the Frontier.
HSÜ LING. Waters of Lung-t'ou, The.
HSÜ PEN. Hermit, The.
HSÜ YING YÜ. Farewell to Spring.
HUANG-FU SUNG. Dream of Chiangnan, A.
HUANG PIEN. Cups of Jade.
Gifts.
Tears.
Yearning.
HUANG WAN CH'IUNG. Flute at Evening, A.
HUBBARD, P. M. To Cynthia, Not to Let Him Read the Ladies' Magazines.
HUBBELL, ROSE STRONG. Mangroves Dance, The.
HUCH, RICARDA. Deep in the Heavens.
HUCKEL, OLIVER. O Mind of God, Broad as the Sky.
Unanswered Prayer.
HUDNUT, WILLIAM HERBERT, SR. In Him Ye Are Made Full.
Quit You like Men.
HUDNUT, WILLIAM HERBERT, JR. No Prisoner of Time.
HUDSON, DENIS. Valse des Fleurs.
HUDSON, FLEXMORE. Song of an Australian.
HUDSON, MARY CLEMMER AMES. *See* CLEMMER, MARY.
HUDSON, THOMAS. Jack Robinson.
HUEFFER, FORD MADOX. *See* FORD, FORD MADOX.
HUERTA, EFRAÍN. Recollection of Love.
Sounds of Dawn, The.
HUESTIS, ANNIE CAMPBELL. Aldaran.
On the Stair.
Will-o'-the-Wisp, The.
HUFF, BARBARA A. Afternoon with Grandmother.
Library, The.
HUGHAN, JESSIE WALLACE. Where the Wood-Thrush Calls.
HUGHES, DANIEL. Damascus Road, The.
HUGHES, DAVE ("Old Arkansaw"). Drifter, The.
HUGHES, DOROTHY. Dusting of the Books, The.
HUGHES, HENRY. Behold great Neptunes risen from the deep, *at.*
Chloris a Constant Comfort.
O I am sick, I am sick to death, tis soe, *at.*
HUGHES, HUGH J. Pards.
HUGHES, JAMES D. My Son.
HUGHES, JOHN. Court of Neptune, The.
Sonnet: "I die with too transporting joy," *tr.*
Ungrateful Cupid, The.
HUGHES, JOHN CEIRIOG ("Ceiriog"). Epilogue to Alun Mabon.
Liberty.
Welsh Lullaby, A.
HUGHES, LANGSTON. Acceptance.
African Dance.
Afro-American Fragment.
Alabama Earth (at Booker Washington's grave).
April Rain Song.
As I Grew Older.
Brass Spittoons.
City; San Francisco.
Cross.
Cycle.
Dream Variation.
Dreams.
Dressed Up.
Drum.
Early Evening Quarrel.
Epigram: " 'Do you not wish to renounce the Devil?' " *tr.*
Epilogue: "I, too, sing America."
Esthete in Harlem.
Fantasy in Purple.
Feet o' Jesus.
Fire.
Florida Road Workers.
From Selma.
Garment.
Gone Boy.
Gypsy Man.
Hard Daddy.
Hard Luck.
Harlem Sweeties.
Havana Dreams.
Heaven; the City Called Heaven.
Homesick Blues.
House in Taos, A.
I, Too.
In Time of Silver Rain.
Jazz Band in a Parisian Cabaret.
Jazzonia.
Last Call.
Late Corner.
Let America Be America Again.
Life Is Fine.
Little Green Tree Blues.
Ma Lord.
Merry-go-round.
Mexican Market Woman.
Moon. *Fr.* A House in Taos.
Mother to Son.
Negro, The.
Negro Speaks of Rivers, The.
New Wind a-Blowin', A.
Personal.
Po' Boy Blues.
Poem: "Night is beautiful, The."
Prayer: "I ask you this."
Proem: "I am a Negro."
Rain. *Fr.* A House in Taos.
Refugee in America.
Sailor.
Saturday Night.
Seascape.
Snail.
Song for a Dark Girl.
Song to a Negro Wash-Woman.
Suicide's Note.
Sun. *Fr.* A House in Taos.
Testament.
To Midnight Nan at LeRoy's.
Trip; San Francisco.
Two Somewhat Different Epigrams.
Weary Blues, The.
When Sue Wears Red.
Where? When? Which?
Wind. *Fr.* A House in Taos.
Winter Sweetness.
Wisdom.
Youth.
For translations from French and Spanish, see AnCL; FaPON; PoNe.
HUGHES, RICHARD. Burial of the Spirit.
Explanation, on Coming Home Late.
Felo de Se.
Glaucopis.
Horse-Trough, The.
Image, The.
Invocation to the Muse.
Lover's Reply to Good Advice.
Old Cat Care.
On Time.
Poets, Painters, Puddings.
Ruin, The.
Sermon, The.
Singing Furies, The.
Tramp.
Walking Road, The.
Winter.
HUGHES, RUPERT. For Decoration Day.
Martyrs of the *Maine,* The.
With a First Reader.
HUGHES, TED. Decay of Vanity, The.
Jaguar, The.
Thrushes.
Witches.
HUGHES, THOMAS. If Ever You Go to Dolgelly.
HUGO PRIMAS OF ORLÉANS. On the Gift of a Cloak.
HUGO, VICTOR. After Six Thousand Years.
Age is Great and Strong, The.
Alcove at Sunrise, An.
Another Song: "Though heaven's gate of light uncloses."
Apparition.
At Dawn.
At Nightfall, on the Wall of Paris.
At Villequier.
Be like the Bird.
Boaz Asleep.
Bright Stars and Dark. *Fr.* Les Contemplations.
Burgraves, Les, *sel.*
Celestial Fête.
Children of the Poor, The.
Choses du soir, *sel.*
Conscience.
Contemplations, Les, *sel.*
Cradle Song: "In the darken'd alcove."
December.
Ecstasy.
Genesis of Butterflies, The.
Good Night.
Grandfather's Ditty, A.
Granny's Nodding.
Grave and the Rose, The.

Heard on the Mountain.
Hernani, *sel.*
House and Home.
In Early Spring.
Indignation.
June Nights.
Kings.
Light and Life. *Fr.* Les Burgraves.
Lion at Noon, The.
Little Music, A.
Love. *Fr.* Ruy Blas.
Luna.
Memory.
More Strong than Time.
Mourning.
My Poems.
My Two Daughters.
New Song to an Old Air.
No Child.
Nocturne: "I walked beside the deep, one night of stars."
O France When Thou Art Prone and Bound.
Oh, Thou, My Lover. *Fr.* Hernani.
Oceano Nox.
Olympio's Sadness.
Our Dead.
Paroles sur la dune, *sel.*
Poet's Simple Faith, The.
Poor Children.
Quia Pulvis Es.
Rayons et les ombres, Les, *sel.*
Republic of the World.
Ruy Blas, *sel.*
Sadness of Olympio, The. *Fr.* Les Rayons et les ombres.
Song: "To what bliss could my spirit aspire."
Song That Lovers Sing, The.
Sowing Season.
Sunset.
To His Dead Daughter.
To My Daughter Adèle.
Toute la Lyre, *sel.*
Trumpets of the Mind, The.
Universal Republic, The.
Vase, The.
Waiting.
When the Child Appears.
Where Goest Thou?
Wings.
Worst Treason, The.
HUIATT, S. R. When the Preacher Comes to Tea.
HUIDOBRO, VICENTE. Art of Poetry, The.
Bewitching Drowned.
Bring Games.
Emigrant to America.
I Am Partly Moon.
In.
Nature vive.
Prelude to Hope.
Round.
Serenade of Laughing Life.
She.
Time of Waiting.
You Have Never Known the Tree of Tenderness.
"HULDA." *See* BENEDIKTSDÓTTIR, UNNUR.
HULL, ELEANOR. Consecration, *tr.*
Dirge on the Death of Art O'Leary, *tr.*
Fairies' Lullaby, The, *tr.*
Four Prayers, *tr.*
Four Prayers, *sels., tr.*
Hymn to the Virgin Mary, *tr.*
I Lie Down with God, *tr.* *Fr.* Four Prayers.
I Rest with Thee, O Jesus, *tr.* *Fr.* Four Prayers.
Lay of Prince Marvan, The, *tr.*
Mary's Vision, *tr.*
May the Sweet Name of Jesus, *tr.*
Night Prayer, *tr.*
Prayer: "Be Thou my vision, O Lord of my heart," *tr.*
Prayer before Going to Sleep, *tr.*
Roisin Dubh, *tr.*
Sacred Trinity, The, *tr.* *Fr.* Four Prayers.
Sleep-Song of Grainne over Dermuid, The, *tr.*
Soul's Desire, The, *tr.*
Straying Sheep, The, *tr.*
HULLAH, J. P. Come with Thy Lute.
HULME, THOMAS ERNEST. Above the Dock.
Autumn.
Conversion.
Embankment, The.
Fantasia of a Fallen Gentleman on a Cold Bitter Night on the Embankment.
Mana Aboda.
HUME, ALEXANDER. Of God's Omnipotencie.
Of the Day Estivall.
Story of a Summer Day, The.
Summer Day, A.
"HUME, ISOBEL" (I. H. Fisher). Homecoming.
Sleeper, The.
Whiteness.
HUME, TOBIAS. Fain Would I Change That Note, *at.*
Song: "Fain would I change that note," *at.*
HUMPHREYS, DAVID. On Disbanding the Army.
Western Emigration.
HUMPHREYS, EMYR. Courage.
Cowardice.
1536–1936.
Nonconformist, A.
Sympathy Explained.
Unloading Hay.
HUMPHRIES, ROLFE. Aeneas and Dido, *tr.* *Fr.* The Aeneid.
Aeneas at the Site of Rome, *tr.* *Fr.* The Aeneid.
Aeneid, The, *sels., tr.*
Camilla, *tr.* *Fr.* The Aeneid.
Carmina Burana, *sel., tr.*
Cynneddf, The.
Down the Field.
Faithless Wife, The, *tr.*
Harp Music.
He Visits a Hospital.
Heresy for a Classroom.
Lower World, The (the Sibyl Speaks), *tr.* *Fr.* The Aeneid.
Odes (*of* Horace), *sel., tr.*
Polo Grounds.
Proteus; or, The Shapes of Conscience.
Render unto Caesar.
Static.
To the Greatest City in the World.
Variation on a Theme by Francis Kilvert.
Vidi Viridi Phyllida sub Tilia, *tr.* *Fr.* Carmina Burana.
War in the Dark, The.
For translations from Spanish, see AnCL.
HUNNIS, WILLIAM. If Thou Desire to Live in Rest.
No Pains Comparable to His Attempt.
Nosegay Always Sweet, for Lovers to Send for Tokens of Love at New Year's Tide, or for Fairings, A, *at.*
Shipmen, The.
HUNT, HELEN. *See* JACKSON, HELEN HUNT.
HUNT, JOSEPHINE SLOCUM. You Kissed Me.
HUNT, JOSIE R. Katie Lee and Willie Grey, *at.*
HUNT, LEIGH. Abou Ben Adhem.
Abou Ben Adhem and the Angel.
Aminta, *sel., tr.*
Amyntas; or, The Impossible Dowry, *sel., tr.*
Bacchus in Tuscany, *sel., tr.*
Blessed Spot, A, *tr.*
Canzone 126: "Clear, fresh, and dulcet streams," *tr.*
Captain Sword.
Complaint, The, *tr.*
Cupid Drowned.
Cupid Swallowed.
Dearest Poets, The.
Dirge for an Infant.
Dream of Venus, A, *tr.*
Epitaph on Erotion.
Essence of Opera, The, *tr.*
Fairies' Song, *tr.* *Fr.* Amyntas; or, The Impossible Dowry.
Fish Answers, A. *Fr.* The Fish, the Man, and the Spirit.
Fish, the Man, and the Spirit, The.
Fish, the Man, and the Spirit, The, *sels.*
Fish to Man. *Fr.* The Fish, the Man, and the Spirit.
Glove and the Lions, The.
Golden Age, The, *tr.* *Fr.* Aminta.
Grasshopper and the Cricket, The.
Home to Sermio, *tr.*
House and Grounds, A.
I Dreamt I Saw Great Venus, *tr.*
Idylls (*of* Theocritus), *sel., tr.*
If You Be a Nun.
Jaffar.
Jenny Kiss'd [*or* Kissed] Me.
Jovial Priest's Confession, The.
Love-Lesson, A, *tr.*
Love-Letters Made in Flowers.
Lover's Prison, The, *tr.*
Madame d'Albert's Laugh, *tr.*
Mahmoud.
Nile, The.
Nun, The.
Nymphs, The, *sel.*
Odyssey, The, *sel., tr.*
On Her Laugh, *tr.*
On the Death of His Son Vincent.
On the Grasshopper and Cricket.
Paying a Debt, *tr.*
Places of Nestling Green. *Fr.* The Story of Rimini.
Poets, The.
Prayer in the Bower, The.
Providence, *tr.*
River Nile, The.
Rondeau: "Jenny kissed me when we met."
Sneezing.
Song of Fairies Robbing an Orchard, *tr.* *Fr.* Amyntas; or, The Impossible Dowry.
Songs and Chorus of the Flowers.
Spring, *tr.*
Story of Rimini, The, *sels.*
To a Child during Sickness.
To [a] Fish. *Fr.* The Fish, the Man, and the Spirit.
To Hampstead.
To John Keats.
To the Grasshopper and the Cricket.
To the Spirit Great and Good.
Trumpets of Doolkarnein, The.
Two Heavens.
Written under the Engraving of a Portrait of Rafael.
Yes and No, *tr.*
HUNT, SARA KEABLES. Two Little Stockings, The.
HUNTER, ANNE (Home). My Mother Bids Me Bind My Hair.
HUNTER, MRS. J. Simile, A.
HUNTER, JOHN. Dreams and Deeds.
HUNTER-DUVAR, JOHN. Adieu to France. *Fr.* De Roberval.
Brawn of England's Lay.
De Roberval, *sels.*
Emigration of the Fairies, The, *sels.*
Gallant Fleet. *Fr.* De Roberval.
La Belle Sauvage. *Fr.* De Roberval.
Ohnáwa. *Fr.* De Roberval.
Twilight Song. *Fr.* De Roberval.
HUNTING, G. F. Help One Another.
HUNTINGTON, ELLEN M. *See* GATES, ELLEN M. HUNTINGTON.
HUNTINGTON, GEORGE. International Hymn.
Peace Hymn for England and America.
HUNTINGTON, GERTRUDE. *See* MCGIFFERT, GERTRUDE HUNTINGTON.
HUNTINGTON, WILLIAM REED. Authority.
Tellus.
HUNTLEY, LYDIA HOWARD. *See* SIGOURNEY, LYDIA HUNTLEY.
HUNTLEY, STANLEY. Annabel Lee.
HURD, HARRY ELMORE. Black and White Shuffle.
Medallion of Saint Francis.
HURDIS, JAMES. Landscape, A, *sel.*
Village Curate, The, *sels.*
HUSSEY, NORAH E. I Spy.
My Garden.

HUSSEY, NORAH E. (*continued*)
Toad the Tailor.
HUSSEY, RUTH ANNE. Little Rain Men.
HUSTED, ELLERY. I Saw a Maid.
HUSTON, FRANCIS. Forty Years Ago, *at.*
Twenty Years Ago, *at.*
HUTCHINSON, ELLEN MACKAY. *See* CORTISSOZ, ELLEN MACKAY HUTCHINSON.
HUTCHINSON, M. M. Dancing on the Shore.
Harvest.
Making Tens.
My New Umbrella.
Ten Little Indian Boys.
Thames, The.
Tug-of-War, A.
Twice.
HUTCHISON, COLLISTER. Winter Night.
HUTCHISON, PERCY. Columbus.
HUTCHISON, PERCY ADAMS. "Bottoms Up" ad Finem.
Methinks the Measure.
HUTT, FRANK. Vacation Time.
HUTTON, JOSEPH. Tomb of the Brave.
HUTTON, LAURENCE. Doves of Venice.
HUXLEY, ALDOUS. Afternoon of a Faun, The, *tr.*
Anniversaries.
Après-Midi d'un faune, L', *tr.*
Canal, The.
Cicadas, The.
Doors of the Temple.
Femmes Damnées, *sel., tr.*
Fifth Philosopher's Song.
First Philosopher's Song.
Frascati's.
Jonah.
Male and Female Created He Them.
Mole.
Ninth Philosopher's Song.
Out of the Window.
Soles Occidere et Redire Possunt, *sel.*
Song of Poplars.
Sunset, A.
Villiers de l'Isle-Adam.
HUXLEY, THOMAS HENRY. Tennyson.
HYBRIAS. Freelance, The.
My wealth's a burly spear and brand.
Soldier's Riches, A.
Song of a Legionnaire.
HYDE, DOUGLAS. Blessed Be the Holy Will of God, *tr.*
Brow of Nephin, The, *tr.*
Bruadar and Smith and Glinn, *tr.*
Cold, Sharp Lamentation.
Colum-Cille's Farewell to Ireland, *tr.*
Cooleen, The.
Farewell to Ireland, *tr.*
He Meditates on the Life of a Rich Man.
I Am Raftery, *tr.*
I Shall Not Die for Thee, *tr.*
Joyce's Repentance, The, *tr.*
Little Child, I Call Thee, *tr.*
My Grief on the Sea, *tr.*
My Love, Oh, She Is My Love, *tr.*
Mystery, The, *tr.*
O King of the Friday, *tr.*
O Youth of the Bound Black Hair, *tr.*
On His Exile to Iona, *tr.*
Poem to Be Said on Hearing the Birds Sing, A.
Priest and the Friars, The, *tr.*
Red Man's Wife, The, *tr.*
Ringleted Youth of My Love, *tr.*
This Weariness and Grief, *tr.*
Though Riders Be Thrown, *tr.*
Troubled Friar, The, *tr.*
Will You Be as Hard?
HYDE, FILLMORE. Philosophical Poem on Cats, A.
HYDE, WILLIAM DE WITT. Creation's Lord, We Give Thee Thanks.
HYMAN, MELANIE. Balance.
What forms of anguish might this pattern show.
HYNSON, GEORGE B. Our Delaware.
HYWEL AB OWAIN GWYNEDD. Love Poem, A.
Ode to a Chosen Girl.
"HYDE, ROBIN" (Iris Guiver Wilkinson). Beaches, The, *sels.*
English Rider, The.
Houses, The, *sels.*
Journey from New Zealand.
Ku Li.
People, The, *sels.*
Sarah.
Sisters.

I

"I., B." Garland of the Blessed Virgin Marie, The.
"I. T." *See* "T., I."
"I. V. S. W." *See* "W., I. V. S."
"I. W." *See* "W., I."
IBÁÑEZ, ROBERTO. Elegy for the Drowned Men Who Return.
IBARBOUROU, JUANA DE. Fleeting Restlessness.
Rainy Night.
Smith, The.
IBN ABD RABBIHI. Favourites.
Modest Blush.
Ritual.
IBN ABDUL GHAFUR. Coat of Mail.
IBN ABDUN. Fate.
Poor Lodgings.
IBN ABDUS. White Horse with a Crimson Flash, A.
IBN ABI BISHR. Sunshine.
IBN ABIL KHAYAL. Alchemy.
IBN ABI RUH. Night of Joy.
IBN ADHA. On Taking Up a Humble Place at Court.
IBN ADIYA, AL-SAMAU'AL. Are We Not the People, *sel.*
Oh, Would That I Knew.
Oh, Ye Censurers.
IBN A'ISHA. Apricot Tree, The.
Violet.
IBN AL-ABBAR. Gilliflower.
Jessamine.
Wheel, The.
IBN ALALAF ALNAHARWANY. To a Cat.
IBN AL-ARABI. Beauty in Rags.
Ode: "They journeyed."
Ode: Who Can Support the Anguish of Love?
Sand.
IBN AL-ATTAR. White and Black.
IBN AL-BAIN. Storm.
Virgin Earth.
IBN AL-BATTI. Eye and Heart.
Hypocrites, The.
Pilgrim.
IBN AL-FARAS. Moon of Beauty.
IBN AL-HADDAD. Apology.
Compliment.
IBN AL-HAJJ. Beard, The.
Clemency.
Odi et Amo.
IBN AL-HAMMARA. Eyelashes.
House, The.
On the Death of His Wife.
IBN AL-IMAM. Hopes.
IBN AL-KHABBAZA. King Who Died Young, The.
Striking of the Tent, The.
IBN AL-LABBANA. Patronage.
IBN AL-MISSISI. Fragment.
IBN AL-QABILA. Gazelle.
IBN AL-QABTURNU. Hawk, The.
Party, The.
IBN AL-QAFFUN. Family Tree.
IBN AL-QUTIYA. Lilies and Roses.
Walnut, The.
IBN AL-RA'I'A. Fountain, The.
IBN AL-RUMI. On a Valetudinarian.
IBN AL-SABUNI. Mirror, The.
Red Gown, The.
IBN AL-TALLA. Artichoke, The.
IBN AL-TARAWA. Saki Refusing to Drink Wine, A.
IBN AL-YAMANI. Wings of Wine.
IBN AL-ZAQQAQ. Bloody Sword, The.
Exposure.
Frankincense.
Night of Bliss.
Portent, The.
Rose-Petals.
Star Flowers.
IBN AMMAR. In Praise of the King.
Poet's Pride.
Ransom.
Spare.
IBN ATIYA. Night Traveller, The.
IBN BAQI. Bacchanal.
Champion, The.
Love's Evidence.
IBN BASSAM. Mist.
IBN BILLITA. Dawn.
Drunken Beauty.
Marguerite.
Sails.
IBN BURD. Blue and Gold.
Daybreak.
Moon in Mist.
IBN CHASDAI, ABRAHAM. Advice to Bores.
Elusive Maid, The.
Meek and the Proud, The.
Poor Scholar, The.
IBN DARRAJ. Lilies.
Night and Day.
Ship in Storm.
IBN DARRAJ AL-ANDALUSI. Wing of Separation, The.
IBN EZRA, ABRAHAM. Ages of Man, The, *at.*
Far Sweeter than Honey.
Freedom.
God Everywhere.
Law, The.
Living God, The.
Out of Luck.
Song of Chess, The, *at.*
IBN EZRA, MOSES. All Ye That Go Astray. *Fr.* The World's Illusion.
Awake, My Soul. *Fr.* Wine-Songs.
Beautiful Is the Loved One.
Beauty of the Stars, The.
Book of Tarshish, The, *sel.*
Bring Me the Cup. *Fr.* Wine-Songs.
Drink, Friends. *Fr.* Wine-Songs.
Dying Wife to Her Husband, A.
Elegy: "In pain she bore the son who her embrace."
Elegy: "My thoughts impelled me to the resting-place."
End of Man Is Death, The.
God That Doest Wondrously.
He That Regards the Precious Things of Earth. *Fr.* The World's Illusion.
Hot Flame of My Grief, The.
I Went Out into the Garden.
In Vain Earth Decks Herself. *Fr.* The World's Illusion.
Joy of Life. *Fr.* The Book of Tarshish.
Man Is a Weaver.
Men Are Children of This World.
My Love Is like a Myrtle.
My Love Sways, Dancing.
On My Sorrowful Life.
Promises of the World, The. *Fr.* The World's Illusion.
Rejoice, O Youth, in the Lovely Hind.
Rosy Days Are Numbered, The. *Fr.* Wine-Songs.
Sorrow Shatters My Heart.
Splendor of Thine Eyes, The.
Strange Love.
Those Beauteous Maids.
To a Plagiarist.
Walk in the Precepts.
When She Plays upon the Harp or Lute.
Why Should I Grieve?
Wine-Songs, *sels.*
With Hopeless Love.
Without My Friends the Day Is Dark.
Works of God, The.
World Is Like a Woman of Folly, The. *Fr.* The World's Illusion.
World's Illusion, The, *sels.*
Ye Anger Earth. *Fr.* The World's Illusion.
Young Dove, The.
IBN FADDAL. Young Pilgrim, The.
IBN FARAJ. Continence.
IBN FARSAN. Battle Song.
IBN GABIROL, SOLOMON. Almighty! What Is Man?

Defiance.
Degenerate Age, A.
"From Thee to Thee."
I Have Sought Thee Daily.
In Praise of Wisdom.
Invitation.
Meditations.
Morning Song.
My God. *Fr.* The Royal Crown.
Night.
Night-Thoughts.
O Soul, with Storms Beset.
Royal Crown, The, *sels.*
Song of the Wind and the Rain.
Stanzas: "With tears thy grief thou dost bemoan."
Two Things Have Met in Me.
Water Song.
Wine and Grief.
IBN GHAIYATH. White Hair.
IBN HAIYUN. Inverted Eyelids.
Moles.
IBN HAMDIN. Ebony and Ivory.
IBN HAMDIS. Early Pleasure.
Flowing Stream.
Moon in Eclipse.
Night Visitor.
Water-Lilies.
IBN HANI. Aspiration.
Aubade.
Royal Bounty.
Victory.
IBN HARIQ. Galley, The.
IBN HAZM. Absent Friends.
Mutability.
Slander.
IBN IYAD. Beardless Youth.
Glance, The.
IBN JAKHA. Serpent Curls.
IBN KHAFAJA. Carousal.
Lovely Maid.
Lovely River.
Roan, The.
Swimmer, The.
Treachery.
IBN KHARUF. Aleppo.
Dancer, The.
Tailor's Apprentice, The.
Wages.
IBN KOLTHUM. Pour Us Wine. *Fr.* The Mu'allaqât.
IBN LUBBAL. Inkstand, The.
Schooners.
IBN MAATUK. Perturbation at Dawn.
IBN MAIMUN. Immunity.
IBN MALIK OF GRANADA. Algeciras Seen over a Stormy Sea.
Sister Sun.
IBN MALIK OF MURCIA. In the Mosque.
IBN MUJBAR. Departure.
Red Wine in a Black Glass.
IBN MUNAKHKHAL. Dialogue.
IBN MUQANA. Dawn.
IBN QADI MILA. Fruit Tree.
Lute, The.
IBN QUZMAN. Radish, The.
IBN RASHIQ. Continuing Love.
Debauch.
Down, The.
Pretences.
Rain at Festival.
IBN SAAD AL-KHAIR. Water.
IBN SABBATAI, JUDAH. Expensive Wife, The. *Fr.* The Gift of Judah the Woman-Hater.
Gift of Judah the Woman-Hater, The, *sel.*
IBN SAFAR. Almeria.
Carousal.
Flow and Ebb.
Ship, The.
Wine at Morning.
IBN SA'ID OF ALCALA LA REAL. Amulet.
Archery.
Betrayal.
Black Horse with a White Breast, A.
Changes.
Comely Warrior, The.
Courtship.
Crow, The.
Dawn Song.
Guardians, The.
Knights, The.
Love's Storm.
Miser, The.
Noblesse Oblige.
Nuptials, The.
Old Toper, The.
Palanquins, The
River, The.
Royal Bounty.
Sea of Night.
Setting Sun, The.
Stolen Penknife, The.
Strategy.
Sunlight on the Sea.
Tale of Battle, The.
Virgin, The.
Wave Wing.
Wind, The.
Wine at Dawn.
Yellow Horse with a Blaze, A.
Yellow Horse with a Blaze and a Black Mane, A.
IBN SA'ID OF SEVILLE. Invitation.
IBN SARA. Aubergines.
Benefactor, The.
Fire.
Oranges.
Quince, The.
Youth, The.
IBN SHAKIL. Ugliness.
IBN SHARAF. Chess.
Concert.
Protector, The.
IBN SHUHAID. Rain and Lightning.
Stolen Pleasure.
Sword and Lance.
IBN TIBBON, JUDAH. Father's Testament, A.
IBNU'L-FARID. Remembrance.
IBN WAHBUN. Fate's Malignity.
On Hearing al-Mutanabbi Praised.
IBN ZAYDUN [*or* ZAIDUN]. Cordova.
Cruel Masters.
Fidelity.
Flirtation.
IBSEN, HENRIK. Agnes. *Fr.* Brand.
Brand, *sels.*
Brand Speaks. *Fr.* Brand.
Burnt Ships.
Eider Duck, The.
In the Album of a Composer.
In the Orchard.
Light-shy.
Miner, The.
Power of Memory.
Stormy Petrel, The.
Swan, A.
Wild Flowers and Potted Plants.
With a Water Lily.
IBYCUS. Autumn Love.
Epilogue to Polycrates, An.
In the Spring.
Love.
Love Looks Tenderly.
Passion without Respite.
Reflections of Spring.
What time soft zephyrs fan the trees.
ICAZA, FRANCISCO A. DE. For the Poor Blind Man.
Golden.
Responding Voice.
Wayfaring.
ICELAND, REUBEN. Over All the Roof Tops.
ICHIHARA, PRINCE. Solitary Pine.
"IDAS." *See* WAYLAND, JOHN ELTON.
IGLESIAS DE LA CASA, JOSÉ. Alexis Calls Me Cruel.
IGNATIUS, SISTER MARY. On a Certain Nun.
Our Lady of the Libraries.
IGNATIUS LOYOLA, SAINT. Anima Christi.
IGNATOW, DAVID. Promenade.
IKHNATON (Amenhotep IV). Hymn to the Sun.
ILOTT, PERCY H. Witch, The.
IMAGE, SELWYN. Her Confirmation.
Meditation for Christmas, A.
Prayer, A: "Dear, let me dream of love."
Protestation, The.
IMBER, NAPHTALI HERZ. Hatikvah—a Song of Hope.
Zionist Marching Song.
IMELDA, SISTER MARY. Etching, An.
IMMANUEL DI ROMA. Elegy: "Floods of tears well from my deepest heart, The."
Happiness amidst Troubles.
Love.
Machberoth, *sel.*
My Sweet Gazelle!
Oh, Let Thy Teachings.
On the Wall.
Paradise.
Virtue. *Fr.* Machberoth.
What Profit?
Worthless Heart, The.
IMR [*or* IMRA] EL KAIS. Assignation, The.
Night Long, The.
Ode: "Weep, ah weep love's losing." *Fr.* The Mu'allaqât.
Storm, The.
Weep Love's Losing. *Fr.* The Mu'allaqât.
INBER, VERA. Dawn in Besieged Leningrad.
Diary of a Journey, *sel.*
Five Days and Nights.
Leningrad: 1943. *Fr.* The Pulkovo Meridian.
Mayakovsky Memory. *Fr.* Diary of a Journey.
Pulkovo Meridian, The, *sel.*
INCHFAWN, FAY. For Martha's Kitchen.
INGALLS, JEREMY. Invasion of Greece, The.
My Head on My Shoulders.
INGALLS, JOHN JAMES. Opportunity.
Tribute to Grass.
INGALLS, MILDRED D. Death of a Friend.
Letter from the Metropolis, A.
INGAMELLS, REX. Forgotten People, *sel.*
Noon Is on the Cattle-Track, The.
Sea-Chronicles.
Ship from Thames.
INGE, CHARLES. Limerick: "Certain young gourmet of Crediton, A," *at.*
On Monsieur Coué.
INGE, WILLIAM RALPH. Limerick: "There was a good Canon of Durham."
INGELEND, THOMAS. Disobedient Child, The, *sel.*
Song, A: "Why doth the world study vain glory to attain." *Fr.* The Disobedient Child.
INGELOW, JEAN. About the Fairies.
Apprenticed. *Fr.* Songs of the Night Watches.
Brides of Enderby, The; or, The High Tide.
Divided.
Dreams That Came True, The, *sel.*
Echo and the Ferry.
For Exmoor.
Four Bridges, The, *sel.*
Heigh Ho! *Fr.* Songs of Seven.
High Tide on the Coast of Lincolnshire, The (1571).
Honors.
I Leaned out My Window.
I Saw in a Vision. *Fr.* The Dreams That Came True.
I Will Trust.
Kinsman.
Like a Laverock in the Lift.
Long White Seam, The.
Longing for Home. *Fr.* Songs of Seven.
Maiden with a Milking-Pail, A.
Maternity. *Fr.* Songs of Seven.
Noble Tuck-Man, The.
One Morning, Oh! So Early.
Playing on the virginals.
Sailing beyond Seas.
Sea-nurtured.
Seven Times Five. *Fr.* Songs of Seven.
Seven Times Four. *Fr.* Songs of Seven.
Seven Times One. *Fr.* Songs of Seven.
Seven Times Seven. *Fr.* Songs of Seven.
Seven Times Six. *Fr.* Songs of Seven.
Seven Times Three. *Fr.* Songs of Seven.

INGELOW, JEAN (*continued*)
Seven Times Two. *Fr.* Songs of Seven.
Singing Lesson, The.
Song for a Babe.
Songs of Seven.
Songs of Seven, *sels.*
Songs of the Night Watches, *sel.*
Sorrows Humanize Our Race.
Supper at the Mill, *sel.*
Sweet Is Childhood.
INGEMANN, BERNHARD SEVERIN. Dannebrog (The Danish Flag).
Lovely the Earth Is.
Pilgrim's Song.
Two Days, The.
INGHAM, JOHN HALL. Genesis.
George Washington.
Phillips Brooks.
Summer Sanctuary, A.
INGHILFREDI, SICILIANO. Canzone: He Rebukes the Evil of That Time, *sel.*
INGIANNI, IGNACE M. Loneliness.
Sea, The.
"INGOLDSBY, THOMAS" (Richard Harris Barham). As I Laye a-Thynkynge.
City Bells. *Fr.* The Lay of St. Aloy's.
Confession, The.
Cynotaph, The, *sel.*
Eheu Fugaces.
Forlorn One, The.
Hand of Glory, The.
Hon. Mr. Sucklethumbkin's Story. *Fr.* Ingoldsby Legends.
Ingoldsby Legends, *sels.*
Jackdaw of Rheims, The.
Knight and the Lady, The.
Last Lines.
Lay of St. Aloy's, The, *sel.*
Lay of St. Cuthbert, The.
Misadventures at Margate.
Mr. Barney Macguire's Account of the Coronation.
More Walks.
Not a Sou Had He Got. *Fr.* The Cynotaph.
Verses Prefixed to the "Lay of St. Gengulphus."
INGRAHAM, CHARLES ANSON. Frightening Death.
Value of Elemental Remedies.
INGRAM, JOHN KELLS. Memory of the Dead, The.
National Presage.
Nationality.
Social Future, The.
Social Heredity.
Sonnet: "Yes! mourn the soul, of high and pure intent."
INGRAM, K. E. Lizard.
INMAN, ARTHUR. Werewolf.
INNES, GUY. It's Three No Trumps.
INNOCENT III, POPE. Golden Sequence, The.
"INNSLEY, OWEN" (Lucy White Jennison). Bondage.
Burden of Love, The.
Dream of Death, A.
INOUE, MITSUKO. Country Pastor.
IONS, MARY CECILE. Letter to the Dead in Spring.
IQBAL. Community.
IRAJ. Epitaph: "Know ye, fair folk who dwell on earth."
Mother.
IRAQI. Gamble.
I Cannot See.
Mystic Cups.
"IRELAND, BARON." *See* SALSBURY, NATE.
"IRELAND, MICHAEL." *See* FIGGIS, DARRELL.
IREMONGER, VALENTIN. Descending.
Dog, The.
Elizabeth.
Evening in Summer.
Going down the Mountain.
Hector.
Icarus.
In New Ross.
In This River.
Recollection in Autumn.
Spring Stops Me Suddenly.
These Apple Trees.
This Houre Her Vigill.
Time, the Faithless.
While the Summer Trees Were Crying.
IRIARTE [*or* YRIARTE], TOMÁS DE. Ass and the Flute, The.
Bear, the Monkey, and the Hog, The.
Bee and the Cuckoo, The.
Flint and the Steel, The.
Sword and the Skewer, The.
IRIS, SCHARMEL. After the Martyrdom.
Fisherman Speaks, A.
Friar of Genoa, The.
IRMA, SISTER MARY. Joy.
Letter from a Postulant.
Young Dead Speak, The.
"IRONQUILL." *See* WARE, EUGENE FITCH.
IRONS, GENEVIEVE M. J. Easter.
IRVIN, ERIC. Brother Ass.
Christmas 1942.
Midnight Patrol.
IRVINE, J. P. August Afternoon, An.
Indian Summer.
Summer Drought.
IRVINE, JOHN. One Haunted Night.
Swans, The.
IRVING, MINNA (Mrs. Harry Michener).
Americans All.
Betsy's Battle-Flag.
His Living Monument.
Lincoln Leads.
Old Year's Prayer, The.
Wedding Gift, The.
IRVING, WASHINGTON. Certain Young Lady, A.
IRWIN, THOMAS CAULFIELD. Antique Glimpses, *sel.*
Autumn.
Caesar, *sel.*
Character, A.
December.
Elizabethan Days, *sel.*
Faerie's Child, The.
Ghost's Promenade, The.
Glints of the Year—from a Window.
Hours I Remember Lonely and Lovely to Me.
Imogen—in Wales.
Iphione.
L'Angelo.
Leaving Troy.
May Sunday, A.
Minnie.
Nature's Key-Notes.
Objects of the Summer Scene, The.
Song: "My dreams were doleful and drear."
Sonnet: "Apples ripen under yellowing leaves, The."
Sonnet: "Awakened, I behold through dewy leaves."
Sonnet: "I walk of grey noons by the old canal."
Sonnet: "Into the wood at close of rainy day."
Sonnet: "Isle of trees full foliaged in a meadow, An."
Sonnet: "Now winter's dolorous days are o'er, and through."
Sonnet: "Rainbow o'er the sea of afternoon, The."
Sonnet: "Regions of soft clear air, of cold green leaves."
Sonnet: "Remote from smoky cities, aged and grey."
Sonnet: "Roadside inn this summer Saturday, A."
Sonnet: "Rough green wealth of wheaten fields that sway, The."
Sonnet: "Upon an upland orchard's sunny side."
Sonnet: "When I had turned Catullus into rhyme."
Sonnet: "Ye two fair trees that I so long have known."
Sonnets (I–XIV).
Spring.
Suire, The.
Swift, *sel.*
To a Skull.
To a Skull, *sel.*
Window Song, A.
Winter Life and Scenery.
Winter Noon in the Woods, *sel.*
With the Dawn.
IRWIN, WALLACE ("Ginger"; "Hashimura Togo"). At the Stevenson Fountain.
Aunt Nerissa's Muffin.
Blow Me Eyes!
Constant Cannibal Maiden, The.
Fate of the Cabbage Rose, The.
From Romany to Rome.
Grain of Salt, A.
Nautical Extravagance, A.
Powerful Eyes o' Jeremy Tait, The.
Reminiscence.
Sea Serpant, The.
Sensitive Sydney.
Song for a Cracked Voice.
Worried Skipper, The.
ISAAC BEN SAMUEL OF DAMPIÈRE. His Hand Shall Cover Us.
ISAACS, JORGE. Nima, The.
ISAHAKIAN, AVETIS. Black Eyes.
Huntsman, That on the Hills Above.
Sun Went Down, The.
Wind Is Howling through the Winter Night, The.
Ye Mountain Bluebells.
ISAKOVSKY, MIKHAIL. He Saw Her Home.
In Woods near the Frontline.
Maiden Meditation.
Twelve Blades of Grass.
Two girls of Ukraine.
ISBELL, HUGH O. Crucifixion.
Faith.
Good Friday.
ISE, LADY. Is it your command/ That we must pass through this life.
Rains of Spring, The.
Wild Geese.
ISHERWOOD, CHRISTOPHER, *and* SWAMI PRABHAVANANDA. *See* PRABHAVANANDA, SWAMI, *and* CHRISTOPHER ISHERWOOD.
ISHERWOOD, CHRISTOPHER, *and* WYSTAN HUGH AUDEN. *See* AUDEN, WYSTAN HUGH, *and* CHRISTOPHER ISHERWOOD.
ISHII. His Grace.
ISHII *and* OBATA. *For translations from Japanese, see* OnPM.
ISHIKAWA, TAKUBOKU [*or* TABUBOKEE]. Feeling inclined toward charity.
I picked up my mother.
Whenever I get angry.
ISHIKAWA KIMIKO. No Spare Time.
ISH-KISHOR, SULAMITH. War.
ISIDORUS. Farmer Lost at Sea, The.
On a Fowler.
Sea Trade.
ISLAND, E. H. L. Penny Whistle Blues.
ISLER, ELIZABETH. Little Things, The.
ISLWYN. Gwel uwchlaw cymylau amser.
Storm, The, *sel.*
ISSA. Another [Beggar Poem] ("For one copper").
Another Beggar Poem ("A bleak day!").
Cherry flowers.
Contrast.
Dear little one,/ I would still your cry.
Death it can bring.
Dews Disappear, The.
Dislike of a Governor.
Haikai.
Haiku: "In my life."
Haiku: "Wild goose, wild goose."
In my life.
Misery of the Beggars at the Gate of Zenkoji, The.
On the Eta, the Untouchables.
Satirical Poems on Daimyos.
Temple That Charged Admission, The.
These cherry flowers.
Tree will soon be hewn, The.
Wild goose, wild goose.
Winter.
ITA, SAINT. Jesukin, *at.*
Saint Ita's Fosterling, *at.*
ITO, SHIZUO. Evening Sea.
Picture Drawn by a Boy.
IVANOV, GEORGE. Roses over against your window.
IVANOV, VYACHESLAV IVANOVICH. Beauty's Nomads.

Complaint.
Fallow Land and Stubble Fields, *sel.*
Funeral.
Holy Rose, The.
Narcissus; a Pompeian Bronze.
Nomads of Beauty.
Now the golden leaves have been beggared.
Road to Emmaus, The.
Seeking of Self, The.
Vespers, *sels.*
Winter Sonnets, *sel.*
IWANO, HOMEI. Sad Love and Sad Song.
IYAD. Corn in the Wind.
IZAN. Homeless beggar, A.
IZARD, FORREST. "Art of Our Necessities Is Strange, The."
IZEMBO. Shower, A.
IZUMI SHIKIBU, LADY. I go out of the darkness.
Will I cease to be.

J

"J., L." Day at the Farm, A.
"J., M." Animal Howl, The.
Deportation.
Funeral, The.
Song of a Jewish Boy.
"J. B. H." *See* "H., J. B."
"J. C." *See* "C., J."
"J. C. C. H., JR." *See* "H., J. C. C., JR."
"J. D." *See* "D., J."
"J. H. S." *See* "S., J. H."
"J. P. H." *See* "H., J. P."
"J. R." *See* "R., J."
"J. T." *See* "T., I. [*or* J.]."
"J. W. G. W." *See* "W., J. W. G."
JACKS, OLIVE CECILIA. Offering, The.
JACKSON, ABRAHAM VALENTINE WILLIAMS. Dream of Dakiki, The, *tr.*
Gathas, *sel., tr.*
Lament in Old Age, *tr.*
Sacred Book, The, *tr. Fr.* Gathas.
Zoroaster Devoutly Questions Ormazd, *tr. Fr.* Gathas.
JACKSON, ADA. Again the Story Is Told.
I Have a Roof.
In Memoriam.
Mary Shakespeare.
Widow-Mother.
JACKSON, BYRON. *See* JACKSON, KATHRYN, *and* BYRON JACKSON.
JACKSON, HELEN HUNT ("H. H."; "Saxe Holm"). Cheyenne Mountain.
Coronation.
Danger.
Day-Star in the East, The.
Doubt.
Down to Sleep.
Dream, A.
Emigravit.
Habeas Corpus.
Last Prayer, A.
Morn.
My Legacy.
Not As I Will.
October's Bright Blue Weather.
Poppies in the Wheat.
Prayer: "Father, I scarcely dare to pray."
September.
September Days Are Here.
Song of Clover, A.
Spinning.
That Things Are No Worse, Sire.
Transplanted.
Two Truths.
JACKSON, HENRY R. My Wife and Child.
JACKSON, KATHRYN, *and* BYRON JACKSON. Noonday Sun.
Open Range.
JACKSON, LEROY F. All Aboard for Bombay.
Buzzy Brown.
Candle, A.
Columbus.
Duckle, Duckle, Daisy.
Grandpa Dropped His Glasses.
Hero, The.
Hippity Hop to Bed.
I've Got a New Book from My Grandfather Hyde.
Kitty Caught a Hornet.
Little Pig Asleep, A.
Off to Yakima.
Old Father Annum.
Sea Gull, The.
Simple Sam.
To China.
Uncle Andy and I.
JACKSON, MAUD FRAZER. Faith.
New Years and Old.
JACKSON, PETER. Afrikaans Homestead.
At the Grave of Cecil Rhodes.
Dombashawa.
Great Zimbabwe.
In Loco.
JACKSON, SARA. Lily McQueen.
Spiritus Sanctus.
JACKSON, SCHUYLER B. To Sylvia, Who Sent Me Music of Her Own Composing.
JACKSON, WINIFRED VIRGINIA. Finality.
JACOB, HILDEBRAND. Writer, The.
JACOB, MAX. Frontispiece.
Infant Moses, The.
It May Be.
Love of One's Neighbor.
Rain.
Ravignan Street.
Real Miracles.
Reply to the Apparition.
Revelation, The.
To Modigliani to Prove to Him That I Am a Poet.
Visitation.
JACOB, VIOLET. Tam i' the Kirk.
JACOBS, CATHERINE HAYDON. Secret.
JACOBS, HENRY. Avon, The.
JACOBSEN, JENS PETER. Dream!
In the Moonlight.
Irmeline Rose.
Moment Inexpressible, The.
No More than a Dream.
Silken Shoe upon Golden Last.
JACOBSEN, JOSEPHINE. Animals, The.
Eyes of Children at the Brink of the Sea's Grasp, The.
For Any Member of the Security Police.
Listen, David!
Mollesse.
Short Short Story.
JACOBSON, ETHEL. Atomic Courtesy.
Limerick: "To smash the simple atom."
Stanzas in the Infrared.
JACOBY, GROVER. Juxta.
JACOPO DA LENTINO. Canzonetta: He will Neither Boast nor Lament to His Lady.
Canzonetta: "My lady mine, I send."
Canzonetta: Of His Lady and of His Making Her Likeness.
No Jewel So Worthy.
Of His Lady's Face.
Sonnet: Of His Lady in Heaven.
Sonnet: Of His Lady's Face.
JACOPONE DA TODI. Cantica: Our Lord Christ; of Order, *at.*
Christ and His Mother at the Cross.
Dialogue of the Body with the Soul [Which Is] Leading It to Judgment.
Highest Wisdom, The.
Little Angels, The.
Nativity Song.
Near the Cross, *at.*
Of Holy Poverty.
Of Impatience Which Brings All Our Gains to Nothing.
Praise of Diseases.
Stabat Mater Dolorosa, *at.*
To Jesus.
JACOT, EMILE. Jack Tar.
Wandering Jack.
Who's That a-Knocking?
JAFFRAY, NORMAN R. Elusive Dove, The, 1946.
JÄGER, MARIA. O World, Be Not So Fair.
JAGO, RICHARD. Absence.
Hamlet's Soliloquy Imitated.
Swallows, The; an Elegy.
JAKUREN (the monk Jakuren). Hanging raindrops, The.
JALALU'D-DIN RUMI. *See* RUMI, JALAL ED-DIN.
JAMES I, KING OF ENGLAND. Enigma of Sleep, An.
Heaven and Earth.
Sonnet: "Azured vault, the crystal circles bright, The."
JAMES I, KING OF SCOTLAND. Coming of Love, The. *Fr.* The Kingis Quair.
Dawn of Love, The. *Fr.* The Kingis Quair.
Good Counsel.
Great Change, The. *Fr.* The Kingis Quair.
He Sees His Beloved. *Fr.* The Kingis Quair.
Kingis Quair, The, *sels.*
Spring Song of the Birds. *Fr.* The Kingis Quair.
Walking under the Tour. *Fr.* The Kingis Quair.
JAMES IV, KING OF SCOTLAND. Gaberlunzie Man, The.
JAMES V, KING OF SCOTLAND. Jolly Beggar, The, *at.*
JAMES, ALICE ARCHER SEWALL. Butterfly, The.
Lullaby: "O'er the haycocks comes the moon."
Processional.
Sinfonia Eroica.
JAMES, THOMAS. Lines on His Companions Who Died in the Northern Seas.
JAMES, WILLIAM. In Panther Gorge.
JAMESON, ANNA BROWNELL. Take Me, Mother Earth.
JAMI. Absál Tempts Salámán. *Fr.* Salámán and Absál.
Baharistan, *sel.*
Bewildered Arab, The. *Fr.* Salámán and Absál.
Birth of Salámán, The. *Fr.* Salámán and Absál.
Burning of Absál, The. *Fr.* Salámán and Absál.
Changing World, The.
Fragment: "Though decked the tray." *Fr.* Baharistan.
Friendship.
Glorious God, The.
God behind the Veil.
Great Idealist, The.
Greeting.
Hidden Truth, The.
Kind Friend, A.
Life within Our Forms, The.
Lovers Flee, The. *Fr.* Salámán and Absál.
Man's Prime Desire.
Morning Air.
Night.
One Heart, One Love.
Preliminary Invocation. *Fr.* Salámán and Absál.
Salámán and Absál, *sels.*
Sequence.
Simple Arab, The. *Fr.* Salámán and Absál.
Solitude.
Song of Mystic Unity, The.
Tears.
Union of Love.
Ways of Love, The.
JAMIESON, ROBERT. Elfer Hill, *tr.*
Mer-Man and Marstig's Daughter, The, *tr.*
My Wife's a Winsome Wee Thing.
JAMIL. Buthaina.
JAMISON, ROSCOE CONKLING. Negro Soldiers, The.
JAMMES, FRANCIS. Alone.
Amsterdam.
Amsterdam, *sel.*

JAMMES, FRANCIS (*continued*)
Child Reads an Almanac, The.
Country Wedding.
Géorgiques Chrétiennes, *sel.*
In the Silence of Night.
Learned Ass, The.
Love.
Palm Sunday.
Prayer That an Infant May Not Die.
Prayer to Go to Paradise with the Asses [*or* Donkeys].
Robinson Crusoe Returns to Amsterdam. *Fr.* Amsterdam.
Room, The.
When You elect to call me, God, O call.
JANIS, ELSIE. My Prayer.
JANSON, KRISTOFER. Aastrid.
JANTA, ALEXANDER. Psalm of the Singing Grave.
JANVIER, FRANCIS DE HAES. God Save Our President.
JANVIER, MARGARET THOMPSON. *See* "VANDEGRIFT, MARGARET."
JANVIER, THOMAS A. Santiago.
JAPP, ALEXANDER HAY. Landor.
Music Lesson, A.
Shelley.
JAQUES [*or* JACQUES], EDNA. In Flanders Now.
Red Cross, The.
To an Old Farmhouse.
JAQUES, FLORENCE PAGE. Goblinade, A.
There Once Was a Puffin.
JAQUITH, W. L. Oh, Golden-Rod.
JARMAN, WRENNE. Letter to Claudia.
Neutral, The.
Plastic Airman.
Valedictory.
JARRELL, RANDALL. Angels at Hamburg, The.
Black Swan, The.
Breath of Night, The.
Burning the Letters.
Camp in the Prussian Forest, A.
Child, The, *tr.*
Childhood, *ad.*
Country Life, A.
Cow Wandering in the Bare Field, The.
Dead in Melanesia, The.
Dead Wingman, The.
Death, *tr.*
Death of the Ball Turret Gunner, The.
Eighth Air Force.
Emancipators, The.
Evening, *tr.*
For an Emigrant.
Game at Salzburg, A.
Girl in a Library, A.
Great Night, The, *tr.*
Grownup, The, *tr.*
Hope.
Jews at Haifa.
Knight, Death, and the Devil, The.
Lady Bates.
Lament: "All is far/ And long gone by," *tr.*
Lines, The.
Loss.
Losses.
Lullaby, A: "For wars his life and half a world away."
Märchen, The.
Metamorphoses, The.
90 North.
Officers' Prison Camp Seen from a Troop-Train, An.
Orient Express, The.
Pilot from the Carrier, A.
Pilots, Man Your Planes.
Port of Embarkation.
Prisoners.
Refugees, The.
Requiem—for the Death of a Boy, *tr.*
2nd Air Force.
Seele im Raum.
Sick Child, A.
Sick Nought, The.
Siegfried.
Sleeping Beauty, The; Variation of the Prince.
Snow-Leopard, The.
Soldier (T. P.)
Soldier Walks under the Trees of the University, The.
State, The.
Utopian Journey, A.
Variations.
Ward in the States, A.
Washing the Corpse.
Woman at the Washington Zoo, The.
JARRY, ALFRED. Fable.
Sonnet: "Across the heath, the monolith's pubic arch."
JARVIS, MURIEL WHITEHEAD. Message from a Little Ghost.
JAVITZ, ALEXANDER. Old Men, The.
JAYADEVA. Gita Govinda, The, *sels.*
Hymn to Vishnu. *Fr.* The Gita Govinda.
Song: "Low whispers the wind from Malaya." *Fr.* The Gita Govinda.
"JAZBO OF OLD DUBUQUE" (John P. Mulgrew). Lines for "Tops."
Wish, A.
JEAN DE MEUN *and* GUILLAUME DE LORRIS. *See* GUILLAUME DE LORRIS *and* JEAN DE MEUN.
JECK, RANDOLPH. Ode of Lament.
JEFFERS, ROBINSON. Age in Prospect.
All the Little Hoofprints.
Answer, The.
Ante Mortem.
Antrim.
Apology for Bad Dreams.
Ascent to the Sierras.
Ave Caesar.
Battle.
Beauty of Things, The.
Birds.
Birth-Dues.
Bixby's Landing.
Black-out.
Bloody Sire, The.
Boats in a Fog.
Broken Balance, The, *sel.*
Caged Eagle's Death Dream, The. *Fr.* Cawdor.
California Vignette, A. *Fr.* Tamar.
Calm and Full the Ocean.
Cassandra.
Cawdor, *sel.*
Clouds of Evening.
Coast-Road, The.
Compensation.
Continent's End.
Credo.
Cruel Falcon, The.
Crumbs or the Loaf.
Cycle, The.
Divinely Superfluous Beauty.
Eagle Valor, Chicken Mind.
Edison.
Evening Ebb.
Excesses of God, The.
Eye, The.
Fawn's Foster-Mother.
Fire on the Hills.
Flight of Swans.
Fog.
Fourth Act.
Gale in April.
Granite and Cypress.
Gray Weather.
Haunted Country.
Hellenistics.
Hurt Hawks.
I Shall Laugh Purely.
Inquisitors, The.
Joy.
Life from the Lifeless.
Love the Wild Swan.
Maid's Thought, The.
Margrave.
May–June, 1940.
Meditation on Saviours.
New Year's Eve.
Night.
Noon.
Not Our Good Luck.
Nova.
November Surf.
Oh, Lovely Rock.
Ocean.
Old Man's Dream after He Died, The. *Fr.* Cawdor.
Original Sin.
Pelicans.
People and a Heron.
Phenomena.
Place for No Story, The.
Post Mortem.
Practical People.
Prescription of Painful Ends.
Promise of Peace.
Purse-Seine, The.
Rearmament.
Reference to a Passage in Plutarch's Life of Sulla.
Return.
Roan Stallion.
Rock and Hawk.
Salmon-fishing.
Science.
Second-best.
Self-Criticism in February.
Shakespeare's Grave.
Shine, Perishing Republic.
Signpost.
Stars Go over the Lonely Ocean, The.
Steelhead.
Still the Mind Smiles.
Suicide's Stone.
Summer Holiday.
Summit Redwood, The.
Tamar, *sels.*
To a Young Artist.
To the Stone-Cutters.
Tor House.
Two Christmas-Cards.
Two Christmas Cards, *sel.*
Watch the Lights Fade.
Wise Men in Their Bad Hours.
Wonder and Joy.
World's Wonders, The.
JEFFERSON, JOSEPH. Immortality.
JEFFERYS, CHARLES. Jeannette and Jeannot.
We Have Lived and Loved Together.
JEFFREY, FRANCIS, LORD JEFFREY. Epitaph: "Here lies the body of Richard Hind."
Epitaph; in Christ Church, Bristol, on Thomas Turner, Twice Master of the Company of Bakers.
Epitaph; in St. Olave's Church, Southwark, on Mr. Munday.
Epitaph; on Peter Robinson.
Epitaphs.
On Peter Robinson.
JEFFRIES, CHRISTIE. Lone Huntsman.
JEHUDAH HALEVI. *See* HALEVI, JUDAH.
JEITTELES, ALOIS. To My Distant Beloved.
JEITTELES, BENEDICT. Epitaph for a Judge.
JEKYLL, JOSEPH. Two Heads Are Better than One.
JELAL ED-DIN RUMI. *See* RUMI, JALAL ED-DIN.
JELLICOE, S. CHARLES. Advice to a Lover.
JENKINS, BURKE. Cowboy to His Friends in Need.
JENKINS, OLIVER. Captain's Walk; Salem.
Merry-go-round.
Ship Comes In, A.
Time Out.
Waterfront.
JENKINS, WILLIAM VAUGHAN. O God of Love, to Thee We Bow.
JENKS, EDWARD A. Going and Coming.
JENKS, TUDOR. Christmas Song, A.
Limerick: " 'It's a very warm day,' observed Billy."
Old Bachelor, An.
On the Road.
Small and Early.
Spirit of the *Maine*, The.
JENKYN, PATTERICKE. To the Sun.
JENNER, EDWARD. Signs of Rain.
JENNETT, SEÁN. And the Dead.
Cycle; Seven War Poems.
Cycle; Seven War Poems, *sel.*
Grey Washer by the Ford, The.
I. H. S.
I Was a Labourer. *Fr.* Cycle; Seven War Poems.
Island, The.
Mahoney.

Merchandise.
My Subtle and Proclamant Song.
Old Joyce.
Omphalos; the Well.
Quick, The.
JENNINGS, ELIZABETH. Afternoon in Florence.
Answers.
Beyond Possession.
Climbers, The.
Communication.
Delay.
Enemies, The.
Escape and Return.
Florence; Design for a City.
Identity.
Idler, The.
In the Night.
Mirrors.
Music and Words.
Not in the Guide-Books.
Song at the Beginning of Autumn.
Way of Looking, A.
Weathercock.
Winter Love.
JENNINGS, LESLIE NELSON. Belden Hollow.
Deep Woods.
Highways.
Lost Harbor.
Strange Meeting.
Wide Front Porch.
Wilderness.
JENNINGS, WILLIAM. *For translations from Chinese, see* BoFr.
JENNISON, LUCY WHITE. *See* "INNSLEY, OWEN."
JENSEN, JOHANNES V. At Memphis Station.
Bathing Girl, A.
Denmark Song.
JENSEN, PETER ANDREAS. In the Storm.
JEPHCOTT, SYDNEY. Dreamers, The.
White Paper.
JEREMY, SISTER MARY. Academy.
Candle-Lighter, The.
Desdemona.
Legend.
Sister Lights the Candles, A.
JEROME, FRA. Dedication to My Gray Lady.
JERVEY, MARY. General Albert Sidney Johnston.
JESSE, FRYNIWYD TENNYSON. Lover's Memory.
Lover's Wish.
Testament.
JEWETT, ELEANORE MYERS. Down among the Wharves.
JEWETT, ELLEN A. Sermon in a Stocking.
JEWETT, JOHN H. Those Rebel Flags.
JEWETT, SARAH ORNE. Caged Bird, A.
Discontent.
JEWETT, SOPHIE ("Ellen Burroughs"). Armistice.
Communion.
If Spirits Walk.
In the Dark.
Least of Carols, The.
Nativity Song, *tr.*
Pearl, The, *tr.*
Shepherds, The.
Sleep.
Smiling Demon of Notre Dame, A.
Soldier, The.
Song: "Thy face I have seen as one seeth."
Thus Far.
When Nature Hath Betrayed the Heart That Loved Her.
"JEWISH SIBYL, THE." Fourth Book of Sibylline Oracles, The, *sel., at.*
There Is a City, *at. Fr.* The Fourth Book of Sibylline Oracles.
JEX, ADA LORRAINE. Father's Birthday Cake.
JIMÉNEZ, JUAN RAMÓN. Above a Snow.
Autumnal Aria, *sel.*
Best That I Have, The.
Dream Nocturne.
Fleeting Return.
Flowers under the Lightning.
Fortunate Being.
Green.
I Would That All My Verses.
Last Journey, The.
Love.
Nocturne.
On the Eve of Departure.
One Night.
Only Rose, The.
Seas.
Shepherd's Star, The.
There Was No One.
Were I Reborn.
What Becomes of a Strain of Music.
Yellow Spring.
You Light.
JOAN, NATALIE. Dicky-Birds.
Kind Mousie, The.
JOCHUMSSON, MATTHÍAS. Ecstasy.
Millennial Hymn of Iceland, The.
New Year's Hymn.
Providence.
JODELLE, ETIENNE. To the Ashes of Claude Colet.
JOHANNES BARBUCALLUS [*or* JOANNES BARBOCOLLAS]. As I looked on my Husband, and felt my last thread was spun.
Desolation of Berytus, The.
Ruined Harbour, A.
JOHANNES SECUNDUS (Jan Nicolai Everaerts). Elegies, *sel.*
Foolish Husband, The.
Gather Ye Roses. *Fr.* Elegies.
Ladies of Bourges, The.
Ode of Johannes Secundus, An.
Seventeenth Kiss, The: Neaera's Lips.
Third Kiss, The: Butterfly Kisses.
Thirteenth Kiss, The: Love, Life and Death.
To a Lady Who Used Cosmetics.
JOHN, ——. Band, The.
JOHN, EDMUND. Fragment: "Give me your hands, and let your strange wild eyes."
Symphonie Symbolique, *sel.*
JOHN, GWEN. Child's Winter Evening.
JOHN DAMASCENE, SAINT. *See* JOHN OF DAMASCUS, SAINT.
JOHN FREDERICK, SISTER MARY. Joculator Domini.
JOHN OF DAMASCUS, SAINT [*or* ST. JOHN DAMASCENE]. Come, ye faithful, raise the strain.
Day of Resurrection, The.
Easter Hymn.
Resurrection.
Risen with Healing in His Wings.
Today in Bethlehem Hear I.
JOHN OF THE CROSS, SAINT. Dark Night of the Soul, The.
Fount That Freely Flows, The.
Living Flame of Love, The.
O Flame of Living Love.
Obscure Night of the Soul, The.
Romance VIII.
Song of the Soul and the Bridegroom.
Songs of the Soul.
Spiritual Canticle between the Soul and Christ.
To Christ Crucified, *at.*
Upon a Gloomy Night.
Verses Written after an Ecstasy of High Exaltation.
Verses Written upon an Ecstasy of High Contemplation.
JOHNS, ORRICK. Answer, The.
Dilemma.
Door, The.
Failure.
Home Fire, The.
Interpreter, The.
Last Night, The.
Little Things.
Mothers and Children.
Sea-Lands, The.
Second Avenue.
Shopping Day.
Song of Youth, The. *Fr.* Songs of Deliverance.
Songs of Deliverance, *sel.*
Spring.
Tree-Toad, The.
Wild Plum.
JOHNSON, ALBERT E. Perjured, The.
Return of the Prodigal.
JOHNSON, BURGES. Contentment.
Glad Young Chamois, The.
Gnu Wooing, The.
I'm Sorry, Love, I Bring So Small a Bone.
In the Study.
Incorrigible.
Jealous Doggerel.
Llyric of the Llama, A.
My Sore Thumb.
Omar Meets a Toy.
Remarks from the Pup.
Rondeau of Remorse, A.
Serenade: "Dogs on a summer night."
Service, The.
Soap, the Oppressor.
Sympathetic.
When Daddy Sings.
Why Doth a Pussy Cat?
JOHNSON, CHARLES BERTRAM. Little Cabin, A.
Negro Poets.
JOHNSON, CHARLES FREDERICK. Modern Romans, The.
Then and Now.
JOHNSON, DOROTHY VENA. Epitaph for a Bigot.
Green Valley.
Palace.
Twinkling Gown.
JOHNSON, EDWARD. Cry unto the Lord to Stay His Hand, A, *sel. Fr.* The Wonder-working Providence of Sions Saviour in New England.
Water-Drinker, The.
Wonder-working Providence of Sions Saviour in New England, The, *sel.*
JOHNSON, EMILY PAULINE ("Tekahion Wake"). As Red Men Die.
At Husking Time.
Brier.
Corn Husker, The.
In the Shadows.
Legend of Qu'Apelle Valley, The.
Lost Lagoon, The.
Lullaby of the Iroquois.
Pilot of the Plains, The.
Shadow River.
Sleeping Giant, The.
Song My Paddle Sings, The.
Songster, The.
Trail to Lillooet, The.
Train Dogs, The.
Vagabonds, The.
JOHNSON, ESTHER ("Stella"). O shield me from his rage, celestial Powers!
To Dr. Swift on His Birthday.
JOHNSON, FENTON. Aunt Jane Allen.
Banjo Player, The.
Children of the Sun.
Drunkard, The.
Lonely Mother, The.
Lost Love, The.
Marathon Runner, The.
Minister, The.
New Day, The.
Puck Goes to Court.
Rulers.
Scarlet Woman, The.
Tired.
Vision of Lazarus, The, *sel.*
When I Die.
Who Is That a-Walking in the Corn?
JOHNSON, GEOFFREY. All Over the World.
Appian Way, The.
Drought.
First of April, The.
Noonday Ghosts.
Peat-Cutters.
Rediscovery.
Windmill, The.
For translations from Latin, see LaP.
JOHNSON, GEORGE W. When You and I Were Young, Maggie.
JOHNSON, GEORGIA DOUGLAS. Benediction.
Dreams of the Dreamer, The.
Guardianship.
Heart of a Woman, The.
Hope.
I Closed My Shutters Fast Last Night.
I Want to Die While You Love Me.

JOHNSON, GEORGIA DOUGLAS (*continued*)
Interracial.
I've Learned to Sing.
Lethe.
Little Son.
Lost Illusions.
My Little Dreams.
Old Black Men.
Proving.
Recessional.
Remember.
Service.
Suppliant, The.
Tomorrow's Men.
Welt.
What Need Have I for Memory?
When I Am Dead.
Youth.
JOHNSON, HELENE. Bottled; New York.
Fulfillment.
Invocation: "Let me be buried in the rain."
Little Brown Boy.
Magalu.
Poem: "Little brown boy."
Remember Not.
Road, The.
Sonnet to a Negro in Harlem.
Summer Matures.
What Do I Care for Morning.
JOHNSON, HERBERT CLARK. Boy's Need, A.
Crossing a Creek.
On Calvary's Lonely Hill.
Willow Bend and Weep.
JOHNSON, HILDA. Ballade of Expansion, The.
Quest of the Purple Cow, The.
JOHNSON, JAKOBINA. *For translations from Icelandic, see* IcP; LiTW.
JOHNSON, JAMES WELDON. Brothers.
Creation, The (a Negro Sermon).
Envoy: "If homely virtues draw from me a tune."
Farewell to My Mother, *tr.*
Fifty Years, 1863-1913.
Glory of the Day Was in Her Face, The.
Go Down Death.
Hostess' Daughter, The, *tr.*
Lift Every Voice and Sing.
Listen, Lord.
My City.
O Black and Unknown Bards.
Plácido's Sonnet to His Mother, *tr.*
Prayer at Sunrise.
Prodigal Son, The.
Sence You Went Away.
White Witch, The.
You's Sweet to Yo' Mammy Jes' de Same.
JOHNSON, JOSEPHINE. Children of Earth.
In This Stern Hour.
Supplication.
There Is a Tide.
Unwilling Gypsy, The.
JOHNSON, JOSEPHINE WINSLOW. Final Autumn.
Lightship, The.
This Is the Trouble with Us All.
Year's End, *sel.*
JOHNSON, LIONEL PIGOT. Age of a Dream, The.
Bagley Wood.
By the Statue of King Charles at Charing Cross.
Cadgwith.
Cadgwith, *sel.*
Child of War.
Christmas and Ireland.
Church of a Dream, The.
Collins.
Coming of War, 1889, The.
Comrades.
Dark Angel, The.
Dark Angel, The, *sel.*
Day of Coming Days, The.
Dead.
Desideria.
Dream of Youth, A.
Escape.
Friend, A.
Friends.
Glories.
In Falmouth Harbour, *sel.*
In Memory, *sel.*
Ireland.
Last Music, The.
London Town.
Lucretius.
Magic, *sel.*
Mystic and Cavalier.
Oracles.
Our Lady of France.
Our Lady of the May.
Our Lady of the Snows.
Oxford.
Oxford Nights.
Parnell.
Precept of Silence, The.
Red Wind, The.
Song: "My windows open to the autumn night."
Sylvan Morfydd.
Te Martyrum Candidatus.
To a Friend.
To a Traveler.
To Morfydd.
To My Patrons.
To Ocean Hazard; Gipsy.
To the Dead of '98.
To Weep Irish.
Upon a Drawing.
Vinum Daemonum.
Visions.
Ways of War.
Westward.
Winchester.
JOHNSON, LOUIS. Cataclysm.
Comedian.
Dirge: "We built our love up like a work of art."
Elegy: "Fond, frozen, first and only lover."
Fable of a Forgotten Woman.
Mother of a Daughter.
Poem in Karori.
Pygmalion.
Sandwich Man, The.
JOHNSON, MARGARET. Around and around a dusty little room.
Day Dreams, or Ten Years Old.
Grandma's Mistake, *at.*
JOHNSON, MARJORIE E. Paul to Peter and John.
JOHNSON, MAURICE C. Headaches 'Jes 'fore School.
JOHNSON, NORMAN M. Hob the Elf.
JOHNSON, PAULINE. *See* JOHNSON, EMILY PAULINE.
JOHNSON, PETER. Sonnet: "Out of this world's imperial terror."
JOHNSON, RAY M. Greatest Work, The.
JOHNSON, ROBERT UNDERWOOD. As a Bell in a Chime.
Blossom of the Soul, The.
Browning at Asolo.
Dewey at Manila.
English Mother, An.
Hearth Song.
I Journeyed South to Meet the Spring.
In Tesla's Laboratory.
Irish Love-Song, An.
Italian Rhapsody.
Leader, The.
Love and Italy.
Love in the Calendar.
Love Once Was like an April Dawn.
Markham.
Star Song.
To My Countrymen.
To Patricia, Eleven.
To the Housatonic at Stockbridge.
To the Returning Brave.
Ursula.
Voice of Webster, The, *sel.*
Wistful Days, The.
Woodrow Wilson.
JOHNSON, ROSSITER. Evelyn.
Ninety-nine in the Shade.
Soldier Poet, A.
JOHNSON, SAMUEL (1709-84). Ambition. *Fr.* The Vanity of Human Wishes.
Anacreon's Dove.
As with My Hat.
Burden of Age, The. *Fr.* The Vanity of Human Wishes.
Burlesque [of Lope de Vega].
Celestial Wisdom, *tr.* *Fr.* Satires.
Charles XII. *Fr.* The Vanity of Human Wishes.
Comets—On the Italian Duke Who Ran Away for Fear of the Comet of 1742.
Dr. Levett.
Epitaph on [*or* upon the Celebrated] Claudy Phillips, a Musician, An.
Hermit Hoar.
Hinted Wish, A, *tr.*
I put my hat upon my head.
If the Man Who Turnips Cries.
Irene, *sel.*
Legacy, A, *tr.*
Life of Ages.
Life's Last Scene. *Fr.* The Vanity of Human Wishes.
Lines on the Death of Mr. Levett.
Lines Written in Ridicule of Certain Poems Published in 1777.
London.
London, *sels.*
London Delights. *Fr.* London.
O Qui Perpetua Mundum Ratione Gubernas, *tr.*
O Thou Whose Pow'r, *tr.*
Odes (*of* Horace), *sel., tr.*
On Hearing Miss Thrale Deliberate about Her Hat.
On the Coming of Age of a Rich Extravagant Young Man, *sel.*
On the Death of Mr. [*or* Dr.] Robert Levet.
On the Death of Mr. Robert Levet, *sel.*
One-and-twenty.
Poverty in London. *Fr.* London.
Prayer: "Where then shall Hope and Fear their objects find?" *Fr.* The Vanity of Human Wishes.
Prologue: "Prest by the load of life, the weary mind." *Fr.* The Good-natur'd Man (*by* Goldsmith).
Prologue Spoken by Mr. Garrick at the Opening of the Theatre Royal.
Prologue Spoken by Mr. Garrick at the Opening of the Theatre Royal, *sels.*
Prologue to "The Good-natur'd Man."
Quiet Life, The.
Rise and Fall, The. *Fr.* The Vanity of Human Wishes.
Satires (*of* Juvenal), *sels., tr.*
Scholar's Life, The. *Fr.* The Vanity of Human Wishes.
Shakespeare and Jonson.
Short Song of Congratulation, A.
Spring's Return, *tr.* *Fr.* Odes.
To a Young Heir.
Tomorrow. *Fr.* Irene.
Translation of Horace.
Turnip Seller, The.
Vanity of Human Wishes, The.
Vanity of Human Wishes, The, *sels.*
Verses: "What hopes, what terrors does thy gift create."
Wits, The. *Fr.* Prologue Spoken by Mr. Garrick at the Opening of the Theatre Royal.
JOHNSON, SAMUEL (1822-82). City of God.
For Divine Strength.
Inspiration.
Prayer for Strength.
JOHNSON, SKULI. *For translations from Icelandic, see* IcP.
JOHNSON, "SPUD." City Birds.
JOHNSON, VICTORIA SAFELLE. Dedication: "Holy Jesus, Thou art born."
JOHNSON, WILLIAM. *See* CORY, WILLIAM JOHNSON.
JOHNSON, WILLIAM KNOX. Anniversary, An.
JOHNSON, WILLIAM MARTIN. On Snowflakes Melting on His Lady's Breast.
JOHNSON, WILLIAM SAMUEL. Chiffons!
JOHNSON, WILLIS FLETCHER. Immortality.
JOHNSON-CORY, WILLIAM. *See* CORY, WILLIAM JOHNSON.
JOHNSTON, ANNA. *See* "CARBERY, ETHNA."

JOHNSTON, BERTHA. Did You Ever Hear an English Sparrow Sing?
JOHNSTON, CHARLES H. L. President, The.
JOHNSTON, MARY. Virginiana.
JOHNSTON, WILLIAM. On the Downtown Side of an Uptown Street.
JOHNSTONE, ARTHUR. Fisher's Apology, A.
JOHNSTONE, D. V. Star of the Morning.
JOHNSTONE, HENRY, LORD JOHNSTONE.
Charm to Call Sleep, A.
Fastidious Serpent, The.
Good-Night Prayer for a Little Child.
Guessing Song.
Snake Story.
JOMEI, EMPEROR. Cry of the Stag.
JONAS, SAMUEL ALROY. Confederate Note, The.
Lines on the Back of a Confederate Note.
Only a Soldier's Grave.
JONES, ALAN PRYCE-. *See* PRYCE-JONES, ALAN.
JONES, AMANDA THEODOSIA. Panama.
JONES, BOB, JR. Worship.
JONES, C. L. Question, A.
JONES, CHARLES L. S. Fort Bowyer.
Hero of Bridgewater, The.
JONES, CULLEN. I Gained a Greater Strength. *Fr.* Sonnets in Wartime.
Now That the Flowers.
Sonnets in Wartime.
While Life Sits Idly. *Fr.* Sonnets in Wartime.
JONES, DAVID. Anathemata, The, *sels.*
Englynion to His Love.
Five Unmistakable Marks, The.
Rite and Fore-Time. *Fr.* The Anathemata.
JONES, DOUGLAS G. Death of a Hornet.
JONES, EBENEZER. Face, The.
Hand, The.
Song of the Kings of Gold.
Ways of Regard, *sels.*
When the World Is Burning.
JONES, EDWARD SMYTH. Song of Thanks, A.
JONES, ELIJAH. How Big Was Alexander?
JONES, EMILY B. C. (Mrs. F. L. Lucas).
Jerked Heartstrings in Town.
Middle-Age.
JONES, EMILY READ. Thanksgiving.
JONES, ERNEST CHARLES. Earth's Burdens.
Song of the Lower Classes, The.
Song of the Wage-Slave, The.
JONES, FREDERICK SCHEETZ. New Haven.
On the Democracy of Yale.
To New Haven.
JONES, GLYN. Beach.
Esyllt.
Gold.
Gull.
Merthyr.
Night.
Park.
Sande.
Song: "I kept neat my virginity."
JONES, HERBERT. True Romance, The.
JONES, HOWARD MUMFORD. Adelheid, *tr.*
Assignation, The, *tr.*
Buthaina, *tr.*
Church Bell at Night, The, *tr.*
Crucifixion, The, *tr.*
Dies Irae, *tr.*
Epitaph: "Fate to beauty still must give," *tr.*
Heartbreak.
In His Will.
Lonely Isle, The, *tr.*
Painted Passion, *tr.*
Sea-God's Song to Bran, The, *tr.*
Singing on the Moselle, *sel.*, *tr.*
Song of Crede, The, *tr.*
To the Cuckoo, *tr.*
JONES, IONE L. Sleep, Baby, Sleep.
JONES, JOHN (*fl.* 1635). Adrasta, *sel.*
Come, Lovers, Bring Your Cares. *Fr.* Adrasta.
JONES, JOHN (1810–69). *See* "TALHAIARN."
JONES, JOSHUA HENRY. To a Skull.
JONES, LAWRENCE M. I Am the Flag.
JONES, LEILA. Colour of October.
Connecticut Trilogy.
Unholy Garden.
JONES, LEROI. For Hettie.
In Memory of Radio.
One Night Stand.
Ostriches & Grandmothers!
To a Publisher . . . Cut-out.
Turncoat, The.
Way Out West.
JONES, LOUISE SEYMOUR. Who Loves a Garden.
JONES, LUCY HAMILTON. *See* HOOPER, LUCY HAMILTON.
JONES, MARGARET WYNNE. Tale from the Garden, A.
JONES, MARY HOXIE. Four Deer, The.
JONES, RALPH M. Bed-Time.
Oxen.
JONES, RICHARD. Printer to the Reader, The, *at.*
JONES, ROBERT. Madrigal: "O I do love, then kiss me."
O I do love, then kiss me.
JONES, RUTH LAMBERT. Epicure.
JONES, T. GWYNN. Grave, The.
Ystrad Fflur.
JONES, THOMAS SAMUEL, JR. After All.
Akhnaton.
April.
As in a Rose-Jar.
Ave atque Vale.
Ave atque Vale, *sel.*
Beyond.
Birds of Whitby, The.
Blessing of Columcille, The. *Fr.* Sonnets of the Saints.
Blind Nun, The.
Brindled Hare, The. *Fr.* Sonnets of the Saints.
Cædmon.
Candle-Light.
Cathedral, The.
Clonard.
Daphne.
Dusk at Sea.
Empedocles.
Ezekiel.
Four Sonnets.
From the Hills.
Garden, The. *Fr.* Four Sonnets.
Gautama.
George Herbert.
Great Refusal, The.
Guardian Angel, The.
Henry Vaughan.
Holy Thorn, The.
I Know a Quiet Vale.
In Excelsis.
In the Fall o' Year.
In Trinity Church-Yard.
Joyous-Gard.
Lao-tse.
Last Spring, The. *Fr.* Four Sonnets.
Leonardo da Vinci.
Little Ghosts, The.
May upon Ictis.
My Soul Is like a Garden-Close.
Noon-Tide.
O little buds all bourgeoning with Spring. *Fr.* Two Songs in Spring.
Old Song, An.
Path of the Stars, The. *Fr.* Four Sonnets.
Pythagoras.
Quatrain: "Here upon earth eternity is won."
Quatrain: "Nothing is judged according to its size."
Richard Crashaw.
Roses of Saint Francis, The.
Saint Teresa.
Saint Thomas Aquinas.
Sanctuary. *Fr.* Four Sonnets.
Sometimes.
Song in Spring, A.
Sonnets of the Saints.
Spinoza.
To Song.
Two Songs in Spring.
Urbs Beata.
Vase of Myrrh, The.
Veil, The.
Way Back, The.
You and I.
Youth.
Zarathustra.
JONES, W. S. HANDLEY. He Is Not Risen.
JONES, SIR WILLIAM. Baby, The, *after* Kalidasa.
Compassion, *tr.*
Epigram: "On parent knees, a naked, new-born child."
Moral Tetrastich, A.
Morning Air, *tr.*
Ode in Imitation of Alcaeus, An.
Ode in Imitation of Alcaeus, An, *sel.*
On Parent Knees, a Naked New-born Child.
Persian Song [of Hafiz], A, *tr.*
Song of the Reed, The, *tr.*
State, The. *Fr.* An Ode in Imitation of Alcaeus.
To an Infant Newly Born.
Turkish Ode of Mesihi, A.
What Constitutes a State? *Fr.* An Ode in Imitation of Alcaeus.
JONSON, BEN. Aeglamour Seeks His Shepherdess. *Fr.* The Sad Shepherd.
Aeglamour's Lament. *Fr.* The Sad Shepherd.
Alchemist, The, *sels.*
All Your Fortunes We Can Tell Ye. *Fr.* The Gypsies Metamorphosed.
Angel Describes Truth, An. *Fr.* Hymenaei.
Answer to Master Wither's Song.
Apollo's Song. *Fr.* The Masque of Augurs.
Beauties, Have Ye Seen This Toy. *Fr.* The Hue and Cry after Cupid.
Begging Another, on Colour of Mending the Former. *Fr.* A Celebration of Charis.
Ben Jonson's Sociable Rules for the Apollo.
Buz [*or* Buzz], Quoth the Blue Fly. *Fr.* Oberon, the Fairy Prince.
Case Is Altered, The, *sel.*
Catch, A: "Buz [*or* Buzz], quoth the blue fly." *Fr.* Oberon, the Fairy Prince.
Celebration of Charis, A, *sels.*
Ceremonies for Candlemas Day, The.
Charm.
Chloridia, *sel.*
Chorus: "Spring all the Graces of the age." *Fr.* Neptune's Triumph.
Claiming a Second Kiss by Desert.
Clerimont's Song. *Fr.* Epicoene.
Come, My Celia, Let Us Prove. *Fr.* Volpone.
Cupid. *Fr.* The Hue and Cry after Cupid.
Cynthia's Revels, *sels.*
Dances Inspired by Love. *Fr.* Love Restored.
Dream, The.
Drink to Me Only with Thine Eyes.
Echo's Dirge for Narcissus. *Fr.* Cynthia's Revels.
Echo's Lament of Narcissus. *Fr.* Cynthia's Revels.
Echo's Song. *Fr.* Cynthia's Revels.
Elegie, An: "Let me be what I am, as Virgil cold."
Elegie, An: "Though Beautie be the marke of praise."
Elegy, An: "Since you must go, and I must bid farewell."
Elegy, An: "Though beauty be the mark of praise."
Epicoene; or, The Silent Woman, *sel.*
Epigram: "Tonight, grave Sir, both my poor house and I."
Epigram of Inigo Jones, An.
Epigram to King Charles for an Hundred Pounds He Sent Me in My Sickness, An.
Epistle Answering to One That Asked to Be Sealed of the Tribe of Ben, An.

JONSON, BEN (*continued*)
Epistle to Elizabeth, Countess of Rutland, *sels.*
Epistle to Lady Rutland, An, *sels.*
Epitaph on Elizabeth, L. H.
Epitaph on S. P. [Salamon *or* Salomon *or* Salathiel Pavy], a Child of Q. El.'s [Queen Elizabeth's] Chapel.
Epitaph on the Countess of Pembroke, *wr. at.*
Epithalamium, *sel.*
Epode.
Execration upon Vulcan, An.
Faeries' Song, The. *Fr.* The Gypsies Metamorphosed.
Fair Phyllis.
Fairy Beam upon You, The. *Fr.* The Gypsies Metamorphosed.
Fame.
Fantasy. *Fr.* The Vision of Delight.
Farewell to the World, A.
Fit of Rime against Rime, A.
Foeda Est in Coitu, *tr.*
Follow a Shadow.
Fools. *Fr.* Volpone.
For What Is Life?
Fortunate Fool.
Fortunate Isles and Their Union, The, *sel.*
Freedom in Dress. *Fr.* Epicoene.
Ghyrlond of the Blessed Virgin Marie, The.
Gipsy Song ("The faery beam upon you"). *Fr.* The Gypsies Metamorphosed.
Gipsy Song ("To the old, long life and treasure"). *Fr.* The Gypsies Metamorphosed.
Glove, The. *Fr.* Cynthia's Revels.
Good and Great God!
Good Life, Long Life. *Fr.* A Pindaric Ode.
Greatness in Littleness. *Fr.* A Pindaric Ode.
Gypsies Metamorphosed, The, *sels.*
Had Those That Dwell in Error Foul. *Fr.* The Second Mask, Which Was of Beauty.
Have You Seen [but] a Bright Lily grow. *Fr.* A Celebration of Charis.
Her Man Described by Her Own Dictamen. *Fr.* A Celebration of Charis.
Her Triumph. *Fr.* A Celebration of Charis.
Here She Was Wont to Go. *Fr.* The Sad Shepherd.
Here's the Rich Peru. *Fr.* The Alchemist.
Hesperus' Hymn [*or* Song] to Cynthia. *Fr.* Cynthia's Revels.
His Excuse for Loving. *Fr.* A Celebration of Charis.
Honour in Bud. *Fr.* A Pindaric Ode.
Hour Glass, The.
How He Saw Her. *Fr.* A Celebration of Charis.
Hue and Cry after Cupid, The, *sel.*
Hymenaei.
Hymn: "Queen and huntress, chaste and fair." *Fr.* Cynthia's Revels.
Hymn on [*or* of *or* for] the Nativity of My Saviour, A.
Hymn to Comus. *Fr.* Pleasure Reconciled to Virtue.
Hymn to Cynthia. *Fr.* Cynthia's Revels.
Hymn to Diana. *Fr.* Cynthia's Revels.
Hymn to God the Father, A.
Hymn to the Belly. *Fr.* Pleasure Reconciled to Virtue.
Hymne, The: "Queene, and Huntress, chaste, and faire." *Fr.* Cynthia's Revels.
Hymne on the Nativitie of My Saviour, A.
Hymne to God the Father, A.
I Follow, Lo, the Footing.
If I Freely May Discover. *Fr.* The Poetaster.
In Defense of Their Inconstancy.
In the Person of Woman Kind.
Inviting a Friend to Supper.
It Is Not Growing like a Tree. *Fr.* A Pindaric Ode.
It Was a Beauty That I Saw. *Fr.* The New Inn.
Jackman's Song, The. *Fr.* The Gypsies Metamorphosed.
Karolin's Song. *Fr.* The Sad Shepherd.
Keeping Endless Holiday, *tr.*
Kiss, The. *Fr.* A Celebration of Charis.
Kiss, The. *Fr.* Cynthia's Revels.
Lady Venetia Digby, The.
Love and Death. *Fr.* The Sad Shepherd.
Love Freed from Ignorance and Folly, *sel.*
Love Restored, *sel.*
Lovel's Song. *Fr.* The New Inn.
Mab the Mistress-Fairy. *Fr.* The Satyr.
Masque of Augurs, The, *sel.*
Masque of Beauty, The, *sel.*
Masque of Christmas, The.
Masque of Oberon, The, *sel.*
Masque of Queens, The, *sel.*
Masque of the Gypsies, The, *sels.*
Masque of the Metamorphosed Gypsies, A, *sels.*
Metamorphosed Gipsies, The, *sels.*
Moon-Goddess, The. *Fr.* Cynthia's Revels.
Mother Maudlin the Witch. *Fr.* The Sad Shepherd.
My Picture, Left in Scotland.
Nano's Song. *Fr.* Volpone.
Neptune's Triumph, *sel.*
New Inn, The, *sels.*
Nightingale, The, *tr.*
Noble Balm, The.
Noble Nature, The. *Fr.* A Pindaric Ode.
Nymph's Passion, A.
Nymph's Secret, A.
O, Do Not Wanton with Those Eyes.
Oh, That Joy So Soon Should Waste. *Fr.* Cynthia's Revels.
Oak and Lily. *Fr.* A Pindaric Ode.
Oberon, the Fairy Prince.
Oberon, the Fairy Prince, *sel.*
Ode, An: "High-spirited friend."
Ode to Himself ("Come leave the loathed stage").
Ode to Himself, An ("Where do'st thou careless lie").
Odes (*of Horace*), *sel., tr.*
Of Life and Death.
Of Pan we sing, the best of singers, Pan. *Fr.* Pan's Anniversary.
On a Lover's Dust, Made Sand for an Hour-Glass.
On His First Sonne.
On Lucy, Countess of Bedford.
On Margaret Ratcliffe.
On My First Daughter.
On My First Son [*or* Sonne].
On Reformed Gamester.
On Something That Walks Somewhere.
On the Countess Dowager of Pembroke, *wr. at.*
On the Portrait of Shakespeare Prefixed to the First Folio Edition, 1623.
On the twenty-second of June, *at.*
Over the Door at the Entrance into the Apollo.
Pan's Anniversary; or, The Shepherd's Holiday, *sel.*
Parasite, The. *Fr.* Volpone.
Particular Entertainment of the Queen and Prince at Althrope, 1603, *sel.*
Patrico's Song. *Fr.* The Gypsies Metamorphosed.
Perfect Life, The. *Fr.* A Pindaric Ode.
Perfection in Small Things. *Fr.* A Pindaric Ode.
Picture of Her Mind, The.
Pindaric Ode, A.
Pindaric Ode, A, *sels.*
Pleasure Reconciled to Virtue, *sel.*
Poetaster, The, *sels.*
Power of Poets, The. *Fr.* Epistle to Elizabeth, Countess of Rutland.
Proportion.
Queen and Huntress, Chaste and Fair. *Fr.* Cynthia's Revels.
Queen Mab. *Fr.* The Satyr.
Reconciliation [of Lovers], *tr.*
Sad Shepherd, The, *sels.*
Satyr, The, *sel.*
Second Mask, Which Was of Beauty, The, *sel.*
See the Chariot at Hand Here of Love. *Fr.* A Celebration of Charis.
Shadow, The.
She. *Fr.* A Celebration of Charis.
Short Measures. *Fr.* A Pindaric Ode.
Silent Woman, The, *sel.*
Simplex Munditiis. *Fr.* Epicoene.
Simplicity [and Sweet Neglect]. *Fr.* Epicoene.
Slow, Slow, Fresh Fount [Keep Time with My Salt Tears]. *Fr.* Cynthia's Revels.
So Sweet Is She. *Fr.* A Celebration of Charis.
So White, So Soft, So Sweet. *Fr.* A Celebration of Charis.
Song: "How near to good is what is fair." *Fr.* Love Freed from Ignorance and Folly.
Song: "If I freely may discover." *Fr.* The Poetaster.
Song: Kiss, The. *Fr.* Cynthia's Revels.
Song: "Kiss me, sweet; the wary lover."
Song: "Oh do not wanton with those eyes."
Song: "O, that joy so soon should waste!" *Fr.* Cynthia's Revels.
Song: "Slow, slow, fresh fount, keep time with my salt tears." *Fr.* Cynthia's Revels.
Song: "Still to be neat, still to be dressed." *Fr.* Epicoene.
Song: That Women Are but Men's Shadows.
Song: "Thus, thus begin the yearly rites." *Fr.* Pan's Anniversary.
Song: To Celia ("Come, my Celia, let us prove"). *Fr.* Volpone.
Song: To Celia ("Drink to me only with thine eyes").
Song: To Celia ("Kiss me, sweet; the wary lover").
Song: To Comus. *Fr.* Pleasure Reconciled to Virtue.
Song: To Cynthia. *Fr.* Cynthia's Revels.
Song: "When love at first did move." *Fr.* The Masque of Beauty.
Song of Echo. *Fr.* Cynthia's Revels.
Song of Zephyrus and the Spring. *Fr.* Chloridia.
Song to Celia ("Come, my Celia, let us prove"). *Fr.* Volpone.
Song to Celia ("Drink to me only with thine eyes").
Still to Be Neat, Still to Be Dressed. *Fr.* Epicoene.
Sweet Neglect. *Fr.* Epicoene.
Swell Me a Bowl. *Fr.* The Poetaster.
Sylvan Catch. *Fr.* The Masque of Oberon.
That Women Are but Men's Shadows.
This is Mab, the mistress-fairy. *Fr.* The Satyr.
Though I Am Young. *Fr.* The Sad Shepherd.
Thus, Thus Begin. *Fr.* Pan's Anniversary.
To Celia ("Come my Celia, let us prove"). *Fr.* Volpone.
To Celia ("Drink to me only with thine eyes").
To Celia ("Kiss me, sweet").
To Censorious Courtling.
To Diana. *Fr.* Cynthia's Revels.
To Doctor Empiric.
To Edward Allen.
To Francis Beaumont.
To Heaven.
To Himself.
To James Warre.
To John Donne ("Donne, the delight of Phoebus, and each muse").
To John Donne ("Who shall doubt, Donne, where I a poet be").
To King James.

To Lucy, Countesse of Bedford, with Mr. Donnes Satyres.
To Mary Lady Wroth.
To My Book.
To My Bookseller.
To My Mere English Censurer.
To My Worthy and Honoured Friend, Mr. George Chapman, on His Translation of Hesiod's "Works and Days."
To Penshurst.
To Penshurst, *sel.*
To Sir Henrie Savile [upon His Translation of Tacitus].
To Sir Robert Wroth.
To the Ghost of Martial.
To the Immortal Memory and Friendship of That Noble Pair, Sir Lucius Cary and Sir H. Morison.
To the Memory of My Beloved Master [*or* the Author] William Shakespeare.
To the Memory of My Beloved Master William Shakespeare, *sels.*
To the Reader.
To the Same.
To Thomas Lord Chancellor.
To Venus, *tr.*
To William Camden.
To William Roe.
Triumph of Charis, The. *Fr.* A Celebration of Charis.
True Balm.
Two Songs to Celia.
Venus' Runaway. *Fr.* The Hue and Cry after Cupid.
Verses Placed over the Door at the Entrance into the Apollo Room at the Devil Tavern.
Vision of Beauty. *Fr.* The New Inn.
Vision of Delight, The.
Vision of Delight, The, *sel.*
Vivamus Mea Lesbia atque Amemus. *Fr.* Volpone.
Volpone, *sels.*
Volpone's Song: To Celia. *Fr.* Volpone.
Why I Write Not of Love.
Wish, A. *Fr.* The Gypsies Metamorphosed.
Witches' Charm. *Fr.* The Masque of Queens.
Witches' Song, The.
Women Men's Shadows.
Wretched and foolish jealousy.
JÓNSSON, KRISTJÁN. Tear, The.
Waterfall, The.
JORDAN, BARBARA LESLIE. Desert Shipwreck.
JORDAN, CAROL. Jealousy of the Gods, The.
JORDAN, CHARLOTTE BREWSTER. Hammock Lullaby.
To Borglum's Seated Statue of Abraham Lincoln.
JORDAN, DAVID STARR. Altruism.
And So at Last.
Men Told Me, Lord!
To Love, at Last, the Victory.
Vivérols.
JORDAN, ETHEL BLAIR. Disarm the Hearts.
JORDAN, THOMAS. Alarm in 1645, An, *sel.*
Careless Gallant, The.
Cavalier's Lullaby for His Mistress, A. *Fr.* An Alarm in 1645.
Coronemus Nos Rosis Antequam Marcescant.
Epicure, The, Sung by One in the Habit of a Town Gallant.
Epitaph: "In this marble, buried lies."
Pym's Anarchy, *at.*
JØRGENSEN, JOHANNES. Meseemed There Called.
Plants Stand Silent Round Me, The.
'Twas at the Bridal Time of Flowers.
JORTIN, JOHN. Epitaphium Felis.
JOSA. Crocuses.
JOSE, ARTHUR WILBERFORCE. Freedom the Goddess.
Pioneers.
Sum of Things, The.
JOSEPH (Chief Joseph). War.
JOSEPH, MICHAEL. To a Siamese Cat.
JOSEPH, MICHAEL KENNEDY. Braque.
Drunken Gunners.
For Any Beachhead.
Lovers and the City, The, *sel.*
Mercury Bay Eclogue, *sel.*
New Moses, The.
Old Montague. *Fr.* The Lovers and the City.
On the Mountain.
Secular Litany.
Vacation Exercise.
Victory March.
JOSEPH OF THE STUDIUM, SAINT. Finished Course, The.
JOSEPHSON, ERNST. Cello, The.
JOSO. Haiku: "Autumn cicada, The."
Winter.
JOSUI. Cuckoo's Song, The.
JOUVE, PIERRE JEAN. Two Witnesses, The.
Woman and Earth.
JOWETT, JOHN HENRY. God's Ferns.
JOYCE, JAMES. All Day I Hear [the Noise of Waters]. *Fr.* Chamber Music.
Alone.
Ballad of Persse O'Reilly, The. *Fr.* Finnegans Wake.
Bid Adieu, Adieu, Adieu. *Fr.* Chamber Music.
Bid Adieu to Girlish Days. *Fr.* Chamber Music.
Bid Adieu to Maidenhood. *Fr.* Chamber Music.
Chamber Music, *sels.*
Ecce Puer.
Finnegans Wake, *sel.*
Flood.
Flower Given to My Daughter, A.
Goldenhair. *Fr.* Chamber Music.
Holy Office, The.
I Hear an Army [Charging upon the Land]. *Fr.* Chamber Music.
I would in that sweet bosom be. *Fr.* Chamber Music.
Memory of the Players in a Mirror at Midnight, A.
My dove, my beautiful one. *Fr.* Chamber Music.
Noise of Waters, The. *Fr.* Chamber Music.
O Sweetheart, Hear You. *Fr.* Chamber Music.
On the Beach at Fontana.
She Weeps over Rahoon.
Simples.
Song: "Lean out of the window." *Fr.* Chamber Music.
Song: "O, it was out by Donnycarney." *Fr.* Chamber Music.
Strings in the Earth [and Air]. *Fr.* Chamber Music.
This Heart That Flutters near My Heart. *Fr.* Chamber Music.
Tutto è Sciolto.
What Counsel Has the Hooded Moon. *Fr.* Chamber Music.
JOYCE, ROBERT DWYER. Blacksmith of Limerick, The.
Crossing the Blackwater.
Fair Maidens' Beauty Will Soon Fade Away.
Fineen the Rover.
Leprahaun, The.
JOYNES, ALICE B. For Those Who Fly.
JUAN DE LA CRUZ, SAN. *See* JOHN OF THE CROSS, SAINT.
JUAN II OF CASTILE. Cancion.
JUANA INÉS DE LA CRUZ, SISTER (*originally* Juana de Asbaje). Amorous of Laura's Loveliness.
Christmas Hymn.
Crimson lute that comest in the dawn.
Describes Rationally the Irrational Effects of Love.
Diuturnal infirmity of hope.
Divine Narcissus, The.
Divine rose, that in a pleasant garden.
First Dream, *sel.*
Green enravishment of human life.
In the Face of Grief.
Redondillas.
Tarry, shadow of my scornful treasure.
This coloured counterfeit that thou beholdest.
This evening when I spake with thee, beloved.
To Celio.
To Her Portrait.
To the Marquesa Mancera.
Verses Expressing the Feelings of a Lover.
"JUDAH." Fragrant Thy Memories.
JUDAH HA-LEVI. *See* HALEVI, JUDAH.
JUDD, SYLVESTER. Light of the World.
JUDSON, ADONIRAM. In Spite of Sorrow.
JUDSON, EMILY CHUBBUCK. *See* "FORESTER, FANNY."
"JUDY." Bells, The.
Imitation of Walt Whitman.
Remember.
Sarah's Halls.
JUDY, SCOTT, *and* "DOC" HAMMOND. Song: "We came to Tamichi in 1880."
JUEL, AXEL. Joy, Sorrow and Happiness.
JUHASZ, GYULA. Wilderness, The.
JULES-BOIS, H. A. India the Magic.
JULIAN, V. M. Mr. Squirrel.
JULIAN THE APOSTATE (Flavius Claudius Julianus). Beer.
JULIANUS [*or* JULIAN THE EGYPTIAN]. Bride of Sixteen, The.
Her Picture.
Laughter to the Last.
Love and Wine.
Old Fisherman.
Old Fishing Net, An.
On Anacreon.
JULIE, SISTER. Zaccheus.
JULIUS POLYAENUS. Life.
"JUNIA." Ballade of a Summer Hotel.
JURICA, ALICE B. Good Friday.
"JUSTI, BEAU." Ol' Hound Dog.
JUSTICE, DONALD. Beyond the Hunting Woods.
Counting the Mad.
In Bertram's Garden.
Sestina.
JUSTUS, MAY. Dress of Spring, The.
Footwear.
Garden Path, A.
Remember September.
Strawberry Jam.
Winds a-Blowing.
Witchwood.
JUVENAL (Decimus Junius Juvenalis). Against Women: Satire VI. *Fr.* Satires.
But you should know what Everywoman does. *Fr.* Satires.
Celestial Wisdom. *Fr.* Satires.
Fair Field for Satire, A. *Fr.* Satires.
In Saturn's Reign. *Fr.* Satires.
Life at Rome. *Fr.* Satires.
Memorial Trees.
Mood and Figure Bride, A. *Fr.* Satires.
New Woman, The. *Fr.* Satires.
On Poets Who Recite in Public—and Other Sinners. *Fr.* Satires.
Rome a Greek City. *Fr.* Satires.
Satires, *sels.*
Tenth Satire of Juvenal, The.
Vanity of Human Wishes, The. *Fr.* Satires.

K

"K." How Firm a Foundation.
"K., A." La Donna e Mobile.
"K., E. H." City Church, The.
"K., R. K." White Opal, The.
KAALUND, HANS VILHELM. In a Sunny Nook.
KABERRY, C. J. "Indian Elephant, The."
KABIR. He Cares.
Hope in Him While Thou Livest.
My Lord Hides Himself.
Songs of Kabir.
Two Songs.

KAGA NO CHIYO. On Her Child's Death.
To Her Husband, at the Wedding.
KAGAWA, TOYOHIKO. As the Sculptor.
Burden, The.
Christ Liveth in Me.
Day's End.
I Call the Swallows.
Japan Can Teach.
Kingdom of God Is within You, The.
Living Christ, The.
Love Means Adventure.
Meditation.
Mirrors.
O Skylarks, Teach Japan to Sing.
One with the Universe.
Only a Flower.
Penniless.
Sculptor of the Soul.
Silence.
Simple Life, The.
Spring.
Waiting for Dawn.
Work.
KAGEKI. Butterflies.
Maiden, A.
KAHANOVITCH, PINHAS. See "DER NISTOR."
KAHN, GUSTAVE. Homage.
Pilgrim from the East, The.
Song: "O lovely April, rich and bright."
You Masks of the Masquerade.
KAHN, HANNAH. To Be Black, to Be Lost.
KALAKAUA, KING OF THE HAWAIIAN ISLANDS. Our Native Land.
KALAR, JOSEPH. Invocation to the Wind.
Paper Mill.
KALIDASA. Aja's Lament over His Dead Wife.
Autumn. *Fr.* The Seasons.
Baby, The.
Cloud-Messenger, The, *sel.*
Early Spring. *Fr.* The Seasons.
Nightfall.
Rains, The. *Fr.* The Seasons.
Salutation of [*or* to] the Dawn, The, *at.*
Seasons, The, *sels.*
Spring. *Fr.* The Seasons.
Summer. *Fr.* The Seasons.
Winter. *Fr.* The Seasons.
Woman.
KALIR. See BEN KALIR, ELEAZAR.
KALLMAN, CHESTER. Little Epithalamium.
Nightmare of a Cook.
Urban History.
KALMAR, BERT, *and* HARRY RUBY. America, I Love You.
KALONYMOS BEN JUDAH. Although Tormented.
KALONYMOS BEN KALONYMOS. Hypocrite, The. *Fr.* The Touchstone.
Touchstone, The, *sels.*
Unfortunate Male, The. *Fr.* The Touchstone.
Yoke, The. *Fr.* The Touchstone.
KALONYMOS BEN MOSES OF LUCCA. His Sovereignty.
KAMAL UD-DIN OF ISFAHAN. O Love, Thy Hair!
KAMBARA, ARIAKE. Oyster Shell, The.
When the Wise Physiognomist Looked at Me.
KAMZON, JACOB DAVID. Very Fair My Lot.
KANBARA, YUMEI. Dark-red Shadow-Spots, The.
KANDA. His Will.
KANE, DOUGLAS V. On the Ferry.
Requiem.
Westering.
KANE, SHERRY. Reminder.
KAN JU YÜ. Incense and Moonlight.
KANTOR, MACKINLAY. Appomattox.
Snow of the Okoboji, The.
KAO ANG. Marching Song, A.
KAO SHIH. Parting and Meeting.
KAO SHUANG. Forsaken.
KAPLAN, MILTON. Circus, The.
Knife, The.
KAPLAN, MORDECAI. God the Life of Nature.
KAPNIST, VASILI. On Julia's Death.
KARAMZIN NIKOLAI MIKHAILOVICH. Autumn.
Where art thou lingering, tell me, thou fair one?
KARIOTAKIS, KOSTAS. Athens.
Diakos.
Michael.
Prevesa.
Sleep.
KARLFELDT, ERIK AXEL. Dalecarlian March.
Dreams and Life.
Flower-Songs, *sel.*
Fridolin's Pleasure-Garden, *sel.*
Hymn to the Harvest Moon.
Imagined Happiness.
In the Elk Season.
Misjudged Fiddler, The.
My Forefathers. *Fr.* Songs of Nature and Love.
Poems on Dalecarlian Paintings, *sel.*
Prelude: "My muse dwelleth not on Parnassus." *Fr.* Fridolin's Pleasure-Garden.
Song after Harvest.
Songs of Nature and Love, *sel.*
Time of Waiting.
Vagrant, A.
Virgin Mary, The. *Fr.* Poems on Dalecarlian Paintings.
KARNI, YEHUDA. Place Me in the Breach.
KARNOSH, LOUIS J. General Paresis.
Melancholia.
Paranoia.
KARTACK, ELSIE F. Pop-Corn Land.
KARVOUNIS, NICHOLAS. Song of the Vanquished, The.
KASA, LADY. I dreamed I held/ A sword against my flesh.
I love and fear him.
Tolling Bells.
KASMUNEH. Overripe Fruit.
Timid Gazelle, The
KÄSTNER, ERIC. Rooming-House Melancholy.
"KATE, RICKETTY" (Mrs. A. J. Filson). Affinity.
KATZIN, OLGA. See "SAGITTARIUS."
KAUFFMAN, REGINALD WRIGHT. Call, The.
Memorial Day, 1898.
Troia Fuit.
Wastrel, The.
KAUFFMAN, RUSSELL E. Christ of God, The.
KAUFFMAN, RUTH WRIGHT. Vagabond at Home, The.
KAUFMAN, GEORGE SIMON. Advice to Worriers.
Lines to a Man Who Thinks that Apple Betty with Hard Sauce Is Food for a Human Being.
KAUFMAN, HERBERT. This Is Your Hour.
KAUFMAN, KENNETH CARLYLE. Tame Duck.
KAUFMAN, SANFORD, *and* MARTIN S. ALLWOOD. See ALLWOOD, MARTIN SAMUEL, *and* SANFORD KAUFMAN.
KAVANAGH, PATRICK. Auditors In.
Christmas Childhood, A.
Epic.
Father Mat.
Father Mat, *sel.*
Glut on the Market, A.
Great Hunger, The, *sel.*
If Ever You Go to Dublin Town.
Memory of Brother Michael.
Pegasus.
Sanctity.
Shancoduff.
Spraying the Potatoes.
Through the Open Door.
KAVANAGH, ROSE. St. Michan's Churchyard.
KAVINOKY, BERNICE. Poet to Dancer.
KAWABUCHI. Thou Art.
"KAY." Christmas Verse, A.
KAY, ELLEN DE YOUNG. Cante Hondo.
Magnanimous, The.
Tiresias' Lament.
To a Blue Hippopotamus.
KAYE-SMITH, SHEILA. Ascension Day.
Lady Day in Harvest.
Optimist, The.
"KAZANOVA, KID." See STACK, PHILIP.
KAZANTZAKIS, GALATEA ("Petroula Psiloriti"). Laborer, The.
Sinner.
KAZANTZAKIS, NICHOLAS. Odyssey, The, *sel.*
KAZIN, VASILI. Bricklayer, The.
Carpenter's Plane, The.
KAZIN, VLADIMIR. Accordionist.
Match's Way, The.
Uncle or Sun.
KEARNEY, PEADAR. Down by the Glenside.
Soldier's Song, The.
Tri-colored Ribbon, The.
Whack fol the Diddle.
KEATING, GEOFFREY. Keen Thyself, Poor Wight.
My Grief on Fál's Proud Plain, *sel.*
O Woman Full of Wile, *at.*
KEATING, JOSEPH, SR. Charles Gustavus Anderson, *vers.* II, *at.*
KEATING, NORMA. Never, Never Can Nothingness Come.
KEATING, WILLIAM. Down, Down, Down.
KEATS, JOHN. Address to the Moon.
Addressed to Haydon.
Adonis in Slumber. *Fr.* Endymion.
After Dark Vapors Have Oppressed Our Plains.
Ars Gratia Artis. *Fr.* The Fall of Hyperion.
Ballad: La Belle Dame sans Merci.
Banquet, The. *Fr.* Lamia.
Bards of Passion and of Mirth.
Beauty Triumphant. *Fr.* Endymion.
Beginning of Love, The. *Fr.* Isabella; or, The Pot of Basil.
Bright Star, Would I Were Steadfast [*or* Stedfast] as Thou Art.
Calidore.
Cast Asleep. *Fr.* Endymion.
Coming of Dian, The. *Fr.* Endymion.
Conclusion; the Decision of the Gods. *Fr.* Endymion.
Credo. *Fr.* Endymion.
Cybele Drawn by Lions. *Fr.* Endymion.
Daisy's Song, The.
Day Is Gone, The.
December.
Dedication: To Leigh Hunt.
Den of the Titans, The. *Fr.* Hyperion.
Devon Maid, The.
Diana. *Fr.* Endymion.
Dove, The.
Dream, after Reading Dante's Episode of Paolo and Francesca, A.
Encounter with Sleep. *Fr.* Endymion.
Endymion, *sels.*
Endymion Chooses Mortal Love. *Fr.* Endymion.
Endymion's Vision. *Fr.* Endymion.
Entrance of Hyperion. *Fr.* Hyperion.
Epistle to Charles Cowden Clark.
Epistle to George Felton Mathew.
Epistle to My Brother George.
Epistle to My Brother George, *sel.*
Epistle to Reynolds, *sel.*
Epitaph: "Here lies one whose name was writ in water."
Eve of St. Agnes, The.
Eve of St. Agnes, The, *sels.*
Eve of Saint Mark, The.
Faery [*or* Fairy] Song.
Fall of Hyperion, The, *sels.*
Fame ("Fame, like a wayward girl, will still be coy"). *Fr.* Two Sonnets on Fame.
Fame ("How fevered is the man"). *Fr.* Two Sonnets on Fame.
Fancy.
Feast of Dian, The. *Fr.* Endymion.
Flight, The. *Fr.* The Eve of St. Agnes.
Forest, The. *Fr.* Endymion.
Four Seasons Fill the Measure.
Fragment of a Sonnet, *tr.*
Fragment of an Ode to Maia [Written on May Day, 1818].

From the Bridge. *Fr.* I Stood Tiptoe upon a Little Hill.
Goldfinches.
Grasshopper and the Cricket, The.
Great Spirits Now on Earth Are Sojourning.
Happy Insensibility.
Happy Is England! I Could be Content.
He Saw Far in the Concave Green of the Sea. *Fr.* Endymion.
Here Is Wine. *Fr.* Endymion.
His Last Sonnet.
How Fevered Is the Man.
How Many Bards Gild the Lapses of Time.
Human Seasons, The.
Hymn to Pan. *Fr.* Endymion.
Hyperion; a Fragment, *sels.*
Hyperion and Saturn. *Fr.* Hyperion.
Hyperion's Arrival. *Fr.* Hyperion.
I Had a Dove.
I Stood Tiptoe upon a Little Hill.
I Stood Tiptoe upon a Little Hill, *sels.*
Imitation of Spenser.
In a Drear-nighted December.
Indian Maid, The. *Fr.* Endymion.
Induction to Endymion.
Invocation to the Power of Love. *Fr.* Endymion.
Isabella; or, The Pot of Basil.
Isabella; or, The Pot of Basil, *sels.*
Keats' Last Sonnet.
Keen, Fitful Gusts Are Whisp'ring Here and There.
Kernel of the Grave, The. *Fr.* Isabella; or, The Pot of Basil.
La Belle Dame sans Merci.
Lamia.
Lamia, *sels.*
Last Sonnet.
Life Again. *Fr.* Endymion.
Lines: "Ay, if a madman could have leave."
Lines: "This living hand, now warm and capable."
Lines on First Looking into Chapman's Homer.
Lines on Seeing a Lock of Milton's Hair.
Lines on the Mermaid Tavern.
Lines to Fanny, *sel.*
Lines Written in the Highlands after a Visit to Burns's Country, *sel.*
Loss of the Mortal Maiden. *Fr.* Endymion.
Love and Friendship. *Fr.* Endymion.
Marigolds. *Fr.* I Stood Tiptoe upon a Little Hill.
Meg Merrilies.
Mermaid Tavern, The.
Minnows. *Fr.* I Stood Tiptoe upon a Little Hill.
Morning. *Fr.* Imitation of Spenser.
Naughty Boy, The.
Nightingale, The. *Fr.* Ode to a Nightingale.
No, no, go not to Lethe, neither twist.
Oh! how I love, on a fair summer's eve.
O Solitude! If I Must with Thee Dwell.
Oceanus. *Fr.* Hyperion.
Ode: "Bards of Passion and of Mirth."
Ode on a Grecian Urn.
Ode on [*or* to] Indolence.
Ode on Melancholy.
Ode on the Poets.
Ode to a Nightingale.
Ode to a Nightingale, *sel.*
Ode to Autumn.
Ode to Fanny, *sel.*
Ode to Psyche.
Ode to Psyche, *sel.*
Old Meg.
On a Dream.
On a Grecian Urn.
On a Picture of Leander.
On Fame ("Fame, like a wayward girl"). *Fr.* Two Sonnets on Fame.
On Fame ("How fevered is the man"). *Fr.* Two Sonnets on Fame.
On First Looking into Chapman's Homer.
On Imagination. *Fr.* Epistle to Reynolds.
On Melancholy.
On Seeing the Elgin Marbles.
On Sitting Down to Read "King Lear" Once Again.
On the Grasshopper and [the] Cricket.
On the Sea.
On the Sonnet.
Poetry of Earth Is Never Dead, The.
Portrait, A.
Procession of Bacchus. *Fr.* Endymion.
Proud Florentines, The. *Fr.* Isabella; or, The Pot of Basil.
Real Woman, A.
Realm of Fancy, The.
Reflection.
Robin Hood.
Roundelay: "O Sorrow, why dost borrow." *Fr.* Endymion.
Sacrifice to Pan, The. *Fr.* Endymion.
Saturn. *Fr.* Hyperion.
Saturn Fallen. *Fr.* Hyperion.
Sea, The.
Season of mists and mellow fruitfulness.
Sharing Eve's Apple.
Shell's Song, The.
Sigh of Silence, The. *Fr.* I Stood Tiptoe upon a Little Hill.
Sleep. *Fr.* Endymion.
Sleep and Poetry.
Sleep and Poetry, *sels.*
Sleeping Youth, A. *Fr.* Endymion.
Solitude.
Song: "I had a dove and the sweet dove died."
Song: "In a drear-nighted December."
Song: "O Sorrow." *Fr.* Endymion.
Song about Myself, A.
Song about Myself, A, *sel.*
Song of Spring.
Song of the Indian Maid. *Fr.* Endymion.
Sonnet: Addressed to Haydon.
Sonnet: After Dark Vapors.
Sonnet: "Bright star! would I were steadfast [*or* stedfast] as thou art."
Sonnet: "How many bards gild the lapses of time!"
Sonnet: "Keen fitful gusts are whispering here and there."
Sonnet: "O Solitude! if I must with thee dwell."
Sonnet: On a Picture of Leander.
Sonnet: On First Looking into Chapman's Homer.
Sonnet: On Seeing the Elgin Marbles.
Sonnet: On the Grasshopper and the Cricket.
Sonnet: To a Friend Who Sent Me Some Roses.
Sonnet: To a Young Lady Who Sent Me a Laurel Crown.
Sonnet: To Chatterton.
Sonnet: To Homer.
Sonnet: "To one who has been long in city pent."
Sonnet: To Sleep.
Sonnet: "When I have fears that I may cease to be."
Sonnet: "Why did I laugh to-night?"
Sonnet: Written at the End of "The Floure and the Lefe."
Sonnet: Written in January, 1818.
Sonnet: Written on a Blank Page in Shakespeare's Poems, Facing "A Lover's Complaint."
Sonnet: Written on the Day that Mr. Leigh Hunt Left Prison.
Sonnet Claims More Freedom, The.
Sonnet on a Picture of Leander.
Sonnet on First Looking into Chapman's Homer.
Sonnet on Seeing the Elgin Marbles.
Sonnet on the Sea.
Sonnet to a Young Lady Who Sent Me a Laurel Crown.
Sonnet to Mrs. Reynolds' Cat.
Sonnet to Sleep.
Sonnet to Solitude.
Sonnet Written at the End of "The Floure and the Lefe."
Specimen of an Induction to a Poem.
Spenserian Stanzas on Charles Armitage Brown.
Stanzas: "In a drear-nighted December."
Sweet Peas. *Fr.* I Stood Tiptoe upon a Little Hill.
Terror of Death, The.
There Was a Naughty Boy.
Thing of Beauty, A [Is a Joy Forever]. *Fr.* Endymion.
To a Cat.
To a Nightingale.
To Ailsa Rock.
To Autumn.
To Byron.
To Charles Cowden Clarke.
To Chatterton.
To Fancy.
To Fanny.
To G. A. W.
To Homer.
To Kosciusko.
To Leigh Hunt, Esq.
To Maia.
To My Brother George.
To My Brothers.
To One Who Has Been Long in City Pent.
To Psyche.
To Sleep.
To Solitude.
To Spenser.
To the Adventurous.
To the Nile.
To the Poets.
Two Sonnets on Fame.
Upon a Hill.
Wayfarer, The.
What Is Life? *Fr.* Sleep and Poetry.
What the Thrush Said.
When I Have Fears That I May Cease to Be.
Where Be You Going, You Devon Maid.
Wherein Lies Happiness. *Fr.* Endymion.
Why Did I Laugh To-Night? No Voice Will Tell.
Wide-spreaded Night. *Fr.* Lamia.
World outside the World, The. *Fr.* Lines Written in the Highlands after a Visit to Burns's Country.
Written in Disgust of Vulgar Superstition.
Written on a Blank Page in Shakespeare's Poems, Facing "A Lover's Complaint."
Written on the Blank Space at the End of Chaucer's Tale of "The Floure and the Lefe."
Written on the Day that Mr. Leigh Hunt Left Prison.

KEBLE, JOHN. As We Pray. *Fr.* Oh, Timely Happy, Timely Wise.
At Hooker's Tomb.
Balaam.
Bathing.
Burial of the Dead.
Christian Year, The, *sel.*
Christmas Bells.
Easter Day.
Effect of Example, The.
Evening, *sel.*
Evening Hymn.
Example.
Fill High the Bowl.
Gardening.
Holy Matrimony.
Morning.
Noontide.
November.
Oh, Timely Happy, Timely Wise.
Oh, Timely Happy, Timely Wise, *sel.*
Oak, The.
Purification, The, *sel.*
Purity of Heart. *Fr.* The Purification.
Rainbow, The.
Red o'er the Forest.
St. Stephen's Day.
Seed Time Hymn.
Sun of my soul, thou Saviour dear.
United States.
Walk to Church.

KEBLE, JOHN (*continued*)
We Need Not Bid, for Cloistered Cell.
What Went Ye Out to See? *Fr.* The Christian Year.
Whitsunday.
Who Runs May Read.
KECHARETZI, KHACHATUR. *See* "FRIK."
KEECH, BENJAMIN. Discovery.
Little Words.
Love Is Kind.
True to the Best.
KEEGAN, CATHLEEN. Fulfillment.
Renunciation. *Fr.* Three Sonnets.
Temptation. *Fr.* Three Sonnets.
Three Sonnets.
KEEGAN, JOHN. Dark Girl by the Holy Well, The.
Irish Reaper's Harvest Hymn, The.
KEELER, CHARLES AUGUSTUS. Black Sailor's Chanty.
Camilla.
Cleaning Ship.
Ocean Lullaby, An.
Pescadero Pebbles.
To an Alaskan Glacier.
KEELER, FRANCIS L. Some Mother's Child.
KEELING, MILDRED. God's World.
KEESING, NANCY. Old Men.
KEITH, GEORGE. How Firm a Foundation, *at.*
KEITH, JOSEPH JOEL. Books.
Crickets and Mice.
Definitions.
Immaculate Palm.
In the First House.
Let Us Not Say the Skin Is Dark.
Little People, The.
Lonely Trek.
She Walks.
Though She Slumbers.
KELLEHER, DANIEL LAWRENCE. For C. K. at His Christening.
Its Name Is Known.
Mother.
Upper Room, An.
KELLER, HELEN. In the Garden of the Lord.
KELLER, MARTHA. Andrew Jackson.
Brady's Bend.
Deadfall.
KELLEY, ANDREW. *See* "MIX, PARMENAS."
KELLEY, ETHEL M. His Dog.
I've Got a Dog.
KELLEY, FRANCIS CLEMENT. Throne of the King, The.
KELLEY, HUBERT. Warrior Passes, The.
KELLGREN, JOHAN HENRIK. Art of Succeeding, The.
KELLOGG, KATE. Lady Moon.
KELLOGG, LEON W. Serenade: "Venus and the young new moon."
KELLY, BLANCHE MARY. Brother Juniper.
Gaelic, The.
Housewife's Prayer, The.
Kingfisher, The.
Mirror, The.
Omniscience.
Silentium Altum.
KELLY, JOHN W. Slide, Kelly, Slide.
Throw Him Down M'Closkey.
KELLY, MARY EVA. Tipperary.
KELLY, PATRICK. Light Shoes.
Sally Ring, The.
KELLY, SAMUEL WALTER. Meditation, A.
KELLY, THOMAS. Cross and the Crown, The.
KELLY, WALT. Boston Charlie.
How Low Is the Lowing Herd.
KELLY, WILLIAM D. Twilight of Thanksgiving, The.
KELSEY, AGNES SMYTH. Our Father, as We Start the Day.
KEMBLE, FRANCES ANNE. Absence.
Absence, *sel.*
Black Wall-Flower, The.
Dream Land.
Faith.
Lament of a Mocking-Bird.
Paola and Francesca.
Trust.
What Shall I Do? *Fr.* Absence.
Woman's Heart, *sel.*
KEMP, HARRY. Alienation.
Blind.
Chant of the Box Cars.
Conquerors, The.
Farewell: "Tell them, O Sky-born, when I die."
Fickleness.
God, the Architect.
Going Down in Ships.
Going of His Feet, The.
Good Morning, America!
He Did Not Know.
Hesperides.
Humming Bird, The.
I Sing the Battle.
In a Storm.
Joses, the Brother of Jesus.
Literary Love.
Love-Faith.
Nicodemus.
Our Thirty Pieces.
Passing Flower, The.
Phantasy of Heaven, A.
Prayer, A: "I kneel not now to pray that Thou."
Prithee, Strive Not.
Remedy, The.
Resurrection.
Seaman's Confession of Faith, A.
Seeker after God, The.
Shakespeare and Later.
Tell All the World.
There's Nothing like a Ship at Sea.
Tide, The.
To God, the Architect.
Tramp's Prayer, A.
Unknown, The.
Voice of Christmas, The.
Whaler's Confession, A.
Wind's Life, The.
KEMPIS, THOMAS À. *See* THOMAS À KEMPIS.
KEN, THOMAS. Anodyne, An.
Awake, My Soul.
Evening Hymn, An.
Evening Prayer.
Glory to Thee This Night.
Morning Hymn.
Now.
Old Hundredth.
Praise God, from whom all blessings flow!
KENDALL, HENRY CLARENCE. Bell-Birds.
Beyond Kerguelen.
Coogee.
Last of His Tribe, The.
Mooni.
Orara.
Prefatory Sonnet.
September in Australia.
To a Mountain.
Voice in the Wild Oak, The.
KENDALL, JOHN KAYE ("Dum-Dum").
Cat That Followed His Nose, The.
Circumstance without Pomp.
Contented Bachelor, The.
Hug Me Tight.
My Last Illusion.
Ode to the Nightingale.
Pipes in the Sty.
Problem of the Poles, The.
Soldier of Weight, A.
KENDALL, LAURA E. Evening Prayer, An.
KENDALL, MAY. Ballad: "He said: 'The shadows darken down.'"
Board School Pastoral, A.
Lay of the Trilobite, The.
Legend, A.
Page of Lancelot, The.
Pure Hypothesis, A.
Seraph and the Snob, The.
Taking Long Views.
KENDALL, TIMOTHE. Dead Childe, A, *tr.*
Frowning fates have taken hence, The, *tr.*
Of Alphus, *tr.*
Of Fuscus, a Drunkard, *tr.*
Quip to the Reader, *tr.*
To a Married Couple That Could Not Agree, *tr.*
To Fidentinus, *tr.*
To Sabidius, *tr.*
To the Reader, *after* Martial.
KENDON, FRANK. Country Life.
I Spend My Days Vainly.
Immigrant, The.
Kernel, The.
Looker-on, The.
Now to the World.
Now You Are in Your Country.
Orange, The.
So Deep Is Death.
Son in December, A.
KENDRICK, JOHN. Fable, A: Mice and Felis, The.
KENDRICK, LUCILE. Not All the Crosses.
KENEALY, EDWARD. Castlehyde.
Dreams of My Youth.
Sweet Castle Hyde.
KENNEDY, CHARLES RANN. Terrible Meek, The, *sel.*
KENNEDY, CHARLES WILLIAM. Approach of Pharaoh, The, *tr. Fr.* Genesis.
Beowulf, *sels., tr.*
Fall of the Angels, The, *tr. Fr.* Genesis.
Gnomic Lines, *tr.*
Grave, The, *tr.*
I've Worked for a Silver Shilling.
Slaughter of Grendel by Beowulf, The, *tr. Fr.* Beowulf.
Wanderer, The, *tr.*
Wife's Lament, The, *tr.*
For other translations from Anglo-Saxon, see AnOE.
KENNEDY, CRAMMOND. Greenwood Cemetery.
KENNEDY, EDWARD D. Strange, Is It Not.
KENNEDY, EDWIN O. Prayer for Charity, A.
KENNEDY, GEOFFREY ANKETELL STUDDERT-. *See* STUDDERT-KENNEDY, GEOFFREY ANKETELL.
KENNEDY, LEO. Calling Eagles.
Epithalamium.
Mad Boy's Song.
Meek Candidates for Grave Space.
Mole Talk.
Of One Dead.
Reflection for a Sunday Morning.
Rite of Spring.
Words for a Resurrection.
KENNEDY, MARION. Tribute to Our Soldiers.
KENNEDY, MARY. Unfortunate Mole, The.
KENNEDY, SARA BEAUMONT. Prayer Rug, The.
With Little Boy Blue.
KENNEDY, THOMAS. Night Dancers.
KENNEDY, WILLIAM SLOANE. Shadows.
KENNET OF THE DENE, EDWARD HILTON YOUNG, 1ST BARON. *See* YOUNG, EDWARD HILTON.
KENNEY, JAMES. Green Leaves All Turn Yellow, The.
Old Story Over Again, The.
KENNON, RUTH. November Furrow.
KENNY, HERBERT A. On a Chasuble with Birds Embroidered.
Pleasure Is Too Surely Found.
KENNY, NICK. Patty-Poem.
KENRICK, DANIEL. To Celia.
KENT, CHARLES. Pope at Twickenham.
KENT, LOUIS. Hunt, The.
Toad, The.
KENYON, BERNICE LESBIA. Cat's World.
Defiance to False Gods.
Homecoming in Storm.
Love-Song, The.
Night of Rain.
Return.
Two Cats on the Hearth.
KENYON, DORIS. Foreknown.
KENYON, JAMES BENJAMIN. Bedouins of the Skies, The.
Bring Them Not Back.
Bylo-Land.
Challenge, A.
Come, O Wind.
Come Slowly, Paradise.
Cricket, The.
Death and Night.

Lullaby: "Sleep, O my babe, not thine a manger."
Play, The.
Racers, The.
Reconciliation, The.
Sleep, Sleep, My Babe.
Sympathy.
Tacita.
Two Spirits, The.
We Shall Attain.
KENYON, JOHN. Champagne Rosée [*or* Rosé].
KENYON, THEDA. City Bird.
For a Library Door.
Heredity.
In a Garden.
Relinquishing.
Stacking the Needles.
KEOHLER, THOMAS. Night's Ancient Cloud.
KEPPEL, LADY CAROLINE. Robin Adair.
KEPPEL, DAVID. Trouble.
KEPPEL, FRANCIS. Silver Tree, The.
KEPPEL, FREDERICK. Plain Man's Dream, A.
KERNAHAN, COULSON. I ran for a catch.
KERNER, JUSTINUS. Home-Sickness.
KEROUAC, JACK (John Kerouac). Chorus: "Big Engines, The." *Fr.* Mexico City Blues.
Chorus: "Essence of Existence, The." *Fr.* Mexico City Blues.
Chorus: "Glenn Miller and I were heroes." *Fr.* Mexico City Blues.
Chorus: "Got up and dressed up." *Fr.* Mexico City Blues.
Chorus: "Love's multitudinous boneyard." *Fr.* Mexico City Blues.
Chorus: "Nobody knows the other side." *Fr.* Mexico City Blues.
Chorus: "Old Man Mose." *Fr.* Mexico City Blues.
Chorus: "Only awake to Universal Mind." *Fr.* Mexico City Blues.
Chorus: "Praised be man, he is existing in milk." *Fr.* Mexico City Blues.
Chorus: "Saints, I give myself up to thee." *Fr.* Mexico City Blues.
Chorus: "Void that's highly embraceable, The." *Fr.* Mexico City Blues.
Chorus: "Wheel of the quivering meat, The." *Fr.* Mexico City Blues.
Mexico City Blues, *sels.*
KERR, HAZEL M. New Gethsemane.
KERR, HUGH THOMSON. Come Thou My Light.
God of Our Life through All the Circling Years.
Thy Will Be Done.
KERR, MINNIE MARKHAM. Nocturne: "There is a stillness in the heart of night."
"KERR, ORPHEUS C." (Robert Henry Newell). American Traveller, The.
Editor's Wooing, The.
Great Fight, A.
Picciola.
Rejected "National Hymns," The.
Rejected "National Hymns," The, *sels.*
KERR, WALTER H. Curtains for a Spinster.
Dignity of Man—Lesson #1, The.
Proud Trees, The.
Villanelle: "Woods we're lost in aren't real, The."
KERR, WATSON. Ancient Thought, The.
KERSH, GERALD. Soldier, A—His Prayer.
KETCHAM, HOWARD. Limerick: "This Bird is the Keel-billed Toucan."
KETCHUM, ANNIE CHAMBERS. Bonnie Blue Flag, The.
Sea-Weeds.
KETCHUM, ARTHUR. Bethlehem.
Candle-lighting Song.
Countersign. *Fr.* Legends for Trees.
Legends for Trees, *sels.*
My Lady Goes to the Play.
Sea-Wind, The.
Spirit of the Birch, The. *Fr.* Legends for Trees.
Traveller's Joy.
KETHE, WILLIAM. Hundredth Psalm, The (*metrical vers.*).
Old Hundredth.
Scotch Te Deum.
KETTLE, THOMAS MICHAEL. Cancel the Past.
Lady of Life, The.
Parnell.
Parnell's Memory.
To My Daughter Betty, the Gift of God.
KEY, FRANCIS SCOTT. Hymn: "Lord, with glowing heart I'd praise thee."
On a Young Lady's Going into a Shower Bath.
Our Rock.
Star-spangled Banner, The.
KEYES, JULIA L. Only One Killed.
Soldier in the Rain, The.
KEYES, SIDNEY. Advice for a Journey.
Against a Second Coming, *sel.*
Alexander Pope at Stanton Harcourt. *Fr.* Sour Land.
Anti-Symbolist, The.
Cruel Solstice, The.
Early Spring.
Elegy: "April again and it is a year again."
Expected Guest, The.
Foreign Gate, The, *sel.*
Gardener, The.
Glaucus.
Grail, The.
Greenwich Observatory.
Holstenwall.
Hope for Those Separated by War, A.
Kestrels, The.
Moonlight Night on the Port.
Neutrality.
Pheasant.
Plowman.
Promised Landscape, The.
Remember Your Lovers.
Rome Remember.
Snow, The.
Sour Land, *sel.*
Spring Night.
Time Will Not Grant.
Walking Woman, The. *Fr.* Against a Second Coming.
Were I to Mount beyond the Field. *Fr.* The Foreign Gate.
Wilderness, The.
William Wordsworth.
KEYNTON, JOHN. Cradle-Boat, The.
KEYSNER, BLANCHE WHITING. Old River Road.
KEZHYN, BRONISLAV. On Volga Banks.
KHANLARI. Eagle, The.
Night the Plunderer.
KHANSA. Tears.
KHAYYAM, OMAR. *See* OMAR KHAYYAM.
KHLEBNIKOV, VIKTOR ("Velemir Khlebnikov"). Death Feast.
Elephants Fought.
Hey, Lads.
"I believe" sang the guns and the squares.
It is time, it is time.
Liberty for All.
Nations, years and every creature.
Priest of the springtime's Koran.
KHODASEVICH, VLADISLAV FELITSYANOVICH. Cork, The.
It Scarcely Seems Worth While.
Monkey, The.
Stanzas: "Brightly lit from above, I am sitting."
Temptation.
What is the use of time and rhyme?
KHOMYAKOV, ALEKSEY. Labourer, The.
KI, PRINCESS. Not Alone.
KIANG KANG-HU, *and* WITTER BYNNER. *See* BYNNER, WITTER, *and* KIANG KANG-HU.
KICKHAM, CHARLES JOSEPH. Irish Peasant Girl, The.
Myles O'Hea.
Rory of the Hill.
St. John's Eve.
"KID KAZANOVA." *See* STACK, PHILIP.
KIDDER, MRS. M. A. Don't Go In.
KIEFFER, PAUL. Limerick: "Yes, theirs was a love that was tidal."
KIELY, FRANCES. In Autumn.
Is Earth My Enemy or No?
Phantoms.
KIERAN, JOHN. Advice from an Expert.
KIJO. I sit alone and listen.
KIKAKU. Fairies.
Haiku: "Blind child, A."
KIKURIO. Daffodils.
KILLIGREW, HENRY. Song: "While Morpheus thus doth gently lay."
KILLIGREW, SIR WILLIAM. Beauty Paramount. *Fr.* Selindra.
Selindra, *sel.*
KILMER, ALINE (Mrs. Joyce Kilmer).
Against the Wall.
Ambition.
Diagonals.
Experience.
For All Ladies of Shalott.
For the Birthday of a Middle-aged Child.
Gift, The.
Heart Knoweth Its Own Bitterness, The.
I Shall Not Be Afraid.
Light Lover.
Masquerader, The.
My Mirror.
Olim Meminisse Juvabit.
One Shall Be Taken and the Other Left.
Prevision.
Remembrance.
Sanctuary.
Shards.
Song against Children.
Stirrup Cup, The.
Things.
To Aphrodite; with a Mirror.
To Sappho, about Her Apple.
To Two Little Sisters of the Poor.
Tribute.
Two Lovers.
Victory.
Vigils.
Wind Rose in the Night, A.
KILMER, JOYCE. Ballade of My Lady's Beauty.
Blue Valentine, A.
Cathedral of Rheims, The, *tr.*
Citizen of the World.
Dave Lilly.
Daw's Dinner.
Easter.
Father Gerard Hopkins, S. J.
Gates and Doors.
His Laureate.
House with Nobody in It, The.
In Fairyland.
Kings.
King's Ballad, The.
Lionel Johnson.
Lullaby for a Baby Fairy.
Main Street.
Martin.
Memorial Day.
Multiplication.
Old Poets.
Peacemaker, The.
Pennies.
Poets.
Prayer of a Soldier in France.
Roofs.
Rouge Bouquet.
Servant Girl and Grocer's Boy.
Singing Girl, The.
Thanksgiving.
Theology.
To a Young Poet Who Killed Himself.
Trees.
Wealth.
White Ships and the Red, The.
KILMER, MRS. JOYCE. *See* KILMER, ALINE.
KILMER, KENTON. Dawn.
Little Serenade.
Yellow.
KIMBALL, HANNAH PARKER. Beyond.
One Way of Trusting.
Soul and Sense.
KIMBALL, HARRIET MCEWEN. All's Well.
Blessed Task, The.
Crickets, The.

KIMBALL, HARRIET MCEWEN (*cont.*)
Evening Prayer, An.
Guest, The.
White Azaleas.
KINDER, CAROLINE M. Watering Trough, The.
KINDIG, L. JAMES. Is It Nothing to You?
KING, ALFRED CASTNER. Miner, The.
Ruined Cabin, The.
KING, ANNA M. Faith and Sight.
KING, BEN. Cultured Girl Again, The.
How Often.
If I Should Die To-Night.
Jane Jones.
Pessimist, The.
That Cat.
KING, DOROTHY. Billy Boy.
Gipsy Man.
Jenny and Johnny.
KING, EDITH. Acorns.
Beetle, The.
Cobwebs.
Duck, The.
Evening Song.
Hedgehog, The.
Holly, The.
Mole, The.
Pebbles.
Rabbit, The.
Robin's Song.
To the Bat.
KING, EDWARD. Captain Loredan.
Tsigane's Canzonet, The.
Woman's Execution, A.
KING, ELIZABETH GRISWOLD. Quester, The.
KING, ELLEN, *and* H. E. ENGLE. *See* ENGLE, H. E., *and* ELLEN KING.
KING, ETHEL. Wood Music.
KING, GEORGIANA GODDARD. Man Called Dante, I Have Heard, A.
Song: "Something calls and whispers, along the city street." *Fr.* The Way of Perfect Love.
Way of Perfect Love, The, *sel.*
KING, HARRIET ELEANOR HAMILTON.
Crocus, The.
Disciples, The, *sel.*
Garden of the Holy Souls. *Fr.* Hours of the Passion.
Hours of the Passion, *sel.*
Love's Strength.
Palermo. *Fr.* The Disciples.
KING, HELEN. Human Touch, The.
KING, HENRY, BISHOP OF CHICHESTER.
Acknowledgment (of a Locket Received) An.
Anniverse, The.
Brave flowers, that I could gallant it like you.
Conjectured to Be upon the Death of Sir Walter Raleigh.
Contemplation upon Flowers, A.
Dirge, The: "What is the existence of man's life."
Double Rock, The.
Elegy upon the Most Incomparable King Charles the First, An, *sel.*
Even Such Is Man.
Exequy, The.
Exequy, The, *sels.*
Exequy on His Wife.
Farewell, A: "Thus kiss I your fair hands, taking my leave."
Go Thou, That Vainly Dost Mine Eyes Invite.
Like to the Falling of a Star.
My Midnight Meditation, *at.*
Of Human Life.
On the Life of Man.
Paradox: That Fruition Destroys Love, *sel.*
Renunciation, A.
Sic Vita.
Sonnet: "Tell me no more how fair she is."
Surrender, The.
Tell Me No More.
That Distant Bliss.
To the Memory of My Friend, Ben Jonson.
Upon a Braid of Hair in a Heart.
Upon the Death of My Ever-desired Friend, Doctor Donne [Dean] of Paul's.
Vow-Breaker, The.
KING, JOHN. My Midnight Meditation, *at.*
KING, MARY (Mrs. Anthony H. White). Mary of Bethlehem.
KING, MARY PERRY. Hymn of Freedom, A.
KING, PHILLIP. Song: "Tell me not I my time misspend," *at.*
KING, STODDARD. Commissary Report.
Etude Géographique.
Mrs. Brown and the Famous Author.
Song of Switzerland.
Wasted Ammunition.
KING, WILLIAM. Art of Cookery, The.
Mountown! Thou Sweet Retreat. *Fr.* Mully of Mountown.
Mully of Mountown, *sel.*
You Say You Love.
KINGSLEY, CHARLES. Airly Beacon.
Alton Locke, *sels.*
Alton Locke's Song [1848]. *Fr.* Alton Locke.
Andromeda, *sels.*
Andromeda and the Sea-Nymphs. *Fr.* Andromeda.
Bad Squire, The. *Fr.* Yeast.
Ballad: A.D. 1400.
Ballad of Earl Haldan's Daughter.
Christmas Day, *sel.*
Clear and Cool. *Fr.* The Water Babies.
Crusader Chorus. *Fr.* Saint's Tragedy.
Dartsiae.
Day of the Lord, The, *sel.*
Dead Church, The.
Do the Work That's Nearest.
Dolcino to Margaret.
Drifting Away.
Easter Week.
Farewell, A: "My fairest child, I have no song to give you."
Great Physician, The.
Guta's Song.
Hey, Nonny!
Instruction sore long time I bore.
Killarney.
Knight's Leap, The.
Last Buccaneer, The.
Lorraine [*or* Lorraine, Lorrèe].
Lost Doll, The. *Fr.* The Water Babies.
Margaret to Dolcino.
Merry Lark, The.
Myth, A.
Night Bird, The.
North-east Wind, The.
O Mary, Go and Call the Cattle Home! *Fr.* Alton Locke.
Ode to the North-east Wind.
Old Buccaneer, The.
Old [Old] Song, The. *Fr.* The Water Babies.
On the Death of a Certain Journal.
Oubit, The.
Pallas in Olympus. *Fr.* Andromeda.
People's Song, 1849. *Fr.* Alton Locke.
Pleasant Isle of Avès, The.
Poetry of a Root Crop, The.
Rough Rhyme on a Rough Matter, A. *Fr.* Yeast.
Saint's Tragedy, The, *sels.*
Sands of Dee, The. *Fr.* Alton Locke.
Sing Heigh-ho!
Song: "Oh! that we two were Maying." *Fr.* The Saint's Tragedy.
Song of the River. *Fr.* The Water Babies.
South Wind, The.
Swan-Neck, The.
There Sits a Bird.
Three Fishers, The.
Tide River, The. *Fr.* The Water-Babies.
To a Child.
To Miss Mitford.
Valentine's Day.
Water Babies, The, *sels.*
Weird Lady, The.
Welcome, A.
When All the World Is Young, Lad. *Fr.* The Water Babies.
When I Was a Greenhorn and Young. *Fr.* The Saint's Tragedy.
Yeast, *sel.*
Young and Old. *Fr.* The Water Babies.
KINGSLEY, HENRY. At Glastonbury.
Magdalen.
KINNELL, GALWAY. Chicago.
First Song.
For the Lost Generation.
Full Moon.
Island of Night.
Leaping Falls.
Near Barbizon.
Passion.
Spring Oak.
To William Carlos Williams.
Told by Seafarers.
Walk in the Country, A.
KINNEY, COATES. Patter of the Rain.
Rain on the Roof.
KINNEY, ELIZABETH CLEMENTINE. Blind Psalmist, The.
Dream, A.
Emerson.
Moonlight in Italy.
Quakeress Bride, The.
To the Boy.
KI NO AKIMINE. Beloved person must, I think, The. *Fr.* Kokin Shu.
KINON, VICTOR. Agnus Dei.
KINOSHITA, MOKUTARO. Ryogoku.
Sherry.
This Side and That Side.
KI NO TOMONORI. In the eternal/ Light of the spring day.
KINSELLA, THOMAS. Baggot Street Deserta.
In the Ringwood.
King John's Castle.
Pause en Route.
Triads of Ireland, The, *sel.*, *tr.*
KINTSUNE (the prime minister Kintsune). Flowers whirl away, The.
KINWELMERSH, FRANCIS. For Christmas Day.
For Whitsunday.
KIOKUSUI. Traveler Caught in a Storm, A.
KIPER, FLORENCE. *See* FRANK, FLORENCE KIPER.
KIPLING, ALICE MACDONALD. At the Dawn.
KIPLING, RUDYARD. All the Mowgli Stories, *sel.*
Anchor Song.
Astrologer's Song, An.
Bagheera's Song. *Fr.* The Second Jungle Book.
Ballad of East and West, The.
Ballad of East and West, The, *sel.*
Ballad of Fisher's Boarding-House, The.
Ballad of the *Bolivar*, The.
Ballad of the *Clampherdown*, The.
Ballad of the King's Jest, The.
Bee-Boy's Song, The.
Barrack-Room Ballads, *sel.*
Batteries Out of Ammunition. *Fr.* Epitaphs of the War.
Beginner, The. *Fr.* Epitaphs of the War.
Bell Buoy, The.
Betrothed, The.
Bombed in London. *Fr.* Epitaphs of the War.
Boots.
Boxing. *Fr.* Verses on Games.
Bridegroom, The.
Bridge-Guard in the Karroo.
Buddha at Kamakura, The.
Burial, The.
Camel's Hump, The. *Fr.* Just-so Stories.
Captive, The.
Certain Maxims of Hafiz, *sel.*
Chant-Pagan.
Charm, A.
Children's Song, The.
Christmas in India.
Cities and Thrones and Powers. *Fr.* Puck of Pook's Hill.
Coastwise Lights, The.
Code of Morals, A.

Cold Iron.
Common Form. *Fr.* Epitaphs of the War.
Commonplaces.
Conundrum of the Workshops, The.
Coward, The. *Fr.* Epitaphs of the War.
Danny Deever.
Dawn Wind, The.
Dead Statesman, A. *Fr.* Epitaphs of the War.
Death-Bed, A, 1918.
Dedication: "Beyond the path of the outmost sun through utter darkness hurled." *Fr.* Barrack-Room Ballads.
Dedication: "If I were hanged." *Fr.* The Light That Failed.
Dedication, A: "My new-cut ashlar takes the light."
Destroyers in Collision. *Fr.* Epitaphs of the War.
Divided Destinies.
Dove of Dacca, The.
Dykes, The.
Eddi's Service.
England. *Fr.* The Return.
English Flag, The.
English Irregular, '99–'02.
Envoy: "There's a whisper down the field where the year has shot her yield."
Envoy: "When Earth's last picture is painted and the tubes are twisted and dried."
Epitaphs of the War, 1914–18, *sels.*
Estunt the Griff.
"Equality of Sacrifice." *Fr.* Epitaphs of the War.
Evarra and His Gods.
Ex-Clerk. *Fr.* Epitaphs of the War.
Explorer, The.
Explorer, The, *sel.*
Fabulists, The.
Fairies' Siege, The.
Fear. *Fr.* The Second Jungle Book.
Feet of the Young Men, The.
Female of the Species, The.
First Friend, The. *Fr.* Just-so Stories.
Five War Epitaphs.
Flag of England, The.
Flight of the Bucket, The.
Flowers, The.
"Follow Me 'Ome."
For All We Have and Are.
For to Admire.
Ford o' Kabul River.
Frankie's Trade.
Fuzzy Wuzzy.
Galley-Slave, The.
Gehazi.
General Summary, A.
Gertrude's Prayer.
Gethsemane.
Giffen's Debt.
Gipsy Trail, The.
Gipsy Vans.
Glory of the Garden, The.
Go! *Fr.* The Explorer.
Grave near Cairo, A. *Fr.* Epitaphs of the War.
Grave of the Hundred Head, The.
Great-Heart.
Gunga Din.
Harp Song of the Dane Women.
Heriot's Ford.
Holy War, The.
Hunting-Song of the Seeonee Pack.
If.
In Quebec.
In the Neolithic Age, *sel.*
Islanders, The.
Jam-Pot, The.
Jane Smith.
Jobson's Amen.
Jungle Book, The, *sels.*
Just-so Stories, *sels.*
King, The.
King Henry VII and the Shipwrights.
La Nuit Blanche.
Ladies, The.
Land, The.
Land of Our Birth. *Fr.* Puck of Pook's Hill.
Last Chantey, The.
Last Ode, The.
Last Rhyme of True Thomas, The.
Law of the Jungle, The. *Fr.* The Second Jungle Book.
Legends of Evil, The.
L'Envoi: "There's a whisper down the field." *Fr.* The Long Trail.
L'Envoi: "What is the moral? Who rides may read."
L'Envoi: "When Earth's last picture is painted."
Lest We Forget!
Lichtenberg.
Light That Failed, The, *sel.*
Limerick: "There was a small boy of Quebec."
Limerick: "There was a young man from Quebec."
Long Trail, The.
Looking-Glass, The.
Love Song of Har Dyal, The.
M. I. (Mounted Infantry of the Line).
M'Andrew's [*or* McAndrew's] Hymn.
Maid of the Meerschaum, The.
Mandalay.
Many Inventions, *sel.*
Mary Gloster, The.
Maxim. *Fr.* Certain Maxims of Hafiz.
Mesopotamia 1917.
Mine Sweepers.
Mother o' Mine. *Fr.* The Light That Failed.
Municipal.
My Boy Jack.
My Father's Chair.
My New-cut Ashlar.
My Rival.
Naaman's Song.
Night-Song in the Jungle.
O Mary Pierced with Sorrow. *Fr.* Song before Action.
On the Road to Mandalay.
Only Son, An.
Overland Mail, The.
Pan in Vermont.
Pink Dominoes.
Plain Tales from the Hills, *sel.*
Playing Robinson Crusoe. *Fr.* Just-so Stories.
Post That Fitted, The.
Power of the Dog, The.
Predestination. *Fr.* Plain Tales from the Hills.
Prelude to "Departmental Ditties" ("I have eaten your bread and salt").
Puck of Pook's Hill, *sels.*
Puck's Song. *Fr.* Puck of Pook's Hill.
Quaeritur.
Queen's Men, The.
Rabbi's Song, The.
Rahere.
Rebirth: 1914–18.
Recall, The.
Recessional.
Refined Man, The. *Fr.* Epitaphs of the War.
Return, The.
Return, The, *sel.*
Rhyme of the Three Captains, The.
Road-Song of the Bandar-Log. *Fr.* The Jungle Book.
Runes on Weland's Sword, The.
St. Helena Lullaby, A.
Salonikan Grave. *Fr.* Epitaphs of the War.
Screw-Guns.
Sea and the Hills, The.
Seal [*or* Seal's] Lullaby. *Fr.* The Jungle Book.
Second Jungle Book, The, *sels.*
Secret of the Machines, The.
Servant, A. *Fr.* Epitaphs of the War.
Sestina of the Tramp-Royal.
Shillin' a Day.
Shiv and the Grasshopper. *Fr.* The Jungle Book.
Sing-Song of Old Man Kangaroo, The.
Sir Richard's Song.
Smuggler's Song, A. *Fr.* Puck of Pook's Hill.
Son, A. *Fr.* Epitaphs of the War.
Song before Action, *sel.*
Song of Diego Valdez, The.
Song of the Banjo, The.
Song of the English, A.
Song of the Galley-Slaves. *Fr.* Many Inventions.
Song of the Little Hunter, The. *Fr.* The Second Jungle Book.
Sons of Martha, The.
Storm Cone, The.
Story of the Gadsbys, the, *sel.*
Story of Uriah, The.
Study of an Elevation, in Indian Ink.
Supplication of the Black Aberdeen.
Sussex.
Theodore Roosevelt.
Thousandth Man, The.
To James Whitcomb Riley.
To-Day.
Tomlinson.
Tommy.
True Royalty. *Fr.* Just-so Stories.
Vampire, The.
Verses on Games, *sel.*
Voortrekker, The.
Way through the Woods, The.
Wet Litany, The.
When Earth's Last Picture Is Painted.
When 'Omer Smote 'Is Bloomin' Lyre.
White Man's Burden, The.
White Seal, The, *sel.* *Fr.* The Jungle Book.
White Seal's Lullaby, The. *Fr.* The Jungle Book.
Wide, Wide World, The. *Fr.* In the Neolithic Age.
Widow at Windsor, The.
Winners, The. *Fr.* The Story of the Gadsbys.
Wishing-Caps, The.
Wonder, The. *Fr.* Epitaphs of the War.

KIRBY, INEZ BARCLAY. Bright Delusion.
Night unto Night.
Silence.
Strange Promise.
Wells of Our Fathers, The.

KIRBY, JEANNIE. Aeroplane, The.
Child's Morning Prayer, A.
I Wonder.
Pigeon's Story, The.
Proud Little Spruce Fir.
Timid Bunnies.
Union Jack, The.

KIRBY, PATRICK F. Compline.
Consecration.
Rain.
Riddles.
Sequel to Finality.
Song for These Days.

KIRILLOV, VLADIMIR TIMOFEEVICH. Iron Messiah, The.
We.

"KIRK, ELEANOR" (Eleanor Maria Easterbrook Ames). Wash Dolly Up like That.

KIRK, RICHARD R. Bees.
Brother Toper.
Cock-a-doodle-doo!
Company.
Conversational Neighbor, A.
Faithful Servant, The.
God's Little Epigrams.
Mice, The.
Old People.
Our Two Gardens.
There May, of Course, Be Mice.
Thrice Blessed.
We Visit My Estate.

KIRK, WILLIAM F. Courtship of Miles Standish, The, *parody.*
Giving.
Goldfish, The.
Lumberyak, The.
Sonnet on Stewed Prunes.

KIRKCONNELL, WATSON. Aimless, *tr.*
Ballad of Tristram, The, *tr.*
Courting of Olga Karg, The.
Crow and the Nighthawk, The.
Golden Elegy, The, *tr.*
Lament: "Snows cloaked," *tr.*
Morning and Evening, *tr.*
Pursuit, *tr.*
Rain, *tr.*
Road to Bethlehem, The.
There Is No Country, *tr.*
Tide of Life, The, *sel.*

KIRKCONNELL, WATSON (*continued*)
To a Polish Mother, *tr.*
To Sleep, *tr.*
Wilderness, The, *tr.*
For translations from Icelandic, see IcP.
"KIRKE, EDMUND." *See* GILMORE, JAMES ROBERTS.
KIRKPATRICK, ELENITA THOMPSON. Beneath the Sanctuary Lamp.
KIRKUP, JAMES. Correct Compassion, A.
Homage to Vaslav Nijinsky.
La Bête Humaine.
Mortally.
Pavement Artist, The.
Ursa Major.
Wreath Makers; Leeds Market.
KIRKWOOD, MARIE. Convent Garden, The.
KIRSANOV, SEMYON OSIPOVICH. Simplicity.
This Will Pass.
This Will Remain.
Wishes.
KIRSCHENBAUM, LEO. Iberia.
KIRWAN, M. Look not upon me, seek no more to stay me.
These are my tears that now you see.
KISA'I OF MERV. Beauty's Queen.
KISER, SAMUEL ELLSWORTH. Bargain Sale, A.
Blessing of Toil.
Boy's King, A.
Fighter, The.
His New Suit.
If Paw Could Have His Way.
It May Be.
Little Prayer, A.
Memorial Day, 1889.
My Creed.
Necho, The.
Unsubdued.
When I Had Need of Him.
When Pa Was a Boy.
KITAGAWA, FUYUHIKO. Faces in the Procession.
Festivals.
Rush Hour, The.
KITAHARA, HAKUSHU. Impression of a Fountain.
Okaru and Kampei.
Precious Music of Heresy, The.
Spinning-Wheel.
KITASONO, KATUE. Bar at Night, A, *tr.*
Bored Mirror, The, *tr.*
Country Pastor, *tr.*
Flesh, The, *tr.*
Green Sunday.
Impression of a Fountain, *tr.*
KITCHEL, MARY EVA. So Runs Our Song.
KITTREDGE, HERMAN EUGENE. Laughter of the Spheres, The.
Reality.
KITTREDGE, WALTER. Tenting on the Old Camp Ground.
Tenting To-Night.
We're Tenting Tonight.
KIYOWARA FUKUYABU. Because river-fog. *Fr.* Shui Shu.
Pure, and fragile and pale.
River-Fog. *Fr.* Shui Shu.
KIZER, CAROLYN. Afterthoughts of Donna Elvira.
To My Friend, behind Walls.
What the Bones Know.
"KLABUND" (Alfred Henschke). Fever.
KLEBNIKOV, VYELEMIR. *See* KHLEBNIKOV, VIKTOR.
KLEIN, ABRAHAM MOSES. Autobiographical.
Baal Shem Tov.
Ballad of the Days of the Messiah.
Bestiary.
Biography.
Bread.
City of Slaughter, The, *tr.*
Dance of Despair, The, *tr.*
Dawn, *tr.*
Design for Mediaeval Tapestry.
Design for Mediaeval Tapestry, *sel.*
Filling Station.
For the Sisters of the Hôtel Dieu.
Frigidaire.
Grain Elevator.
Haggadah.
Heirloom.
In re Solomon Warshawer.
Job Reviles. *Fr.* Design for Mediaeval Tapestry.
Kinnereth, *tr.*
Lone Bather.
Monsieur Gaston.
Montreal.
Political Meeting.
Psalm VI: "And on that day, upon the heavenly scarp." *Fr.* The Psalter of Avram Haktani.
Psalm IX: "I am not of the saints, O Lord, to wear."
Psalm XII: "These were the ones who thanked their God." *Fr.* The Psalter of Avram Haktani.
Psalter of Avram Haktani, The, *sels.*
Rabbi Yom-Tob of Mayence Petitions His God.
Rev Owl.
Rocking Chair, The.
Snowshoers, The.
Spinning Wheel, The.
Still Small Voice, The.
Upon the Heavenly Scarp. *Fr.* The Psalter of Avram Haktani.
Venerable Bee, The.
When the Days Shall Grow Long, *tr.*
Wine, *tr.*
KLEIN, MAYSIE TULEY. Country Churches.
KLEISER, GRENVILLE. Bridge You'll Never Cross, The.
Challenge, The.
I'm the Dog.
Most Vital Thing in Life, The.
My Daily Prayer.
Only a Dog.
Our Refuge and Strength.
Prayer: "God of the sunlight, God of the sea."
We Thank Thee.
"KLINGLE, GEORGE" (Georgiana Klingle Holmes). As Thy Days So Shall Thy Strength Be.
At Dawn of the Year.
Be Patient.
He Will Give Them Back.
Hour by Hour.
Make Thy Way Mine.
Miracle, A.
Palm Sunday Hymn.
Tomorrow's News.
Wounded Christ-Heart, The.
KLINGSOR, TRISTAN. Curtain, The.
Magpie, The.
Old House, The.
KLOPSTOCK, FRIEDRICH GOTTLIEB. Resurrection, The.
KLUYEV, NIKOLAI ALEKSEYEVICH. Cottage Song, A.
On the Firs.
KNAPP, CHARLES R. Woodsman Goes to Sea, A.
KNAPP, CLARENCE HOLLISTER. I'm Going to Start In Writing Letters; a Sob Ballad.
I'm Proud to Admit That I'm Blushing; a Sob Ballad.
KNEVET, RALPH. Rhodon and Iris, *sel.*
KNIBBS, HARRY [*or* HENRY] HERBERT. Charley Lee.
Cowboys' [*or* Cowboy's] Ball, The.
Desert, The.
Long Road West, The.
Lost Range, The.
Oro Stage, The.
Out There Somewhere.
Riders of the Stars.
Roll a Rock Down.
Shallows of the Ford, The.
Trail Makers, The.
Valley That God Forgot, The.
KNIGHT, HENRY COGGSWELL. Lunar Stanzas.
KNIGHT, KATHARINE. Roads.
KNIGHT, NELLIE. Mary.
KNIGHT-ADKIN, JAMES H. No Man's Land.
Patrol, The.
KNIPE, ARTHUR A. Autumn.
Discovery, A.
Thirsty Flowers.
KNISTER, RAYMOND. Boy Remembers in the Field.
Change.
Colt, The.
Feed.
Hawk, The.
Lake Harvest.
Plowman [*or* Ploughman], The.
Plowman's Song.
Stable-Talk.
KNOTT, ETHEL RUNYON. Gone!
KNOTT, WILLIAM F. We'll Fling the Starry Banner Out.
KNOWLES, FREDERIC LAWRENCE. Columbia.
Golgotha.
Hail, America.
If Love Were Jester at the Court of Death.
Last Word, The.
Laus Mortis.
L'Envoi: "O Love triumphant over guilt and sin."
Life.
Love Triumphant.
Memory, A.
My Faith.
Nature, The Artist.
New Age, The.
On a Flyleaf of Burns's Songs.
Out of the Depths.
Pasture, A.
Song of Content, A.
Song of Desire, A.
Survivor, The.
To Jesus of Nazareth.
To Mother Nature.
Victory Which Is Peace, The.
KNOWLES, JAMES SHERIDAN. Switzerland. *Fr.* William Tell.
William Tell, *sel.*
KNOX, EDMUND GEORGE VALPY ("Evoe").
Inspiration.
Limerick: "There was a young curate of Hants."
Mr. A. E. Housman on the Olympic Games.
My Own Simplified Spelling.
Nimble Stag, The.
Stately Homes of England, The.
To the God of Love.
Tryst, The.
KNOX, ETHEL LOUISE. Reporter.
KNOX, ISA CRAIG. Woodruffe, The.
KNOX, J. MASON. Co-operation.
KNOX, JOHN. Lord Is My Shepherd, The.
KNOX, RONALD ARBUTHNOTT. Absolute and Abitofhell.
Limerick: "Clergyman, in want, A."
Limerick: "Evangelical vicar in want."
Limerick: "There once was a man who said: 'God.' "
KNOX, WILLIAM. Mortality.
Oh! Why Should the Spirit of Mortal Be Proud?
KOBBÉ, GUSTAV. From the Harbor Hill.
To a Little Girl.
KOBER, ARTHUR. Evidence.
KOBRIN, STELLA. "Who Ride?"
KOCH, CLAUDE F. Words for Artificers.
KOCH, JAMES H. To a Young Lady Swinging Upside Down on a Birch Limb over a Winter-swollen Creek.
KOCH, KENNETH. Fresh Air.
Mending Sump.
Thank You.
KOCH, KENNETH, *and* GEORGES GUY. *For translations from French, see* AnFP.
KOCHANOWSKI, JAN. To Sleep.
KOEHLER, G. STANLEY. Ground Swell.
New Construction; Bath Iron Works.
Siciliana; the Landings at Gela.
KOGYOKU, EMPRESS. Separation.
KOHEI. Band of beggars out to view, A.
KÖHLER, WILLIBALD. Bridge, The.
KOHN, ANNETTE. Epitaph for the Unknown Soldier.
Old Soldier Dead.
KOHN, WINIFRED. Mood.
Regret.

Ko I. Spring Rain.
KOKA (the stewardess of the empress Koka). For the sake of a night.
KOKO (the emperor Koko). When I went out in.
KOLARS, MARY. If This Old Place.
KOLLAR, JAN. Daughter of the Slava, The, *sel.*
KOLTSOV, ALEKSEY VASILYEVICH. Do not rustle, rye.
Harvest.
Hawk's Thoughts, A.
Nightingale, The.
Old Man's Song, An.
Song: "Oh, my love was more hot."
Song: "Sing not, nightingale."
Song: "Where, my days, are you."
Woman's Song.
Young Reaper, The.
KOOPMAN, HARRY LYMAN. Icarus.
John Brown.
Revealed.
Satirist, The.
Sea and Shore.
KORNAROS, VINCENZO. Erotokritos, *sel.*
KÖRNER, KARL THEODOR. Good Night.
Men and Boys.
Sword Song.
KOTOMICHI. Moon, The.
KOUCHAK, NAHABED [*or* KOUTCHAK, NAHAB]. Birthday Song.
My Heart Is Turned into a Wailing Child.
O Night, Be Long.
Snares, The.
KOVALENKOV, ALEKSANDR. Be near Me.
KRAG, VILHELM. Ecstasy.
My May-Day Bride.
Serenade: "On a mandolin with slender/ Strings."
When You Come.
Young Girl's Song, The.
KRAMER, ARTHUR. Inflamed Disciple, The.
KRAMER, EDGAR DANIEL. Envy.
God's Book.
Good Friday.
New Year Prayer.
Sequence.
Tall Trees.
Youth's Thankfulness.
KRASINSKI, ZYGMUNT [*or* SIGISMUND]. Waiting for Sunrise.
KRAUS, KARL. Express Train.
On the Threshold.
KRESENSKY, RAYMOND. Afternoon in a Church.
Christ on Madison Street.
Comrade, Remember.
Discovery.
End of the World, The.
For the Old Year.
Golgotha's Cross.
Heaven in My Hand.
Jesus Was a Humble Man.
Men Follow Simon.
Prayer of the Unemployed.
Refusal.
Suffering God, The.
To the Tomb.
KREYMBORG, ALFRED. America.
Ants.
Arabs.
Ballad of the Common Man.
Ballad of the Lincoln Penny.
Berceuse Arielles, *sel.*
Bloom.
Call Him High Shelley Now.
Cézanne.
Circe.
Convention.
Credo.
Crocus.
Dawns.
Dirge: "She came."
Ditty the City Sang, The.
Dorothy.
Ego's Dream.
Festoons of Fishes.
Geometry.
Her Body. *Fr.* Dorothy.
Her Eyes. *Fr.* Dorothy.
Her Hair. *Fr.* Dorothy.
Her Hands. *Fr.* Dorothy.
Idealists.
Improvisation.
Indian Sky.
Less Lonely.
Madonna di Campagna.
Man Besmitten So, A.
Man Whom Men Deplore, A.
Manikin and Minikin.
Nun Snow.
Old Manuscript.
Parasite.
Pasts.
Peasant.
Peewee.
Rain Inters Maggiore.
Ribbon Two Yards Wide, A.
Springtime.
There's a Nation.
Threnody: "I have been a snob today."
Tree, The.
Under Glass.
Vista.
Yearning.
KRILOFF, IVAN ANDREIEVICH. *See* KRYLOV, IVAN ANDREYEVICH.
KRISTENSEN, TOM. Diminuendo.
KROUT, MARY HANNAH. Little Brown Hands.
KRUGER, CHARLOTTE M. Beautiful Saviour.
KRUGER, FANIA. In Thine Image; a Negro Speaks.
Passover Eve.
Since I Have Seen Death's Face.
KRUMMACHER, FRIEDRICH ADOLPH. Alpine Heights.
Moss Rose, The.
KRYLOV, IVAN ANDREYEVICH. Peasant and the Sheep, The.
Swan, the Pike, and the Crab, The.
Wolf in the Kennels, The.
KRYSTALLIS, KOSTAS. Embroidery on the Kerchief, The.
I Would Love to Be a Shepherd.
To the Imperial Eagle.
Vintage, The.
KUAN TAO-SHENG. You and I.
KÜCHELBECKER, WILHELM. To Alexander Griboyedow, *sel.*
KÜCKEN, FRIEDRICH WILLIAM. How Can I Leave Thee.
KUDER, BLANCHE BANE. Blue Bowl, The.
KUHN, WALTER J. My Only Plea.
KUJO, TAKEKO. At the time of parting.
How disagreeable it is.
"I bring good news," said Spring.
Shaking gold and silver bells.
KU JO P'U. Gathering Bamboo.
KULBAK, MOYSHE. Driving the Rafts.
Grandma.
Grandma, May She Rest in Peace, Died.
Hay Mowing.
Jew, The. *Fr.* The Secret Saint.
Secret Saint, The, *sel.*
KUMIN, MAXINE W. Halfway.
K'UNG HSIANG SHU. Bell at Evening, A.
K'UNG P'ING CHUNG. Wandering at Night.
KUNITZ, STANLEY JASSPON. Careless Love.
Change.
Daughters of the Horseleech, The.
Deciduous Branch.
End of Summer.
For the Word Is Flesh.
He.
Hemorrhage, The.
In a Strange House.
Mens Creatrix.
Reflection by a Mailbox.
Scourge, The.
Soul's Adventure.
To the Reader, *tr.*
Very Tree.
KURAHASHIBE OTOME. This Needle.
"KÜRENBERG, THE KNIGHT OF." Falcon, The.
Star.
KURT, KIM. Runaway.
Sun-Bather, The.
Vernal Paradox.
Woodlore.
KURTH, PAULA. Association Copy.
KURZ, ISOLDE. First Night, The.
KUSANO, SHIMPEI. Conversation on an Autumn Night.
Frog, The.
Queroqué the Frog; an Autobiography.
KU SHIH. Awakening of Spring, The.
Pool in My Garden, The.
KUSHNIROFF, AARON. Die My Shriek.
KUTHAIYIR. Raven, The.
KUYKENDALL, JOHN M. Veteran Cowboy's Ruminations, A.
KUZMIN, MIKHAIL ALEKSEYEVICH. Alexandrian Songs, *sels.*
Now Dry Thy [*or* Your] Eyes.
This Summer's Love, *sel.*
KVARAN, EINAR HJÖRLEIFSSON. Death Comes Riding. *Fr.* Governor Lenhard.
Governor Lenhard, *sels.*
My Country Lies Wounded. *Fr.* Governor Lenhard.
KWASO. Butterfly.
KWITKO, LEIB. Moods.
You Who Dog My Footsteps.
KYD, THOMAS. Cornelia, *sel.*
Of Fortune. *Fr.* Cornelia.
KYLE, FRANCES. Quilting Party, The.
KYNASTON, SIR FRANCIS. Dear Cynthia, though thou bear'st the name.
Do not conceal thy radiant eyes.
If thou a reason dost desire to know.
Know 'twas well said, that spirits are too high.
To Cynthia.
To Cynthia on Concealment of Her Beauty.
To Cynthia, on Her Changing.
To Cynthia, on Her Embraces.
To Cynthia on His Love after Death.
KYOHAKU. There are no gloomy days.
KYOKO. Far beyond/ White Lilies.
KYOROKU. Above white clouds I hear sweet.
KYOSHI. Butterflies can scarcely find, The.

L

"L., C. G." Master, The.
"L., O." Prayer of the Satirist.
River of Commerce, The.
"L. B." *See* "B., L."
"L. E. L." *See* LANDON, LETITIA ELIZABETH.
"L. G." *See* "G., L."
"L. J." *See* "J., L."
"L. L. O'K." *See* "O'K., L. L."
"L. W." *See* "W., L."
LA BAU, FLORENCE. Sonnet of the Sea.
LABÉ, LOUISE. And If at Last.
Dreams.
Elegy: "Time makes an ending of the Pyramids," *sel.*
Memories.
Povre Ame Amoureuse.
Sonnet: "As soon as I begin to overtake."
What Does It Avail Me?
LABERIUS, DECIMUS. Old Actor Addresses Julius Caesar, An.
LABOMBARD, JOAN. Sibyl, The.
LABRUNIE, GÉRARD. *See* NERVAL, GÉRARD DE.
LACEY, FLORENCE. Promise.
LACHMANN, HEDWIG. Home-Sickness.
Walk, A.
LACKAYE, WILLIAM. Player's Christmas, The.
LA COSTE [*or* LA CONTE], MARIE. Somebody's Darling.
LA COUR, POUL. That Day.
LACY, BETH. Something.
"LADY OF SAKANOYE, THE." *See* SAKANOYE, LADY OTOMO NO.

La Farge, Christopher. If I Am but the Water.
Prayer for Living and Dying.
Prologue, Each to the Other, *sel.*
La Follette, Melvin Walker. Ballad of Red Fox, The.
Blue Horse, The.
Didactic Sonnet.
Hunt.
Summerhouse.
Lafon, André. Prayer, A: "Let me be like that lonely house, O Lord."
La Fontaine, Jean de. Acorn and the Pumpkin, The.
Animals Ill with the Plague, The.
Ape, The.
Bird Wounded by an Arrow, The.
Boy and the Schoolmaster, The.
Castle Builder, The.
Cat and the Fox, The.
Cat Changed into a Woman, The.
Cat into Lady.
Cat, the Weasel, and the Little Rabbit, The.
Cobbler and the Rich Man, The.
Cock and the Pearl, The.
Cockerel, the Cat, and the Young Mouse, The.
Council Held by the Rats, The.
Crow and the Fox, The.
Eagle and the Beetle, The.
Earthen Pot and the Iron Pot, The.
Fox and the Bust, The.
Fox and the Grapes, The.
Grasshopper and the Ant, The.
Glutton, The.
Hag and the Slavies, The.
Hen with the Golden Eggs, The.
Heron, The.
Jay in the Feathers of the Peacock, The.
Lion Grown Old, The.
Lion, the Ape, and the Two Asses, The.
Love and Folly.
Man and the Flea, The.
Milkmaid and the Milk-Jar, The.
Monkey and the Cat, The.
Monkey and the Pard, The.
Oak and the Reed, The.
Old Cat and the Young Mouse, The.
Old Maid, The.
Old Man and the Ass, The.
Oyster and the Litigants, The.
Rat Who Withdrew from the World, The.
Rats Hold Council, The.
Raven and the Fox, The.
Sick Lion and the Fox, The.
Swan and the Cook, The.
Thieves and the Ass, The.
Two Doves, The.
Wallet, The.
Wolf and the Dog, The.
Wolf and the Lamb, The.
Wolf, the Goat, and the Kid, The.
Young Widow, The.
Laforgue, Jules. Another Lament of Lord Pierrot.
Apotheosis.
Approach of Winter, The.
Character and Talent.
Cigarette, The.
Complaint of the King of Thule.
Complaint of the Moon in the Provinces.
Complaint on the Oblivion of the Dead.
End of a Day in the Provinces, The.
First Night, The.
Flash in the Gulf.
For the Book of Love.
Hot Stagnant Evening, A.
I Hear My Sacred Heart Beat.
Impossible, The.
Lament at the Day's End.
Lament of Forgetfulness of the Dead.
Lament of the Organist of Notre-Dame de Nice.
Lament of the Pianos Which Are Overheard in Well-to-do Quarters.
Lament of This Good Moon.
Lightning of the Abyss.
Mid-July Twilight, Eight o'Clock.
Moon Solo.
Pierrots (One Has Principles).
Romance.
Skeptic Christmas.
Song of the Little Hypertrophic Child.
Spring Evening on the Boulevards.
Summer Landscape.
Thunderbolt.
Toad, The, *wr. at. See* Corbière, Tristan.
Twilight.
Winter Is Coming.
Winter Sunset.
Without the Moon.
La Fresnaye, Jean de. *See* Vauquelin de la Fresnaye.
La Fuente Benavides, Rafael de. *See* "Adán, Martín."
Lagerkvist, Pär. Beauty Is Most at Twilight's Close.
Lagerlöf, Selma. Child of Peace, The.
Laidlaw, William. Lucy's Flittin'.
Laight, Frederick E. Soliloquy.
Laighton, Albert. Under the Leaves.
Laing, Alexander, of Brechin. Ae Happy Hour.
My Ain Wife.
Standard on the Braes o' Mar, The.
Laing, Alexander Kinnan. Last Romantic, The.
Lindbergh; a Ballad.
Triolet: "Night is full of the crying, The."
Laing, Allan M. Family Life.
Jack the Ripper.
Samuel Pepys.
When they found Giotto.
"Laird, William" (William Laird Brown). Prayer, A: "Lord, make my childish soul stand straight."
Traümerei at Ostendorff's.
Very Old Song, A.
Lake, George Burt. Birth.
Lake, Stuart N. Dad 'n' Me.
"Lakon." William the Bastard.
Laluah, Aquah. *See* Hayford, Gladys May Casely.
Lamantia, Philip. Man Is in Pain.
Morning Light Song.
Still Poem 9.
Terror Conduction.
Lamar, Mirabeau Buonaparte. Daughter of Mendoza, The.
Lamartine, Alphonse Marie Louis de. Cedars of Lebanon, The.
Crucifix, The.
Hymn to Sorrow.
Lake, The.
Village Bell, The.
Lamb, Charles. Childhood.
Childhood Fled.
Farewell to Tobacco, A.
Free Thoughts on Several Eminent Composers.
Hester.
Hester, *sel.*
Housekeeper, The, *tr.*
I have had playmates, I have had companions.
In My Own Album.
John Woodvil; a Tragedy, *sel.*
Lines on the Celebrated Picture by Leonardo da Vinci, Called the Virgin of the Rocks.
Lines Written in My Album.
Missal, A.
Names, The.
Nonsense Verses.
Old Familiar Faces, The.
On an Infant Dying as Soon as Born.
Snail, The, *tr.*
Triumph of the Whale.
Triumph of the Whale, The, *sel.*
Work.
Written at Cambridge.
Lamb, Charles, *and* Mary Lamb. Anger.
Beasts in the Tower, The.
Breakfast.
Cleanliness.
Crumbs to the Birds.
Dessert, The.
Envy.
Feigned Courage.
First Tooth, The.
Going into Breeches.
Magpie's Nest, The.
Neatness in Apparel.
Orange, The.
Peach, The.
Which Is the Favourite?
Lamb, Mary. Aspiration.
Child, A.
Choosing a Name.
Helen.
In Memoriam.
Maternal Lady with the Virgin Grace.
Parental Recollections.
Two Boys, The.
Lambdin, Sylvia S. January.
Lambert, Clara. Skyscraper Is a City's House.
Summon the Workers.
Lambert, Elisabeth. Brave Old World.
"Lambert, Louis." *See* Gilmore, Patrick Sarsfield.
Lamburn, Joan. Bondage.
Celibate, The.
First Cause.
How Will You Remember Me?
Lamdan, Yitzhak. For the Sun Declined, *sel.*
La Monnoye, Bernard de. Burgundian Carol (Patapan).
Epigram: "To all men thou dost slander me."
Patapan.
La Mothe le Vayer, François. Epitaph on the Duchess of Maine's Cat.
Lampman, Archibald. After Rain.
After the Shower.
Among the Millet.
Among the Orchards.
April in the Hills.
Between the Rapids.
City of the End of Things, The.
Clearer Self, The.
Comfort of the Fields.
Dawn on the Lièvre, The.
Dedication: "Mother to whose valiant will." *Fr.* Lyrics of Earth.
Evening.
Forecast, A.
Frost Elves, The.
Heat.
In March.
In November.
January Morning, A.
Largest Life, The.
Largest Life, The, *sel.*
Late November.
Life and Nature.
Loons, The.
Lyrics of Earth, *sel.*
Midnight.
Midsummer Night.
Morning on the Lièvre.
Nesting Time.
Peccavi, Domine.
Prayer, A: "O Earth, O dewy mother, breathe on us."
Railway Station, The.
September.
Snow.
Solitude.
Song Sparrow, The.
Summer Evening, A.
Sunset at Les Eboulements, A.
There Is a Beauty. *Fr.* The Largest Life.
Thunderstorm, A.
To My Daughter.
Truth, The.
Violinist, The.
Vision of Twilight, A.
Wind's Word, The.
Winter Evening.
Woodcutter's Hut, The.
Lamprey, Louise. Biographer, The.
Days of the Leaders, 1925, *sel.*
Deaf, The. *Fr.* Days of the Leaders, 1925.
Lullaby of the Pict Mother.
Lamprocles. National Anthem, A.
Lampton, William James. New Version, The.
Landau, Zisha [*or* Ziche]. For All That Ever Has Been Ours.
Holy Balshemtov, The.

How through Green-grassed Fields.
Softly Let Us All Vanish.
LANDAUER, HORTENSE (Mrs. Morton H. Sanger). For Emily Dickinson.
LANDELS, THOMAS DURLEY. At Eighty-three, *sel.*
Immanence.
Pilate Remembers. *Fr.* Pontius Pilate.
Pontius Pilate, *sels.*
LANDERS, WARREN P. When We Plant a Tree.
LANDON, LETITIA ELIZABETH ("L. E. L."). Cedars of Lebanon, The.
Death and the Youth.
Factory, The, *sel.*
Female Convict, The.
Necessity.
Wind, The.
LANDOR, ROBERT EYRES. Babylon. *Fr.* The Impious Feast.
Festival, The. *Fr.* The Impious Feast.
Historic Time. *Fr.* The Impious Feast.
Impious Feast, The, *sels.*
Jew's Home, The. *Fr.* The Impious Feast.
Nineveh. *Fr.* The Impious Feast.
Sleep. *Fr.* The Impious Feast.
LANDOR, W. D. Winter.
LANDOR, WALTER SAVAGE. Abertawy.
Absence ("Here, ever since you went abroad").
Absence ("Ianthe! you resolve to cross the sea").
Acon and Rhodope; or, Inconstancy.
Advice.
Aeschylos and Sophocles.
Age.
Aged Man Who Loved to Doze Away, An.
Ah! What Avails the Sceptred Race.
Alas, How Soon [the Hours Are Over].
Alciphron and Leucippe.
Ancient Idyl, The; Europa and Her Mother.
Antony and Octavius, *sel.*
Appeal, The.
Around the Child.
Autumn.
Autumnal Song.
Away my verse, and never fear.
Behold, O Aspasia! I Send You Verses. *Fr.* Pericles and Aspasia.
Burden of an ancient rhyme, The.
Charoba at Her Bath. *Fr.* Gebir.
Child of a Day [Thou Knowest Not].
Children.
Chrysolites and Rubies [Bacchus Brings], The.
Citation and Examination of Shakespeare, The.
Cleone to Aspasia. *Fr.* Pericles and Aspasia.
Commination.
Copy of Verses Sent by Cleone to Aspasia, A. *Fr.* Pericles and Aspasia.
Corinna, from Athens, to Tanagra. *Fr.* Pericles and Aspasia.
Corruption of Power, The. *Fr.* Antony and Octavius.
Corythos, *sel.*
Cowslips.
Crimean Heroes, The.
Critic, A.
Day Returns, My Natal Day, The.
Death, The.
Death of Artemidora, The. *Fr.* Pericles and Aspasia.
Death of Chrysaor, The. *Fr.* The Hellenics.
Death of the Day.
Death Stands above Me.
Death Undreaded.
Defiance.
Dirce. *Fr.* Pericles and Aspasia.
Do You Remember Me?
Dragon-Fly, The.
Dull Is My Verse.
Dying Speech of an Old Philosopher.
End, The.
Envoi: "I strove with none, for none was worth my strife."
Epigram: "Grateful heart for all things blesses, The."
Epigram: "I wonder not that youth remains."
Epigram: "Joy is the blossom, sorrow is the fruit."
Epigram: "No, my own love of other years!"
Epigram: "No truer word, save God's, was ever spoken."
Epigram: Stand Close Around, Ye Stygian Set. *Fr.* Dirce.
Epigram: "Well I remember how you smiled."
Epigram: "Years, many parti-coloured years."
Examination of Shakespeare, The.
Faesulan Idyl.
Farewell to Italy.
Fate! I Have Asked.
Fault Is Not Mine, The.
Fiesolan Idyl, A.
Finis.
Florence.
For a Gravestone in Spain.
For an Epitaph at Fiesole.
Foreign Ruler, A.
Gebir, *sels.*
Genius of Greece, The.
Georges, The.
Gifts Returned.
Give Me the Eyes.
God Scatters Beauty.
Graceful Acacia.
Hamadryad, The. *Fr.* The Hellenics.
Hearts-ease.
Helen and Corythos. *Fr.* Corythos.
Hellenics, The, *sels.*
Her Lips.
Her Name.
His Epitaph.
Honey-Moon, The.
How Many Voices Gaily Sing.
How Often, When Life's Summer Day.
How to Read Me.
I cannot tell, not I, why she.
I entreat you, Alfred Tennyson.
I Held Her Hand. *Fr.* Ianthe.
I Know Not Whether I Am Proud.
I Strove with None.
I Wonder Not That Youth Remains.
Ianthe.
Ianthe, *sels.*
Ianthe's Question.
Ianthe's Troubles.
In After Time.
In Clementina's Artless Mien.
In Clementina's Artless Mien, *sel.*
In Memoriam; Lady Blessington.
In spring and summer winds may blow.
Introduction to "The Last Fruit off an Old Tree."
Invocation, An: "We are what suns and winds."
Iphigeneia. *Fr.* The Hellenics.
Iphigeneia and Agamemnon. *Fr.* The Hellenics.
Ireland.
Ireland Never Was Contented.
Is It Not Better at an Early Hour.
It Often Comes into My Head.
Izaac Walton, Cotton, and William Oldways.
Jealous, I Own It.
Kiss, The.
Lament: "Mild is the parting year, and sweet."
Last Fruit off an Old Tree, The.
Last Fruit off an Old Tree, The, *sels.*
Late Leaves.
Lately Our Poets.
Lately Our Songsters [*or* Poets] Loiter'd [in Green Lanes].
Leaf after Leaf Drops Off.
Leaves are falling, The; so am I.
Lines to a Dragon Fly.
Little Aglaë. *Fr.* Pericles and Aspasia.
Little you think, my lovely friend.
Long awaited day, The. *Fr.* Gebir.
Love's Madness, *tr.*
Lyric, A: "You smiled, you spoke."
Macaulay.
Maid I Love, The.
Maid's Lament, The. *Fr.* The Citation and Examination of Shakespeare.
Man.
Margaret, *tr.*
Masar. *Fr.* Gebir.
Memory.
Menelaus and Helen at Troy.
Mild Is the Parting Year.
Milton.
Milton in Italy.
Mimnermus Incert.
Mother, I Cannot Mind My Wheel.
My Hopes Retire.
My Serious Son.
Myrtis to Aspasia. *Fr.* Pericles and Aspasia.
Nancy's Hair.
Night Airs and Moonshine.
No Longer Could I Doubt Him True.
No Truer Word.
No Word of Fear.
Nymph, The. *Fr.* Gebir.
Of Clementina.
On a Child.
On Catullus.
On Death.
On Himself.
On His Ninth Decade.
On His Own Agamemnon and Iphigeneia.
On His Own Death.
On His Seventy-fifth Birthday. *Fr.* The Last Fruit off an Old Tree.
On Living Too Long.
On Lucretia Borgia's Hair.
On Man.
On Music.
On Seeing a Hair of Lucretia Borgia.
On Southey's Death ("Friends, hear the words").
On the Dead.
On the Death of M. d'Ossoli and His Wife, Margaret Fuller.
On the Death of Southey ("It was a dream").
On the Death of Southey ("Not the last struggles").
On the Hellenics. *Fr.* The Hellenics.
On the Smooth Brow and Clustering Hair.
On Timely Death.
Once a fair city. *Fr.* Gebir.
One Gray Hair, The.
One White Hair, The.
One Year Ago.
Open Grave, An.
Overture. *Fr.* Thrasymedes and Eunoe.
Past Ruin'd Ilion [Helen Lives]. *Fr.* Ianthe.
Pericles and Aspasia, *sels.*
Persistence.
Place Where Soon, The.
Plays.
Pleasure! Why Thus Desert.
Poem: "I cannot tell, not I, why she."
Proem to Hellenics. *Fr.* The Hellenics.
Progress of Evening, *sel.*
Prophecy, A.
Proud Word You Never Spoke.
Provident and wakeful fear, A.
Pursuits! alas, I now have none.
Regeneration.
Remain, Ah Not in Youth Alone.
Reply to Lines by Thomas Moore, A, *sel.*
Resignation.
Rose Aylmer.
Rose Aylmer's Hair, Given by Her Sister.
Sacrifice.
Sappho to Hesperus. *Fr.* Pericles and Aspasia.
Sea-Nymph's Parting, The. *Fr.* Gebir.
Separation.
Shades of Agamemnon and Iphigeneia.
Shakespeare and Milton.
She I love (alas in vain!).
Shells, The. *Fr.* Gebir.
So Late Removed from Him She Swore.

LANDOR, WALTER SAVAGE (*continued*)
So Then, I Feel Not Deeply!
Some of Wordsworth.
Song: "Often I have heard it said."
Stand close around, ye Stygian set. *Fr.* Pericles and Aspasia.
Sweet Was the Song.
Tamar and the Nymph. *Fr.* Gebir.
Tamar's Wrestling. *Fr.* Gebir.
Ternissa! You Are Fled! *Fr.* The Hellenics.
Test, The. *Fr.* Ianthe.
There Are Sweet Flowers.
There Are Who Say.
There Falls with Every Wedding Chime.
Theseus and Hippolyta.
Thou Needst Not Pitch upon My Hat.
Thought, A.
Thrasymedes and Eunoe. *Fr.* The Hellenics.
Thrasymedes and Eunoe, *sel. Fr.* The Hellenics.
Three Roses, The.
Time to Be Wise.
To a Bride.
To a Cyclamen.
To a Painter.
To Age.
To Corinth.
To His Verse.
To Ianthe.
To Joseph Ablett.
To Mary Lamb.
To Miss Arundell.
To My Child Carlino.
To My Ninth Decade.
To Our House-Dog Captain.
To Poets.
To Robert Browning.
To Robert Browning, *sel.*
To Rose.
To Shelley.
To Sleep.
To Southey, 1833.
To the Sister of Elia.
To Varus, *tr.*
To Wordsworth.
To Youth.
True or False, *tr.*
Twenty Years Hence.
Tyrannicide.
Under the Lindens.
Upon a Sweet-Briar. *Fr.* The Citation and Examination of Shakespeare.
Various the Roads of Life.
Verse: "Past ruined Ilion Helen lives."
Verses Why Burnt.
Very True, the Linnets Sing.
Wall-Flower, The.
Well I Remember How You Smiled.
Wert thou but blind, O Fortune, then perhaps.
When Helen first saw wrinkles in her face.
Why.
Why Do Our Joys Depart.
Why, Why Repine.
With Petrarch's Sonnets.
With Rosy Hand.
Wrinkles.
Yacht, The.
Ye little household gods, that make.
Ye walls! sole witnesses of happy sighs.
Years After.
Years, Many Parti-coloured Years.
Yes; I Write Verses.
You Smiled, You Spoke.
Your Pleasures Spring.
LANE, ALEXA. Ghost.
LANE, BERTHA PALMER. Star, The.
LANE, DENNY. Lament of the Irish Maiden, The.
LANE, FRANKLIN K. I Am What You Make Me.
LANE, TEMPLE. Fairy Tree, The.
LANE, WILMOT B. Owning.
LANG, ANDREW. Aesop.
Almae Matres.
Amours de Marie, *sels., tr.*
Amours Diverses, Les, *sel., tr.*
Another Way.
April, *tr.*
April on Tweed.
Arbor Amoris, *tr.*
Aucassin and Nicolete, *tr.*
Ballad of Dead Ladies, The.
Ballad of the Gibbet, *tr.*
Ballad of the Primitive Jest.
Ballade of a Friar, *tr.*
Ballade of Blue China.
Ballade of Dead Ladies.
Ballade of His Choice of a Sepulchre.
Ballade of Middle Age.
Ballade of Primitive Man.
Ballade of the Bookworm.
Ballade of the Gibbet, *tr.*
Ballade of the Primitive Jest.
Ballade of the Southern Cross.
Ballade to Theocritus, in Winter.
Before the Snow.
Bridge of Death, The, *tr.*
Brahma.
But now the dentist cannot die.
Changeful Beauty.
Clevedon Church.
Danaë's Lullaby.
Deadly Kisses, *tr.*
Death, *tr.*
Dream, A.
Dreams.
Endure, My Heart.
Envoy: "Friends, sursum corda, soon or slow."
Erinna.
Fisherman, The, *tr.*
Garden of Regrets, The.
Genesis of Butterflies, The, *tr.*
Golden Eyes, *tr.*
Grave and the Rose, The, *tr.*
Heliodora, *tr.*
Heliodore, *tr.*
Heliodore Dead, *tr.*
Herodotus in Egypt.
His Lady's Death, *tr.*
His Lady's Tomb, *tr.*
Homeric Unity.
Hymn to the Winds, *tr.*
I know not what my secret is.
I'd Leave.
Idylls (*of* Theocritus), *sels., tr.*
In the Spring, *tr.*
Juana, *tr.*
Lady of High Degree, A, *tr.*
Lament for Adonis, The, *tr.*
Lament for Bion, The, *tr.*
Limerick: "There was a young lady of Limerick."
Limerick: "There was an auld birkie ca'ed Milton."
Lost for a Rose's Sake, *tr.*
Lost in Hades.
Lost Love.
Love in Her Hair, *tr.*
Love in May, *tr.*
Man and the Ascidian.
Martial in Town.
Melville and Coghill.
Milk White Doe, The, *tr.*
Moonlight, *tr.*
More Strong than Time, *tr.*
New Shakespeare, A.
Nightingale Weather.
O Gentle Ships, *tr.*
O Joy of Love's Renewing.
Ode: "See, Mignonne, hath not the rose," *tr.*
Odyssey, The.
Of Blue China.
Of His Choice of a Sepulchre.
Of His Death, *tr.*
Of His Lady's Old Age, *tr.*
Of Life.
Of the Book-Hunter.
Old Loves, *tr.*
Old Tune, An, *tr.*
On Calais Sands.
On His Lady's Waking, *tr.*
Père Sévère, Le, *tr.*
Psalm of Life, A.
Rhodanthe, *tr.*
Romance.
Rondel: "Good-by, the tears are in my eyes," *tr.*
Rondel: "Strengthen, my Love, this castle of my heart," *tr.*
Rondel to His Mistress, *tr.*
Ronsard.
Rose, The, *tr.*
Roses, *tr.*
San Terenzo.
Scot to Jeanne d'Arc, A.
Scythe Song.
Sea Dirge, *tr.*
Shadows of His Lady, *tr.*
Sonnet to Heavenly Beauty, *tr.*
Spinning Woman, The, *tr.*
Spring ("Now the bright crocus flames"), *tr.*
Spring ("The year has changed his mantle cold"), *tr.*
Spring in the Students' Quarter, *tr.*
Telling the Bees.
There was an Old Man of Toronto.
Three Captains, *tr.*
Three Portraits of Prince Charles.
To Helen, *tr.*
To His Friend in Elysium, *tr.*
To His Young Mistress, *tr.*
To Sappho, *tr.*
To the Moon, *tr.*
To Theocritus, in Winter.
Trout-fishing on Tweed.
Tusitala.
Twilight on Tweed.
Villon's Ballade, *tr.*
Vow to Heavenly Venus, A, *tr.*
Weeping and wakeful all the night I lie, *tr.*
White Pacha, The.
LANG, ANDREW, *and* SAMUEL HENRY BUTCHER. *See* BUTCHER, SAMUEL HENRY, *and* ANDREW LANG.
LANG, ANDREW, *and* EDWARD BURNETT TYLOR. Double Ballade of Primitive Man.
LANG, ANDREW, WALTER LEAF, *and* ERNEST MYERS. Iliad, The, *sels., tr.*
LANG, ELIZABETH. Honey Bear.
LANG, V. R. Waiting and Peeking.
LANGBRIDGE, FREDERICK. Quite by Chance.
LANGBRIDGE, ROSAMOND. Phosphorescence.
LANGDON, MABEL. Twilight Musing.
LANGE, THOR. To Tell How I Love You.
Were I a Lark So Gay.
LANGE-MÜLLER, EMIL. Summer Lightning.
LANGFORD, DOROTHY J. On Top of Troubled Waters.
Son of Man, The.
LANGFORD, G. W. Speak Gently, *wr. at. See* BATES, DAVID.
LANGHORNE, CHARLES HARTLEY. Theocritus.
LANGHORNE, JOHN. Apology for Vagrants. *Fr.* The Country Justice.
Country Justice, The.
Country Justice, The, *sel.*
Evening Primrose, The. *Fr.* The Fables of Flora.
Fables of Flora, The, *sels.*
Farewell Hymn to the Valley of Irwan, A. *Fr.* Solyman and Almena.
Solyman and Almena, *sel.*
Wail'd the sweet warbler to the lonely shade, *tr.*
Wall-Flower, The. *Fr.* The Fables of Flora.
LANGLAND, JOSEPH. Aria for Flute and Oboe.
Ecclesiastes.
Hunters in the Snow: Brueghel.
Pruners; Conca di Marini.
War.
Willows.
Winter Juniper.
LANGLAND, WILLIAM. Avarice. *Fr.* The Vision of Piers Plowman.
Average Man, The. *Fr.* The Vision of Piers Plowman.
Confession of the Deadly Sins, The. *Fr.* The Vision of Piers Plowman.
Covetousness. *Fr.* The Vision of Piers Plowman.
Crucifixion and the Harrowing of Hell, The. *Fr.* The Vision of Piers Plowman.

Descent into Hell, The. *Fr.* The Vision of Piers Plowman.
Dream, A. *Fr.* The Vision of Piers Plowman.
Fable of Belling the Cat, The. *Fr.* The Vision of Piers Plowman.
Field Full of Folk, The ("In a summer season"). *Fr.* The Vision of Piers Plowman.
Field Full of Folk, A ("What this mountain betokens"). *Fr.* The Vision of Piers Plowman.
Glutton, The. *Fr.* The Vision of Piers Plowman.
Glutton and Bat the Brewer. *Fr.* The Vision of Piers Plowman.
Gluttony. *Fr.* The Vision of Piers Plowman.
Grace for Theology. *Fr.* The Vision of Piers Plowman.
Holy Church. *Fr.* The Vision of Piers Plowman.
Holy Church Speaks. *Fr.* The Vision of Piers Plowman.
Human Soul Speaks, The. *Fr.* The Vision of Piers Plowman.
Incarnation, The. *Fr.* The Vision of Piers Plowman.
Induction, The: "In a summer season." *Fr.* The Vision of Piers Plowman.
Langland's Life. *Fr.* The Vision of Piers Plowman.
Love We as Brothers. *Fr.* The Vision of Piers Plowman.
Maiden Meed, The. *Fr.* The Vision of Piers Plowman.
Palace of Truth, The. *Fr.* The Vision of Piers Plowman.
Palmer, The. *Fr.* The Vision of Piers Plowman.
Piers Plowman, *sels.*
Poor, The. *Fr.* The Vision of Piers Plowman.
Poverty Not All Loss. *Fr.* The Vision of Piers Plowman.
Prayer for the Poor. *Fr.* The Vision of Piers Plowman.
Preaching and Not Doing. *Fr.* The Vision of Piers Plowman.
Prologue, The: "In a somer sesun." *Fr.* The Vision of Piers Plowman.
Providence. *Fr.* The Vision of Piers Plowman.
Search for St. Truth, The. *Fr.* The Vision of Piers Plowman.
Sufferings of the Poor, The. *Fr.* The Vision of Piers Plowman.
Theology. *Fr.* The Vision of Piers Plowman.
This I trow to be truth—who can teach thee better. *Fr.* The Vision of Piers Plowman.
Two Confessions. *Fr.* The Vision of Piers Plowman.
Vision of Jesus, The. *Fr.* The Vision of Piers Plowman.
Vision of Nature, A. *Fr.* The Vision of Piers Plowman.
Vision of Piers Plowman, The, *sels.*
LANGLEY, EVE. Australia.
Native-born.
This Year, before It Ends.
LANGWORTHY, YOLANDE. Drifting Sands and a Caravan.
LANIER, CLIFFORD. Edgar Allan Poe.
LANIER, SIDNEY. Acknowledgment.
Acknowledgment, *sel.*
Ballad of Trees and the Master, A.
Barnacles.
Battle of Lexington, The. *Fr.* The Psalm of the West.
Betrayal. *Fr.* The Jacquerie.
Burn the Stubble!
Centennial Meditation of Columbia, The, *sel.*
Corn.
Cross, The.
Crystal, The.
Crystal, The, *sel.*
Crystal Christ, The. *Fr.* The Crystal.
Dear Land of All My Love. *Fr.* The Centennial Meditation of Columbia.
Dying Words of Stonewall Jackson, The.
Evening Song.
From the Flats.
Harlequin of Dreams, The.
Hound, The.
Hymns of the Marshes, *sel.*
Individuality.
Jacquerie, The, *sels.*
Land of the Wilful Gospel. *Fr.* The Psalm of the West.
Lexington. *Fr.* The Psalm of the West.
Marsh Song—at Sunset.
Marshes of Glynn, The.
Marshes of Glynn, The, *sels.*
Mocking Bird, The.
My Springs.
Night and Day.
Nirvana.
Opposition.
Owl against Robin.
Pine Tree, The, *tr.*
Prayer at a Wedding.
Psalm of the West, The, *sels.*
Raven Days, The.
Resurrection.
Revenge of Hamish, The.
Song: "Hound was cuffed, the hound was kicked, The." *Fr.* The Jacquerie.
Song for "The Jacquerie." *Fr.* The Jacquerie.
Song of the Chattahoochee.
Song of the Future, A.
Stirrup-Cup, The.
Story of Vinland, The. *Fr.* The Psalm of the West.
Struggle.
Sunrise. *Fr.* Hymns of the Marshes.
Sunrise, *sel.* *Fr.* Hymns of the Marshes.
Symphony, The.
Symphony, The, *sels.*
Tampa Robins.
Thar's More in the Man than Thar Is in the Land.
Tournament.
Trees and the Master, The.
Triumph, The. *Fr.* The Psalm of the West.
Waving of the Corn, The.
Wedding-Hymn.
LANIGAN, GEORGE THOMAS. Ahkoond of Swat, The.
Dirge of the Moolla of Kotal.
Gai lon la, gai le rosier, *tr.*
Isabeau s'y promène, *tr.*
Quatrain: "Squeak's heard in the orchestra, A."
Threnody, A: "What, what, what."
Threnody on the Ahkoond of Swat, A.
LANKFORD, FRANCES STOAKLEY. Required Course.
LANNING, JANE MCKAY. Lent.
LANSDOWNE, GEORGE GRANVILLE, BARON. *See* GRANVILLE, GEORGE, BARON LANSDOWNE.
LANUSSE, ARMAND. Epigram: "'Do you not wish to renounce the Devil?'"
LANYON, CARLA LANYON. One Generation to Another.
LANYON, HELEN. Haunted.
LAO-TZU [*or* LAO-TSE]. Endless Self, *at.* *Fr.* Tao Teh King.
Gentle Touch, A, *at.* *Fr.* Tao Teh King.
He Who Feels Punctured, *at.* *Fr.* Tao Teh King.
In a Land, *at.* *Fr.* Tao Teh King.
Knowledge Studies Others, *at.* *Fr.* Tao Teh King.
Lesson of Water, *at.*
Life, *at.* *Fr.* Tao Teh King.
Paradoxes, *at.* *Fr.* Tao Teh King.
Simple Way, The, *sels., at.*
Tao, *at.* *Fr.* Tao Teh King.
Tao Teh King, *sels., at.*
Those Who Know Do Not Tell, *at.* *Fr.* Tao Teh King.
To Be, *at.* *Fr.* Tao Teh King.
True Freedom, *at.* *Fr.* Tao Teh King.
Way of the Sage, The, *at.* *Fr.* Tao Teh King.
LAPSLEY, R. A. Psalm Fifty-one.
LARAMORE, VIVIAN YEISER. First Mother.
Folly.
Talk to Me Tenderly.
LARCOM, LUCY. Apple Blossoms.
Brown Thrush, The.
By the Fireside.
Calling the Violet.
Canticle de Profundis.
Christmas Thought, A.
Day of Joy, The.
Flag, The.
Golden-Rod.
Grace and Her Friends.
Hannah Binding Shoes.
Hymn Written for the Two Hundredth Anniversary of the Old South Church, Beverly, Massachusetts.
In the Tree-Top.
January.
Lily of the Resurrection.
March.
Mistress Hale of Beverly.
Mountains.
Nature's Easter Music.
Nineteenth of April (1861), The.
Our Christ.
Plant a Tree.
Proof, The.
Rain.
Red-Top and Timothy.
Re-enlisted.
Rivulet, The.
Shared.
Sinking of the *Merrimac[k]*, The.
Sir Robin.
Strip of Blue, A.
Thanksgiving, A.
Thanksgiving, A, *sel.*
Thy Will Be Done.
Tolling.
Trees, The.
Two Festivals.
Violets.
Woman's Easter.
LARDNER, RING (Ringgold Wilmer Lardner). Fragment from "Clemo Uti—the Water Lilies."
LARKIN, MARGARET. Good-by—to My Mother.
LARKIN, PHILIP. At Grass.
Born Yesterday.
Church Going.
Deceptions.
Lines on a Young Lady's Photograph Album.
Next, Please.
Places, Loved Ones.
Poetry of Departures.
Toads.
LARMINIE, VERA. In Extremis.
LARMINIE, WILLIAM. Consolation.
Epilogue to "Fand." *Fr.* Fand.
Fand, *sels.*
Killarney.
Moytura, *sel.*
Nameless Doon [*or* Dun], The.
Nameless Ruin, The.
Speech of Emer, The. *Fr.* Fand.
Sword of Tethra, The. *Fr.* Moytura.
LARRABEE, HAROLD ATKINS. Itch to Etch, The.
Professors.
Very Model of a Modern College President, The.
LARREMORE, WILBUR. Blossom Time.
Madam Hickory.
"LARS, CLAUDIA" (Carmen Brannon Beers). Heads and Tails.
Sketch of the Frontier Woman.
LARSEN, THØGER. Summer.
LARSSON, RAYMOND ELLSWORTH. Antique Carved Figures.
Christemasse Carol for Saint Francis' Ears, A.
Epistle for Spring.
O City, Cities! *sel.*
To Our Lady, the Ark of the Covenants.
LART, K. C. Walk in Spring, A.

LASKER-SCHÜLER, ELSE. Always in the Parting Year.
I Have a Blue Piano.
I Know That I Must Die Soon.
Love-Song.
Love's Flight.
My Love-Song.
Rock Crumbles, The.
To Gottfried Benn.
To Senna Hoy.
Zebaoth.
LASYNYS, ELIS WYN O. Death the Great.
"LA T., M." Seaside Nursery Song.
LATCHAW, GLADYS. My Yoke Is Easy.
LATHBURY, MARY ARTEMISIA ("Aunt Mary"). Bread of Life, The.
Break Thou the Bread of Life.
Day Is Dying in the West, The.
Easter Song.
Song of Hope.
Summer Sunshine.
LATHROP, ADELE. Because He Lives.
LATHROP, GEORGE PARSONS. Charity.
Child's Wish Granted, The.
Flown Soul, The.
Keenan's Charge.
Marthy Virginia's Hand.
Name of Washington, The.
Remembrance.
Song-Sparrow, The.
South-Wind.
Sunshine of Thine Eyes, The.
Voice of the Void, The.
LATHROP, LENA. Woman's Question, A.
LATHROP, MARY T. Day Dawn of the Heart.
LATHROP, ONA FREEMAN. Mother's Reward, A.
LATHROP, ROSE HAWTHORNE (Mrs. George Parsons Lathrop; Mother Mary Alphonsa). Clock's Song, The.
Despair. *Fr.* Give Me Not Tears.
Dorothy.
Give Me Not Tears.
Impress of the Crucifix.
Joy. *Fr.* Give Me Not Tears.
Song before Grief, A.
LATIMER, BETTE DARCIE. For William Edward Burghardt DuBois on His Eightieth Birthday.
LA TROBE, JOHN ANTES. Peace of Christ, The.
LATTIMORE, RICHMOND. Father, The.
Max Schmitt in a Single Scull.
Ship Bottom.
Threnody: "Blow out the dying candles one by one."
For translations from French, see AnFP.
For translations from Greek, see GrPo *and* LiTW.
LAUBE, CLIFFORD JAMES. At the Battery Sea-Wall.
Ave, Vita Nostra!
Bees of Christ, The.
Dream across the Dark.
Last Rally.
To Lizard Head.
LAUFER, CALVIN W. Evening Prayer.
Morning Prayer.
Prayer Poem, A.
LAUGHLIN, ELMER OSBORN. Doctor, The.
Expectant Father, The.
Inscription for a Hospital.
Lincoln Circuit, The.
Unknown, The.
LAUGHLIN, JAMES. Busy Day.
Dawn of the Golden Age, *tr. Fr.* Eclogues.
Eclogue IV: "Muses/ Muses of Sicily," *tr. Fr.* Eclogues.
Eclogues (*of* Virgil) *sels., tr.*
Fourth Eclogue, The, *tr. Fr.* Eclogues.
Letter to Hitler, A.
Summons, The.
LAUGHTON, FREDA. At the Party.
Bull, The.
Rain on a Cottage Roof.
To the Spring Sun.
Welcome, The.
When to My Serene Body.
Woman with Child, The.
LAUGHTON, LOUISE M. Word to the Wise, A.
LAUNE, SEIGNIORA. My Neighbor.
LAUREN, JOSEPH. Butterfly and the Caterpillar, The.
Fox and the Grapes, The.
Frogs Who Wanted a King, The.
LAURENCE, ELSIE. Alone.
LAURENCE, RAY. Hollyhocks, The.
"LAUTRÉAMONT, COMTE DE" (Isidore Lucien Ducasse). Song of Maldoror, The, *sel.*
LAVATER, LOUIS. Barrier, The.
Mopoke.
Ocean.
LAVELLE, THOMAS. *See* FLAVELL, THOMAS.
LAW, MARGARET LATHROP. Hands.
Those Who Soar.
LAWLER, ANNE MARY. Lines for Insomnia.
LAWLESS, EMILY. After Aughrim.
Clare Coast.
Dirge of the Munster Forest.
Fontenoy, 1745.
In Spain.
In Spain; Drinking Song.
Spain.
Stranger's Grave, The.
LAWLESS, MARGARET ELWARD. Manhattan.
LAWRENCE, A. H. To Be a Nurse.
LAWRENCE, DAVID HERBERT. All of Roses.
"And Oh!—That the Man I Am Might Cease to Be."
Autumn at Taos.
Aware.
Baby Asleep after Pain, A.
Baby Running Barefoot.
Ballad of Another Ophelia.
Bare Almond Trees.
Bavarian Gentians.
Brooding Grief.
Cherry Robbers.
City-Life.
Collier's Wife, The.
Discord in Childhood.
Don'ts.
Dreams Old and Nascent.
Elephant Is Slow to Mate, The.
End of Another Home Holiday.
Fate and the Younger Generation.
Fidelity.
Fireflies in the Corn.
Giorno dei Morti.
Gloire de Dijon.
Glory.
Green.
Grief.
Hostile Sun, The.
How Beastly the Bourgeois Is.
Humming-Bird.
Hymn to Priapus.
In Trouble and Shame.
Kangaroo.
Kisses in the Train.
Last Words to Miriam.
Let Us Be Men.
Letter from Town; the Almond Tree.
Lightning.
Love on the Farm.
Lucifer.
Man of Tyre, The.
Men in New Mexico.
Moonrise.
Morning Work.
Mosquito, The.
Mountain Lion.
North Country, The.
Nostalgia.
Optimist, The.
Pax.
People.
Piano.
Resurrection.
River Roses.
Sea, The.
Service of All the Dead.
Shadows.
Ship of Death, The.
Ship of Death, The, *sel.*
Sicilian Cyclamens.
Sinners.
Snake.
Song of a Man Who Has Come Through.
Sorrow.
Sphinx.
Spring Morning.
Suburbs on a Hazy Day.
Suspense.
Tell Me a Word.
Tommies in the Train.
Tortoise Family Connections.
Tortoise Shell.
Tortoise Shout.
Trees in the Garden.
Turkey-Cock.
Twilight.
Under the Oak.
Virgin Mother, The, *sel.*
Wedding Morn.
When I Went to the Circus.
Whether or Not.
White Blossom, A.
Wild Common, The.
Winter's Tale, A.
Woman and Her Dead Husband, A.
Work.
Young Wife, A.
Youth Mowing, A.
LAWRENCE, J. B. I Believe.
LAWRENCE, RUTH. Washington's Tomb.
LAWRENCE, THOMAS EDWARD (Thomas Edward Shaw). Dog Argos, The. *Fr.* The Odyssey.
Nausicaa ("Having thus fulfilled her purpose Athene went away"), *tr. Fr.* The Odyssey.
Odyssey, The, *sels., tr.*
Olympus, *tr. Fr.* The Odyssey.
Phaeacian Nights—Demodocus, *tr. Fr.* The Odyssey.
Silence of Ajax, The, *tr. Fr.* The Odyssey.
LAWRENCE, VIRGINIA. Query.
Wisdom.
LAWSON, HENRY. Great Grey Plain, The.
Roaring Days, The.
Sliprails and the Spur, The.
Teams, The.
LAWSON, JAMES GILCHRIST. All Nature Has a Voice to Tell.
O Lord, I Come Pleading.
War!
World Hymn, The.
LAWSON, MARIE A. Halloween.
LAWTON, WILLIAM CRANSTON. Abrim with Dionysos' wine, *tr.*
Athenian Monument, The, *tr.*
From loftiest turret to foundation-stone, *tr.*
How long, upon vain hopes intent, *tr.*
I, Thespis, in dramatic mould, *tr.*
My Fatherland.
Proclos, a silvern gift I send, *tr.*
Song, Youth, and Sorrow.
This wreath, O Rhodocleia, to thee I send, *tr.*
Way to Hades, The, *tr.*
Works and Days, *sel., tr.*
LAXNESS, HALLDÓR. She Was All That You Loved.
LAY, NORMA. Sea Sonnet.
LAYAMON. Arthur's Dream. *Fr.* The Brut.
Arthur's Last Fight [*or* Battle]. *Fr.* The Brut.
Battle of Bath, The. *Fr.* The Brut.
Birth of Arthur, The. *Fr.* The Brut.
Brut, The, *sels.*
Building of London, The. *Fr.* The Brut.
King Arthur. *Fr.* The Brut.
Leir and His Daughters. *Fr.* The Brut.
Prolog, The: "There was a priest in the land." *Fr.* The Brut.
Prophecy of Diana, The. *Fr.* The Brut.
Round Table, The. *Fr.* The Brut.
LAYCOCK, SAMUEL. Welcome, Bonny Brid!
LAYTON, IRVING. Birth of Tragedy, The.
Bull Calf, The.

Composition in Late Spring.
For Louise, Age 17.
Gothic Landscape.
Jewish Main Street.
Newsboy.
Swimmer, The.
Words without Music.
LAYZER, ROBERT. Elegy: "Whenever we touched, I thought of the Lying-in Hospital."
Insult, The.
Lawn Roller, The.
Saint's Parade.
Sleeping Beauty, The.
LAZARUS, BRIAN. Martian Maid, The.
LAZARUS, EMMA. Almighty! What Is Man? *tr.*
And When I Lamented, *tr.* *Fr.* Homeward Bound.
Banner of the Jew, The.
Bar Kochba.
Best Religion, The, *tr.* *Fr.* Tannhäuser.
Cranes of Ibycus, The.
Crowing of the Red Cock, The.
Dearest Friend, Thou Art in Love, *tr.* *Fr.* Homeward Bound.
Defiance, *tr.*
Degenerate Age, A, *tr.*
Elegy: "My thoughts impelled me to the resting-place," *tr.*
Epilogue: "Like the stalks of wheat in the fields," *tr.* *Fr.* The North Sea.
Gifts.
He Cometh, *tr.*
Homeward Bound, *sels.*, *tr.*
I, a Most Wretched Atlas, *tr.* *Fr.* Homeward Bound.
Inscription on the Statue of Liberty. *Fr.* The New Colossus.
Letter to His Friend Isaac, A, *tr.*
Lines on Carmen Sylva.
Longing for Jerusalem, *tr.*
Lorelei, *tr.*
Love Song, *tr.*
Man Is a Weaver, *tr.*
Mater Amabilis.
Meditations, *tr.*
Mirror, The, *tr.*
Mortal, Sneer Not at the Devil, *tr.* *Fr.* Homeward Bound.
My Love Sways, Dancing, *tr.*
My Sweetheart's Dainty Lips, *tr.*
New Colossus, The.
New Colossus, The, *sel.*
New Ezekiel, The.
Night, *tr.*
Night on the Shore, *tr.*
Night-Thoughts, *tr.*
North Sea, The, *sel.*, *tr.*
On the Proposal to Erect a Monument in England to Lord Byron.
Quiet Night, The, *tr.*
Shadow-Love, *tr.* *Fr.* Songs to Seraphine.
Song: "There stands a lonely pine-tree," *tr.*
Songs to Seraphine, *sels.*, *tr.*
Solomon, *tr.*
Sonnet to My Mother, A, *tr.*
Spring Song, *tr.*
Stanzas: "With tears thy grief thou dost bemoan," *tr.*
Tannhäuser, *sel.* *tr.*
This Mad Carnival of Loving, *tr.* *Fr.* To Angélique.
Thou Hast Diamonds, *tr.* *Fr.* Homeward Bound.
Thou Seemest Like a Flower, *tr.* *Fr.* Homeward Bound.
To Angélique, *sel.*, *tr.*
Venus of the Louvre.
Waves Gleam in the Sunshine, The, *tr.* *Fr.* Songs to Seraphine.
Wine and Grief, *tr.*
World's Justice, The.
LEA, FANNIE HEASLIP. Dead Faith, The.
LEA, JOCELYN C. Fly in Church, The.
LEA, JOHN. Silver House, The.
LEACH, BETTY FRYE. Illustrated Booklet on Request.
LEAF, WALTER. Archedike, *tr.*
Breathe, Mountain Pan, a joyous note, *tr.*
Here in the orchard's breezy nook, *tr.*
Lawful Wine, *tr.*
Lion over the Tomb of Leonidas, The, *tr.*
Lost a boy! A runaway! *tr.*
Lost at Sea ("A strange land holds thy bones"), *tr.*
No wasting sickness, but long years of peace, *tr.*
On Those Who Fell at Plataea, *tr.*
Passing Away, *tr.*
Shepherds, ye that haunt these rocks, *tr.*
Swimming, *tr.*
Though men believe it not this thing I know, *tr.*
For other translations from Greek, see OxBG.
LEAF, WALTER, ANDREW LANG, *and* ERNEST MYERS. *See* LANG, ANDREW, WALTER LEAF, *and* ERNEST MYERS.
LEAHY, JACK. How We Built a Church at Ashcroft.
LEAMY, EDMUND. For a Very Little Boy.
Gethsemane.
Ireland.
Lullaby: "Oh, honey, li'l honey, come and lay yo' wooly head."
Music Magic.
My Lips Would Sing.
My Ship.
Three Tarry Men.
Ticket Agent, The.
Visions.
LEAPOR, MARY. Autumn. *Fr.* Colinetta.
Colinetta, *sel.*
Upon Her Play Being Returned to Her Stained with Claret.
LEAR, EDWARD. A. Apple Pie.
A was once an apple-pie.
Akond of Swat, The.
At Dingle Bank.
Author of the "Pobble," The.
Broom, the Shovel, the Poker, and the Tongs, The.
By Way of Preface.
Calico Pie.
Courtship of the Yonghy-Bonghy-Bo, The.
Cummerbund, The.
Dong with a Luminous Nose, The.
Duck and the Kangaroo, The.
How Pleasant to Know Mr. Lear.
Incidents in the Life of My Uncle Arly.
Jumblies, The.
Just as He Feared.
Limerick: "There is a young lady whose nose."
Limerick: "There was a faith-healer of Deal."
Limerick: "There was a young girl of Majorca."
Limerick: "There was a young lady of Bute."
Limerick: "There was a young lady of Corsica."
Limerick: "There was a young lady of Hull."
Limerick: "There was a young lady of Norway."
Limerick: "There was a young lady of Portugal."
Limerick: "There was a young lady of Russia."
Limerick: "There was a young lady of Ryde."
Limerick: "There was a young lady whose bonnet."
Limerick: "There was a young lady whose chin."
Limerick: "There was a young lady whose eyes."
Limerick: "There was a young lady whose nose."
Limerick: "There was a young person of Ayr."
Limerick: "There was a young person of Crete."
Limerick: "There was a young person of Janina."
Limerick: "There was a young person of Smyrna."
Limerick: "There was an old lady of Chertsey."
Limerick: "There was an old lady whose folly."
Limerick: "There was an old man in a barge."
Limerick: "There was an old man in a boat."
Limerick: "There was an old man in a pew."
Limerick: "There was an old man in a tree."
Limerick: "There was an old man of Ancona."
Limerick: "There was an old man of Aosta."
Limerick: "There was an old man of Berlin."
Limerick: "There was an old man of Cape Horn."
Limerick: "There was an old man of Cashmere."
Limerick: "There was an old man of Coblenz."
Limerick: "There was an old man of Kamschatka."
Limerick: "There was an old man of Leghorn."
Limerick: "There was an old man of Madras."
Limerick: "There was an old man of Melrose."
Limerick: "There was an old man of Nepaul."
Limerick: "There was an old man of Peru."
Limerick: "There was an old man of Port Grigor."
Limerick: "There was an old man of Spithead."
Limerick: "There was an old man of the Coast."
Limerick: "There was an old man of the Dargle."
Limerick: "There was an old man of The Hague."
Limerick: "There was an old man of the Isles."
Limerick: "There was an old man of the South."
Limerick: "There was an old man of the West."
Limerick: "There was an old man of Thermopylae."
Limerick: "There was an old man of Vesuvius."
Limerick: "There was an old man of West Dumpet."
Limerick: "There was an old man on the Border."
Limerick: "There was an old man on whose nose."
Limerick: "There was an old man who said, 'How.'"
Limerick: "There was an old man who said, 'Hush!'"
Limerick: "There was an old man who said, 'Well!'"
Limerick: "There was an old man who supposed."
Limerick: "There was an old man, who when little."
Limerick: "There was an old man with a beard,/ Who said: 'It is just as I feared!'"
Limerick: "There was an old man with a beard,/ Who sat on a horse when he reared."
Limerick: "There was an old man with a nose."
Limerick: "There was an old man with a poker."
Limerick: "There was an old party of Lyme."
Limerick: "There was an old person of Anerly."
Limerick: "There was an old person of Blythe."
Limerick: "There was an old person of Bray."

LEAR, EDWARD (*continued*)
Limerick: "There was an old person of Burton."
Limerick: "There was an old person of Cassel."
Limerick: "There was an old person of Dean."
Limerick: "There was an old person of Ewell."
Limerick: "There was an old person of Grange."
Limerick: "There was an old person of Gretna."
Limerick: "There was an old person of Ickley."
Limerick: "There was an old person of Pinner."
Limerick: "There was an old person of Rheims."
Limerick: "There was an old person of Rye."
Limerick: There was an old person of Slough."
Limerick: "There was an old person of Spain."
Limerick: "There was an old person of Sparta."
Limerick: "There was an old person of Tring."
Limerick: "There was an old person of Ware."
Limerick: "There was an old person of Wick."
Limerick: "There was an old person of Wilts."
Limerick: "There was an old person of Woking."
Limerick: "There was an old person whose habits."
Lines to a Young Lady.
M.
Mr. and Mrs. Discobbolos.
Mr. and Mrs. Spikky Sparrow.
Mr. Lear.
Moppsikon Floppsikon Bear, The.
New Vestments, The.
Nonsense Alphabet ("A was an ape").
Nonsense Alphabet ("A was once an apple-pie").
Nutcrackers and the Sugar-Tongs, The.
Old Man with a Beard.
Owl and the Pussy-Cat, The.
Pelican Chorus, The.
Pobble Who Has No Toes, The.
Quangle-Wangle's Hat, The.
Says I to Myself.
Self Portrait.
Self-Portrait of the Laureate of Nonsense.
Sonnet, A: "Cold are the crabs that crawl on yonder hills."
Table and the Chair, The.
There Once Was an Old Man of Lyme.
There Was a Young Lady Whose Nose.
There was an old man of Dumbree.
There Was an Old Person of Bradley.
There was an old person of Diss.
There was an old person of Skye.
There Was an Old Person Whose Habits.
Two Old Bachelors, The.
Yonghy-Bonghy-Bo, The.
Young Lady of Norway, A.
Young Lady, Whose Bonnet, A.
LEAR, OSCAR H. Wide Open Spaces, The.
LEARNED, LEILA SPRAGUE. To My Son, Four Days Old.
LEARNED, WALTER. Explanation, An.
Growing Old.
In Explanation.
Last Reservation, The.
On a Fly-Leaf of a Book of Old Plays.
On the Fly-Leaf of "Manon Lescaut."
Time's Revenge.
To Critics.
With a Spray of Apple Blossoms.
"LEARSI, RUFUS" (Israel Goldberg). Martyrdom.
LEARY, HARRY F. Saint Francis of Assisi.
LEATHER, ROBINSON KAY. Advice to a Boy.
LEAVENS, EMILY. Death on the Rancherie.
LEAVENWORTH, COMAN. Norfolk Memorials.
North Pickenham. *Fr.* Norfolk Memorials.
Rackheath. *Fr.* Norfolk Memorials.
Wendling. *Fr.* Norfolk Memorials.
LEBAR, WINIFRED STODDARD. And Thou Would'st Not!
LEBEDEV, BORIS. Heart, The.
LEBEDEV-KUMACH, VASILI. Christmas Tree.
Comrade, Do Not Forget!
LEBENSOHN, MICAH JOSEPH. Wine.
LEBOURNE, GEORGE. Flying Trapeze, The.
LECA, MATEO VÁZQUEZ DE. Foolish Leander.
LECKY, WILLIAM EDWARD HARTPOLE. Early Thoughts.
On an Old Song.
Say Not That the Past Is Dead.
Sower and His Seed, The.
Unconscious Cerebration.
Undeveloped Lives.
LECLAIRE, GORDON. Chameleon.
Love.
Miser.
Old Seawoman.
LE CLERCQ, J. G. CLEMENCEAU. *See* "TANAQUIL, PAUL."
LE COMPTE, CALVIN. Visitation, The.
LECONTE DE LISLE, CHARLES MARIE RENÉ. Birds of Prey.
Condor's Sleep, The.
Elephants, The.
Elves, The.
Epiphany.
Hialmar Speaks to the Raven.
Hialmar's Heart.
Howlers, The.
Immortal Perfume.
Lines: "Old lover of the sun, who thus made moan."
Lydia.
Manchy, The.
Night.
Pan.
Qaïn, *sel.*
Showmen, The.
Solvet Saeclum.
Three Threads of Gold.
LECRON, HELEN COWLES. Little Charlie Chipmunk.
Little Danny Donkey.
Sally Centipede.
Willie Wolf.
LEDOUX, LOUIS VERNON. At Sunset.
Fulfilment.
Gift, The.
Hymn to Demeter. *Fr.* The Story of Eleusis.
Mater Dolorosa.
Music of a Friend, The.
Only Way, The.
Persephone (Singing).
Slumber Song: "Drowsily come the sheep."
Story of Eleusis, The, *sel.*
LEDWARD, PATRICIA. Evening in Camp.
LEDWIDGE, FRANCIS. Ardan Mór.
August.
Behind the Closed Eye.
Death of Ailill, The.
Desire in Spring.
Dream of Artemis, A, *sel.*
Evening Clouds.
Evening in England, An.
Evening in February.
Fairy Music.
Find, The.
God's Remembrance.
Growing Old.
Had I a Golden Pound.
Herons, The.
Homecoming of the Sheep, The.
In September.
In the Dusk.
June.
Lament for the Poets, 1916.
Lament for Thomas MacDonagh.
Little Boy in the Morning, A.
Lost Ones, The.
Mother's Song, A.
My Mother.
Pan.
Rainy Day in April, A.
Shadow People, The.
Ships of Arcady, The.
Soliloquy.
Song of April, A.
Thomas MacDonagh.
Thoughts at the Trysting Stile.
To a Linnet in a Cage.
To a Sparrow.
Twilight in Middle March, A.
Vision on the Brink, The.
Wedding Morning, The.
Wife of Llew, The.
LEE, AGNES. Christ-Child, The.
Convention.
Enemies.
Ilex Tree, The.
Lonely Man, A.
Mrs. Malooly.
Motherhood.
Numbers.
Old Lizette on Sleep.
Old Woman with Flowers, An.
Peace.
Quest, The.
Radium.
Shakespeare.
Statue in a Garden, A.
Sweeper, The.
Tower, The.
LEE, ALEXANDER. Soldier's Tear, The.
"LEE, ANDY" (W. W. Delaney). Crazy Song to the Air of "Dixie."
LEE, ARTHUR. Prophecy, A.
LEE, EDITH M. Fault Is Mine, The.
LEE, FRANK. He'll See It When He Wakes.
LEE, HARRY. Madness.
My Master.
Valentine for My Mother.
Winged Heels.
LEE, JOSEPH JOHNSTON. German Prisoners.
Requiem.
LEE, LAURIE. April Rise.
Day of These Days.
First Love
Juniper.
Larch Tree.
Milkmaid.
Summer Rain.
Sunken Evening.
Three Winds, The.
Village of Winter Carols.
Wild Trees, The.
Winter 1939-1940.
LEE, LAWRENCE. Bequest to My Daughters.
Fire-Bringers, The.
For a Poet Growing Old.
For Any Lady's Birthday.
Hawk from Cuckoo Tavern, A.
Letters, The.
Subway Builders.
Take Up the Wings.
LEE, LORETTA. Busybody.
LEE, MARION. Rank and File.
Rust on the Latch.
LEE, MARY. *See* CHUDLEIGH, LADY.
LEE, MILTON. When I Go Home.
LEE, MUNA. After Reading Saint Teresa, Luis de Leon and Ramon Lull.
Along my ways of life you never came. *Fr.* Sonnets.
As Helen Once.
Behind the House Is the Millet Plot.
Brother Dog, *tr.*
Choice.
Departed Friend, The, *tr.*
Dirge: "Though you should whisper."
Gifts.
I have a thousand pictures of the sea. *Fr.* Sonnets.
I Have Lost My Shoes, *tr.*
I Look Up Hotels, *tr.*
I make no question of your right to go. *Fr.* Sonnets.

It were easiest to say: "The moon and lake." *Fr.* Sonnets.
It will be easy to love you when I am dead. *Fr.* Sonnets.
January Night, *tr.*
Life of itself will be cruel and hard enough. *Fr.* Sonnets.
Little Girl That Lost a Finger, The, *tr.*
Melilot.
Pamphlet, *tr.*
Parable of Generosity, *tr.*
Reaping the Barley, *tr.*
Rimas, *sel., tr.*
Song: "I am a passion; I am a flame," *tr.*
Song of Happiness, A.
Sonnets, *sels.*
Stroke of One, *tr.*
Tropical Pool.
What other form were worthy of your praise. *Fr.* Sonnets.
When We Shall Be Dust.
Woman's Song, A.
For other translations from Spanish, see AnCL.
LEE, NATHANIEL. Blush Not Redder than the Morning. *Fr.* Caesar Borgia.
Caesar Borgia, *sel.*
Dead Night. *Fr.* Theodosius; or, The Force of Love.
Mithridates, King of Pontus, *sel.*
Semandra's Death. *Fr.* Mithridates, King of Pontus.
Song: "Beneath the poplar's shadow lay me." *Fr.* Sophonisba; or, Hannibal's Overthrow.
Sophonisba; or, Hannibal's Overthrow, *sel.*
Theodosius; or, The Force of Love, *sel.*
Tragedy of Nero, The, *sel.*
Very Dark. *Fr.* The Tragedy of Nero.
LEE-HAMILTON, EUGENE. Baudelaire.
Charles II of Spain to approaching Death.
Death of Puck, The.
Elfin Skates.
Fairy Godmothers.
Flight from Glory, A.
Have dark Egyptians stolen Thee away. *Fr.* Mimma Bella.
Idle Charon.
Ipsissimus.
Izaak Walton to River and Brook.
Lost Years.
Mimma Bella, *sels.*
My Own Hereafter.
Oh, bless the law that veils the future's face. *Fr.* Mimma Bella.
Oh, rosy as the lining of a shell. *Fr.* Mimma Bella.
On His "Sonnets of the Wingless Hours."
One day, I mind me, now that she is dead. *Fr.* Mimma Bella.
Sea-Shell Murmurs.
Sir Walter Raleigh to a Caged Linnet.
Song: "Under the winter, dear."
Sunken Gold.
To My Tortoise 'Ἀνάγκη (Ananke).
To My Tortoise Chronos.
Two springs she saw—two radiant Tuscan springs. *Fr.* Mimma Bella.
What essences from Idumean palm. *Fr.* Mimma Bella.
What the Sonnet Is.
Wood-Song.
LEES, EDWIN. Signs of Christmas.
LEESON, JANE ELIZA. Saviour, Teach Me.
LE FANU, JOSEPH SHERIDAN. Abhrain An Bhuideil.
Beatrice, *sel.*
Drunkard to His Bottle, A.
Fionula. *Fr.* The Legend of the Glaive.
Hymn: "Hush! oh ye billows." *Fr.* Beatrice.
Legend of the Glaive, The.
Legend of the Glaive, The, *sels.*
Shemus O'Brien.
Song of the Spirits, The. *Fr.* The Legend of the Glaive.
LE FORT, GERTRUDE VON. Christmas.
Vigil of the Assumption.
LEFROY, EDWARD CRACROFT. Ageanax. *Fr.* Echoes from Theocritus.
Cleonicos. *Fr.* Echoes from Theocritus.
Cricket Bowler, A.
Echoes from Theocritus, *sels.*
Epitaph of Eusthenes, The. *Fr.* Echoes from Theocritus.
Flute of Daphnis, The. *Fr.* Echoes from Theocritus.
Football-Player, A.
Grave of Hipponax, The. *Fr.* Echoes from Theocritus.
Monument of Cleita, The. *Fr.* Echoes from Theocritus.
On a Spring Board.
Sacred Grove, A. *Fr.* Echoes from Theocritus.
Shepherd Maiden, A. *Fr.* Echoes from Theocritus.
Sicilian Night, A. *Fr.* Echoes from Theocritus.
Summer Day in Old Sicily, A. *Fr.* Echoes from Theocritus.
Sylvan Revel, A. *Fr.* Echoes from Theocritus.
Thyrsis. *Fr.* Echoes from Theocritus.
LEFTWICH, JOSEPH. Tailor, The.
For translations from Yiddish, see TrJP.
LE GALLIENNE, RICHARD. After the War.
All Sung.
As in the Woodland I Walk.
Ballad of London, A.
Ballade Catalogue of Lovely Things, A.
Ballade of Queen's Lace.
Ballade of the Road Unknown.
Ballade of the Things That Remain.
Ballade of the Unchanging Beauty.
Beatus Vir.
Blue eyes, against the whiteness pressed. *Fr.* Fragoletta.
Blue eyes, looking up at me. *Fr.* Fragoletta.
Brooklyn Bridge at Dawn.
Called Away.
Caravan from China Comes, A.
Child's Evensong, A.
Cloister, The.
Cuckoo, The.
Dream Tryst.
Eternal Way, The.
Flos Aevorum.
Fragoletta, blessed one. *Fr.* Songs for Fragoletta.
Frost Fancy, A.
Harvest, *tr.*
I Meant to Do My Work Today.
Illusion of War, The.
Lady April.
Lonely Dancer, The.
Lord Christ Came to Notre Dame, The.
Love's Language, *tr.*
Love's Poor.
May Is Building Her House.
Melton Mowbray Pork-Pie, A.
Never—Ever.
Noon.
November.
Old Man's Song, An.
Orbits.
Passionate Reader to His Poet, The.
Prayer, A: "Out of the deeps I cry to thee, O God!"
Regrets.
Rose Is Not the Rose, The, *tr.*
Second Crucifixion, The.
So Soon Tired.
Song: "She's somewhere in the sunlight strong."
Song: "Take it, love!"
Song of Bread and Honey, A.
Songs for Fragoletta.
Spirit of Sadness.
That, Fragoletta, is the rain. *Fr.* Songs for Fragoletta.
This Is War.
To a Bird at Dawn.
To a Mountain Spring.
War.
War Poem.
Wayfaring.
What of the Darkness?
Wife from Fairyland, The.
Wind's Way, The.
Wonder-Child, The.
Wood Flower.
LEGARÉ, JAMES MATTHEW. Ahab Mohammed.
Amy.
Flowers in Ashes.
Haw-Blossoms.
On the Death of a Kinsman.
Reaper, The.
To a Lily.
LEGEAR, LAURA LOURENE. Unbridled Now.
LÉGER, ALEXIS SAINT-LÉGER. *See* "PERSE, ST.-J."
LEGG, BERNICE HALL. Forest Meditation, A.
LEGGE, JAMES. *For translations from Chinese, see* BoFr.
LEGLER, MARY FERGUSON. Door Between, The.
LEHMAN, HELEN M. Prisoners.
LEHMANN, JOHN. Crimea Red.
Death in Hospital, A.
In a London Terminus.
Last Ascent, The.
Little Distance Off, A.
Looking Within.
Sphere of Glass, The.
This Excellent Machine.
To Penetrate That Room.
LEHMANN, RUDOLPH CHAMBERS. Bird in the Room, The.
Dance, The.
Middle Age.
On Saturday Morning Early.
Plea for a Plural, A.
Singing Water.
LEHMER, DERRICK NORMAN. Riches.
LEHMER, EUNICE MITCHELL. Armistice.
LE HOUX, JEAN. To His Nose, *formerly at. to* Olivier Basselin.
War and Wine, *formerly at. to* Olivier Basselin.
LEIB, MANI (Mani Leib Brahinsky). Be Still.
Door and Window Bolted Fast.
Elijah in the House of Study.
Hush, Hush.
When I See Another's Pain.
LEIGH, AMY E. If I But Knew.
LEIGH, CHANDOS, BARON LEIGH. On Uvedale Price's Essay, *sel.*
LEIGH, FREDERICK, *and* FREDERICK MURRAY. *See* MURRAY, FREDERICK, *and* FREDERICK LEIGH.
LEIGH, HENRY SAMBROOKE. Answer, An.
Ballad of Baby Bunting, The.
Cossimbazar.
Maud.
My Love and My Heart.
Not Quite Fair.
Nursery Legend, A.
Only Seven.
Romaunt of Humpty Dumpty, The.
'Twas Ever Thus.
Twins, The.
LEIGH, RICHARD. Eccho, The.
Her Window.
Sleeping on Her Couch.
LEIGHTON, LOUISE. Earthly Illusion.
LEIGHTON, ROBERT. Books.
Dried-up Fountain, The.
Duty Our Ladder.
LEISER, JOSEPH. Day of Atonement, The, *sel.*
Kol Nidra. *Fr.* The Day of Atonement.
LEISHMAN, J. B., *and* STEPHEN SPENDER. *See* SPENDER, STEPHEN, *and* J. B. LEISHMAN.
LEISNER, DOROTHY ROBERTS. *See* ROBERTS, DOROTHY.
LEITCH, MARY SINTON. April.
Before.
Clues.
Failure.
From Bethlehem Blown.
Glacier.
He Who Has Known a River.

LEITCH, MARY SINTON (*continued*)
"Lee."
Lidice.
Lines to a Dictator.
My Instant.
One Rose.
Pagan, The.
Phantom Rose, The.
Pity the Great.
Poet, The.
River, The.
Sea Words.
Secret, The.
Statue Inscribed "Lee," Richmond.
When Spring Came to Nazareth.
Winter Oak.
LEIVICK, HALPER. Forever.
Night, Stars, Glow-Worms.
LELAND, CHARLES GODFREY ("Hans Breitmann"). Ballad by Hans Breitmann.
Ballad of the Mermaid.
By the Waters of Babylon, *tr.* *Fr.* Hebrew Melodies.
Carey, of Carson.
El Capitan-General.
Fisher's Cottage, The, *tr.*
Flying Dutchman, The.
Hans Breitmann's Party [*or* Barty].
Hebrew Melodies, *sel., tr.*
Legend of Heinz von Stein, The.
Masher, The.
New Jewish Hospital at Hamburg, The, *tr.*
Out and Fight.
Princess Sabbath, *tr.*
Ritter Hugo.
Story of Samuel Jackson, The.
There's a Time to Be Jolly.
Two Friends, The.
Wabanaki Song, *tr.*
Zu fragmentarisch ist Welt und Leben, *tr.*
LELAND, CLARA CARSON. Love's Magic.
LELAND, MARIAN. Sonnet to That Great Mother, Schumann-Heink, A.
LEMAÎTRE, JULES. Cat, A.
LEMARR, D. F. Roving Rebel, The.
LE MESURIER, L. Journey, The.
LEMKE, E. Rhyme for Musicians, A.
LEMON, MARK. How to Make a Man of Consequence.
LEMONT, JESSIE. African Night.
Autumn, *tr.*
Book of Hours, The, *sel., tr.*
Buddha in Glory, *tr.*
Death of the Beloved, *tr.*
Extinguish My Eyes, *tr.*
Flamingos, The, *tr.*
I Praise, *tr.*
I Would Comprehend Thee, *tr.*
Last Evening, *tr.*
Lute, The, *tr*
Neighbor, The, *tr*
Palm of the Hand, *tr.*
Panther, The, *tr.*
Pont du Carrousel, *tr.*
Presaging, *tr.*
Silent Hour, *tr.*
Solitude, *tr.*
Sonnets to Orpheus, *sels., tr.*
Strophes: "There is one who takes all men within his hand," *tr.*
What Stillness around a God! *tr.*
LENART, MARIE. Atonement.
Give Us Great Dreams.
Litany.
LENAU, NIKOLAUS. Autumn Complaint.
Ended!
Entreaty.
Niagara.
Oak Grove, The.
Postilion, The.
Question.
Sedge Songs.
Three Gypsies.
LENGYEL, CORNEL. Fool Song.
LENNEN, ELINOR. Evaluation.
Fellowship.
His Last Week.
Nor House nor Heart.
On Entering a Forest.
Pilgrimage.
Praetorium Scene: Good Friday.
Prayer for a Play House.
LENNGREN, ANNA MARIA. Boy and His Playthings, The.
Castle and Cottage.
Portraits, The.
"LENNOX." Neighbors.
LENSKI, LOIS. Fourth of July Song.
Old Santa Is an Active Man.
People.
LENT, EMMA A. Memorial Day.
Unawares.
LENTINO, JACOPO DA. *See* JACOPO DA LENTINO.
LEO XIII, POPE. Return from Egypt, The.
War Cry: To Mary.
LEÓN, LUIS PONCE DE (Fray Luis de Léon). Ascension, The.
Assumption of the Virgin, The.
At the Ascension.
At the Assumption.
Avarice.
Heavenly Home, The.
Hymn on the Ascension.
Life of the Blessed, The.
Life Removed, The.
Lines on the Wall of His Prison Cell.
Love Song.
Night of Stars.
Night Serene, The.
Ode to Felipe Ruiz.
Ode to Francisco Salinas.
Ode to Retirement.
Ode to Salinas.
On Leaving Prison.
To Retirement.
Valley of the Heavens, The.
Written on the Walls of His Dungeon.
LEONARD, D. S. Not Here.
LEONARD, DOROTHY. Minuet, The.
LEONARD, PRISCILLA. Happiness.
Lost Key, The.
Making of Man, The.
This Is the Making of Man.
Tide Will Win, The.
What Man May Choose.
LEONARD, S. G. Mistress, The.
Moron.
LEONARD, WILLIAM ELLERY. Alone, *tr.*
Ass in the Lion's Skin, The, *tr.*
Beginnings of Civilization, *tr.* *Fr.* Of the Nature of Things.
Beyond Religion, *tr.* *Fr.* Of the Nature of Things.
Buddha, *tr.*
Compensation.
De Rerum Natura, *sels., tr.*
Fatherland Song (Norwegian National Hymn), *tr.*
Flight of Crows.
Forever Dead, *tr.*
Full Moon, *tr.*
Gilgamesh, *tr.*
I will report a twofold truth, *tr.*
Image of Delight, The.
Indian Summer. *Fr.* Two Lives.
Israel.
Lorelei, The, *tr.*
Love, *tr.*
Lynching Bee, The.
May Night.
Mountain in Labor, The, *tr*
Ode to Anactoria, *tr.*
Ode to Aphrodite, *tr.*
Of Human Progress, *tr.* *Fr.* Of the Nature of Things.
Of the Nature of Things (De Rerum Natura), *sels., tr.*
Origins and Savage Period of Mankind, *tr.* *Fr.* Of the Nature of Things.
Origins of Life, The, *tr.* *Fr.* Of the Nature of Things.
Origins of Vegetable and Animal Life, *tr.* *Fr.* Of the Nature of Things.
Quaker Meeting-House, The.
Round about Me, *tr.*
Saecla Ferarum.
Shepherd-Boy and the Wolf, The, *tr.*
Swan and the Goose, The, *tr.*
There is a word of Fate, an old decree, *tr.*
To Himself, *tr.*
To the Dead Doughboys.
To the Victor.
Tom Mooney.
Two Lives, *sels.*
Unpathed Haunts, *tr.* *Fr.* Of the Nature of Things.
Vine and the Goat, The, *tr.*
When We Are No More, *tr.* *Fr.* Of the Nature of Things.
LEONARD, WILLIAM ELLERY, *and* HERMANN RANKE. Gilgamesh Laments the Death of Engidu, *tr.*
LEONARDO DA VINCI. Art and Life.
Perseverance.
LEONIDAS OF ALEXANDRIA. Home.
Menodotis.
On a Picture of an Infant Playing near a Precipice.
LEONIDAS OF TARENTUM. "All Ashore!"
Apelles the Painter.
Asked the Traveller of the Tomb.
Boy's Playthings.
Cleitagoras.
Contentment.
Cricket's Grave, The.
Dead Shepherd, The.
Epitaph of a Sailor.
Erinna, songstress of the honeyed lay.
Farmer's Rest, The.
Fisherman, The.
Goatherds' Thank-offering, The.
Here lies old Theris: death has set him free.
Last Journey, The.
Lightning, *at.*
Measureless time or ever thy years, O man, were reckon'd.
Only Son, An.
Peace to the Tomb, *at.*
Philocles.
Shepherd.
Shepherd's Last Sleep, The.
Shepherds, ye that haunt these rocks.
Spinning Woman, The.
Spring Sailing.
Time.
Tomb of Crethon, The.
Wayside Epigram.
Wayside Grave, A.
LEONTIUS. Picture of a Physician.
Plato, a Musician.
LEOPARDI, GIACOMO. A sè stesso.
Broom, The.
Evening of the Feast-Day, The.
Infinite, The.
Infinito, L'.
Infinity.
To Italy.
Walls and Arches, The.
LEOPOLD, KARL GUSTAF AF. Legacy, A.
LE PAN, DOUGLAS. Canoe-Trip.
Country without a Mythology, A.
Coureurs de Bois.
Finale.
Image of Silenus.
Incident, An.
Nimbus, The.
One of the Regiment.
Rider on the Sands.
Wounded Prince, The.
LERMONTOV, MIKHAIL YUREVICH. After Goethe.
Angel, The.
Ballad: "On high by the sea sat a beautiful maid."
Borodino.
Captive Knight.
Circassian Song.
Clouds.
Composed While under Arrest.
Cossack Cradle-Song.
Crag, The.
Cup of Life, The.
Dagger.
Demon [*or* Daemon], The, *sel.*
Do you remember how together.
Dream.
Gratitude.
Hebrew Melody.
Hope.
How Lonely, How Drear.
I would not have the world to know.
Land of Masters.
Lone, I wander where the pathway glistens.

Monologue.
Mountain, The.
My Country.
My Home.
No, not for you, for you, does my love flame.
Oh gloomy and dreary! and no one to stretch out a hand.
O when afield the waves of yellow corn are swaying.
On the Death of Pushkin.
Poet's Death, The.
Prayer: "When life's oppressive hour is mine."
Prophet, The.
Reed, The.
Sail, A.
See How He Gallops.
Testament.
Thought, A.
Triple Dream, The.
Veteran's Grave, The.
We parted, but my heart still wears.
When o'er the yellowing corn a fleeting shadow rushes.
When the Yellow Rye-Field Billows.
Why.
Wish, The.
LERNER, ALAN JAY. With a Little Bit of Luck.
LERNER, LAURENCE DAVID. Desert Travellers, The.
14 July 1956.
Senchi Ferry; Gold Coast.
LE ROW, CAROLINE B. Bryant Alphabet, A.
Emerson Alphabet, An.
For a Warning.
Holmes Alphabet, A.
Longfellow Alphabet, A.
Lowell Alphabet, A.
"Scallywag."
Song of the Steamer Engine.
Whittier Alphabet, A.
LERSCH, HEINRICH. Brothers.
LESEMANN, MAURICE. City Asleep.
Lost.
Man Walks in the Wind, A.
Noctiflora.
Ranchers.
Sheep Herders.
LESLIE, KENNETH. By Stubborn Stars, *sels.*
Cobweb College.
Escapade.
Halibut Cove Harvest.
Lowlands Low.
Sonnet: "Day slipped out of the web of her fog-wet gown." *Fr.* By Stubborn Stars.
Sonnet: "My love is sleeping." *Fr.* By Stubborn Stars.
Sonnet: "Silver herring throbbed thick in my seine, The." *Fr.* By Stubborn Stars.
Sonnet: "Warm rain whispers, but the earth knows best, A." *Fr.* By Stubborn Stars.
LESLIE, SHANE (Sir John Randolph Shane Leslie). Fleet Street.
Four Winds, The.
Ireland, Mother of Priests.
Monaghan.
Muckish Mountain (The Pig's Back).
On Our Lady of Blachernae, *tr.*
On the Annunciation, *tr.*
Priest or Poet.
Rebel Mother's Lullaby.
Saint Francis of Assisi.
To the Most Holy Mother of God, *tr.*
Two Mothers, The.
LESSING, GOTTHOLD EPHRAIM. I Asked My Fair. One Happy Day.
Mendax.
Names.
To a Slow Walker and Quick Eater.
L'ESTRANGE, SIR ROGER. In Prison.
Liberty and Requiem of an Imprisoned Royalist, The.
Loyalty Confin'd.
Mr. Le Strange His Verses in the Prison at Linn.
LETTS, WINIFRED M. (Mrs. W. H. Foster Verschoyle). Angelic Service.
Boys.
Children's Ghosts, The.
Connaught Rangers, The.
Elfin People Fill the Tubes, The.
For England's Sake Men Give Their Lives.
Grandeur.
Hallows' E'en.
Harbour, The.
In Service.
Kerry Cow, The.
Monkey's Carol, The.
My Blessing Be on Waterford.
Pensioners.
Quantity and Quality.
Says She.
Shops.
Soft Day, A.
Somehow, Somewhere, Sometime.
Spires of Oxford, The.
Spring, the Travelling Man.
Synge's Grave.
Tim, an Irish Terrier.
What Reward?
Winds at Bethlehem, The.
Wishes for William.
LEUTY, HELEN. Apple Harvest.
Night, The.
Poplars.
LEVER, CHARLES JAMES. Bad Luck to This Marching.
Charles O'Malley, the Irish Dragoon, *sels.*
Harry Lorrequer, *sel.*
It's Little for Glory I Care.
Larry M'Hale. *Fr.* Charles O'Malley, the Irish Dragoon.
Man for Galway, The.
Mickey Free's Song. *Fr.* Charles O'Malley, the Irish Dragoon.
Pope [He Leads a Happy Life], The. *Fr.* Harry Lorrequer.
Widow Malone, The. *Fr.* Charles O'Malley, the Irish Dragoon.
LEVERIDGE, LILIAN. Cry from the Canadian Hills, A.
First Robin, The.
LEVERIDGE, RICHARD. Roast Beef of Old England, The.
Song in Praise of Old English Roast Beef, A.
LEVERTIN, OSCAR. Artist, The.
Beatrice.
Ithaca.
Monica.
Old New-Year's Song, An.
Solomon's Hymn to the Moon.
LEVERTOV [*or* LEVERTOFF], DENISE. Anteroom, The.
Autumn Journey.
Barricades, The.
Beyond the End.
Christmas 1944.
Five-Day Rain, The.
Folding a Shirt.
Goddess, The.
Hands, The.
Merritt Parkway.
Pleasures.
Poem: "Some are too much at home in the role of wanderer."
Scenes from the Life of the Peppertrees.
Sharks, The.
Third Dimension, The.
Way Through, The.
LEVI, ADELE. Death of Friends, The.
LEVINE, NORMAN. Cathedral by Sea.
Crabbing.
Wind Harbour, The.
LEVI YITZHOK OF BERDITCHEV. Kaddish.
LEVY, ALBAN A. Out of a Dust.
LEVY, AMY. Between the Showers.
Birch-Tree at Loschwitz, The.
Dove, The, *tr.*
Epitaph: "This is the end of him, here he lies."
In the Mile End Road.
London Plane-Tree, A.
London Poets.
New Love, New Life.
Plane-Tree, The.
Reminiscence, A.
To Vernon Lee.
LEVY, LOUIS. Swallow's Flight, The.
LEVY, NEWMAN. Ballad of Sir Brian and the Three Wishes, The.
Belle of the Balkans, The.
Carmen.
I Wonder What Became of Rand, McNally.
If You Stick a Stock of Liquor.
Midsummer Jingle.
Othello.
Rain.
Reporters, The.
Scandalous Tale of Percival and Genevieve, The.
Thais.
Tristan and Isolda.
LEVY, NEWMAN, *and* NATE SALSBURY. *See* SALSBURY, NATE, *and* NEWMAN LEVY.
LEVY, ROSE FLORENCE. Memorial Day.
LEWIN, LIONEL H. Birds in the Night.
LEWIN, RALPH A. Les Chasse-Neige.
LEWIS, ALONZO. Death Song.
LEWIS, ALUN. After Dunkirk.
All Day It Has Rained.
Bivouac.
Christmas Holiday.
Dawn on the East Coast.
Defeated, The.
In Hospital; Poona.
Jungle, The.
Mid-Winter.
Mine Host, *tr.*
Mountain over Aberdare, The.
On a Bereaved Girl.
Peasants, The.
River Rhondda.
Sentry, The.
Soldier, The.
Song: "First month of his absence, The."
Song (On Seeing Dead Bodies Floating off the Cape).
To a Comrade in Arms.
To Edward Thomas.
Troopship in the Tropics.
Water Music.
LEWIS, CECIL DAY. *See* DAY LEWIS, CECIL.
LEWIS, CLIVE STAPLES. Awake, My Lute.
Passing today by a cottage, I shed tears.
LEWIS, DAVID. Song of the Soul and the Bridegroom, *tr.*
When None Shall Rail.
LEWIS, DOMINIC BEVAN WYNDHAM ("Timothy Shy"). Ballade of [*or* on] the Harrowing of Hell.
Envoi: "I warmed both hands before the fire of Life."
Having a Wonderful Time.
Seated one day at the organ.
Shot at Random, A.
LEWIS, EILUNED. Birthright, The.
Man and His Books.
Reflections on the Fall of France, June, 1940.
We Who Were Born.
LEWIS, GARDNER E. How to Tell Juan Don from Another.
Poem, neither Hillaryous Norgay.
LEWIS, H. H. Farmhands' Refrain.
LEWIS, JANET (Mrs. Yvor Winters). Candle Flame, The.
Hélène (Helen, the Sad Queen), *tr.*
LEWIS, MATTHEW GREGORY. Allan Water.
Alonzo the Brave and Fair Imogine. *Fr.* The Monk.
Maniac, The.
Monk, The, *sel.*
LEWIS, MICHAEL. April Winds.
August.
Chant Royal of Love.
Chart, The.
Dead Liar Speaks, A.
Food for Thought.
Here Lies.
In Spring
January.

LEWIS, MICHAEL (*continued*)
King and the Clown, The, *ad.*
Medley, A.
Moon-Children.
Nonsense Song, *tr.*
Regretful Rondeau, A.
Spring Ring-Jingle.
Triolet, The: "Gesture in space, A."
LEWIS, MICHAEL ARTHUR. Caulker, The.
LEWIS, MURIEL. Pastoral: "Farmer turns for home, The; his team's glad tread."
LEWIS, ROBERT. If You Had a Friend.
LEWIS, SAUNDERS. Café Scene.
LEWIS, SINCLAIR. Cat.
LEWIS, WYNDHAM. One-Way Song, *sel.*
LEWISOHN, JOHN. Rabbit, The.
LEWISOHN, LUDWIG. Heinrich Heine.
Together.
For translations from French and German, see AWP; FaPON; JAWP; LiTW; TrJP; WBP; WoL.
LEYBOURNE, GEORGE. Man on the Flying Trapeze, The.
LEYDEN, JOHN. Daisy, The.
Eagle on a Tombstone, *tr.*
Lords of the Wilderness.
Noontide.
Sabbath Morning, The.
Scenes of Infancy, *sel.*
LEZAMA LIMA, JOSÉ. Rhapsody for the Mule.
LIBAIRE, GEORGE. Limerick: "Half baked potato named Sue, A."
Limerick: "There was [*or* was once] a young curate of Salisbury," *at.*
Limerick: "These places abound in the old."
LIBERO, LIBERO DE. Cicada.
LI CHIH-YI. River-long Love, A.
LI CH'ING-CHAO. Alone in the Night.
Autumn Evening beside the Lake.
Day of Cold Food, The.
Midautumn Festival, The.
Mist.
Mounting the High Balcony.
Quail Sky.
Spring Returns.
To the Tune of "A Sprig of Plum Blossom."
To the Tune of "Like a Dream."
To the Tune, "Plum Blossoms Fall and Scatter."
Two Springs.
LIDDELL, CATHERINE C. Jesus the Carpenter.
Poet in the City, The.
LIDDELL, GEORGE T. Christ of Common Folks, The.
Jesus of Nazareth Passes By.
LIDNER, BENGT. Introduction to "Spastara's Death."
Medea, *sel.*
Song of the Battle-Skald. *Fr.* Medea.
Spastara's Death, *sel.*
LIEBER, FRANCIS. Ship Canal from the Atlantic to the Pacific, The.
LIEBERMAN, ELIAS. Abandoned Tow-Path, An.
Aladdin Throws Away His Lamp.
Brothers.
Caravels of Columbus, The.
Chant of Loyalty.
Classroom in October.
Heart Specialist.
I Am an American.
It Is Time to Build.
Notation in Haste.
Shadows, *tr.*
Sholom Aleichem.
Weary Peddlers.
LIEBHARDT, LOUISE. Now with the Moon.
LIESSIN, ABRAHAM. Spring Nocturne.
LIGHTHALL, WILLIAM DOUW. Battle of La Prairie, The.
Caughnawaga Beadwork Seller, The.
Commandant's Isle.
Confused Dawn, The.
Montreal.
Praeterita ex Instantibus.
Shebear, The.
LIGUORI, ALFONSO MARIA DE'. *See* ALPHONSUS LIGUORI, SAINT.
LI HO. Below the City of P'ing.
Departure of Autumn.
Die for His Majesty.
Great Song, A.
I Pass the Great Hall.
Journey among Ruins.
King Drinks Wine, A.
Lady's Sepulcher, A.
Long Song after Short Songs, A.
Meditation.
Ninth Moon.
Plant No Trees.
Song for the Bronze God.
Song of Chun-k'u.
Song of Heaven, A.
Song of Returning to Kwei-chi.
Song of the Arrowhead.
Sword in the Spring Office, A.
To the Harp Player.
Twelve Moons, The.
LI HUA. Old Battlefield, The.
LI HUNG-CHANG. Shoreless Sea, The.
LI I. Following the Army to the North.
Following the Army to the Northern Expedition.
LI KWANG-T'IEN. Over the Bridge.
LILIENCRON, DETLEV FREIHERR VON. After the Hunt.
Autumn.
Death in the Corn.
Who Knows Where.
LILIENTHAL, JOSEPH. Full Edition, A.
Large Edition, A.
LILLARD, R. W. America's Answer.
America's Reply.
LILLIAT, JOHN. False Love, *at.*
Love, Time and Measure, *at.*
Song: "When love on time and measure makes his ground," *at.*
LILLINGTON, KENNETH. Ballade to My Psychoanalyst.
LI LUNG YÜ. Alone.
LILY, JOHN. *See* LYLY, JOHN.
LIMA, JORGE DE. Big Mystical Circus, The.
Bird, The.
Christian's Poem.
Daddy John.
Paraclete.
Poem of Any Virgin.
LINCOLN, ABRAHAM. Memory.
LINCOLN, JOSEPH CROSBY. Cod-Fisher, The.
Sister's Best Feller.
When the Minister Comes to Tea.
Wood-Box, The.
LINCOLN, MARY W. Kings of France.
LIND, LEVI ROBERT. Autumn Twilight, *tr.*
Joy and Dream, *tr.*
Madrigal: "Eyes that are clear, serene," *tr.*
Shadowy Swallows, *tr.*
To a Recalcitrant Virgin, *tr.*
To Heliodora, Dead, *tr.*
Two Folk Songs, *tr.*
Vine to the Goat, The, *tr.*
For translations from Italian, see LiTW; LyMA; LyPI.
For translations from Latin, see LaP; LiTW.
LINDBERG, GENE. Home Winner, The.
LINDBERGH, ANNE MORROW (Mrs. Charles Augustus Lindbergh). Caprice.
Height.
Stone, The.
LINDEGREN, ERIK. Journey, IV.
Man without a Road, The, X.
LINDORM, ERIK. Life-Boat, The.
LINDSAY, LADY ANNE (Lady Anne Lindsay Barnard). Auld Robin Gray.
East Coast Lullaby.
My Heart Is a Lute, *at.*
Nursery Hour, A.
LINDSAY, CAROLINE BLANCHE ELIZABETH FITZROY, LADY. My Heart Is a Lute, *at.*
Sonnet: "Yea, Love is strong as life; he casts out fear."
LINDSAY [*or* LYNDSAY], SIR DAVID. Ane Supplication in Contemptioun of Syde Taillis.
Carman's Account of a Law-Suit, A.
Childhood of James V, The. *Fr.* The Complaynt of Schir David Lindesay.
Complaint of the Common Weill of Scotland.
Complaynt of Schir David Lindesay, The, *sel.*
Dreme, The, *sel.*
Prologue: "Father and founder of faith and felicity." *Fr.* The Satire of the Three Estates.
Prologue: "In-to the calendis of Januarie." *Fr.* The Dreme.
Satire of the Three Estates, The, *sels.*
So Young ane King.
LINDSAY, JACK. *For translations from Latin, see* LaP; LyMA.
For translations from Russian, see RuPo.
LINDSAY, RUTH TEMPLE. Hunters, The.
LINDSAY, VACHEL. Above the Battle's Front.
Abraham Lincoln Walks at Midnight.
Aladdin and the Jinn.
Alexander Campbell, *sel.*
Angel Sons, The.
Apple-Barrel of Johnny Appleseed, The.
Blacksmith's Serenade, The.
Booker Washington Trilogy, The, *sels.*
Broncho That Would Not Be Broken, The.
Bryan, Bryan, Bryan, Bryan.
Chinese Nightingale, The.
Comet of Going-to-the-Sun, The.
Congo, The.
Congo, The, *sels.*
Curse for the Saxophone, A.
Dandelion, The.
Daniel.
Daniel Jazz, The.
Dirge for a Righteous Kitten.
Dove of New Snow, The.
Dreamer, The.
Eagle That Is Forgotten, The.
Euclid.
Every-Soul Is a Circus, *sel.*
Explanation of the Grasshopper, An.
Factory Windows Are Always Broken.
Fairy Circus, The.
Flower-fed Buffaloes, The.
Flower of Mending, The.
Flute of the Lonely, The.
Foreign Missions in Battle Array.
Franciscan Aspiration.
Gamblers, The.
General William Booth Enters into Heaven.
Ghosts [*or* Ghost] of the Buffaloes, The.
Golden Whales of California, The, *sel.*
Grasshopper, The.
How Samson Bore Away the Gates of Gaza.
Humble Bumble Bee, The.
I Heard Immanuel Singing.
I Want to Go Wandering.
I Went Down into the Desert to Meet Elijah.
In Memory of a Child.
In Praise of Johnny Appleseed.
Indian Summer Day on the Prairie, An.
Jazz of This Hotel, The.
John Brown. *Fr.* The Booker Washington Trilogy.
Johnny Appleseed, *sel.*
Johnny Appleseed Still Further West.
Kallyope Yell, The.
Kansas.
Knight in Disguise, The.
Leaden-eyed, The.
Lincoln. *Fr.* Litany of the Heroes.
Lion, The.
Litany of the Heroes, *sel.*
Little Turtle, The.
Love and Law.
Moon's the North Wind's Cooky, The.
Mouse That Gnawed the Oak-Tree Down, The.
My Fathers Came from Kentucky. *Fr.* Alexander Campbell.
My Lady Is Compared to a Young Tree.
Mysterious Cat, The.

Nancy Hanks, Mother of Abraham Lincoln.
Negro Sermon, A; Simon Legree. *Fr.* The Booker Washington Trilogy.
Net to Snare the Moonlight, A.
Old Horse in the City, The.
Old Old Old Andrew Jackson.
On the Building of Springfield.
Oration, An, Entitled "Old, Old, Old, Old Andrew Jackson."
Poems about the Moon.
Pontoon Bridge Miracle, The. *Fr.* Every Soul Is a Circus.
Potatoes' Dance, The.
Prologue to "Rhymes to Be Traded for Bread."
Rain.
Red Eagle—the Mountain with Wings.
Rhyme about an Electrical Advertising Sign, A.
Rhyme for all Zionists, A.
St. Francis.
Santa Fé Trail, The; a Humoresque.
Santa Fé Trail, The; a Humoresque, *sel.*
Scissors-Grinder, The.
Sense of Humor, A.
Sew the Flags Together.
Simon Legree; a Negro Sermon. *Fr.* The Booker Washington Trilogy.
Star of My Heart.
These Are the Young.
Three Hours.
Three Poems about Mark Twain, *sel.*
To a Golden-haired Girl in a Louisiana Town.
To Reformers in Despair.
Traveler, The.
Unpardonable Sin, The.
Virginia.
Virginians Are Coming Again, The.
Voyage, The.
What Grandpa Mouse Said.
What Semiramis Said.
What the Moon Saw.
What the Rattlesnake Said.
When I Was a Tree.
When Lincoln Came to Springfield.
When the Mississippi Flowed in Indiana. *Fr.* Three Poems about Mark Twain.
Where Is the Real Non-Resistant?
Wild Cats.
Yet Gentle Will the Griffin Be.
LINDSEY, THERESE KAYSER. Man Christ, The.
Radio.
LINDSEY, WILLIAM. En Garde, Messieurs.
Hundred-Yard Dash, The.
LINDSTEDT, MARTHA. Absolution.
LING, J. S. Morning Shower, A.
LING JU JUNG. Night Reverie.
LIN I NING. Good News.
LINK, CAROLYN WILSON. Elements.
Little Death, The.
Sleeping Beauty.
To Be Etched in Silver.
LINK, GORDDEN. Artist and Ape.
LINK, LENORE M. Holding Hands.
LINN, EDITH WILLIS. Downy Owl, The.
Presence.
LINNEY, DOROTHY A. Supplication.
LINSLEY, EDNA E. My Zoölogical Flame.
LINTON, RALPH. Two Towns.
LINTON, WILLIAM JAMES. Brave Women of Tann, The.
Epicurean.
Eviction.
Faint Heart.
Heart and Will.
Love and Youth.
Love's Blindness.
Nature's Gentleman.
Our Cause.
Patience.
Robin Hood.
Silenced Singer, The.
Spring and Autumn.
Threnody, A: In Memory of Albert Darasz, *sel.*
Too Late.
Weep Not! Sigh Not!
LIN YUTANG. Tao Teh King, *sel.*, *tr.*
Weapons of Evil, *tr.* *Fr.* Tao Teh King.
LI PIN. Homeward.
LI PO [*or* LI TAI PO *or in Japanese* RIHAKU]. After Being Separated for a Long Time.
Amusing Myself.
Answer to a Worldly One.
At the River's Edge.
Awakening from Drunkenness on a Spring Day.
Ballad of Ch'ang Kan, A.
Bitter Love, A.
Boating Song.
Bravo of Chao, The.
Bringing in the Wine.
By the Great Wall.
Chang Liang.
Clearing at Dawn.
Conversation in the Mountains.
Crows at Nightfall, The.
Deserted Garden, The.
Dreaming of Wandering through the Tien-mu Mountain.
Drinking Alone by Moonlight ("A cup of wine, under the flowering trees").
Drinking Alone by Moonlight ("If high Heaven had no love for wine").
Drinking Alone by Moonlight ("In the third month the town of Hsien-yang").
Drinking Alone in Moonlight ("If Heaven had no love for wine").
Drinking Alone in the Moonlight ("A pot of wine among flowers").
Drinking Alone under Moonlight ("Holding a jug of wine among the flowers").
Drinking Alone with the Moon ("From a pot of wine among the flowers").
Elegy for Yueh, An.
Encounter in the Field, An.
Endless Yearning.
Exile's Letter.
Farewell Song of White Clouds, A.
Few Words to Meng Hao-jan, A.
Fighting on the South Frontier.
Fisherman, The.
For the Dancer of the King of Wu, When She Is Half Drunk.
Girl of Yueh, The ("She is gathering lotos seed in the river of Yueh").
Girl of Yueh, A ("The waters of Mirror Lake are white like the moon").
Girls of Yueh, The ("The jade faces of the girls on Yueh Stream").
Girls on the Yueh River.
Hearing a Flute on a Spring Night.
In Memoriam; Ho Chi-chang.
In Spring.
In the Mountains on a Summer Day.
Lament for a Dead Wine-Maker.
Lament of the Frontier Guard.
Lao-lao Ting, a Tavern.
Leaving White Emperor City at Dawn.
Lines: "Cool is the autumn wind."
Listening to the Monk of Szechuan Playing on His Lute.
Lonely Wife, The.
Long War, The.
Looking toward Mount Wu.
Maid of Wu.
Meditation on a Quiet Night.
Meeting, A.
Message to Meng Hao-jan, A.
Mirror, The.
Moon at the Fortified Pass, The.
Moon over the Mountain Pass, The.
My Far-off Home.
Nefarious War, The.
Night of Sorrow, The.
Nocturne: "Blue water . . . a clear moon."
On a Journey.
On a Quiet Night.
On Climbing the Phoenix Tower at Chin-ling.
On Hearing a Bamboo Flute.
On Hearing the Sound of Flutes at Loyang on a Spring Night.
On Seeing Off Meng Hao-jan.
Poem for Wang Lung, A.
Poet Mourns His Japanese Friend, The.
Resentment.
River-Merchant's Wife, The; a Letter.
Saying Farewell to a Friend.
Second Song of Chang-kan, A.
Self-Abandonment.
Sigh from a Staircase of Jade, A.
Soldier's Wife, A.
Song before Offering Wine.
Song for the Moon on Mount Omei.
Song of Chang-kan, A.
Song of Ching-ping, A.
Song of the Blue Water.
Song of the Four Seasons, The.
Song of the River.
Song of War, A.
Songs to the Peonies.
Sport-Fellows, The.
Spring Dawn.
Spring Grief and Resentment.
Spring Thoughts.
Summer Day, A.
Summit Temple, The.
Taking Leave of a Friend.
Three with the Moon and His Shadow.
To ——: "When the fair one was here, the house was adorned with flowers."
To a Beautiful Lady Encountered on the Road.
To His Three Friends.
To His Wife on His Departure.
To My Wife from Yeh-lang, the Place of Exile.
To Tan Ch'iu.
To Tu Fu.
To Tu Fu from Sand Hill City.
To Wang Lun.
Verses: "Clean is the autumn wind."
Waking from Drunkenness on a Spring Day.
War.
White Sun and Bright Moon.
Woman of Yueh, A.
Women of Yueh, The.
Yellow Crane Tower, The.
You Have a Yellow Horse.
Youth Rides Forth.
LIPPINCOTT, SARA JANE CLARKE. *See* "GREENWOOD, GRACE."
LIPPITT, LUCILE. He Lives at Last.
LIPPMANN, ARTHUR L. Organ Recital.
LIPPMANN, JULIE MATHILDE. Love and Life.
Pines, The.
Santa Claus' Petition.
Stone Walls.
LI SHANG-YIN. Cicada, A.
Coming and Going.
Fallen Flowers.
Inlaid Psaltery, The.
Letter Home, A.
Lo-yu Tombs, The.
Ma Wei.
Melancholy.
No Title ("So difficult the meeting").
Sent to Home.
Spring Rain.
Thoughts in the Cold.
To One Unnamed.
LI SHIH-MING [*or* T'AI TSUNG]. Song of the Candle, The.
To the Tune of "Horses Drinking by the Great Wall."
LISLE, CHARLES MARIE LECONTE DE. *See* LECONTE DE LISLE, CHARLES MARIE.
LISLE, ROUGET DE. *See* ROUGET DE LISLE, CLAUDE JOSEPH.
LISLE, SAMUEL. When Orpheus Went Down.
LISSAUER, ERNST. Chant of Hate against England, A.
Chant of Hate against England, A, *sel.*
LISTER, RICHARD PERCIVAL. At the Ship.
Gemlike Flame, The.
Human Races, The.
Lament of an Idle Demon.
Musician, The.
LI SUI CH'U. Mirror, The.
LI TAI PO. *See* LI PO.
LITCHFIELD, ADDIE. Flower Lullaby.

LITCHFIELD, GRACE DENIO. Good-by.
My Letter.
My Other Me.
To a Hurt Child.
To My Father.
LITCHFIELD, JESSIE. In the Day's Work.
LITSEY, EDWIN CARLILE. Dreams Ahead, The.
LITTLE, ARTHUR J. Christ Unconquered, *sel.*
Invocation: "Mother of God, mother of man reborn." *Fr.* Christ Unconquered.
LITTLE, KATHARINE DAY. Hazlitt Sups.
LITTLE, LIZZIE M. Life.
LITTLE, PHILIP FRANCIS. Blue Hills.
Three Poplars, The.
To a Dead Infant.
LITTLEFIELD, HAZEL. Not for Its Own Sake.
LITTLEFIELD, MILTON S. Come, O Lord, like Morning Sunlight.
O Son of Man, Thou Madest Known.
LITTLEWOOD, W. E. Heart of God, The.
LITTLEWORT, DOROTHY. Prayer of a Teacher.
LITVINOFF, EMANUEL. All Ruin Is the Same.
Garrison Town.
If I Forget Thee.
Not Revenge . . . but These.
Note from an Intimate Diary.
Poem for the Atomic Age.
Rededication.
War Swaggers.
LIU CHI. Soldier to His Wife, A.
Soldier's Wife to Her Husband, A.
LIU CHIA. Drinking Bout, A.
LIU FANG-P'ING. Spring Heart-break.
LIU HSIAO HSIEN. Melancholy.
LIU HSI CHÜN. Wedded to a Tartar.
LIU HSÜN, WIFE OF. Curtain of the Wedding Bed, The.
LIU PANG (Emperor Kao Ti). Great Wind, The.
LIU PING. Home.
LIU TEH-JEN. Strolling in a Village.
LIU TSUNG-YUAN. Ice in a Stream.
LI TÜAN. On Hearing Her Play the Harp.
LIU TZU HUI. Evening at the Inn of Yün Meng.
Halfway Up the Mountain.
Happy Old Man, A.
LIU YUNG. Farewell to My Love, A.
Thinking of Her.
LIU YÜ SHIH. Peonies.
LIVESAY, DOROTHY. Child Looks Out, The.
City Wife.
Contact.
Epilogue to the Outrider.
Fantasia.
For Federico García Lorca.
Improvisation on an Old Theme.
Inheritors, The.
Interval with Fire.
Lament.
London Revisited—1946.
Of Mourners.
Poem: "Night's soft armor welds me into thought."
Prelude for Spring.
Sea-Flowers.
This Arrow.
Winter.
LIVESAY, FLORENCE RANDAL. Butterfly Weed—Indian Fire.
Captives, The, *tr.*
Floating Barque, The, *tr.*
Fragment: "Ukraina is sad for that she has no place to dwell in," *tr.*
In the Public Ward, *tr.*
Khustina—The Kerchief, *tr.*
Tim, the Fairy.
Violin Calls, The.
Widow, The, *tr.*
LIVINGSTON, EDNA. Question, A.
LIVINGSTON, WILLIAM (1723–90). Wife, The.
Wife, The, *sel.*
LIVINGSTON, WILLIAM (1808–70). Ireland Weeping.
Message to the Bard.
LIVINGSTON, WILLIAM. In Cherry Lane.
LI YI. On Hearing a Flute at Night from the Wall of Shou-hsiang.
LI YU. Angel Enclosed, An.
Before the Pavilion.
Fisherman's Song.
Girl's Yearning, A.
Meditation.
Melancholy.
Native Land.
Past, The.
Spring Blossoms.
Thinking of My Love.
To the Tune of "A Clear Calm Music."
To the Tune of "Breaking through Battle."
To the Tune of "Crows Crying by Night."
To the Tune of "Meeting Happiness."
To the Tune of "Mountain Flowers."
To the Tune of "The South River Song."
Tryst, The.
LLEWELLYN, KARL NICKERSON. Jonathan Smith.
Prairie.
LLOYD, BEATRIX DEMAREST. Love and Time.
Night-Wind.
With Roses.
LLOYD, CECIL FRANCIS. Helen.
March Winds.
Truth.
LLOYD, CHARLES. Essay on the Genius of Pope, An, *sel.*
LLOYD, ELIZABETH. *See* HOWELL, ELIZABETH LLOYD.
LLOYD, ROBERT. Critic's Rules, The. *Fr.* Shakespeare; an Epistle to Mr. Garrick.
Milkmaid, The.
Shakespeare; an Epistle to Mr. Garrick, *sel.*
LLOYD, WILLIAM, BISHOP OF ST. ASAPH. Reflection on the Course of Human Life, A.
LLOYD, WILLIAM F. My Times Are in Thy Hand.
LLUELLYN, MARTIN. Cock-throwing.
LLWYD, JOHN PLUMMER DERWENT. Vestal Virgin, The, *sel.*
LLYWARCH HEN. Tercets.
LLYWARCH THE AGED. Hearth of Urien, The.
LLYWELYN-WILLIAMS, ALUN. When I Was Young.
Ystrad Fflur, *tr.*
"LOCHABER, NETHER." *See* STEWART, ALEXANDER.
LOCHHEAD, MARION. Christmas Night.
Nox Est Perpetua.
LOCHORE, ROBERT. Marriage and the Care o't.
LOCKER-LAMPSON, FREDERICK. At Her Window.
Circumstance.
Cuckoo, The.
Garden Lyric, A.
Jester's Plea, The.
Loulou and Her Cat.
Love, Time and Death.
Mrs. Smith.
My Love Is Always Near.
My Mistress's Boots.
Nice Correspondent, A.
Old Buffer, An.
Old Oak Tree at Hatfield Broadoak, The.
On a Sense of Humor.
On an Old Muff.
Our Photographs.
Rhyme of One, A.
Rotten Row.
St. James's Street.
Skeleton in the Cupboard, The.
Some Ladies.
Susan.
Terrible Infant, A.
To My Grandmother.
To My Mistress.
Unrealized Ideal, The.
Widow's Mite, The.
LOCKHART, JOHN GIBSON. Avenging Childe, The, *tr.*
Bavieca, *tr.*
Beyond.
Captain Paton's Lament.
Cid, The, *sel., tr.*
Cid and the Five Moorish Kings, The, *tr.*
Cid and the Leper, The, *tr.* *Fr.* The Cid.
Count Arnaldos, *tr.*
Death of Don Pedro, The, *tr.*
Flight from Granada, *tr.*
Lament for Capt. Paton.
Lamentation for Celin, The, *tr.*
Lamentation for Celin, The, *sel., tr.*
Lamentation of Don Rodrigo [*or* Roderick], The, *tr.*
Lines: "When youthful faith hath fled."
Lord of Butrago, The, *tr.*
My ornaments are arms, *tr.*
On Peter Robertson.
Serenade: "While my lady sleepeth."
Song of the Galley, The, *tr.*
Wandering Knight's Song, The, *tr.*
When Youthful Faith Hath Fled.
Zara's Ear-Rings, *tr.*
LOCKWOOD, WILLIAM A. Limerick: "There was a trim maiden named Wood."
LODGE, EDITH. Song of the Hill.
LODGE, GEORGE CABOT. Day and Dark.
Exordium.
Song of the Wave, A.
Trumbull Stickney.
Youth.
LODGE, J. SHENTON. Prayer for Any Bride and Groom.
LODGE, THOMAS. Accurst Be Love.
All Things Revive save the Lover. *Fr.* A Margarite of America.
Armistice.
Beauty, Alas, Where Wast Thou Born, *at.*
Blith and Bonny Country Lass, A.
Carpe Diem. *Fr.* Robert, Second Duke of Normandy.
Contents of the Scedule Which Sir John of Bordeaux Gave to His Sons, The. *Fr.* Rosalynde.
Corydon's Song. *Fr.* Rosalynde.
Devoid of reason, thrall to foolish ire. *Fr.* Phyllis.
Dewy, roseate morn had with her hairs, The. *Fr.* Phyllis.
Earth, Late Chok'd with Showers, The. *Fr.* Scillaes Metamorphosis.
Fancy, A ("First shall the heavens want starry light"). *Fr.* Rosalynde.
Fancy, A ("When I admire the rose"). *Fr.* The Life and Death of William Longbeard.
Fatal Star, The.
Fidelity. *Fr.* Phyllis.
Fig for Momus, A, *sel.*
For Pity, Pretty Eyes, Surcease.
Her Rambling. *Fr.* The Life and Death of William Longbeard.
I would in rich and golden-colored rain. *Fr.* Phyllis.
I'll teach thee, lovely Phillis, what love is. *Fr.* Phyllis.
Life and Death of William Longbeard, The, *sels.*
Like Desert Woods.
Love Guards [*or* Guides] the Roses of Thy Lips. *Fr.* Phyllis.
Love in My Bosom like a Bee. *Fr.* Rosalynde.
Lover's Protestation, A. *Fr.* Rosalynde.
Love's Protestation. *Fr.* Rosalynde.
Love's Witchery.
Margarite of America, A, *sel.*
Melancholy. *Fr.* Scillaes Metamorphosis.
Montanus' Sonnet. *Fr.* Rosalynde.
Most Pithy and Pleasant History of Glaucus and Scylla, The. *Fr.* Scillaes Metamorphosis.
My Bonny Lass, Thine Eye.
My Frail and Earthly Bark, by Reason's Guide.
My Mistress. *Fr.* The Life and Death of William Longbeard.

My Phillis hath the morning sun. *Fr.* Phyllis.
No stars her eyes, to clear the wandering night. *Fr.* Phyllis.
O Pleasing Thoughts. *Fr.* Phyllis.
O Shady Vales! O Fair Enrichèd Meads. *Fr.* A Margarite of America.
Ode, An: "Now I find thy looks were feigned." *Fr.* Phyllis.
Of Ceaseless Thoughts My Mind Hath Fram'd His Wings.
Of Rosalind. *Fr.* Rosalynde.
Old Damon's Pastoral.
Passion's Hounds, *tr.*
Phillis ("My Phillis hath the morning sun"). *Fr.* Phyllis.
Phoebe's Sonnet.
Phyllis, *sels.*
Pluck the Fruit and Taste the Pleasure. *Fr.* Robert, Second Duke of Normandy.
Robert, Second Duke of Normandy, *sel.*
Rosader's Second Sonetto. *Fr.* Rosalynde.
Rosader's Sonnet. *Fr.* Rosalynde.
Rosader's Sonnet, Sent to Rosalynde. *Fr.* Rosalynde.
Rosalind. *Fr.* Rosalynde.
Rosalind's Complaint. *Fr.* Rosalynde.
Rosalind's [*or* Rosalynde's] Description. *Fr.* Rosalynde.
Rosalind's [*or* Rosalynde's] Madrigal. *Fr.* Rosalynde.
Rosaline. *Fr.* Rosalynde.
Rosalynde [*or* Rosalind]; or, Euphues' Golden Legacy, *sels.*
Rosalynde's [*or* Rosalind's] Description. *Fr.* Rosalynde.
Rosalynde's [*or* Rosalind's] Madrigal. *Fr.* Rosalynde.
Rose, The. *Fr.* The Life and Death of William Longbeard.
Scillaes [*or* Scilla's *or* Scylla's] Metamorphosis, *sels.*
Solitary Shepherd's Song, The.
Sonetto: "Of all chaste birds the phoenix doth excel." *Fr.* Rosalynde.
Song: "Now I see thy looks were feigned." *Fr.* Phyllis.
Song: "O shadie vales, O faire inriched meades." *Fr.* A Margarite of America.
Sonnet: "Earth, late choked with showers, The." *Fr.* Scillaes Metamorphosis.
Sonnet: "I feele my selfe endaungered beyond reason."
Sonnet: "My Phyllis hath the morning sun." *Fr.* Phyllis.
Sonnet: "O shady vales, O fair enriched meads." *Fr.* A Margarite of America.
Strive No More.
To a Dear Friend Lately Given Over to Covetousness. *Fr.* A Fig for Momus.
To Love.
To Master Everard Digby.
To Master Michael Drayton.
To Phyllis. *Fr.* Phyllis.
To Phyllis, the Fair Shepherdess. *Fr.* Phyllis.
Truth's Complaint over England.
LOESSER, FRANK. Praise the Lord and Pass the Ammunition.
LOEWINSOHN, RON. Insomniac Poem.
Mrs. Loewinsohn &c.
My Sons.
Pastoral: "Death./ The death of a million."
Stillness of the Poem, The.
Thing Made Real, The.
LOFTING, HUGH. Betwixt and Between.
Mister Beers.
Oom-pah.
Picnic.
LOFTON, BLANCHE DE GOOD. Song of the Seasons.
LOFTUS, CECILIA. In the Morning.
LOGAN, GEORGE B., JR. Dawn.
LOGAN, JOHN. Braes of Yarrow, The.
Ode: To the Cuckoo.
Thy Braes Were Bonny.
To the Cuckoo.
LOGAN, JOHN DANIEL. Brock; Valiant Leader.
Cartier; Dauntless Discoverer.
Champlain; First Canadian.
Flute of God.
Heavenly Runaway, The.
Heliodore.
Laval; Noble Educator.
Over-Song of Niagara, The.
Winifred Waters.
LOGAN, JOHN EDWARD ("Barry Dane"). Blood-Red Ring Hung round the Moon, A.
Dead Singer, A.
"Injun, The."
Nor'west Courier, The.
LOGAU, FRIEDRICH VON. Retribution.
LOGUE, CHRISTOPHER. Seven Sonnets.
LOINES, RUSSELL HILLIARD. On a Magazine Sonnet.
LOK, HENRY. It is not, Lord, the sound of many words. *Fr.* Sonnets of Christian Passions.
Sonnets of Christian Passions, *sels.*
Sundry Christian Passions, *sels.*
Words may well want, both ink and paper fail. *Fr.* Sonnets of Christian Passions.
LOM, IAIN (John MacDonald). Day of Inverlochy, The.
To Mackinnon of Strath.
LOMAX, JOHN A. Old Mackenzie Trail, The.
LOMONOSOV, MIKHAIL. Lord and Judge, The.
LONG, ELIZABETH-ELLEN. After-Christmas Poem.
Autumn Song.
Christmas Song.
Discarded Christmas Tree.
Rain Clouds.
LONG, FRANK BELKNAP. Abominable Snow Men, The.
Goblin Tower, The.
Horror on Dagoth Wold, The.
In Mayan Splendor.
Knight of La Mancha, A.
On Reading Arthur Machen.
Sonnet: "Gods are dead, The. The earth has covered them."
LONG, HANIEL. Book of Economics, A.
Butterflies.
Cause of This I Know Not, The.
Dead Men Tell No Tales.
Faun, The.
Girl Athletes.
Herd Boy, The.
His Deaths.
Poet, The.
Song: "Poppies paramour the girls."
Students.
LONG, JOHN D. Prayer, A: "I would, dear Jesus, I could break."
LONG, JOSEPH SCHUYLER. Family Man as a Poet, The.
LONG LANCE (Chief Long Lance). Death-Song.
LONG, R. H. City of God.
Skylark's Nest, The.
Super-Lark, The.
LONG, STEWART I. Was It You?
LONG, WILLIAM. *See* "YATES, PETER."
LONGFELLOW, HENRY WADSWORTH. Aceldama.
Age Is Opportunity. *Fr.* Morituri Salutamus.
Alhambra, The, *tr.*
All-seeing Gods, The. *Fr.* The Masque of Pandora.
Allah, *tr.*
Alone God Sufficeth, *tr.*
April.
Arrow and the Song, The.
Arsenal at Springfield, The.
Arsenal at Springfield, The, *sel.*
Art and Nature, *tr.*
Assumption of the Virgin, The, *tr.*
Auf Wiedersehen, *sel.*
Autumn ("Thou comest Autumn, heralded").
Autumn ("With what a glory comes").
Azrael. *Fr.* Tales of a Wayside Inn.
Ballad of the French Fleet, A.
Battle of Lovell's Pond, The.
Battle of Simancas, The, *tr.* *Fr.* The Life of San Millán.
Bayard Taylor.
Beleaguered City, The.
Belfry of Bruges, The.
Belfry of Bruges, The, *sel.*
Belisarius.
Bell of Atri, The. *Fr.* Tales of a Wayside Inn.
Bells of Lynn, The.
Bells of San Blas, The.
Bernardo's March to Roncesvalles, *tr.*
Beware, *tr.*
Birds of Killingworth, The. *Fr.* Tales of a Wayside Inn.
Blind Bartimeus.
Book of Good Love, The, *sels., tr.*
Bridge, The.
Broken Oar, The.
Brook and the Wave, The.
Builders, The.
Building of the *Long Serpent*, The. *Fr.* Tales of a Wayside Inn.
Building of the Ship, The.
Building of the Ship, The, *sels.*
Burial of the Minnisink.
Carillon. *Fr.* The Belfry of Bruges.
Castle Builder, The, *sel.*
Castle by the Sea, The, *tr.*
Catawba Wine.
Celestial Pilot, The, *tr.* *Fr.* Divina Commedia.
Challenge of Thor, The. *Fr.* Tales of a Wayside Inn.
Challenge to Youth. *Fr.* The Castle Builder.
Chamber over the Gate.
Charlemagne. *Fr.* Tales of a Wayside Inn.
Charles Sumner.
Chaucer.
Childhood, *tr.*
Children.
Children's Hour, The.
Chimes.
Christmas Bells.
Christmas Carol: "When Christ was born in Bethlehem," *tr.*
Christmas Carols, *par.*
Christus; a Mystery, *sels.*
City and the Sea, The.
Come, read to me some poem. *Fr.* The Day Is Done.
Coplas de Manrique, *sel.*
Coplas on the Death of His Father, *tr.*
Courtship of Miles Standish, The.
Courtship of Miles Standish, The, *sels.*
Cross of Snow, The.
Cumberland, The.
Curfew.
Curfew, *sel.*
Dante.
Day Is Done, The.
Day Is Done, The, *sel.*
Day of Sunshine, A.
Daybreak.
Death of Minnehaha, The. *Fr.* The Song of Hiawatha.
Decoration Day.
Dedication: "With favoring winds, o'er sunlit seas." *Fr.* Ultima Thule.
Discoverer of the North Cape, The.
Disembodied Spirit, The, *tr.*
Divina Commedia, *sels., tr.*
Divina Commedia (*poems introductory to the translation*).
Dutch Picture, A.
Einar Tamberskelver. *Fr.* Tales of a Wayside Inn.
Elected Knight, The, *tr.*
Elegiac.
Embarkation, The. *Fr.* Evangeline.
Emperor's Bird's Nest, The.
Endymion.
Equinox, The. *Fr.* Seaweed.
Eternal Word, The.
Evangeline.
Evangeline, *sels.*
Evangeline in Acadie. *Fr.* Evangeline.
Evening Star, The.
Excelsior.
Expedition to Wessagusset, The. *Fr.* The Courtship of Miles Standish.
Eyes So Tristful, *tr.*

LONGFELLOW, HENRY W. (*continued*)
Famine, The. *Fr.* The Song of Hiawatha.
Fate of the Prophets, The. *Fr.* Christus; a Mystery.
Fiftieth Birthday of Agassiz, The.
Fiftieth Birthday of Agassiz, The, *sel.*
Finding of Gabriel, The. *Fr.* Evangeline.
Fire of Drift-Wood, The.
Firefly Song. *Fr.* The Song of Hiawatha.
Flight into Egypt, The. *Fr.* Christus; a Mystery.
Flower-de-Luce.
Flowers.
Foe Within, The.
Follow Me.
Footsteps of Angels.
Four Winds, The. *Fr.* The Song of Hiawatha.
Friar Lubin, *tr.*
Frithiof's Farewell, *tr.* *Fr.* Frithiof's Saga.
Frithiof's Homestead, *tr.* *Fr.* Frithiof's Saga.
Frithiof's Saga, *sels.*
From My Arm-Chair.
Galley of Count Arnaldos, The.
Gaspar Becerra.
Ghosts, The. *Fr.* The Song of Hiawatha.
Giles Corey of the Salem Farms, *sels.*
Giotto's Tower.
Glove of Black in White Hand Bare, *tr.*
God's Acre.
Golden Legend, The, *sel.*
Golden Mile-Stone, The.
Good Shepherd, The, *tr.*
Grave, The, *sel.*, *tr.*
Hanging of the Crane, The.
Harvest Moon, The.
Haunted Houses.
Hawthorne.
He That Doeth the Will.
Heights, The. *Fr.* The Ladder of St. Augustine.
Helen of Tyre.
Hermes Trismegistus.
Hiawatha and Mudjekeewis. *Fr.* The Song of Hiawatha.
Hiawatha's Brothers. *Fr.* The Song of Hiawatha.
Hiawatha's Canoe. *Fr.* The Song of Hiawatha.
Hiawatha's Chickens. *Fr.* The Song of Hiawatha.
Hiawatha's Childhood. *Fr.* The Song of Hiawatha.
Hiawatha's Departure. *Fr.* The Song of Hiawatha.
Hiawatha's Sailing. *Fr.* The Song of Hiawatha.
Hiawatha's Wedding-Feast. *Fr.* The Song of Hiawatha.
Hiawatha's Wooing. *Fr.* The Song of Hiawatha.
Holidays.
Holidays, *sel.*
Home Song.
Household Sovereign, The. *Fr.* The Hanging of the Crane.
How strange the sculptures that adorn these towers! *Fr.* Divina Commedia.
Hunting of Pau-Puk-Keewis, The. *Fr.* The Song of Hiawatha.
Hymn of the Moravian Nuns of Bethlehem.
Hymn to the Night.
Hymn to the Virgin, *tr.* *Fr.* The Book of Good Love.
I enter, and I see thee in the gloom. *Fr.* Divina Commedia.
I Heard the Bells on Christmas Day.
I lift mine eyes, and all the windows blaze. *Fr.* Divina Commedia.
Ideal Beauty, *tr.*
Image of God, The, *tr.*
In the Churchyard at Cambridge.
In the Forest. *Fr.* Evangeline.
Jericho's Blind Beggar.
Jesus at Play with His School-Mates. *Fr.* Christus; a Mystery.
Jewish Cemetery at Newport, The.
John Endicott, *sels.*
Jugurtha.
Keats.
Kéramos.
Kéramos, *sel.*
Killed at the Ford.
King Christian, *tr.*
King Olaf's Death-Drink. *Fr.* Tales of a Wayside Inn.
King Olaf's Return. *Fr.* Tales of a Wayside Inn.
King Olaf's War-Horns. *Fr.* Tales of a Wayside Inn.
King Robert of Sicily. *Fr.* Tales of a Wayside Inn.
King Witlaf's Drinking-Horn.
Ladder of St. Augustine, The.
Ladder of St. Augustine, The, *sel.*
Lakes of the Atchafalaya, The. *Fr.* Evangeline.
Leap of Roushan Beg, The.
Legend Beautiful, The. *Fr.* Tales of a Wayside Inn.
Legend of Rabbi Ben Levi, The. *Fr.* Tales of a Wayside Inn.
Legend of the Cornstalk, The. *Fr.* The Song of Hiawatha.
Let Me Go Warm, *tr.*
Let Nothing Disturb Thee, *tr.*
Let War's Tempests Cease.
Life. *Fr.* A Psalm of Life.
Life of San Millán, The, *sel.*, *tr.*
Light of Stars, The.
Light of Stars, The, *sel.*
Lines Written in Her Breviary, *tr.*
Little Moon, The.
Lives of Great Men All Remind Us. *Fr.* A Psalm of Life.
Loss and Gain.
Lost Youth.
Love and Hate. *Fr.* Christus; a Mystery.
Luck of Edenhall, The, *tr.*
Lullaby of Nokomis. *Fr.* The Song of Hiawatha.
Mad River.
Maidenhood.
Manichaean's Prayer, The. *Fr.* Tales of a Wayside Inn.
Manuscripts of God, The. *Fr.* The Fiftieth Birthday of Agassiz.
Masque of Pandora, The, *sels.*
Message of Peace, A.
Mezzo Cammin.
Midnight Mass for the Dying Year.
Milton.
Miracles of Our Lady, The, *sels.*, *tr.*
Monk of Casal-Maggiore, The.
Moonlight on the Prairie. *Fr.* Evangeline.
Morituri Salutamus.
Morituri Salutamus, *sel.*
Musings.
My Books.
My Cathedral.
My Lost Youth.
My Lost Youth, *sel.*
Nameless Grave, A.
Nativity of Christ, The, *tr.*
Nature.
New Household, A. *Fr.* The Hanging of the Crane.
Night.
Nun of Nidaros, The. *Fr.* Tales of a Wayside Inn.
Nuremberg.
O Ship of State. *Fr.* The Building of the Ship.
O star of morning and of liberty! *Fr.* Divina Commedia.
Ode on the Death of His Father, *tr.*
O'er all the hill-tops, *tr.* *Fr.* Wanderer's Night-Songs.
Oft Have I Seen at Some Cathedral Door. *Fr.* Divina Commedia.
Old Bridge at Florence, The.
Old Clock on the Stairs, The.
Old St. David's at Radnor.
On Dante's "Divine Comedy." *Fr.* Divina Commedia.
On the Atchafalaya. *Fr.* Evangeline.
On the Crucifix, *tr.*
On Translating the "Divina Commedia." *Fr.* Divina Commedia.
Pau-Puk-Keewis. *Fr.* The Song of Hiawatha.
Paul Revere's Ride. *Fr.* Tales of a Wayside Inn.
Peace.
Peace-Pipe, The. *Fr.* The Song of Hiawatha.
Peace through Prayer. *Fr.* Divina Commedia.
Phantom Ship, The.
Poets, The.
Political Chaos in Italy, *tr.*
Potter's Song, The. *Fr.* Kéramos.
Praise of Little Women, *tr.* *Fr.* The Book of Good Love.
Praise of Little Women, *sel.*, *tr.* *Fr.* The Book of Good Love.
Praise of Spring, The, *tr.* *Fr.* The Miracles of Our Lady.
Prelude: "Youth was there, of quiet ways, A." *Fr.* Tales of a Wayside Inn.
President Garfield.
Primeval Forest, The. *Fr.* Evangeline.
Proclamation, The. *Fr.* John Endicott.
Prologue: "Delusions of the days that once have been." *Fr.* Giles Corey of the Salem Farms.
Prologue: "Tonight we strive to read, as we may best." *Fr.* John Endicott.
Prologue to "Evangeline."
Prophets in Their Time. *Fr.* Christus; a Mystery.
Psalm of Life, A.
Psalm of Life, A, *sel.*
Rain in Summer.
Rain in Summer, *sel.*
Rainy Day, The.
Reaper and the Flowers, The.
Republic, The. *Fr.* The Building of the Ship.
Resignation.
Retribution, *tr.*
Return of Spring, The, *tr.*
Revenge of Rain-in-the-Face, The.
Robert Burns.
Rondel: To His Mistress, to Succor His Heart, *tr.*
Saga of King Olaf, The. *Fr.* Tales of a Wayside Inn.
Saga of King Olaf, The, *sels.* *Fr.* Tales of a Wayside Inn.
Sail On, O Ship of State! *Fr.* The Building of the Ship.
Saint Francis' Sermon to the Birds.
St. John's, Cambridge.
Saint Teresa's Book-Mark, *tr.*
San Miguel de la Tumba, *tr.* *Fr.* The Miracles of Our Lady.
Sandalphon.
Santa Filomena.
Santa Teresa's Book-Mark, *tr.*
Scanderbeg. *Fr.* Tales of a Wayside Inn.
Sea Hath Its Pearls, The, *tr.*
Sea Memories. *Fr.* My Lost Youth.
Seaweed [*or* Sea Weed].
Seaweed, *sel.*
Secret of the Sea, The.
Serenade: "Stars of the summer night!" *Fr.* The Spanish Student.
Shakespeare.
Ship of State, The. *Fr.* The Building of the Ship.
Ships That Pass in the Night. *Fr.* Tales of a Wayside Inn.
Sicilian's Tale, The. *Fr.* Tales of a Wayside Inn.
Silent Love, *tr.*
Simon Danz.
Sir Humphrey Gilbert.
Skeleton in Armor, The.
Slave's Dream, The.
Sleep, Comrades, Sleep.
Snow.
Snowflakes.
Some Day, Some Day, *tr.*
Song: "If thou art sleeping, maiden," *tr.*

Song: "Stay, stay at home, my heart, and rest."
Song of Hiawatha, The, *sels.*
Song of the Bell, *tr.*
Song of the Bird, The, *tr.*
Song of the Silent Land, *tr.*
Sonnet: Dante, *tr.*
Sound of the Sea, The.
Spanish Student, The, *sel.*
Spirit of Poetry, The.
Stars of the Summer Night. *Fr.* The Spanish Student.
Stay, Stay at Home, My Heart, and Rest.
Sunset.
Suspiria.
Tales of a Wayside Inn, *sels.*
Tegnér's Drapa, *tr.*
There Was a Little Girl, *at.*
This Is Indeed the Blessed Mary's Land. *Fr.* The Golden Legend.
Thou that from the heavens art, *tr.* *Fr.* Wanderer's Night-Songs.
Thou, Too, Sail On! *Fr.* The Building of the Ship.
Three Friends of Mine.
Three Kings, The.
Three Silences of Molinos, The.
Tide Rises, the Tide Falls, The.
To a Child, *sel.*
To an Old Danish Song-Book.
To Italy, *tr.*
To the Driving Cloud.
To Vittoria Colonna, *tr.*
Tomorrow, *tr.*
Too Late?
Trial, The. *Fr.* Giles Corey of the Salem Farms.
Tristia, *sels., tr.*
Twilight.
Two Angels, The, *sel.*
Two Harvests, The, *tr.*
Ultima Thule, *sel.*
Venice.
Victor and Vanquished.
Victor and Vanquished, *sel.*
Victor Galbraith.
Village Blacksmith, The.
Village School, The. *Fr.* Christus; a Mystery.
Wanderer's Night-Songs, *tr.*
Wanderer's Night-Songs, *sels., tr.*
Wapentake.
Warden of the Cinque Ports, The.
Warning, The.
War-Token, The. *Fr.* The Courtship of Miles Standish.
Wayside Inn, The. *Fr.* Tales of a Wayside Inn.
Weariness.
When War Shall Be No More. *Fr.* The Arsenal at Springfield.
Whither, *tr.*
Who God Possesseth, *tr.*
Windmill, The.
With snow-white veil and garments as of flame. *Fr.* Divina Commedia.
With the Ages. *Fr.* Divina Commedia.
Witnesses, The.
Wreck of the *Hesperus,* The.
LONGFELLOW, SAMUEL. April.
Beneath the Shadow of the Cross.
Christian Life, The.
Church Universal, The.
God of the Earth, the Sky, the Sea.
God, Through All and in You All.
November.
One holy church of God appears.
Peace on Earth.
LONGFORD, EDWARD ARTHUR HENRY PAKENHAM, 6TH EARL OF. Careful Husband, The, *tr.*
Kiss, The, *tr.*
LONGLEY, SNOW. I Dreamed Last Night.
Sonnet: "I dreamed last night I stood with God on high."
LONGSTAFF, W. D. Take Time to Be Holy.
LONGUS. Daphnis. *Fr.* Daphnis and Chloe.
Daphnis and Chloe, *sel.*
LONGWELL, E. ELIZABETH. Pear Tree, The.
LONZANO, MENAHEM BEN JUDAH. Gentleman, The.
LOOKE, JOHN. Famous Sea-Fight, A.
LOOMIS, C. FRANCES. King's Gifts, The.
LOOMIS, CHARLES BATTELL. Jack and Jill.
O-U-G-H.
Propinquity Needed.
Song of Sorrow, A.
Timon of Archimedes.
LOOMIS, EDITH. Little Nun, A.
LOPE DE VEGA CARPIO, FÉLIX. Christmas Cradlesong, A.
Clover.
Country Life.
Estrella de Sevilla, La, *sel.*
Estrella Learns that Her Lover Has Killed Her Brother. *Fr.* La Estrella de Sevilla.
Good Shepherd, The.
Halloa! the Good Ship of Delight.
I always said, shall say, and now do say.
Lullaby, The: "As through the palms ye wander."
Lullaby of the Virgin.
Madonna, to Her Sleeping Child, The.
New Art of Making Plays, The.
Song for [*or* of] the Virgin Mother, A.
Sonnet on a Sonnet.
Tomorrow.
Varied Effects of Love.
Whispering Palms.
LÓPEZ, LUIS. Village Barber, The.
LÓPEZ, LUIS CARLOS. Country Girl, Don't Stay Away.
Mayor, The.
Old Maids.
Rubbish.
To a Dog.
To My Native City.
To Satan.
Tropic Siesta.
Vespers.
Village Night.
LÓPEZ, RAFAEL. Venus Poised.
LÓPEZ DE AYALA, PERO. Concerning Lawyers. *Fr.* Palace Rhymes.
Palace Rhymes, *sel.*
Song to the Virgin Mary.
LÓPEZ MERINO, FRANCISCO. My Cousins, on Sundays.
Song for Afterwards.
LÓPEZ-PENHA, ABRAHAM Z. Dusk.
LÓPEZ VELARDE, RAMÓN. Ants.
Ascension and the Assumption, The.
Gentle Fatherland.
Humbly.
I Honour You in Dread.
In the Wet Shadows.
Malefic Return, The.
My Cousin Agueda.
My Heart Atones.
Now, as Never.
Our Lives Are Pendulums.
Sound of the Heart, The.
Tear, The.
Wet Earth.
Your Teeth.
LORD, CAROLINE A. Song of Street Labor, A.
LORD, EVERETT W. Legend of the Admen, The.
LORD, MAY CARLETON. Old Man with a Mowing Machine.
Prayer: "Keep me from fretting, Lord, today."
LORD, PHILLIPS H. Your Church and Mine.
LORD, WILLIAM WILBERFORCE. Brook, The.
Keats. *Fr.* Ode to England.
Ode to England, *sels.*
On the Defeat of a Great Man.
On the Defeat of Henry Clay.
To Rosina Pico.
Wordsworth. *Fr.* Ode to England.
Worship, *sel.*
LORENTZ, PARE. River, The, *sel.*
LORING, FREDERICK WADSWORTH. Fair Millinger, The.
In the Old Churchyard at Fredericksburg.
"LORRAIN, JEAN" (Paul Duval). Wild Marjorie.
LORRAINE, LILITH. Alien to the Earth.
Beyond the Final Breath.
If He Should Come.
If These Endure.
Into the Endless Night.
Let Dreamers Wake.
Not Made with Hands.
Other People, The.
Stalker of Dreams.
What Will the Stars Remember?
When Planes Outsoar the Spirit.
Who Are the Dead?
Without Regret.
LORRIS, GUILLAUME DE, *and* JEAN DE MEUN. *See* GUILLAUME DE LORRIS *and* JEAN DE MEUN.
LOTAREV, IGOR VASILYEVICH. *See* "SEVERYANIN, IGOR."
"LOTHROP, AMY." *See* WARNER, ANNA BARTLETT.
LOTHROP, HARRIET MULFORD. *See* "SIDNEY, MARGARET."
LOUGÉE, DAVID. Sestina for Cynthia, A.
LOUIS, LOUISE. Wounded, The.
LOUISE, SISTER MARY. To a Nun Violinist.
LOUNKIANOS. Vision, The.
LOVE, ADELAIDE. Alchemy.
Beyond Electrons.
For a Materialist.
Lien, The.
No Sweeter Thing.
Poet's Prayer.
Walk Slowly.
Word to a Dictator.
LOVE, JOHN, JR. Barber, Spare Those Hairs.
LOVE, ROBERTUS. Boy from Hodgensville, The.
LOVECRAFT, HOWARD PHILLIPS. Ancient Track, The.
Continuity.
Fungi from Yuggoth.
Memory, A.
Messenger, The.
Psychopompos.
LOVEJOY, GEORGE NEWELL. Easter Carol: "O Earth! throughout thy borders."
Gift, The.
Mother, The.
LOVELACE, RICHARD. Anniversary, An.
Another.
Elinda's Glove.
Epigrams (*of* Ausonius), *tr.*
Female Glory.
From Prison.
Glove, The.
Going to the Warres [*or* Wars].
Grasshopper, The.
Gratiana Dancing [*or* Dauncing] and Singing.
La Bella Bona Roba.
Lucasta Laughing.
On the Death of Mrs. Elizabeth Filmer.
Ode: Grasshopper, The.
Paradox, A.
Rose, The.
Scrutiny [*or* Scrutinie], The.
Snayl, The.
Song: Scrutiny, The.
Song: To Althea, from Prison.
Song: To Lucasta, Going beyond the Seas.
Song: To Lucasta, Going to the Warres.
Song: "Why should you swear I am forsworn."
Stone Walls Do Not a Prison Make. *Fr.* To Althea from Prison.
Strive Not, Vain Lover, to Be Fine.
That no fair woman will, wonder not why, *tr.*
To Althea from Prison.
To Althea from Prison, *sel.*
To Amarantha, That She Would Dishevel Her Hair.
To Fletcher Reviv'd.
To Lucasta ("I laugh and I sing but cannot tell").

LOVELACE, RICHARD (*continued*)
To Lucasta ("Tell me not, sweet, I am unkind").
To Lucasta, from Prison.
To Lucasta, [on] Going beyond the Seas.
To Lucasta, [on] Going to the Wars.
To Lucasta: Her Reserved Looks.
To Lucasta: The Rose.
To My Truly Valiant, Learned Friend, Who in His Book Resolv'd the Art Gladiatory into the Mathematics.
To the Grasshopper.
To Pentadius, *tr.*
Vintage to the Dungeon, The.
LOVELAND, FRANCES. Why Do You Walk through the Fields with Gloves?
LOVEMAN, ROBERT. April.
April Rain.
Creed and Deed.
Diamond, A.
Georgia.
Hobson and His Men.
March.
Rain Song.
Riches.
Spring.
Sunset, A.
LOVER, SAMUEL. Angel's Whisper, The.
Ask and Have.
Baby Dear.
Barney O'Hea.
Birth of St. Patrick, The.
Fairy Boy, The.
Fairy Tempter, The.
Father Land and Mother Tongue.
Father Molloy.
Handy Andy, *sel.*
How to Ask and Have.
Lanty Leary.
Low-backed Car, The.
Paddy O'Rafther.
Quaker's Meeting, The.
Rory O'More; or, Good Omens.
St. Kevin.
War Ship of Peace, The.
What Will You Do, Love?
Widow Machree. *Fr.* Handy Andy.
LOVETT, ROBERT. Forbidden Drink.
LOW, BENJAMIN ROBBINS CURTIS. Due North.
Locomotive to the Little Boy, The.
To-Day.
White Violets.
LOWATER, NINETTE M. Song of Labor, The.
LOWE, C. M. Hay-Time.
LOWE, JOHN. Mary's Dream.
LOWE, ROBERT, VISCOUNT SHERBROOKE. Song of the Squatter.
LOWELL, AMY. Anticipation.
Apology.
Appuldurcombe Park.
Aquarium, An.
Autumn and Death.
Bombardment, The.
Book of Hours of Sister Clotilde, The.
Chinoiseries: Falling Snow.
Chinoiseries: Hoar-Frost.
Chinoiseries: Reflections.
City of Falling Leaves, The. *Fr.* 1777.
Cornucopia of Red and Green Comfits, The.
Critical Fable, A, *sel.*
Crowned.
Day That Was That Day, The.
Decade, A.
Dinner-Party, The.
Dolphins in Blue Water.
Dracula of the Hills, A.
Dusty Hour-Glass, The.
Evelyn Ray.
Falling Snow.
Flute-Priest Song for Rain, *sel.*
Four Sides to a House.
Fragment: "What is poetry? Is it a mosaic."
Free Fantasia on Japanese Themes.
Frimaire.
Fringed Gentians.
Garden by Moonlight, The.
Gift, A.
Grievance.
Haunted.
Hoar-Frost.
In Excelsis.
Lady, A.
Lamp of Life, The.
Letter, The.
Lilacs.
Little Garden, A.
Little Ivory Figures Pulled with String.
London Thoroughfare Two A.M., A.
Madonna of the Evening Flowers.
Meeting-House Hill.
Merchandise.
Music.
Night Clouds.
Nuit Blanche.
Ombre Chinoise.
On Looking at a Copy of Alice Meynell's Poems, Given Me, Years Ago, by a Friend.
Opera House, An.
Painter on Silk, The.
Paper in the Gate-legged Table, The.
Paper Windmill, The.
Patterns.
Poet, The.
Precinct—Rochester, The.
Prime.
Purple Grackles.
Red Lacquer Music-Stand, The.
Red Slippers.
Reflections.
Rhyme Out of Motley, A.
Rome.
Roxbury Garden, A.
Sea Shell, The.
1777, *sels.*
Shadow, The.
Shooting the Sun.
Sisters, The.
Solitaire.
Taxi, The.
Texas.
Thorn Piece.
To John Keats.
Trades.
Trumpet-Vine Arbour, The. *Fr.* 1777.
Tulip Garden, A.
Vase, The, *tr.*
Venus Transiens.
Vernal Equinox.
Wind and Silver.
Winter Ride, A.
Winter's Turning.
LOWELL, AMY, *and* FLORENCE AYSCOUGH.
After Being Separated for a Long Time, *tr.*
Ai Ai Thinks of the Man She Loves, *tr.*
Blossoms of Lo Yang, The, *tr.*
Blue-green Stream, The, *tr.*
Dancing, *tr.*
Drinking Alone in the Moonlight, *tr.*
Excursion, The, *tr.*
Lonely Wife, The, *tr.*
Mirror, The, *tr.*
Once More Fields and Gardens, *tr.*
Song of Grief, A, *tr.*
Song of the Courtesans, *tr.*
Songs to the Peonies, *tr.*
Spring Grief and Resentment, *tr.*
LOWELL, JACK. Funny and Wise.
LOWELL, JAMES RUSSELL. Abraham Lincoln. *Fr.* Ode Recited at the Harvard Commemoration, July 21, 1865.
After the Burial.
Aladdin.
Ambrose.
America's Gospel.
And what is so rare as a day in June? *Fr.* The Vision of Sir Launfal.
Auf Wiedersehen.
Auspex.
Autograph, An.
Beaver Brook.
Beaver Brook, *sel.*
Bible of the Race, The.
Bibliolatres, *sel.*
Biglow Papers, The, *sels.*
Birch-Tree, The.
Bobolink, The. *Fr.* The Biglow Papers.
Bow Down, Dear Land. *Fr.* Ode Recited at the Harvard Commemoration, July 21, 1865.
Brook in Winter, The. *Fr.* The Vision of Sir Launfal.
Bryant. *Fr.* A Fable for Critics.
Candidate's Creed, The. *Fr.* The Biglow Papers.
Candidate's Letter, The. *Fr.* The Biglow Papers.
Cathedral, The, *sels.*
Chippewa Legend, A.
Christmas Carol, A: "'What means this glory round our feet.'"
Columbus.
Columbus, *sel.*
Commemoration Ode, The.
Commemoration Ode, The, *sel.*
Contrast, A.
Cooper. *Fr.* A Fable for Critics.
Count me o'er earth's chosen heroes. *Fr.* The Present Crisis.
Courtin', The. *Fr.* The Biglow Papers.
Daphne's Embarkation. *Fr.* A Fable for Critics.
Das Ewig-Weibliche.
Day in June, A. *Fr.* The Vision of Sir Launfal.
Debate in the Sennit, The. *Fr.* The Biglow Papers.
December. *Fr.* The Vision of Sir Launfal.
Elegy on the Death of Dr. Channing, *sels.*
Ember Picture, An.
Emerson. *Fr.* A Fable for Critics.
Ez for War. *Fr.* The Biglow Papers.
Fable for Critics, A.
Fable for Critics, A, *sels.*
Fatherland, The.
Finding of the Lyre, The.
First Snowfall, The.
First Snowfall, The, *sel.*
Flawless His Heart. *Fr.* Ode for the Fourth of July, 1876.
For an Autograph.
For an Autograph, *sel.*
Fountain, The.
Fourth of July Ode.
Franciscus de Verulamio Sic Cogitavit.
Freedom ("Are we, then, wholly fallen? Can it be").
Freedom ("Men! whose boast it is that ye"). *Fr.* Stanzas on Freedom.
Freedom ("They are slaves who fear to speak"). *Fr.* Stanzas on Freedom.
Freedom ("We are not free: Freedom doth not consist").
George Washington. *Fr.* Under the Old Elm.
Glance behind the Curtain, A, *sel.*
God Is Not Dumb. *Fr.* Bibliolatres.
Great Virginian, The. *Fr.* Under the Old Elm.
Harvard Commemoration Ode, The.
Hawthorne. *Fr.* A Fable for Critics.
He Gives Nothing. *Fr.* The Vision of Sir Launfal.
Hebe.
Heritage, The.
His Throne Is with the Outcast.
Holmes. *Fr.* A Fable for Critics.
Hosea Biglow's Lament. *Fr.* The Biglow Papers.
I Grieve Not that Ripe Knowledge.
I Would Not Have This Perfect Love of Ours.
Imperial Man. *Fr.* Under the Old Elm.
In a Copy of Omar Khayyám.
In Absence.
In the Twilight.
International Copyright.
Irving. *Fr.* A Fable for Critics.
January. *Fr.* The Vision of Sir Launfal.
Jonathan to John. *Fr.* The Biglow Papers.
Joys.
June. *Fr.* The Vision of Sir Launfal.
Kossuth.
Labor. *Fr.* A Glance behind the Curtain.
Letter from Mr. Ezekiel Biglow of Jaalam to the Hon. Joseph T. Buckingham, A. *Fr.* The Biglow Papers.
Letter from Mr. Hosea Biglow to the

Hon. J. T. Buckingham, A. *Fr.* The Biglow Papers.
Life's Purpose. *Fr.* The Cathedral.
Lincoln ("Nature, they say, doth dote"). *Fr.* Ode Recited at the Harvard Commemoration, July 21, 1865.
Lincoln ("Such was he, our Martyr-Chief"). *Fr.* Ode Recited at the Harvard Commemoration, July 21, 1865.
Love, *sel.*
Lowell. *Fr.* A Fable for Critics.
Maple, The.
Margaret Fuller. *Fr.* A Fable for Critics.
Martyr Chief, The. *Fr.* Ode Recited at the Harvard Commemoration, July 21, 1865.
May and June. *Fr.* Under the Willows.
Mr. Hosea Biglow Speaks. *Fr.* The Biglow Papers.
Mr. Hosea Biglow to the Editor of the Atlantic Monthly. *Fr.* The Biglow Papers.
Monna Lisa.
My Country. *Fr.* Ode Recited at the Harvard Commemoration, July 21, 1865.
My Love.
My Love, I Have No Fear That Thou Shouldst Die.
Mystical Ballad, A, *sel.*
New Year's Eve, 1850.
New-come Chief, The. *Fr.* Under the Old Elm.
Nightingale in the Study, The.
Not Only around Our Infancy. *Fr.* The Vision of Sir Launfal.
Not What We Give. *Fr.* The Vision of Sir Launfal.
Now Is the High-Tide of the Year. *Fr.* The Vision of Sir Launfal.
O Mother State. *Fr.* To John Gorham Palfrey.
Oak, The.
Ode for the Fourth of July, 1876, An.
Ode Recited at the Harvard Commemoration, July 21, 1865.
Ode Recited at the Harvard Commemoration, July 21, 1865, *sels.*
On a Bust of General Grant.
On Himself. *Fr.* A Fable for Critics.
On the Death of a Friend's Child, *sel.*
Once to Every Man and Nation. *Fr.* The Present Crisis.
Oriental Apologue, An.
Origin of Didactic Poetry, The.
Our Country Saved. *Fr.* Ode Recited at the Harvard Commemoration, July 21, 1865.
Our Love Is Not a Fading, Earthly Flower.
Our Martyr-Chief. *Fr.* Ode Recited at the Harvard Commemoration, July 21, 1865.
Ours, and All Men's. *Fr.* Under the Old Elm.
Over His Keys. *Fr.* The Vision of Sir Launfal.
Palinode.
Parable, A.
Petition, The.
Pious Editor's Creed, The. *Fr.* The Biglow Papers.
Poe and Longfellow. *Fr.* A Fable for Critics.
Prelude to Part First. *Fr.* The Vision of Sir Launfal.
Prelude to Part Second. *Fr.* The Vision of Sir Launfal.
Prepared for a Soldiers' and Sailors' Monument in Boston.
Present Crisis, The.
Present Crisis, The, *sel.*
Protest, The.
Rhoecus.
St. Michael the Weigher.
Search, The.
Secret, The.
She Came and Went.
Shepherd of King Admetus, The.
Si Descendero in Infernum, Ades.
Singing Leaves, The.
Sir Launfal and the Leper. *Fr.* The Vision of Sir Launfal.
Sixty-eighth Birthday.
Slaves. *Fr.* Stanzas on Freedom.
Sonnet: "For this true nobleness I seek in vain."
Sonnet: "I cannot think that thou shouldst pass away."
Sonnet: "I thought our love at full, but I did err."
Sonnet: "I would not have this perfect love of ours."
Sonnet: "My Love, I have no fear that thou shouldst die."
Sonnet: "Our love is not a fading, earthly flower."
Sovereign Emblem, The. *Fr.* The Cathedral.
Spring ("O little city-gals, don't never go it"). *Fr.* The Biglow Papers.
Stanzas on Freedom.
Stanzas on Freedom, *sels.*
Stealing.
Street, The.
Sub Pondere Crescit.
Summer Storm.
Sunthin' in the Pastoral Line. *Fr.* The Biglow Papers.
Thing We Long For, The. *Fr.* Longing.
'Tis Sorrow Builds the Shining Ladder Up.
To a Recruiting Sergeant. *Fr.* The Biglow Papers.
To Freedom.
To H. W. L.
To Henry Wadsworth Longfellow.
To His Countrymen. *Fr.* A Fable for Critics.
To John G. Whittier.
To John Gorham Palfrey, *sel.*
To the Dandelion.
To the Dandelion, *sel.*
To the Memory of Hood.
To the Spirit of Keats.
To those who died for her on land and sea.
To Whittier.
True Love.
Truth and Love Abide. *Fr.* Elegy on the Death of Dr. Channing.
Under the Old Elm, *sels.*
Under the Willows, *sels.*
Unwasted Days. *Fr.* Under the Old Elm.
Vision of Sir Launfal, The.
Vision of Sir Launfal, The, *sels.*
War. *Fr.* The Biglow Papers.
Washers of the Shroud, The.
Washington. *Fr.* Under the Old Elm.
Washington under the Old Elm. *Fr.* Under the Old Elm.
We Will Speak Out.
Wendell Phillips.
What Is So Rare as a Day in June. *Fr.* The Vision of Sir Launfal.
What Mr. Robinson Thinks. *Fr.* The Biglow Papers.
What Rabbi Jehosha Said.
When a deed is done for Freedom. *Fr.* The Present Crisis.
Whittier. *Fr.* A Fable for Critics.
Who Now Shall Sneer?
Whom We Revere. *Fr.* Under the Old Elm.
William Lloyd Garrison.
Winter Evening Hymn to My Fire, A.
Winter Morning, A. *Fr.* The Vision of Sir Launfal.
Winter Pictures. *Fr.* The Vision of Sir Launfal.
Without and Within.
Witness of God. *Fr.* The Cathedral.
Work.
Yussouf.
LOWELL, MARIA WHITE (Mrs. James Russell Lowell). Morning-Glory, The.
Opium Fantasy, An.
Song: "O bird, thou dartest to the sun."
LOWELL, ROBERT TRAILL SPENCE (1816–91). After-Comers, The.
Brave Old Ship, the *Orient*, The.
Relief of Lucknow, The.
LOWELL, ROBERT (Traill Spence), JR. (1917–). After the Surprising Conversions.
As a Plane Tree by the Water.
Between the Porch and the Altar.
Bomber, The.
Charles the Fifth and the Peasant.
Children of Light.
Christ Is Here.
Christmas Eve under Hooker's Statue.
Colloquy in Black Rock.
Dead in Europe, The.
Death from Cancer.
Death of the Sheriff, The.
Drunken Fisherman, The.
Exile's Return, The.
Falling Asleep over the Aeneid.
Ghost, The.
Her Dead Brother.
Holy Innocents, The.
In Memory of Arthur Winslow.
Mary Winslow.
Mr. Edwards and the Spider.
Mother Marie Therese.
New Year's Day.
Noli Me Tangere.
North Sea Undertaker's Complaint, The.
On the Eve of the Feast of the Immaculate Conception, 1942.
Orpheus, Eurydice, and Hermes, *ad.*
Our Lady of Walsingham. *Fr.* The Quaker Graveyard in Nantucket.
Quaker Graveyard in Nantucket, The.
Quaker Graveyard in Nantucket, The, *sel.*
Salem.
Shako, The.
Where the Rainbow Ends.
LOWREY, BOOTH. Miss Hen.
Ole Billy William.
Prodjeckin' Son, De.
LOWRY, HENRY DAWSON. Holiday.
LOWRY, MALCOLM. Cain Shall Not Slay Abel Today on Our Good Ground.
He Plays the Piano with a Razor.
In Memoriam; Ingvald Bjorndal and His Comrade.
King Lear Blinded Oedipus in a Dream.
Lupus in Fabula.
Salmon Drowns Eagle.
World of Ghosts Moves Closer Every Hour, The.
LOY, MINA. Human Cylinders.
Love Songs.
LO YIN. I Am Content with Life and at Peace with the World.
LOYOLA, MOTHER. Rabboni! Master!
LOYOLA, SAINT IGNATIUS. *See* IGNATIUS LOYOLA, SAINT.
LUBBOCK, PHYLLIS M. I picked a primrose, pale as death.
LUBKE, BERNICE W. All-sufficient Christ, The.
LUCAN (Marcus Annaeus Lucanus). Cato's Address to His Troops in Lybia. *Fr.* Pharsalia.
Civil War, The, *sels.*
Coracle, The.
Pharsalia, *sels.*
Pompey and Cornelia. *Fr.* Pharsalia.
Portents, The. *Fr.* Pharsalia.
Stoic's Wedding, The. *Fr.* Pharsalia.
LUCAS, ALICE. Prayer before Sleep.
For translations from Hebrew, see TrJP.
LUCAS, DANIEL BEDINGER. In the Land Where We Were Dreaming.
Land Where We Were Dreaming, The.
LUCAS, EDWARD VERRALL. Carpenter.
Cat's Conscience, The. *Fr.* The Nature of the Cat.
Chocolate Cream. *Fr.* Counsel to Those That Eat.
Clay.
Conjuror, The.
Counsel to Those That Eat, *sels.*
Friends.
In Brittany.
In Normandy.
Mr. Coggs.

LUCAS, EDWARD VERRALL (*continued*)
Nature of the Cat, The, *sel.*
O England, Country of My Heart's Desire.
Pedestrian's Plaint, The.
Potatoes. *Fr.* Counsel to Those That Eat.
Stamp Battalion.
Story Books.
Windmill, The.
LUCAS, FRANK LAURENCE. Beleaguered Cities.
Dictator's Holiday.
In Memoriam.
Modernity.
Pipe of Peace, The.
Spain, 1809.
Spring-Song, 1939.
For translations from Greek, see GrL; GrPE; OxBG; *from Latin, see* LaP.
LUCAS, ST. JOHN. Curate Thinks You Have No Soul, The.
Pain.
LUCCHI, LORNA DE'. A sè stesso, *tr.*
Infinito, L', *tr.*
Infinity, *tr.*
Ox, The, *tr.*
Relations, *tr.*
Sonnet: "As I approach the last of all my days," *tr.*
To Dante, *tr.*
What Art Thou, Death? *tr.*
With Dreams of Wealth and Fame, *tr.*
Your Excellency, *tr.*
Youth Is Sweet and Well, *tr.*
LUCE, MORTON. Bow down, my song, before her presence high. *Fr.* Thysia.
Comes the New Year; wailing the north winds blow. *Fr.* Thysia.
Hear, O Self-Giver, infinite as good. *Fr.* Thysia.
How shall I tell the measure of my love? *Fr.* Thysia.
I watch beside you in your silent room. *Fr.* Thysia.
Like some lone miser, dear, behold me stand. *Fr.* Thysia.
So sang I in the springtime of my years. *Fr.* Thysia.
Thysia, *sels.*
Twin songs there are, of joyance, or of pain. *Fr.* Thysia.
LUCIAN (Lucianus). Artificial Beauty.
Committing wrong the chance may be that you elude men's eyes.
Dead Child, A.
Enjoy your goods as if your death were near.
Frowning fates have taken hence, The.
Golden Mean, The.
On a Child.
Passing Away.
Philosopher called Stesichore, A.
Rule of Life, A.
Things owned by mortals needs must mortal be.
Time as Variable.
LUCILLIUS [*or* LUCILIUS]. Atoms are small things, The.
Better to Be Brave.
Champion's Statue, The.
Dead Song-Writer, A.
Eutychides.
Gaius was so very thin.
Little Hermogenes is so small.
Look at Marcus and take warning.
Market Place, The.
Miser, traversing his house, A.
Miser's Entertainment, The.
Nicylla dyes her locks, 'tis said.
On an Old Woman.
Portraitist, The.
They call thee rich; I deem thee poor.
Treasure.
Valentine for a Lady, A.
"LUCIO." Lidice.
LUCIUS APULEIUS. *See* APULEIUS, LUCIUS.
LUCRETIUS (Titus Lucretius Carus). Address to Venus, *tr. by* Spenser. *Fr.* De Rerum Natura.
Against the Fear of Death, *sels., tr. by* Dryden. *Fr.* De Rerum Natura.
Beginnings of Civilization, *tr. by* Leonard. *Fr.* Of the Nature of Things.
Beyond Religion, *sel., tr. by* Leonard. *Fr.* Of the Nature of Things.
Creation of the Infinite Universe, The; How It Is Maintained, *tr. by* Macauley. *Fr.* De Rerum Natura.
De Rerum Natura, *sels.*
Death, *tr. by* Dryden. *Fr.* De Rerum Natura.
Earth, The, *tr. by* Rouse. *Fr.* De Rerum Natura.
Evolution of Life and Society, *tr. by* Rouse. *Fr.* De Rerum Natura.
Fear of Death, The, *tr. by* Dryden. *Fr.* De Rerum Natura.
Fear of Death, *tr. by* Rouse. *Fr.* De Rerum Natura.
From the Shore of Life, *tr. by* Johnson. *Fr.* De Rerum Natura.
Guileful Ocean, The, *tr. by* Salt. *Fr.* De Rerum Natura.
Introduction; Combinations of Atoms; Creation and Destruction of Worlds, *tr. by* Rouse. *Fr.* De Rerum Natura.
Invocation; the Bondage of Religion, *tr. by* Rouse. *Fr.* De Rerum Natura.
Life of Primitive Man, The, *tr. by* McLeod. *Fr.* De Rerum Natura.
No Single Thing Abides, *tr. by* Mallock. *Fr.* De Rerum Natura.
Of Human Progress, *tr. by* Leonard. *Fr.* Of the Nature of Things.
Of the Nature of Things (De Rerum Natura), *sels.*
On Human Ambitions, *tr. by* Lindsay. *Fr.* De Rerum Natura.
Origins and Savage Period of Mankind, *tr. by* Leonard. *Fr.* Of the Nature of Things.
Origins of Life, The, *tr. by* Leonard. *Fr.* Of the Nature of Things.
Origins of Vegetable and Animal Life, *tr. by* Leonard. *Fr.* Of the Nature of Things.
Sickness Which Is Love, The, *tr. by* Highet. *Fr.* De Rerum Natura.
Suave Mari Magno, *tr. by* Mallock. *Fr.* De Rerum Natura.
Unpathed Haunts, *tr. by* Leonard. *Fr.* Of the Nature of Things.
When We Are No More, *tr. by* Leonard. *Fr.* Of the Nature of Things.
LUDERS, CHARLES HENRY. Corsage Bouquet, A.
Four Winds, The.
Haunts of the Halcyon, The.
Heart of Oak.
Mountebanks, The.
My Maiden Aunt.
Old Thought, An.
LUDLOW, FITZ HUGH [*or* FITZHUGH]. Socrates Snooks.
Too Late.
LUDLOW, WILMA C. Imitation of Christ.
LUDLUM, WILLIAM. Business Man's Prayer, A.
Let Us Come before His Presence.
Stairway to the Stars, The.
Thanksgiving.
That Radio Religion.
LUGOVSKOI, VLADIMIR. Bear, The.
Star.
LUHRS, MARIE. Aria in Austria.
LUI CHI. Poet Thinks, A.
LUKE, JEMIMA THOMPSON. Child's Desire, The.
I Think When I Read That Sweet Story of Old.
LUKONIN, MIKHAIL. Morning.
My Friends.
New Day.
LULHAM, HABBERTON. Meeting and a Memory, A.
Nested.
Old Doctor, The.
LULL, RAMON. Lover and the Beloved, The.
Tree of Love, The.
LU LUN. Autumn Leaves.
Dark Night, the Wild Geese Fly High.
On Meeting a Sick Soldier.
On Seeing Ch'ang-an in Spring.
LUMMIS, CHARLES FLETCHER. Cowboy's Valentine, The.
John Charles Frémont.
Lost Child.
Mastery.
Poe-'em of Passion, A.
LUNACHARSKY, ANATOLI VASILYEVICH. Faust and the City, *sel.*
Song of the Old Man in Chains. *Fr.* Faust and the City.
LUND, CHRISTIE. Prayer for a Bride's House.
LUNDBERGH, HOLGER. Interlude.
LUNT, GEORGE. Requiem.
Requiem for One Slain in Battle.
LURIA, ISAAC. Sabbath of Rest, A.
LUSHINGTON, FRANKLIN. No More Words.
LUTHER, MARTIN. All Hail, Thou Noble Guest.
Ane Sang of the Birth of Christ, with the Tune of Baw Lula Low.
Away in a Manger.
Christmas Carol for Children, A.
Cradle Hymn.
Easter.
Hymn: "Mighty fortress is our God."
Martin Luther to His Son, Hans.
Martyrs' Hymn, The.
Mighty Fortress Is Our God, A.
Mother's Evening Hymn, A.
LUTTRELL, HENRY. Advice to Julia, *sels.*
After the Wedding. *Fr.* Advice to Julia.
Dress. *Fr.* Advice to Julia.
Honeymoon, The. *Fr.* Advice to Julia.
Lovers and Friends. *Fr.* Advice to Julia.
Peace, The. *Fr.* Advice to Julia.
LUTZ, GERTRUDE MAY. Prisoner of War.
LU YING SU. Rain at Night.
LU YU. August.
Autobiography.
Autumn ("Like a fairy spirit I leave the gate of the city").
Autumn ("The village wine is sweet and sour").
Autumn Thoughts.
Boating in Autumn.
Clouds, The.
Cries of Birds, The.
Death.
Drinking at the Village.
Dying Spring.
Evening in the Village.
Evening Wind, The.
Flower-Seller, The.
Gazing after Her Husband.
Guest Goes on His Way, The.
Herd Boy, The.
How I Sailed on the Lake till I Came to the Eastern Stream.
I Get Up at Dawn.
I Walk Out into the Country at Night.
Idleness.
Leaving the Monastery Early in the Morning.
Moon over the Pass, The.
Night Rain, The.
Night Thoughts.
Old Age ("Irrigate the high wasteland and the slopes for plowing").
Old Age ("Unbearable is the sickness that invades old age").
Old Apothecary, The.
On Hearing the Flute.
Pedlar of Spells, The.
Phoenix Hairpins.
Prune Flowers.
Prune Trees.
Rain on the River.
Returning at Night.
Roadside Song, A.
Sailing on the Lake to the Ching River.
Strolling under the Moon.
To His Sons.
Wild Flower Man, The.
Wind and the Rain, The.
Yellow River, The.

LU YÜN. Valley Wind, The.
LUZI, MARIO. Excerpts from a "Gothic Notebook." *Fr.* Gothic Notebook.
Gothic Notebook, *sel.*
LUZZATTO, ISAAC. Death, Thou Hast Seized Me.
LUZZATTO, JACK. Solution.
LUZZATTO, MOSES HAYYIM, OF PADUA.
Chorus: "All ye that handle harp and viol and pipe." *Fr.* Unto the Upright Praise.
Unto the Upright Praise, *sel.*
LVOV, NIKOLAY. I Trod upon the Age's Heels.
LYALL, SIR ALFRED COMYN. Badminton. *Fr.* Studies at Delhi.
Hindu Ascetic, The. *Fr.* Studies at Delhi.
Meditations of a Hindu Prince.
Studies at Delhi.
Theology in Extremis.
LYALL, SIR CHARLES JAMES. After the Plague, *tr.*
Bragging Song, *tr.*
Hamasah, *sels., tr.*
He Thinks of His Children, *tr. Fr.* Hamasah.
His Children, *tr. Fr.* Hamasah.
Nusaib, *tr.*
Storm, The, *tr.*
LYCOPHRON. Alexandra, *sels.*
LYDGATE, JOHN. Against Women's Fashions.
Ballad Warning Men to Beware of Deceitful Women, A, *sel.*
Child Jesus to Mary the Rose, The.
Court of Sapience, *sel.*
Dance, The. *Fr.* The Dance of Death.
Dance of Death, The, *sel.*
Fall of Princes, The, *sels.*
Henry before Agincourt: October 25, 1415.
Lament: "Farewell Mercy, farewell thy piteous grace." *Fr.* Court of Sapience.
Lat Noman Booste of Konnyng nor Vertu. *Fr.* The Fall of Princes.
Like a Midsummer Rose. *Fr.* The Fall of Princes.
London Lickpenny [*or* Lackpenny], *at.*
Lover's New Year's Gift, A.
Story of Thebes, The, *sel.*
To the Virgin.
Vox Ultima Crucis.
LYDSTON, DONNA R. Family, The.
LYLE, ROB. Fireworks at the Redentore.
LYLE, THOMAS. Kelvin Grove.
LYLY, JOHN. Alexander and Campaspe, *sels.*
Apelles' Song. *Fr.* Alexander and Campaspe.
Apollo's Song. *Fr.* Midas.
Cards and Kisses. *Fr.* Alexander and Campaspe.
Cupid and Campaspe. *Fr.* Alexander and Campaspe.
Cupid and My Campaspe [Played]. *Fr.* Alexander and Campaspe.
Cupid's Indictment. *Fr.* Galathea.
Daphne. *Fr.* Midas.
Endymion, *sels.*
Fairy Frolic, The.
Fairy Revels. *Fr.* Endymion.
Fairy Song, A. *Fr.* Endymion.
Fools in Love's College. *Fr.* Mother Bombie.
Galathea [*or* Gallathea], *sel.*
Love's Schooling. *Fr.* Mother Bombie.
Midas, *sels.*
Mother Bombie, *sels.*
My Daphne's hair is twisted gold. *Fr.* Midas.
My shag-hair Cyclops, come, let's ply. *Fr.* Sapho and Phao.
Mydas, *sels.*
O Cupid! monarch over kings. *Fr.* Mother Bombie.
Pan's Song. *Fr.* Midas.
Pan's Syrinx Was a Girl. *Fr.* Midas.
Sapho and Phao, *sels.*
Sapho's Song. *Fr.* Sapho and Phao.
Serving Men's Song, A. *Fr.* Alexander and Campaspe.
Sing to Apollo, god of day. *Fr.* Midas.
Song: "It is all one in Venus' wanton school."
Song by Apelles. *Fr.* Alexander and Campaspe.
Song by Fairies. *Fr.* Endymion.
Song in Making of the Arrows, The. *Fr.* Sapho and Phao.
Song of Accius and Silena. *Fr.* Mother Bombie.
Song of Apelles. *Fr.* Alexander and Campaspe.
Song of Daphne to the Lute, A. *Fr.* Midas.
Song of Diana's Nymphs, A. *Fr.* Galathea.
Song to Apollo. *Fr.* Midas.
Spring, The. *Fr.* Alexander and Campaspe.
Spring's Welcome. *Fr.* Alexander and Campaspe.
Syrinx. *Fr.* Midas.
To Welcome in the Spring. *Fr.* Alexander and Campaspe.
Trico's Song. *Fr.* Alexander and Campaspe.
Urchins' Dance, The.
Vulcan's Song. *Fr.* Sapho and Phao.
What Bird So Sings. *Fr.* Alexander and Campaspe.
LYNCH, ANNE CHARLOTTE. *See* BOTTA, ANNE CHARLOTTE LYNCH.
LYNCH, JOHN W. Crucifixion, The.
Woman Wrapped in Silence, A, *sel.*
LYNCH, STANISLAUS. Blue Peter.
LYNCH, THOMAS TOKE. Holy Spirit, Dwell with Me.
Lift Up Your Heads, Rejoice!
Reinforcements.
Thousand Years Have Come, A.
Where Is Thy God, My Soul?
LYNCHE, RICHARD. Diella, *sels.*
End this enchantment, love, of my desires. *Fr.* Diella.
Love's Despair. *Fr.* Diella.
Soon as the azure-colored gates of th' east. *Fr.* Diella.
Weary with serving where I nought could get. *Fr.* Diella.
What sugared terms, what all-persuading art. *Fr.* Diella.
LYND, SYLVIA. Cowper at Olney.
Happy Hour, The.
To Sheila Playing Haydn.
LYNDSAY, SIR DAVID. *See* LINDSAY, SIR DAVID.
LYNN, ETHEL. *See* BEERS, ETHEL LYNN.
LYON, CARRIE WARD. Flowers in a Library.
Hallow Even.
Halloween.
Little Folk.
Wonder Books.
LYON, LILIAN BOWES. *See* BOWES-LYON, LILIAN.
LYON, P. H. B. Envoi: "Earth puts her colours by."
LYON, ROGER H. Keep on Praying.
LYONS, A. NEIL. Fairy Cobbler, The.
LYSAGHT, EDWARD. Garnyvillo.
Kitty of Coleraine, *at.*
LYSAGHT, SIDNEY ROYSE. Beyond the Farthest Horizon.
Deserted Home, A.
First Pathways.
Home. *Fr.* Old Landmarks.
New Horizons.
Old Landmarks, *sel.*
Secret of the Deeps, The.
Test of Faith, The.
LYSTER, MRS. HENRY F. Michigan, My Michigan!
LYTE, HENRY FRANCIS. Abide with Me.
Agnes.
Forgiveness.
Lo, We Have Left All.
Lost Love, A.
Secret Place, The.
Unknown God, The.
LYTE, HENRY FRANCIS, *and* JOHN QUARLES. *See* QUARLES, JOHN, *and* HENRY FRANCIS LYTE.
LYTLE, JAMES T. Rangers' Song, The.
LYTLE, WILLIAM HAINES. Antony to [*or* and] Cleopatra.
In Camp.
Siege of Chapultepec, The.
Volunteers, The.
LYTTELTON, GEORGE, BARON LYTTELTON.
Epistle to Mr. Pope, An.
Ode, in Imitation of Pastor Fido.
Song: "When Delia on the plain appears."
Tell Me, My Heart, if This Be Love.
To the Memory of a Lady.
Written at Mr. Pope's House at Twickenham.
LYTTELTON, LUCY. Quod Semper.
Simon the Cyrenean.
LYTTON, EDWARD GEORGE BULWER-LYTTON, 1ST BARON. *See* BULWER-LYTTON, EDWARD, BARON LYTTON.
LYTTON, EDWARD ROBERT BULWER-LYTTON, 1ST EARL OF. *See* "MEREDITH, OWEN."

M

"M., A. E." Night-driving.
"M., F." Another, of Another Mind.
"M., H. J." Rivers of France, The.
"M., P. S." Dawn.
"M., R." Thyroid Gland, The.
"M., S. M." Surrender.
"M., S. W. D." Lalage.
"M., T. M." My Alma Mater.
"M. E. W." *See* "W., M. E."
"M. J." *See* "J., M."
"M. K. B." *See* "B., M. K."
"M. K. H." *See* "H., M. K."
"M. P. D." *See* "D., M. P."
"M. R." *See* "R., M."
"M. W. S." *See* "S., M. W."
MAAS, WILLARD. Kind Look, The.
Letter to R.
No Season for Our Season.
On Reading Gene Derwood's "The Innocent."
MABBE, JAMES. Celestina, *sels., tr.*
Now Sleep, and Take Thy Rest, *tr. Fr.* Celestina.
You birds whose warblings prove, *tr. Fr.* Celestina.
MABUCHI. Tempest, The.
View of the Sea, A.
MACALEESE, D. Memory, A.
MCALLISTER, CLAIRE. Aeneid.
July in the Jardin des Plantes.
MACALPINE, JAMES. To an Irish Blackbird.
MAC AN BHAIRD, LAOISEACH. Civil Irish and Wild Irish.
Man of Experience, A.
MACANDREW, RACHEL. Pony, The.
Robin Hood.
MACARTHUR, ELINOR. Sanctuary.
Sea-Birds.
Winter Birds.
MACARTHUR, GLORIA. Phineas Pratt.
MCARTHUR, PETER. Corn-planting.
Earthborn.
End of the Drought, The.
Indian Wind Song, An.
Stone, The.
Sugar Weather.
To the Birds.
MACARTNEY, FRANCES. *See* GREVILLE, FANNY.
MACARTNEY, FREDERICK THOMAS BENNETT. Bargain Basement.
You'll Know Love.
MACAULAY, ROSE. Baffled.
Devourers, The.
Many Sisters to Many Brothers.
MACAULAY, THOMAS BABINGTON MACAULAY, 1ST BARON. Armada, The.
Battle, The. *Fr.* Lays of Ancient Rome.
Battle of Ivry, The.
Battle of Lake Regillus, The, *sels. Fr.* Lays of Ancient Rome.

MACAULAY, THOMAS BABINGTON (*cont.*)
Battle of Naseby, The.
Battle of Naseby, The, *sel.*
Country Clergyman's Trip to Cambridge, The.
Death of Herminius, The. *Fr.* The Battle of Lake Regillus.
England's Standard. *Fr.* The Armada.
Epitaph on a Jacobite.
Fight at the Bridge, The. *Fr.* Lays of Ancient Rome.
Fight in the Centre, The. *Fr.* The Battle of Lake Regillus.
Horatius [at the Bridge]. *Fr.* Lays of Ancient Rome.
Horatius [at the Bridge], *sels.* *Fr.* Lays of Ancient Rome.
Ivry.
Jacobite's Epitaph, A.
Last Buccaneer, The.
Lays of Ancient Rome, *sels.*
Milton, *sels.*
Naseby.
Prophecy of Capys, The.
Roman Father's Sacrifice, The. *Fr.* Lays of Ancient Rome.
Sermon in a Churchyard.
Song: "O stay, Madonna! stay."
Spanish Armada, The.
War-Horse, The. *Fr.* Lays of Ancient Rome.
MCAULEY, JAMES PHILLIP. Autumn, *tr.*
Blue Horses, The.
Celebration of Love.
Death of Chiron, The.
Incarnation of Sirius, The.
Late Winter.
Missa Papae Marcelli.
New Guinea Lament.
She like the Moon Arises.
Sleep.
MACBEAN, LACHLAN. Hushaby, Darling.
MACBETH, GEORGE. Thoughts on Choosing.
MCBURNEY, WILLIAM B. ("Carroll Malone"). Croppy Boy, The.
Good Ship *Castle Down*, The.
MCCABE, JAMES H. On the Reported New Outbreak of Christianity.
MCCABE, WILLIAM GORDON. Christmas Night of '62.
Dreaming in the Trenches.
John Pegram.
MACCAIG, NORMAN. Birds All Singing.
Double Life.
Two Musics.
Tyrant Apple Is Eaten, The.
You within Love.
MCCALL, JAMES EDWARD. New Negro, The.
MCCALL, PATRICK JOSEPH. Herself and Myself.
Old Pedhar Carthy from Clonmore.
"MCCALL, SIDNEY." *See* FENOLLOSA, MARY.
MACCALLUM, JOHN BRUCE. Death.
Egotist.
Epitaph: "Spirit of death, so soft, so sweet."
Sleep.
MCCANN, MICHAEL JOSEPH. O'Donnell Aboo.
MCCANN, REBECCA. Fences.
Horizons.
Humane Thought.
MCCARCY, MYRTLE ALICE. Hour of Autumn.
MCCARN, CORNEILLE. Queer Habits.
MCCARROLL, JAMES. Grey Linnet, The.
Irish Wolf, The.
MCCARTHY, DENIS ALOYSIUS. Ah, Sweet Is Tipperary.
Banner of America.
Childher, The.
Christmas Legends.
Fields o' Ballyclare, The.
Green o' the Spring, The.
In the Nuns' Garden.
Land Where Hate Should Die, The.
Poor Man's Daily Bread, The.
Rosa Mystica.
St. Brigid.
Song for the Flag, A.
Sthreets of Home.
Tailor That Came from Mayo, The.
Thought about Saint Francis, A.
Veterans, The.
MACCARTHY, DENIS FLORENCE. Bell-Founder, The, *sel.*
Bless the Dear Old Verdant Land.
"Cease to Do Evil—Learn to Do Well."
Dead Tribune, The.
Foray of Con O'Donnell, The, *sels.*
Ireland.
Irish Wolf-Hound, The. *Fr.* The Foray of Con O'Donnell.
Labor Song. *Fr.* The Bell-Founder.
Lament: "Youth's bright palace."
Love and Time.
Spring Flowers from Ireland.
Summer Longings.
MACCARTHY, DONAL, FIRST EARL CLANCARTY. Body's Speech, The.
MACCARTHY, ETHNA. Ghosts.
Insomnia.
Shrine, The.
Viaticum.
MCCARTHY, FRANK C. Frenchie.
MCCARTHY, HARRY. Bonnie Blue Flag, The.
MCCARTHY, JOHN RUSSELL. I Have Cursed Winter.
Now I Who Saw.
Snake.
So High.
M'CARTHY, JUSTIN HUNTLY. Ballad of Dead Ladies, A. *Fr.* If I Were King.
I Wonder in What Isle of Bliss. *Fr.* If I Were King.
If I Were King, *sels.*
To Omar Khayyám.
MCCARTHY, LEONARD. Breviary on the Subway.
Holy Thursday.
MCCARTNEY, MABEL E. Refuge.
"MACCATHMHAOIL, SEOSAMH." *See* CAMPBELL, JOSEPH.
MCCAULIFF, GEORGE A. Quiet Place, The.
MACCAWELL, HUGH. Christmas Night.
MCCLELLAN, GEORGE MARION. Butterfly in Church, A.
Dogwood Blossoms.
Feet of Judas, The.
Hills of Sewanee, The.
MCCLELLAN, ISAAC. *See* MCLELLAN, ISAAC, JR.
MCCLINTOCK, CHARLES W. Everybody Works but Father.
MCCLURE, JOHN. Apology.
As I Lay Dreaming Abed.
Carol: "Month can never forget the year, The."
Carol Naïve.
Chanson Naïve.
Finis.
Man to Man.
Song: "Oh, you hear sweet music."
To a Lady.
When You Are Old.
MCCLURE, MICHAEL. Breech, The.
Canticle.
Flowers of Politics, The, I.
Flowers of Politics, The, II.
For Artaud.
Hymn to St. Geryon, *sel.*
Ode for Soft Voice.
Peyote Poem, *sel.*
Rug, The.
MCCLUSKY, KATE WISNER. Lullaby, A: "Suppose I put my babe to sleep."
MACCOLL, DUGALD SUTHERLAND. Ballade of Andrew Lang.
Cats, *tr.*
Connoisseurs.
MACCOLMAIN, RUMANN. Song of the Sea, *at.*
MACCONGLINNE. Vision That Appeared to Me, A.
Wheatlet Son of Milklet.
MAC-CON-MARA [*or* MACNAMARA], DONOGH. Fair Hills of Eire, O, The!
MACCONMIDHE, GIOLLABHRIGHDE. Childless.
MCCORD, DAVID. Ascot Waistcoat.
At the Garden Gate.
Axolotl, The.
Baccalaureate, *parody.*
Backstair Ballad.
Big Chief Wotapotami.
Bucket of Bees, A.
Convalescence.
Cow has a cud, The.
Crows.
Dog in a Car.
Double Star, A.
Euterpe; a Symmetric. *Fr.* New Chitons for Old Gods.
Every Time I Climb a Tree.
Fisherman, The.
Fred.
Frost Pane, The.
Go Fly a Saucer.
Go Fly a Saucer, *sel.*
Grasshopper, The.
Hex on the Mexican X, A.
History of Education.
In Grato Jubilo.
Isabel Jones & Curabel Lee.
Joe.
Lacquer Liquor Locker, The.
Lessons in Limericks.
Mr. Macklin's Jack o'Lantern.
Monday morning back to school.
New Chitons for old Gods, *sel.*
Newt, The.
Of Red in Spring.
On a Waiter.
Our Mr. Toad.
Out of November: Speaking for One.
Perambulator Poems.
Pickety fence, The.
Progress.
Rainbow, The.
Reflection in Blue.
Reservation.
Song of the Train.
Spider, The.
Stropshire Lad, A.
Thin ice/ Free advice.
This Is My Rock.
Tiggady Rue.
To a Child.
Waltzing Mice.
Watching the Moon.
Weather Words.
When I Was Christened.
Where Is My Butterfly Net?
MCCORMICK, VIRGINIA TAYLOR. Daedalus Sings in the Dusk; Before the Skyline of New York.
Doubting.
Flower of Quince.
Hepzibah of the Cent Shop.
To a Thorn Tree Blooming on a City Street.
To One Who Died in Autumn.
Twilight.
Yorktown Road, The.
MCCORMICK, WASHINGTON JAY. In Montana.
Rigger, The.
MCCOURT, EDNA WAHLERT. I Have Wandered to a Spring.
MCCOY, C. LINDSAY. Caroline Cricket.
Devil's Darning Needle.
Honey Bee.
Hornets.
Katy-did.
Lady Bug.
Snail.
Whirligig Beetle.
MCCOY, SAMUEL. Thompson Street.
MCCRACKEN, HATTIE B. I Would Be Great.
MCCRAE, DOROTHY FRANCES. Homesick.
September.
Treasure, The.
M'CRAE, GEORGE GORDON. Forby Sutherland.
MCCRAE, HUGH. Ambuscade.
Australian Spring.
Bridal Song, A.
Colombine.
End of Desire, The.
Enigma.
Fantasy.
Fragment: "As if stone Caesar shook."
June Morning.
Mimshi Maiden, The.

Morning.
Never Again.
Song of the Rain.
Song of the Witless Boy.
McCRAE, JOHN. Anxious Dead, The.
Dying of Père Pierre, The.
Harvest of the Sea, The.
In Flanders Fields.
Night Cometh, The.
Pilgrims, The.
Song of the Derelict, The.
McCREA, LILIAN. Boots and Shoes.
Getting Up.
My Toys.
Noises in the Night.
Pussy-Cat and Puppy-Dog.
Rain.
Wash-Day.
McCREARY, FREDERICK R. Before Winter.
Fog, The.
Gray.
Since Christmas.
McCREERY, JOHN LUCKEY. There Is No Death.
There Is No Death, *sel.*
McCRUM, JEAN. Sometime.
McCUAIG, RONALD. Betty by the Sea.
Chanty: "When rain falls, I say."
Daily Round, The.
Is Love Not Everlasting?
Love Me and Never Leave Me.
Mokie's Madrigal.
Passionate Clerk to His Love, The.
McCULLOCH, MARGARET. Aftermath.
McCOLLOUGH, ANNIE WILLIS. Extra Prayer, The.
McCULLOUGH, MARY E. Presence.
Thought for Easter.
McCULLY, LAURA E. Ballad of the Lakes, A.
Canoe Song at Twilight.
Our Little Sister.
MACCUMHAILL, FIONN. In Praise of May, *at.*
MACDARA, SHIEL. Nun, The.
McDERMOT, THOMAS HENRY. *See* "REDCAM, TOM."
McDERMOTH, CORA A. Mother's Prayer, The.
McDERMOTT, JESSIE. April Weather.
MACDERMOTT, MARTIN. Girl of the Red Mouth.
MACDIARMID, BELLE (Mrs. J. Warren Ritchie). I Shall Not Weep.
MACDIARMID, ETHEL. Call of the Plains, The.
"MACDIARMID [*or* McDIARMID], HUGH" (Christopher Murray Grieve). Antenora.
At the Cenotaph.
Birlinn Chlann-Raghnaill, *tr.*
Bonnie Broukit Bairn, The.
Cattle Show.
De Profundis.
Deep-Sea Fishing.
Eemis-Stane, The.
Empty Vessel.
Glen of Silence, The.
Hymn to Sophia; the Wisdom of God.
In the Hedgeback.
Man in the Moon, The.
Milk-Wort and Bog Cotton.
Munestruck.
O Wha's Been Here afore Me, Lass.
On the Oxford Book of Victorian Verse.
Parley of Beasts.
Perfect.
Praise of Ben Dorain, The, *tr.*
Reflections in an Iron Works.
Requiem: To Paula Modersohn-Becker, *tr.*
Scunner.
Skeleton of the Future, The.
Spanish Trilogy, The, *tr.*
To a Sea Eagle.
Two Parents, The.
Water Music.
Watergaw, The.
Wheesht, wheesht, my foolish hert.
With a Lifting of the Head.
MACDONAGH, DONAGH. Childhood.
Dublin Made Me.
Galway.
Going to Mass Last Sunday.
Hungry Grass, The.
Invitation, The.
Love's Language.
On the Bridge of Athlone; a Prophecy.
Prothalamium.
Revel, A.
Veterans, The.
Warning to Conquerors, A.
Wind Blows, The.
MACDONAGH, THOMAS. Ideal, *tr.*
In Paris.
John-John.
Lullaby of the Woman of the Mountain, *tr.*
Night Hunt, The.
Of [*or* On] a Poet Patriot.
Song: "Love is cruel, Love is sweet."
Stars Stand Up in the Air, The, *tr.*
To Death, *tr.*
What Is White?
Wishes for My Son.
Woman, A.
Yellow Bittern, The, *tr.*
MACDONALD, AGNES FOLEY. Eternal.
MACDONALD, ALEXANDER (Alasdair MacMhaighstir Alasdair). Bark of Clanranald, The.
Birlinn Chlann-Raghnaill.
Elegy: On a Pet Dove.
McDONALD, DOROTHY NELL. Birthday Wish, A.
MACDONALD, ELIZABETH ROBERTS. Summons, The.
MACDONALD, FREDERIKA RICHARDSON. New Year's Eve—Midnight.
MACDONALD [*or* MACDONALD], GEORGE. Adela Cathcart, *sel.*
Ane by Ane.
Approaches.
At the Back of the North Wind, *sel.*
Baby, The. *Fr.* At the Back of the North Wind.
By the Cradle.
Carpenter, The.
Christ the Answer.
Christmas Meditation.
Christmas Prayer, A.
Come Down.
De Profundis.
Dorcas.
Earl o' Quarterdeck, The.
Epitaph: "Here lie I, Martin Elginbrodde," *at.*
Evening Hymn, *sel.*
Father's Hymn for the Mother to Sing, The.
Gravestones.
Here lie I, Martin Elginbrodde, *at.*
Hic Jacet, *at.*
I Need Thee.
Light.
Lost and Found.
Mammon Marriage.
Martin Elginbrodde, *at.*
May.
Memorial of Africa, A, *sel.*
O Night, send up the harvest moon. *Fr.* Songs of the Autumn Night.
Obedience.
Oneness with Him.
Over the Hill.
Paul Faber, Surgeon, *sel.*
Phantastes, *sel.*
Prayer, A: "When I look back upon my life nigh spent."
Preacher's Prayer, The.
Rest.
Rondel: "Heart, thou must learn to do without."
Sir Lark and King Sun. *Fr.* Adela Cathcart.
So, like the corn, moon-ripened last. *Fr.* Songs of the Autumn Night.
Song: "I dream'd that I woke from a dream."
Song: "Why do the houses stand."
Song of the Lark, The.
Song of the Spring Days.
Song of the Summer Days.
Sonnet: "This infant world has taken long to make." *Fr.* A Memorial of Africa.
Sweeper of the Floor, The.
Sweet Peril.
That Holy Thing. *Fr.* Paul Faber, Surgeon.
This Infant World. *Fr.* A Memorial of Africa.
To My God.
Travellers' Song.
What Christ Said.
What the Auld Fowk Are Thinkin'.
What Would You See?
Where Did You Come From? *Fr.* At the Back of the North Wind.
Wind and the Moon, The.
Within and Without, *sel.*
Woman Who Came behind Him in the Crowd, The.
World and Soul. *Fr.* A Memorial of Africa.
MACDONALD, GOODRIDGE. Elegy, Montreal Morgue.
Sailor, The.
MACDONALD, GREVILLE. Stars' Song, The.
MACDONALD, HUGH. Birds of Scotland, The.
MACDONALD, JAMES EDWARD HERVEY. Gallows and Cross.
Hanging, The.
Kitchen Window.
MACDONALD, JOHN. *See* LOM, IAIN.
MACDONALD, LUCY MAUD. *See* MONTGOMERY, LUCY MAUD.
McDONALD, NANCY MAY. Quiet Street, The.
Wet Summer; Botanic Gardens.
McDONALD, S. P. Casey—Twenty Years Later.
MACDONALD, WILSON PUGSLEY. Armand Dussault.
Baby Show, De.
Battle of Peace, The.
Cry of the Song Children, The.
Evening Song, An.
Exit.
I Love Old Things.
In a Wood Clearing.
In the Far Years.
John Graydon.
June.
Last Portage, The, *sel.*
Masked Ball, The.
Miracle Songs of Jesus, The.
Moonlight on Lake Sydenham.
Nineteen Twenty-six.
Pierre of Timagami in New York.
Song of the Ski, The.
Teemothy Hatch.
Toll-Gate Man, The.
Whist-Whee.
McDONALL, AMY. Feast Day, The.
MACDONNELL, JAMES FRANCIS CARLIN. *See* CARLIN, FRANCIS.
McDONNELL, THOMAS P. Next Voice You Hear, The.
Psalm for Moderns, A.
MACDONOGH, PATRICK. Be Still as You Are Beautiful.
Dodona's Oaks Were Still.
River, The.
She Walked Unaware.
Snare, The.
Song: "She spoke to me gently with words of sweet meaning."
Song for a Proud Relation.
Soon with the Lilac Fades Another Spring.
This Morning I Wakened among Loud Cries of Seagulls.
Waking.
Widow of Drynam, The.
MACDONOUGH, PATRICK. Bring Home the Poet.
McDONOUGH, PATRICK. Via Longa.
McDOUGAL, VIOLET. Sea Wolf, The.
MACDOUGALL, ARTHUR R., JR. Bitter Question.
Captains of the Years, The.
Death of Christ.
It Isn't Far to Bethlehem.
We Need a King.
McDOUGALL, JEAN. Quarrel.

McDougall, Joseph Easton. For the Records.
New House, The.
Wings.
Macduff, John. Jesus, My Saviour, Look on Me!
McDuffee, Franklin. Hakluyt Unpurchased.
Michelangelo, *sel.*
Mace, Frances Laughton. Alcyone.
Angelus, The.
Easter Morning.
Only Waiting.
Succession, The.
Macedonius. "Betwixt a Sleep and a Sleep."
Dedication of a Ship.
Earth, that gave body! Birth-Goddess, shelter in womb!
Farewell to the Sea.
From loftiest turret to foundation-stone.
Greet All Equally.
Sailor's Dedication, The.
Statue of a Dog.
MacElgun [*or* Mac Giolla Ghunna], Cathal Buidhe. Yellow Bittern, The.
MacEwen, Pearl Forbes. Kite, The.
My Little Dog.
McFadden, Isobel. April.
McFadden, Roy. Address to an Absolute.
Aged Writer, An.
Elegy: "Out on the roads of sky the moon stands poised."
Epithalamium: "So you are married, girl. It makes me sad."
Independence.
Mihailovich.
Orator, The.
Saint Francis and the Birds.
Virgin Country.
White Bird, The.
William Blake Sees God.
MacFarlan, James. Scotland's Tribute to Wallace.
McFarland, John T. Be Merciful.
Journey, The.
McFarlane, Basil. Final Man, The.
McFarlane, Dorothy. Sonnet from an Oil-Field.
McFarlane, J. E. Clare. On National Vanity.
Macfie, Ronald Campbell. Dying-Day of Death, The.
In Memoriam; John Davidson.
Ode Written for the Completion and Opening of the New Buildings, Marischal College, Aberdeen.
MacFie, Roy Campbell. Worship.
McGaffey, Ernest. As the Day Breaks.
Geronimo.
I Fear No Power a Woman Wields.
Little Big Horn.
Mark.
Rise, A.
McGaffin, Audrey R. At Cambridge.
Avalon.
Cemetery Is, The.
Inertia.
Invalid.
Poor Relation, A.
McGarvey, Margaret. D-Dawn.
McGee, Clyde. Cross Makers.
Free Enterprise.
Gratitude.
Mary at the Cross.
McGee, Mrs. M. H. *See* "Halliburton, Maurine."
McGee, Thomas D'Arcy. Apology to the Harp, An.
Arctic Indian's Faith, The.
Celtic Cross, The.
Celts, The.
Dead Antiquary O'Donovan, The.
Exile's Devotion, The.
Infelix Felix.
Irish Wife, The.
Jacques Cartier.
Man of the North Countrie, The.
Salutation to the Kelts.
Sister Margaret Bourgeoys.
Thomas Moore at St. Anne's.
To Ask Our Lady's Patronage for a Book on Columbus.
To Duffy in Prison.
McGeorge, Alice Sutton. Autumn's Fete.
McGiffert, Gertrude Huntington. Azrael.
Garden, The.
Maine Trail, A.
Saint Francis.
MacGill, Patrick. By-the-Way.
Conger Eel, The.
Death and the Fairies.
Dedication: "I speak with a proud tongue of the people who were."
Hipe, The.
It's a Far, Far Cry.
Night before and the Night after the Charge, The.
Slainthe!
Song of the Old Days, A.
MacGillivray, Arthur. Death.
Madonna of the Dons.
Macgillivray, Pittendrigh. Return, The.
Macgillivray, William. Thrush's Song, The, *tr.*
McGinley, Phyllis. All Around the Town, *sels.*
B. *Fr.* All Around the Town.
Ballad of Culinary Frustration.
Ballroom Dancing Class.
B's the Bus. *Fr.* All Around the Town.
Carol with Variations.
Certain Age, A.
Club Woman.
Concert, The.
Confirmation for a Rumor.
Country Club Sunday.
Dido of Tunisia.
E. *Fr.* All Around the Town.
Enigma in Altman's.
F Is the Fighting Firetruck. *Fr.* All Around the Town.
Fourteenth Birthday.
Giveaway, The.
Good Humor Man, The.
Hospital Song.
In Praise of Diversity.
Intimations of Mortality.
Journey toward Evening.
J's the Jumping Jay-Walker. *Fr.* All Around the Town.
Literary Landscape with Dove and Poet.
Midcentury Love Letter.
My Six Toothbrushes.
Portrait of a Girl with Comic Book.
R is for the Restaurant. *Fr.* All Around the Town.
Recipe for an Evening Musicale.
Reflections at Dawn.
Saint Francis Borgia; or, A Refutation for Heredity.
Text for Today.
This Side of Calvin.
Tirade on Tea.
To a Modernistic Christmas Tree.
Trial and Error.
McGinnis, Dan. Jack Haggerty, *at.*
Mac Giolla Ghunna, Cathal Buidhe. *See* MacElgun, Cathal Buidhe.
McGovern, Margaret. Madeline at Jefferson Market Night Court.
MacGowan, Liam. Connolly.
McGowan, R. E. Young Man's Fancy, A, *at.*
MacGowran, Hugh. Description of an Irish Feast, The; or, O'Rourk's Frolic.
O'Rourk's Frolic.
McGrath, Marion. *See* Albertus Magnus, Sister.
McGrath, Thomas. Against the False Magicians.
Ode for the American Dead in Korea.
Odor of Blood, The.
Remembering That Island.
Repeated Journey, The.
McGreevy, Thomas. Aodh Ruadh O Domhnaill.
Dream Nocturne, *tr.*
Gioconda.
Homage to Hieronymus Bosch.
Homage to Jack Yeats.
Red Hugh.
MacGregor, Gertrude. *See* Moffat, Gertrude MacGregor.
MacGregor, Robert Guthrie. Better Eros, The, *tr.*
Four Years Only, *tr.*
He Hopes That Time Will Render Her More Merciful, *tr. Fr.* Sonnets to Laura.
Heliodora's Garland, *tr.*
Muse on Death, *tr.*
Praises of Laura Transcend His Poetic Power, The, *tr. Fr.* Sonnets to Laura.
Rests Charidas beneath this tomb? "Here I," *tr.*
Sacrifice of Youth, *tr.*
Sinister Dialogue, *tr.*
Small Cleodemus, *tr.*
Spring Sailing, *tr.*
To Be and Not to Be, *tr.*
To the Virgin Mary, *tr. Fr.* Sonnets to Laura.
Two Fires, *tr.*
Uncommon, *tr.*
With Two Fair Girls, *tr.*
Zeus! since by Philip scal'd Macynus' wall, *tr.*
McGrew, A. O. Hit at the Times, A.
McGroarty, John Steven. Blow, Bugles, Blow.
King's Highway, The.
Port o' Heart's Desire, The.
McGuire, Harry. Phantoms.
McGuire, Will Victor. College "Oil Cans."
MacGurcaich, Artur. Lay of Norse-Irish Sea-Kings.
Machado, Antonio. Autumn Dawn.
Behold, Lord, Thou Didst Tear from Me.
Clock Struck Twelve, The.
Counsels.
Crime Took Place at Granada, The.
Denuded Is the Land.
Fields of Soria, *sels.*
Figures in the Fields against the Sky.
Frail Sound of a Tunic Trailing, A.
From the Threshold of a Dream.
Iberian God.
Iberian God, *sel.*
Naked is the earth.
Perchance in Dreams.
Poems.
Songs of Several Lands.
To Don Francisco Giner de los Ríos.
To José María Palacio.
We think to create festivals.
Well Belovèd House, The.
Machado, Manuel. Adelphos.
Figurines.
On the Annunciation of Fra Angelico.
Philip the Fourth.
Machar, Agnes Maule. Untrodden Ways.
Machault, Guillaume de. *See* Guillaume de Machault.
Machiavelli, Niccolò. Opportunity.
McHugh, Vincent. Amphimachos the Dandy.
Mantis Friend, The.
Mice at the Door, The.
Natural History of Pliny, The.
Ode in a Night of Overhanging Weather.
MacInnes, Mairi. For a Siamese Cat.
MacInnes, Tom. Amber Lands.
Ballade of Faith.
Ballade of the Mystic and the Mud.
Ballade of Youth Remaining.
Chinatown Chant.
Mirelle of the Good Bed.
Modernists, The.
Nirvana.
Tiger of Desire, The.
To Walt Whitman.
Velvet Sonneteers, The.
White Magic.
Zalinka.
McInnis, Edgar. Fire Burial.
Requiem for a Dead Warrior.
Song against the Evil Days, A.

MacIntosh, Claire Harris. Barn in Winter, The.
Spirit of the *Bluenose*, The.
MacIntyre, Carlyle Ferren. Autumn, *tr.*
Autumn Day, *tr.*
Caesar, *tr.*
Death in the Corn, *tr.*
Faust, *sel., tr.*
Faust Struggles with His Soul, *tr.* *Fr.* Faust.
From a Childhood, *tr.*
Green, *tr.*
Initiation, *tr.*
Lament: "Oh, everything is far," *tr.*
Last Evening, The, *tr.*
O Strassburg, *tr.*
Panther, The, *tr.*
Prelude: "We are those same children who amazed," *tr.*
Solemn Hour, *tr.*
Solitary, The, *tr.*
Solitude, *tr.*
Torso of an Archaic Apollo, *tr.*
Voyage, The, *tr.*
MacIntyre, Duncan Ban. Haunt of the Deer, The. *Fr.* The Praise of Ben Dorain.
Last Leave of the Hills.
Praise of Ben Dorain, The.
Praise of Ben Dorain, The, *sel.*
McIntyre, James. On the High Cost of Dairy Products.
Queen of Cheese.
Shelly.
McIntyre, Robert. In the Carpenter Shop.
Nazareth Shop, The.
"McK., F." Strike the Blow.
Mack, Louise. Before Exile.
To Sydney.
Mack, Robert Ellice. Lullaby, A: "Sleep, baby, sleep, the wind."
"M'K., S. C." Quiet from Fear of Evil.
Mackail, John William. Aeneid, The.
At Pylos, *tr.* *Fr.* The Odyssey.
Etruscan Ring, An.
Home-Coming, *tr.* *Fr.* The Odyssey.
Masque of Balliol, The, *sels.*
Odysseus Puts to Sea, *tr.* *Fr.* The Odyssey.
Odyssey, The, *sels., tr.*
Of His Mother's Shade, *tr.* *Fr.* The Odyssey.
On the Death of Arnold Toynbee.
Penelope Dreams ("But when her heart had had its fill of weeping"), *tr.* *Fr.* The Odyssey.
Penelope Dreams ("So said he and the crone went down the hall"), *tr.* *Fr.* The Odyssey.
Penelope Forlorn, *tr.* *Fr.* The Odyssey.
MacKavanaugh, James L. Greek, Four Credits.
McKay, Brenham. White Peacock.
Mackay, Charles. Bachelor's Monorhyme, A.
Cheer, Boys, Cheer.
Children's Auction, The.
Cleon and I.
Climbing to the Light.
Cynical Ode to an Ultra-cynical Public.
Earl Norman and John Truman.
Good Time Coming, The.
Gourd and the Palm, The, *tr.*
Great and Small.
Holly Bough, The.
I Love My Love.
If I Were a Voice.
Inquiry, The.
Little and [*or* but] Great.
Miller of the Dee, The.
No Enemies.
Noble Work.
Reconciliation.
Sea-King's Burial, The.
Ship, The.
Small Beginnings.
Song: "Men of thought! be up and stirring."
Song of Life.
Tell Me, Ye Winged Winds.
True Freedom.
Tubal Cain.
Two Houses, The.
Under the Holly Bough.
Vixi, *at.*
What Might Be Done.
McKay, Claude. Absence.
After the Winter.
America.
Baptism.
Barrier, The.
Commemoration.
Desolate.
Exhortation: Summer, 1919.
Flame-Heart.
Harlem Dancer, The.
Harlem Shadows.
Heritage.
Home Thoughts.
Homing Swallows.
If We Must Die.
Lynching, The.
Moon Song.
My House.
My Mother.
North and South.
Russian Cathedral.
Song of the Moon, A.
Spanish Needle, The.
Spring in New Hampshire.
Tired Worker, The.
To O. E. A.
To the White Fiends.
Tropics in New York, The.
Two-an'-six.
When Dawn Comes to the City; New York.
White Houses.
Wild Goat, The.
Mackay, Eric. Ecstasy.
In Tuscany.
Mary Arden.
Waking of the Lark, The.
Mackay, Isabel Ecclestone. Bridge Builder, The.
Calgary Station.
Dream People.
Fires of Driftwood.
Helen—Old.
Homesteader, The.
Mother, The.
Prairie School, The.
Unchanged, The.
Wanderlust.
When as a Lad.
McKay, J. T. Making Port.
McKay, James Thompson. Cenotaph of Lincoln, The.
Mackay, Jessie. Burial of Sir John McKenzie, The.
Dunedin in the Gloaming.
For Love of Appin.
Grey Company, The.
In Galilee.
Maisrie.
October in New Zealand.
Ortygia.
Song of the Drift Weed.
McKay, Lois Weakley. Night.
MacKay, Louis Alexander ("John Smalacombe"). Admonition for Spring.
Battle Hymn of the Spanish Rebellion.
Erotica Antiqua, *sel.*
I Wish My Tongue Were a Quiver. *Fr.* The Ill-tempered Lover.
Ill-tempered Lover, The, *sel.*
Look, I Have Thrown All Right.
Non Nobis.
Now There Is Nothing Left.
Nunc Scio, Quid Sit Amor.
Propertian. *Fr.* Erotica Antiqua.
Rend Your Heart and Not Your Garments.
Snow Story.
Mackay, Lydia Miller. Dewdrops, The.
Mackay, Margaret. Asleep in Jesus.
Mackay, Margaret Mackprang. Dog Asleep.
Dog in Chair.
Dog Meets Cat.
Dog Wanted.
MacKaye, Christy. Earth Melody.
MacKaye, Percy. Automobile, The.
France.
Goethals, the Prophet Engineer.
Hymn of the New World.
Look Inland Now.
Mocking-Bird, Misnamed, The.
Old Age.
Ourselves, *sel.*
Prayer of the Peoples, A.
Prayer of the Peoples, A, *sel.*
She Was a Child of February.
Song-Sparrow, The.
Summer Song.
To an Upland Plover.
To Sleep.
Trail, The. *Fr.* Ourselves.
Uriel.
Wilson.
McKee, Gladys. First Geography.
First Reader (Fifth Reading).
Legacy.
Spring Cellar.
McKeehan, Irene Pettit. Closing the Doors.
McKeighan, Irene. Crowd, The.
Mackellar, Dorothea. In a Southern Garden.
Montoro's Song against Count Alvaro de Luna, High Constable of Castile, *tr.*
My Country.
Open Sea, The.
McKellar, John Alexander Ross. Football Field; Evening.
Res Publica.
Retreat from Heaven, The.
Twelve o'Clock Boat.
MacKellar, Thomas. Jesus First and Jesus Last.
To a Troublesome Fly.
McKelway, St. Clair. Boogie-woogie Ballads.
Mackenzie, Compton. Lilies of the Field, The.
Song of Parting, A.
MacKenzie, Donald A. Blue Men of the Minch, The.
My Fairy Lover.
Wee Folk, The.
Mackenzie, H. C. Compton. *See* Mackenzie, Compton.
Mackenzie, Kenneth. Caesura.
Confession.
Legerdemain.
Moonlit Doorway, The.
Snake, The.
Tree at Post 4, The.
Mackenzie, Seaforth. Idas Te Diliget Unam.
Leaf from a Fly-Book, A.
M'Kenzie, William P. Lullaby Song.
Mother's Song, The.
Mackie, Albert D. Molecatcher.
McKinney, Laurence. Compromise.
English Horn.
Hubbub in Hub.
Old School Tie-up, The.
Song to My Love.
MacKinnon, Cecilia. Sea-Garden.
Three Princesses, The.
McKinsey, Folger. He Who Has Vision.
MacKinstry, Elizabeth. Man Who Hid His Own Front Door, The.
Mackintosh, Alan. Death.
Mackintosh, H. S. "Il Est Cocu—le Chef de Gare!"
Mackintosh, Newton. Fin de Siècle.
Limerick: "Cleopatra, who thought they maligned her."
Lucy Lake.
Optimism.
Pessimism.
Mackworth, Cecily. *For translations from French, see* MiFP.
McLachlan, Alexander. Backwoods Hero, A, *sel.*
Emigrant, The, *sels.*
Glasgow Chap's Story, The; or, Confessions over a Bottle.
God, *sel.*
In the Forest. *Fr.* The Emigrant.
O! Come to the Greenwood Shade.
Old Canada; or, Gee Buck Gee.

McLachlan, Alexander (*continued*)
Song: "Old England is eaten by knaves." *Fr.* The Emigrant.
To an Indian Skull, *sel.*
We Live in a Rickety House.
Woman, *sel.*
Young Canada; or, Jack's as Good as His Master.
Maclachlan [*or* McLachlan], H. D. C.
Cattle Round-up, The.
Panhandle Cob.
McLaren, Floris Clark. Crusoe.
Frozen Fire.
No More the Slow Stream.
Tide Trapped.
Visit by Water.
Who Has Gone through the Wood.
Maclaren, Hamish. Carol: "Winter winds have chilled us quite."
Dolphins, The.
Harp in the Rigging.
Sailor and Inland Flower.
Maclean, Nannie Fitzhugh. Lullaby: "My heart makes mock at the long day's harms."
Maclean, Sorley. Dain do Eimhir, *sels.*
Dain Eile, *sel.*
I Walked with My Reason.
Knightsbridge of Libya.
Nightmare, The.
To a Depraved Lying Woman.
MacLeish, Archibald. Against Illuminations.
Ah How the Throat of a Girl. *Fr.* Conquistador.
Air Raid, The.
Alien.
America Was Promises.
America Was Promises, *sel.*
American Letter.
American Letter, *sel.*
. . . & Forty-second Street.
Argument, The. *Fr.* Conquistador.
Ars Poetica.
Background with Revolutionaries. *Fr.* Frescoes for Mr. Rockefeller's City.
Before March.
Bernal Diaz' Preface, *sel. Fr.* Conquistador.
Bernal Diaz' Preface to His Book. *Fr.* Conquistador.
Brave New World.
Burying Ground by the Ties. *Fr.* Frescoes for Mr. Rockefeller's City.
Calypso's Island.
Captured.
Conquistador, *sels.*
Cook County.
Dawn on the Wall-Head There. *Fr.* Conquistador.
Discovery of This Time.
"Dover Beach"—a Note to That Poem.
Dusk.
Einstein.
Einstein, *sel.*
Eleven.
Empire Builders. *Fr.* Frescoes for Mr. Rockefeller's City.
End of the World, The.
Epistle to Be Left in the Earth.
Ever Since.
Ezry.
Fall of the City, The.
Fall of the City, The, *sel.*
Farm, The.
Farm, The, *sels.*
Final Chorus: "Bellies bitter with drinking." *Fr.* Panic.
Frescoes for Mr. Rockefeller's City.
Frescoes for Mr. Rockefeller's City, *sels.*
Geography of This Time.
Hamlet of A. MacLeish, The, *sel.*
Hypocrite Auteur.
Immortal Autumn.
In My Thirtieth Year.
Invocation to the Social Muse.
L'An Trentiesme de Mon Eage.
Land of the Free, *sel.*
Landscape as a Nude. *Fr.* Frescoes for Mr. Rockefeller's City.
Le Secret Humain.
Learned Men, The.
Lines for an Interment.
Memorial Rain.
Memory Green.
Men.
My Naked Aunt.
Night Dream, The.
1933.
"Not Marble nor the Gilded Monuments."
Oil Painting of the Artist as the Artist. *Fr.* Frescoes for Mr. Rockefeller's City.
Old Man to the Lizard, The.
Panic, *sels.*
Poem in Prose.
Poem Should Be Palpable and Mute, A.
Pole Star for This Year.
Pony Rock.
Prologue: "These alternate nights and days, these seasons."
Reasons for Music.
Reconciliation, The.
Reed-Player, The.
Reply to Mr. Wordsworth, *sel.*
Reproach to Dead Poets.
Salute.
Seafarer.
1750. *Fr.* The Farm.
Sheep in the Ruins, The.
Signature for Tempo.
Silence, The.
Silent Slain, The.
Speech to a Crowd.
Speech to Those Who Say Comrade.
Too-late Born, The.
Vicissitudes of the Creator.
Voice of the Announcer ("We are here on the central plaza"). *Fr.* The Fall of the City.
Voice of the Studio Announcer ("Ladies and gentlemen:/This broadcast comes to you from the city"). *Fr.* The Fall of the City.
Voyage West.
We wonder whether the dream of American liberty. *Fr.* Land of the Free.
Weather.
What Riddle Asked the Sphinx.
What the Serpent Said to Adam.
Wildwest. *Fr.* Frescoes for Mr. Rockefeller's City.
Words in Time.
You, Andrew Marvell.
Young Dead Soldiers, The.
McLeish, John A. B. Not without Beauty.
McLellan, Isaac, Jr. Death of Napoleon, The.
New England's Dead.
Pilgrim Fathers, The (*by* John Pierpont), *add. sts.*
M'Lemore, John C. Rappahannock Army Song, The.
What the Village Bell Said.
McLennan, William. En roulant ma boule, *tr.*
Entre Paris et Saint-Denis, *tr.*
Jamais je nourrirai de geai, *tr.*
Malbrouck, *tr.*
Marianson, *tr.*
Pommier doux, Le, *tr.*
McLeod, Crofton Uniacke. Fisher-Wife's Song, The.
"Macleod, Fiona" (William Sharp).
At the Last.
Autumnal Evening, An.
Bells of Youth, The.
Bugles of Dreamland, The.
Coves of Crail, The.
Cross of the Dumb, The.
Cry on the Wind, A.
Death-Child, The.
Deirdre Is Dead.
Desire.
Dim Face of Beauty.
Dream Fantasy.
Dreams within Dreams.
Empire (Persepolis).
End of Aodh-of-the-Songs, The.
Field Mouse, The.
Founts of Song, The.
From the Hills of Dream.
High Noon at Midsummer on the Campagna.
Hushing Song.
Invocation of Peace, *sel.*
Isle of Lost Dreams, The.
Lament of Ian the Proud, The.
Last Aboriginal, The.
Lullaby: "Lennavan-mo."
Madonna Natura.
Mo-Lennav-a-Chree.
Moon-Child, The.
Mystic's Prayer, The.
On a Nightingale in April.
Red Poppies. *Fr.* Sospiri di Roma.
Redeemer, The.
Rose of Flame, The.
Saint Bride's Lullaby.
St. Christopher of the Gael.
Secret Gate, The.
Shule, Shule, Shule, Agrah!
Sleep.
Song: "Love in my heart: oh, heart of me, heart of me!"
Song of Dreams, A.
Sospiri di Roma, *sels.*
Susurro. *Fr.* Sospiri di Roma.
Tryst of Queen Hynde, The.
Undersong, The.
Unknown Wind, The.
Vale, Amor!
Valley of Pale Blue Flowers, The.
Valley of Silence, The.
Valley of White Poppies, The.
Vision, The. *Fr.* Sospiri di Roma.
Washer of the Ford, The.
Wasp, The.
Weaver of Snow, The.
White Peace, The.
White Peacock, The. *Fr.* Sospiri di Roma.
McLeod, Helen Brosi. Dog—Lost, A.
McLeod, Irene Rutherford (Mrs. Aubrey de Sélincourt). He Lives! He Lives!
Is Love, Then, So Simple.
London.
Lone Dog.
Missing.
My Dear Comes Down to Meet Me.
On a Hill.
Prayer, A: "O Love, give me a passionate heart."
Rebel.
Rest.
Sea-Song.
So Beautiful You Are, Indeed.
Song: "How do I love you?"
Song from "April."
Sonnet: "Between my love and me there runs a thread." *Fr.* Sonnets.
Sonnet: "In heaven there is a star I call my own." *Fr.* Sonnets.
Sonnet: "Shall I be fearful thus to speak my mind." *Fr.* Sonnets.
Sonnet: "Sweet, when I think how summer's smallest bird." *Fr.* Sonnets.
Sonnet: "When sane men gather in to talk of love." *Fr.* Sonnets.
Sonnets, *sels.*
Unborn.
When My Beloved Sleeping Lies.
Macleod, Joseph Gordon ("Adam Drinan"). Ecliptic, The: Cancer, or, The Crab, *sel.*
Love Song.
MacLeod, Leroy. Wild Duck, The.
MacLeod, Murdo. Isle of the Heather, The.
Macleod, Norman (1783–1862). Farewell to Fiunary.
Macleod, Norman (1812–72). Creed, A.
Trust in God and Do the Right.
Trust in God and Do the Right, *sel.*
MacLiesh, Archibald Fleming ("Archibald Fleming"). Airman's Certificate—No. 39289—U.S. Civil Aeronautics Authority. *Fr.* Exploration by Air.
Destroyers, The, *sel.*
Exploration by Air.
Jungle, The, *sel.*
Report. *Fr.* The Jungle.

Solo (Teterboro Airport). *Fr.* Exploration by Air.
Summer Shower, A.
"McM." Allegro.
McMahan, Helen. October.
MacMahon, ——. Jack Dempsey's Grave.
MacMahon, Bryan. Corner Boys.
MacManus, Anna Johnston. *See* "Carbery, Ethna."
MacManus, Francis. Pattern of Saint Brendan.
McManus, S. B. My Little Bo-Peep.
MacManus, Seumas. Health to the Birds, A.
Hedge Schoolmasters, The.
In Dark Hour.
Lullaby: "Softly now the burn is rushing."
Resignation.
Shane O'Neill.
MacManus, Theodore F. Cave Sedem!
McMaster, Guy Humphreys. Carmen Bellicosum.
Old Continentals, The.
MacMechan, Archibald. Ballad of *La Tribune*, The.
Ballad of the *Rover*, The.
MacMillan, Alexander. Ich weiss nicht, was soll es bedeuten, *tr.*
Macmillan, Hugh. Wish of the Aged Bard, The, *tr.*
MacMore, Dallan. Carroll's Sword, *at.*
Song of Carroll's Sword, The, *at.*
McMullen, Mary A. Sister Agatha.
MacMurray, Niall. Vanished Night, The.
Macnab, Roy. Child of the Long Grass.
Majuba Hill.
Man of Grass, The, *sel.*
Settler, The.
McNabb, Vincent. Spotless Maid, The.
Macnaghten, Hugh. Idyll: "In Switzerland one idle day."
Macnair, J. H. Household Gods.
MacNamara, Brinsley. On Seeing Swift in Laracor.
Macnamara, Donogh. *See* Mac-Conmara, Donogh.
Macnamara, Francis. Carol of Jesus Child.
Diminutivus Ululans.
MacNamee, Giolla Brighde. To an Anti-poetical Priest.
McNaughton, J. H. Faded Coat of Blue, The.
McNeal-Sweeney, Mildred Isabel. *See* Sweeney, Mildred Isabel McNeal.
MacNeice, Louis. Agamemnon, *sel.*, *tr.*
Alcohol.
Among These Turf-Stacks.
And Love Hung Still.
Aubade.
August.
August Is Nearly Over. *Fr.* Autumn Journal.
Autobiography.
Autumn Journal, *sels.*
Bagpipe Music.
Birmingham.
British Museum Reading Room, The.
Brother Fire.
Carrickfergus.
Chorus from "Agamemnon," *tr.*
Christina.
Circe.
Conversation.
Corner Seat.
County Sligo.
Cradle Song: "Clock's untiring fingers wind the wool of darkness, The."
Cradle Song: "Sleep, my darling, sleep."
Creditor, The.
Death-Wish, The.
Dublin.
Eclogue by a Five-barred Gate.
Eclogue for Christmas, An.
Elegy for Minor Poets.
Entered in the Minutes.
Entirely.
Explorations.
For X.
Galway.
Gardener, The. *Fr.* Novelettes.
Glacier, The.
Good-bye Now, Plato and Hegel. *Fr.* Autumn Journal.
Hebrides, The.
If I Were to Tell of Our Labours, Our Hard Lodging, *tr.* *Fr.* Agamemnon.
Individualist Speaks, The.
Jehu.
Jigsaw III.
June Thunder.
Kingdom, The, *sel.*
Leaving Barra.
Les Sylphides.
Meeting Point.
Mixer, The.
Morning Sun.
Museums.
Nature Morte.
Neutrality.
Nostalgia.
Novelettes, *sel.*
Now We Are Back to Normal. *Fr.* Autumn Journal.
Nuts in May.
Ode: "Tonight is so coarse with chocolate."
Odes (*of* Horace), *sel.*, *tr.*
Perseus.
Prayer before Birth.
Prognosis.
Refugees.
Sleep Serene, Avoid the Backward. *Fr.* Autumn Journal.
Slow Movement.
Snow.
Song: "Sunlight on the garden, The."
Springboard, The.
Strand, The.
Streets of Laredo, The.
Stylite.
Sunday Morning.
Sunlight on the Garden, The.
Their Last Will and Testament.
These Days Are Misty, Insulated. *Fr.* Autumn Journal.
Toast, A.
Turf Stacks.
Valediction.
Venus' Speech.
Wessex Guidebook.
Winter to Spring, *tr.*
Wolves.
You Who Will Soon Be Unrecapturable.
Zone Libre, *tr.*
McNeil, Duncan. Make Me Kind.
MacNeill, Hector. Come under My Plaidie.
I Lo'ed Ne'er a Laddie but Ane.
My Boy Tammy.
McNeill, John Charles. August Meeting, The.
Away Down Home.
Before Bedtime.
Crown of Power, The.
Dew.
Few Days Off, A.
'Ligion.
Lines: "To you dear mother heart."
Mr. Nigger.
Nigger Demus.
Oh, Ask Me Not.
October.
Old Clock, The.
'Possum Time Again.
Punishment.
Spring.
Sunburnt Boys.
Sundown.
To Melvin Gardner; Suicide.
When I Go Home.
Wishing.
MacNeill, Nigel. Dark Winter Is Going, *tr.*
Macourek, Milos. Punching Clock, The.
McPartlin, Catharine. In the Longer Novitiate.
McPeek, James A. S. For Transient Things.
Macpherson, James ("Ossian"). Carthon, a Poem.
Carthon, *sel.*
Cath-Loda, *sel.*
Fingal; an Ancient Epic Poem, *sels.*
Fisherman, The.
Ossian's Address to the Sun. *Fr.* Carthon.
Songs of Selma, The.
Swan, The.
Temora, *sel.*
Woods No More, The.
McQuilland, Louis J. Song of the Open Road, A.
MacVeagh, F. W. Here Ananias lies because he lied.
McVey, Paul B. Her Dilemma.
McWebb, Elizabeth Upham. At Mrs. Appleby's.
Macy, Arthur. Boston Cats, The.
Peppery Man, The.
Rollicking Mastodon, The.
Macy, George. Ballade of Remembered Roses.
Daphne and Apollo.
Macy, John Albert. Vagabonds, The.
Macy, John C. White Brigade, The.
Maddock, Anne Elizabeth. Spring.
Maddow, Ben. City, The.
Madeleva, Sister Mary. As One Finding Peace.
At Winter's End.
Ballad of the Happy Christmas Wind.
Ballade on Eschatology.
Beech Trees.
Christmas in Provence.
Design for a Stream-lined Sunrise.
Dialogue.
Dream of the Road, The, *tr.*
Gates.
I Go to School.
I Visit Carmel.
In Desert Places.
Knights Errant.
Midnight Mass. *Fr.* Christmas in Provence.
Motif for Mary's Dolors.
New Things and Old.
Nun Speaks to Mary, A.
October Birthday.
Of Wounds.
Peace by Night.
Pepper Tree, The.
Question of Lovers, A.
Questions on a Nun's Habit.
Return.
Riddles.
Roses for My King.
Serenade, The: "This age-old church." *Fr.* Christmas in Provence.
Snow Storm.
Things to Be Loved.
Wardrobe.
Madge, Charles. At War.
Ballad of Hope and Fear.
Birds of Tin, The.
Blocking the Pass.
Delusions IV.
Delusions VI.
Delusions VIII.
Fortune.
Hours of the Planets, The.
Hours of the Planets, The, *sel.*
In Conjunction.
Loves of the Lions, The.
Lusty Juventus.
Monument, A.
Nightly Deed, A.
Poem by Stages, *sels.*
Rumba of the Three Lost Souls.
Solar Creation.
Times, The.
To Make a Bridge.
Madison, Dolly. La Fayette.
Mael-Isu. Deus Meus.
Maeterlinck, Maurice. If He Should Come Again.
Last Words, The.
Song: "Three little maidens they have slain."
Magaret, Helene. Aureole.
Impiety, *sel.*
Thoroughbred, The.
Magee, John Gillespie, Jr. High Flight.

MAGEE, WILLIAM KIRKPATRICK. *See* "EGLINTON, JOHN."
"MAGGIE." Passionate Encyclopedia Britannica Reader to His Love, The.
MAGIL, A. B. They Are Ours.
MAGINN, WILLIAM. I Give My Soldier Boy a Blade.
Irishman and the Lady, The.
St. Patrick of Ireland, My Dear!
Soldier-Boy, The.
Waiting for the Grapes.
MAGNÚSSON, EIRÍKUR. King Sverrir, *tr.*
MAGNÚSSON, EIRÍKUR, *and* WILLIAM MORRIS. *See* MORRIS, WILLIAM, *and* EIRÍKUR MAGNÚSSON.
MAGNY, OLIVIER DE. Contentment.
MAGRATH, ANDREW. Andrew Magrath's Reply to John O'Tuomy.
Boatman's Hymn, *at.*
Lament of the Mangaire Sugach.
MAGRUDER, MARY LANIER. Lights.
MAGRUDER, WILLIAM BEANS. Flowers, *sel.*
MAGUIRE, FRANCIS. Address to the Body.
And Rest in a Flame.
Bull, The.
People as Flowers.
Quaint Rider.
Root, The.
Sin, The; a Definition.
Sweet Land.
MAGUIRE, TOM. Bold Robert Emmet.
MAHLMANN, SIEGFRIED AUGUST. Allah.
MAHLMANN, SIEGFRIED AUGUST, *and* WILLIAM EDWARD HICKSON. God Bless Our Native Land.
MAHONEY, LEONARD. Lauds.
MAHONY, FRANCIS SYLVESTER ("Father Prout"). Ad Leuconoen.
Attractions of a Fashionable Irish Watering-Place, The.
Bells of Shandon, The.
Flight into Egypt, The.
Groves of Blarney, The.
In Mortem Venerabilis Andreae Prout Carmen.
L'Envoy to W. L. H. Ainsworth, Esq.
Malbrouck, *tr.*
Panegyric on Geese, A.
Piper's Progress, The.
Popular Recollections of Bonaparte, *tr.*
Red-Breast of Aquitania, The.
Sabine Farmer's Serenade, The.
Shandon Bells, The.
Solvitur Acris Hiems.
MAIANO, DANTE DA. Sonnet: He Craves Interpreting of a Dream of His.
Sonnet: To Dante Alighieri (He Interprets Dante Alighieri's Dream).
MAIKOV, APOLLON NIKOLAYEVICH. Art.
Hay Harvest, The.
Haymaking.
Pan.
Summer Rain.
Swallows.
Swell, The.
Upon This Wild Headland.
MAIR, ALEXANDER WILLIAM. Hesiod, 1908.
In Memoriam.
MAIR, CHARLES. August.
Buffalo Herds, The. *Fr.* Tecumseh.
Dreamland, *sel.*
Enter General Brock and Lefroy. *Fr.* Tecumseh.
Fireflies, The, *sel.*
Iena's Song. *Fr.* Tecumseh.
Lefroy in the Forest. *Fr.* Tecumseh.
Tecumseh, *sels.*
Tecumseh to General Harrison. *Fr.* Tecumseh.
There was a time on this fair continent. *Fr.* Tecumseh.
We left/ The silent forest. *Fr.* Tecumseh.
Winter.
MAIS, ROGER. I, Remembering.
MAISUN, LADY. She Scorns Her Husband the Caliph.
MAITLAND, DOLLIE. *See* RADFORD, DOLLIE.
MAITLAND, SIR RICHARD. Advice to Leesome Merriness.
Against the Thieves of Liddesdale.
Aganis the Thievis of Liddisdale.
Satire on the Toun Ladies.
MALAKASSIS, MILTIADES. Battarias.
Forest, The.
Spring Storm.
Takis Plumis.
MALAM, CHARLES. House Demolished.
Steam Shovel.
MALAN, H. It Is Not Death to Die.
MALAQUAIS, JEAN. Paris-am-Seine.
MALCOLM, GEORGE. Lament: "As I walked under the African moon."
MALESKA, EUGENE T. Assembly; Harlem School.
MALET, DAVID. *See* MALLET, DAVID.
MALHERBE, FRANÇOIS DE. Imitation of a Psalm.
On the Death of Mlle de Conty.
MALINS, JOSEPH. Fence or an Ambulance, A.
MALLALIEU, HERBERT B. Cozzo Grillo.
Look for Me on England.
New Year's Eve.
Next of Kin.
Platform Goodbye.
To Naples.
MALLARMÉ, STÉPHANE. Afternoon of a Faun, The.
Anguish.
Another Fan (of Mademoiselle Mallarmé).
Apparition.
Après-Midi d'un faune, L'.
Azure, The.
Bestowal of the Poem.
Canticle of Saint John.
Chastised Clown, The.
Flowers.
Funeral Toast.
Hérodiade, *sels.*
In Thought.
Insert Myself within Your Story.
Languor.
Little Air, I.
Little Air, II.
Miss Mallarmé's Fan.
My Old Books Closed.
O So Dear from Far Away, So Near and White.
Old-Clothes Woman, The.
Poetry.
Pure Nails Brightly Flashing.
Renouncement.
Royalty.
Saint.
Sea Breeze.
Sea-Wind.
Sea Winds.
Sigh.
Sonnet: "From afar so lov'd and near, so cloudless fair."
Still by the Cloud Stricken.
Swan, The.
This Day, This Pure, Enduring, Beautiful Today.
Throw of the Dice, A.
Toast.
Tomb of Charles Baudelaire, The.
Tomb of Edgar Poe, The.
Tomb [of Paul Verlaine].
Virgin, Bright, and Beautiful To-Day, The.
Weary of Bitter Ease.
When Winter on Forgotten Woods.
White Water Lily, The.
Windows.
Wreathed in Storm-Clouds Overhanging.
MALLET [*or* MALET *or* MALLOCH], DAVID. Birks of Invermay [*or* Endermay], The.
William and Margaret.
MALLET, DAVID, *and* JAMES THOMSON. *See* THOMSON, JAMES, *and* DAVID MALLET.
MALLET, LOLA. City Rain.
MALLOCH, DAVID. *See* MALLET, DAVID.
MALLOCH, DOUGLAS. "Ain't It Fine Today!"
As I Grow Old.
Be the Best of Whatever You Are.
Comrade Rides Ahead, A.
Daddy like Mine, A.
Family Trees.
Father's Prayer, A.
Fun.
Give a Boy a Dawg.
God's Mothers.
If Easter Eggs Would Hatch.
If You Have a Dog.
It's Fine Today.
June.
My Son.
Night Ma Heard the Burglar, The.
Some Youngster's Dad.
Sores.
Things of the Spirit, The.
We Call This Life.
When Dad Takes Me.
When the Drive Goes Down.
You Have to Believe.
MALLOCK, WILLIAM HURRELL. Bridal Hymn, *tr.*
De Rerum Natura, *sels., tr.*
Human Life.
Lines: "Homeless man goes, even on life's sunniest slope."
No Single Thing Abides, *tr.* *Fr.* De Rerum Natura.
On the Nature of Things, *sels., tr.*
Suave Mari Magno, *tr.* *Fr.* De Rerum Natura.
MALLORY, SARAH TROUSDALE. Vesta.
MALLOY, DANIEL. Beaver Island Boys, The, *at.*
MALMSTRÖM, BERNHARD ELIS. Sigh of the Forest, The.
Softly, My Heart!
MALON DE CHAIDE, PEDRO. Conversion of the Magdalene, The, *sel.*
Sonnet: "O patience, that dost wait eternally!"
MALONE, CARMEN. We Thank Thee.
"MALONE, CARROLL." *See* MCBURNEY, WILLIAM B.
MALONE, KEMP. New Year's Hymn, *ad.*
MALONE, WALTER. Agnostic's Creed.
Blend of mirth and sadness, smiles and tears, A.
He Who Hath Loved.
Lincoln.
Masterpiece, The.
October in Tennessee.
Opportunity.
MANCHAN, SAINT, OF LEMANAGHAN IN OFFALY. Hermitage, The, *at.*
MANCHESTER, ——. Mister Angleworm.
MANCHESTER, LESLIE CLARE. Revelation, The.
MANDEL, E. W. Estevan, Saskatchewan.
Job.
MANDELSTAM, OSIP EMILYEVICH. Air Strikes Chill, The.
Meganom.
On Every Still Suburban Street.
Tristia.
Twilight of Liberty, The.
MANDEVILLE, BERNARD. Another Dawn. *Fr.* A Description of the Morning.
Description of the Morning, A, *sel.*
Grumbling Hive, The; or, Knaves Turn'd Honest.
Grumbling Hive, The; or, Knaves Turn'd Honest, *sel.*
Honour. *Fr.* On Honour.
Moral to "The Grumbling Hive," The. *Fr.* The Grumbling Hive.
On Honour, *sel.*
MANGAN, JAMES CLARENCE. Advice against Travel.
Aldfrid's Itinerary through Ireland, *tr.*
And Then No More, *tr.*
Andrew Magrath's Reply to John O'Tuomy.
Book of Rights, *sel., tr.*
Cean-Salla.
Dark Rosaleen, *tr.*
Dawning of the Day, The.
Disaster.
Dream-Pedlary.
Dying Enthusiast, The.
Ellen Bawn, *tr.*
Enthusiasm.
Fair Hills of Eirè, O, The, *tr.*
Farewell, O [*or* to] Patrick Sarsfield, *tr.*
Geraldine's Daughter, The, *tr.*

Geraldine's Daughter, The, *sel.*, *tr.*
Gone in the Wind.
Home-Sickness, *tr.*
Hymn for Pentecost.
Ichabod! Thy Glory Has Departed, *tr.*
Irish Lamentation, An, *tr.*
Karamanian Exile, The.
Kathaleen Ny-Houlahan, *tr.*
Kincora, *tr.*
King Cahal Mór of the Wine-red Hand.
King of Thule, *tr.* *Fr.* Faust.
Lament for Banba, *tr.*
Lament for the Princes of Tyrone [*or* Tir-Owen] and Tyrconnel [*or* Tirconnell], A, *tr.*
Lamentation for the Death of Sir Maurice Fitzgerald, Knight of Kerry, A, *tr.*
Lamentation of Mac Liag for Kincora, *tr.*
Lay of the Captive Count, The, *tr.*
Lines Written in a Nunnery Chapel.
Love.
Lover's Farewell, The.
Lullaby, A: "O hushaby, baby! Why weepest thou?" *tr.*
Maid of Orleans, The, *tr.*
Mariner's Bride, The.
Minstrel, The, *tr.*
Nameless One, The.
Night Is Falling, The.
Night Is Nearing.
Ode to the Maguire, *tr.*
O'Hussey's Ode to the Maguire, *tr.*
O'Tuomy's Drinking Song.
Rose, The.
St. Patrick's Hymn before Tara.
St. Patrick's Hymn before Tara, *sel.*
Shapes and Signs.
Siberia.
Song: "O, strew the way with rosy flowers."
Sonnet: "Bird that discoursest from yon poplar bough."
Soul and Country.
Sunken City, The, *tr.*
Testament of Cathaeir Mor, The, *tr.* *Fr.* Book of Rights.
Three Khalandeers, The.
Three Proverbs.
Time of the Barmecides, The.
To Amine.
To My Friends, *tr.*
To My Native Land.
To My Native Land, *sel.*
To the Ingleezee Khafir, Calling Himself Djann Bool Djenkinzun.
Triplet on the Reign of the Great Sultan, A.
Twenty Golden Years Ago.
Twenty Golden Years Ago, *sel.*
Unrealities, The, *tr.*
Vision of Connaught in the Thirteenth Century, A.
Voice from the Invisible World, *tr.*
Volto Sciolto e Pensieri Stretti.
Welcome to the Prince of Ossory, *tr.*
Woman of Three Cows, The, *tr.*
World, The; a Ghazel.
Written in a Nunnery Chapel.
MANGER, ITZIK [*or* ITZIG]. Adam and Eve.
Alone.
At the Crossroad.
Autumn.
Ballad of the Holy Evening Bread, The.
Binding of Isaac, The.
Cain and Abel.
Hagar's Last Night at Abraham's.
I Am the Autumn.
Jealous Adam.
Love.
Mother Sarah's Lullaby.
Saint Balshemtov.
MANIFOLD, JOHN. Bunyip and the Whistling Kettle, The.
Camouflage.
Defensive Position.
Deserter, The.
Fife Tune.
Griesly Wife, The.
"Heureux Qui Comme Ulysse."
Listening to a Broadcast.
Night Piece.
Ration Party.
Sirens, The.
Suburban Lullaby.
Tomb of Lieutenant John Learmonth, AIF, The.
MANILIUS, MARCUS. Times, The.
MANN, KATHERINE. Château de Monthiers.
From the Virgins.
MANN, LEONARD. At Manly.
Earth, The.
Escape.
Freedom.
Girls and Soldiers Singing.
Love of Swans, The.
Meditation in Winter.
Soldier Overseas.
MANNIN, ETHEL EDITH. Out-of-Doors.
Road That Leads to Home, The.
Secret Voices, The.
Ship-Love.
MANNING, FREDERIC. At Even.
Kore.
Revenants des Enfants.
Sacrifice.
Sign, The.
Trenches, The.
MANNING, JAMES HAROLD. At the Turning of the Tide.
Ode to the Spirit of Life.
Stormy Petrel, The.
What Is Truth? *sel.*
MANNING, RENA M. Little Tramp Dog.
To a Kitten.
MANNING, ROBERT. *See* MANNYNG, ROBERT.
MANNING-SANDERS, RUTH. Come, Wary One.
Margery Daw.
Old City, The.
MANNIX, MARY E. All Souls' Eve.
MANNYNG [*or* MANNING], ROBERT. Bishop's Harp, The.
No thyng ys to man so dere.
Praise of Women.
Round Table, The.
Woman's Love.
MANRIQUE, GÓMEZ. On the Bad Government of Toledo.
To a Lady Going Veiled.
MANRIQUE, JORGE. Coplas on the Death of His Father [the Grandmaster of Santiago].
Ode on the Death of His Father.
MANSEL, W. L. Sun's Perpendicular Rays, The.
MANSFIELD, KATHERINE (Kathleen Beauchamp, Mrs. John Middleton Murry). Arabian Shawl, The. *Fr.* Two Nocturnes.
Gulf, The.
In the Rangitaki Valley.
Little Brother's Secret.
Meeting, The.
Sanary.
Sleeping Together. *Fr.* Two Nocturnes.
To L. H. B.
Two Nocturnes.
Voices of the Air.
MANSFIELD, MARGERY SWETT. Blessing Mrs. Larkin.
Corpus Christi.
This Is New England.
MANSFIELD, RICHARD. Eagle's Song, The.
Voice, The.
MANT, RICHARD, *and* EDWARD CASWALL. At the cross her station keeping, *tr.*
Stabat Mater Dolorosa, *tr.*
MANTON, JOSEPH. On Looking at the School War Memorial.
MANTUAN, BAPTISTA SPAGNUOLI. Eglogs of the Poet B. Mantuan Carmelitan, The, *sel.*
Second Egloge Entituled Fortunatus, The. *Fr.* The Eglogs of the Poet B. Mantuan Carmelitan.
MANVILLE, MARION (Mrs. Marion Manville Pope). Lee's Parole.
Surrender of New Orleans, The.
MANZONI, ALESSANDRO. Fifth of May, The—Napoleon. *Fr.* Ode.
Ode, *sel.*
Soffermati sull' arida sponda, *sel.*
MAO KUANG SHENG. Drunkard, The.
MAO TSE-TUNG. Snow, The.
MAPES, EDITH L. Oh, If They Only Knew!
Shall I Pray On?
MARAGALL, JUAN. Canto Espiritual.
Night of the Immaculate Conception.
MARBLE, EARL. Spelling in the Nursery.
MARCABRUN. At the Fountain.
Pastorela.
MARCELA DE CARPIO DE SAN FELIX, SISTER. Amor Mysticus.
MARCELIN, PHILIPPE THOBY-. *See* THOBY-MARCELIN, PHILIPPE.
MARCH, AUZIAS. What Guardian Counsels?
MARCUS ARGENTARIUS. *See* ARGENTARIUS, MARCUS.
MARECHAL, LEOPOLDO. Cortège.
MARGARET MARIA, SISTER. Martyrs of Nazareth.
MARGARET OF NAVARRE. Recipe for a Happy Life.
MARGARET PATRICIA, SISTER MARY. September 17.
MARGARET TERESA, SISTER. Matthew.
Woodland.
MARGETSON, GEORGE REGINALD. Fledgling Bard and the Poetry Society, The.
MARGOLIS, SILVIA. Never Ask Me Why.
MARI NIGHEAN ALISDAIR RUAIDH. Cumha Mhic Leoid (Lament for the Son of Leod).
"MARIA DEL OCCIDENTE." *See* BROOKS, MARIA GOWEN.
MARIA DEL REY, SISTER. "Haec Est Domus Dei et Porta Coeli."
MARIE DE FRANCE. Chartivel, *sel.*
Sarrazine's Song [to Her Dead Lover]. *Fr.* Chartivel.
Song from "Chartivel."
Would I Might Go Far over Sea.
"MARIE JOSEPHINE." *See* HEMENWAY, ABBY MARIA.
MARIELLA, SISTER. Blue Larkspur.
Jefferson Highway, The.
Sheep Herd, The.
MARIENHOF, ANATOLY BORISOVICH. October.
Savage Nomad Hordes.
MARINETTI, FILIPPO TOMMASO. Against the Hope of Reconstruction.
MARINI, GIAMBATTISTA. Description of Beauty, A.
Fading Beauty.
MARINO, GIOVANNI BATTISTA. *See* MARINI, GIAMBATTISTA.
MARINONI, ROSA ZAGNONI. Ash Wednesday.
At Sunrise.
Crushed Fender.
For a New Home.
Who Are My People?
MARIO, ANTONIO. Thyrsis.
MARIS STELLA, SISTER. Afternoon in a Tree.
Bay Violets.
Cause of Our Joy.
Grapes.
I Who Had Been Afraid.
In Memory of Mother Seraphine Ireland.
It Is the Reed.
Landscape with Children.
Lines for a Feast of Our Lady.
Love Is Not Solace.
Now That Can Never Be Done.
Out of Darkness.
Ox and Donkey's Carol.
Oxford Bells.
Pelicans My Father Sees, The.
San Marco Museum, Florence.
This One Heart-shaken.
Voice, The.
MARJ KUHL. Garden at Sunset.
MARK, RICKMAN. Snow in Town.
"MARK TWAIN." *See* "TWAIN, MARK."

MARKHAM, ANNA CATHERINE (Mrs. Edwin Markham). In an Alameda Field.
MARKHAM, EDWIN. Anchored to the Infinite.
Angelus, The.
Angelus, The, *sel.*
Ann Rutledge.
Ascension, The.
Avengers, The.
Breathless Awe.
Brotherhood.
Call, The.
Child of My Heart.
Christ of the Andes, The.
Christ of the Andes, The, *sel.*
Conscripts of the Dream, *sel.*
Consecration of the Common Way, The.
Courage, All.
Creed, A.
Creed, A, *sel.*
Day and the Work, The.
Dream, The.
Duty.
Earth Is Enough.
Epitaph, An: "Let us not think of our departed dead."
Errand Imperious, The.
Flying Mist.
For the New Year.
Free Nation, A.
Gift of Work, The.
Great Guest Comes, The.
Guard of the Sepulcher, A.
Harvest Song, A.
How Oswald Dined with God.
How Shall We Honor Them?
How the Great Guest Came.
How to Go and Forget.
If He Should Come.
Inbrothered. *Fr.* A Creed.
Invisible Bride, The.
Joy of the Hills, The.
Joy of the Morning.
Last Furrow, The.
League of Love in Action, The.
Let There Be No More Battles!
Lincoln the Great Commoner.
Lincoln, the Man of the People.
Lincoln, the Man of the People, *sel.*
Lincoln Triumphant.
Lion and Lioness.
Little Brothers of the Ground.
Live and Help Live.
Look into the Gulf, A.
Lord of All, The.
Love's Vigil.
Man with the Hoe, The.
Man-making.
My Comrade.
Nail-torn God, The.
Need of the Hour, The.
New Trinity, The.
Night Moths, The.
Opportunity.
Our Dead.
Our Dead, Overseas.
Outwitted.
Panther, The.
Peace.
Pilgrim, The.
Place of Peace, The.
Poet, The.
Poetry.
Power.
Prayer, A: "Teach me, Father, how to go."
Preparedness.
Quatrain: "Here is the Truth in a little creed."
Revelation.
Rhyme for Thanksgiving Day, A.
Right Kind of People, The.
Rules for the Road.
Saint Patrick.
Shine on Me, Secret Splendor.
Song for Heroes, A.
Song of the Shepherds, The.
Song of Victory, A, *sels.*
Song to a Tree.
Task That Is Given to You, The.
Testing, The.
Thanksgiving Rosary, The.
Third Wonder, The.
To Saint Francis.
Toiler, The, *sel.*
Toilers, The.
True Work Is Worship. *Fr.* The Angelus.
Two at a Fireside.
Two Taverns.
Unbelievable, The.
Victory in Defeat.
Virgilia.
Virgilia, *sel.*
Wharf of Dreams, The.
Whirlwind Road, The.
Young Lincoln.
Your Tears.
MARKHAM, LUCIA CLARK. Bluebells.
MARKHAM, VIRGIL. Babylon.
MARKISH, PERETZ. We Reached Out Far.
MARKORAS, GERASIMOS. Dead Maiden's Complaint, A.
Innocent Fears.
Spring Nights, *sel.*
Two.
MARKS, EDWARD B. Little Lost Child, The.
My Mother Was a Lady; or, If Jack Were Only Here.
MARKS, GODFREY. Sailing.
MARKS, JEANNETTE. To Some Philadelphia Sparrows.
MARKS, MARGARET. Chorus for Refusal.
Lady with Arrows.
Tactic.
MARLATT, EARL BOWMAN. Crucifixion.
Icarus.
Paul.
World-Nation, A.
MARLOWE, CHRISTOPHER. Ah faire Zenocrate. *Fr.* Tamburlaine.
Ah, Faustus, now hast thou but one bare hower to live. *Fr.* Dr. Faustus.
Ambition. *Fr.* Tamburlaine.
Amores, *sels., tr.*
And ride in triumph through Persepolis! *Fr.* Tamburlaine.
Barabas in His Counting-House. *Fr.* The Jew of Malta.
Beauty. *Fr.* Tamburlaine.
Blacke Is the Beauty of the Brightest Day. *Fr.* Tamburlaine.
Bloody Conquests of Mighty Tamburlaine, The. *Fr.* Tamburlaine.
Chorus on the Death of Faustus. *Fr.* Dr. Faustus.
Climbing after Knowledge. *Fr.* Tamburlaine.
Come live with me and be my love.
Death of Zenocrate, The. *Fr.* Tamburlaine.
Divine Zenocrate. *Fr.* Tamburlaine.
Dr. Faustus.
Dr. Faustus, *sels.*
Edward the Second, *sels.*
Edward's Death. *Fr.* Edward the Second.
Elegies, *sels., tr.*
Emperor of the Threefold World. *Fr.* Tamburlaine.
End of Faustus, The. *Fr.* Dr. Faustus.
Fair Is Too Foul an Epithet. *Fr.* Tamburlaine.
Faustus to Helen. *Fr.* Dr. Faustus.
Faustus to the Apparition of Helen. *Fr.* Dr. Faustus.
Finale: "Ah, Faustus, now hast thou." *Fr.* Dr. Faustus.
First Sight. *Fr.* Hero and Leander.
Fragment: "I walk'd along a stream, for pureness rare," *at.*
Fye; what a trouble tis to count this trash. *Fr.* The Jew of Malta.
God of war resigns his room to me, The. *Fr.* Tamburlaine.
Helen [of Troy]. *Fr.* Dr. Faustus.
Hero and Leander.
Hero and Leander, *sels.*
Hero the Faire. *Fr.* Hero and Leander.
Holla, ye pampered jades of Asia. *Fr.* Tamburlaine.
I walk'd along a stream for pureness rare, *at.*
I will, with engines never exercised. *Fr.* Tamburlaine.
Idea of Wealth, An. *Fr.* The Jew of Malta.
If All the Pens That Ever Poets Held. *Fr.* Tamburlaine.
Immortal Flowers of Poesy. *Fr.* Tamburlaine.
It lies not in our power to love or hate. *Fr.* Hero and Leander.
Jew of Malta, The, *sels.*
Last Hour of Faustus, The. *Fr.* Dr. Faustus.
Love at First Sight. *Fr.* Hero and Leander.
Milkmaid's Song, The.
Mine Argosy from Alexandria. *Fr.* The Jew of Malta.
Nature That Framed Us of Four Elements. *Fr.* Tamburlaine.
Now Clear the Triple Region of the Air. *Fr.* Tamburlaine.
O Hero, Hero, thus he cry'de full oft. *Fr.* Hero and Leander.
O Lente, Lente, Curite Noctis Equi. *Fr.* Dr. Faustus.
Passionate Shepherd to His Love, The.
Perfect Bliss and Sole Felicity. *Fr.* Tamburlaine.
Pharsalia, *sel., tr.*
Poet's Pen, The. *Fr.* Tamburlaine.
Portents, The, *tr.* *Fr.* Pharsalia.
Precious Stones. *Fr.* The Jew of Malta.
Rudiments of War. *Fr.* Tamburlaine.
Shepherd to His Love, The.
Shepherd's Plea, The.
So from the east unto the farthest west. *Fr.* Tamburlaine.
Song of Ithamore, The. *Fr.* The Jew of Malta.
Spell of Invisibility, A, *at.*
Tamburlaine the Great, *sels.*
Tamburlaine on Poetry. *Fr.* Tamburlaine.
Tamburlaine to Zenocrate. *Fr.* Tamburlaine.
Tamburlaine's Love. *Fr.* Tamburlaine.
Thirst of raigne and sweetness of a crown. *Fr.* Tamburlaine.
To Entertain Divine Zenocrate. *Fr.* Tamburlaine.
To Verse Let Kings Give Place, *tr.* *Fr.* Elegies.
Tragical History of Doctor Faustus, The. *See* Dr. Faustus.
Was This the Face. *Fr.* Dr. Faustus.
What Is Beauty, Saith My Sufferings, Then? *Fr.* Tamburlaine.
Who Ever Loved, That Loved Not at First Sight? *Fr.* Hero and Leander.
World will strive with hosts of men-at-arms, The. *Fr.* Tamburlaine.
MARLOWE, CHRISTOPHER, *and* THOMAS NASHE. I Have an Orchard. *Fr.* The Tragedy of Dido.
Tragedy of Dido, The, *sels.*
MARNAU, FRED. London Elegies, II.
MAROT, CLÉMENT. Ballade of a Friar.
Carol: "Shepherd and a shepherdess, A."
Friar Lubin.
Love-Lesson, A.
Madame d'Albert's [*or* d'Albret's] Laugh.
Of Himself.
Of the Abbot and His Valet.
Of "Yea" and "Nay."
Old-Time Love.
On Her Laugh.
Posy Ring, The.
Song: "If ye would drink delight."
Song of the Vineyard Knife.
To Anne.
Yes and No.
MARQUINA, EDUARDO. Montoro's Song against Count Alvaro de Luna, High Constable of Castile.
MARQUIS, DON (Donald Robert Marquis).
Another Villon-ous Variation.
Archy a Low Brow. *Fr.* Archys Life of Mehitabel.

Archy and Mehitabel, *sels.*
Archy Confesses. *Fr.* Archy and Mehitabel.
Archy Experiences a Seizure. *Fr.* Archys Life of Mehitabel.
Archy, the Cockroach, Speaks. *Fr.* Certain Maxims of Archy.
Archygrams. *Fr.* Archys Life of Mehitabel.
Archys Autobiography. *Fr.* Archys Life of Mehitabel.
Archys Last Name. *Fr.* Archys Life of Mehitabel.
Archys Life of Mehitabel, *sels.*
Artists Shouldn't Have Offspring. *Fr.* Archys Life of Mehitabel.
Awakening, The.
Ballade: "Outcast bones from a thousand biers." *Fr.* Archy and Mehitabel.
Ballade of the Under Side. *Fr.* Archys Life of Mehitabel.
Birth, The.
Bridal Night.
Certain Maxims of Archy.
Certain Maxims of Archy, *sel.*
Chant Royal of the Dejected Dipsomaniac.
Cheerio My Deario. *Fr.* Archy and Mehitabel.
Confession of a Glutton.
Desk Motto, A.
Dog, The.
Down in a Wine Vault.
Flattered Lightning Bug, The. *Fr.* Archy and Mehitabel.
For I am Sad.
From the Bridge.
Gentleman of Fifty Soliloquizes, A.
God-Maker, Man, The.
God-Maker, Man, The, *sels.*
Grotesques, *sels.*
Heir and Surf.
Hen and the Oriole, The. *Fr.* Archy and Mehitabel.
Hero Cockroach, The. *Fr.* Archys Life of Mehitabel.
Honey Bee, The.
Hot-Weather Song, A.
I Have Looked Inward, *sels.*
I rose . . . I rose . . . *Fr.* I Have Looked Inward.
Incendiary Sex, The.
Jokesmith's Vacation, The.
King Cophetua and the Beggar Maid.
Lilies.
Limerick: "There was a young fellow named Sydney."
Little While, A.
Mehitabel Sings a Song. *Fr.* Archy and Mehitabel.
Mystic, The.
Name, The.
Noah an' Jonah an' Cap'n John Smith.
Nobler Lesson, The.
Old Trouper, The. *Fr.* Archy and Mehitabel.
Only Thy Dust.
Pete at the Seashore.
Pete's Holiday.
Pete's Theology.
Prohibition.
Quinks, The.
Rondeau, The: "Your rondeau's tale must be light."
Savage Portraits.
Small Talk.
Song of a Thousand Years, *sel.*
Song of Mehitabel, The. *Fr.* Archy and Mehitabel.
Spinks, The.
Spring Ode.
There was a locked door. *Fr.* I Have Looked Inward.
They Had No Poet.
Those That Come Back.
Time time said old King Tut.
To a Lost Sweetheart, *sel.*
Tomcat [*or* Tom-Cat], The.
Tragedy of the Deep, A.
Transient.
Triolet, The: "Your triolet should glimmer."
Tristram and Isolt.
Unrest.
Wages, The.
Wail of Archy, The, *sel.* *Fr.* Archy and Mehitabel.
Warty Bliggens, the Toad. *Fr.* Archy and Mehitabel.
When One Loves Tensely.
Young Moses, The.
MARR, BARBARA. Prayer: "Lord, make me sensitive to the sight."
MARRIOTT, ANNE. Prairie Graveyard.
Sandstone.
Search.
Wind Our Enemy, The.
Wind Our Enemy, The, *sel.*
Woodyards in the Rain.
MARRIOTT, SIR JAMES. Ode on Lyric Poetry.
MARRIOTT, JOHN. Devonshire Lane, The.
On John Donne's Book of Poems.
MARRIS, SIR WILLIAM. Blackbird, A, *tr.*
Freshet, A, *tr.*
Iliad, The, *sels., tr.*
Odes (*of* Horace), *sel., tr.*
Odyssey, The, *sels., tr.*
Poet's Shield, The, *tr.*
MARRON, OS. Nocturnal.
MARRYAT, FREDERICK. Captain Stood on the Carronade, The. *Fr.* Snarleyyow; or, The Dog Fiend.
Old Navy, The. *Fr.* Snarleyyow; or, The Dog Fiend.
Port Admiral.
Snarleyyow; or, The Dog Fiend, *sel.*
MARS, ANN (Annalita Marsigli). Shadow.
MARSDEN, WILLIAM. What Is Time?
MARSH, DANIEL L. Greatest Person in the Universe, The.
MARSH, E. L. Magic Piper, The.
MARSH, SIR EDWARD. Cat and the Fox, The, *tr.*
Cat into Lady, *tr.*
Coelo Tonantem, *tr.*
Crow and the Fox, The, *tr.*
Piano, The, *tr.*
MARSHAK, SAMUEL. Dictionary.
Long Road Blossoms, The.
MARSHALL, ARCHIBALD. Limerick: "There was a young man of Devizes."
MARSHALL, EDWARD. Leave the Word Alone.
MARSHALL, JAMES (Jim). Oregon Trail, 1851.
MARSHALL, LENORE G. Argument on Immortality.
Invented a Person.
MARSHALL, WILLIAM E. Brookfield.
Brookfield, *sel.*
To a Mayflower.
MARSMAN, HENDRIK. Valley of Sleep, The. *Fr.* The Zodiac.
Zodiac, The, *sel.*
MARSON, UNA. Hunted.
Nightfall.
MARSTON, JOHN. Antonio and Mellida, *sel.*
Antonio's Revenge, *sel.*
Dutch Courtesan, The, *sel.*
Malcontent, The, *sel.*
Nut-brown Ale, The, *at.*
O Love, How Strangely Sweet. *Fr.* The Dutch Courtesan.
Oblivion. *Fr.* The Scourge of Villainy.
Proemium in Librum Primum. *Fr.* The Scourge of Villainy.
Prologue: "Rawish dank of clumsy winter ramps, The." *Fr.* Antonio's Revenge.
Prologue to "Antonio's Revenge."
Satire V: "Ambitious Gorgons," *sel.*
Satire VIII: "Curio, ay me! Thy mistress' monkey's dead!" *Fr.* The Scourge of Villainy.
Satire X: Humors. *Fr.* The Scourge of Villainy.
Satire II: "I cannot hold, I cannot, I, indure." *Fr.* The Scourge of Villainy.
Satire VII: "'Man, a man, a kingdom for a man, A!'" *Fr.* The Scourge of Villainy.
Satire IV: "Vice, from privation of that sacred grace." *Fr.* The Scourge of Villainy.
Scholar and the Dog, The.
Scourge of Villainy, The, *sels.*
Song: "Delicious beauty, that doth lie," *at.*
Song: "O Love, how strangely sweet." *Fr.* The Dutch Courtesan.
To Detraction [I Present My Poesy]. *Fr.* The Scourge of Villainy.
To Everlasting Oblivion. *Fr.* The Scourge of Villainy.
MARSTON, JOHN WESTLAND. Marie de Meranie, *sel.*
Parting of King Philip and Marie, The. *Fr.* Marie de Meranie.
MARSTON, PHILIP BOURKE. After.
After Summer.
At Last.
At the Last.
Garden Fairies.
Greeting, A.
Her Pity.
How My Songs of Her Began.
If You Were Here.
It must have been for one of us, my own.
Love and Music.
Love's Music.
No Death.
Not Thou but I.
Old Churchyard of Bonchurch, The.
Rose and the Wind, The.
Roses' Song. *Fr.* Garden Fairies.
To the Spirit of Poetry.
Vain Wish, A.
Worth Remembrance.
MARSTON, WESTLAND. *See* MARSTON, JOHN WESTLAND.
MARTÍ, JOSÉ. Out of the Goodness of His Heart.
Simple Verses, *sel.*
To Cocola Fernández del Castillo.
MARTIAL (Marcus Valerius Martialis). Against Writers That Carp at Other Men's Books.
Antiquary, The.
Beau, The.
Bee in amber hides, yet gleams unspoiled, The.
Believe me, sir, I'd like to spend whole days.
Bought Locks.
By daily sipping poison Mithridates used to think.
Country Pleasures.
Critics.
Critics and Cooks.
De Coenatione Micae.
Dinner with Ligurinus.
Dude, The.
Dull are the topics you want me to treat in my epigrams, Mister.
"Epic epigram, An," I heard you say.
Epigram: "They say your lady friends have no long life."
Epigrams should, I suppose, please their readers by saying it briefly.
Epitaph on Erotion.
Erotion.
Explanation, An.
From the West.
Generous and jealous, soft and hard of heart.
Golden Sorrow, A.
Gouty-footed Colonel J.
Grammar of Love, The.
Happy Life, The.
He who prefers to grant only half of the total which Linus.
Hinted Wish, A.
How to Raise a Son.
I wasn't well, and at my call.
In All the Humors.
Issa's more full of sport and wanton play.
It's not a case of poisoned cup.
Legacy, A.
Look round: you see a little supper room.
Lover's Play of Words.
Lupus, you question carefully.
Man's Inhumanity to Man.

MARTIAL (*continued*)
Marriage of Claudia.
Martial, the things for to attain.
Martial's Quiet Life.
Means to Attain Happy Life, The.
Mine was the Book, Fidentine, till you ravished it for your recital.
Mr. Flint goes up the West.
Misunderstanding, A.
More than Quit.
Mother and sire, to you do I commend.
Nor a Lender Be.
Nothing you give while alive; but you promise a legacy, Maro.
Now Antoninus, in a smiling age.
Of late our friend has bought a purple-dyed toga.
On a Little Dog.
On the Death of a Young and Favorite Slave.
On your bald, dirty head you wear.
Once a surgeon, Dr. Baker.
Once I used to be called to join your parties.
Outclassed.
Procrastination.
Quip to the Reader.
Reactionary Critic.
Sealed Bags of Ducats.
Seventy-five percent of his debt did the wine-bleared Hylas.
Sextus the Usurer.
Shopper, The.
Smith's seventh wife has joined the batch.
So you would like to become Mrs. Prisca?—Well, I understand that.
Some of these poems are good, some are medium, many are poor stuff.
Tailor Bills.
"Tell me honestly, Marcus, tell me, please do."
Temperament.
That fellow Singer, it is said.
That I now call you by your name.
Thermometrical.
Things That Cause a Quiet Life, The.
Though you never recite, you would like to pass for a poet.
Thus, Prince, of all my goods bereft.
To a Married Couple That Could Not Agree.
To a Poetic Lover.
To a Schoolmaster.
To an Old Fraud.
To bring yourself to be happy.
To Fidentinus.
To His Book.
To His Cousin.
To Lupus.
To Quintus.
To Sabidius.
To Septicianus.
To Sextus.
To-Morrow.
Total Abstainer, A.
Translat. ex Martial.
Un Médecin Malgré Eux.
Unchanged.
Upon the platform Croker.
What Makes a Happy Life.
When Handiman shaves Herr von Wolf.
You, Casey, long a baker.
You serve the best wine always, my dear sir.
You, Vacerra, admire the ancients only.
You've bestowed a suburban farm on me, Sir.
MARTIN, ADA LOUISE. Sleep.
MARTIN, ARTHUR PATCHETT. Cynic of the Woods, The.
Love and War.
MARTIN, C. D. God's Goodness.
MARTIN, EDWARD SANDFORD. Christmas, 1898.
Contemporary Suitor, The.
Egotism.
Girl of Pompeii, A.
Infirm.
Little Brother of the Rich, A.
Mea Culpa.
My Name Is Legion.
Sea Is His, The.
Snow-bound.
Which Is Me?
MARTIN, EVA. Cat and Crocuses.
MARTIN, HERMANN FORD. Home.
Wander-Lure.
MARTIN, JOHN. God's Dark.
MARTIN, MARGARET NICKERSON. Judas Iscariot.
MARTIN, MICHAEL C. Electric Storm.
Guard.
MARTIN, SARAH CATHERINE. Old Mother Hubbard [and Her Dog].
MARTIN, SIR THEODORE. Bore, The, *tr.*
Debate of the Body and the Soul, The, *ad.*
Du bist wie eine Blume, *tr.*
Du schönes Fischer-Mädchen, *tr.*
Farewell to Bithynia, *tr.*
Gazelles, *tr.*
Grenadiers, The, *tr.*
Home to Sirmio, *tr.*
Im Traum sah ich ein Männchen klein und putzig, *tr.*
Integer Vitae, *tr.*
Loreley, *tr.*
Love Is All, *tr.*
Mädchen mit dem rothen Mündchen, *tr.*
Odes (*of Horace*), *sel., tr.*
Purity, *tr. Fr.* Odes.
Reconciliation, The, *tr.*
Thou Lovely Fisher-Maiden, *tr.*
To Aristius Fuscus, *tr.*
To His Cup-Bearer, *tr.*
To Lucius Sestius, *tr.*
Two Songs (*by Heine*), *tr.*
Wenn ich in deine Augen seh', *tr.*
Whene'er I Look into Thine Eyes, *tr.*
With Inky Sails, *tr.*
MARTIN, SIR THEODORE, *and* WILLIAM E. AYTOUN. *See* AYTOUN, WILLIAM EDMONSTOUNE, *and* SIR THEODORE MARTIN.
MARTIN, WILLIAM WESLEY. Apple Orchard in the Spring, The.
MARTÍN CÓDAX. Cantiga de Amigo: "When you know you love a sweetheart."
MARTINDALE, CYRIL CHARLIE. God Leads the Way, *tr.*
MARTINEAU, G. D. Ivan.
Jan.
MARTINEAU, HARRIET. On, On, Forever.
MARTÍNEZ DE LA ROSA, FRANCISCO. Alhambra, The.
Anacreontic.
MARTÍNEZ DE NAVARRETE, JOSÉ MANUEL. Morning.
MARTINSON, HARRY. Visual Memory.
MARTLEY, JOHN. Budget of Paradoxes, A.
Valley of Shanganagh, The.
MARUYAMA, KAORU. Distant View of School.
Gyroscopic Lamp, A.
MARVELL, ANDREW. Ametas and Thestylis Making Hay-Ropes.
Appleton House, *sels.*
Bermudas.
Carrying Their Coracles. *Fr.* Upon Appleton House.
Character of Holland, The, *sel.*
Charles II. *Fr.* Last Instructions to a Painter.
Chorus: "Climb at Court for me that will," *tr. Fr.* Thyestes.
Conclusion. *Fr.* A Dialogue between the Soul and Body.
Coronet, The.
Cromwell Dead. *Fr.* A Poem upon the Death of O. C.
Death of the White Fawn.
Definition of Love, The.
Dialogue between the Resolved Soul and Created Pleasure, A.
Dialogue between the Soul and Body, A.
Dialogue between the Soul and Body, A, *sel.*
Drop of Dew, A.
Dutch in the Medway, The. *Fr.* Last Instructions to a Painter.
Enough; and leave the rest to Fame.
Epitaph, An: "Enough; and leave the rest to fame."
Epitaph upon ——, An.
Execution of King Charles, The. *Fr.* An Horatian Ode upon Cromwell's Return from Ireland.
Eyes and Tears.
Fair Singer, The.
Fair Singer, The, *sel.*
First Anniversary of the Government under His Royal Highness the Lord Protector, The, *sel.*
Fleckno, an English Priest at Rome.
Gallery, The.
Garden, The ("How vainly men").
Garden, The ("How vainly men"), *sels.*
Garden, A ("See how the flowers"). *Fr.* Upon Appleton House.
Girl and Her Fawn, The. *Fr.* The Nymph Complaining for the Death of her Fawn.
Girl Describes Her Fawn, The. *Fr.* The Nymph Complaining for the Death of her Fawn.
Go, intercept some fountain in the vein.
Had we but world enough, and time.
Here at the fountain's sliding foot. *Fr.* The Garden.
Hewel, or Woodpecker, The. *Fr.* Upon Appleton House.
Horatian Ode upon Cromwell's Return from Ireland, An.
Horatian Ode upon Cromwell's Return from Ireland, An, *sels.*
In a Forest. *Fr.* Upon Appleton House.
In Exile.
King Charles upon the Scaffold. *Fr.* An Horatian Ode upon Cromwell's Return from Ireland.
Kingfisher, The. *Fr.* Upon Appleton House.
Last Instructions to a Painter, *sels.*
Loyal Scot, The, *sel.*
Match, The.
Mower against Gardens, The.
Mower to the Glowworms, The.
Mower's Song, The.
Musick's Empire.
Nymph and Her Fawn, The. *Fr.* The Nymph Complaining for the Death of Her Fawn.
Nymph Complaining for the Death of Her Fawn, The.
Nymph Complaining for the Death of Her Fawn, The, *sels.*
On a Drop of Dew.
On [Mr.] Milton's "Paradise Lost."
On Paradise Lost.
On the Lord Mayor and Court of Aldermen, Presenting the Late King and Duke of York Each with a Copy of Their Freedoms, Anno Dom. 1674.
On the Victory Obtained by Admiral Blake.
Picture of Little T. C. in a Prospect of Flowers, The.
Poem upon the Death of His Late Highness the Lord Protector, A, *sels.*
Poem upon the Death of Oliver Cromwell, A.
Quiet Life, The, *tr.*
Senec. Traged. ex Thyeste Chor. 2, *tr.*
Song of the Emigrants in Bermuda [*or* in the Bermudas].
Thoughts in a Garden.
Thoughts in a Garden, *sel.*
Thyestes, *sel., tr.*
To Glow-Worms.
To His Coy Mistress.
To His Coy Mistress, *sel.*
Two Kings.
Upon Appleton House, *sels.*
Upon Appleton House, to My Lord Fairfax.
Young Love.
MARVIN, DWIGHT EDWARDS. Lord, Give Me Faith.
Nearing the Ford.
Sabbath Morning Worship.
Sleeplessness.

Vesper Bells.
Marx, Anne. Lacemaker, The (Vermeer).
Marx, Groucho. You're So Kind.
Mary, Queen of Hungary. Prayer: "O God! though sorrow be my fate."
Mary, Queen of Scots. *See* Mary Queen of Scots.
Mary, E. Sister Ann Raphael.
Mary Catherine, Sister, O.S.U.
Again for You.
New Testament, Revised Edition.
Who Know Thee Best.
Mary Catherine, Sister, S.C. Beside Lilia Dead.
Mary Francis, Sister. Children of Francis, 1953.
Epitaph: "Here lies the ideal of Saint Francis."
Genealogy.
Memorandum to Saint Francis—April 16.
Mary Honora, Sister. After Mardi Gras.
Eighteen.
Land of the Free.
Mary Immaculata, Sister. Spring Comes to Our Garden.
Mary Immaculate, Sister. Ordination.
Mary Monica, Sister. Wolf of Gubbio Speaks to Saint Francis, The.
Mary of the Angels, Sister. Nun's Hobby, A.
Mary of the Visitation, Sister. As One Finding Peace.
Gifts.
In Tenebris.
Profession Song.
Mary Queen of Scots. Farewell to France, *at.*
Prayer before Execution.
Sonnets, *sels.*
Maryanna, Sister. Knight, The.
Meditations in a Museum Cloister.
Paradox.
With One Swift Thought.
Marzials, Frank T. Death as the Fool.
Death as the Teacher of Love-Lore.
Two Sonnet-Songs.
Marzials, Théophile Julius Henry.
Carpe Diem.
Last Night, *tr.*
May Margaret.
Pastoral, A: "Flower of the medlar."
Song: "There's one great bunch of stars in heaven."
Tragedy, A.
Twickenham Ferry.
Masaoka Shiki. Waiting.
Mase, Sidney Warren. It's Simply Great.
Masefield, John. Ah, we are neither heaven nor earth, but men. *Fr.* Sonnets ("Long long ago").
"All Ye That Pass By."
Another Cross. *Fr.* The Everlasting Mercy.
August, 1914.
Ballad of John Silver, A.
Beauty ("I have seen dawn and sunset").
Being Her Friend.
Biography.
Book & Bookplate.
By a Bier-Side.
C. L. M.
Cape Horn Gospel—I.
Cape Horn Gospel—II.
Captain Stratton's Fancy.
Cargoes.
Chanty: "Kneel to the beautiful women who bear us this strange brave fruit." *Fr.* The Tragedy of Pompey the Great.
Chief Centurions, The. *Fr.* The Tragedy of Pompey the Great.
Choice, The. *Fr.* Lollingdon Downs.
Clipper Loitered South, The. *Fr.* Dauber.
Consecration, A.
Countrymen, The. *Fr.* Reynard the Fox.
Creed, A.
Dauber, *sels.*
Dauber Rounds Cape Horn, The. *Fr.* Dauber.
D'Avalos' Prayer.
Dead Knight, The.
Death Warnings, *tr.*
End, The. *Fr.* Sonnets ("Long long ago").
Enslaved, *sels.*
Everlasting Mercy, The.
Everlasting Mercy, The, *sels.*
Flesh, I Have Knocked at Many a Dusty Door. *Fr.* Sonnets ("Long long ago").
Fox Awakes, The. *Fr.* Reynard the Fox.
Fox Hunt, The. *Fr.* Reynard the Fox.
Fragments.
Frontier, The.
Golden City of St. Mary, The.
Her Heart.
How many ways, how many times. *Fr.* Sonnets ("Long long ago").
I could not sleep for thinking of the sky. *Fr.* Lollingdon Downs.
I Never See the Red Rose [Crown the Year]. *Fr.* Sonnets ("Long long ago").
If I Could Come Again to That Dear Place. *Fr.* Sonnets ("Long long ago").
If I could get within this changing I. *Fr.* Sonnets ("Long long ago").
Ignorance.
In the Great Green Commonwealth of Thought.
It May Be So with Us. *Fr.* Sonnets ("Long long ago").
June Twilight.
Kings Go By, The. *Fr.* Lollingdon Downs.
King's Highway, The.
Laugh and Be Merry.
Lemmings, The.
Let that which is to come be as it may. *Fr.* Sonnets ("Long long ago").
Life Is a Miracle. *Fr.* Sonnets ("Long long ago").
Lines: "By this the sun was all one glitter." *Fr.* The Everlasting Mercy.
Lollingdon Downs.
Lollingdon Downs, *sels.*
London Town.
Long long ago, when all the glittering earth. *Fr.* Sonnets ("Long long ago").
Lyrics: "Give me a light that I may see her."
Man has his unseen friend, his unseen twin. *Fr.* Sonnets ("Long long ago").
Mayblossom, The.
Men Are Made Human by the Mighty Fall. *Fr.* Sonnets ("Long long ago").
Mother Carey.
Night [Is] on the Downland.
O little self, within whose smallness lies. *Fr.* Sonnets ("Long long ago").
Old Song Resung, An.
On Eastnor Knoll.
On Growing Old.
On Growing Old, *sel.*
On Malvern Hill.
Open Gate, The. *Fr.* The Everlasting Mercy.
Passing Strange, The.
Ploughman, The. *Fr.* The Everlasting Mercy.
Port of Holy Peter.
Port of Many Ships.
Prayer: "When the last sea is sailed, and the last shallow charted."
Racer, The.
Revelation.
Reynard the Fox, *sels.*
Rider at the Gate, The.
Right Royal.
Rima LXXIII: "They closed her eyes," *tr.* *Fr.* Rimas.
Rimas, *sel., tr.*
Roadways.
Rose of the World, The.
Roses Are Beauty. *Fr.* Sonnets ("Long long ago").
Rounding the Horn. *Fr.* Dauber.
Sea-Change.
Sea-Fever.
Seekers, The.
Ships.
Sonnet: "Ah, we are neither heaven nor earth, but men." *Fr.* Sonnets ("Long long ago").
Sonnet: Death-Warnings, *tr.*
Sonnet: "Flesh, I have knocked at many a dusty door." *Fr.* Sonnets ("Long long ago").
Sonnet: "Go, spend your penny, Beauty, when you will." *Fr.* Sonnets ("Long long ago").
Sonnet: "Here in the self is all that man can know." *Fr.* Sonnets ("Long long ago").
Sonnet: "I could not sleep for thinking of the sky." *Fr.* Lollingdon Downs.
Sonnet: "I never see the red rose crown the year." *Fr.* Sonnets ("Long long ago").
Sonnet: "If I could come again to that dear place." *Fr.* Sonnets ("Long long ago").
Sonnet: "Is there a great green commonwealth of thought." *Fr.* Sonnets ("Long long ago").
Sonnet: "Man has his unseen friend, his unseen twin." *Fr.* Sonnets ("Long long ago").
Sonnet: "Now they are gone with all their songs and sins." *Fr.* Sonnets ("Like bones the ruins of the cities stand").
Sonnet: "O little self, within whose smallness lies." *Fr.* Sonnets ("Long long ago").
Sonnet: "What am I, Life? A thing of watery salt." *Fr.* Sonnets ("Long long ago").
Sonnets ("Like bones the ruins of the cities stand"), *sel.*
Sonnets ("Long long ago"), *sels.*
Sorrow of Mydath.
Spanish Waters.
Tarry Buccaneer, The.
Tewkesbury Road.
There Is No God, as I Was Taught in Youth. *Fr.* Sonnets ("Long long ago").
There, on the Darkened Deathbed [Dies the Brain]. *Fr.* Sonnets ("Long long ago").
They Closed Her Eyes, *tr.*
They Marched over the Field of Waterloo.
To C. L. M.
To His Mother, C. L. M.
To the Seamen.
Tomorrow.
Trade Winds.
Tragedy of Pompey the Great, The, *sels.*
Tree, The.
Truth.
Twilight.
Up on the Downs.
Vagabond.
Valediction, A; Liverpool Docks.
Wanderer, The ("All day they loitered").
Wanderer's Song, A.
Watching by a Sick-Bed.
West Wind, The.
What am I, Life? A thing of watery salt. *Fr.* Sonnets ("Long long ago").
What is this atom which contains the whole. *Fr.* Sonnets ("Long long ago").
Wild Duck, The.
Wood-Pigeons.
Word, The.
Yarn of the *Loch Achray,* The.
Mason, Agnes Louisa Carter. Whenever a Little Child Is Born.
Mason, Caroline Atherton Briggs.
Do They Miss Me at Home?
En Voyage.

MASON, CAROLINE ATHERTON (*cont.*)
En Voyage, *sel.*
Eventide.
Four Winds, The. *Fr.* En Voyage.
God Knows Best.
God's Will Is Best.
Open Secret, An.
President Lincoln's Grave.
Reconciliation.
That Wind Is Best.
When I Am Old.
Whichever Way the Wind Doth Blow.
MASON, EDGAR COOPER. Safe in His Keeping.
Satisfied.
Tear Down the Walls!
MASON, GENEVIEVE W. My Dog and I.
MASON, GUY. Adventure.
Independence.
MASON, JONATHAN. Columbus to Ferdinand, *wr. at. See* FRENEAU, PHILIP.
MASON, MADELINE. Janus.
MASON, MARIE. Mary's Easter.
"MASON, MARK." *See* WINNER, SEPTIMUS.
MASON, MARY AUGUSTA. My Little Neighbor.
Scarlet Tanager, The.
MASON, MARY J. Saviour, Who Died for Me.
MASON, RONALD ALLISON KELLS. After Death.
Be Swift O Sun.
Body of John.
Ecce Homunculus.
Footnote to John II:4.
Fugue.
Judas Iscariot.
On a Dead Cripple.
On the Swag.
Our Love Was a Grim Citadel.
Prelude: "This short straight sword."
Song of Allegiance.
Sonnet of Brotherhood.
Young Man Thinks of Sons, The.
MASON, W. L. My Airedale Dog.
MASON, WALT. Eyes of Lincoln, The.
Little Green Tents.
MASON, WILLIAM. English Garden, The, *sels.*
Landscape. *Fr.* The English Garden.
Making a Garden. *Fr.* The English Garden.
Ode to a Friend.
Ode to a Water Nymph.
Sonnet: Anniversary, February 23, 1795.
MASSEY, GERALD. Around Me Rose the Phantoms of the Dark. *Fr.* Only a Dream.
Captain of the Northfleet, The.
Christie's Portrait.
Deserter from the Cause, The.
England.
His Banner over Me.
"In the Dead Unhappy Midnight."
Lullaby: "Softly sink in slumbers golden."
Marriage Prayer, A.
Men of "Forty-eight," The.
Mother's Idol Broken, The, *sel.*
O, Lay Thy Hand in Mine, Dear!
Only a Dream, *sel.*
Our Wee White Rose. *Fr.* The Mother's Idol Broken.
Parting.
Soldier's Wife, A.
Tale of Eternity, *sel.*
'Tis Weary Waiting.
To-Day and To-Morrow.
Voices of the Loved and Lost.
Young Love.
MASSINGER, PHILIP. Death Invoked. *Fr.* The Emperor of the East.
Emperor of the East, The, *sel.*
Forest's Queen, The.
Maid of Honour, The, *sel.*
Picture, The, *sel.*
Renegado, The, *sel.*
Sad Song, A. *Fr.* The Emperor of the East.
Song: "Blushing rose and purple flower, The." *Fr.* The Picture.
Song: "Why art thou slow, thou rest of trouble, Death." *Fr.* The Emperor of the East.
Song of Pleasure, A. *Fr.* The Picture.
Why art thou slow, thou rest of trouble, Death. *Fr.* The Emperor of the East.
MASSINGER, PHILIP, *and* JOHN FLETCHER. *See* FLETCHER, JOHN, *and* PHILIP MASSINGER.
MASSON, TOM (Thomas Lansing Masson).
Desolation.
Kiss, The.
Red Cross Nurse, The.
When I Get Time.
MASTERMAN, LUCY LYTTELTON. *See* LYTTELTON, LUCY.
MASTERS, EDGAR LEE. Aaron Hatfield. *Fr.* Spoon River Anthology.
Achilles Deatheridge.
Acoma, *sel.*
Alexander Throckmorton. *Fr.* Spoon River Anthology.
Anne Rutledge. *Fr.* Spoon River Anthology.
Archibald Higbie. *Fr.* Spoon River Anthology.
Arielle Grierson. *Fr.* The New Spoon River.
Arlo Will. *Fr.* Spoon River Anthology.
Benjamin Franklin Hazard. *Fr.* The New Spoon River.
Benjamin Pantier. *Fr.* Spoon River Anthology.
Bert Kessler. *Fr.* Spoon River Anthology.
Bertrand Hume. *Fr.* The New Spoon River.
"Butch" Weldy. *Fr.* Spoon River Anthology.
By the Waters of Babylon.
Canticle of the Race.
Carl Hamblin. *Fr.* Spoon River Anthology.
Cassius Hueffer. *Fr.* Spoon River Anthology.
Chandler Nicholas. *Fr.* The New Spoon River.
Christmas at Indian Point.
Cleanthus Trilling. *Fr.* The New Spoon River.
Clipper Ships, The.
Daisy Fraser. *Fr.* Spoon River Anthology.
D'Arcy Singer. *Fr.* The New Spoon River.
Davis Matlock. *Fr.* Spoon River Anthology.
Desolate Scythia.
Doc Hill. *Fr.* Spoon River Anthology.
Doctor Meyers. *Fr.* Spoon River Anthology.
Draw the Sword, O Republic.
Editor Whedon. *Fr.* Spoon River Anthology.
Edmund Pollard. *Fr.* Spoon River Anthology.
Elliott Hawkins. *Fr.* Spoon River Anthology.
Elsa Wertman. *Fr.* Spoon River Anthology.
Emily Sparks. *Fr.* Spoon River Anthology.
English Thornton. *Fr.* Spoon River Anthology.
Epitaph for Us.
Euripides Alexopoulos. *Fr.* The New Spoon River.
Father Malloy. *Fr.* Spoon River Anthology.
Fiddler Jones. *Fr.* Spoon River Anthology.
Garden, The.
George Gray. *Fr.* Spoon River Anthology.
Hamilton Greene. *Fr.* Spoon River Anthology.
Hare Drummer. *Fr.* Spoon River Anthology.
Harmon Whitney. *Fr.* Spoon River Anthology.
Henry C. Calhoun. *Fr.* Spoon River Anthology.
Henry Cogdal. *Fr.* The New Spoon River.
Henry Ditch. *Fr.* The New Spoon River.
Henry Zoll, the Miller. *Fr.* The New Spoon River.
Herman Altman. *Fr.* Spoon River Anthology.
Hill, The. *Fr.* Spoon River Anthology.
Howard Lamson. *Fr.* The New Spoon River.
Hymn to the Sun. *Fr.* Acoma.
Isaiah Beethoven. *Fr.* Spoon River Anthology.
J. Milton Miles. *Fr.* Spoon River Anthology.
Jack Kelso, *sel.*
Jacob Godbey. *Fr.* Spoon River Anthology.
James Garber. *Fr.* Spoon River Anthology.
Jay Hawkins. *Fr.* The New Spoon River.
John Hancock Otis. *Fr.* Spoon River Anthology.
John Horace Burleson. *Fr.* Spoon River Anthology.
John Wasson. *Fr.* Spoon River Anthology.
Johnny Appleseed.
Jonathan Houghton. *Fr.* Spoon River Anthology.
Julia Miller. *Fr.* Spoon River Anthology.
Julius Brink. *Fr.* The New Spoon River.
Knowlt Hoheimer. *Fr.* Spoon River Anthology.
Lake Boats, The.
Lee, *sel.*
Levy Silver. *Fr.* The New Spoon River.
Linford Newman. *Fr.* The New Spoon River.
Lionel Grierson. *Fr.* The New Spoon River.
Loom, The.
Lost Orchard, The.
Louise Hedeen. *Fr.* The New Spoon River.
Lucinda Matlock. *Fr.* Spoon River Anthology.
Mayor Marston. *Fr.* The New Spoon River.
Mrs. Meyers. *Fr.* Spoon River Anthology.
Mrs. Williams. *Fr.* Spoon River Anthology.
Mollie McGee. *Fr.* Spoon River Anthology.
Morgan Oakley. *Fr.* The New Spoon River.
Mourner's Bench, The.
My Light with Yours.
Nathan Suffrin. *Fr.* The New Spoon River.
Neither Faith nor Beauty Can Remain.
New Spoon River, The, *sels.*
No Grief for the Great Ones. *Fr.* Lee.
O You Young Eagles!
Perry Zoll. *Fr.* Spoon River Anthology.
Petit, the Poet. *Fr.* Spoon River Anthology.
Portrait of a Poet. *Fr.* Jack Kelso.
Reuben Pantier. *Fr.* Spoon River Anthology.
Rutherford McDowell. *Fr.* Spoon River Anthology.
Scholfield Huxley. *Fr.* Spoon River Anthology.
Seth Compton. *Fr.* Spoon River Anthology.
Seven Cities of America, The.
Sexsmith the Dentist. *Fr.* Spoon River Anthology.
Silence.
Silence, *sel.*
Simon Surnamed Peter.
Slip-Shoe Lovey.
Sounds Out of Sorrow.
Spoon River Anthology, *sels.*

Starved Rock.
Statue of Liberty, The.
Supplication.
Supplication, *sel.*
Thomas Rhodes. *Fr.* Spoon River Anthology.
Thomas Trevelyan. *Fr.* Spoon River Anthology.
Village Atheist, The. *Fr.* Spoon River Anthology.
Visit to the Sea, A.
Washington McNeeley. *Fr.* Spoon River Anthology.
Webster Ford. *Fr.* Spoon River Anthology.
Week-End by the Sea.
Widows.
William H. Herndon. *Fr.* Spoon River Anthology.
William Jones. *Fr.* Spoon River Anthology.

MASTERS, MARCIA. Country Ways. *Fr.* Impressions of My Father.
Impressions of My Father, *sel.*

MASTERSON, KATE. Modern Rubaiyat, The.

MASTIN, FLORENCE RIPLEY. Flying.
Old Hound.
Return to Spring.

MATCHETT, WILLIAM H. Old Inn on the Eastern Shore.
Packing a Photograph from Firenze.
Spit-Bug, The.
Water Ouzel.

MATHAMS, WALTER J. Now in the Days of Youth.

MATHERS, EDWARD POWYS. Abla, *tr.* *Fr.* The Mu'allaqát.
Abu Nowas for the Barmacides, *tr.* *Fr.* The Thousand and One Nights.
Ballade of Muhammad Din Tilai, *tr.*
Beautiful Boy, The, *tr.* *Fr.* The Thousand and One Nights.
Birds, *tr.* *Fr.* The Thousand and One Nights.
Black Hair, *tr.*
Black Marigolds, *tr.*
Dalliance of Leopards, The, *tr.*
Dates, *tr.* *Fr.* The Thousand and One Nights.
Death, *tr.* *Fr.* The Thousand and One Nights.
Death Sends Me the Flickering of Powdery Lids, *tr.*
Drinking Song, *tr.* *Fr.* The Thousand and One Nights.
Drunken Rose, The, *tr.*
English Girl, *tr.*
Ghazal of Isa Akhun Zada, *tr.*
Great Offence, The, *tr.*
Haroun Al-Rachid for Heart's-Life, *tr.* *Fr.* The Thousand and One Nights.
Haroun's Favorite Song, *tr.* *Fr.* The Thousand and One Nights.
Her Mouth Carelessly Scented, *tr.*
Her Rival for Aziza, *tr.* *Fr.* The Thousand and One Nights.
I Have a Need, *tr.*
I Have No Surety, *tr.*
I Know My Princess, *tr.*
I Know That I Have Savoured, *tr.*
I Love Long Black Eyes, *tr.*
I Mind That I Went Round with Men and Women, *tr.*
I Mind the Coming, *tr.*
I Mind the Time of the Falling of Blossoms, *tr.*
I See Her, *tr.*
I See the Heavy Startled Hair, *tr.*
I Seem to See My Prison Walls, *tr.*
If I See in My Soul, *tr.*
If My Girl with Lotus Eyes, *tr.*
Inscriptions at the City of Brass, *tr.* *Fr.* The Thousand and One Nights.
Inscriptions at the City of Brass, *sel.*, *tr.* *Fr.* The Thousand and One Nights.
Lament, *tr.* *Fr.* The Thousand and One Nights.
Love, *tr.* *Fr.* The Thousand and One Nights.
Love Is a God, *tr.*
Morning Shower, A, *tr.*
Mu'allaqát, The, *sels.*, *tr.*
My Eyes That Hurry to See, *tr.*
Old Scent of the Plum Tree, *tr.*
Pearls Seen through Amber, *tr.* *Fr.* The Thousand and One Nights.
Perturbation at Dawn, *tr.*
Pleased Intimacy, The, *tr.*
Poet Thinks, A, *tr.*
Pour Us Wine, *tr.* *Fr.* The Mu'allaqát.
Power of Love, The, *tr.* *Fr.* The Thousand and One Nights.
Psalm of Battle, *tr.* *Fr.* The Thousand and One Nights.
She Swims Back in the Crowning Hour, *tr.*
She with Young Limbs, *tr.*
Sleeper, The, *tr.* *Fr.* The Thousand and One Nights.
Song: "If you love God, take your mirror between your hands and look," *tr.*
Song of the Narcissus, The, *tr.* *Fr.* The Thousand and One Nights.
Spread We Our Nets, *tr.*
Stainless Fair Appearance, The, *tr.*
Tell Him, O Night, *tr.* *Fr.* The Thousand and One Nights.
Thousand and One Nights, The, *sels.*, *tr.*
To Lighten My Darkness, *tr.* *Fr.* The Thousand and One Nights.
Tumadir Al-Khansa for Her Brother, *tr.* *Fr.* The Thousand and One Nights.
Wazir Dandan for Prince Sharkan, The, *tr.* *Fr.* The Thousand and One Nights.
When All My Heavy Heart, *tr.*
White Frost, The, *tr.*
Woodcutter and the Fisherman Turn Home, The, *tr.*
Your Mouth, *tr.*

MATHESON, ANNIE. Love's Cosmopolitan.
Song of Handicrafts, A.

MATHESON, GEORGE. Christian Freedom.
Christ's Bondservant.
Doors in the Temple, The.
Gather Us In.
O Love That Wilt Not Let Me Go.

MATHESON, MARY. Afterward.
Evening.

MATHEUS, JOHN FREDERICK. Harlem, *tr.*
Requiem.

MATHEW, RAY. For Harry and June.
Genesis.
Let Us Not Pretend.
Picnic.
Poems Come Easier, The.
Young Man's Fancy.

MATHEWS, ALBERT. To an Autumn Leaf.

MATHEWS, CORNELIUS. Poet, The.

MATHEWS, ESTHER. Song: "I can't be talkin' of love, dear."

MATHIAS, EILEEN. All in Red.
Go Out.
In the Wood.
Just Jumbo.
Little Things.
My Hut.
Sea Fairies.
Tall Trees.
Zoo Manners.

MATHIAS, ROLAND. Balloon over the Rhondda.

MATSUYAMA, TAKAYOSHI. God's Word.

MATTAM, DONALD. In a Town Garden.
Table Talk.

MATTHEW, SIR TOBIE. Answer, An.

MATTHEWS, ALICE CLEAR. Of the Mathematician.

MATTHEWS, BRANDER. American Girl, An.
Ballade of Adaptation, The.
Ballade of Fact and Fiction, The.
Rain and Shine.

MATTHEWS, JAMES NEWTON. Ballade of Busy Doctors, A.
Death—What Is It?
Life—What Is It?

MATTHEWS, WASHINGTON. Incantation for Rain, *tr.*
Mountain Chant, *tr.*
Prayer of the Night Chant, A, *tr.*
Therefore I Must Tell the Truth, *tr.*
Voice That Beautifies the Land, The, *tr.*

MATTOCKS, BREWER. Preacher's Mistake, The.

MATUSOVSKY, MIKHAIL LVOVICH. Happiness.
Long Roads.

MAUGHAM, HENRY NEVILLE. Husband of Poverty, The, *sel.*
Knight of Bethlehem, A. *Fr.* The Husband of Poverty.
Song: "There was a Knight of Bethlehem." *Fr.* The Husband of Poverty.

MAURA, SISTER. Blessing of Saint Francis, The.
Deirdre's Song at Sunrise.
Hymn for Laudes; Feast of Our Lady, Help of Christians, *tr.*
Hymn for Laudes; Feast of Our Lady of Good Counsel, *tr.*
O Glory of Virgins, *tr.*
Rosary, The.

MAURA, SISTER MARY. After the Thought of Saint Francis.
Data for Accreditation.
Lucifer at Leisure.
Motif from the Second Shepherd's Play.
Our Lady of the Refugees.
Professor of Medieval Balladry.
Song of the Fire.
To the Queen of Dolors.

MAURER, IRVING. O God, Hear Thou the Nation's Prayer.

"MAURICE, FURNLEY." *See* WILMOT, FRANK.

MAUROPUS, JOHN. Our Lady of the Passion.

MAURRON, CHARLES, *and* JULIAN BELL. *See* BELL, JULIAN, *and* CHARLES MAURRON.

MAVILIS, LORENZO. In Silence.
Lethe.
Noble Parentage.
Olive Tree.
Sweet Death.

MAVITY, NANCY BARR. Prisoners.

MAXTONE, MARY. Skywriting.

MAXWELL, ELINOR. Pop.

MAXWELL, IAN. Vespers.

MAXWELL, JAMES CLERK. In Memory of Edward Wilson, *parody.*
Rigid Body Sings.

MAXWELL, JOSEPH R. N. Old Bard Speaks, The.

MAXWELL, W. F. Disciple Speaks, The.

MAXWELL, WILLIAM. Dance at Silver Valley, The.

MAXWELL, SIR WILLIAM STIRLING. *See* STIRLING-MAXWELL, SIR WILLIAM.

MAXWELL-HALL, AGNES. Jamaica Market.
Lizard.

MAY, BEULAH. Captain of St. Kitts, The.
Deprecating Parrots.
Fishers in the Night.
Prayer for Little Beasts.
Trail's End.

MAY, CURTIS. Tucking the Baby In.

MAY, EDWINA. Haitches!

MAY, JULIA HARRIS. Day by Day.
Kindergarten Orator, A.

MAY, THOMAS. Continuation of Lucan, *sel.*
Dear, do not your fair beauty wrong. *Fr.* The Old Couple.
Death. *Fr.* Continuation of Lucan.
Love's Prime. *Fr.* The Old Couple.
Not He That Knows. *Fr.* The Tragedy of Cleopatra.
Old Couple, The, *sel.*
Song, A: "Not he, that knows how to acquire." *Fr.* The Tragedy of Cleopatra.
Tragedy of Cleopatra, The, *sel.*

MAYA, RAFAEL. Far over Yonder.

MAYAKOVSKY, VLADIMIR. About This, *sel.*
At the Top of My Voice.

MAYAKOVSKY, VLADIMIR (*continued*)
At the Top of My Voice, *sels.*
Death of Lenin, The. *Fr.* Vladimir Ilyich-Lenin.
For the Signboards.
Good! *sel.*
Heinesque.
Home! *sel.*
Hungry Winter. *Fr.* Good!
It's Two o'Clock.
Left March.
Listen.
Man Seven Years Standing, The. *Fr.* About This.
Moonlit Night.
Most Extraordinary Adventure, A.
Our March.
So What?
Tale of How Fadey Learned of the Law Protecting Workingmen, The, *sel.*
Vladimir Ilyich-Lenin, *sel.*
Worker Poet, The.
MAYBIN, PATRICK. April, 1940.
Ballykinlar, May, 1940.
Fallen Tree, The.
Monks at Ards, The.
Thoughts from Abroad.
MAYER, EDWIN JUSTUS. Poet Dreams of the Wings of Death, The.
MAYER, FRANK H. At Timber Line.
MAYHEW, HORACE. Cockney Enigma on the Letter H.
Travesty of Miss Fanshawe's Enigma.
MAYKOV, APOLLON. *See* MAIKOV, APOLLON NIKOLAYEVICH.
MAYNARD, FRANCIS X. Chiseler, The.
MAYNARD, THEODORE. Apocalypse.
Cecidit, Cecidit Babylon Magna!
Certain Rich Man, A.
Desideravi.
Duel, The.
Dwell with Me, Lovely Images.
Earth-bound.
Exile.
Faith.
Faith's Difficulty.
If I Had Ridden Horses.
On the Edge of the Pacific.
Requiem.
Ships, The.
Song of Colours, A.
Song of Laughter, A.
World's Miser, The.
MAYNE, JASPER. Amorous War, The, *sel.*
City Match, The, *sel.*
First Song, Sung by Two Amazons, The. *Fr.* The Amorous War.
Time. *Fr.* The Amorous War.
To the Memory of Ben Johnson, *sel.*
MAYNE, JOHN. Hallowe'en.
Logan Braes.
MAYO, EDWARD LESLIE. Anglo-Saxon.
D Minor, The.
El Greco.
En Route.
I Saw My Father.
In the Web.
Letter to Karl Shapiro.
Mole, The.
Nausea.
Oracle.
Pool, The.
Uninfected, The.
Wagon Train.
MAYO, HERBERT. Induced Current.
"MAYSI, KADRA." *See* SIMONS, KATHERINE DRAYTON MAYRANT.
MA YÜEH LO. Forlorn.
MAZAN, ROSE. I'd Know You!
MEACHAM, HARRY M. To a Young Poet.
MEAD, STELLA. Last Gate, The.
Merry Man of Paris, The.
When We Are Men.
MEADOWCROFT, CLARA PLATT. Night in the Green Hill.
MEANY, EDMOND S. Washington's Song.
MEARNS, HUGHES. Antigonish.
Case, A.
Frustrated Male.
Lady with Technique, The.
Later Antigonishes.
Little Man Who Wasn't There, The.
Perfect Reactionary, The.
Reveille.
MEDARY, ANNA. Hallowe'en.
Learning to Swim.
MEDICI, LORENZO DE'. Carnival Song: Song of the Girls and the Tattlers (Cicadas).
Carnival Song: Triumph of Bacchus and Ariadne.
How can I sing light-souled and fancy-free.
Into a little close of mine I went.
Sonnet: "How fruitless is each human hope, how vain."
Sonnet: "I saw my lady by a cool, fresh stream."
Sonnet: "Let him who wishes seek pomp and honor, follow."
Sonnet: "O sweetest sleep, come now at last to stay."
Youth Is Sweet and Well.
MEDRANO, FRANCISCO DE. Art and Nature.
Two Harvests, The.
MEEHAN, JOHN JAMES. Grant at Rest.
Race of the *Oregon*, The.
MEEK, ALEXANDER BEAUFORT. Balaklava.
Wouldst Thou Have Me Love Thee?
MEEKER, MARJORIE. After Pain.
Before You Came.
Memorial Sonnet.
Prophecy.
Snowfall.
They.
Walls.
When I Am Old.
Where My Step Falters.
MEHLEK, FRANCES BOAL. Sinner Contemplates, A.
MEIDHRE, BRIAN MACGIOLLA. *See* MERRIMAN, BRIAN.
MEIGS, CHARLES D. Home without a Bible, A.
Others.
MEIGS, MILDRED PLEW. Abraham Lincoln.
Chicago.
Gossip (A.D. 1585).
If I Were a One-legged Pirate.
Johnny Fife and Johnny's Wife.
Moon Song.
Organ Grinders' Garden, The.
Pirate Don Durk of Dowdee, The.
Road to Raffydiddle, The.
Shepherd Left Behind, The.
Silver Ships.
Sonnet for Myself.
To Chicago at Night.
MEIJI, EMPEROR. Buried Fire.
MEILIR AP GWALCHMAI. His Delight.
Triumphs of Owen, The.
MEINLOH VON SEVELINGEN. I Serve.
MEÏR OF ROTHENBURG. Burning of the Law, The.
MEI SHENG. Of this day's glorious feast and revel, *at. Fr.* Seventeen Old Poems.
MEISLING, VAUGHN FRANCIS. I Dreamt She Came.
MEI YAO CH'EN. Crescent Moon, The.
Dream at Night, A.
Excuse for Not Returning the Visit of a Friend, An.
Fish Peddler.
Friend Advises Me to Stop Drinking, A.
I Remember the Blue River.
I Remember the River at Wu Sung.
In Broad Daylight I Dream of My Dead Wife.
Melon Girl.
Next Door.
On the Death of a New Born Child.
On the Death of His Wife.
Sorrow.
MELACHRINOS, APOSTOLOS [*or* APPOSTOLOS]. Apollonius, *sel.*
It Is Raining Again.
Magic Refrains. *Fr.* Variations.
Playing the Lyre. *Fr.* Apollonius.
Variations, *sel.*
MELCOMBE, BARON. *See* DODINGTON, GEORGE BUBB, BARON MELCOMBE.
MELEAGER. Against Mosquitoes.
Baby Hare, The.
Beware the Jealous Hand.
Bride, A.
Bride of Death, The.
Child Eros, The.
Child for Sale, A.
Cicada, A.
Coquette, The, *at.*
Cup-Bearer, The.
Draught of Love, The.
Favoritism.
Garland for Heliodora, A.
Gusts of winter are gone, the sky no longer lowers, The.
Heliodora ("Tears for my lady dead").
Heliodora and the Bee.
Heliodora's Garland.
Heliodora's Wreath.
Heliodore ("Pour wine").
Heliodore Dead.
His Anthology.
Hue and Cry after Love.
I'll twine white violets and the myrtle green.
In the Spring.
Irreparable Rose.
"Lenten Ys Come with Love to Toune."
Let him be sold, though still he sleep.
Little Love-God, The.
Lost a boy! A runaway!
Lost Desire.
Love at the Door.
Love for Sale.
Love in Spring.
Love-Messenger.
Love, The Baby.
Love the Rascal.
Love, the Vagrant.
Lover's Curse, A.
Love's Last Sacrament.
Message, The.
Mosquito Turned Messenger, The.
O Gentle Ships.
"O Lente, Lente."
Of Himself.
Of His Death.
On Himself.
Persuasion's Rose.
Runaway Cupid.
Siren, The.
Spring: "Now the bright crocus flames."
Spring: "Now winter's winds are banished from the sky."
Spring Garland, A.
Tears to thee even beneath the earth, my Heliodora.
That morn which saw me made a bride.
To a Caged Grasshopper.
To Heliodora.
To Heliodora; a Fretful Monody.
To Heliodora, Dead.
Toast to Heliodore, A.
Two Fires.
Upon a Maid That Died the Day She Was Married.
Vow, The.
Wreath for Heliodora.
Writ in Water.
Zenophila.
MELÉNDEZ VALDÉS, JUAN. A Jovino: El Melancólico.
Despair.
Juvenilities.
Nisé.
Of Love's Awakening.
Sacred Ode.
Sum of Kisses, A.
Thought, A.
Useless Flight, The.
MELLEN, GRENVILLE. Lonely Bugle Grieves, The. *Fr.* Ode on the Celebration of the Battle of Bunker Hill, June 17, 1825.
Ode on the Celebration of the Battle of Bunker Hill, June 17, 1825, *sel.*
MELLER, WALTER CLIFFORD. Crusader's Song, *tr.*
MELLO, FRANCISCO MANUEL DE. Death's Apology.
On Ascending a Hill Leading to a Convent.

MELTON, WIGHTMAN F. Black Mammy's Lullaby, 1855.
MELTZER, DAVID. 15th Raga: For Bela Lugosi.
Prayerwheel 2.
Revelation.
12th Raga: For John Wieners.
MELVILLE, GEORGE JOHN WHYTE-. See WHYTE-MELVILLE, GEORGE JOHN.
MELVILLE, HERMAN. After the Pleasure Party.
Art.
At the Cannon's Mouth.
Ball's Bluff.
Berg, The.
Billy Budd, Foretopman, *sel.*
Billy in the Darbies. *Fr.* Billy Budd, Foretopman.
Bridegroom Dick, *sel.*
Camoens.
Camoens in the Hospital.
Chattanooga.
Clarel, *sels.*
College Colonel, The.
Crossing the Tropics.
Cumberland, The.
Devotion of the Flowers to Their Lady, The.
Dirge for McPherson, A.
Eagle of the Blue.
Enthusiast, The.
Enviable Isles, The.
Epilogue: "If Luther's day expand to Darwin's year." *Fr.* Clarel.
Fall of Richmond, The.
Falstaff's Lament over Prince Hal Become Henry V.
Far Off-Shore.
Father Mapple's Hymn. *Fr.* Moby Dick.
"Formerly a Slave."
Fragments of a Lost Gnostic Poem of the Twelfth Century.
From the Conflict of Convictions.
Gold in the Mountain.
House-Top, The.
Immolated.
In a Bye-Canal.
In a Church of Padua.
In the Desert.
In the Pauper's Turnip-Field.
In the Prison Pen.
John Marr, *sel.*
Lake, The.
L'Envoi: "My towers at last! these rovings end."
L'Envoi: Return of the Sire de Nesle, The.
Lone Founts.
Maldive Shark, The.
Malvern Hill.
March into Virginia, The.
Mardi, *sel.*
Martyr, The.
Misgivings.
Moby Dick, *sel.*
Monody.
Mound by the Lake, The.
Night-March, The.
Of Rama.
Of Rome. *Fr.* Clarel.
On Mammon. *Fr.* Clarel.
On the Home Guards.
On the Slain at Chickamauga.
Portent, The.
Ravaged Villa, The.
Requiem, A.
Requiem for Soldiers Lost in Ocean Transports, A.
Returned Volunteer to His Rifle, The.
Ribs and Terrors, The. *Fr.* Moby Dick.
Running the Batteries.
Seedsmen of Old Saturn's Land. *Fr.* Clarel.
Sheridan at Cedar Creek.
Shiloh, a Requiem.
Song: "Ribs and terrors in the whale, The." *Fr.* Moby Dick.
Southern Cross.
Stone Fleet, The.
Surrender at Appomattox, The.
Temeraire, The.
Time's Long Ago.
To Ned.
Tuft of Kelp, The.
Ungar and Rolfe. *Fr.* Clarel.
Uninscribed Monument on One of the Battle-Fields of the Wilderness, An.
Victor of Antietam, The.
We Fish. *Fr.* Mardi.
Whale, The. *Fr.* Moby Dick.
Where's Commander All-a-Tanto? *Fr.* Bridegroom Dick.
MENA, JUAN DE. Labyrinth of Fortune, *sel.*
Macías in the Circle of Venus. *Fr.* Labyrinth of Fortune.
MÉNAGE, GILLES. Happy Man, The.
MENAHEM BEN JACOB. Harvesting of the Roses, The.
Martyr's Death, A.
MENAHEM BEN MAKHIR OF RATISBON. How Sweet Thy Precious Gift of Rest.
MENAI, HUW (Hugh Menai Williams). Back in the Return.
Cwm Farm near Capel Curig.
In Our Time.
In the Vale of Glamorgan.
Inexorable, The.
Old Peasant in the Billiard Saloon, The.
Paradox.
Stalingrad.
Stars Look Down, The.
MENANDER. Advice to a Lover. *Fr.* Perikeiromene.
Aid to Self-Knowledge.
Arbitrants, *sels.*
Being a man, ask not release from pain.
Charisius Rebukes Himself. *Fr.* Epitrepontes.
Common Lot, The.
Conscience Doth Make Cowards of Us All.
Defilement Cometh from Within.
Don't talk of birth and family; all those.
Epitrepontes, *sels.*
Family Dinner-Party, The.
Guide Within, The. *Fr.* Epitrepontes.
Here Are Sands, Ignoble Things.
Marriage—Two Views.
Mutes in Life's Chorus, The.
My Own, My Native Land.
Passing Show, The.
Perikeiromene, *sel.*
Plight of a Forsaken Lover. *Fr.* Perikeiromene.
These Stones.
This Defileth a Man.
This World Is All a Fleeting Show.
Threats.
Whom the gods love die young; that man is blest.
MENDELSSOHN, FELIX. Every Day.
Love the Beautiful.
MENDELSSOHN, MOSES. Self-Portrait.
MENDÈS, CATULLE. At Early Morn.
I Go by Road.
Mother, The.
Swans, The.
MENDES, MOSES. Ass, The. *Fr.* The Chaplet.
Chaplet, The, *sels.*
On the Death of a Lady's Owl.
Philanderer, The. *Fr.* The Chaplet.
MENDES, MURILO. Psalm: "I proclaim Thee great and wonderful."
MÉNDEZ, FRANCISCO. Blood on a Stone.
MÉNDEZ DORICH, RAFAEL. Duchess's White Cats, The.
Porcelain of the North.
She Was Carrying the Lamp.
MENDOZA, INIGO DE. Chant of the Ninth Order of Seraphim.
MENÉNDEZ Y PELAYO, MARCELINO. Rome.
MENG CHIA. Friendship.
MENG CHIAO. Song of a Pure-hearted Girl, A.
MENG HAO-JAN. Sleepless.
Stopping at a Friend's Farm-House.
Taking Leave of Wang Wei.
To Chu Ta.
MENG SHU CH'ING. My Sanctuary.
MENTH, ROBERT. Cry from the Battlefield.
MEOGO, PERO. Cantiga de Amigo: "On the greening grasses."
Cossante: "Tell me, daughter, my lovely daughter."
MERCANTINI, LUIGI. Garibaldi Hymn, The.
MERCER, ERNESTINE. Artist.
On Looking Backward.
MERCER, MARGARET. Exhortation to Prayer.
MERCIER, LOUIS. For Those Who Died in Battle.
Notre Dame des Petits.
Vespers.
MERCIER, ROSELLE. See MONTGOMERY, ROSELLE MERCIER.
MEREDITH, GEORGE. All other joys of life he strove to warm. *Fr.* Modern Love.
Am I failing? For no longer can I cast. *Fr.* Modern Love.
Antigone.
Appeasement of Demeter, The.
Appreciation.
Ask, Is Love Divine.
At dinner, she is hostess, I am host. *Fr.* Modern Love.
At last we parley: we so strangely dumb. *Fr.* Modern Love.
"Atkins."
Ballad of Past Meridian, A.
Beauty Rohtraut, *tr.*
Beggar's Soliloquy, The.
Bellerophon.
Breath of the Briar.
Burden of Strength, The.
But where began the change; and what's my crime? *Fr.* Modern Love.
By this he knew she wept with waking eyes. *Fr.* Modern Love.
Certain People, A.
Coin of Pity, The. *Fr.* Modern Love.
Dirge in Woods.
Discipline of Wisdom, The.
Dusty Answer, A. *Fr.* Modern Love.
Earth and Man.
Earth's Secret.
End of Love, The. *Fr.* Modern Love.
Faith on Trial, A, *sel.*
Garden of Epicurus, The.
Grace and Love.
Hard Weather.
He felt the wild beast in him betweenwhiles. *Fr.* Modern Love.
He found her by the ocean's moaning verge. *Fr.* Modern Love.
Head of Bran, The.
Here Jack and Tom Are Paired with Moll and Meg. *Fr.* Modern Love.
Hiding the Skeleton. *Fr.* Modern Love.
How many a thing which we cast to the ground. *Fr.* Modern Love.
Hymn to Color.
I am not of those miserable males. *Fr.* Modern Love.
I must be flattered. *Fr.* Modern Love.
I play for Seasons, not Eternities. *Fr.* Modern Love.
In our old shipwrecked days there was an hour. *Fr.* Modern Love.
In Paris, at the Louvre, there have I seen. *Fr.* Modern Love.
Internal Harmony.
It ended, and the morrow brought the task. *Fr.* Modern Love.
It is the season of the sweet wild rose. *Fr.* Modern Love.
Juggling Jerry.
Kinship with the Stars. *Fr.* Modern Love.
Lark Ascending, The.
Last Words of Juggling Jerry, The.
Lines: "Love within the lover's breast."
Love Dies. *Fr.* Modern Love.
Love in the Valley.
Love in the Valley, *sels.*
Love's Grave. *Fr.* Modern Love.
Lucifer in Starlight.
Manfred.
Mares of the Camargue, *tr. Fr.* The Mirèio.
Marian,

Meredith, George (*continued*)
Mark where the pressing wind shoots javelin-like. *Fr.* Modern Love.
Martin's Puzzle.
Meditation under Stars.
Melampus.
Men and Man.
Mirèio, The, *sel., tr.*
Modern Love.
Modern Love, *sels.*
Nature and Life.
Not solely that the Future she destroys. *Fr.* Modern Love.
O briar-scents, on yon wet wing.
Ode to the Spirit of Earth in Autumn.
Ode to the Spirit of Earth in Autumn, *sel.*
Old Chartist, The.
Old Chartist, The, *sel.*
On Hearing the News from Venice.
On the Danger of War.
One Twilight Hour. *Fr.* Modern Love.
Orson of the Muse, An.
Out in the yellow meadows, where the bee. *Fr.* Modern Love.
Outer and Inner.
Phoebus with Admetus.
Question Whither, The.
Seed-Time.
Sense and Spirit.
Should thy love die.
Society.
Song: "No, no, the falling blossom is no sign."
Song in the Songless.
Song of Theodolinda, The.
Song of Theodolinda, The, *sel.*
Spirit of Shakespeare, The.
State of Age, The.
Stave of Roving Tim, A.
Tardy Spring.
Test of Manhood, The, *sel.*
That was the chirp of Ariel.
Their sense is with their senses all mixed in. *Fr.* Modern Love.
This Little Moment. *Fr.* Modern Love.
This was the woman; what now of the man? *Fr.* Modern Love.
Thou Lovely Fishermaiden, *tr.*
Thrush in February, The.
Thrush in February, The, *sel.*
Thus piteously Love closed what he begat. *Fr.* Modern Love.
'Tis Christmas weather, and a country house. *Fr.* Modern Love.
To a Skylark.
To J. M.
Tragic Memory. *Fr.* Modern Love.
Two Masks, The.
Under yonder beech-tree single on the greensward. *Fr.* Love in the Valley.
We saw the swallows gathering in the sky. *Fr.* Modern Love.
We three are on the cedar-shadowed lawn. *Fr.* Modern Love.
What Are We First?
What may the woman labor to confess? *Fr.* Modern Love.
When I Would Image.
Whimper of Sympathy.
White Owl, The. *Fr.* Love in the Valley.
Will o' the Wisp.
Winter Heavens.
Woodland Peace.
Woods of Westermain, The.
Woods of Westermain, The, *sel.*
World's Advance, The.
Year's Sheddings, The.
Yet it was plain she struggled, and that salt. *Fr.* Modern Love.
Young Reynard.
Youth in Age.
"Meredith, Owen" (Edward Robert Bulwer-Lytton, 1st Earl of Lytton).
Aux Italiens.
Babylonia, *sel.*
Chess-Board, The.
Dinner Hour, The. *Fr.* Lucile.
Forbearance.
Genseric.
Going Back Again.
Heart and Nature, The.
Indian Love-Song.
King Solomon.
Last Lines, *sel.*
Last Wish, The.
Legend of the Dead Lambs, The.
Lucile, *sels.*
Mission of Sister Seraphine, a Sister of Charity, The. *Fr.* Lucile.
Night in Italy, A, *sel.*
One Thing.
Portrait, The. *Fr.* The Wanderer.
Possession.
Since We Parted.
Sister of Charity Comforts a Wounded Soldier, A. *Fr.* Lucile.
Tempora Acta. *Fr.* Babylonia.
True Greatness.
Uriel.
Utmost, The.
Wanderer, The, *sel.*
What We May Live Without. *Fr.* Lucile.
White Anemone, The, *sel.*
Meredith, William. Boon, A.
Chinese Banyan, The.
Do Not Embrace Your Mind's New Negro Friend.
Korean Woman Seated by a Wall, A.
Love Letter from an Impossible Land.
Open Sea, The.
Perhaps the Best Time.
Picture of a Castle.
Rainy Season, The.
Starlight.
Thoughts on One's Head.
Transport.
View of the Brooklyn Bridge, A.
Meredith, William Tuckey. Farragut.
Merezhkovsky, Dmitry Sergeyevich. Nirvana.
Prayer for Wings.
Trumpet Call, The.
Merilaas, Kersti. Saint.
Merington, Marguerite. Christmas Eve.
Hey Nonny No.
Merivale, Herman Charles. Aetate XIX.
Darwinity.
Ready, Ay, Ready.
Thaisa's Dirge.
Town of Nice, The.
Merivale, John Herman. Bows will not avail thee, *tr.*
Child Eros, The, *tr.*
Come then, my friend, and seize the flask, *tr.*
Constitution of Athens, The, *tr.*
Glitters with brass my mansion wide, *tr.*
Leave the gods to order all things, *tr.*
Long, long and dreary is the night, *tr.*
Love, the Master of True Eloquence, *tr.*
Love, the Vagrant, *tr.*
Metaphysician, The, *tr.*
On Those Who Fell, *tr.*
Plant, The, *tr.*
Power of Love, The, *tr.*
Storm, The, *tr.*
To Quintus Dellius, *tr.*
Tomb of Crethon, The, *tr.*
Unmourn'd, unburied, traveller, we lie, *tr.*
Very Torch, The, *tr.*
Vow, The, *tr.*
What time soft zephyrs fan the trees, *tr.*
Wingèd Change, *tr.*
Wishes, *tr.*
Merivale, John Herman, *and* Lord Neaves. Life's Brevity, *tr.*
Merkel, Andrew. Tallahassee, *sel.*
Merrell, Lloyd Frank. Reincarnation.
Resurrection.
Unity.
Merriam, Eve. Away, Your Touch Is Everywhere.
Coward, The.
Restricted.
Wall, The.
Merriam, Lillie Fuller. At the Door.
Merrick, James. Chameleon, The.
Ignorance of Man, The.
Taking of Troy, The, *sel., tr.*
Merrill, Charles Edmund, Jr. Persicos Odi.
Merrill, James. Bed, The.
Black Swan, The.
Cloud Country.
Foliage of Vision.
For a Second Marriage.
Hôtel de l'Univers et Portugal.
Olive Grove.
Transfigured Bird.
Variations: The Air Is Sweetest That a Thistle Guards.
Merrill, Phyllis. Heard on Leaving the Opera.
Mount Holyoke.
Merrill, Stuart. Royalty.
For translations from French, see OnPM.
Merrill, William Pierson. Call to the Strong, The.
Expect!
Festal Song.
Not Alone for Mighty Empire.
People's Thanksgiving, The.
Rise Up, O Men of God.
Merriman, Brian [*or* Brian MacGiolla Meidhre]. Maiden's Complaint, The. *Fr.* The Midnight Court.
Midnight Court, The.
Midnight Court, The, *sel.*
Merritt, Dixon Lanier. Limerick: "Wonderful bird is the pelican, A."
Merryman, Bryan. *See* Merriman, Brian.
Merryman, Mildred Plew. *See* Meigs, Mildred Plew.
Mertins, Louis. Indian Songs.
Merton, Thomas. Argument, An—Of the Passion of Christ.
Blessed Virgin Mary Compared to a Window, The.
Evening of the Visitation, The.
Figure for an Apocalypse.
For My Brother.
Like Ilium.
Messias.
Ode to the Present Century.
St. Agnes; a Responsory.
Two States of Prayer.
Merwin, William Stanley. Autumn, *tr.*
Ballad of John Cable and Three Gentlemen.
Camel.
Colloquy at Peniel.
December: Of Aphrodite.
Leviathan.
Master, The.
Mirabeau Bridge, The, *tr.*
Star, *tr*
Toro.
Two Horses.
Variation on a Line by Emerson.
When I Came from Colchis.
White Goat, White Ram.
Merzlyakov, Aleksey. Song: "Among the level valley lands."
Messenger, Ruth. Fear, A.
Messinger, Robert Hinckley. Give Me the Old.
Winter Wish, A.
Metagenes. This river Crathis rolls us down.
Metastasio, Pierre A. B. D. Without and Within.
Metcalf, Nelson C. Kid in Upper 4, The.
Metcalf, Richard. These Are Not Lost, *at.*
Metcalfe, James J. Visit the Sick.
Metrodorus. In every way of life true pleasure flows.
Metrodorus' Mind to the Contrary.
Meun, Jean de, *and* Guillaume de Lorris. *See* Guillaume de Lorris *and* Jean de Meun.
Meuttman, Margaret Moore. Survival.
Mew, Charlotte. A Quoi Bon Dire.
Absence.
Again.

Beside the Bed.
Call, The.
Changeling, The.
Exspecto Resurrectionem.
Farmer's Bride, The.
Here Lies a Prisoner.
I Have Been through the Gates.
In the Fields.
Ken.
Madeleine in Church, *sel.*
Moorland Night.
Not for That City.
Old Shepherd's Prayer.
On the Asylum Road.
Pedlar [*or* Pedler], The.
Rambling Sailor, The.
Saturday Market.
Saturday Market, *sel.*
Sea Love.
Shade-Catchers, The.
Song: "Love, love today, my dear."
Song: "Oh! Sorrow, Sorrow, scarce I knew."
Spring.
To a Child in Death.
Trees Are Down, The.
MEY, MILDRED T. Quiet Days.
MEYER, F. B. Faith.
MEYER, GERARD PREVIN. Autumn Song, *tr.*
Poor in Church, The, *tr.*
S. T. Coleridge Dismisses a Caller from Porlock.
MEYER, KUNO. *For translations from Irish, see* AnIL; AnIV; FaBoCh; GTIV; LiTW; LoGBV; OnYI; OxBI; SiB.
MEYER, TOVE. I Have Three Pearls.
MEYERS, JEROME. For Dissection.
Old Patient, The.
Sonnet on the Death of Paul Ehrlich, Discoverer of Salvarsan.
MEYERS, ROBERT CORNELIUS V. If I Should Die Tonight, *wr. at. See* SMITH, ARABELLA EUGENIA.
Raggles.
MEYERSTEIN, EDWARD HARRY WILLIAM. Domine, Dirige Nos.
Elegy on the Death of Mme Anna Pavlova, *sel.*
Husband and Wife.
Ode on Nothing.
Phoenix.
Thoughts of a Briton in the Fourth Year of War. *Fr.* Two War Sonnets.
Thus Answered. *Fr.* Two War Sonnets.
Two War Sonnets.
MEYNELL, ALICE (Mrs. Wilfrid Meynell). After a Parting.
At Night.
Changeless.
Chimes.
Christ in the Universe.
Christmas Night.
Cradle Song at Twilight.
Crucifixion, The.
Dead Harvest, A.
Easter Night.
General Communion, A.
"I Am the Way."
I Go by Road, *tr.*
In Early Spring.
In Portugal, 1912.
Lady of the Lambs, The.
Lady Poverty, The.
Letter from a Girl to Her Own Old Age, A.
Maternity.
Modern Mother, The.
Modern Poet, The.
Mother.
My Heart Shall Be Thy Garden.
Newer Vainglory, The.
No Sudden Thing of Glory.
November Blue.
Nurse Edith Cavell.
October Redbreast, The.
One Wept Whose Only Child Was Dead.
Parted.
Poet of One Mood, A.
Poet to the Birds, The.
Rainy Summer, The.
Renouncement.
"Rivers Unknown to Song."
Roaring Frost, The.
San Lorenzo Giustiniani's Mother.
San Lorenzo's Mother.
Shepherdess, The.
"Sœur Monique."
Song: "My Fair, no beauty of thine will last."
Song of Derivations, A.
Song of the Night at Daybreak.
Summer in England 1914.
Thoughts in Separation.
Threshing Machine, The.
Thrush before Dawn, A.
To a Daisy.
To the Beloved.
To the Body.
To the Mother of Christ, the Son of Man.
To W. M.
Two Poets, The.
Unto Us a Son Is Given.
Veneration of Images.
Via, et Veritas, et Vita.
Visiting Sea, The.
Voice of a Bird, The.
Watershed, The.
Wind Is Blind, The.
Young Neophyte, The.
MEYNELL, SIR FRANCIS. Man and Beast.
Permanence.
MEYNELL, VIOLA (Mrs. John Dallyn). Blind Man's Morning, The.
Child to Parents.
Dusting.
Frozen Ocean, The.
Girl, A.
Jonah and the Whale.
Maid in the Rice-Fields, The.
MEYNELL, WILFRID. Folded Flock, The.
Joseph Mary Plunkett.
MEYRICH, GERALDINE. Washington.
MEYSEY-WIGLEY, CAROLINE. *See* CLIVE, CAROLINE.
MEZEY, ROBERT. Bedtime Story, A.
In Defense of Felons.
In the Environs of the Funeral Home.
Salesman, The.
Simpler Thing, a Chair, A.
MEZQUIDA, ANNA BLAKE. Hope.
My House Has Windows.
MIBU NO TADAMI. Yes, I am in love.
MICHAEL, JAMES LIONEL. Eye of the Beholder, The.
MICHAEL MARIE, SISTER. Our Lady on Calvary.
MICHAEL OF KILDARE, FRIAR. Land of Cokaygne, The, *at.*
Satire on the People of Kildare, A, *at.*
Sweet Jesus.
MICHAELIS, ALINE. Lindbergh.
MICHAËLIS, SOPHUS. Night.
Smile, The.
Villa Borghese.
MICHAELS, MOLLY. Dolphins.
Perfect Child, The.
Three Peters, The.
MICHAUX, HENRI. Clown.
Death Chant.
Fate.
I Am Writing You from a Distant Land.
Impulses.
In the Land of Magic.
My Occupation.
Peaceful Man, A.
Plume Travelling.
MICHELANGELO BUONARROTI. Amulet of Love, The.
Beauty and the Artist.
Carnal and Spiritual Love.
Celestial Love.
Come gentle sleep, Death's image tho' thou art.
Dante.
Deathless Flower, A.
Defence of Night, The.
Doom of Beauty, The.
Eternal Lord! Eased of a Cumbrous Load.
Fearful Joy.
For Inspiration.
Garland and the Girdle, The.
Haven and last refuge of my pain, The.
His Great Love on High.
I know not if from uncreated spheres.
If It Be True That Any Beauteous Thing.
Joy May Kill.
Last Refuge.
Love, the Light-Giver.
Love's Entreaty.
Love's Justification.
Madrigal: "If it be true that any beauteous thing."
Madrigal 178: "Lady, up to your high and shining crown."
Madrigal 139: "Led on through many years to my last hours."
Madrigal 109: "Ravished by all that to the eyes is fair."
Madrigal 95: "Though time may prod against me and insist."
Madrigal 86: "While life is running out in me through time."
Might of One Fair Face, The.
Model and the Statue, The.
Night.
No mortal object did these eyes behold.
On Dante Alighieri.
On Rome in the Pontificate of Julius II.
On the Brink of Death.
On the Crucifix.
Prayer for Faith, A.
Prayer for Inspiration.
Prayer for Purification, A.
Prayer for Strength, A.
Ravished by all that to the eyes is fair.
Sacred Night.
Sonnet: Dante.
Sonnet: "From thy fair face I learn, O my loved lord."
Sonnet: "He who created time, and out of nothing."
Sonnet: "I never used to think myself so fine."
Sonnet: "If one pure love, if one supreme devotion."
Sonnet: "No mortal object did these eyes behold."
Sonnet: "Oh, make me see thy face in every place."
Sonnet: Silkworm, The.
Sonnet: "Thou knowest, love, I know that thou dost know."
Sonnet: To Vittoria Colonna.
Sonnet: "Well may sure hope at times, on wings elate."
Sonnet: "With heart and breast of brimstone, flesh of flax."
Sonnet: "Yes! hope may with my strong desire keep pace."
Soul of Dante, The.
Speech of Night, The.
Supplication, A.
Thou Alone Art Good.
To Giovanni da Pistoia on the Painting of the Sistine Chapel, 1509.
To the Supreme Being.
To Vittoria Colonna.
Transfiguration of Beauty, The.
Waiting for Death.
Yes! hope may with my strong desire keep pace.
MICHELSON, MAX. Bird, The.
Hymn to Night.
Love Lyric.
O Brother Tree.
MICHIHIKO. Do you ask for a picture.
MICHITSUNA (the mother of the commander Michitsuna). Have you any idea.
MICHIZANE, SUGAWARA. When I have gone away.
MICKIEWICZ, ADAM. Sages, The.
Spin Love from Out Your Heart.
To a Polish Mother.
MICKLE, WILLIAM JULIUS. And are ye sure the news is true?
Concubine, The, *sels.*
Cumnor Hall.
Cumnor Hall, *sel.*

MICKLE, WILLIAM JULIUS (*continued*)
Evening. *Fr.* The Concubine.
Evening at the Abbey. *Fr.* Pollio; an Elegy.
Flowers and Vegetables. *Fr.* The Concubine.
Mariner's Wife, The.
Ode on Vicissitude, *sel.*
Pollio; an Elegy, *sel.*
Sailor's Wife, The.
Seasons, The. *Fr.* Ode on Vicissitude.
Sir Martyn (The Concubine), *sels.*
Sunset. *Fr.* The Concubine.
There's Nae Luck about the House.
Wild [*or* Wyld] Romantic Dell, A. *Fr.* The Concubine.
MICKLEM, NATHANIEL. On the Frontier.
MIDDLETON, JESSE EDGAR. Ballad of Jack Monroe, The.
Canadian, The.
Debt, The.
For Dominion Day.
Jesous Ahatonhia.
MIDDLETON, RICHARD. Any Lover, Any Lass.
Carol of the Poor Children, The.
Dream Song.
For He Had Great Possessions.
Heyst-sur-Mer.
Lass That Died of Love, The.
Love's Mortality.
On a Dead Child.
Pagan Epitaph.
Serenade: "By day my timid passions stand."
Song of the King's Minstrel, The.
To A. C. M.
MIDDLETON, SCUDDER. Grasses.
Interlude.
Jezebel.
Journey, The.
Mystery.
Poets, The.
Romance.
Wisdom.
Woman, A.
MIDDLETON, THOMAS. Blurt, Master Constable, *sels.*
Changeling, The, *sels.*
Chaste Maid in Cheapside, A, *sel.*
Come, my dainty doxies. *Fr.* More Dissemblers Besides Women.
Give me fortune, give me health. *Fr.* The Widow.
Lips and Eyes. *Fr.* Blurt, Master Constable.
Love for such a cherry lip. *Fr.* Blurt, Master Constable.
Mad World, A, My Masters, *sel.*
Midnight. *Fr.* Blurt, Master Constable.
More Dissemblers Besides Women, *sel.*
O for a Bowl of Fat Canary. *Fr.* A Mad World, My Masters.
Parting. *Fr.* A Chaste Maid in Cheapside.
Song: "Love for such a cherry lip." *Fr.* Blurt, Master Constable.
Song: Love Is like a Lamb. *Fr.* Blurt, Master Constable.
True Love Ditty, A. *Fr.* Blurt, Master Constable.
Weep eyes, break heart! *Fr.* A Chaste Maid in Cheapside.
Widow, The, *sel.*
Women Beware of Women, *sel.*
MIDDLETON, THOMAS (*at.*), *and* JOHN FLETCHER. *See* FLETCHER, JOHN, *and* (*at.*) THOMAS MIDDLETON.
MIDDLETON, THOMAS, *and* WILLIAM ROWLEY. Song: "Trip it gipsies, trip it fine." *Fr.* The Spanish Gipsy.
Spanish Gipsy, The, *sel.*
Trip It, Gipsies. *Fr.* The Spanish Gipsy.
MIDLANE, ALBERT. Little Lamb Went Straying, A.
There's a Friend for Little Children.
MIEGEL, AGNES. Fair Agnete, The.
Ghost.
MIFFLIN, LLOYD. April. *Fr.* The Fields of Dawn.
April Speaks.
Autumn. *Fr.* The Fields of Dawn.
Battle-Field, The.
Doors, The.
Fiat Lux.
Fields of Dawn, The, *sels.*
Flight, The.
Half-Mast.
Harvest Waits, The.
He Made the Night.
Milton.
Sesostris.
Ship, The.
Sovereign Poets.
Sovereigns, The.
Summer. *Fr.* The Fields of Dawn.
Theseus and Ariadne.
To a Maple Seed.
To an Old Venetian Wine-Glass.
To the Milkweed.
Upon the Hearth.
MIHALKOV, SERGEI. *See* MIKHALKOV, SERGEI.
MIKATA SHAMI. Tread Not the Snow.
MIKHALKOV, SERGEI. Drawing.
Elephant Artist, The.
MIKHALKOV, SERGEI, *and* EL-REGISTAN. Hymn of the Soviet Union.
MIKI, ROFU. After the Kiss.
Bell across the Snow.
Native Place.
Song of Departing May.
MILES, ALFRED H. Big and Little Things.
MILES, C. AUSTIN. From Dawn to Evensong.
I come to the garden alone.
MILES, GEORGE HENRY. Marcela.
Raphael's San Sisto Madonna.
Said the Rose.
MILES, JOSEPHINE. Appointment in Doctor's Office.
Belief.
Bombay.
Confessed.
Day the Winds, The.
Driver Saying.
Education.
Enlightenment.
Entry.
For Futures.
Forecast.
Government Injunction [Restraining Harlem Cosmetic Co.].
Halt, The.
Harvest Moon.
Herald.
Housewife.
Idea of Joy.
Kind.
Lark.
Lineman Calling.
Meeting.
Mercury.
Monkey.
Moonrise in City Park.
Opal.
Plastic Glass, The.
Polo Match. Sunday, 2 P.M.
Preliminary to Classroom Lecture.
Pride.
Reason.
Riddle.
Sale.
Savages, The.
Son.
Statute.
Sympathizers, The.
Thoroughgoing, The.
What Followed.
MILLARD, BAILEY. Apache in Ambush, The.
Crotalus, The.
MILLARD, EDITH G. Banbury Fair.
MILLAY, EDNA ST. VINCENT ("Nancy Boyd"). Afternoon on a Hill.
And You as Well Must Die, Belovèd Dust. *Fr.* Unnamed Sonnets.
Anguish, The.
Anselmo Speaks ("There is no peace on earth today save the peace in the heart"). *Fr.* Conversation at Midnight.
Ashes of Life.
Autumn Chant.
Autumn Daybreak.
Ballad of the Harp-Weaver, The.
Before this coiling planet shall be cold. *Fr.* Epitaph for the Race of Man.
Betrothal, The.
Blue-Flag in the Bog.
Bluebeard.
Buck in the Snow, The.
Cameo, The.
Cherish You Then the Hope I Shall Forget. *Fr.* Unnamed Sonnets.
Chorus: "Give away her gowns." *Fr.* Memorial to D. C.
City Trees.
Conversation at Midnight, *sel.*
Counting-out Rhyme.
Curse, The.
Dawn, *tr.*
Departure.
Dirge without Music.
Elaine.
Elegy: "Let them bury your big eyes." *Fr.* Memorial to D. C.
Elegy before Death.
Endymion.
Epitaph: "Heap not on this mound." *Fr.* Memorial to D. C.
Epitaph for the Race of Man, *sels.*
Euclid Alone [Has Looked on Beauty Bare].
Even in the Moment of Our Earliest Kiss.
Exiled.
Fawn, The.
Feast.
First Fig.
God's World.
Grown Not Too High, Grow Not Too Far from Home.
Heart, Have No Pity on This House of Bone.
Here Is a Wound That Never Will Heal.
Here lies, and none to mourn him but the sea. *Fr.* Epitaph for the Race of Man.
Horseshoe, The. *Fr.* A Very Little Sphinx.
Hungry Heart, The.
I Dreamed I Moved among the Elysian Fields.
I Know I Am but Summer to Your Heart.
I Like Americans.
I Shall Go Back.
In the Grave No Flower.
Journal, *sel.*
Journey.
Justice Denied in Massachusetts.
Keen.
King of the Rainy Country, The, *tr.*
Lament: "Listen, children:/ Your father is dead."
Lethe.
Love Is Not All; It Is Not Meat nor Drink.
Memorial to D. C., *sels.*
Memory of England.
Moriturus.
My Candle [Burns at Both Ends].
My Spirit, Sore from Marching.
Never May the Fruit Be Plucked.
Not in a Silver Casket Cool with Pearls.
Not with Libations. *Fr.* Unnamed Sonnets.
O Earth, unhappy planet born to die. *Fr.* Epitaph for the Race of Man.
Oh, Sleep Forever in the Latmian Cave.
Oh, Think Not I Am Faithful to a Vow.
October—an Etching.
On First Having Heard the Skylark.
On Hearing a Symphony of Beethoven.
On the Wide Heath.
Only the diamond and the diamond's dust. *Fr.* Epitaph for the Race of Man.
Passer Mortuus Est.
Pear Tree, The.
Penitent, The.
Philosopher, The.
Pioneer, The.

Pity Me Not [because the Light of Day].
Poet and His Book, The.
Portrait by a Neighbor.
Prayer to Persephone. *Fr.* Memorial to D. C.
Recuerdo.
Renascence.
Renascence, *sel.*
Return, The.
Say What You Will.
Second Fig.
See Where Capella with Her Golden Kids. *Fr.* Epitaph for the Race of Man.
She Is Overheard Singing.
Shroud, The.
Siege.
Singing-Woman from the Wood's Edge, The.
Song for a Lute ("For you there is no song").
Song for a Lute ("Seeing how I love you utterly").
Song of a Second April.
Sonnet: "And you as well must die, belovèd dust." *Fr.* Unnamed Sonnets.
Sonnet: "Cherish you then the hope I shall forget." *Fr.* Unnamed Sonnets.
Sonnet: "Euclid alone has looked on beauty bare."
Sonnet XVIII: "Here lies, and none to mourn him but the sea."
Sonnet XIV: "Him not the golden fang of furious heaven."
Sonnet: "How healthily their feet upon the floor."
Sonnet: "I know I am but summer to your heart."
Sonnet: "Into the golden vessel of great song." *Fr.* Unnamed Sonnets.
Sonnet: "Night is my sister, and how deep in love."
Sonnet: "Not with libations, but with shouts and laughter." *Fr.* Unnamed Sonnets.
Sonnet: "Oh, my beloved, have you thought of this." *Fr.* Unnamed Sonnets.
Sonnet: "Say what you will, and scratch my heart to find."
Sonnet: "What lips my lips have kissed, and where, and why."
Sonnet to Gath.
Spring.
Tavern.
Thou Art Not Lovelier than Lilacs. *Fr.* Unnamed Sonnets.
Thursday.
Time Does Not Bring Relief. *Fr.* Unnamed Sonnets.
To a Young Poet.
To Jesus on His Birthday.
To the Not Impossible Him.
Travel.
Unexplorer, The.
Unnamed Sonnets, *sels.*
Vacation Song.
Very Little Sphinx, A, *sel.*
Weeds.
What Lips My Lips Have Kissed.
What's This of Death.
When Death was young and bleaching bones were few. *Fr.* Epitaph for the Race of Man.
When It Is Over.
When the Year Grows Old.
Wild Swans.
Winter Night.
Wonder Where This Horseshoe Went. *Fr.* A Very Little Sphinx.
Wraith.
MILLAY, KATHLEEN (Mrs. Howard Irving Young). Absent Minded Birch Tree, The.
Discouraged Cherry Tree, The.
Gargoyle in the Snow, The.
Hermit Thrush.
I Must Out and Play Again.
Little Gift of Laughter, The.
Masterpiece, The.
Relativity.
Spinner's Song, The.
Timid Ash Tree, The.
Year In, Year Out.
MILLER, ALBERT G. Pygmalion.
MILLER, ALICE DUER. American to France, An.
Bread and Butter Letter, A.
Consistent Anti to Her Son, A.
If They Meant All They Said.
Song: "Light of spring, The."
Sonnet, A: "Dear, if you love me, hold me most your friend."
White Cliffs, The, *sels.*
MILLER, ALICE DUER, *and* CAROLINE DUER. *See* DUER, CAROLINE, *and* ALICE DUER MILLER.
MILLER, ANTOINETTE. Phantasy of the Sea, A.
MILLER, BETTY. Wind, The.
MILLER, CATHERINE GRAHAM. Fandango for Sorrow.
Hymn Not in Favor of Evolution, A.
MILLER, CINCINNATUS HEINE [*or* HINER]. *See* MILLER, JOAQUIN.
MILLER, EMILY HUNTINGTON. Bluebird, The.
Coast-Guard, The.
Grandpa and Bess.
Granny's Story.
Land of Heart's Desire, The.
New Year Song.
Wood-Dove's Note, The.
MILLER, FRANCESCA FALK. Abraham Lincoln.
George Washington.
Invocation: "Help me to make this working day."
Old Face, An.
MILLER, GRACE MADDOCK. Poetic Tale.
MILLER, HELEN JANET. Only the Wind Says Spring.
MILLER, HELLEN GAY. If There Be Music.
MILLER, HUGH. Babie, The, *wr. at.* *See* RANKIN, JEREMIAH EAMES.
MILLER, JAMES. Italian Opera.
Italian Opera, *sel.*
Life of a Beau, The.
MILLER, JOAQUIN (Cincinnatus Heine [*or* Hiner] Miller). Adios.
Alaska.
Arctic Moon, The. *Fr.* The Yukon.
Army of the Potomac.
At the Grave of Walker.
Bravest Battle, The.
By the Pacific Ocean.
Byron, *sel.*
California Christmas, A.
Charity. *Fr.* Byron.
Christmas Morning.
Columbus.
Crossing the Plains.
Cuba Libre.
Dead in the Sierras.
Defense of the Alamo, The.
Exodus for Oregon.
Exodus for Oregon, *sel.*
For Those Who Fail.
Fortunate Isles, The.
'49.
Greatest Battle That Ever Was Fought, The.
In Men Whom Men Condemn [as Ill]. *Fr.* Byron.
Is It Worth While?
Juanita.
Kit Carson's Ride.
Land That Man Has Newly Trod, A.
Last Supper, The.
Lines: "In men whom men condemn as ill." *Fr.* Byron.
Monkeys. *Fr.* With Walker in Nicaragua.
Mothers of Men, The.
Myrrh, *sel.*
People's Song of Peace, The. *Fr.* Song of the Centennial.
Peter Cooper.
Picture of a Bull.
Rejoice.
Resurge San Francisco.
San Francisco.
Sea-blown.
Song: "There is many a love in the land, my love."
Song of the Centennial, *sel.*
Tantalus—Texas.
That Gentle Man from Boston Town.
That Texan Cattle Man.
To Russia.
Twilight at the Heights.
Vaquero.
Voice of the Dove, The.
Walker in Nicaragua, *sels.*
Westward Ho!
William Brown of Oregon.
With Walker in Nicaragua, *sels.*
Yukon, The.
Yukon, The, *sel.*
MILLER, JOSEPH CORSON. Conan of Fortingall.
Epicedium.
Flying Fish.
Ghost.
Hymn to the Guardian Angel.
Mad Poll.
Market Place, The.
Roses.
St. Thomas Aquinas.
Sleepers.
Song for Love's Coming of Age.
To a Nun Decorated with the Iron Cross.
Traveler, The.
Wind in the Elms, The.
MILLER, JOSEPH DANA. Hymn of Hate, The.
MILLER, KATHERINE WISE. Stevenson's Birthday.
MILLER, MADELEINE SWEENY. How Far to Bethlehem?
In Bethlehem, Today.
Winter Lullaby, A.
MILLER, MARJORIE ALICE. Flood Tide.
MILLER, MARY BRITTON. Camel.
Cat, The.
Here She Is.
Lion.
Shore.
Son just born, A.
MILLER, NELLIE BURGET. Little Day Moon.
Mist, The.
Morning Clouds.
Our House.
Prophecy.
Shack, The.
Shadow on the Loom, The.
Snow, The.
Sun Drops Red, The.
MILLER, OLIVE BEAUPRÉ. Circus Parade, The.
Lilies, *arr.*
Rains of Spring, The, *arr.*
Road to China, The.
Shower, A, *arr.*
MILLER, QUEENA DAVISON. Return.
MILLER, RACHEL E. Silent Wooded Place, The.
MILLER, RUTH. Floating Island, The.
Fruit.
Fundisi.
Honey.
MILLER, THOMAS. Mister Fly.
Mother to Her Infant, The.
My Dearest Baby, Go to Sleep.
Old Baron, The.
Sea-Deeps, The.
Spring Walk, The.
Sun, The.
MILLER, VASSAR. Adam's Footprint.
Apology.
Autumnal Spring Song.
Bout with Burning.
Ceremony.
Epithalamium.
Love Song Out of Nothing.
Paradox.
Reciprocity.
MILLER, W. Dawson's Woman.
MILLER, WILLIAM. John Frost.
Spring, *sel.*
Wee Willie Winkie.
Willie Winkie.
MILLETT, WILLIAM. I Am Ham Melanite.

MILLIGAN, ALICE. Dark Palace, The.
Fainne Gael an Lae.
Song of Freedom, A.
When I Was a Little Girl.
White Wave Following, The.
MILLIGAN, J. LEWIS. Where Is Thy God? *par.*
MILLIKIN, RICHARD ALFRED. Groves of Blarney, The.
MILLS, CLARK. Anonymous Lieutenant, The.
Pastoral for Poland, A.
Valmondois.
MILLS, ELIZABETH RANDALL-. *See* RANDALL-MILLS, ELIZABETH.
MILLS, IDA M. At Breakfast.
In Days Gone By.
MILLS, MARY. Apostasy.
Fable: "Bough will bend, the leaf will sometime fall, The."
Garden Party.
Library, The.
Pedigree.
Postscript.
White Horse, The.
White Peacock, The.
MILMAN, HENRY HART. Beacons, The. *Fr.* Samor.
Burial Hymn.
Crucifixion, The.
Fall of Jerusalem, The, *sel.*
For Palm Sunday.
Hebrew Wedding. *Fr.* The Fall of Jerusalem.
Holy Field, The.
Hymn for the Sixteenth Sunday after Trinity.
Jewish Hymn in Babylon.
Merry Heart, The.
Ride On in Majesty.
Samor, *sel.*
Thanksgiving, *tr.*
MILNE, ALAN ALEXANDER. At the Zoo.
Ballad of Private Chadd, The.
Brownie.
Diana Fitzpatrick Mauleverer James.
Dormouse and the Doctor, The.
End, The.
Four Friends, The.
From a Full Heart.
Furry Bear.
Halfway Down.
Happiness.
Hoppity.
Hums of Pooh. *Fr.* Winnie the Pooh.
In the Fashion.
King's Breakfast, The.
Lines and Squares.
London, 1940.
Market Square.
Miss James.
Missing.
Old Sailor, The.
Puppy and I.
Sand-between-the-Toes.
Three Foxes, The.
Us Two.
Winnie the Pooh, *sel.*
MILNE, ANGELA. *See* "ANDE."
MILNE, EWART. Artificer, The.
Could I Believe.
Deirdre and the Poets.
Diamond Cut Diamond.
Dublin Bay.
Evergreen.
Hills of Pomeroy, The.
In a Valley of This Restless Mind.
Sierran Vigil.
Tinker's Moon.
Vanessa Vanessa.
MILNER, B. E. Christmas Night.
MILNES, RICHARD MONCKTON, 1ST BARON HOUGHTON. Brookside, The.
Columbus and the *Mayflower.*
Enfant perdu, *tr.*
Envoy to an American Lady, A.
Good Night and Good Morning.
In Memoriam.
Lady Moon.
London Churches.
Lost Child, *tr.*
Men of Old, The.
Our Mother Tongue.
Palm-Tree and the Pine, The.
Shadows.
Small Things.
Song: "I wander'd by the brook-side."
Two Angels.
Venetian Serenade, The.
Wie langsam kriechet sie dahin, *tr.*
MILNS, WILLIAM. Federal Constitution, The.
MILTON, BROCK. Night Shower.
MILTON, JOHN (c.1563–1647). Fair Oriana in the Morn.
MILTON, JOHN (1608–1674). Adam and Eve. *Fr.* Paradise Lost.
Adam and Eve in the Garden. *Fr.* Paradise Lost.
Adam Describing Eve. *Fr.* Paradise Lost.
Adam, First Man of Men. *Fr.* Paradise Lost.
Adam to Eve. *Fr.* Paradise Lost.
Adam's Morning Hymn [in Paradise]. *Fr.* Paradise Lost.
All is best, though we oft doubt. *Fr.* Samson Agonistes.
And God Created the Great Whales. *Fr.* Paradise Lost.
Arcades, *sels.*
Areopagitica, *sel.*
Ark, The. *Fr.* Paradise Lost.
Arms and the Muse.
As when a vulture on Imaus bred. *Fr.* Paradise Lost.
At a Solemn Music [*or* Musick].
At a Vacation Exercise.
Athens. *Fr.* Paradise Regained.
Athens the Eye of Greece. *Fr.* Paradise Regained.
Atonement, The. *Fr.* Paradise Lost.
Avenge, O Lord.
Banishment, The. *Fr.* Paradise Lost.
Banishment from Paradise. *Fr.* Paradise Lost.
Battle between the Angels and the Anarchs. *Fr.* Paradise Lost.
Battle of the Angels. *Fr.* Paradise Lost.
Beëlzebub Rises to Speak. *Fr.* Paradise Lost.
Beginning of the Battle of the Angels, The. *Fr.* Paradise Lost.
Blest Pair of Sirens.
Blindness of Samson, The. *Fr.* Samson Agonistes.
Brave Epitaph, A. *Fr.* Samson Agonistes.
But to His Mother Mary. *Fr.* Paradise Regained.
By the rushy-fringèd bank. *Fr.* Comus.
Calm and Sinless Peace. *Fr.* Paradise Regained.
Captain or Colonel, or Knight in Arms.
Challenge of Death, The. *Fr.* Paradise Lost.
Chastity. *Fr.* Comus.
Choruses from "Samson Agonistes."
Christmas Hymn. *Fr.* Ode on the Morning of Christ's Nativity.
Come, come, no time for lamentation now. *Fr.* Samson Agonistes.
Come Pensive Nun. *Fr.* Il Penseroso.
Comus; a Masque Presented at Ludlow Castle, *sels.*
Comus' Invocation to His Revelers. *Fr.* Comus.
Comus Tempts the Lady. *Fr.* Comus.
Comus's Praise of Nature. *Fr.* Comus.
Cottager and His Landlord, The.
Council of Satan, The. *Fr.* Paradise Lost.
Creation of the World, The. *Fr.* Paradise Lost.
Cromwell, Our Chief of Men, Who through a Cloud.
Cyriac, whose Grandsire on the Royal Bench.
Death. *Fr.* Paradise Lost.
Death of Samson. *Fr.* Samson Agonistes.
Delilah. *Fr.* Samson Agonistes.
Deliverer, The. *Fr.* Samson Agonistes.
Departure from Paradise, The. *Fr.* Paradise Lost.
Echo. *Fr.* Comus.
Eden. *Fr.* Paradise Lost.
Epilogue: "All is best, though we oft doubt." *Fr.* Samson Agonistes.
Epitaph, An, on the Admirable Dramatic Poet, William Shakespeare.
Epitaph on the Marchioness of Winchester, An.
Eternal Spring, The.
Eve. *Fr.* Paradise Lost.
Eve and the Serpent. *Fr.* Paradise Lost.
Eve Penitent. *Fr.* Paradise Lost.
Eve Speaks to Adam. *Fr.* Paradise Lost.
Eve to Adam. *Fr.* Paradise Lost.
Evening in Paradise. *Fr.* Paradise Lost.
Eve's Lament. *Fr.* Paradise Lost.
Expulsion from Paradise, The. *Fr.* Paradise Lost.
Eyeless at Gaza. *Fr.* Samson Agonistes.
Fairfax, Whose Name in Arms through Europe Rings.
Faithful Angel, The. *Fr.* Paradise Lost.
Fall, The. *Fr.* Paradise Lost.
Fall of the Angels, The. *Fr.* Paradise Lost.
Fallen Angels, The. *Fr.* Paradise Lost.
Farewell of the Attendant Spirit. *Fr.* Comus.
Fifth Ode of Horace, The, *tr. Fr.* Odes.
Final Chorus: "All is best, though we oft doubt." *Fr.* Samson Agonistes.
First Day of Creation, The. *Fr.* Paradise Lost.
First Temptation, The. *Fr.* Paradise Regained.
Flight of Satan, The. *Fr.* Paradise Lost.
Flowers. *Fr.* Lycidas.
For Whom, Pyrrha? *tr.*
Formation Flight. *Fr.* Paradise Lost.
Free to Serve. *Fr.* Paradise Lost.
Free Will and God's Foreknowledge. *Fr.* Paradise Lost.
Gabriel Meets Satan. *Fr.* Paradise Lost.
Hail Holy Light. *Fr.* Paradise Lost.
Haste thee, Nymph, and bring with thee. *Fr.* L'Allegro.
Haunt of the Sorcerer, The. *Fr.* Comus.
He That Has Light Within. *Fr.* Comus.
Heaven. *Fr.* Paradise Lost.
Hell. *Fr.* Paradise Lost.
Hero in Prison, A. *Fr.* Samson Agonistes.
Heroic Vengeance. *Fr.* Samson Agonistes.
How Soon Hath Time, the Subtle Thief of Youth.
Hymn: "It was the winter wild." *Fr.* Hymn on the Morning of Christ's Nativity.
Hymn on the Morning of Christ's Nativity.
Hymn on the Morning of Christ's Nativity, *sels.*
Hymn to Light ("Hail, holy Light"). *Fr.* Paradise Lost.
Il Penseroso.
Il Penseroso, *sel.*
Immortality. *Fr.* Lycidas.
Inner Light. *Fr.* Paradise Lost.
Invocation: "Of Mans First Disobedience, and the Fruit." *Fr.* Paradise Lost.
Invocation of Comus, The. *Fr.* Comus.
Invocation to Light. *Fr.* Paradise Lost.
Invocation to the Heavenly Muse. *Fr.* Paradise Lost.
Invocation to Urania. *Fr.* Paradise Lost.
Katherine Milton: Died MDCLVIII.
Lady Lost in the Wood, The. *Fr.* Comus.
Lady's Song. *Fr.* Comus.
L'Allegro.

L'Allegro, *sel.*
Last Chorus: "All is best, though we oft doubt." *Fr.* Samson Agonistes.
Late Massacre in Piedmont, The.
Lawrence of Virtuous Father Virtuous Son.
Leave Taking. *Fr.* Paradise Lost.
Let Us with a Gladsome Mind.
Light. *Fr.* Paradise Lost.
Light Within. *Fr.* Comus.
Love Virtue. *Fr.* Comus.
Lucifer. *Fr.* Paradise Lost.
Lycidas.
Lycidas, *sels.*
Magi, The. *Fr.* On the Morning of Christ's Nativity.
Mammon. *Fr.* Paradise Lost.
Man and Woman Made One Unity. *Fr.* Paradise Lost.
Mask, A. *Fr.* Comus.
May Morning.
Messiah, The. *Fr.* Paradise Regained.
Methought I Saw My Late Espoused Saint.
Moon and the Nightingale, The. *Fr.* Paradise Lost.
Morning Hymn in Paradise. *Fr.* Paradise Lost.
Morning Hymn of Adam. *Fr.* Paradise Lost.
Morning Hymn of Adam and Eve. *Fr.* Paradise Lost.
Mustering the Hosts of Hell. *Fr.* Paradise Lost.
Myself Am Hell. *Fr.* Paradise Lost.
New Worlds. *Fr.* Paradise Lost.
Night Falls on Eden. *Fr.* Paradise Lost.
Night Mysteries. *Fr.* Comus.
Now came still evening on, and twilight grey. *Fr.* Paradise Lost.
Nymph of the Severn, The. *Fr.* Comus.
Nymphs and shepherds, dance no more. *Fr.* Arcades.
O Dark, Dark, Dark. *Fr.* Samson Agonistes.
O Earth, How Like to Heav'n. *Fr.* Paradise Lost.
O Foolishnes of Men. *Fr.* Comus.
O how comely it is. *Fr.* Samson Agonistes.
O Nightingale.
O Nightingale That on Yon Bloomy Spray.
Ode on the Morning of Christ's Nativity.
Ode on the Morning of Christ's Nativity, *sel.*
Odes (*of* Horace), *sel., tr.*
O'er the Smooth Enamelled Green. *Fr.* Arcades.
On a May Morning.
On His Being Arrived at [*or* to] the Age of Twenty-three [*or* at His Twenty-third Year].
On His Birthday.
On His Blindness.
On His Deceased Wife.
On His Having Arrived at the Age of Twenty-three.
On His Late Wife.
On His 24th Birthday.
On His Twenty-third Birthday.
On May Morning.
On Shakespeare.
On the Detraction Which Followed upon My Writing Certain Treatises.
On the Late Massacre in Piedmont.
On the Lord Gen. Fairfax at the Siege of Colchester.
On the Morning of Christ's Nativity.
On the Morning of Christ's Nativity, *sel.*
On the New Forcers of Conscience under the Long Parliament.
On the Oxford Carrier.
On the Religious Memory of Mrs. Catherine Thomson.
On the Same.
On the University Carrier (Who Sickn'd in the Time of His Vacancy).
On Time.
Opening Argument, The. *Fr.* Paradise Lost.
Out of Adversity. *Fr.* Samson Agonistes.
Over All the Face of Earth Main Ocean Flowed. *Fr.* Paradise Lost.
Pandemonium and Its Architect. *Fr.* Paradise Lost.
Paradise. *Fr.* Paradise Lost.
Paradise Lost, *sels.*
Paradise Regained, *sels.*
Parthians, The. *Fr.* Paradise Regained.
Passion, The, *sel.*
Peaceful Night, The. *Fr.* On the Morning of Christ's Nativity.
Philosophy. *Fr.* Comus.
Place of the Damned, The. *Fr.* Paradise Lost.
Plan of Salvation, The. *Fr.* Paradise Lost.
Poet-Preacher's Prayer, A. *Fr.* Paradise Lost.
Prologue of the Attendant Spirit in "Comus." *Fr.* Comus.
Praise the Lord.
Prospect of Eden, The. *Fr.* Paradise Lost.
Psalm LXXXIV: "How lovely are thy dwellings fair!" *tr.*
Retreat from Paradise, The. *Fr.* Paradise Lost.
Rivers Arise; a Fragment.
Rome. *Fr.* Paradise Regained.
Sabrina. *Fr.* Comus.
Sabrina Fair. *Fr.* Comus.
Samson Agonistes.
Samson Agonistes, *sels.*
Samson at Gaza; His Last Trial of Strength. *Fr.* Samson Agonistes.
Samson Fallen. *Fr.* Samson Agonistes.
Samson Hath Quit Himself. *Fr.* Samson Agonistes.
Samson on His Blindness. *Fr.* Samson Agonistes.
Satan. *Fr.* Paradise Lost.
Satan and His Host. *Fr.* Paradise Lost.
Satan and the Fallen Angels. *Fr.* Paradise Lost.
Satan Beholds Eve. *Fr.* Paradise Lost.
Satan Defiant. *Fr.* Paradise Lost.
Satan Discovers Eden. *Fr.* Paradise Lost.
Satan Greets Hell. *Fr.* Paradise Lost.
Satan in Sight of Eden. *Fr.* Paradise Lost.
Satan Journeys to the Garden of Eden. *Fr.* Paradise Lost.
Satan Looks upon Adam and Eve in Paradise. *Fr.* Paradise Lost.
Satan on War. *Fr.* Paradise Lost.
Satan Ponders His Fallen State. *Fr.* Paradise Lost.
Satan Rallies the Fallen Angels. *Fr.* Paradise Lost.
Satan Reflects. *Fr.* Paradise Lost.
Satan Speaks. *Fr.* Paradise Lost.
Satan Views the World. *Fr.* Paradise Lost.
Satan's Address to the Sun. *Fr.* Paradise Lost.
Satan's Adjuration. *Fr.* Paradise Lost.
Satan's First Meeting with Death. *Fr.* Paradise Lost.
Satan's Guile. *Fr.* Paradise Regained.
Satan's Kingdom. *Fr.* Paradise Lost.
Satan's Pride. *Fr.* Paradise Lost.
Satan's Soliloquy. *Fr.* Paradise Lost.
Satan's Survey of Greece. *Fr.* Paradise Regained.
Scene in Paradise, A. *Fr.* Paradise Lost.
Scheme of Redemption, The. *Fr.* Paradise Lost.
Second Sonnet on "Tetrachordon."
Sometimes, with Secure Delight. *Fr.* L'Allegro.
Son of God in the Wilderness, The. His Dream. *Fr.* Paradise Regained.
Song: May Morning, A.
Song: "Nymphs and shepherds, dance no more." *Fr.* Arcades.
Song: "O'er the smooth enameled green." *Fr.* Arcades.
Song: "Sabrina fair." *Fr.* Comus.
Song: "Star that bids the shepherd fold, The." *Fr.* Comus.
Song: "Sweet Echo . . ." *Fr.* Comus.
Song: "To the ocean now I fly." *Fr.* Comus.
Song from "Arcades." *Fr.* Arcades.
Song on [a] May Morning.
Songs from "Comus."
Sonnet: Avenge O Lord Thy Slaughter'd Saints.
Sonnet: "Captain or Colonel, or Knight in Arms."
Sonnet: "Cyriack, whose grandsire on the royal bench."
Sonnet: "Daughter to that good Earl, once President."
Sonnet: "How soon hath Time the subtle thief of youth."
Sonnet: "Lawrence of vertuous father vertuous son."
Sonnet: "Methought I saw my late espoused saint."
Sonnet: "O Nightingale, that on yon bloomy spray."
Sonnet: On the Late Massacre in Piedmont.
Sonnet: On the Religious Memorie of Mrs. Catherine Thomason My Christian Friend Deceas'd Dec. 16, 1646.
Sonnet: To Mr. H. Lawes, on his Aires.
Sonnet: To the Nightingale.
Sonnet: "When I consider how my light is spent."
Sonnet on His Being [*or* Having] Arrived at [*or* to] the Age of Twenty-three.
Sonnet on His Blindness.
Sonnet on His Deceased Wife.
Standing on Earth. *Fr.* Paradise Lost.
Star that bids the shepherd fold, The. *Fr.* Comus.
Subject of Heroic Song, The. *Fr.* Paradise Lost.
Sum of Wisdom, The. *Fr.* Paradise Lost.
Summons, The. *Fr.* Paradise Lost.
Superior Fiend, The. *Fr.* Paradise Lost.
Sweet Echo [Sweetest Nymph]. *Fr.* Comus.
Sweet Is the Breath of Morn. *Fr.* Paradise Lost.
Table Richly Spread, A. *Fr.* Paradise Regained.
Temperance and Virginity. *Fr.* Comus.
Tenure of Kings and Magistrates, The. *sel.*
Their Banishment. *Fr.* Paradise Lost.
Their Wedded Love. *Fr.* Paradise Lost.
Then When I Am Thy Captive, Talk of Chains. *Fr.* Paradise Lost.
These Are Thy Glorious Works. *Fr.* Paradise Lost.
To a Flirt, *tr.* *Fr.* Odes.
To a Virtuous Young Lady.
To Cyriack Skinner ("Cyriack, this three years' day").
To Mr. Cyriack Skinner upon His Blindness.
To Mr. H. Lawes on His Airs.
To Mr. Lawrence.
To Oliver Cromwell.
To Pyrrha, *tr.*
To Sir Henry Vane the Younger.
To the Lady Margaret Ley.
To the Lord General Cromwell.
To the Lord General Fairfax.
To the Nightingale.
To the ocean now I fly. *Fr.* Comus.
To the Same (Cyriack Skinner).
Transcendence of God, The. *Fr.* Samson Agonistes.
True and False Glory. *Fr.* Paradise Regained.
Universe of Death, A. *Fr.* Paradise Lost.
Victor, The. *Fr.* Paradise Lost.

MILTON, JOHN (*continued*)
Virgin, daughter of Locrine. *Fr.* Comus.
Vision of Athens. *Fr.* Paradise Regained.
War in Heaven, The. *Fr.* Paradise Lost.
Ways of God to Men, The. *Fr.* Samson Agonistes.
Wedded Love. *Fr.* Paradise Lost.
When I Consider [How My Light Is Spent].
When the Assault Was Intended to the City.
With Them That Rest. *Fr.* Samson Agonistes.
Woman. *Fr.* Samson Agonistes.
World Beautiful, The. *Fr.* Paradise Lost.
Yonder Nether World. *Fr.* Paradise Lost.
"MIMI." *See* DURYEE, MARY BALLARD.
MIMNERMUS. Among the Embers.
Elegiac.
"Gather Ye Rosebuds."
Glad Flow'ring Time.
Labours of the Sun, The.
Never-resting Sun, The.
"Sated Guest, The."
Sine Amore Nil Est Jucundum.
Sun's Golden Bowl, The.
We All Do Fail as a Leaf.
We, like the leaves of many-blossomed Spring.
What is joy of life apart from Venus the golden?
Youth and Age.
MINAMOTO NO KANEMASA. Guardian of the gate/ Of Suma.
MINAMOTO NO MOROTADA. In the mountain village.
MINAMOTO NO MUNEYUKI. I can feel the loneliness.
MINAMOTO NO SANETOMO. If only the world.
MINAMOTO NO SHIGEYUKI. Winter has at last come. *Fr.* Shui Shu.
MINAMOTO NO TORU. Like Michinoku/ Cloth, printed with tangled ferns.
MINAMOTO NO TSUNENOBU. In the evening/ The rice leaves in the garden.
MINER, LEIGH RICHMOND. Dey Don' Know.
Li'l Road to Res', De.
MINER, VIRGINIA SCOTT. Golden Spurs.
MINERS, HAZEL. Plea, A.
MING HUANG. Puppets.
MING TI. Bowl of Wine, A.
MINOR, TENNYSON. Bather's Dirge.
MINOT, JOHN CLAIR. Brook That Runs to France, The.
Little Flags, The.
MINOT, LAURENCE. Burgesses of Calais, The.
How King Edward and His Menge Met with the Spaniards in the Sea.
Sea-Fight at Sluys, The.
Song of Laurence Minot, A.
Winchelsea Fight, or the Humbling of the Spaniards.
"MINSKI [*or* MINSKY], NIKOLAI MAKSIMOVICH" (Nikolai Maksimovich Vilenkin). Force.
Immortality.
MINSTER, LEO. Warsaw, 27 September, 1939.
MIR ALISHIR. Lines from a Ghazel.
MIRIAM, SISTER (Margaret Miriam Gallagher; "F. Kevin Condol"). Carmelite Breaks Silence, A.
Give Me the Sun.
Prometheus Unbound.
Tower of Lowliness, The.
Victim Invisible.
MIRIAM OF THE HOLY SPIRIT, SISTER. *See* POWERS, JESSICA.
MIRIAM TERESA, SISTER. To the Most Holy Crown of Thorns.
MIRICK, EDITH. Last Hill.
Man Plowing.
Miracle.
Two Others, on Either Side.
MISCH, ROBERT J. To J. S.
"MISS X *and* MISS Y." Merry Month, The.
MISTRAL, FRÉDÉRIC. Aliscamp, The.
Cocooning, The. *Fr.* The Mirèio.
Leaf-picking, The.
Mares of the Camargue, The. *Fr.* The Mirèio.
Mirèio, The, *sels.*
"MISTRAL, GABRIELA" (Lucila Godoy Alcayaga). Deep Sleep.
God Wills It.
Hymn for the Day.
Little Girl That Lost a Finger, The.
Night.
Prayer, The: "Thou knowest, Lord, with what flaming boldness."
Teacher's Prayer, The.
Where Shall We Dance?
MITCHELL, AGNES E. When the Cows Come Home.
MITCHELL, ANNA VIRGINIA. Sonnet: "Be secret, heart; and if your dreams have come."
MITCHELL, CYPRUS R. Soul of Jesus Is Restless, The.
MITCHELL, DOROTHY. Clean.
Values.
MITCHELL, GRACE. Lullaby: "Birds in their nests are softly calling."
MITCHELL, JACK. Ballad of the Sailor Ben.
MITCHELL, JOHN. Reply to "In Flanders Fields."
MITCHELL, JOHN HANLON. City Song, A.
Farm Wife.
Sea Hunger.
MITCHELL, JOHN KEARSLEY. To N. Chapman, M.D., *sel.*
MITCHELL, LANGDON ELWYN ("John Philip Varley"). Carol: "Mary, the mother, sits on the hill."
Fear.
Purpose. *Fr.* To a Writer of the Day.
Song: "Mary, the mother, sits on the hill."
Sweets That Die.
Technique. *Fr.* To a Writer of the Day.
To a Writer of the Day, *sels.*
To One Being Old.
Wayside Virgin, The.
Written at the End of a Book.
MITCHELL, LUCY SPRAGUE. Back and Forth.
House of the Mouse, The.
It Is Raining.
Lost Ball, The.
What Is a Brook?
MITCHELL, LULU W. Toiler, Canst Thou Dream?
MITCHELL, RUTH COMFORT (Mrs. William Sanborn Young). Barbara.
Bride, The.
Cherry Way.
Compensation.
El Poniente.
Night Court, The.
Quién Sabe?
Symphony Pathétique.
Travel Bureau, The.
Vinegar Man, The.
MITCHELL, SILAS WEIR. Birth and Death of Pain, The, *sel.*
Decanter of Madeira, Aged 86, to George Bancroft, Aged 86.
Evening.
For a Guest Book.
From Dark to Light.
Good Night.
Herndon.
How the *Cumberland* Went Down.
Idleness.
Kearsarge.
Lincoln.
Of One Who Seemed to Have Failed.
On a Boy's First Reading of "King Henry V."
Quaker Graveyard, The.
Song of the Flags, The.
To a Magnolia Flower in the Garden of the Armenian Convent at Venice.
Vesperal.
Vespers.
MITCHELL, SUSAN L. Descent of the Child, The.
Heart's Low Door, The.
Immortality.
Irish Council Bill, 1907, The [*parody on the* Shan Van Vocht], *sel.*
Living Chalice, The.
Wind Bloweth Where It Listeth, The.
MITCHELL, WALTER. Cheer of the *Trenton*, The.
Reefing Topsails.
Tacking Ship off Shore.
MITCHELL, WILLIAM. Shall We Forget.
MITFORD, JOHN (1781–1859). Roman Legions, The.
MITFORD, JOHN (1782–1831). Adventures of Johnny Newcome in the Navy, The, *sels.*
Fight, The. *Fr.* The Adventures of Johnny Newcome in the Navy.
Gale of Wind, A. *Fr.* The Adventures of Johnny Newcome in the Navy.
MITFORD, MARY RUSSELL. Joy of Life.
Rienzi, *sel.*
Rienzi to the Romans. *Fr.* Rienzi.
Written in July, 1824.
MITSUKUNI. Lotus Leaves.
MITSUNE (Oshikochi no Mitsune). Since I heard. *Fr.* Kokin Shu.
White chrysanthemum, The.
MIU HSI. Bearer's Song.
"MIX, PARMENAS" (Andrew J. Kelley). Accepted and Will Appear.
He Came to Pay.
MIYAMORI. O little insects in my autumn garden.
MIYAMORI, ASATARO. *For translations from Japanese, see* OnPM.
MIYAUCHI. Comfort.
Glorying.
MIYAUCHI, TSURUE. New Year, The.
MIYAZAWA, KENJI. Fantasia under the Clear Sky.
Orchard.
Sapporo City.
Silent Wail.
MIYOSHI. Easter.
God's Plan.
MIYOSHI, TATSUJI. Deer, The.
Nostalgia.
Sea-Gulls.
Snow.
MNASALCAS. Dead Fowler, The.
Mare, A.
Temple, A.
To a Dead Cricket.
MOCKETT, LUELLA MARKLEY. Haymow, The.
MODENA, LEONE DA. Epitaph: "Implacable angel, The."
MOE, JÖRGEN. God Has Put It Away.
Sæter Girl's Sunday, The.
MOERO. Abrim with Dionysos' wine.
Childhood of Zeus, The.
MOFFAT [*or* MOFFATT], GERTRUDE MACGREGOR. All Night I Heard.
Brief as the Snow.
Genius.
Lyric: "I want to be where all is very still."
Out of My Want.
Pine, The.
MOHAMMED. Koran, The, *sel.*
Teaching of Mohammed, The. *Fr.* The Koran.
MOHR, JOSEPH. Silent Night [Holy Night].
Stille Nacht.
MOIR, DAVID MACBETH. Angler, The, *sel.*
Casa Wappy.
Casa's Dirge.
Rustic Lad's Lament in the Town, The.
MOLBECH, CHRISTIAN K. F. Freya's Star.
MOLESWORTH, MARY LOUISA STEWART. Race, A.
MOLIÈRE (Jean Baptiste Poquelin). Men of Religion. *Fr.* Tartuffe.
Tartuffe, *sel.*
To Monsieur de la Mothe le Vayer.
MOLL, ERNEST G. At the Grave of a Land-Shark.

Beware the Cuckoo.
Clearing for the Plough.
Dew-Plants.
Eagles over the Lambing Paddock.
Fishing in the Australian Alps.
Foxes among the Lambs.
On Having Grown Old.
Returned Soldier.
Undertaker's Advertisement, An.
MØLLER, POUL MARTIN. Fair Unknown, The.
MOLLOY, J. L. Little Soldier, The.
MOLLOY, JAMES LYMAN. Bantry Bay.
Kerry Dance, The.
MOLODOWSKY, KADIE. Mother, The.
My "Fatherlands."
Singer, The.
When My Eye Loses Its Hue.
MOLONEY, PATRICK. Sonnets—Ad Innuptam.
MOMBERT, ALFRED. Along the Strand.
Idyl: "And my young sweetheart."
Sleeping They Bear Me.
MOMENT, JOHN J. Best Treasure, The.
New Year.
Palm Sunday.
MONCRIEFF, WILLIAM THOMAS. Waltzing It.
MONEY, SIR LEO. King Cotton, *sel.*
MONEY-COUTTS, FRANCIS BURDETT. Any Father to Any Son.
Dream, The.
Empires.
"Forgive!" *Fr.* A Little Sequence.
Little Sequence, A, *sels.*
Mors, Morituri Te Salutamus.
No wonder you so oft have wept. *Fr.* A Little Sequence.
On a Fair Woman.
On a Wife.
MONICA, SISTER. Reply, The.
Teacher, The.
MONK, MARY. Lines Written on Her Death-Bed.
"MONK OF EIGHT FINGERS." Song of a Soldier.
MONK OF MONTAUDON. Vexational.
MONKHOUSE, COSMO. Dead March, A.
Dead March, A, *sel.*
In Arcady.
Limerick: "Lady there was of Antigua, A."
Limerick: "Poor benighted Hindoo, The."
Limerick: "There once was a girl of New York."
Limerick: "There once was a person of Benin."
Limerick: There once was an old man of Lyme."
Limerick: "There was a young girl of Lahore."
Limerick: "There was a young lady of Niger," *at.*
Night Express, The.
Rebel, The, *tr.*
Secret, The.
Song: "Who calls me bold because I won my love."
Song of the Seasons, A.
Spectrum, The.
There Was a Young Lady of Niger.
To a New-born Child.
MONKMAN, ROBINA. Sea Burial.
MONOD, THEODORE. None of Self and All of Thee.
MONRAD, CALLY. To the Sea.
MONRO, HAROLD. At a Country Dance in Provence.
Bird at Dawn.
Bitter Sanctuary.
Cat's Meat.
Children of Love.
City-Storm.
Clock.
Curate's Christmas Eve, The.
Dawn, *sel.*
Dawn of Womanhood.
Dog.
Dogs.
Earth for Sale, The.
Elm Angel.
Evening.
Every Thing.
Flower Is Looking [through the Ground], A. *Fr.* Strange Meetings.
Fresh Air, The.
From an Old House.
God. *Fr.* Dawn.
Great City.
Guest, The.
Hearthstone.
Holy Matrimony.
Hurrier, The.
If Suddenly a Clod of Earth. *Fr.* Strange Meetings.
Impressions.
Journey, *sel.*
Living.
London Interior.
Man Carrying Bale.
Midnight Lamentation.
Milk for the Cat.
Natural History, The, *sel.*
New Day.
Nightingale near the House, The.
One Blackbird. *Fr.* Strange Meetings.
Overheard on a Saltmarsh.
Real Property.
Rebellious Vine, The.
Romantic Fool.
Rumour.
She Was Young and Blithe and Fair.
Silent Pool, The.
Solitude.
Strange Companion, The.
Strange Meetings, *sels.*
Street Fight.
Suburb.
Terrible Door, The.
Thistledown.
Too Near the Sea.
Trees, *sel.*
Week-End.
Week-End, *sels.*
Wind, The.
Wind in the Dusk.
Youth in Arms.
MONROE, ARTHUR W. Cliff Dwelling, The.
Forest Fire, The.
Lost in a Blizzard.
Man of the Open West, The.
Toll of the Desert, The.
MONROE, HARRIET. April—North Carolina.
Back Home.
Blue Ridge, The.
Commemoration Ode (World's Columbian Exposition, Chicago, 1892), *sels.*
Democracy. *Fr.* Commemoration Ode.
Farewell, A: "Good-bye!—no, do not grieve that it is over."
Fortunate One, The.
Hotel, The.
I Love My Life, but Not Too Well.
In the Beginning.
Inner Silence, The.
Lincoln. *Fr.* Commemoration Ode.
Love Song.
Lullaby: "My little one, sleep softly."
Man of Science Speaks, The.
Meeting, The.
Mother Earth.
Mountain Song.
Nancy Hanks.
Night-blooming Cereus, The.
Now.
On the Porch.
Pain.
Pine at Timber-Line, The.
Radio.
Romney, The.
Shadow Child, The.
Supernal Dialogue.
Thief on the Cross, The.
Turbine, The.
Two Heroes. *Fr.* Commemoration Ode.
Vernon Castle.
Washington. *Fr.* Commemoration Ode.
Water Ouzel, The.
Wonder of It, The.
MONSELL, JOHN SAMUEL BEWLEY. Fight the Good Fight.
In the Garden.
Light of the World,
Litany: "When my feet have wander'd."
On our way rejoicing.
Worship the Lord in the Beauty of Holiness.
MONT, POL DE. Evening Landscape.
MONTAGNE, VICTOR ALEXIS DE LA. Congress, 1878.
MONTAGU, LADY MARY WORTLEY. Caveat to the Fair Sex, A.
Farewell to Bath.
In Answer to a Lady Who Advised Retirement.
Lover, The; a Ballad.
MONTAGUE, JAMES JACKSON. And When They Fall.
Fame.
It's Fun to Be a Pup.
Mollusk, The.
Same Old Story, The.
Scot's Farewell to His Golf Ball, A.
Sleepytown Express, The.
Thanksgiving Day.
To a Katydid.
Vamp Passes, The.
MONTAGUE, MARGARET PRESCOTT. Point of View, The.
MONTALE, EUGENIO. Dora Markus.
Pain of Living, The.
Sunflower, The.
MONTECANTI, GUERZO DI. *See* GUERZO DI MONTECANTI.
MONTEMAYOR, JORGE DE. Diana, *sels.*
Melisea, Her Song in Scorn of Her Shepherd Narcissus. *Fr.* Diana.
Nymph Diana's Song, The. *Fr.* Diana.
Nymph Selvagia, Her Song, The. *Fr.* Diana.
Song: "Shepherd, who can pass such wrong." *Fr.* Diana.
MONTESQUIOU-FEZENSAC, COMTE ROBERT DE. Child's Prayer, The.
MONTGOMERIE, ALEXANDER. Adieu to His Mistress.
Admonition to Young Lassies, An.
Bankis of Helicon, The.
Cherry and the Slae, The, *sel.*
He Bids Adieu to His Mistress.
Hey! Now the Day Dawns!
May-Morn and Cupid. *Fr.* The Cherry and the Slae.
Night [*or* Nicht] Is Near [*or* Neir] Gone, The.
Night [*or* Nicht] Is Near [*or* Neir] Gone, The, *sel.*
Royal Palace of the Highest Heaven, The, *at.*
Solsequium, The.
Sonnet: To His Mistress.
Sweetheart, Rejoice in Mind.
MONTGOMERIE, WILLIAM. Elegy for William Soutar.
MONTGOMERY, ELEANOR ELIZABETH. Adieu.
New Zealand Regret, A.
MONTGOMERY, GEORGE EDGAR. At Night.
Dead Soldier, A.
England.
Lullaby, A: "Sleep, my dear one, sleep."
To a Child.
MONTGOMERY, JAMES. According to Thy Gracious Word.
Angels, from the Realms of Glory.
Arnold von Winkelried.
At Home in Heaven.
Birds. *Fr.* The Pelican Island.
Christ Our Example in Suffering.
Columbus. *Fr.* The West Indies.
Come to Calvary's Holy Mountain.
Common Lot, The.
Coral Reef, The. *Fr.* The Pelican Island.
Daisy, The.
Daisy, The, *sel.*
Earth Is Full of God's Goodness, The.
Field Flower, A.
Forever with the Lord.
Go to Dark Gethsemane.
God Is My Strong Salvation.
Good Tidings of Great Joy to All People.
In the Hour of Trial.
Inspiration, The. *Fr.* The West Indies.

MONTGOMERY, JAMES (*continued*)
King Eternal, The.
Lust of Gold, The. *Fr.* The West Indies.
Make Way for Liberty.
Mother's Love, A.
My Country.
Nativity.
Night.
Ocean, The.
Our Cherished Flag.
Parted Friends.
Patriot's Pass-Word, The.
Pelican, The. *Fr.* The Pelican Island.
Pelican Island, The, *sels.*
Prayer: "Prayer is the soul's sincere desire."
Sea Life. *Fr.* The Pelican Island.
Shepherd of souls, refresh and bless.
Soliloquy of a Water-Wagtail.
Stranger, The.
There Is a Land.
Well Done.
West Indies, The, *sels.*
What Is Prayer?
MONTGOMERY, JAMES STUART. Deep Down.
Deep Water Man, The.
Landlubber's Chantey, The.
Road Song.
Swashbuckler's Song, The.
MONTGOMERY, LESLIE ALEXANDER. *See* "DOYLE, LYNN."
MONTGOMERY, LUCY MAUD (Mrs. Ewan Macdonald). Love's Miracle.
Off to the Fishing Ground.
Old Home Calls, The.
Old Man's Grave, The.
Sunrise along Shore.
When the Dark Comes Down.
MONTGOMERY, P. L. Whence Cometh My Help.
MONTGOMERY, ROSELLE MERCIER. Armistice Day.
Celebration for Neptune, *tr.*
Counsel.
Dawn.
Farmer's Prayer, A.
I Shall Not Make a Garment of My Grief.
Odes (*of* Horace), *sel., tr.*
On the Death of an Aged Friend.
Savannah River.
To Helen, Middle-aged.
Ulysses Returns.
What Does It Mean to Be American?
Woodrow Wilson.
MONTGOMERY, U. M. Grey Brother.
MONTGOMERY, WHITNEY. Even to the Dead.
Last Bob White, The.
Revelation.
Thanksgiving.
Tryst, The.
MONTI, VINCENZO. Ode on Superstition, *sel.*
MONTORO, ANTONIO DE. Ropero, El.
MONTOTO Y RAUTENSTRAUCH, LUIS. Our Poets' Breed.
MONTREUIL, MATHIEU DE. To Madame de Sévigné.
MONTROSE, JAMES GRAHAM, 5TH EARL AND 1ST MARQUESS OF. *See* GRAHAM, JAMES, MARQUESS OF MONTROSE.
MONTROSS, LOIS SEYSTER (Mrs. Lynn Montross). Codes.
Decent Burial.
I Wear a Crimson Cloak To-Night.
MONTROSS, PERCY. Oh, My Darling Clementine.
MOODIE, SUSANNA STRICKLAND (Mrs. John Wedderburn Dunbar Moodie).
Canadian Herd-Boy, The.
Canadian Hunter's Song.
Fisherman's Light, The.
Indian Summer.
MOODY, MINNIE HITE. Cotton Field.
Country Sabbath.
How Fraught with Struggle.
Ohio Farmstead.
Say This of Horses.
MOODY, WILLIAM VAUGHN. Along the earth and up the sky. *Fr.* The Fire-Bringer.
At Assisi. *Fr.* Song-Flower and Poppy.
Because one creature of his breath. *Fr.* The Fire-Bringer.
Brute, The.
Counting Man, The.
Daguerreotype, The.
Death of Eve, The, *sel.*
Faded Pictures.
Fire-Bringer, The, *sels.*
Gloucester Moors.
Gloucester Moors, *sel.*
Golden Journey, The.
Good Friday Night.
Grey Day, A.
Heart's Wild-Flower.
I stood within the heart of God. *Fr.* The Fire-Bringer.
In New York. *Fr.* Song-Flower and Poppy.
Jetsam, *sel.*
No Hint of Stain. *Fr.* An Ode in Time of Hesitation.
Ode in Time of Hesitation, An.
Ode in Time of Hesitation, An, *sels.*
Of Wounds and Sore Defeat. *Fr.* The Fire-Bringer.
On a Soldier Fallen in the Philippines.
Pandora's Song ("I stood within the heart of God"). *Fr.* The Fire-Bringer.
Pandora's Song ("Of wounds and sore defeat"). *Fr.* The Fire-Bringer.
Pandora's Songs. *Fr.* The Fire-Bringer.
Prairie Ride, A.
Quarry, The.
Road-Hymn for the Start.
Robert Gould Shaw. *Fr.* An Ode in Time of Hesitation.
Serf's Secret, The.
Song-Flower and Poppy, *sels.*
Thammuz.
Thousand aeons nailed in pain, A. *Fr.* The Fire-Bringer.
Too far, too far, though hidden in thine arms. *Fr.* The Fire-Bringer.
MOONEY, JAMES. Sacred Formula to Attract Affection, *tr.*
Sacred Formula to Destroy Life, *tr.*
MOORE, AUGUSTUS M. Ballade of Ballade-Mongers, A.
MOORE, CHARLES LEONARD. Disenchantment.
Fourth of July, The.
Or Ever the Earth Was.
Soul unto Soul Glooms Darkling.
Spring Returns, The.
Then Shall We See.
Thou Livest, O Soul!
To England.
MOORE, CLEMENT CLARKE. Night before Christmas, The.
Visit from St. Nicholas, A.
MOORE, EDWARD. Fables for the Ladies, *sel.*
Poet and His Patron, The. *Fr.* Fables for the Ladies.
Song the Eighth.
Song the Ninth.
MOORE, ELLA MAUD. "Rock of Ages," *at.*
MOORE, FRANK. Abraham Lincoln.
MOORE, GEORGE. Rondo: "Did I love thee? I only did desire."
MOORE, J. M. Bookworm, The.
MOORE, JOHN. Christmas Snow.
MOORE, SIR JOHN HENRY. Duke of Benevento, The.
Song: "Indeed, my Caelia, 'tis in vain."
MOORE, JOHN TROTWOOD. Ballad of Emma Samson, A.
Sam Davis.
MOORE, JULIA A. And now, kind friends, what I have wrote.
Departed Friend, A.
Little Libbie.
Sketch of Lord Byron's Life, *sel.*
What I Have Wrote.
Willie's and Nellie's Wish.
MOORE, MARIANNE. Apparition of Splendor.
Armour's Undermining Modesty.
At Rest in the Blast.
Carriage from Sweden, A.
Critics and Connoisseurs.
Dock Rats.
Elephants.
England.
Fish, The.
Four Quartz Crystal Clocks.
Frigate Pelican, The.
Grave, A.
Graveyard, A.
Harp You Play So Well, The.
He Made This Screen.
Hero, The. *Fr.* Part of a Novel, Part of a Poem, Part of a Play.
His Shield.
Icosasphere, The.
In Distrust of Merits.
Jerboa, The.
Keeping Their World Large.
Labors of Hercules, The.
Melancthon.
Mind Is an Enchanting Thing, The.
Monkeys, The.
My Apish Cousins.
Nevertheless.
Nine Nectarines and Other Porcelain.
No Swan So Fine.
O to Be a Dragon.
Pangolin, The.
Paper Nautilus, The.
Part of a Novel, Part of a Poem, Part of a Play.
Part of a Novel, Part of a Poem, Part of a Play, *sel.*
Pedantic Literalist.
Peter.
Poetry.
Poetry, *sel.*
Propriety.
Roses Only.
See in the Midst of Fair Leaves.
Silence.
Snakes, Mongooses, Snake-Charmers and the Like.
Spenser's Ireland.
Staff of Aesculapius, The.
Steeple-Jack, The. *Fr.* Part of a Novel, Part of a Poem, Part of a Play.
Sun!
Talisman, A.
That Harp You Play So Well.
Then the Ermine.
Those Various Scalpels.
To a Chameleon.
To a Snail.
To a Steam Roller.
Values in Use.
Virginia Britannia.
What Are Years?
When I Buy Pictures.
Wood-Weasel, The.
MOORE, MAVOR. Biography.
MOORE, MERRILL. And Then Her Burial.
And to the Young Men.
Answer.
Bees before Winter.
Book of How, The.
Constellation.
Deaf Men.
"Final Status Never Ascertained," Lloyds Registry.
Fire.
Flies, The.
He Said the Facts.
How She Resolved to Act.
Hymn for Water.
It Is Winter, I Know.
Joe Greene.
Just Then the Door.
Les Savants Ne Sont Pas Curieux.
Liquids.
Lucky Strike.
Mr. and Mrs. Alonzo Sidney.
No Envy, John Carter.
Noise That Time Makes, The.
O Mad Spring, One Waits.
Old Men.
Old Men and Old Women Going Home on the Street Car.
Pandora and the Moon.

Poet.
Poet Tells about Nature, The.
Scientia Vincit Omnia.
Shot Who? Jim Lane!
Surgery of the Liver.
There Is a Way of Life.
They Also Stand . . .
Twitter of Swallows.
Unconscious, The.
Unknown Man in the Morgue.
Village Noon; Mid-Day Bells.
Warning to One.
Why He Stroked the Cats.
MOORE, MOLLIE E. *See* DAVIS, MARY EVELYN.
MOORE, NICHOLAS. Act of Love.
Alcestis in Ely.
Fred Apollus at Fava's.
Hair's Breadth, The.
Incidents in Playfair House.
Little Girl, The.
O Rose, O Rainbow.
Phallic Symbol, The.
Poem from "The Year of Loss."
Why the British Girls Give In So Easily.
Winter and Red Berries.
MOORE, RICHARD. Deep Discussion, A.
MOORE, ROSALIE. Catalog.
Gnat.
Imprecation for an Aesthetic Society with Newts, Warts, Waxes and Pins.
MOORE, STURGE. *See* MOORE, THOMAS STURGE.
MOORE, THOMAS. After the Battle.
Alas! How Light a Cause May Move. *Fr.* Lalla Rookh.
All That's Bright Must Fade.
Anacreon, *tr.*
Argument, An.
As a Beam o'er the Face of the Waters May Glow.
As by the Shore at Break of Day.
As Down in the Sunless Retreats.
As Slow Our Ship.
At the Mid Hour of Night.
Away, away, ye men of rules, *tr.*
Before the Battle.
Believe Me if All Those Endearing Young Charms.
Bendemeer. *Fr.* Lalla Rookh.
Bird, Let Loose in Eastern Skies, The.
Black and Blue Eyes.
By Bendemeer's Stream. *Fr.* Lalla Rookh.
Canadian Boat Song, A.
Child's Song.
"Come, Come," Said Tom's Father.
Come, Rest in This Bosom.
Come, Ye Disconsolate.
Cupid Stung.
Dear Fanny.
Dear Harp of My Country.
Did Not.
Duke Is the Lad, The.
Echo[es].
Epigram: "When Eve upon the first of men."
Epigram: "While life was mine, the little hour."
Epigram: "With women and apples both Paris and Adam."
Epistle of Condolence.
Epitaph on a Well-known Poet.
Epitaph on Robert Southey.
Evenings in Greece, *sel.*
Farewell, but Whenever [You Welcome the Hour].
Farewell to Thee, Araby's Daughter. *Fr.* Lalla Rookh.
Fill the Bumper Fair.
Fire-Worshippers, The. *Fr.* Lalla Rookh.
Flight of Fondest Hopes, The. *Fr.* Lalla Rookh.
Fly to the Desert, Fly with Me. *Fr.* Lalla Rookh.
Four Blessings, The, *tr.*
French Cookery. *Fr.* The Fudge Family in Paris.
Fudge Family in Paris, The, *sel.*
Girl's Song, A. *Fr.* Lalla Rookh.
Glory of God in Creation, The.
Go Where Glory Waits Thee.
Hark! the Vesper Hymn Is Stealing.
Harp That Once through Tara's Halls, The.
Has Sorrow Thy Young Days Shaded?
How Dear to Me the Hour.
How Oft Has the Banshee Cried.
Hymn of a Virgin of Delphi at the Tomb of Her Mother.
I Knew by the Smoke That So Gracefully Curled.
I Pray You.
I Saw from the Beach.
I Wish I Was by That Dim Lake.
If You Have Seen.
Ill Omens.
Irish Peasant to His Mistress, The.
Joke Versified, A.
Journey Onwards, The.
Kiss, The.
Lake of the Dismal Swamp, The.
Lalla Rookh, *sels.*
Last Rose of Summer, The.
Legacy.
Let Erin Remember the Days of Old.
Lewis, the Lost Lover.
Light of Other Days, The.
Light of the Haram, The. *Fr.* Lalla Rookh.
Light That Lies, The. *Fr.* The Time I've Lost in Wooing.
Linda to Hafed. *Fr.* Lalla Rookh.
"Living Dog" and "The Dead Lion," The.
Long, Long Be My Heart with Such Memories Filled.
Love and Hate, *tr.*
Love Enslaved, *tr.*
Love Is a Hunter Boy.
Lover's Play of Words, *tr.*
Love's Young Dream.
Lying.
M. P.; or, The Blue Stockings, *sel.*
Meeting of the Ships, The.
Meeting of the Waters, The.
Minstrel Boy, The.
Mountain Sprite, The.
My Birthday.
My Birthday, *sel.*
No, Not More Welcome.
Nonsense.
Oh Blame Not the Bard.
Oh, Breathe Not His Name!
Oh, Come to Me When Daylight Sets.
Oh, my sweet mother, 'tis in vain, *tr.*
Oh, Thou! Who Dry'st the Mourner's Tear.
Odes (*of Anacreon*), *sels., tr.*
Of All the Men.
Oft, in the Stilly Night.
On Music.
On Taking a Wife.
Orator Puff. *Fr.* M. P.; or, The Blue Stockings.
Origin of the Harp, The.
Paddy's Metamorphosis.
Peace Be around Thee.
Peace to the Slumberers!
Poet's Inspiration, The, *tr.*
Prattling Swallows, *tr.*
Pro Patria Mori.
Quantum Est Quod Desit.
Rich and Rare Were the Gems She Wore.
Row Gently Here.
Scotch Air.
She Is Far from the Land.
Snake, The.
Song: "Come, rest in this bosom, my own stricken deer."
Song: "When Time, who steals our years away."
Song: "Where is the nymph, whose azure eye."
Song of Fionnuala, The.
Song of O'Ruark, Prince of Breffni, The.
Sound the Loud Timbrel.
Spring.
Stricken Deer, The.
Sweet Innisfallen.
Syria. *Fr.* Lalla Rookh.
Take Back the Virgin Page.
Tara.
Temperate Drinking, *tr.*
Temple to Friendship, A.
They May Rail at This Life.
This World is All a Fleeting Show.
Those Evening Bells.
Thou Art, O God.
Thoughts on Editors.
Thou'st Had Thy Day, *tr.*
Thro' Grief and thro' Danger.
Time I've Lost in Wooing, The.
'Tis the Last Rose of Summer.
To ——: "When I loved you, I can't but allow."
To a Boy, with a Watch.
To Anacreon, *tr.*
To Campbell.
To Cloe.
To Fanny.
To Ladies' Eyes.
To My Mother.
Torch of Liberty, The.
Two Streams, The. *Fr.* Evenings in Greece.
Upon Being Obliged to Leave a Pleasant Party.
Vale of Avoca, The.
Vale of Cashmere, The. *Fr.* Lalla Rookh.
Verses Written in an Album.
Were Not the Sinful Mary's Tears.
What's My Thought Like?
When He Who Adores Thee.
When I Loved You.
While life was mine, the little hour.
Women tell me every day, The, *tr.*
Wreathe the Bowl.
Yes—loving is a painful thrill, *tr.*
Young May Moon, The.
MOORE, THOMAS STURGE. Beautiful Meals.
Chercheuses de poux, Les, *tr.*
Daughter of Admetus, A.
Days and Nights.
Deed, The.
Duet, A.
Dying Swan, The.
Event, The.
Faun, The.
Faun Tells of the Rout of the Amazons, The.
Gazelles, The.
Home of Helen, The.
Idleness.
Kindness.
Leaden Echo and the Golden Echo, The, *par.*
Light Heart.
Lubber Breeze.
Much Virtue in If.
Renaissance.
Response to Rimbaud's Later Manner.
Rower's Chant.
Sent from Egypt with a Fair Robe of Tissue to a Sicilian Vinedresser.
Shells.
Silence Sings.
Tempio di Venere.
Theseus.
To Giacomo Leopardi.
To Idleness.
Tongues.
Variation on Ronsard.
Vigil, The.
Wind's Work.
"MOORE, TOM, JR." O'Duffy's Ironsides.
MOORE, TOM INGLIS. Druidic Gums.
Kookaburra, *sel.*
No, Not the Owl.
Song for Lovers.
MOORE, VIRGINIA. Courage.
Epic.
Good Ground, The.
I Am Undone.
Joan of Arc, 1926.
My Father.
Rust.
To Spring.
To the Woman I Will Be Fifty Years Hence.
Unconcern.
MOORE, WILLIAM H. A. Dusk Song.
It Was Not Fate.
MORAN, IRENE SHIRLEY. Lilacs for Remembrance.

MORDAUNT, CHARLES, EARL OF PETERBOROUGH. Chloe.
MORDAUNT, THOMAS OSBERT. Call, The.
One Crowded Hour.
Sound, Sound the Clarion.
Verses Written during the War 1756–1763.
MORDECAI BEN ISAAC. Fair Thou Art.
Rock of My Salvation.
MORDEN, PHYLLIS B. Godmother.
MORE, HANNAH. Bas Bleu, *sel.*
Book, A.
Conversation. *Fr.* Bas Bleu.
Riddle, A: Book, A.
Search after Happiness, The, *sel.*
Solitude. *Fr.* The Search after Happiness.
MORE, HELEN F. What's in a Name?
MORE, HENRY. Democritus Platonissans; or, An Essay upon the Infinity of Worlds out of Platonick Principles.
Hymn to Charity and Humility.
Hymne in Honour of Those Two Despised Virtues, Charitie and Humilitie, An.
In Him We Live.
Philosopher's Devotion, The.
Resolution; the Song of Hylobaris Concerning Divine Providence.
MORE, PAUL ELMER. Angler, The, *tr.*
By Shaded Wells, *tr.*
Dilemma, *tr.*
Friend or Stranger, *tr.*
Half-Way Knowledge, *tr.*
Heart in Brahma, The, *tr.*
Indian Epigram, *tr.*
Loaded Ass, The, *tr.*
Love in Moonlight, *tr.*
Nothing and the Soul, *tr.*
Peace, *tr.*
Round Robin, *tr.*
Sign, The, *tr.*
Snake and the Mouse, The, *tr.*
Time, *tr.*
Two as One, *tr.*
MORE, SIR THOMAS (Saint Thomas More). Age.
Childhood.
Consider Well.
Davy, the Dicer. *Fr.* Two Short Ballettes.
Eternal Reward, Eternal Pain.
Fortune. *Fr.* Two Short Ballettes.
Lewis, the Lost Lover. *Fr.* Two Short Ballettes.
Manhood.
Of Fortune.
Of Fuscus, a Drunkard.
Rueful Lamentation on the Death of Queen Elizabeth, A.
VII Properte, The. *Fr.* The XII Properties or Condicyons of a Lover.
X Properte, The. *Fr.* The XII Properties or Condicyons of a Lover.
To Fortune.
XII Properties or Condicyons of a Lover, The, *sels.*
Two Short Ballettes . . . Made for His Pastime While He Was Prisoner in the Tower of London.
MORÉAS, JEAN. Stances, *sel.*
MORELAND, JOHN RICHARD. Autumn.
Beyond.
Birch Trees.
Captive.
Christ Is Crucified Anew.
Coins of Love, The. *Fr.* What of the Night?
Driftwood Fires.
Faith.
Gossip, The.
Grave, A.
Greater Guilt, The.
His Hands.
I Did Not Heed That Spring Was Here.
If a Man Die [Shall He Live Again]?
If I Could Grasp a Wave from the Great Sea.
In April.
Intolerance.
Kings.
Life's Cloudy Quest.
Little House, The.
Minor Poet, A.
Mountains.
O Years Unborn.
One April Day.
Only One King.
Poet.
Priest Is Come and the Candles Burn, The.
Promise Lan', De.
Recompense.
Remembrance.
Resurgam.
Revealment.
Sand Dunes and Sea.
Sea Is Full of Loveliness and Tears, The.
Sea Song, A.
Secret, The.
Song of Thanksgiving.
Splendid Lover, The.
Stranger, The.
Symbols.
To One Who Worshipped Gods of Gold.
Tokens.
What of the Night? *sel.*
Whippoorwill.
White Tree in Bloom, A.
Wind Was Cold, the Sky Steel Gray, The.
Ye Who Fear Death Remember April.
MORELAND, PATRICK DACUS. Compensate.
Crucified.
MORENO, JOSÉ ROSAS. *See* ROSAS MORENO, JOSÉ.
MORENO JIMENO, MANUEL. Damned, The.
MORENO VILLA, JOSÉ. Adventurer, The.
Anguish.
At Dawn.
Discovery.
Eating Nuts and Oranges.
Fire.
Impulse.
Infinity and Motor.
It does not fly, does not sing.
Joy cannot be found in the star.
Kite, The.
Longings.
Magic.
Nothing but Flight.
Opposites.
Power-driven.
To-day the axe has almost touched my being at its source.
Two Loves, Hyacinth!
When?
Where?
MORFORD, SYBIL. Fairies, The.
MORGAN, ANGELA. Awakening, The.
Choice.
Gandhi.
God Prays.
God the Artist, *at.*
God, When You Thought of a Pine Tree, *at.*
Grief.
Hail Man!
Humanitarian, The, *sel.*
Hymn to Labor.
In Spite of War.
In Such an Age.
June Rapture.
Kinship.
Let Us Declare! *sel.*
Lindbergh.
Poet, The.
Poet, The, *sel.*
Reality.
Resurrection.
Song of Life, A.
Song of the New World.
Stand Forth!
Thanksgiving.
Three Green Trees.
Today.
When Nature Wants a Man.
Windows for My Soul.
Work; a Song of Triumph.
MORGAN, BESSIE. 'Spacially [*or* 'Specially] Jim.
MORGAN, EDWIN. Old Print, An.
Prayer: "Now that I know that what I am must be."
For translations from German, see AnGP. *For translations from Italian, see* LyPI.
"MORGAN, EMANUEL." *See* BYNNER, WITTER.
MORGAN, EVAN. Christmas Dawn at Sea, A.
Eel, The.
MORGAN, HENRY VICTOR. World-Man, The.
MORGAN, JAMES APPLETON. Malum Opus.
MORGAN, SYDNEY, LADY MORGAN. Kate Kearney.
MORGENSTERN, CHRISTIAN. Among the Mountains I Had Lost My Way.
And Now Dwell Thou, I Pray.
Ant-ology.
Bim, Bam, Bum.
Cloud Fantasies, I.
Consider, Friend, When We Together Spoke.
Dreamer, The.
Eastcoat, The.
Ex Libris.
Fate.
Gallows' Brother's Song.
Impossible Fact, The.
Knee, The.
Korf's Joke.
Look Not What Others Do.
Mousetrap, The.
Night Song of the Fish.
Noise Protection.
O Give Me Joys That Are Not Bound.
O Night, Thou Starry River!
Palmström to a Nightingale Who Kept Him from Sleeping.
Pike, The.
Pious Giant, The.
Twelve-Elf, The.
Two Asses, The.
Very Grail I Elevate, A.
Vice Versa.
Water.
Wooden Fence, The.
MORGRIDGE, HARRIET S. Jack and Jill. *Fr.* Mother Goose Sonnets.
Mother Goose Sonnets, *sels.*
Simple Simon. *Fr.* Mother Goose Sonnets.
MORIARTY, ELIZA F. New Year's Guest, A.
MORIARTY, HELEN LOUISE. Convent Echoes.
MÖRIKE, EDUARD FRIEDRICH. Beauty Rohtraut.
Butterfly in April.
Departure.
Deserted Maiden, The.
Fair Wildheart.
Forest Idyll.
Forsaken Maid, The.
From a Church Tower.
Girl's Love Song.
Hunter's Song.
In Spring.
Midnight.
My River.
Old Church Cock, The.
On a Lamp.
Peregrina.
Ponder It, O Soul!
Prayer: "Lord, as thou wilt, bestow."
September Morning.
Spring It Is!
Weyla's Song.
Wind's Song, The.
Withdrawal.
MORIN, CATHERINE A. High June.
Lace Pedlar The.
MORIN, MAUD. Bachelors' Buttons.
Shower and Sunshine.
MORITAKE, ARAKIDA. Fallen flowers seemed, The.
Hokku: "I thought I saw the fallen leaves."
I breathe but, "Oh!"
I thought I saw a fallen flower.
MORLAIX, BERNARD DE. *See* BERNARD OF CLUNY [*or* OF MORLAIX].

MORLEY, CHRISTOPHER. Animal Crackers.
At a Window Sill.
At the Dog Show.
At the Mermaid Cafeteria.
Austin Dobson.
Charm, A.
Code, The.
Confession in Holy Week.
Crib, The.
Dandy Dandelion.
Deny Yourself.
Epitaph for Any New Yorker.
Eternity and the Tooth.
Flags on Fifth Avenue, The.
Gospel of Mr. Pepys, The.
Grapes of Wrath, The.
Grub Street Recessional, A.
Hallowe'en Memory, A.
Hero and Leander.
Hero and Leander, *sels.*
I Almost Had Forgotten.
I knew a black beetle, who lived down a drain. *Fr.* Nursery Rhymes for the Tender-hearted.
I Know a Secret.
In an Auction Room.
In Honour of Taffy Topaz.
Love at First Sight.
Mandarin on the Air.
Mar Quong, Chinese Laundryman.
Milkman, The.
Moon-Sheep, The.
My Pipe.
No Coaching.
Nursery Rhymes for the Tender-hearted.
Nursery Rhymes for the Tender-hearted, *sels.*
Of a Child That Had Fever.
Of an Ancient Spaniel in Her Fifteenth Year.
On a Portrait of Dr. Samuel Johnson, LL.D.
Plumpuppets, The.
Poets Easily Consoled.
Power-House, The.
Pre-Raphaelite, A.
Private Enterprise.
Psychoanalysts.
Quickening.
Reading Aloud.
Scuttle, scuttle, little roach. *Fr.* Nursery Rhymes for the Tender-hearted.
Secret Laughter.
Skating Song.
Sleep, *sel.*
Smells.
Smells (Junior).
Song for a Little House.
"Spoken Word, The."
Sun's over the Foreyard, The.
This is all we ever say.
Thoughts for St. Stephen.
Thoughts in the Gulf Stream.
Thoughts on Being Invited to Dinner.
Three Trees.
To a Child.
To a Post-Office Inkwell.
To a Very Young Gentleman.
To the Little House.
Trees, The.
Tryst, The.
Unearned Increment.
Verification.
When Shakespeare Laughed.
MORLEY, GEORGE. Epitaph on Mistress Mary Prideaux, An, *at.*
MORLEY, SYLVANUS GRISWOLD. Amid the Shadows, *tr.*
Concerning Lawyers, *tr. Fr.* Palace Rhymes.
In the Arena, *tr.*
Inner Voice, The, *tr.*
Palace Rhymes, *sel., tr.*
Upon the Whirlwind, *tr.*
MORLEY, THOMAS. Hard by a Crystal Fountain.
"MORO, CÉSAR" (César Quíspez Asín). Illustrated World, The.
Vision of Moth-eaten Pianos Falling to Pieces.
You Come in the Night with the Fabulous Smoke of Your Hair.
MORONELLI DI FIORENZA, PIER. Canzonetta: Bitter Song to His Lady.
MORPEAU, LOUIS. To Madame la Duchesse de Bauffremont.
MORPURGO, RACHEL. Song: "Ah, vale of woe, of gloom and darkness moulded."
Sonnet: "My soul surcharged with grief now loud complains."
MORRELL, EDITH DOROTHEA. Analogy.
MORRILL, BELLE CHAPMAN. Kindly Screen, The.
My Galilees.
To a Japanese Girl Grieved over the War on China.
MORRIS, C. Contrast, The.
MORRIS, CEDRIC. Passage On.
MORRIS, CHARLES. Reason Fair to Fill My Glass, A.
MORRIS, CLAIRE. Memories.
MORRIS, GEORGE HORNELL. Sailor's Prayer, A.
MORRIS, GEORGE POPE. Flag of Our Union Forever, The.
Jeannie Marsh.
Main Truck, The; or, A Leap for Life.
My Mother's Bible.
Near the Lake.
Pocahontas.
Retort, The.
We Were Boys Together.
Where Hudson's Wave.
Woodman, Spare That Tree.
Yankee Doodle.
MORRIS, GOUVERNEUR, JR. D'Artagnan's Ride.
MORRIS, HARRISON SMITH. Always.
Change of Face, A.
Destiny.
Fickle Hope.
Good-Night.
June.
Lonely-Bird, The.
Mohammed and Seid.
Naked Boughs.
Pine-Tree Buoy, A.
Separate Peace.
Walt Whitman.
MORRIS, HARRY. Girod Street Cemetery; New Orleans.
MORRIS, HERBERT. Brahms, The.
North of Wales, The.
Road, The.
This Alice.
Workmen.
MORRIS, HILDA. November.
November Wears a Paisley Shawl.
MORRIS, J. W. Collusion between a Alegaiter and a Water-Snaik.
MORRIS, JOSEPH. Prayer for Courage, A.
MORRIS, SIR LEWIS. At Last.
Beginnings of Faith, The.
Brotherhood, *sels.*
Christmas 1898, *sel.*
God Within Yet Above.
Heathen Hymn, A.
Heathen Hymn, A, *sel.*
On a Thrush Singing in Autumn.
Separation Deed, A.
Song: "Love took my life and thrill'd it."
Surface and the Depths, The.
To a Child of Fancy.
Tolerance.
MORRIS, ROBERT. Cabin Where Lincoln Was Born, The.
Level and the Square, The.
MORRIS, WILLIAM. Agnes and the Hill-Man, *tr.*
Alas! for Saturn's days of gold. *Fr.* The Life and Death of Jason.
Ancient Castle, An. *Fr.* Golden Wings.
Antiphony. *Fr.* The Earthly Paradise.
Apology, An: "Of Heaven or Hell I have no power to sing." *Fr.* The Earthly Paradise.
Atalanta's Defeat. *Fr.* The Earthly Paradise.
Atalanta's Race. *Fr.* The Earthly Paradise.
Atalanta's Victory. *Fr.* The Earthly Paradise.
August. *Fr.* The Earthly Paradise.
Blue Closet, The.
Brooding of Sigurd, The. *Fr.* The Story of Sigurd the Volsung.
Burghers' Battle, The.
Chants for Socialists, *sel.*
Chapel in Lyoness, The.
Concerning Geffray Teste Noire.
Day Is Coming, The.
Day of Days, The.
Day of Love, The. *Fr.* Love Is Enough.
Days That Were, The.
Death Song, A.
Defence of Guenevere, The.
Down among the Dead Men.
Drawing near the Light.
Dream of John Ball, A, *sel.*
Earthly Paradise, The, *sels.*
Echoes of Love's House.
Error and Loss.
Eve of Crécy, The.
Farewell to Kind Hosts and a God-speed, *tr. Fr.* The Odyssey.
February. *Fr.* The Earthly Paradise.
Final Chorus. *Fr.* Love Is Enough.
For the Bed at Kelmscott.
From Far Away.
Garden by the Sea, A. *Fr.* The Life and Death of Jason.
Gilliflower [*or* Gillyflower] of Gold, The.
Gold Hair.
Gold Wings across the Sea. *Fr.* Golden Wings.
Golden Apples, The. *Fr.* The Earthly Paradise.
Golden Wings.
Golden Wings, *sels.*
Gunnar in the Pit of Adders. *Fr.* The Story of Sigurd the Volsung.
Half of Life Gone, The.
Hands.
Haystack in the Floods, The.
Hollow Land, The, *sel.*
I Know a Little Garden Close. *Fr.* The Life and Death of Jason.
Iceland First Seen.
Idle Singer, The. *Fr.* The Earthly Paradise.
In Prison.
In the white-flower'd hawthorn brake. *Fr.* The Earthly Paradise.
Inscription for an Old Bed.
Introduction: "Forget six counties overhung with smoke." *Fr.* The Earthly Paradise.
Invocation to Chaucer. *Fr.* The Life and Death of Jason.
Judgment of God, The.
June. *Fr.* The Earthly Paradise.
King's Visit, The. *Fr.* The Earthly Paradise.
Knight in Prison, The.
Ladies' Gard. *Fr.* Golden Wings.
Lady of the Land, The. *Fr.* The Earthly Paradise.
Laertes, *tr. Fr.* The Odyssey.
Land across the Sea, A. *Fr.* The Earthly Paradise.
L'Envoi: "Here are we for the last time face to face." *Fr.* The Earthly Paradise.
Life and Death of Jason, The, *sels.*
Limbo; the Shades of the Suitors, *tr. Fr.* The Odyssey.
Lines for a Bed at Kelmscott Manor.
Little Tower, The.
Love Is Enough, *sels.*
March. *Fr.* The Earthly Paradise.
March of the Workers, The.
Masters, in This Hall.
May Grown a-Cold.
Meeting in Winter.
Message of the March Wind, The.
Message of the March Wind, The, *sel.*
Midways of a Walled Garden. *Fr.* Golden Wings.
Minstrels and Maids. *Fr.* The Earthly Paradise.
Mother and Son.
Near Avalon.

MORRIS, WILLIAM (*continued*)
No Master.
November. *Fr.* The Earthly Paradise.
Nymph's Song to Hylas, The. *Fr.* The Life and Death of Jason.
O Bitter Sea. *Fr.* The Life and Death of Jason.
"O death, that maketh life so sweet." *Fr.* The Life and Death of Jason.
O love, this morn, when the sweet nightingale. *Fr.* The Earthly Paradise.
O the sweet valley of deep grass. *Fr.* The Life and Death of Jason.
October. *Fr.* The Earthly Paradise.
October, *sel.* *Fr.* The Earthly Paradise.
Odyssey, The, *sels., tr.*
Of Circe, *tr.* *Fr.* The Odyssey.
Of Cyclops and the Ram, *tr.* *Fr.* The Odyssey.
Of Heaven or Hell I have no power to sing. *Fr.* The Earthly Paradise.
Of Noman and Cyclops, *tr.* *Fr.* The Odyssey.
Of the Passing Away of Brynhild. *Fr.* The Story of Sigurd the Volsung.
Ogier the Dane, *sel.*
Old Love.
Orpheus' Song of Triumph. *Fr.* The Life and Death of Jason.
Outlanders, Whence Come Ye Last? *Fr.* The Earthly Paradise.
Praise of My Lady.
Prelude to "The Earthly Paradise." *Fr.* The Earthly Paradise.
Prologue: "Forget six counties overhung with smoke." *Fr.* The Earthly Paradise.
Prologue: "Of Heaven or Hell I have no power to sing." *Fr.* The Earthly Paradise.
Prologue to "The Earthly Paradise."
Proud King, The. *Fr.* The Earthly Paradise.
Rapunzel.
Riding Together.
Sailing of the Sword, The.
Seasons, The.
Shameful Death.
Sheriff, The. *Fr.* A Dream of John Ball.
Sigurd Rideth to the Glittering Heath. *Fr.* The Story of Sigurd the Volsung.
Sigurd the Volsung, *sels.*
Singer's Prelude, The. *Fr.* The Earthly Paradise.
Sir Giles' War-Song.
Slaying, The. *Fr.* The Odyssey.
Slaying of the Niblungs, The. *Fr.* The Story of Sigurd the Volsung.
Slaying of the Suitors, The, *tr.* *Fr.* The Odyssey.
Song: "Christ keep the Hollow Land." *Fr.* The Hollow Land.
Song: "Fair is the night, and fair the day." *Fr.* The Earthly Paradise.
Song: "Gold wings across the sea!" *Fr.* Golden Wings.
Song: To Psyche. *Fr.* The Earthly Paradise.
Song for Music. *Fr.* Love Is Enough.
Song from "Ogier the Dane." *Fr.* The Earthly Paradise.
Song from "The Hill of Venus." *Fr.* The Earthly Paradise.
Song from "The Hollow Land." *Fr.* The Hollow Land.
Song from "The Land East of the Sun and West of the Moon." *Fr.* The Earthly Paradise.
Song from "The Story of Acontius and Cydippe." *Fr.* The Earthly Paradise.
Song from "The Story of Cupid and Psyche." *Fr.* The Earthly Paradise.
Song of Jehane du Castel Beau, The. *Fr.* Golden Wings.
Song of the Argonauts. *Fr.* The Life and Death of Jason.
Songs of Orpheus and the Sirens. *Fr.* The Life and Death of Jason.
Story of Sigurd the Volsung, The, *sels.*
Summer Dawn.
Sweet Song Sung Not Yet to Any Man, A. *Fr.* The Life and Death of Jason.
Tapestry Trees.
Test of the Bow, The, *tr.* *Fr.* The Odyssey.
To Chaucer. *Fr.* The Life and Death of Jason.
To the Muse of the North.
To the Sea. *Fr.* The Life and Death of Jason.
Tune of [the] Seven Towers, The.
Two Red Roses across the Moon.
Voice of Toil, The.
Wind, The.
Winter Weather.
Writing on the Image, The. *Fr.* The Earthly Paradise.
MORRIS, WILLIAM, *and* EIRÍKUR MAGNÚSSON. Counsels of Sigrdrifa, *tr.* *Fr.* The Elder Edda.
Elder Edda, The, *sels., tr.*
First Lay of Gudrun, *tr.* *Fr.* The Elder Edda.
Hell-Ride of Brynhild, The, *tr.* *Fr.* The Elder Edda.
Lay of Sigurd, The, *tr.* *Fr.* The Elder Edda.
Short Lay of Sigurd, The, *tr.* *Fr.* The Elder Edda.
MORRIS-JONES, SIR JOHN. Seagulls, The.
MORRISON, M. T. What the Choir Sang about the New Bonnet.
MORRISON, MARY. Nobody Knows but Mother.
MORRISON, THEODORE. Kindred.
Legend.
MORROW, ANNE SPENCER. *See* LINDBERGH, ANNE MORROW.
MORROW, ELIZABETH. Lot's Wife.
This Pine-Tree.
Wall.
MORSE, B. J. Eventual Birth of Thought.
MORSE, JAMES HERBERT. Brook Song.
His Statement of the Case.
Power of Beauty, The.
Silence.
Wayside, The.
Wild Geese, The.
MORSE, KATHARINE DUNCAN ("Jerry Doane"). Bee Sets Sail, A.
Fairy Frock, The.
To ——: "They could not shut you out of heaven."
MORSE, MADELINE. Christmas Prayer.
MORSE, RICHARD ELY. This Swan.
MORSE, ROBERT. Persephone the Queen.
Queen of Eleusis, The.
MORSE, SAMUEL FRENCH. Track into the Swamp, The.
MORSE, SIDNEY HENRY. Sundered.
Way, The.
MORTENSON, ALICE. Beautiful Lily.
Behold, My Cross Was Gone!
Bethlehem Star, The, Shines On!
Christmas Bells.
He Wore a Crown of Thorns.
He's Come! The Saviour Has Come!
Let Not Your Heart Be Troubled.
O Christ of Calvary, This Lent.
O My Saviour and Redeemer.
Oh, No Cross That I May Carry!
They've Crucified Our Lord.
MORTON, ——. Balloon Man, The.
MORTON, SIR ALBERTUS. Greedy Lover, Pause Awhile.
MORTON, DAVID. Acquaintance.
Adoration.
After Storm.
Attendants.
Boke of Two Ladies, *sel.*
Chorus for Easter.
Daffodils over Night.
Dead, The ("Think you the dead are lonely in that place").
Fields at Evening.
Immortalis.
In a Girls' School.
King in Egypt, A.
Kings are Passing Deathward, The.
Lover to Lover.
Mariners.
Mary Sets the Table.
Moons.
Moths.
Old Ships.
On Hearing a Bird Sing at Night.
Petition for a Miracle. *Fr.* Boke of Two Ladies.
Revelation.
Scars.
Schoolboy Reads His Iliad, The.
Ships in Harbor [*or* Harbour].
Sonnets from a Hospital, *sel.*
Spring. *Fr.* Sonnets from a Hospital.
Symbol.
These Fields at Evening.
Touring.
Visitation.
Where There Is Music.
Who Walks with Beauty.
Wooden Ships.
MORTON, JOHN BINGHAM ("Beachcomber"). Ballade of Charon and the River Girl.
Bonnie Jeanie.
Dancing Cabman, The.
Singing Saint, The.
Song of the Ballet.
Tripe.
MORTON, SARAH WENTWORTH. To Aaron Burr, under Trial for High Treason.
MORTON, THOMAS. New English Canaan, *sel.*
Song, The: "Drink and be merry, merry, merry boys." *Fr.* New English Canaan.
MORUS, HUW. In Praise of a Girl.
MOSCHION. Primitive Man.
MOSCHUS. Aloud for her son Eros, Cypris cries.
Craft of a Keeper of Sheep, The.
Cupid Turned Plowman.
Epitaph of Bion.
Europa and the Bull.
Gleaming Sea, The.
He spoke, and what he spoke was all fulfilled.
I Dreamt I Saw Great Venus, *at.*
Lament for Bion, *at.*
Lament for Bion, *at., sel.*
Land and Sea.
Landsman, The.
Lesson to Lovers, A.
Love-Chain, The.
Love's Lesson.
Mingle your sighs with mine, ye dales, thou Dorian water, *at.*
Not long it was her fate among the flowers.
Ocean, The.
Once to Europa sweetly came a dream.
Soliloquy.
MOSES, W. R. American History.
Angina Pectoris.
MOSHER, M. FLORENCE. It Is Coming.
MOSS, ELIZABETH PATTON. Sermon without Words.
MOSS, HOWARD. Around the Fish; after Paul Klee.
Balcony with Birds, A.
Burning Love Letters.
Chalk from Eden.
Elegy for My Father.
Elizabethan Tragedy; a Footnote.
Gift to Be Simple, The.
Hermit, The.
Horror Movie.
Lesson from Van Gogh, A.
Lie, The.
Summer Gone, A.
Tourists.
Tragedy.
Underwood.
Venice.
Waterwall Blues.
Winter's End.
MOSS, THOMAS. Beggar, The.
MOTHERLY, MRS. Cow, The.
Dickey-Bird, The.
Fishes, The.
Flying Flowers.
Nursery, The.
MOTHERWELL, WILLIAM. Bonnie George Campbell.
Cavalier's Song, The.

I've Plucked the Berry.
Jeanie Morrison.
Last Verses.
My Heid Is Like to Rend, Willie.
Sing On, Blithe Bird!
They Come! The Merry Summer Months!
Water, The! The Water!
MOTOKIYO, SEAMI. Love-Cave, The.
MOTOYOSHI, PRINCE. I am unhappy.
MOTON, CORA BALL. Sight.
MOTT, ADRIAN. Cloud House, The.
MOTTEUX, PETER ANTHONY [*or* PIERRE ANTOINE]. Friendship, *tr.*
London. *Fr.* Love's a Jest.
Love's a Jest, *sel.*
Rondelay, A: "Man is for woman made."
Slaves to London. *Fr.* Love's a Jest.
Song, A: "Slaves to London, I'll deceive you." *Fr.* Love's a Jest.
Town-Rakes, The, *at.*
MOTTRAM, RALPH HALE. Flower of Battle, The.
MOULT, THOMAS. Chayah.
Prayer for This Our Time.
Prelude to Cricket.
MOULTON, LOUISE CHANDLER (Ellen Louise Chandler). Hic Jacet.
House of Death, The.
Last Good-by, The.
Late Spring, The.
Laura Sleeping.
Laus Veneris.
Louisa May Alcott.
Love's Resurrection Day.
Out in the Snow.
Painted Fan, A.
Shadow Dance, The.
Shall I Complain?
Somebody's Child.
Spring Is Late, The.
Summer Wooing, A.
To-Night.
Tryst, A.
We Lay Us Down to Sleep.
Were But My Spirit Loosed upon the Air.
MOULTRIE, JOHN. Dear Little Violets.
Fairy Maimounè, The.
Forget Thee?
Forget Thee? *sel.*
Sir Launfal, *sel.*
Three Sons, The.
Violets.
MOUNTAIN, GEORGE J. Indian's Grave, The.
MOUSLEY, JAMES P. Prayer: "God of light and blossom."
MOWRER, PAUL SCOTT. Mozart's Grave.
MOXON, EDWARD Moonlight.
Nightingale, The.
Similes.
MOXON, FREDERICK. All at Sea.
MUDA. Azaleas.
MUDIE, IAN. Australia Day, 1942; in Memoriam W. J. Miles.
This Land.
Underground.
MUELLER, LISEL. Apples.
For a Nativity.
People at the Party, The.
Sans Souci.
MUHAMMADJI. Black Hair.
MUHLENBERG, WILLIAM. Carol, Brothers, Carol.
MUIR, ALEXANDER. Maple Leaf Forever, The.
MUIR, EDWIN. Animals, The.
Annunciation, The.
Bird, The.
Castle, The.
Child Dying, The.
Childhood.
Combat, The.
Confirmation, The
Enchanted Knight, The.
Enchanted Prince, The.
Escape, The.
Face, The.
Gate, The.
Grass.
Grove, The.
Hölderlin's Journey.
Horses.
Human Fold, The.
In Love for Long.
Interrogation, The.
Journey, The.
Killing, The.
Love in Time's Despite.
Love's Remorse.
Merlin.
Old Gods, The.
Reading in War Time.
Recurrence, The.
Return, The.
Rider Victory, The.
Riders, The. *Fr.* Variations on a Time Theme.
Road, The.
Stationary Journey, The.
Too Much.
Toy Horse, The.
Transfiguration, The.
Transmutation, The.
Trophy, The.
Variations on a Time Theme, *sel.*
Voyage, The.
Wayside Station, The.
West, The.
Window, The.
MUIR, HENRY D. Lullaby: "In this hush of night."
Soldier's Grave, The.
MUIR, JOHN. Camp-Fire in Alaska.
MUIRHEAD, JAMES. Bess the Gawkie.
MU'IZZI, AMUR. To a Young Lover.
MULCHINOCK, WILLIAM PEMBROKE. Rose of Tralee, The.
MULGREW, JOHN P. *See* "JAZBO OF OLD DUBUQUE."
MULHOLLAND, ROSA (Lady Gilbert). Irish Franciscan, The.
Lay of the Famine, A, *at.*
Love and Death.
Saint Brigid.
Sister Mary of the Love of God.
Song: "Silent bird is hid in the boughs, The."
MÜLLER, MAX (Friedrich Maximilian Müller). Rig-Veda, The, *sel.*, *tr.*
Story of Svetaketu, The, *tr.* *Fr.* The Upanishads.
To the Unknown God, *tr.*
Universal Self, The, *tr.* *Fr.* The Upanishads.
Upanishads, The, *sels.*, *tr.*
MÜLLER, WILHELM. Coming of Spring, The.
Song of the Bird, The.
Sunken City, The.
Whither?
MULLINEAUX, MARY. Dragon, The.
MULLINS, HELENE (Helen Gallagher Mullins). Boy Christ, The.
Epithalamium.
Farmers.
Give Heed to the Old.
Harper, The.
Lady and the Violinist, The.
Mountain Comes to Mahomet, The.
Saint Francis Weds the Three Maidens, *after* Sassetta.
Sister Mary Conceptia.
Thirty Pieces of Silver for Jesus.
This, Too.
MULOCK, DINAH MARIA. *See* CRAIK, DINAH MARIA MULOCK.
MULVANY, CHARLES PELHAM. Messalina Speaks.
MUNBY, ARTHUR JOSEPH. Après.
Beauty at the Plough. *Fr.* Dorothy; a Country Story.
Country Kisses. *Fr.* Dorothy; a Country Story.
Doris; a Pastoral.
Dorothy. *Fr.* Dorothy; a Country Story.
Dorothy; a Country Story, *sels.*
Dorothy's Room. *Fr.* Dorothy; a Country Story.
Flos Florum.
Susan; a Poem of Degrees, *sel.*
Sweet Nature's Voice. *Fr.* Susan; a Poem of Degrees.
MUNCH, ANDREAS. Bridal Voyage, The.
Hope.
Iceland.
MUNCH-PETERSEN, GUSTAF. To One.
MUNDAY, ANTHONY. Anthony Munday unto All Young Gentlemen in Commendation of this Gallery and Workmen Thereof.
Beauty Bathing.
Beauty sat [*or* Beautie sate] bathing by a spring.
Colin.
Fedele and Fortunio, *sels.*
Fedele's Song. *Fr.* Fedele and Fortunio.
I Serve a Mistress. *Fr.* Fedele and Fortunio.
If love be like the flower that in the night. *Fr.* Fedele and Fortunio.
Love. *Fr.* Zelanto, the Fountain of Fame.
Primaleon of Greece, *sel.*
To Colin Clout.
Wood-Man's Walk, The.
Zelanto, the Fountain of Fame, *sel.*
MUNDAY, ANTHONY, *and* HENRY CHETTLE. Death of Robert, Earl of Huntingdon, *sel.*
Dirge for Robin Hood. *Fr.* Death of Robert, Earl of Huntingdon.
Song: "Weep, weep, ye woodmen! wail." *Fr.* Death of Robert, Earl of Huntingdon.
Weep, Weep, Ye Woodmen. *Fr.* Death of Robert, Earl of Huntingdon.
MUNDORF, FRANK. Letter from a State Hospital.
Remembering Lincoln.
MUNDY, JOHN. Lightly She Whipped o'er the Dales.
MUNETAKE. On Tsukuda-Isle in July.
Snow.
MUNGER, ROBERT. Derelict, The.
God's Will.
MUNK, KAJ. Being Danish.
Flowers of Nazareth, The.
For Shame!
No Appeasement.
To the King.
MUNKITTRICK, RICHARD KENDALL. At the Shrine.
Autumn Haze.
Ballade of the Engaged Young Man.
Bulb, A.
Ghosts.
Old Beau, An.
To Miguel de Cervantes Saavadra.
Unsatisfied Yearning.
What's in a Name?
Winter Dusk.
MUÑOZ MARÍN, LUIS. Pamphlet.
Proletarians.
MUNRO, JAMES. Dark Winter Is Going.
MUNRO, KATHRYN. Fallen Leaves.
MUNRO, NEIL. Fiddle, The.
Heather, The.
John o' Lorn.
MUNSON, C. C. Dead Past, A, *at.*
MUNSON, IDA NORTON. Assurance.
Bethlehem Road, The.
Easter Light.
Hour Is Late, The.
Launch Out into the Deep.
Malchus.
Mary Knew.
Open Door, The.
Resurrection.
Road to Emmaus, The.
Sight.
Star, The.
Surgeon's Hands, The.
Vision.
MUNSON, MIRIAM OTT. Grandmother's Garden.
MÜNSTERBERG, MARGARETE. Blessed Be the Hour, *tr.*
Falcon, The, *tr.*
Hostess' Daughter, The, *tr.*
Lovely Rose Is Sprung, A, *tr.*
My Favorite Tree.
Oracle, The, *tr.*
Thanksgiving.
Voice in Darkness, *tr.*
MURASAKI SHIKIBU, LADY. Someone passes.

MURASAKI SHIKIBU, LADY (*continued*)
While I walked in the moonlight.
MURGER, HENRY. Old Loves.
Spring in Students' Quarter.
MURO, SAISEI. Lonely Spring.
Susaki Waterfront.
MURPHY, BEATRICE M. Letter, The.
Signs.
MURPHY, DENNIS. Boy with a Silver Plow.
Etching.
Ozark Song.
MURPHY, JOHN MAHER. Family History.
MURPHY, RICHARD. Archaeology of Love, The.
Philosopher and the Birds, The.
MURRAY, ADA FOSTER (Mrs. Henry Mills Alden). Above Salerno.
Ave.
Her Dwelling-Place.
Old-fashioned Poet, An.
One Who Stayed, The.
Prevision.
Psyche's Lamp.
Reveille.
Sacrifice.
Shadowed Star, The.
Unguarded.
When You Came.
MURRAY, CHARLES. Alien, The.
Green Yule, A.
Hint o' Hairst, The.
Lettergae, The.
Whistle, The.
MURRAY, SIR DAVID. Caelia, *sel.*
Sonnet: "Ponder thy cares, and sum them all in one." *Fr.* Caelia.
MURRAY, ELLEN. Shepherd Dog of the Pyrenees, The.
MURRAY, FREDERICK, *and* FREDERICK LEIGH. Charlie Piecan.
MURRAY, GEORGE. Auld Kirk o' Scotland, The.
Lesson of Mercy, A.
To a Humming Bird in a Garden.
MURRAY, GILBERT. *For translations from Greek, see* GrR; OxBG; ShBV-4; UnS.
MURRAY, KENTON FOSTER. Challenge.
MURRAY, PAULI. Without Name.
MURRAY, PHILIP. Carrara.
Cloud of Unknowing, The.
Finches, The.
In the Annals of Tacitus.
Little Litany to St. Francis, A.
Locust Hunt, The.
Turning, The.
MURRAY, ROBERT FULLER. Andrew M'Crie.
December Day, A.
End of April, The.
For Scotland.
Moonlight North and South.
MURTON, JESSIE WILMORE. Ballad of Coronado's Quest.
Strength.
MUSAEUS. Hero and Leander.
Hero and Leander, *sels.*
Leander's Death. *Fr.* Hero and Leander.
MUSET, COLIN. *See* COLIN MUSET.
MUSHIMARO. On Mount Tsukuba.
MUSSER, BENJAMIN FRANCIS. Bell-Birds.
Der Heilige Mantel von Aachen.
Elderly Nun.
Fire Shall Burn before Him, A.
Holy Land of Walsingham, The.
Le Coeur de l'Immaculée.
Poverello, *sel.*
MUSSET, ALFRED DE. Chandelier, Le, *sel.*
Evening Star, The.
Forget Me Not.
Fortunio's Song. *Fr.* Le Chandelier.
Juana.
Malibran.
Mary Singing.
On a Dead Lady.
Pepita.
Song: "Should you, of mirth and hope bereft."
Souvenir.
To Madame N. Ménessier.
To Mr. Victor Hugo.
MU'TAMID, KING OF SEVILLE. Fountain, The.
Great Poet, The.
Handsome Knight, The.
I Traveled with Them.
King's Hand, The.
Letter, The [*or* A].
Moon of Loveliness.
Night by the River.
Tears of the World.
Thy Garden.
Vine, The.
Woo Not the World.
MUTARRIF. Love's Code.
MUTH, EDNA TUCKER. Ruth Goes By.
MUTH, ELEANOR. Night Enchantment.
MYALL, CHARLES. Indian Lullaby.
MYERS, ERNEST. Achilles.
Etsi Omnes, Ego Non.
Fiorentina.
Gordon.
Sea-Maids' Music, The.
Song of the Thames, A.
MYERS, ERNEST, ANDREW LANG, *and* WALTER LEAF. *See* LANG, ANDREW, WALTER LEAF, *and* ERNEST MYERS.
MYERS, FREDERIC WILLIAM HENRY. Advent. *Fr.* Saint Paul.
Alpha and Omega. *Fr.* Saint Paul.
Christ All-sufficient. *Fr.* Saint Paul.
Evanescence.
Experience. *Fr.* Saint Paul.
From God to God, *tr.*
Harold at Two Years Old.
I Saw, I Saw the Lovely Child.
Immortality.
Inner Light, The.
Knowledge. *Fr.* Saint Paul.
Last Appeal, A.
Letter from Newport, A.
Not in Solitude. *Fr.* Saint Paul.
O God, How Many Years Ago.
On a Grave at Grindelwald.
Prayer, A: "O for one minute hark what we are saying!"
Saint Paul.
Saint Paul, *sels.*
Song, A: "Pouring music, soft and strong, The."
Surrender to Christ.
Teneriffe, *sel.*
MYERS, LYLA. Just Plain Dog.
MYERS, ROBERT C. V. *See* MEYERS, ROBERT CORNELIUS V.
MYRINUS. Love the Shepherd.
"MYRTIOTISSA" (Theoni Dracopoulou). Women of Suli.

N

"N. C." *See* "C., N."
NABBES, THOMAS. Beauty no more the subject be. *Fr.* Hannibal and Scipio.
Hannibal and Scipio, *sels.*
Love Sets Order in the Elements. *Fr.* Microcosmus.
Microcosmus, *sel.*
On a Mistress of Whose Affections He Was Doubtful. *Fr.* The Spring's Glory.
Song: "Beauty no more the subject be." *Fr.* Hannibal and Scipio.
Song: "What a dainty life the milkmaid leads!" *Fr.* Tottenham Court.
Spring's Glory, The, *sel.*
Tottenham Court, *sel.*
What a dainty life the milkmaid leads. *Fr.* Tottenham Court.
What though with figures I should raise. *Fr.* The Spring's Glory.
NABOKOV, VLADIMIR. Last Love, *tr.*
Literary Dinner.
Nightfall, *tr.*
Triple Dream, The, *tr.*
NACK, JAMES. Here She Goes, and There She Goes.
NADAUD, GUSTAVE. Carcassonne.
Horse and Rider.
NADEN, CONSTANCE CAROLINE WOODHILL. Pantheist's Song of Immortality, The.
NADIR, MOISHE (Yitzhok Reis). Adjectives.
NADSON, SEMYON YAKOVLEVICH. Brother, The.
I had yesterday happiness gladly rejected.
O tell me not that he is dead—for yet he lives.
NAEVIUS, GNAEUS. Girl from Tarentum, The.
His Own Epitaph.
NAGATA. Autumn.
God's Justice.
Goodness of God, The.
In All Things, Victory.
Leading.
Peace of Prayer, The.
Prayer Reaches Him.
Thought of God, The.
To One in Heaven.
NAGAYASU, SYUICHI. Bored Mirror, The.
NAGEL, S. A. God and Man.
NAGO OKIMARO. Even in the Palace.
NAHMAN OF BRATZLAV. Annul Wars.
Heart of the World, The.
NAHUM. Spring Song.
NAIDU, SAROJINI. Coromandel Fishers.
Cradle Song: "From groves of spice."
Ecstasy.
Illusion of Love, The.
In Salutation to My Father's Spirit.
In the Bazaars of Hyderabad.
Life.
Palanquin Bearers.
Soul's Prayer, The.
To a Buddha Seated on a Lotus.
Transience.
NAIRNE, CAROLINA OLIPHANT, BARONESS. Auld House, The.
Balooloo, My Lammie.
Caller Herrin'.
Charlie Is My Darling.
Heavenward.
Hundred Pipers, The.
Laird o' Cockpen, The.
Land o' the Leal, The.
Lass o' Gowrie, The.
Lullaby: "Baloo, loo, lammy, now baloo, my dear."
Rest Is Not Here.
Rowan Tree, The.
Wha'll Be King but Charlie?
Will Ye No Come Back Again?
NAJARA, ISRAEL. God of the World.
Loved of My Soul.
NÁJERA, FRANCISCO CASTILLO. Remembrance.
NAKANO, SHIGEHARU. Locomotive.
Tokyo Imperial University Students.
NAKATSUKASA. If it were not for the voice. *Fr.* Shui Shu.
O nightingale.
Shui Shu, *sel.*
NALAN HSINTEH. After Seeing Her in a Dream.
Boredom.
Song of the Golden Pavilion for Liang Fen.
To the Tune of "Gathering Mulberry Seeds."
To the Tune of "Pusa Barbarian."
Yearnings of Love.
NALBANDIAN, MICHAEL CHAZARIAN. Liberty.
NALÉ ROXLO, CONRADO. Game, The.
Nocturne: "Forest falls asleep, The."
Unforeseen, The.
NAMDEV. Everlasting to Everlasting, *sel.*
NANCE, BERTA HART. Achievement.
Arizona Nights.
Cattle.
NANDINO, ELIAS. Suicide?
NANMOR, DAFYDD. Ode to Rhys ap Maredudd of Tywyn.
NAOJO. I've not the heart to pick the violets.

NAOYOSHI. Beautiful Night, A.
NAPIER, ELLIOTT. All Men Are Free!
France.
Mater Dolorosa.
Russia.
NARIHIRA (Ariwara no Narihira). Even in the age.
I am so lost.
I have always known.
I knew quite well that some day.
Sudden Call, The.
This is not the moon.
NASH, FLORENCE. Call of the Road, The.
NASH, OGDEN. Admiral Byrd.
Adventures of Isabel.
Among the anthropophagi.
Anatomy of Happiness, The.
And Three Hundred and Sixty-six in Leap Year.
Arthur.
Autres Bêtes, Autres Mœurs.
Bankers Are Just like Anybody Else, except Richer.
Benjamin.
Birds, The. *Fr.* The Carnival of Animals.
Boy Who Laughed at Santa Claus, The.
Camel, The.
Canary, The.
Carnival of Animals, The, *sels.*
Caution to Everybody, A.
Celery.
Centipede, The.
Clean Platter, The.
Cow, The.
Do You Plan to Speak Bantu? or, Abbreviation Is the Thief of Sanity.
Don't Guess. Let Me Tell You.
Duck, The.
Edouard.
Eel, The.
Evening Out, The.
Family Court.
Firefly, The.
Fly, The.
Funebrial Reflections.
Genealogical Reflection.
Gentlemen of the High Command. *Fr.* Heil, Heilige Nacht!
Germ, The.
Golly, How Truth Will Out.
Goodbye Now; or, Pardon My Gauntlet.
I Never Even Suggested It.
I Want to Sit Next to Emily.
I Will Arise and Go Now.
Introduction: "Camille St. Saëns was racked with pains." *Fr.* The Carnival of Animals.
Introduction to Dogs, An.
Introspective Reflection.
Japanese, The.
Jellyfish, The.
Kind of an Ode to Duty.
Kindly Unhitch That Star, Buddy.
Kitten, The.
Lama, The.
Limerick: "There was an old man in a trunk."
Lines in Dispraise of Dispraise.
Lion, The.
More about People.
No Doctors Today, Thank You.
Oh, Please Don't Get Up!
Oh, Stop Being Thankful All Over the Place.
Octopus, The.
One-l lama, The.
Oyster, The.
Panther, The.
Parsnip, The.
People.
Phoenix, The.
Piano Tuner, Untune Me That Tune.
Pig, The.
Portrait of the Artist as a Prematurely Old Man.
Poultries, The.
Private Dining Room, The.
Purist, The.
Reflections on Ice-Breaking.
Requiem.
Rhinoceros, The.
Sea-Gull, The.
Seven Spiritual Ages of Mrs. Marmaduke Moore, The.
Shrew, The.
Song of the Open Road.
Song to Be Sung by the Father of Infant Female Children.
Spring Comes to Murray Hill.
Squirrel, The.
Tableau at Twilight.
Taboo to Boot.
Tale of Custard, the Dragon, The.
Termite, The.
Terrible People, The.
That Reminds Me.
Third Limick.
Thoughts Thought While Waiting for a Pronouncement from a Doctor, a Big Executive, the Department of Internal Revenue, or Any Other Momentous Pronouncer.
To a Small Boy Standing on My Shoes While I Am Wearing Them.
Traveler's Rest.
Turtle, The.
Two and One Are a Problem.
Up from the Egg; the Confessions of a Nuthatch Avoider.
Up from the Wheelbarrow.
Very like a Whale.
Visit, The.
Wapiti, The.
What's the Matter, Haven't You Got Any Sense of Humor?
Who Wants to Travel All Over Europe and See Nothing but a Lot of American Tourists? I do.
Wombat, The.
Yes and No.
NASHE [*or* Nash], THOMAS. Adieu, Farewell Earth's Bliss! *Fr.* Summer's Last Will and Testament.
A-Maying, a-Playing. *Fr.* Summer's Last Will and Testament.
Ambition.
Autumn. *Fr.* Summer's Last Will and Testament.
Beauty is but a flower. *Fr.* Summer's Last Will and Testament.
Birds in Spring, The. *Fr.* Summer's Last Will and Testament.
Clownish Song, A. *Fr.* Summer's Last Will and Testament.
Death's Summons. *Fr.* Summer's Last Will and Testament.
Dust Hath Closed Helen's Eye. *Fr.* Summer's Last Will and Testament.
Fair Summer Droops. *Fr.* Summer's Last Will and Testament.
Harvest. *Fr.* Summer's Last Will and Testament.
In Plague Time. *Fr.* Summer's Last Will and Testament.
In [a] Time of Pestilence. *Fr.* Summer's Last Will and Testament.
Lament [*or* Litany] in Time of Pestilence, A. *Fr.* Summer's Last Will and Testament.
Lord, Have Mercy on Us. *Fr.* Summer's Last Will and Testament.
Rich men, trust not in wealth.
Song, The: "Adieu, farewell, Earth's bliss." *Fr.* Summer's Last Will and Testament.
Sonnet: "Fair room, the presence of sweet beauty's pride."
Spring. *Fr.* Summer's Last Will and Testament.
Spring, the Sweet Spring. *Fr.* Summer's Last Will and Testament.
Summer's Farewell. *Fr.* Summer's Last Will and Testament.
Summer's Last Will and Testament, *sels.*
Waning Summer. *Fr.* Summer's Last Will and Testament.
NASHE, THOMAS, *and* CHRISTOPHER MARLOWE. *See* MARLOWE, CHRISTOPHER, *and* THOMAS NASHE.
NASIR-I KHUSRAU. Message.
NASON, ELIAS. Jesus Only.
NASON, EMMA HUNTINGTON. Child's Question, A.
Cricket's Story, The.
NATHAN, ROBERT. At the Symphony.
Be Not Afraid.
Beauty Is Ever to the Lonely Mind.
Because My Grief Seems Quiet and Apart.
Bells in the Country.
Captain Colin P. Kelly, Jr.
Christmas 1942.
Comes Fall.
Daughter at Evening, The.
Dunkirk.
Ebb Tide.
Epistle: "Christian, be up before the end of day."
Epitaph: "Say he was sad, for there was none to love him."
He Thinks of the Friend of His Youth, and of His Rooms at College. *Fr.* Youth Grows Old.
Heart in Wonder, The.
I Ride the Great Black Horses of My Heart.
Love Hath No Physic for a Grief Too Deep.
Mountain Interval.
Mountaineer, The.
Now from the World the Light of God Is Gone.
Poet Describes His Love, The.
Proem: "Man grows up."
Sonnet: "Because my grief seems quiet and apart."
Sonnet: "God of pity and love, return to this earth."
Sonnet: "Heart in wonder, like a lonely wren, The."
Sonnet: "Now from the world the light of God is gone."
Sonnet: "These are the chosen people. He has set."
There Are Four Doors Which Open on the Skies.
These Are the Chosen People.
To a Young Friend.
Tread Softly, Sorrow.
Watch, America.
When in the Crowd I Suddenly Behold.
Will Beauty Come.
Youth Grows Old, *sel.*
NATHANSON, NATHANIEL. Flanders Grave, A.
NAU, IGNACE. Belle-de-nuit.
NAUDÉ, ADÈLE. Memling's Virgin with Apple.
Oracle of Delphi, The.
NAVAGERO, ANDREA. To Demeter.
NAYADU, SAROJINI. *See* NAIDU, SAROJINI.
NAYLOR, JAMES BALL. Dr. John Goodfellow—Office Upstairs.
King David and King Solomon.
NAZHUN. Blind Man, The.
Riposte.
NEAL, JOHN. Men of the North.
Music of the Night.
NEALE, JOHN MASON. All glory, laud and honor, *tr.*
Art Thou Weary?
Before the ending of the day, *tr.*
Celestial Country, The, *tr. Fr.* De Contemptu Mundi.
Christian, Dost Thou See Them? *tr.*
Come, ye faithful, raise the strain, *tr.*
Darkness Is Thinning, *tr.*
Day of Resurrection, The, *tr.*
De Contemptu Mundi, *sel., tr.*
Fierce Was the Wild Billow, *tr.*
Good Christian Men [Rejoice], *tr.*
Good King Wenceslaus, *tr.*
Hymn to the Holy Cross, *tr.*
Jerusalem, the Golden, *tr. Fr.* De Contemptu Mundi.
Light's Glittering Morn.
Resurgam, *tr.*
NEALE, JOHN MASON, *and others.* Cathemerinon, *sel., tr.*
NEALY, MARY E. Maul, The.
NEARCHOS. *See* "OURANIS, KOSTES."
NEAVES, CHARLES, LORD NEAVES. Let Us All Be Unhappy on Sunday.
Stuart Mill on Mind and Matter.

NEAVES, CHARLES, LORD NEAVES (*cont.*)
For translations from Greek, see GrPo; OnPM.
NEAVES, CHARLES, LORD NEAVES, *and* JOHN HERMAN MERIVALE. *See* MERIVALE, JOHN HERMAN, *and* LORD NEAVES.
NECHAYEV, GEORGI EFIMOVICH. Freedom.
NEDOGONOV, ALEKSEY. Biography.
Soldier's Tale.
NEELE, HENRY. Moan, Moan, Ye Dying Gales.
NEIDHART VON REUENTAL. Bargain, The.
On the Mountain.
Winter-Time.
NEIHARDT, JOHN GNEISENAU. April Theology.
At Beecher's Island. *Fr.* The Song of the Indian Wars.
Ballad of a Child.
Battle Cry.
Child's Heritage, The.
Cry of the People.
Easter 1923.
Envoi: "O seek me not within a tomb."
L'Envoi: "Seek not for me within a tomb."
Let Me Live Out My Years. *Fr.* The Quest.
Lyric Deed, The.
Outward.
Poet's Town, The.
Prairie Fire, The. *Fr.* The Song of Three Friends.
Prayer for Pain.
Quest, The, *sel.*
Roman Nose Ride. *Fr.* The Song of the Indian Wars.
Shooting of the Cup, The. *Fr.* The Song of Three Friends.
Song of the Indian Wars, The, *sels.*
Song of Three Friends, The, *sels.*
Sowing of the Dragon, The. *Fr.* The Song of the Indian Wars.
When I Am Dead.
When I Have Gone Weird Ways.
NEILSON, FRANCIS. Eugenio Pacelli.
NEILSON, JOHN SHAW. Birds Go By, The.
Break of Day, The.
Green Singer, The.
I Spoke to the Violet.
Land Where I Was Born, The.
Love's Coming.
May.
Native Companions Dancing.
O Heart of Spring!
Orange Tree, The.
Poor, Poor Country, The.
Schoolgirls Hastening.
Song Be Delicate.
Stony Town.
'Tis the White Plum Tree.
To a Blue Flower.
Whistling Jack, The.
NEKRASOV, NIKOLAI ALEKSEYEVICH. After Heine.
Burning Letters, The.
Capitals Are Rocked, The.
For him cease in such frenzy to cry.
Freedom.
Good-bye! Forget the days of wane.
Happy that easy-tempered bard I call.
Home.
Hungry One, The. *Fr.* Who Can Be Happy and Free in Russia?
Hymn, A: "Lord, give them freedom who are weak."
Hymn: "O Lord, with good the people dower!"
I thought on war with horrors rife.
Mother, The.
My Verses!
Newlyweds.
Oh tread not the road. *Fr.* Who Can Be Happy and Free in Russia?
On Passing through the Haymarket.
Salt Song, The. *Fr.* Who Can Be Happy and Free in Russia?
Song of the Siberian Exiles, The.
Unreaped Field, The.
Who Can Be Happy and Free [*or* Who Lives Happily] in Russia? *sels.*
Wife's Lament, The. *Fr.* Who Can Be Happy and Free in Russia?
You are kind beyond all emulation.
NELSON, ALICE RUTH DUNBAR. I Sit and Sew.
Snow in October.
Sonnet: "I had no thought of violets of late."
NELSON, FRANK CARLETON. Human Heart, The.
NELSON, HOPE. 'Tis March.
NELSON, LAWRENCE EMERSON. My Pompous Friend.
NELSON, PAULA. House, The.
NELSON, STARR. White Rainbow, The.
NEMEROV, HOWARD. Banquet, The, *sel., tr.*
Chromium-plated Hat, A; Inlaid with Scenes from Siegfried.
Dandelions.
Ecstasies of Dialectic, The.
Fable of the War, A.
Frozen City, The.
Glass Dialectic.
Goose Fish, The.
History of a Literary Movement.
I Only Am Escaped Alone to Tell Thee.
Lives of Gulls and Children, The.
Phoenix, The.
Poem of Margery Kempe, A.
Pond, The.
Redeployment.
Salt Garden, The.
Sanctuary, The.
Sestina on Her Portrait.
Snow Globe, The.
Sonnet at Easter.
Truth.
Vacuum, The.
Winter Lightning [for Paul], The.
Young Woman.
NERSES, SAINT. Annunciation, The.
Arrival of the Crusaders, The.
Assumption, The.
"NERUDA, PABLO" (Neftalí Ricardo Reyes Basualto). Alberto Rojas Jiménez Comes Flying.
Almería.
Battle of the Jarama, The.
Burial in the East.
Death Alone.
International Brigade Arrives at Madrid, The.
Lightless Suburb.
Liturgy of My Legs.
Lone Gentleman.
Nocturnal Collection.
November 7; Ode to a Day of Victories.
No. XVII. *Fr.* Twenty Poems of Love.
Ode of the Sun to the People's Army.
Ode with a Lament.
Return of Autumn.
Savor.
Sexual Water.
Sonata and Destructions.
Twenty Poems of Love, *sel.*
Walking Around.
NERVAL, GÉRARD DE (Gérard Labrunie). All Things Are Sentient.
Anteros.
Artemis.
Black Dot, The.
Cydalises, The.
Dark Blot, The.
Delfica [*or* Delphica].
Desdichado, El.
Fantasia.
Fantasy.
Glorified, The.
Golden Verses.
Horus.
In the Woods.
Myrtho.
Old Tune, An.
NERVO, AMADO. And Thou, Expectant.
Entreaty to the Cloud.
Evocation.
Mystical Poets.
Old Burden, An.
NESBIT, EDITH (Edith Nesbit Bland). All in All.
Baby Seed Song.
Ballad of a Bridal.
Bird's Song in Spring.
Child's Song in Spring.
Denny Misquotes. *Fr.* The Would-be-Goods.
Dream Verses.
If on some balmy summer night.
Mr. Ody met a body.
Sleep, My Treasure.
Summer Song.
Tragedy, A.
Would-be-Goods, The, *sel.*
NESBIT, WILBUR DICK. Anonymous Valentine, The.
Christmas Dusk.
Forever on Thanksgiving Day.
Howdy, Mr. Winter!
Hymn of Thanksgiving, A.
Let Us Smile.
Small Boy Points a Moral, The.
Song of Our Flag, A.
Thanksgiving Night.
Who Hath a Book.
Your Flag and My Flag.
NESJAR, CARL, *and* MARTIN S. ALLWOOD. To One, *tr.*
NESMITH, JAMES ERNEST. Statue of Lorenzo de' Medici, The.
NETHERCLIFT, BERYL. London Trees.
NEVILLE, HELEN. Body's Freedom.
NEVIN, ALICE. God's Will.
NEVIN, EDWIN HENRY. I Am with You Alway.
NEWBOLT, SIR HENRY. Admiral Death.
Admirals All.
Clifton Chapel.
Commemoration.
Craven.
Day's End.
Death of Admiral Blake, The.
Drake's Drum.
End, The.
Felix Antonius.
Fighting *Téméraire,* The.
Final Mystery, The.
Finis.
From Generation to Generation.
Gillespie.
Guides at Cabul, 1879, The.
Hawke.
He Fell among Thieves.
Imogen.
Master and Man.
Messmates.
Minora Sidera.
Moss-Rose, The.
Nightjar, The.
Non-Combatant, The.
Old *Superb,* The.
Only Son, The.
Play the Game.
Rilloby-Rill.
Sacramentum Supremum.
Sailing at Dawn.
St. George's Day—Ypres, 1915.
Song: "Flowers that in thy garden rise, The."
Song of the Children in Paladore.
To a River in the South.
Toy Band, The.
Vitaï Lampada.
Volunteer, The.
War Films, The.
Yattendon.
NEWBURY, COLIN. Epilogue of the Wandering Jew, The.
Letter from Paparua.
New Wine, Old Bottles.
NEWCASTLE, MARGARET CAVENDISH, DUCHESS OF. Convent of Pleasure, The, *sel.*
Dialogue betwixt Peace and War.
Love, how thou'rt tired out with rhyme!
Mirth and Melancholy.
O do not grieve, Dear Heart, nor shed a tear.
O Love, how thou art tired out with rhyme!
Sea-Goddess, The. *Fr.* The Convent of Pleasure.
Soul's Garment, The.
NEWCASTLE, WILLIAM CAVENDISH, DUKE OF. Heaven's Mould, The.

Love's Matrimony.
Love's Vision ("Dear, let us two each other spy").
Love's Vision ("There is no happy life").
Maiden Gown, The.

Newell, Catherine Parmenter. Dream House.

Newell, J. R. Christmas Carol: "From the starry heav'ns descending."

Newell, Mary Elizabeth. For a Valentine.

Newell, Peter. Educated Love Bird, The.
Her Dairy.
Her Polka Dots.
Timid Hortense.
Wild Flowers.

Newell, Robert Henry. *See* "Kerr, Orpheus C."

Newell, William. Seek Those Things Which Are Above.

Newey-Johnson, D. To Let.

Newlin, Edith H. New Baby Calf, The.
Tiger-Cat Tim.

Newman, Francis William. Call to God's Service.

Newman, Israel. Iron Horse, The.

Newman, John Henry, Cardinal. Angel: "My work is done." *Fr.* The Dream of Gerontius.
Angel: "Softly and gently, dearly-ransom'd soul." *Fr.* The Dream of Gerontius.
Angel of the Agony. *Fr.* The Dream of Gerontius.
Angelic Guidance.
Chorus of the Elements.
Discovery, The.
Dream of Gerontius, The, *sels.*
Elements, The.
England.
Fifth Choir of Angelicals. *Fr.* The Dream of Gerontius.
Flowers without Fruit.
Fragment from Saint Gregory Nazianzen, A.
Greek Fathers, The.
Guardian Angel.
Judaism.
Lead, Kindly Light.
Light in the Darkness.
Melchizedek.
Monks.
My Lady Nature and Her Daughters.
Patient Church, The.
Pillar of the Cloud, The.
Praise to the Holiest in the Height. *Fr.* The Dream of Gerontius.
Progress of Unbelief.
Queen of Seasons, The.
Relics of Saints.
Rest.
Reverses.
St. Philip in Himself.
Sensitiveness.
Sign of the Cross, The.
Snapdragon.
Soul before God, The. *Fr.* The Dream of Gerontius.
Substance and Shadow.
Thanksgiving, A.
Trance of Time, The.
Valentine to a Little Girl.
Zeal of Jehu, The.

Newman, Joseph S. Hero and Leander.

Newman, Louis Israel. Voice of God, The.

Newman, Preston. Some Questions to Be Asked of a Rajah, Perhaps by the Associated Press.

Newsome, Mary Effie Lee. Arctic Tern in a Museum.
Baker's Boy, The.
Bats.
Cotton Cat, The.
Cricket and the Star, The.
Little Birches.
Morning Light.
Pansy.
Quilt, The.
Quoits.
Sassafras Tea.
Sky Pictures.
Wild Roses.

Newton, Byron Rufus. Owed to New York.

Newton, Charlotte. Fulfillment.

Newton, Douglas. Gaiety of Descendants.
Invasion Weather.

Newton, Earl L. Skippery Boo, The.

Newton, John. All Our Griefs to Tell.
Come, My Soul, Thy Suit Prepare.
Glorious Things of Thee Are Spoken.
How Sweet the Name of Jesus Sounds.
In Evil Long I Took Delight.
Looking at the Cross.
Name of Jesus, The.
Name of Jesus, The, *sel.*
Nothing to Wish or to Fear.
Precious Name, The.
Safely through another week.

Newton, Joseph Fort. "Follow Me."
White Presence, The.

Newton, Mary Leslie. Queen Anne's Lace.

Newton, Muriel. Death in May.

Newton, Nyleen. Autumn Song.
Woman.

Nicaenetus. Samoan Revel.
Wine and Song.

Nicarchus [*or* Nicarchos]. Demophilus.
Fortunatus the R. A.
On Marcus the Physician.
What's come? The end of Nikon's nose.

Niccolini, Giovanni Battista [*or* Giambattista]. Barbarossa, *sel.*

Niccolò degli Albizzi. Prolonged Sonnet.
Troops Returning from Milan.
When the Troops Were Returning from Milan.

Nichol, H. E. ("Colin Sterne"). Sweet Mary Lulled Her Blessed Child.

Nichol, John. Good Night.
H. W. L.
Love Endures.
Mare Mediterraneum.

Nicholas de [*or* of] Guildford. Owl and the Nightingale, The, *at., sels.*

Nicholl, Louise Townsend. Ark of the Covenant.
Celestial Body.
Choir-Boys on Christmas Eve.
Cigar Smoke, Sunday, after Dinner.
Cleavage.
Color Alone Can Speak.
Creation.
Different Speech, A.
Different Winter.
For a Child Named Katherine.
Improvising.
Incense.
Knowing What Time It Is at Night.
Made Lake, The.
Ornamental Water.
Pediment: Ballet.
Physical Geography.
Recital, *sel.*
Rondel for Middle Age.
Shape of the Heart, The.
Three Persons.
Time in the Sun.
Wild Cherry.

Nicholls, John F. Tommy's Prayer.

Nichols, Carrie May. Boomerang, The.

Nichols, John Bowyer Buchanan. Lines by a Person of Quality.
Masque of Balliol, The, *sel.*
On the Toilet Table of Queen Marie-Antoinette.
Pastoral, A: "My love and I among the mountains strayed."

Nichols, Rebecca S. Reed ("Ellen Kate Cleveland"). Philosopher Toad, The.

Nichols, Robert. Assault, The.
Aurelia.
Battery Moving Up to a New Position from Rest Camp; Dawn.
But piteous things we are—when I am gone. *Fr.* Sonnets to Aurelia.
By the Wood.
Catch for Spring, A.
Come, let us sigh a requiem over love. *Fr.* Sonnets to Aurelia.
Dawn on the Somme.
Day's March, The.
Don Juan's Address to the Sunset.
Flower of Flame, The, *sel.*
Fulfilment.
Full Heart, The.
Harlots' Catch.
I Love a Flower.
Little Pony.
Moon behind High Tranquil Leaves, The.
Nearer.
Night Rhapsody.
Our Dead.
Out of Trenches; the Barn, Twilight.
Pilgrim, The.
Plaint of an Humble Servant.
Plaint of Friendship by Death Broken.
Secret Garden, The.
Sonnet: Our Dead.
Sonnets to Aurelia, *sels.*
Sprig of Lime, The.
Though to your life apparent stain attach. *Fr.* Sonnets to Aurelia.
To ——: "Asleep within the deadest hour of night."
To D'Annunzio: Lines from the Sea.
Water-Lily, The.
When the proud World does most my world despise. *Fr.* Sonnets to Aurelia.

Nichols, Wallace B. Immortal Panoply, The. *Fr.* Prometheus in Piccadilly.
Prometheus in Piccadilly, *sel.*

Nicholson, John. On a Calm Summer's Night.

Nicholson, John Urban. I Would Remember Constant Things.
Old Maid.
Reconciliation.
String Stars for Pearls.
To a Pretty Woman.

Nicholson, L. Bubbles.

Nicholson, Martha Snell. And His Name Shall Be Called Wonderful.
His Promises.
Lo, I Am with You Always.
Look Up.
My Lord.
Suppose that Christ Had Not Been Born.
This Easter Day.
What Are You Doing for Jesus?

Nicholson, Meredith. From Bethlehem to Calvary.

Nicholson, Norman. Blackberry, The.
Burning Bush, The.
Cædmon.
Carol: "Mary laid her Child among."
Cleator Moor.
Cockley Moor, Dockray, Penrith.
For the New Year.
Michaelmas.
Millom Old Quarry.
Motion of the Earth, The.
Now in the Time of This Mortal Life.
Old Man at a Cricket Match.
Poem for Epiphany.
Preachers, The.
Ride to Jerusalem, The.
Rockferns.
Song at Night.
Tame Hare, The.
To a Child before Birth.
To the River Duddon.
Undiscovered Planet, The.
Wales.

Nicholson, Reynold Alleyne. *For translations from Arabic, see* LiTW. *For translations from Persian, see* LiTW; PeP.

Nicias. Fountain at the Tomb, The.
Hermes of the Playground.
Wayside Fount, The.

Nicol, James. Where Quair Rins Sweet amang the Flowers.

Nicolai, Philip. Wake, Awake, for Night Is Flying.

Nicoll, Robert. Bonnie Bessie Lee.
Hero, The.
We Are Brethren A'.
We'll A' Go Pu' the Heather.

NICOLSON, ADELA FLORENCE CORY. *See* "HOPE, LAURENCE."
NICOLSON, ALEXANDER. Bark of Clanranald, The, *tr.*
Skye.
NICOSTRATUS. Prattling Swallows.
NIELSEN, L. C. From Dover.
NIETZSCHE, FRIEDRICH WILHELM. Also sprach Zarathustra, *sel.*
Among Foes.
Seven Seals, The. *Fr.* Also sprach Zarathustra.
Solitary, The.
Star Morals.
NIGHTINGALE, MADELEINE THRIFT. Apple Rhyme, The.
Caravan, The.
Faery Song, A.
Muffin-Man, The.
Ring-a-Ring o' Fairies.
Scissor-Man, The.
Underneath the Clothes.
Waits, The.
NIJLEN, JAN VAN. Master of Time, The.
NIKITIN, IVAN SAVVICH. Night in a Village, A.
NILES, NATHANIEL. American Hero, The.
Bunker Hill.
NIMS, JOHN FREDERICK. Apocalypse.
Barrier.
Clock Symphony.
Consolation.
Dollar Bill.
Fairy Tale.
For My Son.
La Ci Darem la Mano.
Love Poem.
Madrigal: "Beside the rivers of the midnight town."
Midwest.
New Year's Eve, 1938.
Non-Euclidean Elegy.
Odes (*of* Horace), *sels., tr.*
To the Rulers.
Trainwrecked Soldiers.
NININE. Prayer to St. Patrick.
NINOMIYA, TAKAMICHI, *and* DENNIS JOSEPH ENRIGHT. *For translations from Japanese, see* PoLJ.
NISHIWAKI, JUNZABURO. Let the Traveller Pause.
Rain.
NIU HSI-CHI. For Remembrance.
NIVEN, FREDERICK. Indian Dance.
NIXON, JOHN, JR. Through a Fog of Stars.
NIXON, PAUL. *For translations from Latin, see* LiTW; RoL; WoL.
NIZAMI. Death of Kais, The. *Fr.* Lailí and Majnún.
Death of Lailí, The. *Fr.* Lailí and Majnún.
Envoi: "O ye, who thoughtlessly repose." *Fr.* Lailí and Majnún.
Kais Declares His Love. *Fr.* Lailí and Majnún.
Kais in the Desert. *Fr.* Lailí and Majnún.
Lailí and Majnún, *sels.*
Lailí Disconsolate. *Fr.* Lailí and Majnún.
Poet in His Poverty, The.
NJEGOS, PETAR PETROVITCH. Mountain Wreath, The, *sel.*
Speech of Abbot Stephen. *Fr.* The Mountain Wreath.
NOBLE, FAY LEWIS. Prayer for Song.
NOBLE, LUCRETIA GRAY. Stars and Stripes, The.
NOBUTSUNA. Flute, A.
NOE, COTTON (James Thomas Cotton Noe). Daniel Boone.
In the Mountains.
Tip Sams of Kentucky.
Umbrella Jim.
NOEL, CAROLINE MARIA. At the Name of Jesus.
NOEL, HENRY. Beauty Extolled, *at.*
Gaze not on swans in whose soft breast, *at.*
NOEL, RODEN BERKELEY WRIOTHESLEY. Beethoven.
Casual Song, A.
Cradle Song for Summer.
Dying.
I Flung Me round Him. *Fr.* The Water-Nymph and the Boy.
Lady to a Lover, A.
Lament: "I am lying in thy tomb, love."
Merry-go-round, The.
Old, The.
Sea Slumber-Song.
Secret of the Nightingale, The.
Song of the Water-Nymph. *Fr.* The Water-Nymph and the Boy.
Swimmer, The.
"That They All May Be One."
Toy Cross, The.
Vale!
Water-Nymph and the Boy, The, *sel.*
NOEL, THOMAS. Old Winter.
Pauper's Drive, The.
NOGUCHI, YONE. Dark-red Shadow-Spots, The, *tr.*
Hokku: "I thought I saw the fallen leaves," *tr.*
I Have Cast the World.
Lines: "When I am lost in the deep body of the mist on a hill."
Poet, The.
Sad Love and Sad Song, *tr.*
NOIN HOSHI (the monk Noin). After the storm.
As I approach.
Tanka: "In the evening/ Quiet of the country town."
NOLAN, BERTHA. My Mother.
NOLAN, EDWARD. Oxford Is a Stage.
NOLAN, MICHAEL. Little Annie Rooney.
NOMBERG, DAVID. Russian Cradle Song, A.
NONNUS. Chalcomede Prays to Be Saved from Love. *Fr.* Dionysiaca.
Chalcomede Wards Off Her Lover. *Fr.* Dionysiaca.
Dionysiaca, *sels.*
Tyre. *Fr.* Dionysiaca.
NORCROSS, ELLINOR L. Devotions.
NORMAN, CHARLES. Any Town.
Chant of the Old Men in the Woods.
NORRIS, ALFRED. Prayer for Faith, A.
NORRIS, JOHN. Aspiration, The.
Aspiration, The, *sel.*
Canticle: "'Twas my Beloved spake."
Hymn to Darkness.
My Little Saint.
Parting, The.
Retirement, The.
Second Chap. of the Cant. from the 10 Verse to the 13.
To Dr. Plot.
NORRIS, KATHLEEN. Mother.
NORRIS, MARY RACHEL. Pax Beata.
NORSE, HAROLD. Colosseum.
"NORTH, CHRISTOPHER" (John Wilson). Angler's Tent, The, *sel.*
Calm as the Cloudless Heaven.
Come Forth, Come Forth!
Evening Cloud, The.
Garland for Heliodora, A, *tr.*
Rose and the Gauntlet, The.
Sacred Poetry.
Turn Ye to Me.
Wreath for Heliodora, *tr.*
Written on the Banks of Wastwater during a Calm.
NORTH, E. Out of Doors.
NORTH, FRANK MASON. Christ in the City.
City, The.
Waking World, The.
Where cross the crowded ways of life.
NORTH, JESSICA NELSON (Mrs. Reed Inness MacDonald). Balloon Man.
Hibernalia.
Mathematical.
Rainy Morning.
To Duncan.
Truth.
Young Boy, A.
NORTON, A. One More Year.
NORTON, ANDREWS. Hymn for the Dedication of a Church.
NORTON, CAROLINE ELIZABETH SARAH SHERIDAN (*afterwards* Lady Stirling-Maxwell). Arab to His Favorite Steed, The.
Arab's Farewell to His Horse.
Bingen on the Rhine.
Dream, The, *sel.*
I Do Not Love Thee.
I Would the World Were Mine.
King of Denmark's Ride, The.
Love Not.
Mother's Heart, The.
Not Lost, but Gone Before.
Say Not 'Tis Dark.
Soldier's Burial, The.
We Have Been Friends Together.
NORTON, ELEANOUR. Chopin Prelude.
Lake, The.
NORTON, GLENN, *and* L. F. POST. *See* POST, L. F., *and* GLENN NORTON.
NORTON, GRACE FALLOW. Adventure.
Allegra Agonistes.
Deer on the Mountain.
I Give Thanks.
If my dark grandam had but known. *Fr.* Little Gray Songs from St. Joseph's.
Little Gray Songs from St. Joseph's, *sels.*
Love is a Terrible Thing.
Make No Vows.
My little soul I never saw. *Fr.* Little Gray Songs of St. Joseph's.
O Sleep.
Oh, the Burden, the Burden of Love Ungiven.
O World, Be Not So Fair, *tr.*
This Is My Love for You.
White Veil, The.
With cassock black, baret and book. *Fr.* Little Gray Songs from St. Joseph's.
You Say There Is No Love.
NORTON, THOMAS. Against Women either Good or Bad.
Man May Live Thrice Nestor's Life, A.
NORWOOD, EILLE. Limerick: "Pretty young actress, a stammerer, A."
NORWOOD, ROBERT. After the Order of Melchisedec.
Bill Boram, *sel.*
Companion of the highroad, hail! all hail! *Fr.* His Lady of the Sonnets.
His Lady of the Sonnets, *sels.*
I meet you in the mystery of the night. *Fr.* His Lady of the Sonnets.
Man of Kerioth, The, *sels.*
Rahab.
Resurrection and the Life, The.
Why?
Witch of Endor, The, *sel.*
NOSSIS. Pretty Nossis vows that she.
Rose of Love, The.
NOTKER BALBULUS. Cantemus Cuncti Melodum.
Media Vita, *at.*
NOTOPOULOS, JAMES A. New Hampshire Sexton.
NOTT, KATHLEEN. Lines to a Future Historian.
NOTT-BOWER, E. E. Haulage.
Patience.
NOTTAGE, MAY HASTINGS. My Father's Voice in Prayer.
NOVA, SAYAT. I Beheld My Love This Morning.
I Have a Word I Fain Would Say.
Thou Art So Sweet.
Thy Voice Is Sweet.
Without Thee What Are Song and Dance to Me?
"NOVALIS" (Georg Friedrich Philipp von Hardenberg). Hymns to the Night.
Hymns to the Night, *sel.*
I See Thee in a Thousand Pictures. *Fr.* Sacred Songs.
Sacred Songs, *sels.*
There Come Such Troubled Hours. *Fr.* Sacred Songs.
Though All Are Faithless Growing. *Fr.* Sacred Songs.
When in Sad and Weary Hour. *Fr.* Sacred Songs.

When Numbers, Figures, No More Hold the Key.
Yearning for Death. *Fr.* Hymns to the Night.
NOVO, SALVADOR. Departed Friend, The.
Journey.
Poetry.
NOVOSYOLOV, NIKOLAY. Daisy in an Alien Land, A.
NOWELL, M. H. Of Disdainful Daphne.
NOYES, ALFRED. Admiral's Ghost, The.
Apes and Ivory.
Art.
Assisi.
At Kew. *Fr.* The Barrel-Organ.
Avenue of the Allies, The.
Barrel-Organ, The.
Barrel-Organ, The, *sel.*
Betsy Jane's Sixth Birthday.
Bird Song. *Fr.* The Last Voyage.
Black Bill's Honey-Moon. *Fr.* Tales of the Mermaid Tavern.
Call of the Spring, The.
Carol of the Fir Tree, The.
Chimney-Sweeps of Cheltenham, The.
Creation.
Daddy Fell into the Pond.
Dawn of Peace, The. *Fr.* The Wine Press.
Diplomats, The.
Double Fortress, The.
Drake, *sels.*
Epilogue: "Carol, every violet has." *Fr.* The Flower of Old Japan.
Flower of Old Japan, The, *sels.*
Forty Singing Seamen.
Go Down to Kew in Lilac-Time. *Fr.* The Barrel-Organ.
God's Gift.
Highwayman, The.
In the Cool of the Evening.
Kilmeny.
Japanese Love-Song, A.
Last Voyage, The, *sels.*
Lavender.
Lights of Home, The.
Loom of Years, The, *sel.*
Love's Rosary.
May-Tree, The.
Messages. *Fr.* The Last Voyage.
Messenger, The.
Moon Is Up, The.
Mountain Laurel.
Music of the Spheres, The. *Fr.* Watchers of the Sky.
Nestling Church at Ovingdean, The.
New Duckling, The. *Fr.* Touchstone on a Bus.
Niobe.
Odes (*of* Horace), *sels., tr.*
Old Grey [*or* Gray] Squirrel.
Old Man Mountain.
Old Sceptic, The.
On the Death of Francis Thompson.
Our Lady of the Sea.
Outlaw, The.
Pact, The.
Paraclete.
Pirates.
Prayer, A: "Angels, where you soar."
Princeton.
Resurrection.
Seagulls on the Serpentine.
Seven Wise Men. *Fr.* Tales of the Mermaid Tavern.
Sherwood.
Shining Streets of London, The.
Silver Crook, The.
Slumber-Songs of the Madonna.
Snow.
Song: "Fairy band are we, A."
Song: "I came to the door of the House of Love."
Song: "Now the purple night is past." *Fr.* Drake.
Song of Jeppe, The. *Fr.* Watchers of the Sky.
Song of Sherwood, A.
Strange Guest, The.
Strong City, The. *Fr.* The Last Voyage.
Tales of the Mermaid Tavern, *sels.*
Tell Me You That Sing. *Fr.* The Last Voyage.
Thomas Dekker's Song. *Fr.* Tales of the Mermaid Tavern.
To Faunus, *tr.*
Torch Bearers, The. *Fr.* Watchers of the Sky.
Touchstone on a Bus, *sel.*
Unconscious, The. *Fr.* The Last Voyage.
Under the Pyrenees. *Fr.* The Last Voyage.
Unity.
Victory.
Victory Ball, A.
Washington's Last Birthday.
Watchers of the Sky, *sels.*
When Spring Comes Back to England.
Will Shakespeare's out like Robin Hood. *Fr.* Tales of the Mermaid Tavern.
Wine-Press, The, *sel.*
Wizards.
World's May-Queen, The.
You That Sing in the Blackthorn. *Fr.* The Last Voyage.
NUGENT, GERALD. Farewell to Fál, A.
NUGENT, ROBERT, EARL NUGENT. Epigram: "I loved thee beautiful and kind."
I Loved Thee.
NUNAN, THOMAS. Dreamer, The.
NÚÑEZ DE ARCE, GASPAR. Dejection.
Miserere.
NUNN, HELEN GLEAVES. Small Boy's Prayer, A.
NURTON, C. My Doggie.
NUTTER, MEDORA ADDISON. Mountain Creed.
NUTTING, J. K. How the Froggies Go to Sleep, *sel.*

O

"O., G. S." Engine Driver, The.
"O. L." *See* "L. O."
OAKES, PHILIP. Love in Hunger.
OAKES, URIAN. Elegy on the Death of Thomas Shepard, *sel.*
Oh! that I were a poet now in grain! *Fr.* Elegy on the Death of Thomas Shepard.
OAKES-SMITH, ELIZABETH. *See* SMITH, ELIZABETH OAKES.
OAKLEY, EBENEZER S. Thoughts That Move the Heart of Man, The.
OAKS, GLADYS. Anatole France at Eighty.
OATES, ANNA NORMAN. Thy Will Be Done.
OBALDÍA, MARÍA OLIMPIA DE. Wings over Europe.
OBATA, SHIGEYOSHI. By the Great Wall, *tr.*
Crows at Nightfall, The, *tr.*
Encounter in the Field, An, *tr.*
Farewell Song of White Clouds, A, *tr.*
In Memoriam; Ho Chi-chang, *tr.*
Invitation to Li Po, An, *tr.*
Lao-lao Ting, a Tavern, *tr.*
Lines: "Cool is the autumn wind," *tr.*
Maid of Wu, *tr.*
My Far-off Home, *tr.*
Nefarious War, The, *tr.*
Night of Sorrow, The, *tr.*
Nocturne, *tr.*
On a Quiet Night, *tr.*
On Seeing Off Meng Hao-jan, *tr.*
Parting with Li Po on the Tung-ting Lake, *tr.*
Poem Composed at the Imperial Command, *tr.*
Poet Mourns His Japanese Friend, The, *tr.*
Sport-Fellows, The, *tr.*
Summer Day, A, *tr.*
Summit Temple, The, *tr.*
There with the Moon and His Shadow, *tr.*
To His Three Friends, *tr.*
To His Wife on His Departure, *tr.*
To Tu Fu from Sand Hill City, *tr.*
To Wang Lun, *tr.*
Woman of Yueh, A, *tr.*
Women of Yueh, The, *tr.*
OBENCHAIN, ELIZA CALVERT. *See* "HALL, ELIZA CALVERT."
OBERHOLTZER, SARA LOUISA. Come for Arbutus.
O'BOLGER, T. D. Counsels of O'Riordan, the Rann Maker, The.
O'BRIEN, ——. Benny Havens, Oh!
O'BRIEN, ANNE. Gypsy Woman.
O'BRIEN, EDWARD JOSEPH. Her Fairness, Wedded to a Star.
Irish.
Last Piper, The.
Shepherd Boy, The.
Song: "She goes all so softly."
Whisper of Earth, The.
O'BRIEN, FITZ-JAMES. Battledores.
Demon of the Gibbet, The.
Kane.
Legend of the Easter Eggs, The.
Lost Steamship, The.
Minot's Ledge.
Second Mate, The.
Three Gannets, The.
O'BRIEN, JACK. Supai Hill Patrol.
O'BRIEN, KATHARINE. Spring Song.
O'BRIEN, SEUMAS. Poet, The.
O'BRIEN, THOMAS. Always Battling.
International Brigade Dead.
Terror.
OBSTFELDER, SIGBJÖRN. Barcarole.
I Look.
Nocturne: "Wings of the windmill rustle no longer."
Rose, The.
Torture.
"O'BYRNE, DERMOT" (Sir Arnold Bax). Dublin Ballad, A; 1916.
OCAMPO, SILVINA. Sleepless Palinurus.
O'CAROLAN, TURLOUGH. *See* CAROLAN, TURLOUGH.
"OCCIDENTE, MARIA DEL." *See* BROOKS, MARIA GOWEN.
OCCLEVE, THOMAS. *See* HOCCLEVE, THOMAS.
O CLÉIRIGH, CÚ CHONNACHT. Ghost, The.
O'CONNELL, RICHARD. *For translations from Spanish, see* AnCL.
O'CONNER, JOSEPHINE. Violets.
O'CONNOR, ARMEL. Appreciation à la Mode.
Little Black Hen, The.
O'CONNOR, FRANK (*originally* Michael O'Donovan). Autumn, *tr.*
Drowning of Conaing, The, *tr.*
Grey Eye Weeping, A, *tr.*
Harper, The, *tr.*
Hugh Maguire, *tr.*
Kilcash, *tr.*
Lament for Art O'Leary, The, *tr.*
Learned Mistress, A, *tr.*
Liadain and Cuirithir, *tr.*
May, *tr.*
Midnight Court, The, *tr.*
Old Woman of Beare Regrets Lost Youth, The, *tr.*
Prayer for the Speedy End of Three Great Misfortunes, *tr.*
Reverie, The, *tr.*
Sleepless Night, A, *tr.*
Starkness of Earth, The, *tr.*
Student, The, *tr.*
Three Old Brothers.
To Tomaus Costello at the Wars, *tr.*
For other translations from Irish, see KiLC.
O'CONNOR, JOSEPH. General's Death.
What Was My Dream?
O'CONNOR, JULIA CLAIRE. Resignation.
O'CONNOR, MICHAEL. Reveille.
O'CONNOR, PATRICK. In Pace in Idipsum Dormiam et Requiescam.
Mantle of Mary, The.
O'CONNOR, PHILIP. Poems.
O'CONOR, NORREYS JEPHSON. Beside the Blackwater.
For Francis Ledwidge.
Good-bye.

O'CONOR, NORREYS JEPHSON (*cont.*)
In Memoriam; Francis Ledwidge.
In the Monastery.
In the Moonlight.
To a Child.
Viking Ship, The.
O'COTTER, PAT. Malemute Dog, A.
O'CROWLEY, DENIS. Washington.
OCTAVIANUS. Painted Passion, *at.*
O'CURNAIN, DIARMAD. Love's Despair.
O'CURRY, EUGENE. Do You Remember That Night? *tr.*
Feast of Saint Brigid of Kildare, The, *tr.*
Gaelic Litany to Our Lady, The, *tr.*
O'DALA, DONNCHADH MOR. At Saint Patrick's Purgatory, *at.*
O'DALY, CARROL. Eileen Aroon.
Lover and Echo.
O'DALY, MURDOCH (Miuredach "Albanach"). Consecration.
In the Heart of Jesus.
ODELL, JONATHAN ("Camillo Querno").
Birthday Song, A.
Molly Odell on Her Birthday.
On Our Thirty-ninth Wedding Day.
Song for a Fishing Party near Burlington, on the Delaware, in 1776.
ODOEVSKY, ALEKSANDR. Do you know those whom I so loved before.
O'DONNELL, CHARLES LEO. Ad Matrem, in Caelis.
Address to the Crown.
Cloister.
Dead Musician, The.
Forgiveness.
In Praesepio.
On Meeting a Lady.
Poet's Bread, The.
Process.
Prodigals.
Resolution.
Rime of the Rood, A.
Road of Ireland, A.
Security.
Shed, The.
Song of God, The.
Spinner, The.
To St. Joseph.
Trelawny Lies by Shelley.
O'DONNELL, HUGH. Dark Rosaleen.
O'DONNELL, JOHN FRANCIS. Adare, *sel.*
April.
By the Turnstile.
Drifting.
Geraldine's Garden.
Happy Christmases, *sel.*
In the Twilight, *sel.*
July Dawn, A, *sel.*
Lilies, The.
Limerick Town, *sel.*
May, *sel.*
My Jack.
Ossian, *sel.*
Reminiscences of a Day, *sel.*
Spinning Song, A.
Spring, The.
To Spring, *sel.*
O'DONNELL, T. C. If I.
O'DONOVAN, MICHAEL. *See* O'CONNOR, FRANK.
O'DOWD, BERNARD. Australia.
Bush, The, *sels.*
Cow, The.
Last Stanzas of "The Bush." *Fr.* The Bush.
Love and Sacrifice.
Poet, The.
Proletaria.
Quail.
Young Democracy.
O'DUGAN [*or* DUGAN], MAURICE. Coolun, The.
OEHLENSCHLÄGER, ADAM GOTTLOB. Fair Maiden!
Freya's Spinning Wheel.
Korsør. *Fr.* Langelands Rejsen.
Langelands Rejsen, *sel.*
Once More It Is the Springtime.
Rose of Roses, The.
There Is a Charming Land.
OESCH, MARY MAE. Beatitudes for a Housewife.
OEVER, KAREL VAN DEN. Telephone Pole, The.
O'FAOLÁIN, SEÁN. At Saint Patrick's Purgatory, *tr.*
Desire for Hermitage, The, *tr.*
Fand Yields Cuchulain to Emer, *tr.*
Heavenly Banquet, The, *tr.*
Starry Sky, *tr.*
Summer Is Gone, *tr.*
For other translations from Irish, see SiB.
O FARACHÁIN, ROIBÉARD. *See* FARREN, ROBERT.
OFFALY, GERALD FITZGERALD, BARON OF. Gambler's Repentance, The.
O'FLAHERTY, CHARLES. Humours of Donnybrook Fair, The.
OGAREV, NIKOLAY PLATONOVICH. Road.
OGDEN, EDITH. Half Past Tears.
O'GILLAN, ANGUS. Clonmacnoise.
Dead at Clonmacnois, The.
OGILVIE, WILLIAM HENRY. Blades of Harden, The. *Fr.* Whaup o' the Rede.
Drought.
From the Gulf.
Hoofs of the Horses, The.
On a Roman Helmet.
Raiders, The.
Tweedmouth Bar.
Whaup o' the Rede, *sel.*
Witches' Steeds, The.
OGLE, GEORGE. Banks of Banna, The.
Mailligh Mo Stor.
OGMUNDARSON, CORMAC. Two Songs in Praise of Steingerd.
O'GNIVE, FEARFLATHA. Downfall of the Gael, The.
O'GRADY, STANDISH. Emigrant, The, *sels.*
Old Nick in Sorel. *Fr.* The Emigrant.
Winter in Lower Canada. *Fr.* The Emigrant.
O'GRADY, STANDISH JAMES. I Give My Heart to Thee.
Lough Bray.
O'HAGAN, JOHN. Old Story, The.
Ourselves Alone.
Protestant Ascendency.
Song of Roland, The, *sel., tr.*
O'HAGAN, THOMAS. Another Year.
Giotto's Campanile.
Woman.
O'HALLORAN, ELSPETH MCDUFFIE. *See* "ELSPETH."
O'HARA, FRANK. Chez Jane.
Day Lady Died, The.
For James Dean.
Hotel Transylvanie.
In Favor of One's Time.
In Memory of My Feelings.
Ode: "Idea of justice may be precious, An."
Ode: Salute to the French Negro Poets.
Ode to Joy.
Ode to Michael Goldberg's Birth and Other Births.
Poem: "Hate is only one of many responses."
Poem: "Khrushchev is coming on the right day!"
To Hell with It.
Why I Am Not a Painter.
You Are Gorgeous and I'm Coming.
O'HARA, JOHN MYERS. Ad Matrem Amantissimam et Carissimam Filii in Aeternum Fidelitas.
Atropos.
Faun in Wall Street, A.
Golden Pulse.
Greater Mystery, The.
Haunted Room, A.
In Patris Mei Memoriam.
Vespasian's Circus.
O'HARA, THEODORE. Bivouac of the Dead, The.
Bivouac of the Dead, The, *sel.*
Old Pioneer, The.
O'HEARN, WALTER. For They Are England.
O'HEFFERNAN, MAHON. Who Will Buy a Poem?
O'HIGGINS, MYRON. Blues for Bessie.
Sunset Horn.
Two Lean Cats.
Vaticide.
Young Poet.
O'HIGGINS, TOMAS. To Tomas [*or* Tomaus] Costello at the Wars, *at.*
O'HUIGINN, TADHG DALL. First Vision, The.
Second Vision, The.
O'HUIGINN, TADHG O'G. On the Breaking-up of a School.
O'HUSSEY, EOCHADH [*or* EOCHY]. Hugh Maguire, *at.*
Ode to the Maguire, *at.*
O'Hussey's Ode to the Maguire, *at.*
"O'K., L. L." Mary to Her Babe.
O'KANE, T. C. My Mother's Prayer.
O'KEEFFE, ADELAIDE. Beasts, Birds, and Fishes.
Butterfly, The.
Foolish Emily and Her Kitten.
George and the Chimney-Sweeper.
Going to Bed at Night.
Lucy's Canary.
Nimble Dick.
O'KEEFFE, JOHN. Amo, Amas.
Friar of Orders Gray, The. *Fr.* Merry Sherwood.
I Am a Friar of Orders Gray. *Fr.* Merry Sherwood.
Jingle.
Merry Sherwood, *sel.*
O'KELLY, PATRICK. Blessing on Doneraile.
Curse of Doneraile, The.
OKU, PRINCESS. Journeying Alone.
Would I Had Stayed.
OKURA. Because he is young. *Fr.* Manyo Shu.
He is so little, and the way is dim.
Manyo Shu, *sel.*
On the Death of His Child.
ÓLAFSSON, PÁLL. Happy Valley, The.
"OLD ARKANSAW." *See* HUGHES, DAVE.
OLDHAM, G. ASHTON. America First.
OLDHAM, JOHN. Careless Good Fellow, The.
Cup, The.
Infant Roses in Their Bloom. *Fr.* To the Memory of Mr. Charles Morwent.
Mortal Cage, The. *Fr.* To the Memory of Mr. Charles Morwent.
Prologue: "For who can longer hold?" *Fr.* Satires upon the Jesuits.
Quiet Soul, A. *Fr.* To the Memory of Mr. Charles Morwent.
Satire, A, *sel.*
Satire I: Garnet's Ghost Addressing to the Jesuits. *Fr.* Satires upon the Jesuits.
Satire Dissuading from Poetry, A, *sel.*
Satires [*or* Satyrs] upon the Jesuits, *sels.*
Satyr Address'd to a Friend That Is About to Leave the University, and Come Abroad in the World, A, *sel.*
Satyr III: "When shaven Crown, and hallow'd Girdle's Power." *Fr.* Satires upon the Jesuits.
To the Memory of Mr. Charles Morwent, *sels.*
Tranquil Soul, A. *Fr.* To the Memory of Mr. Charles Morwent.
Words from a Wooden Image. *Fr.* Satires upon the Jesuits.
OLDMIXON, JOHN. I Lately Vowed, but 'Twas in Haste.
Prithee, Chloe, Not So Fast.
To Corinna.
OLDS, N. S. Rivets.
OLDYS, WILLIAM. Fly, The.
On a Fly Drinking out of [*or* from] His Cup.
To a Fly.
O'LEARY, CORMAC. Reflections on Cleopathera's Needle.
O'LEARY, EILEEN. Lament for Art O'Leary, The.
O'LEARY, ELLEN. My Old Home.
To God and Ireland True.
O'LEARY, JOSEPH. Whisky, Drink Divine.
O'LEARY, SHAWN. Bayonet, The.

OLESON, HELMER O. Ballad of Johnny Appleseed, A.
OLIER, JEAN JACQUES. O Jesu.
OLIPHANT, CAROLINA. *See* NAIRNE, CAROLINA OLIPHANT, BARONESS.
OLIPHANT, CAROLINE, THE YOUNGER. Oh, Never! No, Never!
OLIPHANT, THOMAS. National Air: Wales, *tr.*
Where Are the Men? *tr.*
OLITSKI, LEIB. My Song to the Jewish People.
OLIVARES FIGUEROA, R. Sower, The.
OLIVER, THADDEUS. All Quiet along the Potomac Tonight, *wr. at. See* BEERS, ETHEL LYNN.
OLIVER, W. H. Beachcomber, The.
Death and the Maiden, *sel.*
Phoenix, The.
Sleep Will Come Singly.
OLIVER, WADE. Christ Speaks.
Estrangement.
Kinship.
Recompense.
Ships with Your Silver Nets.
This Senseless Slug.
Who'll Ride with Me?
OLMEDO, JOAQUÍN DE. Ode to Bolívar, *sel.*
OLNEY, D. A. Just like This.
OLNEY, WILLIAM. What Is This Coming Year?
OLSEN, CHARLES OLUF. Kingdoms.
OLSON, CHARLES. As the Dead Prey upon Us.
Death of Europe, The.
Distances, The.
I, Maximus of Gloucester, to You.
Kingfishers, The.
Lordly and Isolate Satyrs, The.
Maximus, to Himself.
Newly Discovered "Homeric" Hymn, A.
Songs of Maximus, The.
Variations Done for Gerald van de Wiele.
OLSON, ELDER. Essay on Deity.
Jack-in-the-Box.
Knight, with Umbrella.
Night There Was Dancing in the Streets, The.
Plot Improbable, Character Unsympathetic.
Waters.
OLSON, TED (Theodore Olson). For an Argonaut, Age Seven.
Hawk's Way.
Things That Endure.
O'MALLEY, CHARLES J. Poet's Harvesting, The.
O'MALLEY, D. J., *or* D. J. WHITE ("R. J. Stovall"). After the Round-up, *at.*
Charlie Rutledge.
Horse Wrangler, The.
Tenderfoot, The.
When the Work's All Done This Fall.
OMAR B. ABI RABI'A. Damsel, The.
OMAR KHAYYÀM. Ball, The. *Fr.* The Rubáiyát.
Bird of Time, The. *Fr.* The Rubáiyát.
Careless Delight. *Fr.* The Rubáiyát.
Equity with God. *Fr.* The Rubáiyát.
Fatalism. *Fr.* The Rubáiyát.
Fifteen Rubaiyat. *Fr.* The Rubáiyát.
Great Argument. *Fr.* The Rubáiyát.
Heaven and Hell. *Fr.* The Rubáiyát.
I Myself Am Heaven and Hell. *Fr.* The Rubáiyát.
Iram Indeed Is Gone. *Fr.* The Rubáiyát.
Like Snow. *Fr.* The Rubáiyát.
Long While, The. *Fr.* The Rubáiyát.
Master-Knot, The. *Fr.* The Rubáiyát.
Minister of Wine, The. *Fr.* The Rubáiyát.
Moving Finger, The. *Fr.* The Rubáiyát.
New Year, The. *Fr.* The Rubáiyát.
Omar and Death. *Fr.* The Rubáiyát.
Omar's Lament. *Fr.* The Rubáiyát.
Paradise. *Fr.* The Rubáiyát.
Predestination. *Fr.* The Rubáiyát.
Prefer the Cash. *Fr.* The Rubáiyát.
Quatrains. *Fr.* The Rubáiyát.
Ritual of the Grape. *Fr.* The Rubáiyát.
Rubáiyát, The, *tr. by* Fitzgerald.
Rubáiyát, The, *sels., tr. by* Fitzgerald.
Sleep Unbroken. *Fr.* The Rubáiyát.
So Red the Rose. *Fr.* The Rubáiyát.
Soul Is All, The. *Fr.* The Rubáiyát.
There Is No Sin. *Fr.* The Rubáiyát.
This Life Flies. *Fr.* The Rubáiyát.
Wake! *Fr.* The Rubáiyát.
Waste Not Your Hour. *Fr.* The Rubáiyát.
Wish, A. *Fr.* The Rubáiyát.
Worldly Hope, The. *Fr.* The Rubáiyát.
Worldly Wisdom. *Fr.* The Rubáiyát.
O'MULCONRY, PEADAR. Were Not the Gael Fallen.
ONAKATOMI NO YOSHINOBU. Deer on pine mountain, The. *Fr.* Shui Shu.
Deer which lives, The. *Fr.* Shui Shu.
ONDERDONK, H. U. Spirit, in Our Hearts, The.
O'NEIL, DAVID. Modern Orchard, A.
Starvation Peak Evening.
Vernal Showers.
O'NEIL, GEORGE. Adam's Wonder.
Cobbler in Willow Street, The.
Composition.
Events.
Fable: "I led him on into the frosted wood."
Garden Incident.
Homage.
Lucid Interval.
Margot.
Ode to a Frog.
Socrates Prays a Day and a Night.
South Wind.
Where It Is Winter.
White Rooster, The.
Woman Passes the Door, A.
O'NEILL, MARY DEVENPORT. Dead in Wars and in Revolutions.
Galway.
Old Waterford Woman, An.
Scene-Shifter Death.
Tramp's Song, The.
"O'NEILL, MOIRA" (Nesta Higginson Skrine). Beauty's a Flower.
Birds.
Boy from Ballytearim, The.
Broken Song, A.
Bud in the Frost, A.
Corrymeela.
Crusade, The, *tr.*
Cuttin' Rushes.
Fairy Lough, The.
Forgettin'.
Grace for Light.
Grand Match, The.
Johneen.
Lookin' Back.
Sea Wrack.
Song of Glenann, A.
O'NEILL, ROSE. As I Went By.
Betrayed, The, *sel.*
Eagle Hunter, The.
Established.
Faun-taken.
Flying Dead, The.
Gift, The.
I Made a House of Houselessness.
Love-Ending.
Love-Ending, *sel.*
My Darkness.
Owl Sinister.
When the Dead Men Die.
ONITSURA. Cherry-blossoms, more.
ONO, TOSABURO. Nature-Hater.
Winter.
ONO NO KOMACHI. As certain as color.
Imperceptible/ It withers in the world.
Thing which fades, A. *Fr.* Kokin Shu.
Traveller, The.
ONO NO TAKAMURA. Did I ever think. *Fr.* Kokin Shu.
ONO NO YOSHIKI. My love/ Is like the grasses. *Fr.* Kokin Shu.
Unknown. *Fr.* Kokin Shu.
O'NOLAN, BRIAN. Aoibhinn, a leabhráin, do thriall, *tr.*
Scel lem duib, *tr.*
ONSTOTT, MARY BROWN. Expatriate.
"OPDYKE, OLIVER" (John Baker Opdyke). My Road.
Spring Lay, A.
OPHEL, FREDERICK WILLIAM. His Epitaph.
Pioneers.
OPITZ, MARTIN. Beauty of This Earth.
OPPENHEIM, JAMES. Action.
As to Being Alone.
Bread and Roses.
Create Great Peace. *Fr.* 1914—and After.
Death.
For Randolph Bourne.
Future.
Handful of Dust, A.
Hebrews.
Immoral.
Lincoln Child, The.
Lonely Child, The.
My Father's House. *Fr.* Night.
My Land.
New God, The.
New York Skyscraper, A, *sel.*
Night, *sels.*
Night Note.
1914—and After, *sels.*
Not Overlooked.
Pittsburgh.
Priest, The.
Reason, The.
Report on the Planet, Earth.
Runner in the Skies, The.
Saturday Night.
Slave, The.
Slums.
Tasting the Earth.
Where Love Once Was.
Would You End War? *Fr.* 1914—and After.
OPPENHEIMER, JOEL. Bath, The.
Blue Funk.
Bus Trip, The.
Feeding, The.
Mare Nostrum.
OPPER, EMMA A. Charms, The.
OPPIAN. Cynegetica, *sel.*
Dolphin and Seal. *Fr.* Halieuticks.
Dolphin's Death, The. *Fr.* Halieuticks.
Eels, Tortoises, Soles, Lampreys. *Fr.* Halieuticks.
Halieuticks, *sels.*
How Sea-Calves Are Born. *Fr.* Halieuticks.
Ichneumon, The. *Fr.* Cynegetica.
Lions and Dragons. *Fr.* Halieuticks.
Mullet and the Hook, The. *Fr.* Halieuticks.
Shoal of Slime-Fish, The. *Fr.* Halieuticks.
Temptation. *Fr.* Halieuticks.
OQUENDO DE AMAT, CARLOS. Angel and the Rose, The.
Madhouse Poem.
Mother.
Surrealist Poem of the Elephant and the Song.
ORACLE OF SERAPIS. Living God, The.
O'RAHILLY [*or* O'REILLY], EGAN. Brightness of Brightness.
Enchanted Mistress, The.
Geraldine's Daughter, The.
Geraldine's Daughter, The, *sel.*
Grey Eye Weeping, A.
Lament for Banba.
Last Lines.
More Power to Cromwell.
On a Cock Which Was Stolen from a Good Priest.
On a Pair of Shoes Presented to Him, *sel.*
Reverie, The.
Reverie at Dawn.
Sleepless Night, A.
Storm, The, *sel.*
ORDE, JULIAN. Changing Wind, The.
ORDEN, J. RODRÍGUEZ LA. To an Andalusian Fan.
O'REILLY, DOWELL. Australia.
Faith, Love, and Death.
Sea-Grief.
Stars.

O'REILLY, EGAN. *See* O'RAHILLY, EGAN.
O'REILLY, JOHN BOYLE. Art Master, An.
At Best.
At Fredericksburg (Dec. 13, 1862).
Boston.
Builder's Lesson, A, *sel.*
Chicago.
Constancy.
Crispus Attucks.
Cry of the [*or* a] Dreamer, The.
Disappointment.
Experience.
Forever.
In Bohemia.
Infinite, The.
Love Was True to Me.
Lure, The.
Mayflower.
Message of Peace, A.
Midnight—September 19, 1881.
My Native Land.
Name of Mary.
Pilgrim Fathers, The.
Ride of Collins Graves, The.
Savage, A.
Song: "Love was true to me."
To-Day.
Wendell Phillips, *sel.*
What Is Good?
White Rose, A.
O'REILLY, MARY ANNE. Christmas Carol, A: "Night in the far Judean land."
Hush Song.
Lullaby, A: "*Mo cheann ban beag,* lie still and rest."
ORENTE, ROSE J. Master City, The.
ORESHIN, PIOTR VASILYEVICH. Not by Hands Created.
Not Made by Hands.
Tailor, The.
Saviour, The.
ORFORD, HORACE WALPOLE, 4TH EARL OF. *See* WALPOLE, HORACE, 4TH EARL OF ORFORD.
ORIBE, EMILIO. Ode to the Sky of the New Atlantis.
Song to the Glory of the Sky of America.
"ORINDA." *See* PHILIPS, KATHERINE.
O'RIORDAN, CONAL ("Norreys Connell").
Care Is Heavy.
Hymn to the Virgin Mary.
Requiem.
ÖRJASÆTER, TORE. Man Carries Woman.
ORLÉANS, CHARLES, DUC D'. Ah God, How Good She Is to See.
Alons au bois le may cueillir.
Ballade: Hostelry of Thought, The.
Ballade: "Looking one day toward the coast of France."
Ballade: "One day I asked my heart."
Ballade for Peace.
Ballade Written during Captivity in England.
Confession, A.
Dieu Qu'il la fait.
Fairest Thing in Mortal Eyes, The.
Go Get You Gone, Begone, Begone.
Leave Me in Peace to Meditate.
My Gostly fader, I me confess[e].
Of Darts from Lattices Beware.
Return of Spring, The.
Rondeau: Well, The.
Rondeau: "Year his winter cloak lets fall, The."
Rondeau of Spring.
Rondel: "As we look at these gay flowers."
Rondel: "First day of the month of May, The."
Rondel: "Greet all the company for me."
Rondel: "Stephen Le Gout, in the nominative."
Rondel: "Strengthen, my love, this castle of my heart."
Rondel: "Summer has sent his stewards on."
Rondel: "Winter, you're nothing but a lout."
Rondel: "Year has put his cloak away, The."
Rondel to His Mistress.
Song: "Lovers, avoid the shafts that fly."
Spring ("The time hath laid his mantle by").
Spring ("The year has changed his mantle cold").
Summer's Harbingers Are Here, The.
Year Hath Doffed His Cloak To-Day, The.
ORLEANS, ILO. Anatomy Lesson.
Any Bird.
Give me the sky.
I offered the donkey.
I saw a dog.
I thank you, God.
In the Garden.
It isn't hard/ To drive a car.
Little man.
Shoes have tongues.
Sky came tripping, The.
Soap is green.
Soldiers fight by land and air.
Upon the beach.
Water has no color.
ORLOV, SERGEY. Pause on the March.
ORLOVSKY, PETER. Second Poem: "Morning again, nothing has to be done."
ORMSBY, STEPHANIE. Caribbean, The.
O'ROURKE, MAY. Stick, The.
ORR, HUGH ROBERT. Calvary.
Litany of Night.
They Softly Walk.
ORR, JAMES. Irishman, The.
ORR, PATRICK. Annie Shore and Johnnie Doon.
In the Mohave.
ORRED, META. In the Gloaming.
ORRERY, ROGER BOYLE, BARON BROGHILL, 1ST EARL OF. Excellency of Wine, The.
'Tis Wine that inspires.
ORRM. Orrmulum, The, *sel.*
ORTIZ DE MONTELLANO, BERNARDO. Second Dream.
O'RYAN, EDMOND. Ah! What Woes Are Mine.
OSBORN, LAUGHTON. Death of General Pike, The.
OSBORN, MARGOT. Always the Melting Moon Comes.
OSBORN, MARY ELIZBETH. Alma Mater.
Come Not Near.
Exquisite Lady.
Mid-Century.
Old Man in the Park.
Rural Legend.
Thought for the Winter Season.
Water-Images.
OSBORN, MARY I. Every Day.
My Playmate.
Swing, The.
OSBORN, SELLECK. Modest Wit, A.
OSBORNE, CHARLES. So Fly by Night.
OSBORNE, DUFFIELD. Ave! Nero Imperator.
OSBORNE, EDITH D. Popcorn Man, The.
OSBORNE, GENE H. Thanksgiving.
OSBORNE, LOUIS SHREVE. Riding Down from Bangor.
OSBORNE, MARIAN. Dedication: "O say not he is dead! What messenger."
Elf, The.
Folded Wings.
Phaon to Sappho.
Sister.
Trinity, The.
White Violet.
OSCAR II, KING OF SWEDEN. Hoist the Flag!
OSGOOD, FRANCES SARGENT. Calumny.
Celeste Dancing.
Dancing Girl, A.
Labor.
On a Dead Poet.
On Sivori's Violin.
Song: "Your heart is a music-box, dearest!"
To Labor Is to Pray.
To Sleep.
OSGOOD, KATE PUTNAM. Driving Home the Cows.
O'SHAUGHNESSY, ARTHUR WILLIAM EDGAR. Appointment, The, *tr.*
At Her Grave.
Chartivel, *sel., tr.*
Doom.
Enchainment.
Fair Maid and the Sun, The.
Fountain of Tears, The.
Has Summer Come without the Rose?
Hath any loved you well, down there.
If She But Knew.
Love after Death.
Love Symphony, A.
Music-Makers, The.
New Love and the Old, The.
Ode: "We are the music-makers."
Poets, The.
St. John Baptist.
Sarrazine's Song [to Her Dead Lover], *tr. Fr.* Chartivel.
Silences.
Song: "Has summer come without the rose."
Song: "I made another garden, yea."
Song: "When the rose came I loved the rose."
Song from "Chartivel," *tr.*
Struggle, The, *tr.*
We are the music-makers.
Would I Might Go Far over Sea, *tr.*
Zuleika.
O'SHEA, DIARMUID. Prayer at Dawn.
O'SHEEL, SHAEMAS. Exultation.
He Whom a Dream Hath Possessed.
Lover Envies an Old Man, The.
Lover Thinks of His Lady in the North, The.
Mary's Baby.
Replying to the Many Kind Friends Who Ask Me If I No Longer Write Poetry.
Roma Mater Sempaeterna.
They Went Forth to Battle.
While April Rain Went By.
O-SHI-O. When I Think of the Hungry People.
"OSSIAN." *See* MACPHERSON, JAMES.
OSSIAN-NILSSON [*or* OSSIANNILSSON], KARL GUSTAV. Bismarck.
March for Youth, A.
OSTENSO, MARTHA. Farmer's Wife, The.
Return, The.
Unicorn and the Hippogrif, The.
ÖSTERLING, ANDERS. Meeting of Phantoms.
OSTROFF, ANTHONY. River Glideth in a Secret Tongue, The.
So Long Folks, Off to the War.
Sparrows at the Airport, The.
OSTROVOY, SERGEY. Little Birch Tree.
O'SULLIVAN, DANIEL JAMES. Dawn in Inishtrahull.
Drinking Time.
Glaucous-Gull's Death, The.
January.
Lament for Seán.
Moschatel.
Nightfall in Inishtrahull.
O'SULLIVAN, OWEN ROE. Lullaby, A: "O hushaby, baby! Why weepest thou?"
Rodney's Glory.
To the Blacksmith with a Spade.
"O'SULLIVAN, SEUMAS" (James Starkey). Ballad of the Fiddler, The.
Birds.
Credo.
Epitaphium Felis, *tr.*
Half Door, The.
Herdsman, The.
If There Be Any Gods.
Je ne veux de personne auprès de ma tristesse, *tr.*
Lament for Sean MacDermott.
Lamplighter, The.
Land War, The.
Lark's Song.
Lullaby: "Husheen, the herons are crying."
Milkman, The.
Monk, The.
My Sorrow.
Nelson Street.
Night, *tr.*

Others, The.
Petit Chat, Le, *tr.*
Piper, A.
Poplars, The.
Praise.
Rain.
Rosses, The.
Sedges, The.
Sheep, The.
Sketch.
Splendid and Terrible [Your Love].
Starling Lake, The.
Tony's Grave.
Trains, The.
Twilight People, The.
O'SULLIVAN, VINCENT. Norman Cradle-Song.
OTERO REICHE, RAÚL. America.
Night Was Going, The.
Romanza of the Guitarrist.
OTERO SILVA, MIGUEL. Crossroads.
Sowing.
OTHÓN, MANUEL JOSÉ. Elegy: "Along the tangled path and in the red."
Envoy: "On your altars I have spent my incense."
Steppe in the Nazas Country, A.
Wild Idyll.
OTIS, ELIZABETH LINCOLN. "If" for Girls, An.
OTO. I thought my net was full of shining fish.
OTOMO MIYORI. On Again Meeting a Lady.
OTOMO TABITO. Grotesque!
Passing the Cape.
OTSUJI. Winter midnight.
O'TUOMY, JOHN. O'Tuomy's Drinking Song.
OTWAY, THOMAS. Bankrupt, The. *Fr.* Venice Preserved.
Come All Ye Youths. *Fr.* The Orphan.
Enchantment, The.
Friendship in Fashion, *sel.*
Jaffier Parting with Belvidera. *Fr.* Venice Preserved.
Morning. *Fr.* The Orphan.
O Woman! Lovely Woman! *Fr.* Venice Preserved.
Orphan, The, *sels.*
Song: "How blest he appears." *Fr.* Friendship in Fashion.
Venice Preserved, *sels.*
OUAN-TSI. Leaf on the Water, The.
OULD, CHARLES. In Exile, VIII.
"OURANIS, KOSTES" (Nearchos). Prayer to God to Rest All the Unfortunate.
OUTRAM, GEORGE. Annuity, The.
On Hearing a Lady Praise a Certain Rev. Doctor's Eyes.
OU-TY, EMPEROR. *See* WU TI, EMPEROR.
OU-YANG HSIU. Answer to Ting Yuan Ch'en, An.
Cicada, The.
East Wind.
Fisherman.
Green Jade Plum Trees in Spring.
In the Evening I Walk by the River.
Lantern Festival, The.
Old Age.
Reading the Poems of an Absent Friend.
Song of Liang Chou.
Spring Day on West Lake.
Spring Walk to the Pavilion of Good Crops and Peace.
Waiting for News.
When the Moon Is in the River of Heaven.
ÖVERLAND, ARNULF. Little Adam.
We Shall Survive.
You Were Much Too Near.
OVERSTREET, BONARO. Count Ten.
First Day of Teaching.
OVID (Publius Ovidius Naso). Amores, *sels.*
Apollo and Daphne. *Fr.* Metamorphoses.
Baucis and Philemon. *Fr.* Metamorphoses.
Captive of Love, A.
Carmen.
Complaisant Swain, The.
Creation of the World, The. *Fr.* Metamorphoses.
Daedalus and Icarus. *Fr.* Metamorphoses.
Elegies, *sels.*
Epistle from Pontus, *sel.*
Every Lover Is a Soldier. *Fr.* Amores.
Fable of Acis, Polyphemus and Galatea, The, *sel.* *Fr.* Metamorphoses.
Fall of Icarus, The.
Flood, The. *Fr.* Metamorphoses.
Graecinus (well I wot) thou touldst me once. *Fr.* Amores.
I Heard the Ruffian-Shepherd Rudely Blow. *Fr.* Metamorphoses.
I meane not to defend the scapes of any. *Fr.* Amores.
In summers heate and mid-time of the day. *Fr.* Amores.
Lente, Lente.
Love, as a Warrior Lord.
Metamorphoses, *sels.*
Narcissus. *Fr.* Metamorphoses.
Niobe. *Fr.* Metamorphoses.
Now ore the sea from her old Love comes she. *Fr.* Amores.
Now the zephyrs diminish the cold, and the year being ended. *Fr.* Tristia.
Old wood, stands uncut of long yeares space, An. *Fr.* Amores.
Orpheus and Eurydice. *Fr.* Metamorphoses.
Philemon and Baucis. *Fr.* Metamorphoses.
Phoenix Self-born, The. *Fr.* Metamorphoses.
Pygmalion and Galatea. *Fr.* Metamorphoses.
Pyramus and Thisbe. *Fr.* Metamorphoses.
Pyrrha and Deucalion. *Fr.* Metamorphoses.
Should any one there in Rome remember Ovid the exile. *Fr.* Tristia.
Slowly, Slowly.
Story of Phaeton, The. *Fr.* Metamorphoses.
Time Is No Remedy. *Fr.* Tristia.
To a Janitor. *Fr.* Amores.
To His Wife. *Fr.* Tristia.
To Verse Let Kings Give Place. *Fr.* Elegies.
Tristia, *sels.*
Winter at Tomi.
OVSHOVER, JOSEPH. *See* "DAHL, BASIL."
OWARI. Girls in Spring.
OWEN, DORA. Children, Children Don't Forget.
OWEN, EVERARD. Three Hills.
OWEN, GORONWY. Invitation, The.
OWEN, J. ELGAR. Maturity.
OWEN, JOHN. Bed, The. *Fr.* Four Epigrams.
Four Epigrams.
King Arthur's Round Table. *Fr.* Four Epigrams.
Of Labienus. *Fr.* Four Epigrams.
On One Ignorant and Arrogant.
To Polla. *Fr.* Four Epigrams.
OWEN, LOUISE. "Chart Showing Rain, Winds, Isothermal Lines and Ocean Currents."
Shadow.
White of cherry bloom, The.
Words are the silver notes.
OWEN, MOSES. Nothing but Flags.
OWEN, WILFRED. A Terre.
All Sounds Have Been as Music.
Anthem for Doomed Youth.
Apologia pro Poemate Meo.
Arms and the Boy.
Asleep.
Disabled.
Dulce et Decorum Est.
End, The.
Exposure.
Fragment: Abyss of War, The.
From My Diary, July 1914.
Futility.
Greater Love.
Insensibility.
Inspection.
Mental Cases.
Miners.
Next War, The.
On Seeing a Piece of Our Artillery Brought into Action.
Parable of the Old Men and the Young, The.
Send-off, The.
Sentry, The.
Shadwell Stair.
Show, The.
Song of Songs.
Spring Offensive.
Strange Meeting.
To My Friend.
Unreturning, The.
Young Soldier, The.
OWENS, BELLE F. Garden, The.
Good Companion, The.
Upper Room, The.
OWENS, VILDA SAUVAGE. If I Ever Have Time for Things That Matter.
Passing of the Unknown Soldier, The.
OXENHAM, JOHN (*originally* William Arthur Dunkerley). A Dieu! and Au Revoir.
After Work.
Art Thou Lonely?
Break Down the Walls.
Brothers of the Faith.
Chaos—and the Way Out, *sel.*
Coming Day, The.
Credo.
Cross at the Crossways, The.
Crowning Wonder, The.
Dedication for a Home, *wr. at. See* BENSON, LOUIS FITZGERALD.
Dies Irae—Dies Pacis.
Easter.
Face to Face with Reality.
Faith.
Follow Me!
For all the wonder. *Fr.* A Little Te Deum of the Commonplace.
For Beauty, We Thank Thee.
Goal and the Way, The.
God's Sunshine.
Gratitude for Work.
Great Heart.
He Is Risen.
He—They—We.
Hearts Courageous.
High Way and a Low, A.
His Youth.
How—When—Where.
Key, The.
Law of Love, The. *Fr.* Chaos—and the Way Out.
Little Te Deum of the Commonplace, A, *sels.*
Live Christ.
Love.
Love's Prerogative.
Morning Breaks, The.
New Earth, A.
No East or West.
On the Road.
Peace.
Per Ardua ad Astra.
Philosopher's Garden.
Pilgrim Way, The.
Prayer, A: "Lord, when on my bed I lie."
Prayer, A: "Through every minute of this day."
Prayer for Peace, A.
Prayer for the Churches.
Prince of Life, The.
Profit and Loss.
Promotion.
Sacrament of Fire, The.
Sacrament of Love, The.
Sacrament of Work, The.
Seeds.
So Little and So Much.
Some Blesseds.
Spread the Light.
Te Deum of the Commonplace, A, *sels.*
Thanksgiving.
To Whom Shall the World Henceforth Belong?
To Win the World.
Valley of Decision, The.

OXENHAM, JOHN (*continued*)
Vision Splendid, The, *sel.*
Ways, The.
We Break New Seas Today.
We Thank Thee ("For all life's beauties").
We Thank Thee, Lord ("For all thy ministries").
We Thank Thee, Lord ("We thank Thee, Lord").
Where Are You Going, Great-Heart?
Your Place.
OXFORD, EARL OF. *See* VERE, EDWARD DE, EARL OF OXFORD.

P

"P., F. B." Jerusalem, My Happy Home, *at.*
O Mother Dear, Jerusalem, *at.*
Song Made by F. B. P., A, *at.*
"P. H." *See* "H., P."
"P. S. M." *See* "M., P. S."
PACE, CHARLES NELSON. Cross, The.
Prayer for Today, A.
PACK, ROBERT. Anecdote of the Sparrow.
Bird in Search of a Cage, A.
Departure, The.
Faithful Lover, The.
Idyl in Idleness, An.
On the Seventh Anniversary of the Death of My Father.
Poem for You.
Way We Wonder, The.
PACK, SAMUEL MINTURN. Grapevine Swing, The.
PACKARD, FREDERICK. Balearic Idyll.
PACKARD, WINTHROP. Shoogy-Shoo, The.
PACUVIUS, MARCUS. His Own Epitaph.
PAGAN, ISOBEL. Answer, The.
Ca' the Yowes to the Knowes.
PAGAZA, JOAQUÍN ARCADIO. Chest of Perote, The.
Crag, The.
Twilight.
"PAGE, A." (Gerald Michael Joseph Cushing Fitzgerald). Sister, A.
Sister and Nun.
PAGE, A. W. Forest Song.
PAGE, CURTIS HIDDEN. *For translations from French, see* PrPoCR; *from Japanese, see* AWP; JAWP; LiTW; PFE; WBP.
PAGE, EDGAR. I've reached the land of corn and wine.
PAGE, HUBBARD FULTON. Autumn Rain, The.
Come, Gently Stir.
Last Spinning Wheel, The.
Mae Christie.
To a Blind Bird.
PAGE, MYRIAM. Walls.
PAGE, PATRICIA K. Adolescence.
Average.
Bands and the Beautiful Children, The.
Christmas Eve; Market Square.
Cullen.
Election Day.
Element.
Isolationist.
Landlady.
Landscape of Love.
Mole, The.
Puppets.
Stenographers, The.
Summer.
Summer Resort.
PAGE, PAUL D., JR. Fancy.
PAGE, R. W. Sea Gulls.
PAGE, ROSEWELL. General Dabney H. Maury.
PAGE, THOMAS NELSON. Ashcake.
Dragon of the Seas, The.
Uncle Gabe's White Folks.
Valentine Verses.
PAGET-FREDERICKS, JOSEPH. Alone.
Pipings.
PAHLOW, GERTRUDE CURTIS BROWN. Happy Thoughts.
PAIN, BARRY. Bangkolidye.
Macaulay at Tea.
Martin Luther at Potsdam.
Oh! Weary Mother. *Fr.* The Poets at Tea.
Poets at Tea, The.
Poets at Tea, The, *sel.*
Theme with Variations, A.
PAINE, ALBERT BIGELOW. Hills of Rest, The.
In Louisiana.
Little Child, The.
Mis' Smith.
New Memorial Day, The.
Sary "Fixes Up" Things.
Superman, The.
PAINE, ROBERT TREAT. Adams and Liberty.
PAINE, THEODORA L. Danger.
PAINE, THOMAS. Castle in the Air, The.
Liberty Tree.
PAINTON, EDITH PUTNAM (Edith F. A. U. Palmer Painton). Parody, A: "Farewell! A long farewell."
"PAI TA-SHUN." *See* PETERSON, FREDERICK.
PALAGYI, LOUIS. Aimless.
PALAMAS, KOSTES. Altars, The, *sel.*
Arrival, The. *Fr.* The Twelve Songs of the Gypsy.
City and Solitude, *sel.*
Dead Youth, The. *Fr.* Life Immovable.
Fair of Kakava, The. *Fr.* The Twelve Songs of the Gypsy.
Fathers, The. *Fr.* The Altars.
Grave, The, *sel.*
Hymn to Passion.
Laborers, The.
Life Immovable, *sel.*
Love. *Fr.* The Twelve Songs of the Gypsy.
Prophet, The. *Fr.* The Twelve Songs of the Gypsy.
Rose-Fragrance. *Fr.* City and Solitude.
Satyr, The; or, The Song of Nudity.
Twelve Songs of the Gypsy, The, *sels.*
PALEN, JENNIE M. Early Dutch.
Water Front.
PALÉS MATOS, LUIS. Clair de lune.
Elegy of the Duke of Marmalade.
Hurricane, The.
Look Out for the Snake!
Ñáñigo to Heaven.
San Sabas.
Well, The.
PALFREY, R. S. Three o'Clock in the Morning.
PALFREY, SARAH HAMMOND. *See* "FOXTON, E."
PALGRAVE, FRANCIS TURNER. Ancient and Modern Muses, The.
Childless Mother, The.
Child's Evening Hymn, A.
City of God, The.
Creçy.
Danish Barrow, A.
Eutopia.
God Save Elizabeth.
Little Child's Hymn, A.
London Bridge, *sel.*
Margaret Roper's Vision of Her Father, Sir Thomas More. *Fr.* London Bridge.
Pro Mortuis.
Reine d'Amour.
Take Up Thy Cross.
Trafalgar.
William Wordsworth.
PALLADAS [*or* PALLADES]. All the World's a Stage.
Ballet.
End, The.
Eremites.
Freedom.
God's Concern.
In place of fire God a woman gave.
Lacrimae Rerum.
Life a Voyage.
Life is a perilous voyage. The seas o'erwhelm.
Life is but a flying slave.
Muse on Death.
Naked I Came.
Night passes. We are born day after day.
O Man, Remember.
On Maurus the Rhetor.
Praise of Women.
Question of Gender, A.
Rest Is Silence, The.
Sail with the Wind.
"Sailor Home from the Sea, The."
Sentence of Death.
Slaughter-House, The.
Stream that carries you doth carry all, The.
Tell me, and wouldst thou span the ends of earth.
This life a theatre we well may call.
"To-Morrow Is a New Day."
Vanity of Vanities.
We Are Born Every Day.
What Is Man?
Wives are a curse.
World's Stage, The.
Yahoo.
PALLEN, CONDÉ BENOIST. Babe of Bethlehem, The.
Christus Triumphans.
Maria Immaculata.
Raising of the Flag, The.
PALLIS, ALEXANDROS. Girl from Roumely.
Kanaris.
Woman from Samos.
PALMER, ALICE FREEMAN. Butterfly, The.
Communion Hymn.
Hallowed Places.
On a Gloomy Easter.
Parting.
Spring Journey, A.
PALMER, ARTHUR. Epicharis.
PALMER, E. HARRIET. Parterre, The.
Shipwreck, The.
PALMER, ELIZABETH. Hummingbird.
PALMER, GRACE B. Bulwark of Home, The.
PALMER, HERBERT EDWARD. Abélard Tells His Love to Héloise.
Aunt Zillah Speaks.
Easter Poem, An: "Hush harlequin brain . . ."
Hate.
Ishmael.
Nature in War-Time.
Phil, the Black Persian.
Prayer for Rain.
To Some Reviewers Who Have Wilfully Abused Certain True Poets.
Unknown Warrior Sings and Curses in the Street, The.
Woodworkers' Ballad.
Wounded Hawk, The.
PALMER, HORATIO R. Yield not to temptation, for yielding is sin.
PALMER, JOHN F. Band Played On, The.
PALMER, JOHN RANSOM. Drowning.
Emptiness.
Fatigue Attacks the Nerves, the Brain.
Life like a Matador Goes Forth.
Note on the Continuity of Life, A.
PALMER, JOHN WILLIAMSON. Fight at [the] San Jacinto, The.
For Charlie's Sake.
Maryland Battalion, The.
Ned Braddock.
Reid at Fayal.
Stonewall Jackson's Way.
Theodosia Burr; the Wrecker's Story.
Thread and Song.
PALMER, NETTIE. Barrack Yard, The.
Mother, The.
Unsung.
Welcome, The.
PALMER, RAY. Blessed Face, The.
Faith.
I Give My Heart to Thee, *tr.*
I Saw Thee.
Jesus, These Eyes Have Never Seen.
Jesus, Thou Joy of Loving Hearts, *tr.*

My Faith Looks Up to Thee.
O Jesus! Sweet the Tears I Shed.
Soul's Cry, The.
PALMER, SAMUEL. Shoreham.
PALMER, T. H. Try, Try Again, *at.*
PALMER, VANCE. Farmer Remembers the Somme, The.
Pathfinders, The.
Youth and Age.
PALMER, WILLIAM PITT. Smack in School, The.
PALMER, WINTHROP. Arlington Cemetery Looking toward the Capitol.
Dionysus.
House Plant.
PALQUERA, SHEM-TOB BEN JOSEPH. Adapt Thyself.
Mouth and the Ears, The.
PAMAN, CLEMENT. On Christmas Day.
PAMPHILUS. Swallow, The.
PAMPLIN, DON CARLOS. Moonspath.
PANATATTU. God Is One.
PAN CHIEH-YU. Song of Grief, A.
PANDOLPHUS. Description of a Gun.
P'AN I. Deserted Garden on the Road to Hua Chou, A.
PANORMITANUS, IANUS VITALIS (Giano Vitale). Rome.
P'AN SHIH. Waning Moon, The.
PAO CHAO. Devotion.
Red Hills, The.
Scholar Recruit, The.
PAO LIN HUI. Call of Spring, The.
PAO SSU HSIEN. Moonlight on the West Tower.
PAPADAKY, SOPHIA MAVROIDI. Altar of Liberty.
Little Servant, The.
Love Song.
To a Mother.
PAPADOPOULO, GEORGE. *See* "AVGERIS, MARKOS."
PAPONDONIOU, ZACHARIAS. Marigo.
Old Shepherd, The.
Prayer of the Humble, The.
Sad Sunsets.
Serenade at the Window of the Wise Man.
PAPPAS, NICHOLAS. Four Years.
Post-War Roll Call.
PAPPAS, RITA BOUMY. Athens, *sel.*
PARADISE, CAROLINE WILDER FELLOWES. Little Theocritus.
PARAMORE, EDWARD E., JR. Ballad of Yukon Jake, The.
PARAVICINO Y ARTEAGA, HORTENSIO FÉLIX. Divine Passion, The.
PARDO GARCÍA, GERMÁN. Moment, The.
Remoteness.
PARINI, GIUSEPPE. With Dreams of Wealth and Fame.
PARK, JAMES S. Christmas Carol: "So crowded was the little town."
PARK, JOHN. Where Gadie Rins.
PARK, JOHN EDGAR. We Would See Jesus.
PARKE, WALTER. Foam and Fangs.
His Mother-in-Law.
Limerick: "There was a princess of Bengal."
Limerick: "There was a young man who was bitten," *at.*
Limerick: "There was an old stupid who wrote."
My Madeline.
Vague Story, A.
Young Gazelle, The.
PARKER, DOROTHY. Autobiography.
Autumn Valentine.
Ballade of Big Plans.
Ballade of Unfortunate Mammals.
Bohemia.
Coda.
Comment.
Counselor, The.
Danger of Writing Defiant Verse, The.
Dark Girl's Rhyme, The.
Dilemma.
Evening Primrose, The.
Experience.
Fable: "Oh, there once was a lady."
False Friends, The.
Fighting Words.
Gentlest Lady, The.
George Sand.
Godmother.
Incurable.
Inventory.
Little Old Lady in Lavender Silk, The.
Love Song.
Maid-Servant at the Inn, The.
News Item.
Observation.
Of a Woman, Dead Young.
On Being a Woman.
One Perfect Rose.
Philosophy.
Portrait of the Artist.
Prayer for a New Mother.
Prologue to a Saga.
Résumé.
Social Note.
Some Beautiful Letters.
Somebody's Song. *Fr.* Songs of a Markedly Personal Nature.
Song of Perfect Propriety.
Song of the Open Country.
Songs of a Markedly Personal Nature.
"Star Light, Star Bright."
Story.
Theory.
They Part.
Thought for a Sunshiny Morning.
Threnody: "Lilacs blossom just as sweet."
Two-Volume Novel.
Unfortunate Coincidence.
Verse for a Certain Dog.
PARKER, SIR GILBERT. Art. *Fr.* A Lover's Diary.
Envoy: "When you and I have played the little hour." *Fr.* A Lover's Diary.
Invincible. *Fr.* A Lover's Diary.
Little Garaine.
Little House, The.
Love Is Enough.
Lover's Diary, A, *sels.*
Love's Outset. *Fr.* A Lover's Diary.
Red Patrol, The.
Reunited. *Fr.* A Lover's Diary.
Rosleen.
Woman's Hand, A. *Fr.* A Lover's Diary.
World in Making, The.
Yellow Swan, The.
You'll Travel Far and Wide.
PARKER, HELEN ADAMS. Apple Blossoms.
PARKER, HENRY, BARON MORLEY. To His Posterity.
PARKER, HUBBARD. Old Flag.
PARKER, JULIA BENSON. In Remembrance.
Perfect Gift, The.
PARKER, MARTIN. Description of a Strange (and Miraculous) Fish, A.
Keep a Good Tongue in Your Head.
King Enjoys His Own Again, The.
Maunding Soldier, The; or, The Fruits of Warre Is Beggery.
Milkmaid's Life, The.
Neptune's Raging Fury; or, The Gallant Seaman's Sufferings.
Sailors for My Money.
When the King Enjoys His Own Again.
Wooing Maid, The.
PARKER, THEODORE. Higher Good, The.
Jesus.
New Year Prayer, A.
Prayer, A: "O Thou Eternal One, may I commune."
Way, the Truth, and the Life, The.
PARKER, WILLIAM HENRY. Tell Me the Stories of Jesus.
PARKES, SIR HENRY. Weary.
PARKHURST, JOHN. Of Alphus.
PARKWOOD, ROSE. Garden, The.
"PARLEY, PETER." *See* GOODRICH, SAMUEL GRISWOLD.
PARMENIDES. For this shall never prevail, that the things which are not.
Horses bore me as far as my desire, The.
Narrower bands were filled with unmixed Fire, The.
Thou shalt know the nature of the Sky.
Way of Knowledge, The.
PARMENTER, CATHERINE. Christmas.
Christmas Eve.
Crossroads, The.
"Disabled"—Armistice Day.
Discovery.
For a Certain Dog.
Kittens.
Land of Destiny.
Pilgrimage.
San Francesco d'Assisi.
Silent Testimony.
To the Memory of John Burroughs.
PARNELL, FANNY. After Death.
Post-Mortem.
PARNELL, THOMAS. Advice to an Old Beauty. *Fr.* An Elegy: To an Old Beauty.
Anacreontic.
Angel or Woman.
Batrachomyomachia, *sel., tr.*
Elegy, An: To an Old Beauty.
Elegy, An: To an Old Beauty, *sel.*
Hermit, The.
Hymn to Contentment, A.
Night-Piece on Death, A.
Night-Piece on Death, A, *sels.*
On a Lady with Foul Breath.
Small Silver-coloured Bookworm, The.
Song: "My days have been so wondrous free."
Song: "When thy beauty appears."
To Mr. Pope.
Vigil of Venus, The, *tr.*
When Your Beauty Appears.
PARNY, EVARISTE DE. On the Death of a Young Girl.
PARRA, MANUEL DE LA. Well, The.
PARRHASIUS. Artist's Last Word, The.
Though men believe it not this thing I know.
PARRIS, SAMUEL BARTLETT. Anticipations and Recollections, *sel.*
PARRISH, ELSIE. Some Things That Easter Brings.
PARRISH, RANDALL. Your Lad, and My Lad.
PARRISH, WILLIAMINA. Name, The.
PARROT, HENRY. Asperius Nihil Est Humili cum Surgat in Altum.
Brutus, that brave and complete cavalier.
Country farmer had a friend at court, A.
Cutbert our cobbler can no more forbear.
Dupliciter Beatus.
Ebrius Dissimulans.
Epilogus: "Thus have I waded through a worthless task."
Faunus for feats of fencing bears the bell.
Have you not heard of Monsieur Maximus.
Heard ye not yet of Captain Ferdinand?
Humor of Tobacco and the Rest, The.
I cry you mercy, sir, I knew you not.
Impar Impares Odit.
In Obitum Alienius.
Knot of knaves are early met together, A.
Magus would needs, forsooth, this other day.
Musco, that always kept with policy.
Nemo Nascitur Artifex.
Nil Perdunt Mendici.
Nullum Stimulum Ignavis.
Nuptiae post Nummos.
Olim Haec Meminisse Juvabit.
Ortus Novus Urbe Britannus.
Paulus a pamphlet doth in prose present.
Perdat Qui Caveat Emptor.
Peter hath lost his purse, but will conceal it.
Rufus is wondrous rich, but what of that?
Shall Simon Suckegg, simple Simkins' son.
Sic Ars Diluditur Arte.
Silus hath sold his crimson satin suit.

PARROT, HENRY (*continued*)
Sir, can you tell where my young master lives.
Such were those epigrams of elder times.
Suum Cuique Pulchrum.
Tempus Edax Rerum.
To the Ungentilized Censurer.
Tush hang it, have at all, says Curio.
Veniunt Spectentur ut Ipsi.
Videantur Quae Non Sunt.
What tell you me of such a peasant groom.
Would any deem Dacus were now the man.
PARRY, DAVID FISHER. Bachelor's Ballade, The.
Miniver Cheevy, Jr., *parody*.
PARRY, EDWARD ABBOTT. Fisherman on Toast, The.
I Would Like You for a Comrade.
PARRY, JOSEPH. Friends Old and New.
New Friends and Old Friends.
PARRY, R. WILLIAMS. Fox, The.
PARRY, ROBERT. Except I Love, *at. Fr.* The Mirror of Knighthood.
Mirror of Knighthood, The, *sels., at.*
Song: "Fond affection, hence, and leave me!" *at. Fr.* The Mirror of Knighthood.
PARRY-WILLIAMS, SIR THOMAS HERBERT. Words.
PARSON, DONALD. Death of Shelley, The.
Surely the Author.
To an Egyptian Mummy.
PARSONS, EDITH F. Sea-Bird's Cry, The.
PARSONS, KITTY. Station, The.
PARSONS, MARY CATHERINE. My Valentine.
PARSONS, THOMAS WILLIAM. Andrew.
Dirge: For One Who Fell in Battle.
Dirge: "Room for a soldier! lay him in the clover."
Everett.
Groomsman to His Mistress, The.
Her Epitaph.
Into the Noiseless Country.
Like as the lark that, soaring higher and higher.
Mary Booth.
O Ye Sweet Heavens!
Obituary.
On a Bust of Dante.
Paradisi Gloria.
Saint Peray.
Saint Valentine's Day.
Stanzas: "We have forgot what we have been."
To a Lady.
To a Young Girl Dying.
PARTON, MARGARET. Cold.
PARTRIDGE, SYBIL F. (Sister Mary Xavier). Just for Today.
To-Day.
PARTRIDGE, WILLIAM ORDWAY. Creeds.
Nathan Hale.
PARVIN. Man and Wife.
PASCOLI, GIOVANNI. Drayman, The.
Hopes and Memories.
PASQUALIGO, LUIGI. Fedele and Fortunio, *sel.*
I Serve a Mistress. *Fr.* Fedele and Fortunio.
If love be like the flower that in the night. *Fr.* Fedele and Fortunio.
PASSERAT, JEAN. Love in May.
Villanelle: "I have lost my turtle-doo."
PASTERNAK, BORIS LEONIDOVICH. Air is whipped by the frequent rain-drops, The.
Childhood. *Fr.* 1905.
Cocks, The.
Coming of Winter.
Definition of Creativeness.
Definition of the Soul.
Do Not Touch.
Drowsy Garden, The.
Fresh Paint.
Here the Trace.
If I had known what would come later.
If Only, When I Made My Debut.
Improvisation.
In the Breeze.
In the Wood.
January, 1919.
Love is for some a heavy cross.
Lyubka.
May It Be.
1905, *sel.*
Out of Superstition.
Poem: "So they begin. With two years gone."
Roosters.
Rupture.
So they begin. With two years gone.
Sparrow Hills.
Spasskoye.
Spring ("How many buds").
Spring ("It's spring, I leave a street").
Spring ("I've come from the street").
Spring 1944.
Stars raced headlong. Seaward headlands lathered.
Summer.
Summer Day.
Swung down from the fragrant branches.
Three Variations.
To a Friend.
Tragic Tale.
Urals for the First Time, The.
Vorobyev Hills.
Waves, *sels.*
Waving a Bough.
We're Few.
You Pictures Flying.
PATCHEN, KENNETH. At the New Year.
Character of Love Seen as a Search for the Lost, The.
Constant Bridegrooms, The.
Deer and the Snake, The.
Do the Dead Know What Time It Is?
Everlasting Contenders, The.
Fog.
Fox, The.
From My High Love.
In Memory of Kathleen.
In Order To.
Known Soldier, The.
Like a Mourningless Child.
Lute in the Attic, The.
Nice Day for a Lynching.
Origin of Baseball, The.
Pastoral: "Dove walks with sticky feet, The."
Street Corner College.
We Go Out Together.
Who'll That Be.
PATER, WALTER. Mona Lisa.
PATERSON, ANDREW BARTON. Bushman's Song, A.
By the Grey Gulf-Water.
Clancy of The Overflow.
Man from Snowy River, The.
On Kiley's Run.
Waltzing Matilda.
PATKANIAN, RAPHAEL. Cradle Song: "Nightingale, oh, leave our garden."
Cradle Song: "Sweet slumber now creeps o'er thee slow."
Tears of Araxes, The.
PATMORE, COVENTRY KERSEY DIGHTON. Amaranth, The. *Fr.* The Angel in the House.
Angel in the House, The, *sels.*
Arbor Vitae.
Arbor Vitae, *sel.*
Attainment, The. *Fr.* The Angel in the House.
Auras of Delight.
Azalea, The.
Child's Purchase, The.
Constancy. *Fr.* The Angel in the House.
Courtesy. *Fr.* The Angel in the House.
Dean's Consent, The. *Fr.* The Angel in the House.
Deliciae Sapientiae de Amore.
Deliciae Sapientiae de Amore, *sel.*
Departure.
Eros.
Evening Scene, An.
Faint yet Pursuing.
Farewell, A: "With all my will, but much against my heart."
First Spousal, The.
Fool and Wise.
Foreign Land, The. *Fr.* The Angel in the House.
Girl of All Periods, The.
Going to Church. *Fr.* The Angel in the House.
Hail Virgin in Virginity a Spouse. *Fr.* Deliciae Sapientiae de Amore.
Honoria's Surrender. *Fr.* The Angel in the House.
Honour and Desert. *Fr.* The Angel in the House.
I, singularly moved.
Idle poet, here and there, An. *Fr.* The Angel in the House.
If I Were Dead.
Impossibility, The. *Fr.* The Angel in the House.
Joyful Wisdom, The. *Fr.* The Angel in the House.
Kiss, The. *Fr.* The Angel in the House.
Legem Tuam Dilexi.
Life of Life. *Fr.* The Angel in the House.
Love at Large. *Fr.* The Angel in the House.
Love in Action. *Fr.* The Angel in the House.
Love Serviceable. *Fr.* The Angel in the House.
Love, won or lost, is countless gain. *Fr.* The Angel in the House.
Lover, The. *Fr.* The Angel in the House.
Love's Reality. *Fr.* The Angel in the House.
Magna Est Veritas.
Married Lover, The. *Fr.* The Angel in the House.
My memory of Heaven awakes. *Fr.* The Angel in the House.
Nearest the Dearest. *Fr.* The Angel in the House.
Not in the crises of events. *Fr.* The Angel in the House.
Pain.
Parting.
Poet's Confidence, The. *Fr.* The Angel in the House.
Preludes. *Fr.* The Angel in the House.
Prologue, A: "Thou Speaker of all wisdom in a Word."
Prophets Who Cannot Sing.
Regina Coeli.
Remembered Grace.
Revelation, The. *Fr.* The Angel in the House.
River, The, *sel.*
Rose of the World, The. *Fr.* The Angel in the House.
Rosy Bosom'd Hours, The.
Round the Year.
Saint Valentine's Day.
Sensuality. *Fr.* The Angel in the House.
Shadow of Night, The.
Shame. *Fr.* The Angel in the House.
Sly Thoughts. *Fr.* The Angel in the House.
Spirit's Epochs, The. *Fr.* The Angel in the House.
Storm, The.
Sweet Meeting of Desires.
Tamerton Church Tower, *sel.*
Three Witnesses, The.
To the Body.
To the Unknown Eros.
Toys, The.
Tribute, The. *Fr.* The Angel in the House.
Truth.
Truth Is Great, The.
'Twas When the Spousal Time of May. *Fr.* The Angel in the House.
Two Deserts, The.
Unthrift. *Fr.* The Angel in the House.
Warning, A.
Wasteful Woman. *Fr.* The Angel in the House.

Wedding Sermon, The. *Fr.* The Angel in the House.
"Why, having won her, do I woo?" *Fr.* The Angel in the House.
Wind and Wave.
Winter.
Woman. *Fr.* The Angel in the House.
Year, The.
Year's Round, The.
PATMORE, F. J. White Owl, The.
PATON, ALAN. Discardment, The.
Samuel.
Sanna.
To a Small Boy Who Died at Diepkloof Reformatory.
PATON, SIR JOSEPH NOEL. Last of the *Eurydice,* The.
Requiem.
There Is a Wail in the Wind To-Night.
Timor Mortis Conturbat Me.
PATRICK, SAINT. Breastplate of St. Patrick, The, *at.*
Deer's Cry, The, *at.*
Deer's Cry, The, *sels., at.*
God's Blessing on Munster, *at.*
St. Patrick's Breastplate, *at.*
PATRICK, JOHNSTONE G. Closing Prayer.
Grace.
Prayer for Peace.
PATRICK, LUTHER. Sleepin' at the Foot of the Bed.
PATTEN, ARTHUR B. Faith of Our Mothers.
PATTEN, E. W. Headin' Home.
PATTERSON, EMILY. Caravans.
PATTERSON, FRANCES TAYLOR. Harbor View.
PATTISON, THOMAS. Advice to a Clansman, *tr.*
Boatman, The, *tr.*
Dear Islay!
Islesman's Home, The.
Monaltri, *tr.*
PATTON, MARGARET FRENCH (Mrs. Thomas Archer Jones). Comfort.
Easter Even.
Needle Travel.
PAUL, DOROTHY. Captive Ships at Manila, The.
Figurehead.
Heritage.
PAUL, JAY. I Cannot Wait Longer.
Wisdom.
"PAUL, JOHN." *See* WEBB, CHARLES HENRY.
PAUL, LOUIS. Cynical Portraits.
PAUL THE DEACON [*or* PAULUS DIACONUS]. Adelheid.
PAUL THE SILENTIARY. *See* PAULUS SILENTIARIUS.
PAULDING, JAMES KIRKE. Backwoodsman, The, *sel.*
Ode to Jamestown.
Old Man's Carousal, The.
PAULINUS, SISTER MARY. Canticle of Quietness.
Here at the Stable Door.
PAULINUS OF NOLA (Pontius Meropius Anicius Paulinus). For St. Felix Day.
To Ausonius.
PAULL, H. M. Eastern Question, An.
PAULTON, HARRY, *and* CLAXSON BELLAMY. *See* BELLAMY, CLAXSON, *and* HARRY PAULTON.
PAULUS DIACONUS. *See* PAUL THE DEACON.
PAULUS SILENTIARIUS [*or* PAUL THE SILENTIARY]. Broken Tryst.
Dead Ballet-Dancer, The.
Epitaph—and the Reader, The.
Fair girl, I swore to stay apart from you.
"Farewell!" I murmur, and then hold my breath.
Love or Death.
Love-Madness.
Many a Tear.
My name, my country—what are they to thee?
No Matter.
"Rest Is Silence, The."
Soft Venus do I serve, and round the bed.
Stronger than Death.
Tantalos [*or* Tantalus].
Tears of Fear, The.
United.
Vain Farewell, The.
Vanities.
PAVLOVA, KAROLINA KARLOVNA. We Shall Not Overcome Our Sorrows.
While in dark and deadly places.
PAWSEY, IRENE F. Bramble Jam.
Browny Bee.
Browny Hen, The.
Egg for Easter, An.
Eggs for Breakfast.
Found in the Woods.
Greedy Little Pig, The.
Haytime.
June.
Thief, The.
White Horses.
PAXTON, JEAN GRIGSBY. Preparedness.
Release.
PAYN, JAMES. I never had a piece of toast.
PAYNE, ANNE BLACKWELL. After Snow.
Ambition.
At Night.
Definitions for a Tree.
Difference, The.
Fairy Aeroplanes.
Fairy Carpets.
I Must Be Silent.
Little Girl in Bloom, A.
Neighbors.
Prayer before Poems.
Released.
Resolutions for April.
Robin.
Silver Sheep.
To a Young Priest.
Top of Day, The.
PAYNE, JOHN. Ballad: "Lady of Heaven, Regent of the earth," *tr. Fr.* Le Grand Testament.
Ballad of Poor Chimney Sweeps, *tr.*
Cadences.
Christmas Time, *tr. Fr.* Le Petit Testament.
Full Fair, *tr.*
Grand Testament, Le, *sel., tr.*
Kyrielle.
Lake, The, *tr.*
Lesser Testament, The, *tr.*
Love's Autumn.
Merry Ballad of Vintners, A.
My Day and Night.
Of the Choice of His Burial-Place, *tr.*
Of Three Damsels in a Meadow.
Petit Testament, Le, *sel., tr.*
Red Rose, *tr.*
Rococo.
Rondeau Redoublé.
Sibyl.
Song's End.
Stanzas: "Lady fair, if on the page," *tr.*
Thorgerda.
To His Mistress, *tr.*
Villanelle: "I have lost my turtle-doo," *tr.*
PAYNE, JOHN HOWARD. Brutus; or, The Fall of Tarquin, *sel.*
Clari, the Maid of Milan, *sel.*
Home, Sweet Home. *Fr.* Clari.
Lucius Junius Brutus over the Body of Lucretia. *Fr.* Brutus; or, The Fall of Tarquin.
PAYNE, PERCY SOMERS. Rest.
PAYNE, WILLIAM MORTON. "Ej Blot til Lyst."
Incipit Vita Nova.
Lohengrin.
Tannhäuser.
PAZ, OCTAVIO. Oblivion.
Wall, The.
PEABODY, FRANCIS GREENWOOD. Of Such Is the Kingdom.
Venture of Faith, The.
PEABODY, JOSEPHINE PRESTON (Mrs. Lionel Simeon Marks). After Music.
Alms.
Caravans.
Cedars, The.
Changeling Grateful, A.
Cloud, The.
Concerning Love.
Cradle Song: "Lord Gabriel, wilt thou not rejoice."
Enchanted Sheep-Fold, The.
Envoi: "Belovèd, till the day break."
Far-off Rose, A.
Fishers, The.
Forethought.
Found.
House and the Road, The.
Hymn: "Dear Lord, Whose serving-maiden."
In the Silence.
Isolation.
Journey, A.
Man's Bread, A.
Nightingale Unheard, The.
Piper, The.
Prelude: "Words, words, ye are like birds."
Return.
Rubric.
Singing Man, The.
Song of a Shepherd-Boy at Bethlehem, The.
Song of Solomon, A.
Sonnet in a Garden.
Spinning in April.
Stay-at-Home, The.
To a Dog.
Unsaid.
"Vanity, Saith the Preacher."
Wood-Song.
PEABODY, WILLIAM BOURN OLIVER. Lament of Anastasius.
Pussy, Pussy, Do Not Mew.
PEACE, DOROTHY. Sea Change, A.
PEACH, ARTHUR WALLACE. "Cap'n."
Genesis.
Golden Day, The.
Mosaic Worker, The.
My Dog's Tail.
O Youth with Blossoms Laden.
Secret, The.
PEACHAM, HENRY. Nuptial Hymn. *Fr.* The Period of Mourning.
Period of Mourning, The, *sel.*
PEACOCK, THOMAS LOVE. Bacchus. *Fr.* Rhododaphne.
Beneath the Cypress Shade.
Castles in the Air.
Catch, A: "Seamen three! What men be ye?" *Fr.* Nightmare Abbey.
Chorus: "Hail to the Headlong!" *Fr.* Headlong Hall.
Chorus: "If I drink water while this doth last." *Fr.* Crotchet Castle.
Crotchet Castle, *sels.*
Flower of Love, The. *Fr.* Melincourt.
For the Slender Beech and the Sapling Oak. *Fr.* Maid Marian.
Friar's Hunting Song.
Glee—the Ghosts. *Fr.* Melincourt.
Grave of Love, The.
Greatness. *Fr* Crotchet Castle.
Greenwood Tree, The. *Fr.* Maid Marian.
Grey Friar, The.
Gryll Grange, *sel.*
Headlong Hall, *sels.*
In His Last Binn Sir Peter Lies. *Fr.* Headlong Hall.
In the Days of Old. *Fr.* Crotchet Castle.
Larissa. *Fr.* Rhododaphne.
Llyn-y-Dreiddiad-Vrawd; the Pool of the Diving Friar. *Fr.* Crotchet Castle.
Love and Age. *Fr.* Gryll Grange.
Maid Marian, *sels.*
Margaret Love Peacock.
Melincourt, *sels.*
Men of Gotham, The. *Fr.* Nightmare Abbey.
Merlin's Apple-Trees. *Fr.* The Misfortunes of Elphin.
Misfortunes of Elphin, The, *sels.*
Mr. Cypress's Song. *Fr.* Nightmare Abbey.
New Order of Chivalry, A.
Nightmare Abbey, *sels.*
Not Drunk Is He. *Fr.* The Misfortunes of Elphin.

PEACOCK, THOMAS LOVE (*continued*)
Oak and the Beech, The. *Fr.* Maid Marian.
Over, Over. *Fr.* Maid Marian.
Priest and the Mulberry Tree, The. *Fr.* Crotchet Castle.
Quintetto upon the Christmas Pie, *sel. Fr.* Melincourt.
Rhododaphne, *sels.*
Rich and Poor; or, Saint and Sinner.
Robin Hood and the Grey Friars. *Fr.* Maid Marian.
Seamen Three. *Fr.* Nightmare Abbey.
Song: "Drink and sing, and eat and laugh."
Song: "For the tender beech and the sapling oak." *Fr.* Maid Marian.
Song: "In his last bin Sir Peter lies." *Fr.* Headlong Hall.
Song: "It was a friar of orders free." *Fr.* Maid Marian.
Song: "Oh! say not woman's heart is bought," *wr. at.*
Song, by Mr. Cypress. *Fr.* Nightmare Abbey.
Song of Gwythno. *Fr.* The Misfortunes of Elphin.
Song of the Four Winds, The. *Fr.* The Misfortunes of Elphin.
Sun-Dial, The. *Fr.* Melincourt.
There Is a Fever of the Spirit. *Fr.* Nightmare Abbey.
Though I Be Now a Gray, Gray Friar. *Fr.* Maid Marian.
Three Men of Gotham. *Fr.* Nightmare Abbey.
War Song of Dinas Vawr, The. *Fr.* The Misfortunes of Elphin.
Who Is Drunk? *Fr.* The Misfortunes of Elphin.
Wise Men of Gotham, The ("In a bowl to sea went wise men three").
Wise Men of Gotham, The ("Seamen three! What men be ye?"). *Fr.* Nightmare Abbey.
PEACOCKE, ISABEL MAUD. Happy Islands, The.
PEAKE, MERVYN LAURENCE. Cocky Walkers, The.
London, 1941.
Maeve.
PEALE, REMBRANDT. Don't Be Sorrowful, Darling.
Faith and Hope.
PEARCE, J. Heaving the Lead.
PEARCE, NORMAN V. Blind.
PEARCE, ROY GENTRY. Entropy.
New Year, The.
PEARCE, W. By the Deep Nine.
PEARMAN, W. T. Prayer: "When in the morning hour you rise."
PEARSE, MARK GUY. Don't Trouble Trouble.
Facing the New Year.
Grace for Grace.
My Prayer.
Orthodox.
PEARSE, PADRAIC. Farewell to Fál, A, *tr.*
Fool, The.
How Happy the Little Birds, *tr.*
I Am Ireland.
Ideal.
Keen Thyself, Poor Wight, *tr.*
Keening of Mary, The, *tr.*
Little Dark Rose, The, *tr.*
Lullaby of a [*or* the] Woman of the Mountain.
Mother, The.
My Grief on Fál's Proud Plain, *sel., tr.*
O Woman Full of Wile, *tr.*
Rann I Made, A.
Rebel, The.
Sleep Song, A, *tr.*
Tara Is Grass, *tr.*
To Death.
To His Ideal.
Wayfarer, The.
PEARSON, JAMES LARKIN. At the Sorghum-Biln'.
Choice.
Consolation.
Erosion.
Fifty Acres.
Homer in a Garden.
Lincoln.
Utterance.
PEAVYHOUSE, WILLIAM W. Theodore Roosevelt.
PECK, HARRY THURSTON. Heliotrope.
Jefferson Davis.
Jefferson Davis, *sel.*
Other One, The.
Wonderland.
PECK, KATHRYN BLACKBURN. Carpenter's Son, The.
Lord of Heaven to Earth Came Down, The.
Rejoice! He Liveth!
PECK, SAM. *River Lea, The.*
PECK, SAMUEL MINTERN. Autumn's Mirth.
Belinda's Fan.
Bessie Brown, M.D.
Captain's Feather, The.
Cupid at Court.
Grapevine Swing, The.
Kiss in the Rain, A.
Little Kiss When No One Sees, A.
My Drowsy Little Queen.
My Grandmother's Turkey-Tail Fan.
My Little Girl.
Sassafras.
Southern Girl, A.
Spectres.
PEDERSEN, HANS HARTVIG SEEDORFF. Autumn.
Swans from the North, The.
To a Silhouette.
PEDLEY, KATHERINE GREENLEAF. Golgotha.
PEDROSO, REGINO. Opinions of the New Chinese Student.
Opinions of the New Student.
Tomorrow.
PEEL, ARTHUR J. Shadows.
PEEL, DORIS. To Someone in Berlin.
PEELE, GEORGE. Arraignment [*or* Araygnement] of Paris, The, *sels.*
Bathsheba's Song. *Fr.* David and Bethsabe.
Bethsabe Bathing [Sings]. *Fr.* David and Bethsabe.
Bethsabe's Song. *Fr.* David and Bethsabe.
Celanta at the Well of Life. *Fr.* The Old Wives' Tale.
Colin, the Enamored Shepherd, Singeth This Passion of Love. *Fr.* The Arraignment of Paris.
Colin's Passion of Love. *Fr.* The Arraignment of Paris.
Coridon and Melampus' Song. *Fr.* The Hunting of Cupid.
Cupid's Curse. *Fr.* The Arraignment of Paris.
David and Bethsabe, *sels.*
Dirge: "Welladay, welladay, poor Colin." *Fr.* The Arraignment of Paris.
Fair and Fair. *Fr.* The Arraignment of Paris.
Fair Maiden. *Fr.* The Old Wives' Tale.
Farewell, A: "Have doone with care my harts, aborde amaine."
Farewell to Arms, A. *Fr.* Polyhymnia.
Farewell to the Most Famous Generals, Sir John Norris and Sir Francis Drake, Knights, A.
Harvester's Song. *Fr.* The Old Wives' Tale.
Harvestmen a-Singing. *Fr.* The Old Wives' Tale.
His Golden Locks Time Hath to Silver Turn'd. *Fr.* Polyhymnia.
Hot Sun, Cool Fire, Temper'd with Sweet Air. *Fr.* David and Bethsabe.
Hunting of Cupid, The, *sels.*
Lo! here we come a-reaping. *Fr.* The Old Wives' Tale.
Locrine, *sel., at.*
Love. *Fr.* The Hunting of Cupid.
Love of King David and Fair Bethsabe, The. *sels.*
My golden locks, Time hath to silver turnd.
Not Iris in Her Pride. *Fr.* The Arraignment of Paris.
O Gentle Love. *Fr.* The Arraignment of Paris.
Oenone's Complaint. *Fr.* The Arraignment of Paris.
Old Knight, The. *Fr.* Polyhymnia.
Old Wives' Tale, The, *sels.*
Peeping Flowers. *Fr.* The Arraignment of Paris.
Polyhymnia, *sel.*
Shepherd's Dirge, The. *Fr.* The Arraignment of Paris.
Sonet, A: "His golden lockes, Time hath to silver turn'd." *Fr.* Polyhymnia.
Song: "Whenas the rye reach to the chin." *Fr.* The Old Wives' Tale.
Song at the Well, The. *Fr.* The Old Wives' Tale.
Song of Coridon and Melampus. *Fr.* The Hunting of Cupid.
Song of Paris and Oenone. *Fr.* The Arraignment of Paris.
Sonnet: "His golden locks time hath to silver turn'd." *Fr.* Polyhymnia.
Spell, A. *Fr.* The Old Wives' Tale.
Summer Song, A. *Fr.* The Old Wives' Tale.
To the Author. *Fr.* Hecatompathia.
Voice [Speaks] from the Well, A. *Fr.* The Old Wives' Tale.
We cobblers lead a merry life, *at. Fr.* Locrine.
What Thing Is Love? *Fr.* The Hunting of Cupid.
Whenas the Rye Reach to the Chin. *Fr.* The Old Wives' Tale.
PEELE, STEVEN. Letter to Rome, A.
PEGIS, JESSIE CORRIGAN. Eyes of Wonder, The.
Stay Little Always.
PÉGUY, CHARLES. Eve, *sel.*
Freedom, *sel.*
Happy Are Those Who Have Died.
Mystery of the Innocent Saints, The, *sel.*
Night, *sel.*
Paris Twin-Galleys.
Paris Two-banked Galley.
Passion of Our Lady, The, *sel.*
PEI PAO YU LAN. Pine Tree, The.
PELHAM, M. Comical Girl, The.
PELHAM, NETTIE H. Reply to "A Woman's Question."
PELLEW, GEORGE. Death.
On a Cast from an Antique.
PELLICER, CARLOS. Etude.
Sunday.
Third Time.
PELLOW, JOHN DYNHAM CORNISH. After London.
Temple of the Trees, The.
When All Is Said.
PELOUBET, MAURICE E. Eternal Kinship, The.
PELTZ, MARY ELLIS. Straw.
PEMBROKE, MARY SIDNEY HERBERT, COUNTESS OF. Antonius, *sel., tr.*
Chorus: "Alas, with what tormenting fire," *tr. Fr.* Antonius.
Dialogue between Two Shepherds, Thenot and Piers, in Praise of Astrea, A.
Of Death, *tr. Fr.* Antonius.
Psalm CXXXIX: "O Lord, in me there lieth nought," *par.*
Wondrous Love.
PEMBROKE, WILLIAM HERBERT, EARL OF. Disdain Me Still.
Paradox, A.
Song: "Soules joy, now I am gone," *at.*
PEÑA BARRENECHEA, ENRIQUE. Dead Poets.
Elegy for Bécquer.
Man's Road.
PEÑALOSA, JOAQUIN ANTONIO. God's Little Creatures; Foreword.
Lament for a Dead Burro.
Sermon to the Fishes.

P'eng Chien P'u. Glimpse into a Courtyard, A.
Pennant, Edmund. Lost Explorer.
Pennell, Henry Cholmondeley. *See* Cholmondeley-Pennell, Henry.
Penney, William Edward. Town of Nogood, The.
Penny, Lucretia. Beware Our Loving Dog.
Peón y Contreras, José. Echoes.
Peralta, Alejandro. Andean Crossing.
Percival, James Gates. Apostrophe to the Island of Cuba.
Clouds.
Coral Grove, The.
Elegiac.
Graves of the Patriots, The.
It Is Great for Our Country to Die.
May.
Mind, The, *sel.*
New England.
Perry's Victory on Lake Erie.
Seneca Lake.
To Seneca Lake.
"Percy, Florence." *See* Allen, Elizabeth Akers.
Percy, Thomas. Gentle River, Gentle River, *tr.*
O Nancy, Wilt Thou Go with Me?
Song, A: "O Nancy, wilt thou go with me."
Percy, William. Coelia, *sels.*
If it be sin so dearly for to love thee. *Fr.* Coelia.
It shall be said I died for Coelia. *Fr.* Coelia.
Judged by my goddess' doom to endless pain. *Fr.* Coelia.
Receive these writs, my sweet and dearest friend. *Fr.* Coelia.
Relent, my dear yet unkind Coelia. *Fr.* Coelia.
Sonnet: "It shall be said I died for Coelia!" *Fr.* Coelia.
Sonnets to the Fairest Coelia, *sels.*
What is the fair to whom so long I plead? Lead. *Fr.* Coelia.
Percy, William Alexander. Adventure.
Chorus: "Surely in no benignant mood."
Confidants.
Delta Autumn, The.
Dirge: "Tuck the earth, fold the sod."
Enzio's Kingdom, *sel.*
Epilogue: "O God, author of song," *sel.*
Epilogue: "This wind upon my mouth, these stars I see." *Fr.* Enzio's Kingdom.
Farmers.
For Them That Died in Battle.
His Peace.
Holy Women, The.
Home.
Hymn to the Sun.
In an Autumn Wood.
In April Once, *sel.*
In New York.
In New York, *sels.*
In the Night.
Little Page's Song, A.
Little Shepherd's Song, The.
On Sunday Morning.
Overtones.
Page's Road Song, A.
Poppy Fields.
Sappho in Levkas.
Song You Love, The.
Spring of God, The. *Fr.* In April Once.
Stirrup Cup.
To an Old Tune.
To Butterfly.
Unloved to His Beloved, The.
Volunteer's Grave, A.
Wanderer, The.
Weariness.
Wonder and a Thousand Springs.
Pereda Valdés, Ildefonso. Cradle Song to Put a Negro Baby to Sleep.
Peretz, Isaac [*or* Yitzchok] Leibush. All through the Stranger's Wood.
Believe Not.
Eternal Sabbath.
Hope and Faith.
In the Silent Night.
Little People.
Three Seamstresses, The.
Pérez de Ayala, Ramón. She Was a Pretty Little Girl.
Perkins, Fanny Elizabeth. To a Cat.
Perkins, George Matthews. Prophet, The.
Perkins, Jacob Randolph. And the Greatness of These.
Back of God, The.
World's Lone Lover, The.
Perkins, Jeannette Eloise. I Stretch My Thoughts.
Social Hymn for Children.
Perkins, Lucy Alice. Laborers Together with God.
Perkins, Lucy Fitch. Gardener, The.
Honey-Bee.
Perkins, Silas H. Common Road, The.
Perkoff, Stuart Z. Feasts of Death, Feasts of Love.
Flowers for Luis Bunuel.
Recluses, The.
Perrin, John. Rejected Odyssey.
Perronet, Edward. All hail the power of Jesus' Name!
Coronation.
Perry, Eleanore L. Unheeded Vocation.
Perry, George. Siva, Destroyer.
Perry, Josephine Hovey. Hail, Vermont!
Perry, Katherine H. Every-Day Botany.
Perry, Lilla Cabot (Mrs. Thomas Sergeant Perry). Art.
As It Was. *Fr.* Meeting after Long Absence.
As She Feared It Would Be. *Fr.* Meeting after Long Absence.
Death, Life, Fear.
Horseman Springing from the Dark; a Dream.
I love not wine, but shouldst thou wish, *tr.*
Life and Death.
Meeting after Long Absence.
O Life, what refuge have we fleeing thee, *tr.*
Perry, Martha Eugenie. Lonely Shell, The.
Mainspring, The.
Terror in Beauty.
Water-Witch, The.
Perry, Nora. Abraham Lincoln's Christmas Gift.
Balboa.
Coming of [the] Spring, The.
Cressid.
In June.
Love-Knot, The.
Next Year.
Riding Down.
Running the Blockade.
Some Day of Days.
Too Late.
Who Knows?
Yesterday.
"Perse, St.-J." (Alexis Saint-Léger Léger). Anabasis, *sels.*
And You, Seas. *Fr.* Seamarks.
For my soul engaged in far matters. *Fr.* Anabasis.
Seamarks, *sel.*
Song: "I have halted my horse by the tree of the doves." *Fr.* Anabasis.
Song: "Under the bronze leaves a colt was foaled." *Fr.* Anabasis.
Such Is the Way of the World. *Fr.* Anabasis.
Three Sections from "Anabasis."
Thus Was the City Founded. *Fr.* Anabasis.
We Shall Not Dwell Forever in These Yellow Lands. *Fr.* Anabasis.
Persell, George A. On a Pet Cat.
Perses. God of the Lowly, The.
Persius (Aulus Persius Flaccus). Choliambs.
Prologue to the First Satire, The. *Fr.* Satires.
Satire I: "Alas, man's care, and O the vacuity." *Fr.* Satires.
Satire VI: "Has winter brought you to the Sabine fire." *Fr.* Satires.
Satire III: "Still at it? Morning stares between the shutters." *Fr.* Satires.
Satires, *sels.*
Pesado, José Joaquín. Huntress, The.
Pestel [*or* Pestell], Thomas. For Christmas Day.
For the Right Honorable Lucy, Countess of Huntingdon, 1649.
On Tobacco.
Psalm for Christmas Day.
Psalm for Sunday Night, A.
Relief on Easter Eve, The.
Song: "Silly boy, there is no cause."
"Peter." Bus, The.
Saint Wears a Halo, The.
Speed Track, The.
Peter, John. Christmas on Three Continents.
Cypress.
Estrangement.
Heart's Desire.
Reading Tolstoy.
Peterborough, Charles Mordant, Earl of. *See* Mordant, Charles, Earl of Peterborough.
Peter Damian, Saint. Glory of Paradise, The.
Peters, Hugh. Yankee Lyric, A.
Peters, Mary. Jesus, How Much Thy Name Unfolds.
Peters, Phillis Wheatley. *See* Wheatley, Phillis.
Petersen, Nils. Hazard.
Peterson, Arthur. Kelpius's Hymn.
Peterson, Frederick ("Pai Ta-shun"). Bridge, The.
Heredity.
Idiot, The.
In Prison.
Solitude.
Wild Geese.
Peterson, Henry. Death of Lyon, The.
Ode for Decoration Day.
Ode for Decoration Day, *sel.*
Rinaldo.
Petofi, Alexander [*or* Sandor]. In the Forest.
National Song ("Rise, Magyar").
War and Peace.
Petrarch (Francesco Petrarca). Against the Court of Rome. *Fr.* Sonnets to Laura.
Ah Liberty, so lovely, so denied! *Fr.* Sonnets to Laura.
Alas! that liquid look, that lovely face! *Fr.* Sonnets to Laura.
All my green years and golden prime of man. *Fr.* Sonnets to Laura.
Alone, thought-sick, I pace where none has been. *Fr.* Sonnets to Laura.
Already in the east the amorous star. *Fr.* Sonnets to Laura.
Although from falsehood I with all my will. *Fr.* Sonnets to Laura.
Amorous Worms' Meat, The. *Fr.* Sonnets to Laura.
Canzone 126: "Clear, fresh, and dulcet streams." *Fr.* Sonnets to Laura.
Canzone: "Clear, fresh, sweet waters." *Fr.* Sonnets to Laura.
Canzone 129: "From thought to thought, from mountain-peak to mountain." *Fr.* Sonnets to Laura.
Canzone: "It is the evening hour; the rapid sky."
Canzone 128: "O my own Italy! though words are vain."
Complaint by Night of the Lover Not Beloved, A. *Fr.* Sonnets to Laura.
Complaint of a Lover Rebuked. *Fr.* Sonnets to Laura.
Contrarious Passions in a Lover, The. *Fr.* Sonnets to Laura.
Description of the Contrarious Passions in a Lover. *Fr.* Sonnets to Laura.
Distance and Solitude. *Fr.* Sonnets to Laura.

PETRARCH (*continued*)
Ecstasy of thought upraised me where, An. *Fr.* Sonnets to Laura.
Eyes, the face, the limbs of heavenly mould, The. *Fr.* Sonnets to Laura.
Fair Virgin,/ Vestured with the sun! *Fr.* Sonnets to Laura.
Father of heaven! after the days all lost. *Fr.* Sonnets to Laura.
Flying Lesson, The. *Fr.* Sonnets to Laura.
Golden upon the wind her loose hair streaming. *Fr.* Sonnets to Laura.
He Hopes That Time Will Render Her More Merciful. *Fr.* Sonnets to Laura.
He Is Jealous of the Heavens and Earth. *Fr.* Sonnets to Laura.
He Understands the Great Cruelty of Death. *Fr.* Sonnets to Laura.
He Wishes He Might Die and Follow Laura. *Fr.* Sonnets to Laura.
Heart on the Hill. *Fr.* Sonnets to Laura.
Here Rules Love. *Fr.* Sonnets to Laura.
I find no peace and all my war is done. *Fr.* Sonnets to Laura.
I find no peace, yet from all wars abstain me. *Fr.* Sonnets to Laura.
If Amorous Faith. *Fr.* Sonnets to Laura.
If faith most true, a heart that cannot feign. *Fr.* Sonnets to Laura.
If It Be Destined. *Fr.* Sonnets to Laura.
If the lone bird lament or the green leaves. *Fr.* Sonnets to Laura.
If this should not be Love, O God, what shakes me? *Fr.* Sonnets to Laura.
In what bright realm, what sphere of radiant thought. *Fr.* Sonnets to Laura.
In Wintry Midnight, o'er a Stormy Main.
It was the morning of that blessed day. *Fr.* Sonnets to Laura.
Jealous Enemy, The. *Fr.* Sonnets to Laura.
Last Trial, The. *Fr.* Sonnets to Laura.
Laura Waits for Him in Heaven. *Fr.* Sonnets to Laura.
Life ever flies with course that nought may stay. *Fr.* Sonnets to Laura.
Lofty Column and the Laurel fall, The. *Fr.* Sonnets to Laura.
Long love that in my thought doth harbor, The. *Fr.* Sonnets to Laura.
Long Love that is sovereign to my mind, The. *Fr.* Sonnets to Laura.
Love kept me one and twenty years a slave. *Fr.* Sonnets to Laura.
Love, that doth reign and live within my thought. *Fr.* Sonnets to Laura.
Lover Compareth His State to a Ship in Perilous Storm Tossed on the Sea, The. *Fr.* Sonnets to Laura.
Lover for Shamefastness Hideth His Desire within His Faithful Heart, The. *Fr.* Sonnets to Laura.
Love's Fidelity. *Fr.* Sonnets to Laura.
Love's Inconsistency. *Fr.* Sonnets to Laura.
Madrigale 52: "Diana, naked in the shadowy pool."
My galley charged with forgetfulness. *Fr.* Sonnets to Laura.
My mind! prophetic of my coming fate. *Fr.* Sonnets to Laura.
My vessel, cargoed with oblivion, cleaves. *Fr.* Sonnets to Laura.
Nearer I approach that final day, The. *Fr.* Sonnets to Laura.
Ne'er to the son, in whom her age is blest. *Fr.* Sonnets to Laura.
Night. *Fr.* Sonnets to Laura.
Nightingale, The. *Fr.* Sonnets to Laura.
Not skies serene, with glittering stars inlaid. *Fr.* Sonnets to Laura.
O rich and happy flowers forever apart. *Fr.* Sonnets to Laura.
O sweet severity, repulses mild. *Fr.* Sonnets to Laura.
Ode to the Virgin. *Fr.* Sonnets to Laura.
Of His Foolish Passion for Laura. *Fr.* Sonnets to Laura.
Palmer bent, with locks of silver gray, The. *Fr.* Sonnets to Laura.
Place me where herb and flower the sun has dried. *Fr.* Sonnets to Laura.
Poor solitary bird, that pour'st thy lay. *Fr.* Sonnets to Laura.
Praises of Laura Transcend His Poetic Power, The. *Fr.* Sonnets to Laura.
Set Me Where Phœbus' Heat. *Fr.* Sonnets to Laura.
Set Me Whereas the Sun Doth Parch the Green. *Fr.* Sonnets to Laura.
Seven Penitential Psalms, *sel.*
Signs of Love. *Fr.* Sonnets to Laura.
Sonnet: "Ah, had I ever thought the world would care." *Fr.* Sonnets to Laura.
Sonnet: "Alone and ever weary with dark care." *Fr.* Sonnets to Laura.
Sonnet: "Already I grow weary thinking how." *Fr.* Sonnets to Laura.
Sonnet: "Ancient greybeard shoulders on his load, The." *Fr.* Sonnets to Laura.
Sonnet: "As over the fresh grass her golden feet." *Fr.* Sonnets to Laura.
Sonnet: "Determined with one sally to erase." *Fr.* Sonnets to Laura.
Sonnet: "Father in heaven! after the days misspent." *Fr.* Sonnets to Laura.
Sonnet: "Fountain of sorrow, inn of cursed ire." *Fr.* Sonnets to Laura.
Sonnet: Good Friday 1327. *Fr.* Sonnets to Laura.
Sonnet: "I find no peace and bear no arms for war." *Fr.* Sonnets to Laura.
Sonnet: "In what divine ideal, what lofty sphere." *Fr.* Sonnets to Laura.
Sonnet: "Life hurries on, a frantic refugee." *Fr.* Sonnets to Laura.
Sonnet: "More my own poor wishes would commend me, The." *Fr.* Sonnets to Laura.
Sonnet: "Now I go grieving for the days on earth." *Fr.* Sonnets to Laura.
Sonnet: "Now while the wind and earth and heavens rest." *Fr.* Sonnets to Laura.
Sonnet: "O little room, my harbor from the sea." *Fr.* Sonnets to Laura.
Sonnet: "O lovely little bird, I watch you fly." *Fr.* Sonnets to Laura.
Sonnet: "O unforgiving thoughts, I pray you: Peace!" *Fr.* Sonnets to Laura.
Sonnet: On the Death of Cino da Pistoia. *Fr.* Sonnets to Laura.
Sonnet: "Rain fire from Heaven down upon thy head." *Fr.* Sonnets to Laura.
Sonnet: "Set me whereas the sun doth parch the green." *Fr.* Sonnets to Laura.
Sonnet: "She used to let her golden hair fly free." *Fr.* Sonnets to Laura.
Sonnet: "That window where the sun at midday shows." *Fr.* Sonnets to Laura.
Sonnet: "Through savage woods I walk without demur." *Fr.* Sonnets to Laura.
Sonnet: "Through twenty-one long years love held me burning." *Fr.* Sonnets to Laura.
Sonnet: "You who give ear to sorrow, as you scan." *Fr.* Sonnets to Laura.
Sonnet: "Zephyr returns, and scatters everywhere." *Fr.* Sonnets to Laura.
Sonnets on the Death of Laura. *Fr.* Sonnets to Laura: To Laura in Death.
Sonnets to Laura, *sels.*
Soul of my soul, how often you return. *Fr.* Sonnets to Laura.
Spring returns, the spring wind softly blowing, The. *Fr.* Sonnets to Laura.
That nightingale, who weeps so sweetly, grieves. *Fr.* Sonnets to Laura.
That touching pallor which, like a soft cloud. *Fr.* Sonnets to Laura.
Thousand times, O my sweet warrior, A. *Fr.* Sonnets to Laura.
To His Lady. *Fr.* Sonnets to Laura.
To that pure look which honours Paradise. *Fr.* Sonnets to Laura.
To the Virgin Mary. *Fr.* Sonnets to Laura.
To Young Imaginaries in Knowledge. *Fr.* Seven Penitential Psalms.
Translation from Petrarch ("Mine old dear enemy, my froward master"), *tr. by* Wyatt.
Translation from Petrarch, A ("What a grudge I am bearing the earth"), *pr. tr. by* Synge. *Fr.* Sonnets to Laura.
Two glowing roses, fresh from Paradise. *Fr.* Sonnets to Laura.
Valley familiar with my desperate din. *Fr.* Sonnets to Laura.
Visions, The. *Fr.* Sonnets to Laura.
Vow to Love Faithfully [Howsoever He Be Rewarded], A. *Fr.* Sonnets to Laura.
Wail'd the sweet warbler to the lonely shade. *Fr.* Sonnets to Laura.
Weeping, I still regret the years that went. *Fr.* Sonnets to Laura.
What a grudge I am bearing the earth. *Fr.* Sonnets to Laura.
What pity-driven angel proved his speed. *Fr.* Sonnets to Laura.
When Love his flaming image on her brow. *Fr.* Sonnets to Laura.
Who Wishes to Behold.
Whoso List to Hunt. *Fr.* Sonnets to Laura.
Ye, who may listen to each idle strain. *Fr.* Sonnets to Laura.

PETRONIUS ARBITER (Caius Petronius Arbiter). All the Heaven.
Encouragement to Exile.
Foeda Est in Coitu.
Fornication is a filthy business.
Good God, what a night that was.
I had just gone to bed.
In the soldier's helmet doves.
Keeping Endless Holiday.
Malady of Love Is Nerves, The.
O restless, caressing eyes.
Outward looks are not enough.
Satyricon, *sel.*
Snow Ball, The.
So, contrary to Nature's normal ways.
That night will long delight us, Nealce.
This is nobleness, this is the one claim.
Waking, my eyes, and in the night.
We Are Such Stuff as Dreams.
Why do you frown on me, you puritans.
With your beautiful hair and seemly.
You send me apples hot with gold, Martia.

PETROVA, OLGA. To a Child Who Inquires.
PETTEE, G. W. Sleigh Song.
PETTEE, J. T. Prayer and Potatoes.
PETTENGILL, MARGARET MILLER. There Will Be Peace.
PETTINOS, SARAH J. Song of Arbor Day.
PEYRAT, NAPOLÉON. Roland.
PFEFFEL, GOTTLIEB KONRAD. Nobleman and Pensioner, The.
PFEIFFER, EDWARD HEYMAN. Life.
Soul Speaks, The.
PFEIFFER, EMILY (Davis). Song of Winter, A.
To a Moth That Drinketh of the Ripe October.
To the Herald Honeysuckle.
PHAEDIMUS. Lost at Sea.
PHAEDRUS. Aesop at Play.
Dog in the River, The.
Man and the Weasel, The.
Purpose of Fable-writing, The.
PHANOCLES. Orpheus.

PHELON, WILLIAM A. Paul Jones.
PHELPS, ARTHUR LEONARD. Apple Blossoms.
Monk's Day, The.
Old Man's Weariness, An.
On the Eve of All Hallows.
There Was a Rose.
Thoughts.
Wall, The.
PHELPS, CHARLES HENRY. Henry Ward Beecher.
Rare Moments.
Yuma.
PHELPS, MRS. DAWSON M. "Lily's" Thanksgiving, The.
PHELPS, E. J. Essex Junction.
PHELPS, ELIZABETH STUART. *See* WARD, ELIZABETH STUART PHELPS.
PHELPS, GUY FITCH. White Christs, The.
PHELPS, S. D. Something for Jesus.
PHELPS-RIDER, ALICE. On Hearing Jazz.
PHERAIOS [*or* VELESTINLI], RHIGAS. War Hymn.
"PHILARDEE" (Phil R. Davis). To My Father.
PHILEMON. Greatest Tribute, The.
Happy creature is your snail indeed, A!
Happy the animals! they do not bother.
Who Is Free?
PHILETAS. Last Request, The.
Life's Medley.
"Nothing Is Here to Wail."
"PHILIBIN, AN." *See* "PILIBIN, AN."
PHILIP V, KING OF MACEDON. Alcaeus of Messene.
PHILIP, JOHN. Subject of the Bishop's Miracle, The.
PHILIP, SISTER MARY. Air Mail, Special.
Hide and Seek.
Poet's Bread.
To-Day.
PHILIP OF THESSALONICA. Seeing the martyred corpse of Sparta's king.
PHILIPA, PRINCESS. To Holy Jesus.
PHILIPOTT, THOMAS. On a Spark of Fire Fixing on a Gentlewoman's Breast.
PHILIPPE DE THAON [*or* THAUN]. Pelican, The.
Unicorn, The.
PHILIPPS, THOMAS. Peace of the Roses, The.
PHILIPS, AMBROSE. Blest as the Immortal Gods, *tr.*
First Olympionique: To Hiero of Syracuse, *tr.*
Fragment from [*or* of] Sappho, *tr.*
Glittering Frost. *Fr.* A Winter Piece.
Happy Swain, The.
Ocean of Ice, The. *Fr.* A Winter Piece.
Pastoral Landscape. *Fr.* Pastorals.
Pastorals, *sels.*
Sixth Pastoral, The. *Fr.* Pastorals.
Song: "From White's and Will's."
To [Miss] Charlotte Pulteney [in Her Mother's Arms].
To Miss Margaret Pulteney.
To Signora Cuzzoni.
To the Earl of Dorset.
To the Right Honourable Robert Walpole, Esq.
Winter Piece, A.
Winter Piece, A, *sels.*
Wit and Wisdom.
PHILIPS, BARCLAY. Holiday Task, A, *at.*
Polka Lyric, A, *at.*
PHILIPS, JOAN. *See* "EPHELIA."
PHILIPS, JOHN. Splendid Shilling, The.
Thirsty Poet, The. *Fr.* The Splendid Shilling.
PHILIPS, KATHERINE ("Orinda").
Death.
Friendship's Mystery.
I did not live until this time.
Little Hector Philips.
Orinda to Lucasia.
Orinda to Lucasia Parting, October, 1661, at London.
Song: "'Tis true our life is but a long disease."
To a Friend before Taking a Journey.
To Mrs. M. A. upon Absence.
To My Excellent Lucasia, on Our Friendship.
To My Lucasia, in Defence of Declared Friendship.
To One Persuading a Lady to Marriage.
Virgin, The.
Wiston Vault.
PHILITAS. "Man Is Born to Sorrow."
PHILLIMORE, JOHN SWINNERTON. Dying Thief, The.
In a Meadow.
PHILLIP, JOHN. Comedy of Patient and Meek Grissell, The, *sel.*
Lullaby: "Lullaby baby, lullaby baby." *Fr.* The Comedy of Patient and Meek Grissell.
Patient and Meek Grissill, *sel.*
PHILLIPPS, THOMAS. Peace of the Roses, The.
PHILLIPS, CHARLES. Come Up to Umbria.
Music.
Our Native Land.
PHILLIPS, GERTIE STEWART. Prayer: "Oft times I pray with words."
PHILLIPS, HARRY IRVING (H. I. Phillips). Study of a People.
PHILLIPS, HARTIE I. Acrostic (on Abraham Lincoln).
PHILLIPS, L. Z. Marines' Hymn, The, *at.*
PHILLIPS, MARIE TELLO. Sorrow.
PHILLIPS, REDMOND. Butchers.
PHILLIPS, ROSE MYRA. Wanderers.
PHILLIPS, STEPHEN. Apparition, The.
Beautiful Lie the Dead.
Benediction. *Fr.* Herod.
Christ's Reign of Peace.
Dream, A.
Grief and God.
Herod, *sels.*
Homecoming of Ulysses, The. *Fr.* Ulysses.
I in the Grayness Rose.
Marpessa, *sels.*
Paolo and Francesca, *sel.*
Parting of Launcelot and Guinevere, The.
Poet's Prayer, A.
Right of Asylum, The.
To a Lost Love.
To Milton—Blind.
Ulysses, *sel.*
PHILLIPS, SUSAN KELLY. In November.
Rose of Eden, The.
PHILLPOTTS, BERTHA SURTEES. Elder Edda, The, *sel.*, *tr.*
Thor Gets Back His Hammer, *tr. Fr.* The Elder Edda.
PHILLPOTTS, EDEN. Badgers, The.
Experience.
Feline Anyway.
Finis.
Fruit Piece, A.
Gaffer's Song, The.
Hunting, The.
Litany to Pan.
Man's Days.
Puddle, The.
Reveillé.
Two Funerals.
Wasp, The.
PHILODEMUS OF GADARA [*or* PHILODEMOS THE EPICUREAN]. Coquette, The, *at.*
I loved, I played, I drank my wine.
Moonlight.
Moonlit Love.
Philaenion is dark and small.
Remonstrance.
Shine, twy-horned Lady of the Night, shine on!
To Piso from his pet friend.
What feet she has, what legs, what waist, what thighs.
Years of Discretion.
PHILPOT, WILLIAM. Maritae Suae.
PHOCYLIDES. Exception, The.
Exception That Proves the Rule, The.
"In Huts Where Poor Men Lie."
Problem in Logic.
Small City on a Rock, A.
PHRYNICHUS. Sophocles.
PIATT, JOHN JAMES. Child in the Street, The.
Chrysalis, The.
Dear President, The.
Farther.
Guerdon, The.
Honors of War.
Ireland.
Leaves at My Window.
Lost Genius, The.
Mower in Ohio, The.
October Morning.
Purpose.
Rose and Root.
Sonnet in 1862.
Suggested Device of a New Western State.
To a Lady.
To Abraham Lincoln.
Torch-Light in Autumn.
PIATT, SARAH MORGAN BRYAN. After Wings.
Call on Sir Walter Raleigh, A.
Envoy: "Sweet World, if you will hear me now."
In Clonmel Parish Churchyard.
Into the World and Out.
Irish Wild-Flower, An.
My Babes in the Wood.
Term of Death, The.
Tradition of Conquest.
Transfigured.
Watch of a Swan, The.
Witch in the Glass.
Word with a Skylark, A.
PICCHIA, MENOTTI DEL. Bay of Guanabara.
Narrow Street, The.
PICHETTE, HENRI. Apoem I.
PICK [*or* PICKE], SAMUEL. To His Mistress Confined, *at.*
PICKERING [*or* PIKERYNG], JOHN. Farewell, adieu, that courtly life! *Fr.* Horestes.
Haltersick's Song. *Fr.* Horestes.
Horestes, *sel.*
New Interlude of Vice, Containing the History of Horestes, A, *sel.*
Song: "Farewell, adieu, that courtly life." *Fr.* Horestes.
PICKERING, THEODOSIA. *See* GARRISON, THEODOSIA PICKERING.
PICKETT, ELIZABETH. Gay Crimson Leaves.
PICKTHALL, MARJORIE LOWRY CHRISTIE.
Bega.
Bridegroom of Cana, The.
Canada to England.
Child's Song of Christmas, A.
Duna.
Ebb Tide.
Evening.
How Looked She When She Breathed Good-bye?
I Sat among the Green Leaves.
Immortal, The.
Lamp of Poor Souls, The.
Little Fauns to Proserpine, The.
Little Sister of the Prophet, The.
Little Songs.
Lovers of Marchaid, The.
Mary Shepherdess.
Modern Endymion, A.
Mother in Egypt, A.
Père Lalement.
Pool, The.
Quiet.
Resurgam.
Shepherd Boy, The.
Swallow Song.
To a Believer.
PICO DELLA MIRANDOLA, GIOVANNI, CONTE. Consider.
Golden Sestina, The.
PICOT, JAMES. Do You Not Hear?
Finale.
Main Range.
To the Rosella in the Poinsettia Tree.
PIDDINGTON, R. A. Tudor Aspersions.
PIEN CHIH-LIN. Composition of Distances, The.
First Lamp, The.

PIEN CHIH-LIN (*continued*)
History of Communications and a Running Account, The.
Peking.
PIER, R. Statue, A.
PIER MORONELLI, DI FIORENZA. *See* MORONELLI DI FIORENZA, PIER.
PIERCE, DOROTHY MASON. Good Night.
Sprinkling.
PIERCE, EDITH LOVEJOY. Alas, Alas, the Winter.
Certain Saturday, A.
Christmas Amnesty.
Civitas Dei.
Crucifix.
Dirge: "O sad, sad world, O world that knows not love."
Great Powers Conference.
Had There Been Peace.
Hymn to the Perfect.
In the Wilderness.
Incarnation.
Let Me Not Die.
Loyalty Hymn.
O Christ Thou Art within Me like a Sea.
Prayer: "Bear with me, Master, when I turn from Thee."
Prayer for the Useless Days.
Song of the Wise Men.
Sons of Failure.
Supplication.
PIERCE, JASON NOBLE. Which Sword?
PIERPOINT, FOLLIOTT SANDFORD. For the Beauty of the Earth.
PIERPONT, JAMES S. Jingle Bells.
We Conquer or Die.
PIERPONT, JOHN. Ballot, The.
Centennial Hymn.
Evening Hymn for a Child.
Exile at Rest, The.
Fourth of July, The.
Fugitive Slave's Apostrophe to the North Star, The.
General Joseph Warren's Address.
Kidnapping of Sims, The.
My Child.
Not on the Battle-Field.
On Laying the Cornerstone of the Bunker Hill Monument.
Pilgrim Fathers, The.
Sparkling Bowl, The.
Warren's Address [to the American Soldiers].
Warren's Address at Bunker Hill.
Whittling.
PIETY, CHAUNCEY ROSCOE. Come Back, Lincoln.
Gifts.
My World.
New Patriotism, A.
Soul of Lincoln, The.
Thanksliving.
PIGOTT, MOSTYN T. Hundred Best Books, The.
PIKE, ALBERT. Buena Vista.
Dixie.
Song of the Navajo.
To the Mocking-Bird.
Widowed Heart, The.
PIKE, CECILY E. Jack Frost.
PIKERYNG, JOHN. *See* PICKERING, JOHN.
PILCHER, CHARLES VENN. Teachers, The.
"PILIBIN [*or* PHILIBIN], AN" (John Hackett Pollock). Cairn Builders.
Retrospect
PILKINGTON, FRANCIS. O Softly Singing Lute.
PILKINGTON, LAETITIA. Written by the Authoress on Her Death Bed.
PILLSBURY, STANLEY. Shepherdess of the Shell, The.
PIMENTEL CORONEL, RAMÓN. Jesus.
PINCH, ESTHER. City Nature.
Friction.
PINCKNEY, JOSEPHINE. Escape at Moonrise.
In the Barn.
Lonesome Grabeya'ad.
Misses Poar Drive to Church, The.
Peggy Considers Her Grandmothers.
Phyllis and the Philosopher.
Sea-drinking Cities.
Street Cries.
PINDAR. Achilles. *Fr.* Isthmian Odes.
Aetna. *Fr.* Pythian Odes.
After-Life.
Argonauts, The. *Fr.* Pythian Odes.
Asclepius. *Fr.* Pythian Odes.
Athens.
Before the Laureate's Day. *Fr.* Isthmian Odes.
Bellerophon. *Fr.* Olympian Odes.
Bride to the Victor, A. *Fr.* Olympian Odes.
Castor and Polydeuces. *Fr.* Nemean Odes.
Childhood of Achilles, The. *Fr.* Nemean Odes.
Coming of Jason to Iolcus, The. *Fr.* Pythian Odes.
Content at Home.
Cyrene. *Fr.* Pythian Odes.
Delos.
Eclipse, An.
Elysium.
Evadne. *Fr.* Olympian Odes.
Evadne and Her Son. *Fr.* Olympian Odes.
First Olympionique: To Hiero of Syracuse. *Fr.* Olympian Odes.
First Pythian Ode.
For Arkesilas of Kyrene. *Fr.* Pythian Odes.
For Asopichus of Orchomenus. *Fr.* Olympian Odes.
For Hiero [*or* Hieron], Tyrant of Syracuse. *Fr.* Olympian Odes.
For Theron, Tyrant of Akragas. *Fr.* Olympian Odes.
Fortune's Tides. *Fr.* Olympian Odes.
God and Man. *Fr.* Nemean Odes.
Great Heart. *Fr.* Pythian Odes.
Hearken! O Eileithyia. *Fr.* Nemean Odes.
Human Life. *Fr.* Pythian Odes.
Hyperboreans, The. *Fr.* Pythian Odes.
In Praise of Delos.
Infant Heracles, The. *Fr.* Nemean Odes.
Island of the Blest, The. *Fr.* Olympian Odes.
Isthmian Odes, *sels.*
Jason's Father Sees His Returning Son. *Fr.* Pythian Odes.
Life after Death.
Lord of Nature.
Magic of Melody, The. *Fr.* Pythian Odes.
Marriage of Thetis, The. *Fr.* Isthmian Odes.
Mercenary Muse, The. *Fr.* Isthmian Odes.
Moderation. *Fr.* Nemean Odes.
Mortality. *Fr.* Nemean Odes.
Music's Anodyne. *Fr.* Nemean Odes.
Nemean Odes, *sels.*
O Golden Lyre! *Fr.* Pythian Odes.
Odes, *sels.*
Of Gods and Men. *Fr.* Nemean Odes.
Olympian Odes, *sels.*
Only a Dream-Shadow. *Fr.* Pythian Odes.
Orestes. *Fr.* Pythian Odes.
Pathless Briars. *Fr.* Olympian Odes.
Pelops. *Fr.* Olympian Odes.
Poet's Power, The. *Fr.* Isthmian Odes.
Poet's Praise, The. *Fr.* Nemean Odes.
Power of Custom, The.
Power of Music, The. *Fr.* Pythian Odes.
Prize, The. *Fr.* Pythian Odes.
Pythian Odes, *sels.*
Quest of the Golden Fleece, The. *Fr.* Pythian Odes.
Sons of Aeacus, The. *Fr.* Isthmian Odes.
Soul, The.
Spring.
Strepsiades of Thebes. *Fr.* Isthmian Odes.
Tale of the Golden Fleece, The. *Fr.* Pythian Odes.
Taming of Pegasus, The. *Fr.* Olympian Odes.
Theoxenus.
Thrasybulus.
To a Nation's Hero. *Fr.* Isthmian Odes.
To Athens.
To Goddess Luck. *Fr.* Olympian Odes.
Twin Brothers. *Fr.* Nemean Odes.
Wooing of Cyrene, The. *Fr.* Pythian Odes.
"PINDAR, PETER" (John Wolcot). Actor, An.
Apple Dumplings and a King.
Bozzy and Piozzi, *sel.*
Introduction and Anecdotes. *Fr.* Bozzy and Piozzi.
Lines on Dr. Johnson.
Ode: "Astronomers should treat of stars and comets."
Ode, An, to Eight Cats Belonging to Israel Mendez, a Jew.
Pilgrims and the Peas, The.
Razor Seller, The.
Royal Tour, The.
Sleep.
To a Fly.
To a Kiss.
To Chloe.
Tray's Epitaph.
PINEO, J. FRANKLIN. Except Ye Repent.
"PINK." Groaning Board, The.
PINKERTON, H. A. (Mrs. Wesley Trimpi). Degrees of Shade.
Deprivation.
Error Pursued.
Prism, The.
PINKERTON, HELEN. Dido, on the Departure of Aeneas.
Filia Patri.
Green Growing Bush.
Subjectivity.
Two Sonnets; to a Spiritual Entity.
Visible and Invisible.
PINKNEY, DOROTHY COWLES. Dame Liberty Reports from Travel.
PINKNEY, EDWARD COOTE [*or* COATE].
Elysium.
Evergreens.
Health, A.
Melancholy's Curse of Feasts.
On Parting.
Self-Esteem.
Serenade, A: "Look out upon the stars, my love."
Song: "Day departs this upper air."
Song: "We break the glass, whose sacred wine."
Votive Song.
Voyager's Song, The.
Widow's Song, The.
PINTO, VIVIAN DE SOLA. *For translations from Russian, see* BoR; BoRS; LiTW.
PIOZZI, HESTER THRALE. *See* THRALE, HESTER.
PIPER, EDWIN FORD. Bindlestiff.
Church, The.
Gee-up Dar, Mules.
Have You an Eye?
Last Antelope, The.
Prairie Schooner, The.
Six Yoke.
Sweetgrass Range.
PISAN, CHRISTINE DE. If Frequently to Mass.
Rondel: "If I'm at church these days."
PISE, CHARLES CONSTANTINE. American Flag, The.
PITT, CHARLES. Bandit's Grave, The.
PITT, MARIE ELIZABETH JOSEPHINE. Hamilton.
PITT, WILLIAM. Sailor's Consolation, The.
PITTER, RUTH. Bat, The.
Beautiful Negress, The.
Burning the Bee-Tree.
But for Lust.
Coffin-Worm, The.
Come Out of the Lily.
Dear Perfection.
Digdog.
Dun-Colour.
Early Rising, *sel.*
End of Fear, The.
Estuary, The.
Eternal Image, The.

For Sleep or Death.
Help, Good Shepherd.
Hut, The.
If You Came.
Kitten's Eclogue, The.
Matron Cat's Song, The.
Military Harpist, The.
Missal, The.
1938.
O Come Out of the Lily.
Of Silence and the Air.
Paradox, The.
Quorum Porum.
Rainy Summer.
Safety-Valve, The.
Solemn Meditation, A.
Spirit Watches, The.
Stockdove, The.
Strawberry Plant, The.
Swan Bathing, The.
Tall Fruit Trees, The.
Task, The.
Tigress, The.
Time's Fool.
To J. S. Collis.
Train Will Fight to the Pass, The.
Unicorn, The.
Urania.
Viper, The.
Weeping Water.
PITTS, WILLIAM S. Little Brown Church in the Vale, The.
PIXLEY, J. H. Katie Lee and Willie Grey, *at.*
"PLÁCIDO" (Gabriel de la Concepción Valdés). Farewell to My Mother.
Plácido's Sonnet [*or* Farewell] to His Mother.
Prayer to God.
PLANCHÉ, JAMES ROBINSON. Dreadful Story about Harriet and the Matches, The, *tr., at.*
Literary Squabble, A.
Sea-Serpent, The.
Self-evident.
Shock-headed Peter, *tr., at.*
Song: "Three score and ten by common calculation."
Story of Augustus Who Would Not Have Any Soup, The, *tr., at.*
Story of Cruel Frederick, The, *tr., at.*
Story of Fidgety Philip, The, *tr., at.*
Story of Flying Robert, The, *tr., at.*
Story of Johnny Head-in-Air, The, *tr., at.*
Story of Little Suck-a-Thumb, The, *tr., at.*
Story of the Inky Boys, The, *tr., at.*
Story of the Man That Went Out Shooting, The, *tr., at.*
To Mollidusta.
PLANTZ, MYRA GOODWIN. Answered Prayer.
PLARR, VICTOR. Ad Cinerarium.
Che Sara Sara.
Epitaphium Citharistriae.
Stand Not Uttering Sedately.
PLASS, WILLIAM H. Sleep, My Little 'Simmin-colored Coon.
PLATEN [*or* PLATEN-HALLERMUND], AUGUST, GRAF VON. At Least to Be at Peace.
Fain Would I Live in Safest Freedom.
Forfairn's My Hert.
Grave in the Busento, The.
I Roused, Started Up, in the Night.
Love Is My Betrayer.
New Shoots Scatter Their Scent Far Away, The.
Pilgrim at St. Yuste, The.
Pilgrim before St. Just, The.
Sigh in Winter, A.
Time and Space, Torment.
To a Woodbine Tendril.
To Jean Paul.
Tristan.
Truest of Sages Are You to Me.
Venetian Sonnets, *sels.*
Whitely the Lily Wavers.
Who Has Ever Held Life in His Hand.
PLATH, SYLVIA. Hardcastle Crags.
Two Views of a Cadaver Room.
PLATO. Aster ("Thou gazest on the stars").
Aster ("Thou wert the morning-star among the living").
Country Gods.
Country Music.
Dedication of a Mirror.
Dedication to Aphrodite.
Dion of Syracuse.
Ecstasy.
Eretrian Dead, The.
Farewell: "Far from the roar of the Aegean main."
Farewell, A: "Venus take my votive glass."
Farmer and Sailor.
For Priam's queen and daughters at their birth.
Goodbye to the Aegean.
Graces, seeking for a shrine, The.
Irony, An.
Lady Who Offers Her Looking-Glass to Venus, The.
Lais' Mirror.
Lais of the haughty smile.
Love Lies Sleeping.
Love Sleeping.
Lover to His Lady, The, *at.*
Love's Apple.
Morning and Evening Star.
My Star.
On a Seal.
On Alexis.
On Archaeanassa.
On Aristophanes.
On Praxiteles' Statue of Aphrodite at Cnidus.
One to All Men.
Pan's Piping.
"Passing the Love of Women."
"Quand Vous Serez Bien Vieille."
Seaman's Tomb, A.
Star.
Take Thought.
Thou wert the morning star among the living.
Time the Changer.
To Aristophanes.
To Aster.
To Stella.
To the Eretrian Dead.
Young Astronomer, The.
Young Astronomer Dead, The.
PLATT, ANNA M. Crocuses.
PLAUTUS (Titus Maccius Plautus). Amphitryon, *sel.*
Asinaria, *sel.*
Casina, *sel.*
Curculio, *sels.*
Mercator, *sel.*
Miles Gloriosus, *sels.*
Mostellaria, *sel.*
Truculentus, *sel.*
Vertue. *Fr.* Amphitryon.
PLAYFORD, JOHN. Jovial Marriner, The; or, The Sea-Man's Renown.
PLEW, MILDRED. *See* MEIGS, MILDRED PLEW.
PLIMPTON, FLORUS B. Fort Duquesne.
PLIMPTON, HARRIET. Hudson, The.
PLOMER, WILLIAM. Archaic Apollo.
Boer War, The.
Caledonian Market, The.
Death of a Zulu, The.
Devil-Dancers, The.
Explorer, The.
French Lisette.
Headline History.
Johannesburg.
Levantine, A.
Mews Flat Mona.
Namaqualand after Rain.
Pioneers, The; or, Twenty Years After.
Playboy of the Demi-World, The; 1938.
Prisoner, The.
Ruined Farm, The.
Scorpion, The.
September Evening, 1938.
Tattooed.
Transvaal Morning, A.
Traveller's Tale, A.
Victoria Falls, The.
PLOTINUS. We Are Not Cast Away.
PLOUG, PARMO CARL. Unity of the North, The.
PLOWMAN, MAX. Her Beauty.
PLUMB, BEATRICE. Peace.
PLUMMER, MARY E. Pussy Willows.
PLUMMER, MARY WRIGHT. Irrevocable.
PLUMPTRE, EDWARD HAYES. Antigone, *sels., tr.*
Earliest Christian Hymn, *tr.*
Hymn to Christ the Saviour, *tr.*
Hymn to Zeus, *tr.*
Rejoice, ye pure in heart!
PLUNKETT, EDWARD JOHN MORETON DRAX. *See* DUNSANY.
PLUNKETT, JOSEPH MARY. Claim That Has the Canker on the Rose, The.
Dark Way, The.
Epitome.
I See His Blood upon the Rose.
My Lady Has the Grace of Death.
O Sower of Sorrow.
Our Heritage.
Poppies.
See the Crocus' Golden Cup.
"Sic Transit."
Spark, The.
Stars Sang in God's Garden, The.
This Heritage to the Race of Kings.
To G. K. Chesterton.
Wave of the Sea, A.
White Dove of the Wild Dark Eyes.
PLUNKETT, PATRICK MARY. Vale.
PLUTZIK, HYAM. Argumentum ad Hominem.
Begetting of Cain, The.
Divisibility.
Equation, An.
Exhortation to the Artists.
Faustus. *Fr.* Horatio.
For T. S. E. Only.
He Inspects His Armory.
Horatio, *sels.*
Identity.
Mr. Pollington Remembers a Poet.
My Sister.
On the Photograph of a Man I Never Saw.
Ostler, The. *Fr.* Horatio.
Portrait.
Road, The.
PO CHÜ-I. After Collecting the Autumn Taxes.
After Getting Drunk Becoming Sober in the Night.
After Lunch.
After Passing the Examination.
Alarm at First Entering the Yang-tze Gorges.
Almond Blossoms of Chao Village, The.
Arriving at Hsün-yang.
At I-ye Temple.
At the End of Spring.
Beginning of Summer, The.
Being on Duty All Night in the Palace and Dreaming of Hsien-yu Temple.
Being Visited by a Friend during Illness.
Big Rug, The.
Buying Flowers.
Captives from the Western Tribes.
Chancellor's Gravel-Drive, The.
Charcoal-Burner, The.
Charcoal-Seller, The.
Children.
Chrysanthemums in the Eastern Garden, The.
Chuang-tzu, the Monist. *Fr.* The Philosophers.
Chu-ch'en Village.
Climbing the Ling Ying Terrace and Looking North.
Climbing the Terrace of Kuan-yin and Looking at the City.
Cranes, The.
Dragon of the Black Pool, The.
Dream of Mountaineering, A.
Dreaming of Yüan Chen.
Dreaming That I Went with Lu and Yu to Visit Yüan Chen.
Drunk Again.
Early Levée, An.
Ease.
Eating Bamboo-Shoots.

Po Chü-i (*continued*)
Escorting Candidates to the Examination Hall.
Everlasting Sorrow, The.
Farewell in Secret.
Fifteenth Volume, The.
Fishing in the Wei River.
Flower, A?
Flower Market, The.
Forsaken Garden, A.
Getting Up Early on a Spring Morning.
Going Alone to Spend a Night at the Hsien-yu Temple.
Going to the Mountains with a Little Dancing Girl, Aged Fifteen.
Golden Bells.
Good-bye to the People of Hang-chow.
Grain-Tribute, The.
Grand Houses at Lo-yang, The.
Grass.
Harp, The.
Harper of Chao, The.
Hat Given to the Poet by Li Chien, The.
Having Climbed to the Topmost Peak of the Incense-Burner Mountain.
Hearing the Early Oriole.
Heart in Autumn, The.
Heavy Taxes.
I Look Down.
Illness ("Dear friends, there is no cause for so much sympathy").
Illness ("Sad, sad—lean with long illness").
Illness and Idleness.
In Early Summer Lodging in a Temple to Enjoy the Moonlight.
Invitation to Hsiao Chü-shih.
Kept Waiting in the Boat at Chiu-k'ou Ten Days by an Adverse Wind.
Lament for My Son Ts'ui, A.
Lao-tzu.
Last Poem.
Lazy Man's Song.
Letter, The.
Lodging with the Old Man of the Stream.
Lonely Night in Early Autumn.
Looking in the Lake.
Losing a Slave Girl.
Lung Men Temple.
Mad Poem Addressed to My Nephews and Nieces, A.
Madly Singing in the Mountains.
Magic.
Man Who Dreamed of Fairies, The.
Mirror, The.
Mourning for Li San.
My Servant Wakes Me.
Myself.
Night on the West River.
North Garden, The.
Old Age.
Old Harp, The.
Old Man with the Broken Arm, The.
On a Box Containing His Own Works.
On an Ancient Tomb East of the Village.
On Being Removed from Hsün-yang and Sent to Chung-chou.
On Being Sixty.
On Being Stricken with Paralysis.
On Board Ship; Reading Yüan Chen's Poems.
On Hearing Someone Sing a Poem by Yüan Chen.
On His Baldness.
On the Fasting Monk Chu Chuan.
On the Tower Overlooking the River.
On the Way to Hang-chow; Anchored on the River at Night.
Parting from the Winter Stove.
Passing T'ien-men Street in Ch'ang-an and Seeing a Distant View of Chung-nan Mountain.
People of Tao-chou, The.
Philosophers, The.
Pine-Trees in the Courtyard, The.
Planting a Lichi Tree.
Planting Bamboos.
Planting Flowers on the Embankment.
Po Chü-i to Yüan Chen.
Poem on the Wall, The.
Poems in Depression, at Wei Village.
Politician, The.
Prisoner, The.
Pruning Trees.
Rain.
Red Cockatoo, The.
Rejoicing at the Arrival of Ch'en Hsiung.
Releasing a Migrant "Yen" (Wild Goose).
Remembering Golden Bells.
Resignation.
Sand and the Waves, The.
Sauntering through Chao Village at Apricot-blossoming Time.
Seeing Hsia Chan Off by River.
Separation.
Sick Leave.
Silver Spoon, The.
Since I Lay Ill.
Sitting at Night.
Sleeping Alone at the Hsien-yu Temple.
Sleeping on Horseback.
Song of Past Feelings.
Song of the Palace, A.
Song of the Pines.
Spring River, The.
Starting Early from the Ch'u-ch'eng Inn.
Stopping the Night at Jung-yang.
Taoism and Buddhism.
Temple, The.
Thinking of the Past.
To a Portrait Painter Who Desired Him to Sit.
To a Talkative Guest.
To His Brother Hsing-chien.
To Li Chien.
To My Brothers and Sisters Adrift in Troubled Times This Poem of the Moon.
To the Distant One.
Two Red Towers, The.
Visiting the Hermit Cheng.
Visiting the Hsi-lin Temple.
Watching the Reapers.
Whither?
Willow by the River, The.
Winter Night.
Woodpeckers' Song.
Written when Governor of Soochow.

Pocock, Isaac. Heir of Vironi, The, *sel.*
Song: "Oh! say not woman's love is bought." *Fr.* The Heir of Vironi.

Poe, Edgar Allan. Al Aaraaf.
Al Aaraaf, *sels.*
Alone.
Annabel Lee.
Assignation, The, *sel.*
Bells, The.
Bells, The, *sel.*
Bridal Ballad.
City in the Sea, The.
Coliseum, The.
Conqueror Worm, The. *Fr.* Ligeia.
Doomed City, The.
Dream, A.
Dream-Land.
Dream within a Dream, A.
Dream within a Dream, A, *sel.*
Dreams.
Eldorado.
Eulalie; a Song.
Evening Star.
Fairy-Land.
Fall of the House of Usher, The, *sel.*
For Annie.
From Childhood's Hour.
Happiest Day [the Happiest Hour], The.
Haunted Palace, The. *Fr.* The Fall of the House of Usher.
Helen thy beauty is to me.
Hymn: "At morn, at noon, at twilight dim."
Hymn of the Angelus.
Israfel.
Lake, The: To ——.
Lenore.
Ligeia ("Ligeia! Ligeia!"), *poem. Fr.* Al Aaraaf.
Ligeia, *pr. tale, sel.*
'Neath Blue-Bell or Streamer. *Fr.* Al Aaraaf.
Raven, The.
Romance.
Simple Duty, A.
Sleeper, The.
Sleeper, The, *sel.*
Song: "Neath blue-bell or streamer." *Fr.* Al Aaraaf.
Song: "Spirit! that dwellest where." *Fr.* Al Aaraaf.
Song from "Al Aaraaf."
Song of Nesace. *Fr.* Al Aaraaf.
Sonnet to My Mother.
Sonnet to Science. *Fr.* Al Aaraaf.
Sonnet to Zante.
Spirits of the Dead.
Tamerlane.
Tamerlane, *sel.*
To ——: "Bowers whereat, in dreams, I see, The."
To ——: "I heed not that my earthly lot."
To ——: "I saw thee on thy bridal day."
To ——: "Take this kiss upon thy brow!"
To F——.
To Frances S. Osgood.
To Helen ("Helen, thy beauty is to me").
To Helen ("I saw thee once—once only—years ago").
To My Mother.
To One in Paradise. *Fr.* The Assignation.
To Science. *Fr.* Al Aaraaf.
Triumphal Song of the Roman Army, *tr.*
Ulalume.
Valley of Unrest, The.

Poitiers, Guillaume de. *See* Guillaume de Poitiers.

Pokagon, Chief Simon. Hazeleye's Lullaby.

Pol, Wincenty. Song of the Mound.

Poletayev, Nikolai Gavrilovich. Red Square, The.

Politian. *See* Poliziano, Angelo.

Politzer, Heinz. My Language.

Poliziano [*or* Politian], Angelo.
Ballata: "Welcome to May."
Ballata of Myrrha's Eyes.
Dance Song.
Dulce Mihi Quondam Studium Fuit.
Ecce Autem Dulces Labris Pater Ingerit Uvas.
Epitaph for Giotto, the Painter.
Giostra, La, *sel.*
He who knows not what thing is Paradise. *Fr.* Three Ballate.
I found myself one day all, all alone. *Fr.* Three Ballate.
I went a roaming, maidens, one bright day. *Fr.* Three Ballate.
Orfeo, *sel.*
Protinus Extremo cum Jam Boreas Autumno.
Rispetto: "Eyes that without a tongue can speak to me."
Rispetto: "I ask no other vengeance, Love, from you."
Rispetto: "This little girl's so gay and fidgety."
Rispetto: "When, these eyes closed in death, you look on me."
Ruris Opes Saturi, Gnavoque Agitanda Colono.
Sacrifice of the Bacchantes in Honor of Bacchus. *Fr.* Orfeo.
Simonetta. *Fr.* La Giostra.
Three Ballate.

Pollard, Josephine. Demon on the Roof, The.
Strange Experience, A.

Pollard, Lancaster. April's Coming.
Clouds and Sky.
Denial.
Morning Song.

Pollock, Edward. Olivia.

Pollock, Sir Frederick. Six Carpenters' Case, The.

Pollock, John Hackett. *See* "Pilibin, An."

POLLOCK, THOMAS B. Father, into Thy Hands.
POLLOCK, WALTER HERRIES. Below the Heights.
Conquest, A.
Father Francis.
POLLOK, ROBERT. Byron. *Fr.* The Course of Time.
Course of Time, The, *sels.*
Ocean. *Fr.* The Course of Time.
POLONSKY, YAKOV PETROVICH. Blind Preacher, The.
Cosmic Fabric, The.
Swan, The.
POLYAENUS, JULIUS. Deceitful Hope.
Prayer for Home-Coming.
Wanderer, The.
POMBO, RAFAEL. Our Madonna at Home.
To Bolivar.
POMEROY, EDWARD NOYES. Today and Tomorrow.
POMFRET, JOHN. Choice, The.
Choice, The, *sel.*
POMPEIUS. "In Fields Where Roses Fade."
Mycenae.
Mycenae Fallen.
PONCIANO, ANGELO DE. Empties Coming Back.
PONSONBY, A. B. Boy's Prayer.
PONTALAIS, JEHAN DU. Money.
PONTANO, GIOVANNI. Fannia.
PONTING, HERBERT GEORGE. Sleeping-Bag, The.
POOLE, LOUELLA C. Betsey Trotwood's Cat.
Black Friday.
Charles Dickens.
Cricket Singing in the Market-Place.
Metempsychosis.
Parlor Cat, A.
Welcome Home.
POORE, DUDLEY. Bird, The, *tr.*
Brazil, *tr.*
For other translations from Portuguese, see AnCL.
POPE, ALEXANDER. Addison. *Fr.* Epistle to Dr. Arbuthnot.
After the Chariot-Race. *Fr.* The Iliad.
Alps of Poetry, The. *Fr.* An Essay on Criticism.
Alps on Alps. *Fr.* An Essay on Criticism.
Arete; Portrait of a High-born Matron, *tr.* *Fr.* The Odyssey.
Art of Writing, The. *Fr.* An Essay on Criticism.
As the Twig Is Bent. *Fr.* Moral Essays.
Atticus. *Fr.* Epistle to Dr. Arbuthnot.
Author's Miseries, The. *Fr.* Epistle to Dr. Arbuthnot.
Away from London. *Fr.* An Epistle to Martha Blount on Her Leaving Town after the Coronation.
Balance of Europe, The.
Battle of the Curetes and Aetolians, *tr.* *Fr.* The Iliad.
Behold the Child. *Fr.* An Essay on Man.
Belinda. *Fr.* The Rape of the Lock.
Belinda's Morning. *Fr.* The Rape of the Lock.
Bufo. *Fr.* Epistle to Dr. Arbuthnot.
Challenge, The.
Chaos. *Fr.* The Dunciad.
Chaos on Her Throne, or the Triumph of Dullness. *Fr.* The Dunciad.
Characters from the Satires: Atticus. *Fr.* Epistle to Dr. Arbuthnot.
Characters from the Satires: Chloe. *Fr.* Moral Essays.
Characters from the Satires: Sporus. *Fr.* Epistle to Dr. Arbuthnot.
Characters from the Satires: Wharton. *Fr.* Moral Essays.
Charity. *Fr.* An Essay on Man.
Chloe. *Fr.* Moral Essays.
Compliments. *Fr.* Epistle to Dr. Arbuthnot.
Conclusion: "In vain, in vain—the all-composing hour." *Fr.* The Dunciad.
Contented Man, The.
Court of Charles II, The. *Fr.* To Augustus.
Coxcomb Bird, The. *Fr.* Moral Essays.
Craft of Verse, The. *Fr.* An Essay on Criticism.
Dead Is Patroclus, *tr.* *Fr.* The Iliad.
Death of Buckingham, The. *Fr.* Moral Essays.
Death of Gorgythian, The, *tr.* *Fr.* The Iliad.
Death of the Duke of Buckingham, The. *Fr.* Moral Essays.
Descend, ye Nine. *Fr.* Ode for Music on St. Cecilia's Day.
Dire Dilemma, A. *Fr.* Epistle to Dr. Arbuthnot.
Dogs.
Domicile of John, The.
Duke of Buckingham, The. *Fr.* Moral Essays.
Dull, Sullen Prisoners. *Fr.* Elegy to the Memory of an Unfortunate Lady.
Dunciad, The, *sels.*
Dying Christian to His Soul, The.
Ease in Writing. *Fr.* An Essay on Criticism.
Elegy to the Memory of an Unfortunate Lady.
Elegy to the Memory of an Unfortunate Lady, *sels.*
Eloisa. *Fr.* Eloisa to Abelard.
Eloisa to Abelard.
Eloisa to Abelard, *sels.*
Eloisa's Prayer for Abelard. *Fr.* Eloisa to Abelard.
Engraved on the Collar of a Dog, Which I Gave to His Royal Highness.
Epigram: "I am his Highness' dog at Kew."
Epigram: "Should D——s print, how once you robb'd your brother."
Epigram: "Sir, I admit your general rule."
Epigram: "When other Ladies to the Shades go down."
Epigram: "You beat your pate."
Epigram Engraved on the Collar of a Dog.
Epigram on the Toasts of the Kit-Kat Club, Anno 1716.
Epilogue to the Satires, *sels.*
Epistle to a Young Lady on Her Leaving the Town after the Coronation.
Epistle to Burlington, *sel.*
Epistle to Dr. Arbuthnot.
Epistle to Dr. Arbuthnot, *sels.*
Epistle to [Miss *or* Mrs.] Martha Blount on Her Leaving Town after the Coronation.
Epistle to [Miss *or* Mrs.] Martha Blount on Her Leaving Town after the Coronation, *sel.*
Epistle to Miss Blount.
Epistle to Mrs. Blount, with the Works of Voiture.
Epitaph: "Nature and Nature's laws lay hid in night."
Epitaph: "Of manners gentle."
Epitaph Intended for Sir Isaac Newton.
Epitaph on Mrs. Corbet, Who Dyed of a Cancer in Her Breast.
Epitaph on [Sir Isaac] Newton.
Essay on Criticism, An.
Essay on Criticism, An, *sels.*
Essay on Man, An.
Essay on Man, An, *sels.*
Evening in the Capital. *Fr.* The Rape of the Lock.
Faith. *Fr.* An Essay on Man.
Fame. *Fr.* An Essay on Man.
Farewell to London in the Year 1715.
Field Sports. *Fr.* Windsor Forest.
Finality. *Fr.* The Dunciad.
First Epistle of the First Book of Horace Imitated, The, *sel.*
First Epistle of the Second Book of Horace, The.
First Epistle of the Second Book of Horace, The, *sels.*
First Satire of the Second Book of Horace Imitated, The, *sel.*
Flames of Death, The. *Fr.* Windsor Forest.
Fool and the Poet, The.
For One Who Would Not Be Buried in Westminster Abbey.
Fragment, A: "What are the falling rills, the pendent shades."
Fragments from "Essay on Man."
Fufidia (Lady Mary Wortley Montagu). *Fr.* Sober Advice from Horace to the Young Gentlemen about Town.
Future, The. *Fr.* An Essay on Man.
Gem and the Flower, The. *Fr.* Moral Essays.
Glitter. *Fr.* Windsor Forest.
Great Chain of Being, The. *Fr.* An Essay on Man.
Greatness. *Fr.* An Essay on Man.
Happiness. *Fr.* An Essay on Man.
Happy the Man.
Has Life No Sourness? *Fr.* The Second Epistle of the Second Book of Horace.
Heaven's Last Best Work. *Fr.* Moral Essays.
Hector and Andromache, *tr.* *Fr.* The Iliad.
Heights of Arts, The. *Fr.* An Essay on Criticism.
Henry St. John, Viscount Bolingbroke. *Fr.* An Essay on Man.
Homer. *Fr.* An Essay on Criticism.
Homeric Moonlight, A, *tr.* *Fr.* The Iliad.
Homer's Iliad, *sels., tr.*
Honest Fame. *Fr.* The Temple of Fame.
Honest Man, An. *Fr.* An Essay on Man.
Hope ("Hope springs eternal"). *Fr.* An Essay on Man.
Hope Springs Eternal ("Heav'n from all creatures"). *Fr.* An Essay on Man.
Human Folly. *Fr.* An Essay on Man.
Hymn: "Rise, crowned with light, imperial Salem, rise!"
I am His Highness' dog at Kew.
Ideals of Satire, The. *Fr.* First Epistle of the Second Book of Horace.
Iliad, The, *sels., tr.*
Imitation of the Sixth Satire of the Second Book of Horace, An, *sel.*
Immortality of Verse, The.
In Defence of Satire. *Fr.* Epilogue to the Satires.
Inscribed on the Collar of a Dog.
Insects from the Nile. *Fr.* An Essay on Criticism.
Intended for Sir Isaac Newton.
Know Then Thyself [*or* Thy-Self]. *Fr.* An Essay on Man.
Know Thyself. *Fr.* An Essay on Man.
Last Lines of the Dunciad. *Fr.* The Dunciad.
Life's Poor Play. *Fr.* An Essay on Man.
Lines by a Person of Quality, *at.*
Literary Poet to his Patron, A. *Fr.* An Essay on Man.
Little Learning [Is a Dangerous Thing], A. *Fr.* An Essay on Criticism.
Lo, the Poor Indian! *Fr.* An Essay on Man.
Lord Hervey. *Fr.* Epistle to Dr. Arbuthnot.
Love Song, A, *at.*
Man. *Fr.* An Essay on Man.
Man of Ross, The. *Fr.* Moral Essays.
Messiah.
Messiah, *sel.*
Mob, The. *Fr.* The First Satire of the Second Book of Horace Imitated.
Moral Essays, *sels.*
Name No Names. *Fr.* Epilogue to the Satires.
Nature and Nature's laws lay hid in night.
Nature's Chain. *Fr.* An Essay on Man.
Newton and Himself. *Fr.* An Essay on Man.

POPE, ALEXANDER (*continued*)
Nun's Lot, The. *Fr.* Eloisa to Abelard.
Ode: Dying Christian to His Soul, The.
Ode for Music on St. Cecilia's Day.
Ode for Music on St. Cecilia's Day, *sel.*
Ode on [*or* to] Solitude.
Ode to Quinbus Flestrin.
Odes (*of* Horace), *sel.*, *tr.*
Odyssey, The, *sels.*, *tr.*
Of the Characters of Women. *Fr.* Moral Essays.
Of the Characters of Women, *sel.* *Fr.* Moral Essays.
Of the Use of Riches. *Fr.* Moral Essays.
Ombre at Hampton Court. *Fr.* The Rape of the Lock.
On a Certain Lady at Court.
On Mr. Gay; in Westminster Abbey, 1732.
On Mrs. Corbet.
On One Who Made Long Epitaphs.
On the Collar of a Dog [Presented by Mr. Pope to the Prince of Wales].
On the Hon. Simon Harcourt.
One Thousand Seven Hundred and Thirty-eight.
Palace of Alcinous, The, *tr.* *Fr.* The Odyssey.
Paragon of Animals, The. *Fr.* An Essay on Man.
Paraphrase on Thomas à Kempis, A.
Paraphrase on Thomas à Kempis, A, *sel.*
Pastorals, *sel.*
Pedigree. *Fr.* An Essay on Man.
Pheasant, The. *Fr.* Windsor Forest.
Playing Cards, The. *Fr.* The Rape of the Lock.
Pleasure of Hope, The. *Fr.* An Essay on Man.
Poetical Numbers. *Fr.* An Essay on Criticism.
Poet's Friend, The. *Fr.* An Essay on Man.
Poet's Use, The. *Fr.* To Augustus.
Pope on Dryden. *Fr.* The First Epistle of the Second Book of Horace.
Portrait of Atticus. *Fr.* Epistle to Dr. Arbuthnot.
Prayer of St. Francis Xavier.
Preparation of the Pyre for Patroclus, *tr.* *Fr.* The Iliad.
Priam and Achilles, *tr.* *Fr.* The Iliad.
Prologue: Homer Addresses the Muse of Poetry, *tr.* *Fr.* The Iliad.
Prologue to Mr. Addison's Tragedy of Cato.
Prologue to the Satires. *Fr.* Epistle to Dr. Arbuthnot.
Proper Study of Man [*or* Mankind], The. *Fr.* An Essay on Man.
Provocation to Satire. *Fr.* Epilogue to the Satires.
Pyre of Patroclus, The, *tr.* *Fr.* The Iliad.
Quiet Life, The.
Quotations from Pope.
Rape of the Lock, The.
Rape of the Lock, The, *sels.*
Reason and Instinct. *Fr.* An Essay on Man.
Reign of Chaos, The. *Fr.* The Dunciad.
Reverend Sire, A. *Fr.* Moral Essays.
Riddle of the World. *Fr.* An Essay on Man.
Rise, Crowned with Light. *Fr.* The Messiah.
Ruling Passion, The. *Fr.* Moral Essays.
Satire: "Ask you what provocation I have had?" *Fr.* Epilogue to the Satires.
Satire: "Yes; thank my stars! as early as I knew." *Fr.* The Satires of Dr. John Donne, Versified.
Satire on Riches. *Fr.* Moral Essays.
Satires. *Fr.* Epistle to Dr. Arbuthnot.
Satires of Dr. John Donne, Versified, The, *sel.*
Scale of Being, The. *Fr.* An Essay on Man.
Scandal. *Fr.* Epistle to Dr. Arbuthnot.
Science.
Second Duke of Buckingham, The. *Fr.* Moral Essays.
Second Epistle of the Essay on Man, The.
Second Epistle of the Second Book of Horace, The, *sel.*
Shield of Achilles, The, *tr.* *Fr.* The Iliad.
Sir Balaam. *Fr.* Moral Essays.
Sir, I Admit Your General Rule, *at.*
Sirens, Scylla and Charybdis, The, *tr.* *Fr.* The Odyssey.
Sober Advice from Horace to the Young Gentlemen about Town, *sel.*
Solitude.
Song: "'Twas in this shade."
Song by a Person of Quality, *at.*
Soul's Calm Sunshine, The. *Fr.* An Essay on Man.
Sound and Sense. *Fr.* An Essay on Criticism.
Sporus. *Fr.* Epistle to Dr. Arbuthnot.
Strife, War's Sister Urges on the Host, *tr.* *Fr.* The Iliad.
Summer. *Fr.* Pastorals.
Teach me to feel. *Fr.* The Universal Prayer.
Temple of Fame, The, *sel.*
Ten Per Cent; Then as Now. *Fr.* The First Epistle of the First Book of Horace Imitated.
Thick as the Bees. *Fr.* The Temple of Fame.
Timon's Villa. *Fr.* Moral Essays.
To a Blockhead.
To a Lady; of the Characters of Women. *Fr.* Moral Essays.
To a Young Lady.
To a Young Lady on Her Leaving the Town after the Coronation.
To Augustus.
To Augustus, *sels.*
To Dr. Arbuthnot.
To James Craggs, Esq.; Secretary of State.
To Mr. Jervas, with Fresnoy's Art of Painting, Translated by Mr. Dryden.
To Mrs. M. B. on Her Birthday [*or* Birth-Day].
To Robert Earl of Oxford, and Earl Mortimer.
Toilet, The. *Fr.* The Rape of the Lock.
Treatment for Old Jades and Janes, The. *Fr.* An Essay on Criticism.
Triumph of Dulness, The. *Fr.* The Dunciad.
Triumph of Ignorance, The. *Fr.* The Dunciad.
True Worth. *Fr.* An Essay on Man.
Two Mice, The. *Fr.* An Imitation of the Sixth Satire of the Second Book of Horace.
Ulysses and His Dog, *tr.* *Fr.* The Odyssey.
Unity of Nature. *Fr.* An Essay on Man.
Universal Prayer, The.
Universal Prayer, The, *sel.*
Verbal Critics. *Fr.* Epistle to Dr. Arbuthnot.
Verses to the Memory of an Unfortunate Lady.
Vestal, The. *Fr.* Eloisa to Abelard.
Vice. *Fr.* An Essay on Man.
Virtue and Vice. *Fr.* Epilogue to the Satires.
Vision of the Future, A.
Vital Spark of Heavenly Flame.
Wharton. *Fr.* Moral Essays.
Whatever Is, Is Right. *Fr.* An Essay on Man.
Why Did I Write? *Fr.* Epistle to Dr. Arbuthnot.
Windsor Forest, *sels.*
Woman's Ruling Passions. *Fr.* Moral Essays.
POPE, J. R. Word of Encouragement, A.
POPE, WALTER. Old Man's Wish, The.
Old Man's Wish, The, *sel.*
Wish, The.
POQUELIN, JEAN BAPTISTE. *See* MOLIÈRE.
PORDAGE, SAMUEL. To Lucia Playing on Her Lute.
PORGES, DOROTHY DIX. Tell it to God.
"PORPHYRAS, LAMBROS" (Demetrios Sypsomos). Epigram: "Here at this solitary spring."
Lacrimae Rerum.
Last Fairy-Tale, The.
Trip, The.
PORSON, RICHARD. Academic Visit to the Continent, An.
Dido.
Epigram on an Academic Visit to the Continent.
Little garden little Jowett made, A, *at.*
Note on the Latin Gerunds, A.
Nothing.
On a German Tour.
On the Latin Gerunds.
PORTER, ALAN. Dean, The.
Love's Fragility.
River, The.
Signature of Pain, The.
PORTER, ANNA MARIA. Hymn on the Seasons.
PORTER, BRUCE. Limerick: "H was an indigent hen."
PORTER, COLE. Begin the Beguine.
You're the Top.
PORTER, MRS. DAVID. Thou Hast Wounded the Spirit That Loved Thee.
PORTER, H. H. Forty Years Ago.
PORTER, HAL. Bi-focal.
Sheep, The.
PORTER, INA M. Mumford.
Pro Memoria.
PORTER, JENNY LIND. In the Beginning.
PORTER, KATHERINE ANNE. Requiescat.
PORTER, KENNETH WIGGINS. Beaver Sign.
Certainties.
Epitaph for a Man from Virginia City.
Judgment.
Not Kings.
Old Coon-Dog Dreams, The.
Old Thad Stevens.
Oration, An, *sel.* *Fr.* To the Younger Old-Americans.
Poem on a Slippery Sidewalk.
Simon and Judas.
Stone, The
Street Scene—1946.
Thistle, Yarrow, Clover.
To a Prince of the Church.
To the Younger Old-Americans, *sel.*
PORTER, SAMUEL JUDSON. Way; the Truth; the Life, The.
PORTER, THOMAS. Serenade, to Two Ladies. *Fr.* The Villain.
Villain, The, *sel.*
PORTOR, LAURA SPENCER (Mrs. Francis Pope). Christ-Child, The.
Christ Child's Christmas, The.
Gift, The.
Shepherds, The.
Windflowers and the Sage, The.
POSEIDIPPUS [*or* POSIDIPPUS]. Courtesan to Aphrodite, The.
Doricha.
For an Epicurean Club Dinner.
For Doricha the Courtesan.
Man's Life, after Posidonius or Crates, *at.*
No Way Is Good.
Sappho.
Statue by Lysippus, A.
To Philaenis.
Too Near the Waves.
Trust not to tears, Philaenis, nay.
What course of life should wretched mortals take? *at.*
With Bacchus' shower soak us all.
POST, L. F., *and* GLENN NORTON. Gila Monster Route, The.
POTAMKIN, HARRY ALAN. Cargoes of the Radanites.
POTEAT, EDWIN MCNEILL. Barabbas Speaks.

Casualty.
Eternal God Whose Searching Eye Doth Scan.
Faith.
Focus of That Face, The.
Grace at Evening.
He, Too, Loved Beauty.
If Any Man Would Come after Me.
Jericho Road, The.
Legend about Color, A.
Light of the World, How Long the Quest.
Mary Pondered All These Things.
Names.
Orisons.
Palm Sunday and Monday.
Prayer at Dawn.
Prayer for Contentment.
Stigmata.
Two Chalices.
Pothinus, Saint. Epigram on Marcus the Gnostic.
Po T'ing. Carefree.
Pott, Francis. Angel voices, ever singing.
Opening Year, The, *tr.*
Strife is o'er, the battle done, The, *tr.*
Victory, *tr.*
Potter, Ellis M. River, The.
Potter, Henry Codman. Flag, The.
Pottle, Emory. I Have a Son.
Pottle, Juliet Wilbor Tompkins. *See* Tompkins, Juliet Wilbor.
Potts, Margaret. Guenevere at Almesbury.
Potts, Paul. For My Father.
Jean.
Muse to an Unknown Poet, The.
Poulson, Harper. Strange Meeting.
Poulsson, Emilie. Baby's Breakfast.
Bed-Time Song.
Books Are Keys.
Breakfast Song, The.
Chickens in Trouble, *tr.*
Farm Voices.
First Christmas, The.
Judging by Appearances.
Lovable Child, The.
Nutting Time.
Puppy['s] Problem[s], A.
Santa Claus and the Mouse.
Story of Baby's Blanket, The.
Story of Baby's Pillow, The.
While Stars of Christmas Shine.
Pound, Ezra. Age Demanded, The ("For this agility chance found"). *Fr.* Hugh Selwyn Mauberley.
Age demanded an image, The. *Fr.* Hugh Selwyn Mauberley.
Alba Innominata, *tr.*
Alchemist, The.
Ancient Music.
Apparuit.
Au Jardin.
Ballad for Gloom.
Ballad of the Goodly Fere.
Ballata 7: "Being in thought of love I came upon," *tr.*
Ballata 5: "Light do I see within my Lady's eyes," *tr.*
Bath Tub, The.
Brennbaum. *Fr.* Hugh Selwyn Mauberley.
Canto I: "And then went down to the ship."
Canto II: "Hang it all, Robert Browning."
Canto XIII: "Kung walked/ by the dynastic temple."
Canto XIV, *sel.*
Canto XV, *sel.*
Canto XVI, *sel.*
Canto XVII: "So that the vines burst from my fingers."
Canto XX, *sel.*
Canto XXI: "Keep the peace, Borso!"
Canto XXI, *sel.*
Canto XXIX, *sel.*
Canto XLV: "With Usura/ With usura hath no man a house of good stone."
Canto XLVII: "Who even dead, yet hath his mind entire!"
Canto LXXIX, *sel.*
Canto LXXX, *sel.*
Canto LXXXI, *sels.*
Canzo of Bird-Songs and Love, *tr.*
Canzone: Lady Asks Me, A, *tr.*
Chi è questa, *tr.*
Choir Boys, The, *tr.*
Cino.
Coming of War, The; Actaeon.
Commission.
Dance Figure.
Δώρια (Doria).
E. P. Ode pour l'Election de Son Sepulchre. *Fr.* Hugh Selwyn Mauberley.
Envoi: "Go, dumb-born book." *Fr.* Hugh Selwyn Mauberley.
Envoi (1919). *Fr.* Hugh Selwyn Mauberley.
Epilogue: "O chansons foregoing."
Erat Hora.
Exile's Letter, *tr.*
Eyes, The.
Faun, The.
Flame, The.
Francesca.
Further Instructions.
Garden, The.
Garret, The
Girl, A.
Golden Sestina, The, *tr.*
Greek Epigram.
Gypsy, The.
Heimkehr, Die, *sels., tr.*
Histrion.
Homage to Sextus Propertius, *sels.*
House of Splendour, The.
Hugh Selwyn Mauberley.
Hugh Selwyn Mauberley, *sels.*
If you'd have me go on loving you. *Fr.* Impressions of François-Marie Arouet (de Voltaire).
Immorality, An.
Impressions of François-Marie Arouet (de Voltaire), *sel.*
In a Station of the Metro.
Ione, Dead the Long Year.
Ité.
Kung's Wisdom (Canto XIII).
La Fraisne.
Lake Isle, The.
Lament of the Frontier Guard, *tr.*
L'Art, 1910.
Les Millwin.
Light, Light of My Eyes, *tr.*
Lyrics. *Fr.* Hugh Selwyn Mauberley.
Mauberley [1920]. *Fr.* Hugh Selwyn Mauberley.
Me Happy, Night, Night Full of Brightness. *Fr.* Homage to Sextus Propertius.
Medallion. *Fr.* Hugh Selwyn Mauberley.
Meditatio.
Mr. Nixon. *Fr.* Hugh Selwyn Mauberley.
Moeurs Contemporaines.
Na Audiart.
Near Périgord.
Near Périgord, *sel.*
N.Y. ("My City, my beloved").
Night Litany.
Ode pour l'Election de Son Sepulchre. *Fr.* Hugh Selwyn Mauberley.
Ortus.
Pact, A.
Pagani's, November 8.
Phanopoeia, *sel.*
Phyllidula.
Piccadilly.
Piere Vidal Old.
Pisan Cantos, The, *sels.*
Planh for the Young English King, *tr.*
Portrait.
Portrait d'une Femme.
Pour L'Election de Son Sepulchre. *Fr.* Hugh Selwyn Mauberley.
Provincia Deserta.
Pull Down Thy Vanity. *Fr.* Canto LXXXI.
Rest, The.
Return, The.
River Merchant's Wife, The; a Letter, *tr.*
Rome, *tr.*
Rose White, Yellow, Silver. *Fr.* Phanopoeia.
Salutation.
Salutation the Second.
Seafarer, The, *tr.*
Seafarer, The, *sel., tr.*
Sestina; Altaforte.
Shades of Callimachus, Coan ghosts of Philetas. *Fr.* Homage to Sextus Propertius.
"Siena Mi Fe'; Disfecemi Maremma." *Fr.* Hugh Selwyn Mauberley.
Silet.
Song of Battle, *tr.*
Song of [*or* for] the Virgin Mother, A, *tr.*
Sonnet: "I saw the eyes, where Amor took his place," *tr.*
Sonnet: "If I should pray this lady pitiless," *tr.*
Sonnet: "My Lady's face it is they worship there," *tr.*
Sonnet: "Who is she that comes, makyng turn every man's eye," *tr.*
Sonnet: "You, who do breach mine eyes and touch the heart," *tr.*
South-Folk in Cold Country.
Spring, The.
Study in Aesthetics, The.
Taking Leave of a Friend, *tr.*
Tenzone.
These Fought in Any Case. *Fr.* Hugh Selwyn Mauberley.
This villa is raked of winds from fore and aft, *tr.*
Threnos.
Tomb at Akr Çaar, The.
Translations and Adaptations from Heine, *sels.*
Tree, The.
Turning Aside from Battles, *tr.*
Villanelle; the Psychological Hour.
Virginal, A.
Well Pleaseth Me the Sweet Time of Easter, *tr.*
What thou lovest well remains. *Fr.* Canto LXXXI.
When, when, and whenever death closes our eyelids. *Fr.* Homage to Sextus Propertius.
Yeux Glauques. *Fr.* Hugh Selwyn Mauberley.
Powell, Arthur. Welcome, The.
Powell, Frederick York. Ballade: "Pretty maid, The, she died," *tr.*
Last Words, The, *tr.*
Pretty Maid, The, *tr.*
Sailor and the Shark, The, *tr.*
Powell, Harry A. Here We Have Idaho.
Powell, Richard Stillman. I Go Fishin'.
Powell, Ruth. After Reading Milne.
Power, John. Thy Name We Bless and Magnify.
Power, Marguerite, Countess of Blessington. Friend, A.
Power, Marguerite A. Hidden Rose-Tree, A.
Powers, Horatio Nelson. Chimney Swallows.
New Year, The.
Our Sister.
Year Ahead, The.
Powers, Jessica (Sister Miriam of the Holy Spirit). And in Her Morning.
Beauty, Too, Seeks Surrender.
Boundaries.
Celestial Bird.
Cloud of Carmel, The.
Death in Carmel.
Death of Saint Therese of Lisieux.
Doxology.
For One Who Died.
I Would Define My Love.
If You Have Nothing.
Obscurity.
Powers, Rose Mills. I Dare Believe.
Lone Swan.
Sea Sorrow.
Swifts in the Chimney.
Powers, Star. Harvest Time.
Powys, John Cowper. Candle Light.
Hour before Dawn, The.

POWYS, JOHN COWPER (*continued*)
Rider, The.
To One Who Spoke of Eternal Things.
Truth, The?
POYNTER, MARY H. Slumber Song: "Now the golden day is ending."
POZZI, ANTONIA. Mountain Climber, The.
Rendezvous.
PRABHAVANANDA, SWAMI, *and* CHRISTOPHER ISHERWOOD. Bhagavad-Gita, *sels., tr.*
Considerations of Murder, *tr. Fr.* Bhagavad-Gita.
Debate between Arjuna and Sri Krishna, *tr. Fr.* Bhagavad-Gita.
Give Me Your Whole Heart, *tr. Fr.* Bhagavad-Gita.
PRADOS, EMILIO. Constant Friend.
Dream.
Form of Flight, A.
I closed my door to the world.
Invitation to Death.
January Tenth.
My forehead is weary as a river.
Song: "Fleeing I go from death."
PRAED, WINTHROP MACKWORTH. Belle of the Ball-Room, The. *Fr.* Every-Day Characters.
Belle of the Ball-Room, The, *sel. Fr.* Every-Day Characters.
Camp-Bell.
Charade.
Covenanter's Lament for Bothwell Brigg, The.
Epitaph on the Late King of the Sandwich Isles.
Every-Day Characters, *sels.*
Fairy Song.
Good-Night to the Season.
How Am I Like Her?
Intolerance.
Latin Hymn [to the Virgin].
Letter of Advice, A.
Letters from Teignmouth, *sel.*
Love at a Rout.
Marston Moor.
Mater Desiderata.
Newly-wedded, The.
One More Quadrille.
Our Ball. *Fr.* Letters from Teignmouth.
Peace Be Thine.
Portrait of a Lady in the Exhibition of the Royal Academy. *Fr.* Every-Day Characters.
Preface, A, *sel.*
Red Fisherman, The.
Remember Me.
School and Schoolfellows.
Song of Impossibilities, A.
Stanzas on Seeing the Speaker Asleep in His Chair.
Talented Man, The.
Time's Song.
To ——: "We met but in one giddy dance."
To Helen.
Vicar, The. *Fr.* Every-Day Characters.
Voltaire, Cobbett, and Gastronomy. *Fr.* A Preface.
Waterloo.
PRATHER, W. H. Indian Ghost Dance and War, The.
PRATI, GIOVANNI. Holy Viaticum Comes to Me, The.
PRATT, ADELINE. Peace.
PRATT, ANNA MARIA. Early News.
Little Mistake, A.
Mortifying Mistake, A.
PRATT, EDWIN JOHN. Behind the Log, *sel.*
Brébeuf and His Brethren, *sels.*
Burial at Sea. *Fr.* The *Roosevelt* and the *Antinoe*.
Cachalot, The, *sel.*
Come Away, Death.
Come Not the Seasons Here.
Decision, The.
Dunkirk, *sels.*
Erosion.
From Stone to Steel.
Ground-Swell, The.
Iceberg, The. *Fr.* The *Titanic.*
Ice-Floes, The.
In the Skies. *Fr.* Dunkirk.
Invisible Trumpets Blowing. *Fr.* Brébeuf and His Brethren.
Isador and Ida Strauss. *Fr.* The *Titanic.*
Man and the Machine, The.
Newfoundland.
Old Eagle, The.
Prairie Sunset, A.
Prize Cat, The.
Putting Winter to Bed.
Roosevelt and the *Antinoe,* The.
Roosevelt and the *Antinoe,* The, *sel.*
Sea Cathedral, The.
Sea Gulls.
Silences.
Stoics, The.
Titanic, The, *sels.*
To an Enemy.
Way of Cape Race, The.
Witches' Brew, The.
PRATT, FLORENCE EVELYN. Abraham Lincoln.
Courting in Kentucky.
PRATT, HARRY NOYES. For My Fireplace.
Gypsy Heart, The.
Hushabye Sea.
Lullaby-O, By-O, Babe.
My House.
Seventh City of Cibola, The.
Wood of Tara, The.
PRATT, LENORE ALEXANDRA. Blizzard, The.
Midwinter Thaw.
Old Boat, The.
PRATT, SAMUEL JACKSON. Cottage Pictures, *sel.*
PRATT, WILLIAM W. Golden Wedding.
PRAXILLA. At the Window.
Girlish face is what appears through the lattice-slot, A.
Lost World of Adonis, The.
"Neither Maid nor Wife."
No More!
PRAY, BENJAMIN STURGIS. Motorcycle.
PREBLE, GEORGE HENRY. From Texas to Maine.
PRENTICE, GEORGE DENISON. Closing Year, The.
Memories.
New England.
Ocean, The.
PRENTICE, JOHN A. Washington.
PRENTISS, ELIZABETH PAYSON (Mrs. George Lewis Prentiss). Cradle Song: "Sleep, baby, sleep!" *tr.*
Kitty.
Little Kitty.
Long Time Ago.
Now Let Me Lay the Pearl Away.
Sleep, Baby, Sleep, *tr.*
Slumber Song, A, *tr.*
Susy Miller.
PRERADOVIC, PETAR. Ode to Slavdom, *sel.*
PRESCOTT, MARY NEWMARCH. In the Dark, in the Dew.
Lullaby, A: "Hush, hush, rest my sweet."
"PRESLAND, JOHN" (Gladys Skelton). Inn, The.
London Idyll, A.
Spring in Oxford Street.
Street Music.
PRESS, JOHN. Farewell.
PRESSOIR, CHARLES FERNAND. Country Graveyard.
Mambo dans le Hounfort, La.
PRESTON, KEITH. Awful Responsibility, An.
Deep Stuff.
Durable Bon Mot.
First Christmas, The.
Good Reasons.
Humorist, The.
Lapsus Linguae.
Marital Tragedy.
Original Cuss, An.
Responsible William.
Warm Babies.
PRESTON, MARGARET JUNKIN. Acceptation.
Dirge for Ashby.
First Proclamation of Miles Standish, The.
First Thanksgiving Day, The.
Gone Forward.
Grave in Hollywood Cemetery, Richmond, A.
Hero of the Commune, The.
Hymn to the National Flag.
Last Meeting of Pocahontas and the Great Captain, The.
Mystery of Cro-a-tàn, The.
Shade of the Trees, The.
Under the Shade of the Trees.
Virginia Capta.
Vision of the Snow, The.
When Saint Chrysostom Prayed.
PRESTWICH, EDMUND. To Phoebus Seeing a Lady before Sunrise.
PRÉVERT, JACQUES. Late Rising.
PREWETT, FRANK. Out of the Night.
Snow-Buntings.
Somme Valley, The, 1917.
Voices of Women.
When Cuckoo First.
PRICE, DAISY CONWAY. Easter Joy.
Follower, A.
PRICE, JONATHAN. Forked Radish, A.
Tay Toy Babilarde Arondelle, *tr.*
PRICE, LAURENCE. Win at First and Lose at Last; or, A New Game at Cards.
PRICE, NELL GOODALE. School Begins.
PRICE, RICHARD GEOFFREY GEORGE. Who Walks by the Dockside.
PRICE, WILLIAM JAMES. Be Strong.
Open Your Heart.
To-Day.
PRICHARD, JOHN. Easter Poem.
Green Navies, The.
Poem: "In fear of death do not neglect small bounty."
Poem: "Is there virtue in the sweet medium?"
Poem: "When birds and brittle leaves come down."
Swansea Bay.
PRIDEAUX, TOM. Skip-Scoop-Anellie.
PRIDVOROV, YEFIM. *See* "BEDNY, DEMYAN."
PRIEST, NANCY WOODBURY (Nancy Amelia Woodbury Wakefield). Heaven.
Over the River.
"PRIMUS." Far from Somewhere.
PRINCE, FRANK TEMPLETON. At a Parade.
Babiaantje, The.
Chaka.
False Bay.
In a Province.
Question, The.
Soldiers Bathing.
Tears of a Muse in America, A.
To a Friend on His Marriage.
To a Man on His Horse.
Token, The.
PRINGLE, THOMAS. Afar in the Desert.
Desolate Valley, The, *sel.*
Emigrants, The; Introductory Stanzas.
Emigrant's Farewell, The.
Ewe-Buchtin's Bonnie, The.
Hottentot, The.
PRINZIVALLE, DORIA. Canzone: Of His Love.
PRIOR, MATTHEW. Adriani Morientis ad Animam Suam, *tr.*
Alma; or, The Progress of the Mind, *sel.*
Another [Epigram]: "Yes, every Poet is a Fool."
Answer to Cloe [*or* Chloe] Jealous.
Better Answer [to Cloe Jealous], A.
Chloe.
Cloe Jealous.
Cupid [*or* Cupid's] Mistaken.
Cupid Turned Plowman, *tr.*
Dear Cloe, how blubber'd is that pretty face.
Down Hall.

Down Hall, *sel.*
Dutch Proverb, A.
English Ballad, An, on the Taking of Namur by the King of Great Britain, 1695.
English Padlock, An.
Epigram: "Frank carves very ill, yet will palm all the meats."
Epigram: "Sir, I admit your general rule," *at.*
Epigram: "To John I owed great obligation."
Epigram: "When Pontius wished an edict might be passed."
Epigram: "Yes, every Poet is a Fool."
Epitaph, An: "Interred [*or* interr'd] beneath this marble stone."
Epitaph on Himself.
Farewell, A: "Venus take my votive glass."
Female Phaeton, The.
For His Own Tomb-Stone.
For My Own Monument.
For My Own Tomb-Stone.
Fortune-Teller, The.
Garland, The.
Hymn to Zeus, *sel., tr.*
I Sent for Ratcliffe.
In Imitation of Anacreon.
Jinny the Just.
Knowledge; Solomon Discourses. *Fr.* Solomon on the Vanity of the World.
Lady Who Offers Her Looking-Glass to Venus, The.
Lais' Mirror, *tr.*
Letter, A.
Letter to the Hon. Lady Miss Margaret Cavendish-Holles-Harley, A.
Love and Reason. *Fr.* Solomon on the Vanity of the World.
Lover's Anger, A.
Man and the Universe. *Fr.* Solomon on the Vanity of the World.
Merchant, to Secure His Treasure, The.
More than Quit, *tr.*
Nannette.
Nonpareil.
Ode, An: "Merchant, to secure his treasure, The."
On a Pretty Madwoman.
On Beauty; a Riddle.
On Critics.
On Exodus III, 14, I Am That I Am.
On My Birthday, July 21.
Paraphrase from the French, A.
Phillis's [*or* Phyllis's] Age.
Picture of Seneca Dying in a Bath.
Power, *sel. Fr.* Solomon on the Vanity of the World.
Prior's Epitaph.
Protogenes and Apelles.
Question to Lisetta, The.
Quits.
Reasonable Affliction, A.
Remedy Worse than the Disease, The.
Reply, A, *at.*
Secretary, The.
Simile, A.
Sir, I Admit Your General Rule, *at.*
Solomon on the Vanity of the World, *sels.*
Song, A: "If wine and music have the power."
Song, A: "In vain you tell your parting lover."
Song: "Merchant, to secure his treasure, The."
Thief and the Cordelier, The.
To a Child of Noble Birth.
To a Child of Quality [Five Years Old].
To a Lady: She Refusing to Continue a Dispute with Me, and Leaving Me in the Argument.
To Cloe Jealous [a Better Answer].
To Cloe Weeping.
To His Soul, *tr.*
To My Lord Buckhurst, Very Young, Playing with a Cat.
To the Hon. Charles Montague.
True Maid, A.
Written in a Lady's Milton.
Written in the Beginning of Mezeray's History of France.

PRITZKOW, LOUIS W. Take Back Your Gold.

PROBYN, MAY. Bees of Middleton [*or* Myddleton] Manor, The.
Beloved, The.
Christmas Carol: "Lacking samite and sable."
"Is It Nothing to You?"

PROCTER, ADELAIDE ANNE. Angel's Story, The.
Annunciation, The.
Be Strong.
Cleansing Fires.
Cradle-Song of the Poor, The.
Doubting Heart, A.
Fidelis.
Give Me Thy Heart.
Judge Not.
Legend, A.
Legend of Bregenz, A.
Legend of Provence, A, *sel.*
Lost Chord, A.
No Star Is Ever Lost. *Fr.* A Legend of Provence.
One by One.
Our Daily Bread.
Per Pacem ad Lucem.
Pilgrims, The.
Pray for Me!
Present, The.
Requital.
Sacred Heart, The.
Shadows of the Evening Hours, The.
Strive, Wait and Pray.
Thankfulness.
Warrior to His Dead Bride, The.
Who Is the Angel That Cometh?
Woman's Answer, A.
Woman's Question[s], A.

PROCTER, BRYAN WALLER. *See* "CORNWALL, BARRY."

PROCTOR, EDNA DEAN. At Jerusalem.
Brooklyn Bridge, The.
Captive's Hymn, The.
Cid of the West.
Columbia's Emblem.
Columbus Dying.
Forward.
Glory of Toil, The.
Heaven, O Lord, I Cannot Lose.
Heroes.
John Brown.
Lincoln.
Lost War-Sloop, The.
President's Proclamation, The.
Queen of the Year, The.
Sa-Ca-Ga-We-A.
Song of the Ancient People, The, *sel.*
Stripes and the Stars, The.
Take Heart.
Theodore Roosevelt.

PROCTOR, THOMAS. How Time Consumeth All Earthly Things, *at.*
Mirror of Mortality, A.
Proper Sonnet, How Time Consumeth All Earthly Things, A, *at.*
Respice Finem.
Sic Transit, *at.*

PROKOSCH, FREDERIC. And If at Last, *tr.*
Campaign, The.
Chorus from "Medea," *tr.*
Conspirators, The.
Dolls, The.
Eclogue: "No one dies cleanly now."
Etching at Dusk.
Evening Fantasy, *tr.*
Fable: "O the vines were golden, the birds were loud."
Festival, The.
Gray Geese Flying.
Half of Life, The, *tr.*
Medea, *sel., tr.*
Ode: "O happy the huntsman . . ."
Reapers, The
Song from Portugal, 1940.
To Nature, *tr.*
What Does It Avail Me? *tr.*

PROPERTIUS, SEXTUS. Ah Woe Is Me. *Fr.* Elegies.
All that you see here, stranger, where great Rome now stands. *Fr.* Elegies.
And in that faroff age when Amphitryoniades. *Fr.* Elegies.
Arethusa sends this message to her husband Lycotas. *Fr.* Elegies.
At the banquet tables of our social gatherings, I was ridiculed. *Fr.* Elegies.
Cease, Paullus, to oppress my tomb with tears. *Fr.* Elegies.
Complaint of Tarpeia's Door, The.
Corinthian Lais received no such crowds in her home. *Fr.* Elegies.
Cynthia, Cynthia.
Elegies, *sels.*
Happiness, happiness! blessed night! and bless you. *Fr.* Elegies.
Hylas. *Fr.* Elegies.
I am compelled to make the long trip to classic Athens. *Fr.* Elegies.
I, entrance door to Tarpeia's house, swung open, once. *Fr.* Elegies.
Is it true, Cynthia, that throughout Rome you are notorious. *Fr.* Elegies.
Jupiter Feretrius? His origin? I'll make a start: write. *Fr.* Elegies.
Jupiter, have compassion, finally, on that sick girl, my sweetheart. *Fr.* Elegies.
Learn, you who wonder at my many forms. *Fr.* Elegies.
Let others write about you, or leave you all unknown. *Fr.* Elegies.
Let us return, meantime, to the round of song. *Fr.* Elegies.
Light, Light of My Eyes.
Listen to what startled the neighbors, one night. *Fr.* Elegies.
Love Is the God of Peace. *Fr.* Elegies.
Lover's Death, The. *Fr.* Elegies.
May earth, O Acanthis, procuress, cover your grave. *Fr.* Elegies.
May your wellknown mercy, Persephone, remain steadfast. *Fr.* Elegies.
Now, O Bacchus, I turn humbly to your shrine. *Fr.* Elegies.
Plea of Cornelia, The. *Fr.* Elegies.
Priest performs rites: let there be silence during the rites, The. *Fr.* Elegies.
Revenge to Come. *Fr.* Elegies.
Roman Matron to Her Husband, A. *Fr.* Elegies.
Shade of Cornelia Consoles Her Husband, The. *Fr.* Elegies.
Shades are real, The. Death is not the end. *Fr.* Elegies.
Shades of Callimachus, and holy rites of Philetas. *Fr.* Elegies.
She is gone whom I loved so long, my girl that I loved so dear. *Fr.* Elegies.
Tarpeia's grove; Tarpeia's traitor-tomb; capture of. *Fr.* Elegies.
This faith in your beauty, woman, is false. *Fr.* Elegies.
Turning Aside from Battles.
Watering Place, The.
What that man is, I often was: but in time, perhaps. *Fr.* Elegies.
When Thou Must Home.
Who sees you, sins. Who has not seen you, therefore. *Fr.* Elegies.
You who flee to escape a bloody death like mine. *Fr.* Elegies.

PROUDFIT, DAVID LAW ("Peleg Arkwright"). Poor Little Joe.
Prehistoric Smith.
Willis, The.

"PROUT, FATHER." *See* MAHONY, FRANCIS SYLVESTER.

PROVINE, JUNE. Toast, A.

PROVOST, BARBARA JANE. Holland.

PROWSE, WILLIAM JEFFERY NICHOLAS. City of Prague, The.

PRUDENTIUS (Aurelius Clemens Prudentius). Before Sleep.
Burial of the Dead, The.
Cathemerinon, *sel.*

PRUDENTIUS (*continued*)
For the Burial of the Dead.
Holy Innocents, The.
Hymn for Morning. *Fr.* Cathemerinon.
Laudate for Christmas.
O Noble Virgin. *Fr.* Cathemerinon.
Of the Father's Love Begotten.
Per Quinquennia Iam Decem.
PRUDHOMME, SULLY-. *See* SULLY-PRUDHOMME.
PRUITT, J. W. Hell-bound Train, The, *at.*
PRYCE-JONES, ALAN. Said the Captain.
PRYS, THOMAS. Trouble at Sea.
PRYS-JONES, ARTHUR GLYN. Down Channel.
"PSILORITI, PETROULA." *See* KAZANTZAKIS, GALATEA.
PTOLEMY [*or* PTOLEMAEUS]. Scientist, The.
Starry Heavens Without.
PTOLEMY (Claudius Ptolemaeus). Immortality.
PUDNEY, JOHN. After Bombardment.
For Johnny.
Jack Overdue.
Map Reference T994724.
Missing.
To You Who Wait.
PUGLIESI, GIACOMINO. Canzone: Of His Dead Lady.
Canzonetta: Of His Lady in Absence.
PULCI, LUIGI. Appeal for Illumination. *Fr.* Il Morgante maggiore.
Morgante maggiore, Il, *sels.*
Prophecy. *Fr.* Il Morgante maggiore.
PULLEN, ALICE MURIEL. Quest Eternal, The.
PULLEN, ELISABETH JONES CAVAZZA.
Alicia's Bonnet.
Derelict.
Goose à la Mode.
Her Shadow.
Jack and Jill.
Love and Poverty.
Sea-Weed, The.
PULLEN, EUGENE HENRY. Now I Lay Me Down to Sleep.
PULLMAN, GEORGE CONRAD. His Passion.
PULSIFER, HAROLD TROWBRIDGE. Conquest of the Air, The.
Duel, The.
Ecstasy.
Harvest of Time, The.
I Accept.
Immortal Living.
Of Little Faith.
Peace.
Riderless Horse, The.
Thoughts upon a Walk with Natalie, My Niece, at Houghton Farm.
Winged Victory.
PULSIFER, WOODBURY. Who Won the War?
PURCELL, ELSIE B. Distribution.
PURCELL, HENRY. Come Ye Sons of Art, *sel.*
PURDY, ALFRED W. Landscape.
PURNELL, IDELLA. Haloes.
PUROHIT, SWAMI. I Know That I Am a Great Sinner.
Miracle Indeed, A.
Shall I Do This?
PUSHKIN, ALEKSANDR SERGEYEVICH.
Abandoning an Alien Country.
Along the Noisy Streets.
Angel.
Arion.
Autumn.
Avalanche, The.
Beauty, The.
Beneath Her Native Skies.
Bird, The.
Caucasus, The.
City of the Plague, The, *sel.*
Cloud, The.
Coach of Life, The.
Coach of Time, The.
Crucifix, The.
Day's rain is done. The rainy mist of night.
Devils.
Earth and Sea.
Echo.
Elegy: "As leaden as the aftermath of wine."
Elegy: "Mirth, now dead, that once was madly bubbling, The."
Elegy: "Outlived are all my aspirations."
Eremites of Old, The.
Eugene Onegin, *sels.*
Evil Spirits.
For One Last Time.
For the last time I risk caresses.
Foreboding.
Fronting amazed Cythera grows.
Gay Feast.
Gipsies, The, *sel.*
Gipsy's Song. *Fr.* The Gipsies.
Girls' Song. *Fr.* Eugene Onegin.
Grapes.
Gypsies, The.
Heavy clouds at length are scattering, The.
Here's Winter.
I Loved You Once.
I thought my heart had lost the power [*or* quite forgot].
I Visited Again.
In Vain I Seek to Flee.
I've lived to bury my desires.
Lovely Youth.
Madonna.
Man I Was of Old, The.
May 26, 1828.
Message to Siberia.
Monastery on Kazbek [*or* Kasbek].
Monument.
My Critic.
Nereid, A.
Night Piece.
No, Never Think.
O virgin-rose, no blushes.
On Count M. S. Vorontzov.
On the Death of Amalia Riznich.
On the Translation of the Iliad.
Over the Georgian hills the night her mantle throws.
Poet, The.
Portrait.
Prayer, A: "Hermits and blameless women full of grace."
Prisoner, The.
Prologue, A: "Chain hangs down with golden fetters, A."
Prophet, The.
Remembrance[s].
Secular Power.
Song in Time of Plague. *Fr.* The City of the Plague.
Stanzas: "When down the loud streets I go straying."
Storm, The.
Take not away my wits, O God!
Tale of the Golden Cockerel, The.
Tatyana's Letter to Onegin. *Fr.* Eugene Onegin.
Though Soporific Not a Little.
Three Springs.
'Tis Time, My Friend.
To ——: "Bound for your far-off native shore."
To a Brownie.
To A. P. Kern.
To Chaadayev.
To Madame A. P. Kern.
To N. N.
To the Poet.
Unto Myself I Reared a Monument.
Upas Tree, The.
Verses Written during a Sleepless Night.
Wagon of Life, The.
What though life conspire to cheat you.
When in My Arms.
When, Lost in Thought.
When the last great and solemn act was played.
Winter Evening.
Winter Morning.
Winter Road.
With Freedom's Seed.
Work.
PUTINAS. Torches Have Gone Out, The.
PUTNAM, EDITH PALMER. *See* PAINTON, EDITH PUTNAM.
"PUTNAM, ELEANOR" (Mrs. Arlo Bates; Harriet Leonora Bates). Quel Dommage.
PUTNAM, HOWARD PHELPS (Phelps Putnam). About Women.
Ballad of a Strange Thing.
Hasbrouck and the Rose.
Hymn to Chance.
To the Memory of Yale College.
PUTTENHAM, GEORGE. Cruel You Be.
PYKE, B. K. Blacksmith.
PYLE, KATHARINE. Dandelion, The.
How the Little Kite Learned to Fly, *at.*
Sea Princess, The.
September.

Q

"Q." *See* QUILLER-COUCH, SIR ARTHUR THOMAS.
QUARLES, FRANCIS. Argalus and Parthenia, *sels.*
Authour's Dreame, The. *Fr.* Argalus and Parthenia.
Canticle.
Child Jesus, The.
Christmas Carol, A: "Glory to God on high, and jolly mirth." *Fr.* The Shepherd's Oracles.
David's Epitaph on Jonathan.
Delight in God [Only]. *Fr.* Emblems.
Dependence on God.
Divine Care.
Divine Rapture, A. *Fr.* Emblems.
Emblems, *sels.*
Epigram: "Paul's midnight voice prevail'd; his music's thunder." *Fr.* Emblems.
Epigram: Respice Finem.
Even [*or* Ev'n] like Two Little Bank-dividing Brooks. *Fr.* Emblems.
False World, Thou Liest [*or* Ly'st]. *Fr.* Emblems.
Forme of Prayer, A.
God Who Hides, The.
Good Night, A.
He Is Mine. *Fr.* Emblems.
Hos Ego Versiculos. *Fr.* Argalus and Parthenia.
Human Touch, The ("My soul, sit thou a patient looker-on").
I Am My Beloved's, and His Desire Is towards Me.
Like as the Damask Rose, *at.*
Like to the Arctic Needle. *Fr.* Emblems.
Like to the Arctic Needle, *sel.* *Fr.* Emblems.
Lord, When We Leave the World.
Mary and Martha.
My Beloved Is Mine, and I Am His; He Feedeth among the Lillies. *Fr.* Emblems.
My Glass Is Half Unspent.
Mystical Ecstasy, A. *Fr.* Emblems.
O, the Fickle State of Lovers.
O Whither Shall I Fly?
Of Common Devotion.
On Psalm CXIX, 5.
On the Infancy of Our Saviour.
On the Needle of a Sundial.
On the Plough-Man.
On Those That Deserve It.
On Zacheus.
Respice Finem.
Shekel in the Fish's Mouth, The.
Shepherd's Oracles, The, *sel.*
Song: "Oh, the fickle state of lovers!"
Sweet Phosphor, Bring the Day.
Unsettled Soul, The.
Vanity of the World, The. *Fr.* Emblems.
Wherefore Hidest Thou Thy Face, and

Holdest Me for Thy Enemie? *Fr.* Emblems.
Why Dost Thou Shade Thy Lovely Face? O Why. *Fr.* Emblems.
Wilt Thou Set Thine Eyes upon That Which Is Not? *Fr.* Emblems.
World's a Sea, The.
World's Fallacies, The. *Fr.* Emblems.
QUARLES, JOHN, *and* HENRY FRANCIS LYTE. Long Did I Toil.
QUASIMODO, SALVATORE. Ancient Winter.
And Suddenly It's Evening.
High Sailboat, The.
QUAYLE, WILLIAM ALFRED. All's Well.
QUENNELL, PETER. Divers, The.
Flight into Egypt, The.
Hero Entombed, I.
Leviathan.
Leviathan, *sel.*
Procne.
Small Birds.
Sunflower, The.
While I Have Vision.
QUENTAL, ANTERO DE. Amid the Shadows.
In the Arena.
Inner Voice, The.
Upon the Whirlwind.
QUEREMEL, ANGEL MIGUEL. Ballad of Love and Blood.
Manifesto of the Soldier Who Went Back to War.
"QUERNO, CAMILLO." *See* ODELL, JONATHAN.
QUEVEDO Y VILLEGAS, FRANCISCO GÓMEZ DE. Death Warnings.
Letrilla; the Lord of Dollars.
Life's Brevity.
Lisa's Golden Hair.
Lord of Dollars, The.
Madrigal: Restless Lover, The.
My Fortune.
On Lisa's Golden Hair.
Rome in Her Ruins.
Sonnet: Death Warnings.
To a Nose.
QUICK, DOROTHY. Barrier.
Forest God.
Special Place, A.
Strange.
Tree Woman.
Wolves of Egremont, The.
QUILLER-COUCH, SIR ARTHUR THOMAS ("Q"). Alma Mater.
Chant Royal of High Virtue.
De Tea Fabula.
Dolor Oogo.
Famous Ballad of the Jubilee Cup, The.
Lady Jane (Sapphics).
Letter, A.
Lion is a beast to fight, The.
Retrospection.
Sage Counsel.
Saturn.
Splendid Spur, The.
Tim the Dragoon.
Upon Eckington Bridge, River Avon.
Upon New Year's Eve.
Victoria.
White Moth, The.
QUILLET, CLAUDE. Way to Have Handsome Children, The, *sel.*
QUILLEVIC. Monsters.
QUILLINAN, EDWARD. Hour Glass, The.
QUIN, ROGER. To a Skylark, Singing above Barnhill Poorhouse, Glasgow.
QUINN, JOHN. Foxhole for the Night, A.
QUINN, RODERIC. By Momba Tracks.
Camp within the West, The.
Circling Hearths, The.
Fisher, The.
Hidden Tide, The.
Mid-Forest Fear.
QUINTANA, MANUEL JOSÉ. Ode to Spain—after the Revolution of March.
Ode to Spain—after the Revolution of March, *sel.*
QUINTERO, SERAFÍN ALVAREZ, *and* JOAQUÍN ALVAREZ QUINTERO. *See* ALVAREZ QUINTERO.
QUINTUS SMYRNAEUS. Death of Oenone, The. *Fr.* Posthomerica.
Paris Is Dead. *Fr.* Posthomerica.
Posthomerica, *sels.*
Return from Troy, The. *Fr.* Posthomerica.
QUIRINO, GIOVANNI. Sonnet: To Dante Alighieri (He Commends the Work of Dante's Life).
To Dante Alighieri.
QUIRK, CHARLES J. Countersign, The. *Fr.* Quatrains.
On the Parapet of Notre Dame. *Fr.* Quatrains.
QUÍSPEZ ASÍN, CÉSAR. *See* "MORO, CÉSAR."

R

"R., E. H." Big Arm-Chair, The.
"R., E. M. G." Midsummer Moon.
"R., H. T." Salve.
Woman Always Pays, The.
"R., J." Knife, The.
"R., M." Lord, who lovest little children.
"R. D. H." *See* "H., R. D."
"R. H." *See* "H., R."
"R. K. B." *See* "B., R. K."
"R. K. K." *See* "K., R. K."
"R. M." *See* "M., R."
"R. S." *See* ZINSSER, HANS.
"R. W." *See* "W., R."
RAB (Abba Arika). Kingdom of God, The.
RABELAIS, FRANÇOIS. Gargantua, *sel.*
Inscription Set upon the Great Gate of Theleme, The. *Fr.* Gargantua.
RABI'A, DAUGHTER OF KA'B. Curse, A.
"RACHEL" (Rachel Blumstein). Barren.
Dawn.
Jonathan.
Kinnereth.
To My Country.
RACINE, JEAN. Athalie, *sel.*
Bajazet, *sel.*
Chorus: "God whose goodness filleth every clime, The." *Fr.* Athalie.
Conquest of Love, The. *Fr.* Phèdre.
Phaedra Declares Her Love for Her Stepson. *Fr.* Phèdre.
Phaedra Jealous. *Fr.* Phèdre.
Phèdre, *sels.*
RADFORD, DOLLIE (Dollie Maitland). Ah, Bring It Not.
Buttercups.
I could not through the burning day.
If All the World.
Model, A.
My Little Dear.
October.
Spring Song.
RADFORD, ERNEST. Out.
Plymouth Harbour.
Quiet.
RADISHCHEV, ALEKSANDR. Sapphic Stanzas.
RAFFETTO, BERTHA. Home Means Nevada.
RAFFI. Ballad: "Dark forests clothe the mountain-side."
Lake of Van, The.
Parrot's Song, The.
RAFFLES, THOMAS. O Lord! My Hiding Place.
RAFI OF MERV. Roses of Thy Cheeks, The.
RAFTERY, ANTHONY. County Mayo, The.
I Am Raftery.
Mary Hynes.
Peggy Mitchell.
RAFTERY, GERALD. Apartment House.
Lineman.
New Dynamo.
Old Teacher.
On a Dead Teacher.
RAGO, HENRY. Coming of Dusk upon a Village in Haiti, The.
Monster, The.
RAHBEK, KNUD LYHNE. Drinking Song.
"RAIMAR, FREIDMUND." *See* RÜCKERT, FRIEDRICH.
RAINE, KATHLEEN JESSIE. Air.
Crystal Skull, The.
Desire.
Easter Poem.
Envoi: "Take of me what is not my own."
Fall, The.
Fata Morgana.
For Posterity.
Goddess, The.
Heroes.
In Time.
Invocation of Death.
Isis Wanderer.
London Night.
Love Poem.
Message from Home.
Moment, The.
Mourning in Spring, 1943.
Night in Martindale.
Nocturne: "Night comes, an angel stands."
On Leaving Ullswater.
Parting.
Pythoness, The.
Requiem.
Rock, *sel.*
Rose, The.
Seen in a Glass.
Seventh Day.
Shells.
Silver Stag, The.
Spell of Creation.
Spell of Sleep.
Still Life.
Still Pool, The.
"Tu Non Se' in Terra, Si Come Tu Credi . . ."
Water, *sel.*
Worry about Money.
RAINER, DACHINE. Ashokan.
At Eighty-seven.
Double Ritual.
Epithalamium for Cavorting Ghosts.
Night Musick for Thérèse.
Samis Idyll.
Upon Being Awakened at Night by My Four Year Old Daughter.
RAINSFORD, CHRISTINA. Shadbush.
RAIZISS, SONIA. Message Received.
RAK, JÁN. Illusion.
RAKUTEN. For lack of rain.
RALEGH, SIR WALTER. Advice, The.
Affection and Desire.
All the World's a Stage.
Another of the Same.
Answer to Marlowe.
As You [*or* Ye] Came from the Holy Land, *at.*
Author's Epitaph, Made by Himself, The.
Conceit Begotten by the Eyes.
Conclusion, The.
Coracle, The, *tr.*
Description of Love, A.
Diana.
Dulcina, *at.*
Epitaph: "Even such is Time, which takes in trust."
Epitaph on Sir Philip Sidney, *at.*
Epitaph on the Earl of Leicester, *at.*
Epitaph upon the Right Honorable Sir Philip Sidney, Knight, Lord Governor of Flushing, An, *at.*
Even Such Is Time.
Excuse, The.
Faery [*or* Faerie] Queen, The.
False Love.
Farewell, false love, the oracle of lies.
Farewell to False Love, A.
Farewell to the Court.
Farewell to the Court, *sel.*
Give Me My Scallop-Shell of Quiet.
Her Face, Her Tongue, Her Wit, *at.*
Her Reply.
Hermit, The, *at.*
His [Own] Epitaph.
His Petition to Queen Anne of Denmark (1618).
His Pilgrimage.

RALEGH, SIR WALTER (*continued*)
If Cynthia Be a Queen.
In Commendation of George Gascoigne's Steel Glass.
Last Booke of the Ocean to Scinthia, The, *sels.*
Last Lines.
Lie, The.
Like Hermit Poor, *at.*
Like to a [*or* an] Hermit Poor, *at.*
Like Truthless Dreams.
Lines Found in His Bible.
Lines from Catullus.
Lines Written the Night before His Execution.
Love and Time.
Lover's Complaint, A.
Lye, The.
Merit of True Passion, The.
Methought I saw the grave where Laura lay.
My Body in the Walls Captived.
My Pilgrimage.
My Woe Must Ever Last.
Nature, That Wash'd Her Hands in Milk.
Now What Is Love.
Nymph's Reply to the [Passionate] Shepherd, The.
Ocean to Cynthia, The.
Ocean to Cynthia, The, *sel.*
Ocean's Love to Cynthia, The.
Of Spenser's Faery Queen.
On Dulcina, *at.*
On the Life of Man.
On the Snuff of a Candle.
Passionate Man's Pilgrimage, The.
Passionate Man's Pilgrimage, The, *sel.*
Pilgrim to Pilgrim, *at.*
Pilgrimage. *Fr.* The Passionate Man's Pilgrimage.
Pilgrimage, The, *sel.*
Poem, A: "Like to a hermit poor in place obscure," *at.*
Poem Entreating of Sorrow, A.
Poem Put into My Lady Laiton's Pocket, A.
Praised Be Diana's Fair and Harmless Light.
Prognostication upon Cards and Dice, A.
Reply to Marlowe's "The Passionate Shepherd to His Love."
Rise, O My Soul! *at.*
Shepheard, What's Loue? *at.*
Shepherd's Description of Love, The, *at.*
Shepherd's Praise of Diana, The.
Shepherd's Wooing Dulcina, The, *at.*
Silent Lover, The.
Silent Lover, The, *sel.*
Sir Walter Ralegh the Night before His Death.
Sir Walter Raleigh to His Son.
Sir Walter Raleigh to the Queen.
Sir Walter Raleigh's Verses, Found in His Bible in the Gatehouse at Westminster.
Sonet, A: "Her face, her tongue, her wit," *at.*
Sonnet: "Like to an hermit poor, in place obscure," *at.*
Sonnet: "Like truthless dreams, so are my joys expired."
Sorrow Stays.
Soul's Errand, The.
Soul's Pilgrimage, The.
Sweet Unsure.
To His Mistress.
To His Son.
To Jesus, *at.*
To Queen Elizabeth.
To the Queen.
To the Translator of Lucan's Pharsalia (1614).
Verses Found in His Bible in the Gate-House at Westminster.
Verses Made by Sir Walter Raleigh the Night before He Was Beheaded.
Verses Written in His Bible.
Vision upon the "Faery Queen," A.
Vision upon This Conceit [*or* Conceipt] of the Faerie [*or* Faery] Queene, A.
Walsinghame, *at.*
What is our life? A play of passion.
Wood, the Weed, the Wag, The.
Wrong not, sweet [*or* dear] empress of my heart. *Fr.* The Silent Lover.

RALEIGH, SIR WALTER ALEXANDER (1861–1922). Artist, The.
Ballade of the Goth.
Eating Song.
I wish I loved the Human Race.
My Last Will.
Ode to Himself.
Stans Puer ad Mensam.
Wishes of an Elderly Man.

RALPH, NATHAN. When They Grow Old.

RAMAGE, JOYCE. My Companion.

"RAMAL, WALTER." *See* DE LA MARE, WALTER.

RAMIE, MARIAN. Will You, One Day.

RAMÍREZ, IGNACIO. For the Dead Gregorians.

RAMOS, FELIX V. Look, the Soldiers!

RAMSAUR, HUGH WILGUS. Absolute, The.
Enigma.
Epitaph, Found Somewhere in Space.
Gargantua.
Suicide, The.
World-Ruin.

RAMSAY, ALLAN. An Thou Were My Ain Thing.
An Thou Were My Ain Thing, *sel.*
Caterpillar and the Ant, The.
Clock and Dial, The.
Dainty Sang, A. *Fr.* The Gentle Shepherd.
Gentle Shepherd, The, *sels.*
Give Me a Lass.
Katy's Answer.
Lass of Patie's Mill, The.
Lochaber No More.
Look Up to Pentland's Tow'ring Tap.
My Peggy. *Fr.* The Gentle Shepherd.
Ode to Mr. F——, An.
Peggy. *Fr.* The Gentle Shepherd.
Poet's Wish, A [*or* The]; an Ode.
Polwart on the Green.
Sang: "My Peggy is a young thing." *Fr.* The Gentle Shepherd.
Song: "At setting day and rising morn."
Up in the Air.
Waukin' o' the Fauld, The. *Fr.* The Gentle Shepherd.
Widow, The.
Young Laird and Edinburgh Katy, The.

RAMSAY, ALLEN BEVILLE. No teacher I of boys or smaller fry.

"RAMSAY, JOAN" (Louise Wilson). Green Branches.
Saint Francis of Assisi.

RAMSDEN, HOWARD. On a Green Hillock.

RAMSEY, THOMAS WESTON. Caught by Chance.
Power Station.

RANCHIN, JACQUES. King of Triolets, The.

RAND, EDWARD A. Little Ships in the Air.

RAND, KENNETH. Lonely Road, The.

RAND, THEODORE HARDING. Dragonfly, The.
June.
Loon, The.
Sea Music.

RANDALL, JAMES RYDER. After a Little While.
John Pelham.
Lone Sentry, The.
Magdalen.
Maryland, My Maryland.
My Maryland.
Why the Robin's Breast Was Red.

RANDALL, LAURA LEE. Our Circus.

RANDALL, VIRGINIA D. October Winds.

RANDALL, WILLIAM H. Decoration Hymn.

RANDALL-MILLS, ELIZABETH. Crossing the County Line.

RANDOLPH, ANSON DAVIES FITZ. Hopefully Waiting.
Master's Invitation, The.

RANDOLPH, INNES. Good Old Rebel.
I'm a Good Old Rebel.
Rebel, The.

RANDOLPH, JAMES. We sit and talk, and kiss away the hours.

RANDOLPH, THOMAS. Amyntas; or, The Impossible Dowry, *sel.*
Aristippus, *sel.*
Charm, A. *Fr.* The Jealous Lovers.
Come, Spur Away!
Devout Lover, A.
Drinking Song. *Fr.* Aristippus.
Eclogue [*or* Eglogue] to Mr. Johnson, An.
Eclogue to Mr. Johnson, An, *sel.*
Elegie, An: "Love, give me leave to serve thee, and be wise."
Fairies' Song. *Fr.* Amyntas.
Gratulatory to Mr. Ben. Johnson for His Adopting of Him to Be His Son, A.
He Lives Long Who Lives Well.
I have a mistress, for perfections rare.
Jealous Lovers, The, *sel.*
Love and Reverence.
Now come, my boon companions.
Ode on Leaving the Great Town.
Ode to Mr. [*or* Master] Anthony Stafford to Hasten Him into the Country, An.
On a Maide of Honour Seene by a Schollar in Sommerset Garden.
Parley with His Empty Purse, A.
Pastoral Courtship, A, *sel.*
Poetry and Philosophy. *Fr.* An Eclogue to Mr. Johnson.
Poetry Defined.
Song of Fairies Robbing an Orchard. *Fr.* Amyntas.
Straphyla's Lullaby.
To a Lady Admiring Herself in a Looking-Glass.
To One Admiring Herself in a Looking Glass.
Upon His Picture.

RANDS, WILLIAM BRIGHTY ("Matthew Browne"). Ba-ba, black wool. *Fr.* Topsy-turvy World.
Beauty of the World, The.
Black Bunny.
Blue Boy in London, The.
Brown Bee.
Carry and Kate. *Fr.* Topsy-turvy World.
Cat of Cats. *Fr.* The White Princess.
Child's World, The.
Chorus: "Ba-ba, black wool."
Clean Clara.
Dolladine.
Dream of a [Little] Boy Who Lived at Nine-Elms, The.
Dream of a [Little] Girl Who Lived at Seven-Oaks, The.
Dressing the Doll.
Drummer-Boy and the Shepherdess, The.
Father, Now My Prayer Is Said.
First Tooth, The.
Fishing Song, A.
Flowers, The.
Gipsy Jane.
Godfrey Gordon Gustavus Gore.
Great, Wide, Beautiful, Wonderful World.
Gypsy Jane.
Happy World, The.
I Saw a New World.
If black was white. *Fr.* Topsy-turvy World.
If the butterfly courted the bee. *Fr.* Topsy-turvy World.
Kitten Speaks, The. *Fr.* The White Princess.
Kitty; What She Thinks of Herself. *Fr.* The White Princess.
Lavender Beds, The.
Lilliput Levee.
Little Christel.
Love and the Child.
Lullaby: "Baby wants a lullaby."
Lullaby: "Wind whistled loud at the window-pane, The."
Pedlar's [*or* Peddler's] Caravan, The.
Polly.

Polly Pansy.
Praise and Love.
Reformation of Godfrey Gore, The.
Shooting Song, A.
Stalky Jack.
Thought, The.
Topsy-turvy World.
Topsy-turvy World, sels.
White Princess, The, sel.
Wonderful World, The.
World, The; a Child's Song.
RANKE, HERMANN, and WILLIAM ELLERY LEONARD. See LEONARD, WILLIAM ELLERY, and HERMANN RANKE.
RANKIN, JEREMIAH EAMES. Babie, The.
Fairest of Freedom's Daughters.
God Be with You till We Meet Again.
Word of God to Leyden Came, The.
RANKO [or REINKO]. Fall of the Plum Blossoms, The.
Plum Blossoms ("So sweet . . .").
Plum Trees.
RANSOM, JOHN CROWE. Address to the Scholars of New England.
Agitato Ma Non Troppo.
Amphibious Crocodile.
Antique Harvesters.
Armageddon.
Autumn Love.
Bells for John Whiteside's Daughter.
Blackberry Winter.
Blue Girls.
Captain Carpenter.
Conrad in Twilight.
Dead Boy.
Dog.
Emily Hardcastle, Spinster.
Epitaph: "Napoleon took many captures and is dead."
Equilibrists, The.
First Travels of Max.
Her Eyes.
Here Lies a Lady.
Husband Betrayed.
Inland City.
It was beside the fire that I had lit.
Janet Waking.
Judith of Bethulia.
Lady Lost.
Little Boy Blue.
Lover, The.
Man Without Sense of Direction.
Miller's Daughter.
Miss Euphemia.
Morning.
Necrological.
Noonday Grace.
Number Five.
Old Man Playing with Children.
Old Man Pondered.
Old Mansion.
Our Two Worthies.
Painted Head.
Painting; a Head.
Parting at Dawn.
Parting, without a Sequel.
Persistent Explorer.
Philomela.
Piazza Piece.
Prelude to an Evening.
Somewhere Is Such a Kingdom.
Southern Mansion.
Spectral Lovers.
Spiel of the Three Mountebanks.
Survey of Literature.
Swimmer, The.
Tall Girl, The.
Tom, Tom, the Piper's Son.
Triumph.
Two in August.
Two Sonnets, sel.
Under the Locusts.
Vagrant, The.
Vaunting Oak.
Vision by Sweetwater.
What Ducks Require.
Winter Remembered.
Wrestling.
Yea. Fr. Two Sonnets.
RAPLEE, ELIZABETH VIRGINIA. Nostalgia.
Poet Considers Perfection, The.
RAPPOPORT, SOLOMON. See "ANSKY, S."
RASCAS, BERNARD. Love of God, The.

RASHLEY, R. E. Caterpillar.
Portrait of an Indian.
Voyageur.
RASKIN, PHILIP M. Dreams.
Ghetto Cradle-Song, A.
RATCLIFFE, DOROTHY UNA (Mrs. Alfred Phillips). February.
Pirates' Tea-Party, The.
St. Bridget's Lullaby.
Song of Nidderdale, The.
RATHBONE, IRENE. Was There a Summer?
RATHOM, JOHN R. "Unknown" Dead, The.
RAUSCHENBUSCH, WALTER. For This Universe. Fr. For This World.
For This World, sel.
Little Gate to God, The.
RAVENEL, BEATRICE WITTE. Alligator, The.
Coasts. Fr. Tidewater.
Day You Went, The.
Harbor Water. Fr. Tidewater.
Intervals.
Lill' Angels.
Poe's Mother.
Salvage.
Swamp, The.
Tidewater, sels.
RAVENSCROFT, EDWARD. Citizen Turned Gentleman, The, sel.
I Sigh All the Night. Fr. The Citizen Turned Gentleman.
In Derision of a Country Life. Fr. The Italian Husband.
Italian Husband, The, sel.
RAVENSCROFT, THOMAS. Elves' Dance, The.
Hawking for the Partridge.
Madrigal: "My mistress is as fair as fine," at.
Urchins' Dance, The, at.
RAVITCH, MELECH. Today the Nazi Forces Marched.
RAWES, HENRY AUGUSTUS. Last Hour, The.
Veni, Domine Jesu!
RAWNSLEY, HARDWICKE DRUMMOND. Ballad of the Conemaugh Flood, A.
Father, Whose Will Is Life and Good.
Old Parish Church, Whitby, The.
We Meet at Morn.
RAY, LOUISE CRENSHAW. But Still Intrepid Icarus.
Middle-aged Quixote.
Philippine Madonna.
Steel Mills after Midnight.
RAY, MAUDE LOUISE. My Task.
"RAYMOND, GRACE" (Annie Raymond Stillman). Birth.
RAYMOND, ROSSITER WORTHINGTON. Christus Consolator.
Trooper's Death, The, tr.
RAYMUND, BERNARD. Wonder.
READ, HENRI CHARLES. Ghosts.
READ, SIR HERBERT EDWARD. Analysis of Love, The.
Analysis of Love, The, sel.
April. Fr. Eclogues.
Beata l'Alma.
Bombing Casualties in Spain.
Contrary Experience, The.
Cranach.
Curfew. Fr. Eclogues.
Day's Affirmation.
Device.
Eclogues, sels.
End of a War, The.
Falcon and the Dove, The.
Inbetweentimes.
Mutations of the Phoenix.
My Company.
Northern Legion, A.
Ode: Written during the Battle of Dunkirk, May, 1940, sel.
Orchard, The. Fr. Eclogues.
Refugees, The.
Scene of War, The; Fear.
Scene of War, The; the Happy Warrior.
September Fires.
Seven Sleepers, The.
Sic et Non.
Song for the Spanish Anarchists, A.

Sorrow of Unicume, The.
Summer Rain.
Time Regained.
To a Conscript of 1940.
Tourists in a Sacred Place.
White Isle of Leuce, The.
World within a War, A.
READ, JOHN. Down by the Old Mill Stream.
READ, OPIE PERCIVAL. Haug-Eye Man, The.
READ, THOMAS BUCHANAN. Angler, The.
Attack, The.
Blennerhassett's Island. Fr. The New Pastoral.
Brave at Home, The. Fr. The Wagoner of the Alleghanies.
Closing Scene, The.
Drifting.
Eagle and Vulture, The.
Flag of the Constellation, The.
Lines to a Blind Girl.
New Pastoral, The, sel.
Oath, The.
Rising, The. Fr. The Wagoner of the Alleghanies.
Sheridan's Ride.
Stranger on the Sill, The.
Summer Shower, The.
Valley Forge. Fr. The Wagoner of the Alleghanies.
Wagoner of the Alleghanies, The, sels.
Windy Night, The.
REALF, RICHARD. Apocalypse.
"De Mortuis Nil Nisi Bonum."
Defence of Lawrence, The.
Ever-present Spirit, The.
Holy Nation, A. Fr. Of Liberty and Charity.
Indirection.
O Earth! Fr. Symbolisms.
Of Liberty and Charity, sel.
Old Man's Idyl, An.
Symbolisms, sels.
Word, The. Fr. Symbolisms.
World, The. Fr. Symbolisms.
REANEY, JAMES. Chough, The.
Gramophone, The.
Horn, The.
Katzenjammer Kids, The.
Klaxon.
Oracular Portcullis, The.
Plum Tree, The.
Red Heart, The.
Two Kites, The.
REAVEY, GEORGE. This Age, This Faust.
REBOLLEDO, BERNARDINO, CONDE DE. Clora!
REBOLLEDO, EFRÉN. Vampire, The.
RECKE, ERNST VON DER. Angel Touched Your Forehead, An.
Methought.
Oh, Is It Wrought.
You Never Have Cared.
"REDCAM, TOM" (Thomas Henry McDermot). San Gloria.
REDDEN, LAURA CATHERINE. See SEARING, LAURA CATHERINE REDDEN.
REDI, FRANCESCO. Bacchus in Tuscany, sels.
Bacchus on Beverages. Fr. Bacchus in Tuscany.
Bacchus's Opinion of Wine, and Other Beverages. Fr. Bacchus in Tuscany.
Creation of My Lady, The.
REDMAN, BEN RAY. How Could You Know?
REDPATH, BEATRICE (Mrs. William Redpath). But I Shall Weep.
Clown, The.
Convict, The.
Earth Love.
Mother, The.
Ponto the Fool.
Star, The.
REECE, BYRON HERBERT. Fox Hunters of Hell.
REED, ANNA NELSON. Message, A.
REED, EDWARD BLISS. Despair.
Go, Magi, on Your Way, tr.
Heritage, The.
I'll Go to Bethlehem, tr.
Noël de Thevet, tr.
Poplars.

REED, EDWARD BLISS (*continued*)
Prayer: "She cannot tell my name," *sel.*
September.
September Is Here.
REED, HENRY. Chard Whitlow.
Chrysothemis.
Door and the Window, The.
Judging Distances. *Fr.* Lessons of the War.
Lessons of the War.
Lessons of the War, *sels.*
Lives.
Map of Verona, A.
Morning.
Naming of Parts. *Fr.* Lessons of the War.
Place and the Person, The, *sel.*
Sailor's Harbor.
Unarmed Combat. *Fr.* Lessons of the War.
Wall, The.
REED, JOHN. Fog.
Proud New York.
Sangar.
REED, LANGFORD. Limerick: "Consider the lowering Lynx."
Limerick: "Indolent vicar of Bray, An."
REED, MARY DAVIS. One Year to Live.
REED, NAN TERRELL. Forget-me-not Day.
Life.
Vases.
REES, GORONWY. Landscape Fading, The.
Seasons' Fool, The.
REESE, LIZETTE WOODWORTH. After.
After Disaster.
Anne.
Apples.
April Ghost, An.
April Weather.
Arraignment.
At Cockcrow.
Betrayed.
Bible Stories.
Bitters.
Book, A.
Carol, A: "Joseph was an old man."
Carol, A: "Mary the Mother sang to her son."
Chesapeake Marsh, A.
Christmas Folk-Song, A.
Common Lot, The.
Compensation.
Cool of Evening, The.
Credo.
Crows.
Daffodils.
Daffodils of Old Saint Paul's, The.
Dust, The.
Ellen Hanging Clothes.
Flower of Mullein, A.
Ghost Night.
Girl's Mood, A.
Good Friday.
Good Joan, The.
Herbs.
Heroism.
Hester.
His First Love.
His Mother in Her Hood of Blue.
Holiday, A.
House of the Silent Years, The.
Immortality.
In Harbor.
In Praise of Common Things.
In Time of Grief.
Keats.
Lark, The.
Lilac Dusk.
Little Song of Life, A.
Lonely.
Love Came Back at Fall o' Dew.
Love, Weeping, Laid This Song.
Lydia.
Lydia Is Gone This Many a Year.
Miracle.
Old Saul.
On a Colonial Picture.
Ownership.
Pastoral, A: "Oho, my love, oho, my love."
Portrait of a Florentine Lady, The.
Possessions.
Prayer of an Unbeliever.
Puritan Lady, A.
Reserve.
Rhyme of Death's Inn, A.
Road of Remembrance, The.
Roads.
Robert Louis Stevenson.
Scarcity.
Small Things.
Spicewood.
Spring Ecstasy.
Street Scene, A.
Sunrise.
Surety.
Sweet Weather.
Taps.
Tears.
Tell Me Some Way.
Telling the Bees.
That Day You Came.
This Very Hour.
Thistledown.
Thomas à Kempis.
Thrift.
To a Town Poet.
Today.
Tragic Books.
Trust.
Waiting.
Wild Cherry.
Windy Night, A.
Wise.
Women.
Written in a Song-Book.
Young Mother, The.
REESE, LOWELL OTUS. Snagtooth Sal.
REEVES, HENRY. Green Mountain Justice, The.
REEVES, JAMES. Beech Leaves.
Chickamungus, The.
Climbing a Mountain.
Doze, The.
Little Fan.
Old Crabbed Men.
Old Wife and the Ghost, The.
Queer Things.
Song of the Dumb Waiter, The.
Spells.
Three Singing Birds, The.
Visitors to the Waterfall.
W.
REEVES, WILLIAM PEMBER. Albatross, The.
Colonist in His Garden, A.
Dutch Seamen and New Holland, The.
New Zealand.
Nox Benigna.
Passing of the Forest, The.
RÉGNIER, HENRI DE. Autumn Twilight.
Gate of the Armies, The.
Je ne veux de personne auprès de ma tristesse.
Landscape.
Light and Darkness.
Night.
Secret, The.
Towards the Past.
Town of France.
Vase, The.
Voice, The.
RÉGNIER, MATHURIN. Epitaph on Himself.
REICH, MAX ISAAC. One Thing Needful, The.
REID, ALASTAIR. Casa d'Amunt.
Game of Glass, A.
Pigeons.
Question in the Cobweb, The.
To Lighten My House.
Who Can Say.
REID, ALICE. Ragged Robin and Bouncing Bet.
REID, BARRIE. Nothing.
St. Kilda.
REID, DOROTHY E. Men.
Mrs. Winkelsteiner.
Tea.
REID, FORREST. Autumn.
REID, PHYLLIS. Fireworks.
Naked and Alone.
Song of Green, A.
Sonnet: "As a seed deeply sheathed within a cone."
Sonnet: "As one who lingers over some old store."
Sonnet: "Do not be angry with me for the word."
Wind.
REINKO. *See* RANKO.
REINMAR VON HAGENAU. As on the Heather.
Childish Game, A.
Deduction.
Meadow and My Lady, A.
REINMAR VON ZWETER. Fortitude.
I Came a-Riding.
REIS, LINCOLN. North Wind, The.
REIS, YITZHOK. *See* NADIR, MOISHE.
REISEN, ABRAHAM. Burn Out Burn Quick.
Healing.
Two Songs.
Watchman, The.
REISS-ANDERSEN, GUNNAR. Phantoms and Spring.
REITH, E. G. Christmas Today.
"REMUS, UNCLE." *See* HARRIS, JOEL CHANDLER.
RENDALL, ELIZABETH. And of Laughter That Was a Changeling.
Buttercup Cow.
Needs.
Wind, The.
RENFROW, GRACE B. My Choice.
That's Jesus!
Trusting Jesus.
Upheld by His Hand.
RENGETSU. Voices of Pine Trees, The.
RENNELL, JAMES RENNELL RODD, 1ST BARON. *See* RODD, JAMES RENNELL, 1ST BARON RENNELL.
RENTOUL, ANNIE ISOBEL RATTRAY (Mrs. John Laurence Rentoul). Fairy Frolic.
RENTOUL, JOHN LAURENCE. Australia.
RENWICK, MATTIE M. We Thank Thee.
REPPLIER, AGNES. Le Repos en Egypte; the Sphinx.
Sphinx, The.
REQUIER, AUGUSTUS JULIAN. Ashes of Glory.
Baby Zulma's Christmas Carol.
Clouds in the West.
REUENTAL, NEIDHART VON. *See* NEIDHART VON REUENTAL.
REVERDY, PIERRE. Everything Is Dark.
REVERE, PAUL. Unhappy Boston.
REXFORD, EBEN EUGENE. At Fourscore.
Cradle Song: "O lullaby, my baby. The bee has gone to sleep."
On Easter Morning.
Sign of Spring, A.
Silver Threads among the Gold.
Trust; a Song.
REXROTH, KENNETH. Advices from Rexroth's Bestiary. *Fr.* A Bestiary.
Antipater of Thessalonica.
Bestiary, A, *sels.*
Deer. *Fr.* A Bestiary.
Herring. *Fr.* A Bestiary.
Infinite, The, *tr.*
Letter to William Carlos Williams, A.
Lion. *Fr.* A Bestiary.
Lyell's Hypothesis Again.
Marcus Argentarius.
Maximian Elegy V.
Racoon. *Fr.* A Bestiary.
You. *Fr.* A Bestiary.
For translations from Chinese, see HoPM; OnPC.
For translations from Japanese, see HoPM; LiTW; OnPJ.
For translations from Latin, see LaP; LiTW; LyMA.
REYES, ALFONSO. Gulf of Mexico.
Menace of the Flower, The.
Monterrey Sun.
River of Oblivion.
Tarahumara Herbs.
Scarcely . . .
To-and-Fro of Saint Theresa.
REYES BASUALTO, NEFTALÍ RICARDO. *See* "NERUDA, PABLO."
REYNOLDS, ELIZABETH GARDNER. Little Black Dog, The.

REYNOLDS, GEORGE NUGENT. Kathleen O'More.
Mary Le More.
REYNOLDS, HENRY. Aminta, *sel., tr.*
Golden Age, The, *tr. Fr.* Aminta.
Love above Beauty.
Song: "Was it a form, a gait, a grace."
Was It a Form?
REYNOLDS, JOHN. Aminta, *sel., tr., wr.*
Garden's Queen, The.
Golden Age, The, *tr., wr. Fr.* Aminta.
Nosegay, A.
REYNOLDS, JOHN HAMILTON. Farewell to the Muses.
Peter Bell; a Lyrical Ballad.
Sonnet: "Sweet poets of the gentle antique line."
Sonnet to ——.
REYNOLDS, LUCILE HARGROVE. To the New Owner.
REYNOLDS, TOM. Corbitt's Barkentine, *at.*
REZNIKOFF, CHARLES. Group of Verse.
Lamps Are Burning, The.
Te Deum.
RHABANUS MAURUS. Sancte Confessor.
RHINELANDER, PHILIP H. Bathtub Gin.
Hangover.
It's Very Unwise to Kill the Goose.
RHINOW, ARTHUR B. And Yet.
Unknown Soldier, The.
Victory.
RHOADES, JAMES. In Whom We Live and Have Our Being.
RHODES, HUGH. Advice.
RHODES, MARGARET G. Best of All, The.
Carol Singers, The.
RHU, LUCY W. Lord Buffington.
RHYS, ERNEST. Autobiography, An.
Ballads of the Last Prince, The, *sel.*
Brechva's Harp Song.
Clio.
Dagonet's Canzonet.
Diana.
Elegy for Lucy Lloyd, *tr.*
Grave, The, *tr.*
Lament for Urien, The, *tr. Fr.* The Red Book of Hergest.
London.
London Feast.
Lost in France.
Mountain Liberty. *Fr.* The Ballads of the Last Prince.
Old Men, The.
Red Book of Hergest, The, *sel., tr.*
Revenant.
Song of Happiness, A.
Song of the Graves, The, *tr.*
Song of the Wulfshaw Larches.
True Love.
White Roses.
Words.
RHYS, KEIDRYCH. During Lambing Season.
Ephemerae for Bruska.
Good Shepherd, The.
Interlude.
Letter to My Wife.
Life of Man, The.
Poem for a Neighbour.
River Sawdde.
Sheep.
Third and Fourth.
Tragic Guilt.
Youth.
RICE, ALBERT. Black Madonna, The.
To a Certain Woman.
RICE, CALE YOUNG. As the Tide Comes In.
Atavism.
Brother Beasts.
Brother Gian.
Chanson of the Bells of Oseney.
Chant of the Colorado, The.
Contessa to Her Judges, The.
Daniel Boone's Last Look Westward.
Dusk from a Train Window.
From a Felucca.
Great Seducer, The.
Heart's Question, The.
His Widow.
I Know Your Heart, O Sea!
Immortal, The.
In An Oriental Harbour.
Kinchinjunga.
Litany for Latter-Day Mystics, A.
Mary at Nazareth.
Mystic, The.
New Dreams for Old.
Nights on the Indian Ocean.
Old Age.
On the Beach.
On the Moor.
Peace Triumphant.
Pilgrims of Thibet, The.
Providence.
Runaway, The.
Self-Server, A.
Serfs.
Sidmouth Soul, A.
Son and Mother.
Sound of Rain, The.
Spades.
Submarine Mountains.
Swallows.
To a Petrel.
To a Solitary Sea-Gull.
To the Afternoon Moon, at Sea.
When the Wind Is Low.
Wife of Judas Iscariot, The.
Wild Geese Come Over No More, The.
RICE, CARRIE SHAW. New Leaf, A.
RICE, SIR CECIL ARTHUR SPRING-. *See* SPRING-RICE, SIR CECIL ARTHUR.
RICE, EDWARD H. "Rock of Ages," *at.*
RICE, ELIZABETH STANTON. Christmas.
RICE, GRANTLAND. Alumnus Football.
Alumnus Football, *sels.*
As We Grow Older.
Back Home Again.
First Division Marches, The.
Forgotten Wars.
Songs above the Dust.
RICE, HARVEY. Cuba.
RICE, RUTH MASON. Japanese Print, A.
RICE, STEPHEN E. SPRING. *See* SPRING RICE, STEPHEN E.
RICE, WALLACE. *Armstrong* at Fayal, The.
Battle-Song of the *Oregon.*
Blood Is Thicker than Water.
Brooklyn at Santiago, The.
David Glasgow Farragut.
Defeat and Victory.
Destroyer of Destroyers, The.
Dewey and His Men.
End, The.
First American Sailors, The.
First Fruits in 1812.
Immortal Flowers.
Jackson at New Orleans.
Minute-Men of North-Boro', The.
Passing of Richard Somers, The.
Spain's Last Armada.
Sudbury Fight, The.
Sweet Clover.
Under the Stars.
Wheeler's Brigade at Santiago.
RICH, ADRIENNE CECILE. At a Bach Concert.
Bears.
Celebration in the Plaza, The.
Epilogue for a Masque of Purcell.
For the Conjunction of Two Planets.
Living in Sin.
Love in the Museum.
Orient Wheat.
Recorders in Italy.
Versailles.
Walk by the Charles, A.
RICH, BARNABE. Barnabe Rich, Gentleman Soldier, in Praise of the Author.
Epitaph upon the Death of Sir William Drury, An.
RICH, HIRAM. Skipper-Hermit, The.
RICH, RICHARD. Newes from Virginia.
RICHARD, EDWARD. Pastoral Poem, *sel.*
Poet's Welcome, The. *Fr.* Pastoral Poem.
RICHARD CŒUR DE LION (Richard Lion-Heart). Prison Song.
RICHARD OF CHICHESTER. Prayer for the New Year.
RICHARDS, BERESFORD. Guest.
RICHARDS, EDWARD HERSEY. Wise Old Owl, A [*or* The].
RICHARDS, JOSEPH ADDISON. Boat, The.
Master of My Boat, The.
RICHARDS, LAURA ELIZABETH (Mrs. Henry Richards). Advice to Young Naturalists.
Alice's Supper.
Antonio.
At Easter Time.
Baby Goes to Boston, The.
Bird Song.
Bobbily Boo and Wollypotump.
Cave-Boy, The.
Crocodile, The.
Dandy Cat, The.
Difference, The.
Drinking Vessels.
Egg, The.
Eletelephony.
Emily Jane.
Five Little Princesses, The.
Fussy.
Harriet Hutch. *Fr.* Nonsense Verses.
He and His Family.
High Barbaree, The.
In Foreign Parts.
In Samarcand.
Jippy and Jimmy.
Johnny's By-low Song.
Jumbo Jee.
Kindness to Animals.
Legend of [Lake] Okeefinokee, A.
Little Brown Bobby.
Little Cossack, The.
Little John Bottlejohn.
Mermaidens, The.
Mrs. Snipkin and Mrs. Wobblechin.
Molly Pitcher.
Monkeys and the Crocodile, The.
Nicholas Ned. *Fr.* Nonsense Verses.
Nonsense Verses.
Nursery Song, A.
Our Colors.
Owl and the Eel and the Warming-Pan, The.
Party, A.
Ponsonby Perks. *Fr.* Nonsense Verses.
Postman, The.
Prince Tatters.
Punkydoodle and Jollapin.
Sleepyland.
Sleigh-Ride, A.
Some Fishy Nonsense.
Song of the Cornpopper, The.
Song of the Little Winds.
Song of Two Angels, A.
"Talents Differ."
Umbrella Brigade, The.
Valentine, A.
Was She a Witch?
Where Helen Sits.
Why Does it Snow?
Why I No Longer Travel.
Winifred White. *Fr.* Nonsense Verses.
RICHARDSON, CHARLES FRANCIS. Hundred Noble Wishes, A.
Perfect Life, The.
RICHARDSON, DOROTHY M. (Mrs. Alan Odle). Buns for Tea.
RICHARDSON, GEORGE LYNDE. Classical Criticism.
RICHARDSON, ISLA PASCHAL. My Dog and I.
Ownership.
Raindrops.
RICHARDSON, JUSTIN. All Awry.
Back Room Joys.
La Carte
Oocuck, The.
Titles.
What'll Be the Title?
RICHARDSON, MARION MUIR. Gold Seekers, The.
RICHARDSON, NORMAN EGBERT. Prayer for Aviators, A.
Teacher's Prayer, The.
RICHARDSON, ROBERT. Epitaph: "Warm Summer Sun."
Epitaph Placed on His Daughter's Tomb by Mark Twain.
Requiem.
RICHARDSON, SHERMAN D. Denver Jim.
RICHARDSON, THOMAS. Proper New Song Made by a Student in Cambridge, A.

RICHARDSON, THOMAS (*continued*)
Proper New Song Made by a Student in Cambridge, A, *sel.*
Take Heed of Gazing Overmuch. *Fr.* A Proper New Song Made by a Student in Cambridge.
RICHARDT, CHRISTIAN. Forest Wedding, The.
Ninetta's Tom-Cat.
Teach Me!
RICHEPIN, JEAN. Song of Mary-of-the-Angels, The.
RICHMOND, OLIFFE. Delphi.
Moat, The.
"They Also Serve . . ."
RICHTER, MARGARET R. Greek Vase.
Unbowed.
RICKARD, TRUMAN E., *and* ARTHUR UPSON. Hail! Minnesota!
"RICKETTY KATE." *See* "KATE, RICKETTY."
RICKS, PIERSON. Saint Francis of Assisi.
RICKWORD, EDGELL. Cascade, The.
Cosmogony.
Rimbaud in Africa.
RIDDELL, ELIZABETH. Children March, The.
Country Tune.
Forebears.
Lifesaver.
Old Sailor, The.
News of a Baby.
Train in the Night, The.
RIDDELL, HENRY SCOTT. Dowie Dens o' Yarrow, The.
Ours Is the Land.
Scotland Yet.
RIDER, GEORGE T. Sleep, My Infant Saviour.
RIDGE, LOLA. Altitude.
April of Our Desire.
Art and Life.
Bees, The.
Child and Wind.
Death Ray.
Débris.
Edge, The.
Electrocution.
Faces.
Ghetto, The, *sels.*
Iron Wine.
Joy Is in the Morning Veiled, A.
Legion of Iron, The.
Marie.
Memory, A.
Mother.
New Orleans.
Reveille.
Snow-Dance for the Dead.
Song, The: "That day, in the slipping of torsos and straining flanks."
Sons of Belial.
To E. A. R.
Wind in the Alleys.
RIDING, LAURA. After So Much Loss.
As Many Questions as Answers.
Auspice of Jewels.
Because of Clothes.
Dear Possible.
Doom in Bloom.
Earth.
Flowering Urn, The.
For-ever Morning.
Lucrece and Nara.
Map of Places, The.
Not All Immaculate. *Fr.* Three Sermons to the Dead.
O Vocables of Love.
Quids, The.
Respect for the Dead.
Sea, False Philosophy.
Three Sermons to the Dead.
Three Sermons to the Dead, *sel.*
Tiger, The.
Tillaquils, The.
Victory, The.
Way of the Air, The. *Fr.* Three Sermons to the Dead.
Wind Suffers, The.
Wind, the Clock, the We, The.
RIDINGS, J. WILLARD. Thesaurus Nightmare, A.
RIDLER, ANNE. Before Sleep.
Bunhill's Fields.
Christmas and Common Birth.
Deus Absconditus.
Dream Observed, A.
Edlesborough.
For a Child Expected.
For a Christening.
Letter, A.
Mile from Eden, A.
Now as Then.
Now Philippa Is Gone.
O Love, Answer.
Of the Unscathing Fire.
On a Picture by Michele da Verona.
Phoenix Answered, The.
Piero della Francesca.
Poem for a Christmas Broadcast.
Speech of the Dead, The.
Spring Equinox, The.
Zennor.
RIEU, EMILE VICTOR. Lesser Lynx, The.
Meditations of a Tortoise Dozing under a Rosetree near a Beehive at Noon While a Dog Scampers About and a Cuckoo Calls from a Distant Wood.
Night Thought of a Tortoise Suffering from Insomnia on a Lawn.
Soliloquy of a Tortoise on Revisiting the Lettuce Beds after an Interval of One Hour While Supposed to Be Sleeping in a Clump of Blue Hollyhocks.
RIGBY, RALPH. Branding Iron Herd, The.
RIGGS, KATHERINE DIXON. Mockery.
RIGGS, LENORE. Bathtub Bay.
RIGGS, LYNN. Spring Morning—Santa Fé.
RIHAKU. *See* LI PO.
RIIS, CLAUS PAVELS. Yes, I Will Have Me a Heart's-beloved.
RILEY, ATHELSTAN. Ye Watchers and Ye Holy Ones.
RILEY, JAMES WHITCOMB. Away.
Back to Griggsby's Station.
Barefoot Boy, A.
Beetle, The, *sel.*
Bereaved.
Boy's Mother, A.
Brook Song, The.
Days Gone By, The.
Dwainie. *Fr.* The Flying Islands of the Night.
Extremes.
First Bluebird, The.
Flying Islands of the Night, The, *sel.*
Funniest Thing in the World, The.
Glimpse of Pan, A.
God Bless Us Every One.
Going to the Fair.
He Is Not Dead.
He's Just-Away.
His Christmas Sled.
Honey Dripping from the Comb.
Ike Walton's Prayer.
It. *Fr.* A Session with Uncle Sidney.
Just Be Glad.
Kissing the Rod.
Knee-deep in June.
Lawyer and Child.
Let Something Good Be Said.
Life-Lesson, A.
Like His Mother Used to Make.
Lincoln.
Little Orphant Annie.
Little Red Ribbon, The.
Liz-Town Humorist, A.
Longfellow ("The winds have talked").
Love's Prayer.
Lugubrious Whing-Whang, The.
Man by the Name of Bolus, A.
Man in the Moon, The.
Mister Hop-Toad.
Monument for the Soldiers, A.
My Boy.
Name of Old Glory, The.
Old John Henry.
Old Man and Jim, The.
Old Sweetheart of Mine, An.
Old Sweetheart of Mine, An, *sel.*
Old Swimmin'-Hole, The.
Old Times Were the Best, The.
On the Death of Little Mahala Ashcraft.
Our Hired Girl.
Out of the Hitherwhere.
Out to Old Aunt Mary's.
Parting Guest, A.
Prayer Perfect, The.
Prior to Miss Belle's Appearance.
Raggedy Man, The.
Rival, The.
Runaway Boy, The.
Sea-Song from the Shore, A.
Session with Uncle Sidney, A, *sel.*
Spirk Troll-Derisive, The.
Sudden Shower, A.
That Little Dog.
Three Jolly Hunters, The.
Way the Baby Slept, The.
Way the Baby Woke, The.
When She Comes Home.
When the Frost Is on the Punkin.
When the Green Gits Back in the Trees.
Witch of Erkmurden, The.
RILEY, KAY. Home Brunt, The.
RILEY, MAY LOUISE. *See* SMITH, MAY RILEY.
RILKE, RAINER MARIA. Abishag.
Annunciation.
Archaic Torso of Apollo.
Autumn.
Autumn [*or* Autumn's] Day.
Book of Hours, The, *sels.*
Buddha in Glory.
Child, The.
Childhood.
Cornet, The.
Death.
Death Is Great.
Death of the Beloved.
Death of the Poet.
Duino Elegies, The, *sels.*
Eingang (Prelude).
Eva.
Evening.
Extinguish My Eyes.
Flamingos, The.
For, Lord, the Crowded Cities Be.
Four Sonnets to Orpheus. *Fr.* Sonnets to Orpheus.
From a Childhood.
Going Blind.
Goldsmith, The.
Great Night, The.
Grownup, The.
I Praise.
I Was a Child.
I Would Comprehend Thee.
In Memoriam Egon von Rilke.
Initiation.
Insane in the Garden, The.
Interior of the Rose.
Joseph's Suspicion.
Knight, The.
Lament: "All is far/ And long gone by."
Lament: "Oh, everything is far."
Last Evening, The.
Loneliness.
Love Song.
Lute, The.
Neighbor, The.
Ninth Duino Elegy, The.
O Tell Us, Poet.
On the Death of Mary.
Orpheus, Eurydice, and Hermes.
Outcast on the Mountains of the Heart.
Palm of the Hand.
Panther, The.
Poet, The. Fr. Sonnets to Orpheus.
Pont du Carrousel.
Praise.
Prayer of the Maidens to Mary.
Presaging.
Put Out My Eyes, and I Can See You Still.
Remembrance.
Requiem—for the Death of a Boy.
Requiem; to Paula Modersohn-Becker.
Roman Fountain.
Shako, The.
Silent Hour.
Solemn Hour.
Solitary, The.

Solitude.
Song of Love, The.
Sonnets to Orpheus, *sels.*
Spanish Trilogy, The.
Strophes: "There is one who takes all men within his hand."
Tenth Duino Elegy, The.
Third Duino Elegy, The.
To Hölderlin.
To the Angel.
Torso of an Archaic Apollo.
Walk.
Washing the Corpse.
What Stillness around a God!
What Will You Do, God, When I Die?
When the Clocks Strike.
You Are the Future.
Young Girl's Tomb, A.
Youth Dreams, The.

RIMBAUD, ARTHUR. After the Flood.
Alchemy of Words, The.
Antique.
Bally.
Barbarian.
Being Beauteous.
Brussels.
Chastisement of Tartufe, The.
Cherceuses de poux, Les.
Cities.
Dawn.
Departure.
Drunken Boat, The.
Eternity.
Evenings.
Evil.
Feeling.
Flowers.
Gibbet Dance.
Gipsying.
Head of a Faun.
Hunger.
Ill Will.
Lice-Seekers, The.
Lives.
Louse-Catchers, The.
Marine.
Memory.
Michael and Christine.
Morning.
My Bohemia.
Novel.
Ophelia.
Poets Seven Years Old.
Poor in Church, The.
Ravens, The.
Royalty.
Season in Hell, A, *sel.*
Sensation.
Seven-year-old Poet.
Shame.
Sleeper in [*or* of] the Valley, The.
Sly-Boots.
Song of the Highest Tower.
Sonnet: "Dead men of 'ninety-two, also of 'ninety-three."
Stolen Heart, The.
Tear.
Vision, A.
Vowels.
Voyels.
Waifs and Strays.
What to Us, My Heart.
Workers.
Young Couple.

RIMEL, DUANE W. Dreams of Yith.

RIMOS, MOSES, OF MAJORCA. Elegy: "Tumult of death, dizziness hath seized me, The."

RINALDO D'AQUINO. Crusade, The.
Lament for the Sailing of the Crusade.

RINKART, MARTIN. Now Thank We All Our God.

RIOJA, FRANCISCO DE. To the Rose.

RISLEY, RICHARD VOORHEES. Dewey in Manila Bay.

RITA AGNES, SISTER. Limits.
On Moving into a Skylight Room.

RITCHIE, ALEXANDER A. Lullaby, A: "O saftly sleep, my bonnie bairn!"

RITCHIE, CAROL M. Harvest of Dust.

RITO. Tea Flowers.

RITSOS, YIANNIS. Spring Symphony, *sel.*
To My Sister, *sel.*

RITTENHOUSE, JESSIE BELLE (Mrs. Clinton Scollard). Bouton d'Or.
Communion.
Debt[s].
Dragon-Fly, The.
Frost in Spring.
Ghostly Galley, The.
Green Tree in the Fall, The.
Haunted Heart, The.
Hour, The.
Marsh-Grass.
My Father.
My Wage.
Nightingales of Surrey, The.
Onset, The.
Osprey and Eagle.
Paradox.
Patrins.
Radiant Loss, The.
Secret, The.
Seven Times the Moon Came.
Some Star within Orion.
Transformation.
Unto the End.
White Peacocks.
Youth.

RITTER, FANNY RAYMOND. Hottentot Cradle-Song.

RITTER, MARGARET TOD. Faith, I Wish I Were a Leprechaun.
Hero's Invocation to Death.
Indictment.
Release.
Resurgence.
Sonnet to a Plow-Woman of Norway.

RITTER, MARY LOUISE. Perished.
Why?

RIVA PALACIO, VICENTE. To the Wind.

RIVAS, ANGEL DE SAAVEDRA, DUQUE DE. Ode to the Lighthouse at Malta.

RIVES, AMÉLIE (Princess Troubetzkoy). Before the Rain.
Mood, A.
My Laddie.
Sonnet, A: "Take all of me—I am thine own, heart, soul."

RIVOLA, FLORA S. In the Afterglow.

RIZAL, JOSÉ. My Last Thought.

ROADS, HELEN PURCELL. Centurion, The.
Test.

ROBB, ETHEL. Child's Evensong.
Christmas "Good Night."

ROBBINS, HOWARD CHANDLER. Put Forth, O God, Thy Spirit's Might.
Saviour, Whose Love Is like the Sun.
Spirit from Whom Our Lives Proceed.
Via Lucis.

ROBBINS, S. D. Master, The.

ROBERT II, KING OF FRANCE. Strength, Love, Light.
Veni, Sancte Spiritus.

ROBERT, JEANNE. *See* FOSTER, JEANNE ROBERT.

ROBERTS, CECIL EDRIC MORNINGTON. Charing Cross.
Charing Cross, *sel.*
Eyeless and Limbless and Shattered. *Fr.* Charing Cross.
Prayer for a Pilot.
Springtime in Cookham Dean.
Watchmen of the Night.

ROBERTS, SIR CHARLES GEORGE DOUGLAS. Afoot.
Aim, The.
All Night the Lone Cicada.
April Adoration, An.
As Down the Woodland Ways.
At Tide Water.
Autochthon.
Ballad of Manila Bay, A.
Bird's Song, the Sun, and the Wind, The.
Book of the Native, The, *sel.*
Brooklyn Bridge.
Burnt Lands.
Cambrai and Marne.
Canada.
Canada Speaks of Britain.
Child's Prayer at Evening, A.
Cricket, The.
Deserted City, The.
Domine, Cui Sunt Pleiades Curae.
Epitaph: "His fame the mock of shallow wits."
Epitaph for a Sailor Buried Ashore.
Epitaph on a Husbandman, An.
Flight of the Geese, The. *Fr.* Songs of the Common Day.
Frosted Pane, The.
Going Over.
Good Earth, The.
Gray Rocks and Grayer Sea.
Hath Hope Kept Vigil?
Hawkbit, The.
Here on the hill. *Fr.* Hill Top Songs.
Herring Weir, The. *Fr.* Songs of the Common Day.
Hill Top Songs.
Ice.
Iceberg, The.
In an Old Barn.
In Apia Bay.
In the Barn-Yard's Southerly Corner.
In the Night Watches.
In the Wide Awe and Wisdom of the Night.
Isles, The.
Keepers of the Pass, The.
Marsyas.
Monition.
Mowing, The.
Night Sky, The.
O Earth, Sufficing All our Needs.
O Solitary of the Austere Sky.
On the Road.
Pea-Fields, The. *Fr.* Songs of the Common Day.
Philander's Song.
Place of His Rest, The.
Potato Harvest, The.
Recessional, The.
Salt Flats, The.
Sleepy Man.
Solitary Woodsman, The.
Songs of the Common Day, *sels.*
Sower, The.
Summons, The.
Tantramar Revisited.
Under the Pillars of the Sky.
Unknown City, The.
Vagrant of Time, The.
Wayfarer of Earth.
When the Cloud Comes down the Mountain.
When the lights come out in the cottages. *Fr.* Hill Top Songs.
When the Sleepy Man Comes. *Fr.* The Book of the Native.
Wrestler, The.

ROBERTS, DANIEL C. National Hymn: "God of our fathers, whose almighty hand."

ROBERTS, DICK (Richard Edwin Roberts). Duty to Death, LD.

ROBERTS, DOROTHY. Goose Girl, The.
Sisters.

ROBERTS, ELIZABETH MADOX. At the Water.
August Night.
Autumn.
Autumn Fields.
Ballet Song of Mary, A.
Big Brother.
Butterbean Tent, The.
Child Asleep, A.
Christmas Morning.
Cinderella's Song.
Circus, The.
Cornfield, The.
Crescent Moon.
Evening Hymn.
Father's Story.
Firefly.
Grandmother, The.
Hens, The.
Horse.
Little Rain.
Milking Time.
Mr. Wells.
Mumps.
My Heart.
Orpheus.
People, The.
People Going By.
Picnic, The.
Pilaster, The.

ROBERTS, ELIZABETH MADOX (*continued*)
Rabbit, The.
Richest Woman, The.
Shells in Rock.
Sky, The.
Strange Tree.
Stranger.
Twins, The.
Water Noises.
Wolves, The.
Woodcock of the Ivory Beak.
Woodpecker, The.
Worm, The.
ROBERTS, FLORENCE CECILIA. Ambuscade, The.
ROBERTS, FREDERICK T. Cup, The.
ROBERTS, G. D. Old Morgan.
ROBERTS, HOMER. Pa's Chickens.
ROBERTS, JANE ELIZABETH GOSTWYCKE. In the Golden Birch.
ROBERTS, LEVAN. Unemployed, The.
ROBERTS, LLOYD. Changing Year, The.
Dead Days.
Deep Dark River.
Fruit-Rancher, The.
Husbands over Seas.
If I Must.
Madness of Winds, The.
Miss Pixie.
One Morning When the Rain-Birds Call.
Young Blood.
ROBERTS, LYNETTE. Broken Voices.
Circle of C, The.
Englyn.
Heroic Poem, A, *sel.*
Lamentation.
Low Tide.
Poem from Llanybri.
Seasons, The.
Shadow Remains, The.
These Words I Write on Crinkled Tin.
To the Priest of the Middles.
ROBERTS, MARY ELEANOR. Heaven Soaring Lark, The.
Witch-Wife, The.
ROBERTS, MICHAEL. Castle, The.
Caves, The.
Elegy for the Fallen Climbers, *sel.*
Gale Warning.
Green Lake, The.
Hymn to the Sun.
In Our Time.
In the Strange Isle.
In Time of Peace.
Les Planches-en-Montagne.
Midnight.
St. Gervais.
St. Ursanne.
Shining Dark.
Wir Sind Alle Verloren. *Fr.* Elegy for the Fallen Climbers.
World's End, The.
ROBERTS, RICHARD EDWIN. *See* ROBERTS, DICK.
ROBERTS, THEODORE GOODRIDGE. Blind Sailor, The.
Blue Heron, The.
Fiddler's Green.
Hamadryad, The.
Lost Shipmate, The.
Maid, The.
Pernambuco in May.
Wreckers' Prayer, The.
ROBERTS, WALTER ADOLPHE. Boyhood Etchings.
Captains, The.
Cat, The.
For Poets Slain in War.
Maroon Girl, The.
On a Monument to Marti.
Peacocks.
San Francisco.
Tropic Storm. *Fr.* Boyhood Etchings.
Tropic Sunset. *Fr.* Boyhood Etchings.
Vieux Carré.
Villanelle of Poor Pierrot.
Villanelle of the Living Pan.
Villanelle of Washington Square.
ROBERTS, WILLIAM H. I Will Believe.
ROBERTSON, ALEXANDER. Au Revoir.
ROBERTSON, CLYDE. Mistress of the Matchless Mine.
Woman in the Wagon, The.
ROBERTSON, ELLA BROADUS. Prayer for a College Girl.
ROBERTSON, GRACE MARGARET. All is Hidden, Naught Concealed.
ROBERTSON, HARRISON. Kentucky Philosophy.
Two Triolets.
What He Said. *Fr.* Two Triolets.
What She Thought. *Fr.* Two Triolets.
ROBERTSON, JAMES LOGIE ("Hugh Haliburton"). Dave.
Farmer of Westerha', The.
Hughie Seeks to Console a Brother Shepherd, Over-grieving for the Loss of His Son.
Hughie's Advice to Dauvit to Enjoy the Fine Weather.
Ochil Farmer, An.
Quem Tu, Melpomene.
Spring on the Ochils.
ROBERTSON, LEXIE DEAN. Gossip.
I Gave My Love.
New Temples.
Radio Prayer.
ROBERTSON, W. GRAHAM. Glad Day.
Other Side of the Sky, The.
Primroses, The.
Ring o' Roses.
Sand Castles.
Snowdrops.
ROBEY, GEORGE. Limerick: "Eccentric old person of Slough, An."
ROBINDEAU, ——. "Metis" Song of the Buffalo Hunters, The.
ROBINS, HENRY BURKE. Better a Day of Faith.
City of God, The.
Eternal Spirit, Evermore Creating.
Life of Our Life.
Of One Blood Hath God Created.
One Hundred Fifty-first Psalm, A.
ROBINS, TED (Edmund John Robins). Dive, The.
ROBINSON, AGNES MARY FRANCES (Mme Emile Duclaux). Ah, Me, Do You Remember Still.
Ballad of Orleans, A.
Castello.
Celia's Home-coming.
Cockayne Country.
Darwinism.
Dawn-Angels.
Elysium.
Etruscan Tombs.
Idea, The.
Italian Garden, An.
Le Roi Est Mort.
Let Us Forget.
Music.
Orchard at Avignon, An.
Pulvis et Umbra.
Red May.
Retrospect.
Rispetto. *Fr.* Tuscan Cypress.
Rosa Rosarum.
Sometimes When I Sit Musing All Alone.
Temple Garlands.
Tuscan Cypress, *sels.*
Twilight.
ROBINSON, ANNE. April and May.
Conversation.
Drummer, The.
To Laddie.
ROBINSON, ANNIE DOUGLAS GREEN. *See* "DOUGLAS, MARIAN."
ROBINSON, CORINNE ROOSEVELT (Mrs. Douglas Robinson). Belovèd, from the Hour That You Were Born.
By an Open Window in Church.
Call of Brotherhood, The.
Debt.
Forgotten Countersign, The.
Friendship.
Life, a Question.
Lincoln.
Path That Leads to Nowhere, The.
Sagamore.
To Peace, with Victory.
Unfulfilled.
Valiant-for-Truth.
Which.
ROBINSON, EDWIN ARLINGTON. Aaron Stark.
Amaryllis.
Another Dark Lady.
Aretemias.
As It Looked Then.
Ballade by the Fire.
Ballade of a Ship.
Ballade of Dead Friends.
Ben Jonson Entertains a Man from Stratford.
Ben Jonson Entertains a Man from Stratford, *sel.*
Bewick Finzer.
Calvary.
Calverly's.
Captain Craig, *sels.*
Caput Mortuum.
Cassandra.
Charles Carville's Eyes.
Children of the Night, The.
Children of the Night, The, *sel.*
Christmas Sonnet, A.
Clavering.
Clerks, The.
Cliff Klingenhagen.
Corridor, The.
Credo.
Dark Hills, The.
Demos.
Discovery.
Doctor of Billiards.
Doricha, *tr.*
Dust of Timas, The, *tr.*
Erasmus.
Eros Turannos.
Eutychides.
Exit.
False Gods, The.
Field of Glory, The.
Firelight.
Flammonde.
Fleming Helphenstine.
For a Dead Lady.
For Arvia.
Fragment: "Faint white pillars."
George Crabbe.
Gift of God, The.
Growth of Lorraine, The.
Happy Man, A.
Hillcrest.
House on the Hill, The.
How Annandale Went Out.
Inscription by the Sea, An, *tr.*
Isaac and Archibald.
Isaac and Archibald, *sel.*
James Wetherell.
John Evereldown.
John Gorham.
Just as I wonder at the two-fold screen.
Karma.
Klondike, The.
Lais to Aphrodite.
L'Envoi: "Now in a thought, now in a shadowed word." *Fr.* The Children of the Night.
Leonora.
Llewellyn and the Tree.
Long Race, The.
Luke Havergal.
Man against the Sky, The.
Many Are Called.
Master, The.
Mighty Runner, A.
Mill, The.
Miniver Cheevy.
Mr. Flood's Party.
Momus.
Monadnock through the Trees.
Neighbors.
New England.
New Tenants, The.
Nimmo.
Not Always.
Oh for a Poet—for a Beacon Bright.
Octaves, *sels.*
Odes (*of* Horace), *sel., tr.*
Old King Cole.
Old Story, The ("Like many a one when you had gold").
Old Story, An ("Strange that I did not know him then").
Partnership.
Pasa Thalassa Thalassa.
Pilot, The.
Pity of the Leaves, The.

Poor Relation, The.
Prodigal Son, The.
Raven, The, *tr.*
Return of Morgan and Fingal, The.
Reuben Bright.
Revealer, The.
Richard Cory.
Sheaves, The.
Sonnet: "Never until our souls are strong enough."
Sonnet: "When we can all so excellently give."
Souvenir.
Stafford's Cabin.
Tasker Norcross.
There Is One Creed, and Only One.
Thomas Hood.
Three Quatrains.
To-Morrow.
Too Much Coffee.
Torrent, The.
Toussaint L'Ouverture.
Town down the River, The.
Twilight Song.
Two Men.
Uncle Ananias.
Unforgiven, The.
Vain Gratuities.
Valley of the Shadow, The.
Variations of Greek Themes.
Verlaine.
Veteran Sirens.
Vickery's Mountain.
Walt Whitman.
Why He Was There.
Wilderness, The.
Zola.
ROBINSON, EDWIN MEADE. Annual Solution, The.
David Jazz, The.
Disagreeable Feature, A.
Fishers.
How He Turned Out.
How Homer Should Have Written the Iliad. *Fr.* Limericised Classics.
It Happens Often.
Limericised Classics.
Ode to Eve.
Rubaiyat, The. *Fr.* Limericised Classics.
Sad September Sentiments.
Shakespeare Might Have Boiled Othello. *Fr.* Limericised Classics.
Song of the Movie Mexican, A.
Spoon River Anthology. *Fr.* Limericised Classics.
Story of Ug, The.
"To Lucasta, on Going to the Wars." *Fr.* Limericised Classics.
Villanelle of a Villaness.
ROBINSON, ELOISE. To-Day I Saw Bright Ships.
ROBINSON, ELSIE. Beauty as a Shield.
Help Me Today.
Pain.
ROBINSON, GEORGE. One sole baptismal sign.
ROBINSON, GRANT P. I Fights mit Sigel!
ROBINSON, HENRY MORTON. Chantey of Notorious Bibbers.
Cock-Crow; Woodstock.
December Fugitive.
Earth-canonized.
Heaven Tree.
November Fugitive.
Second Wisdom.
Seventh Station, *tr.*
ROBINSON, JOSEPHINE. Universal Language.
ROBINSON, KENNETH ALLAN. American Laughter.
Lines to Dr. Ditmars.
ROBINSON, LUCY CATLIN BULL (Mrs. Tracy Robinson). Ballade of Islands, A.
Fire i' the Flint, The.
"Hic Me, Pater Optime, Fessam De seris."
ROBINSON, MARY K. Brown Frog, The.
Dandelion Puff, The.
Queen Bee, The.
ROBINSON, R. H. Light at Evening Time.
ROBINSON, ROLAND. And Each Man's Leave.
Casuarina.
I Breathed into the Ash.
Rock-Lily's Pale Spray, The.
Tea-Tree and the Lyrebird, The.
To a Mate.
Tumult Ends, The.
ROBINSON, SELMA. Ballad of the Huntsman.
Bus Ride. *Fr.* Ferry Ride.
City Childhood.
Dead, The.
Ferry Ride, *sel.*
Gentle Name.
Harvesting.
Pendulum Rhyme.
Summer Shower.
ROBINSON, TED. April.
Ditty: "Time was long and long ago, The."
Sure.
Unfaith.
ROBINSON, TOM (Thomas Pendleton Robinson). Autumn Color.
Little French Dog, The.
Little Lady Wren.
Look and See.
Pansies.
Rabbit.
Shoes.
Swallow Tails.
ROBINSON, TRACY. Song of the Palm.
ROBINSON, VICTOR. Hasheesh.
Healing Hands, The.
Tuberculosis.
ROBINSON, WEY. Horse & Rider.
ROBISON, ALBERTA. Status.
ROBY, H. A. Red and the Blue, The.
ROCHE, JAMES JEFFREY. "Albemarle" Cushing.
Andromeda.
Boston Lullaby, A.
Constitution's Last Fight, The.
Don't.
Fight of the *Armstrong* Privateer, The.
First Citizen.
Flag, The.
Gettysburg.
Gospel of Peace, The.
If.
Jack Creamer.
Kearsarge, The.
Lament of the Scotch-Irish Exile.
Men of the Alamo, The.
My Comrade.
Nature the False Goddess.
Net of Law, The.
On Rereading Télémaque.
Panama.
Reuben James.
Sailor's Yarn, A.
Skeleton at the Feast, The.
Three Doves.
V-a-s-e, The.
Washington.
Way of the World, The.
ROCHE, PAUL. Courage for the Pusillanimous.
ROCHESTER, JOHN WILMOT, 2D EARL OF. Absent from thee, I languish still!
All my past life is mine no more.
Allusion to Horace, An. The 10th Satire of the 1st Book.
Answer, The.
Bowl, The.
Bully, The, *at.*
Chaste Arabian Bird, The.
Constancy.
Dialogue between Strephon and Daphne, A.
Epitaph on Charles II.
Fall, The.
Farewell: "Tir'd with the noysom follies of the age."
Farewell to the Court, *sel.*
His Mistress.
I Cannot Change as Others Do.
Impromptu on Charles II.
Jealousy.
Julian, *sel.*
King Charles II.
King's Epitaph, The.
Letter, A, *sel.*
Letter from Artemisa in the Town, to Cloe in the Country, A.
Letter from Artemisa in the Town, to Cloe in the Country, A, *sels.*
Love and Life.
Love, as a Warrior Lord, *tr.*
Lovely Lass to a Friar Came, A, *at.*
Maim'd [*or* Maimed] Debauchee, The.
May the Ambitious Ever Find, *at.*
Mistress, The.
Mistress, The, *sel.*
More Dullness. *Fr.* Julian.
My Dear Mistress.
My Light Thou Art.
Nature of Women, The, *sel.*
On Charles II.
Pastoral Courtship, A, *sel.*
Return.
Royal Angler, The, *sel.*
Satire [*or* Satyr] against Mankind, A.
Satire [*or* Satyr] against Mankind, A, *sel.*
Since All the World's Thus Gay and Free.
Song: "Absent from thee, I languish still."
Song: "All my past life is mine no more."
Song: "Give me leave to rail at you."
Song: "I cannot change as others do."
Song: "I promised Sylvia to be true."
Song, A: "Love a woman! you're an ass."
Song, A: "My dear mistress has a heart."
Song: Noble Name of Spark, The.
Song: "Room, room for a blade of the town."
Song: "Too late, alas! I must confess."
Song of a Young Lady to Her Ancient Lover, A.
Spoken Extempore.
To a Lady; in a Letter.
To Chuse a Friend, but Never Marry, *at.*
To His Mistress.
Tragedy of Valentinian, *sel.*
Upon Drinking in a Bowl.
Upon [His] Leaving His Mistress.
Upon Nothing.
While on Those Lovely Looks I Gaze.
Within the Canopy of Leaves. *Fr.* A Pastoral Courtship.
Woman. *Fr.* The Nature of Women.
Wretched Man. *Fr.* A Satire against Mankind.
ROCHFORD, GEORGE BOLEYN, VISCOUNT. *See* BOLEYN, GEORGE, VISCOUNT ROCHFORD.
ROCK, FRANCIS J. "Tell Ye the Faint of Heart."
ROCK, MADELEINE CARON. He Is the Lonely Greatness.
ROCKETT, F. V. Melt the Bells.
ROCKETT, WINNIE LYNCH. Invincible.
Mother before a Soldier's Monument.
Potion, The.
RODD, JAMES RENNELL, 1ST BARON RENNELL. Actea.
Daisy, The.
Evening, *tr.*
Imperator Augustus.
Roman Mirror, A.
Song of Autumn, A.
Then and Now.
When I Am Dead.
RODE, HELGE. Clover.
Early Spring.
RODENBACH, GEORGES. Dead Waters.
Morning Bells.
You Are My Sisters.
RODGER, ALEXANDER. Behave Yoursel' before Folk.
My Auld Breeks.
RODGERS, WILLIAM ROBERT. Airman, The.
Apollo and Daphne.
Autumn.
Awake!
Beagles.
Carol: "Deep in the fading leaves of light."
Christ Walking on the Water.

RODGERS, WILLIAM ROBERT (*continued*)
Direction to a Rebel.
Express.
Fountains, The.
Lent.
Life's Circumnavigators.
Nativity.
Neither Here nor There.
Net, The.
Raider, The.
Sing, Brothers, Sing!
Snow.
Snow, *sel.*
Song for Peace.
Song for War.
Spring.
Spring-Dance.
Stormy Day.
Stormy Day, *sel.*
Stormy Night.
Summer Holidays.
Swan, The.
White Christmas.
Winter's Cold.
RODMAN, FRANCES. Lost Dog.
Spring Cricket.
RODMAN, SELDEN. After Six Thousand Years, *tr.*
Against the Hope of Reconstruction, *tr.*
Cemetery by the Sea, *tr.*
Consuelo at the Country Club.
Daphne.
Dirge for the Barrel-Organ of the New Barbarism, *tr.*
Eadem Mutato Resurgo.
Harpers Ferry.
Late Rising, *tr.*
Lawrence; the Last Crusade, *sel.*
Man, Not His Arms.
Norris Dam.
On a Picture by Pippin, Called "The Den."
Pioneers, The.
Poet, The, *tr. Fr.* Sonnets to Orpheus.
Sleeper in the Valley, The, *tr.*
Sonnets to Orpheus, *sel., tr.*
Three Haitian Creole Moods, *tr.*
V-Letter to Karl Shapiro in Australia.
Zone, *tr.*
RODMAN, THOMAS P. Battle of Bennington, The.
RODRÍGUEZ DEL PADRÓN, JUAN (Juan Rodríguez de la Cámara). Prayer to the Blessed Virgin.
To the Virgin.
RODRÍGUEZ GALVÁN, IGNACIO. Prophecy of Cuauhtémoc, *sel.*
ROE, SIR THOMAS. To My Friend Mr. Jonson.
ROETHKE, THEODORE. Academic.
Bat, The.
Big Wind.
Centaur, The.
Child on Top of a Greenhouse.
Cow, The.
Dance, The. *Fr.* Four for Sir John Davies.
Dolor.
Dream, The.
Elegy for Jane.
Flight, The. *Fr.* The Lost Son.
Forcing House.
Four for Sir John Davies.
Four for Sir John Davies, *sels.*
Frau Bauman, Frau Schmidt, and Frau Schwartze.
Give Way, Ye Gates.
Heron, The.
I Cry, Love! Love!
I Knew a Woman, Lovely in Her Bones.
Interlude.
Lost Son, The.
Lost Son, The, *sel.*
Love's Progress.
Mistake, The.
Moss-gathering.
My Papa's Waltz.
Night Crow.
On the Road to Woodlawn.
Open House.
Partner, The. *Fr.* Four for Sir John Davies.
Pipling.
Poem: "I knew a woman, lovely in her bones."
Prayer before Study.
Root Cellar.
Sensualists, The.
Shape of the Fire, The.
"Shimmer of Evil, The."
Sloth, The.
Song, The: "I met a ragged man."
Song: "Under a southern wind."
Song for the Squeeze-Box.
Vernal Sentiment.
Visitant, The.
Waking, The.
Words for the Wind.
ROGERS, ALEX. Rain Song, The.
Signs of Rain.
Why Adam Sinned.
ROGERS, AMY MAY. Abandoned Roads.
ROGERS, D. H. At Sea.
Homeward Bound.
ROGERS, F. Wishes.
ROGERS, JULIA ANN. Caterpillar Appeal.
ROGERS, ROBERT. Ponteach; or, The Savages of America, *sel.*
ROGERS, ROBERT CAMERON. Dancing Faun, The.
Doubt.
Health at the Ford, A.
In Absence.
Rosary, The.
Shadow Rose, The.
Sleeping Priestess of Aphrodite, A.
Virgil's Tomb.
ROGERS, SAMUEL. Bologna, and Byron. *Fr.* Italy.
Captivity.
Dear Is My Little Native Vale.
Descent, The. *Fr.* Italy.
Epitaph on a Robin Redbreast, An.
Fond Youth. *Fr.* Human Life.
Ginevra. *Fr.* Italy.
Human Life, *sels.*
Inscription on a Grot. *Fr.* The Pleasures of Memory.
Italian Song, An.
Italy, *sels.*
Italy and Bergamo. *Fr.* Italy.
Jorasse. *Fr.* Italy.
Marriage. *Fr.* Human Life.
Naples. *Fr.* Italy.
On a [*or* the] Picture of an Infant, *tr.*
On a Tear.
On J. W. Ward.
Pleasures of Memory, The, *sel.*
Robin's Grave, The.
Rome. *Fr.* Italy.
Sleeping Beauty, The.
Tear, A.
Venice. *Fr.* Italy.
Wish, A.
ROGERS, THOMAS. Spirit of Night, The.
ROJAS, FERNANDO DE. Celestina, *sels.*
Now Sleep, and Take Thy Rest. *Fr.* Celestina.
You birds whose warblings prove. *Fr.* Celestina.
ROKEAH, DAVID. Zealots of Yearning.
"ROKHA, PABLO DE" (Carlos Díaz Loyola). Allegory of Torment.
Elegy for All Ages.
Lament: "Weariness of the bones."
Pale Conquerors, The.
Seafaring Towns.
Subterranean Days and Nights.
Tribal Lay.
"ROKHA, WINÉTT DE" (Luisa Anabalón Sanderson; Señora "Pablo de Rokha"). Song of Thomas, Departed.
Waltz in Yungay Square.
ROLFE, EDWIN. Definition.
Elegy for Our Dead.
No Man Knows War.
Poem to Delight My Friends Who Laugh at Science-Fiction, A.
Song: "Keep the dream alive and growing always."
ROLLE OF HAMPOLE, RICHARD. Love Is Life, *sels.*
My Truest Treasure [*or* Trewest Tresowre].
Song of the Love of Jesus, A.
Song of the Passion, A.
ROLLESTON, THOMAS WILLIAM HAZEN. Clonmacnoise, *tr.*
Cois na Teineadh.
Dead at Clonmacnois, The, *tr.*
Grave of Rury, The.
In Praise of May, *tr.*
Lament of Maev Leith-Dherg, The, *tr.*
Night.
Song of Maelduin.
ROLLINS, ALICE WELLINGTON. Death of Azron, The.
Many Things Thou Hast Given Me, Dear Heart.
Vita Benefica.
ROLNIK, JOSEPH. Thank God.
ROMAINE, HARRY. Ad Coelum.
Unattainable, The.
ROMAINS, JULES. Another Spirit Advances.
Church, The.
ROMANELLI, SAMUELE. From Battle Clamour.
Love.
ROMANES, GEORGE JOHN. Simple Nature.
ROMANO, JENNIE. Old Houses.
ROMANO, LIBORIA E. Lyric Barber.
ROMIG, EDNA DAVIS. For a Shakespearean Garden.
ROMIG, ETHEL. *See* FULLER, ETHEL ROMIG.
ROMILU, MYRTLE. If to Die.
RONALD, ETHEL BOWMAN. When Elizabeth Went Home.
RONSARD, PIERRE DE. Adieu.
Amours de Cassandre, *sels.*
Amours de Marie, *sels.*
Amours Diverses, Les, *sels.*
And Lightly like the Flowers.
Another Winter comes. The last comes soon, I know. *Fr.* Les Amours Diverses.
As in the gardens, all through May, the rose. *Fr.* Amours de Marie.
As the young stag, when lusty Spring supreme. *Fr.* Amours de Cassandre.
As When the Rose. *Fr.* Amours de Marie.
Beauty's Paradigm. *Fr.* Sonnets pour Hélène.
Blissful Bane.
Calmly to wait whatever Chance may give. *Fr.* Odes.
Cassandra Speaks.
Celestial Dream.
Cold Kisses.
Come, boy, and where the grass is thickest pied. *Fr.* Amours de Cassandre.
Count me the stairs I climbed to your retreat. *Fr.* Sonnets pour Hélène.
Cruel, farewell, since I do but annoy thee. *Fr.* Sonnets pour Hélène.
Dance, lovely lady, dance and mask your face. *Fr.* Sonnets pour Hélène.
Deadly Kisses.
Delay Not!
Elegies, *sel.*
Epitaph on Rabelais.
Ere Love from barren Chaos drew the skies. *Fr.* Amours de Cassandre.
Fair flower of fifteen springs, that still. *Fr.* Amours de Marie.
Four Sonnets to Helen.
Fragment of a Sonnet.
Gayetez.
God guard you, and greet you well. *Fr.* Odes.
Good-bye.
Happy Martyrdom.
Hawthorn fair, whose burgeoning. *Fr.* Odes.
Helen, this age, by your exceeding worth. *Fr.* Sonnets pour Hélène.
Helen's Birthday.
Helen's Bosom.
Hide this one night thy crescent, kindly Moon. *Fr.* Amours de Marie.

His Lady's Death. *Fr.* Amours de Marie.
His Lady's Tomb. *Fr.* Amours de Marie.
Hunt, The.
I consecrate this fountain Helen's, praying. *Fr.* Sonnets pour Hélène.
I dragged my life along with sullen sighs. *Fr.* Amours de Cassandre.
I Often Watch Thee Musing Dreamily.
I send to you a nosegay that but now.
I want three days to read the Iliad through!
I Would.
In these long winter nights when moon doth steer. *Fr.* Sonnets pour Hélène.
Lark, The.
Love Indivisible.
Love's an Enchanter.
Love's Own Home.
Madam, when we two walked, the rest unheeding. *Fr.* Sonnets pour Hélène.
Maid of fifteen, in childlike beauty dight. *Fr.* Amours de Cassandre.
Many Joys.
Marie, arise, my indolent sweet saint! *Fr.* Amours de Marie.
More closely than the clinging vine. *Fr.* Les Amours Diverses.
My des Autels, whose true. *Fr.* Odes.
My Golden Helen.
Nature Adorned Cassandra. *Fr.* Amours de Cassandre.
No Other Slave. *Fr.* Sonnets pour Hélène.
No other torch save what my dreams discover. *Fr.* Sonnets pour Hélène.
Oh! but my mind is weary! *Fr.* Odes.
O caves, and you, O springs. *Fr.* Odes.
Ode: "Lovely Venus on a day."
Ode: "See, Mignonne, hath not the rose."
Odes, *sels.*
Of His Lady's Old Age.
Of the Choice of His Burial-Place. *Fr.* Odes.
On His Lady's Waking.
On the Choice of His Sepulchre. *Fr.* Odes.
Only your arm, and nothing more, I found. *Fr.* Sonnets pour Hélène.
Out of her lattice gazing on the leas. *Fr.* Sonnets pour Hélène.
Passion's Hounds.
Pour we roses into wine! *Fr.* Odes.
Return of Spring.
Revenge, The.
Rose, The.
Roses.
Sacred to Helen.
See love, whose kingdom as the world is ample. *Fr.* Sonnets pour Hélène.
Shall I your beauties with the moon compare? *Fr.* Sonnets pour Hélène.
Song: "Good day my heart, my sweetest life good day."
Song: "Since the lily's white is not so white as you."
Sonnet: "As on a branch, in May, we see the rose."
Sonnet: "I fly the crowded roads where thousands hurry."
Sonnet: "O, I could wish, most richly yellowing."
Sonnet: "Two flowers I love, the March-flower and the rose."
Sonnets pour Hélène, *sels.*
Spring. *Fr.* Odes.
Spring Song. *Fr.* Odes.
Stay, woodsman, stay thy hand awhile, and hark. *Fr.* Elegies.
Summer's Revel, The.
Sweet-heart, come see if the rose. *Fr.* Odes.
Take thou this rose, sweet even as thou art. *Fr.* Amours de Cassandre.
Tay Toy Babilarde Arondelle.
That century to century may tell. *Fr.* Sonnets pour Hélène.
That evening when love bad you take the floor. *Fr.* Sonnets pour Hélène.
This is the wood my holy angel-child. *Fr.* Amours de Cassandre.
Though by wide seas and Time we sundered are.
To a Fountain.
To Bellerie Spring.
To Cassandra.
To Corydon.
To Helen.
To His Page.
To His Young Mistress. *Fr.* Amours de Marie.
To Remi Belleau.
To the Moon. *Fr.* Amours de Marie.
To think one thought a hundred hundred ways. *Fr.* Amours de Cassandre.
Twain that were foes, while Mary lived, are fled. *Fr.* Amours de Marie.
Wake Up, Marie. *Fr.* Amours de Marie.
We hold not in our power. *Fr.* Odes.
What boots it me to see this verdure fair.
What though the spirit of man, by Plato taught. *Fr.* Sonnets pour Hélène.
When Nature formed Cassandra, who should move. *Fr.* Amours de Cassandre.
When that your sail bent to the ocean-swell.
When the beauteous Spring I see. *Fr.* Amours de Marie.
When you are very old, by the hearth's glare. *Fr.* Sonnets pour Hélène.
"Who," cried the elders on the Trojan wall. *Fr.* Sonnets pour Hélène.
Wild Beast.
ROOK, ALAN. Dunkirk Pier.
ROONEY, JOHN JEROME. Ave Maria.
Beam of Light, A.
Empire Builder, The.
Homing, The.
Joined the Blues.
McIlrath of Malate.
Marquette on the Shores of the Mississippi.
Men behind the Guns, The.
Râhat, The.
Revelation.
Where Helen Comes.
Woodland Singer, The.
ROONEY, WILLIAM. Dear Dark Head.
Poet, The.
ROOT, EDWARD MERRILL. Birth.
Carpenter of Eternity.
Chicago Idyll.
Eucharist.
Even as the Bird.
Filling Station.
Flames.
Nativity, The.
Phoenix.
Prayer for Dreadful Morning.
Pretty Polly.
Scrub Oak.
Starry Classroom.
Still the Cross.
To Him Who Walks the Water.
War.
Youth and Death.
ROOT, GEORGE FREDERICK. Battle Cry of Freedom, The.
Just before the Battle, Mother.
Tramp, Tramp, Tramp.
ROPE, H. E. G. Mount Alvernia.
ROPER, FLORENCE WILSON. Dusty Answer, *sel.*
Flame against the Wind.
If There Is Thought among the Daffodils.
Ocean, The.
Return of Proserpine, *sel.*
Sonnet: "I heard beneath the quiet stars last night." *Fr.* Return of Proserpine.
Sonnet: "There is a dream that comes to me by night." *Fr.* Dusty Answer.
This Much I Know.
Was It the Wind That Stirred?
ROPES, ARTHUR REED. In Pace.
Lost Pleiad, The.
On the Bridge.
ROPES, P. A. Before Spring.
Bluebells.
Daffodils.
Disappointed Shrimper, The.
Dust.
Glow-Worms.
I Will Keep Christmas.
If.
In February.
Poppies.
Violets.
Watering Rhyme, A.
RORIE, DAVID. Pawky Duke, The.
RORTY, JAMES. Acolyte, The.
Bell, The.
Bell-Ringers, The.
Bird Music.
California Dissonance.
Entry to the Desert.
Escape.
Gray Shore.
Islands, The; Puget Sound.
Lodging for the Night, A.
Not Spring.
Now That These Two.
Rainy Night.
Spring Garland, A.
Sunday Morning.
Winter Noon.
ROS, UILLEAM. *See* ROSS, WILLIAM.
ROSAS MORENO, JOSÉ. Caterpillar and the Butterfly, The.
Mocking Bird and the Donkey, The.
ROSCOE, WILLIAM. Butterfly's Ball, The.
To My Books.
ROSCOE, WILLIAM CALDWELL. Earth.
For Ever.
Master-Chord, The.
Parting.
Poetic Land, The.
Spiritual Love.
To La Sanscoeur.
ROSCOE, WILLIAM STANLEY. To Spring [on the Banks of the Cam].
ROSCOMMON, WENTWORTH DILLON, 4TH EARL OF. Advice. *Fr.* An Essay on Translated Verse.
Art of Poetry, The, *tr.*
Day of Judgment, The ("Dies irae, dies illa"), *tr.*
Essay on Translated Verse, An, *sels.*
More Advice. *Fr.* An Essay on Translated Verse.
On the Day of Judgement.
ROSE, ALEXANDER MACGREGOR ("A. M. R. Gordon"). Hoch! Der Kaiser.
Kaiser & Co.
ROSE, BILLY. Unknown Soldier, The.
ROSE, FRANCIS HOWARD. Martyr's Hymn, The.
ROSE, GRETA LEORA. Spring Is at Work with Beginnings of Things.
ROSE, MARGARET. Autumn Song.
Butterfly, The.
Little Bird's Song, A.
Little Fir Tree, The.
Magic Whistle, The.
November.
ROSE, R. SELDEN, *and* LEONARD BACON. *See* BACON, LEONARD, *and* R. SELDEN ROSE.
ROSE, WILLIAM STEWART. Orlando Furioso, *sels., tr.*
To the Rt. Hon. John Hookham Frere in Malta.
ROSELIEP, RAYMOND FRANCIS. Carmen Paschale, *sel., tr.*
Cathemerinon, *sel., tr.*
Dedication: "Eugenius, thy son, who guards the Rock," *tr.*
Hail, Maiden Root, *tr. Fr.* Carmen Paschale.
Hymn for Second Vespers; Feast of the Apparition of Our Lady of Lourdes, *tr.*
Lady of Letters.
Lullaby: "Slumber, Jesu, lightly dreaming," *tr.*
O Noble Virgin, *tr. Fr.* Cathemerinon.
Salutations: To Mary, Virgin, *tr.*
Symphony in Blue.
To Mary: At the Thirteenth Station.

ROSELIEP, RAYMOND FRANCIS (*cont.*)
War Cry: To Mary, *tr.*
Where Do I Love You, Lovely Maid?
Youth Autumnal.
ROSENBAUM, BENJAMIN. O Pity Our Small Size.
ROSENBAUM, NATHAN. Pictures at an Exhibition.
ROSENBERG, ISAAC. Beauty.
Break of Day in the Trenches.
Burning of the Temple, The.
Chagrin.
Dead Heroes, The.
Dead Man's Dump.
Destruction of Jerusalem by the Babylonian Hordes, The.
Expression.
Female God, The.
God.
I Am the Blood.
If You Are Fire.
Immortals, The.
Jew, The.
Love and Lust.
Midsummer Frost.
Moses; a Play, *sel.*
My Soul Is Robbed.
On a Lady Singing.
On Receiving News of the War.
One Lost, The.
Returning, We Hear the Larks.
Soldier; Twentieth Century.
Spiritual Isolation.
Spring.
Through These Pale Cold Days.
Wedded.
Worm Fed on the Heart of Corinth, A.
ROSENBERG, JAMES NAUMBURG. Darkness.
ROSENBERGER, COLEMAN. Death at Sea.
Goats of Juan Fernandez, The.
Star Gazer.
ROSENFELD, MORRIS JACOB. Another While.
Cry from the Ghetto, A.
Exile Song.
For Hire.
I Know Not Why.
Jewish May, The.
My Camping Ground.
Simchas Torah.
So Long Ago.
ROSENHANE, GUSTAV. Sonnet: "And then I sat me down, and gave the rein."
Sonnet: "Deep in a vale where rocks on every side."
Sonnets.
ROSENZWEIG, EFRAIM. Dreidel Song.
Song of Always, A.
ROSNER, PAUL. Don't Say You Like Tchaikowsky.
ROSS, ABRAM BUNN. Indignant Male, An.
Two in Bed.
ROSS, ALAN. Leave Train.
Mess Deck Casualty.
Portoferraio.
ROSS, ALEXANDER. Bridal o 't, The.
Woo'd and Married and A'.
ROSS, ALLISON. Game Out of Hand.
ROSS, CARY. Sonnet on a Somewhat Inferior Radio Outfit.
ROSS, CHARLES SARSFIELD. Dear Old Mothers.
Old Mothers.
ROSS, DAVID. Book Review.
Broadcast to the Scholars in the Eyrie.
Demosthenes to the Radio Announcer.
Fallen Flyer Aged 19.
He Bloomed among Eagles.
Houses Should Have Homes to Live In.
I Am Your Loaf, Lord.
In My Infancy.
In the Year's Morning.
Lament of Granite.
Man's Need.
News Reel.
Passport beyond Tyranny.
Praised Be the Psalmist.
ROSS, DAVID MACDONALD. Bloody Bill.
ROSS, DELLE OGLESBEE. Pastel, A.
ROSS, GERTRUDE ROBISON. I Was Made of This and This.
ROSS, MARY. Whip of Anger, The.
ROSS, PATIENCE ADRIAN. Robin Hood.
ROSS, SIR RONALD. Anniversary, The.
Cure of Malaria, The.
Father, The.
Half Stun'd I Look Around.
In Exile; Reply.
Indian Fevers.
Lines Written after the Discovery by the Author of the Germ of Yellow Fever.
Power.
Reply.
River, The.
ROSS, W. W. EUSTACE. Dawn, The.
Death, A.
Diver, The.
Fish.
If Ice.
In the Ravine.
On Angels.
On the Supernatural.
Saws Were Shrieking, The.
Stream of Life, The.
Summons, The.
Three Spiritual Sonnets.
Walk, The.
ROSS, WILLIAM [*or* UILLEAM ROS]. Another Song: "It is I that am under sorrow at this time."
ROSSETER, PHILIP. All Is Vanity, *at.*
Vanity of Vanities, *at.*
ROSSETTI, CHRISTINA GEORGINA. Abnegation. *Fr.* Monna Innominata.
Advent.
After Death.
All Heaven Is Blazing Yet.
All the bells were ringing. *Fr.* Sing-Song.
All Things Wait upon Thee.
Aloof. *Fr.* The Thread of Life.
Amor Mundi.
And timid, funny, brisk little bunny. *Fr.* Sing-Song.
Apple Gathering, An.
At Home.
At the Goal.
Autumn ("Care flieth").
Autumn ("I dwell alone").
Baby, Sleep. *Fr.* Sing-Song.
Battle Within, The.
Before the Beginning.
Before the Paling of the Stars.
Better Resurrection, A.
Bird or Beast?
Bird Raptures.
Birthday, A.
Birthday Gift, A. *Fr.* A Christmas Carol: "In the bleak mid-winter."
Blue-eyed phantom far before, A.
Boatman, The. *Fr.* Sing-Song.
Boats Sail on the Rivers. *Fr.* Sing-Song.
Bourne, The.
Bride Song, A ("Through the vales to my love!").
Broken Doll, The.
Brown and Furry. *Fr.* Sing-Song.
Brownie, Brownie, Let Down Your Milk. *Fr.* Sing-Song.
Bruised Reed Shall He Not Break, A.
But Give Me Holly, Bold and Jolly. *Fr.* Sing-Song.
Carol: "In the bleak mid-winter."
Caterpillar, The. *Fr.* Sing-Song.
Cherry Tree.
Child's Talk in April.
Chill, A.
Christ Can Give Thee Heart.
Christ Our All in All, *sel.*
Christmas Carol, A: "Before the paling of the stars."
Christmas Carol, A: "In the bleak mid-winter."
Christmas Carol, A: "In the bleak mid-winter," *sel.*
Christmas Carol, A: "Shepherds had an Angel, The."
Christmas Daybreak.
City Mouse and the Garden [*or* Country] Mouse, The. *Fr.* Sing-Song.
Color. *Fr.* Sing-Song.
Come back to me, who wait and watch for you. *Fr.* Monna Innominata.
Come, Blessèd Sleep.
Come to me in the silence of the night.
Confluents.
Consider.
Convent Threshold, The.
Convent Threshold, The, *sel.*
Cor Mio.
Coral. *Fr.* Sing-Song.
Daisies. *Fr.* Sing-Song.
Daughter of Eve, A.
Days are clear, The. *Fr.* Sing-Song.
De Profundis.
Dead before Death.
December.
Dedicatory Sonnet.
Descent from the Cross, The, *sel.*
Despised and Rejected.
Did any bird come flying.
Dirge, A: "Why were you born when the snow was falling?"
Do You Know? *Fr.* Sing-Song.
Does the road wind up-hill all the way? *Fr.* Up-Hill.
Dream, The.
Dream Land.
Dream-Love.
Easter Carol, An: "Flash forth, thou sun."
Easter Carol, An: "Spring bursts today."
Easter Even.
Easter Tuesday.
Echo.
Echo from Willowwood, An.
Eight o'Clock. *Fr.* Sing-Song.
1880. *Fr.* Valentines to My Mother.
1885. *Fr.* Valentines to My Mother.
1882. *Fr.* Valentines to My Mother.
Eleanor.
Emerald is as green as grass, An. *Fr.* Sing-Song.
End, An.
End of the First Part, The. *Fr.* Three Stages.
Eve.
Exultate Deo.
Face of Jesus Christ, The. *Fr.* The Descent from the Cross.
Fanny's Doves.
Ferry Me across the Water. *Fr.* Sing-Song.
Ferryman, The. *Fr.* Sing-Song.
First Day, The. *Fr.* Monna Innominata.
First Spring Day.
Fluttered Wings.
Fly away, fly away, over the sea. *Fr.* Sing-Song.
Four Pets.
Frisky Lamb, A. *Fr.* Sing-Song.
From House to Home, *sels.*
From Metastasio.
From Sunset to Star Rise.
From the Antique.
Fulfil Thy Will.
Fur and Feather.
Ghost's Petition, The.
Goblin Market.
Goblin Market, *sel.*
Gone were but the winter.
Good Advice.
Good-by.
Good Friday.
Good Friday Evening.
Good Shepherd, The.
Green Cornfield, A.
Growing in the Vale. *Fr.* Sing-Song.
He and She.
Heart Knoweth Its Own Bitterness, The.
Heart's Chill Between.
Heaven Is Heaven. *Fr.* Sing-Song.
Heaven Is Not Far.
Heaven Overarches [Earth and Sea].
Herself a Rose Who Bore the Rose.
Hills Are Tipped with Sunshine, The.
Hold Thou Me Fast.
Holy Innocents.
Hopping Frog.
Horses of the Sea, The. *Fr.* Sing-Song.
House of Cards, A. *Fr.* Sing-Song.

How Many Seconds in a Minute?
Hurt No Living Thing. *Fr.* Sing-Song.
I Bore with Thee, Long, Weary Days.
I cannot tell you how it was. *Fr.* May.
I dream of you, to wake. *Fr.* Monna Innominata.
"I, if I perish, perish." *Fr.* Monna Innominata.
I loved you first. *Fr.* Monna Innominata.
I Thought to Deal the Death-Stroke. *Fr.* Three Stages.
I Will Accept.
I wish I could remember that first day. *Fr.* Monna Innominata.
I'd Laugh Today, *wr. at.*
If a Pig Wore a Wig. *Fr.* Sing-Song.
If I could trust mine own self with your fate. *Fr.* Monna Innominata.
If I Were a Queen. *Fr.* Sing-Song.
If Only.
If So Tomorrow Saves.
If stars dropped out of heaven. *Fr.* Sing-Song.
If There Be Any One.
If we shall live, we live.
Immalee.
In an Artist's Studio.
In Life Our Absent Friend Is Far Away.
In spring I look gay.
In the Bleak Mid-Winter.
In the Round Tower at Jhansi.
Incarnate Love.
Invitation to Sleep.
Irresponsive Silence of the Land, The.
Is It Well with the Child?
Is the Moon Tired? *Fr.* Sing-Song.
It Is Finished.
Italia, Io Ti Saluto!
Judge Not According to the Appearance.
"Kookoorookoo! Kookoorookoo!" *Fr.* Sing-Song.
L. E. L.
Lady Moon. *Fr.* Sing-Song.
Lambs at Play. *Fr.* Sing-Song.
Last Prayer.
Later Life, *sels.*
Lesson, A. *Fr.* Sing-Song.
Let Me Sleep.
Let's Be Merry. *Fr.* Sing-Song.
Lie a-bed. *Fr.* Sing-Song.
Life and Death.
Life Hidden.
Life's Parallels, A.
Lily has a smooth stalk, The. *Fr.* Sing-Song.
Linnet in a Gilded Cage, A.
Little One Weary.
Looking Forward.
Lord, Dost Thou Look on Me.
Lord, Grant Us Calm.
Lord, I Am Here. *Fr.* Christ Our All in All.
Lord, Save Us, We Perish.
Love Is Strong as Death.
Love Is Stronger than Death.
Love me, for I Love you. *Fr.* Monna Innominata.
Love Me—I Love You. *Fr.* Sing-Song.
"Love of Christ Which Passeth Knowledge, The."
Love That Is Dead and Buried.
Lowest Place, The.
Lullaby: "Lullaby, oh lullaby!" *Fr.* Sing-Song.
Luscious and Sorrowful.
Many in aftertimes will say of you. *Fr.* Monna Innominata.
Martyrs' Song.
Marvel of Marvels.
Mary Magdalene and the Other Mary.
Maude Clare.
May.
May-Time. *Fr.* Sing-Song.
Meeting ("If we shall live, we live").
Meeting ("They made the chamber sweet").
Memory.
Milking-Maid, The.
Milking Time. *Fr.* Sing-Song.
Minnie and Mattie. *Fr.* Sing-Song.
Minnie, Mattie and May. *Fr.* Sing-Song.
Mirage.
Mix a Pancake. *Fr.* Sing-Song.
Monna Innominata.
Monna Innominata, *sels.*
Months, The ("January cold"). *Fr.* Sing-Song.
Months, The; a Pageant, *sel.*
Mother Country.
Mother shake the cherry-tree. *Fr.* Sing-Song.
Motherless soft lambkin, A. *Fr.* Sing-Song.
Mother's Song, A. *Fr.* Sing-Song.
My Gift. *Fr.* A Christmas Carol: "In the bleak mid-winter."
My heart is like a singing bird.
Neighboring. *Fr.* Sing-Song.
Nesting-Time. *Fr.* Sing-Song.
New Year Ditty.
Next of Kin.
Noble Sisters.
None Other Lamb.
Not Yours but You.
November.
Nun, A.
O Earth, Lie Heavily upon Her Eyes.
Oh, Fair to See. *Fr.* Sing-Song.
O Lady Moon. *Fr.* Sing-Song.
O My Heart's Heart. *Fr.* Monna Innominata.
O Sailor, Come Ashore. *Fr.* Sing-Song.
O Wind, Where Have You Been? *Fr.* Sing-Song.
O wind, why do you never rest. *Fr.* Sing-Song.
October, *sel.* *Fr.* The Months; a Pageant.
Old and New Year Ditties, *sel.*
On the Death of a Cat, a Friend of Mine Aged Ten Years and a Half.
On the Grassy Banks. *Fr.* Sing-Song.
One Certainty.
P.R.B., The.
Pageant and Other Poems, The.
Pancake, The. *Fr.* Sing-Song.
Paradise.
Paradoxes. *Fr.* Sing-Song.
Passing and Glassing.
Passing Away. *Fr.* Old and New Year Ditties.
Pause, A.
Pause of Thought, A. *Fr.* Three Stages.
Pin Has a Head, A. *Fr.* Sing-Song.
Pocket Handkerchief to Hem, A. *Fr.* Sing-Song.
Portrait, A.
Postman, The. *Fr.* Sing-Song.
Prayer, A: "Clother of the lily, Feeder of the sparrow."
Prayer: "Lord, grant us eyes to see, and ears to hear."
Precious Stones. *Fr.* Sing-Song.
Prince's Progress, The.
Prince's Progress, The, *sel.*
Pussy has a whiskered face. *Fr.* Sing-Song.
Queen Rose.
Remember.
Remember, *sel.*
Requiem.
Rest.
Rose in Jericho, A.
Roses for the Flush of Youth.
Rushes in a Watery Place.
Sea-Sand and Sorrow.
Seasons.
Seldom "can't." *Fr.* Sing-Song.
Send Me.
Shadows To-Day.
She listen'd like a cushat dove.
Shepherds Had an Angel, The.
Sing Me a Song. *Fr.* Sing-Song.
Sing-Song, *sels.*
Sing-Song Verses.
Skylark, The.
Skylark and Nightingale. *Fr.* Sing-Song.
Sleep at Sea.
Sleeping at Last.
Snack, A. *Fr.* Sing-Song.
Somewhere or Other.
Song: "Oh roses for the flush of youth."
Song: "When I am dead, my dearest."
Song for the Least of All Saints, A.
Song of Flight, A.
Sonnet: "Remember me when I am gone away."
Soul, A.
Sound of the Wind, The. *Fr.* Sing-Song.
Sound Sleep.
Spring.
Spring Quiet.
Star Sirius and the Pole Star dwell afar. *Fr.* Later Life.
Stars, The. *Fr.* Sing-Song.
Stay, June, Stay! *Fr.* Sing-Song.
Stitching. *Fr.* Sing-Song.
Summer [Days].
Summer Is Ended, The.
Summer Wish, A.
Sun and Rain.
Swallow, The. *Fr.* Sing-Song.
Sweet Daffadowndilly. *Fr.* Sing-Song.
Testimony.
There is but one May in the year. *Fr.* Sing-Song.
There is one that has a head without an eye. *Fr.* Sing-Song.
There's Nothing like the Rose.
There's Snow on the Fields. *Fr.* Sing-Song.
They Toil Not neither Do They Spin.
Thinking of you, and all that was. *Fr.* Monna Innominata.
Thread of Life, The.
Thread of Life, The, *sel.*
Three Enemies, The.
Three Plum Buns. *Fr.* Sing-Song.
Three Seasons.
Three Stages.
To Love and to Remember: That Is Good.
To My First Love, My Mother.
To the End.
Today for Me.
Too Late for Love. *Fr.* The Prince's Progress.
Tread Softly! [All the Earth Is Holy Ground.] *Fr.* Later Life.
Tree, A., *wr. at.*
Trust. *Fr.* Monna Innominata.
Trust me, I have not earned your dear rebuke. *Fr.* Monna Innominata.
Tune Me, O Lord, into One Harmony.
Twice.
Twilight Calm.
Twilight Calm, *sel.*
Twist Me a Crown. *Fr.* Sing-Song.
Two doves upon the selfsame branch.
Two Pursuits.
Two Thoughts of Death.
Up-Hill [*or* Uphill].
Valentines to My Mother.
Vanity of Vanities.
Watching Angels. *Fr.* Sing-Song.
We lack, yet cannot fix upon the lack. *Fr.* Later Life.
Weary in Well-doing.
Wednesday in Holy Week.
What Do They Do?
What Does the Bee Do? *Fr.* Sing-Song.
What Is It Jesus Saith?
What is pink? A rose is pink. *Fr.* Sing-Song.
When I Am Dead, My Dearest.
When the Cows Come Home. *Fr.* Sing-Song.
White hen sitting, A. *Fr.* Sing-Song.
Who Has Seen the Wind. *Fr.* Sing-Song.
Who Shall Deliver Me?
Wife to Husband.
Wind, The. *Fr.* Sing-Song.
Wind Has Such a Rainy Sound, The. *Fr.* Sing-Song.
Wind of January, The.
Winter ("Bread and milk . . ."). *Fr.* Sing-Song.

ROSSETTI, CHRISTINA GEORGINA (*cont.*)
Winter ("Sweet blackbird . . .").
Wisdom.
Wish, A.
Woolly Lambkins. *Fr.* Sing-Song.
Wrens and Robins in the Hedge. *Fr.* Sing-Song.
Year's Windfalls, A, *sel.*
Yet a Little While.
Young Death.
Youth gone, and beauty gone if ever there. *Fr.* Monna Innominata.
ROSSETTI, DANTE GABRIEL. Alas, So Long!
All my thoughts always speak to me of love, *tr.* *Fr.* La Vita Nuova.
All ye that pass along Love's trodden way, *tr.* *Fr.* La Vita Nuova.
Ardour and Memory. *Fr.* The House of Life.
Aspecta Medusa.
Astarte Syriaca.
At the Grave of Selvaggia, *tr.*
At the Sunrise in 1848.
At whiles (yea oftentimes) I muse over, *tr.* *Fr.* La Vita Nuova.
Autumn Idleness. *Fr.* The House of Life.
Autumn Song.
Ave.
Ballad [*or* Ballade] of Dead Ladies, The, *tr.*
Ballata: Concerning a Shepherd-Maid, *tr.*
Ballata: He Reveals His Increasing Love for Mandetta, *tr.*
Ballata: He Will Gaze upon Beatrice, *tr.*
Ballata: His Talk with Certain Peasant Girls, *tr.*
Ballata: In Exile at Sarzana, *tr.*
Ballata: Of a Continual Death in Love, *tr.*
Ballata: Of His Lady among Other Ladies, *tr.*
Ballata: Of True and False Singing, *tr.*
Ballata: One Speaks of the Beginning of His Love, *tr.*
Ballata: "With other women I beheld my love," *tr.*
Ballata of True and False Spring, *tr.*
Barren Spring. *Fr.* The House of Life.
Beauty, *tr.*
Beauty and Duty, *tr.*
Beauty's Pageant. *Fr.* The House of Life.
Beyond the sphere which spreads to widest space, *tr.* *Fr.* La Vita Nuova.
Birth-Bond, The. *Fr.* The House of Life.
Blessed Damozel, The.
Body's Beauty. *Fr.* The House of Life.
Bridal Birth. *Fr.* The House of Life.
Bride's Prelude, The.
Broken Music. *Fr.* The House of Life.
Burden of Nineveh, The.
Canst thou indeed be he that still would sing, *tr.* *Fr.* La Vita Nuova.
Cantica: Our Lord Christ; Of Order, *tr.*
Canzone: "Eyes that weep for pity of the heart, The," *tr.* *Fr.* La Vita Nuova.
Canzone: He Beseeches Death for the Life of Beatrice, *tr.*
Canzone: He Perceives His Rashness in Love, *tr.*
Canzone: He Rebukes the Evil of That Time, *sel.*, *tr.*
Canzone: He Speaks of His Condition through Love, *tr.*
Canzone: His Lament for Selvaggia, *tr.*
Canzone: His Portrait of His Lady, *tr.*
Canzone: "Ladies that have intelligence in love," *tr.* *Fr.* La Vita Nuova.
Canzone: Of His Dead Lady, *tr.*
Canzone: Of His Love, *tr.*
Canzone: Of the Gentle Heart, *tr.*
Canzone: To Love and to His Lady, *tr.*
Canzonetta: Bitter Song to His Lady, A, *tr.*
Canzonetta: He Will neither Boast nor Lament to His Lady, *tr.*
Canzonetta: "My lady mine, I send," *tr.*
Canzonetta: Of His Lady and of His Making Her Likeness, *tr.*
Canzonetta: Of His Lady in Absence, *tr.*
Card-Dealer, The.
Catch: On a Wet Day, *tr.*
Choice, The. *Fr.* The House of Life.
Cloud and Wind. *Fr.* The House of Life.
Cloud Confines, The.
Dark Day, A. *Fr.* The House of Life.
Dark Glass, The. *Fr.* The House of Life.
Day agone, as I rode sullenly, A, *tr.* *Fr.* La Vita Nuova.
Day of Love, A. *Fr.* The House of Life.
Death, always cruel, Pity's foe in chief, *tr.* *Fr.* La Vita Nuova.
Death-in-Love. *Fr.* The House of Life.
Death's Songsters. *Fr.* The House of Life.
Dialogue: Lover and Lady, *tr.*
Divided Thoughts, *tr.* *Fr.* La Vita Nuova.
Eden Bower.
Equal Troth. *Fr.* The House of Life.
Even as the others mock, thou mockest me, *tr.* *Fr.* La Vita Nuova.
Even So.
Eyes that weep for pity of the heart, The, *tr.* *Fr.* La Vita Nuova.
Farewell to the Glen. *Fr.* The House of Life.
Fiammetta, *tr.*
First Love Remembered.
Five English Poets.
For "A Venetian Pastoral" by Giorgione.
For certain he hath seen all perfectness, *tr.* *Fr.* La Vita Nuova.
For "Our Lady of the Rocks."
For the Holy Family by Michelangelo.
For "The Wine of Circe."
Found.
Fragment: "As balmy as the breath of her you love."
Francesca da Rimini, *tr.* *Fr.* Divina Commedia.
Friar of Orders Grey, The.
From Dawn to Noon. *Fr.* The House of Life.
Genius in Beauty. *Fr.* The House of Life.
Gentle thought there is will often start, A, *tr.* *Fr.* La Vita Nuova.
Gracious Moonlight. *Fr.* The House of Life.
Grand Testament, Le, *sel.*, *tr.*
He and I. *Fr.* The House of Life.
Heart of the Night, The. *Fr.* The House of Life.
Heart's Compass. *Fr.* The House of Life.
Heart's Haven. *Fr.* The House of Life.
Heart's Hope. *Fr.* The House of Life.
Her Gifts. *Fr.* The House of Life.
Her Heaven. *Fr.* The House of Life.
Hero's Lamp. *Fr.* The House of Life.
Hill Summit, The. *Fr.* The House of Life.
His Mother's Service to Our Lady, *tr.*
Hoarded Joy. *Fr.* The House of Life.
Honeysuckle, The.
Hope Overtaken. *Fr.* The House of Life.
House of Life, The.
House of Life, The, *sels.*
Husbandman, The. *Fr.* The House of Life.
I Felt a Spirit of Love Begin to Stir, *tr.* *Fr.* La Vita Nuova.
In Great Bitterness, *tr.*
In Honor of His Mistress, *tr.*
Inclusiveness. *Fr.* The House of Life.
Inscription for a Portrait of Dante, *tr.*
Insomnia.
Jenny.
John Keats. *Fr.* Five English Poets.
John of Tours, *tr.*
King's Tragedy, The.
Kiss, The. *Fr.* The House of Life.
Known in Vain. *Fr.* The House of Life.
La Bella Donna.
Ladies That Have Intelligence in Love, *tr.* *Fr.* La Vita Nuova.
Lady of Heaven, *tr.*
Lamp's Shrine, The. *Fr.* The House of Life.
Landmark, The. *Fr.* The House of Life.
Last Confession, A.
Last Fire. *Fr.* The House of Life.
Life-in-Love. *Fr.* The House of Life.
Life the Beloved. *Fr.* The House of Life.
Like the sweet apple which reddens upon the topmost bough, *tr.*
Lilith.
Limerick: "There is a young artist named Whistler."
Limerick: "There is an old he-wolf named Gambart."
Limerick: "There once was a painter named Scott."
Limerick: "There was a poor chap called Rossetti."
Limerick: "There was once a young fir-tree of Bosnia."
Limerick: "There's a combative artist named Whistler."
Limerick: "There's a Portuguese person named Howell."
Limerick: "There's an Irishman, Arthur O'Shaughnessy."
Little While, A.
Lost Days. *Fr.* The House of Life.
Lost on Both Sides. *Fr.* The House of Life.
Love and Hope. *Fr.* The House of Life.
Love and the gentle heart are one same thing, *tr.* *Fr.* La Vita Nuova.
Love Enthroned. *Fr.* The House of Life.
Love hath so long possessed me for his own, *tr.* *Fr.* La Vita Nuova.
Love in Men and Devils, *tr.*
Love-Letter, The. *Fr.* The House of Life.
Love-Lily.
Love-Moon, The. *Fr.* The House of Life.
Love-Sight [*or* Lovesight]. *Fr.* The House of Life.
Love-Sweetness. *Fr.* The House of Life.
Lovers' Walk, The. *Fr.* The House of Life.
Love's Baubles. *Fr.* The House of Life.
Love's Fatality. *Fr.* The House of Life.
Love's Last Gift. *Fr.* The House of Life.
Love's Lovers. *Fr.* The House of Life.
Love's Nocturn.
Love's pallor and the semblance of deep ruth, *tr.* *Fr.* La Vita Nuova.
Love's Testament. *Fr.* The House of Life.
Madrigal: To His Lady Selvaggia Vergiolesi, *tr.*
Making of Master Messerin, The, *tr.*
March, *tr.*
Mary Magdalene.
Mary Magdalene at the Door of Simon the Pharisee.
Mary's Girlhood. *Fr.* Sonnets for Pictures.
May, *tr.*
Memorial Thresholds. *Fr.* The House of Life.
Michelangelo's Kiss. *Fr.* The House of Life.
Mid-Rapture. *Fr.* The House of Life.

Mine eyes beheld the blessed pity spring, *tr.* *Fr.* La Vita Nuova.
Mirror, The.
Monochord, The. *Fr.* The House of Life.
Moonstar, The. *Fr.* The House of Life.
Morrow's Message, The. *Fr.* The House of Life.
My Father's Close, *tr.*
My Lady Carries Love, *tr.* *Fr.* La Vita Nuova.
My lady looks so gentle and so pure, *tr.* *Fr.* La Vita Nuova.
My Sister's Sleep.
Nevermore, The. *Fr.* The House of Life.
New Year's Burden, A.
Newborn Death. *Fr.* The House of Life.
No Jewel So Worthy, *tr.*
Not as These. *Fr.* The House of Life.
Not Too Deeply in Love, *tr.*
Nuptial Sleep. *Fr.* The House of Life.
O thou who at Love's hour. *Fr.* The House of Life.
Of All He Would Do, *tr.*
Of Caution, *tr.*
Of England, and of Its Marvels, *tr.*
Of Fiammetta Singing.
Of His Lady's Face, *tr.*
Of His Last Sight of Fiammetta, *tr.*
Of Order in Our Lord Christ, *tr.*
Of the Gentle Heart, *tr.*
Of the Months, *tr.*
Of Three Girls and [of] Their Talk, *tr.*
Old Song Ended, An.
On Burns.
On Refusal of Aid between Nations.
On the Death of Beatrice, *tr.* *Fr.* La Vita Nuova.
On the Fitness of Seasons, *tr.*
On the Poet O'Shaughnessy.
On the "Vita Nuova" of Dante.
One Girl, *tr.*
One Hope, The. *Fr.* The House of Life.
Orchard-Pit, The.
Order, *tr.*
Our Lady of the Rocks.
Parted Love. *Fr.* The House of Life.
Passing Away, Saith the World.
Passion and Worship. *Fr.* The House of Life.
Passover in the Holy Family, The.
Past Help, *tr.*
Penumbra.
Percy Bysshe Shelley. *Fr.* Five English Poets.
Portrait, The ("O Lord of all compassionate control"). *Fr.* The House of Life.
Portrait, The ("This is her picture as she was").
Praise, *tr.*
Pride of Youth. *Fr.* The House of Life.
Prolonged Sonnet: When the Troops Were Returning from Milan, *tr.*
Refusal of Aid between Nations.
"Retro Me, Sathana!" *Fr.* The House of Life.
St. Luke the Painter. *Fr.* The House of Life.
Samuel Taylor Coleridge. *Fr.* Five English Poets.
Sea-Limits, The.
Secret Parting. *Fr.* The House of Life.
Sestina; of the Lady Pietra degli Scrovigni, *tr.*
Severed Selves. *Fr.* The House of Life.
Sibylla Palmifera. *Fr.* The House of Life.
Silent Noon. *Fr.* The House of Life.
Sister Helen.
Sleepless Dreams. *Fr.* The House of Life.
Song and Music.
Song of the Bower, The.
Song-Throe, The. *Fr.* The House of Life.
Song, tis my will that thou do seek out love, *tr.* *Fr.* La Vita Nuova.
Sonnet, The ("A sonnet is a moment's monument"). *Fr.* The House of Life.
Sonnet: "Beatrice is gone up into high Heaven," *tr.* *Fr.* La Vita Nuova.
Sonnet: "Because mine eyes can never have their fill," *tr.*
Sonnet: "Beyond the sphere which spreads to widest space," *tr.* *Fr.* La Vita Nuova.
Sonnet: Death Is Not without but within Him, *tr.*
Sonnet: He Argues His Case with Death, *tr.*
Sonnet: He Compares All Things with His Lady, *tr.*
Sonnet: He Craves Interpreting of a Dream of His, *tr.*
Sonnet: He Is Out of Heart with His Time, *tr.*
Sonnet: He Is Past All Help, *tr.*
Sonnet: He Jests Concerning His Poverty, *tr.*
Sonnet: He Rails against Dante, *tr.*
Sonnet: He Speaks of a Third Love of His, *tr.*
Sonnet: He Will Not Be Too Deeply in Love, *tr.*
Sonnet: He Will Praise His Lady, *tr.*
Sonnet: "If I were fire, I'd burn the world away," *tr.*
Sonnet: In Absence from Becchina, *tr.*
Sonnet: Lady Laments for Her Lost Lover, A, *tr.*
Sonnet: "Last All Saints' holy-day, even now gone by," *tr.*
Sonnet: "Mine eyes beheld the blessed pity spring," *tr.*
Sonnet: "My lady carries love within her eyes," *tr.* *Fr.* La Vita Nuova.
Sonnet: "My lady looks so gentle and so pure," *tr.* *Fr.* La Vita Nuova.
Sonnet: Of All He Would Do, *tr.*
Sonnet: Of an Ill-favored Lady, *tr.*
Sonnet: Of Beatrice de Portinari, *tr.*
Sonnet: Of Beauty and Duty, *tr.*
Sonnet: Of Becchina in a Rage, *tr.*
Sonnet: Of Becchina, the Shoemaker's Daughter, *tr.*
Sonnet: Of His Lady in Heaven, *tr.*
Sonnet: Of His Lady's Face, *tr.*
Sonnet: Of His Pain from a New Love, *tr.*
Sonnet: Of Love, in Honor of His Mistress Becchina, *tr.*
Sonnet: Of Love in Men and Devils, *tr.*
Sonnet: Of Moderation and Tolerance, *tr.*
Sonnet: Of the Eyes of a Certain Mandetta, *tr.*
Sonnet: Of the Grave of Selvaggia, *tr.*
Sonnet: Of the Making of Master Messerin, *tr.*
Sonnet: Of the 20th of June, 1291, *tr.*
Sonnet: Of Virtue, *tr.*
Sonnet: Of Why He Is Unhanged, *tr.*
Sonnet: Of Why He Would Be a Scullion, *tr.*
Sonnet: On the Detection of a False Friend, *tr.*
Sonnet: On the 9th of June, 1290, *tr.*
Sonnet: Rapture Concerning His Lady, A, *tr.*
Sonnet: To a Friend Who Does Not Pity His Love, *tr.*
Sonnet: To Brunetto Latini, *tr.*
Sonnet: To Certain Ladies, *tr.*
Sonnet: To Dante Alighieri (He Commends the Work of Dante's Life), *tr.*
Sonnet: To Dante Alighieri (He Conceives of Some Compensation in Death), *tr.*
Sonnet: To Dante Alighieri (He Interprets Dante Alighieri's Dream), *tr.*
Sonnet: To Dante Alighieri (He Interprets Dante's Dream), *tr.*
Sonnet: To Dante Alighieri (He Mistrusts the Love of Lapo Gianni), *tr.*
Sonnet: To Dante Alighieri (He Reports the Successful Issue of Lapo Gianni's Love), *tr.*
Sonnet: To Dante Alighieri (He Writes to Dante, Defying Him), *tr.*
Sonnet: To Dante Alighieri (On the Last Sonnet of the "Vita Nuova"), *tr.*
Sonnet: "To every heart which the sweet pain doth move," *tr.* *Fr.* La Vita Nuova.
Sonnet: To His Lady Joan, of Florence, *tr.*
Sonnet: To Love, in Great Bitterness, *tr.*
Sonnet: To the Lady Pietra degli Scrovigni, *tr.*
Sonnet: To the Same Ladies, *tr.*
Sonnet: Trance of Love, A, *tr.*
Sonnet: "When God had finish'd Master Messerin," *tr.*
Sonnet: "With sighs my bosom always laboureth," *tr.* *Fr.* La Vita Nuova.
Sonnet: "Wonderfully out of the beautiful form," *tr.* *Fr.* La Vita Nuova.
Sonnet: "Ye pilgrim-folk, advancing pensively," *tr.* *Fr.* La Vita Nuova.
Sonnet is a moment's monument, A. *Fr.* The House of Life.
Sonnets for Pictures, *sels.*
Sonnets of the Months, *sels.*, *tr.*
Soothsay.
Soul-Light. *Fr.* The House of Life.
Soul's Beauty. *Fr.* The House of Life.
Soul's Sphere, The. *Fr.* The House of Life.
Spring.
Staff and Scrip, The.
Stay now with me, and listen to my sighs, *tr.* *Fr.* La Vita Nuova.
Stillborn Love. *Fr.* The House of Life.
Stratton Water.
Stream's Secret, The.
Sudden Light.
Sun's Shame, The. *Fr.* The House of Life.
Sunset Wings.
Superscription, A. *Fr.* The House of Life.
Supreme Surrender. *Fr.* The House of Life.
That lady of all gentle memories, *tr.* *Fr.* La Vita Nuova.
Thomas Chatterton. *Fr.* Five English Poets.
Thoughts are broken in my memory, The, *tr.* *Fr.* La Vita Nuova.
Three Shadows.
Through Death to Love. *Fr.* The House of Life.
To Beatrice on All Saints' Day, *tr.*
To Dante Alighieri, *tr.*
To Dante in Paradise, *tr.*
To Death, of His Lady, *tr.*
To every heart that the sweet pain doth move, *tr.* *Fr.* La Vita Nuova.
To One Who Had Censured, *tr.*
Tom Agnew, Bill Agnew.
Transfigured Life. *Fr.* The House of Life.
Trees of the Garden, The. *Fr.* The House of Life.
Tribute to Dante, A, *tr.*
Troops Returning from Milan, *tr.*
Troy Town.
True and False Singing, *tr.*
True Woman. *Fr.* The House of Life.
Twelve Sonnets. *tr.* *Fr.* Of the Months.
Vain Virtues. *Fr.* The House of Life.
Vase of Life, The. *Fr.* The House of Life.
Venetian Pastoral.
Venus Verticordia.
Venus Victrix. *Fr.* The House of Life.
Very bitter weeping that ye made, The, *tr.* *Fr.* La Vita Nuova.
Very pitiful lady, very young, A, *tr.* *Fr.* La Vita Nuova.
Virgin Declares Her Beauties, A, *tr.*
Vita Nuova, La, *sels.*, *tr.*
Weep Lovers, sith Love's very self doth weep, *tr.* *Fr.* La Vita Nuova.

ROSSETTI, DANTE GABRIEL (*continued*)
What smouldering senses in death's sick delay. *Fr.* The House of Life.
Whatever while the thought comes over me, *tr.* *Fr.* La Vita Nuova.
When the Troops Were Returning from Milan, *tr.*
White Ship, The.
William Blake. *Fr.* Five English Poets.
Willowwood. *Fr.* The House of Life.
Winged Hours. *Fr.* The House of Life.
Within Her Eyes, *tr.* *Fr.* La Vita Nuova.
Without Her. *Fr.* The House of Life.
Woe's me! by dint of all these sighs that come, *tr.* *Fr.* La Vita Nuova.
Woodspurge, The.
World's Worth.
Ye pilgrim-folk, advancing pensively, *tr.* *Fr.* La Vita Nuova.
You that thus wear a modest countenance, *tr.* *Fr.* La Vita Nuova.
Young Bride, A, *tr.*
Young Fir-Wood, A.
Youth's Antiphony. *Fr.* The House of Life.
Youth's Spring-Tribute. *Fr.* The House of Life.
ROSSETTI, WILLIAM MICHAEL. Ye Who Taste That Love Is Sweet.
ROSSI, AZARIAH DI. Epitaph: "From out the stormy sea unto the shore."
ROSSLYN, EARL OF. *See* ERSKINE, FRANCIS ROBERT ST. CLAIR.
ROSTAND, EDMOND. Cathedral of Rheims, The.
Cyrano de Bergerac, *sels.*
Cyrano de Bergerac Discusses His Nose. *Fr.* Cyrano de Bergerac.
Petit Chat, Le.
Woman of Samaria, The, *sel.*
ROSTEN, NORMAN. Black Boy.
Out of Our Shame.
This Child.
"ROSTREVOR, GEORGE." *See* HAMILTON, GEORGE ROSTREVOR.
ROTH, C. B. Spring in Florida.
ROTH, SAMUEL. All vision fades, but splendor does not fail.
ROTHERBURGER, LEILA AVERY. Three Crosses.
ROUGET DE LISLE, CLAUDE JOSEPH. Marseillaise, The.
ROUMAIN, JACQUES. Guinea.
Langston Hughes.
When the Tom-tom Beats.
ROUMER, EMILE. Peasant Declares His Love, The.
Three Haitian Creole Moods.
ROUNDS, EMMA. Ballad of the Merry Ferry, The.
Fire Pictures.
Plane Geometry.
Wild Home-Pussy, The.
ROUNDY, WILLIAM NOBLE. Lullaby, A; "Wind is tapping the window-pane, The."
ROUSSEAU, JEAN BAPTISTE. Epigram: "Translator who rhymed the Iliad, The."
ROWBOTHAM, DAVID. Little White Fox.
Moment, The.
ROWE, DOROTHY E. HANBURY. Coal.
Interval.
ROWE, ELIZABETH. Bright Offerings from Shepherds. *Fr.* A Pastoral in Imitation of Drayton's Second Nymphal.
Egyptian Dead, The. *Fr.* The History of Joseph.
God and His Creation.
History of Joseph, The, *sel.*
Hymn: "Glorious armies of the sky, The."
Hymn of the Three Eastern Magi, Adoring Our Saviour at His Nativity, The.
On Heaven, *sel.*
Pastoral in Imitation of Drayton's Second Nymphal, A, *sel.*
Seraphs in Heaven, The. *Fr.* On Heaven.
To a Very Young Gentleman at a Dancing-School.
ROWE, HENRY. Moon.
Sun.
ROWE, JOYCE. Past Song.
Without Syncopation.
ROWE, NICHOLAS. Cato's Address to His Troops in Lybia, *tr.* *Fr.* Pharsalia.
Colin's Complaint.
Fair Penitent, The, *sel.*
Pharsalia, *sels., tr.*
Pompey and Cornelia, *tr.* *Fr.* Pharsalia.
To Lady Jane Wharton, on Her Studying the Globe.
ROWE, RICHARD. Angel of Life, The.
ROWLAND, EVA. Gingerbread Man, The.
ROWLAND, HELEN (Mrs. Frederick Kinney Noyes). Little Things.
ROWLANDS, RICHARD. *See* VERSTEGAN, RICHARD.
ROWLANDS, SAMUEL. Bid me go asleep; I scorn it with my heels.
Glutton.
Idle Housewife.
Melancholy Knight, The, *sels.*
Miserable Merchant.
Poetaster, The. *Fr.* The Melancholy Knight.
Politic Peter meets his friend ashore.
Scholar newly entered marriage life, A.
Severus is extreme in eloquence.
Sir Eglamour [*or* Eglamore]. *Fr.* The Melancholy Knight.
Upstart Courtier.
ROWLES, CATHARINE BRYANT. New Snow.
ROWLEY, SAMUEL, THOMAS DEKKER, *and* JOHN DAY. *See* DEKKER, THOMAS, SAMUEL ROWLEY, *and* JOHN DAY.
ROWLEY, WILLIAM, *and* JOHN FLETCHER. *See* FLETCHER, JOHN, *and* WILLIAM ROWLEY.
ROWLEY, WILLIAM, *and* THOMAS MIDDLETON. *See* MIDDLETON, THOMAS, *and* WILLIAM ROWLEY.
ROWNTREE, MAURICE. O Heart.
ROWSE, ALFRED LESLIE. Remembrance Sunday, Coombe Church, 1940.
ROWSWELL, ALBERT. Should You Go First.
ROYDE-SMITH, NAOMI GWLADYS. Horse, The.
ROYDEN [*or* ROYDON] MATTHEW. Elegy, or Friend's Passion for His Astrophil, An, *sel.*
On Sir Philip Sidney. *Fr.* An Elegy, or Friend's Passion for His Astrophil.
Sir Philip Sidney. *Fr.* An Elegy, or Friend's Passion for His Astrophil.
ROYLE, EDWIN MILTON. Don't You Be What You Ain't.
ROYLE, JOSEPHINE. Bright Spirit.
Deep Peace.
Give Us This Day.
RUBIN, LARRY. Addict, The.
Exile, The.
Lesson, The.
RUBY, HARRY, *and* BERT KALMAR. *See* KALMAR, BERT, *and* HARRY RUBY.
RÜCKERT, FRIEDRICH ("Freimund Raimar"). And Then No More.
Barbarossa.
Gone in the Wind.
Ride round the Parapet, The.
RUDAGI. Lament in Old Age.
RUDDICK, BRUCE. Freighter.
Plaque.
RUDDOCK, MARGOT. Autumn, Crystal Eye.
Child Compassion, The.
I Take Thee, Life.
Love Song.
O Holy Water.
Spirit, Silken Thread.
Take Away.
RUDEL, JAUFRÉ. Quan lo ruis de la fontana.
RUDOLPH, BROTHER. Saint Francis.
RUDYERD [*or* RUDDIER], SIR BENJAMIN. Why Do We Love.
RUFINUS DOMESTICUS. Andante, ma Non Assai.
By all the gods I did not know.
Do not embrace a girl too thin.
Golden Eyes.
Grey Hair.
Happy Mean, The.
Her Only Flaw.
Love the Archer.
Lover's Posy, The.
Rosy Wreath, The.
"This Same Flower That Smiles To-Day."
This wreath, O Rhodocleia, to thee I send.
To Melité.
Very natural girl I hate, A.
RUGGERI, AGNES O'GARA. To the City in the Snow.
RUHNKA, ELIZABETH. To a Passing Gypsy.
RUIZ, JUAN, ARCHPRIEST OF HITA. Archpriest's Prayer, The. *Fr.* The Book of Good Love.
Book of Good Love, The, *sels.*
Disputation between the Greeks and the Romans, The. *Fr.* The Book of Good Love.
Easter Day.
Endrina and Trota-Conventos.
Hymn to the Virgin. *Fr.* The Book of Good Love.
In Praise of Love.
Joys of the Virgin Mary, The. *Fr.* The Book of Good Love.
Lady Sloe.
Lament of a Despised Lover.
Mountain Song.
Power of Money, The. *Fr.* The Book of Good Love.
Praise of Little Women. *Fr.* The Book of Good Love.
Praise of Little Women, *sel.* *Fr.* The Book of Good Love.
Song of the Mountain Girl, The. *Fr.* The Book of Good Love.
Street Song.
Suspicious Truth, The, *sel.*
RUKEYSER, MURIEL. Ajanta.
Antagonists, The. *Fr.* Ninth Elegy.
Beast in View.
Birth, A.
Boy with His Hair Cut Short.
Ceiling Unlimited.
Chapultepec Park.
Charm for Cantinflas, A.
Children, the Sandbar, That Summer.
Children's Elegy. *Fr.* Eighth Elegy.
Citation for Horace Gregory.
City of Monuments.
Cornfield, The, *sel.*
Easter Eve, 1945.
Effort at Speech between Two People.
Eighth Elegy, *sel.*
Even during War. *Fr.* Letter to the Front.
Eyes of Night-Time.
Foghorn in Horror.
From the Duck-Pond to the Carousel.
George Robinson: Blues.
Gibbs, *sel.*
Holy Family.
Homage to Literature.
Ives, *sel.*
Leg in a Plaster Cast, A.
Letter to the Front.
Letter to the Front, *sels.*
Madboy's Song.
Meeting, The.
Motive of All of It, The.
Night Feeding.
Ninth Elegy, *sel.*
Nuns in the Wind.
Reading Time: 1 Minute 26 Seconds.
Return, The.
Rotten Lake Elegy.
Song: "World is full of loss, The."
Soul and Body of John Brown, The.
Structure of the Plane, The.
Study in a Late Subway.
Tenth Elegy: Elegy in Joy.
Then I Saw What the Calling Was.
This Place in the Ways.

To Be a Jew in the Twentieth Century. *Fr.* Letter to the Front.
Trial, The.
Who in One Lifetime.
RUMI, JALAL [*or* JELAL] ED-DIN [*or* DSCHELLALEDDIN]. Artists, The.
As salt resolved in the ocean.
Beauty That All Night Long, A.
Breeze of the morn, The.
Departure.
Descent.
Flowers every night.
Ghazel on the Letter Kiaf.
Happy was I.
He Comes.
He set the world aflame.
He that is my soul's repose.
Heavenly rider passed, The.
I Saw the Winter Weaving.
I sought a soul in the sea.
If life be gone, fresh life to you.
Parrot of Bagdad, The.
Poor Copies.
Progress of Man, The.
Reality and Appearance.
Remembered Music.
Remembering thy lip.
Resurgence.
Song of the Reed, The.
Spirit of the Saints, The.
Thou and I.
Thou who lovest, like a crow.
Though every way I try.
Time bringeth swift to end.
To Heaven Approached a Sufi Saint.
True Sufi, The.
Unseen Power, The.
"Who lifteth up the spirit."
Who was he that said.
RUNCIE, JOHN. Pagan Hymn, A.
RUNEBERG, JOHAN LUDVIG. Beside a Spring.
Girl of the Cottage, The.
Idylls and Epigrams, *sel.*
Laughter.
Morning.
National Anthem.
Our Land.
Soldier Boy, The.
Sven Duva.
Swan, The.
Tears.
Thought.
Trouble Not the Maiden's Soul.
RUNKLE, BERTHA. Song of the Sons of Esau, The.
RUNYON, DAMON. Song of Panama, A.
RUSKIN, JOHN. Awake! Awake! *Fr.* Song of the Dawn.
Song of the Dawn, *sel.*
Trust Thou My Love.
Wreck, The.
RUSS, VIRGINIA. Shape of Autumn, The.
RUSSELL, BERTRAND ARTHUR WILLIAM RUSSELL, 3D EARL. Message for the Nations of the World, A.
RUSSELL, CHARLES EDWARD. Fleet at Santiago, The.
RUSSELL, ETHEL GREEN. Letter from the Vieux Carre.
RUSSELL, FRANCIS ALBERT ROLLO. Laborare Est Orare.
RUSSELL, G. J. It Might Have Been Worse.
RUSSELL, GEORGE WILLIAM. *See* "Æ."
RUSSELL, IRWIN. Blessing [on] the Dance, A. *Fr.* Christmas-Night in the Quarters.
Christmas-Night in the Quarters, *sels.*
First Banjo, The. *Fr.* Christmas-Night in the Quarters.
Furst Banjo, De. *Fr.* Christmas-Night in the Quarters.
Nebuchadnezzar.
Selling a Dog.
RUSSELL, MATTHEW. Thought from Cardinal Newman, A.
RUSSELL, MAUD. Great Outdoors, The.
RUSSELL, PERCY. Birth of Australia, The.
RUSSELL, SOLVEIG PAULSON. Mistletoe Sprites.
RUSSELL, SYDNEY KING. After Hour.
Aftermath.
Death Was a Woman.
Girl in the Subway.
Midsummer.
Pilgrimage.
Portrait.
Prayer: "Let me remember music."
Vachel Lindsay.
Victor, The.
What Does It Matter Now.
RUSSELL, THOMAS (1762–88). Maniac, The.
Philoctetes.
Sonnet: "Could then the Babes from yon unshelter'd cot."
Sonnet: To Oxford.
Sonnet: To Valclusa.
Sonnet Suppos'd to Be Written at Lemnos.
Suppos'd to Be Written at Lemnos.
To Oxford.
RUSSELL, THOMAS (*fl.* 1852). New Testament, The.
Old Testament, The.
RUSTICO DI FILIPPO. Making of Master Messerin, The.
Sonnet: Of the Making of Master Messerin.
Sonnet: "When God had finish'd Master Messerin."
RUTEBEUF. Poet's Poverty, The.
RUTHERFORD, RUTH. Far Off.
RUTLEDGE, ARCHIBALD. Lee.
My Old Hound Pack.
O Mariners!
Peachtree.
Requiem.
Veery, The.
RUTTER, JOSEPH. Hymen. *Fr.* The Shepherd's Holiday.
Shepherd's Holiday, The, *sel.*
RYAN, ABRAM JOSEPH (Father Ryan). Better than Gold.
Cause of the South, The.
Child's Wish, A.
Conquered Banner, The.
Land without Ruins, A.
Rosary of My Tears, The.
Sentinel Songs.
Song of the Mystic.
Southern Soldier Boy, The.
Sword of Robert Lee, The.
RYAN, ANNE. Mary Salome, Widow.
Music.
RYAN, GEORGE. Unsolved Mystery.
RYAN, GEORGE B. Still Undaunted.
RYAN, KATHRYN WHITE. Exile.
Mother, The.
Triumph.
Turquoise Bowl, The.
RYAN, MALACHY. Rose Adair.
RYAN, MARGARET. Twilight.
RYAN, RICHARD. O, Saw Ye the Lass.
RYDBERG, VIKTOR. Bathing Children, The.
Cantata for the Graduation Festival at Upsala, the Sixth of September, 1877.
Dexippos, *sel.*
House-Goblin, The.
Longing.
Psyche.
Shipwreck.
Snowfrid.
Song of the Athenians. *Fr.* Dexippos.
Thy Grief Is Thine.
Two Bells, The.
Vain Quest of Beauty.
RYDER, ARTHUR WILLIAM. Aëtius at Châlons, September, 451.
Aja's Lament over His Dead Wife, *tr.*
Arrows of Love, *tr.*
Better in the Wild, *tr.*
Better Part, The, *tr.*
Cloud-Messenger, The, *sel., tr.*
Dignity, *tr.*
Flaming Banners, *tr.*
In the Days of Thy Youth, *tr.*
Indian Epigrams, *tr.*
Love Grows by What It Feeds On, *tr.*
Love, the Fisher, *tr.*
Nightfall, *tr.*
Panchatantra, The, *sels., tr.*
Seasons, The, *sels., tr.*
Struggling Fancies, *tr.*
Stubborn Fool, The, *tr.*
Sweet and Bitter, *tr.*
When I Knew a Little Bit, *tr.*
Why My Poems Died, *tr.*
Wise Misogynist, The, *tr.*
Women's Eyes, *tr.*
RYLEEV, KONDRATI. *See* RYLEYEV, KONDRATI FEODOROVICH.
RYLENKOV, NIKOLAI. Get Up.
RYLEYEV, KONDRATI FEODOROVICH. Citizen.
Elegy: "End has come to all my yearning, An."
O Liberty, proud inspiration! *at.*
RYMER, THOMAS. Edgar, *sel.*
On Her Absence.
Wit Predominant. *Fr.* Edgar.
RYOKWAN. Murmuring of Pine Trees, The.
RYOTA. Haiku: "No one spoke."
No one spoke.
Way of the World, The.
White Chrysanthemum, The.
RYOTO. Cunning fireflies, The.
Firefly, A/ Flitted by.
RYOZEN (the monk Ryozen). When I am lonely.
RYSKIND, MORRIE ("John P. Wintergreen"). Happy Thought for Some Struggling Nation.
Horace the Wise.
To Natalie.

S

"S., A. H." Lost Voice, The.
"S., A. W." Life That Counts, The.
"S., C. N." Thenot Protests.
"S., E." Being Forsaken of His Friend He Complaineth.
Why should I longer long to live.
"S., J. H." New Year's Wish, A.
"S., M. W." Flag, The.
"S., W. H." Ballad of the Prodigal Son, The.
"S. C. M'K." *See* "M'K., S. C."
"S. M. M." *See* "M., S. M."
"S. W. D. M." *See* "M., S. W. D."
SÁ [*or* SAA] DE MIRANDA, FRANCISCO DE. Where Is Dominga?
SAADI. *See* SADI.
SABIN, EDWIN LEGRAND. Apple-Barrel, The.
Easter.
Mothers.
My Enemy.
Work.
SABIR, ADIB-I. Epitaph for a Tyrannous Governor Who Choked on Wine.
SABOLY, NICOLAS. Boots and Saddles.
Bring a Torch, Jeannette, Isabella, *at.*
Christmas Carol of Provence, *at.*
Shepherd Boys, The.
Shepherd Folk Go to Bethlehem, The.
SACCHETTI, FRANCO. Ballata: His Talk with Certain Peasant Girls.
Catch: On a Wet Day.
SACKVILLE, CHARLES, 6TH EARL OF DORSET. Advice, The.
Bonny Black Bess.
Dorinda.
Fire of Love, The, *at. Fr.* The Amorous Bigot (*by* Thomas Shadwell).
May the Ambitious Ever Find, *at.*
On a Lady Who Fancied Herself a Beauty.
Phillis for Shame Let Us Improve.
Song: "Dorinda's sparkling wit, and eyes."
Song: "Methinks the poor town has been troubled too long."
Song: "Oh, why did e'er my thoughts aspire."
Song: "Phillis, for shame let us improve."
Song: "To all you ladies now at land."
Song, Written at Sea, in the First Dutch War.

SACKVILLE, CHARLES (*continued*)
Written at Sea, in the First Dutch War.
SACKVILLE, LADY MARGARET. Apple, The.
Drownèd Lover, The.
Message, The.
Poet at the Court of Pan, A.
Resurrection.
Sermon, A.
This quiet pillow.
To One Who Denies the Possibility of a Permanent Peace.
SACKVILLE, THOMAS, 1ST EARL OF DORSET. Approach of Winter, The. *Fr.* Induction to "The Mirror for Magistrates."
Complaint of Henrie Duke of Buckinghame, The.
Induction to "The Mirror for Magistrates."
Induction to "The Mirror for Magistrates," *sels.*
Mayster Sackvilles Induction. *Fr.* The Mirror for Magistrates.
Mirror for Magistrates, The, *sels.*
Old Age. *Fr.* Induction to "The Mirror for Magistrates."
Porch of Hell, The. *Fr.* Induction to "The Mirror for Magistrates."
Sleep. *Fr.* Induction to "The Mirror for Magistrates."
Thomas Sackville in Commendation of the Work to the Reader.
Troy. *Fr.* Induction to "The Mirror for Magistrates."
Vision of Sorrow. *Fr.* Induction to "The Mirror for Magistrates."
Vision of War, A. *Fr.* Induction to "The Mirror for Magistrates."
Winter. *Fr.* Induction to "The Mirror for Magistrates."
SACKVILLE-WEST, VICTORIA MARY (Mrs. Harold Nicolson). Autumn, *sel.*
Bee-Master.
Bitterness.
Bull, The.
Dream, A.
Early Love.
Evening.
Full Moon.
Greater Cats, The. *Fr.* King's Daughter.
I Find My God. *Fr.* Solitude.
Idle Thoughts.
King's Daughter.
King's Daughter, *sel.*
Labour. *Fr.* The Land.
Land, The.
Land, The, *sels.*
Mirage, *sel.*
On the Lake.
Peddler and the Reddleman, The. *Fr.* The Land.
Personal Valour.
Ploughing. *Fr.* The Land.
Saxon Song, A.
Sissinghurst.
Solitude, *sel.*
Sometimes When Night.
Song: "I know a room where tulips tall." *Fr.* Mirage.
Song: "If I had only loved your flesh."
Song: "My spirit like a shepherd boy."
Spring. *Fr.* The Land.
Spring Was Late That Year, The. *Fr.* The Land.
Tuscany.
Vintage. *Fr.* The Land.
Weed Month. *Fr.* The Land.
Winter. *Fr.* The Land.
Winter Song. *Fr.* The Land.
Wood-cut.
SADAIYE. Blossoms and Storm.
SADI [*or* SAADI] (Muslih-ud-Din). Adam's Race.
Alas. *Fr.* The Gulistan.
Beneficence.
Bustan, The, *sels.*
Compassion.
Contentment.
Courage. *Fr.* The Gulistan.
Dance.
Dancer, The. *Fr.* The Bustan.
Darweesh, The.
Divine Providence.
Forgiveness.
Friendship. *Fr.* The Gulistan.
From Slavery to Slavery. *Fr.* The Gulistan.
Gift of Speech, The. *Fr.* The Gulistan.
Good Wife, The.
Great Physician, The. *Fr.* The Bustan.
Guardians.
Gulistan, The, *sels.*
He Hath No Parallel. *Fr.* The Gulistan.
Held Fast.
Help. *Fr.* The Gulistan.
Hyacinths to Feed Thy Soul. *Fr.* The Gulistan.
Jesus and the Sinner.
Joy and Sorrow.
Love the Foe.
Love's Last Resource. *Fr.* The Gulistan.
Mesnevi. *Fr.* The Gulistan.
Ode: "Until thine hands clasp girdle-wise the waist of the belov'd."
On the Deception of Appearances. *Fr.* The Gulistan.
On True Worth.
Persian Maxim.
Prudence.
Purgatory May Be Paradise. *Fr.* The Gulistan.
Shiraz.
Sieve, The.
Sooth-Sayer, The. *Fr.* The Gulistan.
Take the Crust. *Fr.* The Gulistan.
Wantoning.
Wealth. *Fr.* The Gulistan.
Wrestler, The. *Fr.* The Gulistan.
SAFFORD, WILLIAM HARRISON. Battle of Muskingum, The.
SAGE, RUFUS B. Night on the Prairie.
Summer on the Great American Desert.
Wanderer's Grave, The.
"SAGITTARIUS" (Olga Katzin). Good King Wenceslas Look'd Out.
Player Queen, The.
Prologue; Written for the Re-opening of the Theatre Royal, Richmond, Yorkshire, 1942.
Romantic, The.
SAGLIO, HUGH T. Snow-Drift.
SA'IB OF ISFAHAN. Cliques and Critics.
SAIDY, FRED. For a Little Lady.
SAIGYO HOSHI. Although I do not know.
In my boat that goes.
Like those boats which are returning.
Mingling my prayer.
Since I am convinced.
Startled/ By a single scream.
Tanka: Reflection, A.
Those ships which left.
SAINT. *See under names of individual saints.*
SAINT-GELAIS, MELLIN DE. Flame and Snow.
On a Detractor, *sel.*
Seeing those mountains, distant and obscure.
Sonnet of the Mountain, The.
ST. JOHN, PETER. Descent on Middlesex, The.
ST. LEGER, WARHAM. False Gallop of Analogies, A.
To My Hairdresser.
ST. MIRIAM OF THE TEMPLE, SISTER. Mater Misericordiae.
ST. VIRGINIA, SISTER MARY. Case of Thomas More, The.
Convent Cemetery—Mount Carmel.
Edmund Campion.
Great Silence.
Nun to Mary, Virgin, A.
Saint Teresa of Avila.
Shrine in Nazareth.
This Sharpening Tension.
SAINTE-BEUVE, CHARLES AUGUSTIN. God's Voice.
Which Was Most Truly Dead?
SAITO, MOKICHI. Dirge, A: "Lacewing has lighted upon the wall, A."
Hospital Verses.
Lunatic, A.
"SAKANOYE, THE LADY OF" (Lady Otomo no Sakanoye). Do not smile to yourself.
Dress that my brother has put on is thin, The. *Fr.* Manyo Shu.
Friends Drinking Together.
My heart, thinking. *Fr.* Manyo Shu.
Unknown love. *Fr.* Manyo Shu.
You say, "I will come."
SALAMAH, SON OF JANDAL. Gone Is Youth. *Fr.* The Mufaddaliyat.
Mufaddaliyat, The, *sel.*
SALAMAN, ESTHER POLIANOWSKY. *See* CORNFORD, FRANCES, *and* ESTHER POLIANOWSKY SALAMAN.
SALAS BARBADILLO, ALONSO JERÓNIMO DE. Disputes.
SALDAÑA, DIEGO DE. Eyes So Tristful.
SALEMME, MARTHA. Next Next Shortest Poem in the World, The.
SALINAS, PEDRO. Distant Sea.
Do you not hear how they ask for reality.
His Triumph.
How Gently You Rock My Child to Sleep.
How many lost things there were.
I am so sure that your presence.
I see you not, though well.
If the voice were perceived with the eyes.
It Might Be Avila.
Not in palaces of marble.
On dry land.
Seeking, Finding.
Shore, The.
Soil. Nothing more.
Swimmer of Night.
Tell me, do you remember.
To think of you to-night.
Truth of Two.
SALINGER, HERMAN. *For translations from German, see* AnGP; LiTW; TwGV.
SALISBURY, HELEN MOLYNEAUX. Refugee, The.
SALIS-SEEWIS, JOHANN GAUDENZ VON. Song of the Silent Land.
SALKELD, BLANAID. Anchises.
Evasion.
Leave Us Religion.
Meditation.
Men Walked To and Fro.
No Uneasy Refuge.
Now Is Farewell.
Optimism.
Peggy.
Templeogue.
Terenure.
That Corner.
Youth.
SALMON, ANDRÉ. Massacre of the Innocents, The.
Ovanuna Believed.
SALOMON, ISIDORE LAWRENCE. Song for the Greenwood Fawn.
SALSBURY, NATE ("Baron Ireland"). Apex.
Big Boss Speaks, The.
Krazy: Reflection No. 5.
Take Nothing for Granite.
SALSBURY, NATE, *and* NEWMAN LEVY. Ballade of the Ancient Wheeze.
SALTILLO, JOSÉ DE. Rio Bravo—a Mexican Lament.
SALTUS, FRANCIS SALTUS. Andalusian Sereno, The.
Bayadere, The.
Ideal, The.
Pastel.
Sphinx Speaks, The.
SALUSBURY, SIR JOHN. Buen Matina.
SALVADORI, GIULIO. Presence of the Spirit, The.
SALVERSON, LAURA GOODMAN. If a Maid Be Fair.
Premonition.
SALZ, HELEN. Late.
SAMAIN, ALBERT. Cleopatra.
From Summer Hours.
My Heart.
Pannyra of the Golden Heel.
Tower, The.
SAMANIEGO, FÉLIX MARÍA DE. Wolf and the Dog, The, *tr.*

Young Philosopher and His Friends, The.
SAMBROOK, JOYCE. Wild Thyme.
Woodpecker, The.
SAMMIS, J. H. All Needs Met.
SAMPLEY, ARTHUR MCCULLOUGH. Dead Earth, The. *Fr.* Fragments of Eternity.
Defender, The.
Eternity. *Fr.* Fragments of Eternity.
Fragments of Eternity, *sels.*
SAMPSON, WILLIAM. Vow Breaker, The, *sel.*
When from the wars I do return. *Fr.* The Vow Breaker.
SAMPTER, JESSIE E. Alone, *tr.*
Blessings for Chanukah.
Grasshopper's Song, The, *tr.*
Kadia the Young Mother Speaks.
Promised Land, The.
Psalm: "They have burned to Thee many tapers."
Queen Sabbath, *tr.*
Summer Sabbath.
SAMUEL HA-NAGID. Proverbs.
SAMUELS, RUTH. Realism.
SAN GARDE, EVELINA. Giant's Cake, A.
SAN GEMINIANO [*or* GEMIGNANO], FOLGORE DA. March. *Fr.* Sonnets of the Months.
May. *Fr.* Sonnets of the Months.
Of the Months.
On Knighthood.
Sonnet: Of Virtue.
Sonnets of the Months, *sels.*
SAN JUAN DE LA CRUZ. *See* JOHN OF THE CROSS, SAINT.
SANA'I. Blind Men and the Elephant, The.
Devil's Complaint, The.
Good Night.
Perfect Love.
Thy Love.
SANBORN, FRANKLIN BENJAMIN. Ariana.
Samuel Hoar.
SÁNCHEZ, LUIS ANÍBAL. Brother Dog.
SANCHEZ QUELL, HIPÓLITO. Praise of Saccarello Street.
"SANCTA-CLARA, ABRAHAM À." St. Anthony's Sermon to the Fishes.
SANDALL, HAROLD C. Song: "Love that is hoarded, moulds at last," *wr. at.* *See* GINSBERG, LOUIS.
SANDBURG, CARL. A.E.F.
Accomplished Facts.
Adelaide Crapsey.
American Yarns. *Fr.* The People, Yes.
Arithmetic.
Arithmetic, *sel.*
At a Window.
Autumn Movement.
Baby Toes.
Bas-Relief.
Best, The. *Fr.* The People, Yes.
Between Worlds.
Blue Island Intersection.
Boy and Father.
Bricklayer Love.
Bringers.
Broken-Face Gargoyles.
Buffalo Dusk.
Bundles.
Caboose Thoughts.
Calls.
Chicago.
Child.
Child of the Romans.
Children of the Wind. *Fr.* The People, Yes.
Choose.
Clean Curtains.
Clocks.
Code arrives, A; language; lingo; slang. *Fr.* Good Morning, America.
Cool Tombs.
Couple, A.
Cumulatives.
Dan.
Death Snips Proud Men.
Early Lynching.
Early Moon.
Electric Sign Goes Dark, An.
Elephants Are Different to Different People.
Evening Waterfall.
Explanations of Love.
Face.
Falltime.
Fence, A.
Finale. *Fr.* Slabs of the Sunburnt West.
Fire-Logs.
Fireborn Are at Home in Fire, The.
Fish Crier.
Five Towns on the B. and O.
Flash Crimson.
Flat Lands.
Fog.
Foolish about Windows.
For You.
Four Brothers, The, *sel.*
Four Preludes on Playthings of the Wind.
From Illinois and Indiana came a later myth. *Fr.* The People, Yes.
From the four corners of the earth. *Fr.* The People, Yes.
Gone.
Good Morning, America, *sel.*
Grass.
Graves.
Great Hunt, The.
Handfuls.
Hangman at Home, The.
Happiness.
Harbor, The.
Harvest Sunset.
Haze.
Helga.
Hoof Dusk.
Hope Is a Tattered Flag. *Fr.* The People, Yes.
Horses and Men in Rain.
House.
I Am the People, the Mob.
Ice Handler.
Jan Kubelik.
Jazz Fantasia.
Joliet.
Joy.
Killers ("I am put high over all others in the city today").
Killers ("I am singing to you").
Kin.
Languages.
Laughing Corn.
Lawyers Know Too Much, The.
Letters to Dead Imagists.
Limited.
Little Candle.
Little Girl, Be Careful What You Say.
Loam.
Localities.
Long Shadow of Lincoln, The.
Look at Six Eggs. *Fr.* Prairie.
Losers.
Lost.
Mammy Hums.
Man-Hunt, The. *Fr.* The Four Brothers.
Man in the Street Is Fed, The. *Fr.* The People, Yes.
Man with the Broken Fingers, The.
Manual System.
Manufactured Gods.
Milk-white Moon, Put the Cows to Sleep.
Mist Forms.
Mr. Attila.
Moist Moon People.
Monotone.
Mysterious Biography.
New Farm Tractor.
Night Stuff.
Nocturne in a Deserted Brickyard.
Old Flagman, The.
Old Timers.
On a Flimmering Floom You Shall Ride.
Ossawatomie.
Our Prayer of Thanks.
People Who Must.
People Will Live On, The. *Fr.* The People, Yes.
People with Proud Chins.
People, Yes, The, *sels.*
Personality.
Phizzog.
Picnic Boat, The.
Places.
Plunger.
Poor, The.
Population Drifts.
Potomac Town in February.
Prairie.
Prairie, *sel.*
Prayers of Steel.
Precious Moments.
Primer Lesson.
Psalm of Those Who Go Forth before Daylight.
Record is a scroll of many indecipherable scrawls, The. *Fr.* The People, Yes.
Redhaw Rain.
Red-headed Restaurant Cashier.
Repetitions.
Road and the End, The.
Sandhill People.
Sea-Wash.
Shenandoah.
Singing Nigger.
Sins of Kalamazoo, The.
Sketch.
Skyscraper.
Slabs of the Sunburnt West.
Slabs of the Sunburnt West, *sels.*
Sleep is a Suspension. *Fr.* The People, Yes.
Slippery.
Smoke and Steel.
Smoke and Steel, *sels.*
Smoke Rose Gold.
Splinter.
Spring Grass.
Stars, Songs, Faces.
Sumach and Birds.
Summer Stars.
Sunsets.
Take a Letter to Dmitri Shostakovitch.
Teamster's Farewell, A.
Ten Definitions of Poetry.
Theme in Yellow.
They All Want to Play Hamlet.
They Have Yarns. *Fr.* The People, Yes.
They Will Say.
Three Spring Notations on Bipeds.
Threes.
To a Contemporary Bunkshooter.
To Beachey, 1912.
To the Ghost of John Milton.
Under a Telephone Pole.
Under the Harvest Moon.
Upstream.
Valley Song.
Washington Monument by Night.
What the people learn out of lifting and hauling. *Fr.* The People, Yes.
Whiffs of the Ohio River at Cincinnati.
Who can make a poem of the depths of weariness. *Fr.* The People, Yes.
Who Shall Speak for the People? *Fr.* The People, Yes.
Wilderness.
Wind Song.
Windy City, The, *sel.*
Work Gangs.
Worms and the Wind.
Yarns of the People. *Fr.* The People, Yes.
Young Sea.
SANDERS, ELSIE DUNCAN. Mother's Diary.
SANDERS, RUTH MANNING-. *See* MANNING-SANDERS, RUTH.
SANDFORD, EGBERT. God Is at the Organ.
SANDFORD, JAMES. Of Love.
SANDOVAL Y ZAPATA, LUIS DE. Beauty on a Western Balcony.
Grievous Peril of a Gallant in Moth Metaphor.
To a Dead Actress.
To Primal Matter.
To the Admirable Transubstantiation of the Roses.
White Lily.
SANDS, ROBERT CHARLES. Green Isle of Lovers, The.
SANDSTROM, FLORA. Stately Lady, The.

SANDYS, GEORGE. Deo Opt. Max. *Fr.*
A Paraphrase on the Psalms of
David.
Lines Written at the Temple of the
Holy Sepulchre.
Paraphrase on the Psalms of David, A,
sels.
Psalme CXXXVII: "As on Euphrates
shady banks." *Fr.* A Paraphrase on
the Psalms of David.
SANGSTER, CHARLES. Autumn Change,
An. *Fr.* The Happy Harvesters.
Brock.
Comet, The.
Evening.
Happy Harvesters, The, *sels.*
Harvest Hymn.
Lost and Found.
Lyric to the Isles.
Mariline.
Plains of Abraham, The.
Rapid, The.
Red Men, The.
St. Lawrence and the Saguenay, The,
sel.
Snows, The.
Soldiers of the Plough, The. *Fr.* The
Happy Harvesters.
Sonnet: "I sat within the temple of
her heart."
Sonnets Written in the Orillia Woods,
sel.
Thousand Islands, The. *Fr.* The St.
Lawrence and the Saguenay.
Wine of Song, The.
SANGSTER, MARGARET ELIZABETH (Mun-
son) (1838-1912). Are the Chil-
dren at Home?
Average Man, The.
Awakening.
Building of the Nest, The.
Christmas Day.
Christmas in the North.
Face to Face with Trouble, *sel.*
From Nazareth.
Mary.
Oh, face to face with trouble. *Fr.*
Face to Face with Trouble.
Our Father's World.
Our Missionaries.
Our Own.
Patience with the Living.
Show Me Thyself.
Sin of Omission, The.
Song for Our Flag, A.
Washington's Name in the Hall of
Fame.
White Carnation, The.
Whittier.
Within the Veil.
Work of Love, The.
SANGSTER, MARGARET ELIZABETH
(1894?-). Armistice.
At Prayer Meeting.
Autumn Day, An.
Blind Man, The.
Campus.
Commencement.
Forgiven.
From a Pet-Shop Window.
Gratitude.
In a Shop Window.
In Gratitude for Friends.
Independence Day To-Day.
Jim-Dog.
Lost Dog.
Mother Speaks, A.
Mother's Prayer, A.
New Year, A.
New Year Is a Banner, A.
Our Flag.
Prayer for Faith, A.
Recognition.
Riveter, The.
Road Song.
Security.
Soul of a Mother, The.
Thanksgivin' Pumpkin Pies.
Thanksgiving ("For the days when
nothing happens").
Thanksgiving ("I think God loves sim-
plicity").
There Is No Dream.
They Never Quite Leave Us.

Vacation Time.
Washington's Birthday.
SANJO, EMPEROR. Involuntary/ I may
live on.
SANKER, LOUIS JOHN. Boy at the Door.
Honey for the Heart.
Trumpet for Yuletide.
SANNAZARO, JACOPO (Actius Sincerus
Sannazarius). Celestial Queen. *Fr.*
De Partu Virginis.
De Partu Virginis, *sel.*
Like to these unmeasurable moun-
tains.
Lover's Life Compared to the Alps,
The.
To Pentadius.
SANNIKOV, GEORG. In Spring.
SANSOM, CLIVE. Dustman, The.
Matthew.
Postman, The.
SANT' ANGELO, BARTOLOMEO DI. Son-
net: He Jests Concerning His Pov-
erty.
SANTAYANA, GEORGE. After Gray Vigils,
Sunshine in the Heart. *Fr.* Son-
nets.
Art, *tr.*
As in the Midst of Battle There Is
Room. *Fr.* Sonnets.
As when the sceptre dangles from the
hand. *Fr.* Sonnets.
Before a Statue of Achilles.
Deem Not, because You See Me. *Fr.*
Sonnets.
Elegies (*of* Tibullus), *sel., tr.*
Faith. *Fr.* Sonnets.
Gathering the echoes of forgotten wis-
dom. *Fr.* Odes.
Have patience; it is fit that in this
wise. *Fr.* Sonnets.
I Sought on Earth. *Fr.* Sonnets.
I Would I Might Forget That I Am
I. *Fr.* Sonnets.
Last Refuge, *tr.*
Light of Faith, The. *Fr.* Sonnets.
Madrigal 109: "Ravished by all that
to the eyes is fair," *tr.*
Minuet on Reaching the Age of Fifty,
A.
My Heart Rebels against My Genera-
tion. *Fr.* Odes.
O Martyred Spirit.
O World [Thou Choosest Not the Bet-
ter Part]. *Fr.* Sonnets.
Ode: "Gathering the echoes of forgot-
ten wisdom." *Fr.* Odes.
Ode: "My heart rebels against my
generation." *Fr.* Odes.
Ode: "Of thee the Northman by his
beachèd [*or* bleachèd] galley." *Fr.*
Odes.
Ode: "Slowly the black earth gains
upon the yellow." *Fr.* Odes.
Ode: "What god will choose me from
this labouring nation." *Fr.* Odes.
Ode to the Mediterranean. *Fr.* Odes.
Odes.
Odes, *sels.*
On a Piece of Tapestry.
On the Death of a Metaphysician.
Prosit Neujahr.
Rustic at the Play, The.
Slow and reluctant was the long de-
scent. *Fr.* Sonnets.
Slowly the black earth gains upon the
yellow. *Fr.* Odes.
Solipsism.
Sonnet: "As when the scepter dangles
from the hand." *Fr.* Sonnets.
Sonnet: "O World, thou choosest not
the better part!" *Fr.* Sonnets.
Sonnet: "'Tis love that moveth the
celestial spheres." *Fr.* Sonnets.
Sonnets, *sels.*
Sorrow. *Fr.* Sonnets.
Souvenir, *tr.*
Sweet are the days we wander with no
hope. *Fr.* Sonnets.
These Strewn Thoughts by the Moun-
tain Pathway Sprung. *Fr.* Sonnets.
To W. P.
To W. P., *sels.*
We Needs Must Be Divided in the
Tomb. *Fr.* Sonnets.

What god will choose me from this
labouring nation. *Fr.* Odes.
What Riches Have You? *Fr.* Son-
nets.
With You a Part of Me. *Fr.* To
W. P.
SANTEUIL, JEAN-BAPTISTE DE. Ascension
Hymn.
SANTIC, ALEKSA. Dalmatian Nocturne.
SANTILLANA, IÑIGO LÓPEZ DE MENDOZA,
MARQUÉS DE. Canción: "Whether
you love me."
On Friendship.
Serranilla VIII: "Early once in Roble-
dillo."
Serranilla: "From Calatrava as I took
my way."
Serranilla VI: "I ne'er on the border."
Sonnet XVIII: "Afar from you and
very near to care."
Villancico for His Three Daughters.
SANTOB [*or* SHEM-TOB] DE CARRION.
Friend, A.
Jewish Poet Counsels a King, A.
Resignation.
Self-Defense.
SANUKI, LADY. Hyaku-Nin-Isshu, The,
sel.
Like a great rock far out at sea. *Fr.*
The Hyaku-Nin-Isshu.
SAPHIER, WILLIAM. Meeting.
SAPPHO. Absent Friend, An.
Adolescence.
Adonis.
Alone.
Andromache's Wedding.
Arignota Remembers.
Bas-Relief.
Beauty.
Beloved, The.
Beyond the Vulgar Reach.
Blest as the Immortal Gods.
Bride of Sardis, The.
Captive, The.
Clais.
Dead Shalt Thou Lie.
E'en the Country Maid.
Evening.
Evensong.
Eventide.
Farewell to Anactoria.
Farewell to Maidenhood.
Flowers for the Graces.
Forever Dead.
Forgotten.
Forsaken.
Fragment from [*or of*] Sappho.
Full Moon.
Garden, A.
Garden of the Nymphs.
Girl, A.
Hesperus, *at.*
Highest Fruit, The.
Hymn to Aphrodite.
Immortal Aphrodite.
Invocation: "Goddess of Cyprus come."
Like the sweet apple which reddens
upon the topmost bough.
Lonely Night.
Lost Friend, The.
Lost Heart.
Lost Maidenhead.
Love.
Maid Unwed, The.
Moon, The.
Moon Has Set, The.
Moon hath left the sky, The.
Mother, I Cannot Mind My Wheel.
Night.
Nightingale, The.
Note to Gongyla.
O Hesperus! Thou bringest all things
home.
Oh, my sweet mother, 'tis in vain.
Ode: "Peer of gods he seemeth to me,
the blissful."
Ode to Anactoria.
Ode to Aphrodite.
One Girl.
Orchard Song.
Parting, The.
Peer of the Gods.
Round about Me.
Silver Moon, The.

Some there are who say that the fairest thing seen.
This dust was Timas'; ere her bridal hour.
Thou art come, it is well, for of thee I am fain.
Thou Happy Bridegroom.
Thou liest dead, and there will be no memory left behind.
Though Youth Be Gone.
Throned in splendor, deathless, O Aphrodite.
Thy Form Is Lovely.
Timas.
To a Bride.
To a Rich Uncultured Woman.
To an Uncultivated Woman.
To Aphrodite.
To Atthis.
To me the Muses truly gave.
To Mnesidice.
Vae Soli.
Wealth that has no share in worth, The.
Wedding Song ("Up with the rafters high").
Wedding Songs ("Maidenhood, O Maidenhood").
Wormwood.
Young Bride, A [*or* The].
Youth and Age.
SAPPINGTON, JAMES COALE, JR. Idealist, The.
SARBIEWSKI, CASIMIR. On the Victory of Poland and Her Allies over the Sultan Osman, 1621.
To Liberty.
SARETT, LEW. Angus McGregor.
Articulate Thrush.
Beat against Me No Longer.
Blacktail Deer.
Blue Duck, The.
Breakers of Broncos.
Brittle World.
Broken Drake.
Chant for the Moon-of-Flowers.
Clipped Wings.
Conjurer, The.
Crazy Medicine.
Dog's Life, A.
Double-Bear Dances. *Fr.* Thunderdrums.
Feather.
Feud.
Five Peas on a Barrelhead.
Four Little Foxes.
Ghost-Wolf Dances. *Fr.* Thunderdrums.
God Is at the Anvil.
Granite.
Granite Mountain, The.
Great Divide, The.
Hang Me among Your Winds.
Iron-Wind Dances. *Fr.* Thunderdrums.
Leave Me to My Own.
Let Me Flower as I Will.
Let Me Go Down to Dust.
Loon, The.
Miscreant Angel, The.
Mountain Hamlet.
Red-Rock, the Moose-Hunter.
Reflection.
Refuge.
Requiem for a Modern Croesus.
Sheepherder, The.
So like a Quiet Rain.
Thunderdrums.
To a Wild Goose over Decoys.
Wailing Lynx.
Weeng; an Indian Slumber Song.
Wind in the Pine.
Wolf Cry, The.
SARGENT, DANIEL. *Ark* and the *Dove*, The.
Change of Subject, A.
Courtesy.
Last Day. The.
Music.
Preference.
SARGENT, EPES. Death of Warren, The.
Deeds of Kindness.
Evening in Gloucester Harbor.
Heart's Summer, The.
Life on the Ocean Wave, A.
Summer Noon at Sea, A.
Sunrise at Sea.
Suppose.
Tropical Weather.
Webster.
SARGENT, H. F. Land of Dreams, The.
SARGENT, LOUISE PEABODY. Thy Will Be Done.
SARGENT, JOHN OSBORNE. Horace.
Odes (*of* Horace), *sel., tr.*
Restorer, The, *tr. Fr.* Odes.
Spring, *tr. Fr.* Odes.
SARGENT, N. B. Building for Eternity.
SARGENT, NETTIE M. Hymn of Trust.
SARGENT, WILLIAM D. Barn-Swallow, The.
Wind-Wolves.
SARMÈD THE YAHUD. Quatrain: "Sarmèd, whom they intoxicated from the cup of love."
Quatrain: "This existence has, without the azure sphere, no reality."
SARONA, F. Dip, Boys, Dip the Oar.
SARSON, H. M. Lovely Things.
Road to Town, The.
SARSON, MAY. I Must Away.
SARTON, MAY. Celebration, A.
Clavichord, The.
Conversation in Black and White.
From Men Who Died Deluded.
Innumerable Friend.
Leaves before the Wind.
Nativity.
Prothalamium.
Sacred Order, The.
Santos; New Mexico.
Summer Music.
Transition.
SARUMARU (the priest Sarumaru). Deep in the mountain.
SASS, GEORGE HERBERT. Ballad of the War, A.
SASSOON, SIEGFRIED. Absolution.
Aftermath.
Aftermath, *sel.*
All Souls' Day.
Alone.
Ancient History.
At the Cenotaph.
At the Grave of Henry Vaughan.
Attack.
Autumn.
Base Details.
Before Day.
"Blighters."
Brevities.
Case for the Miners, The.
Child's Prayer, A.
Cleaning the Candelabrum.
Concert Party, A.
Conclusion.
Counter-Attack.
Credo.
Daybreak in a Garden.
Death-Bed, The.
December Stillness, Teach Me.
Devotion to Duty.
Does It Matter?
Dreamers.
Dug-out, The.
Early Chronology.
Elected Silence.
Eulogy of My House.
Everyman.
Everyone [*or* Every One] Sang.
Falling Asleep.
Fantasia on a Wittelsbach Atmosphere.
Forsaken, The.
General, The.
Gloria Mundi.
Glory of Women, The.
Grandeur of Ghosts.
Heart's Journey, The.
Heart's Journey, The, *sels.*
I Stood with the Dead.
In Barracks.
In Me, Past, Present, Future Meet.
Invocation: "Come down from heaven to meet me when my breath."
It Was the Love of Life.
Kiss, The.
Leaders, New Style: The General (1917).
Limitations.
Local Train of Thought, A.
Long Ago.
Make Them Forget.
Memory.
Monody on the Demolition of Devonshire House.
Morning Express.
Morning Glory.
Musical Critic Anticipates Eternity, A.
My Past Has Gone to Bed.
Mystic as Soldier, A.
Need, The.
Old Huntsman, The.
Old-World Effect, An.
On Passing the New Menin Gate.
On Reading the War Diary of a Defunct Ambassador.
On Reading the War Diary of a Defunct Ambassador, *sel.*
On Scratchbury Camp.
One Who Watches.
Phoenix, The.
Picture-Show.
Power and the Glory, The.
Prayer from 1936, A.
Prehistoric Burials.
Prelude: "Dim gradual thinning of the shapeless gloom."
Prelude: Troops, The.
Presences Perfected.
Rear-Guard, The.
Redeemer, The.
Revisitation.
Road, The.
Sheldonian Soliloquy.
Sick Leave.
Slumber Song: "Sleep; and my song shall build about your bed."
Songbooks of the War.
South Wind.
Stand-to; Good Friday Morning.
Storm on Fifth Avenue.
Strangeness of Heart.
Together.
"They."
To These I Turn, in These I Trust.
Tree and Sky.
Troops, The.
Ultimate Atrocity, The.
Vibrations.
Vigils.
Vigils, *sel.*
When I'm Alone.
Wisdom of the World, The.
Working Party, A.
SATO, HARUO. Song of the Samma.
To a Person.
Wish, A.
SATTERLEE, WALTER. Eve's Cradle-Song.
SATYRUS. Voice of the Hills, The.
SAUL, GEORGE BRANDON. Elizabeth.
Little and Lonely under the Evening Star.
Love Song.
Spring Song.
SAUNDERS, C. R. May.
SAUNDERS, MARY WRIGHT. Remembering Day.
SAUNDERS, RIPLEY DUNLAP. Sunshine and Music.
SAUNDERS, THOMAS. End of Steel.
Horizontal World.
SAUVAGE, CÉCILE. My Little Lover.
SAVAGE, DEREK S. Absent Creation.
Confession.
February.
Living.
Scenario.
Separation.
Wild Swan, The.
Winter Offering.
SAVAGE, FRANCES HIGGINSON. Duck in Central Park.
SAVAGE, HOWARD JAMES. Call of the Sea, The.
SAVAGE, JOHN. Shane's Head.
SAVAGE, MINOT JUDSON. Affirmation, An.
Christmas Question, A.
Decorating the Soldiers' Graves.
Earth's Common Things.
Life's Common Duties.

SAVAGE, MINOT JUDSON (*continued*)
My Birth.
Where Is God?
SAVAGE, PHILIP HENRY. Infinity.
Late Winter.
Morning.
New England.
Silkweed.
Solitude.
SAVAGE, RICHARD. Bastard, The, *sels.*
Bastard's Lot, The. *Fr.* The Bastard.
Cliff and Cloud. *Fr.* The Wanderer.
King-Cups and a Stream. *Fr.* The Wanderer.
Northern Lights, The. *Fr.* The Wanderer.
On Himself. *Fr.* The Bastard.
Sunset and Landscape. *Fr.* The Wanderer.
To a Young Lady.
Wanderer, The, *sels.*
Wintry Sunrise, A. *Fr.* The Wanderer.
SAVAGE, THOMAS JEFFERSON. Alcoholic Goblins.
SAVAGE-ARMSTRONG, GEORGE FRANCIS. Autumn Memories.
De Verdun of Darragh, *sel.*
Father, The.
Gay Provence.
Lugnaquillia, *sel.*
My Guide.
Mystery, The.
One in the Infinite.
Scalp, The.
Through the Solitudes.
Wicklow. *Fr.* De Verdun of Darragh.
Wicklow Scene, A. *Fr.* Lugnaquillia.
SAVILE, JEREMY. Health unto His Majesty, A, *at.*
His Majesty's Health, *at.*
Song: "Here's a health unto His Majesty!" *at.*
SAVONAROLA, GIROLAMO. Good Friday.
Jesus, Refuge of the Weary.
O Star of Galilee.
SAWYER, C. P. I Used to Love my Garden.
SAWYER, CHARLES CARROLL. Weeping, Sad and Lonely.
When This Cruel War Is Over.
SAWYER, FREDERICK WILLIAM. *See* SAWYER, WILLIAM.
SAWYER, MARK. Kite Days.
SAWYER, RUTH (Mrs. Albert C. Durand). Feast o' St. Stephen.
On Christmas Morn, *tr.*
Words from an Old Spanish Carol, *tr.*
SAWYER, WILLIAM. "Caudal" Lecture, A.
Cremation.
Recognition, The.
Turvey Top.
SAXE, JOHN GODFREY. Blind Men and the Elephant, The.
Comic Miseries.
Coquette, The.
Darling, Tell Me Yes.
Do I Love Thee?
Early Rising.
Echo.
Find a Way.
Game of Life, The.
How Cyrus Laid the Cable.
How I Love You.
Justine, You Love Me Not!
Men, dying, make their wills; but wives.
Mourner à la Mode, The.
My Eyes! How I Love You.
My Familiar.
Old Man's Motto, The.
Proud Miss MacBride, The.
Puzzled Census-Taker, The.
Pyramus and Thisbe.
Railroad Rhyme.
Real Riches, The.
Rhyme of the Rail.
Riding on the Rail.
Romance of Nick Van Stann, The.
Solomon and the Bees.
Sonnet to a Clam.
Story of Life, The.
To Lesbia.
To My Love.
Too Candid by Half.
Where There's a Will There's a Way.
Woman's Will.
Wouldn't You Like to Know.
Youth and the Northwind, The.
SAXTON, ANDREW BICE. First Step, The.
SAYANOV, VISSARION. Voice, The.
SAYERS, DOROTHY LEIGH. Choice of the Cross, The. *Fr.* The Devil to Pay.
Devil to Pay, The, *sels.*
Hymn in Contemplation of Sudden Death.
Judgment and Mercy. *Fr.* The Devil to Pay.
War Cat.
Zeal of Thy House, The.
SAYERS, FRANCES CLARKE. *See* CLARKE, FRANCES.
SAYLOR, HENRI DEWITT. Steel.
SAYRES, CORTLANDT W. Bankrupt.
SCANNELL, VERNON. Schoolroom on a Wet Afternoon.
SCANTLEBURY, ELIZABETH E. Hymn of Dedication.
SCARBOROUGH, DOROTHY. Organ Cactus, The.
SCARBOROUGH, GEORGE L. To the Men Who Lose.
SCARBROUGH, GEORGE. Birth by Anesthesia.
SCARFE, FRANCIS. Cats.
Clock, The.
Grotto, The.
Progression.
Tyne Dock.
Window, The.
SCÈVE, MAURICE. Délie, La, *sel.*
SCEVOLA DE SAINTE-MARTHÉ. Art of Bringing Up Children, The, *sel.*
SCHACHT, MARSHALL. First Autumn.
Not to Forget Miss Dickinson.
SCHAUFFLER, HENRY PARK. Easter Sacraments.
SCHAUFFLER, RACHEL CAPEN. Day of Victory, The.
Violet under the Snow, The.
SCHAUFFLER, ROBERT HAVEN. Divers.
Earth's Easter.
Epigram: "*Mayflower* once filled this shore, The."
God's-Eye View.
Great Armistice, The.
Harvest.
Helen of Laughing Ledge.
Homesick in England.
Influence.
Look in Their Eyes, The.
Mirror, The.
Nonsense.
Poetry Cure, The.
Reality.
"Scum o' [*or* of] the Earth."
To Browning, the Music Master.
To My Mother.
Trash.
Two Silences.
Violin Mood, A.
Washington.
White Comrade, The.
With Peter Pan.
Worlds at War.
SCHAUKAL, RICHARD. Images.
SCHAUMANN, RUTH. Evensong.
Fourth Station.
Mary on Her Way to the Temple.
SCHEFFAUER, ETHEL TALBOT. Copper Song.
Reply from the Akond of Swat, A.
SCHEFFAUER, HERMAN. Leper of London, The.
Marta of Milrone.
Miserere.
SCHEFFEL, JOSEPH VIKTOR VON. Lays of Tom-Cat Hiddigeigei.
SCHEFFLER, JOHANNES. *See* "ANGELUS SILESIUS."
SCHEFTEL, GEORGE. Divine Rebel, The.
SCHEIER, ELEANOR OSBORNE. Witch's Moon, The.
SCHERZO, I. O. Threnody: "Truth is a golden sunset far away."
SCHEUER, MARJORIE SOMERS. Fox, The.
SCHEVILL, JAMES. Astonished Listener Hears the Radio Announcer Bat Out the Long Balls of Verbs, Nouns and Adjectives, An.
Birth of Arachne, the Spider, The.
Cheops.
Coastguardsman in the Fog, The.
Confidential Data on the Loyalty Investigation of Herbert Ashenfoot.
D-9.
Dancers with a Hop, The.
Death of a Dove, The.
Dramas of the Rose.
Fabre, the Bughunter.
Guilty Father to His Daughter, A.
Lament for a Man Who Loved God.
Old Pilot Tunnels under the English Channel, The.
Perhaps a Prayer.
Plea for Alias, A.
Seurat.
Song for Old Apis, A.
Turtle, The.
Unnatural, Unusual and Unfair.
Will of Writing, The.
SCHIERLOH, SAMUEL. Bucko-Mate.
SCHIFF, CHARLES. France (June, 1938; June, 1941).
Lidice.
SCHILLER, JOHANN CHRISTOPH FRIEDRICH VON. Braut von Messina, Die, *sel.*
Don Carlos, *sel.*
Friend and Foe.
Friendship.
Hostage, The, *at.*
Hymn to Joy.
Maid of Orleans, The, *play, sel.*
Maid of Orleans, The, *poem.*
Mary Stuart, *sel.*
Metaphysician, The.
Ode to Joy.
Philosophers, The.
Piccolomini, The, *sel.*
Plant, The.
Rainbow, The—a Riddle.
Rousseau.
Song of the Bell.
Song of the Bell, *sel.*
Steer, Bold Mariner, On!
Thekla's Song. *Fr.* The Piccolomini.
Three Lessons.
Three Words of Strength.
Time.
To My Friends.
Unrealities, The.
Where Mortals Dwell. *Fr.* Die Braut von Messina.
William Tell, *poem.*
SCHLEGEL, KATHARINA VON. Be Still.
SCHLESINGER, ——. To the Parotid Gland.
SCHLICHTER, NORMAN C. Sledding Song, A.
SCHLIPF, BENJAMIN. Contentment.
SCHLOERB, ROLLAND WALTER. O Church of God.
O Thou Eternal Source of Life.
Prayer for Peace.
Thou Light of Ages.
SCHMID, CONSTANCE M. Synekdechestai.
SCHMIDT, AUGUSTO FREDERICO. To a Dead Poet (Armando Más Leite).
SCHMOLKE [*or* SCHMOLCK], BENJAMIN. Consecration.
Heavier the Cross.
My Jesus, as Thou Wilt.
SCHMULLER, AARON. Legend of His Lyre.
SCHNECKENBURGER, MAX. Watch on the Rhine, The.
SCHNEIDER, ISIDOR. Ambience of Love, The.
Insects.
Joy of Knowledge.
Riding Song.
Sunday Morning.
Wall, The.
SCHNEOUR, ZALMAN. Besieged.
Cherries.
Forsaken.
Last Words of Don Henriquez, The.
Like Water down a Slope.
Road, The.

Star There Fell, A.
War Comes.
Welcome, Queen Sabbath.
SCHOECK, RICHARD J. Homage (Diptych, 2).
SCHOLES, J. N. He Worked.
SCHOLTEN, MARTIN. Soliloquy by the Shore.
SCHOMBERG, RALPH. Ay or Nay? *Fr.* The Judgment of Paris.
Courtier's a Riddle, A. *Fr.* The Judgment of Paris.
Judgment of Paris, The, *sels.*
Like Birds of a Feather. *Fr.* The Judgment of Paris.
SCHOOLCRAFT, HENRY ROWE. Ojibwa War Songs, *tr.*
SCHOOLCRAFT, LUKE. Shine On.
SCHOONMAKER, BLANCHE W. Wings.
SCHOULTZ, SOLVEIG VON. Deaths, The.
SCHÖYEN, ROLF HJORTH. To Love.
SCHRIEBER, SAMUEL. Rainy Night.
SCHROY, PAULINE. Prayer: "Lord, forgive."
SCHULL, JOSEPH. I, Jones, Soldier, *sel.*
Legend of Ghost Lagoon, The, *sels.*
Pirates' Fight, The. *Fr.* The Legend of Ghost Lagoon.
SCHULTZ, LULU MINERVA. What Price.
SCHULZ, LILLIAN. *See* VANADA, LILLIAN SCHULZ.
SCHUYLER, JAMES. February.
Elizabethans Called It Dying, The.
Freely Espousing.
Salute.
SCHUYLER, LYDIA. Napoleon II.
SCHUYLER, MONTGOMERY. Carlyle and Emerson.
SCHUYLER-LIGHTHALL, WILLIAM DOUW. *See* LIGHTHALL, WILLIAM DOUW.
SCHWARTZ, DELMORE. All Clowns Are Masked. *Fr.* The Repetitive Heart.
All of Us Always Turning Away for Solace. *Fr.* The Repetitive Heart.
At This Moment of Time.
Ballad of the Children of the Czar, The.
Ballet of the Fifth Year, The.
Beautiful American Word, Sure, The.
Being Unused to Joyous Consciousness.
Do They Whisper.
Dog Named Ego [the Snowflakes as Kisses], A. *Fr.* The Repetitive Heart.
Father and Son.
First Morning of the Second World, The.
For One Who Would Not Take His Life in His Hands.
For Rhoda. *Fr.* The Repetitive Heart.
For the One Who Would Take Man's Life in His Hands.
Fulfillment, The.
Genesis, *sel.*
Heavy Bear [Who Goes with Me], The. *Fr.* The Repetitive Heart.
I Wish I Had Great Knowledge or Great Art.
In the Naked Bed, in Plato's Cave.
Let Us Consider Where the Great Men Are. *Fr.* Shenandoah.
Lincoln.
Look, in the Labyrinth of Memory.
Masters of the Heart Touched the Unknown, The.
"Mentrechè il Vento, Come Fa, Si Tace." *Fr.* The Repetitive Heart.
Morning Light for One with Too Much Luck, The.
"One in a Thousand of Years of the Nights."
Prothalamion.
Repetitive Heart, The, *sels.*
Saint, Revolutionist.
Self Unsatisfied Runs Everywhere, The.
She Lives with the Furies of Hope and Despair.
She Was the Girl within the Picture Frame.
Shenandoah, *sel.*
Socrates' Ghost Must Haunt Me Now.
Starlight like Intuition [*or* Starlight's Intuitions] Pierced the Twelve.
"There'll Be Others but Non So for Me."
Time Is the Fire. *Fr.* The Repetitive Heart.
Tired and Unhappy [You Think of Houses].
Today Is Armistice, a Holiday.
True, the Good and the Beautiful, The.
What Is to Be Given.
Will You Perhaps. *Fr.* The Repetitive Heart.
You Are a Jew! *Fr.* Genesis.
SCHWOB, MARCEL. Actions.
Moments.
Things Dead.
SCOLLARD, CLINTON. Ad Patriam.
April Music.
Archer, The.
As I Came Down from Lebanon.
At the Grave of Poe.
At the Tomb of Washington.
Autumn Cricket, The.
Bag-Pipes at Sea.
Ballad of Lieutenant Miles.
Ballad of Paco Town, The.
Ballad of the Thanksgiving Pilgrim.
Ballade of the Golfer in Love.
Barren Easter, The.
Battle of Plattsburg Bay, The.
Be Ye in Love with April-Tide.
Bell, A.
Bells of Christmas, The.
Bethlehem.
Bird's Song in April.
Boasting of Sir Peter Parker, The.
Book Lover, The.
Butterfly, The.
Cricket.
Daffodil Time.
Darley Dale.
Daughter of the Regiment, The.
Dawn in the Desert.
Day for Wandering, A.
Deed of Lieutenant Miles, The.
Deeds of Valor at Santiago.
Dusk.
Eve of Bunker Hill, The.
First Thanksgiving [Day], The.
First Three, The.
For Our Dead.
Grave of Lawrence, The.
Great Voice, The.
Harding Hill.
Hawk.
High Hill, The.
Hill in Picardy, A.
Horizons.
How Miracles Abound.
If Only the Dreams Abide.
In the Library. *Fr.* Lyrics from a Library.
In the Pass.
In the Sultan's Garden.
Khamsin.
King of Dreams, The.
King Philip's Last Stand.
Kris Kringle.
Land of Our Fathers.
Little Brown Wren, The.
Little Town, The.
Lyrics from a Library, *sel.*
Madrigal, A: "Easter-glow and Eastergleam!"
Man, A.
Marathon.
Memnon.
Memorial Day.
Men of the *Maine,* The.
Men of the *Merrimac,* The.
Montgomery at Quebec.
Noureddin, the Son of the Shah.
Old Forge, The.
Old Hickory.
On a Bust of Lincoln.
On an American Soldier of Fortune Slain in France.
On the Eve of Bunker Hill.
One Song More.
Out in the Wood.
Out of Babylon.
Patchwork.
Peace.
Petition.
Prayer, A: "Each day I walk with wonder."
Private Blair of the Regulars.
Quest, The.
Rain Riders.
Reticent Lover.
Ride of Tench Tilghman, The.
Riding with Kilpatrick.
Saint Leger.
Sanctuary.
Sea Shells.
Sidney Godolphin.
Sleeper, The.
Song for Memorial Day.
Song in March.
Southern Whip-Poor-Will, A.
Streams.
Sunflowers.
Supplication, A.
Swimming.
Thanksgiving Song.
There Is a Pool on Garda.
Time.
To William Sharp.
Trumpet of the Dawn, The.
Unreturning, The.
Upon the Stair I See My Lady Stand.
Valor of Ben Milam, The.
Way to Bethlehem, The.
Wayne at Stony Point.
Where White Creek Goes.
Who Goes By.
Winds of God, The.
Wood-Thrush.
SCOLLARD, MRS. CLINTON. *See* RITTENHOUSE, JESSIE BELLE.
SCOLLARD, ELISABETH. Bitter-sweet.
Goldfinches.
He Leads.
I Thought I Had Outlived My Pain.
Robin Song.
SCOLOKER, ANTHONY. Her Praises.
SCOT, MICHAEL. Ballad of the Cats of Bygone Time.
Charcoal Sketch.
Kittens.
SCOTT, ALEXANDER. Bequest of His Heart, A.
Depart, depart, depart!
Hence, Hairt [*or* Heart, with Her That Must Depart].
Lament, A; 1547.
Lament of the Master of Erskine.
Return Thee, Heart.
Rondel of Love, A.
To Love Unloved [*or* Luve Unluvit].
Wha is Perfyte.
SCOTT, ANDREW. Rural Content.
SCOTT, CLEMENT WILLIAM. Lilian Adelaide Neilson.
Oh, Promise Me.
Rus in Urbe.
Women of Mumbles Head, The.
SCOTT, DUNCAN CAMPBELL. Above St. Irénée.
After Battle.
At Delos.
At Gull Lake, August, 1810.
At Les Eboulements.
At the Cedars.
August Mood, An.
Be Strong!
Bells.
Builder, The.
Compline.
Ecstasy.
End of the Day, The.
Fallen, The.
Forsaken, The.
Half-breed Girl, The.
Hymn for Those in the Air.
Idle to Grieve.
In November.
In the Selkirks.
Life and Death.
Lines in Memory of Edmund Morris, *sel.*
Little Song, A.
Memory.
Night Burial in the Forest.
Night Hymns on Lake Nipigon.
O Turn Once More.
Off Rivière du Loup.
Old Olives at Bordighera.

SCOTT, DUNCAN CAMPBELL (*continued*)
On the Way to the Mission.
Onondaga Madonna, The.
Ottawa.
Piper of Arll, The.
Power.
Rapids at Night.
Reed-Player, The.
Road Song, A.
Sailor's Sweetheart, The.
Sea by the Wood, The.
Sleeper, The.
Song, A: "In the air there are no coral-/ Reefs or ambergris."
Spring in the Valley.
Thoughts.
To the Canadian Mothers.
Voice and the Dusk, The.
Watkwenies.
Wood by the Sea, The.
SCOTT, MRS. DUNCAN CAMPBELL. *See* AYLEN, ELISE.
SCOTT, EVELYN ("Ernest Souza"). Autumn Night.
Hawk Afield.
SCOTT, FRANCIS REGINALD. Armageddon, *sel.*
Bedside.
Bonne Entente.
Canadian Authors Meet, The.
Caring.
Conflict.
Dedication: "From those condemned to labour."
Devoir Molluscule.
Eden.
Examiner.
For Brian Priestman.
Full Valleys.
Grain of Rice, A.
Hardest It Is.
Old Song ("Far voices").
Recovery.
Saturday Sundae.
Shock, The. *Fr.* Armageddon.
Someone Could Certainly Be Found, *tr.*
Tourist Time.
Trans Canada.
Windfall.
SCOTT, FRED NEWTON. Romeo and Juliet.
SCOTT, FREDERICK GEORGE. Ad Majorem Dei Gloriam.
Among the Spruces.
Burden of Time, The.
Crucifixion.
Dawn.
Easter Island.
Feud, The.
In the Winter Woods.
In the Woods.
Knowledge.
"Little Friend's" Grave.
Requiescant.
River, The.
Samson.
Sister of Charity, A.
Snowstorm, The.
Sting of Death, The.
Storm, The.
"Te Judice."
Time.
Unnamed Lake, The.
Van Elsen.
Wayside Cross, The.
SCOTT, G. FORRESTER. School Greeting.
SCOTT, GEOFFREY. All Our Joy Is Enough.
Bridge, The.
Faster.
Frutta di Mare.
Here Is Music, Dark and Still.
I Love the Beginning of All Rain.
Skaian Gate, The, *sel.*
What Was Solomon's Mind.
SCOTT, JOE. Plain Golden Band, The, *at.*
SCOTT, LADY JOHN (Alicia Ann Spottiswoode). Comin' o' the Spring, The.
Durisdeer.
Loch Lomond, *at.*
SCOTT, JOHN, OF AMWELL. Amwell; a Descriptive Poem, *sel.*
Drum, The.
On the Ingenious Mr. Jones's Elegant Translations and Imitations of Eastern Poetry, and His Resolution to Decline Translating the Persian Poets.
Retort on the Foregoing.
Rural Scenery—Eclogue I, *sel.*
SCOTT, MARGARETTA. Little Boys.
SCOTT, NANCY BOCKIUS. Little Gopher Man, The.
SCOTT, ROBERT BALGARNIE YOUNG. Doxology for Peace.
O God of Light.
O Voice That Calls to Me.
Prayer at Eventide.
SCOTT, RUBY T. Museum Meteorite.
SCOTT, THOMAS. Angels, Roll the Rock Away!
SCOTT, SIR WALTER. Abbess, The. *Fr.* Marmion.
Abbot, The, *sel.*
Aged Carle, The. *Fr.* The Antiquary.
Alice Brand. *Fr.* The Lady of the Lake.
Allen-a-Dale. *Fr.* Rokeby.
And What though Winter Will Pinch Severe. *Fr.* Old Mortality.
And You Shall Deal the Funeral Dole. *Fr.* The Pirate.
Anna-Marie, love, up is the sun. *Fr.* Ivanhoe.
Annot Lyle's Song: "Birds of omen." *Fr.* The Legend of Montrose.
Answer. *Fr.* Old Mortality.
Antiquary, The, *sels.*
Ave Maria. *Fr.* The Lady of the Lake.
Ballad: Alice Brand. *Fr.* The Lady of the Lake.
Ballad: "'And whither would you lead me then?'" *Fr.* Rokeby.
Ballad, A: "Druid Urien had daughters seven, The."
Bannockburn. *Fr.* The Lord of Isles.
Barefooted Friar, The. *Fr.* Ivanhoe.
Battle, The. *Fr.* Marmion.
Battle of Beal' an Duine. *Fr.* The Lady of the Lake.
Beal' an Dhuine. *Fr.* The Lady of the Lake.
Betrothed, The, *sel.*
Bible, The. *Fr.* The Monastery.
Black Prince, The. *Fr.* Rob Roy.
Boat Song. *Fr.* The Lady of the Lake.
Bold Dragoon, The.
Bonny [*or* Bonnie] Dundee. *Fr.* The Doom of Devorgoil.
Book of Books, The. *Fr.* The Monastery.
Border Ballad [*or* March]. *Fr.* The Monastery.
Breathes There the Man [with Soul So Dead]. *Fr.* The Lay of the Last Minstrel.
Bride of Lammermoor, The, *sels.*
Brignall [*or* Brignal] Banks. *Fr.* Rokeby.
Call, The, *at.* *Fr.* Old Mortality.
Call it not vain; they do not err. *Fr.* The Lay of the Last Minstrel.
Carle, Now the King's Come.
Cavalier, The. *Fr.* Rokeby.
Cavalier Song. *Fr.* Old Mortality.
Challenge. *Fr.* Marmion.
Charge at Waterloo, The. *Fr.* The Field of Waterloo.
Chase, The. *Fr.* The Lady of the Lake.
Christmas [in England]. *Fr.* Marmion.
Christmas in the Olden Time. *Fr.* Marmion.
Clarion, *wr. at.*
Claud Halcro's Song: "And you shall deal the funeral dole." *Fr.* The Pirate.
Cleveland's Song: "Farewell! Farewell!" *Fr.* The Pirate.
Cleveland's Song: "Love wakes and weeps." *Fr.* The Pirate.
Coronach. *Fr.* The Lady of the Lake.
County Guy. *Fr.* Quentin Durward.
Cradle Song: "Oh hush thee, my baby, thy sire was a knight."
Cypress Wreath, The. *Fr.* Rokeby.
Datur Hora Quieti. *Fr.* The Doom of Devergoil.
David Gellatley's Song. *Fr.* Waverley.
Dawn on Lake Katrine. *Fr.* The Lady of the Lake.
Dies Irae, *par.* *Fr.* The Lay of the Last Minstrel.
Dirge of the Lovely Rosabelle, The. *Fr.* The Lay of the Last Minstrel.
Donald Caird.
Doom of Devorgoil, The, *sels.*
Dying Gipsy's Dirge, The. *Fr.* Guy Mannering.
Edmund's Song. *Fr.* Rokeby.
Ellen's Song. *Fr.* The Lady of the Lake.
Erl-King, The, *tr.*
Eve of St. John, The.
Evening. *Fr.* The Doom of Devorgoil.
Fading Autumn. *Fr.* The Lord of the Isles.
False Love. *Fr.* Waverley.
Farewell: "Farewell! Farewell! the voice you hear." *Fr.* The Pirate.
Farewell! Farewell! *Fr.* The Pirate.
Feast was over in Branksome tower, The. *Fr.* The Lay of the Last Minstrel.
Field of Waterloo, The, *sel.*
Fiery Cross, The. *Fr.* The Lady of the Lake.
Fitz-James and Roderick Dhu. *Fr.* The Lady of the Lake.
Flowers and Trees. *Fr.* The Lady of the Lake.
Foray, The.
Friday.
Gallant Ship, The.
Gathering Song of Donald the Black [*or* Donald Dhu *or* Donuil Dhu].
Gellatley's Song to the Deerhounds. *Fr.* Waverley.
Gin by Pailfuls.
Gipsy's Dirge, The. *Fr.* Guy Mannering.
Glee for King Charles. *Fr.* Woodstock.
Glenfinlas; or, Lord Ronald's Coronach.
Guy Mannering, *sels.*
Hail to the Chief Who in Triumph Advances. *Fr.* The Lady of the Lake.
Harlaw. *Fr.* The Antiquary.
Harold the Dauntless, *sel.*
Harold's Song [to Rosabelle]. *Fr.* The Lay of the Last Minstrel.
Harp of the North. *Fr.* The Lady of the Lake.
Harp of the North, Farewell. *Fr.* The Lady of the Lake.
He is gone on the mountain. *Fr.* The Lady of the Lake.
He paused: the listening dames again. *Fr.* The Lay of the Last Minstrel.
Heart of Midlothian, The, *sels.*
Heath This Night Must Be My Bed, The. *Fr.* The Lady of the Lake.
Helvellyn.
Here's a Health to King Charles. *Fr.* Woodstock.
Herring, The. *Fr.* The Antiquary.
Hie Away. *Fr.* Waverley.
Humble boon was soon obtain'd, The. *Fr.* The Lady of the Lake.
Hunting Song.
Hymn for the Dead. *Fr.* The Lay of the Last Minstrel.
Hymn to the Virgin. *Fr.* The Lady of the Lake.
If thou would'st view fair Melrose aright. *Fr.* The Lay of the Last Minstrel.
In Memoriam: Nelson, Pitt, Fox. *Fr.* Marmion.
Innominatus. *Fr.* The Lay of the Last Minstrel.
It was an English ladye bright. *Fr.* The Lay of the Last Minstrel.
Ivanhoe, *sels.*
James Fitz-James and Ellen. *Fr.* The Lady of the Lake.

Jock of [*or* o'] Hazeldean.
Knight's Toast, The, *at.*
Lady Coriskin. *Fr.* The Lord of the Isles.
Lady Heron's Song. *Fr.* Marmion.
Lady of the Lake, The, *sels.*
Last Minstrel, The. *Fr.* The Lay of the Last Minstrel.
Late When the Autumn Evening Fell. *Fr.* Waverley.
Lay of Rosabelle, The. *Fr.* The Lay of the Last Minstrel.
Lay of the Last Minstrel, The, *sels.*
Leaders, Old Style. *Fr.* Marmion.
Legend of Montrose, The, *sels.*
Leonard: "Sun upon the lake is low, The." *Fr.* The Doom of Devorgoil.
Life. *Fr.* The Abbot.
Lighthouse, The.
Like April morning clouds. *Fr.* Marmion.
Lochinvar. *Fr.* Marmion.
Look Not Thou. *Fr.* The Bride of Lammermoor.
Lord of the Isles, The, *sels.*
Love. *Fr.* The Lay of the Last Minstrel.
Love of Country [*or* Fatherland]. *Fr.* The Lay of the Last Minstrel.
Lucy Ashton's Song. *Fr.* The Bride of Lammermoor.
Lullaby of an Infant Chief.
MacGregor's Gathering.
Mackrimmon's Lament.
Maid of Neidpath, The.
Man the Enemy of Man. *Fr.* Rokeby.
March, March [Ettrick and Teviotdale]. *Fr.* The Monastery.
Marmion, *sels.*
Marmion and Douglas. *Fr.* Marmion.
Melrose Abbey. *Fr.* The Lay of the Last Minstrel.
Mermaids and Mermen. *Fr.* The Pirate.
Minstrel, The. *Fr.* The Lay of the Last Minstrel.
Minstrel's Lowly Bower, The. *Fr.* The Lay of the Last Minstrel.
Monastery, The, *sels.*
Monks of Bangor's March, The.
Motto from "Old Mortality."
My [Own, My] Native Land. *Fr.* The Lay of the Last Minstrel.
Native Land. *Fr.* The Lay of the Last Minstrel.
Nativity Chant, The. *Fr.* Guy Mannering.
Nature's Sympathy with the Poet. *Fr.* The Lay of the Last Minstrel.
Nelson, Pitt, Fox. *Fr.* Marmion.
Nora's Vow.
Norham Castle. *Fr.* Marmion.
Nought of the bridal will I tell. *Fr.* The Lay of the Last Minstrel.
November in Ettrick Forest. *Fr.* Marmion.
November's sky is chill and drear. *Fr.* Marmion.
O, Woman! [In Our Hours of Ease]. *Fr.* Marmion.
Old Christmas-Tide. *Fr.* Marmion.
Old Mortality, *sels.*
Omnipotent, The. *Fr.* The Antiquary.
On the Setting Sun.
On Tweed River. *Fr.* The Monastery.
One Crowded Hour, *at.* *Fr.* Old Mortality.
Outlaw, The. *Fr.* Rokeby.
Oyster, The. *Fr.* The Antiquary.
Palmer, The.
Parting of Marmion and Douglas, The. *Fr.* Marmion.
Patriotism. *Fr.* The Lay of the Last Minstrel.
Pibroch of Donuil Dhu.
Pirate, The, *sels.*
Pitt and Fox. *Fr.* Marmion.
Pride of Youth. *Fr.* The Heart of Midlothian.
Proud Maisie. *Fr.* The Heart of Midlothian.
Quentin Durward, *sel.*
Rebecca's Hymn. *Fr.* Ivanhoe.
Red Harlaw, The. *Fr.* The Antiquary.
Rob Roy, *sel.*
Roderick Dhu [and Fitz-James]. *Fr.* The Lady of the Lake.
Rokeby, *sels.*
Rosabelle. *Fr.* The Lay of the Last Minstrel.
Rover, The. *Fr.* Rokeby.
Rover's Farewell [*or* Adieu], The. *Fr.* Rokeby.
St. Swithin's Chair. *Fr.* Waverley.
Savage Grandeur. *Fr.* The Lord of the Isles.
Scotland. *Fr.* The Lay of the Last Minstrel.
Serenade, A: "Ah! County Guy, the hour is nigh." *Fr.* Quentin Durward.
Shepherd [in Winter], The. *Fr.* Marmion.
Sir Walter Scott's Tribute. *Fr.* The Monastery.
Soldier, Rest! [Thy Warfare O'er]. *Fr.* The Lady of the Lake.
Soldier's Song ("Our vicar still preaches . . ."). *Fr.* The Lady of the Lake.
Song: "Ah! County Guy, the hour is nigh." *Fr.* Quentin Durward.
Song: Brignall Banks. *Fr.* Rokeby.
Song: Cavalier, The. *Fr.* Rokeby.
Song: Harp, The. *Fr.* Rokeby.
Song: "Heath this night must be my bed, The." *Fr.* The Lady of the Lake.
Song: "Not faster yonder rowers' might." *Fr.* The Lady of the Lake.
Song: "O Brignall banks are wild and fair." *Fr.* Rokeby.
Song: "Soldier, rest! thy warfare o'er." *Fr.* The Lady of the Lake.
Song: "Weary lot is thine, fair maid, A." *Fr.* Rokeby.
Song: "When friends are met o'er merry cheer." *Fr.* The Doom of Devorgoil.
Song: "Where shall the lover rest." *Fr.* Marmion.
Song of Albert Graeme. *Fr.* The Lay of the Last Minstrel.
Song of Clan-Alpine. *Fr.* The Lady of the Lake.
Song of the Reim-Kennar, The. *Fr.* The Pirate.
Sound, Sound the Clarion, *at.* *Fr.* Old Mortality.
Stag Hunt, The. *Fr.* The Lady of the Lake.
Sun upon the Lake Is Low, The. *Fr.* The Doom of Devorgoil.
Sun upon the Weirdlaw Hill, The.
Sweet Teviot. *Fr.* The Lay of the Last Minstrel.
Tempest, A. *Fr.* The Lord of the Isles.
This morn is merry June, I trow.
Thus while I ape the measure wild. *Fr.* Marmion.
Time. *Fr.* The Antiquary.
'Tis Merry in Greenwood. *Fr.* Harold the Dauntless.
To a Lady [with Flowers from the Roman Wall].
To a Lock of Hair.
To an Oak Tree.
To Britain—after War. *Fr.* The Field of Waterloo.
To William Erskine, Esq. *Fr.* Marmion.
To William Stewart Rose, Esq. *Fr.* Marmion.
Toils Are Pitched, The. *Fr.* The Lady of the Lake.
True-Love, an Thou Be True. *Fr.* The Bride of Lammermoor.
Twist Ye, Twine Ye! Even So. *Fr.* Guy Mannering.
Violet, The.
Waken, Lords and Ladies Gay.
Wasted, Weary, Wherefore Stay. *Fr.* Guy Mannering.
Waverley, *sels.*
Way was long, the wind was cold, The. *Fr.* The Lay of the Last Minstrel.
Weary Lot Is Thine, A. *Fr.* Rokeby.
Western Waves of Ebbing Day, The. *Fr.* The Lady of the Lake.
When dark December glooms the day. *Fr.* Marmion.
Where Shall the Lover Rest. *Fr.* Marmion.
Why Sit'st Thou by That Ruin'd Hall. *Fr.* The Antiquary.
Wild Huntsman, The, *tr.*
William and Helen, *after* Bürger.
Woman's Faith. *Fr.* The Betrothed.
Woodstock, *sel.*
Young Lochinvar. *Fr.* Marmion.

SCOTT, WILLIAM BELL. Below the Old House.
Contentment in the Dark.
Glenkindie.
Hero-Worship.
Love's Calendar.
Lowland Witch Ballad, A.
My Mother.
Norns Watering Yggdrasill, The.
Pygmalion.
To the Dead.
Witch's Ballad, The.
Youth and Age.

SCOTT, WINFIELD TOWNLEY. Annual Legend.
Baldness and the Swan.
Bermuda Suite.
Bermuda Suite, *sel.*
Blue Sleigh.
Codicil for Pvt. John Hogg's Will.
Difference, The.
Exercise in Aesthetics.
Game, The.
Gert Swasey.
Green and Red and Darkness.
Hour Is Late, The.
House, The.
How Shall I Ever Come to Any Good?
Indian Summer—Buffalo Summer.
Landscape as Metal and Flowers.
Memento.
Merrill's Brook.
Mr. Whittier.
Mrs. Severin.
Natural Causes.
Old Talk.
Re-run.
Sonnet: "I watched the sea for hours blind with sun."
Swedish Angel.
Three American Women and a German Bayonet.
To Edwin Arlington Robinson.
To L. B. S.
To Marry Strangers.
U.S. Sailor with the Japanese Skull, The.
Unsexed by the Cold Sea.
We'll All Feel Gay.

SCOTT-GATTY, SIR ALFRED SCOTT. Three Little Pigs, The.

SCOTT-HOPPER, QUEENIE. Amy Elizabeth Ermyntrude Annie.
My Party.
Railway Tunnel, The.
Very Nearly.
What the Thrush Says.

SCOTT MONCRIEFF, CHARLES KENNETH. Last Battle, The, *tr.* *Fr.* The Song of Roland.
Ready They Make Hauberks Sarrazinese, *tr.* *Fr.* The Song of Roland.
Song of Roland, The, *sels., tr.*

SCOTT OF AMWELL, JOHN. *See* SCOTT, JOHN, OF AMWELL.

SCOVELL, E. J. Bloody Cranesbill on the Dunes.
Boy Fishing, The.
Child Waking.
Dark World, A.
Elegy, An: "In early winter before the first snow."
Evening Scene.
First Year, The, *sel.*
Girl to Her Sister, A.
Love's Immaturity.

SCOVELL, E. J. (*continued*)
Midsummer Meadow, The.
Open Air Performance of "As You Like It," An.
Shadows of Chrysanthemums.
Swan's Feet, The.
"SCRACE, RICHARD" (Mrs. J. B. Williamson). At the Place of the Roman Baths.
Auction, The.
Gypsies, The.
Masque of Souls, A.
SCRANTON, BERTHA S. Christmas Thought about Dickens, A.
SCRIVEN, JOSEPH. Unfailing Friend, The.
What a friend we have in Jesus.
SCROPE, SIR CARR. As Amoret with Phyllis Sat. *Fr.* The Man of Mode (*by* Sir George Etherege).
SCRUGGS, ANDERSON M. Christmas 1930.
Christmas Today.
City Trees.
Covered Bridge, The.
Glory to Them.
How Can They Honor Him?
Only the Dream Is Real.
Pines.
Retired Business Man.
Song for Dark Days.
Sonnet on Turning a Radio Dial.
Street Beggar.
SCUDDER, ELIZA. Love of God, The.
Quest, The.
Thou Life within My Life.
To a Young Child.
Who by Searching Can Find Out God?
SCUDDER, VIDA DUTTON. Thy Kingdom, Lord, We Long For.
SEAGER, MILLICENT. Birds' Nests.
SEAGER, RALPH W. Taste of Prayer, The.
SEALEY, MRS. MACEY P. God's Unspeakable Gift.
SEAMAN, HELLENE. Hills Keep Holy Ground, The.
SEAMAN, SIR OWEN. At the Sign of the Cock.
Ballad of a Bun, A.
Between Midnight and Morning.
Bulbul, The.
From "A Vigo-Street Eclogue."
In Praise of Commonplace.
Lines Written by Request.
Ode to Spring in the Metropolis, An.
Of Baiting the Lion.
Of the Stalking of the Stag.
Old Songs, The.
Penalties of Baldness, The.
Plea for Trigamy, A.
Presto Furioso.
Rhyme of the Kipperling, The.
Seamy Side of Motley, The.
Song of Renunciation, A.
To a Boy-Poet of the Decadence.
To Julia in Shooting Togs.
To Julia under Lock and Key.
Uses of Ocean, The.
Victory.
Warrior's Lament, The.
SEARING, LAURA CATHERINE REDDEN ("Howard Glyndon"). Disarmed.
Mazzini.
SEARS, CLARA ENDICOTT. Unfurling of the Flag, The.
SEARS, EDMUND HAMILTON. Angels' Song, The.
Birth Song of Christ, The.
Christmas Song: "Calm on the listening ear of night."
Glorious Song of Old, The.
Gracious Saviour Born of Mary.
It Came upon the Midnight Clear.
Peace on Earth.
SEAVER, EDWIN. To My People.
SECCOMB, JOHN. Father Abbey's Will.
SEDGWICK, HENRY DWIGHT. Leo to His Mistress.
SEDLEY, SIR CHARLES. Advice to the Old Beaux.
Ah Cloris! that I now could sit. *Fr.* The Mulberry Garden.
Alexandra, *sel., tr.*
Ballad to the Tune of Bateman, A.
Child and Maiden. *Fr.* The Mulberry Garden.
Chloris, I cannot say your eyes.
Happy Pair, The, *sel.*
Hears Not My Phyllis.
Indifference, The.
Knotting Song, The.
Love Still Has Something of the Sea.
Mulberry Garden, The, *sel.*
Not, Celia, that I juster am.
Odes (*of* Horace), *sel., tr.*
On a Cock at Rochester.
Out of Lycophron, *tr. Fr.* Alexandra.
Phillis Knotting.
Phillis, let's shun the common fate.
Phyllis.
Phyllis [*or* Phillis] Is My Only Joy.
Song: "Ah Chloris! that I now could sit." *Fr.* The Mulberry Garden.
Song: "Hears not my Phillis, how the birds."
Song: "Love still has something of the sea."
Song: "Not Celia, that I juster am."
Song: "Phillis [*or* Phyllis] is my only joy."
Song: "Smooth was the water, calm the air."
Song: To Chloris. *Fr.* The Mulberry Garden.
Song to Celia, A.
To a Very Young Lady. *Fr.* The Mulberry Garden.
To Celia.
To Chloris. *Fr.* The Mulberry Garden.
Young Coridon and Phillis, *at.*
SEDULIUS, CAELIUS. Apostrophe to Death. *Fr.* Carmen Paschale.
Carmen Paschale [*or* Easter Song], *sels.*
Christ Quiets the Tempest. *Fr.* Carmen Paschale.
Hail, Maiden Root. *Fr.* Carmen Paschale.
Invocation: "Eternal God omnipotent! The One." *Fr.* Carmen Paschale.
Magi Visit Herod, The. *Fr.* Carmen Paschale.
Miracle, The. *Fr.* Carmen Paschale.
Slaughter of the Innocents by Order of King Herod, The. *Fr.* Carmen Paschale.
"SEEDY, WILL." *See* DEMOREST, WILLIAM CURTIS.
SEEGER, ALAN. I Have a Rendezvous with Death.
Message to America, A.
Ode in Memory of the American Volunteers Fallen for France.
Rendezvous, The.
Sonnet: "Oh, love of woman, you are known to be."
Sonnet: "Sidney, in whom the heyday of romance."
Sonnet to Sidney.
To —— in Church.
SEFERIS, GEORGE [*or* GEORGIOS]. Argonautica.
Cistern, The.
Now When So Much Has Passed.
SEFTON, EVA WEAVER. Living Bread.
SEHLSTEDT, ELIAS. Snow-Sparrow, The.
SEIDEL, INA. Marriage.
SEIFFERT, MARJORIE ALLEN ("Elijah Hay"). Ancient Tree, The.
Ballad: "Follow, follow me into the South."
Ballad of Riding, A.
Ballad of the Rag-Bag Heart.
Ballad of Thread for a Needle.
Dream House, The.
Interior.
Iron Fare.
Italian Chest, An.
Japanese Vase Wrought in Metals, A.
Lorenzo's Bas-Relief for a Florentine Chest.
Old Woman, The.
Secret Temple, The.
Winter's Tree, *sel.*
SEI SHONAGON, LADY. Though you can tell me.
SEITZ, DON C. Night at Gettysburg.
SEKULA, IRENE. Mother Goose (circa 2054).
SELANDER, STEN. Withered Tree, The.
SELDEN, ELIZABETH. Duet.
Elemental Rhythm.
Lay Not a Memory Low.
New Day, The.
Song of Nature.
For translations from various languages, see BoFr.
SELDON, FRANK H. To My Setter, Scout.
SELGAS Y CARRASCO, JOSÉ. Empty Cradle, The.
SELIGMAN, ULMA. Truth Has Perished.
SELLAR, WALTER CARRUTHERS, *and* ROBERT JULIAN YEATMAN. How I Brought the Good News from Aix to Ghent (or Vice Versa).
SELVA, SALOMÓN DE LA. Elegy: "My comrade is dead."
Tropical Town.
SELVINSKY, ILYA. Man with an Eagle on His Shoulder, The, *sel.*
Song of Babek. *Fr.* The Man with an Eagle on His Shoulder.
Song of the Cossack Girl.
SEMONIDES (of Amorgos). Dead, The.
In the beginning God made various kinds of women.
On Women.
Some Women.
Women.
SEMPILL, FRANCIS. Maggie Lauder.
SEMPILL, ROBERT. Epitaph of Habbie Simpson, The.
Life and Death of the Piper of Kilbarchan, The.
SENECA (Lucius Annaeus Seneca). Angry Kynges, The. *Fr.* Hercules Furens.
Chorus: "Climb at Court for me that will." *Fr.* Thyestes.
Chorus: "Let th' ayre complayne, and eke the parent great." *Fr.* Hercules Furens.
Chorus: "What sharpe assaultes of cruell Cupids flame." *Fr.* Medea.
End of Being, The.
Hercules Furens, *sels.*
Medea, *sel.*
Of the Meane and Sure Estate. *Fr.* Thyestes.
Quiet Life, The.
There can be slain/ No sacrifice.
Thyestes, *sels.*
SENESH, HANNAH. Blessed Match, The.
SENIOR, WALTER STANLEY. Vita Magistra.
SENNETT, HARRIET. Flamingoes.
Marsh Blackbird, A.
SENNETT, STEPHEN. Twelfth Night Song.
"SERANUS." *See* HARRISON, SUSAN FRANCES.
SEREBROVSKAYA, E. Mines.
SERINI, VITTORIO. Anniversary of Antonia Pozzi's Death by Suicide.
City by Night.
SERRAILLIER, IAN. Fox, The.
Hen and the Carp, The.
Squirrel, The.
SERRANO PLAJA, ARTURO. Banished, The.
SERVASIUS, SULPICIUS LUPERCUS, JR. Rivers level granite mountains.
SERVICE, ROBERT WILLIAM. Call of the Wild, The.
Carry on!
Cremation of Sam McGee, The.
Jean Desprez.
Law of the Yukon, The.
Little Moccasins.
Men That Don't Fit In, The.
My Madonna.
Outlaw, The.
Scribe's Prayer, The.
Shooting of Dan McGrew, The.
Song of the Pacifist, The.
Spell of the Yukon, The.
Wonderer, The.
Young Fellow My Lad.

SETON, ELIZABETH. Mary, Virgin and Mother.
"SETOUN, GABRIEL" (Thomas Nicoll Hepburn). Eyes of God, The.
Happy as a King.
How the Flowers Grow.
Jack Frost.
Mystery, A.
Rain in Spring.
Romance.
Wind's Song, The.
World's Music, The.
SETTLE, ELKANAH. Cambyses, *sel.*
She That with Love Is Not Possessed. *Fr.* Cambyses.
SEVELINGEN, MEINLOH VON. *See* MEINLOH VON SEVELINGEN.
"SEVERYANIN, IGOR" (Igor Vasilyevich Lotarev). Russian Song, A.
Spring Apple Tree.
SEWALL, ALICE ARCHER. *See* JAMES, ALICE ARCHER SEWALL.
SEWALL, FRANK. Roll Out, O Song.
SEWALL, HARRIET WINSLOW. Why Thus Longing?
SEWALL, JONATHAN MITCHELL. Cato, *sel.*
On Independence.
War and Washington. *Fr.* Cato.
SEWARD, ANNA. Execution of Major André.
SEWELL, ELIZABETH. Image Imagination.
SEWELL, GEORGE. Dying Man in His Garden, The.
SEXTON, ANNE. Kind Sir: These Woods.
SEYMOUR, A. J. Over Guiana, Clouds, *sel.*
SEYMOUR, AARON CROSSLEY HOBART. Christ, the Conqueror.
SEYMOUR, EDWARD, DUKE OF SOMERSET. Poor Estate to Be Holden for Best, The, *at.*
SEYMOUR, WILLIAM KEAN. Caesar Remembers.
Foiled Reaper.
To a Mouse, *Eng. vers.*
To Music.
SEYMOUR-SMITH, MARTIN. Green Wall My Grave.
SHABISTARI, SA'D UD-DIN MAHMUD. In the Secret Rose Garden.
SHACKBURG, RICHARD. *See* SHUCKBURG, RICHARD.
SHACKLEFORD, THEODORE HENRY. Big Bell in Zion, The.
SHACKLETT, MILDRED D. Autumn Gloves.
Autumn Train.
Belonging to Summer.
Broadcasting.
Deep in the Woods.
Four Kinds of Wading.
Golden Tacks.
Movies in the Fire.
Mud Cakes.
Sometimes Wish, A.
Swing Ship, The.
Winter Feathers.
Winter Treats.
SHADWELL, BERTRAND. Aguinaldo.
Cervera.
SHADWELL, THOMAS. Amorous Bigot, The, *sel.*
Expostulation, The. *Fr.* The Squire of Alsatia.
Fire of Love, The, *at.* *Fr.* The Amorous Bigot.
Good-Morrow, A. *Fr.* Timon of Athens.
Let Some Great Joys Pretend to Find. *Fr.* The Woman-Captain.
Song: "Fringéd vallance of your eyes advance, The."
Squire of Alsatia, The, *sels.*
Timon of Athens, *sel.*
Victory in Hungary, The. *Fr.* The Squire of Alsatia.
Woman-Captain, The, *sel.*
SHAFER, JULIA BUDD. Table Blessing.
SHAHAZIZ, SMPAD. Dream, The.
SHAHRIYAR. Nocturne: "When I am alone, to dream."
SHAIRP, JOHN CAMPBELL. Ben Dorain, *sel., tr.*
Bush aboon Traquair, The.
Cailleach Bein-y-Vreich.
Haunt of the Deer, The, *tr.* *Fr.* Ben Dorain.
I Have a Life with Christ to Live.
SHAKESPEARE, WILLIAM. Absence. Sonnets, LVII.
Address of Richard III to His Army, The. *Fr.* King Richard III.
After the Battle. *Fr.* King Henry V.
Against my love shall be, as I am now. Sonnets, LXIII.
Agamemnon and Nestor. *Fr.* Troilus and Cressida.
Age and Youth. *Fr.* The Passionate Pilgrim.
Agincourt. *Fr.* King Henry V.
Ah, my young princes! ah, my tender babes! *Fr.* King Richard III.
Airy Nothings. *Fr.* The Tempest.
Alas, 'tis true I have gone here and there. Sonnets, CX.
All the World's a Stage. *Fr.* As You Like It.
All's Well That Ends Well, *sels.*
Ambition. *Fr.* King Henry VIII.
And will he [*or* a'] not come again? *Fr.* Hamlet.
And wilt thou pluck my fair son from my age. *Fr.* King Richard II.
Antony and Cleopatra, *sels.*
Antony on the Death of Caesar. *Fr.* Julius Caesar.
Antony's Oration [over Caesar's Body]. *Fr.* Julius Caesar.
Approach of Age, The. Sonnets, XII.
Approach of the Fairies, The. *Fr.* A Midsummer Night's Dream.
Ariel's Dirge. *Fr.* The Tempest.
Ariel's Last Song. *Fr.* The Tempest.
Ariel's Song: "Come unto these yellow sands." *Fr.* The Tempest.
Ariel's Song: "Full fathom five thy father lies." *Fr.* The Tempest.
Ariel's Song: "Where the bee sucks, there suck I." *Fr.* The Tempest.
Armed. *Fr.* King Henry IV, Pt. I.
As an unperfect actor on the stage. Sonnets, XXIII.
As You Like It, *sels.*
Asleep, my Love? *Fr.* A Midsummer Night's Dream.
Aubade. *Fr.* Cymbeline.
Autolicus's Song. *Fr.* The Winter's Tale.
Ay, but to Die. *Fr.* Measure for Measure.
Balcony Scene, The. *Fr.* Romeo and Juliet.
Balthasar's Song. *Fr.* Much Ado about Nothing.
Banished Duke [Living in the Forest] Speaks to His Retainers, The. *Fr.* As You Like It.
Banishment. *Fr.* King Richard II.
Barge she sat in, like a burnish'd throne, The. *Fr.* Antony and Cleopatra.
Be True. *Fr.* Hamlet.
Beauty Is a Witch. *Fr.* Much Ado about Nothing.
Before Agincourt. *Fr.* King Henry V.
Being your slave, what should I do but tend. Sonnets, LVII.
Beshrew that heart that makes my heart to groan. Sonnets, CXXXIII.
Bitter Song. *Fr.* As You Like It.
Blast of War, The. *Fr.* King Henry V.
Blind Love. Sonnets, CXLVIII.
Blossom, The. *Fr.* Love's Labour's Lost.
Blow, Blow, Thou Winter Wind. *Fr.* As You Like It.
Blow, Winds. *Fr.* King Lear.
Body and Soul. Sonnets, CXLVI.
Bolingbroke. *Fr.* King Richard II.
Boy's Song to Mariana. *Fr.* Measure for Measure.
Brave New World. *Fr.* The Tempest.
Bravery. *Fr.* King Henry IV, Pt. I.
Brutus. *Fr.* Julius Caesar.
Brutus and Portia. *Fr.* Julius Caesar.
But be contented: when that fell arrest. Sonnets, LXXIV.
But Man, Proud Man. *Fr.* Measure for Measure.
But wherefore do not you a mightier waie. Sonnets, XVI.
Caliban. *Fr.* The Tempest.
Caliban on the Island. *Fr.* The Tempest.
Call of the Woods, The. *Fr.* As You Like It.
Cardinal Wolsey's Farewell. *Fr.* King Henry VIII.
Cares of Majesty, The. *Fr.* King Henry IV, Pt. II.
Carpe Diem. *Fr.* Twelfth Night.
Cassius Poisons Brutus' Mind. *Fr.* Julius Caesar.
Charm, The. *Fr.* Macbeth.
Christmas. *Fr.* Hamlet.
Chronicle of Wasted Time. Sonnets, CVI.
Citizens Defend Angiers, The. *Fr.* King John.
Cleopatra. *Fr.* Antony and Cleopatra.
Cleopatra's Barge. *Fr.* Antony and Cleopatra.
Cleopatra's Death. *Fr.* Antony and Cleopatra.
Cleopatra's Lament. *Fr.* Antony and Cleopatra.
Clown's Song. *Fr.* Twelfth Night.
Cod-Piece That Will House, The. *Fr.* King Lear.
Combat, A. *Fr.* King Henry IV, Pt. I.
Come Away, Come Away, Death. *Fr.* Twelfth Night.
Come Night, Come Romeo. *Fr.* Romeo and Juliet.
Come, Thou Monarch [of the Vine]. *Fr.* Antony and Cleopatra.
Come unto These Yellow Sands. *Fr.* The Tempest.
Commonwealth of the Bees, The. *Fr.* King Henry V.
Compliment to Queen Elizabeth. *Fr.* A Midsummer Night's Dream.
Conscience. *Fr.* Macbeth.
Consolation, A. Sonnets, XXIX.
Constant Service of the Antique World, The. *Fr.* As You Like It.
Content. *Fr.* King Henry VI, Pt. III.
Coriolanus, *sels.*
Counsel of Polonius, The. *Fr.* Hamlet.
Country Song. *Fr.* As You Like It.
Course of True Love, The. *Fr.* A Midsummer Night's Dream.
Courser [and the Jennet], The. *Fr.* Venus and Adonis.
Cowards. *Fr.* Julius Caesar.
Crabbed Age and Youth. *Fr.* The Passionate Pilgrim.
Cranmer's Prophecy of Queen Elizabeth. *Fr.* King Henry VIII.
Cymbeline, *sels.*
Daffodils. *Fr.* The Winter's Tale.
Dagger of the Mind, A. *Fr.* Macbeth.
Death of Adonis, The. *Fr.* Venus and Adonis.
Death of Antony. *Fr.* Antony and Cleopatra.
Death of Cleopatra. *Fr.* Antony and Cleopatra.
Death of Cowards, The. *Fr.* Julius Caesar.
Death of Death, The. Sonnets, CXLVI.
Death of Falstaff, The. *Fr.* King Henry V.
Death of Hamlet. *Fr.* Hamlet.
Death of Kings, The. *Fr.* King Richard II.
Death of Lear. *Fr.* King Lear.
Death of Othello. *Fr.* Othello.
Deaths of Antony and Cleopatra, The. *Fr.* Antony and Cleopatra.
Desdemona's Song. *Fr.* Othello.
Despite Time. Sonnets, CXXIII.
Devouring Time, blunt thou the lion's paws. Sonnets, XIX.

SHAKESPEARE, WILLIAM (*continued*)
Did Not the Heavenly Rhetoric of Thine Eye. *Fr.* Love's Labour's Lost.
Dirge: "Come away, come away, death." *Fr.* Twelfth Night.
Dirge: "Fear no more the heat o' the sun." *Fr.* Cymbeline.
Dirge for [*or* of] Love. *Fr.* Twelfth Night.
Discovery of Pity. *Fr.* King Lear.
Ditty: "Full fadom five thy father lies." *Fr.* The Tempest.
Divine Harmony, The. *Fr.* The Merchant of Venice.
Doubts. *Fr.* Measure for Measure.
Dover Cliffs. *Fr.* King Lear.
Dream of Clarence, The. *Fr.* King Richard III.
Dream of Wrecks, A. *Fr.* King Richard III.
Drinking Song, A. *Fr.* Antony and Cleopatra.
Dumain's Rhymes. *Fr.* Love's Labour's Lost.
Duncan's Murder. *Fr.* Macbeth.
Dying Men. *Fr.* King Richard II.
Empty Life, The. *Fr.* Macbeth.
England ("This England never did"). *Fr.* King John.
England ("This royal throne of kings"). *Fr.* King Richard II.
England at Peace; a Vision. *Fr.* King Henry VIII.
England at War. *Fr.* King Henry V.
England at War: Harfleur, England and St. George. *Fr.* King Henry V.
Enobarbus' Description of Cleopatra. *Fr.* Antony and Cleopatra.
Epilogue: "Now my charms are all ore-throwne." *Fr.* The Tempest.
Epilogue: "Now the hungry lion roars." *Fr.* A Midsummer Night's Dream.
Epilogue to "A Midsummer Night's Dream."
Eternal Feminine, The. *Fr.* Antony and Cleopatra.
Eternal Summer. Sonnets, XVIII.
Eve of Agincourt, The. *Fr.* King Henry V.
Everlasting Rest. *Fr.* Romeo and Juliet.
Evil Designs. *Fr.* King Richard III.
Expense of spirit in a waste of shame, The. Sonnets, CXXIX.
Fair Is My Love, *at.* *Fr.* The Passionate Pilgrim.
Fairies' Lullaby, The ("Come, now a roundel"). *Fr.* A Midsummer Night's Dream.
Fairies' Lullaby, The ("You spotted snakes"). *Fr.* A Midsummer Night's Dream.
Fairies' Song, The. *Fr.* A Midsummer Night's Dream.
Fairy Blessing, The. *Fr.* A Midsummer Night's Dream.
Fairy Land. *Fr.* A Midsummer Night's Dream.
Fairy Land. *Fr.* The Tempest.
Fairy Life, The ("Come unto these yellow sands"). *Fr.* The Tempest.
Fairy Life, The ("Where the bee sucks"). *Fr.* The Tempest.
Fairy Lullaby ("Come now a roundel"). *Fr.* A Midsummer Night's Dream.
Fairy Lullaby ("You spotted snakes"). *Fr.* A Midsummer Night's Dream.
Fairy Queen, The. *Fr.* A Midsummer Night's Dream.
Fairy Songs ("Now the hungry lion roars"). *Fr.* A Midsummer Night's Dream.
Fairy Songs ("Now, until the break of day"). *Fr.* A Midsummer Night's Dream.
Fairy Songs ("Over hill, over dale"). *Fr.* A Midsummer Night's Dream.
Fairy Songs ("You spotted snakes with double tongue"). *Fr.* A Midsummer Night's Dream.
Fairy Songs. *Fr.* The Tempest.
Fairy to Puck, The. *Fr.* A Midsummer Night's Dream.
Fairy's Life, A ("Where the bee sucks"). *Fr.* The Tempest.
Fairy's Song. *Fr.* A Midsummer Night's Dream.
Fairy's Wander-Song. *Fr.* A Midsummer Night's Dream.
Fancy. *Fr.* The Merchant of Venice.
Farewell, A: "Now, most noble Brutus." *Fr.* Julius Caesar.
Farewell Content. *Fr.* Othello.
Farewell! thou art too dear for my possessing. Sonnets, LXXXVII.
Farewell to [All My] Greatness. *Fr.* King Henry VIII.
Father and Son. *Fr.* King Henry VI, Pt. I.
Father's Fury, A. *Fr.* King Lear.
Fear No More the Heat o' the Sun. *Fr.* Cymbeline.
Fear of Death. *Fr.* Measure for Measure.
Feste's Songs. *Fr.* Twelfth Night.
Fidele. *Fr.* Cymbeline.
Fidele's Dirge. *Fr.* Cymbeline.
Fie on Sinful Fantasy! *Fr.* The Merry Wives of Windsor.
Flowers ("O Proserpina!"). *Fr.* The Winter's Tale.
Flowers ("Out, alas!"). *Fr.* The Winter's Tale.
Flowers of Middle Summer. *Fr.* The Winter's Tale.
Flowers of Perdita, The. *Fr.* The Winter's Tale.
Food of Love, The. *Fr.* Twelfth Night.
Footpath Way, The. *Fr.* The Winter's Tale.
For a Patriot. *Fr.* King Henry VIII.
For God's Sake, Let Us Sit upon the Ground. *Fr.* King Richard II.
For I the Ballad Will Repeat. *Fr.* All's Well That Ends Well.
For Thy Sweet Love. Sonnets, XXIX.
Forest of Arden, The. *Fr.* As You Like It.
Fortune and Men's Eyes. Sonnets, XXIX.
Fortune's Finger. *Fr.* Hamlet.
Forward violet thus did I chide, The. Sonnets, XCIX.
Frailty, Thy Name Is Woman. *Fr.* Hamlet.
Fraud of Men, The. *Fr.* Much Ado about Nothing.
Friar Laurence's Cell. *Fr.* Romeo and Juliet.
Friar of Orders Grey, The. *Fr.* Hamlet.
Friendship ("Horatio, thou art e'en as just a man"). *Fr.* Hamlet.
Friendship ("When to the sessions of sweet silent thought"). Sonnets, XXX.
From fairest creatures we desire increase. Sonnets, I.
From you have I been absent in the spring. Sonnets, XCVIII.
Frustra. *Fr.* Measure for Measure.
Full Fathom Five [Thy Father Lies]. *Fr.* The Tempest.
Full many a glorious morning have I seen. Sonnets, XXXIII.
Funeral Song. *Fr.* Cymbeline.
Gaunt's Dying Speech. *Fr.* King Richard II.
Gentle Richard. *Fr.* King Richard II.
Give me my robe, put on my crown. *Fr.* Antony and Cleopatra.
Good Deeds. *Fr.* The Merchant of Venice.
Good Deeds Past. *Fr.* Troilus and Cressida.
Good in Everything. *Fr.* As You Like It.
Good Name, A. *Fr.* Othello.
Good Sir, Whose Powers Are These? *Fr.* Hamlet.
Goodness of Things Evil. *Fr.* King Henry V.
Gracious Time, The. *Fr.* Hamlet.
Grand Style, The. *Fr.* The Tempest.
Gratitude. *Fr.* King Henry VI, Pt. II.
Greenwood [Tree], The. *Fr.* As You Like It.
Grief ("Good Hamlet, cast thy nighted color off"). *Fr.* Hamlet.
Grief fills the room up of my absent child. *Fr.* King John.
Had it pleas'd Heaven. *Fr.* Othello.
Hallowed Season, The. *Fr.* Hamlet.
Hamlet, *sels.*
Hamlet Broods over the Death of His Father. *Fr.* Hamlet.
Hamlet Contemplates Death [*or* Suicide]. *Fr.* Hamlet.
Hamlet's Instructions to the Players. *Fr.* Hamlet.
Hamlet's Soliloquy. *Fr.* Hamlet.
Hark, Hark! the Lark. *Fr.* Cymbeline.
Hate the Idle Pleasures. *Fr.* King Richard III.
He Jests at Scars, That Never Felt a Wound. *Fr.* Romeo and Juliet.
He That Has and a Little Tiny Wit. *Fr.* King Lear.
Heavenly Rhetoric, The. *Fr.* Love's Labour's Lost.
Helena and Hermia. *Fr.* A Midsummer Night's Dream.
Henry V at Harfleur. *Fr.* King Henry V.
Henry V before Harfleur. *Fr.* King Henry V.
Henry V to His Soldiers. *Fr.* King Henry V.
Henry Fifth's Address to His Soldiers. *Fr.* King Henry V.
Henry IV's Soliloquy on Sleep. *Fr.* King Henry IV, Pt. II.
Her Beauty. Sonnets, CVI.
Her Infinite Variety. *Fr.* Antony and Cleopatra.
Here lie I, Timon; who, alive, all living men did hate, *tr.*
Here Lies Juliet. *Fr.* Romeo and Juliet.
Hero's Epitaph. *Fr.* Much Ado about Nothing.
Hiems. *Fr.* Love's Labour's Lost.
Higher Loyalty, The. *Fr.* King Henry VIII.
Horse, The. *Fr.* King Henry V.
Horse, A. *Fr.* Venus and Adonis.
Hotspur. *Fr.* King Henry IV, Pt. I.
Hotspur's Description of a Fop. *Fr.* King Henry IV, Pt. I.
How all occasions do inform against me. *Fr.* Hamlet.
How can I then return in happy plight. Sonnets, XXVIII.
How can my Muse want subject to invent. Sonnets, XXXVIII.
How heavy do I journey on the way. Sonnets, L.
How like a winter hath my absence been. Sonnets, XCVII.
How oft when men are at the point of death. *Fr.* Romeo and Juliet.
How oft, when thou, my music, music play'st. Sonnets, CXXVIII.
How Should I Your True Love Know. *Fr.* Hamlet.
How sweet and lovely dost thou make the shame. Sonnets, XCV.
How Sweet the Moonlight Sleeps. *Fr.* The Merchant of Venice.
Hubert and Arthur. *Fr.* King John.
I Am Fire, and Ayre. *Fr.* Antony and Cleopatra.
I Come to Bury Caesar. *Fr.* Julius Caesar.
I Have Lived Long Enough. *Fr.* Macbeth.
I Know a Bank. *Fr.* A Midsummer Night's Dream.
I saw a thousand fearful wrecks. *Fr.* King Richard III.
If It Do Come to Pass. *Fr.* As You Like It.
If Music Be the Food of Love. *Fr.* Twelfth Night.

If there be nothing new, but that which is. Sonnets, LIX.
If thou survive my well-contented day. Sonnets, XXXII.
If we offend it is with our good will. *Fr.* A Midsummer Night's Dream.
If we shadows have offended. *Fr.* A Midsummer Night's Dream.
I'll Live in This Poor Rime. Sonnets, CVII.
Imagination. *Fr.* A Midsummer Night's Dream.
In faith, I do not love thee with mine eyes. Sonnets, CXLI.
In loving thee thou know'st I am forsworn. Sonnets, CLII.
In Such a Night. *Fr.* The Merchant of Venice.
In the Greenwood. *Fr.* As You Like It.
In the old age black was not counted fair. Sonnets, CXXVII.
In Tune with the Infinite. *Fr.* The Merchant of Venice.
Ingratitude. *Fr.* As You Like It.
Inspiration. *Fr.* A Midsummer Night's Dream.
Is it thy will thy image should keep open. Sonnets, LXI.
It Was a Lording's Daughter, *at.* *Fr.* The Passionate Pilgrim.
It Was a Lover and His Lass. *Fr.* As You Like It.
Jealousy. *Fr.* Othello.
Jog On, Jog On. *Fr.* The Winter's Tale.
John of Gaunt's Dying Speech. *Fr.* King Richard II.
Jolly Shepherd, The. *Fr.* King Lear.
Juliet's Yearning. *Fr.* Romeo and Juliet.
Julius Caesar, *sels.*
Julius Caesar's Preference. *Fr.* Julius Caesar.
Justice. *Fr.* King Henry VI, Pt. II.
King Henry. *Fr.* King Henry V.
King Henry before the Field of Saint Crispian. *Fr.* King Henry V.
King Henry IV, Pt. I, *sels.*
King Henry IV, Pt. II, *sels.*
King Henry V, *sels.*
King Henry VI, Pt. I, *sels.*
King Henry VI, Pt. II, *sels.*
King Henry VI, Pt. III, *sels.*
King Henry VI Yearns for the Simple Life. *Fr.* King Henry VI, Pt. III.
King Henry VIII, *sels.*
King Is Dead, A. *Fr.* King Henry VI, Pt. I.
King John, *sels.*
King Lear, *sels.*
King Richard II, *sels.*
King Richard III, *sels.*
King to His Soldiers before Harfleur, The. *Fr.* King Henry V.
King's Army, The. *Fr.* King Henry IV, Pt. I.
Kingship ("Lets talk of graves"). *Fr.* King Richard II.
Kingship ("O God! methinks it were"). *Fr.* King Henry VI, Pt. III.
Lament: "O! wither'd is the garland of the war." *Fr.* Antony and Cleopatra.
Lament for Imogen. *Fr.* Cymbeline.
Lament of Guiderius and Arviragus. *Fr.* Cymbeline.
Lawn as white as driven snow. *Fr.* The Winter's Tale.
Lear and Cordelia. *Fr.* King Lear.
Lear's Speech to Cordelia. *Fr.* King Lear.
Let me confess that we two must be twain. Sonnets, XXXVI.
Let Me Live. *Fr.* Measure for Measure.
Let me not to the marriage of true minds Sonnets, CXVI.
Let Me Play the Fool. *Fr.* The Merchant of Venice.
Let Rome in Tiber melt. *Fr.* Antony and Cleopatra.
Let those who are in favor with their stars. Sonnets, XXV.
Let/ Thy mother rather feel thy pride than fear. *Fr.* Coriolanus.
Life. *Fr.* As You Like It.
Life and Death. *Fr.* Measure for Measure.
Life without Passion, The. Sonnets, XCIV.
Like as the waves make towards the pebbled shore. Sonnets, LX.
Like as, to make our appetites more keen. Sonnets, CXVIII.
Lilies That Fester. Sonnets, XCIV.
Little love-god lying once asleep, The. Sonnets, CLIV.
Living Juliet, The. *Fr.* Romeo and Juliet.
Lo, as a careful housewife runs to catch. Sonnets, CXLIII.
Lo! Here the Gentle Lark. *Fr.* Venus and Adonis.
Lo, in the orient when the gracious light. Sonnets, VII.
Look in thy glass, and tell the face thou viewest. Sonnets, III.
Looke here upon this picture. *Fr.* Hamlet.
Lord of my love, to whom in vassalage. Sonnets, XXVI.
Love ("Tell me where is fancy bred"). *Fr.* The Merchant of Venice.
Love and the Poet. *Fr.* Love's Labour's Lost.
Love Concealed. *Fr.* Twelfth Night.
Love Dissembled. *Fr.* As You Like It.
Love Forsworn. *Fr.* Measure for Measure.
Love-in-Idleness. *Fr.* A Midsummer Night's Dream.
Love in Springtime. *Fr.* As You Like It.
Love Is Not Love Which Alters. Sonnets, CXVI.
Lover's Lament, A. *Fr.* Twelfth Night.
Lovers Love the Spring. *Fr.* As You Like It.
Love's Concession. Sonnets, CXXX.
Love's Despair. *Fr.* Twelfth Night.
Love's Eternity. Sonnets, CXVI.
Love's Labour's Lost, *sels.*
Love's Memory. *Fr.* All's Well That Ends Well.
Love's Not Time's Fool. Sonnets, CXVI.
Love's Perjuries. *Fr.* Love's Labour's Lost.
Lunatic, the Lover, and the Poet, The. *Fr.* A Midsummer Night's Dream.
Lust. Sonnets, CXXIX.
Macbeth, *sels.*
Macbeth Does Murder Sleep. *Fr.* Macbeth.
Macbeth Learns of His Wife's Death. *Fr.* Macbeth.
Macbeth on His Wife's Death. *Fr.* Macbeth.
Macbeth's Murder Meditation. *Fr.* Macbeth.
Macbeth's Words before Murdering. *Fr.* Macbeth.
Madrigal, A: "Crabbed Age and Youth." *Fr.* The Passionate Pilgrim.
Madrigal: "Take, O take those lips away." *Fr.* Measure for Measure.
Madrigal: "Tell me where is Fancy bred." *Fr.* The Merchant of Venice.
Magic. *Fr.* The Tempest.
Man ("Man, proud man"). *Fr.* Measure for Measure.
Man ("This was the noblest Roman of them all"). *Fr.* Julius Caesar.
Man ("What a piece of work is a man!"). *Fr.* Hamlet.
Man New Made. *Fr.* Measure for Measure.
Man's Ingratitude. *Fr.* As You Like It.
Mark Antony's Lament. *Fr.* Julius Caesar.
Mark Antony's Oration. *Fr.* Julius Caesar.
Marriage of True Minds, The. Sonnets, CXVI.
Martial Friendship. *Fr.* Coriolanus.
Master, the Swabber, The. *Fr.* The Tempest.
Measure for Measure, *sels.*
Memory. Sonnets, XXX.
Merchant of Venice, The, *sels.*
Mercutio Describes Queen Mab. *Fr.* Romeo and Juliet.
Mercutio's Queen Mab Speech. *Fr.* Romeo and Juliet.
Mercy ("The quality of mercy is not strained"). *Fr.* The Merchant of Venice.
Mercy ("Your brother is a forfeit of the law"). *Fr.* Measure for Measure.
Merry Heart, A [*or* The]. *Fr.* The Winter's Tale.
Merry Wives of Windsor, The, *sel.*
Methought I Saw a Thousand Fearful Wrecks. *Fr.* King Richard III.
Midnight ("The locks between her chamber"). *Fr.* The Rape of Lucrece.
Midnight Song. *Fr.* A Midsummer Night's Dream.
Midsummer Night's Dream, A, *sels.*
Mind Diseased, A. *Fr.* Macbeth.
Mistress Mine. *Fr.* Twelfth Night.
Moonlight [and Music]. *Fr.* The Merchant of Venice.
Morning Song. *Fr.* Cymbeline.
Mortality. *Fr.* King Henry IV, Pt. II.
Mother, for love of grace. *Fr.* Hamlet.
Motley's the Only Wear. *Fr.* As You Like It.
Much Ado about Nothing, *sels.*
Multitudinous Seas Incarnadine. *Fr.* Macbeth.
Murder, The. *Fr.* Macbeth.
Murder of Julius Caesar. *Fr.* Julius Caesar.
Murder Pact, The. *Fr.* Macbeth.
Murderers, The. *Fr.* Macbeth.
Muse of Fire, A. *Fr.* King Henry V.
Music ("How sweet the moonlight sleeps"). *Fr.* The Merchant of Venice.
Music ("If music be the food of love"). *Fr.* Twelfth Night.
Music ("Orpheus with his lute"), *at. also to* Fletcher. *Fr.* King Henry VIII.
Music of Hounds, The. *Fr.* A Midsummer Night's Dream.
Music's Silver Sound. *Fr.* Romeo and Juliet.
My desolation does begin. *Fr.* Antony and Cleopatra.
My glass shall not persuade me I am old. Sonnets, XXII.
My Liege, I Did Deny No Prisoners. *Fr.* King Henry IV, Pt. I.
My love is as a fever, longing still. Sonnets, CXLVII.
My love is strengthen'd, though more weak in seeming. Sonnets, CII.
My mistress' eyes are nothing like the sun. Sonnets, CXXX.
My Poore Foole. *Fr.* King Lear.
My tongue-tied Muse in manners holds her still. Sonnets, LXXXV.
"Nay, a mother:/ Why not a mother?" *Fr.* All's Well That Ends Well.
Night. *Fr.* Macbeth.
No longer mourn for me when I am dead. Sonnets, LXXI.
No more be grieved at that which thou hast done. Sonnets, XXXV.
No more but in a woman. *Fr.* Antony and Cleopatra.
No More Dams I'll Make. *Fr.* The Tempest.
No, Time, thou shalt not boast that I do change! Sonnets, CXXIII.

SHAKESPEARE, WILLIAM (*continued*)
Noble Friendship, A, Hamlet and Horatio. *Fr.* Hamlet.
Noblest Roman, The. *Fr.* Julius Caesar.
None of Us Cared for Kate. *Fr.* The Tempest.
Not marble, nor the gilded monuments. Sonnets, LV.
Not [*or* Nor] mine own fears, nor the prophetic soul. Sonnets, CVII.
Not Poppy, nor Mandragora. *Fr.* Othello.
Not Thine Own. *Fr.* Measure for Measure.
Novice, A. *Fr.* Measure for Measure.
Now Entertain Conjecture of a Time. *Fr.* King Henry V.
Now (my fairst Friend). *Fr.* The Winter's Tale.
Now the Hungry Lion Roars. *Fr.* A Midsummer Night's Dream.
Now, until the break of day. *Fr.* A Midsummer Night's Dream.
O, call not me to justify the wrong. Sonnets, CXXXIX.
O Foole, I Shall Go Mad. *Fr.* King Lear.
O, for my sake do you with Fortune chide. Sonnets, CXI.
Oh from what power hast thou this powerful might. Sonnets, CL.
O! Full of Scorpions. *Fr.* Macbeth.
O, how much more doth beauty beauteous seem. Sonnets, LIV.
O me! what eyes hath Love put in my head. Sonnets, CXLVIII.
O Mistress Mine. *Fr.* Twelfth Night.
O! never say that I was false of heart. Sonnets, CIX.
O Proserpina. *Fr.* The Winter's Tale.
O that this too too solid flesh would melt. *Fr.* Hamlet.
O! that you were yourself; but, love, you are. Sonnets, XIII.
O thou, my lovely boy, who in thy power. Sonnets, CXXVI.
O we have made a vow to study, Lord. *Fr.* Love's Labour's Lost.
Oberon and Titania to the Fairy Train. *Fr.* A Midsummer Night's Dream.
Of the Death of Kings. *Fr.* King Richard II.
Old Age of Temperance. *Fr.* As You Like It.
Olivia. *Fr.* Twelfth Night.
On a Day—Alack the Day! *Fr.* Love's Labour's Lost.
On Death. *Fr.* Measure for Measure.
On Degree. *Fr.* Troilus and Cressida.
Once More into the Breach, Dear Friends, Once More. *Fr.* King Henry V.
Ophelia's Death. *Fr.* Hamlet.
Ophelia's Songs ("And will he not come again?") *Fr.* Hamlet.
Ophelia's Songs ("How should I your true love know"). *Fr.* Hamlet.
Opportunity. *Fr.* The Rape of Lucrece.
Or I shall live your epitaph to make. Sonnets, LXXXI.
Orlando's Rhymes. *Fr.* As You Like It.
Orpheus, *at. also to* Fletcher. *Fr.* King Henry VIII.
Orpheus with His Lute, *at. also to* Fletcher. *Fr.* King Henry VIII.
Othello, *sels.*
Othello and Desdemona. *Fr.* Othello.
Othello; How He Won the Love of Desdemona. *Fr.* Othello.
Othello Reviews His Career. *Fr.* Othello.
Othello's Death. *Fr.* Othello.
Othello's Defense. *Fr.* Othello.
Othello's Farewell. *Fr.* Othello.
Othello's Remorse. *Fr.* Othello.
Othello's Wooing. *Fr.* Othello.
Our Little Life. *Fr.* The Tempest.
Our Revels Now Are Ended. *Fr.* The Tempest.
Ousel Cock, The. *Fr.* A Midsummer Night's Dream.
Out, Out, Brief Candle! *Fr.* Macbeth.
Outer and the Inner Man, The. Sonnets, CXLVI.
Over Hill, over Dale. *Fr.* A Midsummer Night's Dream.
Pages' Song, The. *Fr.* As You Like It.
Pardon, Goddess of the Night. *Fr.* Much Ado about Nothing.
Passionate Shepherd's Song, The. *Fr.* Love's Labour's Lost.
Past Reason Hunted. Sonnets, CXXIX.
Patience and Sorrow. *Fr.* Much Ado about Nothing.
Patience on a Monument. *Fr.* Twelfth Night.
Pedlar's Song, The. *Fr.* The Winter's Tale.
Perdita's Garden. *Fr.* The Winter's Tale.
Perfect Tribute, The. *Fr.* Julius Caesar.
Pericles [Prince of Tyre], *sel.*
Phoenix and the Turtle, The.
Phoenix and the Turtle, The, *sel.*
Poet Greatly Pictured, The. *Fr.* A Midsummer Night's Dream.
Polonius' Advice to His Son [*or* to Laertes]. *Fr.* Hamlet.
Poor soul, the centre of my sinful earth. Sonnets, CXLVI.
Poor Wat. *Fr.* Venus and Adonis.
Portia's Appeal [*or* Plea] for Mercy. *Fr.* The Merchant of Venice.
Portia's Picture. *Fr.* The Merchant of Venice.
Portrait of Brutus. *Fr.* Julius Caesar.
Portrait of Caesar. *Fr.* Julius Caesar.
Portrait of Cressida. *Fr.* Troilus and Cressida.
Portrait of Helen. *Fr.* Troilus and Cressida.
Post Mortem. Sonnets, XXXII.
Power of Music. *Fr.* The Merchant of Venice.
Prospero. *Fr.* The Tempest.
Prospero Ends the Revels. *Fr.* The Tempest.
Prospero's Epilogue. *Fr.* The Tempest.
Puck Speaks. *Fr.* A Midsummer Night's Dream.
Puck's Song. *Fr.* A Midsummer Night's Dream.
Quality of Mercy, The. *Fr.* The Merchant of Venice.
Queen Mab. *Fr.* Romeo and Juliet.
Rain It Raineth Every Day, The. *Fr.* Twelfth Night.
Rape of Lucrece, The.
Rape of Lucrece, The, *sels.*
Remembrance [of Things Past]. Sonnets, XXX.
Remorse. *Fr.* Macbeth.
Revolutions. Sonnets, LX.
Richard II Banishes Bolingbroke. *Fr.* King Richard II.
Richard II's Dejection. *Fr.* King Richard II.
Romeo and Juliet, *sels.*
Romeo's Last Words. *Fr.* Romeo and Juliet.
Rose Looks Fair, The. Sonnets, LIV.
Royal Barge, A. *Fr.* Antony and Cleopatra.
Sad Stories of the Death of Kings. *Fr.* King Richard II.
Saint Valentine's Day. *Fr.* Hamlet.
Say that thou didst forsake me for some fault. Sonnets, LXXXIX.
Sea Dirge, A. *Fr.* The Tempest.
Sealed in Vain. *Fr.* Measure for Measure.
Seals of Love. *Fr.* Measure for Measure.
Seasons Alter, The. *Fr.* A Midsummer Night's Dream.
Sermons in Stones. *Fr.* As You Like It.
Sessions of Sweet Silent Thought. Sonnets, XXX.
Seven Ages of Man, The. *Fr.* As You Like It.
Shall I compare thee to a summer's day? Sonnets, XVIII.
She Never Told Her Love. *Fr.* Twelfth Night.
She Should Have Died Hereafter. *Fr.* Macbeth.
Shepherd's Life, A. *Fr.* King Henry VI, Pt. III.
Shylock's Defense. *Fr.* The Merchant of Venice.
Sigh No More [Ladies]. *Fr.* Much Ado about Nothing.
Silvia. *Fr.* The Two Gentlemen of Verona.
Since brass, nor stone, nor earth, nor boundless sea. Sonnets, LXV.
Single Famished Kiss, A. *Fr.* Troilus and Cressida.
Sleep ("How many thousand"). *Fr.* King Henry IV, Pt. II.
Sleep ("Methought I heard a voice"). *Fr.* Macbeth.
Sleep—Innocent Sleep. *Fr.* Macbeth.
So am I as the rich, whose blessed key. Sonnets, LII.
So is it not with me as with that Muse. Sonnets, XXI.
So now I have confessed that he is thine. Sonnets, CXXXIV.
So oft have I invoked thee for my Muse. Sonnets, LXXVIII.
So shall I live, supposing thou art true. Sonnets, XCIII.
So Sweet a Kiss. *Fr.* Love's Labour's Lost.
So work the honey-bees. *Fr.* King Henry V.
Soliloquy from "Hamlet."
Soliloquy on Death. *Fr.* Hamlet.
Soliloquy on Sleep. *Fr.* King Henry IV, Pt. II.
Some Flowers o' the Spring. *Fr.* The Winter's Tale.
Song: "And will he not come again?" *Fr.* Hamlet.
Song: "Blow, blow, thou winter wind." *Fr.* As You Like It.
Song: "Come away, come away, death." *Fr.* Twelfth Night.
Song: "Come unto these yellow sands." *Fr.* The Tempest.
Song: "Fear no more the heat o' the sun." *Fr.* Cymbeline.
Song: "Full fathom [*or* fadom] five thy father lies." *Fr.* The Tempest.
Song: "Good morrow, 'tis St. Valentine's day." *Fr.* Hamlet.
Song: "Hark, hark! the lark at heaven's gate sings." *Fr.* Cymbeline.
Song: "How should I your true love know." *Fr.* Hamlet.
Song: "It was a lover and his lass." *Fr.* As You Like It.
Song: "O mistress mine, where are you roaming?" *Fr.* Twelfth Night.
Song: "Orpheus with his lute made trees," *at. also to* Fletcher. *Fr.* King Henry VIII.
Song: "Sigh no more, ladies, sigh no more." *Fr.* Much Ado about Nothing.
Song: Spring and Winter. *Fr.* Love's Labour's Lost.
Song: "Take, O take those lips away." *Fr.* Measure for Measure.
Song, A: "Tell me, where is fancy bred." *Fr.* The Merchant of Venice.
Song: "Tomorrow is Saint Valentine's day." *fr.* Hamlet.
Song: "Under the greenwood tree." *Fr.* As You Like It.
Song: "When daffodils begin to peer." *Fr.* The Winter's Tale.
Song: "When daisies pied and violets blue." *Fr.* Love's Labour's Lost.
Song: "When icicles hang by the wall." *Fr.* Love's Labour's Lost.
Song: "When that I was and a little tiny boy." *Fr.* Twelfth Night.
Song: "Where the bee sucks, there suck I." *Fr.* The Tempest.

Song: "Who is Silvia? what is she." *Fr.* The Two Gentlemen of Verona.
Song: "You spotted snakes with double tongue." *Fr.* A Midsummer Night's Dream.
Song at the Moated Grange, A. *Fr.* Measure for Measure.
Song for Mariana. *Fr.* Measure for Measure.
Song of Ariel. *Fr.* The Tempest.
Song of Autolycus. *Fr.* The Winter's Tale.
Song of Robin Goodfellow, A. *Fr.* A Midsummer Night's Dream.
Song of the Fairy. *Fr.* A Midsummer Night's Dream.
Song of the Holly. *Fr.* As You Like It.
Song of the Musicians ("Hark! hark! the lark"). *Fr.* Cymbeline.
Song of the Musicians ("Who is Silvia?"). *Fr.* The Two Gentlemen of Verona.
Song of the Two Brothers. *Fr.* Cymbeline.
Song of the Two Pages. *Fr.* As You Like It.
Song to Imogen. *Fr.* Cymbeline.
Song to Silvia. *Fr.* The Two Gentlemen of Verona.
Songs: Spring and Winter. *Fr.* Love's Labour's Lost.
Songs of the Greenwood ("Blow, blow, thou winter wind!"). *Fr.* As You Like It.
Songs of the Greenwood ("Under the greenwood tree"). *Fr.* As You Like It.
Sonnet: "Against my love shall be, as I am now." Sonnets, LXIII.
Sonnet: "Ah wherefore with infection should he live." Sonnets, LXVII.
Sonnet: "Alas 'tis true I have gone here and there." Sonnets, CX.
Sonnet: "As an unperfect actor on the stage." Sonnets, XXIII.
Sonnet: "Being your slave, what should I do but tend." Sonnets, LVII.
Sonnet: "Beshrew that heart that makes my heart to groan." Sonnets, CXXXIII.
Sonnet: "But be contented: when that fell arrest." Sonnets, LXXIV.
Sonnet: "Devouring Time, blunt thou the lion's paws." Sonnets, XIX.
Sonnet: "Did not the heavenly rhetoric of thine eye." *Fr.* Love's Labour's Lost.
Sonnet: "Expense [*or* Expence] of spirit in a waste of shame, The." Sonnets, CXXIX.
Sonnet: "Farewell, thou art too dear for my possessing." Sonnets, LXXXVII.
Sonnet: "Forward violet thus did I chide, The." Sonnets, XCIX.
Sonnet: "From fairest creatures we desire increase." Sonnets, I.
Sonnet: "From you I have been absent in the spring." Sonnets, XCVIII.
Sonnet: "Full many a glorious morning have I seen." Sonnets, XXXIII.
Sonnet: "How can my Muse want subject to invent." Sonnets, XXXVIII.
Sonnet: "How heavy do I journey on the way." Sonnets, L.
Sonnet: "How like a winter hath my absence been." Sonnets, XCVII.
Sonnet: "How oft, when thou, my music, music play'st." Sonnets, CXXVIII.
Sonnet: "How sweet and lovely dost thou make the shame." Sonnets, XCV.
Sonnet: "If there be nothing new, but that which is." Sonnets, LIX.
Sonnet: "If thou survive my well contented day." Sonnets, XXXII.
Sonnet: "In faith, I do not love thee with mine eyes." Sonnets, CXLI.
Sonnet: "In loving thee thou know'st I am forsworn." Sonnets, CLII.
Sonnet: "In the old age black was not counted fair." Sonnets, CXXVII.
Sonnet: "Is it thy will thy image should keep open." Sonnets, LXI.
Sonnet: "Let me not to the marriage of true minds." Sonnets, CXVI.
Sonnet: "Let not my love be call'd idolatry." Sonnets, CV.
Sonnet: "Let those who are in favor with their stars." Sonnets, XXV.
Sonnet: "Like as the waves make towards the pebbled shore." Sonnets, LX.
Sonnet: "Little love-god, lying once asleep, The." Sonnets, CLIV.
Sonnet: "Lo, as a careful housewife runs to catch." Sonnets, CXLIII.
Sonnet: "Lo, in the orient when the gracious light." Sonnets, VII.
Sonnet: "Look in thy glass, and tell the face thou viewest." Sonnets, III.
Sonnet: "Lord of my love, to whom in vassalage." Sonnets, XXVI.
Sonnet: "Love is too young to know what conscience is." Sonnets, CLI.
Sonnet: "Music to hear, why hear'st thou music sadly?" Sonnets, VIII.
Sonnet: "My love is as a fever, longing still." Sonnets, CXLVII.
Sonnet: "My love is strengthened, though more weak in seeming." Sonnets, CII.
Sonnet: "My mistress' eyes are nothing like the sun." Sonnets, CXXX.
Sonnet: "No longer mourn for me when I am dead." Sonnets, LXXI.
Sonnet: "No, Time, thou shalt not boast that I do change!" Sonnets, CXXIII.
Sonnet: "Nor mine own fears, nor the prophetic soul." Sonnets, CVII.
Sonnet: "Not from the stars do I my judgment pluck." Sonnets, XIV.
Sonnet: "Not marble, nor the gilded monuments." Sonnets, LV.
Sonnet: "Not mine own fears, nor the prophetic soul." Sonnets, CVII.
Sonnet: "O, call not me to justify the wrong." Sonnets, CXXXIX.
Sonnet: "Oh, for my sake do you with Fortune chide." Sonnets, CXI.
Sonnet: "Oh, how I faint when I of you do write." Sonnets, LXXX.
Sonnet: "Oh, how much more doth beauty beauteous seem." Sonnets, LIV.
Sonnet: "O! lest the world should task you to recite," *sel.* Sonnets, LXXII.
Sonnet: "Oh, never say that I was false of heart." Sonnets, CIX.
Sonnet: "Oh, that you were yourself! but, love, you are." Sonnets, XIII.
Sonnet: "O thou, my lovely boy, who in thy power." Sonnets, CXXVI.
Sonnet: "Poor soul, the centre of my sinful earth." Sonnets, CXLVI.
Sonnet: "Say that thou didst forsake me for some fault." Sonnets, LXXXIX.
Sonnet: "Shall I compare thee to a summer's day?" Sonnets, XVIII.
Sonnet: "Since brass, nor stone, nor earth, nor boundless sea." Sonnets, LXV.
Sonnet: "Sinne of selfe-love possesseth al mine eie." Sonnets, LXII.
Sonnet: "So are you to my thoughts as food to life." Sonnets, LXXV.
Sonnet: "So is it not with me as with that Muse." Sonnets, XXI.
Sonnet: "Sweet love, renew thy force; be it not said." Sonnets, LVI.
Sonnet: "That time of year thou mayst in me behold." Sonnets, LXXIII.
Sonnet: "Then hate me when thou wilt; if ever, now." Sonnets, XC.
Sonnet: "Then let not winter's ragged hand deface." Sonnets, VI.
Sonnet: "They that have power to hurt, and will do none." Sonnets, XCIV.
Sonnet: "Thine eyes I love, and they, as pitying me." Sonnets, CXXXII.
Sonnet: "Those hours that with gentle work did frame." Sonnets, V.
Sonnet: "Those lines that I before have writ do lie." Sonnets, CXV.
Sonnet: "Those pretty wrongs that liberty commits." Sonnets, XLI.
Sonnet: "Thus is his cheek the map of days outworn." Sonnets, LXVIII.
Sonnet: "Thy bosome is indeared with all hearts." Sonnets, XXXI.
Sonnet: "Thy glass will show thee how thy beauties wear." Sonnets, LXXVII.
Sonnet: "Tired [*or* Tyr'd] with all these, for restful death I cry." Sonnets, LXVI.
Sonnet: "Tis better to be vile than vile esteemed." Sonnets, CXXI.
Sonnet: "To me, fair friend, you never can be old." Sonnets, CIV.
Sonnet: "Two loves I have of comfort and despair." Sonnets, CXLIV.
Sonnet: "Was it the proud full sail of his great verse." Sonnets, LXXXVI.
Sonnet: "Weary with toil, I haste me to my bed." Sonnets, XXVII.
Sonnet: "What is your substance, whereof are you made." Sonnets, LIII.
Sonnet: "What potions have I drunk of Siren tears." Sonnets, CXIX.
Sonnet: "When forty winters shall besiege thy brow." Sonnets, II.
Sonnet: "When I consider every thing that grows." Sonnets, XV.
Sonnet: "When I do count the clock that tells the time." Sonnets, XII.
Sonnet: "When I have seen by Time's fell hand defaced." Sonnets, LXIV.
Sonnet: "When in disgrace with fortune and men's eyes." Sonnets, XXIX.
Sonnet: "When in the chronicle of wasted time." Sonnets, CVI.
Sonnet: "When my love sweares that she is made of truth." Sonnets, CXXXVIII.
Sonnet: "When thou shalt be dispos'd to set me light." Sonnets, LXXXVIII.
Sonnet: "When to the sessions of sweet silent thought." Sonnets, XXX.
Sonnet: "Who will believe my verse in time to come." Sonnets, XVII.
Sonnet: "Whoever hath her wish, thou hast thy will." Sonnets, CXXXV.
Sonnet: "Why didst thou promise such a beauteous day." Sonnets, XXXIV.
Sonnet: "Why is my verse so barren of new pride?" Sonnets, LXXVI.
Sonnet: "Woman's face with nature's own hand painted, A." Sonnets, XX.
Sonnets.
Sonnets, *sels.*
Soul and Body. Sonnets, CXLVI.
Spight of Fortune, The. Sonnets, XC.
Spring. *Fr.* Love's Labour's Lost.
Spring and Winter. *Fr.* Love's Labour's Lost.
Spring Flowers. *Fr.* The Winter's Tale.
Staff Officer, The. *Fr.* King Henry IV, Pt. I.
Stephano's Song. *Fr.* The Tempest.
Such Stuff as Dreams Are Made On. *Fr.* The Tempest.
Sunrise on the Sea. *Fr.* A Midsummer Night's Dream.
Suns and Clouds. Sonnets, XXXIII.
Sweet-and-twenty. *Fr.* Twelfth Night.
Sweet Are the Uses of Adversity. *Fr.* As You Like It.
Sweet Love, Renew Thy Force. Sonnets, LVI.
Sweet Music, *at. also to* Fletcher. *Fr.* King Henry VIII.

SHAKESPEARE, WILLIAM (*continued*)
Sweet Rose, Fair Flower, *at*. *Fr.* The Passionate Pilgrim.
Swimmer, A. *Fr.* Julius Caesar.
Sylvia. *Fr.* The Two Gentlemen of Verona.
Take all my loves, my love, yea, take them all. Sonnets, XL.
Take, O Take Those Lips Away. *Fr.* Measure for Measure.
Take Physic, Pomp. *Fr.* King Lear.
Taming of the Shrew, The, *sels.*
Tavern, The. *Fr.* King Henry IV, Pt. II.
Tell Me Where Is Fancy Bred. *Fr.* The Merchant of Venice.
Tempest, The, *sels.*
Temple-haunting Martlet, The. *Fr.* Macbeth.
That Men Should Fear. *Fr.* Julius Caesar.
That thou hast her, it is not all my grief. Sonnets, XLII.
That time of year thou may'st in me behold. Sonnets, LXXIII.
That you were once unkind befriends me now. Sonnets, CXX.
Then hate me when thou wilt; if ever, now. Sonnets, XC.
There Is a Tide [in the Affairs of Men]. *Fr.* Julius Caesar.
These are the forgeries of jealousie. *Fr.* A Midsummer Night's Dream.
These Few Precepts. *Fr.* Hamlet.
These Lines. Sonnets, XXXII.
Theseus and Hippolyta. *Fr.* A Midsummer Night's Dream.
They bore him barefaced on the bier. *Fr.* Hamlet.
They that have power to hurt, and will do none. Sonnets, XCIV.
Thine eyes I love, and they, as pitying me. Sonnets, CXXXII.
This above All. *Fr.* Hamlet.
This England ("This England never did"). *Fr.* King John.
This England ("This royal throne of kings"). *Fr.* King Richard II.
This Royal Throne of Kings. *Fr.* King Richard II.
This Spring of Love. *Fr.* The Two Gentlemen of Verona.
Those pretty wrongs that liberty commits. Sonnets, XLI.
Thrice Armed. *Fr.* King Henry VI, Pt. II.
Thrice the brinded cat hath mewed. *Fr.* Macbeth.
Thus can my love excuse the slow offense. Sonnets, LI.
Thus is his cheek the map of days outworn. Sonnets, LXVIII.
Thus with a Kiss I Die. *Fr.* Romeo and Juliet.
Thy bosom is endeared with all hearts. Sonnets, XXXI.
Time ("Like as the waves"). Sonnets, LX.
Time ("Time hath, my lord, a wallet at his back"). *Fr.* Troilus and Cressida.
Time and Love ("Since brass, nor stone, nor earth, nor boundless sea"). Sonnets, LXV.
Time and Love ("When I have seen by Time's fell hand defaced"). Sonnets, LXIV.
Time to Strike, The. *Fr.* Julius Caesar.
Time's Glory. *Fr.* The Rape of Lucrece.
Timon of Athens, *sels.*
Timon's Epitaph, *tr.*
Tired with all these, for restful death I cry. Sonnets, LXVI.
'Tis Better to Be Vile than Vile Esteemed. Sonnets, CXXI.
Titania's Bower. *Fr.* A Midsummer Night's Dream.
Titus Andronicus, *sel.*
To Be, or Not to Be. *Fr.* Hamlet.
To Dream Again. *Fr.* The Tempest.
To Fidele. *Fr.* Cymbeline.
To Gild Refinèd Gold. *Fr.* King John.
To His Love. Sonnets, XVIII *and* CVI.
To me, fair friend, you never can be old. Sonnets, CIV.
To Silvia. *Fr.* The Two Gentlemen of Verona.
To Thine Own Self Be True. *Fr.* Hamlet.
Tomorrow, and Tomorrow, and Tomorrow. *Fr.* Macbeth.
Tomorrow Is Saint Valentine's Day. *Fr.* Hamlet.
Traitors. *Fr.* King Henry V.
Tricks of Imagination, The. *Fr.* A Midsummer Night's Dream.
Triumph of Death, The. Sonnets, LXXI.
Troilus and Cressida, *sels.*
Troy Depicted. *Fr.* The Rape of Lucrece.
True Friend, A. *Fr.* Hamlet.
True Love. Sonnets, CXVI.
Tu-Whit To-Who. *Fr.* Love's Labour's Lost.
Twelfth Night, *sels.*
Twilight of Love. Sonnets, LXXIII.
Two Gentlemen of Verona, The, *sels.*
Two loves I have of comfort and despair. Sonnets, CXLIV.
Two of Feste's Songs. *Fr.* Twelfth Night.
Two Songs by Amiens. *Fr.* As You Like It.
Ulysses Advises Achilles Not to Let Slip Opportunity. *Fr.* Troilus and Cressida.
Ulysses. On Degree. *Fr.* Troilus and Cressida.
Ulysses. The Instant Way. *Fr.* Troilus and Cressida.
Unarme Eros, the long dayes taske is done. *Fr.* Antony and Cleopatra.
Unchangeable, The. Sonnets, CIX.
Under the Greenwood Tree. *Fr.* As You Like It.
Uneasy Lies the Head. *Fr.* King Henry IV, Pt. II.
Unrequited Love. *Fr.* Twelfth Night.
Uses of Adversity, The. *Fr.* As You Like It.
Valour. *Fr.* Coriolanus.
Vaulting Ambition. *Fr.* Macbeth.
Venus Abandoned. *Fr.* Venus and Adonis.
Venus and Adonis.
Venus and Adonis, *sels.*
Ver and Hiems. *Fr.* Love's Labour's Lost.
Victorious Titus, rue the tears I shed. *Fr.* Titus Andronicus.
Violet Bank, A. *Fr.* A Midsummer Night's Dream.
Vision, The. *Fr.* King Henry VIII.
Was it the proud full sail of his great verse. Sonnets, LXXXVI.
Way to Dusty Death, The. *Fr.* Macbeth.
Weary with toil, I haste me to my bed. Sonnets, XXVII.
What I Am, I Cannot Avoide. *Fr.* The Merry Wives of Windsor.
What is your substance, whereof are you made. Sonnets, LIII.
What potions have I drunk of Siren tears. Sonnets, CXIX.
What Shall He Have That Kill'd the Deer? *Fr.* As You Like It.
What you do, still betters what is done. *Fr.* The Winter's Tale.
When Daffodils Begin to Peer. *Fr.* The Winter's Tale.
When Daisies Pied and Violets Blue. *Fr.* Love's Labour's Lost.
When forty winters shall besiege thy brow. Sonnets, II.
When I consider every thing that grows. Sonnets, XV.
When I do count the clock that tells the time. Sonnets, XII.
When I have seen by Time's fell hand defaced. Sonnets, LXIV.
When Icicles Hang by the Wall. *Fr.* Love's Labour's Lost.
When in disgrace with fortune and men's eyes. Sonnets, XXIX.
When in the chronicle of wasted time. Sonnets, CVI.
When Mercy Seasons Justice. *Fr.* The Merchant of Venice.
When my love swears that she is made of truth. Sonnets, CXXXVIII.
When Priests Are More in Word. *Fr.* King Lear.
When That I Was and a Little Tiny Boy. *Fr.* Twelfth Night.
When to the sessions of sweet silent thought. Sonnets, XXX.
Where art thou, Muse, that thou forget'st so long. Sonnets, C.
Where Is Fancy Bred? *Fr.* The Merchant of Venice.
Where late the sweet birds sang. Sonnets, LXXIII.
Where the bee sucks, there suck I. *Fr.* The Tempest.
Where the Wild Thyme Blows. *Fr.* A Midsummer Night's Dream.
Whilst I alone did call upon thy aid. Sonnets, LXXIX.
Who Is Silvia [*or* Sylvia]. *Fr.* The Two Gentlemen of Verona.
Who will believe my verse in time to come. Sonnets, XVII.
Why didst thou promise such a beauteous day. Sonnets, XXXIV
Why is my verse so barren of new pride. Sonnets, LXXVI.
Why Should a Man. *Fr.* The Merchant of Venice.
Will You Buy Any Tape? *Fr.* The Winter's Tale.
Winter. *Fr.* Love's Labour's Lost.
Winter of Our Discontent. *Fr.* King Richard III.
Winter [*or* Winter's] Song. *Fr.* Love's Labour's Lost.
Winter's Tale, The, *sels.*
Witches' Charm. *Fr.* Macbeth.
Witches' Meeting. *Fr.* Macbeth.
Witches' Song. *Fr.* Macbeth.
Witches' Spell, The. *Fr.* Macbeth.
With a Kiss I Die. *Fr.* Romeo and Juliet.
Wolsey's Advice to Cromwell. *Fr.* King Henry VIII.
Wolsey's Farewell to Cromwell. *Fr.* King Henry VIII.
Wolsey's Farewell to His Greatness. *Fr.* King Henry VIII.
Woman's face, with nature's own hand painted, A. Sonnets, XX.
Words of Faulconbridge, The. *Fr.* King John.
World's Way, The. Sonnets, LXVI.
You Never Can Be Old. Sonnets, CIV.
You Nymphs, Call'd Naiads. *Fr.* The Tempest.
You Spotted Snakes. *Fr.* A Midsummer Night's Dream.
Young Love. *Fr.* The Merchant of Venice.
Youth and Age. *Fr.* The Passionate Pilgrim.
SHAKESPEARE, WILLIAM, *and* JOHN FLETCHER. *See* FLETCHER, JOHN, *and* WILLIAM SHAKESPEARE.
SHAKESPEARE, WILLIAM, *and others.*
Passionate Pilgrim, The, *sels.*
SHAMS TABREZ. Self-Love.
SHANAFELT, CLARA. Invocation: "O Glass-Blower of time."
SHANAHAN, EILEEN. Desolate Lover, The.
Epiphany.
Kilkenny Boy, The.
Shankill.
Three Children near Clonmel, The.
SHANE, ELIZABETH. Herons on Bo Island.
Hush Song.
Mountainy Childer, The.
Sheskinbeg.
Wee Hughie.
SHAN HO YÜ. Fevered Sleep.
Lamp and the Moon, The.

Shanks, Edward. Boats at Night.
Drilling in Russell Square.
Fields Are Full, The.
For Remembrance.
For the Eightieth Birthday of a Great Singer.
Garden Reverie.
Glade, The.
Glow-Worm, The.
Going In to Dinner.
High Germany.
Lady Godiva.
Lonely Place, A.
Memory.
Night Piece, A.
Rainbow, The.
Searchlights.
Sleeping Heroes.
Song: "As I lay in the early sun."
Storm, The.
Swimmers, The.
To the Unimplored Beloved.
To the Unknown Light.
Waste.
Wind, The.
Woman's Song.
Shanly, Charles Dawson. Brier-Wood Pipe, The.
Civil War.
Kitty of Coleraine, *at.*
Walker of the Snow, The.
Shannon, Monica. Coaxing a Fairy Fiddler.
Could It Have Been a Shadow?
Country Trucks.
Cow Time.
Four-Leaf Clover, The.
Gallop, Gallop to a Rhyme.
How to Tell Goblins from Elves.
Only My Opinion.
Our Hired Man (and His Daughter, Too).
Perfect Child, The.
Raking Walnuts in the Rain.
Three Old Cattlemen.
Tree Toad, The.
Uncle Frank.
Shannon, Sheila. Soldier and Girl Sleeping.
Shao Ch'ang Heng. Misery.
Shapiro, Harvey. Heart, The.
Shapiro, Karl. Adam and Eve.
Adam and Eve, *sels.*
Auto Wreck.
Buick.
Christmas Eve; Australia.
Conscientious Objector, The.
Dirty Word, The.
Dome of Sunday, The [*or* A].
Drug Store.
Elegy for a Dead Soldier.
Elegy for Two Banjos.
Elegy Written on a Frontporch.
Epitaph for John and Richard.
Fly, The.
Full Moon; New Guinea.
Geographers, The.
Giantess, *tr.*
Going to School.
Haircut.
Hollywood.
Homecoming.
Interlude, The.
Israfel.
Leg, The.
Love for a Hand.
Midnight Show.
Minute, The.
Mongolian Idiot.
Necropolis.
Nigger.
Nostalgia.
October I.
On Reading Keats in Wartime.
Paradox: The Birds.
Poet.
Potomac, The.
Progress of Faust, The.
Puritan, The.
Recapitulations, *sels.*
Recognition of Eve, The. *Fr.* Adam and Eve.
Scyros.
Sickness of Adam, The. *Fr.* Adam and Eve.
Southerner, The.
Tingling Back, The.
Travelogue for Exiles.
Troop Train.
Twins, The.
University.
V-Letter.
Waitress.
Washington Cathedral.
Sharaf al-Din. Fragment.
Water-Cooler, The.
Sharman, Lyon (Abbie Mary Lyon Sharman). Ballad of a Famous Fisherman, A.
Brasses.
Building of the Sea-Wall, The.
Dragon Sees His Advantage, The.
Dragon's Warning, The.
Great Tides, The.
Old Man Pot.
Sharp, William. *See* "Macleod, Fiona."
Sharpe, R. L. Bag of Tools, A.
Builders.
Sharpe, Richard Scrafton. Dame Wiggins of Lee and Her Wonderful Cats, *at.*
Minute-Gun, The.
Sharpless, Stanley J. In Praise of Cocoa, Cupid's Nightcap.
Shaw, Charles Green. Dissembler.
Shaw, Cuthbert. Monody to the Memory of a Young Lady, *sel.*
Time's Balm. *Fr.* Monody to the Memory of a Young Lady.
Shaw, David T. Columbia, the Gem of the Ocean.
Red, White and Blue, The.
Shaw, Frances. Child's Quest, The.
Cologne Cathedral.
Harp of the Wind, The.
Last Guest, The.
Little Pagan Rain Song.
Ragpicker, The.
Rain.
Star Thought.
Who Loves the Rain.
Shaw, Isabel. Christmas Chant.
Shaw, John. Sleighing Song.
Song: "Who has robbed the ocean cave."
Shaw, Knowles. Handwriting on the Wall, The.
Shaw, Neufville. Drowned Sailor.
Shaw, Thomas Edward. *See* Lawrence, Thomas Edward.
Shaw, Winifred. Fine Clay.
Shchipachev [*or* Shehipachov], Stepan Petrovich. Duel.
Here Sorrow Had No Limit.
Learn Truly.
On the Boulevard.
On the Road to the Sovkoz.
She used to rock the cradle. They would leave her.
Snowflake.
Sunflower.
Three Love Poems.
Tryst.
Shea, John Augustus. Ocean, The.
Shea, Walter. Crusts.
Most Honored Guest.
Sheard, Virna. Ballad of the Quest, The.
Daisy, The.
Exile.
Hallowe'en.
In Solitude.
Nocturne: "Infold us with thy peace, dear moon-lit night."
Shepherd Wind, The.
Slumber Angel, The.
Song of Summer Days, A.
Southern Lullaby, A.
Yak, The.
Sheehan, Patrick Augustine.
S M.S. (Sister Mary Stanislaus, O.P.).
Sheers [*or* Sheeres], Sir Henry. Pastorella. *at*
Sheffield, John, Duke of Buckingham and Normanby. From all Uneasy Passions Free.
Love's Slavery.
On Mr. Hobbs, and His Writings.
On One Who Died Discovering Her Kindness.
Reconcilement, The.
Relapse, The.
Song: "Come, Celia, let's agree at last."
To a Coquet Beauty.
Sheffield, Rena Cary. Ján Ibn Ján.
Sea-Stretch.
Shehabuddin, Jenab. Your Mouth.
Shehipachov, Stepan Petrovich. *See* Shchipachev, Stepan Petrovich.
Shelburne, Mary Willis. Strange Night.
Sheldon, Charles Frederic. Psalm XXXVII: "Trust in the Lord," *par.*
Sheldon, Charles Monroe. Jesus the Carpenter.
Sheldon, Gilbert. St. Anthony's Township.
Shelley, Percy Bysshe. Adonais; an Elegy on the Death of John Keats.
Adonais; an Elegy on the Death of John Keats, *sels.*
Against Oblivion. *Fr.* Adonais.
Alastor; or, The Spirit of Solitude.
Alastor; or, The Spirit of Solitude, *sels.*
Allegory, An: "Portal as of shadowy adamant, A."
Arethusa.
Asia. *Fr.* Prometheus Unbound.
Asia's Song. *Fr.* Prometheus Unbound.
Aster ("Thou wert the morning-star among the living"), *tr.*
Autumn; a Dirge.
Away, Away! *Fr.* To Jane: The Invitation.
Away! The moor is dark beneath the moon.
Beatrice Cenci in Her Cell. *Fr.* The Cenci.
Beatrice's Last Words. *Fr.* The Cenci.
Birth of Hermes, The, *tr.* *Fr.* Homeric Hymns.
Boat on the Serchio, The, *sel.*
Bridal Song, A.
Cattle-Thief, The, *tr.* *Fr.* Homeric Hymns.
Cenci, The.
Cenci, The, *sels.*
Charioteer, The. *Fr.* Prometheus Unbound.
Charles the First, *sel.*
Child of Twelve, A. *Fr.* The Revolt of Islam.
Chorus: "Life may change, but it may fly not." *Fr.* Hellas.
Chorus: "Life of Life! thy lips enkindle." *Fr.* Prometheus Unbound.
Chorus: Love Song, *tr.* *Fr.* Cyclops.
Chorus: "O Slavery! thou frost of the world's prime." *Fr.* Hellas.
Chorus: "World's great age begins anew, The." *Fr.* Hellas.
Chorus: "Worlds on worlds are rolling ever." *Fr.* Hellas.
Chorus of Satyrs, Driving Their Goats, *tr.* *Fr.* Cyclops.
Chorus of Spirits: "From unremembered ages we." *Fr.* Prometheus Unbound.
Closing Lines of "Prometheus Unbound." *Fr.* Prometheus Unbound.
Cloud, The.
Cloud, The, *sels.*
Curse, The. *Fr.* Prometheus Unbound.
Cyclops, *sels., tr.*
Cyclops' Philosophy, A, *tr.* *Fr.* Cyclops.
Cyclops' Views on Life, A, *tr.* *Fr.* Cyclops.
Daemon of the World, The, *sel.*
Darkness has dawned in the East. *Fr.* Hellas.
Day of Liberty, The. *Fr.* Prometheus Unbound.
Day of Love, The. *Fr.* Prometheus Unbound.
Daybreak.

SHELLEY, PERCY BYSSHE (*continued*)
Death.
Defiance. *Fr.* Prometheus Unbound.
Demogorgon's Last Words. *Fr.* Prometheus Unbound.
Demogorgon's Speech. *Fr.* Prometheus Unbound.
Demon Speaks, The, *tr.* *Fr.* El Magico prodigioso.
Desire of the Moth, The.
Dirge, A: "Rough wind, that moanest loud."
Dirge for the Year.
Dream of the Unknown, A.
Earth the Mother of All, *tr.* *Fr.* Homeric Hymns.
Earth, Universal Mother, *tr.* *Fr.* Homeric Hymns.
Eclogues, *sel.*, *tr.*
End of Tyranny, The. *Fr.* Prometheus Unbound.
England in 1819.
Epigram: "Eagle! why soarest thou above that tomb?" *tr.*
Epilogue of "Prometheus." *Fr.* Prometheus Unbound.
Epipsychidion.
Epipsychidion, *sels.*
Evening; Ponte al Mare, Pisa.
Ever as We Sailed. *Fr.* The Revolt of Islam.
Fair Exchange, *tr.* *Fr.* Cyclops.
Fatal Vision, The. *Fr.* The Two Spirits.
Feelings of a Republican on the Fall of Bonaparte.
Final Chorus: "World's great age begins anew, The." *Fr.* Hellas.
Final Victory, The. *Fr.* Prometheus Unbound.
Flight of Love, The.
Fragment: "I went into the deserts of dim sleep."
Fragment: Music.
Fragment: Rain.
Fragment, A: To Music.
Fragment: To the Moon.
Fragment: "To thirst and find no fill —to wail and wander."
Fragment: Vine-Shroud, The.
Fragment: "When soft winds and sunny skies."
Fragment, A: Woodman and the Nightingale, The.
From the Arabic.
From unremembered ages we. *Fr.* Prometheus Unbound.
Fugitives, The.
Garden, A.
Ginevra, *sel.*
Gleaming Sea, The, *tr.*
Go Thou to Rome. *Fr.* Adonais.
Good-Night.
Grave of Keats ("Go thou to Rome"). *Fr.* Adonais.
Hate-Song, A.
He Is Not Dead. *Fr.* Adonais.
Hellas, *sels.*
Homeric Hymns, *sels.*, *tr.*
Hymn of Apollo.
Hymn of Pan.
Hymn to Athena, *tr.* *Fr.* Homeric Hymns.
Hymn to Castor and Pollux, *tr.* *Fr.* Homeric Hymns.
Hymn to Earth the Mother of All, *tr.* *Fr.* Homeric Hymns.
Hymn to Intellectual Beauty.
Hymn to Mercury, *tr.* *Fr.* Homeric Hymns.
Hymn to Selene, *tr.* *Fr.* Homeric Hymns.
Hymn to Selene, *sel.*, *tr.* *Fr.* Homeric Hymns.
Hymn to the Earth, Mother of All, *tr.* *Fr.* Homeric Hymns.
Hymn to the Moon, *tr.* *Fr.* Homeric Hymns.
Hymn to the Spirit of Nature. *Fr.* Prometheus Unbound.
I Arise from Dreams of Thee.
I Fear Thy Kisses, Gentle Maiden.
I love snow and all the forms.
Ideal, The. *Fr.* Prometheus Unbound.
Indian Serenade, The.
Invitation [to Jane], The.
Invocation: "Rarely, rarely, comest thou."
Invocation: To the Spirit of Delight.
Invocation to Misery.
Invocation to Nature. *Fr.* Alastor.
Keen Stars Were Twinkling, The.
Lament, A: "O world! O life! O time!"
Landsman, The, *tr.*
Laon and Cythna (The Revolt of Islam), *sels.*
Lesson to Lovers, A, *tr.*
Letter to Maria Gisborne.
Letter to Maria Gisborne, *sel.*
"Life may change, but it may fly not." *Fr.* Hellas.
Life of Life. *Fr.* Prometheus Unbound.
Lift Not the Painted Veil.
Lines: "Cold earth slept below, The."
Lines: "When the lamp is shattered."
Lines: "When the lamp is shattered," *sel.*
Lines to a Critic.
Lines to an Indian Air.
Lines Written among the Euganean Hills.
Lines Written among the Euganean Hills, *sel.*
Lines Written on Hearing the News of the Death of Napoleon.
Longest Journey, The. *Fr.* Epipsychidion.
Love.
Love Slumbers On.
Love's Philosophy.
Lumen de Lumine. *Fr.* Adonais.
Magic Car Moved On. *Fr.* Queen Mab.
Magico prodigioso, El, *sel.*, *tr.*
Magnetic Lady to Her Patient, The.
Man, one harmonious soul of many a soul. *Fr.* Prometheus Unbound.
Many a green isle needs must be. *Fr.* Lines Written among the Euganean Hills.
Mask [*or* Masque] of Anarchy, The.
Mask [*or* Masque] of Anarchy, The, *sels.*
Memory.
Men of England.
Millennium, The. *Fr.* Prometheus Unbound.
Mont Blanc.
Moon, The ("And, like a dying lady lean and pale").
Moon, The ("Art thou pale for weariness").
Morning. *Fr.* Prometheus Unbound.
Morning and Evening Star, *tr.*
Music ("I pant for the music which is divine").
Music ("Music, when soft voices die").
Music ("Silver key of the fountain of tears").
Music, When Soft Voices Die.
Music's Mastery, *tr.*
Mutability.
My coursers are fed with the lightning. *Fr.* Prometheus Unbound.
My faint spirit was sitting in the light.
My Soul Is an Enchanted Boat. *Fr.* Prometheus Unbound.
Nest of Love, The. *Fr.* Lines: "When the lamp is shattered."
New World, A. *Fr.* Hellas.
Night ("How beautiful this night"). *Fr.* Queen Mab.
Night ("Swiftly walk o'er the western wave").
Oh! There Are Spirits.
O Thou Immortal Deity.
O world, O life, O time!
Ocean, The, *tr.*
Ode to a Skylark.
Ode to Liberty, *sels.*
Ode to Naples.
Ode to the West Wind.
Ode to the West Wind, *sels.*
On a battle-trumpet's blast. *Fr.* Prometheus Unbound.
On a Faded Violet.
On a Painted Woman.
On a Poet's Lips I Slept. *Fr.* Prometheus Unbound.
On Fanny Godwin.
One with Nature. *Fr.* Adonais.
One Word Is Too Often Profaned.
One Word Is Too Often Profaned, *sel.*
Our Sweetest Songs. *Fr.* To a Skylark.
Ozymandias [of Egypt].
Peaks of Life. *Fr.* Prometheus Unbound.
Peter Bell the Third, *sel.*
Plants Decay, The. *Fr.* The Sensitive Plant.
Plato's Tomb, *tr.*
Pocket-Cattle-Thief, *tr.* *Fr.* Homeric Hymns.
Poet's Dream, The.
Poet's World, The. *Fr.* Prometheus Unbound.
Political Greatness.
Power of Music, The. *Fr.* Homeric Hymns.
Prince Athanese, *sel.*
Prologue in Heaven, *tr.* *Fr.* Faust.
Promethean Ideal, The. *Fr.* Prometheus Unbound.
Prometheus. *Fr.* Prometheus Unbound.
Prometheus Unbound.
Prometheus Unbound, *sels.*
Queen Mab, *sels.*
Question, The ("I dreamed that, as I wandered . . .").
Rainbow's Arch, A. *Fr.* Prometheus Unbound.
Rarely, Rarely, Comest Thou.
Recollection, The.
Remembrance.
Remorse.
Revolt of Islam, The, *sels.*
Sensitive Plant, The.
Sensitive Plant, The, *sels.*
Seraph of Heaven. *Fr.* Epipsychidion.
Singing Tortoise, The, *tr.* *Fr.* Homeric Hymns.
Slavery.
Snow upon my lifeless mountains, The. *Fr.* Prometheus Unbound.
Some say, when nights are dry and clear.
Song: "Rarely, rarely, comest thou."
Song, A: "Widow bird sate mourning for her love, A." *Fr.* Charles the First.
Song to the Men of England.
Sonnet: England in 1819.
Sonnet: "Lift not the painted veil which those who live."
Sonnet: Political Greatness.
Sonnet: To Guido Cavalcanti, *tr.*
Sonnet to Byron.
Spirit of Delight.
Spirit of Plato, *tr.*
Spirit's Song in "Prometheus." *Fr.* Prometheus Unbound.
Spring. *Fr.* The Revolt of Islam.
Stanzas: "Away! the moor is dark beneath the moon."
Stanzas—April 1814.
Stanzas Written in Dejection near Naples.
Star, *tr.*
Summer and Winter.
Summer Evening Churchyard, A.
Sun Is Warm, the Sky Is Clear, The.
Sunset. *Fr.* Queen Mab.
Swiftly walk o'er [*or* over] the western wave. *Fr.* To Night.
Thou, Earth, calm empire of a happy soul. *Fr.* Prometheus Unbound.
Thou wert the morning star among the living, *tr.*
Time.
Time Long Past.
To ——: "I fear thy kisses, gentle maiden."
To ——: "Music, when soft voices die."
To ——: "One word is too often profaned."
To ——: "When passion's trance is overpast."
To a Lady, with a Guitar.

To a Singer. *Fr.* Prometheus Unbound.
To a Skylark.
To a Skylark, *sel.*
To Aster, *tr.*
To Byron.
To Coleridge.
To Constantia Singing.
To Dante, *tr.*
To Guido Cavalcanti, *tr.*
To Harriet. *Fr.* Queen Mab.
To Ianthe.
To Ianthe, Sleeping. *Fr.* Queen Mab.
To Jane: The Invitation.
To Jane: The Invitation, *sels.*
To Jane: The Keen Stars were Twinkling.
To Jane: The Recollection.
To Mary (Dedication). *Fr.* The Revolt of Islam.
To Mary Shelley.
To Night.
To Stella, *tr.*
To Suffer Woes Which Hope Thinks Infinite. *Fr.* Prometheus Unbound.
To the Lord Chancellor, *sel.*
To the Moon.
To the Night.
To the Nile.
To William Shelley.
To Wordsworth.
Tomorrow.
Tortoise-Shell, The, *tr.* *Fr.* Homeric Hymns.
Trackless Deeps, The. *Fr.* The Daemon of the World.
Tribute to America.
Triumph of Life, The.
Triumph of Life, The, *sel.*
True Love. *Fr.* Epipsychidion.
Two Spirits, The; an Allegory.
Two Spirits, The; an Allegory, *sel.*
Unfathomable Sea!
Verses on a Cat.
Victory. *Fr.* Prometheus Unbound.
View from the Euganean Hills, North Italy.
Vision of the Sea, A.
Voice in the Air [Singing]. *Fr.* Prometheus Unbound.
Waning Moon, The.
War. *Fr.* Queen Mab.
West Wind, The. *Fr.* Ode to the West Wind.
When Passion's Trance [Is Overpast].
When the Lamp Is Shattered.
Who Reigns? *Fr.* Prometheus Unbound.
Widow Bird [Sate Mourning], A. *Fr.* Charles the First.
Wilt thou not turn/ Those spirit-beaming eyes.
Winter ("A widow bird sat mourning . . ."). *Fr.* Charles the First.
Witch of Atlas, The.
Witch of Atlas, The, *sel.*
With a Guitar: To Jane.
World's Great Age Begins Anew, The. *Fr.* Hellas.
Worlds on worlds are rolling ever. *Fr.* Hellas.
World's Wanderers, The.
Worship. *Fr.* One Word Is Too Often Profaned.
Written among the Euganean Hills.
Written in the Euganean Hills, North Italy.
Ye Hasten to the Grave!
SHELTON, MARION BROWN. Greatest, The.
SHEN CH'ÜAN. Therefore We Preserve Life.
SHEN YO. Dream, A.
Memories.
SHEN YÜ CH'IU. Afloat on the Lake.
SHEN YÜEH. Tryst, The.
SHENSTONE, WILLIAM. Absence. *Fr.* A Pastoral Ballad.
Bloom the Jasmines.
Elegy: He Complains How Soon the Pleasing Novelty of Life Is Over.
He Complains How Soon the Pleasing Novelty of Life Is Over.
Hint from Voiture.
Hope. *Fr.* A Pastoral Ballad.
In Imitation of Spenser. *Fr.* The Schoolmistress.
Inscription: On a Tablet against a Root-House.
Inscription: On the Back of a Gothic Seat.
Kid, The.
Landscape, The.
O Sweet Anne Page.
Ode to a Young Lady, Somewhat Too Solicitous about Her Manner of Expression.
Ode to Memory.
O'er Desert Plains, and Rushy Meers.
Pastoral Ballad, A.
Pastoral Ballad, A, *sels.*
Schoolmistress, The.
Schoolmistress, The, *sels.*
Shepherd's Home, The.
Slender's Ghost.
Song: Landskip, The.
Song: "O'er desert plains, and rushy meers."
Village Schoolmistress, The. *Fr.* The Schoolmistress.
Written at [*or* in] an Inn at Henley.
SHEPARD, ELIZABETH ALSOP. White Fox.
SHEPARD, ODELL. Adventurer, The.
Certain American Poets.
Earth-born.
Elm, The.
Flock at Evening, The.
Gifts, The.
Goldfinch, The.
Hidden Weaver, The.
Home Thoughts.
In the Dawn.
In the Dawn, *sel.*
Love among the Clover.
Nun, The.
Singer's Quest, The.
Sonnet: "We two, O true-heart, who have learned so well."
Thanksgiving.
Vespers.
Vistas.
Whence Cometh My Help.
SHEPARD, SHELDON. Follow Me!
Injustice.
Interpretation.
SHEPHERD, HOPE. Trains.
SHEPHERD, NATHANIEL GRAHAM. Only the Clothes She Wore.
Roll-Call.
SHEPHERD, THOMAS. Alas, My God. *Fr.* For Communion with God.
For Communion with God, *sel.*
Must Jesus bear the cross alone.
SHEPPARD, MURIEL EARLEY. Coquette, The.
Episode, An.
Snake Charmer, The.
SHEPPARD, SAMUEL. Of Death.
SHERBROOKE, VISCOUNT. *See* LOWE, ROBERT, VISCOUNT SHERBROOKE.
SHERBURNE, SIR EDWARD. And She Washed His Feet with Her Tears, and Wiped Them with the Hairs of Her Head.
Christus Matthaeum et Discipulos Alloquitur.
Conscience.
Fountain, The.
Magdalen, The.
Sweetmeat, The.
Violets in Thaumantia's Bosome.
Vow, The.
Weeping and Kissing.
SHERIDAN, C. B. Dreams! cheer the child with sights of joy, *tr.*
Hush, hush, my little babe! *tr.*
Santa Maria! cover the child, *tr.*
SHERIDAN, CAROLINE ELIZABETH SARAH. *See* NORTON, CAROLINE ELIZABETH SARAH SHERIDAN.
SHERIDAN, HELEN SELINA, LADY DUFFERIN. Charming Woman, The.
Irish Emigrant, The.
Lament of the Irish Emigrant.
Love Hath a Language. *Fr.* To My Son.
Terence's Farewell.
To My Dearest Son.
To My Son, *sel.*
SHERIDAN, JOHN D. Each in His Inmost Heart.
SHERIDAN, NIALL. Ad Lesbiam, *tr.*
Poem: "As rock to sun or storm."
SHERIDAN, RICHARD BRINSLEY. Air: "I ne'er could any luster see." *Fr.* The Duenna.
By Coelia's Arbor.
Dry Be That Tear.
Duenna, The, *sels.*
Epigram: "'I would,' says Fox, 'a tax devise.'"
Famous Toast, A. *Fr.* The School for Scandal.
Had I a Heart for Falsehood Framed. *Fr.* The Duenna.
Here's to the Maiden. *Fr.* The School for Scandal.
How Oft, Louisa, Hast Thou Told. *Fr.* The Duenna.
Let the Toast Pass. *Fr.* The School for Scandal.
Literary Lady, The.
Months, The.
Oh, the Days When I Was Young. *Fr.* The Duenna.
Oh Yield, Fair Lids.
Quarrel between Sir Peter and Lady Teazle. *Fr.* The School for Scandal.
School for Scandal, The, *sels.*
Song: "Had I a heart for falsehood framed." *Fr.* The Duenna.
Song: "Here's to the maiden of bashful fifteen." *Fr.* The School for Scandal.
Song: "If a daughter you have, she's the plague of your life." *Fr.* The Duenna.
This Bottle's the Sun of Our Table. *Fr.* The Duenna.
Wife, A.
SHERIDAN, THOMAS. Bookworm's Content, A.
SHERLOCK, PHILLIP M. Dinner Party, 1940.
SHERMAN, ELIZA M. Old Man's Dreams, An.
SHERMAN, FRANCIS. Between the Battles.
Builder, The.
Deserted City, The, *sel.*
Foreigner, The.
House of Colour, The. *Fr.* The Deserted City.
In Memorabilia Mortis.
Let Us Rise Up and Live.
SHERMAN, FRANK DEMPSTER. At Midnight.
Bacchus.
Bees.
Broker Cupid.
Bundle of Letters, A.
Clouds.
Daisies.
Dawn.
Dewdrop, A.
Dies Ultima.
February.
Footprints in the Snow.
Four Winds, The.
Golden Rod, The.
Hollyhock, A.
In Parenthesis.
In the Meadow.
It is my joy in life to find.
Ivy.
January.
Jester Bee.
Kite, A.
Library, The.
Love's Springtide.
Lullaby: "Slumber, slumber, little one, now."
Mary and the Lamb.
May.
Moonrise.
On a Greek Vase.
On Some Buttercups.
Prayer, A: "It is my joy in life to find."
Quatrain, A: "Hark at the lips of the pink whorl of shell."
Real Santa Claus, A.
Rose's Cup, The.
Shadows, The.

SHERMAN, FRANK DEMPSTER (*continued*)
Snow-Bird, The.
Spinning Top.
To a Rose.
Untutored Mind, An.
Waterfall, The.
Winter's Tale, A.
Wish, A.
Witchery.
Wizard Frost.
SHERMAN, JEANIE ROGERS. Thanksgiving.
SHERRINGTON, SIR CHARLES SCOTT. Body of Man, The.
Green and Black.
SHERRY, RUTH FORBES. Promises.
SHERWOOD, ADA SIMPSON. Arbor Day Alphabet.
SHERWOOD, ALICE E. Hymn of Thanksgiving, A.
Into a Mountain Apart.
SHERWOOD, GRACE BUCHANAN. After Laughter.
Now Walks the Devil Up and Down.
SHERWOOD, KATE BROWNLEE. Albert Sidney Johnston.
Drummer Boy of Mission Ridge, The.
Molly Pitcher.
Red, the White, the Blue, The.
States Crowning Washington, The.
Thomas at Chickamauga.
Ulric Dahlgren.
We Keep Memorial Day.
SHERWOOD, MARGARET. In Memoriam—Leo, a Yellow Cat.
SHERWOOD, ROBERT EMMET. Old Hokum Buncombe, The.
SHI-EI. Two slender stalks of black bamboo.
SHIELDS, ELIZABETH MCEWEN. God Is Near.
I'm Glad.
Prayer of a Teacher, The.
SHIELDS, REN. In the Good Old Summer Time.
SHIELDS, SHAEMAS. *See* O'SHEEL, SHAEMAS.
SHIFFRIN, ABRAHAM B. *See* "CHRISTOPHER, ROBIN."
SHIH CH'ENG LE. Call of Spring, The.
SHIH EE. Ch'i Lai' (March of the Volunteers).
SHIH LING YÜ. Garment of Mortality, The.
SHIKI. High noon;/ And on the clouds above.
What kind of men are these.
SHIKO. Flying birds,/ Beware!
Lilies.
Maple Leaves.
Now Autumn comes to me.
SHILLITO, EDWARD. Ave Crux, Spes Unica!
Christmas Tree, The.
Dereliction.
I Am the Last.
Jesus of the Scars.
Life to Come, The.
Lonely Christ, The.
One Love.
Prayer for a Preacher, A.
Prayer of a Modern Thomas.
Untried Door, The.
SHIMAZAKI, TOSON. Coco-Nut, A.
Crafty Fox.
First Love.
In the Birdless Country.
Otsuta.
SHINN, MILICENT WASHBURN. Song and Science.
Washington Sequoia, The, *sel.*
When Almonds Bloom.
Yosemite. *Fr.* The Washington Sequoia.
SHIPLEY, JOSEPH T. Another Spirit Advances, *tr.*
Ballad of the Bells, *sel.*, *tr.*
Epitaph: For Himself, *tr.*
Shadows, *tr.*
Song for a Jewess, *tr.*
SHIPMAN, THOMAS. Epitaph on His Grandfather, An.
Epitaph upon My Grandfather, An.
Resolute Courtier, The.
SHIPP, E. RICHARD. Eighteen-ninety.
SHIPP, HORACE. Everest.
Saint Francis.
SHIPPE, BETTY. Sky.
SHIPPEN, EDWARD. Prayer: "From food when it is hash."
SHIPPEY, LEE. Battle Cry, A.
If We Could Only Be!
Unknown Reporter, The.
SHIPTON, ANNA. Unerring Guide, The.
SHIRER, J. MARION. Our Departed Comrades.
SHIRK, JEANNETTE C. Clock Shop, The.
SHIRLEY, HENRY. Martyred Soldier, The, *sel.*
What are earthly honors. *Fr.* The Martyred Soldier.
SHIRLEY, JAMES. Bard's Chant. *Fr.* Saint Patrick for Ireland.
Calchas before the Body of Ajax. *Fr.* The Contention of Ajax and Ulysses.
Cease, warring thoughts, and let his brain. *Fr.* The Triumph of Beauty.
Changes; or, Love in a Maze, *sel.*
Come away, away, away. *Fr.* The Triumph of Peace.
Commonwealth of Birds, The.
Contention of Ajax and Ulysses, The, *sels.*
Cupid and Death, *sels.*
Cupid Ungodded.
Death the Conqueror ("The glories of our blood and state"). *Fr.* The Contention of Ajax and Ulysses.
Death, the Conqueror ("Victorious men of earth! no more"). *Fr.* Cupid and Death.
Death the Leveller. *Fr.* The Contention of Ajax and Ulysses.
Death's Emissaries. *Fr.* Cupid and Death.
Death's Final Conquest. *Fr.* The Contention of Ajax and Ulysses.
Death's Subtle Ways. *Fr.* Cupid and Death.
Dirge: "Glories of our blood and state, The." *Fr.* The Contention of Ajax and Ulysses.
Glories of Our Blood and State, The. *Fr.* The Contention of Ajax and Ulysses.
Hymn, A: "O fly, my soul! What hangs upon." *Fr.* The Imposture.
Imposture, The, *sels.*
Io. *Fr.* The Imposture.
King of Kings, The. *Fr.* The Contention of Ajax and Ulysses.
Last Conqueror, The. *Fr.* Cupid and Death.
Levelling Dust, The. *Fr.* The Contention of Ajax and Ulysses.
Looking Glass, The.
Love, a Thousand Sweets Distilling. *Fr.* The Witty Fair One.
Love's Victories. *Fr.* Cupid and Death.
Lullaby, A: "Cease, warring thoughts, and let his brain." *Fr.* The Triumph of Beauty.
Maid's Revenge, The, *sel*
Melancholy, hence! go get. *Fr.* Changes; or, Love in a Maze.
More Ways to Kill. *Fr.* Cupid and Death.
O Fly My Soul. *Fr.* The Imposture.
Of Death. *Fr.* The Contention of Ajax and Ulysses.
Our Blood and State. *Fr.* The Contention of Ajax and Ulysses.
Passing Bell, The.
Peace. *Fr.* The Imposture.
Piping Peace. *Fr.* The Imposture.
Saint Patrick for Ireland, *sel.*
Song: "Glories of our blood and state, The." *Fr.* The Contention of Ajax and Ulysses.
Song: "Love a thousand sweets distilling." *Fr.* The Witty Fair One.
Song: "Victorious men of Earth, no more." *Fr.* Cupid and Death.
Song: "You Virgins that did late despair." *Fr.* The Imposture.
Song of Nuns, A. *Fr.* The Imposture.
To His Mistress [*or* Mistris] Confined.
To My Friend, Master John Ford.
To the Excellent Pattern of Beauty and Virtue, Lady Elizabeth, Countess of Ormond.
Triumph of Beauty, The, *sel.*
Triumph of Peace, The, *sel.*
Upon His Mistress Dancing.
Upon Scarlet and Blush-coloured Ribbands, Given by Two Ladies.
Victorious Men of Earth. *Fr.* Cupid and Death.
Witty Fair One, The, *sel.*
You Virgins. *Fr.* The Imposture.
SHIRREFS, ANDREW. Cogie o' Yill, A.
SHISHOVA, ZINAIDA. Unfamiliar Air, An.
SHIVELL, PAUL. In God's Eternal Studios. *Fr.* The Studios Photographic.
Studios Photographic, The, *sel.*
SHIZUMOKI. My Flowers.
SHKULEV, FILIP STEPANOVICH. Revolution, The.
SHLONSKY, ABRAHAM. Grape-gathering.
SHOEMAKER, BLANCHE. *See* WAGSTAFF, BLANCHE SHOEMAKER.
SHOKU, PRINCESS. Hyaku-Nin-Isshu, *sel.*
I would that even now. *Fr.* Hyaku-Nin-Isshu.
SHOLL, ANNA MCCLURE. Wolf of Gubbio to Saint Francis, The.
SHOREY, GEORGE H. Bubbles.
SHORT, JOHN. Carol: "There was a Boy bedded in bracken."
Landmark.
SHORT, MARION. Dead Pussy Cat, The, *at.*
SHORTER, DORA SIGERSON. All Souls' Night.
April.
Ballad of Marjorie, A.
Ballad of the Little Black Hound.
Beware.
Bird from the West, A.
Cean Duv Deelish.
Comforters, The.
Fair Little Maiden, The.
Fairy Thorn-Tree, The.
Fetch, The.
Gypsies' Road, The.
In the Midst of Life.
Ireland.
Kine of My Father, The.
Man Who Trod on Sleeping Grass, The.
Mother's Prayer, The.
New Year, A.
Nora.
One Forgotten, The.
Patchwork Quilt, The.
Piper on the Hill, The.
Rose Will Fade, A.
Sixteen Dead Men.
Wind on the Hills, The.
SHOTOKU, PRINCE. On Seeing a Dead Man.
SHOU. Birds sit and sing among the flowers.
SHOVE, FREDEGOND. Dream in Early Spring, A.
Farmer, The, 1917.
Infant Spring.
New Ghost, The.
Song: "Spring lights her candles everywhere."
Sops of Light.
SHUCKBURG, RICHARD. Yankee Doodle, *at.*
SHUFORD, GENE. Harvest.
SHU HSI. Hot Cake.
SHULTS, GEORGE FRANCIS. Under the Mistletoe.
SHUN-E (the monk Shun-e). All during a night/ Of anxiety I wait.
SHURAIKH. Distich.
SHURTLEFF, ERNEST W. Lead On, O King Eternal.
Old Thanksgiving Days, The.
SHUSTER, GEORGE NAUMAN. Newman.
Poet-Hearts, *tr.*
Returning Spring, *tr.*
What Highway?
SHUTE, EVAN VERE. Luck.
Night Comes Apace.
Poor Fool.
Twenty Years After.

"SHY, TIMOTHY." *See* LEWIS, DOMINIC BEVAN WYNDHAM.

SIBLEY, CHARLES. Plaidie, The.

SICKELS, DAVID BANKS. It Cannot Be. Reincarnation.

SIDEY, JAMES A. Irish Schoolmaster, The.

SIDGWICK, FRANK. Aeronaut to His Lady, The.

Christmas Legend, A.

Corinna Goes a-Singing.

"Form Fours."

Glory of Early Rising, The.

His Hirsute Suit.

Imaginary Correspondence, *parody*.

Sing a Song of Sixpence, *parody*.

When My Ship Comes In, *sel*.

SIDGWICK, HENRY. Goethe and Frederika.

"SIDNEY, MARGARET" (Harriet Mulford Lothrop). Memorial Day.

SIDNEY, MARY, COUNTESS OF PEMBROKE. *See* PEMBROKE, MARY SIDNEY HERBERT, COUNTESS OF.

SIDNEY, Sir PHILIP. Absence.

Advice to the Same. *Fr.* Arcadia.

Against Artifice. *Fr.* Astrophel and Stella.

Ah, bed! the field where joy's peace some do see. *Fr.* Astrophel and Stella.

Alas, have I not pain enough, my friend. *Fr.* Astrophel and Stella.

And do I see some cause a hope to feed. *Fr.* Astrophel and Stella.

Answered Thus by Sir P. S.

Arcadia, *sels*.

As good to write as for to lie and groan. *Fr.* Astrophel and Stella.

Astrophel and Stella.

Astrophel and Stella, *sels*.

Astrophel's Love Is Dead.

Bargain, The. *Fr.* Arcadia.

Be your words made, good Sir, of Indian ware. *Fr.* Astrophel and Stella.

Because I breathe not love to everyone. *Fr.* Astrophel and Stella.

Because I oft in darke abstracted guise. *Fr.* Astrophel and Stella.

Child-Song.

Come, let me write. And to what end? To ease. *Fr.* Astrophel and Stella.

Come Sleep! [O Sleep, the Certain Knot of Peace]. *Fr.* Astrophel and Stella.

Complaint of Love. *Fr.* Arcadia.

Conditional Surrender. *Fr.* Astrophel and Stella.

Contentment. *Fr.* Arcadia.

Countess of Pembroke's Arcadia, The, *sels*.

Country Song, A. *Fr.* Arcadia.

Cupid. *Fr.* Arcadia.

Cupid, because thou shin'st in Stella's eyes. *Fr.* Astrophel and Stella.

Curious wits, seeing dull pensiveness, The. *Fr.* Astrophel and Stella.

Dear, why make you more of a dog than me? *Fr.* Astrophel and Stella.

Delight of Solitariness, The. *Fr.* Arcadia.

Desire. *Fr.* Astrophel and Stella.

Desire, though thou my old companion art. *Fr.* Astrophel and Stella.

Dialogue, A: "Who is it that this dark night." *Fr.* Astrophel and Stella.

Dian, that fain would cheer her friend the night. *Fr.* Astrophel and Stella.

Dirge: "Ring out your bell [e]s."

Dispraise of a Courtly Life.

Ditty: Heart Exchange.

Ditty, A: "My true love hath my heart and I have his." *Fr.* Arcadia.

Dorus His Comparisons. *Fr.* Arcadia.

Dorus's Song. *Fr.* Arcadia.

Double Sestine. *Fr.* Arcadia.

Doubt there hath been, when with his golden chain. *Fr.* Astrophel and Stella.

Doubt You to Whom? *Fr.* Astrophel and Stella.

Echo. *Fr.* Arcadia.

Eleventh Song: "Who is it that this dark night." *Fr.* Astrophel and Stella.

Envious wits, what hath been mine offence. *Fr.* Astrophel and Stella.

Epithalamium: "Let mother earth now deck[e] herself[e] in flowers." *Fr.* Arcadia.

Excellent Sonnet of a Nymph, An.

Farewell, A: "Leave me, O love." *Fr.* Astrophel and Stella.

Farewell, A: "Oft have I mused."

Farewell World. *Fr.* Astrophel and Stella.

Fie, school of Patience, fie! Your lesson is. *Fr.* Astrophel and Stella.

First Song: "Doubt you to whom my muse these notes intended [or entendeth]." *Fr.* Astrophel and Stella.

Fly, fly, my friends, I have my death wound, fly. *Fr.* Astrophel and Stella.

Fourth Song: "Only joy, now here you are." *Fr.* Astrophel and Stella.

Friendship. *Fr.* Arcadia.

Geron and Histor. *Fr.* Arcadia.

Get Hence Foule Griefe. *Fr.* Arcadia.

Go, My Flock. *Fr.* Astrophel and Stella.

Golden Mean, The, *tr. Fr.* Odes.

Graven Thoughts. *Fr.* Arcadia.

Grief, find the words; for thou hast made my brain. *Fr.* Astrophel and Stella.

Having this day my horse, my hand, my lance. *Fr.* Astrophel and Stella.

Heart Exchange. *Fr.* Arcadia.

Highway, The. *Fr.* Astrophel and Stella.

Highway, since you my chief Parnassus be. *Fr.* Astrophel and Stella.

His Lady's Cruelty. *Fr.* Astrophel and Stella.

Hope, art thou true, or dost thou flatter me? *Fr.* Astrophel and Stella.

Hymn to Apollo.

I might—unhappy word—oh me, I might. *Fr.* Astrophel and Stella.

I never drank of Aganippe well. *Fr.* Astrophel and Stella.

I on my horse, and Love on me, doth try. *Fr.* Astrophel and Stella.

If Orpheus' Voice. *Fr.* Astrophel and Stella.

In a Grove Most Rich of Shade. *Fr.* Astrophel and Stella.

In highest way of heaven the Sun did ride. *Fr.* Astrophel and Stella.

In martial sports I had my cunning tried. *Fr.* Astrophel and Stella.

In truth, O love, with what a boyish kind. *Fr.* Astrophel and Stella.

In Vain, Mine Eyes. *Fr.* Arcadia.

In Wonted Walks, Since Wonted Fancies Change.

It is most true, that eyes are form'd to serve. *Fr.* Astrophel and Stella.

Just Exchange. *Fr.* Arcadia.

Late tired with woe, even ready for to pine. *Fr.* Astrophel and Stella.

Leave Me, O Love [Which Reachest but to Dust]. *Fr.* Astrophel and Stella.

Let dainty wits cry on the Sisters nine. *Fr.* Astrophel and Stella.

Like as the Dove.

Lists, The. *Fr.* Astrophel and Stella.

Litany, A: "Ring out your bells . . ."

Lock up, fair lids, the treasure of my heart. *Fr.* Arcadia.

Look into Thy Heart.

Love. *Fr.* Astrophel and Stella.

Love and Jealousy. *Fr.* Arcadia.

Love and Reason. *Fr.* Arcadia.

Love Is Dead.

Love still a boy, and oft a wanton, is. *Fr.* Astrophel and Stella.

Loved I Am, and Yet Complaine of Love. *Fr.* Arcadia.

Lovers' Dialogue. *Fr.* Astrophel and Stella.

Love's Silence. *Fr.* Astrophel and Stella.

Loving in truth, and fain in verse

my love to show. *Fr.* Astrophel and Stella.

Madrigal: "Why dost thou haste away." *Fr.* Arcadia.

Magpies and Swans. *Fr.* Astrophel and Stella.

Moon, The. *Fr.* Astrophel and Stella.

Morpheus, the lively son of deadly sleep. *Fr.* Astrophel and Stella.

Muses, I oft invoked your holy aid. *Fr.* Astrophel and Stella.

My mouth doth water, and my breast doth swell. *Fr.* Astrophel and Stella.

My Muse may well grudge at my heavenly joy. *Fr.* Astrophel and Stella.

My Sheep Are Thoughts. *Fr.* Arcadia.

My True Love Hath My Heart. *Fr.* Arcadia.

Night. *Fr.* Arcadia.

Nightingale [as Soon as April Bringeth], The.

No more, my dear, no more these counsels try. *Fr.* Astrophel and Stella.

Not at the first sight, nor with a dribbed shot. *Fr.* Astrophel and Stella.

Nymph of the Garden Where All Beauties Be. *Fr.* Astrophel and Stella.

O Dear Life, When Shall It Be? *Fr.* Astrophel and Stella.

O Faire! O Sweete!

O grammar rules, O now your virtues show. *Fr.* Astrophel and Stella.

O Happy Thames. *Fr.* Astrophel and Stella.

O joy too high for my low style to show! *Fr.* Astrophel and Stella.

O Night the ease of care the pledge of Pleasure. *Fr.* Arcadia.

O Sweet Woods. *Fr.* Arcadia.

O Words Which Fall like Summer Dew on Me. *Fr.* Arcadia.

O You That Hear This Voice. *Fr.* Astrophel and Stella.

Odes (of Horace), *sel., tr.*

Old Age. *Fr.* Arcadia.

Only Joy! Now Here You Are. *Fr.* Astrophel and Stella.

Philomela.

Reason, in faith thou art well served, that still. *Fr.* Astrophel and Stella.

Rich fools there be whose base and filthy heart. *Fr.* Astrophel and Stella.

Ring Out Your Bells.

Road, The. *Fr.* Astrophel and Stella.

Rural Poesy. *Fr.* Arcadia.

Sapphics. *Fr.* Arcadia.

Sestina. *Fr.* Arcadia.

Shepherd Song. *Fr.* Arcadia.

Shepherdess' Song. *Fr.* Arcadia.

Shepherd's Tale, A. *Fr.* Arcadia.

Since So Mine Eyes. *Fr.* Arcadia.

Sleep ("Come, sleep!"). *Fr.* Astrophel and Stella.

Sleep ("Lock up, fair lids"). *Fr.* Arcadia.

Solitariness. *Fr.* Arcadia.

Some lovers speak, when they their Muses entertain. *Fr.* Astrophel and Stella.

Song: "My true love hath my heart, and I have his." *Fr.* Arcadia.

Song: "No, no, no, no, I cannot hate my foe."

Song: "O fair! O sweet! when I do look on thee."

Song: "Who hath his fancy pleasèd."

Song: "Who is it that, this dark night." *Fr.* Astrophel and Stella.

Sonnet: "Come, Sleep, O Sleep, the certain knot of peace." *Fr.* Astrophel and Stella.

Sonnet: "Highway, since you my chief Parnassus be." *Fr.* Astrophel and Stella.

Sonnet: "I might—unhappy word!—oh me, I might." *Fr.* Astrophel and Stella.

SIDNEY, SIR PHILIP (*continued*)
Sonnet: "In truth, O Love, with what a boyish kind." *Fr.* Astrophel and Stella.
Sonnet: "Late tired with woe, even ready for to pine." *Fr.* Astrophel and Stella.
Sonnet: "Leave me, O Love, which reachest but to dust." *Fr.* Astrophel and Stella.
Sonnet: "Lock up, fair lids, the treasure of my heart." *Fr.* Arcadia.
Sonnet: "Love still a boy, and oft a wanton is." *Fr.* Astrophel and Stella.
Sonnet: "Loving in truth and fain in verse my love to show." *Fr.* Astrophel and Stella.
Sonnet: "My true Love hath my heart, and I have his." *Fr.* Arcadia.
Sonnet: "No more, my dear, no more these counsels try." *Fr.* Astrophel and Stella.
Sonnet: "Not at first sight, nor yet with a dribbed shot." *Fr.* Astrophel and Stella.
Sonnet: "O happy Thames that didst my Stella bear!" *Fr.* Astrophel and Stella.
Sonnet: "Rich fools there be whose base and filthy heart." *Fr.* Astrophel and Stella.
Sonnet: "Stella! since thou so right a princess art." *Fr.* Astrophel and Stella.
Sonnet: "Stella, think not that I by verse seek fame." *Fr.* Astrophel and Stella.
Sonnet: "Thou blind man's mark."
Sonnet: "What have I thus betrayed my libertie?" *Fr.* Astrophel and Stella.
Sonnet: "When nature made her chief work, Stella's eyes." *Fr.* Astrophel and Stella.
Sonnet: "With how sad steps, O Moon, thou climb'st the skies." *Fr.* Astrophel and Stella.
Sonnet: "Your words, my friend, right healthful caustics, blame." *Fr.* Astrophel and Stella.
Soul's joy, bend not those morning stars from me. *Fr.* Astrophel and Stella.
Splendidis Longum Valedico Nugis. *Fr.* Astrophel and Stella.
Stella Looked On. *Fr.* Astrophel and Stella.
Stella Oft Sees the Very Face of Woe. *Fr.* Astrophel and Stella.
Stella since thou so right a princesse art. *Fr.* Astrophel and Stella.
Stella Sleeping. *Fr.* Astrophel and Stella.
Stella, the fullness of my thoughts of thee. *Fr.* Astrophel and Stella.
Stella, the only planet of my light. *Fr.* Astrophel and Stella.
Stella, think not that I by verse seek fame. *Fr.* Astrophel and Stella.
Strephon and Klaius. *Fr.* Arcadia.
Strife is grown between Virtue and Love, A. *Fr.* Astrophel and Stella.
Such maner time there was. *Fr.* Arcadia.
Sweet kiss, thy sweets I fain would sweetly indite. *Fr.* Astrophel and Stella.
Sweeter Saint I Serve, A. *Fr.* Arcadia.
Tale for Husbands, A. *Fr.* Arcadia.
Thou Blind Man's Mark. *Fr.* Astrophel and Stella.
Though dusty wits dare scorn astrology. *Fr.* Astrophel and Stella.
Thought, with good cause thou likest so well the night. *Fr.* Astrophel and Stella.
To a Sparrow. *Fr.* Astrophel and Stella.
To Sleep. *Fr.* Astrophel and Stella.
To Stella. *Fr.* Astrophel and Stella.
To the Moon. *Fr.* Astrophel and Stella.
To You! To You!
Translated Out of Horace Which Begins Rectius Vives, *tr.*
True Love. *Fr.* Arcadia.
Truth Doth Truth Deserve. *Fr.* Arcadia.
Two Pastorals, *sel.*
Underneath My Window. *Fr.* Astrophel and Stella.
Upon His Meeting with His Two Worthy Friends and Fellow-Poets. *Fr.* Two Pastorals.
Virtue, alas, now let me take some rest. *Fr.* Astrophel and Stella.
Voices at the Window. *Fr.* Astrophel and Stella.
What, have I thus betrayed my liberty? *Fr.* Astrophel and Stella.
What may words say, or what may words not say. *Fr.* Astrophel and Stella.
What Tongue Can Her Perfections Tell? *Fr.* Arcadia.
When far-spent night persuades each mortal eye. *Fr.* Astrophel and Stella.
When nature made her chief work, Stella's eyes. *Fr.* Astrophel and Stella.
When to My Deadly Pleasure.
When Two Suns Do Appear. *Fr.* Arcadia.
Whether the Turkish new-moon minded be. *Fr.* Astrophel and Stella.
Who Hath His Fancy Pleased.
Who Is It That This Dark Night. *Fr.* Astrophel and Stella.
Who will in fairest book of Nature know. *Fr.* Astrophel and Stella.
Whose senses in so ill consort their step-dame Nature lays. *Fr.* Astrophel and Stella.
Why dost thou haste away. *Fr.* Arcadia.
Why Fear to Die? *Fr.* Arcadia.
Wisest scholar of the wight most wise, The. *Fr.* Astrophel and Stella.
With how sad steps, O moon, thou climb'st the skies! *Fr.* Astrophel and Stella.
With what sharp checks I in myself am shent. *Fr.* Astrophel and Stella.
Woe having made, with many fights, his own. *Fr.* Astrophel and Stella.
Wooing Stuff.
Wronged Lover, The. *Fr.* Arcadia.
Ye gote-heard gods, that love the grassie mountaines. *Fr.* Arcadia.
Yoke of Tyranny, The. *Fr.* Astrophel and Stella.
You that do search for every purling spring. *Fr.* Astrophel and Stella.
You that with allegory's curious frame. *Fr.* Astrophel and Stella.
Your words, my friend (right healthful caustics), blame. *Fr.* Astrophel and Stella.

SIDONIUS APOLLINARIS. *See* APOLLINARIS SIDONIUS.

SIEGEL, ELI. All the Smoke.
Shortest Poem in the World, The.

SIEGRIST, MARY. League of Nations, The.
Ongoing, The

SIELLER, WILLIAM VINCENT. Windmill on the Cape.

SIERRA, JUSTO. Bucolic Funeral.

SIGEBERT OF GEMBLOUX. Virgin Martyrs, The.

SIGERSON, DORA. *See* SHORTER, DORA SIGERSON.

SIGERSON, GEORGE. Apostrophe to Death, *tr. Fr.* Carmen Paschale.
Blackbird's Nest, The, *tr.*
Blackbird's Song, The, *tr.*
Book of Leinster, *sel., tr.*
Calling, The.
Carmen Paschale [*or* Easter Song], *sels., tr.*
Christ Quiets the Tempest, *tr. Fr.* Carmen Paschale.
Conall's Head, *tr.*
Cuchulainn's Lament for Ferdiad, *tr.*
Cuchullain's Lament over Fardiad, *tr.*
Deus Meus, *tr.*
Dirge of Cael, The, *tr.*
Eileen Aroon, *tr.*
Fairy Lullaby, *tr.*
Far-away.
Heavenly Pilot, The, *tr. Fr.* Book of Leinster.
In the Heart of Jesus, *tr.*
Incantation, The, *tr.*
Invocation: "Eternal God omnipotent! The One," *tr. Fr.* Carmen Paschale.
Jesukin, *tr.*
Lay of Norse-Irish Sea-Kings, *tr.*
Lost Tribune, The.
Lover and Echo, *tr.*
Love's Despair, *tr.*
Lullaby: "I'll put you, myself, my baby, to slumber," *tr.*
My Own Cáilin Donn.
Roving Worker, The, *tr.*
Ruined Nest, The, *tr.*
Silva Gadelica, *sel., tr.*
Slaughter of the Innocents by Order of King Herod, The, *tr. Fr.* Carmen Paschale.
Smith's Song.
Solace in Winter. *Fr.* Silva Gadelica.
Things Delightful, *tr.*
Vision of MacConglinne, The, *tr.*

SIGERSON, HESTER. Mad Song.

SIGMUND, JAY G. Christ in the Street.
Grubber's Day.
Men Have Forged.
Saint Francis of Assisi Talks with a Priest.

SIGNAIGO, J. AUGUSTINE. On the Heights of Mission Ridge.

SIGOURNEY, LYDIA HUNTLEY. Advertisement of a Lost Day.
Alpine Flowers, The.
California.
Camel's Nose, The.
Columbus.
Coral Insect, The.
Go to Thy Rest.
I Must Not Tease My Mother.
Indian Names.
Indian Summer.
Indian's Welcome to the Pilgrim Fathers, The.
Jesus of Nazareth Passeth By.
Man—Woman.
Return of Napoleon from St. Helena, The.
Stars in My Country's Sky—Are Ye All There?

SIGÜENZA Y GÓNGORA, CARLOS DE. Eastern Evangelic Planet, *sel.*
Invocation and Proposition. *Fr.* Eastern Evangelic Planet.

SIGURJÓNSSON, JÓHANN. Greetings to Norway.
Sonnet, A: "Spring has departed; early days' sweet scent."
Sorrow.

SIKELIANOS, ANGELOS [*or* ANGELO]. Acheloos (the River-God).
Daedalus in Crete, *sel.*
Kleisoura.
Letter from the Front.
March of the Spirit.
On Death, *sel.*
Resistance.
Sacred Way, The.
Stygian Oath, The.

"SILAV-NA-MON." *See* DOLLARD, JAMES BERNARD.

SILBERGER, JULIUS. Reply to Nancy Hanks, A.

"SILESIUS, ANGELUS." *See* "ANGELUS SILESIUS."

SILFVERSTOLPE, GUNNAR MASCOLL. Dreamer, The.

SILKIN, JON. Death of a Bird.
Death of a Son.
Death to Us, A.
First It Was Singing.
Space in the Air, A.

SILL, EDWARD ROWLAND. Appreciated.
Baker's Duzzen uv Wize Sawz, A.
Before Sunrise in Winter.
Broken Sword, The.
Coup de Grace, The.

Dare You?
Dead President, The.
Evening.
Five Lives.
Fool's Prayer, The.
Fool's Prayer, The, *sel.*
For the Gifts of the Spirit.
Force.
Future, The.
Her Explanation.
Home.
Life.
Links of Chance, The.
Lover's Song, The.
Moods.
Morning Thought, A.
Opportunity.
Prayer, A: "O God, our Father, if we had but truth."
Prayer for Peace, A.
Reverie.
Solitude.
Tempted.
To a Maid Demure.
Tropical Morning at Sea, A.
SILL, LOUISE MORGAN. Faith.
SILLÉN, MÄRTA AF. Burden, The.
SILLERY, CHARLES DOYNE. She Died in Beauty.
SILVA, JOSÉ ASUNCIÓN. Art.
First Communion.
Lazarus.
Nocturne: "One night."
SILVERA, EDWARD S. Forgotten Dreams.
Jungle Taste.
On the Death of a Child.
South Street.
SILVERMAN, HAROLD. Improvisation III.
SIMEON BEN ISAAC BEN ABUN OF MAINZ.
All the Hosts of Heaven.
I Come to Supplicate.
SIMMIAS [or SIMIAS]. Decoy Partridge, A.
On Sophocles.
On the Tomb of Sophocles.
Sophocles' Tomb.
To Prote.
Wind, gentle evergreen, to form a shade.
SIMMONS, BARTHOLOMEW. Stanzas to the Memory of Thomas Hood.
To the Memory of Thomas Hood.
SIMMONS, JAMES WRIGHT. Sumter's Band.
SIMMONS, LAURA. At Christmastide.
Bartimeus.
Hail to Thee, Blithe Spirit.
I Have Overcome the World.
Lincoln.
May.
Munition-Maker.
New Year Prayer, A.
Next Time.
Noel! Noel!
Othello: Tomcat.
Pentecost.
Rich Young Man, The.
Toast to Poets, A.
Trimmed Lamp, The.
Vigil.
Way, The.
World Conqueror.
SIMMS, WILLIAM GILMORE. Battle of Eutaw, The.
Decay of a People, The.
Edge of the Swamp, The.
Grape-Vine Swing, The.
Lost Pleiad, The.
Mother and Child.
Night Storm.
Shaded Water, The.
Slain Eagle, The.
Song in March.
Sonnet: "We are a part of all things that we see."
Swamp Fox, The.
'Tis True That Last Night I Adored Thee.
SIMON, JOHN. Two Morsels of Profundity from the Minor Pre-Socratics.
SIMONIDES (of Amorgos). See SEMONIDES.
SIMONIDES (of Ceos). Aeschylus, *wr.*
Archedike.

At Thermopylae.
Athenian Dead, The.
Athenian Monument, The.
Backbiter, The.
Boxer, A.
Cenotaph, A.
Climb to Virtue, The.
Cretan Merchant, A.
Danaë.
Danaë Adrift.
Dead of Athens at Chalcis, The.
Dead of Sparta at Plataea, The.
Dead of Sparta at Thermopylae, The.
Dedication for a Spear.
Epitaph of a Thessalian Hound.
Epitaph to a Merchant.
Friend's Grave, A.
Go tell the Spartans, thou that passest by.
Grave, A.
Greek Dead at Thermopylae, The.
Hound, A.
Hound's Grave, The.
Human Imperfection.
Inscription to Spartans Dead at Thermopylae.
Lamentation of Danaë, The.
Life's Best.
Life's Brevity.
Long, long and dreary is the night.
Lost at Sea ("Ah, misty Geraneia, ill crag, thou shouldst stand facing").
Lost at Sea ("From Sparta to Apollo we").
Lost at Sea ("Go, topless Geraneia").
Lost at Sea ("A strange land holds thy bones").
Lost at Sea ("Thou hast but foreign earth, O Cleisthenes, to hide thee").
Mock Epitaph, A.
Monuments Perish.
Not to Die.
Of those who at Thermopylae were slain.
On a Dog.
On the Army of Spartans, Who Died at Thermopylae.
On the Daughter of Hippias, Son of Pisistratus.
On the Lacedaemonian Dead at Plataea.
On the Spartans Who Fell at Thermopylae.
On Those Who Fell at Plataea.
On Those Who Fell at Thermopylae.
On Two Brothers.
Orpheus.
Per Ardua.
Plataea.
Poet's Friend, The.
Poor Man's Epitaph, A.
Prophetic Death.
Sacrifice of Youth.
Sic Transit.
Spartan Monument, The.
Stillness and Sound.
Tegea.
Thermopylae.
Thermopylae Ode, The.
This is the grave of famed Megistias, whom.
Three Hundred, The.
Thus Sang the Chian Singer.
Timocreon.
Timomachus.
To the Honoured Dead.
Turn of a Dragonfly's Wing, The.
Unlooked-for Bargain, The.
When, in the carven chest.
Who that trusts his mind could believe the man of Lindos, Cleobulus.
Wingèd Change.
Winner of the Pentathlon, A.
SIMONIDES, THE YOUNGER. On Those Who Fell.
SIMONOV, KONSTANTIN MIKHAILOVICH.
I've Searched the Year.
Just Wait for Me.
Rainbow, The.
Tears Cost Her Nothing Anyway.
Trance, The.
Wait, and I'll be home again.
You Remember, Alyosha.
SIMONS, JOHN W. Broadcast, The.
Simeon's Light Remembered.

Whale and the Tiger, The.
SIMONS, KATHERINE DRAYTON MAYRANT ("Kadra Maysi"). Old Name, The.
Stella Maris.
SIMPSON, ALBERT BENJAMIN. Glory to the Name of Jesus!
It Is I, Be Not Afraid.
Jesus Only.
Thy Kingdom Come.
Why Doubt God's Word?
SIMPSON, F. A. Lincoln and Liberty.
SIMPSON, GEORGE S. Simpson's Rest.
SIMPSON, HENRY. In February.
SIMPSON, LOUIS. As Birds Are Fitted to the Boughs.
Ash and the Oak, The.
Green Shepherd, The.
Heroes, The.
I Dreamed That in a City Dark as Paris.
John the Baptist.
Man Who Married Magdalene, The.
Memories of a Lost War.
Nine o'Clock.
Silent Generation, The.
Song: "Let's sing a song together once."
Squeal.
To the Western World.
Tom Pringle.
True Weather for Women, The.
SIMPSON, MABEL. Vigil.
SIMPSON, WILLIAM HASKELL. Bareback. *Fr.* In Arizona.
Burdens. *Fr.* In Arizona.
Hopi Ghosts. *Fr.* In Arizona.
In Arizona, *sels.*
Pity Not. *Fr.* In Arizona.
Trees. *Fr.* In Arizona.
SIMROCK, KARL. German Slumber Song.
Go to Sleep.
SIMS, GEORGE ROBERT ("Dagonet").
Billy's Rose.
By Parcels Post.
Christmas Day in the Workhouse.
Old Actor's Story, The.
'Ostler Joe.
Station-Master's Story, The.
SINCLAIR, DONALD. Path of the Old Spells, The.
SINCLAIR, JOHN. Johnny Sands, *at.*
SINCLAIR, KEITH. Ballad of Halfmoon Bay, The, *at.*
Chronicle of Meola Creek, The.
For a Parting.
Lord of All I Survey.
Moors, Angels, Civil Wars.
Mother.
Night Full of Nothing, A.
War with the Weeds, The.
SINCLAIR, MARY CRAIG (Mrs. Upton Sinclair). Beauty.
SINCLAIR, UPTON. Making of the Soul of Man, The.
On a Steamship.
SINGER, BURNS. Marcus Antoninus Cui Cognomen Erat Aurelius.
SINGER, JOHN. Stepney Green.
SINGER, JOSEPH. Ports Astern.
SINGLETON, MARGARET EVELYN. Christmas Rose.
Insubordination.
Master Musician.
SINGLETON, MARY MONTGOMERIE. See "FANE, VIOLET."
SINISGALLI, LEONARDO. Orphic Interior.
SINKS, P. W. Just Like Me.
SINNETT, PERCY F. Song of the Wild Storm-Waves, The.
SINTON, MARY. See LEITCH, MARY SINTON.
SIPE, MURIEL. Good Morning.
SIRAJ. Benevolence.
House of the Heart, The.
Nightfall.
SITWELL, EDITH. Ass-Face.
Aubade.
By the Lake. *Fr.* Façade.
Coat of Fire, The.
Colonel Fantock.
Daphne.
Dark Song. *Fr.* Façade.
Dirge for the New Sunrise.
Drum, The.

SITWELL, EDITH (*continued*)
Façade, *sels.*
Fan, The.
Fête Galante. *Fr.* Façade.
Gardener Janus Catches a Naiad.
Girl and Butterfly.
Gold Coast Customs, *sel.*
Hambone and the Heart, The.
Harvest.
Heart and Mind.
Holiday.
Hornpipe.
How Many Heavens.
Hymn to Venus.
Interlude.
Invocation: "I who was once a golden woman like those who walk."
King of China's Daughter, The.
Lady with the Sewing-Machine, The.
Lament of Edward Blastock, The.
Little Ghost Who Died for Love, The.
Lullaby: "Though the world has slipped and gone."
Madame Mouse Trots. *Fr.* Façade.
Mademoiselle Richarde.
Most Lovely Shade.
Night Piece.
Old Nurse's Song, The.
Old Woman, An.
Old Woman Laments in Springtime, An.
Panope.
Peach Tree, The.
Perpetuum Mobile.
Sailor, What of the Isles?
Satyr in the Periwig, The. *Fr.* Façade.
Shadow of Cain, The.
Sir Beelzebub. *Fr.* Façade.
Sleeping Beauty, The, *sel.*
Solo for Ear Trumpet.
Song: "In summer when the rose-bushes."
Song: "Now that Fate is dead and gone."
Song: "Once my heart was a summer rose."
Spinning Song.
Spring.
Still Falls the Rain.
Street Song.
Swans, The.
Tears.
Three Poems of the Atomic Bomb, *sel.*
Variations on an Old Nursery Rhyme.
Waltz. *Fr.* Façade.
Web of Eros, The.
When Sir Beelzebub. *Fr.* Façade.
You, the Young Rainbow.
Youth with Red-gold Hair, The.
SITWELL, SIR OSBERT. Aubade: Dick, the Donkey-Boy.
Ballad of Sister Anne, The.
Blind Peddler [*or* Pedlar], The.
Clown Pondi.
Elegy for Mr. Goodbeare.
England Reclaimed, *sel.*
Fountains ("Proud fountains, wave your plumes").
Giardino Pubblico.
How Shall We Rise to Greet the Dawn?
Lament for Richard Rolston.
Lament of the Mole-Catcher, The.
London Squares.
Lousy Peter.
Manner, The.
Mrs. Crudeman.
Mrs. Hague.
Mrs. Southern's Enemy.
On the Coast of Coromandel.
Osmund Toulmin.
Silence of God, The.
Three Nocturns.
To Charlotte Corday.
Trippers.
What Was Your Dream, Doctor Murricombe?
Winter the Huntsman.
SITWELL, SACHEVERELL. Agamemnon's Tomb.
Agamemnon's Tomb, *sel.*
Ballad: White Rose.
Battles of the Centaurs, *sel.*
Belle Isis; Ballad of a Rose. *Fr.* Rosario d'Arabeschi; Poems and Rose Portraits.
Centaurs and Lapithae. *Fr.* Battles of the Centaurs.
Cherry Tree.
Dandelions.
Derbyshire Bluebells.
Farnese Hercules, The.
Fisherman.
Fountains ("This night is pure and clear . . .").
Kingcups.
Landscape with the Giant Orion, *sel.*
Magnolia Tree.
O Rose with Two Hearts. *Fr.* Rosario d'Arabeschi; Poems and Rose Portraits.
Orange Tree by Day. *Fr.* The Red-gold Rain.
Orange Tree by Night. *Fr.* The Red-gold Rain.
Orion Seeks the Goddess Diana. *Fr.* Landscape with the Giant Orion.
Outside Dunsandle.
"Psittachus Eois Imitatrix Ales ab Indis."
Red-gold Rain, The.
Red-gold Rain, The, *sels.*
Rio Grande, The.
River God, The.
Rosario d'Arabeschi; Poems and Rose Portraits, *sels.*
Tulip Tree.
Variation on a Theme by John Lyly.
Venus of Bolsover Castle, The.
SIVLE, PER. Land We Must Have, A.
Tord Foleson.
SJÖBERG, BIRGER. Spanish Moonlight.
SKALDASPILLIR, EYVIND FINNSSON. *See* EYVINDR FINSSON.
SKALLAGRIMSSON, EGILL. Loss of My Sons, The.
SKEAT, WALTER WILLIAM. Villanelle: "It's all a trick, quite easy when you know it."
SKELTON, GLADYS. *See* "PRESLAND, JOHN."
SKELTON, JOHN. Against Garnesche, *sel.*
At the Instance of a Noble Lady.
Auncient Acquaintance, Madam, The.
Ballade of the Scottyshe Kynge, A.
Boke of Phyllyp Sparowe, The, *sels.*
Bowge of Court, The.
Colyn Cloute [*or* Colin Clout], *sels.*
Commendations of Mistress Jane Scrope, The. *Fr.* Phyllyp Sparowe.
Dirge for Phyllip Sparowe, A. *Fr.* Phyllyp Sparowe.
Elinor Rumming [*or* Elynour Rummynge].
Elinor Rumming [*or* Elynour Rummynge], *sels.*
Funeral of Philip Sparrow, The. *Fr.* Phyllyp Sparowe.
Garlande of Laurell, The, *sels.*
Gift of a Skull, The.
Gup, Scot!
Here Folowith Divers Balettis and Dities Solacious, Devised by Master Skelton, Laureate.
House of Fame, The. *Fr.* The Garlande of Laurell.
In Praise of Isabel Pennell. *Fr.* The Garlande of Laurell.
Lullay, Lullay.
Magnificence, *sel.*
Mannerly Margery Milk and Ale.
Maystres Jane Scroupe. *Fr.* Phyllyp Sparowe.
Merry Margaret. *Fr.* The Garlande of Laurell.
Mistress Margaret Hussey. *Fr.* The Garlande of Laurell.
Nun's Lament for Philip Sparrow, The, *sel.* *Fr.* Phyllyp Sparowe.
O Cat of Carlish Kind. *Fr.* Phyllyp Sparowe.
On the Death of the Noble Prince King Edward the Fourth.
Parrot, The. *Fr.* Speak, Parrot.
Parrot's Soliloquy. *Fr.* Speak, Parrot.
Phyllyp Sparowe [*or* Philip Sparrow].
Phyllyp Sparowe [*or* Philip Sparrow], *sels.*
Placebo. *Fr.* Phyllyp Sparowe.
Prayer to the Father of [*or* in] Heaven, A.
Prelates, The. *Fr.* Colyn Cloute.
Salutation to Cardinal Wolsey. *Fr.* Speak, Parrot.
Skelton Laureate, upon a Dead Man's Head.
Sparrow's Dirge, The. *Fr.* Phyllyp Sparowe.
Speak [*or* Speke], Parrot, *sels.*
To Mistress Gertrude Statham. *Fr.* The Garlande of Laurell.
To Mistress [*or* Maystres] Isabel Pennell. *Fr.* The Garlande of Laurell.
To Mistress Margaret Hussey. *Fr.* The Garlande of Laurell.
To Mistress Margery Wentworth. *Fr.* The Garlande of Laurell.
To My Lady Mirriel Howard. *Fr.* The Garlande of Laurell.
To the Holy Ghost.
Tragedy of the Sparrow and the Cursing of the Cat, The. *Fr.* Phyllyp Sparowe.
Tunning of Elinour Rumming [*or* Tunnynge of Elynour Rummynge], The.
Tunning of Elinour Rumming, The, *sels.*
Upon a Dead Man's Head.
Why Were Ye Calliope Embrawdred with Letters of Golde?
With Lullay, Lullay, like a Child.
Woefully Arrayed.
Worldly Prelates. *Fr.* Colyn Cloute.
SKELTON, PHILIP. To God, Ye Choir Above.
SKELTON, ROBIN. Twickenham Grotto.
SKENE, DON. After Reading Twenty Years of Grantland Rice.
SKIDMORE, RUTH MATHER. Fantasy.
SKINNER, CHARLES R. Do It Now.
SKINNER, CONSTANCE LINDSAY. Bear's Song, The, *tr.*
Change-Song, The.
Chief's Prayer after the Salmon Catch, The. *Fr.* Songs of the Coast Dwellers.
Incantation for Healing.
Love Song ("Beautiful is she, this woman"), *tr.*
Love Song ("I lie in the tall grass"), *tr.*
Parting Song, *tr.*
Song for Fine Weather, *tr.*
Song of Basket-weaving.
Song of Cradle-making.
Song of the Full Catch. *Fr.* Songs of the Coast Dwellers.
Song of the Long River.
Song of the Search. *Fr.* Songs of the Coast Dwellers.
Song of Whip-plaiting. *Fr.* Songs of the Coast Dwellers.
Songs of the Coast Dwellers, *sels.*
Wild Woman's Lullaby, The.
SKINNER, CORNELIA OTIS. Path to Shottery, The.
To the Sistine Madonna.
SKINNER, JOHN. Ewie wi' the Crookit Horn, The.
John o' Badenyon.
Lizzy Liberty.
Tullochgorum.
SKINNER, MARTYN. Letters to Malaya, *sel.*
SKINNER, MURRAY. Futile Sacrifice.
SKIPIS, SOTORIS. O Sweet Athens.
You Will Remember Me.
SKIPSEY, JOSEPH. Butterfly, The.
Dewdrop [Wind and Sun].
Merry Bee, A.
Miner Laddie, The.
Mother Wept.
Violet and the Rose, The.
SKIRVING, ADAM. Hey Johnnie Cope.
Johnnie Cope.
SKJOLDBORG, JOHAN. Cotter's Song.
Morning Song.
SKRINE, NESTA HIGGINSON. *See* "O'NEILL, MOIRA."

SLADE, MARY B. C. Mount Vernon's Bells.
Sleep, Darling, Sleep.
SLADEN, DOUGLAS BROOKE WHEELTON.
Charles II, *sel.*
Christmas Letter from Australia, A.
Salopia Inhospitalis.
Sunset on the Cunimbla Valley, Blue Mountains.
Tropics, The.
Under the Wattle.
SLATER, ELEANOR. Ballad of Wonder, A.
Bigot.
Cradle Carol.
December Twenty-fourth.
Misdirection.
Petition.
Sight and Insight.
SLATER, FRANCIS CAREY ("Jan van Avond"). Drought, *sels.*
Karroo, The, *sels.*
Lament for a Dead Cow.
Milking Kraal.
Wood-Gatherers, The.
SLATER, JOHN ROTHWELL. Easter Reveille, An.
SLATER, MARY WHITE. Butterfly.
Playmates.
Sandman, The.
SLEDD, BENJAMIN. At Lexington.
Innominata.
L'Inferno.
My Silent Guest.
Vision of the Milk-white Doe, The.
Wind and the Wires, The.
Wraith of Roanoke, The.
SLEIGH, BERNARD. Hazel Dorn.
SLEMP, JOHN CALVIN. I Sought the Living God.
O Christ, Who Died.
SLENDER, PAULINE. Vagrant, The.
SLESSOR, KENNETH. Beach Burial.
Country Towns.
Crow Country.
Earth-Visitors.
Five Bells.
Five Visions of Captain Cook.
Five Visions of Captain Cook, *sel.*
Gulliver.
Last Trams, *sel.*
Mermaids.
Metempsychosis.
Night-Ride, The.
Sensuality.
Sleep.
Stars.
Two Chronometers. *Fr.* Five Visions of Captain Cook.
Waters.
SLOAN, ERROL B. And Yet.
SLOAN, JOCELYN MACY. Eliza Telefair.
SOLONIMSKI, ANTONI. All.
He Is My Countryman.
London Spring.
Morning and Evening.
Remembrance.
"SMALACOMBE, JOHN." *See* MACKAY, LOUIS ALEXANDER.
SMALL, BLANCHE D. Antique Dresden Porcelain, Marked "Do Not Handle."
SMALL, FLOYD B. Root Hog or Die.
SMALL, JAMES G. I've found a Friend, O such a Friend!
SMALL, SAMUEL W. Them Yankee Blankits.
SMÁRI, JAKOB JÓHANNESSON. Harp, The.
SMART, ALEXANDER. Better than Gold, *at.*
Herd Laddie, The.
Last Day of the Year, The.
Still Small Voice, The.
SMART, CHRISTOPHER. Adoration. *Fr.* A Song to David.
Blockhead and Beehive, The, *sel.*
Cat, The. *Fr.* Jubilate Agno.
Catholic Amen, The. *Fr.* A Song to David.
Christmas Day. *Fr.* Hymns and Spiritual Songs.
Dog in the River, The, *tr.*
Easter Day, *sel.*
Flowers. *Fr.* Jubilate Agno.
Flowers Are Great Blessings. *Fr.* Jubilate Agno.
For I Will Consider My Cat Jeoffry. *Fr.* Jubilate Agno.
For the Letter ל Which Signifies God. *Fr.* Jubilate Agno.
Gift of Song, The, *tr.*
Glorious the Sun in Mid Career. *Fr.* A Song to David.
God's Creatures.
Hymns and Spiritual Songs, *sel.*
Hymns for the Amusement of Children, *sel.*
Imagination. *Fr.* Reason and Imagination.
Jubilate Agno, *sels.*
Kneel to the Lord. *Fr.* On the Goodness of the Supreme Being.
Lark's Nest, A. *Fr.* Hymns for the Amusement of Children.
Lass with the Golden Locks, The.
Let Elizur Rejoice with the Partridge. *Fr.* Jubilate Agno.
Let Lotan Rejoice with Sauterelle. *Fr.* Jubilate Agno.
Let Peter Rejoice with the Moon Fish. *Fr.* Jubilate Agno.
Man and the Weasel, The, *tr.*
Man of Prayer, The. *Fr.* A Song to David.
Mermaid's Pap, The. *Fr.* A Song to David.
Mowers, The. *Fr.* A Noon Piece; or, The Mowers at Dinner.
My Cat Jeoffry. *Fr.* Jubilate Agno.
Nativity of Our Lord, The.
Noon Piece, A; or, The Mowers at Dinner, *sel.*
Ode to the Earl of Northumberland, *sel.*
Odes (*of* Horace), *sel., tr.*
On a Bed of Guernsey Lilies. *Fr.* Ode to the Earl of Northumberland.
On the Goodness of the Supreme Being, *sel.*
Paradise.
Patriots of Mankind.
Poet, The. *Fr.* The Blockhead and Beehive.
Praise.
Psalm VIII, *sel., par.*
Psalm CXLVIII, *par.*
Reason and Imagination, *sel.*
Rejoice in God. *Fr.* Jubilate Agno.
Rejoice in the Lamb.
Rejoice in the Lamb, *sel.*
St. Philip and St. James, *sel.*
Search for Pearls, The. *Fr.* Jubilate Agno.
Song: "Where shall Celia fly for shelter."
Song of David, The. *Fr.* A Song to David.
Song to David, A.
Song to David, A, *sels.*
Spring.
Stars, The.
Stars, The, *sel.*
Strength. *Fr.* A Song to David.
Strong Is the Horse upon His Speed. *Fr.* A Song to David.
Swans, Lilies, and Doves.
This Is Thy Gift, O Muse, *tr. Fr.* Odes.
SMART, RICHARD. *See* SMERT, RICHARD.
SMEDLEY, MENELLA BUTE. Little Fair Soul, The.
Wind Me a Summer Crown.
SMEETON, JOHN P. Jack Frost in the Garden.
SMELYAKOV, YAROSLAV. Nazim Hikmet.
SMERT [*or* SMART], RICHARD. Blessed May Thou Be, Sweet Jesus, *at.*
Jesu, Fili Virginis, *at.*
SMERT, RICHARD, *and* JOHN TROULUFFE. *See* TROULUFFE, JOHN, *and* RICHARD SMERT.
SMET, JOACHIM. Rush Hour.
SMETHAM, JAMES. Soul's Departure, The.
SMIBERT, THOMAS. Scottish Widow's Lament, The.
SMILEY, JOSEPH BERT. St. Peter at the Gate.
SMIRNOV, SERGEI. At Night.
Earth.
Waterdrop.
SMIRNOW, LOUIS MAIR. Shortly After.
SMITH, A. BABINGTON. To Saint Francis.
SMITH, A. C. Waif, The.
SMITH, ADA. In City Streets.
SMITH, ALEXANDER. Autumn. *Fr.* A Life-Drama.
Barbara.
Beauty.
Edinburgh.
For Posterity.
Forerunners. *Fr.* A Life-Drama.
Fragment from a Ballad, A.
Glasgow.
King Dying on the Battle-Field, The.
Lady Barbara.
Life-Drama, A, *sels.*
Love.
Minor Poet, A. *Fr.* A Life-Drama.
Night before the Wedding, The; or, Ten Years After.
Quaint Character, A. *Fr.* A Life-Drama.
Scorned.
Sea-Marge. *Fr.* A Life-Drama.
To ——: "Broken moon lay, The."
SMITH, ANNE MAY. At the Zoo.
SMITH, ARABELLA EUGENIA. If I Should Die Tonight.
SMITH, ARTHUR JAMES MARSHALL. Archer, The.
Ballade un Peu Banale.
Brigadier, *tr.*
Face, The.
Far West.
Fountain, The.
Good Friday.
Hyacinth for Edith, A.
Lonely Land, The.
Mermaid, The.
News of the Phoenix.
Noctambule.
Ode: Eumenides, The.
Ode: On the Death of William Butler Yeats.
Plot against Proteus, The.
Prothalamium.
Shadows There Are.
Sonnet: "How all men wrongly death to dignify."
Universe into Stone.
SMITH, BELLE E. *See* SMITH, ARABELLA EUGENIA.
SMITH, CHARD POWERS. Along the Wind.
SMITH, CHARLOTTE. Beachy Head, *sel.*
Elegiac Sonnet.
First Swallow, The.
Gossamer, The.
Nautilus, The.
Sonnet: Written at the Close of Spring.
Swallow, The.
SMITH, CICELY FOX. Afoot.
Hastings Mill.
In Prize.
In the Trades.
Pictures.
Sailor's Delight.
Saint George of England.
Skipper.
Traveller, The.
Traveller's Rest.
What the Old Man Said.
SMITH, CLARK ASHTON. Dream of Beauty, A.
Eldritch Dark, The.
Envoys, The.
Fantaisie d'Antan.
Fragment: "This I remember clearly: from stone to stepping-stone."
Hashish-Eater, The.
Hill-Top, The.
In Thessaly.
Nero, *sel.*
Nightmare.
Nyctalops.
Outlanders.
Resurrection.
Shadows.
Strange Girl.
Town Lights.
Warning.

SMITH, DANIEL. *Donzella* and the *Ceylon*, The, *at.*
SMITH, DEXTER. Our National Banner.
SMITH, DILL ARMOR. Forty Years Ago, *at.*
Twenty Years Ago, *at.*
SMITH, EDGAR. Heaven Will Protect the Working Girl.
Heaven Will Protect the Working Girl, *sel.*
SMITH, ELIZABETH OAKES (Mrs. Seba Smith). Drowned Mariner, The.
Sinless Child, The, *sel.*
SMITH, F. BURGE. Little Golden-hair.
SMITH, FLORENCE. Song: "How pleasant it is that always."
SMITH, FLORENCE MARGARET. *See* SMITH, STEVIE.
SMITH, GOLDIE CAPERS. Dog at the Schoolhouse Door.
Prayer for Dogs, A.
SMITH, GOLDWIN. I'll twine white violets and the myrtle green, *tr.*
Loss after Loss, *tr.*
Nature's Travail, *tr.*
On the Death of a Young and Favorite Slave, *tr.*
Ruins of Corinth, The, *tr.*
This Stone, *tr.*
To Chloe, *tr.*
To Pyrrha, *tr.*
SMITH, GWEN A. Off We Go to Market.
SMITH, HARRY BACHE. Armorer's Song, The.
Her Faults.
I Didn't Like Him.
Idol's Eye, The, *sel.*
Long Night, The.
My Angeline. *Fr.* The Wizard of the Nile.
Same Old Story.
Song of the Turnkey, The.
Tattooed Man, The. *Fr.* The Idol's Eye.
Wizard of the Nile, The, *sel.*
SMITH, HELEN C. Mother's Heritage.
SMITH, HELEN L. Boy and Girl of Plymouth.
Columbus.
September Days.
SMITH, HELEN ROGERS. He Lifted from the Dust.
SMITH, HENRY LEE. Journey's End, The.
SMITH, HILDA WORTHINGTON. Carpenter of Galilee, The.
SMITH, HORACE [*or* HORATIO]. Address to the Mummy [at Belzoni's Exhibition].
Bit of Colour, A.
Gouty Merchant and the Stranger, The.
Hymn to the Flowers.
Jester Condemned to Death, The.
Living Lustres, The.
Moral Cosmetics.
Tale of Drury Lane, A.
SMITH, HORACE [*or* HORATIO], *and* JAMES SMITH. Baby's Debut, The.
Loyal Effusion.
Theatre, The, *sel.*
SMITH, JAMES. Baloo, My Bairnie, Fa Asleep.
Playhouse Musings.
Surnames.
SMITH, JAMES, *and* HORACE SMITH. *See* SMITH, HORACE, *and* JAMES SMITH.
SMITH, JOHN (1580–1631). Sea Mark, The.
SMITH [*or* SMYTH], JOHN (1662–1717). Strephon.
SMITH, JOSEPH. Eulogium on Rum.
SMITH, KAY. Child's Poem.
Eye of Humility, The.
O Light.
What the Madman Sees Looking in the Window.
What Then, Dancer?
When a Girl Looks Down.
SMITH, LANGDON. Evolution.
SMITH, LANTA WILSON. This, Too, Shall Pass Away.
SMITH, LEROY, JR. Salvation Prospect.
Sappho Rehung.
Spring Song.
What Sanguine Beast?
SMITH, LEWIS WORTHINGTON. News from Yorktown.
SMITH, MARION COUTHOUY. King of the Belgians.
Perfect Sign, The.
Star, The; Dedicated to Theodore Roosevelt.
SMITH, MARTIN SEYMOUR. All Devils Fading.
SMITH, MARY BRAINERD. Poor for Our Sakes.
SMITH, MAY RILEY. Child in Me, The.
Christmas Roses.
Departure.
God's Plans.
His Birthday.
If We Knew.
Last Dance, The.
My Life Is a Bowl.
My Uninvited Guest.
O Bells in the Steeple.
Scatter Seeds of Kindness.
Sometime.
Sorrow in a Garden.
Tired Mothers.
Tree-Top Road, The.
Two Valentines.
SMITH, NAOMI GWLADYS ROYDE-. *See* ROYDE-SMITH, NAOMI GWLADYS.
SMITH, NINNA MAY. If Some Grim Tragedy.
SMITH, NORA ARCHIBALD. Feast of the Doll, The.
Haughty Aspen, The.
Meadow Talk.
Morning in the Market.
Neighbors of the Christ Night.
SMITH, NORMA E. Evangeline.
SMITH, OSWALD J. Saviour Can Solve Every Problem, The.
SMITH, PHOEBE. Via Dolorosa.
SMITH, SAMUEL FRANCIS. America.
Daybreak.
Flower-strewn Graves.
Memorial Day. *Fr.* Our Honored Heroes.
Morning Light Is Breaking, The.
Our Honored Heroes.
Our Honored Heroes, *sel.*
Tree-planting.
SMITH, SEBA ("Major Jack Downing").
Frozen Girl, The.
Mother's Sacrifice, The.
Snow Storm, The, *sel.*
Young Charlotte.
SMITH, MRS. SEBA. *See* SMITH, ELIZABETH OAKES.
SMITH, SHEILA KAYE-. *See* KAYE-SMITH, SHEILA.
SMITH, SIDNEY GOODSIR. Can I Forget?
Deevil's Waltz, The.
Defeat o' the Hert.
Exile.
Largo.
Mandrake Hert, The.
Saagin.
Sang: Recoll o Skaith.
Whan the Hert Is Laich.
Ye Spier Me.
SMITH, STEVIE (Florence Margaret Smith). Bereaved Swan, The.
Deathly Child, The.
Ghost, The.
God Speaks to the Man in Despair.
Heavenly City, The.
Le Désert de l'Amour.
Little Boy Lost, The.
River God, The.
To the Tune of the Coventry Carol.
Touch and Go.
Weak Monk, The.
SMITH, SYDNEY. Recipe for a Salad, A.
Salad, A.
SMITH, SYDNEY GOODSIR. *See* SMITH, SIDNEY GOODSIR.
SMITH, VIVIAN. Old Men Are Facts.
SMITH, WALTER. Carpenter of Nazareth, The.
SMITH, WALTER CHALMERS. Best Way, The.
Christian Paradox, The.
Daughters of Philistia. *Fr.* Olrig Grange.
Glenaradale.
Miss Penelope Leith.
Olrig Grange, *sel.*
Scattered.
Self-exiled, The.
Wish, A.
SMITH, WILLIAM. Chloris, *sels.*
Colin, my dear and most entire beloved. *Fr.* Chloris.
Feed, silly sheep, although your keeper pineth. *Fr.* Chloris.
My Love, I Cannot Thy Rare Beauties Place. *Fr.* Chloris.
Notable Description of the World, A, *at.*
Sonnet: "My Love, I cannot thy rare beauties place." *Fr.* Chloris.
To the Most Excellent and Learned Shepherd, Colin Clout. *Fr.* Chloris.
When I more large thy praises forth shall show. *Fr.* Chloris.
Whole showers of tears to Chloris I will pour. *Fr.* Chloris.
SMITH, WILLIAM HART-. *See* HART-SMITH, WILLIAM.
SMITH, WILLIAM JAY. American Primitive.
Antelope.
Asides, *tr.*
At the Tombs of the House of Savoy.
Autumn.
Butterfly.
Cigarette, The, *tr.*
Closing of the Rodeo, The.
Complaint of the King of Thule, *tr.*
Complaint on the Oblivion of the Dead, *tr.*
Convoy.
Cupidon.
Dead Snake.
Death of a Jazz Musician.
Dream.
Elegy: "I stood between two mirrors when you died."
First Night, The, *tr.*
Gull.
Hot Stagnant Evening, A, *tr.*
Hotel Continental.
I Hear My Sacred Heart Beat, *tr.*
Impossible, The, *tr.*
Laughing Time.
Mid-July Twilight, Eight o'Clock, *tr.*
Mr. Smith.
Mrs. Caribou.
Monkey.
Moon Solo, *tr.*
Morning at Arnheim.
Neo-classical Poem.
Opossum.
Over and Under.
Pavane for the Nursery, A.
Persian Miniature.
Plain Talk.
Processional.
Romance, *tr.*
Rondeau: "Lord, I'm done for: now Margot."
Seal.
Spring Evening on the Boulevards, *tr.*
Summer Landscape, *tr.*
Things.
3 for 25.
Thunderbolt, *tr.*
Today I Have Touched the Earth.
Twilight, *tr.*
Wooing Lady, The.
Yak.
Zebra.
SMITH, WILLIAM WYE. Second Concession of Deer, The.
SMITH-DAMPIER, E. M. Avenging Daughters, The, *tr.*
Maiden Hind, The, *tr.*
For other translations from Danish, see BoDaBa.
SMITHYMAN, KENDRICK. Considerations of Norfolk Island, *sel.*
Could You Once Regain.

Defenceless Children, Your Great Enemy.
Dirge for Two Clavichords and Bowler Hat.
Elegy against a Latter Day.
Evening Music.
Icarus.
Incident at Matauri.
Moment, The.
Night Walkers, The.
Personal Poem.
This Blonde Girl.
Waiwera.
Walk Past Those Houses on a Sunday Morning.
SMOLLETT, TOBIAS GEORGE. Independence. *Fr.* Ode to Independence.
Ode to Independence.
Ode to Independence, *sel.*
Ode to Leven Water.
Ode to Sleep.
Tears of Scotland, The.
To Leven Water.
SMULLER, E. A. Thanksgivings of Old.
SMYTH, FLORIDA WATTS. Eternal Contour.
Green Mountain Boy.
North and South.
Unclaimed.
SMYTH, JOHN. *See* SMITH, JOHN (1662–1717).
SMYTHE, ALBERT ERNEST STAFFORD. Anastasis.
Death the Revealer.
November Sunshine.
Seasons of the Gods, The.
Trysting Path, The.
Way of the Master, The.
SMYTHE, DANIEL. From My Thought.
Transcontinental Bus.
SMYTTAN, GEORGE HUNT. Forty days and forty nights.
SNAITH, STANLEY. Birds in the Flax.
Blue Ghosts.
Discovery, The.
Dust.
Gulls.
Hare, The.
Parachute.
Scythe, The.
Stack, The.
To Some Builders of Cities.
SNIDER, P. M. Communion.
SNODGRASS, C. A. Poem for Christmas, A.
SNODGRASS, WILLIAM DEWITT. April Inventory.
Heart's Needle, *sels.*
Marsh, The.
Mousetrap, The, *tr.*
Ten Days Leave.
SNOILSKY, COUNT CARL. Aphrodite and the Knife-Grinder.
Benvenuto Cellini.
Birds on a Telegraph Wire.
Black Swans.
Edelweiss.
Introductory Song: "I stand with roses beside the highway." *Fr.* Travel Scenes.
King Erik.
Noli Me Tangere.
Old China.
Porcelain Factory, The.
Sorrento.
Travel Scenes, *sel.*
SNORRI STURLUSON. Frothi's Meal, *sel.* *Fr.* The Younger Edda.
Younger [*or* Snorra *or* Prose] Edda, The, *sel.*
SNOW, LAURA A. BARTER. God Is In Every Tomorrow.
SNOW, ROGER VINTON. State of Maine Song.
SNOW, SOPHIA P. Annie and Willie's Prayer.
SNOW, WILBERT. Aged Ninety Years.
SNYDER, GARY. Burning. *Fr.* Myths & Texts.
For a Far-out Friend.
Myths & Texts, *sel.*
Praise for Sick Women.
Riprap.
This Tokyo.
SOAMES [*or* SOAME], SIR WILLIAM, *and* JOHN DRYDEN. Art poétique, L', *sels., tr.*
Fantastick Mind, The, *tr.* *Fr.* L'Art poétique.
SOBILOFF, HY. Airship.
Cubism.
My Mother's Table.
Painting of a Lobster by Picasso.
Pittsburgh.
Unquestionable Questions.
Upon Differences of Opinion.
SODERBECK, ELEANOR FOOTE. Great Towers of Steel.
SÖDERBERG, HJALMAR. Darkness Gathers, The.
SÖDERGRAN, EDITH. Moon, The.
SODO. Spring in My Hut.
SOIN. Dewdrops.
SOKAN. Fan, The.
SOLIS-COHEN, SOLOMON. Out of the Beast.
Spiritual Vision.
For translations from Hebrew, see LiTW; TrJP.
"SOLOGUB, FEODOR" (Feodor Kuzmich Teternikov). Amphora, The.
Austere My Verse.
Austere the Music of My Songs.
Devil's Swing, The.
Evil Dragon.
God, who created me from sodden clay.
I came. Cool are the meadows here.
In a Gay Jar.
Jar, The.
Lullaby in Undertones.
She was in a village by a forest side.
Stifling day was harsh and hot, The.
We Are Weary.
When, Tossed upon the Stormy Waters.
SOLOMON, MARVIN. Cat and the Bird, The.
Garden, The.
Giraffe, The.
Lemon Sherbet.
Vole, The.
SOLOMON EPHRAIM BEN AARON OF LENCZICZ. These Things I Do Remember.
SOLOMOS, DIONYSIOS. Cretan, The.
Destruction of Psara, The.
Dream, The, *sel.*
Easter Day. *Fr.* Lambros.
Free Besieged, The, *sels.*
Hymn to Liberty, *sel.*
I Walked the Road of the Dawn. *Fr.* The Free Besieged.
Lambros, *sels.*
Maria's Dream. *Fr.* Lambros.
Maria's Prayer. *Fr.* Lambros.
Temptation. *Fr.* The Free Besieged.
To Francesca Frazer.
SOLOMOS, GEORGE P. Wisdom of the Gazelle.
SOLON. Constitution of Athens, The.
Diversity of Gifts.
Lawgiver's Boast, The.
Nor Gold nor Silver.
O ye splendid children of Memory and Zeus the Olympian.
Protectress of Athens, The.
Rise of Dictatorship, The.
Rule of Fair Play.
Shame of Losing Salamis, The.
Soldier, The.
Which of the aims that spurred me to unite.
SOLOVIEV, VLADIMIR SERGEYEVICH. Dearest One.
Do you not see, Beloved?
L'Onda dal Mar' Divisa.
Once in the misty dawn with timid foot.
With Wavering Feet I Walked.
SOLSTAD, EINAR. Young Girl.
SOMERVILE [*or* SOMERVILLE], WILLIAM. Address to His Elbow-Chair, New Cloath'd, An.
Chace, The, *sel.*
Hare-hunting. *Fr.* The Chace.
Presenting to a Lady a White Rose and a Red, on the Tenth of June.
SONÉ. Blessed.
SOPHOCLES. AJAX, *sels.*
Ajax, before His Suicide. *Fr.* Ajax.
Ajax! to All Farewell! *Fr.* Ajax.
Ajax's Death. *Fr.* Ajax.
Antigone, *sels.*
Antigone Entombed Alive. *Fr.* Antigone.
As It Was in the Beginning Is Now and Ever Shall Be. *Fr.* Antigone.
Before Death. *Fr.* Ajax.
Bitterness. *Fr.* Ajax.
Bitter-sweet is the ailment called love.
Blindness. *Fr.* Oedipus Rex.
Burial Urn, The [*or* A]. *Fr.* Electra.
Buried Alive. *Fr.* Antigone.
Calchas the Seer. *Fr.* Ajax.
Castaway, The. *Fr.* Philoctetes.
Chariot-Race, A. *Fr.* Electra.
Childhood's Immunity from Inward Sorrows. *Fr.* Trachiniae.
Choral Ode: "Numberless are the world's wonders." *Fr.* Antigone.
Choral Ode: "Wonders are many, and none is more wonderful than man." *Fr.* Antigone.
Choral Poem: "Land beloved of horsemen, fair, The." *Fr.* Oedipus at Colonus.
Chorus: "Fair Salamis, the billow's roar." *Fr.* Ajax.
Chorus: "For this one thing above all I would be praised as a man." *Fr.* Oedipus Rex.
Chorus: "Oh, may my constant feet not fail." *Fr.* Oedipus Rex.
Chorus: "What man is he that yearneth." *Fr.* Oedipus at Colonus.
Creon. *Fr.* Oedipus Rex.
"Cursed Be He Who First Taught Grecians War." *Fr.* Ajax.
Death of Jocasta, The. *Fr.* Oedipus Rex.
Decay, Earth's Universal Law. *Fr.* Oedipus at Colonus.
Deianira's Love Charm. *Fr.* Trachiniae.
Deianira's Wooing. *Fr.* Trachiniae.
Doubt Not a Dream. *Fr.* Electra.
Dreams Come True. *Fr.* Electra.
Edge of the World, The.
Electra, *sels.*
Embittered Youth. *Fr.* Philoctetes.
Endure what life God gives and ask no longer span. *Fr.* Oedipus at Colonus.
Everything Decays. *Fr.* Oedipus at Colonus.
Evils of Money, The. *Fr.* Antigone.
Fatal Discovery. *Fr.* Oedipus Rex.
Fortune Is like the Moon.
Girls, look you, Kupris is not Kupris only.
Glories of Athens, The. *Fr.* Oedipus at Colonus.
God and Man. *Fr.* Oedipus Rex.
God of War, The.
Grove of Colonus, The. *Fr.* Oedipus at Colonus.
Hard it is that impious men, of base forebears.
He Sins Not Who Sins Unwittingly. *Fr.* Oedipus at Colonus.
Hecate.
Heracles. *Fr.* Trachiniae.
Heracles' Errant Love. *Fr.* Trachiniae.
Higher Command, The. *Fr.* Antigone.
In Time of Pestilence. *Fr.* Oedipus Rex.
Jocasta's Death. *Fr.* Oedipus Rex.
Last Journey, The. *Fr.* Antigone.
Light and Shadow. *Fr.* Electra.
Love, Conquering and Unconquerable. *Fr.* Antigone.
Lovely Colonus! *Fr.* Oedipus at Colonus.
Man; Creation's Masterpiece. *Fr.* Antigone.
Melting Ice.
Musings on Man's Sad Estate. *Fr.* Ajax.
Night Fears.

SOPHOCLES (*continued*)
Now am I nought—abandoned: oftentimes.
Nuptials of Haemon and Antigone, The. *Fr.* Antigone.
"O Dark, Dark, Dark Amid the Blaze of Noon." *Fr.* Oedipus Rex.
O Welcome! Gentle Death. *Fr.* Ajax.
Oedipus at Colonus, *sels.*
Oedipus, King-Saviour. *Fr.* Oedipus Rex.
Oedipus' Last Hour. *Fr.* Oedipus at Colonus.
Oedipus Rex, *sels.*
Old Age. *Fr.* Oedipus at Colonus.
Old Age the Friendless. *Fr.* Oedipus at Colonus.
Omniscience Granted to No Man. *Fr.* Antigone.
Out of Suffering, Tolerance. *Fr.* Oedipus at Colonus.
Outlaw, The. *Fr.* Oedipus Rex.
Paean of Joy. *Fr.* Trachiniae.
Passing of Oedipus, The. *Fr.* Oedipus at Colonus.
People Pray, The. *Fr.* Oedipus Rex.
Philoctetes, *sels.*
Philoctetes Deserted. *Fr.* Philoctetes.
Philoctetes Robbed of His Bow. *Fr.* Philoctetes.
Pity the Captive Maiden's Lot. *Fr.* Trachiniae.
Plaint of the Nightingale, The. *Fr.* Electra.
Power of Love, The ("My children, know Love is not Love alone").
Power of Love, The ("When Love disputes"). *Fr.* Antigone.
Riddle, A: "Though the goddess made you wonder, do believe the things she said."
Scruple. *Fr.* Philoctetes.
Sleep! *Fr.* Philoctetes.
State versus Conscience, The. *Fr.* Antigone.
Stolen Bow, The. *Fr.* Philoctetes.
Suave Mari Magno.
Tecmessa. *Fr.* Ajax.
Tecmessa's Fruitless Plea. *Fr.* Ajax.
Thebes of the Seven Gates. *Fr.* Antigone.
Trachiniae [*or* Trachinian Maidens], *sels.*
Triumph of Time, The. *Fr.* Oedipus at Colonus.
Unconquerable Love. *Fr.* Antigone.
Undying Law, The. *Fr.* Antigone.
Universal Change. *Fr.* Ajax.
Unpalatable Truths. *Fr.* Ajax.
"Vanity of Vanities; All Is Vanity." *Fr.* Oedipus Rex.
Victory over Aggressors. *Fr.* Antigone.
Void of a Joyless Heart, The. *Fr.* Antigone.
Wanderings of Heracles, The. *Fr.* Trachiniae.
What a Piece of Work Is a Man. *Fr.* Antigone.
When Pestilence Strikes. *Fr.* Oedipus Rex.
Wind in the Poplars.
Womankind.
SORELL, WALTER. All That Matters.
SØRENSEN, POUL. Centaur, The.
SORG, HENRY CHARLES. Praise of Mary, *tr.*
SORLEY, CHARLES HAMILTON. All the Hills and Vales Along.
Expectans Expectavi.
Marlborough, *sel.*
Peer Gynt.
Rooks.
Route March.
Saints have adored the lofty soul of you. *Fr.* Two Sonnets.
Seekers, The.
Song of the Ungirt Runners, The.
Sonnet: "Saints have adored the lofty soul of you." *Fr.* Two Sonnets.
Sonnet: "Such, such is Death: no triumph: no defeat." *Fr.* Two Sonnets.
Such, such is Death: no triumph: no defeat. *Fr.* Two Sonnets.
To Germany.
To Poets.
Two Sonnets.
Two Sonnets on Death.
SORRENTINO, GILBERT. Classic Case, A.
Zoo, The.
SOSEI (Sosei Hoshi). Forgetfulness.
Only because she said.
She said she would come.
You bring no joy, but strange regret.
SOSEKI. How can I tell you, dear.
SOTO DE ROJAS, PEDRO. Penitence.
SOULARY, JOSEPH MARIE [*or* JOSÉPHIN DE]. Ambitious Dreams.
SOUSTER, RAYMOND. Drunk; on Crutches.
Enemies, The.
Ersatz.
Falling of the Snow, The.
Flight of the Roller-Coaster.
Girl Asleep.
Hunter, The.
Mother, The.
Need of an Angel.
Phony War.
Postscript.
Reality.
Search.
Speakers, Columbus Circle.
Sunday Night Walk.
This Poem Will Never Be Finished.
When I See Old Men.
SOUTAR, WILLIAM. Ballad: "O! shairly ye hae seen my love."
Children, The.
Gowk, The.
In the Mood of Blake.
"Nation Shall Speak Peace . . ."
Parable.
Permanence of the Young Men, The.
Poetry.
Revelation.
Song: "Whaur yon broken brig hings owre."
Star, The.
Thocht, The.
Tryst, The.
Wait for the Hour.
SOUTER, CHARLES HENRY. Bound for Sourabaya!
Mallee Fire, The.
SOUTHERNE, THOMAS. Maid's Last Prayer, The, *sel.*
Sir Antony [*or* Anthony] Love, *sel.*
Song: "Pursuing beauty, men descry." *Fr.* Sir Antony Love.
Song in the Second Act, A. *Fr.* Sir Antony Love.
Song, Set by H. Purcell, and Sung by Mrs. Hodgson, A. *Fr.* The Maid's Last Prayer.
Though You Make No Return. *Fr.* The Maid's Last Prayer.
SOUTHESK, EARL OF. *See* CARNEGIE, JAMES, EARL OF SOUTHESK.
SOUTHEY, CAROLINE ANNE BOWLES. *See* BOWLES, CAROLINE ANNE.
SOUTHEY, ROBERT. Abenamar, Abenamar, *tr.*
Absolvers, The. *Fr.* A Vision of Judgement.
After Blenheim.
Among His Books.
Battle of Blenheim, The.
Bishop Hatto [and the Rats].
Bower of Peace, The. *Fr.* Ode Written during the War with America, 1814.
Calm Sea, A.
Cataract of Lodore, The.
Curse of Kehama, The, *sels.*
Emmet's Epitaph.
Father William.
Fountain of the Fairies, The.
God's Judgment [*or* Judgement] on a Wicked Bishop.
God's Judgment on Hatto.
His Books.
Holly Tree, The.
Homeward Bound.
Imitated from the Persian.
Immortality of Love, The. *Fr.* The Curse of Kehama.
Inchcape Rock, The.
Inscription for a Tablet on the Banks of a Stream.
King of the Crocodiles, The.
Legend of Bishop Hatto, The.
Lord, Who Art Merciful, *tr.*
Malice. *Fr.* The Curse of Kehama.
March to Moscow, The.
Mary, the Maid of the Inn.
Morning Mist, The.
My Days among the Dead Are Past [*or* Passed].
Night [in the Desert]. *Fr.* Thalaba the Destroyer.
O God! Have Mercy, in This Dreadful Hour.
Ode, Written during the Negociations with Buonaparte, in January, 1814.
Ode Written during the War with America, 1814, *sel.*
Old Man's Comforts [and How He Gained Them], The.
Old Mansion, The, *sel.*
Old Woman of Berkeley, The.
On the Speech of Robert Emmet.
Pig, The.
Prelude: "Tell us a story, old Robin Gray!"
St. Romuald.
Scholar, The.
Soldier's Wife, The.
Sonnet: "Go, Valentine, and tell that lovely Maid."
Thalaba and the Banquet. *Fr.* Thalaba the Destroyer.
Thalaba and the Magic Thread. *Fr.* Thalaba the Destroyer.
Thalaba the Destroyer, *sels.*
To a Bee.
Traveller's Return, The.
Vision of Judgement, A, *sel.*
Wat Tyler, *sel.*
Well of St. Keyne, The.
Widow, The.
Winter.
Written Immediately after Reading the Speech of Robert Emmet.
Written on a Sunday Morning.
Written on the First of December, 1793.
SOUTHEY, ROBERT, *and* CAROLINE ANNE BOWLES. Greenwood Shrift, The.
SOUTHEY, ROBERT, *and* SAMUEL TAYLOR COLERIDGE. Devil's Thoughts, The.
Devil's Thoughts, The, *sel.*
Devil's Walk on Earth, The.
SOUTHEY, MRS. ROBERT. *See* BOWLES, CAROLINE ANNE.
SOUTHWELL, ROBERT. At Fotheringay.
At Fotheringay, *sels.*
Before My Face the Picture Hangs.
Behold, a silly tender babe.
Burning Babe, The.
Carol, A: "As I in a hoarie, winter's night."
Child My Choice, A.
Christ's Bloody Sweat.
Come to Your Heaven, You Heavenly Choirs!
Content and Rich.
Decease, Release. Dum Morior, Orior.
Elegy for Margaret Howard, Lady Buckhurst.
Ensamples of Our Saviour.
Humble Pomp.
I Die [*or* Dye] Alive.
Image of Death, The, *sel.*
In the wrecks of Walsingham.
Lewd Love Is Loss.
Life Is but Loss.
Look Home.
Loss in Delay[s].
Love's Servile Lot.
Man's Civil War.
Marie Magdalens Complaint at Christs Death.
Martyrdom of Mary, Queen of Scots, The. *Fr.* At Fotheringay.
New Heaven, New War.
New Prince, New Pomp.

Of the Blessèd Sacrament of the Altar.
On the Execution of Mary, Queen of Scots. *Fr.* At Fotheringay.
Our Lady's Salutation.
Saint Peter's Complaint, *sel.*
Scorn Not the Least.
Seek Flowers of Heaven.
Self-pleasing souls that play with beauty's bait.
Stanzas from Saint Peter's Complaint.
Times [*or* Tymes] Go[e] by Turn[e]s.
To the Christian Reader.
Upon the Image of Death.
Virgin Mary to Christ on the Cross, The.
Virgin Mary's Conception, The.
Wassailer's Song.
SOUTHWOLD, STEPHEN. Mother of Men.
"SOUZA, ERNEST." *See* SCOTT, EVELYN.
SPAETH, JOHN DUNCAN ERNST. Beowulf, *mod. vers.*
Christ, The, *sel., tr.*
Phoenix, The, *sel., tr.*
SPAIN, RICHARD LEON. At Timberline.
Easter Island.
Evening by the Sea, the Plovers Fly.
SPALDING, HELEN. Curtain.
Dream, The.
E Tenebris.
SPALDING, JOHN LANCASTER. At the Ninth Hour. *Fr.* God and the Soul.
Believe and Take Heart.
Et Mori Lucrum. *Fr.* God and the Soul.
Forepledged.
God and the Soul, *sels.*
Nature and the Child. *Fr.* God and the Soul.
Silence.
Starry Host, The. *Fr.* God and the Soul.
Void Between, The. *Fr.* God and the Soul.
SPALDING, SUSAN MARR. Fate.
Sea's Spell, The.
Song's Worth, A.
SPARGUR, JILL. Tragedy.
SPAULDING, E. LESLIE. Man with Crow's-Feet round His Eyes, A.
SPEAR, CHARLES. Christoph.
Die Pelzaffen.
1894 in London.
Karl.
Watchers, The.
SPEAR, JOHN EDWARD. If You Keep Faith with Me.
SPEAR, RUSSELL MAYO. To Craske's Statue at Gloucester.
To One Singing.
SPEARS, WOODRIDGE. Restoration.
SPEE, FREDERICK (Friedrich Spee von Langenfeld). Dialogue at the Cross.
SPEED, SAMUEL. Flower, The, *at.*
On Peace, *at.*
Peace, *at.*
SPENCER, ANNE. At the Carnival.
Before the Feast of Shushan.
Creed.
Dunbar.
For Jim, Easter Eve.
I Have a Friend.
Innocence.
Letter to My Sister.
Life-long, Poor Browning.
Lines to a Nasturtium.
Neighbors.
Questing.
Substitution.
Translation.
Wife-Woman, The.
SPENCER, BERNARD. Aegean Islands 1940–41.
Behaviour of Money.
Cold Night, A.
Delos.
Greek Excavations.
Hand, A.
Ill.
Letters.
Notes by a Foreigner.
Olive Trees.
Part of Plenty.
Sarcophagi.
Yachts on the Nile.
SPENCER, BERNARD, *and* NANOS VALAORITIS. Now When So Much Has Passed, *tr.*
SPENCER, CAROLINE S. Living Waters.
SPENCER, CAROLYN. Alone.
SPENCER, HIRAM LADD. Hundred Years to Come, A.
SPENCER, LILIAN WHITE. Aut Caesar aut Nullus.
Fray Serra.
Porpoise, *tr.*
Red Ghosts Chant, The.
Spring Song of Aspens.
SPENCER, THEODORE. Contemporary Song.
Eden; or One View of It.
Entropy.
Epitaph: "She was a high-class bitch and a dandy."
Inflatable Globe, The.
Invocation: "Empty my heart, Lord, of daily vices," *sel.*
Narrative, A.
Phoenix, The.
Reason for Writing, A.
Song: "I who love you bring."
Spring Song.
SPENCER, WILLIAM ROBERT. Beth Gêlert [or the Grave of the Grayhound].
How D'-y'-do and Good-by.
Too Late I Stayed.
Wife, Children, and Friends.
SPENDER, STEPHEN. After They Have Tired.
Already.
Anno Santo.
Auf dem Wasser zu Singen.
Barn, The.
Beethoven's Death Mask.
Bombed Happiness, The.
Childhood, A.
Daybreak.
Discovered in Mid-Ocean.
Double Shame, The.
Elegy for Margaret, *sel.*
Elementary School Classroom [in a Slum], An.
Epilogue: "Time is a thing."
Epilogue to a Human Drama.
Express, The.
Farewell in a Dream.
Fates, The.
Footnote, A.
From All These Events.
Funeral, The.
He Will Watch the Hawk.
"I" Can Never Be a Great Man, An.
I Hear the Cries of Evening.
I Think Continually of Those Who Were Truly Great.
Ice.
In a Garden.
In 1929.
In Railway Halls [on Pavements].
Into Life.
Judas Iscariot.
Labourer in the Vineyard, The.
Landscape near an Aerodrome, The.
Marston.
Mask.
Memento.
Midsummer.
Missing My Daughter.
Moving through the Silent Crowd.
My Parents Kept Me from Children Who Were Rough.
Never Being, but Always at the Edge.
New Year.
Nor Will These Tears Be the Last, *tr.*
North, The.
Not Palaces.
O Night O Trembling Night.
Oh Young Men Oh Young Comrades.
On the Pilots Who Destroyed Germany in the Spring of 1945.
On the Third Day.
Polar Exploration.
Poor Girl.
Port Bou.
Prisoners, The.
Pylons, The.
Rejoice in the Abyss.
Rolled Over on Europe.
Room above the Square, The.
Seascape.
Shapes of Death [Haunt Life], The.
Song: "Stranger, you who hide my love."
Sonnet: "You were born; must die."
Spiritual Explorations, *sel.*
Statistics.
Stopwatch and an Ordnance Map, A.
Swan, The.
Thoughts during an Air Raid.
To a Spanish Poet.
To Poets and Airmen.
Trance, The.
Two Armies.
Two Kisses.
Ultima Ratio Regum.
Vase of Tears, The.
War God, The.
What I Expected.
Whim of Time, A.
Who Live under the Shadow.
Winter and Summer.
Winter Landscape.
Without That Once Clear Aim.
Word.
Your Body Is Stars.
SPENDER, STEPHEN, *and* FRANCES CORNFORD. From Solitude to Solitude towards Life, *tr.*
Our Movement, *tr.*
Through an Embrace, *tr.*
SPENDER, STEPHEN, *and* J. L. GILI. Cazador (Hunter), *tr.*
Lament for Ignacio Sanchez Mejias, *tr.*
Ode to Walt Whitman, *tr.*
Somnambule Ballad, *tr.*
SPENDER, STEPHEN, *and* J. B. LEISHMAN. Third Duino Elegy, The, *tr.*
SPENSER, EDMUND. Address to Venus, *tr. Fr.* De Rerum Natura *and fr.* The Faerie Queene.
After long stormes and tempests sad assay. *Fr.* Amoretti.
After so long a race as I have run. *Fr.* Amoretti.
All This World's Riches. *Fr.* Amoretti.
Amoretti.
Amoretti, *sels.*
And is there care in heaven? and is there love. *Fr.* The Faerie Queene.
Another Element. *Fr.* Amoretti.
April. *Fr.* The Shepheardes Calender.
April, *sel. Fr.* The Shepheardes Calender.
April Smile. *Fr.* Amoretti.
Archimago's Hermitage. *Fr.* The Faerie Queene.
Art of Eyes, The. *Fr.* Amoretti.
Artegall and Radigund. *Fr.* The Faerie Queene.
Astrophel.
Astrophel, *sel.*
At Court. *Fr.* Prosopopoia; or, Mother Hubberd's Tale.
August. *Fr.* The Faerie Queene.
August. *Fr.* The Shepheardes Calender.
Autumn. *Fr.* The Faerie Queene.
Balme. *Fr.* The Faerie Queene.
Be Bold. *Fr.* The Faerie Queene.
Beauty. *Fr.* An Hymne in Honour of Beautie.
Behold, O Man. *Fr.* The Faerie Queene.
Being myself captived here in care. *Fr.* Amoretti.
Bower of Bliss, The. *Fr.* The Faerie Queene.
Bower of Bliss, The, *sel. Fr.* The Faerie Queene.
Bride, The. *Fr.* Epithalamion.
Bright Squadrons, The. *Fr.* The Faerie Queene.
Britomart in the House of Busirane. *Fr.* The Faerie Queene.
Butterfly, The. *Fr.* Muiopotmos.
Cave of Despair, The. *Fr.* The Faerie Queene.
Cave of Mammon, The. *Fr.* The Faerie Queene.

SPENSER, EDMUND (*continued*)
Cave of Sleep, The. *Fr.* The Faerie Queene.
Colin Clout at Court. *Fr.* Colin Clout's Come Home Again.
Colin Clout's Come Home Again, *sel.*
Coming to kiss her lips (such grace I found). *Fr.* Amoretti.
Contempt of Poetry, The. *Fr.* The Shepheardes Calender.
Cymochles and Phaedria. *Fr.* The Faerie Queene.
Cymochles in the Bower of Bliss. *Fr.* The Faerie Queene.
Dame Nature. *Fr.* The Faerie Queene.
Dance, The. *Fr.* The Faerie Queene.
Dance of the Graces, The. *Fr.* The Faerie Queene.
Daphnaida, *sels.*
De Rerum Natura, *sel.*, *tr.*
Death. *Fr.* The Faerie Queene.
Death of Astrophel, The.
Death of the Dragon, The. *Fr.* The Faerie Queene.
December. *Fr.* The Shepheardes Calender.
Despair. *Fr.* The Faerie Queene.
Dido My Dear, Alas, Is Dead. *Fr.* The Shepheardes Calender.
Ditty, A: In Praise of Eliza, Queen of the Shepherds. *Fr.* The Shepheardes Calender.
Ditty, A: "See where she sits upon the grassy green." *Fr.* The Shepheardes Calender.
Doubt which ye misdeem, fair love, is vain, The. *Fr.* Amoretti.
Dragon, The. *Fr.* The Faerie Queene.
Easter [Morning]. *Fr.* Amoretti.
Eftsoons they heard a most melodious sound. *Fr.* The Faerie Queene.
Elisa. *Fr.* The Shepheardes Calender.
Epithalamion: "Ye learned sisters."
Epithalamion: "Ye learned sisters," *sels.*
Faerie [*or* Faery] Queene, The, *sels.*
Fair is my love, when her fair golden hairs. *Fr.* Amoretti.
Fair Proud! now tell me, why should fair be proud. *Fr.* Amoretti.
Famous warriors of the antique world, The. *Fr.* Amoretti.
Fayre eyes, the myrrour of my mazed hart. *Fr.* Amoretti.
Fayre ye be sure, but cruell and unkind. *Fr.* Amoretti.
Februarie. *Fr.* The Shepheardes Calender.
Fight of the Red Cross Knight and the Heathen Sansjoy, The. *Fr.* The Faerie Queene.
Fresh spring, the herald of love's mighty king. *Fr.* Amoretti.
Garden of Adonis, The. *Fr.* The Faerie Queene.
Garden of Proserpina, The. *Fr.* The Faerie Queene.
Gather the Rose. *Fr.* The Faerie Queene.
Gentle Knight was pricking on the plaine, A. *Fr.* The Faerie Queene.
Glorious image of the Maker's beauty, The. *Fr.* Amoretti.
Golden Hook, The. *Fr.* Amoretti.
Great wrong I doe, I can it not deny. *Fr.* Amoretti.
Guardian Angels. *Fr.* The Faerie Queene.
Happy Isle, The. *Fr.* The Faerie Queene.
Happy ye leaves! when as those lily [*or* lilly] hands. *Fr.* Amoretti.
Heavenly Aid. *Fr.* The Faerie Queene.
Her Heards Be Thousand Fishes. *Fr.* Colin Clout's Come Home Again.
Her Name upon the Strand. *Fr.* Amoretti.
His Love's Riches. *Fr.* Amoretti.
Hobbinol's Lay of Fair Elisa, Queen of Shepherds. *Fr.* The Shepheardes Calender.
House of Ate, The. *Fr.* The Faerie Queene.
House of Morpheus, The. *Fr.* The Faerie Queene.
House of Pride, The. *Fr.* The Faerie Queene.
House of Richesse, The. *Fr.* The Faerie Queene.
Huge Leviathan, The. *Fr.* Visions of the World's Vanity.
Hymn in Honor of Beauty, An.
Hymn in Honor of Love, An.
Hymn of Heavenly Love, An.
Hymne in Honour of Beautie, An.
Hymne in Honour of Beautie, An, *sels.*
Hymne of Heavenly Beautie, An.
Hymne of Heavenly Beautie, An, *sel.*
Hymne of Heavenly Love, An.
I joy to see how in your drawn work. *Fr.* Amoretti.
I Saw a Phoenix in the Wood Alone. *Fr.* The Visions of Petrarch.
Iambica.
Iambicum Trimetrum.
Ice and Fire. *Fr.* Amoretti.
Idle Lake, The. *Fr.* The Faerie Queene.
In that proud part, which her so goodly graceth. *Fr.* Amoretti.
Invocation to the Faerie Queene. *Fr.* The Faerie Queene.
Is it her nature or is it her will. *Fr.* Amoretti.
It Fell upon a Holy Eve. *Fr.* The Shepheardes Calender.
January. *Fr.* The Shepheardes Calender.
January Eclogue. *Fr.* The Shepheardes Calender.
Joy of my life! full oft for loving you. *Fr.* Amoretti.
July. *Fr.* The Shepheardes Calender.
June. *Fr.* The Shepheardes Calender.
Kinds of Trees to Plant. *Fr.* The Faerie Queene.
Lacking my love, I go from place to place. *Fr.* Amoretti.
Lament for Daphnaida.
Legend of Sir Guyon, or of Temperaunce, The. *Fr.* The Faerie Queene.
Legend of the Knight of the Red Crosse, or of Holinesse, The. *Fr.* The Faerie Queene.
Like [*or* Lyke] as a huntsman after weary chase [*or* chace]. *Fr.* Amoretti.
Like [*or* Lyke] as a ship that through the ocean wide [*or* wyde]. *Fr.* Amoretti.
Like as the culver, on the barèd bough. *Fr.* Amoretti.
Little lowly hermitage it was, A. *Fr.* The Faerie Queene.
Lo I the man, whose Muse whilome did maske. *Fr.* The Faerie Queene.
Long while I sought to what I might compare. *Fr.* Amoretti.
Love. *Fr.* The Faerie Queene.
Make Haste, Sweet Love. *Fr.* Amoretti.
Malbecco and Hellenore. *Fr.* The Faerie Queene.
Mammon enmovéd was with inward wrath. *Fr.* The Faerie Queene.
Mammon's House. *Fr.* The Faerie Queene.
Mark when she smiles with amiable cheer. *Fr.* Amoretti.
Mask of Mutability, The. *Fr.* The Faerie Queene.
Masque of Cupid, The. *Fr.* The Faerie Queene.
May. *Fr.* The Faerie Queene.
Men call you fair [*or* fayre], and you do[e] credit it. *Fr.* Amoretti.
Mermaids, The. *Fr.* The Faerie Queene.
Merry cuckoo [*or* cuckow], messenger of spring, The. *Fr.* Amoretti.
Ministering Angels [*or* Spirits], The. *Fr.* The Faerie Queene.
Ministry of Angels, The. *Fr.* The Faerie Queene.
More than most fair[e], full of the living fire. *Fr.* Amoretti.
Most glorious Lord of life [*or* lyfe], that on this day. *Fr.* Amoretti.
Mother Hubberd's Tale, *sel.*
Muiopotmos, *sel.*
Music at the Bower of Bliss, The. *Fr.* The Faerie Queene.
Mutability. *Fr.* The Faerie Queene.
My love is like to ice, and I to fire. *Fr.* Amoretti.
Nature. *Fr.* The Faerie Queene.
New yeare forth looking out of Ianus gate. *Fr.* Amoretti.
Next unto Him Was Neptune Pictured. *Fr.* The Faerie Queene.
Noble heart that harbours virtuous thought, The. *Fr.* The Faerie Queene.
November. *Fr.* The Shepheardes Calender.
November, *sel.* *Fr.* The Shepheardes Calender.
Now Strike Your Sailes Ye Jolly Mariners! *Fr.* The Faerie Queene.
Nymphs and Graces Dancing to a Shepherd's Pipe. *Fr.* The Faerie Queene.
Oak and the Brere, The. *Fr.* The Shepheardes Calender.
October. *Fr.* The Shepheardes Calender.
October, *sel.* *Fr.* The Shepheardes Calender.
Of this worlds theatre in which we stay. *Fr.* Amoretti.
Oft when my spirit doth spre[a]d her bolder wing[e]s. *Fr.* Amoretti.
Old January. *Fr.* The Faerie Queene.
One day as I unwarily did gaze. *Fr.* Amoretti.
One day I wrote her name upon the strand. *Fr.* Amoretti.
Pageant of the Seasons and the Months, The. *Fr.* The Faerie Queene.
Pastoral, A: "From thence into the open fields he fled." *Fr.* The Faerie Queene.
Penelope, for her Ulysses' [*or* Ulisses] sake. *Fr.* Amoretti.
Perigot and Willie's [*or* Willye's] Roundelay. *Fr.* The Shepheardes Calender.
Perigot and Willye. *Fr.* The Shepheardes Calender.
Phaedria and the Idle Lake. *Fr.* The Faerie Queene.
Port after Stormie Seas. *Fr.* The Faerie Queene.
Prayer to Venus. *Fr.* The Faerie Queene.
Prince Arthur. *Fr.* The Faerie Queene.
Procession of Cupid, The. *Fr.* The Faerie Queene.
Procession of Times and Seasons, The. *Fr.* The Faerie Queene.
Prologue: "So oft as I with state of present time." *Fr.* The Faerie Queene.
Prosopopoia; or, Mother Hubberd's Tale.
Prothalamion.
Quelling of the Blatant Beast, The. *Fr.* The Faerie Queene.
Red-Cross Knight, The. *Fr.* The Faerie Queene.
Rolling wheel[e], that runneth often round, The. *Fr.* Amoretti.
Rome, *tr.*
Roundelay, A: "It fell upon a holy eve." *Fr.* The Shepheardes Calender.
Rudely thou wrongest my dear heart's desire. *Fr.* Amoretti.
Ruins of Rome, I-VIII, *tr.*
Sea Monsters. *Fr.* The Faerie Queene.
Seasons, The. *Fr.* The Faerie Queene.
Shepheardes [*or* Shepheards *or* Shepherd's] Calender, The, *sels.*
Since I did leave the presence of my love. *Fr.* Amoretti.
Sleep after Toil. *Fr.* The Faerie Queene.
So Let Us Love. *Fr.* Amoretti.

So oft as I her beauty do behold. *Fr.* Amoretti.
Song, The: "So passeth, in the passing of a day." *Fr.* The Faerie Queene.
Sonnet: "After long storms and tempests' sad assay." *Fr.* Amoretti.
Sonnet: "Being my[e]self captived [*or* captyved] here in care." *Fr,* Amoretti.
Sonnet: "Comming to kisse her lyps (such grace I found)." *Fr.* Amoretti.
Sonnet: "Fair is my love, when her fair golden hairs [*or* heares]." *Fr.* Amoretti.
Sonnet: "Fresh spring, the herald of love's mighty king." *Fr.* Amoretti.
Sonnet: "Happy ye leaves! when as those lily [*or* lilly] hands." *Fr.* Amoretti.
Sonnet: "It was the time, when rest, soft sliding downe," *tr. Fr.* Visions.
Sonnet: "Lacking my love, I go from place to place." *Fr.* Amoretti.
Sonnet: "Like [*or* Lyke] as a huntsman after weary chase [*or* chace]." *Fr.* Amoretti.
Sonnet: "Like [*or* Lyke] as a ship, that through the ocean wide [*or* wyde]." *Fr.* Amoretti.
Sonnet: "Mark when she smiles with amiable cheer." *Fr.* Amoretti.
Sonnet: "Men call you fair, and you do credit it." *Fr.* Amoretti.
Sonnet: "Most glorious Lord of life, that on this day." *Fr.* Amoretti.
Sonnet: "My love is like to ice, and I to fire." *Fr.* Amoretti.
Sonnet: "One day I wrote her name upon the strand." *Fr.* Amoretti.
Sonnet: "Rudely thou wrongest my dear heart's desire." *Fr.* Amoretti.
Sonnet: "So oft as I her beauty do[e] behold." *Fr.* Amoretti.
Sonnet: "Sweet is the rose, but grows upon a brere." *Fr.* Amoretti.
Sonnet: "Trust not the treason of those smyling lookes." *Fr.* Amoretti.
Sonnet: "Was it the work of Nature or of Art." *Fr.* Amoretti.
Sonnet: "What guile is this, that those her golden tresses." *Fr.* Amoretti.
Sonnet: "Ye tradeful merchants that, with weary toil." *Fr.* Amoretti.
Soul Is Form. *Fr.* An Hymne in Honour of Beautie.
Sovereign beauty which I do admire, The. *Fr.* Amoretti.
Stanzas from Epithalamion ("Now cease, ye damsels, your delights forepast").
Story of the Red Cross Knight or of Holiness, The. *Fr.* The Faerie Queene.
Summer. *Fr.* The Faerie Queene.
Sweet and Sour. *Fr.* Amoretti.
Sweet is the rose, but grows upon a brere. *Fr.* Amoretti.
Tamed Deer, The. *Fr.* Amoretti.
Tell me when shall these wearie woes have end. *Fr.* Amoretti.
Temple of Venus, The. *Fr.* The Faerie Queene.
Thence passing forth, they shortly doe arryve. *Fr.* The Faerie Queene.
There the most daintie paradise on earth. *Fr.* The Faerie Queene.
This holy season fit to fast and pray. *Fr.* Amoretti.
To Be or Not to Be. *Fr.* The Faerie Queene.
To His Booke. *Fr.* The Shepheardes Calender.
To the Right Noble and Valorous Knight, Sir Walter Raleigh.
To the Right Worshipful, My Singular Good Friend, M[aster] Gabriel Harvey, Doctor of the Laws.
True Fair, The. *Fr.* Amoretti.
Trust not the treason of those smiling looks. *Fr.* Amoretti.
Two Cantos of Mutabilitie. *Fr.* The Faerie Queene.
Una and the Lion. *Fr.* The Faerie Queene.
Una and the Red Cross Knight. *Fr.* The Faerie Queene.
Upon a Day.
Venemous toung, tipt with vile adders sting. *Fr.* Amoretti.
Venus in Search of Cupid, Coming to Diana. *Fr.* The Faerie Queene.
Visions (*of* Du Bellay), *sel., tr.*
Visions of Petrarch, The, *tr. Fr.* Sonnets to Laura.
Visions of the World's Vanity, *sel.*
Was it the work[e] of Nature or of Art. *Fr.* Amoretti.
Weary year[e] his race now having run, The. *Fr.* Amoretti.
What guile [*or* guyle] is this, that those her golden tresses. *Fr.* Amoretti.
What If Some Little Paine the Passage Have. *Fr.* The Faerie Queene.
When I behold that beauty's wonderment. *Fr.* Amoretti.
When I bethinke me on that speech whyleare. *Fr.* The Faerie Queene.
When my abodes prefixed time is spent. *Fr.* Amoretti.
When She Smiles. *Fr.* Amoretti.
Winter. *Fr.* The Faerie Queene.
World that cannot deeme of worthy things, The. *Fr.* Amoretti.
Ye tradeful merchants that, with weary toil [*or* toyle]. *Fr.* Amoretti.
Your Power. *Fr.* Amoretti.
"Speranza." *See* Wilde, Lady.
Speyer, Leonora. A B C's in Green.
Anniversary.
Answer.
April on the Battlefields.
Ballad of a Lost House, The.
Ballad of Old Doc Higgins.
Bavarian Roadside.
Blue Jay.
Crickets at Dawn.
Duet.
Garden under Lightning.
Happy Is He.
Hark! Hark!
Heart Looks On, The.
Heart Recalcitrant, The.
House of Calvin.
I'll Be Your Epitaph.
Kleptomaniac.
Ladder, The.
Let Not My Death Be Long.
Little Lover.
Mary Magdalene.
Measure Me, Sky!
Naturalist on a June Sunday, The.
New Excavations.
Note from the Pipes, A.
Oberammergau.
Of Mountains, *sel.*
One Version.
Pain.
Pan Crucified.
Protest in Passing.
Sardinia from a Liner.
She Says, Being Forbidden.
Snow in April.
Sonnet: "For I have seen this Light. I did not dream." *Fr.* Sonnets for the Beloved.
Sonnets for the Beloved, *sel.*
Squall, The.
Star-Fear.
Suddenly.
Swans.
Tears for Sale.
These Poems I Have So Loved.
Words to Sleep Upon.
X-Ray.
Speyers, Laura Livingston. Poppies.
Sphakianakis, Yiannis. Song of Freedom and the Sea, The.
Spicer, Anne Higginson. City Priest.
Fisherman, The, *tr.*
Hail and Farewell.
Spicer, J. L. Communion.
Spicer, Jack. Imaginary Elegies, I-IV.
Spinden, Herbert Joseph. Lover's Lament, A, *tr.*
Spingarn, Joel Elias. Beauty.
Helios.
Italian Poppies.
Out of the Italian.
Spring Passion.
Spingarn, Lawrence Perry. Museum Piece.
Spire, André. Abishag.
Dust.
Hear, O Israel!
It Was Not You.
Lonely.
Now You're Content.
Nudities.
Spring.
Spitta, Karl Johann Philipp. O Blessèd House, That Cheerfully Receiveth.
O Happy Home.
Unchanging Jesus.
Spofford, Harriet Elizabeth Prescott. Ballad: "In the summer even."
Between the Graves.
Can't.
Christmas Peal, The.
Evanescence.
Every Day Thanksgiving Day.
Flag Song.
Godspeed.
Hereafter.
How We Became a Nation.
Hunt, The.
Mother-Song, A.
Music in the Night.
My Own Song.
Only.
Phantoms All.
Phillips Brooks.
Pines, The.
Sigh, A.
Snowdrop, A.
Vanity.
Voice.
Spottiswoode, Alicia Ann. *See* Scott, Lady John.
Sprague, Charles. Brothers, The.
Centennial Ode, *sel.*
Curiosity, *sels.*
Family Meeting, The.
Fiction. *Fr.* Curiosity.
Fourth of July, The.
Indians. *Fr.* Centennial Ode.
News, The. *Fr.* Curiosity.
Winged Worshippers, The.
Sprat, Thomas. On His Mistress Drown'd.
Sprigg, Christopher St. John. *See* "Caudwell, Christopher."
Springer, Thomas Grant. Giving and Forgiving.
Harmony.
Spring-Rice, Sir Cecil Arthur. Day.
Homeland, The.
I Vow to Thee, My Country.
In Memoriam, A.C.M.L., *sel.*
Masque of Balliol, The, *sels.*
Spring Rice, Stephen E. Early Friendship.
Sproat, Nancy Dennis. Blackberry Girl, The.
Sprod, G. N. Request Number.
Sproull, Lyman H. Emigrant's Child, The.
Stationed Scout, The.
Sprouse, Sarah Elizabeth. Little Song of Work, A.
Squier, George L. O Christ, the Way.
Squire, Sir John Collings ("Solomon Eagle"). Another Generation.
Approaching America.
Ballade of Any Father to Any Son, A.
Ballade of Diminishing Control, A.
Ballade of Soporific Absorption.
Ballade of the Poetic Life.
Birds, The.
Cats, The, *tr.*
Christmas Hymn for Lambeth.
Discovery, The.
Dog's Death, A.
Epitaph, An: "Shiftless and shy, gentle and kind and frail."
Exquisite Sonnet, The.
Fresh Morning, A.
Hands-across-the-Sea Poem, The.
Happy Night, The.

SQUIRE, SIR JOHN COLLINGS (*cont.*)
Honesty at a Fire.
House, A.
How They Do It.
If Gray Had Had to Write His Elegy in the Cemetery of Spoon River Instead of in That of Stoke Poges.
If Pope Had Written "Break, Break, Break."
It did not last; the Devil shouting Ho!
Late Snow.
Lines: "Mine ears have heard your distant moan."
Little Commodore, The.
March, The.
Niagara.
On Oculists.
Passion of Man, The: 1918–1938.
Poor Old Man, The.
Prologue: In Darkness.
Rivers.
Ship, The.
Song: "You are my sky; beneath your circling kindness."
Sonnet: "There was an Indian, who had known no change."
Starlight.
There Was an Indian.
Three Hills, The.
To a Bull-Dog.
To a Roman.
Under.
Winter Nightfall.
SRVANSTIAN, KAREKIN. Lament over the Heroes Fallen in the Battle of Avarair.
SSU-K'UNG SHU. To a Friend Bound North after the Rebellion.
STACK, PHILIP ("Kid Kazanova"). Admonition.
STACKPOLE, S. H. Zebras.
STACKPOLE, S. H., *and* F. S. HOLMES. *See* HOLMES, F. S., *and* S. H. STACKPOLE.
STACPOOLE, HENRY DE VERE. Adonis, *tr.*
Bas-Relief, *tr.*
Captive, The, *tr.*
Clais, *tr.*
Dead Shalt Thou Lie, *tr.*
E'en the Country Maid, *tr.*
Farewell to Maidenhood, *tr.*
Invocation, *tr.*
Lonely Night, *tr.*
Though Youth Be Gone, *tr.*
Thy Form Is Lovely, *tr.*
Timas, *tr.*
To Mnesidice, *tr.*
Youth and Age, *tr.*
STACY, THOMAS H. In Days like These.
STADLER, ERNST. Form Is Delight.
STAFF, LEOPOLD. Golden Elegy, The.
Liberty.
STAFFELDT, A. W. SCHACK VON. At the Rendezvous.
STAFFORD, JUNIATA. My Country's Flag.
STAFFORD, WENDELL PHILLIPS. America Resurgent.
Invocation: "O Thou whose equal purpose runs."
Lincoln.
Lindbergh.
Lullaby: "Sleep, my baby, all the night!"
On the Photograph of a Lynching.
One of Our Presidents.
R. S. S.
Washington and Lincoln.
STAFFORD, WILLIAM. On Being Invited to a Testimonial Dinner.
One Home.
Outside.
Ritual to Read to Each Other, A.
Testimony to an Inquisitor.
STAGNELIUS, ERIK JOHAN. Memory.
Nixie, The.
STALKER, PHILIP A. Talk.
STAM, BETTY SCOTT. Christmas.
STAMPA, GASPARA. Sonnet: Dream, The.
Sonnet: In Absence.
STANDISH, CELIA. New Year's Days.
STANFIELD, LEONTINE. Little Cat Angel, The.
STANFORD, ANN. On a Ship at Sea.
STANFORD, DEREK. Carol for His Darling on Christmas Day.
Tomb of Honey Snaps Its Marble Chains, The.
STANFORD, WILLIAM BEDELL. Angelus-Time near Dublin.
Before Salamis.
Cat and the Partridge, The, *tr.*
To a Greek Ship in the Port of Dublin.
Undertone.
STANHOPE, PHILIP DORMER. *See* CHESTERFIELD, PHILIP DORMER STANHOPE, 4TH EARL OF.
STANLEY, ARTHUR PENRHYN. Teach Us to Die.
STANLEY, EDWARD GEORGE GEOFFREY SMITH, 14TH EARL OF DERBY. *See* DERBY, EARL OF.
STANLEY, M. LIZZIE. Some Years in Washington's Life.
STANLEY, MARY (Mrs. Kendrick Smithyman). Per Diem et per Noctem.
Record Perpetual Loss.
Wife Speaks, The.
STANLEY, THOMAS. All Things Drink.
At the Mid Hour of Night, *tr.*
Beauty.
Combat, The.
Deposition from Beauty, A.
Destiny.
Divorce, The.
Exequies, The.
Expectation.
Far from My Dearest Self, *tr.*
Fruitful Earth Drinks Up the Rain.
Horns to Bulls Wise Nature Lends, *tr.*
I not care for Gyges' sway, *tr.*
If thou dost the number know, *tr.*
La Belle Confidente.
Love Sleeping, *tr.*
Magnet, The.
Of th' Atrides I would sing, *tr.*
Old I Am, *tr.*
On a Seal, *tr.*
On a Violet in Her Breast.
On Archaeanassa, *tr.*
Painter, by unmatch'd desert, *tr.*
Picture, The.
Relapse, The.
Repulse, The.
Roses.
Solitudes, *sel.*, *tr.*
Song: "Fool, take up thy shaft again."
Song: "I prithee let my heart alone."
Song: "When I lie burning in thine eye."
Spring.
Stung, *tr.*
Swallow, The.
Though when I lov'd thee thou wert fair.
To Celia Pleading Want of Merit.
To One That Pleaded Her Own Want of Merit.
To the Swallow, *tr.*
Tombe, The.
Vigil of Venus, The, *tr.*
When I Loved Thee.
Wish, The.
Youthful Age.
STANSBURY, JOSEPH. God Save the King.
Let Us Be Happy as Long as We Can.
Lords of the Main, The.
New Song, A.
Song for a Venison Dinner at Mr. Bunyan's, New York, 1781.
To Cordelia.
To His Wife.
When Good Queen Elizabeth Governed the Realm.
STANSBURY, MARY ANNA PHINNEY. How He Saved St. Michael's.
Surprise at Ticonderoga, The.
STANTON, FRANK LEBBY. Country Philosopher, A.
Good Lawd Know My Name, De.
Graveyard Rabbit, The.
How to Eat Watermelons.
In the Time of Strife.
Just a Wearyin' for You.
Keep a-Goin'.
Little Dreamers, The.
Little Way, A.
Lullaby, A: "Sich a li'l feller."
Mighty Lak' a Rose.
Mocking-Bird, The.
Old Battle-Field, An.
Old Flag Forever, The.
Old Hymns, The.
One Country.
Our Flag Forever.
Plantation Ditty, A.
Regiment Song.
Reunited.
So Many!
Sweetes' Li'l' Feller.
"Tollable Well!"
Volunteer, The.
Warship *Dixie*, The.
Wearyin' for You.
STANTON, HENRY THOMPSON. Moneyless Man, The.
"STANTON, PAUL." *See* WINNER, SEPTIMUS.
STANTON, RUTH EDNA. Farm Life.
STANYHURST, RICHARD. Aeneid, The, *sels.*, *tr.*
Dido to Aeneas. *Fr.* The Aeneid.
Prayer to the [Holy] Trinity, A.
To the Trinity.
STAPP, EMILIE BLACKMORE. Autumn Races.
Learning to Skate.
On the Beach.
Rainy Day, A.
Taking Turns.
Welcome Visitors.
STAPYLTON [*or* STAPLETON], SIR ROBERT. Bard's Song, The.
STAR, BELLE. Bucking Bronco, *at.*
STARBUCK, GEORGE. Bone Thoughts on a Dry Day.
STARBUCK, VICTOR. City Butterfly, A.
David's Song to the Troubled King. *Fr.* Saul, King of Israel.
Dead, The.
Gilboa. *Fr.* Saul, King of Israel.
I Have Found Romance.
If I Come Back.
Jabesh Gilead. *Fr.* Saul, King of Israel.
Moon-Madness.
Night for Adventures.
Pine against the Blue, The.
Quiet Streets.
Saul, King of Israel, *sels.*
Seekers, The.
Two Winds.
Vanity Fair.
Wind, The.
STARCK, MARY. Reign of Peace, The.
STARKEY, JAMES. *See* "O'SULLIVAN, SEUMAS."
STARKWEATHER, PAULINE. Two Mountains Men Have Climbed.
STARKWEATHER, W. C. It Happened So Very Long Ago.
STARR, HATTIE. Little Alabama Coon.
STARRETT, VINCENT. Changeling.
Dancer.
Extraordinary Visit.
God's Riding.
Gooseflesh.
Legend.
My Lord's Motoring.
November 24, 1918.
Sea Story.
221B.
Villon Strolls at Midnight.
Visitation.
Voyage.
STASINOPOULOS, MICHALIS. Chess Knight.
Young Provincial, The.
STATIUS, PUBLIUS PAPINIUS. Silvae, *sel.*
Sleep.
STATYLLIUS FLACCUS. Exchange of Fortune, An.
STAUDE, FRANZ. Farewell in Memory of F. O. Haeller.
STAUFFER, DONALD A. Bulldozer, The.
Lemmings, The.
Time Zones for Forty-four.
STAUFFER, FRANCIS H. Three Little Fishers.
STEAD, WILLIAM FORCE. Festival in Tuscany.

How Infinite Are Thy Ways. *Fr.* Uriel.
I Closed My Eyes To-Day and Saw.
Praise, then, to Uriel, who in unlikely places. *Fr.* Uriel.
Reach forth Thy hand! *Fr.* Uriel.
Sweet Wild April.
Uriel, *sels.*
STEARNS, L. D. Triumph.
STEBBINS, MARY ELIZABETH HEWITT. Harold the Valiant.
Sunflower to the Sun, The.
STEDMAN, EDMUND CLARENCE. Aaron Burr's Wooing.
Abraham Lincoln.
Alice of Monmouth, *sel.*
Aucassin and Nicolette.
Autumn Song.
Betrothed Anew.
Cavalry Song. *Fr.* Alice of Monmouth.
Corda Concordia, *sel.*
Cousin Lucrece.
Cuba.
Custer.
Discoverer, The.
Doorstep, The.
Dutch Patrol, The.
Epitaph of Bion, *tr.*
Falstaff's Song.
Feast of Harvest, The.
Flight of the Birds, The.
Gettysburg.
Going a-Nutting.
Hand of Lincoln, The.
Helen Keller.
Horace Greeley.
How Old Brown Took Harper's Ferry.
Hymn of [*or* to] the West.
Invocation: "Thou—whose enduring hand once laid in sooth."
Israel Freyer's Bid for Gold.
John Brown of Osawatomie.
Kearny at Seven Pines.
Liberty Enlightening the World.
Lullaby of Danaë, The.
Morgan.
Mors Benefica.
Mother's Picture, A.
Odyssey, The, *sel., tr.*
Old Admiral, The.
On a Great Man Whose Mind Is Clouding.
Ordeal by Fire, The, *sel.*
Pan in Wall Street.
Peter Stuyvesant's New Year's Call.
Prelude: "I saw the constellated matin choir."
Provençal Lovers.
Quest. *Fr.* Corda Concordia.
Salem.
Seeking the Mayflower.
Si Jeunesse Savait!
Singer, The.
Song from a Drama.
Star Bearer, The.
Sumter.
Toujours Amour.
Treason's Last Device.
Voice of the Western Wind.
Wanted—a Man.
What the Winds Bring.
Why?
Witchcraft.
World Well Lost, The.
STEDMAN, JANE W. Geologist's Epitaph, A.
STEECE, ARVEL. There Is Yet Time.
World Planners.
STEEL, M. Little Lucy Lester.
STEELE, ANNE. Compassion So Divine.
Great Redeemer Lives, The.
O How Sweet Are Thy Words!
Only Name Given under Heaven, The.
Prayer: "Dear Refuge of my weary soul."
STEELE, JOHN R. Hell in Texas, *at.*
STEELE, SIR RICHARD. Song: "Me Cupid made a happy slave."
Song: "Why, lovely charmer, tell me why." *Fr.* The Tender Husband.
Tender Husband, The, *sel.*
STEELE, S. S. Walk, Jaw-Bone.
STEENDAM, JACOB. Complaint of New Amsterdam, The.
Praise of New Netherland, The.
STEESE, EDWARD. Tenth Reunion.
STEFÁNSSON, DAVÍD. Abba-labba-lá.
I Sail in the Fall.
STEFANSSON, VILHJALMUR. Generosity, *tr.*
Lions and Swine, *tr.*
Winter, *tr.*
STEFFAN, MARGUERITE. Dance of the Gnats.
Negro Student, The.
STEIGMAN, BENJAMIN MORRIS. Opera in English?
STEIN, EVALEEN. Budding-Time Too Brief.
Flood-Time on the Marshes.
In Mexico.
In Youth.
Little Fir-Trees, The.
November Morning.
Wild Beasts.
STEIN, GERTRUDE. Accents in Alsace, *sels.*
Alsace or Alsatians. *Fr.* Accents in Alsace.
Day Lost, A.
Four Saints in Three Acts, *sel.*
Heat, The.
I Am Rose.
Land of Nations, *sel.*
Mother of Us All, The, *sel.*
Page IX.
Sacred Emily, *sel.*
Scenes, *sel.*
Stanzas in Meditation VI (1940).
Watch on the Rhine, The. *Fr.* Accents in Alsace.
STEIN, GLORIA T. Heart's Poverty.
STEIN, KURT M. An Unserer Beach.
Mama's Advice.
Morning Song.
Reflection.
Vor a Gauguin Picture zu Singen.
STEINBERG, ELIEZER. Terrible Thought, A.
STEINBERG, JACOB. Heart, The.
STEINMAN, DAVID BARNARD. Blueprint.
"STELLA." *See* JOHNSON, ESTHER.
STELLA, SISTER MARIS. *See* MARIS STELLA, SISTER.
STEM, THAD, JR. And So It Goes.
Deep Night, Summer.
Fall Freshet.
News from Home.
Not Alone.
STENHOUSE, WILLIAM. Empty Jar, The.
STENNETT, SAMUEL. Majestic Sweetness.
On Jordan's stormy banks I stand.
STEPANCHEV, STEPHEN. Archipelago, The, *tr.*
Beatrice, *tr.*
Benediction, *tr.*
Drunken Boat, The, *tr.*
Inner Brother.
No Furlough.
Strength to War.
STEPHANIE, SISTER MARY. That Far Lone Mountain.
STEPHANSSON, STEPHAN G. At Close of Day.
Evening.
STEPHEN, ALEXANDER MAITLAND.
A. C. S.
Apotheosis.
Bring Torches.
Capilano.
Dryad, The.
Voices.
STEPHEN, JAMES KENNETH. Cynicus to W. Shakespeare [*or* Shakspere].
England and America.
Grievance. A.
Heaven and Hell.
Imitation of Robert Browning.
Imitation of Walt Whitman.
Lapsus Calami.
Last Ride Together, The (from Her Point of View).
Millennium, The.
My Education.
Of W. W. (Americanus).
Old School List, The.
On a Parisian Boulevard. *Fr.* England and America.
On a Rhine Steamer. *Fr.* England and America.
School.
Senex to Matt. Prior.
Sincere Flattery.
Sonnet, A: "Two voices are there; one is of the deep."
Sonnet on Wordsworth, A.
Splinter, The.
Thought, A.
To R. K.
Two Epigrams.
Two Voices Are There.
Wordsworth.
STEPHEN THE SABAITE, SAINT. Art Thou Weary [Art Thou Troubled], *ad. by* J. M. Neale.
STEPHENS, A. G. Babylon.
STEPHENS, ANN S. Polish Boy, The.
STEPHENS, BRUNTON. Dominion of Australia, The (a Forecast, 1877).
STEPHENS, EVAN. Utah, We Love Thee.
STEPHENS, HARRY. Night-herding Song.
STEPHENS, JAMES. Anthony O'Daly.
April Showers.
Autumn.
Barbarians.
Bessie Bobtail.
Blue Blood.
Breakfast Time.
Centaurs, The.
Check.
Cherry Tree, The.
Chill of the Eve.
Christmas in Freelands.
Clann Cartie.
College of Surgeons, The.
Coolin, The.
County Mayo, The, *tr.*
Crest Jewel, The.
Daisies, The.
Dance.
Danny Murphy.
Dark Wings.
Day and Night.
Deirdre.
Egan O Rahilly, *tr.*
Eileen, Diarmuid and Teig.
Etched in Frost.
Evening.
Evening Falls, An.
Fifteen Acres, The.
Fossils.
Fur Coat, The.
Ghost, The, *tr.*
Glass of Beer, A.
Goat Paths, The.
Good and Bad.
Hate.
Hawks.
Hesperus.
I Am Raftery, *tr.*
In the Night.
In the Poppy Field.
In Waste Places.
Inis Fal, *tr.*
Lake, The.
Little Things.
Main-Deep, The.
Night, The.
Night Was Creeping.
Nothing is easy! Pity then.
O'Bruidar [*or* O Bruadair], *tr.*
Odell.
On a Lonely Spray.
Optimist.
Outcast, The.
Peadar Og Goes Courting.
Peggy Mitchell, *tr.*
Pit of Bliss, The.
Psychometrist.
Red-haired Man's Wife, The.
Righteous Anger.
Rivals, The.
Road, The.
Satyr, The.
Seumas Beg.
Shame.
Shell, The.
Snare, The.
Sweet Apple.

STEPHENS, JAMES (*continued*)
Tanist.
Theme.
Theme with Variations, *sel.*
To the Four Courts, Please.
Visit from Abroad, A.
Voice of God, The.
Waste Places, The.
Watcher, The.
Wave of Cliona, The.
Westland Row.
What the Devil Said.
What Tomas [*or* Thomas] an Buile Said in a Pub.
What Tomas Said in a Pub.
When You Walk.
Whisperer, The.
White Fields.
White Window, The.
Why Tomas Cam Was Grumpy.
William O'Kelly.
Wind, The.
Woman Is a Branchy Tree, A.
Wood of Flowers, The.
STEPHENS, JAMES BRUNTON. *See* STEPHENS, BRUNTON.
STEPHENS, SENNETT. Astrology.
Chloris and Corydon.
Lenten Lines to Lydia.
STEPHENS, WILLIAM. Eyes Have It, The.
Standard Forgings Plant.
STERLING, ANDREW B. Wait till the Sun Shines, Nellie.
STERLING, GEORGE. Aldebaran at Dusk.
Ashes in the Sea, The.
At the Grand Canyon.
Autumn in Carmel.
Balance, The.
Ballad of Two Seas.
Black Vulture, The.
Conspiracy.
Coyote.
Deserted Farm, A.
Father Coyote.
Final Faith, The.
First Food, The.
Gardens of the Sea, The.
Guerdon of the Sun, The.
In Autumn.
In Extremis.
Inclusion.
Kindred.
Last Days, The.
Legend of the Dove, A.
Love's Shadow.
Master Mariner, The.
Music at Twilight.
My Songs.
Mystery.
Night of Gods, The.
Omnia Exeunt in Mysterium.
On the Skull of Shakespeare.
Princess of the Headland, The.
Pumas.
Queen Forgets, The.
Sails.
Saul.
Skull of Shakespeare, The.
Slaying of the Witch, The.
Sonnets by the Night Sea, *sel.*
Sonnets on the Sea's Voice.
Spring in Carmel.
Then and Now.
Three Sonnets on Oblivion.
To Pain.
To the Goddess of Liberty.
Willy Smith at the Ball Game.
Wind of Night, The. *Fr.* Sonnets by the Night Sea.
Young Witch, The—1698.
STERLING, JOHN. Alfred the Harper.
From Heaven High I Come to You.
Hero and Leander, *sel.*, *tr.*
Louis XV.
Of those who at Thermopylae were slain, *tr.*
On a Beautiful Day.
Orpheus, *tr.*
Shakespeare.
Song of Eve to Cain, The.
Spice-Tree, The.
To a Child.
STERN, JUDITH. Miriam's Unsaid Speech.
STERN, MICHAEL. Worlds.
STERNBERG, JACOB. Little Birds.
"STERNE, COLIN." *See* NICHOL, H. E.
"STERNE, STUART" (Gertrude Bloede).
My Father's Child.
Night after Night.
Soul, Wherefore Fret Thee?
Tomorrow and Tomorrows.
STERNHOLD, THOMAS. Beati Omnes, *tr.* *Fr.* Psalms.
Beatus Vir, *tr.* *Fr.* Psalms.
Cum Invocarem, *tr.* *Fr.* Psalms.
Domine Quid Multiplicati Sunt, *tr.* *Fr.* Psalms.
Majesty of God, The.
Psalms, *sels.*, *tr.*
STERRY, JOSEPH ASHBY. *See* ASHBY-STERRY, JOSEPH.
STESICHORUS. Palinode on Helen.
Processional.
Setting Sun, The.
Voyage of the Sun.
STETSON, CHARLOTTE PERKINS. *See* GILMAN, CHARLOTTE PERKINS STETSON.
STETSON, GRACE ELLERY CHANNING. *See* CHANNING, GRACE ELLERY.
STEVENS, FRANK. Alley Cat.
STEVENS, GEORGE ALEXANDER. Pastoral, A: "By the side of a green stagnate pool."
Storm, The.
STEVENS, GEORGE W. Organist, The.
STEVENS, H. P. Why.
STEVENS, MARGARET TALBOTT. Carcassone.
STEVENS, MARVIN. Man.
STEVENS, ROWAN. Cradle Song: "Crickets in the corner sing, The."
STEVENS, WALLACE. Academic Discourse at Havana.
Anecdote of Men by the Thousand.
Anecdote of the Jar.
Annual Gaiety.
Another Weeping Woman.
Asides on the Oboe.
Autumn Refrain.
Banjo Boomer.
Bantams in Pine-Woods.
Bethou Me, Said Sparrow. *Fr.* Notes toward a Supreme Fiction.
Bird with the Coppery, Keen Claws, The.
Bouquet of Belle Scavoir.
Bowl.
Candle, The, a Saint.
Comedian as the Letter C, The.
Connoisseur of Chaos.
Continual Conversation with a Silent Man.
Contrary Theses, I.
Conversation with Three Women of New England.
Cortège for Rosenbloom.
Credences of Summer.
Crude Foyer.
Cuisine Bourgeoise.
Dance of the Macabre Mice.
Death of a [*or* the] Soldier, The.
Disillusionment of Ten o'Clock.
Domination of Black.
Dry Loaf.
Earthy Anecdote.
Emperor of Ice-Cream, The.
Esthétique du Mal.
Esthétique du Mal, *sel.*
Evening without Angels.
Extract from Addresses to the Academy of Fine Ideas, An.
Fabliau of Florida.
Flyer's Fall.
Gallant Château.
Girl in a Nightgown.
Glass of Water, The.
Great Statue of the General Du Puy, The.
Hibiscus on the Sleeping Shores.
High-toned Old Christian Woman, A.
Holiday in Reality.
Homunculus et la Belle Etoile.
How Red the Rose That Is the Soldier's Wound. *Fr.* Esthétique du Mal.
Idea of Order at [*or* in] Key West, The.
Idiom of the Hero.
In Battle.
It Feels Good as It Is without the Giant. *Fr.* Notes toward a Supreme Fiction.
It Is the Celestial Ennui of Apartments. *Fr.* Notes toward a Supreme Fiction.
It Must Be Abstract.
Le Monocle de Mon Oncle.
Lion Roars at the Enraging Desert, The. *Fr.* Notes toward a Supreme Fiction.
Load of Sugar Cane, The.
Man with the Blue Guitar, The.
Man with the Blue Guitar, The, *sel.*
Martial Cadenza.
Mechanical Optimist, The.
Men Made Out of Words.
Mrs. Alfred Uruguay.
Motive for Metaphor, The.
Mozart, 1935.
No Possum, No Sop, No Taters.
Nomad Exquisite.
Not Ideas about the Thing but the Thing Itself.
Notes toward a Supreme Fiction, *sels.*
Novel, The.
Nuances of a Theme by Williams.
Of Heaven Considered as a Tomb.
Of Modern Poetry.
Of the Manner of Addressing Clouds.
Of the Surface of Things.
On an Old Horn.
Ordinary Evening in New Haven, An, *sel.*
Ordinary Women, The.
Paltry Nude Starts on a Spring Voyage, The.
Parochial Theme.
Pediment of Appearance, The.
Peter Parasol.
Peter Quince at the Clavier.
Place of the Solitaires, The.
Plain Sense of Things, The.
Pleasures of Merely Circulating, The.
Plot against the Giant, The.
Ploughing on Sunday.
Poems of Our Climate, The.
Poetry Is a Destructive Force.
Postcard from the Volcano, A.
Prejudice against the Past, The.
Prelude to Objects.
Presence of an External Master of Knowledge.
President Ordains the Bee to Be, The.
Prologues to What Is Possible.
Puella Parvula.
Rabbit as King of the Ghosts, A.
Repetitions of a Young Captain.
Restatement of Romance.
Sad Strains of a Gay Waltz.
Sailing after Lunch.
Sea Surface Full of Clouds.
Sense of the Sleight-of-Hand Man, The.
Six Significant Landscapes.
Snow Man, The.
So-and-So Reclining on Her Couch.
Soldier, There Is a War between the Mind. *Fr.* Notes toward a Supreme Fiction.
Soldier's Wound, The. *Fr.* Esthétique du Mal.
Song of Fixed Accord.
Stars at Tallapoosa.
Study of Images, I.
Study of Two Pears.
Sunday Morning.
Sunday Morning, *sels.*
Tattoo.
Tea at the Palaz of Hoon.
Theory.
Thirteen Ways of Looking at a Blackbird.
To the One of Fictive Music.
Two at Norfolk.
Two Figures in Dense Violet Light [*or* Night].
Two Illustrations That the World Is What You Make of It.

We Reason of These Things. *Fr.* Notes toward a Supreme Fiction.
Whistle Aloud, Too Weedy Wren.
Woman in Sunshine, The.
Woman Looking at a Vase of Flowers.
Woman That Had More Babies than That, The.
World as Meditation, The.
World without Peculiarity.
Worms at Heaven's Gates, The.
STEVENS, WILLIAM O. Charm for Swarming Bees, *tr.*
Nine Herbs Charm, *tr.*
STEVENSON, ALEC BROCK. Et Sa Pauvre Chair.
Icarus in November.
STEVENSON, BURTON EGBERT. Henry Hudson's Quest.
Peace Message, The.
STEVENSON, CANDACE THURBER. Public Library.
STEVENSON, JAMES. Gallant Fighting "Joe," The.
STEVENSON, JOHN. Land o' Nae Surprise, The.
STEVENSON, LIONEL. Gulls and Dreams.
In a Desert Town.
Summer Interlude.
STEVENSON, MABEL ROSE. Springtime in Donegal.
STEVENSON, MARY B. Angel Voices.
STEVENSON, MATTHEW. At the Florists' Feast in Norwich.
Stay! O Stay! Ye Winged Howers.
STEVENSON, PATRIC. Anglo-Eire Vignette.
Autumnal Consummation.
Corn Cañon.
Dogrose.
STEVENSON, QUENTIN. Antinous.
Lufoten, *ad.*
Night-Labour.
Victus.
STEVENSON, ROBERT LOUIS. Alcaics; to H. F. B.
Almighty Will, The. *Fr.* It Is Not Yours, O Mother, to Complain.
At the Seaside.
Auntie's Skirts.
Autumn Fires.
Bed in Summer.
Blast . . . 1875, The.
Block City.
Blows the Wind To-Day.
Brave lads in olden musical centuries.
Bright Is the Ring of Words.
Camp, A. *Fr.* Travels with a Donkey.
Camper's Night Song. *Fr.* Travels with a Donkey.
Celestial Surgeon, The.
Child's Thought, A.
Christmas at Sea.
Cow, The.
De Coenatione Micae, *tr.*
Ditty: "Cock shall crow, The."
Dumb Soldier, The.
End of Travel, An.
Envoy: "Go, little book, and wish to all."
Escape at Bedtime.
Evensong.
Fairy Bread.
Far-Farers, The.
Farewell to the Farm.
Flowers, The.
Foreign Children.
Foreign Lands.
From a Railway Carriage.
Gardener, The.
Go, Little Book.
God's Green Inn. *Fr.* Travels with a Donkey.
Good and Bad Children.
Good Play, A.
Happy Thought.
Hayloft, The.
Heather Ale.
Home No More Home to Me.
House Beautiful, The.
I Do Not Fear.
I Have Trod.
I Should Like to Rise and Go.
I Will Make You Brooches.

If This Were Enough.
If This Were Faith.
If This Were Faith, *sel.*
In Memoriam F. A. S.
In the Highlands.
In the Season.
In the States.
It Is Not Yours, O Mother, to Complain.
It Is the Season Now to Go.
Keepsake Mill.
Lad That Is Gone, A.
Lamplighter, The.
Land of Counterpane, The.
Land of Nod, The.
Land of Story-Books, The.
Limerick: "There was an old man of the Cape," *at.*
Little Land, The.
Looking Forward.
Marching Song.
Martial Elegy for Some Lead Soldiers, A.
Mile an' a Bittock, A.
Morning Drum-Call, The.
Mother and Son.
My Bed Is a Boat.
My House.
My Kingdom.
My Shadow.
My Ship and I.
My Task.
My Treasures.
My Valentine.
My Wife.
Nest Eggs.
North-west Passage, *sel.*
Not I.
Over the Sea to Skye.
Pirate Story.
Portrait, A.
Prayer: "I ask good things that I detest."
Rain, The.
Requiem.
Resurgence.
Roadside Fire, The.
Romance.
Shadow March. *Fr.* North-west Passage.
Sick Child, The.
Since Thou Hast Given Me This Good Hope, O God.
Sing a Song of Seasons!
Sing Me a Song.
Singing.
Skerryvore: The Parallel.
Song of a Traveller, The.
Song of the Road, A.
Spaewife, The.
Summer Sun.
Sun's Travels, The.
Swing, The.
System.
There in the night, where none can spy. *Fr.* The Land of Story-Books.
Though He That Ever Kind and True.
Thought, A.
Time to Rise.
To a Gardener.
To Alison Cunningham.
To Andrew Lang.
To Any Reader.
To Doctor Hake.
To My Wife.
To N. V. de G. S.
To S. R. Crockett.
To the Muse.
To Will. H. Low.
Travel.
Travels with a Donkey, *sel.*
Trusty, Dusky, Vivid, True.
Unforgotten, The, II.
Unseen Playmate, The.
Vagabond, The.
Vailima.
Verses Written in 1872.
Visit from the Sea, A.
Wandering Willie.
Wear and Tear.
Whaups, The.
When I am grown to man's estate.
Where Go the Boats?

Whole Duty of Children.
Wind, The.
Windy Nights.
Winter-Time.
Wishes.
Words.
Young Night Thought.
Youth and Love.
STEVENSON, WILLIAM. Back and Side Go Bare, Go Bare, *at. Fr.* Gammer Gurton's Needle.
Gammer Gurton's Needle, *sel., at.*
In Praise of Ale, *at. Fr.* Gammer Gurton's Needle.
Jolly Good Ale and Old, *at. Fr.* Gammer Gurton's Needle.
Of Jolly Good Ale and Old, *at. Fr.* Gammer Gurton's Needle.
STEWART, ALEXANDER ("Nether Lochaber"). Elegy: On a Pet Dove, *tr.*
Lullaby, A: "Hush thee, my baby boy, hush thee to sleep," *tr.*
St. Kilda Maid's Song, The, *tr.*
STEWART, DOUGLAS. Bunyip, The.
Green Lions.
Helmet Orchid.
Lament: "Sigh, wind in the pine."
Mahony's Mountain.
Mending the Bridge.
Native Inhabitant.
Old Iron.
Rock Carving.
Sun Orchids.
Sunflowers, The.
Terra Australis.
Worsley Enchanted, *sels.*
STEWART, EDWARD LOVELLE. Dragons.
STEWART, FIONA. Quadrille.
STEWART, GEORGE DAVID. Don't Cut the String.
Tired Doctor's Prayer, A.
STEWART, GERVASE. I Burn for England with a Living Flame.
Landscape Lies within My Head, The.
Poem: "I burn for England with a living flame."
Poem: "I take four devils with me when I ride."
Red Cross Nurses.
STEWART, HAROLD. Dialogue of the Way.
Flight of Wild Geese, A.
STEWART, JANE G. June.
STEWART, PHILLIPS. Hope.
STEWART, W. Aristocrats of Labor. *Fr.* The True Aristocrat.
True Aristocrat, The.
True Aristocrat, The, *sel.*
STEWART, WINIFRED GRAY. Only the Arrogant Heart.
They Are Forewarned.
STICKNEY, HELEN FRITH. Camouflage.
Habitué.
Hay Wagon.
STICKNEY, TRUMBULL. Age in Youth.
Alone on Lykaion. *Fr.* Sonnets from Greece.
At Sainte-Marguerite.
Be Still. The Hanging Gardens Were a Dream.
Dramatic Fragment.
Driftwood.
Eride, *sel.*
Fidelity.
He Said: "If in His Image I Was Made."
In Ampezzo ("In days of summer let me go").
In Ampezzo ("Only once more and not again").
In the Past.
Leave Him Now Quiet [by the Way].
Live Blindly [and upon the Hour].
Love, I Marvel What You Are.
Mnemosyne.
Mt. [or Mount] Lykaion. *Fr.* Sonnets from Greece.
Near Helikon.
Now in the Palace Gardens. *Fr.* Eride.
On Some Shells Found Inland.
Once.
Six o'Clock.
Sonnets from Greece, *sels.*

STICKNEY, TRUMBULL (*continued*)
Soul of Time, The.
Sunium.
STIDGER, WILLIAM LEROY. Child and the Book, The.
Child's Prayer, A.
Cross and the Tree, The.
Day, A.
I Am the Cross.
I Saw God.
I Saw God Wash the World.
Integrity.
Judean Hills Are Holy.
Lest Thou Forget.
Motherhood.
Outdoor Son of God, The.
Poet of Palestine, The.
Resignation.
Waste of War, The.
We Are the Burden-Bearers!
STIGALL, JOHN. Beggar for God, A.
STILES, NINA. Thank You, God.
STILLINGFLEET, BENJAMIN. Sonnet: True Ambition.
STILLMAN, ALBERT. Ballad of the Faithful Clerk.
Truth about B. F., The.
When I Am Dead.
STILLMAN, ANNIE RAYMOND. *See* "RAYMOND, GRACE."
STILLMAN, HERMAN W. Symphony, The.
STINSON, SAM S. Nothin' Done.
STIRLING, WILLIAM ALEXANDER, EARL OF. Aurora, *sels.*
Darius, *sel.*
I Swear, Aurora, by thy starry eyes. *Fr.* Aurora.
Illusion. *Fr.* Darius.
Madrigal: "When in her face mine eyes I fix." *Fr.* Aurora.
O if thou knew'st how thou thyself dost harm. *Fr.* Aurora.
Robert Burns.
Sonnet: "I envy not Endymion now no more." *Fr.* Aurora.
Sonnet: "Let others of the world's decaying tell." *Fr.* Aurora.
Sonnet: "Oh, if thou knew'st how thou thyself dost harm." *Fr.* Aurora.
Sonnet: "Then whilst that Latmos did contain her bliss." *Fr.* Aurora.
To Aurora. *Fr.* Aurora.
Two in One. *Fr.* Aurora.
STIRLING-MAXWELL, SIR WILLIAM. In Memoriam.
To Anne.
STIRLING-MAXWELL, LADY. *See* NORTON, CAROLINE ELIZABETH SARAH.
STITCH, WILHELMINA. Blessed Are They.
Little Roads to Happiness.
STIVER, MARY WEEDEN. *See* WEEDEN, MARY.
STJERNE, OSCAR. Little One Smiles, The.
Spring-Grass.
STOCK, ELEANOR BAUG. Prayer of the Quest, The.
STOCKARD, HENRY JEROME. As Some Mysterious Wanderer of the Skies.
In the Lighthouse at Point Lookout, North Carolina.
Last Charge at Appomattox, The.
Mocking-Bird, The.
Mollusks.
My Library.
Over Their Graves.
Shakespeare.
Sir Walter Raleigh.
Unattained, The.
STOCKING, JAY THOMAS. O Master Workman of the Race.
STODART, M. A. One Thing at a Time.
STODART-WALKER, ARCHIBALD. Counsel to Girls. *Fr.* The Moxford Book of English Verse.
Early Bacon. *Fr.* The Moxford Book of English Verse.
Inflictis. *Fr.* The Moxford Book of English Verse.
Moxford Book of English Verse, The, *sels.*
STODDARD, CHARLES WARREN. Albatross.
Ave Maria Bells.
Bells of San Gabriel, The.
Cocoa Tree, The.
First Snowfall, The.
Rhyme of Life, A.
Royal Mummy to Bohemia, The.
Stigmata.
Tamalpais, *sel.*
Toast, The.
Wind and Wave.
STODDARD, ELIZABETH. Baby Song, A.
In the Still, Star-lit Night.
Last Days.
Mercedes.
November.
On the Campagna.
Poet's Secret, The.
Summer Night, A.
Unreturning.
STODDARD, HAROLD PATTON. Silent Cockatoo, The.
STODDARD, LAVINIA. Soul's Defiance, The.
STODDARD, RICHARD HENRY. Abraham Lincoln.
Adsum.
Arab Song.
Arrow, The.
At Last.
Birds.
Brahma's Answer.
Catch, A: "Once the head is gray."
Colonel Ellsworth.
Day and Night My Thoughts Incline.
Divan, The.
Dying Lover, The.
Falcon, The.
Flight of the Arrow, The.
Flight of Youth, The.
Gazelle, A.
Horatian Ode, An.
Hymn to the Sea, A.
Imogen.
It Never Comes Again.
Jar, The.
Lincoln's Birthday.
Little Drummer, The.
Lover, The.
Men of the North and West.
Mors et Vita.
Old Song Reversed, An.
Out to Sea.
Proud Lover.
Sea, The.
Shadow, The.
Silent Songs.
Songs: "How are songs begot and bred?"
There Are Gains for All Our Losses.
Threescore and Ten.
Twilight on Sumter.
Two Anchors, The.
Under the Rose.
Wine and Dew.
Witch's Whelp, The.
STODDARD, W. L. Indian Runner, The.
STODDART, THOMAS TOD. Angler's Trysting-Tree, The.
Angler's Vindication, The.
Come When the Leaf Comes.
River, The.
Taking of the Salmon, The.
STOKES, FRANCIS G. Blue Moonshine.
STOKES, WHITLEY. God's Blessing on Munster, *tr.*
King Ailill's Death, *tr.*
Lament for King Ivor.
Man Octipartite, *tr.*
Viking, The.
Vision of Ita, The, *tr.*
STOKES, WHITLEY, JOHN STRACHAN, *and* KUNO MEYER. *For translations from Irish, see* AnIL; OnYI.
STOKES, WILL. Bugs.
STOLITZA, LUBOV NIKITISHNA. Lent.
STOLTZE, JOHN. Across Illinois.
STONE, MRS. C. S. Sly Santa Claus.
STONE, ELIOT KAYS. Days.
Saint Francis.
STONE, FRANCES B. Alas—a Sea Song.
STONE, PHYLLIS M. Mr. Pennycomequick.
Topsy-turvy Land.
STONE, RUTH. Magnet, The.
STONE, SAMUEL JOHN. Church's One Foundation, The.
STONER, WINIFRED SACKVILLE (Countess Charles P. de Bruché). History of the U.S., The.
STONESTREET, MARGIELEA. Galilean.
STOPHER, VASHTI R. Song of Louisiana.
STOPPLE, LIBBY. Calvary.
STORER, AGNES W. Resurrection.
STORER, THOMAS. Rivers.
STOREY, VIOLET ALLEYN. Christmas Trees.
Country Church, A.
Dawn Song—St. Patrick's Day.
Hummingbird.
Ironical.
Neighborly.
Oh, Bring Not Gold!
Poise.
Prayer after Illness, A.
Prayer for a Very New Angel.
Prayer for Broken Little Families, A.
Prayer for the New Year, A.
Prayer in Affliction.
Prayer in Late Autumn, A.
Rainy Day Song.
Silhouette.
Wood of the Cross.
STORK, CHARLES WHARTON. Bronze Statuette of Kwan-yin, A.
Death—Divination.
Flemish Madonna, A.
God, You Have Been Too Good to Me.
Nails, The.
Painter in New England, A.
Rose and God, The.
Silent Folk, The.
Standards.
Statistician, The.
To Rodin.
Troubadour of God, The.
Zuloaga.
For translations from Danish, see BoDS; LiTW; OnPM; *from German, see* TrJP; *from Norwegian, see* AnNoLy; LiTW; *from Swedish, see* AnSL; LiTW; OnPM.
STORNI, ALFONSINA. Ancestral Burden.
Epitaph for My Tomb.
Inheritance.
World of the Seven Wells.
STORY, ROBERT. Whistler, The.
STORY, WILLIAM WETMORE. Cleopatra.
English Language, The.
Henry Wadsworth Longfellow.
I Have My Cruse of Oil. *Fr.* Tired.
Io Victis.
Io Victis, *sel.*
Musical Box, A.
Pan in Love.
Perseverance, *tr.*
Praxiteles and Phryne.
Snowdrop.
Tired, *sel.*
Violet, The.
STOTT, ROSCOE GILMORE. Strong Woman, The.
"STOVALL, R. J." *See* O'MALLEY, D. J.
STOVER, GEORGE H. Oak's Farewell, The.
STOWE, HARRIET BEECHER. Abide in Me, *sel.*
Day in the Pamfili Doria, A.
Hymn: "When winds are raging o'er the upper ocean."
Lines to the Memory of "Annie," Who Died at Milan, June 6, 1860.
Only a Year.
Other World, The.
Still, Still with Thee.
When I Awake, I Am Still with Thee.
STRACHAN, JOHN, WHITLEY STOKES, *and* KUNO MEYER. *For translations from Irish, see* AnIL; OnYI.
STRACHAN, PEARL. Morning Overture: Chorus of Dogs.
STRACHEY, LYTTON. Cat, The.
STRAHAN, SPEER. Holy Communion.

Mad Lover, The.
Poor, The.
Promised Country, The.
STRANAHAN, W. SCOTT. Sortin' the Mail.
STRANDBERG, KARL VILHELM AUGUST. Swedish National Hymn.
STRANGE, MICHAEL (Blanche Marie Louise Oelrichs Tweed). O Listen You to Whom I Meaning Much.
STRATO. "Gather Ye Rosebuds."
STRAUM, AUGUST. Melancholy.
"STRAUSS, YAWCOB." *See* ADAMS, CHARLES FOLLEN.
"STREAMER, COL. D." *See* GRAHAM, HARRY.
STREET, ALFRED BILLINGS. American Independence.
Loon, The.
Nightfall; a Picture.
Settler, The.
STREET, JULIAN, *and* JAMES MONTGOMERY FLAGG. Said Opie Read.
To Be Continued.
STREETER, R. M. Song of the Maple.
STRETTELL, ALMA. Dion of Tarsus, *tr.*
Grapes, *tr.*
Lullaby of the Virgin, *tr.*
Now it grows late—the angel has passed by, *tr.*
Snow, The, *tr.*
Widow's Lullaby, The, *tr.*
STRINDBERG, AUGUST. Esplanade Method, The.
Sabbath Eve.
STRINGER, ARTHUR. At the Comedy.
Caoch O'Lynn.
Celt Speaks, The.
Final Lesson, The.
I'll Niver Go Home Again.
Keeper, The.
Knight Errant, The.
Life-Drunk.
Meeting, The.
Memories.
Morning in the North-West.
Old Garden, The.
Sappho's Tomb.
Seekers, The.
Sod-Breaker, The.
Sour Wine.
Taps at Twilight.
There Is Strength in the Soil.
Wanderer's Litany.
War.
You Bid Me to Sleep.
STRINGER, R. E. C. Sartorial Solecism.
STROBEL, MARION (Mrs. James Herbert Mitchell). Alice Clay and Sally Mitchell.
Daily Prayer.
Day Will Come, The.
Dog over Snow.
Eight Months Old.
Frightened Face.
God for You, A.
Little Things.
Lost City.
Pastoral: "Hill was flowing with sheep, The."
Pitiful in Your Bravery.
To My Children.
We Have a Day.
STRODE, MURIEL. How Shall I Go?
I Am the Cry.
STRODE, WILLIAM. Chloris in the Snow.
Commendation of Music, The.
Devonshire Song, A, *at.*
Floating Island, The, *sel.*
Hence, All You Vain Delights, *at.*
I saw fair Chloris walk alone.
I'll tell you whence the Rose did first grow red.
In Commendation of Music.
Kisses.
On a Gentlewoman Walking in the Snowe.
On Chloris Walking in the Snow.
On His Mistress, *at.*
On Westwall Downes.
Sing aloud, harmonious spheares.
Song: "My limbs I will fling." *Fr.* The Floating Island.
STRODTMANN, ADOLF. O Spring, Come Prettily In.
STRONG, ANNA LOUISE ("Anise"). City of God, The.
Our Country.
STRONG, ARCHIBALD T. Australia, 1905. *Fr.* Sonnets of the Empire.
Australia, 1914. *Fr.* Sonnets of the Empire.
Australia to England. *Fr.* Sonnets of the Empire.
Dawn at Liverpool. *Fr.* Sonnets of the Empire.
Gloriana's England. *Fr.* Sonnets of the Empire.
Grey.
Hawke. *Fr.* Sonnets of the Empire.
Nelson. *Fr.* Sonnets of the Empire.
Oxford. *Fr.* Sonnets of the Empire.
Roses and Rain.
Sonnets of the Empire, *sels.*
STRONG, GEORGE. Epiphany, The.
STRONG, GEORGE A. Hiawatha's Mittens. *Fr.* The Song of Milkanwatha.
Modern Hiawatha, The. *Fr.* The Song of Milkanwatha.
Song of Milkanwatha, The, *sel.*
STRONG, HEZEKIAH. Railroad Crossing.
STRONG, JULIA HURD. Huckster's Horse, The.
Son and Surf.
STRONG, LEONARD ALFRED GEORGE. Brewer's Man, The.
Bride, The.
Childless.
Contrary Joe.
Departure.
Door, The.
Epitaph: "Where she fell swearing, hand to side."
Epitaph on a Sentry.
From the Greek Anthology.
In the Lane.
Knowledgeable Child, The.
Lament, A: "I saw her last night."
Lowery Cot.
Mad Woman of Punnet's Town, The.
Madman, The.
Man's Way.
March Evening.
Memory, A.
Moment, A.
Mysteries, The.
Northern Light.
Old Dan'l.
Old Man at the Crossing, The.
Old Woman outside the Abbey Theater, An.
Return, The.
Rufus Prays.
"Safe for Democracy."
Seals, The.
Sheepstor.
Sunday Morning.
Two Generations.
Washerwoman's Song.
Zeke.
STRONGIN, JOSEPHINE. Poem: "Child—in all the flying sky."
"STRUTHER, JAN" (Joyce Anstruther Maxtone Graham). Biography.
Cat.
Cul-de-Sac, The.
Freedom.
Knowledge.
R. I. P.
To Grow Older.
Travelling America.
STRYKER, CARRIE W. My Friend, the Cat.
STRYKER, LEONORA CLAWSON. Boundless.
Galatea to Pygmalion.
Palpable Silence.
STRYKER, MELANCTHON WOOLSEY. Almighty Lord, with One Accord.
STUART, ALARIC BERTRAND. Jim-Jam King of the Jou-Jous, The.
STUART, FRANCIS. Coogan's Wood.
Ireland.
Southern Summer.
Une Idole du Nord.
Upper Lake, The.
STUART, HENRY LONGAN. Account Me Not.
Complaint to the Moon.
Fountain, The.
Intempestiva.
Resurrexit.
To the Moon.
STUART, JAMES. Distant Prospect of the City of Armagh, The. *Fr.* Morna's Hill.
Morna's Hill, *sel.*
STUART, JESSE. Heart-summoned.
Jenny. *Fr.* Man with a Bull-Tongue Plow.
Kentucky Mountaineer. *Fr.* Man with a Bull-Tongue Plow.
Man with a Bull-Tongue Plow, *sels.*
My Greenup Friends. *Fr.* Man with a Bull-Tongue Plow.
My Land Is Fair for Any Eyes to See.
Sonnets from Camp.
There Is Shrill Music in High Winds at Night. *Fr.* Man with a Bull-Tongue Plow.
Young Kentucky.
STUART, KEITH. Coquette.
STUART, MARY [*or* MARIE]. *See* MARY QUEEN OF SCOTS.
STUART, MURIEL. Common Fires.
In the Orchard.
Lady Hamilton.
Man and His Makers.
Old Saint, The.
Seed Shop, The.
To ——: "When I grow old and my quick blood is chilled."
STUART, ROGER WINSHIP. Countryman's God.
STUART, RUTH MCENERY. Endless Song, The.
Hen-Roost Man, The.
Sea of Peace, The.
STUBBS, CHARLES WILLIAM. Conscience [and Future Judgment].
'Twas Jolly, Jolly Wat.
STUBBS, JANE. Sim Ines.
STUBBS, JOHN HEATH-. *See* HEATH-STUBBS, JOHN.
STUBBS, WILLIAM. Froude informs the Scottish youth.
STUCKENBERG, VIGGO. Morning.
My Mother.
STUDDERT-KENNEDY, GEOFFREY ANKETELL ("Woodbine Willie"). Carpenter, The.
Christian Soldier, The.
Crucifixion, The.
Faith.
Gambler.
"Gone West."
Great Wager, The.
He Was a Gambler Too.
I Thank My God.
Indifference.
Is It a Dream?
It Is Not Finished, Lord.
Kiss of God, The.
Lord of the World, The.
Mother Understands, A.
My Peace I Give unto You.
Patience.
Peace and Joy. *Fr.* The Suffering God.
Rose, The.
Roses in December.
Suffering God, The.
Suffering God, The, *sel.*
Thy Will Be Done.
Unutterable Beauty, The.
We Shall Build On!
When through the Whirl of Wheels.
STULTS, ROBERT MORRISON. Sweetest Story Ever Told, The.
STURGEON, LORENA W. Love's Tribute.
STURGES-JONES, MARION. To the Crocus—with My Love.
STURLUSON, SNORRI. *See* SNORRI STURLUSON.
STURM, CHRISTOPH CHRISTIAN. Christ Is Risen!
STURM, FRANK PEARCE. Accursed, The, *tr.*
Still-Heart.
STYLES, JOHN H., JR. My Altar.
SUASNAVAR, CONSTANTINO. I Have Lost My Shoes. *Fr.* Numbers.
I Look Up Hotels. *Fr.* Numbers.

SUASNAVAR, CONSTANTINO (*continued*)
Numbers, *sels.*
SUCCORSA, JANICE APPLEBY. My Garden.
SU CH'AN I. Welcome Home!
SUCKLING, SIR JOHN. Actuality.
Advice to a Lover. *Fr.* Aglaura.
Against Fruition.
Aglaura, *sels.*
Art of Love, The.
Ballad [*or* Ballade] upon [*or* of] a Wedding, A.
Ballad [*or* Ballade] upon [*or* of] a Wedding, A, *sels.*
Barley-break.
Besieged Heart, The.
Bride, The. *Fr.* A Ballad upon a Wedding.
Constancy.
Constant Lover, The. *Fr.* Aglaura.
Discontented Colonel, The, *sel.*
Doubt of Martyrdom, A.
Encouragements to a Lover.
Hast Thou Seen the Down in the Air?
Honest lover whatsoever.
I Prithee Send Me Back My Heart.
Loving and Beloved.
Loves World.
My dearest Rival, least our love.
O for Some Honest Lover's Ghost.
Of Thee, Kind Boy.
On New-Years Day 1640. To the King.
Orsames' Song. *Fr.* Aglaura.
Out upon it! I Have Loved.
Poem, A: "Out upon it!"
Sad One, The, *sel.*
Session of the Poets, A.
She's Pretty to Walk With. *Fr.* The Discontented Colonel.
Siege, The.
Sir J.S.
Soldier, A.
Song, A: "Hast thou seen the down in the air."
Song: "Honest lover whosoever [*or* whatsoever]."
Song: "I prithee send me back my heart."
Song: "If you refuse me once, and think again."
Song: "No, no, fair heretic[k], it needs must be." *Fr.* Aglaura.
Song: "Of thee, kind boy, I ask no red and white."
Song: "Out upon it, I have loved."
Song: "When, dearest, I but think of thee," *at.*
Song: "Why so pale and wan, fond lover?" *Fr.* Aglaura.
Song to a Lute.
Sonnet: "Dost see how unregarded now."
Sonnet: "Oh! for some honest Lover's ghost."
Sonnet: "Of thee (kind boy) I ask no red and white."
Supplement of an Imperfect Copy of Verses of Mr. Wil. Shakespeare, A.
That None Beguiled Be.
Thinking on thee, thy beauties then.
'Tis Now Since I Sate [*or* Sat] Down.
To My Love.
Wedding, A.
When, Dearest, I but Think of Thee, *at.*
Why So Pale and Wan [Fond Lover]? *Fr.* Aglaura.
SUCKOW, RUTH. Grampa Schuler.
Odd Ones, The.
SUCKOW, W. J. We Would See Jesus.
SUHL, YURI. And the Earth Rebelled.
SUI FU JEN. Return of Spring, The.
SULLAM, SARAH COPIA. My Inmost Hope.
SULLIVAN, ALAN. Brébeuf and Lalemant.
Suppliant.
White Canoe, The.
SULLIVAN, ALOYSIUS MICHAEL. Advice.
Avowal.
Chronometer, The.
Destroyer.
Flying Dutchman, The.
Genesis.
Heritage.
Jet Plane.
Late Autumn.
Measurement.
Monument.
Pilgrim.
Plenitude.
Psalm against the Darkness.
Psalm to the Holy Spirit.
Seismograph.
Sextant, The.
Shadows Are Black.
Smoke Stack.
Stigmata.
Villanelle.
Villanelle of Light.
Whale and the *Essex,* The.
SULLIVAN, ARCHIBALD BERESFORD. Little Gray Lamb, The.
SULLIVAN, JOSEPH J. Where Did You Get That Hat?
SULLIVAN, MARGARET L. Mild Rebuke, A.
SULLIVAN, RICHARD. Stranger, The.
SULLIVAN, RICHARD WEBB. Star of the Sea.
SULLIVAN, TIMOTHY DANIEL. Dear Old Ireland.
God Save Ireland.
Steering Home.
You and I.
SULLY-PRUDHOMME, RENÉ FRANÇOIS ARMAND. Appointment, The.
Custom.
Naked World, The.
Struggle, The.
Wheel, The.
SULPICIA. Later, to Cerinthus.
To Cerinthus: "At last comes such a love that gossip that I conceal it."
To Cerinthus: "Have you no tender thoughts, Cerinthus, for your sweetheart."
To Cerinthus: "I thank you indeed that, sure of me, you assume such license."
To Cerinthus: "May I be, dear love, no more a caution so glowing."
To Cerinthus: "My hateful birthday is coming, and dismally I must spend it."
SULPICIA II. Satire, The, *sel.*
SUMMERS, HAL. Cerne Abbas.
Eclogue: "When all the powers have fallen."
On the Cliff.
Valentine, A.
Wet Through.
Yorkshire Moors, The.
SUMMERS, HOLLIS SPURGEON. Family Reunion.
Valentine.
SUMNER, JEZANIAH. Ode on Science.
SUNG SHIH. Caring for Silkworms.
SUNG TZU-HOU. Song: "On the Eastern Way at the city of Lo-yang."
"SUNSET JOE." Lines on Mountain Villages.
Rivers of the West.
SUN YÜN FENG. Riding at Daybreak.
SUO [*or* SUWO], LADY. That spring night I spent.
SUPERVIELLE, JULES. By Candlelight.
Full Sky.
God Thinks of Man.
Grasp.
Hard Journey, The.
Heart.
How Heavy.
In the Forest.
Insomnia.
Madame.
Point of Flame.
Prophecy.
Sick Man, The.
Song of the Mountebank.
This Pure Child.
Wait for Death, The.
Whisper in Agony.
Worries.
"SURFACEMAN." *See* ANDERSON, ALEXANDER.
SURIKOV, IVAN. In the green garden the nightingale.
Ukrainian Song.
SURKOV, ALEKSEY ALEKSANDROVICH. Girl's Song.
In the Small Stove.
Twenty Years Old.
Whipped On by December.
SURREY, HENRY HOWARD, EARL OF. Aeneid, The, *sels., tr.*
Age of Children Happiest, The.
Alas, so all things now do hold their peace.
Although I had a check.
Another Tribute to Wyatt ("In the rude age, when knowledge was not rife").
As oft as I behold and see.
Bonum Est Mihi Quod Humiliasti Me.
Brittle Beauty.
Brittle beauty, that Nature made so frail.
Certain Books of Virgil's Aeneis, *tr. Fr.* The Aeneid.
Complaint by Night [of the Lover Not Beloved], A.
Complaint of a Lover Rebuked, *tr. Fr.* Sonnets to Laura.
Complaint of a Lover That Defied Love and Was by Love After the More Tormented.
Complaint of the Absence of Her Lover Being upon the Sea.
Complaint of the Lover Disdained.
Complaint That His Ladie after She Knew of His Love Kept Her Face Alway Hidden from Him.
Consolation.
Cornet, The.
Death of Wyatt, The.
Departure of Aeneas from Dido, *tr. Fr.* The Aeneid.
Description and Praise of His Love Geraldine.
Description of Spring [Wherein Each Thing Renews, save Only the Lover].
Dido's Hunting, *tr. Fr.* The Aeneid.
Epitaph on Thomas Clere.
Exhortation to Learn by Others' Trouble.
Fourth Book of Virgil, The, *sel., tr. Fr.* The Aeneid.
Frail Beauty.
Frailty and Hurtfulness of Beauty, The.
From Tuscan Came My Lady's Worthy Race.
Give Place, Ye Lovers.
Golden Gift, The.
Golden Mean, The.
Happy Life, The, *tr.*
His Incomparable Lady.
How Each Thing save the Lover in Spring Reviveth to Pleasure.
How No Age Is Content.
I never saw you, madam, lay apart.
If care do cause men cry, why do not I complain?
If he that erst the form so lively drew.
In Cyprus springs—whereas dame Venus dwelt.
In Praise of Wyatt's Psalms.
In Windsor Castle.
In winter's just return, when Boreas gan his reign.
Lady Again Complains, The.
Lady Complains of Her Lover's Absence, A.
Laid in My Quiet Bed [in Study as I Were].
Lines to Ratclif.
London, Hast Thou Accusèd Me.
Love that liveth and reigneth in my thought, *tr. Fr.* Sonnets to Laura.
Lover Comforteth Himself with the Worthiness of His Love, The.
Love's Fidelity, *tr. Fr.* Sonnets to Laura.
Love's Rebel.
Martial, the things for to attain, *tr.*
Means to Attain Happy Life, The, *tr.*
Night.
Noble Voyage, The.
O happy dames, that may embrace.
O loathsome place! where I.

Of a Lady That Refused to Dance with Him.
Of [*or* On] the Death of Sir Thomas Wyatt [the Elder].
Portrait of Henry VIII, The.
Praise of His Love, Wherein He Reproveth Them That Compare Their Ladies with His, A.
Prisoned in Windsor, He Recounteth His Pleasure There Passed.
Restless Heart, The.
Restless State of a Lover, The.
Sardanapalus.
Satire on London, A.
Seafarer, The.
Second Boke of Virgiles Aenaeis, The, *tr.* *Fr.* The Aeneid.
Set Me Whereas the Sun Doth Parch the Green, *tr.* *Fr.* Sonnets to Laura.
Since fortune's wrath envieth the wealth.
So cruel prison how could betide, alas.
Sonnets to Laura, *sels.*, *tr.*
Soote season, that bud and bloom forth brings, The.
Spring.
Such wayward ways hath Love, that most part in discord.
Summer Comes.
Summer Is Come.
Sun hath twice brought forth the tender green, The.
Things That Cause a Quiet Life, The, *tr.*
Though I regarded not.
To His Lady, *tr.* *Fr.* Sonnets to Laura.
Too dearly had I bought my green and youthful years.
Translation from Virgil's Aeneid.
Tribute to Wyatt ("Wyatt resteth here").
Vow to Love Faithfully, Howsoever He Be Rewarded, *tr.* *Fr.* Sonnets to Laura.
When raging love with extreme pain.
When Summer took in hand the winter to assail.
When Windsor walls sustain'd my wearied arm.
When youth had led me half the race.
Woman's Answer, A, *at.*
Wrapt in my careless cloak, as I walk to and fro.
Wyatt resteth here, that quick could never rest.
Youth and Age.
SU SHIH. *See* SU T'UNG-PO.
SÜSSKIND VON TRIMBERG. O Thought!
Power of Thought, The.
Virtuous Wife, The.
Why Should I Wander Sadly.
SUSUKIDA, KYUKIN. Home Thoughts.
In the Heat of the Day.
Were I in the Province of Yamato.
SUTHERLAND, ANNE. Empty Little House, The.
SUTHERLAND, R. G. Washington at Valley Forge.
SUTPHEN, MARGARET P. Autumn Leaves.
SUTPHEN, ROSS. Gulls over Great Salt Lake.
SUTPHEN, VAN TASSEL. Deep Waters.
SUTSKEEVER, ABRAHAM. Father Dies.
Here I Am.
How?
Like Groping Fingers.
On My Wander Flute.
Secret Town, The, *sel.*
SUTTON, HENRY SEPTIMUS. Inward Light, The.
SUTTON, KATHLEEN. Geese Flying over England.
Lonely Tryst.
Universalism.
SU T'UNG-PO. At Gold Hill Monastery.
At the Washing of My Son.
Autumn.
Begonias.
Boiling Tea.
Bookworm, The.
Dreaming of My Dead Wife.
Echoing Chang Tzu-yeh's "Spring Daylight."
End of the Year, The.
Epigram: "I fish for minnows in the lake."
Farewell to Chao Ta-lin.
Fisherman, The.
For My Brother.
Harvest Sacrifice.
Last Day of the Year, The.
Leaving Ching-k'ou.
Listening to the River.
Looking from the Pavilion over the Lake.
Meditation at Red Cliff.
Midautumn at Huang-chou.
Moon, Flowers, Man.
Moonlight on the Han River.
On the Birth of His Son.
On the Death of His Baby Son.
On the Siu Cheng Road.
On the Tower of Gathering Remoteness.
Poem, A, Written on a Painting Called "The Smoky River and the Folding Peaks" Possessed by Wang Tingkuo.
Purple Peach Tree, The.
Rain in the Aspens.
Red Cliff, The.
Rowing at Night on the West Lake.
Seeking Spring beyond the City.
Shadow of Flowers, The.
Sitting at Night with My Nephew Who Has Just Come from Afar.
Southern Room over the River, The.
Spring.
Spring Night.
Spring Scene.
Temples Built with Hands.
Terrace in the Snow, The.
Thinking of My Brother.
Thoughts in Exile.
Tien-ho Temple.
To a Traveler.
Turning Year, The.
Verses: "I am old, sick, and lonely."
Walk in the Country, A.
Weaker the Wine, The.
SUWO, LADY. *See* SUO, LADY.
SU WU. Since our hair was plaited and we became man and wife.
To a Husband.
To His Wife.
SVETLOV, MIKHAIL ARKADYEVICH. Grenada.
Rider, The.
SWAIN, CHARLES. Field-Path, The.
Home Is Where There Is One to Love Us.
Life.
Rose Thou Gav'st, The.
Smile and Never Heed Me.
Song: "Violet in her lovely hair, A."
Take the World as It Is.
Take the World as It Is, *sel.*
Tripping down the Field-Path.
'Twas Just before the Hay Was Mown.
Violet in Her Hair, A.
SWAN, CAROLINE D. Stars of Cheer.
SWANN, THOMAS BURNETT. Japanese Birthday Wish, A.
SWART, E. V. Casey Jones.
SWARTZ, ROBERTA TEALE. Bittern, The.
Cease Not to Be a Mystery.
Hawthorn Tree, The.
I Do Remember You.
Prayer by Moonlight.
To Engineers.
SWASEY, EVA INGERSOLL. My Love for You, Mother.
SWEANY, MICHAEL. Devil's Meditation, The.
SWEENEY, FRANCIS. April.
Boy Playing an Organ.
In a Class of Moral Theology.
Tanglewood.
SWEENEY, JOHN L. Wind's Head, The.
SWEENEY, MILDRED ISABEL MCNEAL. Chavez.
Poet, The.
Simple Field That I Shall Buy, The.
SWEENEY, THOMAS. Old Earthworks.
Saint Francis of Assisi.
SWEET, FRANK HERBERT. Before It Is Too Late.
SWEETMAN, ELINOR. Orchard by the Shore, The; a Pastoral.
SWEETSER, F. W. Story of the Little Rid Hin, The.
SWENSON, LILLIAN M. Dissenter, The.
SWENSON, MAY. Centaur, The.
Cloud-Mobile, The.
Evolution.
Feel like a Bird.
Frontispiece.
Garden at St. John's, The.
Key to Everything, The.
Question.
Sunday in the Country.
To the Shore.
Was Worm.
SWETT, HERBERT B. Gathering, The.
SWETT, SUSAN HARTLEY. Blue-Jay, The.
It Is July.
July.
SWIFT, HILDEGARDE HOYT. Man of Galilee, The.
Teacher, The.
SWIFT, IVAN. Home.
Humming Bird, The.
Sandpiper, The.
To a Grosbeak in the Garden.
SWIFT, JONATHAN. A E I O U.
Abroad and at Home.
Animal Critics, The. *Fr.* To Mr. Congreve.
Apples. *Fr.* Verses for Fruitwomen.
As the World Turns.
Baucis and Philemon.
Beasts' Confession, The.
Beautiful Young Nymph Going to Bed, A.
Cadenus and Vanessa, *sel.*
Character of Sir Robert Walpole, The.
City Shower, A.
Clever Tom Clinch Going to Be Hanged.
Critick Vermin, The. *Fr.* To Doctor Delany on the Libels Writ against Him.
Critics. *Fr.* On Poetry; a Rhapsody.
Day of Judgement, The.
Description of a City Shower, A.
Description of a City Shower, A, *sels.*
Description of an Irish Feast, The; or, O'Rourk's Frolic, *tr.*
Description of the Morning, A.
Endurance and Faithfulness, *tr.* *Fr.* Odes.
English in Ireland, The. *Fr.* Verses Occasioned by the Sudden Drying Up of St. Patrick's Well.
Epigram: "Who killed Kildare? Who dared Kildare to kill?"
Epistle to a Lady, *sel.*
Excellent New Song on a Seditious Pamphlet, An.
Excellent New Song upon His Grace Our Good Lord Archbishop of Dublin, An.
Fable of Midas, The.
Five, The.
Furniture of a Woman's Mind, The.
Gentle Echo on Woman, A.
Herrings. *Fr.* Verses for Fruitwomen.
Horace, Epistle VII, Book I, Imitated.
Humble Petition of Frances Harris, The.
In a Glass.
In Sickness.
Lesbia Railing, *tr.*
Life and Genuine Character of Dean Swift, The.
Lines by a Person of Quality, *at.*
Love Song, A, *at.*
Mary the Cook-Maid's Letter to Dr. Sheridan.
Mrs. Frances Harris's Petition.
Mrs. Harris's Petition to Their Excellencies the Lords Justices of Ireland.
Mollis Abuti.
Nature and the Poet. *Fr.* Ode to Sir William Temple.
Near Neighbors.
New Song of Wood's Halfpence, A.
Ode to Dr. William Sancroft, *sel.*
Ode to Sir William Temple, *sels.*
Odes (*of* Horace), *sel.*, *tr.*
On a Curate's Complaint of Hard Duty.
On an Ill-managed House.
On an Upright Judge.
On Blenheim, *after* Martial.

SWIFT, JONATHAN (*continued*)
On Censure.
On Fleas.
On Himself.
On His Own Deafness.
On Mrs. Biddy Floyd.
On Poetry; a Rhapsody, *sels.*
On Stella's Birthday.
On the Day of Judgement.
On the Death of Doctor Swift.
On the Upright Judge, Who Condemned the "Drapier's" Printer.
On the World.
Onions. *Fr.* Verses for Fruitwomen.
O'Rourk's Frolic, *tr.*
Our Knowledge. *Fr.* Ode to Sir William Temple.
Phillis; or, The Progress of Love.
Place of the Damn'd, The.
Pleased with an Empty Swelling. *Fr.* Ode to Dr. William Sancroft.
Poets and Poetasters. *Fr.* To Stella, Who Collected and Transcribed His Poems.
Politician and Mr. Gay, The. *Fr.* To Mr. Gay.
Progress of Beauty, The.
Progress of Beauty, The, *sel.*
Progress of Love, The.
Progress of Poetry, The.
Quiet Life and a Good Name, A.
Receipt to Restore Stella's Youth, A.
Rhapsody on Poetry, A. *Fr.* On Poetry; a Rhapsody.
Riddle, A: "We are little airy creatures."
Satirical [*or* Satyrical] Elegy on the Death of a Late Famous General, A (the Duke of Marlborough).
Satirist, The. *Fr.* Epistle to a Lady.
Soldier and a Scholar, A, *sel.*
Song by a Person of Quality, *at.*
Stella's Birthday.
Stella's Birth-Day; March 13, 1726/27.
Stella's Birth-Day, 1720.
Stella's Birth-Day; Written A.D. 1720–21.
Stella's Birthday, Written in the Year 1718.
To a Lady Who Desired I Would Write Some Verses in the Heroic Style, *sel.*
To Doctor Delany on the Libels Writ against Him, *sel.*
To Mr. Congreve, *sel.*
To Mr. Gay, *sel.*
To Stella; March 13, MDCCXXIII-IV.
To Stella, Who Collected and Transcribed His Poems, *sel.*
To Their Excellencies the Lords Justices of Ireland.
Tonis ad Resto Mare.
Twelve Articles.
Verses for Fruitwomen, *sels.*
Verses Occasioned by the Sudden Drying Up of St. Patrick's Well, *sel.*
Verses on Blenheim.
Verses on the Death of Dr. Swift.
Verses on the Death of Dr. Swift, *sels.*
Vowels, The; a Riddle.
Whiter than White.
Who killed Kildare? Who dared Kildare to kill?

SWIGERT, MINERVA FLORENCE. Three Arts, The.

SWINAMER, GEORGE. Gale of August, '27, The.

SWINBURNE, ALGERNON CHARLES.
Adieux à Marie Stuart.
After Death.
After Looking into Carlyle's Reminiscences.
After Sunset, *sel.*
Anactoria.
Anactoria, *sel.*
Appeal, An.
April, *tr.*
At Parting.
Atalanta in Calydon.
Atalanta in Calydon, *sels.*
August.
Ave atque Vale.
Baby, baby bright. *Fr.* Cradle Songs.
Baby, baby dear. *Fr.* Cradle Songs.
Baby's Death, A.
Baby's eyes. *Fr.* Etude Réaliste.
Baby's feet, A. *Fr.* Etude Réaliste.
Baby's hands. *Fr.* Etude Réaliste.
Ballad against the Enemies of France, *tr.*
Ballad of Burdens, A.
Ballad of Death, A.
Ballad [*or* Ballade] of Dreamland, A.
Ballad of François Villon, A.
Ballad of Life, A.
Ballad of the Lords of Old Time, *tr.*
Ballad of the Women of Paris, *tr.*
Ballad Written for a Bridegroom, *tr.*
Beaumont and Fletcher. *Fr.* Sonnets on English Dramatic Poets (1590–1650).
Before Dawn.
Before the Beginning of Years. *Fr.* Atalanta in Calydon.
Before the Mirror.
Before the Mirror, *sel.*
Ben Jonson. *Fr.* Sonnets on English Dramatic Poets (1590–1650).
Between the Sunset and the Sea. *Fr.* Chastelard.
Birds, The, *sel.*, *tr.*
Bothwell, *sel.*
Burns; an Ode.
By the North Sea.
By the North Sea, *sels.*
Channel Passage, A.
Chastelard, *sels.*
Chastelard and Mary Stuart. *Fr.* Chastelard.
Child and Poet.
Children.
Children of the Poor, The, *tr.*
Child's Future, A.
Child's Laughter, A.
Child's Song.
Chorus: "Before the beginning of years." *Fr.* Atalanta in Calydon.
Chorus: "We have seen thee, O Love, thou art fair; thou art goodly, O Love." *Fr.* Atalanta in Calydon.
Chorus: "When the hounds of spring are on winter's traces." *Fr.* Atalanta in Calydon.
Chorus from "Atalanta." *Fr.* Atalanta in Calydon.
Chorus of Birds, *tr.*
Choruses from "Atalanta in Calydon."
Christmas Antiphon[y], A.
Christmas Antiphon[y], A, *sel.*
Christmas Carol, A: "Three damsels in the queen's chamber."
Christopher Marlowe. *Fr.* Sonnets on English Dramatic Poets (1590–1650).
Cleopatra.
Cliffside Path, The.
Complaint of the Fair Armoress, The, *tr.*
Cor Cordium.
Cradle Songs.
De Contemptu Mundi, *tr.*
Death of Meleager, The. *Fr.* Atalanta in Calydon.
Death of Richard Wagner, The.
Death of Urgan, The. *Fr.* Tristram of Lyonesse.
Dedication: "Sea gives her shells to the shingle, The."
Dedication: "Sea of the years that endure not, The."
Dedication to Poems and Ballads, First Series.
Dialogue, A.
Dickens.
Dies Irae, *tr.*
Disappointed Lover, The. *Fr.* The Triumph of Time.
Dispute of the Heart and Body of François Villon, The, *tr.*
Dolores.
Double Ballad of Good Counsel, *tr.*
Eastward.
England; an Ode.
England, Queen of the Waves. *Fr.* The Armada.
Envoi: "Fly, white butterflies, out to sea."
Epistle in Form of a Ballad to His Friends, *tr.*
Epitaph in Form of a Ballad, The, Which Villon Made for Himself and His Comrades, *tr.*
Erotion.
Etude Réaliste.
Eve of Revolution, The, *sel.*
Farewell, A: "There lived a singer in France of old." *Fr.* The Triumph of Time.
Fate. *Fr.* Atalanta in Calydon.
Faustine.
Félise.
Félise, *sel.*
Final Chorus: "Who shall contend." *Fr.* Atalanta in Calydon.
First Footsteps.
For the Feast of Giordano Bruno.
Forsaken Garden, A.
Fortunate Dead, The. *Fr.* Atalanta in Calydon.
Fragment on [*or* of] Death, *tr.*
Garden of Proserpine, The.
Garden of Proserpine, The, *sels.*
Genesis.
Grand Chorus of Birds, *tr.* *Fr.* The Birds.
Heptalogia, The, *sels.*
Hertha.
Hesperia.
Hesperia, *sel.*
Higher Pantheism in a Nutshell, The. *Fr.* The Heptalogia.
Hope and Fear.
Hounds of Spring, The. *Fr.* Atalanta in Calydon.
Huntsman's Chorus, The. *Fr.* Atalanta in Calydon.
Hymn of Man.
Hymn of the Birds, The, *tr.* *Fr.* The Birds.
Hymn to Proserpine.
Hymn to Proserpine, *sel.*
I will go back to the great sweet mother. *Fr.* The Triumph of Time.
If with voice of words or prayers. *Fr.* The Litany of Nations.
Ilicet.
In a Garden.
In a Rosary.
In Guernsey.
In Memory of "Barry Cornwall."
In Memory of Walter Savage Landor.
In the Bay.
In the lower lands of day.
In the Water. *Fr.* A Midsummer Holiday.
In Time of Mourning.
Interlude, An.
Interpreters, The.
Invocation: "Maiden, and mistress of the months and stars." *Fr.* Atalanta in Calydon.
Itylus.
Jacobite in Exile, A.
Jacobite's Exile, 1746, A.
Jacobite's Farewell, A.
John Jones. *Fr.* The Heptalogia.
John Knox's Indictment of the Queen. *Fr.* Bothwell.
John Webster. *Fr.* Sonnets on English Dramatic Poets (1590–1650).
Kissing Her Hair.
Lake of Gaube, The.
Last Oracle, The.
Laud of Saint Catherine, The. *Fr.* Siena.
Laus Veneris.
Leave-taking, A.
Leper, The.
Les Noyades, *sel.*
Let us go hence, my songs; she will not hear. *Fr.* A Leave-taking.
Life of Man, The. *Fr.* Atalanta in Calydon.
Lines on the Monument of Giuseppe Mazzini.
Love and Love's Mates. *Fr.* Atalanta in Calydon.
Love and Sorrow. *Fr.* The Sisters.
Love at Ebb. *Fr.* Chastelard.
Love at Sea.
Love That Is First and Last.
Lyke-Wake Song, A.
Lyric, A: "There's nae lark loves the lift, my dear."
Madonna Mia.

Making of Man, The. *Fr.* Atalanta in Calydon.
Man. *Fr.* Atalanta in Calydon.
Many, The. *Fr.* Sonnets on English Dramatic Poets (1590–1650).
Mary Beaton's Song ("Between the sunset and the sea"). *Fr.* Chastelard.
Mary Stuart, *sel.*
Masque of Queen Bersabe, The, *sel.*
Match, A.
Mater Dolorosa.
Mater Triumphalis.
Messidor.
Midsummer Holiday, A, *sels.*
Nature. *Fr.* Atalanta in Calydon.
Neap-Tide.
Nephelidia. *Fr.* The Heptalogia.
Nephelidia, *sel. Fr.* The Heptalogia.
"Non Dolet."
Northumberland.
Not a Child.
Not as with Sundering of the Earth. *Fr.* Atalanta in Calydon.
Nympholept, A.
Oblation, The.
Of Such Is the Kingdom of Heaven.
Old Saying, An.
Olive.
On a Country Road. *Fr.* A Midsummer Holiday.
On Lamb's Specimens of Dramatic Poets.
On the Cliffs.
On the Death of Robert Browning.
On the Deaths of Thomas Carlyle and George Eliot.
On the Monument Erected to Mazzini at Genoa.
On the South Coast.
On the Verge. *Fr.* A Midsummer Holiday.
Oscar Wilde, *at.*
Peace-Giver, The.
Philip Massinger. *Fr.* Sonnets on English Dramatic Poets (1590–1650).
Pilgrims, The.
Play Then and Sing!
Poet and the Woodlouse, The.
Poor Children, *tr.*
Prelude: "Between the green bud and the red." *Fr.* Songs before Sunrise.
Prelude: "Love that is first and last of all things made." *Fr.* Tristram of Lyonesse.
Prelude: Tristram and Iseult. *Fr.* Tristram of Lyonesse.
Prelude to "Songs before Sunrise."
Proserpine. *Fr.* The Garden of Proserpine.
Queen's Song, The. *Fr.* Chastelard.
Relics.
Return, The. *Fr.* The Triumph of Time.
Rizpah.
Rococo.
Rondel: "Kissing her hair, I sat against her feet."
Rondel: "These many years since we began to be."
Rosamond, *sel.*
Rosamond at Woodstock. *Fr.* Rosamond.
Rose.
Roundel, The: "Roundel is wrought as a ring or a starbright sphere, A."
Salt of the Earth, The.
Sapphics.
Sappho ("All the night sleep came not").
Sappho ("Love's priestess"). *Fr.* On the Cliffs.
Sea, The. *Fr.* The Triumph of Time.
Seaboard, The.
Sequence of Sonnets on the Death of Robert Browning, A.
Seven Years Old.
Shelley. *Fr.* Cor Cordium.
Siena.
Siena, *sel.*
Singing Lesson, A.
Sisters, The, *sels.*
Solitude, A.
Song: "And ye maun braid your yellow hair." *Fr.* Mary Stuart.
Song: "Love laid his sleepless head."
Song in Season, A.
Song in Time of Order, A (1852).
Song of the Standard, The.
Songs before Sunrise, *sel.*
Sonnet for a Picture. *Fr.* The Heptalogia.
Sonnets on English Dramatic Poets (1590–1650), *sels.*
Spring Song.
Stage Love.
Stanzas: "I will go back to the great sweet mother." *Fr.* The Triumph of Time.
Sunbows, The.
Sundew, The.
Sunrise at Sea.
Super Flumina Babylonis.
Super Flumina Babylonis, *sel.*
Swan Song. *Fr.* The Garden of Proserpine.
Swimming. *Fr.* Tristram of Lyonesse.
Thalassius.
There lived a singer in France of old. *Fr.* The Triumph of Time.
There's Nae Lark. *Fr.* The Sisters.
Thomas Decker. *Fr.* Sonnets on English Dramatic Poets (1590–1650).
Three Damsels in the Queen's Chamber.
To a Cat.
To a Seamew.
To Louis Kossuth.
To Victor Hugo.
To Walt Whitman in America.
To Walt Whitman in America, *sel.*
Transfiguration.
Triads.
Tristram and Iseult. *Fr.* Tristram of Lyonesse.
Tristram of Lyonesse, *sels.*
Triumph of Time, The.
Triumph of Time, The, *sels.*
Tyneside Widow, The.
Unto Each His Handiwork.
Up the Spout.
Upon a Child.
Vision of Spring in Winter, A.
Watch in the Night, A.
Way of the Wind, The.
We Have Seen Thee, O Love. *Fr.* Atalanta in Calydon.
When the Hounds of Spring [Are on Winter's Traces]. *Fr.* Atalanta in Calydon.
White Butterflies.
"Whoso Loseth His Life." *Fr.* Super Flumina Babylonis.
William Shakespeare. *Fr.* Sonnets on English Dramatic Poets (1590–1650).
Wilt Thou Yet Take All. *Fr.* Hymn to Proserpine.
Winds, The.
Witch-Mother, The.
Word with the Wind, A.
Year's Burden, A, 1870, *sel.*
Youth of the Year, The. *Fr.* Atalanta in Calydon.
SWINGLER, RANDALL. Letter I.
Letter VIII.
Swans, The.
They Live.
SYLVAIN, NORMIL. Negro Sings, A.
SYLVESTER, FREDERICK OAKES. Picture, The.
SYLVESTER, JOSHUA. Amor Ineluctabilis, *at.*
Autumnus.
Constancy, *at.*
Contented Mind, A.
Contentment.
Du Bartas: His First Week or Birth of the World, *sel.*
First Day of the First Week, The. *Fr.* Du Bartas: His First Week or Birth of the World.
Go, Silly Worm.
Love's Omnipresence, *at.*
Omnia Somnia.
Sonnet: "They say that shadows [*or* shadowes] of deceased ghosts."
Sonnet: "Were I as base as is the lowly plain," *at.*
Surcloying the Stomach. *Fr.* Tetrasticha.
Sweet mouth, that send'st a musky-rosed breath.
Tetrasticha, *sel.*
They Say That Shadows of Deceasèd Ghosts.
Ubique, *at.*
Were I as Base as Is the Lowly Plain, *at.*
SYMONDS, JOHN ADDINGTON. Alas, poor heart, I pity thee, *tr.*
Among the Embers, *tr.*
Amulet of Love, The, *tr.*
Antidote, *tr.*
Ballata of Myrrha's Eyes, *tr.*
Beauty and the Artist, *tr.*
Before my lady's window gay, *tr.*
Being a man, ask not release from pain, *tr.*
Bellerophon, *sel., tr.*
Beneath the branch of the green may, *tr.*
Carmina Burana, *sel., tr.*
Carnal and Spiritual Love, *tr.*
Celestial Love, *tr.*
Christmas Lullaby, A.
Church Triumphant, The.
Coming Day, The.
Danaë, *tr.*
Defence of Night, The, *tr.*
Demetrius Enters Athens, *tr.*
Doom of Beauty, The, *tr.*
Drink, gossips mine, we drink no wine, *tr.*
Drinking Song, *tr.*
Episode, An.
Fair is her body, bright her eye, *tr.*
Fall of a Soul, The.
Farewell: "It is buried and done with."
Farewell: "Thou goest; to what distant place."
Fearful Joy, *tr.*
Flora, *tr.*
Garden Close, A, *tr.*
Garland and the Girdle, The, *tr.*
Gaudeamus Igitur, *tr.*
Girl, A, *tr.*
Girls, look you, Kupris is not Kupris only, *tr.*
Give me thyself! It were as well to cry. *Fr.* Stella Maris.
Giving a Heart, *tr.*
Harvest.
He who knows not what thing is Paradise, *tr. Fr.* Three Ballate.
Hecuba, *sel., tr.*
His Great Love on High, *tr.*
How can I sing light-souled and fancy-free, *tr.*
How often have I now outwatched the night. *Fr.* Stella Maris.
Human Outlook, The.
Hymn to Aphrodite, *tr.*
I found at daybreak yester morn, *tr.*
I found myself one day all, all alone, *tr. Fr.* Three Ballate.
I see the dawn e'en now begin to peer, *tr.*
I went a roaming, maidens, one bright day. *Fr.* Three Ballate.
I would I were a bird so free, *tr.*
Idyll of the Rose, *tr.*
Il Fior Degli Eroici Furori.
In a Green Garden, *tr. Fr.* Three Ballate.
In February.
In the Small Canals. *Fr.* In Venice.
In this merry morn of May, *tr.*
In Venice, *sels.*
Invitation to the Gondola, The. *Fr.* In Venice.
Invitation to Youth, *tr.*
Invocation, An: "O God, unknown, invisible, secure," *sel.*
Invocation, An: "To God, the everlasting, who abides."
Invocation, An: "To God, the everlasting, who abides," *sel.*
It was the morning of the first of May, *tr.*
Joy May Kill, *tr.*

SYMONDS, JOHN ADDINGTON (*cont.*)
Kiss me then, my merry May, *tr.*
Κοινὰ τὰ τῶν φίλων (Koina ta ton Philon).
Lament for Adonis, *tr.*
Lamentation of Danaë, *tr.*
Lauda, *tr.*
Lauriger Horatius, *tr.*
Le Jeune Homme Caressant Sa Chimère.
Lo, I have given thee plumes wherewith to skim, *tr.*
Loftier Race, A.
Loss at Sea, *tr.*
Love at the Door, *tr.*
Love in Dreams.
Love, the Light-Giver, *tr.*
Love's Entreaty, *tr.*
Lullaby for Christmas, A.
Lux Est Umbra Dei.
Maid Marjory sits at the castle gate, *tr.*
Man at Peace, *tr.*
Medieval Norman Songs, *tr.*
Model and the Statue, The, *tr.*
Moon hath left the sky, The, *tr.*
My Love for him shall be, *tr.*
Night.
Night Fears, *tr.*
Nightingale, The.
Now am I nought—abandoned: oftentimes, *tr.*
Now who is he on earth that lives, *tr.*
O love, my love, and perfect bliss! *tr.*
O nightingale of woodland gay, *tr.*
Ode: "Peer of gods he seemeth to me, the blissful," *tr.*
Ode to Aphrodite, *tr.*
On a Picture by Poussin Representing Shepherds in Arcadia.
On Dante Alighieri, *tr.*
On Knighthood, *tr.*
On Rome in the Pontificate of Julius II, *tr.*
On Sunday morning well I knew, *tr.*
On the Brink of Death, *tr.*
Orestes, *sels., tr.*
Orestes and Electra, *tr. Fr.* Orestes.
Passing across the billowy sea, *tr.*
Pastoral, A: "There went out in the dawning light," *tr.*
Pastoral Dialogue, *tr.*
Peace on Earth.
Peer of the Gods, *tr.*
Peer of the gods he seemeth to me, the blissful, *tr.*
People, The, *tr.*
Philosophic Flight, The, *tr.*
Poem of Privacy, A, *tr.*
Popular Songs of Tuscany, *tr.*
Prayer for Faith, A, *tr.*
Prayer for Purification, A, *tr.*
Prayer for Strength, A, *tr.*
Processional for Demetrius Poliorcetes, *tr.*
Sacred Night, *tr.*
Sad, lost in thought, and mute I go, *tr.*
Saon of Acanthus, *tr.*
Seeing the martyred corpse of Sparta's king, *tr.*
Sic Transit, *tr.*
Silver Moon, The, *tr.*
Sleeping or waking, thou sweet face, *tr.*
Song of the Open Road, *tr.*
Sonnet: "From thy fair face I learn," *tr.*
Sonnet: Philosophic Flight, The, *tr.*
Sonnet: Silkworm, The, *tr.*
Sonnet, The: "Sonnet is a fruit which long hath slept, The."
Sonnet: "Thou knowest, love," *tr.*
Sonnet: To Vittoria Colonna, *tr.*
Speech of Night, The, *tr.*
Spurning the Earth, *tr.*
Statue by Lysippus, A, *tr.*
Stella Maris, *sels.*
Strew me with blossoms when I die, *tr.*
Swallow Song, *tr.*
Sweet flower that art so fair and gay.
Sweetness of Spring, The, *tr.*
Terrible Man, A, *tr.*
There Are No Gods, *tr. Fr.* Bellerophon.
There's No Lust like to Poetry.
These Things Shall Be.
They have said evil of my dear, *tr.*
They lied those lying traitors all, *tr.*
This month of May, one pleasant eventide, *tr.*
Thou Alone Art Good, *tr.*
Three Ballate, *tr.*
Thyself. *Fr.* Stella Maris.
Timas, *tr.*
Time's Flying, *tr.*
To Cyrnus, *tr.*
To Giovanni da Pistoia on the Painting of the Sistine Chapel, 1509, *tr.*
To mortal men Peace giveth these good things, *tr.*
To Prote, *tr.*
To Sleep, *tr.*
Tomb of Diogenes, The, *tr.*
Transfiguration of Beauty, *tr.*
Venice. *Fr.* Stella Maris.
Venice, thou Siren of sea-cities, wrought. *Fr.* Stella Maris.
Virtue, to men thou bringest care and toil, *tr.*
Vow to Cupid, The, *tr.*
Waiting for Death, *tr.*
What time I see you passing by, *tr.*
When, in the carven chest, *tr.*
Whom the gods love die young; that man is blest, *tr.*
Wind in the Poplars, *tr.*
Worst Horror, The, *tr.*
Youth and Age, *tr.*
SYMONS, ARTHUR. A Clymène, *tr.*
A la promenade, *tr.*
Absinthe-Drinker, The.
After Love.
Amends to Nature.
Angel of Perugino.
Anguish, *tr.*
Arques—Afternoon.
Art poétique, *tr.*
Asking Forgiveness.
At Burgos.
At Carbis Bay.
At Dawn.
At Fontainebleau.
At the Stage-Door.
Beauty, *tr.*
Before the Squall.
By the Pool at the Third Roses.
Cat and Lady, *tr.*
Cats, The, *tr.*
Chansons d'automne, *tr.*
Clair de lune, *tr.*
Colloque sentimentale, *tr.*
Colombine, *tr.*
Confession, A, *tr.*
Cornish Wind.
Cortège, *tr.*
Cracked Bell, The, *tr.*
Credo.
Crying of Water, The.
Cythère, *tr.*
Dans l'allée, *tr.*
Declaration.
Design for a List of Pictures.
Despair of the Old Woman, The, *tr.*
During Music.
Elegies, *tr.*
Elevation, *tr.*
Emmy.
En bateau, *tr.*
Enemy, The, *tr.*
Epilogue: Credo.
Epilogue: "With heart at rest," *tr.*
Epilogue to Prose Poems, *tr.*
Epithalamium.
Exotic Perfume, *tr.*
Fair Dorothy, The, *tr.*
Fantoches, *tr.*
Femme et chatte, *tr.*
Fisher's Widow, The.
Giantess, The, *tr.*
Gipsy Love.
Grey Wolf, The.
Gypsies on the March, *tr.*
Hallucination.
Hérodiade, *sel., tr.*
Hiboux, Les, *tr.*
Humoradas, *sel., tr.*
Hymn to God.
If a wished-for thing and a thing past hoping for, *tr.*
If, Lord, Thy Love for Me Is Strong, *tr.*
In Fountain Court.
In Kensington Gardens.
In the Bay.
In the Meadows at Mantua.
In the Wood of Finvara.
Javanese Dancers.
Kisses.
La Mélinite; Moulin-Rouge.
Last Memory, The.
Laus Virginitatis.
Let Mine Eyes See Thee, *tr.*
Leves Amores.
Life Is a Dream, *tr.*
Life Is a Dream, *sel., tr.*
Loom of Dreams, The.
Love and Sleep.
Love Song.
Mandoline, *tr.*
Memory.
Mists and Rain, *tr.*
Modern Beauty.
Montserrat.
Nerves.
Night.
No, I Am Not as Others Are, *tr.*
O Flame of Living Love, *tr.*
O woman of my love.
Obscure Night of the Soul, The, *tr.*
Of Charity.
Old Women, The.
On the Beach.
Opals.
Pale Woman, The.
Pantomime, *tr.*
Parfum exotique, *tr.*
Posthumous Coquetry, *tr.*
Prayer to Saint Anthony of Padua, A.
Prologue: Before the Curtain.
Prose Poem: Dog and the Flask, The, *tr.*
Quintia is beautiful, many will tell you: to me, *tr.*
Rain on the Down.
Remorse after Death, *tr.*
Requies.
Return, The.
Roundel of Rest, A.
Sagesse, *sels., tr.*
Sea-Wind, *tr.*
Sed Non Satiata, *tr.*
Shadow, The.
Shepherd, Shepherd, Hark, *tr.*
Sigh, *tr.*
Song of Autumn, *tr.*
Street-Singer, The.
Thee I Adore, *tr.*
To a Portrait.
To a Sea-Gull.
To Night.
To-Day a Shepherd, *tr.*
Turning Dervish, The.
Twilight.
Unloved, The.
Veneta Marina.
Wanderers, The.
Wanderer's Song.
White Magic.
Within a Dainty Garden-Close, *tr.*
Woman and Cat, *tr.*
You wave your fan with such a graceful art, *tr. Fr.* Humoradas.
Zulia.
SYMONS, JULIAN. And the World's Face.
For My Wife.
For the Depressed.
Gladstone.
Hart Crane.
Homage to Our Leaders.
Hospital Observation.
Mr. Symons at Richmond, Mr. Pope at Twickenham.
Pub.
Reflections in Bed.
Second Man, The.
Spring Poem.
Sunday, July 14th; a Fine Day at the Baths.
SYNESIUS. Beloved, glorious, blest.

Hymn: "Ah, what are strength and beauty?"
SYNGE, JOHN MILLINGTON. Beg-Innish.
Curse, The.
Danny.
Dread.
He Is Jealous of the Heavens and Earth, *tr.* *Fr.* Sonnets to Laura.
He Understands the Great Cruelty of Death, *tr.* *Fr.* Sonnets to Laura.
He Wishes He Might Die and Follow Laura, *tr.* *Fr.* Sonnets to Laura.
In Glencullen.
In Kerry.
In May.
I've Thirty Months.
Laura Waits for Him in Heaven, *tr.* *Fr.* Sonnets to Laura.
Old Woman's Lamentations, An, *tr.*
On a Birthday.
On an Anniversary.
On an Island.
Passing of the Shee, The.
Patch-Shaneen.
Prelude: "Still south I went and west and south again."
Queens.
Question, A.
Sonnets to Laura, *sels.*, *tr.*
To the Oaks of Glencree.
Translation from Petrarch, A ("What a grudge I am bearing the earth"), *tr.* *Fr.* Sonnets to Laura.
Translation from Villon, A ("Mother of God that's Lady of the Heavens"), *tr.*
Translation from Walther von der Vogelweide, A ("I never set my two eyes . . ."), *tr.*
Two Translations from Villon, *tr.*
What a grudge I am bearing the earth, *tr.* *Fr.* Sonnets to Laura.
Winter.
SYNNOTT, J. B. Grave of Albert Sidney Johnston.
SYPSOMOS, DEMETRIOS. *See* "PORPHYRAS, LAMBROS."
SYRIAN, AJAN. Syrian Lover in Exile Remembers Thee, Light of My Land, The.

T

"T., A. J." What Is Love?
"T., B. A." Joe Dobson.
"T., B. L." *See* TAYLOR, BERT LESTON.
"T., C. W." Valentine.
"T., I. [*or* J.]." When Stars Are Shrouded.
"T. M. M." *See* "M., T. M."
TA' ABBATA SHARRA. Ever Watchful.
TABB, JOHN BANISTER. All in All.
Annunciation, The.
Anonymous.
Aspiration.
Assumption, The.
At Bethlehem. *Fr.* The Child.
At Lanier's Grave.
Becalmed.
Betrayal.
Boy Jesus, The.
Brother Ass and St. Francis.
Bubble, The.
Bunch of Roses, A.
Butterfly.
Cats.
Child, The.
Child at Bethlehem, The. *Fr.* The Child.
Childhood.
Child's Prayer, A.
Child's Star, The.
Christ and the Pagan.
Christ and the Winds.
Christ the Mendicant.
Clover.
Communion.
Compensation.
Cradle-Song, A: "Sing it, Mother! sing it low."
Dandelion, The.
David and Goliath.
Deep unto Deep.
Departed, The.
Difference, The.
Druid, The.
Evolution.
Faith.
Fame.
Father Damien.
Fern Song.
Fire-Fly, The.
Foot Soldiers.
Fraternity.
God.
Going Blind.
High and Low.
Holy Saturday.
Hospitality.
Humming-Bird, The.
Immaculate Conception, The.
Inconvenience, An.
Indian Summer.
Influence.
Insectarian, An.
Insomnia.
Inspiration.
"Is Thy Servant a Dog?"
Keats.
Kildee.
Lake, The.
Lamb-Child, The.
Leaf and Soul.
Light of Bethlehem, The.
Little Child's Prayer, A.
Lone-Land.
Mater Dolorosa.
Matins.
Missing.
Mouse, a Cat, and an Irish Bull, A.
My Secret.
My Star.
Nekros.
Old Pastor, The.
Out of Bounds.
Overflow.
Pleiads, The.
Poe's Critics.
Precipice, The.
Reaper, The.
Recognition.
Robin Redbreast.
Shakespeare's Mourners.
Sisters, The.
Sleep.
Slumber Song: "Lo, in the west."
Snowbird, The.
Tax-Gatherer, The.
Test, The.
To a Photograph.
To a Rose.
To a Songster.
To a Wood-Violet.
To His Mother. *Fr.* The Child.
To Shelley.
To the Christ.
Transition.
Two Easter Lilies.
Water-Lily, The.
White Jessamine, The.
Wind, The.
Woodpecker, The.
TABER, HARRY PERSONS. Jabberwocky of Authors, The.
TABLADA, JOSÉ JUAN. Alternating Nocturne.
Dawn in the Cockloft.
Haiku of a Day.
Haiku of the Flowerpot.
Idol in the Porch, The.
Parrot, The.
TABLEY, LORD DE. *See* DE TABLEY, JOHN BYRNE LEICESTER WARREN, 3D BARON.
TACHIHARA, MICHIZO. Preface.
TADAMINE (Mibu no Tadamine). Cascade, The.
Since I left her.
TADEMA, LAURENCE ALMA-. *See* ALMA-TADEMA, LAURENCE.
TAGGARD, GENEVIEVE (Mrs. Kenneth Durant). Desert Remembers Her Reasons, The.
Dilemma of the Elm.
Doomsday Morning.
Enamel Girl, The.
Eruption in Utopia.
Everyday Alchemy.
First Miracle.
For Eager Lovers.
Galatea Again.
Gladness.
Hawaiian Hilltop.
Long View.
Millions of Strawberries.
Mood from 3000 B.C.
Quiet Woman, The.
Sea-Change.
Solar Myth.
Song for Unbound Hair.
Still Search, The.
Thoreau.
To the Veterans of the Abraham Lincoln Brigade.
Tropical Girl to Her Garden.
Try Tropic.
Unfaithful, The.
With Child.
TAGGERT, GEORGE. Moth and the Flame, The.
TAGORE, RABINDRANATH. Autumn.
Baby's Way.
Because of Thee. *Fr.* Gitanjali.
Bird, The.
Day after Day. *Fr.* Gitanjali.
Divine Companion, The. *Fr.* Gitanjali.
End, The.
Freedom.
Fruit-gathering, *sels.*
Further Bank, The.
Gardener, The, *sels.*
Gift, The.
Gitanjali, *sels.*
Have you not heard his silent steps? *Fr.* Gitanjali.
Here is thy footstool. *Fr.* Gitanjali.
I Dive Down into the Depth.
I have got my leave. *Fr.* Gitanjali.
I was not aware of the moment. *Fr.* Gitanjali.
If it is not my portion. *Fr.* Gitanjali.
In the Dusky Path of a Dream. *Fr.* The Gardener.
India.
Merchant, The.
My Free Country. *Fr.* Gitanjali.
My Song.
Oarsmen, The, *sel.*
On the slope of the desolate river. *Fr.* Gitanjali.
Paper Boats.
Paper Boats, *sel.*
Prayer for Courage.
Prayer for Strength. *Fr.* Gitanjali.
Recall, The.
Song-Offering, A.
Thou art the sky. *Fr.* Gitanjali.
Thou hast made me known to friends. *Fr.* Gitanjali.
Thy gifts to us mortals. *Fr.* Gitanjali.
Two Songs, *tr.*
Vocation.
When One Knows Thee. *Fr.* Gitanjali.
Where the mind is without fear. *Fr.* Gitanjali.
Yellow Bird Sings, The. *Fr.* The Gardener.
TAHUREAU, JACQUES. Moonlight.
Shadows of His Lady.
TAIGI. Firefly, The.
TAI PING. Climbing Tung Kuan Mountain.
TAIRI NO KANEMORI. Although I hide it.
In spite of my efforts.
T'AI TSUNG. *See* LI SHIH-MING.
T'AI WANG-SHU. Unrequited Lover, The.
TAKAHASHI, SHINKICHI. Fine Rain, The.
Raven, The.
TAKAMOTO. Heaven.
Hills of God, The.
My All.
Your Death.

TAKAMURA, KOTARO. My Poetry.
Rain-beaten Cathedral, The.
Taciturn Sea Captain.
TAKENAKA, IKU. At the Close of Day.
Japan for Sightseeing.
Memory of a Witch.
TALBOT, ELLEN V. Sleepy-Time.
TALBOT, ETHEL. Crab-Apple.
Give Love To-Day.
TALBOTT, CARLTON. Ballyhoo for a Mendicant.
Day Closes, The.
Royal Pickle, A.
Sisters Kastemaloff, The.
TALFOURD, SIR THOMAS NOON. Friend, A.
Ion, *sel.*
Sympathy. *Fr.* Ion.
"TALHAIARN" (John Jones). Where Are the Men?
TALIESIN [*or* TALIESSIN]. Battle of Argoed Llwyfain, The.
Dialogue between Poet and Patron.
Prophecy of Taliesin, The.
Song to the Wind, A.
TALL, GRACE CORNELL. Needle, The.
TALLADAY, JENNIE. Boneset Tea.
TALLANTE, MOSSÈN [*or* MOSEN] JUAN. Prayer to Jesus.
Prayer to the Crucifix.
TALPALAR, MORRIS. True Happiness.
TAMUKE. Love's Fancy.
TANAKA, FUYUJI. Mosquito Net.
Stone Staircase Overlooking the Sea.
TANAKA, KATSUMI. Chance Encounter.
Wilderness.
"TANAQUIL, PAUL" (J. G. Clemenceau Le Clercq). History.
TANASSO, ELDA. Remember That Our Love Moves like the Snow.
TANIKADO. Dawn.
TANNAHILL, ROBERT. Bonnie Wood o' Craigie-lea.
Braes o' Balquhither, The.
Braes o' Gleniffer, The.
By Yon Burn Side.
Flower o' Dumblane, The.
Gloomy Winter's Now Awa'.
Jessie, the Flower o' Dunblane.
Lass o' Arranteenie, The.
Loudoun's Bonnie Woods and Braes.
Midges Dance aboon the Burn, The.
O Are Ye Sleeping, Maggie?
TANSEY, ANNE. There Must Be Silence.
T'AO CH'IEN. *See* TAO YUAN-MING.
TAO YUAN-MING [*or* T'AO CH'IEN]. Beggar, The.
Blaming Sons.
Chill and harsh the year draws to its close.
Chrysanthemums ("The autumn chrysanthemums have the loveliest colors").
Chrysanthemums ("I built my cottage among the habitations of men").
Cold Year, The.
Cozy.
Drunk and Sober.
Elegy for Myself, An.
Empty Boat, The.
Fire Burns Down My Cottage, A.
Flood.
Friendship.
Hermit, The.
I Built My Hut.
In Early Morning.
In the quiet of the morning I heard a knock at my door.
Living in the Country.
Long I Have Loved to Stroll.
Long time ago, A.
Moving House.
New Corn.
Once More Fields and Gardens.
Orchid, The.
Planting Beans.
Poor Scholars, The.
Reading the Book of Hills and Seas.
Reading "The Book of Strange Places and Seas."
Remembering the Ancient Farmstead.
Retrospect.
Return to the Country.
Returning to the Fields.
Shady, Shady.
Substance, Shadow, and Spirit.
Visiting the Chou Family Tombs.
TAO-YÜN. Climbing a Mountain.
TAPLIN, GARDNER, *and* RICHARD EBERHART. *See* EBERHART, RICHARD, *and* GARDNER TAPLIN.
TAPPAN, WILLIAM BINGHAM. Hour of Peaceful Rest, The.
Jesus Prays Alone.
TAPPER, THOMAS. Tides, The.
TARKINGTON, LOUISE FLETCHER. Land of Beginning Again, The.
TARRANT, WILLIAM GEORGE. Master's Man, The.
TASSIN, ALGERNON DE VIVIER. Attainment.
TASSIS, JUAN DE. *See* VILLAMEDIANA.
TASSO, TORQUATO. Aminta, *sels.*
Armida, the Sorceress. *Fr.* Jerusalem Delivered.
Birds and Plants of Love, The. *Fr.* Aminta.
Crusaders Behold Jerusalem, The. *Fr.* Jerusalem Delivered.
Crusaders Reach Jerusalem, The. *Fr.* Jerusalem Delivered.
Epigram: "I'd like to be a bee."
Erminia Wanders in the Fields and Dreams of Love. *Fr.* Jerusalem Delivered.
Far from My Dearest Self.
Godfrey of Bulloigne, *sels.*
Golden Age, The. *Fr.* Aminta.
Jerusalem Delivered, *sels.*
Love.
Love, the Master of True Eloquence.
Madrigal: "What dewdrops or what tears."
Pastoral, A: "Oh happy golden age." *Fr.* Aminta.
Pastoral of Tasso, A.
Pluto's Council. *Fr.* Jerusalem Delivered.
Prayer Brings Rain, A. *Fr.* Jerusalem Delivered.
Shepherd's Song, The. *Fr.* Jerusalem Delivered.
Silent the Forests.
Sonnet: "Arms and the leader I sang whose piety."
Sonnet: Cats of Santa Anna, The.
Sonnet: "Royal spouse, the season is now at hand."
Sonnet: Swallow, The.
To an Ungrateful Friend.
To Don Angelo Grillo.
To His Mistress in Absence.
To the Duke Alphonso.
To the Princesses of Ferrara.
TASSONI, ALESSANDRO. Relations.
TASTU, AMABLE. To the Guardian Angel.
TATE, ALLEN. Advice to a Young Romanticist.
Aeneas at Washington.
Again the Native Hour Lets Down the Locks. *Fr.* More Sonnets at Christmas.
Autumn. *Fr.* Seasons of the Soul.
Buried Lake, The.
Carrion, A, *tr.*
Correspondences, *tr.*
Cross, The.
Death of Little Boys.
Ditty.
Elegy: "No more the white refulgent streets."
Emblems.
Eye, The.
Farewell to Anactoria, *tr.*
Horatian Epode to the Duchess of Malfi.
Idiot.
John Brown.
Jubilo.
Last Days of Alice, The.
Mediterranean, The.
Mr. Pope.
More Sonnets at Christmas.
More Sonnets at Christmas, *sel.*
Mother and Son.
Oath, The.
Obituary: In Mem. S. B. V. 1834–1909.
Ode: "Once more the country calls."
Ode to Fear.
Ode to Our Young Pro-Consuls of the Air.
Ode to the Confederate Dead.
Paradigm, The.
Pauper, A.
Seasons of the Soul.
Seasons of the Soul, *sel.*
Shadow and Shade.
Sonnets at Christmas.
Swimmers, The.
To a Romanticist.
Traveler, The.
Trout Map, The.
Vigil of Venus, The, *tr.*
Winter Mask.
Wolves, The.
TATE, NAHUM. Amorist, The.
Blessed Virgin's Expostulation, The.
Christmas: "While shepherds watch'd their flocks by night."
History of King Richard II, *sel.*
Love's Delights. *Fr.* History of King Richard II.
Song of the Angels.
While Shepherds Watched Their Flocks by Night.
TATE, NAHUM, *and* JOHN DRYDEN. Absalom and Achitophel, Pt. II, *sels.*
TATHAM, JOHN. Ostella, *sel.*
Seeing a Lady. *Fr.* Ostella.
To Philomel.
TATMAN, ADALINE H. Night Meeting, The.
TATNALL, FRANCES DORR SWIFT. Art Thou the Same.
TATYANICHEVA, LUDMILA. Snowstorms Sleep, The.
TAVALLALI. Mary.
Sad Love.
TAVASTSTJERNA, KARL AUGUST. 'Tis Growing So Hushed around Me.
TAYLOR, ANN (Ann Taylor Gilbert). Another Plum-Cake.
Baby, The.
Boy and the Sheep, The.
Jane and Eliza.
Little Girl to Her Dolly, The.
Meddlesome Matty.
My Mother.
My Mother, *sel.*
Pin, The.
Plum-Cake, The.
Sheep, The.
Tumble, The.
Washing and Dressing.
Worm, The.
TAYLOR, ANN *or* JANE. Breakfast and Puss.
Cow, The.
Cruel Boy and the Kittens, The.
Evening Hymn, An.
Evening Hymn for a Little Family, An.
Good Dobbin.
Learning to Draw.
Little Ants, The.
Little Fish That Would Not Do as It Was Bid, The.
Meadows, The.
Of What Are Your Clothes Made?
Pretty Cow.
Sleepy Harry.
Thank You, Pretty Cow.
TAYLOR, BAYARD. America. *Fr.* National Ode, Read at the Celebration in Independence Hall, Philadelphia, July 4, 1876.
Angelo Orders His Dinner.
Arab to the Palm, The.
Ariel in the Cloven Pine.
Bedouin [Love] Song.
By the Sea.
Camerados.
Cantelope, The.
Cimabuella.
Demon of the Mirror, The.
Easter Chorus from Faust, *tr. Fr.* Faust.
Echo Club, The, *sel*
Faust, *sels.*, *tr.*

Fight of Paso Del Mar, The.
Gettysburg Ode, The, *sel.*
Gwendoline.
Hadramaut.
Hassan Ben Khaled, *sel.*
Hiram Hover.
Kilimandjaro.
King of Thule, The, *tr.* *Fr.* Faust.
Lay of Macaroni, The.
Liberty's Latest Daughter. *Fr.* National Ode, Read at the Celebration in Independence Hall, Philadelphia, July 4, 1876.
Lincoln at Gettysburg. *Fr.* Gettysburg Ode.
Marigold.
National Ode, Read at the Celebration in Independence Hall, Philadelphia, July 4, 1876.
Nettle, The.
Night with a Wolf, A.
Nubia.
Ode on a Jar of Pickles.
Palabras Grandiosas. *Fr.* The Echo Club.
Poet's Journal, The, *sel.*
Possession.
Prayer: "Incline, O Maiden," *tr.* *Fr.* Faust.
Promissory Note, The.
Proposal.
Quaker Widow, The.
Return of Spring, The.
Rose, The. *Fr.* Hassan Ben Khaled.
Scott and the Veteran.
Self-Mastery.
Shepherd's Lament, The, *tr.*
Shrimp-Gatherers, The.
Sir Eggnogg.
Soldier's Song, *tr.* *Fr.* Faust.
Song: "Daughter of Egypt, veil thine eyes!"
Song in Camp, The.
Song of the Camp, The.
Storm Song.
Story for a Child, A.
Sunshine of the Gods, The, *sel.*
Three Songs, The.
Through Baltimore.
To M. T.
To the Nile.
Tyre.
Village Stork, The.
TAYLOR, BENJAMIN FRANKLIN. Isle of the Long Ago, The.
Long Ago, The.
TAYLOR, BERT LESTON ("B. L. T.").
Ataraxia.
Ballade of Spring's Unrest, A.
Bards We Quote, The.
Behind the Door.
Busy Music Critic, The.
Bygones.
Canopus.
Cow.
Dinosaur, The.
Farewell: "Farewell! Another gloomy word."
Happy Thought.
Hence These Rimes.
Lazy Writer, The.
Old Stuff.
Post-Impressionism.
Rain.
Reward.
Road to Anywhere, The.
Sundown.
To Lillian Russell.
To What Base Uses! *parody.*
Vanished Fay, The.
"We Have with Us Tonight."
TAYLOR, CHARLES EDWARD. For Sale, a Horse.
TAYLOR, CHARLES S. Scandal among the Flowers, A.
TAYLOR, COLEY BANKS. Chinoiseries.
TAYLOR, CYRIL G. All.
TAYLOR, DEEMS. "Haec Olim Meminisse Iuvabit."
TAYLOR, EDWARD. Accusation of the Inward Man, The. *Fr.* God's Determinations.
Address to the Soul Occasioned by a Rain, An.
Am I Thy Gold? *Fr.* Sacramental Meditations.
Christ's Reply. *Fr.* God's Determinations.
Ebb and Flow, The.
Elegy upon the Death of That Holy Man of God Mr. John Allen, An, *sel.*
Experience, The. *Fr.* Sacramental Meditations.
Glory of and Grace in the Church, The. *Fr.* God's Determinations.
God's Determinations, *sels.*
God's Selecting Love in the Decree. *Fr.* God's Determinations.
Housewifery.
Huswifery.
I Kenning through Astronomy. *Fr.* Sacramental Meditations.
Joy of Church Fellowship [Rightly Attended], The. *Fr.* God's Determinations.
Like to the Marigold. *Fr.* Sacramental Meditations.
Meditation Eight ("I kenning through astronomy divine"). *Fr.* Sacramental Meditations.
Meditation Fifty-six ("Should I with silver tooles delve through the hill"). *Fr.* Sacramental Meditations.
Meditation Seven ("Thy human frame, my glorious Lord, I spy"). *Fr.* Sacramental Meditations.
Meditation Six ("Am I thy gold? Or purse, Lord, for thy wealth"). *Fr.* Sacramental Meditations.
Meditation Ten ("Stupendious Love! all saints astonishment"). *Fr.* Sacramental Meditations.
Meditation Thirty ("Prest down with sorrow, Lord, not for my sin"). *Fr.* Sacramental Meditations.
Meditation Thirty-eight ("Oh! what a thing is man? Lord, who am I?"). *Fr.* Sacramental Meditations.
Meditation Thirty-three ("My Lord, my life, can envy ever bee"). *Fr.* Sacramental Meditations.
Meditations, *sels.*
Oh! What a Thing Is Man. *Fr.* Sacramental Meditations.
Our Insufficiency to Praise God Suitably for His Mercy. *Fr.* God's Determinations.
Outward Man Accused, The. *Fr.* God's Determinations.
Preface: "Infinity, when all things it beheld." *Fr.* God's Determinations.
Reflection [*or* Reflexion], The.
Sacramental Meditations, *sels.*
Souls Groan to Christ for Succour, The. *Fr.* God's Determinations.
Stanzas: "When these assaults proove vain, the Enemy." *Fr.* God's Determinations.
This Dove &/ Olive Branch.
Upon a Spider Catching a Fly.
Upon a Wasp Chilled with Cold.
Upon What Base.
What Love Is This. *Fr.* Sacramental Meditations.
TAYLOR, EMILY. Mother.
TAYLOR, FRANCES BEATRICE. Fruit Vendor, The.
Husbandman, The.
Last Tavern, The.
Old Gardens.
Wayfaring Fools.
Wedgwood Bowl, A.
TAYLOR, GEOFFREY. Bluebell.
Boat-Haven, Co. Mayo.
Country Walk.
Cruel Clever Cat.
English Liberal.
From an Irish-Latin Macaronic.
Limerick: "'I think' thought Sam Butler."
Song: "Rousing to rein his pad's head back."
TAYLOR, GEORGE LANSING. No Slave beneath the Flag.
TAYLOR, HELEN. Come to the Fair.
TAYLOR, SIR HENRY. Aretina's Song.
Athulf and Ethilda. *Fr.* Edwin the Fair.
Characterization, A.
Edwin the Fair, *sels.*
Elena's Song. *Fr.* Philip van Artevelde.
Heart-Rest. *Fr.* Philip van Artevelde.
Hero, The.
John of Launoy. *Fr.* Philip van Artevelde.
Philip van Artevelde, *sels.*
Revolutions. *Fr.* Philip van Artevelde.
Scholar, The. *Fr.* Edwin the Fair.
Song: "Bee to the heather, The."
Song: "Down lay in a nook my lady's brach." *Fr.* Philip van Artevelde.
Song: "Quoth tongue of neither maid nor wife." *Fr.* Philip van Artevelde.
Wife, A. *Fr.* Philip van Artevelde.
Wind in the Pines, The. *Fr.* Edwin the Fair.
Women Singing.
TAYLOR, JANE. Child's Hymn of Praise, A.
Contented John.
Cow and the Ass, The.
Daisy, The.
Dirty Jim.
Employment.
Encouragement for Little Children, *sel.*
Farm, The.
Field Daisy, The.
God Is So Good. *Fr.* Encouragement for Little Children.
Good Night.
I Like [*or* Love] Little Pussy.
Kitty; How to Treat Her.
Little Hymn, A. *Fr.* Encouragement for Little Children.
Little Pussy.
Little Star.
Morning.
Now and Then.
Philosopher's Scales, The.
Pond, The.
Poppy, The.
Pussy.
Recreation.
Snow.
Spider and His Wife, The.
Star, The.
Sweetly Sleep, *at.*
Toad's Journal, The.
Twinkle, Twinkle, Little Star.
Two Little Kittens, *at.*
Violet, The.
See also TAYLOR, ANN *or* JANE.
TAYLOR, JEFFERYS. Dog of Reflection, The.
Lion and the Mouse, The.
Milkmaid, The.
Young Mouse, The.
TAYLOR, JEREMY. Christ's Coming [O Jerusalem] in Triumph.
Heaven.
Hymn for Christmas Day, A ("Awake, my soul, and come away").
Hymn for Christmas Day ("Where is this blessed Babe").
Lord, Come Away!
My Soul Doth Pant towards Thee.
Penitent, The.
Prayer, The: "My soul doth pant towards thee."
TAYLOR, JOHN. Odcomb's Complaint, *sel.*
Sonnet: "Sweet semi-circled Cynthia played at maw." *Fr.* Odcomb's Complaint.
Walking along the streets the other day.
TAYLOR, JOHN W. Chipeta's Ride.
TAYLOR, JOSEPH RUSSELL. Blow Softly, Thrush.
Breath on the Oat.
Dove's Nest.
Flute, The.
Lullaby: "At sunset our white butterflies."
Veery-Thrush, The.
TAYLOR, KATHERINE KELLEY. Flying Fish.

TAYLOR, MORGAN. Limerick: "Lieutenant who went out to shoot, A."
TAYLOR, RACHEL ANNAND. Age Intercedes for Youth.
Body, The.
Ecstasy.
End of the Duel, The.
Impression of Autumn.
Joys of Art, The.
Knights to Chrysola, The.
May-Music.
Princess of Scotland, The.
Question, The.
Roman Road, The.
Unknown Sword-Maker, The.
TAYLOR, SARAH WINGATE. Hope.
Master-Welder, The.
With Metaphor.
TAYLOR, TOM. Abraham Lincoln.
Dance of the Sword, The, *tr.*
Fool's Revenge, The, *sel.*
Jester and His Daughter, The. *Fr.* The Fool's Revenge.
TAYLOR, VIOLA. Babylon.
TCHAIKOVSKY, PETER ILICH. Legend, A: "Christ, when a Child, a garden made."
TCHAN TIOU-LIN. Willow Leaf, The.
TCHERNICHOWSKY, SAUL. Before a [*or* the] Statue of Apollo.
Credo.
Dance of Saul with the Prophets, The.
Death of Tammuz, The.
Grave in Ukraine, A.
I Believe.
This Be Our Revenge.
To Ashtaroth and Bel.
TCHOBANIAN, ARSCHAG. Happiness.
TEASDALE, SARA. After Parting.
Answer, The.
Appraisal.
April.
Arcturus in Autumn.
August Moonrise.
August Night.
Autumn on the Beaches.
Barter.
Beautiful Proud Sea.
Because.
Blue Squills.
Buried Love.
Calm Morning at Sea.
Central Park at Dusk.
Child, Child.
Christmas Carol: "Kings they came from out the south, The."
Cloud, The.
Coin, The.
Come.
Crystal Gazer, The.
Dark Cup, The, *sel.*
Day's Ending.
Debt.
December Day, A.
Doubt.
Effigy of a Nun.
End, An.
Epitaph: "Serene descent, as a red leaf's descending."
Falling Star, The.
Faults.
February Twilight.
Flight, The.
Fontainebleau.
Fountain, The.
Four Winds.
Full Moon; Santa Barbara.
Grace before Sleep.
I Am Not Yours.
I Have Loved Hours at Sea.
I Have Seen the Spring.
I Remembered.
I Shall Live to Be Old.
I Shall Not Care.
I Would Live in Your Love.
If Death Is Kind.
Immortal.
In Memory of Vachel Lindsay.
In the Carpenter's Shop.
In the Wood.
Inn of Earth, The.
Interlude: Songs Out of Sorrow, *sels.*
It Is Not a Word.
It Is Not Far.
June Day, A.
Kind Moon, The.
Kiss, The.
Lamp, The.
Late October.
Leaves.
Lessons. *Fr.* Interlude: Songs Out of Sorrow.
Let It Be Forgotten.
Lights of New York, The.
Like Barley Bending.
Long Hill, The.
Longing.
Look, The.
Lovely Chance.
Mastery. *Fr.* Interlude: Songs Out of Sorrow.
May Day. *Fr.* The Dark Cup.
Message.
Metropolitan Tower, The.
Moods.
Moon's Ending.
Morning.
My Heart Is Heavy.
Mystery, The.
Net, The.
Night.
Night Song at [*or* of] Amalfi.
Not by the Sea.
Old Enemy, The.
On the Dunes.
On the South Downs.
On the Sussex Downs.
Open Windows.
Over the Roofs.
Peace.
Philosopher, The.
Pierrot.
Prayer, The: "My answered prayer came up to me."
Prayer, A: "Until I lose my soul and lie."
Redbirds.
Refuge. *Fr.* Interlude: Songs Out of Sorrow.
Return at Night.
Sappho.
September Day.
Since There Is No Escape.
Solitary, The.
Song: "Let it be forgotten as a flower is forgotten."
Song at Capri.
Song for Colin, The.
Song Making.
Spirit's House. *Fr.* Interlude: Songs Out of Sorrow.
Spring in War-Time.
Spring Night.
Star Map, A.
Stars.
Summer Night, Riverside.
Sunset; St. Louis.
Swallow Flight.
There Will Be Stars.
There Will Come Soft Rains.
Thoughts.
To Dick, on His Sixth Birthday.
To E.
To Rose.
To the Sea.
Truce.
Unchanging, The.
Unseen, The.
Voice, The.
Water-Lilies.
Wayfarer, The.
What Do I Care?
Winter Night Song.
Winter Noon.
Winter Solstice.
Wisdom. *Fr.* Interlude: Songs Out of Sorrow.
Wood Song. *Fr.* Interlude: Songs Out of Sorrow.
TEGNÉR, ESAIAS. Birds of Passage.
Eternal, The.
Farewell to My Lyre.
Frithiof's Farewell. *Fr.* Frithiof's Saga.
Frithiof's Homestead. *Fr.* Frithiof's Saga.
Frithiof's Saga, *sels.*
Giant, The.
Kisses.
Song to the Sun.
Tegnér's Drapa.
TEICHNER, MIRIAM. Awareness.
Struggle, The.
Victory.
TEJADA, JUAN MANUEL GARCIA. To Jesus on the Cross.
"TEKAHIONWAKE." *See* JOHNSON, EMILY PAULINE.
TELEMAQUE, HAROLD. Adina.
Roots.
TELFER, JAMES. Goblin's Song, The.
TEMPLE, ANNA. *See* WHITNEY, ANNA TEMPLE.
TEMPLE, ANNE HUNTER. King Passes, The.
TEMPLETON, J. D. New Year, The.
TENCHI, EMPEROR. Through the thatched roof.
TENNANT, EDWARD WYNDHAM. Home Thoughts in Laventie.
I saw green banks of daffodil.
Light after Darkness.
Reincarnation.
TENNANT, PAMELA. *See* GREY OF FALLODON, PAMELA GREY, VISCOUNTESS.
TENNANT, WILLIAM. Anster Fair, *sels.*
Ode to Peace.
On the Road to Anster Fair. *Fr.* Anster Fair.
TENNYSON, ALFRED TENNYSON, 1ST BARON. Achilles on the Rampart, *tr.* *Fr.* The Iliad.
Achilles' Shout, *tr.* *Fr.* The Iliad.
Again at Christmas did we weave. *Fr.* In Memoriam.
Akbar's Dream, *sel.*
Albert the Good. *Fr.* Idylls of the King.
All in All. *Fr.* Idylls of the King.
Ancient Sage, The.
Ancient Sage, The, *sel.*
And all is well, tho' faith and form. *Fr.* In Memoriam.
And rise, O moon, from yonder down. *Fr.* In Memoriam.
And was the day of my delight. *Fr.* In Memoriam.
April Days. *Fr.* In Memoriam.
Arthur's Disillusionment. *Fr.* Idylls of the King.
As Sometimes in a Dead Man's Face. *Fr.* In Memoriam.
As thro' the Land at Eve We Went. *Fr.* The Princess.
As When a Man. *Fr.* A Dream of Fair Women.
Ask Me No More. *Fr.* The Princess.
Autumn. *Fr.* In Memoriam.
Aylmer's Field, *sels.*
Baby-Song. *Fr.* Sea Dreams.
Balin and Balan. *Fr.* Idylls of the King.
Ballad of Oriana, The.
Ballad of the Fleet, A.
Battle of Brunanburh, The, *tr.*
Be Comforted. *Fr.* The Death of the Duke of Clarence and Avondale.
Be near me when my light is low. *Fr.* In Memoriam.
Becket, *sel.*
Beggar Maid, The.
Bells of Yule. *Fr.* In Memoriam.
Birth of Christ, The. *Fr.* In Memoriam.
Blackbird, The.
Blow, Bugle, Blow. *Fr.* The Princess.
Break, Break, Break.
Brook, The.
Brook, The, *sels.*
Brook's Song, The. *Fr.* The Brook.
Bugle, The. *Fr.* The Princess.
Bugle Song. *Fr.* The Princess.
Buonaparte.
By an Evolutionist.
By an Evolutionist, *sel.*
By night we lingered on the lawn. *Fr.* In Memoriam.
Calm is the morn without a sound. *Fr.* In Memoriam.
Captain, The.
Cast Your Cares on God. *Fr.* Enoch Arden.

Challenge of Life, The. *Fr.* Ulysses.
Charge of the Heavy Brigade at Balaclava, The, *sels.*
Charge of the Light Brigade, The.
Choric Song: "There is sweet music here that softer falls." *Fr.* The Lotos-Eaters.
Choric Song of the Lotos-Eaters. *Fr.* The Lotos-Eaters.
Christmas. *Fr.* In Memoriam.
Christmas Bells. *Fr.* In Memoriam.
Circumstance.
City Child, The.
Claribel.
Cling to Faith. *Fr.* The Ancient Sage.
Columbus Day.
Come Down, O Maid [from Yonder Mountain Height]. *Fr.* The Princess.
Come into the Garden, Maud. *Fr.* Maud.
Come Not, When I Am Dead.
Coming of Arthur, The. *Fr.* Idylls of the King.
Conclusion to the May Queen and New Year's Eve. *Fr.* The May Queen.
Contemplate all this work of Time. *Fr.* In Memoriam.
Cradle Song: "Sweet and low." *Fr.* The Princess.
Cradle Song: "What does little birdie say." *Fr.* Sea Dreams.
Crossing the Bar.
Daisy, The.
Danube to the Severn gave, The. *Fr.* In Memoriam.
Dark House, by Which Once More I Stand. *Fr.* In Memoriam.
Dash Back.
Days That Are No More, The. *Fr.* The Princess.
De Profundis.
Dead Friend, The. *Fr.* In Memoriam.
Dead, Long Dead. *Fr.* Maud.
Dear friend, far off, my lost desire. *Fr.* In Memoriam.
Death of Oenone, The.
Death of the Duke of Clarence and Avondale, The, *sel.*
Death of the Old Year.
Dedication, A: "Dear, near and true —no truer Time himself."
Dedication: "These to His Memory—since he held them dear." *Fr.* Idylls of the King.
Deep Dark Night, The. *Fr.* The Devil and the Lady.
Defence of Lucknow, The.
Demeter and Persephone.
Departure, The. *Fr.* The Day-Dream.
Deserted House, The.
Devil and the Lady, The, *sel.*
Dip down upon the northern shore. *Fr.* In Memoriam.
Do we indeed desire the dead. *Fr.* In Memoriam.
Dora.
Dost Thou Look Back? *Fr.* In Memoriam.
Doubt. *Fr.* In Memoriam.
Doubt and Prayer.
Dragon-Fly, The. *Fr.* The Two Voices.
Dream of Fair Women, A.
Dream of Fair Women, A, *sels.*
Dying Swan, The.
Eagle, The.
Early Spring.
Edward Gray.
Elaine, *sel.* *Fr.* Idylls of the King.
Elaine's Song. *Fr.* Idylls of the King.
England. *Fr.* Maud.
England and America in 1782.
Enid's Song. *Fr.* Idylls of the King.
Enoch Arden.
Enoch Arden, *sel.*
Epic, The (Introduction to "Morte d'Arthur").
Experience. *Fr.* Ulysses
Fair ship, that from the Italian shore. *Fr.* In Memoriam.
Faith. *Fr.* The Ancient Sage.
Far—Far—Away.
Farewell, A: "Flow down, cold rivulet, to the sea."
Fatima.
Federation of the World. *Fr.* Locksley Hall.
Fire of Heaven, The. *Fr.* Idylls of the King.
Flower, The.
Flower in the Crannied Wall.
Follow the Christ. *Fr.* Idylls of the King.
Follow the Gleam. *Fr.* Merlin and the Gleam.
Foolish Virgins, The. *Fr.* Idylls of the King.
Foresters, The, *sel.*
Fortune. *Fr.* Idylls of the King.
Fragment: "Flower in the crannied wall."
"Frater Ave atque Vale."
Freedom ("O thou so fair in summers gone").
Freedom ("Of old sat Freedom").
From "Gareth and Lynette." *Fr.* Idylls of the King.
Gardener's Daughter, The.
Gardener's Daughter, The, *sel.*
Gareth and Lynette. *Fr.* Idylls of the King.
Go Not, Happy Day.
Godiva.
Golden Year, The.
Goose, The.
Guinevere. *Fr.* Idylls of the King.
Hands All Round.
Hands All Round, *sel.*
Hapless Doom of Woman. *Fr.* Queen Mary.
Happy He with Such a Mother.
Harold, *sel.*
Heavy Brigade, The. *Fr.* The Charge of the Heavy Brigade at Balaclava.
Helen and Iphigenia. *Fr.* A Dream of Fair Women.
Hero to Leander.
Hesperides, The.
Higher Pantheism, The.
Holy Grail, The. *Fr.* Idylls of the King.
Home They Brought Her Warrior Dead. *Fr.* The Princess.
Horns of Elfland, The. *Fr.* The Princess.
How many a father have I seen. *Fr.* In Memoriam.
Hymn: "Once again thou flamest heavenward, once again we see thee rise." *Fr.* Akbar's Dream.
I cannot love thee as I ought. *Fr.* In Memoriam.
I cannot see the features right. *Fr.* In Memoriam.
I envy not in any moods. *Fr.* In Memoriam.
I Have Led Her Home. *Fr.* Maud.
I hear the noise about thy keel. *Fr.* In Memoriam.
I held it truth, with him who sings. *Fr.* In Memoriam.
I know that this was Life,—the track. *Fr.* In Memoriam.
I sing to him that rests below. *Fr.* In Memoriam.
I trust I have not wasted breath. *Fr.* In Memoriam.
I vex my heart with fancies dim. *Fr.* In Memoriam.
I Wage Not Any Feud with Death. *Fr.* In Memoriam.
I Would That Wars Should Cease. *Fr.* The Charge of the Heavy Brigade at Balaclava.
Idyl, An: "Come down, O maid, from yonder mountain height." *Fr.* The Princess.
Idylls of the King, *sels.*
If Love Be Ours. *Fr.* Idylls of the King.
Iliad, The, *sels., tr.*
Ilion, Ilion.
In Love, if Love Be Love. *Fr.* Idylls of the King.
In Memoriam A. H. H.
In Memoriam A. H. H., *sels.*
In Memoriam—W. G. Ward.
In the Children's Hospital.
In the Garden at Swainston.
In the Valley of Cauteretz.
Intuition. *Fr.* In Memoriam.
Iphigenia. *Fr.* A Dream of Fair Women.
Is it, then, regret for buried time. *Fr.* In Memoriam.
It Is the Miller's Daughter. *Fr.* The Miller's Daughter.
Jephthah's Daughter.
June Bracken and Heather.
King, The. *Fr.* Idylls of the King.
King Arthur's Order of Chivalry. *Fr.* Idylls of the King.
Kraken, The.
Lady Clara Vere de Vere.
Lady Clara Vere de Vere, *sel.*
Lady Clare.
Lady Clare, *sel.*
Lady of Shalott, The.
Lancelot and Elaine. *Fr.* Idylls of the King.
Lancelot and Elaine, *sel.* *Fr.* Idylls of the King.
Lancelot and the Grail. *Fr.* Idylls of the King.
Larger Hope, The. *Fr.* In Memoriam.
Last Tournament, The. *Fr.* Idylls of the King.
Leolin and Edith. *Fr.* Aylmer's Field.
Letters, The.
Life Not Death. *Fr.* The Two Voices.
Life Shall Live for Evermore. *Fr.* In Memoriam.
Lilian.
Little Birdie. *Fr.* Sea Dreams.
Little Rift within the Lute, The. *Fr.* Idylls of the King.
Locksley Hall.
Locksley Hall, *sels.*
Locksley Hall Sixty Years After.
Locksley Hall Sixty Years After, *sels.*
Lord of Burleigh, The.
Lost Love. *Fr.* In Memoriam.
Lotos-Eaters, The.
Lotos-Eaters, The, *sels.*
Love and Death.
Love is and was my lord and king. *Fr.* In Memoriam.
Love, Pride, and Forgetfulness.
Love Thou Thy Land, with Love Far-brought.
Lover's Tale, The, *sel.*
Low, Lute, Low! *Fr.* Queen Mary.
Lucretius.
Lullaby: "Sweet and low, sweet and low." *Fr.* The Princess.
Lyric from "Maud."
Lyrics from "The Princess."
Making of Man, The.
Mariana.
Mariana, *sel.*
Mariana in the South.
Marriage of Geraint, The. *Fr.* Idylls of the King.
Maud.
Maud, *sels.*
May Queen, The.
May Queen, The, *sel.*
Merlin and the Gleam.
Merlin and the Gleam, *sel.*
Merlin and Vivien, *sel.* *Fr.* Idylls of the King.
Merlin's Riddle. *Fr.* Idylls of the King.
Mermaid, The.
Mermaid, The, *sel.*
Merman, The.
Merman, The, *sel.*
Milkmaid's Song. *Fr.* Queen Mary.
Miller's Daughter, The.
Miller's Daughter, The, *sel.*
Milton.
Minnie and Winnie.
Montenegro.
Morte d'Arthur.
Morte d'Arthur, *sels.*
Move Eastward, Happy Earth.
My Life Is Full of Weary Days.
My Lord and King.
My own dim life should teach me this. *Fr.* In Memoriam.

TENNYSON, ALFRED (*continued*)
Mystic, The.
New Year, The. *Fr.* In Memoriam.
New Year's Eve ("If you're waking, call me early"). *Fr.* The May Queen.
New Year's Eve ("Ring out, wild bells"). *Fr.* In Memoriam.
Nobility. *Fr.* Lady Clara Vere de Vere.
Northern Farmer; New Style.
Northern Farmer; Old Style.
Now fades the last long streak of snow. *Fr.* In Memoriam.
Now Sleeps the Crimson Petal. *Fr.* The Princess.
Now, sometimes in my sorrow shut. *Fr.* In Memoriam.
O days and hours, your work is this. *Fr.* In Memoriam.
O living will that shalt endure. *Fr.* In Memoriam.
O Purblind Race. *Fr.* Idylls of the King.
O sorrow, cruel fellowship. *Fr.* In Memoriam.
O Swallow, Swallow, Flying, Flying South. *Fr.* The Princess.
O That 'Twere Possible. *Fr.* Maud.
Oh yet we trust that somehow good. *Fr.* In Memoriam.
Oak, The.
Ode on the Death of the Duke of Wellington.
Ode on the Death of the Duke of Wellington, *sels.*
Oenone.
Oenone, *sel.*
Of Old Sat Freedom on the Heights.
Of One Dead. *Fr.* In Memoriam.
Old Yew, which graspest at the stones. *Fr.* In Memoriam.
Olivia. *Fr.* The Talking Oak.
One writes, that "other friends remain." *Fr.* In Memoriam.
Our Echoes Roll from Soul to Soul. *Fr.* The Princess.
Our Enemies Have Fallen. *Fr.* The Princess.
Owl, The.
Palace of Art, The.
Passing of Arthur, The. *Fr.* Idylls of the King.
Path by which we twain did go, The. *Fr.* In Memoriam.
Peace, come away: the song of woe. *Fr.* In Memoriam.
Pelleas and Ettarre. *Fr.* Idylls of the King.
Pelleas and Ettarre, *sel.* *Fr.* Idylls of the King.
Poet, The.
Poet, The, *sel.*
Poet's Mind, The.
Poet's Prophecy, A. *Fr.* Locksley Hall.
Poet's Song, The.
Politics.
Prayer: "More things are wrought by prayer." *Fr.* Morte d'Arthur.
Prayer: "The old order changeth, yielding place to new." *Fr.* Idylls of the King.
Prayer, The: "O living will." *Fr.* In Memoriam.
Prayer for the Dead. *Fr.* Morte d'Arthur.
Princess, The, *sels.*
Proem: "Strong Son of God, immortal Love." *Fr.* In Memoriam.
Progress of Spring, The, *sel.*
Prologue: "Strong Son of God, immortal Love." *Fr.* In Memoriam.
Prophecy. *Fr.* Locksley Hall.
Pure Heart, The. *Fr.* Sir Galahad.
Queen Becomes an Abbess, A. *Fr.* Idylls of the King.
Queen Mary, *sels.*
Quest of the Grail, The. *Fr.* Idylls of the King.
Recollections of the Arabian Nights.
Reconciliation, The. *Fr.* The Princess.
Remorse. *Fr.* Idylls of the King.
Retrospection. *Fr.* The Princess.
Revenge, The [a Ballad of the Fleet].
Revival, The. *Fr.* The Day-Dream.
Ring out, wild bells, to the wild sky. *Fr.* In Memoriam.
Rise, Happy Morn. *Fr.* In Memoriam.
Risest thou thus, dim dawn, again. *Fr.* In Memoriam.
Rizpah.
Saint Agnes' Eve.
Saint Francis. *Fr.* Locksley Hall Sixty Years After.
Sea Dreams, *sel.*
Sea-Fairies, The.
Shell, The. *Fr.* Maud.
Shepherd's Song. *Fr.* The Princess.
Silent Voices, The.
Sir Galahad.
Sir Galahad, *sel.*
Sir John Franklin: On the Cenotaph in Westminster Abbey.
Sir Launcelot and Queen Guinevere.
Sisters, The.
Sisters, The, *sel.*
Sleeping House, The. *Fr.* Maud.
Snowdrop, The.
"So careful of the type?" but no. *Fr.* In Memoriam.
Song: "Blow, trumpet, for the world is white with May." *Fr.* Idylls of the King.
Song: "Come down, O maid, from yonder mountain height." *Fr.* The Princess.
Song: "Come into the garden, Maud." *Fr.* Maud.
Song: "Go not, happy day." *Fr.* Maud.
Song: "It is the miller's daughter." *Fr.* The Miller's Daughter.
Song: Miller's Daughter, The.
Song: "Now sleeps the crimson petal." *Fr.* The Princess.
Song: "O diviner air." *Fr.* The Sisters.
Song: "O, let the solid ground." *Fr.* Maud.
Song: Owl, The.
Song: "Spirit haunts the year's last hours, A."
Song: "Splendour falls on castle walls, The." *Fr.* The Princess.
Song: "Sweet and low." *Fr.* The Princess.
Song: "Tears, idle tears, I know not what they mean." *Fr.* The Princess.
Song: "There is no land like England." *Fr.* The Foresters.
Song: "Who can say."
Song at the Ruin'd Inn. *Fr.* The Vision of Sin.
Song from "Maud."
Song of the Brook, The. *Fr.* The Brook.
Song of the Lotos-Eaters. *Fr.* The Lotos-Eaters.
Song of the Milkmaid. *Fr.* Queen Mary.
Songs from "The Princess."
Spirit Haunts the Year's Last Hours, A.
Splendor [*or* Splendour] Falls [on Castle Walls], The. *Fr.* The Princess.
Spring ("Dip down upon the northern shore"). *Fr.* In Memoriam.
Spring ("Now fades the last long streak of snow"). *Fr.* In Memoriam.
Strong Son of God, immortal Love. *Fr.* In Memoriam.
Stronger Faith, A. *Fr.* In Memoriam.
Summer Night. *Fr.* The Princess.
Sunset and evening star.
Supposed Confessions of a Second-rate Sensitive Mind.
Sweet after showers, ambrosial air. *Fr.* In Memoriam.
Sweet and Low. *Fr.* The Princess.
Talking Oak, The, *sel.*
Tears, Idle Tears. *Fr.* The Princess.
Temple, The.
That Which Made Us. *Fr.* Locksley Hall Sixty Years After.
That which we dare invoke to bless. *Fr.* In Memoriam.
Their Conscience as Their King. *Fr.* Idylls of the King.
There Is None like Her. *Fr.* Maud.
There rolls the deep where grew the tree. *Fr.* In Memoriam.
Third of February, The, 1852.
Tho' truths in manhood darkly join. *Fr.* In Memoriam.
Thousand Years of Peace, The. *Fr.* In Memoriam.
Throstle, The.
Thy voice is heard thro' rolling drums. *Fr.* The Princess.
Thy voice is on the rolling air. *Fr.* In Memoriam.
Time draws near the birth of Christ, The. *Fr.* In Memoriam.
'Tis Better to Have Loved and Lost. *Fr.* In Memoriam.
Tithonus.
To ——: "All good things have not kept aloof."
To ——: "I send you here a sort of allegory." *Fr.* The Palace of Art.
To ——, with the Following Poem.
To Christopher North.
To Dante.
To E. [*or* Edward] FitzGerald.
To E. L., on His Travels in Greece.
To General Hamley.
To J. M. K.
To Sleep I give my powers away. *Fr.* In Memoriam.
To the Queen ("O loyal to the royal in thyself"). *Fr.* Idylls of the King.
To the Queen ("Revered, beloved—O you that hold").
To the Queen ("These to His Memory—since he held them dear"). *Fr.* Idylls of the King.
To the Rev. F. D. Maurice.
To Victor Hugo.
To Virgil [*or* Vergil].
To-night the winds begin to rise. *Fr.* In Memoriam.
Too Late. *Fr.* Idylls of the King.
Trojan Camp-Fires, The, *tr.* *Fr.* The Iliad.
Trumpet Song. *Fr.* Idylls of the King.
Truths That Never Can Be Proved, The. *Fr.* In Memoriam.
Turn, Fortune, Turn Thy Wheel. *Fr.* Idylls of the King.
Two Voices, The.
Two Voices, The, *sels.*
Ulysses.
Ulysses, *sels.*
Universal Peace, The. *Fr.* Locksley Hall.
Unwatch'd, the garden bough shall sway. *Fr.* In Memoriam.
Valedictory.
Vastness.
Vision, A. *Fr.* Locksley Hall.
Vision of Sin, The.
Vision of Sin, The, *sel.*
Vision of the World, The. *Fr.* Locksley Hall.
Vivien's Song. *Fr.* Idylls of the King.
Voice, A. *Fr.* Maud.
Voice and the Peak, The.
Voice by the Cedar Tree, A. *Fr.* Maud.
Voyage, The.
Voyage of Maeldune, The.
Wages.
War Song, The. *Fr.* Idylls of the King.
Way to Power, The. *Fr.* Oenone.
We Kiss'd Again with Tears. *Fr.* The Princess.
We Needs Must Love the Highest. *Fr.* Idylls of the King.
Welcome to Alexandra, A.
What a Lovely Shell. *Fr.* Maud.
What Does Little Birdie Say? *Fr.* Sea Dreams.
What Know We Greater than the

Soul? *Fr.* Ode on the Death of the Duke of Wellington.
When Cats Run Home.
When on my bed the moonlight falls. *Fr.* In Memoriam.
When rosy plumelets tuft the larch. *Fr.* In Memoriam.
White Owl, The.
Widow and Child. *Fr.* The Princess.
Wild bird, whose warble, liquid sweet. *Fr.* In Memoriam.
Will.
Winter.
Wish, that of the living whole, The. *Fr.* In Memoriam.
With trembling fingers did we weave. *Fr.* In Memoriam.
Woman and Man. *Fr.* The Princess.
Word, The. *Fr.* In Memoriam.
Word Incarnate, The. *Fr.* In Memoriam.
Work May Yet Be Done. *Fr.* Ulysses.
Worm within a Rose, A. *Fr.* Idylls of the King.
Yet if some voice that man could trust. *Fr.* In Memoriam.
Yew in the Graveyard, The. *Fr.* In Memoriam.
You say, but with no touch of scorn. *Fr.* In Memoriam.

TENNYSON, CHARLES. *See* TURNER, CHARLES TENNYSON.

TENNYSON, FREDERICK. Blackbird, The.
Harvest Home.
Holy Tide, The.
Incident, An.
Iona.
Niobe, *sel.*
Skylark, The.
Thirty-first of May.

TERENCE (Publius Terentius Afer). Dost ask (my dear) what service I will have?

TERESA, SAINT, OF AVILA. *See* THERESA, SAINT, OF AVILA.

TERESA, SANTA, DE JESÚS. *See* THERESA, SAINT, OF AVILA.

TERPANDER. Sparta.
To Apollo and the Muses.
To Zeus.

TERRAL, RUFUS. Chant Royal from a Copydesk.

TERRAZAS, FRANCISCO DE. Sonnet: "I dreamed that I was thrown from a crag."
To a Beautiful but Heartless Coquette.

TERRELL, MYRA BURNHAM. Theodosia Burr.

TERRETT, WILLIAM. Platonic.

TERRY, EDWARD H. S. Kinship.

TERRY, ELLEN. No Funeral Gloom, *wr. at. See* ALLINGHAM, WILLIAM.

TERRY, LILA. Interview.

TERRY, LUCY. Bars Fight.

TERRY. URIAH. Wyoming Massacre, The.

TERZYAN, THOMAS. Chragan Palace, The.

TESSIMOND, ARTHUR SEYMOUR JOHN. British, The.
Cats.
Children Look at the Parents, The.
Daydream.
Earthfast.
La Marche des Machines.
Man in the Bowler Hat, The.
Man of Culture, A.
One Almost Might.
Radio.
Sleep.

TETERNIKOV, FEODOR KUZMICH. *See* "SOLOGUB, FEODOR."

THACKER, MARY AFTON. I Found God.

THACKERAY, WILLIAM MAKEPEACE. Ad Ministram.
After the Storm. *Fr.* The White Squall.
Age of Wisdom, The. *Fr.* Rebecca and Rowena.
At the Church Gate. *Fr.* Pendennis.
Ballad of Bouillabaisse, The.
Betsinda's Bun. *Fr.* The Rose and the Ring.
Cane-bottomed Chair, The.
Chronicle of the Drum, The, *sels.*
Commanders of the Faithful.
Credo, A.
Crystal Palace, The.
Dr. Birch and His Young Friends, *sel.*
End of the Play, The. *Fr.* Dr. Birch and His Young Friends.
Fairy Days.
Garret, The.
Jolly Jack.
King Canute.
King of Brentford, The.
King of Yvetot, The, *tr.*
King on the Tower, The, *tr.*
Larry O'Toole.
Little Billee.
Love at Two Score. *Fr.* Rebecca and Rowena.
Lucy's Birthday.
Mahogany Tree, The.
Minaret Bells, The.
Mr. Molony's Account of the Ball.
Noble Art of Murdering, The.
Old Fashioned Fun.
Pen and the Album, The.
Pendennis, *sel.*
Persicos Odi.
Pocahontas.
Rebecca and Rowena, *sels.*
Ronsard to His Mistress.
Rose and the Ring, The, *sel.*
Sorrows of Werther.
Timbuctoo.
Tragic Story, A, *tr.*
When Moonlike ore [*or* o'er] the Hazure Seas.
Willow-Tree, The.
Wofle New Ballad of Jane Roney and Mary Brown, The.
Yankee Volunteers, The.

THAON [*or* THAUN], PHILIPPE DE. *See* PHILIPPE DE THAON [*or* THAUN].

THAXTER, CELIA (Laighton). As Happy Dwellers by the Seaside Hear.
August.
Chanticleer.
Child and the Year, The.
Christmas Wish, A.
Compensation.
Cradle Song: "In the wingèd cradle of sleep I lay."
Day Shall Yet Be Fair, The.
Flowers for the Brave.
Little Gustava.
Lost.
Lullaby, A: "Sleep, my darling, sleep!"
March.
May Morning.
Nikolina.
On Easter Day.
Sandpiper, The.
Seaward.
Slumber Song: "Thou little child, with tender clinging arms."
Song: "We sail toward evening's lonely star."
Song of Easter, A.
Spring.
Sunrise Never Failed Us Yet, The.
Under the Eaves.
Wild Geese.

THAYER, ERNEST LAWRENCE. Casey at the Bat.

THAYER, JULIA H. Shining Hope, A.

THAYER, LOUIS EDWIN. Hang to Your Grit! *Fr.* Keep Your Grit.
Keep Your Grit.
Keep Your Grit, *sel.*
Little Child's Faith, The.

THAYER, LUCIUS H. Life of Man, The.

THAYER, MARY DIXON (Mrs. Maurice Fremont-Smith). Afterwards.
Bird-Song.
Finding You.
How Nice.
My Jewels.
Prayer, A: "God, is it sinful if I feel."
Prayer, A: "I pray for you, and yet I do not frame."
To Elizabeth.
To Our Lady.
Treasures.
Woman, A.

THAYER, STEPHEN HENRY. Europa.
Poet of Earth.
Waiting Chords, The.

THAYER, WILLIAM ROSCOE ("Paul Hermes"). Last Hunt, The.
Man in Nature.
Violin's Complaint, The.

THAYER, WILLIAM SYDNEY. Old Dogs.
Osler.

THEOCRITUS. Adonis Song, The. *Fr.* Idylls.
Amycus. *Fr.* Idylls.
"And Thou Beside Me Singing in the Wilderness." *Fr.* Idylls.
Bound for the Harvest-Home. *Fr.* Idylls.
Cup, The. *Fr.* Idylls.
Cyclops, The. *Fr.* Idylls.
Cyclops in Love, The. *Fr.* Idylls.
Daphnis. *Fr.* Idylls.
Daphnis Song, The. *Fr.* Idylls.
Death of Daphnis. *Fr.* Idylls.
Dogs at the Homestead, The. *Fr.* Idylls.
Domestic Scene. *Fr.* Idylls.
Dream of a Golden Catch. *Fr.* Idylls.
Fisherman's Hut. *Fr.* Idylls.
Fishermen, The. *Fr.* Idylls.
Fishermen's Hut, The. *Fr.* Idylls.
Giant's Wooing, The. *Fr.* Idylls.
Gift-Card Enclosed. *Fr.* Idylls.
Gorgo and Praxinoa. *Fr.* Idylls.
Harvest-Home. *Fr.* Idylls.
Herdsmen, The. *Fr.* Idylls.
Hunter Hunted, The.
Hylas. *Fr.* Idylls.
Idylls, *sels.*
Ill Merchandise, *at.*
In Praise of Bombyca. *Fr.* Idylls.
Incantation, The. *Fr.* Idylls.
Late Summer in the Country. *Fr.* Idylls.
Lines Written to Accompany the Gift of a Distaff to Theugenis. *Fr.* Idylls.
Love-Magic.
Lovers' Meeting. *Fr.* Idylls.
Lovesick Cyclops, A. *Fr.* Idylls.
Neatherd's Lament, The. *Fr.* Idylls.
Passing of Daphnis, The. *Fr.* Idylls.
Peace to the Tomb, *at.*
Pharmaceutria, The. *Fr.* Idylls.
Polyphemus to Galatea. *Fr.* Idylls.
Reapers' Song. *Fr.* Idylls.
Rustic Serenade. *Fr.* Idylls.
"Season of Mellow Fruitfulness." *Fr.* Idylls.
Second Idyll, The. *Fr.* Idylls.
Serenade ("O beautiful Amaryllis"). *Fr.* Idylls.
Simaetha. *Fr.* Idylls.
Song of the Death of Daphnis, The. *Fr.* Idylls.
Sorceress. The. *Fr.* Idylls.
Summer Joys. *Fr.* Idylls.
Syracusan Women [at the Adonis Festival], The. *Fr.* Idylls.
Thine Early Death.
Transfiguring Love. *Fr.* Idylls.
Transience. *Fr.* Idylls.
Two Boxers. The. *Fr.* Idylls.
Wooing of Daphnis, The. *Fr.* Idylls.

THEODORE OF STUDIUM, SAINT. Canon for Apocreos, The.

THEODORIDES [*or* THEODORIDAS]. On a Shipwrecked Sailor.
Pass On.

THEODULPH OF ORLEANS. All glory, laud and honor.

THEOGNIS. Adder, The.
Advice to Kyrnos.
Against the Demos.
All or Nothing.
All Things to All Men.
Bane of Poverty, The.
Beloved. The.
Better Part, The.
Broken Chain, The.
Café Society.
"Cherchez Fortune Ailleurs."

THEOGNIS (*continued*)
Choosing Friends.
"Crabbed Age and Youth."
Crane's Message, The.
Critics.
Dead Feel Not, The.
Despair.
Dust to Dust.
Enjoyment.
Eugenics.
Eye for an Eye, An.
Faithless Friend, A.
False One, The.
Friendlessness.
Hope.
"Hurler avec les Loups."
Immortality Conferred in Vain.
Lo, I have given thee plumes where-with to skim.
Love in the Springtime.
Love's Blindness.
Loyalty.
May I Drink the Blood of My Enemies.
Nativity.
Nec Odi Nec Amo.
Nostalgia.
Oath, An.
On Choosing Friends.
Plutocracy.
Poverty.
Pride of the Flesh.
Problem, The.
Protective Colouring.
Put Money in Thy Purse.
Race.
Refined Gold.
Refugee, The.
Reproach No Man for Poverty.
Sampler, The.
Stoic, The.
Teetotal?
To Cyrnus.
To rear a child is easy, but to teach.
Truth of It, The.
Unselfish Suitor.
Usurper, The.
Vendetta.
"Vive Hodie."
Wanderer, The.
Weep for Youth's Passing.
Years, The.
THEOPHILUS. "Crabbed Age and Youth."
THERESA [*or* TERESA], SAINT, OF AVILA.
Alone God Sufficeth.
I Die because I Do Not Die.
If, Lord, Thy Love for Me Is Strong.
Let Mine Eyes See Thee.
Let Nothing Disturb Thee.
Life Above, the Life on High, The.
Lines Written in Her Breviary.
Santa [*or* Saint] Teresa's Book-Mark.
Shepherd, Shepherd, Hark.
To-Day a Shepherd.
Who God Possesseth.
THÉRÈSE, SAINT, OF LISIEUX. My Song of Today.
Scattering Flowers.
Unpetalled Rose, The.
THÉRÈSE, SISTER MARY. Arcum Conteret.
Bird, The.
Christmas in Carmel.
I Send Our Lady.
Moment in Ostia.
On a Favorite Poet.
Port-of-Call.
To a Nun-Stigmatist.
To Joan of Arc on D-Day.
Traveler.
THEWLIS, JOHN. Song of a Happy Rising, The.
THIBAUDEAU, COLLEEN. Spring Poem.
THIBAUT IV, COUNT OF CHAMPAGNE [*later* THIBAUT I, KING OF NAVARRE]. Chanson: Leaving on Crusade.
Chanson: "There is no comfort to be found for pain."
Oh, Gentle Beauty.
THIELE, COLIN. Burke and Wills, *sels.*
Final Soliloquy, The. *Fr.* Burke and Wills.
Wills Dies in Solitude. *Fr.* Burke and Wills.
THIELE, ERNEST W. Ludmilla; an Ode on the Occasion of Her Departure from These Shores.
THOBY-MARCELIN, PHILIPPE. Elegies.
THOM, WILLIAM. Blind Boy's Pranks, The.
Mitherless Bairn, The.
Song of the Forsaken.
They Speak o' Wiles.
THOMAS, ALINE. Youth.
THOMAS, BEATRICE LLEWELLYN. To Puck.
THOMAS, CHARLES EDWARD. To a Moth.
THOMAS, CHARLES F., JR. Cowboy Up to Date, The.
THOMAS, CLAIRE RICHCREEK. Flesh will heal and pain will fade.
Heart Wounds.
THOMAS, DYLAN. After the Funeral.
Altarwise by Owl-Light.
Among Those Killed in the Dawn Raid Was a Man Aged One Hundred.
And Death Shall Have No Dominion.
Ballad of the Long-legged Bait.
Before I Knocked and Flesh Let Enter.
Ceremony after a Fire Raid.
Do Not Go Gentle into That Good Night.
Ears in the Turrets Hear.
Especially When the October Wind.
Fern Hill.
Force That through the Green Fuse Drives [the Flower], The.
Grief Ago, A.
Hand That Signed the Paper [Felled a City], The.
Hold Hard, These Ancient Minutes.
Holy Spring.
Hunchback in the Park, The.
I, in My Intricate Image.
I See the Boys of Summer.
In Country Sleep.
In Memory of Ann Jones.
In My Craft or Sullen Art.
In the Beginning.
In the White Giant's Thigh.
Johnnie Crack and Flossie Snail. *Fr.* Under Milk Wood.
Last time I slept with the queen, The.
Light Breaks Where No Sun Shines.
Marriage of a Virgin, The.
Not from This Anger.
Now stamp the Lord's Prayer on a grain of rice. *Fr.* Sonnets.
October. *Fr.* Poem in October.
On No Work of Words.
On the Marriage of a Virgin.
Over Sir John's Hill.
Poem: "Especially when the October wind."
Poem: "Force that through the green fuse drives the flower, The."
Poem: "On no work of words now for three lean months in the bloody."
Poem: "Once it was the colour of saying."
Poem: "Process in the weather of the heart, A."
Poem: "Spire cranes, The. Its statue is an aviary."
Poem: "We lying by seasand, watching yellow."
Poem Five.
Poem for Caitlin.
Poem in October ("Especially when the October wind").
Poem in October ("It was my thirtieth year to heaven").
Poem on His Birthday.
Process in the Weather of the Heart, A.
Prologue: "This day winding down now."
Refusal to Mourn the Death, by Fire, of a Child in London, A.
Should Lanterns Shine.
Song: "Johnnie Crack and Flossie Snail." *Fr.* Under Milk Wood.
Song of the Mischievous Dog, The.
Sonnet: "Altarwise by owl-light in the halfway-house." *Fr.* Sonnets.
Sonnet: "And from the windy West came two-gunned Gabriel." *Fr.* Sonnets.
Sonnet: "Cartoons of slashes on the tide-traced crater." *Fr.* Sonnets.
Sonnet: "Death is all metaphors, shape in one history." *Fr.* Sonnets.
Sonnet: "First there was the lamb on knocking knees." *Fr.* Sonnets.
Sonnet: "From the oracular archives and the parchment." *Fr.* Sonnets.
Sonnet: "Let the tale's sailor from a Christian voyage." *Fr.* Sonnets.
Sonnet: "Now stamp the Lord's Prayer on a grain of rice." *Fr.* Sonnets.
Sonnet: "This was the crucifixion on the mountain." *Fr.* Sonnets.
Sonnet: "What is the metre of the dictionary?" *Fr.* Sonnets.
Sonnets (I–X).
Sonnets, *sels.*
This Bread I Break Was Once the Oat.
This Side of the Truth.
Tombstone Told When She Died, The.
Twenty-four Years.
Two Sonnets.
Under Milk Wood, *sel.*
Vision and Prayer.
Vision and Prayer, *sel.*
When All My Five and Country Senses See.
Why East Wind Chills.
Winter's Tale, A.
THOMAS, EDITH MATILDA. Autumn Fashions.
Babouscka.
Babushka; a Russian Legend.
Baby's Evening-Song.
Betrayal of the Rose, The.
Blooming of the White Thorn, The.
Breath of Hampstead Heath.
Britons and Guests.
Chickadees.
Christopher of the Shenandoah, A.
Courage of the Lost, The.
Cure-All. *Fr.* The Inverted Torch.
Deep-Sea Pearl, The.
Evoe!
Far Cry to Heaven, A.
Fir-Tree, The.
Frost To-Night.
God of Music, The.
Grasshopper, The.
If Still They Live. *Fr.* The Inverted Torch.
In the Lilac-Rain.
Insomnia.
Inverted Torch, The.
Little Boy's Vain Regret, A.
Lyric: "Tell me, is there." *Fr.* The Inverted Torch.
Moly.
Mother England.
Mother Who Died Too, The.
Muses, The.
Music.
Old Soul, The.
On Easter Morn.
Passer-by, The.
Patmos.
Ponce de Leon.
Quiet Pilgrim, The
Rank and File.
Red Cross Nurse, The.
Reply of Socrates, The.
Shoe or Stocking.
Sleepward.
Soul in the Body, The.
Sursum Corda, *sel.*
Talking in Their Sleep.
Tears of the Poplars, The.
Tell Me. *Fr.* The Inverted Torch.
Thefts of the Morning.
To Imagination.
To Spain—a Last Word.
Triumph of Forgotten Things, The.
Valentine.
Vesper Sparrow, The.
Vos Non Vobis.
Water of Dirce, The.

We Are Old.
When in the First Great Hour. *Fr.* The Inverted Torch.
Will It Be So? *Fr.* The Inverted Torch.
Winter Sleep.
THOMAS, EDWARD ("Edward Eastaway"). Adlestrop.
As the Team's Head-Brass.
Aspens.
Beauty.
Bright Clouds.
Brook, The.
Cat, A.
Clouds That Are So Light, The.
Cock-Crow.
Combe, The.
Digging.
Early One Morning.
February Afternoon.
Fifty Faggots.
For These.
Gallows, The.
Glory, The.
Green Roads, The.
Haymaking.
Health.
If I Should Ever by Chance.
In Memoriam; Easter 1915.
It Rains.
Liberty.
Lights Out.
Like the Touch of Rain.
Lob.
Manor Farm, The.
Melancholy.
Mill-Pond, The.
New House, The.
No One Cares Less than I.
No One So Much as You.
November.
October.
Old Man.
Out in the Dark.
Owl, The.
Path, The.
Penny Whistle, The.
Private, A.
Rain.
Sedge Warblers.
Sign-Post, The.
Snow.
Sowing.
Sun Used to Shine, The.
Swedes.
Tale, A.
Tall Nettles.
Tears.
Thaw.
There's Nothing like the Sun.
This Is No Case of Petty Right or Wrong.
Trumpet, The.
Two Houses.
Two Pewits.
Under the Woods.
Unknown, The.
Unknown Bird, The.
What Shall I Give?
When First I Came Here.
Will You Come?
Women He Liked.
Word, The.
THOMAS, EDWIN. Warrior Bold, A.
THOMAS, ELIZABETH H. Once upon a Time.
THOMAS, EVAN. Laborer, The.
THOMAS, FREDERICK WILLIAM. Song: "'Tis said that absence conquers love!"
THOMAS, GILBERT. Across the Fens.
Cup of Happiness, The.
Invocation: "There is no balm on earth."
Ploughman, The.
Red Sky at Morning.
Unseen Bridge, The.
THOMAS, JAMES B. Eagle.
Flute of Krishna, The.
Song of the Hermit Thrush, The.
THOMAS, KENETHA. Night Lies Silently.
THOMAS, LETTA EULALIA. What America Means to Me.
THOMAS, LOUISA CARROLL. What Is Charm?
THOMAS, MARTHA BANNING. Chirrupy Cricket, The.
Gentle Storm.
THOMAS, OLIVIA. Southern Republic, The.
THOMAS, ORMOND. Let Us Break Down the Barriers.
Poem in February.
Strange within the Dividing.
THOMAS, PERCY. Give Me a Gentle Heart.
THOMAS, PHILIP EDWARD. *See* THOMAS, EDWARD.
THOMAS, RONALD STUART. Affinity.
Enigma.
Farm Child.
Hill Farmer Speaks, The.
Madrigal: "Your love is dead, lady, your love is dead."
Peasant, A.
Question, The.
Village, The.
Welsh Hill Country, The.
THOMAS, T. E. Roosevelt.
THOMAS, WRIGHT. When Shrill Winds Shriek.
THOMAS À KEMPIS. Imitation of Christ, *sels.*
Immunity. *Fr.* Imitation of Christ.
Joys of Heaven, The.
Man Proposes. *Fr.* Imitation of Christ.
Of Love of Silence and of Solitude. *Fr.* Imitation of Christ.
Thoughts of Christ, The. *Fr.* Imitation of Christ.
THOMAS AQUINAS, SAINT. Adoro Te Devote.
Hymn: "Sing, my tongue, the Saviour's glory."
Hymn for Corpus Christi Day.
Lauda Sion.
Rhythmus ad SS. Sacramentum.
THOMAS AQUINAS, SISTER. Arbor Una Nobilis.
THOMAS MORE, SAINT. *See* MORE, SIR THOMAS.
THOMAS OF CELANO. Day of Judgment, The.
Dies Irae.
THOMAS OF HALES. Love Letter, A.
Love-Song, A.
Luve Ron, A.
Luve Ron, A, *sel.*
Where Is Paris and Heleyne? *Fr.* A Luve Ron.
THOMAS OF STRENGNAES. Ode to Freedom.
"THOMOND, BARD OF." *See* HOGAN, MICHAEL.
THOMPSON, ANN LOUISE. Leafless Tree, A.
THOMPSON, D'ARCY WENTWORTH. In London-town Dame Trottypeg. *Fr.* Nursery Nonsense.
Inquisitive Cock Sparrow, An. *Fr.* Nursery Nonsense.
Nursery Nonsense, *sels.*
Once upon a Time.
Poor Dear Grandpapa.
There lived an old man in a garret. *Fr.* Nursery Nonsense.
Two little dogs went out for a walk. *Fr.* Nursery Nonsense.
Two Magpies Sat on a Garden Rail.
THOMPSON, DONALD. On the Relative Merit of Friend and Foe, Being Dead.
THOMPSON, DOROTHY BROWN. Arbor Day.
Autosonic Door.
Boy Washington, The.
City and the Trucks, The.
Escape.
Fifth Wheel.
Getting Back.
I Like House Cleaning.
Lemonade Stand.
Maps.
Our House.
Parlor Car.
Round and Round.
This Is Halloween.
Youth Seekers, The.
THOMPSON, DUNSTAN. Articles of War.
In All the Argosy of Your Bright Hair.
Knight of Ghosts and Shadows, A.
Largo.
Lay of the Battle of Tombland, The.
Moment of the Rose, The.
Nor Mars His Sword.
This Loneliness for You Is like the Wound.
THOMPSON, EDITH OSBORNE. Monkeys, The.
THOMPSON, EDWARD. Author Writes His Own Epitaph, The.
Epilogue: "With words as counters."
Harbour Music.
THOMPSON, EVERARD V. Diversity.
THOMPSON, FRANCIS. Ad Castitatem.
After Woman, The.
All Flesh.
All's Vast.
And now, O shaken from thine antique throne. *Fr.* Ode to the Setting Sun.
Anthem of Earth, An, *sel.*
Any Saint.
Arab Love-Song, An.
Assumpta Maria.
Before Her Portrait in Youth.
"By Reason of Thy Law."
Carmen Genesis.
Child's Kiss, A.
Child's Prayer, A.
Contemplation.
Contemplation, *sel.*
Correlated Greatness.
Corymbus for Autumn, A, *sel.*
Counsel of Moderation, A.
Daisy.
Daisy, *sel.*
Dead Astronomer, A.
Dedication: "If the rose in meek duty."
Desiderium Indesideratum.
Dread of Height, The.
Dream-Tryst.
Envoy: "Go, songs, for ended is our brief, sweet play."
Epilogue: "Heaven, which man's generations draws." *Fr.* A Judgment in Heaven.
Epilogue: "Virtue may unlock hell." *Fr.* A Judgment in Heaven.
Ex Ore Infantium.
Fair Inconstant, The.
Fallen Yew, A.
Field-Flower.
Franciscus Christificatus.
From the Night of Forebeing.
From the Night of Forebeing, *sels.*
Grace of the Way.
Grace of the Way, *sel.*
Heart, The.
Heart, The, *sel.*
Hound of Heaven, The.
Hound of Heaven, The, *sel.*
House of Sorrows, The.
Hunchèd camels of the night, The.
In Her Paths.
In No Strange Land.
Judgment [*or* Judgement] in Heaven, A, *sels.*
Kingdom of God, The.
Kiss, A? for a child's kiss? *Fr.* Sister Songs.
Lilium Regis.
Lines for a Drawing of Our Lady of the Night.
Little Jesus.
Love and the Child.
Making of Viola, The.
May Burden, A.
Messages.
Mistress of Vision, The.
New Year's Chimes.
Nocturn.
Non Pax—Expectatio.
Now of that vision I, bereaven. *Fr.* Grace of the Way.
Ode for the Diamond Jubilee of Queen Victoria, 1897, *sel.*
Ode to the Setting Sun.

THOMPSON, FRANCIS (*continued*)
Ode to the Setting Sun, *sels.*
Orient Ode.
Orient Ode, *sel.*
Pastoral.
Poppy, The.
Prelude: "Wailful sweetness of the violin, The." *Fr.* Ode to the Setting Sun.
St. Monica.
Singer Saith of His Song, The.
Sister Songs, *sels.*
Sun, The. *Fr.* Ode to the Setting Sun.
To a Poet Breaking Silence.
To a Snowflake.
To Daisies.
To My Godchild [Francis M. W. Meynell].
To Olivia.
To Stars.
To the Dead Cardinal of Westminster.
To the English Martyrs.
To W. M.
Tokens, The. *Fr.* Daisy.
Veteran of Heaven, The.
Veteran of Heaven, The, *sel.*
Whereto Art Thou Come?
THOMPSON, FREDERIC. Ave Maria, *tr.*
Constant.
Heaven and Earth.
Plan for a Novel.
THOMPSON, IRENE. Caravans.
Country Child, The.
Feet.
Holiday Train, The.
Penny Wish, A.
Rainy Nights.
Secret Places.
Swinging.
Town Child, The.
Welcome to Spring.
THOMPSON, J. W. Work.
THOMPSON, JAMES MAURICE. *See* THOMPSON, MAURICE.
THOMPSON, JIM. Road and a Memory, A.
THOMPSON, JOHN. Chess.
Letter to a Friend.
Lyric: "Songs of adolescence, The."
Refuge.
THOMPSON, JOHN, JR. Birthday Poem, November 4th.
Eclogue I: "You to your beech tree, Tityrus, withdraw," *tr.* *Fr.* Eclogues.
Eclogues (*of* Virgil), *sel., tr.*
Love for Patsy, A.
THOMPSON, JOHN B. Chiaroscuro.
THOMPSON, JOHN BEAUCHAMP. Passover.
THOMPSON, JOHN REUBEN. Ashby.
Battle Rainbow, The.
Burial of Latané, The.
Captain Latané.
Carcassonne, *tr.*
Lee to the Rear.
Music in Camp.
Obsequies of Stuart.
On to Richmond.
THOMPSON, JOHN W. That I Shall Die.
THOMPSON, LESLIE. There Are So Many Ways of Going Places.
THOMPSON, LESLIE P. Song of Satisfaction on Completing an Overhauling of Fishing Tackle, A.
THOMPSON, LEWIS. Black Angel.
Rose.
THOMPSON, LULU E. In Hardin County, 1809.
THOMPSON, MAURICE. At Lincoln's Grave. *Fr.* Lincoln's Grave.
Atalanta.
Ballad of Chickamauga, The.
Blue Heron, The.
Bluebird, The.
Creole Slave-Song, A.
Dropping Corn.
Early Bluebird, An.
Flight Shot, A.
He Is Not Dead. *Fr.* Lincoln's Grave.
Humming Bird, The.
In the Haunts of Bass and Bream.
Lincoln.
Lincoln's Grave, *sels.*
Lion's Cub, The.
On a Fly-Leaf of Theocritus.
Prelude, A: "Spirit that moves the sap in spring."
Prophecy, A. *Fr.* Lincoln's Grave.
Spring's Torch-Bearer.
Wild Honey.
Written on a Fly-Leaf of Theocritus.
THOMPSON [*or* THOMSON], MORTIMER NEAL. Power of the Pen, The.
THOMPSON, PHILLIPS. Failed.
THOMPSON, STITH. Battle of Brunanburh, The, *tr.*
Seafarer, The, *tr.*
Wanderer, The, *tr.*
THOMPSON, VANCE. Linen Bands.
Symbols.
THOMPSON, WILL HENRY. Come Love or Death.
Fold the Banners. *Fr.* The High Tide at Gettysburg.
High Tide at Gettysburg, The.
High Tide at Gettysburg, The, *sel.*
THOMPSON, WILLIAM. Happy Life, The, *sel.*
On Laurel Hill, *sel.*
THOMSEN, GRÍMUR. Iceland's Song.
King Sverrir.
THOMSON, ——. Song to Mary.
THOMSON, CLAIRE AVEN. Tranquil Sea.
THOMSON, EDWARD WILLIAM. Aspiration.
Canadian Rossignol, The.
Mandan Priest, The.
Peter Ottawa, *sel.*
Thunderchild's Lament.
THOMSON, JAMES (1700–1748). Angling. *Fr.* The Seasons: Spring.
Approach of Winter. *Fr.* The Seasons: Winter.
Autumn. *Fr.* The Seasons.
Autumn, *sels.* *Fr.* The Seasons.
Bathing. *Fr.* The Seasons: Summer.
Birds in Spring. *Fr.* The Seasons: Spring.
Britannia, *sels.*
Britannia. *Fr.* The Seasons: Summer.
Britannia's Empire. *Fr.* Britannia.
British Commerce. *Fr.* Liberty.
Castle of Indolence, The, *sels.*
Coming of the Rain, The. *Fr.* The Seasons: Spring.
Connubial Life. *Fr.* The Seasons: Spring.
Domestic Birds. *Fr.* The Seasons: Spring.
Enchanted Ground. *Fr.* The Castle of Indolence.
Finis: "As those we love decay, we die in part." *Fr.* On the Death of Mr. William Aikman.
For Ever, Fortune.
Frost at Night. *Fr.* The Seasons: Winter.
Happy Britannia. *Fr.* The Seasons: Summer.
He Heard Her Sing, *sel.*
Hymn, A: "These, as they change, Almighty Father! these." *Fr.* The Seasons.
Hymn on Solitude.
Hymn on Solitude, *sel.*
Hymn on the Seasons, A. *Fr.* The Seasons.
Indifference to Fortune. *Fr.* The Castle of Indolence.
Land of Indolence, The. *Fr.* The Castle of Indolence.
Lavinia. *Fr.* The Seasons: Autumn.
Liberty, *sel.*
Lisy's Parting with Her Cat.
Lo! from the Livid East. *Fr.* The Seasons: Winter.
Lost Shepherd, The. *Fr.* The Seasons: Winter.
Love of Nature. *Fr.* The Seasons: Autumn.
Moonlight. *Fr.* The Seasons: Autumn.
Moonlight in Autumn. *Fr.* The Seasons: Autumn.
Newton Fixes the Moon. *Fr.* A Poem Sacred to the Memory of Sir Isaac Newton.
Newton on Light. *Fr.* A Poem Sacred to the Memory of Sir Isaac Newton.
Nightingale Bereaved, The. *Fr.* The Seasons: Spring.
Ode: "Tell me, thou soul of her I love."
On the Death of a Particular Friend.
On the Death of Mr. William Aikman the Painter, *sel.*
Plea for the Animals. *Fr.* The Seasons: Spring.
Poem Sacred to the Memory of Sir Isaac Newton, A.
Poem Sacred to the Memory of Sir Isaac Newton, A, *sels.*
Praise of Industry, The. *Fr.* The Castle of Indolence.
Prelude: "North-east spends his rage, The." *Fr.* The Seasons: Spring.
Sea-Birds.
Seasons, The, *sels.*
Sheep Shearing, The. *Fr.* The Seasons: Summer.
Sheep-washing, The. *Fr.* The Seasons: Summer.
Snow Scene, A. *Fr.* The Seasons: Winter.
Solitude. *Fr.* Hymn on Solitude.
Song: "One day the god of fond desire."
Song of Indolence. *Fr.* The Castle of Indolence.
Songsters, The. *Fr.* The Seasons: Spring.
Spring, *sels.* *Fr.* The Seasons.
Spring Flowers. *Fr.* The Seasons: Spring.
Stag Hunt, The. *Fr.* The Seasons: Autumn.
Storm, The. *Fr.* The Seasons: Summer.
Storm, The. *Fr.* The Seasons: Winter.
Storm in Harvest. *Fr.* The Seasons: Autumn.
Storm in Winter, A. *Fr.* The Seasons: Winter.
Summer, *sels.* *Fr.* The Seasons.
Summer Evening and Night. *Fr.* The Seasons: Summer.
Summer Morning. *Fr.* The Seasons: Summer.
Swan, Turkey, Dove, and the Bull in the Broom. *Fr.* The Seasons: Spring.
Tell Me, Thou Soul of Her I Love.
Ten Thousand, The.
To Amanda.
To Fortune.
To the Memory of Sir Isaac Newton, *sel.*
To the Reverend Mr. Murdoch.
Vale of Indolence, The. *Fr.* The Castle of Indolence.
Venus Shines Out. *Fr.* The Seasons: Summer.
Verses Occasioned by the Death of Dr. Aikman.
War for the Sake of Peace. *Fr.* Britannia.
Winter. *Fr.* The Seasons.
Winter, *sels.* *Fr.* The Seasons.
Winter Scene, A. *Fr.* The Seasons.
Winter Storm, A. *Fr.* The Seasons.
Winter Winds. *Fr.* The Seasons.
Witching Song, A. *Fr.* The Castle of Indolence.
Wondrous Show, A. *Fr.* The Castle of Indolence.
Woodland Choir, The. *Fr.* The Seasons: Spring.
THOMSON, JAMES (1700–1748), *and* DAVID MALLET [*or* MALET *or* MALLOCH]. Alfred, a Masque, *sel.*
Ode, An: "When Britain first, at heaven's command." *Fr.* Alfred, a Masque.
Rule, Britannia! *Fr.* Alfred, a Masque.
THOMSON, JAMES ("B. V." *or* "Bysshe Vanolis"). Art.
Art, *sels.*

As I Came through the Desert. *Fr.* The City of Dreadful Night.
As We Rush, as We Rush in the Train. *Fr.* Sunday at Hampstead.
Blauen Veilchen der Äugelein, Die, *tr.*
Bridge, The. *Fr.* Sunday up the River.
City Is of Night, The. *Fr.* The City of Dreadful Night.
City of Dreadful Night, The.
City of Dreadful Night, The, *sels.*
E. B. B.
Es stehen unbeweglich, *tr.*
Exile, *tr.*
Fichtenbaum steht einsam, Ein, *tr.*
Fire That Filled My Heart of Old, The.
Fisher Maiden, The, *tr.*
For I Must Sing of All I Feel and Know.
Forlornly, *tr.*
Gifts. *Fr.* Sunday up the River.
Give a Man a Horse He Can Ride. *Fr.* Sunday up the River.
If you have a carrier-dove. *Fr.* Art.
In the Room.
In the Train. *Fr.* Sunday at Hampstead.
L'Ancien Régime.
Let My Voice Ring Out. *Fr.* Sunday up the River.
Life's Hebe.
Lotosblume ängstigt, Die, *tr.*
Lotus-Flower, The, *tr.*
Love Dead, *tr.*
Madonna, A, *tr.*
Mater Tenebrarum.
Mein Herz, mein Herz, ist traurig, *tr.*
Mein Liebchen, wir sassen zusammen, *tr.*
Melancholia. *Fr.* The City of Dreadful Night.
Mermaidens, The, *tr.*
Midsummer Courtship. *Fr.* Richard Forest's Midsummer Night.
Mir träumte wieder der alte Traum, *tr.*
Mond ist aufgegangen, Der, *tr.*
Oh, What Are You Waiting For. *Fr.* Sunday up the River.
On a Broken Pipe.
Once in a Saintly Passion.
Philosophy, *tr.*
Picture, The, *tr.*
Prayer, A: "My darling, thou art flowerlike," *tr.*
Proem: "Lo, thus, as prostrate, 'In the dust I write.'" *Fr.* The City of Dreadful Night.
Reflection.
Requiem, A.
Richard Forest's Midsummer Night, *sel.*
Sag', wo ist dein schönes Liebchen. *tr.*
Singing is sweet; but be sure of this. *Fr.* Art.
Song: "Let my voice ring out and over the earth." *Fr.* Sunday up the River.
Song: "Like violets pale i' the spring o' the year." *Fr.* Sunday up the River.
Song: "My love is the flaming sword." *Fr.* Sunday up the River.
Song of Sighing, A.
Sphinx, The. *Fr.* The City of Dreadful Night.
Striving to sing glad songs, I but attain. *Fr.* Two Sonnets.
Sunday at Hampstead, *sels.*
Sunday up the River, *sels.*
Superfluous Bite. *tr.*
This is the Heath of Hampstead. *Fr.* Sunday at Hampstead.
To Our Ladies of Death.
Two Sonnets.
Two Sonnets, *sel.*
Vine, The. *Fr.* Sunday up the River.
Voice from the Nile, A.
Welt ist dumm, die Welt ist blind, Die, *tr.*
What precious thing are you making fast. *Fr.* Art.
Why Are Your Songs All Wild and Bitter Sad. *Fr.* Two Sonnets.
William Blake.
Wine of Love is Music, The. *Fr.* Sunday up the River.
Withered Heart, The, *tr.*
World Is Dull, The, *tr.*

THOMSON, MORTIMER NEAL. *See* THOMPSON, MORTIMER NEAL.

THOMSON, MRS. ROBERT. Texas Cowboy, The.

THOMSON, ROSAMOND DARGAN. Panic.

THOMSON OF CARDINGTON, CHRISTOPHER BIRDWOOD THOMSON, 1ST BARON. Questions.

THORARENSEN, BJARNI. Lines to Sigrún.
Winter.

THORARENSEN, JAKOB. Cathedral in Trondheim, The.
Desert Dangers.

THOREAU, HENRY DAVID. All Things Are Current Found. *Fr.* A Week on the Concord and Merrimack Rivers.
Among the Worst of Men That Ever Lived.
At Midnight's Hour I Raised My Head.
Atlantides, The. *Fr.* A Week on the Concord and Merrimack Rivers.
Between the Traveller and the Setting Sun.
Conscience. *Fr.* A Week on the Concord and Merrimack Rivers.
Epitaph on the World.
Fall of the Leaf, The.
Fisher's Boy, The.
For Though the Caves Were Rabbited.
Forever in My Dream and in My Morning Thought.
Free Love.
Great Adventure, The.
Great Friend.
Great God, I Ask Thee for No Meaner Pelf.
Haze. *Fr.* A Week on the Concord and Merrimack Rivers.
I Am a Parcel [of Vain Strivings Tied].
I Was Born upon Thy Bank, River.
I Was Made Erect and Lone.
I'm Thankful that My Life Doth Not Deceive.
In the Busy Streets, Domains of Trade.
Independence.
Inspiration.
Inspiration, *sel.*
Inward Morning, The.
It Is No Dream of Mine.
Light-winged Smoke [Icarian Bird]. *Fr.* Walden.
Lines: "Though all the Fates should prove unkind."
Love.
Low-anchored Cloud. *Fr.* A Week on the Concord and Merrimack Rivers.
Men Say They Know Many Things.
Mist.
Moon Now Rises [to Her Absolute Rule], The.
Mountains.
My Books I'd Fain Cast Off, I Cannot Read.
My Prayer.
Nature.
Old Marlborough Road, The.
On the Sun Coming Out in the Afternoon.
Pray to What Earth Does This Sweet Cold Belong.
Prayer: "Great God! I ask thee for no meaner pelf."
Respectable Folks, The.
Rumors from an Aeolian Harp.
Sic Vita.
Smoke. *Fr.* Walden.
Smoke in Winter.
Stanzas: "Nature doth have her dawn each day."
Summer Rain.
Sympathy.
Tall Ambrosia.
Thaw, The.
To a Marsh Hawk in Spring.
To the Maiden in the East.
To the Mountains.
Travelling.
Walden.
Walden, *sels.*
Week on the Concord and Merrimack Rivers, A, *sels.*
What's the Railroad to Me?
Who Sleeps by Day and Walks by Night.
Winter Memories.
Within the Circuit of This Plodding Life.
Woof of the Sun. *Fr.* A Week on the Concord and Merrimack Rivers.

THORLEY, WILFRID. Buttercups.
Chant for Reapers.
Child-Thought, A.
Fan, the Filly.
Grocer and the Gold-Fish, The.
Hansom Cabbies.
Happy Sheep, The.
Harvest Elves, The.
Norse Sailor's Joy.
Of a Spider.
Of the Abbot and His Valet, *tr.*
Old Inn-Sign, The.
Roger Francis.
Song for a Ball-Game.
Sound of the Horn, The, *tr.*
Wild Marjorie, *tr.*

THORN, JOHN. Man's Flitting Life Finds Surest Stay.

THORNBURY, GEORGE WALTER. Cavalier's Escape, The.
Court Historian, The.
Death of Marlborough, The.
Death of Oberon, The.
Dirge on the Death of Oberon, the Fairy King.
Jacobite on Tower Hill, The.
Jester's Sermon, The.
La Tricoteuse.
Melting of the Earl's Plate.
Old Grenadier's Story, The.
Pompadour, The.
Riding to the Tournament, The.
Sally from Coventry, The.
Three Scars, The.
Three Troopers, The.
White Rose over the Water, The.

THORNE, ANNA H. Dawn of the Century.
Peace Universal.

THORNE, META E. B. Autumn. *Fr.* Songs of the Seasons.
Songs of the Seasons.
Spring. *Fr.* Songs of the Seasons.
Summer. *Fr.* Songs of the Seasons.
Winter. *Fr.* Songs of the Seasons.

THORNELY, THOMAS. Atom, The.
Patronage.
Presage.

THORNTON, ELIZA. Reign of Peace, The.

THORNTON, EMILY. Dying Newsboy, The.

THORNTON, FRANCIS BEAUCHESNE. Snow Meditation.

THORNTON, JAMES. Irish Jubilee, The.

THORNTON, LALIA MITCHELL. Blue Ribbon Cats.
Change.
Forgive.

THORNTON, M. B. Limerick: "All young men should take note of the case."
Limerick: "There once was a popular crooner."

THORNTON, NATHANIEL. To Virginia Woolf.

THORP, H. M. Finger Folk.

THORP, N. HOWARD ("Jack"). Little Joe, the Wrangler, *at.*

THORPE, ROSE HARTWICK. Curfew Must Not Ring Tonight.

THORSON, INEZ CLARK. Dog Abandoned.
Progression.

THORSTEINSSON, STEINGRÍMUR. At Sunset.
Epigrams.
Generosity. *Fr.* Epigrams.
Lions and Swine. *Fr.* Epigrams.
Love Song, A.
Mountain and Hillock. *Fr.* Epigrams.
Swansong on the Moorlands.
Voice of Song.

THRALE, HESTER LYNCH (Mme Piozzi). Three Warnings, The.
THRING, EDWARD. Hymn for the Nativity.
THRING, GODFREY. Fierce raged the tempest o'er the deep.
I heard a sound of voices.
Jesus Comes on Clouds Triumphant.
THUCYDIDES. Epitaph on Euripides, *at.*
Euripides, *at.*
To Hellas' bard all Hellas gives a tomb, *at.*
THURLOW, EDWARD HOVELL-THURLOW, 2D BARON. *See* HOVELL-THURLOW, EDWARD.
THURLOW, EDWARD THURLOW, 1ST BARON. On Beholding Bodiam Castle.
THURSTON, CHARLOTTE W. Thanksgiving Philosophy.
THWAITES, MICHAEL. Prophetic Hour, The.
THYILLUS. Dead Dancer, The.
THYMOCLES. "And Left the Thorn."
TIBULLUS, ALBIUS. Cerinthus Forgiven; Once More Tibullus Speaks for the Girl.
Elegies. *sels.*
Elegy, An: "Let others pile their yellow ingots high." *Fr.* Elegies.
He Need Speak No Longer in Behalf of Sulpicia and Cerinthus.
He Speaks for the Girl, on Cerinthus' Birthday.
Hoards let others heap of tawny gold. *Fr.* Elegies.
How well I'd bear the break, my anger spoke it. *Fr.* Elegies.
Hush, all. Our crops, our lands we purify. *Fr.* Elegies.
I see enslavement to a mistress closing on me. *Fr.* Elegies.
If you had already resolved to blight my joyless love. *Fr.* Elegies.
Intercession, on Sulpicia's Birthday, to Her Guardian Spirit.
Macer has joined the army, and what's to become of peaceable Cupid? *Fr.* Elegies.
Matronalia, March 1, The.
No Harm to Lovers.
Pastoral Elegy, A.
Plea and Counsel.
Recantation, The.
Sulpicia's Rival.
What man first forged the terrifying blade? *Fr.* Elegies.
You will sail the dancing Aegean, Messalla, without me. *Fr.* Elegies.
TICHBORNE [*or* TICHBOURNE], CHIDIOCK. Elegy: "My prime of youth is but a frost of cares."
Lament the Night before His Execution, A.
Lines Written by One in the Tower.
My prime of youth is but a frost of cares.
On the Eve of His Execution.
Poem, Written on the Eve of Execution.
Retrospect.
Tichborne's Elegy, Written [with His Own Hand] in the Tower before His Execution, 1586.
Untimely End, The.
Verses Written in the Tower the Night before He Was Beheaded.
Written on the Eve of Execution.
Written the Night before His Execution.
TICKELL, THOMAS. Addison's Funeral in the Abbey. *Fr.* To the Earl of Warwick on the Death of Mr. Addison.
Colin and Lucy.
Fairies. *Fr.* Kensington Garden.
Kensington Garden, *sels.*
Lucy and Colin.
Ode Inscribed to the Earl of Sunderland at Windsor, An.
To a Lady before Marriage, *sel.*
To the Earl of Warwick on the Death of Mr. Addison.
To the Earl of Warwick on the Death of Mr. Addison, *sel.*
Tulips, The. *Fr.* Kensington Garden.
TICKENER, H. M. Reddened Road, The.
TICKNOR, FRANCIS ORRERY [*or* ORRAY]. Albert Sidney Johnston.
Battle Ballad, A.
Little Giffen.
Our Left.
Our Treasure in Heaven.
Song for the Asking, A.
Virginians of the Valley, The.
TIECK, JOHANN LUDWIG. Autumn Song.
Love.
TIEMER-WILLE, GERTRUDE. Repast.
TIEMPO, CÉSAR (*originally* Israel Zeitlin). Harangue on the Death of Chayim Nachman [*or* Hayyim Nahman] Bialik.
I Tell of Another Young Death.
Israelite Graveyard.
Prayer: "Moon, mother of the Sabbath, transfuse your loving."
Weeping and Singing.
TIEN CH'IEN. Children's Festival.
More than a Hundred.
TIETJENS, EUNICE. April.
Bacchante to Her Babe, The.
City Wall, The.
Completion.
Drug Clerk, The.
Fun with Fishing.
Graduating Class, The.
Great Man, The.
Imprisoned.
Most-sacred Mountain, The.
Moving.
My Mother's House.
Old Friendship.
Old Maps.
On the Height.
Parting after a Quarrel.
Psalm to My Belovèd.
Sonnet: "Oh, breath is sweet, here in this mountain land!"
Steam Shovel, The.
Tanka: "Blossoms of the plum," *tr.*
Thaw.
To My Friend, Grown Famous.
TIFFANY, ESTHER B. Applied Astronomy.
TIGERSCHIÖLD, HUGO. Smelting Furnace, The.
TIGHE, MARY. Sonnet: "As one who late hath lost a friend adored."
To a Little Girl Gathering Flowers.
TIKHONOV, NIKOLAI. Ballad of Nails, The.
Before the Aragva at Night.
Bridge, The.
Dawn in London.
Enemy has forced an entry, The.
Epoch, The.
Fire, a hawser, bullets and an axe, A.
Fire, the Rope [*or* Noose].
Flanders Roses.
From Gombor.
I was born at night on the crossways.
In the Humpbacked Sky.
Kirov Is with Us.
Long Was the Road.
My Mother.
Nelly.
Not yesterday did the blacksmith hammer.
Our Rooms.
Reckless Devil-may-care.
Snow of the Crane.
We Have Unlearned.
TILDEN, ETHEL ARNOLD. Dedication: "We dedicate a church today."
TILDEN, STEPHEN. Braddock's Fate, with an Incitement to Revenge.
British Lyon Roused, The.
TILLER, TERENCE. Bathers.
Beggar.
End of the Story, The.
Epithalamion: "Wind in the street, and sadness of unknown walkers."
Europa.
Image in a Lilac Tree.
Killed in Action.
No Time.
Perfumes.
Poem: "Grecian tulip and the gothic rose, The."
Prothalamion.
Vase, The.
TILLETT, WILBUR FISK. Incarnate Love.
My Father Knows.
TILLEY, LUCY EVANGELINE. When Even Cometh On.
TILNEY, CHARLES. Cobbler's Song, The, *at.* *Fr.* Locrine.
Locrine, *sel.*, *at.*
TILTON, THEODORE. Cœur de Lion to Berengaria.
Even This Shall Pass Away.
Flight from the Convent, The.
Fly, The.
French with a Master.
God Save the Nation.
Great Bell Roland, The.
King's Ring, The.
No and Yes.
Sir Marmaduke's Musings.
TIMOCREON. Evil Genius, The.
God of Wealth, The.
Themistocles.
TIMOTHEUS. Contemporaneity.
Manifesto, A.
Persae, *sels.*
Sea-Fight, A. *Fr.* Persae.
TIMROD, HENRY. At Magnolia Cemetery.
Carolina.
Charleston.
Christmas.
Cotton Boll, The.
Cry to Arms, A.
Decoration Day at Charleston.
Elusive Nature.
Ethnogenesis; Written during the Meeting of the First Southern Congress, at Montgomery, February, 1861.
Hark to the Shouting Wind.
Hymn for Memorial Day.
I Know Not Why, but All This Weary Day.
I Scarcely Grieve, O Nature!
Love.
Love and Life.
Magnolia Cemetery.
Most Men Know Love But as a Part of Life.
Ode: "Sleep sweetly in your humble graves."
Ode for Decoration Day.
Ode Sung on the Occasion of Decorating the Graves of the Confederate Dead, at Magnolia Cemetery, Charleston, S.C.
Quatorzain.
Serenade: "Hide, happy damask, from the stars."
Sonnet: At Last, Beloved Nature.
Sonnet: I Know Not Why.
Sonnet: "Most men know love but as a part of life."
Spring [in Carolina].
Trifle, A.
Two Armies, The.
Unknown Dead, The.
Why Silent.
TINCKOM-FERNANDEZ, W. G. Beloved Vagabond, The.
Road Song.
TINDLEY, C. A. Nothing Between.
TING LIU NIANG. Ai Ai Thinks of the Man She Loves.
Blossoms of Lo Yang, The.
Song of the Courtesans.
TINKER, CHAUNCEY BREWSTER. Beowulf, *tr.*
Beowulf, *sels.*, *tr.*
Brussels Cross Inscription, *tr.*
Death of Grendel's Mother, The, *tr.* *Fr.* Beowulf.
Ruined City, The, *tr.*
Slaying of Grendel, The, *tr.* *Fr.* Beowulf.
"TIPCUCA." *See* WILSON, T. P. CAMERON.
TIPLADY, THOMAS. Above the Hills of Time.
Grace, A.
Hymn of the Unemployed.
Prayer for the Presence of Christ, A.
Wedding Hymn, A.
Wedding Hymn, A, *sel.*
When Life's Day Closes.

When the Daylight Wanes.
TIPPETT, JAMES STERLING. Autumn Woods.
Building a Skyscraper.
Busy Carpenters.
Circus Parade.
Counting the Days.
Do Not Open until Christmas.
Ducks at Dawn.
Elevated Train, The.
Engine.
Familiar Friends.
Ferry-Boats.
First Zeppelin, The.
Freight Boats.
George Washington.
Green Bus, The.
Hang Out the Flags.
I Like Christmas.
My Taxicab.
Old Log House.
Park, The.
River Bridge, The.
"Sh."
Sleet Storm.
Spider Webs.
Sunning.
Trains.
Trucks.
Tugs.
Underground Rumbling.
Up in the Air.
TIPPLE, E. H. Hot Weather in the Plains—India.
TITHERINGTON, RICHARD HANDFIELD. Faithful unto Death.
TIVNAN, E. P. To My Nun Sister.
TOBIAS, RUBY WEYBURN. Cross, The.
Food.
Gifts for the New Year.
Prayer Time.
True Apostolate, The.
TOBIN, JAMES EDWARD. Conversation in Clichés.
Cradle Song of a Celtic Queen.
Madonna of the Exiles.
Song above Death.
For translations from German, see AnGP.
TODD, ALICE. If.
Postman, The.
TODD, EARL D. Resurrection and Ascension.
TODD, JOHN F. Prayer for Mothers, A.
TODD, RUTHVEN. Lonely Month, The.
Personal History; for my Son.
Six Winters.
To a Very Beautiful Lady.
Various Ends.
Watching You Walk.
TODHUNTER, JOHN. Aghadoe.
Banshee, The.
Beethoven.
Black Knight, The.
Druid Song of Cathvah, The.
Fairy Gold.
Fate of the Sons of Usna, The. *Fr.* The First Duan: The Coming of Deirdre.
First Duan, The: The Coming of Deirdre, *sel.*
Lamentation for the Three Sons of Turann, Which Turann, Their Father, Made over Their Grave, The.
Laurella, *sel.*
Maureen.
Moment, A.
Morning in the Bay of Naples. *Fr.* Laurella.
O Mighty, Melancholy Wind.
Song: "Bring from the craggy haunts of birch and pine."
TOELLE, GERVASE. Fra Carmelo's Morning Sacrifice.
TOFTE, ROBERT. Alba, *sel.*
As burnish'd gold, such are my sovereign's hears. *Fr.* Laura.
Down from the neck unto that dainty breast. *Fr.* Laura.
In love his kingdom great, two fools there be. *Fr.* Laura.
Laura, *sels.*
Love's Labour Lost. *Fr.* Alba.
Strange is this thing! My horse I cannot make. *Fr.* Laura.
Two winds, one calm, another fierce to see. *Fr.* Laura.
Unto thy favor, which when nature formed. *Fr.* Laura.
What time with brow the loveliest gins to scowl. *Fr.* Laura.
When I did part from thee the other night. *Fr.* Laura.
When she was born she came with smiling eye. *Fr.* Laura.
"TOGO, HASHIMURA." *See* IRWIN, WALLACE.
TOLESON, M. BEAUNURUS. *See* TOLSON, MELVIN BEAUNEARUS.
TOLKIEN, JOHN RONALD RENEL. Goblin Feet.
Roads Go Ever Ever On [*or* Ever On and On].
Sing All Ye Joyful.
There Is an Inn, a Merry Old Inn.
Troll Sat Alone on His Seat of Stone.
TOLLER, ERNST. Book I Held Grew Cold, The.
Corpses in the Wood.
Marching Song.
O Heavy Step of Slow Monotony.
O Master Masons.
O My Swallows!
One Who Struggles, The.
To the Dead of the Revolution.
To the Living.
To the Mothers.
TOLLET, ELIZABETH. On this resemblance—where we find.
TOLSON, MELVIN BEAUNEARUS. Dark Symphony.
John Henry in Harlem.
TOLSTOY, ALEKSEY KONSTANTINOVICH. At dusk the torrid day grew pale with mood elusive.
At times 'mid daily toils and tumults unrelenting.
Believe me not, friend, when in grief's unreason.
By chance, at the ball, in the welter.
Convicts, The.
Do you remember, Mary.
In the leaves the raindrops gently.
It chanced when the dance was pealing.
It was an early day of spring.
John Damascene, *sel.*
Land of mine, where I was bred.
Mistrust me, when, distraught by grief's unreason.
My Little Almond Tree.
O Autumn! Thou hast strewn and heaped our garden bare.
Outside it is blowing and raining.
Soldier of Neither Camp.
Through the slush and the ruts of the highway.
Troparion. *Fr.* John Damascene.
'Twas on an early day of spring.
Well, A.
West is lost in space that rosy pallors fill.
When I Am Plagued.
Where boughs above the pool are swinging.
TOMKIS, THOMAS. Gordian Knot, The, *at. Fr.* Lingua.
Lingua, *sel., at.*
TOMLINSON, CHARLES. Nine Variations in a Chinese Winter Setting.
TOMPKINS, HARRIET HARTRIDGE. Silent Stars Go By, The.
TOMPKINS, JULIET (Juliet Wilbor Tompkins Pottle). When the Minister Comes to Tea.
TOMPSON, BENJAMIN. Alarming Progress of Luxury in New England, The. *Fr.* New England's Crisis.
New England's Crisis, *sels.*
On a Fortification at Boston Begun by Women.
"TOMSON, GRAHAM R." *See* WATSON, ROSAMUND MARRIOTT.
TONESS, LOUISE H. Is This Presumption?
TONNA, CHARLOTTE ELIZABETH. Maiden City, The.
TOOKER, LEWIS FRANK. "He Bringeth Them unto Their Desired Haven."
His Quest.
Homeward Bound.
Last Fight, The.
Old Conservative, The.
Sea-King, The.
Sleep.
TOOMER, JEAN. Beehive.
Cotton Song.
Evening Song.
Face.
Georgia Dusk.
November Cotton Flower.
Reapers.
Song of the Son.
TOPELIUS, ZAKARIAS. Little Maia.
Milky Way, The.
My Mother.
Rose-Marie.
TOPLADY, AUGUSTUS MONTAGUE. Ah! Give Me, Lord, the Single Eye.
Compared with Christ.
Deathless Principle, Arise.
Happiness Found, *sel.*
Lord! It Is Not Life to Live. *Fr.* Happiness Found.
Prayer, Living and Dying, A.
Rejoicing in Hope.
Rock of Ages.
TORIN. Nightingale sat singing out his heart, A.
TORLINO. Therefore I Must Tell the Truth.
TORMEY, MICHAEL. Ancient Race, The.
TORNA. Lament for Corc and Niall of the Nine Hostages, *at.*
TORRENCE, RIDGELY. Adam's Song of the Visible World.
Bird and the Tree, The.
Carpe Diem. *Fr.* The House of a Hundred Lights.
Compensation. *Fr.* The House of a Hundred Lights.
Conclusion of the Whole Matter, The. *Fr.* The House of a Hundred Lights.
Evensong.
Eye-Witness.
House of a Hundred Lights, The, *sels.*
Invitation.
Legend.
Lesser Children, The.
Santa Barbara Beach.
Singers in a Cloud, The.
Son, The.
Three o'Clock—Morning.
Tramp Sings, The. *Fr.* Eye-Witness.
Young Lovers, The. *Fr.* The House of a Hundred Lights.
Youth and Age. *Fr.* The House of a Hundred Lights.
TORRES BODET, JAIME. April.
City.
Core.
Dance.
Love.
Noon.
TORREY, BRADFORD. Not So in Haste, My Heart.
TOULET, PAUL [*or* PIERRE] JEAN. Contrarimes, *sel.*
Simple Things.
TOUMANIAN, HAROUTUNE. Morning.
TOUMANIAN, HOVHANNES. Crane, The.
Earth and Sky.
TOURIAN, BEDROS. Complaints.
Day After, A.
Little Lake, The.
Love One Another.
My Death.
TOURNEUR, CYRIL. Atheist's Tragedy, The, *sels.*
Drowned Soldier, A. *Fr.* The Atheist's Tragedy.
Epitaph on a Soldier. *Fr.* The Atheist's Tragedy.
I Was the Man. *Fr.* The Revenger's Tragedy.
Revenger's Tragedy, The, *sels.*
Soldier's Death, A. *Fr.* The Atheist's Tragedy.
To His Mistress' Skull. *Fr.* The Revenger's Tragedy.
Walking Next Day upon the Fatal Shore. *Fr.* The Atheist's Tragedy.

TOUSSAINT-L'OUVERTURE, ISAAC. Farewell: "Shores of my native land."
TOVEY, DUNCAN. Last Pilot, The.
TOWNE, CHARLES HANSON. Around the Corner.
At Nightfall.
Baboon.
Ballad of the Circus, A.
Best Road of All, The.
Beyond the Stars.
Carouse.
City, The. *Fr.* Manhattan.
City Roofs.
Deathless Tale, The.
Easter.
Easter Canticle, An: "In every trembling bud and bloom."
Easter Prayer, An.
How Will It Seem?
In Summer.
Last Sleep, The.
Light Love.
Love's Ritual.
Manhattan, *sels.*
Memories.
Messed Damozel, The.
Messengers.
Needs.
Nightfall.
Of One Self-Slain.
Pilot and Prophet.
Prayer for the Old Courage, A.
Prayer to the Giver.
Quiet Singer, The.
Renewal.
Roof-Tops.
Roosevelt—Pilot and Prophet!
Silence.
Song: "I saw the day's white rapture."
Song at Easter, A.
Spring in Town. *Fr.* Manhattan.
Thanksgiving.
Theodore Roosevelt—Pilot and Prophet!
Time-Clock, The.
To a Certain Little Boy.
To One Self-slain.
Victors, The.
When We Were Poor in Paris.
TOWNE, FRANK M. Reconciliation.
TOWNLEY, MARY. Rose in October, The.
TOWNSEND, ANNIE LAKE. Sursum Corda.
TOWNSEND [*or* TOWNSHEND], AURELIAN.
Constant Lover, The.
Dialogue betwixt Time and a Pilgrim, A.
Loves Victory.
Rock Constancy.
Song: "Though regions far divided."
Though Regions Far Divided.
'Tis not how witty, nor how free.
To the Countesse of Salisbury.
To the Lady May.
Upon Kind and True Love.
Youth and Beauty.
TOWNSEND, F. H. To the Cuckoo.
TOWNSEND, GEORGE ALFRED. Army Correspondent's Last Ride.
In Rama.
TOWNSEND, LILBURN H. Hand of Labor.
TOWNSEND, MARY ASHLEY ("Xariffa").
At Set of Sun.
Creed.
Dead Singer, The.
Down the Bayou.
Embryo.
Georgia Volunteer, A.
Her Horoscope.
Reserve.
Virtuosa.
TOWNSHEND, AURELIAN. *See* TOWNSEND, AURELIAN.
TOWNSHEND, CHAUNCEY HARE. Thy Joy in Sorrow.
TOYNBEE, LAWRENCE. Castle Howard. November 11th, 1942.
TOYO. I gathered in my rod and line.
TRACY, NEIL. Ballade Morale.
I Doubt a Lovely Thing Is Dead.
Prelude: "Thing long sought, A."
TRAHERNE, THOMAS. Amendment.
Apostasy, The, *sel.*
Approach, The.
Approach, The, *sel.*
Bible, The.
Childhood.
Choice, The.
Christendom.
Christendom, *sel.*
Christian Ethics, *sels.*
Consummation.
Contentment Is a Sleepy Thing.
Desire.
Dreams.
Eden.
Enquiring Soul, The.
For giving me desire.
For Man to Act.
Fullness.
Hosanna.
Infant's Eye, An.
Innocence.
Insatiableness.
Love.
Mankind Is Sick.
Measure. *Fr.* Christian Ethics.
My Spirit.
News.
On Christmas-Day.
On Christmas-Day, *sel.*
On Leaping over the Moon.
On Leaping over the Moon, *sel.*
On News.
Person, The, *sel.*
Poverty.
Preparative, The.
Rapture, The.
Recovery, The.
Right Apprehension.
Salutation, The.
Salutation, The, *sels.*
Shadows in the Water.
Solitude.
Solitude, *sel.*
Thanksgivings for the Beauty of His Providence.
Thanksgiving for the Body.
To the Same Purpos.
Walking.
Wonder.
World, The.
TRAILL, HENRY DUFF. After Dilettante Concetti.
Drawing-Room Ballad, A.
TRAKL, GEORG. Amen. *Fr.* Rosary Songs.
Birth.
Caspar Hauser Song.
Childhood.
De Profundis.
Desolation.
Eastern Front.
Elis.
Evening.
Grodek.
In Hellbrunn.
Lament: "Sleep and death, the darkling eagles."
Limbo.
Nearness of Death. *Fr.* Rosary Songs.
Nocturne: "Beneath the stars a man alone."
On the Mönchsberg.
On the Way.
Peace and Silence.
Rats, The.
Rest and Silence.
Rosary Songs, *sels.*
Sebastian in Dream.
Soul's Springtime, The.
South Wind.
Sun, The.
To One Who Died Young.
To Sister. *Fr.* Rosary Songs.
To the Boy Elis.
Wayfaring.
Whispered to the Afternoon.
Winter Night.
TRAPNELL, EDNA VALENTINE. Fiddle, The.
TRASK, KATRINA (Kate Nichols Trask).
Aidenn.
Army of the Red Cross, The.
At Last.
Love.
New Banner, The.
Sorrow.
TRAUBEL, HORACE LOGO. Chants Communal, *sel.*
Epicedium.
How Are You, Dear World, This Morning?
I Served in a Great Cause.
If All the Voices of Men.
What Can I Do? *Fr.* Chants Communal.
TREBOR, NEVAH. Illusion.
TREE, IRIS (Mrs. Curtis Moffat). To My Father.
You Preach to Me of Laws.
TREE, MAUD HOLT, LADY (Mrs. Beerbohm Tree). There is many a slipton.
TREECE, HENRY. Ballad: "Oh, come my joy, my soldier boy."
Birdwatcher.
Christ Child.
Crimson Cherry Tree, The.
Dyke-Builder, The.
Haunted Garden, The.
Heart's Wild Geese, The.
House, The.
In the Beginning Was the Bird.
In the Third Year of War.
Love Song.
Poem: "Death walks through the mind's dark woods."
Poem: "In the dark caverns of the night."
Poem: "Through the dark aisles of the wood."
Prayer in Time of War.
Second Coming 1942.
Waiting Watchers, The.
Walking at Night.
War Poem.
Y Ddraig Goch.
TRENCH, HERBERT. Charge, A.
Come, Let Us Make Love Deathless.
Come, Let Us Make Love Deathless, *sel.*
I Heard a Soldier.
I Seek Thee in the Heart Alone.
Jean Richepin's Song.
Love. *Fr.* Come, Let Us Make Love Deathless.
Musing on a Great Soldier.
O Dreamy, Gloomy, Friendly Trees!
Old Anchor Chanty.
Paean of Dawn in May.
Requiem of Archangels for the World.
She Comes Not When Noon Is on the Roses.
Shepherds Who Pastures Seek.
Song: "She comes not when noon is on the roses."
Song of the Larks at Dawn.
To Arolilia, *sel.*
Trees, The.
What Bids Me Leave.
Who Art Thou, Starry Ghost?
TRENCH, RICHARD CHENEVIX. After the Battle.
Century of Couplets, *sel.*
Cross, The, *tr.*
Different Minds.
Elegy: "This winter eve how soft! how mild!"
Gibraltar.
God Our Refuge.
Harmosan.
Hour with Thee, An.
If There Had Anywhere Appeared.
In Thy Presence.
Kingdom of God, The.
Life through Death.
Life's a Dream, *sel.*, *tr.*
Lord, Many Times I Am Aweary Quite.
Love Found Me.
Not Thou from Us!
Power of Prayer, The.
Prayer: "Lord, what a change within us one short hour."
Prevailing Prayer.
Recollections of Burgos.
Retirement.
Some Murmur When Their Sky Is Clear.
Sonnet: "All beautiful things bring sadness, nor alone."
Sonnet: "I stood beside a pool, from whence ascended."

Sonnet: "Lord, what a change within us one short hour."
Sonnet: "Open wound which has been healed anew, An."
Sonnet: "Wretched thing it were, to have our heart, A."
Sonnet in a Pass of Bavaria.
This Were to Pray.
To an Infant Sleeping.
TRENT, LUCIA (Mrs. Ralph Cheyney).
All Too Slowly.
Architects of Dream.
Armistice Day [1926].
Blessed Agitator, The.
Bread of Brotherhood.
Dreamers Cry Their Dream, The.
From Beyond.
Give Me No Lover Young with Love.
It Is Not Too Late.
Lady in a Limousine.
Mary's Son.
Master Surgeon.
Prayer: "Oh, kneel to that God force of love."
Query.
Salt Tides.
Society Woman.
Song for Tomorrow.
There is so much of loneliness.
These Are My People.
Thought on a News Item.
To Young Dreamers.
TRENT, LUCIA, *and* RALPH CHEYNEY.
Ten Years After, *sel.*
Toward a True Peace. *Fr.* Ten Years After.
True Peace, A. *Fr.* Ten Years After.
TREVELYAN, HERBERT. Song for a May Morning.
TREVELYAN, ROBERT CALVERLEY. Evening of the Feast-Day, The, *tr.*
For translations from Greek and Latin, see GrR; LiTW; OxBG.
TRIEM, EVE. Gardens Are All My Heart.
TRIMM, RIETTA. Autumn.
Touch Not a Leaf.
TRIMPI, W. WESLEY. Affliction.
Asteria.
Contingency.
Dwarf, The.
Elegy: "Forgotten playground, grave."
Glass Swan, The.
Growth of Perseus, The.
Leda.
Lines for a Wedding Gift.
Oedipus to the Oracle.
On a Bas-Relief.
Phlegm.
Pygmalion.
Sea Wall, The.
Search for Perfection.
Silent Piano.
Sonnet: "Mole, which sleeps beneath the woven peat, The."
To Giotto.
TRINE, GRACE HYDE. Coming and Going.
Echo, An.
TROTT, HARLAN. Out from Gloucester.
TROTT, NORMAN L. No Time for God.
TROTT, PERIENT. Negro Spiritual.
TROTTER, BERNARD FREEMAN. Altars.
"Ici Repose."
Poplars, The.
Road to Tartary, The.
Smoke, *sels.*
Songs We Need, The.
TROTTER, MARY JOSEPHINE. *See* BENSON, MARY JOSEPHINE.
"TROUBADOUR." Law of Averages, The.
Reversible Metaphor, The.
TROUBETZKOY, AMÉLIE RIVES, PRINCESS. *See* RIVES, AMÉLIE.
TROUBETZKOY, ULRICH. Christmas Lullaby.
Out of the Wilderness
TROULUFFE [*or* TRUELOVE], JOHN, *and* RICHARD SMERT [*or* SMART]. Jesu, Fili Dei, *at.*
TROWBRIDGE, JOHN TOWNSEND. At Sea.
Boy I Love, The.
Columbus at the Convent.
Cup, The.
Darius Green and His Flying-Machine.
Dorothy in the Garret.
Evening on [*or* at] the Farm.
Farm-Yard Song.
Lincoln.
Midsummer.
Midwinter.
Pewee [*or* Peewee], The.
Trouting.
Vagabonds, The.
Widow Brown's Christmas.
TROY, GRACE E. Pastor's Prayer, A.
Pastor's Prayer for His Congregation, A.
TRUEBA Y LA QUINTANA, ANTONIO DE. Nightfall.
TRUELOVE, JOHN, *and* RICHARD SMERT. *See* TROULUFFE, JOHN, *and* RICHARD SMERT.
TRUMBULL, ANNIE ELIOT. To O. S. C.
TRUMBULL, JOHN. Aging Coquette, The. *Fr.* The Progress of Dulness.
Amorous Temper, An. *Fr.* The Progress of Dulness.
Country Clown, The.
Elegy on the Times.
Essay on the Fine Arts, *sel.*
Future of American Literature, The. *Fr.* Essay on the Fine Arts.
Harriet Simper Has Her Day. *Fr.* The Progress of Dulness.
Liberty Pole, The. *Fr.* M'Fingal.
M'Fingal, *sels.*
Progress of Dulness, The, *sels.*
Tom Brainless as Student and Preacher. *Fr.* The Progress of Dulness.
Tom Brainless at College. *Fr.* The Progress of Dulness.
Tom Brainless Seeks a Wife. *Fr.* The Progress of Dulness.
Town Meeting, The. *Fr.* M'Fingal.
TRUMBULL, ROSE. Mary.
TRYPANIS, CONSTANTINE. Theonichos and Mnesarete.
TRYPHIODORUS. Taking of Troy, The, *sel.*
TSANG CHIH. Song: "I was brought up under the Stone Castle."
TS'AO CHIH. Cock-Fight, The.
Homeless.
Ruins of Lo-yang, The.
Vision, A.
TS'AO HO. Impatience.
TS'AO SUNG. Protest in the Sixth Year of Ch'ien Fu, A (A.D. 879).
TSCHAIKOVSKY, PETER ILICH. *See* TCHAIKOVSKY, PETER ILICH.
TSE NAN. Happy Farmer, The.
TS'EN TS'AN. Farewell: "North wind sweeps over the land, The."
Homesick.
Horsemen on the Great Szechuan Road.
Ode to a Monk on the Tai-pei Mountains.
On Meeting a Messenger to the Capital.
Song of White Snow, A.
Spring Dreams.
Two Songs for General Chao.
TSO SSU. Day Dreams.
Scholar in the Narrow Street, The.
TSOU HAO. Pool, The.
TSUCHII, BANSUI. Fair Japan.
Moon on the Ruined Castle, The.
TS'UEI HAO. Song of Ch'ang-kan, A.
TS'UI SHU. Parting in the Rain.
TS'UI TSUNG-CHI. Invitation to Li Po, An.
TS'UI YING YING. Waiting.
TSUNG WAN SHENG. Mother, The.
TSUN TSAO. Shadows on the Wall.
TSURAYUKI (Ki no Tsurayuki). Avenue of Trees, The.
Elegy, An: "So frail our life, perchance to-morrow's sun."
Flowers of Snow.
Heron cries in sorrow, The.
Most fragile of all is the cherry-bloom.
No, the human heart/ Is unknowable.
Out in the marsh reeds.
Tanka: Cry of the Crane, The.
Time I went to see my sister, The.
Wake, The.
TSURU. Willows in the Snow.
TUBBS, ARTHUR LEWIS. Moment in the Morning, A.
TU CHIU NIANG. Wise Age to Youth.
TUCK, CLYDE EDWIN. Good Shepherd, The.
TUCK, EDWARD. Age, *at.*
TUCKER, BEVERLEY RANDOLPH. Capt. Sally Tompkins, C.S.A.
Hallucinations?
TUCKER, PAUL. Heavenly Friend, A.
TUCKER, ST. GEORGE. Days of My Youth.
Resignation.
Southern Cross, The.
TUCKERMAN, FREDERICK GODDARD. And So the Day Drops By.
Roll On, Sad World!
Sometimes, When Winding Slow.
Tall Stately Plants with Spikes and Forks of Gold.
Two Sonnets.
Under the Mountain.
Upper Chamber in a Darkened House, An.
Yet Vain, Perhaps, the Fruits.
TUCKERMAN, HENRY THEODORE. All Hearts Are Not Disloyal.
Courage and Patience.
Desolation.
Newport Beach.
Washington's Statue.
TU FU. Advent of Spring.
After Rain.
Alone in Her Beauty.
Another Spring.
Arrival of a Guest, The.
At the Frontier.
Autumn Countryside.
Banquet at the Tso Family Manor.
Beautiful Woman, The.
Bride's Song, The.
Brimming Water.
By the Winding River ("Every day on the way home").
By the Winding River ("Everywhere petals are flying").
Chariots Go Forth to War, The.
Chengtu.
Clear after Rain.
Clear Evening after Rain.
Cocks Are Crowing.
Country Cottage.
Cricket, The.
Dawn over the Mountains.
Day Comes.
Emperor, The.
Empty Purse, The.
Excursion, The.
Exile.
Far Up the River.
Farewell Once More: To My Friend Yen at Feng Chi Station.
Farewell to Han So.
Farewell, A, to Ho Yung on His Leaving Min Valley for the Capital.
Fireflies, The.
Full Moon.
Homecoming—Late at Night.
I Pass the Night at General Headquarters.
In Absence.
In My Late Age.
Jade Flower Palace.
Journey to the North.
Lament for a Quince Tree Uprooted by the Storm.
Little Rain, The.
Loneliness.
Love of a King, The.
Meeting, A.
Mongolian Horse, The.
Moon Festival.
My Brother.
New Moon.
Night in the House by the River.
Night in the Villa by the River.
Night Thoughts while Travelling.
Night Vigil in the Left Court of the Palace, A.
On a Historic Landmark.
On a Moonlight Night.

TU FU (*continued*)
On a Pine Tree Shown to Me by the Taoist Scholar Li.
On Climbing the Heights on the Ninth Day of the Ninth Moon.
On Hearing that Our Arms Have Captured Honan and Hupeh.
On Leaving the Tomb of Premier Fang.
On Meeting Li Kuei-nien down the River.
Overlooking the Desert.
Overnight in the Apartment by the River.
Painting of an Eagle, The.
Parrot, The.
Parting from My Old Wife.
Prelude: "This fugitive between the earth and sky."
Quatrain: "Before you praise spring's advent, note."
Rain.
Rain at Night, The.
Recruiting Officer, The.
Restless Night in Camp, A.
Return, The.
Riding in a Boat on the Day before the Spring Festival.
Roof Whirled Away by Winds, The.
Seeing Li Po in a Dream.
Snow Storm.
Soldier-Statesman Returns, The.
Song of Autumn.
Song of Dagger-Dancing, A, *sel.*
Song of the Vermeil Phoenix.
South Wind.
Spring.
Stars and Moon on the River.
Staying at the Official Residence on a Spring Night.
Summer Night.
Sunset.
Temple, The.
Thinking of Li Po.
Thinking of My Brothers [on a Moonlit Night].
To Cheng on His Deposal.
To Li Po.
To Li Po on a Spring Day.
To My Retired Friend Wei.
To My Youngest Son.
To Pi Ssu Yao.
To Wei Pa, a Retired Scholar.
Travelling Northward.
Unexpected Visit, An.
View of T'ai-shan, A.
Village and the River, The.
Visiting Tsan, Abbot of Ta-yun.
Visitors.
Waiting for Audience on a Spring Night.
War.
White Horse, The.
Willow, The.
Winter Dawn.
With Her Beauty.
Written on the Wall at Chang's Hermitage.
TU HSÜN HAO. Man and the Sea.
Taoist Monk, The.
Taxes.
TULKOURANTZI, HOVHANNES. Concerning Death.
TULL, JEWELL BOTHWELL. Plea for a Cat.
Sport for Gods.
TULLAR, GRANT COLFAX. As Thy Days.
TU MU. Bestowed in Farewell.
Garden of the Gold Valley, The.
Gold Rivers and Jade Gates.
Happy Regret.
Morning at Chien-wei River.
Nightingales, The.
Red Bridge, The.
Separation.
Silk Curtain, The.
To Hen Chu, Magistrate of Yangchow.
TUNSTALL, VIRGINIA LYNE (Mrs. Robert Baylor Tunstall). "Brother."
Evening on the Harbor.
Macroom on Market Day.
Old April. *Fr.* Sonnets of an Old Town.
Point of View.
Porcelaine de Saxe.
Sonnets of an Old Town.
Spinster Song.
Spring Dusk in Williamsburg. *Fr.* Sonnets of an Old Town.
They Sleep So Quietly. *Fr.* Sonnets of an Old Town.
TUPPER, HELEN ISABELLA. Give Thanks.
Thanks for Everything.
TUPPER, KATHRYN MUNRO. *See* MUNRO, KATHRYN.
TUPPER, MARTIN FARQUHAR. Of Cruelty to Animals. *Fr.* Proverbial Philosophy.
Proverbial Philosophy, *sel.*
Wood Finches, *tr.*
TURBERVILLE [*or* TURBERVILE], GEORGE. Eglogs of the Poet B. Mantuan Carmelitan, The, *sel.*, *tr.*
George Turbervile in Praise of the Translator of This Book.
He Declares That Albeit He Were Imprisoned in Russia, Yet His Mind Was at Liberty and Did Daily Repair to His Friend.
I Wot Full Well that Beauty Cannot Last.
Lover Abused Renounceth Love, The, *sel.*
Lover Exhorteth His Lady to Take Time While Time Is, The.
Lover Extolleth the Singular Beauty of His Lady, The.
Lover to His Lady, The.
Lover to the Thames of London to Favour His Lady Passing Thereon, The.
Lover, The, Whose Mistresse Feared a Mouse, Declareth That He Would Become a Cat, if He Might Have His Desire.
My Girl, Thou Gazest Much, *tr.*
Of Drunkenness.
Others as Fair, but Not So Faithful.
Pine to the Mariner, The.
Second Egloge Entituled Fortunatus, The, *tr.* *Fr.* The Eglogs of the Poet B. Mantuan Carmelitan.
That Death Is Not So Much to Be Feared as Daily Diseases Are.
That He Findeth Others as Fair, but Not So Faithful as His Friend.
To a Fair Gentlewoman, False to Her Friend.
To His Friend [Promising That Though Her Beauty Fade, Yet His Love Shall Last].
To His Friend Riding to Londonward.
To His Love.
To His Ring, Given to His Lady.
Unable by Long and Hard Travel to Banish Love, Returns Her Friend.
Verse in Praise of Lord Henry Howard, Earl of Surrey.
TURBYFILL, MARK. Apollo Alone Approves.
Benediction.
Prayer for Sophistication.
Shapes.
Song for Souls under Fire, A.
Strangers.
Things Not Seen.
TURGENEV, IVAN SERGEYEVICH. Ballad: "He, before the captain, still and silent stood."
On the Road.
TURNBULL, ELEANOR L. Canticle of the Creatures, The, *tr.*
For translations from Spanish, see AnSpL-2; CoSP; LiTW; OnPM; TeCS.
TURNBULL, MONICA PEVERIL. Lullaby, A: "Sleep soft, baby mine!"
TURNER, CHARLES TENNYSON. Brilliant Day, A.
Buoy-Bell, The.
Charming of the East Wind, The.
Forest Glade, The.
Her First-born.
Home Field, The; Evening.
Lachrymatory, The.
Lattice at Sunrise, The.
Letty's Globe.
Lion's Skeleton, The.
Mary Queen of Scots.
Ocean, The.
Orion.
Rookery, The.
Steam Threshing-Machine, The.
Summer Twilight, A.
To the Gossamer-Light.
Vacant Cage, The.
Why Should We Weep for Those Who Die.
TURNER, ELIZA SPROAT. Little Goose, A.
TURNER, ELIZABETH. Bird-Catcher, The.
Bird's Nest, The.
Canary, The.
Good Girl, The. *Fr.* Mrs. Turner's Object-Lessons.
How to Write a Letter.
Letter, The. *Fr.* Mrs. Turner's Object-Lessons.
Lost Pudding, The.
Miss Sophia.
Mrs. Turner's Object-Lessons, *sels.*
New Book, The.
Politeness.
Rebecca's After-Thought.
Result of Cruelty, The.
Rudeness.
TURNER, ETHEL. Boat on the Sea, A.
Christ-Child Day in Australia, A.
TURNER, EVA MOAD. Testimony.
TURNER, LEO C. Boy's Trust, A.
TURNER, MARTHA PROVINE LEACH. Good Friday.
TURNER, MATILDA HUTCHINSON. Joy.
With the Winds.
TURNER, NANCY BYRD. Adventure.
Alley Cat, An.
Armistice Day, 1918–1928.
Autumn!
Bagpipe Man, The.
Best Time of All, The.
Black and Gold.
Books.
Boy, Bare Your Head.
Buccaneer, The.
Careless Fairy, The.
Chaireplane Chant.
Christmas.
Christmas Star, The.
Click o' the Latch.
Concerning Brownie.
Contrary Mary.
Courage Has a Crimson Coat.
Dark-eyed Lad Columbus.
Death Is a Door.
Down a Sunny Easter Meadow.
Easter Joy.
Easter Prayer.
Extraordinary Dog, The.
Fellowship of Prayer, The.
First Christmas Night of All.
First Thanksgiving, The.
First Thanksgiving of All.
Flame Song.
God with Us.
Going Up to London.
Good-Night.
I Wish.
Immigrants.
League of Nations.
Legacy.
Let Us Have Peace.
Lincoln.
Lines for a Girl's Study.
Little Girl That Mother Used to Be.
Little Road, The.
London Rain.
Mongrel Pup, A.
More than Flowers We Have Brought.
Notation on Immortality.
Old Man Long Ago.
Old Quin Queeribus.
Ordinary Dog, The.
Planting a Tree.
Poem for Little Dogs, A.
Pop Corn Song, A.
Prayer, A: "Lord, give us more of faith."
Prayer at Christmas Time, A.
Prayer at New Year's.
Prayer at Thanksgiving Time.
Prayer on Christmas Eve.
Prayer on Fourth of July.
Prince Peter.
Resolute Cat, The.
Ships.

Sing a Song of Books.
Sister Mary Veronica.
Snowlight.
Spring Wind.
Sure Sign, A.
Teacher's Prayer, The.
To a Staring Baby in a Perambulator.
Twenty Foolish Fairies.
Washington.
Weather.
Weather Factory, The.
When Abraham Went Out of Ur.
When Young Melissa Sweeps.
Whenever I Say "America."
Wings and Wheels.
With Regard to Dogs.
Word about Woodpiles, A.
Words.
TURNER, TOM. Communion.
TURNER, WALTER JAMES. Dancer, The.
Death and Despair.
Death's Men.
Death's Men, *sel.*
Dragon Flies.
Ecstasy.
Ecstasy, *sel.*
Epithalamium, *sel.*
Forest-Bird, The.
Formal Lyric.
Giraffe and Tree.
Hero, The.
Hunter, The.
Hymn to Her Unknown.
In the Caves of Auvergne.
In Time like Glass.
India.
Land, The.
Life and Death.
Lion, The.
Love-Song, A.
Men Fade like Rocks.
Music of a Tree, The.
Navigators, The.
Poetry and Science.
Princess, The.
Reflection.
Robber, The.
Romance.
Seven Days of the Sun, The, *sel.*
Silence.
Song: "Can the lover share his soul." *Fr.* Epithalamium.
Song: "Fortunate are the feet of the swallow."
Song: "Lovely hill-torrents are."
Sun, The.
Talking with Soldiers.
Tragic Love.
Under a grey October sky. *Fr.* Death's Men.
Word Made Flesh, The.
TURNER, WILLIAM. Turners Dish of Lentten Stuffe; or, A Galymaufery.
TUSIANI, JOSEPH. Anticipation.
Rest O Sun I Cannot.
TUSSER, THOMAS. As True as Thy Faith, This Riddle Thus Saith.
Author's Life, The.
Christmas.
Christmas Husbandly Fare.
Description of an Envious and Naughty Neighbor, The.
Description of Life and Riches, A.
Description of the Properties of Winds All [*or* at All] the Times of the Year, A.
Description of Time and the Year, A.
Digression from Husbandry to a Point or Two of Huswifery, A.
Digression to Hospitality, A.
Hundreth good points of good husbandry, A.
July.
Ladder to Thrift, The.
March.
October's Husbandry.
Posies for Thine Own Bedchamber.
Praise of Husbandry, The.
Preface to the Book of Housewifery, The.
Preface to the Buyer of This Book, A.
Saint Bernard's Verses, *tr.*
September.
Sonnet upon the Author's First Seven Years Service, A.
Upon the Author's First Seven Years' Service.
TUTTLE, EDITH M. Three Thousand Years After.
TUTTLE, STELLA WESTON. Quickening, The.
TUTWILER, JULIA S. Alabama.
TUWIM, JULIAN [*or* JULJAN]. Epos.
Prayer, A: "I pray Thee O Lord."
Pursuit.
Request for a Song.
There Is No Country.
TVARDOVSKY, ALEKSANDR TRIFONOVICH. Land of Muravia, The, *sel.*
Starling, The.
"TWAIN, MARK" (Samuel Langhorne Clemens). Adventures of Huckleberry Finn, The, *sel.*
Adventures of Tom Sawyer, The, *sel.*
Epitaph Placed on His Daughter's Tomb, *ad.*
Missouri Maiden's Farewell to Alabama, A. *Fr.* The Adventures of Tom Sawyer.
Ode to Stephen Dowling Bots, Dec'd. *Fr.* The Adventures of Huckleberry Finn.
Requiem, *ad.*
Right.
TWEEDSMUIR, JOHN BUCHAN, 1ST BARON. *See* BUCHAN, JOHN.
TWEEDY, HENRY HALLAM. Christmas at Babbitt's.
Eternal God, Whose Power Upholds.
Prayer: "Eternal God, whose power upholds."
TWELLS, HENRY. At Even, when the Sun Was Set.
TWIG, JOHN. Ballade of the Nurserie, A.
TWYNHAM, LEONARD. Old Dog.
TYCHBORN, CHIDIOCK. *See* TICHBORNE, CHIDIOCK.
TYLEE, EDWARD SYDNEY. Outward Bound.
TYLER, INEZ M. Call to Pentecost, A.
TYLER, PARKER. To a Photograph.
TYLER, ROYALL. Independence Day.
Sweet child of woe! who pour'st thy love-lorn lays.
TYLOR, EDWARD BURNETT, *and* ANDREW LANG. *See* LANG, ANDREW, *and* EDWARD BURNETT TYLOR.
TYMNES. Maltese Dog, A.
TYNAN, ANNIE E. Sleep Fairy.
TYNAN, KATHARINE (Katharine Tynan Hinkson). All Souls.
Ass Speaks, The.
August Weather.
Aux Carmélites.
Beloved, The.
Bethlehem.
Call, The.
Chanticleer.
Children of Lir, The.
Choice, The.
Christmas Eve in Ireland.
Convent Garden, The.
Cuckoo.
Cuckoo Song.
Daffodil.
De Profundis.
Dead Coach, The.
Desire, The.
Doves, The.
Drought.
Easter.
Epitaph, The: "Write on my grave when I am dead."
Farewell: "Not soon shall I forget."
Flying Wheel, The.
Footpath Way, The.
Girl's Song, A.
I was born under a kind star.
In Time of Need.
Island Fisherman, An.
Lambs.
Larks.
Last Voyage, The.
Leaves.
Little Ghost, The.
Little House, The.
Little Red Lark, The.
Lux in Tenebris.
Maker, The.
Making of Birds, The.
Man of the House, The.
Mater Dei.
Memory, A.
Menace.
Michael the Archangel.
Modereen Rue.
Nightingale, The.
Oak Said to the Eagle, The, *tr.*
Of an Orchard.
Old Love, The.
Old Soldier, The.
Old Song Re-sung, An.
Passiontide Communion.
Pink Almond.
Planting Bulbs.
Prayer, A: "Now wilt me take for Jesus' sake."
Quiet Nights, The.
Sad Mother, The.
St. Francis and the Wolf.
Saint Francis to the Birds.
She Asks for New Earth.
Sheep and Lambs.
Singing Stars.
Slow Spring.
Song for the Season, A.
Summer-sweet.
Ten Lepers, The.
Turn o' the Year.
Waiting.
Wild Geese.
Winter Evening.
Witch, The.
Would God I Were the Tender Apple Blossom.
TYPALDOS, JULIUS. Execution of the Klepht, The.
TYRRELL, HENRY. Lincoln.
Lincoln's Way.
Masterful Man, The.
TYRRELL, ROBERT YELVERTON. Johnny, I Hardly Knew Ye: In Swinburnese, *parody.*
TYRTAEUS. "Dulce et Decorum."
From never-vanquished Hercules ye boast.
How Can Man Die Better.
Man I would not name, I would not prize, A.
Marching Song.
Pro Patria.
Refugee, The.
Young Hero, The.
TYRWHITT, RICHARD ST. JOHN. Glory of Motion, The.
TYTLER, JAMES. Bonnie Bruckit Lassie, The.
I Hae Laid a Herring in Saut.
TYUTCHEV, FEODOR IVANOVICH. All day she lay in deep oblivious dream.
As Ocean Holds the Globe.
As Ocean's Stream.
Autumn Evening.
By the open highway I betake me.
Dear one, I love thine eyes, amazed.
I Knew Her.
July, 1850.
July 14, at Night.
Last Love.
'Mid letters heaped upon the floor.
Nay, in a poet put no trust.
Night was dark with indignation, The.
Night Wind.
Nightfall.
No sickness of the flesh is ours today.
Not with the Mind.
O Love, how deadly beats thy measure.
Oh, Wizard Soul.
On the horizon rises holy Night.
Presdestination.
Service of the Lutherans, The.
She lay unconscious there through all the day.
She sat upon the ground; there lay.
Silentium.
Sorry Hamlets.
Spring.
Spring Thunder.
Spring Waters.
Tears.
These poor hamlets, humbly faring.

TYUTCHEV, FEODOR IVANOVICH (*cont.*)
This day, just fifteen years ago, was dated.
Twilight.
Vouchsafe, O Lord, Thy consolation.
What mind shall fathom Russia? None.
Why Do You Howl So Madly, Wind of Night?
Why, O willow, to the river.
TZARA, TRISTAN. Forbidden Fire, The.
TZU YEH. Constancy.
Drums of Night, The.
Fragrant Blossoms, The.
Frost, The.
Regrets.
Song, A: "Is it only to-day."
Song of Cherry-Time, A.
Song of Songs.
Through Your Window.
To Him I Love.
Weaving.
Youth.
TZVETAYEVA, MARINA IVANOVNA. No Longer Now.

U

UBADA. Drinking Song.
UBERTI, FAZIO DEGLI. *See* FAZIO DEGLI UBERTI.
UDA, EMPEROR. Like a wave crest/ Escaped and frozen.
UDALL [*or* UDAL], NICHOLAS. I Mun Be Married a Sunday. *Fr.* Ralph Roister Doister.
Minion Wife, A. *Fr.* Ralph Roister Doister.
Ralph Roister Doister, *sels.*
UFFORD, EDWARD SMITH. Throw Out the Lifeline.
UGGA BYAN. Her Absent Lord, *sel.*
UHLAND, LUDWIG (Johann Ludwig Uhland). Castle by the Sea, The.
Durand of Blonden.
Good Comrade, The.
Hostess' Daughter, The.
Ichabod! Thy Glory Has Departed.
In a Lovely Garden Walking.
King on the Tower, The.
Landlady's Daughter, The.
Leaf, A.
Lost Church, The.
Luck of Edenhall, The.
Passage, The.
Spirits Everywhere.
UKON, LADY. It does not matter/ That I am forgotten.
ULRICH VON LICHTENSTEIN [*or* LIECHTENSTEIN]. Love, Whose Month Was Ever May.
UMAKI. At an Old Battlefield.
UNAMUNO, MIGUEL DE. Beauty.
Brazier Coals, The.
Castile.
Christ of Velazquez, The, *sels.*
Domestic Scenes.
On Gredos.
Salamanca.
Sleep, My Soul, Sleep.
Sow Your Self!
When the Shades of Night Have Come.
UNDERHILL, EVELYN (Mrs. Stuart Moore). Corpus Christi.
English Easter, 7 A.M.
Friday Night.
Immanence.
Introversion.
Lady Poverty, The.
Supersensual.
Theophany.
UNDERWOOD, EDNA WORTHLEY. To an Attic Marble.
For translations from French (of Haitian poets), see PoNe.
UNDERWOOD, EDNA WORTHLEY, *and* CHI HWANG CHU. *See* CHI HWANG CHU *and* EDNA WORTHLEY UNDERWOOD.
UNDERWOOD, ELLEN H. I Shall Not Pass again This Way.
UNDERWOOD, JOHN CURTIS. Central.
Central, *sel.*
Down Fifth Avenue.
Strong, The.
Wave, The.
Weak, The.
UNDERWOOD, PIERSON. Talk Is a Candle.
UNDERWOOD, WILBUR. Cattle of His Hand, The.
Cor Cordium.
To the Brave Soul.
White Sisters of Culion, The.
UNGARETTI, GIUSEPPE. Island, The.
San Martino del Carso.
Soldiers, The.
UNTERMEYER, JEAN STARR. Altar, The.
Autumn.
Birthday.
Bitter Bread and Weak Wine.
Clay Hills.
Country of No Lack.
Dew on a Dusty Heart.
End of Summer.
False Enchantment.
From the Day-Book of a Forgotten Prince.
Glimpse in Autumn.
Gothic.
High Tide.
Lake Song.
Last Plea.
Little Dirge.
Lullaby for a Man-Child.
Man, A ("Often, when I would sit").
Mater in Extremis.
Nature Cure.
Old Nurse Winter.
One Kind of Humility.
Passionate Sword, The.
Possession.
Rain.
Sinfonia Domestica.
Sung on a Sunny Morning.
Thaw.
Undedicated.
White Armour.
UNTERMEYER, LOUIS. Against Time.
Anno 1829, *tr.*
Any Sunset.
Apocryphal Soliloquies.
Arctic Agrarian.
Arise! Arise!
At the Bottom of the Well.
Audivere, Lyce, *tr.*
Birds and Francis, The.
Boy and Tadpoles.
Boy and the Wolf, The, *ad.*
Briar-Rose, *tr.*
Brief, den du geschrieben, Der, *tr.*
Burning Bush.
Caliban in the Coal Mines.
Catalogue.
Cell-Mates.
Coal Fire.
Coffin, The, *tr.*
Come, O Friend, to Greet the Bride, *tr.*
Dark Chamber, The.
Daybreak.
Day-Dreamer, *ad.*
Dick Said.
Disenchanted.
Disenchantment.
Dog at Night.
Early Mornings, *tr.*
Edgar A. Guest Considers "The Old Woman Who Lived in a Shoe" and the Good Old Verities at the Same Time.
Einstein among the Coffee-Cups.
Embarrassed Amorist, The.
Epilog, *tr.* *Fr.* The North Sea.
Fairies.
Fantasy.
Feuerzauber.
First Words before Spring.
Folk-Song: "Back she came through the trembling dusk."
Food and Drink.
Food and Drink, *sel.*
Frustrate.
Fürchte Nichts, geliebte Seele, *tr.*
German Slumber Song, *ad.*
Glad Day.
Go to Sleep.
God's Youth.
Goliath and David.
Good Advice, *ad.*
Good Fortune, *tr.*
Greedy Fox and the Elusive Grapes, The, *ad.*
Hands.
Heart, The, *ad.*
How Much of Godhood.
Hymn of the Soviet Union, *tr.*
Ich weiss nicht, was soll es bedeuten, *tr.*
In the Subway.
Infidelity.
Irony.
Jerusalem Delivered.
Jewish Lullaby.
Just Home.
King David, *tr.*
Koheleth.
Landscapes.
Last Words before Winter.
Laughers, The.
Lesson from a Sun-Dial, *ad.*
Let the Pulse Speak.
Leviathan.
Little Sandman's Song, *tr.*
Lonely Pine Is Standing, A, *tr.*
Long Feud.
Loreley, The, *tr.*
Love.
Maiden Lies in Her Chamber, A, *tr.*
Man, A ("I listened to them talking").
Mandy's Lay.
Matter.
Meeting, A, *tr.*
Mockery.
Morning Bird.
Mother Goose Up-to-Date.
Motto, *ad.*
Munitions Plant.
My Songs Are Poisoned, *tr.*
Oh Lovely Fishermaiden, *tr.*
Obituary.
Old German Mottos, *ad.*
On the Birth of a Child.
On the Eve of New Wars.
On the Palisades.
Only of Thee and Me.
Owen Seaman.
Pilgrimage, The.
Plaza Square.
Portrait of a Child.
Portrait of a Machine.
Portrait of an Old Cathedral.
Prayer: "God, though this life is but a wraith."
Prayer for a New House.
Prayer for Courage.
Prayer for This House.
Proverbs, *tr.*
Questioning Lydia ("Lydia, dic, per omnis"), *tr.*
Questions at Night.
Religion, *tr.*
Return to Birds.
Reveille.
Revenge, *tr.*
Road Song.
Robert Frost.
Roman Lullaby, *ad.*
Round: "Worlds, you must tell me."
Sandman, The, *tr.*
Scarcely Spring.
Shoes.
Short Sermon, *ad.*
Side Street, A.
Spanish Lullaby, *ad.*
Spratt vs. Spratt.
Spring.
Spring Song of a Super-Blake.
Song Tournement: New Style.
Stars Look at Love, The, *tr.*
Steel Mill.
Storm, The, *tr.*
Summons, *sel.*
Supplication.
Swimmers.
Ten Brothers, *ad.*
Ten Years Old.
Tendency, The, *tr.*
Three Things, *ad.*
To a Dead Cricket, *ad.*

To a Pomeranian Puppy Valued at 2500 Dollars.
Transfigured Swan.
Twelve-Elf, The, *ad.*
Twilight, *tr.*
Unreasoning Heart.
Victory in the Cabarets.
Voices.
W. H. Davies Simplifies the Simplicities He Loves.
Warning, A, *tr.*
Waters of Babylon.
Weavers, The, *tr.*
What Every Gardener Knows, *ad.*
When Two Are Parted, *tr.*
Wise Woman, The.
With Energy Renewed. *Fr.* Summons.
Yes and No.
Yet Nothing Less.
Young Mystic, The.
UNTERMEYER, LOUIS, *and others.* Important People.
UNTERMEYER, RICHARD, *and* LOUIS UNTERMEYER. Concerning a Storm.
Storm, The.
UPDIKE, JOHN. I Like to Sing Also.
Mirror.
Ode, An: "I'm going to write a novel, hey."
Party Knee.
Quilt.
Youth's Progress.
UPHAM, THOMAS COGSWELL. Song of the Pilgrims.
UPHOFF, L. S. Far Away from Flanders Field.
"UPPER, JOSEPH" (Joseph Upper Harris). Artist.
October Prelude.
UPSON, ARTHUR. After a Dolmetsch Concert.
After All.
Agamede's Song. *Fr.* The City.
City, The, *sels.*
Euchenor Chorus. *Fr.* The City.
Ex Libris.
Failures.
Gospel of the Fields.
Incurables, The.
Old Gardens.
Say, Little Maiden.
Since We Said Good-bye.
Song: "Flame at the core of the world."
Strange.
Vers la Vie.
UPSON, ARTHUR, *and* TRUMAN E. RICKARD. *See* RICKARD, TRUMAN E., *and* ARTHUR UPSON.
UPSON, ELIZABETH F. Washday.
UPTON, JAMES. Lass of Richmond Hill, The.
UPTON, MINNIE LEONA. Street Car Miracle, A.
Tabitha Soliloquizes.
Traveling Light.
UPWARD, ALLEN. Pear Tree, The, *tr.* *Fr.* Shi King.
Scented Leaves from a Chinese Jar.
URBINA, LUIS G. Ancient Tear, The.
Centaur's Bath, The.
Dayspring.
Our Lives Are Rivers.
Silent Day, The.
URMY, CLARENCE THOMAS. Arrow, The.
As I Came Down Mount Tamalpais.
At the Edge of the Day.
Blondel.
I Lay My Lute beside Thy Door.
Old Year, The.
Woodland Revel, A.
URQUHART, GERTRUDE BOUGHTON. Coming of Mary Louise, The.
USCHOLD, MAUD E. Casual Gold.
March Wind.
Moonlight.
November Rain.
USHAKOV, NIKOLAI. Craftsmanship.
Spring Poem.
Wine.
USHER, JOHN. Pipe of Tobacco, The, *at.*
USHER, LEILA. I Am the Cat.
USSERY, BERNICE. Table Blessing.
UTKIN, IOSIF. Guitar.
Nurse, The.
UTSUNOMIYA. Prayer: "Oh, make my heart so still, so still."
UTTER, ROBERT PALFRY. Swan Boat, A.

V

"V. B.' *See* THOMSON, JAMES (1834–1882).
VAIL, CLARA WARREN. Bed during Exams.
VALAORITIS, ARISTOTELIS. Athanase Diakos, *sel.*
Creeping Vine, The.
Kera Phrosini, *sel.*
Photinos the Plowman, *sel.*
VALAORITIS, NANOS, *and* BERNARD SPENCER. *See* SPENCER, BERNARD, *and* NANOS VALAORITIS.
VALDÉS, GABRIEL DE LA CONCEPCIÓN. *See* "PLÁCIDO."
VALDIVIELSO, JOSÉ DE. Seguidilla.
VALENCIA, CONSUELO. After Christmas.
VALENCIA, GUILLERMO. Sursum.
VALENTINE, EDWARD ABRAM UFFINGTON. Helen.
Spirit of the Wheat, The.
VALÉRY, PAUL. Asides.
Bee, The.
Buried Lady, The.
Caesar.
Cemetery by the Sea, The.
Dawn.
Footsteps, The.
Friendly Wood, The.
Girdle, The.
Graveyard by the Sea, The.
Helen.
Helen, the Sad Queen.
Hélène.
Insinuation.
Interior.
Jeune Parque, La, *sel.*
Lost Wine, The.
Marine Cemetery, The.
Narcissus.
Palm.
Poesy.
Pomegranates.
Secret Ode.
Seeming Dead, The.
Serpent, The, *sel.*
Song of the Columns.
Steps, The.
Sylph, The.
VALLE, ADRIANO DEL. Cradle Song of the Elephants.
VALLE, ISABEL. Very Minor Poet Speaks, A.
VALLE, RAFAEL HELIODORO. Thirsting Amphora.
VALLEJO, CÉSAR. Anger.
Black Messengers, The.
Distant Footsteps.
Dregs.
Grown-ups, The.
Hymn to the Volunteers of the Republic, *sel.*
If It Rained Tonight.
Little Responsory for a Republican Hero.
Masses.
Miners, The.
Nine Monsters, The.
Pedro Rojas.
Second of November Tolls, The.
Spain, Take from Me This Cup.
Spider, The.
Trilce, XVIII, XXVIII, XLIV.
VALLIS, VAL. For This, the Tide.
Michael.
VANADA, LILLIAN SCHULZ. Fuzzy wuzzy, creepy crawly.
VAN ALSTYNE, FRANCES JANE CROSBY. *See* CROSBY, FANNY.
"VAN AVOND, JAN." *See* SLATER, FRANCIS CAREY.
VAN BRAKLE, JOHN. Easter.
Easter Message.
VANBRUGH, SIR JOHN. Aesop, *sel.*
Nightingale, The. *Fr.* Aesop.
Philira. *Fr.* The Provoked Wife.
Provoked Wife, The, *sel.*
Song: "Fly, fly, you happy shepherds, fly." *Fr.* The Provoked Wife.
VAN BUREN, D. B. Eternal Question, The.
VANCE, ABNER. Vance Song, The.
VANCE, R. B. Southern Homes in Ruin, The.
VAN CLEVE, FLORENCE. Books.
Star of Bethlehem.
"VANDEGRIFT, MARGARET" (Margaret Thomson Janvier). Clown's Baby, The.
Little Wild Baby.
Sandman, The.
VANDERBILT, JOHN. Highways and Byways.
VAN DER VEER, JUDY. Calf in the Goldenrod.
Christmas Calf, The.
Cows.
Little Woodland God.
VAN DE WATER, FREDERIC F. Last Tourney, The.
VAN DE WOESTIJNE, KAREL. *See* WOESTIJNE, KAREL VAN DE.
VAN DOREN, MARK. Above the Battle.
April, 1942.
Autonomous.
Axle Song.
Bitten.
Bore, The.
Bystanders, The.
Civil War.
Close Clan, The.
Comedy.
Company Gone.
Confinement, The.
Crisis.
Crow.
Deduction.
Defeated Farmer.
Deserted Hollow.
Difference, The.
Distant Runners, The.
End, The.
Epitaphs: For a Fickle Man.
Escape, The.
Exaggerator.
Faith of Appearances.
First Night Alone.
Foreclosure.
Former Barn Lot.
Friendship, The.
God of Galaxies, The.
Going Home.
Good Fates, The.
Good Night.
His Trees.
If Any God.
If They Spoke.
Immortal.
It Should Be Easy.
Marriage.
Memories.
Morning Worship.
Music God.
Night Lilac.
No Faith.
Now the Sky.
Old Hundred.
Orchard Ghost, The.
Our Lady Peace.
Private Worship.
Proper Clay.
Pulse, The.
Return to Ritual.
Runaways, The.
Tall Tale God.
That Day.
This Amber Sunstream.
To a Child with Eyes.
Tourist.
Tower, The.
Tragedy.
Translation, The.
Traveling Storm.
Turkey-Buzzards.
Two of You.
When the World Ends.
Whisperer, The.

VAN DOREN, MARK (*continued*)
Why, Lord.
Winter Tryst.
Wit.
Young Woman at a Window.
VAN DORN, RALPH. Look at Life, A.
VAN DUSEN, RUTH B. Prayer in a Country Church.
VAN DUYN, MONA. Gentle Snorer, The.
VAN DYKE, HENRY. America.
America for Me.
America for Me, *sel.*
America's Prosperity.
America's Welcome Home.
Ancestral Dwellings, The.
Angler's Reveille, The. *Fr.* The Toiling of Felix.
Angler's Wish, An.
Bedtime Prayer.
Builders, The.
Builders, The, *sel.*
Child in the Garden, The.
Christ of Everywhere.
Envoy: "Legend of Felix is ended, the toiling of Felix is done, The." *Fr.* The Toiling of Felix.
Face of a Friend, The.
Four Things [to Do].
God of the Open Air, *sels.*
God's Message to Men.
Gospel of Labor, The, *sels.*
Great River, The.
Home Thoughts from Europe.
Hymn of Joy.
If All the Skies [were Sunshine].
In Lucem Transitus, October, 1892.
Indian Summer.
Jesus, Thou Divine Companion.
Legend of Service, A.
Life. *Fr.* The Three Best Things.
Light between the Trees.
Lily of Yorrow, The.
Little Boatie.
Longfellow.
Lost Word of Jesus, A.
Love. *Fr.* The Three Best Things.
Lover's Envy, A.
Mare Liberum.
Maryland Yellowthroat, The.
Matins.
Mile with Me, A.
Mother's Birthday, A.
My April Lady.
Nativity, The. *Fr.* To the Child Jesus.
Night-Watch Prayer.
1904's Sundial at Wells College.
Pan Learns Music.
Peace.
Prayer: "Lord, the newness of this day."
Prayer: "These are the gifts I ask of thee."
Red Cross, The.
Reliance.
Roslin and Hawthornden.
Salute to Trees, A.
Shelley.
Song Sparrow, The.
Spring in the South.
Stars and Stripes, The.
Tennyson.
Texas.
These Are the Gifts I Ask.
They Tell Me Thou Art Rich.
This Is the Gospel of Labour.
Three Best Things, The.
Three Best Things, The, *sels.*
Thy Sea Is Great, Our Boats Are Small.
To the Child Jesus.
To the Child Jesus, *sel.*
Toiling of Felix, The, *sels.*
Trees.
Valley of Vain Verses, The.
Veery, The.
Voyagers.
Way, The.
When Tulips Bloom.
Whippoorwill, The.
Who Follow the Flag.
Wind of Sorrow, The.
Work. *Fr.* The Three Best Things.
Zest of Life, The.
VAN DYKE, TERTIUS. Laughter and Tears.
Love of Life.
VANDYNE, MARY E. Bald-headed Tyrant, The.
Nation's Birthday, The.
VANHOMRIGH, ESTHER ("Vanessa"). Hail, blushing goddess, beauteous Spring!
VAN NOPPEN, LEONARD CHARLES. Man of Men, A.
Martyrdom.
"VANOLIS, BYSSHE." *See* THOMSON, JAMES (1834–1882).
VAN PLATTENHAUS, LOUISA. Love to My Lord.
VAN RENSSELAER, MARIANA GRISWOLD (Mrs. Schuyler Van Rensselaer).
At Bedtime.
Cradle-Song: "How do we know."
Dolly's Lullaby.
Love's Prisoner.
Manners.
Typewriter, The.
Whispering Pine Tree, The.
VAN RENSSELAER, PEYTON. At Twilight.
VAN RENSSELAER, MRS. SCHUYLER. *See* VAN RENSSELAER, MARIANA GRISWOLD.
VANSITTART, ROBERT GILBERT VANSITTART, 1ST BARON. Greece.
Moonlight.
VAN SLYKE, BEREN. Shepherds, The.
VAN STOCKUM, HILDA. Hut, The.
VAN TASSEL, ETTA MAY. Joy as Old as Breathing, A.
Splendid Flower, The.
VAN VOORHIS, LINDA LYON. Ad Matrem in Coelis.
"That Which Hath Wings Shall Tell."
To a Humble Bug.
VAN VORST, MARIE (Mrs. Gaetano Cogiati). Sing Again.
Slumber Song: "When the low flying wind, awake."
VAN WINKLE, GERTRUDE. Magic Waves.
Microphone, The.
My Radio.
Static.
VAN WYNEN, PETER. May God Give Strength.
VAN ZILE, EDWARD SIMS. Close Up the Ranks.
VARALLANOS, JOSÉ. Mob of Mountains.
"VARLEY, JOHN PHILIP." *See* MITCHELL, LANGDON ELWYN.
VARNALIS, KOSTAS. Ballad of Andrew, The.
Doomed.
"Good" People, The.
Mother of Christ, The.
Pains of the Virgin Mary, The.
VASALIS, M. Sea Dike, The.
VASILIKOS, PETROS. *See* "HATZOPOULOS, KOSTES."
VÁSQUEZ, EMILIO. Indian Girl.
VAUGHAN, GRACE. When I Am Old.
VAUGHAN, H. A. Nocturne: "Wind is blowing from the hill, The."
Old Convict, The.
VAUGHAN, HENRY. Affliction.
And do they so? have they a sense.
As time one day by me did pass.
Ascension-Day.
Ascension-Hymn.
Awake! Glad Heart!
Beyond the Veil.
Bird, The.
Book, The.
Burial of an Infant, The.
Buriall.
Childhood.
Christ's Nativity.
Cock-crowing.
Come, come, what doe I here?
Constellation, The.
Constellation, The, *sel.*
Corruption.
Daughter of Herodias, The.
Dawning, The.
Dear, beauteous Death! the jewel of the just.
Dear Night, This World's Defeat.
Departed Friends.
Dwelling-Place, The.
Early Rising and Prayer.
Easter Hymn.
Eclipse, The.
Eternity. *Fr.* Nature, Man, Eternity.
Evening Watch, The; a Dialogue.
Favour, The.
Flower, The.
Fragment: "Walk with thy fellow-creatures: note the hush."
Friends Departed.
Friends in Paradise.
Garland, The.
Happy those early days, when I.
Hidden Flower, The.
Holy Fire.
I Walked the Other Day.
Idle Verse.
Jews, The.
Joy of My Life!
Knot, The.
Lamp, The.
Love and Discipline.
Man.
Metrum V.
Midnight.
Morning Watch, The.
Mount of Olives.
My soul, there is a country.
Nature, Man, Eternity.
Night, The.
O thou art such, that I could be.
Palm-Sunday.
Palm-Sunday, *sel.*
Paulinus. Versus Apud Epist. XXXII. 17.
Peace.
Pursuit, The.
Queer, The.
Quickness.
Regeneration.
Regeneration, *sel.*
Religion.
Retirement.
Retreat, The.
Retreat, The, *sel.*
Revival, The.
Rhapsody, A.
Rom. Cap. 8. Ver. 19.
Search, The.
Seed Growing Secretly, The.
Shall these early fragrant hours.
Shepherds, The.
Shower, The.
Silence and Stealth of Dayes!
Silex Scintillans.
Since Thou Art Gone.
Son-Dayes.
Song to Amoret, A.
Starre, The.
Stone, The.
Sweet Peace.
They Are All Gone [into the World of Light].
Timber, The.
To Amoret Gone from Him.
To His Books.
To His Retired Friend, *sel.*
Triumphant Entry, The. *Fr.* Palm-Sunday.
Unprofitableness.
Upon Mr. Fletchers Playes, Published, 1647.
Upon the Priory Grove, His Usual Retirement.
Vanity of Spirit.
Vision, A. *Fr.* The World.
Waterfall, The.
Waterfall, The, *sel.*
When Night Comes.
Whole Duty of Man, The.
World, The.
World, The, *sel.*
VAUGHAN, LOIS GIVENS. Aged Couple Gives Thanks, An.
Thanksgiving for Benefits Received.
VAUGHAN, THOMAS. Stone, The.
VAUGHN, F. E. Ballad of Chicken Bill, The.
VAUGHN, JANET. Our Cat.
Our Dog.
Stormy Sea.
VAUQUELIN DE LA FRESNAYE, JEAN.

Idyll: "Among the flowers, among the lilies."
Religion.
VAUX, THOMAS, 2D BARON VAUX OF HARROWDEN. Aged Lover Renounceth Love, The.
Bethinking Himself of His End, Writeth Thus.
Content.
Death in Life.
I Loathe That I Did Love.
Image of Death, The.
In His Extreme Sickness.
Latter Day, The.
Lover, Disdained, Complaineth, A.
No Pleasure without Some Pain.
Of [or On] a Contented Mind.
Of the Mean Estate.
Sins of Youth, The.
Youth.
VAVAL, DURACINÉ. Mangoes, The.
VAZAKAS, BYRON. All the Farewells.
Midsummer Night's Dream.
Pavilion on the Pier, The.
Progress of Photography, The.
Skyscraper.
VEDDER, DAVID. To Orkney.
VEDDER, MIRIAM. Epitaph for a Kitten.
VEEL, MARY COLBORNE-. *See* COLBORNE-VEEL, MARY.
VEGA, GARCILASO DE LA. *See* GARCILASO DE LA VEGA.
VEGA CARPIO, LOPE DE. *See* LOPE DE VEGA CARPIO.
VEITCH, JOHN. Laird of Schelynlaw, The.
VELESTINLI, RHIGAS. *See* PHERAIOS, RHIGAS.
VELEY, MARGARET. First or Last?
VENABLE, WILLIAM HENRY. Battle Cry.
El Emplazado.
Forest Song.
Founders of Ohio, The.
John Filson.
Johnny Appleseed.
My Catbird.
National Song: "America, my own!"
School Girl, The.
Teacher's Dream, The.
Welcome to "Boz," A.
VENANTIUS FORTUNATUS. *See* FORTUNATUS.
VENEVITINOV, DMITRI VLADIMIROVICH. Fatherland, *at.*
I feel that deep within me burns.
Three Roses.
VERDAGUER, JACINTO. Five Roses.
VERE, EDWARD DE, 17TH EARL OF OXFORD. Choice, A.
Doubtful Choice, A.
Epigram: "Were I a king, I could command content."
Fair Fools.
His Good Name Being Blemished, He Bewaileth.
If Women Could Be Fair.
Lover Rejected Complaineth, A.
Of the Birth and Bringing Up of Desire.
Of the Mighty Power of Love.
Pains and Gains.
Renunciation, A.
Were I a King.
What Cunning Can Express.
White and Red.
Who Taught Thee First to Sigh?
VERGIL. *See* VIRGIL.
VERHAEREN, EMILE. Cathedral of Rheims, The.
Fishermen, The.
I Bring to You as Offering Tonight.
Mill, The.
November.
Old Masters, The.
Poor, The.
She of the Garden.
Snow, The.
VERLAINE, PAUL. A Clymène.
A la promenade.
Amour, *sel.*
And I Have Seen Again the Marvelous Child.
Anguish.
Apathy.
Art of Poetry, The.
Art poétique.
Autumn Song.
Cat and Lady.
Celestial Hour.
Chanson d'automne.
Clair de lune.
Colloque sentimental.
Columbine.
Confession, A.
Cortège.
Cythère.
Dance the Jig.
Dans l'allée.
Easter.
En bateau.
Exile.
Expiation.
Fantoches.
Femme et chatte.
From a Prison.
Give Ear to the Very Faint Song.
God Said.
Great Dark Sleep, A.
Green.
Her Name.
I Know Not Why.
Il pleut doucement sur la ville.
In the Unending Tedium.
In the Woods.
Kindred Harmonies.
Mandoline.
Mandolines.
Moonlight.
Muted.
My Familiar Dream.
My God Has Spoken.
My Recurring Dream.
Mystical Dialogue.
Nightingale, The.
Noise of the Cabarets, The.
Oh Sad, Sad Was My Soul.
Pantomime.
Parsifal. *Fr.* Amour.
Piano, The.
Sagesse.
Sagesse, *sels.*
Sentimental Colloquy.
Sentimental Dialogue.
Shepherd's Hour, The.
Simple Song.
Sky above the Roof, The.
Sky Is Up Above the Roof, The.
Song of Autumn.
Sonnet: "And I have seen again the marvellous child."
Spleen.
Tears.
Tears and Rain.
Tears Fall within Mine Heart.
Tears Flow in My Heart.
Two Voices.
White Moon, The.
Wild Past.
Wind in the Wood.
Woman and Cat.
Women's Loveliness.
VERLON, RENE. Was It for This?
VERNÈDE, ROBERT ERNEST. Petition, A.
VERNON, WEIR. Colors.
VERPLANCK, GULIAN. Prophecy.
VERRY, ISABEL WILLIAMS. Alcestis.
VERSTEGAN [or VERSTEGEN], RICHARD (Richard Rowlands). Lullaby: "Upon my lap my sovereign sits."
Our Blessed Lady's Lullaby.
Our Lady's Lullaby.
Upon My Lap My Sovereign Sits.
Vision of the World's Instability, A.
VERWEY, ALBERT. Bridge, The.
VERY, JONES. Ark, The.
Branch, The.
Coming of the Lord, The.
Cottage, The.
Created, The.
Day.
Dead, The.
Earth, The.
Enoch.
Garden, The.
Gifts of God, The.
Hand and Foot, The
Health of Body Dependent on Soul.
Idler, The.
In Him We Live.
Lament of the Flowers, The.
Latter Rain, The.
Light from Within, The.
Morning.
Nature.
New Birth, The.
New World, The.
Night.
October.
Old Road, The.
Prayer, The: "Wilt Thou not visit me?"
Present Heaven, The.
Robin, The.
Soldier, The.
Spirit-Land, The.
Strangers, The.
Thy Brother's Blood.
To the Painted Columbine.
Tree, The.
War, The.
Wild Rose of Plymouth, The.
Wind-Flower, The.
Yourself.
"VESTAL, STANLEY" (Walter Stanley Campbell). Fandango.
Kit Carson's Last Smoke.
Oliver Wiggins.
VIAU, THÉOPHILE DE. Sleep.
VIBE, JØRGEN. Song of Sprats, A.
VICENTE, GIL. Angelic Vilancete, The. *Fr.* The Auto of the Four Seasons.
Auto of the Bark of Purgatory, The, *sel.*
Auto of the Four Seasons, The, *sel.*
Cantiga: "Take away from me my eyes."
Cantiga: "White and crimson, cheek and breast."
Cassandra's Song of Celibacy.
Esparsa.
Flerida and Don Duardos.
Grace and Beauty Has the Maid.
Hymn of the Angels and Sibyls.
I Come from the Rose Garden, Mother.
In the Garden Blossoms the Rose.
Nightingale, The.
Rose Song, The.
Song: "Grace and beauty has the maid."
Song: "If thou art sleeping, maiden."
Song of the Three Angels. *Fr.* The Auto of the Bark of Purgatory.
VIDA, MARCO GIROLAMO. De Bombycibus, *sel.*
Silkworm, The. *Fr.* De Bombycibus.
VIDAL, PEIRE. Song of Breath.
VIDAME DE CHARTRES. *See* CHARTRES, VIDAME DE.
VIELÉ, HERMAN KNICKERBOCKER. Borderland.
Good Inn, The. *Fr.* The Inn of the Silver Moon.
Inn of the Silver Moon, The, *sel.*
Stop Thief.
VIELÉ-GRIFFIN, FRANCIS. Hours Grey.
VIERECK, GEORGE SYLVESTER. After the Battle.
Buried City, The.
Candle and the Flame, The.
Haunted House, The.
Hymn of Armageddon, The.
On Broadway.
Prayer: "I stood upon the threshold."
Salutation.
Slaves.
Wanderers.
VIERECK, PETER. Affirmations.
Before You Now, My Tyrant-Sorrow, *tr.*
Blindman's Buff.
Counter-Serenade; She Invokes the Autumn Instant.
Crass Times Redeemed by Dignity of Souls.
Crass Times Redeemed by Dignity of Souls, *sel.*
Day's No Rounder than Its Angles Are, The.
Don't Look Now but Mary Is Everybody.
For Two Girls Setting Out in Life.
From Ancient Fangs.

VIERECK, PETER (*continued*)
Kilroy [Was Here].
Love Song to Eohippus.
Now Kindness.
Poet.
Slacker Apologizes, The.
Small Perfect Manhattan.
Some Lines in Three Parts.
Stop Pondering on Things Imponderable, *tr.*
To a Sinister Potato.
Twilight of the Outward Life, *tr.*
Vale from Carthage (Spring, 1944).
Walk on Snow, A.
Why, in Drunken Blend of Flute and Bugle, *tr.*
You All Are Static; I Alone Am Moving.
VIGNALE, PEDRO JUAN. Dead Grenadier, The.
VIGNY, ALFRED DE. Anger of Samson, The.
Fates, The.
Horn, The.
My Torn Heart.
Nature.
Silence.
Snow.
Sound of the Horn, The.
VILARAS, YIANNIS. Spring.
VILAS, FAITH VAN VALKENBURGH. Mother on Her Daughter's Wedding Day, A.
VILDRAC, CHARLES. After Midnight.
VILENKIN, NIKOLAI MAKSIMOVICH. *See* "MINSKI, NIKOLAI MAKSIMOVICH."
VILLA, JOSÉ GARCÍA. Be Beautiful, Noble, like the Antique Ant.
Between God's Eyelashes.
Divine Poems, *sels.*
God Said, "I Made a Man."
Mostly Are We Mostless.
My Most. My Most. O My Lost! *Fr.* Divine Poems.
My Mouth Is Very Quiet.
Now, If You Will Look in My Brain.
Poem: "Distinction is in Fire and Division, The."
Poem: "Living, giant, all, in, little, pieces, A."
Saw God Dead but Laughing.
There Came You Wishing Me.
Way My Ideas Think Me, The.
VILLAMEDIANA, JUAN DE TASSIS Y PERALTA, CONDE DE. To a Cloistress.
VILLAURRUTIA, XAVIER. Angel-Nocturne.
Nocturne in Which Death Speaks.
VILLEGAS, ANTONIO. Love's Extremes.
VILLIERS, GEORGE, 2D DUKE OF BUCKINGHAM. *See* BUCKINGHAM, GEORGE VILLIERS, 2D DUKE OF.
VILLON, FRANÇOIS. All Things except Myself I Know.
Arbor Amoris.
Ballad: "Lady of Heaven, Regent of the earth."
Ballad: Things of No Account, The.
Ballad against the Enemies of France.
Ballad of Dead Ladies, The.
Ballad of Poor Chimney Sweeps.
Ballad of the Gibbet.
Ballad of the Lords of Old Time.
Ballad of the Women of Paris.
Ballad Written for a Bridegroom.
Ballade: "I die of thirst beside the fountain's brim."
Ballade of Fair Ladies of Olden Time.
Ballade of the Gibbet.
Ballade of the Hanged Men.
Ballade of the Women of the Past.
Ballade That Villon Made at the Request of His Mother to Intercede with Our Lady.
Christmas Time. *Fr.* Le Petit Testament.
Complaint of the Fair Armoress, The.
Dispute of the Heart and Body of François Villon, The.
Double Ballad of Good Counsel, A.
Epistle in Form of a Ballad to His Friends.
Epitaph: "Here lies, in this small chamber."
Epitaph in Form of a Ballad, The, Which Villon Made for Himself and His Comrades, Expecting to Be Hanged Along with Them.
Fragment on [*or* of] Death.
His Mother's Service to Our Lady.
If I Were King.
Lament of "La Belle Heaulmière," The.
Lament of the Lovely Helmet-Dealer.
Lament of the Old Woman Remembering Her Youth.
Lesser Testament, The.
Lines on Death, and Ballade.
Little Testament, The.
No, I Am Not as Others Are.
Old Woman's Lamentations, An.
Petit Testament, Le.
Petit Testament, Le, *sel.*
Prayer, Made in Ballat Form bi Villon for His Mither, The.
Quatrain: "As I'm French born, I'm pained to say."
Rondel: "Death, I denounce thy cruelty."
Rondel: "Good-by, the tears are in my eyes."
Rondel: "Grant him eternal rest, poor wight!"
Rondel: "Johnny of the Avenue."
Testament, The, *sels.*
To Death of His Lady.
Translation from Villon, A, *by* Synge.
Two Translations from Villon, *by* Synge.
Villon's Ballade.
Villon's Epitaph in Ballade Form.
Villon's Straight Tip to All Cross Coves.
Would I Be Shrived?
VINAL, HAROLD. Dead Enchantress.
Enduring Music, The.
Flight.
Ghostly Reaper.
Hymnal: "Bringer of sun, arrower of evening, star-begetter and moonriser."
Judas.
Lesbia Sewing.
Miser.
Nights Remember, The.
Of Mariners.
Prescience.
Quest, The.
Satan in Profile.
Sea Born.
Sea Longing.
To One with Hands of Sleep.
VINCENT, CLARENCE A. Heaven.
VINCENTE, GIL. *See* VICENTE, GIL.
VINCI, LEONARDO DA. *See* LEONARDO DA VINCI.
VINES, SHERARD. Prayer for Singleness of Vision, A.
Prophet, The.
VINJE, AASMUND OLAFSSON. Day Will Not Come, The.
Only Thing That Is Left to Do, The.
Recollections.
VIOLANTE DO CEO, SISTER. Night of Marvels, The.
While to Bethlehem We Are Going.
VIRGIL [*or* VERGIL] (Publius Vergilius Maro). Aeneas and Dido. *Fr.* The Aeneid.
Aeneas at the Site of Rome. *Fr.* The Aeneid.
Aeneid, The, *sels.*
After the Rain. *Fr.* Georgics.
Battle of Actium. *Fr.* The Aeneid.
Blest Abode, A. *Fr.* The Aeneid.
Camilla. *Fr.* The Aeneid.
Certain Books of Virgil's Aeneis. *Fr.* The Aeneid.
Copa; the Barmaid.
Corydon. *Fr.* Eclogues.
Corydon and Thyrsis. *Fr.* Eclogues.
Dawn of the Golden Age. *Fr.* Eclogues.
Death of Turnus, The. *Fr.* The Aeneid.
Departure of Aeneas from Dido. *Fr.* The Aeneid.
Destruction of Troy, The. *Fr.* The Aeneid.
Dido among the Shades. *Fr.* The Aeneid.
Dido's Hunting. *Fr.* The Aeneid.
Eclogues, *sels.*
Entrance to Hell, The. *Fr.* The Aeneid.
Entrance to Tartarus, The. *Fr.* The Aeneid.
Fall of Troy, The. *Fr.* The Aeneid.
Fatal Blindness. *Fr.* Eclogues.
Fourth Eclogue, The, *sel.*
From God to God.
Georgics, *sels.*
Honey-Farm, The. *Fr.* Georgics.
Ibant Obscuri; Vision of Aeneas. *Fr.* The Aeneid.
Jupiter Sends a Fury to Baffle Turnus in Battle. *Fr.* The Aeneid.
Lower World, The (the Sibyl Speaks). *Fr.* The Aeneid.
Lycidas and Moeris. *Fr.* Eclogues.
Marcellus. *Fr.* The Aeneid.
Messiah, The. *Fr.* Eclogues.
On Some Verses of Virgil. *Fr.* The Aeneid.
Prelude: "What makes a plenteous harvest." *Fr.* Georgics.
Rang'd on the Line Opposed, Antonius Brings. *Fr.* The Aeneid.
Return of the Golden Age, with the Birth of Pollio, The. *Fr.* Eclogues.
Sad Dido. *Fr.* The Aeneid.
Sex among Lions. *Fr.* Georgics.
Shepherd's Gratitude, The. *Fr.* Eclogues.
Shipwreck of the Trojans; Landing at Carthage. *Fr.* The Aeneid.
Sibylline Prophecy, The. *Fr.* Eclogues.
Snake, The. *Fr.* Georgics.
Stateliest Measure, The. *Fr.* Georgics.
Sunt Lacrimae Rerum. *Fr.* The Aeneid.
Venus the Goddess. *Fr.* The Aeneid.
Vision of Rome's Destiny. *Fr.* The Aeneid.
We Have Paid Enough Long Since in Our Own Blood. *Fr.* Georgics.
Welcome to the Sun. *Fr.* The Aeneid.
With Wound Still Fresh. *Fr.* The Aeneid.
VIRTUE, VIVIAN L. Atlantic Moonrise.
Gleaner, The.
To Claude McKay.
VISITATION, SISTER MARY OF THE. *See* MARY OF THE VISITATION, SISTER.
VISSCHER, MARIA TESSELSCHADE. Nightingale, The.
VITALE, GIANO. *See* PANORMITANUS, IANUS VITALIS.
VITTORELLI, JACOPO. On a Nun.
Sonnet: Addressed by a Father Mourning His Recently Deceased Married Daughter to the Father Whose Daughter Had Entered a Convent.
VIVIAN, MARY. Four Scarlet Berries.
Snowdrops.
VIVIEN, GEOFFREY. Song of Self-Pity, A.
VIZINOS, GEORGIOS. Dream, The.
Hidden Sorrow, The.
"VLASTOS, PETROS" (Ermonas). To My Mother.
Village of Love, The.
VOGELWEIDE, WALTHER VON DER. *See* WALTHER VON DER VOGELWEIDE.
VOGT, ANTON. For a Child's Drawing.
For England, in Grateful Appreciation, *sel.*
VOGT, NILS COLLETT. February Morning on the Gulf.
Moonlight.
Song of the Billows, The.
VOITURE, VINCENT. Rondeau: "By Jove, 'tis done with me, for Isabeau."
VOLLMOELLER, KARL GUSTAV. Nocturne in G Minor.
VOLOSHIN, MAXIMILIAN ALEKSANDROVICH. Cimmerian Twilight.
Lunaria, *sel.*
Terror.
Under Sail.
VOLTAIRE (François Marie Arouet). Inscription for a Statue of Love.

Last night in sleep I seemed a king.
On a Christ in Jesuit Robes.
On His Portrait between Two Others.
On Jean Fréron.
On the Phrase, "To Kill Time."
To Madame Lullin.
VONDEL, JOOST VAN DEN. Adam's Hymn in Paradise.
Chorus of Batavian Women.
Hymn of Adam, The.
On the Passing of My Little Daughter.
VON SCHLICHTEN, HENRY J. Lost, but Won.
Prayer of a Patriot.
VON TILZER, HARRY, *and* WILL DILLON. *See* DILLON, WILL, *and* HARRY VON TILZER.
VOORHEES, DAYTON. Limerick: "There was an old man of Nantucket."
VORIES, WILLIAM MERRELL. Life.
VOSS, CHARLES HANNIBAL. Yet Love Was Born.
VOSS, J. H. Who Does Not Love Wine, Women and Song.
VREPONT, BRIAN. Apple Tree, The.
Bomber, The.
Earth.
Fishers, The.
Heron, The.
Net-Menders, The.
Peace.
Song-Bird.
VRETTAKOS, NICEPHORUS. Athens.
Child of the Wind with the Harmonica.
Elegy on the Grave of a Small Fighter.
Just One More Spring.
33 Days, *sel.*
VRIESLAND, VICTOR VAN. Ars Poetica.
Evening.
VULGARIUS, EUGENIUS. Metrum Parhemiacum Tragicum.
VYAZEMSKY, PIOTR ANDREYEVICH, PRINCE. Spring.
Thou art my bright star in a world half-hidden.
When youth still made my spirit bold.

W

"W., A." Bright shines the sun; play, beggars, play!
Desire's Government.
Dispraise of Love [and Lovers' Follies].
Fiction, A.
Give Me Leave.
Hopeless Desire Soon Withers and Dies.
In Praise of a Beggar's Life.
In Praise of the Sun.
Ladies' Eyes Serve Cupid Both for Darts and Fire.
Petition to Have Her Leave to Die.
Play, Beggars, Play!
Sweet Love, Mine Only Treasure.
To Time.
Upon Visiting His Lady by Moonlight.
When will the fountain of my tears be dry?
Where His Lady Keeps His Heart.
"W., C. H." Preface to Confessional.
"W., E." Folkways of Sodom, The.
"W., I." Quiet Things.
"W., I. V. S." Snowfall.
"W., J. W. G." Lost Ape, The.
"W., L." All Things Be Dear but Poor Mens Labour; or, The Sad Complaint of Poor People.
"W., M. E." To Slumber Town.
"W., R." Evening Hymn.
"W. A. G." *See* "G., W. A."
"W. B." *See* "B., W."
"W. H. S." *See* "S., W. H."
WABNITZ, WILLIAM S. Hinds of Kerry, The.
WADDELL, ELIZABETH. Crusaders.
WADDELL, HELEN. Appendix Vergiliana, *tr.*
Before Sleep, *tr.*
Burial of the Dead, The, *tr.*
Carmina Burana, *sels., tr.*
David's Lament for Jonathan, *tr.*
Dawn-Song to Waken the Lovers, *tr.*
Day of Wrath, The, *tr.*
De Ramis Cadunt Folia, *tr. Fr.* Carmina Burana.
Dum Diane Vitrea, *tr.*
Evening on the Moselle, *tr.*
For St. Felix' Day, *tr.*
Good Friday: The Third Nocturn, *tr.*
His Epitaph, *tr.*
How Goes the Night, *tr. Fr.* Shi King.
I Wait My Lord, *tr. Fr.* Shi King.
Lament for Alcuin, *tr.*
Love Song ("Herself hath given back my life to me"), *tr.*
Maiden's Complaint in Spring-Time, A, *tr.*
MS of Benedictbeuern, *tr.*
MS of St. Martial of Limoges, *tr.*
Metrum Parhemiacum Tragicum, *tr.*
Morning Glory, The, *tr. Fr.* Shi King.
Obmittamus Studia, *tr. Fr.* Carmina Burana.
On Newblown Roses, *tr.*
Petronius Arbiter, *tr.*
Shi King, *sels., tr.*
Si Vis Celsi Iura Tonantis, *tr.*
This Discord in the Pact of Things, *tr.*
To Ausonius, *tr.*
To His Friend in Absence, *tr.*
To His Wife, *tr.*
Under the Pondweed, *tr. Fr.* Shi King.
Venantius Fortunatus, *tr.*
Virgin Martyrs, The, *tr.*
Volo Virum Vivere Viriliter, *tr. Fr.* Carmina Burana.
Winter Love Song, *tr.*
WADDELL, JEAN PERCIVAL. Half-Light.
Rhythm.
WADDING, LUKE. Christmas Day Is Come.
WADDINGTON, MIRIAM. Cadenza.
Circles.
Gimli.
Investigator.
Lovers.
Lullaby: "Hush dove the summer."
Night in October.
Portrait.
Restricted.
Wonderful Country.
WADDINGTON, PATRICK D. Lines to the Unborn.
WADDINGTON, SAMUEL. Inn of Care, The.
Morning.
Mors et Vita.
Soul and Body.
WADDY, R. W. Old Friends.
WADE, BLANCHE ELIZABETH. Song of the Christmas Trees.
WADE, JAMES PALMER. Hymn to No One Body, A.
WADE, JOHN. Leather Bottel, The.
WADE, THOMAS. Birth and Death.
Half-asleep, The.
Net-Braiders, The.
True Martyr, The.
"WADSWORTH, OLIVE A." (Katherine Floyd Dana). Over in the Meadow.
Wonderful Meadow, The.
WAFU. Some ears are tuned to catch.
WAGNER, CHARLES ABRAHAM. Three City Cantos.
Unknown Soldier, The.
When I Loved You.
WAGNER, CHARLES L. H. Let's Forget.
WAGNER, JOHN A. Carolina.
WAGNER, MADGE MORRIS. To the Colorado Desert.
WAGNER, MARY BOYD. Lethal Thought, The.
WAGON, BILL. O-Bar Cowboy, *at.*
WAGONER, DAVID. Gift of a Mirror to a Lady.
News from the Court.
"Tan Ta Ra, Cries Mars . . ."
WAGSTAFF, BLANCHE SHOEMAKER. All Paths Lead to You.
Pilgrimage.
Quiet Waters.
Wildness.
WAID, WILLA MAE. When It's Iris Time in Tennessee.
WAIN, JOHN. Eighth Type of Ambiguity.
Letter to Santa Claus.
Reason for Not Writing Orthodox Nature Poetry.
WAINWRIGHT, VERA. When we are older and the hidden fires.
WAITE, ARTHUR EDWARD. At the End of Things.
WAITE, SHIRLEY DILLON. Cross, The.
WAKE, WILLIAM BASIL. Saying Not Meaning.
WAKEFIELD, NANCY AMELIA WOODBURY. *See* PRIEST, NANCY WOODBURY.
WAKEFORD, AMELIA. Thou Alone Canst Save.
WAKELEY, CHARLES RUSSELL. Gethsemane.
Love.
WAKLEY, THIRZA. Easter Chick, An.
Mouse, The.
Spring Work at the Farm.
WALAFRID [*or* WILAFRID] STRABO. To His Friend in Absence.
WALDECK, HEINRICH SUSO. Cleansing.
WALDHEIM, FRANKLIN. Help Wanted.
WALDO, ROSE. Camp Chums.
Kite Tales.
Sing-Time.
Take Care.
Welcome.
WALDREN, ——. To Chloris, *at.*
WALEY, ARTHUR. After Passing the Examination, *tr.*
Although I do not know, *tr.*
Autumn Wind, The, *tr.*
Battle, The, *tr.*
Because he is young, *tr.*
Because river-fog, *tr.*
Bones of Chuang Tzu, The, *tr.*
Book of Odes, The, *sels., tr.*
Bright Night, A, *tr.*
Burial Song, *tr.*
Business Men, *tr.*
By way of pretext, *tr.*
Censorship.
Charcoal-Seller, The, *tr.*
Ch'in Chia's Farewell, *tr.*
Ch'in Chia's Wife's Reply, *tr.*
Cicada, The, *tr.*
Civilization, *tr.*
Clearing at Dawn, *tr.*
Cock-Crow Song, *tr.*
Cranes, The, *tr.*
Crossing the Mountain Alone, *tr.*
Dance Song, *tr.*
Dreaming that I Went with Lu and Yu to Visit Yüan Chen, *tr.*
Elms of the Eastern Gate, *tr. Fr.* Shi King.
Fallen Leaves, *tr. Fr.* Shi King.
Farming, *tr. Fr.* Shi King.
Ferry, The, *tr.*
Fighting South of the Castle, *tr.*
Fighting South of the Ramparts, *tr.*
Flood, *tr.*
Flower Market, The, *tr.*
Folk Song: "Hat you loved, the damask-trimmed reed-hat, The," *tr.*
For my Sister's sake, *tr.*
Gentle Wind, A, *tr.*
Girl in the Carriage, The, *tr. Fr.* Shi King.
Glimpse of a Plain Cap, The, *tr. Fr.* Shi King.
Good-bye to the People of Hang-chow, *tr.*
Great Summons, The, *tr.*
Harper of Chao, The, *tr.*
Hat Given to the Poet by Li-chien, The, *tr.*
Hearing That His Friend Was Coming Back from the War, *tr.*
Hearing the Early Oriole, *tr.*
Herd Boy, The, *tr.*
Hot Cake, *tr.*
I Built My Hut, *tr.*
I have got her, *tr.*
I Look Down, *tr.*
I sent out invitations, *tr.*
If Along the Highroad, *tr. Fr.* Shi King.

WALEY, ARTHUR (*continued*)
If only, when one heard, *tr.*
Illness, *tr.*
In Early Summer Lodging in a Temple to Enjoy the Moonlight, *tr.*
In my boat that goes, *tr.*
In Our Lane, *tr. Fr.* Shi King.
In the Mountains on a Summer Day, *tr.*
In the ocean of the sky, *tr.*
Kokin Shu, *sels., tr.*
Lady and the Magpie, The, *tr.*
Lao-tzu, *tr.*
Letter, The, *tr.*
Li Fu-jen, *tr.*
Like those boats which are returning, *tr.*
Little Cart, The, *tr.*
Little Lady of Ch'ing-hsi, The, *tr.*
Lodging with the Old Man of the Stream, *tr.*
Long time ago, A, *tr.*
Losing a Slave-Girl, *tr.*
Love's Terror, *tr.*
Lo-yang, *tr.*
Lychee, The, *tr.*
Madly Singing in the Mountains, *tr.*
Manyo Shu, *sels., tr.*
Men of Valor, The, *tr.*
Mingling my prayer, *tr.*
My heart, thinking, *tr.*
My love/ Is like the grasses, *tr.*
O nightingale, *tr.*
Oath of Friendship ("If you were riding in a coach"), *tr.*
Oath of Friendship ("Shang Ya!/ I want to be your friend"), *tr.*
Old and New, *tr.*
Old Chinese Poem: "At the beginning of winter," *tr.*
Old Chinese Poem: "Bright moon illumines the night-prospect, A," *tr.*
Old Chinese Poem: "Cold, cold the year draws to its end," *tr.*
On Being Sixty, *tr.*
On Going to a Tavern, *tr.*
On the Birth of His Son, *tr.*
On this night that is cold, *tr.*
People Hide Their Love, *tr.*
People of Tao-chou, The, *tr.*
Philosopher, The, *tr.*
Pitcher, The, *tr.*
Plucking the Rushes, *tr.*
Po Chü-i to Yüan Chen, *tr.*
Pretext, *tr.*
Prisoner, The, *tr.*
Protest, A, in the Sixth Year of Ch'ien Fu (A.D. 879), *tr.*
Red Cockatoo, The, *tr.*
Rejoicing at the Arrival of Ch'en Hsiung, *tr.*
Remembering Golden Bells, *tr.*
Returning to the Fields, *tr.*
River-Fog, *tr.*
Sailing Homeward, *tr.*
Satire on Paying Calls, *tr.*
Scholar in the Narrow Street, The, *tr.*
Scholar Recruit, The, *tr.*
Shady, Shady, *tr.*
Shall we make love, *tr.*
Shi King, *sels., tr.*
Shui Shu, *sels., tr.*
Since I am convinced/ That reality, *tr.*
Since our hair was plaited and we became man and wife, *tr.*
Sleeping on Horseback, *tr.*
Soldier Thought Dead Returns Home, The, *tr. Fr.* Shi King.
Song of Lo-fu, The, *tr.*
Song of Snow-white Heads, *tr.*
Sound of her silk skirt has stopped, The, *tr.*
South, The, *tr.*
South of the Great Sea, *tr.*
Startled/ By a single scream, *tr.*
Summer Song, *tr.*
Sun in the East, *tr. Fr.* Shi King.
Tanka: Cry of the Crane, The, *tr.*
Tanka: "Men of valor, The," *tr.*
Tanka: Reflection, A, *tr.*
Tell Me Now, *tr.*
Temple, The, *tr.*
They say there is, *tr.*
Those ships which left, *tr.*
To His Wife, *tr.*
To Li Chien, *tr.*
To Tan Ch'iu, *tr.*
"Tzu-Yeh" Song, A: "All night I could not sleep," *tr.*
"Tzu-Yeh" Song, A: "I heard my love was going to Yang-chou, *tr.*
Valley Wind, The, *tr.*
Wake, The, *tr.*
Wedding Song, *tr. Fr.* Shi King.
What Should a Man Want? *tr.*
When evening comes, *tr.*
Whirlpool, *tr.*
Winter Night, *tr.*
With a rocking, *tr.*
Woman, *tr.*
For other translations from Chinese, see TrCh.
WALFORD, WILLIAM W. Sweet Hour of Prayer.
WALKER, ARCHIBALD STODART-. *See* STODART-WALKER, ARCHIBALD.
WALKER, DEE LAWRENCE. Et Cetera.
WALKER, E. M. To America, on Her First Sons Fallen in the Great War.
WALKER, MARGARET. For Mary McLeod Bethune.
For My People.
Harriet Tubman.
Molly Means.
October Journey.
We Have Been Believers.
WALKER, MARION MITCHELL. Chickadee.
Crocus.
Lilies of the Valley.
Meadow Lark.
Oriole.
Sleepy Tulips, The.
WALKER, RAYMOND W. Junior's Foxy Friends, The.
My Bess.
WALKER, WILLIAM SIDNEY. Death's Alchemy.
Too solemn for day, too sweet for night.
WALL, ARNOLD. Going Upstairs.
WALLACE, EDNA KINGSLEY. Christmas Eve.
Growing Up.
Wishes.
WALLACE, FRANCES REVETT. Only Then.
WALLACE, JAMES COWDEN. God [the Omniscient].
WALLACE, JOHN AIKMAN. Power of Prayer, The.
WALLACE, LEW. Ben-Hur, *sel.*
Song: "Wake not, but hear me, love!" *Fr.* Ben-Hur.
Table Blessing.
WALLACE, ROBERT. Crayfish, The.
WALLACE, W. V. Speak Gently, *wr. at. See* BATES, DAVID.
WALLACE, WILLIAM ROSS. Hand That Rocks the Cradle Is the Hand That Rules the World, The.
Hand That Rules the World, The.
Sword of Bunker Hill, The.
What Rules the World.
WALLER, EDMUND. Apology for Having Loved Before, An.
At Penshurst.
Battle of the Summer Islands, The.
Battle of the Summer Islands, The, *sel.*
Chloris and Hylas.
Chloris Farewell.
Dancer, The.
From "Divine Poems." *Fr.* Of the Last Verses in the Book.
Go, Lovely Rose.
Last Verses.
Of a Fair Lady Playing with a Snake.
Of English Verse.
Of His Divine Poems.
Of His Majesties Receiving the News of the Duke of Buckingham's Death.
Of My Lady Isabella Playing on the Lute.
Of the Last Verses in the Book.
Of the Last Verses in the Book, *sel.*
Old Age [and Death]. *Fr.* Of the Last Verses in the Book.
On a Girdle.
On Her Coming to London.
On St. James's Park, as Lately Improved by His Majesty.
On the Head of a Stag.
On the Last Verses in His Book of Poems.
Panegyrick to My Lord Protector, A.
Panegyrick to My Lord Protector, A, *sel.*
Say, Lovely Dream.
Self-banished, The.
Song: "Chloris farewell; I now must go."
Song: "Go lovely Rose."
Song: "Stay, Phoebus, stay!"
Soul's Dark Cottage, The. *Fr.* Of the Last Verses in the Book.
Stay, Phoebus!
Story of Phoebus and Daphne, Applied, The.
That which her slender waist confined.
To a Fair Lady Playing with a Snake.
To a Lady Singing a Song of His Own Composing.
To a Very Young Lady.
To Amoret.
To Flavia.
To Mr. Henry Lawes, Who Had Then Newly Set a Song of Mine, in the Year 1635.
To My Young Lady Lucy Sidney.
To Phyllis.
To the King on His Navy.
Under a Lady's Picture.
Upon Ben. Johnson.
Upon Mr. John Fletcher's Playes.
Upon Our Late Loss of the Duke of Cambridge.
Why came I so untimely forth.
WALLER, JOHN. Enemy, The.
Legend.
Limb and Mind.
Oscar Wilde and Aubrey Beardsley.
When Sadness Fills a Journey.
WALLER, JOHN FRANCIS. Dance Light.
Kitty Neil.
Spinning Wheel, The.
Spinning-Wheel Song, The.
WALLIN, JOHAN OLOF. Angel of Death, The, *sel.*
WALLIS, CLAIRE. Mode Atmospheric, The.
WALLIS, ELEANOR GLENN. Deathless Ones, The.
Hunter, The.
In a City Square.
Iulus.
"Trade" Rat.
WALLIS, GEORGE B. Lovely Rivers and Lakes of Maine, The.
WALLIS, JOHN. Twister Twisting Twine, *at.*
WALLIS, S. TEACKLE. Prayer for Peace, A.
WALPOLE, HENRY. Martyrdom of Father Campion, The.
Song of Mary the Mother of Christ, The, *at.*
WALPOLE, HORACE, 4TH EARL OF ORFORD. Anne Grenville, Countess Temple, Appointed Poet Laureate to the King of the Fairies.
Countess Temple, Appointed Poet Laureate to the King of the Fairies.
Epitaph on Lady Ossory's Bullfinch.
To Lady Ann Fitzpatrick, When about Five Years Old.
WALSH, DONALD DEVENISH. *For translations from French and Spanish, see* AnCL; FaPON; LiTW; OnPM; TrJP; WoL.
WALSH, EDWARD. Dawning of the Day, The, *tr.*
Fairy Nurse, The.
Have You Been at Carrick? *tr.*
Kitty Bhan.
Lament: "When the folk of my household," *tr.*
Lament of the Mangaire Sugach, *tr.*
Mairgread ni Chealleadh.
Mo Craoibhin Cno.
My Hope, My Love, *tr.*
WALSH, ERNEST. Doctor Bill Williams.
Lazarus Walks in the Alps.
WALSH, J. PATRICK. For the Magi.

Now That You Are Gone.
WALSH, JOHN. Drimin Donn Dilis.
To My Promised Wife.
WALSH, MARY M. Quality of Mercy, The.
WALSH, THOMAS. Abbey, The, *tr.*
Art, *tr.*
At the Ascension, *tr.*
At the Assumption, *tr.*
Birds, The, *tr.*
Blind, The.
Brazier Coals, The, *tr.*
Calling, The, *tr.*
Cantiga, *tr.*
Canto Espiritual, *tr.*
Caravan, The, *tr.*
Cathedral of Rheims, The, *tr.*
Christ and His Mother at the Cross, *tr.*
Christmas Carol: "Land grew bright in a single flower, The," *tr.*
Coelo et in Terra.
Conversion of the Magdalene, The, *sel.*, *tr.*
Coplas on the Death of His Father, the Grandmaster of Santiago, *tr.*
Counsels, *tr.*
Death Warnings, *tr.*
Death-Bed Hymn of Saint Anthony of Padua, *tr.*
Divine Passion, The, *tr.*
Domestic Scenes, *tr.*
Dusk, *tr.*
Egidio of Coimbra—1597 A.D.
Empty Cradle, The, *tr.*
Envying a Little Bird, *tr.*
Fan, The, *tr.*
Feast of Padre Chala, The.
First Communion, *tr.*
Five Roses, *tr.*
Fourth Eclogue, The, *sel.*, *tr.*
Friar, The, *tr.*
Garden Prayer, A.
Holy Eclogue, The, *tr.*
Hymn of the Angels and Sibyls, *tr.*
In Provence, *tr.*
In the Depths of Night, *tr.*
In the Face of Grief, *tr.*
In the Mushroom Meadows.
India the Magic, *tr.*
Inscription on a Shrine near Ischl, *tr.*
Jolly Supper, The, *tr.*
Letrilla; the Lord of Dollars, *tr.*
Lines on the Wall of His Prison Cell, *tr.*
Lord, The, *tr.*
Lord of Dollars, The, *tr.*
Love ("Clouded vision, light obscure"), *tr.*
Love Song, *tr.*
Lullaby, The: "As through the palms ye wander," *tr.*
Madonna's Lamp, The, *tr.*
Manchy, The, *tr.*
Miserere, *tr.*
Mother Most Powerful, *tr.*
Mystical Poets, *tr.*
Night of the Immaculate Conception, *tr.*
Night Serene, The, *tr.*
Nightfall, *tr.*
Nisé, *tr.*
Nocturne: "One night," *tr.*
Ode—Imitated from the Pslams, *tr.*
Ode to Spain—after the Revolution of March, *sel.*, *tr.*
On the Annunciation of Fra Angelico, *tr.*
On the Bad Government of Toledo, *tr.*
One Night, *tr.*
Our Little House.
Our Poets' Breed, *tr.*
Parish Church, The, *tr.*
Portico, *tr.*
Prayer: "Spirit of Christ my sanctification," *tr.*
Prayer to the Crucifix, *tr.*
Presence of the Spirit, The, *tr.*
Queen of the Angels, The, *tr.*
Rann of the Tree, The, *tr.*
Rimas, *tr.*
Rose, The, *tr.*
Rune of Hospitality, The, *tr.*
Russian Spring Song with Minaiev, A.
Secret, The, *tr.*
Seguidilla, *tr.*
Sibylline Prophecy, The, *tr.* *Fr.* The Fourth Eclogue.
Snares, The, *tr.*
Song to the Virgin Mary, *tr.*
Stabat Mater Dolorosa, *tr.*
Stabat Mater Speciosa, *tr.*
Stille Nacht, *tr.*
Street of Doctors, The.
Such Is Love, *tr.*
Sum of Kisses, A, *tr.*
Sursum, *tr.*
Tears against the Moon.
To a Lady Going Veiled, *tr.*
To an Andalusian Fan, *tr.*
To an English Setter.
To Christ Crucified, *tr.*
To Holy Jesus, *tr.*
To Jesus on the Cross, *tr.*
To Our Lord, *tr.*
To Our Saviour, *tr.*
To Retirement, *tr.*
Toledo ("No more the jousts"), *tr.*
Toledo ("Perched on its yellow peak"), *tr.*
Traditions, *tr.*
Valley of the Heavens, The, *tr.*
Village Barber, The, *tr.*
Villancico, *tr.*
Vision, The, *tr.*
Waiting Harp, The, *tr.*
What Guardian Counsels, *tr.*
When the Shades of Night Have Come, *tr.*
Written on the Walls of His Dungeon, *tr.*
You Are My Sisters, *tr.*
WALSH, WILLIAM. Death; a Sonnet.
Despairing Lover, The.
Elegy: Unrewarded Lover, The.
Grant Me Peace, *tr.*
Rivalry [*or* Rivals] in Love.
Rivals.
Song: "Of all the torments, all the cares."
Sonnet: Death.
Sonnet on Death.
To His Book.
To His Mistress.
Unrewarded Lover, The.
Upon a Favour Offered.
WALSH, WILLIAM F. Conversation.
WALSH, WILLIAM THOMAS. Marriage Song.
Requiem.
WALTER, HOWARD ARNOLD. I Would Be True.
My Creed.
WALTER OF CHATILLON. Love's Temperature.
WALTERS, LETTICE D'OYLY. All Is Spirit and Part of Me.
Seville.
WALTERS, LILA V. He Shall Speak Peace unto the Nations.
WALTERS, MEURIG. Rhondda.
Seminary.
WALTHER VON DER VOGELWEIDE. Awake! Awake! The Day Is Coming Now.
Blessed Be the Hour.
For One of Low Degree.
Maria Bright.
Oracle, The.
Song: "Under the lime-tree, on the daisied ground."
Tandaradei.
There Is a Lady Conquering [with Glances].
Translation, A, *by* J. M. Synge.
Uncourtly Love.
Under the Lime Tree.
Under the Linden.
With a Rod No Man Alive.
WALTON, ALFRED GRANT. First Impressions.
Recipe for Living.
Sincere Man, The.
World We Make, The.
WALTON, EDA LOU. Leda, the Lost.
WALTON, GEORGE LINCOLN. Erasistratus Forbear, *sel.*
WALTON, IZAAK. Angler's Wish, The. *Fr.* The Compleat Angler.
Compleat Angler, The, *sel.*
WALTON, MILLY. Dog's Life, A.
WANDREI, DONALD. Sonnets of the Midnight Hours.
WANG AN SHIH. Evening at Chung Shan.
Greetings!
Night in Spring, A.
Plum Tree, The.
WANG CHANG-LING. Under the Frontier Post.
WANG CHI. On Going to a Tavern.
Success.
Tell Me Now.
What Should a Man Want?
White Frost, The.
WANG CHIEN. Hearing that His Friend Was Coming Back from the War.
South, The.
Visit, A.
WANG CHIH HUAN. Grand Canal, The.
WANG CHIN CHU. Doubt.
WANG CHI-WEN. Going beyond the Jade Gate Pass.
WANG HAN. Song of Liangchow, The.
WANG I. Autumn Moon.
Lychee, The.
WANG JUNG. Since You Are Gone.
Song of the Four Colors.
WANG MOU FANG. Flute, The.
Hostess, The.
WANG SHIH CHENG. Autumn Sunset.
WANG T'AI CH'ING. Song of Mo Shang Sang, A.
WANG TS'ANG-LING. Recruiting Song.
Young Wife, The.
WANG WEI. After Long Rain.
Answering Vice-Prefect Chang.
Beautiful Hsi-shih, The.
Beside the Lake.
Cold Mountain, The.
Departure.
Desolation.
In a Bamboo Grove.
In the Hills.
Meditation.
Morning.
My Lodge at Wang-ch'uan after a Long Rain.
My Retreat at Mount Chung-nan.
Nature and Man.
News from Home?
No News.
On Going Away.
On Passing a Friend's House.
Parting, A.
"So Farewell."
Song for Wei City, A.
Thinking of My Brother in Shantung on the Ninth Day of the Ninth Moon.
To Chi Wu Ch'ien Bound Home after Failing in an Examination.
Verses: "You who come from the old village."
Walking at Leisure.
WANLEY, NATHANIEL. Casket, The.
Fall, The.
Human [*or* Humaine] Cares.
Invitation, The.
Resurrection, The.
Royal [*or* Royall] Presents.
Royal Presents, *sel.*
Sigh, The.
WAN TSE. Jewel, The.
WAN YÜAN CHANG. Faith.
"WARD, ARTEMUS" (Charles Farrar Browne). Uncle Simon and Uncle Jim.
WARD, C. C. Onion, The.
WARD, EDWARD. Ballad on the Taxes, A.
Hudibras Redivivus, *sel.*
In a London Street. *Fr.* Hudibras Redivivus.
WARD, ELIZABETH STUART PHELPS. Afterward.
Conemaugh.
Eternal Christmas.
Generous Creed, A.
Gloucester Harbor.
Little Mud-Sparrows, The; Jewish Legend.
Lost Colors, The.
Message, A.
Prayer at the Close of a Marred Day.
Room's Width, The.

WARD, JEAN. Autumn Healing.
WARD, KENNETH. Investor's Soliloquy.
WARD, LEO. Four Friends.
Last Communion, The.
WARD, LEO L. Marginalia for Pentecost.
WARD, LYDIA AVERY COONLEY. Baby Corn.
Flag Song.
Heredity.
Song for Flag Day, A.
To-Day.
WARD, MARION. I Love to Love.
WARD, MAY WILLIAMS. My House.
Wet Summer.
WARD, SAMUEL. Proem, A: "When in my walks I meet some ruddy lad."
WARD, TERENCE. Kevin Barry.
WARD, WILLIAM HAYES. New Castalia, The.
To John Greenleaf Whittier.
WARDLAW, MARY HOGE. Easter.
WARE, EUGENE FITCH ("Ironquill").
Aztec City, The.
He and She.
Jackpot, The.
John Brown.
Manila.
Violet Star, The.
Whist.
WARE, MARY. Song of Our Glorious Southland.
WARFIELD, CATHERINE ANNE. Beauregard.
Manassas.
WARING, ANNA LAETITIA. In Heavenly Love Abiding.
My Times Are in Thy Hand.
WARING, H. C. Quite the Cheese.
WARLOW, HALLE W. Dawn in the Everglades.
WARMAN, CY. Creede.
Doing Railroads for *The Rocky Mountain News.*
Memorial Day.
Old Red Hoss Mountain.
Rise and Fall of Creede, The.
Sweet Marie.
WARNER, ANNA BARTLETT ("Amy Lothrop"). Daffy-down-dilly.
Jesus loves me, this I know.
Let Us See Jesus.
WARNER, C. E. Inn by the Road, The.
WARNER, CHARLES DUDLEY. Bookra.
WARNER, EVA. Irony of God.
WARNER, L. G. Friends.
WARNER, REX. Argonautica, *tr.*
Lapwing.
Mallard.
Sonnet: "How sweet only to delight in lambs."
Sonnet: "Understanding of a medical man, The."
WARNER, SYLVIA TOWNSEND. Absence, The.
After He Had Gone.
Alarum, The.
Building in Stone.
Country Thought.
Elizabeth.
Epitaph: "After long thirty years re-met."
Epitaph: "Her grieving parents cradled here."
Epitaph: "I, an unwedded wandering dame."
Epitaph: "I, Richard Kent, beneath these stones."
Epitaph: "John Bird, a laborer, lies here."
Green Valley, The.
Image, The.
Killing No Murder.
Maid's Tragedy, The.
Modo and Alciphron.
Nelly Trim.
Rival, The.
Sad Green.
Sailor, The.
Song: "She has left me, my pretty."
Song from the Bride of Smithfield.
Triumph of Sensibility.
Tudor Church Music.
Willow.
WARNER, WILLIAM. Albion's England, *sels.*
Armada, The, *at.*
Defeat of the Spanish Armada, The, *at.*
Fate of Narcissus, The. *Fr.* Albion's England.
My Mistress.
Spanish Armado, The, *at.*
WARR, BERTRAM J. Death of an Elephant.
Deviator, The.
End of the World, The.
Heart to Carry On, The.
Murder, The.
On a Child with a Wooden Leg.
Poets in Time of War.
There Are Children in the Dusk.
Trees, Who Are Distant.
War Widow.
Winter Stalks.
Working Class.
WARREN, EDGAR L. Schemer, A.
WARREN, GEORGE F. Lord Guy.
WARREN, GRETCHEN O. Peace.
WARREN, HAMILTON. Requiem: "Let the mountains stand forth!"
WARREN, JAMES EDWARD, JR. Beneath Such Rains.
Schoolroom: 158.
WARREN, JOHN BYRNE LEICESTER, BARON DE TABLEY. *See* DE TABLEY, JOHN BYRNE LEICESTER WARREN, BARON.
WARREN, JOSEPH. Free America, *at.*
WARREN, MERCY. Lines Written after a Very Severe Tempest Which Cleared Up Extremely Pleasant.
Massachusetts Song of Liberty.
Squabble of the Sea Nymphs, The, or the Sacrifice of the Tuscararoes.
WARREN, ROBERT PENN. Aubade for Hope.
Ballad of Billie Potts, The.
Bearded Oaks.
Cardinal, The. *Fr.* Kentucky Mountain Farm.
Crime.
Croesus in Autumn.
Eidolon.
End of Season.
For a Friend Who Thinks Himself Urbane.
Grandfather Gabriel.
History among the Rocks. *Fr.* Kentucky Mountain Farm.
Kentucky Mountain Farm.
Kentucky Mountain Farm, *sels.*
Letter from a Coward to a Hero.
Letter of a Mother.
Letter to a Friend.
Mexico Is a Foreign Country, *sels.*
Monologue at Midnight.
Original Sin; a Short Story.
Owl, The.
Pondy Woods.
Pro Sua Vita.
Pursuit.
Revelation.
Small Soldiers with Drum in Large Landscape. *Fr.* Mexico Is a Foreign Country.
Terror.
To a Little Girl, One Year Old, in a Ruined Fortress.
To a Little Girl, One Year Old, in a Ruined Fortress, *sel.*
Variation: Ode to Fear.
World Comes Galloping, The; a True Story. *Fr.* Mexico Is a Foreign Country.
Wrestling Match, The.
WARREN, SIR THOMAS HERBERT. Lines for a Sundial.
May-Day on Magdalen Tower.
WARTON, JOSEPH. Charms of Nature, The. *Fr.* The Enthusiast; or, The Lover of Nature.
Enthusiast, The; or, The Lover of Nature.
Enthusiast, The; or, The Lover of Nature, *sels.*
Epistle from Thomas Hearn, Antiquary, An.
Invocation to Fancy. *Fr.* Ode to Fancy.
Ode to Evening.
Ode to Fancy.
Ode to Fancy, *sel.*
WARTON, THOMAS, THE ELDER. American Love-Ode, An.
Retirement, an Ode, *sel.*
Runic Ode, A.
WARTON, THOMAS, THE YOUNGER. Crusade, The.
Goodbye to Mr. Pope. *Fr.* The Pleasures of Melancholy.
Grave of King Arthur, The.
Inscription in a Hermitage.
Ode: Solitude, at an Inn.
Ode to a Friend on His Leaving a Favourite Village in Hampshire, *sel.*
Ode Written at Vale-Royal Abbey in Cheshire.
On Bathing.
On the Approach of Summer, *sel.*
Pleasures of Melancholy, The.
Pleasures of Melancholy, The, *sels.*
Retirement.
Solemn Noon of Night, The. *Fr.* The Pleasures of Melancholy.
Sonnet: On King Arthur's Round Table at Winchester. *Fr.* Sonnets.
Sonnet: To the River Lodon [*or* Loddon]. *Fr.* Sonnets.
Sonnet: Written after Seeing Wilton-House.
Sonnet: Written at Stonehenge. *Fr.* Sonnets.
Sonnet: Written in a Blank Leaf of Dugdale's Monasticon. *Fr.* Sonnets.
Sonnet to the River Lodon. *Fr.* Sonnets.
Sonnets, *sels.*
Sunshine after a Shower. *Fr.* On the Approach of Summer.
To Mr. Gray.
To the River Lodon. *Fr.* Sonnets.
Verses on Sir Joshua Reynolds's Painted Window at New-College, Oxford.
Wet Morning, The. *Fr.* The Pleasures of Melancholy.
Written in a Blank Leaf of Dugdale's "Monasticon." *Fr.* Sonnets.
WASHBOURNE, THOMAS. Casting All Your Care upon God, for He Careth for You.
God's Two Dwellings, *sel.*
Humility. *Fr.* God's Two Dwellings.
Prayer: "What a commanding power."
Upon a Passing Bell.
WASHBURN, CHARLES CAMPBELL. In the Meadow.
WASHBURN, HENRY STEVENSON. Song of the Harvest.
Vacant Chair, The.
WASON, HARRIET L. Slide at the Empire Mine, The.
WASSALL, IRMA. Singing in the Dark.
Stone from the Gods.
WASSE, WALTER. Hunting of the Gods, The.
WASSON, DAVID ATWOOD. All's Well.
Joy-Month.
Love against Love.
WASTELL, SIMON. Man's Mortality. *Fr.* Microbiblion.
Microbiblion, *sel.*
Of Man's Mortalitie. *Fr.* Microbiblion.
WATERHOUSE, GILBERT. This Is the Last.
WATERMAN, NIXON. Far from the Madding Crowd.
I Got to Go to School.
If I Knew You and You Knew Me.
If We Didn't Have to Eat.
If We Didn't Have to Eat, *sel.*
Johnny's Hist'ry Lesson.
Making a Man.
Recompense.
Rose to the Living, A.
Second Table, The.
Tame Animals I Have Known.
"To Know All Is to Forgive All."
Today.
Two Towns.

Understanding.
Vacation.
What Have We Done Today?
When the Train Comes In.
WATERSTON, ROBERT CASSIE. Jesus Is Near.
WATKINS, LUCIAN B. Star of Ethiopia.
To Our Friends.
Two Points of View.
WATKINS, VERNON. Ballad of the Equinox.
Cave-Drawing, The.
Christening Remembered, A.
Collier, The.
Dead Words, The.
Discoveries.
Feather, The.
Fire in the Snow, The.
First Joy.
Foal.
From My Loitering.
Gravestones.
Healing of the Leper, The.
Heron, The.
Indolence.
Infant Noah.
Lady with the Unicorn, The.
Llewelyn's Chariot.
Mother and Child, The.
Mummy, The.
Music of Colours: The Blossom Scattered.
Music of Colours—White Blossom.
Ophelia.
Peace in the Welsh Hills.
Returning to Goleufryn.
Shooting of Werfel, The.
Song of the Good Samaritan, The.
Spoils of War, The.
Sunbather, The.
Sycamore.
Turning of the Leaves, The.
Yeats' Tower.
Yew-Tree, The.
Zacchaeus in the Leaves.
For translations from French, see AnFP; LiTW.
For translations from German, see AnGP; LiTW.
WATKYNS, ROWLAND. Wedding Garment, The.
WATSON, ALBERT DURRANT. Beauty Everywhere.
Breeze and Billow.
Colonial Song, A.
Crow, The.
Galileo.
God and Man.
Hymn for Canada, A.
Kepler.
Listen.
One Consciousness.
Priest and Pagan.
Song of the Storm.
Soul Lifted.
Twenty.
Under the Open Sky.
WATSON, EDWARD WILLARD. Absolution.
Hades of Science, The.
WATSON, FLORA WILLIS. Calendar Rhyme.
WATSON, JAMES WREFORD ("James Wreford"). Early Willows.
Gatineaus, The.
Heads and Tails of Love, The.
Kirkland Lake.
Our Love Shall Be the Brightness.
Riding the Rims.
Sic Transit Gloria Mundi.
Stay, Time.
Warm Front and the Cold, The.
We Shall Have Far to Go.
Wild Willow.
Winter Weather.
WATSON, JOHN WHITTAKER. Beautiful Snow, The.
Wounded to Death.
WATSON, MINOR. Constancy.
WATSON, ROSAMUND MARRIOTT ("Graham R. Tomson"; "R. Armytage").
Arsinoë's Cats.
Ave atque Vale.
Deid Folks' Ferry.
Farm on the Links, The.
Finis.
Hereafter.
Last Fairy, The.
Le Mauvais Larron.
Les Roses Mortes.
Omnia Somnia.
Optimist, The.
Requiescat.
South Coast Idyll, A.
To My Cat.
WATSON, THOMAS. Come, Gentle Death! *Fr.* Hecatompathia.
Ditty of the Six Virgins' Song, The. *Fr.* The Honourable Entertainment Given to the Queen's Majesty in Progress at Elvetham, 1591.
Hecatompathia, *sels.*
Here Lieth Love. *Fr.* Hecatompathia.
Honourable Entertainment Given to the Queen's Majesty in Progress at Elvetham, 1591, The, *sel.*
I curse the time, wherein these lips of mine.
If Cupid Were a Child. *Fr.* Hecatompathia.
Love's Grave. *Fr.* Hecatompathia.
Marigold so likes the lovely sun, The.
My Love Is Past. *Fr.* Hecatompathia.
Passion: "If Jove himself be subject unto love." *Fr.* Hecatompathia.
Questo di Verde.
Some That Report. *Fr.* Hecatompathia.
Sonnet: "I saw the object of my pining thought." *Fr.* The Tears of Fancy.
Speak, gentle heart, where is thy dwelling place?
Tears of Fancy, The, *sels.*
Time. *Fr.* Hecatompathia.
Vezzosi Augelli.
With Fragrant Flowers We Strew the Way. *Fr.* The Honourable Entertainment Given to the Queen's Majesty in Progress at Elvetham, 1591.
WATSON, WILFRED. Canticle of Darkness, *sel.*
Contempt for Dylan Thomas, A.
In the Cemetery of the Sun.
Juniper Tree, The.
O My Poor Darling.
WATSON, SIR WILLIAM. After Reading "Tamburlaine the Great."
April, April.
At a Burial.
Autumn.
Ballad of Semmerwater, The.
Beasts in field are glad, and have not wit, The.
Byron the Voluptuary.
Church Today, The.
Criticism.
Dawn on the Headland.
Domine, Quo Vadis?
Dürer's "Melancholia."
England My Mother.
Epigram: "Captains and conquerors leave a little dust."
Epigram: "Children romp within the graveyard's pale, The."
Epigram: "Love, like a bird, hath perch'd upon a spray."
Epigram: "Momentous to himself as I to me."
Epigram: "Poet gathers fruit from every tree, The."
Epigram: "Statue, The—Buonarroti said—doth wait."
Epigram: "When whelmed are altar, priest, and creed."
Estrangement.
Eternal Search, The.
Exit: "In mid whirl of the dance of Time ye start."
Faithless and the Constant, The.
First Skylark of Spring, The.
For metaphors of man we search the skies.
God-seeking.
Great Misgiving, The.
Heaven and Hell.
His friends he loved. His direst earthly foes.
History.
Hope of the World, The.
Hymn to the Sea.
Inscription: "Sea-fowls build in wrinkles on my face, The."
Invention.
Key-Board, The.
Lacrimae Musarum.
Leavetaking.
Love. *Fr.* Two Epigrams.
Mighty Denier, The.
Nightmare (Written during Apparent Imminence of War).
Ode in May.
On Dürer's "Melencolia."
Play of "King Lear," The.
Playmates, The.
Poet, The. *Fr.* Two Epigrams.
Prince's Quest, The, *sel.*
Sculpture and Song.
Shakespeare.
Shelley and Harriet Westbrook.
Shelley's Centenary.
So, without overt breach, we fall apart.
Song: "April, April,/ Laugh thy girlish laughter."
Song: "O, like a queen's her happy tread."
Song in Imitation of the Elizabethans.
Song to April.
Song's Apostasy.
Sonnet: "If I had never known your face at all." *Fr.* Sonnets to Miranda.
Sonnets to Miranda, *sels.*
Sovereign Poet, The.
"Things That Are More Excellent, The."
Think not thy wisdom can illume away.
Thomas Hood.
To a Foolish Wise Man.
To a Friend.
To a Seabird.
To Christina Rossetti.
To the Sultan.
Trial of Orthodoxy, A.
Turk in Armenia, The.
Two Epigrams.
Unknown God, The.
Visitor Abhorred, The.
Vita Nuova.
Woman with the Serpent's Tongue, The.
Wordsworth's Grave.
World in Armor, The.
World-Strangeness.
WATT, FREDERICK B. Inspection, The.
WATT, LAUCHLAN MACLEAN. I Bind My Heart.
In the Way of Peace.
Long Last Mile, The.
Reapers, The.
Tryst, The.
WATT, T. S. From My Rural Pen.
WATT, W. W. Summer Song.
WATTLES, WILLARD AUSTIN. Acceptance.
Builder, The.
Comrades of the Cross.
Courage, Mon Ami!
Creeds.
Devil Is Dying, The.
Discovery of No Importance, A.
Family of Nations, The.
From the Parthenon I Learn.
Gabriel.
Hrolf's Thrall, His Song.
Hugh, the Carter, Tarries.
I Thought Joy Went by Me.
Jericho.
Page from America's Psalter, A.
Pisgah.
Thy Kingdom Come!
War at Home, The.
WATTS, ALARIC ALEXANDER. Alliteration; or, The Siege of Belgrade, *at.*
Austrian Army, An, *at.*
Siege of Belgrade, The, *at.*
WATTS, ISAAC. Accept Our Tribute.
Against Idleness and Mischief.
Against Idleness and Mischief, *sel.*
Against Quarrelling and Fighting.
Alas! and did my Saviour bleed.

WATTS, ISAAC (*continued*)
Am I a soldier of the cross.
Bee, The.
Begin, my tongue, some heavenly theme.
Busy Bee, The.
Christ hath a garden walled around.
Christ Is the Substance of the Levitical Priesthood.
Come, Holy Spirit, heavenly Dove.
Come, we who love the Lord.
Comparison and Complaint, The.
Cradle Hymn, A.
Cradle Hymn, A, *sels.*
Cross, The.
Crucifixion to the World, by the Cross of Christ. *Fr.* When I Survey the Wond'rous Cross.
Day of Judgement [*or* Judgment], The.
Dead, The. *Fr.* The Death and Burial of a Saint.
Death and Burial of a Saint, The, *sel.*
Eternal, The.
Evening Prayer, An.
Felicity.
Flying Fowl and Creeping Things, Praise Ye the Lord, *sel.*
God's Dominion and Decrees.
Hazard of Loving the Creatures, The.
Heaven.
Horace Paraphrased.
How Doth the Little Busy Bee.
Hush, My Dear, Lie Still and Slumber.
Hymn: "Our God, our help in ages past."
Incomprehensible, The.
Inscriptions on Dials, *sel.*
Insignificant Existence.
Jesus Shall Reign Where'er the Sun.
Joy to the World! The Lord Is Come.
King Triumphant.
Let Dogs Delight to Bark and Bite.
Little Busy Bee.
Love between Brothers and Sisters.
Man Frail and God Eternal.
Meditation in a Grove.
My dear Redeemer and my Lord.
Our God, Our Help in Ages Past.
Prospect of Heaven Makes Death Easy.
Quarrelling.
Recessional.
Seeking the Pastures of Christ the Shepherd.
Serpents. *Fr.* Flying Fowl and Creeping Things, Praise Ye the Lord.
Shepherds Rejoice.
Shortness of Life, and the Goodness of God, The.
Sincere Praise.
Sincere Praise, *sel.*
Sluggard, The.
Summer Evening, A.
Sweet Muse.
There is a land of pure delight.
Thus Steal the Silent Hours Away. *Fr.* Inscriptions on Dials.
True Greatness.
True Riches.
Universal Hallelujah, The, *sel.*
When I Survey the Wondrous Cross.
When I Survey the Wondrous Cross, *sel.*
Where-e'er My Flatt'ring Passions Rove.
With songs and honors sounding loud.
WATTS, MARJORIE SEYMOUR. New Shoes.
Parade, The.
Policeman, The.
WATTS-DUNTON, THEODORE. Breath of Avon, The.
Coleridge.
Coming of Love, The, *sels.*
First Kiss, The.
John the Pilgrim.
Mother Carey's Chicken.
Natura Maligna.
Ode to Mother Carey's Chicken.
Sonnet's Voice, The.
Toast to Omar Khayyám.
Wassail Chorus at the Mermaid Tavern.
WAUGH, EDWIN. Dule's i' This Bonnet o' Mine, The.
Owd Pinder.
Sweetheart Gate, Th'.
WAVELL, ARCHIBALD PERCIVAL WAVELL, 1ST EARL. Sonnet for the Madonna of the Cherries.
WAXMAN, PERCY. Mother.
WAY, ARTHUR SANDERS. *For translations from Greek, see* GrL; GrPo; GrR; WoL.
WAYLAND, JOHN ELTON ("Idas"). Epilogue at Wallack's, An.
WAYNE, ROBERT. From Inward Shining.
WEARE, MESHECH. Blasted Herb, The.
WEARING, THOMAS. New Year.
WEATHERLY, FREDERIC EDWARD. Bell's Dream.
Bird in the Hand, A.
Carol, A: "Angels to the shepherds sang, The."
Cats' Tea-Party, The.
Cherries.
Darby and Joan.
Door at the End of Our Garden, The.
Douglas Gordon.
Dustman, The.
Gray Dove's Answer, The.
Holy City, The.
Limerick: "My name's Mister Benjamin Bunny."
Lobster and the Maid, The.
London Bridge.
London River.
My Garden.
Nancy Lee.
"Peg Away."
Song of the Wood, The.
Tale of a Tart, The.
Thursday.
Usual Way, The.
When the Christ Child Came.
WEAVER, BENNETT. To Mother—in Heaven.
WEAVER, JOHN VAN ALSTYN. Drugstore.
Ghost.
Legend.
My Son Stands Alone.
Nocturne: " 'Nothin' or everythin' it's got to be.' "
Old.
To My Son.
To Youth.
Two Ways.
WEAVER, ROBERT. *See* WEVER, R.
WEAVER, T. B. Boy with the Hoe, The.
WEAVING, WILLOUGHBY. Star, The.
WEBB, CHARLES DAVID. And Dust to Dust.
Jardin des Fleurs.
Monasteries.
Orestes Pursued.
Threshold.
WEBB, CHARLES HENRY ("John Paul").
Dictum Sapienti.
Dum Vivimus Vigilamus.
Gil, the Toreador.
King and the Pope, The.
Little Mamma.
Lost Word, The.
March.
What She Said about It.
With a Nantucket Shell.
WEBB, FRANCIS. Captain of the Oberon, The. *Fr.* A Drum for Ben Boyd.
Cartier at St. Malo. *Fr.* A View of Montreal.
Drum for Ben Boyd.
Drum for Ben Boyd, A, *sel.*
For My Grandfather.
Gunner, The.
Laid Off.
Morgan's Country.
Pioneer of Monaro, A.
View of Montreal, A, *sel.*
WEBB, FREDERICK G. Dash for the Colors, The.
WEBB, MARION ST. JOHN. Nugly Little Man, The.
Sunset Garden, The.
WEBB, MARY. Anne's Book.
Bounty.
Colomen.
Fallen Poplar, The.
Foxgloves.
Green Rain.
Hazel Buds.
Land Within, The.
Market Day.
Secret Joy, The.
Shell, The.
Water-Ousel, The.
Why?
WEBB, PHYLLIS. Sprouts the Bitter Grain.
WEBB, TEDDY. Apology to a Small Dog.
WEBB, TESSA SWEAZY. Bright Abandon.
Love's Unveiling.
WEBB, THOMAS HARRY BASIL. Ancient Prayer, An.
Prayer, A: "Give me a good digestion, Lord."
WEBB, WINIFRED. Heartening, The.
WEBBE, CHARLES. Against Indifference.
More Love or More Disdain.
Sweet, Be No Longer Sad.
WEBER, HELEN. Lessons.
WEBSTER, AUGUSTA DAVIES ("Cecil Home"). Day Is Dead.
Deaths of Myron and Klydone, The. *Fr.* In a Day.
In a Day, *sel.*
Message of Victory, The.
News to the King.
Pine, The.
Seeds.
Tell Me Not of Morrows, Sweet.
'Tween Earth and Sky.
Violet and the Rose, The.
WEBSTER, DANIEL. Immortal Craftsmen.
Memory of the Heart, The.
On the Death of My Son Charles.
WEBSTER, JOHN. All Is Vanity. *Fr.* The Devil's Law Case.
All the Flowers of the Spring. *Fr.* The Devil's Law Case.
Burial, The. *Fr.* The Devil's Law Case.
Call for the Robin Redbreast [and the Wren]. *Fr.* The White Devil.
Cornelia's Song. *Fr.* The White Devil.
Devil's Law Case, The, *sels.*
Dirge, A: "Call for the robin redbreast and the wren." *Fr.* The White Devil.
Dirge: "Hark, now everything is still." *Fr.* The Duchess of Malfi.
Duchess of Malfi, The, *sels.*
Funeral Dirge for Marcello. *Fr.* The White Devil.
General Mist of Error, A. *Fr.* The Duchess of Malfi.
Hark, now everything is still. *Fr.* The Duchess of Malfi.
Heart-Cry of the Duchess, The. *Fr.* The Duchess of Malfi.
Land Dirge, A. *Fr.* The White Devil.
Madman's Song, The. *Fr.* The Duchess of Malfi.
Nets to Catch the Wind. *Fr.* The Devil's Law Case.
Oh, Let Us Howl Some Heavy Note. *Fr.* The Duchess of Malfi.
Shrouding of the Duchess of Malfi, The. *Fr.* The Duchess of Malfi.
So have I seen a silver swan, *at.*
Song: "All the flowers of the spring." *Fr.* The Devil's Law Case.
Song: "Call for the Robin-redbreast and the wren." *Fr.* The White Devil.
Summons to Execution. *Fr.* The Duchess of Malfi.
Survey our progress from our birth.
Vanitas Vanitatum. *Fr.* The Devil's Law Case.
Vanitas Vanitatum, *sel.* *Fr.* The Devil's Law Case.
White Devil [*or* Divel], The, *sels.*
WEBSTER, LOUISE. Tombs.

WEBSTER, MRS. M. M. Marriage of Pocahontas, The.
WEBSTER, WINIFRED FRY. Virtuous Clam, The.
WEDDERBURN, JAMES, JOHN WEDDERBURN, *and* ROBERT WEDDERBURN. Balulalow.
Cradle Song: "Oh my deir hert, young Jesus sweit."
Nativity Carol.
WEDDERBURN, JOHN. Ane Sang of the Birth of Christ, with the Tune of Baw Lula Low.
In Dulci Jubilo [*or* Iubilo].
Now Let Us Sing with Joy and Mirth.
WEDGEFARTH, W. DAYTON. Bum.
Mother in gladness, Mother in sorrow.
Mother's Hands.
WEEDEN, HOWARD. Banjo of the Past, The.
Borrowed Child, The.
WEEDEN, LULA LOWE. Dance.
Have You Seen It.
Little Dandelion, The.
Me Alone.
Robin Red Breast.
Stream, The.
WEEDEN, MARY (Mary Weeden Stiver).
Steep Slopes of Morning, The.
WEEKES, CHARLES. In Brittany.
Poppies.
Solstice.
That.
Think.
WEEKS, NAN F. Our Thanks.
WEEKS, ROBERT KELLEY. In May.
Man and Nature.
Medusa.
Moral, The.
Song for Lexington, A.
Undersong.
WEEVER, JOHN. Ad Gulielmum Shakespeare.
Ad Gulielmum Warner.
Ad Jo. Marston & Ben. Jonson.
Ad Lectorem.
Ad Michaelem Drayton.
Ad Samuelem Daniel.
De Se.
In Ed. Allen.
In Nigellum.
In Obitum Ed. Spenser Poetae Prestaniss.
In Rudionem.
In Tumulum Abrahami Simple.
In Tumulum Avari.
Translat. ex Martial.
WEEVER, ROBERT. *See* WEVER, R.
WEI CHUANG. Nanking.
Spring Sorrow.
WEIL, JAMES L. At a Loss.
WEIN, JULES ALAN. Genesis.
WEINHEBER, JOSEF. Unknown Woman.
WEIR, ARTHUR. Christmas Lullaby, A.
Snowshoeing Song.
WEIR, HARRISON. English Robin, The.
WEISMILLER, EDWARD. Burial.
Deer Come Down, The, *sels.*
Epitaph: "It seemed that he would rather hear."
To the Woman in Bond Street Station.
Trail, The.
Winter Breath.
World, Defined.
WEISS, MICHAEL. Resurrection Hymn.
WEISS, THEODORE. Barracks Apt. 14.
Greater Music, The.
WEISSMANN, MARIA LOUISE. Robinson, *sel.*
Robinson Finds Friday. *Fr.* Robinson.
WEIST, CARL S. Cross on a Hill, A.
Crucifixion.
Symbol of Hope.
WEI TING. On Hearing a Blackbird at Ch'ang An.
WEI WEN-TI. Campaign against Wu, The.
On the Death of His Father.
WEI YING-WU. Cuckoo Sings, The.
Riding to Tsan Shih.
To His Brother.
WELBY, AMELIA B. COPPUCK. Old Maid, The.
Twilight at Sea.
WELCH, LEW. After Anacreon.
Chicago Poem.
WELCH, MARIE DE L. Chipmunk.
Harvests.
Lord of Eden.
Saint Francis and the Cloud.
WELCH, MYRA BROOKS. Greater Glory, The.
Touch of the Master's Hand, The.
WELCH, SARAH. Digger's Grave, The.
WELCOME, L. O. Phantom Mail Coach, The.
WELDON, CHARLES. Poem of the Universe, The.
WELHAVEN, JOHAN SEBASTIAN CAMMERMEYER. Afternoon on the Water.
Bird-Notes.
Cup Reversed, The.
Ganymede.
Like an April Day.
Lotus, The.
My Saint.
Night Thoughts, *sel.*
Nixie, The.
Norway's Highlands.
Singer's Prayer, A.
Soul of Poetry, The.
WELLES, WINIFRED. Actual Willow.
Angel in the Apple Tree, The.
Aunt Eliza's Slow Ear.
Behind the Waterfall.
Boy.
Child's Song to Her Mother, A.
Climb.
Cobweb.
Cruciform.
Curious Something.
Dog Who Ate a Pond Lily, A.
Dogs and Weather.
From a Chinese Vase.
Gesture.
"God's First Creature Was Light."
Golden Outline.
Green Grass and White Milk.
Green Moth.
Harvest Dust.
Heart of Light, The.
Hesitant Heart, The.
Indian Pipes.
Language.
Last Night of Winter, The.
Lifetime.
Love Song from New England.
Lucky Snail, The.
Man with a Little Pleated Piano, A.
Merciful Medusa.
Nosegay for a Young Goat.
Old Ellen Sullivan.
One Voice.
River Skater.
School.
Second Growth.
Silence.
Skipping Along Alone.
Starfish.
Stocking Fairy.
Three Lovely Holes.
Tree at Dusk, A.
Trinket.
Twanging Gold.
White Fear.
Winter Apples.
WELLESLEY, DOROTHY, DUCHESS OF WELLINGTON. As Lambs into the Pen.
Asian Desert.
Buried Child, The.
Deserted House, *sel.*
Docks.
Fire.
Fishing.
Horses.
I Think Myself to Be Alive.
In Memory of Rex Whistler.
Late Love.
Lenin, *sel.*
Matrix, *sel.*
Morning After, The.
Traffic Problem in East Anglia, The.
WELLESLEY, HENRY. Demophilus, *after* Nicarchus.
WELLINGTON, ALICE. *See* ROLLINS, ALICE WELLINGTON.
WELLINGTON, DOROTHY WELLESLEY, DUCHESS OF. *See* WELLESLEY, DOROTHY.
WELLS, AMOS RUSSEL. Glorious Name, The.
Inn That Missed Its Chance, The.
Mothers—and Others.
People's Prayer, The.
Pray!
Pray for Me.
Prayer for the President.
Prayer Meeting, The.
Thanksgiving for Thanksgiving.
WELLS, ANNA MARIA. Cow-Boy's Song, The.
WELLS, CAROLYN. Abbie Ben Adams.
All Hallow Eve.
Alone.
Arch Armadillo, The.
Baby's Omar, The.
Ballade of a Conspicuous Omission from "The Book of Humorous Verse."
Ballade of Old Loves, A.
Canner, Exceedingly Canny, A.
Cupid's Failure.
Diversions of the Re-Echo Club.
Dresscessional, A.
Grandiloquent Goat, The.
Happy Hyena, The.
How to Tell [*or* Know] the Wild Animals.
Limerick: "Canner, exceedingly canny, A."
Limerick: "Miss Minnie McFinney of Butte," *at.*
Limerick: "Said a bad little youngster named Beauchamp," *at.*
Limerick: "There once was a happy hyena."
Limerick: "There once was an arch armadillo."
Limerick: "There was a young fellow named Tate," *at.*
Limerick: "Tutor who tooted a flute, A."
Non-returnable.
One Week.
Overworded Elocutionist, An.
Oyster-Crabs.
Penitential Week, A.
Poets at a House-Party, The.
Policy.
Possibility, A.
Poster Girl, The.
Pussy-Cat Who Visited the Queen, The.
Serious Question, A.
Styx River Anthology.
Thanksgiving, A.
To a Baked Fish.
To a Poet.
Travelogue, A; Clovelly.
Tutor, The.
Tutor Who Tooted the [*or* a] Flute, A.
Universal Favorite, The.
Whist-Player's Soliloquy, The.
Young America.
WELLS, CHARLES JEREMIAH. Envy.
Joseph and His Brethren, *sels.*
Patriarchal Home, The. *Fr.* Joseph and His Brethren.
Phraxanor to Joseph. *Fr.* Joseph and His Brethren.
Rachel. *Fr.* Joseph and His Brethren.
Triumph of Joseph, The. *Fr.* Joseph and His Brethren.
WELLS, ELEANOR. For the Undefeated.
WELLS, FAITH. More than We Ask.
WELLS, ROLLIN J. As We Grow Older.
Growing Old[er].
WELSH, ANNE. Body's Eye, The.
Sight.
Victoria Dancing.
WELSH, ROBERT GILBERT. Azrael.
WELSH, W. K. Name for My Love, A.
WELSHIMER, HELEN. Dusk.
Light.
On Parting with Spot.
Prayer for a Bride.
Pretense.
Worship.

WELSTED, LEONARD. Epigram: "I owe," says Metius, much to Colon's care."
WENCESLAS, KING OF BOHEMIA. Proffered Rose, The.
WENDELL, W. G. Inscription in a Library.
WEN I-TO. *See* WEN YI-TUO.
WENNERBERG, GUNNAR. Hymn: "O God, Who guid'st the fate of nations."
WEN T'ING-YUN. Beyond the Tower.
She Sighs on Her Jade Lute.
WENTWORTH, WILLIAM CHARLES. Australasia, *sel.*
WEN YI-TUO [*or* WEN I-TO]. Confession, The.
Dead Water, The.
Desk, The.
Early Summer Night.
God of Love, The.
WERFEL, FRANZ. Eternal Road, The, *sel.*
Exaltation.
For I Have Done a Good and Kindly Deed.
I Am a Grown Man.
Indolent Heart.
Kiss, The.
Litany of the Rooms of the Dead.
Loneliness.
Song of Life, A.
Spiritual Song, A.
Strangers Are We All upon the Earth.
Teach Us to Mark This, God.
To a Lark in War-Time.
Ye Sorrowers. *Fr.* The Eternal Road.
WERGELAND, HENRIK. At Bjerregaard's Grave.
First Butterfly, The.
Flower, The.
Freedom of the Press, The.
Jewess, The, *sel.*
Last Voyage, The.
Morning Worship.
My Wife's Return.
Sunset Clouds.
To My Gillyflower.
To Spring.
Wall-Flower, The.
With a Nosegay.
WERLEIGH, CHRISTIAN. Poet of Farewell.
WERNER, ALICE. Bannerman of the Dandenong.
Song of Fleet Street, A.
WERTHEIMER, PAUL. Souls.
WESCOTT, GLENWAY. I, in My Pitiful Flesh.
Poet at Night-Fall, The.
These Are the Subtle Rhythms.
Without Sleep.
WESLEY, CECIL COBB. As Night Comes On.
WESLEY, CHARLES. Bid Me Sin No More.
Break My Heart of Stone.
Charge to Keep I Have, A.
Christ, the Good Physician.
Christ the Lord Is Risen Today.
Christ, Whose Glory Fills the Skies.
Christmas Day.
Claiming the Promise.
Come, Lord Jesus.
Come, O Thou Traveller Unknown.
Conquering Love of Jesus, The.
Covenant of His Grace, The.
Cup of Blessing, The.
Dedication: "Lord, in the strength of grace."
Divine Love.
Divine Lover, The.
Draw Me, Saviour, after Thee.
Draw Near, O Son of God.
Dying That I Might Live.
Easter Day.
Easter Hymn.
Father, How Wide Thy Glories Shine.
Fly Back to Christ.
Fly to Jesus.
For Christmas-Day.
For Easter-Day.
For One Retired into the Country.
For Perfect Peace.
For the Peace of Jerusalem.
Gentle Jesus [Meek and Mild].
Graven on the Palms of His Hands.
Great Shepherd of the Sheep.
Hark! the Herald Angels Sing.
Hymn: "O Thou who camest from above."
I know that my Redeemer lives.
In Temptation.
Jesus [*or* Jesu], Lover of My Soul.
Jesus the Name Most High.
Jesus, the Soul of Our Joys.
Jesus, Thou Art the King.
Light Yoke and Easy Burden, The.
Loadstone of His Love, The.
Love Divine.
Morning Hymn, A.
Nativity, The.
Now Is the Accepted Time.
O for a heart to praise my God.
O for a thousand tongues to sing.
O Thou Who Camest from Above.
Only Jesus Will I Know.
Rejoice, the Lord is King!
Soldiers of Christ, arise.
Speak the Word.
Still, O Lord, for Thee I Tarry.
Thy Conquering Name.
Thy Glorious Face Above.
Times without Number Have I Pray'd.
Triumph of His Grace.
Walking with Him in White.
Wash Me Whiter than Snow.
Well of Living Water, The.
Wrestling Jacob.
Ye servants of God, your Master proclaim.
WESLEY, JOHN. Courage, *tr.*
Hope Springing Up.
Hymn: "Thou hidden love of God, whose height."
I Believe Thy Precious Blood.
John Wesley's Rule.
Love of God Supreme, The.
My Light! My Way! *tr.*
Rule, A.
What to Do.
WESLEY, SAMUEL (1691–1739). Epigram on Miltonicks.
From a Hint in the Minor Poets.
Hymn to God the Father.
On Butler's Monument.
On the Setting Up [of] Mr. Butler's Monument in Westminster Abbey.
Saviour, The.
WEST, A. White-throated Sparrow, The.
WEST, DON. My South.
WEST, ELIZABETH DICKINSON. *See* DOWDEN, ELIZABETH DICKINSON WEST.
WEST, ELWYN CHAUNCEY. Names (for Mother).
WEST, JESSAMYN. Song of the Settlers.
WEST, JOHN, 1ST EARL DE LA WARR. Fair Hebe.
WEST, KENYON. "Thou Shouldst Be Living at This Hour!"
WEST, LILIAN BAYNE. May Basket, A.
WEST, PAUL. Cumberbunce, The.
WEST, V. SACKVILLE-. *See* SACKVILLE-WEST, VICTORIA MARY.
WESTBROOK, JOHN T. Summer Bayou.
WESTCOTT, JOSEPH L. Legend of Grand Lake, The.
WESTENDORF, THOMAS P. I'll Take You Home Again, Kathleen.
WESTMORLAND, MILDMAY FANE, 2D EARL OF. In Praise of Fidelia.
WESTON, MILDRED. Argument.
Bleat of Protest.
Echo.
Hat Bar.
Hotel Lobby.
Pastorale: "Only cows can loll at ease."
Song for Thrift Week.
To a Lady Holding the Floor.
WESTON, REBECCA J. Father, We Thank Thee, *at.*
Morning Prayer, *at.*
Prayer, A: "Father, we thank Thee for the night," *at.*
WESTON, ROBERT. Honest Doubt.
WESTON, STELLA. For All Fathers.
WESTPHALEN, EMILIO ADOLFO VON. As Time Goes On.
WESTRUP, J. M. Best of All.
Flying.
Furry Home, The.
Growing Rhyme, A.
Leaves.
My Little House.
Poor Snail, The.
Vision Clear, The.
WESTWOOD, HORACE. Psalm of Confidence, A.
WESTWOOD, THOMAS. Bee and the Lily, The.
In the Golden Morning of the World.
Lark's Grave, The.
Little Bell.
Lost Lamb, The.
Mine Host of "The Golden Apple."
Night of Spring.
O Wind of the Mountain!
Under My Window.
WETHERALD, ETHELWYN. At Waking.
Earth's Silences.
Hay Field, The.
House of the Trees, The.
If One Might Live.
In April.
Indigo Bird, The.
Legacies.
My Orders.
Screech-Owl, The.
Snow Storm, The.
Song Sparrow's Nest, The.
To February.
Wind of Death, The.
Woodland Worship.
WETTE, ADELHEID. Hansel and Gretel, *sel.*
Witch's Ride, The. *Fr.* Hansel and Gretel.
WEVER, R. In a herber green, asleep whereas I lay. *Fr.* Lusty Juventus.
In Youth Is Pleasure. *Fr.* Lusty Juventus.
Lusty Juventus, *sel.*
Of Youth He Singeth. *Fr.* Lusty Juventus.
Youth. *Fr.* Lusty Juventus.
WEXIONIUS, OLOF. On the Death of a Pious Lady.
WEYBURN, RUBY E. [*or* T.]. *See* TOBIAS, RUBY WEYBURN.
WHALEN, PHILIP. Denunciation; or, Unfrock'd Again.
For C.
Forty-five Years Since the Fall of the Ch'ing Dynasty.
Martyrdom of Two Pagans.
Same Old Jazz, The.
Sourdough Mountain Lookout.
Take I, 4: II: 58
2 Variations: All about Love.
WHALER, JAMES. Monsieur Pipereau.
Pond, The. *Fr.* Runaway.
Runaway, *sel.*
WHALLEY, GEORGE. Commandos Embarking.
Night Flight.
We Who Are Left.
WHAN, EDGAR WILLIAM. Christ, The.
WHARTON, EDITH. Battle Sleep.
Experience.
Lyrical Epigram, A.
With the Tide.
Yet for One Rounded Moment.
You and You.
Young Dead, The.
WHARTON, GORDON. Errors of Observation.
WHARTON, HENRY MARVIN. Our Confederate Dead.
WHARTON, MORTON BRYAN. Christmas of Long Ago, A.
Our Dead Heroes.
Southern Dead, The.
To a Dejected Friend.
WHARTON, THOMAS WHARTON, 1ST MARQUESS OF. Lilli Burlero.
New Song, A; or, Lilliburlero.
WHARTON, WILLIAM H. Ben Milam.
WHEATLEY, PHILLIS. Hymn to the Evening, An.
Hymn to the Morning.
On Imagination.

To the Right Honorable William, Earl of Dartmouth.
WHEATLEY, VERA. Credo.
WHEELER, CHARLES ENOCH. Adjuration.
Tumult.
WHEELER, CURTIS. Armistice Night.
Lest We Forget.
WHEELER, EDWARD JEWETT. Night's Mardi Gras.
WHEELER, KATHARINE WELLES. Circle, The.
WHEELER, KATHLEEN. New Leaf, The [*or* A].
WHEELER, RUTH WINANT. Christmas Song, A.
Legacy.
Nurse's Prayer, A.
Prayer for Shut-Ins.
WHEELOCK, JOHN HALL. Afternoon; Amagansett Beach.
All afternoon the passion of heaven spent. *Fr.* The Divine Fantasy.
Autumn along the Beaches.
Black Panther, The.
Bonac.
By the Gray Sea.
Dark Memory, The.
Dark Wood, The.
Dawn on Mid-Ocean.
Dear Mystery, The.
Dialectics of Flight.
Divine Fantasy, The, *sel.*
Divine Insect, The.
Earth.
Ernest Dowson.
Exile from God.
Far Land, The.
Fish-Hawk, The.
For Them All.
Hippopotamothalamion.
Holy Light.
Hour of the Morning-Star, The.
I Do Not Love to See Your Beauty Fire.
I Lift My Gaze.
Immensity.
Imprisoned.
Legend.
Letter, The.
Life.
Like Music.
Lion-House, The.
Love and Liberation.
Love Knocks at the Door.
Mozart Perhaps.
Night Thoughts in Age.
Nirvana.
Once in a Lonely Hour.
Pitiless Beauty.
Prayer: "Have pity on us, Power just and severe."
Prayer to the Sun.
Random Reflections on a Cloudless Sunday.
Reconciliation.
Sea Is Wild, The.
Sea-Voyage.
Silence.
Song: "All my love for my sweet."
Sound of the Sea, The.
Spent Wave.
Sun Men Call It, The.
Sunday Evening in the Common.
Symphony: First Movement.
Thanks from Earth to Heaven.
Thanks from Earth to Heaven, *sel.*
This Quiet Dust.
Thunder-Shower, The.
To the Modern Man.
Triumph of Love.
Triumph of the Singer, The.
Unison.
Unknown Beloved, The.
Valediction.
Vaudeville Dancer.
Victory, The.
Wood-Thrush.
Years, The.
WHEELWRIGHT, JOHN. Apocryphal Apocalypse.
Ave Eva.
Fish Food.
From Gestures to the Dead.
Huntsman, The.
Paul and Virginia.
Seed Pods.
There Is No Opera like "Lohengrin."
Train Ride.
Why Must You Know?
WHEELWRIGHT, WILLIAM B. Widow, The.
WHETSTONE, GEORGE. Cressid's Complaint.
Description of Cozeners.
Epilogus.
Gentlewoman Forsweareth, A.
Give Me My Work.
WHEWELL, WILLIAM. Physics.
WHICHER, GEORGE FRISBIE. *For translations from Latin, see* LaP; LyMA.
WHICHER, GEORGE MEASON. Bacchylides.
On Coming to an End.
To the Frivolous Muse.
WHINERY, VERNA. This Day Is Thine.
WHIPPLE, WADE. Diffidence.
WHISENAND, EMMA BOGE. Open Your Eyes.
WHISTLER, JAMES ABBOTT MCNEILL. Limerick: "There is a creator named God."
WHISTLER, LAURENCE. Flight.
In Time of Suspense.
In Time of Suspense, *sel.*
No Answer.
Shape of a Bird, The.
WHITAKER, ROBERT. Abraham Lincoln.
Easter.
"For God So Loved the World."
Holy Week.
My Country.
My Country Is the World, *at.*
No Room.
O Mothers of the Human Race.
Out-of-Doors.
Prayer of Penitence, A.
Rivals, The.
Starred Mother, The.
Upon This Rock.
Whence Cometh War?
Worship.
WHITCHER, FRANCES MIRIAM BERRY. K. K. Can't Calculate.
Widow Bedott Papers, The, *sel.*
Widow Bedott to Elder Sniffles. *Fr.* The Widow Bedott Papers.
WHITE, ADELINE. Autumn Morning.
Christmas Party, The.
Colour.
Over the Fields.
WHITE, ALAN. Poem for Combatants.
WHITE, ANTONIA. Epitaph: "By man came death."
WHITE, BLANCO. *See* WHITE, JOSEPH BLANCO.
WHITE, COOL. Lubly Fan.
WHITE, D. J. *See* O'MALLEY, D. J.
WHITE, EDWARD LUCAS. Genius.
Last Bowstrings, The.
WHITE, ELWYN BROOKS. Affidavit in Platitudes.
Apostrophe to a Pram Rider.
Apostrophic Notes from the New-World Physics.
Circus, The.
Classic Waits for Me, A.
Commuter[s].
Fashions in Dogs.
Father Does His Best, A.
I Marvel at the Ways of God.
I Paint What I See.
Marble-Top.
Natura in Urbe.
Nugatory.
To a Lady across the Way.
WHITE, EUGENE RICHARD. Of the Lost Ship.
WHITE, GILBERT. Invitation to Selborne, The, *sel.*
Natural History of Selborne, The, *sel.*
WHITE, GLEESON JOSEPH WILLIAM. Ballade of Playing Cards, A.
Primrose Dame, A.
Sufficiency.
WHITE, HARRIET R. Uffia.
WHITE, HENRY KIRKE. Description of a Summer's Eve.
Early Primrose, The.
Fragment: "O pale art thou, my lamp, and faint."
Lullaby of a Female Convict to Her Child, the Night Previous to Execution, The.
Man's Littleness in Presence of the Stars.
Pastoral Song, A.
Song from Fragment of an Eccentric Drama.
To an Early Primrose.
To My Mother.
To the Harvest Moon.
Verses: "When pride and envy, and the scorn."
WHITE, HERVEY. I Saw the Clouds.
WHITE, HINTON. I've Travelled Far in Many Lands.
World Is One, The.
WHITE, JAMES TERRY. Consummation.
If Hearts Are Dust.
Not by Bread Alone.
We Shall Remember Them.
WHITE, JON MANCHIP. Captain, The.
Count Orlo in England.
Orlo's Valediction.
Rout of San Romano, The.
WHITE, JOSEPH BLANCO. Mysterious Night.
Night [and Death].
Sonnet to Night, A.
To Night.
To Night, *sel.*
WHITE, RAELENE NEWELL. Rain-Talk.
WHITE, RICHARD. Discovery of San Francisco Bay.
WHITE, TERENCE HANBURY. Reading Giraldus Cambrensis.
WHITE, VIOLA CHITTENDEN. Dutch Slumber Song.
Litany of the Comfortable, The.
WHITE, WILLIAM ALLEN. Intermezzo for the Fourth Act, An.
WHITE, WILLIAM ANTHONY PARKER. *See* "BOUCHER, ANTHONY."
WHITEFIELD, GEORGE. Oh, Lovely Appearance of Death.
WHITEHEAD, CHARLES. As Yonder Lamp.
Lamp, The.
Summer Storm, A.
WHITEHEAD, PAUL. Apollo and Daphne, *sel.*
Hunting Song. *Fr.* Apollo and Daphne.
WHITEHEAD, WILLIAM. Enthusiast, The; an Ode.
Je Ne Sçay [*or* Sais] Quoi, The.
On Friendship.
On the Birthday of a Young Lady.
WHITELEY, OPAL. Words, The.
WHITELOCK, WILLIAM WALLACE. Cats.
WHITESIDE, MARY BRENT. Acolyte.
After All Splendors.
Again, Sappho.
Alien.
Lost—an April.
Renunciation.
Stone Mountain.
Who Has Known Heights.
WHITFIELD, FREDERICK. I Need Thee.
There Is a Name I Love to Hear.
WHITING, CHARLES GOODRICH. Blue Hills beneath the Haze.
Eagle's Fall, The.
Way to Heaven, The.
WHITING, LILIAN. Lost Cat, The.
Mystery, The.
Three Poets, The.
WHITING, NATHANIEL. Il Insonio Insonnado, *sel.*
Le Hore di Recreatione; or, The Pleasant Historie of Albino and Bellama, *sel.*
Office of Poetry, The. *Fr.* Il Insonio Insonnado.
Tinker and the Monks, The. *Fr.* Le Hore di Recreatione.
WHITING, SEYMOUR W. Alamance.
WHITING, WILLIAM. Eternal Father, Strong to Save.

WHITMAN, JAMES I. Incident of French History, An.
WHITMAN, S. W. October.
WHITMAN, SARAH HELEN. Day of the Indian Summer, A.
If thy sad heart, pining for human love. *Fr.* Sonnets from the Series Relating to Edgar Allan Poe.
Lost Church, The, *par.*
Oft since thine earthly eyes have closed on mine. *Fr.* Sonnets from the Series Relating to Edgar Allan Poe.
On our lone pathway bloomed no earthly hopes. *Fr.* Sonnets from the Series Relating to Edgar Allan Poe.
Sonnets from the Series Relating to Edgar Allan Poe, *sels.*
Still Day in Autumn, A.
To Edgar Allan Poe. *Fr.* Sonnets from the Series Relating to Edgar Allan Poe.
When first I looked into thy glorious eyes. *Fr.* Sonnets from the Series Relating to Edgar Allan Poe.
WHITMAN, WALT. Aboard at a Ship's Helm.
Adieu to a Soldier.
Afoot and Light-hearted. *Fr.* Song of the Open Road.
After an Interval.
After the Dazzle of Day.
After the Sea-Ship.
After the Supper and Talk.
American Feuillage.
Animals. *Fr.* Song of Myself.
Annual Drama, The. *Fr.* The Return of the Heroes.
Are You the New Person Drawn toward Me?
Army Corps on the March, An.
As Adam Early in the Morning.
As at Thy Portals Also Death.
As I Ebb'd with the Ocean of Life.
As I Lay with My Head in Your Lap Camerado.
As I Pondered in Silence.
As Toilsome I Wander'd Virginia's Woods.
Ashes of Soldiers.
Assurances.
Bare-bosom'd Night. *Fr.* Song of Myself.
Base of All Metaphysics, The.
Battle of the *Bonhomme Richard* and the *Serapis*. *Fr.* Song of Myself.
Be Not Afraid. *Fr.* Song of the Open Road.
Beasts, The. *Fr.* Song of Myself.
Beat! Beat! Drums!
Beautiful Women.
Beginners.
Beginning My Studies.
Beholding God. *Fr.* Song of Myself.
Birds of Passage, *sel.*
Bivouac on a Mountain Side.
Broad-Axe, The. *Fr.* Song of the Broad-Axe.
Broadway.
Brotherhood. *Fr.* Passage to India.
Brown Bird, The.
By Blue Ontario's Shore, *sels.*
By the Bivouac's Fitful Flame.
Camps of Green.
Cavalry Crossing a Ford.
Chanting the Square Deific.
Child, A, Said, What Is the Grass? *Fr.* Song of Myself.
City Dead-House, The.
City of Ships.
Clear Midnight, A.
Come Lovely and Soothing Death. *Fr.* When Lilacs Last in the Dooryard Bloom'd.
Come Muse Migrate from Greece and Ionia. *Fr.* Song of the Exposition.
Come, Said My Soul.
Come Said the Muse. *Fr. various poems.*
Come Up from the Fields Father.
Commonplace, The.
Continuities.
Crossing Brooklyn Ferry.
Crossing Brooklyn Ferry, *sel.*
Dalliance of the Eagles, The.
Darest Thou Now, O Soul.
Dazzling and Tremendous How Quick the Sun-Rise Would Kill Me. *Fr.* Song of Myself.
Death Carol. *Fr.* When Lilacs Last in the Dooryard Bloom'd.
Delicate Cluster! Flag of Teeming Life!
Dirge for Two Veterans.
Dismantled Ship, The.
Drayman, The. *Fr.* Song of Myself.
Dresser, The.
Dying Fireman. *Fr.* Song of Myself.
Dying Heroes. *Fr.* Song of Myself.
Earth at Night. *Fr.* Song of Myself.
Earth, My Likeness.
Eidolons.
Eighteen Sixty-one.
Epitaph for Lincoln.
Ethiopia Saluting the Colours.
Europe.
Faces.
Faces, *sel.*
Facing West from California's Shores.
Farm Picture, A.
First Dandelion, The.
First O Songs for a Prelude.
For Religion's Sake. *Fr.* Starting from Paumanok.
For You, O Democracy.
From Paumanok Starting I Fly Like a Bird.
From Pent-up Aching Rivers.
Full of Life Now.
Give Me the Splendid Silent Sun.
Glimpse, A.
Gods.
Good-bye, My Fancy!
Grass. *Fr.* Song of Myself.
Great City, The. *Fr.* Song of the Broad-Axe.
Great Mother, The. *Fr.* A Song of the Rolling Earth.
Had I the Choice.
Halcyon Days.
Hand-Mirror, A.
Have You Learned Lessons Only of Those Who Admired You?
Heroes. *Fr.* Song of Myself.
Hub for the Universe, A.
Human Progress. *Fr.* Song of the Open Road.
Hush'd Be the Camps To-Day (May 4, 1865). *Fr.* Memories of President Lincoln.
Hymn to America.
I Am an Acme of Things Accomplished. *Fr.* Song of Myself.
I Am He That Walks [with the Tender and Growing Night]. *Fr.* Song of Myself.
I Celebrate Myself. *Fr.* Song of Myself.
I Dote upon Myself. *Fr.* Song of Myself.
I Dream'd in a Dream.
I Hear America Singing.
I Hear and See Not Strips of Cloth Alone.
I Hear It Was Charged against Me.
I Heard You, Solemn-sweet Pipes of the Organ.
I Know I Am Deathless. *Fr.* Song of Myself.
I Saw in Louisiana a Live-Oak Growing.
I Saw Old General at Bay.
I Saw the Vision of Armies.
I Sing the Body Electric.
I Sit and Look Out.
I Think I Could Turn. *Fr.* Song of Myself.
I Tramp a Perpetual Journey. *Fr.* Song of Myself.
Imprisoned Soul, The.
In Cabin'd Ships at Sea.
In Paths Untrodden.
In This Earth, Perfection. *Fr.* Birds of Passage.
Indian Woman, The. *Fr.* The Sleepers.
Infinity. *Fr.* Song of Myself.
Italian Music in Dakota.
Joy, Shipmate, Joy!
Justified Mother of Men, The. *Fr.* Faces.
Keep heart, O comrade, God may be delayed.
L. of G.'s Purport.
Last Invocation, The.
Leaf for Hand in Hand, A.
Leaf of Grass, A. *Fr.* Song of Myself.
Leaves of Grass. *Fr.* Song of Myself.
"Leaves of Grass's" Purport.
Letters from God. *Fr.* Song of Myself.
Lines: "Child, A, said '*What is the grass?*'" *Fr.* Song of Myself.
Lo, Victress on the Peaks.
Long, Too Long America.
Look Down Fair Moon.
Manhattan Arming.
Mannahatta ("I was asking . . .").
March in the Ranks Hard-prest, and the Road Unknown, A.
Me Imperturbe.
Memories of President Lincoln.
Microcosm, The. *Fr.* Song of Myself.
Miracles ("I believe a leaf of grass . . ."). *Fr.* Song of Myself.
Miracles ("Why, who makes much of a miracle?")
Mocking Bird, The. *Fr.* Out of the Cradle Endlessly Rocking.
Muse in the New World, The. *Fr.* Song of the Exposition.
My Barbaric Yawp. *Fr.* Song of Myself.
Myself. *Fr.* Song of Myself.
Myself and Mine.
Mystic Trumpeter, The.
Native Moments.
Necessity of Religion, The. *Fr.* Starting from Paumanok.
Night on the Prairies.
No Labor-saving Machine.
Noiseless, Patient Spider, A.
Not Heat Flames Up and Consumes.
Not Heaving from My Ribb'd Breast Only.
Not the Pilot.
Not Youth Pertains to Me.
O Captain! My Captain! *Fr.* Memories of President Lincoln.
O Magnet-South.
O Star of France.
O Tan-faced Prairie-Boy.
Of Him I Love Day and Night.
Of the Terrible Doubt of Appearances.
Old-Time Sea-Fight, An. *Fr.* Song of Myself.
Old War-Dreams.
On the Beach at Night.
Once I Pass'd through a Populous City.
One Hour to Madness and Joy.
One's-Self I Sing.
Open Road, The. *Fr.* Song of the Open Road.
Others May Praise What They Like.
Out of the Cradle Endlessly Rocking.
Out of the Rolling Ocean the Crowd.
Over the Carnage Rose Prophetic a Voice.
Ox-Tamer, The.
Oxen That Rattle the Yoke and Chain. *Fr.* Song of Myself.
Passage to India.
Passage to India, *sel.*
Patrolling Barnegat.
Peaceful Death.
Pensive on Her Dead Gazing.
Perpetual Journey, The. *Fr.* Song of Myself.
Pioneers! O Pioneers!
Poem of Joys, The, *sels.*
Poet, The. *Fr.* By Blue Ontario's Shore.
Poets to Come.
Prairie-Grass Dividing, The.
Prairie Sunset, A.
Prayer of Columbus.
Prayer of Columbus, *sels.*

Quicksand Years.
Race of Veterans.
Reconciliation.
Recorders Ages Hence.
Respondez!
Return of the Heroes, The, *sel.*
Roots and Leaves Themselves Alone.
Runaway Slave, The. *Fr.* Song of Myself.
Runner, The.
Salut au Monde.
Salut au Monde, *sel.*
Sea-Fight, A. *Fr.* Song of Myself.
Sea of Faith, The. *Fr.* Passage to India.
Ship Starting, The.
Shut Not Your Doors.
Sight in Camp [in the Daybreak Gray and Dim], A.
Singer in the Prison, The.
Sleepers, The.
Sleepers, The, *sel.*
So Long!
Sometimes with One I Love.
Song for All Seas, All Ships.
Song for the States, A.
Song of Joys, A. *Fr.* A Poem of Joys.
Song of Myself.
Song of Myself, *sels.*
Song of the Broad-Axe.
Song of the Broad-Axe, *sels.*
Song of the Exposition, *sels.*
Song of the Open Road.
Song of the Open Road, *sels.*
Song of the Rolling Earth, A, *sel.*
Song of the Universal, *sels.*
Soon Shall the Winter's Foil Be Here.
Sparkles from the Wheel.
Spirit That Form'd This Scene.
Spirit Whose Work Is Done.
Spontaneous Me.
Starting from Paumanok.
Starting from Paumanok, *sels.*
Still Though the One I Sing.
Tears.
Thanks in Old Age.
There Was a Child Went Forth.
There Was a Child Went Forth, *sel.*
Thick-sprinkled Bunting.
This Compost.
This Dust Was Once the Man. *Fr.* Memories of President Lincoln.
This Moment Yearning and Thoughtful.
Thou Mother with Thy Equal Brood.
Thou Mother with Thy Equal Brood, *sel.*
Thought.
To a Certain Civilian.
To a Common Prostitute.
To a Foil'd European Revolutionaire, *sel.*
To a Locomotive in Winter.
To Abraham Lincoln.
To Foreign Lands.
To Him That Was Crucified.
To Old Age.
To Rich Givers.
To the East and to the West.
To the Man-of-War-Bird.
To the Man-of-War-Bird, *sel.*
To Think of Time.
To Those Who've Failed.
To You ("Stranger, if you passing meet me").
To You ("Whoever you are, I fear").
To-Day and Thee.
Twenty-eight Young Men Bathe by the Shore. *Fr.* Song of Myself.
Two Veterans.
Unexpress'd, The.
Untold Want, The.
Vigil Strange I Kept on the Field One Night.
Voyage of Democracy, The. *Fr.* Thou Mother with Thy Equal Brood.
Walt Whitman.
Walt Whitman, a kosmos, of Manhattan the son. *Fr.* Song of Myself.
Weave In, My Hardy Life.
What Best I See in Thee.
What Endures? *Fr.* Song of the Broad-Axe.
What Is the Grass? *Fr.* Song of Myself.
When I Heard at the Close of the Day.
When I Heard the Learn'd Astronomer.
When I Peruse the Conquer'd Fame.
When Lilacs Last in the Dooryard Bloom'd. *Fr.* Memories of President Lincoln.
When Lilacs Last in the Dooryard Bloom'd, *sel.*
Whispers of Heavenly Death.
Whitman's Mother. *Fr.* Faces.
Who Learns My Lesson Complete?
Whoever You Are Holding Me Now in Hand.
With Antecedents.
With Husky-haughty Lips, O Sea.
With Music Strong I Come. *Fr.* Song of Myself.
World below the Brine, The.
World Take Good Notice.
Wound-Dresser, The.
Wounded Person, The. *Fr.* Song of Myself.
Year that Trembled and Reel'd beneath Me.
Years of the Modern.
Yonnondio.
You Sea! *Fr.* Song of Myself.
Youth, Day, Old Age, and Night.
WHITMELL, LUCY. Christ in Flanders.
WHITNEY, ADELINE DUTTON TRAIN. Equinoctial.
February.
Humpty Dumpty. *Fr.* Mother Goose for Grown Folks.
Jack Horner. *Fr.* Mother Goose for Grown Folks.
Mother Goose for Grown Folks, *sels.*
Peace.
Sparrows.
WHITNEY, ANNA TEMPLE. Kneeling Camel, The.
Rest and Work.
Submission and Rest.
WHITNEY, ERNEST. Nightingale and the Lark, The.
Ute Pass.
WHITNEY, GEFFREY. Content.
In Crystal Towers.
WHITNEY, HELEN HAY (Mrs. Payne Whitney). Cat, The.
Does the Pearl Know?
Love's Kiss.
Man, The.
Sigh Not for Love.
Song: "We only ask for sunshine."
To Diane.
Was There Another Spring?
Woman's Pride, A.
WHITNEY, JOSEPH ERNEST. Drop of Ink, A.
WHITNEY, S. N. Voice of an Alumnus, The.
WHITTAKER, FREDERICK. Custer's Last Charge.
WHITTEMORE, ELIZABETH. My Friends Are Little Lamps to Me.
WHITTEMORE, REED. Abbreviated Interviews with a Few Disgruntled Literary Celebrities.
After Some Day of Decision.
Alfred, Lord Tennyson.
American Takes a Walk, An.
Day with the Foreign Legion, A.
Line of an American Poet, The.
Projection, A.
Shakespeare, Possibly, in California.
Spring, etc.
Treasure, A.
Week of Doodle, A.
WHITTIER, JOHN GREENLEAF. Abraham Davenport.
Adjustment.
All's Well.
Among the Hills, *sel.*
Amy Wentworth.
Andrew Rykman's Prayer, *sel.*
Angel of Patience, The.
Angels of Buena Vista, The.
Arisen at Last.
Astraea.
Astraea at the Capitol.
At Last.
At Port Royal.
At Port Royal, *sel.*
At School-Close.
Autograph, An.
Barbara Frietchie.
Barclay of Ury.
Barefoot Boy, The.
Barefoot Boy, The, *sel.*
Bartholdi Statue, The.
Battle Autumn of 1862, The.
Bayard Taylor.
Benedicite.
Bible, The. *Fr.* Miriam.
Book Our Mothers Read, The. *Fr.* Miriam.
Brewing of Soma, The.
Brewing of Soma, The, *sel.*
Brotherhood.
Brown Dwarf of Rügen, The.
Brown of Ossawatomie.
Bryant on His Seventieth Birthday.
Burial of Barber.
Burns.
Cable Hymn, The.
Cassandra Southwick.
Centennial Hymn, The.
Chicago.
Christian Slave, The.
Christmas Carmen, A.
Clerical Oppressors.
Conductor Bradley.
Corn Song, The. *Fr.* The Huskers.
Crisis, The.
Dead Feast of the Kol-Folk, The.
Dead Ship of Harpswell, The.
Dear Lord and Father of Mankind. *Fr.* The Brewing of Soma.
Dedication: "I would the gift I offer here." *Fr.* Songs of Labor.
Democracy.
Destiny. *Fr.* Raphael.
Disarmament.
Disarmament, *sel.*
Divine Compassion.
Emancipation Group, The.
Emancipation Group, The, *sel.*
Epitaph: "Bathsheba: To whom none ever said scat."
Eternal Good. *Fr.* Eventide.
Eternal Goodness, The.
Eternal Goodness, The, *sels.*
Eve of Election, *sel.*
Evening. *Fr.* Summer by the Lakeside.
Eventide, *sel.*
Exile's Departure, The.
Expostulation.
Faith in Time of Darkness. *Fr.* Snow-bound.
Farewell, The: "Gone, gone—sold and gone."
Female Martyr, The.
Firelight. *Fr.* Snow-bound.
Fireside, The. *Fr.* Snow-bound.
First-Day Thoughts.
Fishermen, The.
Fitz-Greene Halleck.
For an Autumn Festival.
For an Autumn Festival, *sel.*
For Righteousness' Sake.
Forgive.
Forgiveness.
Friend's Burial, The.
Friend's Burial, The, *sel.*
Frost Spirit, The.
Garrison ("The storm and peril").
Garrison of Cape Ann, The.
Gift of Tritemius, The.
Hampton Beach.
Harvest Hymn. *Fr.* For an Autumn Festival.
Healer, The.
Healer, The, *sel.*
Henchman, The.
Hive at Gettysburg, The.
Hunters of Men, The.
Huskers, The.
Huskers, The, *sel.*
Husking, The. *Fr.* Mabel Martin.
Hymn from the French of Lamartine, *sel.*

WHITTIER, JOHN GREENLEAF (*cont.*)
I bow my forehead to the dust. *Fr.* The Eternal Goodness.
I Call the Old Time Back. *Fr.* Mabel Martin.
I know not what the future hath. *Fr.* The Eternal Goodness.
Ichabod.
In Earthen Vessels. *Fr.* The Friend's Burial.
In Memory of James T. Fields.
In School-Days.
In School-Days, *sel.*
In the "Old South."
Indian Summer. *Fr.* The Eve of Election.
James Russell Lowell.
John Charles Frémont.
John Underhill.
Joseph Sturge.
Joy of Giving, The.
July, *at.*
Kallunborg Church.
Kansas Emigrants, The.
King's Missive, The.
Last Walk in Autumn, The.
Laus Deo!
Le Marais du Cygne.
Legacy, A.
Letter from a Missionary.
Lexington.
Library, The.
Life and Love. *Fr.* Snow-bound.
Light That Is Felt, The.
Lines: "Sun that brief December day, The." *Fr.* Snow-bound.
Lines: "Unwarmed by any sunset light." *Fr.* Snow-bound.
Lost Occasion, The.
Lumbermen, The.
Mabel Martin; a Harvest Idyl.
Massachusetts to Virginia.
Maud Muller.
Maud Muller, *sel.*
Meeting, The.
Memories.
Miriam, *sel.*
Moral Warfare, The.
Mother. *Fr.* Snow-bound.
Mulford.
My Playmate.
My Psalm.
My Triumph.
My Trust.
My Trust, *sel.*
Mystery, A.
New Challenge, The.
New England in Winter. *Fr.* Snow-bound.
New Wife and the Old, The.
Noon. *Fr.* Summer by the Lakeside.
Norembega.
Norsemen, The.
O Brother Man.
On the Big Horn.
Our Autocrat.
Our Master.
Our Master, *sel.*
Our mother, while she turned her wheel. *Fr.* Snow-bound.
Over-Heart, The.
Over-Heart, The, *sel.*
Palatine, The.
Palestine.
Palm-Tree, The.
Parson Avery.
Pentucket.
Pipes at Lucknow, The.
Poor Voter on Election Day, The.
Prayer of Agassiz, The.
Prelude: "Along the roadside, like the flowers of gold." *Fr.* Among the Hills.
Pressed Gentian, The.
Proclamation, The.
Proem: "I love the old melodious lays."
Prophetess. *Fr.* Snow-bound.
Pumpkin, The.
Quaker of the Olden Time, The.
Randolph of Roanoke.
Raphael, *sel.*
Reformer, The ("All grim and soiled").
Reformers, The ("O pure reformers!").
Rendition, The.
Requirement.
Saddest Words, The. *Fr.* Maud Muller.
St. Elizabeth of Hungary.
St. John.
Schoolmaster, The. *Fr.* Snow-bound.
Sea Dream, A.
Shadow and the Light, The, *sel.*
Ship-Builders, The.
Shoemakers, The. *Fr.* Songs of Labor.
Sister. *Fr.* Snow-bound.
Sisters, The.
Skipper Ireson's Ride.
Slave-Ships, The.
Snow, The. *Fr.* Snow-bound.
Snow-bound; a Winter Idyl.
Snow-bound; a Winter Idyl, *sels.*
Snow-Storm, The. *Fr.* Snow-bound.
Song of Slaves in the Desert.
Song of the Negro Boatman. *Fr.* At Port Royal.
Song of the Slaves in the Desert.
Songs of Labor, *sels.*
Summer by the Lakeside.
Sumner.
Sun That Brief December Day, The. *Fr.* Snow-bound.
Sunset on the Bearcamp.
Swan Song of Parson Avery, The.
Telling the Bees.
Tent on the Beach, The, *sel.*
Texas.
Thanksgiving Ode. *Fr.* For an Autumn Festival.
Three Bells [of Glasgow], The.
Thy Will Be Done.
To Children of Girard, Pa.
To Her Absent Sailor. *Fr.* The Tent on the Beach.
To John C. Frémont.
To Paths Unknown.
To Ronge.
To the Thirty-ninth Congress.
To William H. Seward.
To William Lloyd Garrison ("Champion of those").
Trailing Arbutus, The.
Two Angels, The.
Two Rabbins, The.
Uncle, The. *Fr.* Snow-bound.
Undying Soul, The.
Vanishers, The.
Vesta.
Vow of Washington, The.
Vow of Washington, The, *sel.*
Waiting, The.
Washington's Vow.
We Live by Faith.
Winter Day. *Fr.* Snow-bound.
Winter Night. *Fr.* Snow-bound.
Wishing Bridge, The.
Witch's Daughter, The. *Fr.* Mabel Martin.
World Sits at the Feet of Christ, The. *Fr.* The Over-Heart.
World Transformed, The. *Fr.* Snow-bound.
Worship of Nature, The.
Wreck of Rivermouth, The.
Yet Love Will Dream. *Fr.* Snow-bound.
WHITTLE, DANIEL W. Moment by Moment.
WHITWORTH, WILLIAM HENRY. Time and Death.
WHYTE-MELVILLE, GEORGE JOHN. Good-bye!
WHYTHORNE, THOMAS. Now That the Truth Is Tried.
WICKHAM, ANNA (Mrs. Patrick Hepburn). Affinity, The.
After Annunciation.
Cherry-Blossom Wand, The.
Choice.
Contemplative Quarry, The.
Creatrix.
Dedication of the Cook.
Divorce.
Domestic Economy.
Egoist, The.
Envoi: "God, thou great symmetry."
Fired Pot, The.
Fresh Start, The.
Friend Cato.
Gift to a Jade.
Last Round, The.
Man with a Hammer, The.
Marriage.
Meditation at Kew.
Mummer, The.
Nervous Prostration.
O heavenly fool! thy most kiss-worthy face.
Prayer for Miracle.
Recompense, The.
Sehnsucht.
Self-Analysis.
Self-Esteem.
Ship near Shoals.
Silence, The.
Singer, The.
Song: "I was so chill, and overworn, and sad."
Song-Maker, The.
Song of the Child, The.
Song of Women, A.
Soul's Liberty.
Tired Man, The.
Tired Woman, The.
To a Crucifix.
To Men.
Vanity.
Weapons.
Wife's Song, The.
WICKHAM, JOHN. Song: To a Lady with Many Names.
WIDDEMER, MARGARET. As I Lay Quiet.
Awakened War God, The.
Barter.
Bear Hunt, The.
Beggars, The.
Belinda's Window.
Boy of the Ghetto, A.
Carnations.
Certainties.
Comfort.
Country Carol, A.
Cyprian Woman, A.
Daisy Field, The.
Dark Cavalier, The.
Dialogue.
Factories, The.
Faithless Flowers, The.
Father-Prayer.
Fiddlers' Green.
God and the Strong Ones.
Greek Folk Song.
Holly Carol.
Hymn for Grief.
If You Should Tire of Loving Me.
Invisible Playmate, The.
Irish Love Song.
Little Carved Bowl, The.
Looking-Glass Pussy, The.
Mary, Helper of Heartbreak.
Masters, The.
Modern Woman to Her Lover, The.
Mother-Prayer.
New Victory, The.
No Words Are Lost.
Not unto the Forest.
Old Books.
Old Road to Paradise, The.
Other Shepherd, The.
Pageant.
Prescience.
Procession, The.
Remembrance; Greek Folk-Song.
Revisitants.
Sea Call.
Search.
Secret Cavern, The.
Song: "Going down the old way."
Song: "Spring will come when the year turns, The."
Song from a Masque.
Teresina's Face.
Under Dusky Laurel Leaf.
Warning.
Watcher [—Mother], The.
Whistle—Fantasy.
Willow Cats, The.

Wind-Litany.
Winter Branches.
WIECHERT, ERNST. Child Cried at Night, A.
WIENERS, JOHN. Poem for Museum Goers, A.
Poem for Painters, A.
Poem for the Insane, A.
Poem for the Old Man, A.
Poem for Trapped Things, A.
WIEWEL, JANICE. King of Elves, The.
WIGGAM, LIONEL. He Climbs a Hill and Turns His Face.
Mathematics.
WIGGIN, KATE DOUGLAS. Child and the World, The.
Cuddle Down, Dolly.
Romance of a Christmas Card, The.
WIGGLESWORTH, MICHAEL. Damnation of the Infants. *Fr.* The Day of Doom.
Day of Doom, The, *sels.*
Heathen and the Infants, The. *Fr.* The Day of Doom.
Infants' Petition, The. *Fr.* The Day of Doom.
Men of Good Works. *Fr.* The Day of Doom.
Sounding of the Last Trump. *Fr.* The Day of Doom.
Summons, The. *Fr.* The Day of Doom.
Vanity of Vanities.
WIGHTMAN, RICHARD. Pilgrim, The.
Servants, The.
WIJESINHE, S. HELEN. Sanskrit Stanza, A.
WILBERFORCE, ROBERT. "Peace Is the Tranquillity of Order."
WILBERFORCE, SAMUEL. If I Were a Cassowary, *at.*
Just for Today, *wr. at. See* PARTRIDGE, SYBIL F.
Some Cannibal, *at.*
WILBUR, RICHARD. After the Last Bulletins.
All These Birds.
Apoem I, *tr.*
Apology.
At Year's End.
Baroque Wall-Fountain in the Villa Sciarra, A.
Beasts.
Beautiful Changes, The.
Bell Speech.
Beowulf.
Black November Turkey, A.
Castles and Distances.
Ceremony.
Cicadas.
Cigales.
Death of a Toad, The.
Driftwood.
Epistemology.
Exeunt.
Folk-Tune.
For the New Railway Station in Rome.
Grace.
In a Bird Sanctuary.
In the Elegy Season.
Invitation to the Voyage, *tr.*
Juggler.
La Rose des Vents.
Lamarck Elaborated.
Lament: "Nashe's old queens who bartered young and fair."
Lightness.
Looking into History.
Love Calls Us to the Things of This World.
Marché aux Oiseaux.
Merlin Enthralled.
Mind.
Museum Piece.
O.
Pangloss' Song.
Pardon, The.
Pelican, The, *tr.*
Potato.
Simile for Her Smile, A.
Speech for the Repeal of the McCarran Act.
Still, Citizen Sparrow.
Terrace, The.
Then When the Ample Season.
Two Voices in a Meadow.
Tywater.
Voice from under the Table, A.
Winter Spring.
World without Objects Is a Sensible Emptiness, A.
Years-End.
WILCOX, CARLOS. God Everywhere in Nature.
Northern Lights.
Sights and Sounds of the Night.
Spring in New England.
Summer Noon, A.
WILCOX, DORA. At Evening.
Blue and Gold.
Liebesweh.
WILCOX, ELLA WHEELER. Accept My Full Heart's Thanks.
Ad Finem.
Attainment.
Barbarous Chief, The.
Beautiful Land of Nod, The.
Better, Wiser and Happier.
Beyond, The.
Building.
Christian's New-Year Prayer, The, *sel.*
Conquest.
Faith.
Five Little Brothers.
Friendship.
Friendship after Love.
Gethsemane.
Goal, The.
Growing Old.
How Salvator Won.
I Love You.
Illusion.
Inspiration, An.
Interlude.
Laugh, and the World Laughs with You.
Leaners or Lifters.
Life.
Life's Forest Trees.
Life's Magnet.
Life's Scars.
Lifting and Learning.
Love much. Earth has enough of bitter in it.
Love Thyself Last.
Midsummer.
Mistakes.
Morning Prayer, A.
My Love Ship.
New Year's Resolve.
One Need, The.
One of Us Two.
One Ship Drives East.
Optimism.
Pin, A.
Price He Paid, The.
Progress.
Queen's Last Ride, The.
Recrimination.
Solitude.
Sonnet: "Methinks ofttimes my heart is like some bee."
Talk Faith.
Talk Happiness.
Talk not of strength.
They Say.
Those We Love the Best.
To know thy bent and then pursue.
True Brotherhood.
Two Glasses, The.
Two Kinds of People.
Unanswered Prayers.
Universal Language, The.
Uselessness.
Was, Is, and Yet-to-be.
Way of the World, The.
Whatever Is—Is Best.
Will.
Windows of the Soul. *Fr.* Progress.
Winds of Fate, The.
World's Need, The.
Worth While.
You and Today.
You Never Can Tell.
WILD [*or* WILDE], ROBERT. Epitaph: "Here lies a piece of Christ; a star in dust."
Epitaph, An, for a Godly Man's Tomb.
WILDE, JANE FRANCESCA, LADY ("Speranza"). Famine Year, The.
Voice of the Poor, The.
WILDE, OSCAR. Apologia.
Ave Imperatrix!
Ave Imperatrix! *sel.*
Ave Maria, Gratia Plena.
Ballad of Reading Gaol, The.
Ballad of Reading Gaol, The, *sels.*
Ballade de Marguerite, *tr.*
Burden of Itys, The, *sel.*
Clouds, The, *sel., tr.*
Dole of the King's Daughter, The, *tr.*
E Tenebris.
East a-Callin', The. *Fr.* Ave Imperatrix!
Easter Day in Rome.
Endymion.
For Our Sakes.
Garden, The.
Grave of Keats, The.
Harlot's House, The.
Hélas!
Hope. *Fr.* The Ballad of Reading Gaol.
Humanitad, *sels.*
Impression: Le Réveillon.
Impression du Matin.
Impressions.
Impressions, *sels.*
In Prison. *Fr.* The Ballad of Reading Gaol.
In Reading Gaol by Reading Town. *Fr.* The Ballad of Reading Gaol.
In the Gold Room.
Joy. *Fr.* Humanitad.
La Fuite de la Lune. *Fr.* Impressions.
Le Jardin.
Le Jardin des Tuileries.
Les Silhouettes. *Fr.* Impressions.
Magdalen Walks.
Midwinter. *Fr.* Humanitad.
On the [Recent] Sale by Auction of Keats' Love Letters.
"Quia Multum Amavi."
Requiescat.
Rome Unvisited, *sel.*
Serenade: "Western wind is blowing fair, The."
Song of the Clouds, *tr. Fr.* The Clouds.
Sonnet on Hearing the *Dies Irae* Sung in the Sistine Chapel.
Sonnet on Holy Week.
Sonnet to Liberty.
Sphinx, The.
Sphinx, The, *sel.*
Symphony in Yellow.
Theocritus.
To Milton.
True Knowledge, The.
Yet Each Man Kills the Thing He Loves. *Fr.* The Ballad of Reading Gaol.
WILDE, RICHARD HENRY. Farewell to America, A.
Hesperia, *sel.*
Life.
My Life Is Like the Summer Rose.
Stanzas: "My life is like the summer rose."
To Lord Byron.
To the Mocking Bird.
WILDE, ROBERT. *See* WILD, ROBERT.
WILDENVEY, HERMAN. Love.
O Still to Be.
Selma.
Two Stanzas about Eve.
WILDER, AMOS NIVEN. Alive for Evermore.
And with No Language but a Cry.
De Profundis.
If I Have Lifted Up Mine Eyes to Admire.
Prayer: "Omnipotent confederate of all good."
Thanksgiving.
To Pulpit and Tribune.

WILDER, JOHN NICHOLS. Stand by the Flag.
"WILDGOOSE, OSCURO." More Impressions.
WILDMAN, JOHN HAZARD. To Pius X at Easter.
WILE, FRANCES WHITMARSH. All Beautiful the March of Days.
WILEY, ALMA ADAMS. Lincoln Memorial, The.
Memorial Day.
Nation's Shrine, The.
Washington Monument, The.
WILEY, SARA KING. Faun, The.
WILFRID, SISTER MARY. Nun's Vow, The.
WILHELM, PRINCE OF SWEDEN. Madonna's Lamp, The.
WILKES, JOHN. Epitaph on the Lap-Dog of Lady Frail.
WILKES, WETENHALL. Bellville, *sel.*
Pigeon House, A. *Fr.* Bellville.
WILKIE, A. C. Old Song by New Singers, An.
WILKINS, ALICE. Ducks, The.
Elephant's Trunk, The.
Fairies' Lights.
Fun on the Beach.
Leaves Drink, The.
Little Brown Bear.
Little Frog, A.
My Funny Umbrella.
New Shoes.
Snow.
Ways of Traveling.
WILKINS, EITHNE. Anabasis.
And Only Our Shadow Walks with Us.
Barbed Wire.
Cockcrow.
Dreamers and the Sea, The. *Fr.* Parzival.
Eye, The.
Failure.
High Place, A.
Parzival, *sel.*
Passage of an August.
Shark's Fin.
Spoken through Glass.
Variations on a Theme by Sidney Keyes.
WILKINS, MARY E. *See* FREEMAN, MARY ELEANOR WILKINS.
WILKINS, WILLIAM. Actaeon, *sel.*
Disillusion.
Engine Driver's Story, The.
Magazine Fort, Phoenix Park, Dublin, The.
WILKINSON, ANNE. For Dinah, the Adeneys' Cat.
In June and Gentle Oven.
Lens.
Poet's Eye-View, A.
Summer Acres.
WILKINSON, ELIZABETH HAYS. Good-Night.
Land of Nod, The.
WILKINSON, FLORENCE. *See* EVANS, FLORENCE WILKINSON.
WILKINSON, GRACE. Light.
WILKINSON, H. E. Bread.
Topsy-turvy Land.
What Is It?
WILKINSON, IRIS GUIVER. *See* "HYDE, ROBIN."
WILKINSON, MARGUERITE OGDEN BIGELOW. Before Dawn in the Woods.
Chant Out of Doors, A.
Christ and the Common Day.
Comrade to Comrade.
End, The. *Fr.* Songs of an Empty House.
Ghosts.
Guilty.
His Cross.
Incantation, An.
Jane Addams.
Never Hurt the Proud.
New City, The.
Pawnbrokers.
Peace.
Proud Song, A.
Psalm to the Son, A.
Robber in England, The.
Scatheless.
Somerset Farmer, The.
Song for My Mate, A.
Song of Light, A.
Song of Two Wanderers, A.
Songs of an Empty House.
Time.
To Failure.
To My Country.
To the Lighted Lady Window.
Toast, A.
Victory.
Vista. *Fr.* Songs of an Empty House.
Waking Thought.
Woman's Beloved, A.
WILKINSON, WILLIAM CLEAVER. At Marshfield. *Fr.* Webster, an Ode.
Webster, an Ode, *sel.*
WILLARD, EMMA HART. Cradle of the Deep, The.
Rocked in the Cradle of the Deep.
WILLETTE, FLORENCE HYNES. For a Girl in Love.
WILLIAM OF SHOREHAM. Hours of the Passion, *sel.*
WILLIAMS, BERTYE YOUNG. Friend Who Just Stands By, The.
Like Flakes of Snow.
Prayer, A: "Oh, not for more or longer days, dear Lord."
Prayer of Busy Hands, A.
Sonnet in Sorrow.
Trus' an' Smile.
Washington.
Who Are the Wise Men?
Your House of Happiness.
WILLIAMS, CHARLES. After Ronsard.
At Dawn.
At the "Ye That Do Truly."
Crowning of Arthur, The.
Divorce.
Dream, A.
Mount Badon.
Night Song.
Night Song for a Child!
Taliessin's Song of Lancelot's Mass.
Taliessin's Song of the Unicorn.
Theobalds' Roads.
To Michael Meditating a New Costume.
Walking Song.
WILLIAMS, SIR CHARLES HANBURY. Come, Chloe, and Give Me Sweet Kisses.
Epigram of Martial, Imitated.
Isabella, *sel.*
Ode on Miss Harriet Hanbury at Six Years Old, An.
Old General, The. *Fr.* Isabella.
WILLIAMS, EUGENE. Story of the Alchemist, The.
WILLIAMS, EVELYN M. Chestnut Buds.
WILLIAMS, FRANCIS HOWARD. Electra.
Song: "Bird in my bower, A."
Walt Whitman.
WILLIAMS, FRANKLIN B. Spirit Muses.
WILLIAMS, GWYN. *For translations from Welsh, see* LoGBV; LyMA; PrWP.
WILLIAMS, HARRIET B. Guidance.
WILLIAMS, HELEN MARIA. Julia, a Novel, *sel.*
To Hope. *Fr.* Julia, a Novel.
WILLIAMS, JESSIE E. Submission.
WILLIAMS, JOHN. Dead, The.
For My Students, Returning to College.
History, A.
Leaf, The.
Meaning of Violence, The.
Skaters, The.
WILLIAMS, JONATHAN. Distances to the Friend, The.
Fast Ball.
Little Tumescence, A.
Switch Blade, The; or, John's Other Wife.
Those Troublesome Disguises.
WILLIAMS, JOSEPHINE. Tides.
WILLIAMS, LUCY ARIEL. *See* HOLLOWAY, ARIEL WILLIAMS.
WILLIAMS, MARION. Peach-Blooms.
WILLIAMS, MICHAEL. Michael the Archangel.
WILLIAMS, OSCAR. Borrower of Salt, The. *Fr.* Variations on a Theme.
By Fiat of Adoration.
Children's Playground, The.
Dinner Guest.
Dwarf of Disintegration.
Editor's Private Cocktail Party, The.
Elements, The.
First Born, The.
Gray.
Hub, The.
I Sing an Old Song.
In Postures That Call.
Jeremiad.
Last Supper, The.
Leg in the Subway, The.
Man Coming toward You, The.
Man Coming toward You, The, *sel.*
Man in That Airplane, The.
Milk at the Bottom of the Sea.
Mirage, The.
On Meeting a Stranger in a Bookshop.
On the Couch.
On the Death of an Acquaintance. *Fr.* Variations on a Theme.
One Morning the World Woke Up.
Paper in the Meadow, The.
Praying Mantis Visits a Penthouse, The.
Road from Election to Christmas, The.
Seesaw, The.
Shopping for Meat in Winter.
Spring.
Spritely Dead, The. *Fr.* Variations on a Theme.
Total Revolution, A.
Variations on a Theme.
Wooden Horse of Myth, The.
WILLIAMS, RICHARD D'ALTON. Dying Girl, The.
Extermination.
Munster War-Song, The.
WILLIAMS, ROGER. Boast Not, Proud English. *Fr.* A Key into the Language of America.
Brother Indian, The.
Courteous Pagan Shall Condemn, The. *Fr.* A Key into the Language of America.
God Makes a Path.
Key into the Language of America, A; or, An Help to the Language of the Natives, *sels.*
Shelter, Food, and Company.
WILLIAMS, RUTH M. Conqueror, The.
God Incarnate.
Living Water.
WILLIAMS, SARAH. Deep Sea Soundings.
Is It True? *at.*
Old Astronomer to His Pupil, The.
Old Astronomer to His Pupil, The, *sel.*
Omar and the Persian.
Youth and Maidenhood.
WILLIAMS, SPENCER. Mountain Top Blues.
WILLIAMS, SUSAN ADGER. Concerning Cookies.
Pockets.
WILLIAMS, THEODORE CHICKERING. Aeneas and Dido, *tr. Fr.* The Aeneid.
Aeneid, The, *sels., tr.*
Fall of Troy, The, *tr. Fr.* The Aeneid.
Shipwreck of the Trojans; Landing at Carthage, *tr. Fr.* The Aeneid.
Thy Brother.
WILLIAMS, SIR THOMAS HERBERT PARRY-. *See* PARRY-WILLIAMS, SIR THOMAS HERBERT.
WILLIAMS, TREVOR. Girl I Took to the Cocktail Party, The.
WILLIAMS, WILLIAM. Arglwydd Arwain.
Christian Pilgrim's Hymn, The.
Divine Hand, The.
Guide Me, O Thou Great Jehovah.
WILLIAMS, WILLIAM CARLOS. Apology: Why Do I Write Today?
Artist, The.
At the Ball Game.
Before the grass is out the people are out. *Fr.* Paterson.
Botticellian Trees, The.

Bull, The.
Burning the Christmas Greens.
By the Road to the Contagious Hospital.
Calypso.
Catholic Bells, The.
Children, The.
Classic Scene.
Clouds, The.
Complaint.
Crowd at the Ball Game, The.
Daisy.
Dance, The.
Danse Russe.
Dawn.
Death.
Descent, The.
Desert Music, The, *sel.*
Desolate Field, The.
Drink.
El Hombre.
Elegy for D. H. Lawrence, An.
Elsie.
Fine Work with Pitch and Copper.
Flight to the City.
Flowers by the Sea.
Folded Skyscraper, A, *sel.*
Forgotten City, The.
Gift, The.
Goodnight, A.
Gulls.
Hemmed-in Males.
Hero.
Hounded Lovers, The.
How Strange You Are. *Fr.* Paterson.
Illegitimate Things.
In the American Grain, *sel.*
Intelligent Sheep-Man and the New Cars, The.
January.
John Landless Leads the Caravan, *tr.*
Le Médecin Malgré Lui.
Library, The. *Fr.* Paterson.
Love Song.
Man in a Room.
Metric Figure.
Monstrous Marriage, The.
Nantucket.
On Gay Wallpaper.
Pastoral: "Little sparrows, The."
Pastoral: "When I was younger."
Paterson, *sels.*
Peace on Earth.
Poem: "As the cat."
Poem: "By the road to the contagious hospital."
Poor, The.
Portrait of a Lady.
Postlude.
Preface: "To make a start." *Fr.* Paterson.
Pure Products of America, The.
Queen-Ann's-Lace.
Rain.
Red Wheelbarrow, The.
Right of Way, The.
Rigmarole.
St. Francis Einstein of the Daffodils.
Sappho, Be Comforted.
Sea-Elephant, The.
Shadow, The.
Signs Everywhere of Birds Nesting, While. *Fr.* Paterson.
Sir Walter Raleigh. *Fr.* In the American Grain.
Slow Movement.
Smell.
Sort of a Song, A.
Spring and All.
Sub Terra.
Sunday in the Park. *Fr.* Paterson.
Term, The.
These.
This Is Just to Say.
This Is Pioneer Weather.
To a Dog Injured in the Street.
To a Poor Old Woman.
To Daphne and Virginia.
To Elsie.
To Flossie.
To Waken an Old Lady.
Tract.
Unison, A.
Wanderer, The.
Widow's Lament in Springtime, The.
Willow Poem.
Winds, The.
Winter Trees.
Yachts, The.
Yellow Season, The.
WILLIAMSON, BRUCE. Afternoon in Anglo-Ireland.
For M——.
Homage of War.
Thought for My Love, A.
WILLIAMSON, FRANK S. Dew.
Magpie's Song, The.
She Comes as Comes the Summer Night.
WILLIAMSON, MRS. J. B. *See* "SCRACE, RICHARD."
WILLIS, ELLEN H. Wild White Rose, The.
WILLIS, HELEN CECILIA. Little Love Song, A.
WILLIS, NATHANIEL PARKER. Absence.
André's Request to Washington.
Belfry Pigeon, The.
Chamber Scene.
David's Lament for Absalom.
Death of Harrison, The.
Declaration, The.
Execution of Major André.
Healing of the Daughter of Jairus, The.
January 1, 1828.
Leper, The.
Love in a Cottage.
Mephibosheth.
On the Picture of a "Child Tired of Play."
Parrhasius.
To Giulia Grisi.
To Helen in a Huff.
To Laura W——, Two Years Old.
Torn Hat, The.
Two Women.
Unseen Spirits.
WILLOBY, HENRY. To Avisa, *at. Fr.* Willobie His Avisa.
Willobie His Avisa, *sel., at.*
WILLS, WILLIAM GORMAN. Charles the First, *sel.*
Cromwell and Henrietta Maria. *Fr.* Charles the First.
I'll Sing Thee Songs of Araby.
WILLSON, ARABELLA M. Appeal for Are to the Sextant of the Old Brick Meetinouse, A.
To the "Sextant."
WILLSON, DIXIE. Mist and All, The.
Mr. Rabbit.
Rainbows.
She Would.
Smiling.
Tip-Toe Tale.
WILLSON, FORCEYTHE. Boy Brittan.
In State.
Old Sergeant, The.
WILLY, MARGARET. Cathedral Verger, The.
Dunster Church.
Gargoyles at Oxford.
Heathcliffe Mourns for Cathy.
Inviolable.
Old Labourer, An.
To a Medieval Workman; Winchester.
WILMOT, FRANK ("Furnley Maurice").
Beauty of the World.
Fellow-Passengers.
Gully, The, *sels.*
Last Port, The.
Melbourne and Memory, *sel.*
Melbourne Ode, A; the Agricultural Show, Flemington, Victoria.
1914.
Progress.
To God, from the Warring Nations.
To God, from the Warring Nations, *sel.*
Towers at Evening, The. *Fr.* Melbourne and Memory.
Victoria Markets Recollected in Tranquillity, The, *sels.*
WILMOT, JOHN, EARL OF ROCHESTER. *See* ROCHESTER, JOHN WILMOT, 2D EARL OF.
WILSON, ALEXANDER. Blue-Bird, The.
Fisherman's Hymn, The.
WILSON, ANNE ELIZABETH. In a Museum.
WILSON, ANNE GLENNY. Fairyland.
Travel Song.
WILSON, ANTOINETTE. Wit's End Corner.
"WILSON, CHARLOTTE." *See* BAKER, KARLE WILSON.
WILSON, DEDIE HUFFMAN. Speak to the Sun.
WILSON, DOROTHY CLARKE. Christ of the World's Highway, The.
God's Way.
WILSON, MRS. E. V. Children We Keep, The.
WILSON, EDMUND. Elegies for a Passing World.
House of the Eighties, A.
On Editing Scott Fitzgerald's Papers.
Riverton.
Rose Found in a Greek Dictionary, A.
Voice, The.
When All the Young Were Dying.
White Sand, The.
WILSON, ELEANOR ROBBINS. Modern Columbus, A.
WILSON, FLORENCE M. Green Hunters, The.
WILSON, JAMES. Casey's Revenge.
WILSON, JOHN (1627?–1696). Belphegor; or, The Marriage of the Devil, *sel.*
Were I to Take Wife. *Fr.* Belphegor; or, The Marriage of the Devil.
WILSON, JOHN (1785–1854). *See* "NORTH, CHRISTOPHER."
WILSON, LOUISE. *See* "RAMSAY, JOAN."
WILSON, MCLANDBURGH. Hushaby.
Memorial Day.
Round Trip, The.
Theodore Roosevelt.
WILSON, MARGARET ADELAIDE. Road to Babylon, The.
WILSON, MARJORIE. From the Train.
Gates to England, The.
Jungle Trees, The.
Lighthouse, The.
Little Things That Happen, The.
Through the Porthole.
Tide, The.
WILSON, PATRICK SEYMOUR. Anchorage, The.
Childhood Church, The.
Cuvier Light.
Farewell, The.
Precious Pearl, The.
Tree, The.
WILSON, ROBERT. Conscience's Song. *Fr.* The Three Ladies of London.
New Brooms. *Fr.* The Three Ladies of London.
Simplicity's Song. *Fr.* The Three Ladies of London.
Three Ladies of London, The, *sels.*
WILSON, ROBERT BURNS. Ballad of the Faded Field.
Battle Song.
Cut the Cables.
Dead Player, The.
It Is in Winter That We Dream of Spring.
Passing of March, The.
Such Is the Death the Soldier Dies.
Sunrise of the Poor, The.
To a Crow.
When in the Night We Wake and Hear the Rain.
WILSON, ROBERT NOBLE DENISON. Enemies.
Saint Apollinare in Classe.
Woodcut.
WILSON, ROSE CECIL O'NEILL. *See* O'NEILL, ROSE.
WILSON, SAMUEL N. My Mother.
WILSON, T. P. CAMERON ("Tipcuca").
City Tramp, The, *sel.*
Dulce et Decorum.
In the City. *Fr.* The City Tramp.
Life.
London.
Magpies in Picardy.
Sportsmen in Paradise.

WILSON, V. B. Ticonderoga.
WILTON, RICHARD. Hymn to the Holy Spirit.
WINANT, RUTH G. Thanksgiving Prayer, A.
WINCHILSEA, ANNE FINCH, COUNTESS OF. Adam Posed.
All Is Vanity.
Aminta, *sel., tr.*
Ardelia to Melancholy.
Atheist and the Acorn, The.
Bird, The.
Birds and Plants of Love, The, *tr. Fr.* Aminta.
Birthday of Catharine Tufton, The, *sel.*
Cautious Lovers, The, *sel.*
Celia, thy sweet angels face, *at.*
Consolation, The.
Fragment: "So here confin'd, and but to female clay."
Greater Trial, The.
Hope.
Invitation to Daphnis, An, *sel.*
Jealousy.
Letter to Daphnis [*or* Dafnis], A.
Nature's Colours. *Fr.* An Invitation to Daphnis.
Nocturnal Reverie, A.
On Love.
On Myself.
Petition for an Absolute Retreat, The.
Petition for an Absolute Retreat, The, *sel.*
Portrait, The. *Fr.* The Birthday of Catharine Tufton.
Sigh, A.
Soldier's Death, The.
Song, A: "If for a woman I would die."
Song, A: "Love, thou art best of human joys."
Song, A: "'Tis strange, this heart within my breast."
Spleen, The, *sel.*
To Death.
To Silvia. *Fr.* The Cautious Lovers.
To the Echo; in a Clear Night upon Astrop Walks.
To the Nightingale.
Trail All Your Pikes.
Tree, The.
WINDEATT, MARY FABYAN. Nuptial.
WINDES, MARGARET A. Poem I Should Like to Write, The.
WINDOLPH, FRANCIS LYMAN. Sonnet: "Upon our fullness shines the dawning day."
WINDOM, W. H. Fatal Wedding, The.
WINDSOR, FANNIE. Never Trouble Trouble.
WING, G. C. December Prayer, A.
WING, HELEN. Apple Blossoms.
Clouds.
Crickets.
Hallowe'en.
March Wind.
Midnight Performance, A.
Monday Morning.
Neighbors.
Other Children.
Rain.
Rock-a-bye Song, A.
Turtle Town.
WINGATE, MARY. Washington.
When Shall We See Thy Like Again?
WINGFIELD, SHEILA. Lines for the Margin of an Old Gospel.
Odysseus Dying.
Poisoned in Search of the Medicine of Immortality.
Winter.
WINKWORTH, CATHERINE. All My Heart This Night Rejoices, *tr.*
I Am the Rose of Sharon.
Nothing Fair on Earth I See, *tr.*
Now Thank We All Our God, *tr.*
To God on high be thanks and praise, *tr.*
Veni Sancte Spiritus, *tr.*
WINNER, SEPTIMUS ("Alice Hawthorne"; "Percy Cruger"; "Mark Mason"; "Paul Stanton"). Abraham's Daughter.
Listen to the Mocking-Bird.
What Is Home without a Mother?
WINSLOW, ANNE GOODWIN. Alpine Village, An.
Beaten Path, The.
Lesson, The.
Masque of Loved Ladies, A.
Outdoor Theatre, The.
Qui Vive!
WINSLOW, HELEN MARIA. August.
Hope's Song.
WINSLOW, HORATIO. Polite Petrarch Peck.
WINSOR, FREDERICK. Limerick: "At the village emporium in Woodstock."
WINSTANLEY, GERRARD. Diggers' Song, The.
WINSTANLEY, JOHN. Upon a Friend's Pet Cat, Being Sick.
WINTCHEVSKY, MORRIS. Child-King, The.
If I Felt Less.
WINTER, CHARLES E. Miner's Song, The.
Wyoming.
WINTER, MARY. Blessing the Hounds.
Lower Forms of Life.
WINTER, WILLIAM. Adelaide Neilson.
After All.
Age.
Arthur.
Asleep.
Beauty.
Heart's Anchor, The.
Heaven's Hour.
I. H. B.
My Queen.
Night Watch, The.
On the Verge.
Passing Bell at Stratford, The.
Queen, The.
Refuge.
Rubicon, The.
Unwritten Poems.
"WINTERGREEN, JOHN P." *See* RYSKIND, MORRIE.
WINTERS, YVOR. Before Disaster.
By the Road to the Air-Base.
Death Goes before Me.
Grave, The.
Heracles.
Immobile Wind, The.
John Sutter.
Journey, The.
Marriage, The.
Ode on the Despoilers of Learning in an American University (1947), An.
Orpheus.
Prayer for My Son, A.
Priesthood, The.
Quod Tegit Omnia.
Sir Gawaine and the Green Knight.
Sonnet to the Moon.
Spring Serpent, A.
Summer Commentary, A.
Summer Noon, 1941.
To a Military Rifle, 1942.
To the Holy Spirit.
Two Songs of Advent.
Vision, A.
Walker, The.
WINTERS, MRS. YVOR. *See* LEWIS, JANET.
WINTHER, CHRISTIAN. At the Manor House.
Had I Some Magic Power.
Last Night.
Longing.
My Home.
WINTHROP, THEODORE. But Once.
WINTLE, WALTER D. Thinking.
WINTON, ELIZABETH. Little Valentine, A.
Special Delivery.
Summer Walk, A.
Surprise, A.
WINWAR, FRANCES. Autumn.
"WIOLAR." Resolution.
WIPO. Victimae Paschali.
Victimae Paschali Laudes.
WIRSÉN, CARL DAVID AF. Books and Love.
Moonbeams.
WISDOME [*or* WISDOM], ROBERT. Religious Use of Taking Tobacco, A, *at.*
Turk and Pope.
WISE, WILLIAM. After the Party.
Grownups.
Little Miss Pitt.
Telegram.
What to Do.
WISEMAN, GEORGE W. Easter Must Be Reclaimed.
Youth's Prayer.
WISTER, OWEN. Said Aristotle unto Plato.
WITHEFORD, HUBERT. Alone.
At the Discharge of Cannon Rise the Drowned.
Elegy in the Orongorongo Valley.
Invasion.
Magnolia Tree, The.
WITHER, GEORGE. Ah Me! Am I the Swaine.
Amaryllis I did woo.
Aspiration.
Author's Resolution [in a Sonnet], The. *Fr.* Fair Virtue, *and also in* Fidelia.
Brittan's Remembrancer, *sel.*
Choice, The.
Christmas Carol, A: "So, now is come our joyfullest feast."
Christmas Carol, A: "So, now is come our joyfullest feast," *sel.*
Christmas Day.
Collection of Emblemes, Ancient and Moderne, A, *sel.*
Conquered King, The, *sel.*
Divided Heart, The. *Fr.* Fair Virtue.
Eclogue IV, *sels. Fr.* The Shepherd's Hunting.
Fair Virtue, the Mistress of Philarete, *sels.*
Farewell, Sweet Groves. *Fr.* Fair Virtue.
Fidelia, *sels.*
For a Musician. *Fr.* Hallelujah.
Fourth Eglogue, The. *Fr.* The Shepherd's Hunting.
Hallelujah, or Britain's Second Remembrancer, *sels.*
Hence, Away, You Sirens! *Fr.* Fair Virtue, *and also in* Fidelia.
Her Fairness. *Fr.* Fair Virtue.
Her true beauty leaves behind. *Fr.* Fair Virtue.
Her Virtue. *Fr.* Fair Virtue.
Hymn L: Rocking Hymn, A. *Fr.* Hallelujah, or Britain's Second Remembrancer.
Hymn for a Widower or a Widow Deprived of a Loving Yoke-Fellow.
Hymne I: Generall Invitation to Praise God, A. *Fr.* Hallelujah, or Britain's Second Remembrancer.
I Loved a Lass.
I Wandered Out. *Fr.* Fair Virtue.
Lord! When Those Glorious Lights I See.
Love Sonnet, A.
Lover's Resolution, The. *Fr.* Fair Virtue, *and also in* Fidelia.
Lullaby, A: "Sweet baby, sleep! what ails my dear." *Fr.* Hallelujah.
Manly Heart, The. *Fr.* Fair Virtue, *and also in* Fidelia.
Marigold, The.
Old Christmas.
On the Muse of Poetry. *Fr.* The Shepherd's Hunting.
Our Joyful Feast. *Fr.* A Christmas Carol.
Philarete Praises Poetry. *Fr.* The Shepherd's Hunting.
Protector, The, *sel.*
Resolution, The. *Fr.* Fair Virtue.
Rocking Hymn, A. *Fr.* Hallelujah.
Shall I, Wasting In Despair. *Fr.* Fair Virtue, *and also in* Fidelia.
Shepherd's Hunting, The, *sels.*
Shepherd's Resolution, The. *Fr.* Fair Virtue, *and also in* Fidelia.
Sleep, Baby, Sleep.
Soldier, The.
Song: Who Finds a Woman Good and Wise.

Sonnet: "Hence away, you sirens, leave me." *Fr.* Fair Virtue.
Sonnet: "I wandered out a while agone." *Fr.* Fair Virtue.
Sonnet: "Shall I, wasting in despair." *Fr.* Fair Virtue, *and also in* Fidelia.
Sonnet upon a Stolen Kiss. *Fr.* Fair Virtue.
Stolen Kiss, A. *Fr.* Fair Virtue.
Tired Petitioner, The, *sel.*
To a Musician. *Fr.* Hallelujah.
What Care I. *Fr.* Fair Virtue, *and also in* Fidelia.
When We Are upon the Seas. *Fr.* Hallelujah.
Widow's Hymn.
WITHERBY, DIANA. Casualty.
Childhood and Age.
WITHERS, CARL. Charlie Chaplin Went to France, *at.*
WITHERSPOON, NAOMI LONG. Refugee.
WITTENBERG, ERNEST. Sub-average *Time* Reader, The.
WITTLIN, JOZEF [*or* JOSEPH]. Stabat Mater.
WODEHOUSE, E. A. Afforestation.
WODEHOUSE, PELHAM GRENVILLE.
Printer's Error.
Song about Whiskers.
Time like an Ever-rolling Stream.
WOESTIJNE, KAREL VAN DE. Elegy: "Child, your white face is chanting memories."
Sailors, The.
WOJTALEWICZ, MILDRED. Sanctuary.
WOLCOT, JOHN. *See* "PINDAR, PETER."
WOLF, ROBERT LEOPOLD. Eve.
Man in the Dress Suit, The.
Pagan Reinvokes the Twenty-third Psalm, A.
WOLFE, CHARLES. After Corunna.
Burial of Sir John Moore after [*or* at] Corunna, The.
Go, Forget Me.
Lines Written to Music.
Song: "Oh say not that my heart is cold."
Song: To Mary.
Sonnet Written during His Residence in College.
To Mary.
WOLFE, FFRIDA. Choosing Shoes.
Four and Eight.
Hidden.
Poppies in the Garden, The.
What the Toys Are Thinking.
WOLFE, HUMBERT. A. E. Housman and a Few Friends.
Aphrodite of Praxiteles, The, *tr.*
Baudelaire.
Beware lest, Love, too often with your stings, *tr.*
Blackbird, The.
Boy in the Dusk.
Bright Hair, Grow Dim.
British Journalist, The.
Child for Sale, A, *tr.*
Count me the stairs I climbed to your retreat, *tr.* *Fr.* Sonnets pour Hélène.
Cruel, farewell, since I do but annoy thee, *tr.* *Fr.* Sonnets pour Hélène.
Dance, lovely lady, dance and mask your face, *tr.* *Fr.* Sonnets pour Hélène.
Dead Fiddle, The.
Dead Locust, A, *tr.*
Dead Song-Writer, A, *tr.*
Do you remember, Joan. *Fr.* Requiem.
End of Sorrow, The, *tr.* *Fr.* The Wall of Weeping.
Endymion.
Feathers in a fan, The. *Fr.* Requiem.
Fiddle and the Bow, The.
Fishes.
Fool Hath Said in His Heart, The.
For Omar.
Four Sonnets to Helen, *tr.*
From the Greek Anthology, *tr.*
G. K. Chesterton.
Gray Squirrel, The.
Green Candles.
Green Parrot, The.
Helen, this age, by your exceeding worth, *tr.* *Fr.* Sonnets pour Hélène.
High Song, The. *Fr.* Requiem.
I consecrate this fountain Helen's, praying, *tr.* *Fr.* Sonnets pour Hélène.
I saw no doctor, but, feeling queer inside, *tr.*
Iliad.
In these long winter nights when moon doth steer, *tr.* *Fr.* Sonnets pour Hélène.
Journey's End.
Laburnum.
Lamb.
Lilac, The.
Listen!
Love and Timarion matched their wings and eyes, *tr.*
Love in Jeopardy.
Love Is a Keeper of Swans.
Madam, when we two walked, the rest unheeding, *tr.* *Fr.* Sonnets pour Hélène.
Man. *Fr.* Requiem.
Marcus, when running in the armored race, *tr.*
Mary and Darnley.
My Desk.
My Golden Helen, *tr.*
No other torch save what my dreams discover, *tr.* *Fr.* Sonnets pour Hélène.
Not for My Tears.
Old Lady, The.
On Dean Inge.
Only your arm, and nothing more, I found, *tr.* *Fr.* Sonnets pour Hélène.
Out of her lattice gazing on the leas, *tr.* *Fr.* Sonnets pour Hélène.
Palace, The.
Queen Victoria.
Reading Hesiod, *tr.*
Requiem, *sels.*
Return of the Fairy, The.
Road, The.
Robert Bridges.
Ronsard and Hélène.
Rose, The.
Saint, The, *sels.* *Fr.* Requiem.
See love, whose kingdom as the world is ample, *tr.* *Fr.* Sonnets pour Hélène.
Shall I your beauties with the moon compare? *tr.* *Fr.* Sonnets pour Hélène.
Silence.
Snow.
Soldier, The ("Down some cold field"). *Fr.* Requiem.
Soldier, The ("I do not ask God's purpose"). *Fr.* Requiem.
Song's Indenture.
Sonnet: "I fly the crowded roads where thousands hurry," *tr.*
Sonnets pour Hélène, *sels.*, *tr.*
Swallow, The, *tr.*
That evening when love bad you take the floor, *tr.* *Fr.* Sonnets pour Hélène.
Things Lovelier.
This Blind Rose.
This House was built for Zeus, *tr.*
This Is Not Death.
Thrushes.
To Aristophanes, *tr.*
Tulip.
Two Sparrows.
Wall of Weeping, The, *sels.*, *tr.*
Wandering Jew Comes to the Wall, The, *tr.* *Fr.* The Wall of Weeping.
Waters of Life, The.
What though the spirit of man, by Plato taught, *tr.* *Fr.* Sonnets pour Hélène.
White Dress, The.
"Who," cried the elders on the Trojan wall, *tr.* *Fr.* Sonnets pour Hélène.
You need no torch to light your lamp, *tr.*
Zoo, The.
WOLFE, JAMES. How Stands the Glass Around?
WOLFE, THOMAS CLAYTON. Something Has Spoken to Me in the Night.
Toward Which.
What Are We?
WOLFF, DAVID. While We Slept.
WOLFRAM VON ESCHENBACH. Fealty.
His Own True Wife.
Hope for Miracles.
WOLFSKEHL, KARL. And Yet We Are Here!
Shekhinah.
To Be Said at the Seder.
We Go.
WOLKER, JIRI. Epitaph: "Here lies the poet Wolker, lover of the world."
Love Poem.
On This My Sick-Bed Beats the World.
Pillar-Box, The.
WOOD, ALFRED E. Fight at Dajo, The.
WOOD, ANNA HAMILTON. Anvil of God's Mercy, The.
WOOD, CHARLES ERSKINE SCOTT. Desert, The. *Fr.* The Poet in the Desert.
Devil's Auction, The.
First Snow.
Goats.
It Is Spring and All Is Well.
Mammon Monster, The.
Poet in the Desert, The, *sels.*
Sunrise. *Fr.* The Poet in the Desert.
Sweat-Shop Slaves.
When I Walk Alone.
WOOD, CLEMENT. Berkshires in April.
Black Rose, The.
Eagle Sonnets, *sels.*
Flower of the dust am I: for dust will flower. *Fr.* Eagle Sonnets.
Glory Road, De.
How pretty, then, the me above the you. *Fr.* Eagle Sonnets.
I am a tongue for beauty. *Fr.* Eagle Sonnets.
I Cannot Know That Other Men Exist.
I have been sure of three things all my life. *Fr.* Eagle Sonnets.
I Pass a Lighted Window.
If the Seas Dry.
Longing.
Minstrel of God, The, *sel.*
O bitter moon, O cold and bitter moon. *Fr.* Eagle Sonnets.
O sweet strange minstrel of the joyous singing. *Fr.* The Minstrel of God.
Old Men and the Young Men, The.
Prayer in Time of Blindness, A.
Singing Saviors, The.
Tipsiness.
To All People.
Voyager's Song.
We are the singing shadows beauty casts. *Fr.* Eagle Sonnets.
When down the windy vistas of the years. *Fr.* Eagle Sonnets.
Wide Haven.
WOOD, MRS. CLEMENT. *See* GODDARD, GLORIA.
WOOD, EDNA D. Bumblebee.
Firefly.
WOOD, STANLEY. Homes of the Cliff Dwellers.
WOOD, URSULA. Lazarus.
Penelope.
WOODBERRY, GEORGE EDWARD. Agathon, *sel.*
At Gibraltar.
Between my eyes and her so thin the screen. *Fr.* Ideal Passion.
Beyond Good and Evil.
Child, The. *Fr.* Wild Eden.
Comrades.
Daisies, The.
Divine Awe. *Fr.* Wild Eden.
Edith Cavell.
England, I stand on thy imperial ground. *Fr.* At Gibraltar.
Essex Regiment March.
Evil thing is honor, once of old, An. *Fr.* Ideal Passion.

WOODBERRY, GEORGE EDWARD (*cont.*)
Farewell, my Muse! for, lo, there is no end. *Fr.* Ideal Passion.
Flight, The.
Homeward Bound. *Fr.* Wild Eden.
I never muse upon my lady's grace. *Fr.* Ideal Passion.
Ideal Passion.
Immortal Love, too high for my possessing. *Fr.* Ideal Passion.
In what glorious substance did they dream. *Fr.* Ideal Passion.
Islands of the Sea, The.
Life, A.
Love's Rosary.
My Country, *sels.*
My lady ne'er hath given herself to me. *Fr.* Ideal Passion.
Oh, how with brightness hath Love filled my way. *Fr.* Ideal Passion.
O, Inexpressible as Sweet. *Fr.* Wild Eden.
O Land Beloved. *Fr.* My Country.
O, Struck beneath the Laurel. *Fr.* Wild Eden.
Old House, The.
On a Portrait of Columbus.
Our First Century.
Roamer, The, *sel.*
Rose of Stars, The. *Fr.* Wild Eden.
Seaward. *Fr.* Wild Eden.
Secret, The. *Fr.* Wild Eden.
So Slow to Die. *Fr.* Wild Eden.
Sodoma's Christ Scourged.
Song: "O, inexpressible as sweet."
Song of Eros. *Fr.* Agathon.
Sonnets Written in the Fall of 1914.
When First I Saw Her. *Fr.* Wild Eden.
Why, Love, beneath the fields of asphodel. *Fr.* Ideal Passion.
Wild Eden.
Wild Eden, *sels.*
"WOODBINE WILLIE." *See* STUDDERT-KENNEDY, GEOFFREY ANKETELL.
WOODBOURNE, HARRY. Flute of May, The.
WOODBRIDGE, BENJAMIN. Upon the Tomb of John Cotton.
WOODBURY, IDA SUMNER VOSE. Lincoln's Birthday.
WOODCOCK, GEORGE. Hero, The.
Imagine the South.
Island, The.
Landore.
Merthymawr.
Poem from London, 1941.
Sonnet: "Looking into the windows that doom has broken."
Southerndown Beach.
Steel Valley, 1938.
Sunday on Hampstead Heath.
Tree Felling.
White.
WOODROW, CONSTANCE DAVIES. To a Vagabond.
WOODRUFF, DONALD M. Night Attack.
WOODRUM, LON R. King of Kings, The.
Prophecy, The.
WOODS, BERTHA GERNEAUX. At His Table.
Dedication of a Home.
Francis of Assisi.
Open My Eyes.
Patient Scientists, The.
Prayer for Faith in Peace.
Prayer on Entering Church.
WOODS, CHARLES COKE. Robin in the Rain, The.
WOODS, JAMES CHAPMAN. Soul Stithy, The.
World's Death-Night, The.
WOODS, MARGARET LOUISA. "Again I Saw Another Angel."
Eastern Legend, An.
Facing the Gulf. *Fr.* The Return.
Gaudeamus Igitur.
Genius Loci.
Ghosts.
If All the Tears Thou Madest Mine.
March Thoughts from England.
Mariners, The.
Now Sleeps the Lord.
Rest.
Return, The, *sel.*
To the Forgotten Dead.
Weep No More.
Young Windebank.
WOODS, WILLIAM HERVEY. House of Broken Swords, The, *sel.*
Prayer of Beaten Men, The. *Fr.* The House of Broken Swords.
WOODSON, MARY BLAKE. Workers.
WOODWARD, GEORGE RATCLIFFE. Before the Ikon of the Mother of God, *tr.*
Horologium, *sel., tr.*
Maid, Out of Thine Unquarried Mountain-Land, *tr.*
Mother of God, The, *tr. Fr.* Horologium.
WOODWORTH, FRANCIS CHANNING. Snow-Bird's Song, The.
WOODWORTH, NELLY HART. Hermit Thrush, The.
WOODWORTH, SAMUEL. Bucket, The.
Hunters of Kentucky, The.
Loves She like Me?
Needle, The.
Old Oaken Bucket, The.
Old Oaken Bucket, The, *sel.*
WOOLEY, CELIA PARKER. Refracted Lights.
WOOLNER, THOMAS. Given Over.
My Beautiful Lady.
WOOLSEY, SARAH CHAUNCEY. *See* "COOLIDGE, SUSAN."
WOOLSEY, THEODORE DWIGHT. Eclipse of Faith, The.
WOOLSON, CONSTANCE FENIMORE. Kentucky Belle.
Wild March.
Yellow Jessamine.
WOOTON, SIR HENRY. *See* WOTTON, SIR HENRY.
WORDSWORTH, C. W. V. Song in Praise of Paella.
WORDSWORTH, CHRISTOPHER. Giver of All.
Giving to God.
O Day of Rest and Gladness.
Ship in the Midst of the Sea, The.
WORDSWORTH, DOROTHY. Address to a Child during a Boisterous Winter Evening.
Address to a Child during a Boisterous Winter Evening, *sel.*
Cottager to Her Infant, The.
Cottager's Lullaby, The.
Loving and Liking.
Mother's Return, The.
Wind, The. *Fr.* Address to a Child.
WORDSWORTH, WILLIAM. Admonition to a Traveller.
Affliction of Margaret, The.
After-Thought. *Fr.* The River Duddon.
Alice Fell.
Alpine Descent. *Fr.* The Prelude.
Among All Lovely Things My Love Had Been.
Among the Stars. *Fr.* Peter Bell.
Anecdote for Fathers.
Animal Tranquillity and Decay.
April Morning, An. *Fr.* Poems on the Naming of Places.
As If Awakened, Summoned. *Fr.* The Prelude.
At Sunset.
At the Grave of Burns.
At This Farewell.
Band of Military Officers, A. *Fr.* The Prelude.
Behold her single in the field.
Between Namur and Liége.
Blest Statesman He, Whose Mind's Unselfish Will.
Blest the Infant Babe. *Fr.* The Prelude.
Blind Highland Boy, The.
Books. *Fr.* The Prelude.
Books a Substantial World. *Fr.* Personal Talk.
Boyhood. *Fr.* The Prelude.
Brook and road, The. *Fr.* The Prelude.
Brothers, The.
By Moscow Self-devoted to a Blaze.
By the Sea.
Cambridge and the Alps. *Fr.* The Prelude.
Cathedrals, etc.
Change in the Year, A. *Fr.* To My Sister.
Character of the Happy Warrior.
Characteristics of a Child Three Years Old.
Childhood. *Fr.* The Prelude.
Childhood and School-Time. *Fr.* The Prelude.
Childless Father, The.
Christmas Carol, The: "Minstrels played their Christmas tune, The."
Church Decking at Christmas.
Churchyard among the Mountains, The. *Fr.* The Excursion.
Cock Is Crowing, The.
Come, gentle Sleep, Death's image though thou art, *tr.*
Communion. *Fr.* The Excursion.
Communion with Nature ("For I would walk alone"). *Fr.* The Prelude.
Communion with Nature ("Think you . . ."). *Fr.* Expostulation and Reply.
Complaint, A.
Complaint of a Forsaken Indian Woman, The.
Composed at Neidpath Castle, the Property of Lord Queensberry, 1803.
Composed by the Sea-Side, near Calais, August, 1802.
Composed by the Side of Grasmere Lake.
Composed in One of the Catholic Cantons.
Composed in the Valley near Dover [on the Day of Landing].
Composed on a May Morning, 1838.
Composed upon an Evening of Extraordinary Splendor and Beauty.
Composed upon the Beach near Calais [August, 1802].
Composed upon Westminster Bridge, September 3, 1802.
Conclusion. *Fr.* The Prelude.
Continued (King's College Chapel). *Fr.* Ecclesiastical Sonnets.
Crescent Boat, The. *Fr.* Peter Bell.
Crossing the Alps. *Fr.* The Prelude.
Cuckoo and the Nightingale, The, *tr.*
Cuckoo at Laverna, The, *sel.*
Daffodils [The].
Daisy, The. *Fr.* So Fair, So Sweet, Withal So Sensitive.
Dear Child of Nature, let them rail.
Dear Native Regions.
Deathless Flower, A, *tr.*
Dedicated Spirit, A. *Fr.* The Prelude.
Demobilized Soldier, The. *Fr.* The Prelude.
Desideria.
Desire We Past Illusions to Recall?
Despondency Corrected. *Fr.* The Excursion.
Destined to war from very infancy, *tr. Fr.* Epitaphs.
Destiny.
Devotional Incitements.
Dion.
Discourse of the Wanderer, and an Evening Visit to the Lake. *Fr.* The Excursion.
Diverging now (as if his quest had been). *Fr.* The Excursion.
Down the Simplon Pass. *Fr.* The Prelude.
Eagles. Composed at Dunolly Castle.
Earth Has Not Anything to Show More Fair.
Ecclesiastical Sonnets, *sels.*
Education of Nature, The.
1811.
Elegiac Stanzas [Suggested by a Picture of Peele Castle in a Storm].
Emigrant Mother, The.
England and Switzerland, 1802.
England, 1802.
Enough of Humble Arguments. *Fr.* The Prelude.
Eternal Lord! Eased of a Cumbrous Load, *tr.*
Evening on Calais Beach.

Evening Voluntary.
Evening Walk, An.
Evening Walk, An, *sels.*
Excursion, The, *sels.*
Expostulation and Reply.
Expostulation and Reply, *sel.*
Extempore Effusion upon the Death of James Hogg.
Extempore Effusion upon the Death of James Hogg, *sel.*
Extract from the Conclusion of a Poem, Composed in Anticipation of Leaving School.
Extract from the Conclusion of a Poem, Composed in Anticipation of Leaving School, *sel.*
Fair seed-time had my soul. *Fr.* The Prelude.
Faith. *Fr.* The Excursion.
Faith and Freedom.
Favourite pleasure, A. *Fr.* The Prelude.
Feelings of the Tyrolese.
Fidelity.
For I have learn'd. *Fr.* Lines Composed a Few Miles above Tintern Abbey.
For I would walk alone. *Fr.* The Prelude.
For Inspiration, *tr.*
Force of Prayer, The, *sel.*
Founding of Bolton Priory, The.
Fountain, The.
Fragment: "Up, up! My friend and quit your books." *Fr.* The Tables Turned.
France. *Fr.* The Prelude.
Francesco Ceni, *tr.*
French and [the] Spanish Guerrillas, The.
French Revolution, The. *Fr.* The Prelude.
From low to high doth dissolution climb.
Gladness of the May, The.
Glen-Almain, the Narrow Glen.
Glow-Worm, The. *Fr.* The Prelude.
Goody Blake and Harry Gill.
Gracious spirit o'er this earth presides, A. *Fr.* The Prelude.
Great Men Have Been Among Us.
Green Linnet, The.
Guilt and Sorrow, *sel.*
Happy Warrior, The.
Hart-Leap Well.
Hast Thou Seen with Flash Incessant.
He Remembers the Vista of a Towering Peak. *Fr.* The Prelude.
Here Pause: the Poet Claims at Least This Praise.
Horn of Egremont Castle, The.
I Grieved for Buonaparté.
I Have Felt a Presence. *Fr.* Lines Composed a Few Miles above Tintern Abbey.
I have learn'd. *Fr.* Lines Composed a Few Miles above Tintern Abbey.
I have seen a curious child. *Fr.* The Excursion.
I Saw the Figure of a Lovely Maid.
I see around me here. *Fr.* The Excursion.
I thought of thee, my partner and my guide. *Fr.* The River Duddon.
I Traveled among Unknown Men.
I Wandered Lonely as a Cloud.
Ideal.
Idiot Boy.
If This Great World of Joy and Pain.
If Thou Indeed Derive Thy Light from Heaven.
Imagination. *Fr.* The Prelude.
Imagination and Taste, How Impaired and Restored. *Fr.* The Prelude.
In a Child's Album.
In a throng, a festal company. *Fr.* The Prelude.
In Childhood and Youth. *Fr.* The Prelude.
In London, September 1802.
In March.
In One of Those Excursions. *Fr.* The Prelude.
In Sight of the Town of Cockermouth, Where the Author Was Born, and His Father's Remains Are Laid.
Incident Characteristic of a Favorite Dog.
Influence of Natural Objects. *Fr.* The Prelude.
Inner Vision, The.
Inside of King's College Chapel, Cambridge. *Fr.* Ecclesiastical Sonnets.
Intimations of Immortality.
Intimations of Immortality, *sels.*
Introduction—Childhood and School-Time. *Fr.* The Prelude.
It Is a Beauteous Evening, Calm and Free.
It Is Not to Be Thought Of.
It Was an April Morning.
I've watched you now a full half-hour.
King's College Chapel, Cambridge. *Fr.* Ecclesiastical Sonnets.
Kitten and Falling Leaves, The.
Kitten at Play, The.
Kitten Playing with the Falling Leaves, The.
Laodamia.
Last of the Flock, The.
Leech-Gatherer, The.
Lesson, A.
Let Nature Be Your Teacher. *Fr.* The Tables Turned.
Liberty, *sel.*
Lines: "Nay, traveller! rest."
Lines: "Slumber did my spirit seal, A."
Lines Composed a Few Miles above Tintern Abbey.
Lines Composed a Few Miles above Tintern Abbey, *sels.*
Lines Composed at Grasmere.
Lines Left upon a Seat in a Yew-Tree.
Lines Written above Tintern Abbey.
Lines Written in Early Spring.
Lines Written near Richmond, upon the Thames, at Evening.
London, 1802.
Lost Love, The.
Louisa.
Love. *Fr.* The Prelude.
Love's Justification, *tr.*
Lucy: "I traveled among unknown men."
Lucy: "She dwelt among the untrodden ways."
Lucy: "She dwelt among the untrodden ways," *sel.*
Lucy: "Slumber did my spirit seal, A."
Lucy: "Strange fits of passion have I known."
Lucy: "Three years she grew in sun and shower."
Lucy: "Three years she grew in sun and shower," *sel.*
Lucy Gray; or, Solitude.
Majestic Intellect. *Fr.* The Prelude.
Man Is Dear to Man: the Poorest Poor.
March.
Margaret; or, The Ruined Cottage. *Fr.* The Excursion.
Mary Queen of Scots Landing at the Mouth of the Derwent, Workington.
Maternal Grief.
Matthew.
Memory.
Memory of one particular hour, The. *Fr.* The Prelude.
Merry Month of March, The.
Michael.
Milton.
Ministration.
Mist Opening in the Hills. *Fr.* The Excursion.
Most Sweet It Is [with Unuplifted Eyes].
Motherland, The.
Mutability. *Fr.* Ecclesiastical Sonnets.
My Heart Leaps Up [When I Behold].
Nature ("I have learned"). *Fr.* Lines Composed a Few Miles above Tintern Abbey.
Nature ("The world is too much with us").
Nature and the Poet.
Nature, Love, and Man. *Fr.* The Prelude.
Nature's Gifts to Lucy. *Fr.* Three Years She Grew in Sun and Shower.
Nature's Healing. *Fr.* The Prelude.
Nature's Ministry. *Fr.* The Prelude.
Near Dover, September, 1802.
Near the Spring of the Hermitage.
Newton. *Fr.* The Prelude.
Night in June, A. *Fr.* Lines after Tea at Grasmere.
Night-Piece, A.
Nightingale, The.
No mortal object did these eyes behold, *tr.*
Noble, The. *Fr.* The Prelude.
Not in the Lucid Intervals of Life.
Not Love, Not War, nor the Tumultuous Swell.
Not Seldom, Clad in Radiant Vest.
Not without heavy grief of heart did he, *tr.* *Fr.* Epitaphs.
November, 1806.
November 1.
Nuns Fret Not at Their Convent's Narrow Room.
Nutting.
Oh, Blank Confusion. *Fr.* The Prelude.
O Day of Rest and Gladness.
O flower of all that springs from gentle blood, *tr.* *Fr.* Epitaphs.
O Friend! I know not which way I must look.
Oh! Mystery of Man. *Fr.* The Prelude.
O Nightingale.
O pleasant exercise of hope and joy! *Fr.* The Prelude.
O thou who movest onward with a mind, *tr.* *Fr.* Epitaphs.
Oh! yet a few short years. *Fr.* The Prelude.
October, 1803.
Ode: Intimations of Immortality from Recollections of Early Childhood.
Ode: Intimations of Immortality from Recollections of Early Childhood, *sels.*
Ode on [the] Intimations of Immortality from Recollections of Early Childhood.
Ode to Duty.
Of His Daughter Catherine Dead Long Since.
Of the Sonnet.
Oft have I heard the Nightingale and Thrush. *Fr.* The Cuckoo at Laverna.
Old Cumberland Beggar, The.
Old inventive poets, had they seen, The. *Fr.* The River Duddon.
Old Man, An.
On Burns.
On Revisiting Dunolly Castle.
On the Beach at Calais.
On the Departure of Sir Walter Scott from Abbotsford (for Naples, 1831).
On the Extinction of the Venetian Republic.
On the Frozen Lake. *Fr.* The Prelude.
On the Sea-Shore near Calais.
On the Sonnet.
On the Subjugation of Switzerland.
On the Swiss.
One evening (surely I was led by her). *Fr.* The Prelude.
One Summer Evening. *Fr.* The Prelude.
Parsonage, The. *Fr.* The Excursion.
Pass of Kirkstone, The.
Pause, courteous spirit!—Balbi supplicates, *tr.* *Fr.* Epitaphs.
Perfect Woman.
Perhaps some needful service of the state, *tr.* *Fr.* Epitaphs.
Personal Talk.
Personal Talk, *sels.*
Persuasion. *Fr.* Ecclesiastical Sonnets.

WORDSWORTH, WILLIAM (*continued*)
Pet Lamb, The.
Peter Bell, *sel.*
Pilgrim Fathers, The.
Places of Worship.
Plain of Donnerdale, The. *Fr.* The River Duddon.
Poems on the Naming of Places, *sels.*
Poet and the French Revolution. *Fr.* The Prelude.
Poet, A!—He Hath Put His Heart to School.
Poet's Epitaph, A.
Poor Susan's Dream.
Prayer for Inspiration, A, *tr.*
Prefatory Sonnet.
Prelude, The.
Prelude, The, *sels.*
Presences of Nature in Boyhood. *Fr.* The Prelude.
Primrose of the Rock, The.
Progress of Poets, The. *Fr.* Resolution and Independence.
Prospectus. *Fr.* The Recluse.
Protest against the Ballot.
Rainbow [in the Sky], The.
Raven's Nest, The. *Fr.* The Prelude.
Reaper, The.
Recluse, The.
Recluse, The, *sel.*
Recollections of Early Childhood. *Fr.* Ode: Intimations of Immortality.
Redbreast Chasing a Butterfly, The.
Remembrance of Collins.
Residence in France. *Fr.* The Prelude.
Residence in France (Continued). *Fr.* The Prelude.
Residence in London. *Fr.* The Prelude.
Resolution and Independence.
Resolution and Independence, *sel.*
Retrospect—Love of Nature Leading to Love of Man. *Fr.* The Prelude.
Return, Content! for fondly I pursued. *Fr.* The River Duddon.
Reverie of Poor Susan, The.
River Duddon, The, *sels.*
Ruth.
Ruth, *sel.*
Sailor's Mother, The.
Same, The (King's College Chapel). *Fr.* Ecclesiastical Sonnets.
Same, The ("Milton! thou shouldst be living at this hour").
Same, The ("What awful perspective! while from our sight"). *Fr.* Ecclesiastical Sonnets.
School-Time. *Fr.* The Prelude.
Scorn Not the Sonnet.
September, 1815.
September, 1819.
September, 1802. Near Dover.
September, 1802 (Upon the Same Occasion).
September 1, 1802.
Serving No Haughty Muse.
Seven Sisters, The; or, The Solitude of Binnorie.
She Dwelt among the Untrodden Ways.
She Dwelt among the Untrodden Ways, *sel.*
She Was a Phantom of Delight.
Simon Lee [the Old Huntsman].
Simplon Pass, The. *Fr.* The Prelude.
Single tree there was, A. *Fr.* The Prelude.
Sister, A.
Skating. *Fr.* The Prelude.
Sky after Storm. *Fr.* The Excursion.
Sleep.
Sleeplessness.
Slumber Did My Spirit Seal, A.
Small Celandine, The.
Small Service.
So Fair, So Sweet, Withal So Sensitive.
So Fair, So Sweet, Withal So Sensitive, *sel.*
Sole listener, Duddon! to the breeze that played. *Fr.* The River Duddon.
Solitary, The. *Fr.* The Excursion.
Solitary Reaper, The.
Solitude. *Fr.* The Prelude.
Song at the Feast of Brougham Castle.
Song for the Spinning Wheel.
Sonnet: "Ambition—following down this far-famed slope."
Sonnet: Composed after a Journey across the Hamilton Hills, Yorkshire.
Sonnet: Composed by the Side of Grasmere Lake.
Sonnet: Composed upon Westminster Bridge, September 3, 1802.
Sonnet: Composed While the Author Was Engaged in Writing a Tract Occasioned by the Convention of Cintra.
Sonnet: "Earth has not anything to show more fair."
Sonnet: 1811.
Sonnet: "Fair star of evening, splendor of the west."
Sonnet: French and the Spanish Guerrillas, The.
Sonnet: "From low to high doth dissolution climb."
Sonnet: "How sweet it is, when mother Fancy rocks."
Sonnet: "I saw the figure of a lovely maid."
Sonnet: "I thought of thee, my partner and my guide."
Sonnet: "It is a beauteous evening, calm and free."
Sonnet: "It is not to be thought of that the flood."
Sonnet: "Milton! thou shouldst be living at this hour."
Sonnet: "No mortal object did these eyes behold," *tr.*
Sonnet: "Nuns fret not at their convent's narrow room."
Sonnet, The: "Scorn not the Sonnet; critic, you have frowned."
Sonnet: September, 1815.
Sonnet: September, 1802.
Sonnet: September 1, 1802.
Sonnet: "Sole listener, Duddon! to the breeze that played." *Fr.* The River Duddon.
Sonnet: "Surprised by joy—impatient as the wind."
Sonnet: There Is a Bondage Worse.
Sonnet: "There is a little unpretending rill."
Sonnet: Thought of a Briton on the Subjugation of Switzerland.
Sonnet: To ——.
Sonnet: To the Lady Beaumont.
Sonnet: Where Lies the Land.
Sonnet: Wild Duck's Nest, The.
Sonnet, A: "World is too much with us, The."
Sonnet: Written in London, September, 1802.
Sonnet: "Yes! hope may with my strong desire keep pace," *tr.*
Sonnet Composed upon Westminster Bridge, September 3, 1802.
Sonnet on Catherine Wordsworth.
Sonnet on the Sonnet.
Sonnet-Prison, The.
Sonnet to an Octogenarian.
Sonnet to the Virgin.
Sparrow's Nest, The.
Speak!
Springtime with One Love. *Fr.* The Excursion.
Stanzas Written in My Pocket Copy of Thomson's "Castle of Indolence."
Stepping Westward.
Stern Daughter of the Voice of God. *Fr.* Ode to Duty.
Stolen Boat, The. *Fr.* The Prelude.
Strange Fits of Passion Have I Known.
Such was the boy. *Fr.* The Excursion.
Summer Vacation. *Fr.* The Prelude.
Sun Has Long Been Set, The.
Sunset and Sea.
Sunset in the Lake Country. *Fr.* An Evening Walk.
Supplication ("The prayers I make will then be sweet indeed"), *tr.*
Surprised by Joy—Impatient as the Wind.
Swans. *Fr.* An Evening Walk.
Swiss Peasant, The.
Tables Turned, The.
Tables Turned, The, *sel.*
Tenour which my life holds, The. *Fr.* The Excursion.
There Is a Little Unpretending Rill.
There Is an Eminence.
There never breathed a man, who, when his life, *tr.* *Fr.* Epitaphs.
"There!" Said a Stripling.
There Was a Boy. *Fr.* The Prelude.
These Helps Solicit. *Fr.* The Excursion.
They Dreamt Not of a Perishable Home.
This Prayer I Make. *Fr.* Lines Composed a Few Miles above Tintern Abbey.
Thorn, The.
Thought [*or* Thoughts] of a Briton on the Subjugation of Switzerland.
Three Cottage Girls, The.
Three Years She Grew in Sun and Shower.
Three Years She Grew in Sun and Shower, *sel.*
Tidings of Invisible Things. *Fr.* The Excursion.
Timothy.
Tintern Abbey.
'Tis Said That Some Have Died for Love.
'Tis Said That Some Have Died for Love, *sel.*
To ——: "O dearer far than light and life are dear."
To a Butterfly ("I've watched you").
To a Butterfly ("Stay near me").
To a Child.
To a Distant Friend.
To a Highland Girl.
To a Skylark ("Ethereal minstrel!").
To a Skylark ("Up with me!").
To a Snowdrop.
To a Young Lady.
To B. R. Haydon.
To Catherine Wordsworth 1808-1812.
To Duty.
To H. C.
To Hartley Coleridge.
To M. H.
To Milton.
To My Sister.
To My Sister, *sel.*
To Sleep.
To the Cuckoo.
To the Daisy ("Bright flower! whose home is everywhere").
To the Daisy ("In youth from rock to rock I went").
To the Daisy ("With little here").
To the Highland Girl of Inversneyde.
To the Men of Kent.
To the Poet, John Dyer.
To the Same Flower (Celandine).
To the Same Flower (Daisy).
To the Skylark ("Ethereal minstrel!").
To the Small Celandine.
To the Small Celandine, *sel.*
To the Supreme Being, *tr.*
To Toussaint L'Ouverture.
To Toussaint L'Ouverture, *sel.*
Trailing Clouds of Glory. *Fr.* Ode: Intimations of Immortality.
Trosachs, The.
True is it that Ambrosio Salinero, *tr.* *Fr.* Epitaphs.
'Twere Long to Tell. *Fr.* The Prelude.
Twilight.
Two April Mornings, The.
Two Victories. *Fr.* Song at the Feast of Brougham Castle.
Two Voices Are There.
Universal Heart of Man, The. *Fr.* The Prelude.
Unknown Poets. *Fr.* The Excursion.
Unremitting Voice of Nightly Streams, The.
Up! Up! My Friend, and Quit Your Books.
Upon the Sight of a Beautiful Picture.
Upon Westminster Bridge.

Valedictory Sonnet to the River Duddon. *Fr.* The River Duddon.
Venice.
Violet, The.
Virgin, The.
Waggoner, The, *sel.*
Walk in Meditation.
Walton's Book of Lives. *Fr.* Ecclesiastical Sonnets.
Wanderer, The. *Fr.* The Excursion.
Waterfall and the Eglantine, The.
We Are Seven.
Weak Is the Will of Man, His Judgment Blind.
Weep not, beloved friends! nor let the air, *tr. Fr.* Epitaphs.
Westminster Bridge.
What Man Has Made of Man.
When First I made. *Fr.* The Prelude.
When I Have Borne in Memory [What Has Tamed].
When, to the Attractions of the Busy World.
Where Lies the Land [to Which Yon Ship Must Go]?
Whirl-Blast from behind the Hill, A.
Who Ponders National Events Shall Find.
Why Art Thou Silent?
Wild Duck's Nest, The.
Winander Lake. *Fr.* The Prelude.
Wings Have We. *Fr.* Personal Talk.
Wisdom and Spirit of the Universe. *Fr.* The Prelude.
With How Sad Steps.
With Ships the Sea Was Sprinkled.
Within King's College Chapel, Cambridge. *Fr.* Ecclesiastical Sonnets.
Within the Soul a Faculty Abides. *Fr.* The Excursion.
World, The. *Fr.* The World Is Too Much with Us.
World Is Too Much with Us, The.
World Is Too Much with Us, The, *sel.*
Worldliness.
Wren's Nest, A.
Written after the Death of Charles Lamb, *sel.*
Written in Early Spring.
Written in London, September, 1802.
Written in March.
Written in the Album of a Child.
Written in Very Early Youth.
Yarrow Revisited.
Yarrow Unvisited.
Yarrow Visited.
Yes! hope may with my strong desire keep pace, *tr.*
Yes, It Was the Mountain Echo.
Yew-Trees.
WORK, HENRY CLAY. Come Home, Father.
Father, Dear Father, Come Home with Me Now.
Grandfather's Clock.
Kingdom Come.
Marching through Georgia.
Ship That Never Returned, The.
Year of Jubilo [*or* Jubilee].
WORKS, AUSTIN MELVIN. Song of Youth.
WORRELL, EDNA RANDOLPH. Christmas Legend.
WORSLEY-BENISON, H. Song of the Engine, The.
WORTH, KATHARINE. Trees That Shade a House.
WORTH, KATHRYN. Circus Elephant. Smells.
"WORTH, PATIENCE." Lullaby: "Dream, dream, thou flesh of me!"
WORTHING, MRS. E. Prayer for the Dogs in War, A.
WORTHINGTON, KIM. I Held a Lamb.
WORTMAN, DENIS. God of the Prophets.
WOTTON, SIR HENRY. Character of a Happy Life, The.
"D. O. M."
De Morte, *at.*
Description of the Spring, A.
Dialogue betwixt God and the Soul, A, *at.*
Elegy, An: "O faithless world, and thy most faithless part."
Elizabeth of Bohemia.
Eternall Mover.
Happy Life, The.
How Happy Is He Born.
Hymn Made When He Was an Ambassador at Venice, in the Time of a Great Sickness There.
Hymn to My God in a Night of My Late Sicknesse, A.
In Praise of Angling.
It Is Finished.
Lord of Himself.
May Day, A.
Of a Woman's Heart.
On a [*or* the] Bank as I Sat [*or* Sate] a-Fishing.
On His Mistress [*or* Mistris], the Queen of Bohemia.
On the Bank as I Sat a-Fishing.
On the Death of Sir Albert Morton's Wife.
To His Mistress, Elizabeth of Bohemia.
Upon the Death of Sir Albert Morton's Wife.
Upon the Sudden Restraint of the Earle of Somerset, Then Falling from Favor.
WOTTON, SIR JOHN. Damaetas' Jig.
In Praise of His Daphnis.
In Praise of His Love.
WRAFTER, DENIS. Braggart!
Old Man to His Scythe, The.
On Hearing a Broadcast of Ceremonies in Connection with Conferring of Cardinals' Hats.
Sabbath Reflection.
WRATISLAW, THEODORE. Expectation.
Music-Hall, The.
Vain Desire, A.
WRAY, ANGELINA. Autumn Leaves.
WREDE, PRINCESS GABRIELLE. Before the Crucifix.
WREFORD, HEYMAN. Christ Is Coming.
"WREFORD, JAMES." *See* WATSON, JAMES WREFORD.
WREFORD, JOHN R. Lord, While for All Mankind [We Pray].
WREN, LOWE W. Dog's Howl, A.
WRENN, PHILIP. To a Cafeteria Rubber-Plant.
WRIGHT, BRUCE MCM. African Affair, The.
Journey to a Parallel.
WRIGHT, CATHARINE MORRIS. Hillside Pause.
WRIGHT, CELESTE TURNER. Thumbprint. Today.
WRIGHT, DAVID. Canons Ashby.
Monologue of a Deaf Man.
Moral Story II.
Seven South African Poems.
Verses to St. Cecilia.
Voyage to Africa, A, *sel.*
Walking to Dedham.
WRIGHT, DAVID MCKEE. Arlington.
Duff, The.
Earth Song.
In the Moonlight.
Shearing.
While the Billy Boils.
WRIGHT, ELIZUR. Ape, The, *tr.*
Bird Wounded by an Arrow, The, *tr.*
Boy and the Schoolmaster, The, *tr.*
Cock and the Pearl, The, *tr.*
Cockerel, the Cat, and the Young Mouse, The, *tr.*
Fox and the Bust, The, *tr.*
Fox and the Grapes, The, *tr.*
Glutton, The, *tr.*
Hen with the Golden Eggs, The, *tr.*
Jay in the Feathers of the Peacock, The, *tr.*
Lion Grown Old, The, *tr.*
Man and the Flea, The, *tr.*
Old Man and the Ass, The, *tr.*
Oyster and the Litigants, The, *tr.*
Raven and the Fox, The, *tr.*
Sick Lion and the Fox, The, *tr.*
Thieves and the Ass, The, *tr.*
Wolf and the Dog, The, *tr.*
WRIGHT, ERNEST VINCENT. When Father Carves the Duck.
WRIGHT, FREDERICK ADAM. Letter to the City Clerk.
For translations from Latin, see LaP.
WRIGHT, GLADYS YOAKUM. Texas, Our Texas.
WRIGHT, IVAN LEONARD. Want of You, The.
WRIGHT, JAMES. Assignation, The.
At the Slackening of the Tide.
On the Skeleton of a Hound.
Paul.
To a Defeated Saviour.
To the Ghost of a Kite.
WRIGHT, JUDITH. Ancestors, The.
Bora Ring.
Builders, The.
Bullocky.
Company of Lovers, The.
Country Dance.
Legend.
Night and the Child.
Old Prison, The.
South of My Days.
To a Child.
Trapped Dingo.
Unborn, The.
Woman to Man.
Woman's Song.
WRIGHT, MERLE ST. CROIX. Cradle Song: "Winds are whispering over the sea, The."
WRIGHT, RICHARD. Between the World and Me.
I Have Seen Black Hands.
WRIGHT, WILLARD HUNTINGTON. Song against Women.
WRIGHT, WILLIAM BULL. Brook, The, *sel.*
WRIGHTON, W. T. Dearest Spot on Earth, The.
WROTH [*or* WROATH], LADY MARY. Countess of Montgomery's Urania, The, *sel.*
Love, What Art Thou? *Fr.* The Countess of Montgomery's Urania.
WU MOU CH'IEN. Fleeting Years, The.
WURDEMANN, AUDREY (Mrs. Joseph Auslander). Enduring Word, The.
Little Black Man with a Rose in His Hat.
WURTZBAUGH, JEWEL. Peon's Mother, The.
WU SHANG YEH. Slave, The.
WU TI, EMPEROR. Autumn Wind [*or* Winds], The.
Liberator, The.
Li Fu-jen.
People Hide Their Love.
Sound of her silk skirt has stopped, The.
Summer Song.
To One Who Has Passed.
WU TSUNG AI. Memories of Childhood.
Separation.
WU WEN TI. Rejected.
WU YUNG. Love.
WYATT, EDITH FRANKLIN. City Afternoon, A.
On the Great Plateau.
To F. W.
WYATT, SIR THOMAS. A! My Herte, A! What Aileth The.
Abused Lover Seeth His Folly and Entendeth to Trust No More, The.
Against the Court of Rome, *tr.*
Alas! Madam, for Stealing of a Kiss.
All heavy minds.
And wilt thou leave me thus?
Appeal, The.
Betrayal.
Blame Not My Lute.
Comparison of Love to a Streame Falling from the Alpes.
Complaint for True Love Unrequited.
Constancy.
Contrarious Passions in a Lover, The, *tr. Fr.* Sonnets to Laura.
Courtier's Life, The.
Deme as Ye List upon Goode Cause.
Description of a Gun, *tr.*
Description of Such a One as He Would Love, A.
Description of the Contrarious Passions in a Lover, *tr. Fr.* Sonnets to Laura.

WYATT, SIR THOMAS (*continued*)
Deserted Lover Consoleth Himself, The.
Disdain ("If in the world").
Disdain Me Not without Desert.
Divers Doth Use, as I Have Heard and Know.
Earnest Suit to His Unkind Mistress Not to Forsake Him, An.
Epigram: "Enemy of life, decayer of all kind, The."
Epigram: "Face that should content me wonders well, A."
Epigram: "Fruit of all the service that I serve, The."
Epigram: "Lux my fair falcon, and your fellows all."
Epigram: "Sighs are my food, drink are my tears."
Epigram: "Who hath heard of such cruelty before?"
Epigrams.
Epitaph, An, of Sir Thomas Gravener, Knight.
Face that should content me wondrous well, A.
Farewell: "What should I say."
Farewell, Love.
Farewell, Unkist.
Forget Not Yet.
Fortune.
Galley, The, *tr.* *Fr.* Sonnets to Laura.
Hate Whom Ye List.
He Ruleth Not though He Reign over Realms That Is Subject to His Own Lusts.
Help Me to Seek.
Hind, The.
His Lady's Hand.
His Reward.
Honesty.
How Like You This?
How Should I Be So Pleasant?
I abide and abide and better abide.
I Find No Peace, *tr.*
If in the World There Be More Woe.
In Eternum I Was Once Determed.
In Spain.
Is It Possible?
Liberty.
Like to these unmeasurable mountains, *tr.*
Long love that in my thought doth harbor, The, *tr.*
Lover Beseecheth His Mistress Not to Forget His Steadfast Faith and True Intent, The.
Lover Compareth His Heart to the Overcharged Gun, The.
Lover Compareth His State to a Ship in Perilous Storm Tossed on the Sea, The, *tr.* *Fr.* Sonnets to Laura.
Lover Complaineth the Unkindness of His Love, The.
Lover Describeth His Being Striken with Sight of His Love, The.
Lover for Shamefastness Hideth His Desire within His Faithful Heart, The, *tr.* *Fr.* Sonnets to Laura.
Lover Like to a Ship Tossed on the Sea, The, *tr.* *Fr.* Sonnets to Laura.
Lover Rejoiceth [That He Hath Broken the Snares of Love], The.
Lover Rejoiceth the Enjoying of His Love, The.
Lover Renounceth Love, The.
Lover Sendeth Sighs to Move His Suit, The.
Lover Showeth [*or* Sheweth] How He Is Forsaken of Such as He Sometime Enjoyed, The.
Lover to His Bed, with Describing of His Unquiet State, The, *after* Petrarch.
Lover's Appeal, The.
Lover's Life Compared to the Alps, The, *tr.*
Love's Inconsistency, *tr.* *Fr.* Sonnets to Laura.
Love's Snare.
Luckes, my faire falcon, and your fellowes all.
Lute Obeys, The.
Madame, withouten many words.
Marvel No More.
May Time.
Mine own John Poins, since ye delight to know.
My Galley Charged with Forgetfulness, *tr.* *Fr.* Sonnets to Laura.
My lute, awake! perform the last.
O Goodly Hand.
Of Dissembling Words.
Of His Love Called Anna.
Of His Love That Pricked Her Finger with a Needle.
Of His Return from Spain.
Of Such as Had Forsaken Him.
Of the Courtier's Life. *Fr.* Satires.
Of the Mean and Sure Estate ("My mother's maids"). *Fr.* Satires.
Of the Mean and Sure Estate ("Stand whoso list"), *tr.* *Fr.* Thyestes.
Patience.
Perdye I Saide Yt Not.
Promise, A.
Protest, A.
Remembrance.
Renouncing of Hardly Escaped Love, A.
Renouncing of Love, A.
Resignation.
Revocation, A.
Rondeau: "Help me to seek, for I lost it there."
Rondeau: "What? No, perdie! ye may be sure."
Satire: "Mine own John Poynz."
Satires, *sels.*
Say Nay.
Since you will needs [*or* Sins you will nedes] that I shall sing.
Sonnet: "Divers doth use (as I have heard and know)."
Sonnet: "Each man me telleth I change most my devise."
Sonnet: "Farewell, Love, and all thy laws for ever."
Sonnet: "I abide and abide and better abide."
Sonnet: "I find no peace, and all my war is done."
Sonnet: "My galley chargèd with forgetfulness."
Sonnet: "My love took scorn my service to retain."
Sonnet: "To rail or jest, ye know I use it not."
Sonnet: "Whoso list to hunt, I know where is an hind."
Sonnet: "You that in love find luck and abundaunce."
Sonnets to Laura, *sels.*, *tr.*
Steadfastness.
Stond [*or* Stand] Who So List upon the Slipper Toppe [*or* Top], *tr.* *Fr.* Thyestes.
Supplication, A.
Tagus, farewell, that westward with thy streams.
Tangled I Was.
That Speaking or Proffering Brings Alway Speeding.
They Flee from Me.
Thyestes, *sel.*, *tr.*
To a Lady to Answer Directly with Yea or Nay.
To Cause Accord or to Agree.
To His Heart.
To His Lady.
To His Lute.
To His Pen.
To Sir Francis Brian. *Fr.* Satires.
Translation from Petrarch ("Mine old dear enemy, my froward master").
Treizaine.
Unstable Dream, According to the Place.
Varium et Mutabile.
Vixi Puellis Nuper Idoneus.
What No, Perdy.
What rage is this? what furor of what kind?
What should I say.
Whoso List to Hunt.
With Serving Still.
Wyatt Being in Prison, to Bryan.
Ye Know My Heart.
You That in Love Find Luck and Abundance.
Ys Yt Possyble.
WYCHERLEY, WILLIAM. Drinking Song, A, against All Sorts of Disputes in Drinking.
Love in a Wood, *sel.*
Song, A: In the Name of a Lover, to His Mistress.
Spouse I Do Hate, A. *Fr.* Love in a Wood.
To a Good Physician.
To a Witty Man of Wealth and Quality.
To His Mistress, Who Said She Hated Him for His Grey Hairs.
Upon the Most Useful Knowledge, Craft or Cunning, Which Is More Wisdom, as 'Tis Less Wit.
Wife I Do Hate, A.
WYETH, JOHN ALLAN. Air Raid.
Hospital.
Hospital Train.
WYLIE, ELINOR. Address to My Soul.
Atavism.
August.
Beauty.
Bells in the Rain.
Benvenuto's Valentine.
Birthday Sonnet.
Castilian.
Children and Dogs Are Subject.
Coast Guard's Cottage, The.
Cold-blooded Creatures.
Confession of Faith.
Country Song.
Demon Lovers.
Desolation Is a Delicate Thing.
Doomsday.
Down to the Puritan marrow of my bones. *Fr.* Wild Peaches.
Drowned Woman.
Eagle and the Mole, The.
Epitaph: "For this she starred her eyes with salt."
Escape.
Farewell, Sweet Dust.
Felo de Se.
Full Moon.
Golden Bough.
Heroics.
House Sonnet. *Fr.* One Person.
How Many Faults.
Hymn to Earth.
I Hereby Swear That to Uphold Your House. *Fr.* One Person.
Innocent Landscape.
Innocents, The.
King Honor's Eldest Son.
Knight Fallen on Evil Days, The.
Last Supper.
Lavish Kindness.
Let No Charitable Hope.
Lion and the Lamb, The.
Little Elegy.
Little Joke.
Lucifer Sings in Secret.
Madman's Song.
Malediction upon Myself.
Minotaur.
Miranda's Supper.
My honoured lord, forgive the unruly tongue. *Fr.* One Person.
Nameless Song.
Nebuchadnezzar.
Now Am I Orson to Your Valentine.
O love, how utterly am I bereaved. *Fr.* One Person.
O Virtuous Light.
On a Singing Girl.
One Person, *sels.*
Parting Gift.
Pebble, The.
Pegasus Lost.
Peregrine.
Peter and John.
Poor Old Cannon, The.
Pretty Words.
Prophecy.
Proud Lady, A.
Puritan Sonnet. *Fr.* Wild Peaches.
Puritan's Ballad, The.
Red Carpet for Shelley, A.
Sanctuary.

Sea Lullaby.
Sequence.
Shepherd's Holiday.
Sleeping Beauty.
Sonnet: "Down to the Puritan marrow of my bones." *Fr.* Wild Peaches.
Sonnet: "I hereby swear that to uphold your house." *Fr.* One Person.
Sonnet: "My honoured lord, forgive the unruly tongue." *Fr.* One Person.
Sonnet: "When I perceive the sable of your hair." *Fr.* One Person.
Sonnet: "You are the faintest freckles on the hide."
Sonnets from "One Person."
Spring Pastoral.
Sunset on the Spire.
This Corruptible.
To a Book.
To Claudia Homonoea.
To His Soul, *tr.*
Tortoise in Eternity, The.
True Vine.
Twelfth Night.
Unfinished Portrait.
Velvet Shoes.
What Other Name Had Half Expressed.
When I Perceive the Sable of Your Hair. *Fr.* One Person.
Where, O, Where?
Wild Peaches.
Wild Peaches, *sels.*
Winter Sleep.

WYN, EIFION. Son of the Mountain.

WYN, HEDD. War.

WYNDHAM, CHARLES, 2D EARL OF EGREMONT. Fair Thief, The.

WYNNE, ANNETTE. Airplane, The.
Book, Book.
Books Are Soldiers.
Cars Go Fast.
Chairs.
Christopher Columbus.
Columbus.
Elephant, The.
Excuse Us, Animals in the Zoo.
Fairy Shoes.
Happy Oxen in a Stall.
Harebells in June.
Hearts Were Made to Give Away.
House Cat, The.
I Heard It in the Valley.
I Keep Three Wishes Ready.
I Wonder if the Lion Knows.
I'm Wishing the Whole World Christmas.
Indian Children.
Letter Is a Gypsy Elf, A.
Lions Running over the Green.
Little Folks in the Grass.
Little Maid of Far Japan.
Memorial Day.
My Book Holds Many Stories.
Once When You Were Walking.
Outside the Door.
Palos, Spain, 1492.
People Buy a Lot of Things.
Pilgrims Came, The.
Ring around the World.
Song of the Snowflakes.
Teacher, The.
Telegraph, The.
Thanksgiving Day.
Tree Stands Very Straight and Still, The.
Wires Are So Still and High, The.
Wish Is Quite a Tiny Thing, A.

WYNNE, FRANCES. Lesson in Geography, A.

X

"X, BROTHER." *See* "BROTHER X."

XAMMAR, LUIS FABIO. Spring, The.

"XARIFFA." *See* TOWNSEND, MARY ASHLEY.

XAVIER, SISTER MARY. *See* PARTRIDGE, SYBIL F.

XENOPHANES. Agnostic, The.
Anthropomorphism.
Athleticism.
Now the floor is clean, and our hands.
Pythagoras and the Dog.
Rainbow.
Why, if one should win a victory in the foot-race.
Wickedness of Poets.

Y

YAHA. I thrilled to hear the heavenly singing of the nightingale.
Quiet.

YAKAMOCHI (Otomo no Yakamochi). Blossoms.
By way of pretext. *Fr.* Manyo Shu.
Cry of the stag, The.
Deer and Echo.
Dream encounters.
Echo.
Frost lies white, The.
Gazing at the Moon while Journeying Homewards.
I lie long abed.
I send you a box/ Of glowing pearls.
I will come to you.
In the spring garden.
Manyo Shu, *sels.*
Mist floats on the spring meadow.
Night;/ And a doorway left ajar.
Now to meet only in dreams.
On this night that is cold.
Pretext.
This Hill.
Vain Wish.
We were together.
When evening comes. *Fr.* Manyo Shu.
When I see the first/ New moon.
Wind rustles the bamboos, The.

YALE, ELSIE DUNCAN. Uncuddled Baby, The.

YALE, MARGARET. Some Things There Are.

YAMAGUCHI. Thoughtfulness.

YAMAMURA, BOCHO. Curve, The.
In the Blue Sky.
Old Pond, An.
Solo.

YAMAMURA, JUN. Gay Summertime.
Story of a Dream, The.

YAMAMURO, GUMPEI. Carpenter, The.

YAMAMURO, TAMIKO. Flood.
In Prison.
New Year Bride, A.
Night.
So Cold.

YAMANAKA, TIROUX. Flesh, The.

YAMATOHIME, EMPRESS. Others may forget you, but not I.

YANAGIWARA, AKIKO. Falling flowers! Heaven and earth.
If a woman be loved, hated, and envied.
Today I met a stranger.
When you are gone.

YANG CH'U-YUAN. East of the City, Early Spring.

YANG KUEI-FEI. Dancing.
Eventide.

YANG-TI, EMPEROR. Flowers and Moonlight on the Spring River.

YANG W'AN-LI. Lines Written in a Small Inn While Staying in the Capital in the Late Spring.
Sleeping on a Summer Day.
Temple Bells of Yün Sui, The.

YANNAI. And It Came to Pass at Midnight.

YARMOLINSKY, AVRAHM, *and* BABETTE DEUTSCH. *See* DEUTSCH, BABETTE, *and* AVRAHM YARMOLINSKY.

YASHIN, ALEKSANDR. Alyona.
On the Altai.
To My Fellow Writers.

YASIMI. Socrates' House.

YASUHIDE. Flowers of the Sea.

YATES, EDMUND. All Saints'.

YATES, JOHN H. Old Man in the Model Church, The.

YATES, L. E. Strange Talk.

"YATES, PETER" (William Long). Smelling the End of Green July.
Star of Eternal Possibles and Joy.
Thought and the Poet.

YATES, PETER B., JR. Isolte of Brittany.

YAUGER, FAY MCCORMICK. Planter's Charm.

YAZYKOV, NIKOLAI. Bard's Song.
Elegy: "Blest, who upon night's bed can lie."
O Liberty, proud inspiration!
Who sings not when the wine-cups throng.

YBARRA, THOMAS RUSSELL. Appeal to the Goddess A, An.
Christian, A.
Christian Is a Man Who Feels, A.
Lay of Ancient Rome.
Limerick: "Mussolini's pet Marshal, Graziani."
Limerick: "There was a young fellow from Fife."
Little Swirl of Vers Libre, A.
Ode to Work in Springtime.
Prose and Poesy; a Rural Misadventure.
Yarn of the *Let-Her-Rip*, The.

YEATMAN, JENNETTE. Exile.
Four Men.

YEATMAN, ROBERT JULIAN, *and* WALTER CARRUTHERS SELLAR. *See* SELLAR, WALTER CARRUTHERS, *and* ROBERT JULIAN YEATMAN.

YEATS, WILLIAM BUTLER. Acre of Grass, An.
Adam's Curse.
Aedh Tells of the Rose in His Heart.
Aedh Wishes for the Cloths of Heaven.
After Long Silence.
Against Unworthy Praise.
All Souls' Night. *Fr.* A Vision.
Among School Children.
Ancestral Houses. *Fr.* Meditations in Time of Civil War.
Apparitions, The.
Appointment, An.
Arrow, The.
At the Hawk's Well, *sel.*
Baile and Ailinn.
Ballad of Father Gilligan, The.
Ballad of Moll Magee, The.
Ballad of the Foxhunter, The.
Black Tower, The.
Blood and the Moon.
Bronze Head, A.
Brown Penny.
Byzantium.
Cap and Bells, The.
Cat and the Moon, The.
Celtic Twilight, *sel.*
Certain Artists Bring Her Dolls and Drawings. *Fr.* Upon a Dying Lady.
Choice, The.
Chorus: "For this one thing above all I would be praised as a man," *tr.* *Fr.* Oedipus Rex.
Circus Animals' Desertion, The.
Coat, A.
Cold Heaven, The.
Collar-Bone of a Hare, The.
Come Gather round Me, Parnellites.
Coming of Wisdom with Time, The.
Consolation.
Coole and Ballylee, 1931.
Coole Park, 1929.
Courage Equal to Desire. *Fr.* No Second Troy.
Cradle Song, A: "Angels are stooping, The."
Cradle Song, A: "Danaan children laugh, in cradles of wrought gold, The."
Crazy Jane and Jack the Journeyman.
Crazy Jane and the Bishop.
Crazy Jane Grown Old Looks at the Dancers.
Crazy Jane on God.

YEATS, WILLIAM BUTLER (*continued*)
Crazy Jane on the Day of Judgment.
Crazy Jane on the Mountain.
Crazy Jane Reproved.
Crazy Jane Talks with the Bishop.
Cuchulain Comforted.
Cuchulain's Fight with the Sea.
Curse of Cromwell, The.
Dancer at Cruachan and Cro-Patrick, The.
Dark under Froth. *Fr.* The Fisherman.
Dawn, The.
Death.
Death of Cuchulain, The.
Dedication to a Book of Stories Selected from the Irish Novelists, The.
Deep-sworn Vow, A.
Deirdre, *sels.*
Dialogue of Self and Soul, A.
Dolls, The.
Down by the Salley Gardens.
Dream of a Blessed Spirit, A.
Dream of Death, A.
Drinking Song, A.
Easter, 1916.
Ego Dominus Tuus.
End of Day, The. *Fr.* Upon a Dying Lady.
Everlasting Voices, The.
Faeries' Song. *Fr.* The Land of Heart's Desire.
Faery Song, A ("We who are old . . .").
Fairy Song ("The wind blows out of the gates of the day"). *Fr.* The Land of Heart's Desire.
Fallen Majesty.
Fascination of What's Difficult, The.
Father Gilligan.
Fergus and the Druid.
Fiddler of Dooney, The.
First Love. *Fr.* A Man Young and Old.
Fisherman, The.
Fisherman, The, *sel.*
Folk of the Air, The.
Folly of Being Comforted, The.
Fool by the Roadside, The.
For Anne Gregory.
For His Own Epitaph. *Fr.* Under Ben Bulben.
Friends.
Friends, *sel.*
Friends of His Youth, The. *Fr.* A Man Young and Old.
Gratitude to the Unknown Instructors.
Hanrahan and Cathleen the Daughter of Hoolihan, *sel.*
Happy Townland, The.
Hawk, The.
He Bids His Beloved Be at Peace.
He Gives His Beloved Certain Rhymes.
He Mourns for the Change That Has Come upon Him and His Beloved, and Longs for the End of the World.
He Remembers Forgotten Beauty.
He Thinks of His Past Greatness When a Part of the Constellations of Heaven.
He Wishes for the Cloths of Heaven.
Heart of the Woman, The.
Her Courage. *Fr.* Upon a Dying Lady.
Her Courtesy. *Fr.* Upon a Dying Lady.
Her Friends Bring Her a Christmas Tree. *Fr.* Upon a Dying Lady.
Her Praise.
Her Race. *Fr.* Upon a Dying Lady.
Host of the Air, The.
Hosting of the Sidhe, The.
Hound Voice.
Human Dignity. *Fr.* A Man Young and Old.
"I Am of Ireland."
I See Phantoms of Hatred and of the Heart's Fullness and of the Coming Emptiness. *Fr.* Meditations in Time of Civil War.
In Memory of Con and Eva Gore-Booth.
In Memory of Eva Gore-Booth and Con Markiewicz.
In Memory of Major Robert Gregory.
In the Seven Woods.
Indian Song, A.
Indian upon God, The.
Into the Twilight. *Fr.* Celtic Twilight.
Irish Airman Foresees His Death, An.
Island of Sleep. *Fr.* The Wanderings of Oisin, The.
It Is Time That I Wrote My Will. *Fr.* The Tower.
John Kinsella's Lament for Mrs. Mary Moore.
Lady's Third Song, The. *Fr.* The Three Bushes.
Lake Isle of Innisfree, The.
Lamentation of the Old Pensioner.
Land of Heart's Desire, The.
Land of Heart's Desire, The, *sels.*
Lapis Lazuli.
Last Confession, A.
Leaders of the Crowd, The.
Leda and the Swan.
Let All Things Pass Away, *sel.*
Long-Legged Fly.
Lover Mourns for the Loss of Love, The.
Lover Tells of the Rose in His Heart, The.
Lullaby: "Beloved, may your sleep be sound."
Mad as the Mist and Snow.
Madness of King Goll, The.
Magi, The.
Man and the Echo, The.
Man Who Dreamed of Faeryland, The.
Man Young and Old, A, *sels.*
Meditations in Time of Civil War.
Meditations in Time of Civil War, *sel.*
Men Improve with the Years.
Mermaid, The. *Fr.* A Man Young and Old.
Michael Robartes Remembers Forgotten Beauty.
Mother of God, The.
Municipal Gallery Revisited, The.
My Descendants. *Fr.* Meditations in Time of Civil War.
My House. *Fr.* Meditations in Time of Civil War.
My Table. *Fr.* Meditations in Time of Civil War.
Never Give All the Heart.
New Faces, The.
News for the Delphic Oracle.
Nineteen Hundred and Nineteen.
No Second Troy.
No Second Troy, *sel.*
Oedipus at Colonus, *sel., tr.*
Oedipus Rex, *sel., tr.*
Old Memory.
Old Men Admiring Themselves in the Water, The.
Old Song Resung, An.
On a Political Prisoner.
On Being Asked for a War Poem.
On Hearing That the Students of Our New University Have Joined the Agitation against Immoral Literature.
On Woman.
Only Jealousy of Emer, The, *sel.*
Pardon, Old Fathers. *Fr.* Responsibilities.
Parting.
Paudeen.
People, The.
Pity of Love, The.
Players Ask for a Blessing on the Psalteries and on Themselves, The.
Politics.
Prayer for My Daughter, A.
Prayer for Old Age, A.
Priest of Coloony, The.
Ragged Wood, The.
Reconciliation.
Red Hanrahan's Song about Ireland. *Fr.* Hanrahan and Cathleen the Daughter of Hoolihan.
Remorse for Intemperate Speech.
Renowned Generations, The.
Responsibilities, *sels.*
Resurrection, The, *sel.*
Road at My Door, The.
Rose of Peace, The.
Rose of the World, The.
Rose Tree, The.
Running to Paradise.
Sad Shepherd, The.
Sailing to Byzantium.
Salley Gardens, The.
Salt Sea Wind. *Fr.* At the Hawk's Well.
Scholars, The.
Second Coming, The.
Secret Rose, The.
September 1913.
She Turns the Dolls' Faces to the Wall. *Fr.* Upon a Dying Lady.
So Great a Sweetness. *Fr.* Friends.
Solomon to Sheba.
Song, A: I Thought No More Was Needed.
Song: "Wind blows out of the gates of day, The." *Fr.* The Land of Heart's Desire.
Song from a Play. *Fr.* The Resurrection.
Song from "The Only Jealousy of Emer."
Song of the Faeries [*or* Fairies], The. *Fr.* The Land of Heart's Desire.
Song of the Happy Shepherd, The.
Song of the Old Mother, The.
Song of Wandering Ængus, The.
Sorrow of Love, The.
Stare's Nest by My Window, The. *Fr.* Meditations in Time of Civil War.
Statesman's Holiday, The.
Statues, The.
Stolen Child, The.
Stream and Sun at Glendalough.
Swift's Epitaph.
Symbols.
That the Night Come.
Those Dancing Days Are Gone.
Those Images.
Three Bushes, The.
Three Bushes, The, *sel.*
Three Hermits, The.
Three Things.
To a Child Dancing in the Wind.
To a Friend Whose Work Has Come to Nothing.
To a Shade.
To a Squirrel at Kyle-na-no.
To a Young Beauty.
To a Young Girl.
To an Isle in the Water.
To Be Carved on a Stone.
To His Heart, Bidding It Have No Fear.
To Ireland in the Coming Times.
To the Rose upon the Rood of Time.
Tom O'Roughley.
Tom the Lunatic.
Tower, The.
Tower, The, *sel.*
Two Songs from a Play. *Fr.* The Resurrection.
Two Songs of a Fool, *sel.*
Two Trees, The.
Two Years Later.
Under Ben Bulben.
Under Ben Bulben, *sel.*
Under the Moon.
Upon a Dying Lady.
Vacillation.
Vacillation, *sel.*
Valley of the Black Pig, The.
Vision, A, *sels.*
Voice, The.
Wanderings of Oisin, The, *sel.*
Waters of the Boyne. *Fr.* Responsibilities.
What Then?
What Was Lost.
Wheel, The.
When Helen Lived.
When You Are Old.
Where My Books Go.
White Birds, The.
Who Goes with Fergus?
Wild Old Wicked Man, The.
Wild Swans at Coole, The.
Witch, The.

Youth and Age.
"YEHOASH" (Solomon Bloomgarden [*or* Blumgarten]). Angelus.
At the Tomb of Rachel.
Harp of David, The.
Hunting.
Jephthah's Daughter.
Mystery.
Old Song, An.
Prayer, A: "Eternal God, our life is but."
Prophet, The.
Psalm: "Happy is the man whom Thou hast set apart."
Shadows.
Song, A: "Song of grass, A,/ A song of earth."
Song as Yet Unsung, A.
Strongest, The.
Terror.
Thanksgiving.
That Is All I Heard.
Tool of Fate, The.
Wanderer, The.
Withered Rose, A.
Yang-se-fu.
YEISER, VIVIAN. *See* LARAMORE, VIVIAN YEISER.
YELLAND, EDNA HOLROYD. Damascus.
YELLEN, SAMUEL. Cloisters, The.
Discourse on the Real.
Grisaille with a Spot of Red.
Prognostic.
Time of Light, a Time of Shadow, A.
Wood of the Self-Destroyers, The.
Wooden Tiger, The.
YESENIN [*or* ESENIN], SERGEI ALEKSANDROVICH. Autumn.
Confession of a Hooligan.
Droves.
Herd of Horses, The.
Hopes, Painted.
I am the last village-poet.
In the Clear Cold.
Jordan Dove, The, *sel.*
Last Lines.
Little thatched house I was born in, The.
Moony Thin Desolation, A.
Not Vain the Winds.
O fields of corn, O fields of corn.
Oh, Listen.
Song about a Bitch.
Transfiguration, *sel.*
Wake Me Tomorrow.
Where Dawn Is Sprinkling.
Where, my childhood's home, art thou.
YESTER, LORD. Tweedside.
YIN SHIN. Autumn Rain.
YO FEI. Full River Red.
YOFFIE, LEAH RACHEL. Kiddush.
YORK, ESTHER BALDWIN. Stranger at the Peace Table.
YORK, EVA ROSE. I Shall Not Pass This Way Again.
YOSANO, AKIKO. Abandoned on the beach.
Here is a little girl.
I saw a white bird once.
Like five moving fingers.
More rapid than hail.
My old self.
Out of the dear dark years.
Wave of coldness, A.
White iris, The.
YOSHIKI. *See* ONO NO YOSHIKI.
YOUNG, ANDREW. Bee-Orchis, The.
Bird, The.
Black Rock of Kiltearn, The.
By a British Barrow.
Chalk-Cliff, The.
Christmas Day.
Conversion. *Fr.* Nicodemus.
Cuckoo.
Cuckoos.
Dead Crab, The.
Elm Beetle, The.
Evening Walk, An.
Fairy Ring, The.
Fear, The.
Field-Glasses.
Flood, The.
Go Now, My Song.
Hard Frost.
Idleness.
In December.
Lane, The.
Last Snow.
Late Autumn.
March Hares.
Nest, The.
Nicodemus, *sel.*
On Middleton Edge.
Prehistoric Camp, A.
Round Barrow, The.
Ruined Chapel, The.
Scarecrow, The.
Secret Wood, The.
Sheaf, The.
Shepherd's Hut, The.
Stay, Spring.
Stockdoves, The.
Swans, The.
Walking in Beech Leaves.
Wiltshire Downs.
Windy Day, A.
Wood and Hill.
YOUNG, ARTHUR J. Good Friday.
Moschatel.
YOUNG, BARBARA. Being a Gypsy.
Changeling.
Common Things, The.
Earth Angel.
I Go a-Walking.
I Hear It Said.
Little Stones of Arlington, The.
Road Fellows.
Sophisticate.
Town Child.
Wait's Carol: "Give ye good-den."
When I Shall Hear You Coming.
YOUNG, BARTHOLOMEW. Diana, *sels., tr.*
Melisea, Her Song in Scorn of Her Shepherd Narcissus, *tr. Fr.* Diana.
Nymph Diana's Song, The, *tr. Fr.* Diana.
Nymph Selvagia, The, Her Song, *tr. Fr.* Diana.
Song: "Shepherd, who can pass such wrong," *tr. Fr.* Diana.
YOUNG, CHARLOTTE. Evening.
YOUNG, DOROTHY M. Thoughts in School.
YOUNG, DOUGLAS. Ice-Flumes Owregie Their Lades.
Last Lauch.
YOUNG, EDITH LILLIAN. Disappointment—His Appointment.
YOUNG, EDWARD (1683–1765). Art Thou Dejected? *Fr.* Night Thoughts.
At Home among the Stars. *Fr.* Night Thoughts.
Black Militia of the Pen, The. *Fr.* Epistles to Mr. Pope.
Chambers of Death, The. *Fr.* A Paraphrase on Part of the Book of Job.
Characters of Women. *Fr.* Love of Fame.
Complaint, The; or, Night Thoughts, *sels.*
Criminality of War, The.
Day of Judgement, The.
Epistles to Mr. Pope Concerning the Authors of the Age, *sels.*
Extempore to Voltaire Criticising Milton.
Fame and Envy. *Fr.* Epistles to Mr. Pope.
Fruits of Friendship, The. *Fr.* Night Thoughts.
Happiness an Art. *Fr.* Night Thoughts.
Introduction: "Tired Nature's sweet restorer, balmy sleep!" *Fr.* Night Thoughts.
Lament of the Damned in Hell, The.
Lapse of Time, The. *Fr.* Night Thoughts.
Last Day, The, *sel.*
Leviathan. *Fr.* A Paraphrase on Part of the Book of Job.
Love of Fame, the Universal Passion, *sels.*
Love of Praise, The. *Fr.* The Love of Fame.
Man. *Fr.* Night Thoughts.
Narcissa. *Fr.* Night Thoughts.
Night ("These thoughts, O night!"). *Fr.* Night Thoughts.
Night ("Tired Nature's sweet restorer, balmy sleep!"). *Fr.* Night Thoughts.
Night Thoughts, *sels.*
Ocean, an Ode, *sel.*
Ocean and Stars. *Fr.* Ocean, an Ode.
Paraphrase on Part of the Book of Job, A, *sels.*
Procrastination. *Fr.* Night Thoughts.
Smart Lady, The. *Fr.* The Love of Fame.
This Life and the Next. *Fr.* Night Thoughts.
Time. *Fr.* Night Thoughts.
YOUNG, EDWARD (b. 1818). Under the Violets.
YOUNG, EDWARD HILTON, 1ST BARON KENNET OF THE DENE. Boy Was Born at Bethlehem, A.
Christmas.
YOUNG, ELEANOR G. R. Man from Sangamon at Gettysburg, The.
YOUNG, ELLA. Bed Time.
Greeting.
Holiday.
Invitation.
Rain.
Shape-Changer.
Unicorn, The.
YOUNG, ETHEL FANNING. Remembering Calvary.
YOUNG, FRANCIS BRETT. Atlantic Charter; 1942. *Fr.* The Island.
Bête Humaine.
Dhows, The.
February.
Five Degrees South.
Island, The, *sel.*
104° Fahrenheit.
Prothalamion.
Seascape.
Song at Santa Cruz.
Song of the Dark Ages.
YOUNG, GEOFFREY WINTHROP. Cragsman, The.
Mountain Speed.
YOUNG, GEORGE W. Lips That Touch Liquor Must Never Touch Mine, The.
YOUNG, MARGUERITE. Death by Rarity.
Noah's Ark.
Speculative Evening.
Whales, The.
White Rat, The.
YOUNG, PEARCE. At the Grave of My Grandfather.
Country Church, A.
Exhortation.
Invective.
Litany for Peace, A.
October Garden.
Rational Man, The.
Sonnet: "Evening bends upon a stubborn day, The."
To a Giant Sequoia, Fallen and Enshrined in Calaveras County, California.
Upon Reading an Old Book.
Winter Flood, The.
Yet in Time.
YOUNG, ROLAND. Ape, The.
Flea, The.
Goat, The.
Happy Bounding Flea, The.
Jungle Pest, The.
Miscegeneous Zebra, The.
Owl, The.
Zebra, The.
YOUNG, RUTH COMFORT MITCHELL. *See* MITCHELL, RUTH COMFORT.
YOUNG, SAMUEL HALL. Into the Sunset.
Let Me Die Working.
YOUNG, STANLEY. Epitaph for a Concord Boy.
YOUNG, VIRGINIA BRADY. Teacher, The.
YOUNG, WILLIAM. Bells, The. *Fr.* Wishmakers' Town.
Bridal Pair, The. *Fr.* Wishmakers' Town.
Conscience-Keeper, The. *Fr.* Wishmakers' Town.

YOUNG, WILLIAM (*continued*)
Flower-Seller, The. *Fr.* Wishmakers' Town.
Judith.
Losers, The. *Fr.* Wishmakers' Town.
Pawns, The. *Fr.* Wishmakers' Town.
Philomel to Corydon.
Victor, The.
Wishmakers' Town, *sels.*
YOUNGS, MARY FANNY. Edge of the World, The.
In the Cove.
YOZEI, EMPEROR. Falling from the ridge.
YRIARTE, TOMÁS DE. *See* IRIARTE, TOMÁS DE.
YÜAN CHEN. Deserted Temple, A.
Elegy, An: "O youngest, best-loved daughter of Hsieh."
Farewell to Po Chü I.
Lonely Old Age.
Pitcher, The.
YÜAN CHI. Regret.
Speaking My Mind.
Strange Bird.
YÜAN CHIEH. Civilization.
Stone Fish Lake.
YÜAN K'AI. Letter from Home, A.
YUAN MEI. In an Old Library.
YÜAN TI. Confession.
Rejected Wife, The.
YUD, NACHUM. Like the Eyes of Wolves.
YUHARA, PRINCE. Dialogue.
What am I to do with my Sister? *Fr.* Manyo Shu.
YÜ HSIN. To Hsü Ling.
YÜ HSÜAN CHI. West River, The.
YUKE, PRINCE. With a rocking.
YULE, SIR HENRY. *Birkenhead,* The.
Birkenhead, The, *sel.*
YULE, PAMELIA VINING. Littlewit and Loftus.
YU MIN-CHUAN. Lady Macbeth.

Z

ZABEL, MORTON DAUWEN. Herakles Archer.
Homage to Mürren.
Nettle, the Flower, The.
Scène à Faire.
Storm at Nightfall, The.
Teufelsdröckh Minor.
Traitors, The.
ZANGWILL, ISRAEL. At the Worst.
At the Zoo.
Death's Transfiguration.
Despair and Hope.
Dreams.
Evolution.
I Have Sought Thee Daily, *tr.*
In the City.
In the Morgue.
Inexhaustible.
Israel.
Jehovah.
Jehovah, *sel.*
"Might Is Right."
Moses and Jesus.
Redeeming Mercy, The. *Fr.* Jehovah.
Royal Crown, The, *tr.*
Seder-Night.
Sundered.
Tabernacle Thought, A.
Theodor Herzl.
To a Pretty Girl.
Two Things Have Met in Me, *tr.*
Vanitas Vanitatum.
Vision.
Why Do We Live?
Yom Kippur.
For translations from Hebrew, see TrJP.
ZARATHUSTRA. *See* ZOROASTER.
ZATURENSKA, MARYA ALEXANDROVNA (Mrs. Horace Gregory). Castaways, The.
Chorale for Autumn.
Daisy, The.
Death and Transfiguration.
Elegies over John Reed.
Elegy of the Kremlin Bells. *Fr.* Elegies over John Reed.
False Summer, The.
Girl Takes Her Place among the Mothers, The.
Head of Medusa.
Lightning for Atmosphere.
Lovers, The.
Old Tale, An.
Song for Saint Cecelia, A.
Song of a Factory Girl.
Song of the Scarlet Banners over John Reed. *Fr.* Elegies over John Reed.
Spinners at Willowsleigh.
Tempest, The.
They Bury Him. *Fr.* Elegies over John Reed.
Variations on a Theme by George Herbert.
White Dress, The.
Woman at the Piano.
Written in a Volume of "The Imitation of Christ."
ZEB-UN-NISSA, PRINCESS. Lament: "Within my bosom stirs once more tonight."
ZECH, PAUL. Factory Street in Daylight.
Forest, The.
Houses Have Open Eyes.
ZEITLIN, AARON. Salvation.
Text.
ZEITLIN, ISRAEL. *See* TIEMPO, CÉSAR.
ZELDIS, CHAYYIM. Holy Ones, the Young Ones, The.
ZENKEVICH, MIKHAIL ALEXANDROVICH. Belated Sunflowers.
ZENODOTUS. Statue of Love, A, *at.*
ZEREA JACOB, EMPEROR OF ABYSSINIA. Hymn to Mary.
Salutation.
ZHUKOVSKY, VASILY ANDREYEVICH. Remembrance.
Sea, The.
To Her.
You were before me.
ZIMMERMAN, ELEANOR HALBROOK. Little Samaritan, The.
ZINSSER, HANS ("R. S."). Two Sonnets, *sel.*
ZINZENDORF, NIKOLAUS LUDWIG, GRAF VON. Lowly Bethlehem.
My Light! My Way!
ZIZZAMIA, ALBA. Vehicles.
Wanderlust.
ZOLA, EMILE. My Wishes.
ZONAS OF SARDIS. End of a Venture, The.
Harvest-Home.
"Lip of This Poor Earthen Urn, The."
Little Ghost, The.
ZOROASTER [*or* ZARATHUSTRA]. Divine Songs to Ahura Mazda.
Gathas, *sel., at.*
O Great Creator, *at.* *Fr.* Gathas.
Sacred Book, The, *at.* *Fr.* Gathas.
Zoroaster Devoutly Questions Ormazd, *at.* *Fr.* Gathas.
ZORRILLA Y MORAL, JOSÉ. Boabdil.
Christian Lady and the Moor, The.
Oriental.
Toledo.
ZORRO, JOAN. Barcarola: "Along by the sea and the river."
ZOUCHE, RICHARD. Prayer for an Airman.
ZUCKER, ANNE. Waiting Mothers.
ZUCKMAYER, CARL. My Death.
ZWEIG, STEFAN. Chosen of God. *Fr.* Jeremiah.
Flowering without End. *Fr.* Jeremiah.
Jeremiah, *sels.*
ZWICKER, KENNETH. Shantyboys' Song, The.

SUBJECT INDEX

Aachen, Germany. Aix-la-Chappelle, 1945. Edgar Bowers.
Abbey Asaroe, Ireland. Abbey Asaroe. Allingham.
Abbey Theatre, Dublin. Old Woman, An, Outside the Abbey Theater. L. A. G. Strong.
Abel
Abel. Capetanakis.
Ancient History. Sassoon.
Abelard, Peter
Eloisa's Prayer for Abelard. Pope.
Sic et Non. Read.
Abishag. Abishag. Spire, *tr. fr. French by* Eisenberg.
Abolitionists
Abolitionist, The. Conquest.
John Brown's Prayer. *Fr.* John Brown's Body. S. V. Benét.
Abraham
Abraham. E. V. Cooke.
When Abraham Went Out of Ur. N. B. Turner.
Absalom
David's Lament for Absalom. *Fr.* Absalom. Willis.
David's Reconciliation with Absalom. "Michael Field."
Dispraise of Absalom, The. *Tr. fr. Irish by* Flower.
Acacia
Acacia Leaves, The. *Fr.* Scented Leaves from a Chinese Jar. Upward.
Wattle and Myrtle. Cuthbertson.
Whisperings in Wattle-Boughs. A. L. Gordon.
Young Acacia, The. Bialik, *tr. fr. Hebrew by* Frank.
Acadia
Acadia, *sel.* ("In ev'ry thought, in ev'ry wish I own"). Joseph Howe.
Evangeline. Norma E. Smith.
Acadians
Emigration of the Fairies, The, *sel.* ("A few days more they drifted, ever west"). Duvar.
Evangeline. Longfellow.
Indian Massacre, The. *Fr.* Acadia. Joseph Howe.
Accordion. Man with a Little Pleated Piano, A. Welles.
Achilles
Achilles. Myers.
Achilles. Pindar, *tr. fr. Greek by* Billson.
Achilles Rejects the Embassy. *Fr.* The Iliad. Homer, *tr. fr. Greek by* Lucas.
Achilles' Remorse. *Fr.* The Iliad. Homer, *tr. fr. Greek by* Lucas.
Achilles' Shield. *Fr.* The Iliad. Homer, *tr. fr. Greek by* Chapman.
Before a Statue of Achilles. Santayana.
Epitaph on Achilles. *Unknown, tr. fr. Greek by* Hardinge.
Vulcan Forges the Shield of Achilles. *Fr.* The Iliad. Homer, *tr. fr. Greek by* Chapman.
Wrath of Achilles, The. *Fr.* The Iliad. Homer, *tr. fr. Greek by* Lucas.
Aconite. Aconite, The. Graham.
Acorns
Acorn, The. *Unknown.*
Acorns. King.
Actaeon
Actaeon. Heppenstall.
Actaeon, *sel.* ("It was on the Mount Cithaeron"). Wilkins.
Acting and Actors
Ballade of Dead Actors. Henley.
They All Want to Play Hamlet. Sandburg.
When Burbadge Played. Dobson.
Adam
Adam and Eve. Manger, *tr. fr. Yiddish by* Sonntag.
Adam and Eve. Shapiro.
Adam Lay I-Bowndyn. *Unknown.*
Adam Posed. Countess of Winchilsea.
Ancient History. Sassoon.
Begetting of Cain, The. H. Plutzik.
Exile, The. De la Mare.
Jealous Adam. Manger, *tr. fr. Yiddish by* Sonntag.
"O Felix Culpa!" *Unknown.*
Old Adam, The. W. R. Benét.
Temptation and Fall of Man, The. *Fr.* Genesis. *Unknown, tr. fr. Anglo-Saxon by* Kennedy.
Adamastor. Voyage to Africa, A, *sel.* ("Adamastor, whom Camoens and the sea"). David Wright.
Adams, Franklin Pierce ("F.P.A."). Lines Written on November 15, 1933, by a Man Born November 14, 1881, to Another Born November 15, 1881. Clayton Hamilton.
Adams, John Quincy. John Quincy Adams. S. V. Benét.
Addams, Jane. Jane Addams. Wilkinson.
Addison, Joseph
Atticus. *Fr.* Epistle to Dr. Arbuthnot. Pope.
To the Earl of Warwick on the Death of Mr. Addison. Tickell.
Adlestrop, England. Adlestrop. E. Thomas.
Adonis
Adonis. Doolittle ("H. D.").
Lament for Adonis. Bion, *tr. fr. Greek.*
Shepherd's Song of Venus and Adonis, The. Henry Constable.
Venus and Adonis. Shakespeare.
Adur (river), England. Flood, The. Andrew Young.
Advent
Advent. J. G. Fletcher.
Advent. C. G. Rossetti.
No Sudden Thing of Glory. Alice Meynell.
Two Songs of Advent. Winters.
Advertising. Lucky Strike. Merrill Moore.
Aegean Sea. Archipelago, The. Hölderlin, *tr. fr. German by* Stepanchev.
Aeneas
Aeneas at Washington. Tate.
Aeneid, The, *sels.* Virgil, *tr. fr. Latin.*
Staye, staye Aeneas, for thyne owne sake staye. *Unknown.*
Aeneid, The (Virgil)
Concerning Virgil's Aeneids. Grimald.
Falling Asleep Over the Aeneid. Robert Lowell.
Ængus. Song of Wandering Ængus, The. Yeats.
Aeschylus. Aeschylos and Sophocles. Landor.
Aesop
Aesop. Lang.
Aesop at Play. Phaedrus, *tr. fr. Latin by* Smart.
Africa
Afar in the Desert. Pringle.
Africa. Lewis Alexander.
African Dance. Langston Hughes.
Congo, The. Lindsay.
Invocation to the African Muse. *Fr.* The Flaming Terrapin. Roy Campbell.
Memorial of Africa, A. George Macdonald.
Scorpion, The. William Plomer.
Book of South African Verse, A (BoSA). Guy Butler, ed.
Afternoon
City Afternoon, A. Wyatt.
Post-Meridian. Garrison.
Afton (river), Scotland. Flow Gently, Sweet Afton. Burns.
Agamemnon. Agamemnon's Tomb. Sacheverell Sitwell.
Agassiz, Louis
Farewell to Agassiz, A. Holmes.
Fiftieth Birthday of Agassiz, The. Longfellow.
Three Friends of Mine. Longfellow.
Age. *See* Middle age; Old age.
Aghadoe, Ireland. Aghadoe. Todhunter.
Agincourt, battle of
Agincourt. Drayton.
Agincourt Song of Victory. *Unknown.*
Before Agincourt. *Fr.* Henry V. Shakespeare.
Agnes, Saint. St. Agnes; a Responsory. Merton.
Agnosticism
Agnostic's Creed, The. Malone.
Agnosto Theo. Hardy.
Biography of an Agnostic. Louis Ginsberg.
Agricola, Johannes. Johannes Agricola in Meditation. Robert Browning.
Aguinaldo, Emilio. Aguinaldo. Shadwell.
Aikman, William. On the Death of Mr. William Aikman the Painter. James Thomson.
Ailsa Craig, Scotland. To Ailsa Rock. Keats.
Air
Air. Denby.
Day the Winds, The. Josephine Miles.
Air raids
Bombers. C. Day Lewis.
Bombing Casualties in Spain. Read.
Fury of Aerial Bombardment, The. Eberhart.
Hills. Apollinaire, *tr. fr. French by* Fitts.
Losses. Jarrell.

AIR RAIDS (*continued*)
On the Pilots Who Destroyed Germany in the Spring of 1945. Spender.
Raider, The. W. R. Rodgers.
Refusal to Mourn the Death, by Fire, of a Child in London, A. Dylan Thomas.
Still Falls the Rain. Edith Sitwell.
Watching Post. C. Day Lewis.
AIR WARFARE
Death of the Ball Turret Gunner, The. Jarrell.
Irish Airman Foresees His Death, An. Yeats.
Pilots, Man Your Planes. Jarrell.
2nd Air Force. Jarrell.
AIRPLANES
Aeroplane. Green.
Airplane, The. Bennett.
Cockpit in the Clouds. Dorrance.
Jet Plane. Sullivan.
Landscape near an Aerodrome, The. Spender.
Night Plane. Frances Frost.
Prayer for a Pilot. Cecil Roberts.
Riding in an Airplane. Baruch.
Silver Ships. Meigs.
Taking Off. Green.
To Beachey, 1912. Sandburg.
Up in the Air. Tippett.
Wishes. Kirsanov, *tr. fr. Russian by* Lindsay.
AJANTA, INDIA. Ajanta. Rukeyser.
AJAX (Telamonian Ajax). Leaving Troy. Irwin.
AKHNATON. *See* IKHNATON.
ALABAMA (state). Alabama. Tutwiler.
ALABAMA (ship)
Alabama, The. Maurice Bell.
Eagle and Vulture, The. T. B. Read.
Kearsarge and *Alabama*. *Unknown.*
ALAMEDA, CALIFORNIA. In an Alameda Field. Markham.
ALAMO
Defense [*or* Defence] of the Alamo, The. Joaquin Miller.
Men of the Alamo, The. Roche.
Within the Alamo. Baker.
ALARIC I
Dirge of Alaric the Visigoth. Everett.
Grave in the Busento, The. Platen, *tr. fr. German by* Durling.
ALASKA
Alaska. Joaquin Miller.
Alaska. *Unknown.*
Cremation of Sam McGee, The. Service.
Shooting of Dan McGrew, The. Service.
To an Alaskan Glacier. Keeler.
Trail Makers, The. Knibbs.
ALBATROSS
Albatross, The. Baudelaire, *tr. fr. French.*
Albatross. Charles Burgess.
Albatross, The. W. P. Reeves.
Albatross. Stoddard.
ALBERT I, KING OF THE BELGIANS. King of the Belgians. Smith.
ALCESTIS. Alcestis. Verry.
ALCHEMY AND ALCHEMISTS. Alchemist, The, *sel.* ("I will have all my beds blown up"). Jonson.
ALCOTT, LOUISA MAY. Louisa May Alcott. Moulton.
ALCUIN. Alcuin; His Epitaph. Waddell.
ALDEN, JOHN, AND PRISCILLA ALDEN. American History. Adams.
ALDER TREES. White Alder, The. *Unknown.*
ALE
Ale. W. H. Davies.
Back and Side Go Bare, Go Bare. *Fr.* Gammer Gurton's Needle. *At. to* William Stevenson.
In Praise of Ale. Bonham.
Mannerly Margery Milk and Ale. John Skelton.
Tunning of Elinour Rumming, The. John Skelton.
ALEICHEM, SHOLOM. Sholom Aleichem. Lieberman.
ALEXANDER JANNAEUS, KING OF JUDAH. Alexander Jannai. Cavafy, *tr. fr. Greek by* Chasen.
ALEXANDER THE GREAT
Alexander the Great. *Unknown.*
Alexander's Feast; or, The Power of Music. Dryden.
ALEXANDRA, QUEEN OF ENGLAND. Welcome to Alexandra, A. Tennyson.
ALFRED THE GREAT
Alfred the Harper. Sterling.
Ballad of the White Horse, The. Chesterton.
ALHAMBRA. *See* GRANADA.
ALIENS
Alien. Frazee-Bower.
Alien. MacLeish.
Alien, The. Charles Murray.
America Greets an Alien. *Unknown.*
ALL FOOLS' DAY. *See* APRIL FOOLS' DAY.
ALL SAINTS' EVE. *See* HALLOWEEN.
ALL SOULS' DAY. Pray for the Dead. A. D. H. Eaton.
ALL SOULS' NIGHT
All Souls' Night. Shorter.
All Souls' Night. *Fr.* A Vision. Yeats.
On Kingston Bridge. Cortissoz.
ALLEN, EDWARD
In Ed. Allen. Weever.
To Edward Allen. Jonson.
ALLEN, ETHAN. Green Mountain Boy. F. W. Smyth.
ALLIGATORS. Alligator, The. Ravenel.
ALMOND TREES
Almond Blossom. Sir Edwin Arnold.
Almond Blossoms. *Fr.* Three Pictures. Dalmon.
Pink Almond. Tynan.
When Almonds Bloom. Shinn.
ALNWICK CASTLE, ENGLAND. Alnwick Castle. Halleck.
ALOES. Aloe Plant, The. Harbaugh.
ALPHEUS
Alpheus and Arethusa. E. H. Daly.
Arethusa. Shelley.
ALPS
Alpine Flowers, The. Sigourney.
Alpine Heights. Krummacher, *tr. fr. German by* Brooks.
Alpine Village, An. Winslow.
ALTGELD, JOHN PETER. Eagle That Is Forgotten, The. Lindsay.
ALTOLAGUIRRE, MANUEL. To a Spanish Poet. Splender.
ALUMNI. Tenth Reunion. Steese.
AMERICA (United States of). *See* UNITED STATES.
AMERICAN REVOLUTION
Ballad for a Boy, A. Cory.
Bonhomme Richard and *Serapis*, The. Freneau.
Bunker Hill. Calvert.
Carmen Bellicosum. McMaster.
Chester. Billings.
Concord Hymn. Emerson.
Cornwallis's Surrender. *Unknown.*
Cruise of the *Fair American*. *Unknown.*
Daughter's Rebellion, The. Francis Hopkinson.
Epitaph for a Concord Boy. Stanley Young.
Green Mountain Boys, The. Bryant.
Hospital Prison Ship, The. *Fr.* The British Prison Ship. Freneau.
Independence Bell—July 4, 1776. *Unknown.*
Lexington. *Fr.* The Psalm of the West. Lanier.
Lexington. Whittier.
Liberty-Pole, The. *Fr.* M'Fingal. Trumbull.
Little Black-eyed Rebel, The. Carleton.
Maryland Battalion, The. Palmer.
Minute-Men of North-Boro', The. Rice.
Modern Jonas, The. *Unknown.*
Molly Maguire at Monmouth. Collins.
Molly Pitcher. Richards.
Morgan Stanwood. Rich.
Mugford's Victory. Chadwick.
New England's Chevy Chase. E. E. Hale.
New England's Dead. McLellan.
News from Yorktown. L. W. Smith.
Northern Soldier, The. Freneau.
Off from Boston. *Unknown.*
On a Hessian Debarkation. Freneau.
On Disbanding the Army. Humphreys.
On Independence. Sewell.
On the Departure of the British from Charleston. Freneau.
On the Eve of Bunker Hill. Scollard.
Paul Revere's Ride. *Fr.* Tales of a Wayside Inn. Longfellow.
Poem Containing Some Remarks on the Present War, A. *Unknown.*
Progress of Sir Jack Brag, The. *Unknown.*
Riflemen's Song at Bennington. *Unknown.*
Rodney's Ride. Brooks.
Royal Adventurer, The. Freneau.
Running the Blockade. Nora Perry.
Seventy-six. Bryant.
Storming of Stony Point, The. Guiterman.
Swamp Fox, The. Simms.
Ticonderoga. V. B. Wilson.
To the Memory of the Brave Americans. Freneau.
Town-Meeting, A. *Fr.* M'Fingal. Trumbull.
Trip to Cambridge, The. *Unknown.*
Wagoner of the Alleghanies, The, *sels.* Read.
War and Washington. *Fr.* Cato. Sewall.
Warren's Address at Bunker Hill. Pierpont.
What a Court Hath Old England. *Unknown.*
Yankee Doodle's Expedition to Rhode Island. *Unknown.*
Yankee Privateer, The. Arthur Hale.
AMERICANS
American Laughter. K. A. Robinson.
Americans All. Irving.
Ave Caesar. Jeffers.
Blood Is Thicker than Water. Rice.
Coming American, The. Foss.
England and America in 1782. Tennyson.
I Am an American. Lieberman.
I Hear America Singing. Whitman.

I Like Americans. Boyd.
I, Too, Sing America. Langston Hughes.
Men of America, Answering the Call. Borland.
New Englanders Are Maples. Coffin.
Over the Carnage Rose Prophetic a Voice. Whitman.
People, Yes, The, *sels.* Sandburg.
Peregrine White and Virginia Dare. Rosemary *and* S. V. Benét.
"Scum o' the Earth." Schauffler.
To America. Alfred Austin.
To the Younger Old-Americans. Kenneth Porter.
Two 'Mericana Men. Daly.
What Does It Mean to Be American? Montgomery.
Yanks. Foley.
See also UNITED STATES.
AMSTERDAM, HOLLAND
Amsterdam. Jammes, *tr. fr. French by* Bithell.
Robinson Crusoe Returns to Amsterdam. *Fr.* Amsterdam. Jammes, *tr. fr. French by* Bithell.
ANACREON
Elegie upon Anacreon. Cowley.
To Anacreon. Antipater of Sidon, *tr. fr. Greek by* Moore.
ANCESTORS AND ANCESTRY
Ancestors, The. Judith Wright.
Ancestry. *Fr.* The Black Riders. Stephen Crane.
Children of Light. Robert Lowell.
Forebears. Gibbon.
Forebears. Elizabeth Riddell.
Forefathers. Blunden.
On the Photograph of a Man I Never Saw. Plutzik.
To Our Forefathers. Hamlet.
With Antecedents. Whitman.
ANCHISES. Anchises. Salkeld.
ANCHORS
Anchor: "Oft I must strive with wind and wave." *Fr.* Riddles. *Unknown, tr. fr. Anglo-Saxon by* Kennedy.
Forging of the Anchor, The. Ferguson.
ANDALUSIA, SPAIN
Andalusian Sereno, The. Saltus.
Little Town. García Lorca, *tr. fr. Spanish by* Turnbull.
ANDERSEN, HANS CHRISTIAN. Hans Christian Andersen. Gosse.
ANDRÉ, JOHN
André. C. F. Bates.
André's Request to Washington. Willis.
Brave Paulding and the Spy. *Unknown.*
ANDREWES, LANCELOT. Upon Bishop Andrewes His Picture before His Sermons. Crashaw.
ANDROMEDA
Andromeda. *Fr.* Pauline. Robert Browning.
Andromeda, *sels.* Kingsley.
Andromeda. Roche.
ANEMONE
To a Wind Flower. Cawein.
White Anemone, The. "Owen Meredith."
Windflower, A. Carman.
Wind-Flower, The. Very.
ANGELUS
Angelus, The. Mace.
Angelus Domini. *Unknown.*
ANGER
He That Is Slow to Anger. Proverbs, Bible, *O.T.*
Poison Tree, A. *Fr.* Songs of Experience. Blake.
ANIMALS
About Animals. Hilda Conkling.
Allie. Robert Graves.
Animal Fair. *Unknown.*
Animal Store, The. Rachel Field.
Animal Tranquillity and Decay. Wordsworth.
Animals, The. Josephine Jacobsen.
Animals, The. Muir.
Animals. *Fr.* Song of Myself. Whitman.
Ariel. David Campbell.
At the Zoo. A. A. Milne.
Auguries of Innocence. Blake.
Beasts. Wilbur.
Beasts, Birds and Fishes. O'Keefe.
Bells of Heaven, The. Hodgson.
Bestiary, A, *sels.* Rexroth.
Christmas Folk Song, A. Reese.
Circus-postered Barn, The. Coatsworth.
Color. Rowena Bennett.
Earthy Anecdote. Wallace Stevens.
Familiar Friends. Tippett.
Family, The. *Unknown, tr. fr. German by* Fyleman.
Feather or Fur. John Becker.
Four Friends, The. A. A. Milne.
Friendly Beasts, The. *Unknown.*
How to Tell the Wild Animals. Carolyn Wells.
Kindness to Animals. *Unknown.*
Little Things. James Stephens.
Menagerie, The. Moody.
Native Inhabitant. Douglas Stewart.
Nature's Friend W. H. Davies.
Over in the Meadow. Wadsworth.
Pangolin, The. Marianne Moore.
Parley of Beasts. "Hugh MacDiarmid."
Peaceable Kingdom, The. Isaiah, Bible, *O.T.*
Spangled Pandemonium, The. Palmer Brown.
Tame Animals I Have Known. Nixon Waterman.
Wild Beasts. Evaleen Stein.
Under the Tent of the Sky (UTS). John E. Brewton, comp.
ANN, CAPE, MASSACHUSETTS
Garrison of Cape Ann, The. Whittier.
Landscapes. T. S. Eliot.
ANNE, QUEEN OF ENGLAND
On Queen Anne's Death. *Unknown.*
Queen Anne. *Unknown.*
ANNE OF DENMARK. His Petition to Queen Anne of Denmark (1618). Ralegh.
ANNUNCIATION OF THE VIRGIN. *See* MARY, THE VIRGIN.
ANTARCTICA. Worsley Enchanted, *sel.* ("White, said Worsley, and glistening, the ridgy plain"). Douglas Stewart.
ANTELOPES
Antelope. W. J. Smith.
Antelopes, The. J. K. Baxter.
Last Antelope, The. E. F. Piper.
ANTHONY, SAINT. Temptation of St. Anthony, The. Gales, *ad. fr. Old French.*
ANTHONY OF PADUA, SAINT
Death-Bed Hymn of Saint Anthony of Padua. St. Anthony of Padua, *tr. fr. Latin by* Walsh.
Prayer to Saint Anthony of Padua, A. Symons.
ANTIETAM CAMPAIGN. Victor of Antietam, The. Melville.
ANTIGONE. Antigone, *sels.* Sophocles.
ANTIQUES. Antique Shop. Carmer.
ANTONY (Marc Antony)
Antony and Cleopatra. Heredia, *tr. fr. French by* Coulette.
Antony and Cleopatra. Heredia, *tr. fr. French by* Conder.
Antony to Cleopatra. Lytle.
Death of Antony. *Fr.* Antony and Cleopatra. Shakespeare.
Mark Antony. Cleveland.
ANTS
Ant, The. Al-Tulaitili, *tr. fr. Arabic by* Arberry.
Ant, The. Herford.
Ant and the Cricket, The. *Unknown.*
Ant Battle. Dresbach.
Ant Explorer, The. Dennis.
Ant Village, The. Edey *and* Grider.
Ants. Kreymborg.
Bee, the Ant, and the Sparrow, The. Cotton.
By an Ant-Heap. Terence Heywood.
Departmental. Robert Frost.
Wandering Ant, The. Corydon Bell.
APACHE INDIANS
Apache in Ambush, The. Millard.
Dance of the Maskers. *Tr. fr. Apache Indian by* Austin.
APELLES. Apelles the Painter. Leonidas of Tarentum, *tr. fr. Greek by* Lord Neaves.
APHRODITE
Aphrodite. "Æ."
Aphrodite and the Knife-Grinder. Snoilsky, *tr. fr. Swedish by* Stork.
Hymn to Aphrodite. *Fr.* Homeric Hymns. *Unknown, tr. fr. Greek.*
Immortal Aphrodite. Sappho, *tr. fr. Greek by* Hubbell.
To Aphrodite. Sappho, *tr. fr. Greek by* Lucas.
See also VENUS.
APIA, WESTERN SAMOA. In Apia Bay. C. G. D. Roberts.
APOLLO
Apollo. Chivers.
Apollo Alone Approves. Turbyfill.
Apollo and Daphne. *Fr.* Metamorphoses. Ovid, *tr. fr. Latin by* Highet.
Before a Statue of Apollo. Tchernichovsky, *tr. fr. Hebrew by* Kahn.
Callicles' Song. *Fr.* Empedocles on Etna. Matthew Arnold.
Consolation, The. Countess of Winchilsea.
Hunting Song. *Fr.* Apollo and Daphne. Whitehead.
Hymn of Apollo. Shelley.
Hymn to Apollo. Callimachus, *tr. fr. Greek.*
Hymn to Apollo. Sidney.
Hymn to the Delian Apollo. *Fr.* Homeric Hymns. *Unknown, tr. fr. Greek by* Lucas.
Many Are Called. E. A. Robinson.
Phoebus, Arise! Drummond of Hawthornden.
Phoebus with Admetus. George Meredith.
Shepherd of King Admetus, The. J. R. Lowell.
Song to Apollo. *Fr.* Midas. Lyly.
Stay, Phoebus! Waller.
Sun-God, The. A. T. De Vere.
To Apollo. *Unknown, tr. fr. Greek by* Lindsay.
Torso of an Archaic Apollo. Rilke, *tr. fr. German by* MacIntyre.
APOSTLES
Christus Matthaeum et Discipulos Alloquitur. Sir Edward Sherburne.

APOSTLES (*continued*)
Conversion. *Fr.* Nicodemus. Andrew Young.
Last Supper, The. Oscar Williams.
Starlight's Intuitions Pierced the Twelve, The. Schwartz.
APPIAN WAY. Appian Way, The. Johnson.
APPLE TREES
Appile Tree, De. J. C. Harris.
Apple Blossom. K. L. Brown.
Apple Blossoms. Bergengren.
Apple Blossoms. H. A. Parker.
Apple Blossoms. A. L. Phelps.
Apple Blossoms. Helen Wing.
Apple Gathering, An. C. G. Rossetti.
Apple Harvest. Leuty.
Apple Season. Frances Frost.
Apple Tree, The. B. C. Brown.
Apple-Tree, The. Nancy Campbell.
Apple Tree, The. Gogarty.
Apple Tree, The. *Unknown, tr. fr. Armenian by* Boyajian.
Apples in New Hampshire. Gilchrist.
Mine Host of the "Golden Apple." Westwood.
Planting of the Apple-Tree, The. Bryant.
With a Spray of Apple Blossoms. Learned.
APPLES
After Apple-picking. Robert Frost.
Apple, The. Sackville.
Apple Season. Frances Frost.
Apple Song. Frances Frost.
Apples. Mueller.
Moonlit Apples. Drinkwater.
Sunday Morning Apples. Hart Crane.
APPLESEED, JOHNNY. *See* CHAPMAN, JOHN.
APPOMATTOX, VIRGINIA
Last Charge at Appomattox, The. Stockard.
Surrender at Appomattox, The. Melville.
APRIL
Alone in April. Cabell.
Altered look about the hills, An. Emily Dickinson.
April. Auringer.
April. Belleau, *tr. fr. French.*
April. Cheney.
April. Theodosia Garrison.
April. Florence Hamilton.
April. T. S. Jones, Jr.
April. Leitch.
April. H. W. Longfellow.
April. Samuel Longfellow.
April. Loveman.
April. McFadden.
April. *Fr.* Fields of Dawn. Mifflin.
April. O'Donnell.
April. Ted Robinson.
April. Shorter.
April. *Fr.* The Shepheardes Calender. Spenser.
April. Sweeney.
April. Teasdale.
April. Tietjens.
April. Torres Bodet, *tr. fr. Spanish by* Castellón.
April. Sir William Watson.
April Adoration, An. C. G. D. Roberts.
April—and Dying. A. R. Aldrich.
April and May. *Fr.* May-Day. Emerson.
April and May. Anne Robinson.
April, April. Sir William Watson.
April! April! Are You Here? Goodale.
April Day, An. C. A. Bowles.
April Day, An. J. S. Cotter, Jr.
April Days. *Fr.* In Memoriam A. H. H. Tennyson.
April Earth, The. Max Eastman.
April, 1885. Robert Bridges.
April Fantasie. Cortissoz.
April Fools. Brégy.
April in the Hills. Lampman.
April Inventory. Snodgrass.
April Morning, An. Carman.
April Morning. Elliston.
April Mortality. Léonie Adams.
April Music. Scollard.
April—North Carolina. Harriet Monroe.
April of the Ages, The. Dolben.
April on the Battlefields. Speyer.
April Rain. Blind.
April Rain. Loveman.
April Rain Song. Langston Hughes.
April Rise. Lee.
April Showers. M. E. W. Freeman.
April Smile. *Fr.* Amoretti. Spenser.
April Speaks. Mifflin.
April Theology. Neihardt.
April Weather. Carman.
April Weather. McDermott.
April Weather. Reese.
April Winds. Michael Lewis.
April's Amazing Meaning. George Dillon.
April's Coming. Pollard.
Awakening, An. Angela Morgan.
Berkshires in April. Clement Wood.
Birds in April. Henley.
Bird's Song in April. Scollard.
Blue Squills. Teasdale.
Cherry Tree. C. G. Rossetti.
Concert, The. McGinley.
Day before April, The. M. C. Davies.
Early April. Robert Frost.
First of April, The. Mortimer Collins.
First Warm Days. Denby.
Heigh-ho, April! Farjeon.
Home Thoughts from Abroad. Robert Browning.
How Long till April? Fields.
In April. E. A. Allen.
In April. E. G. Arnold.
In April. Ashley.
In April. Moreland.
In April. Wetherald.
In the April Rain. Mary Anderson.
In the month of April. *Unknown.*
In Two Months Now. Dillon.
Invitation to the Country, An. Bryant.
Lady April. Le Gallienne.
Lost—an April. M. B. Whiteside.
My Lady April. Dowson.
Now the Noisy Winds Are Still. M. M. Dodge.
One April Day. Moreland.
One Distant April. Gertrude Hall.
Prayer in April. S. H. Hay.
Prologue to "The Canterbury Tales." Chaucer.
Rain in April. Eleanor Hammond.
Rainy Day in April, A. Ledwidge.
Renewal. Towne.
Shore Roads of April. "Bill" Adams.
Sign of Spring, A. Rexford.
Song: "April, April, / Laugh thy girlish laughter." Sir William Watson.
Song: "O lovely April, rich and bright." Kahn, *tr fr. French by* Lewisohn.
Song from "April." McLeod.
Song of April, A. Ledwidge.
Spring Song. Carman.
Street in April, A. Dudek.
Succession of the Four Sweet Months, The. Herrick.
Sweet Wild April. Stead.
Switch Cut in April, A. Dyment.
This Fevers Me. Eberhart.
Wasted Hours. Addison.
West Wind, The. Masefield.
APRIL FOOLS' DAY
All Fool's Day. *Unknown.*
April Fool. Coatsworth.
April Fool. Hammond.
April Fool's Day. *Unknown.*
First of April, The. Hone.
First of April, The. Geoffrey Johnson.
First of April, some do say, The. *Unknown.*
AQUARIUMS. At the Aquarium. Max Eastman.
ARABIA. Arabia. De la Mare.
ARABS
Arab to His Favorite Steed, The. C. E. S. Norton.
Arab to the Palm, The. Bayard Taylor.
Arabs. Kreymborg.
Moorish Poetry; a Translation of The Pennants (MooP). A. J. Arberry, ed. and tr.
ARACHNE. Birth of Arachne, the Spider, The. Schevill.
ARAN ISLANDS, IRELAND. Aran. *Unknown, tr. fr. Old Irish.*
ARARAT. Before Ararat. J. R. Anderson.
ARAS (river), TURKEY, RUSSIA, AND IRAN
Araxes Came Devouringly. Hovhannessian, *tr. fr. Armenian by* Boyajian.
Tears of Araxes, The. Patkanian, *tr. fr. Armenian by* Blackwell.
ARBOR DAY
Arbor Day. D. B. Thompson.
Arbor Day Song. Heermans.
Arbor Day Tree, An. *Unknown.*
Child's Song in Spring. Nesbit.
City Trees. Dargan.
Cross and the Tree, The. Stidger.
Fir Forest. E. R. Fuller.
Forest Meditation, A. Legg.
Heart of the Tree, The. Bunner.
Hymn for Arbor Day, A. H. H. Hay.
On Entering a Forest. Lennen.
Plant a Tree. Larcom.
Prayer, A: "Teach me Father, how to go." Markham.
Song of Arbor Day. Pettinos.
Temple of the Trees, The. Pellow.
They All Belong to Me. Eliza Cook.
Tree-building. Cable.
Tree Feelings. Stetson.

Trees. T. C. Clark.
What Do We Plant? Abbey.
White Tree in Bloom, A. Moreland.
Woodman, Spare That Tree. G. P. Morris.
Arbor Day (Our American Holidays Series) (ADAH). Robert Haven Schauffler, ed.
ARBUTUS
Come for Arbutus. Oberholtzer.
May Flowers. Garrison.
To a Mayflower. W. E. Marshall.
Trailing Arbutus. Henry Abbey.
Trailing Arbutus, The. Whittier.
ARCTIC
Arctic Agrarian. Untermeyer.
Arctic Vision. Harte.
Wolf Cry, The. Sarett.
ARCTURUS
Arcturus in Autumn. Teasdale.
Under Arcturus. Cawein.
ARDEN FOREST, ENGLAND. Thirteenth Song, The. *Fr.* Poly-olbion. Drayton.
ARES. *See* MARS.
ARETHUSA
Alpheus and Arethusa. E. H. Daly.
Arethusa. Shelley.
ARIADNE. Theseus and Ariadne. Mifflin.
ARIOSTO, LUDOVICO. Serious Sonnets: Sleep, Ariosto! Aretino, *tr. fr. Italian by* Putnam.
ARISTOPHANES. On Aristophanes. *Unknown, tr. fr. Greek by* Lord Neaves.
ARITHMETIC. *See* MATHEMATICS.
ARIZONA
Arizona. Clifford.
Arizona. S. M. Hall.
Arizona. *Unknown.*
Arizona Boys and Girls, The. *Unknown.*
Arizona Nights. Nance.
Arizona Poems, *sels.* J. G. Fletcher.
New Mexico and Arizona. Canterbury.
Painted Hills of Arizona, The. Curran.
ARK
Ark, The. Milton.
One More River. *Unknown.*
ARKANSAS
Arkansas Traveler, The. *At. to* Sanford C. Faulkner.
Farewell, The. "Plumed hills of Arkansas." J. G. Fletcher.
ARLINGTON NATIONAL CEMETERY
Arlington Cemetery Looking toward the Capitol. Winthrop Palmer.
Little Stones of Arlington, The. Barbara Young.
ARMADA. *See* SPANISH ARMADA.
ARMADILLOS. Armadillo, The. Gordon.
ARMAGH, IRELAND. Distant Prospect of the City of Armagh, A. *Fr.* Morna's Hill. James Stuart.
ARMENIA
Turk in Armenia, The. Sir William Watson.
Armenian Legends and Poems (ArmLP). Zabelle C. Boyajian, comp.
ARMISTICE DAY
"And There Was a Great Calm." Thomas Hardy.
Architects of Dream. Trent.
Armistice. Going.
Armistice. Lehmer.
Armistice. Sangster.
Armistice Day. R. M. Montgomery.
Armistice Day. Trent.
Armistice Day Vow. Gould.
Armistice Night. Wheeler.
At the Cenotaph. Sassoon.
Blow, Bugle! T. C. Clark.
Brotherhood. Markham.
Challenge. T. C. Clark.
Day, The. Bynner.
Dedication: "'They shall not die in vain,' we said." Gustafson.
Design for Peace. Bangs.
"Disabled"—Armistice Day. Parmenter.
Dreamers Cry Their Dream, The. Trent.
Everyone Sang. Sassoon.
For the Fallen. Binyon.
Goal and the Way, The. Oxenham.
Golden Day, The. Peach.
Great Armistice, The. Schauffler.
Great Powers Conference. E. L. Pierce.
Hymn of Hate, The. J D. Miller.
It Shall Not Be Again! T. C. Clark.
Lessons. Weber.
Lest We Forget. Wheeler.
Let Dreamers Wake. Lorraine.
Let Us Declare. Angela Morgan.
Litany for Peace. L. S. Clark.
Make Way! Comfort.
Memorial Rain. MacLeish.
Message of Peace, The. Howe.
New City, The. Wilkinson.
New Song, The. A. G. Field.
Next Time. Simmons.
No Armistice in Love's War. Cheyney.
November Eleventh. Burton.
Peace. Pulsifer.
Peace. G. O. Warren
Peace Call, The. Hampton.
Peace Triumphant. C. Y. Rice.
Peace Universal A. H. Thorne.
Prepare. Bynner.
Preparedness. Paxton.
Reign of Peace, The. Thornton.
Requiem. T. C. Clark.
Song for Tomorrow. Trent.
This Is the Last. Waterhouse.
Today Is Armistice, a Holiday. Schwartz.
Tournament of Man, The. Crosby.
True Freedom. Mackay.
Valley of Decision, The. Oxenham.
Victory Bells. Conkling.
Victory Parade. Hoffman.
Waste of War, The. Stidger.
We Who Build Visions. Coblentz.
When the Cannon Booms [No More]. Carruth.
Where Are You Going, Great-Heart? Oxenham.
Which Sword? J. N. Pierce.
Wild Weather. K. L. Bates.
Without Regret. Lorraine.
World Planners. Steece.
Armistice Day (Our American Holidays Series) (AOAH). A. P. Sanford *and* Robert Haven Schauffler, eds.
ARMSTRONG, JOHN OR JOHNIE. Johnie Armstrong. *Unknown.*
ARMSTRONG, WILLIAM. Kinmont Willie. *Unknown.*
ARNOLD, BENEDICT
Arnold at Stillwater. English.
Arnold, the Vile Traitor. *Unknown.*
Arnold's Departure. Freneau.
Epigram: "Quoth Satan to Arnold." *Unknown.*
ARNOLD, MATTHEW. Pax Paganica. Guiney.
ARNOLD, THOMAS. Rugby Chapel, November, 1857. Matthew Arnold.
AROOSTOOK WAR. Annie McConkus. A. B. Adams.
ART
Accident in Art. Hovey.
Ajanta. Rukeyser.
Andrea del Sarto. Robert Browning.
Ars Victrix. Dobson.
Art. Emerson.
Art. Gautier, *tr. fr. French.*
Art. Melville.
Art. Noyes.
Art. Perry.
Art. *Unknown.*
Art and Life. Ridge.
Birth of Arachne, the Spider, The. Schevill.
Craftsman, The. Christian.
Cubism. Sobiloff.
Exercise in Aesthetics. W. T. Scott.
Gaspar Becerra. Longfellow.
Hugh Selwyn Mauberley, *sel.* ("The age demanded an image"). Pound.
Humanities. Conquest.
I would not paint a picture. Emily Dickinson.
Japanese Print, A. R. M. Rice.
Japanese Vase Wrought in Metal, A. Seiffert.
Joys of Art, The. R. A. Taylor.
Let dainty wits cry on the Sisters nine. *Fr.* Astrophel and Stella. Sir Philip Sidney.
Louvre. Rhys Davies.
Marble Statuette Harpist. S. A. V. Allen.
Ode on a Grecian Urn. Keats.
On Seeing the Elgin Marbles. Keats.
Palace of Art, The. Tennyson.
Pavement Artist, The. Kirkup.
Pictures of the Gone World, *sel.* ("Sarolla's women in their picture hats"). Ferlinghetti.
Ransom, The. Baudelaire, *tr. fr. French by* Conder.
Technique. Burnham Eaton.
To the Stone-Cutters. Jeffers.
When I Buy Pictures. Marianne Moore.
Why I Am Not a Painter. Frank O'Hara.
Woodcut. R. N. D. Wilson.
ARTEMIS
Artemis. Nerval, *tr. fr. French by* Howes.
Artemis Prologizes. Robert Browning.
See also DIANA.
ARTEVELDE, PHILIP VAN. Philip van Artevelde, *sels.* Sir Henry Taylor.
ARTHURIAN LEGEND
Brut, The, *sels.* Layamon.
Camelot. Dalmon.
Defence of Guenevere, The. Morris.
Grave of Arthur, The. Chesterton.

Arthurian legend (*continued*)
Grave of King Arthur, The. Thomas Warton.
Hunting Song. *Fr.* King Arthur. Hovey.
Idylls of the King, *sels.* Tennyson.
King Arthur, *sels.* Dryden.
King Arthur and King Cornwall. *Unknown.*
King Arthur's Death. *Unknown.*
King Arthur's Dream. *Unknown.*
Lady of Shalott, The. Tennyson.
Lancelot. Bontemps.
Lancelot and Guinevere. Gould.
Marriage of Sir Gawain, The. *Unknown.*
Morte Arthure (*Alliterative*), *sels. Unknown.*
Morte d'Arthur, The. Blunt.
Morte d'Arthur. Tennyson.
Myth of Arthur, The. Chesterton.
Parting of Launcelot and Guinevere, The. Phillips.
Round Table, The. Mannyng.
Sir Galahad. Tennyson.
Sir Gawain and the Green Knight. *Unknown, tr. fr. Middle English.*
Sir Launfal. Chester.
Sir Launfal, *sel.* ("But here at starting"). Moultrie.
Ylen's Song. *Fr.* The Birth of Galahad. Hovey.
Artichokes. Artichoke, The. Ibn al-Talla, *tr. fr. Arabic by* Arberry.
Ascanius. Iulus. E. G. Wallis.
Ascension Day
Ascension Day. Kaye-Smith.
At the Ascension. Luis de León, *tr. fr. Spanish by* Walsh.
Eve of Ascension Day, The. Demirjian, *tr. fr. Armenian by* Boyajian.
Ash trees
Ash Trees. *Unknown, tr fr. Chinese.*
Timid Ash Tree, The. Kathleen Millay.
Ash Wednesday
Ash Wednesday. T. S. Eliot.
Ash Wednesday. Erskine.
Ash Wednesday. Marinoni.
Ashby, Turner. Ashby. Thompson.
Asia. Source of the Danube, The. Hölderlin, *tr. fr. German by* Hull.
Aspen trees
Aspens. Edward Thomas.
Spring Song of Aspens. L. W. Spencer.
Asses
Brother Ass. Eric Irvin.
Burro, The. Gibbons.
Burro with the Long Ears. *Tr. fr. Navajo Indian by* Wetherill.
Donkey, The. Chesterton.
Lament for a Dead Burro. Peñalosa, *tr. fr. Spanish by* Train.
Little Danny Donkey. Le Cron.
Me and Prunes. Sherwood.
Ol' Jinny Mine, The. Detrick.
When You elect to call me, God, O call. Jammes, *tr. fr. French by* Conder.
Assisi, Italy
Assisi. Noyes.
At Assisi. *Fr.* Song-Flower and Poppy. Moody.
Assumption of the Virgin. *See* Mary, the Virgin.
Astarte. To Ashtaroth and Bel. Tchernichowsky, *tr. fr. Hebrew by* Snowman.
Astrology
Astrologer's Song, An. Kipling.
Astrology. Sennett Stephens.
Though dusty wits dare scorn astrology. *Fr.* Astrophel and Stella. Sidney.
Astronomers and astronomy
Astronomer, The. Doherty.
Fantasia under the Clear Sky. Miyazawa, *tr. fr. Japanese by* Ninomiya *and* Enright.
Uranus. Clough.
When I Heard the Learn'd Astronomer. Whitman.
Atalanta
Atalanta. Maurice Thompson.
Atalanta in Calydon, *sels.* Swinburne.
Atheism. Atheist and the Acorn, The. Finch.
Athens, Greece
Athens. Kariotakis, *tr. fr. Modern Greek by* Dalven.
Athens, *sel.* ("Athens is critically ill"). Pappas, *tr. fr. Modern Greek by* Dalven.
Athens. Vrettakos, *tr. fr. Modern Greek by* Dalven.
O Sweet Athens. Skipis, *tr. fr. Modern Greek by* Dalven.
To Athens. Pindar, *tr. fr. Greek.*
Athletes
Runner, The. Whitman.
To an Athlete Dying Young. A. E. Housman.
Atlanta, Georgia. Litany at Atlanta, A. DuBois.
Atlantic Ocean. Atlantic. Florit, *tr. fr. Spanish by* Hays.
Atlantis
Atlantis. Bottomley.
Atlantis. *Fr.* The Bridge. Hart Crane.
Song at Santa Cruz. Young.
Atom
Atom, The. Thornely.
Presage. Thornely.
They Have Blown the Trumpet. Converse.
Atomic bomb
Dirge for the New Sunrise. *Fr.* Three Poems of the Atomic Bomb. Edith Sitwell.
There Is Yet Time. Steece.
Atoyac (river), Mexico. To the Atoyac. Altamirano, *tr. fr. Spanish by* Beckett.
Attis. Across the roaring ocean, with heart and with eye of flame. Catullus, *tr. fr. Latin by* Allen.
Attucks, Crispus. Crispus Attucks. O'Reilly.
Auburn, Ireland. Deserted Village, The. Goldsmith.
Auden, Wystan Hugh
Just a Smack at Auden. Empson.
Their Last Will and Testament. MacNeice.
Aughrim, Ireland
After Aughrim. Georghegan.
After Aughrim. Lawless.
August
August. Fallon.
August. Gallagher.
August. Ledwidge.
August. Michael Lewis.
August. MacNeice.
August. Mair.
August. *Fr.* The Shepheardes Calender. Spenser.
August. Swinburne.
August. Thaxter.
August. H. M. Winslow.
August. Elinor Wylie.
August Afternoon. Edey.
August Afternoon, An. Irvine.
August Evening. Dargan.
August Mood, An. D. C. Scott.
August Moonrise. Teasdale.
August Night. E. M. Roberts.
August Smiles. Coatsworth.
August Weather. Tynan.
Golden Month, The. Marion Doyle.
In August. Howells.
Mid-August. Driscoll.
Month of Falling Stars, The. Ella Higginson.
Augustine, Saint
Passage in the Life of St. Augustine. *Unknown.*
Petitions of Saint Augustine. *Unknown.*
Augustus. Fugal Chorus. *Fr.* For the Time Being. Auden.
Aurora borealis
Aurora. Emily Dickinson.
Northern Lights. Benediktsson, *tr. fr. Icelandic by* Johnson.
Northern Lights, The. Savage.
Northern Lights, The. B. F. Taylor.
Sights and Sounds of the Night. Wilcox.
Ausonius. To Ausonius. Paulinus of Nola, *tr. fr. Latin by* Waddell.
Austen, Jane. Anemones for Miss Austen. Bergonzi.
Austin, Texas. Some Towns of Texas. Baker.
Australia
Australia. Hope.
Australia. Rentoul.
Australia to England. *Fr.* Sonnets of the Empire. Strong.
Australian Federation. William Gay.
Ballade of the Southern Cross. *Fr.* Ballades in Blue China. Lang.
Birth of Australia, The. Russell.
Dominion of Australia, The. Stephens.
Dutch Seamen and New Holland, The. W. P. Reeves.
Midsummer Noon in the Australian Forest, A. Harpur.
September in Australia. H. C. Kendall.
Book of Australian and New Zealand Verse, A (BoAu). Walter Murdoch, ed.
Book of Australian Verse, A (BoAV). Judith Wright, comp.
Modern Australian Poetry (MoAuPo). H. M. Green, comp.
New Land, New Language (NeLNL). Judith Wright, comp.
Australians
Australian Girl, An. Castilla.
Boundary Rider, The. Heney.
Circling Hearths, The. Quinn.
Last Aboriginal, The. "Fiona Macleod."
Austria. House of Sorrows, The. Francis Thompson.
Authors and authorship
Author to Her Book, The. Bradstreet.
Canadian Authors Meet, The. F. R. Scott.
Messire Geoffrey Chaucer to His Editor. Guiterman.
Mrs. Brown and the Famous Author. Stoddard King.
On Some South African Novelists. Roy Campbell.
To a Writer of the Day. "John Philip Varley."
To an Author. Freneau.
To His Book. *Fr.* Amoretti. Spenser.
Upon Her Play Being Returned to Her Stained with Claret. Leapor.
Veld Eclogue, A; the Pioneers, *sel.* ("But 'nameless somethings' and 'unbounded spaces' "). Roy Campbell.
Writer to His Book, The. Campion.

AUTOMOBILES
Auto Wreck. Shapiro.
Automobile, The. Mackaye.
Automobile and the Cat, The. **Coatsworth.**
Buick. Shapiro.
Hildebrand. Belloc.
Klaxon. Reaney.
Meeting, The. Monroe.
Motor Cars. R. B. Bennett.
Night-driving. "A. E. M."
One, Two, Three. Albert.
Pedestrian's Plaint, The. **E. V. Lucas.**
Reason. Josephine Miles.
Song for a Blue Roadster. **Rachel Field.**
This Dim and Ptolemaic Man. **J. P. Bishop.**
AUTUMN
Adios. D. C. Babcock.
Against the Cold. Bynner.
Alms in Autumn. Fyleman.
Autumn. Apollinaire, *tr. fr. French by* **Merwin.**
Autumn. Roy Campbell.
Autumn. Carman.
Autumn. Carruth.
Autumn. Clare.
Autumn. Curran.
Autumn. De la Mare.
Autumn, The. *Fr.* Autumn in the West. Gallagher.
Autumn. Gorostiza, *tr. fr. Spanish by* Hays.
Autumn. *Fr.* Works and Days. Hesiod, *tr. fr. Greek by* Lucas.
Autumn. Hoatson.
Autumn ("I saw old Autumn"). Hood.
Autumn. Hulme.
Autumn. Irwin.
Autumn. Karamzin, *tr. fr. Russian by* Bowring.
Autumn. Knipe.
Autumn. *Fr.* Colinetta. Leapor.
Autumn. Liliencron, *tr. fr. German by* Lewisohn.
Autumn ("Thou comest, Autumn, heralded by the rain"). Longfellow.
Autumn ("With what a glory comes"). Longfellow.
Autumn. Manger, *tr. fr. Yiddish by* Leftwich.
Autumn. *Fr.* The Fields of Dawn. Mifflin.
Autumn. Moreland.
Autumn. *Fr.* Summer's Last Will and Testament. **Nashe.**
Autumn. Pushkin, *tr. fr. Russian.*
Autumn. Reid.
Autumn. Rilke, *tr. fr. German by* **Flores.**
Autumn. E. M. Roberts.
Autumn. Rodgers.
Autumn. Sassoon.
Autumn. B. H. Smith.
Autumn. W. J. Smith.
Autumn. James Stephens.
Autumn. Su T'ung-po, *tr. fr. Chinese by* Rexroth.
Autumn. Tagore.
Autumn. *Fr.* The Seasons. James Thomson.
Autumn. Trimm.
Autumn. *Unknown, tr. fr. Irish by* Frank O'Connor.
Autumn. J. S. Untermeyer.
Autumn. Sir William Watson.
Autumn. Winwar.
Autumn. Yesenin, *tr. fr. Russian by* **Bowra.**
Autumn; a Dirge. Shelley.
Autumn along the Beaches. **Wheelock.**
Autumn; an Ode. Gullans.
Autumn and Death. Amy Lowell.
Autumn and Winter. Chatterton.
Autumn at Taos. D. H. Lawrence.
Autumn Bird. Corning.
Autumn Breeze, An. Hayne.
Autumn Chant. Millay.
Autumn Color. Tom Robinson.
Autumn Complaint. Lenau, *tr. fr. German by* **Durling.**
Autumn Cricket, An. Scollard.
Autumn, Crystal Eye. Ruddock.
Autumn Day. Rilke, *tr. fr. German by* MacIntyre.
Autumn Day, An. Sangster.
Autumn Daybreak. Millay.
Autumn Eve. Andriello.
Autumn Evening. Tyutchev, *tr. fr. Russian.*
Autumn Evening beside the Lake. Li Ch'ing-chao, *tr. fr. Chinese by* Rexroth.
Autumn Fancies. *Unknown.*
Autumn Fashions. E. M. Thomas.
Autumn Fields. E. M. Roberts.
Autumn Fires. R. L. Stevenson.
Autumn, Forsake These Hills. **F. E. Hill.**
Autumn Fruits. *Fr.* Aella. **Chatterton.**
Autumn Garden, An. Carman.
Autumn Gloves. Shacklett.
Autumn Haze. Munkittrick.
Autumn Healing. Ward.
Autumn Hour. George Chapman.
Autumn in Carmel. Sterling.
Autumn in the Highlands. Clough.
Autumn in the West. Gallagher.
Autumn in Wartime. Gilean Douglas.
Autumn Is a Season. Cotter.
Autumn Leaves. J. S. Heyward.
Autumn Leaves. M. C. Hopkins.
Autumn Leaves. Lu Lun, *tr. fr. Chinese by* **Hart.**
Autumn Leaves. Sutphen.
Autumn Leaves. *Unknown.*
Autumn Leaves. Wray.
Autumn Memories. Savage-Armstrong.
Autumn Morning, An. *Unknown.*
Autumn Morning. Adeline White.
Autumn Morning at Cambridge. **Cornford.**
Autumn Movement. Sandburg.
Autumn Night. Evelyn Scott.
Autumn Riddle, An. *Unknown.*
Autumn Road, An. Dresbach.
Autumn Rose-Tree, An. Earls.
Autumn Song. Griffith.
Autumn Song. P. C. Horton.
Autumn Song. E. E. Long.
Autumn Song. Nyleen Newton.
Autumn Song. Margaret Rose.
Autumn Song. D. G. Rossetti.
Autumn Song. Tieck, *tr. fr. German by* Mangan.
Autumn Song. *Unknown, tr. fr. Old Irish by* **Colum.**
Autumn Train. Shacklett.
Autumn Twilight. Régnier, *tr. fr. French by* **Lind.**
Autumn Wind, The. Wu Ti, *tr. fr. Chinese by* **Waley.**
Autumn Woods. Bryant.
Autumn Woods. Tippett.
Autumnal, The. *Fr.* Elegies. **Donne.**
Autumnal. Gilchrist.
Autumnal Clouds. J. G. Fletcher.
Autumnal Consummation. Patric Stevenson.
Autumnal Evening, An. "Fiona Macleod."
Autumnal Spring Song. Vassar Miller.
Autumn's Day. Rilke, *tr. fr. German by* **Flores.**
Autumn's Fete. McGeorge.
Autumn's Mirth. Peck.
Autumn's Processional. Craik.
Autumnus. Sylvester.
Battle Autumn of 1862, The. **Whittier.**
Blue Smoke. Frances Frost.
Bonny Harvest Moon, The. Barr of Craigielee.
Bright moon illumines the night-prospect, A. *Fr.* Seventeen Old Poems. *Unknown, tr. fr. Chinese by* **Waley.**
Burning of the Leaves, The. Binyon.
Calvinist Autumnal. Harrod.
Carouse. Towne.
Chansons d'Automne. Verlaine, *tr. fr. French by* **Symons.**
Chant for Skippers. Gallagher.
Chorale for Autumn. Zaturenska.
Colour. Adeline White.
Come, Little Leaves. George Cooper.
Come to the Park They Say Is Dead and See. George, *tr. fr. German by* Gee.
Comes Fall. Nathan.
Contemplations, *sel.* ("Some time now past in the autumnal tide"). Bradstreet.
Counter-Serenade; She Invokes the Autumn Instant. Viereck.
Days like These. Egbert.
Death of the Flowers, The. **Bryant.**
Delta Autumn, The. Percy.
Disillusion. **Sister Mary Edwardine.**
Early Autumn. Fairthorne.
End of Summer. **Kunitz.**
Fall, The. Barnes.
Fall. A. L. Fisher.
Fall Days. Conger.
Fall, Leaves, Fall. **Emily Brontë.**
Fall of the Year. Ellison.
Falltime. Sandburg.
Farmer. L. H. Bailey.
First Autumn, The. **Schacht.**
Friends. L. G. Warner.
Glimpse in Autumn. **J. S. Untermeyer.**
Harvest Moon, The. **Longfellow.**
Hound, The. Deutsch.
How the Leaves Came Down. **"Susan Coolidge."**
Hurrahing in Harvest. Hopkins.
I Am the Autumn. Manger, *tr. fr. Yiddish by* **Leftwich.**
Immortal Autumn. MacLeish.
In an Autumn Wood. Percy.
In Autumn. Kiely.
In Autumn. Sterling.
In Coventry. J. J. Daly.
In the Elegy Season. Wilbur.
In the Fall o' Year. **T. S. Jones, Jr.**
Indian Summer. A. S. Draper.
Joys of the Road, The. Carman.
Last Rose of Summer, The. **Thomas Moore.**
Last Walk in Autumn, The. **Whittier.**

AUTUMN (*continued*)
Late Autumn. Allingham.
Late Autumn. Hagiwara, *tr. fr. Japanese by* Ninomiya *and* Enright.
Late Autumn. A. M. Sullivan.
Late Autumn. Andrew Young.
Load. Hewitt.
Memory Green. MacLeish.
Merry Autumn Days. Dickens.
Mild Is the Parting Year. Landor.
Mist and All, The. Willson.
Mnemosyne. Stickney.
Morns are meeker than they were, The. Emily Dickinson.
Mosquito Net. Tanaka, *tr. fr. Japanese by* Ninomiya *and* Enright.
My Autumn Walk. Bryant.
My Wind Is Turned to Bitter North. Clough.
Naseby; Late Autumn. Dowling.
Nature's Miracle. Fallon.
O Amber Day, amid the Autumn Gloom. Allison.
October, *sel.* ("O, the sweet melancholy of the time"). Gray.
October's Husbandry. Tusser.
Ode to Autumn. Keats.
Ode to the West Wind. Shelley.
Old Age. C. Y. Rice.
Pirate Wind. Carr.
Pity of the Leaves, The. E. A. Robinson.
Plants Decay, The. *Fr.* The Sensitive Plant. Shelley.
Poem in October. Dylan Thomas.
Protinus Extremo cum Jam Boreas Autumno. Politian, *tr. fr. Latin by* Allen.
Red in Autumn. Gould.
Rich Days. W. H. Davies.
Scene in a Garden. *Fr.* Paracelsus. Robert Browning.
Seed-Time. George Meredith.
Shape of Autumn, The. Russ.
Sick Autumn. Apollinaire, *tr. fr. French by* Conder.
Sigh. Mallarmé, *tr. fr. French by* Morgan.
Something Told the Wild Geese. Rachel Field.
Song: "Feathers of the willow, The." R. W. Dixon.
Song: "It Autumne was, and on our Hemispheare." Drummond of Hawthornden.
Song: "Spirit haunts the year's last hours, A." Tennyson.
Song: "Why fadest thou in death." R. W. Dixon.
Song at the Beginning of Autumn. Elizabeth Jennings.
Song in Autumn, A. Garrison.
Song of Autumn, A. A. L. Gordon.
Song of Autumn, A. Rodd.
Song of Autumn. Verlaine, *tr. fr. French by* Symons.
Song of Early Autumn, A. R. W. Gilder.
Songs of the Autumn Night. MacDonald.
Spring and Autumn. Linton.
Still Day in Autumn, A. S. H. Whitman.
Summer Is Gone. *Unknown, tr. fr. Old Irish by* O'Faoláin.
Tell Me Not Here. Housman.
Theme in Yellow. Sandburg.
Thief, The. Pawsey.
Third of November, The. Bryant.
Threnody: "Red leaves fall upon the lake, The." Farrar.
To Autumn. Keats.
Torch-Light in Autumn. Piatt.
Unparalleled Autumn, An. "Anna Akhmatova," *tr. fr. Russian by* Deutsch.
Unreaped Field, The. Nekrasov, *tr. fr. Russian by* Phillimore.
Vagabond Song, A. Carman.
Watching the Moon. McCord.
When the Frost Is on the Punkin. Riley.
When unto Nights of Autumn Do Complain. Cummings.
Wind of Fall, A. Léonie Adams.
AUVERGNE, FRANCE. In the Caves of Auvergne. W. J. Turner.
AVIATION AND AVIATORS
Aeroplane, The. *Fr.* The Bridge: Cape Hatteras. Hart Crane.
Airman's Alphabet, The. *Fr.* Journal of an Airman. Auden.
Airplane, The. R. B. Bennett.
Airplane, The. Wynne.
Aviator, The. Blok, *tr. fr. Russian by* Loomis.
Ceiling Unlimited. Rukeyser.
Chavez. M. M. Sweeney.
Conquest of the Air, The. Pulsifer.
Crash at Leithfield. Curnow.
Dead Aviator. Akins.
Dead Aviator, The. Hackett.
Death of the Ball Turret Gunner, The. Jarrell.
Eagle Youth. K. W. Baker.
Epitaph for an American Bomber. Bertram.
First Flight. Coffin.
Flight, The. *Fr.* A Time to Dance. Day Lewis.
Flyers, The. F. E. Hill.
Flying. Mastin.
High Flight. J. G. Magee, Jr.
Hymn for Those in the Air. D. C. Scott.
Icarus. Iremonger.
Irish Airman Foresees His Death, An. Yeats.
London to Paris by Air. Gorell.
Losses. Jarrell.
Norfolk Memorials. Leavenworth.
Nox Mortis. Bewsher.
Ongoing, The. Siegrist.
P-51. Ciardi.
Prayer for a Pilot. Cecil Roberts.
Sparrows at the Airport, The. Ostroff.
Third Time. Pellicer, *tr. fr. Spanish by* Fitts.
To Poets and Airmen. Spender.
Trans Canada. F. R. Scott.
Poetry of Flight, The (PoF). Selden Rodman, ed.
AVIGNON, FRANCE. Orchard at Avignon, An. A. M. F. Robinson.
AVOCA (river), IRELAND. Meeting of the Waters, The. Thomas Moore.
AVON (river), ENGLAND. Upon Eckington Bridge, River Avon. Quiller-Couch.
AVON (ship, War of 1812). Ocean-Fight, The. *Unknown.*
AYR, SCOTLAND. Brigs of Ayr, The, *sel.* ("When heavy, dark"). Burns.
AZALEAS
Azalea, The. *Fr.* The Unknown Eros. Patmore.
Azaleas. Muda, *tr. fr. Japanese by* Erickson.
White Azaleas. Kimball.
AZRAEL
Azrael. Longfellow.
Azrael. McGiffert.
Azrael. Welsh.
AZTEC. Aztec City, The. Ware.

B

BAAL. To Ashtaroth and Bel. Tchernichowsky, *tr. fr. Hebrew by* Snowman.
BABEL, TOWER OF. Babel and Bethel. Buchanan.
BABIES
Alcove at Sunrise, An. Hugo, *tr. fr. French by* Conder.
Baby, The. M. R. S. Andrews.
Baby. E. G. Eastman.
Baby. Frank.
Baby. George Macdonald.
Baby, The. Ann Taylor.
Baby Asleep after Pain, A. D. H. Lawrence.
Baby at Play. *Unknown.*
Baby Girl, The. Florit, *tr. fr. Spanish by* Walsh.
Baby's Feet, A. Swinburne.
Bacchante to Her Babe, The. Tietjens.
Blessing for the Blessed, A. Alma-Tadema.
Blest the Infant Babe. *Fr.* The Prelude. Wordsworth.
Cradle Song: "Sleep, sleep, beauty bright." Blake.
Cradle Song: "Sweet slumber now creeps o'er thee slow." Patkanian, *tr. fr. Armenian by* Boyajian.
Cradle Song: "What is the little one thinking about?" *Fr.* Bitter-sweet. Holland.
Eskimo Baby, An. Diamond.
Etude Réaliste. Swinburne.
For a Child Expected. Ridler.
For My Son. Nims.
In Go-Cart So Tiny. Greenaway.
Infant Joy. Blake.
Johneen. "Moira O'Neill."
Kadia the Young Mother Speaks. Sampter.
King of the Cradle, The. Ashby-Sterry.
Little. Aldis.
Little Brown Baby. Dunbar.
Little One Smiles, The. Stjerne, *tr. fr. Swedish by* Stork.
Little Papoose. Hilda Conkling.
Methinks 'Tis Pretty Sport. Bastard.
Modern Baby, The. Doane.
Mundus et Infans. Auden.
My Little Lover. Sauvage, *tr. fr. French by* Conder.
New Arrival, The. Cable.
New-born, The. Hoyt.
New-born Baby's Song, The. Cornford.
News of a Baby. Riddell.
No Baby in the House. Dolliver.
Only a Baby Small. Barr.
Slippery. Sandburg.
To a New-born Baby Girl. Hilda Conkling.
To a New-born Child. Monkhouse.
To a Staring Baby in a Perambulator. N. B. Turner.
Weight Gainer. Guest.
Where Did You Come From? George Macdonald.
Wonder-Child, The. La Gallienne.
BABOONS
Baboon. Towne.

Big Baboon, The. Belloc.
BABYLON. Babylon. Hodgson.
BACCHUS
Bacchus. Sherman.
Bacchus' Opinion of Wine, and Other Beverages. *Fr.* Bacchus in Tuscany. Redi, *tr. fr. Italian by* Hunt.
Elegies, *sel.* ("Now, O Bacchus, I turn humbly to your shrine"). Propertius, *tr. fr. Latin by* Fletcher.
Sacrifice of the Bacchantes in Honor of Bacchus. *Fr.* Orfeo. Poliziano, *tr. fr. Italian by* Creekmore.
BACH, JOHANN SEBASTIAN
Considerations on Certain Music of J. S. Bach, *sel.* ("Meditating in silence after the last note"). Beaglehole.
Four Friends. Ward.
BACHELORS
Bachelor Hall. Eugene Field.
Bachelor's Dream, The. Hood.
Bachelor's Hall. Finley.
Bachelor's Mono-Rhyme, A. Mackay.
Bachelor's Soliloquy, The. *Unknown.*
Batchelors Song, The. Flatman.
Where the Single Men Go in Summer. Bourne.
BACON, FRANCIS. Franciscus de Verulamio Sic Cogitavit. J. R. Lowell.
BADGERS. Badger. Clare.
BAGPIPES
Bagpipe Man, The. N. B. Turner.
Bag-Pipes at Sea. Scollard.
BALACLAVA, CRIMEA
Charge of the Light Brigade, The. Tennyson.
Heavy Brigade, The. Tennyson.
BALBOA, VASCO NÚÑEZ DE. Balboa. Perry.
BALDER (Norse god of light). Balder Dead, *sels.* Matthew Arnold.
BALDNESS
Baldness and the Swan. W. T. Scott.
On His Baldness. Po Chü-i, *tr. fr. Chinese by* Waley.
Penalties of Baldness, The. Seaman.
BALE, JOHN. To Doctor Bale. Barnabe Googe.
BALL, JOHN
Sermon to the Rebels at Blackheath. Ball.
Song of the Plow, The, *sel.* ("He loathed his bond, but could not stir"). Hewlett.
BALLADS AND FOLK SONGS
American Ballads and Folk Songs (ABF). John A. Lomax *and* Alan Lomax, eds.
American Ballads and Songs (ABS). Louise Pound, ed.
American Songbag, The (AS). Carl Sandburg, comp.
Ballad Book, The (BaBo). MacEdward Leach, ed.
Book of Danish Ballads, A (BoDaBa). Axel Olrik, ed.
Cowboy Songs and Other Frontier Ballads (CSF). John A. Lomax, ed.
Cowboy Songs and Other Frontier Ballads (CoSo). John A. Lomax *and* Alan Lomax, eds.
English and Scottish Popular Ballads (ESPB). Helen Child Sargent *and* George L. Kittredge, eds.
Our Singing Country (OuSiCo). John A. Lomax *and* Alan Lomax, eds.
Oxford Book of Ballads, The (OBB). Arthur Quiller-Couch, ed.
Saucy Sailor and Other Dramatized Ballads, The (SaSa). Alice M. G. White *and* Janet E. Tobitt, comps.
Songs of American Folks (SoAF). Satis H. Coleman *and* Adolph Bregman, eds.
Songs of the Cattle Trail and Cow Camp (SCC). John A. Lomax, ed.
Steamboatin' Days (StDa). Mary Wheeler, comp.
Treasury of American Song, A (TrAS). Olin Downes *and* Elie Siegmeister, comps.
See also SEA CHANTEYS.
BALLET
I cannot dance upon my toes. Emily Dickinson.
Pediment: Ballet. Nicholl.
Song of the Ballet. J. B. Morton.
To Potapovitch. Hart Crane.
BALLIOL COLLEGE, OXFORD
Balliol Rooks, The. F. S. Boas.
To the Balliol Men Still in Africa. Belloc.
BALLOONS
Balloon Man, The. Fyleman.
Balloon Man, The. Morton.
Balloon Man. North.
In Soapsuds Street. Bandeira, *tr. fr. Portuguese by* Poore.
Progress of Balloons, The. Freneau.
BALL'S BLUFF, BATTLE OF. Ball's Bluff. Melville.
BALLYSHANNON, IRELAND
Adieu to Belashanny. Allingham.
Song of Ballyshannon. J. R. Foster.
Winding Banks of Erne, The. Allingham.
BALSHEMTOV, YISROEL
Holy Balshemtov, The. Landau, *tr. fr. Yiddish by* Betsky.
Saint Balshemtov. Manger, *tr. fr. Yiddish by* Betsky.
BALTIC, BATTLE OF THE. Battle of the Baltic, The. Thomas Campbell.
BALTIMORE, IRELAND. Sack of Baltimore, The. T. O. Davis.
BALTIMORE, MARYLAND
Battle of Baltimore, The. *Unknown.*
Incident. Cullen.
Streets of Baltimore. *Unknown.*
Through Baltimore. Bayard Taylor.
BANANAS. Banana. C. G. Bell.
BANCROFT, GEORGE. Decanter of Madeira, Aged 86, to George Bancroft, Aged 86, Greeting, A. Mitchell.
BANDITS
Bandit, The. R. P. Baker.
Bandit Peter Mancino's Death, The. *Unknown, tr. fr. Italian by* Graham.
Bandit's Grave, The. Pitt.
BANDS. Band, The. John.
BANJOS
Banjo of the Past, The. Weeden.
Banjo Player, The. Fenton Johnson.
Song of the Banjo, The. Kipling.
BANKING AND BANKERS. Bankers Are Just like Anybody Else, except Richer. Nash.
BANNERS. *See* FLAGS.
BANNOCKBURN, BATTLE OF. Scots Wha Hae. Burns.
BAPTISM. On the Baptized Ethiopian. Crashaw.
BAR KOKBA, SIMON. Bar Kochba. Lazarus.
BARABBAS. Barabbas. W. E. Brooks.
BARDS
Good Tradition, The. *Unknown, tr. fr. Early Modern Irish by* Flower.
On the Breaking-up of a School. Tadhg O'g O'Huiginn, *tr. fr. Late Middle Irish by* Bergin.
Were Not the Gael Fallen. Peadar O'Mulconry, *tr. fr. Early Modern Irish by* Flower.
Who Will Buy a Poem? Mahon O'Heffernan, *tr. fr. Early Modern Irish by* Jackson.
BAREBONE, PRAISE-GOD. Praise-God Barebones. Cortissoz.
BARLEY
Barley Fields, The. Blewett.
Barley-Mowers' Song, The. Howitt.
Like Barley Bending. Teasdale.
BARNACLES
Barnacle, The. A. P. Herbert.
Barnacles. Lanier.
BARNEGAT BAY, NEW JERSEY. Patrolling Barnegat. Whitman.
BARNS
Barn, The. Blunden.
Barn, The. Coatsworth.
Barn, The. Spender.
Barn in Winter, The. MacIntosh.
Hayloft, The. Stevenson.
BARNYARD. Barnyard, The. Burnham.
BARRY, KEVIN. Kevin Barry. Ward.
BARRYMORE, JOHN. Requiescat. Freund.
BARTON, ANDREW. Sir Andrew Barton. *Unknown.*
BASEBALL
Baseball's Sad Lexicon. F. P. Adams.
Casey at the Bat. Thayer.
Casey's Revenge. James Wilson.
Cobb Would Have Caught It. Robert Fitzgerald.
Greata Basaball, Da. Daly.
Origin of Baseball, The. Patchen.
Pitcher. Robert Francis.
Polo Grounds. Humphries.
Slide, Kelly, Slide. J. W. Kelly.
Umpire, The. Gibson.
Willy Smith at the Ball Game. George Sterling.
BASS, SAM. Sam Bass. *Unknown.*
BASTILLE. Bastille, The. Cowper.
BATH, ENGLAND
Farewell to Bath. Montagu.
New Bath Guide, The, *sels.* Anstey.
BATHS AND BATHING. Bath, The. Oppenheimer.
BATS
Bat, The. Pitter.
Bat, The. Roethke.
Bats, The. Hillyer.
BATTERY PARK, NEW YORK CITY. Battery Park. Cline.
BAUDELAIRE, CHARLES
Ave atque Vale. Swinburne.
Baudelaire. Lee-Hamilton.
Baudelaire. Wolfe.
Tomb of Charles Baudelaire, The. Mallarmé, *tr. fr. French by* Bennett.
BAVARIA
Bavarian Roadside. Speyer.
Sonnet in a Pass of Bavaria. Trench.
BEARDSLEY, AUBREY. Oscar Wilde and Aubrey Beardsley. John Waller.
BEAN, ROY. Roy Bean. *Unknown, at. to* Finger.
BEARCAMP RIVER, NEW HAMPSHIRE. Sunset on the Bearcamp. Whittier.
BEARS
Bear, The. Robert Frost.
Bear, The. Lugovskoi, *tr. fr. Russian by* Lindsay.
Bear Hunt, The. Widdemer.

BEARS (*continued*)
Bear in the Hill, The. *Unknown.*
Bears. Guiterman.
Brown Bear, The. Mary Austin.
Fox, the Wolf, and the Bear, The. *Unknown, tr. fr. Armenian by* Boyajian.
Grizzly Bear. Mary Austin.
Little Brown Bear. Alice Wilkins.
Shebear, The. Lighthall.
BEATRICE PORTINARI
Beatrice. Baudelaire, *tr. fr. French by* Stepanchev.
Canzone: "Eyes that weep for pity of the heart, The." Dante, *tr. fr. Italian by* D. G. Rossetti.
To Beatrice on All Saints' Day. Dante, *tr. fr. Italian by* D. G. Rossetti.
BEAUMONT, FRANCIS
Bards of Passion and of Mirth. Keats.
On Mr. Francis Beaumont (Then Newly Dead). Corbet.
To Francis Beaumont. Jonson.
BEAUMONT, FRANCIS, AND JOHN FLETCHER
Beaumont and Fletcher. *Fr.* Sonnets on English Dramatic Poets (1590–1650). Swinburne.
To the Memory of the Incomparable Paire of Authors Beaumont and Fletcher. *Unknown.*
BEAUREGARD, PIERRE GUSTAVE TOUTANT. Beauregard. Warfield.
BEAUTY
Barter. Teasdale.
Beauté, La. Baudelaire, *tr. fr. French.*
Beauty. Binyon.
Beauty. Cowley.
Beauty. E-Yeh-Shure'.
Beauty. Hille, *tr. fr. German by* Bithell.
Beauty. *Fr.* Tamburlaine the Great. Marlowe.
Beauty. Masefield.
Beauty. Isaac Rosenberg.
Beauty. Spingarn.
Beauty. Edward Thomas.
Beauty. Winter.
Beauty. Wylie.
Beauty and Terror. Harford.
Beauty crowds me till I die. Emily Dickinson.
Beauty Is Ever to the Lonely Mind. Nathan.
Beauty of the World. Wilmot.
Beauty, sweet love, is like the morning dew. *Fr.* To Delia. Daniel.
Beauty's a Flower. O'Neill.
Beauty's Hands Are Cool. K. W. Baker.
Body's Beauty. *Fr.* The House of Life. D. G. Rossetti.
Brittle beauty, that Nature made so frail. Earl of Surrey.
Changeful Beauty. Lang.
Color. W. W. Gibson.
Colours of Love, The. Devlin.
Definition of Beauty, The. Herrick.
Description of Beauty, A. Marino, *tr. fr. Italian by* Daniel.
Dim Face of Beauty. "Fiona Macleod."
Each and All. Emerson.
Earth's Common Things. Savage.
Euclid Alone Has Looked on Beauty Bare. Edna St. Vincent Millay.
Exhortation to the Artists. Plutzik.
Frailty and Hurtfulness of Beauty, The. Earl of Surrey.
Gascoigne's Arraignment. Gascoigne.
Give Beauty All Her Right. Campion.
Gloire de Dijon. D. H. Lawrence.
Great Breath, The. "Æ."
He Remembers Forgotten Beauty. Yeats.
Here Is the Place Where Loveliness Keeps House. Cawein.
Hymn to Intellectual Beauty. Shelley.
Hymne in Honour of Beautie, An. Spenser.
Hymne of Heavenly Beautie, An. Spenser.
I died for beauty. Emily Dickinson.
I Hear the Woodlands Calling. Cawein.
I Never See the Red Rose Crown the Year. Masefield.
Immortal, The. Pickthall.
Impiety, *sel.* ("Lord, I have not time to pray"). Magaret.
Like Music. Wheelock.
Little Things. Johns.
Lord of the Far Horizons. Carman.
Merciles Beaute. Chaucer.
Modern Beauty. Symons.
New Inn, The, *sel.* ("It was a beauty that I saw"). Jonson.
Not Our Good Luck. Jeffers.
Ode on a Grecian Urn. Keats.
Ode to Beauty. Emerson.
On a Lamp. Mörike, *tr. fr. German by* Flores.
Perilous Light. Gore-Booth.
Pied Beauty. Hopkins.
Pitiless Beauty. Wheelock.
Prayer, A: "Each day I walk with wonder." Scollard.
Prayer: "Lord, make me sensitive to the sight." Marr.
Primer of Plato. Garrigue.
Rose of the World, The. Yeats.
Say Not That Beauty. Flower.
Scribe, The. De la Mare.
Snare, The. Davison.
Soul's Beauty. *Fr.* The House of Life. D. G. Rossetti.
Testament of Beauty, The, *sel.* ("'Twas at thatt hour of beauty when the setting sun"). Robert Bridges.
Thing of Beauty, A [Is a Joy Forever]. *Fr.* Endymion. Keats.
This Is the Shape of the Leaf. *Fr.* Priapus and the Pool. Aiken.
Tristan. Platen, *tr. fr. German by* Cotterell.
Unutterable Beauty, The. Studdert-Kennedy.
Vale. Plunkett.
Wayfarer, The. Pearse.
Who Pilots Ships. Hicky.
Who Walks with Beauty. David Morton.
BECERRA, GASPAR. Gaspar Becerra. Longfellow.
BEDFORD, COUNTESS OF. *See* RUSSELL, LUCY, COUNTESS OF BEDFORD.
BEECH TREES
Beech, The. Daeubler, *tr. fr. German by* Cambon.
Beech Trees. Sister Mary Madeleva.
Beech Tree's Petition, The. Thomas Campbell.
To My Totem. Beeching.
BEECHER, HENRY WARD
Henry Ward Beecher. Phelps.
Said a great Congregational preacher. *At. to* O. W. Holmes.
BEECHER ISLAND (Colo.), BATTLE OF. Beecher Island. Chapman.
BEER
Beer. *Unknown.*
Glass of Beer, A. James Stephens.
BEES
Bee, The ("Like trains of cars on tracks of plush"). Emily Dickinson.
Bee, The. Fandel.
Bee, The. Fitzgeffry.
Bee, The. Hawkins.
Bee, The. *Unknown.*
Bee, The. Isaac Watts.
Bee and the Lily, The. Westwood.
Bee in amber hides, yet gleams unspoiled, The. Martial, *tr. fr. Latin by* Johnson.
Bee-Master. Sackville-West.
Bee Sets Sail, A. Morse.
Bee, the Ant, and the Sparrow, The. Cotton.
Bees. Chute.
Bees, The. Gibbon.
Bees. Kirk.
Bees, The. Ridge.
Bees. Sherman.
Bees before Winter. Moore.
Bees of Myddleton Manor, The. Probyn.
Bees' Song, The. De la Mare.
Browny Bee. Pawsey.
Bumblebee. E. D. Wood.
Bumble-Bee and Clover. *Unknown.*
Butterfly and the Bee, The. Bowles.
Flowers. Behn.
Forth, My Gallant Honey-Bees! Holstein, *tr. fr. Danish by* Stork.
Happy World, The. Rands.
Honey. Ruth Miller.
Honey Bee. McCoy.
Honey-Bee. Perkins.
Honey Harvest. Armstrong.
How Doth the Little Busy Bee. Isaac Watts.
Humble-Bee, The. Emerson.
Humble Bumble Bee, The. Lindsay.
Merry Bee, A. Skipsey.
More Ancient Mariner, A. Carman.
Near Dusk. Auslander.
Nestling Church at Ovingdean, The. Noyes.
On a Honey Bee Drinking from a Glass of Wine and Drowned Therein. Freneau.
Pedigree of Honey, The. Emily Dickinson.
Riddle: "As I went over Tipple Tyne." *Unknown.*
Song of the Bees. Gould.
Swarm of bees in May, A. *Unknown.*
Tax-Gatherer, The. Tabb.
Telling the Bees. Lang, *after the Greek.*
Telling the Bees. Reese.
Telling the Bees. Whittier.
There Was an Old Man in a Tree. Lear.
To a Bee. Southey.
Venerable Bee, The. Klein.
What Does the Bee Do? *Fr.* Sing-Song. C. G. Rossetti.
Where the Bee Sucks. *Fr.* The Tempest. Shakespeare.
Wild Bees. J. K. Baxter.
BEETHOVEN, LUDWIG VAN
Beethoven. F. E. Allen.
Beethoven. Edward Carpenter.
Beethoven. Noel.
Beethoven. Todhunter.
Beethoven Andante, A. Conkling.

Beethoven's Death Mask. Spender.
Four Friends. Ward.
On First Hearing Beethoven. George Barker.
BEETLES
Beetle, The. Aleixandre, *tr. fr. Spanish by* Turnbull.
Beetle, The. Edith King.
Beetle, The. J. W. Riley.
Riddle: "Wee man o' leather." *Unknown.*
BEGGING AND BEGGARS
Beggar, The. Bruner.
Beggar, The. Doak.
Beggar. Flint.
Beggar, The. Moss.
Beggar. Tiller.
Beggar Laddie, The. *Unknown.*
Beggar to Burgher. Fairburn.
Beggars. Rhys Carpenter.
Beggars. Francis Davidson.
Beggars. Higginson.
Beggars, The. Widdemer.
Cante Hondo. Kay.
Cast Our Caps and Cares Away. *Fr.* Beggars' Bush. Fletcher.
Happy Beggarman, The. *Unknown.*
In Praise of a Beggar's Life. "A. W."
Jolly Beggar, The. *At. to* James V, King of Scotland.
Loving Mad Tom. *Unknown.*
Maunding Souldier, The; or, The Fruits of Warre Is Beggery. *Unknown*
Old Cumberland Beggar, The. Wordsworth.
On a Fair Beggar. Ayres.
Song of the Beggars. Brome.
Street Beggar. Scruggs.
Three Beggars, The. De la Mare.
Tom o' Bedlam's Song. *Unknown.*
West London. Matthew Arnold.
BELGIUM
Homeland, The. Cammaerts, *tr. fr. French by* Bynner.
Moon and the Night and the Men, The. Berryman.
BELGRADE, YUGOSLAVIA. Siege of Belgrade, The. *Unknown, at. to* Watts.
BELISARIUS. Belisarius. Longfellow.
BELLBIRDS. Bell-Birds. H. C. Kendall.
BELLEAU, REMY. To Remi Belleau. Ronsard, *tr. fr. French by* Currey.
BELLEROPHON. Bellerophon. George Meredith.
BELLS
Ave Maria Bells. C. W. Stoddard.
Bell, The. Rorty.
Bell, A. Scollard.
Bell-Ringers, The. Rorty.
Bell Speech. Richard Wilbur.
Bell Tower. Léonie Adams.
Bells, The. Fogazzaro, *tr. fr. Italian.*
Bells, The. Poe.
Bells. D. C. Scott.
Bells, The. *Unknown.*
Bells across the Snow. Havergal.
Bell's Dream. Weatherly.
Bells in the Country. Nathan.
Bells in the Rain. Wylie.
Bells of London, The. *Unknown.*
Bells of Shandon, The. Mahony.
Bells of Youth, The. "Fiona Macleod."
Bredon Hill. Housman.
Broken Tower, The. Hart Crane.
Burro Bells in the Moonlight. Dresbach.
Carillon, The. Castro, *tr. fr. Spanish by* Strane.
Chanson of the Bells of Oseney. Rice.
Children's Bells, The. Farjeon.
Chimes. Longfellow.
Chimes. Alice Meynell.
Christmas Bells. Longfellow.
Church Bell in the Night, The. *Unknown, tr fr. Old Irish by* Meyer.
Cracked Bell, The. Baudelaire, *tr. fr. French by* Watkins.
Little Bell. Westwood.
London Bells. *Unknown.*
Merry Are the Bells. *Unknown.*
Minaret Bells, The. Thackeray.
Oxford Bells. Sister Maris Stella.
Passing Bell, The. Shirley.
Passing-Bell, The. *Unknown.*
Passing Bell at Stratford, The. Winter.
Reflection for a Sunday Morning. Leo Kennedy.
Those Evening Bells. Thomas Moore.
Two Bells. The. Rydberg, *tr. fr. Swedish by* Stork.
Upon a Ring of Bells. Bunyan.
Victory Bells. Conkling.
BELSHAZZAR. Vision of Belshazzar, The. Byron.
BEN BULBEN, IRELAND. Under Ben Bulben. Yeats.
BENBOW, ADMIRAL JOHN
Admiral Benbow. *Unknown.*
Death of Admiral Benbow, The. *Unknown.*
BENDEMEER, WALES. By Bendemeer's Stream. *Fr.* Lalla Rookh. Thomas Moore.
BENÉT, STEPHEN VINCENT. S. V. B. W. R. Benét.
BENNINGTON, BATTLE OF
Battle of Bennington, The. Rodman.
Rifleman's Song at Bennington, The. *Unknown.*
BENTLEY, RICHARD. Stanzas to Mr. Bentley. Thomas Gray.
BEOWULF. Beowulf. Wilbur.
BERENGARIA, QUEEN. Cœur de Lion to Berengaria. Tilton.
BERKSHIRE, ENGLAND. Berkshire Holiday, A. Bax.
BERKSHIRE HILLS, MASSACHUSETTS
Berkshires in April. Clement Wood.
Monument Mountain. Bryant.
Whole Duty of Berkshire Brooks, The. G. H. Conkling.
BERKSHIRE SYMPHONIC FESTIVAL. Tanglewood. Francis Sweeney.
BERMUDA
Battle of the Summer-Islands, The. Waller.
Bermuda Suite. W. T. Scott.
Bermudas. Marvell.
BERNADETTE, SAINT. Canticle of Bernadette, The. *Unknown.*
BERNARDO DEL CARPIO
Bernardo del Carpio. Hemans.
Bernardo's March to Roncesvalles. *Unknown, tr. fr. Spanish by* Longfellow.
BETH GÊLERT. Beth Gêlert. Spencer.
BETHLEHEM, ISRAEL
At Bethlehem. Tabb.
Bethlehem. Canton.
Bethlehem. Carman, *ad. fr. the French of* Guilbert.
Bethlehem. Farrington.
Bethlehem. Tynan.
Bethlehem Road, The. Munson.
Bethlehem-Town. Eugene Field.
Birds of Bethlehem, The. Gilder.
How Far to Bethlehem? M. S. Miller.
In Bethlehem, Today. M. S. Miller.
Light of Bethlehem, The. Tabb.
Little Town, The. Scollard.
O Little Town of Bethlehem. Phillips Brooks.
Once in Royal David's City. C. F. Alexander.
While to Bethlehem We Are Going. Sister Violante do Ceo, *tr. fr. Portuguese by* Bowring.
BETHUNE, MARY MCLEOD. For Mary McLeod Bethune. Walker.
BEVERLY, MASSACHUSETTS. Hymn Written for the 200th Anniversary of The Old South Church, Beverly, Mass. Larcom.
BIALIK, HAYYIM NAHMAN. Harangue on the Death of Hayyim Nahman Bialik. Tiempo, *tr. fr. Spanish by* Walsh.
BIBLE
Bible, The, *sel.* ("Thou, Zion, old and suffering"). Levi, *tr. fr. Italian by* Craig.
Bible, The. Traherne.
Bible, A. *Fr.* Riddles. *Unknown, tr. fr. Anglo-Saxon by* Thompson.
Bible, The. *Fr.* Miriam. Whittier.
Holy Bible, Book Divine. Burton.
In the Beginning Was the Word. Branch.
Inscription on the Flyleaf of a Bible. Abse.
Knowledge. *Unknown.*
Lines on a Re-reading of Parts of the Old Testament, *sel.* ("Sublimity! Sublimity! I lay thee down"). W. W. Campbell.
Living Book, The. Bates.
My Old Bible. *Unknown.*
New Testament, The. Thomas Russell.
Old Testament, The. Thomas Russell.
Shakespeare Reads the King James Version. Burton.
BICYCLES
Different Bicycles. Baruch.
Going down Hill on a Bicycle. Beeching.
Gol-darned Wheel, The. *Unknown.*
BIDDLE, NICHOLAS. On the Death of Captain Nicholas Biddle. Freneau.
BIG BETHEL, VIRGINIA. Bethel. Duganne.
BIG THOMPSON CANYON, COLORADO. Big Thompson Canon. J. M. Gower.
BILLY THE KID. Billy the Kid ("I'll sing you a true song of Billy the Kid"). *Unknown.*
BINDWEED. Bind-Weed. "Susan Coolidge."
BINGEN, GERMANY. Bingen on the Rhine. Norton.
BION
Epitaph of Bion. Moschus, *tr. fr. Greek by* Stedman.
Lament for Bion. *Unknown, tr. fr. Greek by* Lucas.
BIRCH TREES
Absent Minded Birch Tree, The. Kathleen Millay.
Birch Stream. Averill.
Birch-Tree, The. J. R. Lowell.
Birch-Tree at Loschwitz, The. Amy Levy.
Birch Trees. Moreland.
Birches. Robert Frost.
Birks of Invermay, The Mallet.
Little Birches. Newsome.

Birds
Afternoon in a Tree. Sister Maris Stella.
All These Birds. Wilbur.
Angler's Reveille, The. Van Dyke.
Answer to a Child's Question. S. T. Coleridge.
Any Bird. Ilo Orleans.
Ariel. David Campbell.
Asian Birds. Bridges.
At Common Dawn. Ellis.
Autumn Flitting, An. Cotterell.
Balcony with Birds, A. Howard Moss.
Beasts, Birds and Fishes. O'Keeffe.
Berceuse for Birds. Auslander.
Bird, The. Allingham.
Bird, The. Hoffenstein.
Bird, The. Michelson.
Bird, The. Tagore, *tr. fr. Bengali by* Tagore.
Bird, The. Sister Mary Thérèse.
Bird, The. Vaughan.
Bird, The. Countess of Winchilsea.
Bird at Dawn, The. Monro.
Bird came down the walk, A. Emily Dickinson.
Bird from the West, A. Shorter.
Bird in a Cage, The. Bowles.
Bird in a Cage, The. *Unknown.*
Bird, Let Loose in Eastern Skies, The. Thomas Moore.
Bird Music. Rorty.
Bird Omens. George, *tr. fr. German by* Passage.
Bird-Parliament, The, *sels.* Ferid ed-Din Attar, *tr. fr. Persian by* Fitzgerald.
Bird Raptures. C. G. Rossetti.
Bird Sings at Night, A. Flanner.
Bird Song. John Hay.
Bird Trades. *Unknown.*
Bird Was Singing, A. Dietmar von Aist, *tr. fr. German by* Bithell.
Birds, The, *sels.* Aristophanes, *tr. fr. Greek.*
Birds, The. Blake.
Birds. Dearmer.
Birds, The. Dracontius, *tr. fr. Latin by* Walsh.
Birds, The. Gorman.
Birds. Jeffers.
Birds. "Moira O'Neill."
Birds, The. Squire.
Birds. Stoddard.
Birds All Singing. MacCaig.
Birds and Francis, The. Louis Untermeyer.
Birds' Courting Song, The. *Unknown.*
Birds Go By, The. Neilson.
Birds in April. Henley.
Birds in Summer. Howitt.
Birds in the Fens. *Fr.* Polyolbion. Drayton.
Birds of Passage, The. Hemans.
Birds of Passage. Tegnér, *tr. fr. Swedish by* Stork.
Bird's Song at Morning. Dawson.
Bird's Song in April. Scollard.
Blinded Bird, The. Thomas Hardy.
Broken Pinion, The. Butterworth.
Caged Bird, A. Jewett.
Cat and the Bird, The. Solomon.
Children of the Wind. *Fr.* The People, Yes. Sandburg.
Choir of Day, The. *Fr.* Milton. Blake.
Choristers, The. Carman.
Come Not Near. M. E. Osborn.
Crumbs to the Birds. Charles *and* Mary Lamb.
Death of a Bird. Silkin.
Dream, The. *Fr.* The Book of the Duchesse. Chaucer.
Educated Love Bird, The. Newell.
Faithful Bird, The. Cowper.
Fifteen Acres, The. Stephens.
Firetail's Nest, The. Clare.
Four Birds. *Unknown.*
Green Rain. Mary Webb.
Hark! Hark! Speyer.
In a Bird Sanctuary. Wilbur.
In Glencullen. Synge.
In the Woods. Nerval, *tr. fr. French by* Conder.
Introduction: "'Twas late in my long journey, when I had clomb to where." *Fr.* The Testament of Beauty. Robert Bridges.
Invitation. Harry Behn.
Joe. McCord.
Joy of the Morning. Edwin Markham.
Kookaburra, *sel.* ("Over the multiple terrors of Mars"). T. I. Moore.
Little Birds. *Fr.* Sylvie and Bruno Concluded. "Lewis Carroll."
Little Birds. Sternberg, *tr. fr. Yiddish by* Leftwich.
L'Oiseau Bleu. M. E. Coleridge.
Lord of the Island, The. George, *tr. fr. German by* Passage.
Making of Birds. Tynan.
Marché aux Oiseaux. Wilbur.
Migrants. D. G. Davies.
Minor Bird, A. Robert Frost.
Mopoke. Lavater.
Morning Bird. Louis Untermeyer.
My Little Birds. *Unknown, tr. by* Siksek-Su'ad.
Native Companions Dancing. Neilson.
Never Again Would Birds' Song Be the Same. Robert Frost.
Night Bird, The. Kingsley.
Night Walkers, The. Smithyman.
Nightjar, The. Newbolt.
O Bird, So Lovely. Louis Golding.
Of the Child with the Bird at the Bush. Bunyan.
Old Man in the Park. M. E. Osborn.
Orphan's Song, The. Dobell.
Our Native Birds. Dole.
Our Singing Strength. Robert Frost.
Oven Bird, The. Robert Frost.
Pack, Clouds, Away. *Fr.* The Rape of Lucrece. Thomas Heywood.
Paradox; the Birds. Shapiro.
Parlement of Foules, The, *sels.* Chaucer.
Pretty Wantons. *Unknown.*
Rivals, The. James Stephens.
Saint Francis and the Birds. R. H. Benson.
Saint Francis' Sermon to the Birds. Longfellow.
Saint Francis to the Birds. Clement Cook.
Saint Francis to the Birds. Tynan.
Sea Bird, The. Keith Douglas.
Seed-Eaters, The. Robert Francis.
Shag Rookery. Hart-Smith.
Shore Birds. Vi Gale.
Silver Bird of Herndyke Mill, The. Blunden.
Sing On, Blithe Bird! Motherwell.
Small Birds. Quennell.
Song-Bird. Vrepont.
Speak with the Sun. David Campbell.
Tea-Tree and the Lyrebird, The. Roland Robinson.
That Is All I Heard. "Yehoash," *tr. fr. Yiddish by* Goldstick.
To a Bird at Dawn. Le Gallienne.
To a Blind Bird. Page.
To A. D. Henley.
To a Waterfowl. Bryant.
To the Birds. McArthur.
Trail of the Bird, The. Courthope.
Unknown Bird, The. Edward Thomas.
Warblers. Hartley.
What Bird So Sings. *Fr.* Alexander and Campaspe. Lyly.
Whistling Jack, The. Neilson.
Widow Bird, A. *Fr.* Charles the First. Shelley.
Windhover, The; to Christ Our Lord. Hopkins.
Yellow Warblers. K. L. Bates.
You That Sing in the Blackthorn. Noyes.
Bird-Lover's Anthology, The (BLA). Clinton Scollard *and* Jessie B. Rittenhouse, comps.
Where Birds Sing (WhBS). Ada L. F. Snell, comp.

Birds' nests
Bird's Nest, A. E. A. Allen.
Bird's Nest, The. Drinkwater.
Bird's Nest, The. Elizabeth Turner.
Bird's Nest in Winter, A. "John Crichton."
Birds' Nests, The. *Unknown.*
Discovery, The. Snaith.
Nest, The. Elliot.
Nests in Elms. "Michael Field."
Ruined Nest, The. *Unknown, tr. fr. Irish by* Sigerson.
Snow-filled Nest, The. Cooke.
Turtle-Dove's Nests, The. *Unknown, at. to* Hawkshaw.
What Robin Told. Cooper.
Who Stole the Bird's Nest? Child.

Birds of paradise
Bird of Paradise, The. Laura Benét.
Bird of Paradise, The. W. H. Davies.

Birkenhead (ship). Loss of the *Birkenhead,* The. Doyle.

Birmingham, England. Birmingham. MacNeice.

Birth
Birth. Raymond.
Birth. Root.
Birth, A. Rukeyser.
Birth. Trakl, *tr. fr. German by* Middleton.
In My Infancy. David Ross.
Out of a Dust . . . Levy.
Prime. Auden.

Birthdays
Betsy Jane's Sixth Birthday. Noyes.
Birthday, The. Bynner.
Birthday, A. Rachel Field.
Birthday, A. C. G. Rossetti.
Birthday Child, The. Fyleman.
Birthday Gifts. Asquith.
Birthday Song, A. Gilder.
Birthday Song. Kouchak, *tr. fr. Armenian by* Boyajian.
Birthday Song, A. Odell.
Birthdays. Chute.

My Birthday. Thomas Moore.
My Gift. *Fr.* A Christmas Carol. C. G. Rossetti.
Our Birthday. Edey.
Party, A. L. E. Richards.
Poem in October. Dylan Thomas.
Poem on His Birthday. Dylan Thomas.
Seven Times One. Ingelow.
BISCAY, BAY OF. Bay of Biscay, The. Cherry.
BISHOP, JOHN PEALE. Beyond Connecticut, beyond the Sea. Bishop.
BISMARCK, OTTO VON
Bismarck. Ossian-Nilsson, *tr fr. Swedish by* Stork.
Lines on the Death of Bismarck. J. J. Chapman.
BITTERNS. Bittern, The. Swartz.
BJÖRNSON, BJÖRNSTJERNE. To Björnstjerne Björnson. Hamsun, *tr. fr. Norwegian by* Stork.
BLACKBIRDS
Blackbird, The. Barnes.
Blackbird, The. Beeching.
Blackbird, The. Alice Cary.
Blackbird, The. Craik.
Blackbird, The. Drinkwater.
Blackbird, The. Gautier, *tr. fr. French by* Conder.
Blackbird, The. Henley.
Blackbird, The. Frederick Tennyson.
Blackbird, The. *Unknown, tr. fr. Middle Irish by* Meyer.
Blackbird, The. Humbert Wolfe.
Blackbird by Belfast Lough, The. *Unknown, tr. fr. Irish by* O'Connor.
Blackbird in the Town, The. Gogarty.
Blackbird Song, The. Christmas.
Blackbird Suddenly, A. Auslander.
Blackbirds in the Rain Wet June; England. Horner.
Blackbird's Song, The. *Unknown, tr. fr. Irish by* Sigerson.
I Watched a Blackbird. Hardy.
Marsh Blackbird, A. Sennett.
Neutral, The. Jarman.
O What If the Fowler. Dalmon.
One Blackbird. *Fr.* Strange Meetings. Monro.
Ruined Nest, The. *Unknown, tr. fr. Irish by* Sigerson.
There Were Two Blackbirds. Mother Goose.
Thirteen Ways of Looking at a Blackbird. Wallace Stevens.
To an Irish Blackbird. MacAlpine.
Vespers. T. E. Brown.
BLACKHEATH, LONDON. Sermon to the Rebels at Blackheath. Ball.
BLACKSMITHS
Blacksmith, The. *Unknown, tr. fr. German.*
Blacksmith of Limerick, The. R. D. Joyce.
Legend. Judith Wright.
Smith's Song. Sigerson, *ad. fr. the Irish.*
Village Blacksmith, The. Longfellow.
BLACKWATER (river), IRELAND
Beside the Blackwater. O'Conor.
Crossing the Blackwater. Joyce.
BLAKE, ROBERT. Death of Admiral Blake, The. Newbolt.
BLAKE, WILLIAM
Blake. J. G. Fletcher.
Canto XVI, *sel.* ("And before hell mouth; dry plain"). Pound.
Mad Blake. W. R. Benét.
To William Blake. Dargan.
William Blake. *Fr.* Five English Poets. D. G. Rossetti.
William Blake. James Thomson.
William Blake Sees God. McFadden.
Wiser than the Children of Light. Gibbon.
BLANC, MONT, SWITZERLAND. *See* MONT BLANC.
BLASPHEMY. For All Blasphemers. S. V. Benét.
BLENHEIM, BATTLE OF
Battle of Blenheim, The. Southey.
Blenheim. *Fr.* The Campaign. Addison.
BLENHEIM PARK, ENGLAND
On Blenheim House. Evans.
Verses on Blenheim. Swift, *after the Latin of* Martial.
BLENNERHASSET ISLAND, WEST VIRGINIA. Blennerhasset's Island. *Fr.* The New Pastoral. T. B. Read.
BLINDNESS
Blind. N. V. Pearce.
Blind Boy, The. Cibber.
Blind Highland Boy, The. Wordsworth.
Blind Man at the Fair, The. Joseph Campbell.
Blind Man Lay beside the Way. *Unknown.*
Blindness of Samson, The. *Fr.* Samson Agonistes. Milton.
Cease thy wishes gentle boy. *Unknown.*
For the Poor Blind Man. Icaza, *tr. fr. Spanish by* Beckett.
Going Blind. Higginson.
Going Blind. Rilke, *tr. fr. German by* Salinger.
Going Blind. Tabb.
On a Blind Girl. Baha Ad-din Zuhayr, *tr. fr. Arabic by* Palmer.
On His Blindness. Milton.
BLIZZARDS
Lost in a Blizzard. A. W. Monroe.
Snowstorm, The. Pearl Riggs Crouch.
BLOCK, ADRIAEN. Adrian Block's Song. E. E. Hale.
BLOCK ISLAND. *Palatine,* The. Whittier.
BLONDEL DE NESLE. Blondel. Urmy.
BLOODHOUNDS
Bloodhound, The. Edward Anthony.
Ol' Rattler. *Unknown.*
BLOODROOT. Blood-Root. "E. S. F."
BLUE JAYS
Blue Jay, The. Driscoll.
Blue Jay. Speyer.
Blue-Jay, The. Swett.
BLUE RIDGE MOUNTAINS. Blue Ridge, The. Monroe.
BLUEBELLS
Bluebell, The. Emily Brontë.
Bluebells. De la Mare.
Bluebells. Enoch.
Bluebells. Ewing.
Bluebells. Markham.
Bluebells. Ropes.
Bluebells of Scotland, The. *Unknown.*
To a Bluebell. Emily Brontë.
To a Bluebell. Coleman.
BLUEBIRDS
Advice to a Blue-Bird. Bodenheim.
Bluebird, The. *Fr.* Spring in New England. T. B. Aldrich.
Bluebird. Conkling.
Bluebird, The ("Before you thought of spring"). Emily Dickinson.
Bluebird, The. E. H. Miller.
Bluebird, The. Maurice Thompson.
Blue-Bird, The. Alexander Wilson.
Bluebirds. Egerton.
Early Bluebird, An. Maurice Thompson.
First Bluebird, The. Riley.
Last Word of a Bluebird, The. Robert Frost.
L'Oiseau Bleu. M. E. Coleridge.
Sign of Spring, A. Rexford.
BLUENOSE (ship). Spirit of the *Bluenose,* The. C. H. MacIntosh.
BOADICEA. Boadicea. Cowper.
BOATS
Boats. R. B. Bennett.
Boats at Night. Shanks.
Boats in a Fog. Jeffers.
Crescent Boat, The. *Fr.* Peter Bell. Wordsworth.
Freight Boats. Tippett.
Kayak, The. *Unknown.*
Old Boat, The. Lenore Pratt.
Paper Boats. Tagore.
Riding in a Motor Boat. Baruch.
Where Go the Boats. Stevenson.
Whistles. Rachel Field.
See also SHIPS.
BOBOLINKS
Bobolink, The. Thomas Hill.
Bobolinks, The. Cranch.
O'Lincoln Family, The. Flagg.
Robert of Lincoln. Bryant.
BOBWHITES
Bob White. George Cooper.
Bob White. Goodale.
BOER WAR
Boer War, The. Plomer.
Drummer Hodge. Hardy.
Rank and File. Dobson.
BOGS. Bog Lands, The. Byrne.
BOHEMIA. My Bohemia. Rimbaud, *tr. fr. French by* Varèse.
BOLEYN, ANNE. Anne Boleyn. Bingley.
BOLÍVAR, SIMON. To Bolívar. Pombo, *tr. fr. Spanish by* Blackwell.
BOLL WEEVILS. Ballet [*or* Ballit] of de Boll Weevil, De. *Unknown.*
BOLTON PRIORY, ENGLAND. Founding of Bolton Priory, The. Wordsworth.
BOMBAY, INDIA. Bombay. Josephine Miles.
BOMBERS
Bomber, The. Vrepont.
BOMBS AND BOMBING. *See* AIR RAIDS.
BONHOMME RICHARD (ship)
Bonhomme Richard and *Serapis,* The. Freneau.
Paul Jones. *Unknown.*
BONNIE DUNDEE. *See* DUNDEE, JOHN GRAHAM OF CLAVERHOUSE, 1ST VISCOUNT.
BONNIE PRINCE CHARLIE. *See* STUART, CHARLES EDWARD.
BONNIVARD, FRANÇOIS DE. Prisoner of Chillon, The. Byron.
BONONCINI, GIOVANNI BATTISTA. Epigram on Handel and Bononcini. Byrom.
BOOKS
Author to Her Book, The. Bradstreet.
Book, A. More.
Book, A. Reese.
Book, The. Vaughan.
Book Is an Enchanted Gate, A. Beer.

BOOKS (*continued*)
Book-Lover, The. Scollard.
Books. Ch'en Shih-tao, *tr. fr. Chinese.*
Books. Conkling.
Books. *Fr.* The Library. Crabbe.
Books. Farjeon.
Books. Hesse, *tr. fr. German by* Salinger.
Books. John Higgins.
Books. Keith.
Books. *Unknown.*
Books. Van Cleve.
Books Are Keys. Poulsson.
Bookworm, The. De la Mare.
Bookworm, The. Su T'ung-po, *tr. fr. Chinese by* Hart.
Bookworms, The. Burns.
Child and the Book, The. Stidger.
Concerning the Honour of Books. *At. to* Florio.
Dedication on the Gift of a Book to a Child. Belloc.
Dickens in Camp. Harte.
Discovery, The. M. C. Davies.
Envoy: "Go, little book, and wish to all." R. L. Stevenson.
Ex Libris. Morgenstern, *tr. fr. German by* Hull.
First Geography. McKee.
First Reader (Fifth Reading). McKee.
Golden Spurs. Miner.
"Good from a Book." *Fr.* Aurora Leigh. E. B. Browning.
He ate and drank the precious words. Emily Dickinson.
If I did not love you more than my very eyes. Catullus, *tr. fr. Latin by* Fletcher.
I've Got a New Book from My Grandfather Hyde. L. F. Jackson.
Land of Story-Books, The. R. L. Stevenson.
Letter to Hitler, A. Laughlin.
Lines to a Book Borrower. "F. C."
Man and His Books. Eiluned Lewis.
My Books. Dobson.
My Books. Longfellow.
My Books. *Unknown.*
My Books I'd Fain Cast Off, I Cannot Read. Thoreau.
My Days among the Dead Are Past. Southey.
My Library. Stockard.
New Book, The. Elizabeth Turner.
O for a Booke. *Unknown.*
Of the Book-Hunter. Lang.
Old Books. Widdemer.
Old Books Are Best. Chew.
Old Susan. De la Mare.
On Opening a New Book. A. F. Brown.
On the Detraction Which Followed upon My Writing Certain Treatises. Milton.
Precious, mouldering pleasure 'tis, A. Emily Dickinson.
Reading in War Time. Muir.
Shut Not Your Doors. Whitman.
Sibrandus Schafnaburgensis. *Fr.* Garden Fancies. Robert Browning.
Sing a Song of Books. N. B. Turner.
Solace of Books, The. *Unknown.*
Tables Turned, The. Wordsworth.
There is no frigate like a book. Emily Dickinson.
To His Book. Martial, *tr. fr. Latin by* Herrick.
To His Book. Walsh.
To His Books. Vaughan.
To My Book. Freneau.
To My Book. Jonson.
To My Books. Roscoe.
To My Bookseller. Jonson.
To the Lady with a Book. *Unknown, tr. fr. Irish by* O'Connor.
To the Reader. *Unknown.*
Tragic Books. Reese.
"Treasure Island." Chalmers.
Upon Reading an Old Book. Pearce Young.
Valediction, A; of the Booke. Donne.
Where My Books Go. Yeats.
Who Hath a Book. Nesbit.
Wonder Books. Lyon.
Magic of Books, The (Our American Holidays Series) (MOB). A. P. Sanford *and* Robert Haven Schauffler, eds.
BOONE, DANIEL
Daniel Boone. S. V. Benét.
Daniel Boone. Guiterman.
Daniel Boone. Noe.
Daniel Boone's Last Look Westward. Rice.
BOOTH, EDWIN
Edwin Booth. Alice Brown.
Sargent's Portrait of Edwin Booth at "The Players." Aldrich.
BOOTH, JOHN WILKES. Pardon. Howe.
BOOTH, WILLIAM. General William Booth Enters into Heaven. Lindsay.
BORDEN, LIZZIE. Crimes of Lizzie Borden, The ("Lizzie Borden with an axe"). *Unknown.*
BORDIGHERA, ITALY. Old Olives at Bordighera. Scott.
BORGIA, LUCREZIA. On Seeing a Hair of Lucretia Borgia. Landor.
BORODINO, BATTLE OF. Borodino. Lermontov, *tr. fr. Russian by* Cornford.
BOSCÁN ALMOGÁVER, JUAN. Epistle to Boscán. Garcilaso de la Vega, *tr. fr. Spanish by* Wiffen.
BOSTON, MASSACHUSETTS
Ballad of the Boston Tea-Party, A. O. W. Holmes.
Boston. Emerson.
Boston. O'Reilly.
Boston. *Unknown.*
Boston Common—Three Pictures. O. W. Holmes.
Boston Toast, A. Bossidy.
Calf-Path, The. Foss.
Church of the Revolution, The. Butterworth.
In the "Old South." Whittier.
Off from Boston. *Unknown.*
On a Fortification at Boston Begun by Women. Benjamin Tompson.
Poem Containing Some Remarks on the Present War, A. *Unknown.*
Seven Cities of America, The. Masters.
Sunday Evening in the Common. Wheelock.
Thanksgiving in Boston Harbor, The. Butterworth.
BOSTON EVENING TRANSCRIPT. Boston Evening Transcript, The. T. S. Eliot.
BOSTON MASSACRE. Unhappy Boston. Paul Revere.
BOSTON SYMPHONY ORCHESTRA. Boston Symphony Orchestra, The. J. F. Cooper.
BOSTON TEA PARTY. New Song, A. *Unknown.*
BOTANY BAY, AUSTRALIA. Botany Bay. *Unknown.*
BOTHWELL, JAMES HEPBURN, 4TH EARL OF. Earl Bothwell. *Unknown.*
BOTHWELL, SCOTLAND
Bothwell Bridge. *Unknown.*
Covenanter's Lament for Bothwell Brigg, The. Praed.
BOUNCING BET (plant). Ragged Robin and Bouncing Bet. Alice Reid.
BOURGEOISIE
How Beastly the Bourgeois Is. D. H. Lawrence.
Lament of the Pianos Which Are Overheard in Well-to-do Quarters. Laforgue, *tr. fr. French by* Bennett.
BOWDOIN COLLEGE. Morituri Salutamus. Longfellow.
BOWERY, THE, NEW YORK CITY. Bowery, The. Hoyt.
BOWLES, WILLIAM LISLE. To the Reverend W. L. Bowles. S. T. Coleridge.
BOYHOOD. *See* YOUTH.
BOYNE, BATTLE OF THE. Boyne Water, The. *Unknown.*
BOYNE, IRELAND
Boyne Walk, The. F. R. Higgins.
Father and Son. F. R. Higgins.
BOYS. *See* YOUTH.
BOZZARIS, MARCO. Marco Bozzaris. Halleck.
BRADDOCK, EDWARD
Braddock's Defeat. *Unknown.*
Braddock's Fate, with an Incitement to Revenge. Tilden.
Ned Braddock. Palmer.
Song of Braddock's Men, The. *Unknown.*
BRADSTREET, ANNE. Homage to Mistress Bradstreet, *sels.* Berryman.
BRAHE, TYCHO. Old Astronomer to His Pupil, The. Williams.
BRAHMA
Brahma. Emerson.
Brahma. J. G. Fletcher.
BRAHMS, JOHANNES. Brahms, The. Herbert Morris.
BRANCUSI, CONSTANTIN. Overheard at a Sculpture Show at a Museum. *Unknown.*
BRAQUE, GEORGES. Braque. M. K. Joseph.
BRAY, IRELAND. Lough Bray. O'Grady.
BRAZIL. Brazil. Carvalho, *tr. fr. Portuguese by* Poore.
BREAD
Bread. Burnshaw.
Bread. A. M. Klein.
BRÉBEUF, JEAN DE
Brébeuf and His Brethren, *sels.* Pratt.
Brébeuf and Lalement. Sullivan.
BREGENZ, AUSTRIA. Legend of Bregenz, A. Procter.
BRENDAN, SAINT
Burial of Saint Brendan, The. Padraic Colum.
Pattern of Saint Brendan. MacManus.
Saint Brandan. Matthew Arnold.
BRIAN BORU. Lamentation of Mac Liag for Kincora. *Unknown, tr. fr. Middle Irish by* Mangan.
BRIDES. *See* MARRIAGE.
BRIDGER, JAMES. Mountain Liars. Hafen.
BRIDGES, ROBERT
Robert Bridges. Humbert Wolfe.
To R. B. G. M. Hopkins.
BRIDGES
Bridge, The. Hart Crane.
Bridge. Damon.
Bridge, The. Köhler, *tr. fr. German by* Shuster.
Bridge, The. Longfellow.

Bridge, The. **Peterson.**
Bridge, The. Tikhonov, *tr. fr. Russian by* Lindsay.
Bridge of Arta, The. *Unknown, tr. fr. Modern Greek by* Dalven.
Covered Bridge, The. Cawein.
Covered Bridge, The. Scruggs.
Oh, What Are You Waiting For. *Fr.* **Sunday up the River.** James Thomson.
River Bridge, The. Tippett.
BRIDGET, SAINT
Feast of Saint Brigid of Kildare, The. *At. to* St. Brigid, *tr. fr. Middle Irish by* O'Curry.
Giveaway, The. McGinley.
I Should Like to Have a Great Pool of Ale. *At. to* St. Bridget, *tr. fr. Middle Irish by* Jackson.
St. Brigid. McCarthy
BRIGHT, JOHN. **John Bright. Gummere.**
BRISTOL, ENGLAND. Last Verses. Chatterton.
BRISTOL, RHODE ISLAND. Bombardment of Bristol, The. *Unknown.*
BRITAIN, BATTLE OF. So I Praise Thee. John Pudney.
BRITISH EMPIRE
At Gibraltar. Woodberry
Ballade of the Southern Cross. *Fr.* **Ballades in Blue China.** Lang.
BRITISH GUIANA. Over Guiana, Clouds. Seymour.
BRITISH MUSEUM, LONDON
At the British Museum. Aldington.
British Museum Reading Room, The. **MacNeice.**
BROADWAY, NEW YORK CITY
Broadway. Hagedorn.
Broadway. Whitman.
Broadway's Canyon. J. G. Fletcher.
Rhyme about an Electrical Advertising Sign, A. **Lindsay.**
BROCK, SIR ISAAC
Brock. Sangster.
Brock; Valiant Leader. Logan.
Come All You Bold Canadians. *Unknown.*
BRONTË, ANNE. On the Death of Anne Brontë. Charlotte Brontë.
BRONTË, BRANWELL. Wanderer from the Fold, The. Emily Brontë.
BRONTË, CHARLOTTE. For Charlotte Brontë. Emily Dickinson.
BRONTË, EMILY
Emily Brontë. Day Lewis.
Grace. J. G. Patrick.
BRONX, NEW YORK CITY. Bronx. **Drake.**
BROOKE, RUPERT
Going, The. W. W. Gibson.
Rupert Brooke. **Dollard.**
BROOKLYN, NEW YORK CITY
Crossing Brooklyn Ferry. Whitman.
To a Portrait of Whistler in the Brooklyn Art Museum. E. R. Cox.
BROOKLYN (ship). *Brooklyn* at Santiago, The. **Wallace Rice.**
BROOKLYN BRIDGE
Bridge, The. Hart Crane.
Brooklyn Bridge. Clapp.
Brooklyn Bridge, The. E. D. Proctor.
Brooklyn Bridge. C. G. D. Roberts.
Brooklyn Bridge at Dawn. Le Gallienne.
View of the Brooklyn Bridge, A. **William Meredith.**
BROOKS, PHILLIPS
Phillips Brooks. Ingham.
Phillips Brooks. Spofford.
BROOKS
Beaver Brook. J. R. Lowell.
Brook, The. W. W. Lord.
Brook, The. Tennyson.
Brook, The. Edward Thomas.
Brook and the Wave, The. Longfellow.
Brook in the City, A. Robert Frost.
Brook Song. J. H. Morse.
Brook Song, The. J. W. Riley.
Brook's Song, The. *Fr.* The Brook. **Tennyson.**
Brookside, The. Milnes.
Country-Brook. Bodenheim.
Hyla Brook. Robert Frost.
Inversnaid. G. M. Hopkins.
Meadow Brook Runs Over, The. Corning.
Pretty Brook Was Running at Play, A. *Unknown.*
Rivulet, The. Larcom.
Runaway Brook. Follen.
That Is All I Heard. "Yehoash," ***tr. fr. Yiddish by*** **Goldstick.**
There Is a Little Unpretending Rill. Wordsworth.
Valley Brook, The. Bryant.
Water, The! the Water! Motherwell.
West-running Brook. Robert Frost.
What Is a Brook? Mitchell.
Whole Duty of Berkshire Brooks, The. G. H. Conkling.
Winter Pictures. *Fr.* The Vision of Sir Launfal. J. R. Lowell.
BROOM (flower)
Broom Flower, The. Howitt.
Broom of Cowdenknows, The ("Oh the broom, the bonnie, bonnie broom"). *Unknown.*
BROOMS. Broom. Farrar.
BROTHERHOOD
All Hail, the Pageant of the Years. Holmes.
Ballad of East and West, The. Kipling.
Brother, The. Nadson, *tr. fr. Russian by* **Badanes.**
Brotherhood. *Fr.* Jerusalem. Blake.
Brotherhood. O. S. Davis.
Brotherhood. Markham.
Brotherhood, *sel.* ("There shall arise"). **Morris.**
Brothers. G. E. Day.
Brothers. Lersch, *tr. fr. German by* Salinger.
Brothers of the Faith. Oxenham.
Creed, A. Markham.
Creed and Deed. Loveman.
Dance of Saul with the Prophets, The. Tchernichowsky, *tr. fr. Hebrew by* Lask.
Day Is Coming, The. **William Morris.**
Fatherland, The. J. R. Lowell.
Gentle Park, A. Moss Herbert.
German Prisoners. J. J. Lee.
Goliath and David. Louis Untermeyer.
He Is My Countryman. **Slonimski,** ***tr. fr. Polish by*** **Notley.**
I Believe. Tchernichowsky, *tr. fr. Hebrew by* Feldman.
I Must to Prayer. Buchanan.
In the City. Zangwill.
Is It a Dream? Studdert-Kennedy.
Liberty for All. Garrison.
Like Water down a Slope. Schneour, *tr. fr. Hebrew by* Fein.
Little Black Boy, The. *Fr.* Songs of Innocence. Blake.
London Spring. Slonimski, *tr. fr. Polish by* Notley.
Love. Immanuel di Roma, *tr. fr. Italian by* Chotzner.
Love We as Brothers. Langland.
Lying in the Grass. Gosse.
Man unto His Fellow Man. *Fr.* On a Note of Triumph. Corwin.
Modern Saint, The. Burton.
New Jewish Hospital at Hamburg, The. Heine, *tr. fr. German by* Leland.
New Patriotism, A. Piety.
New York Skyscraper, A. *sel.* ("O sprawling city! worlds in a world!"). Oppenheim.
Nihil Humani Alienum. Coan.
O Brother Man. Whittier.
On a Note of Triumph, *sel.* ("Lord God of trajectory and blast"). Corwin.
Out of Our Shame. Rosten.
Prayer for Brotherhood, A. Hoyland.
Pronouns. K. W. Baker.
Speech to Those Who Say Comrade. MacLeish.
Spiritual Song, A. Werfel, *tr. fr. German by* Selden.
Street Scene—1946. Kenneth Porter.
This Moment Yearning and Thoughtful. Whitman.
Thy Brother. T. C. Williams.
To Edom. Heine, *tr. fr. German.*
To Life I Said Yes. Grade, *tr. fr. Yiddish by* Leftwich.
Tomorrow. Pedroso, *tr. fr. Spanish by* Fitts.
True Brotherhood. E. W. Wilcox.
Universal Republic, The. Hugo, *tr. fr. French.*
We Are Brethren A'. Nicoll.
What Doth the Lord Require of Thee. Cross.
When I See Another's Pain. Leib, *tr. fr. Yiddish by* Leftwich.
Where Is Thy Brother? *Unknown.*
Who Is So Low. Harlow.
BROWN, JOHN
Battle of Charlestown, The. Brownell.
Brown of Osawatomie. Whittier.
How Old Brown Took Harper's Ferry. Stedman.
John Brown. Koopman.
John Brown. *Fr.* Booker Washington Trilogy. Vachel Lindsay.
John Brown. E. D. Proctor.
John Brown. Tate.
John Brown. E. F. Ware.
John Brown's Body, *sels.* S. V. Benét.
John Brown's Body. *Unknown, at. to* **Hall** *and to* **Bishop.**
Portent, The. Melville.
BROWNING, ELIZABETH BARRETT
E. B. B. James Thomson.
Her "Last Poems." Emily Dickinson.
On the Death of Mrs. Browning. Dobell.
Sisters, The. Amy Lowell.
BROWNING, ROBERT
Browning at Asolo. R. U. Johnson.
Burial of Robert Browning, The. "Michael Field."
Life-long, Poor Browning. Anne Spencer.
On Hearing the News from Venice. George Meredith.
On the Death of Robert Browning. Swinburne.
To Browning, the Music Master. Schauffler.
To Robert Browning. Bynner.

BROWNING, ROBERT (*continued*)
To Robert Browning. Landor.
BRUCE, ROBERT
Bruce and the Spider. Barton.
Freedom. *Fr.* The Bruce. Barbour.
King Bruce and the Spider. Eliza Cook.
Scots Wha Hae. Burns.
BRUEGHEL, PIETER
Breughel's Winter. De la Mare.
Dance, The. W. C. Williams.
BRUGES, BELGIUM. Belfry of Bruges, The. Longfellow.
BRUNANBURH, BATTLE OF. Battle of Brunanburh. *Unknown, tr. fr. Anglo-Saxon.*
BRUNO, GIORDANO. For the Feast of Giordano Bruno. Swinburne.
BRUSSELS, BELGIUM. Brussels. Rimbaud, *tr. fr. French by* Varèse.
BRUT (legendary founder of Britain)
Albion's England, *sels.* William Warner.
First Song, The. *Fr.* Polyolbion. Drayton.
BRUTUS (Marcus Junius Brutus). Noblest Roman, The. *Fr.* Julius Caesar. Shakespeare.
BRYAN, WILLIAM JENNINGS. Bryan, Bryan, Bryan, Bryan. Lindsay.
BRYANT, WILLIAM CULLEN
Bryant. *Fr.* A Fable for Critics. J. R. Lowell.
Bryant Dead. Hayne.
Bryant on His Seventieth Birthday. Whittier.
William Cullen Bryant. Halleck.
BUBER, MARTIN. Martin Buber in the Pub. Max Harris.
BUCKINGHAM, GEORGE VILLIERS, 2D DUKE OF
Death of the Duke of Buckingham, The. *Fr.* Moral Essays. Pope.
Duke of Buckingham, The. *Fr.* Absalom and Achitophel. Dryden.
BUDDHA
Buddha. Holz, *tr. fr. German by* Leonard.
Buddha at Kamakura, The. Kipling.
Buddha in Glory. Rilke, *tr. fr. German by* Lemont.
Proofs of Buddha's Existence. *Unknown.*
BUENA VISTA, BATTLE OF
Angels of Buena Vista, The. Whittier.
Buena Vista. Pike.
Buena Vista Battlefield. *Unknown.*
BUFFALO BILL (William Frederick Cody). Portrait. Cummings.
BUFFALOES
Buffalo. Daniells.
Buffalo Dusk. Sandburg.
Buffalo Hunters, The. *Unknown.*
Buffalo Skinners, The. *Unknown.*
Call to Freedom. H. H. Harris.
Flower-fed Buffaloes, The. Lindsay.
Ghosts of the Buffaloes, The. Lindsay.
Passing of the Buffalo, The. Garland.
BUGLES
Bugle Song. *Fr.* The Princess. Tennyson.
Call of the Bugles, The. Hovey.
No One Cares Less than I. Edward Thomas.
Words for Army Bugle Calls. *Unknown.*
BULL RUN, BATTLES OF
Manassas. Warfield.
Our Left. Ticknor.
Run from Manassas Junction, The. *Unknown.*
Upon the Hill before Centreville. Boker.
BULLFIGHTS AND BULLFIGHTERS
Juan Belmonte, Torero. Finkel.
Lament for Ignacio Sanchez Mejias. García Lorca, *tr. fr. Spanish by* Spender *and* Gili.
BULLS
Bull, The. Hodgson.
Bull, The. Sackville-West.
Bull, The. Williams.
Hoosen Johnny. *Unknown.*
BUNDLING. Whore on the Snow Crust, The. *Unknown.*
BUNKER HILL, BATTLE OF
American Hero, The. Niles.
Ballad of Bunker Hill, The. *At. to* Hale.
Battle of Bunker's Hill, The. Cozzens.
Bunker Hill. Calvert.
Eve of Bunker Hill, The. Scollard.
Grandmother's Story of Bunker Hill Battle. Holmes.
Lonely Bugle Grieves, The. *Fr.* Ode on the Celebration of the Battle of Bunker Hill, June 17, 1825. Mellen.
On the Eve of Bunker Hill. Scollard.
Poem of Bunker Hill, The, *sel.* ("Then once more men's ears were full of 'Yankee Doodle'"). Harry Brown.
Sword of Bunker Hill, The. W. R. Wallace.
Warren's Address at Bunker Hill. Pierpont.
BUNKER HILL MONUMENT. On Laying the Corner-Stone of the Bunker Hill Monument. Pierpont.
BUNTINGS
Snow-Bunting, The. Erlingsson, *tr. fr. Icelandic by* Fjeldsted.
Snow-Buntings. Prewett.
BUNYAN, PAUL. Paul Bunyan. Bourinot.
BUOYS
Bell Buoy, The. Kipling.
Buoy-Bell, The. Turner.
BURBAGE, RICHARD. When Burbadge [*or* Burbage] Played. Dobson.
BURGHLEY OR BURLEIGH, WILLIAM CECIL, 1ST BARON. Lord of Burleigh, The. Tennyson.
BURGOS, SPAIN
At Burgos. Symons.
Recollections of Burgos. Trench.
BURGOYNE, JOHN
Fate of John Burgoyne, The. *Unknown.*
Progress of Sir Jack Brag, The. *Unknown.*
Surrender of Burgoyne, The. De Peyster.
BURKE, EDMUND. Retaliation. Goldsmith.
BURMA
Burma Hills. Gutteridge.
Mandalay. Kipling.
BURNS, ROBERT
At the Grave of Burns. Wordsworth.
Bard of Auld Lang Syne. J. M. Dixon.
Bard's Epitaph, A. Burns.
Burns. Halleck.
Burns. Whittier.
Burns; an Ode. Swinburne.
On Burns. D. G. Rossetti.
On Burns. Wordsworth.
Poet's Epitaph, A. Elliott.
Robert Burns. William Alexander.
Robert Burns. Longfellow.
BURR, AARON
Aaron Burr. S. V. Benét.
Aaron Burr's Wooing. Stedman.
Colonel B. Carrier.
To Aaron Burr, under Trial for High Treason. Morton.
BURR, THEODOSIA
Priest and the Pirate, The. Hervey Allen.
Theodosia Burr. Terrell.
Theodosia Burr; the Wrecker's Story. Palmer.
BURROS. *See* ASSES.
BURROUGHS, JOHN. To the Memory of John Burroughs. Parmenter.
BUSHMEN
By Momba Tracks. Roderic Quinn.
Man from Snowy River, The. A. B. Paterson.
BUSINESS MEN. Business Men. Chen Tzu-ang, *tr. fr. Chinese by* Waley.
BUSSES
B's the Bus. *Fr.* All Around the Town. McGinley.
Bus Ride. *Fr.* Ferry Ride. Selma Robinson.
BUTLER, SAMUEL
English Liberal. Geoffrey Taylor.
On the Setting Up Mr. Butler's Monument in Westminster Abbey. Samuel Wesley.
BUTT, ISAAC. Lost Tribune, The. Sigerson.
BUTTERCUPS
Advice to a Buttercup. Bodenheim.
Buttercup, A. *Unknown.*
Buttercups. Louis Ginsberg.
Buttercups. Radford.
Buttercups. Thorley.
Buttercups and Daisies. Howitt.
On Some Buttercups. Sherman.
BUTTERFLIES
Butterflies. Chu Miao Tuan, *tr. fr. Chinese by* Hart.
Butterflies. John Davidson.
Butterflies. Kageki, *tr. fr. Japanese by* Miyamori Asataro.
Butterflies. Haniel Long.
Butterfly. Hilda Conkling.
Butterfly, The. A. A. James.
Butterfly, The. O'Keeffe.
Butterfly, The. A. F. Palmer.
Butterfly, The. Scollard.
Butterfly, The. Skipsey.
Butterfly. Slater.
Butterfly. W. J. Smith.
Butterfly, The. *Fr.* Muiopotmos. Spenser.
Butterfly, The. Tabb.
Butterfly and the Bee, The. Bowles.
Butterfly and the Caterpillar, The. Lauren.
Butterfly and the Snail, The. John Gay.
Butterfly in April. Mörike, *tr. fr. German by* Tobin.
Butterfly's Ball, The. Roscoe.
Butterfly's First Flight, The. *Unknown.*
Caterpillar and the Butterfly, The. Moreno, *tr. fr. Spanish by* Bryant.
City Butterfly, A. Starbuck.
First Butterfly, The. Wergeland, *tr. fr. Norwegian by* Stork.
Flying Crooked. Graves.
From a Chinese Vase. Winifred Welles.
Genesis of Butterflies, The. Hugo, *tr. fr. French by* Lang.

Hokku: "I thought I saw the fallen leaves." Moritake, *tr. fr. Japanese by* Noguchi.
Ode to a Butterfly. Higginson.
Redbreast Chasing a Butterfly, The. Wordsworth.
To a Butterfly. Hastings.
To a Butterfly ("I've watched you"). **Wordsworth.**
To Butterfly. Percy.
Tuft of Flowers, The. Robert Frost.
Was Worm. **May Swenson.**
White Butterflies. Swinburne.
BUTTERFLY WEED. Butterfly Weed—Indian Fire. **Livesay.**
BUZZARDS
Buzzards, The. Armstrong.
Turkey-Buzzards. Van Doren.
BYGDÖ, NORWAY. Viking Ship, The. O'Conor.
BYRD, RICHARD EVELYN. Admiral Byrd. Nash.
BYRON, GEORGE GORDON NOEL BYRON, 6TH BARON
Byron. C. W. Hill.
Byron. Joaquin Miller.
Byron the Voluptuary. Sir William Watson.
Damnation of Byron, The. Hope.
Letter to Lord Byron, *sels.* Auden.
Memorial Verses. Matthew Arnold.
On the Proposal to Erect a Monument in England to Lord Byron. Lazarus.
On This Day I Complete My Thirty-sixth Year. Byron.
Sketch of Lord Byron's Life, *sel.* ("Lord Byron was an Englishman"). J. A. Moore.
Sonnet to Byron. Shelley.
Stanzas from the Grande Chartreuse, *sel.* ("What helps it now, that Byron bore"). Matthew Arnold.
To Byron. Keats.
To Byron. Shelley.
To Lord Byron. R. H. Wilde.
BYZANTIUM
Byzantium. Yeats.
Sailing to Byzantium. **Yeats.**

C

CABOT, JOHN. First Voyage of John Cabot, The. K. L. Bates.
CABUL, PALESTINE. Guides at Cabul, 1879, The. Newbolt.
CACTUS
Cactus. Terence Heywood.
Cactus, The. *Unknown.*
Organ Cactus, The. Scarborough.
CADE, JACK. How Jacke Cade Traiterously Rebelling agaynst His Kyng . . . *Fr.* A Mirror for Magistrates. *At. to* William Baldwin.
CADIZ, SPAIN, BATTLE OF (1596). Winning of Cales, The. Deloney.
CÆDMON
Cædmon. T. S. Jones, Jr.
Cædmon. Nicholson.
CAESAR, JULIUS
Antony's Oration over Caesar's Body. *Fr.* Julius Caesar. Shakespeare.
Caesar, *sel.* ("Within the dim"). Irwin.
Caesar. Valéry, *tr. fr. French by* MacIntyre.
Caesar Remembers. Seymour.
Fragment: "As if stone Caesar shook." McCrae.
Old Actor Addresses Julius Caesar, An. Laberius, *tr. fr. Latin by* Cunningham.
Pharsalia, *sel.* ("Wars worse then civil on Thessalian plains"). Lucan, *tr. fr. Latin by* Marlowe.
Rider at the Gate, The. Masefield.
CAIN AND ABEL
Abel. Capetanakis.
Ancient History. Sassoon.
Cain and Abel. Manger, *tr. fr. Yiddish by* Betsky.
Conscience. Hugo, *tr. fr. French by* Conder.
CALAIS, FRANCE
Burgesses of Calais, The. Laurence Minot.
On Calais Sands. Lang.
CALGARY, ALBERTA. Calgary Station. Mackay.
CALIBAN
Caliban. *Fr.* The Tempest. Shakespeare.
Caliban upon Setebos; or, Natural Theology in the Island. Robert Browning.
CALIFORNIA
California. T. L. Harris.
California. Sigourney.
California. *Unknown.*
California Christmas, A. Joaquin Miller.
California Dissonance. Rorty.
California Trail. *Unknown.*
Exile. Maynard.
Golden Whales of California, The, *sel.* ("Yes, I have walked in California"). Lindsay.
CALLIOPE (goddess). Why Were Ye Calliope Embrawdred with Letters of Golde? Skelton.
CALLIOPE (circus)
Calliope. *Unknown.*
Kallyope Yell, The. Lindsay.
CALVARY
Calvary. Hallet.
Calvary. W. D. Howells.
Calvary. Orr.
Calvary. E. A. Robinson.
Calvary. *Unknown.*
Calvary and Easter. "Susan Coolidge."
CALVES
New Baby Calf, The. Newlin.
Our Little Calf. Aldis.
Young Calves, The. Coffin.
CALVIN, JOHN
Calvinist Autumnal. Harrod.
House of Calvin. Speyer.
CALVINISM
Holy Willie's Prayer. Burns.
Johannes Agricola in Meditation. Robert Browning.
To the Rev. John M'Math. Burns.
CAMBRIDGE, ENGLAND
Autumn Morning at Cambridge. Cornford.
Devourers, The. Macaulay.
CAMBRIDGE, MASSACHUSETTS. Cambridge Ladies, The. Cummings.
CAMBRIDGE UNIVERSITY
In the Backs. Cornford.
Inside of King's College Chapel, Cambridge. Wordsworth.
On Bertrand Russell's "Portraits from Memory." Davie.
St. John's, Cambridge. Longfellow.
Written at Cambridge. Charles Lamb.
CAMDEN, WILLIAM. To William Camden. Jonson.
CAMELLIAS. White Camellia, A. Fawcett.
CAMELOT. Camelot. Dalmon.
CAMELS
Camel. M. B. Miller.
Camel, The. Ogden Nash.
Camel's Nose, The. Sigourney.
Dromedary, The. A. Y. Campbell.
Exile. Sheard.
Legend of the First Cam-u-el, The. Guiterman.
Plaint of the Camel, The. C. E. Carryl.
Song of the Camels. Coatsworth.
CAMERON, DONALD. Lochiel's Warning. Campbell.
CAMÕES [*or* CAMOENS], LUÍS DE
Camoens. Melville.
Camoens in the Hospital. Melville.
Luis de Camões. Roy Campbell.
CAMPAGNA DI ROMA, ITALY
High Noon at Midsummer on the Campagna. "Fiona Macleod."
On the Campagna. Stoddard.
View across the Roman Campagna, A. E. B. Browning.
CAMPAIGNS, POLITICAL
Autumn. E. M. Roberts.
Bryan, Bryan, Bryan, Bryan. Vachel Lindsay.
What Mr. Robinson Thinks. *Fr.* The Biglow Papers. J. R. Lowell.
CAMPANULA. Bed of Campanula, A. "John Crichton."
CAMPBELL, ALEXANDER. My Fathers Came from Kentucky. *Fr.* Alexander Campbell. Lindsay.
CAMPBELL, ROY
In Memoriam: Roy Campbell. Currey.
Seven South African Poems. David Wright.
CAMPBELL, THOMAS
Camp-Bell. Praed.
To Campbell. Thomas Moore.
CAMPING
Black Ashes. M. H. Clark.
Bunyip and the Whistling Kettle, The. Manifold.
Camper's Night Song. *Fr.* Travels with a Donkey. R. L. Stevenson.
Camp-Fire, The. W. H. Clemons.
Camping Song. Carman.
Have You? Dean.
Wanderers. Hebblethwaite.
CAMPION, EDMUND
Edmund Campion. Sister Mary St. Virginia.
Martyrdom of Father Campion. Henry Walpole.
CANA, GALILEE. Cana. J. F. Clarke.
CANADA
Between Two Furious Oceans, *sel.* ("You have asked me, 'What am I?' "). Dick Diespecker.
Canada. C. G. D. Roberts.
Canada; Case History. Birney.
Canada Speaks of Britain. C. G. D. Roberts.
Canada to England. Pickthall.
Canadian Boat Song, A. Thomas Moore.
Canadian Boat Song. *Unknown, at. to* Galt.

CANADA (*continued*)
Canadian Hunter's Song. S. S. Moodie.
East Coast—Canada. Elizabeth Brewster.
For Dominion Day. J. E. Middleton.
Hymn for Canada, A. A. D. Watson.
Old Canada; or, Gee Buck Gee. McLachlan.
Poem on Canada, *sels.* Anderson.
Book of Canadian Poetry, The (BoCaPo). A. J. M. Smith, ed.
Canadian Poetry in English (CaP). Bliss Carman, Lorne Pierce, *and* V. B. Rhodenizer, eds.
Canadian Poets (CPG). John W. Garvin, ed.
Our Canadian Literature (OCL). Bliss Carman *and* Lorne Pierce, eds.
Penguin Book of Canadian Verse, The (PeCV). Ralph Gustafson, ed.
Twentieth Century Canadian Poetry (TwCaPo). Earle Birney, ed.
CANADIANS
Canadian, The. J. E. Middleton.
Champlain; First Canadian. Logan.
Nice Leetle Canadienne, De. W. H. Drummond.
Old Habitant, An. Call.
CANARIES
Canary, The. Ogden Nash.
Canary, The. Elizabeth Turner.
My Canary's Rhapsody. Ackerman.
CANCER (disease)
Cancer Cells, The. Eberhart.
Death from Cancer. Robert Lowell.
CANDLEMAS
Candlemas. H. F. Blunt.
Candlemas. Alice Brown.
Candlemas. *Unknown.*
Carol, for Candlemas Day. *Unknown.*
Ceremony for Candlemas Day, A. Herrick.
Ceremonies for Candlemas Day, The. Jonson.
Ceremonies for Candlemass Eve ("Down with the rosemary and bays"). Herrick.
Simeon's Light Remembered. J. W. Simons.
CANOES AND CANOEING
Canoe, The. I. V. Crawford.
Canoe Song at Twilight. McCully.
Lullaby: "Long canoe, The." Hillyer.
Silver Canoe, The. Guiterman.
Song My Paddle Sings, The. E. P. Johnson.
White Canoe, The. Alan Sullivan.
CANONICUS. Canonicus and Roger Williams. *Unknown.*
CANTERBURY, NEW ZEALAND. Canterbury. Dowling.
CANUTE, KING
Canute the Great, *sel.* ("She dared not wait"). "Michael Field."
King Canute. Thackeray.
CAPE OF GOOD HOPE. Rounding the Cape. Roy Campbell.
CAPITALISM
After They Have Tired of the Brilliance of Cities. Spender.
Deserted Village, The. Goldsmith.
Empire Builders. MacLeish.
Latest Decalogue, The. Clough.
CAPITOL (Washington)
Smoke Rose Gold. Sandburg.
View of the Capitol from the Library of Congress. Elizabeth Bishop.
CAPRI, ITALY. Song at Capri. Teasdale.
CARCASSONNE, FRANCE
At Carcassonne. Garrison.
Carcassonne. Nadaud, *tr. fr. French by* Thompson.
CARDINAL (bird)
Cardinal, The. *Fr.* Kentucky Mountain Farm. R. P. Warren.
Cardinal Bird, The. Gallagher.
Redbirds. Teasdale.
CARIBBEAN SEA. Caribbean, The. Ormsby.
CARLOS, PRINCE OF THE ASTURIAS. Don Carlos, *sel.* ("I understood thy hint"). Schiller, *tr. fr. German.*
CARLYLE, THOMAS
After Looking into Carlyle's Reminiscences. Swinburne.
As I was laying on the green. *Unknown.*
Carlyle and Emerson. Schuyler.
On the Deaths of Thomas Carlyle and George Eliot. Swinburne.
Thomas Carlyle. *Unknown.*
CARMAN, BLISS. Welcome to Bliss Carman, A. Herriman.
CARMARTHENSHIRE, WALES. Grongar Hill. John Dyer.
CARMEL, CALIFORNIA
Autumn in Carmel. Sterling.
Spring in Carmel. Sterling.
CARNATIONS
Carnations. Ken Etheridge.
Carnations. Widdemer.
White Carnation, The. Sangster.
CARPENTERS
Busy Carpenters. Tippett.
Carpenter. Lucas.
Carpenter's Plane, The. Kazin, *tr. fr. Russian by* Deutsch.
CARRICKFERGUS, NORTHERN IRELAND. Carrickfergus. MacNeice.
"CARROLL, LEWIS." In Memory of Lewis Carroll. *Unknown.*
CARROTS. Poetry of a Root Crop. Kingsley.
CARROUSELS
Merry-go-round. Baruch.
Merry-go-round. Rachel Field.
Merry-go-round. Oliver Jenkins.
Merry-go-round, The. Noel.
CARS. *See* AUTOMOBILES.
CARSON, KIT
Kit Carson. Guiterman.
Kit Carson's Last Smoke. Vestal.
Kit Carson's Ride. Joaquin Miller.
CARTHAGE. Carthage. deFord.
CARTHUSIANS. Carthusians. Dowson.
CARTIER, JACQUES
Cartier Arrives at Stadacona. W. T. Allison.
Cartier: Dauntless Discoverer. J. D. Logan.
Jacques Cartier. McGee.
CASABIANCA, LOUIS. Casabianca. Hemans.
CASEMENT, ROGER DAVID. On the Death of Roger Casement. Colum.
CASHEL, IRELAND. Rock of Cashel, The. Sir Aubrey De Vere.
CASSANDRA. Cassandra. Bogan.
CASTIGLIONE, BALDASSARE, CONTE. Thomas Sackville in Commendation of the Work to the Reader. Sackville.
CASTILE, SPAIN. Castile. Unamuno, *tr. fr. Spanish by* Turnbull.
CASTLE, VERNON. Vernon Castle. Monroe.
CASTLECONNELL, IRELAND. Castleconnell. Sir Aubrey De Vere.
CASTLEREAGH, ROBERT STEWART, 2D VISCOUNT
Dedication: "Bob Southey! You're a poet—Poet-laureate." *Fr.* Don Juan. Byron.
Epigrams on Castlereagh. Byron.
CASTLES. Castles and Distances. Wilbur.
CATALPA TREES. Catalpa Tree. Colum.
CATARACTS. *See* WATERFALLS.
CATBIRDS
Catbird. Crombie.
My Catbird. Venable.
To the Catbird. *Unknown.*
CATERPILLARS
Butterfly and the Caterpillar, The. Lauren.
Caterpillar, The. Robert Graves.
Caterpillar, The. C. G. Rossetti.
Caterpillar and the Butterfly, The. Rosas Moreno, *tr. fr. Spanish by* Bryant.
Caterpillars. John Freeman.
Caterpillar's Apology for Eating a Favorite Gladiolus, A. Dalmon.
Caterpillars' Conversation. Findlater.
Only My Opinion. Shannon.
Oubit, The. Kingsley.
Tired Caterpillar, The. *Unknown.*
CATFISH
Catfish. John Farrar.
Catfish, The. Herford.
CATHERINE OF SIENA, SAINT
Laud of Saint Catherine, The. *Fr.* Siena. Swinburne.
To Saint Catherine. Constable.
CATHOLICISM
Catholic Faith, The. Digby.
Christ Brought Home. *Unknown.*
Hind and the Panther, The, *sels.* Dryden.
I hold as faith. *Unknown.*
Patient Church, The. Newman.
Popish Plot, The. *Fr.* Absalom and Achitophel. Dryden.
Religio Laici. Dryden.
To the Noblest and Best of Ladies, the Countess of Denbigh. Crashaw.
Anthology of Catholic Poets, An (ACP). Shane Leslie, ed.
Catholic Anthology, The (CAW). Thomas Walsh, ed.
Golden Book of Catholic Poetry, The (GoBC). Alfred Noyes, ed.
I Sing of a Maiden (ISi). Sister M. Thérèse, ed.
Joyce Kilmer's Anthology of Catholic Poets (JKCP). Joyce Kilmer, ed.
Poetry and Life (PoLi). F. J. Sheed, comp.
Praise of Nuns, In (PraNu). James M. Hayes, ed.
CATILINE. Catiline to the Roman Army. *Fr.* Catiline. Croly.
CATO THE YOUNGER
Cato, *sels.* Addison.
Cato's Way of Life. Bibaculus, *tr. fr. Latin by* Johnson.
Stoic's Wedding, The. *Fr.* The Civil War. Lucan, *tr. fr. Latin by* Highet.
CATS
Ad-dressing of Cats, The. T. S. Eliot.
All the Cats. Greenaway.
Alley Cat. Georges.
Alley Cat, An. N. B. Turner.

Bad Kittens, The. Coatsworth.
Black Cat. Dunetz.
Cat. Baruch.
Cat, The. Baudelaire, *tr. fr. French.*
Cat, The. *Fr.* Sad Memories. Calverley.
Cat, The. Richard Church.
Cat. Sinclair Lewis.
Cat. M. B. Miller.
Cat, The. W. A. Roberts.
Cat. "Jan Struther."
Cat, The. Whitney.
Cat and the Bird, The. Solomon.
Cat and the Moon, The. Yeats.
Cat Ballerina Assoluta. Glen.
Cat-Goddesses. Robert Graves.
Cat on the Porch at Dusk. Harriman.
Cat to Her Kittens, A. Eliza Grove.
Catalog. Rosalie Moore.
Cats, The. Baudelaire, *tr. fr. French.*
Cats. Tessimond.
Cat's Meat. Monro.
Catts as other creatures doe, The. *Unknown.*
Colubriad, The. Cowper.
Country Cat. Coatsworth.
Cruel Clever Cat. Geoffrey Taylor.
Diamond Cut Diamond. Ewart Milne.
Dinah. Gale.
Duel, The. Eugene Field.
Epitaph on a Pet Cat. Du Bellay, *tr. fr. French by* Currey.
Five Eyes. De la Mare.
For a Siamese Cat. MacInnes.
Garden-Lion. Evelyn Hayes.
Gardener's Cat, The. Chalmers.
Greater Cats, The. Sackville-West.
Growltiger's Last Stand. T. S. Eliot.
Gus, the Theatre Cat. T. S. Eliot.
Hearth. Peggy Bacon.
House Cat, The. Wynne.
I Like Little Pussy. Jane Taylor.
In Honor of Taffy Topaz. Morley.
Kilkenny Cats, The. *Unknown.*
Kitten, The. Baillie.
Kitten, A. Farjeon.
Kitten, The. Ogden Nash.
Kitten at Play, The. *Fr.* The Kitten and the Falling Leaves. Wordsworth.
Kittens, The. Hey.
Kitty. Prentiss.
Kitty: What She Thinks of Herself. Rands.
Last Words to a Dumb Friend. Hardy.
Lat Take a Cat. *Fr.* The Canterbury Tales: The Maunciple's Tale. Chaucer.
Long Time Ago. Prentiss.
Macavity, the Mystery Cat. T. S. Eliot.
Milk for the Cat. Monro.
Monk and His Pet Cat, The. *Unknown, tr. fr. Old Irish.*
My Cat Jeoffry. *Fr.* Jubilato Agno. Smart.
Mysterious Cat, The. Lindsay.
Night. L. W. McKay.
O Cat of Carlish Kind. *Fr.* Phyllyp Sparowe. John Skelton.
Ode on the Death of a Favourite Cat, Drowned in a Tub of Goldfishes. Thomas Gray.
Old Gumbie Cat, The. T. S. Eliot.
On a Night of Snow. Coatsworth.
On a Pet Cat. Persell.
Our Cat. Janet Vaughn.
Owl and the Pussy-Cat, The. Lear.
Pangur Bán. *Unknown, tr. fr. Old Irish by* Flower.
Poem: "As the cat/climbed over." W. C. Williams.
Prize Cat, The. E. J. Pratt.
Pussy, Pussy, Do Not Mew. Peabody.
Pussy Sits beside the Fire. *Unknown.*
Retired Cat, The. Cowper.
Rum Tum Tugger, The. T. S. Eliot.
Scholar and the Cat, The. *Unknown, tr. fr. Irish by* O'Connor.
Skimbleshanks, the Railway Cat. T. S. Eliot.
Song of Mehitabel, The. *Fr.* Archy and Mehitabel. Marquis.
Song of the Jellicles, The. T. S. Eliot.
Sonnet: Cats of Santa Anna, The. Tasso, *tr. fr. Italian by* Lind.
Sunday. Coatsworth.
That Cat. Ben King.
There was a Presbyterian cat. *Unknown.*
Three Little Kittens, The. Follen.
Tiger-Cat Tim. Newlin.
To a Cat. Keats.
To My Cat. R. M. Watson.
Tomcat, The. Marquis.
Tortoiseshell Cat, The. Chalmers.
Tracks in the Snow. Coatsworth.
V Is for Victory, as You Can Plainly See. Hartley.
What the Gray Cat Sings. Guiterman.
Who's that ringing at my doorbell? *Unknown.*
Witch Cat. Rowena Bennett.
Cat in Verse, The (CIV). Carolyn Wells *and* Luella D. Everett, comps.
Poet's Cat, The (PoC). Mona Gooden, comp.

CATTAILS. When We Went Gathering Cat-Tails. Rachel Field.

CATTLE
Branding Iron Herd, The. Rigby.
Buttercup Cow. Rendall.
Cattle. Banko, *tr. fr. Japanese.*
Cattle Round-Up, The. McLachlan.
Cow, The. Motherly.
Cow, The. O'Dowd.
Cow, The. Roethke.
Cow, The. R. L. Stevenson.
Cow, The. Ann *or* Jane Taylor.
Cow at Sullington, A. Dalmon.
Cow in Apple-Time, The. Robert Frost.
Cow Time. Shannon.
Cows. Van der Veer.
Driving Home the Cows. Osgood.
Drover, A. Padraic Colum.
Eighteen-ninety. E. R. Shipp.
From the Gulf. Ogilvie.
Highland Cattle, *sel.* ("Down the wintry mountain"). Craik.
Kerry Cow, The. Letts.
Lament for a Dead Cow. F. C. Slater.
Milk-white Moon, Put the Cows to Sleep. Sandburg.
Milking Kraal. F. C. Slater.
Moo! Hillyer.
Moo-Cow-Moo, The. E. V. Cooke.
Pastoral: "Farmhouse skyline, draped with trees, The." Creighton.
Purple Cow, The. Gelett Burgess.
Riddle, A: "Four stiff-standers." *Unknown.*
Round-up, The. S. E. Howard.
Stampede, The. Brininstool.
Stampede, The. Coburn.
Whoopee Ti Yi Yo, Git Along, Little Dogies. *Unknown.*
Woman of Llyn y Fan's Call to Her Cattle, The. *Unknown, tr. fr. Welsh by* Jones.
Yoke of Steers, A. Heyward.
See also BULLS; CALVES; OXEN.

CATULLUS. On Catullus. Landor.

CAUCASUS. Caucasus, The. Pushkin, *tr. fr. Russian by* Bowra.

CAUTERETS VALLEY, FRANCE. In the Valley of Cauteretz. Tennyson.

CAVALCANTI, GUIDO. Sonnet: To Guido Cavalcanti. Dante, *tr. fr. Italian by* Shelley.

CAVALIERS
Cavalier Tunes. Robert Browning.
Come drawer some wine or wele pull downe your signe. *Unknown.*
Melting of the Earl's Plate. Thornbury.
Old Cavalier, The. Doyle.
Young Windebank. Woods.

CAVALRY. Cavalry Crossing a Ford. Whitman.

CAVELL, EDITH
Edith Cavell. Woodberry.
Nurse Edith Cavell. Alice Meynell.

CAVES. Caves, The. Michael Roberts.

CECILIA, SAINT. Verses to St. Cecilia. David Wright.

CEDAR TREES
Cedars, The. Peabody.
Cedars of Lebanon, The. Lamartine, *tr. fr. French by* Dutt.
Cedars of Lebanon, The. Landon.

CELANDINE
Lesson, A. Wordsworth.
To the Small Celandine. Wordsworth.

CELERY. Celery. Ogden Nash.

CELIBACY. Cassandra's Song of Celibacy. Vicente, *tr. fr. Spanish by* Ticknor.

CELLINI, BENVENUTO. Benvenuto Cellini. Snoilsky, *tr. fr. Swedish by* Stork.

CELLOS
Cello, The. R. W. Gilder.
Cello, The. Josephson, *tr. fr. Swedish by* Stork.

CELTS. Celts, The. McGee.

CEMETERIES
Cemetery by the Sea, The. Valéry, *tr. fr. French by* Gibbs.
Cemetery Is, The. McGaffin.
Churchyard of St. Mary Magdalene, Old Milton. Heath-Stubbs.
God's-Acre. Longfellow.
Grave, The. Robert Blair.
Graves of a Household, The. Hemans.
Graves of Infants. Clare.
Gravestone, A. Allingham.
Graveyard, The. Bialik, *tr. fr. Hebrew by* Beinkinstadt.
In Clonmel Parish Churchyard. Piatt.
Island Cemetery, The. Auden.

CEMETERIES (*continued*)
Jewish Cemetery at Newport, The. Longfellow.
Mountain Cemetery, The. Bowers.
On the Road to Woodlawn. Roethke.
Prairie Graveyard. Marriott.
Quaker Graveyard, The. Mitchell.
This quiet dust was gentlemen and ladies. Emily Dickinson.
CENTAURS
Centaur, The. Roethke.
Centaur Song. Doolittle ("H. D.").
Centaurs, The. James Stephens.
Centaurs and Lapithae. *Fr.* Battles of the Centaurs. Sacheverell Sitwell.
Centaur's Bath, The. Urbina, *tr. fr. Spanish by* Beckett.
Centaurs' Flight. Heredia, *tr. fr French by* Conder.
CENTIPEDES
Centipede, The. A. P. Herbert.
Centipede, The. Ogden Nash.
Centipede, A. *Unknown.*
Puzzled Centipede, The. *Unknown.*
CENTRAL PARK, NEW YORK CITY. Central Park at Dusk. Teasdale.
CERES. *See* DEMETER.
CERVANTES SAAVEDRA, MIGUEL DE. To Miguel de Cervantes Saavadra. Munkitrick.
CEYLON. Ceylon. A. H. Fisher.
CÉZANNE, PAUL
Cézanne. Kreymborg.
Oh, You Wholly Rectangular. E. R. Cole.
CHAFFINCHES. Chaffinch's Nest at Sea, The. Cowper.
CHALEUR BAY, CANADA. Phantom Light of the Baie des Chaleurs, The. A. W. H. Eaton.
CHAMELEONS
Chameleon. Delius.
Chameleon. Engle.
Chameleon, The. A. P. Herbert.
Chameleon, The. Merrick, *after* Des la Matte.
To a Chameleon. Marianne Moore.
CHAMOIS. Glad Young Chamois, The. Burges Johnson.
CHAMONIX, FRANCE. Chamonix. Hookham.
CHAMPLAIN, SAMUEL DE. Champlain; First Canadian. Logan.
CHAMPLAIN, LAKE, BATTLE OF. Battle of Lake Champlain, The. Freneau.
CHANCELLORSVILLE, BATTLE OF. Keenan's Charge. Lathrop.
CHANGE
Harvest Moon. Josephine Miles.
Locksley Hall Sixty Years After. Tennyson.
Mutability. Shelley.
Sonnet: "World, that all contains, is ever moving, The." *Fr.* Caelica. Greville.
Two Cantos of Mutabilitie. *Fr.* The Faerie Queene. Spenser.
Van Winkle. *Fr.* The Bridge. Hart Crane.
CHANNING, WILLIAM HENRY. Channing. Alcott.
CHANTEYS. *See* SEA CHANTEYS.
CHANTICLEER. *See* COCKS.
CHAPMAN, GEORGE
On First Looking into Chapman's Homer. Keats.
To George Chapman. Freeman.
To My Worthy and Honoured Friend, Mr. George Chapman, on His Translation of Hesiod's Works and Days. Jonson.
To My Worthy Friend Mr. George Chapman, and His Translated Hesiod. Drayton.
CHAPMAN, JOHN (Johnny Appleseed)
Apple-Barrel of Johnny Appleseed, The. Lindsay.
Apple-Seed John. L. M. Child.
Ballad of Johnny Appleseed, A. Oleson.
In Praise of Johnny Appleseed. Lindsay.
Johnny Appleseed. Rosemary *and* S. V. Benét.
Johnny Appleseed. Bourinot.
Johnny Appleseed, *sel.* Lindsay.
Johnny Appleseed. Masters.
Johnny Appleseed. Venable.
CHAPMAN, NATHANIEL. To N. Chapman, M.D. Mitchell.
CHAPULTEPEC, MEXICO
Chapultepec Park. Rukeyser.
Siege of Chapultepec, The. Lytle.
CHARING CROSS, LONDON
As I Was Going by Charing Cross. *Unknown.*
Charing Cross. C. E. M. Roberts.
CHARLEMAGNE
Charlemagne. Longfellow.
Opening of the Tomb of Charlemagne, The. De Vere.
CHARLES V, EMPEROR
Charles the Fifth and the Peasant. Robert Lowell.
Pilgrim before St. Just, The. Platen, *tr. fr. German.*
CHARLES I, KING OF ENGLAND
As I was going by Charing Cross. *Unknown.*
Bright soule, instruct poore mortalls how to mourne. *Unknown.*
By the Statue of King Charles at Charing Cross. Lionel Johnson.
Cavalier Tunes. Robert Browning.
Elegy upon the Most Incomparable King Charles the First, An, *sel.* ("Thou from th' en'throned martyrs blood-stain'd line"). King.
Epigram to King Charles for an Hundred Pounds He Sent Me in My Sickness, An. Jonson.
Execution of King Charles, The. Marvell.
Fall, The. *Fr.* Il Pastor Fido. Fanshawe.
Here lyes Charles the first the great. *Unknown.*
King Charles upon the Scaffold. *Fr.* An Horatian Ode upon Cromwell's Return from Ireland. Marvell.
On the Death of Charles I. James Graham, Marquess of Montrose.
Pastoral on the King's Death, The. Written in 1648. Brome.
CHARLES II, KING OF ENGLAND
Absalom and Achitophel, Pt. I. Dryden.
Astraea Redux. Dryden.
Epitaph on Charles II. Earl of Rochester.
Here's a Health to King Charles. *Fr.* Woodstock. Scott.
Impromptu on Charles II. Earl of Rochester.
In Good King Charles's Golden Days. *Unknown.*
Last Instructions to a Painter: Charles II. Marvell.
On the Lord Mayor and Court of Aldermen. Marvell.
Royal Angler, The, *sel.* ("Methinks, I see our mighty Monarch stand"). Earl of Rochester.
To His Sacred Majesty, a Panegyrick on His Coronation, 1661, *sel.* ("Time seems not now"). Dryden.
Will Ye No Come Back Again? Lady Nairne.
CHARLES II, KING OF SPAIN. Charles II of Spain to Approaching Death. Lee-Hamilton.
CHARLES XII, KING OF SWEDEN. Charles XII. *Fr.* The Vanity of Human Wishes. Johnson.
CHARLESTON, SOUTH CAROLINA
At Magnolia Cemetery. Timrod.
Battle of Charleston Harbor, The. Hayne.
Charleston. Gilder.
Charleston. Hayne.
Charleston. Timrod.
Charleston Garden, A. Bellamann.
Seven Cities of America, The. Masters.
Song about Charleston, A. *Unknown.*
CHARLETON, WALTER. To My Honored Friend, Dr. Charleton. Dryden.
CHARTISM
Alton Locke, *sels.* Kingsley.
Chartist Song. Cooper.
Old Chartist, The. George Meredith.
CHATTAHOOCHEE RIVER, GEORGIA. Song of the Chattahoochee. Lanier.
CHATTANOOGA CAMPAIGN. Chattanooga. Melville.
CHATTERTON, THOMAS
Five English Poets: Thomas Chatterton. D. G. Rossetti.
Last Verses. Chatterton.
Monody on the Death of Chatterton. S. T. Coleridge.
Resolution and Independence, *sel.* ("I thought of Chatterton, the marvellous boy"). Wordsworth.
To Chatterton. Keats.
CHAUCER, GEOFFREY
Chaucer. Brawley.
Chaucer. Cummings.
Chaucer. Longfellow.
Chaucers Word[e]s unto Adam, His Owne Scriveyn. Chaucer.
Description of Sir Geoffrey Chaucer. *Fr.* Greene's Vision. Robert Greene.
Dream of Fair Women, A, *sel.* ("I read, before my eyelids dropt their shade"). Tennyson.
Faerie Queene, The, *sel.* ("Whylome, as antique stories tellen us"). Spenser.
Fall of Princes, The, *sel.* ("Sith of our language he was the lode-star"). Lydgate.
For a Statue of Chaucer at Woodstock. Akenside.
For Maister Geoffrey Chaucer. Hillyer.
Garlande of Laurell, The, *sel.* ("O noble Chaucer"). Skelton.
Invocation to Chaucer. *Fr.* The Life and Death of Jason. William Morris.
Lament for Chaucer. *Fr.* De Regimine Principum. Hoccleve.
O Reverend Chaucer! Rose of Rhetoris All. Dunbar.
Sir Geoffrey Chaucer. *Fr* Greene's Vision. Robert Greene.
Sonnet Written at the End of "The Floure and the Lefe." Keats.
To Chaucer. *Fr.* De Regimine Principum. Hoccleve.
CHEETAHS. Cheetah. Eglington.
CHEOPS, PHARAOH OF EGYPT. Cheops. Schevill.
CHERRY TREES
Cherries. Weatherly.
Cherry Tree. Claudius, *tr. fr. German by* Salinger.
Cherry Tree. Eastwick.
Cherry Tree, The. James Stephens.
Crimson Cherry Tree, The. Treece.
Discouraged Cherry Tree, The. Millay.

Hokku: "Wayside cherry tree, A." Basho, *tr. fr. Japanese by* Porter.
Japanese Cherries. Brégy.
Legend of Cherries, A. Dalmon.
Loveliest of Trees, the Cherry Now. *Fr.* A Shropshire Lad. Housman.
Now Is the Cherry in Blossom. M. E. W. Freeman.
Oh, fair to see. *Fr.* Sing-Song. C. G. Rossetti.
Wild Cherry. J. R. Foster.
CHESAPEAKE (ship)
Chesapeake and *Shannon*. *Unknown.*
Shannon and the *Chesapeake,* The. Bouvé.
CHESS
Chess Knight. Stasinopoulos, *tr. fr. Modern Greek by* Dalven.
Duel in the Park. Grenelle.
Game of Chess, The. D. S. Foster.
Song of Chess, The. *At. to* Abraham ibn Ezra, *tr. fr. Hebrew by* Salaman.
CHESTERTON, GILBERT KEITH
G. K. Chesterton. Humbert Wolfe.
In Memory of G. K. Chesterton. De la Mare.
To G. K. Chesterton. Plunkett.
CHESTNUT TREES. Horse Chestnut Tree, The. Eberhart.
CHIANG KAI-SHEK, MADAME. For Madame Chiang Kai-shek. A. B. Hall.
CHICAGO, ILLINOIS
Chicago. Anderson.
Chicago. Harte.
Chicago. Kinnell.
Chicago. O'Reilly.
Chicago. Sandburg.
Chicago. Whittier.
Chicago Poem. Lew Welch.
Dawn Patrol; Chicago. Durham.
Seven Cities of America, The. Masters.
Tenement Room; Chicago. F. M. Davis.
To Chicago at Night. Meigs.
CHICKADEES
Chickadee. M. H. Clark.
Chickadee. Hilda Conkling.
Chickadee, The. Emerson.
Chickadee. M. M. Walker.
Chickadees. E. M. Thomas.
Song of the Chickadee. *Unknown.*
Titmouse, The. Emerson.
CHICKAMAUGA, BATTLE OF
Chickamauga. Ferris.
Chickamauga. *Unknown.*
Chickamauga—1898. *Unknown.*
Memorials on the Slain at Chickamauga. Melville.
CHICKENS
Blue Ribbon at Amesbury, A. Robert Frost.
Chickens, The. *Unknown.*
Five Little Chickens. *Unknown.*
Poultries, The. Ogden Nash.
CHILD LABOR
Child Labor. Gilman.
Chimney Sweeper, The. *Fr.* Songs of Experience. Blake.
Cry of the Children, The. E. B. Browning.
Factory Children. Burton.
Golf Links, The. Cleghorn.
CHILDHOOD AND CHILDREN
Address to a Child during a Boisterous Winter Evening. Dorothy Wordsworth.
Among School Children. Yeats.
Around the Child. Landor.
Baal-Shem Tov. A. M. Klein.
Baby Running Barefoot. D. H. Lawrence.
Barren. "Rachel," *tr fr. Hebrew by* Snowman.
Bathers. Tiller.
Bathing Children, The. Rydberg, *tr. fr. Swedish by* Stork.
Carol of the Poor Children, The. Middleton.
Centaur, The. Swenson.
Certain Age, A. McGinley.
Characteristics of a Child Three Years Old. Wordsworth.
Child, The. Sara Coleridge.
Child, A. Gilder.
Child, The. Rilke, *tr fr. German by* Jarrell.
Child. Sandburg.
Child and Poet. Swinburne.
Child and the World, The. Wiggin.
Child and the Year, The. Thaxter.
Child in the Garden, The. Van Dyke.
Child in the House, The. Cawein.
Child Looks Out, The. Livesay.
Child Next Door, The. Fyleman.
Child of a Day. Landor.
Child of My Heart. Markham.
Child of To-Day, A. Buckham.
Child on Top of a Greenhouse. Roethke.
Child to the Father, The. Robert Bridges.
Child Waking. Scovell.
Childher, The. McCarthy.
Childhood. Baggesen, *tr. fr. Danish by* Longfellow.
Childhood. Drummond de Andrade, *tr. fr. Portuguese by* Poore.
Childhood. Louis Ginsberg.
Childhood. Lamb.
Childhood. More.
Childhood. Muir.
Childhood. Rilke, *ad. fr. German by* Jarrell.
Childhood. Tabb.
Childhood. Trakl, *tr. fr. German by* Middleton.
Childhood. Vaughan.
Childhood and Age. Witherby.
Childhood and School-Time. *Fr.* The Prelude. Wordsworth.
Childhood Church, The. Pat Wilson.
Childhood Fled. Charles Lamb.
Childless. Giollabhrighde Mac Conmidhe, *tr. fr. Irish by* O'Connor.
Children, The. C. M. Dickinson, *wr. at. to* Dickens.
Children, The. Dyment.
Children. Longfellow.
Children. Po Chü-i, *tr. fr. Chinese by* Waley.
Children. Swinburne.
Children Look at the Parents, The. J. Tessimond.
Children of the Poor. Hugo, *tr. fr. French.*
Children's Hour, The. Longfellow.
Children's Song. F. M. Ford.
Child's Laughter, A. Swinburne.
Child's Song Overheard. G. H. Conkling.
Chronicle of Meola Creek, The. Keith Sinclair.
City Childhood. Selma Robinson.
Cradle Song, A: "Sleep, sleep, beauty bright." Blake.
Cry of the Children. E. B. Browning.
Daughter at Evening, The. Nathan.
David. Walker Gibson.
Days Gone By, The. Riley.
Elementary School Class Room in a Slum, An. Spender.
Eleven. MacLeish.
Eyes of Wonder, The. Pegis.
Fern Hill. Dylan Thomas.
Fern House, Kew. Dehn.
For a Child. Glover.
For a Child Expected. Ridler.
For a Child Who Died. J. G. E. Hopkins.
Gardener, The. R. L. Stevenson.
Going into Breeches. Charles *and* Mary Lamb.
Good and Bad Children. R. L. Stevenson.
Grownup, The. Rilke, *tr. fr. German by* Jarrell.
Grown-ups, The. Vallejo, *tr. fr. Spanish by* Walsh.
Happy Child, The. W. H. Davies.
Hiding. Aldis.
Holy Thursday. *Fr.* Songs of Innocence. Blake.
I Remember, I Remember. Hood.
In Defense of Children. Guiterman.
In the Children's Hospital. Tennyson.
Indoor Games near Newbury. Betjeman.
Invitation. Torrence.
Jemima. *Unknown.*
Jenny White and Johnny Black. Farjeon.
Jo Jo, My Child. *Unknown, tr fr. Hebrew by* Olsvanger.
Land of Our Birth. *Fr.* Puck of Pook's Hill. Kipling.
Lice Seekers, The. Rimbaud, *tr. fr. French by* Koch *and* Guy.
Lilliput Levee. Rands.
Little Boy Blue. Eugene Field.
Little Boy in the Morning, A. Ledwidge.
Little Blue-Ribbons. Dobson.
Little Chap Who Follows Me, The. *Unknown.*
Little Child, The. Paine.
Little Child, I Call Thee. *Unknown, tr. fr. Irish by* Hyde.
Little Children, The. Granich.
Little Children. Howitt.
Little Orphant Annie. Riley.
Little Rebel, The. Ashby-Sterry.
Lives of Gulls and Children, The. Nemerov.
Lonely Child, The. Oppenheim.
Long Time a Child. Hartley Coleridge.
Lullaby: "O! hush thee, my darling, sleep soundly my son." *Unknown, tr. fr. Yiddish by* Lucas.
Mein Kind, wir waren Kinder. Heine, *tr. fr. German by* E. B. Browning.
Minnie and Mattie. C. G. Rossetti.
Monday's child is fair of face. *Unknown.*
Motherless Child, The. Barnes.
Mountainy Childer, The. Shane.
My Child. Pierpont.
My Kingdom. R. L. Stevenson.
My Parents Kept Me from Children Who Were Rough. Spender.
Now Once Your Garden in the Early Haze. George, *tr. fr. German by* Luke.
Nurse's Song. *Fr.* Songs of Innocence. Blake.
Ode: Intimations of Immortality from Recollections of Early Childhood. Wordsworth.

CHILDHOOD AND CHILDREN (*continued*)
Ode on a Distant Prospect of Eton College. Thomas Gray.
Ode on Miss Harriet Hanbury at Six Years Old, An. Sir C. H. Williams.
Of a Small Daughter Walking Outdoors. Frances Frost.
Old Man, The. Herford.
On a Dead Child. Robert Bridges.
On Children. *Fr.* The Prophet. Gibran.
On the Death of My Child. Eichendorff, *tr. fr. German by* Flores.
On the Mountain. M. K. Joseph.
One, Two, Three. Bunner.
Other Children. Wing.
Paper Roses. Burnet.
Paper Windmill, The. Amy Lowell.
Parental Ode to My Son, Aged Three Years and Five Months, A. Hood.
Parental Recollections. Mary Lamb.
Party. Carrier.
Peregrine White and Virginia Dare. Rosemary *and* S. V. Benét.
Poor Children, The. Hugo, *tr. fr. French by* Swinburne.
Requiem—for the Death of a Boy. Rilke, *tr. fr. German by* Jarrell.
Retreat, The. Vaughan.
Rhenish Autumn. Apollinaire, *tr. fr. French by* Aldan.
Ring-a-Ring. Greenaway.
Sebastian in Dream. Trakl, *tr. fr. German by* Flores.
Sephestia's Song to Her Child. *Fr.* Menaphon. Greene.
Sick Child, A. Jarrell.
Snow Globe, The. Nemerov.
So Long Folks, Off to the War. Ostroff.
Song about Myself, A. Keats.
Song against Children. Aline Kilmer.
Song at Summer's End. Fairburn.
Song of the Little Hypertrophic Child. Laforgue, *tr. fr. French by* Watkins.
South Wind. Trakl, *tr. fr. German by* Luke.
Squatter's Children. Elizabeth Bishop.
System. R. L. Stevenson.
There Was a Boy. Wordsworth.
There Was a Child Went Forth. Whitman.
There Was a Little Girl. Longfellow.
These Children Singing. Cummings.
Third Duino Elegy, The. Rilke, *tr. fr. German by* Hull.
Three Children near Clonmel, The. Shanahan.
Three Years She Grew. Wordsworth.
Time of Light, a Time of Shadow, A. Yellen.
To a Child. Montgomery.
To a Child. Morley.
To a Child Dancing in the Wind. Yeats.
To a Child of Quality. Prior.
To a Hurt Child. Litchfield.
To a Young Child. Scudder.
To His Saviour, a Child; a Present by a Child. Herrick.
To One Who Died Young. Trakl, *tr. fr. German by* Middleton.
Town Child. Barbara Young.
Toys, The. *Fr.* The Unknown Eros. Patmore.
Two Children. Guillén, *tr. fr. Spanish by* Hays.
Walk, The. Leonard Clark.
Warning to Children. Robert Graves.
When I Was a Little Girl. Milligan.
When I Was Six. Zora Cross.
When the Child Appears. Hugo, *tr. fr. French by* Conder.
Whole Duty of Children. R. L. Stevenson.
Wishes for My Son. MacDonagh.
CHILDREN'S CRUSADE. "Children's Crusade," The. De Vere.
CHILDREN'S VERSE
All Day Long (AlDL). Pamela Whitlock, comp.
Book of Children's Literature, A (BoChLi). Lillian Hollowell, ed.
Boy's Book of Verse, The (BBV). Helen Dean Fish, comp.
Bridled with Rainbows (BrR). Sara Brewton *and* John E. Brewton, eds.
Cambridge Book of Poetry for Children, The (CBPC). Kenneth Grahame, ed.
Children's Garland, The (CG). Conventry Patmore, ed.
Come Hither (CH). Walter de la Mare, ed.
Days and Deeds (DD). Burton Egbert Stevenson *and* Elizabeth E. Stevenson, comps.
Faber Book of Children's Verse, The (FaBoCh). Janet Adam Smith, comp.
Four and Twenty Blackbirds (FTB). Helen Dean Fish, ed.
Gaily We Parade (GaP). John E. Brewton, comp.
Girl's Book of Verse, The (GBV). Mary Gould Davis, comp.
Golden Book of Poetry, The (GoBP). Jane Werner, ed.
Golden Flute, The (GFA). Alice Hubbard *and* Adeline Babbitt, comps.
Golden Numbers (GN). Kate Douglas Wiggin *and* Nora Archibald Smith, eds.
Golden Treasury of Poetry, The (GoTP). Louis Untermeyer, comp.
Magic Circle, The (MaC). Louis Untermeyer, ed.
Magic World, A (MW). Margery Gordon *and* Marie B. King, eds.
Merry Meet Again (MeMeAg). Elizabeth Hough Sechrist, ed.
More Silver Pennies (MoSiPe). Blanche Jennings Thompson, comp.
One Hundred and Ten Favorite Children's Poems (OnHT). H. G. Platt, ed.
One Thousand Poems for Children (OTPC). Roger Ingpen, ed. (1923); Elizabeth Hough Sechrist, ed. (1946).
Oxford Nursery Rhyme Book, The (OxNR). Iona Opie *and* Peter Opie, comps.
Pocketful of Rhymes, A (PoRh). Katherine Love, ed.
Poems Every Child Should Know (PECK). Mary E. Burt, ed.
Poems for the Children's Hour (PCH). Josephine Bouton, comp.
Posy Ring, The (PRWS). Kate Douglas Wiggin *and* Nora Archibald Smith, eds.
Rainbow Gold (RG). Sara Teasdale, comp.
Rainbow in the Sky (RIS). Louis Untermeyer, ed.
Ring-a-Round (RAR). Mildred P. Harrington, comp.
Silver Pennies (SP). Blanche Jennings Thompson, comp.
Sing a Song of Seasons (SiSoSe). Sara *and* John E. Brewton, comps.
Stars to Steer By (StaSt). Louis Untermeyer, ed.
Story and Verse for Children (StVeCh). Miriam Blanton Huber, ed.
Sugar and Spice (SAS). Mary Wilder Tileston, comp.
Sung under the Silver Umbrella (SUS). Association for Childhood Education.
This Singing World for Younger Children (TSWC). Louis Untermeyer, ed.
Time for Poetry (TiPo). May Hill Arbuthnot, ed.
Treasury of Verse for Little Children, A (TVC). M. G. Edgar, ed.
CHILLINGHAM, ENGLAND. Chillingham. Coleridge.
CHILLON CASTLE, SWITZERLAND
Prisoner of Chillon, The. Bryon.
Sonnet on Chillon. Byron.
CHILTERN HILLS, ENGLAND. Chilterns, The. Davidson.
CHIMBORAZO, ECUADOR. Romance. Turner.
CHIMNEY SWEEPERS. Chimney Sweeper, The. *Fr.* Songs of Innocence. Blake.
CHIMPANZEES. Chimpanzee, The. Herford.
CHINA
Children's Festival. Tien Ch'ien, *tr. fr. Chinese.*
Hands off China. Mayakovsky, *tr. fr. Russian.*
Snow, The. Mao Tse-tung, *tr. fr. Chinese.*
South, The. Wang Chien, *tr. fr. Chinese by* Waley.
One Hundred Poems from the Chinese (OnPC). Kenneth Rexroth, tr.
Poems of the Hundred Names (PoHN). Henry H. Hart, ed. and tr.
Translations from the Chinese (TrCh). Arthur Waley, tr.
White Pony, The (WhP). Robert Payne, ed.
CHINA, GREAT WALL OF. At the Great Wall of China. Blunden.
CHINAWARE
Ballade of Blue China. Lang.
On a Nankin Plate. Dobson.
To a Lady on Her Passion for Old China. Gay.
CHIPETA (wife of Ute chief Ouray)
Chipeta. Eugene Field.
Chipeta's Ride. J. W. Taylor.
CHIPMUNKS
Chipmunk. Welch.
Little Charlie Chipmunk. LeCron.
CHISHOLM TRAIL
Mesa Trail. Bard.
Old Chisholm Trail, The. *Unknown.*
CHOPIN, FRÉDÉRIC FRANÇOIS. Chopin Prelude. Norton.
CHRIST. *See* JESUS CHRIST.
CHRIST OF THE ANDES. Christ of the Andes, The. Markham.
CHRISTIAN X, KING OF DENMARK. To the King. Munk, *tr. fr. Danish by* Stork.
CHRISTMAS
Above the Stable. Duffy.
Al the Meryere. *Unknown.*
Alchemy. Love.
All You That in This House Be Here. *Unknown.*
"And Lo, the Star!" Haley.
Ane Sang of the Birth of Christ, with the Tune of Baw Lula Low. Luther, *tr. fr. German by* Wedderburn.
Angelic Chorus, The. D. J. Donahoe.
Angels, The. Drummond of Hawthornden.
As I Sat on a Sunny Bank. *Unknown.*
As Joseph Was a-Walking. *Unknown.*
At Christmastide. Simmons.
At Christmas Time. Clapp.
Awake! Glad Heart! Vaughan.
Babe of Bethlehem, The. Beer.
Babe of Bethlehem, The. Pallen.

Babushka; a Russian Legend. E. M. Thomas.
Barn, The. Coatsworth.
Before Dawn. De la Mare.
Before the Paling of the Stars. C. G. Rossetti.
Beggar's Rhyme. *Unknown.*
Bethlehem-Town. Eugene Field.
Birth, The. Marquis.
Brightest and Best of the Sons of the Morning. Heber.
Bundles. Farrar.
Burning Babe, The. Southwell.
Can I Not Sing. *Unknown.*
Carol, A: "Angels to the shepherds sang, The." Weatherly.
Carol, Bringing in the Boar's Head, A. *Unknown.*
Carol, Brothers, Carol. Muhlenberg.
Carol for Christmas Day, A. *Unknown.*
Carol for Christmas Day before Dawn, A. Bottomley.
Carol for His Darling on Christmas Day. Stanford.
Carol of the Poor Children, The. Middleton.
Carol Singers, The. Rhodes.
Catch by the Hearth, A. *Unknown.*
Ceremonies for Christmas ("Come, bring with a noise"). Herrick.
Cherry-Tree Carol, The. *Unknown.*
Childlike Heart. Catlin.
Children's Song of the Nativity. Frances Chesterton.
Child's Christmas Carol, A. Chaundler.
Child's Christmas Song. T. A. Daly.
Child's Song of Christmas, A. Pickthall.
Choir-Boys on Christmas Eve. Nicholl.
Christ Candle, The. K. L. Brown.
Christ Child, The. L. S. Portor.
Christ Child at Christmas, The. Drinkwater.
Christ-Child Lay on Mary's Lap, The. Chesterton.
Christ Was Born on Christmas Day. *At. to* Helmore.
Christmas. Avison.
Christmas. Bryant.
Christmas. Chute.
Christmas. George Herbert.
Christmas. Parmenter.
Christmas. Timrod.
Christmas. N. B. Turner.
Christmas. *Unknown.*
Christmas. Sir E. H. Young.
Christmas Amnesty. Pierce.
Christmas and Common Birth. Ridler.
Christmas and Ireland. Lionel Johnson.
Christmas Antiphon. Swinburne.
Christmas at Babbitt's. Tweedy.
Christmas at Sea. R. L. Stevenson.
Christmas Bells. George Cooper.
Christmas Bells. Longfellow.
Christmas Candle, The. K. L. Brown.
Christmas Carols. *See* Christmas Carol *in* Title and First Line Index.
Christmas Chant. Isabel Shaw.
Christmas Child, The. *Unknown, tr. fr. Spanish by* Clay.
Christmas Childhood, A. Kavanagh.
Christmas Cradlesong, A. Lope de Vega, *tr. fr. Spanish by* Ticknor.
Christmas Dawn at Sea. Evan Morgan.
Christmas Day. Sangster.
Christmas Day. *Fr.* Hymns and Spiritual Songs. Smart.
Christmas Day. Andrew Young.
Christmas Day in the Workhouse. Sims.
Christmas Day Is Come. Wadding.
Christmas Dusk. Nesbit.
Christmas, 1898. E. S. Martin.
Christmas Encyclical. Auslander.
Christmas Eve. Brockman.
Christmas Eve. Cole.
Christmas Eve. John Davidson.
Christmas Eve. Drinkwater.
Christmas Eve. Edey.
Christmas Eve. Eugene Field.
Christmas Eve. Parmenter.
Christmas Eve. Wallace.
Christmas Eve—Another Ceremony. Herrick.
Christmas Eve—Another to the Maids. Herrick.
Christmas Eve Choral, A. Carman.
Christmas Eve in France. Fauset.
Christmas Eve; Market Square. P. K. Page.
Christmas Everywhere. Phillips Brooks.
Christmas Folk-Song, A. Reese.
Christmas Greeting. *Unknown.*
Christmas Holly, The. Eliza Cook.
Christmas Husbandly Fare. Tusser.
Christmas Hymn. Domett.
Christmas Hymn, A. Gilder.
Christmas Hymn for Lambeth. Squire.
Christmas in Freelands. James Stephens.
Christmas in Provence. Sister Mary Madeleva.
Christmas in the Heart. *Unknown.*
Christmas in the North. Sangster.
Christmas in the Olden Time. *Fr.* Marmion. Scott.
Christmas in the Woods. Frances Frost.
Christmas Is Remembering. Binns.
Christmas Legend, A. Sidgwick.
Christmas Lullaby, A. Symonds.
Christmas Lullaby. Troubetzkoy.
Christmas Morning. Joaquin Miller.
Christmas Morning. E. M. Roberts.
Christmas Night. Lochhead.
Christmas Night. MacCawell, *tr. fr. Irish by* O'Connor.
Christmas Night. Alice Meynell.
Christmas Night in the Quarters. Irwin Russell.
Christmas Night of '62. McCabe.
Christmas, 1943. Bax.
Christmas, 1943. James Boyd.
Christmas 1942. Irvin.
Christmas, 1942. Nathan.
Christmas, 1917. B. D. Allinson.
Christmas, 1930. Scruggs.
Christmas of Long Ago, A. Wharton.
Christmas on Three Continents. Peter.
Christmas Party, A. Bailey.
Christmas Party, The. Adeline White.
Christmas Pastoral. Hillyer.
Christmas Peal, The. Spofford.
Christmas Prayer, A. Baugher.
Christmas Prayer, A. Haley.
Christmas Prayer, A. Hines.
Christmas Prayer. Macdonald.
Christmas Prayer. Morse.
Christmas Rede. Barlow.
Christmas Silence, The. Deland.
Christmas Singing. E. W. Chandler.
Christmas Song. Brayton.
Christmas Song. Carman.
Christmas Song. Eugene Field.
Christmas Song. E. E. Long.
Christmas Song, A. Wheeler.
Christmas Song for Three Guilds, A. Chesterton.
Christmas Sonnet, A. E. A. Robinson.
Christmas, the Year One, A.D. S. H. Hay.
Christmas Thought, A. Larcom.
Christmas Tree, The. Day Lewis.
Christmas Tree, The. Freeman.
Christmas Tree. Lebedev-Kumach, *tr. fr. Russian by* Lindsay.
Christmas Tree, The. Savitzsky.
Christmas Tree, The. Shillito.
Christmas Tree in the Nursery, The. Gilder.
Christmas-Tree Song, A. Rodney Bennett.
Christmas Trees, The. Butts.
Christmas Trees. Robert Frost.
Christmas Wish, A. Fyleman.
Christ's Nativity. Vaughan.
Come, Holy Babe! Bangham.
Come, Ride with Me to Toyland. Rowena Bennett.
Cradle Hymn: "Away in a manger, no crib for a bed." Luther, *tr. fr. German.*
Crossroads, The. Parmenter.
Dame, Get up and Bake Your Pies. *Unknown.*
David, Aged Four. *Unknown.*
Day Dawn of the Heart. *Unknown.*
Dogs of Bethlehem, The. K. L. Bates.
Earth Has Grown Old with Its Burden of Care, The. Phillips Brooks.
Earth Listens. K. L. Bates.
Eclogue for Christmas, An. MacNeice.
Eddi's Service. Kipling.
Eighth Street West. Rachel Field.
End of the Play, The. *Fr.* Dr. Birch and His Young Friends. Thackeray.
Epic, The. Tennyson.
Eternal Christmas. Phelps.
Everywhere, Everywhere Christmas Tonight. Phillips Brooks.
Falcon, The. *Unknown.*
Festum Nativitatis. De Vere.
First Christmas, The. St. Luke, Bible, *N.T.*
First Christmas, The. Poulsson.
First Christmas Night of All. N. B. Turner.
First Nowell, The. *Unknown.*
For Christmas. Rachel Field.
For Christmas Day. Farjeon.
For Christmas Day. Kinwelmarsh.
For Christmas Eve—a Prayer. *Unknown.*
Forgotten Star, The. T. C. Clark.
From Bethlehem Blown. Leitch.
From the Starry Heav'ns Descending. "Orpheus C. Kerr."
Gates and Doors. Joyce Kilmer.
Gift, The. Portor.
Glad Day. W. G. Robertson.
God Bless the Master of This House. *Unknown.*
God Rest You Merry, Gentlemen. *Unknown.*
God with Us. N. B. Turner.
Good King Wenceslaus. *Unknown, tr. fr. Latin by* Neale.

CHRISTMAS (*continued*)
Gracious Time, The. *Fr.* Hamlet. Shakespeare.
Green Yule, A. Murray.
Happy Christmases, *sels.* O'Donnell.
Hark! the Herald Angels Sing. Wesley.
Hayll, Comly and Clene. *Unknown.*
"He Is Our Peace." Haley.
Heart Is Bethlehem, The. Gertrude Hanson.
Here Have I Dwelt. *Unknown.*
Here We Come a-Caroling. *Unknown.*
Holly and the Ivy, The. *Unknown.*
Holy Night. N. A. Benson.
House of Christmas, The. Chesterton.
Humble Pomp. Southwell.
Hymn for Christmas. Hemans.
Hymn for Christmas Day. Byrom.
Hymn for Christmas Day, A. Chatterton.
Hymn of the Three Eastern Magi, The, Adoring Our Saviour at His Nativity. Rowe.
Hymne on the Nativitie of My Saviour, A. Jonson.
I Pray You, Be Merry and Sing with Me. *Unknown.*
I Saw Three Ships. *Unknown.*
I Will Keep Christmas. Ropes.
If. Bailey.
I'm Wishing the Whole World Christmas. Wynne.
In Dulci Jubilo. *Unknown, tr. fr. German by* Wedderburn.
In the Holy Nativity of Our Lord God a Hymn Sung as by the Shepheards. Crashaw.
In the Week When Christmas Comes. Farjeon.
Indignation Dinner, An. Corrothers.
Instead of Neat Inclosures. *Fr.* An Ode of the Birth of Our Saviour. Herrick.
It Came upon the Midnight Clear. Sears.
It Isn't Far to Bethlehem. Macdougall.
It Was Not Strange. Hagg.
Jesous Ahatonhia. J. E. Middleton, *after* Brébeuf.
Jest 'fore Christmas. Eugene Field.
Journey of the Magi. T. S. Eliot.
Kolendy for Christmas. *Unknown, tr. fr. Polish by* Dalgiewicz.
Lacking Samite and Sable. Probyn.
Land Grew Bright in a Single Flower, The. Sister Francisca Josefa del Castillo, *tr. fr. Spanish by* Walsh.
Laudate for Christmas. Prudentius, *tr. fr. Latin by* Henry.
Legend of Noël. Frances Frost.
Legend of the Christmas Rose, The. F. B. Davis.
Life. *Fr.* Christmas-Eve and Easter-Day. Robert Browning.
Light of Bethlehem, The. Tabb.
Little Christ Child. E. M. Fowler.
Little Christmas Tree, The. "Susan Coolidge."
Little Fir Tree, The. Rose.
Little Gottlieb. Cary.
Little Ones, The. W. H. Davies.
Long, Long Ago. *Unknown.*
Lord of the World, The. Studdert-Kennedy.
Lordings, Listen to Our Lay. *Unknown.*
"Los Pastores." Agnew.
Maid-Servant at the Inn, The. Dorothy Parker.
Make Me Merry Both More and Less. *Unknown.*
Mary's Baby. O'Sheel.
Masters, in This Hall. William Morris.
Meditation for Christmas, A. Image.
Merry Christmas and a Glad New Year, A. George Cooper.
Merry Christmas Time, The. George Arnold.
Miracle Dreams, The. Best.
More Sonnets at Christmas. Allen Tate.
My Gift. *Fr.* A Christmas Carol. C. G. Rossetti.
My Master. Harry Lee.
Nativity. Hayford
Nativity, The. L. P. Hopkins.
Nativity, The. E. M. Root.
Nativity Ode. St. Cosmas, *tr. fr. Greek by* Neale.
Nativity of Christ, The. Góngora, *tr. fr. Spanish by* Longfellow.
Nativity of Our Lord. Smart.
Nativity Song. Jacopone da Todi *ad. fr. Latin by* Jewett.
Neighbors of Bethlehem. *Unknown, tr. fr. French.*
New Prince, New Pompe. Southwell.
New Things and Old. Sister Mary Madeleva.
Night in the Far Judean Land. O'Reilly.
No Sweeter Thing. Love.
Noel. Belloc.
Noel. Burket.
Noel. Feeney.
Noël. Gilder.
Noel! *Unknown.*
Noel; Christmas Eve, 1913. Robert Bridges.
Noel! Noel! Laura Simmons.
Nor House nor Heart. Lennen.
Now Every Child. Farjeon.
Now Thrice Welcome, Christmas. *Unknown.*
Nowel. Gautier, *tr. fr. French by* Conder.
Nowell, Nowell. Robert Finch.
Nowell Sing We. *Unknown.*
O Come, All Ye Faithful. *Unknown, tr. fr. Latin by* Oakeley.
O Little Town of Bethlehem. Phillips Brooks.
O Years Unborn. Moreland
Ode on Christmas. Clinton.
Ode on the Birth of Our Saviour, An. Herrick.
Of a Rose, a Lovely Rose. *Unknown.*
Old Christmas. Howitt.
Old Christmas ("Those Christmas bells as sweetly chime"). *Unknown.*
Old Christmas Greeting, An. *Unknown.*
Old Christmastide. Sir Walter Scott.
Old Shepherds, The. Farjeon.
On Christmas Day. Paman.
On the Day after Christmas. F. P. Adams.
On the Morning of Christ's Nativity. Milton.
On the Nativity of Christ Our Lord. Joseph Bennett.
Once in Royal David's City. C. F. Alexander.
Our Christmas Hymn. J. D. Bruns.
Our Joyful Feast. Wither.
Outlanders, Whence Come Ye Last? William Morris.
Ox and Donkey's Carol. Sister Maris Stella.
Oxen, The. Hardy.
Peace on Earth. Marie Barton.
Perfect Gift, The. J. B. Parker.
Perpetual Christmas. A. G. Field.
Pilgrimage. Lennen.
Player's Christmas, The. Lackaye.
Poem for Christmas, A. Snodgrass.
Prayer: "Last night I crept across the snow." John Farrar.
Prayer at Christmas Time, A. N. B. Turner.
Prayer on Christmas Eve. N. B. Turner.
Psalm for Christmas Day. Pestell.
Quem Pastores Laudaverunt. *Unknown, tr. fr. Latin by* Hodge.
Riding of the Kings, The. Farjeon.
Romance of a Christmas Card, The. Wiggin.
Rorate Coeli Desuper. William Dunbar.
Second Shepherds' Play, The. *Unknown.*
Shepherd and the King, The. Farjeon.
Shepherd Speaks, The. Erskine.
Shepherds, The. Portor.
Shepherds' Hymn, The. Crashaw.
Shepherds Went Their Hasty Way, The. S. T. Coleridge.
Silent Night! Holy Night! Mohr, *tr. fr. German.*
Silver Bells. Hendry.
Since Christmas. McCreary.
Skeptic Christmas. Laforgue, *tr. fr. French by* Flores.
Sleep, Holy Babe. Caswall.
Snow at Christmas. Granlund, *tr. fr. Swedish by* Stork.
Song: "Why do bells for Christmas ring?" Eugene Field.
Song of the Wise Men. Pierce.
Sonnet for Christmas. V. G. Burns.
Sonnets at Christmas. Allen Tate.
Star, The. Munson.
Star of the East. Eugene Field.
Stars of Cheer. Swan.
Stay, Christmas! Eastwick.
Swedish Angel. W. T. Scott.
Tell Me What Is This Innumerable Throng. Gilder.
Ten Little Christmas Trees. Rodney Bennett.
There's a Song in the Air! Holland.
This day our Savior Christ was born. *Unknown.*
Through the Ages. Hope.
Tidings of Great Joy. St. Luke, Bible, *N.T.*
Time draws near the birth of Christ, The. *Fr.* In Memoriam. Tennyson.
Tis Christmas now, 'tis Christmas now. *Unknown.*
To Jesus on His Birthday. Millay.
Today in Bethlehem Hear I. St. John of Damascus, *tr. fr. Greek.*
Trumpet for Yuletide. Sanker.
Tryste Noel. Guiney.
Twelve Days of Christmas, The. *Unknown.*
Two Christmas Cards, *sel.* ("For an hour on Christmas eve"). Jeffers.
Two Inscriptions for the Christmas Candle. Branch.
Under the Holly Bough. Mackay.
Unto Us a Son Is Given. Alice Meynell.
Visit from St. Nicholas, A. Moore.
Wait's Carol: "Give ye good-den." Young.
Wassail Chorus at the Mermaid Tavern. Watts-Dunton.
We Have Seen His Star in the East. Haley.
What Child Is This? Dix.
What Sweeter Music Can We Bring. Herrick.
What the Christmas Tree Thinks. M. C. Davies.
When Christ was born in Bethlehem. *Unknown, tr. fr. Italian.*
When Christ Was Born of Mary Free. *Unknown.*
When the Herds Were Watching. Canton.
While Shepherds Watched Their Flocks by Night. Nahum Tate.
White Christmas. Rodgers.
Why Do the Bells of Christmas Ring? Eugene Field.

Widow Brown's Christmas. Trowbridge.
Words from an Old Spanish Carol. *Unknown, tr. fr. Spanish by* Sawyer.
Yule Days, The. *Unknown.*
Yule Log, The. Hayne.
Yuletide. Furlong.
Yule-Tide Fires. *Unknown.*
Ancient English Christmas Carols (AnEC). Edith Rickert, ed.
Beautiful Poems on Jesus (BePJ). Basil Miller, comp.
Christmas (Our American Holidays Series) (COAH). Robert Haven Schauffler, ed.
Christmas Bells Are Ringing (ChBR). Sara Brewton *and* John E. Brewton, eds.
Christmas Book of Legends and Stories, The (ChrBoLe). Elva Sophronia Smith *and* Alice Isabel Hazeltine, eds.
Christmas in Legend and Story (CLS). Elva S. Smith *and* Alice I. Hazeltine, eds.
Stardust and Holly (SDH). Dorothy Middlebrook Shipman, comp.
Story of Jesus in the World's Literature, The (StJW). Edward Wagenknecht, ed.
Yale Carol Book, The (YaCaBo). H. Frank Bozyan *and* Sidney Lovett, eds.
See also SANTA CLAUS.
CHRISTOPHER, SAINT. St. Christopher of the Gael. "Fiona Macleod."
CHRYSANTHEMUMS
Chrysanthemums. M. M. Dodge.
Chrysanthemums in the Eastern Garden, The. Po Chü-i, *tr. fr. Chinese by* Waley.
Last Chrysanthemum, The. Hardy.
Shadows of Chrysanthemums. Scovell.
CHURCH OF ENGLAND. *See* ENGLAND, CHURCH OF.
CHURCHES
At Church Next Sunday. *Unknown.*
Auld Kirk o' Scotland, The. George Murray.
Cathedral in Trondheim, The. Thorarensen, *tr. fr. Icelandic by* Kirkconnell.
Cathedral of Rheims, The. Rostand, *tr. fr. French by* Walsh.
Cathedral of Rheims, The. Verhaeren, *tr. fr. French by* Kilmer.
Childhood Church, The. Pat Wilson.
Church, The. E. F. Piper.
Church Going. Larkin.
Church Today, The. Sir William Watson.
Church Universal, The. Longfellow.
Churches. *Unknown.*
Churches of Rome and of England, The. *Fr.* The Hind and the Panther. Dryden.
City Church, The. "E. H. K."
Country Church. Coffin.
Country Church, A. Pearce Young.
Country Churches. M. T. Klein.
How Amiable Are Thy Tabernacles! Bryant.
How We Built a Church at Ashcroft. Leahy.
I Am a Little Church (No Great Cathedral). Cummings.
I Love Thy Kingdom, Lord. Dwight.
In a Church of Padua. Melville.
Little Brown Church in the Vale, The. Pitts.
Mightier Church, A. H. B. Carpenter.
Morwennae Statio. Hawker.
My Church ("My church has but one temple"). "E. O. G."
My Church ("On me nor Priest nor Presbyter nor Pope"). *Unknown.*
New England Church, A. W. A. Barrett.
New England Gothic. Rachel Field.
New England Steeple. Frances Frost.
Old St. David's at Radnor. Longfellow.
Parish Church, The. Herrera y Reissig, *tr. fr. Spanish by* Walsh.
Places of Worship. Wordsworth.
Prayer in a Country Church. Van Dusen.
Russian Cathedral. McKay.
St. Saviour's, Aberdeen Park, Highbury, London, N. Betjeman.
Sunday Afternoon Service in St. Enodoc Church, Cornwall. Betjeman.
When the Church Is No Longer Regarded. *Fr.* The Rock. T. S. Eliot.
CHURCHILL, WINSTON LEONARD SPENCER
Homage to Our Leaders. Julian Symons.
"Spoken Word, The." Morley.
CIBOLA. Seventh City of Cibola, The. H. N. Pratt.
CICADAS
All Night the Lone Cicada. C. G. D. Roberts.
Cicada, A. Meleager, *tr. fr. Greek by* Headlam.
Cicada, The. Ou-yang Hsiu, *tr. fr. Chinese by* Waley.
Cicada. *Unknown, tr. fr. Greek.*
Cicadas, The. Huxley.
Cicadas. Wilbur.
CICERO (Marcus Tullius Cicero)
Marcus Tullius Cicero's Death. Grimald.
Of all the sons of Romulus who walk the earth. Catullus, *tr. fr. Latin by* Gregory.
CID *or* CID CAMPEADOR
Bavieca. *Unknown, tr. fr. Spanish by* Lockhart.
Cid, The, *sels. Unknown, tr. fr. Spanish by* Rose *and* Bacon.
Cid and the Five Moorish Kings, The. *Unknown, tr. fr. Spanish by* Lockhart.
Cid's Rising, The. Hemans.
CIGARETTES. Blind, I Speak to the Cigarette. De Longchamps.
CINCINNATI, OHIO. Whiffs of the Ohio River at Cincinnati. Sandburg.
CINDERELLA
Cinderella's Song. E. M. Roberts.
Coach. Farjeon.
CINQUE PORTS. Cinque Port, A. Davidson.
CINTRA, PORTUGAL. On Revisiting Cintra after the Death of Catarina. Camões, *tr. fr. Portuguese by* Garnett.
CIRCE
Circe. De Tabley.
Circe. *Fr.* The Odyssey. Homer, *tr. fr. Greek.*
Circe. Kreymborg.
Circe. MacNeice.
Circe Remembers. Sherman Conrad.
Circe's Palace. T. S. Eliot.
For the Wine of Circe; a Picture by Edward Burne-Jones. D. G. Rossetti.
CIRCUS
At the Circus. Aldis.
Circus, The. F. S. Davis.
Circus, The. Milton Kaplan.
Circus, The. E. M. Roberts.
Circus Garland, A, *sels.* Rachel Field.
Circus Parade, The. O. P. Miller.
Circus Parade. Tippett.
Cirque d'Hiver. Elizabeth Bishop.
Our Circus. L. L. Randall.
When I Went to the Circus. D. H. Lawrence.
CITIES
Beleaguered Cities. F. L. Lucas.
Broadway's Canyon. J. G. Fletcher.
Cities. Rimbaud, *tr. fr. French by* Morgan.
City. Langston Hughes.
City-Life. D. H. Lawrence.
City Lights. K. W. Baker.
City Lights. Rachel Field.
For, Lord, the Crowded Cities Be. Rilke, *tr. fr. German by* Lewisohn.
From the Country to the City. Elizabeth Bishop.
In the Busy Streets, Domains of Trade. Thoreau.
Master City, The. Orente.
Mockery. Louis Untermeyer.
Native Son. Gertrude Callaghan.
Noise of the Cabarets, The. Verlaine, *tr. fr. French by* Flores.
Purse-Seine, The. Jeffers.
Rudolph Is Tired of the City. Gwendolyn Brooks.
Unwilling Guest, The; an Urban Dialogue. Horace Gregory.
Up at a Villa—Down in the City. Robert Browning.
Urban History. Kallman.
Waving of the Corn, The. Lanier.
Winter Evening, The. *Fr.* The Task. Cowper.
CIVIL WAR, AMERICAN
Abraham's Daughter. Winner.
All Quiet along the Potomac. Beers.
Apocalypse. Realf.
Army Corps on the March, An. Whitman.
Army Correspondent's Last Ride. Townsend.
Army of the Potomac, *abr.* Joaquin Miller.
As Toilsome I Wander'd Virginia's Woods. Whitman.
Ashes of Soldiers. Whitman.
At Fredericksburg—December 13, 1862. O'Reilly.
At Magnolia Cemetery. Timrod.
Ball's Bluff. Melville.
Barbara Frietchie. Whittier.
Battle Autumn of 1862, The. Whittier.
Battle-Hymn of the Republic. J. W. Howe.
Bay Fight, The. Brownell.
Beauregard. Warfield.
Bivouac on a Mountain Side. Whitman.
Black Regiment, The. Boker.
Blue and the Gray, The. Finch.
Brother Jonathan's Lament for Sister Caroline. Holmes.
By the Bivouac's Fitful Flame. Whitman.
Capt. Sally Tompkins, C.S.A. Tucker.
Cavalry Crossing a Ford. Whitman.
Charleston. Timrod.
Civil War. Mark Van Doren.
Cleburne. *Unknown.*
Come Up from the Fields Father. Whitman.
Cumberland, The. Longfellow.
Death the Peacemaker. E. H. Flagg.

CIVIL WAR, AMERICAN (*continued*)
Dixie. Emmett.
Dying Soldier, The. *Unknown.*
Eagle and Vulture, The. T. B. Read.
Eagle's Song, The. Richard Mansfield.
Eighteen Sixty-one. Whitman.
1861–1865. *Fr.* For Decoration Day. Rupert Hughes.
Ethnogenesis. Timrod.
Farragut. W. T. Meredith.
First O Songs for a Prelude. Whitman.
From Potomac to Merrimac. E. E. Hale.
Garfield's Ride at Chickamauga. Butterworth.
Grant at Appomattox. Claytor.
High Tide at Gettysburg, The. W. H. Thompson.
John Brown's Body, *sels.* S. V. Benét.
Joined the Blues. Rooney.
Jonathan to John. *Fr.* The Biglow Papers. J. R. Lowell.
Keenan's Charge. G. P. Lathrop.
Kentucky Belle. Woolson.
Last Charge at Appomattox, The. Stockard.
Last Fierce Charge, The. *Unknown.*
Lee in the Mountains. Donald Davidson.
Lincoln. Schwartz.
Little Giffen. Ticknor.
Long, Too Long America. Whitman.
Malvern Hill. Melville.
Manassas. Warfield.
March in the Ranks Hard-prest and the Road Unknown, A. Whitman.
March into Virginia, The. Melville.
Memorials on the Slain at Chickamauga. Melville.
Men of the North and West. Stoddard.
Misgivings. Melville.
Mosby at Hamilton. Cawein.
Mumford. I. M. Porter.
Nameless Grave, A. Longfellow.
Nineteenth of April (1861), The. Larcom.
Not the Pilot. Whitman.
Ode Recited at the Harvard Commemoration, July 21, 1865. J. R. Lowell.
Ode to the Confederate Dead. Allen Tate.
On the Home Guards. Melville.
On to Richmond. J. R. Thompson.
Our Country's Call. Bryant.
Picket-Guard, The. Beers, *sometimes at. to* Fontaine.
Portent, The. Melville.
Rebel, The. Randolph.
Rebel Soldier, The. *Unknown.*
Reveillé, The. Harte.
River-Fight, The. Brownell.
Romance. Henley.
Run from Manassas Junction, The. *Unknown.*
Running the Batteries. Melville.
Shenandoah. Sandburg.
Sheridan's Ride. T. B. Read.
Shiloh. Melville.
Sight in Camp, A. Whitman.
Spirit Whose Work Is Done. Whitman.
Stonewall Jackson's Way. J. W. Palmer.
Sumter. Brownell.
Surrender at Appomattox, The. Melville.
Three Hundred Thousand More. Gibbons.
Through Baltimore. Bayard Taylor.
Uninscribed Monument on One of the Battle-Fields of the Wilderness, An. Melville.
Unknown Dead, The. Timrod.
Unsung Heroes, The. P. L. Dunbar.
Upon the Hill before Centreville. Boker.
Varuna, The. Boker.
Vicksburg; a Ballad. Hayne.
Victor of Antietam, The. Melville.
Vigil Strange I Kept on the Field One Night. Whitman.
When Johnny Comes Marching Home. Gilmore.
With Corse at Allatoona. Byers.
Wound-Dresser, The. Whitman.
Year of Jubilo, The. Work.
Year That Trembled and Reel'd Beneath Me. Whitman.
Zagonyi. Boker.
Zollicoffer. Flash.
Blue and the Gray, The (BlG). Claudius Meade Capps, ed.
CIVIL WAR, SPANISH
Ballad of the Spanish Civil Guard. Garcia Lorca, *tr. fr. Spanish by* Kemp.
Banished, The. Serrano Plaja, *tr. fr. Spanish by* Humphries.
Battle Hymn of the Spanish Republic. L. A. Mackay.
Bombing Casualties in Spain. Read.
International Brigade Arrives at Madrid, The. "Pablo Neruda," *tr. fr. Spanish by* Flores.
Little Responsory for a Republican Hero. Vallejo, *tr. fr. Spanish by* Hays.
Look, the Soldiers! Ramos, *tr. fr. Spanish by* Rukeyser.
November 7; Ode to a Day of Victories. "Pablo Neruda," *tr. fr. Spanish by* Fitts.
Ode of the Sun to the People's Army. "Pablo Neruda," *tr. fr. Spanish by* Hays.
Pedro Rojas. Vallejo, *tr. fr. Spanish by* Hays.
Spain 1937. Auden.
To a Spanish Poet. Spender.
To the International Brigade. Alberti, *tr. fr. Spanish by* Chapin.
To the Veterans of the Abraham Lincoln Brigade. Taggard.
Two Armies. Spender.
CLAMS
Covering the Subject. Armour.
Mess of Clams, A. Coffin.
CLARE, SAINT
Epitaph: "Here lies the ideal of Saint Francis." Sister Mary Francis.
Genealogy. Sister Mary Francis.
St. Clare Hears St. Francis. Cleghorn.
September 17. Sister M. Margaret Patricia.
CLARE ISLAND, IRELAND. Clare Coast. Emily Lawless.
CLARKE, CHARLES COWDEN. Epistle: To Charles Cowden Clarke. Keats.
CLASS STRUGGLE
Thirty Bob a Week. Davidson.
Tunnel, The. *Fr.* The Bridge. Hart Crane.
CLAY, HENRY. On the Defeat of Henry Clay. Lord.
CLEBURNE, PATRICK RONAYNE. Cleburne. *Unknown.*
CLEMENS, SAMUEL LANGHORNE. *See* "TWAIN, MARK."
CLEOPATRA
Antony and Cleopatra. Heredia, *tr. fr. French.*
Antony and Cleopatra, *sels.* Shakespeare.
Antony to Cleopatra. Lytle.
Cleopatra. *Fr.* All for Love. Dryden.
Cleopatra. Samain, *tr. fr. French by* Flint.
Cleopatra. Story.
Cleopatra. Swinburne.
Cleopatra and Antony. *Fr.* All for Love. Dryden.
Cleopatra Dying. T. S. Collier.
Cleopatra Embarking on the Cydnus. T. K. Hervey.
Dead Cleopatra Lies in a Crystal Casket. *Fr.* Discordants. Aiken.
Death of Cleopatra, The. *Fr.* Odes. Horace, *tr. fr. Latin.*
In Praise of a Gentlewoman Who, though She Were Not Very Fair, Yet Was She as Hard-favored as Might Be. Gascoigne.
Mark Antony. John Cleveland.
CLERGY
Aaron. George Herbert.
Amorous Temper, An. *Fr.* The Progress of Dullness. Trumbull.
Ballad of Father Gilligan, The. Yeats.
Bishop Orders His Tomb at Saint Praxed's Church, The. Robert Browning.
Blind Preacher, The. Polonsky, *tr. fr. Russian by* Phillimore.
Clerical Oppressors. Whittier.
Colin Clout, *sels.* John Skelton.
Collar, The. George Herbert.
Curé's Progress. Dobson.
Father Mat. Kavanagh.
High Priest, The. *Unknown, tr. fr. Hebrew by* Davis.
Of Clergymen and Their Livings. Harington.
On a Curate's Complaint of Hard Duty. Swift.
On Clergymen Preaching Politics. Byrom.
Parson, The. *Fr.* The Canterbury Tales: Prologue. Chaucer.
Portrait of a Vicar. *Fr.* The Borough. Crabbe.
Prayer for a Priest. *Unknown.*
Preachment for Preachers. *Fr.* The Ship of Fools. Barclay.
Priest, A. Norman Gale.
Priest and Pagan. A. D. Watson.
Priest Is Come and the Candles Burn, The. Moreland.
Priest or Poet. Leslie.
Priesthood, The. Yvor Winters.
Priests and Soldiers, The. *Unknown.*
Priests and the Friars, The. *Unknown, tr. fr. Irish by* Hyde.
Priest's Lament, The. R. H. Benson.
Priest's Prayer, A. Bianchi.
Problem, The. Emerson.
Prosopopoia; or, Mother Hubberd's Tale. Spenser.
Rival Curates, The. W. S. Gilbert.
Servants of the Great Adventure. Dearmer.
Smooth Divine, The. Dwight.
This Side of Calvin. McGinley.
To a Young Priest. Payne.
Tom Brainless as Student and Preacher. *Fr.* The Progress of Dulness. Trumbull.
True Preacher, The. *Fr.* The Task. Cowper.
Two Red Towers, The. Po Chü-i, *tr. fr. Chinese by* Waley.
Unfrocked Priest, The. Joseph Campbell.
Vicar, The. *Fr.* Every-Day Characters. Praed.
Village Preacher, The. *Fr.* The Deserted Village. Goldsmith.
CLEVEDON, ENGLAND. Clevedon Church. Lang.

Cleveland, Grover
Cleveland. W. G. Brown.
Grover Cleveland. Joel Benton.
Cliff dwellers
Cliff Dwelling, The. A. W. Monroe.
Homes of the Cliff Dwellers. Wood.
Clifton, England
Clifton. T. E. Brown.
Clifton Chapel. Newbolt.
Clinton, Sir Henry
On Sir Henry Clinton's Recall. *Unknown.*
Sir Henry Clinton's Invitation to the Refugees. Freneau.
Clive, Robert. Clive. Bentley.
Clocks
Clock. Monro.
Clock and Dial, The. Allan Ramsay.
Clock Shop, The. Shirk.
Clocks. Louis Ginsberg.
Clocks. Sandburg.
Clock's Song, The. R. H. Lathrop.
Cuckoo Clock, The. John Farrar.
Eight-Day Clock, The. Cochrane.
Grandfather's Clock. Work.
Kitchen Clock, The. Cheney.
Old Clock, The. J. C. McNeill.
Old Clock on the Stairs, The. Longfellow.
Old Kitchen Clock, The. Hawkshaw.
Our Clock. Eakman.
Sad Tale of Mr. Mears, The. *Unknown.*
Song for a Little Cuckoo Clock. Coatsworth.
Ticking Clocks. Rachel Field.
Cloisters, the (New York city). Cloisters, The. Yellen.
Clonmacnoise, Ireland
Dead at Clonmacnois, The. O'Gillan, *tr. fr. Middle Irish by* Rolleston.
End of Clonmacnois, The. *Unknown, tr. fr. Irish by* O'Connor.
Clonmel, Ireland. In Clonmel Parish Churchyard. Piatt.
Clothing
Beau's Receipt for a Lady's Dress, The. *Unknown.*
Braid Claith. Robert Fergusson.
Delight in Disorder. Herrick.
First Aid. Hopegood.
Lady's Receipt for a Beau's Dress, The. *Unknown.*
New Vestments, The. Lear.
Simplex Munditiis. Jonson.
Think of Dress in Every Light. *Fr.* Achilles. Gay.
Upon Julia's Clothes. Herrick.
"Vanity, Saith the Preacher." Peabody.
Clouds
Among the Millet. Lampman.
Cloud, The. Herford.
Cloud, The. Pushkin, *tr. fr. Russian by* Bowra.
Cloud, The. Shelley.
Cloud, The. Teasdale.
Cloud Country. James Merrill.
Clouds. Angell.
Clouds. Ault.
Clouds. Rupert Brooke.
Clouds. J. J. Chapman.
Clouds, The. Croswell.
Clouds. W. H. Davies.
Clouds. F. E. Hill.
Clouds. Percival.
Clouds. F. D. Sherman.
Clouds. *Unknown, wr. at. to* C. G. Rossetti.
Clouds. Wing.
Clouds and Sky. Pollard.
Clouds Have Left the Sky, The. Robert Bridges.
Clouds Have Wings, The. Gerald Gould.
Clouds That Are So Light, The. Edward Thomas.
Evening Cloud, The. "Christopher North."
Evening Clouds. Ledwidge.
Low-anchored Cloud. Thoreau.
Night Clouds. Amy Lowell.
Rain Clouds. Long.
Song of the Clouds. *Fr.* The Clouds. Aristophanes, *tr. fr. Greek.*
Summer Sky. R. M. Gordon.
Watching Clouds. John Farrar.
When clouds appear like rocks and towers. *Unknown.*
When the Cloud Comes down the Mountain. C. G. D. Roberts.
Clough, Arthur Hugh
Thyrsis. Matthew Arnold.
To a Republican Friend, 1848. Matthew Arnold.
Clover
Clover, The. Deland.
Clover. Rode, *tr. fr. Danish by* Stork.
Clover. Tabb.
Four-Leaf-Clover. Higginson.
Four-Leaf Clover, The. Shannon.
Song of Clover, A. H. H. Jackson.
There is a flower that bees prefer. Emily Dickinson.
Weed Month. *Fr.* The Land. Sackville-West.
Clowns
Chastised Clown, The. Mallarmé, *tr. fr. French by* Flores.
Circus Clown, The. John Ferguson.
Clown, The. Anthias, *tr. fr. Modern Greek by* Dalven.
Clown, The. Bruner.
Clown, The. Redpath.
Clown's Baby, The. "Margaret Vandegrift."
Dusk. Apollinaire, *tr. fr. French by* Fitts.
Quoth John to Joan. *Unknown.*
Clyde, Firth of. Mother's Malison, The; or, Clyde's Waters. *Unknown.*
Coal. Coal. Rowe.
Coast Guard. Coast-Guard, The. E. H. Miller.
Cobbett, William. Elegy on William Cobbett. Ebenezer Elliott.
Cobblers
Cobbler. Peggy Bacon.
Cobbler, The. *Unknown.*
Cobbler in Willow Street, The. O'Neil.
Shoe-Maker, The. *Unknown.*
Shoemakers, The. *Fr.* Songs of Labor. Whittier.
Shoemaker's Holiday, The, *sel.* ("Cold's the wind, and wet's the rain"). Dekker.
Cobequid Bay, Nova Scotia. By Cobequid Bay. A. L. Fraser.
Cobras
Lower Animals. Alan Anderson.
To a Pet Cobra. Roy Campbell.
Cobwebs
Cobweb. Welles.
Cobwebs. *Unknown.*
Cochiti, New Mexico. Dance for Rain, A. Bynner.
Cockaigne, land of
Cokaygne. *Unknown.*
Cockayne Country. A. M. F. Robinson.
Cockatoos. Red Cockatoo, The. Po Chü-i, *tr. fr. Chinese by* Waley.
Cockermouth, England. In Sight of the Town of Cockermouth, Where the Author Was Born, and His Father's Remains Are Laid. Wordsworth.
Cockfighting. Cock-Fight, The. Ts'ao Chih, *tr. fr. Chinese by* Waley.
Cockroaches
Ballade of the Under Side. Marquis.
Nursery Rhyme for the Tender-hearted. Morley.
To a Humble Bug. Van Voorhis.
Cocks
Chanticleer. John Farrar.
Chanticleer. Thaxter.
Chanticleer. Tynan.
Cock, The. Farjeon.
Cock, The. Fyleman.
Cock and Hens. Follen.
Cock-Crow. A. H. Evans.
I Have a Gentil Cok. *Unknown.*
Nun's Priest's Tale, The. *Fr.* The Canterbury Tales. Chaucer.
Roosters. Elizabeth Bishop.
To Be or Not to Be. *Unknown.*
White Rooster, The. O'Neil.
Cocoa. In Praise of Cocoa, Cupid's Nightcap. Sharpless.
Coconuts. Coconut, The. "Ande."
Cody, William Frederick. *See* Buffalo Bill.
Cold
Cold. Robert Francis.
Cold. Parton.
Twenty Below. R. A. D. Ford.
Cole, Thomas. To Cole, the Painter, Departing for Europe. Bryant.
Coleridge, Hartley. To H. C. Wordsworth.
Coleridge, Samuel Taylor
Coleridge. De Vere.
Coleridge. Hellman.
Coleridge. Watts-Dunton.
Epitaph: "Stop, Christian passer-by!—Stop, child of God." Coleridge.
On the Late S. T. Coleridge. Allston.
S. T. Coleridge Dismisses a Caller from Porlock. G. P. Meyer.
Samuel Taylor Coleridge. *Fr.* Five English Poets. D. G. Rossetti.
To S.T.C. on His 179th Birthday, October 12th, 1951. Maurice Carpenter.
Coliseum. *See* Colosseum.
Colleges
Alma Mater, Forget Me. William Cole.
University. Shapiro.
Views of the Favorite Colleges. Brinnin.
Collies. Collies, The. Edward Anthony.
Collins, Michael. Tomb of Michael Collins, The. Devlin.
Collins, William. Remembrance of Collins. Wordsworth.
Cologne, Germany
Cologne. Bate.

COLOGNE, GERMANY *(continued)*
Cologne Cathedral. Frances Shaw.
On My Joyful Departure from the City of Cologne. S. T. Coleridge.
COLONNA, VITTORIA. To Vittoria Colonna. Michelangelo, *tr. fr. Italian by* Longfellow.
COLORADO (state)
Colorado. Dillenback.
Land Where the Columbines Grow. Fynn.
To the Colorado Desert. M. M. Wagner.
COLORADO (river)
Chant of the Colorado, The. C. Y. Rice.
Rivers of the West. "Sunset Joe."
Song of the Colorado, The. S. M. Hall.
COLOSSEUM
Coliseum, The ("Arches on arches"). *Fr.* Childe Harold's Pilgrimage. Byron.
Coliseum, The ("Stars are forth, The"). *Fr.* Manfred; a Dramatic Poem. Byron.
Coliseum, The. Poe.
Colosseum. Norse.
Vespasian's Circus. O'Hara.
COLUMBA, SAINT. *See* COLUMCILLE, SAINT.
COLUMBINES
Colombine. McCrae.
Columbines. Guiterman.
To the Painted Columbine. Very.
COLUMBUS, CHRISTOPHER
Ave Maria. *Fr.* The Bridge. Hart Crane.
Boy Columbus, The. *Unknown.*
Caravels of Columbus, The. Lieberman.
Christopher Columbus. F. P. Adams.
Christopher Columbus. Rosemary *and* S. V. Benét.
Christopher Columbus. Wynne.
Columbian Ode. P. L. Dunbar.
Columbus. Clough.
Columbus. Coates.
Columbus. Delavigne, *tr. fr. French by* Conder.
Columbus. Going.
Columbus. E. E. Hale.
Columbus. Hutchison.
Columbus. L. F. Jackson.
Columbus. J. R. Lowell.
Columbus. Joaquin Miller.
Columbus. *Fr.* The West Indies. James Montgomery.
Columbus. Sigourney.
Columbus. H. L. Smith.
Columbus. Wynne.
Columbus and the *Mayflower.* Milnes.
Columbus at the Convent. Trowbridge.
Columbus Day. Tennyson.
Columbus Dying. E. D. Proctor.
Columbus Goes West. Hart-Smith.
Columbus in Chains. Freneau.
Columbus Never Knew. Burket.
Columbus the World-Giver. Egan.
Columbus to Ferdinand. Freneau.
Dark-eyed Lad Columbus. N. B. Turner.
Discoverer, The. A. G. Field.
Discovery, The. Squire.
Final Struggle, The. *Fr.* The New World. Block.
Homage to Columbus. Horace Gregory.
Immortal Morn. Butterworth.
Light in the Darkness. Aileen Fisher.
Mysterious Biography. Sandburg.
On a Portrait of Columbus. Woodberry.
Palos, Spain, 1492. Annette Wynne.
Passage to India. Whitman.
Prayer of Columbus, The. Whitman.
Psalm of the West, *sels.* Lanier.
Space. Hart-Smith.
Thanksgiving for America, The. Butterworth.
There Was an Indian. Squire.
To Columbus. J. G. Fletcher.
COLUMCILLE, SAINT
Blessing of Columcille, The. *Fr.* Sonnets of the Saints. T. S. Jones, Jr.
Columcille the Scribe. *At. to* Saint Columcille, *tr. fr. Middle Irish by* Meyer.
Cross of the Dumb, The. "Fiona Macleod."
St. Columcille's Island Hermitage. *Unknown, tr. fr. Middle Irish by* Jackson.
COMETS
Comet. Fullerton.
Comet, The. Sangster.
COMMENCEMENT
At Graduating Time. *Unknown.*
Commencement. Sangster.
Graduating Class, The. Tietjens.
Invocation: "Help me to make this working day." F. F. Miller.
Parody, A: "Farewell! A long farewell to all our school days!" Painton.
Ruth Goes By. Muth.
There Is No Dream. Sangster.
Graduation Day (Our American Holidays Series) (GDAH). A. P. Sanford *and* Robert Haven Schauffler, eds.
COMMUNISM
Communism? *Fr.* The Ecclesiazusae. Aristophanes, *tr. fr. Greek by* Rogers.
Dostoievsky to a Young Communist. Honan.
H——y P——tt. *Unknown.*
Wandering Rats, The. Heine, *tr. fr. German by* Issawi.
COMOX, VANCOUVER ISLAND, CANADA. Lairdless Place, The. K. R. Archer.
CONCENTRATION CAMPS
Camp in the Prussian Forest. Jarrell.
Cradle Song: "Sleep, my child, my little daughter." *Unknown, tr. fr. Yiddish by* Leftwich.
From Tomorrow On. *Unknown, tr. fr. Yiddish by* Leftwich.
Funeral, The. "M. J.," *tr. fr. Polish by* Glanz-Leyeless.
Memento. Spender.
Shipment to Maidanek. Fogel.
CONCORD, MASSACHUSETTS
Concord Hymn. Emerson.
Emerson; Last Days at Concord. Horace Gregory.
CONDORS. Condor's Sleep, The. Leconte de Lisle, *tr. fr. French by* Conder.
CONEMAUGH (river), PENNSYLVANIA
By the Conemaugh. Coates.
Conemaugh. Phelps.
CONFEDERACY
At Magnolia Cemetery. Timrod.
Bonnie Blue Flag, The. Ketchum.
Confederacy, The. J. T. H. Cross.
Conquered Banner, The. A. J. Ryan.
Heroes of the South. Hayne.
Lines on the Back of a Confederate Note. Jonas.
Ode to the Confederate Dead. Allen Tate.
Resurgam. M. B. Clarke.
Southern Republic, The. Olivia Thomas.
We Conquer or Die. Pierpont.
CONFEDERATE CRUISERS. Eagle and Vulture, The. T. B. Read.
CONFUCIANISM. Wilderness. Tanaka, *tr. fr. Japanese by* Ninomiya *and* Enright.
CONGREVE, WILLIAM. To My Dear Friend, Mr. Congreve, on His Comedy Call'd "The Double-Dealer." Dryden.
CONNAUGHT, IRELAND. Vision of Connaught in the Thirteenth Century, A. Mangan.
CONNECTICUT (state)
Connecticut Road Song. Branch.
Connecticut Trilogy. Leila Jones.
State We Honor, The. F. J. Crosby.
CONNECTICUT RIVER. To the Connecticut River. Brainard.
CONNOLLY, JAMES. Connolly. MacGowan.
CONQUISTADORS
Bernal Diaz' Preface to His Book. MacLeish.
Conquistador. Coatsworth.
CONSCIENTIOUS OBJECTORS. *See* PACIFISM AND PACIFISTS.
CONSTANTINE I (Constantine the Great). Constantine's Vision of the Cross. *Fr.* Elene. Cynewulf, *tr fr. Anglo-Saxon by* Kennedy.
CONSTANTINOPLE, TURKEY. Fall of Constantinople, The. *Unknown, tr. fr. Modern Greek by* Dalven.
CONSTELLATION (ship). *Constellation* and the *Insurgente,* The. *Unknown.*
CONSTITUTION (ship)
Constitution and the *Guerrière,* The. *Unknown.*
Constitution's Last Fight, The. Roche.
Old Ironsides. Holmes.
CONTENTMENT
Ah, sweet content, where is thy mild abode? *Fr.* Parthenophil and Parthenophe. Barnabe Barnes.
Art thou poor, yet hast thou golden slumbers? *Fr.* The Pleasant Comedy of Patient Grissell. Dekker *and others.*
Careless Content. Byrom.
Character of a Happy Life. Wotton.
Cheerfulness Taught by Reason. E. B. Browning.
Content. Campion.
Content. *Fr.* The Black Riders. Stephen Crane.
Content. Earl of Essex.
Content. Norman Gale.
Content. *Fr.* Farewell to Folly. Greene.
Content and Rich. Southwell.
Contented at Forty. Cleghorn.
Contented Mind, A. Sylvester.
Contented wi' Little. Burns.
Contentment. Al-Tutili, *tr. fr. Arabic by* Arberry.
Contentment. Calverley.
Contentment. Cowper.
Contentment. *Fr.* The Autocrat of the Breakfast Table. Holmes.
Contentment. Magny, *tr. fr. French by* Conder.
Contentment. Sadi, *tr. fr. Persian by* Costello.
Contentment. Schlipf.
Contentment; or, the Happy Workman's Song. Byrom.

Coridon's Song. Chalkhill.
Cottager, The, *sel.* ("True as the church clock"). Clare.
Ease. Po Chü-i, *tr. fr. Chinese by* Waley.
Fain Would I Live in Safest Freedom. Platen, *tr. fr. German by* Morgan.
Golden Mean, The. *Fr.* Odes. Horace, *tr. fr. Latin by* Sidney.
Golden Mean, The. Earl of Surrey.
Hermit and the King, The. *Unknown, tr. fr. Old Irish by* O'Faoláin.
His Content in the Country. Herrick.
His Grange, or Private Wealth. Herrick.
Hymn to Contentment, A. Thomas Parnell.
If Thou Desire. Hunnis.
Man of Life Upright, The. Campion.
Means to Attain a Happy Life. Martial, *tr. fr. Latin by* Surrey.
Merry Heart, The. Milman.
My Mind to Me a Kingdom Is. Dyer.
Oh, Sweet Content. W. H. Davies.
Ode on Solitude. Pope.
Of a Contented Mind. Vaux.
Of Content. William Dunbar.
On Peace. Speed.
On Retirement. Freneau.
Prayer for Contentment. Poteat.
Quiet Life, The. Seneca, *tr. fr. Latin by* Marvell.
Reading the Book of Hills and Seas. T'ao Ch'ien, *tr. fr. Chinese by* Waley.
Rural Content. Andrew Scott.
Shepherd Boy's Song in the Valley of Humiliation, The. *Fr.* The Pilgrim's Progress. Bunyan.
Some Murmur When Their Sky Is Clear. Trench.
Sweet Are the Thoughts That Savor of Content. *Fr.* Greene's Farewell to Folly. Greene.
They of the Meane Estate Are Happiest. *Unknown.*
Vanity of Riches, The. *Fr.* Odes. Horace, *tr. fr. Latin by* Clark.
Wish, The. Godfrey.

CONVENTS
Convent Echoes. Moriarty.
Hawkesyard. Sister Mary Benvenuta.
Lines Written in a Nunnery Chapel. Mangan.
Mountain Convent. Laura Benét.

CONWAY, WALES. With a Rose from Conway Castle. Dorr.
COOK, JAMES. Five Visions of Captain Cook. Slessor.
COOKING AND COOKS
Art of Cookery, The. William King.
Aunt Nerissa's Muffin. Irwin.
Ballad of Culinary Frustration. McGinley.
Roundup Cook, The. R. V. Carr.
Ship's Cook, a Captive Sings, The. Hofmannsthal, *tr. fr. German by* Stork.
This and That. F. B. Davis.

COOLE, IRELAND
Coole Park, 1929. Yeats.
Wild Swans at Coole, The. Yeats.

COOPER, JAMES FENIMORE. Cooper. *Fr.* A Fable for Critics. J. R. Lowell.
COOPER, PETER. Peter Cooper. Joaquin Miller.
COPENHAGEN, BATTLE OF. Battle of the Baltic, The. Thomas Campbell.
CÓRDOBA, SPAIN
Cordova. Ibn Zaydun, *tr. fr. Arabic by* Gibb.
Quién Sabe? Mitchell.
Rider's Song. García Lorca, *tr. fr. Spanish by* Turnbull.

CORINTH, GREECE
Siege of Corinth, The. Byron.
To Corinth. Landor.

CORK, IRELAND. Bells of Shandon, The. Mahony.
CORMAC MAC ART
Burial of King Cormac, The. Sir Samuel Ferguson.
Song of the Heads, The. *Unknown, tr. fr. Irish by* O'Connor.

CORMORANTS. Common Cormorant, The. *Unknown.*
CORN
America Is Corn. Coffin.
Columbia's Emblem. E. D. Proctor.
Corn. Lanier.
Corn-planting. McArthur.
Corn Song, The. *Fr.* The Huskers. Whittier.
Cornfield. Leo Cox.
Cornfield, The. E. M. Roberts.
Cornfields. Howitt.
Last Corn Shock, The. Dresbach.
Laughing Corn. Sandburg.
Legend of the Cornstalk, The. Longfellow.
Maize, The. W. W. Fosdick.
Ploughman, The. Bottomley.
Story of the Corn. K. Fisher.
To Mother Corn. *Tr. fr. Pawnee Indian.*
Waving of the Corn, The. Lanier.

CORN LAWS (Great Britain). Corn-Law Hymn. Ebenezer Elliott.
CORNCRAKES
Corn-Crake, The. David Gray.
First Corncrake. Hewitt.
Landrail, The. De Vere.

CORNFLOWERS. Ragged Sailors. *Unknown.*
"CORNWALL, BARRY" (Bryan Waller Procter). In Memory of "Barry Cornwall." Swinburne.
CORNWALL, ENGLAND
Cornish Wind. Symons.
Song of the Western Men, The. Hawker.

CORNWALLIS, CHARLES CORNWALLIS, 1ST MARQUIS
Cornwallis's Surrender. *Unknown.*
Lord Cornwallis and a Carolina Spring. Bevington.

COROMANDEL COAST, INDIA
Coromandel Fishers, The. Naidu.
On the Coast of Coromandel. Sir Osbert Sitwell.

CORONADO, FRANCISCO VÁSQUEZ DE
Ballad of Coronado's Quest. Murton.
Quivira. Guiterman.

CORTÉS, HERNÁN. With Cortez in Mexico. W. W. Campbell.
CORUÑA, LA, SPAIN. Burial of Sir John Moore. Charles Wolfe.
COSMETICS. Government Injunction Restraining Harlem Cosmetic Co. Josephine Miles.
COTOPAXI, ECUADOR. Romance. W. J. Turner.
COTSWOLD HILLS, ENGLAND. Cotswold Hills. Colbourne-Veel.
COTTON, CHARLES. Grasshopper, The. Lovelace.
COTTON, JOHN. Upon the Tomb of John Cotton. Woodbridge.
COTTON
Cotton Boll, The. Timrod.
Cotton Field Song. *Unknown.*
Cotton Song. Toomer.

COUNTRY DANCES. Dance by the Roadside, The. Fröding, *tr. fr. Swedish by* Stork.
COUNTRY LIFE
A La Belle Etoile. Birchall.
Baucis and Philemon. Swift.
Birthright, The. Eiluned Lewis.
Bright Abandon. T. S. Webb.
Burials. *Fr.* The Parish Register. Crabbe.
Call, The. Guest.
Come Spur Away. Randolph.
Coridon's Song. Chalkhill.
Country Life. *Fr.* Epodes. Horace, *tr. fr. Latin by* Dryden.
Country Pleasures. Martial, *tr. fr. Latin by* Wright.
Country Reverie. Coates.
Country Summer. Léonie Adams.
Country Summer Pastoral, A. Foss.
Country Tune. Riddell.
Country Wedding. Jammes, *tr. fr. French by* Conder.
Cwm Farm near Capel Curig. Huw Menai.
Denial. Pollard.
Deserted Village, The. Goldsmith.
Early Morning at Bargis. Hagedorn.
Elegy Written in a Country Churchyard. Thomas Gray.
Far from the Madding Crowd. Waterman.
Fire of Drift-Wood, The. Longfellow.
For One Retired into the Country. Charles Wesley.
For These. T. E. Thomas.
Georgics, *sels.* Virgil, *tr. fr. Latin.*
Happy Is the Country Life. *Unknown.*
His Content in the Country. Herrick.
In Derision of a Country Life. *Fr.* The Italian Husband. Ravenscroft.
Jack and Joan. Campion.
Journey. Millay.
Letter from the Country, A. Howard Baker.
Merry Country Lad, The. *Fr.* The Passionate Shepherd. Breton.
Minnie and Mattie. *Fr.* Sing-Song. C. G. Rossetti.
No One Knows the Countryside. Struthers Burt.
Ode to Mr. Anthony Stafford to Hasten Him into the Country, An. Thomas Randolph.
Old Man near Verona Who Never Left His Farm, The. Ausonius, *tr. fr. Latin by* Lindsay.
Pastoral 2: "Who can live in heart so glad." *Fr.* The Passionate Shepherd. Breton.
Pasture, The. Robert Frost.
Poor, Poor Country, The. Neilson.
Rebellion. Chalmers.
Remembering the Ancient Farmstead. Tao Yuan-ming, *tr. fr. Chinese.*
Retirement. Vaughan.
Return to the Country. Tao Yuan-ming, *tr. fr. Chinese.*
Returning to the Fields. T'ao Ch'ien, *tr. fr. Chinese by* Waley.
Rudolph Is Tired of the City. Gwendolyn Brooks.
Ruris Opes Saturi, Gnavoque Agitanda Colono. Politian, *tr. fr. Latin by* Allen.
Sojourner, The. Birchall.
Song of the Open. Birchall.
Streams. Scollard.

COUNTRY LIFE (*continued*)
To a Friend in the Country. Gogarty.
To My Honoured Kinsman John Dryden of Chesterton. Dryden.
To One Who Has Been Long in City Pent. Keats.
Traveller's Rest. C. F. Smith.
Tree-Top Road, The. M. R. Smith.
Up at a Villa—Down in the City. Robert Browning.
Upon Himself. Herrick.
Village, The, *sels.* Crabbe.
Village, The. R. S. Thomas.
Winter. *Fr.* The Land. Sackville-West.
Winter Evening, The. *Fr.* The Task. Cowper.

COURAGE
Battle Cry, A. Shippey.
Besieged. Schneour, *tr. fr. Yiddish by* Leftwich.
Captain Death. *Unknown.*
Courage. "Anna Akhmatova," *tr. fr. Russian by* Deutsch.
Courage. Matthew Arnold.
Courage. Stopford Brooke.
Courage. Earhart.
Courage. Frazee-Bower.
Courage. Gerhardt, *tr. fr. German by* Wesley.
Courage. *Fr.* The Church Porch. George Herbert.
Courage. Virginia Moore.
Courage, All. Markham.
Courage and Patience. Tuckerman.
Courage Has a Crimson Coat. N. B. Turner.
Courage of the Lost, The. E. M. Thomas.
Courage to Live. Crowell.
Endurance and Faithfulness. *Fr.* Odes. Horace, *tr. fr. Latin by* Swift.
Inevitable, The. Bolton.
Invictus. Henley.
Leak in the Dike, The. Phoebe Cary.
Losers. Sandburg.
Never Admit the Pain. Mary Gilmore.
Prayer for Courage. Tagore.
Resolution and Independence. Wordsworth.
To fight aloud is very brave. Emily Dickinson.

COUREURS DE BOIS. Coureurs de Bois. Le Pan.

COURTIER, THE (Castiglione). Thomas Sackville in Commendation of the Work to the Reader. Sackville.

COURTIERS
Of the Mean and Sure Estate. Wyatt.
Old and the New Courtier, The. *Unknown.*
Prosopopoia; or, Mother Hubberd's Tale. Spenser.
Up-Start Courtier. Rowlands.

COVENTRY, ENGLAND. Sleeping Now in Coventry. Bourinot.

COWBOYS
At a Cowboy Dance. J. B. Adams.
Breakers of Broncos. Sarett.
Closing of the Rodeo, The. W. J. Smith.
Country Tune. Riddell.
Cowboy, The. Antrobus.
Cowboy, The ("He wears a big hat"). *Unknown.*
Cowboy Boasting Chants. *Unknown.*
Cowboy Song. Causley.
Cowboy Song ("One night as I lay on the prairie"). *Unknown.*
Cowboy to Pitching Bronco. *Unknown.*
Cowboys' Christmas Ball, The. Chittenden.
Cowboy's Dream, The. C. J. Finger.
Cowboy's Dream, The. *Unknown.*
Cowboys' Gettin'-up Holler. *Unknown.*
Cowboy's Lament, The. *Unknown.*
Cowboy's Life, The. *At. to* J. B. Adams.
Cowboy's Prayer, The. C. B. Clark, Jr.
Cow-Boy's Song, The. A. M. Wells.
Dying Cowboy, The. *Unknown.*
I Want to Be a Cowboy. *Unknown.*
Last Cowboy, The. Dresbach.
O Bury Me Not on the Lone Prairie. *Unknown.*
Old Chisholm Trail, The. *Unknown.*
Pards. H. J. Hughes.
Poor Lonesome Cowboy. *Unknown.*
Vaquero. Dorn.
Vaquero. Joaquin Miller.
Whoopee Ti Yi Yo, Git Along Little Dogies. *Unknown.*
Zebra Dun. *Unknown.*
Cowboy Songs and Other Frontier Ballads (CSF). John A. Lomax, ed. (1916)
Cowboy Songs and Other Frontier Ballads (CoSo). John A. Lomax *and* Alan Lomax, eds. (1938)
Poems of the Old West; a Rocky Mountain Anthology (PoOW). Levette J. Davidson, ed.
Songs of the Cattle Trail and Cow Camp (SCC). John A. Lomax, ed.

COWDENKNOWES, SCOTLAND. Cowdenknowes. Robert Crawford.

COWLEY, ABRAHAM
Cowley. Addison.
On Mr. Abraham Cowley, His Death and Burial amongst the Ancient Poets. Denham.

COWPENS, BATTLE OF. Battle of the Cowpens, The. English.

COWPER, WILLIAM
Cowper. Clare.
Cowper at Olney. Lynd.
Cowper's Grave. E. B. Browning.
Homage to William Cowper. Davie.

COWS. *See* CATTLE.

COWSLIPS
Bunch of Cowslips, A. *Unknown.*
With Rosy Hand. Landor.

COYOTES
Coyote. George Sterling.
Coyote and the Locust, The. *Tr. fr. Zuni Indian by* Cushing.
Prairie Wolves. R. V. Carr.

CRAB APPLE TREE. Crab Tree, The. Gogarty.

CRABBE, GEORGE
English Bards and Scotch Reviewers, *sel.* ("There be who say, in these enlighten'd days"). Byron.
George Crabbe. E. A. Robinson.

CRABS
Crab, The. Avianus, *tr. fr. Latin by* Lindsay.
Dead Crab, The. Andrew Young.
Old Chang, the Crab. *Unknown, tr. fr. Chinese by* Headland.

CRACOW, POLAND. Waiting for Death. Gebirtig, *tr. fr. Yiddish by* Leftwich.

CRAIL, SCOTLAND. Coves of Crail, The. "Fiona Macleod."

CRANE, HART
Fish Food. Wheelwright.
Hart Crane. Julian Symons.

CRANES (birds)
Crane, The. J. R. Anderson.
Cranes of Ibycus, The. Lazarus.
Herald Crane, The. Garland.
Pet Crane, A. *Unknown, tr. fr. Old Irish by* Dillon.
Sandhill Crane, The. Mary Austin.
Tanka: Cry of the Crane, The. Tsurayuki, *tr. fr. Japanese by* Waley.
To a Captive Crane. Garland.

CRASHAW, RICHARD
On the Death of Mr. Crashaw. Cowley.
Richard Crashaw. T. S. Jones, Jr.

CRAZY HORSE (Indian chief). Wildwest. *Fr.* Frescoes for Mr. Rockefeller's City. MacLeish.

CREATION
Beginning and the End, The. *Fr.* The Elder Edda. *Unknown, tr. fr. Old Norse by* Bellows.
Carmen Genesis. Francis Thompson.
Chant Out of Doors, A. Marguerite Wilkinson.
Creation, The. C. F. Alexander.
Creation. Bierce.
Creation, The. J. W. Johnson.
Creation. Nicholl.
Creation. Noyes.
Creation of the World, The. *Fr.* Metamorphoses. Ovid, *tr. fr. Latin by* Hankins.
First Day of the First Week, The. *Fr.* Du Bartas: His First Week or Birth of the World. Sylvester.
Eve. Flores, *tr. fr. Spanish by* Beckett.
Forest Hymn, A, *sel.* ("Father, thy hand"). Bryant.
Genesis. Geoffrey Hill.
Genesis. A. M. Sullivan.
Glory of God in Creation, The. Thomas Moore.
God, through All and in You All. Samuel Longfellow.
Hymn of Creation. *Fr.* The Rigveda. *Unknown, tr. fr. Sanskrit by* Macdonnell.
Hymn of the World's Creator, The. Cædmon.
In the Beginning Was the Bird. Treece.
Morning Hymn of Adam. *Fr.* Paradise Lost. Milton.
Over All the Face of Earth Main Ocean Flowed. *Fr.* Paradise Lost. Milton.
Pastoral Hymn, A. John Hall.
Preface: "Infinity, when all things it beheld." *Fr.* God's Determinations. Edward Taylor.
Pulley, The. George Herbert.
Reconciliation, *sel.* ("God of the Granite and the Rose!"). Doten.
Room, The. Aiken.
Sincere Praise, *sel.* ("Almighty Maker God"). Isaac Watts.
Spacious Firmament on High, The. Addison.
Spell of Creation. Raine.
Thou Art, O God. Thomas Moore.
Tiger, The. *Fr.* Songs of Experience. Blake.
To God, the Architect. Kemp.
Walam Olum, The; a Lenape Legend. *Tr. by* Brinton.

CRÉCY, BATTLE OF
Creçy. Palgrave.
Eve of Crécy, The. William Morris.

CREEDE, COLORADO
Creede. Warman.
Rise and Fall of Creede, The. Warman.

CRESSIDA. *See* TROILUS AND CRESSIDA.

CRETE
Paranoia in Crete. Corso.
Tomb of Lt. John Learmonth, AIF, The. Manifold.
Withdrawal from Crete. A. A. Brown.
CRICKETS
Ant and the Cricket, The. *Unknown.*
Autumn Cricket, An. Scollard.
Chirrupy Cricket, The. M. B. Thomas.
Cricket, The. Barrows.
Cricket, The. Bourne, *tr. fr. Latin by* Cowper.
Cricket, The. Kenyon.
Cricket, The. C. G. D. Roberts.
Cricket. Scollard.
Cricket, The. Tu Fu, *tr. fr. Chinese by* Chi Hwang Chu *and* Edna Worthley Underwood.
Crickets, The. Kimball.
Crickets. Wing.
Crickets at Dawn. Speyer.
Cricket's Story, The. Nason.
O Cricket, From Your Cheery Cry. Basho, *tr. fr. Japanese by* Page.
On the Grasshopper and Cricket. Keats.
Singing. D. K. Aldis.
Splinter. Sandburg.
Spring Cricket. Frances Rodman.
To a Cricket. W. C. Bennett.
To an Obscure Poet Who Lives on My Hearth. Hildreth.
To the Grasshopper and the Cricket. Leigh Hunt.
When Plaintively and Near the Cricket Sings. French.
CRIMEAN WAR
Charge of the Light Brigade, The. Tennyson.
Heavy Brigade, The. Tennyson.
Song of the Camp, The. Bayard Taylor.
CRITICISM AND CRITICS
Ballade of a Book-Reviewer, A. Chesterton.
Critic, A. Landor.
Criticaster, A. *Fr.* The Rosciad. Charles Churchill.
Criticism. Sir William Watson.
Critics. *Fr.* On Poetry; a Rhapsody. Swift.
Critics and Cooks. Martial, *tr. fr. Latin by* Harington.
English Bards and Scotch Reviewers, *sels.* Byron.
Essay on Criticism, An. Pope.
His Defense against the Idle Critic. Drayton.
Lines to a Critic. Shelley.
Obituary. Brode.
On Critics. Prior.
Pipling. Roethke.
Reactionary Critic. Martial, *tr. fr. Latin by* Fuller.
To Some Reviewers Who Have Wilfully Abused Certain True Poets. Herbert Palmer.
Verbal Critics. *Fr.* Epistle to Dr. Arbuthnot. Pope.
CRIVELLI, CARLO. Detail from an Annunciation by Crivelli. Rosemary Dobson.
CROCKETT, SAMUEL RUTHERFORD. To S. R. Crockett. R. L. Stevenson.
CROCODILES
Amphibious Crocodile. Ransom.
Crocodile, A. *Fr.* The Last Man. Beddoes.
Crocodile, The. *Fr.* Alice in Wonderland. "Lewis Carroll."
Crocodile, The. L. E. Richards.
Lady and Crocodile. Charles Burgess.
Lower Animals. Alan Anderson.
Monkeys and the Crocodile, The. L. E. Richards.
CROCUSES
Crocus, The. Walter Crane.
Crocus. S. J. Day.
Crocus, The. Mary Elliott.
Crocus, The. H. E. H. King.
Crocus. Kreymborg.
Crocus ("Warm sunshine came down"). *Unknown.*
Crocus. M. M. Walker.
Crocuses. Josa, *tr. fr. Japanese.*
Crocuses. Platt.
Crocuses. *Unknown, tr. fr. Japanese by* Porter.
Crocuses in [the] Grass. John Gray.
CROMWELL, OLIVER
Cromwell and Henrietta Maria. *Fr.* Charles the First. Wills.
Cromwell Dead. *Fr.* A Poem upon the Death of O. C. Marvell.
First Anniversary of the Government under His Royal Highness the Lord Protector. Marvell.
Heroic Stanzas, Consecrated to the Memory of His Highness, Oliver, Late Protector of This Commonwealth. Dryden.
Horatian Ode upon Cromwell's Return from Ireland, An. Marvell.
More Power to Cromwell. O'Rahilly, *tr. fr. Modern Irish by* Dinneen *and* O'Donoghue.
Panegyrick to My Lord Protector, A. Waller.
Poem, A, upon the Death of His Late Highness the Lord Protector, *sels.* Marvell.
Protector, The. Wither.
To the Lord General Cromwell. Milton.
CROMWELL, THOMAS
Cromwell, I Did Not Think to Shed a Tear. *Fr.* Henry VIII. Shakespeare.
Thomas Cromwell. *Unknown.*
CROSS
Ballad of Trees and the Master, A. Lanier.
Cathedral, The, *sel.* ("Whatsoever/ The form of building or the creed professed"). J. R. Lowell.
Cross, The. Braden.
Cross, The. Calderón, *tr. fr. Spanish by* Trench.
Cross, The. Gore-Booth.
Cross, The. Tobias.
Cross, The. Waite.
Cross and the Tree, The. Stidger.
Dream of the Rood, The. *Unknown, tr. fr. Anglo-Saxon.*
Golgotha's Cross. Kresensky.
Holy Cross, The. *Unknown.*
I Am the Cross. Stidger.
I Saw Death Slain. Capell.
Sign of the Cross, The. Newman.
Symbol of Hope. Weist.
Two Crosses. Hedrick.
Waking Thought. M. O. B. Wilkinson.
CROWS
Crow, The. Alexander.
Crow, The. Burroughs.
Crow, The. Canton.
Crow, The. Ibn Sa'id of Alcala La Real, *tr. fr. Arabic by* Arberry.
Crow. Mark Van Doren.
Crow, The. A. D. Watson.
Crow and Pie. *Unknown.*
Crow and the Fox, The. La Fontaine, *tr. fr. French by* Marsh.
Crow Country. Slessor.
Crows, The. Bogan.
Crows, The. McCord.
Crows. Reese.
Crows, The. *Unknown.*
Crows in Spring. Clare.
Crows in the Garden. *Unknown.*
Old Crow. Drinkwater.
Old Crow, The. *Unknown.*
Over in the Meadow. *Unknown.*
To a Crow. R. B. Wilson.
To Be or Not to Be. *Unknown.*
Twa Corbies, The. *Unknown.*
CRUCIFIXION, THE
Calvary. Hallet.
Calvary. E. A. Robinson.
Calvary. Stopple.
Christ Crucified. Crashaw.
Christ Is Crucified Anew. Moreland.
Christ Tells of His Passion. *Fr.* Christ. Cynewulf.
Crucifix, The. Lamartine, *tr. fr. French by* Stuart.
Crucifix, The. Pushkin, *tr. fr. Russian by* Cornford *and* Salaman.
Crucifixion, The. Chivers.
Crucifixion. Gore-Booth.
Crucifixion. Isbell.
Crucifixion, The. J. W. Lynch.
Crucifixion, The. Alice Meynell.
Crucifixion. F. G. Scott.
Crucifixion, The ("At the cry of the first bird"). *Unknown, tr. fr. Irish.*
Crucifixion, The ("They crucified my Lord"). *Unknown.*
Crucifixion and the Harrowing of Hell, The. *Fr.* The Vision of Piers Plowman. Langland.
Crucifixion to the World, by the Cross of Christ. Watts.
Dream of the Rood, The. *Unknown, tr. fr. Anglo-Saxon.*
Early Lynching. Sandburg.
Earth Worshiped, The! C. C. Coblentz.
Gambler. Studdert-Kennedy.
Good Friday. C. G. Rossetti.
Him I Follow. *Fr.* Will Shakespeare. "Clemence Dane."
His Garments. Hagg.
Holy Mother at the Cross, The. R. W. Dixon.
Holy Thorn. T. S. Jones, Jr.
I. H. S. Jennett.
Indifference. Studdert-Kennedy.
Jesus of Nazareth. Colwell.
Killing, The. Muir.
Martyr, The. Flohr.
Ninth Hour, The. Hazard.
O King of the Friday. Hyde, *tr. fr. Irish.*
O My Harte Is Wo. *Unknown.*
Pastoral: "Dove walks with sticky feet, The." Patchen.
Resurgam. J. R. Moreland.
Sacrifice, The. George Herbert.
Sunset on Calvary. *Unknown.*
There Is a Man on the Cross. Cheney.
Upon a Hill. Crouse.

Crucifixion, the (*continued*)
Upon the Body of Our Blessed Lord, Naked and Bloody. Crashaw.
Upon the Ensignes of Christes Crucifyinge. Alabaster.
Veteran of Heaven, The. Francis Thompson.
Crusades
Arrival of the Crusaders, The. St. Nerses Shnorhali, *tr. fr. Armenian by* Boyajian.
Crusade. Belloc.
Crusade, The. Thomas Warton, the Younger.
Crusaders. Waddell.
Crusaders Reach Jerusalem, The. *Fr.* Jerusalem Delivered. Tasso, *tr. fr. Italian by* Wiffen.
Crusaders' Song. *Unknown, tr. fr. French by* Meller.
God Wills It. Grady.
Jerusalem Delivered, *sels.* Tasso, *tr. fr. Italian.*
Lepanto. Chesterton.
Victory in Hungary, The. *Fr.* The Squire of Alsatia. Shadwell.
Cuba
Apostrophe to the Island of Cuba. Percival.
Cuba. Harvey Rice.
Cuba. Stedman.
Cuba Libre. Joaquin Miller.
Cuba to Columbia. Will Carleton.
Farewell to Cuba. M. G. Brooks.
Cuchulain (Irish legendary hero)
Cuchulain's Fight with the Sea. Yeats.
Death of Cuchulain. Cox.
Fand Yields Cuchulain to Emer. *Unknown, tr. fr. Old Irish by* O'Faoláin.
Cuckoos
Amoretti, *sel.* ("The merry cuckoo, messenger of spring"). Spenser.
Beware the Cuckoo. Moll.
Cuckoo! Belloc.
Cuckoo, The. Carlin.
Cuckoo, The. Chalmers.
Cuckoo, The. Fyleman.
Cuckoo, The. G. M. Hopkins.
Cuckoo, The. Le Gallienne.
Cuckoo, The. Locker-Lampson.
Cuckoo. Tynan.
Cuckoo, The. *Unknown.*
Cuckoo: "In former days my father and mother." *Fr.* Riddles. *Unknown, tr. fr. Anglo-Saxon by* Kennedy.
Cuckoo. Andrew Young.
Cuckoo Song. Doolittle ("H. D.").
Cuckoo's Song, The. Josui, *tr. fr. Japanese by* Porter.
Fragment, A: "Repeat that, repeat." G. M. Hopkins.
Gowk, The. Soutar.
Late Winter. McAuley.
O Cuckoo. *Fr.* Kokin Shu. *Unknown.*
Ode to the Cuckoo. Bruce.
Oocuck, The. Justin Richardson.
Spring ("When daisies pied and violets blue"). *Fr.* Love's Labour's Lost. Shakespeare.
Sumer Is Icumen In. *Unknown.*
To the Cuckoo. Alcuin, *tr. fr. Latin by* Jones.
To the Cuckoo. F. H. Townsend.
To the Cuckoo. Wordsworth.
When Cuckoo First. Prewett.
When daisies pied and violets blue. *Fr.* Love's Labour's Lost. Shakespeare.
Culloden, battle of
Lochiel's Warning. Thomas Campbell.
Old Scottish Cavalier, The. Aytoun.
Cumberland, Margaret Clifford, Countess of. To the Lady Margaret, Countess of Cumberland. Daniel.
Cumberland (ship)
Cumberland, The. Longfellow.
Cumberland, The. Melville.
Cumberland's Crew, The. *Unknown.*
How the *Cumberland* Went Down. Weir Mitchell.
On Board the *Cumberland* (March 7, 1862). Boker.
Cupid
Ah Cupid, I Mistook Thee. Francis Davison.
Alexander and Campaspe, *sels.* Lyly.
Beauties, Have Ye Seen. *Fr.* The Hue and Cry after Cupid. Jonson.
Cheat of Cupid, The; or, The Ungentle Guest. Herrick.
Children of Love. Harold Monro.
Cupid. Blake.
Cupid. *Fr.* Arcadia. Sir Philip Sidney.
Cupid. *Unknown.*
Cupid Abroad was Lated. *Fr.* Greene's Orpharion. Greene.
Cupid at Court. Peck.
Cupid in a Bed of Roses. *Unknown.*
Cupid Mistaken. Prior.
Cupid Stung. Thomas Moore.
Cupid Swallowed. Leigh Hunt, *after the Greek of* Anacreon.
Cupid Ungodded. Shirley.
Cupid's Darts. *Unknown.*
Cupid's Indictment. *Fr.* Galathea. Lyly.
Damon and Cupid. Gay.
Dream of Venus, A. Bion, *tr. fr. Greek by* Hunt.
Ερως (Eros). Robert Bridges.
Eros. Patmore.
Eros and Psyche, *sel.* ("His skin is brilliant . . ."). Apuleius, *tr. fr. Latin by* Bridges.
Eros Does Not Always Smite. "Michael Field."
O Cupid! Monarch over Kings. *Fr.* Mother Bombie. Lyly.
O Gentle Love. *Fr.* The Arraignment of Paris. Peele.
Of His Cynthia. *Fr.* Caelica. Greville.
To Cupid. Davison.
To Cupid. Drayton.
When I Was Fair and Young. Elizabeth I, Queen of England.
Wily Cupid. *Unknown, tr. fr. Spanish by* Gibson.
Wounded Cupid, The. Herrick, *after the Greek of* Anacreon.
Curfew
Curfew. Longfellow.
Curfew Must Not Ring To-Night. Thorpe.
Curlews
Curlew Calling. W. W. Gibson.
Curlew's Call, A. Jane Barlow.
Curran, Sarah. She Is Far from the Land. Thomas Moore.
Cushing, Harvey. Dedicated to Dr. Harvey Cushing. Fay.
Cushing, William Barker
"Albemarle" Cushing. Roche.
At the Cannon's Mouth. Melville.
Custer, George Armstrong
Custer. Stedman.
Custer's Last Charge. Whittaker.
Death of Custer, The. J. W. Crawford.
Revenge of Rain-in-the-Face, The. Longfellow.
Cyclamen
Cyclamen, The. Bates.
Sicilian Cyclamens. D. H. Lawrence.
To a Cyclamen. Landor.
Cyclone. Cyclone at Sea, A. Hayne.
Cyclops
Cyclops, *sels.* Euripides, *tr. fr. Greek by* Shelley.
Lotus-Land and the Cyclops' Cave. *Fr.* The Odyssey. Homer, *tr. fr. Greek by* Lucas.
Polyphemus and Galatea, *sel.* ("Cyclops—terrific son of Ocean's God!"). Góngora, *tr. fr. Spanish by* Roscoe.
Song of the Cyclops. *Fr.* London's Tempe. Dekker.
Cypress trees
Cypress. John Peter.
Cypress Tree, The. Blackburn.
Czechoslovakia. Salute, Czechoslovakia! W. R. Benét.

D

Dachshunds. Dachshund, The. Edward Anthony.
Daffodils
Daffodil. Tynan.
Daffodil Time. Scollard.
Daffodils. Ballantyne.
Daffodils. Harding.
Daffodils. Kikurio, *tr. fr. Japanese.*
Daffodils. Reese.
Daffodils. *Unknown, tr. fr. Japanese.*
Daffodils over Night. David Morton.
Daffodil's Return. Carman.
Daffy-down-dilly. A. B. Warner.
Divination by a Daffodil. Herrick.
Growing in the Vale. *Fr.* Sing-Song. C. G. Rossetti.
I Wandered Lonely as a Cloud. Wordsworth.
Lent Lily, The. *Fr.* A Shropshire Lad. Housman.
To Daffodils. Dobson.
To Daffodils. Herrick.
Dahlgren, Ulric. Ulric Dahlgren. Sherwood.
Dahlias. Dahlias. Padraic Colum.
Daisies
Buttercups and Daisies. Howitt.
Daisies. Carman.
Daisies. Hilda Conkling.
Daisies, The. Greenaway.
Daisies. F. D. Sherman.
Daisies, The. James Stephens.
Daisies, The. Woodberry.
Daisy, The. Clare.
Daisy, The. Good.
Daisy, The. Leyden.
Daisy, The. Montgomery.
Daisy, The. Rodd.
Daisy, The. Sheard.

Daisy, The. Tennyson.
Daisy. Francis Thompson.
Daisy. W. C. Williams.
Daisy's Song, A. Keats.
Field Daisy, The. Jane Taylor.
I'd Choose to Be a Daisy. *Unknown.*
Moon Daisies. Jacquetta Hawkes.
Of all the floures in the mede. *Fr.* The Legend of Good Women. Chaucer.
To a Daisy. Hartley.
To a Daisy. Alice Meynell.
To a Mountain Daisy. Burns.
To Daisies. Francis Thompson.
To Daisies, Not to Shut So Soon. Herrick.
To the Daisy ("With little here to do or see"). Wordsworth.
Where innocent, bright-eyed daisies are. C. G. Rossetti.
DALLAS, TEXAS
Cities. House.
Some Towns of Texas. K. W. Baker.
DAMASCUS, SYRIA. Gates of Damascus. Flecker.
DAMIEN, FATHER. Father Damien. Tabb.
DAMS. Bucyrus. John Holmes.
DANAË. Danae. Simonides, *tr. fr. Greek.*
DANCING AND DANCERS
African Dance. Hughes.
At a Cowboy Dance. J. B. Adams.
Ballroom Dancing Class. McGinley.
Bill Haller's Dance. R. V. Carr.
Cowboy's Ball, The. Knibbs.
Dance, The. Robert Duncan.
Dance, The. Lehmann.
Dance, The. Roethke.
Dance. Weeden.
Dance, The. W. C. Williams.
Dance for Rain, A. Bynner.
Dance of the Maskers. *Tr. fr. Apache Indian by* Austin.
Dancer, The. Joseph Campbell.
Dancer, The. Ibn Kharuf, *tr. fr. Arabic by* Arberry.
Dancers with a Hop, The. Schevill.
Dancing. Yang Kuei-fei, *tr. fr. Chinese by* Ayscough *and* Lowell.
Dancing Girl, A. Osgood.
Fancy's Knell. Housman.
Fiddler of Dooney, The. Yeats.
Gratiana Dancing and Singing. Lovelace.
Green Corn Dance, The. Corbin.
Javanese Dancers. Arthur Symons.
Little Dancers, The. Binyon.
Minuet, The. M. M. Dodge.
Minuet, The. Dorothy Leonard.
Minuet on Reaching the Age of Fifty, A. Santayana.
My Cousin German Came from France. *Unknown.*
Negro Reel. *Unknown.*
Off the Ground. De la Mare.
Orchestra; or, A Poem of Dancing. Sir John Davies.
Reminiscences of a Dancing Man. Hardy.
Re-run. W. T. Scott.
Seeing Her Dancing. Robert Heath.
Spring-Dance. Rodgers.
Tarantella. Belloc.
Upon His Mistress Dancing. Shirley.
War Dance, The. R. V. Carr.
When Dutchy Plays the Mouth Harp. R. V. Carr.
Untune the Sky (UnS). Helen Plotz, comp.
DANDELIONS
Casual Gold. Uschold.
Dandelion. Annan.
Dandelion. K. L. Brown.
Dandelion, The. Richard Church.
Dandelion. Hilda Conkling.
Dandelion. Garabrant.
Dandelion, The. Vachel Lindsay.
Dandelion, The. Katharine Pyle.
Dandelion, The ("O dandelion, yellow as gold"). *Unknown.*
Dandelion ("There was a pretty dandelion"). *Unknown.*
Dandelions. Albee.
Dandelions, The. Cone.
Dandelions. Sacheverell Sitwell.
Dandelions, The. *Unknown.*
First Dandelion, The. Whitman.
Little Dandelion. Bostwick.
Little Dandelion, The. Weeden.
To the Dandelion. J. R. Lowell.
Young Dandelion, The. Craik.
DANES, THE
Being Danish. Munk, *tr. fr. Danish by* Stork.
King of Ulster, The. *Unknown, tr. fr. Irish by* O'Connor.
Murrough Defeats the Danes, 994. *Unknown, tr. fr. Irish by* O'Connor.
DANIEL. Daniel Jazz, The. Lindsay.
DANIEL, SAMUEL
Ad Samuelem Danielem. Bastard.
Remembrance of Some English Poets, A. Barnfield.
To Samuel Daniel, Prince of English Poets. Francis Davison.
D'ANNUNZIO, GABRIELE. To D'Annunzio: Lines from the Sea. Nichols.
DANTE ALIGHIERI
Dante. Bryant.
Dante ("Tuscan, that wanderest"). Longfellow.
Dante. Michelangelo, *tr. fr. Italian by* Longfellow.
Dante was naïf, although he had an inkling. *Fr.* Sonnets. Leonard Bacon.
Dante's Scourge. Fukao, *tr. fr. Japanese by* Ninomiya *and* Enright.
Elegy: "Floods of tears well from my deepest heart, The." Immanuel di Roma, *tr. fr. Italian by* Chotzner.
Fiammetta. Boccaccio, *tr. fr. Italian by* D. G. Rossetti.
Inscription for Portrait of Dante. Boccaccio, *tr. fr. Italian by* D. G. Rossetti.
Man Called Dante, I Have Heard, A. King.
On a Bust of Dante. T. W. Parsons.
On Dante Alighieri. Michelangelo, *tr. fr. Italian by* Symonds.
On the "Vita Nuova" of Dante. D. G. Rossetti.
Out of the Italian. Spingarn.
Sonnet: Dante. Michelangelo, *tr. fr. Italian by* Longfellow.
Sonnet: To Dante Alighieri (He Commends the Work of Dante's Life). Quirino, *tr. fr. Italian by* D. G. Rossetti.
Sonnet: To Dante Alighieri (He Conceives of Some Compensation in Death). Pistoia, *tr. fr. Italian by* D. G. Rossetti.
Sonnet: To Dante Alighieri (He Interprets Dante's Dream). Cavalcanti, *tr. fr. Italian by* D. G. Rossetti.
Sonnet: To Dante Alighieri (He Interprets Dante's Dream). Pistoia, *tr. fr. Italian by* D. G. Rossetti.
Sonnet: To Dante Alighieri (He Mistrusts the Love of Lapo Gianni). Cavalcanti, *tr. fr. Italian by* D. G. Rossetti.
Sonnet: To Dante Alighieri (He Reports the Successful Issue of Lapo Gianni's Love). Cavalcanti, *tr. fr. Italian by* D. G. Rossetti.
Sonnet: To Dante Alighieri (He Writes to Dante, Defying Him). Cecco Angiolieri da Siena, *tr. fr. Italian by* D. G. Rossetti.
Sonnet: To Dante Alighieri (On the Last Sonnet of the "Vita Nuova"). Cecco Angiolieri da Siena, *tr. fr. Italian by* D. G. Rossetti.
Soul of Dante, The. Michelangelo, *tr. fr. Italian by* Symonds.
Testament of Beauty, The, *sel.* ("In higher natures, poetic or mystical"). Bridges.
To Dante. Alfieri, *tr. fr. Italian by* De' Lucchi.
To Dante. Cavalcanti, *tr. fr. Italian by* Shelley.
To Dante. Tennyson.
DANUBE (river). Danube River, The. Aïdé.
DAPHNE
Apollo and Daphne. *Fr.* Metamorphoses. Ovid, *tr. fr. Latin by* Highet.
Hunting Song. *Fr.* Apollo and Daphne. Whitehead.
Story of Phoebus and Daphne Applied, The. Waller.
DARE, VIRGINIA
For Virginia Dare. Crisp.
Peregrine White and Virginia Dare. Rosemary *and* S. V. Benét.
DAVENANT, SIR WILLIAM. To Sir William Davenant upon His Two First Books of Gondibert. Cowley.
DAVID (Bible)
Abishag. Spire, *tr. fr. French by* Eisenberg.
Apocryphal Soliloquies. Louis Untermeyer.
David. Guy Butler.
David. E. V. Cooke.
David. M. C. Davies.
Davideis, *sels.* Cowley.
David's Epitaph on Jonathan. Quarles.
David's Lament for Absalom. Willis.
David's Reconciliation with Absalom. "Michael Field."
Goliath and David. Louis Untermeyer.
Harp of David, The. Jacob Cohen, *tr. fr. Hebrew by* Kahn.
Harp of David, The. "Yehoash," *tr. fr. Yiddish by* Brody.
In Honour of St. David's Day. *Unknown.*
King David. S. V. Benét.
King David. Heine, *tr. fr. German by* Untermeyer.
King Solomon and King David. *Unknown.*
Listen, David! Josephine Jacobsen.
Saul. Robert Browning.
Song to David, A. Smart.
DAVIDSON, JOHN. In Memoriam; John Davidson. Macfie.
DAVIES, SIR JOHN
Four for Sir John Davies. Roethke.
To Mr. John Davies. Harington.
DAVIES, WILLIAM. I am the Poet Davies, William. William Davies.
DAVIS, JEFFERSON
Elegy: "No more the white refulgent streets." Tate.
Jeff Davis. *Unknown.*
Jefferson D. Cornwell.
Jefferson Davis. W. M. Bell.

DAVIS, JEFFERSON (*continued*)
Jefferson Davis. H. T. Peck.
Our Dead Heroes. M. B. Wharton.
DAVIS, THOMAS OSBORNE. Lament for the Death of Thomas Davis. Sir Samuel Ferguson.
DAVY, SIR HUMPHRY. Sir Humphry Davy. Bentley.
DAWN
Angel of Dawn, The. Cutler.
At Dawn. Hugo, *tr. fr. French by* Conder.
At Dawn. Symons.
At Dawn. Moreno Villa, *tr. fr. Spanish by* Turnbull.
Awake! Awake! *Fr.* Song of the Dawn. Ruskin.
Before Dawn. Chipp.
Before Dawn. Swinburne.
Before Dawn in the Woods. Marguerite Wilkinson.
Beginnings of Day, The. *Fr.* Dryades. Diaper.
Break of Day, The. Neilson.
Cellach's Poem to the Dawn. *Unknown, tr. fr. Old Irish by* O'Faoláin.
Cock-Crow. Edward Thomas.
Coming of Dawn, The. Dennen.
Dawn. "Æ."
Dawn. Ibn Muqana, *tr. fr. Arabic by* Arberry.
Dawn. Logan.
Dawn. Rimbaud, *tr. fr. French by* Flores.
Dawn, The. W. W. E. Ross.
Dawn, The. *Unknown.*
Dawn. W. C. Williams.
Dawn, The. Yeats.
Dawn and Dark. Norman Gale.
Dawn Has Yet to Ripple In. Cane.
Dawn in Inishtrahull. O'Sullivan.
Dawn in London. Tikhonov, *tr. fr. Russian by* Lindsay.
Dawn in the Everglades. Warlow.
Dawn of Day. *Fr.* The Shepherd's Pipe. William Browne.
Dawn on Mid-Ocean. Wheelock.
Dawn on the Headland. Sir William Watson.
Dawn on the Lievre, The. Lampman.
Dawn over the Mountains. Tu Fu, *tr. fr. Chinese by* Rexroth.
Dawning, The. Vaughan.
Dawning of the Day, The. Mangan.
Dawning of the Day, The. *Unknown, tr. fr. Irish by* Walsh.
Day came slow, till five o'clock, The. Emily Dickinson.
Daybreak. De la Mare.
Daybreak. Ibn Burd, *tr. fr. Arabic by* Arberry.
Daybreak. Longfellow.
Daybreak. Shelley.
Daybreak. Louis Untermeyer.
Daybreak Call, The. Haste.
Dayspring. Urbina, *tr. fr. Spanish by* Beckett.
Early Light. L. B. Lyon.
Early News. A. M. Pratt.
Fields of Dawn, The, *sels.* Mifflin.
Getting Up Early on a Spring Morning. Po Chü-i, *tr. fr. Chinese by* Waley.
Hark! Hark! the Lark. *Fr.* Cymbeline. Shakespeare.
Hour before Dawn, The. J. C. Powys.
Hymn for Morning. *Fr.* Cathemerinon. Prudentius, *tr. fr. Latin by* Blackett.
I Walked the Road of the Dawn. *Fr.* The Free Besieged. Solomos, *tr. fr. Modern Greek by* Dalven.
Improvisation III. Silverman.
In the Naked Bed, in Plato's Cave. Schwartz.
Lark Now Leaves His Wat'ry Nest, The. Davenant.
Miracle of the Dawn, The. Cawein.
Morning Light Is Breaking. The. S. F. Smith.
Morning Twilight. Baudelaire, *tr. fr. French by* Gibbs.
Music of the Dawn. V. B. Harrison.
Night Is Near Gone, The. Montgomerie.
Paean of Dawn in May. Trench.
Perturbation at Dawn. Ibn Maatuk, *tr. fr. Arabic by* Mathers.
Phoebus, Arise! Drummond of Hawthornden.
Prayer at Dawn. Poteat
Song of the Night at Day-Break. Alice Meynell.
Starting Early from the Ch'u-ch'eng Inn. Po Chü-i, *tr. fr. Chinese by* Waley.
Summer Dawn. William Morris.
Sunrise. Rowena Bennett.
To a Bird at Dawn. Le Gallienne.
Trumpet of the Dawn, The. Scollard.
With the Dawn. T. C. Irwin.
DAY
Break of Day. Donne.
Carol: "All this night shrill chanticler." William Austin.
Day and Night. Victor Daley.
Hymns to the Night. "Novalis," *tr. fr. German by* Cotterell.
My Day and Night. Payne.
Night and Day. Asadi, *tr. fr. Persian by* Browne.
Night and Day. M. M. Dodge.
Night and Day. Ibn Darraj, *tr. fr. Arabic by* Arberry.
Stoush o' Day, The. Dennis.
DEAFNESS
On His Deafness. *Fr.* Les Amours. Du Bellay, *tr. fr. French by* Conder.
Rhapsody of the Deaf Man. Corbière, *tr. fr. French by* McElroy.
DEAN, JAMES. For James Dean. Frank O'Hara.
DEATH
Address to Death. Fet, *tr. fr. Russian by* Deutsch.
Adieu, Farewell Earth's Bliss! *Fr.* Summer's Last Will and Testament. Nashe.
Admiral Death. Newbolt.
Affinities. Heine, *tr. fr. German by* Salinger.
After Death. R. A. K. Mason.
After Death. Swinburne.
Afterwards. Hardy.
All Men Are Free. Napier.
All the Hills and Vales Along. Sorley.
And Death Shall Have No Dominion. Dylan Thomas.
And the Earth Rebelled. Suhl, *tr. fr. Yiddish by* Rosenfeld.
And There Shall Be No More Death, *sel.* ("That which the long scythe whispered to the grass"). Ruth Gilbert.
And You as Well Must Die, Belovéd Dust. Millay.
Anniversary. George, *tr. fr. German by* Phelps.
Ante Mortem. Jeffers.
Apostrophe to Death. *Fr.* Carmen Paschale. Sedulius, *tr. fr. Latin by* Sigerson.
Argumentum ad Hominem. Plutzik.
Arrival, The. W. R. Benét.
At Last. Whittier.
At Parting. Heine, *tr fr. German by* Durling.
Auto Wreck. Shapiro.
Away, Delights! *Fr.* The Captain. Beaumont *and* Fletcher.
Ay, but to Die. *Fr.* Measure for Measure. Shakespeare.
Babylonian Sorrows. Heine, *tr. fr. German by* Salinger.
Baby's Death, A. Swinburne.
Ballad: White Rose. Sacheverell Sitwell.
Ballad of Past Meridian, A. Meredith.
Ballad of Sister Anne, The. Sir Osbert Sitwell.
Ballad of the Outer Life. Hofmannsthal, *tr. fr. German by* Hamburger.
Bearer's Song. Miu Hsi, *tr. fr. Chinese by* Waley.
Beautiful Lie the Dead. Stephen Phillips.
Because I could not stop for Death. Emily Dickinson.
Before a Corpse. Acuña, *tr. fr. Spanish by* Beckett.
Bells for John Whiteside's Daughter. Ransom.
Beside Lilia Dead. Sister Mary Catherine.
Beside the Bed. Mew.
Bird of Paradise, The. W. H. Davies.
Blind Date./ Aiken.
Bridge of Sighs, The. Hood.
Broken Ring, The. Eichendorff, *tr. fr. German by* Cotterell.
Buck in the Snow, The. Millay.
Bull, The. Ralph Hodgson.
Burn Out Burn Quick. Reisen, *tr. fr. Yiddish by* Leftwich.
Bustle in a house, The. Emily Dickinson.
Cabin-Kid. Corbière, *tr. fr. French by* Fitts.
Cavalier. Richard Bruce.
Child Dying, The. Edwin Muir.
Children's Elegy. *Fr.* Eighth Elegy. Rukeyser.
Choricos. Aldington.
Chorus: "Alas, with what tormenting fire." *Fr.* Antonius. Garnier.
City of the Dead, The. Richard Burton.
Closing Prayer. J. G. Patrick.
Coastguardsman in the Fog, The. Schevill.
Colloquy in Black Rock. Robert Lowell.
Come Away. Death. E. J. Pratt.
Come Away, Death. *Fr.* Twelfth Night. Shakespeare.
Comparison of Life and Death. *Unknown.*
Complaint on the Oblivion of the Dead. Laforgue, *tr. fr. French by* W. J. Smith.
Concerning Death. Tulkourantzi, *tr. fr. Armenian by* Boyajian.
Condemned to Die, The. Espronceda, *tr. fr. Spanish by* Kennedy.
Conversation in the Forest. Eichendorff, *tr. fr. German by* Salinger.
Cool Tombs. Sandburg.
Coplas on the Death of His Father. Jorge Manrique, *tr. fr. Spanish by* Longfellow.
Corpses in the Wood. Toller, *tr. fr. German by* Roberts.
Could I Believe. Ewart Milne.
Crossing the Bar. Tennyson.
Cydalises, The. Nerval, *tr. fr. French by* Aldan.
Cry, A. H. E. Clarke.
Dance of Death, The. Dobson.
Dancing Partners. Philip Child.
Dark Cat, The. A. A. Brown.
Dark Cavalier, The. Widdemer.
D'Avalos' Prayer. Masefield.
Dead, The. Rupert Brooke.

Dead, The. John Williams.
Dead Boy. Ransom.
Dead Man's Dump. Rosenberg.
Death. M. D. Babcock.
Death. Bodenheim.
Death. Emily Brontë.
Death. Cawein.
Death. Coates.
Death. George Herbert.
Death. Hood.
Death. Rilke, *tr. fr. German by* Jarrell.
Death. Yeats.
Death Alone. "Pablo Neruda," *tr. fr. Spanish by* Flores.
Death and Resurrection. Croly.
Death and the Maiden, *sel.* ("Mourn her in the valleys, you young lovers, and throughout your gloom"). W. H. Oliver.
Death and the Maiden. *Unknown, tr. fr. Irish by* O'Connor.
Death, Be Not Proud. *Fr.* Holy Sonnets. Donne.
Death-Bed, The. Sassoon.
Death-Chant of the Centaurs, *sel.* ("Close his eyes with the coins"). S. V. Benét.
Death Comes Riding. Kvaran, *tr. fr. Icelandic by* Johnson.
Death—Divination. Stork.
Death Ends All Woe. Herrick.
Death Fugue. Celan, *tr. fr. German by* Greenberg.
Death in Bed. *Unknown.*
Death in Hospital, A. John Lehmann.
Death Inevitable. *Fr.* Odes. Horace, *tr. fr. Latin by* Creech.
Death Invoked. *Fr.* The Emperor of the East. Massinger.
Death Is a Blessed Thing. "Angelus Silesius," *tr. fr. German by* Carus.
Death is a dialogue. Emily Dickinson.
Death Is at Hand. Heine, *tr. fr. German by* Salinger.
Death Is but Death. Will Dyson.
Death Is Great. Rilke, *tr. fr. German by* Salinger.
Death Is the Chilly Night. Heine, *tr. fr. German by* Flores.
Death May Be Very Gentle. Gogarty.
Death of a Bird. Silkin.
Death of a Dove, The. Schevill.
Death of a Son. Silkin.
Death of an Old Man, The. Hamburger.
Death of Friends, The. Levi.
Death of the Poet. Rilke, *tr. fr. German by* Watkins.
Death Speaks. Calderón de la Barca, *tr. fr. Spanish by* Brenan.
Death Stands above Me, Whispering Low. Landor.
Death the Great. Elis Wyn o Lasynys, *tr. fr. Welsh by* Borrow.
Death the Leveller. *Fr.* The Contention of Ajax and Ulysses. Shirley.
Death the Peacemaker. E. H. Flagg.
Death, Thou Hast Seized Me. Luzzatto, *tr. fr. Hebrew by* Salaman.
Death Was a Woman. S. K. Russell.
Death—What Is It? J. N. Matthews.
Death's Delight. Eichendorff, *tr. fr. German by* Cotterell.
Death's Transfiguration. Zangwill.
Death's Warning to Beauty. *Unknown, tr. fr. Early Modern Irish by* Flower.
Departed Friends. Vaughan.
Departure. Hagedorn.
Departure. *Fr.* The Unknown Eros. Patmore.
Devil's Dream. Fearing.
Dirge: "Never the nightingale." Crapsey.
Dirge in the Woods. Meredith.
Dirge without Music. Millay.
Discoverer, The. Stedman.
Disquisition on Death, *sel.* ("I went through the market-place crying, There is no death"). Fairburn.
Do Not Go Gentle into That Good Night. Dylan Thomas.
Dominus Illuminatio Mea. Blackmore.
Downe downe afflicted soule and paie thy due. *Unknown.*
Dream of a Decent Death. Borgese.
Dream of Gerontius, The. Cardinal Newman.
Dream of the World without Death, The. *Fr.* The Book of Orm. Robert Buchanan.
Dying Christian to His Soul, The. Pope.
Dying Enthusiast, The. Mangan.
Dying Stockman, The. *Unknown.*
Early Death. Hartley Coleridge.
Early Death and Fame. Matthew Arnold.
East Coker. *Fr.* Four Quartets. T. S. Eliot.
Elegy: "Fled is the swiftness of all the white-footed ones." Auslander.
Elegy: "Tumult of death, dizziness hath seized me, The." Moses Rimos of Majorca, *tr. fr. Hebrew by* Abrahams.
Elegy against a Latter Day. Smithyman.
Elegy on Gordon Barber. Derwood.
Elegy over a Tomb. Lord Herbert of Cherbury.
Emperor of the East, The, *sel.* ("Why art thou slow, thou rest of trouble, Death"). Massinger.
Emptiness. J. R. Palmer.
End, The. Wilfred Owen.
End of Man Is Death, The. Moses ibn Ezra, *tr. fr. Hebrew by* Solis-Cohen.
Epilogue: "At the midnight in the silence of the sleep-time." *Fr.* Asolando. Robert Browning.
Epitaph: "Man who in his life trusts in this world, A." *Unknown.*
Epitaph: "This is the end of him, here he lies." Amy Levy.
Epitaph of Graunde Amoure, The. *Fr.* The Pastime of Pleasure. Hawes.
Epitaph on Salomon Pavy, a Child of Queen Elizabeth's Chapel. Jonson.
Epistle to be Left in the Earth. MacLeish.
"Ex Libris." Upson.
Exhortation to the Artists. Plutzik.
Exile from God. Wheelock.
Exit. W. P. MacDonald.
Experience. Hofmannsthal, *tr. fr. German by* Schwarz.
Falstaff's Song. Stedman.
Fantasy in Purple. Langston Hughes.
Farewell. John Press.
Father Dies. Sutskever, *tr. fr. Yiddish by* Betsky.
Fear No More the Heat o' the Sun. *Fr.* Cymbeline. Shakespeare.
For a Dead Lady. E. A. Robinson.
For My Funeral. A. E. Housman.
For Sleep, or Death. Pitter.
For the Burial of the Dead. Prudentius, *tr. fr. Latin by* Blackett.
Forever. O'Reilly.
Fragment on Death. Villon, *tr. fr. French by* Swinburne.
Friends Beyond. Hardy.
Friends Departed. Vaughan.
French Polisher, The. Constance Davies.
Frozen City, The. Nemerov.
Funeral. Murray Bennett.
Funeral, The. "M. J.," *tr. fr. Polish by* Glanz-Leyeless.
Futility. Wilfred Owen.
Gallows' Brother's Song. Morgenstern, *tr. fr. German by* Hull.
Garden of Proserpine, The. Swinburne.
Gardener, The. Laurence Housman.
Gee I Like to Think of Dead. E. E. Cummings.
Geist's Grave. Matthew Arnold.
Gift of a Skull, The. Skelton.
Giorno dei Morti. D. H. Lawrence.
Go Down, Death. J. W. Johnson.
Golden Falcon. Coffin.
Grandma, May She Rest in Peace, Died. Kulbak, *tr. fr. Yiddish by* Betsky.
Grave, The. Robert Blair.
Grave, The. T. G. Jones, *tr. fr. Welsh by* Rhys.
Grave, A. Marianne Moore.
Grave, The. *Unknown, tr. fr. Anglo-Saxon by* Kennedy.
Grave, The. Winters.
Grave in Ukraine, A. Tchernichowsky, *tr. fr. Hebrew by* Snowman.
Gravestones. Vernon Watkins.
Graveyard, The. *Fr.* Burial Songs. *Unknown, tr. fr. Chinese by* Waley.
Green and Red and Darkness. W. T. Scott.
Grey Washer by the Ford, The. Jennett.
Guest. Beresford Richards.
Hath any loved you well, down there. O'Shaughnessy.
Hence flattring hopes. Cease longing and give ore. *Unknown.*
Here Lies a Lady. Ransom.
Hero Song. Robert Duncan.
High Song, The. *Fr.* Requiem. Humbert Wolfe.
His Winding-Sheet. Herrick.
Hos Ego Versiculos. *Fr.* Argalus and Parthenia. Quarles.
Hours, The. J. P. Bishop.
House of Night, The, *sels.* Freneau.
How Great unto the Living Seem the Dead! Heavysege.
How Sleep the Brave. De la Mare.
Hymn to Death. Bryant.
I Am the Reaper. Henley.
I Die Alive. Southwell.
I Die, Being Young. David Gray.
I died for Beauty—but was scarce. Emily Dickinson.
I felt a funeral in my brain. Emily Dickinson.
I. H. S. Jennett.
I Have a Rendezvous with Death. Seeger.
I Have Never Been Here Before. Glatstein, *tr. fr. Yiddish by* Betsky.
I heard a fly buzz when I died. Emily Dickinson.
I never hear that one is dead. Emily Dickinson.
I Stood with the Dead. Sassoon.
I Tell of Another Young Death. Tiempo, *tr. fr. Spanish by* Walsh.

DEATH (*continued*)
I Wage Not Any Feud with Death. *Fr.* In Memoriam A. H. H. Tennyson.
Ignorance of Death. Empson.
Ilicet. Swinburne.
Imagining How It Would Be to Be Dead. Eberhart.
Immortal is an ample word. Emily Dickinson.
In a Time of Pestilence. *Fr.* Summer's Last Will and Testament. Nashe.
In Battle. Wallace Stevens.
In Hellbrunn. Trakl, *tr. fr. German by* Flores.
In the subtraction of my yeares. *Unknown.*
In the Year's Morning. David Ross.
Invocation of Death. Raine.
Invocation to Death. Carnevali.
Irony. Louis Untermeyer.
Is It Far to Go. Day Lewis.
It Is Not Death to Die. Bethune.
I've seen a dying eye. Emily Dickinson.
Journey's End. Humbert Wolfe.
Juggling Jerry. George Meredith.
Jugurtha. Longfellow.
Keys of Morning, The. De la Mare.
Knight, The. Rilke, *tr. fr. German by* Issawi.
Lament: "Listen, children:/Your father is dead." Millay.
Lament for the Makaris. William Dunbar.
Land o' the Leal. Nairne.
Landscape with Figures. Keith Douglas.
Last Conqueror, The. *Fr.* Cupid and Death. Shirley.
Last Invocation, The. Whitman.
Last Journey, The. Leonidas, *tr. fr. Greek by* Merivale.
Last Journey. González Martínez, *tr. fr. Spanish by* Beckett.
Last Lines: "No coward soul is mine." Emily Brontë.
Last Lines, *sel.* ("Lord! if in love, though fainting oft, I have tended thy gracious Vine"). Owen Meredith.
Last night that she lived, The. Emily Dickinson.
Last Plea. J. S. Untermeyer.
Let Me Go Down to Dust. Sarett.
Let Me Live Out My Years. Neihardt.
Let Me Not Die. E. L. Pierce.
Letter from Mexico. Corbière, *tr. fr. French by* Flores.
Libel of Divorce, A. Gascoigne.
Life and Death. L. C. Perry.
Life and Death. C. G. Rossetti.
Life and Death. D. C. Scott.
Life Is Short. *Fr.* Odes. Horace, *tr. fr. Latin by* Deazeley.
Lights Out. Edward Thomas.
Lines: "Sights o'er yonder snowy range." De Vere.
Litany of the Rooms of the Dead. Werfel, *tr. fr. German by* Snow.
Lo! I am Death! With aim as sure as steady. *Fr.* The Dance of Death. *Unknown, tr. fr. Spanish.*
Locust Swarm, The. Hsu Chao, *tr. fr. Chinese by* Rexroth.
Lone Prairie, The. *Unknown.*
Lord! Within Thy Peace I Rest Me. Brentano, *tr. fr. German by* Cotterell.
Luke Havergal. E. A. Robinson.
Man's Mortality. *Unknown.*
Meditation, A. Eberhart.
Memento for Mortality, A. *At. to* William Basse.
Memorial Rain. MacLeish.
Mirror of Mortality, A. Thomas Proctor.
Miserere. Scheffauer.
Missing. Tabb.
Moriturus. Millay.
Mortuary Parlors. S. V. Benét.
Mother Marie Therese. Robert Lowell.
Mother's Lament for the Death of Her Son, A. Burns.
Mrs. Southern's Enemy. Sir Osbert Sitwell.
My Death. Tourian, *tr. fr. Armenian by* Boyajian.
My Death. Zuckmayer, *tr. fr. German by* Ashton.
My life closed twice before its close. Emily Dickinson.
My Sister. Plutzik.
Necrological. Ransom.
News. Elton.
Next of Kin. C. G. Rossetti.
Night-Piece on Death, A. Thomas Parnell.
No Death. Marston.
Non Dolet. Gogarty.
O Death, Rock Me Asleep. *At. to* George Boleyn, *also to* Anne Boleyn.
Oh Death Will Find Me. Rupert Brooke.
Oh, for the Time When I Shall Sleep. *Fr.* The Philosopher. Emily Brontë.
Oh, Let Us Howl Some Heavy Note. *Fr.* The Duchess of Malfi. Webster.
O Mariners! Rutledge.
O Mors! Quam Amara Est Memoria Tua Homini Pacem Habenti in Substantiis Suis. Dowson.
Oh, Thou! Who Dry'st the Mourner's Tear. Thomas Moore.
Obituary. Louis Untermeyer.
Ode on the Death of His Father. Jorge Manrique, *tr. fr. Spanish by* Longfellow.
Ode to the Confederate Dead. Allen Tate.
Of Death. *Fr.* Antonius. Garnier.
Of the Progresse of the Soule, *sels.* Donne.
Old Age. Eichendorff, *tr. fr. German by* Watkins.
Old Man's Dream after He Died, The. *Fr.* Cawdor. Jeffers.
Omnia Somnia. Sylvester.
On a Dead Child. Robert Bridges.
On a Dead Lady. Musset, *tr. fr. French by* Loir.
On a Dying Boy. William Bell.
On Coming to an End. Whicher.
On Death. Landor.
On Death. *Fr.* Measure for Measure. Shakespeare.
On the Acequia Madre. Corbin.
On the Brink of Death. Michelangelo, *tr. fr. Italian by* Symonds.
On the Death of a Recluse. Darley.
On the Death of His Baby Son. Su T'ung-po, *tr. fr. Chinese by* Rexroth.
On the Death of His Son. Lewis Glyn Cothi, *tr. fr. Welsh by* Williams.
On the Death of My Child. Eichendorff, *tr. fr. German by* Flores.
On the Eve of His Execution. Tichborne.
On the Tombs in Westminster Abbey. *At. to* Francis Beaumont, *also to* William Basse.
On the Verge. Winter.
One Who Watches. Sassoon.
Open, Time. Guiney.
Orpheus, Eurydice, and Hermes. Rilke, *ad. fr. German by* Lowell.
Out of the Cradle Endlessly Rocking. Whitman.
Overtures to Death. Day Lewis.
Pardon, The. Wilbur.
Passer Mortuus Est. Millay.
Patchwork Quilt, The. Shorter.
Pause en Route. Kinsella.
Peaceful Death. Whitman.
People Has No Obituary, The. Eunice Clark.
Per Iter Tenebricosum. Gogarty.
Plaint. Ebenezer Elliott.
Poem: "And when I pay death's duty." Blaser.
Poem: "When birds and brittle leaves come down." Prichard.
Ponder It, O Soul! Mörike, *tr. fr. German by* Flores.
Posthumous Remorse. Baudelaire, *tr. fr. French by* Gibbs.
Postscript. Souster.
Prayer: "God, I fain would pray with fervor." Eichendorff, *tr. fr. German by* Cotterell.
Prayer in the Prospect of Death, A. Burns.
Precipice, The. Tabb.
Presence, The. Robert Graves.
Prospice. Robert Browning.
Pure Death. Robert Graves.
Quaker Graveyard in Nantucket, The. Robert Lowell.
Rain on a Grave. Hardy.
Reaper, The. Robert Duncan.
Reapers, The. Watt.
Refusal to Mourn the Death, by Fire, of a Child in London, A. Dylan Thomas.
Remembrance. Emily Brontë.
Requiem—for the Death of a Boy. Rilke, *tr. fr. German by* Jarrell.
Requiescat. Matthew Arnold.
Requiescat. Oscar Wilde.
Respice Finem. Thomas Proctor.
Resurgam. Burt.
Returning Home. Eichendorff, *tr. fr. German by* Cotterell.
Rhenish Autumn. Apollinaire, *tr. fr. French by* Aldan.
Rich men, trust not in wealth. Nashe.
Rima LXXIII: "They closed her eyes." *Fr.* Rimas Bécquer, *tr. fr. Spanish by* Masefield.
Rumination. Eberhart.
Sea of Death, The. Hood.
Secret Gate, The. "Fiona Macleod."
Sense of Death, The. Helen Hoyt.
Separation. Laurence Housman.
Sestina: "I die, no matter what I do I die." Eberhart.
Shadow, The. De la Mare.
Shapes of Death Haunt Life. Spender.
Ship of Death, The. D. H. Lawrence.
Show, The. Wilfred Owen.
Silver swan, who living had no note, The. *Unknown.*
Simplify Me When I'm Dead. Keith Douglas.
Sleep and His Brother Death. W. H. Hayne.
Sleepe O sleepe thou sacred dust. *Unknown.*
Sleepe, sleepe faire virgin, sleepe in peace. *Unknown.*
Snow Globe, The. Nemerov.
Something Has Spoken to Me in the Night. Thomas Wolfe.
Song: "Victorious men of Earth, no more." *Fr.* Cupid and Death. Shirley.

Song from "Chartivel." Marie de France, *tr. fr. French by* O'Shaughnessy.
Song of the Little Hypertrophic Child. Laforgue, *tr. fr. French by* Watkins.
Song to Death. Escrivá, *tr. fr. Spanish by* Peers.
Songs of La Mouche. Head.
Sonnet: "How all men wrongly death to dignify." A. J. M. Smith.
Sonnet: You Were Born; Must Die. Spender.
Soon at Last My Sighs and Moans. Louis Ginsberg.
Sorrow. Mei Yao Ch'en, *tr. fr. Chinese by* Rexroth.
Soul's Garment, The. Duchess of Newcastle.
Space in the Air, A. Silkin.
Speech of the Dead, The. Ridler.
Stand Close Around. Landor.
Stane wi Its Rune Rises frae the Sea, The. Heine, *tr. fr. German into Scottish by* Morgan.
Stirrup-Cup, The. Lanier.
Strange Meeting. Wilfred Owen.
Strangers Are We All upon the Earth. Werfel, *tr. fr. German by* Snow.
Substance, Shadow, and Spirit. T'ao Ch'ien, *tr. fr. Chinese by* Waley.
Suffering. Ehrenstein, *tr. fr. German by* Deutsch.
Suicide's Stone. Jeffers.
Suppose in Perfect Reason. Howard Griffin.
Surrender. Grimké.
Tenth Duino Elegy, The. Rilke, *tr. fr. German by* Speirs.
Text. Zeitlin, *tr. fr. Yiddish by* Betsky.
Thanatopsis. Bryant.
That Death Is Not So Much to Be Feared as Daily Diseases Are. Turberville.
That such have died enables us. Emily Dickinson.
There Is No Death. McCreery.
There Is No Death. *Unknown.*
Therefore, We Thank Thee, God. Grossman, *tr. fr. Hebrew by* Snowman.
They Are All Gone. Vaughan.
Things Dead. Schwob, *tr. fr. French by* Meloney.
Thought. Whitman.
Thought in Two Moods, A. Hardy.
Thought of Death, A. Flatman.
To a Child during Sickness. Leigh Hunt.
To a Child in Death. Mew.
To an Athlete Dying Young. Housman.
To Be or Not to Be. *Fr.* Hamlet. Shakespeare.
To Claudia Homonoea. Elinor Wylie.
To Death. C. A. Bowles.
To Death. Gluck, *tr. fr. German.*
To Death. Herrick.
To Death. Countess of Winchilsea.
To know just how he suffered would be dear. Emily Dickinson.
To One Who Died Young. Trakl, *tr. fr. German by* Middleton.
Twa Corbies, The. *Unknown.*
'Twas warm at first, like us. Emily Dickinson.
Two Garden Scenes. Charles Burgess.
Ultima Ratio Regum. Spender.
Unillumined Verge, The. Robert Bridges.
Unquiet Grave, The. *Unknown.*
Upon a Dead Man's Head. Skelton.
Upon the Image of Death. Southwell.
Upon the Thought of Age and Death. Habington.
Vacillation. Yeats.
Valley of the Shadow. Galsworthy.
Vergissmeinnicht. Keith Douglas.
Verses Written in a Lady's Sherlock "Upon Death." Earl of Chesterfield.
Vesta. Whittier.
Vision, A. Hofmannsthal, *tr. fr. German by* Stork.
Wake All the Dead! What Ho! What Ho! Davenant.
Warning and Reply. Emily Brontë.
We Are Seven. Wordsworth.
We Lay Us Down to Sleep. Moulton.
Welcome, Thou Safe Retreat. Habington.
What Am I Who Dare. Habington.
What Is It to Die? Earle.
What Profit? Immanuel di Roma, *tr. fr. Hebrew by* Chotzner.
When I am Dead, My Dearest. C. G. Rossetti.
When I Have Fears That I May Cease to Be. Keats.
When I Have Gone Weird Ways. Neihardt.
When Lilacs Last in the Dooryard Bloomed. Whitman.
When the Day Comes. Gutiérrez Nájera, *tr. fr. Spanish by* Beckett.
When the Grass Shall Cover Me. Coolbrith.
Where the Dead Men Lie. Boake.
Who's Most Afraid of Death? Thou. E. E. Cummings.
Why Fear to Die? *Fr.* Arcadia. Sidney.
Wills Dies in Solitude. *Fr.* Burke and Wills. Thiele.
Wind of Death, The. Wetherald.
Wreath, A, *sel.* ("When tongues will tax me in the public ear"). Baylebridge.
Written by the Authoress on Her Death Bed. Pilkington.
Yearning for Death. *Fr.* Hymns to the Night. "Novalis," *tr. fr. German by* Cotterell.
Years-End. Wilbur.
You Need Not Fear. Frieseke.
Poems of Death (PoD). Phoebe Pool, comp.

DECATUR, STEPHEN
How We Burned the *Philadelphia.* Barrett Eastman.
On the Death of Decatur. Crafts.

DECEMBER
December. Joel Benton.
December. Blodgett.
December. Aileen Fisher.
December. L. P. Hopkins.
December. Hugo, *tr. fr. French by* Conder.
December. T. C. Irwin.
December. C. G. Rossetti.
December Day, A. R. F. Murray.
December Day, A. Teasdale.
I Heard a Bird Sing. Oliver Herford.
Long Night Moon, The, December. Frances Frost.
Shepheardes Calender, The: December. Spenser.
Stanzas: "In a drear-nighted December." Keats.
Yard in December, The. Ficke.

DECLARATION OF INDEPENDENCE. Emancipation from British Dependence. Freneau.

DECORATION DAY. *See* MEMORIAL DAY.

DEER
Blacktail Deer. Sarett.
Buck in the Snow, The. Millay.
Crystal Moment. Coffin.
Deer. Mary Austin.
Deer. Drinkwater.
Deer, The. Miyoshi, *tr. fr. Japanese by* Ninomiya *and* Enright.
Deer. *Fr.* A Bestiary. Rexroth.
Deer Come Down, The. Weismiller.
Deer of Ireland, The. Padraic Colum.
Deer on the Mountain. G. F. Norton.
Fallow Deer at the Lonely House, The. Hardy.
Fawn in the Snow, The. W. R. Benét.
Fawn's First Snow, A. Dresbach.
Four Deer, The. M. H. Jones.
Milk White Doe, The. *Unknown, tr. fr. French by* Lang.
Nimble Stag, The. Knox.
Nymph Complaining for the Death of Her Fawn, The. Marvell.
Old Man Said, An. Padraic Colum.
Runnable Stag, A. John Davidson.
Song for the Greenwood Fawn. Salomon.
Vision of the Milk-white Doe, The. Sledd.
White-footed Deer, The. Bryant.

DEERFIELD, MASSACHUSETTS. Sack of Deerfield, The. English.

DEIRDRE
Deirdre. *Fr.* Deirdre. Sir Samuel Ferguson.
Deirdre. James Stephens.
Deirdre, *sel.* Yeats.
Deirdre Is Dead. "Fiona Macleod."
Deirdre's Farewell to Alba. *Unknown, tr. fr. Middle Irish by* Ferguson.
Deirdre's Lament for the Sons of Usnach. *Unknown, tr. fr. Irish by* Ferguson.
Foretelling of Cathbad the Druid at Deirdre's Birth, The. *Unknown, tr. fr. Middle Irish by* Lady Gregory.

DEKKER, THOMAS. Thomas Decker. *Fr.* Sonnets on English Dramatic Poets. Swinburne.

DE LA MARE, WALTER. Mr. Walter de la Mare Makes the Little Ones Dizzy. Hoffenstein.

DELAWARE (state). Our Delaware. Hynson.

DELAWARE (river). Across the Delaware. Will Carleton.

DELPHI, ORACLE OF
Oracle at Delphi. Bagg.
Oracle of Delphi, The. Naudé.

DEMETER. Demeter and Persephone. Tennyson.

DEMOCRACY
Democracy. *Fr.* Commemoration Ode. Harriet Monroe.
Demos. E. A. Robinson.
For You, O Democracy. Whitman.
Hymn to Democracy, A. *Fr.* The Highland Call. Paul Green.
Starting from Paumanok. Whitman.
Young Democracy. O'Dowd.

DEMOCRITUS. Democritus. Robert Bridges.

DEMOSTHENES. Demosthenes to the Radio Announcer. Ross.

DENMARK
Ninth of April, The. Gelsted, *tr. fr. Danish.*
There Is a Charming Land. Oehlenschlager, *tr. fr. Danish by* Hillyer.
Book of Danish Ballads, A (BoDaBa). Axel Olrik, ed.
Book of Danish Verse, A Second (BoDS). Charles Wharton Stork, tr.

DENTISTS. Ode to a Dental Hygienist. Hooton.

DENVER, COLORADO
Camels Have Come, The. *Unknown.*

DENVER, COLORADO (*continued*)
Carrier's Address. *Unknown.*
Curtain, The (Old Tabor Grand Opera House). J. M. Gower.
Doing Railroads for *The Rocky Mountain News.* Warman.
Grand Opening of the People's Theatre. Goldrick.
DESCARTES, RENÉ. Theological. Fadiman.
DESERTS
Asian Desert. Wellesley.
Dawn in the Desert. Scollard.
Desert, The. Knibbs.
Desert Remembers Her Reasons, The. Taggard.
Desert Shipwreck. B. L. Jordan.
Deserts. Hanes.
Entry to the Desert. Rorty.
In the Day's Work. Litchfield.
In the Desert. Corbin.
Loves of the Lions, The. Madge.
Toll of the Desert, The. A. W. Monroe.
Two Deserts, The. *Fr.* To the Unknown Eros. Patmore.
DE SOTO, HERNANDO
Distant Runners, The. Van Doren.
Fall of Maubila, The. English.
DESPAIR
Another While. Rosenfeld, *tr. fr. Yiddish.*
Beatrice Cenci in Her Cell. *Fr.* The Cenci. Shelley.
Carrion Comfort. G. M. Hopkins.
Castaway, The. Cowper.
Dance of Despair, The. Bialik, *tr. fr. Hebrew by* Klein.
Darkling Thrush, The. Hardy.
Despair. E. B. Reed.
Despair. *Fr.* The Faerie Queene. Spenser.
Die My Shriek. Kushniroff, *tr. fr. Yiddish by* Leftwich.
Flow my teares fau from your springs. *Unknown.*
I Wake and Feel the Fell of Dark. G. M. Hopkins.
Interlude, for a Solitary Flute, *sel.* ("Little I knew, when morning-white"). Hoffenstein.
Knife, The. Milton Kaplan.
Leaden Echo and the Golden Echo, The. G. M. Hopkins.
When They Have Lost. Day Lewis.
DEUTSCHLAND (ship). Wreck of the *Deutschland,* The. G. M. Hopkins.
DEVIL. *See* SATAN.
DEVONSHIRE, ENGLAND
Dean-bourn, a Rude River in Devon, by Which Sometimes He Lived. Herrick.
Devon to Me. Galsworthy.
Devonshire Lane, A. Marriott.
Devonshire Rhyme, A. *Unknown.*
Devonshire Song, A. *Unknown.*
Discontents in Devon. Herrick.
Frolic Mariners of Devon The. *Fr.* Britannia's Pastorals. William Browne.
DEW
Dew. Williamson.
Dewdrop, A. Sherman.
Dewdrop, Wind and Sun. Skipsey.
Dewdrops, The. Mackay.
Diamond, A. Loveman.
Drop of Dew, A. Halkin, *tr. fr. Yiddish by* Sonntag.
On a Drop of Dew. Marvell.
Prayer for Dew. Eleazar ben Kalir, *tr. fr. Hebrew by* Zangwill.
Quick-falling Dew. Basho, *tr. fr. Japanese by* Page.
When the Dews Are Earliest Falling. Clough.
DEWEY, GEORGE
Dewey and His Men. Wallace Rice.
Dewey at Manila. R. U. Johnson.
Dewey in Manila Bay. Risley.
Manila. Ware.
DIANA (goddess)
Diana. A. A. Brown.
Diana. Ralegh.
Hymn to Diana. Catullus, *tr. fr. Latin by* Jebb.
Hymn to Diana. *Fr.* The Golden Age. Heywood.
Hymn to Diana. *Fr.* Cynthia's Revels. Jonson.
Orion Seeks the Goddess Diana. *Fr.* Landscape with the Giant Orion. Sacheverell Sitwell.
See also ARTEMIS.
DÍAZ DEL CASTILLO, BERNAL. Bernál Díaz's Preface to His Book. *Fr.* Conquistador. MacLeish.
DICKENS, CHARLES
Charles Dickens. L. C. Poole.
Dickens. Swinburne.
Dickens in Camp. Harte.
Owed to Dickens, 1956. Burroway.
DICKINSON, EMILY
Emily Dickinson. Melville Cane.
Emily Dickinson. Paul Engle.
For Emily Dickinson. Landauer.
Not to Forget Miss Dickinson. Schacht.
Sisters, The. Amy Lowell.
To Emily Dickinson. Hart Crane.
DICTATORS. Litany for Dictatorships. S. V. Benét.
DIEPPE, FRANCE. Road to Dieppe, The. Finley.
DIES IRAE. *See* JUDGMENT DAY.
DIGBY, LADY VENETIA
Lady Venetia Digby, The. Jonson.
Picture of Her Mind, The. Jonson.
DIKES. Leak in the Dike, The. Phoebe Cary.
DINAS VAWR. War-Song of Dinas Vawr, The. *Fr.* The Misfortunes of Elphin. Peacock.
DINGOES. Trapped Dingo. Judith Wright.
DIOCLETIAN. Great Diocletian. *Fr.* The Garden. Cowley.
DIOGENES
Diogenes. Max Eastman.
Tomb of Diogenes, The. *Unknown, tr. fr. Greek by* Symonds.
DIPLOMACY AND DIPLOMATS
I Had a Duck-billed Platypus. Barrington.
On Reading the War Diary of a Defunct Ambassador. Sassoon.
DIRIGIBLES. Dirigible, The. Bergengren.
DISRAELI, BENJAMIN. Old Pilot Tunnels under the English Channel, The. Schevill.
DITMARS, RAYMOND LEE. Lines to Dr. Ditmars. K. A. Robinson.
DIVES
Dives and Lazarus. *Unknown.*
Dives Asking a Drop. Crashaw.
On Dives. Crashaw.
DIVORCE. *See* MARRIAGE.
DOBSON, AUSTIN
Austin Dobson. Morley.
To Austin Dobson. Gosse.
DOCTORS. *See* PHYSICIANS.
DOGS
Abandoned Dog, The. Aubigné, *tr. fr. French by* Selden.
Allendale Dog. Bowes-Lyon.
Animal Store, The. Rachel Field.
At Breakfast. I. M. Mills.
At the Dog Show. Christopher Morley.
Bandog, The. De la Mare.
Beth Gêlert. W. R. Spencer.
Beyond the Grave. Bruner.
Bishop Doane on His Dog. Doane.
Come Hither, Little Puppy-Dog. *Unknown.*
Death of Argus, The. *Fr.* The Odyssey. Homer, *tr. fr. Greek by* Lucas.
Dog, The. Marquis.
Dog. Monro.
Dog and the Water-Lily, The. Cowper.
Dog at Night. Louis Untermeyer.
Dog Who Ate a Pond Lily. Welles.
Dogs and Weather. Welles.
Dog's Cold Nose, The. Guiterman.
Duel, The. Eugene Field.
Elegy on the Death of a Mad Dog. Goldsmith.
Epitaph on a Pet Dog. Du Bellay, *tr. fr. French by* Currey.
Epitaph to a Newfoundland Dog. Byron.
Extraordinary Dog, The. N. B. Turner.
Faithful Dog, A. Richard Burton.
Fashions in Dogs. E. B. White.
Fidelity. Wordsworth.
Geist's Grave. Matthew Arnold.
Hairy Dog, The. Herbert Asquith.
Harper, The. Thomas Campbell.
His friends he loved. His direst earthly foes. Sir William Watson.
Hound, The. Lanier.
Hound on the Church Porch. Coffin.
Hounds, The. John Freeman.
I Think I Know No Finer Things than Dogs. H. C. Brent.
Incident Characteristic of a Favorite Dog. Wordsworth.
Introduction to Dogs, An. Nash.
Island Dogs. C. G. Bell.
Joy Meets Boy. Coffin.
Kaiser Dead. Matthew Arnold.
Little Dog's Day, The. Rupert Brooke.
Little Lost Pup. Guiterman.
Little Puppy. *Tr. fr. Navajo Indian by* Wetherill.
Lone Dog. I. R. McLeod.
Lonely Dog, The. Bruner.
Lost Dog. Frances Rodman.
Lugete O Veneres Cupidinesque. Elton.
Malemute Dog, A. O'Cotter.
Maltese Dog, A. Tymnes, *tr. fr. Greek by* Blunden.
Morning Overture; Chorus of Dogs. Strachan.
My Airedale Dog. W. L. Mason.
My Dog. J. K. Bangs.
My Dog. Chute.
My Dog Tray. Byrom.
My Dog Tray. Thomas Campbell.
My Last Terrier. Halsham.
My Old Dog Tray. S. C. Foster.
Obituary. T. W. Parsons.
Old Dog, An. Duffin.

Old Dogs. Thayer.
Old Hound. Mastin.
On a Puppy. Feng Chih, *tr. fr. Chinese by* Chu K'an.
Ordinary Dog, The. N.B. Turner.
Our Dog. Janet Vaughn.
Pardon, The. Wilbur.
Pup een da Snow, Da. T. A. Daly.
Puppy and I. A. A. Milne.
Road to Vagabondia, The. Dana Burnet.
Shepherd and His Dog, The. Bowles.
Shepherd Dog of the Pyrenees, The. Ellen Murray.
Song of the Mischievous Dog, The. Dylan Thomas.
Span of Life, The. Robert Frost.
Subverted Flower, The. Robert Frost.
Sunning. Tippett.
Tim, an Irish Terrier. Letts.
To a Black Dog, Bereaved. Coatsworth.
To a Black Greyhound. Julian Grenfell.
To a Bull-Dog. Squire.
To a Dog. Branch.
To a Dog Injured in the Street. W. C. Williams.
To an English Setter. Thomas Walsh.
To Flush, My Dog. E. B. Browning.
To My Auld Dog Dash. Barr of Craigielee.
To My Setter, Scout. Seldon.
To My Terrier Rex. A. K. Gray.
To Our House-Dog Captain. Landor.
Train Dogs, The. E. P. Johnson.
Vern. Gwendolyn Brooks.
Woodman's Dog, The. Cowper.
All the Best Dog Poems (AIBD). Edwin Burtis, comp.

DOGWOOD
Dogwood Blossoms. McClellan.
Who Plants a Dogwood Tree. Mabel Brown.

DOLLS
Dolladine. Rands.
Doll's Cradle-Song. *Unknown, tr. fr. German.*
Doll's House, The. Barbauld.
Doll's Wooing, The. Eugene Field.
Dolly's Lullaby. J. H. Ewing.
Dolly's Lullaby. Van Rensselaer.
Dressing the Doll. Rands.
Lost Doll, The. *Fr.* The Water Babies. Kingsley.

DOLPHINS
Dolphins, The. Maclaren.
Dolphins. Molly Michaels.
Dolphins in Blue Water. Amy Lowell.

DON JUAN. Don Juan Declaims. Flecker.

DON QUIXOTE
Don Quixote. Betts.
Don Quixote. Dobson.
Don Quixote. Ficke.

DONEGAL, IRELAND. Springtime in Donegal. M. R. Stevenson.

DONKEYS. *See* ASSES.

DONNE, JOHN
Dr. Donne. Alling.
Elegie upon the Death of the Deane of Pauls, Dr. John Donne, An. Carew.
John Donne's Defiance. J. R. Hervey.
On Donne's Poetry. S. T. Coleridge.
On John Donne's Book of Poems. Marriott.
To John Donne ("Donne, the delight of Phoebus, and each Muse"). Jonson.
To John Donne ("Who shall doubt, Donne, where I a Poet bee"). Jonson.
Upon the Death of My Ever Desired Friend Doctor Donne Dean of Paul's. Henry King.

DONNYBROOK FAIR, DUBLIN, IRELAND
Humours of Donnybrook Fair, The. O'Flaherty.
Humours of Donnybrook Fair, The. *Unknown.*

DORDRECHT, HOLLAND. Nightfall in Dordrecht. Eugene Field.

DOUGLAS, STEPHEN ARNOLD. Lecompton's Black Brigade. Halpine.

DOUGLASS, FREDERICK. Frederick Douglass. Hayden.

DOURO (river). *See* DUERO.

DOVER, ENGLAND
Cliffs of Dover, The. Hemans.
Dover Beach. Matthew Arnold.
Dover Cliff. Home.
Dover Cliffs. W. L. Bowles.
Dover Cliffs. *Fr.* King Lear. Shakespeare.

DOVES
Considerations of Norfolk Island, *sel.* ("High in the afternoon the dove"). Smithyman.
Dove, The. Abul Hasan of Seville, *tr. fr. Arabic by* Arberry.
Dove and the Wren, The. *Unknown.*
Doves. Guiney.
Doves, The. Tynan.
Dove's Nest. J. R. Taylor.
Hawk and the Dove, The. *Unknown, tr. fr. Armenian by* Boyajian.
Literary Landscape with Dove and Poet. McGinley.
Mourning Dove, The. Christman.
My Doves. E. B. Browning.
Song: "I had a dove, and the sweet dove died." Keats.
Stockdove, The. Pitter.
Two Doves Upon the Selfsame Branch. C. G. Rossetti.
Voice of the Dove, The. Joaquin Miller.

DOWNS
Downs, The. Bridges.
Downs, The. Galsworthy.

DOWSON, ERNEST. Ernest Dowson. Wheelock.

DRAGONFLIES
Devil's Darning Needle. McCoy.
Dragon Flies. W. J. Turner.
Dragon-Fly, A. Farjeon.
Dragon-Fly, The. Landor.
Dragonfly, The. Rand.

DRAGONS
Dragon, The. *Fr.* The Faerie Queene. Spenser.
Dragon's Warning, The. Sharman.
O to Be a Dragon. Marianne Moore.
Serious Omission. John Farrar.
Sir Eglamour, That Worthy Knight. *Fr.* The Melancholy Knight. Rowlands.
Tale of Custard the Dragon, The. Nash.

DRAKE, SIR FRANCIS
Admiral's Ghost, The. Noyes.
Dragon of the Seas. T. N. Page.
Drake. Noyes.
Drake's Drum. Newbolt.
Epigram: On Sir Francis Drake. *Unknown.*
Farewell to Sir John Norris and Sir Francis Drake, A. Peele.
First American Sailors, The. Wallace Rice.
Last Voyage of Sir Francis Drake, and Sir John Hawkins, The. Fitzgeffrey.
Of the Great and Famous Sir Francis Drake. Hayman.
On Sir Francis Drake. Fitzgeffrey.
Sir Francis Drake Reviv'd. *Fr.* The History of Sir Francis Drake. Davenant.
Taking of Cartagena, The. *Fr.* The True and Perfecte Newes of the Worthy Enterprises of Sir Francis Drake, 1586. Greepe.
To the Noble Sir Francis Drake. Beedome.
Upon Sir Francis Drake's Return from His Voyage about the World, and the Queen's Meeting Him. *Unknown.*

DRAKE, JOSEPH RODMAN. On the Death of Joseph Rodman Drake. Halleck.

DRAYTON, MICHAEL
Ad Michaelem Drayton. Weever.
Funeral Elegy on the Death of His Very Good Friend, Mr. Michael Drayton. Cokayne.
Remembrance of Some English Poets, A. Barnfield.
To Master Michael Drayton. Thomas Lodge.

DREAMING AND DREAMS
Adventure. Laura Benét.
All Is Well. Clough.
Apparition. Mallarmé, *tr. fr. French by* Flores.
Awake, My Lute! C. S. Lewis.
Bad Dreams. Robert Browning.
Cry of the Dreamer, The. O'Reilly.
Dark Chateau. De la Mare.
Dream. Mary Austin.
Dream, A. Blake.
Dream. Branch.
Dream, The. Donne.
Dream, A. Gaston.
Dream. M. E. Hamilton.
Dream, A. Poe.
Dream. W. J. Smith.
Dream-Bearer. M. C. Davies.
Dream-Land. Poe.
Dream Love. C. G. Rossetti.
Dream-Pedlary. Beddoes.
Dream the Great Dream. Coates.
Dreamer, The. Bax.
Dreamer, The. Morgenstern, *tr. fr. German by* Hull.
Dreamers. J. B. Hope.
Dreamers, The. Jephcott.
Dreamers of Dreams. Carruth.
Dreaming That I Went with Lu and Yu to Visit Yüan Chēn. Po Chü-i, *tr. fr. Chinese by* Waley.
Dreams. C. F. Alexander.
Dreams. Herrick.
Dreams. Langston Hughes.
Dreams. Poe.
Dreams. Traherne.
Dreams within Dreams. "Fiona Macleod."
Give Us Great Dreams. LeNart.
Harlequin of Dreams, The. Lanier.
He Whom a Dream Hath Possessed. O'Sheel.
Hold Fast Your Dreams! Driscoll.
If Only the Dreams Abide. Scollard.
Isle of Lost Dreams. "Fiona Macleod."
Kubla Khan. Coleridge.

DREAMING AND DREAMS (*continued*)
Land of Nod, The. R. L. Stevenson.
New Dreams for Old. C. Y. Rice.
Ode: "We are the music-makers." O'Shaughnessy.
Only in Dreams. Holland.
Orchard-Pit, The. D. G. Rossetti.
Plain Man's Dream, A. Keppel.
Reverie at Dawn. O'Rahilly, *tr. fr. Irish by* O'Connor.
Say, Lovely Dream. Waller.
Shepherd's Dream, A. Breton.
Snow Globe, The. Nemerov.
Soft, lovely, rose-like lips, conjoined with mine. Barnabe Barnes.
Song: "Don't Tell Me What You Dreamt Last Night." F. P. Adams.
Song of Dreams, A. "Fiona Macleod."
Supposing I Dreamed This. E. E. Cummings.
'Tis Sair to Dream. Gilfillan.
To Young Dreamers. Trent.
Trance, The. Spender.
Vision, A. Ts'ao Chih, *tr. fr. Chinese by* Waley.
Wharf of Dreams, The. Markham.
What Was My Dream? O'Connor.
Youth Dreams, The. Rilke, *tr. fr. German by* Lewisohn.

DRIFTWOOD
Driftwood. Wilbur.
Fires of Driftwood. MacKay.

DRINKING
Alcibiades to a Jealous Girl. Ficke.
Alcohol. MacNeice.
Bacchus on Beverages. Redi, *tr. fr. Italian by* Hunt.
Back and Side Go Bare, Go Bare. *Fr.* Gammer Gurton's Needle. *At. to* William Stevenson.
Be Drunk. Baudelaire, *tr. fr. French by* Davis.
Bee quick my boyes drinke off your wine. *Unknown.*
Beer. Calverley.
Blood thirsty care goe packe. *Unknown.*
Captain Stratton's Fancy. Masefield.
Careless Gallant, The. Thomas Jordan.
Catch, A: "If all be true that I do think." Henry Aldrich.
"Come, Fill the Cup." *Fr.* Anacreontea. *Unknown, tr. fr. Greek by* Lucas.
Come, Thou Monarch. *Fr.* Antony and Cleopatra. Shakespeare.
Crown high the cup and pass it round. Hedylus, *tr. fr. Greek by* Pott.
Cruiskeen Lawn, The. *Unknown.*
Drink Today, and Drown All Sorrow. *Fr.* The Bloody Brother. John Fletcher, *and others.*
Drinker. Patrick Anderson.
Drinking. Cowley, *after the Greek of* Anacreon.
Drinking. Hsin Chi'i-chi, *tr. fr. Chinese by* Ching Ti.
Drinking Alone in the Moonlight. Li Po, *tr. fr. Chinese.*
Drinking Bout, A. Liu Chia, *tr. fr. Chinese by* Hart.
Drinking Song. "The Archpoet of Cologne," *tr. fr. Latin by* Symonds.
Drinking-Song, A. Carey.
Drinking Song, The. *Fr.* The Bloody Brother. John Fletcher, *and others.*
Drinking Song. Ubada, *tr. fr. Arabic by* Arberry.
Drinking Song. *Unknown.*
Drinking Song, A, against All Sorts of Disputes in Drinking. Wycherley.
Drinking Song for Present-Day Gatherings. Morris Bishop.
Drunk Again. Po Chü-i, *tr. fr. Chinese by* Hart.
Empty Jar, The. Stenhouse.
Epigram: "He is not drunk who, from the floor." Eugene Field.
Fill fill the bowele the lusty wyne will dye. *Unknown.*
Five Reasons for Drinking, The. Henry Aldrich.
Food and Drink. Louis Untermeyer.
Friend Advises Me to Stop Drinking, A. Mei Yao Ch'en, *tr. fr. Chinese by* Rexroth.
If thou doest not love sacke. *Unknown.*
In Taberna Quando Sumus. *Fr.* Carmina Burana. *Unknown, tr. fr. Latin by* Whicher.
John Barleycorn. Burns.
Let the Toast Pass. R. B. Sheridan.
Liquor and Longevity. *Unknown.*
Little Brown Jug. *Unknown.*
Little Vagabond, The. Blake.
Logical Vegetarian, The. Chesterton.
Miniver Cheevy. E. A. Robinson.
Of Drunkenness. Turberville.
Old Toper, The. Ibn Sa'id of Alcala la Real, *tr. fr. Arabic by* Arberry.
On Going to a Tavern. Wang Chi, *tr. fr. Chinese by* Waley.
O'Tuomy's Drinking Song. O'Tuomy, *tr. fr. Modern Irish by* O'Daly, *vers. by* Mangan.
Potatores Exquisiti. *Fr.* Carmina Burana. *Unknown, tr. fr. Latin by* Blackett.
Pox on pelfe why should we love it. *Unknown.*
Reasons for Drinking ("If all be true"). Henry Aldrich.
R-e-m-o-r-s-e. Ade.
She Stoops to Conquer, *sel.* ("Let schoolmasters puzzle their brain"). Goldsmith.
Some love Marce and some love Venus. *Unknown.*
Song: "Who tames the lion now?" Beddoes.
Stirrup-Cup, A. Ainslie.
Stirrup-Cup, The. John Hay.
Stirrup Cup, The. Aline Kilmer.
Stirrup-Cup, The. Lanier.
Stirrup Cup, The. W. A. Percy.
Swell Me a Bowl. *Fr.* The Poetaster. Jonson.
Temperate Drinking. Anacreon, *tr. fr. Greek by* Moore.
To His Cup Bearer. Catullus, *tr. fr. Latin by* Lamb.
Toast. Mallarmé, *tr. fr. French by* Bennett.
Two Drinking Songs. Alcaeus, *tr. fr. Greek by* Bowra.
Upon Drinking in a Bowl. Earl of Rochester.
Villon's Straight Tip to All Cross Coves. Henley.
Waking from Drunkenness on a Spring Day. Li Po, *tr. fr. Chinese by* Waley.
War and Wine. Le Houx, *formerly at. to* Basselin, *tr. fr. French by* Currey.
Wassell wassell wassell wassell. *Unknown.*
Whisky, Drink Divine. O'Leary.
Why, Liquor of Life? Carolan, *tr. fr. Modern Irish by* D'Alton.
Willie Brewed a Peck o' Maut. Burns.
Wine and Water. G. K. Chesterton.

DROMEDARIES. *See* CAMELS.

DROUGHT
Drought. Darlow.
Drought. Ogilvie.
Drought. Tynan.
Drouth. Mary Austin.
Dry Time. Norma Davis.
End of the Drought, The. McArthur.
Soliloquy. Laight.
Sun Drops Red, The. N. B. Miller.
Western Wind, When Wilt Thou Blow? *Unknown.*
Wind Our Enemy, The. Marriott.

DRUG ADDICTION. Addict, The. Rubin.

DRUG STORES
Drug Store. Shapiro.
Drug Store. Weaver.

DRUMS
African Dance. Langston Hughes.
Drum, The. John Farrar.

DRUNKARDS
Drunkard, The. Mao Kuang Sheng, *tr. fr. Chinese by* Hart.
Drunkard, The. Proverbs, Bible, *O.T.*
Drunkard to His Bottle. A. Le Fanu.
Drunkard's Hell, The. *Unknown.*
Drunken Man on Highgate Hill, A. Hasluck.
Hemmed-in Males. W. C. Williams.
I'll Never Get Drunk Any More. *Unknown.*

DRURY, SIR WILLIAM. Epitaph upon the Death of Sir William Drury, An. Barnabe Rich.

DRURY LANE, LONDON. Tale of Drury Lane, A. Smith.

DRURY LANE THEATER, LONDON. Prologue Spoken by Mr. Garrick at the Opening of the Theatre Royal, 1747. Johnson.

DRYDEN, JOHN
Account of the Greatest English Poets, An. Addison.
Canons Ashby. David Wright.
Pope on Dryden. *Fr.* The First Epistle of the Second Book of Horace. Pope.
Progress of Poesy, The. Thomas Gray.

DUBLIN, IRELAND
Back to Dublin. R. A. D. Ford.
Dublin. MacNeice.
Dublin Made Me. MacDonagh.
Georgian Dublin. M. J. Craig.
Magazine Fort, Phoenix Park, Dublin. Wilkins.

DUBOIS, WILLIAM EDWARD BURGHARDT. For William Edward Burghardt Dubois on His Eightieth Birthday. Latimer.

DUCKS
Blue Duck, The. Sarett.
Broken Drake. Sarett.
Dame Duck's First Lecture on Education. Hawkshaw.
Duck, The. Edith King.
Duck, The. Nash.
Duck in Central Park. F. H. Savage.
Ducks. Ault.
Ducks. Daniells.
Ducks. F. W. Harvey.
Ducks, The. Alice Wilkins.
Ducks at Dawn. Tippett.
Duck's Ditty. *Fr.* The Wind in the Willows. Grahame.
Eider Duck, The. Ibsen, *tr. fr. Norwegian by* Stork.
Four Ducks on a Pond. Allingham.
Mallard. Rex Warner.
New Duckling, The. Noyes.
Quack! De la Mare.
Sing-Song Rhyme. *Unknown.*

Wild Duck, The. Masefield.
Wild Duck and Her Brood, The. Grahame.
Wild Duck's Nest, The. Wordsworth.
DUDDON (river), ENGLAND. To the River Duddon. Norman Nicholson.
DUERO *or* DOURO (river). Ballad of the River Duero. Diego, *tr. fr. Spanish by* Turnbull.
DUFFY, SIR CHARLES GAVAN. To Duffy in Prison. McGee.
DUGDALE, SIR WILLIAM. Sonnet: Written in a Blank Leaf of Dugdale's "Monasticon." *Fr.* Sonnets. Warton.
DULLES, JOHN FOSTER. Just Dropped In. William Cole.
DUMAS, ALEXANDRE. Lines Written at the Grave of Alexandre Dumas. G. B. Bennett.
DUNBAR, PAUL LAURENCE
Dunbar. Anne Spencer.
For Paul Laurence Dunbar. Cullen.
Paul Laurence Dunbar. Corrothers.
DUNCAN, ISADORA. Photograph of Isadora Duncan, A. Hayden.
DUNDEE, JOHN GRAHAM OF CLAVERHOUSE, 1ST VISCOUNT (Bonnie Dundee)
Bonnie Dundee. *Fr.* The Doom of Devergoil. Sir Walter Scott.
Upon the Death of the Earl of Dundee. Dryden.
DUNEDIN, NEW ZEALAND. Dunedin in the Gloaming. Mackay.
DUNES
On the Dunes. Teasdale.
Sand Dunes and Sea. Moreland.
DUNKIRK, FRANCE
After Dunkirk. Alun Lewis.
Dunkirk. Nathan.
Dunkirk. E. J. Pratt.
Dunkirk Pier. Rook.
Little Boats of Britain, The. Carsley.
To the Seamen. Masefield.
DUNS SCOTUS, JOHN. Duns Scotus's Oxford. G. M. Hopkins.
DUPREE, FRANK. Dupree. *Unknown.*
DUQUESNE, FORT. Fort Duquesne. Plimpton.
DÜRER, ALBRECHT
Dürer's "Melencolia." Sir William Watson.
Steeple-Jack, The. Marianne Moore.
DUSK
At Twilight. Van Rensselaer.
Close of Day, The. Curtwright.
Dusk. Grimké.
Dusk. DuBose Heyward.
Dusk. Lopez-Penha, *tr. fr. Spanish by* Walsh.
Dusk. MacLeish.
Dusk. Scollard.
Dusk at Sea. T. S. Jones, Jr.
Dusk from a Train Window. C. Y. Rice.
Dusk in the Low Country. DuBose Heyward.
Dusk Song. W. H. A. Moore.
In the Dusk. Ledwidge.
In the Gloaming. Bayles.
Near Dusk. Auslander.
Song of Twilight, A. *Unknown.*
Twilight. Custance.
Twilight. Heavysege.
Twilight. Heine, *tr. fr. German by* Untermeyer.
Twilight. D. H. Lawrence.
Twilight. Longfellow.
Twilight. McCormick.
Twilight. Pagaza, *tr. fr. Spanish by* Blackwell.
Twilight. A. M. F. Robinson.
Twilight. Ryan.
Twilight. Symons.
Twilight. Tyutchev, *tr. fr. Russian by* Deutsch.
Twilight at Sea. Welby.
Twilight at the Heights. Joaquin Miller.
Twilight Calm. C. G. Rossetti.
Twilight in Middle March, A. Ledwidge.
Twilight on Tweed. Lang.
Twilight Song. E. A. Robinson.
Written in Very Early Youth. Wordsworth.
DUST STORMS. Colorado Sand Storm, A. Eugene Field.
DUTCH WARS
Last Instructions to a Painter, *sels.* Marvell.
Written at Sea, in the First Dutch War. Charles Sackville.
DUTY
Duty Emerson.
Duty. Hooper.
Duty. Markham.
Duty. *Unknown.*
Duty—That's to Say Complying. Clough.
Kind of an Ode to Duty. Nash.
Ode to Duty. Wordsworth.
Reward of Service. *Fr.* A Drama of Exile. *At. to* E. B. Browning.
So Nigh Is Grandeur to Man. Cook.
DYER, JOHN. To the Poet, John Dyer. Wordsworth.
DYER, SIR WILLIAM. Epitaph on the Monument of Sir William Dyer at Colmworth, 1641. Lady Catherine Dyer.

E

EAGLES
Dalliance of the Eagles, The. Whitman.
Dead Eagle, The. Thomas Campbell.
Eagle, The. Tennyson.
Eagle. J. B. Thomas.
Eagle and the Mole, The. Elinor Wylie.
Eagle Trail, The. Garland.
Eagles. Bashkin, *tr. fr. Russian by* Deutsch.
Eagle's Love, The. Gourghinian, *tr. fr. Armenian by* Boyajian.
Eagle's Nature, The. *Fr.* The Bestiary. *Unknown.*
Eagle's Song, The. Mary Austin.
Osprey and Eagle. J. B. Rittenhouse.
Painting of an Eagle, The. Tu Fu, *tr. fr. Chinese.*
Salmon Drowns Eagle. Lowry.
Sea and the Eagle, The. Clouts.
Slain Eagle, The. Sims.
EARTH
Dartsiae. Kingsley.
Earth. Bryant.
Earth, The. Emerson.
Earth. J. G. Fletcher.
Earth, The. Leonard Mann.
Earth. Roscoe.
Earth, The. Very.
Earth. Wheelock.
Earth and Sky. Toumanian, *tr. fr. Armenian by* Boyajian.
Earth Breath, The. "Æ."
Earth in Spring, The. Halevi, *tr. fr. Hebrew by* King.
Earth Listens. K. L. Bates.
Earth Love. Redpath.
Earth Melody. Christy MacKaye.
Earth Song. D. McK. Wright.
Eye, The. Jeffers.
False World, Thou Ly'st. *Fr.* Emblems. Quarles.
First Morning of the Second World, The. Schwartz.
Golden Elegy, The. Staff, *tr. fr. Polish by* Kirkconnell.
Hamatreya. Emerson.
Hymn of the Earth. Channing.
Hymn to Earth. Elinor Wylie.
Hymn to Earth the Mother of All. *Unknown, tr. fr. Greek by* Shelley.
I Saw God Wash the World. Stidger.
Last Man, The. Thomas Campbell.
Mother Earth. Harriet Monroe.
Notable Description of the World, A. *At. to* William Smith.
O Earth, Sufficing All Our Needs. C. G. D. Roberts.
O Sweet Spontaneous Earth. E. E. Cummings.
Poetry of Earth, The. Coates.
Praise of Earth. E. B. Browning.
Salutation, The. Traherne.
Soil. Nothing more. Salinas, *tr. fr. Spanish by* Turnbull.
Song of the Earth. *Tr. fr. Navajo Indian by* Curtis.
To an Old Lady. Empson.
Wonder. Traherne.
Wonderful World, The. Rands.
World, The. Drummond of Hawthornden.
World, The. George Herbert.
World, The. *Fr.* Symbolisms. Realf.
World, The. Vaughan.
World, The ("This the best world"). *Unknown.*
World a Game. Drummond of Hawthornden.
World, The; a Ghazel. Mangan.
World in Making, The. Sir Gilbert Parker.
World Music. Bushnell.
World without Peculiarity. Wallace Stevens.
EAST WIND
Charming of the East Wind, The. C. T. Turner.
East Wind, The. Going.
EASTER
As It Began to Dawn. G. E. Hoffman.
Assurance. Crowell.
Assurance. Munson.
At Easter Time. Blanden.
At Easter Time. L. E. Richards.
Calvary and Easter. "Susan Coolidge."
Christ Has Risen. "Susan Coolidge."
Dawn. Crouse.
Day of Resurrection, The. St. John of Damascus, *tr. fr. Greek by* Neale.
Down a Sunny Easter Meadow. N. B. Turner.
Early, Early Easter Day. Aileen Fisher.
Easter. Coatsworth.
Easter. Hilda Conkling.

EASTER (*continued*)
Easter. M. C. Davies.
Easter. Gilder.
Easter. George Herbert.
Easter. Joyce Kilmer.
Easter. Miyoshi, *tr. fr. Japanese by* Erickson.
Easter. Oxenham.
Easter. Sabin.
Easter. Towne.
Easter. Tynan.
Easter ("Sing, soul of mine"). *Unknown.*
Easter ("This is the time Man hath overcome"). *Unknown.*
Easter. Van Brakle.
Easter. Verlaine, *tr. fr. French by* Conder.
Easter. Wardlaw.
Easter. Whitaker.
Easter Advent. Boner.
Easter Canticle, An: "In every trembling bud and bloom." Towne.
Easter Carol, An: "Flash forth, thou sun." C. G. Rossetti.
Easter Carol: "O Earth, throughout thy borders." G. N. Lovejoy.
Easter Carol, An: "Spring bursts to-day." C. G. Rossetti.
Easter Chorus: "Christ is arisen." *Fr.* Faust. Goethe, *tr. fr. German by* Coxe.
Easter Day. Clough.
Easter Day. Crashaw.
Easter Day. Jasper Heywood.
Easter Day. Juan Ruiz, Archpriest of Hita, *tr. fr. Spanish by* Farnell.
Easter Day, *sel.* ("Ye that for psalmody contend"). Smart.
Easter Day. *Fr.* Lambros. Solomos, *tr. fr. Modern Greek by* Dalven.
Easter Day, Naples, 1849. Clough.
Easter Eve, 1945. Rukeyser.
Easter Gloves. *Unknown.*
Easter Hymn. *Fr.* Faust. Goethe, *tr. fr. German.*
Easter Hymn. A. E. Housman.
Easter Hymn. St. John of Damascus, *tr. fr. Greek by* Neale.
Easter Hymn, An. Le Gallienne.
Easter Hymn. Vaughan.
Easter Hymn. Wesley.
Easter in the Woods. Frances Frost.
Easter Joy. Price.
Easter Joy. N. B. Turner.
Easter Light. Munson.
Easter Message. Van Brakle.
Easter Monday. William Barnes.
Easter Morn. *Fr.* Christ's Victory and Triumph. Giles Fletcher.
Easter Morning. Phillips Brooks.
Easter Morning. Garrison.
Easter Music. Deland.
Easter Night. Alice Meynell.
Easter, 1923. Neihardt.
Easter Poem, An. Palmer.
Easter Poem. Prichard.
Easter Poem. Raine.
Easter Praise. Rodney Bennett.
Easter Prayer, An. C. M. Davis.
Easter Prayer, An. Towne.
Easter Prayer. N. B. Turner.
Easter Prayer, An. *Unknown.*
Easter Sacraments. Schauffler.
Easter Snowfall. Behn.
Easter Song. Alishan, *tr. fr. Armenian by* Blackwell.
Easter Song. Lathbury.
Easter Thought. Leo Cox.
Easter Tuesday. C. G. Rossetti.
Easter Week. Kingsley.
Easter-Wings. George Herbert.
Easter Zunday. William Barnes.
English Easter, 7 A.M. Underhill.
Follow Me. Longfellow.
For Easter. Havergal.
For Our Sakes. Oscar Wilde.
From Bethlehem to Calvary. Nicholson.
Good Friday in My Heart. M. E. Coleridge.
His Last Week. Lennen.
If a Man Die, Shall He Live Again? Moreland.
If Easter Be Not True. Barstow.
Jesus Lives, and So Shall I. Gellert.
Lacking my love, I go from place to place. *Fr.* Amoretti. Spenser.
Legend of the Easter Eggs, The. O'Brien.
Mary. Margaret Sangster.
Meeting the Easter Bunny. R. B. Bennett.
Most Glorious Lord of Lyfe. *Fr.* Amoretti. Spenser.
My Easter Prayer. *Unknown.*
My Risen Lord. *Unknown.*
Nature's Easter Music. Larcom.
O Bells in the Steeple. M. R. Smith.
Of the Resurrection of Christ. William Dunbar.
On Easter Day. Thaxter.
On Easter Morning. Rexford
Rest Remaineth. *Fr.* Christmas-Eve and Easter-Day. Robert Browning.
Resurrection, The. J. H. Brooks.
Resurrection. I. N. Munson.
Resurrection Hymn. Weiss.
Softly through the Mellow Starlight. *Unknown.*
Some Things That Easter Brings. Parrish.
Song at Easter, A. Towne.
Song of Easter. Thaxter.
Sonnet at Easter. Nemerov.
That Nature Is a Heraclitean Fire and of the Comfort of the Resurrection. G. M. Hopkins.
They Saw and Believed. Hagg.
This Easter Day. Nicholson.
To Piux X at Easter. Wildman.
What Does Easter Mean to You? Conrad.
Easter (Our American Holidays Series) (EOAH). Susan Tracy Rice *and* Robert Haven Schauffler, eds.

EATING. *See* FOOD.

ECHO
Bugle Song, The. *Fr.* The Princess. Tennyson.
Echo. E. G. Bishop.
Echo. De la Mare.
Echo. Viscountess Grey.
Echo. Thomas Moore.
Echo. Saxe.
Echo. *Fr.* Arcadia. Sidney.
Echo. Tennant.
Echo. *Unknown.*

ECHO (nymph)
Narcissus. Alistair Campbell.
Sad nymph, Gaho, followed to the shadie woods, The. *Unknown.*
Song: "Sweet Echo, sweetest nymph, that liv'st unseen." *Fr.* Comus. Milton.

EDELWEISS. Edelweiss. Snoilsky, *tr. fr. Swedish by* Stork.

EDEN, WILLIAM. Rondeau Humbly Inscribed to the Right Hon. William Eden Minister Plenipotentiary of Commercial Affairs at the Court of Versailles. *At. to* George Ellis.

EDINBURGH, SCOTLAND
Edinburgh. Guiterman.
Edinburgh. Noyes.
Edinburgh. Alexander Smith.
From a Window in Princes Street. Henley.
Written in Edinburgh. Arthur Hallam.

EDISON, THOMAS ALVA
And Yet Fools Say. G. S. Holmes.
Edison. Jeffers.
Modern Columbus, A. E. R. Wilson.

EDUCATION
Elementary School Classroom in a Slum, An. Spender.
Modern Ode to the Modern School. Erskine.
Pains of Education, The. Churchill.
Tables Turned, The. Wordsworth.
Trusty Learning A, B, C. Follen.

EDWARD I, KING OF ENGLAND. Bard, The. Thomas Gray.

EDWARD II, KING OF ENGLAND. Mortimeriados, *sels.* Drayton.

EDWARD IV, KING OF ENGLAND
King Edward the Fourth and a Tanner of Tamworth. *Unknown.*
On the Death of the Noble Prince King Edward the Fourth. Skelton.

EDWARD VII, KING OF ENGLAND
Death of King Edward VII, The. *Unknown.*
Elegy on Albert Edward the Peacemaker. *Unknown.*
New Song on the Birth of the Prince of Wales, A. *Unknown.*

EDWARD THE CONFESSOR. Edward the Confessor. *Unknown.*

EDWARDS, JONATHAN. Mr. Edwards and the Spider. Robert Lowell.

EDWARDS, RICHARD. Of Edwards of the Chapel. Googe.

EELS
Bucket of Sea-Serpents. Ant.
Eel, The. Nash.
Eels, Tortoises, Soles, Lampreys. *Fr.* Halieuticks. Oppian, *tr. fr. Greek by* Diaper.

EGERTON, THOMAS. *See* ELLESMERE, THOMAS EGERTON, BARON.

EGYPT
De Rosis Hibernis. Gosse.
Egypt. Doolittle ("H. D.").
Egypt's Might Is Tumbled Down. M. E. Coleridge.
Herodotus in Egypt. Lang.

EGYPTIAN LOTUS (flower). Egyptian Lotus, The. A. W. H. Eaton.

EHRLICH, PAUL. Sonnet on the Death of Paul Ehrlich, Discoverer of Salvarsan. Jerome Meyers.

EINSTEIN, ALBERT
Einstein. MacLeish.
Gift to Be Simple, The. Moss.

Elands. Seele im Raum. Jarrell.
Eleanor of Aquitaine
Queen Eleanor's Confession. *Unknown.*
Rose of the World, The. Masefield.
Elephants
Blind Men and the Elephant, The. Saxe.
Circus Elephant. Worth.
Cradle Song of the Elephants. Adriano del Valle, *tr. fr. Portuguese by* Malkus.
Death of an Elephant. Warr.
Dignity. Bhartrihari, *tr. fr. Sanskrit by* Ryder.
Elephant, The. Herbert Asquith.
Elephant, The. Belloc.
Elephant. Brettell.
Elephant, The. *Fr.* A Circus Garland. Rachel Field.
Elephant, An. J. G. Francis.
Elephant! Scherman.
Elephant The. Wynne.
Elephant Is Slow to Mate, The. D. H. Lawrence.
Elephants, The. Leconte de Lisle, *tr. fr. French by* Conder.
Elephants. Marianne Moore.
Elephants Are Different to Different People. Sandburg.
Elephant's Trunk. Alice Wilkins.
Eletelephony. L. E. Richards.
Holding Hands. Link.
Indian Elephant, The. Kaberry.
Melancthon. Marianne Moore.
Elgin Marbles. On Seeing the Elgin Marbles. Keats.
Elijah
Angel, The. Alfred Hayes.
Elijah in the House of Study. Leib, *tr. fr. Yiddish by* Betsky.
"Eliot, George." On the Deaths of Thomas Carlyle and George Eliot. Swinburne.
Eliot, Thomas Stearns
Critical Fable, A, *sel.* ("The expatriates"). Amy Lowell.
For T. S. E. Only. Plutzik.
Verses for the 60th Birthday of T. S. Eliot. George Barker.
Elizabeth, Queen of Austria. House of Sorrows, The. Francis Thompson.
Elizabeth, Queen of Bohemia. On His Mistress, the Queen of Bohemia. Wotton.
Elizabeth I, Queen of England
Ad Reginam Elizabetham ("Live long, Elisa, that the wolf of Spain"). Thomas Bastard.
Ad Reginam Elizabetham ("Mother of England, and sweet nurse of all"). Thomas Bastard.
Author to Queen Elizabeth, in Praise of Her Reading, The. Harington.
Ballad to Queen Elizabeth, A. Dobson.
Dedication: "To that clear majesty which in the north." *Fr.* Nosce Teipsum. Sir John Davies.
Drake. Noyes.
Elizabeth. Saul.
Fair Oriana in the Morn. Milton.
Hard by a Crystal Fountain. *Unknown.*
Hymns of Astraea, *sels.* Sir John Davies.
Looking-Glass, The. Kipling.
Poem from "The Year of Loss." Nicholas Moore.
Queen Elizabeth at Tilbury. Deloney.
Silent Lover, The. Ralegh.
Songe betwene the Quenes Majestie and Englande, A. Birche.
Sorrowful Verses Made on the Death of Our Most Sovereign Lady Queen Elizabeth My Gracious Mistress. Churchyard.
To My Most Gracious Dread Sovereign. *Fr.* Nosce Teipsum. Sir John Davies.
To Queen Elizabeth. Ralegh.
When Good Queen Elizabeth Governed the Realm. Stansbury.
With Fragrant Flowers We Strew the Way. Thomas Watson.
Elizabeth, Queen Consort of Henry VII
English Epitaph on Queen Elizabeth, Wife of Henry VII. *Unknown.*
I Pray to Venus. Elizabeth of York.
Rueful Lamentation on the Death of Queen Elizabeth, A. More.
Elizabeth, Saint
Plain Chant of the Hill Country. Sister Mary David.
St. Elizabeth of Hungary. Whittier.
Elks. In the Elk Season. Karlfeldt, *tr. fr. Swedish by* Stork.
Ellesmere, Thomas Egerton, Baron
To Sir Thomas Egerton. Daniel.
To Thomas Lord Chancellor. Jonson.
Ellsworth, Elmer Ephraim
Colonel Ellsworth. Stoddard.
Ellsworth. *Unknown.*
Elm trees
Dilemma of the Elm. Taggard.
Elm, The. Belloc.
Elm, The. Odell Shepard.
Elves. *See* Fairies.
Ely, City of, England. Merrily Sang the Monks in Ely. *Unknown, wr. at. to* King Cnut.
Emancipation Proclamation (1863)
Fifty Years, 1863–1913. J. W. Johnson.
Laus Deo! Whittier.
No Slave beneath the Flag. G. L. Taylor.
Proclamation, The. Whittier.
Slav'ry Chain. *Unknown.*
Emerson, Ralph Waldo
Carlyle and Emerson. Montgomery Schuyler.
Emerson. A. B. Alcott.
Emerson. C. L. Betts.
Emerson. M. M. Dodge.
Emerson. E. C. Kinney.
Emerson. *Fr.* A Fable for Critics. J. R. Lowell.
Emerson; Last Days at Concord. Horace Gregory.
Emmet, Robert
Bold Robert Emmet. Maguire.
O, Breathe Not His Name! Thomas Moore.
She Is Far From the Land. Thomas Moore.
Written Immediately after Reading the Speech of Robert Emmet. Southey.
Empson, William. Just a Fishing Smack at Empson. George Barker.
Endecott, John. John Endicott. Longfellow.
Endymion
Endimion and Phoebe, *sels.* Drayton.
Endymion, *sels.* Keats.
Endymion. Longfellow.
Oh, Sleep Forever in the Latmian Cave. Millay.
Song by Fairies. *Fr.* Endymion. Lyly.
England
Albion's England, *sels.* William Warner.
America. Dobell.
And Did Those Feet in Ancient Time. *Fr.* Milton. Blake.
August, 1914. Masefield.
Australia to England. *Fr.* Sonnets of the Empire. A. T. Strong.
Battle of Maldon, The. *Unknown, tr. fr. Anglo-Saxon.*
Britannia. *Fr.* The Seasons: Summer. James Thomson.
Brumana. Flecker.
Canada Speaks of Britain. C. G. D. Roberts.
Channel Crossing. George Barker.
Chant of Hate against England, A. Lissauer, *tr. fr. German by* Henderson.
Chant of Love for England, A. Cone.
Coastwise Lights, The. Kipling.
Colonist in His Garden, A. W. P. Reeves.
Come to Britain; a Humble Contribution to the Movement. A. P. Herbert.
Composed by the Sea-Side, Near Calais. Wordsworth.
Distant View of England from the Sea. W. L. Bowles.
Dying Patriot, The. Flecker.
Elegy in a Country Churchyard. Chesterton.
England. Binyon.
England. W. W. Campbell.
England. *Fr.* The Task. Cowper.
England. R. E. Day.
England. Massey.
England. G. E. Montgomery.
England. Marianne Moore.
England. Cardinal Newman.
England; an Ode. Swinburne.
England and America in 1782. Tennyson.
England and Switzerland, 1802. Wordsworth.
England, Arise! Edward Carpenter.
England in 1819. Shelley.
England—June, 1940. Gorell.
England, My England. Henley.
England My Mother. Sir William Watson.
England! once Europs envye now her scorne. *Unknown.*
England's Sovereigns in Verse. *Unknown.*
English Fog, The. *Fr.* The Fleece. John Dyer.
English Garden, The, *sels.* William Mason.
English Hills. John Freeman.
English Weather. *Fr.* The Fleece. John Dyer.
Englishman, The. De la Mare.
Evening in England, An. Ledwidge.
Exile. Maynard.
Fair England. Cone.
Fears in Solitude. S. T. Coleridge.
For England. J. D. Burns.
For England, in Grateful Appreciation, *sel.* ("I was five when we moved to England"). Vogt.
For England's Sake Men Give Their Lives. Letts.
Gates to England, The. Marjorie Wilson.
Going towards Spain. Googe.
Green Fields of England! *Fr.* Songs in Absence. Clough.
Grongar Hill. John Dyer.
Hands All Round. Tennyson.
Home Thoughts. Glover.

ENGLAND (*continued*)
Home Thoughts from Abroad. Robert Browning.
Home-Thoughts from the Sea. Robert Browning.
Home Thoughts in Laventie. Tennant.
Homes of England, The. Hemans.
How Sleep the Brave. De la Mare.
I Looked at England. M. E. Allan.
Jerusalem. Blake.
Landscape with Figures. Fairburn.
Last Buccaneer, The. Kingsley.
Letter from Italy, A. Addison.
London, 1802. Wordsworth.
Look for Me on England. Mallalieu.
Look, Stranger, on This Island Now. Auden.
Love Thou Thy Land with Love Far-brought. Tennyson.
Mask of Anarchy, The. Shelley.
Memory of England. Millay.
Merry Green Fields of England. *Unknown.*
Mother England. E. M. Thomas.
Motherland. Wordsworth.
Nightmare (Written during Apparent Imminence of War). Sir William Watson.
No! Hood.
Now Where To? Heine, *tr. fr. German by* Gruenthal.
O England, Country of My Heart's Desire. Lucas.
Ode Written in the Beginning of the Year 1746. William Collins.
Of England and of Its Marvels. Uberti, *tr. fr. Italian by* Rossetti.
Old Chartist, The. George Meredith.
Old Vicarage, The, Grantchester. Rupert Brooke.
On Wenlock Edge. A. E. Housman.
Polyolbion, *sels.* Drayton.
Puck's Song. *Fr.* Puck of Pook's Hill. Kipling.
Ready, Ay, Ready. Merivale.
Refrain, A: "Tell the tune his feet beat." Cripps.
Rolling English Road, The. G. K. Chesterton.
Rule, Britannia. James Thomson.
Soldier, The. *Fr.* 1914. Rupert Brooke.
Song: "Old England is eaten by knaves." McLachlan.
Song of the Bow, The. *Fr.* The White Company. A. Conan Doyle.
Song to the Men of England. Shelley.
Sonnet: England in 1819. Shelley.
Sonnet: On a Distant View of England. W. L. Bowles.
Sonnet to Britain. Aytoun.
South Country, The. Belloc.
Spring in England. Going.
Summer in England 1914. Alice Meynell.
Third of February, 1852, The. Tennyson.
This England. *Fr.* King Richard II. Shakespeare.
This Is England. Binyon.
This Is No Case of Petty Right or Wrong. Edward Thomas.
Thought of a Briton on the Subjugation of Switzerland. Wordsworth.
To a River in the South. Newbolt.
To Britain—after War. *Fr.* The Field of Waterloo: Conclusion. Sir Walter Scott.
To England. Boker.
To England. C. L. Moore.
To the English Martyrs. Francis Thompson.
Truth's Complaint over England. Lodge.
Upon Eckington Bridge, River Avon. Quiller-Couch.
Volunteer Song, A. Baillie.
Whack Fol the Diddle. Kearney.
What Constitutes a State? *Fr.* An Ode in Imitation of Alcaeus. Sir William Jones.
You Ask Me, Why, tho' Ill at Ease. Tennyson.
You That Love England. Day Lewis.
English, Scottish, and Welsh Landscape, 1700–c.1860 (ENSW). John Betjeman *and* Geoffrey Taylor, comps.
ENGLAND, CHURCH OF
Churches of Rome and of England, The. *Fr.* The Hind and the Panther. Dryden.
Hippopotamus, The. T. S. Eliot.
I hold as faith. *Unknown.*
ENGLISH, THE
British, The. Tessimond.
Britons and Guests. E. M. Thomas.
Dunkirk. Nathan.
England and America in 1782. Tennyson.
England, Unprepared for War. *Fr.* An Ode to the Country Gentleman of England. Akenside.
For They Are England. O'Hearn.
Gloriana's England. *Fr.* Sonnets of the Empire. A. T. Strong.
It Is Not to Be Thought Of. Wordsworth.
Mad Dogs and Englishmen. Coward.
Men of England. Thomas Campbell.
Minora Sidera. Newbolt.
Private of the Buffs, A. Doyle.
Secret People, The. Chesterton.
Song of the English, A. Kipling.
Study of a People. H. I. Phillips.
To America. Alfred Austin.
To the Men of Kent. Wordsworth.
Trafalgar Day, 1940. "Clemence Dane."
Tragic Guilt. Rhys.
True-born Englishmen, The, *sels.* Defoe.
Vitaï Lampada. Newbolt.
Why Should I Care for the Men of Thames? Blake.
World Is a Bundle of Hay, The. Byron.
ENGLISH CHANNEL
Channel Crossing. George Barker.
Channel Passage, A. Swinburne.
Moat, The. Richmond.
ENGLISH LANGUAGE. *See* LANGUAGE.
ENNA, ITALY. Night on the Fields of Enna. Golding.
EPICUREANS. Epicure, The. Cowley.
EPICURUS. Garden of Epicurus, The. George Meredith.
EPIGRAMS
"Epic epigram, An," I heard you say. Martial, *tr. fr. Latin by* Cunningham.
What Is an Epigram? S. T. Coleridge.
EPIPHANY. *See* TWELFTH NIGHT.
EPPING FOREST, ENGLAND. Epping Forest. *Fr.* November. Davidson.
ERASMUS. Erasmus. E. A. Robinson.
ERCELDOUNE, THOMAS OF. *See* THOMAS THE RHYMER.
ERIE, LAKE, BATTLE OF
Battle of Erie, The. *Unknown.*
Perry's Victory. *Unknown.*
Perry's Victory on Lake Erie. Percival.
ERIE CANAL
Erie, The: "We were forty miles from Albany." *Unknown.*
Erie Canal, The. W. S. Allen.
Erie Canal: "It was a long, long trip on the Erie." *Unknown.*
Erie Canal Ballad, The. *Unknown.*
Trip on the Erie, A. *Unknown.*
ERNE (river), IRELAND. Winding Banks of Erne, The; or, The Emigrant's Adieu to Ballyshannon. Allingham.
EROS. *See* CUPID.
ERSKINE, JOHN (1509–91). Lament of the Master of Erskine. Alexander Scott.
ESCALATORS. E. *Fr.* All Around the Town. McGinley.
ESCORIAL. Escorial, The. Gautier, *tr. fr. French by* Conder.
ESKIMO
Eskimo Baby, An. Diamond.
For an Eskimo. A. C. Dalton.
Immoral Arctic, The. Morris Bishop.
Kayak, The. *Unknown.*
ESSEX, ROBERT DEVEREUX, 2D EARL OF. Lementable New Ballad upon the Earle of Essex Death, A. *Unknown.*
ESSEX, ENGLAND. Essex. Cripps.
ETERNITY
Eternity. Rimbaud, *tr. fr. French by* Golffing.
Frozen City, The. Nemerov.
Waters. Slessor.
World, The. Vaughan.
ETHIOPIA
On the Baptized Ethiopian Crashaw.
Star of Ethiopia. L. B. Watkins.
ETIQUETTE
Etiquette. W. S. Gilbert.
Etiquette. Guiterman.
Table Manners for the Hostess. Meun, *tr. fr. French by* Grebanier.
ETNA (mountain). To Mount Aetna. Corbière, *tr. fr. French by* Fitts.
ETON COLLEGE
Founder's Day. Bridges.
Ode on a Distant Prospect of Eton College. Thomas Gray.
To the School at War. Alington.
ETRUSCAN CIVILIZATION. Etruscan Warrior's Head. Henze.
ETTRICK WATER, SCOTLAND. Ettrick Banks. *Unknown.*
EUCHARIST
Eucharist. E. M. Root.
O Salutaris Hostia. St. Thomas Aquinas, *tr. fr. Latin.*
Of the Holy Eucharist. *Unknown.*
Sacrament. Harsen.
To the Blessed Sacrament. Constable.
EUCLID
Euclid. Lindsay.
Euclid Alone Has Looked on Beauty Bare. Millay.
EURIPIDES
Balaustion's Adventure, *sel.* ("So were we at destruction's very edge"). Robert Browning.
On Euripides. *Unknown, tr. fr. Greek by* Lord Neaves.
EUROPE
Channel Crossing. George Barker.
Europe. Whitman.
Home Thoughts. Guy Butler.
To Cole, the Painter, Departing for Europe. Bryant.
To Walt Whitman in America. Swinburne.
Zone. Apollinaire, *tr. fr. French by* Fitts.

EUROPEANS. Some Europeans. *Unknown.*
EURYDICE
Eurydice. Bourdillon.
Eurydice to Orpheus. Robert Browning.
Orpheus, Eurydice, and Hermes. Rilke, *ad. fr. German by* Lowell.
Orpheus, O Orpheus, gently touch thy Lesbyan lyre. *Unknown.*
Thus sang Orpheus to his strings. *Unknown.*
EURYDICE (ship). Last of the *Eurydice*, The. Paton.
EUTAW SPRINGS, SOUTH CAROLINA
Battle of Eutaw, The. Simms.
To the Memory of the Brave Americans. Freneau.
EVE
Adam and Eve. Manger, *tr. fr. Yiddish by* Sonntag.
Adam and Eve. Shapiro.
Begetting of Cain, The. Plutzik.
Eva. Rilke, *tr. fr. German by* Salinger.
Eve. Flores, *tr. fr. Spanish by* Beckett.
Eve. Ralph Hodgson.
Eve. C. G. Rossetti.
Eve's Lament. *Unknown, tr. fr. Middle Irish.*
Jealous Adam. Manger, *tr. fr. Yiddish by* Sonntag.
Legend of the Dove, A. Sterling
EVENING
After Sunset. G. H. Conkling.
As Day Begins to Wane. Helena Coleman.
At Close of Day. Stephansson, *tr. fr. Icelandic by* Johnson.
At Evening. *Unknown.*
August Evening. Dargan.
Autumn Evening. Tyutchev, *tr. fr. Russian.*
Autumnal Evening, An. "Fiona Macleod."
Child's Evening Prayer, A. S. T. Coleridge.
Clear Evening after Rain. Tu Fu, *tr. fr. Chinese by* Rexroth.
Cool of Evening, The. Reese.
Cricket sang, The. Emily Dickinson.
Day; a Pastoral. John Cunningham.
Day Is Done, The. Longfellow.
Day's End. Binyon.
Day's Ending. Teasdale.
Descend, Fair Sun! *Fr.* The Masque of the Middle Temple and Lincoln's Inn. George Chapman.
Description of a Summer's Eve. H. K. White.
End of a Day in the Provinces, The. Laforgue, *tr. fr. French by* Crosland.
End of the Day, The. D. C. Scott.
Evenen in the Village. William Barnes.
Evening. Aldington.
Evening, An. Allingham.
Evening. Harry Behn.
Evening. Robert Bridges, *after* Blake.
Evening. *Fr.* Don Juan. Byron.
Evening. Doolittle ("H. D.").
Evening, The. *Fr.* Trivia. Gay.
Evening. Lampman.
Evening. Matheson.
Evening. Pickthall.
Evening. Rilke, *tr. fr. German by* Jarrell.
Evening. Sackville-West.
Evening. Sangster.
Evening. Sill.
Evening. Stephansson, *tr. fr. Icelandic by* Johnson.
Evening. James Stephens.
Evening. Trakl, *tr. fr. German by* Luke.
Evening. Vriesland, *tr. fr. Dutch by* Barnouw.
Evening, and Maidens. William Barnes.
Evening Darkens Over, The. Robert Bridges.
Evening Ebb. Jeffers.
Evening Falls, An. James Stephens.
Evening Hymn, *sel.* ("O God, whose daylight leadeth down"). George Macdonald.
Evening in England, An. Ledwidge.
Evening in Paradise. *Fr.* Paradise Lost. Milton.
Evening in Tyringham Valley. Gilder.
Evening Landscape. Pol de Mont, *tr. fr. Flemish by* Bithell.
Evening on the Farm. Trowbridge.
Evening on the Harbor. Tunstall.
Evening; Ponte al Mare, Pisa. Shelley.
Evening Quatrains. Cotton.
Evening Song. C. F. Alexander.
Evening Song. F. S. Davis.
Evening Song. *Fr.* The Faithful Shepherdess. John Fletcher.
Evening Song. Wilson MacDonald.
Evening Songs. Cheney.
Evening Sun The. Emily Brontë.
Evening Voluntary. Wordsworth.
Evening Walk, An, *sels.* Wordsworth.
Evening Wind, The. Bryant.
Evensong. Aiken.
Even-Song, An. Dobell.
Evensong. Schaumann, *tr. fr. German by* Shuster.
Evensong. R. L. Stevenson.
Grace before Sleep. Teasdale.
Harmonie du soir. Baudelaire, *tr. fr. French.*
Hot Stagnant Evening, A. Laforgue, *tr. fr. French by* Smith.
Hours. González León, *tr. fr. Spanish by* Beckett.
Hymn to the Evening, An. Wheatley.
I Hear the Cries of Evening, While the Paw. Spender.
In the Cool of the Evening. Noyes.
It Is a Beauteous Evening, Calm and Free. Wordsworth.
Lines on an Autumnal Evening. Coleridge.
Morning and Evening. P. P. Frost.
Morning and Evening. Slonimski, *tr. fr. Polish by* Kirkconnell.
Mountain Evenings. Holme.
Nurse's Song. *Fr.* Songs of Experience. Blake.
Ode to Evening. William Collins.
Ode to Evening. Joseph Warton.
On a Calm Summer's Night. John Nicholson.
On a Midsummer Eve. Hardy.
On Eastnor Knoll. Masefield.
Post-Meridian. W. P. Garrison.
Prelude: "Winter evening settles down, The." Preludes, I. T. S. Eliot.
Recollections after an Evening Walk. Clare.
Rural Evening. De Tabley.
Shadows of the Evening Hours. A. A. Procter.
Softly Now the Light of Day. Doane.
Sonnet: "Evening, as slow thy placid shades descend." W. L. Bowles.
Summer Evening. De la Mare.
Summer Evening, A. Lampman.
This Is My Rock. McCord.
Twilight. Laforgue, *tr. fr. French by* Smith.
Vespers. S. Weir Mitchell.
Vespers. Shepard.
Western Waves of Ebbing Day, The. *Fr.* The Lady of the Lake. Sir Walter Scott.
When Even Cometh On. Tilley.
When on the Marge of Evening. Guiney.
Winter Evening. *Fr.* The Task. Cowper.
Winter Evening. Lampman.
Winter Evening. Pushkin, *tr. fr. Russian by* Deutsch.
Winter Evening. Tynan.
Winter Evening Hymn to My Fire, A. J. R. Lowell.
EVENING PRIMROSES
Evening Primrose, The. Clare.
Evening Primrose, The. Langhorne.
Evening Primrose, The. Dorothy Parker.
EVENING STAR
Evening Star, The. Clare.
Evening Star, The. Musset, *tr. fr. French by* Conder.
Evening Star. Poe.
To the Evening Star. Blake.
To the Evening Star ("Gem of the crimson-colour'd Even"). Thomas Campbell.
To the Evening Star ("Star that bringest home the bee"). Thomas Campbell.
EVERGLADES, FLORIDA. Dawn in the Everglades. Warlow.
EVOLUTION
By an Evolutionist. Tennyson.
Darwinism. A. M. F. Robinson.
Evolution. Langdon Smith.
Love Song to Eohippus. Viereck.
Similar Cases. C. P. S. Gilman.
EXECUTIONS
Ballade of the Hanged Men. Villon, *tr. fr. French by* Fitzgerald.
Condemned to Die, The. Espronceda, *tr. fr. Spanish by* Kennedy.
Culprit, The. A. E. Housman.
Eight o'Clock. A. E. Housman.
Gallows, The. Edward Thomas.
On Moonlit Heath. A. E. Housman.
Summons to Execution. *Fr.* The Duchess of Malfi. Webster.
Tichborne's Elegy, Written in the Tower before His Execution. Tichborne.
Upon the Image of Death. Southwell.
EXILE
Along the sand of the beach. Altolaguirre, *tr. fr. Spanish by* Turnbull.
Ballade Written during Captivity in England. Charles d'Orléans, *tr. fr. French by* Conder.
Before Exile. Mack.
Canadian Boat Song. *Unknown.*
Canadian Exile, The. Gérin Lajoie, *tr. fr. French-Canadian by* Boyd.
Castaways, The. Zaturenska.
Come to Me, Dearest. Brennan.
Dublin. MacNeice.
Emigrant Song. "S. Ansky," *tr. fr. Yiddish by* Leftwich.
Exile. Rex Browne.

Exile (*continued*)
Exile, The. Robert Graves.
Exile. Heine, *tr. fr. German by* Thomson.
Exile. K. W. Ryan.
Exile. Tu Fu, *tr. fr. Chinese by* Chi Hwang Chu *and* E. W. Underwood.
Exile at Rest, The. Pierpont.
Exile of Erin, The. Thomas Campbell.
Exile Song. Rosenfeld, *tr. fr. Yiddish by* Leftwich.
Exiled Mother, The. Boucicault.
Exiles. Hayne.
Exile's Devotion, The. McGee.
Exile's Letter. Li Po, *tr. fr. Chinese by* Pound.
Exile's Song, The. Gilfillan.
Exile's Song, The. *Unknown, tr. fr. Armenian by* Boyajian.
Flower of Exile. Max Dunn.
From Exile. Hsü Chu, *tr. fr. Chinese by* Hart.
Impression of Exile. Cernuda, *tr. fr. Spanish by* Turnbull.
In Exile. Baughan.
In Exile. M. E. Blake.
Lament of the Scotch-Irish Exile. Roche.
Lives. Rimbaud, *tr. fr. French by* Flores.
On His Exile to Iona. St. Columcille, *tr. fr. Old Irish by* Hyde.
Sea Breeze. Mallarmé, *tr. fr. French by* Flores.
Song of the Siberian Exiles, The. Nekrasov, *tr. fr. Russian by* Bianchi.
Thoughts in Exile. Su T'ung-po, *tr. fr. Chinese by* Rexroth.
Travelogue for Exiles. Shapiro.
Wanderer, The. Eugene Field.
Existentialism. Existentialism. Frankenberg.
Exmoor, England. For Exmoor. Ingelow.
Exodus from Egypt
Exodus from Egypt, The. Ezekielos of Alexandria, *tr. fr. Greek by* Gifford.
Flowering without End. *Fr.* Jeremiah. Zweig, *tr. fr. German by* Eden *and* Cedar Paul.
Go Down, Moses. *Unknown.*
Parting of the Red Sea, The. *Fr.* Exodus. *Unknown, tr. fr. Anglo-Saxon by* Kennedy.
Sound the Loud Timbrel. Thomas Moore.
Explorers and exploring
Discoverer of the North Cape, The. Longfellow.
Explorer, The. Delius.
Explorer, The. Plomer.
Hakluyt Unpurchased. McDuffee.
Polar Quest, The. Richard Burton.
Projection, A. Whittemore.
Sonnet: "There was an Indian, who had known no change." Squire.
Southward Sidonian Hanno. Hervey Allen.
Terra Australis. Douglas Stewart.
Ulysses. Tennyson.
Verses Supposed to Be Written by Alexander Selkirk. Cowper.
Extreme Unction
Extreme Unction. Dowson.
In Extremis. Chavez.
Ezekiel
Ezekiel. T. S. Jones, Jr.
Road of Suffering, The. Grade, *tr. fr. Yiddish by* Betsky.

F

Factories. Factory Windows Are Always Broken. Lindsay.
Fair American (ship). Cruise of the *Fair American. Unknown.*
Fairfax, Thomas Fairfax, 3d Baron. To the Lord General Fairfax. Milton.
Fairies
About the Fairies. Ingelow.
Apple-Elf, The. Braine.
Arming of Pigwiggen, The. *Fr.* Nymphidia. Drayton.
Best Game the Fairies Play, The. Fyleman.
By the Moon We Sport and Play. *Fr.* The Mayde's Metamorphosis. *Unknown.*
Child and the Fairies, The. *Unknown.*
Come unto These Yellow Sands. *Fr.* The Tempest. Shakespeare.
Confession in Holy Week. Christopher Morley.
Could It Have Been a Shadow? Shannon.
Crab-Apple. Talbot.
Culprit Fay, The. Drake.
Differences. Fyleman.
Door at the End of Our Garden, The. Weatherly.
Dream Fairy, The. *Fr.* Queen Mab. Hood.
Dream Song. Richard Middleton.
Elf, The. Marian Osborne.
Elf and the Dormouse, The. Herford.
Elf Singing, The. Allingham.
Elfin Plane, The. Rowena Bennett.
Elves' Dance, The. *Fr.* The Mayde's Metamorphosis. *Unknown.*
Emigration of the Fairies, The, *sel.* ("A few days more they drifted, ever west"). Duvar.
Enchanted Garden, The. Barrows.
Epilogue to "A Midsummer Night's Dream." Shakespeare.
Explanation of the Grasshopper, An. Vachel Lindsay.
Faerie Fair, The. Harrison.
Faëry Reaper, The. Robert Buchanan.
Faery Song: "Shed no tear!" Keats.
Fairies, The. Allingham.
Fairies. Hilda Conkling.
Fairies. Fyleman.
Fairies, The. Herndon.
Fairies, The. Herrick.
Fairies, The. Morford.
Fairies. *Fr.* Kensington Garden. Tickell.
Fairies' Dance, The ("Dare you haunt our hallow'd green?"). *Unknown.*
Fairies' Farewell, The. Corbet.
Fairies Feast, The. Doughty.
Fairies Have Never a Penny to Spend, The. Fyleman.
Fairies in New Ross, The. *Unknown.*
Fairies' Lights. Alice Wilkins.
Fairies' Lullaby, The. *Unknown, tr. fr. Irish by* Hull.
Fairies of the Caldon-Low, The. Howitt.
Fairies' Recall. Hemans.
Fairies' Shopping, The. Deland.
Fairies' Song. Leigh Hunt.
Fairy Book, The. A. F. Brown.
Fairy Book, The. Gale.
Fairy Boy, The. Lover.
Fairy Bread. R. L. Stevenson.
Fairy Carpets. Payne.
Fairy Child, The. Anster.
Fairy Days. Thackeray.
Fairy Faces. *Unknown.*
Fairy Folk, The. Bird.
Fairy Frilly. Hoatson.
Fairy Frock, The. Katharine Morse.
Fairy Frolic. Rentoul.
Fairy Godmothers. Lee-Hamilton.
Fairy Gold. Todhunter.
Fairy Harpers, The. Dollard.
Fairy Host, The. *Tr. fr. Irish by* Graves.
Fairy in Armor, A. *Fr.* The Culprit Fay. J. R. Drake.
Fairy King, The. Allingham.
Fairy Lough, The. "Moira O'Neill."
Fairy Lullaby. *Unknown, tr. fr. Irish by* Sigerson.
Fairy Maimounè, The. Moultrie.
Fairy Midir's Invitation to Etain, The. *Unknown, tr. fr. Old Irish by* O'Faoláin.
Fairy Music. Fyleman.
Fairy Nurse, The. *Unknown, tr. fr. Irish by* Walsh.
Fairy Queen, The ("Come, follow, follow me"). *Unknown.*
Fairy Ring, The. *Unknown.*
Fairy Shoemaker, The. Allingham.
Fairy Shoes. Wynne.
Fairy Song, A. Dillingham.
Fairy Song. Hemans.
Fairy Song. Praed.
Fairy Tailor, The. Fyleman.
Fairy Tempter, The. Lover.
Fairy Thorn, The. Sir Samuel Ferguson.
Fairy Thrall, The. May Byron.
Fairy Umbrellas. Diamond.
Fairy Voyage, A. *Unknown.*
Fairy Went a-Marketing, A. Fyleman.
Fairy Wings. Howard.
Fairy-Land. Poe.
Fairy's Wander-Song. *Fr.* A Midsummer Night's Dream. Shakespeare.
Farewell to the Fairies. Corbet.
Five Little Fairies, The. Maud Burnham.
Fountain of the Fairies, The. Southey.
Goblin, The. Fyleman.
Goblin Goose, The. *Unknown.*
Goblin Market. C. G. Rossetti.
Goblinade, A. Jaques.
Green Gnome, The. Robert Buchanan.
Have You Watched the Fairies? Fyleman.
Host of the Air, The. Yeats.
House-Goblin, The. Rydberg, *tr. fr. Swedish by* Stork.
How to Tell Goblins from Elves. Shannon.
I Keep Three Wishes Ready. Wynne.
I'd Love to Be a Fairy's Child. Robert Graves.
Kallundborg Church. Whittier.
La Belle Dame sans Merci. Keats.
Lake and a Fairy Boat, A. Hood.
Last Voyage of the Fairies, The. W. H. D. Adams.
Leprahaun. R. D. Joyce.

Light-hearted Fairy, The. *Unknown.*
Little Elf, The. Bangs.
Little Men, The. Fearne.
Little Orphant Annie. Riley.
Man Who Hid His Own Front Door, The. MacKinstry.
Mickleham Way. Eastwick.
Midnight Performance, A. Wing.
Midsummer Magic. Eastwick.
Midsummer Night's Dream, A, *sels.* Shakespeare.
Mountain Sprite, The. Thomas Moore.
Mountain Trolls. Fröding, *tr. fr. Swedish by* Stork.
Now the Hungry Lion Roars. *Fr.* A Midsummer Night's Dream. Shakespeare.
Nymphidia; or, The Court of Fairy. Drayton.
Oh! Where Do Fairies Hide Their Heads. Bayly.
Others, The. "Seumas O'Sullivan."
Overheard on a Saltmarsh. Monro.
Palace of the Fairies, The. Drayton.
Passing of the Sidhe. Dollard.
Plea of the Midsummer Fairies, The, *sels.* Hood.
Plumpuppets, The. Morley.
Queen Mab. Hood.
Queen Mab. *Fr.* The Satyr. Jonson.
Queen Mab. *Fr.* Romeo and Juliet. Shakespeare.
Queen of Elfland's Nourice, The. *Unknown.*
Return of the Fairy, The. Humbert Wolfe.
Robin Goodfellow. *Unknown.*
Sea Fairies. Mathias.
Shadow People, The. Ledwidge.
Sir Olaf. Herder, *tr. fr. German by* Craigmyle.
Song: "Lake and a fairy boat, A." Hood.
Song by Fairies. *Fr.* Endymion. Lyly.
Song of the Elfin Miller. Allan Cunningham.
Song of the Elfin Steersman. George Hill.
Stocking Fairy. Welles.
Stolen Child, The. Yeats.
There Was a Little Goblin. Herbertson.
Thomas the Rhymer. *Unknown.*
Three Beggars, The. De la Mare.
Tim, the Fairy. Livesay.
To a Brownie. Pushkin, *tr. fr. Russian by* Elton.
To Mother Fairie. Alice Cary.
To the Leanan Sidhe. Boyd.
Very Nearly. Scott-Hopper.
Vision. Fyleman.
Visitor, The. Rachel Field.
Water-Lilies. Hemans.
When a Ring's around the Moon. M. J. Carr.
Where the Bee Sucks. *Fr.* The Tempest. Shakespeare.
Wind Blows Out of the Gates of Day, The. *Fr.* The Land of the Heart's Desire. Yeats.
Yesterday in Oxford Street. Fyleman.

FAITH
After the Surprising Conversions. Robert Lowell.
Al-Maumin. Sir Edwin Arnold.
Apostasy. Aus of Kuraiza, *tr. fr. Arabic by* Hirschfeld.
Argument, An—of the Passion of Christ. Merton.
As a Plane Tree by the Water. Robert Lowell.
Belief. Josephine Miles.
Bishop Blougram's Apology. Robert Browning.
Blind Preacher, The. Polonsky, *tr. fr. Russian by* Phillimore.
Captains of the Years, The. MacDougall.
Credo. Jeffers.
Credo. Kreymborg
Credo. "Seumas O'Sullivan."
Credo. Oxenham.
Credo. E. A. Robinson.
Credo. Symons.
Credo, A. Thackeray.
Credo. Wheatley.
Creed, A. Norma Gale.
Creed, A. Masefield.
Creed. Anne Spencer.
Creeds. K. W. Baker.
Dominus Illuminatio Mea. Blackmore.
Dover Beach. Matthew Arnold.
Dying Hymn. Alice Cary.
Eclipse of Faith, The. Woolsey.
Epi-Strauss-ium. Clough.
Eternal Goodness, The. Whittier.
Faith. Chivers.
Faith. Preston Clark.
Faith. D. E. Edwards.
Faith. W. D. Howells.
Faith. Isbell.
Faith. Maynard.
Faith. F. B. Meyer.
Faith. Moreland.
Faith. Oxenham.
Faith. E. M. Poteat.
Faith. L. M. Sill.
Faith. Tabb.
Faith. *Fr.* The Ancient Sage. Tennyson.
Faith. *Unknown.*
Faith. E. W. Wilcox.
Faith and Freedom. *Fr.* It Is Not to Be Thought of. Wordsworth.
Faith and Science. T. C. Clark.
Faith and Sight. *Fr.* Not Knowing. A. M. King.
Faith, Hope and Love. *Unknown.*
Faith is a fine invention. Emily Dickinson.
Faith of Christ's Freemen, The. T. C. Clark.
Faith of Our Fathers. Faber.
Faith on Trial, A, *sel.* ("Dream is the thought in the ghost"). George Meredith.
Faith Trembling. "Madeline Bridges."
Faith's Difficulty. Theodore Maynard.
Faith's Vista. Abbey.
Firm Belief. *Unknown.*
Happy Change. Cowper.
Hind and the Panther, The, *sel.* ("A milk-white Hind, immortal and unchanged"). Dryden.
His Creed. Herrick.
Homeward Journey, The. Aaronson.
Hymn for Atonement Day. Halevi, *tr. fr. Hebrew by* Solis-Cohen.
I Am the Way. Alice Meynell.
I in Thee, and Thou in Me. Cranch.
I never saw a moor. Emily Dickinson.
I Saw a Monk of Charlemaine. *Fr.* Jerusalem. Blake.
If This Were Faith. R. L. Stevenson.
Impercipient, The. Hardy.
Implicit Faith. *Fr.* May Carols. De Vere.
Last Lines. Emily Brontë.
Last Man, The. Thomas Campbell.
Leaden Echo and the Golden Echo, The. G. M. Hopkins.
Light Shining Out of Darkness. Cowper.
Love Song, A. Halevi, *tr. fr. Hebrew by* Salaman.
Meditation on Communion with God. Halevi, *tr. fr. Hebrew by* Solis-Cohen.
My Faith. Acharya.
My Faith. Knowles.
My Faith Looks Up to Thee. Ray Palmer.
My Times Are in Thy Hand. C. N. Hall.
No Coward Soul Is Mine. Emily Brontë.
Noble Voyage, The. Earl of Surrey.
Not Knowing. Brainard.
O World, Thou Choosest Not the Better Part. Santayana.
Oh Yet We Trust that Somehow Good. *Fr.* In Memoriam A. H. H. Tennyson.
Old Sceptic, The. Noyes.
Pastoral Hymn. Addison.
Poet's Simple Faith, The. Hugo, *tr. fr. French by* Dowden.
Prayer for Faith, A. Michelangelo, *tr. fr. Italian by* Symonds.
Prisoner, The. Emily Brontë.
Readings, Forecasts, Personal Guidance. Fearing.
Religio Laici. Dryden.
Return, The. Rukeyser.
Say Not the Struggle Nought Availeth. Clough.
Second Crucifixion, The. Le Gallienne.
Shema Yisrael. *Unknown.*
Supposed Confessions of a Second-rate Sensitive Mind. Tennyson.
That There Are Powers above Us I Admit. Clough.
There Is No Unbelief. Case.
Tide of Faith, The. *Fr.* A Minor Prophet. "George Eliot."
To My Children. Strobel.
Trust. F. A. Kemble.
Trust. Reese.
Trust—a Song. Rexford.
Trust and Obedience. *Unknown.*
When Gathering Clouds. Robert Grant.
Why Are Ye Afraid, O Ye of Little Faith? Crashaw.

FALA (dog). Fala. Gate.

FALCONS
Falcon. W. R. Benét.
Falcon, The. Blunt.
Gay Goss-Hawk, The. *Unknown.*
Golden Falcon. Coffin.
Windhover, The. G. M. Hopkins.

FALMOUTH, ENGLAND
In Falmouth Harbour. Lionel Johnson.
O Falmouth Is a Fine Town. Henley.

FAME
Earth's Immortalities. Robert Browning.
Eve of the Festival, The. George, *tr. fr. German by* Gee.
Fame. Cantus.
Fame. Jonson.
Fame. J. J. Montague.
Fame. Tabb.
Fame Is a Food That Dead Men Eat. Dobson.
Fame Makes Us Forward. Herrick.
How Sleep the Brave. Drummond.
Inquisition upon Fame and Honour, An. Fulke Greville.
Not marble, nor the gilded monuments. *Fr.* Sonnets. Shakespeare.

Fame (*continued*)
Perry Zoll. *Fr.* Spoon River Anthology. Masters.
Pillar of Fame, The. Herrick.
Public Acclaim. Hölderlin, *tr. fr. German by* Flores.
Stanzas Written on the Road between Florence and Pisa. Byron.
Substance, Shadow, and Spirit. T'ao Ch'ien, *tr. fr. Chinese by* Waley.
To an Athlete Dying Young. A. E. Housman.
Two Sonnets on Fame. Keats.
Whilst thus my pen strives to eternize thee. *Fr.* Idea. Drayton.
Wrestler, The. George, *tr. fr. German by* Luke.
You that do search for every purling spring. *Fr.* Astrophel and Stella. Sidney.
Family life
Autobiographical. A. M. Klein.
Cotter's Saturday Night, The. Burns.
Family, The. Lydston.
Family, The. *Unknown, tr. fr. German by* Fyleman.
Family Court. Nash.
Family Meeting, The. Sprague.
Folded Flock, The. Wilfrid Meynell.
From a Childhood. Rilke, *tr. fr. German by* MacIntyre.
Love between Brothers and Sisters. Watts.
Famine
Famine Year, The. Lady Wilde.
Song of the Times. Adler, *tr. fr. Yiddish by* Betsky.
Farmer, George. Ballad for a Boy, A. Cory.
Farming and farmers
Agriculture; a Poem, *sel.* ("See where the farmer"). Dodsley.
Canadian Farmer. Bartole.
City Wife. Livesay.
Code, The. Robert Frost.
Country Summer. Léonie Adams.
Crafty Farmer, The. *Unknown.*
Day at the Farm, A. "L. J."
Death of the Hired Man, The. Robert Frost.
Defeated Farmer. Mark Van Doren.
Digression from Husbandry to a Point or Two of Huswifery, A. Tusser.
Drinking Time. O'Sullivan.
Evening at the Farm. Trowbridge.
Farewell to the Farm. R. L. Stevenson.
Farm, The. Jane Taylor.
Farm Life. Stanton.
Farm Picture, A. Whitman.
Farm Wife. J. H. Mitchell.
Farmer. L. H. Bailey.
Farmer. Fallon.
Farmer, The. *Unknown.*
Farmer and the Farmer's Wife, The. Hiebert.
Farmer Comes to Town, The. *Unknown.*
Farmers. Helene Mullins.
Farmer's Boy, The, *sels.* Bloomfield.
Farmer's Ingle, The. Robert Fergusson.
Farmer's Prayer, A. R. M. Montgomery.
Farmer's Round, The. *Unknown.*
Farming. *Fr.* Shi King. *Unknown, tr. fr. Chinese by* Waley.
Fruit Rancher, The. Lloyd Roberts.
Good Farmer, The. *Unknown, tr. fr. Greek by* Hodgson and Bland.
Good Year, A. Carrión, *tr. fr. Spanish by* Fitts.
Happy Farmer, The. Tse Nan, *tr. fr. Chinese by* Hart.
Happy Farmer, The. *Unknown.*
Hay Mowing. Kulbak, *tr. fr. Yiddish by* Betsky.
Hayfield, The. *Fr.* The Flowing Summer. Bruce.
Haying. Herbin.
Haymaking. Edward Thomas.
Herd Laddie, The. Alexander Smart.
Hill Farmer Speaks, The. R. S. Thomas.
Hillside Farmer A. J. C. Farrar.
Hock-Cart, or Harvest Home, The. Herrick.
Hundreth good points of good husbandry, A. Tusser.
I Will Go with My Father a-Ploughing. Joseph Campbell.
In a Sunny Nook. Kaalund, *tr. fr. Danish by* Stork.
July. Tusser.
Man with the Hoe; a Reply. Cheney.
Manor Farm, The. Edward Thomas.
March. Tusser.
Mowers, The. Allingham.
Northern Farmer: New Style. Tennyson.
Northern Farmer: Old Style. Tennyson.
Ochil Farmer, An. Robertson.
October's Husbandry. Tusser.
Old Farmer Alone. Coffin.
On Our Farm. Antin.
Peter Simson's Farm. Dyson.
Planting Beans. T'ao Ch'ien, *tr. fr. Chinese by* C. W. Luh.
Plowman, The. Knister.
Praise of Husbandry, The. Tusser.
Putting in the Seed. Robert Frost.
Ranchers. Lesemann.
Reaper, The. L. H. Allen.
Rival, The. S. T. Warner.
Seed. Bosman.
September. Tusser.
Sharecropper. Stewart Atkins.
Sheep-Washing, The. *Fr.* The Seasons: Summer. James Thomson.
Soldiers of the Plough, The. *Fr.* The Happy Harvesters. Charles Sangster.
Somerset Farmer, The. Marguerite Wilkinson.
Sower, The. Figueroa, *tr. fr. Spanish by* Fitts.
Sower, The. Sir C. G. D. Roberts.
Sower and His Seed, The. Lecky.
Sower's Song, The. Carlyle.
Sowing. Edward Thomas.
Sowing Season. Hugo, *tr. fr. French by* Conder.
Steel Glass, The, *sel.* ("Behold him, priests, and though he stink of sweat"). Gascoigne.
Testament of Beauty, The, *sel.* ("How was November's melancholy endear'd to me"). Robert Bridges.
Times Have Altered, The. *Unknown.*
Watching the Reapers. Po Chü-i, *tr. fr. Chinese by* Waley.
See also Fields and pastures
Farragut, David Glasgow
David Glasgow Farragut. Wallace Rice.
Farragut. W. T. Meredith.
River Fight, The. Brownell.
Through Fire in Mobile Bay. *At. to* Farragut.
Fate
As I Gird On for Fighting. Housman.
At the Crossroads. Hovey.
Dice Were Loaded, The. Mary Gilmore.
Eros Turannos. E. A. Robinson.
Fate. L. J. Block.
Fate. J. F. Cooper.
Fate. Emerson.
Fate. Harte.
Fate. Ibn Abdun, *tr. fr. Arabic by* Arberry.
Fate. Morgenstern, *tr. fr. German by* Hull.
Fate. S. M. Spalding.
Genseric. "Owen Meredith."
Hap. Hardy.
Hymn to Chance. H. P. Putnam.
Inevitable, The. S. K. Bolton.
Throw of the Dice, A. Mallarmé, *tr. fr. French by* Aldan.
To Leuconoë. Horace, *tr. fr. Latin.*
Wanderer, The. *Unknown, tr. fr. Anglo-Saxon.*
Fathers
Anecdote for Fathers. Wordsworth.
Celebration, A. Sarton.
Daddy. Fyleman.
Dedicatory. Mary Gilmore.
Elegy for My Father. Howard Moss.
Elegy on My Father. Curnow.
Epitaph on My Father. Burns.
Father. Frances Frost.
Father, The. W. W. Gibson.
Father, The. Ronald Ross.
Father and Son. Higgins.
Father Dies. Sutskever, *tr. fr. Yiddish by* Betsky.
Father Does His Best, A. E. B. White.
Father Is Coming. Howitt.
Father Knows, The. "F. L. H."
Fathers and Sons. *Unknown, tr. fr. Irish by* O'Connor.
Father's Prayer, A. *Unknown.*
Father's Story. E. M. Roberts.
Father's Testament, A. Ibn Tibbon, *tr. fr. Hebrew by* Abrahams.
Forgetful Pa. Guest.
Guilty Father to His Daughter, A. Schevill.
Her Great Secret. Gillilan.
I Sit with My Dolls. *Unknown, tr. fr. Yiddish by* Leftwich.
In the Year's Morning. David Ross.
Lament of a Man for His Son. *Tr. fr. Paiute Indian by* Austin.
Lines to My Father. Daiken.
My Dad's Dinner Pail. Harrigan.
My Father. Drennan.
My Father. Rittenhouse.
My Father Moved through Dooms of Love. E. E. Cummings.
My Father's Child. "Stuart Sterne."
My Father's Voice in Prayer. Nottage.
My Papa's Waltz. Roethke.
My Son. Malloch.
On My First Son. Jonson.
On the Death of His Father. Wei Wen-ti, *tr. fr. Chinese by* Waley.
On the Death of His Son. Glyn Cothi, *tr. fr. Welsh by* Williams.
On the Seventh Anniversary of the Death of My Father. Pack.

Poet to His Father, A. M. L. Fisher.
Radio, The. Guest.
Russian Cradle Song, A. Nomberg, *tr. fr. Yiddish by* Alter Brody.
Secret Heart, The. Coffin.
Shabby Old Dad. Anne Campbell.
Sohrab and Rustum. Matthew Arnold.
To My Father. Baxter.
To My Father. Drummond.
To My Father. Iris Tree.
To My Son, Aged Three Years and Five Months. Hood.
To the Reverend Shade of His Religious Father. Herrick.
Way to Know a Father, The. Coffin.
What Father Knows. *Unknown.*
When Father Carves the Duck. E. V. Wright.
When Father Played Baseball. Guest.
When He Goes to Play with the Boys. Gillilan.
Wonderful Man, A. Aileen Fisher.
Father; an Anthology of Verse (FAOV). Margery Doud *and* Cleo M. Parsley, comps.
FAUNS. Afternoon of a Faun, The. Mallarmé, *tr. fr. French.*
FAUST
Dr. Faustus, *sels.* Marlowe.
Faust, *sels.* Goethe, *tr. fr. German.*
Faustus. *Fr.* Horatio. Plutzik.
FAWKES, GUY. Guy Fawkes. *Unknown.*
FAWN. *See* DEER.
FEAR
Appointment in Doctor's Office. Josephine Miles.
Ballad of Sister Anne, The. Sir Osbert Sitwell.
Fear. Kipling.
Fears and Scruples. Robert Browning.
Fears in Solitude. S. T. Coleridge.
Last Night I Woke. Gosse.
Lost Son, The. Roethke.
Ode to Fear. William Collins.
Ode to Fear. Allen Tate.
Scene of War, The; Fear. Sir Herbert Read.
Variation: Ode to Fear. R. P. Warren.
FEBRUARY
Anatomy o Winter, The. *Fr.* Work and Days. Hesiod, *tr. fr. Greek by* Garioch.
Evening in February. Ledwidge.
February. A. L. Hayes.
February. *Fr.* The Earthly Paradise. William Morris.
February. Ratcliffe.
February. F. D. Sherman.
February. *Unknown.*
February. A. D. T. Whitney.
February. F. B. Young.
February, Tall and Trim. A. N. Gilmore.
February Twilight. Teasdale.
First Words before Spring. Louis Untermeyer.
In February. Ropes.
In February. Henry Simpson.
In February. Symonds.
In the Month of February. *Unknown.*
Last Week of February. Robert Bridges.
Late Winter. Savage.
Poem in February. Ormond Thomas.
Snowdrop, The. Tennyson.
Swallow Song. *Unknown.*
To February. Wetherald.
When. Aldis.
FEDERAL CONSTITUTIONAL CONVENTION
Convention Song. *Unknown.*
Federal Convention. *Unknown.*
To the Federal Convention. Dwight.
FELTON, CORNELIUS CONWAY. Three Friends of Mine. Longfellow.
FERNÁNDEZ DE CÓRDOBA, FRANCISCO. Bernal Diaz' Preface to His Book. MacLeish
FERNS
Ferns. *Unknown.*
New Fern, A. "A."
Petrified Fern, The. Branch.
FERRY BOATS
Back and Forth. L. S. Mitchell.
Ferry, The. Emperor Ch'ien Wen-ti, *tr. fr. Chinese by* Waley.
FIDDLES AND FIDDLERS
Green Fiddler, The. Rachel Field.
Mountain Whippoorwill, The. S. V. Benét.
'Tis I Go Fiddling, Fiddling. Nora Hopper.
FIELD, CYRUS WEST. How Cyrus Laid the Cable. Saxe.
FIELDING, HENRY. Henry Fielding. Dobson.
FIELDS, JAMES T. In Memory of James T. Fields. Whittier.
FIELDS AND PASTURES
Beanfield, The. Clare.
Deserted Pasture, The. Carman.
Desolate Field, The. W. C. Williams.
Fallow Field, The. J. C. R. Dorr.
Field-Path, The. Swain.
Fields, The. Bynner.
Fields Are Full, The. Shanks.
Green Cornfield, A. C. G. Rossetti.
In the Field. H. L. Davis.
In the Fields. Mew.
Meadow Talk. N. A. Smith.
Meadows, The. Ann *or* Jane Taylor.
Mower's Song, The. Marvell.
Old Meadows. Hervey Allen.
Out in the Fields with God. *At. to* Guiney *and to* E. B. Browning.
Over in the Meadow. "Olive A. Wadsworth."
Pasture, The. Robert Frost.
Pasture, A. Knowles.
Poplar Field, The. Cowper.
Real Property. Monro.
Return, The. Ostenso.
Return to the Country. Tao Yuan-ming, *tr. fr. Chinese.*
Simple Field That I Shall Buy, The. McNeal.
To Meadows. Herrick.
To One Who Has Been Long in City Pent. Keats.
When You Will Walk in the Field. Leah Goldberg, *tr. fr. Hebrew by* Halkin.
White Fields. James Stephens.
FIESOLE, ITALY. Fiesolan Idyl. Landor.
FINANCIERS. New Order of Chivalry, A. Peacock.
FINCHES
Epitaph on Lady Ossory's Bullfinch. Horace Walpole.
Finches, The. Philip Murray.
Wood Finches. Boethius, *tr. fr. Latin by* Tupper.
FINK, MIKE. Shooting of the Cup, The. *Fr.* The Song of Three Friends. Neihardt.
FINLAND. Our Land. Runeberg, *tr. fr. Swedish by* Stork.
FINN MAC CUMHAIL (Finn MacCool). Death of Dermid, The. Sir Samuel Ferguson.
FINNSBURG, BATTLE OF. Battle of Finnsburg, The. *Unknown, tr. fr. Anglo-Saxon by* Kennedy.
FIR TREES
Fir-Tree, The. E. M. Thomas.
Firwood. Clare.
Little Fir-Trees, The. Evaleen Stein.
Little Firs, The. *Unknown.*
Ryton Firs. Abercrombie.
To the Fir-Tree. *Unknown, tr. fr. German.*
Young Fir-Wood, A. D. G. Rossetti.
FIRE
Adolphus Elfinstone. Gelett Burgess.
Barnfire during Church. Bly.
Brother Fire. MacNeice.
Execration upon Vulcan, An. Jonson.
Fire, The. Burford.
Fire, A. Rachel Field.
Fire. Ibn Sara, *tr. fr. Arabic by* Arberry.
Fire. Moreno Villa, *tr. fr. Spanish by* Turnbull.
Honesty at a Fire. Squire.
Movies in the Fire. Shacklett.
Sacrament of Fire, The. Oxenham.
Winter Evening Hymn to My Fire, A. J. R. Lowell.
Winter Fire, The. Howitt.
FIRE OF LONDON (1666). Fire of London, The. *Fr.* Annus Mirabilis. Dryden.
FIREFLIES
Fireflies. Coplen.
Fireflies. Carolyn Hall.
Fireflies, The. Mair.
Fireflies, The. Tu Fu, *tr. fr. Chinese by* Hart.
Fireflies in the Corn. D. H. Lawrence.
Firefly, The. Nash.
Firefly. E. M. Roberts.
Fire-Fly, The. Tabb.
Firefly, The. Taigi, *tr. fr. Japanese by* Henderson.
FIRST WORLD WAR. *See* WORLD WAR, FIRST.
FISH
Alas, Alack! De la Mare.
At the Aquarium. Max Eastman.
Average. P. K. Page.
Beasts, Birds and Fishes. O'Keeffe.
Description of a Strange (and Miraculous) Fish, A. Martin Parker.
Eels, Tortoises, Soles, Lampreys. *Fr.* Halieuticks. Oppian, *tr. fr. Greek by* Diaper.
Fish, The. Elizabeth Bishop.
Fish! Ch'en Te Chien, *tr. fr. Chinese by* Hart.
Fish. W. W. E. Ross.
Fish, the Man, and the Spirit, The. Leigh Hunt.
Flying Fish. Fenollosa.
Flying Fish. J. C. Miller.
Flying Fish. K. K Taylor.
Heaven. Rupert Brooke.
In the Blue Sky. Yamamura, *tr. fr. Japanese by* Ninomiya *and* Enright.
Leviathan. M. R. Gould.
Minnows. *Fr.* I Stood Tiptoe upon a Little Hill. Keats.
Pike, The. Blunden.

FISH (*continued*)
Piscatores Vocat. *Fr.* Epigrammata Sacra. Crashaw, *tr. fr. Latin by* Allen.
Purse-Seine, The. Jeffers.
Sermon to the Fishes. Peñalosa, *tr. fr. Spanish by* Train.
To the Immortal Memory of the Halibut, on Which I Dined This Day, Monday, April 26, 1784. Cowper.
FISH HAWKS. Fish-Hawk, The. Wheelock.
FISHER, JOHN, CARDINAL (Saint John Fisher). Cardinal Fisher. John Heywood.
FISHING AND FISHERMEN
Angler, The (*in* Izaak Walton's The Compleat Angler). Chalkhill.
Angler. I. F. Conant.
Angler, The. T. B. Read.
Angler's Ballad, The. Cotton.
Angler's Invitation, The. Stoddart.
Angler's Reveille, The. *Fr.* The Toiling of Felix. Van Dyke.
Angler's Song, The (*in* Izaak Walton's The Compleat Angler). Basse.
Angler's Song, The. *Fr.* The Secrets of Angling. Dennys.
Angler's Trysting-Tree, The. Stoddart.
Angler's Vindication, The. Stoddart.
Angler's Wish, An. Van Dyke.
Angler's Wish, The. *Fr.* The Compleat Angler. Walton.
April on Tweed. Lang.
At the Fishhouses. Elizabeth Bishop.
Awful Lot to Fishin', An. Calloway.
Bonny Tweed for Me, The. W. A. Foster.
Boston Come-All-Ye, The. *Unknown.*
Boy Fishing, The. Scovell.
Cod-Fisher, The. Lincoln.
Coromandel Fishers. Naidu.
Crabbing. Levine.
De Piscatione. Bastard.
Drunken Fisherman, The. Robert Lowell.
Epigram: "I fish for minnows in the lake." Su T'ung-po, *tr. fr. Chinese by* Rexroth.
Fish, The. Elizabeth Bishop.
Fisherman, The. A. F. Brown.
Fisherman, The. McCord.
Fisherman. Ou Yang Hsiu, *tr. fr. Chinese by* Rexroth.
Fisherman. Sacheverell Sitwell.
Fisherman, The. *Unknown, tr. fr. Portuguese by* Spicer.
Fisherman, The. Yeats.
Fisherman's Chant, The. Burnand.
Fisherman's Hymn, The. Alexander Wilson.
Fisherman's Light, The. Susanna Moodie.
Fisherman's Luck. W. W. Gibson.
Fisherman's Prayer. E. R. Fuller.
Fisherman's Song, The. D'Urfey.
Fishermen, The. Theocritus, *tr. fr. Greek.*
Fishermen, The. Whittier.
Fisher's Life, The. *Unknown.*
Fishing. Guest.
Fishing in the Wei River. Po Chü-i, *tr. fr. Chinese by* Waley.
Fishing Pole, The. M. C. Davies.
Fishing Song, A. Rands.
Fun with Fishing. Tietjens.
Gamblers, The. Delius.
Ike Walton's Prayer. J. W. Riley.
In Praise of Angling. Wotton.
In the Haunts of Bass and Bream. Maurice Thompson.
Island Fisherman, An. Tynan.
Net-Menders, The. Vrepont.
Off to the Fishing Ground. L. M. Montgomery.
Old Angler, The. De la Mare.
Old Fisherman, The. *Unknown, tr. fr. Chinese by* Luh.
Skipper-Hermit, The. Rich.
Sockeye Salmon. Hambleton.
Song of Sprats, A. Vibe, *tr. fr. Danish by* Stork.
Taking of the Salmon, The. Stoddart.
Three Fishers, The. Kingsley.
Trouting. Trowbridge.
Two Fishers. *Unknown.*
We Fish. *Fr.* Mardi. Melville.
We'll Go to Sea No More. *Unknown.*
Words Are Never Enough. Charles Bruce.
FISK, JAMES. Jim Fisk. *Unknown.*
FITZGERALD, EDWARD. To E. FitzGerald. Tennyson.
FITZGERALD, SIR MAURICE. Lamentation for the Death of Sir Maurice Fitzgerald, Knight of Kerry, A. Pierce Ferriter, *tr. fr. Late Middle Irish by* Mangan.
FITZGERALD, F. SCOTT. On Editing Scott Fitzgerald's Papers. Edmund Wilson.
FITZGERALDS, THE. Geraldines, The, *sel.* ("The Geraldines! the Geraldines!—'tis full a thousand years"). T. O. Davis.
FIVE FORKS. Army Correspondent's Last Ride. Townsend.
FLAGS, CONFEDERACY
Bonnie Blue Flag, The ("Come, brothers! rally for the right"). Ketchum.
Bonnie Blue Flag, The ("We are a band of brothers"). McCarthy.
Conquered Banner, The. A. J. Ryan.
FLAGS, DENMARK. Dannebrog (The Danish Flag). Ingemann, *tr. by* Stork.
FLAGS, GREAT BRITAIN
English Flag, The. Kipling.
Flag of Old England, The. Joseph Howe.
"Injun, The." Logan.
Union Jack, The. Kirby.
FLAGS, SWEDEN. Hoist the Flag! Oscar II, King of Sweden, *tr. by* Stork.
FLAGS, UNITED STATES
American Boy, The. *Unknown.*
American Flag, The. J. R. Drake.
Banner of America. D. A. McCarthy.
Battle-Plane in France, A. O. C. A. Child.
Betsy's Battle Flag. Minna Irving.
Boy, Bare Your Head. N. B. Turner.
Call to the Colors, The. Guiterman.
Delicate Cluster! Flag of Teeming Life! Whitman.
Flag, The. Boker.
Flag, The. Flash.
Flag, The. Horton.
Flag, The. Larcom.
Flag, The. Roche.
Flag Goes By, The. H. H. Bennett.
Flag of Our Union Forever, The. G. P. Morris.
Flag of the *Constellation*, The. T. B. Read.
Flag of the Free. W. T. Field.
Flag of the Free. *Unknown.*
Flag Song. L. A. C. Ward.
Flag Speaks, The. E. G. Balch.
Flag We Fly, The. Aileen Fisher.
Flags on Fifth Avenue. Christopher Morley.
Flower of Liberty, The. Holmes.
God Bless the Flag. *Unknown.*
God Save the Flag. O. W. Holmes.
Good Morning, America! Kemp.
Hang Out the Flags. Tippett.
I Am the Flag. L. M. Jones.
I Am What You Make Me. F. K. Lane.
Little Flags, The. Minot.
My Country Is the World. Robert Whitaker.
My Country's Flag. Stafford.
Name of Old Glory, The. J. W. Riley.
New Banner, The. Trask.
Ode to the Flag. Crellin.
Old Flag, The. Bunner.
Old Flag. Hubbard Parker.
Old Flag Forever, The. Stanton.
Our Cherished Flag. James Montgomery.
Our Flag. F. C. Hamlet.
Our Flag. M. E. Sangster.
Raising of the Flag, The. Pallen.
Red, the White, the Blue, The. K. B. Sherwood.
Service Flag, The. Herschell.
Song for Our Flag, A. M. E. Sangster.
Song for the Flag, A. D. A. McCarthy.
Song of Liberty. L. A. Garnett.
Stand by the Flag. Wilder.
Star-spangled Banner, The. Key.
Thick-sprinkled Bunting. Whitman.
To the Flag of Stars. T. C. Clark.
Under the Stars. Wallace Rice.
Unfurling of the Flag, The. C. E. Sears.
World Take Good Notice. Whitman.
Your Flag and My Flag. Nesbit.
Flag Day (*Our American Holidays Series*) (FOAH). Robert Haven Schauffler, ed.
FLAMINGOS
Flamingoes. Sennett.
Flamingos, The. Rilke, *tr. fr. German by* Lemont.
Turtle and Flamingo, The. J. T. Fields
FLANDERS, BELGIUM
Another Reply to "In Flanders Fields." Galbreath, *sometimes at. to* Armstrong.
Flanders Grave, A. Nathanson.
Flanders Poppies. Colvin.
How They Brought the Good News from Ghent to Aix. Robert Browning.
In Flanders Fields. John McCrae.
In Flanders Fields. *Unknown.*
In Flanders Now. Jaques.
Old Houses of Flanders, The. F. M. Ford.
FLAX
Flax. Bunin, *tr. fr. Russian by* Deutsch *and* Yarmolinsky.
Flax Flower, The. Howitt.
FLEAS
Flea, The. Donne.
Flea, The. Roland Young.
Flea and a fly in a flue, A. *Unknown.*
Fleas, The. De Morgan.
Partners. Castiello.

FLEET STREET, LONDON. Song of Fleet Street, A. Werner.
FLETCHER, JOHN
Bards of Passion and of Mirth. Keats.
To Fletcher Reviv'd. Lovelace.
Upon Master Fletchers Incomparable Playes. Herrick.
Upon Mr. Fletchers Playes, Published, 1647. Vaughan.
Upon Mr. John Fletcher's Playes. Waller.
Upon the Dramatick Poems of Mr. John Fletcher. Cartwright.
FLEUR-DE-LIS. *See* IRIS.
FLIES
Blue-Fly, The. Robert Graves.
Death to Us, A. Silkin.
Flea and a fly in a flue, A. *Unknown.*
Flies. Aldis.
Fly, The. *Fr.* Songs of Experience. Blake.
Fly, The. Nash.
Fly, The. Shapiro.
Near Dusk. Auslander.
On a Fly Drinking from His Cup. Oldys.
Spider and the Fly, The. Howitt.
FLODDEN FIELD, ENGLAND
Flodden. *Fr.* Marmion Sir Walter Scott.
Flodden Field. *Unknown.*
Flowers of the Forest. Elliot.
FLOODS
Flood. Ethel Anderson.
Flood. M. G. Charles.
Flood, The. *Fr.* Metamorphoses. Ovid, *tr. fr. Latin by* Dryden.
Flood. T'ao Ch'ien, *tr. fr. Chinese by* Waley.
FLORENCE, ITALY
Casa Guidi Windows, *sels.* E. B. Browning.
Florence. Landor.
Giotto's Tower. Longfellow.
Old Bridge at Florence, The. Longfellow.
Old Pictures in Florence. Robert Browning.
Road to Firenze, A. A. K. Gray.
San Marco Museum, Florence. Sister Maris Stella.
Santa Maria del Fiore. G. H. Clarke.
FLORIDA
Florida. Elizabeth Bishop.
Florida Road Workers. Langston Hughes.
Spring in Florida. Roth.
Swanee River. S. C. Foster.
FLOWERS
Alpine Flowers, The. Sigourney.
Behold, O Man. *Fr.* The Faerie Queene. Spenser.
Birth of the Flowers, The. Fenollosa.
Bloom. Kreymborg.
Blossom, The. Blake.
Blossom, The. Donne.
Buttercups and Daisies. Howitt.
Chanted Calendar, A. *Fr.* Balder. Dobell.
Charm for Spring Flowers, A. Rachel Field.
Cheddar Pinks. Robert Bridges.
Choir of Day, The. *Fr.* Milton. Blake.
City Child, The. Tennyson.
Contemplation upon Flowers, A. Henry King.
Cycle. Langston Hughes.
Devotion of the Flowers to Their Lady, The. Melville.
Down in a Valley. William Browne.
Evening. Doolittle ("H. D.").
Faithless Flowers, The. Widdemer.
Fear of Flowers, The. Clare.
Field Flowers. Thomas Campbell.
First Spring Flowers. Howland.
Flower, The. L. W. Dodd.
Flower, The. George Herbert.
Flower, The. Tennyson.
Flower-Cart Man, The. Rachel Field.
Flower Chorus. *Unknown, wr. at. to* Emerson.
Flower Dreams. *Unknown.*
Flower Factory. F. W. Evans.
Flower in the Crannied Wall. Tennyson.
Flower Market, The. Po Chü-i, *tr. fr. Chinese by* Waley.
Flowers. Behn.
Flowers. Hood.
Flowers. Longfellow.
Flowers. Mallarmé, *tr. fr. French by* Conder.
Flowers. Rimbaud, *tr. fr. French by* Flores.
Flowers. *Fr.* Jubilate Agno. Smart.
Flowers, The. R. L. Stevenson.
Flowers, The. *Unknown.*
Flowers and Moonlight on the Spring River. Emperor Yang-ti, *tr. fr. Chinese by* Waley.
Flowers by the Sea. W. C. Williams.
Flowers in the Valley. *Unknown.*
Flower's Name, The. *Fr.* Garden Fancies. Robert Browning.
Flowers of Perdita, The. *Fr.* The Winter's Tale. Shakespeare.
Flowers of the Forest, The. Jane Elliot.
How the Flowers Grow. "Gabriel Setoun."
I Walked the Other Day. Vaughan.
Idle Flowers, The. Robert Bridges.
Lesson of the Flowers, The. Hafiz, *tr. fr. Persian by* Palmer.
Nosegay Always Sweet, A, for Lovers to Send for Tokens of Love at New Year's Tide, or for Fairings. *At. to* Hunnis.
Path Flower. Dargan.
Picture of Little T. C. in a Prospect of Flowers, The. Marvell.
Planting Flowers on the Embankment. Po Chü-i, *tr. fr. Chinese by* Waley.
Roadside Flowers. Carman.
Scandal among the Flowers, A. C. S. Taylor.
Seek Flowers of Heaven. Southwell.
Song: "Primrose in the green forest, The." Thomas Delaney.
Song in Spring. Louis Ginsberg.
Sonnets to Orpheus, *sel.* ("Our kinship is with flower, vine leaf, fruit"). Rilke, *tr. fr. German by* Hull.
Some Flowers o' the Spring. *Fr.* The Winter's Tale. Shakespeare.
Spring Flowers. *Fr.* The Seasons. James Thomson.
Spring Flowers from Ireland. D. F. McCarthy.
Spring Garland, A. Rorty.
Subverted Flower, The. Robert Frost.
Suscipe Flos Florem. *Fr.* Carmina Burana. *Unknown, tr. fr. Latin by* Lind.
Thirsty Flowers. Knipe.
Time to Go. "Susan Coolidge."
'Tis But a Little Faded Flower. Howarth.
To a Blue Flower. Neilson.
To a Woodbine Tendril. Platen, *tr. fr. German by* Cotterell.
To Blossoms. Herrick.
To Primroses Fill'd with Morning-Dew. Herrick.
Valley of Pale Blue Flowers, The. "Fiona Macleod."
Violets, daffodils. Coatsworth.
Wild Blossoms. W. H. Davies.
Window Boxes. Farjeon.
Woman Looking At a Vase of Flowers. Wallace Stevens.
Yasmin. *Fr.* Hassan. Flecker.
FLUTES
Amateur Flute, The. *Unknown.*
Flute, The. Chénier, *tr. fr. French by* Conder.
Flute of the Lonely, The. Vachel Lindsay.
Hearing a Flute on a Spring Night. Li Po, *tr. fr. Chinese by* Christy.
Musical Instrument, A. E. B. Browning.
FLYCATCHERS. Flycatchers. Robert Bridges.
FLYING DUTCHMAN
Flying Dutchman, The. A. M. Sullivan.
Flying Dutchman, The. *Unknown.*
FLYING SAUCERS. Go Fly a Saucer. McCord.
FLYING SQUIRRELS. Flying Squirrel, The. M. E. Burt.
FOG
Boats in a Fog. Jeffers.
Coastguardsman in the Fog, The. Schevill.
English Fog, The. Dyer.
Fog, The. Coffin.
Fog, The. W. H. Davies.
Fog. Jeffers.
Fog. McCreary.
Fog. Sandburg.
Fog-Horn. G. H. Clarke.
Mist. Ficke.
Morning Mist, The. Southey.
New England Fog. Callaghan.
River-Fog. Kiyowara, *tr. fr. Japanese by* Waley.
See also HAZE; MIST.
FOLK SONGS. *See* BALLADS AND FOLK SONGS.
FONTAINEBLEAU, FRANCE
At Fontainebleau. Symons.
Fontainebleau. Teasdale.
FONTENOY, BATTLE OF
Fontenoy. T. O. Davis.
Fontenoy, 1745. Lawless.
FOOD
Food and Drink. Louis Untermeyer.
Hasty Pudding, The, *sels.* Barlow.
Hymn to the Belly. Jonson.
If We Didn't Have to Eat, *sel.* ("Life would be an easy matter"). Waterman.
Inviting a Friend to Supper. Jonson.
Jolly Supper, The. Alcázar, *tr. fr. Spanish by* Walsh.
Lucile, *sel.* ("We may live without poetry, music and art"). "Owen Meredith."
Nightmare of a Cook. Kaliman.
Spectator ab Extra. Clough.
Table Richly Spread, A. *Fr.* Paradise Regained. Milton.
Thoughts of Loved Ones. Fishback.
To a Baked Fish. Carolyn Wells.

FOOLS
Ship of Fools, The, *sels.* Brandt, *tr. fr. German by* Barclay.
Volpone, *sel.* (Fools, They Are the Only Nation). Jonson.
FOOTBALL. Under the Goal Posts. Guiterman.
FORBES, EDWARD. Epigram on the Death of Edward Forbes. Dobell.
FORD, JOHN
To My Friend, Master John Ford. Shirley.
Upon Ford's Two Tragedies, "Loves Sacrifice" and "The Broken Heart." Crashaw.
FOREST FIRES. Forest Fire, The. A. W. Monroe.
FOREST RANGERS
Forest Ranger, The. Mary Austin.
Song of the Forest Ranger, The. Bashford.
FORESTS
Advice to a Forest. Bodenheim.
Bonnie Wood o' Craigie-lea. Tannahill.
Burned Forests. Call.
Deep in the Woods. Shacklett.
Deep Woods. Jennings.
English Wood, An. Robert Graves.
Font in the Forest, The. Léonie Adams.
Forest. H. G. Blackwell.
Forest Glade, The. C. T. Turner.
Forest Hymn, A. Bryant.
Forest Song. A. W. Page.
Forest Song. Venable.
Green Inn, The. Garrison.
In the Forest. *Fr.* The Emigrant. McLachlan.
In the Forest. Supervielle, *tr. fr. French by* Conder.
In the Wood of Finvarra. Symons.
In the Woods. Dorothy Baker.
In the Woods. F. G. Scott.
In the Woods. Verlaine, *tr. fr. French by* Kittel.
Inscription for the Entrance to a Wood. Bryant.
Midsummer Noon in the Australian Forest, A. Harpur.
O Sweet Woods. *Fr.* Arcadia. Sidney.
O Woodland Cool. Brentano, *tr. fr. German by* Cotterell.
Over My Head the Forest Wall. *Unknown, tr. fr. Irish by* Flower.
Passing of the Forest, The. W. P. Reeves.
Plants Stand Silent Round Me, The. Jorgensen, *tr. fr. Danish by* Hillyer.
Solitary Woodsman, The. C. G. D. Roberts.
Solitude. Lampman.
Stopping by Woods on a Snowy Evening. Robert Frost.
Sylvan Ode. Chocano, *tr. fr. Spanish by* Rice.
Under the Greenwood Tree. *Fr.* As You Like It. Shakespeare.
Waldeinsamkeit. Emerson.
Way through the Woods, The. Kipling.
Who Has Gone through the Wood. McLaren.
Wood by the Sea, The. Duncan Scott.
Wood Song, A. Hodgson.
Woodland. Sister Margaret Teresa.
Woodland Peace. George Meredith.
Woodland Revel, A. Urmy.
Woodland Worship. Wetherald.
Woodlands, The. William Barnes.
Woodnotes, I. Emerson.
Woods. Auden.
Woods, The. Bandeira, *tr. fr. Portuguese by* Poore.
Woods and Kestrel. Julian Bell.
Woods Are Still, The. "Michael Field."
Woods of Westermain, The. George Meredith.
FORGET-ME-NOTS. Forget-me-not, The. *Unknown.*
FORT LARAMIE TRAIL. Laramie Trail. Hanson.
FORT WORTH, TEXAS
Beauty Is Elsewhere. House.
Cities. House.
FORTUNE
Casino. Auden.
Comming of Good Luck, The. Herrick.
Davy, the Dicer. *Fr.* Two Short Ballettes. Sir Thomas More.
For Ever, Fortune. James Thomson.
Fortune ("The Lady Fortune is both friend and foe"). *Unknown.*
Fortune ("Weal, thou art a crooked thing"). *Unknown.*
Fortune. Wyatt.
Fortune Smiles. *Fr.* Old Fortunatus. Dekker.
Fortune's Treachery. Halevi, *tr. fr. Hebrew by* Solis-Cohen.
Fortune's Wheel. De Tabley.
From a Hint in the Minor Poets. Samuel Wesley.
Hap. Hardy.
Hard Luck. Langston Hughes.
Lewis, the Lost Lover. *Fr.* Two Short Ballettes. Sir Thomas More.
Lovely Chance. Teasdale.
Of Fortune. Sir Thomas More.
Of Fortune's Power. Richard Edwards.
Politician, The. Po Chü-i, *tr. fr. Chinese by* Waley.
Times Go by Turns. Southwell.
To Fortune. Herrick.
To Fortune. Sir Thomas More.
Wert Thou But Blind, O Fortune, Then Perhaps. Landor.
Winters Morning Muse, A. Thomas Howell.
FORTUNE TELLERS. Spaewife, The. R. L. Stevenson.
FORTY-NINERS. '49. Joaquin Miller.
FOTHERINGAY, ENGLAND. At Fotheringay. Southwell.
FOUNTAINS
Dried-up Fountain. Leighton.
Fountain, The. Fyleman.
Fountain, The. Gorman.
Fountain, The. J. R. Lowell.
Fountain, The. Mu'tamid, King of Seville, *tr. fr. Arabic by* Smith.
Fountain, The. H. Stuart.
Fountain, The. Teasdale.
Fountain, The. Wordsworth.
Fountains, The. Rodgers.
Roman Fountain. Rilke, *tr. fr. German by* Luke.
To a Fountain. Ronsard, *tr. fr. French by* Currey.
To the Fountain of Bandusia. Horace, *tr. fr. Latin.*
FOURTH OF JULY
After the Fourth of July. M. P. Dawson.
American Independence. Street.
Centennial Meditation of Columbia, The. Lanier.
Chester. Billings.
Choice. Farrar.
Emancipation from British Dependence. Freneau.
Flower of Liberty, The. O. W. Holmes.
Fourth of July. Chute.
Fourth of July. Rachel Field.
Fourth of July, The. Pierpont.
Fourth of July Night. Aldis.
Fourth of July Ode. J. R. Lowell.
Fourth of July Song. Lenski.
Freedom, Our Queen. O. W. Holmes.
Freedom's Natal Day. Griswold.
Grandfather Watts's Private Fourth. Bunner.
Independence Bell—July 4, 1776. *Unknown.*
Independence Day. Royall Tyler.
Independence Day To-Day. M. E. Sangster.
I've Got a Rocket. *Unknown.*
Nation's Birthday, The. Vandyne.
Ode: Sung in the Town Hall, Concord, July 4, 1857. Emerson.
Ode for the Fourth of July, 1876, An. J. R. Lowell.
Ode to the Fourth of July. George.
Independence Day (Our American Holidays Series) (IDAH). Robert Haven Schauffler, ed.
FOX, CHARLES JAMES. Nelson, Pitt, Fox. *Fr.* Marmion. Sir Walter Scott.
FOXES
Ballad of Red Fox, The. La Follette.
Ballad of the Fox.
Crow and the Fox, The. La Fontaine, *tr. fr. French by* Marsh.
False Fox, The. *Unknown.*
Four Little Foxes. Sarett.
Fox. Dyment.
Fox, The. Hesketh.
Fox, The. Parry, *tr. fr. Welsh by* Williams.
Fox, The. Scheuer.
Fox, The. Serraillier.
Fox, The (*ballad*). *Unknown.*
Fox, The. *Unknown, tr. fr. Armenian by* Boyajian.
Fox and the Grapes, The. La Fontaine, *tr. fr. French by* Wright.
Fox and the Grapes, The. Lauren.
Fox at the Point of Death, The. Gay.
Fox Awakes, The. *Fr.* Reynard the Fox. Masefield.
Fox Hunt, The. *Fr.* Reynard the Fox. Masefield.
Fox, the Wolf, and the Bear, The. *Unknown, tr. fr. Armenian by* Boyajian.
Foxes among the Lambs. Moll.
Hunt, The. Louis Kent.
Little White Fox. Rowbotham.
Lost Fox. Frances Frost.
Modereen Rue. Tynan.
Night of Wind. Frances Frost.
Owl and the Fox, The. *Unknown.*
Raven and the Fox, The. La Fontaine, *tr. fr. French by* Wright.
Sycophantic Fox and the Gullible Raven, The. G. W. Carryl.
Two Foxes, The. *Unknown.*
FOXGLOVE. Foxgloves. Webb.
FRANCE, ANATOLE. Anatole France at Eighty. Oaks.
FRANCE
For Those Who Died in Battle. Mercier, *tr. fr. French by* Conder.
France. Mackaye.
France. Napier.
France; an Ode. S. T. Coleridge.

In France. Cornford.
Liberté, Égalité, Fraternité. Converse.
Luna. Hugo, *tr. fr. French by* Conder.
O France When Thou Art Prone and Bound. Hugo, *tr. fr. French by* Thorley.
O Star of France. Whitman.
On the Prospect of a Revolution in France. Freneau.
Provincia Deserta. Pound.
Reflections on the Fall of France, June, 1940. Eiluned Lewis.
Republic to Republic. Bynner.
Rioupéroux. Flecker.
Road to France, The. Daniel Henderson.
Spell of France, The. Blunden.
Third of February, 1852, The. Tennyson.
To France. Ralph Chaplin.
Vichy. D. G. Davies.
Vive la France. C. H. Crawford.
Zone. Apollinaire, *tr. fr. French by* Strachan.
Formal Spring; French Renaissance Poems (FoS). R. N. Currey, tr.
Mid-Century French Poets (MiCF). Wallace Fowlie, ed. and tr.
Mirror for French Poetry, A, 1840–1940 (MiFP). Cecily Mackworth, ed.
Treasury of French Poetry, A (TrFP). Alan Conder, ed. and tr.
FRANCIS BORGIA, SAINT. Saint Francis Borgia; or, A Refutation for Heredity. McGinley.
FRANCIS OF ASSISI, SAINT
Blessing of St. Francis, The. Sister Maura.
Claribel's Way to God, *sel.* ("I met a friar in a hood"). Doolittle ("H. D.").
Ecco il Santo. K. L. Bates.
Little Litany to St. Francis, A. Philip Murray.
Old Man in the Park. M. E. Osborn.
Return. Hawling.
Saint Francis and the Birds. McFadden.
St. Francis and the Wolf. Tynan.
Saint Francis of Assisi. Ramsay.
St. Francis' Sermon to the Birds. Longfellow.
Vocation of St. Francis, The. Sister Mary Eleanore.
Saint Francis and the Poet (SaFP). Elizabeth B. Patterson, ed.
FRANCIS XAVIER, SAINT. Invocation and Proposition. *Fr.* Eastern Evangelic Planet. Sigüenza y Góngora, *tr. fr. Spanish by* Beckett.
FRANCISCANS
Franciscans. Blocker.
Irish Franciscan, The. Mulholland.
Saint Francis' Lesson to His Brothers, *sel.* ("My Brothers, when the north wind bites us sharply"). *Unknown.*
FRANCK, CÉSAR
At the Symphony. Nathan.
César Franck. Auslander.
Four Friends. Ward.
FRANCO-PRUSSIAN WAR. In Time of "The Breaking of Nations". Hardy.
FRANKLIN, BENJAMIN
Benjamin Franklin, 1706–1790. Rosemary Benét *and* Stephen Vincent Benét.
Benjamin Franklin. Coates.
Ben Franklin's Head (1728). M. A. Howe.
Epistle; from Dr. Franklin (Deceased) to His Poetical Panegyrists on Some of Their Absurd Compliments. Freneau.
On the Death of Dr. Benjamin Franklin. Freneau.
FRANKLIN, SIR JOHN
Lady Franklin's Lament. *Unknown.*
Sir John Franklin; On the Cenotaph in Westminster Abbey. Tennyson.
FRASER (river), BRITISH COLUMBIA. Trail to Lillooet, The. E. P. Johnson.
FREDERICKSBURG, VIRGINIA. In the Old Churchyard at Fredericksburg. Loring.
FREDERICKSBURG, BATTLE OF
At Fredericksburg. O'Reilly.
Crossing at Fredericksburg, The. Boker.
Fredericksburg. Aldrich.
FREEDOM
All Men Are Free. Napier.
Ante-Bellum Sermon, An. P. L. Dunbar.
Antiquity of Freedom, The. Bryant.
As by the Shore at Break of Day. Thomas Moore.
At the Zoo. Zangwill.
Boston Hymn. Emerson.
Breshkovskaya, *sel.* ("Mother of power"). Elsa Barker.
Country Justice, The. Langhorne.
Dame Liberty Reports from Travel. D. C. Pinkney.
Fain Would I Live in Safest Freedom. Platen, *tr. fr. German by* Morgan.
1536–1936. Emyr Humphreys.
Flower of Liberty, The. O. W. Holmes.
France; an Ode. S. T. Coleridge.
Freedom. *Fr.* The Bruce. Barbour.
Freedom. J. R. Lowell.
Freedom. Leonard Mann.
Freedom. Nekrasov, *tr. fr. Russian by* Deutsch.
Freedom. Tennyson.
Freedom, Our Queen. O. W. Holmes.
Harp That Once through Tara's Halls, The. Thomas Moore.
Hymn to Liberty, *sel.* ("I know you by the blade"). Solomos, *tr. fr. Modern Greek by* Dalven.
In After Days. G. F. Cameron.
Independence. Fullerton.
Independence. *Fr.* Ode to Independence. Smollett.
Independence. Thoreau.
Lake of Van, The. Raffi, *tr. fr. Armenian by* Green.
Liberator, The. Wu-ti, *tr. fr. Chinese by* Waley.
Liberty. John Hay.
Liberty. Nalbandian, *tr. fr. Armenian by* Boyajian.
Liberty for All. Khlebnikov, *tr. fr. Russian by* Bowra.
Liberty Song. John Dickinson.
Liberty Tree. Paine.
Lo, Victress on the Peaks. Whitman.
London 1802. Wordsworth.
Loyalty Confin'd. L'Estrange.
Moral Warfare, The. Whittier.
My Political Faith. G. F. Cameron.
No Master. W. H. Davies.
Notes for My Son. Comfort.
O Liberty, proud inspiration. Yazykov, *tr. fr. Russian by* Bowra.
Ode: "God save the Rights of Man!" Freneau.
Ode: "O tenderly the haughty day." Emerson.
Ode to Liberty. *Fr.* Goddwyn. Thomas Chatterton.
Ode to Liberty. Shelley.
Of Old Sat Freedom on the Heights. Tennyson.
Of True Liberty. Sir John Beaumont.
On the Detraction Which Followed upon My Writing Certain Treatises. Milton.
On the Subjugation of Switzerland. Wordsworth.
Our Cause. Linton.
Present Crisis, The. J. R. Lowell.
Pride. Josephine Miles.
Republican Genius of Europe, The. Freneau.
Returning to the Fields. T'ao Ch'ien, *tr. fr. Chinese by* Waley.
Song, A: "Hark! 'tis Freedom that calls, come, patriots, awake!" *Unknown.*
Song of Freedom, A. Milligan.
Song of Liberty, A. Blake.
Song of the Settlers. Jessamyn West.
Sonnet to Liberty. Oscar Wilde.
Sonnet Written While in Prison for Denouncing the Domestic Slave-Trade. Garrison.
Stanzas on Freedom. J. R. Lowell.
To Althea, from Prison. Lovelace.
To Freedom. Barlow.
To Toussaint L'Ouverture. Wordsworth.
To Walt Whitman in America. Swinburne.
Torch of Liberty, The. Thomas Moore.
Unknown Citizen, The. Auden.
Wanderers. Hebblethwaite.
War Hymn. Pheraios, *tr. fr. Modern Greek by* Dalven.
Why I Am a Liberal. Robert Browning.
Winter Morning Walk, The. *Fr.* The Task. Cowper.
Wolf and the Dog, The. Samaniego, *tr. fr. Spanish.*
Poetry of Freedom, The (PoFr). William Rose Benét *and* Norman Cousins, eds.
FREEMASONRY. Lodge Room over Simpkins' Store, The. Greenleaf.
FRÉMONT, JOHN CHARLES
John Charles Frémont. Lummis.
On Recrossing the Rocky Mountains after Many Years. Frémont.
To John C. Frémont. Whittier.
FRENCH, THE. Women Will Soon Knit Again, The. Burlingame.
FRENCH AND INDIAN WARS. Captives' Hymn, The. E. D. Proctor.
FRENCH BROAD RIVER, NORTH CAROLINA. Racing Water. M. B. Clarke.
FRENCH REVOLUTION
Carmagnole, La. *Unknown, tr. fr. French by* Oxenford.
France; an Ode. S. T. Coleridge.
French Revolution, The. Blake.
French Revolution, The. Erasmus Darwin.
French Revolution, The. *Fr.* The Prelude. Wordsworth.
Girondins, The. Dumas, *tr. fr. French by* Oxenford.
Ode: "God save the Rights of Man!" Freneau.
On the Anniversary of the Storming of the Bastille, at Paris, July 14th, 1789. Freneau.
FREUD, SIGMUND
In Memory of Sigmund Freud. Auden.
Return from the Freudian Islands, The. Hope.

FREUD, SIGMUND (*continued*)
Song: "Don't Tell Me What You Dreamt Last Night." F. P. Adams.
FRIARS
Friar of Orders Gray, The. John O'Keeffe.
Friar's Hunting Song. Peacock.
FRIENDS, SOCIETY OF
First-Day Thoughts. Whittier.
For the Quakers. Bianca Bradbury.
Quaker Meeting-House. W. E. Leonard.
Quaker Widow, The. Bayard Taylor.
Quakerdom. C. G. Halpine.
Quakeress Bride, The. E. C. Kinney.
Quaker's Meeting, The. Samuel Lover.
FRIENDSHIP
After They Have Tired of the Brilliance of Cities. Spender.
Amantium Irae Amoris Redintegratio Est. Richard Edwards.
Arrow and the Song, The. Longfellow.
Auld Lang Syne. Burns.
Being Visited by a Friend during Illness. Po Chü-i, *tr. fr. Chinese by* Waley.
Bright moon illumines the night-prospect, A. *Fr.* Seventeen Old Poems. *Unknown, tr. fr. Chinese by* Waley.
Comrades. Woodberry.
Confide in a Friend. *Unknown.*
Consider, Friend, When We Together Spoke. Morgenstern, *tr. fr. German by* Hutchins *and* Grahl.
Departed Friends. Vaughan.
Do They Whisper. Schwartz.
Early Friendship. Spring Rice.
Fame and Friendship. Dobson.
Farewell Once More: To My Friend Yen at Feng Chi Station. Tu Fu, *tr. fr. Chinese by* Rexroth.
Friend, A. *Fr.* Proverbios Morales. Santob de Carrion.
Friend, A. Lionel Johnson.
Friend, A. Marguerite Power.
Friend, A. *Unknown.*
Friend Who Just Stands By, The. B. G. Williams.
Friends Old and New. Joseph Parry.
Friendship. *Fr.* The Testament of Beauty. Robert Bridges.
Friendship. Craik.
Friendship. Emerson.
Friendship. *Unknown.*
Friendship, The. Mark Van Doren.
Friendship after Love. E. W. Wilcox.
Gone. M. E. Coleridge.
Great Friend. Thoreau.
Hare and Many Friends, The. Gay.
I Love a Flower. Heine, *tr. fr. German by* Salinger.
I Tell of Another Young Death. Tiempo, *tr. fr. Spanish by* Walsh.
If You Had a Friend. Robert Lewis.
If You Have a Friend. *Unknown.*
La Belle Confidente. Stanley.
Letter, The. Po Chü-i, *tr. fr. Chinese by* Waley.
Love and Friendship. Emily Brontë.
My Comrade. Roche.
My Frends Are Little Lamps to Me. Whittemore.
O Tan-faced Prairie-Boy. Whitman.
Oaths of Friendship. *Unknown, tr. fr. Chinese by* Waley.
Ode, An: "As it fell upon a day." Barnfield.
Of Frendship. Grimald.
Of Friendship. Harington, *after* Martial.
Of Perfect Friendship. *At. to* Cheke.
Old Familiar Faces, The. Charles Lamb.
Old Friends. Hsü Chi, *tr. fr. Chinese by* Hart.
Old Friends. Waddy.
Old Friendship. Tietjens.
On Friendship. Whitehead.
On Parting with Moses ibn Ezra. Halevi, *tr. fr. Hebrew by* Solis-Cohen.
Only Way to Have a Friend, The. *Unknown.*
Others as Fair, but Not So Faithful. Turberville.
Plain Description of Perfect Friendship, A. *Unknown.*
Plaint of Friendship by Death Broken. R. M. Nichols.
Qua Cursum Ventus. Clough.
Rejoicing at the Arrival of Ch'en Hsiung. Po Chü-i, *tr. fr. Chinese by* Waley.
Sincere Man, The. A. G. Walton.
Speech to Those Who Say Comrade. MacLeish.
Starting from Paumanok. Whitman.
Stimulus of Friendship, The. *Unknown.*
Temple to Friendship. Thomas Moore.
To a Friend. Gullans.
To a Friend in the Wilderness, *sel.* ("Old friend, dear friend"). Fairburn.
To a Run-away Pupil. Alcuin, *tr. fr. Latin by* Lindsay.
To My Friend. Anne Campbell.
To the Immortal Memory and Friendship of That Noble Pair, Sir Lucius Cary and Sir H. Morison. Jonson.
To Thomas Moore. Byron.
To Wei Pa, a Retired Scholar. Tu Fu, *tr. fr. Chinese by* Rexroth.
Two Friends, The. Leland.
We Have Been Friends Together. C. E. S. Norton.
Whirlpool, The. *Unknown.*
With Rue My Heart Is Laden. A. E. Housman.
Without My Friends the Day Is Dark. Moses ibn Ezra, *tr. fr. Hebrew by* Solis-Cohen.
Book of Friendship, The (BoFr). Elizabeth Selden, comp.
FRIETCHIE, BARBARA. Barbara Frietchie. Whittier.
FRITH, JOHN. From William Tyndale to John Frith. Edgar Bowers.
FRITHJOF. Frithiof's Saga. Tegner, *tr. fr. Swedish by* Longfellow.
FRÖDING, GUSTAF. Burial of Gustaf Fröding, The. Heidenstam, *tr. fr. Swedish by* Stork.
FROGS
Brown Frog, The. M. K. Robinson.
Frog, The. Belloc.
Frog, The. *Unknown.*
Frogs' Song The. *Fr.* The Frogs. Aristophanes, *tr. fr. Greek.*
Grandfather Frog. Bechtel.
Ode to a Frog. O'Neil.
Queroqué the Frog; an Autobiography. Kusano, *tr. fr. Japanese by* Ninomiya *and* Enright.
There Was a Frog Lived in a Well. *Unknown.*
Toad and the Frog, The. *Unknown.*
FRONTIERS
Frontier, The. Masefield.
Geography of This Time. MacLeish.
Last Frontier, The. J. G. Fletcher.
Lay of the Last Frontier. Hersey.
FRONTIERSMEN
Old Scout's Lament, The. Drannan.
Shooting of the Cup, The. *Fr.* The Song of Three Friends. Neihardt.
Stationed Scout, The. Sproull.
Texas Types—"The Bad Man." Chittenden.
Tough Cuss from Bitter Creek, A. J. B. Adams.
FROST, ROBERT
Frostbite. Aiken.
Letter to Robert Frost, A. Hillyer.
Robert Frost. Louis Untermeyer.
FROST
Apparently with no surprise. Emily Dickinson.
Black Frost. Hoisington.
Devonshire Rhyme, A. *Unknown.*
Fairy Artist, The. Garabrant.
First Frost. Curran.
Frost. E. R. Fuller.
Frost, The. H. F. Gould.
Frost. E. M. Thomas.
Frost in Spring. Rittenhouse.
Frost Pane, The. McCord.
Frost Spirit, The. Whittier.
Frosted Pane, The. C. G. D. Roberts.
Glittering Frost. *Fr.* A Winter Piece. Ambrose Philips.
Hard Frost. Andrew Young.
Hoar-Frost. Amy Lowell.
Jack Frost. H. B. Davis.
Jack Frost. C. E. Pike.
Jack Frost. "Gabriel Setoun."
Jack Frost in the Garden. Smeeton.
John Frost. William Miller.
White Frost, The. Wang Chi, *tr. fr. Chinese by* Mathers.
Who Is It? *Unknown.*
FRUIT
Fruit. Ruth Miller.
Sonnets to Orpheus, *sel.* ("Our kinship is with flower, vine leaf, fruit"). Rilke, *tr. fr. German by* Hull.
FRY, ELIZABETH. Friendly Address, A. Hood.
FUCHSIA. Fuchsia Hedges in Connacht. Colum.
FULLER, MARGARET
Margaret Fuller. A. B. Alcott.
Margaret Fuller. *Fr.* A Fable for Critics. J. R. Lowell.
On the Death of M. d'Ossoli and His Wife, Margaret Fuller. Landor.
FUNDISI (lake), AFRICA. Fundisi. Ruth Miller.
FUNDY, BAY OF. Arnold, Master of the *Scud.* Carman.
FUNERALS
After the Funeral. Dylan Thomas.
Bucolic Funeral. Sierra, *tr. fr. Spanish by* Beckett.
Funeral, The. De la Mare.
Funeral, The. Donne.
Tract. W. C. Williams.

G

GAGE, THOMAS. Tom Gage's Proclamation. Flucker.
GALATEA

Galatea Again. Taggard.
Galatea to Pygmalion. Stryker.
Pygmalion and Galatea. *Fr.* Metamorphoses. Ovid, *tr. fr. Latin by* Highet.
Pygmalion to Galatea. Robert Graves.
Question, A. Edna Livingston.
GALILEE, PALESTINE. In Galilee. Butts.
GALILEO. Galileo. A. D. Watson.
GALLEY SLAVES
Press-Gang, The. *Unknown.*
Song of the Galley-Slaves. Kipling.
GALLIÉNI, JOSEPH SIMON. General Galliéni. Hillyer.
GALUPPI, BALDASSARE. Toccata of Galuppi's, A. Robert Browning.
GALVESTON, TEXAS
High noon; Galveston Beach. Babb.
Sailor's Song, A. Harris.
GALWAY, IRELAND
Galway. MacNeice.
Galway. M. D. O'Neill.
GAMBLING
Casino. Auden.
Gambler, The. *Unknown.*
Gambler's Repentance, The. Gerald, Baron of Offaly.
Impression at Reno. C. R. Holmes.
Plain Language from Truthful James. Harte.
GANDHI, MOHANDAS KARAMCHAND
Gandhi. Angela Morgan.
Vaticide. O'Higgins.
GANNETS. Long-billed Gannets. Emery.
GARCÍA LORCA, FEDERICO
Ballad of Federico García Lorca. Cardoza y Aragón, *tr. fr. Spanish by* Walsh.
Crime Took Place in Granada, The. Machado, *tr. fr. Spanish.*
Federico. Guillén, *tr. fr. Spanish by* Carruthers.
For Federico García Lorca. Livesay.
Garcia Lorca. Dudek.
In Memory of Garcia Lorca. Grier.
Responsory for García Lorca. Castro Z., *tr. fr. Spanish by* Fitts.
GARCILASO DE LA VEGA
Elegy for Garcilaso. Alberti, *tr. fr. Spanish by* Turnbull.
On the Death of Garcilaso. Boscán Almogáver, *tr. fr. Spanish by* Wiffen.
GARDA, LAKE, ITALY. There Is a Pool on Garda. Scollard.
GARDENS
A B C's in Green. Speyer.
Au Jardin. Ezra Pound.
Benedictine Garden, A. Alice Brown.
Bulbs. Driscoll.
Child's Song: "I have a garden of my own." Thomas Moore.
Choice, The. Tynan.
Colonist in His Garden, A. W. P. Reeves.
Eleven. MacLeish.
Flower's Name, The. *Fr.* Garden Fancies. Robert Browning.
For a Shakespearean Garden. Romig.
Forsaken Garden, A. Swinburne.
Garden, The Joseph Beaumont.
Garden A. T. E. Brown.
Garden, The. *Fr.* The Task. Cowper.
Garden, The. Giltinan.
Garden, The. Grimald.
Garden, The. Marvell.
Garden, A ("See how the flowers, as at parade"). *Fr.* Upon Appleton House. Marvell.
Garden, The. Masters.
Garden, The. Very.
Garden by Moonlight, The. Amy Lowell.
Garden Fancies. Robert Browning.
Garden Incident. O'Neil.
Garden Lyric, A. Locker-Lampson.
Garden of Proserpine, The. Swinburne.
Garden Path, A. Justus.
Garden Prayer, A. Thomas Walsh.
Garden-Song. Cabell.
Garden Song, A. Dobson.
Gardens. Guillén, *tr. fr. Spanish by* Turnbull.
Gardens. *Unknown.*
Gardens Are All My Heart. Triem.
Grace for Gardens. Driscoll.
In a Garden. Swinburne.
In a Glorious Garden Grene. *Unknown.*
In a Lovely Garden Walking. Uhland, *tr. fr. German by* MacDonald.
In a Rose Garden. John Bennett.
In a Southern Garden. Mackellar.
In Green Old Gardens. "Violet Fane."
In My Garden. A. L. Gray.
In the Garden. Ernest Crosby.
In the Garden. F. S. Flint.
Le Jardin. Oscar Wilde.
Little Dutch Garden, A. Durbin.
Little Garden, A. Amy Lowell.
May Garden. Drinkwater.
Merrill's Garden. John Freeman.
Midways of a Walled Garden. *Fr.* Golden Wings. William Morris.
Mower against Gardens, The. Marvell.
Mutability in Gardens. *Fr.* In Memoriam A. H. H. ("Unwatch'd, the garden bough"). Tennyson.
My Garden. T. E. Brown.
My Garden. Emerson.
My Garden. Succorsa.
My Garden. Weatherly.
My Garden Is a Pleasant Place. Driscoll.
My Mother's Garden. A. E. Allen.
Ode to a Garden. A. C. Dalton.
Old-fashioned Garden, The. J. R. Hayes.
Old Garden, The. Stringer.
Old Gardens, The. Eichendorff, *tr. fr. German by* Cotterell.
Old Gardens. F. B. Taylor.
Old Gardens. Upson.
Poet of Gardens, The. Daniel Henderson.
Return to the Country. T'ao Yuan Ming, *tr. fr. Chinese by* Ayscough *and* Lowell.
Salt Garden, The. Nemerov.
Secrets of Our Garden, The. Holland.
Sensitive Plant, The. Shelley.
Some Starlit Garden Gray with Dew. *Fr.* Rhymes and Rhythms. Henley.
Spring Arithmetic. *Unknown.*
Sunken Garden, The. De la Mare.
Sunset Garden, The. Webb.
Tale from the Garden, A. A. W. Jones.
Thy Garden. Mu'tamid, King of Seville, *tr. fr. Arabic by* Smith.
Trees in the Garden. D. H. Lawrence.
Unholy Garden. Leila Jones.
Vision. William Browne.
Way Over in the Blooming Garden. *Unknown.*
Who Loves a Garden. L. S. Jones.
GARFIELD, JAMES ABRAM
At the President's Grave. Gilder.
Bells at Midnight, The. T. B. Aldrich.
Charles Guiteau [*or* James Garfield]. *Unknown.*
Garfield's Ride at Chickamauga. Butterworth.
Midnight—September 19, 1881. O'Reilly.
On the Death of President Garfield. O. W. Holmes.
President Garfield. Longfellow.
GARRICK, DAVID. Retaliation. Goldsmith.
GARRISON, WILLIAM LLOYD
Garrison. A. B. Alcott.
To William Lloyd Garrison. Whittier.
William Lloyd Garrison. J. R. Lowell.
GATINEAU (river), CANADA
Gatineau Point. *Fr.* Down the River. S. F. Harrison.
Nicolas Gatineau. Bourinot.
GAUGUIN, PAUL
Gauguin. M. E. Hamilton.
Vor a Gauguin Picture zu Singen. K. M. Stein.
GAUTIER, THÉOPHILE. Funeral Toast. Mallarmé, *tr. fr. French by* Creekmore.
GAY, JOHN
Epistle to Dr. Arbuthnot, *sel.* ("Bless'd be the great! for those they take away"). Pope.
On Mr. Gay: in Westminster-Abbey, 1732. Pope.
GAZA, PALESTINE. How Samson Bore Away the Gates of Gaza. Lindsay.
GEESE
Flight of the Geese, The. Sir C. G. D. Roberts.
Flight of the Wild Geese. W. E. Channing.
Flight of Wild Geese, A. Harold Stewart.
Geese in Autumn. *Unknown, tr. fr. Japanese by* Chamberlain.
Gray Geese Flying. Prokosch.
Grey Goose, The. *Unknown.*
Night Flight. Whalley.
Out of the Night. Prewett.
Panegyric on Geese, A. Mahony.
Releasing a Migrant "Yen" (Wild Goose). Po Chü-i, *tr. fr. Chinese by* Waley.
Some Geese. Herford.
Something Told the Wild Geese. Rachel Field.
Swan and the Goose, The. Aesop, *tr. fr. Greek by* Leonard.
Wild Geese. Chipp.
Wild Geese. Ise, *tr. fr. Japanese by* Chamberlain.
Wild Cheese, The. J. H. Morse.
Wild Geese. Thaxter.
Wild Geese. Tynan.
Wild Geese in Midwinter. Babb.
GENÊT, EDMOND CHARLES EDOUARD. Ode: "God save the Rights of Man!" Freneau.
GENGHIS KHAN. *See* JENGHIZ KHAN.
GENTIANS
Bavarian Gentians. D. H. Lawrence.

GENTIANS (*continued*)
Fringed Gentians. Amy Lowell.
Gentian. E. G. Crane.
God made a little gentian. Emily Dickinson.
To the Fringed Gentian Bryant.
GEOGRAPHY AND GEOGRAPHERS
Geographers. *Fr.* The Ship of Fools. Alexander Barclay.
Geography. *Fr.* Songs of Education. Chesterton.
Geography. Farjeon.
GEORGE, SAINT. Saint George of England. Fox-Smith.
GEORGE III, KING OF ENGLAND
Absolvers, The. *Fr.* A Vision of Judgement. Southey.
George the Third. *Fr.* The Vision of Judgment. Byron.
Royal Tour, The. "Peter Pindar."
Vision of Judgment, The. Byron
GEORGIA
Georgia. Loveman.
Georgia Dusk. Toomer.
Georgia Volunteer, A. M. A. Townsend.
Georgia Waters. Chivers.
GERANIUMS
Geraniums. W. W. Gibson.
Red Geraniums. M. H. Clark.
GERMANS. Ode to the Germans. Thomas Campbell.
GERMANY
Cost, The. Colman.
German Fatherland, The. Arndt, *tr. fr. German.*
High Germany. Shanks.
Now Where To? Heine, *tr. fr. German by* Gruenthal.
On a German Tour. Porson.
To Germany. Sorley.
Wars of Germany, The. *Unknown.*
Weavers, The. Heine, *tr. fr. German.*
Twentieth-Century German Verse (TwGV). Herman Salinger, ed. and tr.
GERMS. Germ, The. Nash.
GERONIMO. Geronimo. McGaffey.
GETHSEMANE
Ballad of Trees and the Master, A. Lanier.
Canticle of Darkness, *sel.* ("Stand gentle in my words"). Wilfred Watson.
Christ's Prayer in Gethsemane. *Unknown.*
Gethsemane. Bontemps.
Gethsemane. Droste-Hülshoff, *tr. fr. German by* Shuster.
Gethsemane. Leamy.
Gethsemane. Wakeley.
Gethsemane. E. W. Wilcox.
Gethsemane Now. Bobb Hamilton.
GETTYSBURG, PENNSYLVANIA. Night at Gettysburg. Seitz.
GETTYSBURG, BATTLE OF
Battle of Gettysburg. *Fr.* John Brown's Body. S. V. Benét.
Battlefield, The. Mifflin.
Gettysburg. Roche.
Gettysburg. Stedman.
Gettysburg Ode, The. Bayard Taylor.
High Tide at Gettysburg, The. Will Thompson.
Hive at Gettysburg, The. Whittier.
John Burns of Gettysburg. Harte.
Lincoln at Gettysburg. *Fr.* The Gettysburg Ode. Bayard Taylor.
GHETTOS. Ghetto Song. Glatstein, *tr. fr. Yiddish by* Betsky.
GHOST DANCE. Indian Ghost Dance and War, The. Prather.
GHOSTS
Apparition, The. Donne.
Body and Spirit. W. H. Davies.
Eidolon. R. P. Warren.
Garden Seat, The. Hardy.
Ghost, The. De la Mare.
Ghost. Alexa Lane.
Ghost, The. Robert Lowell, *after* Propertius.
Ghost, The. Cú Chonnacht O Cléirigh, *tr. fr. Irish by* Stephens.
Ghost. Weaver.
Ghost That Jim Saw, The. Harte.
Ghost's Moonshine, The. Beddoes.
Ghost's Promenade, The. T. C. Irwin.
Old Wife and the Ghost, The. James Reeves.
Phantom. S. T. Coleridge.
Phantoms. Ashe.
Phantoms. Kiely.
Phantoms. McGuire.
Phantoms All. Spofford.
Specter, The. Hardt, *tr. fr. German by* Bithell.
Spectres. S. M. Peck.
Suffolk Miracle, The. *Unknown.*
Sweet William's Ghost. *Unknown.*
To a Persistent Phantom. Horne.
To a Shade. Yeats.
Unquiet Grave, The. *Unknown.*
Dark of the Moon (DaM). August Derleth, ed.
Unseen Wings; the Living Poetry of Man's Immortality (UnW). Stanton A. Coblentz comp.
GIBBON, EDWARD
Card of Invitation to Mr. Gibbon, at Brighthelmstone, A. Hayley.
Lausanne. Hardy.
Voltaire and Gibbon. *Fr.* Childe Harold's Pilgrimage. Byron.
GIBBS, JOSIAH WILLARD. Gibbs, *sel.* ("It was much later in his life he rose"). Rukeyser.
GIBRALTAR
At Gibraltar. Woodberry.
Gibraltar. Blunt.
Gibraltar. Trench.
GILBERT, SIR HUMPHREY
First American Sailors, The. Wallace Rice.
Sir Humphrey Gilbert. Longfellow.
GILDER, RICHARD WATSON. To Richard Watson Gilder. Dobson.
GINER DE LOS RIOS, FRANCISCO. To Don Francisco Giner de los Rios. Machado, *tr. fr. Spanish by* Farnell.
GIOTTO DI BONDONE
Giotto's Campanile. O'Hagan.
Giotto's Tower. Longfellow.
GIPSIES. *See* GYPSIES.
GIRAFFES
Giraffe, The. Dearmer.
Giraffe, The. Gumilev, *tr. fr. Russian by* Hornstein.
Giraffe, The. Solomon.
Giraffe and Tree. W. J. Turner.
Giraffes. Brettell.
Giraffes, The. Fuller.
GIRLS. *See* YOUTH.
GLACIERS. Glacier. Leitch.
GLASGOW, SCOTLAND. Glasgow. Alexander Smith.
GLASTONBURY THORN
Blooming of the White Thorn, The. E. M. Thomas.
Thorn of Somerset, The. Coleman.
GLOBE THEATRE. Sonnet upon the Pitiful Burning of the Globe Playhouse in London, A. *Unknown.*
GLOUCESTER, MASSACHUSETTS
Evening in Gloucester Harbor. Sargent.
Gloucester Harbor. E. S. Phelps.
Gloucester Moors. W. V. Moody.
Out from Gloucester. Trott.
GLOWWORMS
Dream, A. Blake.
Glow-Worm, The. W. L. Bowles.
Glow-Worm, The. Shanks.
Glow-Worms, The. Hawkshaw.
Mower to the Glow-Worms, The. Marvell.
GLUTTONY AND GLUTTONS
Glutton, The. *Fr.* The Vision of Piers Plowman. William Langland.
Inscription for a Smyrna Privy Agathias Scholasticus, *tr. fr. Greek by* Fitts.
GNATS. Gnat. Rosalie Moore.
GNUS. G. Belloc.
GOATS
All Goats. Coatsworth.
Billy Goats Chew. Emery.
Goat Paths, The. James Stephens.
Goats. C. E. S. Wood.
Nosegay for a Young Goat. Welles.
Sad Goat, The. *Unknown.*
Smile of the Goat, The. Herford.
GOBLINS. *See* FAIRIES.
GOD
Aeterne Rerum Conditor. St. Ambrose, *tr. fr. Latin by* Cunningham.
All the Hosts of Heaven. Simeon ben Isaac ben Abun of Mainz, *tr. fr. Hebrew by* Salaman.
Allah. Mahlmann, *tr. fr. German by* Longfellow.
And Now Dwell Thou, I Pray. Morgenstern, *tr. fr. German by* Barrett.
Antiphon: "Let all the world in every corner sing." George Herbert.
Anvil, The—God's Word. Clifford.
Approaching God. A. B. Alcott.
"Are You There?" Gillilan.
Author of Light. Campion.
Autumn. Rilke, *tr. fr. German by* Flores.
Ave Maria. *Fr.* The Bridge. Hart Crane.
Bless Him. *Unknown, tr. fr. Hebrew by* Abrahams.
Brahma. Emerson.
Canticle of the Sun, The. St. Francis of Assisi, *tr. fr. Latin.*
Celestial Surgeon, The. R L. Stevenson.
Cherubim, The, *sel.* ("I have wandered"). Heywood.
Child's Thought of God, A. E. B. Browning.
City, The. "Æ."
Conversion. Angermayer.
Crazy Jane on God. Yeats.
Credo. Reese.
Dawning. The. Vaughan
Delight in God Only. Quarles.
Divine Image, The. *Fr.* Songs of Innocence. Blake.

Divine Presence, The. *Fr.* May Carols. De Vere.
Divinity, The. Matthew Arnold.
Each in His Own Tongue. Carruth.
Elements, The. Cardinal Newman.
Eternal Goodness, The. Whittier.
Eternal Jew, The. Jacob Cohen, *tr. fr. Hebrew by* Lask.
Even-Song. George Herbert.
Excesses of God, The. Jeffers.
Exit God. Gamaliel Bradford.
Experience, The. *Fr.* Sacramental Meditations. Edward Taylor.
Father, The. Savage-Armstrong.
First Autumn, The. Schacht.
For the Letter 7 Which Signifies God. *Fr.* Jubilate Agno. Smart.
From Glowing Purple Spoke the Wrath of Heaven. George, *tr. fr. German by* Hull.
Glory of God in Creation, The. Thomas Moore.
God. Gamaliel Bradford.
God. C. C. Coblentz.
God. Derzhavin, *tr. fr. Russian by* Bowring.
God, *sel.* ("Hail, Thou great mysterious Being!"). McLachlan.
God. *Fr.* The Upanishads. *Unknown, tr. fr. Hindu by* Mukerji.
God and Man. A. D. Watson.
God Be in My Head. *Unknown.*
God Cares. "Marianne Farningham."
God Everywhere. Abraham ibn Ezra, *tr. fr. Hebrew by* "D. E. de L."
God-forgotten. Hardy.
God Is at the Anvil. Sarett.
God Is at the Organ. Sandford.
God Is Love. Bowring.
God Makes a Path. Roger Williams.
God of love my shepperd is, The. *Unknown.*
God of Might, God of Right. *Unknown, tr. fr. French.*
God Scatters Beauty. Landor.
God, the Artist. *At. to* Angela Morgan.
God the Life of Nature. Kaplan.
God the Omniscient. J. C. Wallace.
God, Whom Shall I Compare to Thee? Halevi, *tr. fr. Hebrew by* Lucas.
God with Us. *Fr.* Saul. Robert Browning.
God's Grandeur. G. M. Hopkins.
Higher Pantheism, The. Tennyson.
Highest Divinity. *Unknown, tr. fr. Hebrew by* Zangwill.
His Hand Shall Cover Us. Isaac ben Samuel of Dampière, *tr. fr. Hebrew by* Salaman.
His Sovereignty. Kalonymos ben Moses of Lucca, *tr. fr. Hebrew by* Salaman.
Holy of Holies. Chesterton.
Hound of Heaven, The. Francis Thompson.
Hymn of Unity. *Unknown, tr. fr. Hebrew by* Adler.
Hymn to God the Father, A. Donne.
Hymnos Ahymnos. Clough.
Image of God, The. Aldana, *tr. fr. Spanish by* Longfellow.
Prayer: "In the bright bay of your morning, O God." Goll, *tr. fr. German by* Deutsch *and* Yarmolinsky.
In the Desert. Melville.
Incarnatio Est Maximum donum Dei. Alabaster.
Indian upon God, The. Yeats.
Kingdom of God, The. Rab, *tr. fr. Hebrew.*
Kingdom of God, The. Francis Thompson.
Laus Deo. Dobell.
Laus Deo! Whittier.
Light Shining Out of Darkness. Cowper.
Little Gate to God, The. Rauschenbusch.
Living God, The. Abraham ibn Ezra, *tr. fr. Hebrew by* Lucas.
Living God, The. Daniel ben Judah, *tr. fr. Hebrew by* Zangwill.
Loneliness. Father Essex.
Lord Is King, The. *Unknown, tr. fr. Hebrew by* Solis-Cohen.
Lord of the World. *Unknown, tr. fr. Hebrew by* de Sola.
Majesty and Mercy of God, The. Sir Robert Grant.
Mihi Adhaerere Deo Bonum Est. *Unknown.*
My Father Knows. Tillett.
My God Has Spoken. Verlaine, *tr. fr. French by* Gray.
My God, How Wonderful Thou Art. Faber.
Mystery, The. *Tr. fr. Irish by* Douglas Hyde.
O God, Our Help in Ages Past. Isaac Watts.
O God, The Rock of Ages. Bickersteth.
O God to Thee I Yield. T. E. Brown.
O, How the Thought of God Attracts. Faber.
Oak Grove, The. Lenau, *tr. fr. German by* Durling.
Of God's Omnipotencie. Hume.
On the Universality and Other Attributes of the God of Nature. Freneau.
"Pater Noster," The. *Unknown.*
Peace. Vaughan.
Pillar of the Cloud, The. Cardinal Newman.
Preface: "Infinity, when all things it beheld." *Fr.* God's Determinations. Edward Taylor.
Providence. Jochumsson, *tr. fr. Icelandic by* Johnson.
Revival, The. Vaughan.
Royal Crown, The, *sels.* Ibn Gabirol, *tr. fr. Hebrew by* Zangwill.
Sacred Ode. Meléndez Valdés, *tr. fr. Spanish.*
Salutation, The. Traherne.
Scribe, The. De la Mare.
Sculptor, The. *Unknown.*
Search for God, The. *Fr.* Hierarchie for the Blessed Angel. Thomas Heywood.
Seeking God. Dowden.
Shape God Wears, The. S. H. Hay.
Sighs and Grones. George Herbert.
Song of David, The. *Fr.* A Song to David. Smart.
Song of the Creatures, The. St. Francis of Assisi, *tr. fr. Italian by* Arnold.
Song of the Wind and the Rain. Ibn Gabirol, *tr. fr. Hebrew by* Solis-Cohen.
Spacious Firmament on High, The. Addison.
Sonnet XI: "Is God invisible? This very room." Greeff.
Sun! Marianne Moore.
"There Is No God," the Wicked Saith. Clough.
This is My Father's World. Babcock.
Though Mine Eye Sleep Not. *Fr.* The Dead Sea Scrolls. *Unknown, tr. fr. Hebrew by* Gaster.
Through All the World. *Unknown.*
To God. Herrick.
To God the Father. Constable.
To His Dear God. Herrick.
To the Supreme Being. Michelangelo, *tr. fr. Italian by* Wordsworth.
Vestigia. Carman.
Vision of God, The. *Fr.* Divina Commedia. Dante, *tr. fr. Italian by* Binyon.
What Tomas Said in a Pub. James Stephens.
Wherefore Hidest Thou Thy Face, and Holdest Me for Thy Enemie? *Fr.* Emblems. Quarles.
Whose Hand. *Unknown, tr. fr. Hebrew by* Davis.
Zebaoth. Lasker-Schüler, *tr. fr. German by* Bithell.

GODFREY, THOMAS
Elegy to the Memory of My Beloved Friend, Mr. Thomas Godfrey. Nathaniel Evans.
Ode to My Ingenious Friend, Mr. Thomas Godfrey. Nathaniel Evans.

GODIVA, LADY
Godiva. Tennyson.
Lady Godiva. Shanks.

GODOLPHIN, SIDNEY, 1ST EARL GODOLPHIN. Sidney Godolphin. Scollard.
GODWIN, MARY. To Mary. Shelley.
GODWIN, WILLIAM. Letter to Maria Gisborne. Shelley.
GOETHALS, GEORGE WASHINGTON. Goethals, the Prophet Engineer. Percy MacKaye.

GOETHE, JOHANN WOLFGANG VON
Memorial Verses. Matthew Arnold.
Sorrows of Werther, The. Thackeray.
Written in a Volume of Goethe. Emerson.

GOLD
Arrowtown. Glover.
Gold Seekers, The. M. M. Richardson.
Gold Seeker's Song, The. *Unknown.*
Song for the Pike's Peaker. *Unknown.*
Yellow Witch of Caribou, The. Clyde Robertson.

GOLD MINING AND MINERS
Ballad of Chicken Bill, The. F. E. Vaughn.
Dow's Flat. Harte.
Gold-Seekers, The. Garland.
Hit at the Times, A. McGrew.
In the Summer of Sixty. *Unknown.*
Little Johnny Mine, The. Detrick.
Me and Prunes. Rupe Sherwood.
Mistress of the Matchless Mine. Clyde Robertson.
Ol' Jinny Mine, The. Detrick.
Pike's Peakers, The. Greenleaf.
Slide at the Empire Mine, The. Wason.
Soliloquy of the Returned Gold Adventurer. *Unknown.*
Song: "We came to Tamichi in 1880." Scott Judy *and* "Doc" Hammond.

GOLDENROD
Golden-Rod. Larcom.
Golden Rod, The. F. D. Sherman.
Oh, Golden-Rod. Jaquith.

GOLDFINCHES
Goldfinch, The. Shepard.
Goldfinches. Keats.
Goldfinches. Scollard.
On a Goldfinch, Starved to Death in His Cage. Cowper.

GOLDFISH. Goldfish, The. A. A. Brown.
GOLIATH. Apocryphal Soliloquies. Louis Untermeyer.

GOOD FRIDAY
Good Friday. Abelard, *tr. fr. Latin by* Lindsay.
Good Friday. Vincent Holme.

GOOD FRIDAY (*continued*)
Good Friday. Isbell.
Good Friday. Jurica.
Good Friday. Kramer.
Good Friday. Reese.
Good Friday. C. G. Rossetti.
Good Friday. Savonarola.
Good Friday. A. J. M. Smith.
Good Friday. Elizabeth Turner.
Good Friday. *Unknown.*
Good Friday. A. J. Young.
Good Friday Evening. C. G. Rossetti.
Good Friday in My Heart. S. T. Coleridge.
Good Friday Night. W. V. Moody.
Good Friday; Rex Tragicus, or Christ Going to His Cross. Herrick.
Good Friday, 1613; Riding Westward. Donne.
Good Friday Song. Coffin.
Praetorium Scene; Good Friday. Lennen.
GORDON, CHARLES GEORGE. White Pacha, The. Lang.
GORE-BOOTH, EVA. In Memory of Eva Gore-Booth and Con Markiewicz. Yeats.
GOSSE, SIR EDMUND. Fame Is a Food That Dead Men Eat. Dobson.
GOULD, BENJAMIN APTHORP. Welcome to Dr. Benjamin Apthorp Gould, A. O. W. Holmes.
GOVERNMENT
Builders of the State. R. W. Gilder.
God Give Us Men! J. G. Holland.
Grain-Tribute, The. Po Chü-i, *tr. fr. Chinese by* Waley.
Politician, The. Po Chü-i, *tr. fr. Chinese by* Waley.
GOYA Y LUCIENTES, FRANCISCO JOSÉ DE. Coney Island of the Mind, A, *sel.* ("In Goya's greatest scenes we seem to see"). Ferlinghetti.
GRACKLES
Purple Grackles. F. M. Frost.
Purple Grackles. Amy Lowell.
GRADUATION. *See* COMMENCEMENT.
GRAHAM, JAMES, 5TH EARL OF MONTROSE. *See* MONTROSE, JAMES GRAHAM, 5TH EARL OF.
GRANADA, SPAIN
Alhambra, The. Martínez de la Rosa, *tr. fr. Spanish by* Longfellow.
Ay de mi Alhama. *Unknown, tr. fr. Spanish by* Byron.
Conquest of Granada, The, *sels.* Dryden.
Flight from Granada. *Unknown, tr. fr. Spanish by* Lockhart.
Moorish King Who Lost Alhama, The. *Unknown, tr. fr. Spanish by* Byron.
GRAND CANYON, ARIZONA
At the Grand Canyon. Sterling.
Grand Canyon, The. Crapsey.
Grand Canyon of the Colorado, The. J. G. Fletcher.
GRAND LAKE, COLORADO. Legend of Grand Lake, The. Westcott.
GRAND PRÉ, NOVA SCOTIA. Low Tide on Grand Pré. Carman.
GRANDFATHERS
Grandfather Watts's Private Fourth. Bunner.
I've Got a New Book from My Grandfather Hyde. L. F. Jackson.
GRANDMOTHERS
Afternoon with Grandmother. B. A. Huff.
Cupboard, The. De la Mare.
Flattering Grandma. *Unknown.*
Grandma. Kulbak, *tr. fr. Yiddish by* Betsky.
Grandmamma's Birthday. Belloc.
Grandmother and Child. Dallas.
Sea Lavender. Bowman.
To My Grandmother. Locker-Lampson.
GRANT, ULYSSES SIMPSON
Aged Stranger, The. Harte.
Appomattox. House.
Burial of Grant, The. Gilder.
Death of Grant, The. Bierce.
In Memory of General Grant. Henry Abbey.
Lee's Parole. Manville.
On a Bust of General Grant. J. R. Lowell.
Ulysses S. Grant. Bliss.
Vanquished. F. F. Browne.
What Best I See in Thee. Whitman.
GRANTCHESTER, ENGLAND. Old Vicarage, Grantchester, The. Rupert Brooke.
GRAPES
American Vineyard. Cousens.
Catawba Wine. Longfellow.
Grapes. Pushkin, *tr. fr. Russian by* Yarmolinsky.
Grapes. Sister Maris Stella.
Grapes. *Unknown, tr. fr. Greek by* Strettell.
Grapes Making. Léonie Adams.
Hunting Muscadines. Boner.
Vintage, The. Krystallis, *tr. fr. Modern Greek by* Dalven.
GRASMERE, ENGLAND. Two Long Vacations; Grasmere. A. G. Butler.
GRASS
Blade of Grass Sings to the River, The. Leah Goldberg, *tr. fr. Hebrew by* Friend.
Blades of Grass, The. *Fr.* The Black Riders. Stephen Crane.
Grass. Muir.
Grass. Sandburg.
Grass. *Fr.* Song of Myself. Whitman.
Grass Fingers. Grimké.
Grass on the Mountain, The. *Tr. fr. Paiute Indian by* Austin.
Grass, so little has to do, The. Emily Dickinson.
Grasses. Scudder Middleton.
In the Grass. Droste-Hülshoff, *tr. fr. German by* Tobin.
In the Grass. Garland.
Long Feud. Louis Untermeyer.
Said a Blade of Grass. Gibran.
Song the Grass Sings, A. Blanden.
Spring Grass. Sandburg.
Tribute to Grass. Ingalls.
Turn to the Grass. Mary Gilmore.
Voice of the Grass, The. Boyle.
GRASSHOPPERS
Explanation of the Grasshopper, An. Lindsay.
Grasshopper, The. *At. to* Anacreon, *tr. fr. Greek by* Cowley.
Grasshopper, The. Belleau, *tr. fr. French by* Conder.
Grasshopper, The. Lovelace.
Grasshopper, The. McCord.
Grasshopper, The. E. M. Thomas.
Grasshopper Green. *Unknown.*
Grasshoppers, The. Aldis.
Grasshopper's Song, The. Bialik, *tr. fr. Hebrew by* Sampter.
My What-is-it. Robert Frost.
On the Grasshopper and Cricket. Keats.
To the Grasshopper and the Cricket. Leigh Hunt.
GRAVES
Ah, Are You Digging on My Grave? Hardy.
In the Grave No Flower. Millay.
Simpson's Rest. G. S. Simpson.
Wanderer's Grave, The. Sage.
We do not play on graves. Emily Dickinson.
GRAVEYARDS. *See* CEMETERIES.
GRAY, THOMAS
Sketch of His Own Character. Gray.
To Mr. Gray. Garrick.
To Mr. Gray. Warton.
GREAT BRITAIN
America to Great Britain. Allston.
Britannia, *sels.* Thomson.
England and America in 1782. Tennyson.
I Vow to Thee, My Country. Spring Rice.
Peace Hymn for England and America. Huntington.
To America. Alfred Austin.
See also ENGLAND.
GREAT LAKES. Lake Boats, The. Masters.
GREAT SALT LAKE, UTAH. Gulls over Great Salt Lake. Sutphen.
GREAT SMOKY MOUNTAINS
Evening in the Great Smokies. DuBose Heyward.
On Clingman Dome. Dargan.
GREAT SUGARLOAF (mountain), WICKLOW, IRELAND. On Great Sugarloaf. G. A. Greene.
GREATNESS
Grey Company, The. Mackay.
I Think Continually of Those Who Were Truly Great. Spender.
Song of Greatness, A. *Tr. fr. Chippewa Indian by* Austin.
GRECO, EL. El Greco. E. L. Mayo.
GREECE
April, 1941. Bax.
Archipelago, The. Hölderlin, *tr. fr. German by* Stepanchev.
Constitution of Athens. The. Solon, *tr. fr. Greek by* Merivale.
Cleon. Robert Browning.
Delphi. Richmond.
Greece. Breyfogle.
Greece. *Fr.* The Giaour. Byron.
Greece. Vansittart.
Hellas, *sels.* Shelley.
Invasion of Greece, The. Ingalls.
Isles of Greece, The. *Fr.* Don Juan. Byron.
On This Day I Complete My Thirty-sixth Year. Byron.
Salute to Greece. "Clemence Dane."
To a Greek Ship in the Port of Dublin. Stanford.
Voices of Hellas, The. Binyon.
Greek Literature in Translation (GrL). Whitney Jennings Oates *and* Charles Theophilus Murphy, eds.
Greek Poetry for Everyman (GrPE). F. L. Lucas, tr. *and* ed.
Greek Poets, The (GrPo). Moses Hadas, ed.
Greek Reader, The (GrR). A. L. Whall, ed.
Modern Greek Poetry (MoGP). Rae Dalven, tr. *and* ed.

Oxford Book of Greek Verse in Translation, The (OxBG). T. F. Higham *and* C. M. Bowra, eds.
Greek War of Independence (1821). To The Sacred Battalion. Calvos, *tr. fr. Modern Greek by* Dalven.
Greeley, Horace. Horace Greeley. Stedman.
Green Mountains. Again among the Hills. Hovey.
Greene, Nathanael. To the Memory of the Brave Americans. Freneau.
Greene, Robert
Due Commendation of the Quipping Autor, A. *Fr.* Four Letters and Certain Sonnets. Gabriel Harvey.
His Admonition to Greene's Companions. *Fr.* Greene's Memorial. Gabriel Harvey.
Greenfield Hill, Connecticut. Greenfield Hill, *sels.* Dwight.
Greenland
Greenland Whale Fishery, The. *Unknown.*
Greenland Winter, A. Diamond.
Gregory, Horace. Citation for Horace Gregory. Rukeyser.
Gregory, Robert. In Memory of Major Robert Gregory. Yeats.
Grenfell, Julian. Julian Grenfell. Baring.
Grenville, Sir Richard
First American Sailors, The. Wallace Rice.
Revenge, The. Tennyson.
Sir Richard Grenville's Farewell, on His Sailing for Foreign Parts in the Year 1585. *Unknown.*
Greyhounds. To a Black Greyhound. Grenfell.
Griboyedov, Aleksandr Sergeyevich. To Alexander Griboyedow. Küchelbecker, *tr. fr. Russian.*
Grief
Alone. De la Mare.
Amphora, The. Sologub, *tr. fr. Russian by* Deutsch *and* Yarmolinsky.
Ancient Tear, The. Urbina, *tr. fr. Spanish by* Beckett.
Angel of Patience, The. Whittier.
Another Weeping Woman. Wallace Stevens.
Astrophel and Stella, *sel.* ("Grief, find the words; for thou hast made my brain"). Sidney.
Because my Grief Seems Quiet and Apart. Nathan.
Before You Now, My Tyrant-Sorrow. George, *tr. fr. German by* Viereck.
Break, Break, Break. Tennyson.
Canzone: "Eyes that weep for pity of the heart, The." Dante, *tr. fr. Italian by* D. G. Rossetti.
Come Sorrow wrap me in thy sable cloake. *Unknown.*
Cypress Curtain of the Night Is Spread, The. Campion.
Desdichado, El. Nerval, *tr. fr. French by* Lattimore.
Dirge: "Sorrow, lie still and wear." Beddoes.
Elegy: "Floods of tears well from my deepest heart, The." Immanuel di Roma, *tr. fr. Italien by* Chotzner.
Flow my teares fau from your springs. *Unknown.*
Flow Not So Fast, Ye Fountains. *Unknown.*
Folded Power. Gladys Cromwell.
Forsaken. Schneour, *tr. fr Yiddish by* Leftwich.
Fraternity. A. R. Aldrich.
From a Car-Window. R. G. Harding.
Ghost, The. De la Mare.
Grey Eye Weeping, A. O'Rahilly, *tr. fr. Irish by* O'Connor.
Grief. E. B. Browning.
Grief. Díaz Mirón, *tr. fr. Spanish by* Beckett.
Grief. Ehrenstein, *tr. fr. German by* Cambon.
Grief. D. H. Lawrence.
Grief and God. Stephen Phillips.
Grodek. Trakl, *tr. fr. German by* Flores.
Has Sorrow Thy Young Days Shaded? Thomas Moore.
I, a Most Wretched Atlas. *Fr.* Homeward Bound. Heine, *tr. fr. German by* Lazarus.
I measure every grief I meet. Emily Dickinson.
I rise, & greive. *Unknown.*
In Sorrow. Thomas Hastings.
In sorrowes drown'd I wast my weary dayes. *Unknown.*
In Time of Grief. L. W. Reese.
In Time of Mourning. Swinburne.
It's such a little thing to weep. Emily Dickinson.
Lachrimae. *Unknown.*
Lament: "Sleep and death, the darkling eagles." Trakl, *tr. fr. German by* Flores.
Lament of Hsi-chün. Hsi-chün, *tr. fr. Chinese by* Waley.
Lamentations. Brody.
Let Us Break Down the Barriers. Ormond Thomas.
Lynmouth Widow, A. Burr.
Maid's Lament, The. *Fr.* The Citation and Examination of William Shakespeare. Landor.
My Grief on the Sea. *Unknown, tr. fr. Irish by* Hyde.
Minstrel's Song. *Fr.* Aella. Chatterton.
No Worst, There Is None. G. M. Hopkins.
Oh Sad, Sad Was My Soul. Verlaine, *tr. fr. French by* Kittel.
Oh, Thou! Who Dry'st the Mourner's Tear. Thomas Moore.
Of My Dear Son, Gervase Beaumont. Sir John Beaumont.
On a Grave in Christ-Church, Hants. O. F. Adams.
On My First Son. Jonson.
On My Sorrowful Life. Moses ibn Ezra, *tr. fr. Hebrew by* Solis-Cohen.
Orphan, The. *Unknown, tr. fr. Chinese by* Waley.
Pale inke, thou art not black enough of hew. *Unknown.*
Portrait, The ("This is her picture"). D. G. Rossetti.
Remembering Golden Bells. Po Chü-i, *tr. fr. Chinese by* Waley.
Remembrance. Emily Brontë.
Sephestia's Song to Her Child. *Fr.* Menaphon. Greene.
Sleepless Night, A. O'Rahilly, *tr. fr. Irish by* O'Connor.
Song, The: "Have pity (Grief) I can not pay." *Fr.* The Rival Friends. Hausted.
Song: Slow, Slow, Fresh Fount. *Fr.* Cynthia's Revels. Jonson.
Song: "Spirit haunts the year's last hours, A." Tennyson.
Song: "When I was young, I said to Sorrow." De Vere.
Song before Grief, A. R. H. Lathrop.
Song of Grief, A. Pan Chieh-yu, *tr. fr. Chinese by* Ayscough *and* Lowell.
Sonnet: "Because my grief seems quiet and apart." Robert Nathan.
Sonnet: Grief. T. H. Chivers.
Sorrow. De Vere.
Sorrow. H. P. Eden.
Sorrow. R. C. Eva.
Sorrow. D. H. Lawrence.
Sorrow. M. T. Phillips.
Sorrow. Trask.
Sorrow. *Unknown, tr. fr. Russian by* Ralston.
Sorrow Seldom Killeth Any. Francis Davison.
Stanzas: "With tears thy grief thou dost bemoan." Ibn Gabirol, *tr. fr. Hebrew by* Lazarus.
Tear, The. López Velarde, *tr. fr. Spanish by* Beckett.
Tears Flow in My Heart. Paul Verlaine, *tr. fr. French by* Kittel.
Tenth Duino Elegy, The. Rilke, *tr. fr. German by* Speirs.
Time and Grief. W. L. Bowles.
Time and Space, Torment. Platen, *tr. fr. German by* Morgan.
Time Is No Remedy. *Fr.* Tristia. Ovid, *tr. fr. Latin by* Johnson.
To Mary. Cowper.
Vesta. Whittier.
Weepe O Mine Eyes. *Unknown.*
Weep You No More, Sad Fountains. *Unknown.*
When Lilacs Last in the Dooryard Bloom'd. Whitman.
Wine and Grief. Ibn Gabirol, *tr. fr. Hebrew by* Lazarus.
Grimald [*or* Grimalde *or* Grimoald], Nicholas. Epitaph of the Death of Nicholas Grimald, An. Googe.
Grindelwald, Switzerland. On a Grave at Grindelwald. F. W. H. Myers.
Grocers. Song against Grocers, The. Chesterton.
Grongar Hill, Wales. Grongar Hill. Dyer.
Grosbeaks. To a Grosbeak in the Garden. Swift.
Groundhogs. Groundhog, The. Eberhart.
Guadalupe, Spain. Guadalupe. G. H. Conkling.
Guérin, Maurice de. Maurice de Guérin. Egan.
Guernsey. In Guernsey. Swinburne.
Guerriere (ship)
Constitution and the *Guerriere,* The. *Unknown.*
On the Capture of the *Guerrière.* Freneau.
Guided missiles. Guided Missiles Experimental Range. Conquest.
Guilt
Crisis. Auden.
Fish in the Unruffled Lakes. Auden.
Rime of the Ancient Mariner, The. S. T. Coleridge.
To Pontius Washing His Hands. Crashaw.
Guitars
Guitar, The. García Lorca, *tr. fr. Spanish by* Trapier.
Guitar Song. Barris.
Six Strings. García Lorca, *tr. fr. Spanish by* Turnbull.
Guiteau, Charles J. Charles Guiteau. *Unknown.*
Gulf Stream
Gulf Stream, The. Bellamann.
Gulf Stream. "Susan Coolidge."
Song of the Gulf Stream. Ford.
Thoughts in the Gulf Stream. Christopher Morley.
Gulls
Alien. MacLeish.
Dialectics of Flight. Wheelock.
Gull. Glyn Jones.
Gull. W. J. Smith.
Gull Goes Up, A. Léonie Adams.
Gulls. W. C. Williams.
Gulls and Dreams. Lionel Stevenson.
Gulls in an Aëry Morrice. Henley.
Gulls over Great Salt Lake. Sutphen.
Gulls, The. Provincetown Harbor. Botkin.
Harbor, The. Sandburg.
Lines Addressed to a Seagull, Seen Off the Cliffs of Moher, in the County of Clare. Griffin.

GULLS (*continued*)
Lives of Gulls and Children, The. Nemerov.
Pater Vester Pascit Illa. Hawker.
Sea-Birds. E. A. Allen.
Sea-Gull. M. C. Davies.
Sea-Gull, The. Mary Howitt.
Sea Gull. The. L. F. Jackson.
Sea-Gull, The. Nash.
Sea Gull. The. *Unknown, tr. fr. Irish.*
Sea gull curves his wings, The. Coatsworth.
Sea-Gulls. N. M. Holland.
Sea-Gulls. Miyoshi *tr. fr. Japanese by* Ninomiya *and* Enright.
Sea Gulls. R. W. Page.
Sea Gulls. E. J. Pratt.
Seagulls on the Serpentine. Noyes.
Sea-Mew, The. E. B. Browning.
Self Unsatisfied Runs Everywhere, The. Schwartz.
Signal, The. Florit, *tr. fr. Spanish by* Hays.
To a Sea-Gull. Symons.
To a Sea-Gull in the Steamer's Wake. Fallström, *tr. fr. Swedish by* Stork.
To a Seamew. Swinburne.
To a Solitary Sea-Gull. C. Y. Rice.
Visit from the Sea, The. R. L. Stevenson.
Winged Mariner. G. C. Hoves.
GUNPOWDER PLOT. Canto I: "Of Men, nay Beasts: worse, Monsters: worst of all." *Fr.* The Locusts, or Apollyonists. Phineas Fletcher.
GUNS. Description of a Gun. Wyatt.
GUSTAVUS II (Gustavus Adolphus), KING OF SWEDEN. Battle Hymn. Altenburg, *tr. fr. German by* Winkworth.
GUTHLAC, SAINT. Death of Saint Guthlac. *Fr.* Guthlac. Cynewulf.
GWYN [*or* GWYNN], ELEANOR. Nell Gwynne's Looking-Glass. Blanchard.
GYPSIES
Being a Gypsy. Barbara Young.
Fair of Kakava, The. *Fr.* The Twelve Songs of the Gypsy. Palamas, *tr. fr. Modern Greek by* Dalven.
Gipsies. Clare.
Gipsy Camp, The. Clare.
Gipsy Girl, The. Hodgson.
Gipsy Jane. Rands.
Gipsy Song. Birchall.
Gipsy Trail, The. Kipling.
Gipsy Vans. Kipling.
Gipsy Wedding, The. Birchall.
Gypsies. *Fr.* The Flight of the Duchess. Robert Browning.
Gypsies. Rachel Field.
Gypsies, The. Pushkin, *tr. fr. Russian by* Kisch.
Gypsies, The. "Richard Scrace."
Gypsies on the March. Baudelaire, *tr. fr. French by* Symons.
Gypsies' Road, The. Shorter.
Gypsy, The. Farjeon.
Gypsy, The. Pound.
Gypsy Children. Rachel Field.
Gypsy Countess, The. *Unknown.*
Gypsy Girl, The. Alford.
Gypsy Heart, The. H. N. Pratt.
Gypsy Laddie, The. *Unknown.*
Gypsy Man. Langston Hughes.
Gypsy Women. O'Brien.
Gypsying, The. Theodosia Garrison.
Idlers, The. Blunden.
Johnnie Faa. *Unknown.*
Meg Merrilies. Keats.
Mendicants, The. Carman.
Princess and the Gypsies, The. Cornford.
Scholar-Gypsy, The. Matthew Arnold.
Three Gypsies. Lenau, *tr. fr. German by* Durling.
To a Passing Gypsy. Ruhnka.
Trip It, Gipsies. *Fr.* The Spanish Gipsy. Middleton *and* Rowley.
Where Do the Gipsies Come From? Bashford.
Wraggle Taggle Gipsies, The. *Unknown.*

H

HAAKON I, KING OF NORWAY. Death Song of Haakon the Good. Eyvindr Finsson, *tr. fr. Old Norse by* Oliver.
HAFIZ
To Hafiz. T. B. Aldrich.
To Hafiz of Shiraz. G. L. Bell.
HAGAR. Hagar's Last Night at Abraham's. Manger, *tr. fr. Yiddish by* Betsky.
HAGGARD, HENRY RIDER. To R. K. J. K. Stephen.
HAGIA SOPHIA. Fall of Constantinople, The. *Unknown, tr. fr. Modern Greek by* Dalven.
HAIDA INDIANS. Bear's Song, The. *Tr. fr. Haida Indian song by* Skinner.
HAIR. More Hair. Hoffenstein.
HAIRCUTS. Haircut. Shapiro.
HAITI
Coming of Dusk upon a Village in Haiti, The. Rago.
Drums of Haiti. Christian.
HALE, NATHAN
Nathan Hale. F. M. Finch.
Nathan Hale. W. O. Partridge.
Nathan Hale. *Unknown.*
HALIBURTON, THOMAS CHANDLER ("Sam Slick"). Toast, A. Howe.
HALLAM, ARTHUR HENRY. In Memoriam A. H. H. Tennyson.
HALLECK, FITZ-GREENE. Fitz-Greene Halleck. Whittier.
HALLEY'S COMET. Stella Flammarum. W. W. Campbell.
HALLOWEEN
All Hallow Eve. Carolyn Wells.
Black and Gold. N. B. Turner.
Hag, The. Herrick.
Hallowe'en. Behn.
Halloween. Joel Benton.
Hallowe'en. Burns.
Hallowe'en. Coxe.
Hallowe'en. Frances Frost.
Halloween. M. A. Lawson.
Hallowe'en. Mayne.
Hallowe'en. Medary.
Hallowe'en. Sheard.
Hallowe'en. *Unknown.*
Hallowe'en. Helen Wing.
Halloween Concert. Aileen Fisher.
Hallowe'en Memory, A. Christopher Morley.
Litany for Halloween. *Unknown.*
Mr. Macklin's Jack o'Lantern. McCord.
On the Eve of All Hallows. A. L. Phelps.
One Forgotten, The. Shorter.
Theme in Yellow. Sandburg.
This Is Halloween. D. B. Thompson.
Hallowe'en (*Our American Holidays Series*) (HOAH). Robert Haven Schauffler, ed.
HAMILTON, EMMA, LADY. Lady Hamilton. Muriel Stuart.
HAMILTON, NEW ZEALAND. Hamilton. Pitt.
HAMPSTEAD HEATH, LONDON
Breath of Hampstead Heath. E. M. Thomas.
On Hampstead Heath. *Fr.* Thoroughfares. W. W. Gibson.
Sunday at Hampstead, *sels.* James Thomson.
Sunday on Hampstead Heath. Woodcock.
HAMPTON, NEW HAMPSHIRE. Hampton Beach. Whittier.
HAMPTON COURT PALACE, ENGLAND. Holiday at Hampton Court. Davidson.
HAMPTON ROADS, VIRGINIA. *Cumberland,* The. Longfellow.
HANDEL, GEORGE FRIDERIC. Epigram on Handel and Bononcini. Byrom.
HANGING
Tyburn and Westminster. John Heywood.
See also EXECUTIONS.
HANKS, NANCY
Fire-Logs. Sandburg.
I Saw a Ghost. Boilleau.
Nancy Hanks. Rosemary Benét.
Nancy Hanks. Monroe.
Nancy Hanks, Mother of Abraham Lincoln. Lindsay.
Reply to Nancy Hanks, A. Silberger.
HANNO. Southward Sidonian Hanno. Hervey Allen.
HANUKKAH
Blessings for Chanukah. Sampter.
Dreidel Song. Rosenzweig.
For Hanukkah. Bialik.
HAPPINESS
Happiness. Beeman.
Happiness. Priscilla Leonard.
Happiness. Tchobanian, *tr. fr. Armenian by* Boyajian.
Happiness Betrays Me. Hoyt.
Her Merriment. W. H. Davies.
I Stumbled upon Happiness. DuBose Heyward.
Interlude. Duggan.
Means to Attain Happy Life, The. Martial, *tr. fr. Latin by* the Earl of Surrey.
Song of Happiness, A. Muna Lee.
Song of Happiness, A. Rhys.
They of the Mean Estate Are Happiest. *Unknown.*
True Happiness. Talpalar.
Wish, The. *Fr.* The Mistress. Cowley.
HARBORS
Bay, The; December. Clapp.
Harbor, The. Letts.
Harbor, The. Sandburg.
Waiwera. Smithyman.

HARDY, THOMAS
Birthday Poem for Thomas Hardy. Day Lewis.
To Thomas Hardy. Laurence Housman.
HAREBELLS. Harebells in June. Wynne.
HARES
Epitaph on a Hare. Cowper.
Hare, The. De la Mare.
Hare and Many Friends, The. Gay.
March Hares. Andrew Young.
On Seeing a Wounded Hare Limp by Me. Burns.
See also RABBITS.
HARFLEUR, FRANCE, BATTLE OF. Once More unto the Breach, Dear Friends, Once More. *Fr.* King Henry V. Shakespeare.
HARLEM, NEW YORK CITY
Esthete in Harlem. Langston Hughes.
Harlem. Brierre, *tr. fr. French by* Matheus.
Harlem Dancer, The. Claude McKay.
Harlem Shadows. Claude McKay.
Harlem Sweeties. Langston Hughes.
Lady from Harlem, The. Malcolm Cowley.
Lenox Avenue. Sidney Alexander.
Sonnet to a Negro in Harlem. Helene Johnson.
HARLEM HEIGHTS, BATTLE OF. Haarlem Heights. Guiterman.
HARLEY, ROBERT, 1ST EARL OF OXFORD AND EARL MORTIMER.
To Robert Earl of Oxford and Earl Mortimer. Pope.
HAROLD, KING OF ENGLAND. Battle of Hastings, *sel.* ("And now Duke William"). Chatterton.
HARPERS FERRY, WEST VIRGINIA
Harpers Ferry. Rodman.
How Old Brown Took Harpers Ferry. Stedman.
HARPS
Aeolian Harp. Allingham.
Aeolian Harp, An. "Michael Field."
Bishop's Harp, The. Robert Manning.
Dear Harp of My Country. Thomas Moore.
Harp That Once through Tara's Halls, The. Thomas Moore.
Harper, The. *Unknown, tr. fr. Early Modern Irish by* O'Connor.
In Praise of a Harp. *Unknown, tr. fr. Old Irish by* Bergin.
Minstrel Boy, The. Thomas Moore.
Origin of the Harp, The. Thomas Moore.
HARRISON, WILLIAM HENRY
Death of Harrison, The. Willis.
Old Tippecanoe. *Unknown.*
HARVARD UNIVERSITY
Fair Harvard. Gilman.
Song for the Centennial Celebration of Harvard College, 1836, A. O. W. Holmes.
HARVEST
Antique Harvesters. J. C. Ransom.
At Harvest. Joseph Campbell.
At Husking Time. E. P. Johnson.
Child's Thought of Harvest, A. "Susan Coolidge."
Cocooning, The. *Fr.* The Mirèio. Frédéric Mistral, *tr. fr. Provençal by* Preston.
Dead Harvest, A. Alice Meynell.
Harvest. Cortissoz.
Harvest. Gore-Booth.
Harvest. Hutchinson.
Harvest. Koltsov, *tr. fr. Russian by* Bowra.
Harvest. Schauffler.
Harvest Dust. Winifred Welles.
Harvest Home. Alford.
Harvest Home. Guiterman.
Harvest-Home Song. John Davidson.
Harvest Hymn. *Fr.* For an Autumnal Festival. Whittier.
Harvest Sacrifice. Su T'ung-po, *tr. fr. Chinese by* Rexroth.
Harvest Song. Dehmel, *tr. fr. German by* Lewisohn.
Harvest Song. *Fr.* King Arthur. Dryden.
Harvest Song. Holty, *tr. fr. German by* Brooks.
Harvest Song, A. Markham.
Harvest Song. *Unknown.*
Harvest Time. Star Powers.
Hay Harvest. Chalmers.
Hay Harvest, The. Maikov, *tr. fr. Russian by* Cornford *and* Salaman.
Haying. Herbin.
Haymaking. Maikov, *tr. fr. Russian by* Kisch.
Hock-Cart, or Harvest Home, The. Herrick.
Huskers, The. Whittier.
Irish Reaper's Harvest Hymn, The. Keegan.
Load. Hewitt.
Mowers, The. M. B. Benton.
Potato Harvest, The. C. G. D. Roberts.
Praise of Ceres. *Fr.* The Silver Age. Heywood.
Reapers, The. Toomer.
Reaping the Barley. Carrera Andrade, *tr. fr. Spanish by* Lee.
Ripe and Bearded Barley, The. *Unknown.*
Singing the Reapers Homeward Come. *Unknown.*
Solitary Reaper, The. Wordsworth.
Song of Apple Gathering, A. Bottomley.
Song of the Harvest. Washburn.
Story of the Corn. K. Fisher.
Valley Harvest, The. H. L. Davis.
Winnowers, The. Robert Bridges.
HARVEY, GABRIEL. To the Right Worshipful, My Singular Good Friend, M[aster] Gabriel Harvey, Doctor of the Laws. Spenser.
HASTINGS, WARREN. Fifth Day. R. D. FitzGerald.
HASTINGS, BATTLE OF. Battle of Hastings, *sel.* ("And now Duke William"). Chatterton.
HATE
Hate. James Stephens.
Hate-Song, A. Shelley.
Hatred. Gwendolyn Bennett.
Love and Hate. *Unknown, tr. fr. Irish by* O'Connor.
Poison Tree, A. *Fr.* Songs of Experience. Blake.
HATHAWAY, ANNE. Anne Hathaway ("Would ye be taught, ye feathered throng"). *Unknown.*
HATS
Hat Bar. Mildred Weston.
Hattage. A. P. Herbert.
HATTERAS, CAPE
Cape Hatteras. *Fr.* The Bridge. Hart Crane.
Hatteras. Freneau.
Hatteras. J. W. Holden.
HAVANA, CUBA. Havana Dreams; Havana. Langston Hughes.
HAWAII
In Hawaiian Seas. Gessler.
Our Native Land. Kalakaua, King of the Hawaiian Islands, *tr. fr. Hawaiian by* Sheldon.
HAWKE OF TOWTON, EDWARD HAWKE, 1ST BARON
Hawke. Newbolt.
Hawke. *Fr.* Sonnets of the Empire. Strong.
HAWKINS, SIR JOHN
First American Sailors, The. Wallace Rice.
Last Voyage of Sir Francis Drake, and Sir John Hawkins, The. *Fr.* Sir Francis Drake. Fitzgeffrey.
HAWKS
Fish-Hawk, The. Wheelock.
Hawk, The. A. C. Benson.
Hawk, The. Clouts.
Hawk, The. W. H. Davies.
Hawk, The. Knister.
Hawk. Scollard.
Hawk Afield. Evelyn Scott.
Hawk and the Dove, The. *Unknown, tr. fr. Armenian by* Boyajian.
Hawks. James Stephens.
Hawk's Nest, The. Harte.
Hurt Hawks. Jeffers.
Night-Hawk. Coffin.
Shepherd and the Hawk, The. Hart-Smith.
To a Marsh Hawk in Spring. Thoreau.
To the Man-of-War-Bird. Whitman.
Wounded Hawk, The. Herbert Palmer.
HAWTHORN
Hawthorn, The. *Unknown.*
Hawthorn Tree, The. Cather.
Hawthorn Tree, The. Swartz.
Old Saul. Reese.
To a Thorn Tree Blooming on a City Street. Virginia McCormick.
HAWTHORNE, NATHANIEL
Hawthorne. A. B. Alcott.
Hawthorne. Longfellow.
Hawthorne. *Fr.* A Fable for Critics. J. R. Lowell.
HAYDEN PLANETARIUM (New York city). Ode to the Hayden Planetarium. Guiterman.
HAYDON, BENJAMIN ROBERT
Addressed to Haydon. Keats.
To B. R. Haydon. Wordsworth.
HAYLEY, WILLIAM
Sonnet to William Hayley. Cowper.
To William Hayley. Blake.
HAZE
Haze. Thoreau.
See also FOG; MIST.
HEAT. Heat. Lampman.
HEATHER. Heather, The. Neil Munro.
HEAVEN
Ballad of Heaven, A. John Davidson.
Description of Elysium. Agee.
Dick Said. Louis Untermeyer.
Heaven. Rupert Brooke.
Heaven Is Heaven. C. G. Rossetti.
Heaven Overarches. C. G. Rossetti.
Home at Last. Chesterton.
Homeland, The. H. R. Haweis.
I never saw a moor. Emily Dickinson.
Lament of This Good Moon. Laforgue, *tr. fr. French by* Bennett.
Life of the Blessed, The. Luis de León, *tr. fr. Spanish by* Bryant.
My Ain Countree. Demarest.
Paradiso, *sels.* *Fr.* Divina Commedia. Dante, *tr. fr. Italian.*

HEAVEN (*continued*)
Promised Country, The. Strahan.
Prospect of Heaven Makes Death Easy, A. Isaac Watts.
Seek Flowers of Heaven. Southwell.
Song: Endymion Porter and Olivia. Davenant.
Where Is Heaven? *Fr.* Here and Now. Carman.
White Island, The; or, The Place of the Blest. Herrick.
World, The. Vaughan.
See also PARADISE.
HEBE. Hebe. J. R. Lowell.
HECTOR
Grave of Hector, The. Ausonius, *tr. fr. Latin.*
Hector. Iremonger.
Hector to Andromache. *Fr.* The Iliad. Homer, *tr. fr. Greek by* Chapman.
Last Parting of Hector and Andromache, The. *Fr.* The Iliad. Homer, *tr. fr. Greek by* Dryden.
HEDGEHOGS
Hedgehog, The. Laura Benét.
Hedgehog, The. Clare.
Hedgehog, The. King.
Hedgehog and His Coat, The. Fleming.
HEINE, HEINRICH
Heine's Grave. Matthew Arnold.
Heinrich Heine. Lewisohn.
Letter to Heine. Louis Ginsberg.
HELEN OF TROY
Helen. Doolittle ("H. D.").
Helen. *Fr.* The Iliad. Homer, *tr. fr. Greek.*
Helen. Lloyd.
Helen. *Fr.* Dr. Faustus. Marlowe.
Helen. Valentine.
Helen—Old. I. E. MacKay.
Hélène (Helen, the Sad Queen). Valéry, *tr. fr. French by* Lewis.
Helen's Rape. Thom Gunn.
Menelaus and Helen at Troy. Landor.
Oenone. Tennyson.
Paris and Oenone, *sel.* ("Who in this desert calls on Paris?"). Binyon.
Past Ruin'd Ilion. Landor.
Priam and Helen on the Wall. *Fr.* The Iliad. Homer, *tr. fr. Greek by* Lucas.
To Helen. Poe.
Troy Town. D. G. Rossetti.
Was This the Face. *Fr.* Dr. Faustus. Marlowe.
HELIOTROPES. Heliotrope. H. T. Peck.
HELL
Ballad of Hell, A. John Davidson.
Inferno, *sels.* *Fr.* Divina Commedia. Dante, *tr. fr. Italian.*
Lament of an Idle Demon. Lister.
Place of the Damned, The. *Fr.* Paradise Lost. Milton.
HENRY I, KING OF ENGLAND. White Ship, The. D. G. Rossetti.
HENRY II, KING OF ENGLAND. Rose of the World, The. Masefield.
HENRY V, KING OF ENGLAND
Agincourt. Drayton.
Henry before Agincourt: October 25, 1415. Lydgate.
King Henry V, *sels.* Shakespeare.
King Henry Fifth's Conquest of France. *Unknown.*
HENRY VIII, KING OF ENGLAND
Ballade of the Scottyshe Kynge, A. Skelton.
Henry VIII. Eleanor Farjeon *and* Herbert Farjeon.
Portrait of Henry VIII, The. Earl of Surrey.
HENRY IV, KING OF FRANCE. Ivry. Macaulay.
"HENRY, O." (William Sydney Porter). Knight in Disguise, The. Vachel Lindsay.
HENRY FREDERICK, PRINCE OF WALES. Lamentation, A. Campion.
HENS
Clucking Hen, The. Hawkshaw.
Cock and Hens. Follen.
Complete Hen, The. Coatsworth.
Hen, The. Claudius, *tr. fr. German.*
Hens, The. E. M. Roberts.
Janet Waking. Ransom.
HENSCHEL, SIR GEORGE. For the Eightieth Birthday of a Great Singer. Shanks.
HEPATICAS. Blue Hepatica. "John Crichton."
HERBERT, GEORGE
George Herbert. T. S. Jones, Jr.
On George Herbert's "The Temple" Sent to a Gentlewoman. Crashaw.
HERBS
Herbs. Reese.
On His Mistress's Garden of Herbs. *Unknown.*
HERESY AND HERETICS
Cold heritique. *Unknown.*
Precious Music of Heresy, The. Kitahara, *tr. fr. Japanese by* Ninomiya *and* Enright.
HERMIT THRUSHES. *See* THRUSHES.
HERMITS
And Here the Hermit Sat, and Told His Beads. W. E. Channing.
Desire for Hermitage, The. *Unknown, tr. fr. Old Irish by* O'Faoláin.
Eremites, The. Robert Graves.
Hermit, The. "Æ."
Hermit, The. Baxter.
Hermit, The. Howard Moss.
Hermitage, The. *Unknown, at. to* St. Manchan of Lemanaghan in Offaly, *tr. fr. Irish by* O'Connor.
Hermit's Song, The. *Unknown, tr. fr. Irish by* O'Connor.
Seraphion. Baxter.
HERO AND LEANDER
Hero and Leander. Marlowe.
Shall I come, if I swim? wide are the waves, you see. Campion.
Sonnet: "Fair and lovely maid, look from the shore." *Fr.* To Delia. Daniel.
HEROD THE GREAT
St. Stephen and Herod. *Unknown.*
Slaughter of the Innocents by Order of King Herod, The. *Fr.* Carmen Paschale. Sedulius, *tr. fr. Latin by* Sigerson.
HERODOTUS. Herodotus in Egypt. Lang.
HEROES AND HEROINES
At the Cedars. D. C. Scott.
Ballad of Hell, A. John Davidson.
Ballad of Heroes, A. Dobson.
Gee-up Dar, Mules. Piper.
He Fell among Thieves. Newbolt.
Hero, The. Bierce.
Hero, The. Nicoll.
Hero, The. Henry Taylor.
Hero, The. W. J. Turner.
Hero. W. C. Williams.
Heroes. Laurence Housman.
Heroes, The. Louis Simpson.
Heroism. Emerson.
Hervé Riel. Robert Browning.
I Think Continually of Those Who Were Truly Great. Spender.
John Maynard. Horatio Alger, Jr.
Little Giffen. Ticknor.
Of a Poet Patriot. MacDonagh.
Private of the Buffs, The. F. H. Doyle.
Pro Patria. Tyrtaeus, *tr. fr. Greek by* Thomas Campbell.
Red Thread of Honour, The. F. H. Doyle.
Revenge, The. Tennyson.
Sixteen Dead Men. Shorter.
Song for Heroes, A. Markham.
Strong Swimmer, The. W. R. Benét.
HERONS
Ardan Mór. Ledwidge.
Blue Heron, The. T. G. Roberts.
Blue Heron, The. Maurice Thompson.
Carolina Herons. Brockman.
Eden. Corke.
Heron. Philip Booth.
Heron, The. Donaghy.
Heron, The. Hovell-Thurlow.
Heron, The. Howitt.
Heron, The. Roethke.
Heron, The. Vrepont.
Heron, The. Watkins.
Heron in Swamp. F. M. Howard.
Herons, The. Ledwidge.
Herons. *Unknown, tr. fr. Japanese.*
Herons on Bo Island, The. Shane.
HERRICK, ROBERT
End-Piece for His Book, An. Herrick.
For a Copy of Herrick. Dobson.
With a Copy of Herrick. Gosse.
HERRING. Herring. *Fr.* A Bestiary. Rexroth.
HERVEY, WILLIAM. On the Death of Mr. William Hervey. Cowley.
HERZL, THEODOR. Theodor Herzl. Zangwill.
HEYWOOD, JOHN
Ad Modernos Epigrammatistas. John Heath.
Of Heywood. John Heywood.
To Old John Heywood the Epigrammatist, Wheresoever. John Davies of Hereford.
HIGHLANDS OF SCOTLAND
Canadian Boat Song. *Unknown.*
In the Highlands. R. L. Stevenson.
My Heart's in the Highlands. Burns.
HIKMET, NAZIM. Nazim Hikmet. Smelyakov, *tr. fr. Russian by* Lindsay.
HILLS AND MOUNTAINS
Afternoon on a Hill. Millay.
At Timberline. Spain.
Blue Hills, The. Little.
Cliff, The. J. H. Boner.
Coming Back to Mountains. Bradbury.
Cry of the Hillborn, The. Carman.
David. Birney.

English Hills. John Freeman.
Grass on the Mountain, The. *Tr. fr. Paiute Indian by* Austin.
Hemlock Mountain. Cleghorn.
Hill Hunger. Auslander.
Hills, The. Braley.
Hills. Hilda Conkling.
Hills, The. Cornford.
Hills, The. Garrison.
Hills. Guiterman.
Hills and the Sea. W. W. Campbell.
Hills of Home. Bynner.
Holy Hill, A. "Æ."
Hymn before Sunrise, in the Vale of Chamouni. S. T. Coleridge.
I Stood Tiptoe upon a Little Hill. Keats.
In a Desert Town. Lionel Stevenson.
In the Highlands. R. L. Stevenson.
In the Mountains. Noe.
In the Mountains on a Summer Day. Li Po, *tr. fr. Chinese by* Waley.
In the Selkirks. D. C. Scott.
Joy of the Hills, The. Markham.
Kinchinjunga. C. Y. Rice.
Main Range. Picot.
Most-sacred Mountain, The. Tietjens.
Mountain, The, *sel.* ("In this sweet solitude"). Channing.
Mountain, The. Robert Frost.
Mountain, The. Lermontov, *tr. fr. Russian by* Eastman.
Mountain Air. Galsworthy.
Mountain and River. Louis Ginsberg.
Mountain Evenings. J. S. Holme.
Mountain Gateway, A. Carman.
Mountain Heart's-Ease, The. Harte.
Mountain in the Sky, The. Corning.
Mountain Lake, The. Richard Church.
Mountain Night. Cheyney.
Mountain sat upon the plain, The. Emily Dickinson.
Mountain Song. Monroe.
Mountain Speed. G. W. Young.
Mountain to the Pine, The. Hawkes.
Mountain Top, The. Hitomaro, *tr. fr. Japanese by* Ives.
Mountain Wind, A. "Æ."
Mountaineer, The. Nathan.
Mountains. A. N. Clark.
Mountains. Larcom.
Mountains. Moreland.
Mountains. Thoreau.
Mountains grow unnoticed, The. Emily Dickinson.
Old Man Mountain. Noyes.
Old Mountains, The. Aasen, *tr. fr. Norwegian by* Stork.
On a Hill. McLeod.
On the Heights. Dowden.
Passing T'ien-men Street in Ch'ang-an and Seeing a Distant View of Chung-nan Mountain. Po Chü-i, *tr. fr. Chinese by* Waley.
Pause. Bethell.
Peaks, The. *Fr.* War Is Kind. Stephen Crane.
Praise of Engineers. J. J. Donohue.
Red Eagle—the Mountain with Wings. Vachel Lindsay.
Song to the Mountains. *Tr. fr. Pawnee Indian by* Fletcher.
Sunset on the Cunimbla Valley, Blue Mountains. Sladen.
That Far Lone Mountain. Sister Mary Stephanie.
Three Hills, The. Squire.
To a Mountain. Kendall.
To Walk on Hills. Robert Graves.
Up a Hill and a Hill. F. S. Davis.
Visitors to the Waterfall. Reeves.
Who Knows a Mountain? E. R. Fuller.
HINDUS. Indian upon God, The. Yeats.
HIPPOPOTAMUSES
Habits of the Hippopotamus. Guiterman.
Hippopotamothalamion. Wheelock.
Hippopotamus, The. Belloc.
Hippopotamus, The. Durston.
Hippopotamus, The. Herford.
I Had a Hippopotamus. Barrington.
To a Blue Hippopotamus. Kay.
HIROSHIMA, JAPAN. Shadow of Cain, The. Edith Sitwell.
HISTORY AND HISTORIANS
Lines to a Future Historian. Kathleen Nott.
Looking into History. Wilbur.
HITLER, ADOLF. Letter to Hitler, A. Laughlin.
HOBART, TASMANIA. Old Sandhills, Hobart, The. Hubert Church.
HOBBES, THOMAS. To Mr. Hobbes. Cowley.
HOBSON, RICHARD PEARSON. Hobson and His Men. Robert Loveman.
HOBY, SIR THOMAS. Thomas Sackville in Commendation of the Work to the Reader. Sackville.
HOGG, JAMES
Extempore Effusion upon the Death of James Hogg. Wordsworth.
Letter to Maria Gisborne. Shelley.
HOGUE, LA, BATTLE OF. Hervé Riel. Robert Browning.
HOHENLINDEN, BATTLE OF. Hohenlinden. Thomas Campbell.
HOKUSAI. Laughing Hyena, by Hokusai, The. Enright.
HÖLDERLIN, JOHANN CHRISTIAN FRIEDRICH
Holderlin's Journey. Muir.
To Hölderlin. Rilke, *tr. fr. German by* Luke.
HOLIDAY, BILLIE (Eleanora Fagan McKay). Day Lady Died, The. Frank O'Hara.
HOLIDAYS
Highdays and Holidays (HH). Florence Adams *and* Elizabeth McCarrick, comps.
Our Holidays in Poetry (OHIP). Mildred P. Harrington *and* Josephine H. Thomas, comps.
Pieces for Every Day the Schools Celebrate (PEDC). Norma H. Deming *and* Katharine I. Bemis, eds.
Pieces for Every Occasion (PEOR). Caroline B. Le Row, ed.
Poems for Red Letter Days (PoRL). Elizabeth Hough Sechrist, comp.
Poems for Special Days and Occasions (PSO). Thomas Curtis Clark, comp.
Poems for the Great Days (PGD). Thomas Curtis Clark *and* Robert Earle Clark, comps.
See also specific holidays.
HOLLAND. *See* NETHERLANDS.
HOLLY
Aunt Mary. Hawker.
But Give Me Holly, Bold and Jolly. C. G. Rossetti.
Green Groweth the Holly. Henry VIII, King of England.
Holly. Bevington.
Holly, The. Edith King.
Holly and Ivy ("Holly bereth beris"). *Unknown.*
Holly and Ivy Made a Great Party. *Unknown.*
Holly and the Ivy, The ("The holly and the ivy,/ When they are both full grown"). *Unknown.*
Holly Fairies. Aileen Fisher.
Holly-Tree. Southey.
HOLLYHOCKS
Hollyhock, A. F. D. Sherman.
Hollyhocks, The. Betts.
Hollyhocks, The. Laurance.
HOLLYWOOD, CALIFORNIA
Hollywood. Blanding.
Hollywood. Shapiro.
HOLMES, OLIVER WENDELL (1809–94)
Holmes. *Fr.* A Fable for Critics. J. R. Lowell.
Oliver Wendell Holmes. W. H. Hayne.
To O. W. Holmes. P. H. Hayne.
HOLY FAMILY
Cherry-Tree Carol, The. *Unknown.*
Flight into Egypt, The. "Father Prout."
Flight into Egypt. *Fr.* Cursor Mundi. *Unknown.*
Return from Egypt, The. Pope Leo XIII, *tr. fr. Latin by* Henry.
HOLY GRAIL. Holy Grail, The. *Fr.* Idylls of the King. Tennyson.
HOME
Autumn. *Fr.* Seasons of the Soul. Allen Tate.
Back Home. Harriet Monroe.
Better than Gold. Ryan.
Broken and Desolate. Boner.
Come Home, Come Home! and Where Is Home for Me. Clough.
Cup of Happiness, The. Gilbert Thomas.
Dearest Spot on Earth, The. Wrighton.
Death of the Hired Man, The. Robert Frost.
Dedication: "O thou whose gracious presence blest." L. F. Benson.
Dedication of a Home. Woods.
Deserted Home, A. Lysaght.
Fifty Acres. J. L. Pearson.
For a New Home. Marinoni.
God Bless Our Home. Robert Freeman.
Going Home. Van Doren.
Golden Mile-Stone, The. Longfellow.
Good-bye. Emerson.
Hame, Hame, Hame. Allan Cunningham.
Hearthstone. Harold Monro.
Heureux qui, comme Ulysse. Du Bellay, *tr. fr. French.*
Home. Greenwell.
Home. Guest.
Home. J. B. Harris.
Home. Heidenstam, *tr. fr. Swedish by* Stork.
Home. Hines.
Home. House.
Home. *Fr.* Old Landmarks. Lysaght.
Home. Nekrasov, *tr. fr. Russian by* Elton.
Home. Sill.
Home Fire, The. Johns.
Home Is Where There Is [*or* There's] One to Love Us. Swain.
Home No More Home to Me. R. L. Stevenson.
Home on the Range, A. *Unknown.*
Home Song. Longfellow.

HOME (*continued*)
Home, Sweet Home. Payne.
Home Thoughts. Susukida, *tr. fr. Japanese by* Ninomiya *and* Enright.
Homecoming in Storm. Kenyon.
Homing Song. Cushman.
House, The. Treece.
House and Home. Joseph Beaumont.
House and Home. Hugo, *tr. fr. French.*
House Blessing. Guiterman.
Hymn for a Household. Daniel Henderson.
I Am the Only Being. Emily Brontë.
I saw green banks of daffodil. Tennant.
Lights of Home, The. Noyes.
Little Bird, The. De la Mare.
Long Voyage, The. Cowley.
My Ain Fireside. Elizabeth Hamilton.
My Early Home. Clare.
My Home. Winther, *tr. fr. Danish by* Stork.
My House. *Fr.* Regrets. Du Bellay, *tr. fr. French by* Conder.
My Little Lodge. *Unknown, tr. fr. Old Irish by* Robinson.
My Mother's House. Tietjens.
My Old Home. O'Leary.
News from Home. Stem.
O Happy Home. Spitta.
Old Folks at Home. S. C. Foster.
Old Home, The. Cawein.
Old Home Calls, The. L. M. Montgomery.
Old Homes. Blunden.
Old Place, The. Baughan.
Old Woman of the Roads, An. Colum.
Our Homestead. Phoebe Cary.
Our House. D. B. Thompson.
Pilgrim from the East, The. Gustave Kahn. *tr. fr. French by* Bithell.
Prayer for a Little Home, A. Bone.
Prayer for Our Home. Hoyland.
Prayer for the Home, *sel.* ("Lord, this humble house we'd keep"). Guest.
Prayer for This House. Louis Untermeyer.
Returning Home. Du Bellay, *tr. fr. French by* Stirling.
Search. Marriott.
Shiny Little House, The. N. M. Hayes.
So Long as There Are Homes. Crowell.
So Long Had I Travelled. W. W. Gibson.
Sometimes a Little House Will Please. Coatsworth.
Song for a Little House. Christopher Morley.
Sun Rises Bright in France, The. Allan Cunningham.
Thanksgiving to God for His House, A. Herrick.
This Is No My Ain House. *Unknown.*
Traveller's Return, The. Southey.
Urn, The. Malcolm Cowley.
What Makes a Home? *Unknown.*
When a Man Turns Homeward. D. W. Hicky.
When I Go Home. J. C. McNeill.
Young and Old. *Fr.* The Water Babies. Kingsley.
HOMER
After Reading Homer. Dolben.
By Deputy. Adcock.
Homer. Alpheus of Mitylene, *tr. fr. Greek by* Lucas.
Homer. Ehrenstein, *tr. fr. German by* Deutsch *and* Yarmolinsky.
Homer in a Garden. Pearson.
Iliad. Humbert Wolfe.
Life through Verse. Alpheus of Mitylene, *tr fr. Greek by* Lord Neaves.
On First Looking into Chapman's Homer. Keats.
Sir Francis Drake, *sel.* ("Heart-stealing Homer, marrow of the Muses"). Fitzgeffrey.
To a Friend. Matthew Arnold.
To Homer. Bulloch.
To Homer. Keats.
Tourist. Van Doren.
HOMESICKNESS
City Clerk, The. Ashe.
Homesick Blues. Langston Hughes.
Homesick in England. Schauffler.
HONESTY
Be True. Bonar.
Honest Man, An. *Fr.* An Essay on Man. Pope.
HONEY
History of Honey, The. Nathalia Crane.
Honey. Ruth Miller.
Honey Harvest. Martin Armstrong.
HONEYSUCKLE
Honeysuckle, The. D. G. Rossetti.
Spray of Honeysuckle, A. M E. Bradley.
To the Herald Honeysuckle. Pfeiffer.
Wild Honeysuckle, The. Freneau.
HONOR
Definitions. J. J. Keith.
Inquisition upon Fame and Honour, An. Greville.
Prison Sonnet. Blunt.
Vitaï Lampada. Newbolt.
HOOD, THOMAS
Thomas Hood. E. A. Robinson.
Thomas Hood. Sir William Watson.
To the Memory of Hood. J. R. Lowell.
To the Memory of Thomas Hood. Bartholomew Simmons.
HOOKER, JOSEPH. Hooker's Across. Boker.
HOOKER, RICHARD. At Hooker's Tomb. Keble.
HOPE
Against Hope. Cowley.
Answer for Hope. Crashaw.
Assassination, The. Hillyer.
"Bottle Should Be Plainly Labeled 'Poison.'" S. H. Hay.
Climbing to the Light. Charles Mackay.
Darkling Thrush, The. Hardy.
Diuturnal Infirmity of Hope. Sister Juana Inés de la Cruz, *tr. fr. Spanish by* Beckett.
For Hope. Crashaw.
Hope. Fanshawe.
Hope. W. D. Howells.
Hope. Jarrell.
Hope. S. W. Taylor.
Hope. Theognis, *tr. fr. Greek by* Frere.
Hope and Fear. Swinburne.
Hope in Failure. "Æ."
Hope is the thing with feathers. Emily Dickinson.
In Praise of Hope. Cowley.
Leaden Echo and the Golden Echo, The. G. M. Hopkins.
Pleasure of Hope, The. *Fr.* An Essay on Man. Pope.
Pleasures of Hope, The, *sel.* ("At summer eve, when Heaven's ethereal bow"). Thomas Campbell.
Prime. Auden.
Put Forth Thy Leaf, Thou Lofty Plane. Clough.
Say Not the Struggle Nought Availeth. Clough.
Song of Hope. Lathbury.
What We, When Face to Face We See. Clough.
HOPI INDIANS
Dance for Rain, A. Bynner.
In Arizona. W. H. Simpson.
HOPKINS, GERARD MANLEY
Breakfast with Gerard Manley Hopkins. Brode.
Father Gerard Hopkins, S.J. Joyce Kilmer.
HORACE
After Horace. Godley.
Allusion to Horace, An. The Tenth Satire of the First Book. Earl of Rochester.
Childe Harold's Pilgrimage, *sel.* ("Then farewell, Horace; whom I hated so"). Byron.
Essay on Criticism, An, *sel.* ("Horace still charms with graceful negligence"). Pope.
Horace. Sargent.
Last Ode, The. Kipling.
Ode: Allusion to Horace. Akenside.
To Q. H. F. Dobson.
HORATIUS. Horatius. *Fr.* Lays of Ancient Rome. Macaulay.
HORN, CAPE
Coming around the Horn. *Unknown.*
Round Cape Horn. *Unknown.*
Rounding the Horn. *Fr.* Dauber. Masefield.
HORNETS. White-tailed Hornet, The. Robert Frost.
HORNS (musical instrument). Sound of the Horn, The. Vigny, *tr. fr. French by* Carrington.
HORSE CHESTNUT TREES. Horse-Chestnut Tree. Bynner.
HORSE RACING
At Grass. Larkin.
Beautiful Horses, The. Donald Hall.
Camptown Races, De. S. C. Foster.
How the Old Horse Won the Bet. O. W. Holmes.
Morning Workout. Deutsch.
Racing-Man, The. A. P. Herbert.
HORSES
Black Horse with a White Breast, A. Ibn Sa'id of Alcala la Real, *tr. fr. Arabic by* Arberry.
Blood Horse, The. "Barry Cornwall."
Blue Horse, The. La Follette.
Broncho That Would Not Be Broken, The. Vachel Lindsay.
Cadences. Clover.
Colt, The. Knister.
Daniel Webster's Horses. Coatsworth.
Distant Runners, The. Van Doren.
Duchess. Bowes-Lyon.
Flash; the Fireman's Story. Carleton.
For Sale, a Horse. C. E. Taylor.
Horse, The. Job, Bible, *O.T.*
Horse. E. M. Roberts.
Horse, The. Royde-Smith.
Horse, The. *Fr.* King Henry V. Shakespeare.
Horse, A. *Fr.* Venus and Adonis. Shakespeare.
Horse and His Master, The. P. F. Allen.
Horse Thief, The. W. R. Benét.
Horses. Muir.
Horses. Dorothy Wellesley.
Horses and Men in Rain. Sandburg.
Horses Chawin' Hay. Garland.
Horses of the Sea, The. C. G Rossetti.

Horses on the Camargue. Roy Campbell.
Huckster's Horse, The. J. H. Strong.
Kentucky Belle. C. F. Woolson.
Last Leap, The. A. L. Gordon.
Man from Snowy River, The. A. B. Paterson.
Mares of the Camargue, The. *Fr.* The Mirèio. Frédéric Mistral, *tr. fr. Provençal by* Meredith.
Milk-Cart Pony, The. Farjeon.
Mongolian Horse, The. Tu Fu, *tr. fr. Chinese by* Chi Hwang Chu *and* E. W. Underwood.
My Bonny Black Bess. *Unknown.*
My Little Pony. *Unknown.*
My Pony. "A."
Noonday Sun. Kathryn Jackson *and* Byron Jackson.
Old Brown Horse, The. W. K. Holmes.
Old Major. Bradbury.
Poor Old Horse. *Unknown.*
Roan Stallion. Jeffers.
Runaway, The. Robert Frost.
Say This of Horses. M. H. Moody.
Song of the Horse. *Tr. fr. Navajo Indian by* Curtis.
Stable-Talk. Knister.
Take Her, Break Her. Anacreon, *tr. fr. Greek by* Headlam.
Tartar Horse, A. Gorman.
There Was a Little Nobby Colt. *Unknown.*
Thoroughbred, The. Magaret.
To a Man on His Horse. Prince.
To My Mouse-colored Mare. Corbière, *tr. fr. French by* Fitts.
Together. Sassoon.
War God's Horse Song, The. *Tr. fr. Navajo Indian by* Dane Coolidge *and* M. R. Coolidge.
What a Proud Dreamhorse. E. E. Cummings.
White Horses. Winifred Howard.
Wild Horse Jerry's Story. S. E. Howard.
Yellow Horse with a Blaze and a Black Mane, A. Ibn Sa'id of Alcala la Real, *tr. fr. Arabic by* Arberry.
HORTON, GEORGE MOSES. George Moses Horton, Myself. Horton.
HOSACK, DAVID. King of the Doctors, The. Drake.
HOSPITALS
Anywhere Out of the World. Baudelaire, *tr. fr. French by* Davis.
Hospital. Funk.
Hospital Observation. Symons.
In Hospital. Henley.
In the Children's Hospital. Tennyson.
In the Hospital. Patrick Anderson.
In the Hospital. Guiterman.
In the Hospital. Howland.
In the Public Ward. Livesay.
Red Cross Nurses. Stewart.
Reflections in a Hospital. Eisenberg.
Spring. *Fr.* Sonnets from a Hospital. David Morton.
Viaticum. Ethna MacCarthy.
HOTELS
Casey's Table d'Hote. Eugene Field.
There Is an Inn, a Merry Old Inn. Tolkien.
HOUSATONIC RIVER. To the Housatonic at Stockbridge. R. U. Johnson.
HOUSE OF THE SEVEN GABLES, SALEM, MASSACHUSETTS. Hepzibah of the Cent Shop. McCormick.
HOUSEKEEPING
Digression from Husbandry to a Point or Two of Huswifery, A. Tusser.
Housewife, The. C. C. Coblentz.
Hundreth good points of good husbandry, A. Tusser.
HOUSES
After Reading in a Letter Proposals for Building a Cottage. Clare.
Ancestral Dwellings, The. Van Dyke.
Consecration of the House. Fairbridge.
Deserted House, The. M. E. Coleridge.
Deserted House, The. Tennyson.
Directive. Robert Frost.
Grand Houses at Lo-yang, The. Po Chü-i, *tr. fr. Chinese by* Waley.
House, A. Squire.
House and Grounds, A. Leigh Hunt.
House and Home. Joseph Beaumont.
House and the Road, The. J. P. Peabody.
House at Evening, The. W. R. Benét.
House Blessing. Guiterman.
House in Wartime, A. Church.
House of the Eighties, A. Edmund Wilson.
House on the Hill, The. E. A. Robinson.
House That Was, The. Binyon.
House to the Man. J. G. Fletcher.
House with Nobody in It, The. Joyce Kilmer.
I know some lonely houses. Emily Dickinson.
I Like Housecleaning. D. B. Thompson.
Little House, The. Struthers Burt.
Little House, A. Cresson.
Little House, The. Moreland.
Little House, The. Sir Gilbert Parker.
Little House, The. Tynan.
My House. H. H. Hall.
My House. Claude McKay.
My House. H. N. Pratt.
My House. R. L. Stevenson.
My House. M. W. Ward.
My House Has Windows. Mazquida.
My Little House. May Byron.
My Little House. H. H. Harris.
New House, The. Edward Thomas.
New Houses. G. N. Crowell.
O Blessed House, That Cheerfully Receiveth. Spitta, *tr. fr. German by* Schaeffer.
O Thou Whose Gracious Presence Blest. L. F. Benson.
Old House, The. William Barnes.
Old House, The. Klingsor, *tr. fr. French by* Conder.
Old House, The. Woodberry.
Old Houses. Struthers Burt.
Old Houses. D'Lettuso.
Old Houses. Romano.
Old Houses of Flanders, The. F. M. Ford.
Old Mansion. Ransom.
Our House. N. B. Miller.
Our Little House. Thomas Walsh.
Out of the Old House, Nancy. Will Carleton.
Prayer, A: "Let me be like that lonely house, O Lord." Lafon, *tr. fr. French by* Conder.
Prayer for a New House. Louis Untermeyer.
Ruined Cabin, The. A. C. King.
Song for a Little House. Christopher Morley.
Song of the House. *Unknown, tr. fr. Navajo.*
Suburbs, The. Derham.
Thanksgiving to God for His House, A. Robert Herrick.
To an Old Farmhouse. Jaques.
To the Little House. Christopher Morley.
To the New Owner. Reynolds.
Two Houses, The. Hardy.
Two Houses, The. Charles Mackay.
Vacant Farmhouse, The. De la Mare.
Your House. *Unknown.*
HOUSMAN, ALFRED EDWARD. A. E. Housman and a Few Friends. Humbert Wolfe.
HOUSTON, TEXAS
Cities. House.
Some Towns of Texas. K. W. Baker.
HOWARD, SIR ROBERT. To My Honor'd Friend Sir Robert Howard, on His Excellent Poems. Dryden.
HUDSON, HENRY. Henry Hudson's Quest. B. E. Stevenson.
HUDSON RIVER
Hudson, The. Hellman.
Hudson, The. Plimpton.
Scene on the Banks of the Hudson, A. Bryant.
HUDSON'S BAY COMPANY. "Injun, The." Logan.
HUGO, VICTOR
To Mr. Victor Hugo. Musset, *tr. fr. French by* Selden.
To Victor Hugo. Swinburne.
To Victor Hugo. Tennyson.
HUGUENOTS
Huguenot, A. M. E. Coleridge.
Psalm, The. Robert Bridges.
HULL, WILLIAM. Hull's Surrender. *Unknown.*
HUMMINGBIRDS
Humming Bird. Coffin.
Humming Bird, A. Fawcett.
Humming-Bird, The. Howitt.
Hummingbird, The. Kemp.
Humming-Bird. D. H. Lawrence.
Hummingbird. Elizabeth Palmer.
Humming Bird, The. Ivan Swift.
Humming-Bird, The. Tabb.
Humming Bird, The. Maurice Thompson.
Route of evanescence, A. Emily Dickinson.
To a Humming Bird in a Garden. George Murray.
Within my garden rides a bird. Emily Dickinson.
HUMOROUS VERSE
Anthology of Light Verse (ALV). Louis Kronenberger, ed.
Book of Humorous Verse, The (BOHV). Carolyn Wells, comp.
Book of Nonsense, The (BoN). Roger Lancelyn Green, ed.
Century of Humorous Verse, 1850–1950, A (CenHV). Roger Lancelyn Green, ed.
Fireside Book of Humorous Poetry, The (FiBHP). William Cole, ed.
Innocent Merriment (InMe) Franklin P. Adams, comp.
Laughing Verse (LauV). Fairfax Downey, comp.
Little Book of American Humorous Verse, A (LHV). T. A. Daly, ed.
Little Book of Limericks, The (LiBL). H. I. Brock, ed.
Little Book of Necessary Nonsense, A (LBN). Burges Johnson, ed.
Little Laughter, A (LiL). Katherine Love, comp.

HUMOROUS VERSE (*continued*)
Moon Is Shining Bright as Day, The (MoShBr). Ogden Nash, ed.
Nonsense Anthology, A (NA). Carolyn Wells, ed.
Oxford Book of Light Verse, The (OxBoLi). W. H. Auden, comp.
Parody Anthology, A (PA). Carolyn Wells, ed.
Silver Treasury of Light Verse, The (SiTL). Oscar Williams, ed.
What Cheer (WhC). David McCord, ed.
HUNGARY. Music of Hungary. A. R. Aldrich.
HUNGER
Hunger. Binyon.
Hunger. Hazel Hall.
Hunger. Rimbaud, *tr. fr. French by* Rickword.
Hunger and Thirst. Louis Ginsberg.
Hungry One, The. *Fr.* Who Can Be Happy and Free in Russia? Nekrasov, *tr. fr. Russian by* Soskice.
Little Cart, The. Ch'en Tzu-lung, *tr. fr. Chinese by* Waley.
Long time ago, A. Tao Yuan-ming, *tr. fr. Chinese by* Waley
HUNT, LEIGH
Letter to Maria Gisborne. Shelley.
Sonnet: Written on the Day That Mr. Leigh Hunt Left Prison. Keats.
HUNTING AND HUNTERS
Badger. Clare.
Bear Hunt, The. Widdemer.
Canadian Hunter's Song. S. S. Moodie.
Castles and Distances. Wilbur.
Cazador (Hunter). García Lorca, *tr. fr. Spanish by* Spender *and* Gili.
Chevy Chase [*or* Chace]. *Unknown.*
Eagle Hunter, The. Rose O'Neill.
For Little Dinogad. *Unknown, tr. fr. Welsh by* Bell.
Fox Hunt, The. *Fr.* Reynard the Fox. Masefield.
Hunt, The. Christian.
Hunt, The. Deutsch.
Hunt. La Follette.
Hunt, The. Louis Kent.
Hunt, The. Spofford.
Hunt Is Up, The. William Gray.
Hunt of Sliabh Truim, The, *sel. Unknown, tr. fr. Late Middle Irish.*
Hunter, A. Ray Ellis.
Hunter, The. W. J. Turner.
Hunter of the Prairies, The. Bryant.
Hunters, The. R. T. Lindsay.
Hunters of Kentucky, The. Woodworth.
Hunter's Song, The. "Barry Cornwall."
Hunting, The. Phillpotts.
Hunting Song. *Fr.* Zapolya. S. T. Coleridge.
Hunting Song. Finkel.
Hunting Song. *Fr.* King Arthur. Hovey.
Hunting Song. Sir Walter Scott.
Hunting-Song. *Unknown, tr. fr. Navajo Indian by* Curtis.
Hunting Song, The ("Come, come my hearts, a-hunting let us wend"). *Unknown.*
Huntsmen, The. De la Mare.
King's Hunt Is Up, The. William Gray.
Like as a huntsman after weary chase. *Fr.* Amoretti. Spenser.
"Metis" Song of the Buffalo Hunters, The. Robindeau.
Mountain Lion. D. H. Lawrence.
Old Squire, The. Blunt.
Red-Rock, the Moose-Hunter. Sarett.
Reynard the Fox. *Unknown.*
Rousing Canoe Song, The. Fraser, *ad. fr. Skittagetan Indian song.*
Runnable Stag, A. John Davidson.
Three Jolly Hunters, The. Riley.
Three Jolly Huntsmen. *Unknown.*
Wild Huntsman, The. Bürger, *tr. fr. German by* Scott.
Wild Huntsmen, The. Hamerton.
Windsor Forest, *sel.* ("See! from the brake the whirring pheasant springs"). Pope.
Yolp, Yolp, Yolp, Yolp. *Unknown.*
HURRICANE
Hurricane, The. Bryant.
Hurricane, The. Hart Crane.
Hurricane, The. Freneau.
Hurricane, The. Matos.
HUSBANDS. *See* MARRIAGE.
HUTCHINSON, ANNE. Anne Hutchinson's Exile. E. E. Hale.
HUTTON, LAURENCE. To Laurence Hutton. Dobson.
HYACINTHS
Admonition for Spring. L. A. MacKay.
Babiaantje, The. Prince.
Hyacinth. L. M. Bowman.
Hyacinths to Feed Thy Soul. *Fr.* The Gulistan. Sadi, *tr. fr. Persian.*
HYDERABAD, INDIA. In the Bazaars of Hyderabad. Naidu.

I

IBN EZRA, ABRAHAM BEN MEIR. Rabbi Ben Ezra. Robert Browning.
IBN EZRA, MOSES. On Parting with Moses ibn Ezra. Halevi, *tr. fr. Hebrew by* Solis-Cohen.
IBYCUS. Cranes of Ibycus, The. Lazarus.
ICARUS
Daedalus and Icarus. *Fr.* Metamorphoses. Ovid, *tr. fr. Latin by* Croxall.
Icarus. Bellinger.
Icarus. Desportes, *tr. fr. French by* Conder.
Icarus. Iremonger.
Icarus. Koopman.
Icarus. Marlatt.
Icarus. Smithyman.
Icarus. *Unknown.*
Icarus in November. A. B. Stevenson.
Light-winged Smoke, Icarian Bird. Thoreau.
Musée des Beaux Arts. Auden.
ICE
Ice. Aldis.
Ice. C. G. D. Roberts.
Ice-Floes, The. E. J. Pratt.
ICEBERGS
Berg, The. Melville.
Iceberg, The. *Fr.* The *Titanic.* E. J. Pratt.
Iceberg, The. C. G. D. Roberts.
Icebergs. W. P. Foster.
Imaginary Iceberg, The. Elizabeth Bishop.
Worsley Enchanted, *sel.* ("White, said Worsley, and glistening, the ridgy plain"). Douglas Stewart.
ICE CREAM. Ice-Cream Man, The. Rachel Field.
ICELAND
Iceland. Munch, *tr. fr. Norwegian by* Stork.
Iceland First Seen. William Morris.
Iceland's Song. Thomsen, *tr. fr. Icelandic by* Johnson.
Icelandic Poems and Stories (IcP). Richard Beck, ed.
ICELANDERS. What Lack We? Fridjónsson, *tr. fr. Icelandic by* Johnson.
IDAHO
Here We Have Idaho. H. A. Powell.
On the Trail to Idaho. *Unknown.*
IKHNATON. Akhnaton. T. S. Jones, Jr.
ILLINOIS
Across Illinois. Stoltze.
El-a-noy. *Unknown.*
Illinois. C. H. Chamberlain.
ILLNESS
Anywhere Out of the World. Baudelaire, *tr. fr. French by* Davis.
Being Visited by a Friend during Illness. Po Chü-i, *tr. fr. Chinese by* Waley.
I wasn't well, and at my call. Martial, *tr. fr. Latin by* "G. I. C."
Illness. Po Chü-i, *tr. fr. Chinese by* Waley.
Land of Counterpane, The. R. L. Stevenson.
Pastoral. *Fr.* In Hospital. Henley.
Since I Lay Ill. Po Chü-i, *tr. fr. Chinese by* Waley.
To Mary. Cowper.
Utopian Journey, A. Jarrell.
IMAGINATION
Idols of Imagination. Eberhart.
Pleasures of Imagination, The, *sel.* ("With what attractive charms this goodly frame"). Akenside.
IMMIGRANTS
My Father. Dalven.
New Colossus, The. Lazarus.
"Scum o' the Earth." Schauffler.
IMMORTALITY
Argument on Immortality. L. G. Marshall.
Because I could not stop for death. Emily Dickinson.
Brahma's Answer. Stoddard.
Cato's Soliloquy. *Fr.* Cato. Addison.
Christus Triumphans. Pallen.
Cities and Thrones and Powers. *Fr.* Puck of Pook's Hill. Kipling.
Death, Be Not Proud. *Fr.* Holy Sonnets. Donne.
Demeter and Persephone. Tennyson.
Human Life; on the Denial of Immortality. S. T. Coleridge.
I Vex Me Not with Brooding of the Years. T. B. Aldrich.
Immortal. Teasdale.
Immortality. "Æ."
Immortality. Matthew Arnold.
Immortality. R. H. Dana.
Immortality. W. W. Gibson.
Immortality. A. S. Hardy.

Immortality. Frank Horne.
Immortality. Joseph Jefferson.
Immortality. Minski, *tr. fr. Russian by* Deutsch.
Immortality. S. L. Mitchell.
Immortality. F. W. H. Myers.
Immortality. Ptolemy, *tr. fr. Greek by* Bridges.
Immortality. Reese.
Immortality. *Unknown, tr. fr. Greek by* Hay.
It is an honorable thought. Emily Dickinson.
Let us return, meantime, to the round of song. Propertius, *tr. fr. Latin by* Fletcher.
Man's Mortality. *Fr.* Microbiblion. *At. to* Wastell.
Meditation, A. S. W. Kelly.
My Sun Sets to Rise Again. *Fr.* At the Mermaid. Robert Browning.
No Death. Marston.
Ode: Intimations of Immortality from Recollections of Early Childhood. Wordsworth.
Of the Soul of Man and the Immortality Thereof. *Fr.* Nosce Teipsum. Sir John Davies.
Of the Terrible Doubt of Appearances. Whitman.
One Generation to Another. Lanyon.
One Immortality. Norbert Engels.
Pantheist's Song of Immortality, The. Naden.
Paradox, The. Pitter.
Past Ruin'd Ilion Helen Lives. *Fr.* Ianthe. Landor.
Phoenix, The. A. A. Brown.
Question Whither, The. George Meredith.
Sailing to Byzantium. Yeats.
Shades of Callimachus, and holy rites of Philetas. Propertius, *tr. fr. Latin by* Fletcher.
Song of the Universal, *sel.* ("All, all for immortality"). Whitman.
Song's Eternity. Clare.
Sonnet: "Not marble, nor the gilded monuments." *Fr.* Sonnets. Shakespeare.
There Is No Death. McCreery.
There Is No Death. *Unknown.*
We thirst at first—'tis nature's act. Emily Dickinson.
What Is It to Die? Earle.
When Coldness Wraps This Suffering Clay. Byron.
While Immortality Endures. Ernest Briggs.
White Island, The; or, Place of the Blest. Herrick.
Who Hath His Fancy Pleased. Sidney.
Unseen Wings; The Living Poetry of Man's Immortality (UnW). Stanton A. Coblentz, comp.

IMPERIALISM
Scythians, The. Blok, *tr. fr. Russian by* Lindsay.
White Man's Burden, The. Kipling.
INAUGURATION DAY. Inauguration Day. R. W. Gilder.
INCENSE. Incense. Essayan, *tr. fr. Armenian by* Boyajian.
INDEPENDENCE DAY. *See* FOURTH OF JULY.
INDEPENDENCE HALL, PHILADELPHIA. Nation's Shrine, The. A. A. Wiley.

INDIA
Half Stun'd I Look Around. Ronald Ross.
Hot Weather in the Plains—India. Tipple.
India. Coates.
India. Tagore.
India the Magic. Jules-Bois, *tr. fr. French by* Walsh.
Passage to India. Whitman.
Studies at Delhi. Sir A. C. Lyall.
INDIAN PIPE (flower). Indian Pipe and Moccasin Flower. Guiterman.

INDIAN SUMMER
Day of the Indian Summer. S. H. Whitman.
Indian Summer, The. Bryant.
Indian Summer. Bumstead.
Indian Summer. W. W. Campbell.
Indian Summer. Helena Coleman.
Indian Summer. Hannum.
Indian Summer. Irvine.
Indian Summer. S. S. Moodie.
Indian Summer. Tabb.
Indian Summer. Van Dyke.
Indian Summer—Buffalo Summer. W. T. Scott.
Indian Summer Day on the Prairie, An. Vachel Lindsay.
These are the days when birds come back. Emily Dickinson.
Vermont; Indian Summer. Philip Booth.

INDIANA
Midwest. Nims.
On the Banks of the Wabash, Far Away. Dresser.

INDIANS, AMERICAN
Aged Indian, The. *Unknown.*
As Red Men Die. E. P. Johnson.
Brother Indian, The. Roger Williams.
Caughnawaga Beadwork Seller, The. Lighthall.
Courteous Pagan Shall Condemn, The. *Fr.* A Key into the Language of America. Roger Williams.
Dance for Rain, A; Cochiti. Bynner.
Feet of the Young Men, The. Kipling.
Flower-fed Buffaloes, The. Vachel Lindsay.
Gathering on the Plains, The. W. T. Butler.
Ghosts of the Buffaloes, The. Vachel Lindsay.
Half-Breed Girl, The. D. C. Scott.
Hiawatha's Childhood. *Fr.* The Song of Hiawatha. Longfellow.
Indian, The. Bourinot.
Indian Burying Ground, The. Freneau.
Indian Children. Wynne.
Indian Ghost Dance and War, The. Prather.
Indian Hunter, The. Eliza Cook.
Indian Names. Sigourney.
Indian Sky. Kreymborg.
Indian Student, The. Freneau.
Indian Summer—Buffalo Summer. W. T. Scott.
Indians. *Fr.* Centennial Ode. Sprague.
Indians Come Down from Mixco, The. Asturias, *tr. fr. Spanish by* Walsh.
"Injun, The." Logan.
Lament of a Man for His Son. *Tr. fr. Paiute Indian by* Austin.
Last Reservation, The. Learned.
Little Papoose. Hilda Conkling.
Missouri Traveller Writes Home, A, 1830. Bly.
Navajo Prayer. *Tr. fr. Navaho Indian by* Austin.
Pilot of the Plains, The. E. P. Johnson.
Portrait of an Indian. Rashley.
Red Men, The. Charles Sangster.
Seventh City of Cibola, The. H. N. Pratt.
Song of Greatness, A. *Tr. fr. Chippewa Indian by* Austin.
Song of the Indian Mother. J. G. Clark.
Song of the Indian Wars, The, *sels.* Neihardt.
Song of the Micmac, The. Joseph Howe.
Sonnet: "There was an Indian, who had known no change." Squire.
Tecumseh, *sel.* ("Once we were strong"). Mair.
There Came an Ancient Huron. *Unknown.*
To the Driving Cloud. Longfellow.
Ute Lover, The. Garland.
War Dance, The. R. V. Carr.
Watkwenies. D. C. Scott.
Western Trail, The. R. V. Carr.
White Man's Road, The. Arthur Chapman.
INDIGO BUNTINGS. Indigo Bird, The. Wetherald.

INDUSTRIAL REVOLUTION
Deserted Village, The. Goldsmith.
Symphony, The. Lanier.
INFANTS. *See* BABIES.
INGE, WILLIAM RALPH. On Dean Inge. Humbert Wolfe.

INJUSTICE
Chancellor's Gravel-Drive, The. Po Chü-i, *tr. fr. Chinese by* Waley.
Charcoal-Seller, The. Po Chü-i, *tr. fr. Chinese by* Waley.
Jericho Road, The. Poteat.
That God Made. Herford.
INNISFREE, IRELAND. Lake Isle of Innisfree, The. Yeats.
INNS. *See* HOTELS.
INSANITY. *See* MADNESS.

INSECTS
Ant Explorer, The. Dennis.
Divine Insect, The. Wheelock.
Hurt No Living Thing. *Fr.* Sing-Song. C. G. Rossetti.
Little Black Bug. M. W. Brown.
Near Dusk. Auslander.
INSURGENTE (ship). *Constellation* and the *Insurgente,* The. *Unknown.*

INTELLECT
Brain is wider than the sky, The. Emily Dickinson.
First Philosopher's Song. Aldous Huxley.
Freedom for the Mind. W. L. Garrison.
Heart and Mind. Edith Sitwell.
Hymn to Intellectual Beauty. Shelley.
In a Hard Intellectual Light. Eberhart.
Mind. Wilbur.
Mind Is an Enchanting Thing, The. Marianne Moore.
My Mind to Me a Kingdom Is. Dyer.
Of a Contented Mind. Thomas, Lord Vaux.
Riddles. Kirby.
Send Forth the High Falcon. Léonie Adams.
Stop Pondering on Things Imponderable. George, *tr. fr. German by* Viereck.
Substance and Shadow. Cardinal Newman.
Thought. Emerson.
INTERNATIONAL BRIGADE. *See* CIVIL WAR, SPANISH.
INVESTORS AND INVESTMENTS. Investor's Soliloquy. Ward.

IONA, SCOTLAND
Iona. A. C. Coxe.
Iona. Tennyson.
IOWA. Song of Iowa, The. Byers.
IRAN. *See* PERSIA.

IRELAND
After Death. F. I. Parnell.
Andromeda. J. J. Roche.
Back to Dublin. R. A. D. Ford.

IRELAND (*continued*)
Christmas and Ireland. Lionel Johnson.
Corrymeela. "Moira O'Neill."
County of Mayo, The. Lavelle, *tr. fr. Irish by* Fox.
Cradle Song of a Celtic Queen. J. E. Tobin.
Dark Rosaleen. *Unknown, tr. fr. Irish by* Mangan.
Dear Harp of My Country. Thomas Moore.
Deer of Ireland, The. Colum.
Easter, 1916. Yeats.
Erin. Digby.
Fair Hills of Eiré, The. Colum, *after the Irish.*
Fair Hills of Eiré, O, The! Mangan, *after the Irish.*
Fair Hills of Ireland, The. *Unknown, tr. fr. Irish by* Ferguson.
Famine Year, The. Lady Wilde.
Farewell to Ireland. *At. to* St. Columcille, *tr. fr. Middle Irish by* Hyde.
Harbor, The. Letts.
Harp That Once through Tara's Halls, The. Thomas Moore.
I Am Ireland. Pearse, *tr. fr. Irish by* Gregory.
I Am of Ireland. Yeats.
Ich Am of Irlonde. *Unknown.*
Inis Fal. *Unknown, tr. fr. Irish by* Stephens.
Ireland. Gwynn.
Ireland. Lionel Johnson.
Ireland. Leamy.
Ireland. D. F. MacCarthy.
Ireland. Piatt.
Ireland. Shorter.
Ireland, Mother of Priests. Shane Leslie.
Ireland Never Was Contented. Landor.
Ireland Weeping. Livingston, *tr. fr. Irish.*
Irish Dancer, The. *Unknown.*
Irish Rapparees, The. Duffy.
Island, The. Jennett.
Kathaleen Ny-Houlahan. *Tr. fr. Irish by* Mangan.
King Cahal Mór of the Wine-red Hand. Mangan.
Lady Day in Ireland. P. J. Carroll.
Let Erin Remember the Days of Old. Thomas Moore.
Little Black Rose, The. De Vere.
Little Waves of Breffny, The. Gore-Booth.
Minstrel Boy, The. Thomas Moore.
Mountown! Thou Sweet Retreat. *Fr.* Mully of Mountown. W. King.
Municipal Gallery Revisited, The. Yeats.
My Land. T. O. Davis.
My Native Land. J. B. O'Reilly.
Neutrality. MacNeice.
Of the Warres in Ireland. Harrington.
On His Exile to Iona. St. Columcille, *tr. fr. Old Irish by* Hyde.
On Not Hearing the Birds Sing in Ireland. Colum.
Poem Written in a Time of Trouble by an Irish Priest Who Had Taken Orders in France, A. *Unknown, tr. fr. Irish by* Lady Gregory.
Portrait with Background. Gogarty.
Red Hanrahan's Song about Ireland. Yeats.
Road of Ireland, A. O'Donnell.
Rose Tree, The. Yeats.
September, 1913. Yeats.
Shan Van Vocht, The. *Unknown.*
Sixteen Dead Men. Shorter.
Soggarth Aroon. Banim.
Song of the Little Villages. Dollard.
Spenser's Ireland. Marianne Moore.
Spring Flowers from Ireland. D. F. McCarthy.
Sthreets of Home. D. A. McCarthy.
Sweet Castle Hyde. Kenealy.
Sweet Innisfallen. Thomas Moore.
To God and Ireland True. O'Leary.
To the Dead of '98. Lionel Johnson.
Valediction. MacNeice.
Wearin' of the Green. *Unknown, add. words by* Boucicault.
Whack Fol the Diddle. Kearney.
Year of Sorrow, The: Ireland 1849. De Vere.
Anthology of Irish Literature, An (AnIL). David H. Greene, ed.
Anthology of Irish Verse, An (AnIV). Padraic Colum, ed.
Golden Treasury of Irish Verse, A (GTIV). Lennox Robinson, ed.
Irish Poets of the Nineteenth Century (IrPN). Geoffrey Taylor, ed.
Kings, Lords & Commons; an Anthology from the Irish (KiLC). Frank O'Connor, tr.
New Irish Poets (NeIP). Devin A. Garrity, ed.
1000 Years of Irish Poetry (OnYI). Kathleen Hoagland, ed.
Oxford Book of Irish Verse; XVIIth Century-XXth Century (OxBI). Donagh MacDonagh *and* Lennox Robinson, comps.
Silver Branch, The (SiB). Seán O'Faoláin, comp.
Treasury of Irish Poetry, A (TIP). Stopford A. Brooke *and* T. W. Rolleston, eds.

IRIS (flower)
Beds of Fleur-de-Lys, The. C. P. Gilman.
Iris, The. Gasetsu, *tr. fr. Japanese.*
Iris. "Michael Field."
Iris. Hooke.
Iris. *Unknown, tr. fr. Japanese by* Porter.
Iris Flowers. Fenollosa.
White Iris, A. Barrington.

IRISH
Civil Irish and Wild Irish. Laoiseach Mac an Bhaird, *tr. fr. Late Middle Irish by* Jackson.
Connachtman, A. Colum.
Cremona. Doyle.
Downfall of the Gael. O'Gnive, *tr. fr. Irish by* Ferguson.
Fighting Race, The. J. I. C. Clarke.
Gods and Heroes of the Gael. E. R. Cox.
I'll Wear a Shamrock. M. C. Davies.
Irish, The. Carlin.
Irish. E. J. O'Brien.
Irish Grandmother. Edelman.
Lament of the Irish Emigrant. Dufferin.
My Irish Great-Grandfather, Patrick O'Flyng. House.
Native Irishman, The. *Unknown.*
O'Bruidar. James Stephens.
On Behalf of Some Irishmen Not Followers of Tradition. "Æ."
Peaceable Race. T. A. Daly.
Slainthe! MacGill.
Written on the Sense of Isolation in Contemporary Ireland. Greacen.

IRONSIDES (ship). *See* CONSTITUTION.

IRVING, WASHINGTON. Irving. *Fr.* A Fable for Critics. J. R. Lowell.

ISAAC. Binding of Isaac, The. Manger, *tr. fr. Yiddish by* Betsky.

ISCHL, AUSTRIA. Inscription on a Shrine near Ischl. Elizabeth, Empress of Austria-Hungary, *tr. fr. German by* Walsh.

ISHMAEL. Ishmael. H. E. Palmer.

ISRAEL
But We Shall Bloom. Guri, *tr. fr. Hebrew by* Kuselewitz.
Pictures at an Exhibition. Rosenbaum.

ITALIANS
Boy from Rome, Da. T. A. Daly.
Cigarette for the Bambino. Ewart.
Modern Romans, The. C. F. Johnson.

ITALY
Ah Me, Do You Remember Still. H. M. F. Robinson.
Daisy, The. Tennyson.
Dear Is My Little Native Vale. Samuel Rogers.
Englishman in Italy, The. Robert Browning.
Farewell to Italy. Landor.
In Ampezzo. Trumbull Stickney.
Italia, Io Ti Saluto! C. G. Rossetti.
Italian Rhapsody. R. U. Johnson.
Italy. *Fr.* Beppo. Byron.
Italy. Filicaja, *tr. fr. Italian by* Byron.
Italy, *sels.* Samuel Rogers.
Letter from Italy, A. Addison.
Lines Written among the Euganean Hills. Shelley.
Night in Italy, A, *sel.* ("Sweet are the rosy memories"). "Owen Meredith."
Non Dolet. Swinburne.
Political Chaos in Italy. Dante, *tr. fr. Italian by* Longfellow.
Song of the Standard, The. Swinburne.
Street Melody, A. Belle Cooper.
Super Flumina Babylonis. Swinburne.
To Italy. Guidiccioni, *tr. fr. Italian by* Longfellow.
To Italy. Leopardi, *tr. fr. Italian by* Rendel.
Walls and Arches, The. Leopardi, *tr. fr. Italian by* De' Lucchi.
Lyric Poetry of the Italian Renaissance (LyPI). L. R. Lind, comp.

IVES, CHARLES. Ives, *sel.* ("This is Charles Ives"). Rukeyser.

IVRY-LA-BATAILLE, FRANCE. Ivry. Macaulay.

IVY
Holly and Ivy ("Holly bereth beris"). *Unknown.*
Holly and Ivy Made a Great Party. *Unknown.*
Holly and the Ivy, The ("The holly and the ivy,/ When they are both full grown"). *Unknown.*
Ivy. F. D. Sherman.
Ivy Green, The. *Fr.* The Pickwick Papers. Dickens.

J

JACK-IN-THE-PULPIT (plant)
Jack-in-the-Pulpit. Rowena Bennett.
Jack-in-the-Pulpit. Eastwick.

Jack-in-the-Pulpit. Holland.
JACKSON, ANDREW
Andrew Jackson. S. V. Benét.
Andrew Jackson. *Fr.* The Tall Men. Donald Davidson.
Andrew Jackson. Martha Keller.
Jackson at New Orleans. Wallace Rice.
Old Hickory. Scollard.
Oration, An, Entitled "Old, Old, Old, Old Andrew Jackson." Vachel Lindsay.
JACKSON, HELEN HUNT. Helen Hunt Jackson. Coolbrith.
JACKSON, THOMAS JONATHAN (Stonewall Jackson)
Dying Words of Stonewall Jackson, The. Lanier.
Stonewall Jackson. Flash.
Stonewall Jackson's Way. J. W. Palmer.
Stonewall's Requiem. Deeves.
Under the Shade of the Trees. M. J. Preston.
JACOB
Jacob, *sel.* ("Come near to me"). Clough.
Wrestling Jacob. Charles Wesley.
JACOBITES
Jacobite on Tower Hill, The. Thornbury.
Jacobite's Exile, 1746, A. Swinburne.
Jacobite's Farewell, A. Swinburne.
Old Scottish Cavalier, The. Aytoun.
Standard on the Braes o' Mar. Laing.
JACOPONE DA TODI. Jacopone da Todi. Matthew Arnold.
JAGUARS. Jaguar, The. Ted Hughes.
JAMAICA, BRITISH WEST INDIES
I Shall Remember. Carberry.
Nature. Carberry.
Slave, The. Horne.
JAMES I, KING OF ENGLAND
Gratulatory Elegy of the Peaceable Entry of King James, A. Harington.
To His Late Majesty, Concerning the True Form of English Poetry. Sir John Beaumont.
To King James. Jonson.
JAMES II, KING OF ENGLAND. King James II. *Fr.* The Hind and the Panther. Dryden.
JAMES I, KING OF SCOTLAND. King's Tragedy, The. D. G. Rossetti.
JAMES IV, KING OF SCOTLAND. Ballade of the Scottyshe Kynge, A. Skelton.
JAMES V, KING OF SCOTLAND. Childhood of James V, The. *Fr.* The Complaynt of Schir David Lindesay. Sir David Lindsay.
JAMES, HENRY
At the Grave of Henry James. Auden.
Jacobean. Fadiman.
JAMES, JESSE
Jesse James. W. R. Benét.
Jesse James. *Unknown.*
JAMES, REUBEN. Reuben James. Roche.
JAMESTOWN, VIRGINIA
Burning of Jamestown, The. English.
Ode to Jamestown. Paulding.
JANUARY
In January. Bottomley.
January. R. E. Jones.
January. Lambdin.
January. Larcom.
January. Michael Lewis.
January. *Fr.* The Vision of Sir Launfal. J. R. Lowell.
January. F. D. Sherman.
January. W. C. Williams.
January Is Here. Fawcett.
January Morning, A. Lampman.
January Snow. Aileen Fisher.
On the Wind of January. *Fr.* A Year's Windfalls. C. G. Rossetti.
Winter Morning, A. *Fr.* The Vision of Sir Launfal. J. R. Lowell.
JANUS. Janus. Madeline Mason.
JAPAN
Japan. Hecht.
Japanesque. Herford.
Walk in Kyoto, A. Birney.
One Hundred Poems from the Japanese (OnPJ). Kenneth Rexroth, tr.
Poetry of Living Japan, The (PoLJ). Takamichi Ninomiya *and* D. J. Enright, trs.
Songs from the Land of Dawn (SoLD). Lois J. Erickson, tr.
JAPANESE, THE. Japanese, The. Ogden Nash.
JASMINE
January Jasmine. Brockman.
Jessamine. Ibn al-Abbar, *tr. fr. Arabic by* Arberry.
White Jessamine, The. Tabb.
Yasmin. *Fr.* Hassan. Flecker.
Yellow Jessamine. Woolson.
JAZZ
Jazz Fantasia. Sandburg.
Jazz of This Hotel, The. Vachel Lindsay.
JEALOUSY
He Desires Her Husband's Death. Dafydd ap Gwilym, *tr. fr. Welsh by* Bell.
I Can't Think What He Sees in Her. A. P. Herbert.
Jealous Man, A. *Unknown, tr. fr. Irish by* O'Connor.
Jealousy. M. E. Coleridge.
Tale for Husbands, A. Sidney.
JEANNE D'ARC. *See* JOAN OF ARC.
JEFFERSON, THOMAS
Ballad of the Common Man. Kreymborg.
Brave New World. MacLeish.
Death of Jefferson, The. Butterworth.
Jefferson and Liberty. *Unknown.*
Thomas Jefferson, 1743–1826. Rosemary Benét *and* Stephen Vincent Benét.
JEFFREYS OF WEM, GEORGE JEFFREYS, 1ST BARON
Lord Chancellours Villanies Discovered, The; or, His Rise and Fall in the Four Last Years. *Unknown.*
Sir T. J.'s Speech to His Wife and Children. *Unknown.*
JENGHIZ KHAN. Tower of Genghis Khan, The. Hervey Allen.
JEREMIAH
Jeremiah. Bynner.
Prophet Jeremiah and the Personification of Israel, The. *At. to* Eleazer ben Kalir, *tr. fr. Hebrew by* Salaman.
JEREZ DE LA FRONTERA, SPAIN. Ballad of the Spanish Civil Guard. García Lorca, *tr. fr. Spanish by* Turnbull.
JERUSALEM
At Jerusalem. E. D. Proctor.
By the Rivers of Babylon. Psalms, Bible, *O.T.*
By the Waters of Babylon. *Fr.* Hebrew Melodies. Heine, *tr. fr. German by* Leland.
Destruction of Jerusalem by the Babylonian Hordes, The. Rosenberg.
Holy City. Weatherley.
If I Forget Thee. Litvinoff.
In the Old City. Fichman, *tr. fr. Hebrew by* Kahn.
Jerusalem. Drummond of Hawthornden.
Jerusalem. *Unknown.*
Jerusalem Delivered, *sels.* Tasso, *tr. fr. Italian.*
Jerusalem Delivered. Louis Untermeyer.
Jerusalem, Rejoice for Joy! *At. to* Dunbar.
Jerusalem the Dismembered. *Fr.* Jerusalem. Uri Zvi Greenberg, *tr. fr. Hebrew by* Cowen.
Jerusalem, the Golden. *Fr.* De Contemptu Mundi. Bernard of Cluny, *tr. fr. Latin by* Neale.
Longing for Jerusalem. Halevi, *tr. fr. Hebrew by* Lazarus.
Mater Hierusalem Civitas Sancta Dei. *Unknown.*
New Jerusalem, The. *Unknown.*
Prayer for Redemption. *Unknown.*
Prisoner's Song of Jerusalem, A. *Unknown.*
Wandering Jew Comes to the Wall, The. *Fr.* The Wall of Weeping. Fleg, *tr. fr. French by* Wolfe.
JESTERS. Fool, The. Baerlein.
JESUITS
Canto I: "Of Men, nay Beasts: worse, Monsters: worst of all." *Fr.* The Locusts, or Apollyonists. Phineas Fletcher.
Prologue: "For who can longer hold?" *Fr.* Satires upon the Jesuits. Oldham.
JESUS CHRIST
Advent. Brother Antoninus.
After the Agony in the Garden. Hine.
Agonie, The. George Herbert.
Ah My Dere. *Unknown.*
Al the Meryere. *Unknown.*
And I Have Seen Again the Marvelous Child. Verlaine, *tr. fr. French by* Watkins.
Annunciation. Etheridge.
Argument, An—of the Passion of Christ. Merton.
Ave Verum Corpus Natum. *Unknown, tr. fr. Latin.*
Ballad of the Goodly Fere. Pound.
Ballad of Trees and the Master, A. Lanier.
Ballade of Illegal Ornaments. Belloc.
Barnfloor and Winepress. G. M. Hopkins.
Beautiful Gift, The. G. N. Crowell.
Better Part, The. Matthew Arnold.
Bitter Withy, The. *Unknown.*
Blind Man's Cries. Corbière, *tr. fr. French by* Koch *and* Guy.
Burning Babe, The. Southwell.
Cantica: Our Lord Christ. St. Francis of Assisi, *tr. fr. Italian by* D. G. Rossetti.
Carpenter, The. Studdert-Kennedy.
Carpenter, The. Yamamuro, *tr. fr. Japanese by* Erickson.
Celebration of Peace. Hölderlin, *tr. fr. German by* Golffing *and* Opitz.
Charitas Nimia; or, The Dear Bargain. Crashaw.
Child Jesus to Mary the Rose, The. Lydgate.
Child My Choice, A. Southwell.
Child's Prayer, A. Francis Thompson.
Christ, *sels.* Cynewulf, *tr. fr. Anglo-Saxon.*
Christ and His Mother at the Cross. Jacopone da Todi, *tr. fr. Italian by* Walsh.
Christ and the Little Ones. Gill.
Christ and the Mourners. Conway.

Jesus Christ (*continued*)
Christ and the Pagan. Tabb.
Christ-Child, The. St. Gregory of Narek, *tr. fr. Armenian by* Blackwell.
Christ-Child, The. Agnes Lee.
Christ Crucified. Crashaw.
Christ in the Universe. Alice Meynell.
Christ of Common Folks, The. Liddell.
Christ of the Andes. Coates.
Christ of the Andes, The. Markham.
Christ on the Cross ("He that seeth on the rood"). *Unknown.*
Christ on the Cross ("They raised him on the rood"). *Unknown.*
Christ Our Example in Suffering. James Montgomery.
Christ Quiets the Tempest. *Fr.* Carmen Paschale. Sedulius, *tr. fr. Latin by* Sigerson.
Christ the Comrade. Colum.
Christ, the Fleur-de-Lis. *Unknown.*
Christ Walking on the Water. Rodgers.
Christ's Bloody Sweat. Southwell.
Christ's Nativity. Vaughan.
Christ's Victory and Triumph, *sels.* Giles Fletcher.
Come to Your Heaven, You Heavenly Choirs! Southwell.
Come, Wandering Sheep, O Come! Góngora, *tr. fr. Spanish by* Bowring.
Coming of Christ, The. *Unknown.*
Comrade Jesus. Cleghorn.
Corpus Christi. M. S. Mansfield.
Dream of the Rood, The. *Unknown, tr. fr. Anglo-Saxon by* Sister Mary Madeleva.
Earliest Christian Hymn. Clement of Alexandria, *tr. fr. Greek.*
Ecce Homo. Gascoyne.
Ecce Homunculus. R. A. K. Mason.
Evening Thought, An. Hammon.
Expected Guest, The. Sidney Keyes.
Eye-Witness. Torrence.
Feet of Judas, The. McClellan.
God Said. Verlaine, *tr. fr. French by* Kittel.
Going of His Feet, The. Kemp.
Good Shepherd, The. Lope de Vega, *tr. fr. Spanish by* Longfellow.
Good Shepherd with the Kid, The. Matthew Arnold.
Guest, The. *Unknown.*
Hayll, Comly and Clene. *Unknown.*
He. Kunitz.
He Made Us Free. Egan.
His Are the Thousand Sparkling Rills. C. F. Alexander.
Holy Eclogue, The. Sister Francisca Josefa del Castillo, *tr. fr. Spanish by* Walsh.
Holy Name of Jesus, The. Crashaw.
Holy Well (Sweet Jesus), The. *Unknown.*
Hora Christi. Alice Brown.
Hound of Heaven, The. Francis Thompson.
Hymn for Morning. *Fr.* Cathemerinon. Prudentius, *tr. fr. Latin by* Blackett.
Hymn on the Ascension. Luis de León, *tr. fr. Spanish by* Ticknor.
Hymn to the Holy Cross. Fortunatus, *tr. fr. Latin.*
Hymns to the Night, V. "Novalis," *tr. fr. German by* Cotterell.
I Heard Immanuel Singing. Vachel Lindsay.
I know that my Redeemer lives & I. *Unknown.*
I See His Blood upon the Rose. Plunkett.
If He Should Come. Lorraine.
In Galilee. Jessie Mackay.
In the Heart of Jesus. O'Daly, *tr. fr. Irish by* Sigerson.
In the Name of Jesus Christ. Cranston.
In the Wilderness. Robert Graves.
Inasmuch! W. E. Brooks.
Jesu. George Herbert.
Jesu Christ, sooth God, sooth man. *Fr.* Prison Songs. *Unknown.*
Jesu Dulcis. St. Bernard of Clairvaux, *tr. fr. Latin.*
Jesu, Dulcis Memoria. *Unknown, tr. fr. Latin.*
Jesus. Eliyia, *tr. fr. Modern Greek by* Dalven.
Jesus. Theodore Parker.
Jesus. Pimentel Coronel, *tr. fr. Spanish by* Clarke.
Jesus. *Unknown.*
Jesus of the Scars. Shillito.
Jesus the Carpenter. Liddell.
Jesus, the Carpenter. Sheldon.
Jesus, Thou Joy of Loving Hearts. St. Bernard of Clairvaux, *tr. fr. Latin.*
Jesus! thy Crucifix. Emily Dickinson.
Killing, The. Muir.
La Corona. Donne.
Lachrymae. Gascoyne.
Last Supper; Jesus to Judas. Damon.
Last Words of Don Henriquez, The. Schneour, *tr. fr. Yiddish by* Leftwich.
Let Mine Eyes See Thee. St. Theresa of Avila.
Life of the Blessed, The. Luis de León, *tr. fr. Spanish by* Bryant.
Little Jesus. Francis Thompson.
Live Christ. Oxenham.
Living Christ, The. Kagawa, *tr. fr. Japanese by* Erickson.
Lord, The. Gabriel y Galán, *tr. fr. Spanish by* Walsh.
Lord Christ Came to Notre Dame, The. Le Gallienne.
Lord! Within Thy Peace I Rest Me. Brentano, *tr. fr. German by* Cotterell.
Lulla, My Sweet Little Baby. *Unknown.*
Lullaby: "Baby child of Mary, The." *Unknown, tr. fr. Spanish.*
Man Christ, The. Therese Lindsey.
Marigold, The. Wither.
Mary's Baby. O'Sheel.
May the Sweet Name of Jesus. *Unknown, tr. fr. Irish by* Hull.
Messias. Merton.
Mithraic Emblems, *sel.* ("Oh let your shining orb grow dim"). Roy Campbell.
Moses and Jesus. Zangwill.
Most glorious Lord of life, that on this day. *Fr.* Amoretti. Spenser.
Mother of Christ, The. Varnalis, *tr. fr. Modern Greek by* Dalven.
Mount of Olives. Vaughan.
My Christ Ever Faithful. *Unknown, tr. fr. Irish by* Flower.
My Risen Lord. *Unknown.*
Name of Jesus, The. John Newton.
New Heaven, New Warre. Southwell.
New Prince New Pomp. Southwell.
Night, The. Vaughan.
Night Song. Charles Williams.
O King of the Friday. *Unknown, tr. fr. Irish by* Hyde.
O Master, Let Me Walk with Thee. Gladden.
Of the Resurrection of Christ. William Dunbar.
On the Infancy of Our Saviour. Quarles.
On the Miracle of Loaves. Crashaw.
On the Safe Side. Lord Dunsany.
On the Swag. R. A. K. Mason.
Our Christ. Farrington.
Our Lord and Our Lady. Belloc.
Our Two Worthies. Ransom.
Patmos. Hölderlin, *tr. fr. German by* Hull.
Phantom, The. Díaz Mirón, *tr. fr. Spanish by* Beckett.
Poet Lived in Galilee, A. Bynner.
Quia Amore Langueo. *Unknown.*
Rabboni! Master! Mother Loyola.
Religious Musings, *sel.* ("Lovely was the death"). S. T. Coleridge.
Rime of the Rood, A. O'Donnell.
Rorate Coeli Desuper. William Dunbar.
Rosa Mystica. *Unknown.*
Sacramental Meditations, *sels.* Edward Taylor.
Sacred Songs, *sel.* ("Though all are faithless growing"). "Novalis," *tr. fr. German by* Hutchins.
Sacrifice, The. George Herbert.
St. Patrick's Breastplate. *At. to* St. Patrick, *tr. fr. Irish.*
Sapphics upon the Passion of Christ. *Unknown.*
Saviour, The. Oreshin, *tr. fr. Russian by* Patrick.
Second Crucifixion, The. Le Gallienne.
Sheep and Lambs. Tynan.
Shine Out, Fair Sun, with All Your Heat. *Fr.* The Masque of the Twelve Months. *Unknown, at. to* George Chapman.
Signum Cui Contradicetur. Sister Mary Angelita.
Son of God, The. O'Donnell.
Song to the Most Holy Name of Jesus. Córdova y Bocanegra, *tr. fr. Spanish by* Beckett.
Springtime—a Humble Cry from the Depths. Brentano, *tr. fr. German by* Cotterell.
Still Falls the Rain. Edith Sitwell.
Sunset on Calvary. *Unknown.*
Terly Terlow. *Unknown.*
Testament of Beauty, The, *sel.* ("So it was when Jesus came in his gentleness"). Robert Bridges.
There Is a Floure Sprung of a Tree. *Unknown.*
This Endernight I Saw a Sight. *Unknown.*
To Christ Crucified. *At. to* St. John of the Cross, *tr. fr. Spanish.*
To Crucify the Son. Guevara, *tr. fr. Spanish by* Beckett.
To Holy Jesus. Princess Philipa, *tr. fr. Portuguese by* Walsh.
To Jesus Christ on His Birthday. Millay.
To Jesus on the Cross. Tejada, *tr. fr. Spanish by* Walsh.
To Our Blessed Lord upon the Choice of His Sepulchre. Crashaw.
To the Nativity. González de Eslava, *tr. fr. Spanish by* Beckett.
To the Young Man Jesus. Dalton.
Transfiguration, The. J. M. Hayes.
Upon the Body of Our Blessed Lord Naked and Bloody. Crashaw.
Veni, Coronaberis. *Unknown.*
Veni, Domine Jesu! Rawes.
Very Grail I Elevate, A. Morgenstern, *tr. fr. German by* Barrett.
Vexilla Regis Prodeunt. Fortunatus, *tr. fr. Latin by* Cook.
Virgin's Song, The. *Unknown.*

Vision of Ita, The. *Unknown, tr. fr. Old Irish by* Stokes.
Vision of Jesus, The. *Fr.* The Vision of Piers Plowman. Langland.
Voice of Christmas, The. Kemp.
Wake oh my Soule awake & raise. *Unknown.*
What Went Ye Out to See? *Fr.* The Christian Year. Keble.
Windhover, The. G. M. Hopkins.
Woefully Arrayed. Skelton.
Yet if His Majesty, our sovereign Lord. *Unknown.*
Beautiful Poems on Jesus (BePJ). Basil Miller, comp.
Christ in Poetry (ChIP). Thomas Curtis Clark *and* Hazel Davis Clark, eds.
Story of Jesus in the World's Literature, The (StJW). Edward Wagenknecht, ed.

JEWEL, JOHN, BISHOP OF SALISBURY. Epitaph upon the Death of the Right Reverent Father in God J. Jewel, An. Bourman.

JEWS
Autobiographical. A. M. Klein.
Banner of the Jew, The. Lazarus.
Boy of the Ghetto, A. Widdemer.
Design for Mediaeval Tapestry. A. M. Klein.
Epilogue of the Wandering Jew, The. Newbury.
Exile Song. Rosenfeld, *tr. fr. Yiddish by* Leftwich.
For All That Ever Has Been Ours. Landau, *tr. fr. Yiddish by* Syrkin.
Hebrews. Oppenheim.
In re Solomon Warshawer. A. M. Klein.
In the Time of the Persecution. Aaronson.
Israel. Leonard.
Israelite Graveyard. Tiempo, *tr. fr. Spanish by* Humphries, Walsh, *and* Fitts.
Jew, The. Isaac Rosenberg.
Jew to Jesus, The. F. K. Frank.
Jew Wrecked in the German Cell, The. Auden.
Jewish Cemetery at Newport, The. Longfellow.
Jewish Conscript, The. F. K. Frank.
Jewish Hymn in Babylon. Milman.
Jewish Lullaby. Louis Untermeyer.
Jewish Main Street. Layton.
Jews, The. Vaughan.
Jews at Haifa. Jarrell.
Judaism. Cardinal Newman.
Lay of the Levite, The. Aytoun.
Mathmid, The. Bialik, *tr. fr. Hebrew by* Samuel.
Moses and Jesus. Zangwill.
Old Jew, The. Bodenheim.
One of the Jews (50 A.D.). Cavafy, *tr. fr. Modern Greek by* Dalven.
Our Torah. Eliyia, *tr. fr. Modern Greek by* Dalven.
Portrait. Plutzik.
Sound the Loud Timbrel. Thomas Moore.
Still Small Voice, The. A. M. Klein.
To Russia. Joaquin Miller.
Wandering Jew, The. *Unknown.*
Weeping and Singing. Tiempo, *tr. fr. Spanish by* Walsh.
World's Justice, The. Lazarus.
Onions and Cucumbers and Plums (OnCuPl). Sarah Zweig Betsky, ed. *and* tr.
Treasury of Jewish Poetry, A (TrJP). Nathan Ausubel *and* Marynn Ausubel, eds.

JEZEBEL. Song for the Clatter-Bones. Higgins.

JOAN OF ARC
Good Joan, The. Reese.
Joan of Arc at Domremy. Going.
Joan of Arc to the Tribunal. Frisch.
Maid, The. Brégy.
Maid, The. T. G. Roberts.
Maid of Arc, The. Bottomley.
Maid of Orleans, The, *play, sel.* ("Farewell, ye mountains, and ye much-loved paths"). Schiller, *tr. fr. German by* Drinkwater-Bethune.
Maid of Orleans, The, *poem.* Schiller, *tr. fr. German by* Dwight.
One Day at Rouen. Sister Mary Bernetta.
Prayer to Jehanne of France. Auslander.
Saint, The. *Fr.* Requiem. Humbert Wolfe.
Saint Jeanne. Garrison.
Scot to Jeanne d'Arc, A. Lang.
To Joan of Arc on D-Day. Sister Mary Thérèse.

JOB (Bible)
Job. S. T. Coleridge.
Job Reviles. *Fr.* Design for Mediaeval Tapestry. A. M. Klein.

JOGUES, SAINT ISAAC. Knowest Thou Isaac Jogues? F. W. Grey.

JOHANNESBURG, SOUTH AFRICA. Johannesburg. Plomer.

JOHN, KING OF ENGLAND. King John and the Abbot of Canterbury. *Unknown.*

JOHN HENRY
John Henry. *Unknown.*
Old John Henry. J. W. Riley.

JOHN OF AUSTRIA. Lepanto. Chesterton.

JOHN THE BAPTIST, SAINT
For the Baptist. Drummond of Hawthornden.
John the Baptist. Louis Simpson.
St. John Baptist. O'Shaughnessy.
Salome. Apollinaire, *tr. fr. French by* Fitts.

JOHNSON, ANDREW. Mr. Johnson's Policy of Reconstruction. Halpine.

JOHNSON, LIONEL
In Memory of Major Robert Gregory. Yeats.
Lionel Johnson. Joyce Kilmer.

JOHNSON, SAMUEL
Epitaph on Dr. Johnson. Cowper.
Lines on Dr. Johnson. "Peter Pindar."
Postscript to "Retaliation," A. Dobson.

JOHNSTON, ALBERT SIDNEY
Albert Sidney Johnston. Sherwood.
Albert Sidney Johnston. Ticknor.
General Albert Sidney Johnston. Jervey.
Grave of Albert Sidney Johnston. Synnott.

JOHNSTOWN FLOOD. Man Who Rode to Conemaugh. Bowen.

JONAH
Jonah. Aldous Huxley.
Jonah. *Fr.* Patience. *Unknown.*
Jonah and the Whale. Alice Meynell.
Meditation Thirty ("Prest down with sorrow, Lord, not for my sin"). *Fr.* Sacramental Meditations. Edward Taylor.
Song of Jonah in the Whale's Belly, The. *Fr.* The Harmony of the Church. Drayton.

JONES, CASEY (John Luther Jones). Casey Jones. *Unknown.*

JONES, JOHN PAUL
Battle of the *Bonhomme Richard* and the *Serapis. Fr.* Song of Myself. Whitman.
Bonhomme Richard and *Serapis,* The. Freneau.
John Paul Jones. R. W. Gilder.
Paul Jones. Phelon.
Paul Jones ("An American frigate from Baltimore came"). *Unknown.*
Paul Jones ("A song unto Liberty's brave buccaneer"). *Unknown.*
Paul Jones—a New Song. *Unknown.*
Paul Jones' Victory. *Unknown.*
Yankee Man-of-War, The. *Unknown.*

JONES, SIR WILLIAM. On the Ingenious Mr. Jones's Elegant Translations and Imitations of Eastern Poetry . . . John Scott of Amwell.

JONSON, BEN
Ad Jo. Marston et Ben. Jonson. Weever.
Ben Jonson. *Fr.* Sonnets on English Dramatic Poets. Swinburne.
Ben Jonson's Commonplace Book. Lucius Cary.
Eclogue to Mr. Johnson, An. Randolph.
Elegy on Ben. Jonson, An. Cleveland.
Epistle Answering to One That Asked to Be Sealed of the Tribe of Ben, An. Jonson.
Gratulatory to Mr. Ben Johnson for His Adopting of Him to Be His Son, A. Randolph.
His Prayer to Ben Jonson. Herrick.
Master Francis Beaumont's Letter to Ben Jonson. Beaumont.
Ode for Ben Jonson, An. Herrick.
Ode: To Himself. Jonson.
On Ben Jonson. Cleyton.
Prologue Spoken by Mr. Garrick at the Opening of the Theatre in Drury Lane, 1747. Samuel Johnson.
To Ben. Jonson. Carew.
To My Friend Mr. Jonson. Roe.
To the Memory of Ben Johnson, *sel.* ("Scorne then their censure"). Mayne.
To the Memory of My Friend, Ben Jonson. Henry King.
Upon Ben Jonson. Herrick.
Upon Ben. Johnson. Waller.

JOSEPH (Bible, *O.T.*). Joseph and His Brethren. C. J. Wells.

JOSEPH, SAINT
Father, The. Ballard.
Man of the House, The. Tynan.
To St. Joseph. O'Donnell.
Vigil of Joseph, The. Elsa Barker.

JUDAS ISCARIOT
Descent for the Lost. Child.
Entrance into Heaven. S. H. Hay.
Judas. Gamaliel Bradford.
Judas. Corning.
Judas. *Unknown.*
Judas. Vinal.
Judas Iscariot. *Fr.* The Ballad of Judas Iscariot. Robert Buchanan.
Judas Iscariot. M. N. Martin.
Judas Iscariot. R. A. K. Mason.
Judas Iscariot. Spender.
Last Supper; Jesus to Judas. Damon.
Simon and Judas. K. W. Porter.
Wife of Judas Iscariot, The. C. Y. Rice.

JUDE, SAINT. *See* SIMON, SAINT, AND SAINT JUDE.

JUDGMENT DAY
Day of Doom, The. Wigglesworth.
Day of Judgement, The. Swift.

JUDGMENT DAY (*continued*)
Day of Judgement, The. Watts.
Day of Judgment, The. Buchanan, *tr. fr. Irish.*
Dialogue of the Body with the Soul, Which Is Leading It to Judgment. Jacopone da Todi, *tr. fr. Italian by* Creekmore.
Dies Irae. J. L. Duff.
Dies Irae. Hagerup, *tr. fr. Norwegian by* Allwood.
Dies Irae. Thomas of Celano, *tr. fr. Latin.*
Eternal Justice, The. A. R. Aldrich.
Human Race Comes to Be Judged, The. *Fr.* Christ. Cynewulf.
Judgment Day. W. D. Howells.
Last Judgment, The. *Fr.* Christ 3. *Unknown, tr. fr. Anglo-Saxon by* Kennedy.
Lyke-Wake Dirge, A. *Unknown.*
Poet's Resurrection. *Fr.* To the Pious Memory of Mrs. Anne Killigrew. Dryden.
JUDITH (Apochrypha). Judith of Bethulia. Ransom.
JUGGLERS
Juggler, The. Carman.
Juggler. Wilbur.
JULIAN THE APOSTATE
Julian the Apostate. Denny.
Last Oracle, The. Swinburne.
JULY
July. Clare.
July. Swett.
July. *At. to* Whittier.
July Dawn, A, *sel.* ("We left the city, street and square"). J. F. O'Donnell.
July Meadow. Louise Driscoll.
Labor of Fields. Coatsworth.
Mid-July Twilight, Eight o'Clock. Laforgue, *tr. fr. French by* Smith.
Succession of the Four Sweet Months, The. Herrick.
That's July. Butts.
JUNE
Adlestrop. Edward Thomas.
Dawning of the Day, The. Mangan.
Full early in the morning. *Unknown.*
In June. Nora Perry.
June. Bryant.
June. M. C. Davies.
June. Hopper.
June. Ledwidge.
June. *Fr.* The Vision of Sir Launfal. J. R. Lowell.
June. Wilson MacDonald.
June. Malloch.
June. William Morris.
June. Pawsey.
June. Rand.
June. J. G. Stewart.
June. *Unknown.*
June Bracken and Heather. Tennyson.
June Morning. Hugh McCrae.
June Night. Hazel Hall.
June Nights. Hugo, *tr. fr. French by* Conder.
June Rapture. Angela Morgan.
June Thunder. MacNeice.
Knee-deep in June. Riley.
May and June. *Fr.* Under the Willows. J. R. Lowell.
Naturalist on a June Sunday, The. Speyer.
Night in June, A. *Fr.* The Sun Has Long Been Set. Wordsworth.
Spring Lilt, A. *Unknown.*
Stay, June, Stay! C. G. Rossetti.
Succession of the Four Sweet Months, The. Herrick.
That's June. Butts.
To a June Breeze. Bunner.
What Is So Rare as a Day in June. *Fr.* The Vision of Sir Launfal. J. R. Lowell.
When June Is Come. Robert Bridges.
JUNGFRAU (mountain) Jungfrau's Cry, The. S. A. Brooke.

K

KANE, ELISHA KENT. Kane. Fitz-James O'Brien.
KANGAROOS
I Saw the Beauty Go. Mary Gilmore.
Kangaroo, The. Coatsworth.
Kangaroo. D. H. Lawrence.
Native-born. Langley.
Sing-Song of Old Man Kangaroo, The. Kipling.
KANSAS
Home on the Range, A. Lomax.
Kansas. Vachel Lindsay.
Kansas Emigrants, The. Whittier.
KANT, IMMANUEL. Third Wonder, The. Markham.
KASHMIR, INDIA. Light of the Haram, The. *Fr.* Lalla Rookh. Thomas Moore.
KATHARINE OF ARAGON, QUEEN OF ENGLAND. Ballad for Katharine of Aragon, A. Causley.
KATYDIDS
Katy-did. Lindsay McCoy.
To a Caty-did. Freneau.
To a Katydid. Montague.
To an Insect. O. W. Holmes.
KAYAKS. Kayak, The. *Unknown.*
KAZBEK, MOUNT, CAUCASIA. Monastery on Kazbék. Pushkin, *tr. fr. Russian by* Kisch.
KEARNY, PHILIP. Kearny at Seven Pines. Stedman.
KEARSARGE (ship)
Eagle and Vulture, The. T. B. Read.
Kearsarge. S. W. Mitchell.
Kearsarge, The. Roche.
Kearsarge and *Alabama. Unknown.*
KEATS, JOHN
Adonais. Shelley.
After a Lecture on Keats. O. W. Holmes.
Association Copy. Kurth.
At Lulworth Cove a Century Back. Hardy.
Five English Poets: John Keats. D. G. Rossetti.
For John Keats, Apostle of Beauty. Countee Cullen.
Grave of Keats, The. Oscar Wilde.
John Keats. T. A. Daly.
Keats. Longfellow.
Keats. *Fr.* Ode to England. Lord.
Keats. Reese.
Keats. Tabb.
October XXIX, 1795 (Keats' Birthday). Braithwaite.
Of Melodies Unheard. M. L. Fisher.
On Reading Keats in Wartime. Shapiro.
On the Recent Sale by Auction of Keats's Love-Letters. Oscar Wilde.
Popularity. Robert Browning.
Rome. Hardy.
To John Keats. Leigh Hunt.
To John Keats. Amy Lowell.
To John Keats, Poet. At Springtime. Countee Cullen.
To Keats. Lord Dunsany.
To the Spirit of Keats. J. R. Lowell.
Who Kill'd John Keats? Byron.
KELLY, CAPTAIN COLIN P., JR. Captain Colin P. Kelly, Jr. Nathan.
KEMBLE, JOHN MITCHELL. To J. M. K. Tennyson.
KEMPE, MARGERY. Poem of Margery Kempe, A. Nemerov.
KEMPENFELT, RICHARD. On the Loss of the *Royal George.* Cowper.
KENSINGTON GARDENS, LONDON
Dead Harvest, A. Meynell.
Kensington Garden, *sels.* Tickell.
Kensington Gardens, *sels.* Humbert Wolfe.
Lines Written in Kensington Gardens. Matthew Arnold.
KENT, ENGLAND. Memory of Kent, The. Blunden.
KENTUCKY
Kentucky Mountaineer. *Fr.* Man with a Bull-Tongue Plow. Jesse Stuart.
Kentucky Philosophy. Harrison Robertson.
My Old Kentucky Home. S. C. Foster.
Young Kentucky. Jesse Stuart.
KERGUELEN (islands), INDIAN OCEAN. Beyond Kerguelen. H. C. Kendall.
KEVIN, SAINT. By That Lake Whose Gloomy Shore. Thomas Moore.
KEW GARDENS, LONDON. Barrel Organ, The. Noyes.
KEY WEST, FLORIDA. Key West. Hart Crane.
KIDD, WILLIAM. Captain Kidd. *Unknown.*
KILCASH, IRELAND. Kilcash. *Unknown, tr. fr. Irish by* O'Connor.
KILIMANJARO (mountain). Kilimandjaro. Bayard Taylor.
KILKENNY, IRELAND. Ould Kilkinny. Dollard.
KILLARNEY, IRELAND
Killarney. Falconer.
Killarney. *Fr.* Fand. Larminie.
KILLIECRANKIE, BATTLE OF. Battle of Killiecrankie, The. Aytoun.
KILLIGREW, ANNE. Ode, An, to the Pious Memory of the Accomplished Young Lady, Mrs. Anne Killigrew. Dryden.
KILMALLOCK, IRELAND. Kilmallock. De Vere.
KILMER, JOYCE. Joyce Kilmer. Burr.
KILPATRICK, HUGH JUDSON. Riding with Kilpatrick. Scollard.
KIMBERLEY, UNION OF SOUTH AFRICA. Outside Kimberley. Brettell.
KING, EDWARD
Lycidas. Milton.
On the Memory of Mr. Edward King, Drown'd in the Irish Seas. Cleveland.
KING, HENRY. Henry King. Belloc.
KING, WILLIAM, ARCHBISHOP OF DUBLIN. Excellent New Song upon His Grace Our Good Lord Archbishop of Dublin, An. Swift.

King Philip's War. Lamentable Ballad of the Bloody Brook. E. E. Hale.
Kingcups. Kingcups. Farjeon.
Kingfishers
Kingfisher, The. W. H. Davies.
Kingfisher, The. B. M. Kelly.
Kingfisher, The. *Fr.* Upon Appleton House. Marvell.
There Are Still Kingfishers. A. Y. Campbell.
Kings
Of the Death of Kings. *Fr.* Richard II. Shakespeare.
There Lived a King. W. S. Gilbert.
Thyestes, *sel.* ("Wealth can never produce a king"). Seneca, *tr. fr. Latin by* Hughes.
King's Mountain, battle of. Battle of King's Mountain, The. *Unknown.*
Kipling, Rudyard
Rhyme of the Kipperling, The. Seaman.
To R. K. J. K. Stephen.
Kit-Kat Club. Epigram on the Toasts of the Kit-Kat Club, Anno 1716. Pope.
Kites
How the Little Kite Learned to Fly. *Unknown.*
Kite, The. Behn.
Kite, The. Fang Che Chai, *tr. fr. Chinese by* Hart.
Kite, The. MacEwen.
Kite, The. Moreno Villa, *tr. fr. Spanish by* Turnbull.
Kite, A. *Unknown.*
Kite Days. Mark Sawyer.
Kite-flying. Fenollosa.
Kite Tales. Waldo.
My Kite. Beatrice Brown.
Klondike
Klondike, The. E. A. Robinson.
Klondike Miner, The. *Unknown.*
Knighthood and knights
Astrophel and Stella, *sel.* ("Having this day my horse, my hand, my lance"). Sidney.
False Knight upon the Road, The. *Unknown.*
Flowers in the Valley. *Unknown.*
New Order of Chivalry, A. Peacock.
Riddling Knight, The. *Unknown.*
True Knight, The. *Fr.* The Pastime of Pleasure. Hawes.
Korea
Korea. Vincent Buckley
Ode for the American Dead in Korea. McGrath.
Korsør, Denmark. Korsør. Oehlenschläger, *tr. fr. Danish by* Stork.
Kosciusko, Thaddeus
Koskiusko. S. T. Coleridge.
To Kosciusko. Keats.
Kossuth, Louis
Kossuth. J. R. Lowell.
To Louis Kossuth. Swinburne.
Ku Klux Klan
Ku Kluck Klan. Gellert.
Ku Klux. Cawein.
Kubelik, Jan. Jan Kubelik. Sandburg.
Kuan Yin (Chinese goddess of mercy). Bronze Statuette of Kwan-yin, A. Stork.
Kyoto, Japan. Home Thoughts. Susukida, *tr. fr. Japanese by* Ninomiya *and* Enright.

L

Labor and laborers
All Life Moving to One Measure. W. W. Gibson.
Artisan, The. Alice Brown.
Blessing of Toil. Kiser.
Bricklayer, The. Kazin, *tr. fr. Russian.*
Building a Skyscraper. Dudek.
Burying Ground by the Ties. MacLeish.
Carpenter's Plane, The. Kazin, *tr. fr. Russian by* Deutsch.
Case for the Miners, The. Sassoon.
Child of the Romans. Sandburg.
Clinker, The. *Unknown.*
Day and the Work, The. Markham.
Dedication: "I would the gift I offer here." *Fr.* Songs of Labor. Whittier.
Diggers' Song, The. Winstanley.
Dignity of Labor, The. *Unknown.*
Do Thy Day's Work. *Unknown.*
Equipment. P. L. Dunbar.
Factories, The. Widdemer.
Factory Whistles. Gastev, *tr. fr. Russian by* Deutsch.
Felix Randal. G. M. Hopkins.
Florida Road Workers. Langston Hughes.
Glory to Them. Scruggs.
God and the Strong Ones. Widdemer.
Golf Links, The. Cleghorn.
Gospel of Labor, The. Van Dyke.
Hand of Labor. L. H. Townsend.
Harvest Song, A. Markham.
How Doth the Little Busy Bee. Isaac Watts.
I Was a Labourer. *Fr.* Cycle; Seven War Poems. Jennett.
Ice Handler. Sandburg.
Labor. F. S. Osgood.
Labor ("Labor is wealth"). *Unknown.*
Labor ("We have fed you all"). *Unknown.*
Laborer, The. Clare.
Laborer, The. Dehmel, *tr. fr. German by* Bithell.
Laborer, The. Gallagher.
Laborer, The. Heredia, *tr. fr. French by* Thorley.
Laborer, The. Kazantzakis, *tr. fr. Modern Greek by* Dalven.
Laborer, The. Evan Thomas.
Laborers, The. Palamas, *tr. fr. Modern Greek by* Dalven.
Labour. Sackville-West.
Lay of the Laborer. Hood.
Life-Mosaic. Havergal.
Machine, The. W. W. Gibson.
Man, the Metal-Worker. Bridson.
Man with the Hoe, The. Markham.
March of the Workers, The. William Morris.
Me Johnny Mitchell Man. *Unknown.*
Morning Work. D. H. Lawrence.
Noble Work. Charles Mackay.
O Son of Man, Thou Madest Known. Littlefield.
Old Flagman, The. Sandburg.
On Work. *Fr.* The Prophet. Gibran.
Pittsburgh. Oppenheim.
Platelayer, The. W. W. Gibson.
Prayer, A: "Let me work and be glad." Garrison.
Psalm of Those Who Go Forth before Daylight. Sandburg
Quiet Work. Matthew Arnold.
Reflections in an Iron Works. "Hugh MacDiarmid."
Reveille. Ridge.
Riveter, The. Auslander.
Riveter, The. M. E. Sangster.
Rivets. Olds.
Serf, The. Roy Campbell.
Sheffield Dawn. Bridson.
Six o'Clock. Stickney.
Song of a Factory Girl. Zaturensky.
Song of Christian Workingmen. T. C. Clark.
Song of Labor, The. Lowater.
Song of Street Labor, A. C. A. Lord.
Song of the Lower Classes, The. Ernest Jones.
Song of the Shirt, The. Hood.
Song of the Wage-Slave The. E. C. Jones.
Song of Work, A. Mary Blake.
Song to a Negro Wash-Woman. Langston Hughes.
Song to the Men of England. Shelley.
Stevedores, The. *Fr.* Down the Mississippi. J. G. Fletcher.
Street Scene—1946. Kenneth Porter.
Structural Iron Workers. MacKnight Black.
Sweat-Shop Slaves. C. E. S. Wood.
Tale of How Fadey Learned of the Law Protecting Workingmen, The, *sel.* Mayakovsky *and others, tr. fr. Russian by* Deutsch.
Thinker, The. Braley.
Time-Clock, The. Towne.
Tired Worker, The. Claude McKay.
To Iron-Founders and Others. Bottomley.
Toil. *Unknown.*
Toil Away. J. J. Chapman.
Toiler, The. Markham.
True Aristocrat, The. W. Stewart.
Two Tramps in Mud Time. Robert Frost.
Village Blacksmith, The. Longfellow.
Voice of Toil, The. William Morris.
Washer-Woman, The. Bohanan.
We Are the Burden-Bearers! Stidger.
When Smoke Stood Up from Ludlow. A. E. Housman.
Work. L. J. Block.
Work. E. B. Browning.
Work. Kenyon Cox.
Work. D. H. Lawrence.
Work. J. R Lowell.
Work. Pushkin, *tr. fr. Russian by* Deutsch *and* Yarmolinsky.
Work. J. W. Thompson.
Work. *Fr.* The Three Best Things. Van Dyke.
Work; a Song of Triumph. Angela Morgan.
Workers. Rimbaud, *tr. fr. French by* Flores.
Workers, The. Woodson.
Working Man's Song, The. Blackie.
Workman. *Unknown, tr. fr. Chinese by* Hart.
World Is Waiting for You The. Calkins.
Labor Unions. *See* Unions, Labor.
Labrador. Labrador Night. Leo Cox.
Laburnum. Laburnum. Humbert Wolfe.

LADYBIRDS
Clock-a-clay. Clare.
Lady-Bird. C. A. Bowles.
Lady Bug. C. L. McCoy.
To the Lady-Bird. *Unknown.*
LA FAYETTE, MARIE JOSEPH, MARQUIS DE
La Fayette. S. T. Coleridge.
La Fayette. Dolly Madison.
LAKES AND PONDS
Composed by the Side of Grasmere Lake. Wordsworth.
Lake, The. L. O. Coxe.
Lakes. Auden.
Little Lake, The. Tourian, *tr. fr Armenian by* Blackwell.
Little Lough, The. Hewitt.
Pond, The. Droste-Hülshoff, *tr. fr. German by* Salinger.
Pond, The. Nemerov.
Pond, The. Jane Taylor.
Pool, The. Alice Corbin.
Pool, The. Pickthall.
Shaded Pool, The. Norman Gale.
Spell of the Pool, The. L. B. Crane.
Spring Pools. Robert Frost.
To Leven Water. Smollett.
To the Lakes. W. W. Campbell.
Tropical Pool. Muna Lee.
Unnamed Lake, The. F. G. Scott.
LALEMANT, GABRIEL
Brébeuf and Lalemant. Alan Sullivan.
Père Lalement. Pickthall.
LAMB, CHARLES
Charles Lamb. Beatty.
This Lime-Tree Bower My Prison. S. T. Coleridge.
Written after the Death of Charles Lamb. Wordsworth.
LAMB, MARY. To the Sister of Elia. Landor.
LAMBS
For a Lamb. Eberhart.
I Held a Lamb. Worthington.
Lamb, The. *Fr.* Songs of Innocence. Blake.
Lamb, The. Greenaway.
Lamb, The. *Unknown.*
Lamb. Humbert Wolfe.
Lambs. Tynan.
Lambs at Play. Bloomfield.
Lambs in the Meadow. Alma-Tadema.
Little Lamb Went Straying, A. Midland.
Little Young Lambs, The. Chalmers.
Mary and Her Lamb. S. J. Hale.
On the Grassy Banks. *Fr.* Sing-Song. C. G. Rossetti.
Pet Lamb, The. Wordsworth.
Sheep and Lambs. Tynan.
Young Lambs. Clare.
LAMPLIGHTERS
Lamplighter, The. R. L. Stevenson.
Light the Lamps Up, Lamplighter. Farjeon.
LAMPMAN, ARCHIBALD. Bereavement of the Fields. W. W. Campbell.
LAMPS. On a Lamp. Mörike, *tr. fr. German by* Flores.
LANCELOT DU LAC
Lancelot and Elaine. *Fr.* Idylls of the King. Tennyson.
Parting of Launcelot and Guinevere. Phillips.
Taliessin's Song of Lancelot's Mass. Charles Williams.
LANDOR, WALTER SAVAGE
In Memory of Walter Savage Landor. Swinburne.
Landor. Albee.
Landor. Japp.
LANDRAILS. *See* CORNCRAKES.
LANG, ANDREW
Ballade of Andrew Lang. MacColl.
To Andrew Lang. R. L. Stevenson.
LANGUAGE
Conversational Reformer, The. Harry Graham.
English Language, The. W. W. Story.
Languages. Sandburg.
Latin Tongue, The. J. J. Daly.
Letter to a Teacher of English. Hillyer.
Our Anglo-Saxon Tongue. J. B. Hope.
Our Mother Tongue. R. M. Milnes.
Pretty Words. Elinor Wylie.
Rhyme for a Phonetician. Cornford.
Upon Dr. Davies' British Grammar. James Howell.
LANIER, SIDNEY. At Lanier's Grave. Tabb.
LAOCOON. Laocoon. Donald Hall.
LAO-TZE. Lao-tzu. Po Chü-i, *tr. fr. Chinese by* Waley.
LAPRAIK, JOHN. Epistle to John Lapraik, an Old Scottish Bard. Burns.
LA PRAIRIE, BATTLE OF. Battle of La Prairie, The. Lighthall.
LAPWINGS. O Lapwing! Blake.
LARCH TREES
Larch Trees. Faber.
Larch Wood Secrets. Eastwick.
Song of the Wulfshaw Larches. Rhys.
LARKS
Address to the Woodlark. Burns.
Caged Sylark, The. G. M. Hopkins.
Ecstatic, The. Day Lewis.
First Skylark of Spring, The. Sir William Watson.
Green Cornfield, A. C. G. Rossetti.
Hark! Hark! the Lark. *Fr.* Cymbeline. Shakespeare.
Heaven Soaring Lark, The. M. E. Roberts.
Lark. Josephine Miles.
Lark, The. Reese.
Lark, The. Ronsard, *tr. fr. French by* Conder.
Lark, The. *Unknown.*
Lark and the Nightingale, The. Hartley Coleridge.
Lark and the Rook, The. *Unknown.*
Lark Ascending, The. George Meredith.
Lark Descending. Blunden.
Lark in the Morning, The. *Unknown.*
Lark Now Leaves His Wat'ry Nest, The. Davenant.
Larks. Tynan.
Lark's Grave, The. Westwood.
Lark's Nest, A. Smart.
Lark's Song, The. "Seumas O'Sullivan."
Late Lark, A. Henley.
Little Red Lark, The. A. P. Graves.
Merry Lark, The. Kingsley.
O Skylarks, Teach Japan to Sing. Kagawa, *tr. fr. Japanese by* Erickson.
On First Having Heard the Skylark. Millay.
Over Salève. G. H. Clarke.
Sea and the Skylark, The. G. M. Hopkins.
Shelley's Skylark. Hardy.
Shepherds Who Pastures Seek. Trench.
Sir Lark and King Sun. *Fr.* Adela Cathcart. George Macdonald.
Skylark, The. James Hogg.
Skylark, The. C. G. Rossetti.
Skylark, The. Frederick Tennyson.
Song of the Lark, The. George Macdonald.
Super-Lark, The. R. H. Long.
To a Lark in War-Time. Werfel, *tr. fr. German by* Snow.
To a Skylark. Shelley.
To a Skylark ("Ethereal minstrel!"). Wordsworth.
To a Skylark ("Up with me!"). Wordsworth.
To a Skylark, Singing above Barnhill Poorhouse, Glasgow. Quin.
To the Lark. Herrick.
Upon the Lark and the Fowler. Bunyan.
Violinist, A. Bourdillon.
Waking of the Lark, The. Eric Mackay.
Word with a Skylark, A. Piatt.
LARKSPUR
Blue Larkspur. Sister Mariella.
Wild Larkspur. Dalton.
LATIN. Latin. *Unknown.*
LAUGHTER. Laughter. I. V. Crawford.
LAUNDRY AND LAUNDERING
Alvorada: "Girl arose so lovely, The." King Dinis, *tr. fr. Portuguese by* Thornton.
Old Ellen Sullivan. Winifred Welles.
LAURELS
Laurels and Immortelles. *Unknown.*
To Laurels. Herrick.
LAURENTIAN MOUNTAINS, QUEBEC. Laurentians, The. Bourinot.
LAVAL, FRANÇOIS XAVIER DE. Laval; Noble Educator. J. D. Logan.
LAVENDER
Lavender. Noyes.
Lavender Beds, The. Rands.
Lavender Bush, The. Fleming.
Lavender's Blue. *Unknown.*
Lavender's for Ladies. Chalmers.
LAWES, HENRY
To Mr. H. Lawes on His Airs. Milton.
To M. Henry Lawes, the Excellent Composer, of His Lyrics. Herrick.
To Mr. Henry Lawes, Who Had Then Newly Set a Song of Mine, in the Year 1635. Waller.
LAWRENCE, DAVID HERBERT. Elegy for D. H. Lawrence, An. W. C. Williams.
LAWRENCE, JAMES. Grave of Lawrence, The. Scollard.
LAWRENCE, THOMAS EDWARD. Lawrence; the Last Crusade, *sel.* ("Out of the East the plane spun"). Selden Rodman.
LAWRENCE, KANSAS. Defense of Lawrence, The. Realf.
LAWRENCE JUSTINIAN, SAINT. San Lorenzo Giustiniani's Mother. Alice Meynell.
LAWYERS AND LAW
Concerning Lawyers. *Fr.* Palace Rhymes. López de Ayala, *tr. fr. Spanish by* Morley.
Law like Love. Auden.
Laws of God, the Laws of Man, The. A. E. Housman.
Lawyer's Farewell to His Muse, The. Blackstone.
Lawyer's Invocation to Spring. Brownell.
Lawyers Know Too Much, The. Sandburg.
Statute. Josephine Miles.

You, Casey, long a baker. Martial, *tr. fr. Latin by* "T. W. M."
LAZARUS
Convert, The. Chesterton.
Dives and Lazarus. *Unknown.*
Epistle, An, Containing the Strange Medical Experience of Karshish, the Arab Physician. Robert Browning.
Lazarus. Ursula Wood.
Lazarus Walks in the Alps. Ernest Walsh.
Vision of Lazarus, The, *sel.* ("Another sate near him"). Fenton Johnson.
LEADERSHIP
God, Give Us Men! Holland.
Leader, A. "Æ."
Masters. Amis.
LEAGUE OF NATIONS
League of Nations, The. Siegrist.
League of Nations. N. B. Turner.
LEAR, KING
Albion's England, *sel.* ("Now of the conqueror this isle had Brutain unto name"). Warner.
King Lear, *sels.* Shakespeare.
Lear. Hood.
On Sitting Down to Read "King Lear" Once Again. Keats.
LEAR, EDWARD
By Way of Preface. Lear.
Edward Lear. Auden.
How Pleasant to Know Mr. Lear. Lear.
Self-Portrait of the Laureate of Nonsense. Lear.
LEARNING
After Passing the Examination. Po Chü-i, *tr. fr. Chinese by* Waley.
Father's Testament, A. Judah ibn Tibbon, *tr. fr. Hebrew by* Abrahams.
Learning. Barnes.
Learning. Fullerton.
Little Learning Is a Dangerous Thing, A. *Fr.* An Essay on Criticism. Pope.
Musophilus. Daniel.
On the Prospect of Planting Arts and Learning in America. George Berkeley.
To a Boy. *Unknown, tr. fr. Irish by* O'Connor.
To Young Imaginaries in Knowledge. *Fr.* Seven Penitential Psalms. Petrarch, *tr. fr. Italian by* Chapman.
LEAVES
Burning Leaves. C. E. Eaton.
Burning of the Leaves, The. Binyon.
City of Falling Leaves, The. Amy Lowell.
College of Surgeons, The. James Stephens.
Come, Little Leaves. George Cooper.
Fallen Leaves. Tupper.
How the Leaves Came Down. "Susan Coolidge."
Leaf-Treader, A. Robert Frost.
Leaves. Rowena Baker.
Leaves. W. H. Davies.
Leaves. Teasdale.
Leaves. Tynan.
Leaves, The. *Unknown.*
Leaves. Westrup.
Leaves at My Window. Piatt.
Leaves Drink, The. Alice Wilkins.
Maple Leaves. T. B. Aldrich.
To an Autumn Leaf. Albert Mathews.
Windfall. F. R. Scott.
LEDA
Leda and the Swan. Gogarty.
Leda and the Swan. Yeats.
LEDO ROAD. Conversation Piece. Dawless.
LEDWIDGE, FRANCIS
For Francis Ledwidge. O'Conor.
Francis Ledwidge. Hilda Conkling.
In Memoriam: Francis Ledwidge. O'Conor.
LEE, NATHANIEL. Nat Lee's Images. *Fr.* To Mr. Lee, on His Alexander. Dryden.
LEE, ROBERT EDWARD
Lee. Archibald Rutledge.
Lee in the Mountains. Donald Davidson.
Lee to the Rear. J. R. Thompson.
Lee's Parole. Manville.
Our Dead Heroes. M. B. Wharton.
Robert E. Lee. J. W. Howe.
Statue Inscribed "Lee," Richmond. Leitch.
Sword of Robert Lee, The. A. J. Ryan.
LEGREE, SIMON. Simon Legree—a Negro Sermon. Vachel Lindsay.
LEICESTER, ROBERT DUDLEY, EARL OF. Epitaph on the Earl of Leicester. Ralegh.
LEIDEN, HOLLAND. Word of God to Leyden Came, The. Rankin.
LEIF ERICSSON. Saga of Leif the Lucky. Hervey Allen.
LEIGH, AUGUSTA. Stanzas to Augusta. Byron.
LEINSTER, IRELAND. In Leinster. Guiney.
LEISURE
Leisure. W. H. Davies.
Walking at Leisure. Wang Wei, *tr. fr. Chinese.*
LEMONADE. Lemonade Stand. D. B. Thompson.
LENIN, VLADIMIR ILYICH
Death of Lenin, The. *Fr.* Vladimir Ilyich-Lenin. Mayakovsky, *tr. fr. Russian by* Lindsay.
Five Days and Nights. Inber, *tr. fr. Russian by* Lindsay.
Lenin, *sel.* ("So I came down the steps"). Wellesley.
No One Knew. "Demyan Bedny," *tr. fr. Russian.*
Skeleton of the Future, The. "Hugh MacDiarmid."
LENT
Easter. Whitaker.
Lent. Rodgers.
Stanzas for Lent. James Howell.
To Keep a True Lent. Herrick.
Two Old Lenten Rhymes. *Unknown.*
LEON, LUIS DE. After Reading Saint Teresa, Luis de Leon, and Ramon Lull. Muna Lee.
LEONARDO DA VINCI
Leonardo da Vinci. T. S. Jones, Jr.
There Lived a Lady in Milan. W. R. Benét.
LEONIDAS
Imaginary Dialogue. Fitts.
Leonidas. Croly.
LEOPARDI, GIACOMO. To Giacomo Leopardi. T. S. Moore.
LEOPOLD III, KING OF THE BELGIANS. Moon and the Night and the Men, The. Berryman.
LEPANTO, BATTLE OF. Lepanto. Chesterton.
LEPERS
Leper, The. Swinburne.
Leper, The. Willis.
Leper of London, The. Scheffauer.
Leper Island. Avis.
LESBOS (island), GREECE
Lesbos. Baudelaire, *tr. fr. French by* Gibbs.
Night in Lesbos, A. George Horton.
L'ESTRANGE, SIR ROGER. Loyalty Confin'd. L'Estrange.
LETTERS
Letter, The. Amy Lowell.
Letters. Emerson.
Letters, The. Tennyson.
Letters Found near a Suicide. Horne.
Missive, The. Gosse.
My letters! all dead paper, mute and white! *Fr.* Sonnets from the Portuguese. E. B. Browning.
Night Mail. Auden.
Pillar-Box, The. Wolker, *tr. fr. Czech by* Selver.
Postman's Bell Is Answered Everywhere, The. Horace Gregory.
Way I read a letter's this, The. Emily Dickinson.
LEVEN (river), SCOTLAND. Ode to Leven Water. Smollett.
LEVETT [*or* LEVET], ROBERT. On the Death of Mr. Robert Levet. Samuel Johnson.
LEWIS, MERIWETHER. On the Discoveries of Captain Lewis. Joel Barlow.
LEXINGTON, BATTLE OF
Lexington. O. W. Holmes.
Lexington. *Fr.* The Psalm of the West. Lanier.
Lexington. Whittier.
New England's Chevy Chase. E. E. Hale.
Song for Lexington, A. R. K. Weeks.
LIBERALISM AND LIBERALS
Lost Leader, The. Robert Browning.
Why I Am a Liberal. Robert Browning.
LIBERTY. *See* FREEDOM.
LIBERTY, STATUE OF
Bartholdi Statue, The. Whittier.
Fairest of Freedom's Daughters. Rankin.
Liberty Enlightening the World. Van Dyke.
New Colossus, The. Lazarus.
Statue of Liberty, The. Crooke.
Statue of Liberty, The. Masters.
To the Goddess of Liberty. Sterling.
LIBRARIES
British Museum Reading Room, The. MacNeice.
In a Library. Richard Burton.
In an Old Library. Yuan Mei, *tr. fr. Chinese by* Cranmer-Byng.
In the Library. *Fr.* Lyrics from a Library. Scollard.
In the Public Library. Alderson.
Library, The, *sels.* Crabbe.
Library, The. B. A. Huff.
Library, The. F. D. Sherman.
Library, The. Whittier.
My Library. Stockard.
Precious, mouldering pleasure 'tis, A. Emily Dickinson.
Public Library. C. T. Stevenson.
LICE
Louse Crept Out of My Lady's Shift, A. Bottomley.
To a Louse. Burns.
LIDICE, CZECHOSLOVAKIA
Lady of Lidice. Chavez.
Lidice. Leitch.
Lidice. "Lucio."
Lidice. Schiff.

LIÈGE, BELGIUM. Between Namur and Liège. Wordsworth.
LIÈVRE (river), QUEBEC. Dawn on the Lièvre, The. Lampman.
LIFE
Any Man's Advice to His Son. Fearing.
Anyone Lived in a Pretty How Town. E. E. Cummings.
Ballad of the Outer Life. Hofmannsthal, *tr. fr. German by* Hamburger.
Comparison of Life and Death. *Unknown.*
Dying Enthusiast, The. Mangan.
For an Autograph. J. R. Lowell.
For Life I Had Never Cared Greatly. Hardy.
I Am a Parcel of Vain Strivings Tied. Thoreau.
I Ponder on Life. Ehrmann.
In My End Is My Beginning. Rosemary Dobson.
Life. Barbauld
Life. Bonar.
Life. Charlotte Brontë.
Life. Alice Brown.
Life. "Barry Cornwall."
Life. Crabbe.
Life. P. L. Dunbar.
Life. George Herbert.
Life. Naidu.
Life. Sill.
Life. Wheelock.
Life, a Question. C. R. Robinson.
Life and Death. L. C. Perry.
Life and Death. C. G. Rossetti.
Life and Death. D. C. Scott.
Life in her creaking shoes. Henley.
Life Is a Dream, *sel.* ("We live, while"). Calderón de la Barca, *tr. fr. Spanish by* Symons.
Life is a poet's fable. *Unknown.*
Life Is Struggle. Clough.
Madrigal: "This life, which seems so fair." Drummond of Hawthornden.
May It Be. Pasternak, *tr. fr. Russian by* Bowra.
Meditation, A. Eberhart.
Mother of Us All, The, *sel.* ("We cannot retrace our steps"). Gertrude Stein.
My life had stood a loaded gun. Emily Dickinson.
Of Human Life. Henry King.
Of Life. Lang.
Our Lives Are Rivers. Urbina, *tr. fr. Spanish by* Beckett.
Our share of night to bear. Emily Dickinson.
Permanency of Life, The. Drummond of Hawthornden.
Psalm of Life, A. Longfellow.
Responding Voice. Icaza, *tr. fr. Spanish by* Beckett.
Sic Vita. Braithwaite.
Sic Vita. Henry King.
Song of Life. Hofmannsthal, *tr. fr. German by* Durling.
Song of Life, A. Werfel, *tr. fr. German by* Snow.
Sonnet: "You were born; must die." Spender.
Story of Life, The. Saxe.
Substance, Shadow, and Spirit. Tao Yuan-ming, *tr. fr. Chinese by* Waley.
Sunday Morning. Wallace Stevens.
Triumph of Life, The. Shelley.
Various the Roads of Life. Landor.
Voyage, The. Baudelaire, *tr. fr. French by* Gibbs.
Voyage of Life, The. *Fr.* Christ 2. Cynewulf, *tr. fr. Anglo-Saxon by* Kennedy.
Voyage to Cythera, A. Baudelaire, *tr. fr. French by* Morgan.
Weaker the Wine, The. Su T'ung-po, *tr. fr. Chinese by* Rexroth.
What Is Our Life? Ralegh.
When I Consider Life. *Fr.* Aureng-Zebe. Dryden.
Who Has Ever Held Life in His Hand. Platen, *tr. fr. German by* Morgan.
LIFFEY (river), IRELAND. To the Liffey with the Swans. Gogarty.
LIGHT
Hymn: To Light. Cowley.
Light at Equinox. Léonie Adams.
LIGHTHOUSES
Flannan Isle. W. W. Gibson.
I'd Like to Be a Lighthouse. Rachel Field.
Lighthouse, The. Sir Walter Scott.
Light-House, The. *Unknown.*
Lighthouse, The. Marjorie Wilson.
Ode to the Lighthouse at Malta. Duque de Rivas, *tr. fr. Spanish.*
LIGHTNING
Lightning is a yellow fork, The. Emily Dickinson.
Young Mystic, The. Louis Untermeyer.
LILACS
Beyond. T. S. Jones, Jr.
Lilac, The. William Barnes.
Lilac. Flint.
Lilac, The. Humbert Wolfe.
Lilac Dusk. Reese.
Lilacs. Hilda Conkling.
Lilacs. Amy Lowell.
Night Lilac. Van Doren.
When Lilacs Last in the Dooryard Bloom'd. Whitman.
With Lilacs. Crandall.
LILIES
Lilies. Colum.
Lilies. Ibn Darraj, *tr. fr. Arabic by* Arberry.
Lilies. Marquis.
Lilies. Shiko, *tr. fr. Japanese.*
Lilies and Roses. Ibn al-Qutiya, *tr. fr. Arabic by* Arberry.
Little White Lily. George Macdonald.
Mariposa Lily, The. Coolbrith.
On Easter Day. Thaxter.
Song of the Lilies, The. Wheelock.
Tiger-Lilies. T. B. Aldrich.
White Lily. Sandoval y Zapata, *tr. fr. Spanish by* Beckett.
Whitely the Lily Wavers. Platen, *tr. fr. German by* Morgan.
LILIES OF THE VALLEY
Lilies of the Valley. M. M. Walker.
Lily of the Valley, The. Beddoes.
LILITH
Body's Beauty. *Fr.* The House of Life. D. G. Rossetti.
Eden Bower. D. G. Rossetti.
LIMERICK, IRELAND
Blacksmith of Limerick, The. R. D. Joyce.
Limerick Town, *sel.* ("Here I've got you, Philip Desmond, standing in the market-place"). J. F. O'Donnell.
LIMERICKS. *Little Book of Limericks, The* (LiBL). H. I. Brock, ed.
LINCOLN, ABRAHAM
Abraham Lincoln. A. S. Ames.
Abraham Lincoln. Auslander.
Abraham Lincoln. S. V. Benét.
Abraham Lincoln. Joel Benton.
Abraham Lincoln. V. F. Boyle.
Abraham Lincoln. H. H. Brownell.
Abraham Lincoln. Bryant.
Abraham Lincoln. S. V. Cole.
Abraham Lincoln, *sel.* ("Kinsmen, you shall behold"). Drinkwater.
Abraham Lincoln. Meigs.
Abraham Lincoln. F. F. Miller.
Abraham Lincoln. Stedman.
Abraham Lincoln ("Not as when some great captain falls"). Stoddard.
Abraham Lincoln ("This man whose homely face"). Stoddard.
Abraham Lincoln. Tom Taylor (*sometimes wr. at. to* Lemon *or* Brooks).
Abraham Lincoln. Whitaker.
Abraham Lincoln, the Master. T. C. Clark.
Abraham Lincoln Walks at Midnight. Vachel Lindsay.
Anne Rutledge. *Fr.* Spoon River Anthology. E. L. Masters.
At the Lincoln Memorial. W. E. Brooks.
Ballad of the Lincoln Penny. Kreymborg.
Cenotaph of Lincoln, The. J. T. McKay.
Death of Lincoln, The. Bryant.
Farmer Remembers Lincoln, A. Bynner.
February Twelfth. Hepburn.
For February Twelfth. Gessner.
Glory of Lincoln, The. T. C. Clark.
Hand of Lincoln, The. Stedman.
His Living Monument. Minna Irving.
House in Springfield. Burket.
How Shall We Honor Lincoln? T. C. Clark.
Hush'd Be the Camps Today. Whitman.
If Lincoln Should Return. Bruner.
In Hardin County, 1809. L. E. Thompson.
John Brown's Body, *sel.* ("Lincoln, six feet one in his stocking feet"). S. V. Benét.
Kentucky Birthday; February 12, 1815. Frances Frost.
Lincoln. *Fr.* Our Heroic Times. Boker.
Lincoln. J. V. Cheney.
Lincoln. J. G. Clark.
Lincoln. Ditmars.
Lincoln. P. L. Dunbar.
Lincoln. J. G. Fletcher.
Lincoln. J. L. Hardy.
Lincoln. C. W. Hill.
Lincoln. J. W. Howe.
Lincoln. Walter Malone.
Lincoln. S. W. Mitchell.
Lincoln. J. L. Pearson.
Lincoln. J. W. Riley.
Lincoln. C. R. Robinson.
Lincoln. Schwartz.
Lincoln. Laura Simmons.
Lincoln. W. P. Stafford.
Lincoln. Maurice Thompson.
Lincoln. Trowbridge.
Lincoln. N. B. Turner.

Lincoln. Tyrrell.
Lincoln ("Lincoln, when men"). *Unknown.*
Lincoln and Liberty. Simpson.
Lincoln at Gettysburg. T. C. Clark.
Lincoln at Gettysburg. *Fr.* The Gettysburg Ode. Bayard Taylor.
Lincoln Calls for Volunteers. *Fr.* John Brown's Body. S. V. Benét.
Lincoln Child, The. Oppenheim.
Lincoln Circuit, The. Laughlin.
Lincoln, Come Back. T. C. Clark.
Lincoln Memorial. A. A. Wiley.
Lincoln Portrait. Copland.
Lincoln Statue, The. W. F. Collins.
Lincoln, the Man of the People. Markham.
Lincoln Triumphant. Markham.
Lincoln's Birthday. J. K. Bangs.
Lincoln's Birthday. Dole.
Lincoln's Birthday. Stoddard.
Lincoln's Birthday. Woodbury.
Lincoln's Grave, *sels.* Maurice Thompson.
Lord Lovel (B *vers., parody*). *Unknown.*
Man of Men, A. Van Noppen.
Man of Peace, The. Carman.
Martyr, The. Melville.
Master, The. E. A. Robinson.
Master, Make Us One! *Fr.* Lincoln; an Ode. Hagedorn.
Nancy Hanks. Rosemary Benét.
O Captain! My Captain! Whitman.
Ode Recited at the Harvard Commemoration, July 21, 1865. J. R. Lowell.
Old Abe Lincoln. *Unknown.*
On a Bust of Lincoln. Scollard.
On a Picture of Lincoln. Cheney.
On the Life-Mask of Abraham Lincoln. Gilder.
One of Our Presidents. Stafford.
Parricide. J. W. Howe.
People, Yes, The, *sel.* ("Lincoln?/He was a mystery in smoke and flags"). Sandburg.
Prairie. Llewellyn.
President Lincoln's Grave. C. A. Mason.
Remembering Lincoln. Mundorf.
Snarlers, The. Guiterman.
Soliloquy of Lincoln before Manassas. *Fr.* John Brown's Body. S. V. Benét.
Soul of Lincoln, The. Piety.
Star of Sangamon, The. L. W. Allen.
This Dust Was Once the Man. *Fr.* Memories of President Lincoln. Whitman.
"Thou Shouldst Be Living at This Hour." West.
Three Hundred Thousand More. Gibbons.
To Abraham Lincoln. Piatt.
To Borglum's Seated Statue of Abraham Lincoln. C. B. Jordan.
To the Memory of Abraham Lincoln. Bryant.
Tolling. Larcom.
Tribute, A ("Lincoln, the man who freed the slave"). *Unknown.*
Warning for Abraham Lincoln, A. Fombona Pachano, *tr. fr. Spanish by* Flores.
Washington and Lincoln. Stafford.
When Lilacs Last in the Dooryard Bloom'd. Whitman.
Young Lincoln. Markham.
Your Glory, Lincoln. Goodman.
Lincoln's Birthday (Our American Holidays Series) (LBAH). Robert Haven Schauffler, ed.
LINCOLN CATHEDRAL, ENGLAND. At Lincoln. O. F. Adams.
LINCOLNSHIRE, ENGLAND
High Tide on the Coast of Lincolnshire, The. Ingelow.
Lincolnshire Remembered. Cornford.
LIND, JENNY. Aquarium. Gorostiza, *tr. fr. Spanish by* Walsh.
LINDBERGH, CHARLES
Lindbergh. Michaelis.
Lindbergh. Angela Morgan.
Lindbergh. Stafford.
Lindbergh; a Ballad. Laing.
Lyric Deed, The. Neihardt.
Skoal! Charles Lindbergh, Skoal! *Unknown.*
LINDSAY, VACHEL
In Memory of Vachel Lindsay. Teasdale.
Vachel Lindsay. S. K. Russell.
LINNETS
Green Linnet, The. Wordsworth.
Grey Linnet, The. McCarroll.
I Heard a Linnet Courting. Robert Bridges.
Linnet, The. De la Mare.
Linnet in a Gilded Cage, A. C. G. Rossetti.
Linnet on the Bough, The. *Fr.* Dione. Gay.
Sir Walter Raleigh to a Caged Linnet. Lee-Hamilton.
To a Linnet. Robert Allan.
To a Linnet in a Cage. Ledwidge.
Young Linnets, The. Hawkshaw.
LIONS
Captive Lion, The. W. H. Davies.
Lion, A. J. G. Francis.
Lion, The. Howitt.
Lion, The. Vachel Lindsay.
Lion. M. B. Miller.
Lion, The. Nash.
Lion. *Fr.* A Bestiary. Rexroth.
Lion, The. W. J. Turner.
Lion and Lioness. Markham.
Lion at Noon, The. Hugo, *tr. fr. French by* Martin.
Lion Grown Old, The. La Fontaine, *tr. fr. French by* Wright.
Lion-House, The. Wheelock.
Lion Path, The. C. P. Gilman.
Lion's Cub, The. Maurice Thompson.
Lion's Nature, The. *Fr.* The Bestiary. *Unknown.*
Lion's Ride, The. Freiligrath, *tr. fr. German.*
Lions Running over the Green. Wynne.
Lion's Skeleton, The. C. T. Turner.
Plains, The. Roy Fuller.
LI PO
Invitation to Li Po, An. Ts'ui Tsung-chi, *tr. fr. Chinese by* Shigeyoshi Obata.
Li Po. Ruth Gilbert.
Thinking of Li Po. Tu Fu, *tr. fr. Chinese.*
To Li Po. Tu Fu, *tr. fr. Chinese.*
To Li Po on a Spring Day. Tu Fu, *tr. fr. Chinese.*
LISMORE, IRELAND. Old Church at Lismore, The. Downing.
LITTLE BIGHORN, BATTLE OF
Death of Custer, The. J. W. Crawford.
Down the Little Big Horn. Francis Brooks.
Little Big Horn. McGaffey.
Miles Keogh's Horse. John Hay.
Revenge of Rain-in-the-Face, The. Longfellow.
LIVE-OAK TREES. I Saw in Louisiana a Live-Oak Growing. Whitman.
LIVERPOOL, ENGLAND. Dawn at Liverpool. *Fr.* Sonnets of the Empire. Strong.
LIVINGSTONE, DAVID. David Livingstone. *Unknown.*
LIZARD HEAD, ENGLAND. To Lizard Head. Laube.
LIZARDS
Lizard, The. A. F. Brown.
Lower Animals. Alan Anderson.
Old Man to the Lizard, The. MacLeish.
LLAMAS
In Praise of Llamas. Guiterman.
Llama, The. Belloc.
LOBSTERS. Lobster, The. *Unknown.*
LODGE, THOMAS. Barnabe Rich, Gentleman Soldier, in Praise of the Author. Barnabe Rich.
LOCOMOTIVES
Locomotive. Nakano, *tr. fr. Japanese by* Ninomiya *and* Enright.
To a Locomotive in Winter. Whitman.
LOCUSTS
Coyote and the Locust, The. *Tr. fr. Zuni Indian by* Cushing.
Four Things. Proverbs, Bible, *O.T.*
Locust Hunt, The. Philip Murray.
Locust Swarm, The. Hsu Chao, *tr. fr. Chinese by* Rexroth.
No King. Guiterman.
LODORE, ENGLAND. Cataract of Lodore, The. Southey.
LOGAN, JOHN ALEXANDER. Logan at Peach Tree Creek. Garland.
LONDON, ENGLAND
After London. Pellow.
Annus Mirabilis, *sel.* ("But ah! how unsincere are all our joys!"). Dryden.
At Piccadilly Circus. Pinto.
Ballad of the Londoner. Flecker.
Barrel-Organ, The. Noyes.
Bells of London, The. *Unknown.*
Building of London, The. *Fr.* The Brut. Layamon, *tr. fr. Middle English.*
City Show, The. Farjeon.
Composed upon Westminster Bridge, September 3, 1802. Wordsworth.
Dawn in London. Tikhonov, *tr. fr. Russian by* Lindsay.
Description of a City Shower, A. Swift.
East London. Matthew Arnold.
Farewell to London in the Year 1715, A. Pope.
Fleet Street. Arthur Adams.
Fleet Street. Shane Leslie.
Going Up to London. N. B. Turner.
Hay's Wharf. Richard Church.
His Return to London. Herrick.
Impression de Nuit; London. Lord Alfred Douglas.
In Honour of the City of London. William Dunbar.
In Lady Street. Drinkwater.
In Regent's Park. Ridler.
In the Mile End Road. Amy Levy.
Lines to a Dictator. Leitch.
London. *Fr.* Songs of Experience. Blake.
London. John Davidson.

LONDON, ENGLAND (*continued*)
London. F. S. Flint.
London. Samuel Johnson.
London. I. R. McLeod.
London. Rhys.
London. T. P. C. Wilson.
London Bridge. Weatherly.
London Churches. R. M. Milnes.
London Despair. Cornford.
London, 1802. Wordsworth.
London Feast. Rhys.
London Idyll, A. "John Presland."
London Interior. Harold Monro.
London Is a Fine Town. *Unknown.*
London Lickpenny. *Unknown.*
London Nightfall. J. G. Fletcher.
London, 1941. Peake.
London Revisited—1946. Livesay.
London River. Weatherly.
London Sad London. *Unknown.*
London Snow. Robert Bridges.
London Squares. Sir Osbert Sitwell.
London Thoroughfare Two A.M., A. Amy Lowell.
London Town. Lionel Johnson.
London Town. Masefield.
London under Bombardment. Briggs.
London Voluntaries. Henley.
Margaret Roper's Vision of Her Father, Sir Thomas More. *Fr.* London Bridge. F. T. Palgrave.
New London, The. *Fr.* Annus Mirabilis. Dryden.
November Blue. Alice Meynell.
Oh, Blank Confusion. *Fr.* The Prelude. Wordsworth.
Of London Bridge, and the Stupendous Sight, and Structure Thereof. James Howell.
On the Lord Mayor and Court of Aldermen. Marvell.
Parliament Hill. Bashford.
Piccadilly. Thomas Burke.
Primrose Hill. Custance.
Quo Ruis ab Demens? London's Progress. Thomas Freeman.
Rotten Row. Locker-Lampson.
Satire on London, A. Earl of Surrey.
Shining Streets of London, The. Noyes.
Slaves to London. Motteux.
Song: "Closes and courts and lanes." John Davidson.
Spring in Oxford Street. Presland.
Streets of Laredo, The. MacNeice.
To the City of London. William Dunbar.
Trivia; or, The Art of Walking the Streets of London, *sels.* Gay.
Troynovant. *Fr.* Entertainment to James. Thomas Dekker.
West London. Matthew Arnold.
Which is the way to London Town. *Unknown.*
Ye Flags of Piccadilly. Clough.
Yesterday in Oxford Street. Fyleman.
LONDONDERRY, NORTHERN IRELAND. Maiden City, The. Tonna.
LONELINESS
Alone. Manger, *tr. fr. Yiddish by* Betsky.
Bereft. Robert Frost.
Buried Life, The. Matthew Arnold.
Desert Places. Robert Frost.
Invitation to Hsiao Chü-shih. Po Chü-i, *tr. fr. Chinese by* Waley.
Loneliness. Edwin Essex.
Loneliness. *Fr.* The Hill Wife. Robert Frost.
Loneliness. Rilke, *tr. fr. German by* Flores.
Loneliness. Werfel, *tr. fr. German by* Snow.
Lonely. Reese.
Lonely. Spire, *tr. fr. French by* Bithell.
Lonely Child, The. Ernest Briggs.
Lonely Night in Early Autumn. Po Chü-i, *tr. fr. Chinese.*
Lonely Wife, The. Li Po, *tr. fr. Chinese by* Ayscough *and* Lowell.
Mnemosyne. Stickney.
Mr. Flood's Party. E. A. Robinson.
On Being Removed from Hsün-yang and Sent to Chungchou. Po Chü-i, *tr. fr. Chinese by* Waley.
Watch-Tower of the Soul, The. Branch.
LONG, CRAWFORD WILLIAMSON. Crawford Long and William Morton. Rosemary *and* S. V. Benét.
LONG, HUEY. Road, The. Plutzik.
LONGFELLOW, HENRY WADSWORTH
H. W. L. John Nichol.
Henry Wadsworth Longfellow. Dobson.
Henry Wadsworth Longfellow. W. W. Story.
Longfellow. T. B. Aldrich.
Longfellow. Betts.
Longfellow. Riley.
Longfellow. Van Dyke.
Poe and Longfellow. *Fr.* A Fable for Critics. J. R. Lowell.
To Henry Wadsworth Longfellow. J. R. Lowell.
To Longfellow. Hayne.
LONGSPURS. To the Lapland Longspur. Burroughs.
LOOKOUT MOUNTAIN, BATTLE OF
Battle in the Clouds, The. W. D. Howells.
Battle of Lookout Mountain, The. Boker.
LOONS
Loon, The. T. H. Rand.
Loon, The. Sarett.
Loon, The. A. B. Street.
Loons, The. Lampman.
Night Laughter. Leonard Bacon.
LORELEI
Conversation in the Forest. Eichendorff, *tr. fr. German by* Salinger.
Lore Lay. Brentano, *tr. fr. German by* Cotterell.
Lorelei, The. Heine, *tr. fr. German.*
LORENZO DI CREDI. Italian Chest, An. Seiffert.
LOTUS
Lotos-Eaters, The. Tennyson.
Lotus-Flower, The. Heine, *tr. fr. German by* Thomson.
Lotus Leaves. Mitsukuni, *tr. fr. Japanese by* Miyamori.
LOUIS XV, KING OF FRANCE. Louis XV. Sterling.
LOUISBURG, NOVA SCOTIA
Louisburg. *Unknown.*
On the Late Successful Expedition against Louisbourg. Francis Hopkinson.
LOUISE, MADAME (daughter of Louis XV of France). Aux Carmélites. Tynan.
LOUISIANA
In Louisiana. A. B. Paine.
Song of Louisiana. Stopher.
LOUSE. *See* LICE.
LOVE
Chinese Love Poems (ChLP). D. J. Klemer, ed.
English Love Poems (EnLoPo). John Betjeman *and* Geoffrey Taylor, eds.
Eternal Passion in English Poetry (EtPaEn). Edith Wharton *and* Robert Norton, comps.
Little Treasury of Love Poems, A (LiTL). John Holmes, ed.
Love (LO). Walter de la Mare, ed.
Love Poems of Six Centuries (LoPS). Helen Husted, ed.
Love Poems, Old and New (LoPo). Catharine Connell, comp.
Love's Enchantment (LoEn). Helen Ferris, comp.
LOW, WILL HICOK. To Will H. Low. R. L. Stevenson.
LOWELL, JAMES RUSSELL
James Russell Lowell ("This is your month"). O. W. Holmes.
James Russell Lowell ("Thou shouldst have sung the swan-song for the choir"). O. W. Holmes.
James Russell Lowell. Whittier.
James Russell Lowell's Birthday Festival. O. W. Holmes.
Lowell. *Fr.* A Fable for Critics. J. R. Lowell.
LUCIFER. *See* SATAN.
LUCKNOW, INDIA
Defence of Lucknow, The. Tennyson.
Pipes at Lucknow, The. Whittier.
LUCRETIUS
Lucretius. Lionel Johnson.
Lucretius. Tennyson.
LUDDITES
Framework-Knitters Lamentation, The. *Unknown.*
Framework-Knitters Petition, The. C. Briggs.
Ode to the Framers of the Frame Bill, An. Byron.
Song for the Luddites. Byron.
LUDLOW, ENGLAND. Poppies in Ludlow Castle. Cather.
LUKE, SAINT. Saint Luke the Painter. *Fr.* The House of Life. D. G. Rossetti.
LULL, RAMON. After Reading Saint Teresa, Luis de Leon and Ramon Lull. Muna Lee.
LULLABIES. *Book of Lullabies, A* (BOL). Elva S. Smith, comp.
LUMBERING AND LUMBERMEN
Buffalo Skinners, The. *Unknown.*
Jack Haggerty. Dan McGinnis.
Jam on Gerry's Rock, The. *Unknown.*
James Whaland. *Unknown.*
Lumbermen, The. Whittier.
On Meesh-e-gan. *Unknown.*
Saws Were Shrieking, The. W. W. E. Ross.
When the Drive Goes Down. Malloch.
Shantymen and Shantyboys (ShS). William Main Doerflinger, comp.
LUNDY'S LANE, BATTLE OF. Battle of Bridgewater, The. *Unknown.*
LUSITANIA (ship). White Ships and the Red. Joyce Kilmer.
LUTES
Blame Not My Lute. Wyatt.
Lute, The. Ibn Qadi Mila, *tr. fr. Arabic by* Arberry.
Lute, The. Rilke, *tr. fr. German by* Lemont.
O Softly Singing Lute. Pilkington.
On a Lute Found in a Sarcophagus. Gosse.
LUXURY
On Luxury. Horace, *tr. fr. Latin by* Gladstone.
Persian Luxury. Horace, *tr. fr. Latin by* Cowper.

Vanity of Riches, The. Horace, *tr. fr. Latin by* Clark.
LYAUTEY, LOUIS HUBERT GONZALVE. Marshal Lyautey. Currey.
LYNCHING
Bird and the Tree, The. Torrence.
Black Boy. Rosten.
Brothers. J. W. Johnson.
Haunted Oak, The. P. L. Dunbar.
Litany at Atlanta, A. DuBois.
Lynched Negro. Bodenheim.
Lynching Bee, The. W. E. Leonard.
Nice Day for a Lynching. Patchen.
On the Photograph of a Lynching. Stafford.
Plaint. C. H. Ford.
So Quietly. L. P. Hill.
Swimmers, The. Allen Tate.
LYNN, MASSACHUSETTS. Bells of Lynn, The. Longfellow.
LYNX
Lesser Lynx, The. Rieu.
Lynx. R. A. D. Ford.
Wailing Lynx. Sarett.
LYON, NATHANIEL. Death of Lyon. Peterson.
LYONESSE
Chapel in Lyoness, The. William Morris.
Lyonesse. Bradby.
Sunk Lyonesse. De la Mare.
When I Set Out for Lyonnesse. Hardy.
LYRE. Listen to the Lyre! Darley.
LYREBIRDS. Tea-Tree and the Lyrebird, The. Roland Robinson.

M

MACCARTHY, DENIS FLORENCE. Florence MacCarthy's Farewell to His English Love. De Vere.
MACAULAY, THOMAS BABINGTON. Macaulay. Landor.
MCCLELLAN, GEORGE BRINTON
How McClellan Took Manassas. *Unknown.*
Victor of Antietam, The. Melville.
MACDONAGH, THOMAS. Thomas MacDonagh. Ledwidge.
MACDONALD, FLORA. Lament of Flora Macdonald, The. Hogg.
MACDONOUGH, THOMAS. Blue Hen's Chickens, The. Guiterman.
MACEDONIAN (ship)
United States and *Macedonian,* The ("Banner of Freedom high floated unfurled"). *Unknown.*
United States and *Macedonian,* The ("How flows each patriot bosom that boasts a Yankee heart"). *Unknown.*
MCGEE, SAM. Cremation of Sam McGee, The. Service.
MCHENRY, FORT
Fort McHenry. *Unknown.*
Star-spangled Banner, The. Key.
MACHINERY
Brute, The. W. V. Moody.
Machine, The. W. W. Gibson.
Machine Hand, A. Ashe.
Machines. Hicky.
Ode to Machines. Louis Ginsberg.
Poems of the Machine Age. MacKnight Black.
Portrait of a Machine. Louis Untermeyer.
Power. *Fr.* The Bridge. Hart Crane.
Secret of the Machines, The. Kipling.
Steam Shovel, The. Tietjens.
Steam Threshing-Machine, The. Tennyson-Turner.
Turbine, The. Harriet Monroe.
Work. D. H. Lawrence.
MCKAY, CLAUDE. To Claude McKay. Virtue.
MCKENZIE, SIR JOHN. Burial of Sir John McKenzie, The. Jessie Mackay.
MCKINLEY, WILLIAM
Buffalo. Coates.
Faithful unto Death. Titherington.
McKinley. *Unknown.*
"MACLEOD, FIONA" (William Sharp). To William Sharp. Scollard.
MACNEICE, LOUIS. Their Last Will and Testament. MacNeice.
MCNEILL, JOHN CHARLES. To John Charles McNeill. Stewart Atkins.
MCPHERSON, JAMES BIRDSEYE. Dirge for McPherson, A. Melville.
MACSWINEY, TERENCE JAMES. Terence MacSwiney. "Æ."
MADNESS
Counting the Mad. Justice.
General Paresis. Karnosh.
I Am. Clare.
Letter from a State Hospital. Mundorf.
Madman, The. L. A. G. Strong.
Madman's Song. Elinor Wylie.
Maniac, The. M. G. Lewis.
Maniac, The. Thomas Russell.
Maud. Tennyson.
Meeting and a Memory, A. Lulham.
Mental Cases. Wilfred Owen.
Modern Endymion, A. Pickthall.
Much madness is divinest sense. Emily Dickinson.
Scene in a Madhouse. De Vere.
Song of the Mad Prince, The. De la Mare.
Sonnet Found in a Deserted Madhouse. *Unknown.*
To One in Bedlam. Dowson.
Tom o' Bedlam's Song. *Unknown.*
MADRID, SPAIN
Segovia and Madrid. R. T. Cooke.
Winter in Castile. Dos Passos.
MADROÑA. Madroño. Harte.
MAECENAS. To Maecenas ("Descended of an ancient line"). *Fr.* Odes. Horace, *tr. fr. Latin by* Dryden.
MAGELLAN, FERDINAND. Magellan. Curnow.
MAGI
Caravans. Emily Patterson.
Different Way, A. Hagg.
Epiphany. Heber.
Hymn of the Three Eastern Magi, The, Adoring Our Saviour at His Nativity. Rowe.
Journey of the Magi. T. S. Eliot.
Kings from the East, The. Heine, *tr. fr. German.*
Kings of the East, The. K. L. Bates.
Kings, They Came from the South, The. Teasdale.
Magi. L. S. Clark.
Magi, The. *Fr.* On the Morning of Christ's Nativity. Milton.
Magi Visit Herod, The. Caelius Sedulius, *tr. fr. Latin by* Henry.
Mystic Magi, The. Hawker.
Out of the Orient Crystal Skies. *Unknown.*
Riding of the Kings, The. Farjeon.
Song of the Wise Men. Pierce.
Take Frankincense, O God. *Fr.* Holy Transportations. Fitzgeffry.
Three Kings, The. Longfellow.
Three Kings of Cologne, The. Eugene Field.
Three Magi, The. R. T. House.
Three Wise Kings. W. E. Brooks.
Three Wise Men, The. John Finley.
Waiting for the Kings. Gales.
Wise Men Seeking Jesus. East.
MAGIC
La Belle Dame sans Merci. Keats.
Magic. John Farrar.
Magic, *sel.* ("They wrong with ignorance"). Lionel Johnson.
Magic. Po Chü-i, *tr. fr. Chinese by* Waley.
Man Who Dreamed of Fairies, The. Po Chü-i, *tr. fr. Chinese by* Waley.
Story of the Alchemist, The. Eugene Williams.
Poems of Magic and Spells (PoMS). William Cole, ed.
MAGNA CARTA
Barons Bold, The. W. J. Fox.
Magna Charta. *Unknown.*
MAGNOLIAS
Magnolia Tree. Sacheverell Sitwell.
Magnolia Tree, The. Witheford.
To a Magnolia Flower in the Garden of the Armenian Convent at Venice. S. W. Mitchell.
MAGPIES
Magpies and Swans. *Fr.* Astrophel and Stella. Sidney.
Magpie's Nest. Charles *and* Mary Lamb.
Magpie's Song, The. Williamson.
MAGUIRE, HUGH, LORD OF FERMANAGH. O'Hussey's Ode to the Maguire. *At. to* Eochadh O'Hussey, *tr. fr. Late Middle Irish by* Mangan.
MAGUIRE, MOLLY. Molly Maguire at Monmouth. William Collins.
MAIMONIDES, MOSES. Duel with Verses over a Great Man, *sels. Unknown, tr. fr. Hebrew.*
MAINE (state)
Down East and Up Along. Grover.
Lovely Rivers and Lakes of Maine, The. Wallis.
Maine Trail, A. McGiffert.
Maine Woods in Winter. G. H. Conkling.
State of Maine Song. R. V. Snow.
Sunrise; Maine Coast. Coffin.
MAINE (ship)
Battle Song. R. B. Wilson.
Half-Mast. Mifflin.
Martyrs of the *Maine,* The. Rupert Hughes.
Men of the *Maine,* The. Scollard.
Spirit of the *Maine,* The. Jenks.
MALAGA, BATTLE OF. Famous Fight at Malago, The; or, The Englishmen's Victory over the Spaniards. *Unknown.*
MALDON (England), BATTLE OF. Battle of Maldon, The. *Unknown, tr. fr. Anglo-Saxon.*

MALTA. Ode to the Lighthouse at Malta. Duque de Rivas, *tr. fr. Spanish.*
MAN
Autonomous. Van Doren.
Average Man, The. *Fr.* The Vision of Piers Plowman. Langland, *mod. by* H. M. Wells.
Before the Beginning of Years. *Fr.* Atalanta in Calydon. Swinburne.
But Man, Proud Man. *Fr.* Measure for Measure. Shakespeare.
Choral Ode: "Wonders are many, and none is more wonderful than man." *Fr.* Antigone. Sophocles, *tr. fr. Greek.*
Dialogue between the Soul and Body, A. Marvell.
Dirge: "Man born of desire." *Fr.* Ode to Music. Robert Bridges.
Elements, The. Cardinal Newman.
Enough of Humble Arguments. *Fr.* The Prelude. Wordsworth.
Epitaph for the Race of Man, *sel.* ("Here lies, and none to mourn him but the sea"). Millay.
Essay on Man, An, *sels.* Pope.
Faces. Whitman.
First Chorus, The. *Fr.* The Glass of Government. Gascoigne.
Fish, the Man, and the Spirit, The. Leigh Hunt.
For metaphors of man we search the skies. Sir William Watson.
From the Shore of Life. *Fr.* De Rerum Natura. Lucretius, *tr. fr. Latin by* Johnson.
Human Races, The. Lister.
Human Soul Speaks, The. *Fr.* The Vision of Piers Plowman. Langland, *mod. by* H. M. Wells.
In Harmony with Nature. Matthew Arnold.
Inquisitors, The. Jeffers.
Know Yourself, *sels.* Arbuthnot.
Last Man, The. Thomas Campbell.
Man. *Fr.* Aurora Leigh. E. B. Browning.
Man. H. L. Cook.
Man. *Fr.* Nosce Teipsum. Sir John Davies.
Man. Greenberg.
Man. George Herbert.
Man. Hölderlin, *tr. fr. German by* Hull.
Man ("What a piece of work is a man!"). *Fr.* Hamlet. Shakespeare.
Man. *Fr.* Atalanta in Calydon. Swinburne.
Man, A. Louis Untermeyer.
Man. Vaughan.
Man, The. H. H. Whitney.
Man. Humbert Wolfe.
Man a Microcosm. Collop.
Man against the Sky, The. E. A. Robinson.
Man and Nature. R. K. Weeks.
Man in the Bowler Hat, The. Tessimond.
Man Is a Prisoner. *Fr.* The Angel in the Cloud. E. W. Fuller.
Man, Man, Man. *Unknown.*
Man Said to the Universe, A. *Fr.* War Is Kind. Stephen Crane.
Man, The Feeblest of Earth's Creatures. *Fr.* The Odyssey. Homer, *tr. fr. Greek by* Cowper.
Man Was Made to Mourn, a Dirge. Burns.
Man's a Man for A' That. Burns.
Man's Mortality. *Unknown.*
Man's Need. David Ross.
Man's Roots, *sel.* ("Man's roots are not in earth; while trees and flowers"). Currey.
Many Truly. Hofmannsthal, *tr. fr. German by* Watkins.
Men. MacLeish.
Men. D. S. Reid.
Men of Old, The. R. M. Milnes.
Monkey. Josephine Miles.
On Human Ambitions. *Fr.* De Rerum Natura. Lucretius, *tr. fr. Latin by* Lindsay.
On Man. Landor.
On the Life of Man. Ralegh.
One's-Self I Sing. Whitman.
Original Sin. Jeffers.
Out of the Beast. Solis-Cohen.
Pity This Busy Monster, Manunkind. E. E. Cummings.
Progress of Man, The. Jalal ed-Din Rumi, *tr. fr. Persian by* Nicholson.
Salutation, The, *sel.* ("From dust I rise"). Traherne.
Satire against Mankind, A. Earl of Rochester.
Sic Vita. Henry King.
Sirens, The, *sels.* Binyon.
So, Man? Derwood.
Sonnet: "Blast of wind, a momentary breath, A." *Fr.* A Divine Century of Spiritual Sonnets. Barnabe Barnes.
To the Lady Margaret Countesse of Cumberland, *sel.* ("Knowing the heart of man is set to be"). Daniel.
Vanity. George Herbert.
Weak Is the Will of Man, His Judgment Blind. Wordsworth.
What Are We? Thomas Wolfe.
Years That Go to Make Me Man, The. Christopher Brennan.
MANASSAS, BATTLES OF. *See* BULL RUN, BATTLES OF.
MANCHOULI, MANCHURIA. Manchouli. Empson.
MANDEVILLE, SIR JOHN. Part of Mandevil's Travels. Empson.
MANGAN, JAMES CLARENCE. Nameless One, The. Mangan.
MANGROVES. Mangroves Dance, The. Hubbell.
MANHASSET, NEW YORK. Limerick: "Then the pair followed Pa to Manhasset." *Unknown.*
MANHATTAN. *See* NEW YORK (city).
MANILA, PHILIPPINE ISLANDS
Battle of Manila, The. Hovey.
Captive Ships at Manila, The. Paul.
Manila. Eugene Ware.
Manila Bay. Arthur Hale.
MANNING, HENRY EDWARD
Cardinal Manning. De Vere.
To the Dead Cardinal of Westminster. Francis Thompson.
MANSFIELD, MOUNT, VERMONT. Sunrise on Mansfield Mountain. Alice Brown.
MANTIS
Chance, The. John Holmes.
Mantis. Terence Heywood.
Mantis Friend, The. McHugh.
Praying-Mantis, The. A. C. Dalton.
Praying Mantis Visits a Penthouse, The. Oscar Williams.
MAPLE SYRUP. Maple Feast. Frances Frost.
MAPLE TREES
Five-fingered Maple, The. K. L. Brown.
Maple, The. J. R. Lowell.
Sleepy Maple Trees, The. Eleanor Hammond.
Song of the Maple. R. M. Streeter.
MAPS
Map, The. Elizabeth Bishop.
Maps. D. B. Thompson.
Old Maps. Tietjens.
Quilt. Updike.
MARAIS DU CYGNE (river), KANSAS. Le Marais du Cygne. Whittier.
MARATHON, BATTLE OF. Persian Version, The. Robert Graves.
MARBLE. Island Quarry. Hart Crane.
MARC ANTONY. *See* ANTONY.
MARCH
Change in the Year, A. *Fr.* To My Sister. Wordsworth.
Counting-out Rhyme for March. Frances Frost.
Dear March, come in. Emily Dickinson.
Earliest Spring. W. D. Howells.
First Smile of Spring. Gautier, *tr. fr. French by* Conder.
Flower Chorus. Emerson.
In March. Lampman.
March. Bryant.
March. Cawein.
March. Coatsworth.
March. I. V. Crawford.
March. Camilla Doyle.
March. Guiterman.
March. Hammond.
March. Holden.
March. Hopper.
March. A. E. Housman.
March. Larcom.
March. Loveman.
March. *Fr.* The Earthly Paradise. William Morris.
March. C. H. Webb.
March brings the lamb. *Unknown.*
March Evening. Strong.
March Thoughts from England. M. L. Woods.
March Wind. Uschold.
March Wind, The. *Unknown.*
March Wind. Wing.
March Winds, The. Houghton.
March Winds. C. F. Lloyd.
Merry Month of March, The. Wordsworth.
One March Day. *Unknown.*
Passing of March, The. R. B. Wilson.
Song in March. Scollard.
Song in March. W. G. Simms.
Swallow Song. *Unknown, tr. fr. Greek.*
'Tis March. Hope Nelson
Twilight in Middle March, A. Ledwidge.
Wild March. Woolson.
Written in March. Wordsworth.
MARCUS AURELIUS. Marcus Antonius cui cognomen erat Aurelius. Burns Singer.
MARGARET, SAINT. To Saint Margaret. Constable.
MARGATE, ENGLAND. Misadventures at Margate. "Thomas Ingoldsby."
MARIA CHRISTINA, QUEEN OF SPAIN. Cristina. Robert Browning.
MARIE ANTOINETTE, QUEEN OF FRANCE
Lines: "And this was she! the peerless and the bright." Holford.

On the Toilet Table of Queen Marie-Antoinette. Nichols.
MARIGOLDS
Marigold, The. William Forrest.
Marigold. Richard Garnett.
Marigold. Bayard Taylor.
Marigold, The. *Fr.* Scented Leaves from a Chinese Jar. Upward.
Marigold, The. Wither.
Marigold So Likes the Lovely Sunne, The. Thomas Watson.
Marigolds. Carman.
Marigolds. Driscoll.
MARINES. *See* UNITED STATES MARINE CORPS.
MARION, FRANCIS
Song of Marion's Men. Bryant.
Swamp Fox, The. Simms.
MARISCHAL COLLEGE (Aberdeen, Scotland). Ode Written for the Completion and Opening of the New Buildings, Marischall College, Aberdeen. Macfie.
MARK ANTONY. *See* ANTONY.
MARKIEWICZ, CONSTANCE GEORGINE, COUNTESS. In Memory of Eva Gore-Booth and Con Markiewicz. Yeats.
MARLBOROUGH JOHN CHURCHILL, 1ST DUKE OF
Death of Marlborough, The. Thornbury.
Satirical Elegy on the Death of a Late Famous General, A. Swift.
MARLOWE, CHRISTOPHER
Christopher Marlowe. *Fr.* To Henry Reynolds, of Poets and Poesy. Drayton.
Christopher Marlowe. *Fr.* Sonnets on English Dramatic Poets. Swinburne.
MARQUETTE, JACQUES. Marquette on the Shores of the Mississippi. Rooney.
MARRIAGE
Any Wife or Husband. Haynes.
Arise, get up, my dear love, rise, make haste, begone thee! *Unknown.*
At the Wedding March. G. M. Hopkins.
Bachelor's Song, The. Flatman.
Ballad of the Despairing Husband. Creeley.
Ballad upon a Wedding, A Suckling.
Before and After Marriage. Anne Campbell.
Bride's Song, The. Tu Fu, *tr. fr. Chinese by* Underwood *and* Chi Hwang Chu.
Bridge Instead of a Wall, A. *Unknown.*
Careful Husband, The. *Tr. fr. Irish by* the Earl of Longford.
Conformers, The. Hardy.
Contention, A, betwixt a Wife, a Widow, and a Maid. Sir John Davies.
Counsel upon Marriage. Chaucer.
Curate's Kindness, The. Hardy.
Downe too farre usurping day. *Unknown.*
Dying Wife to Her Husband, A. Moses ibn Ezra.
Epithalamion, An. Donne.
Epithalamion. Spenser.
Epithalamion Teratus. *Fr.* Hero and Leander. George Chapman.
Family Life. Laing.
Farmer's Bride, The. Mew.
Fisherman Husband. Chamberlain.
For a Marriage. Bogan.
For a Second Marriage. Merrill.
Fortitude. Reinmar von Sweter, *tr. fr. German by* Bithell.
Good & Bad Wives. *Unknown.*
Hector to Andromache. *Fr.* The Iliad. Homer, *tr. fr. Greek by* Chapman.
Holy Matrimony. Keble.
Honeymoon. S. L. Albert.
Husband and Wife. Guiterman.
Hymen hath together tyed. *Unknown.*
I Am Your Wife. *Unknown.*
Incorporation, The. George, *tr. fr. German by* Luke.
Is 5, *sel.* ("It really must/ be Nice"). Cummings.
Jack and Joan. Campion.
Jeane's Wedden Day in Mornen. William Barnes.
Les Sylphides. MacNeice.
Letter. Bergman.
Love in a Life. Robert Browning.
Man May Live Thrice Nestor's Life, A. Thomas Norton.
Marriage. Austin Clarke.
Marriage. Corso.
Marriage. Deutsch.
Marriage. W. W. Gibson.
Marriage. Donald Hall.
Marriage. Van Doren.
Marriage. Wickham.
Marriage, The. Winters.
Marriage and the Care o't. Lochore.
Marriage of Two. Day Lewis.
Marriage Ring, A. Crabbe.
Marriage Song. *Fr.* Emblems of Love. Abercrombie.
Marriage Song. Halevi, *tr. fr. Hebrew by* Lucas.
Midnight Court, The. Brian Merriman, *tr. fr. Modern Irish by* O'Connor.
Minion Wife, A. *Fr.* Ralph Roister Doister. Udall.
Modern Love. George Meredith.
New Wine, Old Bottles. Newbury.
Newly-wedded, The. Praed.
No Love, to Love of Man and Wife. Eedes.
Now You're Married You Must Obey. *Unknown.*
Nox. Diaz Mirón, *tr. fr. Spanish by* Beckett.
Nun's Priest's Tale, The. *Fr.* The Canterbury Tales. Chaucer.
Nuptiall Song, or Epithalmie, A. Herrick.
O, the Marriage! T. O. Davis.
Of Man and Wife. Eedes.
On Marriage. Crashaw.
On Marriage. Flatman.
On the Marriage of a Virgin. Dylan Thomas.
Ou Phrontis. Causley.
Peggy's Wedding. T. E. Brown.
Prayer for a Marriage, A. M. C. Davies.
Prothalamion. Spenser.
Rejoice, O Bridegroom! *Unknown, tr. fr. Hebrew by* Abrahams.
Sanctum, The. T. A. Daly.
Sonnet for a Marriage. Hayes.
This Winter's Weather It Waxeth Cold. *Unknown.*
Three Seamstresses, The. Peretz, *tr. fr. Yiddish by* Leftwich.
'Tis the White Plum Tree. Neilson.
To a Lady on Her Marriage. William Bell.
To a Mate. Roland Robinson.
To His Wife on the Sixteenth Anniversary of Her Wedding-day, with a Ring. Samuel Bishop.
To My Dear and Loving Husband. Bradstreet.
Together. Lewisohn.
Wedded Love. *Fr.* Paradise Lost. Milton.
Wedding-Hymn. Lanier.
Wedding Morn. D. H. Lawrence.
Wife of Bath's Prologue, The. *Fr.* The Canterbury Tales. Chaucer.
Wife of Bath's Tale, The. *Fr.* The Canterbury Tales. Chaucer.
You who dwell upon Helicon. Catullus, *tr. fr. Latin by* Lind.
Young Bride's Dream, The. Coghill.
MARS (god)
Ares. Ehrenstein, *tr. fr. German by* Deutsch *and* Yarmolinsky.
To Mars. *Unknown, tr. fr. Greek by* Chapman.
MARS (planet). Light of Stars, The. Longfellow.
MARSH MARIGOLDS. Marsh Marigolds. Bradby.
MARSHES
Edge of the Swamp, The. Simms.
Flood-Time on the Marshes. Evaleen Stein.
Marsh-Grass. Rittenhouse.
Marsh Song—at Sunset. Lanier.
Marshes of Glynn, The. Lanier.
One Remembering the Marshes. Eiseley.
Swamp, The. Ravenel.
MARSTON, JOHN. Ad Jo. Marston & Ben. Jonson. Weever.
MARSTON MOOR, ENGLAND. Marston Moor. Praed.
MARTHA'S VINEYARD, MASSACHUSETTS. Making Port. J. T. McKay.
MARTIAL
De Poeta Martiali. Bastard.
Martial in Town. Lang.
MARTIN, SAINT. St. Martin and the Beggar. Thom Gunn.
MARTYRS
City of Slaughter, The. Bialik, *tr. fr. Hebrew by* Klein.
Da Silva Gives the Cue. Blumenthal.
Elegy: "I die for Your holy word without regret." A. E. Gomez, *tr. fr. Spanish.*
Here Followeth the Songe of the Death of Mr. Thewlis. *Unknown.*
Last Words of Don Henriquez, The. Schneour, *tr. fr. Yiddish by* Leftwich.
Martyrdom. Learsi.
Martyrdom. Van Noppen.
Martyrdom of Father Campion. Walpole.
Martyr's Death, A. Menahem ben Jacob, *tr. fr. Hebrew.*
Martyr's Hymn, The. Luther, *tr. fr. German by* Fox.
Martyr's Mass, A. Alfred Barrett.
Martyr's Memorial. Guiney.
O Martyrs Numberless. *Unknown.*
Song of Four Priests Who Suffered Death at Lancaster, A. *Unknown.*
Song of Theodolinda, The, *sel.* ("In their heaven the sainted hosts"). George Meredith.
Theology in Extremis. Lyall.
These Things I Do Remember. Solomon Ephraim ben Aaron of Lenczicz, *tr. fr. Hebrew by* Salaman.
Thy Faithful Sons. Eleazar, *tr. fr. Hebrew.*
To the English Martyrs. Francis Thompson.
True Martyr, The. Wade.
Virgin Martyrs, The. Sigebert of Gembloux. *tr. fr. Latin by* Waddell.

MARVELL, ANDREW. Poet of Gardens. Daniel Henderson.
MARY, THE VIRGIN
Against Women's Fashions. Lydgate.
Ah, My Dere. *Unknown.*
Ah (You Say), This Is Holy Wisdom. Doolittle ("H. D.").
Aishah Shechinah. Hawker.
Annunciation, The. M. D. Conway.
Annunciation. *Fr.* La Corona. Donne.
Annunciation, The. Procter.
Annunciation. Rilke, *tr. fr. German by* Leishman.
Annunciation Night. K. E. Conway.
Annunciation to All Women. Foote.
Assumption, The. Sir John Beaumont.
Assumption, The. St. Nerses, *tr. fr. Armenian by* Kent.
Assumption of the Virgin, The. Luis de León, *tr. fr. Spanish by* Longfellow.
Ave. D. G. Rossetti.
Ave (*in mod. Eng.*). *Fr.* Three Devout Fragments. *Unknown.*
Ave Maria. Charasson, *tr. fr. French by* Thompson.
Ave Maria. Rooney.
Ave Maria! *Unknown.*
"Ave Maria Gratia Plena." Oscar Wilde.
Ave, Maris Stella. *Unknown.*
Ave Regina. *Unknown.*
Ave Sanctissima. *Unknown.*
Ballad of Our Lady. William Dunbar.
Ballade of Illegal Ornaments. Belloc.
Ballade to Our Lady of Czestochowa. Belloc.
Bee, The. Henry Hawkins.
"Behold Thy Mother and Thy Brother" (*in mod. Eng.*). Heribert.
Black Madonna, The. Albert Rice.
Blessed Virgin Compared to the Air We Breathe, The. G. M. Hopkins.
Cantiga. Vicente, *tr. fr. Spanish by* Walsh.
Carol: Five Joys of the Virgin, The. *Unknown.*
Cherry-Tree Carol, The ("Joseph was an old man"). *Unknown.*
Dei Genitrix. De Vere.
Epithalamium. Crashaw.
Evening Prayer, An. *Unknown.*
Expectation, The. *Fr.* Our Lady's Expectation. Faber.
Flemish Madonna, A. Stork.
Gaelic Litany to Our Lady, The. *Unknown, tr. fr. Irish by* O'Curry.
Ghyrlond of the Blessed Virgin Marie, The. Jonson.
Grandeurs of Mary, The. Faber.
He Meets His Mother. *Fr.* The Stations of the Cross. Donaghy.
His Mother's Service to Our Lady. Villon, *tr. fr. French by* D. G. Rossetti.
Holy Mother at the Cross, The. R. W. Dixon.
Hymn to the Virgin. Juan Ruiz, Archpriest of Hita, *tr. fr. Spanish by* Longfellow.
Hymn to the Virgin, A. *Unknown.*
I Sing of a Maiden. *Unknown.*
Joys of the Virgin Mary, The. *Fr.* The Book of Good Love. Juan Ruiz, Archpriest of Hita, *tr. fr. Spanish by* Kane.
Lamentation of the Virgin, A. *Unknown.*
Latin Hymn to the Virgin. Praed.
Lulla, la lulla, lulla lullaby./ My sweet little baby. *Unknown.*
Lullaby: "Upon my lap my sovereign sits." "Richard Rowlands."
Lullaby of the Virgin. Lope de Vega, *tr. fr. Spanish by* Ticknor.
Madonna Remembers. Sister Mary Edwardine.
Maiden Ring-adorned, A. Cynewulf, *tr. fr. Anglo-Saxon.*
Maria Immaculata. Pallen.
Maris Stella. Drane.
Mary. Eleanor Downing.
Mary. S. H. Hay.
Mary. Nellie Knight.
Mary. Rose Trumbull.
Mary at the Cross. McGee.
Mary Immaculate. E. C. Donnelly.
Mary Pondered All These Things. Poteat.
Mary, Virgin and Mother. E. Seton.
Mary Weeps for Her Child. *Unknown.*
Mary's Girlhood. *Fr.* Sonnets for Pictures. D. G. Rossetti.
Mater Christi. *Fr.* May Carols. De Vere.
Mater Dolorosa. John Fitzpatrick.
Mater Dolorosa. Grimstone.
Mater Dolorosa. Ledoux.
Mater Misericordiae. Sister St. Miriam of the Temple.
May Magnificat, The. G. M. Hopkins.
Mother and Child. Eastwick.
Mother Most Powerful. Dominici, *tr. fr. Italian by* Walsh.
Mother of God. Gorell.
Mother of God, The. Yeats.
Mother, White as Lily Flower. *Unknown.*
Name of Mary. J. B. O'Reilly.
O Mighty Lady. *Unknown.*
O Mooder Mayde. *Fr.* The Canterbury Tales: The Prioress's Tale. Chaucer.
Of a Rose, a Lovely Rose. *Unknown.*
On the Feast of the Assumption. Eleanor Downing.
On the Glorious Assumption of Our Blessed Lady. Crashaw.
On the Infancy of Our Saviour. Quarles.
Our Lady. Robert Bridges.
Our Lady. M. E. Coleridge.
Our Lady in the Middle Ages. Faber.
Our Lady of Walsingham. *Fr.* The Quaker Graveyard in Nantucket. Robert Lowell.
Our Lady's Assumption. Sister Agnes.
Our Lady's Death. B. D. Hill.
Our Lady's Lullaby. Verstegan.
Our Lady's Song. *Unknown.*
Our Lord and Our Lady. Belloc.
Pains of the Virgin Mary, The. Varnalis, *tr. fr. Greek by* Dalven.
Pieta. Guy Butler.
Prayer, Made in Ballat Form bi Villon for His Mither, The. Villon, *tr. fr. French into Scots by* Scott.
Prayer to the Virgin. *Unknown, tr. fr. Middle Irish by* Strachan *and* Meyer.
Prologue, A: "Thou Speaker of all wisdom in a Word." Patmore.
Quaerit Jesum Suum Maria. Crashaw.
Quia Amore Langueo. *Unknown.*
Quickening, The. S. W. Tuttle.
Regina Coeli. Patmore.
Regina Coeli. *Fr.* The Office of the Blessed Virgin. *Unknown.*
Return of Eve, The. Chesterton.
Rosa Mystica. G. M. Hopkins.
St. Bernard's Prayer to the Virgin Mary. *Fr.* Divina Commedia: Paradiso. Dante, *tr. fr. Italian.*
Saint Francis' Salute to Our Lady. St. Francis of Assisi, *tr. fr. Latin by* Habig.
Song to the Virgin, A. *Unknown.*
Sonnet for the Madonna of the Cherries. Wavell.
Spinner, The. O'Donnell.
Stabat Mater Dolorosa. *At. to* Da Todi, *tr. fr. Latin.*
Stabat Mater Speciosa. *At. to* Da Todi, *tr. fr. Latin by* Walsh.
Star of the Sea. *Fr.* The Ship of Fools. Barclay.
Sweet Mary Lulled Her Blessed Child. Nichol.
Sweet was the song the Virgin sung. *Unknown.*
Tears of Mary, The. Garrison.
Thirteenth Station, The. Giltinan.
To Mary, Mother of Christ. Harsen.
To Our Blessed Lady. Constable.
To Our Lady. Henryson.
To the Virgin. Lydgate.
To the Virgin Mary. *Fr.* Sonnets to Laura. Petrarch, *tr. fr. Italian by* Armi.
Two Carols to Our Lady. *Unknown.*
Veni, Coronaberis. *Unknown.*
Venite Adoremus. Cannon.
Vigil of the Immaculate Conception. Egan.
Virgin, The. Wordsworth.
Virgin Mary, The. Bowers.
Virgin Mary, The. Herrick.
Virgin Mary, The. Karlfeldt, *tr. fr. Swedish by* Stork.
Virgin Mary's Conception, The. Southwell.
Virgin's Song, The. *Unknown.*
Vow to Heavenly Venus, A. Du Bellay, *tr. fr. French by* Lang.
Wayside Virgin, The. L. E. Mitchell.
Well of Pity, The. *Fr.* An A. B. C. Chaucer.
When Mary thro' the Garden Went. M. E. Coleridge.
I Sing of a Maiden (ISi). Sister M. Thérèse, ed.
MARY I, QUEEN OF ENGLAND
Christ Brought Home. *Unknown.*
Marigold, The. William Forrest.
Queen Mary, *sel.* ("O God! I have been too slack, too slack"). Tennyson.
MARY MAGDALEN
And She Washed His Feet with Her Tears. Sherburne.
At Glastonbury. Henry Kingsley.
Conversion of the Magdalene, The, *sel.* ("Encircling Thee Thy holy brides"). Malon de Chaide, *tr. fr. Spanish by* Walsh.
For the Magdalene. Drummond of Hawthornden.
Lent. Rodgers.
Magdalen. Henry Kingsley.
Magdalen. Randall.
Magdalen, The. Sherburne.
Mary Knew. Munson.
Mary Magdalene. Richard Burton.
Mary Magdalene. *Fr.* Sonnets on Pictures. D. G. Rossetti.
Mary Magdalene. Speyer.
Mary Magdalene at the Door of Simon the Pharisee. D. G. Rossetti.

"Multum Dilexit." Hartley Coleridge.
Spoil. W. E. Brooks.
To Mary Magdalen. Argensola, *tr. fr. Spanish by* Bryant.
To St. Mary Magdalen. Constable.
To St. Mary Magdalen. B. D. Hill.
Weeper, The. Crashaw.
Woman. E. S. Barrett.
MARY QUEEN OF SCOTS
Adieux à Marie Stuart. Swinburne.
Alas! Poor Queen. Angus.
At Fotheringay. Southwell.
Decease, Release. Dum Morior, Orior. Southwell.
Martyrdom of Mary, Queen of Scots, The. Southwell.
Mary and Darnley. Humbert Wolfe.
Mary, Queen of Scots. H. G. Bell.
Mary Queen of Scots. Burns.
Mary Queen of Scots. C. T. Turner.
Mary Queen of Scots Landing at the Mouth of the Derwent, Workington. Wordsworth.
Tragic Mary Queen of Scots, The. "Michael Field."
MARYLAND
Maryland Battalion, The. J. W. Palmer.
Maryland Resolves. *Unknown.*
My Maryland. Randall.
MASHONALAND, AFRICA. Mashona Husbandman, A. Cripps.
MASSACHUSETTS. Massachusetts to Virginia. Whittier.
MASSINGER, PHILIP. Philip Massinger. *Fr.* Sonnets on English Dramatic Poets. Swinburne.
MATHEMATICS
Arithmetic. Sandburg.
Equation, An. Plutzik.
Of the Mathematician. A. C. Mathews.
Seven Times One. Ingelow.
Imagination's Other Place (ImOP). Helen Plotz, comp.
MATHER, COTTON. Ben Franklin's Head (1728). M. A. D. Howe.
MATISSE, HENRI. Picasso and Matisse. Robert Francis.
MATTHEW, SAINT. Christus Matthaeum et Discipulos Alloquitur. Sherburne.
MATTHEWS, BRANDER. In Vain Today. Dobson.
MAXWELL, JOHN, 9TH BARON MAXWELL. Lord Maxwell's Last Goodnight. *Unknown.*
MAY
A-Maying, a-Playing. *Fr.* Summer's Last Will and Testament. Nashe.
Apple Blossoms. Larcom.
April and May. *Fr.* May-Day. Emerson.
April and May. Anne Robinson.
Archer, The. Scollard.
As It Fell upon a Day. Barnfield.
Ballata: "Welcome to May." Poliziano, *tr. fr. Italian by* Lind.
Corinna's Going a-Maying. Herrick.
Eidolon. R. P. Warren.
Fairy Music. Ledwidge.
First of May, The. A. E. Housman.
Flute of May, The. Woodbourne.
For Good Luck. Ewing.
Gardener, The. Perkins.
Gladness of the May, The. Wordsworth.
Glycine's Song. *Fr.* Zapolya. S. T. Coleridge.
Here We Come a-Piping. *Unknown.*
In May. W. H. Davies.
In May. *Unknown.*
In May. R. K. Weeks.
In Obitum M.S., X Maii, 1614. William Browne.
In Praise of May. *At. to* Fionn MacCumhaill, *tr. fr. Old Irish by* Rolleston.
In This Merry Morn of May. *Unknown, tr. fr. French by* Symonds.
Jewish May, The. Rosenfeld, *tr. fr. Yiddish by* Stokes *and* Frank.
M. Edwards' May. Richard Edwards.
May. Barnes.
May. S. M. Bird.
May. Cornwell.
May. Macdonald.
May. Neilson.
May. Percival.
May. Laura Simmons.
May, *sel.* ("Open, sweet flowers, your eyes"). J. F. O'Donnell.
May. *Fr.* The Faerie Queene. Spenser.
May. *Unknown, tr. fr. Old Irish by* O'Connor.
May and Death. Robert Browning.
May and June. *Fr.* Under the Willows. J. R. Lowell.
May Basket, The. Goodale.
May Basket, A L. B. West.
May Carol ("In vain thy altars do they heap"). De Vere.
May Day. *Unknown, tr. fr. Old Irish by* Rolleston.
May-Day at Sea. Finerty.
May Day Garland, The. Blurden.
May-Day on Magdalen Tower. T. H. Warren.
May Is Building Her House. Le Gallienne.
May-Lure. Richard Burton.
May Magnificat, The. G. M. Hopkins.
May Morning. Barrows.
May Morning. Milton.
May Morning. Thaxter.
May Mornings. Eastwick.
May Night. W. E. Leonard.
May Queen, The. Tennyson.
May Song, A. "Violet Fane."
May Sun Sheds an Amber Light, The. Bryant.
May upon Ictis. T. S. Jones, Jr.
Maytime. *Fr.* The Shoemaker's Holiday. Dekker.
May-Time. Gant.
May-Time. *Unknown.*
Month of May, The. *Fr.* The Knight of the Burning Pestle. Beaumont *and* Fletcher.
O Lusty May. *Unknown.*
Oh, the Month of May! *Fr.* The Shoemaker's Holiday. Dekker.
Ode in May. Sir William Watson.
Old May Song ("All in this pleasant evening"). *Unknown.*
On a Bank as I Sat a-Fishing. *Fr.* A Description of the Spring. Wotton.
On Mayday we dance. *Unknown.*
Perennial May. T. A. Daly.
Poem in May. Hewitt.
Queen of Seasons, The. Cardinal Newman.
Resurgam. Struthers Burt.
Rhyme for Remembrance of May. Richard Burton.
Rondel: "First day of the month of May, The." Orléans, *tr. fr. French by* Currey.
Sing All Ye Joyful. Tolkien.
Song, The: "Drink and be merry, merry, merry boys." *Fr.* New England Canaan. Morton.
Song: "Now is the month of maying." *Unknown.*
Song for a May Morning. Trevelyan.
Song for May Day, A. Adler.
Song of Departing May. Miki, *tr. fr. Japanese by* Ninomiya *and* Enright.
Song on May Morning. Milton.
Succession of the Four Sweet Months, The. Herrick.
Summer Is Nigh. *Unknown.*
There is but one May in the Year. *Fr.* Sing-Song. C. G. Rossetti.
This Month of May, One Pleasant Eventide. *Unknown, tr. fr. French by* Symonds.
Welcome to May. *Unknown.*
Why It Was Cold in May. H. R. Eliot.
Wonderful Country. Waddington.
Young May Moon, The. Thomas Moore.
MAYAKOVSKY, VLADIMIR. Mayakovsky Memory. *Fr.* Diary of a Journey. Inber, *tr. fr. Russian by* Lindsay.
MAYFLOWER. *See* ARBUTUS.
MAYFLOWER (ship)
Columbus and the *Mayflower.* R. M. Milnes.
Mayflower, The. Ellsworth.
Mayflower. O'Reilly.
MAYO, IRELAND
County Mayo, The. Raftery, *tr. fr. Irish.*
County of Mayo, The. *At. to* Flavell, *tr. fr. Modern Irish by* Fox.
Summer Is Coming, The. Guinness.
MAZEPPA. Mazeppa. Byron.
MAZZINI, GIUSEPPE. Lines on the Monument Erected to Mazzini at Genoa. Swinburne.
MEADOW LARKS
Meadow Lark, The. Garland.
Meadow Lark. M. M. Walker.
Meadow Lark Sang, A. Commerford.
MEADOWS. *See* FIELDS AND PASTURES.
MEATH, IRELAND
Boyne Walk, The. F. R. Higgins.
Father and Son. F. R. Higgins.
MECKLENBURG DECLARATION OF INDEPENDENCE. Mecklenburg Declaration, The. Elam.
MEDEA. Jason and Medea, *sel.* ("The Flees he tok and goth to Bote"). *Fr.* Confessio Amantis. Gower.
MEDICI, LORENZO DE'. Statue of Lorenzo de' Medici, The. Nesmith.
MEDITERRANEAN SEA
Mare Mediterraneum. Nichol.
Mediterranean, The. Allen Tate.
Ode: "Of Thee the Northman." Santayana.
MEDUSA. Medusa. Bogan.
MEIGS, FORT, OHIO. Old Fort Meigs. *Unknown.*
MELAMPUS. Melampus. George Meredith.
MELANCHOLY
Melancholy. *Fr.* The Nice Valour. John Fletcher.
Melancholy. Li Shang-yin, *tr. fr. Chinese by* Jenyns.
Ode on Melancholy. Keats.
Rondeau: Well, The. Charles d'Orléans, *tr. fr. French by* Howes.
MELBOURNE, AUSTRALIA. Towers at Evening, The. *Fr.* Melbourne and Memory. Wilmot.

MELROSE ABBEY, SCOTLAND. Inscription on Melrose Abbey. *Unknown.*
MELTON MOWBRAY, ENGLAND. Melton Mowbray Pork-Pie, A. Le Gallienne.
MELVILLE, HERMAN
At Melville's Tomb. Hart Crane.
Herman Melville. Auden.
MEMLING, HANS. Memling's Virgin with Apple. Naudé.
MEMORIAL DAY
Aftermath. McCulloch.
America's Answer. Lillard.
Ballad of Heroes, A. Dobson.
Bitter Question. Macdougall.
Bivouac of the Dead, The. O'Hara.
Blue and the Gray, The. F. M. Finch.
Comrade, Remember. Kresensky.
Confederate Memorial Day. *Unknown.*
Criminality of War, The. Edward Young.
Crosses. Mabel Hicks.
Dead, The. *Fr.* 1914. Rupert Brooke.
Debt, The. Theodosia Garrison.
Decorating the Soldiers' Graves. Savage.
Decoration Day. G. H. Barbour.
Decoration Day. Wallace Bruce.
Decoration Day. J. W. Howe.
Decoration Day. Longfellow.
Decoration Day Prayer. Bemis.
Decoration Hymn. Randall.
For Decoration Day. Rupert Hughes.
For Our Dead. Scollard.
For Those Who Died. T. C. Clark.
From Beyond. Trent.
Graves of the Patriots, The. Percival.
High Flight. Magee.
How Shall We Honor Them? Markham.
How Sleep the Brave. William Collins.
Hymn to the Victorious Dead. Hagedorn.
I Have a Son. Pottle.
If These Endure. Lorraine.
In Memoriam. Ada Jackson.
In the Name of Our Sons. Dorothy Gould.
It Is Not Too Late. Trent.
Knot of Blue and Gray, A. *Unknown.*
Lament of the Voiceless, The. L. B. Everett.
Little Flags, The. Minot.
Memorial. Goodman.
Memorial Day. W. E. Brooks.
Memorial Day. Dunning.
Memorial Day. Theodosia Garrison.
Memorial Day. Guiney.
Memorial Day. Joyce Kilmer.
Memorial Day. E. A. Lent.
Memorial Day. Margaret Sidney.
Memorial Day. Warman.
Memorial Day. A. A. Wiley.
Memorial Day. McL. Wilson.
Memorial Day. Wynne.
Memorial Day, 1889. Kiser.
Memorials on the Slain at Chickamauga. Melville.
Monument for the Soldiers, A. Riley.
Mother before a Soldier's Monument, A. Rockett.
New Banner, The. Trask.
New Memorial Day, The. Paine.
No More the Thunder of Cannon. Dorr.
Ode for Decoration Day, *sel.* ("O gallant brothers of the generous South"). Henry Peterson.
Ode for Decoration Day. Timrod.
Ode to the Confederate Dead. Allen Tate.
On a World War Battlefield. T. C. Clark.
Parade, The. Badley.
Remembering Day. Saunders.
Requiem for a Dead Warrior. McInnis.
Soldier-Dead. Emery.
Soldier, Rest! *Fr.* The Lady of the Lake. Sir Walter Scott.
Song for Decoration Day. H. C. Bacon.
Song for Heroes, A. Markham.
Song for Memorial Day. Scollard.
Taps at Twilight. Stringer.
Their Victory Won. Coates.
There Will Be Peace. Pettengill.
Thus Speak the Slain. Holliday.
Tribute to Our Soldiers. Kennedy.
True Peace, A. *Fr.* Ten Years After. Trent *and* Cheyney.
Veterans, The. McCarthy.
We Shall Remember Them. J. T. White.
We Who Are Dead. Benjamin.
We Whom the Dead Have Not Forgiven. S. B. Field.
Memorial Day (*Our American Holidays Series*) (MDAH). Robert Haven Schauffler, ed.
MEMORY
Cities Drowned. Newbolt.
Days That Were, The. William Morris.
Empty Jar, The. Stenhouse.
Essay on Memory. R. D. Fitzgerald.
Four Ducks on a Pond. Allingham.
I Remember, I Remember. Hood.
Inscription on a Grot. *Fr.* The Pleasures of Memory. Rogers.
Light of Other Days, The. Thomas Moore.
Memory, A. Coolbrith.
Memory. Erskine, Earl of Rosslyn.
Memory. Helen Hoyt.
Memory, A. Knowles.
Memory. Abraham Lincoln.
Memory, A. MacAleese.
Memory, A. Ridge.
Memory. Rimbaud, *tr fr. French by* Varèse.
Memory. Sassoon.
Memory. Shanks.
Memory. Stagnelius, *tr. fr. Swedish by* Gosse.
Memory. Symons.
Memory. Wordsworth.
Memory of Earth, A. "Æ."
Memory of the Dead, The. Ingram.
Most Quietly at Times. Flaischlen, *tr. fr. German by* Bithell.
Ode to Memory. Shenstone.
Old Familiar Faces, The. Charles Lamb.
Old Man's Carousal, The. Paulding.
Pictures of Memory. Alice Cary.
Remember. C. G. Rossetti.
Remembrance. Emily Brontë.
Remembrance. Slonimski, *tr. fr. Polish by* Notley.
Song: "Memory, hither come." Blake.
To Memory. M. E. Coleridge.
What Need Have I for Memory? G. D. Johnson.
MEMPHIS, TENNESSEE
At Memphis Station. Jensen, *tr. fr. Danish by* Damon.
Memphis Blues. S. A. Brown.
MENAGERIES. *See* ZOOS.
MENDIP HILLS, ENGLAND. Mendip Hills over Wells, The. Alford.
MENELAUS
Menelaus. Clarence Day.
Menelaus and Helen at Troy. Landor.
MENKURE, PHARAOH OF EGYPT. Mycerinus. Matthew Arnold.
MEPHIBOSHETH. Mephibosheth. Willis.
MEPHISTOPHELES. *See* SATAN.
MERCY. Mercy. *Fr.* The Merchant of Venice. Shakespeare.
MEREDITH, GEORGE. George Meredith. Hardy.
MERLIN
Merlin. Emerson.
Merlin. Muir.
MERMAID TAVERN
Lines on the Mermaid Tavern. Keats.
Thomas Dekker's Song. *Fr.* Tales of the Mermaid Tavern. Noyes.
Wassail Chorus at the Mermaid Tavern. Watts-Dunton.
MERMAIDS AND MERMEN
Ballad of the Mermaid. Leland.
Clark Colven. *Unknown.*
Elegy on a Dead Mermaid Washed Ashore at Plymouth Rock. Hillyer.
Enchanted Island, The. Conolly.
Figure-Head, The. Garstin.
Fisher, The. Goethe, *tr. fr. German by* Brooks.
Fisherman's Blunder off New Bedford, Massachusetts. Annemarie Ewing.
Forsaken Merman, The. Matthew Arnold.
Great Silkie of Sule Skerrie, The. *Unknown.*
If on Some Balmy Summer Night. Edith Nesbit.
Little John Bottlejohn. L. E. Richards.
Mermaid, The. A. J. M. Smith.
Mermaid, The. Tennyson.
Mermaid, The. *Unknown.*
Mermaid, The. *Fr.* A Man Young and Old. Yeats.
Mermaid of Margate, The. Hood.
Mermaiden, A. Hennell.
Mermaidens, The. Heine, *tr. fr. German by* Thomson.
Mermaidens, The. L. E. Richards.
Mermaidens' Vesper Hymn, The. Darley.
Mermaids. Slessor.
Mermaids, The. *Fr.* The Faerie Queene. Spenser.
Mermaids and Mermen. *Fr.* The Pirate. Sir Walter Scott.
Merman, The. Tennyson.
Moon-Child, The. "Fiona Macleod."
Neckan, The. Matthew Arnold.
Old Angler, The. De la Mare.
Sea-Maiden, The. De Forest.
Sea-Maids' Music, The. Ernest Myers.
Song of the Mermaids. Darley.
Vision of the Mermaids, A, *sel.* ("Rowing, I reach'd a rock—the sea was low"). G. M. Hopkins.
MERRIMAC (ship)
Men of the *Merrimac*, The. Scollard.

Sinking of the *Merrimac[k]*. Larcom.
Turtle, The. *Unknown.*
MERRITT PARKWAY, CONNECTICUT. Merritt Parkway. Levertov.
MERRY-GO-ROUNDS. *See* CARROUSELS.
MESSIAH
Ballad of the Days of the Messiah. A. M. Klein.
Hush, Hush. Leib, *tr. fr. Yiddish by* Leftwich.
O Hark to the Herald. Eleazar ben Kalir, *tr. fr. Hebrew by* Zangwill.
When the Days Shall Grow Long. Bialik, *tr. fr. Hebrew by* Klein.
MEXICAN WAR
Angels of Buena Vista, The. Whittier.
Battle of the King's Mill [Molino del Rey]. English.
Biglow Papers, The, 1st Series, *sels.* J. R. Lowell.
Buena Vista. Pike.
Buena Vista Battlefield. *Unknown.*
Crisis, The. Whittier.
Monterey. C. F. Hoffman.
Siege of Chapultepec, The. Lytle.
MEXICANS
Mexican Soldiers. Estrada, *tr. fr. Spanish by* Walsh.
Muy Vieja Mexicana. Corbin.
MEXICO
Bernal Diaz' Preface. *Fr.* Conquistador. MacLeish.
Dawn on the Wall-Head There. *Fr.* Conquistador. MacLeish.
Epitaph to the Liberty of America. Fernández de Lizardi, *tr. fr. Spanish by* Blackwell.
Gentle Fatherland. López Velarde, *tr. fr. Spanish by* Hays.
Hex on the Mexican X, A. McCord.
In Mexico. Evaleen Stein.
Indians Come Down from Mixco, The. Asturias, *tr. fr. Spanish by* Walsh.
Mexican Market Woman. Langston Hughes.
Mexican Serenade. Guiterman.
Ode to the Fatherland. Flores, *tr. fr. Spanish by* Blackwell.
Small Soldiers with Drum in Large Landscape. *Fr.* Mexico Is a Foreign Country. R. P. Warren.
Spanish Ships Reach Mexico, The. *Fr.* The Indian Emperor. Dryden.
Anthology of Mexican Poetry (AnMP). Octavio Paz, comp.
MEXICO, GULF OF. Gulf of Mexico. Reyes, *tr. fr. Spanish by* Trend.
MEYNELL, ALICE. On Looking at a Copy of Alice Meynell's Poems, Given Me, Years Ago, by a Friend. Amy Lowell.
MICE
Change of Heart, A. Valine Hobbs.
City Mouse and the Garden Mouse, The. *Fr.* Sing-Song. C. G. Rossetti.
Field-Mouse, The. Blyton.
Field Mouse, The. "Fiona Macleod."
Four III. E. E. Cummings.
House of the Mouse, The. L. S. Mitchell.
I was lying still in a field one day. Zhenya Gay.
Mice. Fyleman.
Mice, The. R. R. Kirk.
Mice. *Unknown, tr. fr. Greek by* Butler.
Mice of Spain, The. Coatsworth.
Missing. A. A. Milne.
Mouse, The. Coatsworth.
Mouse. Hilda Conkling.
Mouse, The. Wakley.
Mouse, a Cat, and an Irish Bull, A. Tabb.
Mouse and the Cake, The. Eliza Cook.
Mouse That Gnawed the Oak-Tree Down, The. Vachel Lindsay.
Mouse's Nest. Clare.
Mouse's Petition, The. Barbauld.
Mousetrap, The. Morgenstern, *tr. fr. German by* Snodgrass.
Prince, The. De la Mare.
Taill of the Uponlandis Mous and the Burges Mous, The. Henryson.
There May, of Course, Be Mice. R. R. Kirk.
To a Mouse, on Turning Her Up in Her Nest with the Plough, November, 1785. Burns.
Two Mice, The. *Fr.* An Imitation of the Sixth Satire of the Second Book of Horace. Pope.
Wood-Mouse, The. Howitt.
Young Mouse, The. Jeffrey Taylor.
MICHAEL, THE ARCHANGEL
Michael the Archangel. Tynan.
Michael the Archangel. Michael Williams.
St. Michael the Weigher. J. R. Lowell.
MICHELANGELO. Michelangelo, *sel.* ("He spoke, and death"). McDuffee.
MICHIGAN. Michigan, My Michigan! Lyster.
MICHIGAN, LAKE. Cook County. MacLeish.
MIDAS. Fable of Midas, The. Swift.
MIDDLE AGE
Autumnal, The. Donne.
End of Summer. Kunitz.
Middle-Age. E. B. C. Jones.
Middle Age. Lehmann.
Rondel for Middle Age. Nicholl.
MIGNONETTE. Mignonette. Geijer, *tr. fr. Swedish by* Stork.
MILAM, BEN. Valor of Ben Milam, The. Scollard.
MILKING
Milker, The. Duggan.
Milking Pails. *Unknown.*
Milking Time. E. M. Roberts.
Milking Time. C. G. Rossetti.
Milkmaid. Laurie Lee.
MILKWEED
Silkweed. Savage.
To the Milkweed. Mifflin.
Two Voices in a Meadow. Wilbur.
MILKY WAY
Milky Way, The. Topelius, *tr. fr. Swedish by* Stork.
Milky Way, The. *Fr.* Scented Leaves From a Chinese Jar. Upward
MILL, JOHN STUART. J. S. Mill. Bentley.
MILLET, JEAN FRANÇOIS. Angelus, The. Coates.
MILLINGTON, EDWARD. Edward Millington. Richard Church.
MILLS
Lesson of the Water-Mill, The. *Fr.* The Man o' Airlie. Doudney.
Water Mill, The. Hawkshaw.
MILTON, JOHN
Afternoon in Artillery Walk, An; Mary Milton Loquitur. Leonard Bacon.
How Could You Know? Redman.
Johannes Milton, Senex. Robert Bridges.
Lines on Seeing a Lock of Milton's Hair. Keats.
Lines Printed under the Engraved Portrait of Milton. Dryden.
London, 1802 ("Milton! Thou shouldest be living at this hour"). Wordsworth.
Milton. Aytoun.
Milton, *sel.* ("And did those feet in ancient time"). Blake.
Milton. Landor.
Milton. Longfellow.
Milton. Mifflin.
Milton. Tennyson.
Milton's Prayer of Patience. E. L. Howell.
On His Blindness. Milton.
On Paradise Lost. Marvell.
Progress of Poesy, The. Thomas Gray.
Shakespeare and Milton. Landor.
To Milton. Oscar Wilde.
To Milton—Blind. Stephen Phillips.
To the Ghost of John Milton. Sandburg.
MILTON, KATHERINE. Katherine Milton: Died MDCLVIII. Milton.
MILWAUKEE, WISCONSIN. Milwaukee Fire, The. *Unknown.*
MIND. *See* INTELLECT.
MINERALS. Mineral Collection. A. H. Evans.
MINER'S HOTEL, GOLD HILL, COLORADO. Casey's Table d'Hote. Eugene Field
MINING AND MINERS
Avondale Mine Disaster, The. *Unknown.*
Back in the Return. Huw Menai.
Caliban in the Coal Mines. Louis Untermeyer.
Cleator Moor. Norman Nicholson.
Coal-Owner and the Pitman's Wife, The. *Unknown.*
Collier, The. Watkins.
Cornish Miner, The. Gries.
Down in a Coal Mine. Geoghegan.
Drilling Missed Holes. Cameron.
Klondike Miner, The. *Unknown.*
Miner, The. Bodenheim.
Miner, The. A. C. King.
Miner's Protégée, The. *Unknown.*
Miner's Song, The. C. E. Winter.
Mother Wept. Skipsey.
Song of the Leadville Mine Boss. Cameron.
Worked-out Mine, The. Dyson.
See also GOLD MINING AND MINERS.
MINNESOTA. Hail! Minnesota! Rickard *and* Upson.
MINOT, LAURENCE. Song of Laurence Minot. Minot.
MINSTRELS
Christmas Carol: "Minstrels played their Christmas tune, The." Wordsworth.
Complaint of the Minstrel's Life. Muset, *tr. fr. French by* Legge.
Deor's Lament. *Unknown, tr. fr. Anglo-Saxon by* Kennedy.
Dialogue between Poet and Patron. Taliesin, *tr. fr. Welsh by* Evans.
Minstrel, The. Goethe, *tr. fr. German by* Mangan.
Minstrel Boy, The. Thomas Moore.
Minstrel's Song. *Fr.* Aella. Chatterton.
Poet's Poverty, The. Rutebeuf, *tr. fr. French by* Legge.
Widsith, the Minstrel. *Fr.* Widsith. *Unknown, tr. fr.*

MINSTRELS (*continued*)
Anglo-Saxon by Kennedy.
MIRACLES
How Miracles Abound. Scollard.
Miracle, The. De la Mare.
Miracle, A. "George Klingle."
Miracle, The. *Fr.* Carmen Paschale. Sedulius, *tr. fr. Latin by* Henry.
Miracle for Breakfast, A. Elizabeth Bishop.
Miracles. Helton.
Miracles. E. M. Root.
Miracles. Whitman.
MIRAGE
Mirage. Blackmur.
Mirage. De la Mare.
Yon Far Country. A. E. Housman.
MIRRORS
Mirror, The. Li Po, *tr. fr. Chinese by* Ayscough *and* Lowell.
Mirror. John Updike.
MISANTHROPES
Complete Misanthropist, The. Morris Bishop.
Desperate. Cino da Pistoia, *tr. fr. Italian by* Lind.
MISSILES (weapon). *See* GUIDED MISSILES.
MISSIONARIES. Man of Grass, The, *sel.* ("India became his jasmined youth, Goa"). Macnab.
MISSISSIPPI (state). Way Down South in Mississippi. Verne Barnes.
MISSISSIPPI RIVER
Down the Mississippi. J. G. Fletcher.
Marquette on the Shores of the Mississippi. Rooney.
On the Mississippi. Garland.
River, The. *Fr.* The Bridge. Hart Crane.
MISSOURI (state). Missouri. Dier.
MISSOURI RIVER
Foreclosure. S. A. Brown.
Missouri Traveller Writes Home, A, 1830. Bly.
Shenandoah. *Unknown.*
MIST
Haze. *Fr.* A Week on the Concord and Merrimack Rivers. Thoreau.
Mist, The. N. B. Miller.
Mist. *Fr.* A Week on the Concord and Merrimack Rivers. Thoreau.
Mist, The. *Unknown, formerly at. to* Dafydd ap Gwilym, *tr. fr. Welsh by* Borrow.
Mist and All, The. Willson.
Mist Opening in the Hills. *Fr.* The Excursion. Wordsworth.
Night Mists. Hayne.
See also FOG.
MISTLETOE
Mistletoe Bough, The. Bayly.
Mistletoe Sprites. S. P. Russell.
MOBILE BAY, BATTLE OF
Bay Fight, The. Brownell.
Craven. Newbolt.
Farragut. W. T. Meredith.
Through Fire in Mobile Bay. *Unknown.*
MOCKINGBIRDS
Epitaph on a Pet Mocking Bird. Gaston.
Lament of a Mocking-Bird. Kemble.
Look at Six Eggs. *Fr.* Prairie. Sandburg.
Mocking Bird, The. Bacheller.
Mocking Bird, A. Bynner.
Mocking-Bird, The. Hayne.
Mocking Bird, The. Hovey.
Mocking Bird, The. Lanier.
Mocking Bird, The. *Fr.* Out of The Cradle Endlessly Rocking. Whitman.
Mocking Bird and the Donkey, The. Rosas, *tr. fr. Spanish by* Bryant.
Mocking-Bird, Misnamed, The. Percy Mackaye.
Moonlight Song of the Mocking-Bird. Hayne.
To the Mocking-Bird. Pike.
To the Mocking-Bird. R. H. Wilde.
MODERATION. Golden Mean, The. *Fr.* Odes. Horace, *tr. fr. Latin by* Sidney.
MOHAVE DESERT. In the Mohave. Orr.
MOLES
All but Blind. De la Mare.
Eagle and the Mole, The. Elinor Wylie.
Mole, The. Clare.
Mole, The. F. W. Harvey.
Mole. Aldous Huxley.
Mole, The. Edith King.
Mole, The. E. L. Mayo.
Mole, The. P. K. Page.
Mole Catcher. Blunden.
Unfortunate Mole, The. Mary Kennedy.
MONA LISA
Mona Lisa. J. R. Lowell.
Mona Lisa. Pater.
MONADNOCK, MOUNT, NEW HAMPSHIRE. Monadnock through the Trees. E. A. Robinson.
MONASTERIES
Decayed Monastery, A. Dermody.
In the Monastery. O'Conor.
MONEY
As I Sat at the Café, I Said to Myself. *Fr.* Dipsychus. Clough.
Avarice. George Herbert.
Away with this cash. *Unknown.*
Behaviour of Money. Bernard Spencer.
Certain Examples of the Power Which Sir Money Possesses. *Fr.* The Book of Good Love. Juan Ruiz, Archpriest of Hita, *tr. fr. Spanish by* Kane.
Evils of Money, The. Sophocles, *tr. fr. Greek by* Campbell.
Fatigue. Belloc.
Hardship of Accounting, The. Robert Frost.
Hero in the Land of Dough, A. Clairmont.
Investor's Soliloquy. Kenneth Ward.
Jack of Newbury, *sel.* ("My masters, I thank you, it's time to pack home"). Deloney.
Lady Pecunia; or, The Praise of Money, *sel.* ("I sing not of Angelica the fair"). Barnfield.
Letrilla; the Lord of Dollars. Quevedo y Villegas, *tr. fr. Spanish by* Walsh.
Money. Armour.
Money. W. H. Davies.
Money. Pontalais, *tr. fr. French by* Carrington.
Money. *Unknown.*
Money and a Friend. *Unknown.*
Penny Problem. Farrar.
"Put Money in Thy Purse" (*in. mod. Eng.*). Unknown.
Quatrains for a Bank Cashier. DeWitt
Render unto Caesar. Humphries.
Rule of Money, The. *Unknown.*
Song of Cash, A. *Unknown, tr. fr. Latin by* Lindsay.
Spectator ab Extra. Clough.
Ye tradeful merchants, that with weary toil. *Fr.* Amoretti. Spenser.
MONICA, SAINT. St. Monica. Francis Thompson.
MONITOR (ship). Cruise of the *Monitor*, The. Boker.
MONKEYS
Monkey, The. Nancy Campbell.
Monkey, The. Howitt.
Monkey. Josephine Miles.
Monkey. W. J. Smith.
Monkey and the Cat, The. La Fontaine, *tr. fr. French.*
Monkeys. *Fr.* Walker in Nicaragua. Joaquin Miller.
Monkeys, The. E. O. Thompson.
Monkeys and the Crocodile, The. L. E. Richards.
Monkey's Carol, The. Letts.
Monkey's Glue, The. Goldwin Goldsmith.
Sonnet on [*or* to] a Monkey, A. Marjorie Fleming.
Three Wise Monkeys, The. F. B. Davis.
MONKS
Carthusians. Dowson.
Listening to the Monk of Szechuan Playing on His Lute. Li Po, *tr. fr. Chinese by* Chiang Shao-yi.
Merrily Sang the Monks of Ely, The. *Unknown.*
Monasteries. C. D. Webb.
Monastic Scribe, The. T. B. Aldrich.
Monk, The. "Seumas O'Sullivan."
Monk and His Pet Cat, The. *Unknown, tr. fr. Old Irish.*
Monk in the Garden, The. Crapsey.
Monk in the Kitchen, The. Branch.
Monk of Casal-Maggiore, The. Longfellow.
Monks. Cardinal Newman.
Monks at Ards, The. Maybin.
Monk's Day, The. A. L. Phelps.
Monks of Bangor's March, The. Sir Walter Scott.
Monk's Vision. *Unknown.*
Ode to a Monk on the Tai-pei Mountains. Ts'en Ts'an, *tr. fr. Chinese by* Yuan Chia-hua.
On the Fasting Monk Chu Chuan. Po Chü-i, *tr. fr. Chinese by* Ching Ti.
Palmer, The. Sir Walter Scott.
Pangur Ban. *Unknown, tr. fr. Old Irish by* Flower.
Poor Monk of Skara, A. Fröding, *tr. fr. Swedish by* Stork.
San Lorenzo Giustiniani's Mother. Alice Meynell.
Soliloquy of the Spanish Cloister. Robert Browning.
MONMOUTH, JAMES SCOTT, DUKE OF
Dutchess of Monmouth's Lamentation for the Loss of Her Duke, The. *Unknown.*
England's Darling; or, Great Britain's Joy and Hope on That Noble Prince James, Duke of Monmouth. *Unknown.*
MONMOUTH, BATTLE OF
Battle of Monmouth, The. English.
Battle of Monmouth, The. "R. H."
Molly Maguire at Monmouth. William Collins.
MONT BLANC

Hymn before Sunrise, in the Vale of Chamouni. Coleridge.
Mont Blanc. Shelley.
MONTANA
In Montana. McCormick.
Montana. Cohan.
MONTENEGRO. Montenegro. Tennyson.
MONTERREY, MEXICO. Monterey. C. F. Hoffman.
MONTGOMERY, RICHARD. Montgomery at Quebec. Scollard.
MONTHS
Garden Year, The. Sara Coleridge.
Marjorie's Almanac. T. B. Aldrich.
Months, The. C. G. Rossetti.
Months, The. R. B. Sheridan.
Sonnets of the Months. San Geminiano, *tr. fr. Italian by* D. G. Rossetti.
Succession of the Four Sweet Months, The. Herrick.
MONTREAL, CANADA
Bonne Entente. F. R. Scott.
Cartier at St. Malo. *Fr.* A View of Montreal. Francis Webb.
Montreal. A. M. Klein.
Montreal. Lighthall.
Psalm of Montreal, A. Samuel Butler.
Winter in Montreal. Patrick Anderson.
MONTROSE, JAMES GRAHAM, 5TH EARL OF
Execution of Montrose, The. Aytoun.
Verses Composed on the Eve of His Execution. James Graham, Marquess of Montrose.
MONTSERRAT (monastery), SPAIN. Monserrat. W. E. Collin.
MOON
African Moonrise. Roy Campbell.
Arctic Moon, The. *Fr.* The Yukon. Joaquin Miller.
At a Luner Eclipse. Hardy.
Bonny Harvest Moon, The. Barr of Craigielee.
Cat and the Moon, The. Yeats.
Clair de Lune. F. M. Ford.
Clair de Lune. Verlaine, *tr. fr. French by* Symons.
Complaint to the Moon. H. L. Stuart.
Crescent Moon. Basho, *tr. fr. Japanese by* Henderson.
Crescent Moon. E. M. Roberts.
Cruel Moon, The. Robert Graves.
Diana. Ralegh.
Early Moon. Sandburg.
Fair Moon, Who with Thy Cold and Silver Shine. Drummond of Hawthornden.
Fields Are Spread, The. Coatsworth.
Folly. Laramore.
Fragment: To the Moon. Shelley.
Full Moon. De la Mare.
Full Moon. *Fr.* Down the Mississippi. J. G. Fletcher.
Full Moon. Kinnell.
Full Moon. Elinor Wylie.
Full Moon; Santa Barbara. Teasdale.
Hymn to the Harvest Moon. Karlfeldt, *tr. fr. Swedish by* Stork.
Hymn to the Moon. *Fr.* Homeric Hymns. *Unknown, tr. fr. Greek by* Shelley.
I Have Cared for You, Moon. G. H. Conkling.
In Dispraise of the Moon. M. E. Coleridge.
In the Moonlight. Hardy.
In the Moonlight. O'Conor.
In the Moonlight. D. M. Wright.
In the Night of the Full Moon. Busse, *tr. fr. German by* Bithell.
Is the Moon Tired? *Fr.* Sing-Song. C. G. Rossetti.
It Was the Lovely Moon. John Freeman.
July Dawn. Bogan.
Lady Moon. R. M. Milnes.
Lament of This Good Moon. Laforgue, *tr. fr. French by* Bennett.
Little Day Moon. N. B. Miller.
Look Down Fair Moon. Whitman.
Man in the Moon, The. *Unknown.*
Milk-white Moon, Put the Cows to Sleep. Sandburg.
Mr. Moon. Carman.
Mockery. K. D. Riggs.
Modern Endymion, A. Pickthall.
Moon, The. Azumamaro, *tr. fr. Japanese by* Asataro Miyamori.
Moon, The. Bhasa, *tr. fr. Sanskrit by* Keith.
Moon, The. W. H. Davies.
Moon, The. Camilla Doyle.
Moon, The. Follen.
Moon, The. Herford.
Moon, The. Kotomichi, *tr. fr. Japanese by* Asataro Miyamori.
Moon. Henry Rowe.
Moon, The ("And like a dying lady"). Shelley.
Moon, The ("Art thou pale for weariness"). Shelley.
Moon, The. Södergran, *tr. fr. Finnish by* Wahlgren *and* Allwood.
Moon-Bathers. John Freeman.
Moon behind High Tranquil Leaves, The. Robert Nichols.
Moon-Children. Michael Lewis.
Moon Compasses. Robert Frost.
Moon Festival. Tu Fu, *tr. fr. Chinese by* Rexroth.
Moon in Eclipse. Ibn Hamdis, *tr. fr. Arabic by* Arberry.
Moon in Mist. Ibn Burd, *tr. fr. Arabic by* Arberry.
Moon It Shines, The. *Unknown, tr. fr. German.*
Moon Looked into My Window, The. E. E. Cummings.
Moon-Madness. Starbuck.
Moon Magic. Hanes.
Moon of Brooklyn, The. Nathalia Crane.
Moon Rider. W. R. Benét.
Moon Ship, The. *Unknown, tr. fr. Japanese.*
Moon, So Round and Yellow. Matthias Barr.
Moon Song. Hilda Conkling.
Moon Spell. Aylen.
Moon was but a chin of gold, The. Emily Dickinson.
Moon Worshippers, The. E. R. Dodds.
Moonbeam. Hilda Conkling.
Moonbeams. Wirsén, *tr. fr. Swedish by* Stork.
Moonlight. De la Mare.
Moonlight. Moxon.
Moonlight. Tahureau, *tr. fr. French by* Lang.
Moonlight. *Unknown.*
Moonlight. Vansittart.
Moonlight. Verlaine, *tr. fr. French by* Kittel.
Moonlight in Italy. Kinney.
Moonlight North and South. R. F. Murray.
Moonlight on Lake Sydenham. Wilson MacDonald.
Moonrise. *Fr.* Contemplation; a Nightpiece. Cunningham.
Moonrise. Doolittle ("H. D.").
Moonrise. Droste-Hülshoff, *tr. fr. German by* Salinger.
Moonrise. A. H. Evans.
Moonrise. G. M. Hopkins.
Moonrise. D. H. Lawrence.
Moonrise. F. D. Sherman.
Moonrise in the Rockies. R. P. Bradley.
Moons. David Morton.
Moon's Orchestra, The. *Fr.* Down the Mississippi. J. G. Fletcher.
Moon's the North Wind's Cooky, The. Vachel Lindsay.
Moonspath. Pamplin.
New Moon, The. Bryant.
Nocturne, A: "Moon has gone to her rest, The." Blunt.
O for a Moon to Light Me Home. De la Mare.
O Lady Moon. C. G. Rossetti.
Ocean to Cynthia, The. Ralegh.
Ode to the Moon. Hood.
On a Moonlight Night. Tu Fu, *tr. fr. Chinese by* Bynner.
On the Telescopic Moon. Drennan.
Phases of the Moon. *Fr.* One Word More. Robert Browning.
Phosphorescence. Langbridge.
Poetic Thought. *Unknown.*
Possum and the Moon, The. David Campbell.
Prayer by Moonlight. Swartz.
Purity of the moonlight, The. *Unknown, tr. fr. Japanese by* Rexroth.
Rising of the Moon, The, A.D. 1798. J. K. Casey.
Roustabout Moon, The. D. M. Davis.
Runaway, The. C. Y. Rice.
Sadness of the Moon. Baudelaire, *tr. fr. French by* Conder.
Satyrs and the Moon, The. H. S. Gorman.
Silver. De la Mare.
Silver Road, The. Hendry.
Sing a Song of Moonlight. Eastwick.
Solomon's Hymn to the Moon. Levertin, *tr. fr. Swedish by* Stork.
Song for the Moon on Mount Omei. Li Po, *tr. fr. Chinese.*
Song of the Moon, A. Claude McKay.
Sonnet: "O bitter moon, O cold and bitter moon." Clement Wood.
Sonnet of the Moon, A. Charles Best.
To the Afternoon Moon, at Sea. C. Y. Rice.
To the Harvest Moon. H. K. White.
To the Moon. Hardy.
To the Moon. Ronsard, *tr. fr. French.*
To the Moon. Shelley.
To the Moon. H. L. Stuart.
Under the Harvest Moon. Sandburg.
Under the Moon. Yeats.
Waning Moon, The. Shelley.
Welcome to the Moon. *Unknown.*
White Moon, The. Verlaine, *tr. fr. French by* Flores.
White Window, The. James Stephens.
Wind and the Moon, The. George Macdonald.
Winter Moonlight. Gillespie Evans.
With How Sad Steps, O Moon. *Fr.* Astrophel and Stella. Sidney.
Young May Moon, The. Thomas Moore.
MOONEY, TOM (Thomas J. Mooney). Tom Mooney. W. E. Leonard.
MOONFLOWERS. To the Moonflower. Betts.

MOONSHINERS
Blockader, The. DuBose Heyward.
Mountain Still, The. Cawein.
MOORE, SIR JOHN. Burial of Sir John Moore after Corunna, The. Charles Wolfe.
MOORE, MARIANNE. Invitation to Miss Marianne Moore. Elizabeth Bishop.
MOORE, THOMAS
On Thomas Moore's Poems. *Unknown.*
Reply to Lines by Thomas Moore, A, *sel.* ("Will you come to the bower I have shaded for you?"). Landor.
Thomas Moore at St. Anne's. McGee.
To Thomas Moore ("My boat is on the shore"). Byron.
To Thomas Moore ("What are you doing now"). Byron.
MOORS
Barren Moors, The. Channing.
Gloucester Moors. W. V. Moody.
On Westwall Downes. Strode.
Owre the Muir amang the Heather. Glover.
MORALITY. There Are Roughly Zones. Robert Frost.
MORE, SIR THOMAS (Saint Thomas More)
Ballad of St. Thomas, A. C. A. Brady.
Case of Thomas More, The. Sister Mary St. Virginia.
Margaret Roper's Vision of Her Father, Sir Thomas More. *Fr.* London Bridge. F. T. Palgrave.
MORGAN, SIR HENRY. Morgan. Stedman.
MORGAN, JOHN HUNT. Kentucky Belle. C. W. Woolson.
MORNING
Awake, Mine Eyes. *Unknown.*
Bird's Song at Morning. Dawson.
Call of the Morning, The. Darley.
Cock-Crow Song. *Unknown, tr. fr. Chinese by* Waley.
Cock-crowing. Vaughan.
Description of the Morning, A. Swift.
Early Morn. W. H. Davies.
Early Morning, The. Belloc.
Early Morning at Bargis. Hagedorn.
Early Morning in a Glade. Dresbach.
Early Morning Meadow Song. Dalmon.
Good Morning. Baillie.
Hail, Fair Morning. *Fr.* The Life of St. Cellach of Killala. *Unknown, tr. fr. Late Middle Irish by* O'Grady.
Herald. Josephine Miles.
Hymn to the Morning. Phillis Wheatley.
I Stood Tiptoe upon a Little Hill. Keats.
In the Morning. Loftus.
Joy of the Morning. Markham.
Keys of Morning, The. De la Mare.
Lark Now Leaves His Wat'ry Nest, The. Davenant.
Mattens. George Herbert.
Morn. H. H. Jackson.
Morning. Blake.
Morning. Hilda Conkling.
Morning. John Cunningham.
Morning. D. H. Gallagher.
Morning, A. Garrison.
Morning, The. *Fr.* Trivia. Gay.
Morning. Keble.
Morning. Lukonin, *tr. fr. Russian by* Lindsay.
Morning. Hugh McCrae.
Morning. Martinez de Navarrete, *tr. fr. Spanish by* Beckett.
Morning. Ransom.
Morning. Rimbaud, *tr. fr. French by* Davis.
Morning. Runeberg, *tr. fr. Swedish by* Stork.
Morning. Savage.
Morning. Stuckenberg, *tr. fr. Danish by* Stork.
Morning. Jane Taylor.
Morning. Teasdale.
Morning. Toumanian, *tr. fr. Armenian by* Boyajian.
Morning. Very.
Morning. Waddington.
Morning and Evening. P. P. Frost.
Morning and Evening. Slonimski, *tr. fr. Polish by* Kirkconnell.
Morning at the Beach. John Farrar.
Morning at the Window. T. S. Eliot.
Morning Breaks, The. Oxenham.
Morning Clouds. N. B. Miller.
Morning Hymn. Alexander.
Morning Hymn. St. Gregory the Great, *tr. fr. Latin by* Caswall.
Morning Hymn. Ken.
Morning Hymn. Wesley.
Morning in the Market. N. A. Smith.
Morning in the North-West. Stringer.
Morning Light. Newsome.
Morning Light for One with Too Much Luck, The. Schwartz.
Morning Meditations. Hood.
Morning Mist, The. Southey.
Morning on the Lièvre. Lampman.
Morning Song. K. W. Baker.
Morning Song. Fet, *tr. fr. Russian by* Eastman.
Morning Song. Pollard.
Morning Song of Senlin. *Fr.* Senlin, a Biography. Aiken.
Morning Twilight. Baudelaire, *tr. fr. French by* Gibbs.
Morning-Watch, The. Vaughan.
Mornin's Mornin', The. Gerald Brennan.
Nocturnal Eclogue, *sel.* ("Hark! the shrill cock, the rising morn proclaims"). Moses Browne.
One Morning When the Rain-Birds Call. Lloyd Roberts.
Pack, Clouds, Away. *Fr.* The Rape of Lucrece. Heywood.
Parting at Morning. Robert Browning.
Prayer for Dreadful Morning. E. M. Root.
Rainy Morning. J. N. North.
Reveille. A. E. Housman.
September Morning. Mörike, *tr. fr. German by* Tobin.
Sister, Awake! *Unknown.*
Summer Morning, A. Rachel Field.
Sung on a Sunny Morning. J. S. Untermeyer.
Time to Rise. R. L. Stevenson.
To Morning. Blake.
Tropical Morning at Sea, A. Sill.
Upon Westminster Bridge. Wordsworth.
Waking Time. Eastwick.
Will there really be a morning? Emily Dickinson.
Yonder See the Morning Blink. A. E. Housman.
MORNING GLORIES
Morning-Glory, The. Coates.
Morning-Glory, The. M. G. Lowell.
MOROCCO. Morocco. Currey.
MORRIS, WILLIAM
To William Morris. W. C. Greene.
William Morris. Idris Davies.
MORTON, WILLIAM THOMAS GREEN. Crawford Long and William Morton. Rosemary *and* S. V. Benét.
MOSBY, JOHN SINGLETON. Mosby at Hamilton. Cawein.
MOSCOW, USSR
Little Thatched House I Was Born in, The. Yesenin, *tr. fr. Russian by* Hewitt.
Red Square, The. Poletaev, *tr. fr. Russian.*
MOSES
Angels Came a-Mustering, The. *Unknown, tr. fr. Hebrew by* Zangwill.
Burial of Moses. C. F. Alexander.
Death of Moses, The. *Unknown, tr. fr. Hebrew by* Lucas.
Moses and Jesus. Zangwill.
Young Moses, The. Marquis.
MOSQUITOES
Mosquito, The. D. H. Lawrence.
Mosquitoes. Al-Sumaisir, *tr. fr. Arabic by* Arberry.
To a Mosquito. Bryant.
MOTHER
As at Thy Portals Also Death. Whitman.
Autumn. J. S. Untermeyer.
Beautiful Hands. E. M. H. Gates.
Between the Porch and the Altar. Robert Lowell.
Blind Child, The. *Unknown.*
Boy's Mother, A. Riley.
C. L. M. Masefield.
Cradle Song: "Sleep, my child, my little daughter." *Unknown, tr. fr. Yiddish by* Leftwich.
Day After, A. Tourian, *tr. fr. Armenian by* Boyajian.
Dear Old Mothers. C. S. Ross.
Definition. G. N. Crowell.
Echo of a Song, The. Foley.
English Mother, An. R. U. Johnson.
Epitaph on My Dear and Ever Honoured Mother, An. Bradstreet.
First Aid. Hopegood.
For You, Mother. Hilda Conkling.
Funeral Song upon the Decease of Annes, His Mother, A. Grimald.
Gift, The. *Unknown.*
God's Mothers. Malloch.
Greatest Battle That Ever Was Fought. Joaquin Miller.
Hand That Rocks the Cradle Is the Hand That Rules the World, The. W. R. Wallace.
Happy He with Such a Mother. *Fr.* The Princess. Tennyson.
Her Hands. *Fr.* Songs for My Mother. Branch.
Her Little Boy. *Unknown.*
Her Words. *Fr.* Songs for My Mother. Branch.
Hide of My Mother, The. Dorn.
How's My Boy? Dobell.
I Must Not Tease My Mother. Sigourney.
Identity. Sister Mary Helen.
Irish Mother in the Penal Days, The. Banim.
Irish Mother's Lament, The. C. F. Alexander.
Jean Richepin's Song. Trench.
Like Mother, like Son. Grafflin.
Little Girl That Mother Used to Be. N. B. Turner.
Little Mother. "M. P. D."
Lonesome. P. L. Dunbar.
Love. Manger, *tr. fr. Yiddish by* Betsky.
Love's Tribute. Sturgeon.
Mary at the Cross. McGee.

Ma's Tools. *Unknown.*
Mater Amabilis. Lazarus.
Maternity. Deutsch.
Maternity. Alice Meynell.
Message, A. A. N. Reed.
Modern Mother, The. Alice Meynell.
Mother, The. S. L. Arnold.
Mother, The. Wilfred Campbell.
Mother, The. Sara Coleridge.
Mother. George Cooper.
Mother. Ehrmann.
Mother. Sister M. Eulalia.
Mother. Fyleman.
Mother. Helburn.
Mother. Iraj, *tr. fr. Persian by* Arberry.
Mother. Kelleher.
Mother. Lovejoy.
Mother, The. I. E. Mackay.
Mother, The. Molodowsky, *tr. fr. Yiddish by* Betsky.
Mother, The. Nekrasov, *tr. fr. Russian by* Kisch.
Mother. Oquendo de Amat, *tr. fr. Spanish by* Hays.
Mother, The. Palmer.
Mother, The. Redpath.
Mother. Ridge.
Mother, The. K. W. Ryan.
Mother. Keith Sinclair.
Mother. Emily Taylor.
Mother ("Each day to her a miracle"). *Unknown.*
Mother, The ("From out the South the genial breezes sigh"). *Unknown, tr. fr. Chinese by* Barrow.
Mother ("Whenever I look in her kind eyes"). *Unknown.*
Mother. Waxman.
Mother—a Portrait. E. R. Fuller.
Mother and Son. William Morris.
Mother and Son. Allen Tate.
Mother, Home, Heaven. W. G. Brown.
Mother in gladness, Mother in sorrow. Wedgefarth.
Mother in the House, The. Hagedorn.
Mother Love. Alford.
Mother o' Mine. *Fr.* The Light That Failed. Kipling.
Mother of a Daughter. Louis Johnson.
Mother of Men. Hooker.
Mother of Men. Southwold.
Mother of the House. Proverbs, Bible, *O.T.*
Mother Thought, A. Guest.
Mother to a Baby. M. E. Coleridge.
Mother to Her Infant, The. Thomas Miller.
Mother to Her Sick Child, A. W. H. Davies.
Mother to Son. Langston Hughes.
Mother Understands, A. Studdert-Kennedy.
Mother Who Died Too, The. E. M. Thomas.
Motherhood. J. D. D. Bacon.
Motherhood. Calverley.
Motherhood. Chworowsky.
Motherhood. Agnes Lee.
Motherhood. Stidger.
Mothers, The. J. P. Bishop.
Mothers. Sabin.
Mothers. *Unknown.*
Mothers—and Others. A. R. Wells.
Mother's Birthday, A. Van Dyke.
Mother's Day. Muth.
Mother's Diary. E. D. Sanders.
Mother's Hands. Wedgefarth.
Mother's Hymn, The. Bryant.
Mother's Lament for the Death of Her Son, A. Burns.
Mother's Love. R. B. Clapp.
Mother's Love. James Montgomery.
Mother's Love ("Her Love is like an island"). *Unknown.*
Mother's Name, A. *Unknown.*
Mothers of Men. A. J. Burr.
Mothers of Men, The. Joaquin Miller.
Mothers of the Earth, The. G. N. Crowell.
Mothers of the West, The. Gallagher.
Mother's Prayer, The. McDermoth.
Mother's Prayer, A. Sangster.
Mother's Prayer, The. Shorter.
Mother's Reward, A. O. F. Lathrop.
Mother's Song, The. Cloud.
Mother's Song ("My Heart is like a fountain true"). *Unknown.*
Mother's Soul, The. I. V. Crawford.
Mother's Trust, The. *Unknown.*
My Altar. Styles.
My Love for You, Mother. Swasey.
My Mother. A. J. Burr.
My Mother. Creelman.
My Mother. M. L. Fisher.
My Mother. Ledwidge.
My Mother. Bertha Nolan.
My Mother. Stuckenberg, *tr. fr. Danish by* Stork.
My Mother. Tikhonov, *tr. fr. Russian by* Lindsay.
My Mother. Ann *and* Jane Taylor.
My Mother. Topelius, *tr. fr. Swedish by* Stork.
My Mother. S. N. Wilson.
My mother and your mother. *Unknown.*
My Mother's Garden. A. E. Allen.
My Mother's House. Tietjens.
My Mother's Prayer. O'Kane.
My Trundle Bed. J. G. Baker.
My Trust. Whittier.
Name of Mother, The. Fetter.
Night and Morning. Aldis.
Nobody Knows—but Mother. *Unknown.*
Now That Can Never Be Done. Sister Maris Stella.
O Mothers of the Human Race. Whitaker.
Old Arm-Chair, The. Eliza Cook.
Old Face, An. F. F. Miller.
Old Mother, The. *Unknown.*
Old Mothers. C. S. Ross.
On the Receipt of My Mother's Picture Out of Norfolk. Cowper.
One Who Struggles, The. Toller, *tr. fr. German by* Roberts.
Only One Mother. George Cooper.
Our Mother. George Cooper.
Our Mother. *Unknown.*
Our Mothers. *Unknown.*
Our Mother's Tunes. Farjeon.
Over the Hill to the Poor-House. Will Carleton.
People, The, *sel.* ("How she grew old happened in fine-darned places"). "Robin Hyde."
Plácido's Sonnet to His Mother. Plácido, *tr. fr. Spanish.*
Prayer for a New Mother. Dorothy Parker.
Prayer for Mothers, A. Todd.
Queen of the World. *Unknown.*
Reading Mother, The. Gillilan.
Remembrance. Bruner.
Rock Me to Sleep. E. A. Allen.
Sailor's Mother, The. Wordsworth.
Second Life of My Mother. Carrera Andrade, *tr. fr. Spanish by* Lee.
Shrine, The. Dolben.
Somebody's Mother. Brine.
Son and Mother. C. Y. Rice.
Song of the Old Mother, The. Yeats.
Songs for My Mother. Branch.
Sonnet to My Mother. George Barker.
Soul of a Mother, The. Sangster.
Starred Mother, The. Whitaker.
To a Mother. Papadaky, *tr. fr. Modern Greek by* Dalven.
To a Polish Mother. Mickiewicz, *tr. fr. Polish by* Parish *and* Noyes.
To C. L. M. Masefield.
To His Mother. Heine, *tr. fr. German by* Marcus.
To Mother. Fessenden.
To Mother—in Heaven. Weaver.
To My First Love, My Mother. C. G. Rossetti.
To My Mother. Heine, *tr. fr. German.*
To My Mother. Henley.
To My Mother. Thomas Moore.
To My Mother. Poe.
To My Mother. "Petros Vlastos," *tr. fr. Modern Greek by* Dalven.
To My Son. Deutsch.
To the Mothers. Toller, *tr. fr. German by* Roberts.
Waiting Mothers. Zuker.
Watcher, The. Widdemer.
What Is Home without a Mother? Alice Hawthorne.
What Rules the World. W. R. Wallace.
When Mother Reads Aloud. *Unknown.*
When Mother Scrubs. *Unknown.*
Which Loved Her Best? "Jay Allison."
White Carnation, The. Sangster.
Wondrous Motherhood. *Unknown.*
You Mean My Mother. *Unknown.*
Young Mother, The. Reese.
Mothers' Anthology, The (MotAn). William Lyon Phelps, comp.
Mothers' Day (*Our American Holidays Series*) (MOAH). Robert Haven Schauffler, ed.

MOTHERS-IN-LAW. His Mother-in-Law. Parke.

MOTHS
Green Moth. Welles.
Moth, The. De la Mare.
Moth Miller. Aileen Fisher.
Moth-Song. Cortissoz.
Moth-Terror. De Casseres.
Moths. David Morton.
Near Dusk. Auslander.
Night Moths, The. Markham.
To a Moth. C. E. Thomas.
To a Moth that Drinketh of the Ripe October. Pfeiffer.

MOTION PICTURES
Essay in Defense of the Movies. Walker Gibson.
Horror Movie. Howard Moss.
Motion Picture Show. Cheyney.
Movies, The. F. K. Frank.
Song of the Movie Mexican, A. E. M. Robison.

MOTLEY, JOHN LOTHROP. In Memory of John Lothrop Motley. Bryant.
MOTORCYCLES. Motorcycle. Pray.
MOUNT HOLYOKE COLLEGE, MASSACHUSETTS. Mount Holyoke. Phyllis Merrill.
MOUNT VERNON, VIRGINIA
Inscription at Mount Vernon. *Unknown.*
Mount Vernon, the Home of Washington. William Day.
Mount Vernon's Bells. Slade.
MOUNTAIN ASH TREES. Rowan Tree, The. Nairne.
MOUNTAIN CLIMBING
Ascent of F 6, The, *sel.* ("At last the secret is out"). Auden *and* Isherwood.
Climbers. Birney.
Climbing a Mountain. Reeves.
Climbing a Mountain. Tao-yün, *tr. fr. Chinese by* Waley.
David. Birney.
De Gustibus. Hankin.
Having Climbed to the Topmost Peak of the Incense-Burner Mountain. Po Chü-i, *tr. fr. Chinese by* Waley.
Mountain Climber, The. Pozzi, *tr. fr. Italian by* Cambon.
On a Grave at Grindelwald. F. W. H. Myers.
On the Heights. L. H. Foote.
Spring Mountain Climb. Eberhart.
Wir Sind Alle Verloren. *Fr.* Elegy for the Fallen Climber. Michael Roberts.
MOUNTAIN LAUREL. Mountain Laurel. Noyes.
MOUNTAIN LIONS. Mountain Lion. D. H. Lawrence.
MOUNTAINEERS. Men of Harlan. Bradley.
MOUNTAINS. *See* HILLS AND MOUNTAINS.
MOUSE. *See* MICE.
MOVIES. *See* MOTION PICTURES.
MOVING. Moving Day. H. M. Hartman.
MOZART, WOLFGANG AMADEUS
For W. A. Mozart. Edgar Bowers.
Four Friends. Leo Ward.
From J. Haydn to Constanze Mozart (1791). Edgar Bowers.
Mozart in Heaven. Bandeira, *tr. fr. Portuguese by* Poore.
Mozart, 1935 Wallace Stevens.
Mozart's Grave. Mowrer.
MULBERRY TREES. Banjo Boomer. Wallace Stevens.
MULES
Cincirinella Had a Mule. *Unknown, tr. fr. Italian by* Cimino.
Ever Since. Coatsworth.
Old Balaam. *Unknown.*
MUMPS. Mumps. E. M. Roberts.
MUNITIONS
Munition-Maker. Laura Simmons.
Munitions Plant. Louis Untermeyer.
MUNSTER, IRELAND
Cashel of Munster. *Unknown, tr. fr. Irish by* Ferguson.
Munster War-Song, The. R. D. Williams.
MURAT, JOACHIM. Murat. *Fr.* Ode from the French. Byron.
MURFREESBORO, BATTLE OF. Battle of Murfreesboro, The. Cornwallis.
MUSEUMS
In a Museum. Deutsch.
In a Museum. A. E. Wilson.
In the Art Museum. Gertrude Hall.
Meditations in a Museum Cloister. Sister Maryanna.
Municipal Gallery Revisited, The. Yeats.
Museums. MacNeice.
Poem for Museum Goers, A. Wieners.
San Marco Museum, Florence. Sister Maris Stella.
MUSHROOMS
Mushroom is the elf of plants, The. Emily Dickinson.
MUSIC
Abt Vogler. Robert Browning.
After a Dolmetsch Concert. Arthur Upson.
After a Symphony Concert. Hayden.
After Music. J. P. Peabody.
Alexander's Feast; or, The Power of Music. Dryden.
Asia. *Fr.* Prometheus Unbound. Shelley.
At a Solemn Music. Milton.
At the Symphony. Nathan.
Ballad of Heaven, A. John Davidson.
Barrel-Organ, The. Noyes.
Beethoven Andante A. G. H. Conkling.
Boy Playing an Organ. Sweeney.
Choral Symphony Conductor. Coates.
Church-Music. George Herbert.
Elegy on the Death of Scots Music. Robert Fergusson.
Envoy: "Go, songs, for ended is our brief, sweet play." Francis Thompson.
Fiddler Jones. *Fr.* Spoon River Anthology. Masters.
Fiddler of Dooney, The. Yeats.
Four Friends. Leo Ward.
God of Music. E. M. Thomas.
Harper, The. *Unknown, tr. fr. Early Modern Irish by* O'Connor.
Harper of Chao, The. Po Chü-i, *tr. fr. Chinese by* Waley.
Haunting Fingers. Hardy.
How oft, when thou, my music, music play'st. *Fr.* Sonnets. Shakespeare.
In Gusts of Music. Sister Davida.
Italian Music in Dakota. Whitman.
Italian Opera. James Miller.
Jazz Fantasia. Sandburg.
L'Envoi: "Now in a thought, now in a shadowed word." E. A. Robinson.
Lines on Hearing the Organ. Calverley.
Lost Chord, A. A. A. Procter.
Man with a Little Pleated Piano, A. Welles.
Military Harpist, The. Pitter.
Music. Baudelaire, *tr. fr. French by* Fitzgerald.
Music. G. K. Chesterton.
Music. Hilda Conkling.
Music. Alice Corbin.
Music. De la Mare.
Music. Du Maurier, *after* Sully-Prudhomme.
Music. Emerson.
Music. Farjeon.
Music. Amy Lowell.
Music. Charles Phillips.
Music. Anne Ryan.
Music ("I pant"). Shelley.
Music and Memory. Albee.
Music at Twilight. Sterling.
Music Comes. John Freeman.
Music I Heard with You. *Fr.* Discordants. Aiken.
Music in Camp. J. R. Thompson.
Music in the Night. Spofford.
Music in the Street. *Unknown.*
Music Magic. Leamy.
Music of a Friend, The. Ledoux.
Music of Hungary. A. R. Aldrich.
Musician. Bax.
Musick in time. *Unknown.*
Musicks Duell. Crashaw.
Musick's Empire. Marvell.
Night Concert. Virginia Earle.
O Black and Unknown Bards. J. W. Johnson.
Ode for Music on St. Cecilia's Day. Pope.
Ode to Francisco Salinas. Luis de León, *tr. fr. Spanish by* Farnell.
Of this day's glorious feast and revel. *Fr.* Seventeen Old Poems. *At. to* Mei Sheng, *tr. fr. Chinese by* Waley.
Old Harp, The. Po Chü-i, *tr. fr. Chinese by* Waley.
On Christmas Day. Paman.
On Hearing a Symphony of Beethoven. Millay.
On Music. Landor.
On Music. Thomas Moore.
Orpheus with His Lute. *Fr.* King Henry VIII. *At. to* Fletcher *and to* Shakespeare.
Passions, The; an Ode for Music. William Collins.
Peter Quince at the Clavier. Wallace Stevens.
Piano, The. Verlaine, *tr. fr. French by* Marsh.
Piano Recital. Deutsch.
Piper, The. Rachel Field.
Piper's Progress, The. "Father Prout."
Ragtime. W. W. Gibson.
Remembered Music. Jalal ed-Din Rumi, *tr. fr. Persian by* Nicholson.
Rubinstein Staccato Etude, The. Dett.
Serenade: "Harken how the flute complains." Brentano, *tr. fr. German by* Salinger.
Soft Musick. Herrick.
Song for St. Cecilia's Day, 1687, A. Dryden.
Song of Shadows, The. De la Mare.
Song of the Banjo, The. Kipling.
Song, to the Gods, Is Sweetest Sacrifice. Annie Fields.
Splendour Falls, The. *Fr.* The Princess. Tennyson.
Stanzas for Music: "There be none of Beauty's daughters." Byron.
Symphony, The. Lanier.
Take a Letter to Dmitri Shostakovitch. Sandburg.
Tanglewood. Francis Sweeney.
Thus sang Orpheus to his strings. *Unknown.*
To a Scarlatti Passepied. Hillyer.
To His Friend Master R. L., in Praise of Music and Poetry. Barnfield.
To Melody. G. L. Allen.
To Music, to Becalm His Fever. Herrick.
To Music. W. K. Seymour.
To Sheila Playing Haydn. Lynd.
To Song. T. S. Jones, Jr.
To the One of Fictive Music. Wallace Stevens.
Toccata of Galuppi's, A. Robert Browning.
Verses to St. Cecilia. David Wright.
Violinist, The. Lampman.
Voice, The. Matthew Arnold.
With a Guitar, to Jane. Shelley.
You muses nurses of delights. *Unknown.*
Untune the Sky (UnS). Helen Plotz, comp.
MUSSELBURGH, SCOTLAND. Musselburgh Field. *Unknown.*
MUSSET, ALFRED DE. Alfred de Musset. *Unknown.*

MYCENAE, GREECE. Mycenae. Alphaeus, *tr. fr. Greek by* Greet.
MYSTICISM
Mystic, The. C. Y. Rice.
Mystic's Prayer, The. "Fiona Macleod."
Song of the Mystic. A. J. Ryan.
MYTHOLOGY
He Inspects His Armory. Plutzik.
Hellenics, The, *sels.* Landor.
Myths. Guy Butler.

N

NABARA (ship). *Nabara*, The. Day Lewis.
NACOGDOCHES, TEXAS. Some Towns of Texas. K. W. Baker.
NAMAQUALAND, AFRICA. Namaqualand after Rain. Plomer.
NAMES
American Names. S. V. Benét.
Choosing a Name. Mary Lamb.
NAMUR, BELGIUM
Between Namur and Liège. Wordsworth.
English Ballad, An, on the Taking of Namur by the King of Great Britain, 1695. Prior.
NANTASKET BEACH, MASSACHUSETTS. Nantasket, *sel.* ("Fair is thy face"). Ames.
NANTUCKETT, MASSACHUSETTS
Alarmed Skipper, The. J. T. Fields.
Nantucket Whalers. Daniel Henderson.
Quaker Graveyard in Nantucket, The. Robert Lowell.
That Nantucket Limerick, and What Followed. *Unknown.*
With a Nantucket Shell. C. H. Webb.
NAOMI. At the Crossroad. Manger, *tr. fr. Yiddish by* Betsky.
NAPLES, ITALY
City of Beggars, The. Alfred Hayes.
Een Napoli. T. A. Daly.
Map of Verona, A. Henry Reed.
Ode to Naples. Shelley.
To Naples. Mallalieu.
Written in Naples. Emerson.
NAPOLEON I.
Advice to a Raven in Russia, December, 1812. Joel Barlow.
Boney. *Unknown.*
Buonaparte. Tennyson.
Death of Napoleon, The. McClellan.
Fifth of May, The—Napoleon. *Fr.* Ode. Manzoni.
Funeral of Napoleon I. Hagarty.
Hop-o-My-Thumb. *Fr.* Ballads on Napoleon. *Unknown.*
I Grieved for Buonaparté. Wordsworth.
Incident of the French Camp. Robert Browning.
Lines Written on Hearing the News of the Death of Napoleon. Shelley.
March to Moscow, The. Southey.
Napoleon. De la Mare.
Napoleon and the British Sailor. Thomas Campbell.
Napoleon's Farewell. Byron.
October, 1803 ("When, looking on the present face of things"). Wordsworth.
Ode to Napoleon Bonaparte. Byron.
Ode, Written during the Negociations with Buonaparte, in January, 1814. Southey.
Return of Napoleon from St. Helena, The. Sigourney.
St. Helena Lullaby, A. Kipling.
Sonnet: "Ambition—following down this far-famed slope." Wordsworth.
Thought of a Briton on the Subjugation of Switzerland. Wordsworth.
To Napoleon in Exile. Channing.
Vendémiaire. Apollinaire, *tr. fr. French by* Fitts.
NAPOLEON II. Napoleon II. Lydia Schuyler.
NAPOLEONIC WARS
Borodino. Lermontov, *tr. fr. Russian by* Cornford.
By Moscow Self-devoted to a Blaze. Wordsworth.
Here Pause: The Poet Claims at Least This Praise. Wordsworth.
Incident of the French Camp. Robert Browning.
November, 1806. Wordsworth.
On the Emperor's Departure, December 7, 1812. Derzhavin, *tr. fr. Russian by* Deutsch.
NARCISSUS (flower)
Narcissus. Cowper.
Narcissus Fields. Farjeon.
NARCISSUS (mythology)
Narcissus. Alistair Campbell.
Narcissus. Gullans.
Narcissus. *Fr.* Metamorphoses. Ovid, *tr. fr. Latin by* Addison.
Narcissus. Valéry, *tr. fr. French by* Shipley.
Narcissus; a Pompeian Bronze. Ivanov, *tr. fr. Russian by* Deutsch.
Sad nymph, Gaho, followed to the shadie woods, The. *Unknown.*
NASEBY, NEW ZEALAND. Naseby; Late Autumn. Dowling.
NASEBY, BATTLE OF. Battle of Naseby, The. Macaulay.
NASH, RICHARD (Beau Nash). On Beau Nash's Picture, Which Once Stood between the Busts of Newton and Pope. Brereton.
NASTURTIUMS
Big Nasturtiums, The. R. B. Hale.
Lines to a Nasturtium. Anne Spencer.
Nasturtiums, The. *Unknown.*
NATIVITY, THE. *See* CHRISTMAS.
NATURE
Again Rejoicing Nature Sees. Burns.
Alastor. Shelley.
And Do They So? Vaughan.
Art and Nature. Medrano, *tr. fr. Spanish by* Longfellow.
Beyond the End. Levertov.
Bonac. Wheelock.
Book of the World, The. Drummond of Hawthornden.
By the Bridge. A. W. H. Eaton.
Celebration of Peace. Hölderlin, *tr. fr. German by* Golffing *and* Opitz.
Chant Out of Doors, A. Marguerite Wilkinson.
Comparison and Complaint, The. Isaac Watts.
Composed While under Arrest. Lermontov, *tr. fr. Russian by* Eastman.
Contemplation, *sel.* ("The river has not any care"). Francis Thompson.
Correspondences. Baudelaire, *tr. fr. French by* Flores.
Dry Loaf. Wallace Stevens.
Enthusiast, The; or, The Lover of Nature. Joseph Warton.
Eternity of Nature. Clare.
Evil Landscape. Corbière, *tr. fr. French by* Koch *and* Guy.
Expostulation and Reply. Wordsworth.
Fain Would I Live in Safest Freedom. Platen, *tr. fr. German* by Morgan.
Fern Hill. Dylan Thomas.
Flood Tide. Hagedorn.
Forest Hymn, A, *sel.* ("Father, thy hand"). Bryant.
Forest of Arden, The. *Fr.* Polyolbion: The Thirteenth Song. Drayton.
From the Shore of Life. *Fr.* De Rerum Natura. Lucretius, *tr. fr. Latin by* Johnson.
Gentian weaves her fringes, The. Emily Dickinson.
Gladness of Nature, The. Bryant.
God, through All and in You All. Samuel Longfellow.
God's Grandeur. G. M. Hopkins.
Green Inn, The. Garrison.
Green Symphony. J. G. Fletcher.
Hard Weather. George Meredith.
Hymn on the Seasons, A. *Fr.* The Seasons. James Thomson.
I taste a liquor never brewed. Emily Dickinson.
In Ampezzo. Stickney.
In Harmony with Nature. Matthew Arnold.
Landscapes. Louis Untermeyer.
Lines Composed a few Miles above Tintern Abbey, on Revisiting the Banks of the Wye during a Tour. Wordsworth.
Maid's Thought, The. Jeffers.
Man and Nature. R. K. Weeks.
Morning Hymn of Adam. *Fr.* Paradise Lost. Milton.
Morning Watch, The. Vaughan.
My Books I'd Fain Cast Off, I Cannot Read. Thoreau.
My Heart Leaps Up When I Behold. Wordsworth.
Natura Naturata. Denham.
Natural Magic. "Æ."
Nature. Binyon.
Nature ("The rounded world"). Emerson.
Nature ("She is gamesome and good"). Emerson.
Nature ("A subtle choice of countless rings"). Emerson.
Nature ("Winters know"). Emerson.
Nature. George Herbert.
Nature. Longfellow.
Nature. Thoreau.
Nature. Vigny, *tr. fr. French by* Jourdain.
Nature and Life. George Meredith.
Nature Doth Have Her Dawn Each Day. Thoreau.
Nature-Hater. Ono, *tr. fr. Japanese by* Ninomiya *and* Enright.
Nature Note. Guiterman.
Nature, the Artist. Knowles.
Nature the False Goddess. Roche.
Nature's Creed. *Unknown.*
Nature's Key-Notes. T. C. Irwin.
Nature's Questioning. Hardy.
Nature's Travail. *Unknown, tr. fr. Greek by* Smith.
O the Fierce Delight. Garland.
On the Religion of Nature. Freneau.
On the Uniformity and Perfection of Nature. Freneau.
Out-of-Doors. Robert Whitaker.

NATURE (*continued*)
Pastoral Hymn, A. John Hall.
Pied Beauty. G. M. Hopkins.
Poem on His Birthday. Dylan Thomas.
Prayer, A: "O Earth, O dewy mother, breathe on us." Lampman.
Prayer, A: "Tend me my birds, and bring again." Norman Gale.
Prelude, The, *sel.* ("The stationary blasts of waterfalls"). Wordsworth.
Quiet Work. Matthew Arnold.
Reason for Not Writing Orthodox Nature Poetry. Wain.
Revival, The. Vaughan.
Saint Francis' Wood. A. J. Cody.
Sky is low, the clouds are mean, The. Emily Dickinson.
Sofa, The, *sel.* ("For I have lov'd the rural walk through lanes"). *Fr.* The Task. Cowper.
Song of Nature. Emerson.
Song Tournement: New Style. Louis Untermeyer.
Sonnet: "At last, beloved nature." Timrod.
Spring, The. *Fr.* The Mistress. Cowley.
Starting from Paumanok. Whitman.
Sweetness of Nature, The. *Unknown, tr. fr. Irish by* O'Connor.
Tables Turned, The ("Up! up! my friend, and quit your books"). Wordsworth.
Testament of Beauty, The, *sel.* ("How was November's melancholy endear'd to me"). Robert Bridges.
Thanatopsis. Bryant.
That Nature Is a Heraclitean Fire and of the Comfort of the Resurrection. G. M. Hopkins.
This is my letter to the world. Emily Dickinson.
Thou Art, O God. Thomas Moore.
To God, the Architect. Kemp.
To Mother Nature. Knowles.
To Nature. S. T. Coleridge.
To Nature. Hölderlin, *tr. fr. German by* Prokosch.
'Twere Long to Tell. *Fr.* The Prelude. Wordsworth.
Vantage Point, The. Robert Frost.
Voice of Nature, The. Robert Bridges.
Wabanaki Song. *Unknown, tr. fr. Wabanaki Indian by* Brown.
Waldeinsamkeit. Emerson.
When Serpents Bargain. E. E. Cummings.
Why, Lord. Van Doren.
Wind in the Pine. Sarett.
Within the Circuit of This Plodding Life. Thoreau.
World, The. *Fr.* Symbolisms. Realf.
Nature Lover's Knapsack, The (NLK). Edwin Osgood Grover, ed.
Songs of Nature (SN). John Burroughs, ed.

NAUTILUS
Chambered Nautilus, The. O. W. Holmes.
To the Nautilus. Hartley Coleridge.

NAVAJO INDIANS
Before Rain. *Tr. from Navajo Indian by* Austin.
Hunting-Song. *Tr. fr. Navajo Indian by* Curtis.
Mountain Chant. *Tr. fr. Navajo Indian by* Matthews.
Navajo Prayer. *Tr. fr. Navajo Indian by* Austin.
Song of the Navajo. Albert Pike.

NAVARINO, BATTLE OF
Battle of Navarino, The. *Unknown.*
Glorious Victory of Navarino, The! *Unknown.*

NAVY, FRANCE. Hervé Riel. Robert Browning.

NAVY, GREAT BRITAIN
All's Well. *Fr.* The British Fleet. Dibdin.
Ballad of the *Clampherdown*, The. Kipling.
Battle of the Baltic, The. Thomas Campbell.
Captain Death. *Unknown.*
Captain Stood on the Carronade, The. Marryat.
Essay on the Fleet Riding in the Downes, An. "J. D."
Famous Fight at Malago, The; or, The Englishmen's Victory over the Spaniards. *Unknown.*
Fighting *Téméraire*, The. Newbolt.
Hawke. Newbolt.
In the Skies. *Fr.* Dunkirk. E. J. Pratt.
Joyfull New Ballad, A. Deloney.
Kilmeny. Noyes.
Loss of the *Birkenhead*, The. F. H. Doyle.
Minora Sidera. Newbolt.
New Song on Lord Nelson's Victory at Copenhagen, A. *Unknown.*
On the Loss of the *Royal George*, The. Cowper.
Revenge, The; a Ballad of the Fleet. Tennyson.
Sailing at Dawn. Newbolt.
To the King on His Navy. Waller.
Ye Mariners of England. Thomas Campbell.

NAVY, HOLLAND. Famous Sea-Fight, A. Looke.

NAVY, SPAIN. Famous Sea-Fight, A. Looke.

NAVY, UNITED STATES
Bay Fight, The. Brownell.
Blood Is Thicker than Water. Wallace Rice.
Constitution and the *Guerrière*, The. *Unknown.*
Cumberland, The. Longfellow.
Farragut. W. T. Meredith.
Fleet at Santiago, The. C. E. Russell.
How We Burned the *Philadelphia*. Barrett Eastman.
Men behind the Guns, The. Rooney.
Old Ironsides. O. W. Holmes.
River Fight, The. Brownell.
Running the Batteries. Melville.
Strong Swimmer, The. W. R. Benét.
When the Great Gray Ships Come in. G. W. Carryl.
Yankee Privateer, The. Arthur Hale.

NAZIS
Ballad: "He did not kill." Glatstein, *tr. fr. Yiddish by* Betsky.
Today the Nazi Forces Marched. Ravitch, *tr. fr. Yiddish by* Betsky.

NEBRASKA. My Nebraska. Diers.

NEBUCHADNEZZAR. Warm Babies. Keith Preston.

NEGRO SPIRITUALS. *Books of American Negro Spirituals, The* (BoAN). James Weldon Johnson *and* J. Rosamond Johnson.

NEGROES
Ancestry. W. A. Donaghy.
And What Shall You Say? J. S. Cotter, Jr.
Ante-Bellum Sermon, An. P. L. Dunbar.
Astraea at the Capitol. Whittier.
Beautiful Negress, The. Pitter.
Big-lipped Negro. Guillén, *tr. fr. Spanish by* Hays.
Black Boy. Rosten.
Black Boys, The. James Boyd.
Black Magdalens. Cullen.
Black Regiment, The. Boker.
Black Tambourine. Hart Crane.
Colored Band, The. P. L. Dunbar.
Congo, The. Vachel Lindsay.
Crispus Attucks. O'Reilly.
Ethiopia Saluting the Colors. Whitman.
For My People. Margaret Walker.
Gee-up Dar, Mules. Piper.
George Robinson; Blues. Rukeyser.
Hard to Be a Nigger. *Unknown.*
I, Too. Langston Hughes.
In Thine Image; a Negro Speaks. Kruger.
Incident. Cullen.
Learned Negro, The. *Unknown.*
Litany of the Dark People. Cullen.
Little Black Boy, The. *Fr.* Songs of Innocence. Blake.
Mr. Nigger. McNeill.
Negro Speaks of Rivers, The. Langston Hughes.
Negro Spirituals. Rosemary *and* S. V. Benét.
Negro Student, The. Steffan.
Nigger. Shapiro.
Ode in Time of Hesitation, An. W. V. Moody.
Old Thad Stevens. Kenneth Porter.
Plaint. C. H. Ford.
Poem: "I am a Negro." Langston Hughes.
Poem: "Little brown boy." Helene Johnson.
September 1, 1802 ("We had a female Passenger"). Wordsworth.
Singing Nigger. Sandburg.
To a Brown Girl. Cullen.
Two-an-Six. Claude McKay.
Unsung Heroes, The. Dunbar.
Book of American Negro Poetry, The (BANP). James Weldon Johnson, ed.
Books of American Negro Spirituals, The (BoAN). James Weldon Johnson *and* J. Rosamond Johnson, eds.
Caroling Dusk. (CDC). Countee Cullen, ed.
Golden Slippers (GoSL). Arna Bontemps, comp.
Poetry of the Negro, The, 1746–1949 (PoNe). Langston Hughes *and* Arna Wendell Bontemps, eds.

NEIGHBORS
Near Neighbors. Swift, *after the Latin of* Martial.
Neighbors, The. Garrison.
Neighbors. A. B. Payne.
Neighbors. Anne Spencer.
Neighbors. Wing.
Portrait by a Neighbor. Millay.
This and That. F. B. Davis.

NEILSON, ADELAIDE
Adelaide Neilson. William Winter.
Lilian Adelaide Neilson. Clement Scott.

NELSON, HORATIO NELSON, VISCOUNT
Admiral's Ghost, The. Noyes.
Ballad of the Good Lord Nelson, A. Durrell.
Battle of the Baltic. Thomas Campbell.
Character of the Happy Warrior. Wordsworth.
Death of Nelson, The. *Unknown.*
1805. Robert Graves.
Nelson. *Fr.* Sonnets of the Empire. Strong.
New Song Composed on the Death of Lord Nelson, A. *Unknown.*
New Song on Lord Nelson's Victory at Copenhagen, A. *Unknown.*
Night of Trafalgar, The. *Fr.* The Dynasts. Hardy.

To William Stewart Rose, Esq. *Fr.* Marmion. Sir Walter Scott.
NEPTUNE
Court of Neptune, The. John Hughes.
Homeric Hymn to Neptune. *Unknown, tr. fr. Greek by* Chapman.
Hymn in Praise of Neptune, A. Campion.
Next unto Him Was Neptune Pictured. *Fr.* The Faerie Queene. Spenser.
NERI, FILIPPO DE'. *See* PHILIP NERI, SAINT.
NERO
Ave! Nero Imperator. Duffield Osborne.
Nero, *sel.* ("I would I were a God"). C. A. Smith.
NETHERLANDS
Character of Holland, The, *sel.* ("Holland, that scarce deserves the name of land"). Marvell.
Dutch Picture, A. Longfellow.
Holland. Provost.
Leak in the Dike, The. Phoebe Cary.
Little Toy Land of the Dutch, The. *Unknown.*
Lowlands o' Holland, The. *Unknown.*
NETLEY ABBEY, SOUTHAMPTON, ENGLAND. Sonnet: Netley Abbey. Bowles.
NETTLES
Nettle, the Flower, The. Zabel.
Tall Nettles. Edward Thomas.
With Seed the Sowers Scatter. A. E. Housman.
NEVADA
Home Means Nevada. Raffetto.
Nevada. Gurney.
NEW ENGLAND
Having New England Fathers. O. W. Holmes.
Hundred Collars, A. Robert Frost.
Late Comer. Fanny de Groot Hastings.
Lilacs. Amy Lowell.
New England. Percival.
New England. G. D. Prentice.
New England. E. A. Robinson.
New England. Savage.
New England Fog. Callaghan.
New England Is New England Is New England. B. H. Green.
New England's Annoyances. *Unknown.*
New England's Chevy-Chase. E. E. Hale.
New England's Crisis. Tompson.
Praise of New England. Chubb.
Refugee in New England. Frances Frost.
Spring in New England. Wilcox.
Stone Crop, The. Coffin.
This Is New England. Margery Mansfield.
NEW GUINEA. New Guinea Lament. McAuley.
NEW HAMPSHIRE
Apples in New Hampshire. Gilchrist.
New Hampshire. *Fr.* Landscapes. T. S. Eliot.
New Hampshire. Robert Frost.
New Hampshire Boy, A. Morris Bishop.
New Hampshire Sexton. Notopoulos.
Old New Hampshire. J. F. Holmes.
Spring in New Hampshire. Claude McKay.
NEW HAVEN, CONNECTICUT. On the Democracy of Yale. F. S. Jones.
NEW JERSEY
Legend. Weaver.
Ode to New Jersey. E. F. Carr.
NEW MEXICO
From the Cliffs at Puye, New Mexico. Hayden.
Men in New Mexico. D. H. Lawrence.
New Mexico. Boyden.
New Mexico and Arizona. Canterbury.
O, Fair New Mexico. Elizabeth Garrett.
On the Great Plateau. E. F. Wyatt.
Railroad Cars Are Coming, The. *Unknown.*
NEW ORLEANS, LOUISIANA
Girod Street Cemetery; New Orleans. Harry Morris.
New Orleans. Ridge.
New Orleans Balcony, A. Haight.
Seven Cities of America, The. Masters.
Vieux Carré. W. A. Roberts.
Zulu King, The; New Orleans. Copeland.
NEW ORLEANS, BATTLE OF
Battle of New Orleans, The. English.
Jackson at New Orleans. Wallace Rice.
Surrender of New Orleans, The. Manville.
To the Defenders of New Orleans. Drake.
NEW SOUTH WALES, AUSTRALIA. Lichtenberg. Kipling.
NEW YEAR
Address to the New Year. Craik.
Amoretti, *sel.* ("New year, forth looking out of Janus' gate"). Spenser.
Another Year. O'Hagan.
Another Year Is Dawning. Havergal.
At Dawn of the Year. "George Klingle."
At the New Year. Patchen.
At the Portal. Havergal.
Bells of New Year. A. G. Field.
Book of the New Year, The. *Unknown.*
Closing Year, The. Prentice.
Dawning o' the Year, The. M. E. M. Blake.
Death of the Old Year. Tennyson.
Diaries. Fuller.
Dying Year, The. C. W. Hill.
Facing the New Year. M. G. Pearse.
Facing the New Year. *Unknown.*
Farewell and Hail! T. C. Clark.
Farewell to the Old Year. Farjeon.
For the New Year. Markham.
Greeting on New Year's Morning, A. *Unknown.*
Here We Come a-Caroling. *Unknown.*
Here We Come a-Wassailing. *Unknown.*
Here We Come a-whistling. *Unknown.*
Higher Good, The. Theodore Parker.
Hymn for the Eve of the New Year. Gerondi, *tr. fr. Hebrew by* Solis-Cohen.
I Am the New Year. *Unknown.*
Imagination. *Fr.* New Year's Eve. John Davidson.
In Trust. M. M. Dodge.
Last Day of the Year, The. Smart.
Merry Christmas and a Glad New Year, A. George Cooper.
Message of the Bells, The. T. C. Clark.
Message of the New Year, The. *Unknown.*
Midnight Mass for the Dying Year. Longfellow.
New Leaf, A. Wheeler.
New Year. Barton.
New Year, The. D. E. Cooke.
New Year, The. George Cooper.
New Year, The. Charles Cotton.
New Year, The. Craik.
New Year, A. M. C. Davies.
New Year. Fujita, *tr. fr. Japanese by* Erickson.
New Year, The. Gard.
New Year, The. Homer-Dixon.
New Year, The. Miyauchi, *tr. fr. Japanese by* Erickson.
New Year. Moment.
New Year, The. H. N. Powers.
New Year, A. Sangster.
New Year, A. Shorter.
New Year, The. Templeton.
New Year, The ("I am the little New Year, ho, ho!"). *Unknown.*
New Year, The ("Oh! I'm the New Year,/Come, look at my wares"). *Unknown.*
New Year ("Over the threshold a gallant newcomer"). *Unknown.*
New Year, The ("With gladness hail the dawning year"). *Unknown.*
New Year. Wearing.
New Year Carol, A: "Here we bring new water." *Unknown.*
New Year Ditty. C. G. Rossetti.
New Year Is a Banner, The. Sangster.
New Year Is Begun, The. *Unknown.*
New-Year Prayer. E. D. Kramer.
New Year Prayer, A. Laura Simmons.
New Year Song. E. H. Miller.
New Year Wish, A. Havergal.
New Years and Old. M. F. Jackson.
New Year's Day. Crashaw.
New Year's Day. Rachel Field.
New Year's Day. *Unknown.*
New Year's Eve. Bartleson.
New Year's Eve. Wyn Griffith.
New Year's Eve. Hardy.
New Year's Eve, 1850. J. R. Lowell.
New Year's Eve—Midnight. F. R. Macdonald.
New Year's Eve, 1913. Bottomley.
New Year's Eve, 1938. Nims.
New Year's Gift to the King, A. William Dunbar.
New Year's Guest, A. Moriarty.
New Year's Hymn. Jochumsson, *ad. fr. Icelandic by* Malone.
New Year's Morning. *Unknown.*
New Year's Promise, A. *Unknown.*
New Year's Resolve. Wilcox.
New Year's Thoughts. Lillian Gray.
New Year's Wish, A. "J. H. S."
New Year's Wish, A. *Unknown.*
New Year's Wishes. Havergal.
News! News! Farjeon.
Old Father Annum. L. F. Jackson.
Old New-Year's Song, An. Levertin, *tr. fr. Swedish by* Stork.
Old Year, The. Clare.
Old Year, The. Urmy.
Old Year's Prayer, The. Minna Irving.
On New Year's Day. *Unknown.*
On the Threshold. A. H. Baldwin.
Passing Year, The. *Unknown.*

NEW YEAR (*continued*)
Peter Stuyvesant's New Year's Call. Stedman.
Prayer: "Bless Thou this year, O Lord!" A. S. C. Clarke.
Prayer for the New Year, A. Armitage.
Prayer for the New Year. Richard of Chichester.
Reconsecration. Dorothy Gould.
Ring, Joyful Bells! Violet Fuller.
Ring Out Wild Bells. *Fr.* In Memoriam A. H. H. Tennyson.
Song for December Thirty-first. Frances Frost.
Song for New Year's Eve, A. Bryant.
Sonnet: "Comes the New Year; wailing the north winds blow." *Fr.* Thysia. Luce.
Thought for a New Year. Burket.
To the New Yeere. Drayton.
Upon New Year's Eve. Quiller-Couch.
Vow for New Year's, A. M. C. Davies.
Way to a Happy New Year, A. Beattie.
Welcome to the New Year. Farjeon.
What cheer? Good cheer! Good cheer! Good cheer! *Unknown.*
When the Year Grows Old. Millay.
Years-End. Wilbur.
NEW YORK (state). Praise of New Netherland, The. Steendam.
NEW YORK (city)
Alternating Nocturne. Tablada, *tr. fr. Spanish by* Beckett.
. . . & Forty-second Street. MacLeish.
Aquarium. Gorostiza, *tr. fr. Spanish by* Walsh.
Bleat of Protest. Mildred Weston.
Bottled; New York. Helene Johnson.
Bowery, The. Hoyt.
Broadway. Hagedorn.
Broadway's Canyon. J. G. Fletcher.
City Birds. Spud Johnson.
Complaint of New Amsterdam, The. Steendam.
Crossing Brooklyn Ferry. Whitman.
Daedalus Sings in the Dusk. Virginia McCormick.
Down Fifth Avenue. Underwood.
Early Dutch. Palen.
First O Songs For a Prelude. Whitman.
From a Downtown Skyscraper. Funk.
Give Me the Splendid Silent Sun. Whitman.
Good Green Bus. Rachel Field.
I'd rather listen to a flute. Hoffenstein.
In New York. *Fr.* Song-Flower and Poppy. W. V. Moody.
In New York. Percy.
Letter to New York. Elizabeth Bishop.
Lights of New York, The. Teasdale.
Manhattan. Beer.
Manhattan. J. G. Fletcher.
Manhattan. Lawless.
Manhattan, *sels.* Towne.
Manhattan Menagerie. Cherwinski.
Mannahatta ("I was asking for something specific . ."). Whitman.
My City. J. W. Johnson.
N. Y. Pound.
New York. "Æ."
New York. Gilder.
New York. Guiterman.
New York City. Abbe.
New York City. Bodenheim.
New York Skyscraper, A, *sel.* ("O sprawling city!"). Oppenheim.
Owed to New York. B. R. Newton.
Peter Stuyvesant's New Year's Call. Stedman.
Proud New York. John Reed.
School Days in New Amsterdam. Guiterman.
Second Avenue. Johns.
Seven Cities of America, The. Masters.
Sidewalks of New York, The. J. W. Blake.
Sky-Signs. Clapp.
Speakers, Columbus Circle. Souster.
Storm on Fifth Avenue. Sassoon.
Sunset on Sixth Avenue. Cadden.
To the Greatest City in the World. Humphries.
Towers of New York, The. Auslander.
Tropics in New York. The; New York. Claude McKay.
Tunnel, The. Hart Crane.
When Dawn Comes to the City; New York. Claude McKay.
NEW YORKER, THE (magazine)
Talk of the Town, The. Ed Fisher.
NEW ZEALAND
In the Rangitaki Valley. Katherine Mansfield.
New Zealand Regret, A. E. E. Montgomery.
October in New Zealand. Jessie Mackay.
Anthology of New Zealand Verse, An (AnNZ). Robert Chapman *and* Jonathan Bennett, eds.
Book of Australian and New Zealand Verse, A (BoAn). Walter Murdock, ed.
NEWFOUNDLAND
Gazeteer of Newfoundland. Michael Harrington.
Newfoundland. E. J. Pratt.
NEWGATE PRISON (London). Friendly Address. A. Hood.
NEWMAN, JOHN HENRY, CARDINAL. Newman. Shuster.
NEWPORT, RHODE ISLAND
Jewish Cemetery at Newport, The. Longfellow.
Letter from Newport, A. F. W. H. Myers.
Newport Beach. Tuckerman.
Newport Street, E. Goldring.
NEWSPAPERS
Boston Evening Transcript, The. T. S. Eliot.
Carrier's Address. *Unknown.*
Doing Railroads for *The Rocky Mountain News.* Warman.
Fleet Street. Leslie.
Headline History. Plomer.
Herald. Josephine Miles.
Newspaper, A. *Fr.* War Is Kind. Stephen Crane.
Pious Editor's Creed, The. *Fr.* The Biglow Papers. J. R. Lowell.
Song of the Press, The. Hillyer.
NEWTON, SIR ISAAC
Epitaph Intended for Sir Isaac Newton. Pope.
Merry Old Souls. Morris Bishop.
Newton. *Fr.* The Prelude. Wordsworth.
Newton to Einstein. Chappell.
Poem Sacred to the Memory of Sir Isaac Newton, A. James Thomson.
NIAGARA FALLS
At the Leap of the Waters. Garesché.
Fall of Niagara, The. Brainard.
Niagara. Garesché.
Niagara. Lenau, *tr. fr. German by* Durling.
Niagara. Squire.
Over-Song to Niagara. J. D. Logan.
NIBELUNGEN LEGENDS
Attila the Hun. *Unknown, tr. fr. Icelandic by* Bellows.
Fall of the Nibelungs, The. *Fr.* The Song of the Nibelungs. *Unknown, pr. tr. fr. Middle High German by* Armour.
First Lay of Gudrun, The. *Fr.* The Elder Edda. *Unknown, tr. fr. Icelandic by* Morris *and* Magnússon.
Norns Watering Yggdrasill, The. W. B. Scott.
Sigurth in Faeroëse. *Unknown, tr. fr. Icelandic by* Smith-Dampier.
NICARAGUA. With Walker in Nicaragua, *sels.* Joaquin Miller.
NIGHT
Acquainted with the Night. Robert Frost.
Allah's Tent. Arthur Colton.
At Night. Cornford.
At Night. Eichendorff, *tr. fr. German by* Cotterell.
At Night. Alice Meynell.
At Night. G. E. Montgomery.
At Night. A. B. Payne.
At Night. Smirnov, *tr. fr. Russian by* Lindsay.
At Night in the Wood. N M. Hayes.
At Nightfall. Towne.
At Nightfall, on the Wall of Paris. Hugo, *tr. fr. French by* Conder
At One o'Clock in the Morning. Baudelaire, *tr. fr. French by* Leefmans.
Be Not Afraid. Nathan.
Beautiful Foreign Land. Eichendorff, *tr. fr. German by* Cotterell.
Beautiful Night, A. *Fr.* Fragments Intended for the Dramas. Beddoes.
Black pitchy night, companion of my woe. *Fr.* Idea's Mirrour. Drayton.
Breath of Night, The. Jarrell.
Check. James Stephens.
Curfew. Longfellow.
Darkness. Peggy Bacon.
Day and Night. Victor Daley.
Day Is Done, The. Longfellow.
Deep Night, Summer. Thad Stem, Jr.
Defence of Night, The. Michelangelo, *tr. fr. Italian by* Symonds.
Draw On, Sweet Night. *Unknown.*
Drowzy night hir wings has spred, The. *Unknown.*
End, The. Newbolt.
Entreaty. Lenau, *tr. fr. German by* Durling.
Evening in Paradise. *Fr.* Paradise Lost. Milton.
First Dream, *sel.* ("But Venus first"). Sister Juana Inés de la Cruz, *tr. fr. Spanish by* Beckett.
First Night, The. Laforgue, *tr. fr. French by* Smith.
First Night Alone. Van Doren.
Four Glimpses of Night. F. M. Davis.
Full Heart, The. Robert Nichols.
Good Night. D. M. Pierce.
Great Night, The. Rilke, *tr. fr. German by* Jarrell.
Hermit, The. Eichendorff, *tr. fr. German by* Cotterell.
Homecoming—Late at Night. Tu Fu, *tr. fr. Chinese by* Rexroth.
Hymn to Night. Cane.
Hymn to Night, A. Michelson.
Hymn to Night. *Fr.* The Rigveda. *Unknown, tr. fr. Sanskrit by* Griffith.

Hymn to the Night. Longfellow.
Hymns to the Night. "Novalis," *tr. fr. German by* Cotterell.
I Roused, Started Up, in the Night. Platen, *tr. fr. German by* Durling.
In the Azure Night. Galindez.
In the Night. Elizabeth Jennings.
In the Night. James Stephens.
In the Night. *Unknown.*
In the Still, Star-lit Night. Stoddard.
In the Wide Awe and Wisdom of the Night. C. G. D. Roberts.
Knowing What Time It Is at Night. Nicholl.
Light the Lamps Up, Lamplighter. Farjeon.
Lighted Night. Guillén, *tr. fr. Spanish by* Turnbull.
Looking Down on Mesopotamia. Bethell.
Lux in Tenebris. Tynan.
Midnight. Dryden.
Midnight. Lampman.
Midnight. *Fr.* Blurt, Master Constable. Thomas Middleton.
Midnight. Mörike, *tr. fr. German by* Cotterell.
Midnight. Michael Roberts.
Midnight. Sackville.
Midnight. Vaughan.
Midnight Prayer. Bialik, *tr. fr. Hebrew by* Frank.
Midsummer Night. Lampman.
Moment Musicale. Carman.
Moon-Night. Eichendorff, *tr. fr. German by* Cotterell.
Music of the Night. John Neal.
My Day and Night. John Payne.
Natura in Urbe. E. B. White.
Night, The. Belloc.
Night. Bialik, *tr. fr. Hebrew by* Samuel.
Night. *Fr.* Songs of Innocence. Blake.
Night. William Browne.
Night. Bullwinkle.
Night. *Fr.* The Shadow of Night. Chapman.
Night. D. J. Hayes.
Night. Heavysege.
Night. Hesse, *tr. fr. German by* Lewisohn.
Night. Ibn Gabirol, *tr. fr. Hebrew by* Lazarus.
Night. Jami, *tr. fr. Persian by* Robinson.
Night. Jeffers.
Night, The. Leuty.
Night. Leconte de Lisle, *tr. fr. French by* Conder.
Night. Longfellow.
Night. L. W. McKay.
Night. James Montgomery.
Night, *sels.* Oppenheim.
Night, *sel.* ("Nights follow each other and are linked"). Péguy, *tr. fr. French by* Anne Green *and* Julian Green.
Night. Regnier, *tr. fr. French by* "Seumas O'Sullivan."
Night. Rolleston.
Night. *Fr.* Queen Mab. Shelley.
Night. *Fr.* Thalaba the Destroyer. Southey.
Night. Symonds.
Night. Symons.
Night. Teasdale.
Night, The. Vaughan.
Night. Very.
Night and Day. Asadi, *tr. fr. Persian by* Browne.
Night and Day. M. M. Dodge.
Night and Day. Ibn Darraj, *tr. fr. Arabic by* Arberry.
Night and the Madman. Gibran.
Night and the Soul, *sel.* ("I should be wretched"). Bigg.
Night Blossoms. Eichendorff, *tr. fr. German by* Cotterell.
Night Cometh. Sidney Dyer.
Night Cometh, The. John McCrae.
Night Enchantment. Muth.
Night Falls on Eden. *Fr.* Paradise Lost. Milton.
Night for Adventures. Starbuck.
Night in a Village, A. Nikitin, *tr. fr. Russian by* Matheson.
Night in Camp. Bashford.
Night in Italy, A, *sel.* ("Sweet are the rosy memories"). "Owen Meredith."
Night in the Green Hill. Meadowcroft.
Night Is Beautiful, The. Langston Hughes.
Night Is Darkening, The. Emily Brontë.
Night Is Near Gone, The. Montgomerie.
Night Lies Silently. Kenetha Thomas.
Night Magic. A. J. Burr.
Night on the Downland. Masefield.
Night on the Prairie. Sage.
Night Rhapsody. Nichols.
Night Serene, The. León, *tr. fr. Spanish by* Walsh.
Night the Plunderer. Khanlari, *tr. fr. Persian by* Arberry.
Night Watch, A. *Fr.* The Passionate Pilgrim. *Unknown.*
Night Will Never Stay, The. Farjeon.
Night-Wind. B. D. Lloyd.
Nightfall. Hsiang Ssu, *tr. fr. Chinese by* Hart.
Nightfall. Kalidasa, *tr. fr. Sanskrit by* Ryder.
Nightfall. Siraj, *tr. fr. Arabic by* Arberry.
Nightfall. Trueba, *tr. fr. Spanish by* Walsh.
Nightfall. Tyutchev, *tr. fr. Russian by* Nabokov.
Nightfall; a Picture. Street.
Nightfall before Syracuse. Hauk.
Nightfall in Dordrecht. Eugene Field.
Night-Ride, The. Slessor.
Night's Mardi Gras. E. J. Wheeler.
Nights Remember, The. Vinal.
Nocturne: "I wander through the silent night." Eichendorff, *tr. fr. German by* Salinger.
Nocturne: "Infold us with thy peace, dear moon-lit night." Sheard.
Nocturne: "Keen winds of cloud and vaporous drifts." Richard Garnett.
Nocturne: "Red flame flowers bloom and die, The." Garstin.
Nocturne: "Softly blow lightly." D. J. Hayes.
Nocturne: "This cool night is strange." Gwendolyn Bennett.
Now through Night's Caressing Grip. Auden.
Now while the Night her sable veil hath spread. Drummond of Hawthornden.
Now Winter Nights Enlarge. Campion.
Nox Benigna. W. P. Reeves.
Nox Nocti Indicat Scientiam. Habington.
O Night, Thou Starry River! Morgenstern, *tr. fr. German by* Hutchins.
Old Adam, The. W. R. Benét.
Orange Tree by Night. *Fr.* The Red-gold Rain. Sacheverell Sitwell.
Out in the Dark. Edward Thomas.
Questions at Night. Louis Untermeyer.
Quiet Street, The. Nan McDonald.
Rainy Night. James Rorty.
Rainy Night. Schrieber.
Sacred Night. Michelangelo, *tr. fr. Italian by* Symonds.
Samarian Nights. Fichman, *tr. fr. Hebrew by* Vardi.
Serenade: "Stars of the summer night." *Fr.* The Spanish Student. Longfellow.
Shadow of Night, The. Patmore.
Shadow of the Night, A. T. B. Aldrich.
Shepherd's Hour, The. Verlaine. *tr. fr. French by* Kittel.
Silver. De la Mare.
Sleepless Night. Droste-Hülshoff, *tr. fr. German by* Salinger.
Song: "My Windows open to the autumn night." Lionel Johnson.
Song: "Night is an ancient sorceress, The." Frug, *tr. fr. Yiddish by* Goldberg.
Song to Night. Coatsworth.
Songs of the Autumn Night. George Macdonald.
Southern Night, A. Matthew Arnold.
Speak from the Distance. Brentano, *tr. fr. German by* Cotterell.
Star That Bids the Shepherd Fold, The. *Fr.* Comus. Milton.
Starlight Night, The. G. M. Hopkins.
Stars and Moon on the River. Tu Fu, *tr. fr. Chinese by* Rexroth.
Stoush o' Day, The. Dennis.
Summer Night, A. Matthew Arnold.
There Are Sweet Flowers. Landor.
There Is Shrill Music in High Winds at Night. Jesse Stuart.
Tiptoe Night. Drinkwater.
To Night. Shelley.
To Night. Symons.
To Night. *Unknown.*
To Night. J. B. White.
Tom o' Bedlam's Song. *Unknown.*
Train in the Night, The. Riddell.
Tryst of the Night, The. Gillington.
'Twas Night. *Unknown.*
Venetian Night, A. Hofmannsthal, *tr. fr. German by* Lewisohn.
Village Night. López, *tr. fr. Spanish by* Walsh.
Waiting for Audience on a Spring Night. Tu Fu, *tr. fr. Chinese by* Rexroth.
Winter Night, A, *sel.* ("When biting Boreas"). Burns.
Winter Night. Millay.
Winter Nightfall. Squire.
NIGHT-BLOOMING CEREUS. Night-blooming Cereus, The. Monroe.
NIGHTINGALE, FLORENCE. Santa Filomena. Longfellow.
NIGHTINGALES
Canadian Rossignol, The. E. W. Thomson.
Concerning the Rose and the Nightingale. Grigoris of Aghtamar, *tr. fr. Armenian by* Boyajian.
Damascus Nightingale, A. Crombie.
Eden. Corke.
Fairford Nightingales. Drinkwater.
Fields Abroad with Spangled Flowers, The. *Unknown.*
Hast Thou Heard the Nightingale? Gilder.
I Love a Flower. Heine, *tr. fr. German by* Salinger.
Itylus. Swinburne.
Lark and the Nightingale, The. Hartley Coleridge.

NIGHTINGALES (*continued*)
Music's Duel. Crashaw.
Nightingale, The. Barnfield.
Nightingale, The. Elizabeth Belloc.
Nightingale, The. Brathwaite.
Nightingale. Chaffee.
Nightingale, The Gerald Griffin.
Nightingale, The. Guillén, *tr. fr. Spanish by* Turnbull.
Nightingale, The. Moxon.
Nightingale, The. Petrarch, *tr. fr. Italian by* Lemesurier.
Nightingale, The. Sidney
Nightingale, The. Symonds.
Nightingale, The. Tynan.
Nightingale, The ("The little pretty nightingale"). *Unknown.*
Nightingale, The. Verlaine, *tr. fr. French by* Kittel.
Nightingale, The. Vicente, *tr. fr. Portuguese by* Bowring.
Nightingale, The. Visscher, *tr. fr. Dutch by* Bowring.
Nightingale, The. Wordsworth.
Nightingale and the Lark, The. Whitney.
Nightingale in the Study, The. J. R. Lowell.
Nightingale near the House, The. Harold Monro.
Nightingale of Avarair, The. Alsihan, *tr. fr. Armenian by* Boyajian.
Nightingale Unheard, The. J. P. Peabody.
Nightingale Weather. Lang.
Nightingales. Robert Bridges.
Nightingales. *Fr.* The Nightingale. S. T. Coleridge.
Nightingales. G. H Conkling.
O Nightingale of Woodland Gay. *Unknown, tr. fr. French by* Symonds.
Ode, An: "As it fell upon a day." Barnfield.
Ode to a Nightingale. Keats.
Ode to the Evening Star. Akenside.
On a Nightingale in April. "Fiona Macleod."
Owl and the Nightingale, The. *At. to* Guildford, *tr. fr. Middle English.*
Palmström to a Nightingale Who Kept Him from Sleeping. Morgenstern, *tr. fr. German by* Gruenthal.
Philomela. Matthew Arnold.
Secret of the Nightingale, The. Noel.
Singing Lesson, The. Ingelow.
To a Nightingale. Drummond of Hawthornden.
To the Nightingale. Ayres.
To the Nightingale. Milton.
To the Nightingale. Countess of Winchilsea.
Whenas the nightingale chanted her vespers. Cleveland.
Where is the nightingale. *Fr.* Songs from Cyprus. Doolittle ("H. D.").
NIJINSKY, VASLAV
For Nijinsky's Tomb. Cornford.
Grand Ballet. Cornford.
Homage to Vaslav Nijinsky. Kirkup.
Nijinsky. Ferne.
NIJMEGEN, NETHERLANDS. Road to Nijmegen. Birney.
NINEVEH, ASSYRIA. Burden of Nineveh, The. D. G. Rossetti.
NILE (river)
Nile, The. Leigh Hunt.
To the Nile. Keats.
To the Nile. Shelley.
To the Nile. Bayard Taylor.
NIOBE. Niobe. *Fr.* Metamorphoses. Ovid, *tr. fr. Latin by* Croxall.
NIPIGON, LAKE, ONTARIO. Night Hymns on Lake Nipigon. D. C. Scott.
NOAH
Before Ararat. J. R. Anderson.
Missing Link, The. Herford.
Noah. *Fr.* The Flaming Terrapin. Roy Campbell.
Noah's Ark. *Unknown.*
Noah's Flood. *Fr.* Genesis. *Unknown, tr. fr. Anglo-Saxon by* Kennedy.
NOISE. Noise Protection. Morgenstern, *tr. fr. German by* Gruenthal.
NONSENSE VERSE. *See* HUMOROUS VERSE.
NOON
Midsummer Noon in the Australian Forest, A. Harpur.
Noon. Clare.
Noon. Le Gallienne.
Noon Is on the Cattle-Track, The. Ingamells.
Noonday. Fan Tseng Hsiang, *tr. fr. Chinese by* Hart.
Noon-Tide. T. S. Jones, Jr.
Noontide. Keble.
Noontide. Leyden.
Winter Noon. Rorty.
NORFOLK, ENGLAND. Norfolk. Betjeman.
NORMANDY. In Normandy. Lucas.
NORRIS, SIR JOHN. Farewell to Sir John Norris and Sir Francis Drake, A. Peele.
NORTH, FREDERICK, 2D EARL OF GUILFORD AND 8TH BARON NORTH. Lord North's Recantation. *Unknown.*
NORTH CAPE, NORWAY. Discoverer of the North Cape, The. Longfellow.
NORTH CAROLINA
April—North Carolina. Harriet Monroe.
Ho! for Carolina! Harrell.
Old North State, The. Gaston.
Tar Heel. Bevington.
NORTH DAKOTA. North Dakota Hymn. Foley.
NORTH POLE. 90 North. Jarrell.
NORTH WIND
Blow, Northern Wind. *Unknown.*
North Wind, The. Gradon.
North Wind, The. Reis.
North Wind Came Up Yesternight, The. Robert Bridges.
North Wind in October. Robert Bridges.
"North Wind, North Wind—Oh, whither so fast?" *Unknown.*
NORTHBORO', MASSACHUSETTS. Minute-Men of North-Boro', The. Wallace Rice.
NORTHERN LIGHTS. *See* AURORA BOREALIS.
NORTHUMBERLAND, ENGLAND. Northumberland. Swinburne.
NORUMBEGA. Norembega. Whittier.
NORWAY
Greetings to Norway. Sigurjónsson, *tr. fr. Icelandic by* Johnson.
Land We Must Have, A. Sivle, *tr. fr. Norwegian by* Stork.
Man with the Broken Fingers, The. Sandburg.
Norway's Highlands. Welhaven, *tr. fr. Norwegian by* Stork.
Anthology of Norwegian Lyrics (AnNoLy). Charles Wharton Stork, ed. and tr.
NORWEGIANS
We Shall Come Back. Grieg, *tr. fr. Norwegian by* Stork.
We Shall Survive. Överland, *tr. fr. Norwegian by* Stork.
NOTRE DAME DE PARIS
On the Parapet of Notre Dame. *Fr.* Quatrains. Quirk.
Rain-beaten Cathedral, The. Takamura, *tr. fr. Japanese by* Ninomiya *and* Enright.
Smiling Demon of Notre Dame, A. Jewett.
NOVA SCOTIA. Flag of Old England, The. Joseph Howe.
NOVEMBER
Epping Forest. *Fr.* November. Davidson.
Hearth Song. R. U. Johnson.
In November. A. R. Aldrich.
In November. Lampman.
In November. S. K. Phillips.
In November. D. C. Scott.
Late November. Lampman.
Mist and All, The. Willson.
My November Guest. Robert Frost.
No! Thomas Hood.
November. Robert Bridges.
November. Alice Cary.
November. Cleaveland.
November. Coatsworth.
November. *Fr.* Sonnets on the Seasons. Hartley Coleridge.
November. Aileen Fisher.
November. M. L. Fisher.
November. Flinn.
November. Keble.
November. Le Gallienne.
November. Samuel Longfellow.
November. William Morris.
November. Rose.
November. C. G. Rossetti.
November. Stoddard.
November. Edward Thomas.
November. Verhaeren, *tr. fr. French by* Lewisohn.
November Afternoons. Sister Mary Madeleva.
November Blue. Alice Meynell.
November Dusk. Ficke.
November Evening. *Fr.* The Cotter's Saturday Night. Burns.
November Eves. Flecker.
November Furrow. Kennon.
November Garden. Louise Driscoll.
November Morning. Evaleen Stein.
November Night. Crapsey.
November Rain. Uschold.
November Sunshine. Smythe.
November Surf. Jeffers.
November Wears a Paisley Shawl. Hilda Morris.
November's Cadence. Carnegie.
Out of November: Speaking for One. McCord.
Weather Vanes. Frances Frost.
NUBIA, AFRICA. Nubia. Bayard Taylor.
NUDISTS. L'Ile du Levant; the Nudist Colony. Barbara Howes.
NUNS
Ballad of a Nun, A. John Davidson.
Effigy of a Nun. Teasdale
Heaven-Haven. G. M. Hopkins.
Hymn of the Moravian Nuns of Bethlehem. Longfellow.
Maid of Honour, The. Massinger.
Mother Marie Therese. Robert Lowell.

Nun, A. Odell Shepard.
Nuns at Eve. Brinnin.
Nuns Fret Not at Their Convent's Narrow Room. Wordsworth.
Nuns in the Wind. Rukeyser.
Nuns of the Perpetual Adoration. Dowson.
Old Nuns. J. M. Hayes.
On a Nun. Vittorelli, *tr. fr. Italian by* Byron.
To a Cloistress. Tassis, *tr. fr. Spanish by* Hemans.
To the Nun. Dafydd ap Gwilym, *tr. fr. Welsh by* Bell.
Vestal, The. *Fr.* Eloisa to Abelard. Pope.
Wreck of the *Deutschland*, The. G. M. Hopkins.
In Praise of Nuns (PraNu). James M. Hayes, ed.
NUREMBERG, GERMANY
Nuremberg. Longfellow.
Old Nürnberg. G. H. Conkling.
NURSES
Nurse's Song. *Fr.* Songs of Experience. Blake.
Old Nurse, The. Cornford.
Santa Filomena. Longfellow.
Staff-Nurse: New Style. *Fr.* In Hospital. Hanley.
Staff-Nurse: Old Style. *Fr.* In Hospital. Hanley.
To Be a Nurse. A. H. Lawrence.
NYMPHS
Afternoon of a Faun, The. Mallarmé, *tr. fr. French by* Morgan.
Nymph and a Swain, A. *Fr.* Love for Love. Congreve.
Nymph Complaining for the Death of Her Fawn, The. Marvell.
Nymph of the Severn, The ("There is a gentle nymph"). *Fr.* Comus. Milton.
Nymphs, The, *sel.* ("There are the fair-limbed Nymphs"). Hunt.
Ode to a Water Nymph. William Mason.
Oenone. Tennyson.
Overheard on a Saltmarsh. Monro.
Sea-Nymph's Parting, The. *Fr.* Gebir. Landor.
Water-Nymph and the Boy, The, *sel.* ("I flung me round him"). Noel.

O

OAK TREES
Bearded Oaks. R. P. Warren.
Brave Old Oak, The. Chorley.
Fall of the Oak, The. George Hill.
Fate of the Oak, The. "Barry Cornwall."
Girt Woak Tree That's in the Dell, The. William Barnes.
Great Oak. Bennett Chapple.
Inscription: "Other stones the aera tell." Cowper.
Oak. Philip Child.
Oak, The. Dryden.
Oak, The. Mary Elliott.
Oak, The. Keble.
Oak, The. Tennyson.
Oak and Olive. Flecker.
Oak Grove, The. Lenau, *tr. fr. German by* Durling.
Oak Leaves. Coatsworth.
Oak's Farewell, The. Stover.
Old Oak Tree at Hatfield Broadoak, The. Locker-Lampson.
Scrub Oak. Root.
Spring Oak. Kinnell.
Three Trees. Christopher Morley.
To an Oak Tree. Sir Walter Scott.
Voice in the Wild Oak, The. Kendall.
Yardley-Oak. Cowper.
OATES, TITUS. Ballad upon the Popish Plot, A. Gadbury.
OBERAMMERGAU, GERMANY. Oberammergau. Speyer.
OBERON. Death of Oberon, The. Thornbury.
OBLIVION. To Everlasting Oblivion. *Fr.* The Scourge of Villany. Marston.
O'CONAIRE, PADRAIC. Padraic O'Conaire—Gaelic Storyteller. F. R. Higgins.
O'CONNELL, DANIEL. Dead Tribune, The. D. F. MacCarthy.
O'CONNOR, RORY. Grave of Rury, The. Rolleston.
OCTOBER
Birthday. J. S. Untermeyer.
Colour of October. Leila Jones.
Fall. Aileen Fisher.
Harvest Home. Guiterman.
In October. Carman.
In the Month of Green Fire. Himmell.
Late October. S. K. Carleton.
Late October. Teasdale.
North Wind in October. Robert Bridges.
October. T. B. Aldrich.
October. Bryant.
October. Bullett.
October. T. A. Daly.
October. Robert Frost.
October. Fyleman.
October. Hooley.
October. H. H. Jackson.
October. Helen McMahan.
October. McNeill.
October. *Fr.* The Earthly Paradise. William Morris.
October. Radford.
October. *Fr.* The Months. C. G. Rossetti.
October. *Fr.* The Shepheardes Calender. Spenser.
October. Edward Thomas.
October. Very.
October. Whitman.
October Ending. Price Day.
October Garden. Pearce Young.
October in New Zealand. Jessie Mackay.
October in Tennessee. Walter Malone.
October Morning. Piatt.
October Night. A. L. Dean.
October of the Angels. J. J. Daly.
October Prelude. "Joseph Upper."
October Winds. V. D. Randall.
October's Bright Blue Weather. H. H. Jackson.
October's Husbandry. Tusser.
October's Party. George Cooper.
Old October. Constable.
Poem in October. Dylan Thomas.
Sonnet: "October's gold is dim—the forests rot." David Gray.
Vagabond Song, A. Carman.
Woodbines in October. C. F. Bates.
OCTOPUSES. Octopus. A. C. Hilton.
ODIN. Descent of Odin, The. Thomas Gray.
O'DONNELL, HUGH ROE. Aodh Ruadh Ó Domhnaill. McGreery.
ODYSSEUS. *See* ULYSSES.
ODYSSEY. Odyssey, The. Lang.
OEDIPUS. Oedipus. Blackburn.
OHIO (state). Founders of Ohio, The. Venable.
OHIO (river). Whiffs of the Ohio River at Cincinnati. Sandburg.
OJIBWA INDIANS. Ojibwa War Songs. *Tr. fr. Ojibwa Indian by* Schoolcraft.
OKEFENOKEE SWAMP, GEORGIA and FLORIDA. Legend of Lake Okeefinokee. L. E. Richards.
OKLAHOMA. Oklahoma. Camden.
OLD AGE
Acre of Grass, An. Yeats.
Adios. Babcock.
Age. Cowley, *after the Greek of* Anacreon.
Age. Richard Garnett.
Age. Landor.
Age. Sir Thomas More.
Age. William Winter.
Age in Prospect. Jeffers.
Age Intercedes for Youth. R. A. Taylor.
Aged, Aged Man, The. *Fr.* Through the Looking-Glass. "Lewis Carroll."
Aged Lover Renounceth Love, The. Vaux.
Aged Man Who Loved to Doze Away, An. Landor.
Aged Ninety Years. Snow.
Ancient Sage, The. Tennyson.
Ancient to Ancients, An. Hardy.
As I Grow Old. Douglas Malloch.
As I Grow Old. *Unknown.*
As We Grow Older. R. J. Wells.
At Eighty. "Katherine Hale."
At Eighty-three. Landels.
At Seventy-two. English.
At the Doors. "Der Nistor," *tr. fr. Yiddish by* Leftwich.
Bedtime Story, A. Mezey.
Blaming Sons. Tao Yuan-ming, *tr. fr. Chinese by* Waley.
Burden of Age, The. *Fr.* The Vanity of Human Wishes. Samuel Johnson.
Changed. Calverley.
Childhood and Age. Witherby.
Come, Captain Age. Cleghorn.
Comfort. Widdemer.
Crabbed Age and Youth. *Fr.* The Passionate Pilgrim. Shakespeare.
Curate's Kindness, The. Hardy.
Danny Murphy. James Stephens.
Days of My Youth. St. George Tucker.
Descending. Iremonger.
Do Not Go Gentle into That Good Night. Dylan Thomas.
Double Ritual. Rainer.
Dregs. Dowson.
Fawn's Foster Mother. Jeffers.
Flight of Youth. Stoddard.
Former Beauties. *Fr.* At Casterbridge Fair. Hardy.
Frailty of Beauty, The. "J. C."
Frost-Morning. William Alexander.
Garadh. Colum.

Old age (*continued*)
Gascoigne's Lullaby. Gascoigne.
Gerontion. T. S. Eliot.
Give Heed to the Old. Mullins.
Goodness of Age. *Unknown, tr. fr. Japanese by* Ishii *and* Obata.
Great-Grandmother, The. Robert Graves.
Green Leaves All Turn Yellow, The. Kenney.
Growing Gray. Dobson.
Growing Old. Matthew Arnold.
Growing Old. "Vandyke Brown."
Growing Old. Learned.
Growing Old. Ledwidge.
Growing Old. *Unknown, tr. fr. Irish by* O'Connor.
Healing. Reisen, *tr. fr. Yiddish by* Leftwich.
His Golden Locks Time Hath to Silver Turn'd. *Fr.* Polyhymnia. Peele.
How Old Are You? *At. to* Edward Tuck *and to* H. S. Fritsch.
I Get Up at Dawn. Lu Yu, *tr. fr. Chinese by* Rexroth.
I Loathe That I Did Love. Vaux.
I Look into My Glass. Hardy.
In Tempore Senectutis. Dowson.
Is It Not Better at an Early Hour. Landor.
Isaac and Archibald. E. A. Robinson.
I've Lived to Bury My Desires. Pushkin, *tr. fr. Russian by* Baring.
John Anderson, My Jo. Burns.
Lament in Old Age. Rudagi, *tr. fr. Persian by* Jackson.
Lament of the Lovely Helmet-Dealer. Villon, *tr. fr. French by* Creekmore.
Lament of the Old Woman Remembering Her Youth. Villon, *tr. fr. French by* Currey.
Lamentation of the Old Pensioner. Yeats.
Last Leaf, The. O. W. Holmes.
Late Leaves. Landor.
Leaden Echo and the Golden Echo, The. G. M. Hopkins.
Leitrim Woman, A. Donaghy.
Let Me Grow Lovely. K. W. Baker.
Letter. Bergman.
Letter from a Girl to Her Own Old Age, A. Alice Meynell.
Light and Dark. Barbara Howes.
Lines for an Old Man. T. S. Eliot.
Litany for Old Age, A. Harsen.
Little Old Lady in Lavender Silk, The. Dorothy Parker.
Little Old Women, The. Baudelaire, *tr. fr. French by* Gibbs.
Lonely, The. "Æ."
Lonely Old Age. Yüan Ch'en, *tr. fr. Chinese by* Hart.
Long Hill, The. Teasdale.
Minuet on Reaching the Age of Fifty, A. Santayana.
Mr. Flood's Party. E. A. Robinson.
My Birthday. Thomas Moore.
Night Is Falling, The. Mangan.
Night Thoughts in Age. Wheelock.
Nod. De la Mare.
Of His Lady's Old Age. Ronsard, *tr. fr. French by* Lang.
Of the Last Verses in the Book. Waller.
Oisin. *Unknown, tr. fr. Irish by* O'Connor.
Old. Ralph Hoyt.
Old, The. Noel.
Old Age. Anacreon, *tr. fr. Greek by* Higham.
Old Age. Bodenheim.
Old Age. Eichendorff, *tr. fr. German by* Watkins.
Old Age. Percy Mackaye.
Old Age. Ou Yang Hsiu, *tr fr. Chinese by* Rexroth.
Old Age. Po Chü-i, *tr. fr. Chinese by* Waley.
Old Age. C. Y. Rice.
Old Age. *Fr.* Arcadia. Sidney.
Old Age. *Fr.* Oedipus at Colonus. Sophocles, *tr. fr. Greek.*
Old Age Pensioner, The. Joseph Campbell.
Old and Young. Bourdillon.
Old Are Sleepy, The. H. L. Davis.
Old Black Men. G. D. Johnson.
Old Crabbed Men. Reeves.
Old Familiar Faces, The. Charles Lamb.
Old Habitant, An. F. O. Call.
Old Knight, The. *Fr.* Polyhymnia. Peele.
Old Labourer, An. Willy.
Old Lady, The. Humbert Wolfe.
Old Man, An. Wordsworth.
Old Man Dreams, The. O. W. Holmes.
Old Man's Comforts and How He Gained Them, The. Southey.
Old Man's Motto, The. Saxe.
Old Man's Weariness, An. A. L. Phelps.
Old Man's Winter Night, An. Robert Frost.
Old Man's Wish, The. Walter Pope.
Old Men, The. De la Mare.
Old Men, The. Javitz.
Old Men. Keesing.
Old Men. Merrill Moore.
Old Men, The. Rhys.
Old Men Admiring Themselves in the Water, The. Yeats.
Old Men and the Young Men, The. Clement Wood.
Old Men and Young Men. John Holmes.
Old Men Are Facts. Vivian Smith.
Old Men on the Blue. Ferril.
Old Men, White-haired, Beside the Ancestral Graves. Basho, *tr. fr. Japanese by* Page.
Old Mr. Tatterlock. Cheyne.
Old People. R. R. Kirk.
Old Seawoman. LeClaire.
Old Song Reversed, An. Stoddard.
Old Woman, The. Bunker.
Old Woman, The. Joseph Campbell.
Old Woman Laments in Springtime, An. Edith Sitwell.
Old Woman of Beare [Regrets Lost Youth], The. *Unknown, tr. fr. Middle Irish.*
Old Woman of the Roads, An. Colum.
Old Woman with Flowers, An. Agnes Lee.
Old Woman's Lamentations, An. Villon, *tr. fr. French by* Synge.
Old Women. Deutsch.
Old Women, The. Symons.
Omnia Somnia. R. M. Watson.
On a Valetudinarian. Ibn al-Rumi, *tr. fr. Arabic by* Carlyle.
On an Old Woman. Lucillius, *tr. fr. Greek by* Cowper.
On and on, always on and on. *Fr.* Seventeen Old Poems. *Unknown, tr. fr. Chinese by* Waley.
On Being Sixty. Po Chü-i, *tr. fr. Chinese by* Waley.
On Growing Old. Masefield.
On Having Grown Old. Moll.
One White Hair, The. Landor.
Out of November: Speaking for One. McCord.
Over the Hill to the Poor-House. Will Carleton.
Philosopher, The. Teasdale.
Piazza Piece. Ransom.
Pigeon-Feeders in Battery Park, The. Altrocchi.
Pity of the Leaves, The. E. A. Robinson.
Portrait of a Very Old Man. Carsley.
Portrait of an Old Woman. Ficke.
Praise of Age, The. Henryson.
Prayer: 'Lord God of the oak and the elm." Villiers.
Prayer for Old Age, A. Yeats.
Prologue: "Poet's age is sad, The: for why?" *Fr.* Asolando. Robert Browning.
Promise of Peace. Jeffers.
Provide, Provide. Robert Frost.
Rabbi Ben Ezra. Robert Browning.
Retirement. *Unknown, tr. fr. Irish by* O'Connor.
Sestina of Youth and Age. Gelett Burgess.
Silver Threads among the Gold. Rexford.
Simon Lee. Wordsworth.
Sing Me a Song. R. L. Stevenson.
Song of the Old Man. J. G. Fletcher.
Song of the Old Mother, The. Yeats.
Superannuation. Sister Mary Eleanore.
Superseded, The. Hardy.
Terminus. Emerson.
Thanks in Old Age. Whitman.
That time of year thou mayst in me behold. *Fr.* Sonnets. Shakespeare.
Thesis and Antithesis. Clough.
Third of November, The. Bryant.
Threescore and Ten. Stoddard.
To Age. Landor.
To an Old Lady. Empson.
To My Ninth Decade. Landor.
To Old Age. Whitman.
To One Being Old. L. E. Mitchell.
To the Woman I Will Be Fifty Years Hence. Virginia Moore.
To Wei Pa, a Retired Scholar. Tu Fu, *tr. fr. Chinese by* Rexroth.
Tower, The. Yeats.
'Twas Just before the Hay Was Mown. Swain.
Twenty Golden Years Ago. Mangan.
Two Old Men. Driscoll.
Upon His Picture. Thomas Randolph.
Upon the Thought of Age and Death. Habington.
Uselessness. E. W. Wilcox.
We Are Never Old. *Fr.* The World-Soul. Emerson.
We Are Old. E. M. Thomas.
We That Are Old. Gwynn.
Welcome Eild. *Unknown.*
When forty winters shall besiege thy brow. *Fr.* Sonnets. Shakespeare.
When Helen first saw wrinkles in her face. Landor.
When I Am Old. C. A. Mason.
When I Am Old. Meeker.
When I See Old Men. Souster.
When They Grow Old. Ralph.
When You Are Old. Henley.
When You Are Old. Yeats.
When Youth Still Made My Spirit Bold. Vyazemsky, *tr. fr. Russian by* Bowra.

Whisperer, The. Arthur Bullen.
Years, The. Wheelock.
Young and Old. Campion.
Young and Old. *Fr.* The Water Babies. Kingsley.
Young Woman. Nemerov.
Youth and Age. George Arnold.
Youth and Age. S. T. Coleridge.
Youth and Age. Mimnermus, *tr. fr. Greek by* Symonds.
Youth and Age. Vance Palmer.
Youth and Age. W. B. Scott.
Old South Meetinghouse, Boston
Church of the Revolution, The. Butterworth.
In the "Old South." Whittier.
Oldham, John. To the Memory of Mr. Oldham. Dryden.
O'Leary, arthur. Lament for Art O'Leary. *Unknown, tr. fr. Irish by* O'Connor.
Olive trees
Olive Tree, The. Baring-Gould.
Olive Trees. Colum.
Olive Trees. Spencer.
Omar Khayyám
For Omar. Humbert Wolfe.
In a Copy of Omar Kháyyám. J. R. Lowell.
To Omar Khayyám. J. H. McCarthy.
Toast to Omar Khayyám. Theodore Watts.
O'More, Rory. Dirge of Rory O'More. De Vere.
O'Neill, Owen Roe. Lament for the Death of Owen Roe O'Neill. T. O. Davis.
O'Neill, Shane. Shane O'Neill. MacManus.
Onions. Onions. *Fr.* Verses for Fruitwomen. Swift.
Opal. Opal. Josephine Miles.
Opera. Carmen. Newman Levy.
Ophelia
Ballad of Another Ophelia. D. H. Lawrence.
Ophelia. Rimbaud, *tr. fr. French by* Hill.
Ophelia. Vernon Watkins.
Opossums
Opossum. W. J. Smith.
Possum and the Moon, The. David Campbell.
Opportunity
Eternity ("He who bends [or binds] to himself a joy"). Blake.
Opportunity. Cawein.
Opportunity. P. L. Dunbar.
Opportunity. Ingalls.
Opportunity. Machiavelli, *tr. fr. Italian by* Flecker.
Opportunity. Walter Malone.
Opportunity. Markham.
Opportunity. Sill.
Oranges
Orange, The. Charles *and* Mary Lamb.
Orange Tree, The. Neilson.
Orange Tree by Day. *Fr.* The Red-gold Rain. Sacheverell Sitwell.
Orange Tree by Night. *Fr.* The Red-gold Rain. Sacheverell Sitwell.
Oranges. Ibn Sara, *tr. fr. Arabic by* Arberry.
Orchards
Among the Orchards. Lampman.
Apple Howling Songs ("Here's to thee, old apple tree"). *Unknown.*
Crowns, The. John Freeman.
In the Orchard. Ibsen, *tr. fr. Norwegian by* Gosse.
In the Orchard. Muriel Stuart.
Little Green Orchard, The. De la Mare.
Lost Orchard, The. Masters.
Of an Orchard. Tynan.
Orchard. Doolittle ("H. D.").
Orchard by the Shore, The; a Pastoral. Sweetman.
Overheard in an Orchard. Cheney.
Tall Fruit Trees, The. Pitter.
Orchids. Sun Orchids. Douglas Stewart.
Oregon (state)
Exodus for Oregon. Joaquin Miller.
Oregon State Song. Buchanan.
Oregon (ship)
Battle-Song of the *Oregon.* Wallace Rice.
Race of the *Oregon,* The. Meehan.
Rush of the *Oregon,* The. Guiterman.
Oregon Trail
Oregon Trail, The. W. R. Benét.
Oregon Trail, 1851. James Marshall.
Oregon Trail, The, 1843. Guiterman.
Organists
Organist, The. G. W. Stevens.
Organist, The. *Unknown.*
Organist in Heaven, The. T. E. Brown.
Over His Keys. *Fr.* The Vision of Sir Launfal. J. R. Lowell.
Orient (ship). Brave Old Ship, *The Orient,* The. R. T. S. Lowell.
Original sin
Adam Lay Ibounden. *Unknown.*
Corruption. Vaughan.
Eva's Lament, *sel.* ("Alas! that ever that speche was spoken"). *Unknown.*
Original Sin; a Short Story. R. P. Warren.
Orioles
Hearing the Early Oriole Po Chü-i, *tr. fr. Chinese by* Waley.
Oriole. Fawcett.
Oriole. M. M. Walker.
Song the Oriole Sings, The. W. D. Howells.
To an Oriole. Fawcett.
To hear an oriole sing. Emily Dickinson.
Orion (mythology). Orion Seeks the Goddess Diana. *Fr.* Landscape with the Giant Orion. Sacheverell Sitwell.
Orion (constellation). Orion. C. T. Turner.
Oriskany, battle of. Battle of Oriskany. Helmer.
Orkney Islands, Scotland
In Orknay. Fowler.
To Orkney. Vedder.
Ormonde, Elizabeth Preston Butler, Countess of. To the Excellent Pattern of Beauty and Virtue, Lady Elizabeth, Countess of Ormond. Shirley.
Orphans
Little Orphant Annie. Riley.
Nobody's Child. P. H. Case.
Orphan, The, *sels.* Otway.
Orphan, The. *Unknown, tr. fr. Irish by* O'Connor.
Orphan, The. *Unknown, tr. fr. Chinese by* Waley.
Orphan Born. Burdette.
Orphans, The. W. W. Gibson.
Orpheus
Eurydice to Orpheus. Robert Browning.
Greater Music, The. Weiss.
Orpheus. Winters.
Orpheus and Eurydice. *Fr.* Metamorphoses. Ovid, *tr. fr. Latin by* Congreve.
Orpheus, Eurydice, and Hermes. Rilke, *ad. fr. German by* Lowell.
Orpheus, O Orpheus, gently touch thy Lesbyan lyre. *Unknown.*
Orpheus with His Lute. *Fr.* King Henry VIII. *At. to* Shakespeare *and to* Fletcher.
Thus sang Orpheus to his strings. *Unknown.*
Osgood, Frances S. To Fr——s S. O——d. Poe.
Osler, Sir William. Osler. Thayer.
Ospreys. Osprey and Eagle. Rittenhouse.
Ossian. Ossian, *sel.* ("Spoke my heart in the dearth of the night"). J. F. O'Donnell.
Ostend, Belgium. Bells of Ostend, The. W. L. Bowles.
Ostriches. Ostrich Is a Silly Bird, The. M. E. W. Freeman.
O'Sullivan Beare, Donall. Dirge of O'Sullivan Bear. J. J. Callanan.
Otago, New Zealand. There's Nae Place like Otago Yet. Barr of Craigielee.
Othello. Cataclysm. Brettell.
Ottawa (city), Canada. Ottawa. D. C. Scott.
Ottawa (river), Canada
Deep Dark River. Lloyd Roberts.
To the Ottawa. Bourinot.
Otter (river), Devon. Sonnet: To the River Otter. S. T. Coleridge.
Otterbourne [*or* Otterburn], battle of
Battle of Otterbourne [*or* Otterburn], The. *Unknown.*
Chevy Chase. *Unknown.*
Hunting of the Cheviot, The. *Unknown.*
Ouray, Colorado. Lines on Mountain Villages. "Sunset Joe."
Outdoor life
Hill Song, A. Egerton.
My Hope, My Love. *Unknown, tr. fr. Irish by* Walsh.
Song of the Open Road. Ogden Nash.
Song of the Open Road, A. *Unknown, tr. fr. Latin by* Symonds.
Song of the Open Road. Whitman.
Song of Wandering, A. Lord Dunsany.
Toil of the Trail, The. Garland.
Up a Hill and a Hill. F. S. Davis.
When in the Woods I Wander All Alone. Hovell-Thurlow.
Nature Lover's Knapsack, The (NLK). Edwin Osgood Grover, ed.
Ovenbirds
Oven-Bird, The. Bolles.
Oven Bird, The. Robert Frost.
Overland Trail. Dust of the Overland Trail, The. J. B. Adams.
Owain Gwynedd, prince of North Wales. Triumphs of Owen, The. Gwalchmai, *tr. fr. Welsh by* Gray.
Owls
Downy Owl, The. E. W. Linn.
Great Brown Owl, The. Hawkshaw.
Hunter, The. E. G. Wallis.
Owl, The. "Barry Cornwall."
Owl, The. De la Mare.
Owl, The. Tennyson.

OWLS (continued)
Owl, The. Edward Thomas.
Owl, The. *Unknown, tr. fr. German.*
Owl, The. Roland Young.
Owl and the Fox, The. *Unknown.*
Owl and the Nightingale, The. *At. to* Guildford, *tr. fr. Middle English.*
Owl and the Pussy-Cat, The. Lear.
Owl-Critic, The. J. T. Fields.
Screech Owl, The. *Unknown.*
Sweet Suffolk Owl. *Unknown.*
There Was an Old Owl. *Unknown.*
White Owl, The. *Fr.* Love in a Valley. George Meredith.
White Owl, The. Tennyson.
Wind and an Eagle Owl, *sel.* ("We rode out with the pealing day before us"). Brettell.
Winter. *Fr.* Love's Labour's Lost. Shakespeare.
Wise Old Owl, A. E. H. Richards.
OXEN
Bullocks, The. Comfort.
Draught-Ox, The. Addaeus, *tr. fr. Greek by* Neaves.
I Have Twelve Oxen. *Unknown.*
Meeting, The. Monroe.
Ox, The. Carducci, *tr. fr. Italian by* Cambon.
Ox-Tamer, The. Whitman.
Oxen, The. Hardy.
Oxen. R. M. Jones.
Partners. Castiello.
Pensioned Ox, The. Addaeus, *tr. fr. Greek by* Lucas.
Red Oxen. García Lorca, *tr. fr. Spanish by* Turnbull.
Teams, The. Lawson.
OXFORD, ENGLAND
Above the High. Grigson.
Alma Mater. Quiller-Couch.
Duns Scotus's Oxford. G. M. Hopkins.
Epilogue Spoken at Oxford by Mrs. Marshall. Dryden.
Gargoyles at Oxford. Willy.
Letter, A. Quiller-Couch.
Oxford. Gerald Gould.
Oxford. Lionel Johnson.
Oxford. *Fr.* Sonnets of the Empire. Strong.
Oxford Bells. Sister Maris Stella.
Oxford Idyll, An. T. E. Brown.
Oxford Is a Stage. Edward Nolan.
Oxford Nights. Lionel Johnson.
Prologue and Epilogue to the University of Oxford (*spoken by Mr. Hart at the acting of* "The Silent Woman"). Dryden.
Sonnet: To Oxford. Thomas Russell.
Spires of Oxford, The. Letts.
To Oxford. *Fr.* Low Sunday and Monday. G. M. Hopkins.
To the University of Oxford, 1674. Dryden.
Verses on Sir Joshua Reynolds's Painted Window at New-College, Oxford. Warton.
Vision of Oxford, A, *sel.* ("Methought I met"). William Alexander.
OYSTERS
Oyster, The. Ogden Nash.
Oyster Crabs. Carolyn Wells.
Oyster Shell, The. Kambara, *tr. fr. Japanese by* Ninomiya *and* Enright.
Precious Pearl, The. Pat Wilson.
OZARK MOUNTAINS. Ozark Song. Dennis Murphy.

P

PACIFIC OCEAN
By the Pacific. Herbert Bashford.
By the Pacific Ocean. Joaquin Miller.
Chart of the Pacific. Gessler.
Eye, The. Jeffers.
On the Edge of the Pacific. Theodore Maynard.
Once by the Pacific. Robert Frost.
Pacific Door. Birney.
PACIFISM AND PACIFISTS
Conscientious Objector, The. Shapiro.
I Sing of Olaf. E. E. Cummings.
Pacifist, The. Belloc.
Pacifists. M. A. Howe.
Poltroon, The. Cleghorn.
Song of the Pacifist, The. Service.
PAGET, VIOLET ("Vernon Lee"). To Vernon Lee. Amy Levy.
PAIN
After great pain a formal feeling comes. Emily Dickinson.
Christian's New-Year Prayer, The, *sel.* ("If my vain soul needs blows and bitter losses"). E. W. Wilcox.
I dreaded that first robin, so. Emily Dickinson.
Never Admit the Pain. Mary Gilmore
90 North. Jarrell.
Pain. Elsie Robinson.
Pain has an element of blank. Emily Dickinson.
Place of Pain in the Universe, The. Hecht.
Prayer for Pain. Neihardt.
Process. C. L. O'Donnell.
Security. C. L. O'Donnell.
Sympathizers, The. Josephine Miles.
To Be. Gutiérrez Nájera, *tr. fr. Spanish by* Beckett.
PAINE, THOMAS
On Mr. Paine's "Rights of Man." Freneau.
Tom Paine. Byron.
PAINTING AND PAINTERS
Andrea del Sarto. Robert Browning.
Bather in a Painting, A. Ashton Greene.
Detail from an Annunciation by Crivelli. Rosemary Dobson.
Episode, An. Symonds.
For a Venetian Pastoral. D. G. Rossetti.
For "The Wine of Circe." D. G. Rossetti.
"Found." D. G. Rossetti.
Fra Lippo Lippi. Robert Browning.
Gallery, The. Marvell.
I Paint What I See. E. B. White.
Large Bad Picture. Elizabeth Bishop.
Musée des Beaux Arts. Auden.
Old Pictures in Florence. Robert Browning.
On the Picture of the Three Fates in the Palazzo Pitti, at Florence. A. H. Hallam.
Painter in New England, A. C. W. Stork.
Paul Veronese: Three Sonnets. Sir Samuel Ferguson.
Pictor Ignotus. Robert Browning.
Portrait of a Cree. "Katherine Hale."
Quatrains: "Brushes and Paint are all I have." G. B. Bennett.
Raphael's San Sisto Madonna. G. H. Miles.
Romney, The. Harriet Monroe.
Sargent's Portrait of Edwin Booth at "The Players." T. B. Aldrich.
Sunday Morning Apples. Hart Crane.
To a Famous Painter. *Fr.* Epistle to a Famous Painter. John Dyer.
To a Painter. *Unknown, tr. fr. Greek by* Edmonds.
To a Portrait Painter Who Desired Him to Sit. Po Chü-i, *tr. fr. Chinese by* Waley.
Unpraised Picture, An. Richard Burton.
Upon the Sight of a Beautiful Picture. Wordsworth.
PALESTINE
Judean Hills Are Holy. W. L. Stidger.
Palestine. Whittier.
See also ISRAEL; ZION.
PALFREY, JOHN GORHAM. O Mother State. *Fr.* To John Gorham Palfrey. J. R. Lowell.
PALINURUS. Palinurus. George Cronyn.
PALISADES, NEW YORK *and* NEW JERSEY. On the Palisades. Louis Untermeyer.
PALM SUNDAY
Donkey, The. G. K. Chesterton.
For Palm Sunday. H. H. Milman.
Little Catkins. Blok, *tr. fr. Russian by* Deutsch.
Palm Sunday. Jammès, *tr. fr. French by* Yung.
Palm Sunday. J. J. Moment.
Palm Sunday and Monday. E. M. Poteat.
Palm-Sunday. Vaughan.
Palm Sunday Hymn. "George Klingle."
Riding through Jerusalem. M. S. Campbell.
Triumphant Entry, The. Vaughan.
PALM TREES
Palm House, Botanic Gardens. Hetherington.
Palm-Tree, The. Abd-ar-Rahman I, *tr. fr. Arabic by* Trend.
Palm Tree, The. Hemans.
Palm-Tree, The. Whittier.
Palm-Tree and the Pine, The. R. M. Milnes.
Song of the Palm. Tracy Robinson.
PALOMAR, MOUNT. Two Mountains Men Have Climbed. Starkweather.
PALOS, SPAIN. Palos, Spain, 1492. Annette Wynne.
PAN (god)
Dead Pan, The. E. B. Browning.
God of Sheep, The. *Fr.* The Faithful Shepherdess. John Fletcher.
Hymn of Pan. Shelley.
Hymn to Pan. *Fr.* Endymion. Keats.
Hymn to Pan. *Fr.* Homeric Hymns. *Unknown, tr. fr. Greek by* Lucas.
Litany to Pan. Eden Phillpotts.
Musical Instrument, A. E. B. Browning.
Pan. Emerson.
Pan. Ledwidge.
Pan. Leconte de Lisle, *tr. fr. French by* Conder.
Pan. Maikov, *tr. fr. Russian by* Phillimore.

Pan. *Unknown, tr. fr. Greek by* Butler.
Pan and the Cherries. Fort, *tr. fr. French by* Bithell.
Pan Crucified. Leonora Speyer.
Pan-Pipes. P. R. Chalmers.
Pan Pipes. *Unknown.*
Pan with Us. Robert Frost.
Pan's Syrinx was a girl indeed. *Fr.* Midas. Lyly.
Pipe of Pan, The. E. A. Allen.
Song for a Forgotten Shrine to Pan. John Farrar.
To Pan ("Pan, who hast to thy command"). *Unknown, tr. fr. Greek by* Higham.
To Pan. *Fr.* Homeric Hymns. *Unknown, tr. fr. Greek by* Way ("Sing me of Hermes beloved son") *and by* Lindsay ("Muse, tell of Pan").
To Pan ("Twy-horn Pan, the ridgy hills"). *Unknown, tr. fr. Greek by* Lothian.
Villanelle of the Living Pan. W. A. Roberts.
Winter-Song for Pan. John Erskine.
PANAMA
Panama. A. T. Jones.
Panama. J. J. Roche.
PANAMA CANAL
Goethals, the Prophet Engineer. MacKaye.
Song of Panama, A. Damon Runyon.
PANDORA. Pandora. *Fr.* Works and Days. Hesiod, *tr. fr. Greek.*
PANGOLINS. Pangolin, The. Marianne Moore.
PANSIES
Pansy. M. E. L. Newsome.
Pansy and the Prayer-Book, The. Betham-Edwards.
Yellow Pansy, A. H. G. Cone.
PANTHERS
Black Panther, The. J. H. Wheelock.
Panther, The. Markham.
Panther, The. Ogden Nash.
Panther, The. Rilke, *tr. fr. German.*
PARACHUTES. Parachute. Snaith.
PARADES
Parade, The. M. E. Badley.
Triumphal March. *Fr.* Coriolan. T. S. Eliot.
PARADISE
Glory of Paradise, The. St. Peter Damian, *tr. fr. Latin by* Blackett.
Paradise. C. G. Blanden.
Paradise. F. W. Faber.
Paradise. C. G. Rossetti.
Paradise Lost, *sels.* Milton.
Paradise Regained, *sels.* Milton.
Paradisi Gloria. T. W. Parsons.
Tiare Tahiti. Rupert Brooke.
See also HEAVEN.
PARAKEETS. Bird with the Coppery, Keen Claws, The. Wallace Stevens.
PARANOIA. Paranoia. Karnosh.
PARENTHOOD
Andre. Gwendolyn Brooks.
Any Father to Any Son. Money-Coutts.
Birthnight Candle, A. J. H. Finley.
Child to Parents. Viola Meynell.
Eight Months Old. Marion Strobel.
Expectant Father, The. E. O. Laughlin.
Fatherhood. H. C. Beeching.
For a Child Expected. Anne Ridler.
I Had a Fair Young Son. S. B. Field.
If I Had a Boy. *Unknown.*
If We Could Only Be! Lee Shippey.
Little Chap Who Follows Me, The. *Unknown.*
Little Son. G. D. Johnson.
Mother Fear. Ditlevsen, *tr. fr. Danish by* Stork.
On My First Daughter. Jonson.
On My First Son. Jonson.
On the Birth of a Child. Louis Untermeyer.
On the Birth of His Son. Su T'ung-po, *tr. fr. Chinese by* Waley.
Parental Ode to My Son, Aged Three Years and Five Months, A. Hood.
Parental Recollections. Charles *and* Mary Lamb.
Parenthood. John Farrar.
Personal History; for My Son. Ruthven Todd.
Poems for My Daughter. Horace Gregory.
Poet's Welcome to His Love-begotten Daughter, A. Burns.
Prayer for My Daughter, A. Yeats.
To a New Daughter-in-Law. *Unknown.*
To His Son, Vincent Corbet. Richard Corbet.
To My Daughter. Lampman.
To My Daughter Betty, The Gift of God. T. M. Kettle.
To My Firstborn. B. I. Durward.
To My Son. Drinkwater.
To My Son. M. J. Griffin.
Toys, The. Patmore.
Two Parents, The. "Hugh MacDiarmid."
Two Sons. Robert Buchanan.
Which Shall It Be? E. L. Beers.
Wishes for My Son. Thomas MacDonagh.
PARIS, FRANCE
A Fauxbourg. *Fr.* Paris in 1815. George Croly.
Babylonian Sorrows. Heine, *tr. fr. German by* Salinger.
In Paris. Thomas MacDonagh.
In the Place de la Bastille. Richard Burton.
Mirabeau Bridge, The. Apollinaire, *tr. fr. French by* Merwin.
Paris. *Fr.* Aurora Leigh. E. B. Browning.
Paris-am-Seine. Malaquais, *tr. fr. French by* Macdonald.
Paris at Night. Corbière, *tr. fr. French by* Koch *and* Guy.
Paris; the Seine at Night. Charles Divine.
Paris; This April Sunset Completely Utters. Cummings.
Public Holiday; Paris. Horner.
Seven Old Men, The. Baudelaire, *tr. fr. French by* Gibbs.
Spring in the Student's Quarter. Murger, *tr. fr. French by* Lang.
Unromantic Song. Brode.
When We Were Poor in Paris. C. H. Towne.
Zone. Apollinaire, *tr. fr. French.*
PARKER, SIR PETER. New War Song by Sir Peter Parker, A. *Unknown.*
PARKS
Come to the Park They Say Is Dead and See. George, *tr. fr. German by* Gee.
False Summer, The. Zaturenska.
From the Duck-Pond to the Carousel. Rukeyser.
Sunday in the Park. *Fr.* Paterson. W. C. Williams.
PARLIAMENT (Great Britain)
Cavalier Tunes. Robert Browning.
Free Parliament Litany, A. *Unknown.*
On the New Forcers of Conscience under the Long Parliament. Milton.
Ye Parliament of England. *Unknown.*
PARNELL, CHARLES STEWART
Come Gather round Me, Parnellites. Yeats.
Parnell. Lionel Johnson.
Parnell's Memory. Kettle.
PARNELL, THOMAS. Epitaph on Dr. Parnell. Oliver Goldsmith.
PARODIES
Parody Anthology, A. (PA). Carolyn Wells, comp.
See also the special parody sections in:
Anthology of Light Verse, An (ALV). Louis Kronenberger, ed.
Book of Humorous Verse, The (BOHV). Carolyn Wells, comp.
Home Book of Verse, The (HBV). Burton Egbert Stevenson, ed.
Innocent Merriment (InMe). Franklin P. Adams, comp.
What Cheer (WhC). David McCord, ed.
PARROTS
Deprecating Parrots. Beulah May.
Parrot, The. Thomas Campbell.
Parrot, The. Flecker.
Parrot, The. W. W. Gibson.
Parrot, The. Tablada, *tr. fr. Spanish by* Beckett.
Parrot, The. Tu Fu, *tr. fr. Chinese by* Hart.
Parrots, The. W. W. Gibson.
Parrot's Soliloquy. *Fr.* Speak, Parrot. Skelton.
Parrot's Song, The. Raffi, *tr. fr. Armenian by* Boyajian.
Pretty Polly. E. M. Root.
"Psittachus Eois Imitatrix Ales ab Indis." Sacheverell Sitwell.
Sailor to His Parrot, The. W. H. Davies.
Song of the Parrot. Coatsworth.
PARTRIDGES. Song of the Partridge, The. *Unknown, tr. fr. Armenian by* Boyajian.
PASSAGE WEST, IRELAND. Attractions of a Fashionable Irish Watering-Place, The. Mahony.
PASSIONFLOWERS
Passion Flower, The. C. G. Blanden.
Passion-Flower, The. M. W. Fuller.
PASSOVER
Angel, The. Alfred Hayes.
Mother in Egypt, A. Pickthall.
Passover Eve. Fania Kruger.
Passover in the Holy Family, The. D. G. Rossetti.
Pesach Has Come to the Ghetto Again. Heller, *tr. fr. Yiddish by* Rosenfeld.
PASTURES. *See* FIELDS AND PASTURES.
PATER, WALTER. Gemlike Flame, The. Lister.
PATERSON, NEW JERSEY. Paterson, *sels.* W. C. Williams.
PATIENCE
Patient Griselda. *Fr.* The Canterbury Tales: The Clerk's Tale. Chaucer.
Sonnet: "Patience, hard thing! the hard thing but to pray." G. M. Hopkins.
PATRICK, SAINT
At Saint Patrick's Purgatory. *At. to* Donnachadh mor O'Dala, *tr. fr. Middle Irish by* O'Faoláin.
Bard's Chant. *Fr.* Saint Patrick for Ireland. Shirley.
Birth of Saint Patrick, The. Lover.
Blackbird of Derrycairn, The. *Unknown, tr. fr. Old Irish by* O'Faoláin.

PATRICK, SAINT (*continued*)
Breastplate of St. Patrick, The. *At. to* St. Patrick, *tr. fr. Irish.*
Dawn Song—St. Patrick's Day. Storey.
I'll Wear a Shamrock. M. C. Davies.
Praise of Fionn, The. *Unknown, tr. fr. Irish by* O'Connor.
Prayer to St. Patrick. Ninine, *tr. fr. Old Irish by* Stokes *and* Strachan.
Saint Patrick. H. H. Bennett.
Saint Patrick. Markham.
St. Patrick Was a Gentleman. Henry Bennett.
Saint Patrick's Day. Eleanor Hammond.
Saint Patrick's Treasure. P. J. Carroll.
Wearing of the Green. Aileen Fisher.
PATRIOTIC SONGS, AMERICAN
Adams and Liberty. R. T. Paine.
America. S. F. Smith.
America for Me. Henry van Dyke.
America the Beautiful. K. L. Bates.
Battle Cry of Freedom, The. G. F. Root.
Battle Hymn of the Republic. J. W. Howe.
Columbia. Timothy Dwight.
Columbia, the Gem of the Ocean. D. T. Shaw.
Hail, Columbia! Joseph Hopkinson.
Liberty Song, The. John Dickinson.
Marching through Georgia. H. C. Work.
National Song ("America, my own!"). W. H. Venable.
O Beautiful, My Country. F. L. Hosmer.
Ode: "God save the Rights of Man!" Freneau.
Ode on Science. Sumner.
Song for Our Flag, A. Sangster.
Star-spangled Banner, The. F. S. Key.
Tenting on the Old Camp Ground. Walter Kittredge.
Three Hundred Thousand More. J. S. Gibbons.
Yankee Doodle. *Unknown.*
Yorktown Centennial Lyric. P. H. Hayne.
I Hear America Singing (IHA). Ruth Barnes, ed.
Patriotic Anthology, The (PaA). Introduced by Carl Van Doren.
Poems of American Patriotism (PAP). Brander Matthews, ed.
See also PATRIOTIC SONGS, CONFEDERATE.
PATRIOTIC SONGS, CANADIAN. Maple Leaf Forever, The. Alexander Muir.
PATRIOTIC SONGS, CHINESE
Battle Hymn of the Chinese Revolution. *Unknown, tr. fr. Chinese.*
Ch'i Lai' (March of the Volunteers). Shih Ee, *tr. fr. Chinese by* Li Pao-sheng *and* Liu Liang-mo.
PATRIOTIC SONGS, CONFEDERATE
Bonnie Blue Flag, The ("Come, brothers! rally for the right"). A. C. Ketchum.
Bonnie Blue Flag, The ("We are a band of brothers"). Harry McCarthy.
Dixie ("I wish I was in de land ob cotton"). D. D. Emmett.
Dixie ("Southrons, hear your country call you!"). Albert Pike.
My Maryland. J. R. Randall.
PATRIOTIC SONGS, DANISH. King Christian. Evald, *tr. fr. Danish by* Longfellow.
PATRIOTIC SONGS, ENGLISH
God Save the King. *Unknown, at. to* Carey.
Ready, Ay, Ready. H. C. Merivale.
Rule Britannia. *Fr.* Alfred, a Masque. James Thomson.
Song: "There is no land like England." *Fr.* The Foresters. Tennyson.
PATRIOTIC SONGS, FINNISH. National Anthem. Runeberg, *tr. fr. Swedish by* Gorden.
PATRIOTIC SONGS, FRENCH
Ça ira! *Unknown, tr. fr. French by* Oxenford.
Marseillaise, The. Rouget de Lisle, *tr. fr. French by* Kerr.
PATRIOTIC SONGS, GERMAN. Watch on the Rhine. Schneckenburger, *tr. fr. German.*
PATRIOTIC SONGS, GREEK. Greek War-Song. *Unknown, tr. fr. Greek by* Byron.
PATRIOTIC SONGS, HUNGARIAN. National Song. Petőfi, *tr. fr. Hungarian by* Loew.
PATRIOTIC SONGS, ICELANDIC
Iceland's Song. Thomsen, *tr. fr. Icelandic by* Johnson.
Millennial Hymn of Iceland, The. Jochumsson, *tr. fr. Icelandic by* Johnson.
PATRIOTIC SONGS, ITALIAN. Garibaldi Hymn, The. Mercantini, *tr. fr. Italian.*
PATRIOTIC SONGS, NORWEGIAN. Fatherland Song. Björnson, *tr. fr. Norwegian by* Leonard.
PATRIOTIC SONGS, POLISH. Polish National Hymn. Felsinki, *tr. fr. Polish by* Soboleski.
PATRIOTIC SONGS, RUSSIAN. Hymn of the Soviet Union. Mihalkov *and* El-Registan, *tr. fr. Russian by* Untermeyer.
PATRIOTIC SONGS, SWEDISH. Swedish National Hymn. Strandberg, *tr. fr. Swedish by* Stork.
PATRIOTIC SONGS, WELSH. Men of Harlech. *Unknown, tr. fr. Welsh.*
PATRIOTISM
Ad Patriam. Scollard.
Barbara Frietchie. Whittier.
Border March. *Fr.* The Monastery. Sir Walter Scott.
Breathes There the Man with Soul So Dead. *Fr.* The Lay of the Last Minstrel. Sir Walter Scott.
Bruce to His Men at Bannockburn. Burns.
Call of the Bugles, The. Richard Hovey.
Celebrations. Austin Clarke.
Children's Song, The. Kipling.
Dear Harp of My Country. Thomas Moore.
Dulce et Decorum Est. Wilfred Owen.
Fatherland, The. J. R. Lowell.
Flag Goes By, The. H. H. Bennett.
Flags on Fifth Avenue. Christopher Morley.
I Am an American. Lieberman.
I Hear America Singing. Whitman.
Nationality. Mary Gilmore.
Nation's Strength, A. Emerson.
Oh, Breathe Not His Name! Thomas Moore.
Our Country's Call. Bryant.
Patriot, The. Robert Browning.
Patriotism. "Susan Coolidge."
Petition, A. Vernède.
Pro Patria. Tyrtaeus, *tr. fr. Greek by* Campbell.
Pro Patria Mori. Thomas Moore.
Rallying Song. Callinus, *tr. fr. Greek by* Coleridge.
Sail On, O Ship of State! *Fr.* The Building of the Ship. Longfellow.
Scots Wha Hae. Burns.
Soldier, The. *Fr.* 1914. Rupert Brooke.
There Is a Land. James Montgomery.
Yesterday. Ethel Anderson.
Patriotic Anthology, The (PaA). Introduced by Carl Van Doren.
Poems of American Patriotism (PAP). Brander Mathews, ed.
Poetry of Freedom, The (PoFr). William Rose Benét *and* Norman Cousins, eds.
PATRONS. Miserly Patron, A. *Unknown, tr. fr. Old Irish by* Dillon.
PAUL, SAINT
Our Two Worthies. Ransom.
Paul. Earl Marlatt.
To St. Peter and St. Paul. Constable.
PAVLOVA, ANNA. Elegy on the Death of Mme Anna Pavlova, *sel.* ("The glory and the ardour of the stage"). Meyerstein.
PAWNSHOPS. Pawnshop Window. Grenville.
PEACE
And They Shall Beat Their Swords into Plowshares. Micah, Bible, *O.T.*
Ballade for Peace. Orléans, *tr. fr. French by* Currey.
Bells of Peace, The. Aileen Fisher.
Bugle Song of Peace. T. C. Clark.
Celebration of Peace. Hölderlin, *tr. fr. German by* Golffing *and* Opitz.
Christ of the Andes, The. Markham.
Disarmament. Whittier.
Dover Beach. Matthew Arnold.
Even during War. *Fr.* Letter to the Front. Rukeyser.
Flag of Peace, The. C. P. Gilman.
Gospel of Peace, The. J. J. Roche.
He Shall Speak Peace. T. C. Clark.
He Shall Speak Peace unto the Nations. L. V. Walters.
History of Peace, A. Robert Graves.
Hush, All Ye Sounds of War. W. H. Draper.
Hymn to Peace. Joel Barlow.
Hymnal: "Bringer of sun, arrower of evening, star-begetter and moon-riser." Vinal.
In the End of Days. Isaiah, Bible, *O.T.*
In the Way of Peace. L. M. Watt.
Lines for Those Invited in T. George, *tr. fr. German by* Phelps.
Love Is the God of Peace. *Fr.* Elegies. Propertius, *tr. fr. Latin by* Nott.
Man unto His Fellow Man. *Fr.* On a Note of Triumph. Corwin.
Message of Peace, The. J. W. Howe.
Message of Peace, A. J. B. O'Reilly.
More than Flowers We Have Brought. N. B. Turner.
New Mars, The. Coates.
New Victory, The. Widdemer.
Ode to Peace. William Tennant.
Ode to Peace. *Unknown.*
On a Note of Triumph, *sel.* ("Lord God of trajectory and blast"). Corwin.
Pax Beata. M. R. Norris.
Peace. Bhartrihari, *tr. fr. Sanskrit by* P. E. More.
Peace. *Fr.* 1914. Rupert Brooke.
Peace. Phoebe Cary.
Peace. Charles De Kay.
Peace. De la Mare.
Peace. Edman.
Peace. Greenberg.

Peace. George Herbert.
Peace. G. M. Hopkins.
Peace. Agnes Lee.
Peace. Markham.
Peace. Oxenham.
Peace. Pulsifer.
Peace. Scollard.
Peace. Vaughan.
Peace. G. O. Warren.
Peace. A. D. T. Whitney.
Peace. Marguerite Wilkinson.
Peace Message, The. B. E. Stevenson.
Peace Must Come as a Troubadour. Marie Drennan.
Peace on Earth. Bacchylides, *tr. fr. Greek by* Symonds.
Peace on Earth. H. W. Cole.
Peace on Earth. Robert Freeman.
Peace on Earth. Samuel Longfellow.
Peace on Earth. E. H. Sears.
Peace Triumphant. C. Y. Rice.
Peace Universal. A. H. Thorne.
Per Pacem ad Lucem. A. A. Procter.
Prepare. Bynner.
Prince of Peace, The. H. E. Fosdick.
Reconciliation. Wheelock.
Reign of Peace, The. Starck.
Reign of Peace, The. Eliza Thornton.
Restorer, The. Horace, *tr. fr. Latin by* Sargent.
Said the Captain. A. P. Jones.
Scythians, The. Blok, *tr. fr. Russian by* Lindsay.
Shalom Aleichem. *Unknown, tr. fr. Hebrew.*
To Men Unborn. D. O. Hamilton.
To Peace. R. W. Dixon.
Vision of Peace, The. N. H. Dole.
Vision of the Future, A. *Fr.* Messiah. Pope.
When the Cannon Booms No More. W. H. Carruth.
When the Great Grey Ships Come In. G. W. Carryl.
When War Shall Be No More. *Fr.* The Arsenal at Springfield. Longfellow.
Where the Rainbow Ends. Robert Lowell.
Winds of God, The. Scollard.
PEACH TREES
Peach, The. A. F. Brown.
Peach, The. Charles *and* Mary Lamb.
Peachtree. Archibald Rutledge.
Peach Tree, The. Edith Sitwell.
PEACOCK, THOMAS LOVE. Letter to Maria Gisborne. Shelley.
PEACOCKS
Peacocks. W. A. Roberts.
White Peacock, The. "Fiona Macleod."
PEARY, ROBERT EDWIN. Frozen Grail, The. Elsa Barker.
PEAS. Peas. *Unknown.*
PEASANTS
Exiled Mother, The. Boucicault.
Forebears. Monk Gibbon.
French Peasants. Monk Gibbon.
Hungry One, The. *Fr.* Who Can Be Happy and Free in Russia? Nekrasov, *tr. fr. Russian by* Soskice.
Peasant. Kreymborg.
Peasant, A. R. S. Thomas.
Peasant and the Sheep, The. Kriloff, *tr. fr. Russian by* Coxwell.
Peon's Mother, The. Wurtzbaugh.
Photinos the Plowman, *sel.* ("Out of the black fog comes a rider"). Valaoritis, *tr. fr. Modern Greek by* Dalven.
Plougher, The. Colum.
Song of the Peasants. *Fr.* The Fountain of Old Poems. *Unknown, tr. fr. Chinese.*
PEDDLERS AND PEDDLING
Connecticut Peddler. The. *Unknown.*
Pedlar, The. Mew.
Pedlar's Caravan, The. W. B. Rands.
Weary Peddlers. Lieberman.
PEEWEES. *See* PEWEES.
PEGASUS
Pegasus. Day Lewis.
Pegasus. Kavanagh.
PEKING, CHINA. Peking. Pien Chih-lin.
PELHAM, JOHN. Band in the Pines, The. J. E. Cooke.
PELICANS
Eden. Corke.
Frigate Pelican, The. Marianne Moore.
Pelican, The. Thaun, *tr. fr. French by* Wilbur.
Pelican Chorus, The. Lear.
Pelican Island, The, *sels.* James Montgomery.
Pelicans My Father Sees, The. Sister Maris Stella.
PEMBROKE, MARY SIDNEY HERBERT, COUNTESS OF
On the Countess Dowager of Pembroke. William Browne.
To the Right Honorable, the Lady Mary, Countess of Pembroke. *Fr.* Delia. Daniel.
PENGUINS
My Penguin Playmate. D. E. Cooke.
Penguin, A. Herford.
PENITENTES, ORDER OF. Penance by Whipping. *Tr. fr. Spanish by* Austin.
PENNSYLVANIA
Ode to the Inhabitants of Pennsylvania. *Unknown.*
Pennsylvania. Bucher.
PENSHURST, ENGLAND
At Penshurst. Edmund Waller.
To Penhurst. Jonson.
PENTECOST
Call to Pentecost, A. I. M. Tyler.
Hymn for Pentecost. Mangan.
Pentecost. Coats.
PENTLAND HILLS, SCOTLAND. Look Up to Pentland's Tow'ring Tap. Allan Ramsay.
PEONIES. Songs to the Peonies. Li Po, *tr. by* Ayscough *and* Lowell.
PEPPER TREES
Pepper Tree, The. Sister M. Madeleva.
Scenes from the Life of the Peppertrees. Levertov.
PEQUOT INDIANS. Assault on the Fortress, The. Timothy Dwight.
PERFUME. Vial, The. Baudelaire, *tr. fr. French by* Flores.
PERNAMBUCO, BRAZIL. Pernambuco in May. T. G. Roberts.
PERRY, OLIVER HAZARD
On the Death of Commodore Oliver H. Perry. Brainard.
Perry's Victory. *Unknown.*
Perry's Victory on Lake Erie. J. G. Percival.
PERSEPHONE
Demeter and Persephone. Tennyson.
Garden of Proserpina, The. *Fr.* The Faerie Queene. Spenser.
Garden of Proserpine, The. Swinburne.
Hark, All You Ladies That Do Sleep! Campion.
Hymn to Proserpine. Swinburne.
Persephone (Singing). L. V. Ledoux.
Persephone the Queen. Robert Morse.
Proserpine at Enna. Bottrall.
PERSEUS. Perseus. MacNeice.
PERSIA
Hassan; or, The Camel Driver. *Fr.* Persian Eclogues. William Collins.
Persian Poems (PeP). A. J. Arberry, ed.
PERUGIA, ITALY. Perugia. A. J. Burr.
PERUGINO. Angel of Perugino, An. Symons.
PESSIMISM. Pessimist, The. *Unknown.*
PETER, SAINT
Domine, Quo Vadis? *Unknown.*
Focus of That Face, The. Poteat.
In the Servants' Quarters. Hardy.
Lord Turned, and Looked upon Peter, The. E. B. Browning.
Meaning of the Look, The. E. B. Browning.
St. Peter. Eileen Duggan.
St. Peter at the Gate. J. B. Smiley.
Simon and Judas. K. W. Porter.
Simon Surnamed Peter. Masters.
To St. Peter and St. Paul. Constable.
Upon This Rock. J. L. Duff.
PETER THE GREAT. Lament of the Troops on the Death of Peter the Great. *Unknown, tr. fr. Russian by* Chadwick.
PETERLOO MASSACRE
Song to the Men of England. Shelley.
Sonnet: England in 1819. Shelley.
PETRARCH
Italy, *sel.* ("There is, within three leagues and less of Padua"). Samuel Rogers.
Petrarch. Carducci, *tr. fr. Italian by* Foulke.
Praise of Petrarch and of Laura, His Lady, A. *Unknown.*
With Petrarch's Sonnets. Landor.
PETRELS
Lines to the Stormy Petrel. *Unknown.*
Stormy Petrel, The. "Barry Cornwall."
Stormy Petrel, The. Ibsen, *tr. fr. Norwegian by* Stork.
Stormy Petrel, The. J. H. Manning.
To a Petrel. C. Y. Rice.
PETRILLO, JAMES CAESAR. Petrillo, *parody.* "Gilbertulus."
PETRONIUS. To Petronius Arbiter. Gogarty.
PEWEES
Peewee. Kreymborg.
Pewee, The. Trowbridge.
Two Pewits. Edward Thomas.
PHEASANTS
Pheasant, The. Coffin.
Pheasant. Keyes.
Pheasant, The. Pope.
PHILADELPHIA, PENNSYLVANIA. Independence Square, Christmas 1783. Guiterman.
PHILADELPHIA (ship). How We Burned the *Philadelphia.* Barrett Eastman.
PHILIP, KING (American Indian chief). King Philip's Last Stand. Scollard.
PHILIP IV, KING OF SPAIN. Philip the Fourth. Machado, *tr. fr. Spanish by* Proske.
PHILIP NERI, SAINT. St. Philip in Himself. Cardinal Newman.

PHILIPHAUGH, BATTLE OF. Battle of Philiphaugh, The. *Unknown.*
PHILIPPINE ISLANDS
My Last Thought. Rizal, *tr. fr. Spanish by* Halstead.
On a Soldier Fallen in the Philippines. W. V. Moody.
PHILLIPS, WENDELL
Monody on the Death of Wendell Phillips. T. B. Aldrich.
Wendell Phillips. A. B. Alcott.
Wendell Phillips. J. R. Lowell.
Wendell Phillips, *sel.* ("What shall we mourn? For the prostrate tree?"). J. B. O'Reilly.
PHILOSOPHY AND PHILOSOPHERS
Business Men. Chen Tzu-ang. *tr. fr. Chinese by* Waley.
Coronet for His Mistress Philosophy, A, *sel.* ("Muses that Fame's loose feathers beautify"). Chapman.
Homage to the Philosopher. Deutsch.
Philosopher and Her Father, The. Shirley Brooks.
PHLOX. Phlox. Louise Driscoll.
PHOEBES. To a Phoebe Bird. Bynner.
PHOEBUS APOLLO. *See* APOLLO.
PHOENIX
Eden. Corke.
I Saw a Phoenix in the Wood Alone. *Fr.* The Visions of Petrarch. Spenser.
Phoenix, The. A. C. Benson.
Phoenix, The. *Fr.* Nepenthe. Darley.
Phoenix, The. Ogden Nash.
Phoenix, The. W. H. Oliver.
Phoenix, The. Sassoon.
Phoenix, The. Theodore Spencer.
Phoenix, The, *sels. Unknown, tr. fr. Anglo-Saxon.*
Phoenix Self-born, The. *Fr.* Metamorphoses. Ovid, *tr. fr. Latin by* Dryden.
PHOTOGRAPHS
Our Photographs. Locker-Lampson.
Photograph. Galvin.
PHYSICIANS
And Can the Physician Make Sick Men Well. *Unknown.*
Correct Compassion, A. Kirkup.
Crawford Long and William Morton. Rosemary *and* S. V. Benét.
Dispensary, The. Sir Samuel Garth.
Epistle, An, Containing the Strange Medical Experience of Karshish, the Arab Physician. Robert Browning.
New Physician, The. Stephen Chalmers.
Surgeons must be very careful. Emily Dickinson.
That Holy Thing. *Fr.* Paul Faber, Surgeon. George Macdonald.
To a Good Physician. William Wycherley.
Poet Physicians (PoP). Mary Lou McDonough, comp.
PICASSO, PABLO
Father, The. Lattimore.
Picasso and Matisse. Robert Francis.
PICKETT, GEORGE EDWARD
Charge of Pickett's Brigade, The. *Unknown.*
Pickett's Charge. *Fr.* John Brown's Body. S. V. Benét.
PICKPOCKETS. Of Pick-Pockets. *Fr.* Trivia. Gay.
PICNICS
Archaeological Picnic, The. Betjeman.
Let's Have a Picnic Out-of-Doors. M. C. Davies.
Picnic, The. Aldis.
Picnic. Hugh Lofting.
Picnic, The. E. M. Roberts.
Picnic Day. Rachel Field.
Song of Bread and Honey, A. Le Gallienne.
PIEDMONT, ITALY. On the Late Massacre in Piedmont. Milton.
PIERO DELLA FRANCESCA
Nativity. Sarton.
Piero della Francesca. Ridler.
PIGEONS
Belfry Pigeon. N. P. Willis.
Cazador (Hunter). García Lorca, *tr. fr. Spanish by* Spender *and* Gili.
Courtyard Pigeons, The. Giltinan.
Message Received. Raiziss.
Mrs. Peck-Pigeon. Farjeon.
Pigeons, The. Burnham.
Pigeons. Dillon.
Pigeons. Reid.
Pigeons and Snow. Andrew Hewitt.
Pigeons Just Awake. Hilda Conkling.
Wood-Pigeons. Masefield.
PIGS
If I Were a Pig. Elizabeth Fleming.
Ode to the Pig: His Tail. W. R. Brooks.
Pig, The. Ogden Nash.
Pig, The. Southey.
Pig-Tale. *Fr.* Sylvie and Bruno Concluded. "Lewis Carroll."
Poor Man's Pig, The. Blunden.
Silver Sty, The. *Unknown.*
Unknown Color, The. Cullen.
PIKE, ZEBULON MONTGOMERY. Death of General Pike, The. Laughton Osborn.
PIKE'S PEAK
Gold Seeker's Song, The. *Unknown.*
Hit at the Times, A. McGrew.
In the Summer of Sixty. *Unknown.*
Pikes Peak. *Unknown.*
Pike's Peakers, The. Greenleaf.
Soliloquy of the Returned Gold Adventurer. *Unknown.*
Song for the Pike's Peaker. *Unknown.*
To Pikes Peak. Hills.
Ute Pass. Whitney.
PILATE. *See* PONTIUS PILATE.
PILGRIM FATHERS
Atlantic Charter: 1942. *Fr.* The Island. F. B. Young.
Boston Hymn. Emerson.
Children of Light. Robert Lowell.
Courtship of Miles Standish, The. Longfellow.
First Proclamation of Miles Standish, The. M. J. Preston.
If I Were a Pilgrim Child. Rowena Bennett.
Indian's Welcome to the Pilgrim Fathers, The. Sigourney.
Landing of the Pilgrim Fathers in New England. Hemans.
Pilgrim Fathers, The. Leonard Bacon.
Pilgrim Fathers, The. J. B. O'Reilly.
Pilgrim Fathers, The. John Pierpont.
Pilgrim Fathers, The. Wordsworth.
Pilgrim Song. Coates.
Pilgrims Came, The. Annette Wynne.
Song of the Pilgrims, The. Rupert Brooke.
Song of the Pilgrims. Upham.
Twenty-second of December, The. Bryant.
Twenty-second of February, The. Bryant.
Word of God to Leyden Came, The. Rankin.
PILGRIMS AND PILGRIMAGES
As You Came from the Holy Land. *Unknown, sometimes at. to* Ralegh.
At Saint Patrick's Purgatory. Donnachadh mor O'Dala, *tr. fr. Old Irish by* O'Faoláin.
Palmer, The. *Fr.* The Vision of Piers Plowman. Langland.
Passionate Man's Pilgrimage, The. Ralegh.
Pilgrim, The. *Fr.* The Pilgrim's Progress. Bunyan.
Pilgrim, The. Eleanor Downing.
Pilgrim, The. "E. Foxton."
Pilgrim and the Herdboy, The. Robert Buchanan.
Pilgrim at Rome, The. *Unknown, tr. fr. Old Irish by* Meyer.
Pilgrim Way, The. Oxenham.
Pilgrimage, The. George Herbert.
Prologue to "The Canterbury Tales." Chaucer.
Quiet Pilgrim, The. E. M. Thomas.
Sailing of the Pilgrims from Sandwich towards St. James of Compostella, The. *Unknown.*
PINDAR. Praise of Pindar, The. Cowley.
PINE TREES
Aspects of the Pines. P. H. Hayne.
Canadian Pine, The. W T. Allison.
Choosing a Mast. Roy Campbell.
Christmas Tree, The. M. E. W. Freeman.
Family Trees. Douglas Malloch.
Fichtenbaum steht einsam, Ein. Heine, *tr. fr. German.*
God, When You Thought of a Pine Tree. *Unknown.*
Hill Pines Were Sighing, The. Robert Bridges.
Murmuring of Pine Trees, The. Ryokwan, *tr. fr. Japanese by* Miyamori.
My Cathedral. Longfellow.
O Pine-tree Standing. *Fr.* Manyo Shu. Hakutsu.
Old Pine Trees. L. B. Hanes.
Palm-Tree and the Pine, The. R. M. Milnes.
Pine, The. G. M. Moffatt.
Pine, The. A. G. Webster.
Pine against the Blue, The. Starbuck.
Pine at Timber-Line, The. Harriet Monroe.
Pine Tree, The. Pei Pao Yu Lan, *tr. fr. Chinese by* Hart.
Pine Tree, The. *Unknown.*
Pine-Tree Buoy, A. H. S. Morris.
Pine Tree for Diana, The. *Fr.* Odes. Horace, *tr. fr. Latin by* Untermeyer.
Pine Trees and the Sky: Evening. Rupert Brooke.
Pine-Trees in the Courtyard, The. Po Chü-i, *tr. fr. Chinese by* Waley.
Pine Woods, The. Lord John Hanmer.
Pines, The. Lippmann.
Pines. Scruggs.
Pines, The. Spofford.
Pine's Mystery, The. P. H. Hayne.
Snowing of the Pines, The. T. W. Higginson.
Solitary Pine. Prince Ichihara, *tr. fr. Japanese by* Ishii *and* Obata.
Song of the Pine, The. Buckham.
This Pine-Tree. Elizabeth Morrow.
Three Trees. Christopher Morley.
Voices of Pine Trees, The. Rengetsu, *tr. fr. Japanese by* Miyamori.

Whispering Pine Trees, The. Van Rensselaer.
Ye Noble Old Pine Tree. *Unknown.*
PINKHAM, LYDIA. Lydia Pinkham. *Unknown.*
PIONEERS
American History. W. R. Moses.
American Laughter. K. A. Robinson.
Axe, The. I. V. Crawford.
Backwoodsman, The, *sel.* ("Glory and Danger are allied"). J. K. Paulding.
Ballad of William Sycamore, The. S. V. Benét.
Cleary Pioneer, A. Crewe.
Early Days, The. Dowling.
Emigrant's Child, The. Sproull.
Emigrants, The: Introductory Stanzas. Pringle.
Exodus for Oregon. Joaquin Miller.
Final Soliloquy, The. *fr.* Burke and Wills. Thiele.
Founders of Ohio, The. W. H. Venable.
Home Winner, The. Lindberg.
Homesteader, The. I. E. Mackay.
Indiana. *Fr.* The Bridge. Hart Crane.
Kansas Emigrants, The. Whittier.
Man from Snowy River, The. Paterson.
Mothers of the West, The. W. D. Gallagher.
Mountain in the Sky, The. H. M. Corning.
New England's Annoyances. *Unknown.*
New Mexico and Arizona. Canterbury.
Old Log House. Tippett.
Old Pioneer, The. Theodore O'Hara.
On the Emigration to America and Peopling the Western Country. Freneau.
Oregon Trail, The. W. R. Benét.
Oregon Trail, 1851. James Marshall.
Pathfinders, The. Vance Palmer.
Pioneer, The. Eugene Field.
Pioneer, The. Guiterman.
Pioneer Mother, The. E. R. Fuller.
Pioneer Woman. V. P. Crawford.
Pioneers. Badger Clark.
Pioneers. Garland.
Pioneers. Gunderson.
Pioneers. A. W. Jose.
Pioneers. Ophel.
Pioneers. *Unknown.*
Pioneers! O Pioneers. Whitman.
Pioneers, The; or, Twenty Years After. Plomer.
Prairie Schooner, The. E. F. Piper.
Roaring Days, The. Henry Lawson.
Root Hog or Die. Small.
Settler, The. Macnab.
Settler, The. A. B. Street.
Silhouette in Sepia. R. V. Carr.
Song of the Forerunners. K. W. Baker.
Teams, The. Henry Lawson.
Trail Makers, The. Knibbs.
Two Hundred Years Ago. W. H. Drummond.
Voortrekker, The. Kipling.
Westward Ho! Joaquin Miller.
Whalin' Up the Lachlan. Esson.
Where the Dead Men Lie. Boake.
Who Is the Pioneer? *Fr.* Of Mountains. Speyer.
Woman in the Wagon, The. Clyde Robertson.
PIRAEUS, GREECE. Toward the Piraeus. Doolittle ("H. D.").
PIRATES AND PIRACY
Ballad of John Silver, A. Masefield.
Ballad of O'Bruadir, The. F. R. Higgins.
Captain Kidd. *Unknown.*
Captain Ward and the *Rainbow.* *Unknown.*
Derelict. Y. E. Allison.
Downfall of Piracy, The. Benjamin Franklin.
Dutch Picture, A. Longfellow.
Flying Cloud, The. *Unknown.*
Henry Martyn. *Unknown.*
If I Were a One-legged Pirate. Meigs.
Last Buccaneer, The. Kingsley.
Last Buccaneer, The. Macaulay.
Morgan. E. C. Stedman.
Pirate Don Durk of Dowdee, The. Meigs.
Pirate Story. R. L. Stevenson.
Pirate Treasure. A. F. Brown.
Pirates. Coatsworth.
Pirates. Noyes.
Pirates' Fight, The. *Fr.* The Legend of Ghost Lagoon. Schull.
Pirate's Song. Espronceda, *tr. fr. Spanish by* McVan.
Sack of Baltimore, The. T. O. Davis.
Sack of Old Panama, The. Dana Burnet.
Salcombe Seaman's Flaunt to the Proud Pirate, The. *Unknown.*
Sir Andrew Barton. *Unknown.*
Song of the Pirates. *Unknown.*
Tarry Buccaneer, The. Masefield.
PISA, ITALY. Evening; Ponte al Mare, Pisa. Shelley.
PITCHER, MOLLY
Molly Pitcher. L. E. Richards.
Molly Pitcher. K. B. Sherwood.
PITT, WILLIAM
Nelson, Pitt, Fox. *Fr.* Marmion. Sir Walter Scott.
Pitt. Reginald Heber.
PITTSBURGH, PENNSYLVANIA
Fort Duquesne. F. B. Plimpton.
Pittsburgh. James Oppenheim.
PIUS X, POPE. To Pius X at Easter. Wildman.
PIUS XII, POPE. Eugenio Pacelli. Neilson.
PLACE NAMES
American Names. S. V. Benét.
American Traveller, The. "Orpheus C. Kerr."
Indian Names. Sigourney.
Maiden of Passamaquoddy, The. James De Mille.
Names. A. F. Brown.
Poems on the Naming of Places, *sels.* Wordsworth.
Rivers of the West. "Sunset Joe."
PLAGUE. Litany in Time of Plague. *Fr.* Summer's Last Will and Testament. Nashe.
PLAINS
Call of the Plains. Ethel MacDiarmid.
Crossing the Plains. Joaquin Miller.
Great Grey Plain, The. Henry Lawson.
On the Plains. *Fr.* Intaglios. Francis Brooks.
Summer on the Great American Desert. Sage.
PLAINS OF ABRAHAM, QUEBEC. Plains of Abraham, The. Charles Sangster.
PLANE TREES
Little Sycamore, The. *Unknown, tr. fr. the Turin Papyrus by* Baikie.
London Plane-Tree, A. Amy Levy.
Plane-Tree. F. S. Flint.
Sycamore. Watkins.
PLANETS. Undiscovered Planet, The. Norman Nicholson.
PLATO
Plato, a Musician. Leontius, *tr. fr. Greek by* Butler.
Plato to Theon. Freneau.
Plato's Tomb. *Unknown, tr. fr. Greek by* Shelley.
Spirit of Plato. *Unknown, tr. fr. Greek by* Shelley.
PLATTSBURG, BATTLE OF
Battle of Plattsburg The. *Unknown.*
Battle of Plattsburg Bay, The. Scollard.
PLATYPUSES
I Had a Duck-billed Platypus. Barrington.
Platypus, The. Herford.
PLEIADES. Pleiades, The. Coatsworth.
PLOUGHING. *See* PLOWING.
PLOVERS
Golden Plover, The. Hallgrimsson, *tr. fr. Icelandic by* Kirkconnell.
Plover. Luella Boynton.
PLOWING
Autumn Ploughing. *Fr.* Works and Days. Hesiod, *tr. fr. Greek by* Lucas.
I Will Go with My Father a-Ploughing. Joseph Campbell.
Lute and Furrow. Dargan.
Ploughboy, The. Clare.
Plougher, The. Colum.
Ploughing on Sunday. Wallace Stevens.
Ploughman, The. K. W. Baker.
Ploughman, The. O. W. Holmes.
Ploughman, The. Gilbert Thomas.
Ploughman at the Plough. Louis Golding.
Plow: "My beak is bent downward, I burrow below." *Fr.* Riddles. *Unknown, tr. fr. Anglo-Saxon by* Kennedy.
Plowing; a Memory. Garland.
Plowman, The. Knister.
Plowman of Today, The. Garland.
Plowman's Song. Knister.
Sod-Breaker, The. Stringer.
Song of Ploughing. *Unknown.*
Sonnet to a Plow-Woman of Norway. M. T. Ritter.
Spring Ploughing. *Fr.* Works and Days. Hesiod, *tr. fr. Greek by* Lucas.
Time When I Was Plowing, The. Maxwell Anderson.
Useful Plough, The. *Unknown.*
When Smoke Stood Up from Ludlow. A. E. Housman.
See also FARMING AND FARMERS.
PLUM TREES
Fall of the Plum Blossoms, The. Ranko, *tr. fr. Japanese.*
Old Scent of the Plum Tree. Ietaka, *tr. fr. Japanese by* Mathers.
Plum Blossoms ("Far across hill and dale"). Basho, *tr. fr. Japanese.*
Plum Tree, The. Reaney.
Plum Tree, The. Wang An Shih, *tr. fr. Chinese by* Hart.
Plum Tree by the House, The. Gogarty.
Plum Trees. Ranko, *tr. fr. Japanese.*
To an Early Plum. Hsieh Hsieh, *tr. fr. Chinese by* Hart.
PLUTARCH. Plutarch. Agathias, *tr. fr. Greek by* Dryden.
PLUTO (planet). Undiscovered Planet, The. Norman Nicholson.

PLYMOUTH, ENGLAND. Plymouth Harbor. Dollie Radford.
POCAHONTAS
Last Meeting of Pocahontas and the Great Captain, The. M. J. Preston.
Marriage of Pocahontas, The. M. M. Webster.
Pocahontas. Thackeray.
POE, EDGAR ALLAN
At the Grave of Poe. Scollard.
Edgar Allan Poe. Clifford Lanier.
Israfel. Shapiro.
Poe and Longfellow. *Fr.* A Fable for Critics. J. R. Lowell.
Poe Cottage, The. Nathalia Crane.
Poe's Cottage at Fordham. J. H. Boner.
Poe's Critics. Tabb.
Poe's Mother. Beatrice Ravenel.
Sonnets from the Series Relating to Edgar Allan Poe, *sels.* S. H. Whitman.
Streets of Baltimore. *Unknown.*
Tomb of Edgar Poe, The. Mallarmé, *tr. fr. French by* Conder.
POETRY AND POETS
Abbreviated Interviews with a Few Disgruntled Literary Celebrities. Whittemore.
Achievement. M. A. Beer.
Acolyte, The. Rorty.
Adam's Curse. Yeats.
Against the Dispraisers of Poetry. Barnfield.
Albatross, The. Baudelaire, *tr. fr. French by* Flores.
Alchemy of Words, The. Rimbaud, *tr. fr. French by* Leefmans.
Alli Veri Figlioli Delle Muse. *Fr.* Zepheria. *Unknown.*
Apologia. Gascoyne.
Apparition of His Mistress Calling Him to Elysium, The. Herrick.
Argument of His Book, The. Herrick.
Ars Poetica. Horace, *tr. fr. Latin.*
Ars Poetica. MacLeish.
Ars Poetica. Vriesland, *tr. fr. Dutch by* Barnouw.
Art of Poetry, The. Huidobro, *tr. fr. Spanish by* Davis.
Art Poétique. Verlaine, *tr. fr. French by* Symons.
As other men, so I myself do muse. *Fr.* Idea. Drayton.
At the Top of My Voice. Mayakovsky, *tr. fr. Russian.*
Atlantis. Bottomley.
Austerity of Poetry, The. Matthew Arnold.
Bantams in Pine-Woods. Wallace Stevens.
Bards, The. Robert Graves.
Bards of Passion and of Mirth. Keats.
Bards We Quote, The. B. L. Taylor.
Bestowal of the Poem. Mallarmé, *tr. fr. French by* Stern.
Bookshop Idyll, A. Amis.
Brief History. O. H. Briggs.
Broken Tower, The. Hart Crane.
Caution to Poets, A. Matthew Arnold.
Certain American Poets. Shepard.
Changeless. Alice Meynell.
Child and Poet. Swinburne.
Chinese Poet, A. F. O. Call.
Choliambs. Persius, *tr fr. Latin by* Brooks.
Classical Criticism. G. L. Richardson.
Cliques and Critics. Sa'ib of Isfahan, *tr. fr. Persian by* Browne.
Coat, A. Yeats.
Come, Poet, Come. Clough.
Commission. Pound.
Comparison of the Sonnet and the Epigram. Harington.
Coney Island of the Mind, A, *sel.* ("Constantly risking absurdity"). Ferlinghetti.
Confession, The. Wen Yi-tuo, *tr. fr. Chinese.*
Correspondences. Baudelaire, *tr. fr. French by* Flores.
Crowned Poet, A. A. R. Aldrich.
Crystal, The Lanier.
Day Is Done, The. Longfellow.
Dead Poet, The. Lord Alfred Douglas.
Dead Poets. Peña Barrenechea, *tr. fr. Spanish by* Davis.
Dearest Poets, The. Leigh Hunt.
Death of the Poet. Rilke, *tr. fr. German by* Watkins.
Dedication: "Bob Southey! You're a poet—Poet laureate." *Fr.* Don Juan. Byron.
Dedication: "I would the gift I offer here." *Fr.* Songs of Labor. Whittier.
Dedication: "I've love songs of my springtime pride." Drachmann, *tr. fr. Danish by* Stork.
Dedication, A: "Life of my learning, fire of all my Art." M. E. Coleridge.
Didactic Poem, The. Richard Garnett.
Divining Rod, The. Eichendorff, *tr. fr. German by* Cotterell.
Drawing-Room Ballad, A. Traill.
Dunciad, The, *sel.* ("The mighty mother, and her son, who brings"). Pope.
Earth. Wheelock.
East Coker. *Fr.* Four Quartets. T. S. Eliot.
Eclogue to Mr. Johnson, An. Thomas Randolph.
Editor's Private Cocktail Party, The. Oscar Williams.
Egoist, The. Wickham.
Elegy for Minor Poets. MacNeice.
Elegy on the Death of Scots Music. Robert Fergusson.
Embryo. M. A. Townsend.
Enamored Architect of Airy Rhyme. T. B. Aldrich.
English Bards and Scotch Reviewers, *sels.* Byron.
Envoy: "If homely virtues draw from me a tune." J. W. Johnson.
Envoy: "So, at the last, I think that we must follow." DuBose Heyward.
Epic. Kavanagh.
Epic, The. Tennyson.
Epigram: "Poet gathers fruit from every tree, The." Sir William Watson.
Epigram: "Yes, every Poet is a Fool." Prior.
Epilogue: "Pretty task, A; and so I told the fool." *Fr.* Aureng-Zebe. Dryden.
Epistemology of Poetry. Conquest.
Epistle to Dr. Arbuthnot. Pope.
Essay on Criticism, An, *sels.* Pope.
Fable for Critics, A. J. R. Lowell.
False Poets and True. Hood.
Fantastick Mind, The. *Fr.* L'art poétique. Boileau-Despreaux, *tr. fr. French by* Dryden *and* Soames.
Fit of Rime against Rime, A. Jonson.
For a Poet Growing Old. Lawrence Lee.
For Poets Slain in War. W. A. Roberts.
Forerunners, The. George Herbert.
Fourth Egloge of Alexander Barclay, The. Barclay.
Fresh Air. Koch.
Fresh Start, The. Anna Wickham.
Frightened Ploughman, The. Clare.
Further Instructions. Pound.
Gift of Song, The. Horace, *tr. fr. Latin by* Smart.
Golden Verses. Nerval, *tr. fr. French by* Aldan.
Gonzalo's Song. *Fr.* The Sea and the Mirror. Auden.
Grandeur of Ghosts. Sassoon.
Had I the Choice. Whitman.
Hear the Voice of the Bard. *Fr.* Songs of Experience. Blake.
His Poetry and His Pillar. Herrick.
His Prayer for Absolution. Herrick.
Home! *sel.* ("I don't want"). Mayakovsky, *tr. fr. Russian by* Deutsch.
How Fraught with Struggle. M. H. Moody.
How It Strikes a Contemporary. Robert Browning.
How Many Bards Gild the Lapses of Time! Keats.
Hugh Selwyn Mauberley. Pound.
Humanities. Conquest.
I Am Raftery. Raftery, *tr. fr. Irish.*
I Broke the Spell That Held Me Long. Bryant.
I Cannot Forget with What Fervid Devotion. Bryant.
I Have Known Poets. Mary Austin.
I Offer You This Verse. Baudelaire, *tr. fr. French by* Watkins.
I Sing an Old Song. Oscar Williams.
I Think Continually of Those Who Were Truly Great. Spender.
I Would That All My Verses. Jiménez, *tr. fr. Spanish by* Trend.
If All the Pens That Ever Poets Held. *Fr.* Tamburlaine the Great. Marlowe.
If I Were a Poet. Baath, *tr. fr. Swedish by* Stork.
Image, The. Roy Fuller.
Image-Maker, The. Gogarty.
Immortality of Verse, The. Pope, *after the Latin of* Horace.
Impression. Gosse.
In a Poem. Robert Frost.
In Memory of W. B. Yeats. Auden.
In My Craft or Sullen Art. Dylan Thomas.
In My Old Verses. Guérin, *tr. fr. French by* Shipley.
Ingrateful Beauty Threatened. Carew.
Invocation: "American muse, whose strong and diverse heart." *Fr.* John Brown's Body. S. V. Benét.
Invocation to the Muse. Richard Hughes.
Invocation to the Social Muse. MacLeish.
January 1940. Roy Fuller.
Jester's Plea, The. Locker-Lampson.
Jocosa Lyra. Dobson.
Jordan ("When first my lines of heavenly joys made mention"). George Herbert.
Jordan ("Who says that fictions only and false hair"). George Herbert.
Lament for a Poor Poet. Myles Connolly.
Lament for the Poets: 1916 Ledwidge.
Landscape. Baudelaire, *tr. fr. French by* Watkins.
Last Mathematician. Edelstein.
Lately Our Poets. Landor.
Laureate, The. Robert Graves.
"Leaves of Grass's" Purport. Whitman.
Letter to a Young Poet. George Barker.

Line of an American Poet, The. Whittemore.
Lines on the Mermaid Tavern. Keats.
Literary Landscape with Dove and Poet. McGinley.
Lives. Rimbaud, *tr. fr. French by* Flores.
London Poets. Amy Levy.
Love-sicke Poet, The. *Fr.* Satires. Joseph Hall.
Lyric Barber. Romano.
Madly Singing in the Mountains. Po Chü-i, *tr. fr. Chinese by* Waley.
Man as God. *Fr.* A Ballad in Blank Verse of the Making of a Poet. John Davidson.
Masters of the Heart Touched the Unknown, The. Schwartz.
Mens Creatrix. Kunitz.
Merlin, I ("Thy trivial harp"). Emerson.
Merlin, II ("The rhyme of the poet"). Emerson.
Metrical Feet. S. T. Coleridge.
Minor Poet, A. J. A. Moreland.
Mirror, The. Hess.
Mirror for Poets, A. Gunn.
Mr. Pollington Remembers a Poet. Plutzik.
Modest Poet, The. *Unknown.*
Muse, The. Thomas Blackburn.
Musophilus. Samuel Daniel.
My Desk. Humbert Wolfe.
My Poetry. Takamura, *tr. fr. Japanese by* Ninomiya *and* Enright.
My Study. P. H. Hayne.
My Voice. "Demyan Bedny," *tr. fr. Russian by* Lindsay.
Mystical Poets. Nervo, *tr. fr. Spanish by* Walsh.
Nay, in a poet put no trust. Tyutchev, *tr. fr. Russian by* Phillimore.
Negro Poets. C. B. Johnson.
New Poet, A. William Canton.
Ninth Duino Elegy, The. Rilke. *tr. fr. German by* Hull.
No Labor-saving Machine. Whitman.
No Uneasy Refuge. Salkeld.
Nothing Is Easy! Pity Then. James Stephens.
Oh for a Poet—for a Beacon Bright. E. A. Robinson.
O Poesy! for Thee I Grasp My Pen. *Fr.* Sleep and Poetry. Keats.
O Tell Us, Poet. Rilke, *tr. fr. German by* Salinger.
Ode, An: "Awake fair Muse for I intend." William Browne.
Ode: "We are the music-makers." O'Shaughnessy.
Ode on Lyric Poetry. Marriott.
Ode on the Poetical Character. William Collins.
Ode on the Poets. Keats.
Ode to Himself, An. Jonson.
Of English Verse. Waller.
Of Modern Poetry. Wallace Stevens.
Old Bard Speaks, The. J. R. N. Maxwell.
Old-Fashioned Poet, An. A. F. Murray.
Old Poets. Joyce Kilmer.
On a Dead Poet. F. S. Osgood.
On a Magazine Sonnet. Loines.
On a Miscellany of Poems. Gay.
On a Young Poetess's Grave. Robert Buchanan.
On Board Ship; Reading Yüan Chen's Poems. Po Chü-i, *tr. fr. Chinese by* Waley.
On First Looking into Chapman's Homer. Keats.
On His "Sonnets of the Wingless Hours." Lee-Hamilton.
On Lamb's Specimens of Dramatic Poets. Swinburne.
On No Work of Words. Dylan Thomas.
On Poetry. Dudek.
On Poetry; a Rapsody, *sel.* ("All human race wou'd fain be wits"). Swift.
On Reading A Poet's First Book. Bunner.
On the Future of Poetry. Dobson.
On the Oxford Book of Victorian Verse. "Hugh MacDiarmid."
On the Sonnet. Keats.
Origin of Didactic Poetry, The. J. R. Lowell.
Orpheus in the Underworld. Gascoyne.
Orson of the Muse, An. George Meredith.
Our Poets' Breed. Montoto y Rautenstrauch, *tr. fr. Spanish by* Walsh.
Outcast on the Mountains of the Heart. Rilke, *tr. fr. German by* Flores.
Over the Door at the Entrance into the Apollo. Jonson.
Pangur Ban. *Unknown, tr fr. Old Irish by* Flower.
Peasant Poet, The. Clare.
Pegasus. Day Lewis.
Perpetuam Mobile. Edith Sitwell.
Persistency of Poetry. Matthew Arnold.
Petit, the Poet. *Fr.* Spoon River Anthology. Masters.
Picture, The. F. O. Sylvester.
Pinch of Salt. Robert Graves.
Piping down the Valleys Wild. *Fr.* Songs of Innocence. Blake.
Plea. Duggan.
Poem: "Supremest fictions grow with fungus speed." Boyars.
Poem I Should Like to Write, The. Windes.
Poem on the Wall, The. Po Chü-i, *tr. fr. Chinese by* Waley.
Poems. Hilda Conkling.
Poems Come Easier, The. Mathew.
Poems of Our Climate, The. Wallace Stevens.
Poet, The. Joel Benton.
Poet, The. Bosman.
Poet, The. E. B. Browning.
Poet, The. Bryant.
Poet, The. Coolbrith.
Poet, The. G. N. Crowell.
Poet, The. T. A. Daly.
Poet, The. Emerson.
Poet, The. Grannis.
Poet, A. Hardy.
Poet, A. Daniel Henderson.
Poet. Nat Henry.
Poet, The. Leitch.
Poet, The. Haniel Long.
Poet, The. Amy Lowell.
Poet, The. Markham.
Poet, The. Cornelius Mathews.
Poet. Merrill Moore.
Poet, The. Angela Morgan.
Poet, The. Noguchi.
Poet, The. Seumas O'Brien.
Poet, The. O'Dowd.
Poet, The. Pushkin, *tr. fr. Russian by* Bowra.
Poet, The. William Rooney.
Poet. Shapiro.
Poet, The. Tennyson.
Poet. Viereck.
Poet, The. *Fr.* By Blue Ontario's Shore. Whitman.
Poet and His Book, The. Millay.
Poet and His Patron, The. *Fr.* Fables for the Ladies. Edward Moore.
Poet and His Song, The. Branch.
Poet and His Song, The. P. L. Dunbar.
Poet and Lark. "Madeline Bridges."
Poet and the Bird, The. E. B. Browning.
Poet and the Child, The. Winifred Howells.
Poet and the People, The. *Fr.* The Acharnians. Aristophanes, *tr. fr. Greek by* Rogers.
Poet and the Wood-Louse, The. H. P. Eden.
Poet at Night-Fall, The. Glenway Wescott.
Poet at the Breakfast Table, The, *sels.* O. W. Holmes.
Poet Confides, The. H. T J. Coleman.
Poet Describes His Love, The. Robert Nathan.
Poet Dreams of the Wings of Death, The. E. J. Mayer.
Poet, A!—He Hath Put His Heart to School. Wordsworth.
Poet-Hearts. Eichendorff, *tr. fr. German by* Shuster.
Poet in the City, The. C. C. Liddell.
Poet in the Desert, The, *sels.* C. E. S. Wood.
Poet Lived in Galilee, A. Bynner.
Poet of Earth. S. H. Thayer.
Poet of Gardens, The. Daniel Henderson.
Poet of One Mood, A. Alice Meynell.
Poet Prays, The. G. N. Crowell.
Poet Songs. K. W. Baker.
Poet Tells about Nature, The. Merrill Moore.
Poet Thinks, A. Lui Chi, *tr. fr. Chinese by* Mathers.
Poet to His Father, A. M. L. Fisher.
Poet to His Love, The. Bodenheim.
Poet to the Birds, The. Alice Meynell.
Poeta Fit, Non Nascitur. "Lewis Carroll."
Poeta Nascitur. Thomas Ashe.
Poetic Land, The. W. C. Roscoe.
Poetic Pains. Cowper.
Poetical Economy. Harry Graham.
Poetics. Robert Browning.
Poetry. L. H. Foote.
Poetry. Ella Heath.
Poetry. *Fr.* Theogony. Hesiod, *tr. fr. Greek by* Lucas.
Poetry. Mallarmé, *tr. fr. French by* Conder.
Poetry. Markham.
Poetry. Marianne Moore.
Poetry. Novo, *tr. fr. Spanish by* Walsh.
Poetry. Soutar.
Poetry and Learning. *Fr.* The Epistle Dedicatory to Chapman's Translation of the Iliad. George Chapman.
Poetry and Philosophy. *Fr.* An Eclogue to Mr. Johnson. Thomas Randolph.
Poetry and Science. W. J. Turner.
Poetry and Thoughts on Same. F. P. Adams.
Poetry Cure, The. R. H. Schauffler.
Poetry Is a Destructive Force. Wallace Stevens.
Poetry Is Happiness. Wrey Gardiner.
Poets. Flexner.
Poets, The. Longfellow.
Poets, The. Scudder Middleton.
Poets and Linnets. Hood.
Poets and Poetasters. *Fr.* To Stella, Who Collected and Transcribed His Poems Swift.
Poet's Bread, The. C. L. O'Donnell.

POETRY AND POETS (*continued*)
Poet's Bread. Sister Mary Philip.
Poet's Bread, The. *Unknown.*
Poet's Dream, The. *Fr.* Prometheus Unbound. **Shelley.**
Poet's Fate, The. Hood.
Poet's Grave, A. T. B. Aldrich.
Poet's Harvesting. C. J. O'Malley.
Poets in Time of War. Warr.
Poet's Lot, The. O. W. Holmes.
Poet's Mind, The. Tennyson.
Poet's Power, The. *Fr.* Isthmian Odes. **Pindar,** *tr. fr. Greek by* Lucas.
Poet's Prayer. Adelaide Love.
Poet's Prayer, A. Stephen Phillips.
Poet's Pride. Ibn Ammar, *tr. fr. Arabic by* Arberry.
Poet's Progress, A. Hamburger.
Poet's Protest. Hedges.
Poet's Secret, The. Elizabeth Stoddard.
Poets Seven Years Old. Rimbaud, *tr. fr. French by* Koch *and* Guy.
Poet's Simple Faith, The. Hugo, *tr. fr. French by* Dowden.
Poet's Song, The. Tennyson.
Poet's Thought, A. "Barry Cornwall."
Poets to Come. Whitman.
Poet's Town, The. Neihardt.
Poet's Voice, The. Blake.
Poet's Wish, A; an Ode. Allan Ramsay.
Pomegranates. Valery, *tr. fr. French by* Flores.
Poor Poet's Lullaby, The. J. H. Finley.
Portrait of a Poet. *Fr.* Jack Kelso. Masters.
Post-Obits and the Poets. Martial, *tr. fr. Latin by* Byron.
Power of the Bards, The, *sel.* ("And owe we not these visions"). P. P. Cooke.
Prayer before Poems. A. B. Payne.
Prayer for All Poets at This Time. Edman.
Prayer for Song. F. L. Noble.
Prefatory Sonnet. Henry Kendall.
Prelude: "What in these lines doth ripened stand." Brentano, *tr. fr. German by* Cotterell.
Printer to the Reader, The. *Unknown.*
Proem: "I love the old melodious lays." **Whittier.**
Progress of Poesy, The. Matthew Arnold.
Progress of Poesy, The. Thomas Gray.
Progress of Poetry, The. Swift.
Progress of Poets, The. *Fr.* Resolution and Independence. Wordsworth.
Prologue, The: "Famous poets with the muses nine, The." *Fr.* Certain Eclogues. Barclay.
Prologue: "Our Author by experience finds it true." *Fr.* Aureng-Zebe. Dryden.
Prologue, The: "To sing of wars, of captains, and of kings." *Fr.* The Four Elements, the Four Humours, the Four Ages, and the Four Seasons. Anne Bradstreet.
Prologue to "Love Triumphant." Dryden.
Prologue to "Secret-Love; or, The Maiden Queen." Dryden.
Reading the Poems of an Absent Friend. Ou Yang Hsiu, *tr. fr. Chinese by* Rexroth.
Reaper, The. Robert Duncan.
Remembrance of Some English Poets, A. Barnfield.
Replying to the Many Kind Friends Who Ask Me If I No Longer Write Poetry. Shaemus O'Sheel.
Reproach to Dead Poets. MacLeish.
Requiem: To Paula Modersohn-Becker. Rilke, *tr. fr. German by* "Hugh MacDiarmid."
Rhymeless. John Freeman.
Rima IV: "Say not that, its treasure exhausted." Bécquer, *tr. fr. Spanish by* Allison.
Road to the Bow, The. Corrothers.
Roundel, The: "Roundel is wrought as a ring or a starbright sphere, A." Swinburne.
Sacred Poetry. "Christopher North."
Sacrifice to Apollo, The. Drayton.
Salutation the Second. Pound.
Satire: "Satire, my friend ('twixt me and you)." Geddes.
Satire Dissuading from Poetry, A, *sel.* John Oldham.
Scorn Not the Sonnet. Wordsworth.
Scribe, The. De la Mare.
Scribe's Prayer, The. Guiterman.
Scribe's Prayer, The. Service.
Self-Criticism in February. Jeffers.
Self Unsatisfied Runs Everywhere, The. Schwartz.
Serving No Haughty Muse. Wordsworth.
Session of the Poets, A. Suckling.
Shepherds, The. Van Slyke.
Sisters, The. Amy Lowell.
Six Poets in Search of a Lawyer. Donald Hall.
Sleep and Poetry, *sels.* Keats.
Some of these poems are good, some are medium, many are poor stuff. Martial, *tr. fr. Latin by* Schnorr.
Song Maker, The. Fairbridge.
Song Tournement: New Style. Louis Untermeyer.
Sonnet: "How many paltry, foolish, painted things." *Fr.* Idea. Drayton.
Sonnet: "Like as the waves make towards the pebbled shore." Shakespeare.
Sonnet: "Not marble, nor the gilded monuments." Shakespeare.
Sonnet: "Not my own fears, nor the prophetic soul." Shakespeare.
Sonnet: "One day I wrote her name upon the strand." *Fr.* Amoretti. Spenser.
Sonnet: "So is it with me as with that Muse." Shakespeare.
Sonnet, The: "Sonnet is a fruit which long hath slept, The." Symonds.
Sonnet: "Sweet poets of the gentle antique line." J. H. Reynolds.
Sonnet: "Was it the proud full sail of his great verse. Shakespeare.
Sonnet, The: "What is a sonnet? 'Tis the pearly shell." R. W. Gilder.
Sonnet: "When in the chronicle of wasted time." Shakespeare.
Sonnet: "Why is my verse so barren of new pride." Shakespeare.
Sonnet on a Sonnet. Lope de Vega, *tr. fr. Spanish by* Gibson.
Sonnets of the Christian Passions, *sel.* ("Words may well want, both ink and paper fail"). Lok.
Sonnets to Orpheus, *sel.* ("Praise is the thing! Like one destined for singing"). Rilke, *tr. fr. German by* Hull.
Sonnet's Voice, The. Watts-Dunton.
Soul of Poetry, The. Welhaven, *tr. fr. Norwegian by* Stork.
Sound and Sense. *Fr.* An Essay on Criticism. Pope.
Sovereign Poet, The. Sir William Watson.
Spirit of Poetry, The. Longfellow.
Stillness of the Poem, The. Loewinsohn.
Strike among the Poets, A. *Unknown.*
Succession, The. F. L. Mace.
Survey of Literature. Ransom.
Ten Definitions of Poetry. Sandburg.
Tenzone. Pound.
Terence, This Is Stupid Stuff. A. E. Housman.
Test, The. Emerson.
There Is a Poem Everywhere. Charles Davies.
There is no frigate like a book. Emily Dickinson.
There's No Lust Like to Poetry. *Unknown, tr. fr. Latin by* Symonds.
These Are the Live. Fearing.
These Poems I Have So Loved. Leonora Speyer.
This is my letter to the world. Emily Dickinson.
Thought and the Poet. Peter Yates.
Threnody for a Poet. Bliss Carman.
Title to Fame. Horace, *tr. fr. Latin by* Gladstone.
To a Boy-Poet of the Decadence. Sir Owen Seaman.
To a Poet. Sister Mary Angelita.
To a Poet a Thousand Years Hence. Flecker.
To a Town Poet. L. W. Reese.
To a Young Poet. Meacham.
To a Young Poet. Millay.
To an Author. Freneau.
To an Unknown Poet. Cullen.
To Detraction I Present My Poesy. *Fr.* The Scourge of Villainy. Marston.
To His Friend Master R. L., in Praise of Music and Poetry. Barnfield.
To His Late Majesty, Concerning the True Forme of English Poetry. Sir John Beaumont.
To His Muse. Herrick.
To His Pen. Wyatt.
To His Reader. Samuel Daniel.
To Live Merrily, and to Trust to Good Verses. Herrick.
To Mary Unwin. Cowper.
To Music Bent Is My Retired Mind. Campion.
To My Book. Jonson.
To My Fellow Writers. Yashin, *tr. fr. Russian by* Lindsay.
To My Most Dearly Loved Friend, Henry Reynolds, Esquire. Of Poets and Poesy. Drayton.
To My Readers. O. W. Holmes.
To Pi Ssu Yao. Tu Fu, *tr. fr. Chinese by* Rexroth.
To Poets. C. H. Sorley.
To R. B. G. M. Hopkins.
To the Fates. Hölderlin, *tr. fr. German by* Gruenthal.
To the Muses. Blake.
To the Poet. Pushkin, *tr. fr. Russian.*
To the Spirit of Poetry. P. B. Marston.
To the Stone-Cutters. Jeffers.
To Verse Let Kings Give Place. Ovid, *tr. fr. Latin by* Marlowe.
Toast to Poets, A. Laura Simmons.
True and False Singing. *Unknown, tr. fr. Italian by* D. G. Rossetti.
Two Poets, The. Alice Meynell.
Unto Myself I Reared a Monument. Pushkin, *tr. fr. Russian by* Deutsch.
Unutterable Beauty, The. Studdert-Kennedy.

Upon a Sweet-Briar. *Fr.* The Citation and Examination of Shakespeare. Landor.
Valedictory. Jarman.
Velvet Sonneteers, The. MacInnes.
Verse: "What should we know." Gogarty.
Verses Why Burnt. Landor.
Very Minor Poet Speaks, A. Isabel Valle.
Very Seldom. Cavafy, *tr. fr. Modern Greek by* Dalven.
Villanelle. Henley.
Villanelle of the Poet's Road. Dowson.
Virgidemiarum, *sel.* ("With some pot-fury, ravished from their wit"). Joseph Hall.
Volunteer's Reply to the Poet, The. *Fr.* Talking Bronco. Roy Campbell.
Wapentake. Longfellow.
"Wen Gott Betrügt, Ist Wohl Betrogen." Clough.
What the Sonnet Is. Lee-Hamilton.
When He Would Have His Verses Read. Herrick.
When I Have Fears That I May Cease to Be. Keats.
Who Does Not Love True Poetry. H. C. Hall.
Whoever You Are Holding Me Now in Hand. Whitman.
Whole Duty of a Poem, The. Guiterman.
Why My Poems Died. Bhartrihari, *tr. fr. Sanskrit by* Ryder.
Wild Strawberries. Robert Graves.
Will of Writing, The. Schevill.
Windows. Mallarmé, *tr. fr French by* Aldan.
Wiser than the Children of Light. Gibbon.
Wish, A. Sato, *tr. fr. Japanese by* Ninomiya *and* Enright.
Words. Parry-Williams, *tr. fr. Welsh by* Williams.
Words in Time. MacLeish.
Worker Poet, The. Mayakovsky, *tr. fr. Russian by* Deutsch.
Poet to Poet (PtP). Houston Peterson *and* William S. Lynch, eds.
See also names of individual poets.
POINT LOBOS, CALIFORNIA
Land's End. Coblentz.
Point Lobos, California. E. W. Barker.
POINT LOOKOUT, NORTH CAROLINA. In the Lighthouse at Point Lookout, North Carolina. Stockard.
POINT PLEASANT, BATTLE OF. Battle of Point Pleasant, The. *Unknown.*
POISON IVY. Poison Ivy! Katharine Gallagher.
POLAND
On the Victory of Poland and Her Allies over the Sultan Osman, 1621. Sarbiewski, *tr. fr. Latin by* Mahony.
Pastoral for Poland, A. Clark Mills.
Song of the Mound. Pol, *tr. fr. Polish by* Soboleski.
Stabat Mater. Wittlin, *tr fr. Polish by* Davidman.
To a Polish Mother. Mickiewicz, *tr. fr. Polish by* Kirkconnell.
POLES, THE. All. Slonimski, *tr. fr. Polish by* Coleman.
POLICEMEN. Bobby Blue. Drinkwater.
POLITICS AND POLITICIANS
Bryan, Bryan, Bryan, Bryan. Vachel Lindsay.
Candidate's Creed, The. *Fr.* The Biglow Papers. J. R. Lowell.
Dead Statesman, A. *Fr.* Epitaphs of the War. Kipling.
Epitaph on the Politician. Belloc.
God Give Us Men! J. G. Holland.
Mayor, The. López, *tr. fr. Spanish by* Hays.
Monsieur Gaston. A. M. Klein.
Political Balance, The. Freneau.
Political Meeting. A. M. Klein.
Politician, The. Bierce.
Politician Is an Arse Upon, A. E. E. Cummings.
Politics. Tennyson.
Snapshot: Politician. Garrett.
Time's Changes. *Fr.* The Art of Politicks. Bramston.
Tom Dunstan; or, The Politician. Robert Buchanan.
Town Meeting, The. John Trumbull.
What Mr. Robinson Thinks. *Fr.* The Biglow Papers. J. R. Lowell.
What the Moon Saw. Vachel Lindsay.
POLO, MARCO. Marco Polo. Clarence Day.
POLO. Polo Match. Sunday, 2 P.M. Josephine Miles.
POLONIUS. Polonius. De la Mare.
POMEGRANATES. Pomegranates. Roy Campbell.
POMPADOUR, MARQUISE DE
On a Fan That Belonged to the Marquise de Pompadour. Dobson.
Pompadour, The. G. W. Thornbury.
POMPEII, ITALY. New Excavations. Speyer.
POMPEY. Tragedy of Caesar and Pompey, The, *sel.* ("As nature works in all things to an end"). George Chapman.
PONCE DE LEÓN, JUAN. Ponce de Leon. E. M. Thomas.
PONTIUS PILATE
He Is Condemned. *Fr.* The Stations of the Cross. W. A. Donaghy.
Pilate Remembers. *Fr.* Pontius Pilate. Landels.
To Pontius Washing His Hands. Crashaw.
POORHOUSE
Christmas Day in the Workhouse. G. R. Sims.
Curate's Kindness, The. Hardy.
Over the Hill to the Poor-House. Will Carleton.
POPCORN. Pop Corn Song, A. N. B. Turner.
POPE, ALEXANDER
Alexander Pope at Stanton Harcourt. *Fr.* Sour Land. Sidney Keyes.
Dialogue to the Memory of Mr. Alexander Pope, A. Dobson.
Epistle to Mr. Pope, An. George Lyttelton.
Essay on the Genius of Pope, An, *sel.* ("'Tis not so much"). Charles Lloyd.
Fame and Envy. *Fr.* Epistles to Mr. Pope Concerning the Authors of the Age. Edward Young.
Mr. Pope. Allen Tate.
Mr. Pope's Welcome from Greece. Gay.
On Laurel Hill, *sel.* ("O Pope! the sweetest of the tuneful race"). William Thompson.
Pope at Twickenham. Charles Kent.
To Mr. Pope. Thomas Parnell.
Written at Mr. Pope's House at Twickenham. George Lyttelton.
POPLAR TREES
Binsey Poplars (Felled 1879). G. M. Hopkins.
Black Poplar-Boughs. John Freeman.
Fallen Poplar, The. Mary Webb.
In France. Frances Cornford.
Poplar, The. Aldington.
Poplar-Field, The. Cowper.
Poplar Tree. Colum.
Poplars. Hilda Conkling.
Poplars, The. Theodosia Garrison.
Poplars. Leuty.
Poplars, The. "Seumas O'Sullivan."
Poplars. E. B. Reed.
Poplars, The. B. F. Trotter.
Song of Poplars. Aldous Huxley.
Three Trees. Christopher Morley.
POPOCATAPETL. Romance. W. J. Turner.
POPPIES
Italian Poppies. Spingarn.
Poppies. Bellamann.
Poppies. Plunkett.
Poppies. Ropes.
Poppies. Laura L. Speyers.
Poppies. *Unknown, tr. fr. Japanese by* Porter.
Poppies in Ludlow Castle. Cather.
Poppies in the Garden, The. ffrida Wolfe.
Poppies in the Wheat. H. H. Jackson.
Poppy, The. Jane Taylor.
Poppy, The. Francis Thompson.
Poppy Fields. W. A. Percy.
Poppy Grows upon the Shore, A. Robert Bridges.
Red Poppies in the Corn. Galbraith.
Valley of White Poppies, The. "Fiona Macleod."
PORTLAND, MAINE. My Lost Youth. Longfellow.
PORTRAITS
Portrait of a Florentine Lady, The. L. W. Reese.
Portrait of a Lady in the Exhibition of the Royal Academy. *Fr.* Every-Day Characters. Praed.
Three Portraits of Prince Charles. Andrew Lang.
To a Photographer. Braley.
To a Portrait. Symons.
To a Portrait of Whistler in the Brooklyn Art Museum. E. R. Cox.
PORTS
Cinque Port, A. John Davidson.
Plymouth Harbour. Dollie Radford.
Ports Astern. Joseph Singer.
POSEIDON. *See* NEPTUNE.
POTATOES
Potato. Wilbur.
Potatoes. E. V. Lucas.
Potatoes' Dance, The. Vachel Lindsay.
Spraying the Potatoes. Kavanagh.
To a Sinister Potato. Viereck.
POTOMAC (river)
By the Potomac. T. B. Aldrich.
Picket-Guard, The. E. L. Beers.
POUND, EZRA
Critical Fable, A, *sel.* ("The expatriates/Come next"). Amy Lowell.
Ezry. MacLeish.
Study: For Ezra Pound. Hellings.
POVERTY
All Things Be Dear but Poor Mens Labour; or, The Sad Complaint of Poor People. *Unknown.*
Bane of Poverty, The. Theognis, *tr. fr. Greek by* Higham.
Beggar lad, The—dies early. Emily Dickinson.
Bread-Line, The. Dana Burnet.
Charcoal-Seller, The. Po Chü-i, *tr. fr. Chinese by* Waley.
Children of the Poor. Hugo, *tr. fr. French by* Conder.
Cloister. C. L. O'Donnell.
Come Live with Me and Be My Love. Day Lewis.
Country Justice, The. Langhorne.

POVERTY (*continued*)
Dedication to My Gray Lady. Fra Jerome.
Devil's Auction. C. E. S. Wood.
Down on My Luck. Fairburn.
Dry Loaf. Wallace Stevens.
Dulce Mihi Quondam Studium Fuit. Politian, *tr. fr. Latin by* Allen.
Eastern Gate, The. *Unknown, tr. fr. Chinese by* Waley.
Franciscan Dream, A. Dinnis.
Holy Poverty. A. S. Cripps.
Holy Thursday. *Fr.* Songs of Experience. Blake.
Hunger. M. C. Davies.
If Lincoln Should Return. M. E. Bruner.
In the Pauper's Turnip-Field. Melville.
Is There for Honest Poverty? Burns.
Lady Poverty, The. Alice Meynell.
Lady Poverty, The. Underhill.
Landore. Woodcock.
Lines from "London." *Fr.* London. Samuel Johnson.
London Lickpenny. *Unknown.*
Lousy Peter. Sir Osbert Sitwell.
Map of Mock-Begger Hall, The. *Unknown.*
Masses. Sandburg.
Of Holy Poverty. Jacopone da Todi, *tr. fr. Italian by* Beck.
On a Fair Beggar. Ayres.
On Lydia Distracted. Ayres.
Other Side of the Valley, The. *Unknown, tr. fr. Chinese by* Waley.
Paradox. Sister Maryanna.
Parley with His Empty Purse, A. Thomas Randolph.
People's Petition, The. W. M. W. Call.
Poet's Poverty, The. Rutebeuf, *tr. fr. French by* Legge.
Poor, The. Strahan.
Poor, The. Verhaeren, *tr. fr. French by* Lewisohn.
Poor, The. W. C. Williams.
Poor Children. Hugo, *tr. fr. French by* Swinburne.
Poor Girl's Meditation, The. *Unknown, tr. fr. Irish by* Colum.
Poor Man, The. Francis Carlin.
Poor Man's Daily Bread, The. D. A. McCarthy.
Poor Old Man, The. Squire.
Poverty. Theognis, *tr. fr. Greek by* Frere.
Poverty ("All poor men and humble"). *Unknown, tr. fr. Welsh by* Roberts.
Poverty in London. *Fr.* London. Samuel Johnson.
Poverty Not All Loss. *Fr.* The Vision of Piers Plowman. William Langland, *mod. by* H. W. Wells.
Prayer for the Poor. *Fr.* The Vision of Piers Plowman. William Langland, *mod. by* H. W. Wells.
Prayer to Saint Francis for Poverty. Brophy.
Proletaria. O'Dowd.
Reproach No Man for Poverty. Theognis, *tr. fr. Greek by* Higham.
Saint Francis of Assisi. Leary.
Sonnet XXI: "Almighty God, whose justice like a sun." Belloc.
Sonnet: He Jests concerning His Poverty. Sant' Angelo, *tr. fr. Italian by* Rossetti.
Steel Valley, 1938. Woodcock.
Sufferings of the Poor, The. *Fr.* The Vision of Piers Plowman. William Langland, *mod. by* H. W. Wells.
Symphony, The. Lanier.
Third Wonder, The. Markham.
Thirty Bob a Week. John Davidson.
Through Streets Where Crooked Wicklow Flows. Horace Gregory.
Two Red Towers, The. Po Chü-i, *tr. fr. Chinese by* Waley.
Village, The, *sel.* ("The village life, and every care that reigns"). Crabbe.
Visit to a Tenement. Guillén, *tr. fr. Spanish by* Fitts.
Voice of the Poor, The. Lady Wilde.
Wagon of the Little Sisters, The. H. F. Blunt.
Wandering Rats The. Heine, *tr. fr. German by* Issawi.
We Live in a Rickety House. Alexander McLachlan.
Winter Offering. D. S. Savage.
Wooing of Saint Francis, The. Blocker.
POZZI, ANTONIA. Anniversary of Antonia Pozzi's Death by Suicide. Serini, *tr. fr. Italian by* Cambon.
PRAGUE, CZECHOSLOVAKIA. Beleaguered City, The. Longfellow.
PRAIRIE DOGS. Prairie-Dog Town. Mary Austin.
PRAIRIE SCHOONER. Prairie Schooner, The. E. F. Piper.
PRAIRIES
Across Illinois. Stoltze.
My Prairies. Garland.
Night on the Prairie. Sage.
Night on the Prairies. Whitman.
Prairie. Herbert Bates.
Prairie. Sandburg.
Prairie Birth. Coates.
Prairie Fires. Garland.
Prairie-Grass Dividing, The. Whitman.
Prairie Ride, A. W. V. Moody.
Prairie Sunset, A. E. J. Pratt.
Prairie Sunset, A. Whitman.
Prairies, The. Bryant.
Songs of the Plains (I-IV) Dresbach.
To make a prairie it takes a clover and one bee. Emily Dickinson.
Wind of the Prairie. G. C. Howes.
PRAXITELES
Praxiteles. *Unknown, tr. fr. Greek.*
Praxiteles and Phryne. W. W. Story.
PRAYER
Cell, The. Hamilton.
Forme of Prayer, A. Quarles.
I Dare Not Pray to Thee. Baring.
Larger Prayer, The. E. D. Cheney.
Prayer: "God, I fain would pray with fervor." Eichendorff, *tr. fr. German by* Cotterell.
Prayer: "Prayer, the church's banquet, angel's age." George Herbert.
Proof. E. R. Fuller.
Qui Laborat, Orat. Clough.
Right Use of Prayer, The. Sir Aubrey De Vere.
Saying a Prayer. Rowena Bennett.
Sonnet: "Lord, what a change within us one short hour." R. C. Trench.
Sweet Hour of Prayer. Walford.
Taste of Prayer, The. R. W. Seager.
Universal Prayer, The. Pope.
What Is Prayer? James Montgomery.
Prayer Poems (PraP). O. V. Armstrong *and* Helen Armstrong, comps.
PRAYING MANTIS. *See* MANTIS.
PREDESTINATION. Johannes Agricola in Meditation. Robert Browning.
PRIDE
Poem of Margery Kempe, A. Nemerov.
Pride. Josephine Miles.
Tower, The, *sel.* ("It is time that I wrote my will"). Yeats.
PRIESTS. *See* CLERGY.
PRIMITIVE MAN
Double Ballade of Primitive Man. Tylor *and* Lang.
Life of Primitive Man, The. *Fr.* De Rerum Natura. Lucretius, *tr. fr. Latin by* McLeod.
PRIMROSES
Evening Primrose. Clare.
Primroses. Alfred Austin.
To a Primrose. Clare.
To an Early Primrose. H. K. White.
To Primroses Fill'd with Morning-Dew. Herrick.
PRINCETON, BATTLE OF. Trenton and Princeton. *Unknown.*
PRINCETON UNIVERSITY. Princeton. Noyes.
PRINTING AND PRINTERS. Printer's Error. Wodehouse.
PRIOR, MATTHEW. For My Own Monument. Prior.
PRISONS AND PRISONERS
Ballad of Reading Gaol, The. Oscar Wilde.
Captives from the Western Tribes. Po Chü-i, *tr. fr. Chinese by* Ching Ti.
Chesspieces. Joseph Campbell.
Convict of Clonmel, The. *Unknown, tr. fr. Modern Irish by* Callanan.
Convicts, The. Tolstoy, *tr. fr. Russian.*
Elegy Wrote in the Tower, 1554. Sir John Harington.
Epistle in Form of a Ballad to His Friends. Villon, *tr. fr. French by* Swinburne.
Five Peas on a Barrelhead. Sarett.
German Prisoners. Joseph Lee.
Gorse, The. W. W. Gibson.
Hospital Prison Ship, The. *Fr.* The British Prison Ship. Freneau.
Imprisoned Revolutionist, The. Damadian, *tr. fr. Armenian by* Blackwell.
In Prison. William Morris.
In Prison. Frederick Peterson.
In Prison. Yamamuro, *tr. fr. Japanese by* Erickson.
In the Prison Pen. Melville.
London, Hast Thou Accused Me. Earl of Surrey.
Loyalty Confin'd. L'Estrange.
Message to Siberia. Pushkin, *tr. fr. Russian.*
My Body in the Walls Captived. Ralegh.
Officers' Prison Camp Seen from a Troop-Train, An. Jarrell.
Old Prison, The. Judith Wright.
Prison. *Unknown, tr. fr. Spanish by* Ellis.
Prison Song. Richard Coeur de Lion, *tr. fr. Old French by* Adams.
Prison Sonnet. W. S. Blunt.
Prisoned in Windsor, He Recounteth His Pleasure There Passed. Earl of Surrey.
Prisoner, The. Emily Brontë.
Prisoner, The. Fet, *tr. fr. Russian by* Bowra.
Prisoner, The. Plomer.
Prisoner, The. Po Chü-i, *tr. fr. Chinese by* Waley.
Prisoner, The. Pushkin, *tr. fr. Russian by* Bowra.

Prisoner, The. *Unknown, tr. fr. Spanish by* Entwistle.
Prisoner Freed, A. Dutton.
Prisoner of Chillon, The. Byron.
Prisoner of War. Lutz.
Prisoners. H. M. Lehman.
Prisoner's Song. Horace Gregory.
Prisoner's Song of Jerusalem, A. *Unknown.*
Seven Long Years in State Prison. *Unknown.*
Song of the Old Man in Chains. Lunacharsky, *tr. fr. Russian by* Magnus *and* Walter.
Sonnet on Chillon. Byron.
To Althea, from Prison. Lovelace.
Tramp, Tramp, Tramp. G. F. Root.
Walker, The. Giovannitti.
Written on the Walls of His Dungeon. Luis de León, *tr. fr. Spanish by* Walsh.
PROGRESS. Thoughts on Progress. Daiches.
PROMETHEUS
Prometheus. Byron.
Prometheus. W. W. Gibson.
Prometheus. Goethe, *tr. fr. German by* Dwight.
Prometheus Bound. Aeschylus, *tr. fr. Greek by* E. B. Browning.
Prometheus Unbound. Sister Miriam.
Prometheus Unbound. Shelley.
PROPERTIUS, SEXTUS
Ghost, The. Robert Lowell, *after* Propertius.
Homage to Sextus Propertius, *sels.* Pound.
PROSERPINA *or* PROSERPINE. *See* PERSEPHONE.
PROSPECTORS. *See* GOLD MINING AND MINERS.
PROVENCE, FRANCE
At a Country Dance in Provence. Monro.
In Provence. Aicard, *tr. fr. French by* Walsh.
PROVINCETOWN, MASSACHUSETTS Gulls, The; Provincetown Harbor. Botkin.
PSARA (island), GREECE. Destruction of Psara, The. Solomos, *tr. fr. Modern Greek by* Dalven.
PSYCHE
Eros and Psyche. Apuleius, *tr. fr. Latin by* Bridges.
Ode to Psyche. Keats.
Psyche. Rydberg, *tr. fr. Swedish by* Stork.
Psyche's Lamp. A. F. Murray.
PSYCHOANALYSIS. Ballade to My Psychoanalyst. Lillington.
PUCK
Death of Puck, The. Lee-Hamilton.
To Puck. B. L. Thomas.
PUERTO RICO. Puerto Rican Side-Street. Dudek.
PUGET SOUND. Islands, The; Puget Sound. James Rorty.
PUMA. Pumas. George Sterling.
PUMPKINS
Mr. Macklin's Jack o'Lantern. McCord.
Pumpkin, The. Whittier.
Theme in Yellow. Sandburg.
PUPPETS
Marionettes, The. De la Mare.
Marionettes. "Michael Field."
Puppet Player, The. Grimké.
Sherry. Kinoshita, *tr. fr. Japanese by* Ninomiya *and* Enright.
PURCELL, HENRY
Henry Purcell. G. M. Hopkins.
On the Death of Mr. Purcell. Dryden.
PURGATORY. Purgatorio, *sels. Fr.* Divina Commedia. Dante.
PURITANS AND PURITANISM
Cavalier Tunes. Robert Browning.
Come drawer some wine or wele pull downe your signe. *Unknown.*
Grasshopper The. Lovelace.
Hudibras, *sels.* Samuel Butler.
On Those That Deserve It. Quarles.
Religio Laici. Dryden.
Say puritan ist come to passe. *Unknown.*
PUSHKIN, ALEKSANDR SERGEYEVICH
On the Death of Pushkin. Lermontov, *tr. fr. Russian by* Bianchi.
Unto Myself I Reared a Monument. Pushkin, *tr. fr. Russian by* Bowra.
PUSSY WILLOWS
Pussy Willow. K. L. Brown.
Pussy Willows. R. B. Bennett.
Pussy-Willows. Guiterman.
Pussy Willows. M. E. Plummer.
Pussy Willows ("There are willow pussies"). *Unknown.*
Willow Cats, The. Widdemer.
PUTNAM, ISRAEL. Death and General Putnam. Guiterman.
PYGMALION
Pygmalion. Louis Johnson.
Pygmalion. W. B. Scott.
Pygmalion and Galatea. *Fr.* Metamorphoses. Ovid, *tr. fr. Latin by* Highet.
Pygmalion to Galatea. Robert Graves.
PYGMIES. Ogres and Pygmies. Robert Graves.
PYM, JOHN. Pyms Anarchy. *At. to* Thomas Jordan.
PYRAMIDS
Egyptian Dead, The. *Fr.* The History of Joseph. Elizabeth Rowe.
Pelters of Pyramids. R. H. Horne.
Sunrise over the Pyramids. Dietrichson, *tr. fr. Norwegian by* Stork.
PYTHONS
Python, The. Belloc.
Python. G. H. Conkling.

Q

QUAKER LADIES (flower). Quaker Ladies. Cortissoz.
QUAKERS. *See* FRIENDS, SOCIETY OF.
QUANTRILL, WILLIAM CLARKE. Quantrell. *Unknown.*
QUEBEC, CANADA. At Quebec. Jean Blewett.
QUEEN ANNE'S LACE (flower)
Queen Anne's Lace. Georgia Benedict.
Queen Anne's Lace. M. L. Newton.
Queen-Anne's-Lace. W. C. Williams.
QUEENSTOWN, BATTLE OF. Battle of Queenstown, The. William Banker, Jr.
QUIVIRA. Quivira. Guiterman.

R

RABBIS
Rabbi's Song, The. Kipling.
Two Rabbins, The. Whittier.
RABBITS
Four Things. Proverbs, Bible, *O.T.*
Mr. Rabbit. Dixie Willson.
Perfect Life, The. Carrera Andrade, *tr. fr. Spanish by* Fitts.
Rabbit, The. W. H. Davies.
Rabbit, The. G. R. Durston.
Rabbit, The. Edith King.
Rabbit, The John Lewisohn.
Rabbit, The. E. M. Roberts.
Rabbit. Tom Robinson.
Rabbit, The. *Unknown.*
Rabbits. Baruch.
Rabbits, The. *Unknown, tr. fr. German.*
Snare, The. James Stephens.
Song of the Rabbits outside the Tavern. Coatsworth.
To a Jack Rabbit. S. O. Barker.
Tracks. John Farrar.
White Season. Frances M. Frost.
See also HARES.
RABELAIS, FRANÇOIS. Epitaph on Rabelais. Ronsard, *tr. fr. French by* Currey.
RACCOONS
Diary of a Raccoon. G. R. Bennett.
Raccoon on the Road. J. P. Brennan.
Racoon. Rexroth.
RACE, CAPE, NEWFOUNDLAND. Way of Cape Race, The. E. J. Pratt.
RACHEL (Bible). Rachel. Ruth Gilbert.
RACING. *See* HORSE RACING.
RADCLIFFE, JAMES, 3D EARL OF DERWENTWATER. Lord Derwentwater. *Unknown.*
RADIO
Broadcast, The. J. W. Simons.
In Memory of Radio. LeRoi Jones.
Microphone, The. Van Winkle.
My Radio. Van Winkle.
Next Voice You Hear, The. T. P. McDonnell.
Radio, The. Guest.
Radio. Theresa Lindsey.
Radio. Harriet Monroe.
Radio. Tessimond.
Sonnet on Turning a Radio Dial. Scruggs.
RADISHES. Radish, The. Ibn Quzman, *tr. fr. Arabic by* Arberry.
RAGGED ROBIN (plant). Ragged Robin and Bouncing Bet. Alice Reid.
RAGWORT. Ragwort, The. Clare.
RAHAB (Bible). Rahab. Robert Norwood.
RAILROAD TRAINS. *See* TRAINS.
RAILROADS
Burying Ground by the Ties. *Fr.* Frescoes for Mr. Rockefeller's City. MacLeish.
Casey Jones. *Unknown.*

RAILROADS *(continued)*
D.L. and W.'s Phoebe Snow, The. *Unknown.*
Finnigan to Flannigan. Gillilan.
I've Been Workin' on the Railroad. *Unknown.*
Joseph Mica. *Unknown.*
Pacific Railway, The. C. R. Ballard.
Paddy Works on the Railway. *Unknown.*
Rail-road crossing. *Unknown.*
Railway Tunnel, The. Scott-Hopper.
There's Many a Man Killed on the Railroad. *Unknown.*
What's the Railroad to Me? Thoreau.
Wreck of the Old 97, The. *Unknown.*
RAIN
After the Rain. T. B. Aldrich.
After the Rain. Corbière, *tr. fr. French by* Koch *and* Guy.
All Night I Heard. G. M. Moffatt.
April Puddle. Rowena Bennett.
April Rain. Loveman.
April Rain Song. Langston Hughes.
April Showers. James Stephens.
Autumn Rain, The. H. F. Page.
Before Rain. *Tr. fr. Navajo Indian by* Austin.
Before the Rain. T. B. Aldrich.
Before the Rain. Rives.
City Rain. Rachel Field.
Conversation with Rain. L. D. Gunn.
Dance for Rain, A; Cochiti. Bynner.
Description of a City Shower in Imitation of Virgil's Georgics, A. Swift.
Down the Rain Falls. Coatsworth.
Fine Rain, The. Takahashi, *tr. fr. Japanese by* Ninomiya *and* Enright.
Green Rain. Mary Webb.
I Saw God Wash the World. Stidger.
In Time of Silver Rain. Langston Hughes.
Invocation to Rain in Summer. W. C. Bennett.
It Is Raining. L. S. Mitchell.
It Is Raining Again. Melachrinos, *tr. fr. Modern Greek by* Dalven.
It Rains. Edward Thomas.
June Thunder. MacNeice.
Latter Rain, The. Very.
Like the Touch of Rain. Edward Thomas.
Little Pagan Rain Song. Frances Shaw.
Little Rain. E. M. Roberts.
Little Rain, The. Tu Fu, *tr. fr. Chinese by* Cranmer-Byng.
Little Rain Men. R. A. Hussey.
Little Raindrops. Hawkshaw.
Mad Girl's Song. L. E. F. Barry.
Memorial Rain. MacLeish.
Night of Rain. Kenyon.
O! Do You Hear the Rain. Custance.
Ode to Rain. *Unknown, tr. fr. Russian.*
Old Man Rain. Cawein.
Old Woman Rain. Louise Driscoll.
On a Wet Summer. Bampfylde.
Our Hold on the Planet. Robert Frost.
Prayer for Rain. Herbert Palmer.
Rain. K. S. Alling.
Rain. Benediktsson, *tr. fr. Icelandic by* Kirkconnell.
Rain. *At. to* M. F. Butts, *also at. to* Larcom.
Rain. Ch'en Fu Liang, *tr. fr. Chinese by* Hart.
Rain. Coatsworth.
Rain, The. W. H. Davies.
Rain. P. F. Kirby.
Rain. Newman Levy.
Rain. Nishiwaki, *tr. fr. Japanese by* Ninomiya *and* Enright.
Rain. "Seumas O'Sullivan."
Rain. Po Chü-i, *tr. fr. Chinese by* Waley.
Rain. Frances Shaw.
Rain. R. L. Stevenson.
Rain. B. L. Taylor.
Rain. Tu Fu, *tr. fr. Chinese by* Chi Hwang Chu *and* Edna Worthley Underwood.
Rain, The ("Open the window"). *Unknown.*
Rain, The ("The rain came down"). *Unknown.*
Rain. J. S. Untermeyer.
Rain. W. C. Williams.
Rain. Helen Wing.
Rain. Ella Young.
Rain and Shine. Brander Matthews.
Rain at Night. Homan.
Rain at Night. Helen Hoyt.
Rain at Night, The. Tu Fu, *tr. fr. Chinese.*
Rain in April. Eleanor Hammond.
Rain in Summer. Longfellow.
Rain in the City. Rachel Field.
Rain in the Hills. C. B. Going.
Rain in the Night. A. J. Burr.
Rain Music. J. S. Cotter, Jr.
Rain on a Grave. Hardy.
Rain on the Down. Symons.
Rain on the Roof. Coates Kinney.
Rain or Shine. *Unknown.*
Rain, Rain. Zoë Akins.
Rain, Rain! *Unknown, tr. fr. Russian by* Ralston.
Rain Riders. Scollard.
Rain Song, The. Alex Rogers.
Rain-Songs from the Rio Grande Pueblos. *Tr. fr. Pueblo Indian by* Austin.
Rain-Talk. R. N. White.
Raindrops. *Unknown.*
Rains of Spring, The. Lady Ise, *tr. fr. Japanese.*
Rainy Day Song. Storey.
Rainy Summer, The. Alice Meynell.
Redhaw Rain. Sandburg.
Reprieve. Cormack.
Rhyme of Rain. John Holmes.
Shower, The. Vaughan.
Signs of Rain. *Fr.* Phaenomena. Aratus, *tr. fr. Greek by* Lucas.
Signs of Rain. Jenner.
Song of the Rain. Hugh McCrae.
Song of the Rain-Chant. *Tr. fr. Navajo Indian by* Curtis.
Sower, The. Figueroa, *tr. fr. Spanish by* Fitts.
Spring Rain. Behn.
Spring Rain. Chute.
Squall. Speyer.
Storm, The. Shanks.
Sudden Squall, A. Gascoyne.
Summer Rain. Laurie Lee.
Summer Rain. Sir Herbert Read.
Summer Rain, The. Thoreau.
Sun and Rain. C. G. Rossetti.
Sunshine after a Shower. *Fr.* On the Approach of Summer. Thomas Warton, the Younger.
Sweet, Low Speech of the Rain, The. Ella Higginson.
Tears Flow in My Heart. Verlaine, *tr. fr. French by* Kittel.
There Will Come Soft Rain. Teasdale.
Tumult Ends, The. Roland Robinson.
Umbrellas. Rowena Bennett.
Way Through, The. Levertov.
What Could Be Lovelier than to Hear. Coatsworth.
What to Do. Wise.
When in the Night We Wake and Hear the Rain. R. B. Wilson.
Who Likes the Rain? C. D. Bates.
Who Loves the Rain. Frances Shaw.
Woodyards in Rain. Marriott.
RAIN-IN-THE-FACE (Indian chief)
On the Big Horn. Whittier.
Revenge of Rain-in-the-Face, The. Longfellow.
RAINBIRDS
Rain-Crow, The. Cawein.
Rain Bird, The. Carman.
RAINBOWS
Boats sail on the rivers. *Fr.* Sing-Song. C. G. Rossetti.
Lord of the World, The. Studdert-Kennedy.
My Heart Leaps Up. Wordsworth.
Rainbow, The. Colby.
Rainbow, The. De la Mare.
Rainbow, The. Keble.
Rainbow, The. McCord.
Rainbow, The. Shanks.
Rainbow Fairies, The. Hadley.
Rainbows. Dixie Willson.
To the Rainbow. Thomas Campbell.
Weather Wisdom. *Unknown.*
RAINIER, MOUNT. Mount Rainier. Bashford.
RALEGH [*or* RALEIGH], SIR WALTER
Author's Epitaph, The. Ralegh.
Call on Sir Walter Raleigh, A. Piatt.
Conclusion, The. Ralegh.
Conjectured to Be Upon the Death of Sir Walter Raleigh. Henry King.
Elizabethan Days, *sel.* ("'Tis pleasant, stretched on grassy lawn"). T. C. Irwin.
Epitaph: On Sir Walter Rawleigh at His Execution. *Unknown.*
First American Sailors, The. Wallace Rice.
Silent Lover The. Ralegh.
Sir Walter Ralegh the Night before His Death. Ralegh.
Sir Walter Raleigh. H. J. Stockard.
Sir Walter Raleigh. *Fr.* In the American Grain. W. C. Williams.
Sir Walter Raleigh to a Caged Linnet. Lee-Hamilton.
Sir Walter Rauleigh His Lamentation. *Unknown.*
To the Right Noble and Valorous Knight, Sir Walter Raleigh. Spenser.
RANCHING AND RANCHERS. *See* FARMING AND FARMERS.
RANDOLPH, JOHN. Randolph of Roanoke. Whittier.
RAPHAEL. Written under the Engraving of a Portrait of Rafael. Leigh Hunt.
RATS
Jerboa, The. Marianne Moore.
Pied Piper of Hamelin, The. Robert Browning.
Rats, The. Trakl, *tr. fr. German by* Sigler.

Rats Away! *Unknown.*
"Trade" Rat. E. G. Wallis.
RATTLESNAKES. Rattlesnake, The. R. V. Carr.
RAVENNA, ITALY. Ravenna. Blok, *tr. fr. Russian by* Elton.
RAVENS
Advice to a Raven in Russia. Joel Barlow.
Raven, The. Kuthaiyir, *tr. fr. Arabic by* Arberry.
Raven, The. Poe.
Raven, The. E. A. Robinson, *after the Greek of* Nicarchus.
Raven, The. Takahashi, *tr. fr. Japanese by* Ninomiya *and* Enright.
Raven and the Fox, The. La Fontaine, *tr. fr. French by* Wright.
Raven and the Oak, The. S. T. Coleridge.
Ravens, The. Rimbaud, *tr. fr. French by* Conder.
Sycophantic Fox and the Gullible Raven, The. G. W. Carryl.
Three Ravens, The. *Unknown.*
Twa Corbies, The. *Unknown.*
READING
On a Boy's First Reading of "King Henry V." S. W. Mitchell.
On Reading. T. B. Aldrich.
Passionate Reader to His Poet, The. Le Gallienne.
To Any Reader. R. L. Stevenson.
REASON
Mock on, Mock on, Voltaire, Rousseau. Blake.
Reason. Josephine Miles.
Reason and Imagination. *Fr.* Milton. Blake.
Reason, in faith thou art well served, that still. *Fr.* Astrophel and Stella. Sidney.
See also INTELLECT.
RECIFE, BRAZIL. Salute to Recife. Bandeira, *tr. fr. Portuguese by* Poore.
RECONSTRUCTION, UNITED STATES
Mr. Johnson's Policy of Reconstruction. Halpine.
Old Thad Stevens. Kenneth Porter.
To the Thirty-ninth Congress. Whittier.
RED CROSS
Army of the Red Cross, The. Trask.
Compensation. R. C. Mitchell.
Great Cross of Mercy, The. Theodosia Garrison.
If Ever Time Shall Come. Alison Brown.
League of Love in Action, The. Markham.
Medical Corps, The. Beatrice Barry.
Red Cross, The. Jacques.
Red Cross, The. Van Dyke.
Red Cross Christmas Seal, The. Theodosia Garrison.
Red Cross Nurse, The. E. M. Thomas.
Red Cross Nurses, The. Masson.
Red Cross Spirit Speaks, The. J. H. Finley.
Soldier of the Silences, The. Herschell.
Somebody's Boy. K. L. Bates.
Three Crosses, The. E. V. Cooke.
Under the Red Cross. Hickox.
Your Cross and My Cross. E. F. Cox.
RED JACKET (Indian Chief). Red Jacket. Fitz-Greene Halleck.
RED SEA. Parting of the Red Sea, The. *Fr.* Exodus. *Unknown, tr. fr. Anglo-Saxon by* Kennedy.
REDBIRDS. *See* CARDINAL.
REDWOOD TREES. Summit Redwood, The. Jeffers.
REED, JOHN. Elegies over John Reed. Zaturenska.
REFUGEES
Banished, The. Serrano Plaja, *tr. fr. Spanish by* Humphries.
From Distant Lands. Hellings.
Grey Uncles. Auerbach, *tr. fr. Yiddish by* Betsky.
One Race, One Flag. Fairburn.
Refugee. *Fr.* Phoenician Maidens. Euripides, *tr. fr. Greek by* Way.
Refugee, The. H. M. Salisbury.
Refugee. Witherspoon.
Refugee Blues. Auden.
Refugee in New England. Frances Frost.
Refugees. G. H. Conkling.
Refugees, The. Jarrell.
Refugees. MacNeice.
Refugees, The. H. E. Read.
REINDEER. Lost Dream, The. F. S. Davis.
RELIGION
Ballade of the Heresiarchs. Belloc.
Dissent; a Fable. Davie.
Garden of Love, The. *Fr.* Songs of Experience. Blake.
Hind and the Panther, The, *sels.* Dryden.
New Sinai, The. Clough.
Of Religion. Gibran.
Religio Laici. Dryden.
Religion. Bierce.
Religion. Dolson.
Religion. Vauquelin de la Fresnaye, *tr. fr. French by* Thorley.
Satire III: On Religion. *Fr.* Satires. Donne.
Sir Hudibras's Religion. *Fr.* Hudibras. Samuel Butler.
Sunday Morning. Wallace Stevens.
There was a Presbyterian cat. *Unknown.*
RELIGIOUS VERSE
Anthology of Catholic Poets, An (ACP). Shane Leslie, ed.
Best Loved Religious Poems, The (BLRP). James Gilchrist Lawson, comp.
Catholic Anthology, The (CAW). Thomas Walsh, ed.
Golden Book of Catholic Poetry, The (GoBC). Alfred Noyes, ed.
Joyce Kilmer's Anthology of Catholic Poets (JKCP). Joyce Kilmer, ed.
Masterpieces of Religious Verse (MaRV). James Dalton Morrison, ed.
Mentor Book of Religious Verse, The (MeRV). Horace Gregory *and* Marya Zaturenska, eds.
Oxford Book of Christian Verse, The (OxBoCh). Lord David Cecil, ed.
Prayer Poems (PraP). O. V. Armstrong *and* Helen Armstrong, comps.
Questing Spirit, The (QS). Halford E. Luccock *and* Frances Brentano, eds.
Treasury of Poems for Worship and Devotion, A (TrPWD). Charles L. Wallis, ed.
Unseen Wings; the Living Poetry of Man's Immortality (UnW). Stanton A. Coblentz, comp.
World's Great Religious Poetry, The (WGRP). Caroline Miles Hill, ed.
See also CATHOLICISM; CHRISTMAS; EASTER; JESUS CHRIST; MARY THE VIRGIN.
RENAISSANCE
Exodus from a Renaissance Gallery. Acton.
Renaissance. Avrett.
Renaissance. Idris Davies.
RENO, NEVADA. Impression at Reno. C. R. Holmes.
RESTAURANTS. R is for the Restaurant. McGinley.
RESURRECTION, THE. *See* EASTER.
RETIREMENT. To Retirement. Luis de León, *tr. fr. Spanish by* Walsh.
REVENGE (ship). *Revenge,* The. Tennyson.
REVERE, PAUL. Paul Revere's Ride. *Fr.* Tales of a Wayside Inn. Longfellow.
REVOLUTION
Song of Babek. *Fr.* The Man with an Eagle on His Shoulder. Selvinsky, *tr. fr. Russian by* Lindsay.
Total Revolution, A. Oscar Williams.
REVOLUTION OF 1848. At the Sunrise in 1848. D. G. Rossetti.
REVOLUTIONARY WAR, AMERICAN. *See* AMERICAN REVOLUTION.
REYNOLDS, HENRY. To My Most Dearly-loved Friend, Henry Reynolds, Esquire, of Poets and Poesy. Drayton.
REYNOLDS, SIR JOSHUA
Retaliation. Goldsmith.
Sir Joshua Reynolds. Blake.
Verses on Sir Joshua Reynolds's Painted Window at New-College, Oxford. Thomas Warton, the Younger.
RHEIMS CATHEDRAL
Cathedral of Rheims, The. Rostand, *tr. fr. French by* Walsh.
Cathedral of Rheims, The. Verhaeren, *tr. fr. French by* Kilmer.
Rheims Cathedral. G. H. Conkling.
Smile of Reims, The. F. E. Coates.
RHINE (river). On the Rhine. W. L. Bowles.
RHINOCEROS
Rhinoceros. Belloc.
Rhinoceros, The. Ogden Nash.
RHODE ISLAND. Rhode Island. T. C. Brown.
RHODES, CECIL JOHN
At the Grave of Cecil Rhodes. Peter Jackson.
Burial, The. Kipling.
Resurgat. Cripps.
RHODOPE MOUNTAINS, GREECE. Mount Rhodope. Griparis, *tr. fr. Modern Greek by* Dalven.
RHODORA. Rhodora, The. Emerson.
RHYS, ERNEST. Autobiography, An. Ernest Rhys.
RICHARD I, KING OF ENGLAND (Richard Coeur de Lion)
Coeur de Lion to Berengaria. Tilton.
Crusade, The. Thomas Warton, the Younger.
Prison Song. Richard Coeur de Lion, *tr. fr. Old French by* Adams.
RICHARD II, KING OF ENGLAND. Richard II as Captive. *Fr.* The Civil Wars. Samuel Daniel.
RICHARD III, KING OF ENGLAND. Tudor Rose, The. *Fr.* The Ship of Fools. Barclay.
RICHARD, EARL OF CORNWALL. Song of Lewes, The. *Unknown.*
RICHES. *See* WEALTH.
RICHMOND, VIRGINIA. Fall of Richmond, The. Melville.
RIENZI, COLA DI. Rienzi to the Romans. *Fr.* Rienzi. M. R. Mitford.
RIFLES. Springfield Calibre Fifty, The. J. M. Hanson.
RILEY, JAMES WHITCOMB
To James Whitcomb Riley. Bide Dudley.
To James Whitcomb Riley. Kipling.

RIMBAUD, ARTHUR
Preludes for Memnon, *sel.* ("Rimbaud and Verlaine, precious pair of poets"). Aiken.
Response to Rimbaud's Later Manner. T. Sturge Moore.
Rimbaud. Auden.
Rimbaud in Africa. Rickword.
RIO DE JANEIRO, BRAZIL
River of Oblivion. Reyes, *tr. fr. Spanish by* Beckett.
Third Time. Pellicer, *tr. fr. Spanish by* Fitts.
RIVERA, DIEGO. I Paint What I See. E. B. White.
RIVERS
Blade of Grass Sings to the River, The. Leah Goldberg, *tr. fr. Hebrew by* Friend.
Clear and Gentle Stream. Robert Bridges.
Flowers and Moonlight on the Spring River. Emperor Yang-ti, *tr. fr. Chinese by* Waley.
Growing River, The. Rodney Bennett.
Mad River. Longfellow.
My River. Mörike, *tr. fr. German by* Hughes.
Negro Speaks of Rivers, The. Langston Hughes.
Night Journey of a River, The. Bryant.
Repose of Rivers. Hart Crane.
River, The. Ibn Sa'id of Alcala la Real, *tr. fr. Arabic by* Arberry.
River, The. Alan Porter.
River Glideth in a Secret Tongue, The. Ostroff.
Rivers. Squire.
Rivers. Thomas Storer.
Rivers Arise; a Fragment. Milton.
Rivers of the West. "Sunset Joe."
Rivers Unknown to Song. Alice Meynell.
Song of the Long River. C. L. Skinner.
Spring River, The. Po Chü-i, *tr. fr. Chinese by* Waley.
Thus the Mayne Glideth. *Fr.* Paracelsus. Robert Browning.
To a River in the South. Newbolt.
Where Runs the River? Bourdillon.
RIVIÈRE DU LOUP, QUEBEC. Off Rivière du Loup. D. C. Scott.
ROADS
Abandoned Roads. A. M. Rogers.
Best Road of All, The. C. H. Towne.
Call of the Road, The. Florence Nash.
Creek-Road, The. Cawein.
I Like Wood Roads. *Unknown.*
Joys of the Road, The. Carman.
King's Highway, The. McGroarty.
Little Road, The. N. B. Turner.
Mountain Road, The. Derham.
My Road. Opdyke.
Old Coach Road, The. Rachel Field.
Old Road, The. Very.
Path, The. Edward Thomas.
Road, The. J. G. Fletcher.
Road, The. Helene Johnson.
Road, The. Ogarev, *tr. fr. Russian by* Matheson.
Road, The. Sassoon.
Road Not Taken, The. Robert Frost.
Road Song. J. S. Montgomery.
Road Song, A. D.C. Scott.
Road Song. Tinckom-Fernandez.
Road Song, A. *Unknown.*
Road Song. Louis Untermeyer.
Road to Town, The. Sarson.
Roads. Ruth Dallas.
Roads. Rachel Field.
Roads. Katharine Knight.
Roads Go Ever Ever On. Tolkien.
Roadways. Masefield.
Rolling English Road, The. Chesterton.
Roman Road, The. R. A. Taylor.
Sea Road, The. M. H. Clarke.
Song of the Open Road, *sel.* ("Afoot and light-hearted"). Whitman.
Tewkesbury Road. Masefield.
Threnody: "There's a grass-grown road." R. G. Harding.
Tree-Top Road, The. M. R. Smith.
Turn of the Road, The. A. R. Coe.
Turn of the Road, The. F. S. Davis.
Walking Road, The. Richard Hughes.
Way through the Woods, The. Kipling.
ROANOKE ISLAND, NORTH CAROLINA
Mystery of Cro-a-tàn, The. M. J. Preston.
Wraith of Roanoke, The. Sledd.
ROBERT I *or* ROBERT THE BRUCE, KING OF SCOTLAND. *See* BRUCE, ROBERT.
ROBERT I, DUKE OF NORMANDY. Fame and Fortune. *Fr.* The Legend of Robert, Duke of Normandy. Drayton.
ROBIN GOODFELLOW. Robin Goodfellow. *Unknown.*
ROBIN HOOD
Birth of Robin Hood, The. *Unknown.*
Bold Peddler and Robin Hood, The. *Unknown.*
Death of Robin Hood, The. W. R. Benét.
Death of Robin Hood, The. Eugene Field.
Death of Robin Hood, The. *Unknown.*
Gest of Robyn Hood, A. *Unknown.*
How Robin Hood Rescued the Widow's Sons. *Unknown.*
In Sherwood Lived Stout Robin Hood. *Unknown.*
Jolly Pinder of Wakefield, The. *Unknown.*
Little John a Begging. *Unknown.*
Noble Fisherman, The; or, Robin Hood's Preferment. *Unknown.*
Robin Hood. Keats.
Robin Hood and Allan-a-Dale. *Unknown.*
Robin Hood and Guy of Gisborne. *Unknown.*
Robin Hood and Little John. *Unknown.*
Robin Hood and Maid Marian. *Unknown.*
Robin Hood and Queen Katherine. *Unknown.*
Robin Hood and the Beggar, I ("Come light and listen, you gentlemen all"). *Unknown.*
Robin Hood and the Beggar, II ("Lyth and listen, gentlemen"). *Unknown.*
Robin Hood and the Bishop. *Unknown.*
Robin Hood and the Bishop of Hereford. *Unknown.*
Robin Hood and the Butcher. *Unknown.*
Robin Hood and the Curtal Friar. *Unknown.*
Robin Hood and the Golden Arrow. *Unknown.*
Robin Hood and the Monk. *Unknown.*
Robin Hood and the Pedlars. *Unknown.*
Robin Hood and the Potter. *Unknown.*
Robin Hood and the Prince of Aragon. *Unknown.*
Robin Hood and the Ranger. *Unknown.*
Robin Hood and the Scotchman. *Unknown.*
Robin Hood and the Shepherd. *Unknown.*
Robin Hood and the Tanner. *Unknown.*
Robin Hood and the Three Squires. *Unknown.*
Robin Hood and the Tinker. *Unknown.*
Robin Hood and the Valiant Knight. *Unknown.*
Robin Hood and the Widow's Three Sons. *Unknown.*
Robin Hood Newly Revived. *Unknown.*
Robin Hood Rescuing the Widow's Three Sons. *Unknown.*
Robin Hood Rescuing Three Squires. *Unknown.*
Robin Hood Rescuing Will Stutly. *Unknown.*
Robin Hood's Birth, Breeding, Valor, and Marriage. *Unknown.*
Robin Hood's Chase. *Unknown.*
Robin Hood's Death. *Unknown.*
Robin Hood's Delight. *Unknown.*
Robin Hood's End. *Unknown.*
Robin Hood's Golden Prize. *Unknown.*
Robin Hood's Progress to Nottingham. *Unknown.*
Song of Sherwood, A. Noyes.
True Tale of Robin Hood, A. *Unknown.*
Weep, Weep, Ye Woodmen. *Fr.* Death of Robert, Earl of Huntingdon. Munday *and* Chettle.
ROBINS
Autumn Robin, The. Clare.
Birds. "Moira O'Neill."
Come Here Little Robin. *Unknown.*
Come Hither, Sweet Robin. *Unknown.*
Death and Burial of Cock Robin, The. *Unknown.*
English Robin, The. Weir.
Epitaph on a Robin Redbreast, An. Samuel Rogers.
First Robin, The. Leveridge.
Gay Robin Is Seen No More. Robert Bridges.
Golden-Robin's Nest, The. J. W. Chadwick.
Little Robin Redbreast. *Unknown.*
Lost—Three Little Robins. *Unknown.*
Redbreast Chasing a Butterfly, The. Wordsworth.
Robin, The. Alma-Tadema.
Robin, The. O. M. Bent.
Robin. A. B. Payne.
Robin, The. *Unknown.*
Robin, The. Very.
Robin and the Cows, The. W. D. Howells.
Robin and the Wren, The. *Unknown.*
Robin in the Rain, The. C. C. Woods.
Robin is the one, The. Emily Dickinson.
Robin Redbreast. Allingham.
Robin Redbreast. G. W. Doane.
Robin Red Breast. Weeden.
Robin Redbreasts, The. Hawkshaw.
Robin Song. Scollard.
Robin to His Mate, The. A. A. G. Carter.
Robin's Come. W. W. Caldwell.
Robin's Egg, The. A. C. Dalton.
Robin's Secret. K. L. Bates.
Robin's Song. Rodney Bennett.
Robin's Song. E. L. M. King.
Secret, The. *Unknown.*
Sir Robin. Larcom.
Song of the Robin, The. Bergquist.
Tampa Robins. Lanier.
Three Things to Remember. Blake.
To a Robin. T. A. Daly.
To Robin Red-Breast. Herrick.
What Robin Told. George Cooper.
When the Snow Is on the Ground. *Unknown.*

Why the Robin's Breast Was Red. J. R. Randall.
Wrens and Robins [in the Hedge]. *Fr.* Sing-Song. C. G. Rossetti.
ROBINSON, EDWIN ARLINGTON. To Edwin Arlington Robinson. W. T. Scott.
ROBINSON CRUSOE
Crusoe. F. C. McLaren.
Robinson Crusoe Returns to Amsterdam. *Fr.* Amsterdam. Jammes, *tr. fr. French by* Bithell.
Robinson Crusoe's Story. C. E. Carryl.
Robinson Finds Friday. Weissmann.
ROCHESTER CATHEDRAL, ENGLAND. Precinct—Rochester, The. Amy Lowell.
ROCKEFELLER CENTER, NEW YORK CITY. I Paint What I See. E. B. White.
ROCKS. *See* STONES AND ROCKS.
ROCKY MOUNTAINS
David. Earle Birney.
Lines on Mountain Villages. "Sunset Joe."
On Recrossing the Rocky Mountains after Many Years. Frémont.
RODERICK (last Visigothic king in Spain). Lamentation of Don Roderick, The. *Unknown, tr. fr. Spanish by* Lockhart.
RODIN, AUGUSTE. To Rodin. Stork.
RODNEY, CAESAR. Rodney's Ride. E. S. Brooks.
RODNEY, GEORGE BRYDGES RODNEY, 1ST BARON
Admiral Rodney's Triumph on the 12th of April. *Unknown.*
Rodney's Glory. O. R. O'Sullivan.
ROLVAAG, OLE EDVART. No Gull's Wings. Paul Engle.
ROMAN CATHOLIC CHURCH. *See* CATHOLICISM.
ROME, ITALY
Aeneas at the Site of Rome. *Fr.* The Aeneid. Virgil, *tr. fr. Latin by* Humphries.
Against the Court of Rome. Petrarch, *tr. fr. Italian by* Wyatt.
Amours de Voyage. Clough.
Antiquities of Rome, *sels.* Du Bellay, *tr. fr. French by* Conder.
Appian Way, The. Geoffrey Johnson.
Boy from Rome, Da. T. A. Daly.
Easter Day in Rome. Oscar Wilde.
Oh Rome! My Country! *Fr.* Childe Harold's Pilgrimage. Byron.
On Old Rome. Philip Ayres.
Pharsalia, *sel.* ("Wars worse then civil on Thessalian plains"). Lucan, *tr. fr. Latin by* Marlowe.
Roma Mater Sempaeterna. O'Sheel.
Rome. Du Bellay, *tr. fr. French.*
Rome. Menendez y Pelayo, *tr. fr. Spanish by* Gill.
Rome. Vitale, *tr. fr. Latin by* Cunningham.
Rome a Greek City. Juvenal, *tr. fr. Latin by* Gifford.
Rome in Her Ruins. Quevedo, *tr. fr. Spanish by* Hemans.
Rome Remember. Sidney Keyes.
Ruins of Rome. Du Bellay, *tr. fr. French by* Spenser.
Ruins of Rome. John Dyer.
Sonnet: "He who would like to see what art and nature." Du Bellay, *tr. fr. French by* Currey.
Sonnet: "Newcomer, you who look in Rome for Rome." Du Bellay, *tr. fr. French by* Currey.
Villa Sciarra; Rome. C. T. Curtis.
Vision of Rome's Destiny. *Fr.* The Aeneid. Virgil, *tr. fr. Latin by* Dryden.
Written at Rome. Emerson.
ROMNEY, GEORGE. Sonnet to George Romney. Cowper.
ROMNEY MARSH, ENGLAND. In Romney Marsh. John Davidson.
RONSARD, PIERRE DE
Ronsard. M. A. deFord.
Ronsard. Lang.
ROOKS
Balliol Rooks, The. F. S. Boas.
Rook Sits High, The. Eliza Cook.
Rooks; New College Gardens. L. I. Guiney.
ROOSEVELT, FRANKLIN DELANO
At Warm Springs. W. R. Benét.
Homage to Our Leaders. Symons.
ROOSEVELT, QUENTIN. Ongoing, The. Siegrist.
ROOSEVELT, THEODORE
Close Up the Ranks. E. S. Van Zile.
Great-Heart. Kipling.
Man, A. Scollard.
Our Colonel. Guiterman.
Pilgrimage. Catherine Parmenter.
Pilot and Prophet. C. H. Towne.
Prophet, The. T. C. Clark.
Roosevelt. R. H. Davis.
Roosevelt. Fandel.
Roosevelt. T. E. Thomas.
Sagamore. C. R. Robinson.
Star, The: Dedicated to Theodore Roosevelt, Following his Death, January 6, 1919. M. C. Smith.
Theodore Roosevelt. S. V. Cole.
Theodore Roosevelt. McLandburgh Wilson.
To Theodore Roosevelt. Darío, *tr. fr. Spanish by* Hills.
Valiant for Truth. C. R. Robinson.
With the Tide. Edith Wharton.
ROOSTERS. *See* COCKS.
ROSAMUND (Fair Rosamund)
Becket, *sel.* ("O I see now your purpose is to fright me"). Tennyson.
Complaint of Rosamond, The. Daniel.
ROSEMARY
Rosemary Spray, The. Góngora, *tr. fr. Spanish by* Churton.
There's Rosemary. O. T. Dargan.
ROSES
Ah me, if I grew sweet to man. Michael Field.
Autumn Rose-Tree, An. Earls.
Ballad: White Rose. Sacheverell Sitwell.
Black Rose, The. Clement Wood.
Bowl of Roses, A. Henley.
Branch of the Sweet and Early Rose. Drennan.
Briar-Rose. *Unknown, tr. fr. German by* Untermeyer.
Brier-Rose. Boyesen.
Bunch of Roses, A. Tabb.
Cliff Rose, The. Fewster.
Concerning the Rose and the Nightingale. Grigoris of Aghtamar, *tr. fr. Armenian by* Boyajian.
Divine rose, that in a pleasant garden. Sister Juana Inés de la Cruz, *tr. fr. Spanish by* Beckett.
Dramas of the Rose. Schevill.
Fancy from Fontenelle, A. Dobson.
Florist Rose, The. Robert Graves.
Gold-of-Ophir Roses. G. A. Dennen.
Green and Red and Darkness. W. T. Scott.
How Roses Came Red. Herrick.
I Never See the Red Rose Crown the Year. Masefield.
I'll Tell You Whence the Rose Did First Grow Red. William Strode.
Interior of the Rose. Rilke, *tr. fr. German by* Flores.
Landscape as Metal and Flowers. W. T. Scott.
Legend of the Christmas Rose, The. F. B. Davis.
Lilies and Roses. Ibn al-Qutiya, *tr. fr. Arabic by* Arberry.
Little Rose Is Dust, My Dear, The. G. H. Conkling.
Little Rose Tree, The. Rachel Field.
Moss Rose, The. Krummacher, *tr. fr. German.*
Moss-Rose, The. Newbolt.
Of Roses. M. C. Davies.
On a Rosebud Sent to Her Lover. *Unknown.*
Overnight, a Rose. Giltinan.
Poor Withered Rose. Robert Bridges.
Red Rose. Hafiz, *tr. fr. Persian by* Payne.
Rosary, The. Herrick.
Rose, A. Arlo Bates.
Rose, The. *Fr.* Visions. William Browne.
Rose, The. Cowper.
Rose, A. Fanshawe.
Rose, The. Goethe, *tr. fr. German by* Lang.
Rose, The. William Hammond.
Rose, The. Thomas Howell.
Rose, The. Lovelace.
Rose, The. Ronsard, *tr. fr. French by* Lang.
Rose. Swinburne.
Rose. Lewis Thompson.
Rose and Root. Piatt.
Rose and the Thorn, The. P. H. Hayne.
Rose and the Wind, The. P. B. Marston.
Rose in Jericho, A. C. G. Rossetti.
Rose in October, The. Townley.
Rose Is a Royal Lady, The. Blanden.
Rose Song, The. Gil Vicente, *tr. fr. Spanish by* Bowring.
Rosebush. Claudius, *tr. fr. German by* Salinger.
Roses. Al-Ghassani, *tr. fr. Arabic by* Arberry.
Roses. "George Eliot."
Roses. Ronsard, *tr. fr. French.*
Roses. Thomas Stanley, *after the Greek of* Anacreon.
Roses. *Unknown.*
Roses Are Beauty, but I Never See. Masefield.
Roses in December. Studdert-Kennedy.
Roses Only. Marianne Moore.
Sick Rose, The. *Fr.* Songs of Experience. Blake.
Song: "When the Rose came I loved the Rose." O'Shaughnessy.
Sonnet: "O, how much more doth beauty beauteous seem." Shakespeare.
Sweet is the rose, but growes upon a brere. *Fr.* Amoretti. Spenser.
Sweet Violets, Love's Paradise. *Unknown.*
There Was a Rose. A. L. Phelps.
There's Nothing like the Rose. C. G. Rossetti.
'Tis the Last Rose of Summer. Thomas Moore.
To a Rose. F. D. Sherman.
To a Rose. Tabb.
To a Wild Rose Found in October. E. P. Clarke.
To a Withered Rose. J. K. Bangs.
To Roses in the Bosom of Castara. *Fr.* Castara. Habington.

ROSES (*continued*)
To the Rose. *Fr.* Hymns of Astraea. Sir John Davies.
To the Rose. Rioja, *tr. fr. Spanish by* Farnell.
To the Rose; a Song. Herrick.
To the Rose upon the Rood of Time. Yeats.
Violet and the Rose, The. Skipsey.
Violet and the Rose, The. A. D. Webster.
White Roses. Fabbri.
White Roses. Ernest Rhys.
Wild Rose. Allingham.
Wild Rose of Plymouth, The. Very.
Wild Roses. Fawcett.
Wild Roses. M. E. L. Newsome.
Wild White Rose, The. E. H. Willis.
ROSS, BETSY. Betsy's Battle Flag. Minna Irving.
ROSSETTI, CHRISTINA GEORGINA
To Christina Rossetti. Greenwell.
To Christina Rossetti. Sir William Watson.
ROSSETTI, DANTE GABRIEL
At the Grave of Dante Gabriel Rossetti. Mackenzie Bell.
Voice of D.G.R., The. Gosse.
ROUSSEAU, JEAN JACQUES
Mock On, Mock On, Voltaire, Rousseau. Blake.
Rousseau. Schiller, *tr. fr. German by* Bulwer-Lytton.
ROWAN TREES. *See* MOUNTAIN ASH TREES.
ROYAL GEORGE (ship). On the Loss of the *Royal George.* Cowper.
ROYAL SCOTS FUSILIERS. In Praise of the Royal Scots Fusiliers. Buchan.
ROYAL SOCIETY
Satire on the Royal Society, A. Samuel Butler.
To the Royal Society. Cowley.
RUBBER PLANTS. To a Cafeteria Rubber-Plant. Wrenn.
RUBINSTEIN, ANTON GRIGORYEVICH. Rubinstein Staccato Etude, The. Dett.
RUSSELL, LUCY, COUNTESS OF BEDFORD
On Lucy, Countess of Bedford. Jonson.
To Lucy, Countess of Bedford, with Mr. Donne's Satires. Jonson.
To the Countesse of Bedford on New-Yeares Day. Donne.
To the Excellent and Most Accomplish'd Lady, Lucy, Countess of Bedford. *Fr.* Mortimeriados. Drayton.
To the Lady Lucy, Countess of Bedford. Daniel.
RUSSIA
Advice to a Raven in Russia, December, 1812. Joel Barlow.
At the Top of My Voice. Mayakovsky, *tr. fr. Russian by* Marshall.
Capitals Are Rocked, The. Nekrasov, *tr. fr. Russian by* Deutsch *and* Yarmolinsky.
Hymn, A: "Lord, give them freedom who are weak." Nekrasov, *tr. fr. Russian by* Cornford *and* Salaman.
Land of Masters. Lermontov, *tr. fr. Russian.*
My Country. Lermontov, *tr. fr. Russian.*
November 7; Ode to a Day of Victories. "Pablo Neruda," *tr. fr. Spanish by* Fitts.
Now Where to? Heine, *tr. fr. German by* Gruenthal.
Russia. Blok, *tr. fr. Russian by* Deutsch *and* Yarmolinsky.
Russia. N. H. Dole.
Russia. Elliott Napier.
Take a Letter to Dmitri Shostakovitch. Sandburg.
To Russia. Joaquin Miller.
Book of Russian Verse, A. (BoR). C. M. Bowra, ed.
Book of Russian Verse, A Second (BoRS). C. M. Bowra, ed.
Russian Poetry, 1917–1955 (RuPo). Jack Lindsay, ed.
Treasury of Russian Verse, A (TrRV). Avrahm Yarmolinsky, ed.
Wagon of Life, The (WaL). Sir Cecil Kisch, tr.
See also UNION OF SOVIET SOCIALIST REPUBLICS.
RUSSIAN REVOLUTION
Mowers in the Line of Fire. Bryusov, *tr. fr. Russian by* Lindsay.
Native Land. "Andrei Bely," *tr. fr. Russian by* Lindsay.
Now All Is Sold. "Anna Akhmatova," *tr. fr. Russian by* Lindsay.
October. Marienhof, *tr. fr. Russian by* Deutsch.
Remote, in a Closed Space. Bryusov, *tr. fr. Russian by* Lindsay.
Revolution, The. Shkulev, *tr. fr. Russian by* Patrick.
Sons of Our Sons, The. Ehrenburg, *tr. fr. Russian by* Lindsay.
To Comrade Intellectuals. Bryusov, *tr. fr. Russian by* Lindsay.
Twelve, The. Blok, *tr. fr. Russian.*
RUSSIANS
Ivan. G. D. Martineau.
Rostov. G. S. Fraser.
We Grow Out of Iron. Gastev, *tr. fr. Russian by* Deutsch.
RUTLEDGE, ANN
Ann Rutledge. Markham.
Anne Rutledge. *Fr.* Spoon River Anthology. Masters.
RYDAL WATER, ENGLAND. Sunrise on Rydal Water. Drinkwater.

S

SABBATH
Come, O Friend, to Greet the Bride. Heine, *tr. fr. German by* Untermeyer.
Country Sabbath. M. H. Moody.
How Sweet Thy Precious Gift of Rest. Menahem ben Makhir of Ratisbon, *tr. fr. Hebrew by* Loewe.
In Soft Moss, Muted Steps. Einhorn, *tr. fr. Yiddish by* Betsky.
Keep Ye Holy Sabbath Rest. *Unknown, tr. fr. Hebrew by* Loewe.
Light and Rejoicing to Israel. *Unknown, tr. fr. Hebrew by* Abrahams.
May Sunday, A. T. C. Irwin.
O Day of Rest and Gladness. Christopher Wordsworth.
Outgoing Sabbath. *Unknown, tr. fr. Yiddish by* Leftwich.
Princess Sabbath. Heine, *tr. fr. German by* Leland.
Queen Sabbath. Bialik, *tr. fr. Hebrew by* Sampter.
Sabbath, The. James Grahame.
Sabbath Eve. Strindberg, *tr. fr. Swedish by* Stork.
Sabbath Morning, The. John Leyden.
Sabbath, My Love. Halevi, *tr. fr. Hebrew by* Solis-Cohen.
Sabbath of Rest, A. Luria, *tr. fr. Hebrew by* Salaman.
Sabbath Sonnet. Hemans.
Sæter Girl's Sunday, The. Moe, *tr. fr. Norwegian by* Stork.
Safely through Another Week. John Newton.
Some keep the sabbath going to church. Emily Dickinson.
Son-Days. Vaughan.
Summer Sabbath. Sampter.
Sunday. George Herbert.
Sunday Bells. Allingham.
Sunday Morning. MacNeice.
Sunday Morning. James Rorty.
Sunday Morning. Wallace Stevens.
Thou Beautiful Sabbath. *Unknown, tr. fr. Yiddish by* Myers.
Welcome, Queen Sabbath. Schneour, *tr. fr. Hebrew by* Fein.
SACAJAWEA. Sa-Ca-Ga-We-A. E. D. Proctor.
SACCO-VANZETTI CASE. Justice Denied in Massachusetts. Millay.
SAGAMORE HILL, OYSTER BAY, LONG ISLAND. Sagamore. C. R. Robinson.
SAGITTARIUS (constellation). Sagittarius or the Archer. J. G. Macleod.
SAHARA DESERT. Desert Travellers, The. L. D. Lerner.
SAILING AND SAILORS
Alarmed Skipper, The. J. T. Fields.
Anchor Song. Kipling.
Argonaut, The; or, Lost Adventurer. Freneau.
At Sea. D. H. Rogers.
Ave Sanctissima. *Unknown.*
Ballad of the *Bolivar,* 1890, The. Kipling.
Barge Wife, A. John Farrar.
Bark of Clanranald, The. MacDonald, *tr. fr. Gaelic.*
Beach Burial. Slessor.
Becalmed. Blight.
Bloody Bill. D. M. Ross.
Boatman's Hymn. *At. to* Magrath, *tr. fr. Modern Irish by* Ferguson.
Cheer Up, My Mates. Cowley.
Child and the Mariner, The. W. H. Davies.
Clipper Captain. Shirley Barker.
Coasters, The. T. F. Day.
Coming around the Horn. *Unknown.*
Compliment to Mariners. G. H. Dillon.
Deep Down. J. S. Montgomery.
Deep Water Man, The. J. S. Montgomery.
Drowned Mariner, The. E. O. Smith.
Drowned Seaman, The. Maude Goldring.
Dutch Seamen and New Holland, The. W. P. Reeves.
End, The. Corbière, *tr. fr. French by* Flores.
Epitaph for a Sailor Buried Ashore. C. G. D. Roberts.
Fiddler's Green. T. G. Roberts.
First American Sailors, The. Wallace Rice.
Flying Cloud, The. *Unknown.*
Forging of the Anchor, The. Ferguson.
Forty Singing Seamen. Noyes.
Frankie's Trade. Kipling.
Good Play, A. R. L. Stevenson.
Greenwich Pensioner, The. *Unknown.*
Hakluyt Unpurchased. McDuffee.
Harp Song of the Dane Women. Kipling.
Homeward Bound. Allingham.
Homeward Bound. D. H. Rogers.
"How's My Boy?" Dobell.
I Sail in the Fall. Stefánsson, *tr. fr. Icelandic by* Kirkconnell.

In the Trades. C. F. Smith.
John Winter. Binyon.
Jovial Marriner, The; or, The Sea-Man's Renown. Playford.
Landfall in Unknown Seas. Curnow.
Life on the Ocean Wave, A. Epes Sargent.
Long Trail, The. Kipling.
Lords of the Main. Joseph Stansbury.
Mariners. David Morton.
Mariners, The. M. L. Woods.
Mariner's Adieu, The. George Hill.
Mariner's Dream, The. Dimond.
Mariners' Song. *Fr.* Death's Jest Book. Beddoes.
Mariner's Song, The. Sir John Davies.
Mariner's Wife, The. *Unknown.*
Men behind the Guns. J. J. Rooney.
Messmates. Newbolt.
Nanny's Sailor Lad. Allingham.
Norse Sailor's Joy. Wilfrid Thorley.
O, Falmouth Is a Fine Town. Henley.
Ode for a Master Mariner Ashore. Guiney.
Of Mariners. Vinal.
Old Grey Squirrel. Noyes.
Old Quartermaster, The. Gordon Grant.
Out to Sea. R. H. Stoddard.
Pageant of Seamen, The. May Byron.
Peg-Leg's Fiddle. Bill Adams.
Quaker Graveyard in Nantucket, The. Robert Lowell.
Rambling Sailor, The. Mew.
Rime of the Ancient Mariner, The. S. T. Coleridge.
Rounding the Horn. *Fr.* Dauber. Masefield.
Sail, A. Lermontov, *tr. fr. Russian.*
Sailing at Dawn. Newbolt.
Sailing beyond Seas. Ingelow.
Sailor, The. Allingham.
Sailor. Langston Hughes.
Sailor, The. Goodridge MacDonald.
Sailor, The. S. T. Warner.
Sailor Boy, The. Tennyson.
Sailors. Patric Dickinson.
Sailors. Gautier, *tr. fr. French by* Conder.
Sailors, The. Woestijne, *tr. fr. Dutch by* Barnouw.
Sailor's Consolation, The. Pitt, *wr. at. to* Dibdin.
Sailor's Delight. C. F. Smith.
Sailors for My Money. Martin Parker.
Sailor's Wife, A. Bernhardt.
Sailor's Wife, The. Mickel, *sometimes at. to* Adams.
Salcombe Seaman's Flaunt to the Proud Pirate, The. *Unknown.*
Say That He Loved Old Ships. D. W. Hicky.
Sea-Fever. Masefield.
Sea Gypsy, The. Hovey.
Sea Song, A. Allan Cunningham.
Sea Urge. *Unknown.*
Seafarer, The. *Unknown, tr. fr. Anglo-Saxon.*
Seumas Beg. James Stephens.
Shipman, The. *Fr.* The Canterbury Tales. Chaucer.
Silence of God, The. Sir Osbert Sitwell.
Son of the Sea, A. Carman.
Song: "To all you ladies now at land." Sackville.
Song for All Seas, All Ships. Whitman.
Southerly. E. J. Brady.
Spring Sailing. Leonidas, *tr. fr. Greek by* Macgregor.
Symphony in Gray Major. Dario, *tr. fr. Spanish by* McVan.
Tacking Ship off Shore. Walter Mitchell.
To the Seamen. Masefield.
Voyage, The. Tennyson.
Wet Sheet and a Flowing Sea, A. Allan Cunningham.
Where Lies the Land? Clough.
Who Pilots Ships. D. W. Hicky.
Windlass Song. Allingham.
Worsley Enchanted, *sel.* ("It's cold, says Crean at the tiller"). Douglas Stewart.
Yankee Privateer, The. Arthur Hale.
Yankee Thunders. *Unknown.*
Ye Mariners of England. Thomas Campbell.
Eternal Sea, The; an Anthology of Sea Poetry (EtS) W. M. Williamson, ed.
Sailor's Garland, A (SG). John Masefield, ed.
See also SEA CHANTEYS.
SAINT AGNES'S EVE
Eve of St. Agnes, The. Keats.
St. Agnes' Eve. Tennyson.
SAINT BARTHOLOMEW'S EVE. For St. Bartholomew's Eve. Cowley.
SAINT BEE'S HEAD, ENGLAND. St. Bee's Head. T. E. Brown.
ST. CLAIR, ARTHUR. Sainclare's Defeat. *Unknown.*
SAINT CROIX [*or* DOCHET] ISLAND, MAINE. L'Ile Sainte Croix. W. H. Eaton.
SAINT CROIX (island), VIRGIN ISLANDS. Beauties of Santa Cruz, The. Freneau.
SAINT JOHN, NEW BRUNSWICK
Port of Saint John, The. H. A. Cody.
Saint John, The. G. F. Clarke.
Ships of Saint John, The. Carman.
SAINT KEYNE'S WELL, CORNWALL. Well of St. Keyne, The. Southey.
SAINT LEGER, BARRY. Saint Leger. Scollard.
SAINT LOUIS, MISSOURI. Sunset: St. Louis. Teasdale.
SAINT MICHAEL'S MOUNT, ENGLAND. St. Michael's Mount. John Davidson.
SAINT PETER [*or* PIERRE], LAKE, QUEBEC. Wreck of the *Julie Plante*, The. W. H. Drummond.
SAINT VALENTINE'S DAY. *See* VALENTINE'S DAY.
SAINTE ANNE DES MONTS, QUEBEC. Bells of Ste. Anne des Monts, The. Leo Cox.
SAINTE THÉRÈSE, QUEBEC. At Ste. Thérèse. S. F. Harrison.
SAINTS
Any Saint. Francis Thompson.
Nameless Saints, The. E. E. Hale.
Why Do I Use My Paper, Ink, and Pen. *Unknown.*
SALAMANCA, SPAIN. Salamanca. Unamuno, *tr. fr. Spanish by* Turnbull.
SALAMIS, BATTLE OF. Salamis. *Fr.* Persians. Aeschylus, *tr. fr. Greek.*
SALEM, MASSACHUSETTS
Salem. Robert Lowell.
Salem. E. C. Stedman.
Ship Comes In, A. Oliver Jenkins.
SALERNO, ITALY. Above Salerno. A. F. Murray.
SALINAS, FRANCISCO. Ode to Francisco Salinas. Luis de León, *tr. fr. Spanish by* Farnell.
SALMON
Salmon Drowns Eagle. Malcolm Lowry.
Sockeye Salmon. Hambleton.
Taking of the Salmon, The. T. T. Stoddart.
SALOME
Daughter of Herodias, The. Vaughan.
Salome. Apollinaire, *tr. fr. French by* Fitts.
SALT LAKE CITY, UTAH. Seven Cities of America, The. Masters.
SALVATION ARMY
General William Booth Enters into Heaven. Vachel Lindsay.
Roll the Chariot. *Unknown.*
SAMARKAND. Golden Journey to Samarkand, The. Flecker.
SAMSON (Bible)
How Samson Bore Away the Gates of Gaza. Lindsay.
Samson. F. G. Scott.
Samson Agonistes. Milton.
Who'll Toll the Knell? Alvarez.
SAMUEL (Bible). Saul, *sel.* ("What now? Thou look'st surprised"). Heavysege.
SAN ANTONIO, TEXAS
Cities. Boyce House.
Some Towns of Texas. K. W. Baker.
SAN BLAS, MEXICO. Bells of San Blas, The. Longfellow.
SAN FRANCISCO, CALIFORNIA
City; San Francisco. Langston Hughes.
Resurge San Francisco. Joaquin Miller.
San Francisco. J. V. Cheney.
San Francisco. Joaquin Miller.
San Francisco. W. A. Roberts.
Seven Cities of America, The. Masters.
To San Francisco. S. J. Alexander.
Trip; San Francisco. Langston Hughes.
SAN GABRIEL, MISSION OF, CALIFORNIA. Bells of San Gabriel, The. C. W. Stoddard.
SAN JACINTO, BATTLE OF. Fight at San Jacinto, The. J. W. Palmer.
SAN JUAN CAPISTRANO, CALIFORNIA. San Juan Capistrano. A. C. Cooper.
SANCHO II, KING OF CASTILE. King Don Sancho. *Unknown, tr. fr. Spanish by* Adams.
SANCHO PANZA. Sancho. W. E. Collin.
SAND, GEORGE
George Sand. Dorothy Parker.
Sonnets to George Sand, *sels.* E. B. Browning.
SAND
Sand. Guillén, *tr. fr. Spanish by* Turnbull.
Sand-between-the-Toes. A. A. Milne.
SANDPIPERS
Sandpiper, The. Bynner.
Sandpiper, The. Ivan Swift.
Sandpiper, The. Celia Thaxter.
Sandpipers. H. M. Egerton.
SANDSTONE. Sandstone. Anne Marriott.
SANDY HOOK, NEW JERSEY. Sandy Hook. George Houghton.
SANDYS, GEORGE. To My Worthy Friend Master George Sandys. Carew.
SANTA BARBARA, CALIFORNIA
Santa Barbara. F. F. Browne.
Santa Barbara Beach. Torrence.
SANTA CLAUS
Boy Who Laughed at Santa Claus, The. Ogden Nash.
Conversation between Mr. and Mrs. Santa Claus. Rowena Bennett.

SANTA CLAUS (*continued*)
Kris Kringle. Scollard.
Kriss Kringle. T. B. Aldrich.
Letter to Santa Claus. Wain.
Old Santa Is an Active Man. Lenski.
Real Santa Claus, A. F. D. Sherman.
Santa Claus. *Unknown.*
Santa Claus and the Mouse. Poulsson.
Visit from St. Nicholas, A. C. C. Moore.
When Santa Claus Comes. *Unknown.*
SANTA FE, NEW MEXICO. Spring Morning—Santa Fé. Lynn Riggs.
SANTA FÉ TRAIL. Old Santa Fé Trail, The. Richard Burton.
SANTA SOPHIA. *See* HAGIA SOPHIA.
SANTAYANA, GEORGE. Upon the Death of George Santayana. Hecht.
SANTIAGO DE COMPOSTELA. Sailing of the Pilgrims from Sandwich towards St. James of Compostella, The. *Unknown.*
SANTIAGO DE CUBA
Charge at Santiago, The. W. H. Hayne.
Deeds of Valor at Santiago. Scollard.
Santiago. T. A. Janvier.
Spain's Last Armada. Wallace Rice.
SANTOS, BRAZIL. Arrival at Santos. Elizabeth Bishop.
SAPPHO
Sapphics. Swinburne.
Sappho. Catullus, *tr. fr. Latin by* Leonard.
Sappho. Poseidippus, *tr. fr. Greek by* Lucas.
Sappho. Teasdale.
Sappho in Levkas. W. A. Percy.
Sappho Rehung. LeRoy Smith, Jr.
Sappho's Tomb. Stringer.
Sisters, The. Amy Lowell.
To Sappho. Antipater of Sidon, *tr. fr. Greek by* Lang.
To Sappho, about Her Apple. Aline Kilmer.
SARACENS. War Song of the Saracens, The. *Fr.* Hassan. Flecker.
SARATOGA, NEW YORK. Field of the Grounded Arms, The. Halleck.
SARDINIA. Sardinia from a Liner. Speyer.
SARSFIELD, PATRICK, EARL OF LUCAN
Ballad of Sarsfield, A. De Vere.
Farewell, O Patrick Sarsfield. *Unknown, tr. fr. Modern Irish by* Mangan.
Patrick Sarsfield, Lord Lucan. *Unknown, tr. fr. Irish by* O'Connor.
SARTO, ANDREA DEL. Andrea del Sarto. Robert Browning.
SARTON, GEORGE. Celebration, A. May Sarton.
SASSAFRAS
Sassafras. S. M. Peck.
Witchwood. Justus.
SATAN
Address to the Deil. Burns.
Courage, Mon Ami. Wattles.
Dark Angel, The. Lionel Johnson.
Devil and the Angel, The, *sels.* Rosemary Dobson.
Devil at Home, The. *Fr.* The Devil's Progress. Hervey.
Devil's Walk on Earth, The. Southey.
Fall of Satan, The. *Fr.* The Flaming Terrapin. Roy Campbell.
Faust, *sels.* Goethe, *tr. fr. German.*
Lucifer. D. H. Lawrence.
Lucifer in Starlight. George Meredith.
Man's Amazement. *Unknown.*
Whale, The. *Fr.* Physiologus. *Unknown, tr. fr. Anglo-Saxon by* Kennedy.
SATIRE
Fair Field for Satire, A. Juvenal, *tr. fr. Latin by* Gifford.
Satire: "Satire, my friend ('twixt me and you)." Geddes.
Virgidemiarum, *sel.* ("I first adventure, with foolhardy might"). Joseph Hall.
Virgidemiarum, *sel.* ("The satire should be like the porcupine"). Joseph Hall.
SATIRIC VERSE
Absalom and Achitophel, Pt. I Dryden.
Absalom and Achitophel, Pt. II, *sels.* Nahum Tate *and* John Dryden.
Absolute and Abitofhell. R. A. Knox.
All Men Are Free! Elliott Napier.
American Primitive. W. J. Smith.
Anatomy of Humor, The. Morris Bishop.
Anno 1829. Heine, *tr. fr. German by* Calverley.
Anthologistics. Guiterman.
Antichrist, or the Reunion of Christendom, an Ode. Chesterton.
Art for Art's Sake. *Fr.* The Cradle Will Rock. Blitzstein.
Ataraxia. B. L. Taylor.
Avarice. León, *tr. fr. Spanish by* Bell.
Awake! Walther von der Vogelweide, *tr. fr. German by* Bithell.
Babylon and Sion. Camões, *tr. fr. Portuguese by* Garnett.
Bagpipe Music. MacNeice.
Baker's Duzzen uv Wize Sawz, A. E. R. Sill.
Ballad of the Good Lord Nelson, A. Durrell.
Ballade of Suicide, A. Chesterton.
Ballade of Unfortunate Mammals. Dorothy Parker.
Bankers Are Just Like Anybody Else, except Richer. Ogden Nash.
Base Details. Sassoon.
Battle of Blenheim, The. Southey.
Bear, the Monkey, and the Hog, The. Iriarte, *tr. fr. Spanish by* Kennedy.
Beasts' Confession, The. Swift.
Beau's Receipt for a Lady's Dress, The. *Unknown.*
Bells of Heaven, The. Ralph Hodgson.
Bewick Finzer. E. A. Robinson.
Book of How, The. Merrill Moore.
Boy and the Schoolmaster, The. La Fontaine, *tr. fr. French by* Wright.
Brass Spittoons. Langston Hughes.
Britannia Rules of Orthography. "Firth."
Bunthorne's Song. *Fr.* Patience. W. S. Gilbert.
Cambridge Ladies, The. E. E. Cummings.
Canadian Authors Meet, The. F. R. Scott.
Canopus. B. L. Taylor.
Captain Carpenter. Ransom.
Chancellor's Gravel-Drive, The. Po Chü-i, *tr. fr. Chinese by* Waley.
Charcoal-Seller, The. Po Chü-i, *tr. fr. Chinese by* Waley.
Child of the Romans. Sandburg.
Clean Curtains. Sandburg.
Clever Tom Clinch Going to Be Hanged. Swift.
Cockerel, the Cat, and the Young Mouse, The. La Fontaine, *tr. fr. French by* Wright.
Coda. Dorothy Parker.
Cologne. S. T. Coleridge.
Come Live with Me and Be My Love. Day Lewis.
Companions. Calverley.
Congress, 1878. Montagne, *tr. fr. Flemish by* Bithell.
Contentment. *Fr.* The Autocrat of the Breakfast Table. O. W. Holmes.
Conundrum of the Workshops, The. Kipling.
Cottage Pictures, *sel.* ("No village dames and maidens now are seen"). S. J. Pratt.
Country Justice, The. Langhorne.
Crocodile, The. *Fr.* Alice's Adventures in Wonderland. "Lewis Carroll."
Crossroads. Otero Silva, *tr. fr. Spanish by* Walsh.
Cultural Notes. Fearing.
Dawn. Baudelaire, *tr. fr. French by* Millay.
Debutantrum. W. R. Benét.
Departed Friend, The. Novo, *tr. fr. Spanish.*
Dirge: "1-2-3 was the number he played but today the number came 3-2-1." Fearing.
Discovery. Freneau.
Don'ts. D. H. Lawrence.
Dragon of the Black Pool, The. Po Chü-i, *tr. fr. Chinese by* Waley.
Drugstore. J. V. A. Weaver.
Duke of Plaza-Toro, The. *Fr.* The Gondoliers. W. S. Gilbert.
During Lambing Season. Keidrych Rhys.
Enfant perdu. Heine, *tr. fr. German by* Milnes.
England and America. J. K. Stephen.
English Bards and Scotch Reviewers, *sels.* Byron.
Epistle to Dr. Arbuthnot. Pope.
Etiquette. W. S. Gilbert.
Evening Primrose, The. Dorothy Parker.
Exit God. Gamaliel Bradford.
Experience. Dorothy Parker.
Fable: "Mountain and the squirrel, The." Emerson.
Family Fool, The. *Fr.* The Yeoman of the Guard. W. S. Gilbert.
Farmhands' Refrain. H. H. Lewis.
Fighting Words. Dorothy Parker.
Flower Market, The. Po Chü-i, *tr. fr. Chinese by* Waley.
For One Who Would Not Be Buried in Westminster Abbey. Pope.
"Forever." Calverley.
Frescoes for Mr. Rockefeller's City. MacLeish.
Friar Lubin. Marot, *tr. fr. French by* Longfellow.
Friend of Humanity and the Knife Grinder, The. Canning *and* Frere.
Golf Links, The. Cleghorn.
Good and Bad Luck. John Hay.
Heaven. Rupert Brooke.
Here Lies a Lady. Ransom.
Homage. Fearing.
Horace Paraphrased. Isaac Watts.
Horrors of Civil War, The. Horace, *tr. fr. Latin by* De Vere.
House of Lords, The. *Fr.* Iolanthe. W. S. Gilbert.
How Beastly the Bourgeois Is. D. H. Lawrence.
How to Raise a Son. Martial, *tr. fr. Latin by* Lind.
Hudibras, *sels.* Samuel Butler.

I Paint What I See. E. B. White.
I Wonder What Became of Rand, McNally. Newman Levy.
Immigrants. N. B. Turner.
In Ciprium. Sir John Davies.
In Gerontem. Sir John Davies.
In Hardin County, 1809. L. E. Thompson.
In Haywodum. Sir John Davies.
In Rufum. Sir John Davies.
In Severum. Sir John Davies.
In the Great Metropolis. Clough.
In Titum. Sir John Davies.
In Westminster Abbey. Betjeman.
Indignation. Hugo, *tr. fr. French.*
Italy. Filicaja, *tr. fr. Italian by* Byron.
Japan for Sightseeing. Takenaka, *tr. fr. Japanese by* Ninomiya *and* Enright.
Japanese, The. Ogden Nash.
Joe Greene. Merrill Moore.
Journey to Exeter, A. Gay.
King of the Rainy Country, The. Baudelaire, *tr. fr. French by* Millay.
Ko-Ko's Song. *Fr.* The Mikado. W. S. Gilbert.
Latest Decalogue, The. Clough.
Let Us Now Praise Famous Men. Day Lewis.
Letrilla; the Lord of Dollars. Quevedo y Villegas, *tr. fr. Spanish by* Walsh.
Letter from a Missionary. Whittier.
Letter to Hitler, A. James Laughlin.
Lie, The. Sir Walter Ralegh.
Little Billee. Thackeray.
London. *Fr.* Songs of Experience. Blake.
London, *sel.* ("By numbers here from shame or censure free"). Samuel Johnson.
London Is a Fine Town. *Unknown.*
MacFlecknoe; or, A Satire upon the True-Blue Protestant Poet, T. S. Dryden.
Male and Female Created He Them. Aldous Huxley.
Man in the Bowler Hat, The. Tessimond.
Man of Culture, A. Tessimond.
Man Who Dreamed of Fairies, The. Po Chü-i, *tr. fr. Chinese by* Waley.
Memorial Rain. MacLeish.
Memorial to the Great Big Beautiful Self-sacrificing Advertisers. Ebright.
Message to Siberia. Pushkin, *tr. fr. Russian.*
Mews Flat Mona. Plomer.
Miniver Cheevy. E. A. Robinson.
Miniver Cheevy, Jr., *parody.* D. F. Parry.
Mrs. Brown and the Famous Author. Stoddard King.
Mrs. Frances Harris's Petition. Swift.
Modern Major-General, The. *Fr.* The Pirates of Penzance. W. S. Gilbert.
Museums. MacNeice.
My Country 'Tis of Thee. Bierce.
Nephelidia. Swinburne.
Next to of Course God. E. E. Cummings.
Nobody Loses All the Time. E. E. Cummings.
Now You're Content. Spire, *tr. fr. French by* Burnshaw.
Obit on Parnassus. F. S. Fitzgerald.
Ode Inscribed to W. H. Channing. Emerson.
Of the Characters of Women. *Fr.* Moral Essays. Pope.
Of Tabacco. Sir John Davies.
Of the Mean and Sure Estate. Wyatt.
Old Grimes. A. G. Greene.
Old Man with the Broken Arm, The. Po Chü-i, *tr. fr. Chinese by* Waley.
On a Curate's Complaint of Hard Duty. Swift.
On an Old Woman. Lucilius, *tr. fr. Greek by* Cowper.
On Rereading Télémaque. J. J. Roche.
On Some South African Novelists. Roy Campbell.
On the Bad Government of Toledo. Manrique, *tr. fr. Spanish by* Walsh.
On the Birth of His Son. Su T'ung-po, *tr. fr. Chinese by* Waley.
Pamphlet. Muñoz Marín, *tr. fr. Spanish by* Lee.
Parley of Beasts. "Hugh MacDiarmid."
Passion of M'Phail, The, *sels.* Horace Gregory.
People, The. Campenella, *tr. fr. Italian by* Symonds.
Petit Testament, Le. Villon, *tr. fr. French by* Payne.
Pity This Busy Monster, Manunkind. E. E. Cummings.
Plato Told. E. E. Cummings.
Playboy of the Demi-World, The, 1938. Plomer.
Poem for Mother's Day. Fishback.
Poem, or Beauty Hurts Mr. Vinal. E. E. Cummings.
Poems in Praise of Practically Nothing, *sels.* Hoffenstein.
Political Chaos in Italy. Dante, *tr. fr. Italian by* Longfellow.
Poor, The. Verhaeren, *tr. fr. French by* Lewisohn.
Portrait. Fearing.
Post-Impressionism. B. L. Taylor.
Progress of Beauty, The. Swift.
Progress of Dullness, The, *sels.* Trumbull.
Rape of the Lock, The. Pope.
Razor Seller, The. "Peter Pindar."
Recitation and Song. *Fr.* Patience. W. S. Gilbert.
Refugee Blues. Auden.
Relations. Tassoni, *tr. fr. Italian by* Lucchi.
Restricted. Eve Merriam.
Rich Man, The. F. P. Adams.
Richard Cory. E. A. Robinson.
Romance of the Rose, *sel.* ("Zeuxis, the painter, strove in vain"). Jean de Meun, *tr. fr. French by* Ellis.
Russia. Blok, *tr. fr. Russian by* Deutsch *and* Yarmolinsky.
SOS. Fearing.
Sabbath-Day Chace. Freneau.
Sail, A. Lermontov, *tr. fr. Russian.*
Salesman Is an It That Stinks Excuse, A. E. E. Cummings.
Satire on Paying Calls. Ch'eng Hsiao, *tr. fr. Chinese by* Waley.
Satirical Letrilla. José Cadalso, *tr. fr. Spanish.*
Satirical Letrillas. Bretón de los Herreros, *tr. fr. Spanish by* Kennedy.
Satires, *sels.* Donne.
Satires, *sels.* Horace, *tr. fr. Latin.*
Satires, *sels.* Juvenal, *tr. fr. Latin.*
Satires, *sels.* Persius, *tr. fr. Latin.*
Satires of Circumstance, *sels.* Hardy.
Satyr Address'd to a Friend That Is About to Leave the University, and Come Abroad in the World, A, *sel.* ("If you for Orders"). Oldham.
Satyrical Elegy on the Death of a Late Famous General, 1722, A. Swift.
Scarlet Woman, The. Fenton Johnson.
Scourge of Villany, The, *sels.* Marston.
Season 'Tis, My Lovely Lambs, The. E. E. Cummings.
Ship of Fools, The, *sels.* Sebastian Brandt.
Siege of Ismail, The. *Fr* Don Juan. Byron.
Sir Christopher Wren. E. C. Bentley.
Sir Joseph's Song. *Fr.* H.M.S. Pinafore. W. S. Gilbert.
Skialetheia, *sels.* Guilpin.
Soldier Boy, The. Runeberg, *tr. fr. Swedish by* Stork.
Some Beautiful Letters. Dorothy Parker.
Song to the Men of England. Shelley.
Sorrows of Werther. Thackeray.
Spider and the Fly, The, *sel.* ("In season what time every growing thing"). John Heywood.
Steel Glass, The, *sel.* ("For whiles I mark this weak and wretched world"). Gascoigne.
Strong Hand, A. Aaron Hill.
Stupidity Street. Hodgson.
Syracusan Women, The. *Fr.* Idylls. Theocritus, *tr. fr. Greek by* Chapman.
Thalia. T. B. Aldrich.
There Lived a King. *Fr.* The Gondoliers. W. S. Gilbert.
Thought, A. Lermontov, *tr. fr. Russian by* Eastman.
Thrushes. Humbert Wolfe.
To a Fat Lady Seen from the Train. Cornford.
To a Louse [on Seeing One on a Lady's Bonnet at Church]. Burns.
To a Plagiarist. Moses ibn Ezra, *tr. fr. Hebrew by* Solis-Cohen.
To an Ungentle Critic. Robert Graves.
To Italy. Leopardi, *tr. fr. Italian by* Rendel.
To Master Everard Digby. Lodge.
To Theodore Roosevelt. Darío, *tr. fr. Spanish by* Hills.
Tourist Time. F. R. Scott.
Town-Meeting, A. *Fr.* M'Fingal. John Trumbull.
Tract. W. C. Williams.
Travel Bureau, The. R. C. Mitchell.
Tropic Siesta. López, *tr. fr. Spanish by* Walsh.
Trumpets of the Mind, The. Hugo, *tr. fr. French.*
Two Confessions. *Fr.* The Vision of Piers Plowman. William Langland, *mod. by* H. W. Wells.
Two Red Towers, The. Po Chü-i, *tr. fr. Chinese by* Waley.
Under Which Lyre. Auden.
Unknown Citizen, The. Auden.
Upon a Dead Man's Head. Skelton.
Valentine for a Lady, A. Lucilius, *tr. fr. Greek by* Fitts.
Vanity of Human Wishes, The. Samuel Johnson.
Verses on the Death of Doctor Swift. Swift.
Virgidemiarum, *sels.* Joseph Hall.
Vision of Judgment, The. Byron.
Waifs and Strays. Rimbaud, *tr. fr. French by* Bithell.
Warning for Abraham Lincoln, A. Fombona Pachano, *tr. fr. Spanish by* Flores.
Wayzgoose, The, *sel.* ("Attend my fable if your ears be clean"). Roy Campbell.
We Have Been Here Before. Morris Bishop.
What Mr. Robinson Thinks. *Fr.* The Biglow Papers. J. R. Lowell.
Where the Cedars. Glatstein, *tr. fr. Yiddish by* Leftwich.
White Christmas. W. R. Rodgers.
Wine and Water. *Fr.* The Flying Inn. Chesterton.
With Freedom's Seed. Pushkin, *tr. fr. Russian by* Deutsch.
Woman. Fu Hsüan, *tr. fr. Chinese by* Waley.
Young Forest, The. "Demyan Bedny," *tr. fr. Russian by* Deutsch.

SATIRIC VERSE (*continued*)
Your Excellency. Giusti, *tr. fr. Italian by* Lucchi.
Book of Humorous Verse, The (BOHV). Carolyn Wells, comp.
Innocent Merriment; an Anthology of Light Verse (InMe). Franklin P. Adams, comp.
Silver Treasury of Light Verse, The (SiTL). Oscar Williams, ed.
See also PARODIES.
SATSUMA PENINSULA, JAPAN. Sunrise in the Hills of Satsuma. Fenollosa.
SATURN (planet). Saturn. Quiller-Couch.
SATYRS
Satyr, The. James Stephens.
Satyrs and the Moon, The. H. S. Gorman.
SAUL (Bible)
Dance of Saul with the Prophets, The. Tchernichowsky, *tr. fr. Hebrew by* Lask.
David's Song to the Troubled King. *Fr.* Saul, King of Israel. Starbuck.
In guilty night & hid in false disguise. *Unknown.*
Saul. Alterman, *tr. fr. Hebrew by* Vardi.
Saul. Robert Browning.
Saul, *sel.* ("What now? Thou look'st surprised"). Heavysege.
Saul. George Sterling.
Song of Saul before His Last Battle. Byron.
SAVANNAH (city), GEORGIA
About Savannah. *Unknown.*
Savannah. A. S. Burroughs.
SAVANNAH (river), GEORGIA. Savannah River. R. M. Montgomery.
SAVILE, HENRY. To Sir Henrie Savile. Jonson.
SAWDDE (river), WALES. River Sawdde. Keidrych Rhys.
SCHILLER, JOHANN CHRISTOPH FRIEDRICH VON. To the Author of "The Robbers." S. T. Coleridge.
SCHOLARS AND SCHOLARSHIP
Andrew M'Crie. R. F. Murray.
Clerk of Oxenford, The. *Fr.* The Canterbury Tales. Chaucer, *mod. by* Hill.
End of April, The. R. F. Murray.
Euthymiae Raptus, *sel.* ("But this is Learning; to have skill to throwe"). George Chapman.
For My Students, Returning to College. John Williams.
Grammarian's Funeral, A. Robert Browning.
"If, Jerusalem, I Ever Should Forget Thee." Heine, *tr. fr. German by* Armour.
In the Lecture Room. *Fr.* Cressida. Baxter.
Letter to a Teacher of English. Hillyer.
My Days among the Dead are Past [*or* Passed]. Southey.
Poor Scholar, The. Ibn Chasdai, *tr. fr. Hebrew by* Chotzner.
Poor Scholar of the Forties, A. Colum.
Scholar, The. Southey.
Scholar and the Cat, The. *Unknown, tr. fr. Irish by* O'Connor.
Scholar-Gypsy, The. Matthew Arnold.
Scholar in the Narrow Street, The. Tso Ssu, *tr. fr. Chinese by* Waley.
Scholars, The. Yeats.
Scholar's Life, The. *Fr.* The Vanity of Human Wishes. Samuel Johnson.
Sons of Our Sons, The. Ehrenburg, *tr. fr. Russian by* Deutsch.
Talmud Student, The. Bialik, *tr. fr. Hebrew by* Frank.
SCHOOL
At School-Close. Whittier.
At This Farewell. Wordsworth.
Big Brother. E. M. Roberts.
Classroom in October. Lieberman.
Country School. Curnow.
Country School, The. *Unknown.*
Departed Friend The. Novo, *tr. fr. Spanish by* Mallan.
Distant View of School. Maruyama, *tr. fr. Japanese by* Ninomiya *and* Enright.
Education. Josephine Miles.
Elementary School Classroom in a Slum, An. Spender.
First Departure. Frances Frost.
Getting Back. D. B. Thompson.
Going Back to School. S. V. Benét.
He Thinks of the Friend of His Youth, and of His Rooms at College. *Fr.* Youth Grows Old. Nathan.
In a Girls' School. David Morton.
In School-Days. Whittier.
Monday morning back to school. McCord.
Old Brown Schoolhouse, The. *Unknown.*
Patrick Goes to School. Aspinwall.
Prairie School, The. I. E. Mackay.
School and Schoolfellows. Praed.
School Begins. N. G. Price.
School-Bell. Farjeon.
School Boy Reads His *Iliad*, The. David Morton.
School Fencibles. William Cory.
Schoolboys in Winter. Clare.
Schoolmistress, The. Shenstone.
Schoolroom on a Wet Afternoon. Scannell.
School's Out. W. H. Davies.
Sing-Song Rhyme. *Unknown.*
Some Old School-Books. *Unknown.*
Tom Brainless at College. *Fr.* The Progress of Dulness. John Trumbull.
Under All This Slate. Hayford.
SCHOOLMASTERS
Schoolmaster, The. *Fr.* Snow-bound. Whittier.
Village Schoolmaster, The. *Fr.* The Deserted Village. Goldsmith.
SCIENCE
Epitaph: "Nature and Nature's laws lay hid in night." Pope.
Hymn to Science. Akenside.
In an Age of Science. T. C. Clark.
Man of Science Speaks, The. Harriet Monroe.
Mock On, Mock On, Voltaire, Rousseau. Blake.
New Sinai, The. Clough.
Old Astronomer to His Pupil, The. Sarah Williams.
Patient Scientists, The. B. G. Woods.
Sonnet to Science. Poe.
To My Honoured Friend Dr. Charleton. Dryden.
Imagination's Other Place (ImOP). Helen Plotz, comp.
SCORPIONS. Scorpion, The. Plomer.
SCOTLAND
Before Bannockburn. Burns.
Birds of Scotland, The. Hugh Macdonald.
Bluebells of Scotland, The. *Unknown.*
Complaint of the Common Weill of Scotland. Sir David Lindsay.
Cotter's Saturday Night, The. Burns.
Deirdre's Farewell to Alba. *Unknown, tr. fr. Old Irish by* O'Faoláin.
Elegy on the Death of Scots Music. Robert Fergusson.
In City Streets. Ada Smith.
Meditation of a Patriot. Fraser.
My Heart's in the Highlands. Burns.
Ode on the Popular Superstitions of the Highlands of Scotland, An. William Collins.
On Scotland. John Cleveland.
Scotland. *Fr.* The Prophecy of Famine. Charles Churchill.
Scotland. Alexander Gray.
Scots Wha Hae. Burns.
Tears of Scotland, The. Smollett.
Wish, The. Lermontov, *tr. fr. Russian by* Kisch.
Book of Scottish Verse, A (BSV). R. L. Mackie, ed.
Edinburgh Book of Scottish Verse, The (*1300–1900*) (EBSV). W. MacNeile Dixon, comp.
English, Scottish, and Welsh Landscape, 1700–c.1860 (EnSW). John Betjeman *and* Geoffrey Taylor, comps.
Golden Treasury of Scottish Poetry, The (GoTS). Hugh MacDiarmid, ed.
SCOTT, SIR WALTER. On Scott's Poem "The Field of Waterloo." Thomas, Lord Erskine.
SCOTT, WINFIELD
Hero of Bridgewater. C. L. S. Jones.
Scott and the Veteran. Bayard Taylor.
SCOTTISH BORDER. Lock the Door, Lariston. Hogg.
SCOTTSBORO CASE
Communication to Nancy Cunard, A. Kay Boyle.
They Are Ours. Magil.
Trial, The. Rukeyser.
SCRIBES. Scribe, The. *Unknown, tr. fr. Old Irish by* Meyer.
SCUDDER, VIDA DUTTON. To Vida D. Scudder. Converse.
SCULPTURE AND SCULPTORS
Carrara. Philip Murray.
On Seeing the Elgin Marbles. Keats.
Statuette: Late Minoan. Day Lewis.
Torso of an Archaic Apollo. Rilke, *tr. fr. German by* MacIntyre.
Venus of Bolsover Castle, The. Sacheverell Sitwell.
SEA
And You, Seas. "St.-J. Perse."
As the Tide Comes In. C. Y. Rice.
At Sainte-Marguerite. Stickney.
At Sea. D. H. Rogers.
At the Seaside. R. L. Stevenson.
Bathymeter. Hart-Smith.
Beautiful Proud Sea. Teasdale.
Break, Break, Break. Tennyson.
By the Gray Sea. Wheelock.
Call of the Sea, The. H. J. Savage.
Cemetery by the Sea, The. Valéry, *tr. fr. French by* Gibbs.
Christmas at Sea. R. L. Stevenson.
Coming Homeward Out of Spain. Googe.
Coquette Keith Stuart.
Crab. Blight.
Dancing Sea, The. *Fr.* Orchestra. Sir John Davies.
Distant Sea. Salinas, *tr. fr. Spanish by* Turnbull.
Dover Beach. Matthew Arnold.
Drama. Hart-Smith.
Dreams of the Sea. W. H. Davies.

East Anglian Bathe. Betjeman.
End, The. Corbière, *tr. fr. French by* Flores.
Evening Sea. Ito, *tr. fr. Japanese by* Ninomiya *and* Enright.
Everywhere of silver, An. Emily Dickinson.
Eye, The. Jeffers.
Face, The. Muir.
Face of the Waters, The. R. D. Fitzgerald.
Father's Testament, A. Ibn Tibbon, *tr. fr. Hebrew by* Abrahams.
Five Visions of Captain Cook. Slessor.
Forgotten Objects on a Beach Excell.
Grave, A. Marianne Moore.
Gray Rocks and Grayer Sea. C. G. D. Roberts.
Had I the Choice. Whitman.
Harbury. Louise Driscoll.
He Who Loves the Ocean. Leitch.
Her Heards Be Thousand Fishes. *Fr.* Colin Clout's Come Home Again. Spenser.
Hills and the Sea. W. W. Campbell.
Horses of the Sea, The. C. G Rossetti.
I Know Your Heart, O Sea! C. Y. Rice.
I started early, took my dog. Emily Dickinson.
Iphione. T. C. Irwin.
Kraken, The. Tennyson.
Last Chantey, The. Kipling.
Leave-taking, A. Broome.
Lighthouse Keeper's Offspring, The. Broughton.
Lord, I Am Here. C. G. Rossetti.
Man Whom the Sea Kept Awake, The. Bly.
Memories. Hölderlin, *tr. fr. German by* Watkins.
Michael. Vallis.
Northern Seas. Howitt.
November Surf. Jeffers.
Ocean, The ("Roll on, thou deep and dark blue Ocean—roll!"). *Fr.* Childe Harold's Pilgrimage. Byron.
Ocean. Jeffers.
Ocean, The. James Montgomery.
Ocean, The. Moschus, *tr. fr. Greek by* Shelley.
Ocean, The. C. T. Turner.
Ocean Burial, The. E. H. Chapin.
Ocean Spills, The. Hoffenstein.
Ocean to Cynthia, The. Ralegh.
Ode: "I am the spirit of the morning sea." R. W. Gilder.
Ode to the Sea. Howard Baker.
On the Seas. Keats.
Open Sea, The. Dorothea Mackellar.
Open Sea, The. William Meredith.
Out of the Cradle Endlessly Rocking. Whitman.
Pagan Hymn, A. Runcie.
Phantasy of the Sea, A. Antoinette Miller.
Quaker Graveyard in Nantucket, The. Robert Lowell.
Rime of the Ancient Mariner, The. S. T. Coleridge.
Salt Garden, The. Nemerov.
Sea, The. Alberti, *tr. fr. Spanish by* Turnbull.
Sea, The. Bernard Barton.
Sea, The. Björnson, *tr. fr. Norwegian by* Stork.
Sea, The. "Barry Cornwall."
Sea, The. Hart Crane.
Sea, The. Frankenberg.
Sea, The. Gorter, *tr. fr. Dutch by* Barnouw.
Sea, The. Nora Hopper.
Sea, The. *Fr.* Seaward. Hovey.
Sea, The. Ingianni.
Sea, The. D. H Lawrence.
Sea, The. R. H. Stoddard.
Sea, The. *Fr.* The Triumph of Time. Swinburne.
Sea, The. *Unknown, tr. fr. Irish by* O'Connor.
Sea, The. Zhukovsky, *tr. fr. Russian by* Bowra.
Sea and Shore. Koopman.
Sea and the Eagle, The. Clouts.
Sea and the Skylark, The. G. M. Hopkins.
Sea Born. Vinal.
Sea by the Wood, The. D. C. Scott.
Sea Call. Widdemer.
Sea-Change. Masefield.
Sea Change, A. Peace.
Sea-Change. Taggard.
Sea-Chronicles. Ingamells.
Sea Dirge. Archias of Byzantium, *tr. fr. Greek by* Lang.
Sea Dirge, A. "Lewis Carroll."
Sea Dream, A. Whittier.
Sea Fever. Masefield.
Sea Gods. Doolittle ("H. D.").
Sea Irony. J. L. Heaton.
Sea Is Full of Loveliness and Tears, The. J. R. Moreland.
Sea Is Wild, The. Wheelock.
Sea Island Miscellany, *sels.* Blackmur
Sea-Limits, The. D. G. Rossetti.
Sea Longing. Vinal.
Sea Longings. T. B. Aldrich.
Sea Ritual, The. Darley.
Sea Road, The. M. H. Clark.
Sea Song. *Fr.* Death's Jest Book. Beddoes.
Sea-Song. M. H. Clark.
Sea Song. Allan Cunningham.
Sea Song. Norah Holland.
Sea-Song. I. R. McLeod.
Sea Song, A. J. R. Moreland.
Sea-Song from the Shore, A. J. W. Riley.
Sea Sonnet. Lay.
Sea Surface Full of Clouds. Wallace Stevens.
Sea, the Sea, The. Alberti, *tr. fr. Spanish by* Turnbull.
Sea Urge. *Unknown.*
Sea Variations. E. J. Pratt.
Sea-Way. Cortissoz.
Sea-Wind, The. Arthur Ketchum.
Sea-Wind. Mallarmé, *tr. fr. French.*
Seaboard, The. Swinburne.
Seafarer, The. *Unknown, tr. fr. Anglo-Saxon.*
Sea's Spell, The. S. M. Spalding.
Seascape. Spender.
Seascape. F. B. Young.
Sea-Shore. Emerson.
Seaward. Gillespy.
Seaward. Thaxter.
Seaweed. Longfellow.
Secret of the Sea, The. Longfellow.
Shell, The. James Stephens.
Ship and the Sea, The. Baughan.
Shore, The. Salinas, *tr. fr. Spanish by* Turnbull.
Silent Day, The. Urbina, *tr. fr. Spanish by* Beckett.
Son of the Sea, A. Carman.
Song for All Seas, All Ships. Whitman.
Song from the Ship. *Fr.* Death's Jest Book. Beddoes.
Song of the Sea. Richard Burton.
Song of the Sea. *Unknown, at. to* MacColmain, *tr. fr. Middle Irish by* Meyer.
Song of the Wave, A. G. C. Lodge.
Sonnet of the Sea. La Bau.
Sorrow of the Sea, The. *Unknown.*
Sound of the Sea, The. Longfellow.
Southerly. E. J. Brady.
Stane wi Its Rune Rises frae the Sea, The. Heine, *tr. fr. German into Scottish by* Morgan.
Stone-Age Sea, The. Helen Hoyt.
Storm, The. Donne.
Storm at Sea, A. *Unknown, tr. fr. Old Irish by* Flower.
This Air That Blows In from the Sea. Coatsworth.
Tide Rises, the Tide Falls, The. Longfellow.
To Sea! To Sea! *Fr.* Death's Jest Book. Beddoes.
Told by Seafarers. Kinnell.
Twilight at Sea. Welby.
Two Old Men Look at the Sea. Hervey.
Undersong, The. "Fiona Macleod."
Upon the Shore. Robert Bridges.
Uses of Ocean. Sir Owen Seaman.
View of the Sea, A. Mabuchi, *tr. fr. Japanese by* Miyamori.
Visiting Sea, The. Alice Meynell.
Wanderer's Song, A. Masefield.
Waves. Emerson.
Waves Gleam in the Sunshine, The. *Fr.* Songs to Seraphine. Heine, *tr fr. German by* Lazarus.
Waves on the Sea-Shore, The. Hawkshaw.
Wet Sheet and a Flowing Sea, A. Allan Cunningham.
When the Gulls Come In. Egerton.
Who Pilots Ships. Hicky.
With Husky-haughty Lips, O Sea. Whitman.
Wood by the Sea, The. D. C. Scott.
World below the Brine, The. Whitman.
Would I Might Go Far over Sea. O'Shaughnessy, *after* Marie de France.
Young Sea. Sandburg.
Zennor. Ridler.
Eternal Sea, The (EtS). W. M. Williamson, ed.
SEA CHANTEYS
American Sea Songs and Chanteys (AmSS). Frank Shay, ed.
Shantymen and Shantyboys (ShS). William Main Doerflinger, comp.
Songs of American Sailormen (SoAmSa). Joanna C. Colcord, ed.
SEA GULLS. *See* GULLS.
SEA SERPENT. Sea Serpant, The. Wallace Irwin.
SEA SHELLS. *See* SHELLS.
SEA VOYAGES. *See* VOYAGES.
SEALS
Dancing Seal, The. W. W. Gibson.
Ice-Floes, The. E. J. Pratt.
Performing Seal, The. Rachel Field.
Seal. W. J. Smith.
Seal Lullaby. Kipling.
Seals, The. Aldis.
SEASONS
Four Seasons. Rowena Bennett.
Frost at Midnight. S. T. Coleridge.
Human Seasons, The. Keats.
Hymn on the Seasons. A. M. Porter.

SEASONS (continued)
Is Life Worth Living? Alfred Austin.
Message of the Snowdrop, The. *Unknown.*
Procession, The. Widdemer.
Seasons, The. J. V. Cheney.
Seasons, The, *sels.* Kalidasa, *tr. fr. Sanskrit by* Ryder.
Seasons, The. *Fr.* Ode on Vicissitude. Mickle.
Seasons, The. William Morris.
Seasons, The. Lynette Roberts.
Seasons. C. G. Rossetti.
Seasons of the Soul. Allen Tate.
Sing a Song of Seasons! R. L. Stevenson.
Song for the Seasons, A. "Barry Cornwall."
Song of the Four Seasons, A. Dobson.
Song of the Four Seasons, The. Li Po, *tr. fr. Chinese.*
Song of the Seasons. Lofton.
Song of the Seasons, A. Monkhouse.
Songs of the Seasons. M. E. B. Thorne.
Sonnet: "Quickly and pleasantly the seasons blow." Hillyer.
Summer sunshine,/ Autumn gold. Lathbury.
Three Seasons. C. G. Rossetti.
Twelve Moons, The. Li Ho, *tr. fr. Chinese by* Ho Chih-yuan.
While Immortality Endures. Ernest Briggs.
Year, The. Patmore.
Year's Round, The. Patmore.
Sing a Song of Seasons (SiSoSe). Sara Brewton *and* John E. Brewton, comps.
Year Around, The (YeAr). Alice I. Hazeltine *and* Elva S. Smith, eds.
SEBASTIAN, KING OF PORTUGAL. Ode on the Death of Don Sebastian. Herrera, *tr. fr. Spanish by* Herbert.
SECOND WORLD WAR. *See* WORLD WAR, SECOND.
SEDITION. Medal, The; a Satire against Sedition. Dryden.
SEED
Baby Seed Song. Edith Nesbit.
Chance-fallen Seed. Gilchrist.
Little Brown Seed in the Furrow, The. Benham.
Seed Shop, The. Muriel Stuart.
Seeds. De la Mare.
Seeds. A. D. Webster.
Sowing Seeds. Ursula Cornwall.
To a Maple Seed. Lloyd Mifflin.
SEGOVIA, SPAIN. Segovia and Madrid. R. T. Cooke.
SELKIRK, ALEXANDER. Verses Supposed to be Written by Alexander Selkirk. Cowper.
SELKIRK MOUNTAINS, BRITISH COLUMBIA. In the Selkirks. D. C. Scott.
SEMMERWATER (lake), ENGLAND. Ballad of Semmerwater, The. Sir William Watson.
SENANCOUR, ETIENNE PIVERT DE. Stanzas in Memory of the Author of "Obermann." Matthew Arnold.
SENECA
Picture of Seneca Dying in a Bath. Prior.
Seneca's Epitaph. Hildebert of Lavardin, *tr. fr. Latin by* Lind.
SENECA LAKE, NEW YORK. To Seneca Lake. Percival.
SENNACHERIB, KING OF ASSYRIA. Destruction of Sennacherib, The. Byron.
SEPARATION
After Being Separated for a Long Time. Li Po, *tr. fr. Chinese by* Ayscough *and* Lowell.
After the Supper and Talk. Whitman.
Autumn Wind, The. Wu-ti, *tr. fr. Chinese by* Waley.
Ballad of the Western Island in the North Country. *Unknown, tr. fr. Chinese by* Waley.
By Return Mail. Aldridge.
Eastern Gate, The. *Unknown, tr. fr. Chinese by* Waley.
Farewell, A. Fairburn.
Forsaken. Schneour, *tr. fr. Yiddish by* Leftwich.
In Exile. Baughan.
Journey Onwards. Thomas Moore.
Meeting, The. Rukeyser.
On Parting with Moses ibn Ezra. Halevi, *tr. fr. Hebrew by* Solis-Cohen.
Parting. "Æ."
Parting, The. *Fr.* Cressida. Baxter.
Parting, The. Drayton.
Parting. Halevi, *tr. fr. Hebrew by* Salaman.
Parting. Massey.
Parting, The. John Norris.
Parting. A. F. Palmer.
Parting. Roscoe.
Parting after a Quarrel. Tietjens.
Parting Gift. Elinor Wylie.
People Hide Their Love. Wu-ti, *tr. fr. Chinese by* Waley.
Separation. Po Chü-i, *tr. fr. Chinese by* Waley.
Strange. Burnshaw.
Sundered. Zangwill.
To His Wife. *At. to* General Su Wu, *tr. fr. Chinese by* Waley.
To Li Chien. Po Chü-i, *tr. fr. Chinese by* Waley.
V-Letter. Shapiro.
SEPTEMBER
In a September Night. F. W. Home.
In September. Eleanor Hammond.
In September. Ledwidge.
Man's Bread, A. Peabody.
Remember September. Justus.
Rondel for September. K. W. Baker.
September. George Arnold.
September. Birchall.
September. Fallis.
September. Mary Howitt.
September. H. H. Jackson.
September. Lampman.
September. E. B. Reed.
September Afternoon. M. H. Carpenter.
September Day. Teasdale.
September Days. H. L. Smith.
September, 1819. Wordsworth.
September Fires. Sir Herbert Read.
September in Australia. H. C. Kendall.
September Morning. Mörike, *tr. fr. German by* Tobin.
To the Month of September. *Fr.* Hymns of Astraea. Sir John Davies.
SEQUOIA TREES
Thumbprint. C. T. Wright.
To a Giant Sequoia, Fallen and Enshrined in Calaveras County, California. Pearce Young.
Washington Sequoia, The, *sel.* Shinn.
SERFS. *See* SLAVERY.
SETTLE, ELKANAH. Og and Doeg. *Fr.* Absalom and Achitophel. Dryden.
SEURAT, GEORGES. Seurat. Schevill.
SEVASTOPOL, USSR. Sebastopol. *Unknown.*
SEVERN (river), ENGLAND
Playmates, The. Sir William Watson.
Severn, The. *Fr.* The Baron's War. Drayton.
SEVIER, JOHN. John Sevier. *Fr.* The Tall Men. Donald Davidson.
SÉVIGNÉ, MARIE DE RABUTIN-CHANTAL, MARQUISE DE. To Madame de Sévigné. Montreuil.
SEVILLE, SPAIN. Seville. L. D'O. Walters.
SEWALL, SAMUEL. Samuel Sewall. Hecht.
SEWARD, WILLIAM HENRY. To William H. Seward. Whittier.
SEWING
Instruction. Hazel Hall.
My Needle Says. Hazel Hall.
Needle, The. Samuel Woodworth.
Needle Travel. M. F. Patton.
Pocket Handkerchief to Hem, A. *Fr.* Sing-Song. C. G. Rossetti.
Three Seamstresses, The. Peretz, *tr. fr. Yiddish by* Leftwich.
SEYMOUR, EDWARD, DUKE OF SOMERSET. On Edward Seymour, Duke of Somerset. *Unknown.*
SEYMOUR, JANE. Death of Queen Jane, The. *Unknown.*
SHADOWS
Could It Have Been a Shadow? Shannon.
I Heard a Noise and Wished for a Sight. *Unknown.*
Lecture upon the Shadow, A. Donne.
My Shadow. R. L. Stevenson.
My Swinging Shadow. Coplen.
Shadow. Richard Bruce.
Shadow. William Griffith.
Shadow. Louise Owen.
Shadow, The. R. H. Stoddard.
Shadow Dance. Eastwick.
Shadow to Shadow. Hervey Allen.
Shadows, The. M. L. Duncan.
Shadows. W. S. Kennedy.
Shadows Are Black. A. M. Sullivan.
Shadows in the Water. Traherne.
SHADWELL, THOMAS
MacFlecknoe; or, A Satire upon the True-Blue Protestant Poet, T. S. Dryden.
Og and Doeg. *Fr.* Absalom and Achitophel. Dryden.
SHAFTESBURY, ANTHONY ASHLEY COOPER, 1ST EARL OF
Achitophel. *Fr* Absalom and Achitophel. Dryden.
Ballad upon the Popish Plot, A. Gadbury.
Dutchess of Monmouth's Lamentation for the Loss of Her Duke, The. *Unknown.*
SHAKERS (religious group). Meditation by Mascoma Lake. Babcock.
SHAKESPEARE, WILLIAM
Ad Gulielmum Shakespeare. John Weever.
Armenia's Love to Shakespeare. Boyajian.
At Shakespeare's Grave. Irving Browne.
At Stratford-on-Avon. Mackenzie Bell.
Ben Jonson Entertains a Man from Stratford. E. A. Robinson.
Breath of Avon, The. Watts-Dunton.
By Deputy. Adcock.
Charms of Nature, The. Joseph Warton.
Critic's Rules, The. *Fr.* Shakespeare; an Epistle to Mr. Garrick. Robert Lloyd.
Elegy on Shakespeare. Basse.

For a Shakespearean Garden. Romig.
Gossip (A.D. 1585). Meigs.
Guilielmus Rex. T. B. Aldrich.
Mary Shakespeare. Ada Jackson.
Names, The. Robert Browning.
On Shakespeare. Milton.
On Sitting Down to Read "King Lear" Once Again. Keats.
On the Portrait of Shakespeare Prefixed to the First Folio Edition, 1623. Jonson.
On the Skull of Shakespeare. George Sterling.
Progress of Poesy, The. Thomas Gray.
Prologue Spoken by Mr. Garrick at the Opening of the Theatre in Drury Lane, 1747. Samuel Johnson.
Prologue to "The Tempest." Dryden.
Remembrance of Some English Poets, A. Barnfield.
Schoolroom: 158. J. E. Warren, Jr.
Shakespeare. Matthew Arnold.
Shakespeare. Blood.
Shakespeare. A. M. Hickey.
Shakespeare. Agnes Lee.
Shakespeare. Longfellow.
Shakespeare. John Sterling.
Shakespeare. Stockard.
Shakespeare. Sir William Watson.
Shakespeare and Milton. Landor.
Shakespeare Dead. Hugh Holland.
Shakespeare, Possibly, in California. Whittemore.
Shakespeare's Grave. Jeffers.
Shakespeare's Mourners. Tabb.
Sonnet to Shakespeare. Hugh Holland.
Spirit of Shakespeare, The. George Meredith.
To Master W. Shakespeare. Thomas Freeman.
To Our English Terence, Mr. Will. Shakespeare. John Davies of Hereford.
To Shakespeare. Hartley Coleridge.
To Shakespeare. Hart Crane.
To Shakespeare. R. E. Day.
To Shakespeare. Hardy.
To the Memory of My Beloved Master William Shakespeare. Jonson.
To the Portrait of Shakespeare. Jonson.
Two Argosies. Wallace Bruce.
William Shakespeare. *Fr.* Sonnets on English Dramatic Poets. Swinburne.
William Shakespeare to Mrs. Anne, Regular Servant to the Rev. Mr. Precentor of York. Thomas Gray.

SHAMROCKS
Green Little Shamrock of Ireland, The. Andrew Cherry.
Shamrock, The. *Unknown.*

SHANNON (ship)
Chesapeake and *Shannon*. *Unknown.*
Shannon and the *Chesapeake*, The. Bouvé.

SHAPIRO, KARL. V-Letter to Karl Shapiro in Australia. Rodman.

SHARECROPPERS. Sharecropper. Atkins.

SHARKS
Maldive Shark, The. Melville.
Sharks, The. Levertov.

SHARP, WILLIAM. *See* "MACLEOD, FIONA."

SHAW, ROBERT GOULD
My Hero; to Robert Gould Shaw. Brawley.
Ode, An: On the Unveiling of the Shaw Memorial on Boston Common. T. B. Aldrich.
Ode in Time of Hestitation, An. W. V. Moody.

SHAYS'S REBELLION. Radical Song of 1786, A. Honeywood.

SHEEP
Ariel. David Campbell.
As I was going to Derby. *Unknown.*
Black Sheep. Richard Burton.
Child's Pet, A. W. H. Davies.
Derby Ram, The. *Unknown.*
Eighteen-ninety. Shipp.
Happy Sheep, The. Thorley.
Homecoming of the Sheep, The. Ledwidge.
Rocky Mountain Sheep, The. Mary Austin.
Shearing. D. M. Wright.
Sheep. W. H. Davies.
Sheep. Hoffenstein.
Sheep, The. "Seumas O'Sullivan."
Sheep, The. Hal Porter.
Sheep, The. Ann *and* Jane Taylor.
Sheep and Lambs. Tynan.
Sheep Fair, The. Hardy.
Sheep in the Shade. William Barnes.
Sheep-Washing, The. *Fr.* The Seasons. James Thomson.

SHEFFIELD, ENGLAND. Sheffield Dawn. Bridson.

SHELLEY, PERCY BYSSHE
Burdens of Unrest. T. H. Chivers.
Cor Cordium. Swinburne.
Death of Shelley, The. Donald Parson.
Man Whom Men Deplore, A. Kreymborg.
Memorabilia. Robert Browning.
Out of the Italian. Spingarn.
Pauline, *sel.* ("I ne'er had ventured e'en to hope for this Robert Browning.
Percy Bysshe Shelley. *Fr.* Five English Poets. D. Rossetti.
Red Carpet for Shelley, A. Elinor Wylie.
Rome. Hardy.
Shelley. P. H. Hayne.
Shelley. Japp.
Shelley. Van Dyke.
Shelley and Harriet Westbrook. Sir William Watson.
Shelley's Centenary. Sir William Watson.
Shelley's Skylark. Hardy.
To Shelley. Tabb.
Wiser than the Children of Light. Gibbon.

SHELLS
Chambered Nautilus, The. *Fr.* The Autocrat of the Breakfast Table. O. W. Holmes.
Enduring Music, The. Vinal.
Frutta di Mare. Geoffrey Scott.
Lonely Shell, The. M. E. Perry.
Sea Shell. E. S. Hardy.
Sea Shell, The. Amy Lowell.
Sea-Shell Murmurs. Lee-Hamilton.
Sea Shells. Scollard.
Shell, The. James Stephens.
Shell, The. Tennyson.
Shells. Raine.
Shell's Song, The. Keats.
With a Nantucket Shell. C. H. Webb.

SHENANDOAH VALLEY, VIRGINIA. Shenandoah. Sandburg.

SHEPHERDS AND SHEPHERDESSES
Blow, shepherds, blow your pipes with gladsome glee resounding. *Unknown.*
Chloris, *sel.* ("Colin, my dear and most entire beloved"). William Smith.
Colin Clout's Come Home Again, *sels.* Spenser.
Damon and Cupid. Gay
Eclogues, *sels.* Virgil, *tr. fr. Latin.*
Egloga Secunda: "My beasts, go feed upon the plain." Googe.
Eighth Eclogue, The. *Fr.* The Shepherd's Garland. Drayton.
Endymion and Phoebe, *sel.* ("In Ionia whence sprang old poets' fame"). Drayton.
Fourth Egloge of Alexander Barclay, The. Barclay.
Friday; or, The Dirge. *Fr.* The Shepherd's Week. Gay.
Gentle Shepherd, The, *sels.* Allan Ramsay.
Herd Boy, The. Haniel Long.
Herd Laddie, The. Smart.
Herdsman, The. "Seumas O'Sullivan."
Herdsman, The. *Fr.* The Idylls. Theocritus, *tr. fr. Greek.*
I Would Love to Be a Shepherd. Krystallis, *tr. fr. Modern Greek by* Dalven.
Lame Shepherd, The. K. L. Bates.
Little Shepherd's Song, The. W. A. Percy.
Long, Long Ago. *Unknown.*
Michael. Wordsworth.
Nod. De la Mare.
Nymph's Reply to the Shepherd, The. Ralegh.
Old Shepherd, The. Papondoniou, *tr. fr. Modern Greek by* Dalven.
Passionate Shepherd to His Love, The. Marlowe.
Pastoral. *Fr.* The Passionate Shepherd. Breton.
Phillida's Love-Call to Her Corydon, and His Replying. *Unknown.*
Saturday; or, The Flights. *Fr.* The Shepherd's Week. Gay.
Second Shepherds' Play, The. *Unknown.*
Sheepheards Daffadill, The. Drayton.
Sheep-Herder, The. C. B. Clark, Jr.
Sheepherder, The. Sarett.
Sheep Herders. Lesemann.
Shepheardes Calender, The, *sels.* Spenser.
Shepherd, The. *Fr.* Songs of Innocence. Blake.
Shepherd. Blunden.
Shepherd and His Dog. W. L. Bowles.
Shepherd and the Hawk, The. Hart-Smith.
Shepherd Boy, The. E. J. O'Brien.
Shepherd Boy, The. Pickthall.
Shepherd Boys, The. Saboly, *tr. fr. Provençal.*
Shepherd Boy's Day, The. George, *tr. fr. German by* Luke.
Shepherd of Meriador, The. W. R. Childe.
Shepherd Speaks, The. John Erskine.
Shepherdess, The. Alice Meynell.
Shepherds, The. Drummond of Hawthornden.
Shepherds, The. L. S. Portor.
Shepherds, The. Vaughan.
Shepherd's Conceit of Prometheus, The. Sir Edward Dyer.
Shepherd's Dream, A. Breton.
Shepherd's Gift, A. Anyte, *tr. fr. Greek by* Burgon.
Shepherd's Holiday. Elinor Wylie.
Shepherd's Hut, The. Andrew Young.
Shepherd's Lament, The. Goethe, *tr. fr. German by* Taylor.
Shepherd's Song, The. Baillie.

).
G.
SHEPHERDESSES (*continued*)
ree, The. Clare.
Wife's Song, The. *Fr.* Greene's Mourning Gar-
reene.
Mountain. Eifion Wyn, *tr. fr. Welsh by* Wil-
ne day the god of fond desire." James Thomson.
Thus, thus begin the yearly rites." *Fr.* Pan's Anni-
ry. Jonson.
estern Night. Chavez.
Terlow. *Unknown.*
edown. Reese.
rsday; or, The Spell. *Fr.* The Shepherd's Week. Gay.
nown Shepherd's Complaint, The. Barnfield.
ealthy Shepherd, The. L. M. Bowman.
hat Pleasure Have Great Princes. *Unknown.*
ERIDAN, PHILIP HENRY
Sheridan at Cedar Creek. Melville.
Sheridan's Ride. T. B. Read.
HERIDAN, THOMAS. Mary the Cook-Maid's Letter to Dr. Sheridan. Swift.
SHERMAN, WILLIAM TECUMSEH
Marching through Georgia. H. C. Work.
Sherman. R. W. Gilder.
Sherman's in Savannah. O. W. Holmes.
Sherman's March to the Sea. Byers.
Song of Sherman's Army, The. Halpine.
SHILOH, BATTLE OF. Shiloh. Melville.
SHIPS
Aboard at a Ship's Helm. Whitman.
After the Sea-Ship. Whitman.
Boating Song. *At. to* St. Columcille, *tr. fr. Latin by* Lindsay.
Building of the Ship, The. Longfellow.
By the Deep Nine. Pearce.
Cargoes. Masefield.
Clinker, The. *Unknown.*
Clipper-Ships. J. G. Fletcher.
Clipper Ships, The. Masters.
Common Conditions, *sel.* ("Lustily, lustily, lustily let us sail forth"). *Unknown.*
Dismantled Ship, The. Whitman.
Famous Fight at Malago, The; or, The Englishmen's Victory over the Spaniards. *Unknown.*
Forging of the Anchor, The. Ferguson.
Freighter. Ruddick
George Aloe and the *Sweepstake*, The. *Unknown.*
Going Down in Ships. Kemp.
Golden Vanity, The. *Unknown.*
High Barbaree. *Unknown.*
I Watch the Ships. A. W. H. Eaton.
Joyfull New Ballad, A. Deloney.
Kilmeny. Noyes.
Leave-taking, A. Broome.
Lover Compareth His State to a Ship in Perilous Storm Tossed on the Sea, The. Wyatt.
Merchantmen, The. John Davidson.
My Brigantine. *Fr.* The Water Witch. J. F. Cooper.
My Ship. E. A. Allen.
My Ship. Leamy.
Nocturne of the Wharves. Bontemps.
O Gentle Ships. Meleager, *tr. fr. Greek by* Lang.
O Ship, Ship, Ship. *Fr.* Songs in Absence. Clough.
Old Ships, The. Flecker.
Old Ships. Louis Ginsberg.
Old Ships. David Morton.
Passer-by, A. Robert Bridges.
"S.S.R., Lost at Sea."—The Times. Gustafson.
Sails. Ibn Billita, *tr. fr. Arabic by* Arberry.
Schooner, The. T. E. Brown.
Schooners. Ibn Lubbal, *tr. fr. Arabic by* Arberry.
Ship, The. Richard Church.
Ship, The. Charles Mackay.
Ship, The. Lloyd Mifflin.
Ship, The. Squire.
Ship and Her Makers, The. Masefield.
Ship and the Sea, The. Baughan.
Ship Bottom. Lattimore.
Ship Comes In, A. Oliver Jenkens.
Ship-Love. Mannin.
Ship near Shoals. Wickham.
Ship of Rio, The. De la Mare.
Ship Sails Up to Bideford, A. Herbert Asquith.
Ship Starting, The. Whitman.
Ship That Never Returned, The. *Unknown.*
Ship That Sails, The. *Unknown.*
Ships. Barrington.
Ships, The. J. J. Bell.
Ships. Masefield.
Ships. N. B. Turner.
Ships at Sea. Barry Gray.
Ships in Harbour. David Morton.
Ships of Yule, The. Carman.
Silver Ships. Meigs.
Sir Andrew Barton. *Unknown.*
Song for All Seas, All Ships. Whitman.
Song of Myself, *sel.* ("Would you hear of an old-time sea-fight?"). Whitman.
South Street. Falkenbury.
Stone Fleet, The. Melville.
Tacking Ship off Shore. Walter Mitchell.
There's Nothing like a Ship at Sea. Kemp.
Viking Ship, The. N. J. O'Conor.
Walloping Window-Blind, The. C. E. Carryl.
Where Lies the Land? Clough.
Where Lies the Land to Which Yon Ship Must Go? Wordsworth.
With Ships the Sea Was Sprinkled Far and Nigh. Wordsworth.
Wooden Ships. David Morton.
Eternal Sea, The; an Anthology of Sea Poetry (EtS). W. M. Williamson, ed.
See also BOATS; YACHTS.
SHIPWRECKS
Alec Yeaton's Son. T. B. Aldrich.
Berg, The. Melville.
Brave Old Ship, the *Orient*, The. R. T. S. Lowell.
Convergence of the Twain, The. Hardy.
Dream of Wrecks, A. *Fr.* Richard III. Shakespeare.
End, The. Corbière, *tr. fr. French by* Flores.
Fisherman Husband. Brenda Chamberlain.
Full Fathom Five. *Fr.* The Tempest. Shakespeare.
In Memory of the Circus Ship *Euzkera*, Wrecked in the Caribbean Sea, 1 September 1948. Walker Gibson.
In Wintry Midnight, o'er a Stormy Main. Petrarch, *tr. fr. Italian by* Barnes.
Inchcape Rock, The. Southey.
Inscription by the Sea, An. *Unknown, tr. fr. Greek by* Robinson.
Loss of the *Birkenhead*, The. Sir F. H. Doyle.
Loss of the *Cedar Grove*, The. *Unknown.*
Lost Steamship, The. Fitz-James O'Brien.
Mary Ross, The. Baughan.
Odyssey, The, *sel.* ("This spoke, a huge wave took him by the head"). Homer, *tr. by* Chapman.
Roosevelt and the *Antinoe*, The. E. J. Pratt.
Sea Story, A. E. H. Hickey.
Shipwreck, The. *Fr.* Don Juan. Byron.
Shipwreck, The, *sels.* Falconer.
Shipwreck. Rydberg, *tr. fr. Swedish by* Stork.
Silent Tower of Bottreaux, The. R. S. Hawker.
Sir Patrick Spens. *Unknown.*
Skipper Ireson's Ride. Whittier.
Still by the Cloud Stricken. Mallarmé, *tr. fr. French by* Flores.
Three Bells, The. Whittier.
Titanic, The. *Unknown.*
Trouble at Sea. Thomas Prys, *tr. fr. Welsh by* Williams.
White Ship, The. D. G. Rossetti.
Wreck, The. Ruskin.
Wreck of Rivermouth, The. Whittier.
Wreck of the *Deutschland*, The. G. M. Hopkins.
Wreck of the *Hesperus*, The. Longfellow.
Wreck of the *Julie Plante*, The. W. H. Drummond.
Yarn of the *Loch Achray*, The. Masefield.
SHOEMAKERS. *See* COBBLERS.
SHOES
Footwear. Justus.
I Have Lost My Shoes. Suasnavar, *tr. fr. Spanish by* Lee.
It's fun to go out and buy new shoes to wear. Hoberman.
Sale. Josephine Miles.
SHOOTING GALLERY. Travelogue in a Shooting-Gallery. Fearing.
SHOPPING. Shopper, The. Martial, *tr. fr. Latin by* Nixon.
SHORE, JANE. How Shore's Wife, Edward the Fourth's Concubine, Was by King Richard Despoiled of All Her Goods . . . *Fr.* A Mirror for Magistrates. Churchyard.
SHOSTAKOVICH, DMITRI. Take a Letter to Dmitri Shostakovitch. Sandburg.
SHREWS
Masked Shrew, The. Isabella Gardner.
Shrew, The. Ogden Nash.
SIBELIUS, JEAN JULIUS CHRISTIAN
Baldness and the Swan. W. T. Scott.
Program Note on Sibelius. Babcock.
SIBERIA
Message to Siberia. Pushkin, *tr. fr. Russian by* Eastman.
Siberia. Mangan.
Song of the Siberian Exiles, The. Nekrasov, *tr. fr. Russian by* Bianchi.
SIBYL. Sibyl, The. LaBombard.
SICILY
Bare Almond Trees. D. H. Lawrence.
Siciliana; the Landings at Gela. Koehler.
SICKNESS. *See* ILLNESS.
SIDNEY, SIR PHILIP

Colin Clout's Come Home Again, *sel.* ("The Shepheards boy best knowen by that name"). Spenser.
Epitaph on Sir Philip Sidney. Lord Herbert of Cherbury.
Epitaph on Sir Philip Sidney. *At. to* Sir Walter Ralegh.
Epitaph upon the Death of Sir Philip Sidney, Knight, Lord-Governor of Vlissing, An. Barnfield.
Epitaph upon the Right Honorable Sir Philip Sidney, An. Greville.
Funerall Song, A: "Come to me, grief for ever." *Unknown.*
Of Sir Philip Sidney. Beaumont.
On Sir Philip Sidney. *Fr.* An Elegy, or Friend's Passion for His Astrophil. Royden.
On the Death of Sir Philip Sidney. Constable.
Sir Philip Sidney. Eleanor Farjeon *and* Herbert Farjeon.
To Sir Philip Sidney's Soul. Constable.
SIEGFRIED. Battle-Flag of Sigurd, The. Dora Greenwell.
SIENA, ITALY. Siena. Swinburne.
SIERRA NEVADA
Ascent to the Sierras. Jeffers.
Dead in the Sierras. Joaquin Miller.
SIGNORELLI, LUCA. Episode, An. Symonds.
SILENCE
Faint Music. De la Mare.
Hound at Night. L. A. Garnet.
Lonely. Reese.
Of Silence and the Air. Pitter.
Silence. M. C. Barnett.
Silence. Hood.
Silence, The. MacLeish.
Silence. Masters.
Silence. Marianne Moore.
Silence. J. H. Morse.
Silence. J. L. Spalding.
Silence. Winifred Welles.
Silence, The. Anna Wickham.
Silence. Humbert Wolfe.
Silence Sings. T. S. Moore.
Sonnet: Silence. Poe.
Sweet Silence after Bells. Christopher Brennan.
There Must Be Silence. Tansey.
This Is the Shape of the Leaf. Aiken.
Valley of Silence, The. "Fiona Macleod."
SILKWORMS. Silkworms. Mary Elliott.
SIMEON (Bible). Song for Simeon, A. T. S. Eliot.
SIMHATH TORAH
Simchas Torah. Rosenfeld, *tr. fr. Yiddish.*
Simhat Torah. J. L. Gordon, *tr. fr. Hebrew by* Lucas *and* Frank.
This Feast of the Law. *Unknown, tr. fr. Hebrew by* Zangwill.
SIMILES. New Song of New Similes, A. Gay.
SIMON, SAINT. Men Follow Simon. Kresensky.
SIMON, SAINT, AND SAINT JUDE. St. Simon and St. Jude's Day. C. F. Alexander.
SIMON OF CYRENE
Simon of Cyrene. Harkness.
Simon the Cyrenian Speaks. Glen Baker.
Simon the Cyrenian Speaks. Cullen.
SIMONY. Certain Examples of the Power Which Sir Money Possesses. *Fr.* The Book of Good Love. Juan Ruiz, Archpriest of Hita, *tr. fr. Spanish by* Kane.
SIMPLICITY. Ode to Simplicity. William Collins.
SIN
Sin's Round. George Herbert.
Vision of Sin, The. Tennyson.
SINGING AND SINGERS
Celia Singing. Carew.
Everyone Sang. Sassoon.
I Hear America Singing. Whitman.
M., Singing. Bogan.
O Black and Unknown Bards. J. W. Johnson.
Of Ballad-Singers. *Fr.* Trivia. Gay.
Of Corinna's Singing. Campion.
Schmaltztenor. M. W. Branch.
Singer, The. Molodowsky, *tr. fr. Yiddish by* Betsky.
Singer, The. E. C. Stedman.
Singer Asleep, A. Hardy.
Singer Saith of His Song, The. Francis Thompson.
Singer's Quest, The. Odell Shepard.
Singing-Time. Fyleman.
Solitary Reaper, The. Wordsworth.
Song about Singing, A. A. R. Aldrich.
To a Lady Playing and Singing in the Morning. Hardy.
To a Lady Who Did Sing Excellently. Lord Herbert of Cherbury.
To Constantia Singing. Shelley.
Why Should I Wander Sadly. Süsskind von Trimberg, *tr. fr. Middle High German.*
Untune the Sky (UnS). Helen Plotz, comp.
SIOUX INDIANS. Remember the Promise, Dakotah. R. V. Carr.
SITWELL, EDITH. Thin Façade for Edith Sitwell, A. Brinnin.
SIVA. Siva Destroyer. George Perry.
SKATING AND SKATES
Elfin Skates. Lee-Hamilton.
Roller Skates. John Farrar.
Skaters, The. John Williams.
Skating. Asquith.
Skating. *Fr.* The Prelude. Wordsworth.
Skating Song. Christopher Morley.
To Kate, Skating Better than Her Date. Daiches.
SKELTON, JOHN. Praise to John Skelton. Horace Gregory.
SKIING
Canadian Ski Song. Bourinot.
Mountain Speed. G. W. Young.
Ski Train. Patrick Anderson.
Skiers, The. Frisch.
Song of the Ski, The. Wilson MacDonald.
SKUNKS
Skunk, The. Coffin.
Wood-Weasel, The. Marianne Moore.
SKY
Azure, The. Mallarmé, *tr. fr. French by* Flores.
Earth and Sky. Toumanian, *tr. fr. Armenian by* Boyajian.
God Said: Let There Be Sky. J. J. Donohue.
Heaven Tree. H. M. Robinson.
Night Sky, The. C. G. D. Roberts.
Now the Sky. Van Doren.
Sky. Betty Shippe.
Sky, The. R. H. Stoddard.
Sky Is Up above the Roof, The. Verlaine, *tr. fr. French by* Dowson.
Spacious Firmament on High, The. Addison.
Testament of Beauty, The. *sel.* ("The sky's unresting cloudland, that with varying play"). Robert Bridges.
Winter Heavens. George Meredith.
SKYE (island), SCOTLAND. Skye. Alexander Nicolson.
SKYLARKS. *See* LARKS.
SKYSCRAPERS
Crucifixion of the Skyscraper. J. G. Fletcher.
Elegy on an Empty Skyscraper. J. G. Fletcher.
Skyscraper. Sandburg.
Skyscraper Is a City's House. Clara Lambert.
Skyscrapers. Rachel Field.
Towers at Evening, The. *Fr.* Melbourne and Memory. Wilmot.
SLANDER
To Detraction I Present My Poesy. *Fr.* The Scourge of Villainy. Marston.
To the Detracted. John Andrewes.
SLAVERY
African Chief, The. Bryant.
Blue-Tail Fly, The. *Unknown.*
Boston Hymn. Emerson.
Christian Slave, The. Whittier.
Clerical Oppressors. Whittier.
Curse for a Nation, A. E. B. Browning.
Death of Slavery, The. Bryant.
Enslaved, *sel.* ("The Khalif's fury raged"). Masefield.
Farewell, The. Whittier.
For Righteousness' Sake. Whittier.
Massachusetts to Virginia. Whittier.
On Liberty and Slavery. G. M. Horton.
Present Crisis, The. J. R. Lowell.
Runaway Slave at Pilgrim's Point, The. E. B. Browning.
Serf, The. Roy Campbell.
Slave, The. R. H. Horne.
Slave, The. Oppenheim.
Slave Auction, The. F. E. W. Harper.
Slave Chase, The. *Unknown.*
Slave Ship, The. Heine, *tr. fr. German by* Feise.
Slave-Ships, The. Whittier.
Slaver, The. *Fr.* John Brown's Body. S. V. Benét.
Slavery. Shelley.
Slaves. G. S. Viereck.
Slave's Complaint, The. G. M. Horton.
Slave's Dream, The. Longfellow.
Song of Myself, *sel.* ("The runaway slave came to my house and stopt outside"). Whitman.
Song of Slaves in the Desert. Whittier.
Stanzas on Freedom. J. R. Lowell.
Sympathy. P. L. Dunbar.
Witnesses, The. Longfellow.
Wounded Person, The. *Fr.* Song of Myself. Whitman.
SLEDS. Sledding Song, A. Schlichter.
SLEEP
And on My Eyes Dark Sleep by Night. "Michael Field."
Before Sleep. Prudentius, *tr. fr. Latin by* Waddell.
Before Sleeping. *Unknown.*
Care-charmer Sleep [Son of the Sable Night]. *Fr.* To Delia. Daniel.
Care-charming Sleep. *Fr.* The Tragedy of Valentinian. Fletcher.
Come, Blessèd Sleep. C. G. Rossetti.
Come, Gentle Sleep, Death's Image tho' thou Art. Michelangelo, *tr. fr. Italian by* Wordsworth.
Come, Heavy Sleep. *Unknown.*

SLEEP (*continued*)
Come, Sleep. *Fr.* The Woman-Hater. Francis Beaumont.
Come, Sleep! O Sleep, the Certain Knot of Peace. *Fr.* Astrophel and Stella. Sidney.
Come to Me, Gentle Sleep! Hemans.
Cradle Song, A: "Sleep, Sleep, beauty bright." Blake.
Cypress Curtain of the Night, The. Campion.
Deep Sleep. "Gabriela Mistral," *tr. fr. Spanish by* "K. G. C."
Disillusionment of Ten o'Clock. Wallace Stevens.
Down to Sleep. H. H. Jackson.
Dreamland, *sel.* ("We are not wholly blest who use the earth"). Mair.
Evening Watch, The; a Dialogue. Vaughan.
Falling Asleep. Sassoon.
For Sleep, or Death. Pitter.
For Sleep When Overtired. Cleghorn.
Golden Slumbers [Kiss Your Eyes]. *Fr.* The Pleasant Comedy of Patient Grisell. Dekker, *and others.*
Good Night. Hood.
Good-Night, A. Quarles.
Grania. *Unknown, tr. fr. Irish by* O'Connor.
Great Dark Sleep, A. Verlaine, *tr. fr. French by* Flores.
Hymns to the Night. "Novalis," *tr. fr. German by* Cotterell.
In Sleep. Richard Burton.
Insomnia. Corbière, *tr. fr. French by* Koch *and* Guy.
Insomnia. Tabb.
Kazoo. Corbière, *tr. fr. French by* Flores.
Land of Nod, The. R. L. Stevenson.
Lights Out. Edward Thomas.
Lines for a Drawing of Our Lady of the Night. Francis Thompson.
Lonely Are the Fields of Sleep. M. N. Baldwin.
Lotos-Eaters, The. Tennyson.
Lullaby: "Sleep, mouseling, sleep." Coatsworth.
Nocturne: "Sleep that like the couched dove." Gerald Griffin.
Now through Night's Caressing Grip. Auden.
O Sleep. G. F. Norton.
Oh, Sleep, Fond Fancy. *Unknown.*
Ode to Sleep. P. H. Hayne.
Ode to Sleep. Fernando de Herrera, *tr. fr. Spanish by* Turnbull.
Ode to Sleep. Smollett.
Old Lizette on Sleep. Agnes Lee.
On a Quiet Conscience. Charles I, King of England.
Pool of Sleep, The. Arlo Bates.
Silvae, *sel.* ("What was my crime, youthful most gentle god"). Statius, *tr. fr. Latin by* Cunningham.
Sleep. Alcázar, *tr. fr. Spanish by* Bowring.
Sleep. T. B. Aldrich.
Sleep. Alice Brown.
Sleep, The. E. B. Browning.
Sleep. Jewett.
Sleep. "Fiona Macleod."
Sleep. McAuley.
Sleep. A. L. Martin.
Sleep, *sel.* ("Yet, in the end"). Christopher Morley.
Sleep. "Peter Pindar."
Sleep. Tabb.
Sleep. Tooker.
Sleep. Viau, *tr. fr. French by* Gosse.
Sleep and His Brother Death. W. H. Hayne.
Sleep and Poetry, *sel.* ("What is more gentle than a wind in summer?"). Keats.
Sleep, Baby, Sleep. Corbière, *tr. fr. French by* Flores.
Sleep Is a Reconciling. *Unknown.*
Sleep, My Child. Sholom Aleichem, *tr. fr. Yiddish by* Brody.
Sleep Sweet. E. M. Gates.
Sleep the Mother. Kiper.
Sleep, This Is the Time for Sleep. *Unknown, ad. fr. German by* Untermeyer.
Sleep Will Come Singly. W. H. Oliver.
Sleeper, The. Clouts.
Sleeper, The. De la Mare.
Sleeper, The. "Isobel Hume."
Sleeper, The. Scollard.
Sleeper of the Valley, The. Rimbaud, *tr. fr. French by* Lewisohn.
Sleepers. J. C. Miller.
Sleeping on Her Couch. Leigh.
Sleeping on Horseback. Po Chü-i, *tr. fr. Chinese by* Waley.
Slumber Song: "Sleep; and my song shall build about your bed." Sassoon.
Soliloquy on Sleep. *Fr.* King Henry IV, Pt. II. Shakespeare.
Somnus, the Humble God. Denham.
Song: "Sleep, O Sleep." Gay.
Song: "While Morpheus thus doth gently lay." Killigrew.
Sonnet: "Sleep, Silence' Child, sweet father of soft rest." Drummond of Hawthornden.
Sound Sleep. C. G. Rossetti.
Spell of Sleep. Raine.
Sweet and Low. *Fr.* The Princess. Tennyson.
To Sleep. Giovanni della Casa, *tr. fr. Italian by* Symonds.
To Sleep. Maybury Fleming.
To Sleep, *sel.* ("But thou, O Sleep, bend down and give"). Norman Gale.
To Sleep. Keats.
To Sleep. Landor.
To Sleep. Percy MacKaye.
To Sleep. F. S. Osgood.
To Sleep. Wordsworth.
Weep You No More, Sad Fountains. *Unknown.*
When the Proficient Poison of Sure Sleep. E. E. Cummings.
With the Dawn. T. C. Irwin.
SLEET. Sleet Storm. Tippett.
SLEIGHS
Sleigh Bells at Night. Coatsworth.
Sleighride. Patrick Anderson.
SLOTHS. Sloth, The. Roethke.
SLUGS. Slug in Woods. Birney.
SLUMS
Cherry Way. R. C. Mitchell.
Elementary School Class Room in a Slum, An. Spender.
Slums. Oppenheim.
SMART, CHRISTOPHER. Parleyings with Certain People of Importance. Robert Browning.
SMILES. Simile for Her Smile, A. Wilbur.
SMITH, HORACE. Letter to Maria Gisborne. Shelley.
SMITH, JOHN
John Smith's Approach to Jamestown. J. B. Hope.
Last Meeting of Pocahontas and the Great Captain, The. M. J. Preston.
SMITH, SIR SIDNEY. Sir Sidney Smith. Dibdin.
SMOKE
Smoke. Thoreau.
Smoke, *sels.* B. F. Trotter.
Smoke in Winter. Thoreau.
Trails of Smoke. Rowena Bennett.
SMUGGLERS. Smuggler, The. *Unknown.*
SMUTS, JAN CHRISTIAAN. Jan. G. D. Martineau.
SNAILS
Butterfly and the Snail, The. Gay.
Housekeeper, The. Bourne, *tr. fr. Latin by* Lamb.
Little Snail. Hilda Conkling.
Lucky Snail, The. Winifred Welles.
Poor Snail, The. Westrup.
Snail, The. Bourne, *tr. fr. Latin by* Cowper.
Snail, The. G. H. Conkling.
Snail, The. Cowper.
Snail. Langston Hughes.
Snail, The. Charles Lamb.
Snail. G. L. McCoy.
Snail, The ("Little snail"). *Unknown, tr. fr. Chinese by* Headland.
Snail, The ("The snail he lives"). *Unknown.*
Snail's Dream, The. Herford.
Snayl, The. Lovelace.
To a Snail. Marianne Moore.
To a Snail in the Cemetery. S. H. Hay.
Upon the Snail. Bunyan.
SNAKES
Colubriad, The. Cowper.
Crotalus. Bret Harte.
Crotalus, The. Bailey Millard.
Five Serpents. Charles Burgess.
In a Garden. D. C. Babcock.
In winter, in my room. Emily Dickinson.
Massasauga, The. Hamlin Garland.
Narrow fellow in the grass, A. Dickinson.
Rattlesnake, The. R. V. Carr.
Serpent's Nature, The. *Fr.* The Bestiary. *Unknown.*
Silent Snake, The. *Unknown.*
Snake. D. H. Lawrence.
Snake. J. R. McCarthy.
Snake, The. Mackenzie.
Snake, The. Thomas Moore.
Snake Charmer, The. M. E. Sheppard.
Snake Story. Henry Johnstone.
Spring Serpent, A. Winters.
To a King Snake. Doughty.
Viper, The. Pitter.
SNAPDRAGONS. Snapdragon. Cardinal Newman.
SNOW
After Snow. A. B. Payne.
Beautiful Snow, *parody. Unknown.*
Beautiful Snow, The. J. W. Watson.
Before the Snow. Lang.
Cynthia in the Snow. Gwendolyn Brooks.
Deep Snow. L. M. Bowman.
Devonshire Rhyme, A. *Unknown.*
Dust of Snow. Robert Frost.
Easter Snowfall. Behn.

Falling of the Snow, The. Souster.
Falling Snow. Amy Lowell.
Falling Snow. *Unknown.*
Fire in the Snow, The. Vernon Watkins.
First Snow. M L. Allen.
First Snow. Eastwick.
First Snow. C. E. S. Wood.
First Snowfall. Carducci, *tr. fr. Italian by* Hughes.
First Snowfall, The. J. R. Lowell.
Flowers of Snow. Tsurayuki, *tr. fr. Japanese by* Chamberlain.
For Snow. Farjeon.
Girl in the Snow, A. Conquest.
Hillside Thaw, A. Robert Frost.
In the Ravine. W. W. E. Ross.
It sifts from leaden sieves. Emily Dickinson.
January. Coatsworth.
Late Snow. J. C. Squire.
Little Ships in the Air. E. A. Rand.
London Snow. Robert Bridges.
New Snow. Rowles.
On a Gentlewoman Walking in the Snow. Strode.
Presence of Snow. Melville Cane.
Pup in the Snowstorm. Frances Frost.
Riddle: "White bird floats down through the air, A." *Unknown.*
Slushy snow splashes and sploshes, The. Hoberman.
Snow. Aldis.
Snow. E. A. Allen.
Snow. Cawein.
Snow. Coatsworth.
Snow, The. Dyment.
Snow, The. F. A. Elliott.
Snow. Robert Frost.
Snow, The. W. W. Gibson.
Snow. Guillén, *tr. fr. Spanish by* Turnbull.
Snow. Lampman.
Snow, The. N. B. Miller.
Snow. Miyoshi, *tr. fr. Japanese by* Ninomiya *and* Enright.
Snow. Alfred Noyes.
Snow. W. R. Rodgers.
Snow. Jane Taylor.
Snow. Edward Thomas.
Snow. *Unknown.*
Snow, The. Verhaeren, *tr. fr French by* Strettell.
Snow. Alice Wilkins.
Snow. Humbert Wolfe.
Snow—a Winter Sketch. Ralph Hoyt.
Snow Anthology. Bourinot.
Snow Fell with a Will. Richard Gillman.
Snow-Gardens, The. Zoë Akins.
Snow in October. A. D. Nelson.
Snow in the City. Rachel Field.
Snow in the Suburbs. Hardy.
Snow in Town. Rickman Mark.
Snow Lies Light, The. W. W. Christman.
Snowlight. N. B. Turner.
Snow Man, The. Wallace Stevens.
Snowman. *Unknown.*
Snow-Messengers, The. P. H. Hayne.
Snow-Shower, The. Bryant.
Snow toward Evening. Cane.
Snow Water. F. E. Hill.
Snow-bound; a Winter Idyl. Whittier.
Snow-Drift. Saglio.
Snowfall. Carducci, *tr. fr. Italian by* Rendel.
Snowfall. Marjorie Meeker.
Snowflake, The. De la Mare.
Snow-flake Song. Hilda Conkling.
Snowflakes. R. M. Arthur.
Snowflakes. Behrend.
Snowflakes ("Little white feathers"). M. M. Dodge.
Snowflakes ("Whenever a snowflake leaves the sky"). M. M. Dodge.
Snow-Flakes. Longfellow.
Snows, The. Charles Sangster.
Snowstorm, The. Emerson.
Snow Storm. Sister Mary Madeleva.
Snowstorm, The. F. G. Scott.
Snow Storm, The. Wetherald.
Snowy Day, A. Dafydd ap Gwilym, *tr. fr. Welsh by* Bell.
Soft Snow. Blake.
Song of White Snow, A. Ts'en Ts'an, *tr. fr. Chinese by* Bynner.
Stopping by Woods on a Snowy Evening. Robert Frost.
Terrace in the Snow, The. Su T'ung-po, *tr. fr. Chinese by* Rexroth.
There Blooms No Bud in May. De la Mare.
To a Snowflake. Francis Thompson.
Under the Snow. Robert Collyer.
Velvet Shoes. Elinor Wylie.
Waiting. Behn.
Weaver of Snow, The. "Fiona Macleod."
White Fields. James Stephens.
White Snow. Apollinaire, *tr. fr. French by* Fitts.
Why Does It Snow? L. E. Richards.

SNOWBIRDS
Snow-Bird, The. Butterworth.
Snow-Bird, The. F. D. Sherman.
Snowbird, The. Tabb.
Snow-Bird's Song, The. F. C. Woodworth.
Southern Snow-Bird, The. W. H. Hayne.

SNOWDON, WALES. Conclusion: "It was a close, warm, breezeless summer night." *Fr.* The Prelude. Wordsworth.

SNOWDROPS
Snow-Drop, The. S. T. Coleridge.
Snowdrop. De Bary.
Snowdrop, A. Spofford.
Snowdrop. W. W. Story.
Snowdrop. Tennyson.
Snowdrops. Alma-Tadema.
Snowdrops. W. G. Robertson.
Snowdrops. Mary Vivian.

SNOWSHOEING. Snowshoeing Song. Arthur Weir.

SOCCER. Football Field: Evening. McKellar.

SOCIALISM.
Day Is Coming, The. William Morris.
Day of Days, The. William Morris.
Death Song, A. William Morris.
Down among the Dead Men. William Morris.
Emigrant Song. "S. Ansky," *tr. fr. Yiddish by* Leftwich.
Man with the Hoe, The. Markham.
No Master. William Morris.
Voice of Toil, The. William Morris.

SOCIETY FOR THE PREVENTION OF CRUELTY TO ANIMALS
S.P.C.A. Sermon. Hemsley.

SOCRATES
Reply of Socrates, The. E. M. Thomas.
Socrates' House. Yasimi, *tr. fr. Persian by* Arberry.
Socrates Prays a Day and a Night. George O'Neil.

SODOM
Sodom. Grade, *tr. fr. Yiddish by* Leftwich.
This Place Rumord to Have Been Sodom. Robert Duncan.

SOJOURNER TRUTH. *See* TRUTH, SOJOURNER.

SOLDIERS
Air Sentry, The. Barrington.
All the Hills and Vales Along. C. H. Sorley.
American Soldier, The. Freneau.
American Soldier's Hymn, The. *Unknown.*
America's Welcome Home. Van Dyke.
Anthem for Doomed Youth. Wilfred Owen.
Apologia pro Poemate Meo. Wilfred Owen.
Aristocrats. Keith Douglas.
Arms and the Boy. Wilfred Owen.
As Toilsome I Wander'd Virginia's Woods. Whitman.
"Atkins." George Meredith.
Ballad: "O what is that sound which so thrills the ear." Auden.
Barrack Yard, The. Nettie Palmer.
Battery Moving Up to a New Position from Rest Camp: Dawn. Robert Nichols.
Before Action. Gellert.
Before the Battle. Thomas Moore.
Biography. Nedogonov, *tr. fr. Russian by* Lindsay.
Bivouac on a Mountain Side. Whitman.
Boots. Kipling.
Bridge-Guard in the Karroo. Kipling.
By the Bivouac's Fitful Flame. Whitman.
Caisson Song, The. E. L. Gruber.
Cavalier's Song, The. Motherwell.
Cavalry Crossing a Ford. Whitman.
City Lieutenant, The. Fröding, *tr. fr. Swedish by* Stork.
Connaught Rangers, The. W. M. Letts.
Conscript, The. W W Gibson.
Cornet, The. Rilke, *tr. fr. German by* Fitz Gibbon.
Danny Deever. Kipling.
Dead Soldier. Guillén, *tr. fr. Spanish by* Hughes.
Death-Bed, A, 1918. Kipling.
Death of the Ball Turret Gunner, The. Jarrell.
Death of the Soldier, The. Wallace Stevens.
Deserter, The. A. E. Housman.
Dirge: For One Who Fell in Battle. T. W. Parsons.
Dirge for Two Veterans. Whitman.
Dreamers. Sassoon.
Drill, The. Harry Brown.
Dry Loaf. Wallace Stevens.
Duke of Plaza-Toro, The. *Fr.* The Gondoliers. W. S. Gilbert.
Dulce et Decorum Est. Wilfred Owen.
Elegy for a Dead Soldier. Shapiro.
Elegy for an Unknown Soldier. Baxter.
Epicedium. J. C. Miller.
Epitaph on an Army of Mercenaries. A. E. Housman.
Exposure. Wilfred Owen.
Fable of the War, A. Nemerov.
Fallen, The. D. C. Scott.

SOLDIERS (*continued*)
Farewell, adieu, that court-like life! *Fr.* Horestes. Pickering.
Fighting South of the Castle. *Unknown, tr fr. Chinese by* Waley.
Five Souls. W. N. Ewer.
Foot Soldiers. Tabb.
For Soldiers. Humphrey Gifford.
For the Blinded Soldiers. Dobson.
For the Fallen. Binyon.
Forced Recruit, The. E. B. Browning.
Foxhole for the Night, A. John Quinn.
General, The. Sassoon.
Greater Love. Wilfred Owen.
Grodek. Trakl, *tr. fr. German by* Flores.
Gunga Din. Kipling.
Hialmar. Roy Campbell.
Homecoming of the Sheep, The. Ledwidge.
Hospital Train. J. A. Wyeth.
How Sleep the Brave. De la Mare.
Hugh Selwyn Mauberley, *sel.* ("These fought in any case"). Pound.
I Stood with the Dead. Sassoon.
In a London Terminus. Lehmann.
In Praise of the Royal Scots Fusiliers. Buchan.
In the Trench. Gellert.
Incident of the French Camp. Robert Browning.
Insensibility. Wilfred Owen.
Into Battle. Julian Grenfell.
Jewish Conscript, The. F. K. Frank.
Jimmy's Enlisted; or, The Recruited Collier. *Unknown.*
Just behind the Battle, Mother. *Unknown.*
Kid in Upper 4, The. Metcalf.
Lancashire Lads. *Unknown.*
Lancer. A. E. Housman.
Last Thoughts of a Fighting Man. *Unknown.*
Leg, The. Shapiro.
Lessons of the War. Henry Reed.
Let the youth hardened by a sharp soldier's life. Horace, *tr. fr. Latin by* Taplin *and* Eberhart.
Little Giffen. Ticknor.
Lost in France. Ernest Rhys.
Lullaby, A: "For wars his life and half a world away." Jarrell.
Man He Killed, The. Hardy.
Marching Song, A. Kao Ang, *tr. fr. Chinese by* Hart.
Maunding Souldier, The; or, the Fruits of Warre Is Beggery. *Unknown.*
Memorial Rain. MacLeish.
Men in Green. David Campbell.
Men Who March Away. Hardy.
Monument for the Soldiers, A. J. W. Riley.
More than Flowers We Have Brought. N. B. Turner.
Negro Soldiers, The. R. C. Jamison.
1918–1941. R. D. Fitzgerald.
Noble Art of Murdering, The. Thackeray.
Ode for the American Dead in Korea. McGrath.
Ode to the Confederate Dead. Allen Tate.
Ode Written in the Beginning of the Year 1746. William Collins.
Old Sergeant, The. Forceythe Willson.
Old Soldier. Colum.
Old Soldiers. Garstin.
Old Souldier of the Queens, An. *Unknown.*
Old Timers. Sandburg.
On a Soldier Fallen in the Philippines. W. V. Moody.
On a Very Young, Very Dead Soldier. Gillman.
One of the Regiment. Le Pan.
Our Modest Doughboys. A. C. Andrews.
Out of Trenches; the Barn, Twilight. Robert Nichols.
Over the Heather the Wet Wind Blows. Auden.
Pause on the March. Orlov, *tr. fr. Russian by* Deutsch.
Peace to the Slumberers. Thomas Moore.
Picket-Guard, The. E. L. Beers.
Pipes o' Gordon's Men. J. S. Glasgow.
Praise of Our Soldiers, The. Churchyard.
Prayer: "Thy blessing on the boys—for time has come." Guri, *tr. fr. Hebrew by* Lask.
Prayer of a Soldier in France. Joyce Kilmer.
Prelude: Troops, The. Sassoon.
Private Blair of the Regulars. Scollard.
Private of the Buffs, The. Sir F. H. Doyle.
Rank and File. Dobson.
Rebel Soldier, The. *Unknown.*
Recruit, The. R. W. Chambers.
Recruiting Drive. Causley.
Returned Soldier. Moll.
Rudiments of War. *Fr.* Tamburlaine the Great. Christopher Marlowe.
Scene of War, The; the Happy Warrior. Sir Herbert Read.
Scott and the Veteran. Bayard Taylor.
Sentry, The. Alun Lewis.
Shillin' a Day. Kipling.
Soldier, The. *Fr.* 1914. Rupert Brooke.
Soldier, A. Robert Frost.
Soldier, The. Sophie Jewett.
Soldier, The. Alun Lewis.
Soldier, A. Suckling.
Soldier, The. Very.
Soldier, The ("Down some cold field"). *Fr.* Requiem. Humbert Wolfe.
Soldier, The ("I do not ask God's purpose"). *Fr.* Requiem. Humbert Wolfe.
Soldier and a Scholar, A, *sel.* ("Thus spoke to my Lady the Knight full of care"). Swift.
Soldier-Dead. Gilbert Emery
Soldier from the Wars Returning. A. E. Housman.
Soldier Going to the Field, The. Davenant.
Soldier, I Can't Figure Why. Guillén, *tr. fr. Spanish by* Hays.
Soldier, Rest! *Fr.* The Lady of the Lake. Sir Walter Scott.
Soldier: Twentieth Century. Rosenberg.
Soldier, What Did You See? Blanding.
Soldiers. Bodenheim.
Soldiers, The. Ungaretti, *tr. fr. Italian by* Cambon.
Soldiers Bathing. Prince.
Soldier's Burial, The. C. E. S. Norton.
Soldier's Dream, The. Thomas Campbell.
Soldier's Farewell to Manchester, The. *Unknown.*
Soldier's Friend, The. Canning.
Soldier's Grave, A. Albee.
Soldier's Grave, The. Muir.
Soldier's Prayer, A. Robert Freeman.
Soldier's Return, The. Bloomfield.
Soldier's Return, The. S. T. Coleridge.
Soldier's Song. David Campbell.
Soldier's Song, The. *Unknown.*
Soldier's Tale. Nedogonov, *tr. fr. Russian by* Lindsay.
Soldier's Tear, The. Alexander Lee.
Soldier's Wife, The. Southey.
Soldier's Wife to Her Husband, A. Liu Chi, *tr. fr. Chinese by* Hart.
Somebody's Darling. Lacoste.
Song for the Heroes. Comfort.
Song of the Camp, The. Bayard Taylor.
Souldiers Farewel to His Love, The. *Unknown.*
Such Is the Death the Soldier Dies. R. B. Wilson.
Spring Offensive. Wilfred Owen.
Strange Meeting. Wilfred Owen.
Sven Duva. Runeberg, *tr. fr. Swedish by* Stork.
Ten Days Leave. Snodgrass.
These Men. Gellert.
Tommies in the Train. D. H. Lawrence.
Tommy. Kipling.
Trooper Temple Pulvermacher. Branford.
Two Armies. Spender.
Ultima Ratio Regum. Spender.
Valley of the Shadow. Galsworthy.
Vergissmeinnicht. Keith Douglas.
Victory March. M. K. Joseph.
Volunteer, The. Asquith.
Volunteer Song, A. Baillie.
Volunteer's Reply to the Poet, The. *Fr.* Talking Bronco. Roy Campbell.
Warrior to His Dead Bride, The. A. A. Procter.
Warrior's Prayer, A. P. L. Dunbar.
We'll All Feel Gay. W. T. Scott.
Which Side Am I Supposed to Be On? Auden.
Widow at Windsor, The. Kipling.
Yankee Volunteers, The. Thackeray.
You who flee to escape a bloody death like mine. Propertius, *tr. fr. Latin by* Hughes.
Young Soldier, The. Wilfred Owen.
Youth in Arms. Monro.
Soldiers' Verse (SoV). Patric Dickinson, comp.
See also WAR.

SOLITUDE
Alastor; or, The Spirit of Solitude. Shelley.
Beata Solitudo. Dowson.
Charcoal-Burner, The. Gosse.
Going Alone to Spend a Night at the Hsien-yu Temple. Po Chü-i, *tr. fr. Chinese by* Waley.
Hymn on Solitude. James Thomson.
In Solitude. Sheard.
Ode on Solitude. Pope.
Of Solitude. Cowley.
Solitude. Allingham.
Solitude. *Fr.* Retirement. Beattie.
Solitude. Clare.
Solitude. De la Mare.
Solitude. Deutsch.
Solitude. Jami, *tr. fr. Persian by* Weston.
Solitude. Frederick Peterson.
Solitude. Rilke, *tr. fr. German by* Lemont.
Solitude. P H. Savage.
Solitude, A. Swinburne.

Solitude. Traherne.
Solitude. E. W. Wilcox.
Thrice Happy He. Drummond of Hawthornden.
To Solitude. Keats.
Valley Wind, The. Lu Yün, *tr. fr. Chinese by* **Waley.**
SOLOMON
King Solomon. "Owen Meredith."
King Solomon and King David. *Unknown.*
Love and Reason. *Fr.* Solomon. Prior.
Solomon. Hagedorn.
Solomon. Heine, *tr. fr. German by* **Lazarus.**
Solomon, *sels. Unknown.*
Solomon and the Bees. Saxe.
Solomon to Sheba. Yeats.
SOLWAY FIRTH, SCOTLAND *and* ENGLAND
Solway Ford. W. W. Gibson.
Solway Sands. Craigmyle.
SOMERSET, ROBERT CARR, EARL OF. Upon the Sudden Restraint of the Earl of Somerset, Then Falling from Favour. Wotton.
SOMME (river), FRANCE. Somme Valley, 1917, The. Prewett.
SOPHOCLES
Aeschylos and Sophocles. Landor.
On the Tomb of Sophocles. Simmias of Thebes, *tr. fr. Greek.*
To a Friend. Matthew Arnold.
SORDELLO. Sordello, *sel.* ("That autumn eve was stilled"). Robert Browning.
SORRENTO, ITALY. Sorrento. Snoilsky, *tr. fr. Swedish by* Stork.
SORROW. *See* GRIEF.
SOUFRIÈRE (volcano), ST. VINCENT. After Soufrière. "Michael Field."
SOUTH, THE
I Sigh for the Land of the Cypress and Pine. S. H. Dickson.
Resurgam. M. B. Clarke.
Southerner, The. Shapiro.
Stricken South to the North, The. Hayne.
Utterance. Pearson.
Lyric South (LS). Addison Hibbard, ed.
SOUTH AFRICA, UNION OF
On Some South African Novelists. Roy Campbell.
Seven South African Poems. David Wright.
Wayzgoose, The, *sel.* ("Attend my fable if your ears be clean"). Roy Campbell.
SOUTH AMERICA
To Theodore Roosevelt. Darío, *tr. fr. Spanish by* Hills.
Anthology of Contemporary Latin-American Poetry (AnCL). Dudley Fitts, ed.
SOUTH CAROLINA
Brother Jonathan's Lament for Sister Caroline. O. W. Holmes.
Carolina. Timrod.
Carolina. J. A. Wagner.
Carolina Spring Song. Hervey Allen.
South Carolina to the States of the North. P. H. Hayne.
SOUTH CAROLINA (ship). *South Carolina,* The. *Unknown.*
SOUTH DAKOTA. Hail! South Dakota. Hammitt.
SOUTH POLE. Southerly. E. J. Brady.
SOUTH WIND
South Wind, The. Charles Kingsley.
South-Wind. G. P. Lathrop.
South Wind. George O'Neil.
South Wind. Sassoon.
SOUTHERN CROSS (constellation). Southern Cross. Melville.
SOUTHEY, ROBERT
Dedication: "Bob Southey! You're a poet—Poet-laureate." *Fr.* Don Juan. Byron.
Epitaph on Robert Southey. Thomas Moore.
On the Death of Southey ("It was a dream"). Landor.
On the Death of Southey ("Not the last struggles"). Landor.
Southey and Wordsworth. *Fr.* Don Juan. Byron.
To Southey, 1833. Landor.
Vision of Judgment, The. Byron.
SPACE (outer space)
Among the Stars. *Fr.* Peter Bell. Wordsworth.
Autosonic Door. D. B. Thompson.
SPAIN
Coming Homeward out of Spain. Googe.
In Spain. Lawless.
In Spain. Wyatt.
Ode to Spain—after the Revolution of March. Quintana, *tr. fr. Spanish by* Walsh.
Of His Return from Spain. Wyatt.
On Gredos. Unamuno, *tr. fr. Spanish by* Turnbull.
Song from Old Spain, A. Alice Corbin.
Spain, 1937. Auden.
Spain, Take from Me This Cup. Vallejo, *tr. fr. Spanish by* Walsh.
Spanish Alleluja. Galvin.
To Spain—a Last Word. E. M. Thomas.
Winter in Castile. Dos Passos.
Anthology of Spanish Literature in English Translation, An (AnSpL 1-2). Seymour Resnick *and* Jeanne Pasmantier, eds.
Contemporary Spanish Poetry (CoSP). Eleanor L. Turnbull, tr.
Ten Centuries of Spanish Poetry (TeCS). Eleanor L. Turnbull, ed.
SPANISH-AMERICAN WAR
Battle Cry. W. H. Venable.
Battle Song. R. B. Wilson.
Brooklyn at Santiago, The. **Wallace Rice.**
Hobson and His Men. Loveman.
McIlrath of Malate. J. J. Rooney.
Martyrs of the *Maine,* The. Rupert Hughes.
"Mene, Mene, Tekel, Upharsin." Cawein.
Off Manilly. E. V. Cooke.
On a Soldier Fallen in the Philippines. **W. V. Moody.**
Rush of the *Oregon,* The. Guiterman.
Santiago. Janvier.
Spain's Last Armada. Wallace Rice.
To the Dead of '98. L. P. Johnson.
Wheeler at Santiago. J. L. Gordon.
Wheeler's Brigade at Santiago. Wallace Rice.
When the Great Grey Ships Come in. G. W. Carryl.
SPANISH ARMADA
Armada, The. Macaulay.
Armada, *sel.* Swinburne.
Ballad to Queen Elizabeth, A. Dobson.
Defeat of the Spanish Armada, The. *Unknown, at. to* William Warner.
Drake. Noyes.
King Philip's Men. A. A. Brown.
Some years of late, in eighty-eight. *Unknown.*
SPANISH CIVIL WAR. *See* CIVIL WAR, SPANISH.
SPANISH MAIN. Song of the Spanish Main, The. John Bennett.
SPANISH NEEDLES (flower). Spanish Needle, The. Claude McKay.
SPANISH POINT, IRELAND. Spanish Point. De Vere.
SPARROWS
Bee, the Ant, and the Sparrow, The. Cotton.
Dead Sparrow, The. William Cartwright.
Dead Sparrow, The. Catullus, *tr. fr. Latin.*
Did You Ever Hear an English Sparrow Sing? Bertha Johnston.
English Sparrow, The. M. I. Forsyth.
First Song-Sparrow, The. *Unknown.*
Fox Sparrow, The. W. W. Christman.
Golden Crown Sparrow of Alaska. John Burroughs.
Little Cock Sparrow, A. *Unknown.*
Northern Lass, The, *sel.* ("A bonny, bonny bird I had"). Brome.
Pastoral: "Little sparrows, The." W. C. Williams.
Song Sparrow, The. Lampman.
Song-Sparrow, The. G. P. Lathrop.
Song-Sparrow, The. Percy MacKaye.
Song Sparrow, The. Van Dyke.
Song Sparrow's Nest, The. Wetherald.
Sparrow. S. V. Benét.
Sparrows. A. D. T. Whitney.
Sparrows at the Airport, The. Ostroff.
To a Hedge-Sparrow. *Unknown.*
To a Sparrow. Ledwidge.
To Some Philadelphia Sparrows. Jeannette Marks.
Two Sparrows. Humbert Wolfe.
Vesper Sparrow, The. E. M. Thomas.
White-Throat, The. *Unknown.*
White-Throat Sings, A. W. P. Eaton.
White-throated Sparrow, The. A. West.
SPENDER, STEPHEN. To Stephen Spender. Corsellis.
SPENSER, EDMUND
In Obitum Ed. Spenser Poetae Prestaniss. John Weever.
Of Spenser's Fairy Queen. Thomas Freeman.
Remembrance of Some English Poets, A. Barnfield.
To Spenser. Keats.
To the Learned Shepheard. Gabriel Harvey.
Vision upon This Conceipt of the Faerie Queene, A. Ralegh.
SPHINX
Le Repos en Egypte; the Sphinx. Repplier.
Sphinx, The. Brownell.
Sphinx, The. Lord Alfred Douglas.
Sphinx, The. Emerson.
Sphinx, The. Oscar Wilde.
Sphinx Speaks, The. Saltus.
SPICEWOOD. Spicewood. Reese.
SPIDERS
Arachne. R T. Cooke.
Arachne. Empson.
Design. Robert Frost.
Image, The. Roy Fuller.
Little City. Horan
Mr. Edwards and the Spider. Robert Lowell.

SPIDERS (*continued*)
Noiseless Patient Spider, A. Whitman.
Of a Spider. Thorley.
Spider, The. Coffin.
Spider, The. A. P. Herbert.
Spider, The. McCord.
Spider, The. Vallejo, *tr. fr. Spanish by* Walsh.
Spider and His Wife, The. Jane Taylor.
Spider and the Fly, The, *sel.* ("In season what time every growing thing"). John Heywood.
Spider and the Fly, The. Mary Howitt.
Spider Web, The. Hausgen.
Spider Webs. Tippett.
Spider's Web, The. C. D. Cole.
Study of a Spider, The. De Tabley.
Vowel Englyn to the Spider. *Unknown, tr. fr. Welsh by* Borrow.
Voyage. Donaghy.
SPINNING
Spinners at Willowsleigh. Zaturenska.
Spinner's Song, The. Kathleen Millay.
Spinning. H. H. Jackson.
Spinning in April. J. P. Peabody.
Spinning Song, A. J. F. O'Donnell.
Spinning-Wheel. Kitahara, *tr. fr. Japanese by* Ninomiya *and* Enright.
Spinning Wheel, The. A. M. Klein.
Spinning Woman, The. Leonidas of Tarentum, *tr. fr. Greek by* Lang.
SPINOZA, BARUCH. Spinoza. T. S Jones, Jr.
SPOHR, LUDWIG. Violinist, The. Lampman.
SPRING
Abishag. Fichman, *tr. fr. Hebrew by* Kahn.
Admonition for Spring. L. A. MacKay.
After Winter. C. S. Bailey.
Air in Spring, The. Dowling.
All the Flowers of the Spring. *Fr.* The Devil's Law Case. John Webster.
Alone in Spring. Giltinan.
Alons au bois le may cueillir. Orléans, *tr. fr. French by* Henley.
American Spring Song. Sherwood Anderson.
Apple Orchard in the Spring, An. W. W. Martin.
Approach of Spring. Clare.
A-Roving. Victor Daley.
As It Fell upon a Day. Barnfield.
At the Edge of the Bay. Chubb.
At Winter's End. Sister Mary Madeleva.
Australian Spring. Hugh McCrae.
Autumnal Spring Song. Vassar Miller.
Awakening of Spring, The. Ku Shih, *tr. fr. Chinese by* Hart.
Barrel Organ, The. Noyes.
Before Spring. Ropes.
Before You Now, My Tyrant-Sorrow. George, *tr. fr. German by* Viereck.
Bells of Youth, The. "Fiona Macleod."
Call of the Spring, The. Noyes.
Catch for Spring, A. Robert Nichols.
Chanson Innocent. E. E. Cummings.
Chanted Calendar, A. *Fr.* Balder. Dobell.
Child's Song in Spring. Edith Nesbit.
City Wife. Livesay.
Cold Spring, A. Elizabeth Bishop.
Come, Love, Let's Walk. *Unknown.*
Comin' o' the Spring, The. Lady John Scott.
Coming of Spring, The. Mary Howitt.
Coming of Spring, The. Müller, *tr. fr. German.*
Coming of Spring, The. Nora Perry.
Coming of Spring, The. *Unknown.*
Darling! Because My Blood Can Sing. E. E. Cummings.
Day before April, The. M. C. Davies.
Day of Sunshine, A. Longfellow.
Days Too Short. W. H. Davies.
Débutante, The. G. W. Carryl.
Description of Spring, Wherein Each Thing Renews, save Only the Lover. Earl of Surrey.
Dress of Spring, The. Justus.
Eager Spring. Bottomley.
Earliest Spring. W. D. Howells.
Early Spring. W. H. Davies.
Early Spring. Rode, *tr. fr. Danish by* Stork.
Early Spring. Tennyson.
Earth in Spring, The. Halevi, *tr. fr. Hebrew by* King.
Echoing Green, The. *Fr.* Songs of Innocence. Blake.
Epistle for Spring. Larsson.
Evening Walk in Spring, An. Clough.
Farewell to Spring. Hsü Ying Yü, *tr. fr. Chinese by* Hart.
First Smile of Spring. Gautier, *tr. fr. French by* Conder.
First Spring Day, The. C. G. Rossetti.
First Spring Morning. Robert Bridges.
First Words before Spring. Louis Untermeyer.
Flower Chorus. *Unknown, wr. at. to* Emerson.
Flowers ("O Proserpina!"). *Fr.* The Winter's Tale. Shakespeare.
Four Ducks on a Pond. Allingham.
Fresh spring, the herald of love's mighty king. *Fr.* Amoretti. Spenser.
Getting Up Early on a Spring Morning. Po Chü-i, *tr. fr. Chinese by* Waley.
Glad Earth. E. C. Forbes.
Golden Spring Redeems the Withered Year, The. Hillyer.
Green Jade Plum Trees in Spring. Ou Yang Hsiu, *tr. fr. Chinese by* Rexroth.
Green Lady, The. C. D. Cole.
Green o' the Spring, The. D. A. McCarthy.
Gully, The, *sel.* ("There breaks upon my sight"). Wilmot.
Gusts of Winter are gone, the sky no longer lowers, The. Meleager, *tr. fr. Greek by* Chamberlayne.
Hawk and the Dove. *Unknown, tr. fr. Armenian by* Boyajian.
Hello! L. A. Garnett.
Here We Come a-Piping. *Unknown.*
Holy Spring. Dylan Thomas.
Home Thoughts from Abroad. Robert Browning.
Hope and Faith. Peretz, *tr. fr. Yiddish by* Goodman.
Hound of Heaven, The. Thompson.
How Each Thing Save the Lover in Spring Reviveth to Pleasure. Earl of Surrey.
Hymn to Spring. Caspari, *tr. fr. Norwegian by* Stork.
"I Bring Good News," Said Spring. Kujo, *tr. fr. Japanese by* Hughes *and* Iwasaki.
I dreaded that first robin, so. Emily Dickinson.
I Journeyed South to Meet the Spring. R. U. Johnson.
Immortal, The. C. Y. Rice.
Immortal Springtime and Its Tokens. *Fr.* Grandeza Mexicana. Balbuena, *tr. fr. Spanish by* Beckett.
In Earliest Spring. W. D. Howells.
In Early Spring. Victor Hugo, *tr. fr. French by* Conder.
In Early Spring. Alice Meynell.
In Hellbrunn. Trakl, *tr. fr. German by* Flores.
In Spring. Mörike, *tr. fr. German by* Watkins.
In Spring. Sannikov, *tr. fr. Russian by* Bowra.
In Spring-Time. W. H. Davies.
In the Haunts of Bass and Bream. Maurice Thompson.
In the Spring. Meleager, *tr. fr. Greek by* Lang.
In Two Months Now. Dillon.
It Might as Well Be Spring. Hammerstein.
It Is in Winter That We Dream of Spring. R. B. Wilson.
It Is Spring and All Is Well. C. E. S. Wood.
It Was a Lover and His Lass. *Fr.* As You Like It. Shakespeare.
Jonathan Bing Dances for Spring. B. C. Brown.
Joy. *Fr.* Humanitad. Oscar Wilde.
Kite Days. Mark Sawyer.
Land, The, *sels.* Sackville-West.
Last Week of February, 1890. Robert Bridges.
Late Spring, The. L. C. Moulton.
Lenten Is Come. *Unknown.*
Letter to His Friend Isaac, A. Halevi, *tr. fr. Hebrew by* Lazarus.
Light exists in spring, A. Emily Dickinson.
Lines Written in Early Spring. Wordsworth.
Lines Written in March. Wordsworth.
Little Song of Spring, A. Mary Austin.
Little Te Deum of the Commonplace, A, *sel.* ("With hearts responsive"). Oxenham.
Loveliest of Trees. A. E. Housman.
Love's Emblems. *Fr.* The Tragedy of Valentinian. John Fletcher.
Magic Piper, The. E. L. Marsh.
Miracle. L. H. Bailey.
Miracle of Spring, The. Bahar, *tr. fr. Persian by* Arberry.
Morning Song. Pollard.
My Lady Spring. *Unknown.*
New-born Year, The. Hovey.
Night of Spring. Thomas Westwood.
Now Fades the Last Long Streak of Snow. *Fr.* In Memoriam. Tennyson.
Now That the Winter's Gone. Carew.
O Heart of Spring. Neilson.
O Spring, Come Prettily In. Strodtmann.
O Sweet Spontaneous. E. E. Cummings.
Ode on the Spring. Thomas Gray.
Of Red in Spring. McCord.
On a Bank as I Sat a-Fishing. Wotton.
On a Hill. I. R. McLeod.
On a Lane in Spring. Clare.
On the Mountain. Neidhart von Reuental, *tr. fr. German by* Bithell.
Once More It Is the Springtime. Oehlenschläger, *tr. fr. Danish by* Stork.
One Morning When the Rain-Birds Call. Lloyd Roberts.
Open Secret, An. *Unknown.*
Our Singing Strength. Robert Frost.
Outside. Chesterman.
Over the Wintry Threshold. Carman.

Page's Road Song, A. Percy.
Parting from the Winter Stove. Po Chü-i, *tr. fr. Chinese by* Waley.
Pastoral. *Fr.* In Hospital. Henley.
Pippa's Song. *Fr.* Pippa Passes. Robert Browning.
Poem on Spring, The. Guiterman.
Prairie Spring. Fallis.
Prayer for This Day. Flanner.
Prayer in Spring, A. Robert Frost.
Prelude for Spring. Livesay.
Prologue to "The Canterbury Tales." Chaucer.
Promise. Lacey.
Put Forth Thy Leaf, Thou Lofty Plane. Clough.
Rains of Spring, The. Lady Ise, *tr. fr. Japanese.*
Return of Spring. Ronsard, *tr. fr. French.*
Returning Spring. Eichendorff, *tr. fr. German by* Shuster.
Revival, The. Vaughan.
Rondel: "Summer has sent his stewards on." Orléans, *tr. fr. French by* Currey.
Rondel: "Year has put his cloak away, The." Orléans, *tr. fr. French by* Currey.
Russian Spring. Bunin, *tr. fr. Russian by* Deutsch.
Russian Spring Song with Minaiev, A. Thomas Walsh.
Secret, The. J. R. Moreland.
Secret Voices, The. Mannin.
Shadow, The. W. C. Williams.
Skies Again Are Deep and Bare. Fet, *tr. fr. Russian by* Elton.
Slender Spring. Guillén, *tr. fr. Spanish by* Turnbull.
Slow Spring. Tynan.
Slumber in Spring. Elizabeth Gould.
Smells. Kathryn Worth.
Song: "Light of spring, The." A. D. Miller.
Song: "Spring lights her candles everywhere." Shove.
Song: "Spring will come when the year turns, The." Widdemer.
Song: "That Zephyr every year." Drummond of Hawthornden.
Song in Spring. Louis Ginsberg.
Song in Spring, A. T. S. Jones, Jr.
Song of Green, A. Phyllis Reid.
Song of the Spring Days. George Macdonald.
Song of the Stork, The. *Unknown, tr. fr. Armenian by* Boyajian.
Song of Waking, A. K. L. Bates.
Song of Zephyrus and the Spring. *Fr.* Chloridia. Jonson.
Sonnet: "Sweet Spring, thou turn'st with all thy goodly train." Drummond of Hawthornden.
Sonnet Written at the Close of Spring. Charlotte Smith.
Soon Shall the Winter's Foil Be Here. Whitman.
Soon with the Lilac Fades Another Spring. MacDonogh.
South Wind. Tu Fu, *tr. fr. Chinese by* Rexroth.
Spring. Allingham.
Spring, The. William Barnes.
Spring. Behn.
Spring. Beshigtashlian, *tr. fr. Armenian by* Boyajian.
Spring. *Fr.* Songs of Innocence. Blake.
Spring. *Fr.* The Four Seasons of the Year. Anne Bradstreet.
Spring. Carew.
Spring. J. A. Carpenter.
Spring, The. Chang Chung-sur, *tr. fr. Chinese.*
Spring. Chute.
Spring. Cornish.
Spring, The. *Fr.* The Mistress. Cowley.
Spring. Ebenezer Elliott.
Spring. *Fr.* The Tragedy of Valentinian. John Fletcher.
Spring. Norman Gale.
Spring, The. Gautier, *tr. fr. French by* Conder.
Spring. Giltinan.
Spring. Gislason, *tr. fr. Icelandic by* Johnson.
Spring. Guarini, *tr. fr. Italian by* Hunt.
Spring. Hafstein, *tr. fr. Icelandic by* Johnson.
Spring. G. M. Hopkins.
Spring. *Fr.* Odes. Horace, *tr. fr. Latin by* Sargent.
Spring. Hovey.
Spring. Hovhannessian, *tr. fr. Armenian by* Boyajian.
Spring. T. C. Irwin.
Spring. Richard Loveman.
Spring. McNeill.
Spring. Maddock.
Spring. Millay.
Spring. Thomas Moore, *after the Greek of* Anacreon.
Spring. *Fr.* Sonnets from a Hospital. David Morton.
Spring. *Fr.* Summer's Last Will and Testament. Nashe.
Spring ("The year has changed his mantle cold"). Orléans, *tr. fr. French by* Lang.
Spring. Pindar, *tr. fr. Greek by* Lucas.
Spring, The. Pound.
Spring. W. R. Rodgers.
Spring. C. G. Rossetti.
Spring. *Fr.* Love's Labour's Lost. Shakespeare.
Spring. Edith Sitwell.
Spring. *Fr.* St. Philip and St. James. Smart.
Spring. Spire, *tr. fr. French by* Bithell.
Spring. Thomas Stanley, *after the Greek of* Anacreon.
Spring. Su T'ung-po, *tr. fr. Chinese by* Rexroth.
Spring. Thaxter.
Spring. Timrod.
Spring. Tu Fu, *tr. fr. Chinese.*
Spring. Tyutchev, *tr. fr. Russian by* Bowra.
Spring ("When from her winter-prison"). *Unknown, tr. fr. Japanese.*
Spring ("When the nightingale singeth the woods waxen green"), *mod. Unknown.*
Spring. Louis Untermeyer.
Spring. Vilaras, *tr. fr. Modern Greek by* Dalven.
Spring. Vyazemsky, *tr. fr. Russian by* Deutsch.
Spring Air. Derwood.
Spring and All. W. C. Williams.
Spring and Autumn. Linton.
Spring & Co. Carrera Andrade, *tr. fr. Spanish by* O'Connell.
Spring and Fall: To a Young Child. G. M. Hopkins.
Spring Comes to Our Garden. Sister Mary Immaculata.
Spring-Dance. W. R. Rodgers.
Spring Doggerel. Coghill.
Spring Ecstasy. Reese.
Spring Equinox, The. Ridler.
Spring, etc. Whittemore.
Spring Evening on the Boulevards. Laforgue, *tr. fr. French by* Smith.
Spring Garland, A. Rorty.
Spring Goeth All in White. Robert Bridges.
Spring Has Come. *Unknown.*
Spring in Carmel. George Sterling.
Spring in England. Going.
Spring in Florida. C. B. Roth.
Spring in Hiding. Frances Frost.
Spring in New England. Carlos Wilcox.
Spring in New Hampshire. Claude McKay.
Spring in New Zealand. Hubert Church.
Spring in Oxford Street. "John Presland."
Spring in the Student's Quarter. Murger, *tr. fr. French by* Lang.
Spring in the Valley. D. C. Scott.
Spring in Town. Bryant.
Spring Is at Work with Beginnings of Things. Rose.
Spring Is Coming by a Many Signs, The. Clare.
Spring Is in the Making. N. K. Duffy.
Spring Is like a Perhaps Hand. E. E. Cummings.
Spring It Is. Mörike, *tr. fr. German by* Passage.
Spring Journey, A. A. F. Palmer.
Spring Lilt, A. *Unknown.*
Spring Market. Louise Driscoll.
Spring Morning. William Browne.
Spring Morning, A. Clare.
Spring Morning. Cornford.
Spring Morning—Santa Fé. Riggs.
Spring, My Dear, The. Henley.
Spring Nocturne. Liessin, *tr. fr. Yiddish.*
Spring Ode. Marquis.
Spring of the Year, The. Allan Cunningham.
Spring on the Ochils. J. L. Robertson.
Spring Poem. Ushakov, *tr. fr. Russian by* Lindsay.
Spring Quiet. C. G. Rossetti.
Spring Returns, The. C. L. Moore.
Spring Signs. M. B. Armstrong.
Spring Song. Baïf, *tr. fr. French by* Conder.
Spring Song. Carman.
Spring Song. John Davidson.
Spring Song. De Vere.
Spring Song. *Fr.* The Spanish Gypsy. "George Eliot."
Spring Song. William Griffith.
Spring Song. Hesse, *tr. fr. German by* Lewisohn.
Spring Song, A. Mary Howitt.
Spring Song. Nahum, *tr. fr. Hebrew by* Lazarus.
Spring Song. Katharine O'Brien.
Spring Song. Dollie Radford.
Spring Song. Ronsard, *tr fr. French by* Conder.
Spring Song. Swinburne.
Spring Song ("Spring, beautiful spring"). *Unknown, tr. fr. Russian.*
Spring Song ("Spring is come to town with love"). *Unknown.*
Spring Song in the City. Robert Buchanan.
Spring Song of Aspens. L. W. Spencer.
Spring Song of the Birds. *Fr.* The Kingis Quair. James I, King of Scotland.
Spring Sows Her Seeds. M. C. Davies.
Spring, the Sweet Spring. *Fr.* Summer's Last Will and Testament. Nashe.
Spring, the Travelling Man. Letts.
Spring Thoughts. Li Po, *tr. fr. Chinese by* Christy.
Spring Thunder. Tyutchev, *tr. fr. Russian by* Pinto.
Spring Walk, The. Thomas Miller.
Spring Was Late That Year, The. *Fr.* The Land. Sackville-West.
Spring Waters. Tyutchev, *tr. fr. Russian by* Bowra.

SPRING (*continued*)
Spring Wind, The. Ho Hung. *tr. fr. Chinese by* Hart.
Spring Wind. N. B. Turner.
Spring Work at the Farm. Wakley.
Spring's Answer. Grover.
Spring's Arrival. *Unknown.*
Spring's Delights. Sterry.
Spring's Immortality. Mackenzie Bell.
Spring's Saraband. Carman.
Springtime. Kreymborg.
Springtime—a Humble Cry from the Depths. Brentano, *tr. fr. German by* Cotterell.
Springtime in Cookham Dean. Cecil Roberts.
Stay, Spring. Andrew Young.
Sudden Spring. Coulby.
Swallow-Song, The. *Unknown, tr. fr. Greek by* Blake-Reed.
Sweet Weather. Reese.
Sweetness of Spring, The. *Unknown, tr. fr. Latin by* Symonds.
Talking in Their Sleep. E. M. Thomas.
Tardy Spring. George Meredith.
Time of Waiting. Karlfeldt, *tr. fr. Swedish by* Stork.
To Spring. Blake.
To Spring, *sel.* ("From the grey wicket of the morn"). O'Donnell.
To Spring. Roscoe.
To Spring. Wergeland, *tr. fr. Norwegian by* Stork.
To the Spring. *Fr.* Hymns of Astraea. Sir John Davies.
To the Spring Sun. Laughton.
To-day I saw a butterfly. Hooley.
Triumph of Spring, The. M. B. Clarke.
Turkish Ode of Mesihi, A. Sir William Jones.
Turn o' the Year. Tynan.
Two Sewing. Hazel Hall.
Two Springs. Li Ch'ing Chao, *tr. fr. Chinese by* Rexroth.
Vagabond at Home, The. R. W. Kauffman.
Ver Redit Optatum. *Fr.* Carmina Burana. *Unknown, tr. fr. Latin by* Whicher.
Vernal Equinox. Amy Lowell.
Vernal Sentiment. Roethke.
Vision of Spring in Winter, A. Swinburne.
Voice before April, A. B. N. Busch, Jr.
Voice of Spring, The. Hemans.
Waking of Spring, The. Custance.
Waking Up. *Unknown.*
Walk in Spring, A. K. C. Lart.
Walk in the Country, A. Su T'ung-po, *tr. fr. Chinese by* Rexroth.
Walking at Night. Hare.
Was There Another Spring? Helen Hay.
Welcome to Spring. Irene Thompson.
What an Evening! Streamlets Run. Fet, *tr. fr. Russian by* Bowra.
When Daffodils Begin to Peer. *Fr.* The Winter's Tale. Shakespeare.
When Daisies Pied and Violets Blue. *Fr.* Love's Labour's Lost. Shakespeare.
When Green Buds Hang in the Elm. A. E. Housman.
When Spring Comes Back to England. Noyes.
When the Hounds of Spring [Are on Winter's Traces]. *Fr.* Atalanta in Calydon. Swinburne.
When the Nyhtegale Singes, the Wodes Waxen Grene. *Unknown.*
Who Calls? F. C. Sayers.
Winter and Spring. *Unknown.*
Winter is Past, The. Song of Solomon, Bible, *O.T.*
Winter Spring. Wilbur.
Winter to Spring. Horace, *tr. fr. Latin by* MacNeice.
Wise Johnny. Fallis.
Wistful Days, The. R. U. Johnson.
Wonder and a Thousand Springs. W. A. Percy.
Woodland Choir, The. *Fr.* The Seasons: Spring. James Thomson.
Written in Early Spring. Wordsworth.
Written in March. Wordsworth.
Year, The. Patmore.
Year's Awakening, The. Hardy.
Yellow Spring. Jiménez, *tr. fr. Spanish by* Turnbull.
SPRINGFIELD, ILLINOIS
Abraham Lincoln Walks at Midnight. Vachel Lindsay.
House in Springfield. Burket.
On the Building of Springfield. Vachel Lindsay.
SPRINGFIELD, MASSACHUSETTS. Arsenal at Springfield, The. Longfellow.
SPRINGS
To a Mountain Spring. Le Gallienne.
Ye Bubbling Springs That Gentle Music Makes. *Unknown.*
SPRUCE TREES
Among the Spruces. F. G. Scott.
Proud Little Spruce Fir. Kirby.
Spruce Tree, The. Herriman.
SQUASH (sport). After a Game of Squash. S. L. Albert.
SQUIRRELS
Five Little Squirrels. *Unknown.*
Fred. McCord.
Grey Squirrels, The. William Howitt.
Joe. McCord.
Mr. Squirrel. V. M. Julian.
Mountain and the Squirrel, The. Emerson.
My Little Neighbor. M. A. Mason.
On a Squirrel Crossing the Road in Autumn, in New England. Eberhart.
Squirrel, The. Bernard Barton.
Squirrel, The. Cowper.
Squirrel, The. Mary Howitt.
Squirrel, The. Ogden Nash.
Squirrel, The. Serraillier.
Squirrel, The *Unknown.*
Squirrel and the Wind, The. *Unknown.*
Story of the Baby Squirrel, The. Aldis.
To a Squirrel at Kyle-na-no. Yeats.
STAGECOACHES. Baldy Green. *Unknown.*
STAIRS
Halfway Down. A. A. Milne.
On the Staircase. Farjeon.
Stairs. Herford.
STALIN, JOSEPH. Homage to Our Leaders. Symons.
STALINGRAD, USSR
"Spoken Word, The." Christopher Morley.
Stalingrad. Huw Menai.
STANDISH, MILES. Courtship of Miles Standish, The. Longfellow.
STANLEY, ARTHUR PENRHYN. Westminster Abbey. Matthew Arnold.
STARFISH
Starfish, The. Coffin.
Starfish. Winifred Welles.
Stonefish and Starfish. Blight.
STARK, JOHN. Marching Song of Stark's Men, The. E. E. Hale.
STARLINGS
Dead Starling, The. Catullus, *tr. fr. Latin by* Coleridge.
Starling's Spring Rondel, A. J. H. Cousins.
STARS
A la Belle Etoile. Birchall.
Aldebaran at Dusk. George Sterling.
And Each Man's Leave. Roland Robinson.
Baby Toes. Sandburg.
Beauty of the Stars, The. Ibn Ezra, *tr. fr. Hebrew by* Solis-Cohen.
Canopus. B. L. Taylor.
Celestial Fête. Hugo, *tr. fr. French by* Conder.
Choose Something like a Star. Robert Frost.
Comfort of the Stars, The. Richard Burton.
Constellation, The, *sel.* ("Fair, order'd lights"). Vaughan.
Daisies. F. D. Sherman.
Es stehen unbeweglich. Heine, *tr. fr. German by* Thomson.
Escape at Bedtime. R. L. Stevenson.
Fallen Star, The. Darley.
Falling Star, The. Teasdale.
Heavy Clouds at Length Are Scattering, The. Pushkin, *tr. fr. Russian by* Jerrold.
Hymn to the North Star. Bryant.
If Stars Dropped Out of Heaven. *Fr.* Sing-Song. C. G. Rossetti.
Light of Stars, The. Furness.
Light of Stars, The. Longfellow.
Like as a ship that through the ocean wide. *Fr.* Amoretti. Spenser.
Meditation under Stars. George Meredith.
Morning and Evening Star. Plato, *tr. fr. Greek by* Shelley.
My Star. Robert Browning.
Noctiflora. Leseman.
North Star. Zona Gale.
Nox Nocti Indicat Scientiam. Habington.
O Ye Sweet Heavens. T. W. Parsons.
On the Beach at Night. Whitman.
Pleiades, The. Coatsworth.
Pole Star. MacLeish.
Silver Sheep. A. B. Payne.
Softly through the Mellow Starlight. *Unknown.*
Song: "Stars are with the voyager, The." Hood.
Song: "There's one great bunch of stars in heaven." Marzials.
Star, The. G. H. Conkling.
Star, The. George Herbert.
Star, The. Redpath.
Star, A ("A star has stopped"). *Unknown.*
Star, The. Weaving.
Star in the West, The. Butterworth.
Star in the West, The. Eliza Cook.
Star Sirius and the Pole Star Dwell Afar. *Fr.* Later Life. C. G. Rossetti.
Star Song. R. U. Johnson.
Star-Splitter, The. Robert Frost.
Star-Talk. Robert Graves.
Star Thought. Frances Wells.

Starlight. J. W. Chadwick.
Starlight. H. L. Cook.
Starlight. William Meredith.
Starlight Night, The. G. M. Hopkins.
Starlighter, The. Guiterman.
Stars. Bacmeister.
Stars, The. "Barry Cornwall."
Stars, The. M. C. Davies.
Stars, The. M. M. Dodge.
Stars. Carolyn Hancock.
Stars, The. Smart.
Stars. Teasdale.
Stars ("I'm glad the stars"). *Unknown.*
Stars ("A little boy"). *Unknown.*
Stars Are Glittering in the Frosty Sky, The. Heavysege.
Stars at Tallapoosa. Wallace Stevens.
Stars Begin to Fall. *Unknown.*
Stars, I Have Seen Them Fall. A. E. Houseman.
Stars Sang in God's Garden, The. Plunkett.
Stars Stand Up in the Air, The. *Unknown, tr. fr. Irish by* McDonagh.
Starscape, A. Bellenden.
Summer Stars. Sandburg.
There Will Be Stars. Teasdale.
To the Evening Star. Blake.
To the Evening Star. Thomas Campbell.
To the Evening Star. Edgar Fawcett.
Twilight at Sea. Welby.
Twinkle, Twinkle, Little Star. Jane Taylor.
Until We Built a Cabin. Aileen Fisher.
Wanderers. De la Mare.
When I Heard the Learn'd Astronomer. Whitman.
STARVED ROCK, ILLINOIS. Starved Rock. Masters.
STATUE OF LIBERTY. *See* LIBERTY, STATUE OF.
STEEL
Prayers of Steel. Sandburg.
Smoke and Steel, *sels.* Sandburg.
Steel. Auslander.
Steel. Saylor.
Steel Mill. Louis Untermeyer.
Steel Mills after Midnight. L. C. Ray.
STEEPLES. Steeple-Jack, The. Marianne Moore.
STEERS. *See* OXEN.
STENOGRAPHERS. Stenographers, The. P. K. Page.
STEPHEN, SAINT
St. Stephen and Herod. *Unknown.*
St. Stephen's Word. Heppenstall.
STEPINAC, ALOYSIUS. To Archbishop Stepinac. Sister Mary Eulalia.
STERLING, GEORGE. Phantom Rose, The. Leitch.
STEVENS, THADDEUS. Old Thad Stevens. Kenneth Porter.
STEVENSON, ROBERT LOUIS
Apparition. *Fr.* In Hospital. Henley.
At the Stevenson Fountain. Wallace Irwin.
Robert Louis Stevenson. Reese.
Saint R. L. S. Cleghorn.
Seamark, A. Carman.
Stevenson's Birthday. Katherine Miller.
To R. L. S. *Fr.* Echoes. Henley.
STEWART, CHARLES. Old Admiral. E. C. Stedman.
STOCKBRIDGE, MASSACHUSETTS. To the Housatonic at Stockbridge. R. U. Johnson.
STOCKHOLM, SWEDEN. Stockholm in White. Fallström, *tr. fr. Swedish by* Stork.
STOICISM. Old Stoic, The. Emily Brontë.
STONE MOUNTAIN, GEORGIA. Stone Mountain. M. B. Whiteside.
STONEFISH. Stonefish and Starfish. Blight.
STONEHENGE, ENGLAND
Sonnet IV: Written at Stonehenge. *Fr.* Sonnets. Thomas Warton, the Younger.
To My Honour'd Friend, Dr. Charleton. Dryden.
STONES AND ROCKS
How happy is the little stone. Emily Dickinson.
Rock, The. Hovhannessian, *tr. fr. Armenian by* Boyajian.
This is My Rock. McCord.
Two Voices in a Meadow. Wilbur.
STONINGTON, BATTLE OF. Battle of Stonington on the Seaboard of Connecticut, The. Freneau.
STONY POINT, NEW YORK. Storming of Stony Point, The. Guiterman.
STORKS
Song of the Stork. The. *Unknown, tr. fr. Armenian by* Boyajian.
Stork, The. Al-Hajjam, *tr. fr. Arabic by* Arberry.
Village Stork, The. Bayard Taylor.
STORMS
After the Storm. Elizabeth Bartlett.
Arnold, Master of the *Scud.* Carman.
Awful tempest mashed the air, An. Emily Dickinson.
Ballad of the Strange and Wonderful Storm of Hail, A. *Unknown.*
Ballad of the Tempest. J. T. Fields.
Before the Squall. Symons.
Before the Storm. A. S. Davis.
Before the Storm. Dehmel, *tr. fr. German by* Lewisohn.
City-Storm. Monro.
Concerning a Storm. Richard Untermeyer *and* Louis Untermeyer.
December Storm. John Hay.
During the Storm. Gautier, *tr. fr. French by* Conder.
Equinox, The. *Fr.* Seaweed. Longfellow.
Gale, The. *Fr.* Sand and Spray; a Sea Symphony. J. G. Fletcher.
High o'er the Poop the Audacious Seas Aspire. Falconer.
Lines Written after a Very Severe Tempest Which Cleared Up Extremely Pleasant. Mercy Warren.
Night Storm. W. G. Simms.
O the Fierce Delight. Garland.
Presage of Storme. *Fr.* Eugenia. George Chapman.
Reefing Topsails. Walter Mitchell.
Song of the Storm. A. D. Watson.
Song of the Wild Storm-Waves, The. Sinnett.
Stanzas Occasioned by the Ruins of a Country Inn Unroofed and Blown Down by the Storm. Freneau.
Storm, The. Alcaeus, *tr. fr. Greek by* Merivale.
Storm, The. "Robin Christopher."
Storm, The. Donne.
Storm. Doolittle ("H. D.").
Storm, The. Heine, *tr. fr. German by* Untermeyer.
Storm, The. Patmore.
Storm, The. F. G. Scott.
Storm, The. Edward Shanks.
Storm, The. G. A. Stevens.
Storm, A, I, II, *and* III. *Fr.* Riddles. *Unknown, tr. fr. Anglo-Saxon by* Thompson.
Storm at Sea, A. *Unknown, tr. fr. Middle Irish by* Flower.
Storm Cone, The. Kipling.
Storm in the Distance, A. P. H. Hayne.
Storm Is Over, The. Robert Bridges.
Storm Song. Bayard Taylor.
Summer Storm. J. R. Lowell.
Summer Storm, A. Charles Whitehead.
Tempest, The. Zaturenska.
That Is All I Heard. "Yehoash," *tr. fr. Yiddish by* Goldstick.
Thunder Shower. Hilda Conkling.
Thunder-Shower, The. Wheelock.
Thunderstorm, A. Lampman.
Viking Terror, The. *Unknown, tr. fr. Irish by* O'Connor.
White Squall, The. "Barry Cornwall."
Winter Storm at Sea, The. *Fr.* The Borough. Crabbe.
See also BLIZZARDS.
STOWE, HARRIET BEECHER. Harriet Beecher Stowe. P. L. Dunbar.
STRADIVARI, ANTONIO. Working with God. *Fr.* Stradivarius. "George Eliot"
STRASBOURG, ALSACE-LORRAINE. O Strassburg. *Unknown, tr. fr. German by* MacIntyre.
STRATFORD-UPON-AVON, ENGLAND. Stratford upon Avon. Ivor Brown.
STRAWBERRIES
Millions of Strawberries. Taggard.
Netted Strawberries. Bottomley.
Strawberry Jam. Justus.
With Strawberries. Henley.
STREETS. Quiet Street, The. Nan McDonald.
STRIKES AND STRIKERS
Bread and Roses. Oppenheim.
Wanderer, The. W. C. Williams.
STUART, CHARLES EDWARD, THE YOUNG PRETENDER
Bonnie Prince Charlie. James Hogg.
Charlie Is My Darling. Lady Nairne.
Moy Castle. *Unknown.*
O'er the Water to Charlie. Burns.
Old Scottish Cavalier, The. Aytoun.
Three Portraits of Prince Charles. Lang.
Wae's Me for Prince Charlie. William Glen.
Wha'll Be King but Charlie. Lady Nairne.
STUART, JAMES EWELL BROWN (Jeb Stuart). Obsequies of Stuart. J. R. Thompson.
STUART, JAMES FRANCIS EDWARD, THE OLD PRETENDER. New Song Entitled the Warming Pan, A. *Unknown.*
STUDENTS
After Passing the Examination. Po Chü-i, *tr. fr. Chinese by* Waley.
Elementary School Class Room in a Slum, An. Spender.
Student, The. *Unknown, tr. fr. Early Modern Irish by* O'Connor.
Tokyo Imperial University Students. Nakano, *tr. fr. Japanese by* Ninomiya *and* Enright
STURMINSTER NEWTON, ENGLAND. On Sturminster Foot-Bridge. Hardy.
STUYVESANT, PETER. Peter Stuyvesant's New Year's Call. E. C. Stedman.
SUBMARINES. Mare Liberum. Van Dyke.
SUBURBS. Do It Yrself. Eigner.

SUBWAYS
In a Station of the Metro. Pound.
On a Subway Express. Firkins.
Subway, The. Beer.
Subway Builders. Lawrence Lee.
Tunnel, The. *Fr.* The Bridge. Hart Crane.
SUCCESS
Don't Give Up. *Unknown.*
Success is counted sweetest. Emily Dickinson.
Villanelle: "Woods we're lost in aren't real, The." W. H. Kerr.
SUCKLING, SIR JOHN. Sir John Suckling's Campaign. *Unknown.*
SUFFRAGE
Ballot, The. John Pierpont.
Protest against the Ballot. Wordsworth.
SUICIDE
After the Surprising Conversions. Robert Lowell.
At the Crossroad Lies Buried. Heine, *tr. fr. German by* Watkins.
Bridge of Sighs, The. Hood.
Empedocles on Etna. Matthew Arnold.
Felo-de-Se. Flecker.
Felo de Se. Richard Hughes.
Mill, The. E. A. Robinson.
Of One Self-Slain. C. H. Towne.
Richard Cory. E. A. Robinson.
Suicide's Stone. Jeffers.
To Be or Not to Be. *Fr.* Hamlet. Shakespeare.
Two Voices, The. Tennyson.
SUMMER
As imperceptibly as grief. Emily Dickinson.
Beginning of Summer, The. Po Chü-i, *tr. fr. Chinese by* Waley.
Belonging to Summer. Shacklett.
Body of Summer, The. "Odysseus Elytis," *tr. fr. Modern Greek by* Friar.
Boy's Summer Song, A. P. L. Dunbar.
Comfort of the Fields. Lampman.
Country Summer. Léonie Adams.
Credences of Summer. Wallace Stevens.
Description of a Summer's Eve. H. K. White.
Dirge for Summer, A. Sebastian Evans.
Ear Is Not Deaf. Dayton.
End of Summer. J. S. Untermeyer.
End-of-Summer Poem. Rowena Bennett.
Fair Summer Droops. *Fr.* Summer's Last Will and Testament. Nashe.
Farewell to Summer. George Arnold.
Flowers of Middle Summer. *Fr.* The Winter's Tale. Shakespeare.
Halves of Life. Hölderlin, *tr. fr. German by* Flores.
Heat. Lampman.
Heaven Is Heaven. C. G. Rossetti.
High Summer. Hishiyama, *tr. fr. Japanese by* Ninomiya *and* Enright.
Hock-Cart, or Harvest Home, The. Herrick.
If on Some Balmy Summer Night. Edith Nesbit.
In Summer. C. H. Towne.
In Summer Time. *Fr.* Robin Hood and the Monk. *Unknown.*
In the Elegy Season. Wilbur.
In the Heat of the Day. Susukida, *tr. fr. Japanese by* Ninomiya *and* Enright.
Invocation to Rain in Summer. W. C. Bennett.
Joy of Life. M. R. Mitford.
Landscape, A. John Cunningham.
Lanes in Summer. Hemphrey.
Level of Abstraction, A. Conquest.
Midsummer. Allingham.
Midsummer. *Fr.* Thyrsis. Matthew Arnold.
Midsummer. Calverley.
Midsummer. Hesse, *tr. fr. German by* Salinger.
Midsummer. O. W. Holmes.
Midsummer. S. K. Russell.
Midsummer. J. T. Trowbridge.
Midsummer. E. W. Wilcox.
Midsummer Holiday, A, *sels.* Swinburne.
Midsummer Invitation. M. B. Benton.
Midsummer Madness. *Unknown.*
Midsummer Night. Elizabeth Gould.
Midsummer Noon in the Australian Forest, A. Harpur.
Midsummer Song, A. R. W. Gilder.
Night Enchantment. Muth.
Now Welcome, Somer. *Fr* The Parlement of Foules. Chaucer.
O Summer Sun. Binyon.
On a Midsummer Eve. Hardy.
On a Wet Summer. Bamfylde.
On the Unusual Cold and Rainie Weather in the Summer, 1648. Roberth Heath.
Poet at the Court of Pan, A. Lady Margaret Sackville.
Qui Bien Aime à Tard Oublie. Chaucer.
Rainy Summer, The. Alice Meynell.
Rainy Summer. Pitter.
Secret. E. H. Doolittle.
Song: "In summer when the rose-bushes." Edith Sitwell.
Song: "O spirit of the Summertime!" Allingham.
Song of Summer. P. L. Dunbar.
Song of Summer Days. J. W. Foley.
Song of Summer Days, A. Sheard.
Song of the Summer Days. George Macdonald.
Soote Season, The. Earl of Surrey.
Succession of the Four Sweet Months, The. Herrick.
Sumer Is Icumen In. *Unknown.*
Summer. *Fr.* Dumb in June. Richard Burton.
Summer. John Davidson.
Summer. *Fr.* Works and Days. Hesiod, *tr. fr. Greek by* Lucas.
Summer. *Fr.* The Fields of Dawn. Lloyd Mifflin.
Summer. P. K. Page.
Summer. *Fr.* Pastorals. Pope.
Summer. *Fr.* The Seasons. James Thomson.
Summer. *Unknown.*
Summer Afternoon. Dowling.
Summer and Winter. G. S Fraser.
Summer and Winter. Shelley
Summer by the Lakeside. Whittier.
Summer Comes. Agnew.
Summer Comes Petrarch, *tr. fr. Italian by* the Earl of Surrey.
Summer Commentary, A. Winters.
Summer Day, A. H. C. Beeching.
Summer Day, A. Florence Harrison.
Summer Day. Alexander Hume.
Summer Days. W. M. W. Call.
Summer Days. Daniells.
Summer Days. C. G. Rossetti.
Summer Drought. J. P. Irvine.
Summer Evening. Clare.
Summer Evening. De la Mare.
Summer Evening, A. Lampman.
Summer Has Come. *Unknown, tr. fr. Middle Irish by* Meyer.
Summer has two beginnings. Emily Dickinson.
Summer Idyll. George Barker.
Summer Images. Clare.
Summer in England 1914. Alice Meynell.
Summer Is Coming, The. Guinness.
Summer Is Gone. *Unknown, tr. fr. Old Irish by* O'Faoláin.
Summer Landscape. Laforgue, *tr. fr. French by* Smith.
Summer Longings. D. F. MacCarthy.
Summer Lullaby, A. Bumstead.
Summer Magic. L. P. Hill.
Summer Matures. Helene Johnson.
Summer Music. Sarton.
Summer Night, A. "Æ."
Summer Night, A. Elizabeth Stoddard.
Summer Night, Riverside. Teasdale.
Summer Noon, A. Carlos Wilcox.
Summer Noon at Sea, A. Epes Sargent.
Summer Pool, The. Robert Buchanan.
Summer Rain. Laurie Lee.
Summer Sabbath. Sampter.
Summer Sanctuary, A. Ingham.
Summer Shower, The. T. B. Read.
Summer Song. Percy MacKaye.
Summer Song. Edith Nesbit.
Summer Song. Wu Ti, *tr fr. Chinese by* Waley.
Summer Stars. Sandburg.
Summer Storm, A. Lord Alfred Douglas.
Summer-sweet. Tynan.
Summer Twilight, A. C. T. Turner.
Summer Wish. John Farrar.
Summer Wish, A. C. G. Rossetti.
Sunshine after a Shower. *Fr* On the Approach of Summer. Thomas Warton, the Younger.
Tell All the World. Kemp.
These are the days when birds come back. Emily Dickinson.
They Come! The Merry Summer Months. Motherwell.
Thistledown. Reese.
Throstle, The. Tennyson.
Time of Roses. Hood.
To Summer. Blake.
Touring. David Morton.
Vacation Song. Millay.
What Could Be Lovelier than to Hear. Coatsworth.
When Summer's End Is Nighing. A. E. Housman.
Wet Summer. M. W. Ward.
SUMNER, CHARLES
Charles Sumner. Longfellow.
Sumner. Whittier.
Three Friends of Mine. Longfellow.
SUMTER, FORT, SOUTH CAROLINA
Battle of Morris' Island, The. *Unknown.*
Fight at Fort Sumter, The. *Unknown.*
On Fort Sumter. *Unknown.*
Sumter. H. H. Brownell.

Sumter. E. C. Stedman.
Sumter; a Ballad of 1861. *Unknown.*
Sumter's Band. J. W. Simmons.
Twilight on Sumter. R. H. Stoddard.
SUN
Canticle of the Sun. St. Francis of Assisi, *tr. fr. Latin.*
Carol: "All this night shrill chanticler." William Austin.
Cockerel Sun. Rosemary Dobson.
Druids' Hymn to the Sun. *Fr.* The Dawn in Britain. Doughty.
Energy of Light, The. John Hay.
Forecast. Josephine Miles.
Give Me the Splendid Silent Sun. Whitman.
Glory, Glory to the Sun. John Alford.
Hint from Voiture. Shenstone.
Hostile Sun, The. D. H. Lawrence.
Hymn to Light. Cowley.
Hymn to the Sun. Darley.
Hymn to the Sun. Espronceda, *tr. fr. Spanish by* Farnell.
Hymn to the Sun. Ikhnaton, *tr. fr. Egyptian by* Breasted.
Hymn to the Sun. Percy.
In the Desert. Melville.
Last Man, The. Thomas Campbell.
Light Is Sweet, The. Ecclesiastes, Bible, *O.T.*
Marigold So Likes the Lovely Sunne, The. Thomas Watson.
Monterrey Sun. Reyes, *tr. fr. Spanish by* Beckett.
On a cleere morne as Phoebus run his race. *Unknown.*
On Mt. Iron. Brasch.
Pale Sun, The. Clare.
Prayer to the Sun. Wheelock.
Riddle: "On yonder hill there is a red deer." *Unknown.*
Rising Sun, The. Al-Haitham, *tr. fr. Arabic by* Arberry.
Salute. MacLeish.
September Sun, 1947. Gascoyne.
Setting Sun, The. Ibn Sa'id of Alcala la Real, *tr. fr. Arabic by* Arberry.
Song to the Sun. Tegnér, *tr. fr. Swedish by* Stork.
Sonnet: "Full many a glorious morning have I seen." Shakespeare.
Sun, The. Baudelaire, *tr. fr. French by* Paul.
Sun, The. John Davis.
Sun, The. Drinkwater.
Sun, The. Thomas Miller.
Sun! Marianne Moore.
Sun. Henry Rowe.
Sun, The. *Fr.* Ode to the Setting Sun. Francis Thompson.
Sun, The. Trakl, *tr. fr. German by* Middleton.
Sun and Rain. C. G. Rossetti.
Sun God, The. De Vere.
Sun Rising, The. Donne.
Sunlight on the Sea. Ibn Sa'id of Alcala la Real, *tr. fr. Arabic by* Arberry.
Sunning. Tippett.
Sun's Travels, The. R. L. Stevenson.
There's Nothing like the Sun. Edward Thomas.
To Father Sun (from the Hako Ceremony). *Unknown, tr. fr. Pawnee Indian.*
To the Sun. Gezelle, *tr. fr. Flemish by* Bithell.
Wan Sun Westers, Faint and Slow, The. Henley.
Welcome to the Sun. *Fr.* The Aeneid. Virgil, *tr. fr. Latin by* Douglas.
SUNDAY. *See* SABBATH.
SUNDERLAND, CHARLES SPENCER, 3D EARL OF. Ode Inscribed to the Earl of Sunderland at Windsor, An. Tickell.
SUNDIAL. On the Needle of a Sundial. Quarles.
SUNFLOWERS
Ah Sunflower. *Fr.* Songs of Experience. Blake.
Sunflower, The. Durant, *tr. fr. French by* Conder.
Sunflower, The. Montale, *tr. fr. Italian by* Cambon.
Sunflower, The. Quennell.
Sunflower. Shchipachev, *tr. fr. Russian by* Deutsch.
Sunflower to the Sun, The. Stebbins.
Sunflowers. Scollard.
Sunflowers, The. Douglas Stewart.
SUNRISE
Day came slow, till five o'clock, The. Emily Dickinson.
Deirdre's Song at Sunrise. Sister Maura.
Design for a Stream-lined Sunrise. Sister Mary Madeleva.
I'll tell you how the sun rose. Emily Dickinson.
Prayer at Sunrise. J. W. Johnson.
Reveille. A. E. Housman
Sing a Song of Sunshine. Eastwick.
Sun Rising, The. Donne.
Sunrise. Guest.
Sunrise. *Fr.* Hymns of the Marshes. Lanier.
Sunrise. Reese.
Sunrise. C. E. S. Wood.
Sunrise along Shore. L. M. Montgomery.
Sunrise at Sea. Atherstone.
Sunrise at Sea. Epes Sargent.
Sunrise at Sea. Swinburne.
Sunrise Never Failed Us Yet, The. Thaxter.
Sunrise Trumpets. Auslander.
SUNSET
After Sunset. Allingham.
Allie. Robert Graves.
Any Sunset. Louis Untermeyer.
At Set of Sun. M. A. Townsend.
At Sunset. Ledoux.
At Sunset. Thorsteinsson, *tr. fr. Icelandic by* Johnson.
Day's End. *Fr.* Songs from the Rockies. Hagedorn.
Fire in the Heavens. Christopher Brennan.
Into the Sunset. S. H. Young.
Looking Down on Mesopotamia. Bethell.
Ode to the Setting Sun. Francis Thompson.
Of the Going Down of the Sun. Bunyan.
Prairie Sunset, A. E. J. Pratt.
Prairie Sunset, A. Whitman.
Sundown. Léonie Adams.
Sunset. Bashford.
Sunset. Bialik, *tr. fr. Hebrew by* Frank.
Sunset. Hölderlin, *tr. fr. German by* Gruenthal.
Sunset, A. Hugo, *tr. fr. French.*
Sunset, A. Loveman.
Sunset and Landscape. *Fr.* The Wanderer. Savage.
Sunset on an English Hill. Acton-Bond.
Sunset Wings. D. G. Rossetti.
Sunsets. Aldington.
Testament of Beauty, The, *sel.* ("'Twas at thatt hour of beauty when the setting sun"). Robert Bridges.
Village before Sunset. Cornford.
Walk at Sunset, A. Bryant.
SUPERB (ship). Old *Superb*, The. Newbolt.
SUPERIOR, LAKE
Lake Superior. S. G. Goodrich.
Memory of Lake Superior. George Dillon.
SURGEONS. *See* PHYSICIANS.
SURREY, HENRY HOWARD, EARL OF
Henry Howard, Earl of Surrey, to the Lady Geraldine. *Fr.* England's Heroical Epistles. Drayton.
Verse in Praise of Lord Henry Howard, Earl of Surrey. Turberville.
SUSANNA (Bible)
Peter Quince at the Clavier. Wallace Stevens.
Susanna Fair, Sometime of Love Requested. *Unknown.*
SUSSEX, ENGLAND
Chanclebury Ring. W. S. Blunt.
Day in Sussex, A. W. S. Blunt.
South Country, The. Belloc.
Sussex. Kipling.
SUTTER, JOHN. John Sutter. Winters.
SWALLOWS
Barn-Swallow, The. William Sargent.
Chimney Swallows. H. N. Powers.
Departure of the Swallow, The. William Howitt.
First Swallow, The. Charlotte Smith.
Homing Swallows. Claude McKay.
Itylus. Swinburne.
O Master Masons. Toller, *tr. fr. German by* Dukes.
O My Swallows! Toller, *tr. fr. German by* Dukes.
Swallow, The. Aird.
Swallow, The. John Burroughs.
Swallow, The. Clare.
Swallow, The. Cowley.
Swallow, The. Ralph Hodgson.
Swallow, The. *Fr.* Sing-Song. C. G. Rossetti.
Swallow, The. Thomas Stanley, *after the Greek of* Anacreon.
Swallow Flight. Teasdale.
Swallow Song. Pickthall.
Swallow-Song, The. *Unknown, tr. fr. Greek by* Blake-Reed.
Swallow Tails. Tom Robinson.
Swallows, The. Sir Edwin Arnold.
Swallows, The. Patric Dickinson.
Swallows. Maikov, *tr. fr. Russian by* Kisch.
Swallows. C. Y. Rice.
Swallows, The; an Elegy. Jago.
Swallow's Flight, The. Louis Levy, *tr. fr. Danish by* Alwood *and* Kaufman.
Swallow's Nest, The. Sir Edwin Arnold.
To a Swallow Building under Our Eaves. J. W. Carlyle.
Twitter of Swallows. Merrill Moore.
What the Swallows Say. Gautier, *tr. fr. French by* Conder.
SWAN LAKE (ballet). Swan, The. Spender.
SWANNANOA (river), NORTH CAROLINA. Swannanoa. *Unknown.*
SWANS
Black Swan, The. Jarrell.
Black Swans. Snoilsky, *tr. fr. Swedish by* Stork.
Dark World, A. Scovell.
Dying Swan, The. T. S. Moore.
Dying Swan, The. *Unknown.*
Goe bidd the swan in silence dye. *Unknown.*
Gray Swan, The. Alice Cary.
Icebound Swans, The. *Unknown, tr. fr. Old Irish by* O'Faoláin.
Lone Swan. R. M. Powers.
Love of Swans, The. Leonard Mann.

SWANS (*continued*)
Riddle, A: "Clothes make no sound when I tread ground." *Unknown, tr. fr. Anglo-Saxon.*
Romance of the Swan's Nest, The. E. B. Browning.
Silver Swan, The. *Unknown.*
Swan, The. Baudelaire, *tr. fr. French by* Bennett.
Swan, The. Coatsworth.
Swan, The. J. G. Fletcher.
Swan, The. F. S. Flint.
Swan, The. Guillén, *tr. fr Spanish by* Turnbull.
Swan, The. Jay Macpherson.
Swan, The. Polonsky, *tr. fr. Russian by* Phillimore.
Swan, The. W. R. Rodgers.
Swan, The. Runeberg, *tr. fr. Swedish by* Stork.
Swan, A. *Fr.* Riddles. *Unknown, tr. fr. Anglo-Saxon.*
Swan and the Goose, The. Aesop, *tr. fr. Greek by* Leonard.
Swan Bathing, The. Pitter.
Swan Boat, A. Utter.
Swans. Durrell.
Swans, The. Dyment.
Swans. Speyer.
Swans at Night, *sel.* ("Within the night, above the dark"). Mary Gilmore
Swans from the North, The. Pedersen, *tr. fr. Danish by* Stork.
This Day, This Pure, Enduring, Beautiful Today. Mallarmé, *tr. fr. French by* Bennett.
This Swan. R. E. Morse.
To the Liffey with the Swans. Gogarty.
Transfigured Swan. Louis Untermeyer.
Two Swans, The. Hood.
Watch of a Swan, The. Piatt.
Wild Swan: "My attire is noiseless when I tread the earth." *Fr.* Riddles. *Unknown, tr. fr. Anglo-Saxon by* Kennedy.
Wild Swans at Coole, The. W. B. Yeats.
Yellow Swan, The. Sir Horatio Parker.
SWANSEA, WALES. Swansea Bay. Prichard.
SWEDEN
Carriage from Sweden, A. Marianne Moore.
Anthology of Swedish Lyrics, from 1750 to 1925 (AnSL). Charles Wharton Stork, ed.
SWEDENBORG, EMANUEL. On a Book Called Unitarian Theology. Freneau.
SWEET CLOVER. Sweet Clover. Wallace Rice.
SWEET PEAS. Sweet Peas. Keats.
SWEETBRIER
Breath of the Briar. Meredith.
Upon a Sweet-Briar. *Fr.* The Citation and Examination of Shakespeare. Landor.
SWIFT, JONATHAN
Life and Genuine Character of Dean Swift, The. Swift.
On Seeing Swift in Laracor. MacNamara.
Swift, *sel.* ("Two women loved him, shapes of Heaven"). T. C. Irwin.
Swift's Epitaph. Yeats.
To Dr. Swift on His Birthday. Esther Johnson ("Stella").
Verses on the Death of Dr. Swift. Swift.
SWIFTS. Swifts in the Chimney. Powers.
SWIMMING AND SWIMMERS
Bathers. Tiller.
Diver, The. Herbin.
Idea of a Swimmer. Bloch, *tr. fr. French by* "S. P."
Lone Bather. A. M. Klein.
Merrill's Brook. W. T. Scott.
Mother, May I Go Out to Swim? *Unknown.*
Our Silly Little Sister. Aldis.
Swimmer. Robert Francis.
Swimmer, The. Layton.
Swimmer, The. Roden Noel.
Swimmer, The. Ransom.
Swimming. Scollard.
SWINBURNE, ALGERNON CHARLES. Singer Asleep, A. Hardy.
SWINGS
Swing, The. R. L. Stevenson.
Swing Song, A. Allingham.
Swinging Song, A. Mary Howitt.
SWISS, THE. Swiss Peasant, The. Wordsworth.
SWITHIN, SAINT. St. Swithin. Daniel Henderson.
SWITZERLAND
Arnold von Winkelreid. James Montgomery.
England and Switzerland, 1802. Wordsworth.
Switzerland. *Fr.* William Tell. J. S. Knowles.
Thought of a Briton on the Subjugation of Switzerland. Wordsworth.
SYCAMORES. *See* PLANE TREES.
SYMBOLS
Correspondences. Baudelaire, *tr. fr. French by* Flores.
Vowels. Rimbaud, *tr. fr. French by* Varèse.
SYDNEY, AUSTRALIA. To Sydney. Louise Mack.
SYMPHONY. At the Symphony. Nathan.
SYNGE, JOHN MILLINGTON
In Memory of Major Robert Gregory. Yeats.
Synge's Grave. Letts.
SYRACUSE, SICILY. Syracuse. Coatsworth.

T

T. V. A. T. V. A., The. *Unknown.*
TABOR, ELIZABETH MCCOURT. Mistress of the Matchless Mine. Clyde Robertson.
TABOR, HORACE AUSTIN WARNER. Ballad of Chicken Bill, The. F. E. Vaughn.
TABOR GRAND OPERA HOUSE (Denver, Colo.). Curtain, The (Old Tabor Grand Opera House). J. M. Gower.
TADOUSSAC, CANADA. Tadoussac. Charles Bancroft.
TADPOLES
Boy and Tadpoles. Louis Untermeyer.
Tadpole, The. Elizabeth Gould.
TAGUS (river), SPAIN *and* PORTUGAL. Tagus, farewell, that westward with thy streams. Wyatt.
TAHITI
Tiare Tahiti. Rupert Brooke.
Vor a Gauguin Picture zu Singen. K. M. Stein.
TAI, CHINA. Most-sacred Mountain, The. Tietjens.
TAILORS
Tailor, The. "S. Ansky," *tr. fr. Yiddish by* Leftwich.
Tailor, The. De la Mare.
Tailor, The. Leftwich.
TALIESIN
Prophecy of Taliesin, The. Taliesin, *tr. fr. Welsh by* Borrow.
Taliesin, *sels.* Hovey.
TALLAPOOSA, GEORGIA. Stars at Tallapoosa. Wallace Stevens.
TALMUD, THE
Talmud, The. Frug, *tr. fr. Yiddish by* Blackwell.
Talmud Student, The. Bialik, *tr. fr. Hebrew by* Frank.
TAMALPAIS, MOUNT, CALIFORNIA
As I Came down Mount Tamalpais. Urmy.
Tamalpais, *sel.* ("The hollow moon"). C. W. Stoddard.
TAMERLANE
Tamburlaine the Great, *sels.* Marlowe.
Tamerlane. Poe.
TAMMUZ. Death of Tammuz, The. Tchernichowsky, *tr. fr. Hebrew by* Snowman.
TAMPICO, MEXICO. Tampico. G. H. Conkling.
TANAGERS
Scarlet Tanager, The. Joel Benton.
Scarlet Tanager, The. M. A. Mason.
To a Scarlet Tanager. Dresbach.
TANGLEWOOD, MASSACHUSETTS. *See* BERKSHIRE SYMPHONIC FESTIVAL.
TANNHÄUSER. Tannhäuser. W. M. Payne.
TAOS, NEW MEXICO
Autumn at Taos. D. H. Lawrence.
House in Taos, A. Langston Hughes.
TAPESTRY
Beyond the Tapestries. Farber.
Tapestry Weavers, The. A. G. Chester.
TARA, IRELAND
Harp That Once through Tara's Halls, The. Thomas Moore.
Tara. *Fr.* Dinnshenchas. *Unknown, tr. fr. Middle Irish by* Gwynn.
Tara Is Grass. *Unknown, tr. fr. Modern Irish by* Pearse.
TARAHUMARA INDIANS. Tarahumara Herbs. Reyes, *tr. fr. Spanish by* Beckett.
TASMANIA. Van Dieman's Land. *Unknown.*
TASSO, TORQUATO
Ferrara! in thy wide and grass-grown street. *Fr.* Childe Harold's Pilgrimage. Byron.
To Torquato Tasso. Grillo, *tr. fr. Italian by* Selden.
TAXES. Ballad on the Taxes, A. Edward Ward.
TAXIS
After Anacreon. Lew Welch.
Taxis. Rachel Field.
TAYLOR, BAYARD
Bayard Taylor. T. B. Aldrich.
Bayard Taylor. Longfellow.
Bayard Taylor. Whittier.
TEA
Boiling Tea. Su T'ung-po, *tr. fr. Chinese by* Yu Min-chuan.
Tea Flowers. Rito, *tr. fr. Japanese by* Porter.
Tea Trader, The. Daniel Henderson.
TEACHING AND TEACHERS
Air Mail, Special. Sister Mary Philip.
Education. Guiterman.
Examiner. F. R. Scott.
First Day of Teaching. Overstreet.
Flycatchers. Robert Bridges.
Jolly Old Pedagogue, The. George Arnold.
Old Brown Schoolhouse, The. *Unknown.*
Old Teacher. Gerald Raftery.
Pedagogical Principles. Amoss.
Prayer of a Beginning Teacher. Dunnam.
Prayer of a Teacher. Littlewort.
Professor of Medieval Balladry. Sister Mary Maura.

Schoolmistress, The. Shenstone.
Teacher, The. L. P. Hill.
Teachers, The. Pilcher.
Teacher's Dream, The. Venable.
Teacher's "If," The. R. J. Gale.
Teacher's Prayer, The. "Gabriela Mistral," *tr. fr. Spanish by* McLean.
TEARS
Lachrymae. Gascoyne.
Saint Mary Magdalene; or, The Weeper. Crashaw.
Tears, Idle Tears. *Fr.* The Princess. Tennyson.
TECUMSEH (Indian chief)
Fall of Tecumseh, The. *Unknown.*
Tecumseh, *sels.* Mair.
Tecumseh and the Eagles. Carman.
TEETH. Your Teeth. López Velarde, *tr. fr. Spanish by* Beckett.
TELEGRAMS. Telegram. William Wise.
TELL, WILLIAM. Archer, The. Scollard.
TEMERAIRE (ship). *Temeraire,* The. Melville.
TEMPERANCE
Face upon the Floor, The. H. A. D'Arcy.
Health, *sel.* ("Would you extend your narrow span"). Nathaniel Cotton.
Temperance ("Wine taken with excess"). *Unknown.*
Temperance, or the Cheap Physician. Crashaw.
TENERIFFE (island), CANARY ISLANDS. Teneriffe, *sel.* ("Atlandtid islands, phantom-fair"). F. W. H. Myers.
TENNESSEE
October in Tennessee. Malone.
Tennessee. V. F. Boyle.
Tennessee. *Fr.* Intaglios. Francis Brooks.
When It's Iris Time in Tennessee. Waid.
TENNIS
Near the Base Line. S. L. Albert.
Tennis. Avison.
TENNYSON, ALFRED TENNYSON, 1ST BARON
Alfred, Lord Tennyson. Whittemore.
Alfred Tennyson. Blunt.
I Entreat You, Alfred Tennyson. Landor.
Lacrimae Musarum. Sir William Watson.
Tennyson. T. B. Aldrich.
Tennyson. F. E. Coates.
Tennyson. T. H. Huxley.
To a Critic of Tennyson. Bierce.
Wapentake. Longfellow.
TEREK (river), USSR. Avalanche, The. Pushkin, *tr. fr. Russian by* Morison.
TERESA, SAINT. *See* THERESA, SAINT.
TERMITES
Termite, The. Ogden Nash.
Termites. C. G. Bell.
TEVIOT (river), SCOTLAND. And There Will I Be Buried. Thomas Davidson.
TEXAS
Cattle. Nance.
Cowboy's Lament, The. *Unknown.*
Homage to Texas. Robert Graves.
Lasca. Desprez.
Little Boys of Texas. Coffin.
Ranger's Song, The. Lytle.
Red Earth. G. N. Crowell.
Some Towns of Texas. K. W. Baker.
Song of Texas. Hosmer.
Song of the Forerunners. K. W. Baker.
Texas. Daugherty.
Texas. Amy Lowell.
Texas. Van Dyke.
Texas. Whittier.
Texas, Our Texas. G. Y. Wright.
Texas Rangers. *Unknown.*
Texas Trains and Trails. Mary Austin.
Texas Types—"The Bad Man." Chittenden.
THALIA (mythology). Thalia. T. B. Aldrich.
THAMES (river), ENGLAND
Bab-Lock-Hythe. Binyon.
Lover to the Thames of London to Favour His Lady Passing Thereon, The. Turberville.
Song of the River Thames, A. *Fr.* Albion and Albanius. Dryden.
Song of the Thames, A. Ernest Myers.
Thames, The. M. M. Hutchinson.
Thames from Cooper's Hill, The. *Fr.* Cooper's Hill. Sir John Denham.
There Is a Hill beside the Silver Thames. Robert Bridges.
THANKSGIVING
Another Grace for a Child. Herrick.
Child's Grace, A. Burns.
For Beauty, We Thank Thee. Oxenham.
Give Thanks. H. I. Tupper.
God, You Have Been Too Good to Me. Stork.
Grace. Emerson.
Grace, A. Tiplady.
Grace and Thanksgiving. Elizabeth Gould.
Grace at Evening. Guest.
Grace at Evening. Poteat.
How Are Thy Servants Blest. Addison.
Hymn: "For Summer's bloom and Autumn's blight." *Fr.* Bitter-sweet. J. G. Holland.
Hymn in Contemplation of Sudden Death. Sayers.
Hymn of Thanksgiving, A. A. E. Sherwood.
Hymn of Thanksgiving. *Unknown.*
I Have a Roof. Ada Jackson.
I Thank You God. E. E. Cummings.
In Thankfull Remembrance for My Dear Husband's Safe Arrivall Sept. 3, 1662. Bradstreet.
Let Us Give Thanks. Farningham.
Morning Thanksgiving. Drinkwater.
Not Alone for Mighty Empire. W. P. Merrill.
Our Prayer. George Herbert.
People's Thanksgiving, The. W. P. Merrill.
Poet's Grace, A. Burns.
Prayer before Meat. Harsen.
Prayer for Thanksgiving, A. Auslander.
Song of Thanks, A. E. S. Jones.
Song of Thanksgiving. J. R. Moreland.
Te Deum of the Commonplace, A. Oxenham.
Thankfulness. A. A. Procter.
Thanks. Norman Gale.
Thanks Be to God. Janie Alford.
Thanks in Old Age. Whitman.
Thanks to My World for the Loan of a Fair Day. Stella Benson.
Thanksgiving, A. J. K. Bangs.
Thanksgiving. A. E. Barr.
Thanksgiving. S. M. Best.
Thanksgiving. F. E. Coates.
Thanksgiving. Louise Driscoll.
Thanksgiving. W. D. Howells.
Thanksgiving, A, *sel.* ("For the rosebud's break of beauty"). Larcom.
Thanksgiving. Angela Morgan.
Thanksgiving, A. Cardinal Newman.
Thanksgiving. G. H. Osborne.
Thanksgiving. Oxenham.
Thanksgiving. Odell Shepard.
Thanksgiving. C. H. Towne.
Thanksgiving. A. N. Wilder.
Thanksgiving Day. Robert Bridges.
Thanksgiving for Thanksgiving. A. R. Wells.
Thanksgiving for the Earth. Goudge.
Thanksgiving Hymn ("The Lord above, in tender love"). *Unknown.*
Thanksgiving Prayer, A. *Unknown.*
Thanksgiving Prayer, A. Winant.
Thanksgiving Rosary, A. Markham.
Thanksgiving Song. Scollard.
Thanksgiving to God for His House, A. Herrick.
Thanksgivings of Old. Smuller.
Things I Miss, The. Higginson.
To the Spirit Great and Good. Leigh Hunt.
We Plow the Fields. Claudius, *tr. fr. German by* Campbell.
We Thank Thee. Kleiser.
We Thank Thee. Oxenham.
We Thank Thee. *Unknown.*
Youth's Thankfulness. E. D. Kramer.
Thanksgiving (*Our American Holidays Series*) (TOAH). Robert Haven Schauffler, ed.
THANKSGIVING DAY
Every Day Thanksgiving Day. Spofford.
Feast Day, The. McDonall.
First Thanksgiving Day, The. Brotherton.
First Thanksgiving Day, The. M. J. Preston.
First Thanksgiving of All. N. B. Turner.
For an Autumn Festival. Whittier.
Forever on Thanksgiving Day. W. D. Nesbit.
Giving Thanks. *Unknown.*
Gratitude. Sangster.
Harvest Hymn. *Fr.* For an Autumnal Festival. Whittier.
Hymn of Thanksgiving, A. W. D. Nesbit.
Hymn Written for the 200th Anniversary of the Old South Church, Beverly, Mass. Larcom.
If I Were a Pilgrim Child. Rowena Bennett.
Let Us Come before His Presence. Ludlum.
Old Thanksgiving Days, The. Shurtleff.
Thanksgiving. Brotherton.
Thanksgiving, A. Larcom.
Thanksgiving. Münsterberg.
Thanksgiving. M. E. Sangster.
Thanksgiving ("Oh! Give thanks"). *Unknown.*
Thanksgiving Day. L. M. Child.
Thanksgiving Day. J. J. Montague.
Thanksgiving Day. Annette Wynne.
Thanksgiving Day Grace. L. B. Cross.
Thanksgiving Fable, A. Herford.
Thanksgiving in Boston Harbor, The. Butterworth.
Thanksgiving Magic. R. B. Bennett.
Thanksgiving Night. W. D. Nesbit.
Thanksgiving Time ("When all the leaves are off the boughs"). *Unknown.*

THANKSGIVING DAY (*continued*)
Thanksliving. Piety.
Turkey Time ("Thanksgiving Day will soon be here"). *Unknown.*
We Thank Thee ("For glowing autumn's brimming yield"). T. C. Clark.
We Thank Thee ("Not for our lands, our wide-flung prairie wealth"). T. C. Clark.
We Thank Thee. Renwick.
Thanksgiving (*Our American Holidays Series*) (TOAH). Robert Haven Schauffler, ed.
THEATER
At the Theater. Rachel Field.
Clown Pondi. Sir Osbert Sitwell.
"Ej Blot til Lyst." W. M. Payne.
Grand Opening of the People's Theatre. Goldrick.
New Art of Making Plays, The. Lope de Vega, *tr. fr. Spanish by* Lord Holland.
Ode to Himself. Jonson.
Old Trouper, The. Marquis.
Outdoor Theatre, The. A. G. Winslow.
Theatre, The, *sel.* ("John Richard William Alexander Dwyer"). Horatio *and* James Smith.
Virgidemiarum, *sel.* ("With some pot-fury, ravished from their wit"). Joseph Hall.
THEBES, EGYPT. Story of Thebes, The, *sel.* ("At a posterne forth they gan to ryde"). Lydgate.
THEOCRITUS
Ballade to Theocritus, in Winter. Lang.
For a Copy of Theocritus. Dobson.
Theocritus. Annie Fields.
Theocritus. Gosse.
Theocritus. Langhorne.
Theocritus. Oscar Wilde.
Written on a Fly-Leaf of Theocritus. Maurice Thompson.
THEOLOGY
On a Book Called Unitarian Theology. Freneau.
Theology. Kilmer.
THERA (island), GREECE. Santorin. Flecker.
THERESA, SAINT, OF AVILA
After Reading Saint Teresa, Luis de Leon and Ramon Lull. Muna Lee.
Flaming Heart, The. Crashaw.
Hymn to the Name and Honour of the Admirable Saint Teresa, A. Crashaw.
To-and-Fro of Saint Theresa. Reyes, *tr. fr. Spanish by* Beckett.
THERMOPYLAE, BATTLE OF
Greek Dead at Thermopylae, The. Simonides, *tr. fr. Greek.*
Thermopylae. Simonides, *tr. fr. Greek.*
THESEUS
Theseus. Price Day.
Theseus. T. S. Moore.
Theseus and Ariadne. Mifflin.
Theseus and Hippolyta. Landor.
THIRTY YEARS WAR. Ode, upon Occasion of His Majesties Proclamation in the Year 1630, An. *Fr.* Il Pastor Fido. Fanshawe.
THISTLES
Roadside thistle, eager, The. Basho, *tr. fr. Japanese by* Page.
Thistledown. Monro.
THOMAS, DYLAN
Contempt for Dylan Thomas, A. Wilfred Watson.
When a Warlock Dies. Isabella Gardner.
THOMAS, EDWARD. To Edward Thomas. Alun Lewis.
THOMAS, GEORGE HENRY. Thomas at Chickamauga. K. B. Sherwood.
THOMAS À BECKET, SAINT
Becket's Diadem. *Unknown.*
Murder of Saint Thomas of Kent, The. *Unknown.*
THOMAS À KEMPIS
Paraphrase on Thomas à Kempis. Pope.
Thomas à Kempis. Bowker.
Thomas à Kempis. Reese.
Written in a Volume of "The Imitation of Christ." Zaturenska.
THOMAS AQUINAS, SAINT
Master-Welder, The. S. W. Taylor.
Saint Thomas Aquinas. T. S. Jones, Jr.
St. Thomas Aquinas. J. C. Miller.
THOMAS THE RHYMER (Thomas of Erceldoune)
Thomas the Rhymer. *Unknown.*
True Thomas. *Unknown.*
THOMPSON, FRANCIS
On the Death of Francis Thompson. Noyes.
Quiet Singer, The. Towne.
THOMSON, JAMES (1700–1748). Ode on the Death of Mr. Thomson. William Collins.
THOMSON, TOM. Tom Thomson. Bourinot.
THOREAU, HENRY DAVID
Savages, The. Josephine Miles.
Thoreau. A. B. Alcott.
Thoreau. Taggard.
Thoreau's Flute. L. M. Alcott.
THORODDSEN, THORVALDUR. Thorvaldur Thoroddsen. Gíslason, *tr. fr. Icelandic by* Johnson.
THOUSAND ISLANDS, NEW YORK *and* ONTARIO. Thousand Islands, The. *Fr.* The St. Lawrence and the Saguenay. Charles Sangster.
THREE HOLY CHILDREN. Warm Babies. Keith Preston.
THREE KINGS. *See* MAGI.
THROSTLES. Throstle, The. Tennyson.
THRUSHES
Articulate Thrush. Sarett.
Blow Softly, Thrush. J. R. Taylor.
Brown Thrush, The. Larcom.
Darkling Thrush, The. Hardy.
Hermit Thrush. Kathleen Millay.
Hermit Thrush, The. N. H. Woodworth.
Hermit Thrush in the Catskills, A. William Griffith.
Might these be thrushes climbing through almost. E. E. Cummings.
My Thrush. Mortimer Collins.
On a Thrush Singing in Autumn. Sir Lewis Morris.
Overflow. Tabb.
Singer, The. Dowden.
Song of the Hermit Thrush, The. J. B. Thomas.
Song of the Thrush, The. T. A. Daly.
Thrush, The. Laura Benét.
Thrush, The. Corsellis.
Thrush, The. John Duffy.
Thrush Sings, A. Henley.
Thrushes. K. W. Baker.
Thrushes. Humbert Wolfe.
Thrush's Nest, The. Clare.
Thrush's Song, The. *Unknown, tr. fr. Gaelic by* Macgillivray.
To a Tawny Thrush. Max Eastman.
To a Thrush. T. A. Daly.
What the Thrush Said. Keats.
What the Thrush Says. Scott-Hopper.
Where the Wood-Thrush Calls. Hughan.
Wise Thrush, The. Robert Browning.
Wood Thrush, The. Cheney.
THULE. Complain of the King of Thule. Laforgue, *tr. fr. French by* Smith.
THYME. Wild Thyme. Sambrook.
TIBET. Pilgrims of Thibet, The. C. Y. Rice.
TIBULLUS. On the Death of Tibullus. Domitius Marsus, *tr. fr. Latin by* Creekmore.
TICHBORNE [*or* TICHBOURNE], CHIDIOCK. On the Eve of His Execution. Tichborne.
TICONDEROGA, BATTLE OF
On the Defeat at Ticonderoga or Carilong. *Unknown.*
Surprise at Ticonderoga, The. Stansbury.
Ticonderoga. V. B. Wilson.
TIDE
As the Tide Comes in. C. Y. Rice.
Flowing Tide, The. Bradby.
High-Tide on the Coast of Lincolnshire. Ingelow.
Tide, The. J. W. Holden.
Tide, The. Kemp.
Tide Rises, the Tide Falls, The. Longfellow.
Tides, The. Tapper.
Tides. Josephine Williams.
TIGERS
Here She Is. M. B. Miller.
India. W. J. Turner.
Tiger, The. *Fr.* Songs of Experience. Blake.
Tigress, The. Pitter.
Young Lady of Niger, The. *Unknown.*
TILGHMAN, TENCH. Ride of Tench Tilghman, The. Scollard.
TIMBER LINE
At Timber Line. F. H. Mayer.
Timber Line Trees. Holme.
TIME
After Lunch. Po Chü-i, *tr. fr. Chinese by* Waley.
Alas, How Soon the Hours. Landor.
All That's Bright Must Fade. Thomas Moore.
As Time Goes On. Westphalen, *tr. fr. Spanish by* Hays.
August. MacNeice.
Burnt Norton. *Fr.* Four Quartets. T. S. Eliot.
Carpe Diem. *Fr.* Odes. Horace, *tr. fr. Latin by* Hawkins.
Chronometer, The. A. M. Sullivan.
Cities and Thrones and Powers. *Fr.* Puck of Pook's Hill. Kipling.
Clock, The. Baudelaire, *tr. fr. French by* Conder.
Clock. Monro.
Coach of Time, The. Pushkin, *tr. fr. Russian by* Bowra.
Cold Fall. Richard Eberhart.
Days. Emerson.
Description of Time and the Year, A. Tusser.
Dialogue betwixt Time and a Pilgrim, A. Townshend.
Earthly Illusion. Leighton.
End of the Year, The. Su T'ung-po, *tr. fr. Chinese by* Rexroth.
Enemy, The. Baudelaire, *tr. fr. French by* Watkins.

Evanescence. Hofmannsthal, *tr. fr. German by* Salinger.
Even Such Is Time. Ralegh.
Father Time. Ault.
Gone in the Wind. Mangan.
Hours. Corbière, *tr. fr. French by* Koch *and* Guy.
How Many Seconds in a Minute? C. G. Rossetti.
I drive my chariot up to the Eastern Gate. *Fr.* Seventeen Old Poems. *Unknown, tr. fr. Chinese by* Waley.
If you were coming in the fall. Emily Dickinson.
In Railway Halls, on Pavements. Spender.
Indefinite Time. Hofmannsthal, *tr. fr. German by* Hamburger.
Influence of Time on Grief. W. L. Bowles.
Isle of Long Ago, The. B. F. Taylor.
Jade Flower Palace. Tu Fu, *tr. fr. Chinese by* Rexroth.
Last Day of the Year, The. Droste-Hülshoff, *tr. fr. German by* Tobin.
Last Leaf, The. O. W. Holmes.
Love and Time. Ralegh.
Meditation on Time. Sister Mary Athanasius.
Minute, The. Shapiro.
Mount, The. Léonie Adams.
My Father's Watch. J. G. Fletcher.
Noise That Time Makes, The. Merrill Moore.
O Heavy Step of Slow Monotony. Toller, *tr. fr. German by* Dukes.
Old Gardener Time. Rachel Field.
On Time. Milton.
One by One. Hazel Hall.
Our Bias. Auden.
Palinode. Gogarty.
Paradox of Time, The. Dobson *after the French of* Ronsard.
Petition to Time, A. "Barry Cornwall."
Proper Sonnet, How Time Consumeth All Earthly Things, A. *Unknown, sometimes at. to* Proctor.
Quod Tegit Omnia. Winters.
River of Life, The. Thomas Campbell.
Song: "On the Eastern Way at the city of Lo-yang." Sung Tzu-hou, *tr. fr. Chinese by* Waley.
Sonnet: "Devouring Time, blunt thou the lion's paws." Shakespeare.
Sonnet: "Like as the waves make towards the pebbled shore." Shakespeare.
Sonnet: "Since brass, nor stone, nor earth, nor boundless sea." Shakespeare.
Sonnet: "When I consider every thing that grows." Shakespeare.
Sonnet: "When I do count the clock that tells the time." Shakespeare.
Sonnet: "When I have seen by Time's fell hand defaced." Shakespeare.
Take Time while Time Doth Last. *Unknown.*
There Isn't Time. Farjeon.
Thumbprint. C. T. Wright.
Time. Bhartrihari, *tr. fr. Sanskrit by* More.
Time. T. S. Collier.
Time. Hilda Conkling.
Time. Curnow.
Time. Robert Graves.
Time. Jasper Mayne.
Time. Schiller, *tr. fr. German.*
Time. Scollard.
Time. F. G. Scott.
Time. Marguerite Wilkinson.
Time and Death. Whitworth.
Time and Grief. W. L. Bowles.
Time and Spirit. Léonie Adams.
Time, Cruel Time, Come and Subdue That Brow. *Fr.* To Delia. Samuel Daniel.
Time Eating. Keith Douglas.
Time Has Come, the Clock Says Time Has Come, The. *Fr.* Preludes for Memnon. Aiken.
Time Is No Remedy. *Fr.* Tristia. Ovid, *tr. fr. Latin by* Johnson.
Time Lags Abed. Cresswell.
Time, Real and Imaginary. S. T. Coleridge.
Time stands still, with gazing on her face! *Unknown.*
Time, the Faithless. Iremonger.
Time to Die. Dandridge.
Time wasteth years, and months, and days, and hours. *Fr.* Hecatompathia. Thomas Watson.
Time, You Old Gipsy Man. Hodgson.
Timers. Arnstein.
Time's Bright Sand. Finch.
Time's Revenge. Learned.
Time's Revenges. Robert Browning.
To His Coy Mistress. Marvell.
To His Watch, When He Could Not Sleep. Lord Herbert of Cherbury.
To the Virgins, to Make Much of Time. Herrick.
To Time. "A. W."
Trumpet, The. Ehrenburg, *tr. fr. Russian by* Hornstein.
What if a Day or a Month or a Year. Campion.
What Time of Day? *Unknown.*
Who Was It, Tell Me. Heine, *tr. fr. German by* Garnett.
Years of a lifetime do not reach a hundred, The. *Fr.* Seventeen Old Poems. *Unknown, tr. fr. Chinese by* Waley.

TIME (magazine)
Sub-average *Time* Reader, The. Wittenberg.
Time like an Ever-rolling Stream. Wodehouse.

TIMES SQUARE, NEW YORK CITY. City Birds. "Spud" Johnson.

TIPPECANOE, BATTLE OF. Battle of Tippecanoe, The. *Unknown.*

TIPPERARY, IRELAND
Ah, Sweet Is Tipperary. D. A. McCarthy.
Tipperary. M. E. Kelly.
Tipperary Recruiting Song. *Unknown.*

TIRESIAS. Tiresias. George Garrett.

TITANIC (ship)
Convergence of the Twain, The. Hardy.
Titanic, The, *sels.* E. J. Pratt.
Titanic, The. *Unknown.*

TITMICE. *See* CHICKADEES.

TOADS
At the Garden Gate. McCord.
Death of a Toad, The. Wilbur.
Friend in the Garden, A. J. H. Ewing.
Little Horned Toad. *Tr. fr. Navajo Indian by* Wetherill.
Lullaby for a Baby Toad. Stella Gibbons.
Mister Hop-Toad. J. W. Riley.
Our Mr. Toad. McCord.
Song of Mr. Toad, The. *Fr.* The Wind in the Willows. Grahame.
Song of the Toad, The. Burroughs.
Toad, The. Corbière, *tr. fr. French by* Watkins.
Toad, A. Fawcett.
Toad, The. Louis Kent.
Toad and the Frog, The. *Unknown.*
Toad's Journal, The. Jane Taylor.
Tree Toad, The. Shannon.
Warty Bliggens, the Toad. Marquis.

TOBACCO
Farewell to Tobacco, A. Charles Lamb.
Humor of Tobacco and the Rest, The. Parrot.
O Metaphysical Tobacco. *Unknown.*
Ode to Tobacco. Calverley.
On Tobacco. Pestel.
Pernicious Weed. Cowper.
Pipe of Tobacco, A, *sels.* Browne.
Pipe of Tobacco, The. *At. to* Usher.
Religious Use of Taking Tobacco, A. *At. to* Wisdome.
Technogamia; or, The Marriage of the Arts, *sel.* ("Tobacco's a musician"). Holiday.
Tobacco. *Unknown.*

TOKYO, JAPAN. Susaki Waterfront. Muro, *tr. fr. Japanese by* Ninomiya *and* Enright.

TOKYO UNIVERSITY. Tokyo Imperial University Students. Nakano, *tr. fr. Japanese by* Ninomiya *and* Enright.

TOLEDO, SPAIN
Toledo. Restrapo, *tr. fr. Spanish by* Walsh.
Toledo. Zorilla, *tr. fr. Spanish by* Walsh.
Toledo, July 1936. Roy Campbell.

TOLLER, ERNST. In Memory of Ernst Toller. Auden.

TOLSTOY, LEO. Reading Tolstoy. Peter.

TOMI, RUMANIA. Winter at Tomi. Ovid, *tr. fr. Latin by* Wright.

TOMPKINS, SALLY. Capt. Sally Tompkins, C.S.A. B. R. Tucker.

TONE, THEOBALD WOLFE. Tone's Grave. T. O. Davis.

TONSON, JACOB. Jacob Tonson, His Publisher. Dryden.

TOOTHBRUSHES. My Six Toothbrushes. McGinley.

TORAH, THE
Angels Came a-Mustering, The. *Unknown, tr. fr. Hebrew by* Zangwill.
Simhat Torah. J. L. Gordon, *tr. fr. Hebrew by* Lucas *and* Frank.
Talmud Student, The. Bialik, *tr. fr. Hebrew by* Frank.
This Feast of the Law. *Unknown, tr. fr. Hebrew by* Zangwill.

TORTOISES
Eels, Tortoises, Soles, Lampreys. *Fr.* Halieuticks. Oppian, *tr. fr. Greek by* Diaper.
Legend of the Tortoise, The. Tennant.
Meditations of a Tortoise Dozing under a Rosetree near a Beehive . . . Rieu.
Night Thought of a Tortoise Suffering from Insomnia on a Lawn. Rieu.
Soliloquy of a Tortoise on Revisiting the Lettuce Beds . . . Rieu.
To My Tortoise ΑΝΑΓΚΗ (Ananke). Lee-Hamilton.
To My Tortoise Chronos. Lee-Hamilton.
Tortoise, The. Herbert Asquith.
Tortoise. Hagiwara, *tr. fr. Japanese by* Ninomiya *and* Enright.
Tortoise Family Connections. D. H. Lawrence.
Tortoise in Eternity, The. Elinor Wylie.

TOURISTS
Arrival at Santos. Elizabeth Bishop.
Tourists. Howard Moss.
Who Wants to Travel All Over Europe and See Nothing but a Lot of American Tourists? I do. Ogden Nash.
TOUSSAINT L'OUVERTURE, FRANÇOIS DOMINIQUE
To Toussaint L'Ouverture. Wordsworth.
Toussaint L'Ouverture. E. A. Robinson.
TOYNBEE, ARNOLD. On the Death of Arnold Toynbee. Mackail.
TOYOKUNI UTAGAWA. Ballade of a Toyokuni Color-Print. Henley.
TOYS
Block City. R. L. Stevenson.
Boy and His Playthings, The. Lenngren, *tr. fr. Swedish by* Stork.
Cirque d'Hiver. Elizabeth Bishop.
Duel, The. Eugene Field.
Dumb Soldier, The. R. L. Stevenson.
Land of Counterpane, The. R. L. Stevenson.
Little Boy Blue. Eugene Field.
Lost Doll, The. *Fr.* The Water Babies. Kingsley.
Toys, The. Patmore.
What the Toys Are Thinking. ffrida Wolfe.
TRACTORS
Caterpillar Tractor, A. *Unknown.*
New Farm Tractor. Sandburg.
Tractor. Hart-Smith.
TRAFALGAR, BATTLE OF
Battle of Trafalgar, The. *Unknown.*
Night of Trafalgar, The. *Fr.* The Dynasts. Hardy.
Trafalgar. William Canton.
Trafalgar. Palgrave.
Trafalgar. *Unknown.*
TRAFALGAR SQUARE, LONDON. Trafalgar Square. Fyleman.
TRAHERNE, THOMAS. Of Thomas Traherne and the Pebble Outside. Clouts.
TRAILING ARBUTUS. *See* ARBUTUS.
TRAINS
As We Rush, as We Rush in the Train. *Fr.* Sunday at Hampstead. James Thompson.
Beautiful Train, The. Empson.
Box-Car Letters. K. W. Baker.
Child in the Train, The. Farjeon.
Express, The. Spender.
Express Trains. Macknight Black.
From a Railway Carriage. R. L. Stevenson.
From the Train. Marjorie Wilson.
I like to see it lap the miles. Emily Dickinson.
In the Train. Bax.
Iron Horse, The. Israel Newman.
Journey, *sel.* ("Oh the wild engine! Every time I sit"). Monro.
Landscape as Metal and Flowers. W. T. Scott.
Limited. Sandburg.
Modern Dragon. A. R. B. Bennett.
Morning Express. Sassoon.
Night Express. MacKnight Black.
Night Express, The. Monkhouse.
Night-Ride, The. Slessor.
Night Train. Hagiwara, *tr. fr. Japanese by* Ninomiya *and* Enright.
Railroad Cars Are Coming, The. *Unknown.*
Rhyme of the Rail. Saxe.
Rush Hour, The. Kitagawa, *tr. fr. Japanese by* Ninomiya *and* Enright.
Shunting. Dowling.
Snow at Midnight; the Elevated. F. M. Clapp.
Song of the Train. McCord.
To a Locomotive in Winter. Whitman.
Train, The. M. E. Coleridge.
Train in the Night, The. Riddell.
Train Will Fight to the Pass, The. Pitter.
Train Window. Robert Finch.
Trains. Tippett.
Trains at Night. Frances Frost.
Travel. Millay.
Ways of Trains, The. Coatsworth.
TRAMPS. *See* VAGABONDS.
TRANSCENDENTALISM. Transcendentalism; a Poem in Twelve Books. Robert Browning.
TRANSVAAL, SOUTH AFRICA. Lichtenberg. Kipling.
TRAUBEL, HELEN. I Like to Sing Also. Updike.
TRAVEL
Advice against Travel. Mangan.
End of Travel, An. R. L. Stevenson.
Flight, The. *Fr.* A Time to Dance. Day Lewis.
I am compelled to make the long trip to classic Athens. Propertius, *tr. fr. Latin by* Fletcher.
Journey, The. Winters.
Missouri Traveller Writes Home, A, 1830. Bly.
Naughty Boy, The. Keats.
On First Looking into a Circular for a Student's Around-the-World-Cruise. "B. A. D."
On the Advantages of Travel. *Unknown.*
On the Move. Thom Gunn.
Over 2000 Illustrations and a Complete Concordance. Elizabeth Bishop.
Sailing Homeward. Chan Fang-sheng, *tr. fr. Chinese by* Waley.
St. Gervais. Michael Roberts.
Song of the Open Road. Whitman.
Song of the Road, A. R. L. Stevenson.
Starting from Paumanok. Whitman.
There Are So Many Ways of Going Places. Leslie Thompson.
To a Poet Who Has Never Travelled. Causley.
To Sir Henry Goodyere. Donne.
Travel. Millay.
Travel. R. L. Stevenson.
Travelers' Song. Hofmannsthal, *tr. fr. German by* Hamburger.
Traveller's Tale, A. Plomer.
Travelling. Gradon.
Travelling. Thoreau.
Travels. W. W. Gibson.
Two Travelers. Day Lewis.
TREASON. Of Treason. Harington.
TREE TOADS
Tree-Toad. Hilda Conkling.
Tree-Toad, The. Johns.
Tree Toad, The. Monica Shannon.
TREES
A B C's in Green. Speyer.
Above the Battle. Van Doren.
Ancient Tree, The. Seiffert.
Autumn Fashions. E. M. Thomas.
Autumnal Spring Song. Vassar Miller.
Ballad of Trees and the Master, A. Lanier.
Be Different [*or* Deferent] to Trees. M. C. Davies.
Brooms. Aldis.
Bushfeller, The. Duggan.
Child's Song in Spring. Edith Nesbit.
City Tree, The. I. V. Crawford.
City Trees. Millay.
City Trees. Scruggs.
Coming of the Trees, The. Guiterman.
Cross and the Tree, The. Stidger.
Cut It Down. M. E. Coleridge.
Definitions for a Tree. A. B. Payne.
Detail. Bethell.
Evergreens. E. C. Pinkney.
Every time I climb a tree. McCord.
For the Slender Beech and the Sapling Oak. *Fr.* Maid Marian. Peacock.
Forest Song. Venable.
Forest Trees, The. Eliza Cook.
Good Company. K. W. Baker.
Green Councillors. H. M. Corning.
Heart of the Tree, The. Bunner.
Heresy for a Class Room. Rolfe Humphries.
Hill-Side Tree. Bodenheim.
House of the Trees, The. Wetherald.
I Planted Little Trees To-Day. Carrington.
Iced Branches. Alling.
In a Wood. *Fr.* The Woodlanders. Hardy.
Jungle Trees, The. Marjorie Wilson.
Leafless Tree, A. A. L. Thompson.
Legends for Trees. Ketchum.
Long Road Blossoms, The. Marshak, *tr. fr. Russian by* Lindsay.
Motto for a Tree-planting. R. W. Gilder.
Mountain Tree, The. Hugh Connell.
O Brother Tree. Michelson.
O Dreamy, Gloomy, Friendly Trees. Herbert Trench.
Oak and the Beech, The. Peacock.
Old Mansion, The, *sel.* ("Aye, master! fine old trees"). Southey.
Paradigm. Deutsch.
Plant a Tree. Larcom.
Planting a Tree. N. B. Turner.
Proud Trees, The. W. H. Kerr.
Pruned Trees. Goddard.
Pruning Trees. Po Chü-i, *tr. fr. Chinese by* Waley.
Reflection. Allonby.
Roots. Louis Ginsberg.
Salute to Trees, A. Van Dyke.
Song of the Forest Trees. *Unknown, tr. fr. Middle Irish by* O'Grady.
Song of the Trees. Colborne-Veel.
Song of the Wood, The. Weatherly.
Song to a Tree. Markham.
Sound of Going in the Tops of the Mulberry Trees, A. Bellamann.
Sound of the Trees, The. Robert Frost.
Strange Tree. E. M. Roberts.
Tall Trees. E. D. Kramer.
Tapestry Trees. William Morris.

Three Green Trees. Angela Morgan.
Three Trees. C. H. Crandall.
Three Trees. Christopher Morley.
Timber Line Trees. Holme.
To a Tree in Bloom. Flanner.
To the Wayfarer. *Unknown.*
Tree, The. Björnson, *tr. fr. Norwegian.*
Tree, The. Ehrenburg, *tr. fr. Russian by* Deutsch.
Tree, The. Kreymborg.
Tree, The. Masefield.
Tree, A. C. G. Rossetti.
Tree, The. Very.
Tree, The. Pat Wilson.
Tree, The. Countess of Winchilsea.
Tree and Sky. Sassoon.
Tree at Dusk, A. Winifred Welles.
Tree at My Window. Robert Frost.
Tree Birthdays. M. C. Davies.
Tree Design, A. Bontemps.
Tree Feelings. C. P. Gilman.
Tree in the Desert, The. Hebbel, *tr. fr. German by* Herman Salinger *and* Marion Salinger.
Tree on the Hill. *Unknown.*
Tree-planting. S. F. Smith.
Tree Planting. *Unknown.*
Tree Shadows. *Unknown, tr. fr. Japanese.*
Tree Stands Very Straight and Still, The. Annette Wynne.
Trees. Behn.
Trees. Carman.
Trees. T. C. Clark.
Trees, The. S. V. Cole.
Trees. Sara Coleridge.
Trees. De la Mare.
Trees. Gumilev, *tr. fr. Russian by* Hornstein.
Trees. Kilmer.
Trees, The. Larcom.
Trees, *sel.* ("There are some men, of course, some men, I know"). Monro.
Trees, The. Christopher Morley.
Trees and Fairies. Fyleman.
Trees Are Down, The. Mew.
Trees' Choice, The. G. B. Carter.
Trees in the Garden. D. H. Lawrence.
Trees That Shade a House. Katharine Worth.
Trees, Who Are Distant. Warr.
Twilight of the Wood. Léonie Adams.
Very Tree. Kunitz.
What Do We Plant? Abbey.
Winter Night. Collister Hutchison.
Winter Trees. W. C. Williams.
Wood-Lot Hill. Frances Frost.
Wood Music. Ethel King.
Wood to Burn and Not to Burn. *Unknown, tr. fr. Old Irish by* O'Grady.
Woodman, Spare That Tree. G. P. Morris.
Year In, Year Out. Kathleen Millay.
Arbor Day (*Our American Holidays Series*) (ADAH). Robert Haven Schauffler, ed.

TRELAWNY, EDWARD JOHN. Trelawny Lies by Shelley. C. L. O'Donnell.

TRELAWNY, SIR JONATHAN. Song of the Western Men, The. Hawker.

TRENTON, BATTLE OF
Battle of Trenton, The. *Unknown.*
Trenton and Princeton. *Unknown.*

TRILLIUM. Red Trillium. "John Crichton."

TRINIDAD, BRITISH WEST INDIES. Trinidad Market. Carvalho, *tr. fr. Portuguese by* Poore.

TRINITY, THE. Trinity, The. *Unknown.*

TRISTAN DA CUNHA (islands). Tristan da Cunha. Roy Campbell.

TRISTRAM
Tristram and Iseult. Matthew Arnold.
Tristram of Lyonnesse, *sels.* Swinburne.
Tristram's End. Binyon.

TROILUS AND CRESSIDA
Comparison of His Love with the Faithful and Painful Love of Troilus to Cressid, A. *Unknown.*
Cressid's Complaint. Whetstone.
Troilus and Cressida. De Vere.
Troilus and Cressida, *sels.* Dryden.
Troilus and Cressida, *sels.* Shakespeare.
Troilus and Criseyde, *sels.* Chaucer.

TROJAN WAR
Fall of Troy, The. *Fr.* The Aeneid. Virgil, *tr. fr. Latin by* Williams.
Iliad, The, *sels.* Homer, *tr. fr. Greek.*
Laodamia, *sel.* ("At dawn they launched the ships; and all went well"). A. A. Brown.
Leaving Troy. T. C. Irwin.
Menelaus and Helen. Rupert Brooke.
Prayer of Calcas, The. *Fr.* Troelus a Chresyd. *Unknown, tr. fr. Welsh by* Williams.
War. Patric Dickinson.

TRONDHEIM, NORWAY. Cathedral in Trondheim, The. Thorarensen, *tr. fr. Icelandic by* Kirkconnell.

TROPICS
Tropical Town. Selva.
Tropics, The. Sladen.

TROUT
Heritage. A. M. Sullivan.
Sanctuary, The. Nemerov.

TROY
Ilion, Ilion. Tennyson.
Palladium. Matthew Arnold.
Troy. *Fr.* Trojan Women. Euripides, *tr. fr. Greek.*
Troy. Robin Flower.
Troy. *Fr.* A Mirror for Magistrates. Sackville.

TRUCKS
Country Trucks. Shannon.
Grumbling Truck, The. R. B. Bennett.
Trucks. Tippett.

TRUTH, SOJOURNER (*originally* Isabella Van Wagener). Oriflamme. Fauset.

TRUTH
Clues. Leitch.
Faustus. *Fr.* Horatio. Plutzik.
I died for beauty. Emily Dickinson.
Invocation: "Truth, be more precious to me than the eyes." Max Eastman.
Lie, The. Ralegh.
Ostler, The. *Fr.* Horatio. Plutzik.
Search for Truth, The. Boethius, *tr. fr. Latin by* Lindsay.
Simple Faith. *Fr.* Truth. Cowper.
Tell all the truth but tell it slant. Emily Dickinson.
To James Warre. *Fr.* Hymenaei. Jonson.
Truth. "Æ."
Truth, The. Lampman.
Truth. C. F. Lloyd.
Truth. Masefield.
Truth. J. N. North.
Truth, The? J. C. Powys.
Truth Crushed to Earth. *Fr.* The Battlefield. Bryant.
Truth Never Dies. *Unknown.*
Ultima Veritas. Gladden.
Wayfarer, The. *Fr.* War Is Kind. Stephen Crane.
"With Whom Is No Variableness, neither Shadow of Turning." Clough.
Winter Lightning, The. Nemerov.

TRUXTON, THOMAS. Truxton's Victory. *Unknown.*

TSAI YUAN-PEI. Many, without discrimination, mention your name. Feng Chih, *tr. fr. Chinese by* Chu K'an.

TU FU. For Tu Fu. Feng Chih, *tr. fr. Chinese by* Chu K'an.

TUBEROSE. Tuberose. L. J. Block.

TUBMAN, HARRIET. Harriet Tubman. Margaret Walker.

TUILERIES, PARIS. Le Jardin des Tuileries. Oscar Wilde.

TULIP TREES. Tulip Tree. Sacheverell Sitwell.

TULIPS
Sleepy Tulips, The. M. M. Walker.
Stately Lady, The. Sandstrom.
Tulip Garden, A. Amy Lowell.
Tulip Queens. H. M. Hooke.
Tulips. Colum.
Tulips. M. B. Houston.

TURBERVILLE, GEORGE. Epitaph in Commendation of George Turberville, a Learned Gentleman, An. Harington.

TURKEYS
Black November Turkey, A. Wilbur.
Melancholy Lay, A. Marjorie Fleming.
Three Turkeys. Marjorie Fleming.

TURNIPS. Mr. Finney's Turnip. *Unknown.*

TURPIN, RICHARD (Dick Turpin)
Dick Turpin and the Lawyer. *Unknown.*
My Bonny Black Bess. *Unknown.*

TURTLE DOVES. Turtle-Dove's Nests, The. *Unknown, sometimes at. to* Hawkshaw.

TURTLES
Covering the Subject. Armour.
Little Turtle, The. Lindsay.
Turtle, The. Ogden Nash.
Turtle, The. Schevill.
Turtle and Flamingo, The. J. T. Fields.

TUSCANY, ITALY
Festival in Tuscany. W. F. Stead.
In Tuscany. Eric Mackay.
Tuscany. Sackville-West.

TUSKEGEE INSTITUTE. Tuskegee. L. P. Hill.

"TWAIN, MARK" (Samuel Langhorne Clemens). Mark Twain; a Pipe Dream. Herford.

TWEED (river), SCOTLAND *and* ENGLAND
April on Tweed. Lang.
Twilight on Tweed. Lang.

TWELFTH NIGHT
Epiphany. Heber.
Here We Come a-Whistling. *Unknown.*
Twelfth Night. J. P. Bishop.
Twelfth Night. Philip Booth.

TWELFTH NIGHT (*continued*)
Twelfth Night. Elinor Wylie.
Twelfth Night Carol. *Unknown.*
Twelfth Night Song. Sennett.
Twelve Days of Christmas, The. *Unknown.*
TWICKENHAM, ENGLAND
Twickenham Ferry. Marzials.
Twickenham Grotto. Robin Skelton.
Written at Mr. Pope's House at Twickenham. George Lyttelton.
TWILIGHT
Approach of Evening. Croly.
As Soon as Ever Twilight Comes. De la Mare.
Children's Hour, The. Longfellow.
In the Twilight, *sel.* ("I row in my boat in the twilight, half-purple, half-grey, overhead"). J. F. O'Donnell.
Twilight. Ch'en Yün, *tr. fr. Chinese by* Hart.
Twilight. Custance.
Twilight. Tyutchev, *tr. fr. Russian by* Deutsch *and* Yarmolinsky.
Winter Twilight, A. Arlo Bates.
Winter Twilight. G. T. Elliot.
TWINS. Twins, The. H. S. Leigh.
TYBURN GALLOWS, LONDON. Tyburn and Westminster. John Heywood.
TYLER, WAT. Wat Tyler, *sel.* ("When Adam delved and Eve span"). Southey.
TYNDALE, WILLIAM. From William Tyndale to John Frith. Edgar Bowers.
TYRANNY
Antiquity of Freedom, The. Bryant.
England in 1819. Shelley.
Song to the Men of England. Shelley.
TYRCONNEL, RICHARD TALBOT DUKE AND EARL OF. Lilliburlero. Thomas, Lord Wharton.
TYRE. Tyre. Bayard Taylor.
TYRINGHAM, MASSACHUSETTS. Evening in Tyringham Valley. R. W. Gilder.

U

UCCELLO, PAOLO. Uccello. Corso.
ULYSSES
Canto I: "And then went down to the ship." Pound.
Haunted Odysseus; the Last Testament. Horace Gregory.
Homecoming, The. Baxter.
Odysseus Dying. Wingfield.
Odyssey, The, *sels.* Homer, *tr. fr. Greek.*
Odyssey, The. Lang.
Old Ships, The. Flecker.
Return, The. Muir.
Ulysses. Robert Graves.
Ulysses, *sel.* Stephen Phillips.
Ulysses. Tennyson.
Ulysses and the Siren. Samuel Daniel.
Ulysses in Autumn. Auslander.
Ulysses Returns. R. M. Montgomery.
UMBRELLAS. Umbrellas. R. B. Bennett.
UMBRIA, ITALY. Come Up to Umbria. Charles Phillips.
UNDERHILL, JOHN. John Underhill. Whittier.
UNEMPLOYMENT
Come Live with Me and Be My Love. Day Lewis.
Hymn of the Unemployed. Tiplady.
Laid off. Francis Webb.
Prayer of an Unemployed Man. Ackerly.
Prayer of the Unemployed. *Unknown.*
Unemployed, The. LeVan Roberts.
UNICORNS
Inhuman Henry. A. E. Housman.
Unicorn, The. *Fr.* Nepenthe. Darley.
Unicorn, The. Philippe de Thaon, *tr. fr. French by* Beaumont.
Unicorn, The. Pitter.
Unicorn, The. Ella Young.
Unicorn and the Hippogrif, The. Ostenso.
UNION OF SOUTH AFRICA. *See* SOUTH AFRICA, UNION OF.
UNION OF SOVIET SOCIALIST REPUBLICS
November 7; Ode to a Day of Victories. "Pablo Neruda," *tr. fr. Spanish by* Fitts.
Song to the Soviet Union. Crespo, *tr. fr. Spanish by* Lee.
See also RUSSIA.
UNIONS, LABOR. My Master and I. *Unknown.*
UNITED STATES
Ad Patriam. Scollard.
America. D. C. Babcock.
America. *Fr.* The Torchbearers. Arlo Bates.
America. *Fr.* John Brown's Body. S. V. Benét.
America. Coates.
America. Dobell.
America. Kreymborg.
America. McKay.
America. S. F. Smith.
America. *Fr.* National Ode . . . at the Celebration . . . July 4, 1876. Bayard Taylor.
America First. Oldham.
America for Me. Van Dyke.
America Greets an Alien. *Unknown.*
America Is Corn. Coffin.
America, my country, can the mind. *Fr.* Journals. Emerson.
America the Beautiful. Bates.
America to Great Britain. Allston.
America Was Promises. MacLeish.
America Was Schoolmasters. Coffin.
American Feuillage. Whitman.
American Freedom, The. Biller.
American Letter. MacLeish.
American Names. S. V. Benét.
America's Answer. Lilliard.
America's Prosperity. Van Dyke.
Ancestral Dwellings, The. Van Dyke.
And thou America,/ thy offspring towering e'er so high. *Fr.* Song of the Exposition. Whitman.
Approaching America. Squire.
Axe Has Cut the Forest Down, The. Coatsworth.
Background with Revolutionaries. MacLeish.
Building of the Ship, The. Longfellow.
By Blue Ontario's Shore, *sels.* Whitman.
Centennial Hymn. John Pierpont.
Columbia. Timothy Dwight.
Eagle's Song, The. Richard Mansfield.
Elegy on the Times. Trumbull.
Empire Builders. MacLeish.
England and America in 1782. Tennyson.
For thou art founded in the eternal fact. *Fr.* My Country. Woodberry.
Free America. *At. to* Joseph Warren.
From Paumanok Starting I Fly like a Bird. Whitman.
Gift Outright, The. Robert Frost.
Great Land, The. W. R. Benét.
History of the U.S., The. W. S. Stoner.
Howl. Allen Ginsberg.
Hymn of the New World. Percy MacKaye.
I Hear America Singing. Whitman.
I, Too. Langston Hughes.
In the States. R. L. Stevenson.
Invocation: "American muse, whose strong and diverse heart." *Fr.* John Brown's Body. S. V. Benét.
Land of Destiny. Parmenter.
Land of the Free. Hosking.
Land of the Free. MacLeish.
Land Where Hate Should Die, The. D. A. McCarthy.
Last Whiskey Cup, The. Paul Engle.
Let America Be America Again. Langston Hughes.
Localities. Sandburg.
Long, Too Long America. Whitman.
Map of My Country. John Holmes.
Men. MacLeish.
My America. T. C. Clark.
My Country. G. E. Woodberry.
My Country, Right. T. C. Clark.
My Land. T. O. Davis.
My Land. Oppenheim.
New Colossus, The. Lazarus.
Next to of Course God. E. E. Cummings.
Now Where to? Heine, *tr. fr. German by* Gruenthal.
O Beautiful, My Country. Hosmer.
O Mother of a Mighty Race. Bryant.
Ode Inscribed to W. H. Channing. Emerson.
On an Invitation to the United States. Hardy.
On the Emigration to America. Freneau.
On the Prospect of Planting Arts and Learning in America. Berkeley.
One Country. F. L. Stanton.
Our Country. J. W. Howe.
Our Country. A. L. Strong.
Our Country's Call. Bryant.
Our Nation Forever. Wallace Bruce.
Over the Carnage Rose Prophetic a Voice. Whitman.
Passage to India. Whitman.
People's Prayer, The. A. R. Wells.
Prairie-Grass Dividing, The. Whitman.
Prairies, The. Bryant.
Quilt. Updike.
Race of Veterans. Whitman.
Refugee in America. Langston Hughes.
Santa-Fé Trail, The. Vachel Lindsay.
Shine, Perishing Republic. Jeffers.
Ship of State, The. *Fr.* The Building of the Ship. Longfellow.
Sleep, My Child. Sholom Aleichem, *tr. fr. Yiddish by* Brody.

Song for the States, A. Whitman.
Song of the Universal. Whitman.
Starting from Paumanok. Whitman.
Sweet Land. Maguire.
There Is a Land. James Montgomery.
This Is America. T. C. Clark.
To America. Alfred Austin.
To America. R. Garnett.
To Cole, the Painter, Departing for Europe. Bryant.
To My Countrymen. R. U. Johnson.
To the East and to the West. Whitman.
To the United States of America. Robert Bridges.
Toast to Our Native Land, A. Robert Bridges ("Droch").
Travelling America. "Jan Struther."
Triumph America! Thomas Burke.
USA. Engle.
Under the Stars. Wallace Rice.
Union and Liberty. O. W. Holmes.
United States. Keble.
Verses on the Prospect of Planting Arts and Learning in America. Berkeley.
Watch, America. Nathan.
What America Means to Me. L. E. Thomas.
Flag Day (*Our American Holidays Series*) (FOAH). Robert Haven Schauffler, ed.
Great Americans, as Seen by the Poets (GA). Burton Egbert Stevenson, ed.
My Country (MC). Burton Egbert Stevenson, ed.
Patriotic Anthology, The (PaA). Introduced by Carl Van Doren.
Poems of American History (PAH). Burton Egbert Stevenson, ed.
Poems of American Patriotism (PAP). Brander Matthews, ed.
UNITED STATES (ship)
United States and *Macedonian,* The ("The Banner of Freedom high floated unfurled"). *Unknown.*
United States and *Macedonian,* The ("How glows each patriot bosom that boasts a Yankee heart"). *Unknown.*
UNITED STATES AIR FORCE. U. S. Air Force, The. Robert Crawford.
UNITED STATES MARINE CORPS. Marines' Hymn, The. *Unknown.*
UNKNOWN SOLDIER
Epitaph for the Unknown Soldier. Kohn.
Passing of the Unknown Soldier, The. V. S. Owens.
Unknown, The. Laughlin.
Unknown Soldier. A. B. Dunn.
Unknown Soldier, The. Virginia Eaton.
Unknown Soldier, The. Rhinow.
Unknown Soldier, The. Billy Rose.
UNWIN, MARY. To Mary Unwin. Cowper.
UPSON, ARTHUR. Ave atque Vale. T. S. Jones, Jr.
URANIA (mythology)
Urania. Matthew Arnold.
Urania. De Vere.
Urania. Pitter.
URIEL. Uriel. Percy MacKaye.
URSA MAJOR. Ursa Major. Kirkup.
USK, ENGLAND. Landscapes. T. S. Eliot.
USURY. Ditty of the Pen Inveighing against Usury and False Dealing, A. John Hall.
UTAH. Utah, We Love Thee. Evan Stephens.
UTE INDIANS
Chipeta. Eugene Field.
Chipeta's Ride. J. W. Taylor.
Legend of Grand Lake, The. Westcott.
Red Ghosts Chant, The. L. W. Spencer.
UTOPIA
Eruption in Utopia. Taggard.
Rumors from an Aeolian Harp. Thoreau.

V

VACATION
After Vacation. *Unknown.*
Far from the Madding Crowd. Nixon Waterman.
School Is Out. Frances Frost.
Thy Blessing, Lord, on All Vacation Days! M. A. Haley.
Vacation Time. Rowena Bennett.
Vacation Time. M. E. Sangster.
VAGABONDS
Amber Lands. Tom MacInnes.
Beloved Vagabond, The. Tinckom-Fernandez.
In Praise of a Beggar's Life. "A. W."
Mendicants, The. Carman.
Needle Travel. M. F. Patton.
Sestina of the Tramp-Royal. Kipling.
To a Vagabond. Woodrow.
Tramp. Richard Hughes.
Traveller, The. C. F. Smith.
Vagabond, The. Guest.
Vagabond, The. R. L. Stevenson.
Vagabond at Home, The. Kauffman.
Vagabond House. Blanding.
Vagabondia. Hovey.
Vagabonds. Birchall.
Vagabonds, The. E. P. Johnson.
Vagabonds, The. J. A. Macy.
Vagabonds, The. J. T. Trowbridge.
Vagrant, The. Ransom.
Vagrant, The. Slender.
VALENTINE'S DAY
Anonymous Valentine, The. Nesbit.
Ditty, A: "My true-love hath my heart, and I have his." Sidney.
Hail, Bishop Valentine. *Fr.* An Epithalamion. Donne.
Hearts Were Made to Give Away. Annette Wynne.
My Valentine. M. C. Parsons.
Romance. R. L. Stevenson.
St. Valentine's Day. *Fr.* The Love Sonnets of Proteus. W. S. Blunt.
St. Valentine's Day. T. H. Hill.
Saint Valentines Day. T. W. Parsons.
Saint Valentine's Day. Patmore.
Sonnet: "Go, Valentine, and tell that lovely Maid." Southey.
Special Delivery. Winton.
Sure Sign, A. N. B. Turner.
To Clarastella on St. Valentines Day Morning. Robert Heath.
To His Valentine. Drayton.
To St. Valentine. J. B. Hartswick.
To-morrow Is Saint Valentine's Day. *Fr.* Hamlet. Shakespeare.
Valentine, A. Betham-Edwards.
Valentine. Blanden.
Valentine. Blodgett.
Valentine. "C. W. T."
Valentine, A. Eugene Field.
Valentine, A. Eleanor Hammond.
Valentine, A. L. E. Richards.
Valentine. E. M. Thomas.
Valentine for My Mother. Harry Lee.
Valentine to a Little Girl. Cardinal Newman.
Valentine to One's Wife. John Erskine.
Valentine Verses. T. N. Page.
Valentine's Day. Aileen Fisher.
Valentine's Message, The. M. J. Hill.
Valentines to My Mother. C. G. Rossetti.
When You Send a Valentine. M. J. Hill.
VALKYRIES
Death Song of Haakon the Good. Eyvindr Finsson, *tr. fr. Old Norse by* Oliver.
Song of the Norns, The. *Unknown, tr. fr. Old Norse by* Hollander.
Three Valkyries, The. Ewald, *tr. fr. Danish by* Stork.
VALPARAISO, BATTLE OF. Battle of Valparaiso, The. *Unknown.*
VAN (lake), TURKEY. Lake of Van, The. Raffi, *tr. fr. Armenian by* Green.
VAN DIEMEN'S LAND. *See* TASMANIA.
VANBRUGH, SIR JOHN. Epitaph On Sir John Vanbrugh. Abel Evans.
VANCOUVER, BRITISH COLUMBIA. Vancouver Lights. Birney.
VANE, SIR HENRY. To Sir Henry Vane the Younger. Milton.
VARUNA (ship). *Varuna,* The. G. H. Boker.
VASES
Japanese Vase Wrought in Metal, A. Seiffert.
V-a-s-e, The. Roche.
VAUDEVILLE. Vaudeville Dancer. Wheelock.
VAUGHAN, HENRY
At the Grave of Henry Vaughan. Sassoon.
Henry Vaughan. T. S. Jones, Jr.
VEERIES
Veery, The. Van Dyke.
Veery-Thrush, The. J. R. Taylor.
VEGA, GARCILASO DE LA. *See* GARCILASO DE LA VEGA.
VEGETABLES. Vegetables. Farjeon.
VEGETARIANS
Logical Vegetarian, The. Chesterton.
Pike, The. Morgenstern, *tr. fr. German by* Hull.
VELÁZQUEZ, DIEGO RODRÍGUEZ DE SILVA Y. Castilian. Elinor Wylie.
VELD
Nocturne: "Red flame flowers bloom and die." Garstin.
Veld Eclogue, A; the Pioneers, *sel.* ("But 'nameless somethings' and 'unbounded spaces' "). Roy Campbell.
VENDÉMIAIRE. Vendémiaire. Apollinaire, *tr. fr. French by* Fitts.
VENICE, ITALY
Academy at Venice, The. Clough.
Doves of Venice, The. Laurence Hutton.

VENICE, ITALY (*continued*)
Fireworks at the Redentore. Lyle.
For "A Venetian Pastoral" by Giorgione. *Fr.* Sonnets on Pictures. D. G. Rossetti.
Lines Written among the Euganean Hills. Shelley.
Night Litany. Pound.
Ode on Venice. Byron.
On the Extinction of the Venetian Republic. Wordsworth.
Toccata of Galuppi's, A. Robert Browning.
Venetian Night, A. Hofmannsthal, *tr. fr. German by* Lewisohn.
Venetian Serenade, The. Milnes.
Venetian Sonnets. Platen, *tr. fr. German by* Morgan.
Venice. Longfellow.
Venice. Symonds.
Venice Preserved, *sels.* Otway.
Water-Colour of Venice, A. Durrell.
VENUS (goddess)
Address to Venus. *Fr.* De Rerum Natura *and fr.* The Fairie Queene. Lucretius, *tr. fr. Latin by* Spenser.
Birth of Venus, The. *Unknown.*
First Dream, *sel.* ("But Venus first"). Sister Juana Inés de la Cruz, *tr. fr. Spanish by* Beckett.
Laus Veneris. Swinburne.
Queen of Paphos, Erycine, The. *Unknown.*
Shepherd's Song of Venus and Adonis, The. Constable.
Song of Venus. *Fr.* King Arthur. Dryden.
To Venus. Horace, *tr. fr. Latin by* Jonson.
Venus and Adonis. *Fr.* Britannia's Pastorals. William Browne.
Venus and Adonis. Shakespeare.
Venus Verticordia. D. G. Rossetti.
See also APHRODITE.
VENUS (planet)
Evening Sky, The. John Freeman.
Morning Star, The. Emily Brontë.
Ode to the Evening Star. Akenside.
Venus Shines Out. *Fr.* The Seasons. James Thomson.
VERCHÈRES, MARIE MADELEINE JARRET DE. Madeleine Verchères. W. H. Drummond.
VERGIL. *See* VIRGIL.
VERLAINE, PAUL
Preludes for Memnon, LVI: "Rimbaud and Verlaine, precious pair of poets." Aiken.
Tomb [of Paul Verlaine]. Mallarmé, *tr. fr. French by* Flores.
Verlaine. E. A. Robinson.
VERMEER, JAN. Lacemaker, The (Vermeer). Anne Marx.
VERMONT
Hail, Vermont! J. H. Perry.
Vermont. Cleghorn.
Vermont; Indian Summer. Philip Booth.
VERONA, ITALY. Map of Verona, A. Henry Reed.
VERONESE, PAOLO. Paul Veronese: Three Sonnets. Sir Samuel Ferguson.
VERSAILLES, FRANCE
Versailles. Bradby.
Versailles. S. A. Brooke.
Versailles. A. C. Rich.
VIATICUM. Viaticum. H. S. Gorman.
VICKSBURG CAMPAIGN
Before Vicksburg. Boker.
Running the Batteries. Melville.
Vicksburg (a Ballad). P. H. Hayne.
VICTORIA, QUEEN OF ENGLAND
Mr. Barney Maguire's Account of the Coronation. *Fr.* The Ingoldsby Legends. "Thomas Ingoldsby."
Old Pilot Tunnels under the English Channel, The. Schevill.
Queen Victoria. *Unknown.*
To the Queen ("Revered, beloved—O you that hold"). Tennyson.
VICTORIA FALLS, AFRICA. Victoria Falls, The. Plomer.
VICTORY OF SAMOTHRACE (statue). Winged Victory. Pulsifer.
VIGILANTES
Lay of the Vigilantes, The. *Unknown.*
Vigilantes, The. Ashmun.
VIKINGS
Battle of Maldon, The. *Unknown, tr. fr. Anglo-Saxon.*
Discoverer of the North Cape, The. Longfellow.
Heritage, The. E. B. Reed
O'er the Wild Gannet's Bath. Darley.
Sea-King's Burial, The. Charles Mackay.
Skeleton in Armor, The. Longfellow.
Viking, The. Whitley Stokes.
Viking Terror, The. *Unknown, tr. fr. Old Irish by* Robinson.
Vikings, The. *Unknown.*
VILLIERS DE L'ISLE-ADAM, PHILIPPE AUGUSTE MATHIAS, COMTE DE. Villiers de l'Isle-Adam. Aldous Huxley.
VILLON, FRANÇOIS
Ballad of François Villon, A. Swinburne.
Dispute of the Heart and Body of François Villon, The. Villon, *tr. fr. French by* Swinburne.
Epitaph: "Here lies, in this small chamber." Villon, *tr. fr. French by* Currey.
Villon Strolls at Midnight. Starrett.
Would I Be Shrived? Villon, *tr. fr. French by* Swain.
VILNA, LITHUANIA
Like Groping Fingers. Sutzkever, *tr. fr. Yiddish by* Leftwich.
Secret Town, The, *sel.* ("Remember the sun in the autumn, its rays"). Sutzkever, *tr. fr. Yiddish by* Sonntag.
We Survive! Glick, *tr. fr. Yiddish by* Rubin.
VINEYARDS
Song of the Vineyard Knife. Marot, *tr. fr. French by* Currey.
Vintage. Sackville-West.
VIOLETS
Bay Violets. Sister Maris Stella.
Calling the Violet. Larcom.
How Violets Came Blue. Herrick.
I Spoke to the Violet. Neilson.
On a Faded Violet. Shelley.
September Violet, A. *Unknown.*
She Dwelt among the Untrodden Ways. Wordsworth.
Sonnet: "I had no thought of violets of late." A. D. Nelson.
Sweet Violets, Love's Paradise. *Unknown.*
To a Wood-Violet. Tabb.
To Violets. Herrick.
Violet, The. W. W. Story.
Violet, The. Jane Taylor.
Violet and the Rose, The. Skipsey.
Violet and the Rose, The. A. D. Webster.
Violet under the Snow, The. R. C. Schauffler.
Violets, The. *Fr.* War Is Kind. Stephen Crane.
Violets. Moultrie.
Violets. Josephine O'Conner.
Violets. Ropes.
Violets. *Unknown.*
White Violet. Marian Osborne.
White Violets. B. R. Low.
Wild Violet, The. H. F. Gould.
Yellow Violet, The. Bryant.
VIOLINS
Neighbor, The. Rilke, *tr. fr. German by* Lemont.
Old Amati, The. O. W. Holmes.
Old Violin, The. M. F. Egan.
Violin, The. R. W. Gilder.
Violin Calls, The. Livesay.
Violin's Complaint, The. W. R. Thayer.
VIOLONCELLOS. *See* CELLOS.
VIRGIL
Odes, *sel.* ("Wave-born Queen of the Cyprian foam"). Horace, *tr. fr. Latin by* Noyes.
Sonnet: Death of Virgil, The. Angelo di Costanzo, *tr. fr. Italian by* Wright.
Thinking of a Master. Richard Church.
To Virgil. Tennyson.
Virgil's Tomb. R. C. Rogers.
VIRGIN MARY. *See* MARY, THE VIRGIN.
VIRGINIA
As Toilsome I Wander'd Virginia's Woods. Whitman.
Carry Me Back to Old Virginny. J. A. Bland.
Landscapes. T. S. Eliot.
Life-long, Poor Browning. Anne Spencer.
Massachusetts to Virginia. Whittier.
Newes from Virginia. Richard Rich.
To the Virginian Voyage. Drayton.
Virginia. Vachel Lindsay.
Virginia Britannia. Marianne Moore.
Virginia Capta. M. J. Preston.
Virginiana. Mary Johnston.
Virginians Are Coming Again, The. Vachel Lindsay.
Virginians of the Valley, The. Ticknor.
VISHNU. Gita Govinda, The. Jayadeva, *tr. fr. Sanskrit by* Arnold.
VOGLER, GEORG JOSEPH. Abt Vogler. Robert Browning.
VOLTAIRE
Mock On, Mock On, Voltaire, Rousseau. Blake.
Voltaire and Gibbon. *Fr.* Childe Harold's Pilgrimage. Byron.
Voltaire at Ferney. Auden.
VOORTREKKERS. Voortrekker, The. Kipling.
VOTERS AND VOTING
Ballot, The. John Pierpont.
Poor Voter on Election Day The. Whittier.
VOYAGES
Arrival and Departure. Eglington.
Coming Homeward out of Spain. Googe.
Dedication: "With favoring winds, o'er sunlit seas." *Fr.* Ultima Thule. Longfellow.
Invitation to the Voyage. Baudelaire, *tr. fr. French by* Wilbur.
It Should Be Easy. Van Doren.
Ode to the Virginian Voyage. Drayton.
Passage to India. Whitman.
Pilgrims, The. Delius.
Qua Cursum Ventus. Clough.
Ulysses. Tennyson.

Voyage, The. Baudelaire, *tr. fr. French by* Gibbs.
Voyage, The. Tennyson.
Voyage to Cythera, A. Baudelaire, *tr. fr. French by* Morgan.
Voyages, *sels.* Hart Crane.
Where Lies the Land to Which the Ship Would Go? Clough.
Would I Might Go Far over Sea. O'Shaughnessy, *after* Marie de France.
VOWELS
Genesis of Vowels. Broughton.
Vowels. Rimbaud, *tr. fr. French by* Varèse.
VULCAN
Shield of Achilles, The. *Fr.* The Iliad. Homer, *tr. fr. Greek.*
Song in Making of the Arrows, The. *Fr.* Sapho and Phao. Lyly.
VULTURES
Song of the Vulture, The. Demirjibashian, *tr. fr. Armenian by* Boyajian.
Vultures. Al-Hajjam, *tr. fr. Arabic by* Arberry.

W

WAGNER, RICHARD
Death of Richard Wagner, The. Swinburne.
Wagner. Rupert Brooke.
WAITERS. To a Junior Waiter. A. P. Herbert.
WALDENSES
Hymn of the Waldenses. Bryant.
On the Late Massacre in Piedmont. Milton.
WALES
Bard, The. Thomas Gray.
Days That Have Been. W. H. Davies.
In the Valley of the Elwy. G. M. Hopkins.
Liberty. J. C. Hughes.
Wales. Norman Nicholson.
We Who Were Born. Eiluned Lewis.
English, Scottish, and Welsh Landscape, 1700–c.1860 (EnSW). John Betjeman *and* Geoffrey Taylor, comps.
Modern Welsh Poetry (MoWP). Keidrych Rhys, ed.
Presenting Welsh Poetry (PrWP). Gwyn Williams, ed.
WALKER, WILLIAM. With Walker in Nicaragua, *sels.* Joaquin Miller.
WALL STREET, NEW YORK CITY. Pan in Wall Street. E. C. Stedman.
WALLACE, SIR WILLIAM
Gude Wallace. *Unknown.*
Scotland's Tribute to Wallace. James MacFarlan.
Wallace, The, *sels.* Henry the Minstrel.
WALLFLOWERS
Black Wall-Flower, The. F. A. Kemble.
Place Where Soon, The. Landor.
Wall-Flower, The. Wergeland, *tr. fr. Norwegian by* Gosse.
WALLS
Divisibility. Plutzik.
Mending Wall. Robert Frost.
Old Grey Wall, The. Carman.
Stone Walls. J. M. Lippmann.
Wall, The. A. L. Phelps.
Wall, The. Schneider.
Walls. Cavafy, *tr. fr. Modern Greek by* Dalven.
Walls. Robert Francis.
Walls. Gore-Booth.
Walls. Marjorie Meeker.
WALNUTS
Raking Walnuts in the Rain. Shannon.
Riddle: "I am within as white as snow." *Unknown.*
WALPOLE, ROBERT, 1ST EARL OF ORFORD
Character of Sir Robert Walpole, The. Swift.
Letter to Sir Robert Walpole, A. Fielding.
To the Right Honourable Robert Walpole, Esq. Ambrose Philips.
WALRUSES. Smile of the Walrus, The. Herford.
WALSINGHAM, ENGLAND
As You Came from the Holy Land of Walsingham. *Unknown, sometimes at. to* Sir Walter Ralegh.
Lament for Our Lady's Shrine at Walsingham. *Unknown.*
Lament for the Priory of Walsingham, A, *sel.* ("Bitter was it, Oh to view"). *Unknown.*
WALTON, IZAAK
Ike Walton's Prayer. J. W. Riley.
Izaak Walton to River and Brook. Lee-Hamilton.
To My Dear and Most Worthy Friend, Mr. Isaac Walton. Cotton.
WANDERLUST
Connecticut Road Song. A. H. Branch.
Down on My Luck. Fairburn.
Early One Morning. Edward Thomas.
Far-away. Sigerson.
Feet of the Young Men, The. Kipling.
Long Trail, The. Kipling.
Over the Hills and Far Away. Henley.
Road Song. J. S. Montgomery.
Road Song. Tinckom-Fernandez.
Sea Gypsy, The. Hovey.
Song: "Something calls and whispers, along the city street." *Fr.* The Way of Perfect Love. G. G. King.
Song of the Open Road, A. McQuilland.
Song of the Open Road. Whitman.
Visions. Leamy.
Wander-Lovers, The. Hovey.
Wander Lure, The. Banning.
Wanderers, The. Symons.
Wanderlust. I. C. Mackay.
Wanderlust. Zizzamia.
Wander-Thirst. Gerald Gould.
WAR
A Terre. Wilfred Owen.
Ad. Fearing.
Aftermath. Sassoon.
All, All of a Piece Throughout. *Fr.* The Secular Masque. Dryden.
All Quiet along the Potomac. E. L. Beers.
Alliteration; or, The Siege of Belgrade. *Unknown.*
Amphitryo, *sel.* ("Then the armies came out"). Plautus, *tr. fr. Latin by* Wright.
Angels at Hamburg, The. Jarrell.
Anthem for Doomed Youth. Wilfred Owen.
Apologia pro Poemate Meo. Wilfred Owen.
Apparition of War. *Fr.* The Columbiad. Joel Barlow.
Apparitions. T. C. Clark.
April on the Battlefields. Speyer.
Ares. Ehrenstein, *tr. fr. German by* Deutsch *and* Yarmolinsky.
Arms and the Boy. Wilfred Owen.
Arsenal at Springfield, The. Longfellow.
At the Cenotaph. "Hugh MacDiarmid."
Awakened War God, The. Widdemer.
Ballad of Nails, The. Tikhonov, *tr. fr. Russian by* Lindsay.
Battle. Ch'ü Yüan, *tr. fr. Chinese by* Waley.
Battle of Blenheim, The. Southey.
Battle of Brunanburh, The. *Unknown, tr. fr. Old English.*
Battle of the Summer Islands, The, *sel.* ("Aid me, Bellona, while the dreadful fight"). Edmund Waller.
Battle Sleep. Edith Wharton.
Battle Song. Ebenezer Elliott.
Beach Burial. Slessor.
Beat! Beat! Drums! Whitman.
Before Action. Gellert.
Before Bannockburn. Burns.
Biography. Nedogonov, *tr. fr. Russian by* Lindsay.
Brave Old World. Lambert.
Break of Day in the Trenches. Isaac Rosenberg.
Brother Dog. L. A. Sanchez, *tr. fr. Spanish by* Lee.
But We Shall Bloom. Guri, *tr. fr. Hebrew by* Kuselewitz.
Campaign against Wu, The. Wei Wen-ti, *tr. fr. Chinese by* Waley.
Carol with Variations. Phyllis McGinley.
Carroll's Sword. Dallan MacMore, *tr. fr. Irish by* O'Connor.
Channel Firing. Hardy.
Charing Cross. Cecil Roberts.
Chariots Go Forth to War, The. Tu Fu, *tr. fr. Chinese by* Hart.
Chronicler, The. Bergman.
Combat, The. Thomas Stanley, *after the Greek of* Anacreon.
Company Commander. Apollinaire, *tr. fr. French by* Fitts.
Cornet, The. Rilke, *tr. fr. German by* Fitz Gibbon.
Counter-Attack. Sassoon.
Criminality of War, The. Edward Young.
Cry to Arms, A. Timrod.
David's Lament. *Fr.* Second Samuel, Bible, *O.T.*
Dead Man's Dump. Rosenberg.
Death of the Ball Turret Gunner, The. Jarrell.
Destruction of Sennacherib, The. Byron.
Disabled. Wilfred Owen.
"Disabled"—Armistice Day. Parmenter.
Do not weep, maiden, for war is kind. *Fr.* War Is Kind. Stephen Crane.
Does It Matter. Sassoon.
Dry Loaf. Wallace Stevens.
Dug-out, The. Sassoon.
Dulce et Decorum Est. Wilfred Owen.
Elegies, *sel.* ("What man first forged the terrifying blade?"). Tibullus, *tr. fr. Latin by* Lindsay.
Elegy for a Dead Soldier. Shapiro.
Elegy on Gordon Barber. Derwood.
End of a War, The. Sir Herbert Read.
Epitaph for an American Bomber. Bertram.
Epitaph on an Army of Mercenaries. A. E. Housman.

WAR (*continued*)
Epodes, *sel.* ("Whither, curs'd rabble, do you rush? Why show"). Horace, *tr. fr. Latin by* Lindsay.
Evening Meal in the Twentieth Century. John Holmes.
Exposure. Wilfred Owen.
Extras. Richard Burton.
Fable of the War, A. Nemerov.
Fata Morgana. K. J. Raine.
Fears in Solitude, *sel.* (". . . Oh! my countrymen!"). S. T. Coleridge.
Fife Tune. Manifold.
Fighting South of the Castle. *Unknown, tr. fr. Chinese by* Waley.
Five Souls. Ewer.
Flanders Roses. Tikhonov, *tr. fr. Russian by* Lindsay.
Flight to Australia. Day Lewis.
For the Fallen. Binyon.
Foxhole for the Night, A. John Quinn.
Fruits of War, The. Gascoigne.
Fury of Aerial Bombardment, The. Eberhart.
Futility. Wilfred Owen.
Galway. MacNeice.
Glories of Our Blood and State, The. *Fr.* The Contention of Ajax and Ulysses. Shirley.
Glory of Women, The. Sassoon.
Granada. Svetlov, *tr. fr. Russian by* Lindsay.
Greater Love. Wilfred Owen.
Guitar. Utkin, *tr. fr. Russian by* Lindsay.
Gunner, The. Francis Webb.
Hialmar. Roy Campbell.
Hills. Apollinaire, *tr. fr. French by* Fitts.
Hohenlinden. Thomas Campbell.
Holy Innocents, The. Robert Lowell.
Home in War-Time. Dobell.
Horses, The. Muir.
How Is the Gold Become Dim. *Fr.* Jeremiah, Bible, *O.T.*
How the Women Will Stop War. *Fr.* Lysistrata. Aristophanes, *tr. fr. Greek by* Rogers.
I Hear an Army Charging upon the Land. *Fr.* Chamber Music. Joyce.
I Pass the Night at General Headquarters. Tu Fu, *tr. fr. Chinese by* Rexroth.
I Sing of Olaf. E. E. Cummings.
In Distrust of Merits. Marianne Moore.
In the Trench. Gellert.
In Time of "The Breaking of Nations." Hardy.
In Time of War, *sel.* ("Here war is simple like a monument"). Auden.
Insensibility. Wilfred Owen.
Invocation: "There is no balm on earth." Gilbert Thomas.
It's a Queer Time. Robert Graves.
I've Heard Them Lilting at Loom and Belting. Day Lewis.
I've Searched the Year. Simonov, *tr. fr. Russian by* Lindsay.
Jewish Conscript, The. F. K. Frank.
Jumbled in the Common Box. Auden.
Karl. Charles Spear.
King of Ulster, The. *Unknown, tr. fr. Irish by* O'Connor.
Knee, The. Morgenstern, *tr. fr. German by* Gruenthal.
Korea. Buckley.
Lament: "We who are left, how shall we look again." W. W. Gibson.
Laughers, The. Louis Untermeyer.
Let War's Tempests Cease. Longfellow.
Letter from the Front. Sikelianos, *tr. fr. Modern Greek by* Dalven.
Liberator, The. Wu-ti, *tr. fr. Chinese by* Waley.
Little Cart, The. Ch'en Tzu-lung, *tr. fr. Chinese by* Waley.
Long Was the Road. Tikhonov, *tr. fr. Russian by* Lindsay.
Losses. Jarrell.
Lost Legion, The. Aneirin, *tr. fr. Welsh by* Evans.
Madam Rumour. Wyn Griffith.
Man He Killed, The. Hardy.
March, The. Squire.
Men in Green. David Campbell.
Mental Cases. Wilfred Owen.
Metal Checks, The. Louise Driscoll.
Miles Gloriosus, *sel.* ("See that upon my shield the sheen is brighter"). Plautus, *tr. fr. Latin by* Highet.
Mine Sweepers. Kipling.
Moon Festival. Tu Fu, *tr. fr. Chinese by* Rexroth.
Mud. Richard Church.
Munich Elegy No. 1. George Barker.
Murrough Defeats the Danes, 994. *Unknown, tr. fr. Irish by* O'Connor.
My Friends. Lukonin, *tr. fr. Russian by* Lindsay.
Naming of Parts. *Fr.* Lessons of the War. Henry Reed.
Nationality. Mary Gilmore.
Nature in War-Time. Herbert Palmer.
New Day. Lukonin, *tr. fr. Russian by* Lindsay.
New Mars, The. Coates.
Next Time. Laura Simmons.
Night before and the Night after the Charge, The. Patrick MacGill.
Night Road. R. A. Donaldson.
Nightmare (Written during Apparent Imminence of War). Sir William Watson.
No Man Knows War. Rolfe.
Northern Legion, A. Sir Herbert Read.
Not to Keep. Robert Frost.
Nuns in the Wind. Rukeyser.
Nurse, The. Utkin, *tr. fr. Russian by* Lindsay.
Oh Stay at Home, My Lad. A. E. Housman.
Old Man with the Broken Arm, The. Po Chü-i, *tr. fr. Chinese by* Waley.
Old Poem. *Unknown, tr. fr. Chinese by* Waley.
On Being Asked for a War Poem. Yeats.
On Limited Warfare. *Unknown.*
On the Danger of War. George Meredith.
On the Eve of New Wars. Louis Untermeyer.
On the Eve of War. Dandridge.
One Morning the World Woke Up. Oscar Williams.
Other Side of the Valley, The. *Unknown, tr. fr. Chinese by* Waley.
Our Orders. J. W. Howe.
Out of Our Shame. Rosten.
Pact, The. Noyes.
Parable of the Old Men and the Young. Wilfred Owen.
Perhaps a Prayer. Schevill.
Permanence of the Young Men, The. Soutar.
Peter Ottawa, *sel.* ("Count up the dead"). E. W. Thomson.
Pharsalia, *sel.* ("Wars worse then civil on Thessalian plains"). Lucan, *tr. fr. Latin by* Marlowe.
Poem: "If there be time enough before the slaughter." Wyn Griffith.
Poem: "Progress in the peaceable blue of a sky in summer." G. E. Evans.
Prayer during Battle. Hagedorn.
Prayer for Light. Coblentz.
Prayer for the Age. Broomell.
Prayer from 1936, A. Sassoon.
Prayer of the Peoples, A, *sel.* ("God of us who kill our kind!"). Percy MacKaye.
Prelude: Troops, The. Sassoon.
Pretty Redhead, The. Apollinaire, *tr. fr. French by* Flores.
Prospect. T. C. Clark.
Protest in the Sixth Year of Ch'ien Fu. Ts'ao Sung, *tr. fr. Chinese by* Waley.
Reapers, The. L. M. Watt.
Rearmament. Jeffers.
Rebel, The. Belloc.
Recalling War. Robert Graves.
Red Hills, The. Pao Chao, *tr. fr. Chinese by* Waley.
Regret. Yüan Chi, *tr. fr. Chinese by* Waley.
Rend Your Heart and Not Your Garments. L. A. MacKay.
Return, The. J. P. Bishop.
Revelation. Soutar.
Rondeau in Wartime. Bertram.
Scapegoats. Breed.
Scyros. Shapiro.
Scythians, The. Blok, *tr. fr. Russian by* Lindsay.
Security. Glover.
Sestina; Altaforte. Pound.
Show, The. Wilfred Owen.
Sick Nought, The. Jarrell.
Silent Slain, The. MacLeish.
Silent Testimony. Parmenter.
Silver Jubilee. Wyn Griffith.
Small Soldiers with Drum in Large Landscape. *Fr.* Mexico Is a Foreign Country. R. P. Warren.
Soldier, What Did You See? Blanding.
Song for the New Year. Auden.
Song of the Borderguard, The. Robert Duncan.
Song of the Child, The. Anna Wickham.
Song of the Cossack Girl. Selvinsky, *tr. fr. Russian by* Lindsay.
Song of the Men of Chin-ling. Hsieh T'iao, *tr. fr. Chinese by* Waley.
Songbooks of the War. Sassoon.
Sons of Our Sons, The. Ehrenburg, *tr. fr. Russian by* Deutsch.
Spires of Oxford, The. Letts.
Spring Offensive. Wilfred Owen.
Strange Meeting. Wilfred Owen.
Streak of Blood, A. George, *tr. fr. German by* Closs.
Take Your Gun. Bronowski.
"Tan Ta Ra, Cries Mars . . ." Wagoner.
There Are Children in the Dusk. Warr.
There Will Come Soft Rains. Teasdale.
These Men. Gellert.
This Is War. Le Gallienne.
To God: From the Warring Nations, *sel.* ("We pray for pity, Lord, not justice, we"). Wilmot.
To His Wife. *At. to* General Su Wu, *tr. fr. Chinese by* Waley.
To the Mothers. Toller, *tr. fr. German by* Roberts.
Tomb of Lt. John Learmonth, A.I.F., The. Manifold.
Too-late Born, The. MacLeish.

Triumphal March. T. S. Eliot.
Triumphal Song of the Roman Army. *Fr.* Aurelian. *Unknown, tr. fr. Latin by* Poe.
Two Armies. Spender.
Ultima Ratio Regum. Spender.
Under the Frontier Post. Wang Chang-ling, *tr. fr. Chinese by* Alley.
Unpardonable Sin, The. Vachel Lindsay.
Vale from Carthage. Viereck.
Valley of the Black Pig, The. Yeats.
Vampire, The. Aiken.
Victory. Duggan.
Vision of War, A. *Fr.* Induction to "The Mirror for Magistrates." Sackville.
Voices of Heroes. Horace Gregory.
Volunteer's Reply to the Poet, The. *Fr.* Talking Bronco. Roy Campbell.
Wage-Slaves to the War-Makers. Cheyney.
War. Fullerton.
War. J. C. Hall.
War. Ish-Kishor.
War! J. G. Lawson.
War. Li Po, *tr. fr. Chinese.*
War. E. M. Root.
War. Stringer.
War. Tu Fu, *tr. fr. Chinese by* Hart.
War, The. Very.
War. Hedd Wyn, *tr. fr. Welsh by* Williams.
War Comes. Schneour, *tr. fr. Yiddish by* Leftwich.
War Films, The. Newbolt.
War Is Kind. Stephen Crane.
War Song. *Unknown.*
War-Song of Dinas Vawr, The. *Fr.* The Misfortunes of Elphin. Peacock.
War Song to Englishmen, A. *Fr.* King Edward the Third. Blake.
Ways of War. Lionel Johnson.
We Who Are about to Die. Fey.
We Who Are Left. Whalley.
What Is Truth? *sel.* ("I have been,/ Three separate times, in war"). J. H. Manning.
What to Us, My Heart. Rimbaud, *tr. fr. French by* Varèse.
Which Side Am I Supposed to Be On? Auden.
While We Slept. Wolff.
White Horse, The. Tu Fu, *tr. fr. Chinese by* Alley.
Women at the Corners Stand, The. Louis Golding.
Wound-Dresser, The. Whitman.
Youth. K. L. Bates.
Youth in Arms. Monro.
Armistice Day (*Our American Holidays Series*) (AOAH). A. P. Sanford *and* Robert Haven Schauffler, eds.
Memorial Day (*Our American Holidays Series*) (MDAH). Robert Haven Schauffler, ed.
Soldiers' Verse (SoV). Patric Dickinson, comp.
War and the Poet (WaaP). Richard Eberhart *and* Selden Rodman, eds.
War Poets, The (WaP). Oscar Williams, ed.
See also SOLDIERS; WORLD WAR, FIRST; WORLD WAR, SECOND.
WAR OF 1812
A-Marching to Quebec. *Unknown.*
Battle of Baltimore, The. *Unknown.*
Battle of Bridgewater, The. *Unknown.*
Blue Hen's Chickens, The. Guiterman.
Bower of Peace, The. *Fr.* Ode Written during the War with America, 1814. Southey.
Come All You Bold Canadians. *Unknown.*
Halifax Station. *Unknown.*
Jackson at New Orleans. Wallace Rice.
Ocean-Fight, The. *Unknown.*
On the British Invasion. Freneau.
Perry's Victory. *Unknown.*
Perry's Victory—a Song. *Unknown.*
Perry's Victory on Lake Erie. J. G. Percival.
Reid at Fayal. J. W. Palmer.
To the Defenders of New Orleans. J. R. Drake.
United States and *Macedonian*, The ("The Banner of Freedom high floated unfurled"). *Unknown.*
United States and *Macedonian*, The ("How glows each patriot bosom that boasts a Yankee heart"). *Unknown.*
Yankee Thunders. *Unknown.*
Ye Parliament of England. *Unknown.*
WARBLERS
Maryland Yellow-Throat, The. Van Dyke.
Warblers. Marsden Hartley.
WARD, JOHN. Captain Ward and the Rainbow. *Unknown.*
WARD, WILLIAM GEORGE. Valedictory. Tennyson.
WARNER, WILLIAM. Ad Gulielmum Warner. Weever.
WARREN, JOSEPH
Death of Warren, The. Epes Sargent.
Warren's Address at Bunker Hill. John Pierpont.
WARSAW, POLAND
Pesach Has Come to the Ghetto Again. Heller, *tr. fr. Yiddish by* Rosenfeld.
Warsaw, 27 September, 1939. Minster.
WARTON, JOSEPH. Wartons, The. Blunden.
WARTON, THOMAS, THE YOUNGER
Lines Written in Ridicule of Certain Poems Published in 1777. Samuel Johnson.
Wartons, The. Blunden.
WASHING
Old Ellen Sullivan. Winifred Welles.
Washing. Drinkwater.
WASHINGTON, BOOKER TALIAFERRO
Alabama Earth. Langston Hughes.
Booker Washington Trilogy, The. Vachel Lindsay.
WASHINGTON, GEORGE
André's Request to Washington. N. P. Willis.
At Mount Vernon. T. C. Clark.
At the Tomb of Washington. Scollard.
Boston Common—Three Pictures. O. W. Holmes.
Boy Washington, The. D. B. Thompson.
Cincinnatus of the West, The. *Fr.* Ode to Napoleon Buonaparte. Byron.
Crown Our Washington. Butterworth.
Ever Since. Coatsworth.
Footnote to History. Coatsworth.
George Washington. Rosemary Benét *and* Stephen Vincent Benét.
George Washington ("Only a baby, fair"). *At. to* Eliza Cook.
George Washington. Ingham.
George Washington. F. F. Miller.
George Washington. Tippett.
George Washington ("By broad Potomac's"). *Unknown.*
George Washington ("In seventeen hundred thirty-two"). *Unknown, at. to* M. A. Bryant.
His Excellency General Washington. Phillis Wheatley.
His Task—and Ours. Dorothy Gould.
Inscription at Mount Vernon. *Unknown.*
Leetla Giorgio Washeenton. T. A. Daly.
Man, A. Scollard.
Mount Vernon, the Home of Washington. William Day.
Name of Washington, The. A. G. Field.
Name of Washington, The. G. P. Lathrop.
Occasioned by General Washington's Arrival in Philadelphia, on His Way to His Residence in Virginia. Freneau.
Ode for Washington's Birthday. O. W. Holmes.
Our Washington. Durbin.
Picture People. Rowena Bennett.
Snarlers, The. Guiterman.
Song for a Venison Dinner at Mr. Bunyan's, New York, 1781. Stansbury.
Stanzas: "No tongue can tell, no pen describe." Freneau.
Star in the West, The. Eliza Cook.
Tribute to Washington. *Unknown.*
Twenty-second of February, The. Bryant.
Under the Old Elm, *sels.* J. R. Lowell.
Vow of Washington, The. Whittier.
War and Washington. *Fr.* Cato. Sewall.
Washington. *Fr.* Ode to Napoleon Buonaparte. Byron.
Washington. M. W. Goodman.
Washington. Meyrich.
Washington. *Fr.* Commemoration Ode. Harriet Monroe.
Washington. O'Crowley.
Washington. J. A. Prentice.
Washington. J. J. Roche.
Washington. Schauffler.
Washington. N. B. Turner.
Washington. B. Y. Williams.
Washington. Wingate.
Washington and Lincoln. W. P. Stafford.
Washington, man of mystery. *Unknown.*
Washington's Birthday. Burdick.
Washington's Birthday. Butterworth.
Washington's Birthday. M. E. Sangster.
Washington's Last Birthday. Noyes.
Washington's Statue. Tuckerman.
Washington's Tomb. Ruth Lawrence.
Young Washington. Guiterman.
Washington's Birthday (*Our American Holidays Series*) (WOAH). Robert Haven Schauffler, ed.
WASHINGTON (state). Washington's Song. E. S. Meany.
WASHINGTON, D.C.
Aeneas at Washington. Allen Tate.
City of Monuments. Rukeyser.
Washington Cathedral. Shapiro.
WASHINGTON MONUMENT
Washington Monument, The. A. A. Wiley.
Washington Monument by Night. Sandburg.
Washington's Monument. *Unknown.*
WASHINGTON SQUARE, NEW YORK CITY. Villanelle of Washington Square. W. A. Roberts.
WASP (ship, War of 1812)
Ocean-Fight, The. *Unknown.*
Wasp's Frolic, The. *Unknown.*
WASPS
New Hampshire, February. Eberhart.

WASPS (*continued*)
Queen Wasp, A. De la Mare.
Upon a Wasp Chilled with Cold. Edward Taylor.
Wasp, The. "Fiona Macleod."
WASTWATER, ENGLAND. Written on the Banks of Wastwater during a Calm. "Christopher North."
WATER
Bucyrus. John Holmes.
Like Water down a Slope. Schneour, *tr. fr. Hebrew by* Fein.
Shadows in the Water. Traherne.
Water. Hilda Conkling.
Water. Morgenstern, *tr. fr. German by* Gruenthal.
Water, *sel.* ("There is a stream that flowed before the first beginning"). Raine.
Water-Images. M. E. Osborn.
Water Noises. E. M. Roberts.
Water Song. Ibn Gabirol, *tr. fr. Hebrew by* Abrahams.
Wine and Water. Chesterton.
WATER LILIES
Cherwell Waterlily, The. F. W. Faber.
Dog and the Water-Lily. Cowper.
Water-Lilies. Hemans.
Water-Lilies. Teasdale.
Water Lily. John Farrar.
Water-Lily, The. Robert Nichols.
Waterlily, The. Tabb.
WATER OUZELS
Water-Ousel, The. Mary Webb.
Water Ouzel. Matchett.
Water Ouzel, The. Harriet Monroe.
WATERFALLS
By the Waterfall. Friedrich Adler, *tr. fr. German by* Bithell.
Cataract of Lodore, The. Southey.
Leaping Falls. Kinnell.
Waterfall, The. Jónsson, *tr. fr. Icelandic by* Fjeldsted.
Waterfall, The. F. D. Sherman.
Waterfall, The. Vaughan.
Waterfall and the Eglantine, The. Wordsworth.
WATERFORD, IRELAND. My Blessing Be on Waterford. Letts.
WATERFOWL. To a Waterfowl. Bryant.
WATERLOO, BATTLE OF
Field of Waterloo, The. *Fr.* The Dynasts. Hardy.
Waterloo. *Fr.* Childe Harold's Pilgrimage. Byron.
Waterloo. Sir Aubrey De Vere.
Waterloo. Praed.
WAYNE, ANTHONY
Anthony Wayne. Guiterman.
Wayne at Stony Point. Scollard.
WEALTH
Of the Use of Riches. *Fr.* Moral Essays. Pope.
Rich fools there be whose base and filthy heart. *Fr.* Astrophel and Stella. Sidney.
Rich Man, The. F. P. Adams.
Wealth. *Fr.* The Gulistan. Sadi, *tr. fr. Persian by* Arnold.
WEASELS. Weasel, The. *Unknown.*
WEATHER
As to the Weather. *Unknown.*
August Weather. Tynan.
Final Thoughts on the Weather in England during 1953. Daiches.
Hard Weather. George Meredith.
Hot Weather. Aldis.
Hydrographic Report. Frances Frost.
I love snow and all the forms. Shelley.
Oh, to Be in England Now the Weather's There! *Unknown.*
Song on the Way, The. *Unknown.*
Sun and Wind. Farjeon.
Weather. Bethell.
Weather. Hilda Conkling.
Weather, The. N. B. Turner.
Weather Rule, A. *Unknown.*
Weather Signs. *Unknown.*
Weathers. Hardy.
What the Weather Does. Hendry.
WEAVERS
Weaver, The. W. H. Burleigh.
Weaver, The ("I sat at my loom in silence"). *Unknown.*
Weavers. Heine, *tr. fr. German.*
Weaver's Song, The. *Unknown.*
WEBSTER, DANIEL
At Marshfield. *Fr.* Webster, an Ode. W. C. Wilkinson.
Birthday of Daniel Webster. O. W. Holmes.
Daniel Webster's Horses. Coatsworth.
Ichabod. Whittier.
Voice of Webster, The, *sel.* ("Silence was envious"). R. U. Johnson.
Webster. Epes Sargent.
WEBSTER, JOHN
John Webster. *Fr.* Sonnets on English Dramatic Poets. Swinburne.
Whispers of Immortality. T. S. Eliot.
WEDDINGS. *See* MARRIAGE.
WELLINGTON, ARTHUR WELLESLEY, 1ST DUKE OF
He Said That He Was Not Our Brother. Banim.
Ode on the Death of the Duke of Wellington. Tennyson.
Warden of the Cinque Ports, The. Longfellow.
Wellington. *Fr.* Don Juan. Byron.
Wellington. Disraeli.
WELLS COLLEGE (Aurora, N.Y.). 1904's Sundial at Wells College. Van Dyke.
WELSH, THE
Tragic Guilt. Keidrych Rhys.
Welshmen of Tirawley, The. Sir Samuel Ferguson.
Where Are the Men? "Talhairan," *tr. fr. Welsh by* Oliphant.
WENCESLAUS, SAINT. Good King Wenceslaus. *Unknown, tr. fr. Latin by* Neale.
WEREWOLVES
Were-Wolf. Julian Hawthorne.
Were-Wolves, The. W. W. Campbell.
WERFEL, FRANZ. Shooting of Werfel, The. Vernon Watkins.
WESLEY, JOHN. John Wesley's Rule. John Wesley.
WESSEX, ENGLAND. Wessex Heights. Hardy.
WEST, BENJAMIN. To Benjamin West. Allston.
WEST, RICHARD. On the Death of Mr. Richard West. Thomas Gray.
WEST (United States)
Breakers of Broncos. Sarett.
Coney Island of the Mind, A, *sel.* ("The wounded wilderness of Morris Graves"). Ferlinghetti.
Étude Géographique. Stoddard King.
Hymn of the West. E. C. Stedman.
Long Road West, The. Knibbs.
Man of the Open West, The. A. W. Monroe.
Others May Praise What They Like. Whitman.
Out Where the West Begins. Arthur Chapman.
Prairie Schooner, The. E. E. Dale.
Redhaw Rain. Sandburg.
Road of Midnight Pageants. The. Greer.
Ruin of Bobtail Bend, The. J. B. Adams.
Slabs of the Sunburnt West. Sandburg.
Spanish Johnny. Cather.
Westering. D. V. Kane.
Western Wagons. S. V. Benét.
Westward Ho! Joaquin Miller.
Poems of the Old West (PoOW). Levette J. Davidson, ed.
WEST INDIES. West Indies. The, *sels.* James Montgomery.
WEST POINT, NEW YORK. Benny Havens, Oh! O'Brien.
WEST VIRGINIA. West Virginia Hills, The. Ellen King *and* H. E. Engle.
WEST WIND
Ode to the West Wind. Christmas.
Ode to the West Wind. Shelley.
Spring Wind. N. B. Turner.
To the West Wind. G. F. Cameron.
To the Western Wind. Halevi, *tr. fr. Hebrew by* Solis-Cohen.
To the Western Wind. Herrick.
West Wind, The. Masefield.
WESTMINSTER ABBEY
On First Entering Westminster Abbey. Guiney.
On the Tombs in Westminster Abbey. *At. to* Beaumont, *also to* Basse.
Tennyson. T. H. Huxley.
WHALES AND WHALING
And God Created the Great Whales. *Fr.* Paradise Lost. Milton.
Brand Fire New Whaling Song Right from the Pacific Ocean. *Unknown.*
Cachalot, The. E. J. Pratt.
Coast of Peru, The. *Unknown.*
Father Mapple's Hymn. *Fr.* Moby Dick. Melville.
Greenland Whale Fishery, The. *Unknown.*
Jonah and the Whale. Viola Meynell.
Leviathan. Merwin.
Nantucket Whalers. Daniel Henderson.
Quaker Graveyard in Nantucket, The. Robert Lowell.
Song of the Hatteras Whale, A. *Unknown.*
There She Blows! *Unknown.*
Triumph of the Whale, The. Charles Lamb.
Whale. W. R. Benét.
Whale, The. Erasmus Darwin.
Whale, The. *Fr.* The Progress of the Soul. Donne.
Whale, The ("Now I will fashion the tale of a fish"). *Fr.* Physiologus. *Unknown, tr. fr. Anglo-Saxon by* Kennedy.
Whale, The ("'Tis a hundred years"). *Unknown.*
Whale and the *Essex*, The. A. M. Sullivan.
Whale's Nature, The. *Fr.* The Bestiary. *Unknown.*
WHEAT
Color in the Wheat. Garland.
Spirit of the Wheat, The. E. A. U. Valentine.
Wind-swept Wheat, The. "Madeline Bridges."
WHEELER, JOSEPH
Wheeler at Santiago. J. L. Gordon.
Wheeler's Brigade at Santiago. Wallace Rice.

Whigs (English political party). Absalom and Achitophel, Pt. I. Dryden.
Whippoorwills
Mountain Whippoorwill, The. S. V. Benét.
Southern Whip-Poor-Will, A. Scollard.
Whippoorwill. J. R. Moreland.
Whippoorwill, The. Van Dyke.
Whisky. Rye Whisky. *Unknown.*
Whistler, James Abbott McNeill
To a Portrait of Whistler in the Brooklyn Art Museum. E. R. Cox.
To James McNeill Whistler. Henley.
Whitby, England
Birds of Whitby, The. T. S. Jones, Jr.
Old Parish Church, Whitby, The. Rawnsley.
White, Peregrine. Peregrine White and Virginia Dare. Rosemary *and* S. V. Benét.
White, William Allen. To William Allen White. Ferber.
Whitman, Marcus. Whitman's Ride for Oregon. Butterworth.
Whitman, Walt
Cape Hatteras. *Fr.* The Bridge. Hart Crane.
Fast Ball. Jonathan Williams.
Imitation of Walt Whitman. "Judy."
Imitation of Walt Whitman. J. K. Stephen.
Ode to Walt Whitman. S. V. Benét.
Ode to Walt Whitman. García Lorca, *tr. fr. Spanish by* Spender *and* Gili.
Pact, A. Pound.
Somebody Called Walt Whitman. *Fr.* The New World. Bynner.
Song of Myself. Whitman.
Supermarket in California, A. Allen Ginsberg.
To Walt Whitman. MacInnes.
To Walt Whitman in America. Swinburne.
Walt Whitman. Zona Gale.
Walt Whitman. Honig.
Walt Whitman. H. S. Morris.
Walt Whitman. E. A. Robinson.
Walt Whitman. F. H. Williams.
Whittier, John Greenleaf
Autograph, An. Whittier.
John Greenleaf Whittier. Phoebe Cary.
John Greenleaf Whittier. J. C. Grant.
Mr. Whittier. W. T. Scott.
My Triumph. Whittier.
Three Silences of Molinos, The. Longfellow.
To John G. Whittier. J. R. Lowell.
To John Greenleaf Whittier. W. H. Ward.
White Magic; an Ode. Braithwaite.
Whittier. *Fr.* A Fable for Critics. J. R. Lowell.
Whittier. M. E. Sangster.
Widecombe Fair. Widdecombe [or Widdicombe] Fair. *Unknown.*
Widows and widowers. Fount of Freshness. *Unknown, tr. fr. Spanish by* Bowring.
Wilberforce, William. Sonnet to William Wilberforce, Esq. Cowper.
Wilde, Oscar
Arrest of Oscar Wilde at the Cadogan Hotel, The. Betjeman.
Dead Poet, The. Lord Alfred Douglas.
Oscar Wilde. *At. to* Swinburne.
Oscar Wilde and Aubrey Beardsley. John Waller.
Wildebeests. Wildebeest, The. June Daly.
William II, Emperor of Germany. Kaiser & Co. A. M. Rose.
William I, King of England. *See* William the Conqueror.
William III, King of England (William of Orange). New Song of an Orange, A. *Unknown.*
William IV, King of England. Royal Adventurer, The. Freneau.
William P. Frye (ship). *William P. Frye,* The. J. R. Foster.
William the Conqueror
Ballad of Val-ès-Dunes, The, *sel.* ("The Horse from Cleres and Valery"). Belloc.
Battle of Hastings, *sel.* ("And now Duke William"). Chatterton.
William I—1066. Farjeon.
Williams, Roger
Canonicus and Roger Williams. *Unknown.*
Roger Williams. Butterworth.
Williams, William Carlos
Doctor Bill Williams. Ernest Walsh.
Letter to William Carlos Williams, A. Rexroth.
To William Carlos Williams. Kinnell.
Willow trees
Green Willow, The. *Unknown.*
To the Willow-Tree. Herrick.
Weeping Willow. Aldridge.
Willow, The. De la Mare.
Willow, The. Tu Fu, *tr. fr. Chinese by* Rexroth.
Willow Poem. W. C. Williams.
Willow-Tree, The. Thackeray.
Willows, The. W. P. Eaton.
Willows. Joseph Langland.
Willows in the Snow. Tsuru, *tr. fr. Japanese by* Porter.
Wills. Woman's Will. Saxe.
Wilson, Woodrow
Wilson. Percy MacKaye.
Woodrow Wilson. S. O. Barker.
Woodrow Wilson. K. L. Bates.
Woodrow Wilson. E. P. Davis.
Woodrow Wilson. Gillies.
Woodrow Wilson. R. U. Johnson.
Woodrow Wilson. R. M. Montgomery.
Winchester, Virginia. Sheridan's Ride. T. B. Read.
Winchester Cathedral, England
To a Medieval Workman; Winchester. Margaret Willy.
Winchester. L. P. Johnson.
Wind
Adventurer, The. Moreno Villa, *tr. fr. Spanish by* Turnbull.
Blow, Blow, Thou Winter Wind. *Fr.* As You Like It. Shakespeare.
Blow, Northern Wind. *Unknown.*
Cook County. MacLeish.
Dawn Wind, The. Kipling.
Description of the Properties of Winds at All Times of the Year, A. Tusser.
Evening Wind, The. Bryant.
Four Winds, The. Shane Leslie.
Four Winds, The. Luders.
Four Winds, The. F. D. Sherman.
Four Winds. Teasdale.
Gale. John Holloway.
Gale Warning. Michael Roberts.
Gentle Wind, A. Fu Hsuan, *tr. fr. Chinese by* Waley.
Happy Wind. W. H. Davies.
Hark to the Shouting Wind. Timrod.
I saw the wind to-day. Colum.
Immobile Wind, The. Winters.
Listen! Humbert Wolfe.
Little Wind. Greenaway.
Lubber Breeze. T. S. Moore.
Madness of Winds, The. Lloyd Roberts.
March Winds, The. Houghton.
My Lady Wind. *Unknown.*
Night Wind, The. Eugene Field.
O Wind of the Mountain! Westwood.
O wind, why do you never rest. *Fr.* Sing-Song. C. G. Rossetti.
Ode to the North-East Wind. Kingsley.
Pirate Wind. M. J. Carr.
Prairie Winds. Helena Coleman.
Roaring Frost, The. Alice Meynell.
Sea-Wind, The. Ketchum.
Song: "Bring from the craggy haunts of birch and pine." Todhunter.
Song of Zephyrus and the Spring. *Fr.* Chloridia. Jonson.
Song to the Wind, A. Taliesin, *tr. fr. Welsh by* Graves.
South Wind. Sassoon.
South Wind. Trakl, *tr. fr. German by* Luke.
Stormy Day, *sel.* ("O look how the loops and balloons of bloom"). W. R. Rodgers.
Summer Wind. Bryant.
Summer Winds. Darley.
That Wind, I used to Hear. Emily Brontë.
There came a wind like a bugle. Emily Dickinson.
There Is a Wail in the Wind To-night. Paton.
Three Winds, The. Laurie Lee.
To the Thawing Wind. Robert Frost.
To the Wind. Palacio, *tr. fr. Spanish by* Beckett.
To the Winds. Philip Ayres.
To the Winter Wind. J. G. Fletcher.
Two Winds. Starbuck.
Unknown Wind, The. "Fiona Macleod."
Way of the Wind, The. Swinburne.
We Are the Voices of the Whispering Wind. Sir Edwin Arnold.
What the Winds Bring. E. C. Stedman.
Which Way Does the Wind Blow? Lucy Aikin.
Whichever Way the Wind Doth Blow. C. A. Mason.
Who Has Seen the Wind? C. G. Rossetti.
Wild Winds. Butts.
Wind, The. Farjeon.
Wind. Feeney.
Wind. Galsworthy.
Wind, The. Louis Ginsberg.
Wind, The. Ibn Sa'id of Alcala la Real, *tr. fr. Arabic by* Arberry.
Wind, The. L. E. Landon.
Wind, The. Betty Miller.
Wind, The. William Morris.
Wind. Phyllis Reid.
Wind, The. Rendall.
Wind, The. Shanks.

WIND (*continued*)
Wind, The. Starbuck.
Wind, The. James Stephens.
Wind, The. R. L. Stevenson.
Wind. *Fr.* Riddles. *Unknown, tr. fr. Anglo-Saxon by* Kennedy.
Wind among the Reeds, The. Nora Hopper.
Wind and the Moon, The. George Macdonald.
Wind and the Wires, The. Sledd.
Wind and Wave. Patmore.
Wind and Wave. C. W. Stoddard.
Wind and Window-Flower. Robert Frost.
Wind has such a rainy sound, The. *Fr.* Sing-Song. C. G. Rossetti.
Wind in a Frolic, The. William Howitt.
Wind in the Dusk. Monro.
Wind in the Elms, The. J. C. Miller.
Wind in the Pines, The. Cawein.
Wind-Litany. Widdemer.
Wind on the Hills, The. Shorter.
Wind on the Wold, The. Henley.
Wind Our Enemy, The. Marriott.
Wind Song. Sandburg.
Wind tapped like a tired man, The. Emily Dickinson.
Wind Weather. Brasier.
Wind, Wind. Alling.
Wind-Wolves. W. D. Sargent.
Winds, The. Cawein.
Winds, The. "John Eglinton."
Winds, The. Swinburne.
Winds, The. W. C. Williams
Winds a-Blowing. Justus.
Wind's Song, The. Mörike, *tr. fr. German by* Hughes.
Wind's Song, The. "Gabriel Setoun."
Wind's Way, The. G. H. Conkling.
Wind's Way, The. Le Gallienne.
Wind's Word, The. Lampman.
Wind's Work. T. S. Moore.
Windy Day, A. Andrew Young.
Windy Morning. Behn.
Windy Nights. R. L. Stevenson.
Winter Night. Butts.
Word with the Wind, A. Swinburne.
See also EAST WIND; NORTH WIND; SOUTH WIND; WEST WIND.
WINDHOVERS. *See* FALCONS.
WINDMILLS
Windmill. John Farrar.
Windmill, The. Geoffrey Johnson.
Windmill, The. Longfellow.
Windmill, The. E. V. Lucas.
Windmill on the Cape. Sieller.
Windmills, The. J. G. Fletcher.
WINDOWS. Windows. Mallarmé, *tr. fr. French by* Aldan.
WINDSOR CASTLE, ENGLAND. Prisoned in Windsor, He Recounteth His Pleasure There Passed. Earl of Surrey.
WINDSOR FOREST, ENGLAND. Windsor Forest, *sels.* Pope.
WINE
Anacreontic. Martínez de la Rosa, *tr. fr. Spanish by* Kennedy.
Bacchus. Emerson.
Bacchus in Tuscany, *sels.* Redi, *tr. fr. Italian.*
Bubbling Wine. Abu Zakariya, *tr. fr. Arabic by* Arberry.
Catawba Wine. Longfellow.
Curculio, *sel.* ("To my nose there came a whiff"). Plautus, *tr. fr. Latin by* Wright.
Dithyrambic on Wine, A. Thomas Godfrey.
Drinking Alone by Moonlight. Li Po, *tr. fr. Chinese by* Waley.
Drinking Song. Rahbek, *tr. fr. Danish by* Stork.
Ecce Autem Dulces Labris Pater Ingerit Uvas. Politian, *tr. fr. Latin by* Allen.
England's Triumph; or, The Subjects' Joy. *Unknown.*
Five Arabic Verses in Praise of Wine. *Unknown, tr. fr. Arabic by* Hirschfeld.
His Farewell to Sack. Herrick.
If thou doest not love sacke. *Unknown.*
Magian Wine. Abu Jaafar, *tr. fr. Arabic by* Arberry.
Man in the Moon Drinks Clarret, The. *Unknown.*
Now, O Bacchus, I turn humbly to your shrine. *Fr.* Elegies. Propertius, *tr. fr. Latin by* Fletcher.
Song and Wine. Bacchylides, *tr. fr. Greek by* Bowra.
Spirit of Wine, The. *Fr.* Echoes. Henley.
Tippler's Philosophy. *Unknown, tr. fr. Greek by* Girdlestone.
To His Cup-Bearer. Catullus, *tr. fr. Greek by* Lamb.
Under Leafy Bowers. Al-Harizi, *tr. fr. Hebrew.*
Vinum Daemonum. L. P. Johnson.
Welcome to Sack, The. Herrick.
Wine. Carlin.
Wine. Dakiki, *tr. fr. Persian by* Nicholson.
Wine. Lebensohn, *tr. fr. Hebrew by* Klein.
Wine and Dew. Stoddard.
Wine and Water. Chesterton.
Wine, My Love. Abu Jaafar, *tr. fr. Arabic by* Arberry.
Wine-Songs. Ibn Ezra, *tr. fr. Hebrew by* Solis-Cohen.
Wings of Wine. Ibn al-Yamani, *tr. fr. Arabic by* Arberry.
Would you be a man in fashion? *Unknown.*
WINKELRIED, ARNOLD VON. Arnold von Winkelried. James Montgomery.
WINNIPEG, CANADA. Winnipeg at Christmas. Fyleman.
WINSLOW, JOHN ANCRUM. Eagle and Vulture, The. T. B. Read.
WINTER
Ancient Music. Pound.
Answer to Ting Yuan Ch'en, An. Ou Yang Hsiu, *tr. fr. Chinese by* Rexroth.
Approach of Winter, The. Laforgue, *tr. fr. French by* Bennett.
Approach of Winter, The. *Fr.* Induction to "The Mirror for Magistrates." Sackville.
Autumn and Winter. *Fr.* Elegy to the Memory of Mr. Thomas Philips of Fairford. Chatterton.
Before Sunrise in Winter. Sill.
Before Winter. F. R. McCreary.
Blow, Blow, Thou Winter Wind. *Fr.* As You Like It. Shakespeare.
Cold winter now is in the wood. Coatsworth.
Coming, The. Delius.
Coming of Winter. Pasternak, *tr. fr. Russian by* Lindsay.
Dark Winter Is Going. Munro, *tr. fr. Gaelic by* MacNeill.
Elegy, An: "In early winter before the first snow." Scovell.
Emmonsail's Heath in Winter. Clare.
Frost at Night. *Fr.* The Seasons. James Thomson.
Frost Fancy, A. Le Gallienne.
Frost-Morning. William Alexander.
Glee for Winter, A. Domett.
Greenland Winter, A. Diamond.
Here's Winter. Pushkin, *tr. fr. Russian by* Deutsch.
How One Winter Came in the Lake Region. W. W. Campbell.
Howdy, Mr. Winter! Nesbit.
In the Barn-Yard's Southerly Corner. Sir C. G. D. Roberts.
In the Winter Woods. F. G. Scott.
In the Wood. Mathias.
Jack Frost. "Gabriel Setoun."
Jingle Bells. James Pierpont.
Kernel, The. Kendon.
Last Night of Winter, The. Welles.
Late Winter. Hazel Hall.
Meditation in Winter. Leonard Mann.
Meeting in Winter. William Morris.
Midwinter. Trowbridge.
Midwinter Thaw. Lenore Pratt.
Million Little Diamonds, A. Butts.
New Year's Days. Celia Standish.
Night Is Freezing Fast, The. A. E. Housman.
Nine Variations in a Chinese Winter Setting. Charles Tomlinson.
No Possum, No Sop, No Taters. Wallace Stevens.
No Songs in Winter. T. B. Aldrich.
Now Comes the Blast of Winter. *Unknown.*
Now the Winter's Come to Stay. *Unknown.*
Now Winter Nights Enlarge. Campion.
O Winter! Wilt Thou Never Go? David Gray.
Ode to Winter. Thomas Campbell.
Old Man's Winter Night, An. Robert Frost.
Old Nurse Winter. J. S. Untermeyer.
Old Winter. Thomas Noel.
Outside. Hugh Chesterman.
Pacific Winter. Flanner.
Pray to What Earth Does This Sweet Cold Belong. Thoreau.
Prelude: "Winter for a moment takes the mind; the snow." *Fr.* Preludes for Memnon. Aiken.
Putting Winter to Bed. E. J. Pratt.
Remembering the Winter. Rowena Bennett.
Schoolboys in Winter. Clare.
Sigh in Winter, A. Platen, *tr. fr. German by* Morgan.
Signs of Winter. Clare.
Snow Man, The. Wallace Stevens.
Snow-bound. Whittier.
Solace in Winter. *Fr.* Silva Gadelica. *Unknown, tr. fr. Irish by* Sigerson.
Something Told the Wild Geese. Rachel Field.
Song of the Stork, The. *Unknown, tr. fr. Armenian by* Boyajian.
Song of Winter, A. Pfeiffer.
Song of Winter, A. *Unknown, tr. fr. Middle Irish by* Meyer.
Spring and Winter. *Fr.* Love's Labour's Lost. Shakespeare.
Stanzas: "In a drear-nighted December." Keats.
Stopping by Woods on a Snowy Evening. Robert Frost.
Summer and Winter. G. S. Fraser.

Summer and Winter. Shelley.
Summer Is Gone. *Unknown, tr. fr. Old Irish.*
Terrace in the Snow, The. Su T'ung-po, *tr. fr. Chinese by* Rexroth.
There's a certain slant of light. Emily Dickinson.
There's Snow on the Fields. *Fr.* Sing-Song. C. G. Rossetti.
Thin ice/ Free advice. McCord.
Three Trees at Solstice. Finnin.
To Hampstead. Leigh Hunt.
Up in the Morning Early. Burns.
Walk on a Winter Day. S. V. A. Allen.
What Is Winter? Blunden.
When Icicles Hang by the Wall. *Fr.* Love's Labour's Lost. Shakespeare.
Where It Is Winter. George O'Neil.
Whirl-Blast from behind the Hill, A. Wordsworth.
White Fields. James Stephens.
Widow Bird, A. *Fr.* Charles the First. Shelley.
Winter. Blyton.
Winter. J. H. Bryant.
Winter. Clare.
Winter. Cotton.
Winter. *Fr.* The Task. Cowper.
Winter. De la Mare.
Winter. Gawin Douglas.
Winter. *Fr.* Works and Days. Hesiod, *tr. fr. Greek by* Lucas.
Winter. *Fr.* Odes. Horace, *tr. fr. Latin by* Dryden.
Winter. Richard Hughes.
Winter. Joso, *tr. fr. Japanese by* Henderson.
Winter. Landor.
Winter. Livesay.
Winter. Mair.
Winter. *Fr.* The Unknown Eros. Patmore.
Winter. C. G. Rossetti.
Winter. Southey.
Winter. *Fr.* The Faerie Queene. Spenser.
Winter. Synge.
Winter. Tennyson.
Winter. *Fr.* The Seasons. James Thomson.
Winter. Thorarensen, *tr. fr. Icelandic by* Stefansson.
Winter ("Keen is the wind"). *Fr.* The Black Book of Carmarthen. *Unknown, tr. fr. Welsh by* Jackson.
Winter ("Old Winter is a sturdy one"). *Unknown.*
Winter; a dirge. Burns.
Winter among the Days. Raymond Holden.
Winter and Spring. *Unknown.*
Winter at Tomi. Ovid, *tr. fr. Latin by* Wright.
Winter Circus. Aileen Fisher.
Winter Days. Henry Abbey.
Winter Eden, A. Robert Frost.
Winter Evening, The. *Fr.* The Task. Cowper.
Winter Evening. Pushkin, *tr. fr. Russian by* Deutsch.
Winter Evening. Tynan.
Winter Evening Hymn to My Fire, A. J. R. Lowell.
Winter Feast. Frances Frost.
Winter Galaxy, The. Heavysege.
Winter Garden. Gascoyne.
Winter Has Come. *Unknown, tr. fr. Old Irish by* Jackson.
Winter in Durnover Field. Hardy.
Winter in Lower Canada. Standish O'Grady.
Winter in the Wood. Eastwick.
Winter Is Coming. W. T. Carmichael.
Winter Is Coming. Laforgue, *tr. fr. French by* Conder.
Winter Joys. Gradon.
Winter Lakes, The. W. W. Campbell.
Winter Life and Scenery. T. C. Irwin.
Winter Lightning, The. Nemerov.
Winter Memories. Thoreau.
Winter Night, A. William Barnes.
Winter Night, A, *sel.* ("When biting Boreas"). Burns.
Winter Night. Butts.
Winter Night. Fairburn.
Winter Night. Millay.
Winter Night. Trakl, *tr. fr. German by* Luke.
Winter-Night Song. F. M. Ford.
Winter Nightfall. Robert Bridges.
Winter Nightfall. Squire.
Winter Noon. Rorty.
Winter Noon. Teasdale.
Winter Noon in the Woods, *sel.* ("With witchlike branches, barren, bleak, and drear"). T. C. Irwin.
Winter Pictures. *Fr.* Vision of Sir Launfal. J. R. Lowell.
Winter Piece, A. Bryant.
Winter-Piece, A. Ambrose Philips.
Winter Ride, A. Amy Lowell.
Winter Rune. Coatsworth.
Winter Scene, The. Carman.
Winter Sketch. Bourinot.
Winter Sleep. E. M. Thomas.
Winter Sleep. Elinor Wylie.
Winter Song, A. W. C. Bennett.
Winter Song. Hölty, *tr. fr. German by* Brooks.
Winter Song. *Fr.* The Land. Sackville-West.
Winter Song: "Drop down, drop down, white snowflakes!" *Unknown, tr. fr. Bohemian.*
Winter-Song for Pan. John Erskine.
Winter Spring. Wilbur.
Winter Storm at Sea, The. *Fr.* The Borough. Crabbe.
Winter Storms, The. Davenant.
Winter Streams. Carman.
Winter the Huntsman. Sir Osbert Sitwell.
Winter Treats. Shacklett.
Winter Westerlies. Devaney.
Winter with the Gulf Stream. G. M. Hopkins.
Winter's Beauty. W. H. Davies.
Winter's Cold. W. R. Rodgers.
Winter's Spring, The. Clare.
Winter's Tale, A. Dylan Thomas.
Winter's Troops. *Fr.* Winter. Cotton.
Winter-Time. R. L. Stevenson.
Wintry Day. *Unknown.*
Wisdom in Winter. *Fr.* The Black Book of Carmarthen. *Unknown, tr. fr. Welsh by* Williams.
Wizard Frost. F. D. Sherman.
Words of Finn, The. *Unknown.*
Workers. Rimbaud, *tr. fr. French by* Flores.
Works and Days, *sel.* ("Beware the January month: beware"). Hesiod, *tr. fr. Greek by* Elton.
Written on the First of December, 1793. Southey.
Years-End. Wilbur.
Book of the Winter, A (BoW). Edith Sitwell, comp.

WINTHROP, THEODORE. Dirge: For One Who Fell in Battle. T. W. Parsons.
WISE MEN. *See* MAGI.
WISHES
My Wishes. Healy, *tr. fr. Modern Irish by* D'Alton.
Rathers. Mary Austin.
Sam's Three Wishes; or, Life's Little Whirligig. De la Mare.
Sometimes Wish, A. Shacklett.
Spring Wish. John Farrar.
Wish, A. Matthew Arnold.
Wish, The. Cowley.
Wish, A. Garland.
Wish, A. "Jazbo of Old Dubuque."
Wish, A. *Fr.* The Gypsies Metamorphosed. Jonson.
Wish, A. C. G. Rossetti.
Wish, A. F. D. Sherman.
Wish, A. W. C. Smith.
Wish, The. Stanley, *after the Greek of* Anacreon.
Wish Is Quite a Tiny Thing, A. Annette Wynne.
Wish of the Aged Bard, The. *Unknown, tr. fr. Gaelic by* Macmillan.
Wishes. Ault.
Wishes of Youth. S. L. Blanchard.
Wishing. Allingham.
WISTERIA. Wisteria. Ahern.
WIT. Ode: Of Wit. Cowley.
WITCHCRAFT
Alison Gross. *Unknown.*
Country Witch, A. William Barnes.
Fatal Sisters, The. Thomas Gray.
Hag, The. Herrick.
In guilty night & hid in false disguise. *Unknown.*
Memory of a Witch. Takenaka, *tr. fr. Japanese by* Ninomiya *and* Enright.
Mistress Hale of Beverly. Larcom.
Mother Maudlin the Witch. *Fr.* The Sad Shepherd. Jonson.
Ride-by-Nights, The. De la Mare.
Salem Witch, A. E. P. Clarke.
Slaying of the Witch, The. George Sterling.
Sorceress, The. *Fr.* Idylls. Theocritus, *tr. fr. Greek by* Lucas.
Tam o' Shanter. Burns.
Twist Ye, Twine Ye! Even So. *Fr.* Guy Mannering. Sir Walter Scott.
White Witch, The. J. W. Johnson.
Witch, A. William Barnes.
Witch, The. L. M. Bowman.
Witch, The. M. E. Coleridge.
Witch, The. Lord Alfred Douglas.
Witch, The. Tynan.
Witch-Mother, The. Swinburne.
Witch of Coös, The. Robert Frost.
Witch of Endor, The, *sel.* ("One word!"). Norwood.
Witch of Willowby Wood, The. Rowena Bennett.
Witch-Wife, The. M. E. Roberts.
Witches. Ted Hughes.
Witches, The. *Unknown.*
Witches' Song. Coatsworth.
Witches' Song. *Fr.* Macbeth. Shakespeare.
Witches' Steeds, The. Ogilvie.
Witches' Town. *Unknown.*

WITCHCRAFT (*continued*)
Witch's Ballad, The. W. B. Scott.
Witch's Charm, A. *Fr.* The Masque of Queens. Jonson.
Witch's Daughter, The. *Unknown, tr. fr. Modern Greek by* Dalven.
Witch's Moon, The. Scheier.
Wreck of Rivermouth, The. Whittier.
Young Witch—1698, The George Sterling.
Dark of the Moon (DaM). August Derleth, ed.
WITTGENSTEIN, LUDWIG. Philosopher and the Birds, The. Richard Murphy.
WIVES. *See* MARRIAGE.
WOLFE, CHARLES. In Clonmel Parish Churchyard. Piatt.
WOLFE, JAMES
Brave Wolfe. *Unknown.*
Death of Wolfe, The. *Unknown.*
WOLSEY, THOMAS, CARDINAL
Cardinal Wolsey's Farewell. *Fr.* King Henry VIII. Shakespeare.
Colyn Cloute, *sels.* Skelton.
How Thomas Wolsey Did Arise unto Great Authority and Government . . . *Fr.* A Mirror for Magistrates. Churchyard.
Speak, Parrot, *sels.* Skelton.
WOLVES
Fox, the Wolf, and the Bear, The. *Unknown, tr. fr. Armenian by* Boyajian.
Night with a Wolf. Bayard Taylor.
Wolf, The. Durston.
Wolf Cry, The. Sarett.
Wolf, the Hornet and the Nightingale, The. Coblentz.
Wolves, The. E. M. Roberts.
Wolves, The. Allen Tate.
WOMBATS. Wombat, The. Ogden Nash.
WOMEN
Against Blame of Women. Gerald, Earl of Desmond, *tr. fr. Late Middle Irish by* the Earl of Longford.
Against Them Who Lay Unchastity to the Sex of Woman. Habington.
Against Women. *Fr.* The Satires. Juvenal, *tr. fr. Latin by* Dryden.
Amateur Bard on Woman, The. *Unknown.*
As Joe Gould says. E. E. Cummings.
Ballad Warning Men to Beware of Deceitful Women, A, *sel.* Lydgate.
Beatitudes for a Housewife. Oesch.
C. L. M. Masefield.
Caveat to the Fair Sex, A. Lady Montagu.
Choice, The. Pomfret.
Colours of Love, The. Devlin.
Creatrix. Wickham.
Dawn of Womanhood. Monro.
December: Of Aphrodite. Merwin.
Delectable Dream, A, *sel.* ("A woman's face is full of wiles"). Gifford.
Dream of Fair Women, A. Amis.
Evening Out, The. Ogden Nash.
Eve's Daughter. Sill.
Farm Wife. J. H. Mitchell.
Former Beauties. *Fr.* At Casterbridge Fair. Hardy.
Free Woman, The. Theodosia Garrison.
Garment of Good Ladies, The. Henryson.
Gert Swasey. W. T. Scott.
Good Wife, The. Sadi, *tr. fr. Persian by* Davie.
Holy Women. W. A. Percy.
Home Winner, The. Lindberg.
Housewife, The; Winter Afternoon. K. W. Baker.
How the Women Will Stop War. Aristophanes, *tr. fr. Greek by* Rogers.
I Am as Light as Any Roe. *Unknown.*
I Never Even Suggested It. Ogden Nash.
If Women Could Be Fair. Edward de Vere.
In Defense of Their Inconstancy. Jonson.
Indifferent, The. Francis Beaumont.
Korean Woman Seated by a Wall, A. William Meredith.
La Femme de quarante ans. Cloete.
Ladies, The. Kipling.
Legend of Good Women, *sels.* Chaucer.
Legend of Viable Women, A. Eberhart.
Let the Toast Pass. *Fr.* The School for Scandal. Sheridan.
Lonely Woman, The. M. Forrest.
Lovely Woman, A. W. H. Davies.
Mrs. Frances Harris's Petition. Swift.
Mrs. Severin. W. T. Scott.
Mistresses. *Unknown, tr. fr. Irish by* O'Connor.
Modern Woman to Her Lover, The. Widdemer.
Mountain Woman, The. Heyward.
New Woman, The. *Fr.* Satires. Juvenal, *tr. fr. Latin by* Gifford.
No Fault in Women. Herrick.
Oh, Please Don't Get Up! Ogden Nash.
Oh, what is longer than the way? *Unknown.*
Of the Characters of Women. *Fr.* Moral Essays. Pope.
Of Women. Richard Edwards.
Of Women No More Evil. *Unknown, tr. fr. Late Middle Irish by* Flower.
Old and New. *Unknown, tr. fr. Chinese by* Waley.
Old Woman, The. Joseph Campbell.
Old Women, The. Symons.
On Woman. Yeats.
Personal Poem. Smithyman.
Peter Parasol. Wallace Stevens.
Pioneer Woman. V. P. Crawford.
Plaint of the Wife. *Unknown, tr. fr. Russian by* Ralston.
Portrait d'une Femme. Pound.
Praise of Little Women. *Fr.* The Book of Good Love. Juan Ruiz, Archpriest of Hita, *tr. fr. Spanish by* Longfellow.
Praise of Women. Mannyng.
Praise of Women. Palladas, *tr. fr. Greek by* Fitts.
Prayer for My Daughter, A. Yeats.
Red-haired Man's Wife, The. James Stephens.
Rights of Women, The. Barbauld.
Satirical Letrilla. Cadalso Vazquez, *tr. fr. Spanish.*
Shack, The. N. B. Miller.
She Walked Unaware. MacDonogh.
She Was a Phantom of Delight. Wordsworth.
Sisters. "Robin Hyde."
Sisters, The. Amy Lowell.
Sketch of the Frontier Woman. "Claudia Lars," *tr. fr. Spanish by* Walsh.
Song: That Women Are but Men's Shadows. Jonson.
Song: "When lovely woman stoops to folly." *Fr.* The Vicar of Wakefield. Goldsmith.
Song: "Woman's face is full of wiles, A." Humfrey Gifford.
Song of Liang Chou. Ou Yang Hsiu, *tr. fr. Chinese by* Rexroth.
Sun Was Slumbering in the West, The. Hood.
That Reminds Me. Ogden Nash.
These Women All. —— Heath.
Thought, A. J. K. Stephen.
Three American Women and a German Bayonet. W. T. Scott.
To a Lady. Pope.
To a Pretty Girl. Zangwill.
To a Woman. Glover.
To Daphne and Virginia. W. C. Williams.
To Onpreise Womene It Were a Shame. *Unknown.*
To the New Women. Davidson.
To Women. Binyon.
Triolet: "All women born are so perverse." Robert Bridges.
Tunnynge of Elynour Rummynge, The. Skelton.
Two Wives, The. W. D. Howells.
Unseen Spirits. N. P. Willis.
Upon the Loss of His Mistresses. Herrick.
Villon's Straight Tip to All Cross Coves. Henley.
Virtuous Wife, The. Trimberg, *tr. fr. Middle High German.*
Virtuous Woman, The. Proverbs, Bible, *O.T.*
Washer-Woman, The. Bohanan.
What One May and May Not Call a Woman. *Unknown.*
When Lovely Woman. Phoebe Cary.
When Nettles in Winter Bring Forth Roses Red. *Unknown.*
Wife Speaks, The. Mary Stanley.
Wise Woman, The. Louis Untermeyer.
Woman. E. S. Barrett.
Woman. Conant.
Woman. Ellis.
Woman. Fu Hsüan, *tr. fr. Chinese by* Waley.
Woman! Hagiwara, *tr. fr. Japanese by* Ninomiya *and* Enright.
Woman. Kalidasa, *tr. fr. Sanskrit by* Wilson.
Woman, A. Thomas MacDonagh.
Woman, *sel.* ("When my gloomy hour comes on me"). Alexander McLachlan.
Woman, A. Scudder Middleton.
Woman. Nyleen Newton.
Woman. Thomas O'Hagan.
Woman. *Fr.* The Nature of Women. Earl of Rochester.
Woman, A. M. D. Thayer.
Woman. *Fr.* Shi King. *Unknown, tr. fr. Chinese by* Giles.
Woman ("When Eve brought woe to all mankind"). *Unknown.*
Woman and Her Dead Husband, A. D. H. Lawrence.
Woman I Am, The. Glen Allen.
Woman in Sunshine, The. Wallace Stevens.
Woman in the Rye, The. Hardy.
Woman in the Wagon, The. Clyde Robertson.
Woman of Three Cows, The. *Unknown, tr. fr. Irish by* Mangan.
Woman of Words, A. A. B. Hall.
Woman on the Walls, The. Cody.
Woman Passes the Door, A. George O'Neil.

Woman with the Serpent's Tongue, The. Sir William Watson.
Womankind. Sophocles, *tr. fr. Greek by* Bowra.
Woman's Execution, A. Edward King.
Woman's looks, A/ Are barbed hooks. *Unknown.*
Woman's Love. Mannyng.
Woman's Pride, A. H. H. Whitney.
Woman's Question, A. A. A. Procter.
Woman's Shortcomings, A. E. B. Browning.
Woman's Song, A. Muna Lee.
Woman's Thoughts, A. R. W. Gilder.
Woman's Will. Saxe.
Woman's Will. *Unknown.*
Women. Bogan.
Women. Semonides, *tr. fr. Greek by* Lucas.
Women at the Corners Stand, The. Louis Golding.
Women Folk, The. Hogg.
Women Toilers, The. G. B. Evans.
Women Will Soon Knit Again, The. Burlingame.
Young Acacia, The. Bialik, *tr. fr. Hebrew by* Frank.
Young Woman. Nemerov.

WOODBINE. Woodbines in October. C. F. Bates.

WOODCHUCKS
Drumlin Woodchuck, A. Robert Frost.
Jolly Woodchuck, The. Edey *and* Grider.

WOODPECKERS
Downy Woodpecker, The. John Burroughs.
Hewel, or Woodpecker, The. *Fr.* Upon Appleton House. Marvell.
Legend of the Northland. Phoebe Cary.
Visit with a Woodpecker, A. Comerford.
Woodpecker, The. Richard Church.
Woodpecker, The. E. M. Roberts.
Woodpecker, The. Sambrook.
Woodpecker, The. Tabb.

WOODS. *See* FORESTS.

WOOL. Wool Trade, The. *Fr.* The Fleece. John Dyer.

WOOLF, VIRGINIA.
Elegy on the Death of Virginia Woolf. Hambleton.
To Virginia Woolf. Nathaniel Thornton.

WORDSWORTH, CATHERINE. To Catherine Wordsworth 1808–1812. Wordsworth.

WORDSWORTH, WILLIAM.
Lost Leader, The. Robert Browning.
Memorial Verses. Matthew Arnold.
On a Portrait of Wordsworth. E. B. Browning.
On Wordsworth. Hartley Coleridge.
On Wordsworth. *Unknown.*
Some of Wordsworth. Landor.
Sonnet on Wordsworth, A. J. K. Stephen.
Southey and Wordsworth. *Fr.* Don Juan. Byron.
Stanzas in Memory of the Author of "Obermann." Arnold.
To William Wordsworth. S. T. Coleridge.
To Wordsworth. Landor.
To Wordsworth. Shelley.
William Wordsworth. Sidney Keyes.
William Wordsworth. Palgrave.
With Wordsworth at Rydal. J. T. Fields.
Wordsworth. *Fr.* Ode to England. W. W. Lord.
Wordsworth's Grave. Sir William Watson.
Youth of Nature, The. Matthew Arnold.

WORK. *See* LABOR AND LABORERS.

WORLD. *See* EARTH.

WORLD FEDERATION
For I Dipped into the Future, Far as Human Eye Could See. *Fr.* Locksley Hall. Tennyson.
Universal Republic, The. Hugo, *tr. fr. French.*

WORLD WAR, FIRST
A. E. F. Sandburg.
Aftermath. Sassoon.
"And There Was a Great Calm." Hardy.
Anxious Dead, The. John McCrae.
Apologia pro Poemate Meo. Wilfred Owen.
Armistice. Going.
Armistice Day. R. M. Montgomery.
Assault Heroic, The. Robert Graves.
At the Front. John Erskine.
Attack. Sassoon.
August, 1914. Masefield.
Back Home Again. Grantland Rice.
Break of Day in the Trenches. Rosenberg.
Cambrai and Marne. C. G. D. Roberts.
Casualties. W. W. Gibson
Corpses in the Wood. Toller, *tr. fr. German by* Roberts.
Dawn. Aldington.
Dead, The. *Fr.* 1914. Rupert Brooke.
Draw The Sword, O Republic. Masters.
Dulce et Decorum Est. Wilfred Owen.
Eastern Front. Trakl, *tr. fr. German by* Middleton.
Exposure. Wilfred Owen.
Farmer Remembers the Somme, The. Vance Palmer.
First Division Marches, The. Grantland Rice.
Flanders Roses. Tikhonov, *tr. fr. Russian by* Lindsay.
For Them That Died in Battle. W. A. Percy.
General Galliéni. Hillyer.
Grodek. Trakl, *tr. fr. German by* Flores.
Guards Came Through, The. A. C. Doyle.
I Sing of Olaf Glad and Big. E. E. Cummings.
In Flanders Fields. John McCrae.
In Flanders Now. Jaques.
It Shall Not Be Again! T. C. Clark.
March, The. Squire.
Mare Liberum. Van Dyke.
Memorial Day. W. E. Brooks.
Mesopotamia 1917. Kipling.
Ode in Memory of the American Volunteers Fallen for France. Seeger.
Our Dead, Overseas. Markham.
Parable of the Old Men and the Young, The. Wilfred Owen.
Recalling War. Robert Graves.
Republic to Republic. Bynner.
Road to France, The. Daniel Henderson.
Sentry, The. Wilfred Owen.
Smoke-blue Plains, The. Badger Clark.
Somme Valley, 1917, The. Prewett.
Song-Books of the War. Sassoon.
Sonnets Written in the Fall of 1914. G. E. Woodberry.
There's About Two Million Fellows. A. J. Cook.
This Is No Case of Petty Right or Wrong. Edward Thomas.
To a Conscript of 1940. Sir Herbert Read.
To a Young Leader of the First World War. George, *tr. fr. German by* Ashton.
To America, on Her First Sons Fallen in the Great War. E. M. Walker.
To the School at War. C. A. Alington.
Unscarred Fighter Remembers France, The. Alling.
White Ships and the Red. Kilmer.
William P. Frye, The. J. R. Foster.
World War I. *Unknown.*

WORLD WAR, SECOND
Address to Tragedy. Berggolts, *tr. fr. Russian by* Lindsay.
After Dunkirk. Alun Lewis.
Ballad: "He did not kill." Glatstein, *tr. fr. Yiddish by* Betsky.
Battle. Jeffers.
Before Invasion, 1940. Betjeman.
Behind the Log, *sel.* ("Whatever doubt the eye might have imposed"). E. J. Pratt.
Black-out. Jeffers.
Commandos Embarking. Whalley.
Conversation Piece. Dawless.
D-Dawn—June 6, 1944. McGarvey.
Dawn in Besieged Leningrad. Inber, *tr. fr. Russian by* Lindsay.
Death of the Ball Turret Gunner, The. Jarrell.
Drunken Gunners. M. K. Joseph.
Duel. Shehipachov, *tr. fr. Russian by* Lindsay.
Dunkirk. Nathan.
Dunkirk Pier. Rook.
Eighth Air Force. Jarrell.
Four Men of God. Guest.
Four Years. Pappas, *tr. fr. Modern Greek by* Dalven.
Fourth Act. Jeffers.
Full Moon; New Guinea. Shapiro.
Homecoming. Shapiro.
In the Skies. *Fr.* Dunkirk. E. J. Pratt.
In Woods near the Frontline. Isakovsky, *tr. fr. Russian by* Lindsay.
Kirov Is with Us. Tikhonov, *tr. fr. Russian by* Lindsay.
Landscape with Figures. Keith Douglas.
Letters to Malaya, IV, *sel.* ("Then came Dunkirk to mitigate the news"). Skinner.
Little Boats of Britain, The. Carsley.
Long Roads. Matusovsky, *tr. fr. Russian by* Deutsch.
Losses. Jarrell.
Man unto His Fellow Man. *Fr.* On a Note of Triumph. Corwin.
May–June, 1940. Jeffers.
Moon and the Night and the Men, The. Berryman.
Mourning in Spring, 1943. Raine.
Neutrality. MacNeice.
New Moses, The. M. K. Joseph.
Ninth of April, The. Gelsted, *tr. fr. Danish.*
Norfolk Memorials. Leavenworth.
Ode to Our Young Pro-Consuls of the Air. Allen Tate.
On the Pilots Who Destroyed Germany in the Spring of 1945. Spender.
Poland, October. *Fr.* Nineteen Thirty-nine. Brasch.
Psalm of the Singing Grave. Janta, *tr. fr. Polish by* White *and* Janta.
Reflections on the Fall of France, June, 1940. Eiluned Lewis.
Remembering That Island. Thomas McGrath.
Road to Nijmegen. Birney.

WORLD WAR, SECOND (*continued*)
Rye Unharvested, The. Drunina, *tr. fr. Russian by* Lindsay.
Scyros. Shapiro.
Second Air Force. Jarrell.
September 1, 1939. Auden.
Siciliana; the Landings at Gela. Koehler.
Snow in Europe. Gascoyne.
"Spoken Word, The." Morley.
Spring, 1944. Pasternak, *tr. fr. Russian by* Bowra.
Spring, 1942. Roy Fuller.
Streets of Laredo, The. MacNeice.
There Is Yet Time. Steece.
To a Conscript of 1940. Sir Herbert Read.
Tragic Tale. Pasternak, *tr. fr. Russian by* Lindsay.
Twenty Years Old. Surkov, *tr. fr. Russian by* Lindsay.
U.S. Sailor with the Japanese Skull, The. W. T. Scott.
War. Joseph Langland.
Wartime Dawn, A. Gascoyne.
We Shall Come Back. Grieg, *tr. fr. Norwegian by* Stork.
Whipped On by December. Surkov, *tr. fr. Russian by* Deutsch.
Winter 1939–1940. Laurie Lee.
World War II. *Unknown.*
You Remember, Alyosha. Simonov, *tr. fr. Russian by* Lindsay.
New Treasury of War Poetry, The (NeTW). George Herbert Clark, ed.
WORLD WAR, THIRD
News of World War III. George Barker.
World War III. *Unknown.*
WORMS
Fishing Song, A. Rands.
Our Little Kinsmen. Emily Dickinson.
Worm, The. Bergengren.
Worms and the Wind. Sandburg.
WORMWOOD. Tall Ambrosia. Thoreau.
WORSHIP
Joy of Church Fellowship Rightly Attended, The. *Fr.* God's Determinations. Edward Taylor.
Morning Worship. Wergeland, *tr. fr. Norwegian by* Stork.
Worship. Emerson.
Worship, *sel.* ("For them, O God who only worship"). W. W. Lord.
Worship. R. C. MacFie.
Worship. Welshimer.
WOTTON, SIR HENRY
Ad Henricum Wottonum ("Wotton, the country and the country swain"). Thomas Bastard.
Letter to Sir H. Wotton at His Going Ambassador to Venice. Donne.
WREN, SIR CHRISTOPHER
Said Sir Christopher Wren. *Unknown.*
Sir Christopher Wren. Bentley.
WRENS
Bird's Nest, A. E. A. Allen.
Dove and the Wren, The. *Unknown.*
Jenny Wren. W. H. Davies.
Little Brown Wren, The. Scollard.
Little Lady Wren. Tom Robinson.
Netted Strawberries. Bottomley.
Robin and the Wren, The. *Unknown.*
When Jenny Wren Was Young. Mother Goose.
Wrens and Robins. *Fr.* Sing-Song. C. G. Rossetti.
Wren's Nest, A. Wordsworth.
WRESTLING
Wrestler, The. George, *tr. fr. German by* Luke.
Wrestling Match, The. R. P. Warren.
WRIGHT, ORVILLE, *and* WILBUR WRIGHT
Aeroplane, The. *Fr.* The Bridge: Cape Hatteras. Hart Crane.
Wilbur Wright and Orville Wright. Rosemary Benét *and* S. V. Benét.
WYATT, SIR THOMAS
Another Tribute to Wyatt. Earl of Surrey.
Death of Wyatt, The. Earl of Surrey.
In Praise of Wyatt's Psalms. Earl of Surrey.
On the Death of Sir Thomas Wyatt. Earl of Surrey.
Tribute to Wyatt, A. Earl of Surrey.
WYE (river), WALES *and* ENGLAND. Playmates, The. Sir William Watson.
WYOMING. Wyoming. C. E. Winter.
WYOMING MASSACRE. Wyoming Massacre, The. Uriah Terry.
WYRE FOREST, ENGLAND. As through the Wild Green Hills of Wyre. A. E. Housman.

X

XENOPHANES. Xenophanes. Emerson.

Y

YACHTS
Lament for the Great Yachts. Patric Dickinson.
Yachts, The. W. C. Williams.
Yachts on the Nile. Bernard Spencer.
YAKS
Yak, The. Belloc.
Yak, The. Sheard.
Yak. W. J. Smith.
YALE UNIVERSITY
On the Democracy of Yale. F. S. Jones.
To the Memory of Yale College. Phelps Putnam.
YANGTZE (river), CHINA. Alarm at First Entering the Yangtze Gorges. Po Chü-i, *tr. fr. Chinese by* Waley.
YARROW *or* YARROW WATER, SCOTLAND
Braes of Yarrow, The. Hamilton.
Braes of Yarrow, The. John Logan.
Yarrow Revisited. Wordsworth.
Yarrow Unvisited. Wordsworth.
Yarrow Visited. Wordsworth.
YEATS, JOHN BUTLER. John Butler Yeats. J. R. Foster.
YEATS, WILLIAM BUTLER
Bring Home the Poet. MacDonough.
Death of Yeats, The. George Barker.
For His Own Epitaph. *Fr.* Under Ben Bulben. Yeats.
In Memory of W. B. Yeats. Auden.
Ode: On the Death of W. B. Yeats. A. J. M. Smith.
To W. B. Yeats Who Says That His Castle of Ballylee Is His Monument. Gogarty.
YEW TREES
Old Yew, Which Graspest at the Stones. *Fr.* In Memoriam. Tennyson.
Yew Trees. Wordsworth.
YOGI. Yogi. Casseres.
YOM KIPPUR
Kol Nidra. *Fr.* The Day of Atonement. Leiser.
Yom Kippur. Zangwill.
YORKSHIRE, ENGLAND. Yorkshire Moors, The. Hal Summers.
YOUNG, BRIGHAM. Brigham Young. *Unknown.*
YOUTH
Advice to a Boy. Leather.
Age Intercedes for Youth. R. A. Taylor.
Alas for Youth. Firdausi, *tr. fr. Persian by* Nicholson.
At the Doors. "Der Nistor," *tr. fr. Yiddish by* Leftwich.
Ball Poem, The. Berryman.
Ballade of Youth and Age. Henley.
Barefoot Boy, The. Whittier.
Being Young. John Holmes.
Birches. Robert Frost.
Blessing on Little Boys. Guiterman.
Boy. Allingham.
Boy, The. Eugene Field.
Boy. Welles.
Boy and a Pup, A. Guiterman.
Boy and Father. Sandburg.
Boy and His Stomach, A. Guest.
Boy and His Top, The. Frere.
Boy and Tadpoles. Louis Untermeyer.
Boy Fourteen. A. B. Hall.
Boy Out of Church, The. Graves.
Boy's Prayer, A. H. C. Beeching.
Boy's Song, A. Hogg.
Cherries. Schneour, *tr. fr. Yiddish by* Leftwich.
Chestnut Casts His Flambeaux, The. A. E. Housman.
Country Tune. Riddell.
Crabbed Age and Youth. *Fr.* The Passionate Pilgrim. Shakespeare.
Days of Our Youth. *Unknown, tr. fr. Arabic by* Blunt.
Departed Friend, The. Novo, *tr. fr. Spanish by* Lee.
English Schoolboy, The. *Fr.* The Play of the Weather. John Heywood.
Extremes. J. W. Riley.
Fair Seed-Time Had My Soul. *Fr.* The Prelude. Wordsworth.
Fern Hill. Dylan Thomas.
Flight of Youth, The. R. H. Stoddard.
Flood Tide. S. V. Benét.
Funeral of Youth, The: Threnody. Rupert Brooke.
Girl, A. Deutsch.
Girl Athletes. Haniel Long.
Girl in a Tree. F. M. Frost.
Girl of All Periods, The. Patmore.
Girl of Dunbwy, The. T. O. Davis.
Girl of Pompeii, A. E. S. Martin.
Girl of the Red Mouth. Martin MacDermott.
Girlhood. *Unknown.*
Girl's Mood, A. Reese.
Has Sorrow Thy Young Days Shaded? Thomas Moore.

Horse Chestnut Tree, The. Eberhart.
How No Age Is Content. Earl of Surrey.
I Heard the Old Men. Edward Davison.
I Remember. Glover.
I Saw from the Beach. Thomas Moore.
Invitation to Youth. *Unknown, tr. fr. Latin by* Symonds.
Invocation to Youth. Binyon.
It Was My June. Duke.
Just Sixteen. Hsü Chien, *tr. fr. Chinese by* Hart.
Lads in Their Hundreds, The. A. E. Housman.
Lightly like Music Running. Garrigue.
Lines on a Young Lady's Photograph Album. Philip Larkin.
Little Girl, A. Angoff.
Lost Shipmate, The. T. G. Roberts.
Lusty Juventus. Wever.
Maidenhood. Longfellow.
My Lost Youth. Longfellow.
Not Youth Pertains to Me. Whitman.
O Boys! O Boys! Gogarty.
O Tan-faced Prairie-Boy. Whitman.
O Youth Whose Hope Is High. Robert Bridges.
O Youth with Blossoms Laden. Peach.
Old and Young. Bourdillon.
Old Man's Comforts and How He Gained Them, The. Southey.
Old Men and the Young Men, The. Clement Wood.
Old Swimmin'-Hole, The. J. W. Riley.
On a Seventeenth Birthday. A. P. L. Field.
Orange Tree, The. Neilson.
Prayer after Youth. Maxwell Anderson.
Rejoyce whyle in thy youth thou art. *Unknown.*
Retreat, The. Vaughan.
Rules for the Road. Markham.
Salute to Recife. Bandeira, *tr. fr. Portuguese by* Poore.
Schoolboy, The. *Fr.* Songs of Experience. Blake.
Schoolgirls Hastening. Neilson.
Seein' Things. Eugene Field.
Sestina of Youth and Age. Gelett Burgess.
Since Youth Is All for Gladness. Dresbach.
Small Boy, The. *Unknown, tr. fr. Chinese.*
Snow of the Crane. Tikhonov, *tr. fr. Russian by* Lindsay.
Song about Myself, A. Keats.
Song for Youth. Burnet.
Song of Youth, The. *Fr.* Songs of Deliverance. Johns.
Song of Youth. Works.
Sunburnt Boys. J. C. McNeill.
There Was a Boy. *Fr.* The Prelude. Wordsworth.
There Was a Lad. Burns.
These Are the Young. Vachel Lindsay.
Thesis and Antithesis. Clough.
To Youth. Landor.
To Youth. J. V. A. Weaver.
Torn Hat, The. Willis.
Two Boys, The. Mary Lamb.
Two Brothers, The. *Unknown.*
When I Was Fair and Young. Elizabeth, Queen of England.
When I Was One-and-twenty. A. E. Housman.
Wishes of Youth. Laman Blanchard.
Wonder. Traherne.
Young and Old. Campion.
Young and Old. *Fr.* The Water Babies. Kingsley.
Young Boy, A. J. N. North.
Youth. K. L. Bates.
Youth. Preston Clark.
Youth. V. W. Cloud.
Youth. *Fr.* Heracles. Euripides, *tr. fr. Greek.*
Youth. Helburn.
Youth. T. S. Jones, Jr.
Youth. G. C. Lodge.
Youth. J. B. Rittenhouse.
Youth. Salkeld.
Youth. Tzu Yeh, *tr. fr. Chinese by* Hart.
Youth. *Unknown.*
Youth. Lord Vaux.
Youth and Age. George Arnold.
Youth and Age. S. T. Coleridge.
Youth and Age. Mimnermus, *tr. fr. Greek by* Symonds.
Youth and Age. Vance Palmer.
Youth and Age. W. B. Scott.
Youth and Calm. Matthew Arnold.
Youth and Death. E. M. Root.
Youth and Love. R. L. Stevenson.
Youth and Maidenhood. Sarah Williams.
Youth Dreams, The. Rilke, *tr. fr. German by* Lewisohn.

YUCATAN, MEXICO. Hunter, the. W. J. Turner.
YUCCA. Yucca in the Moonlight. Dresbach.
YUKON TERRITORY
Law of the Yukon, The. Service.
Spell of the Yukon, The. Service.
YUMA, ARIZONA. Yuma. C. H. Phelps.

Z

ZACCHAEUS. On Zacheus. Quarles.
ZANTE (island), GREECE
Lover of His Country, The. Calvos, *tr. fr. Modern Greek by* Dalven.
Sonnet to Zante. Poe.
ZEBRAS
Zebra. W. J. Smith.
Zebras, The. Roy Campbell.
Zebras. Stackpole.
ZEPPELIN (airship). Zeppelin, The. R. B. Bennett.
ZEUS
Hymn to Zeus. Cleanthes, *tr. fr. Greek.*
Leda and the Swan. Yeats.
ZION
By the Waters of Babylon. *Fr.* Hebrew Melodies. Heine, *tr. fr. German by* Leland.
Hatikvah—a Song of Hope. Imber, *tr. fr. Hebrew by* Snowman.
Kadia the Young Mother Speaks. Sampter.
Last Words of Don Henriquez, The. Schneour, *tr. fr. Yiddish by* Leftwich.
Light and Rejoicing to Israel. *Unknown, tr. fr. Hebrew by* Abrahams.
My Heart Is in the East. Halevi, *tr. fr. Hebrew.*
Ode to Zion. Halevi, *tr. fr. Hebrew by* Salaman.
Prayer for Redemption. *Unknown.*
Promised Land, The. Sampter.
Road, The. Schneour, *tr. fr. Yiddish by* Leftwich.
Song: "There stands a lonely pine-tree." Heine, *tr. fr. German by* Lazarus.
Theodor Herzl. Zangwill.
Through These Pale Cold Days. Rosenberg.
To the Western Wind. Halevi, *tr. fr. Hebrew by* Solis-Cohen.
To Zion. Halevi, *tr. fr. Hebrew by* Samuel.
Zionist Marching Song. Imber, *tr. fr. Hebrew by* Zangwill.
ZOLA, ÉMILE. Zola. E. A. Robinson.
ZOOS
At the Zoo. A. A. Milne.
Excuse Us, Animals in the Zoo. Wynne.
Menagerie, The. W. V. Moody.
Van Amburgh's Menagerie. *Unknown.*
Zoo, The. Humbert Wolfe.
Zoo in the City, The. S. V. A. Allen.
Zoo Manners. Mathias.
ZULU
Death of a Zulu, The. Plomer.
Zulu Girl, The. Roy Campbell.